The New Encyclopædia Britannica

Volume 13

MACROPÆDIA

Knowledge in Depth

FOUNDED 1768
15 TH EDITION

Encyclopædia Britannica, Inc.
Robert P. Gwinn, Chairman, Board of Directors
Peter B. Norton, President
Robert McHenry, Editor in Chief

Chicago
Auckland/Geneva/London/Madrid/Manila/Paris
Rome/Seoul/Sydney/Tokyo/Toronto

THE UNIVERSITY OF CHICAGO

"Let knowledge grow from more to more
and thus be human life enriched."

The *Encyclopædia Britannica* is published with the editorial advice of the faculties of the University of Chicago.

Additional advice is given by committees of members drawn from the faculties of the Australian National University, the universities of Adelaide (Australia), British Columbia (Can.), Cambridge (Eng.), Edinburgh (Scot.), Florence (Italy), London (Eng.), Marburg (Ger.), Melbourne (Australia), Montreal (Can.), Oxford (Eng.), the Ruhr (Ger.), Sussex (Eng.), Sydney (Australia), Toronto (Can.), Victoria (Can.), Waterloo (Can.), and Western Australia; the Complutensian University of Madrid (Spain); La Trobe University (Australia); the Max Planck Institute for Biophysical Chemistry (Ger.); the New University of Lisbon (Port.); the School of Higher Studies in Social Sciences (Fr.); Simon Fraser University (Can.); the State University of Leiden (Neth.); and York University (Can.).

First Edition	1768–1771
Second Edition	1777–1784
Third Edition	1788–1797
Supplement	1801
Fourth Edition	1801–1809
Fifth Edition	1815
Sixth Edition	1820–1823
Supplement	1815–1824
Seventh Edition	1830–1842
Eighth Edition	1852–1860
Ninth Edition	1875–1889
Tenth Edition	1902–1903

Printed in U.S.A.

Library of Congress Catalog Card Number: 91-75907
International Standard Book Number: 0-85229-571-5

CONTENTS

1 Accounting
9 Aesthetics
25 Afghanistan
37 Africa
121 African Arts
168 Agricultural Sciences
172 The History of Agriculture
195 Alcohol and Drug Consumption
224 Alexander the Great
229 Alexandria
234 Algae
244 Algebra
301 American literature
312 Arts of Native American Peoples
349 Native American Peoples
418 Amphibians
436 Amsterdam
441 Analysis (in Mathematics)
523 Physical and Chemical Analysis and Measurement
603 Angiosperms: The Flowering Plants
766 Animals
778 Annelids
788 Antarctica
805 Antwerp
808 Arabia
853 Arachnids
872 Archimedes
874 The Art of Architecture
901 The History of Western Architecture

Accounting

The purpose of accounting is to provide information about the economic affairs of an organization. This information may be used in a number of ways: by the organization's managers to help them plan and control the organization's operations; by owners and legislative or regulatory bodies to help them appraise the organization's performance and make decisions as to its future; by owners, lenders, suppliers, employees, and others to help them decide how much time or money to devote to the organization; and by governmental bodies to determine how much tax the organization must pay.

Accounting provides information for all these purposes through the maintenance of files of data and the preparation of various kinds of reports. Most accounting information is historical—that is, the accountant observes the things that the organization does, records their effects, and prepares reports summarizing what has been recorded.

Accounting information can be developed for any kind of organization, not just for privately owned, profit-seeking businesses. One branch of accounting deals with the economic operations of entire nations. The remainder of this article, however, will be devoted primarily to business accounting.

The article is divided into the following sections:

Company financial statements 1
- The balance sheet 1
- The income statement 1
- The statement of changes in retained earnings 2
- The statement of changes in financial position 2
- Consolidated statements 3
- Disclosure and auditing requirements 3

Measurement principles 3
- Asset value 3
- Asset cost 3
- Net income 4
- Problems of measurement 4

Managerial accounting 5
- Cost finding 5
- Distribution cost analysis 6
- Budgetary planning and performance reporting 6
- Cost and profit analysis 7

Other purposes of accounting systems 7

Bibliography 8

COMPANY FINANCIAL STATEMENTS

Some accounting reports are issued only to the company's management or to tax agencies (see below *Managerial accounting* and *Other purposes of accounting systems*); others are sent to investors and others outside the management group. The reports most likely to go to investors are called the company's financial statements, and their preparation is the province of the branch of accounting known as financial accounting. Four kinds of financial statements will be discussed: the balance sheet, the income statement, the statement of changes in retained earnings, and the statement of changes in financial position.

The balance sheet. A balance sheet describes the resources that are under the company's control on a specified date and indicates where these resources have come from. It consists of three major sections: (1) the assets: valuable rights owned by the company; (2) the liabilities: the funds that have been provided by outside lenders and other creditors in exchange for the company's promise to make payments or to provide services in the future; and (3) the owners' equity: the funds that have been provided by the company's owners or on their behalf (as retained earnings, for example).

The list of assets shows the forms in which the company's resources are lodged; the lists of liabilities and the owners' equity indicate where these same resources have come from. The balance sheet, in other words, shows the company's resources from two points of view, and the following relationship must always exist: total assets equals total liabilities plus total owners' equity.

This same identity is also expressed in another way: total assets minus total liabilities equals total owners' equity. In this form, the equation emphasizes that the owners' equity in the company is always equal to the net assets (assets minus liabilities). Any increase in one will inevitably be accompanied by an increase in the other, and the only way to increase the owners' equity is to increase the net assets.

Assets and liabilities

Assets are ordinarily subdivided into current assets and noncurrent assets. The former include cash, amounts receivable from customers, inventories, and other assets that are expected to be consumed or can be readily converted into cash during the next operating cycle (production, sale, and collection). Noncurrent assets may include noncurrent receivables, fixed assets (such as land and buildings), and long-term investments.

The liabilities are similarly divided into current liabilities and noncurrent liabilities. Most amounts payable to the company's suppliers (accounts payable), to employees (wages payable), or to governments (taxes payable) are included among the current liabilities. Noncurrent liabilities consist mainly of amounts payable to holders of the company's long-term bonds and such items as obligations to employees under company pension plans.

The difference between the total of the current assets and the total of the current liabilities is known as net current assets, or working capital.

Owners' equity

The owners' equity of a U.S. company is divided between paid-in capital and retained earnings. Paid-in capital represents the amounts paid to the corporation in exchange for shares of the company's preferred and common stock. The major part of this, the capital paid in by the common shareholders, is usually divided into two parts, one representing the par value, or stated value, of the shares, the other representing the excess over this amount. The amount of retained earnings is the difference between the amounts earned by the company in the past and the dividends that have been distributed to the owners.

A slightly different breakdown of the owners' equity is used in most of continental Europe and in other parts of the world. The classification distinguishes between those amounts that cannot be distributed except as part of a formal liquidation of all or part of the company (capital and legal reserves) and those amounts that are not restricted in this way (free reserves and undistributed profits).

A simple balance sheet is shown in Table 1. Because the two sides of this balance sheet represent two different aspects of the same entity—the corporation's capital—the totals must always be identical. Thus, a change in the amount for one item must always be accompanied by an equal change in some other item. For example, if the company pays $40 to one of its trade creditors, the cash balance will go down by $40, and the balance in accounts payable will go down by the same amount.

The income statement. The company uses its assets to produce goods and services. Its success depends on whether it is wise or lucky in the assets it chooses to hold and in the ways it uses these assets to produce goods and services.

Net income

The company's success is measured by the amount of profit it earns—that is, the growth or decline in its stock of assets from all sources other than contributions or

Table 1: Any Company, Inc.: Balance Sheet as of Dec. 31, 19__

assets			liabilities and owners' equity		
Current assets			Current liabilities		
Cash		$100	Wages payable		$ 20
Marketable securities		50	Accounts payable		160
Accounts receivable		150	Total current liabilities		$180
Inventories		180	Long-term bonds payable		80
Total current assets		$480	Total liabilities		$260
			Owners' equity		
Long-term investments		70	Common stock	$100	
Plant and equipment			Additional paid-in capital	150	
Original cost	$300		Retained earnings	230	
Less: accumulated depreciation	110	190	Total owners' equity		480
Total assets		$740	Total liabilities and owners' equity		$740

withdrawals of funds by owners and creditors. Net income is the accountant's term for the amount of profit that is reported for a particular time period.

The company's income statement for a period of time shows how the net income for that period was derived. For example, the first line in Table 2 shows the company's sales revenues for the period: the assets obtained from customers in exchange for the goods and services that constitute the company's stock-in-trade. The second line summarizes the company's revenues from other sources.

The income statement next shows the expenses of the period: the assets that were consumed while the revenues were being created. The expenses are usually broken down into several categories indicating what the assets were used for. In Table 2, six expense items are distinguished, starting with the cost of the merchandise that was sold during the period and continuing down through the provision for income taxes.

Table 2: Any Company, Inc.: Income Statement for the Year Ended Dec. 31, 19__

Net sales revenues		$800
Interest and other revenues		14
Total revenues		$814
Expenses		
Cost of merchandise sold	$492	
Salaries of employees	116	
Depreciation	30	
Interest expense	4	
Other expenses	78	
Provision for taxes on ordinary income	47	767
Operating income		$ 47
Gain on sale of investment (less applicable income taxes)		5
Net income		$ 52

The bottom portion of the income statement in this case shows the result of the company's sale of some of its long-term investments for more than their original purchase price. Because this was not part of the company's normal operations, the sale price, costs, and taxes on the sale were kept separate from the operating revenue and expense totals; the income statement shows only a single number, the net gain on the sale.

Net income summarizes all of the gains and losses recognized during the period, including both the results of the company's normal, day-by-day activities and any other events. If net income is negative, it is referred to as a net loss.

The statement of changes in retained earnings. Like the income statement, the statement of changes in retained earnings refers to a period of time rather than to a single date. It explains the change from one balance sheet date to the next in the amount shown as retained earnings.

The retained earnings statement is the link between the income statement and the balance sheet. This relationship can be demonstrated by rewriting the accounting equation in the following way: assets minus liabilities equals paid-in capital plus retained earnings. When the company reports net income, this means that more assets came in as revenues than went out as expenses; more precisely, it means that the net asset total (assets minus liabilities) increased. Therefore, if the accounting equation is to remain balanced, an amount equal to net income must be added to retained earnings.

The distribution of cash dividends reduces net assets, and this change is balanced by a reduction in the retained earnings. Thus the typical statement of changes in retained earnings consists of the items shown in Table 3.

Table 3: Any Company, Inc.: Statement of Changes in Retained Earnings for the Year Ended Dec. 31, 19__

Retained earnings, Jan. 1, 19__	$213
Net income earned during 19__	52
	$265
Less: dividends distributed to shareholders during 19__	35
Retained earnings, Dec. 31, 19__	$230

Starting with retained earnings of $213 at the beginning of the year, the company added $52 in net income during the year (from Table 2). Dividends amounting to $35 were distributed to shareholders during the year, leaving a year-end balance of $230. This is the amount on the year-end balance sheet (Table 1).

The statement of changes in financial position. The statement of changes in financial position, or funds statement, identifies the major flows of funds during the period. In many corporate reports, "funds" means working capital. The idea is easier to understand, however, if the flow of funds means simply the flow of cash. For example, if a salesman receives $48,000 in salary and commission, from which he pays $15,000 for airline tickets, hotel rooms, meals, and other travel expenses, his operations have provided him with funds amounting to $33,000. Further investigation reveals that he borrowed $5,000 from the bank during this same year, bought a car for $11,000, purchased stock for $4,000, and spent $24,000 on ordinary living expenses. At the end of the year, he had $1,000 less in his bank account than he had had at the beginning. A funds statement for the year would show the following:

The flow of funds

sources of funds		uses of funds	
from operations	$33,000	to purchase car	$11,000
from bank borrowing	5,000	to buy stock	4,000
from past savings	1,000	to pay living expenses	24,000
total sources	$39,000	total uses	$39,000

This is very different from an income statement. The sources of funds include amounts borrowed from the bank and taken from past personal savings. These are not current revenues. Similarly, the purchases of stock and of the car are not current expenses: the purchases are made in the expectation of future benefits, not mainly to produce current revenues.

The amount referred to as funds from operations ($33,000) comes from the income statement, but it is not the same as net income. For example, the salesman may say that his expenses should include some recognition of depreciation on the automobile that he used in his business. If depreciation is estimated to be $1,500 for the year, his net income would be $31,500, not $33,000.

The purpose of the funds statement is to permit an examination of the company's financial activities during the period. For example, Table 4 shows that $77 flowed in from ordinary operations, $20 came from the issuance of the company's own bonds, and $13 came from the sale of securities that the company had held as a long-term investment. Almost half of these funds were used to buy a new plant and equipment. Another $35 went to stockholders in the form of dividends, and the remaining $25 was invested in working capital.

Table 4: Any Company, Inc.: Statement of Changes in Financial Position for the Year Ended Dec. 31, 19__

Sources of funds	
From ordinary operations	$ 77
From sale of investments	13
From sale of bonds	20
Total sources of funds	$110
Uses of funds	
To pay dividends	$ 35
To acquire plant and equipment	50
To increase working capital	25
Total uses of funds	$110

The statement itself serves merely to identify existing relationships. It reveals, for instance, that operations did not generate enough funds to cover the company's dividend and capital investment requirements. An observer may reasonably ask whether this seems to be the result of an aggressive and imaginative expansion program or the product of competitive weaknesses that limit the company's fund-generating capacity. Similarly, the amount of funds going into working capital is a statement of fact; whether it is good or bad depends on the reasons for it.

Consolidated statements. Most large corporations in the United States and other industrialized countries own other corporations. Their primary financial statements are consolidated statements, reflecting the total assets, liabilities, owners' equity, net income, and funds flows of all the corporations in the group. Thus, for example, the consolidated balance sheet of the parent corporation (the corporation that owns the others) does not list its investments in its subsidiaries (the companies it owns) as assets; instead, it includes their assets and liabilities with its own.

Some subsidiary corporations are not wholly owned by the parent; that is, some shares of their common stock are owned by others. The equity of these minority shareholders in the subsidiary companies is shown separately on the balance sheet. For example, if Any Company, Inc., had minority shareholders in one or more subsidiaries, the owners' equity section of its December 31, 19__ balance sheet might appear as follows:

Minority interests in subsidiaries		$ 30
Shareholders' equity:		
Common stock	$100	
Additional paid-in capital	150	
Retained earnings	200	450

The consolidated income statement also must show the minority owners' equity in the earnings of a subsidiary as a deduction in the determination of net income. For example:

Income before minority interest	$52
Minority interest in earnings	3
Net income	$49

Government regulation

Disclosure and auditing requirements. A corporation's obligations to issue financial statements are prescribed in the company's own statutes or bylaws and in public laws and regulations. The financial statements of most large and medium-sized companies in the United States fall primarily within the jurisdiction of the federal Securities and Exchange Commission (SEC). The SEC has a good deal of authority to prescribe the content and structure of the financial statements that are submitted to it.

A company's financial statements are ordinarily prepared initially by its own accountants. Outsiders review, or audit, the statements and the systems the company used to accumulate the data from which the statements were prepared. In most countries, including the United States, these outside auditors are selected by the company's shareholders. The audit of a company's statements is ordinarily performed by professionally qualified, independent accountants who bear the title of Certified Public Accountants (CPA) in the United States. In the United Kingdom and many other countries with British-based accounting traditions, they are members of government-chartered organizations. Their primary task is to investigate the company's accounting figures and methods carefully enough to permit them to give their opinion that the financial statements are complete and that the figures have been arrived at through the use of acceptable measurement principles.

MEASUREMENT PRINCIPLES

In preparing financial statements, the accountant has several measurement systems to choose from. Assets, for example, might be measured at what they cost in the past or what they could be sold for now, to mention only two possibilities. To enable users to interpret statements with confidence, companies in similar industries should use the same measurement concepts or principles.

In some countries these concepts or principles are prescribed by government bodies; in the United States they are embodied in "generally accepted accounting principles" (GAAP), which represent partly the consensus of experts and partly the work of the Financial Accounting Standards Board (FASB), a private body. The principles or standards issued by the FASB can be overridden by the SEC. In practice, however, the SEC generally requires corporations within its jurisdiction to conform to the standards of the FASB.

Asset value. One principle that accountants might adopt would be to measure assets at their value to their owners. Under this principle, the economic value of an asset is the maximum amount that the company would be willing to pay for it. This amount depends on what the company expects to be able to do with it. For business assets, these expectations are usually expressed in terms of forecasts of the inflows of cash the company will receive in the future. If, for example, the company believes that by spending $1 on advertising and other forms of sales promotion it can sell a certain product for $5, then this product is worth $4 to the company.

Economic value

When cash inflows are expected to be delayed, value is less than the anticipated cash flow. For example, if the company has to pay interest at the rate of 10 percent a year, an investment of $100 in a one-year asset today will not be worthwhile unless it will return at least $110 a year from now ($100 plus 10 percent interest for one year). In this example, $100 is the present value of the right to receive $110 one year later. Present value is the maximum amount the company would be willing to pay for a future inflow of cash after deducting interest on the investment at a specified rate for the time the company has to wait before it receives its cash.

Value, in other words, depends on three factors: (1) the amount of the anticipated future cash flows, (2) their timing, and (3) the interest rate. The lower the expectation, the more distant the timing, or the higher the interest rate, the less valuable the asset will be.

Value may also be represented by the amount the company could obtain by selling its assets. This sale price is seldom a good measure of the assets' value to the company, however, because few companies are likely to keep many assets that are worth no more to the company than their market value. Continued ownership of an asset implies that its present value to the owner exceeds its market value, which is its apparent value to outsiders.

Asset cost. Accountants are traditionally reluctant to accept value as the basis of asset measurement in the going concern. Although monetary assets such as cash or accounts receivable are usually measured by their value, most assets are measured at cost. The reason is that the accountant finds it difficult to verify the forecasts upon which a generalized value measurement system would have to be based. As a result, the balance sheet does not pretend to show how much the company's assets are worth; it shows how much the company has invested in them.

Historical cost

The historical cost of an asset is the sum of all the expenditures the company made to acquire it. This amount is not always easily measurable. If, for example, a company has built a special-purpose machine in one of its own factories for use in manufacturing other products, and the project required logistical support from all parts of the factory organization, from purchasing to quality control, then a good deal of judgment must be reflected in any estimate of how much of the costs of these logistical activities should be "capitalized" (*i.e.*, placed on the balance sheet) as part of the cost of the machine.

Net income. From an economic point of view, income is defined as the change in the company's wealth during a period of time, from all sources other than the injection or withdrawal of investment funds. Income is the amount the company could consume during the period and still have as much real wealth at the end of the period as it had at the beginning. For example, if the value of the net assets (assets minus liabilities) has gone from $1,000 to $1,200 during a period and dividends of $100 have been distributed, income measured on a value basis would be $300 ($1,200 minus $1,000, plus $100).

Accountants generally have rejected this approach for the same reason that they have found value an unacceptable basis for asset measurement: such a measure would rely too much on estimates of what will happen in the future, estimates that would not be readily susceptible to independent verification. Instead, accountants have adopted what might be called a transactions approach to income measurement. They recognize as income only those increases in wealth that can be substantiated from data pertaining to actual transactions that have taken place with persons outside the company. In such systems, income is measured when work is performed for an outside customer, when goods are delivered, or when the customer is billed.

Transactions approach

Recognition of income at this time requires two sets of estimates: (1) revenue estimates, representing the value of the cash that the company expects to receive from the customer; and (2) expense estimates, representing the resources that have been consumed in the creation of the revenues. Revenue estimation is the easier of the two, but it still requires judgment. The main problem is to estimate the percentage of gross sales for which payment will never be received, either because some customers will not pay their bills or because they will demand and receive credit for returned merchandise or defective work.

Expense estimates are generally based on the historical cost of the resources consumed. Net income, in other words, is the difference between the value received from the use of resources and the cost of the resources that were consumed in the process. As with asset measurement, the main problem is to estimate what portion of the cost of an asset has been consumed during the period in question.

Some assets give up their services gradually rather than all at once. The cost of the portion of these assets the company uses to produce revenues in any period is that period's depreciation expense, and the amount shown for these assets on the balance sheet is their historical cost less an allowance for depreciation, representing the cost of the portion of the asset's anticipated lifetime services that has already been used. To estimate depreciation, the accountant must predict both how long the asset will continue to provide useful services and how much of its potential to provide these services will be used up in each period.

Depreciation is usually computed by some simple formula. The two most popular formulas in the United States are straight-line depreciation, in which the same amount of depreciation is recognized each year, and declining-charge depreciation, in which more depreciation is recognized during the early years of life than during the later years, on the assumption that the value of the asset's service declines as it gets older.

The role of the independent accountant (the auditor) is to see whether the company's estimates are based on formulas that seem reasonable in the light of whatever evidence is available and that these formulas are applied consistently from year to year. Again, what is "reasonable" is clearly a matter of judgment.

Depreciation is not the only expense for which more than one measurement principle is available. Another is the cost of goods sold. The cost of goods available for sale in any period is the sum of the cost of the beginning inventory and the cost of goods purchased in that period. This sum then must be divided between the cost of goods sold and the cost of the ending inventory:

$$\text{Beginning inventory} + \text{Purchases} = \text{Cost of goods sold} + \text{Ending inventory}$$

Accountants can make this division by any of three main inventory costing methods: (1) first in, first out (FIFO), (2) last in, first out (LIFO), or (3) average cost. The LIFO method is widely used in the United States, where it is also an acceptable costing method for income tax purposes; companies in most other countries measure inventory cost and the cost of goods sold by some variant of the FIFO or average cost methods. Average cost is very similar in its results to FIFO; so only FIFO and LIFO need be described.

FIFO and LIFO

Each purchase of goods constitutes a single batch, acquired at a specific price. Under FIFO, the cost of goods sold is determined by adding the costs of the various batches of the goods available, starting with the oldest batch in the beginning inventory, continuing with the next oldest batch, and so on until the total number of units equals the number of units sold. The ending inventory, therefore, is assigned the costs of the most recently acquired batches. For example, suppose the beginning inventory and purchases were as follows:

Inventory, January 1	1,000 units × $5.00	$ 5,000
Purchases, March 19	800 units × $5.25	4,200
Purchases, September 12	1,200 units × $5.50	6,600
Total goods available	3,000 units	$15,800

The company sold 1,900 units during the year and had 1,100 units remaining in inventory at the end of the year. The FIFO cost of goods sold is:

Oldest batch,	1,000 units × $5.00	$5,000
Next oldest batch,	800 units × $5.25	4,200
Next oldest batch,	100 units × $5.50	550
Total cost of goods sold	1,900 units	$9,750

The ending inventory consists of 1,100 units at a FIFO cost of $5.50 each (the price of the last 1,100 units purchased), or $6,050.

Under LIFO, the cost of goods sold is the sum of the most recent purchase, the next most recent, and so on, until the total number of units equals the number sold during the period. In the example, the LIFO cost of goods sold is:

Most recent purchase,	1,200 units × $5.50	$ 6,600
Next most recent purchase,	700 units × $5.25	3,675
Total cost of goods sold	1,900 units	$10,275

The LIFO cost of the ending inventory is the cost of the oldest units in the cost of goods available. In this simple example, assuming the company adopted LIFO at the beginning of the year, the ending inventory cost is the 1,000 units in the beginning inventory at $5 each ($5,000), plus 100 units from the first purchase during the year at $5.25 each ($525), a total of $5,525.

Problems of measurement. Accounting income does not include all of the company's holding gains or losses (increases or decreases in the market values of its assets). For example, construction of a superhighway may increase the value of a company's land, but neither the income statement nor the balance sheet will report this holding gain. Similarly, introduction of a successful new product increases the company's anticipated future cash flows, and this increase makes the company more valuable. Those additional future sales show up neither in the conventional income statement nor in the balance sheet.

Holding gains and losses

Accounting reports have also been criticized on the grounds that they confuse monetary measures with the underlying realities when the prices of many goods and services have been changing rapidly. For example, if the wholesale price of an item has risen from $100 to $150 between the time the company bought it and the time it is sold, many accountants and businessmen claim that $150 is the better measure of the amount of resources consumed by the sale. The $50 is simply a holding gain that should not be classified as ordinary income.

Price changes

When inventory purchase prices are rising, LIFO inventory costing keeps many gains from the holding of inventories out of net income. If purchases equal the quantity sold, the entire cost of goods sold will be measured at the higher current prices; the ending inventory will be measured at the lower prices shown for the beginning-of-year inventory. The difference between the LIFO inventory cost and the replacement cost at the end of the year is an unrealized (and unreported) holding gain.

In the inventory example cited earlier, the LIFO cost of goods sold ($10,275) exceeded the FIFO cost of goods sold ($9,750) by $525. In other words, LIFO kept $525 more of the inventory holding gain out of the income statement than FIFO did. Furthermore, the replacement cost of the inventory at the end of the year was $6,050 (1,100 × $5.50), which was just equal to the inventory's FIFO cost; under LIFO, in contrast, there was an unrealized holding gain of $525 ($6,050 minus the $5,525 LIFO inventory cost).

The amount of inventory holding gain that is included in net income is usually called the "inventory profit." The implication is that this is a component of net income that is less "real" than other components because it results from the holding of inventories rather than from trading with customers.

Purchasing power

When most of the changes in the prices of the company's resources are in the same direction, the purchasing power of money is said to change. Conventional accounting statements are stated in nominal currency units (dollars, francs, lire, etc.), not in units of constant purchasing power. Changes in purchasing power—that is, changes in the average level of prices of goods and services—have two effects. First, net monetary assets (essentially cash and receivables minus liabilities calling for fixed monetary payments) lose purchasing power as the general price level rises. These losses do not appear in conventional accounting statements. Second, holding gains measured in nominal currency units may merely result from changes in the general price level. If so, they represent no increase in the company's purchasing power.

In 1980 the FASB began requiring major corporations in the United States to report the effects of some changes in specific and general price levels, but these measurements are not incorporated in the primary financial statements. In other countries that have experienced severe and prolonged inflation, companies have been allowed or even required to restate their assets to reflect the more recent and higher levels of purchase prices. The increment in the asset balances in such cases has not been reported as income, but depreciation thereafter has been based on these higher figures.

MANAGERIAL ACCOUNTING

Although published financial statements are the most widely visible products of business accounting systems and the ones with which the public is most concerned, they are only the tip of the iceberg. Most accounting data and most accounting reports are generated solely or mainly for the company's managers. Reports to management may be either summaries of past events, forecasts of the future, or a combination of the two. Preparation of these data and reports is the focus of managerial accounting, which consists mainly of three broad functions: (1) cost finding, (2) budgetary planning and performance reporting, and (3) cost and profit analysis.

Cost finding. Cost finding is the process by which the company obtains estimates of the costs of producing a product, providing a service, performing a function, or operating a department. Some of these estimates are historical—how much did it cost?—while others are predictive—what will it cost?

The most fully developed methods of cost finding are used to estimate the costs that have been incurred in a factory to manufacture specific products. The simplest of these methods is known as process costing. In this method, the accountant first accumulates the costs of each separate production operation or process for a specified period of time. The total of these costs is then restated as an average by dividing it by the total output of the process during the same period.

Process costing

Process costing can be used whenever the output of individual processes is reasonably uniform or homogeneous, as in cement manufacturing, flour milling, and other relatively continuous production processes.

Job order costing

A second method, job order costing, is used when individual production centres or departments work on a variety of products rather than just one during a typical time period. Two categories of factory cost are recognized under this method: prime costs and factory overhead costs. Prime costs are those that can be traced directly to a specific batch, or job lot, of products. These are the direct labour and direct materials costs of production. Overhead costs, on the other hand, are those that can be traced only to departmental operations or to the factory as a whole and not to individual job orders. The salary of a departmental supervisor is an example of an overhead cost.

Direct materials and direct labour costs are recorded directly on the job order cost sheets, one for each job. Although not traceable to individual jobs, overhead costs are generally assigned to them by means of overhead rates—*i.e.,* the ratio of total overhead cost to total production volume for a given time period. A separate overhead rate is usually calculated for each production department, and, if the operations of a department are varied, it is often subdivided into a set of more homogeneous cost centres, each with its own overhead rate. Separate overhead rates are sometimes used even for individual processing machines within a department if the machines differ widely in such factors as power consumption, maintenance cost, and depreciation.

Because output within a cost centre is not homogeneous, production volume must be measured by something other than the number of units of product, such as the number of machine hours or direct labour hours. Once the overhead rate has been determined, a provision for overhead cost can be entered on each job order cost sheet on the basis of the number of direct labour hours or machine hours used on that job. For example, if the overhead rate is $3 a machine hour and Job No. 7128 used 600 machine hours, then $1,800 would be shown as the overhead cost of this job.

Most overhead rates are predetermined—that is, they represent the average planned overhead cost at some production volume. The main reason for this is that actual overhead cost averages depend on the total volume and efficiency of operations and not on any one job alone. The relevance of job order cost information will be impaired if these external fluctuations are allowed to change the amount of overhead cost assigned to a particular job.

Variable costing

The methods of cost finding described in the preceding paragraphs are known as full, or absorption, costing methods, in that the overhead rates are intended to include provisions for all manufacturing costs. Both process and job order costing methods can also be adapted to variable, or direct, costing in which only variable manufacturing costs are included in product cost. Variable costs are those that will be greater in total in the upper portions of the company's normal range of volumes than in the lower portion. Total fixed costs, in contrast, are the same at all volume levels within the normal range.

Unit cost under variable costing represents the average variable cost of making the product. The main argument for the variable costing approach is that average variable cost is more relevant to many managerial decisions than average full cost. In deciding whether to manufacture goods in large lots, for example, management needs to estimate the cost of carrying larger amounts of finished goods in inventory. More variable costs will have to be incurred to build the inventory to a higher level; fixed manufacturing costs presumably will be unaffected.

Furthermore, when a management decision changes the company's fixed costs, the change is unlikely to be proportional to the change in volume; therefore, average fixed cost is seldom a valid basis for estimating the cost effects of such decisions. Variable costing eliminates the temptation to assume without question that average fixed cost can be used to estimate changes in total fixed cost.

Estimates of product costs can be built up in exactly the same way as historical averages. Once the route that the product will take through the factory is known, estimates of the amounts of materials, labour, and overhead required at each stage can be written down, totalled, and averaged.

Many systems go even further than this. Estimates of the average costs of each type of material, each operation, and each product are prepared routinely and identified as standard costs. These standard cost figures are then readily available whenever estimates are needed and also serve as an important element in the company's performance reporting system, as described below.

Distribution cost analysis. Similar methods of cost finding can be used to determine or estimate the cost of providing services rather than physical goods. Most advertising agencies and consulting firms, for example, maintain some form of job cost records, either as a basis for billing their clients or as a means of estimating the profitability of individual jobs or accounts.

Service cost estimates

The unit cost of distributing the company's products or of providing administrative and supporting services is more difficult to estimate. Any such estimates are likely to be prepared on the basis of special studies, mostly centring on observations of how employees spend their time during selected test periods. Providing these estimates is the task of distribution cost analysis.

Budgetary planning and performance reporting. The second major component of internal accounting systems for management's use is the company's budgetary planning and performance reporting system. This consists of two highly interrelated elements: (1) establishing budgetary plans and setting performance standards and (2) measuring actual results and reporting differences between actual performance and the plans.

The simplified diagram in Figure 1 illustrates the interrelationships between these elements. Planning leads to plans, which then are translated into action. The results of these actions are compared with the plans and reported in comparative form. Management can then respond to substantial deviations from plan, either by taking corrective action or, if outside conditions differ from those predicted or assumed in the plans, by preparing revised plans.

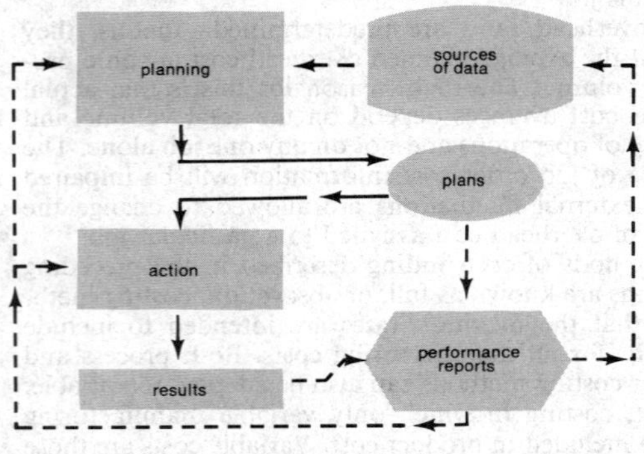

Figure 1: Budget planning and performance reporting.

Although plans can be either broad, strategic outlines of the company's future or schedules of the inputs and outputs associated with specific independent programs, most business plans are periodic plans—that is, they refer to company operations for a specified period of time. These periodic plans are summarized in a series of projected financial statements, or budgets.

The profit plan

The two principal budget statements are the profit plan and the cash forecast. The profit plan is an estimated income statement for the budget period. It summarizes the planned level of selling effort, shown as selling expense, and the results of that effort, shown as sales revenue and the accompanying cost of goods sold. Separate profit plans are ordinarily prepared for each major segment of the company's operations.

The details underlying the profit plan are contained in departmental sales and cost budgets, each part identified with the executive or group responsible for carrying out that part. Figure 2 shows the essence of this relationship: the company's profit plan is really the integrated product of the plans of its two major product divisions. The arrows connecting the two divisional plans represent the coordinative communications that tie them together on matters of mutual concern.

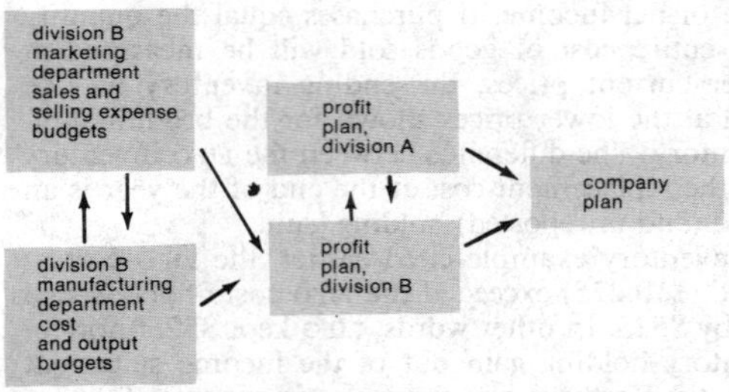

Figure 2: Relationship of company profit plan to responsibility structure.

The exhibit also goes one level farther down, showing that division B's profit plan is really a coordinated synthesis of the plans of the division's marketing department and manufacturing department. Arrows again emphasize the necessary coordination between the two. Each of these departmental plans, in turn, is a summary of the plans of the major offices, plants, or other units within the division. A complete representation of the company's profit plan would require an extension of the diagram through several layers to encompass every single responsibility centre in the entire company.

If standard costs have been established, they are shown in the factory cost budgets and in the standard cost of goods sold on the summary profit plans, with anticipated deviations, or variances, from standard cost budgeted separately. Many companies also prepare alternative budgets for operating volumes other than the volume anticipated for the period. A set of such alternative budgets is known as the flexible budget. The practice of flexible budgeting has been adopted widely by factory management to facilitate evaluation of cost performance at different volume levels and has also been extended to other elements of the profit plan.

The cash forecast

The second major component of the annual budgetary plan, the cash forecast or cash budget, summarizes the anticipated effects on cash of all of the company's activities. It lists the anticipated cash payments, cash receipts, and the amount of cash on hand, month by month throughout the year. In most companies, responsibility for cash management rests mainly in the head office rather than at the divisional level. For this reason, divisional cash forecasts tend to be less important than divisional profit plans.

Company-wide cash forecasts, on the other hand, are just as important as company profit plans. Preliminary cash forecasts are used in deciding how much money will be made available for the payment of dividends, for the purchase or construction of buildings and equipment, and for other programs that do not pay for themselves immediately. The amount of short-term borrowing or short-term investment of temporarily idle funds is then generally geared to the requirements summarized in the final, adjusted forecast.

Other elements of the budgetary plan, in addition to the profit plan and the cash forecast, include capital expenditure budgets, manpower budgets, production budgets, and budgeted balance sheets. They all serve the same purpose: to help management decide upon a course of action and to serve as a point of reference against which to measure subsequent performance.

Planning is a management responsibility, not an accounting function. To plan is to decide, and only the manager has the authority to choose the direction the company is to take. Accounting personnel are nevertheless deeply involved in the planning process. First, they administer the budgetary planning system, establishing deadlines for the completion of each part of the process and seeing that these deadlines are met. Second, they analyze data and help management at various levels compare the estimated effects of different courses of action. Third, they are responsible for collating the tentative plans and proposals coming from the individual departments and divisions and then reviewing them for consistency and feasibility and sometimes for desirability as well. Finally, they must draw up the final plans and see that these plans are understood by the operating executives.

Performance measurement

Once the budgetary plan has been adopted, accounting's next task is to prepare information on the results of company activities and make it available to management. The manager's main interest in this information centres on three questions: Have his or her own actions had the results expected, and, if not, why not? How successful have subordinates been in managing the activities entrusted to them? What problems and opportunities seem to have arisen since the budgetary plan was prepared? For these purposes, the information must be comparative, relating actual results to the level of results that management regards as satisfactory. In each case, the standard for comparison is provided by the budgetary plan.

Much of this information is contained in periodic financial reports. At the top management and divisional levels, the most important of these is the comparative income statement, one of which is illustrated in Table 5. This shows the profit that was planned for this period, the actual results received for this period, and the differences, or variances, between the two. It also gives an explanation of some of the reasons for the difference between a planned and an actual income.

Table 5: Any Company, Inc.: Comparative Income Statement for the Month of October 19__
(in $000,000)

	actual	planned	difference
Divisional profit contribution			
Division A	$100	$120	$(20)
Division B	70	65	5
Division C	140	150	(10)
Total profit contribution	$310	$335	$(25)
Head office expenses	110	105	(5)
Income before taxes	$200	$230	$(30)

Comments

(1) An industry-wide strike in customer factories caused a slowdown in division A deliveries, reducing profit by $24,000,000.

(2) Demand continued strong in division B, reflected in increased volume and a stronger price structure.

(3) Division C's unfavourable results were the result of production losses due to the model change and heavy introductory costs for the new line. These losses should be recovered by the end of the year.

(4) Salary increases account for most of the variance in head office expense. The methods department is seeking ways to offset this.

The report in this exhibit employs the widely used profit contribution format, in which divisional results reflect sales and expenses traceable to the individual divisions, with no deduction for head office expenses. Company net income is then obtained by deducting head office expenses as a lump sum from the total of the divisional profit contributions.

Measuring variances

A similar format can be used within the division, reporting the profit contribution of each of the division's product lines, with divisional headquarters expenses deducted at the bottom. By far the greatest number of reports, however, are cost or sales reports, mostly on a departmental basis. Departmental sales reports usually represent comparisons of actual sales with the volumes planned for the period. Departmental cost performance reports, in contrast, typically compare actual costs incurred with standards or budgets that have been adjusted to correspond to the actual volume of work done during the period. This practice reflects a recognition that volume fluctuations generally originate outside the department and that the department head's responsibility is ordinarily limited to minimizing cost while meeting the delivery schedules imposed by higher management.

For example, a factory department's output consists entirely of a single product, with a standard materials cost of $3 a unit and standard labour cost of $16. Materials cost represents three pounds of raw materials at $1 a pound; standard labour cost is two hours of labour at $8 an hour. Overhead costs in the department are budgeted at $10,000 a month plus $2 a unit. Under normal conditions, volume is 7,000 units a month, but during October only 6,000 units were produced. The cost standards for the month would be as follows:

materials 6,000 units × 3 lb × $1.00 per lb = $18,000
labour 6,000 units × 2 hr × $8.00 per hr = $96,000
overhead 6,000 units × $2.00 + $10,000 = $22,000

The actual cost this month was $17,850 for materials (17,000 pounds at $1.05), $101,250 for labour (12,500 hours at $8.10 an hour), and $23,000 for overhead. A summary report would show the following:

	actual	standard	variance
materials	$17,850	$18,000	$150
labour	101,250	96,000	(5,250)
overhead	23,000	22,000	(1,000)
total	$142,100	$136,000	$(6,100)

These variances are usually analyzed even further in order to identify the underlying causes. The labour variance, for example, can be seen to be the result of both high wage rates ($8.10 instead of $8.00) and high labour usage (12,500 hours instead of 12,000). The factory accountant ordinarily would measure the effect of the rate change in the following way:

actual labour cost = 12,500 × $8.10 = (actual hours × actual wage rate)	$101,250
actual labour hours at standard wage rate = 12,500 × $8.00 =	100,000
labour rate variance	$(1,250)

The labour usage variance would then be obtained as follows:

actual labour hours × standard wage rate = 12,500 × $8	$100,000
standard labour cost (standard labour hours × standard wage rate) = 6,000 × 2 × $8	96,000
labour usage variance	$(4,000)

In most cases, the labour rate variance would not be reported to the department head, because it is not subject to his or her control.

Cost and profit analysis. Accountants share with many other people the task of analyzing cost and profit data in order to provide guidance in managerial decision making. Even if the analytical work is done largely by others, they have an interest in analytical methods because the systems they design must collect data in forms suitable for analysis.

Managerial decisions are based on comparisons of the estimated future results of the alternative courses of action that the decision maker is choosing among. Recorded historical accounting data, in contrast, reflect conditions and experience of the past. Furthermore, they are absolute, not comparative, in that they show the effects of one course of action but not whether these were better or worse than those that would have resulted from some other course.

For decision making, therefore, historical accounting data must be examined, modified, and placed on a comparative basis. Even estimated data, such as budgets and standard costs, must be examined to see whether the estimates are still valid and relevant to managerial comparisons. To a large extent, this job of review and restatement is an accounting responsibility. Accordingly, a major part of the accountant's preparation for the profession is devoted to the study of methods and principles of analysis for managerial decision making.

OTHER PURPOSES OF ACCOUNTING SYSTEMS

Accounting systems are designed mainly to provide information that managers and outsiders can use in decision making. They also serve other purposes: to produce operating documents, to protect the company's assets, and to provide data for company tax returns.

Document preparation

The accounting organization is responsible for preparing documents that contain instructions for a variety of tasks, such as payment of customer bills or preparing employee payrolls. It also must prepare documents that serve what might be called private information purposes, such as the employees' own records of their salaries and wages. Many of these documents also serve as sources of data for other accounting purposes, but they would have to be prepared even if no information reports were necessary. Measured by the number of people involved and the amount of time required, document preparation is one of accounting's biggest jobs.

Accounting systems must provide means of reducing the chance of losses of assets due to carelessness or dishonesty on the part of employees, suppliers, and customers. Asset protection devices are often very simple; for example, many restaurants use numbered meal checks so that waiters will not be able to submit one check to the customer and another, with a lower total, to the cashier. Other devices entail a partial duplication of effort or a division of tasks between two individuals to reduce the opportunity for unobserved thefts.

Internal controls

These are all part of the company's system of internal controls. Another important element in the internal control system is internal auditing. The task of internal auditors is to see whether prescribed data handling and asset protection procedures are being followed. To accomplish this, they usually observe some of the work as it is being performed and examine a sample of past transactions for accuracy and fidelity to the system. They may insert a set of fictitious data into the system to see whether the resulting output meets a predetermined standard. This technique is particularly useful in testing the validity of the programs that are used to process data through electronic computers.

Tax returns

Finally, the accounting system must provide data for use in the completion of the company's tax returns. This function is the concern of tax accounting. In some countries financial accounting must obey rules laid down for tax accounting by national tax laws and regulations, but no such requirement is imposed in the United States, and figures prepared for tax purposes often diverge from those submitted to shareholders and others. "Taxable income" is a legal concept rather than an accounting concept. Tax laws include incentives to encourage companies to do certain things and discourage them from doing others. Accordingly, what is "income" or "capital" to a tax agency may be far different from the accountant's measures of these same concepts.

BIBLIOGRAPHY

Classics: R. GENE BROWN and KENNETH S. JOHNSTON, *Paciolo on Accounting* (1963, reprinted 1984), an annotated translation of the treatise, published in 1494, that is widely accepted as the foundation stone of modern accounting and bookkeeping systems, with biographical notes and a reproduction of the original manuscript; A.C. LITTLETON, *Accounting Evolution to 1900* (1933, reprinted 1981), a scholarly, well-written analysis of the development of accounting from the Renaissance to modern times; JOHN B. CANNING, *Economics of Accountancy* (1929, reprinted 1978), an early landmark in the development of 20th-century accounting thought and one of the first systematic attempts to build a structure of accounting on the basis of economic theory; E. SCHMALENBACH, *Dynamic Accounting* (1959, reprinted 1980), a translation of the 12th ed. of the most influential accounting book published in Germany in the first half of the 20th century, which had a measurable impact on the accounting systems in use in most continental European countries and shaped many of the uniform accounting schemes that have been proposed or adopted in individual European countries. EDGAR O. EDWARDS and PHILIP W. BELL, *The Theory and Measurement of Business Income* (1961), a critical review of conventional accounting measurements, with a detailed examination of possible alternative measurement systems.

Current references: ROBERT N. ANTHONY, *Essentials of Accounting*, 3rd ed. (1983), an easy-to-follow, self-teaching guide to accounting fundamentals, using the programmed-learning approach; GORDON SHILLINGLAW and PHILIP E. MEYER, *Accounting: A Management Approach*, 7th ed. (1983), a concept-oriented introductory textbook covering both financial and managerial accounting; ELDON S. HENDRIKSEN, *Accounting Theory*, 4th ed. (1982), a textbook providing a historical survey and a critical examination of the measurement systems underlying business financial statements; CHARLES T. HORNGREN, *Cost Accounting: A Managerial Emphasis*, 5th ed. (1982), a popular textbook covering managerial accounting in depth.

(G.Sh.)

Aesthetics

Aesthetics (or esthetics) may be vaguely defined as the philosophical study of beauty and taste. To define its subject matter more precisely is, however, immensely difficult. Indeed, it could be said that self-definition has been the major task of modern aesthetics. We are acquainted with an interesting and puzzling realm of experience: the realm of the beautiful, the ugly, the sublime, and the elegant; of taste, criticism, and fine art; and of contemplation, sensuous enjoyment, and charm. In all these phenomena we believe that similar principles are operative and that similar interests are engaged. If we are mistaken in this impression, we will have to dismiss such ideas as beauty and taste as having only peripheral philosophical interest. Alternatively, if our impression is correct and philosophy corroborates it, we will have discovered the basis for a philosophical aesthetics.

This article seeks to clarify the nature of modern aesthetics and to delineate its underlying principles and concerns. Although the article focusses on Western aesthetic thought and its development, it surveys some of the seminal features of Marxist and Eastern aesthetics.

The article is divided into the following sections:

The nature and scope of aesthetics 9
  Three approaches to aesthetics 9
  The aesthetic recipient 10
  The aesthetic object 10
  The aesthetic experience 11
  The role of imagination 13
  Emotion, response, and enjoyment 14
The work of art 15
  Understanding art 15
  Representation, expression, and symbolism 15
  Form 16
  The ontology of art 17
  The value of art 18
Taste, criticism, and judgment 18
The development of Western aesthetics 20
  The contributions of the ancient Greeks 20
  Medieval aesthetics 20
  The origins of modern aesthetics 20
Marxist aesthetics 22
Eastern aesthetics 23
  India 23
  China 23
  Japan 23
Bibliography 23

THE NATURE AND SCOPE OF AESTHETICS

Aesthetics is broader in scope than the philosophy of art, which comprises one of its branches. It deals not only with the nature and value of the arts but also with those responses to natural objects that find expression in the language of the beautiful and the ugly. A problem is encountered at the outset, however, for terms such as beautiful and ugly seem too vague in their application and too subjective in their meaning to divide the world successfully into those things that do, and those that do not, exemplify them. Almost anything might be seen as beautiful by someone or from some point of view; and different people apply the word to quite disparate objects for reasons that often seem to have little or nothing in common. It may be that there is some single underlying belief that motivates all of their judgments. It may also be, however, that the term beautiful has no sense except as the expression of an attitude, which is in turn attached by different people to quite different states of affairs.

Moreover, in spite of the emphasis laid by philosophers on the terms beautiful and ugly, it is far from evident that they are the most important or most useful either in the discussion and criticism of art or in the description of that which appeals to us in nature. To convey what is significant in a poem we might use such terms as ironical, moving, expressive, balanced, and harmonious. Likewise, in describing a favourite stretch of countryside, we may find more use for peaceful, soft, atmospheric, harsh, and evocative, than for beautiful. The least that should be said is that beautiful belongs to a class of terms from which it has been chosen as much for convenience' sake as for any sense that it captures what is distinctive of the class.

At the same time, there seems to be no clear way of delimiting the class in question—not at least in advance of theory. Aesthetics must therefore cast its net more widely than the study either of beauty or of other aesthetic concepts if it is to discover the principles whereby it is to be defined. We are at once returned, therefore, to the vexing question of our subject matter: What should a philosopher study in order to understand such ideas as beauty and taste?

Problem of identifying subject of study

Three approaches to aesthetics. Three broad approaches have been proposed in answer to that question, each intuitively reasonable:

1. The study of the aesthetic concepts, or, more specifically, the analysis of the "language of criticism," in which particular judgments are singled out and their logic and justification displayed. In his famous treatise *On the Sublime and Beautiful* (1757), Edmund Burke attempted to draw a distinction between two aesthetic concepts, and, by studying the qualities that they denoted, to analyze the separate human attitudes that are directed toward them. Burke's distinction between the sublime and the beautiful was extremely influential, reflecting as it did the prevailing style of contemporary criticism. In more recent times, philosophers have tended to concentrate on the concepts of modern literary theory—namely, those such as representation, expression, form, style, and sentimentality. The study invariably has a dual purpose: to show how (if at all) these descriptions might be justified, and to show what is distinctive in the human experiences that are expressed in them.

2. A philosophical study of certain states of mind—responses, attitudes, emotions—that are held to be involved in aesthetic experience. Thus, in the seminal work of modern aesthetics *Kritik der Urteilskraft* (1790; *The Critique of Judgment*), Immanuel Kant located the distinctive features of the aesthetic in the faculty of "judgment," whereby we take up a certain stance toward objects, separating them from our scientific interests and our practical concerns. The key to the aesthetic realm lies therefore in a certain "disinterested" attitude, which we may assume toward any object and which can be expressed in many contrasting ways.

More recently, philosophers—distrustful of Kant's theory of the faculties—have tried to express the notions of an "aesthetic attitude" and "aesthetic experience" in other ways, relying upon developments in philosophical psychology that owe much to G.W.F. Hegel, the Phenomenologists, and Ludwig Wittgenstein (more precisely, the Wittgenstein of the *Philosophical Investigations* [1953]). In considering these theories (some of which are discussed below) a crucial distinction must be borne in mind: that between philosophy of mind and empirical psychology. Philosophy is not a science, because it does not investigate the causes of phenomena. It is an a priori or conceptual investigation, the underlying concern of which is to identify rather than to explain. In effect, the aim of the philosopher is to give the broadest possible description of the things themselves, so as to show how we must understand them and how we ought to value them. The two most prominent current philosophical methods—Phenomenology and conceptual analysis—tend to regard this aim as distinct from, and (at least in part) prior to, the aim of science. For how can we begin to explain what we have yet to identify? While there have been empirical studies of aesthetic experience (exercises in the psychology of beauty), these form no part of aesthetics as considered in this article. Indeed, the remarkable paucity of their conclusions may reasonably be attributed to their attempt to provide a theory of phenomena that have yet to be properly defined.

3. The philosophical study of the aesthetic object. This approach reflects the view that the problems of aesthetics exist primarily because the world contains a special class of objects toward which we react selectively and which we describe in aesthetic terms. In effect, the existence of such objects constitutes the prime phenomenon; aesthetic experience should thus be described according to them and the meaning of aesthetic concepts be determined by them. The usual class singled out as prime aesthetic objects is that comprising works of art. All other aesthetic objects (landscapes, faces, *objets trouvés*, and the like) tend to be included in this class only because, and to the extent that, they can be seen as art (or so it is claimed).

If we adopt such an approach, then there ceases to be a real distinction between aesthetics and the philosophy of art; and aesthetic concepts and aesthetic experience deserve their names through being, respectively, the concepts required in understanding works of art and the experience provoked by confronting them. Thus Hegel, perhaps the major philosophical influence on modern aesthetics, considered the main task of aesthetics to reside in the study of the various forms of art and of the spiritual content peculiar to each. Much of recent aesthetics has been similarly focussed on artistic problems, and it could be said that it is now orthodox to consider aesthetics entirely through the study of art.

The third approach to aesthetics does not require this concentration upon art. Even someone who considered art to be no more than one manifestation of aesthetic value—perhaps even a comparatively insignificant manifestation—may believe that the first concern of aesthetics is to study the objects of aesthetic experience and description and to find in them the true distinguishing features of the aesthetic realm. Unless we restrict the domain of aesthetic objects, however, it becomes extremely difficult to maintain that they have anything significant in common beyond the fact of inspiring a similar interest. This means that we should be compelled to adopt the second approach to aesthetics after all. And there seems no more plausible way of restricting the domain of aesthetic objects than through the concept of art.

The three approaches may lead to incompatible results. Alternatively, they may be in harmony. Once again, it can only be at the end point of our philosophy that we shall be able to decide. Initially, it must be assumed that the three approaches may differ substantially, or merely in emphasis, and thus that each question in aesthetics has a tripartite form.

The aesthetic recipient. Whichever approach we take, however, there is an all-important question upon the answer to which the course of aesthetics depends: the question of the recipient. Only beings of a certain kind have aesthetic interests and aesthetic experience, produce and appreciate art, employ such concepts as those of beauty, expression, and form. What is it that gives these beings access to this realm? The question is at least as old as Plato but received its most important modern exposition in the philosophy of Kant, who argued, first, that it is only rational beings who can exercise judgment—the faculty of aesthetic interest—and, second, that until exercised in aesthetic judgment rationality is incomplete. It is worth pausing to examine these two claims.

Kant's notion of judgment

Rational beings are those, like us, whose thought and conduct are guided by reason; who deliberate about what to believe and what to do; and who affect each other's beliefs and actions through argument and persuasion. Kant argued that reason has both a theoretical and a practical employment, and that a rational being finds both his conduct and his thought inspired and limited by reason. The guiding law of rational conduct is that of morality, enshrined in the categorical imperative, which enjoins us to act only on that maxim which we can at the same time will as a universal law.

By virtue of practical reason, the rational being sees himself and others of his kind as subject to an order that is not that of nature: he lives responsive to the law of reason and sees himself as a potential member of a "kingdom of ends" wherein the demands of reason are satisfied. Moreover, he looks on every rational being—himself included—as made sacrosanct by reason and by the morality that stems from it. The rational being, he recognizes, must be treated always as an end in himself, as something of intrinsic value, and never as a mere object to be disposed of according to purposes that are not its own.

The capacity to see things as intrinsically valuable, irreplaceable, or ends in themselves is one of the important gifts of reason. But it is not exercised only practically or only in our dealings with other reasoning beings. It may also be exercised contemplatively toward nature as a whole. In this case, practical considerations are held in abeyance, and we stand back from nature and look on it with a disinterested concern. Such an attitude is not only peculiar to rational beings but also necessary to them. Without it, they have only an impoverished grasp of their own significance and of their relation to the world in which they are situated through their thoughts and actions. This disinterested contemplation and the experiences that arise from it acquaint us, according to Kant, with the ultimate harmony that exists between the world and our faculties. They therefore provide the ultimate guarantee, both of practical reasoning and of the understanding, by intimating to us directly that the world answers to our purposes and corresponds to our beliefs.

Kant's conception of aesthetic experience

Disinterested contemplation forms, for Kant, the core of aesthetic experience and the ultimate ground of the judgment of beauty. He thus concludes (1) that only rational beings have aesthetic experience; (2) that every rational being needs aesthetic experience and is significantly incomplete without it; and (3) that aesthetic experience stands in fundamental proximity to moral judgment and is integral to our nature as moral beings.

Modern philosophers have sometimes followed Kant, sometimes ignored him. Rarely, however, have they set out to show that aesthetic experience is more widely distributed than the human race. For what could it mean to say of a cow, for example, that in staring at a landscape it is moved by the sentiment of beauty? What in a cow's behaviour or mental composition could manifest such a feeling? While a cow may be uninterested, it cannot surely be disinterested, in the manner of a rational being for whom disinterest is the most passionate form of interest. It is in pondering such considerations that one comes to realize just how deeply embedded in human nature is the aesthetic impulse, and how impossible it is to separate this impulse from the complex mental life that distinguishes human beings from beasts. This condition must be borne in mind by any philosopher seeking to confront the all-important question of the relation between the aesthetic and the moral.

The aesthetic object. The third approach to aesthetics begins with a class of aesthetic objects and attempts thereafter to show the significance of that class to those who selectively respond to it. The term aesthetic object, however, is ambiguous, and, depending on its interpretation, may suggest two separate programs of philosophical aesthetics.

Two types of objects

The expression may denote either the "intentional" or the "material" object of aesthetic experience. This distinction, a legacy of the Scholastic philosophers of the Middle Ages, has played a major role in recent Phenomenology. It may be briefly characterized as follows: When someone responds to object *O*, his response depends upon a conception of *O* that may, in fact, be erroneous. *O* is then the material object of his response, while his conception defines the intentional object. (The term intentional comes from the Latin *intendere*, "to aim.") To cite an example: A person is frightened by a white cloth flapping in a darkened hall, taking it for a ghost. Here, the material object of the fear is the cloth, while the intentional object is a ghost. A philosophical discussion of fear may be presented as a discussion of things feared, but if so, the phrase denotes the class of intentional objects of fear and not the (infinitely varied and infinitely disordered) class of material objects. In an important sense, the intentional object is part of a state of mind, whereas the material object always has independent (and objective) existence. If the expression "aesthetic object" is, therefore, taken in its intentional construction, the study of the aesthetic object becomes the study, not of an independently existing class of things, but of the aesthetic experience itself. It is in this sense that the term occurs in the writings of Phenomenologists (*e.g.,* Mikel Dufrenne, *La Phénoménologie de l'expérience esthétique* [1953; *The Phenomenology of Aesthetic Experience*] and Roman Ingarden, *Das literarische Kunstwerk* [1931; *The Literary Work of Art*]), whose studies of the aesthetic object exemplify not the third, but the second, of the approaches considered above.

Which of those two approaches should be adopted? We can already see one reason for adopting the approach that puts the aesthetic experience first and examines the aesthetic object primarily as the intentional object of that experience. It is, after all, to experience that we must turn if we are to understand the value of the aesthetic realm—our reason for engaging with it, studying it, and adding to it. Until we understand that value, we will not know why we ought to construct such a concept as the aesthetic, still less why we should erect a whole branch of philosophy devoted to its analysis.

A further reason also suggests itself for rejecting the approach to aesthetics that sees it merely as the philosophy of art, because art, and the institutions that sustain it, are mutable and perhaps inessential features of the human condition. While we classify together such separate art forms as poetry, the novel, music, drama, painting, sculpture, and architecture, our disposition to do so is as much the consequence of philosophical theory as its premise. Would other people at other times and in other conditions have countenanced such a classification or seen its point? And if so, would they have been motivated by similar purposes, similar observations, and similar beliefs? We might reasonably be skeptical, for while there have been many attempts to find something in common—if only a "family resemblance"—between the various currently accepted art forms, they have all been both contentious in themselves and of little aesthetic interest. Considered materially (*i.e.,* without reference to the experiences that we direct to them), the arts seem to have little in common except for those properties that are either too uninteresting to deserve philosophical scrutiny (the property, for example, of being artifacts) or else too vast and vague to be independently intelligible.

Consider the theory of Clive Bell (*Art,* 1914) that art is distinguished by its character as "significant form." Initially attractive, the suggestion crumbles at once before the skeptic. When is form "significant"? The only answer to be extracted from Bell is this: "when it is art." In effect, the theory reduces to a tautology. In any normal understanding of the words, a traffic warden is a significant form, at least to the motorist who sees himself about to receive a ticket. Thus, to explain Bell's meaning, it is necessary to restrict the term significant to the significance (whatever that is) of art.

Moreover, it is of the greatest philosophical importance to attend not only to the resemblances between the art forms but also to their differences. It is true that almost anything can be seen from some point of view as beautiful. At the same time, however, our experience of beauty crucially depends upon a knowledge of the object in which beauty is seen. It is absurd to suppose that I could present you with an object that might be a stone, a sculpture, a box, a fruit, or an animal, and expect you to tell me whether it is beautiful before knowing what it is. In general we may say—in opposition to a certain tradition in aesthetics that finds expression in Kant's theory—that our sense of beauty is always dependent upon a conception of the object in the way that our sense of the beauty of the human figure is dependent upon a conception of that figure. Features that we should regard as beautiful in a horse—developed haunches, curved back, and so on—we should regard as ugly in a man, and those aesthetic judgments would be determined by our conception of what men and horses generally are, how they move, and what they achieve through their movements. In a similar way, features that are beautiful in a sculpture may not be beautiful in a work of architecture, where an idea of function seems to govern our perceptions. In every case, our perception of the beauty of a work of art requires us to be aware of the distinctive character of each art form and to put out of mind, as largely irrelevant to our concerns, the overarching category of art to which all supposedly belong. But if that is so, it is difficult to see how we could cast light upon the realm of aesthetic interest by studying the concept of art.

Factors involved in the perception of beauty

Whether or not that concept is a recent invention, it is certainly a recent obsession. Medieval and Renaissance philosophers who approached the problems of beauty and taste—*e.g.,* St. Thomas Aquinas, Peter Abelard, and even Leon Battista Alberti—often wrote of beauty without reference to art, taking as their principal example the human face and body. The distinctively modern approach to aesthetics began to take shape during the 18th century, with the writings on art of Jean-Jacques Rousseau, Charles Batteux, and Johann Winckelmann and the theories of taste proposed by the 3rd Earl of Shaftesbury, Francis Hutcheson, Lord Kames (Henry Home), and Archibald Alison. This approach materialized not only because of a growing interest in fine art as a uniquely human phenomenon but also because of the awakening of feelings toward nature, which marked the dawn of the Romantic movement. In Kant's aesthetics, indeed, nature has pride of place as offering the only examples of what he calls "free beauty"—*i.e.,* beauty that can be appreciated without the intermediary of any polluting concept. Art, for Kant, was not merely one among many objects of aesthetic interest; it was also fatally flawed in its dependence upon intellectual understanding.

Even without taking that extreme position, it is difficult to accept that the fragile and historically determined concept of art can bear the weight of a full aesthetic theory. Leaving aside the case of natural beauty, we must still recognize the existence of a host of human activities (dress, decoration, manners, ornament) in which taste is of the essence and yet which seems totally removed from the world of fine art. It has been common, following the lead of Batteux, to make a distinction between the fine and the useful arts, and to accommodate the activities just referred to under the latter description; but it is clear that this is no more than a gesture and that the points of similarity between the art of the dressmaker and that of the composer are of significance only because of a similarity in the interests that these arts are meant to satisfy.

The aesthetic experience. Such considerations point toward the aforementioned approach that begins with the aesthetic experience as the most likely to capture the full range of aesthetic phenomena without begging the important philosophical questions about their nature. Can we then single out a faculty, an attitude, a mode of judgment, or a form of experience that is distinctively aesthetic? And if so, can we attribute to it the significance that would make this philosophical enterprise both important in itself and relevant to the many questions posed by beauty, criticism, and art?

Taking their cue from Kant, many philosophers have defended the idea of an aesthetic attitude as one divorced from practical concerns, a kind of "distancing," or standing back, as it were, from ordinary involvement. The classic statement of this position is Edward Bullough's "'Psychical Distance' as a Factor in Art and an Aesthetic Principle," an essay published in the *British Journal of Psychology* in 1912. While there is certainly something of interest to be said along those lines, it cannot be the whole story. Just what kind of distance is envisaged? Is the lover distanced from his beloved? If not, by what right

The notion of distance

does he call her beautiful? Does distance imply a lack of practical involvement? If such is the case, how can we ever take up an aesthetic attitude to those things that have a purpose for us—things such as a dress, building, or decoration? But if these are not aesthetic, have we not paid a rather high price for our definition of this word—the price of detaching it from the phenomena that it was designed to identify?

Kant's own formulation was more satisfactory. He described the recipient of aesthetic experience not as distanced but as disinterested, meaning that the recipient does not treat the object of enjoyment either as a vehicle for curiosity or as a means to an end. He contemplates the object as it is in itself and "apart from all interest." In a similar spirit, Arthur Schopenhauer argued that a person could regard anything aesthetically so long as he regarded it in independence of his will—that is, irrespective of any use to which he might put it. Regarding it thus, a person could come to see the Idea that the object expressed, and in this knowledge consists aesthetic appreciation (*Die Welt als Wille und Vorstellung* [1819; *The World as Will and Idea*]).

Art as play

Of a piece with such a view is the popular theory of art as a kind of "play" activity, in which creation and appreciation are divorced from the normal urgencies of existence and surrendered to leisure. "With the agreeable, the good, the perfect," wrote Friedrich Schiller, "man is merely in earnest, but with beauty he plays" (*Briefe über die ästhetische Erziehung des Menschen* [1794–95; *Letters on the Aesthetic Education of Man*]).

Such thoughts have already been encountered. The problem is to give them philosophical precision. They have recurred in modern philosophy in a variety of forms—for example, in the theory that the aesthetic object is always considered for its own sake, or as a unique individual rather than a member of a class. Those particular formulations have caused some philosophers to treat aesthetic objects as though they were endowed with a peculiar metaphysical status (see below *The work of art*). Alternatively, it is sometimes argued that the aesthetic experience has an intuitive character, as opposed to the conceptual character of scientific thought or the instrumental character of practical understanding.

The simplest way of summarizing this approach to aesthetics is in terms of two fundamental propositions:

1. The aesthetic object is an object of sensory experience and enjoyed as such: it is heard, seen, or (in the limiting case) imagined in sensory form.

2. The aesthetic object is at the same time contemplated: its appearance is a matter of intrinsic interest and studied not merely as an object of sensory pleasure but also as the repository of significance and value.

The first of these propositions explains the word aesthetic, which was initially used in this connection by the Leibnizian philosopher Alexander Baumgarten in *Meditationes Philosophicae de Nonnullis ad Poema Pertinentibus* (1735; *Reflections on Poetry*). Baumgarten borrowed the Greek term for sensory perception (*aisthēsis*) in order to denote a realm of concrete knowledge (the realm, as he saw it, of poetry), in which a content is communicated in sensory form. The second proposition is, in essence, the foundation of taste. It describes the motive of our attempt to discriminate rationally between those objects that are worthy of contemplative attention and those that are not.

Almost all of the aesthetic theories of post-Kantian Idealism depend upon those two propositions and try to explain the peculiarities of aesthetic experience and aesthetic judgment in terms of the synthesis of the sensory and the intellectual that they imply—the synthesis summarized in Hegel's theory of art as "the sensuous embodiment of the Idea." Neither proposition is particularly clear. Throughout the discussions of Kant and his immediate following, the "sensory" is assimilated to the "concrete," the "individual," the "particular," and the "determinate," while the "intellectual" is assimilated to the "abstract," the "universal," the "general," and the "indeterminate"—assimilations that would nowadays be regarded with extreme suspicion. Nevertheless, subsequent theories have repeatedly returned to the idea that aesthetic experience involves a special synthesis of intellectual and sensory components, and that both its peculiarities and its value are to be derived from such a synthesis.

Antinomy of taste

The idea at once gives rise to paradoxes. The most important was noticed by Kant, who called it the antinomy of taste. As an exercise of reason, he argued, aesthetic experience must inevitably tend toward a reasoned choice and therefore must formulate itself as a judgment. Aesthetic judgment, however, seems to be in conflict with itself. It cannot be at the same time aesthetic (an expression of sensory enjoyment) and also a judgment (claiming universal assent). Yet all rational beings, by virtue of their rationality, seem disposed to make these judgments. On the one hand, they feel pleasure in some object, and this pleasure is immediate, not based, according to Kant, in any conceptualization or in any inquiry into cause, purpose, or constitution. On the other hand, they express their pleasure in the form of a judgment, speaking "as if beauty were a quality of the object," and so representing their pleasure as objectively valid. But how can this be so? The pleasure is immediate, based in no reasoning or analysis. So what permits this demand for universal agreement?

However we approach the idea of beauty, we find this paradox emerging. Our ideas, feelings, and judgments are called aesthetic precisely because of their direct relation to sensory enjoyment. Hence, no one can judge the beauty of an object that he has never encountered. Scientific judgments, like practical principles, can be received "second hand." I can, for example, take you as my authority for the truths of physics or for the utility of railways. But I cannot take you as my authority for the merits of Leonardo or Mozart if I have not seen or heard works by either artist. It would seem to follow from this that there can be no rules or principles of aesthetic judgment, since I must feel the pleasure immediately in the perception of the object and cannot be talked into it by any grounds of proof. It is always experience, and never conceptual thought, that gives the right to aesthetic judgment, so that anything that alters the experience of an object alters its aesthetic significance as well. As Kant put it, aesthetic judgment is "free from concepts," and beauty itself is not a concept.

Such a conclusion, however, seems to be inconsistent with the fact that aesthetic judgment is a form of judgment. When I describe something as beautiful, I do not mean merely that it pleases me: I am speaking about it, not about myself, and, if challenged, I try to find reasons for my view. I do not explain my feeling but give grounds for it by pointing to features of its object. Any search for reasons has the "universalizing" character of rationality: I am in effect saying that others, insofar as they are rational, ought to feel exactly the same delight as I feel. Being disinterested, I have put aside my interests, and with them everything that makes my judgment relative to me. But, if that is so, then "the judgment of taste is based on concepts, for otherwise there could be no room even for contention in the matter, or for the claim to the necessary agreement of others."

In short, the expression aesthetic judgment seems to be a contradiction in terms, denying in the first term precisely that reference to rational considerations that it affirms in the second. This paradox, which we have expressed in Kant's language, is not peculiar to the philosophy of Kant. On the contrary, it is encountered in one form or another by every philosopher or critic who takes aesthetic experience seriously, and who therefore recognizes the tension between the sensory and the intellectual constraints upon it. On the one hand, aesthetic experience is rooted in the immediate sensory enjoyment of its object through an act of perception. On the other, it seems to reach beyond enjoyment toward a meaning that is addressed to our reasoning powers and that seeks judgment from them. Thus criticism, the reasoned justification of aesthetic judgment, is an inevitable upshot of aesthetic experience. Yet, critical reasons can never be merely intellectual; they always contain a reference to the way in which an object is perceived.

Two related paradoxes also emerge from the same basic conception of the aesthetic experience. The first was given extended consideration by Hegel, who argued, in his *Vorlesungen über die Aesthetik* (1832; "Lectures on

Aesthetics"; Eng. trans., *Philosophy of Fine Art*), roughly as follows: Our sensuous appreciation of art concentrates upon the given "appearance"—the "form." It is this that holds our attention and that gives to the work of art its peculiar individuality. Because it addresses itself to our sensory appreciation, the work of art is essentially concrete, to be understood by an act of perception rather than by a process of discursive thought. At the same time, our understanding of the work of art is in part intellectual; we seek in it a conceptual content, which it presents to us in the form of an idea. One purpose of critical interpretation is to expound this idea in discursive form—to give the equivalent of the content of the work of art in another, nonsensuous idiom. But criticism can never succeed in this task, for, by separating the content from the particular form, it abolishes its individuality. The content presented then ceases to be the exact content of that work of art. In losing its individuality, the content loses its aesthetic reality; it thus ceases to be a reason for attending to the particular work of art that first attracted our critical attention. It cannot be this that we saw in the original work and that explained its power over us. For this content, displayed in the discursive idiom of the critical intellect, is no more than a husk, a discarded relic of a meaning that eluded us in the act of seizing it. If the content is to be the true object of aesthetic interest, it must remain wedded to its individuality: it cannot be detached from its "sensuous embodiment" without being detached from itself. Content is, therefore, inseparable from form and form in turn inseparable from content. (It is the form that it is only by virtue of the content that it embodies.)

Hegel's conception of form

Relationship between form and content

Hegel's argument is the archetype of many, all aimed at showing that it is both necessary to distinguish form from content and also impossible to do so. This paradox may be resolved by rejecting either of its premises, but, as with Kant's antinomy, neither premise seems dispensible. To suppose that content and form are inseparable is, in effect, to dismiss both ideas as illusory, since no two works of art can then share either a content or a form—the form being definitive of each work's individuality. In this case, no one could ever justify his interest in a work of art by reference to its meaning. The intensity of aesthetic interest becomes a puzzling, and ultimately inexplicable, feature of our mental life. If, on the other hand, we insist that content and form are separable, we shall never be able to find, through a study of content, the reason for attending to the particular work of art that intrigues us. Every work of art stands proxy for its paraphrase. An impassable gap then opens between aesthetic experience and its ground, and the claim that aesthetic experience is intrinsically valuable is thrown in doubt.

The "heresy of paraphrase"

A related paradox is sometimes referred to as the "heresy of paraphrase," the words being those of the U.S. literary critic Cleanth Brooks (*The Well Wrought Urn*, 1949). The heresy is that of assuming that the meaning of a work of art (particularly of poetry) can be paraphrased. According to Brooks, who here followed an argument of Benedetto Croce, the meaning of a poem consists precisely in what is not translatable. Poetic meaning is bound up with the particular disposition of the words—their sound, rhythm, and arrangement—in short, with the "sensory embodiment" provided by the poem itself. To alter that embodiment is to produce either another poem (and therefore another meaning) or something that is not a work of art at all, and which therefore lacks completely the kind of meaning for which works of art are valued. Hence no poetry is translatable, and no critic can do better than to point to the objective features of the poem that most seem to him to be worthy of attention. Yet, that result too is paradoxical. For what does the critic see in those objective features and how is his recommendation to be supported? Why should we attend to poetry at all if nothing can be said about its virtues save only "look!"? Why look at a poem rather than an advertisement, a mirror, or a blade of grass? Everything becomes equally worthy of attention, since nothing can be said that will justify attention to anything.

The role of imagination. Such paradoxes suggest the need for a more extensive theory of the mind than has been so far assumed. We have referred somewhat loosely to the sensory and intellectual components of human experience but have said little about the possible relations and dependencies that exist between them. Perhaps, therefore, the paradoxes result only from our impoverished description of the human mind and are not intrinsic to the subject matter of aesthetic interest.

Many modern philosophers have at this point felt the need to invoke imagination, either as a distinct mental "faculty" (Kant) or as a distinctive mental operation by virtue of which thought and experience may be united. For Empiricist philosophers (such as David Hume, Joseph Addison, Archibald Alison, and Lord Kames), imagination involves a kind of "associative" process, whereby experiences evoke ideas, and so become united with them. For Kant and Hegel, imagination is not associative but constitutive—part of the nature of the experience that expresses it.

Once again it is useful to begin from Kant, who distinguished two uses of the imagination: the first in ordinary thought and perception, the second in aesthetic experience. When I look before me and see a book, my experience, according to Kant, embodies a "synthesis." It contains two elements: the "intuition" presented to the senses and the "concept" ("book"), contributed by the understanding. The two elements are synthesized by an act of the imagination that constitutes them as a single experience—the experience of seeing a book. Here imagination remains bound by the concepts of the understanding, which is to say that how I see the world depends upon my disposition to form determinate beliefs about it—in this case, the belief that there is a book before me. In aesthetic experience, however, imagination is free from concepts and engages in a kind of free play. This free play of the imagination enables me to bring concepts to bear on an experience that is, in itself, free from concepts. Thus there are two separate ways in which the content of experience is provided: one in ordinary perception, the other in aesthetic experience. In both cases the operative factor, in holding thought and sensation together, is the imagination.

Whether such theories can cast light on the mysterious unity between the intellectual and the sensory that we observe in aesthetic experience remains doubtful. The argument for saying that there is a single process of imagination involved in all perception, imagery, and remembering seems to consist only in the premise (undoubtedly true) that in these mental processes thought and experience are often inseparable. But to suppose therefore that there is some one "faculty" involved in forging the connection between them is to fail to take seriously the fact that they are inseparable.

Nevertheless, even if we find this general invocation of imagination, as the "synthesizing force" within perception, vacuous or unilluminating, we may yet feel that the imagination has some special role to play in aesthetic experience and that the reference to imagination has some special value in explaining the precise way in which a content and an experience become "fused" (to use George Santayana's term). Whether or not Kant was right to refer to a free play of imagination in aesthetic experience, there certainly seems to be a peculiarly creative imagination that human beings may exercise and upon which aesthetic experience calls. It is an exercise of creative imagination to see a face in a picture, since that involves seeing in defiance of judgment—seeing what one knows not to be there. It is not in the same sense an imaginative act to see a face in something that one also judges to *be* a face. This creative capacity is what Jean-Paul Sartre is referring to in *L'Imaginaire: Psychologie phénoménologique de l'imagination* (1940; "The Imaginary: The Phenomenological Psychology of the Imagination"; Eng. trans., *The Psychology of Imagination*) when he describes imagining as "the positing of an object as a nothingness"—as not being. In memory and perception we take our experience "for real." In imagination we contribute a content that has no reality beyond our disposition to "see" it, and it is clear that this added content is frequently summoned by art when, for example, we see the face in a picture or hear the emotion in a piece of music.

Creative imagination

Recent work in aesthetics, to some extent inspired by the

seminal writings of Sartre and Wittgenstein, has devoted considerable attention to the study of creative imagination. The hope has been to provide the extra ingredient in aesthetic experience that bridges the gap between the sensory and the intellectual and at the same time shows the relation between aesthetic experience and the experience of everyday life—an enterprise that is in turn of the first importance for any study that seeks to describe the moral significance of beauty.

Consider, for example, the spectator at Shakespeare's *King Lear*. He sees before him an actor who, by speaking certain lines and making certain gestures, earns his bread. But that is not all that he sees. He also sees a hoary king, cast down by age, pride, and weakness, who rages against the depravity of man. Yet the spectator knows that, in a crucial sense, there is no such king before him. It is intellectual understanding, not psychical distance, that prevents him from stepping onto the stage to offer his assistance. He knows that the scene he enjoys is one that he contributes, albeit under the overwhelming compulsion induced by the actor and his lines. The spectator is being shown something that is outside the normal commerce of theoretical and practical understanding, and he is responding to a scene that bears no spatial, temporal, or causal relation to his own experience. His response is quintessentially aesthetic. For what interest could he have in this scene other than an interest in it for its own sake, for what it is in itself? At the same time, what it is in itself involves what it shows in general. In imaginatively conjuring this scene the spectator draws upon a wealth of experience, which is brought to mind and, as it were, condensed for him into the imaginative perception of the play. (Hence, Aristotle believed poetry is more general than history, since its concreteness is not that of real events, but rather of imaginary episodes constructed so as to typify human destiny in exemplary representations.)

Such an exercise of the imagination clearly has much to tell us about the nature of aesthetic experience. Whether or not it could found a theory of the "missing link" between sensory enjoyment and intellectual understanding, it at least provides a paradigm of the relation between aesthetic experience and the experience of everyday life. The former is an imaginative reconstruction of the latter, which becomes interesting for its own sake precisely because—however realistic—it is not real.

Emotion, response, and enjoyment. It is natural to suppose that a spectator's response to *King Lear* is at least in part emotional, and that emotion plays a crucial role both in the enjoyment of art and in establishing the value of art. Moreover, it is not only art that stirs our emotions in the act of aesthetic attention: the same is or may be true of natural beauty whether that of a face or of a landscape. These things hold our attention partly because they address themselves to our feelings and call forth a response which we value both for itself and for the consolation that we may attain through it. Thus we find an important philosophical tradition according to which the distinctive character of aesthetic experience is to be found in distinctively "aesthetic" emotions.

This tradition has ancient origins. Plato banished the poets from his ideal republic partly because of their capacity to arouse futile and destructive emotions, and in his answer to Plato, Aristotle argued that poetry, in particular tragic poetry, was valuable precisely because of its emotional effect. This idea enabled Aristotle to pose one of the most puzzling problems in aesthetics—the problem of tragedy—and to offer a solution. How can I willingly offer myself to witness scenes of terror and destruction? And how can I be said to enjoy the result, set store by it, or accord to it a positive value? Aristotle's answer is brief. He explains that by evoking pity and fear a tragedy also "purges" those emotions, and that is what we enjoy and value:

Aristotle's interpretation of tragedy

> Tragedy, then, is an imitation of an action that is serious, complete, and of a certain magnitude; in language embellished with each kind of artistic ornament, the several kinds being found in separate parts of the play; in the form of action, not of narrative; through pity and fear effecting the proper purgation of these emotions.

Aristotle implies that this purgation (*katharsis*) is not unpleasant to us precisely because the fictional and formalized nature of the action sets it at a distance from us. We can allow ourselves to feel what we normally shun to feel precisely because no one is really threatened (or at least no one real is threatened).

Attractive though that explanation may seem, it immediately encounters a serious philosophical problem. It is a plausible tenet of philosophical psychology that emotions are founded on beliefs: fear on the belief that one is threatened, pity on the belief that someone is miserable, jealousy on the belief that one has a rival, and so forth. In the nature of things, however, these beliefs do not exist in the theatre. Confronted by fiction, I am relieved precisely of the pressure of belief, and it is this condition that permits the Aristotelian *katharsis*. How, then, can I be said to experience pity and fear when the beliefs requisite to those very emotions are not present? More generally, how can my responses to the fictions presented by works of art share the structure of my everyday emotions, and how can they impart to those emotions a new meaning, force, or resolution?

Various answers have been proposed to that question. Samuel Taylor Coleridge, for example, argued that our response to drama is characterized by a "willing suspension of disbelief," and thus involves the very same ingredient of belief that is essential to everyday emotion (*Biographia Literaria,* 1817). Coleridge's phrase, however, is consciously paradoxical. Belief is characterized precisely by the fact that it lies outside the will: I can command you to imagine something but not to believe it. For this reason, a suspension of disbelief that is achieved "willingly" is at best a highly dubious example of belief. In fact, the description seems to imply, not belief, but rather imagination, thus returning us to our problem of the relation between emotions directed to reality and those directed to merely imaginary scenes.

The relation between aesthetic and everyday experience

This is part of a much larger problem—namely, that of the relation between aesthetic and everyday experience. Two extreme positions serve to illustrate this problem. According to one, art and nature appeal primarily to our emotions: they awaken within us feelings of sympathy, or emotional associations, which are both pleasant in themselves and also instructive. We are made familiar with emotional possibilities, and, through this imaginative exercise, our responses to the world become illuminated and refined. This view, which provides an immediate and satisfying theory of the value of aesthetic experience, has been espoused in some form or other by many of the classical British Empiricists (Shaftesbury, Hume, Addison, Lord Kames, Alison, and Burke, to cite only a few). It is also related to the critical theories of writers such as Coleridge, Matthew Arnold, and F.R. Leavis, whose criticism would make little or no sense without the supposition that works of art have the power to correct and corrupt our emotions.

According to the opposite view, aesthetic interest, because it focusses on an object for its own sake, can involve no interest in "affect." To be interested in a work of art for the sake of emotion is to be interested in it as a means and, therefore, not aesthetically. In other words, true aesthetic interest is autonomous, standing outside the current of ordinary human feeling—an attitude of pure contemplation or pure "intuition" that isolates its object from the stream of common events and perceives it in its uniqueness, detached, unexplained, and inexplicable. This position has been taken in modern times by Benedetto Croce and, following him, by R.G. Collingwood, whose resolute defense of the autonomy of aesthetic experience was also associated with a theory of the autonomy of art. Art is not only seen as an end in itself but it is an end in itself, in a profound and significant sense that distinguishes art from all its false substitutes (and, in particular, from craft, which for Collingwood is not an end but merely a means).

Collingwood's defense of the autonomy of aesthetic experience

Between those two poles, a variety of intermediate positions might be adopted. It is clear, in any case, that many questions have been begged by both sides. The aesthetic of sympathy, as Croce called it, has enormous difficulties in describing the emotions that are awakened in aesthetic experience, particularly the emotions that we are supposed to feel in response to such abstract arts as music. With what am I sympathizing when I listen to a string quartet or a symphony? What emotion do I feel? Moreover, the position encounters all the difficulties already noted in forging a link between the imaginary and the real.

The aesthetic of autonomy, as we may call it, encounters complementary difficulties and, in particular, the difficulty of showing why we should value either aesthetic experience itself or the art that is its characteristic object. Moreover, it assumes that whenever I take an emotional interest in something, I am interested in it for the sake of emotion, a false inference that would imply equally that the lover is interested only in his love or the angry man only in his anger. Collingwood thus dismisses "amusement art," on the spurious ground that to be interested in a work of art for the sake of amusement is to be interested not in the work but only in the amusement that it inspires. That is to say, it is to treat the work as a means to feeling rather than as an end in itself. Such a conclusion is entirely unwarranted. Amusement is, in fact, a species of interest in something for its own sake: I laugh not for the sake of laughter, but for the sake of the joke. While I may be interested in an object for the sake of the emotion that it arouses, the case is peculiar—the case, in fact, of sentimentality, often dismissed by moralists as a spiritual corruption and equally by critics as a corruption of the aims of art.

The difficulties for both views are brought out by a fundamental aesthetic category: that of enjoyment. Whatever the ultimate value of aesthetic experience, we pursue it in the first instance for enjoyment's sake. Aesthetic experience includes, as its central instance, a certain kind of pleasure. But what kind of pleasure? While our emotions and sympathies are sometimes pleasurable, this is by no means their essential feature; they may equally be painful or neutral. How then does the aesthetic of sympathy explain the pleasure that we take, and must take, in the object of aesthetic experience? And how does the aesthetic of autonomy avoid the conclusion that all such pleasure is a violation of its strict requirement that we should be interested in the aesthetic object for its own sake alone? Neither theory seems to be equipped, as it stands, either to describe this pleasure or to show its place in the appreciation of art.

THE WORK OF ART

As the above discussion illustrates, it is impossible to advance far into the theory of aesthetic experience without encountering the specific problems posed by the experience of art. Whether or not we think of art as the central or defining example of the aesthetic object, there is no doubt that it provides the most distinctive illustration both of the elusive nature and the importance of aesthetic interest. With the increasing attention paid to art in a corrupted world where little else is commonly held to be spiritually significant, it is not surprising that the philosophy of art has increasingly begun to displace the philosophy of natural beauty from the central position accorded to the latter by the philosophers and critics of the 18th century. Nor is this shift in emphasis to be regretted; for the existence of art as a major human institution reminds us of the need for a theory that will attribute more to aesthetic experience than enjoyment and that will explain the profundity of the impressions that we receive from beauty—impressions that may provide both meaning and solace to those who experience them. It is thus worth reviewing some of the special problems in the philosophy of art that have most influenced contemporary aesthetics.

Emphasis on the philosophy of art

Understanding art. The use of the concept of understanding in describing the appreciation of art marks out an interesting distinction between art and natural beauty. A person may understand or fail to understand T.S. Eliot's *Four Quartets,* Michelangelo's "David," or Beethoven's *Ninth Symphony,* but he cannot understand or fail to understand the Highlands of Scotland, even when he finds them beautiful or ugly. Understanding seems to be a prerequisite to the full experience of art, and this has suggested to many critics and philosophers that art is not so much an object of sensory experience as an instrument of knowledge. In particular, art seems to have the power both to represent reality and to express emotion, and some argue that it is through appreciating the properties of representation and expression that we recognize the meaning of art. At least, it might be supposed that, if we speak of understanding art, it is because we think of art as having content, something that must be understood by the appropriate audience.

The most popular approach to this concept of understanding is through a theory of art as a form of symbolism. But what is meant by this? Is such symbolism one thing or many? Is it a matter of evocation or convention, of personal response or linguistic rule? And what does art symbolize—ideas, feelings, objects, or states of affairs?

Representation, expression, and symbolism. Various theories have been proposed in answer to these questions, the most popular being that the forms of art are similar to language and are to be understood as language is understood, in terms of conventions and semantic rules. A few examples of contemporary theories that have described art in this way include Ernst Cassirer's philosophy of symbolic forms, Susanne K. Langer's theory of presentational symbols, and the works on semiology and semiotics, largely inspired by the writings of Roland Barthes, that have been fashionable in continental Europe. It seems important to review some of the arguments that have been employed both for and against the overall conception of art that such theories share.

In favour of the view, it is undeniable that many works of art are about the world in somewhat the way that language may be about the world. This is evident in the case of literature (which is itself an instance of natural language). It is no less evident in the case of painting. A portrait stands to its sitter in a relation that is not unlike that which obtains between a description and the thing described. Even if the majority of pictures are of, or about, entirely imaginary people, scenes, and episodes, this is no different from the case of literature, in which language is used to describe purely imaginary subjects. This relation between a work of art and its subject, captured in the word "about," is sometimes called representation—a term that owes its currency in aesthetics to Croce and Collingwood, who used it to draw the familiar contrast between representation and expression.

Expression in art

The concept of expression is variously analyzed. Its principal function in modern aesthetics, however, is to describe those aspects and dimensions of artistic meaning that seem not to fall within the bounds of representation, either because they involve no clear reference to an independent subject matter or because the connection between the subject and the artistic form is too close and inextricable to admit description in the terms appropriate to representation. Therefore, it is widely recognized that abstract art forms—music, abstract painting, architecture—may yet contain meaningful utterances, and most frequently philosophers and critics use terms such as expression in order to describe these elusive meanings. Music, in particular, is often said to be an expression of emotion and to gain much of its significance from that. Expression in such a case is unlike representation, according to many philosophers, in that it involves no descriptive component. An expression of grief does not describe grief but rather presents it, as it might be presented by a face or a gesture.

Expression must be distinguished from evocation. To say that a piece of music expresses melancholy is not to say that it evokes (arouses) melancholy. To describe a piece of music as expressive of melancholy is to give a reason for listening to it; to describe it as arousing melancholy is to give a reason for avoiding it. (Music that is utterly blank expresses nothing, but it may arouse melancholy.) Expression, where it exists, is integral to the aesthetic character and merit of whatever possesses it. For similar reasons, expression must not be confused with association, in spite of the reliance on the confusion by many 18th-century Empiricists.

The distinction between representation and expression is one of the most important conceptual devices in contem-

Distinction between representation and expression

porary philosophy of art. Croce, who introduced it, sought to dismiss representation as aesthetically irrelevant and to elevate expression into the single, true aesthetic function. The first, he argued, is descriptive, or conceptual, concerned with classifying objects according to their common properties, and so done to satisfy our curiosity. The second, by contrast, is intuitive, concerned with presenting its subject matter (an "intuition") in its immediate concrete reality, so that we see it as it is in itself. In understanding expression, our attitude passes from mere curiosity to that immediate awareness of the concrete particular that is the core of aesthetic experience.

Later philosophers have been content merely to distinguish representation and expression as different modes of artistic meaning, characterized perhaps by different formal or semantic properties. Nelson Goodman of the United States is one such philosopher. His *Languages of Art* (1968) was the first work of analytical philosophy to produce a distinct and systematic theory of art. Goodman's theory has attracted considerable attention, the more so in that it is an extension of a general philosophical perspective, expounded in works of great rigour and finesse, that embraces the entire realm of logic, metaphysics, and the philosophy of science.

Goodman's theory of symbolism

Goodman, like many others, seeks the nature of art in symbolism and the nature of symbolism in a general theory of signs. (This second part of Goodman's aim is what Ferdinand de Saussure called semiology, the general science of signs [*Cours de linguistique générale,* 1916; *Course of General Linguistics*]). The theory derives from the uncompromising Nominalism expounded in Goodman's earlier works, a Nominalism developed under the influence of two other U.S. philosophers, Rudolf Carnap and W.V. Quine, but also showing certain affinities with the later philosophy of Wittgenstein. According to Goodman's general theory of signs, the relation between signs and the world can be described, like any relation, in terms of its formal structure, the objects related, and its genealogy. But, apart from that formal and factual analysis, there is nothing to be said. Words are labels that we attach to things, but the attempt to justify that practice merely repeats it: in using words, it presupposes precisely the justification that it aims to provide.

A corollary of this view is that relations of identical logical structure and identical genealogy between relevantly similar terms are really one and the same relation. Thus, if we assume that paintings, like words, are signs, then portraits stand to their subjects in the same relation as proper names to the objects denoted by them. (This is the substance of Goodman's proof that representation is a species of denotation.) We should not worry if that leads us to no new understanding of the relation (*e.g.,* if it leads to no procedure for decoding the painted sign), for Goodman believes the search for such procedure is incoherent. The meaning of a sign is simply given, along with the artistic practice that creates it.

Goodman proceeds to generalize his theory of symbolism, using the word reference to express the relation between word and thing. (We might well characterize this relation as labelling.) Denotation is the special case of reference exemplified by proper names and portraits—a case in which a symbol labels one individual. When a single label picks out many things, then we have not a name but a predicate.

Sometimes the process of labelling goes both ways. A colour sample is a sign for the colour it possesses—say, the colour red. It therefore refers to the label red, which in turn refers back to the sample. In this case, the predicate red and the sample mutually label each other. Goodman calls this relation exemplification, and analyzes expression as a special case of it—namely, the case where the exemplification of a predicate proceeds by metaphor. For example, a piece of music may refer to sadness; it may also be metaphorically sad. In this case, Goodman argues, we may speak of the music as expressing sadness.

The economy and elegance of Goodman's theory are matched by its extreme inscrutability. On the surface it seems to provide direct and intelligible answers to all the major problems of art. What is art? A system of symbols. What is representation? Denotation. What is expression? A kind of reference. What is the value of art? It symbolizes (displays) reality. What is the distinction between art and science? A distinction between symbol systems but not between the matters they display. Yet, at each point we feel at a loss to know what we are learning about art in being told that it is essentially symbolic.

In this respect, Goodman's theory is similar to many semantic theories of art: it proves that expression, for example, describes a symbolic relation only by giving a theory of symbolism that is so general as to include almost every human artifact. It becomes impossible to extract from the result a procedure of interpretation—a way of understanding a work of art in terms of its alleged symbolic function. In particular, we cannot extend to the discussion of art those theories that show how we understand language in terms of its peculiar syntactic and semantic structure, for such theories always seem to rely precisely on what is peculiar to language and what distinguishes language from, say, music, painting, and architecture.

Langer's semantic theory of art

A similar result can be found in an earlier theory upon which Goodman's is to some extent modelled—the one proposed by Langer in her *Philosophy in a New Key* (1942) and *Feeling and Form* (1953). She argues that works of art symbolize states of mind ("feelings"), but that the relation is not to be explained in terms of any rule of reference such as operates in language. Works of art are, Langer says, "presentational symbols" whose relation to their objects is purely morphological. The symbol and its object are related by virtue of the fact that they possess the same "logical form." It follows that what the symbol expresses cannot be restated in words; words do not present the "logical form" of individuals but rather that of the properties and relations that characterize them. (Here again is the familiar view that art presents the individuality of its subject matter and is therefore not conceptual or descriptive.) With such a view we can no longer explain why we say that a work of art expresses a feeling and not that the feeling expresses the work; for the relation of expression, explained in these morphological terms, is clearly symmetrical. Moreover, like other semantic theories, Langer's analysis provides no procedure for interpretation, nothing that would give application to the claim that in understanding a work of art we understand it as a symbol.

Notwithstanding these difficulties for semantic theories of art, most philosophers remain convinced that the three categories of representation, expression, and understanding are all-important in making sense of our experience of art. They have become increasingly persuaded, however, with Croce and Collingwood, that the differences between representation and expression are more important than the similarities. In particular, while representation may be secured by semantic rules (as in language itself), there cannot be rules for the production of artistic expression. To think otherwise is to imagine that the difference between a Mozart and a Salieri is merely a difference of skill. Expression occurs in art only where there is expressiveness, and expressiveness is a kind of success to be measured by the response of the audience rather than by the grammar of the work. This response crucially involves understanding, and no theory of expression that is not also a theory of how expression is understood can be persuasive.

Form. Expression and representation form part of the content of a work of art. Nonetheless, it is not only content that is understood (or misunderstood) by the attentive recipient. There is also form, by which term we may denote all those features of a work of art that compose its unity and individuality as an object of sensory experience. Consider music. In most cases when a listener complains that he does not understand a work of music, he means, not that he has failed to grasp its expressive content, but that the work has failed to cohere for him as a single and satisfying object of experience. He may put the point (somewhat misleadingly) by saying that he has failed to grasp the language or logic of the composition he hears. What matters, however, is that the appreciation of music (as of the other arts) depends upon the perception of certain "unities" and upon feeling the inherent order and reasonableness in a sequence (in this case, a sequence of tones). It is this perception of order that is fundamental to understanding art, whether abstract or representational, and that to many philosophers and critics has seemed more basic than the understanding of content. When Clive Bell wrote of art as "significant form," he really meant to defend the view, first, that form is the essence of art and, second, that form must be understood and therefore understandable (*i.e.,* significant). Other philosophers have espoused one or another version of formalism, according to which the distinguishing feature of art—the one that determines our interest in it—is form. Part answers part, and each feature aims to bear some cogent relation to the whole. It is such facts as these that compel our aesthetic attention.

Art as form

The study of form must involve the study of our perception of form. A considerable amount of work on this subject has been inspired by the theories of the Gestalt psychologists Max Wertheimer, Wolfgang Köhler, and Kurt Koffka, whose semiempirical, semiphilosophical researches into the perception of form and pattern seem to make direct contact with many of the more puzzling features of our experience of art. The influence of the Gestalt psychologists is also apparent in works of visual aesthetics; *e.g.,* Rudolf Arnheim's *Art and Visual Perception* (1954), which explores the significance of such well-known Gestalt phenomena as the figure-ground relationship and the perception of completed wholes for our understanding of pictures.

Impact of Gestalt psychology on formalism

Fruitful though this emphasis on the "good Gestalt" has been, it cannot claim to have covered in its entirety the immensely complex subject of artistic form. For one thing, the theories and observations of the Gestalt psychologists, while evidently illuminating when applied to music and painting, can be applied to our experience of literature only artificially and inconclusively. Furthermore, it is impossible either to subsume all formal features of music and literature under the idea of a Gestalt or to demonstrate why, when so subsumed, the emotional effect and aesthetic value of form is made intelligible. Too much of aesthetic importance is left unconsidered by the study of the Gestalt, so that formalist critics and philosophers have begun to look elsewhere for an answer to the questions that concern them.

One recurring idea is that the operative feature determining our perception of form is "structure," the underlying, concealed formula according to which a work of art is constructed. This idea has had considerable influence in two areas, music theory and literary criticism, the former through the Austrian music theorist Heinrich Schenker and the latter through the Russian formalists and the structuralist linguists of Prague and Paris. Schenker argued in *Harmonielehre* (1906–35; *Harmony*) that musical form can be understood as generated out of musical "cells," units that are expanded, repeated, and built upon in ways that create a web of significant relationships, including a background and a foreground of musical movement. Certain structuralist critics, notably Tzvetan Todorov and Roland Barthes, have tried to perceive the unity of works of literature in terms of a similar development of literary units, often described tendentiously as "codes," but perhaps better understood as themes. These units are successively varied and transposed in ways that make the whole work into a logical derivation from its parts.

Significance of structure

Against this approach it has been argued that in neither case does structural analysis succeed in making contact with the real source of artistic unity. This unity lies within the aesthetic experience itself and so cannot be understood as a structural feature of the work of art. Once again the temptation has been to enshrine in a body of rules what lies essentially beyond the reach of rules: a unity of experience that cannot be predicted but only achieved. Structuralist aesthetics has therefore come under increasing criticism, not only for its pedantry but also for its failure to make genuine contact with the works of art to which it is applied.

In general, the study of artistic form remains highly controversial and fraught with obstacles that have yet to be overcome. This area of the theory of art remains difficult and inaccessible equally to the critic and the philosopher, both of whom have therefore tended to turn their attention to less intractable problems.

The ontology of art. One such problem is that of the ontological status of the work of art. Suppose that A has on the desk before him *David Copperfield.* Is *David Copperfield* therefore identical with this book that A can touch and see? Certainly not, for another copy lies on B's desk, and a single work of art cannot be identical with two distinct physical things. The obvious conclusion is that *David Copperfield*, the novel, is identical with no physical thing. It is not a physical object, any more than is a piece of music, which is clearly distinct from all its performances. Perhaps the same is true of paintings. For could not paintings be, in principle at least, exactly reproduced? And does not that possibility show the painting to be distinct from any particular embodiment in this or that area of painted canvas? With a little stretching, the same thought experiment might be extended to architecture, though the conclusion inevitably becomes increasingly controversial.

The problem of the nature of the work of art is by no means new. Such an argument, however, gives it a pronounced contemporary flavour, so that both Phenomenologists and Analytical philosophers have been much exercised by it, often taking as their starting point the clearly untenable theory of Croce. According to Croce, the work of art does not consist in a physical event or object but rather in a mental "intuition," which is grasped by the audience in the act of aesthetic understanding. The unsatisfactory nature of this theory, sometimes called the "ideal" theory of art, becomes apparent as soon as we ask how we would identify the intuition with which any given work of art is supposedly identical. Clearly, we can identify it only in and through a performance, a book, a score, or a canvas. These objects give us the intuition that cannot exist independently of them. (Otherwise we should have to say that the world contains an uncountable number of great works of art whose only defect is that they have never been transcribed.)

Clearly then, the physical embodiment of the work—in sounds, language, scores, or other inscriptions—is more fundamentally a part of it (of its "essence") than the ideal theory represents it to be. What then is the work of art, and what is its relation to the objects in which it is embodied? These questions have been discussed by Richard Wollheim in *Art and Its Objects* (1968), and again by Goodman in *Languages of Art* (see above). Wollheim argues that works of art are "types" and their embodiments "tokens." The distinction here derives from the U.S. philosopher and logician C.S. Peirce, who argued that the letter *a,* for example, is neither identical with any particular token of it (such as the one just written) nor distinct from the class of such tokens. Peirce therefore calls *a* a type (*i.e.,* a formula for producing tokens).

Wollheim's theory is open to various objections. For example, works of architecture are not, as things stand, tokens of types but physical objects, and to make them into types by endlessly reproducing them would be to destroy their aesthetic character. To identify an object in terms of a process that destroys its character is not in any evident sense to identify it. The theory, moreover, seems to be unable to distinguish a musical performance containing a wrong note from a performance of a new work of music containing precisely that note as part of its type.

Goodman's theory is more technical and displaces the question of the nature of art in favour of that of the nature of an inscription: Just what is it for a particular set of marks to identify a work of art? Other philosophers have concentrated on the question of identity: What makes this work of art the same as that one? Some argue, for example, that works of art have a distinct criterion of identity, one that reflects the peculiar nature and demands of aesthetic interest. Others dismiss the search for a criterion of identity as both aesthetically insignificant and illusory in itself. Still others, notably the Phenomenologist Roman Ingarden, argue that the work of art exists on several levels, being identical not with physical appearance but with totality of interpretations that secure the various formal and semantic levels that are contained in it.

Question of identity

Questions that so obviously lend themselves to the procedures of modern philosophy have naturally commanded considerable attention. But whether they are aesthetically significant is disputed, and some philosophers go so far as to dismiss all questions of ontology and identity of art as peripheral to the subject matter of aesthetics. The same could not be said, however, of the question of the value of art, which, while less discussed, is evidently of the first importance.

Extrinsic and intrinsic theories

The value of art. Theories of the value of art are of two kinds, which we may call extrinsic and intrinsic. The first regards art and the appreciation of art as means to some recognized moral good, while the second regards them as valuable not instrumentally but as objects unto themselves. It is characteristic of extrinsic theories to locate the value of art in its effects on the person who appreciates it. Art is held to be a form of education, perhaps an education of the emotions. In this case, it becomes an open question whether there might not be some more effective means to the same result. Alternatively, one may attribute a negative value to art, as Plato did in his *Republic,* arguing that art has a corrupting or diseducative effect on those exposed to it.

The extrinsic approach, adopted in modern times by Leo Tolstoy in *Chto takoye iskusstvo?* (1896; *What Is Art?*), has seldom seemed wholly satisfactory. Philosophers have constantly sought for a value in aesthetic experience that is unique to it and that, therefore, could not be obtained from any other source. The extreme version of this intrinsic approach is that associated with Walter Pater, Oscar Wilde, and the French Symbolists, and summarized in the slogan "art for art's sake." Such thinkers and writers believe that art is not only an end in itself but also a sufficient justification of itself. They also hold that in order to understand art as it should be understood, it is necessary to put aside all interests other than an interest in the work itself.

Between those two extreme views there lies, once again, a host of intermediate positions. We believe, for example, that works of art must be appreciated for their own sake, but that, in the act of appreciation, we gain from them something that is of independent value. Thus a joke is laughed at for its own sake, even though there is an independent value in laughter, which lightens our lives by taking us momentarily outside ourselves. Why should not something similar be said of works of art, many of which aspire to be amusing in just the way that good jokes are?

The analogy with laughter—which, in some views, is itself a species of aesthetic interest—introduces a concept without which there can be no serious discussion of the value of art: the concept of taste. If I am amused it is for a reason, and this reason lies in the object of my amusement. We thus begin to think in terms of a distinction between good and bad reasons for laughter. Amusement at the wrong things may seem to us to show corruption of mind, cruelty, or bad taste; and when it does so, we speak of the object as not truly amusing, and feel that we have reason on our side.

Similarly, we regard some works of art as worthy of our attention and others as not. In articulating this judgment, we use all of the diverse and confusing vocabulary of moral appraisal; works of art, like people, are condemned for their sentimentality, coarseness, vulgarity, cruelty, or self-indulgence, and equally praised for their warmth, compassion, nobility, sensitivity, and truthfulness. (The same may apply to the object of natural beauty.) Clearly, if aesthetic interest has a positive value, it is only when motivated by good taste; it is only interest in appropriate objects that can be said to be good for us. All discussion of the value of art tends, therefore, to turn from the outset in the direction of criticism: Can there be genuine critical evaluation of art, a genuine distinction between that which deserves our attention and that which does not? (And, once again, the question may be extended to objects of natural beauty.)

TASTE, CRITICISM, AND JUDGMENT

All aesthetic experience, whether of art or nature, seems to be informed by and dependent upon an exercise of taste. We choose the object of aesthetic experience, and often do so carefully and deliberately. Moreover, we are judged by our choices, not only of works of art but also of colour schemes, dresses, and garden ornaments, just as we are judged by our manners and our sense of humour. By his taste an individual betrays himself: not merely a small part of himself but the whole. Yet, the relation between taste and morality is by no means straightforward. There seems, in fact, to be a puzzling question as to the precise nature of the relation between aesthetic and moral values, and between the good taste that discerns the first and the good conduct that responds to the second. If there is no relation, the enormous amount of human energy that is invested in art and criticism may begin to seem rather pointless. If the relation is too close, however, the result is an intolerable moral elitism that makes refinement the sole standard of acceptable conduct, as for example, the elitism depicted by Villiers de L'Isle-Adam in *Axel,* by J.K. Huysmans in *À Rebours,* and by Oscar Wilde in *The Picture of Dorian Gray.* The aesthete is one who puts aesthetic values above all others and who seeks for a morality that conforms to them. But like his opposite, the philistine, he fails to see that the relation between the aesthetic and the moral is not one of priority; each informs and is informed by the other, without taking precedence and without dictating the choice that belongs within the other's sphere.

Contemporary aesthetics has been less disposed to discuss the idea of taste than that of criticism. But clearly, the two ideas are so closely related that anything said about the one has a direct bearing on the other. In both cases, the approach has been the first of those outlined at the beginning of this article: the approach that starts with a study of the concepts and modes of argument employed in discussing beauty and tries to grasp the distinctive problems of aesthetics through a study of the logical and ideological puzzles that these concepts and arguments arouse.

Interpretative and evaluative criticism

Philosophers often distinguish between two kinds of critical discussion—the interpretative and the evaluative—and two classes of concepts corresponding to them. In describing an object of natural beauty or a work of art, we may use a host of so-called aesthetic terms, terms that seem to have a particular role when used in this context and that articulate the aesthetic impression which it is the first task of criticism to convey. Among such terms we may notice affective terms—moving, frightening, disturbing; terms denoting emotional qualities—sad, lively, mournful, wistful; terms denoting the expressive or representational content of a work of art, its formal features, and its overall artistic genre—comic, tragic, ironic. Some of these terms can be applied meaningfully only to works of art; others may be applied to the whole of nature in order to articulate an aesthetic experience. The examination of their logic has had an increasingly important role in analytical aesthetics. Frank N. Sibley, for example, has argued that such terms are used in aesthetic judgment in a peculiar way, without conditions (*i.e.,* without a reasoned basis), and in order to describe aesthetic properties that are discernible only by the exercise of taste. This sophisticated reminder of Kant's theory that aesthetic judgment is free from concepts has been criticized as creating too great a gap between the language of criticism and the language of everyday life. But it is of considerable interest in itself in attempting to revive a conception of taste that was highly influential in 18th-century aesthetics. As noted above, taste is, according to this conception, a faculty not of evaluation but of perception.

In aesthetics, however, evaluative judgments are inescapable. Theories avoiding the implication that taste is a form of discrimination, which naturally ranks its objects according to their merit, are peculiarly unsatisfying, not the least because they have so little bearing on the practice of criticism or the reasons that lead us to assign such overwhelming importance to art.

What then of the concepts employed in aesthetic evaluation? Burke introduced a famous distinction between two kinds of aesthetic judgment corresponding to two orders of aesthetic experience: the judgment of the beautiful and that of the sublime. The judgment of beauty has its origin in our social feelings, particularly in our feelings toward the other sex, and in our hope for a consolation through love and desire. The judgment of the sublime has its origin in our feelings toward nature, and in our intimation of our ultimate solitude and fragility in a world that is not of our own devising and that remains resistant to our demands. In Burke's words,

> Whatever is fitted in any sort to excite the ideas of pain, and danger, that is to say, whatever is in any sort terrible, or is conversant about terrible objects, or operates in a manner analogous to terror, is a source of the sublime; that is, it is productive of the strongest emotion which the mind is capable of feeling.

Burke's distinction emerges as part of a natural philosophy of beauty: an attempt to give the origins of our sentiments rather than to explain the logic of the judgments that convey them. In Kant, the distinction is recast as a distinction between two categories of aesthetic experience and two separate values that attach to it. Sometimes when we sense the harmony between nature and our faculties, we are impressed by the purposiveness and intelligibility of everything that surrounds us. This is the sentiment of beauty. At other times, overcome by the infinite greatness of the world, we renounce the attempt to understand and control it. This is the sentiment of the sublime. In confronting the sublime, the mind is "incited to abandon sensibility"—to reach over to that transcendental view of things that shows to us the immanence of a supersensible realm and our destiny as subjects of a divine order. Thus, from the presentiment of the sublime, Kant extracts the ultimate ground of his faith in a Supreme Being, and this is for him the most important value that aesthetic experience can convey.

The distinction between the sublime and the beautiful is now less frequently made than at the time of Burke and Kant. Nevertheless, it is undeniable that aesthetic judgment exists in many contrasting forms, of both praise and condemnation. A philosopher who sought to account for the idea of beauty without attending to those of the elegant, the refined, the great, the delicate, the intelligent, the profound, and the lovely would be unlikely to provide us with much understanding of the nature and function of criticism. There may be, however, something that these judgments have in common which might be used in order to cast light on all of them. Kant certainly would have thought so, since he argued that all such judgments share the distinctive features of taste revealed in his antinomy. In other words, they are all grounded in an immediate ("subjective") experience, while at the same time being "universal"—*i.e.,* held forth as valid for all rational beings irrespective of their particular interests and desires. Thus, the critic tries to justify his aesthetic judgments, seeking reasons that will persuade others to see what he sees as elegant or beautiful in a similar light.

Taste as a common denominator of aesthetic judgments

Could there be a genuine critical procedure devoted to that enterprise of providing objective grounds for subjective preferences? This question is integrally connected to another that we have already discussed: the question of the value of aesthetic experience. If aesthetic experience is valueless, or if it has no more value than attaches to idle enjoyment, then it becomes far less plausible to insist on the existence of objective evaluation than if aesthetic experience has the kind of importance attributed to it by Kant.

Modern considerations of this exceedingly difficult question tend to concentrate on the criticism of art and on the role of the critic of art. What is a critic doing when he discusses a work of art, what does he look for, and with what purpose? It might be said that a critic should first of all study the artist's intention, since this will show the real meaning of his work, the real content that he is trying to communicate. The U.S. critics W.K. Wimsatt and Monroe C. Beardsley, however, argue that there is a fallacy (the so-called intentional fallacy) involved in this approach. What is to be interpreted is the work of art itself, not the intentions of the artist, which are hidden from us and no subject for our concern. If judgment is to be aesthetic, it must concern itself with the given object, and the meanings that we attribute to the object are those that we see in it, whatever the artist intended.

The intentional fallacy

The existence of an intentional fallacy has been doubted. Some argue, for example, that Wimsatt and Beardsley make too sharp a distinction between an intention and the act that expresses it, assuming the intention to be a kind of private mental episode forever hidden from an observer rather than a revealed order in the work itself. But when a critic refers to the artistic intention, it is not clear whether he means anything more than the general purposiveness of the work of art, which can be interpreted by a critic without supposing there to be some intention beyond that of producing the precise work before him. (Indeed, in Kant's view, there can be purposiveness without purpose, and this phenomenon provides the central object of aesthetic interest whether in art or in nature.) The dispute here is tortuous and obscure. Nevertheless, the move away from intentionalism, as it is called, has been regarded as imperative by most modern critics, who tend to see the role of criticism in either one of two ways: (1) criticism is devoted to the study and interpretation of the aesthetic object rather than of the artist or the recipient; and (2) criticism is devoted to the articulation of a response to the work of art and to the justification of a particular way of seeing it.

The role of modern criticism

Underlying both these conceptions is the fashionable preoccupation with art as the principal object of critical judgment. Nevertheless, in suggesting that the choice which lies before the critic is between the aesthetic object and the experience that it arouses, the two views ensure that the artist is kept hidden. As a consequence, it is not difficult to adapt them to a wider view of aesthetic judgment and aesthetic experience—to a view that makes room for natural beauty and for the aesthetics of everyday life, as it is manifested in dress, manners, decoration, and the other useful arts.

It might be thought that only the first of the two conceptions can give rise to an objective critical procedure, since it alone requires that criticism focus on an object whose existence and nature is independent of the critic. The most important contemporary defense of an objective criticism, that of the British literary critic F.R. Leavis, has relied heavily on the second idea, however. In a celebrated controversy with his U.S. counterpart, René Wellek, Leavis argued that it is precisely because criticism is devoted to the individual response that it may achieve objectivity. Although there may be objectivity in the scientific explanation of the aesthetic object—*i.e.,* in the classification and description of its typology, structure, and semiotic status—this is not, according to Leavis, the kind of objectivity that matters, for it will never lead to a value judgment and will therefore never amount to an objective criticism. Value judgments arise out of, and are validated by, the direct confrontation in experience between the critical intelligence and the aesthetic object, the first being informed by a moral awareness that provides the only possible ground for objective evaluation.

If criticism were confined to the study of nature, it would look very peculiar. It is only because of the development of artistic and decorative traditions that the habit of aesthetic judgment becomes established. Accordingly, contemporary attempts to provide a defense of aesthetic judgment concentrate almost exclusively on the criticism of art, and endeavour to find principles whereby the separate works of art may be ordered according to their merit, or at least characterized in evaluative terms. Leavis' "objective" criticism is expressly confined to the evaluation of literary works taken from a single tradition. The reason for this narrowness can be put paradoxically as follows: Criticism can be objective only when it is based in subjectivity. Criticism is the justification of a response, and such justification requires a frame of reference that both the critic and his reader can readily recognize. The successful communication and justification of a response are possible only by reference to the canon of works accepted within a common culture. The canonical works—what Matthew Arnold called the touchstones of criticism—provide the context of relevant comparisons, without which no amount of detailed analysis could convey the quality of the individual work. Critical reasoning is an attempt to place works of art in relation to one another, so that the perceived greatness of the one will provide the standard of

Leavis' method of literary criticism

measurement for the other. At the same time, the individual quality of feeling in each work must be elicited and discussed exactly as we might discuss the quality of feeling in everyday life, praising it for its intensity, exactness, and generosity, and criticizing it for its sentimentality, obscurity, or lack of seriousness. All of the moral categories that we apply to human feeling and character we may therefore apply equally to art, and the basis of an objective criticism will be no different from the basis (whatever it might be) for an objective morality. The value of art, on this account, resides partly in the fact that it gives exemplary expression to human feeling and character, and so enables us to measure our own lives and aspirations against their imaginary counterparts.

These ideas are vague and have been frequently criticized for their moralistic overtones as well as for the seeming narrowness of their application. Even if they apply to the criticism of literature, what do we say about the criticism of music, of architecture, of dress and decor, of natural beauty? In the nonliterary arts much criticism is directed first to form, style, and workmanship, and only secondly to the moral content of the works under consideration. There are exceptions to this rule, and once again the principal exception is English—namely, John Ruskin's profoundly moralized criticism of architecture. Nevertheless, the extreme difficulty experienced in extending the Leavisite procedures of practical criticism (in which the reader's response becomes the principal focus of critical attention) to the nonliterary arts has given sustenance to the view that this "moralized" criticism is really only one kind of criticism and not necessarily the most widely applicable or the most important. If such is the case, it cannot really claim to have discovered a basis for the objective exercise of taste.

THE DEVELOPMENT OF WESTERN AESTHETICS

Plato and Aristotle

The contributions of the ancient Greeks. The two greatest Greek philosophers, Plato and Aristotle, shared a sense of the importance of aesthetics, and both regarded music, poetry, architecture, and drama as fundamental institutions within the body politic. Plato notoriously recommends the banning of poets and painters from his ideal republic and in the course of his argument provides an extended theory of imitation (*mimesis*), along with spurious reasons for thinking that imitation derogates both from the laws of morality and from the rational cognition of the world. Much of Aristotle's extended and diverse reply to Plato is concerned with rehabilitating imitation as the foundation of moral education (*Ethica Nicomachea*), as the origin of a necessary *katharsis* (*Poetica*), and as the instrument—through music, dance, and poetry—of character formation (*Politica*).

Plato's more mystical writings, notably the *Timaeus,* contain hints of another approach to aesthetics, one based on the Pythagorean theory of the cosmos that exerted a decisive influence on the Neoplatonists. Through the writings of St. Augustine, Boethius, and Macrobius, the Pythagorean cosmology and its associated aesthetic of harmony were passed on to the thinkers of the Middle Ages. The Aristotelian theory of imitation and the concern with the expressive and emotionally educative aspect of aesthetic experience were not truly influential until the 17th century. At that time much attention was also paid to another classical work, the Hellenistic treatise on the sublime ascribed to Longinus, which is perhaps the most interesting and extended piece of antique literary criticism to have been passed on to the modern world.

Medieval aesthetics. St. Thomas Aquinas devoted certain passages of his *Summa Theologiae* (*c.* 1266–73) to the study of beauty. To his thinking, man's interest in beauty is of sensuous origin, but it is the prerogative of those senses that are capable of "contemplation"—namely, the eye and the ear. Aquinas defines beauty in Aristotelian terms as that which pleases solely in the contemplation of it and recognizes three prerequisites of beauty: perfection, appropriate proportion, and clarity. Aquinas' position typifies the approach to aesthetics adopted by the Scholastics. More widely diffused among medieval thinkers was the Neoplatonist theory, in which beauty is seen as a kind of divine order conforming to mathematical laws: the laws of number, which are also the laws of harmony. Music, poetry, and architecture all exhibit the same conformity to a cosmic order, and, in experiencing their beauty, we are really experiencing the same order in ourselves and resonating to it as one string to another. This theory, expounded in treatises on music by St. Augustine and Boethius, is consciously invoked by Dante in his *Convivio* (*c.* 1304–07; *The Banquet*). In this piece, generally considered one of the first sustained works of literary criticism in the modern manner, the poet analyzes the four levels of meaning contained in his own poems.

Neoplatonist conception of beauty

The Neoplatonist emphasis on number and harmony dominated aesthetics during the early Renaissance as well and was reaffirmed by Leon Alberti in his great treatise on architecture, *De Re Aedificatoria* (1452; *Ten Books on Architecture*). Alberti also advanced a definition of beauty, which he called *concinnitas,* taking his terminology from Cicero. Beauty is for Alberti such an order and arrangement of the parts of an object that nothing can be altered except for the worse. This kind of definition can hardly stand alone as a basis for aesthetics, for what does the word worse mean? The obvious answer, "less beautiful," at once reduces the definition to circularity.

The origins of modern aesthetics. Francis Bacon wrote essays on beauty and deformity, but he confined his remarks to the human figure. René Descartes produced a treatise on music, although it contains little that would be recognized as aesthetics in the modern sense. During the first decades of modern philosophy, aesthetics flourished, not in the works of the great philosophers, but in the writings of such minor figures as Baltasar Gracián, Jean de La Bruyère (who began the study of taste that was to dominate aesthetics for a century), and Georges-Louis Leclerc, comte de Buffon.

It was not until the end of the 17th century that the distinctive concerns of modern aesthetics were established. At that time, taste, imagination, natural beauty, and imitation came to be recognized as the central topics in aesthetics. In Britain the principal influences were the 3rd Earl of Shaftesbury and his disciples Francis Hutcheson and Joseph Addison. Shaftesbury, a follower of the political and educational philosopher John Locke, did more than any of his contemporaries to establish ethics and aesthetics as central areas of philosophical inquiry. As a naturalist, he believed that the fundamental principles of morals and taste could be established by due attention to human nature, our sentiments being so ordered that certain things naturally please us and are naturally conducive to our good (*Characteristiks of Men, Manners, Opinions, Times,* 1711). Taste is a kind of balanced discernment, whereby a person recognizes that which is congenial to his sentiments and therefore an object of pleasurable contemplation. Following Locke, Shaftesbury laid much emphasis on the association of ideas as a fundamental component in aesthetic experience and the crucial bridge from the sphere of contemplation to the sphere of action. Addison adopted this position in a series of influential essays, "The Pleasures of the Imagination" in *The Spectator* (1712). He defended the theory that imaginative association is the fundamental component in our experience of art, architecture, and nature, and is the true explanation of their value to us.

Imaginative association in aesthetic experience

Francis Hutcheson was perhaps the first to place the problem of aesthetic judgment among the central questions of epistemology: How can we know that something is beautiful? What guides our judgment and what validates it? His answer was decidedly Empiricist in tone: aesthetic judgments are perceptual and take their authority from a sense that is common to all who make them. In *An Inquiry into the Original of our Ideas of Beauty and Virtue* (1725), Hutcheson explained: "The origin of our perceptions of beauty and harmony is justly called a 'sense' because it involves no intellectual element, no reflection on principles and causes."

The significance of Baumgarten's work. Such a statement would have been vigorously repudiated by Hutcheson's contemporary Alexander Baumgarten, who, in his aforementioned *Reflections on Poetry,* introduced the term aesthetic in its distinctively modern sense. Baumgarten was a pupil of Christian Wolff, the Rationalist philosopher who had created the orthodox philosophy of the German Enlightenment by building the metaphysical ideas of Gottfried Wilhelm Leibniz into a system. He was thus heir to a tradition that dismissed the senses and the imagination as incapable of providing a genuine cognition of their objects and standing always to be corrected (and replaced) by rational reflection. Baumgarten, however, argued that poetry is surely cognitive: it provides insight into the world of a kind that could be conveyed in no other way. At the same time, poetic insights are perceptual ("aesthetic") and hence imbued with the distinctive character of sensory and imaginative experience. According to Baumgarten, the ideas conveyed by poetry are "clear and confused," as opposed to the "clear and distinct" ideas of reason in the sense that they had been described by Descartes and the 17th-century Rationalists. Baumgarten held that the aesthetic value of a poem resides in the relative preponderance of clarity over confusion. Accordingly, his theory of the value of art was ultimately cognitive.

Baumgarten's theory of the value of art

It was some decades before Baumgarten's coinage became philosophical currency. But there is no doubt that his treatise, for all its pedantry and outmoded philosophical method, deserves its reputation as the founding work of modern aesthetics.

Major concerns of 18th-century aesthetics. The development of aesthetics between the work of Baumgarten and that of Immanuel Kant, who had been influenced by Baumgarten's writings, was complex and diverse, drawing inspiration from virtually every realm of human inquiry. Yet, throughout this period certain topics repeatedly received focal attention in discussions pertaining to aesthetic questions.

One such topic was the faculty of taste, the analysis of which remained the common point among German, French, and English writers. Taste was seen either as a sense (Hutcheson), as a peculiar kind of emotionally inspired discrimination (Hume), or as a part of refined good manners (Voltaire). In an important essay entitled "Of the Standard of Taste" (in *Four Dissertations,* 1757), Hume, following Voltaire in the *Encyclopédie,* raised the question of the basis of aesthetic judgment and argued that "it is natural for us to seek a standard of taste; a rule by which the various sentiments of men may be reconciled; at least, a decision afforded, confirming one sentiment, and condemning another." But where is this standard of taste to be found? Hume recommends an ideal of the man of taste, whose discriminations are unclouded by an emotional distemper and informed by a "delicacy of imagination . . . requisite to convey a sensibility of . . . finer emotions." For, Hume argues, there is a great resemblance between "mental" and "bodily" taste—between the taste exercised in aesthetic discrimination and that exercised in the appreciation of food and drink, which can equally be deformed by some abnormal condition of the subject. Hume proceeded to lay down various procedures for the education of taste and for the proper conduct of critical judgment. His discussion, notwithstanding its skeptical undercurrent, has proved lastingly influential on the English schools of criticism, as well as on the preferred Anglo-Saxon approach to the questions of aesthetics.

Analysis of taste

A second major concern of 18th-century writers was the role of imagination. Addison's essays were seminal, but discussion of imagination remained largely confined to the associative theories of Locke and his followers until Hume gave to the imagination a fundamental role in the generation of commonsense beliefs. Kant attempted to describe the imagination as a distinctive faculty, active in the generation of scientific judgment as well as aesthetic pleasure. Between them, Hume and Kant laid the ground for the Romantic writers on art: Johann Gottfried von Herder, Friedrich Schiller, Friedrich Schelling, and Novalis (pseudonym of Friedrich Leopold, Freiherr von Hardenberg) in Germany, and Samuel Taylor Coleridge and William Wordsworth in England. For such writers, imagination was to be the distinctive feature both of aesthetic activity and of all true insight into the human condition. Meanwhile, Lord Kames and Archibald Alison had each provided full accounts of the role of association in the formation and justification of critical judgment. Alison, in particular, recognized the inadequacies of the traditional Empiricist approach to imaginative association and provided a theory as to how the feelings aroused by a work of art or a scene of natural beauty may become part of its appearance—qualities of the object as much as of the subject (*Essays on the Nature and Principles of Taste* [1790]).

The concept of imitation, introduced into the discussion of art by Plato and Aristotle, was fundamental to the 18th-century philosophy of art. Imitation is a vague term, frequently used to cover both representation and expression in the modern sense. The thesis that imitation is the common and distinguishing feature of the arts was put forward by James Harris in *Three Treatises* (1744) and subsequently made famous by Charles Batteux in a book entitled *Les Beaux Arts réduits à un même principe* (1746; "The Fine Arts Reduced to a Single Principle"). This diffuse and ill-argued work contains the first modern attempt to give a systematic theory of art and aesthetic judgment that will show the unity of the phenomena and their common importance. "The laws of taste," Batteux argued, "have nothing but the imitation of beautiful nature as their object"; from which it follows that the arts, which are addressed to taste, must imitate nature. The distinction between the fine and useful arts (recast by Collingwood as the distinction between art and craft) stems from Batteux.

Concept of imitation

Still another characteristic of 18th-century aesthetics was the concern with the distinction between the sublime and the beautiful. Burke's famous work, *On the Sublime and Beautiful,* has already been discussed. Its influence was felt throughout late 18th-century aesthetics. For example, it inspired one of Kant's first publications, an essay on the sublime. Treatises on beauty were common, one of the most famous being *The Analysis of Beauty* (1753) by the painter William Hogarth, which introduces the theory that beauty is achieved through the "serpentine line."

The view that art is expression emerged during the 1700s. Rousseau put forth the theory of the arts as forms of emotional expression in an essay dealing with the origin of languages. This theory, regarded as providing the best possible explanation of the power of music, was widely adopted. Treatises on musical expression proliferated during the late 18th century. One illustrative example of such writings is James Beattie's *Essay on Poetry and Music as They Affect the Mind* (1776), in which the author rejects the view of music as a representational (imitative) art form and argues that expression is the true source of musical excellence. Another example is provided by Denis Diderot in his didactic novel *Le Neveu de Rameau* (1761–74; *Rameau's Nephew and Other Works*). The theory of expression was inherited by the German Romantics, especially by Schelling, Schiller, and Herder. It was, furthermore, developed in a novel direction by the Italian philosopher Giambattista Vico in his *Scienza nuova* (1725–44; *New Science*). Vico integrated art into a comprehensive theory of the development and decline of civilization. According to him, the cyclical movement of culture is achieved partly by a process of successive expression, through language and art, of the "myths" that give insight into surrounding social conditions.

Art as expression

Kant, Schiller, and Hegel. As previously noted, Kant's *Kritik der Urteilskraft* introduced the first full account of aesthetic experience as a distinct exercise of rational mentality. The principal ingredients of Kant's work are the following: the antinomy of taste, the emphasis on the free play of the imagination, the theory of aesthetic experience as both free from concepts and disinterested, the view that the central object of aesthetic interest is not art but nature, and the description of the moral and spiritual significance of aesthetic experience, which opens to us a transcendental point of view of the world of nature and enables us to see the world as purposive, but without purpose. In that perception, observes Kant, lies the deepest intimation of our nature and of our ultimate relation to a "supersensible" realm.

Schiller's *Briefe über die ästhetische Erziehung des Menschen,* inspired by Kant, develops further the theory of the disinterested character of the aesthetic. Schiller argues that through this disinterested quality aesthetic experience becomes the true vehicle of moral and political education, providing man both with the self-identity that is his fulfillment and with the institutions that enable him to flourish: "What is man before beauty cajoles from him a delight in things for their own sake, or the serenity of form tempers the savagery of life? A monotonous round of ends, a constant vacillation of judgment; self-seeking, and yet without a self; lawless, yet without freedom; a slave, and yet to no rule."

Aesthetic experience as a vehicle of moral and political education

Schiller's *Briefe* exerted a profound influence on Hegel's philosophy in general and on his *Vorlesungen über die Aesthetik* in particular. In discussions of remarkable range and imaginative power, Hegel introduces the distinctively modern conception of art as a request for self-realization, an evolving discovery of forms that give sensuous embodiment to the spirit by articulating in concrete form its inner tensions and resolutions. For Hegel, the arts are arranged in both historical and intellectual sequence, from architecture (in which *Geist* ["spirit"] is only half articulate and given purely symbolic expression), through sculpture and painting, to music and thence to poetry, which is the true art of the Romantics. Finally, all art is destined to be superseded by philosophy, in which the spirit achieves final articulation as Idea. The stages of art were identified by Hegel with various stages of historical development. In each art form a particular *Zeitgeist* (*i.e.,* spirit of the time) finds expression, and the necessary transition from one art form to its successor is part of a larger historical transformation in which all civilization is engaged.

The incidental discussions of Hegel's *Vorlesungen* introduce most of the themes of contemporary philosophy of art, though in the peculiar language of Hegelian Idealism. Nineteenth-century Idealist aesthetics can reasonably be described as a series of footnotes to Hegel, who was, however, less original than he pretended. Many of the individual thoughts and theories in his lectures on aesthetics were taken from the contemporary literature of German Romanticism (in particular, the writings of Herder, Jean Paul [pseudonym of Johann Paul Friedrich Richter] and Novalis) and from the works of German critics and art historians (notably G.E. Lessing and Johann Winckelmann) who had forged the link between modern conceptions of art and the art of antiquity. The influence of Hegel was, therefore, the influence of German Romanticism as a whole, and it is not surprising that the few who escaped it lost their audience in doing so.

Post-Hegelian aesthetics. Little of 19th-century aesthetics after Hegel has proved of lasting interest. Perhaps the most important exception is the controversial literature surrounding Richard Wagner, particularly the attack on the expressive theory of music launched by Wagner's critic Eduard Hanslick in his *Vom musikalisch-Schönen* (1854; *On the Beautiful in Music*). With this work modern musical aesthetics was born, and all the assumptions made by Batteux and Hegel concerning the unity (or unity in diversity) of the arts were thrown in doubt.

The most impressive work on aesthetics of the late 1800s was George Santayana's *The Sense of Beauty* (1896), which shows a welcome move away from the 19th-century obsession with art toward more fundamental issues in the philosophy of mind. Santayana argues against Kant's theory of the disinterested and universal quality of aesthetic interest, and defends the view that pleasure is the central aesthetic category, beauty being "pleasure regarded as the quality of a thing." All human functions and experiences may contribute to the sense of beauty, which has two broad categories of object: form and expression. In his theory of expression Santayana again takes up the problem raised by the theory of the association of ideas, and argues that in aesthetic pleasure the associative process achieves a kind of fusion between the response aroused and the object which arouses it, and that this is the fundamental experience of expression.

Expressionism. After Kant and Hegel, the most important influence on modern aesthetics has been Croce. His oft-cited *Estetica come scienza dell' espressione e linguistica generale* (1902; *Aesthetic as Science of Expression and General Linguistics,* or *Aesthetic*) presents, in a rather novel idiom, some of the important insights underlying the theories of his predecessors. In this work, Croce distinguishes concept from intuition: the latter is a kind of acquaintance with the individuality of an object, while the former is an instrument of classification. Art is to be understood first as expression and second as intuition. The distinction between representation and expression is ultimately identical with that between concept and intuition. The peculiarities of aesthetic interest are really peculiarities of intuition: this is what explains the problem of form and content, and what gives the meaning of the idea that the object of aesthetic interest is interesting for its own sake and not as a means to an end.

Croce's conception of art

Croce conceived his expressionism as providing the philosophical justification for the artistic revolutions of the 19th century and, in particular, for the Impressionist style of painting, in which representation gives way to the attempt to convey experience directly onto the canvas. His extreme view of the autonomy of art led him to dismiss all attempts to describe art as a form of representation or to establish direct connections between the content of art and the content of scientific theories. Croce's disciple R.G. Collingwood (*Principles of Art,* 1938) was similarly dismissive of representation and similarly concerned with presenting a theory of art that would justify the revolutionary practice of his contemporaries (in this case, the post-Symbolist poetry of T.S. Eliot's *The Waste Land*). As pointed out earlier, Collingwood distinguishes craft, which is a means to an end, from art, which is an end in itself. But since art is also, for Collingwood, expression, expression too must be an end in itself. It cannot be construed as the giving of form to independently identifiable states of mind. The feeling must reside in the form itself and be obtainable exclusively in that form. If it were otherwise, art would be simply another kind of craft—the craft of giving expression to preexisting and independently identifiable states of mind. Therefore, like Croce, Collingwood opposes expression in art to description: expression gives us the particularity and not the generality of states of mind.

Collingwood sets his aesthetics within the context of a theory of the imagination, in which he shows the influence of the British Empiricists as well as of the Idealist metaphysicians who had influenced Croce. A similar attempt to unite the theory of art with a philosophy of the imagination had been made by the French philosopher Alain in his *Système des beaux-arts* (1920, revised 1926; "System of the Fine Arts"), a work that is distinguished by its detailed attention to dress, fashion, manners, and the useful arts, and by its idea of the artist as *artisan d'abord.* Along with John Dewey's *Art As Experience* (1934), in which aesthetic experience is presented as integral to the organic completion of human nature, these works provide the culminating expression of a now defunct view of the subject as central to the understanding not of art alone but of the human condition as well.

MARXIST AESTHETICS

Many attempts have been made to develop a specifically Marxist aesthetics, one that would incorporate the Marxian theory of history and class consciousness and the critique of bourgeois ideology, so as to generate principles of analysis and evaluation and show the place of art in the theory and practice of revolution. William Morris in England and Georgy V. Plekhanov in Russia both attempted to unite Marx's social criticism with a conception of the nature of artistic labour. Plekhanov's *Iskusstvo i obshchestvennaya zhizn* (1912; *Art and Social Life*) is a kind of synthesis of early Marxist thought and attempts to recast the practices of art and criticism in a revolutionary mold. The ideology of "art for art's sake," Plekhanov argues, develops only in conditions of social decline when artist and recipient are in "hopeless disaccord with the social environment in which they live." Drawing on Kant and Schiller, Plekhanov presents a theory of the origins of art in play; play, however, must not be understood in isolation. It is indissolubly linked to labour, of which it is the complementary opposite. An art of play will be the

Plekhanov's theory of the origins of art in play

"free" art of the revolution, of mankind returned to social harmony, but only because play and labour will then be reunited and transcended. In place of their opposition will be a harmonious whole in which art is continuous with labour.

The aesthetic theories of the Russian Revolution owe something to Plekhanov; something to the school of Formalist criticism, typified by the proto-Structuralist M. Bakhtin; and something to the anti-aesthetic propaganda of the Russian Constructivists, who believed in an art expressive of man's dominion over raw materials—an art that would be destructive of all existing patterns of subordination. The official approach to art in the Soviet Union, however, has been typified, first, by the persecution of all those who have expressed adherence to those theories, and, second, by the adoption under Stalin of Socialist Realism (the view that art is dedicated to the "realistic" representation of proletarian values and proletarian life) as the sole legitimate basis for artistic practice.

Benjamin and Lukács

Subsequent Marxist thinking about art has been largely influenced by two major central European thinkers: Walter Benjamin and György Lukács. Both are exponents of Marxist humanism, who see the important contribution of Marxian theory to aesthetics in the analysis of the condition of labour and in the critique of the alienated and "reified" consciousness of man under capitalism. Benjamin's collection of essays *Das Kunstwerk im Zeitalter seiner technischen Reproduzierbarkeit* (1936; *The Work of Art in the Age of Mechanical Reproduction*) attempts to describe the changed experience of art in the modern world, and sees the rise of Fascism and mass society as the culmination of a process of debasement, whereby art ceases to be a means of instruction and becomes instead a mere gratification, a matter of taste alone. "Communism responds by politicizing art"—that is, by making art into the instrument by which the false consciousness of the mass man is to be overthrown.

Lukács developed a multifaceted approach to literary criticism, in which the historical condition of society and the reality of class consciousness are singled out as the ideological agenda of works of literature and the major source of their appeal. This position is set forth in such works as *Die Theorie des Romans* (1920; *The Theory of the Novel*). Neither Lukács nor Benjamin produced a coherent aesthetics as defined in this article, although each has been immensely influential on the practice of modern literary criticism whether Marxist or not in its ultimate inspiration. (Ro.Sc.)

EASTERN AESTHETICS

India. The disparagement of the sensory realm as mere illusion ("the veil of Maya"), characteristic of much Indian religion, went hand in hand with a philosophy of embodiment (karma), which gave a distinctive role to art both as an instrument of worship and as an earthly delight. The legends of the great god Krishna abound in exaggerated fantasies of erotic and physical power; the art of the temples testifies to a sensuality that belies the mystical gestures of renunciation which form the commonplaces of Hindu morality. In providing theories of such art, and of the natural beauty that it celebrates, Indian philosophers have relied heavily on the concept of aesthetic flavour, or *rasa,* a kind of contemplative abstraction in which the inwardness of human feelings irradiates the surrounding world of embodied forms.

Theory of *rasa*

The theory of *rasa* is attributed to Bharata, a sage-priest who may have lived about AD 500. It was developed by the rhetorician and philosopher Abhinavagupta (*c.* AD 1000), who applied it to all varieties of theatre and poetry. The principal human feelings, according to Bharata, are delight, laughter, sorrow, anger, fear, disgust, heroism, and astonishment, all of which may be recast in contemplative form as the various *rasa*s: erotic, comic, pathetic, furious, terrible, odious, marvellous, and quietistic. These *rasa*s comprise the components of aesthetic experience. The power to taste *rasa* is a reward for merit in some previous existence.

Confucian aesthetics

China. Confucius (551–479 BC) emphasized the role of aesthetic enjoyment in moral and political education, and, like his near contemporary Plato, was suspicious of the power of art to awaken frenzied and distracted feelings. Music must be stately and dignified, contributing to the inner harmony that is the foundation of good behaviour, and all art is at its noblest when incorporated into the rituals and traditions that enforce the stability and order of social life.

Lao-tzu, the legendary founder of Taoism, was even more puritanical. He condemned all art as a blinding of the eye, a deafening of the ear, and a cloying of the palate. Later Taoists were more lenient, however, encouraging a freer, more intuitive approach both to works of art and to nature. The philosophy of beauty presented in their works, and in the writings of the Ch'an (Zen) Buddhists who succeeded them, is seldom articulate, being confined to epigrams and short commentaries that remain opaque to the uninitiated.

The same epigrammatic style and the same fervent puritanism can be discerned in the writings of Mao Tse-tung, who initiated in the Cultural Revolution the most successful war against beauty that has been waged in modern history.

Japan. The practice of literary commentary and aesthetic discussion was extensively developed in Japan and is exemplified at its most engaging in the great novel *Genji monogatari* (*c.* 1000; *Tale of Genji*), written by Murasaki Shikibu, lady-in-waiting to the Empress. Centuries of commentary on this novel, as well as on the court literature that it inspired, on the Nō and puppet plays, and on the lyrical verses of the haiku poets, led to the establishment of an aesthetics of supreme refinement. Many of the concepts of this form of aesthetics were drawn from the writings of Zeami Motokiyo (1363–1443), a playwright and actor-manager. Zeami argued that the value of art is to be found in *yūgen* ("mystery and depth"), and that the artist must follow the rule of *sōō* ("consonance"), according to which every object, gesture, and expression has to be appropriate to its context.

The concepts of *yūgen* and *sōō*

The domination of aesthetic scruples over Japanese life has, as its culminating instance, the tea ceremony—a marvel of constrained social ballet—to the study of which whole lives have been devoted. Associated with this triumph of manners is an art of mood and evocation, in which significance is found in the small, concentrated gesture, the sudden revelation of transcendent meaning in what is most ordinary and unassuming. In the late 18th century, Motoori Norinaga, a leading literary scholar, summed up the essence of Japanese art and literature as the expression of a touching intimation of transience, which he captured in the famous phrase *mono no aware,* meaning roughly "the sensitivity to the sadness of things." Other aesthetic qualities emphasized by classical scholars and critics are *en* ("charming"), *okashi* ("amusing"), and *sabi* (having the beauty of old, faded, worn, or lovely things). In all such aesthetic categories, we can sense the resonance of the Taoist and Buddhist ideas of renunciation.

(Th.M./Ro.Sc.)

BIBLIOGRAPHY. Two of the most useful anthologies of contemporary aesthetics are ELISEO VIVAS and MURRAY KRIEGER (eds.), *The Problems of Aesthetics* (1953); and JOSEPH MARGOLIS (ed.), *Philosophy Looks at the Arts,* rev. ed. (1978). See also JOHN HOSPERS, *Introductory Readings in Aesthetics* (1969); and HAROLD OSBORNE, *Aesthetics* (1972), the latter of which contains a particularly useful bibliography. MONROE C. BEARDSLEY, *Aesthetics: Problems in the Philosophy of Criticism,* 2nd ed. (1981), provides a broad, scholarly overview of the subject; RICHARD WOLLHEIM, *Art and Its Objects* (1968; 2nd ed., 1980), is more narrow. For the definition of aesthetics, the above texts are relevant, as is ROGER SCRUTON, *The Aesthetics of Architecture* (1979; 2nd printing with corrections, 1980). See also PAUL ZIFF, "The Task of Defining a Work of Art," *Philosophical Review,* 62:58–78 (1953); and GEORGE DICKIE, *Aesthetics: An Introduction* (1971).

The first approach to the subject (see article) is exemplified in JOHN CASEY, *The Language of Criticism* (1966); the second in ROGER SCRUTON, *Art and Imagination* (1974, reissued 1982); and the third in RICHARD WOLLHEIM (see above). The classical study of the aesthetic recipient remains that of IMMANUEL KANT, *Kritik der Urteilskraft* (1790); to which one may add BERNARD BOSANQUET, *Three Lectures on Aesthetic* (1915, reprinted 1968). The aesthetic object is dealt with in considerable detail by

ROMAN INGARDEN, *The Literary Work of Art* (1973; originally published in German, 1931); and MIKEL DUFRENNE, *The Phenomenology of Aesthetic Experience* (1973; originally published in French, 1953). For the differences between the various art forms, see JOHN DEWEY, *Art As Experience* (1934, reissued 1980); and SUSANNE K. LANGER, *Feeling and Form* (1953). In addition to the works already cited, the following are particularly important discussions of paradoxes: LUDWIG WITTGENSTEIN, *Lectures and Conversations on Aesthetics, Psychology and Religious Belief,* ed. by CYRIL BARRETT (1966); F.N. SIBLEY and MICHAEL TANNER, "Objectivity and Aesthetics," *The Aristotelian Society: Supplementary Volume 42* (1968), proceedings. Some philosophical approaches to imagination are summarized in MARY WARNOCK, *Imagination* (1976). The most important 20th-century texts are JEAN-PAUL SARTRE, *The Psychology of the Imagination* (1948, reprinted 1978; originally published in French, 1940); and LUDWIG WITTGENSTEIN, *Philosophical Investigations* (1953), pt. 2. For a later attempt to describe the place of imagination in aesthetic experience as a whole, see SCRUTON, *Art and Imagination* (above). The matters of emotion, response, and enjoyment are considered in some depth by BERNARD BOSANQUET, "On the Nature of Aesthetic Emotion," in *Science and Philosophy and Other Essays* (1927, reprinted 1967); and CASEY (above). For a detailed bibliography on the understanding of art, see the section *Philosophy of art* in the article PHILOSOPHIES OF THE BRANCHES OF KNOWLEDGE.

Many of the individual problems are discussed in WOLLHEIM (above); and in ROGER SCRUTON, *The Aesthetic Understanding* (1983). See also SUSANNE K. LANGER, *Philosophy in a New Key* (1972, reissued 1979); ROLAND BARTHES, *Elements of Semiology* (1967; originally published in French, 1965); BENEDETTO CROCE, *Aesthetic* (1909; originally published in Italian, 1902); R.G. COLLINGWOOD, *Principles of Art* (1938); NELSON GOODMAN, *Languages of Art,* 2nd ed. (1976); P.F. STRAWSON, "Aesthetic Appraisal and Works of Art," in his *Freedom and Resentment* (1974); and OSCAR WILDE, *The Critic As Artist* (1925). For discussions of the logic of music, see RUDOLF ARNHEIM, *Art and Visual Perception,* new, rev. ed. (1974); HEINRICH SCHENKER, *Harmony* (1954, reissued 1973; originally published in German, 1906); ROLAND BARTHES, *S/Z* (1974; originally published in French, 1970); and ROGER SCRUTON, "Understanding Music," in his *The Aesthetic Understanding* (above).

Criticism and aesthetic judgment are dealt with in F.N. SIBLEY, "Aesthetic Concepts," *Philosophical Review,* 68:421–450 (1959), and "Aesthetic and Non Aesthetic," *Philosophical Review,* 74:135–159 (1965); W.K. WIMSATT and MONROE C. BEARDSLEY, "The Intentional Fallacy," in W.K. WIMSATT, *The Verbal Icon* (1954); and F.R. LEAVIS, "Literary Criticism and Philosophy," in his *The Common Pursuit* (1952). For a discussion of some contemporary problems, see ANTHONY SAVILE, *The Test of Time* (1982).

An idiosyncratic but useful historical summary is provided in MONROE C. BEARDSLEY, *Aesthetics from Classical Greece to the Present* (1966, reprinted 1975). A full summary, in an outmoded idiom, is given by W. TATARKIEWICZ, *History of Aesthetics,* 3 vol. (1970–74; originally published in Polish, 1960). For additional information pertaining to ancient aesthetics, see the *Macropædia* entries PLATONISM and ARISTOTELIANISM. For Marxist aesthetics, see also MAYNARD SOLOMON (ed.), *Marxism and Art* (1974, reprinted 1979).

For Eastern aesthetics, see THOMAS MUNRO, *Oriental Aesthetics* (1965), which includes a comparison of Eastern and Western attitudes and beliefs (with many bibliographic notes). Other informative studies are NIHAR-RANJAN RAY, *Indian Aesthetics and Art Activity* (1968); MAI-MAI SZE, *The Tao of Painting,* 2 vol. (1956); and MAKOTO UEDA, *Literary and Art Theories of Japan* (1967).

(Ro.Sc.)

Afghanistan

Afghanistan is located in the heart of south-central Asia. The country is officially named the Republic of Afghanistan (Dari Persian: Jomhūrī-ye Afghānestān; Pashto: Da Afghānestān Jamhawrīyat). It has an area of some 251,825 square miles (652,225 square kilometres) and is completely landlocked, the nearest coast lying along the Arabian Sea, about 300 miles to the south. Its longest border, of 1,125 miles (1,810 kilometres), is with Pakistan, to the east and south. The 510-mile border in the west separates Afghanistan from Iran, and there is a 200-mile border with the part of Jammu and Kashmir claimed by Pakistan. The combined length of Afghanistan's northern borders with Turkmenistan, Uzbekistan, and Tajikistan is 1,050 miles. The shortest border—of 50 miles—is with the Uighur Autonomous Region of Sinkiang of the People's Republic of China, at the end of the long, narrow Vākhān (Wakhan Corridor), in the extreme northeast. The capital of Afghanistan is its largest city, Kabul, which is located in the east-central part of the country at an altitude of about 5,900 feet (1,800 metres). The city is connected by road to most Afghan provinces and neighbouring countries to the north and east.

The boundaries of Afghanistan were established in the late 19th century in the context of rivalry between Britain and Russia. Modern Afghanistan became a pawn in struggles over political ideology and commercial influence. In the late 20th century Afghanistan suffered ruinous effects of prolonged civil war, invasion by the Soviet Union (1979), and Soviet military presence (1979–89).

This article is divided into the following sections:

Physical and human geography 25
The land 25
Relief
Drainage
Soils
Climate
Plant and animal life
Settlement patterns
The people 29
Ethnolinguistic groups
Religion
Demographic trends
The economy 29
Management of the economy
Resources
Agriculture
Industry
Finance
Trade
Transportation
Administration and social conditions 30
Government
Armed forces
Education
Health and welfare
Social divisions
Cultural life 31
History 31
Prehistory 31
Historical beginnings (to the 7th century AD) 31
The Achaemenians and the Greeks
The Kushāns
The Sāsānians and Hephthalites
Medieval period (7th–18th century) 32
The first Muslim dynasties
The Mongol invasion
Later medieval dynasties
Last Afghan empire 32
Overthrow of foreign rule
The Durrānī dynasty
The rise of the Bārakzay
Afghanistan since 1973 35
The Republic of Afghanistan (1973–78)
The Afghan Civil War
Bibliography 36

Physical and human geography

THE LAND

Relief. Afghanistan's shape has been compared to a leaf, of which the Vākhān strip forms the stem. The outstanding geographic feature of Afghanistan is its mountain range, the Hindu Kush (in Afghanistan, Hendū Kosh). This formidable range is a barrier between the comparatively fertile northern provinces and the rest of the country, and it creates the major pitch of Afghanistan from northeast to southwest. The Hindu Kush, when it reaches a point some 100 miles north of Kabul, spreads out and continues westward under the names of Bābā, Bāyan, Safīd Kūh (Paropamisus), and others, each section in turn sending spurs in different directions. One of these spurs is the Torkestān Mountains, which extend northwestward. Other important ranges include the Kasa Murgh, south of the Harī River; the Ḥeṣār Mountains, which extend northward; and two formidable ranges, the Mazar and the Khurd, extending in a southwestern direction. On the eastern frontier with Pakistan, several mountain ranges effectively isolate the interior of the country from the rain-laden winds that blow from the Indian Ocean, accounting for the dryness of the climate.

Hindu Kush

Geographic regions

The Hindu Kush and subsidiary ranges divide Afghanistan into three distinct geographic regions, which roughly can be designated as the Central Highlands, the Northern Plains, and the Southwestern Plateau. The Central Highlands, actually a part of the Himalayan chain, include the main Hindu Kush range. Its area of about 160,000 square miles is a region of deep, narrow valleys and lofty mountains, some peaks of which rise above 21,000 feet. High mountain passes, generally situated between 12,000 and 15,000 feet above sea level, are of great strategic importance and include the Shebar Pass, located northwest of Kabul where the Bābā Mountains meet the Hindu Kush, and the Khyber Pass, which leads to the Indian subcontinent, on the Pakistan border southeast of Kabul. The Badakhshān area in the northeastern part of the Central Highlands is the location of the epicentres for many of the 50 or so earthquakes that occur in the country each year.

The Northern Plains region, north of the Central Highlands, extends eastward from the Iranian border to the foothills of the Pamirs, near the border with Tajikistan. It comprises 40,000 square miles of plains and fertile foothills sloping gently toward the Amu River (the ancient Oxus River). This area is a part of the much larger Central Asian steppe, from which it is separated by the Amu River. The average elevation is about 2,000 feet. The Northern Plains region is intensively cultivated and densely populated. In addition to fertile soils, the region possesses rich mineral resources, particularly deposits of natural gas.

The Southwestern Plateau, south of the Central Highlands, is a region of high plateaus, sandy deserts, and semideserts. The average altitude is about 3,000 feet. The Southwestern Plateau covers about 50,000 square miles, one-fourth of which forms the sandy Rīgestān Desert. The smaller Māргow Desert of salt flats and desolate steppe lies west of the Rīgestān Desert. Several large rivers cross

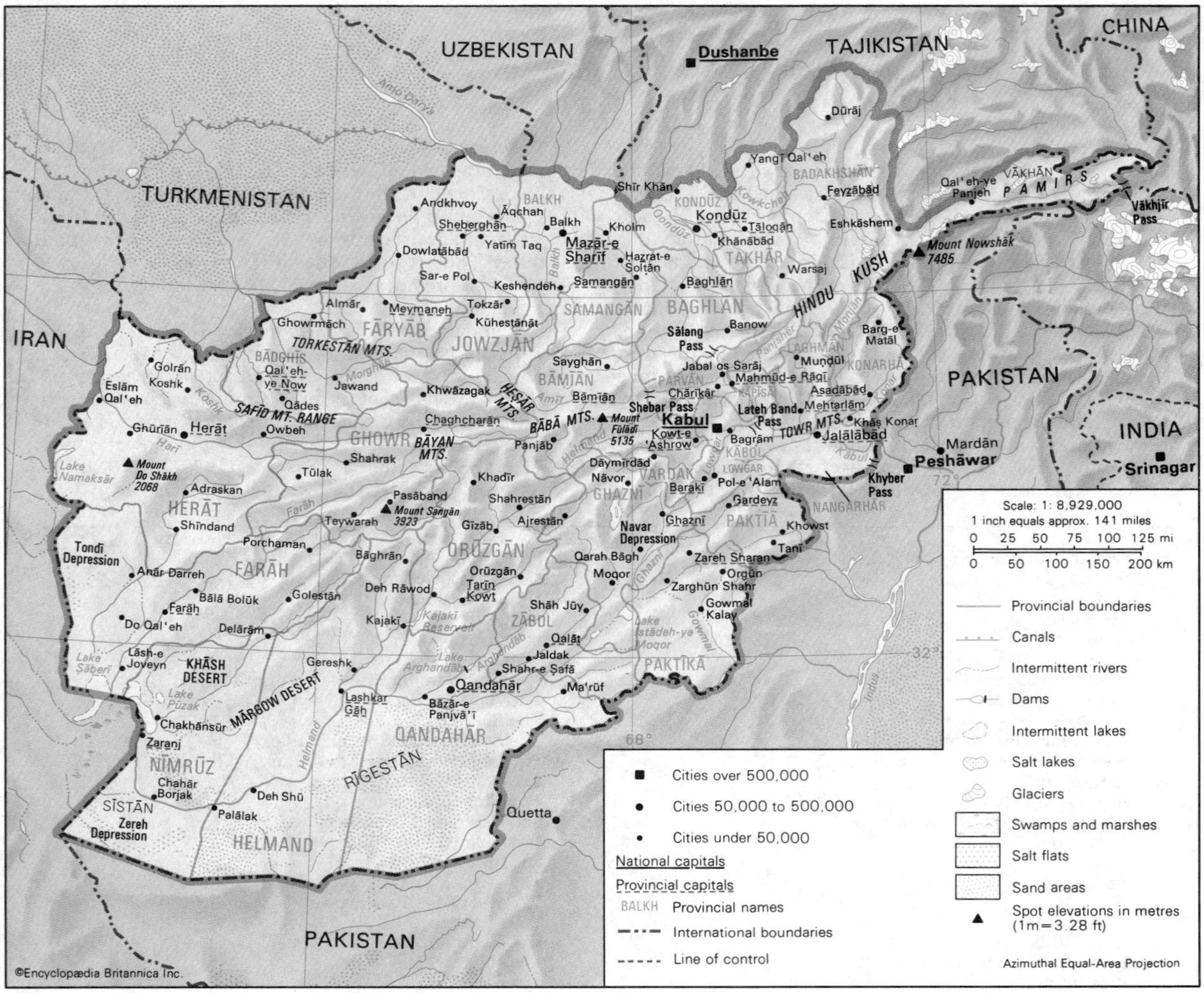

MAP INDEX

Political subdivisions

Badakhshān .....36 45 N 72 00 E
Bādghīs (Bādghisāt) .....35 00 N 63 45 E
Baghlān ....35 45 N 69 00 E
Balkh ....36 30 N 67 00 E
Bāmiān ....34 45 N 67 15 E
Farāh ....33 00 N 62 30 E
Fāryāb (Fariab) ...36 00 N 65 00 E
Ghaznī ....33 00 N 68 00 E
Ghowr (Ghor) ....34 00 N 65 00 E
Harāt, see Herāt
Helmand ....31 00 N 64 00 E
Herāt (Harāt) .....34 30 N 62 00 E
Jowzjān (Jawzjan) ....36 30 N 66 00 E
Kābol (Kabul) ....34 30 N 69 25 E
Kandahār, see Qandahār
Kāpīsā ....34 45 N 69 30 E
Konarhā (Konar, Kunarha) ....35 15 N 71 00 E
Kondūz (Qondūz) ..36 45 N 68 30 E
Kunarha, see Konarhā
Laghmān ....35 00 N 70 15 E
Lowgar ....33 50 N 69 00 E
Nangarhār (Nangrahar, Ningrahar) ......34 45 N 70 50 E
Nīmrūz (Seistan) ..30 30 N 62 00 E
Ningrahar, see Nangarhār
Orūzgān (Uruzgān) ......33 15 N 66 00 E
Paktīā ....33 35 N 69 35 E
Paktīkā ....32 25 N 68 45 E
Parvān (Parwān) ..35 15 N 69 30 E
Qandahār (Kandahār) .....31 00 N 65 45 E
Qondūz, see Kondūz
Samangān ....36 15 N 67 40 E
Seistan, see Nīmrūz
Takhār ....36 30 N 69 30 E
Uruzgān, see Orūzgān
Vardak (Wardak) ..34 15 N 68 00 E
Zābol (Zabul) ....32 00 N 67 15 E

Cities and towns

Adraskan ....33 39 N 62 16 E
Ajrestān ....33 31 N 67 11 E
Almār ....35 50 N 64 32 E
Anār Darreh .....32 46 N 61 39 E
Andkhvoy ....36 56 N 65 08 E
Āq Koprūk, see Keshendeh
Āqchah ....36 56 N 66 11 E
Asadābād ....34 52 N 71 09 E
Āybak, see Samangān
Bactra, see Balkh
Baghlān ....36 13 N 68 46 E
Bāghrān ....33 04 N 65 05 E
Bagrām ....34 58 N 69 17 E
Bālā Bolūk ....32 38 N 62 28 E
Balkh (Bactra) ....36 46 N 66 54 E
Bāmiān (Bāmyān) ..34 50 N 67 50 E
Banow ....35 38 N 69 15 E
Barakī ....33 58 N 68 58 E
Barg-e Matāl .....35 40 N 71 21 E
Bāzār-e Panjvā'ī ...31 32 N 65 28 E
Bust, see Lashkar Gāh
Chaghcharān ....34 31 N 65 15 E
Chahār Borjak ....30 17 N 62 03 E
Chakhānsūr ......31 10 N 62 04 E
Chārīkār ....35 01 N 69 11 E
Dāymīrdād ......34 13 N 68 19 E
Deh Rāwod ......32 37 N 65 27 E
Deh Shū ....30 26 N 63 19 E
Delārām ....32 11 N 63 25 E
Do Qal'eh ....32 08 N 61 27 E
Dowlatābād ......36 26 N 64 55 E
Dūrāj ....37 56 N 70 43 E
Eshkāshem ......36 42 N 71 34 E
Eslām Qal'eh .....34 40 N 61 04 E
Faizābād, see Feyẕābād
Farāh (Farrah, Ferah) ....32 22 N 62 07 E
Feyẕābād (Faizābād) ......37 06 N 70 34 E
Gardeyz (Gardēz) ....33 37 N 69 07 E
Gereshk ....31 48 N 64 34 E
Ghaznī ....33 33 N 68 26 E
Ghowrmāch .....35 44 N 63 47 E
Ghūriān ....34 21 N 61 30 E
Gīzāb ....33 23 N 66 16 E
Golestān ....32 37 N 63 39 E
Golrān ....35 06 N 61 41 E
Gowmal Kalay ....32 31 N 68 51 E
Harāt, see Herāt
Ḥazrat-e Solṭān ...36 27 N 67 54 E
Herāt (Harāt) .....34 20 N 62 12 E
Jabal os Sarāj ....35 07 N 69 14 E
Jalālābād ....34 26 N 70 28 E
Jaldak ....31 58 N 66 43 E
Jawand ....35 04 N 64 09 E
Kabul ....34 31 N 69 12 E
Kajakī ....32 16 N 65 03 E
Kandahār, see Qandahār
Keshendeh (Āq Koprūk) ....36 05 N 66 51 E
Khadīr ....33 55 N 65 56 E
Khānābād ....36 41 N 69 07 E
Khāṣ Konaṛ (Konar-e Khāṣ) ...34 39 N 70 54 E
Kholm ....36 42 N 67 41 E
Khowst ....33 22 N 69 57 E
Khwāzagak ......34 53 N 65 18 E
Konar-e Khāṣ, see Khāṣ Konaṛ
Kondūz (Qondūz) ..36 45 N 68 51 E
Koshk ....34 57 N 62 15 E
Kowt-e 'Ashrow (Maidanshar) ....34 27 N 68 48 E
Kūhestānāt ......35 49 N 65 52 E
Lāsh-e Joveyn ....31 43 N 61 37 E
Lashkar Gāh (Bust) ....31 35 N 64 21 E
Maḥmūd-e Rāqī ...35 01 N 69 20 E
Maidanshar, see Kowt-e 'Ashrow
Maimāna, see Meymaneh
Ma'rūf ....31 34 N 67 03 E
Mazār-e Sharīf ....36 42 N 67 06 E
Mehtarlām ....34 39 N 70 10 E
Meymaneh (Maimāna) ......35 55 N 64 47 E
Moqor ....32 52 N 67 47 E
Munḍūl ....35 17 N 70 10 E

Nāvor 33 53 N 67 57 E
Orgūn 32 57 N 69 11 E
Orūzgān 32 56 N 66 38 E
Owbeh 34 22 N 63 10 E
Palālak 30 14 N 62 54 E
Panjāb 34 22 N 67 01 E
Pasāband 33 41 N 64 51 E
Pol-e ʿAlam 33 59 N 69 02 E
Porchaman 33 08 N 63 51 E
Qādes 34 48 N 63 26 E
Qalāt 32 07 N 66 54 E
Qalʿeh-ye Now 34 59 N 63 08 E
Qalʿeh-ye Panjeh 37 00 N 72 35 E
Qandahār (Kandahār) 31 35 N 65 45 E
Qarah Bāgh 33 12 N 68 06 E
Qondūz, see Kondūz
Sabzevār, see Shīndand
Samangān (Āybak) 36 16 N 68 01 E
Sar-e Pol 36 14 N 65 55 E
Sayghān 35 11 N 67 42 E
Shāh Jūy 32 31 N 67 25 E
Shahrak 34 06 N 64 18 E
Shahr-e Ṣafā 31 50 N 66 22 E
Shahrestān 33 41 N 66 33 E
Sheberghān (Shebirghan, Shibarghān) 36 41 N 65 45 E
Shīndand (Sabzevār) 33 18 N 62 08 E
Shīr Khān 37 11 N 68 36 E
Tāloqān 36 44 N 69 33 E
Tanī 33 15 N 69 49 E
Tarīn Kowt 32 38 N 65 52 E
Teywarah 33 21 N 64 25 E
Tokzār 35 52 N 66 26 E
Tūlak 33 58 N 63 44 E
Warsaj 36 12 N 70 02 E
Yangī Qalʿeh 37 28 N 69 36 E
Yatīm Taq 36 41 N 65 56 E
Zaranj 30 58 N 61 53 E
Zareh Sharan 33 08 N 68 47 E
Zarghūn Shahr 32 51 N 68 25 E

Physical features and points of interest

Amīr, *river* 35 12 N 66 30 E
Amu (Āmū, Oxus), *river* 37 00 N 68 00 E
Arghandāb, *river* 31 27 N 64 23 E
Arghandāb, Lake 31 53 N 65 55 E
Arius, see Harī
Bābā Mountains 34 30 N 67 30 E
Balkh, *river* 36 39 N 66 56 E
Bāyan Mountains 34 20 N 65 30 E
Cophes, see Kābul
Do Shākh, Mount 34 05 N 61 32 E
Erymandrus, see Helmand
Farāh, *river* 31 29 N 61 24 E
Fūlādī, Mount 34 38 N 67 32 E
Ghaznī, *river* 32 35 N 67 58 E
Gowmal (Gumal), *river* 31 56 N 70 22 E
Harī (Arius), *river* 37 24 N 60 38 E
Helmand (Erymandrus, Helmund, Hilmand), *river* 31 12 N 61 34 E
Hendū Kosh, see Hindu Kush
Ḥeṣār Mountains 34 50 N 66 30 E
Hilmand, see Helmand
Hindu Kush (Hendū Kosh), *mountains* 35 00 N 71 00 E
Īstādeh-ye Moqor, Lake 32 32 N 67 57 E
Kābul (Cophes), *river* 33 55 N 72 14 E
Kajakī Reservoir 32 22 N 65 16 E
Khāsh Desert 31 50 N 62 30 E
Khyber Pass (Khaybar, Kowtal-e) 34 05 N 71 10 E
Konar, *river* 34 25 N 70 32 E
Koshk, *river* 36 03 N 62 47 E
Kowkcheh, *river* 37 10 N 69 23 E
Lateh Band Pass 34 30 N 69 34 E
Lowgar, *river* 34 33 N 69 17 E
Mārgow Desert 30 45 N 63 10 E
Monjān, *river* 36 01 N 70 43 E
Morghāb, *river* 38 18 N 61 12 E
Namaksār, Lake 34 00 N 60 30 E
Nāvar Depression 33 44 N 67 45 E
Nowshāk, Mount 36 26 N 71 50 E
Oxus, see Amu
Pamirs, *mountains* 38 00 N 73 00 E
Panjshēr, *river* 34 38 N 69 42 E
Pūzak, Lake 31 30 N 61 45 E
Qondūz, *river* 37 00 N 68 16 E
Rīgestān, *region* 31 00 N 65 00 E
Ṣāberī, Lake 31 30 N 61 20 E
Safīd Mountain Range 34 30 N 63 30 E
Sālang Pass 35 22 N 69 04 E
Sangān, Mount 33 33 N 64 55 E
Shebar Pass 34 54 N 68 14 E
Siāh, see Towr Mountains
Sīstān, *region* 30 30 N 62 00 E
Tondī Depression 32 26 N 60 59 E
Torkestān Mountains 35 25 N 64 15 E
Towr (Siāh) Mountains 34 27 N 70 13 E
Vākhān (Wakhan Corridor), *region* 37 00 N 73 00 E
Vākhjīr (Wakhjir) Pass 37 06 N 74 29 E
Wakhan Corridor, see Vākhān
Wakhjir, see Vākhjīr
Zereh Depression 29 45 N 61 50 E

the Southwestern Plateau; among them are the Helmand River and its major tributary, the Arghandāb.

Most of Afghanistan lies between 2,000 and 10,000 feet in elevation. Along the Amu River in the north and the delta of the Helmand River in the southwest, the altitude is about 2,000 feet. The Sīstān depression of the Southwestern Plateau, 1,500 to 1,700 feet in elevation, was the seat of a flourishing ancient civilization that was ended in the 14th century by Timur (Tamerlane).

The Sīstān depression

Drainage. Practically the entire drainage system of Afghanistan is enclosed within the country. Only the rivers in the east, which drain an area of 32,000 square miles, reach the sea. The Kābul River, the major eastern stream, flows into the Indus River in Pakistan, which empties into the Arabian Sea of the Indian Ocean. Almost all the other important rivers of the country originate in the Central Highlands region and empty into inland lakes or dry up in sandy deserts. The major drainage systems are those of the Amu, Helmand, Kābul, and Harī.

The Amu, a 1,578-mile-long river originating in the glaciers of the Pamirs, drains an area of approximately 93,000 square miles in the northeastern and northern parts of the country. It forms the frontier between Afghanistan and the republics of Tajikistan and Uzbekistan for about 600 miles of its upper course. Two of its major Afghan tributaries, the Kowkcheh and the Qondūz, rise in the mountains of Badakhshān and Kondūz provinces. The Amu becomes navigable from its confluence with the Kowkcheh, 60 miles west of the city of Feyẕābād. It empties into the Aral Sea in Uzbekistan.

The northwestern drainage system is dominated by the Harī River, originating on the western slopes of the Bābā Mountains, at an altitude of 9,000 feet. The river flows westward, just south of Herāt and across the broad Herāt Valley. After irrigating the fertile lands of the valley, the Harī River turns north about 80 miles west of Herāt and forms the border between Afghanistan and Iran for a distance of 65 miles. It then crosses into Turkmenistan and disappears in the Kara-Kum Desert.

Helmand River

The principal river in the southwest is the 715-mile-long Helmand, which rises in the Bābā Mountains, about 50 miles west of Kabul. With its many tributaries, mainly the Arghandāb, it drains more than 100,000 square miles. The river empties into the Ṣāberī, an inland lake. In its course through the southern region of the country, the Helmand flows north of the Rīgestān Desert and then crosses the Mārgow Desert until it reaches a region of seasonal lakes in the Sīstān depression.

The largest drainage system in the southeastern region is that of the Kābul River, which flows eastward from the slopes of the Mazar Range to join the Indus River at Attock, Pak. Its major tributary in the south is the Lowgar.

Afghanistan has few lakes of any considerable size. The two most important are Lake Ṣāberī in the southwest and the saline Lake Īstādeh-ye Moqor, situated 60 miles south of Ghaznī in the southeast. There are five small lakes in the Bābā Mountains known as the Amīr lakes; they are noted for their unusual shades of colour, from milky white to dark green, caused by the underlying bedrock.

Soils. The country possesses extremes in the quality of its soils. The Central Highlands have desert-steppe or meadow-steppe types of soil. The Northern Plains have extremely rich, fertile, loesslike soils, while the Southwestern Plateau has infertile desert soils except along the rivers in the southwest, where alluvial deposits can be found. Erosion is very much in evidence in the Central Highlands, especially in the regions affected by seasonal monsoons and heavy precipitation.

Climate. In general, Afghanistan has extremely cold winters and hot summers, typical of a semiarid steppe climate. There are many regional variations, however. While the mountain regions of the northeast have a subarctic climate with dry, cold winters, the mountainous areas on the border of Pakistan are influenced by the Indian monsoons, usually coming between July and September and bringing maritime tropical air masses with humidity and rains. In addition, strong winds blow almost daily in the southwest during the summer.

Local variation is also produced by differences in altitude. The weather in winter and early spring is strongly influenced by cold air masses from the north and the Atlantic low depression from the northwest; these two air masses bring snowfall and severe cold in the highlands and rain in the lower altitudes.

Afghanistan has a wide range of temperatures. High temperatures over 95° F (35° C) have been recorded in the drought-ridden Southwestern Plateau region. In Jalālābād, one of the hottest localities in the country, the highest temperature of 120° F (49° C) has been recorded in July. January temperatures may drop to 5° F (−15° C) and below in the high mountain areas, while at the city of Kabul, located at an altitude of 5,900 feet, the lowest temperature has been recorded at −24° F (−31° C).

In the mountains the annual mean precipitation increases from west to east; there, as in the southeastern monsoon region, it averages about 16 inches (400 millimetres). The

The Amīr lakes in the Bābā Mountains.
Daniele Pellegrini—Photo Researchers

extremes of precipitation have been recorded in the Sālang Pass of the Hindu Kush, with the highest annual precipitation of 53 inches, and in the arid region of Farāh in the west, with only three inches a year. Most of the country's precipitation occurs from December to April; in the highlands snow falls from December to March, while in the lowlands it rains intermittently from December to April or May. The summer months are hot, dry, and cloudless everywhere but in the monsoon region.

Plant and animal life. Vegetation is sparse in the southern part of the country, particularly toward the west, where dry regions and sandy deserts predominate. Trees are rare, and only in the rainy season of early spring is the soil covered with flowering grasses and herbs. The plant cover becomes more dense toward the north, where precipitation is more abundant; and at higher altitudes the plants are almost luxuriant, particularly in the mountainous region north of Jalālābād, where the climate is influenced by the monsoons. The high mountains abound in large forest trees, among which conifers, such as pine and fir, predominate. Some of these trees are 180 feet high. The average altitude for the fir line is over 10,000 feet. At lower altitudes, somewhere between 5,500 and 7,200 feet, cedar is abundant; below the fir and cedar lines, oak, walnut, alder, ash, and juniper trees can be found. There are also shrubs, several varieties of roses, honeysuckle, hawthorn, and currant and gooseberry bushes.

Most of the wild animals of the subtropical temperate zone inhabit Afghanistan. Large mammals, formerly abundant, are now greatly reduced in numbers. The Siberian tiger, which inhabited the banks of the Amu River, has all but disappeared, as have the tigers that inhabited the southeastern region. There is still a great variety of wild animals roaming the mountains and foothills, including wolves, foxes, striped hyenas, and jackals. Gazelles, wild dogs, and wild cats, such as snow leopards, are widespread. Wild goats, including the markhor (prized for its long, twisted horns) and the ibex (with long, backward-curving horns), can be found in the Pamirs, and wild sheep, including the urial and argali (or Marco Polo sheep), in the Pamirs and the Hindu Kush. Brown bears are found in the mountains and forests. Smaller animals, such as mongooses, moles, shrews, hedgehogs, bats, and several species of kangaroo rat (jerboas), may be found in the many isolated, sparsely populated areas.

Birds of prey include vultures, which occur in great numbers, and eagles. Migratory birds abound during the spring and fall seasons. There are also many pheasant, quail, cranes, pelicans, snipe, partridge, and crows.

There are many varieties of freshwater fish in the rivers, streams, and lakes, but their numbers are not great except on the northern slopes of the Hindu Kush, where the rivers are well stocked with brown trout.

Settlement patterns. The Hindu Kush divides the country into northern and southern regions, which can be further subdivided on the basis of topography, national and ethnolinguistic settlement patterns, or historical tradition. Northern Afghanistan, for example, may be subdivided into the Badakhshān–Vākhān region in the east and the Balkh–Meymaneh region in the west. The east, which is mainly a conglomeration of mountains and high plateaus, is inhabited chiefly by Tajiks, while the west, which is mostly plains of comparatively low altitude, contains a mixture of peoples in which Uzbeks and Turkmens of Turkic origin predominate.

Southern Afghanistan

Southern Afghanistan can be subdivided into four subregions—those of Kabul, Qandahār, Herāt, and Hazārajāt. The Kabul region combines the area drained by the Kābul River and the high plateau of eastern Afghanistan, bounded in the south by the Gowmal (Gumal) River. This region is inhabited by Pashtuns (formerly called Pathans, a term now considered to be derogatory), Tajiks, and Nūristānis. This region is the main corridor connecting the other regions and their peoples.

The Qandahār region consists of the sparsely populated southern part of Afghanistan. The people inhabiting this region belong principally to the Durrānī branch of the Pashtuns. In addition, there is a small number of Baluch and Brahui peoples. The city of Qandahār is located in a fertile oasis near the Arghandāb River.

The region of Herāt, or western Afghanistan, is inhabited by a mixture of Tajiks, Pashtuns, and Chahar Aimaks. The life of the region revolves around the city of Herāt.

The mountainous region of Hazārajāt occupies the central part of the country and is inhabited principally by the Ḥazāras. Although Hazārajāt is located in the heart of the country, its high mountains and poor communication facilities make it the most isolated part of Afghanistan.

Urban settlement. Most urban settlements have grown along the road that runs from Kabul southwestward to Qandahār, then northwest to Herāt, northeast to Mazār-e Sharīf, and southeast back to Kabul. The rural population of farmers and nomads is distributed unevenly over the rest of the country, mainly concentrated along the rivers. The most heavily populated part of the country is between the cities of Kabul and Chārīkār. Other concentrations of people can be found east of the city of Kabul near Jalālābād, in the Herāt oasis and the valley of the Harī River in the northwest, and in the valley of the Qondūz River in the northeast. The high mountains of the central part of the country and the deserts in the south and southwest are sparsely populated or uninhabited.

Major cities

The major cities of Afghanistan are Kabul, Qandahār, Herāt, Baghlān, Jalālābād, Kondūz, Chārīkār, and Mazār-e Sharīf. Kabul is the administrative capital of the country, located south of the Hindu Kush at the crossroads of the trade routes between the Indian subcontinent and Central Asia and between the Middle and Far East. It is built on both sides of the Kābul River and is the main centre of economic and cultural activity. Qandahār, second to Kabul in population, is located on the Asian Highway in the south-central part of the country, between Kabul and Herāt. Qandahār became the first capital of modern Afghanistan in 1747 under Aḥmad Shāh Durrānī.

Rural settlement. Sedentary farmers usually live in small villages, most of them scattered near irrigated land in the valleys of major rivers. These villages, as a rule, are built in the form of small forts. Each fort-village contains several mud houses inhabited by closely connected families who form a defensive community.

The semisedentary farmers, who breed livestock and raise a few crops, live in the high alpine valleys. Since cultivable land there is scarce, they live in scattered isolated hamlets. Each household owns a few head of livestock, which are moved in summer to the highland pastures. The people usually divide themselves into two groups in summer: one group remains in the hamlet to tend the crops, while the other accompanies the livestock to the highlands.

The nomads are mainly Pashtun herdsmen; there are also several thousand Baluch and Kyrgyz nomads. They move in groups (tribes or clans) from summer to winter pasturages, living in tents and, while on the move, packing their belongings on the backs of camels, donkeys, and cattle. Between one-sixth and one-fifth of the total population may be classified as nomadic. Since 1977, however, some nomads have been settled in the plains north of the Hindu Kush or in the area of the Helmand Valley (irrigation) Project.

THE PEOPLE

Ethnolinguistic groups. The people of Afghanistan form a mosaic of ethnic and linguistic groups. Pashto (Pushtu) and Dari, a dialect of Persian (Fārsī), are Indo-European languages; they are the official languages of the country. About half of the population speaks Pashto, the language of the Pashtuns, while about a third of the population speaks Dari, the language of the Tajik, Ḥazāra, Chahar Aimak, and Kizilbash peoples. Other Indo-European languages, spoken by smaller groups, include Western Dardic (Nūristāni or Kafiri), Baluchi, and a number of Indic and Pamiri languages spoken principally in isolated valleys in the northeast. Turkic languages, a subfamily of the Altaic languages, are spoken by the Uzbek and Turkmen peoples, the most recent settlers, who are related to peoples from the steppes of Central Asia. The Turkic languages are closely related; within Afghanistan they include Uzbek, Turkmen, and Kyrgyz, the last spoken by a small group in the extreme northeast.

The present population of Afghanistan contains a number of elements, which, in the course of history and as a result of large-scale migration and conquests, have been superimposed upon each other. Dravidians, Indo-Aryans, Greeks, Scythians, Arabs, Turks, and Mongols have at different times inhabited the country and influenced its culture and ethnography. Intermixture of the two principal linguistic groups is evident in such peoples as the Ḥazāras and Chahar Aimaks, who speak Indo-European languages but have pronounced Mongoloid physical characteristics and cultural traits usually associated with Central Asia.

Pashtuns

The Pashtuns of Afghanistan principally inhabit the southern and eastern parts of the country but are also well represented in the west and north. They are divided into a number of tribes, some sedentary and others nomadic. The traditional homeland of the Pashtuns lies in an area east, south, and southwest of Kabul; many live in contiguous territory of Pakistan. The two most important groups of the Pashtun tribal confederation are the Durrānīs, who live in the area around the city of Qandahār, and the Ghilzays, who inhabit the region between Kabul and Qandahār. The Durrānīs formed the traditional nucleus of Afghanistan's social and political elite.

The Tajiks, mostly farmers and artisans, live in the Kābol and Badakhshān provinces of the northeast and the Herāt region in the west; there are also pockets of Tajiks in other areas. They are sedentary in the plains and semisedentary in the higher valleys. The Tajiks are not divided into clear-cut tribal groups.

The Nūristānis, who speak Western Dardic, inhabit an area of some 5,000 square miles in Laghmān, Nangarhār, and Konarhā provinces, north and east of Kabul. The Ḥazāras traditionally occupy the central mountainous region of Hazārajāt. Because of the scarcity of land, however, many have migrated to other parts of the country. The Ḥazāras speak a Dari dialect that contains a number of Turkish and Mongolian words.

The Chahar Aimaks are probably of Turkic or Turco-Mongolian origin, judging by their Mongoloid physical appearance and their housing of Mongolian-style yurts. They are located mostly in the western part of the central mountain region. The Uzbeks and Turkmens inhabit a region north of the Hindu Kush, and there are small numbers of Kyrgyz in the Vākhān in the extreme northeast. The Uzbeks are usually farmers, while the Turkmens and Kyrgyz are mainly seminomadic herdsmen. The Uzbeks are the largest Turkic-speaking group in Afghanistan. There are also other smaller Turco-Mongolian groups.

Uzbeks and Turkmens

Afghanistan has very small ethnic groups of Dravidian and Semitic speakers. Dravidian languages are spoken by the Brahuis, residing in the extreme south. There is also a small number of Jews, most of whom speak Dari in their daily lives but use Hebrew for religious ceremonies.

Religion. About 99 percent of the people of Afghanistan are Muslims, of whom some three-fourths are members of the Sunnī sect (Ḥanafī branch). The others, particularly the Ḥazāras, Kizilbash, and a few Ismāʿīlīs, follow Shīʿite Islām. The Nūristānis are descendants of a large ethnic group, the Kafirs, who were forcibly converted to Islām in 1895; the name of their region was then changed from Kafiristan ("Land of the Infidels") to Nūristān ("Land of Light"). There are also a few thousand Hindus and Sikhs.

Demographic trends. The establishment of the Democratic Republic of Afghanistan in 1978 and the Soviet invasion of the country the following year disrupted the country's population patterns. Civil war and the destruction of towns and villages caused mass movements of people in two major directions—emigration, mainly to Pakistan and Iran, or escape to the relative safety of the capital city, Kabul. By some estimates almost 3,000,000 people escaped to Pakistan and some 1,850,000 to Iran; the population of Kabul is estimated to have doubled in size. Kabul has grown to encompass almost half of the urban population of the country. Afghanistan's population is mainly rural; almost half of the population is under 15 years of age. Life expectancy is less than 40 years.

THE ECONOMY

When Afghanistan began to plan the development of its economy in the mid-1950s, it lacked not only the necessary social organization and institutions for modern economic activities but also managerial and technical skills. The country was at a much lower stage of economic development than most of its neighbours. Between 1956 and 1979, however, the country's economic growth was guided by several five-year and seven-year plans and was aided by extensive foreign assistance, primarily from the Soviet Union and the United States. Roads, dams, power plants, and factories were constructed, irrigation projects carried out, and education broadened.

The Soviet invasion in 1979 and the subsequent civil war severely disrupted Afghanistan's economic development. Agricultural production declined and food shortages were reported and, with the exception of natural gas production and some other industries considered essential by the Soviet Union, industrial output stagnated. Thus, Afghanistan remains economically one of the world's poorest countries.

Management of the economy. The Socialist government is committed to developing a mixed, guided economy by means of a series of five-year plans. In practice, the effectiveness of such a policy has been limited by the paucity of government resources, by a cumbersome bureaucracy, and by a shortage in technical personnel.

Before the Soviet invasion, the government budget was divided into two parts, ordinary and development. The former covered administrative activities and the latter investment expenditures, incorporated into the national plans of development. Total domestic revenue was usually exceeded by expenditures; the difference was covered through deficit financing and foreign loans and grants. Following the Soviet invasion, a balanced budget was achieved with revenue derived principally from the sale of natural gas and from foreign loans and grants. Expenditures were mainly for governmental ministries, the developmental budget, and foreign debt service.

The private sector engages primarily in agriculture and livestock breeding. There formerly was a mixed pattern of small, medium, and large landholdings, but this system underwent drastic change, particularly after 1978. The bulk of the trade and transport and most manufacturing were in the hands of private entrepreneurs until the late 1970s when these sectors of the economy were nationalized. Public enterprise formerly was confined to a section of the foreign trade, to mining, and to some industries.

Because most of the population is engaged in agriculture, the industrial labour force is insignificant, and labour unions have failed to develop. Traditional loyalties to families and tribes are stronger than those to workers' organizations.

Resources. *Mineral resources.* Extensive surveys have revealed the existence of a number of minerals of economic importance. The most important discovery has been that of natural gas, with large reserves near Sheberghān in Jowzjān province, near the Turkmen border, about 75 miles west of Mazār-e Sharīf. The Khvājeh Gūgerdak and Yatīm Taq fields are major producers, with storage and refining facilities. Pipelines deliver natural gas to Uzbekistan and Tajikistan and to a thermal power plant and chemical fertilizer plant in Mazār-e Sharīf.

Natural gas

Petroleum resources have proved to be insignificant. Many coal deposits have been found in the northern slopes of the Hindu Kush. Major coal fields are at Karkar and Eshposhteh, in Baghlān province, and Fort Sarkārī, in Balkh province.

High-grade iron ore, with an iron content of 62–63 percent, has been discovered at Ḥājīgak, 60 miles northwest of Kabul. Copper is mined at 'Aynak, near Kabul, and uranium is extracted in the mountains near Khvājeh Rawāsh, east of Kabul. There are also deposits of copper, lead, and zinc near Kondūz; beryllium in Khāṣ Konaṛ; chrome ore in the Lowgar valley near Herāt; and the semiprecious stone lapis lazuli in Badakhshān. Afghanistan also has deposits of rock salt, beryl, barite, fluorspar, bauxite, lithium, tantalum, gold, silver, asbestos, mica, and sulfur.

Biological resources. Afghanistan is essentially a pastoral country. Only 12 percent of the total land area is arable, and only about half of the arable acreage is cultivated annually. Much of the arable area consists of fallow cultivable land or steppes and mountains that serve as pastureland. In addition, a large area is desert.

Forests cover about 3 percent of the total land area; they are found mainly in the eastern part of the country and on the southern slopes of the Hindu Kush. Those in the east consist mainly of conifers, providing timber for the building industry as well as some wild nuts for export. Other trees, especially oaks, are used as fuel. North of the Hindu Kush are pistachio trees, the nuts of which are exported.

Power resources. Afghanistan is potentially rich in hydroelectric resources. However, the seasonal flow of the country's many streams and waterfalls—torrential in spring, when the snow melts in the mountains, but negligible in summer—necessitates the costly construction of dams and reservoirs in remote areas. The nation's negligible demand for electricity renders such projects unprofitable except near large cities or industrial centres. The potential of hydroelectricity has been tapped substantially only in the Kabul–Jalālābād region.

Agriculture. Agriculture and animal husbandry, much of which consists of subsistence farming and pastoral nomadism, are by far the most important items of the gross national product, accounting for more than half of its total value. Since much of the land is arid or semiarid, about half of the cultivated land is irrigated.

Irrigation

Most of the cultivated land is planted with cereals. Of these, wheat is the chief crop and the staple food of the population. The other food grains are corn (maize), rice, and barley. Cotton is important, both for the domestic textile industry and for export. Fruits and nuts are also important items of export. Opium poppy and cannabis are grown for the illegal international drug trade.

Animal husbandry produces meat and dairy products for local consumption; skins, especially the famous karakul, and wool (both for export and for domestic carpet weaving) are also important products. Livestock includes sheep, cattle, goats, donkeys, horses, camels, buffalo, and mules. About two-thirds of the annual milk production is from cows, the rest from sheep and goats.

Industry. Industry is based mainly on agricultural and pastoral raw materials. Most important is the cotton textile industry. The country also produces rayon and acetate fibres. Other industrial products are cement, sugar, vegetable oil, furniture, soap, shoes, and woolen textiles. A nitrogenous fertilizer plant, based on natural gas, has been constructed in Mazār-e Sharīf, and phosphate fertilizers are also produced. In addition, Afghanistan has a number of traditional handicrafts, which account for a fair proportion of the country's export earnings.

Finance. In 1975 the government nationalized all banks. The largest bank in the country, the Bank of Afghanistan, is the centre of the formal banking system. It is the sole bank of issue, and it plays an important role in determining and implementing the government's financial policies. There are private money traders who provide nearly all the services of a commercial bank.

Trade. Total annual imports usually exceed exports. Roughly two-thirds of Afghanistan's exports go to the former Soviet republics to the north, and one-seventh to the United Kingdom and Germany. The Soviet Union was traditionally the leading source of imports, followed by Japan, Germany, Hong Kong, and the United Kingdom. The principal export is natural gas, which for many years went mainly to the Soviet Union. In addition, dried fruit, nuts, carpets, wool, and karakul pelts are exported. Imports include vehicles, petroleum products, sugar, textiles, processed animal and vegetable oils, and tea.

Transportation. Being a landlocked country, Afghanistan is primarily dependent on transit facilities from its neighbours for its international trade. Lacking railways and with few navigable rivers, it relies on roads as the mainstay of its transport system. These factors produce high transport costs and also add to the difficulty of integrating the transport system of the country with those of its neighbours. Nevertheless, in the 1960s major efforts were directed toward upgrading the highway system and connecting the main trading centres of the country with one another, as well as with the railheads or road networks of neighbouring countries.

The road network of Afghanistan now connects railheads in Kushka, Turkmenistan, and Termez, Uzbekistan, with those at Chaman and Peshāwar, Pak., respectively, and provides for direct overland transit between the nations to the north and the Indo-Pakistani subcontinent. The most important Afghan highways are those connecting Kabul with Shīr Khān, on the northern border, and with Peshāwar. Other paved roads link Qandahār, Herāt, and Mazār-e Sharīf with Kabul and with frontier towns of Pakistan, Iran, Turkmenistan, and Uzbekistan.

Major highways

Despite the rapid development of motor transport, camels and donkeys are still commonly used as draft animals. In the countryside many people have not abandoned their cherished horses, which are important for prestige.

Civil aviation has increased in importance. Almost all provincial centres have at least a seasonally operable airport, while there are international airports at Kabul and Qandahār. (V.P.P.)

ADMINISTRATION AND SOCIAL CONDITIONS

Government. Until the middle of the 20th century, Afghanistan was ruled by the absolute power of the king. Two constitutions were promulgated, in 1923 and 1931, both affirming the power of the monarchy. The constitution of 1964, however, provided for a constitutional monarchy, based on the separation of executive, legislative, and judicial authorities. A military coup in 1973 overthrew the monarchy, abolished the constitution of 1964, and established the Republic of Afghanistan. The Grand National Assembly (*Loya Jirgah*) adopted a new constitution in February 1977, but it was abrogated in 1978 when another coup established the Democratic Republic of Afghanistan, governed by the Afghan Revolutionary Council. Political turmoil continued, marked by a third coup in September 1979, a massive invasion of troops from the Soviet Union, and the installation of a socialist government in December 1979. A new constitution promulgated in 1987 changed the name of the country back to the Republic of Afghanistan and reaffirmed its nonaligned status, strengthened the post of president, and permitted other parties to participate in government.

The highest government authority is vested in the Grand National Assembly, a body defined as "the highest manifestation of the will of the people of Afghanistan" and made up of members of the executive, legislative, and judicial branches. The Grand National Assembly has the power to elect the president, amend and interpret the constitution, declare war, and adopt decisions on "the most important questions concerning the country's national destiny." The head of state and commander in chief of the armed forces is the president, who is elected for a seven-year term. The Council of Ministers is the highest executive body and is responsible for domestic and foreign policy. The National Assembly is the highest legislative body and comprises a 192-member council of elders and a 234-member council of representatives.

Afghanistan has a centralized system of local government. For administrative purposes the country is divided into provinces, each administered by a centrally appointed governor. The provinces are further subdivided into districts and subdistricts, headed by appointed commissioners.

Armed forces. Regular army officers are trained in a military school in Kabul. There is a small air force, equipped with modern Soviet aircraft and with bases at Bagrām and Shīndand. A secret police force was organized in the late 1970s. (V.P.P./Ed.)

Education. Education is free at all levels, and elementary education is officially compulsory wherever it is provided by the state. Nonetheless, fewer than one-fourth of all Afghan children attend school. There are primary schools throughout the country but secondary schools only in the provincial and in some district centres. Less than one-fourth of the population is literate. Kabul University was founded in 1946 by the incorporation of a number of faculties, the oldest of which is the faculty of medicine, established in 1932. The University of Nangarhār was formed in Jalālābād in 1963.

Health and welfare. Health care and the availability of hospitals, doctors, and nurses in Afghanistan are greatly deficient. Medical training is almost nonexistent, and the medical aid that is available is provided mainly by foreign countries. The major proportion of medical services is concentrated in Kabul, and many rural areas do not have hospitals or doctors. The lack of health care accounts for a high mortality rate among young children. Welfare measures offered by the government are minimal.

Social divisions. The bulk of the population in the rural areas consists of small farmers exploiting their tiny plots of land. The majority of the city and town dwellers are artisans, small traders, or government employees. The industrial labour force, though small, has grown. There is also a business community of merchants and industrialists. Since the 1960s the wearing of a veil by women has been voluntary, and women have found employment in offices and shops. Some Afghan women have received a university education.

CULTURAL LIFE

Afghanistan has a rich cultural heritage, covering more than 5,000 years. Because of almost complete isolation from the outside world, however, little in art, literature, or architecture was produced between the 16th and early 20th centuries. Because most Afghans live outside the cities, their mode of living can be described as that of a peasant tribal society. Kinship is the basis of social life and determines the patriarchal character of the community. Religion plays a very important role.

Archaeological research carried out since 1922 has uncovered many fine works of art of the pre-Islāmic and Islāmic periods. A revival of the traditional arts and an interest in new forms of expression have given a new dynamism to artistic creation. Of the new painters, some draw direct inspiration from the Herāt school of the 15th-century Timurid period; others are influenced by Western styles. Through government initiative, some of the old monuments of architectural value are being restored and redecorated. The School of Fine Arts was established in Kabul in the 1930s. In architecture, the traditional Timurid techniques are preserved, particularly in the design of the exterior walls of mosques or tombs. Handicrafts include the world-renowned Afghan carpets and copper utensils.

Theatre as known in the West has flourished only since about 1960. Adaptations of European classics were introduced at first, but the present trend favours the didactic treatment of themes from everyday Afghan life. In addition to city theatres such as those in Kabul, Herāt, or Qandahār, there are traveling companies that take plays to provincial centres or country fairs.

In music and dance, a revival of traditional folksinging has gone hand in hand with the imitation of modern Western and Indian music. Afghan music is different from Western music in many ways, particularly in its scales, note intervals, pitch, and rhythm, but it is closer to Western than to Asian music. Afghans celebrate their religious or national feast days, and particularly weddings, by public dancing. The performance of the *attan* dance in the open air has long been a feature of Afghan life. It is the national dance of the Pashtuns and now of the nation.

The *attan* dance

The Afghan Historical Society is devoted to disseminating information on Afghan history. It publishes *Aryana,* a monthly, in Pashto and Dari. The society also arranges for the publication of research works on Afghan history, manuscripts, and historical sites and monuments. The Pashto Society works for the development of Pashto literature and for its promotion among the non-Pashto-speaking population. It publishes the monthly *Kābul* and arranges for the publication of old Pashto manuscripts as well as of works on Pashto linguistics and literature.

For statistical data on the land and people of Afghanistan, see the *Britannica World Data* section in the BRITANNICA WORLD DATA ANNUAL. (V.P.P.)

History

Variations on the word "Afghan" may go back as early as a 3rd-century-AD Sāsānian reference to "Abgan." The earliest Muslim reference to the Afghans probably dates to AD 982, but tribes related to the modern Afghans have lived in the region for many generations. For millennia, the land now called Afghanistan has been the meeting place of four cultural and ecological areas: the Middle East, Central Asia, South Asia, and the Far East.

PREHISTORY

Paleolithic peoples probably roamed Afghanistan as early as 100,000 BC. The earliest definite evidence of human occupation was found in the cave of Darra-i-Kur in Badakhshān, where a transitional Neanderthal skull fragment in association with Mousterian-type tools was discovered; the remains are of the Middle Paleolithic, dating about 30,000 years ago. Caves near Āq Koprūk yielded evidence of an early Neolithic culture (*c.* 9000–6000 BC) based on domesticated animals. Archaeological research since World War II has revealed Bronze Age sites, dating both before and after the Indus Valley (or Harappān) civilization of the 3rd to the 2nd millennium BC. There was trade with Bronze Age Mesopotamia and Egypt, the main export from the Afghan area being lapis lazuli from the mines of Badakhshān. In addition, a site with definite links to the Harappān civilization has been excavated at Shortugai near the Amu River, northeast of Kondūz.

HISTORICAL BEGINNINGS (TO THE 7TH CENTURY AD)

The Achaemenians and the Greeks. In the 6th century BC the Achaemenian ruler Cyrus II the Great established his authority over the area. Darius I the Great consolidated Achaemenian rule of the region through the provinces, or satrapies, of Aria (in the region of modern Herāt), Bactria (Balkh), Sattagydia (Ghaznī to the Indus River), Arachosia (Qandahār), and Drangiana (Seistan).

Alexander the Great overthrew the Achaemenians and conquered most of the Afghan satrapies before he left for India in 327 BC. Ruins of an outpost Greek city founded about 325 BC were discovered at Ay Khānom, at the confluence of the Amu and Kowkcheh rivers. Excavations there produced inscriptions and transcriptions of Delphic precepts written in a script influenced by cursive Greek. Greek decorative elements dominate the architecture, including an immense administrative centre, a theatre, and

Alexander the Great

a gymnasium. A nomadic raid about 130 BC ended the Greek era at Ay Khānom.

After Alexander's death in 323 BC, the eastern satrapies passed to the Seleucid dynasty, which ruled from Babylon. In about 304 BC the territory south of the Hindu Kush was ceded to the Maurya dynasty of northern India. Bilingual rock inscriptions in Greek and Aramaic (the official language of the Achaemenians) found at Qandahār and Laghmān (in eastern Afghanistan) date from the reign of Aśoka (*c.* 265–238 BC, or *c.* 273–232 BC), the Maurya dynasty's most renowned emperor. Diodotus, a local Greco-Bactrian governor, declared the Afghan plain of the Amu River independent about 250 BC; Greco-Bactrian conquerors moved south about 180 BC and established their rule at Kabul and in the Punjab. The Parthians of eastern Iran also broke away from the Seleucids, establishing control over Seistan and Qandahār in the south.

The Kushāns. About 135 BC a loose confederation of five Central Asian nomadic tribes known as the Yüeh-chih wrested Bactria from the Bactrian Greeks. These tribes united under the banner of the Kushān (Kuṣāṇa), one of the five tribes, and conquered the Afghan area. The zenith of Kushān power was reached in the 2nd century AD under King Kaniṣka (*c.* AD 78–144), whose empire stretched from Mathurā in north-central India beyond Bactria as far as the frontiers of China in Central Asia.

Kushān art

The Kushāns were patrons of the arts and of religion. A major branch of the Silk Road carrying luxury goods and ideas between Rome, India, and China passed through Afghanistan, where a transshipment centre existed at Balkh. Indian pilgrims traveling the Silk Road introduced Buddhism to China during the early centuries AD, and Buddhist Gandhāra art flourished during this period. The world's largest Buddha figures (175 feet and 120 feet tall) were carved into a cliff at Bāmīān in the central mountains of Afghanistan during the 3rd and 4th centuries AD. Further evidence of the trade and cultural achievement of the period has been recovered at the Kushān summer capital of Bagrām, north of Kabul; it includes painted glass from Alexandria; plaster matrices, bronzes, porphyries, and alabasters from Rome; carved ivories from India; and lacquers from China. A massive Kushān city at Delbarjin, north of Balkh, and a major gold hoard of superb artistry near Sheberghān, west of Balkh, also have been excavated.

The Sāsānians and Hephthalites. The Kushān Empire did not long survive Kaniṣka, though for centuries Kushān princes continued to rule in various provinces. Persian Sāsānians established control over parts of Afghanistan, including Bagrām, in AD 241. In AD 400 a new wave of Central Asian nomads under the Hephthalites took control, only to be defeated in AD 565 by a coalition of Sāsānians and Western Turks. From the 5th through the 7th century many Chinese Buddhist pilgrims continued to travel through Afghanistan. The pilgrim Hsüan-tsang (Xüanzang) wrote an important account of his travels, and several of the religious centres he visited, including Hadda, Ghazna, Kondūz, Bāmīān, Shotorak, and Bagrām, have been excavated.

MEDIEVAL PERIOD (7TH–18TH CENTURY)

Under the Hephthalites and Sāsānians, many of the Afghan princedoms were influenced by Hinduism. The Hindu kings (Shāhī) were concentrated in the Kabul and Ghaznī areas. Excavated sites of the period include a major Hindu Shāhī temple north of Kabul and a chapel in Ghaznī that contains both Buddhist and Hindu statuary, indicating that there was a mingling of these two religions.

The first Muslim dynasties. Islāmic armies defeated the Sāsānians in AD 642 at Nahāvand (near modern Hamadān, Iran) and moved on to the Afghan area, but they were unable to hold the territory; cities submitted, only to rise in revolt, and the hastily converted returned to their old beliefs once the armies had passed. The 9th and 10th centuries witnessed the rise of numerous local Islāmic dynasties. One of the earliest was the Ṭāhirids of Khorāsān, whose kingdom included Balkh and Herāt; they established virtual independence from the ʿAbbāsid caliphate in AD 820. The Ṭāhirids were succeeded in 867–869 by a native dynasty from Seistan, the Ṣaffārids. Local princes in the north soon became feudatories of the powerful Sāmānids, who ruled from Bukhara. From 872 to 999 Bukhara, Samarkand, and Balkh enjoyed a golden age under Sāmānid rule. (L.Du./N.H.D.)

The Ghaznavids. In the middle of the 10th century a former Turkish slave named Alptegin seized Ghazna (Ghaznī). He was succeeded by another former slave, Subüktigin, who extended the conquests to Kabul and the Indus. His son was the great Maḥmūd of Ghazna, who came to the throne in 998. Maḥmūd conquered the Punjab and Multan and carried his raids into the heart of India. The hitherto obscure town of Ghazna became a splendid city, as did the second capital at Bust (Lashkar Gāh).

Maḥmūd of Ghazna

The Ghūrids. Maḥmūd's descendants continued to rule over a gradually diminishing empire until 1150, when ʿAlāʾ-ud-Dīn Ḥusayn of Ghūr, a mountain-locked region in central Afghanistan, sacked Ghazna and drove the last Ghaznavid out to India. ʿAlāʾ-ud-Dīn's nephew, Muʿizz-ud-Dīn Muḥammad, known as Muḥammad of Ghūr, first invaded India in 1175. After his death in 1206, his general, Quṭb-ud-Dīn Aybak, became the sultan of Delhi.

The Khwārezm-Shāhs. Shortly after Muḥammad of Ghūr's death, the Ghurīd Empire fell apart, and Afghanistan was occupied by Sultan ʿAlāʾ ad-Dīn Muḥammad, the Khwārezm-Shāh. The territories of the Khwārezm-Shāh dynasty extended from Chinese Turkistan in the east to the borders of Iraq in the west. (F.R.Al.)

The Mongol invasion. Genghis Khan invaded the eastern part of ʿAlāʾ ad-Dīn's empire in 1219. Avoiding a battle, ʿAlāʾ ad-Dīn retreated to a small island in the Caspian Sea, where he died in 1220. Soon after ʿAlāʾ ad-Dīn's death, his energetic son Jalāl ad-Dīn Mingburnu rallied the Afghan highlanders at Parwan (modern Jabal os Sarāj), near Kabul, and inflicted a crushing defeat on the Mongols under Kutikonian. Genghis Khan, who was then at Herāt, hastened to avenge the defeat and laid siege to Bāmīān. There Mutugen, the Khān's grandson, was killed, an event so infuriating to Genghis Khan that when he captured the citadel he ordered that no living being be spared. Bāmīān was utterly destroyed. Advancing on Ghazna, Genghis won a great victory over Jalāl ad-Dīn, who then fell back toward the Indus (1221), where he made a final but unsuccessful stand.

Later medieval dynasties. After his death in 1227, Genghis Khan's vast empire fell to pieces. In Afghanistan some local chiefs succeeded in establishing independent principalities, and others acknowledged Mongol princes as suzerains. This state of affairs continued until the end of the 14th century, when Timur (Tamerlane) conquered a large part of the country.

Timur's successors, the Timurids, were great patrons of learning and the arts who enriched their capital city of Herāt with fine buildings. Under their rule (1404–1507) Afghanistan enjoyed peace and prosperity.

The Mughals

Early in the 16th century the Turkic Uzbeks rose to power in Central Asia under Muḥammad Shaybānī, who took Herāt in 1507. In late 1510 the Ṣafavid *shāh* Esmāʿīl besieged Shaybānī in Merv and killed him. Bābur, a descendant of Genghis Khan and Timur, had made Kabul the capital of an independent principality in 1504. He captured Qandahār in 1522, and in 1526 he marched on Delhi. He defeated Ibrāhīm, the last of the Lodī Afghan kings of India, and established the Mughal Empire, which lasted until the middle of the 19th century and included all of eastern Afghanistan south of the Hindu Kush. The capital was at Āgra. Nine years after his death in 1530, the body of Bābur was taken to Kabul for burial.

During the next 200 years Afghanistan was parceled between the Mughals of India and the Ṣafavids of Persia—the former holding Kabul north to the southern foothills of the Hindu Kush and the latter Herāt and Farāh. Qandahār was for many years in dispute.

LAST AFGHAN EMPIRE

Overthrow of foreign rule. Periodic attempts were made to gain independence. In 1709 Mīr Veys Khān, a leader of the Hotaki Ghilzay tribe, led a successful rising against Gorgīn Khān, the Persian governor of Qandahār.

The Hotakis. Mīr Veys Khān governed Qandahār until his death in 1715. In 1716 the Abdālīs of Herāt, encouraged by his example, took up arms against the Persians and under their leader, Asadullāh Khān, succeeded in liberating their province. Maḥmūd, Mīr Veys's young son and successor, was not content with holding Qandahār, and in 1722 he led some 20,000 men against Isfahan; the Ṣafavid government surrendered after a six-month siege.

Shāh Ashraf

Maḥmūd died in 1725 and was succeeded by Ashraf, who had to contend with Russian pressure from the north and Ottoman Turk advances from the west. Shāh Ashraf halted both the Russian and Turkish onslaughts, but a brigand chief, Nāder Qolī Beg, defeated the Afghans at Dāmghān in October 1729 and drove them from Persia. During the retreat Ashraf was murdered, probably on orders from his cousin, who was then holding Qandahār.

Nāder Shāh. Nāder Qolī Beg took Herāt in 1732 after a desperate siege. Impressed by their courage, Nāder recruited many Herātis to serve in his army. He was elected *shāh* of Persia, with the name Nāder Shāh, in 1736.

In 1738, after a year's siege, the city of Qandahār fell to Nāder Shāh's army of 80,000 men. Nāder Shāh seized Ghazna and Kabul and occupied the Mughal capital at Delhi in 1739. His booty included the Koh-i-noor diamond and the Peacock Throne. He was assassinated at Khabushan in 1747, which led to the disintegration of his empire and the rise of the last great Afghan empire.

Aḥmad Shāh Durrānī

The Durrānī dynasty. The commander of the Shāh's 4,000-man Afghan bodyguard was Aḥmad Khān Abdālī, who returned to Qandahār where he was elected king (*shāh*) by a tribal council. He adopted the title Durr-i Durrān ("Pearl of Pearls"). Supported by most tribal leaders, Aḥmad Shāh Durrānī extended Afghan control from Meshed to Kashmir and Delhi, from the Amu River to the Arabian Sea. The Durrānī was the second greatest Muslim empire in the second half of the 18th century, surpassed in size only by the Ottoman.

Aḥmad Shāh died in 1772 and was succeeded by his son, Tīmūr Shāh, who received but nominal homage from the tribal chieftains. Much of his reign was spent in quelling their rebellions. Because of this opposition, Tīmūr shifted his capital from Qandahār to Kabul in 1776.

Zamān Shāh (1793–1800). After the death of Tīmūr in 1793, his fifth son, Zamān, seized the throne with the help of Sardār Pāyenda Khān, a chief of the Bārakzay. Zamān then turned to India with the object of repeating the exploits of Aḥmad Shāh. This alarmed the British, who induced Fatḥ ʿAlī Shāh of Persia to bring pressure upon the Afghan king and divert his attention from India. The *shāh* went a step further, helping Maḥmūd, governor of Herāt and a brother of Zamān, with men and money and encouraging him to advance on Qandahār. Maḥmūd, assisted by his vizier, Fatḥ Khān Bārakzay, eldest son of Sardār Pāyenda Khān, and by Fatḥ ʿAlī Shāh, took Qandahār and advanced on Kabul. Zamān, in India, hurried back to Afghanistan. There he was handed over to Maḥmūd, blinded, and imprisoned (1800). The Durrānī Empire had begun to disintegrate after 1798, when Zamān Shāh appointed a Sikh, Ranjit Singh, as governor of Lahore.

Shāh Maḥmūd (1800–03; 1809–18). Shāh Maḥmūd left affairs of state to Fatḥ Khān. Some of the chiefs who had grievances against the King or his ministers joined forces and invited Zamān's brother Shāh Shojāʿ to Kabul. The intrigue was successful. Shāh Shojāʿ occupied the capital, and Maḥmūd sued for peace.

Shāh Shojāʿ (1803–09; 1839–42). The new king, Shāh Shojāʿ, ascended the throne in 1803. The chiefs had become powerful and unruly, and the outlying provinces were asserting their independence. The Sikhs of the Punjab were encroaching upon Afghan territories from the east, while the Persians were threatening from the west.

Napoleon, then at the zenith of his power in Europe, proposed to Alexander I of Russia a combined invasion of India. A British mission, headed by Mountstuart Elphinstone, met Shāh Shojāʿ at Peshāwar to discuss mutual defense against this threat, which never developed.

Treaty with the British

A treaty of friendship was concluded (June 7, 1809), the *shāh* promising to oppose the passage of foreign troops through his dominions. Shortly after the mission left Peshāwar news was received that Kabul had been occupied by the forces of Maḥmūd and Fatḥ Khān. Shāh Shojāʿ's troops were routed, and he withdrew from Afghanistan and found asylum with the British at Ludhiāna in 1815.

The rise of the Bārakzay. The Bārakzay were now dominant. This situation incited the jealousy of Kāmrān, Maḥmūd's eldest son, who seized and blinded Fatḥ Khān. Later, Shāh Maḥmūd had him cut to pieces.

Dōst Moḥammad (1826–39; 1843–63). Advancing from Kashmir in 1818, Dōst Moḥammad, younger brother of Fatḥ Khān, took Peshāwar and Kabul and drove Shāh Maḥmūd and Kāmrān from all their possessions except Herāt, where they maintained a precarious footing for a few years. Balkh was seized by the ruler of Bukhara; the trans-Indus Afghan districts were occupied by the Sikhs; and the outlying provinces of Sind and Baluchistan assumed independence. Ghazna, Kabul, and Jalālābād fell to Dōst Moḥammad.

Dōst Moḥammad established the Bārakzay (or Moḥammadzai) dynasty. His position secure after he assumed the title of *amīr* in 1826 at Kabul, he decided to recover Peshāwar from the Sikhs. Declaring a jihād, or Islāmic holy war, in 1836, he advanced on Peshāwar. The Sikh leader Ranjit Singh, however, sowed dissension in Dōst Moḥammad's camp, the invading army melted away, and Peshāwar was permanently lost to the Afghans.

In November 1837 Moḥammad Shāh of Persia laid siege to Herāt, which the British saw as the key to India. The Russians supported the Persians. The British, fearful that Persia was falling completely under Russian influence, entered into alliances with the rulers of Herāt, Kabul, and Qandahār. A British mission to Kabul under Captain (later Sir) Alexander Burnes in 1837 was welcomed by Dōst Moḥammad, who hoped the British would help him recover Peshāwar. Burnes could not give him the required assurances; and when a Russian agent appeared in Kabul, the British left for India.

First Anglo-Afghan War, 1839–42

With the failure of Burnes's mission, the governor general of India, Lord Auckland, ordered an invasion of Afghanistan, with the object of restoring Shāh Shojāʿ to the throne. In April 1839, after suffering great privations, the British Army entered Qandahār; Shāh Shojāʿ was then crowned *shāh*. Ghazna was captured in the following July, and in August Shāh Shojāʿ was installed at Kabul. Dōst Moḥammad escaped first to Balkh, then to Bukhara, where he was arrested. The Afghans, however, would tolerate neither a foreign occupation nor a king imposed on them by a foreign power, and insurrections broke out. Dōst Moḥammad escaped from prison and returned to Afghanistan to lead his partisans against the British. In a battle at Parwan on Nov. 2, 1840, Dōst Moḥammad had the upper hand, but the next day he surrendered to the British in Kabul. He was deported to India with the greater part of his family.

Outbreaks continued throughout the country, and the British eventually found their position untenable. Terms for their withdrawal were discussed with Akbar Khān, Dōst Moḥammad's son, but Sir William Hay Macnaghten, the British political agent, was killed during a parlay with the Afghans. On Jan. 6, 1842, some 4,500 British and Indian troops, with 12,000 camp followers, marched out of Kabul. Bands of Afghans swarmed around them, and the retreat ended in a blood bath. Shāh Shojāʿ was killed after the British left Kabul.

Though in the summer of the same year British forces reoccupied Kabul, the new governor general, Lord Ellenborough, decided on the evacuation of Afghanistan. In 1843 Dōst Moḥammad returned to Kabul. During the next 20 years Dōst Moḥammad consolidated his rule by occupying Qandahār (1855), Balkh and the northern Khanates (1859), and Herāt (1863), the last less than a month before his death in June 1863.

Shīr ʿAlī (1863–66; 1868–79). Shīr ʿAlī Khān, Dōst Moḥammad's third son, then became *amīr*, but his two elder brothers took the throne from him in May 1866.

Second Anglo-Afghan War, 1878–80

Shīr ʿAlī regained his throne in September 1868. Shīr ʿAlī's reception of a Russian mission at Kabul and his refusal to receive a British one, on British terms, led directly to the war of 1878–80. Shīr ʿAlī, leaving his son, Yaʿqūb Khān, as his regent in Kabul, sought help from the Russians, but they advised him to make peace. Shīr ʿAlī died in Mazār-e Sharīf on Feb. 21, 1879.

Yaʿqūb Khān (*1879*). The Treaty of Gandamak (Gandomak; May 26, 1879) recognized Yaʿqūb Khān as *amīr*, and he subsequently agreed to receive a permanent British embassy at Kabul. In addition, he agreed to conduct his foreign relations with other states in accordance "with the wishes and advice" of the British government. This British triumph, however, was short-lived. On Sept. 3, 1879, the British envoy and his escort were murdered in Kabul. British forces were again dispatched, and before the end of October they occupied Kabul. Yaʿqūb abdicated and was given exile in India, where he died in 1923.

(M.Al./L.Du./N.H.D.)

ʿAbdor Raḥmān Khān (*1880–1901*). The British finally withdrew from Qandahār in April 1881. In 1880 ʿAbdor Raḥmān Khān, a cousin of Shīr ʿAlī, had returned from exile in Central Asia and proclaimed himself *amīr* of Kabul. During the reign of ʿAbdor Raḥmān, the boundaries of modern Afghanistan were drawn by the British and the Russians. The Durand Line of 1893 divided zones of responsibility for the maintenance of law and order between British India and the kingdom of Afghanistan; it was never intended as a de jure international boundary. Afghanistan, therefore, although never dominated by a European imperial government, became a buffer between Tsarist Russia and British India.

ʿAbdor Raḥmān exerted his influence, if not actual control, over the various ethnolinguistic groups inside Afghanistan, fighting some 20 small wars to convince them that a strong central government existed in Kabul. ʿAbdor Raḥmān was so successful that, at his death, his designated successor and eldest son, Ḥabībollāh Khān, succeeded to the throne as Ḥabībollāh I without the usual fratricidal fighting. ʿAbdor Raḥmān can be considered the founder of modern Afghanistan.

Ḥabībollāh Khān (*1901–19*). The introduction of modern European technology begun by ʿAbdor Raḥmān was furthered by Ḥabībollāh. Western ideals and styles penetrated the Afghan royal court and upper classes. An Afghan nationalist, Maḥmūd Beg Ṭarzī, published (1911–18) the periodical *Serāj ol-Akbār* ("Torch of the News"), which had political influence far beyond the boundaries of Afghanistan.

Ḥabībollāh Khān visited British India in 1907 as guest of the viceroy of India, Gilbert Elliot, 4th earl of Minto. Impressed with British power, Ḥabībollāh resisted pressures from Ṭarzī, Amānollāh (Ḥabībollāh's third son, who had married Soraya, a daughter of Ṭarzī), and others to enter World War I on the side of the Central Powers (Germany, Austria-Hungary, the Ottoman Empire, and Bulgaria). The peace ending World War I brought death to Ḥabībollāh; he was murdered on Feb. 20, 1919, by persons associated with the anti-British movement, and Amānollāh seized power.

Third Anglo-Afghan War, 1919

Amānollāh (*1919–29*). Amānollāh launched the inconclusive Third Anglo-Afghan War in May 1919. The month-long war gained the Afghans the conduct of their own foreign affairs. The Treaty of Rāwalpindi was signed on Aug. 8, 1919, and amended in 1921. Before signing the final document with the British, the Afghans concluded a treaty of friendship with the new Bolshevik regime in the Soviet Union; Afghanistan thereby became one of the first nations to recognize the Soviet government, and a "special relationship" evolved between the two governments and lasted until December 1979, when the Soviet Union invaded Afghanistan.

Amānollāh changed his title from *amīr* to *padshah* ("king") in 1923 and inaugurated a decade of reforms—including constitutional and administrative changes, removal of the veil from women, and coeducational schools—that offended conservative religious and tribal leaders.

Civil war broke out in November 1928, and a Tadzhik folk hero called Baccheh Saqow (Bacha Saqqao; "Son of a Water Carrier") occupied Kabul. Amānollāh abdicated on Jan. 14, 1929, in favour of his elder brother, Inayatollāh, but Baccheh Saqow proclaimed himself Ḥabībollāh Ghāzī (or Ḥabībollāh II), *amīr* of Afghanistan. Amānollāh failed to retrieve his throne and went into exile in Italy. He died in 1960 in Zürich.

Moḥammad Nāder Shāh (*1929–33*). Ḥabībollāh II was driven from the throne by Moḥammad Nāder Khān and his brothers, distant cousins of Amānollāh. On Oct. 10, 1929, Ḥabībollāh II was executed along with 17 of his followers. A tribal assembly elected Nāder Khān as *shāh*, and the opposition was bloodily persecuted.

Nāder Shāh produced a new constitution in 1931 that was modeled on Amānollāh's constitution of 1923 but was more conservatively oriented to appease Islāmic religious leaders. The national economy developed in the 1930s under the leadership of several entrepreneurs who began small-scale industrial projects. Nāder Shāh was assassinated on Nov. 8, 1933, and the 19-year-old crown prince, Zahir, succeeded his father.

Mohammad Zahir Shah (*1933–73*). The first 20 years of Zahir Shah's reign were characterized by cautious policies of national consolidation, an expansion of foreign relations, and internal development using Afghan funds alone. World War II brought about a slowdown in development processes, but Afghanistan maintained its traditional neutrality. The "Pashtunistan" problem regarding the political status of those Pashtun living on the British (Pakistani) side of the Durand Line developed after the independence of Pakistan in 1947.

The Pashtunistan problem

Shah Mahmud, prime minister from 1946 to 1953, sanctioned free elections and a relatively free press, and the so-called Liberal Parliament functioned from 1949 to 1952. Conservatives in government, however, encouraged by religious leaders, supported the seizure of power in 1953 by Lieutenant General Mohammad Daud Khan.

Prime Minister Daud Khan (1953–63) took a stronger line on Pashtunistan, and, to the surprise of many, turned to the Soviet Union for economic and military assistance. The Soviets ultimately became Afghanistan's major aid-and-trade partner. The Afghans refused to take sides in the Cold War, and Afghanistan became an "economic Korea," testing the Western (particularly U.S.) will and capability to compete with the Soviet bloc in a nonaligned country. Daud Khan successfully introduced several far-reaching educational and social reforms, such as the voluntary removal of the veil from women and the abolition of purdah (the practice of secluding women from public view), which theoretically increased the labour force by about 50 percent. The regime remained politically repressive, however, and tolerated no direct opposition.

The Pashtunistan issue precipitated Daud Khan's downfall. In retaliation for Afghan agitation, Pakistan closed the border with Afghanistan in August 1961. A prolongation of the closure led to Afghan dependence on the Soviet Union for trade and in-transit facilities. To reverse the trend, Daud Khan resigned in March 1963, and the border was reopened in May. The Pashtunistan problem still existed, however.

Constitutional monarchy

Zahir Shah and his advisers instituted an experiment in constitutional monarchy. In 1964 the National Assembly approved a new constitution, under which the House of the People was to have 216 elected members, and the House of the Elders was to have 84 members, one-third elected by the people, one-third appointed by the king, and one-third elected indirectly by new provincial assemblies.

Elections for both houses of the legislature were held in 1965 and 1969. Several unofficial parties ran candidates with beliefs ranging from fundamentalist Islām to the extreme left. National politics became increasingly polarized, a situation reflected in the appointment by the King of five successive prime ministers between September 1965 and December 1972. The King refused to promulgate the Political Parties Act, the Provincial Councils Act, and the Municipal Councils Act, thereby effectively blocking the institutionalization of the political processes guaranteed in the constitution. Struggles for power developed between the legislative and the executive branches, and an independent Supreme Court, as called for in the 1964 constitution, was never appointed.

Mohammad Daud Khan, the former prime minister and a brother-in-law and first cousin of Zahir Shah, sensed the stagnation of the constitutional processes and seized power on July 17, 1973, in a virtually bloodless coup. Leftist military officers and civil servants of the Banner (Parcham) Party assisted in the overthrow. Daud Khan abolished the constitution of 1964 and established the Republic of Afghanistan, with himself as chairman of the Central Committee of the Republic and prime minister.

AFGHANISTAN SINCE 1973

The Republic of Afghanistan (1973–78). During Daud Khan's second tenure as prime minister, he attempted to introduce socioeconomic reforms, to write a new constitution, and to effect a gradual movement away from the socialist ideals his regime initially espoused. Afghanistan broadened and intensified its relationships with other Muslim countries, trying to move away from its dependency on the Soviet Union and the United States. In addition, Daud Khan and Zulfikar Ali Bhutto, the prime minister of Pakistan, reached tentative agreement on a solution to the Pashtunistan problem.

Daud Khan received approval in 1977 of his new constitution from the National Assembly, which wrote in several new articles and amended others. In March 1977 Daud Khan, then president of Afghanistan, appointed a new Cabinet composed of sycophants, friends, sons of friends, and even collateral members of the royal family. The two major leftist organizations, the People's (Khalq) and Banner parties, then reunited against Daud Khan after a 10-year separation. There followed a series of political assassinations, massive antigovernment demonstrations, and arrests of major leftist leaders. Before his arrest Hafizullah Amin, a U.S.-educated People's Party leader, contacted party members in the armed forces and devised a makeshift but successful coup. Daud Khan and most of his family were killed, and the Democratic Republic of Afghanistan was born on April 27, 1978.

Nur Mohammad Taraki

The Afghan Civil War. Nur Mohammad Taraki was elected president of the Revolutionary Council, prime minister of the country, and secretary general of the combined People's Democratic Party of Afghanistan (PDPA). Babrak Karmal, a Banner leader, and Hafizullah Amin were elected deputy prime ministers. The leaders of the new government insisted that they were not controlled by the Soviet Union and proclaimed their policies to be based on Afghan nationalism, Islāmic principles, socioeconomic justice, nonalignment in foreign affairs, and respect for all agreements and treaties signed by previous Afghan governments.

Unity between the People's and Banner factions rapidly faded as the People's Party emerged dominant, particularly because their major base of power was in the military. Karmal and other selected Banner leaders were sent abroad as ambassadors, and there were systematic purges of any Banner members or others who might oppose the regime.

The Taraki regime announced its reform programs, including the elimination of usury, equal rights for women, land reforms, and administrative decrees in classic Marxist-Leninist rhetoric. The people in the countryside, familiar with Marxist broadcasts from Soviet Central Asia, assumed that the People's Party was Communist and pro-Soviet. The reform program—which threatened to undermine basic Afghan cultural patterns—and political repression antagonized large segments of the population, but major violent responses did not occur until the uprising in Nūrestān late in the summer of 1978. Other revolts, largely uncoordinated, spread throughout all of Afghanistan's provinces, and periodic explosions rocked Kabul and other major cities. On Feb. 14, 1979, U.S. Ambassador Adolph Dubs was killed, and the elimination of U.S. assistance to Afghanistan was guaranteed.

Hafizullah Amin became prime minister on March 28, 1979, although Taraki retained his posts as president of the Revolutionary Council and secretary general of the PDPA. The expanding revolts in the countryside, however, continued, and the Afghan Army collapsed. The Amin regime asked for and received more Soviet military aid.

Taraki was killed in a confrontation between Taraki and Amin supporters on Sept. 14, 1979. Amin then tried to broaden his internal base of support and to again interest Pakistan and the United States in Afghan security. Despite his efforts, on the night of Dec. 24, 1979, the Soviets began their invasion of Afghanistan, and Amin and many of his followers were killed on December 27.

(L.Du./N.H.D.)

Babrak Karmal returned to Afghanistan from the Soviet Union and became prime minister, president of the Revolutionary Council, and secretary general of the PDPA. Opposition to the Soviets and Karmal spread rapidly, urban demonstrations and violence increased, and resistance escalated in all regions. By early 1980, several regional groups, collectively known as mujahideen (from the Persian word meaning "warriors"), had united inside Afghanistan, or across the border in Peshāwar, to resist the Soviet invaders and the Soviet-backed Afghan Army. Friction among the Banner and People's members heightened in 1980 when Karmal removed Assadullah Sarwari, a member of the People's Party, from his position as first deputy prime minister and replaced him with a Banner leader, Sultan Ali Keshtmand. Banner Party dominance was broadened again in June 1981 when Karmal, retaining his other offices, resigned as prime minister and was succeeded by Keshtmand.

On May 4, 1986, Mohammad Najibullah, former head of the secret police, replaced Karmal as secretary general of the PDPA, and in November 1986 Karmal was relieved of all his government and party posts. Friction among the Banner and People's parties continued. A national reconciliation campaign approved by the Politburo in September 1986, which included a unilateral six-month cease-fire to begin on Jan. 15, 1987, met with little response inside Afghanistan and was rejected by resistance leaders in Pakistan.

The 1987 constitution

In November 1987 a new constitution changed the name of the country back to the Republic of Afghanistan and allowed other political parties to participate in the government. Najibullah was elected to the newly strengthened post of president. Despite renewals of the official cease-fire, Afghan resistance to the Soviet presence continued, and the effects of the war were felt in neighbouring countries: Afghan refugees in Pakistan and Iran numbered in the millions. Morale in the Afghan military was low. Men were drafted only to desert at the earliest opportunity, and the Afghan military dropped from its 1978 strength of 105,000 to about 20,000–30,000 by 1987. The Soviets attempted new tactics, but the resistance always devised countertactics. For example, the use of the Spetsnaz (special forces) was met by counter-ambushes.

The only weapons systems that solidly continued to bedevil the resistance were combat helicopter gunships and jet bombers. Toward the end of 1986, however, the resistance fighters began to receive more and better weapons from the outside world—particularly from the United States, the United Kingdom, and China—via Pakistan, the most important of these being shoulder-fired ground-to-air missiles. The Soviet and Afghan air forces then began to suffer considerable casualties.

Unity in the Afghan resistance

Pressure from the Pakistanis, from outside supporters, and from the guerrilla commanders had forced the seven major resistance groups based in Peshāwar to form an alliance in May 1985. Inside Afghanistan, neighbouring ethnolinguistically oriented resistance groups united for military and political purposes within their various regions. Internal struggles for leadership also occurred in certain areas where the Soviets had little influence, such as Hazārajāt and Nūrestān. Although no national liberation front existed, the resistance groups began to feel that they were part of an overall effort to liberate Afghanistan.

During the 1980s talks between the foreign ministers of Afghanistan and Pakistan were held in Geneva under the auspices of the United Nations, the primary stumbling blocks being the timetable for the withdrawal of Soviet troops and the cessation of arms supplies to the mujahideen. Peace accords were finally signed in April 1988. General Secretary Mikhail Gorbachev subsequently carried out an earlier promise to begin withdrawing Soviet troops in May of that year; troops began pulling out as scheduled, and the last Soviet soldier left Afghanistan on Feb. 15, 1989. The civil war continued, however, despite predictions of an early collapse of the Najibullah government upon the withdrawal of the Soviets. The mujahideen formed an interim government in Pakistan and steadfastly resisted efforts of reconciliation by Najibullah.

Najibullah was finally ousted from power in 1992, and a coalition of rebel forces set up a fragile interim government. General peace and stability remained a distant hope for the war-torn nation, as rival militias vied for influence, interethnic tensions flared, and the economy lay in chaos. With the fall of the Communist government, Afghanistan appeared to be on a course of Islāmicization; the interim government banned the sale of alcohol and pressured women to cover their heads in public and adopt traditional Muslim dress.

For later developments in the history of Afghanistan, see the *Britannica Book of the Year* section in the BRITANNICA WORLD DATA ANNUAL. (L.Du./N.H.D./Ed.)

BIBLIOGRAPHY

Physical and human geography: Overviews are provided by RICHARD F. NYROP and DONALD M. SEEKINS, *Afghanistan: A Country Study,* 5th ed. (1986); LOUIS DUPREE, *Afghanistan* (1973, reprinted 1980); LUDWIG W. ADAMEC (ed.), *Historical and Political Gazetteer of Afghanistan,* 6 vol. (1972–85); and ARNOLD FLETCHER, *Afghanistan: Highway of Conquest* (1965, reprinted 1982). JOHANNES HUMLUM, *La Géographie de l'Afghanistan: etude d'un pays aride* (1959), is a comprehensive geography. The first four chapters of W. BARTHOLD, *An Historical Geography of Iran* (1984; originally published in Russian, 1971), discuss Afghan regions. Also useful is *General Atlas of Afghanistan* (1973?). MOUNTSTUART ELPHINSTONE, *An Account of the Kingdom of Caubul, and Its Dependencies in Persia, Tartary, and India* (1815, reprinted 1969), is the first detailed account of Afghanistan by an English observer. Photographs of the country are provided in ROLAND MICHAUD and SABRINA MICHAUD, *Afghanistan* (1980; originally published in French, 1980); and CAMILLE MIREPOIX (STEGMULLER), *Afghanistan in Pictures* (1971). Additional sources of information may be found in KEITH MCLACHLAN and WILLIAM WHITTAKER, *A Bibliography of Afghanistan* (1983); and M. JAMIL HANIFI, *Annotated Bibliography of Afghanistan,* 4th ed. rev. (1982).

Ethnographic studies include RICHARD TAPPERR (ed.), *The Conflict of Tribe and State in Iran and Afghanistan* (1983); THOMAS J. BARFIELD, *The Central Asian Arabs of Afghanistan: Pastoral Nomadism in Transition* (1981); M. NAZIF MOHIB SHAHRANI, *The Kirghiz and Wakhi of Afghanistan: Adaptation to Closed Frontiers* (1979); DONALD NEWTON WILBER *et al., Afghanistan: Its People, Its Society, Its Culture* (1962); and OLAF CAROE, *The Pathans, 550 B.C.–A.D. 1957* (1958, reprinted 1983).

Administrative and social policies are the subject of ANTHONY ARNOLD, *Afghanistan's Two-Party Communism: Parcham and Kalq* (1983); BEVERLEY MALE, *Revolutionary Afghanistan: A Reappraisal* (1982); and RONALD W. O'CONNOR, *Managing Health Systems in Developing Areas: Experiences from Afghanistan* (1980), a study of the country's health problems and traditional health systems. MAXWELL J. FRY, *The Afghan Economy: Money, Finance, and the Critical Constraints to Economic Development* (1974), is still valuable.

Afghanistan's archaeological discoveries are recounted in VIKTOR SARIANIDI, *The Golden Hoard of Bactria: From the Tillyatepe Excavations in Northern Afghanistan* (1985), a lavishly illustrated account of grave goods excavated from an early Kushān princedom cemetery; JEANNINE AUBOYER, *The Art of Afghanistan* (1968; originally published in French, 1968); and BENJAMIN ROWLAND, JR., *Ancient Art from Afghanistan: Treasures of the Kabul Museum* (1966, reprinted 1976). Traditional culture is explored in MARK SLOBIN, *Music in the Culture of Northern Afghanistan* (1976); HIROMI LORRAINE SAKATA, *Music in the Mind: The Concepts of Music and Musician in Afghanistan* (1983); and STANLEY IRA HALLET and RAFI SAMIZAY, *Traditional Architecture of Afghanistan* (1980).

History: F.R. ALLCHIN and NORMAN HAMMOND (eds.), *The Archaeology of Afghanistan from Earliest Times to the Timurid Period* (1978), is an excellent series of essays on all major archaeological periods. See also LOUIS DUPREE *et al., Prehistoric Research in Afghanistan (1959–1966)* (1972). W.W. TARN, *The Greeks in Bactria & India,* 3rd ed. updated by FRANK LEE HOLT (1985); and A.K. NARAIN, *The Indo-Greeks* (1957, reissued 1980), are discussions of the aftermath of Alexander's campaigns in the East. ABDUR REHMAN, *The Last Two Dynasties of the Šahis: An Analysis of Their History, Archaeology, Coinage, and Palaeography* (1979), is a discussion of the neglected historic period of the Hindu Shāhī. Particularly recommended for the early Muslim period are the seminal works of CLIFFORD EDMUND BOSWORTH, *Sīstān Under the Arabs, from the Islamic Conquest to the Rise of the Ṣaffārids (30–250/651–864)* (1968), *The Ghaznavids: Their Empire in Afghanistan and Eastern Iran, 994:1040,* 2nd ed. (1973), and *The Later Ghaznavids: Splendour and Decay: The Dynasty in Afghanistan and Northern India 1040–1186* (1977). LAURENCE LOCKHART, *The Fall of the Safavī Dynasty and the Afghan Occupation of Persia* (1958), is also germane. See also V. MINORSKY (trans.), *Hudūd al-ʿĀlam: "The Regions of the World": A Persian Geography, 377 A.H.–982 A.D.,* trans. from Persian (1937, reprinted 1980).

For modern Afghanistan, HASAN KAWUN KAKAR, *Government and Society in Afghanistan: The Reign of Amir ʿAbd al-Rahman Khan* (1979), is an excellent study of the late 19th century. LUDWIG W. ADAMEC, *Afghanistan, 1900–1923: A Diplomatic History* (1967), and *Afghanistan's Foreign Affairs to the Mid-Twentieth Century: Relations with the USSR, Germany, and Britain* (1974), are well-documented accounts of 20th-century diplomatic history. See also MAY SCHINASI, *Afghanistan at the Beginning of the Twentieth Century: Nationalism and Journalism in Afghanistan: A Study of Seraj ul-Akhbar (1911–1918)* (1979); LEON B. POULLADA, *Reform and Rebellion in Afghanistan, 1919–1929: King Amanullah's Failure to Modernize a Tribal Society* (1973); RHEA TALLEY STEWART, *Fire in Afghanistan, 1914–1929: Faith, Hope and the British Empire* (1973); VARTAN GREGORIAN, *The Emergence of Modern Afghanistan: Politics of Reform and Modernization, 1880–1946* (1969); and LOUIS DUPREE and LINETTE ALBERT (eds.), *Afghanistan in the 1970s* (1974).

Accounts and analyses of the history of Afghanistan since 1978 include J. BRUCE AMSTUTZ, *Afghanistan: The First Five Years of Soviet Occupation* (1986); HENRY S. BRADSHER, *Afghanistan and the Soviet Union,* new and expanded ed. (1985); JOSEPH J. COLLINS, *The Soviet Invasion of Afghanistan: A Study in the Use of Force in Soviet Foreign Policy* (1986); EDWARD GIRARDET, *Afghanistan: The Soviet War* (1985); THOMAS T. HAMMOND, *Red Flag over Afghanistan: The Communist Coup, the Soviet Invasion, and the Consequences* (1984); ANTHONY HYMAN, *Afghanistan Under Soviet Domination, 1964–83* (1984); RALPH H. MAGNUS (ed.), *Afghan Alternatives: Issues, Options, and Policies* (1985); HAFEEZ MALIK (ed.), *Soviet-American Relations with Pakistan, Iran and Afghanistan* (1986); OLIVIER ROY, *Islam and Resistance in Afghanistan* (1986; originally published in French, 1985); and M. NAZIF SHAHRANI and ROBERT L. CANFIELD (eds.), *Revolutions & Rebellions in Afghanistan: Anthropological Perspectives* (1984). For the Soviet viewpoint, see *Afghanistan: Past and Present,* trans. from Russian (1981), published by the U.S.S.R. Academy of Sciences.

(V.P.P./L.Du./N.H.D.)

Africa

Africa is the second largest continent, being smaller only than Asia and covering about one-fifth of the total land surface of the world. The continent is bounded on the west by the Atlantic Ocean, on the north by the Mediterranean Sea, on the east by the Red Sea and the Indian Ocean, and on the south by the mingling waters of the Atlantic and Indian oceans.

Africa's total land area is approximately 11,667,000 square miles (30,217,000 square kilometres), and the continent measures about 5,000 miles (8,000 kilometres) from north to south and about 4,600 miles from east to west. Its northern extremity is Al-Ghīrān Point, near Al-Abyaḍ Point (Cape Blanc), Tun.; its southern extremity is Cape Agulhas, S.Af.; its farthest point east is Xaafuun (Hafun) Point, near Cape Gwardafuy (Guardafui), Somalia; and its western extremity is Almadi Point (Pointe des Almadies), on Cape Verde (Cap Vert), Senegal. In the northeast, Africa was joined to Asia by the Sinai Peninsula until the construction of the Suez Canal. Paradoxically, the coastline of Africa—18,950 miles in length—is shorter than that of Europe, because there are few inlets and few large bays or gulfs.

Off the coasts of Africa a number of islands are associated with the continent, of which Madagascar, one of the largest islands in the world, is the most significant. Other smaller islands include the Seychelles, Socotra, and other islands to the east; the Comoros, Mauritius, Réunion, and other islands to the southeast; Ascension, St. Helena, and Tristan da Cunha to the southwest; Cape Verde, the Bijagós Islands, Bioko, and São Tomé and Príncipe to the west; and the Azores and the Madeira and Canary islands to the northwest.

The continent is cut almost equally in two by the equator, so that most of Africa lies within the tropical region, bounded on the north by the tropic of Cancer and on the south by the tropic of Capricorn. Because of the bulge formed by western Africa, the greater part of Africa's territory lies north of the equator. Africa is crossed from north to south by the prime meridian (0° longitude), which passes a short distance to the east of Accra, Ghana.

In antiquity, the Greeks are said to have called the continent Libya and the Romans to have called it Africa, perhaps from the Latin *aprica* ("sunny") or the Greek *aphrike* ("without cold"). The name Africa, however, was chiefly applied to the northern coast of the continent, which was, in effect, regarded as a southern extension of Europe. The Romans, who for a time ruled the North African coast, are also said to have called the area south of their settlements Afriga, or the Land of the Afrigs—the name of a Berber community south of Carthage.

The whole of Africa can be considered as a vast plateau rising steeply from narrow coastal strips and consisting of ancient crystalline rocks. The plateau's surface is higher in the southeast and tilts downward toward the northeast. In general, the plateau may be divided into a southeastern portion and a northwestern portion. The northwestern part, which includes the Sahara (desert) and that part of North Africa known as the Maghrib, has two mountainous regions—the Atlas Mountains in northwestern Africa, which are believed to be part of a system that extends into southern Europe, and the Ahaggar (Hoggar) Mountains in the Sahara. The southeastern part of the plateau includes the Ethiopian Plateau, the East African Plateau, and—in eastern South Africa, where the plateau edge falls downward in a scarp—the Drakensberg range. One of the most remarkable features in the geologic structure of Africa is the East African Rift System, which lies between 30° and 40° E. The rift itself begins northeast of the continent's limits and extends southward from the Ethiopian Red Sea coast to the Zambezi River basin.

Africa contains an enormous wealth of mineral resources, including some of the world's largest reserves of fossil fuels, metallic ores, and gems and precious metals. This richness is matched by a great diversity of biological resources that includes the intensely lush equatorial rain forests of central Africa and the world-famous populations of wildlife of the eastern and southern portions of the continent. Although agriculture (primarily subsistence) still dominates the economies of most African countries, the exploitation of these resources has become the most significant economic activity in Africa in the 20th century.

Climatic and other factors have exerted considerable influence on the patterns of human settlement in Africa. While some areas appear to have been inhabited more or less continuously since the dawn of humanity, enormous regions—notably the desert areas of northern and southwestern Africa—have been largely unoccupied for prolonged periods of time. Thus, although Africa is the second largest continent, it contains only about 10 percent of the world's population and can be said to be underpopulated. The greater part of the continent has long been inhabited by black peoples, but in historic times there have also occurred major immigrations from both Asia and Europe. Of all foreign settlements in Africa, that of the Arabs has made the greatest impact. The Islāmic religion, which the Arabs carried with them, spread from North Africa into many areas south of the Sahara, so that many western African peoples are now largely Islāmized.

(D.S.H.W.N./Ed.)

This article treats the physical and human geography of Africa, followed by discussion of geographic features of special interest. For discussion of individual countries of the continent, see the articles EGYPT; MADAGASCAR; SOUTH AFRICA; and SUDAN, THE. Other African countries are treated in articles on regions under the titles CENTRAL AFRICA, EASTERN AFRICA, NORTH AFRICA, SOUTHERN AFRICA, and WESTERN AFRICA; these articles also contain the principal treatment of African historical and cultural development. For discussion of major cities of the continent, see the articles ALEXANDRIA, CAIRO, CAPE TOWN, JOHANNESBURG, and KINSHASA. Related topics are discussed in the articles AFRICAN ARTS; EGYPTIAN ARTS AND ARCHITECTURE, ANCIENT; ISLĀM, MUḤAMMAD AND THE RELIGION OF; ISLĀMIC ARTS; and ISLĀMIC WORLD, THE. For further references, see also the *Index*.

The article is divided into the following sections:

Physical and human geography 38
- Geologic history 38
  - General considerations
  - Rock types and structural evolution
    - The Precambrian
    - The Paleozoic Era
    - The Mesozoic Era
    - The Cenozoic Era
- The land 45
  - Relief
  - Drainage
  - Soils
    - Soil types
    - Soil problems
- Climate
  - Factors influencing the African climate
  - Climatic regions
- Plant life
  - Ecological relationships
  - Vegetational zones
  - Long-term changes in vegetation
- Animal life
  - Genera and distribution
  - The effects of humans

Ecology
The people 59
Cultural areas
Northern Africa
Western Africa
West-central Africa
Eastern Africa
Central and southern Africa
Madagascar
Cultural patterns
Languages
Religions
Domestic groupings
Demographic patterns
Population distribution
Settlement patterns
Migrations
The economy 64
Resources
Mineral resources
Water resources
Biological resources
Agriculture
Principal crops
Livestock and fishing
Industry
Power
Trade
Internal trade
External trade
Transportation
Animal transport
Motor transport
Rail transport
Air transport
Navigation
African geographic features of special interest 73
Landforms 73
Atlas Mountains
East African mountains
Ituri Forest
Kalahari
Namib
Sahara
Veld
Drainage systems and waterways 92
Lake Chad
Congo River
East African lakes
Niger River
Nile River
Orange River
Sénégal River
Suez Canal
Zambezi River
Bibliography 118

PHYSICAL AND HUMAN GEOGRAPHY

Geologic history

GENERAL CONSIDERATIONS

The five cratons

The African continent essentially consists of five ancient Precambrian cratons (Kaapvaal, Zimbabwe, Tanzania, Congo, and West African) that were formed between about 3.6 and 2.0 billion years ago and that basically have been tectonically stable since that time; these cratons are bounded by younger fold belts formed between 2.0 billion and 300 million years ago. All these rocks have been extensively folded and metamorphosed (that is, they have been modified in composition and structure by heat and pressure). Precambrian rock outcrops appear on some 57 percent of the continent's surface, while the rest of the surface consists of largely undeformed younger sediments and volcanic rocks.

The oldest rocks are of Archean age (more than 3.6 to 2.5 billion years old) and are found in the so-called granite-gneiss-greenstone terrains of the Kaapvaal, Zimbabwe, and Congo cratons. They consist of gray, banded gneisses, various granitoids, and rather well-preserved volcanic rocks that show evidence of submarine extrusion (*i.e.,* emission of rock material in molten form) and formation under high temperatures. The rock type komatiite is particularly diagnostic of these volcanic sequences and is almost exclusively restricted to the Archean Eon. The cratons were tectonically stabilized by voluminous granite intrusions toward the end of the Archean and were then covered by clastic sediments, some of which contain economically important gold and uranium deposits (*e.g.,* the Witwatersrand System in South Africa).

The Proterozoic Eon (2.5 billion to 570 million years ago) is characterized by the formation of several mobile belts, which are long, narrow zones of strongly deformed and metamorphosed rocks that occur between the cratons and probably resulted from the collision between the cratons due to plate tectonic processes. The oldest mobile belts are found in Archean rocks, such as the Limpopo belt separating the Kaapvaal from the Zimbabwe craton. Younger belts were formed during a continentwide thermotectonic event known as the Eburnian (2.2 to 1.8 billion years ago), which gave rise to the Birimian assemblage in western Africa, the Ubendian assemblage in east-central Africa, and large volumes of rocks in Angola. Still younger belts of the Kibaran thermotectonic event (1.2 billion to 950 million years ago) are found in eastern and southern Africa.

The end of the Precambrian was marked by a major event of mobile-belt formation known as the Pan-African episode (*c.* 950 to 550 million years ago), which generated long fold belts, such as the Mozambique belt along the east coast of Africa, the Damara and Katanga belts extending from Namibia into Zaire and Zambia, the West Congo belt between Angola and Gabon, the Dahomey-Ahaggar belt between Ghana and Algeria, and the Mauritanide belt from Senegal to Morocco.

The Arabian-Nubian Shield

A unique late Precambrian evolution is recorded in the so-called Arabian-Nubian Shield of northeastern Africa and Arabia. There, large volumes of volcanic and granitoid rocks were generated in an island-arc, marginal-basin setting—an environment similar to that of the present southwestern Pacific Ocean. Rocks were accreted onto the ancient African continent, the margin of which was then near the present Nile River, by subduction processes identical to those observed today. (Subduction involves the descent of the edge of one lithospheric plate beneath that of another where two such plates collide.)

The interiors of the ancient cratons were not affected by the above tectonic events, and intracratonic sedimentary and volcanic sequences accumulated in large basins. The most important of these are the Transvaal basin on the Kaapvaal craton that contains economically important iron ore deposits; the Congo basin; and the West African basin, with its thick late-Proterozoic sediments including a prominent tillite horizon that marks a major glaciation event at the end of the Precambrian.

After the Precambrian, Africa's geologic history is characterized by the following events: the formation of fold belts in the Paleozoic Era (570 to 245 million years ago) in South Africa (the Cape fold belt), Morocco (the Anti-Atlas belt), and Mauritania (the Mauritanide belt) bordering the older cratons; voluminous basaltic volcanism some 230 to 200 million years ago in South Africa, Namibia, and East Africa, known as the Karoo System, that was probably related to the beginning of the breakup of the Gondwana supercontinent; the formation of a young mountain belt in northwestern Africa some 100 to 40 million years ago as a result of collision between the African and European plates, together with the closure of the ancestral Mediterranean Sea (the Tethys Sea); and the development of the East African Rift System during and after the Tertiary Period (*i.e.,* the last 66.4 million years), leading to the opening of the Red Sea, the northeast drift of the Arabian Plate, and the fracturing of the ancient crust of Africa along several long rift valleys, accompanied by extensive volcanism.

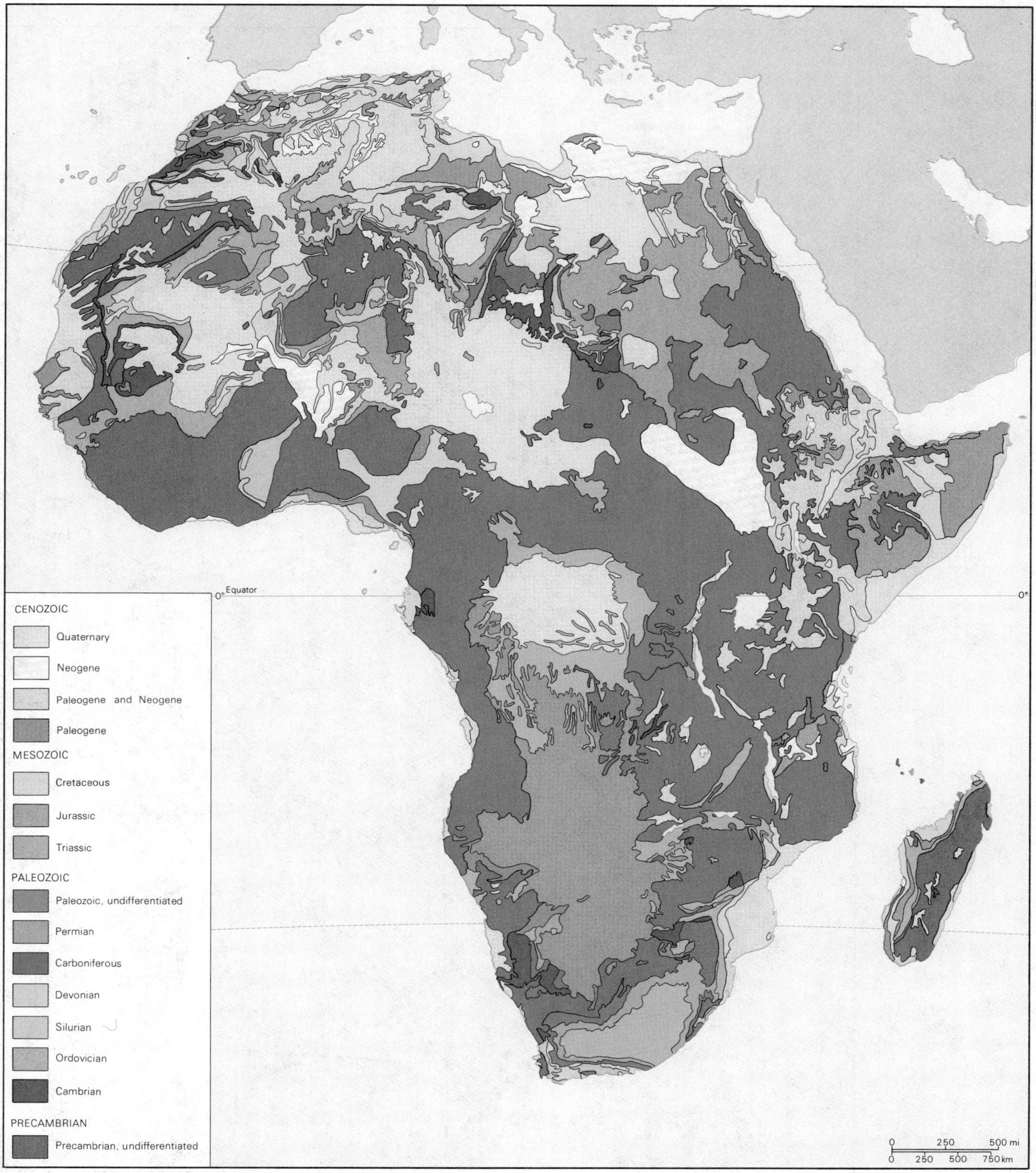

Geologic structure of Africa.

ROCK TYPES AND STRUCTURAL EVOLUTION

The Precambrian. The oldest rocks consist of gneisses, granites, metasediments, and metavolcanic rocks 3.6 to 2.5 billion years old; all are variably deformed and metamorphosed to some degree. The best-preserved assemblages occur in the Kaapvaal and Zimbabwe cratons and contain large deposits of gold and sulfide minerals. The volcanic suites are dominated by basaltic and komatiitic lavas, often interlayered with metasediments and generally referred to as greenstone belts. These are often found together with layered gneisses, or they are intruded by granitoid plutons. Several generations of greenstones have been recognized. The oldest formed about 3.4 billion years ago, the second some 3.0 to 2.9 billion years ago, and the third some 2.7 to 2.6 billion years ago. Some of the oldest traces of life are preserved as unicellular algae in Precam-

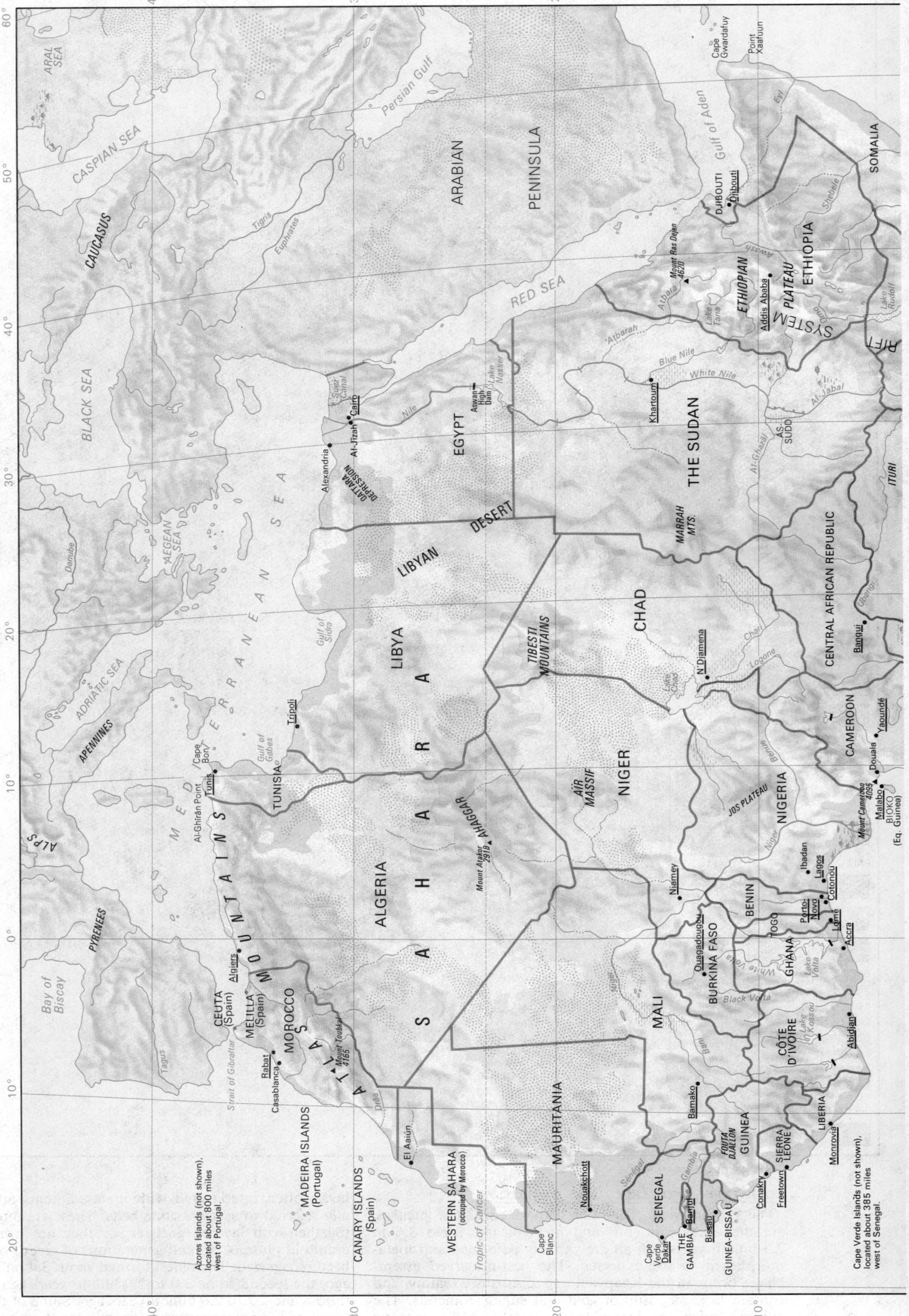

ARAL SEA
CASPIAN SEA
Persian Gulf
ARABIAN
PENINSULA
Gulf of Aden
Cape Gwardafuy
Point Xaafuun
SOMALIA
DJIBOUTI
Djibouti
ETHIOPIA
ETHIOPIAN PLATEAU
Mount Ras Dejen 4620
Addis Ababa
Lake Tana
RED SEA
CAUCASUS
Tigris
Euphrates
BLACK SEA
Suez Canal
Cairo
Al-Jizah
Alexandria
QATTARA DEPRESSION
EGYPT
Aswan High Dam
Lake Nasser
Nile
Atbarah
Blue Nile
White Nile
Khartoum
THE SUDAN
AS SUDD
MARRAH MTS.
ITURI
LIBYAN DESERT
MEDITERRANEAN SEA
AEGEAN SEA
Danube
LIBYA
Gulf of Sidra
Tripoli
Gulf of Gabes
CHAD
TIBESTI MOUNTAINS
N'Djamena
Lake Chad
Chari
Logone
CENTRAL AFRICAN REPUBLIC
Bangui
Ubangi
CAMEROON
Yaoundé
Douala
Mount Cameroon 4095
Malabo
BIOKO (Eq. Guinea)
ADRIATIC SEA
APENNINES
Cape Bon
Tunis
TUNISIA
Al-Ghirān Point
ALPS
NIGER
AÏR MASSIF
AHAGGAR
Mount Atakor 2918
JOS PLATEAU
NIGERIA
Niger
Ibadan
Lagos
Cotonou
Porto-Novo
BENIN
TOGO
Lomé
Accra
GHANA
Lake Volta
White Volta
Black Volta
Niamey
Ouagadougou
BURKINA FASO
ALGERIA
SAHARA
ATLAS MOUNTAINS
Algiers
PYRENEES
Bay of Biscay
Tagus
Strait of Gibraltar
CEUTA (Spain)
MELILLA (Spain)
MOROCCO
Rabat
Casablanca
Mount Toubkal 4165
Drâa
MALI
Bani
CÔTE D'IVOIRE
Lake Kossou
Abidjan
Bamako
GUINEA
FOUTA DJALLON
LIBERIA
Monrovia
SIERRA LEONE
Freetown
Conakry
GUINEA-BISSAU
Bissau
THE GAMBIA
Banjul
Gambia
SENEGAL
Senegal
Dakar
Cape Verde
MAURITANIA
Nouakchott
Cape Blanc
WESTERN SAHARA (occupied by Morocco)
El Aaiún
Tropic of Cancer
MADEIRA ISLANDS (Portugal)
CANARY ISLANDS (Spain)
Azores Islands (not shown), located about 800 miles west of Portugal.
Cape Verde Islands (not shown), located about 385 miles west of Senegal.
60°
50°
40°
30°
20°
10°
0°

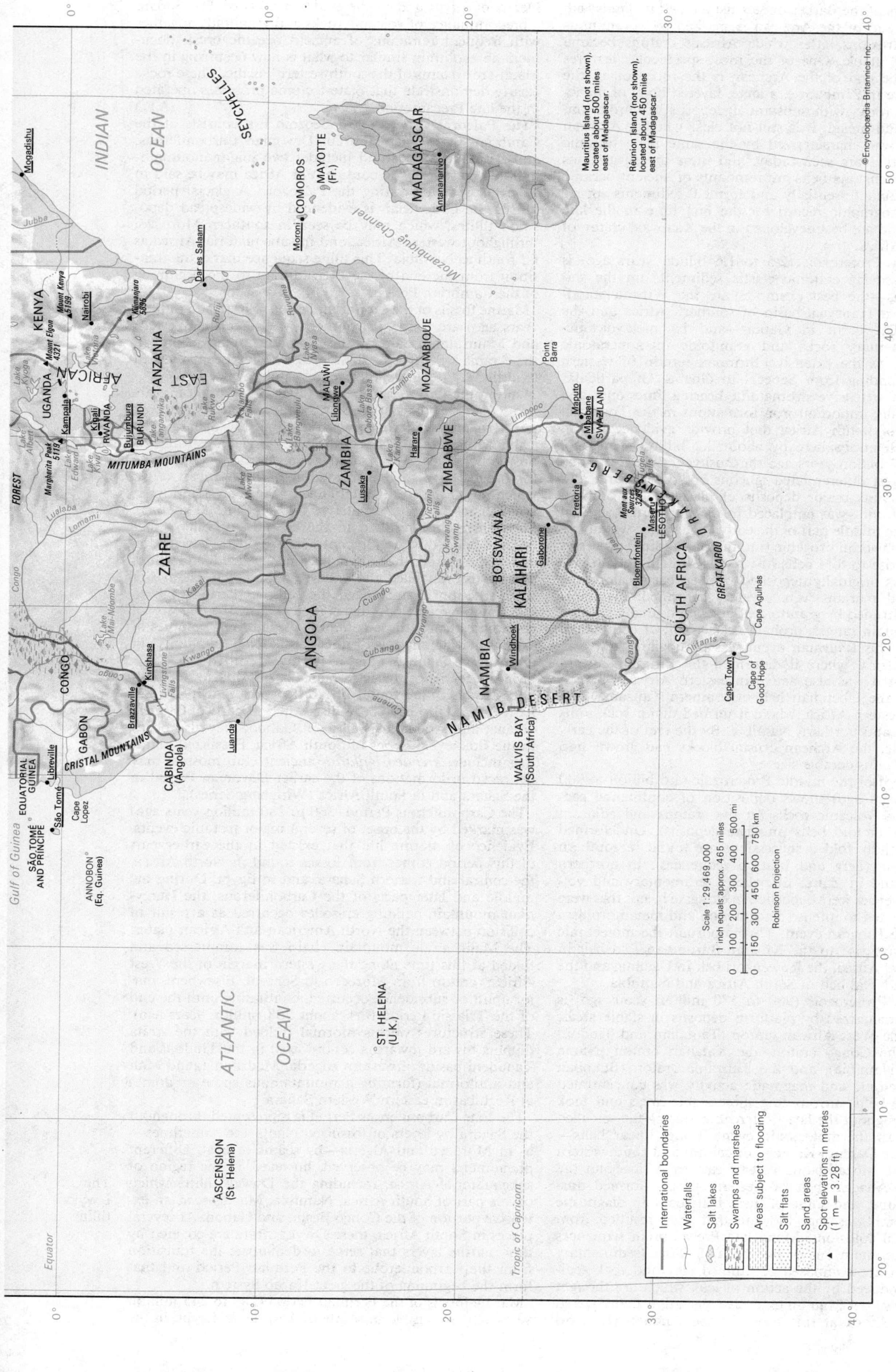
INDIAN
OCEAN
ATLANTIC
OCEAN
Gulf of Guinea
Mozambique Channel
Equator
Tropic of Capricorn
SEYCHELLES
COMOROS
Moroni
MAYOTTE
(Fr.)
MADAGASCAR
Antananarivo
Mauritius Island (not shown), located about 500 miles east of Madagascar.
Reunion Island (not shown), located about 450 miles east of Madagascar.
© Encyclopædia Britannica Inc.
Magadishu
Jubba
KENYA
Mount Kenya
5199
Nairobi
Kilimanjaro
5895
Mount Elgon
4321
Dar es Salaam
UGANDA
Kampala
Lake Victoria
Lake Kyoga
Lake Albert
Lake Edward
Lake Kivu
Lake Tanganyika
Lake Rukwa
Lake Nyasa
Lake Mweru
Lake Bangweulu
Lake Kariba
Lake Cabora Bassa
Lake Mai-Ndombe
AFRICAN
EAST
TANZANIA
RWANDA
Kigali
BURUNDI
Bujumbura
Margherita Peak
5119
MITUMBA MOUNTAINS
FOREST
Lualaba
Lomami
Congo
Kasai
Kwango
Cuando
Cubango
Okavango
Cunene
Zambezi
Limpopo
Orange
Vaal
Olifants
Ruvuma
Rufiji
MALAWI
Lilongwe
MOZAMBIQUE
Maputo
Point Barra
ZAMBIA
Lusaka
Victoria Falls
ZIMBABWE
Harare
Chambo Falls
ZAIRE
Kinshasa
Livingstone Falls
CONGO
Brazzaville
GABON
Libreville
CRISTAL MOUNTAINS
EQUATORIAL GUINEA
SÃO TOMÉ AND PRINCIPE
São Tomé
Cape Lopez
ANNOBON
(Eq. Guinea)
CABINDA
(Angola)
ANGOLA
Luanda
Okavango Swamp
BOTSWANA
KALAHARI
Gaborone
NAMIBIA
Windhoek
NAMIB DESERT
WALVIS BAY
(South Africa)
SOUTH AFRICA
Pretoria
Mbabane
SWAZILAND
DRAKENSBERG
Mont aux Sources
3299
Tugela Falls
Maseru
LESOTHO
Bloemfontein
GREAT KAROO
Cape Agulhas
Cape Town
Cape of Good Hope
ST. HELENA
(U.K.)
ASCENSION
(St. Helena)
Scale 1:29,469,000
1 inch equals approx. 465 miles
0 100 200 300 400 500 mi
0 150 300 450 600 750 km
Robinson Projection
International boundaries
Waterfalls
Salt lakes
Swamps and marshes
Areas subject to flooding
Salt flats
Sand areas
Spot elevations in metres
(1 m = 3.28 ft)
0°
10°
20°
30°
40°
50°

brian cherts of the Barberton greenstone belt in Transvaal, S.Af. The end of the Archean is marked by voluminous granite intrusions, after which Africa's cratons became tectonically stable. One of the most spectacular features marking the end of the Archean is the intrusion of the Great Dyke in Zimbabwe, a large, layered body of mafic-ultramafic rocks with substantial deposits of chromium, asbestos, and nickel. It is still not clear whether Archean evolution was characterized by the same plate tectonic processes that are seen today, and there are suggestions that the greenstone belts are remnants of ancient oceanic crust. Cratonic (essentially undeformed) sediments appear in the stratigraphic record for the first time in the late Archean and are best developed in the Kaapvaal craton of southern Africa.

Cratonic sediments

The early Proterozoic (2.5 to 1.6 billion years ago) is characterized by cratonic clastic sediments on the stable cratons—the best examples are the Witwatersrand-Ventersdorp-Transvaal basin of southern Africa and the Francevillian basin in Gabon—and by metavolcanic-metasedimentary rocks and granitoids in noncratonic areas such as the extensive Birimian terrain of western Africa extending from Senegal to Ghana. Of particular interest are extensive stromatolite-bearing limestones and economically important iron formations in the Transvaal sequence of South Africa that provide evidence for an oxygen-rich atmosphere by about 2.2 billion years ago. At about 2 billion years ago the Bushveld Complex—one of the largest differentiated igneous bodies on Earth and which contains major deposits of platinum, chromium, and vanadium—was emplaced in the northern Kaapvaal craton. The middle part of the early Proterozoic was dominated by powerful orogenic (mountain-building) processes that gave rise to fold belts in which sedimentary and volcanic rocks originally deposited in deep basins along the continental margins were severely deformed, metamorphosed, intruded by granitoid plutons, and finally uplifted into mountain ranges, probably as a result of continental collision. This Eburnian event was particularly active in western Africa, where it deformed the Birimian assemblages; but it was also active in eastern Africa, where it generated the Ubendian belt in southern Tanzania, and in southwestern Africa, where it formed major rock units in Angola and northern Namibia. By the end of the early Proterozoic, the Archean crustal blocks had grown into cratons of considerable size.

The record of the middle Proterozoic (1.6 billion to 900 million years ago) shows deposition of continental sediments and volcanic rocks on the cratons and adjacent to the earlier fold belts (molasse deposits). Undeformed or only mildly folded successions are found in southern Africa (Waterberg and Matsap sequences), in northern Zambia, and in Zaire. Elsewhere, sedimentary and volcanic sequences were deposited in elongate basins that were later subjected to intense deformation and metamorphism during the Kibaran event. This important thermotectonic episode gave rise to the Kibaran-Burundian fold belt in east-central Africa, the Ruwenzori belt in Uganda, and the Namaqua-Natal belt in South Africa and Namibia.

The late Proterozoic (900 to 570 million years ago) is again characterized by platform deposits in stable areas, such as the West African craton (Taoudeni and Tindouf basins), the Congo craton, the Kalahari craton (Nama basin of Namibia), and the Tanzania craton (Bukoban beds). Tectonic and magmatic activity was concentrated in mobile belts surrounding these stable areas and took place throughout the late Proterozoic, during the so-called Pan-African thermotectonic event. Long, linear belts—such as the Damara-Katanga of central and southwestern Africa, the Mozambique belt of eastern Africa, and the Dahomey-Ahaggar belt of western Africa—formed during this time, and some of these belts contain diagnostic rock assemblages that indicate that they resulted from continental collisions. Many late Precambrian sequences of Africa contain one or two beds of tillites (sedimentary rocks that are composed of lithified clay and rock sediments produced by the action of ice), which are thought to have resulted from an extensive glaciation that covered much of Africa at this time. In the Arabian (Eastern) Desert of Egypt and in the Red Sea Hills of The Sudan, a predominance of volcanic rocks and granitoids, together with frequent remnants of ancient oceanic crust, document an evolution similar to what is now occurring in the island-arc systems of the southwestern Pacific. These rocks clearly demonstrate that plate tectonic processes operated in the late Precambrian. (A.K.)

The Paleozoic Era. The Paleozoic Era consists of the Cambrian, Ordovician, Silurian, Devonian, Carboniferous, and Permian periods and includes two major mountain-building episodes. The continent of Africa may be said to have taken shape during the Paleozoic. A glacial period during the Ordovician is evidenced by widespread deposition tillites, which may be seen in southern Morocco, throughout western Africa, and in subequatorial Africa as far south as Namibia. This tillite sequence marks the transition from the end of the Precambrian to the beginning of the Cambrian Period.

Marine fossils of the Cambrian Period (570 to 505 million years ago) are found in southern Morocco, the Western and Mauritanian Sahara, and Namibia. In Egypt and in the Arabian Peninsula, their presence has been revealed by drilling. Elsewhere, they remain unknown.

Marine fossils

During the Ordovician Period (505 to 438 million years ago), fossiliferous marine sandstone completely covered northern and western Africa, including the Sahara. The Table Mountain sandstone of South Africa constitutes its only other trace. This period is, in addition, remarkable for broad, large-scale deformation of the African crust, which raised the continental table of the central and western Sahara by approximately 5,000 feet (1,500 metres). Each emergence resulted in the creation of valleys that became flooded when the continent subsided. Toward the end of the period, the Sahara became glaciated, and tillites and sandstones filled the valleys. A complete change of sedimentation characterized the Silurian Period (438 to 408 million years ago); this is indicated by the deposits of graptolitic shales (those containing small fossil colonies of extinct marine animals of uncertain zoological affinity) in the Arabian Peninsula and in northwestern Africa.

Marine fossils of the Devonian Period (408 to 360 million years ago) are found in North Africa and in the Sahara. Traces also have been discovered in parts of Guinea, Ghana, and Arabia, as well as in Gabon; they also occur in the Bokkeveld Series of South Africa. Fossilized plants that include *Archaeosigillaria* (ancient club mosses) may be traced in formations of the earlier Devonian Period in the Sahara and in South Africa (Witteberg Series).

The Carboniferous Period (360 to 286 million years ago) was marked by the onset of several major tectonic events. Evidence of marine life that existed in the earlier part of this period comes from fossils found in North Africa, the central and western Sahara, and in Egypt. During the middle and later parts of the Carboniferous, the Hercynian mountain-building episodes occurred as a result of collision between the North American and African plates. The Mauritanide mountain chain was compressed and folded at this time along the western margin of the West African craton from Morocco to Senegal. Elsewhere, major uplift or subsidence occurred, continuing until the end of the Triassic Period (*i.e.,* about 208 million years ago). These structures were synformal (folded with the strata dipping inward toward a central axis) in the Tindouf and Taoudeni basins of western Algeria, Mauritania, and Mali and antiformal (forming a mountainous spine or dome) at Reguibat in eastern Western Sahara.

The Late Carboniferous Period is represented throughout the Sahara by layers of fossilized plants and sometimes—as in Morocco and Algeria—by seams of coal. Different phenomena may be observed, however, in the region of subequatorial Africa, including the Dwyka tillite, which covers part of South Africa, Namibia, Madagascar, an extensive portion of the Congo Basin, and Gabon. At several places in South Africa, these Dwyka strata are covered by thin marine layers that serve to demarcate the transition from the Carboniferous to the Permian Period and that form the beginning of the great Karoo System.

The Dwyka tillite

Marine fossils of the Permian Period (286 to 245 million years ago) are visible in southern Tunisia, in Egypt, in the

Arabian Peninsula, on the coasts of Tanzania, and in the Mozambique Channel. Elsewhere, traces of the Permian are of continental rather than marine origin and are included in the Karoo System in South Africa. There, the Lower Permian strata are known as the Ecca Series and are divided into three groups: the Lower Ecca (containing almost 1,000 feet of shales), the Middle Ecca (some 1,650 feet of sandstone, seams of coal, and fossilized plants), and the Upper Ecca (about 650 feet of shales again).

The Upper Permian is represented by the lower part of the Beaufort Series, which continued forming into the Early Triassic Period. The Beaufort Series is almost 10,000 feet thick and is famous for its amphibian and reptile fossils; a similar series is also found in the southern Soviet Union. Other Permian formations, not as rich in coal, occur in Zaire, Tanzania, Kenya, Uganda, Zambia, Zimbabwe, Mozambique, and Madagascar.

The absence of primary marine formations throughout southern Africa should be emphasized. It is not yet known whether this absence is due to a hiatus in deposition or to erosion.

The Mesozoic Era. The Mesozoic Era (245 to 66.4 million years ago) is divided into three periods—the Triassic, Jurassic, and Cretaceous—and is remarkable for the transgression of ancient seas and for the emergence of massive land formations containing interesting fossil remains.

Marine formations. During the Triassic Period (245 to 208 million years ago), ancient seas left deposits of marine formations in North Africa, the southern Sahara, Egypt, Arabia, and parts of Tanzania and northern Madagascar. Deposits from the Jurassic Period (208 to 144 million years ago) extend to the Atlantic basins of the Río de Oro region of Western Sahara and Senegal along the northwest coast of the continent. In the middle of the Jurassic a great transgression of the Indian Ocean extended over Somalia and much of Ethiopia. In the Cretaceous Period (144 to 66.4 million years ago) this was followed by a series of marine transgressions, including those along the coasts of equatorial Africa when Gondwana broke up and the present Atlantic and Indian oceans took shape; during one transgression a shallow sea covered much of the northern and central Sahara and Egypt as far south as The Sudan; and a later one again covered the same areas, as well as western Arabia and the west coast of Madagascar.

Continental formations. In Africa north of the equator and in Arabia, Mesozoic continental formations covered

Adapted from *Carte tectonique de l'Afrique* (1968); UNESCO/ASGA

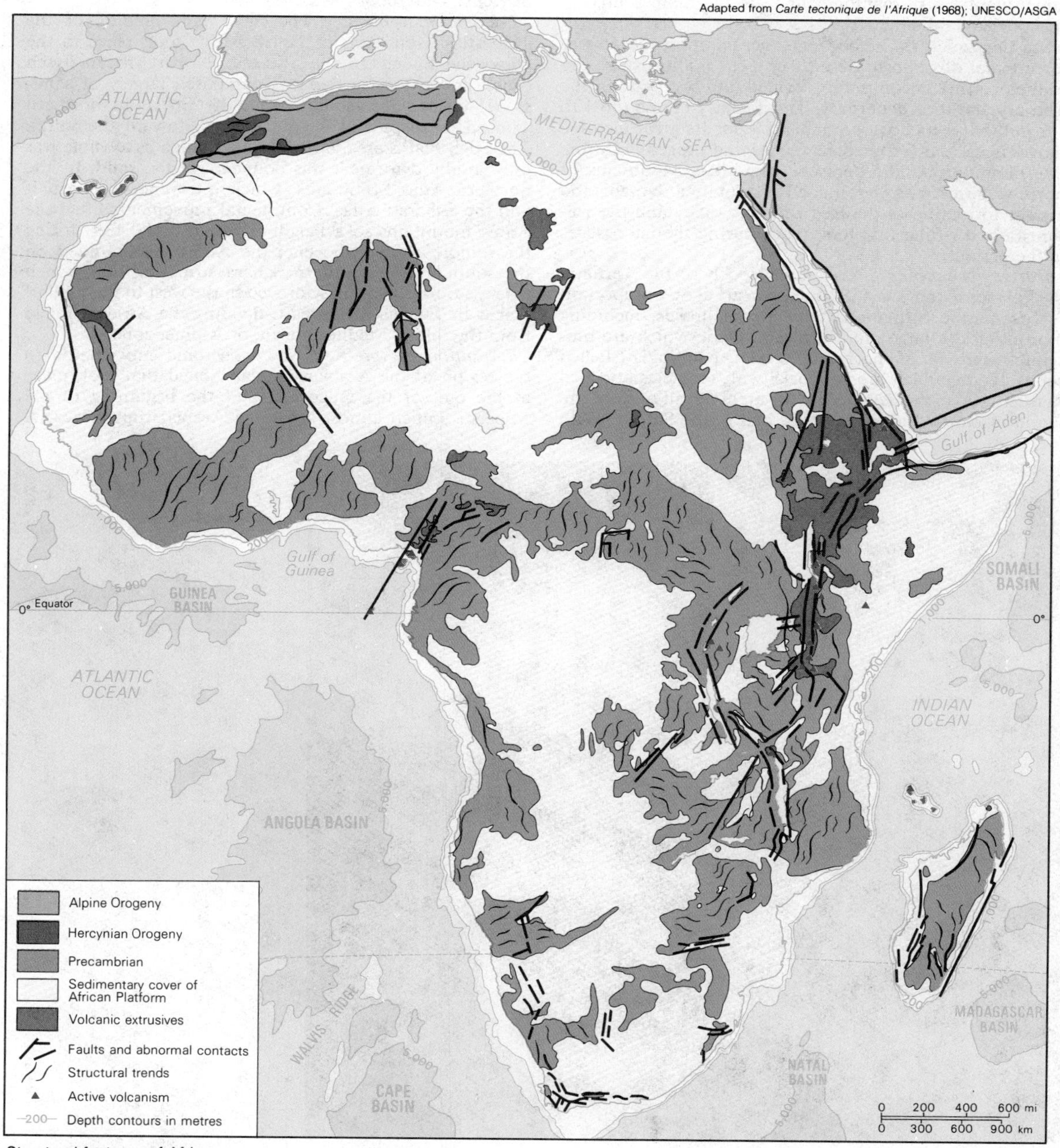

Structural features of Africa.

large areas. During the Triassic the Saharan Zarzaitine Series, containing dinosaur and other reptilian fossil remains, was deposited. The Saharan Taouratine Series, containing fossils of vegetation and of great reptiles, was laid down during the Jurassic. In the upper Karoo System of subequatorial Africa, formed during the Early Triassic Period, the Beaufort Series contains fossils of fish, amphibians, and reptiles. The final stages of the Triassic and the Early Jurassic periods were characterized by the terminal folding of the Cape mountain chain, by subsidence in the Karoo basin, by fracturing, and by widespread upwelling of Karoo basaltic lavas through fissures, creating formations some 4,000 feet thick, such as the Drakensberg range along the eastern border of Lesotho and in South Africa.

During the Jurassic and the Cretaceous periods, widespread sediments were deposited that contain fossilized plants, dinosaurs, and smaller reptiles. Certain unique eruptions occurred during the Cretaceous that led to the creation of kimberlite pipes (near-cylindrical rock bodies, usually approximately vertical and derived from melting at great depth in the upper mantle) in southern and central Africa; some of these, particularly in South Africa, Botswana, Namibia, Angola, and Zaire, contain large quantities of diamonds and are the main source of this precious mineral.

Kimberlite pipes

The Cenozoic Era. The Cenozoic, the most recent major interval of geologic time (from 66.4 million years ago to the present), is commonly divided into two periods: the Tertiary and the Quaternary. The Tertiary Period (66.4 to 1.6 million years ago) is remarkable for its great tectonic movements, that resulted in the Alpine orogeny. During this mountain-building episode, the Atlas Mountains of northwestern Africa were folded and uplifted. Notable too are the formation of the Red Sea Rift valley and the volcanism and rifting that took place during the later stages of the period.

Marine formations. The initial epoch of the Tertiary, the Paleocene (66.4 to 57.8 million years ago), is important for its marine formations with animal fossils, including nummulites (a large kind of foraminifera, which are unicellular animals of macroscopic size), nautiloids (shelled cephalopods, which are mollusks with tentacles attached to their heads), and echinoids (sea urchins); all of these are found in North and West Africa and in the Sahara. With the exception of the Sahara, nummulites of the Eocene Epoch (57.8 to 36.6 million years ago) are found in the same places, as well as on the African coasts of the Indian Ocean. There also are lepidocyclines (foraminifera) of the Oligocene Epoch (36.6 to 23.7 million years ago) and of the Miocene Epoch (23.7 to 5.3 million years ago).

Continental formations. Several levels may sometimes be distinguished in the continental formations of the Tertiary Period. They include lower Eocene levels containing *Pseudoceratodes* (a genus of gastropod) and *Dyrosaurus* (a type of reptile), as well as upper Eocene and Oligocene levels containing silicified wood and fossilized fish, turtles, crocodiles, snakes, and mammals. In Egypt the Oligocene deposits found in the Al-Fayyūm area contain mammals, birds, turtles, and crocodiles. Sediments of the Lower Miocene, which are found on the banks of Lakes Rudolf and Victoria in East Africa, contain mastodon (a large elephant-like mammal) and *Proconsul africanus* (a large ape). Central Asian hipparions (three-toed ancestors of the horse), which simultaneously entered Africa and Europe during the Late Miocene Epoch (11.2 to 5.3 million years ago), also left their fossilized remains in this region, as did genera of hominoid (manlike) apes—*e.g., Kenyapithecus* of Kenya—at about the same time.

Miocene fossils

Tectonic movements. The first major folding of the Tell Atlas Mountains of North Africa took place in the Oligocene Epoch. In the Miocene, North African flysch (thick and extensive deposits composed largely of sandstone) formed layers that, from the Er-Rif to northern Tunisia, were pushed from the north toward the south. The High Plains area, farther south, which as a whole was only mildly deformed, was bounded on the south by the northern Atlas Mountains, which intervened between it and the Saharan Atlas. Continental movements lifted the Aurès mountains to a height of about 3,300 feet during the middle of the Miocene; the Aurès are bounded on the south by the northern Sahara structural line, which extends from Agadir in Morocco in the west to the Gulf of Gabes in Tunisia in the east, dividing the African Shield from the folded Mediterranean, or Alpine, zone.

Formation of the Red Sea. Tectonic movements in the region of the Arabian-Nubian Shield that took place at the end of the Oligocene and the beginning of the Miocene Epoch almost separated Arabia from Africa. A

Photo Almasy

Simen Mountains, rising above the Ethiopian Plateau in northwestern Ethiopia.

trough (fault-bounded depression) developed because of divergence in the crust between northeastern Africa and western Arabia, and the Mediterranean Sea swept into the resulting rift valley, forming a gulf that extended to Yemen. The gulf was prevented from joining the Indian Ocean only by an isthmus that stretched from Djibouti in the west to Aden in the east.

At the end of the Miocene the Isthmus of Suez was formed, and the gulf became a saline lake at the bottom of which thick evaporites (sediments formed as a result of evaporation) were laid down. The isthmus permitted Asian animal life to pass into Africa during part of the Pliocene Epoch (5.3 to 1.6 million years ago). Subsidence of the Djibouti-Aden isthmus, also during the Pliocene, permitted the Indian Ocean to flow into the Red Sea as far as the Isthmus of Suez.

Volcanism and rifting. Tectonic movements during the Miocene and Pliocene scored the African continent with a network of faults that generally trended northeast to southwest and northwest to southeast. Volcanic eruptions and basaltic upwellings accompanied fracturing in the Ahaggar area of southern Algeria, in the Tibesti area of Libya and Chad, in Ethiopia, throughout East Africa, and in Cameroon, as well as in the islands of Bioko (formerly Fernando Po) and São Tomé and Príncipe in the Gulf of Guinea.

Pleistocene and Holocene developments. The Quaternary Period is divided into the Pleistocene Epoch (1,600,000 to 10,000 years ago) and the Holocene, or Recent, Epoch (the last 10,000 years). It represents a phase of continuing volcanic activity that caused the basement rocks of the Ahaggar and Tibesti mountains of the central Sahara to rise. The activity manifested itself in eruptions, in the deepening of the Saharan valleys, and in the extrusion of flood basalt.

During the cold humid periods called pluvials, which correspond to the glacial phases of the Northern Hemisphere, the glaciers that covered the high mountains of East Africa were from 3,000 to 5,000 feet thicker than those remaining in the summit zones today. Elsewhere, the desert zones of the Sahara and the Kalahari were alternately subjected first to humid and then to dry and arid phases that expanded the desert surface at the expense of adjacent forested zones.

Hominid fossils

The oldest levels at which hominid remains have been found are known as the Villafranchian-Kaguerian Series and are recognized in Africa in Ethiopia and Kenya. These levels date to approximately three to four million years ago and contain fossils of the genus *Australopithecus*. The Kaguerian-Kamasian Interpluvial levels, which date to about 500,000 years ago, contain the remains of *Homo erectus* at Olduvai Gorge (Tanzania) and in Morocco, Algeria, and Chad.

The Kamasian, or Second, Pluvial of the Middle Pleistocene Epoch (900,000 to 130,000 years ago) corresponds to the Mindel in Europe. A dry but not a desert climate is implied by the Kamasian-Kanjeran Interpluvial levels at Olduvai Gorge. The Kanjeran, or Third, Pluvial occurred during the Middle Pleistocene and corresponds to the Riss Pluvial in Europe.

An arid phase, which greatly reduced forest land, is revealed in the Kanjeran-Gamblian Interpluvial levels, lasting from about 60,000 to 55,000 years ago. This period corresponds to an important tectonic phase marked by uplift and subsidence in North Africa and activity along all the faults, in particular those in eastern Africa. It was at this time that eastern Africa assumed its present topographic character.

During the Gamblian, or Fourth, Pluvial, which occurred from approximately 30,000 to 15,000 years ago, three distinct humid phases are separated by drier intervals. During these phases the dimensions of Lake Chad and those of the glaciers of Mount Kenya and of Kilimanjaro diminished rapidly. The postpluvial phase that followed this period, equivalent to the postglacial phase of the Northern Hemisphere, was marked by a succession of alternating dry and humid stages and by the desertification of both the Sahara and the Kalahari, a process that began about 3,000 BC. (A.K.)

The land

RELIEF

The physiography of Africa is essentially a reflection of the geologic history and geology that is described in the previous section. The continent, composed largely of a vast rigid block of ancient rocks, has geologically young mountains at its extremities in the highlands of the Atlas Mountains in the northwest and the Cape ranges in the south. Between these mountainous areas is a series of plateau surfaces, with huge areas that are level or slightly undulating, above which stand occasional harder and more resistant rock masses. Surrounding these surfaces is a zone of plateau slopes below which are narrow coastal belts widening along the Mediterranean coast, the coastlands of Tanzania and Mozambique, a narrow belt between the Niger and Kunene rivers, and an area northward of the Gambia and Sénégal rivers.

Highest and lowest points

Kilimanjaro (19,340 feet [5,895 metres]) is the highest point on the continent; the lowest is Lake Assal (502 feet [153 metres] below sea level) in Djibouti. In proportion to its size, Africa has fewer high mountains and fewer lowland plains than any other continent. The limited areas above 8,000 feet are either volcanic peaks or resistant massifs. All the land below 500 feet occurs within 500 miles of the coast, except for two small basins in the Sahara.

The higher areas of the south and east are in marked contrast to the considerably lower elevation of the western and northern parts of the continent. South of a line drawn from near the mouth of the Congo (Zaire) River to the Gulf of Aden, most of the land lies 1,000 feet or more above sea level, and much of it exceeds 3,000 and even 4,000 feet. North of the line there is relatively little land above 3,000 feet, most of the area being between 500 and 1,000 feet above sea level; there are also broad coastal lowlands, except in the region of the Atlas Mountains and, in the east, beyond the Nile.

The highest extensive areas are to be found in Ethiopia, parts of which exceed 15,000 feet. Southward the East African Plateau is highest in Kenya, where it is often 8,000 feet or more above sea level; there are occasional volcanic peaks that are much higher, such as Kilimanjaro, Mount Kenya (17,058 feet), Meru (14,978 feet), and Elgon (14,178 feet). The Ruwenzori (Rwenzori) Range—sometimes called the Mountains of the Moon—which reaches its highest elevation at Margherita Peak (16,763 feet) on the borders of Zaire and Uganda, is not volcanic in origin. From East Africa the plateau extends southward, often with a well-defined, though not continuous, escarpment particularly noticeable in the Drakensberg of southern Africa, where Ntlenyana, or Ntshonyana, is 11,425 feet and Mont aux Sources is 10,822 feet. There, the plateau edges are especially marked, because the rock formations are hard and horizontal, whereas in Ethiopia they are conspicuous because of faulting. Where the rocks are softer and less resistant, the escarpment is not so pronounced and so forms less of a barrier to climatic influences and to human movement.

To the north and west of the plateau area of the southern parts of the continent there is a general descent to the lower areas of the basins of the Congo, Niger, and Nile rivers. The only large areas that extend above 3,000 feet are in the folded ranges of the Atlas Mountains and in the central Sahara, where resistant granites form the massifs of Ahaggar and Tibesti. The interior uplands of West Africa and of Cameroon consist of ancient crystalline rocks, reaching considerable heights only in the Fouta Djallon plateau in Guinea, in the Guinea Highlands, which also extend over the borders of Sierra Leone and Liberia, in the Jos Plateau in Nigeria, in the Adamawa region of Nigeria and Cameroon, and in the Cameroon Highlands. There are extensive low-lying areas near the coast and in the basins of the Sénégal, Gambia, Volta, and Niger–Benue rivers. The high areas of Darfur in The Sudan (more than 10,000 feet) and of Mount Cameroon (13,435 feet) are volcanic in origin and are evidence of the same tensions that have resulted in rifting and volcanism in East Africa.

The East African Rift System constitutes the most striking

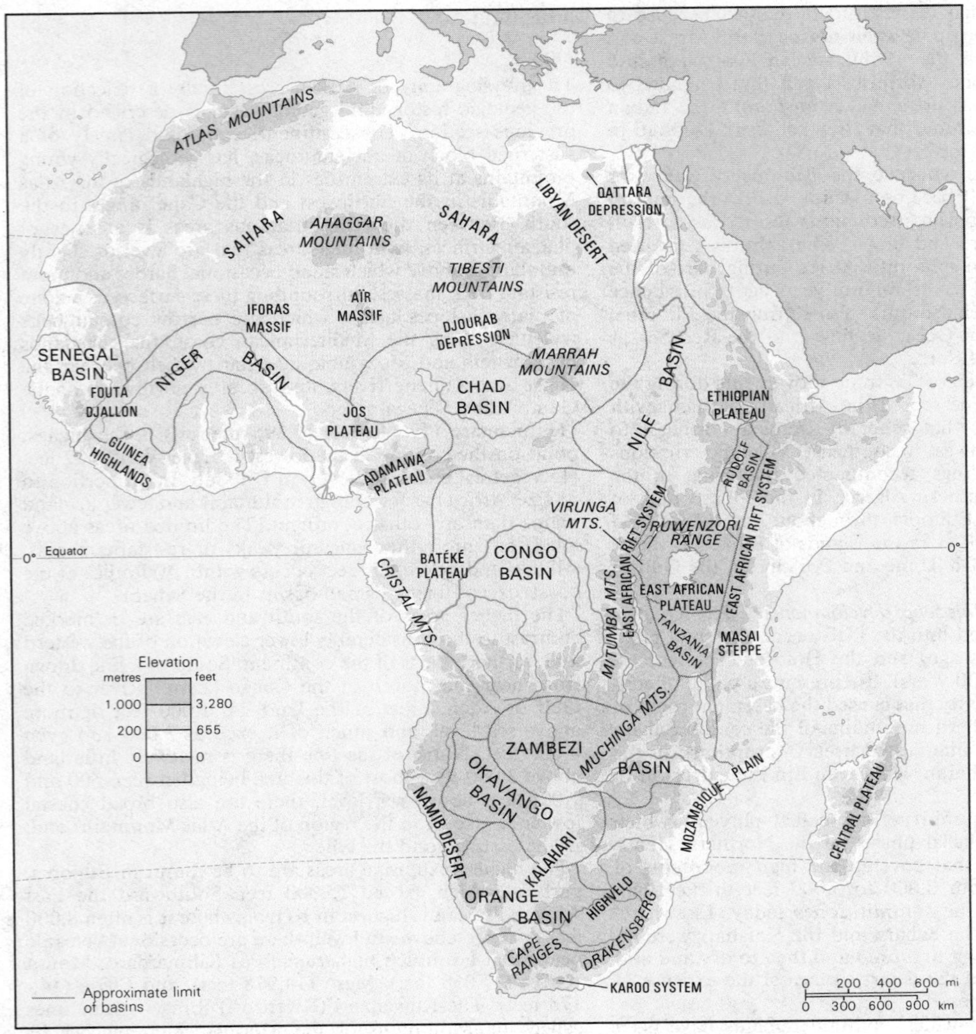

Physiographic regions of Africa.

and distinctive relief feature of the continent. Associated with its formation was the volcanic activity responsible for most of the higher peaks of East Africa, including Kilimanjaro, which is always snowcapped despite its nearness to the equator. Seismic and volcanic disturbances are still recorded in the western portions of the rift valley system. In the Virunga Mountains, northeast of Lake Kivu, there are periodic outbursts (about every 10 or 12 years) that have created a series of lava flows. One of these volcanoes dammed the rift valley and converted a large area, formerly drained by a tributary of the Nile, into Lake Kivu.

Volcanic activity

The rift valley extends for about 4,000 miles, its course being clearly marked out by many of the lakes of East Africa as well as by the adjacent volcanic peaks. From the Gulf of Aqaba it can be traced southward along the Red Sea and into the Ethiopian Plateau to Lakes Rudolf, Naivasha, and Magadi in Kenya. Farther south, through Tanzania, the line of the rift is not quite so obvious. The walls that constitute the eastern rim have been more easily eroded, while the lakes of this area are generally smaller and not in line, and some of them are only waterless salt beds. The largest of these lakes are Natron and Manyara, with Eyasi in a side branch of the main rift. The edges are obvious enough to the south in Malaŵi, where a huge crusted block collapsed along the parallel faults that constitute the steeply rising slopes of Lake Nyasa (Malaŵi). The lake is 360 miles long but never more than 50 miles wide; it has a maximum depth of 2,310 feet. The rift then follows the line of the Shire Valley to reach the Indian Ocean near Beira, Mozambique.

The western branch, or Western Rift Valley, extends from the northern end of Lake Nyasa in a great arc, taking in Lakes Rukwa, Tanganyika (after Lake Baikal in Siberia the deepest lake in the world), Kivu, Edward, and Albert. Subsidiary branches of this valley include the basins in which lie Lakes Mweru and Upemba.

Most of the lakes that occur along the course of the rift valley lie well below the general level of the plateau, ranging from about 1,300 to 3,000 feet above sea level. They are generally very deep and bear a striking resemblance to fjords; some have floors that are below sea level, even though their surfaces are hundreds of feet above sea level.

In complete contrast is Lake Victoria, the largest of all African lakes, which occupies a shallow depression on a plateau 3,720 feet above sea level between the major branches of the rift valley. Its greatest depth is only 270 feet, but, with an area of 26,828 square miles, it is the third largest of the world's lakes, after the Caspian Sea and Lake Superior.

Detailed discussion of the Atlas Mountains, East African mountains, Ituri Forest, Kalahari, Namib, Sahara, and Veld can be found in *African geographic features of special interest* at the end of this article. (Ro.W.St.)

DRAINAGE

The uplifting and warping of the surface of the African continent that occurred during the Pliocene and Pleistocene epochs produced a number of structural basins; these are now either individually occupied by, or are linked up with, drainage systems. With the exception of the Chad basin, all the major drainage basins have outlets to the sea. In addition, minor drainage basins, similar to that of Lake Chad, are situated in the East African Rift Valley. Some, again like Lake Chad, constitute the focus of centripetal drainage (drainage directed toward the centre), while others are linked to river systems. Although the East African lakes are climatically and economically important, relatively little is known of their hydrological characteristics.

Climate, geology, and the history of tectonic activity have imparted certain common characteristics to African rivers. Spatial variations in the incidence and amount of rainfall are reflected in their hydrological regimes. In areas that have one rainfall season, for example, and have pronounced drought throughout the rest of the year, the rivers flood in the rainy season and shrink in the dry season.

Whatever their hydrological regimes, all the important African rivers are interrupted by rapids, cataracts, and waterfalls. This is explained by several factors, the most important of which is the past tectonic activity, or regional land movements, that caused ridges to be formed across the courses of the major rivers. Waterfalls are often found where the rivers are still engaged in cutting downward as they flow across these ridges; Cabora-Bassa (falls) on the Zambezi and the Augrabies Falls on the Orange River are examples. Another factor that contributes to the creation of rapids or falls is the incidence of rock strata that have proved resistant to the erosive effect of the rivers' flow. (Tropical rivers do not generally carry large quantities of stone or rock; instead, they have a tendency to carry loads of fine silt, produced by chemical weathering.)

Although the Nile, the Zambezi, and the Niger rivers have large deltas, their size does not compare with, for example, the enormous delta region of the Ganges and Brahmaputra rivers. In Africa the generally poor development of deltas is mainly because of the restricted extent of the coastal plain, together with the relatively narrow continental shelf, which provides neither sufficient room nor shallow enough water for the deposition of delta-forming material. The great speed with which most of the rivers flow into the sea is another factor inhibiting delta formation.

Major drainage basins

The major drainage basins of Africa are those of the Nile, the Niger, the Congo, the Zambezi, and the Orange rivers and of Lake Chad.

The Nile basin. There are two theories concerning the development of the Nile, which, it appears, originally consisted of two sections. The first theory is that the lower Nile had its source at about latitude 20° N, whence it flowed directly into the sea, while the upper Nile, issuing from Lake Victoria, flowed into an inland lake that covered the As-Sudd region in what is now The Sudan. The lake became filled with water, which then spilled over at its northern end and flowed into what is now the upper Nile. According to the second theory, the upper section originally flowed into a vast lake between Mount as Silsilah (near Luxor, Egypt) and what is now Aswān; this was tapped by the lower section of the Nile after the so-called Sebile erosion (which takes its name from the fact that the breakthrough by the lower Nile was identified at Sebile).

The Nile, which is about 4,132 miles long, is the longest river in the world. From Lake Victoria it flows, as the Victoria Nile, into Lake Albert, from which it emerges as the Albert Nile. Further north it is known as the Al-Jabal River. Thereafter, having received several tributaries, it becomes the White Nile, and finally the Nile, emptying at last into the Mediterranean Sea. Its major left-bank tributary is the Al-Ghazāl, and the largest right-bank tributaries are the Sobat, Blue Nile, and Atbara. Because of the numerous rapids and waterfalls, the Nile descends fairly rapidly from source to mouth, as do its major right-bank tributaries. This is especially true of the Blue Nile, which, after issuing from Lake Tana on the Ethiopian Plateau at a height of approximately 6,000 feet, flows for most of its length through a steep gorge. Swamps also interrupt the river's course. Of these, the largest is the As-Sudd, a vast area of floating swamp reeds, mostly papyrus.

The river's regime is now controlled by a series of dams situated on the Nile itself or on one of its various tributaries; of these, the largest is the Aswan High Dam on the main Nile.

The Niger basin. The Niger basin is the largest river basin of western Africa. The Niger River, which rises in the mountains of Guinea, enters the sea through its delta in southern Nigeria; it is about 2,600 miles in length. Rapids interrupt its course at several points, although some of these (such as below Bamako, Mali) have been submerged in waters impounded by dams.

The Niger receives its largest tributary, the Benue, which flows in from its left bank, in Nigeria. The valleys of both the Niger downstream from Taoussa and of the Benue appear to be faulted troughs dating from the Early Cretaceous Period. Originally, the middle Niger was separate from the upper Niger, which flowed into an inland lake, the remnants of which now form the inland Niger delta. The middle Niger flowed southeastward to the sea; its valley eroded toward its headwaters, eventually tapping the inland lake and linking the middle with the upper Niger.

The Congo basin. With a total area of about 1,335,000 square miles, the Congo basin consists of a vast shallow depression that rises by a series of giant steps to an almost circular rim of highlands through which the river has cut a narrow exit into the Atlantic Ocean. The present exit is geologically relatively recent, the previous exit being to the north of the present one.

Boyoma (Stanley) Falls

The Congo River is some 2,900 miles in length. Its many waterfalls and rapids cause its valley, like that of the Nile, to lose elevation quickly. The river's course is often constricted by gorges. The best-known are the Boyoma (Stanley) Falls at Kisangani, where the river swings through an arc to flow westward; in fact, the Boyoma Falls are no more than a series of unevenly spaced rapids at no great height, extending along a 60-mile stretch of the river. Downstream from Kisangani, the Congo is joined first by the Ubangi from the right and then by the Kasai—which rivals the Ubangi in the size of its drainage basin—from the left. Below its confluence with the Kasai, the main river cuts through the Cristal Mountains in a deep gorge, which at one point expands into Malebo (Stanley) Pool, a shallow lake measuring 22 miles in length and 14 miles in width. The Congo enters the sea through a swampy estuary that is about 6 miles wide at its mouth.

The Zambezi basin. The Zambezi River is about 2,200 miles in length; it occupies a basin with an approximate area of 463,000 square miles. Originally, there were two rivers, corresponding to the upper and lower courses of the present river; the valley of the lower section eroded toward the headwaters until it captured the waters of the upper section. Although there are stretches of the river where the gradient is very gentle—a drop of only about three inches to the mile—the valley as a whole has a fairly steep gradient. There are numerous waterfalls, the most spectacular of which is the Victoria Falls. After these falls, the river winds through a number of deep gorges cut out of basalt and, after flowing through a broad valley, enters Kariba Gorge, which is more than 16 miles in length and is cut through paragneiss (a gneiss, or coarse-grained rock, in which bands rich in granular minerals alternate with bands containing schistose minerals, formed out of sedimentary rock). The Kafue and the Luangwa, the two main tributaries, which both flow through gorges, join the Zambezi on its left bank downstream from Kariba. At the mouth of the main river is a delta about 37 miles wide.

The Orange basin. The Orange River is the longest in South Africa. Flowing across almost the entire width of the country, it makes its way from the highlands in the east through the Kalahari depression in the west to empty into the South Atlantic Ocean. Its major tributary, the Vaal River, is one of its northern headwaters; the two rivers together have a combined length of about 1,300 miles. Together with other major rivers on the continent, the Orange–Vaal river system shares the characteristic of flowing over steep gradients for numerous stretches of its course. The largest drop (about 400 feet) occurs at the Augrabies Falls.

The Chad basin. The Chad basin constitutes the largest inland drainage area in Africa. Lake Chad, a large sheet of fresh water with a mean depth between 3.5 and 4 feet, lies at the centre of the basin but not in its lowest part. Lake Chad is fed by three major streams, the Komadugu Yobe, Logone, and Chari, but these are in danger of having their waters captured by the drainage systems of rivers that flow in opposite directions. Lake Chad itself, with an area of only some 5,000 square miles, was formerly much more extensive.

Detailed discussion of Lake Chad, the Congo River, the East African lakes, the Niger River, the Nile River, the Orange River, the Sénégal River, the Suez Canal, and the Zambezi River can be found in *African geographic features of special interest* at the end of this article.

SOILS

Soil types. In general, soil types on the African continent may be divided into five or six broad categories. There are desert soils; chestnut-brown soils, which border the deserts; and chernozem-like soils (dark black soils rich in humus and carbonates), which are found immediately south of the chestnut soils from The Sudan westward to just beyond the Niger Bend (the bend in the middle course of the Niger River), and pockets of which are also found in East Africa, Zambia, Zimbabwe, and South Africa. In addition, there are black soils (often grouped with chernozems and found on the Accra Plains of Ghana); red tropical soils and laterites (leached red iron-bearing soils), which occur in the tropical wet-and-dry and equatorial climatic zones; and Mediterranean soils, found in the Atlas Mountains of North Africa and the Cape region of South Africa.

Factors affecting soil formation

The most important factors that affect soil formation are climate, parent material, relief, drainage, vegetation cover, and the passage of time. Where the land has been generally stable and fairly flat for prolonged periods, as in Africa, the climate becomes the major determinant of the soil groups. The different rocks are deeply weathered and are broken down into their common component elements to produce broadly similar soils under the same climatic conditions. Given sufficient time under a tropical climate, the differences in humus content of the great soil groups, which are introduced by vegetation types, are minimized. But within these groups there will naturally be differences in soil types as a function of local differences in physical factors.

Desert soils. These soils are characterized by the general lack of organic content; by the types of rock reflected in them, the chemical weathering of which has been inhibited by the lack of water; and by the crusts or concretions of soluble salts on or just below their surface. While these crusts are in general thought to have been formed as a result of evaporation, it is nevertheless possible that they may have been formed under a wetter climate during the Pleistocene Epoch.

Chestnut-brown soils. In the semiarid areas bordering the desert, increased rainfall makes grass vegetation more plentiful, results in rocks becoming more weathered than in the desert, and produces better developed soils with a higher humus content. It is the humus content that, according to the amount present, gives the chestnut soils their characteristic light or dark brown colour. Chestnut soils also differ from desert soils because they receive enough water to wash out some of the salt accumulations either on the surface or immediately below it.

Chernozem-like and black soils. An unfailing characteristic of the chernozem is the presence of a subsurface zone of calcium carbonate, sometimes accompanied by calcium sulfate, which is left behind after all the soluble salts have been washed out. Grouped with them are the

After S.J. Schokalskaja, reproduced by permission of UNESCO

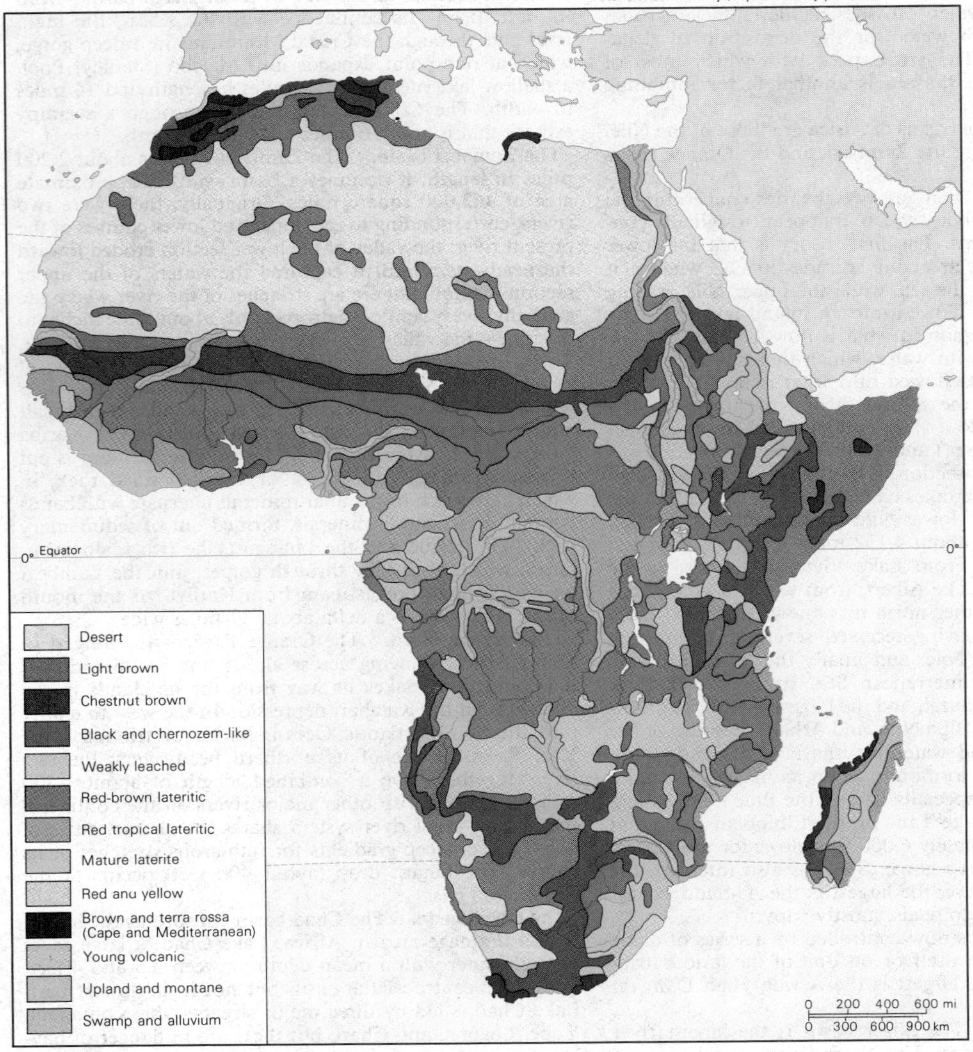

Soils of Africa.

black soils, which should, perhaps, be differently classified, for their black colour is not necessarily due to high humus content but rather to the presence of certain minerals, as in the black soils of the Accra Plains, in Ghana.

Red tropical soils and laterites. The majority of tropical soils have shades of colour varying from yellow and brown to red. The reddish colour reflects the presence of iron oxides that form as a result of chemical weathering. At one time all tropical red earths or soils were indiscriminately referred to as laterites, but it is now clear that the term laterite should be confined to those tropical soils with large concentrations of iron and aluminum sesquioxides (insoluble compounds) that have formed a hard pan at or just below the surface. At the most advanced state of laterization, bauxite, from which aluminum is extracted, is formed. Most tropical soils are in varying stages of laterization, which is to say they are at various stages of accumulating insoluble compounds as the soluble elements are leached out. The compounds accumulate more readily in areas with a pronounced dry season and where the water table is not too far below the surface. If the top horizons (layers) of the soils should erode, the subsurface concentrations of sesquioxides are then exposed to the atmosphere, whereupon they crystallize irreversibly to form true laterite concretions.

Laterization of soils

Mediterranean soils. Mediterranean soils are generally deficient in humus, not so much because of sparse vegetation cover as because of the slowness of the chemical processes that convert the vegetable matter to humus. Low rainfall, occurring when temperatures are lowest, retards chemical weathering. The uneven surface relief of the regions where these soils occur also makes it difficult for mature soils to develop, since the land, except in the valley bottoms, is not sufficiently flat over wide enough areas to allow the soil-forming (parent) materials to remain in place and thus to be thoroughly weathered.

Soil problems. Soil is the foundation of Africa's economic life, and as such its detailed study is most important. Failure to appreciate the physical and chemical properties of the soils has led to disastrous results for several projects for agricultural improvement.

In studying the soils of Africa, it is essential not to lose sight of the importance of such social factors as the ability or inability of mostly uneducated farmers to judge the quality of the soil. Thus, schemes for transforming traditional systems of farming that are based on soil classification but that do not take into account local perception may have little chance of success.

For desert soils to be productive they must be irrigated, as they are on the desert margins of North Africa; their excessive salinity or alkalinity must also be reduced. Compared to desert soils, the chestnut-brown soils are easier to work and are more productive under irrigation. Black soils tend to have a markedly crumbly structure and are sometimes difficult to plow. In the wet season, the black soils of the Accra Plains swell and become slippery, while in the dry season they shrink once more and crack to such an extent that they are said to plow themselves. Red tropical soils need careful handling. Despite their luxuriant vegetation cover, high temperatures coupled with humidity promote the rapid decay of organic matter and keep the humus content low. Erosion is a constant threat if the soils are exposed to the elements for any length of time; the soils remain cultivable only if the sesquioxides remain below the surface.

In the Atlas and Cape regions, there is a clearer relationship between soil characteristics and parent material than in the humid tropical areas. Over expanses of limestone, for example, the soils contain large amounts of calcium compounds, some of which must be washed away or neutralized before the soils can become fully productive.

CLIMATE

Factors influencing the African climate. A number of factors influence the climate of the African continent. First, most of the continent—which extends from latitude 35° S to about latitude 37° N—lies within the tropics. Second, the near bisection of the continent by the equator results in a largely symmetrical arrangement of climatic zones on either side. This symmetry is, however, imperfect because of a third factor—the great east–west extent of the continent north of the equator, in contrast to its narrow width to the south. In consequence, the influence of the sea extends farther inland in southern Africa. Moreover, a quasi-permanent subtropical high-pressure cell (the Saharan anticyclone) develops in the heart of northern Africa, while in southern Africa the belt of high pressure on land weakens during the time of high sun (the season when the Sun is overhead—in December and January in the south). A fourth factor consists of the cool ocean currents, which chill the winds that blow over them and thereby influence the climate of the neighbouring shores. Fifth, because of the extensive plateau surfaces of the continent and the absence of high and long mountain ranges comparable to, for example, the Andes in South America or the Himalayas in Asia, climatic zones in Africa tend to shade into one another, rather than to change abruptly from place to place. Finally, the high mountains have climatic zones of their own that vary with altitude.

While these factors help to account for the broad climatic patterns of the African continent, there are, nevertheless, numerous local variations to be found from place to place within the same climatic zone. Urban areas, for example, have climates that often differ in many respects from those of the surrounding countryside. Typically experiencing higher average temperatures, urban areas also frequently have less wind and lower relative humidity; there is too little relevant data from Africa, however, to permit a detailed study of urban climates.

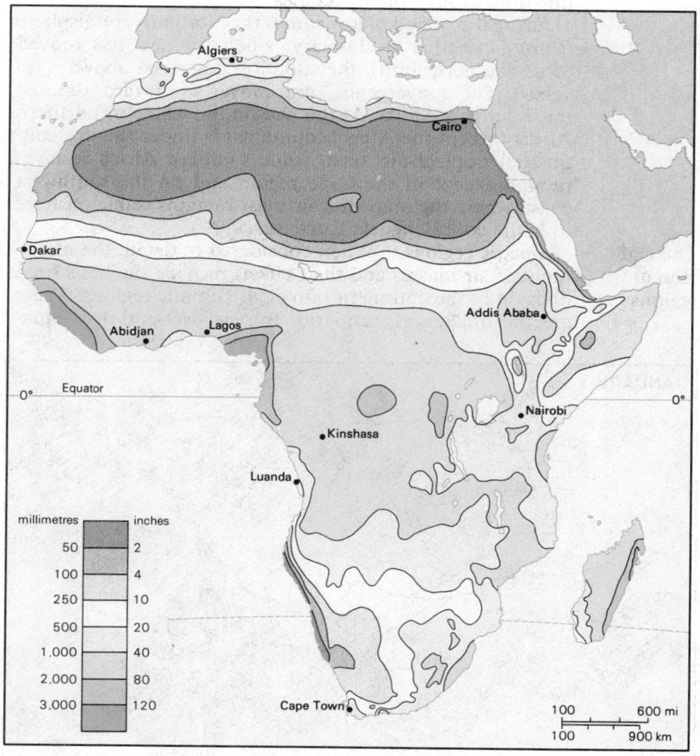

Average annual precipitation for Africa.

The most important differentiating climatic element is rainfall; this, together with several other climatic elements, depends upon the characteristics of the dominating air mass. The air masses of relevance to the African climate may be broadly classified as maritime tropical, maritime equatorial, continental tropical, maritime polar, and continental polar. Of these, the least important are the continental polar air masses, which may occasionally bring intense cold to northern Egypt in December and January, and the maritime polar air masses, which are associated with rain-bearing depressions over the northern and southern extremities of the continent during the winter. With the exception of these, the continent is affected both by a

The air masses

continental tropical air mass to the north and by maritime tropical and maritime equatorial air masses to the south.

These northern and southern air masses meet at the intertropical convergence zone (ITCZ). The hot, dry continental tropical air mass, which is present in the upper levels of the atmosphere, descends to the ground only at the convergence zone. Less hot than the continental tropical are the maritime tropical and maritime equatorial air masses, which originate from the Indian and South Atlantic oceans, respectively; they differ only in that the maritime equatorial air mass is unstable and brings rain, while the maritime tropical air mass, when fully developed, is stable and does not normally bring rain unless it is forced to rise by a high mountain.

In July the ITCZ—following the sun—moves northward toward the area of low pressure over the Sahara; there, the maritime and continental tropical air masses converge, with the maritime air masses swinging inland from the sea. There is no rainfall on the northern side of the convergence zone, since the region is completely under the dry continental tropical air mass originating over the Sahara. At the ITCZ itself, however, precipitation is prolonged and intense as air converges between the maritime and continental air masses and is forced aloft. Immediately south of the convergence zone, rainfall is heavy because of the unstable nature of maritime tropical air over a heated land surface. South of the equator, at yet greater distance from the convergence zone, the maritime air masses are less heated, thick, and stable, and they bring hardly any rainfall, except over some of the East African highlands. Only the southern tip of South Africa receives rainfall at this time, from winter cyclones.

During the period of low sun in the Northern Hemisphere (from December to January, when the sun has moved to its southern limit), the situation described above is reversed. The convergence zone moves southward, dipping into southern Africa. At this season the whole of northern Africa (except the Atlas Mountains) is under the dry continental tropical air mass, while southern Africa receives rainfall except in the Cape region and on the southwest coast, where the maritime air mass remains stable offshore over the cool Benguela Current.

The eight climatic regions

Climatic regions. When considered in detail, the movement of air masses and their effects provide the basis for a division of the continent into eight climatic regions. These are the hot desert, semiarid, tropical wet-and-dry, equatorial (tropical wet), Mediterranean, humid subtropical marine, warm temperate upland, and mountain regions.

The hot desert region consists of the Sahara and Kalahari deserts, which are always under the influence of dry continental tropical air masses, and the northern Kenya–Somali desert, the aridity of which is principally caused by the stable nature of the maritime air masses that pass over it throughout the year. The stability of these maritime air masses is induced by their passing over the cool body of water offshore. In addition to aridity, the desert climate is characterized by high mean monthly temperatures; the diurnal (daily) temperature range is, however, greater than the annual range of the mean monthly temperature.

Semiarid climatic regions fringe the desert areas and include the greater part of the land south of the Zambezi River. They differ from true desert regions in being just within reach of the ITCZ in the course of its seasonal movement and therefore receiving more rainfall. Temperatures are about the same as those in the desert regions.

The tropical wet-and-dry region is often called the savanna climatic region; this implies, incorrectly, that all areas with savanna vegetation have this type of climate. This region covers a little less than half of the total surface area of the continent, extending toward the equator from the semiarid areas. The great distinguishing feature of this climatic region is the seasonal character of its rainfall. During the period of high sun the maritime air masses produce up to six months of rainfall—the length of the rainy season depending on nearness to the equator. The rest of the year is dry. In a few places—for example, on the coast of Mauritania and Senegal—there is also a little rainfall in the period of low sun. As in the desert and semiarid climatic zones, mean monthly temperatures show less variation than daily temperatures. In western Africa the period of low sun corresponds to the harmattan season. The harmattan is a warm, dry northeasterly or easterly wind that blows out of the southern Sahara and is frequently laden with large quantities of sand and dust.

Regions with the equatorial, or tropical wet, type of climate, or variants thereof, are the wettest in Africa. There are two peak periods of rainfall corresponding to the double passage of the ITCZ. Because areas with an equatorial climate are constantly covered by warm maritime air masses, variations in their monthly and daily temperatures are less pronounced than in the tropical wet-and-dry regions.

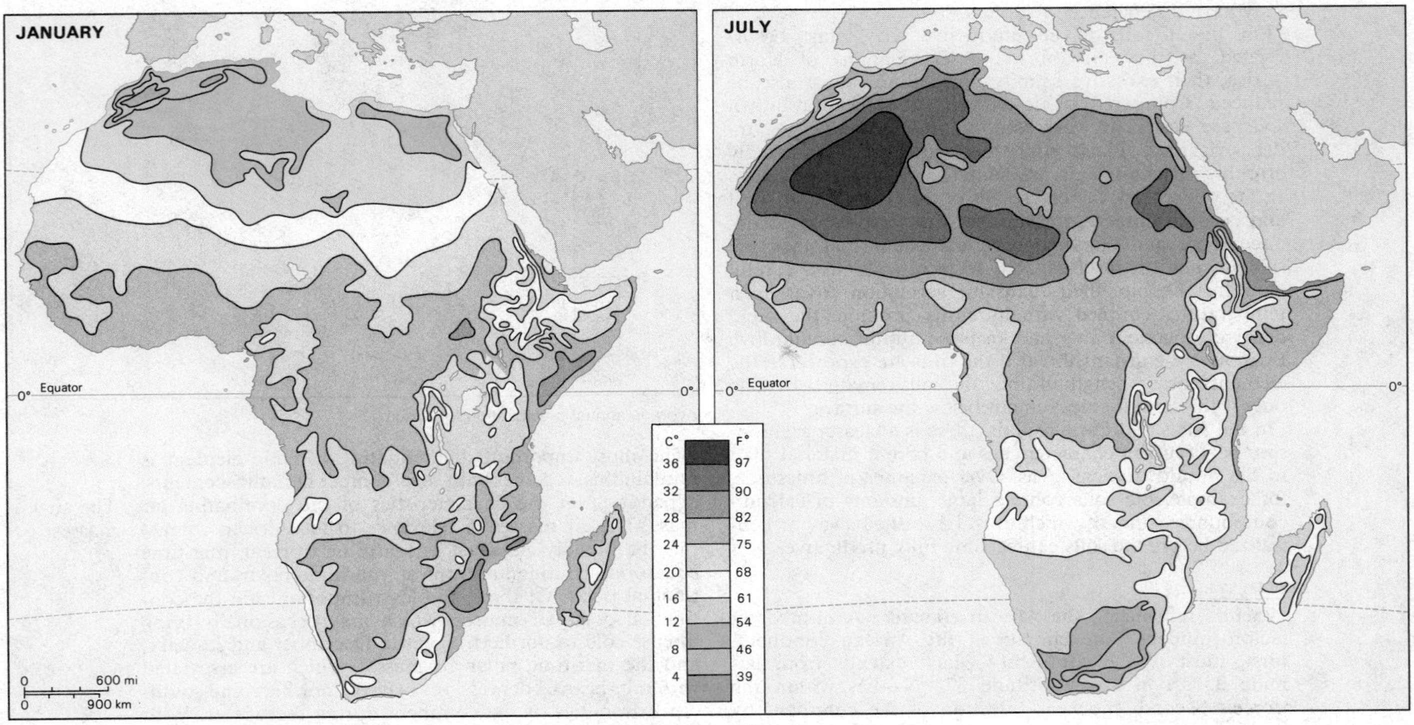

Average temperatures for January (left) and July (right) in °C for Africa.

Marked variations in the rhythm of equatorial climate sometimes occur; for example, the rainfall may be monsoonal and the second rainy season may be all but nonexistent. But the most notable anomaly can be observed on the West African coast from around Cape Three Points, Ghana, eastward to Benin, where, although the bimodal rainfall regime prevails, the total annual precipitation is less than 40 inches (1,000 millimetres). Among the many explanations that have been suggested are that the presence of a cold body of water offshore chills the lower layers of the maritime air mass and makes it stable; that the body of cold air that forms offshore diverts the incoming airstreams to the west and east of the anomalously dry area; that there is a strong tendency for the winds to blow parallel to the shore during the rainy seasons; that the absence of highlands deprives the region of orographic (mountain) rainfall; that fluctuations in the offshore, moisture-bearing winds occur during the rainy season and reduce rainfall; and that local meteorological peculiarities of thunderstorms contribute to the reduction in rainfall.

The Mediterranean climatic zone

In the northern and southern extremities of the continent there is a dry summer subtropical, or Mediterranean, type of climate. Rain falls only in winter (December–January in North Africa, June–July in southern Africa), although in some localities it may fall in autumn (September in North Africa, April in southern Africa). Mean monthly temperatures are lower than in tropical climates, dropping to about 50° F (10° C) in winter, while summer (June–July in North Africa, and December–January in southern Africa) temperatures may sometimes exceed those of tropical climates. Clear blue skies are characteristic.

The humid subtropical marine climate is restricted to the southeast coast of Africa. This region is characterized by rainfall throughout the year, but it is heaviest in summer. In South Africa, south of Natal, the winter rainfall is more pronounced, and the temperatures are a little lower than in the north. Thus, at Port Elizabeth there are six months when temperatures are below 62° F (17° C), while at Durban mean monthly temperatures do not fall below 64° F (18° C).

The warm temperate upland climatic region is found on the Highveld of southern Africa. Its rainfall regime is similar to that of the tropical wet-and-dry climate, but temperatures are greatly modified by the altitude; frost, for example, occasionally occurs in Lesotho. Toward the coast the climate shows maritime characteristics, and there is a tendency toward winter rainfall.

The mountain climatic region includes the high mountain areas of Ethiopia and the lake region of East Africa. In some respects the climate is similar to the warm, temperate upland climate, except that temperatures are even lower and snow occurs on the tops of the highest peaks, such as Kilimanjaro. The rainfall regime is similar to that of the adjacent lowland areas. (K.B.D.)

PLANT LIFE

African vegetation develops in direct response to the interacting effects of rainfall, temperature, topography, and

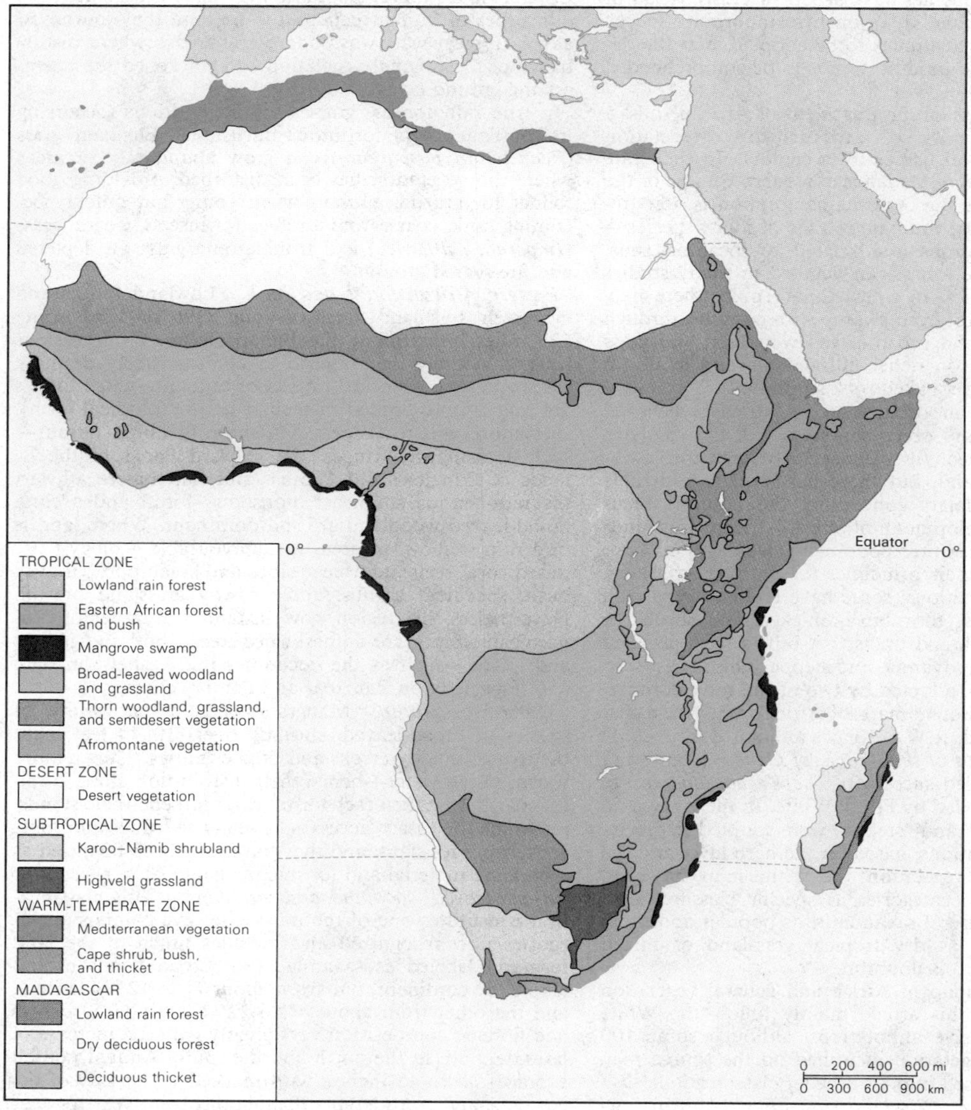

Vegetation zones of Africa.

type of soil; it is further modified by the incidence of fire, human agriculture, and grazing and browsing by livestock. Of the total land area of the continent, forests cover about one-fifth; woodlands, bushlands, grasslands, and thickets about two-fifths; and deserts and their extended margins the remaining two-fifths.

Ecological relationships. Until about two million years ago Africa's vegetation had always been controlled by the interactions of climate; geology, soil, and groundwater conditions (edaphic factors); and the activities of animals (biological factors). The addition of humans to the latter group, however, has increasingly rendered unreal the concept of a fully developed "natural" vegetation—*i.e.,* one approximating the ideal of a vegetational climax. Nevertheless, in broad terms, climate remains the dominant control over vegetation. Zonal belts of precipitation, reflecting latitude and contrasting exposure to the Atlantic and Indian oceans and their currents, give some reality to related belts of vegetation. Early attempts at mapping and classifying Africa's vegetation stressed this relationship: sometimes the names of plant zones were derived directly from climates. In this discussion the idea of zones is retained only in a broad descriptive sense.

Classifying African flora

As more has become known of the many thousands of African plant species and their complex ecology, naming, classification, and mapping have also become more particular, stressing what was actually present rather than postulating about climatic potential. In addition, over time more floral regions of varying shape and size have been recognized. Many schemes have arisen successively, all of which have had to take views on two important aspects: the general scale of treatment to be adopted, and the degree to which human modification is to be comprehended or discounted.

Once, as with the scientific treatment of African soils, a much greater uniformity was attributed to the vegetation than would have been generally acceptable in the same period for treatments of the lands of western Europe or the United States. Quite the opposite assumption is now frequently advanced. An intimate mosaic of many species—in complex associations and related to localized soils, slopes, and drainage—has been detailed in many studies of the African tropics. In a few square miles there may be a visible succession from swamp with papyrus, through swampy grassland and broad-leaved woodland and grass to a patch of forest on richer hillside soil, and finally to succulents on a nearly naked rock summit.

The span of human occupation in Africa is believed to exceed that of any other continent. All the resultant activities have tended, on balance, to reduce tree cover and increase grassland; but there has been considerable dispute among scholars concerning the natural versus human-caused development of most African grasslands at the regional level. Correspondingly, classifications have differed greatly in their principles for naming, grouping, and describing formations: some have chosen terms such as forest, woodland, thornbush, thicket, and shrub for much of the same broad tracts that others have grouped as wooded savanna, savanna, and steppe. This is best seen in the nomenclature adopted by two of the most comprehensive and authoritative maps of Africa's vegetation that have been published: R.W.J. Keay's annotated *Vegetation Map of Africa South of the Tropic of Cancer* (1959) and its more widely based successor, *The Vegetation Map of Africa* (1983), compiled by Frank White. In the Keay map the terms "savanna" and "steppe" were adopted as precise definitions of formations, based on the herb layer and the coverage of woody vegetation; the White map, however, discarded these two categories as specific classifications. Yet any rapid demise of savanna in its popular and more general sense (*i.e.,* as dry tropical grassland or mixed woods and grassland) is doubtful.

The vegetational map of Africa and general vegetation groupings used in this article mainly follow the White map and its extensive annotations, although some 100 specific types of vegetation identified on the source map have been compressed into 14 broader classifications.

Vegetational zones. *Lowland rain forest.* African lowland rain forests occur along the Guinea Coast of West Africa and in the Congo basin. The full development of this tropical formation requires continuously warm conditions and an annual rainfall exceeding 50 to 60 inches (1,270 to 1,520 millimetres) distributed fairly evenly over the year. The vertical limit is about 3,500 to 4,000 feet. This multistoried, highly diverse, extensive, and potentially self-perpetuating assemblage has been described by some as the source of virtually all tropical floristic diversity. No other part of the world sustains a greater biomass (total weight of organic matter in a given surface area) than lowland tropical rain forests. Even though the speciation (proliferation of distinct types of plant) within the African rain forests is notably poorer than that of its counterparts in Southeast Asia and the Amazon basin of South America, these forests sustain a huge multiplicity of life forms, occupying different strata (generalized levels of plant height) and niches (separate, small-scale habitats).

Structure of the forest

Characteristically, tropical rain forest is composed of a ground story, from 6 to 10 feet tall, of shrubs, ferns, and mosses; a middle story of trees and palms 20 to 60 feet in height; and a dominant top canopy consisting of trees up to 150 feet high with straight unbranched trunks, buttressed roots, and spreading crowns of perennial leafage. The large branches of these crowns provide niches for epiphytes, including orchids, ferns, and mosses. Lianas tie trees to one another, parasitic species cling to trunks and branches, and strangler figs (*Ficus pretoriae*) put down aerial taproots. Nevertheless, these are not "impenetrable" jungles. It has been suggested that some early European travelers and pioneer botanists may have exaggerated the difficulties of human penetration because they journeyed along atypical waterways and along tracks where disturbance of the original vegetation had thickened the regenerating ground layer.

In true rain forests, grasses are adventitious (occurring in consequence of fortuitous intrusions). Elephant grass (*Pennisetum purpureum*) can grow abundantly in areas where the vegetation has been disturbed, providing good fodder for grazing animals when young but quickly becoming rank, coarse, and a refuge for insects. Cogon grass (*Imperata cylindrica*) is a troublesome grass on depleted and fire-seared ground.

Eastern African forest and bush. Lowland forests and evergreen bushland form a long belt of land some 125 miles broad along the Indian Ocean. From various causes—notably the monsoonal climate, freely draining soils, and long historical impact of humans—these forests are much more limited in their structure (physical form), speciation, and robustness. On more favoured terrain—such as estuarine fringes, the seaward flanks of the islands of Zanzibar and Pemba, and hill masses athwart the rain-bearing southeast monsoon—forest and a close broad-leaved woodland are still dominant. Where land is in a rain shadow, in areas of unfavourable geology (*e.g.,* raised coral reefs), and near cities and small ports, thorny bush, succulent shrubs, and scrawny grassland prevail. Nevertheless, the region now sustains a number of economically important domesticated trees—both indigenous and exotic—such as the coconut palm, cashew, mango, and (especially on Zanzibar and Pemba) clove.

Mangrove swamp. Mangroves include a variety of species of broad-leaved, shrubby trees (10–40 feet high) that fringe muddy creeks and tidal estuaries. They require warm, saline water—hence their distribution along tropical coastlines. Often they form nearly impenetrable stands, for which the easiest access is by sea. The trunks and roots are termite-resistant, and they have long been favoured as a building material and for making charcoal.

Broad-leaved woodland and grassland. This classification constitutes one of the most extensive composite categories now recognized and includes much of the land formerly labeled as savanna. Two broad bands extend across the continent, one from about 7° to 12° N latitude and the other from about 8° to 22° S latitude. Structure and floristic composition vary greatly with the increase of latitude, both in the north and the south. Annual rainfall averages 35 to 45 inches, with marked seasonality of occurrence and considerable fluctuations from year to year, both in total rainfall and in the onset of rainy periods.

Baobab trees growing in the wooded-grassland area of Senegal in West Africa.
K. Scholz—Shostal/EB Inc.

The woodlands of western Africa strikingly resemble those south of the equator. In both areas, undulating wooded interfluves on light soils successively alternate with swampy, clay-based valley grasslands (called *fadamas* in Nigeria and *dambos* in Zambia and Malaŵi) in a topographically linked sequence of soils called a catena.

Trees, 30 to 50 feet high, are typically deciduous and often fire-resistant, since much of this land is burned annually. Common West African species include types of *Isoberlinia* (a spreading leguminous tree of the pea family), *Daniellia* (a leguminous tree with white bark), and *Lophira* (a tree with strap-shaped leaves that is said to yield the most durable timber in the region). Other hardwoods, forming distinct communities, are *Combretum* and *Terminalia,* which are better suited to the drier areas. Prevalent southern equivalents include *Brachystegia* (a leguminous hardwood, the bark of which formerly was used to make cloth) and *Julbernardia* (another plant of the pea family resembling *Isoberlinia*). Over much of the interior of Tanzania, in areas of reduced rainfall and poorer soils, a light-canopied, sustained woodland called Miombo forest rises above a rather scrawny ground layer. This is an excellent habitat for bees, and honey has long been gathered there.

Typical tree species

Because of periodic burning, tall grasses have become dominant over large expanses of plateau land, which sometimes contains few, if any, of its original trees. The tall, coarse red grass *Hyparrhenia* can form prominent stands, but it makes poor grazing land and often harbours insects that spread disease. Much better for the pastoralists are induced swards of *Themeda.*

For centuries humans have selectively retained certain economically important tree species in areas cleared for farming; the effect has been to create what is called "farmed parkland," in which a few favoured trees rise above the fields. Examples include the shea butter nut tree (*Butyrospermum*), common in Ghana and Côte d'Ivoire; *Acacia albida,* found in Senegal and Zambia; and the truly domesticated baobab (*Adansonia digitata*), which is perhaps the most widely distributed.

Thorn woodland, grassland, and semidesert vegetation. Toward the margins of the tropics the vegetation cover becomes lower and thinner as the fluctuating transition to desert vegetation ensues. In the same progression the concept of an annual rainfall (nominally 5 to 20 inches) yields to the reality of extreme unreliability in both incidence and expectation. Under such restraints a definitive "boundary" with the desert becomes meaningless. Moreover, there appears to have been a trend toward declining precipitation in the last half of the 20th century, and human impact certainly has enhanced the natural deprivation of plant life in the marginal regions. The southern margin of the Sahara—roughly between the latitudes of 15° and 20°—is called the Sahel (Arabic: *Sāḥil;* "shore," or "edge"), the word being extended by implication to comprehend the fluctuating margins of the great sand seas of the Sahara to the north. The southern equivalent covers much of the Kalahari, which is often called a desert but is more properly a thirstland.

Thorn woodland displays a predominance of xerophytic, sometimes succulent or semisucculent trees, such as acacia, *Commiphora* (the myrrh tree), or *Boscia* (an evergreen hard-leaved tree). The occurrence of the bunched and thorny desert date (*Balanites*) seems to accompany land impoverishment. A relatively luxuriant shrub layer, often forming dense thickets, is found in conjunction with succulents, such as aloes, *Sansevieria* (a fibrous species), and *Adenium,* or desert rose (a succulent shrub with smooth grey bark, a huge water-storing base, and beautiful red or pink flowers), and smaller euphorbias.

Farther toward the desert, tree growth and perennial grass—surviving in narrow strips along watercourses—separate much larger areas of sparse annual grasses (*Cenchrus* in western Africa, *Eragrostis* south of the equator, and *Chrysopogon* on the margins) and scattered low shrubs, often mainly acacias. Shrubs may often be salt-tolerant. While shrubs may die from inadequate moisture, they are little affected by the rare fires that occur.

Afromontane vegetation. All high mountains exhibit azonality; *i.e.,* their vegetation differs from that found in the climatic zones from which they rise. The differences manifest themselves as progressive modifications, which are usually well stratified and reflect altitude-dependent climatic changes. Generally, as elevation increases temperature decreases (to the point where frost and even glaciation can occur) and precipitation increases (although above a certain level precipitation decreases markedly). Mountainous terrain can retain ancient climatic conditions—making possible, for example, the survival of relict species—and the relative inaccessibility of the higher elevations to humans has helped preserve more of the vegetal patterns of the past.

Azonality of high mountains

Vegetation strata typically are skewed with regard to slope orientation (aspect). This is mainly due to a contrast between exposure to rain-bearing winds and shadowing from them but may also reflect long-term history. If lower slopes rise abruptly from the base (as they often do in Africa), then a distinct boundary between vegetation formations may be clearly distinguished; if the rise is gentle, vegetations merge (as in the western Kenyan highlands). (All the circumstances mentioned above are represented in the African mountain systems, but for purposes of illustration the vegetational map identifies only areas of altitudinal modification. Thus, some areas that are included are not tropical, such as parts of the Red Sea Hills and the mountains of South Africa and Lesotho.)

Afromontane moorland of tussocky grasses, giant groundsel, and lobelias on the slope of Mount Kenya.
Caroline Weaver—Ardea London

Altitudinal modifications of vegetation are clearly discernible on the high East African peaks near the equator (*e.g.*, Kilimanjaro and Mounts Kenya and Elgon), and a rich forest belt—much reduced upslope by human activities, except where the land has been reserved—clothes the zone that receives the maximum rainfall and is free of frosts (up to about 5,000 to 6,000 feet). Such mountains have great human importance as watersheds and as repositories of native plants.

Desert vegetation. The Sahara has one of the lowest species densities in the world, and a sustained vegetation cover (which can include trees and bushes) occurs only in the massifs and oases. Elsewhere, the vegetation is discontinuous and consists of two main types: perennials with huge root systems and sparse aerial parts, often protected by waxy cuticles, thorns, and hairs; and ephemerals with slight root systems and little foliage but with the ability to flower profusely immediately after occasional storms and then to seed quickly and abundantly. The stony and rocky expanses give more hold for plants than do the vast areas of shifting sands. In some areas with slightly more rainfall, grass tufts may grow 50 yards apart. *Aristida* is the dominant grass, and for brief periods it can yield a nutritious forage called *ashab.*

The Namib is one of the world's driest deserts. The area along the coast, however, is almost always foggy, and succulent shrubs (such as aloes) manage to survive on this moisture. The Namib also contains the strange tumboa, or welwitschia (*Welwitschia mirabilis*), which may live 100 years or more.

Karoo-Namib shrubland. In this drought-prone land, soils are often shallow, even saline. The low shrubs that grow there can be divided into two groups: woody plants, such as species of *Acacia* and *Pentzia* and the saltbush (*Atriplex*); and succulents, including aloes, euphorbias, and *Mesembryantheum. Aristida* and *Themeda* are characteristic grasses. Every year the blossoms of bulbous plants lay short-lived carpets of colour. Being both drought-resistant and high in minerals, many of the shrubs can provide useful grazing for goats and sheep.

Highveld grassland. The grassland classification is restricted to regions with 10 percent or less woody plant cover. The Highveld meets this definition and probably owes much to unaided nature for its creation and perpetuation, since fires caused by lightning strikes are relatively frequent. Its extent has always been fairly precisely defined: areas with more than 15 inches of rainfall during the summer. Highveld vegetation, though modified considerably by human activity, traditionally has been differentiated into sweet veld (dominated by *Themeda*) or sour veld (*Andropogon* and *Eragrostis*), the latter making poorer pasturage.

Mediterranean vegetation. This zone is determined chiefly by its climate, which is characterized by very dry summers and mild, rainy winters, but it has long been much differentiated by its inhabitants; large tracts have been degraded into maquis (macchie), garigue, or dry semidesert (steppe) vegetation. Maquis consists of dense scrub growths of xerophytic (drought-resistant) and sclerophyllous (leathery) shrubs and small trees, which are often fire-resistant. Garigue characteristically is found on limestone soils and has more woody growth, including evergreen and cork oaks (*Quercus suber*). The higher slopes of the Atlas Mountains once carried large stands of pine and cedar, but they have been much depleted. Typical grasses, progressing from the coast to the desert, are *Ampelodesmos, Phalaris,* and *Stipa.*

Cape shrub, bush, and thicket. This region constitutes the southern counterpart of the Mediterranean zone, although (with the exception of the Atlas Mountains) it is richer in its vegetation potential. There were once considerable enclaves of true evergreen bushland, which have reverted to shrubland (*fynbos*). Sclerophyllous foliage and proteas abound. Although grassy tracts occur on the mountains, they are characteristically unusual lower down. Beyond the Cape Ranges, *fynbos* grades into karoo.

Endemic species of Madagascar

Madagascar. Physically and biologically, Madagascar has long formed a separate entity. White has identified eastern and western regions of endemic (unique) vegetation. In the eastern centre, about one-sixth of the plant genera and more than three-fourths of the thousands of

Carol Hughes—Bruce Coleman Ltd.

Tree aloes and other succulents growing in the Karoo-Namib shrubland in Namaqualand, S.Af.

Village along the White Nile in the As-Sudd region, The Sudan.
© Klaus D. Francke—Peter Arnold, Inc.

species are regarded as endemic. The Madagascar rain forest has shorter trees and a somewhat drier climate than its equatorial counterpart and contains its own dwarf palms (*Dypsis*) and bamboos (*Ochlandra*). The western deciduous forest stands in the rain shadow; some of its trees resemble Mediterranean oaks. The southern thickets have prominent euphorbias and species of the Didiereaceae family. The island has much degraded secondary forest (locally called *savoka*) along the eastern and northern coasts.

Sudd. In addition to the major types of vegetation described above, a special vegetation called sudd (literally meaning "barrier") occurs in the great Nile, Niger, and Zambezi drainage systems of the African interior plateau. Characteristic is the sudd along the White Nile River in The Sudan and Uganda. Sedges (especially papyrus), reeds, and other water plants—including the floating Nile cabbage (*Pistia stratiotes*)—form masses of waterlogged plant material that are largely unproductive and are a nuisance to fishing and navigation. *Pistia* has become an unwelcome invader of Lake Kariba, the body of water formed by the impounding (1959) of the Zambezi River in the Kariba Gorge.

Long-term changes in vegetation. Africa's basic vegetational zones are believed to have existed in approximately the same climatically controlled series and with the same characteristically developed species for a long period of time; and, indeed, some ancient African plant families—such as the cycads, which evolved some 200 million years ago—still have living representatives. Nonetheless, the continent's vegetation has been altered continuously by geologic and climatic changes and by the movement of the caloric (heat) equator. The past million years have been a time of unusually rapid changes, with major consequences for Africa's vegetation.

The vegetational history of Africa is of great scientific relevance. Studying the lichens growing in the high East African mountains, for example, may yield a better understanding of the continent's climatic trends, and a knowledge of past conditions in the Sahel might help explain what influence natural phenomena have had on the disastrous droughts of the region since the late 1960s.

Geologic influences. The two most important geologic modifications of vegetation have been the very ancient separation of Madagascar from the mainland, which gave rise to the distinct speciation of the island's flora, and the long-continuing faulting and vulcanism along East Africa's huge rift system that has thrown up high ranges (*e.g.,* the Ruwenzori between Uganda and Zaire) and great vol-

(Left) © Mark Pidgeon—Oxford Scientific Films Ltd; (right) © David Curl—Oxford Scientific Films Ltd.

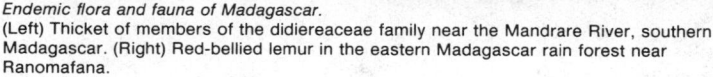

Endemic flora and fauna of Madagascar.
(Left) Thicket of members of the didiereaceae family near the Mandrare River, southern Madagascar. (Right) Red-bellied lemur in the eastern Madagascar rain forest near Ranomafana.

canoes (Kilimanjaro) and has thus created and reshaped Afromontane flora.

Climatic influences. The repercussions of the great Pleistocene Ice Ages of Europe have constituted the most notable climatic influence on African flora in relatively recent geologic history. These consisted of a succession of colder periods marked by glacial advances, interrupted by warmer, drier interglacials; the last series of these ended between about 5,000 and 10,000 years ago. Tropical Africa experienced contemporaneous fluctuations in its climate, although it is misleading to infer any simple equivalences between these fluctuations and the European periods of glacial advances and retreats.

Effects of the Ice Ages

During the wetter times (pluvials) in Africa equatorial forests spread, separating northern woodlands from their southern counterparts (with consequent species differentiation); mountain vegetation descended onto the plateaus; and there is evidence that the Saharan climate was greatly ameliorated, much to the advantage of humans. During the warmer, drier interpluvials the existing vegetation was degraded in many zones. Dunes spread from the Sahara and over the Kalahari, for example, and their fossilized alignments—now vegetated—can be traced across the thorny woodlands and grasslands of Niger, Nigeria, Namibia, and Botswana.

Human influences. The greater part of the reduction of Africa's natural vegetation has happened in the last 2,000 years—probably since the late 19th century for the tropical portions—the time during which humans have been most numerous and active. Pastoralism, agriculture, the rapid growth of human and livestock populations, the expansion of cities and towns, and the external demands for primary resources have made ever-greater demands upon the land for sustenance and perceived economic betterment. Much is known of the detailed processes of vegetation modification along the Mediterranean, since they have been observed and studied since classical times, and a good deal is also known from the more than three centuries of study of the Cape area of South Africa; but until the late 19th century very little was understood about these processes in tropical Africa. Indeed, the time scale of actual human impact on African vegetation may be causally linked to the awareness of it by Europeans.

Within the tropical forests and woodlands, fire undoubtedly has been the great human agent of clearance and degradation, of far greater efficacy than felling, barkringing, or uprooting—at least until the introduction of modern plantation agriculture and logging. Hunters, pastoralists, and cultivators have all fired the land for centuries and have gathered wild foodstuffs, thatch timber for construction, and fuelwood from the volunteer (*i.e.,* uncultivated or self-generating) vegetation. The long-term effects of such activity bear directly upon the debated question of the origin of the savannas.

In earlier times, African cultivators found the fabric of the tropical rain forest comparatively difficult to modify substantially. In the 20th century, however, it has been greatly reduced in extent (such as in Sierra Leone), patched and frayed (Nigeria), and exploited for timber exports (Gabon). Moreover, many of tropical Africa's largest cities and busy seaports are in this zone. The most diverse and seemingly inexhaustible floral realm in Africa has therefore become a cause for widespread concern.

Conserving the vegetation. Perceptions of the need for environmental conservation in Africa held by those outside the continent are sometimes expressed in terms that seem opposed to the legitimate priorities and aspirations of African peoples (in meeting which agriculture and livestock management must remain crucial). It is not surprising that projections based upon the assumptions from these external sources frequently end in pessimism. A more constructive approach is to identify ways in which to more fully integrate wild plant life, crops, and animals, which can be expressed in the concept of productive countryside. The capacity and precision of resource surveys have been greatly enhanced by remote sensing, and this has been coupled with the worldwide transmissibility of information. Research and interest in agroforestry have expanded and become institutionalized. Above all, however, confidence must be put in the capacities of many millions of African farmers to expand agriculture while working toward the reintegration with wild plant life.

ANIMAL LIFE

Africa includes parts of two of the Earth's six main zoogeographic regions: the Ethiopian region, which comprises the continent south of the Sahara and the southwestern part of Arabia, as well as Madagascar; and a southern part of the Palaearctic (Old World) subregion of the Holarctic region (*i.e.,* the lands of the Northern Hemisphere), consisting of North and northwestern Africa south to roughly the tropic of Cancer.

Zoogeographic regions

Genera and distribution. Africa is best known for the enormous diversity and richness of its wildlife. It has a

John Rushmer—Ostman Agency

Typical southern African herbivores at a watering hole in the Transvaal, S.Af.

greater variety of large ungulates, or hoofed mammals (some 90 species), and freshwater fish (2,000 species) than any other continent.

Mammals. The main group of herbivores are the African antelope, which belong to four subfamilies of the ox family (Bovidae). The first subfamily is the oxlike Bovinae, which is further subdivided into the African buffalo and the twist-horned antelope, including the eland (the largest of all antelope), kudu, nyala, and bushbuck. The second subfamily is the duiker, a small, primitive bovid that lives in the thickets, bush, and forests. Third is the "horse antelope," further divided into sabre-horned sable, roan, and oryx antelope; the "deer antelope," kongonis, hartebeest, topi, gnu (wildebeest), and blesbok, all mostly inhabitants of the open plains; and the "marsh antelope," waterbuck, lechwe, kob, puku, and reedbuck. The fourth subfamily is the antelope proper, divided into two distinct tribes, the first of which includes royal, dikdik, klipspringer, oribi, steenbok, and grysbok and the second, gazelle, impala, springbok, and gerenuk. Other well-known large African herbivores include the zebra, giraffe, hippopotamus, rhinoceros, and African elephant.

Probably no group of animals is more identified with Africa than its Carnivora (the order of flesh-eating mammals), of which there are more than 60 species. In addition to the better-known big (or roaring) cats—the lion, leopard, and cheetah—are the wild dog, hyena, serval (a long-limbed cat), wildcat, jackal, fox, weasel, civet, and mongoose. These predators and scavengers are vital in maintaining the ecological equilibrium of the areas that they inhabit.

The primates include some 45 species of Old World monkeys, as well as two of the world's great apes: the chimpanzee and the world's largest ape, the gorilla. Presimian primates—such as pottos (African lemurs) and galagos (bush babies, or small arboreal lemurs), as well as Lorisidae (a family of arboreal lemurs, moving with a slow, delicate crawl)—are mainly small and nocturnal, but in Madagascar, where there are no true monkeys, the world's most diverse assemblage of large and small diurnal and nocturnal presimian lemurs survives.

Marine mammals include one Mediterranean and one South African seal (the Cape fur seal) and two Sirenia (an order of aquatic herbivores)—the dugong and the manatee. In addition, whales, porpoises, and dolphins frequent Africa's coastal waters.

Endemic mammals

Africa's large number of endemic mammal species is second only to that of South America. These include several families of the ungulate order Artiodactyla (composed of mammals with an even number of toes), such as giraffes and hippopotamuses. Some families of Carnivora—such as civets (of the Viverridae family), their smaller relations the genets, and hyenas—are chiefly African. The rodent family of jumping hares (Pedetidae) is endemic, and one order, the aardvark (Tubulidentata)—a large nocturnal burrowing mammal, with one species—is exclusively African. Madagascar also has a remarkable insect-eating family, the tenrecs (animals with long pointed snouts, some of which are spiny and tailless).

Birds. South of the Sahara the birdlife includes nearly 1,500 resident species, to which must be added another 275 species that are either resident in northwestern Africa or else are Palaearctic winter migrants; the migrants once totaled perhaps two billion individuals, but their numbers have been reduced considerably by severe droughts and by human land use and predation. Birds are mainly of Old World families, but of those that are endemic the most noteworthy are perhaps the ostrich, shoebill, hammerkop (a brown heronlike bird), and secretary bird (a large long-legged predatory bird) and the touracos (brightly coloured birds, some with helmetlike crests). Other families, such as bustards, sand grouse, honey guides (small dull-coloured birds, several species of which are noted for leading people to the nests of honeybees, in order to feed on them after the nests have been broken), and larks are predominantly African. There are many avian predators of land mammals, including eagles, hawks, and owls; more of fish, such as storks, waders, and a few species of kingfishers; and even more of insects, this latter group usually being of benefit to humans. Scavengers include vultures and the large marabou stork.

Reptiles and amphibians. Reptiles, of which there are few endemic families, have mainly Old World affinities. Those most likely to be seen include lizards of the agamid family, skinks (a family of lizards characterized by smooth overlapping scales), crocodiles, and tortoises. Endemic reptiles include girdle-tailed and plated lizards. Within the African realm lizards of the iguana family and boa constrictors occur only in Madagascar. Large vipers are abundant and varied; certain species have extremely toxic venom, but they are seldom encountered. A wealth of both colubrine snakes (with fangs at the posterior end of the upper jaw) and elapine snakes (with fixed poison fangs at the front of the upper jaw) include such highly venomous elapine species as mambas.

Amphibians also belong mainly to Old World groups. Salamanders and hylid tree frogs (having teeth in the upper jaw) are confined to the Palaearctic northwest. Abundant commoner frogs and toads include such oddities as the so-called hairy frog of Cameroon, whose hairs are auxiliary respiratory organs. The frog subfamily Phrynomerinae is exclusively African.

Arthropods. Africa possesses an abundant and varied population of arthropods (which include insects and other segmented invertebrates). Among them are found large butterflies of the *Charaxes* (brush-footed) and *Papilio* (swallow-tailed) genera, stick insects, and mantises, grasshoppers, driver, or safari, ants (tropical ants that travel in vast, serried ranks), termites, and dung beetles. Spiders abound throughout the continent, and scorpions and locusts can also be plentiful locally. Periodically huge swarms of locusts spread over wide areas, causing enormous destruction to vegetation. Other serious pests are mosquitoes, which act as vectors in the spread of such human diseases as malaria, and tsetse flies, which transmit the parasite that causes African trypanosomiasis (sleeping sickness) in humans and nagana in livestock.

Archaic fish species

Aquatic life. Freshwater fish include both remarkable archaic forms and examples of rapid recent evolution. Among the ancient forms are lungfish (*Protopterus*), bichirs, or lobefins (*Polypterus*), and reedfish (*Calamoichthys*), all of which can breathe air—a property also possessed by certain catfish (Clariidae), which are able to travel overland for some distance in wet weather. Characteristic of more recent evolutionary trends are the approximately 200 species of fish found in Lake Nyasa, four-fifths of which occur only there.

The coelacanth, an archaic marine form believed extinct for more than 60 million years, was discovered to be alive off the east coast of South Africa in 1938, and since then many others have been found. A rich and varied invertebrate animal life on the east and west coasts includes marine organisms typical of the Indo-Pacific and Atlantic oceans. Coral reefs and associated organisms are mainly found in the warm waters of Africa's east coast, while the southwest and west coasts—washed, respectively, by the cold Benguela and Canary currents—abound in fish.

Origin and adaption of African fauna. At one time most African fauna was thought to derive from elsewhere. There is no doubt, however, that as little as 15,000 years ago an amelioration of the present Saharan climate enabled such typical Ethiopian forms as clariid catfish to reach the river systems of North Africa. Likewise, Palaearctic animal life and vegetation appear to have extended far south into the Sahara, and the white rhinoceros apparently lived beside elklike, typically Palaearctic deer.

Within the Ethiopian region, repeated climatically controlled expansion and contraction of vegetational zones resulted first in organisms establishing themselves in numerous specialized ecological communities (niches) of plants and animals and second in the proliferation of those species that successfully adapted themselves to the prevailing conditions. The spread of forests during the pluvials, separating northern and southern wooded grasslands, led to the evolution of such closely related northern and southern species of antelope as the kob and puku, the Nile and common lechwe, and the northern and southern forms of white rhinoceros.

Some subfamilies of Bovidae, like the spiral-horned antelope (Tragelaphinae), have adapted to almost every ecological environment—forest, woodland, grassland, Afro-Alpine zones, and even to sudd vegetation. Others, like the hartebeests (Alcelaphinae), which inhabit savannas and grasslands, are less adaptable.

Freshwater fishes demonstrate the existence of the relation to one another of former river systems and lakes. Large rivers containing Ethiopian fish evidently existed quite recently in the northern Sahara. The fish life of the now-isolated Lake Rudolf (Lake Turkana), in East Africa, demonstrates that the lake was once connected to the Nile, though Lake Victoria, the present source of the White Nile, was not. Lake Kivu, too, was formerly connected with the Nile, but as a result of volcanic activity it is now part of the Congo drainage system.

In earlier periods the animal life was even more remarkable than today. Fossil deposits have revealed sheep as big as present-day buffalo, huge hippopotamuses, giant baboons, and other types similar to existing species. These huge types probably lived in pluvial periods, dying out as aridity increased. Smaller types survived.

The effects of humans. Until they acquired firearms, humans made relatively little impact on animal numbers or—with some exceptions—their range. From the last half of the 19th century, however, and particularly since 1940, direct or indirect human wastage of Africa's animal life has been intense and has reduced stocks considerably. The antelope known as the Zambian black lechwe, for example, believed to have numbered 1,000,000 in 1900, had been reduced to less than 8,000 by the late 20th century, and the population of African elephants declined from 2,000,000 in the early 1970s to some 600,000 by 1990, largely because of poaching for the ivory trade. The African white rhinoceros reached the verge of extinction in 1980.

Depletion of wildlife

Though European hunters and colonists were rightly blamed for much of the decline at its onset, hunting and destruction and the disturbance of habitats by Africans have become more important. Rinderpest, an acute, and usually fatal, infectious disease of livestock, entered Africa with domestic stock in the 1890s and ravaged herds of indigenous ungulates. The accelerated spread of agriculture and stock raising involving the destruction of forests, as well as heavy grazing and burning of vegetation, eliminated large animals from wide tracts. In the southern Sudan, for example, political strife and warfare in the 1960s entirely eliminated wildlife from some areas. The demand for fancy leather and fur has also endangered the Nile crocodile and the leopard.

Humans, however, have been of benefit to many smaller species. Dams and irrigation schemes, for example, have provided habitats for waterfowl, frogs, and fish, and the spread of grain crops has encouraged certain pests. Even the patchy cultivation of forests has resulted in the development of a mosaic of habitats that can provide new, if small, niches for some species.

Ecology. There are still sufficiently large tracts of relatively unspoiled country in which animal life may be studied in its environment. The complementary roles of wild ungulates, for example, show that in any area inhabited by a wide variety of species, the grass is grazed in regular succession and at different stages of growth—for example, by zebra, gnu, hartebeest, and gazelle—while specific adaptations enable a still greater variety to survive. A much smaller variety of domestic stock cannot duplicate such effects. Overpopulation by domestic or wild species may upset the delicate natural balance, as may be seen by the example of elephant overpopulation in Murchison Falls (Kabalega) National Park, Uganda, and in Tsavo National Park, Kenya; whether the elephants survive or not, they have ineradicably altered the environment to the detriment of many other typical species.

Animal life of particular interest. Animal life of particular interest to humans includes four main groups that are not mutually exclusive. They are: (1) species potentially or actually useful to humans as food (large ungulates), (2) dangerous or pest species that may have to be controlled or eliminated (locusts, tsetse flies, *Quelea* finches or black-faced diochs—which do immense damage to grain crops—and some ungulates or carnivores), (3) species that provide a spectacle and bring economic benefit (elephants, the larger plain ungulates, primates, or carnivores), and (4) endangered, rare, or unique species.

Much of the study of African wildlife has been addressed to the first two groups described above. For example, after it was learned that the feeding habits of domesticated livestock and wild ungulates are complementary, it became possible to incorporate the ungulates into pastoral and mixed-farming systems. This has happened on limited scales with the oryx (which was domesticated by the ancient Egyptians), the springbok (which has been run with cattle for decades in southern Africa), and the African buffalo and eland. Similarly, much attention has been given to controlling pests. In the 1950s and '60s considerable progress was made in the control of mosquitoes and locust swarms, although these achievements have been partially lost by governmental instability and mismanagement and by warfare between states. Infestation by the tsetse fly remains as one of tropical Africa's most critical problems, not only because the tsetse spreads disease but also because—by effectively restricting livestock farming—it denies relief of the chronic protein shortage of many African peoples. Control of the tsetse is possible, but it is complex and requires a coordinated effort within and between countries.

Attempts to control pests

Much research has also been carried out on animals in the third and fourth groups. Studies of predators, such as the lion, for example, have shown that they do not generally control the numbers of ungulates to the same degree as do disease or starvation. It has also been established that the hyena is as much a potent predator as a scavenger. Intensive studies have been made of such primates as baboons, Ethiopian geladas (to which baboons are related), and especially chimpanzees and gorillas; of great interest has been learning what associations there are between human and other primate behaviour and psychology.

Conservation. Many countries have now set aside large tracts as national parks, game reserves, or forest reserves. Of these parks, only some are large enough to be self-contained ecosystems, and most have been set aside to accommodate large mammals. In East Africa there are also sanctuaries for birds and marine organisms. The conservation of vegetation is undertaken mainly in forest reserves but also in national parks. In addition, a number of countries are attempting to conserve wildlife by refusing export licenses for certain kinds of skins, especially those of the leopard, cheetah, and zebra.

The oldest and best-known national park is the Kruger National Park in South Africa, where representative populations of most savanna species are maintained. The Kalahari Gemsbok National Park, which South Africa shares with Botswana, conserves a tract of arid country with such associated types of antelope as springbok and gemsbok; smaller reserves and parks conserve particular species. Only one large mammal species, the blaubok (or blaauwbok), has become extinct, though several subspecies have nearly disappeared; one such subspecies—the quagga, a race of zebra—has vanished. East and central African countries have large national parks, which have been expanded in size or have increased in number as a result of the economic benefits of tourism. Kenya's parks include Tsavo, one of the largest, with an area of more than 8,000 square miles, Lake Nakuru National Park for flamingos, several montane parks, and a marine park. Uganda has three large national parks. Tanzania has the famous Serengeti National Park, with its unrivaled populations of plains ungulates, and the parks of Ngorongoro, Lake Manyara, Arusha, and others. Other countries with notable national parks and game reserves are Botswana, Malaŵi, Namibia, Zambia, and Zimbabwe. All parks in these countries preserve representative woodland, thornbush, grassland, and succulent-desert habitats and species.

Parks of East and central Africa

Elsewhere the situation is less satisfactory. In Zaire, national parks were all seriously depleted after independence. Zaire now has seven major national parks, including the Virunga National Park (3,100 square miles). Though The Sudan is one of the countries with the largest numbers of remaining ungulates, their status is little known, and the country is not served by an adequate park network. Ethiopia has nine parks developed largely during the 1970s, while Somalia has only a rudimentary system consisting mostly of game reserves and one area (Luc Badana) nominally a national park but failing to meet UN criteria for such parks. The "W" park is shared between Burkina Faso (formerly Upper Volta), Niger, and Benin, but most West African countries have only small national parks if any at all.

Animals not protected in parks are not necessarily threatened. Many large species are still plentiful in forest or game reserves or in controlled-hunting areas. Well-managed forest reserves in particular provide secure habitats for many smaller unprotected forms.

Animals affecting land usage. Historically, the abundance of elephants and other large ungulates may have stimulated some individuals—notably West African hunters in the forests and Europeans in southern Africa—to occupy certain areas. Trade routes were established and early hunter-explorers were influenced by the availability of elephants, whose ivory tusks slaves could carry.

Large or small animals now affect humans by competing with them or with their livestock. They may prey on people or on livestock or carry diseases affecting either. The bilharzia snail and the *Simulium* fly (host to an organism causing blindness), the tsetse fly, and the mosquito collectively affect human beings and their livestock far more than do such individually large or formidable species as lions or elephants.

The larger ungulates may compete with domestic livestock for forage, but they are more keenly resented and hunted by those agriculturists whose crops they eat. Pastoralists are much more concerned about lions that occasionally kill cattle than they are about locusts or rats, which, by depleting forage, indirectly cause the death of much livestock; such perceptions may hinder eradication or better control of these pests.

Diseases

Danger to humans from large animals—carnivorous or otherwise—has been greatly exaggerated, but disease carried by living organisms has remained a serious problem. Diseases have reduced crop productivity, spoiled harvests, and acted as a curb on the better integration of land use and on the extension of pastoralism and mixed farming into underused areas. (D.N.McM.)

The people

Africa is now widely recognized as the birthplace of Hominidae (the family to which modern humans belong). Archaeological evidence indicates that the continent has been inhabited by humans and their hominid forebears for some four million years or more. Anatomically modern African peoples are believed to have appeared about 100,000 years ago in sub-Saharan Africa and somewhat later in northern Africa. Exactly how and when the modern races emerged is not known, though the northern and southern groups are believed to have been distinct for some time; nonetheless, Africa is now overwhelmingly populated by the European geographic race in the north and the African geographic race in the south, the great majority being sub-Saharan peoples. Some rough generalizations about these geographic races can be made based on physical appearances (*e.g.,* people in northern Africa tend to have less skin pigmentation than those in sub-Saharan Africa), but the real distinctions between them are largely biochemical (*e.g.,* differences in blood types).

In all African countries the majority of the population is indigenous. In South Africa there are large numbers of Europeans (about 20 percent of the population). Other countries with significant European populations are Zimbabwe, Zambia, Namibia, Mozambique, Kenya, and Senegal. Other substantial minority groups are Asian peoples (chiefly in southern and East Africa), Arabs (in West and East Africa), and people of mixed origin.

CULTURAL AREAS

The basic units of African society have been—and in much of sub-Saharan Africa still are—the ethnic groups, tribes, or peoples. They number almost 3,000. Most are not politically or economically independent social units but rather groups that have a common sense of culture and identity, especially in terms of a distinct language and religion. Boundaries between them are usually not clearly defined, and frequently it is difficult to know whether a collection of very similar communities should be regarded as one tribal group or as many tribal groups. It is convenient to classify these peoples by languages and by the main outlines of their cultures.

Classifications of culture areas

There have been many attempts at cultural classifications of African peoples based on the concept of a culture area consisting of a number of societies with certain common features. Although to some extent useful, the generally accepted culture areas for Africa are too large to be very meaningful because each includes widely differing forms of social and political organization. The best-known of many older classifications is that by the American anthropologist Melville J. Herskovits (1924), which is still referred to despite its inadequacies. A later classification (1959), by another American, G.P. Murdock, takes as units relatively small clusters of peoples, who are grouped largely on linguistic and ethnohistorical grounds. Murdock divided the continent into 55 clusters of tribes, forming 11 main groupings, some of which are defined by livelihood (such as hunting or pastoralism) rather than by ethnic or linguistic affiliation. If one chooses to ignore these rather numerous divisions, then the principal cultural regions are northern, western, west-central, eastern, and central and southern Africa; Madagascar should also be included on this list.

Northern Africa. Africa north of the Sahara is inhabited primarily by peoples who speak languages that belong to the Hamito-Semitic, or Afro-Asian, group. These peoples include, for example, the Berbers of Morocco, Algeria, and Tunisia. The Berbers are most numerous in Morocco and least in Tunisia, where, as a result of culture contact and intermarriage, they have become largely assimilated into the Semitic-speaking Arabs who migrated into North Africa from Arabia in a number of waves; the first of these waves occurred in the 7th century AD. The distinctive nature of Maghrebian, or western Arab, culture resulted from this admixture. In the Sahara, such Arab peoples as the Shuwa live side by side with such Berber peoples as the Tuareg.

Western Africa. Western Africa contains a remarkable diversity of ethnic and cultural groups in the two east–west-trending zones of the savanna along the southern Saharan borderland and the rain forest along the Atlantic coastline. Most of the larger and more powerful of the traditional societies are kingdoms, each surrounded by lesser and politically weaker communities.

Societies of western Africa

Among the more important of the savanna peoples are the three main clusters known as Mande (in Senegal and Mali and including the Bambara, Malinke, and Soninke); the Voltaic group in the savanna zone to the east (including the Senufo, Lobi, Gurunsi, Dogon, and Mossi); and in northern Nigeria, Niger, and Cameroon the many small, mainly non-Muslim tribes of the plateau and highland areas. Throughout this region live the many groups of the Fulani (known also as Fulbe and Peul), a cattle-keeping Muslim people who have either conquered indigenous peoples (such as the numerous Hausa) or live in a symbiotic relationship with agricultural peoples. In the Sahara fringe are the many Berber-speaking groups collectively known as the Tuareg, the Kanuri of Lake Chad, and the many Semitic-speaking Bedouin Arab peoples. Many of the kingdoms are successor states to those of the Middle Ages.

The larger societies in the coastal zone are also mostly kingdoms. In Nigeria are the Igbo (Ibo) and Ibibio, organized into many autonomous polities; the Tiv; the Edo; and the several powerful kingdoms of the Yoruba. Westward are the Fon of Benin; the various peoples of the Akan confederacy, mostly in Ghana, the largest group being the Ashanti (Asante); the Ewe, Ga, Fanti (Fante), and Anyi (Agni) of the coast; the Mende and Temne of Sierra Leone; the Kru of Liberia; the Wolof, Serer, Dyula, and others of Senegal; and the Creoles of Sierra Leone and

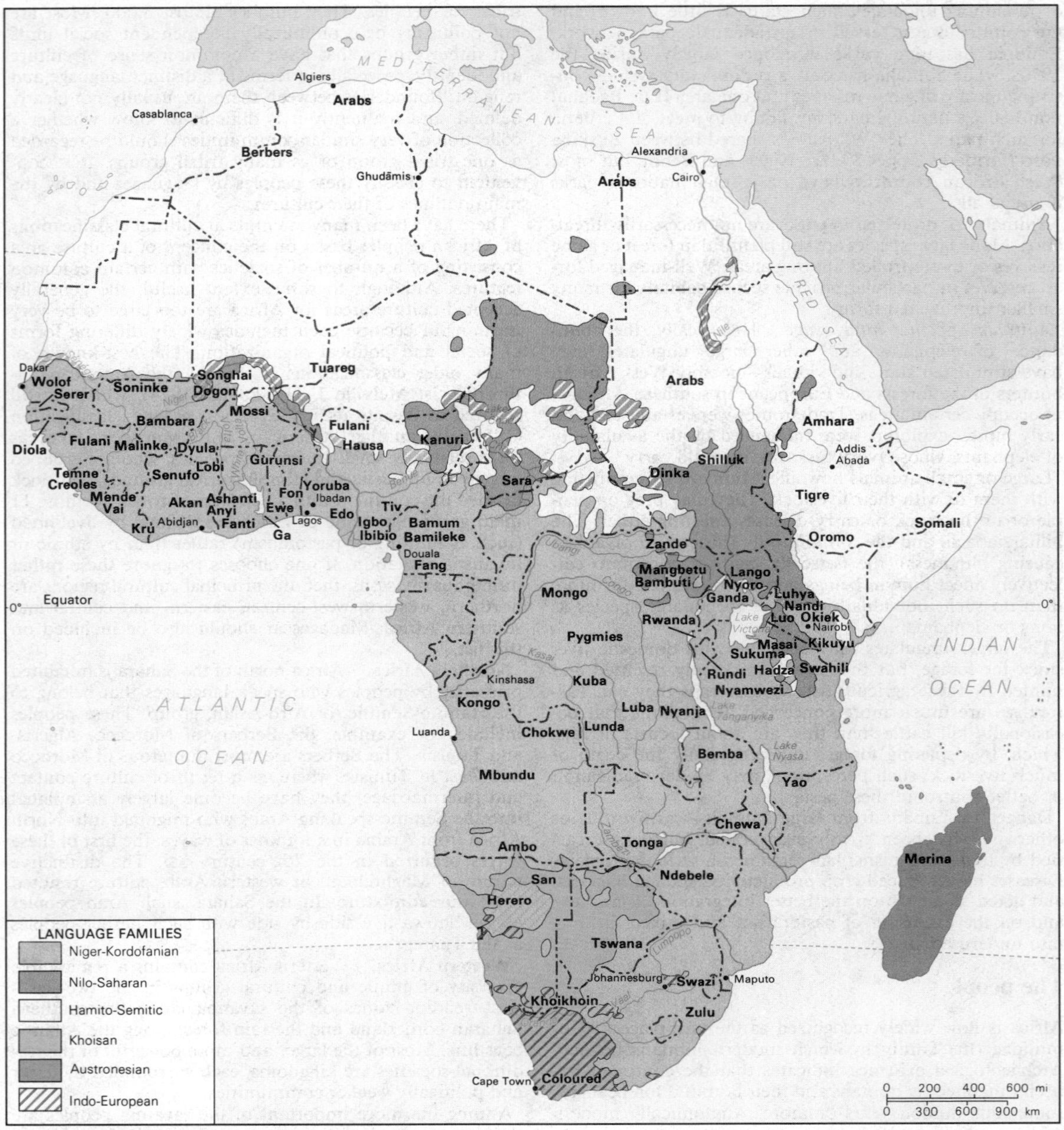

Major language families and peoples of Africa.

Liberia, descendants of freed slaves from the New World or of those who were on their way there.

West-central Africa. Geographically, west-central Africa may be considered as an eastern extension of western Africa: in the north are the savannas of Chad, the Central African Republic, and The Sudan, stretching to the Nile River, and in the south is the largely forested area of the Congo basin. It is ethnically very mixed, with Arabs in the north, Pygmies in the Congo and Gabon, and Sudanic- and Bantu-speaking peoples in the more southern areas. Agriculture is the basic economy of virtually the entire region. The savanna includes many peoples of the Cameroon area, divided into many small kingdoms, of which the Bamileke tribes are the most numerous. Between Cameroon and the Nile are many large Sudanic-speaking peoples, such as the Sara, Mangbetu, and Azande. Southward are Bantu peoples, of which the more important include the Fang of Gabon and the Kongo, Mongo, Kuba, Luba, Lunda, and Chokwe of Zaire and Angola.

Eastern Africa. Eastern Africa contains several ecological and cultural areas. In the north and east are the arid Sudan and Somalia separated by the Ethiopian Plateau; in the centre are the fertile areas of the East African lakes—Victoria, Albert (Mobutu Sese Seko), Tanganyika, Nyasa (Malaŵi)—and the highlands around Mounts Kenya and Kilimanjaro. The remainder consists of savanna, with the depression of the East African Rift Valley running from north to south. The areas of densest population are the more fertile highlands.

This ethnically complex region includes the Eastern Sudanic-speaking pastoralists of the Nile valley (Shilluk, Dinka, Luo, Lango, and others, formerly called Nilotes), those of the central plains (Masai, Nandi, and others, formerly known as Nilo-Hamites), and the Cushitic-speaking Somali and Oromo (Galla) of the Horn of Africa. In Ethiopia also are the Semitic-speaking Amhara, Tigre, and others. Most of the remaining peoples of the region are Bantu speakers who, although they vary widely in other ways, are all peasant farmers. Near the East African lakes are several formerly powerful Bantu kingdoms (Ganda, Nyoro, Rwanda, Rundi, and others). In the Kenya highlands are the Kikuyu, Luhya, and others. On the coast are the various Swahili-speaking tribes, while in Tanzania are the Bantu-speaking Chaga (Chagga), Nyamwezi, Sukuma, and many more. There are also remnants of other groups: the hunting Okiek (Dorobo), Hadza, and some Pygmies. And on the coast are the remnants of the once politically powerful Arabs, formerly based on Zanzibar.

Ethnic complexity of East Africa

Central and southern Africa. Central and southern Africa may be considered as forming a single large culture area. Most of it consists of open and dry savanna grasslands: to the northwest are the edges of the Congo forests; the southwest is very arid; and the coastline of South Africa and Mozambique is more fertile, most of it with subtropical or Mediterranean climate.

The region was once populated by San (Bushmen) and Khoikhoin (Hottentots), both Khoisan-speaking peoples, the former being hunters and the latter pastoralists. The San are today restricted to the arid areas of southwestern Africa and Botswana, and most of the Khoikhoin are merged into the racially mixed Coloured people of the Cape Province of the Republic of South Africa, with European and Asian admixtures. The other indigenous groups are all Bantu-speaking peoples, originally from the area of Cameroon, who dispersed across this region some 2,000 years ago. The vanguard, known linguistically as the Southern Bantu, drove the Khoisan before them and adopted some of their click gutturals into their own languages. After contact with Europeans in the 18th and 19th centuries, the Bantu speakers turned upon one another, establishing the conquest states of the Zulu, Swazi, Tswana, Ndebele (Matabele), Sotho, and others. To the north are the Central Bantu speakers of Zaire, Zimbabwe, Malaŵi, and Tanzania, as well as farmers with many kinds of political systems but who differ markedly from the Southern Bantu speakers in their kinship systems; they include the Bemba, Tonga, Chewa (Cewa), Nyanja, and Yao. In southwestern Africa are the Southwestern Bantu, including the Ovambo and Herero.

Madagascar. Finally, the island of Madagascar forms a distinct culture area. The various Malagasy ethnic groups, of which the politically most important is the Merina, are mainly of Indonesian origin, following migrations across the Indian Ocean probably during the 5th and 6th centuries AD. (R.K.A.G./J.F.M./J.I.C.)

CULTURAL PATTERNS

Languages. Many attempts to classify the languages of Africa have been inadequate because of the great complexity of the languages and because of a confusion between language, race, and economy; for example, there was once a spurious view of pastoralism as related to cultures whose members spoke Hamitic languages and were descendants of ancient Egyptians. The knowledge of most of the individual languages of the continent is still very inadequate, but there are known to be at least 1,000 distinct languages.

Linguistic classifications

One of the most recent and accurate attempts to classify African languages, prepared by the American linguist Joseph Greenberg, is based on the principles of linguistic analysis used for Indo-European languages rather than on geographic, racial, or other nonlinguistic criteria. The four main language families, or phyla, of the continent according to this classification (not totally accepted by all specialists) are the following: Niger-Kordofanian, Nilo-Saharan, Hamito-Semitic (Afro-Asiatic), and Khoisan.

The Niger-Kordofanian is the most widespread family and consists of two subfamilies, Niger-Congo and Kordofanian. These languages are found from Senegal to the Cape of Good Hope, with a geographically widespread extension due to relatively recent migrations over eastern and southern Africa. Niger-Congo covers most of central and southern Africa and includes the West Atlantic, Mande, Voltaic, Kwa, Benue-Congo, and Adamawa-Eastern subgroups; Kordofanian includes subgroups all spoken within a very small area of western Sudan. The most original point in this classification is the group called Benue-Congo, which linguistically subsumes all the Bantu languages found dispersed over most of eastern, central, and southern Africa. This dispersal is attributable to the rapid expansion of people from the area of the Bight of Benin from the beginning of the second millennium AD onward: the vanguard, the Southern Bantu speakers, had not reached the Cape of Good Hope when the Dutch arrived there in the 17th century. The close linguistic similarity among the Bantu languages points to the speed of this vast migration. Swahili, grammatically Bantu but with much Arabic in its vocabulary, is widely used as a lingua franca in eastern Africa; as the language of the people of Zanzibar and the east coast, it was spread by 19th-century Arab slavers in the hinterland as far as the Congo.

The Nilo-Saharan family classification is perhaps the most controversial—because of inadequate research—and the family is the most scattered. It comprises languages spoken along the savanna zone south of the Sahara from the middle Niger to the Nile, with outlying groups among the Para-Nilotic pastoralists of eastern Africa. Its subgroups are Songhai, Saharan, Maban, Fur, Chari-Nile (including the large clusters of Eastern and Central Sudanic), and Koman.

The Hamito-Semitic family includes languages both from Africa and the Middle East: Semitic (including Arabic, Amharic, and Tigrinya), Ancient Egyptian (extinct), Berber, Cushitic, and Chadic (*e.g.,* Hausa). It is found over much of northern Africa and eastward to the Horn of Africa. Arabic is both the official and unofficial language in states north of the Sahara, as well as in The Sudan. In many other countries it is the language of Islām. Amharic is the official language of Ethiopia. Hausa and Fulani are also widely spoken as lingua francas along the northern fringe of sub-Saharan West Africa, a wide area that encompasses many ethnic and political boundaries.

The Khoisan, or Click, family comprises the languages of the San and Khoikhoin, who are now limited to the arid parts of southwestern Africa, and perhaps of the outlying Hadza and Sandawe peoples of northern Tanzania.

The Austronesian (Malayo-Polynesian) family is represented by the various dialects of Malagasy in Madagascar.

Lingua francas of Africa

There are also many widespread trade languages and lingua francas in addition to those mentioned above. Some were imported and used by administrators, missionaries, and traders during the colonial period. They include English, French, and other languages of the former colonial powers; some of them are today the national languages of independent nation-states, and, with the spread of formal education, they are gaining greater acceptance. Between the Sahara and the Zambezi River, either English or French is widely understood. French is the official language in the states that formerly made up French West Africa and French Equatorial Africa, as well as in Madagascar (Malagasy is also an official language) and Zaire. Similarly, English is the official language, or is widely spoken, in the states of West, central, and East Africa formerly under British administration and is also the official language in Liberia. Portuguese is the language, officially and otherwise, in the countries formerly under Portugal. In South Africa, Afrikaans (which developed out of a colloquial version of 17th-century Dutch) and English are both official. Hindi, Gujarati, Urdu, and other languages of the Indian subcontinent are spoken among the Asian communities. In West Africa forms of Creole (Krio) and Pidgin are widespread in the coast towns of very heterogeneous ethnic composition. In southern Africa, Fanagalo, a mixture of English and local Bantu tongues, is spoken in mining areas.

The great majority of African languages have no indigenous forms of writing, although today governments and missions have been reducing them to writing. Many African languages (such as Swahili) have for centuries been written in Arabic script. There are exceptions, however. The best known are those of the Vai of Sierra Leone, the Mum of Cameroon, and the Tuareg and other Berber groups of the southern Sahara, all of whom invented their own scripts.

Religions. In general, northern Africa is predominantly Islāmic and southern Africa largely Christian, although their distributions are not discrete. For example, the Coptic church is found in Egypt and Ethiopia, and Islām is common along the coast of eastern Africa and is expanding southward in western Africa. Many of the Sudanic peoples—such as the Malinke, Hausa, Songhai, and Bornu—are Islāmized, and the religion has also achieved substantial gains among such Guinea Coast people as the Yoruba of Nigeria and the Temne of Sierra Leone. Much conversion to Christianity also has occurred, most notably to Roman Catholicism and in the coastal regions of sub-Saharan Africa.

In most of the rest of sub-Saharan Africa the people practice a variety of traditional religions, which have certain common features. All of those known include the notion of a high or creator God, remote from humans and beyond their comprehension or control. This God is typically not attributed a sex but in some cases is male or female; often God is given an immanent and visible aspect as well. The most important "spiritual" powers are usually associated with things or beings with which people have day-to-day contact or that they know from the past. Thus, there may be many kinds and levels of spirits of the air, of the earth, of rivers, and so on. There may be ancestors and ghosts of the dead who have achieved a partial divinity. There may be mythical heroes who led the people to their present land and founded their society as it is known today.

Traditional religions

The ritual functionaries found in most African societies include priests, lineage and clan elders, rainmakers, diviners, prophets, and others. Very few of these are specialists; typically they hold ritual authority by virtue of age, genealogy, or political office and are primarily responsible for the ritual well-being only of the members of the social groupings that they head; their congregations consist of their joint families, lineages, clans, local village communities, chieftaincies, or the like. Their ritual authority is thus a sanction for their secular and domestic authority.

A central element of every indigenous African religion is its cosmology—which tells of tribal origins and early migrations and explains the basic ideological problems of any culture, such as the origin of death, the nature of society, the relationship of men and women and of living and dead, and so on. Social values are typically expressed in myths, legends, folktales, and riddles; the overt meanings of these various oral statements frequently conceal sociological and historical meanings not easily apparent to outsiders.

In the past, witchcraft and sorcery were given widespread credence and served to explain or control the misfortunes of people who were aware of their lack of mastery and understanding of nature and society. Travelers' tales of African people living in fear of witchcraft, however, were of course grossly exaggerated; the colonial powers usually assumed (incorrectly) that witch doctors were socially harmful and prohibited them. Although belief in witchcraft is receding, it is still important in both rural and urban areas, often serving as a means of explaining the misfortunes that beset urban dwellers and labour migrants who find themselves in new and confusing social milieus. There have been many cases in modern times of "epidemics" of beliefs in witches, and there have arisen a number of evanescent cults led by various kinds of prophets and evangelists. Such manias arise in periods of radical change and its resultant uncertainty and stress.

Nativistic movements

Social and religious changes in Africa have often been accompanied by the appearance of prophets who advocate the expulsion of the Europeans or the eradication of epidemic diseases threatening the traditional ways of life. More recently, also, the spread of Christianity and, to a lesser extent, Islām has given rise to Christian prophets and to leaders of separatist movements repudiating European-controlled mission churches for nationalistic, tribalistic, or racial reasons. Such prophets lead their own cults and establish their own churches, typically gaining new political power sanctioned by their presumed direct links with God. These new churches have been reported in almost all parts of the continent.

Domestic groupings. The forms of the family found in Africa are consistent with the forms of economic production. Throughout most of the rural areas the typical domestic group is the joint or extended family consisting of several generations of kin and their spouses, the whole being under the authority of the senior male. The size of the group varies, but it typically consists of three to five generations of kin. It provides a stable and long-lasting domestic unit able to work as a single cooperative group, to defend itself against others, and to care for all of its members throughout their lifetimes. Polygyny is traditionally widespread as an ideal, its extent depending on the status and wealth of the husband: chiefs and rulers need many wives to give them a mark of high position and to enable them to offer hospitality to their subjects.

In most of Africa these residential groups are based upon descent groups known as clans and lineages, the latter being segments of the former. The significance given to descent groups varies, but they are important in providing for heirs, successors, and marital partners.

In the second half of the 20th century this pattern has been changing, rapidly in the urban and poverty-stricken areas, more slowly in those areas less affected by economic and political development. In cities and in major labour-supplying areas, such as most of southern Africa, the joint or extended family is giving way to the independent nuclear family of husband, wife, and children. There is also a tendency toward the breakdown of family structure because of labour migration—the younger men moving to the cities, leaving women, older men, and children in the impoverished homelands. (J.F.M./J.I.C.)

DEMOGRAPHIC PATTERNS

Africa has the most rapidly expanding population of any region in the world, even though the continent's birth and death rates are also the world's highest. There has been some decline in overall death rates in the latter half of the 20th century; but infant and child mortality rates have remained high, and gains in life expectancy have been smaller than in other developing regions of the world. On average, Africa's population is increasing at about 3 percent per annum, and this growth rate is associated with an increasingly youthful population: in nearly every African country more than 40 percent of the population is less than 15 years of age.

The great majority of the working population is still engaged in subsistence agriculture and in the production of cash crops. In most countries the proportion of the total population dependent on agriculture is at least 60 percent.

The remainder of the working population is divided mainly between a rapidly growing service sector (including civil servants, members of the armed forces, police, teachers, health workers, and those engaged in commerce and communications) and an increasing number of mining and industrial projects; in only a few countries, however, do these latter activities employ more than 10 percent of the work force. Underemployment, particularly in the agricultural sector, is widespread, and unemployment has risen, especially in urban areas. Participation in labour by women varies considerably from country to country. Women in paid employment are generally fewer than men, though a large proportion of women in sub-Saharan countries are engaged in subsistence agriculture—if only part of the time. Women are also employed in the civil service, in trading (especially in western Africa), in domestic service, and to an increasing extent in light industry.

Women in the labour force

Population distribution. Africa has more than 10 percent of the total population of the world, distributed over a land area representing slightly more than one-fifth of the total land surface. Such desert areas as the Sahara, Kalahari, and Namib, however, reduce the amount of habitable land, and such factors as climate, vegetation, and disease have tended to limit the evolution of densely populated areas where agriculture is practiced. With the advent of the colonial era the African continent was divided into small geographically and politically based units that took little or no account of ethnic distribution. These political boundaries persisted, and the continent continued to be characterized by a large number of countries with predominantly small populations.

Wide variations in density occur from country to country in Africa and within countries. In general, the most densely populated areas are found bordering the lakes, in the river basins (especially those of the Nile and Niger), along the coastal belts of North and West Africa, and in certain highland areas, while settlement is the most sparse in the desert and savanna areas. Thus, Rwanda and Burundi, situated in the East African highlands, are the most densely populated countries in Africa, while Western Sahara, Mauritania, and Libya in the Sahara and Botswana and Namibia in the Kalahari and Namib are the least densely populated.

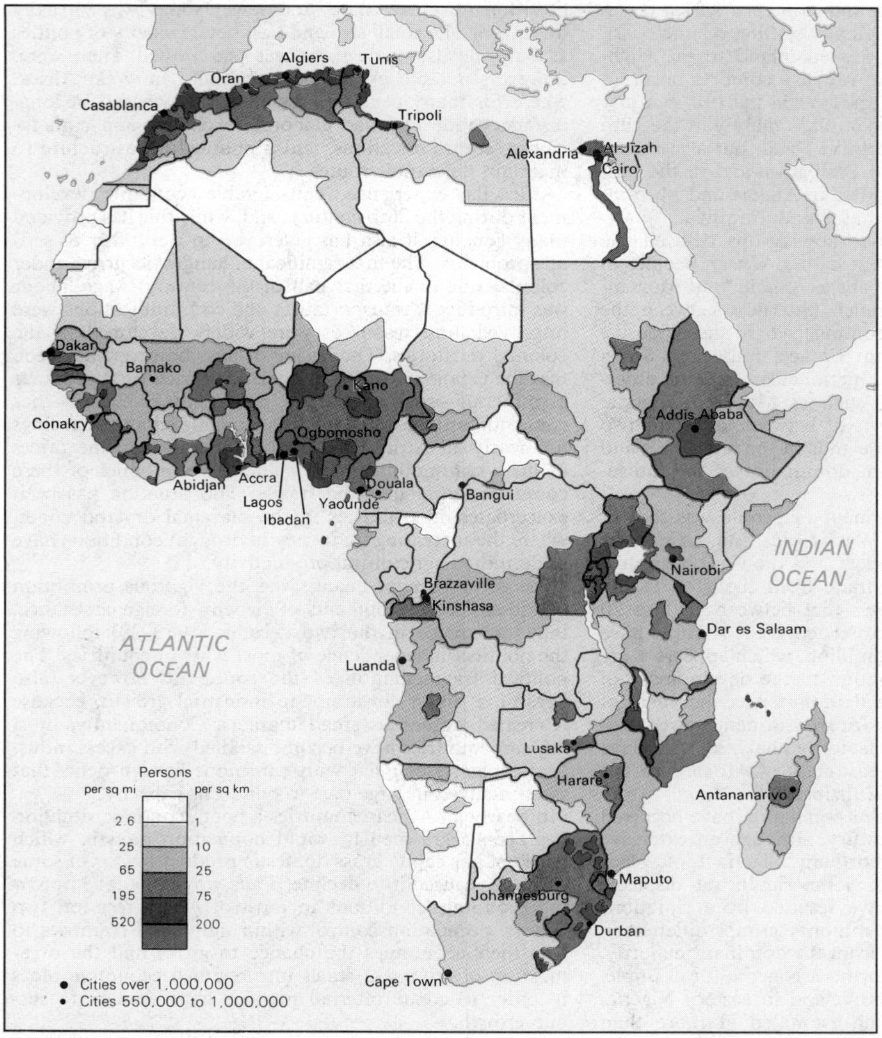

Population density of Africa.

Settlement patterns. Traditional African patterns of settlement vary with differences in landscape and ecology, communications, and warfare. The most widespread pattern has been that of scattered villages and hamlets—the homesteads of joint and extended families—large enough for defense and domestic cooperation but rarely permanent because of the requirements of shifting cultivation and the use of short-lived building materials. In much of the western African savanna, large mud-adobe villages are traditional, but over most of Africa housing consists of mud and wattle with roofs of thatch or palm leaves.

Characteristics of old and new towns

Large towns, however, were not widespread in the continent until the 20th century. Towns dating from precolonial times are found mainly along the Nile valley and the Mediterranean fringe of North Africa—where many date from classical times (*e.g.,* Alexandria, Egypt) and the Middle Ages (*e.g.,* Fès, Mor.)—and also in western Africa, in both forest and savanna zones, where they were the seats of governments of kingdoms. Timbuktu, Djenné, Kano, and others date from the Middle Ages; some, such as Benin and the Yoruba cities of Ibadan and Oyo, are more recent but certainly many centuries old. In eastern Africa there are such medieval Arab coastal towns as Mombasa.

The more traditional towns differ in form, function, and even population characteristics from the many towns and cities established under colonial rule as administrative, trading, or industrial centres and ports. These latter cities are found throughout Africa and include Johannesburg, Lusaka, Harare (formerly Salisbury), Kinshasa, Lubumbashi, Nairobi, Dakar, Freetown, Abidjan, and many others; often, as in the case of Lagos or Accra, they are built onto traditional towns. Typically the focus of in-migration from an impoverished hinterland, they are ethnically heterogeneous. Many have grown to become the largest cities in their respective countries, dominating their national urban hierarchies in size as well as in function.

Mostly rural for centuries, Africa has rapidly become more urbanized. Although it is still the least urbanized of the continents, Africa has the fastest rate of urbanization: about 5 percent annually. Thus, the total population living in towns—which was only about 15 percent in 1950—grew to nearly 35 percent by 1990 and may exceed 40 percent by the year 2000. Generally, the level of urbanization is highest in the north and south, and it is higher in the west than in the east and nearer the coasts than in the interior.

The largest cities include Cairo, Alexandria, and Al-Jīzah, Egypt; Kinshasa, Zaire; Lagos, Nigeria; Casablanca, Mor.; Johannesburg, S.Af.; Addis Ababa, Eth.; and Algiers. Many other large cities are seaports along the coasts or central marketing towns, linked by rail or river with a coast. Examples of seaports are Accra, Ghana; Lagos; and Cape Town. Ibadan and Ogbomosho, Nigeria; Nairobi, Kenya; and Addis Ababa are examples of large inland cities.

Migrations. There have been many movements of population within the African continent, from outside into the continent, and from the continent outward. The major movement within the continent in historic times has been that of the Bantu-speaking peoples, who, as a result of a population explosion that is not fully understood, spread over most of the continent south of the equator.

European settlement

The major movements into the continent in the past few centuries have been of European settlers into northern Africa and of European and Asian settlers in southern

Africa. The Dutch migrations into southern Africa began in the mid-17th century. Originally settling on the coast, the Dutch—or Boers—later moved inland to the Highveld region, where a series of military conflicts occurred between them and the Bantu speakers in the 19th century. Other European settlement took place mainly in the 19th century: the British particularly in Natal, but also inland in what are now Zambia and Zimbabwe and in the East African highlands; the Portuguese in Angola and Mozambique; and the Germans in what is now Namibia.

The presence of large settler populations delayed the achievement of self-government by the African peoples of South Africa, Namibia, Zimbabwe, Angola, and Mozambique and has resulted in much bitterness between the races. In North Africa, by contrast, where the extensive settlement of Europeans from France, Italy, and Spain occurred, the growth of Arab nationalism and the emergence of independent states such as Morocco, Algeria, and Tunisia led to the return of between one and two million colonists to their homelands in the late 1950s and early '60s and to the political dominance of the indigenous peoples.

The greatest outward movement of people was that of Africans—particularly from West Africa and, to a lesser extent, Angola—to the Americas and the Caribbean during the period of the slave trade from the 16th to the 19th century. Earlier estimates that between 15 and 20 million Africans were transported across the Atlantic have been revised to a figure of 10 million, which appears more realistic. While their contribution to the development of the New World was of crucial importance, the effect of the loss of manpower to the African continent was considerable and has yet to be satisfactorily analyzed. The slave trade was also active on the east coast of Africa, where it was centred on the island of Zanzibar.

Population displacements

Few permanent movements of population have occurred within Africa in the 20th century, although an extensive settlement of Hausa from northern Nigeria took place in what is now The Sudan. Some significant displacements of population also have resulted from situations of conflict, usually involving minority groups different in religion, ethnicity, or culture from the dominant majority. In 1966 the Igbo people of northern Nigeria, for example, returned en masse to their homeland in eastern Nigeria, the number of refugees being estimated at more than 500,000. The conflicts in the Horn of Africa since the 1960s have caused similar displacements. Indeed, Africa has millions of refugees, especially in Somalia, The Sudan, Zaire, Burundi, and Tanzania. These refugees are among the poorest and most vulnerable people in the world, and their numbers are substantially augmented by those fleeing drought and famine. The countries to which these people flee often find it extremely difficult to cope with them.

Most movement occurs across uncontrolled borders and between people of the same tribal groups. Much is seasonal, in any case, and is restricted to migrant labourers and nomadic herdsmen. Controlled immigration and emigration are generally negligible; contemporary examples, however, include the employment of mine workers in South Africa, the forced emigration of Asians from East Africa, and the expulsion of people from neighbouring West African states caused by such actions as the enforcement of the Alien Compliance Order of 1969 in Ghana. (R.K.A.G./D.S.H.W.N./J.F.M./J.I.C.)

The economy

With the exception of South Africa and the countries of North Africa, all of which have diversified production systems, the economy of most of Africa can be characterized as underdeveloped. Africa as a whole has abundant natural resources, but much of its economy has remained predominantly agricultural, and subsistence farming still engages more than 60 percent of the population.

Until the beginning of the 20th century this system of farming relied on simple tools and techniques, as well as on traditional organization of the family or community for its labour. Because of poor transport and communications, production was largely for domestic use. There was little long-distance trade, and wage labour was virtually unknown. The small size and vast heterogeneity of polities at that time also made exchanges very limited. There were, however, notable exceptions, especially in West Africa, where for many centuries societies had engaged in long-distance trade and had elaborate exchange and craft facilities, communications, and a political infrastructure to maintain their trade routes.

Development in the 20th century

Africa has experienced considerable economic development during the 20th century; and, while this has provided many benefits, it also has given rise to a number of serious problems. The first significant changes occurred under colonial rule in the first half of the century: wage labour was introduced, transportation and communications were improved, and resources were widely developed in the colonial territories. The legacy of this, however, has been that the export of two or three major agricultural products or minerals—such as peanuts, petroleum, or copper—has come to provide most of the foreign-exchange earnings for nearly all African nations. Fluctuations in the prices of these commodities have made the economies of these countries vulnerable and fragile. The situation has been exacerbated in countries in the marginal dryland zones, where the increasing frequency of drought conditions have undermined agricultural productivity.

The second major change was the vigorous promotion of industrial development, often with foreign assistance, that took place in the two decades (1960–80) following the political independence of most African countries. The political fragmentation of the continent, however, also became a major constraint to industrial growth, because it created numerous small markets. Consequently, most African countries have become saddled with excess industrial capacity, coupled with enormous foreign debts that were incurred in large part to build this capacity.

In nearly all African countries a poor economic situation has been aggravated by rapid population growth, which has kept per capita gross domestic product low or in some cases has caused it to decline. Thus, any hope for improving economic conditions in most of Africa rests on two factors: population control within individual countries to give their economies the chance to grow; and the organization of groups of states into regional economic blocs in order to create internal markets large enough to sustain growth.

RESOURCES

Mineral resources. Africa's known mineral wealth places it among the world's richest continents. Its very large share of the world's mineral resources includes coal, petroleum, natural gas, uranium, radium, low-cost thorium, iron ores, chromium, cobalt, copper, lead, zinc, tin, bauxite, titanium, antimony, gold, platinum, tantalum, germanium, lithium, phosphates, and diamonds.

Major deposits of coal are confined to four groups of coal basins—in southern Africa, North Africa, Zaire, and Nigeria. Proved petroleum reserves in North Africa occur in Libya, Algeria, Egypt, and Tunisia. Exploration has been concentrated north of the Aïr–Ahaggar massifs; there may also be major Saharan reserves to the south. The other major oil reserves are in the West African coastal basin—principally in Nigeria and also in Cameroon, Gabon, and the Congo—and in Angola. Africa's natural gas reserves are concentrated in basins of North and coastal central Africa.

Southern Africa is said to be one of the world's seven major uranium provinces. In South Africa the unusual degree of knowledge of reserves derives from the joint occurrence of uranium with gold, a condition that also decreases the cost of production. Other countries with significant uranium deposits are Niger, Gabon, Zaire, and Namibia.

Metallic deposits. In North Africa reserves of iron ore are concentrated in the Atlas Mountains and in western Sahara. Egypt, however, has medium-grade reserves, of which the most important are at the Al-Wāḥāt al-Baḥrīyah Oasis. The ore deposits in Morocco and Tunisia, which were once of considerable importance, have been severely depleted. Africa's most significant iron reserves are to be found in western and southern Africa. It is the sedimen-

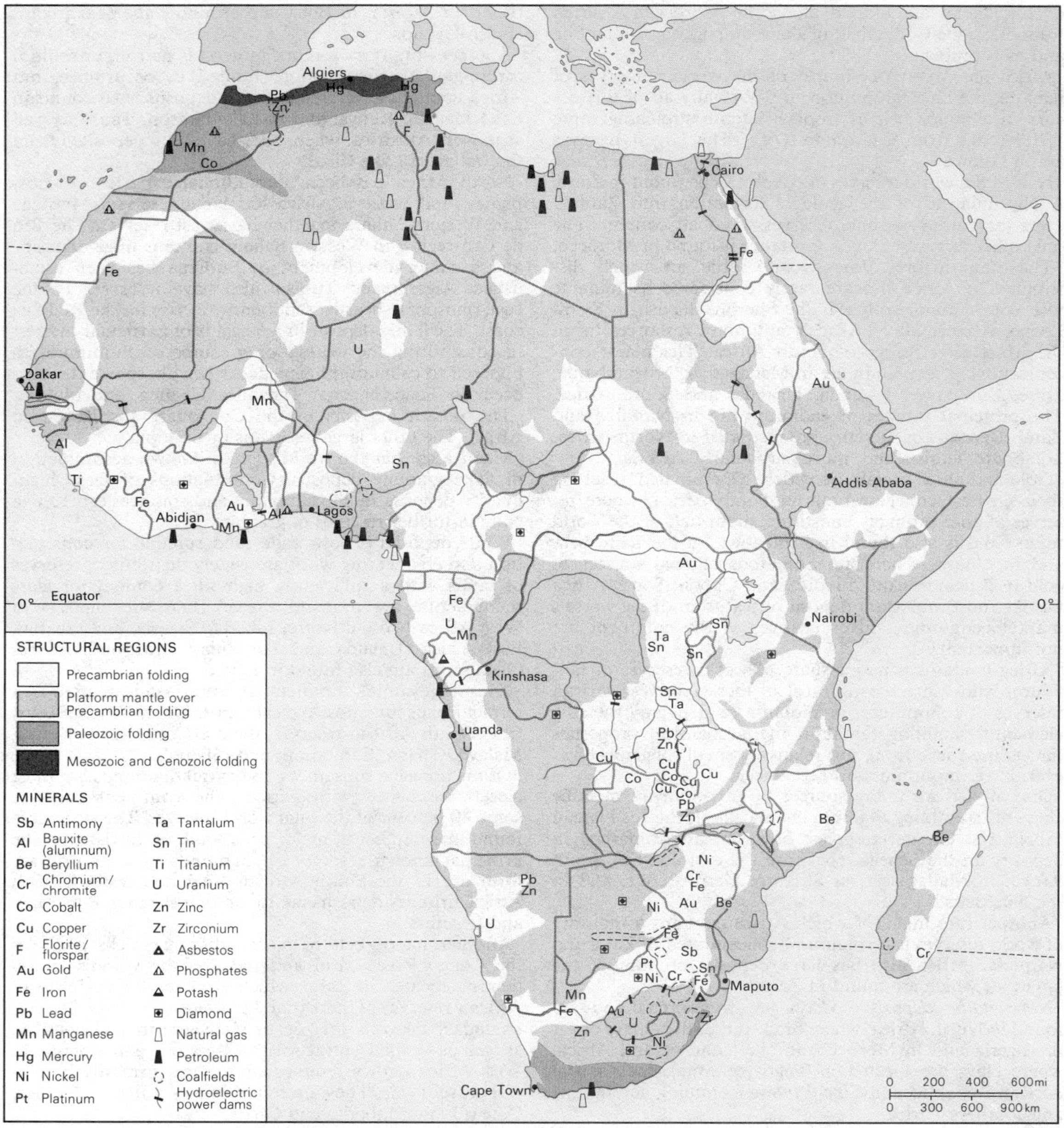

Basic structural regions and principal mineral and hydroelectric sites of Africa.

tary Precambrian rocks, particularly in western Africa, that have proved the basis of Africa's role as a major world producer of iron ore. The most significant deposits are in Liberia in the Bomi Hills, Bong and Nimba ranges, and the Mano valley; in the extension into Guinea of the Nimba–Simandou ranges, where hematites have been located; in Nigeria and Mauritania, which have large deposits of low-grade ore; and in Gabon, where extensive reserves are present in the northeast. In southern Africa most iron ore reserves lie in South Africa itself. The chief deposits are at Postmasburg, in the Bushveld Complex, at Thabazimbi, and in the vast, low-grade deposits of Pretoria. There are also substantial reserves in Zimbabwe.

Ferro-alloy metals

Africa's reserves of minerals used as ferroalloys in the steel industry are even more striking than its enormous share of world iron ore reserves. This is particularly true of chromium. Almost the entire world reserve of chromium is found in southern and, to a much lesser extent, in western and northeastern Africa. The highest concentrations are found in Zimbabwe, at Great Dyke. South Africa contains the largest deposits of chromite. As compared with these two sources, reserves elsewhere in Africa are relatively small.

Manganese reserves are also considerable. In South Africa reserves of contained manganese are found in the Kalahari Manganese Field and elsewhere. The Mouanda deposit in southeastern Gabon is thought to be among the largest in the world. Ghana is another important source of manganese, having both low-grade and high-grade reserves. Elsewhere in West Africa, manganese deposits are situated in Burkina Faso and Côte d'Ivoire, as well as in Zaire and Cameroon. In North Africa manganese is found in Morocco and Algeria.

Africa's contribution to world resources of other ferroalloys is, by comparison, insignificant. Nickel is of some importance, occurring in other metalliferous ores in southern Africa.

Most of Africa's copper is contained in the Central African Copperbelt, stretching across Zambia and into the Shaba area of Zaire. Accompanying minerals vary with the geologic layer, but cobalt dominates. Outside the Copperbelt a number of countries have lesser but still significant reserves of copper.

Only Nigeria, Zaire, and South Africa contain tin reserves of any significance. Although it is difficult to consider Africa's reserves of lead and zinc separately, of the two, lead ores are considerably more widespread. North Africa is the largest traditional producing region. African reserves of zinc metal are located along the Moroccan-Algerian frontier, in the Copperbelt in Zaire, in Nigeria, in Zambia, and in Namibia.

Africa has about one-fourth of the world's reserves of bauxite, the chief aluminum ore. Virtually all of this occurs in a major belt of tropical laterite stretching some 1,200 miles from Guinea to Togo. The largest reserves are in Guinea.

Half of the world reserves of cobalt can be found in Zaire. A continuation of the geologic formation into Zambia gives the country sizable reserves of cobalt content. The only other deposit of any importance is found in Morocco.

The titanium ores, ilmenite and rutile, are widely distributed in Africa but are rarely considered as minable reserves. A major source is the Sherbro deposit in Sierra Leone. Almost all of Africa's antimony resources lie in the Murchison Range of South Africa. The major concentrations of beryllium are in Madagascar, Mozambique, Zaire, Zimbabwe, Rwanda, Uganda, and South Africa. The principal sources of cadmium are in Namibia and Zaire. Deposits of mercury are restricted to North Africa, notably to Tunisia and, more particularly, Algeria.

Precious metals

Gold and allied metals are widely disseminated, reaching their greatest concentrations in South Africa, where reserves of gold probably constitute about half of the world total. Gold is also found in Zimbabwe, in the Zaire belt, and in Ghana. There are numerous alluvial sources of gold in Burundi, Côte d'Ivoire, and Gabon. South Africa has the most important deposit of platinum of the world's market economies. Silver reserves of the continent are not important.

Africa contains a major share of world reserves of tantalum, with Zaire having most of these reserves. African reserves of columbium, or niobium (a steel-gray metallic element resembling tantalum in its chemical properties that is used in alloys), are relatively small. Nigeria, however, is an important world producer.

One of Africa's many sources of zirconium (a metallic element resembling titanium chemically) is the Jos Plateau in Nigeria. Greater reserves, however, are contained in deposits on the Senegal coast; on the east coast of South Africa; in Madagascar; at Sherbro, Sierra Leone; and in the Nile delta.

Another rare metal of which Africa contains a majority of world reserves is germanium, concentrated in Zaire and Namibia. Africa also has large deposits of lithium, the largest of which are found in Zaire.

Nonmetallic deposits. Clays are widespread and are found in North Africa, where brick and pottery clays occur in Algeria and in Morocco; in West and central Africa, where clays are located in Togo (ceramic), the Central African Republic, and Côte d'Ivoire (ceramic); and in East and southern Africa.

Kaolin (china clay) occurs in Algeria. Outside North Africa it is widespread. In West Africa it occurs most notably in Nigeria's Jos Plateau, as well as in Mali, in Ghana, and in Guinea. Similar deposits occur in central and East Africa, as well as in southern Africa.

Bentonite (a clay formed from decomposed volcanic ash, which is able to absorb large quantities of water and to expand to several times its usual size) is found in the Moroccan Atlas Mountains and in Tanzania, Kenya, and South Africa. The continent's principal reserve of fuller's earth (an absorbent clay) is in Morocco.

Economically important mica deposits occur primarily in southern Africa (South Africa, Zimbabwe, and Tanzania) and in Madagascar.

Sulfur and salt

Africa has none of the world's major reserves of sulfur. It reaches economic concentrations only in South Africa's Witwatersrand, in Zambia's Copperbelt, and in Morocco. Large quantities of sodium deposits remain to be evaluated. Sodium chloride is the principal salt, the largest deposit being in the Danakil Plain of Ethiopia. The principal sources of salt in Africa, however, are inland or coastal basins, from which it is extracted by the evaporation of saltwater. Major coastal reserves of this type lie along the North African Mediterranean coast and along Red Sea and Indian Ocean coasts of East Africa and Madagascar. Inland, the chief reserves are in the Oran Sebkha, a salt-pan region in Algeria; in Botswana around Lake Makarikari; and in Uganda.

Another important sodium mineral is natron, or sodium carbonate. Natron is more limited in occurrence, but Africa contains several significant deposits. It is found in Lake Magadi, Kenya, and in Lake Natron, Tanz., as well as in western Africa, where beds have been deposited from the waters of Lake Chad.

North Africa has been a traditional exporter of phosphates, and western Africa has large reserves. Morocco and Western Sahara together have vast reserves. The Río de Oro region in Western Sahara contains huge deposits, and a major development at Bu-Craa has been established. Algeria and Tunisia also have reserves. To the east, phosphate-bearing sediments outcrop on the Red Sea coast. The Thiès deposit in Senegal is of particular interest in constituting the world's only source of aluminum (as opposed to calcium) phosphate. Other phosphate deposits occur in Togo, Nigeria, Tanzania, Uganda, and Malaŵi.

The potash deposits in the Congo are the largest in Africa. The other large reserve is in Ethiopia.

Madagascar has the world's largest known accumulation of flake graphite deposits. Continuations of these high-quality deposits in Mozambique and southeastern Kenya contain further reserves of graphite.

While deposits of low-grade sand suitable for construction and engineering work are widely distributed, reserves of sands with a sufficiently high silica content for glass manufacture are more localized. There are deposits in West Africa (Côte d'Ivoire, Liberia, Nigeria, and Ghana), East Africa (Uganda and Tanzania), and South Africa. Glass sands are also found in Egypt.

Kyanite (cyanite), a mineral aluminum silicate used as a refractory, occurs most typically in southern Africa. Apart from South African reserves, there are deposits in Kenya, Malaŵi, Ghana, Cameroon, and Liberia.

Industrial diamonds

Of the abrasive substances, industrial diamonds are most closely associated with Africa. The continent contains some 40 percent of the total world reserves. The stones are found in a number of major belts south of the Sahara. The principal known reserves of diamonds in their primary form are in the South African Vaal belt. Elsewhere in Africa, primary deposits are found in Tanzania, Botswana, and Lesotho.

Another major belt of diamondiferous rocks encircles the Congo River basin and includes the world's largest deposit, located in Zaire, which contains the majority of Africa's reserves of industrial diamonds. The same belt has secondary deposits that occur elsewhere in that country, as well as in the Central African Republic and Angola. In West Africa known reserves are located primarily in alluvial gravel fields. They are found in Sierra Leone, Guinea, Côte d'Ivoire, Liberia, and Ghana.

A considerable proportion of the world reserves of corundum (a common mineral, aluminum oxide, notable for its hardness) is located in southern Africa. The principal deposits are in Zimbabwe, South Africa, Mozambique, Madagascar, and Malaŵi.

Pumice is found in areas of volcanic activity such as the Atlantic islands, the coastal Atlas Mountains of northeastern Morocco, and in the East African Rift System, notably in Kenya, Tanzania, and Malaŵi. Joint reserves constitute, however, only a small percentage of the world total.

Reserves of building materials are characterized by their wide distribution, to such an extent that the commercial status of such deposits depends more on their location relative to areas of development than on their extent and quality. While almost all African countries have reserves of building materials, knowledge of such reserves is strictly related to the country's level of development, and no meaningful estimate of the size of reserves can be made.

Granite is located in Morocco and Nigeria, and there are vast reserves in Burkina Faso. Quartzite (a granular rock, consisting essentially of quartz) is important as a building stone in Uganda and Zaire. Dolerite (a coarse-grained basalt) is produced in South Africa, and basalt, which is crushed for use in road construction, in Senegal. Marble is found in Mali, Togo, Nigeria, and South Africa.

Limestone is important because of its use in the cement

industry, and deposits are fairly widespread. North Africa is a particularly important source. In western Africa a belt of limestone runs from the Central African Republic to the Atlantic coasts, with major outcrops in northern Nigeria, Niger, Burkina Faso, and Mali. Elsewhere there are deposits in Nigeria, Benin, Togo, and Ghana. East African deposits include those in Kenya, Tanzania, Uganda, and Zambia; there are also deposits in South Africa.

North Africa has major reserves of gypsum on the Mediterranean coast, as well as in outcrops along the Gulf of Suez and the Red Sea. Somalia has one of the largest known deposits. Eastern Africa and Madagascar have further reserves, and in southern and western Africa superficial deposits are particularly important—for instance, north of Nouakchott, Mauritania.

Gems

Many of the major deposits of the most important commercial gem mineral, the diamond, have already been described above in the discussion of industrial diamonds. One major deposit, however—that of Namibia—consists almost entirely of gem diamonds.

There is no other gem mineral in Africa of comparable importance to these diamond reserves. Deposits of a number of such stones are found, however, especially in southern and eastern Africa, where diamond fields contain beryl, garnets, amethyst, rose quartz, topaz, opal, jasper, emeralds, and other stones. Madagascar contains a large deposit of garnet. Tourmaline is found in Madagascar and Namibia. Agate is particularly associated with the volcanic areas of eastern and southern Africa and malachites with the Shaba Copperbelt, while sapphires are found with diamonds in Ghana.

Africa contains no major world deposits of talc, but the mineral is found in Morocco, Nigeria, The Sudan, Zimbabwe, and South Africa. Reserves of asbestos are much more important, and southern Africa has a number of deposits of world significance.

Major deposits of fluorite, or fluorspar (a common mineral, calcium fluoride, used as a flux in metallurgy), are particularly associated with deposits of lead and zinc. In South Africa the chief deposit is in the Transvaal. North African reserves lie primarily in Tunisia and Morocco.

Africa produces a very small share of the world supply of diatomite (a fine siliceous earth, used as an abrasive). The most important deposit is in Kenya.

Water resources. In general, the seasonal distribution of river flow in Africa reflects the seasonal rainfall pattern; the amount of groundwater entering the river channels during the dry season is comparatively small. Important modifications in the flow of some rivers are caused by the presence of large lakes and swamps, which act as natural storage reservoirs, by the construction of dams on their courses, and by the incidence and severity of drought.

Surface water. Although the surface area of Africa is about one-fifth of the Earth's land surface, the combined annual flow of African rivers is only about 7 percent of the world's river flow reaching the oceans.

North Africa's few perennial rivers originate in the mountains of the Maghrib, and their water is used extensively for irrigation. The large number of wadis, or ephemeral watercourses, to be found throughout the Sahara and the eastern Mediterranean coastal lands become filled with water as a result of the rare and erratic storms that occur over mountainous areas; otherwise they remain dry.

From the relatively well-watered areas of western and equatorial Africa, the Sénégal, the Niger, the Logone–Chari, and the Nile rivers flow through the drier inland zones. Of these, the Niger River, originating in the Fouta Djallon region of Guinea, is retarded in the lake and swamp area south of Timbuktu in Mali, and the Logone–Chari feeds Lake Chad.

The Nile, the world's longest river, receives more than 60 percent of its water from the Ethiopian Plateau, although its source is much farther south in the mountains of Burundi. Since the completion of the Aswan High Dam, only a small proportion of the river's total flow reaching Egypt enters the Mediterranean Sea.

A number of rivers flowing in a more or less southerly direction into the Atlantic Ocean drain the southern part of western Africa. Many flow rapidly over bedrock before entering the coastal plains, draining into the system of lagoons and creeks along the coast. During the dry season the upper reaches of these rivers are without water; but in Guinea, Sierra Leone, and Liberia, where the dry season is fairly short, the rivers flow throughout the year.

In the well-watered western part of equatorial Africa the total average annual flow of the Congo River is enormous: some 44 trillion cubic feet. River flow at the lower end of the basin has two maxima: one that corresponds with the rainy season north of the equator, the other with the rainy season that occurs when it is summer in the Southern Hemisphere. The waters in the lower reaches of the river are slightly acid after traversing the large swamps situated in the centre of the basin.

East African lakes

East Africa's many lakes stretch along the East African Rift Valley from the Red Sea to the mouth of the Zambezi River. Evaporation from most of them exceeds their surface rainfall, and in consequence their outflow is less than the quantities brought in annually by their tributaries. They often govern river flow by acting as storage reservoirs—decreasing the flood flow and increasing the dry-season flow. A number of the rift valley lakes are situated in closed basins and contain high percentages of dissolved salts. The largest of these are Lakes Rudolf (Turkana), Natron, and Eyasi.

Rainfall over much of southern Africa is small, and the majority of the rivers originating there have an intermittent flow. Some large perennial rivers (*e.g.,* the Okavango, the Zambezi, and the Orange) flow from areas of abundant rainfall into the drier zones.

Groundwater. The conditions under which groundwater is found and the quantity and quality of groundwater reserves are closely related to geologic structure. Large inland depressions in Africa's basement rock, having been filled with sedimentary layers of continental origin, sometimes form important groundwater reservoirs, notably those in the Taoudeni–Niger region, in the central Sahara between the Atlas and Ahaggar mountains; in the Libyan Desert; and in Chad, the Congo basin, the Karoo area of South Africa, and the Kalahari.

The East African plateaus usually contain little or no quantities of groundwater, and aquifers (geologic formations containing water)—generally of local importance—are found only in humid areas where the crystalline rock is weathered or fractured.

The chalky shales (rocks of laminated structure formed by the consolidation of clays) and dolomitic limestones (those containing calcium magnesium carbonate), which sporadically cover the basement rock, may contain important aquifers; those in Zambia and South Africa are major sources of water.

"Fossil" water layers

In the Sahara a rock stratum called the Continental Intercalary series, which dates from the early Cretaceous Period and which includes the Nubian sandstones of southern Egypt, is the most important water-bearing layer. It extends over very large areas and reaches a thickness of more than 3,000 feet; in Egypt and Algeria it is a major source of artesian water. In The Sudan it sometimes lies directly on the Precambrian bedrock and contains underground water layers of local importance. Overlaying the Continental Intercalary series, but generally separated from it by a thick marine deposit, is a younger Tertiary layer called the Continental Terminal, which is the second largest aquifer in this area. Both these layers contain "fossil" water—*i.e.,* water that entered the layers when rainfall in and around the Sahara was much more abundant than today. Near the surface, aquifers are found in such geologically recent deposits as alluvial deposits and sand dunes.

In the coastal areas of Senegal, Côte d'Ivoire, Ghana, Togo, Benin, Nigeria, Cameroon, Gabon, the Congo, Angola, Mozambique, the East African countries, and Madagascar, aquifers are found in sandstone, limestone, and sand and gravel sediments. Intensive exploitation, however, may result in saltwater intrusions.

The Jurassic limestones of the mountainous area of the Maghrib are much more abundant in water sources than are dolomitic limestones. Around the cape in South Africa, sandstones and limestones contain very little water.

Yields from aquifers with good porosity, such as coastal

sedimentary rocks or alluvial deposits, vary from a few cubic feet per hour in the fine-grained sands found in many parts of the continent to 35,000 cubic feet (990 cubic metres) per hour in the coarse gravels of the Nile delta. The capacity of wells in the Continental Terminal is generally somewhat lower, and those in the Continental Intercalary and the Karoo formations can also deliver moderate to high yields.

In North Africa limestones containing many cracks and fissures may yield thousands of cubic feet of water per hour, while in Zaire, Zambia, and South Africa large yields are drawn from dolomitic limestones.

The harder sandstones, sandy shale, and quartzites of Precambrian and Paleozoic age are not generally very porous, and water is obtained only from fractured or weathered deposits. West African, Angolan, and Tanzanian wells in these formations produce only a few cubic feet per hour. Crystalline and metamorphic rocks are almost impermeable except where fractured or weathered. Volcanic rock, especially the basalts, may yield up to 1,060 cubic feet per hour.

Most of the exploited groundwater is generally fit for consumption because the dissolved minerals in water from shallow wells, particularly in the sandy aquifers of West Africa, are quite low. Groundwater from deeper marine layers, however—such as occurs in parts of North Africa, Mozambique, Ethiopia, and South Africa—may have a high content of dissolved salts. In moist, tropical countries water from Precambrian rocks generally contains only small amounts of dissolved minerals, whereas in the volcanic areas of East Africa groundwater may have so high a content of fluorine as to make it unfit for human consumption. There, and elsewhere in Africa, hot (possibly medicinal) springs with high mineral contents occur.

Availability for human use. The pronounced seasonal character of rainfall and the fact that many rivers stop flowing during the dry season have necessitated the development of groundwater for human use, and the tapping of local aquifers has become important in many parts of the continent.

Irrigation

Large-scale irrigation has long been practiced mainly in North Africa, Egypt, The Sudan, South Africa, Mali, Zimbabwe, and Mozambique. Medium-scale irrigation projects have been operated in Madagascar, Senegal, Somalia, and Ethiopia. In Côte d'Ivoire, Burkina Faso, Kenya, Nigeria, Ghana, and Zambia, medium- to small-scale projects have been constructed.

More than 50 river and lake basins are shared by two or more countries, and the development of their resources requires the cooperation of the basin states and several intergovernmental agencies—such as the Organization for the Development of the Sénégal River, the Niger Basin Authority, and the Lake Chad Basin Commission.

Several large reservoirs were built in the late 20th century, such as the Aswan High Dam, Roseires, and Khashm al-Qirbah reservoirs in the Nile basin, Kainji on the Niger, Akosombo on the Volta, Kariba on the Zambezi, Cabora Bassa on the Zambezi in Mozambique, Kossou on the Bandama in Côte d'Ivoire, Kafue on the Kafue in Zambia, and Inga I and II on the Congo River in Zaire. At a number of man-made lakes, research centres have been set up to study resettlement problems, the full use of ecological conditions, and the control of health hazards that sometimes occur.

Biological resources. Africa's naturally occurring biological resources—its immensely varied vegetational cover, vast insect life, and diverse animal life—have been described above. When combined with cultivated crops and domestic animals, these resources represent the great bulk of the continent's economic wealth.

Botanical resources. The two most economically important types of vegetation are forests and grasslands. Among the forested areas, the tropical forests contain much of the valuable timber. The vast equatorial lowland rain forest has the greatest variety of tree species, but the species most commercially in demand are found in the zones of broad-leaved woodlands and tropical highland forests. The true value of the forested areas, however, cannot be ascertained exactly, as original forests are progressively being converted to farming areas, and few governments have undertaken comprehensive land-use surveys to determine their present extent.

A large proportion of the land surface of Africa bears vegetation in which grass is an essential feature. This abundance of grass has made possible the continent's enormous and varied populations of herbivorous mammals, both wild and domesticated. The tall and fibrous invasive grasses in forest environments and in large tracts of wooded grasslands are seldom very palatable to livestock; but in those parts of the continent where good forage grows naturally or has been introduced, livestock raising is of great economic importance.

The importance of the Albida acacia tree

The Albida acacia tree of the "farmed parkland" areas of West Africa is of special economic importance. Unlike almost all other dry woodland trees, whose leaf shedding normally occurs at the onset of the dry season, the Albida appears to have a period of partial dormancy during the rainy season and springs to life only at the beginning of the dry season. At such periods its foliage is abundant and—being a palatable leguminous species—is much prized as browse for sheep, goats, and cattle. The smaller leafy branches are frequently fed to stock. The tree flowers and produces fruits, which are harvested, dried, and fed as a protein concentrate to stock at the height of the dry season.

Animal resources. Although water buffalo, oxen, horses, mules, donkeys, and camels are used primarily as draft, pack, or riding animals in Africa, they also provide milk, meat, hides, or skins.

The water buffalo is an offshoot of the Asiatic buffalo (*Bubalus bubalis*); it arrived in Africa in relatively recent times and is now found almost exclusively in Egypt. The domesticated African water buffalo is used to cultivate irrigated land (mainly in the Nile delta) and to provide milk and meat. Because of its intractability and wild nature, however, the African elephant—unlike the Asian elephant—is not used for draft or haulage purposes.

Oxen are widely used in Africa for agricultural purposes, especially for plowing and cultivation; they are also trained to thresh grain, pump water, and act as pack animals. Bullock (castrated oxen) plowing is well developed in the countries of North Africa, in Ethiopia and The Sudan, and farther west in Chad, in northern Nigeria, and in the savanna climatic zone of West Africa. Plowing and cultivation by oxen is also well developed in areas of eastern and southern Africa free of the deadly tsetse fly. Females used for work may also be milked. Work oxen are often used for meat and to provide hides.

Horses and ponies are principally found in Morocco, Algeria, Tunisia, Chad, Ethiopia, Mali, Niger, Nigeria, Senegal, Burkina Faso, Egypt, South Africa, and Lesotho. Horses are used as riding or pack animals and in a number of areas are bred with donkeys to produce mules. Few are kept in areas where tsetse flies are present. Five main types of horses inhabit Africa: the Darfur pony, the Dongola horse, the Ethiopian-Galla horse, the Somalia pony, and the South African horse (including the Basuto pony). In North Africa, types also have evolved as a result of selection and crossing with exotic Arab, Barb (Barbary), and Thoroughbred horses. Arab and Thoroughbred influence may also be noted in southern Africa.

The distribution of the ass roughly corresponds to that of the horse, except that it also extends into the livestock areas of eastern and central Africa. Mules are found in Algeria, Ethiopia, Morocco, Somalia, South Africa, and Tunisia, where they provide farm draft power and are used as pack animals and for riding. The ability of mules to perform work in hot, dry climates is superior to that of most other farm animals.

Camels

The Arabian camel, or dromedary, is widely dispersed in the drier regions of northern and eastern Africa. Although used principally as a pack animal, it also is used for land cultivation, water pumping, and human transportation. The camel is essentially a bush browser and, if reasonably well fed and watered, may produce about 11 to 13 pounds (5 to 6 kilograms) of milk daily, in addition to that fed to the calf. The milk is prized by the camel herders and their families. Camel meat and camel hides find a ready market among Muslim communities.

Cattle provide hides, and sheep, goats, and pigs provide skins. Skins of the Maradi, Sokoto, and Kano red goats from Niger and Nigeria are greatly prized by the Morocco leather trade. In the areas north and south of the tropical zone, African sheep are covered with wool, but in the tropics they are hairy. In elevated areas, such as Ethiopia, where temperatures are modified by altitude, some sheep may be partially wooled, at least on the back and buttocks. The wooled sheep of North Africa are largely of the woolly Barbary type, which was originally introduced to Africa from the Middle East.

The great herds of wild African herbivores include the principal game animals. African antelope have been important throughout human history as sources of meat and such by-products as hides and bone; and they, along with other large mammals, became prized by trophy hunters. African elephants have been sought for centuries for the ivory in their tusks, but the severe reduction of their numbers by the late 20th century has led to a total ban on hunting them in most African countries.

The most economically useful fish found in the African waters include many species of freshwater fish. Important among the marine fish are flounder, halibut, sole, redfish, bass, conger, jack, mullet, herring, sardine, and anchovy. Crustaceans are important for local consumption and for export, as are oysters (for pearls), trochus shells, corals, and sponges. The most economically important aquatic mammal is the Southern, or Cape, fur seal.

AGRICULTURE

Agriculture is by far the single most important economic activity in Africa. It provides employment for about two-thirds of the continent's working population and for each country contributes an average of 30 to 60 percent of gross domestic product and about 30 percent of the value of exports. Nonetheless, arable land and land under permanent crops occupy only about 6 percent of Africa's total land area.

Land tenure and ownership

Except for countries with sizable populations of European descent—such as South Africa, Zimbabwe, and Kenya—agriculture has been largely confined to subsistence farming and has been considerably dependent on the inefficient system of shifting cultivation, in which land is temporarily cultivated with simple implements until its fertility decreases and then abandoned for a time to allow the soil to regenerate. In addition, over most of Africa arable land generally has been allocated through a complex system of communal tenure and ownership rather than through individually acquired title, and peasant farmers have had rights to use relatively small and scattered holdings. This system of land ownership has tended to keep the intensity of agricultural production low and has inhibited the rate at which capital has been mobilized for modernizing production. A number of countries have made efforts to raise productive levels by selecting better varieties of seeds and planting materials, using tractors and other mechanized equipment, or increasing the use of mineral fertilizers and insecticides. Such measures, however, have been relatively limited, and they have raised concerns about their part in accelerating soil erosion and desertification. In areas of cash-crop production, land has become private rather than community property, and cultivation is intensive.

The persistence of relatively low-productivity agricultural systems over large parts of the continent also stems from

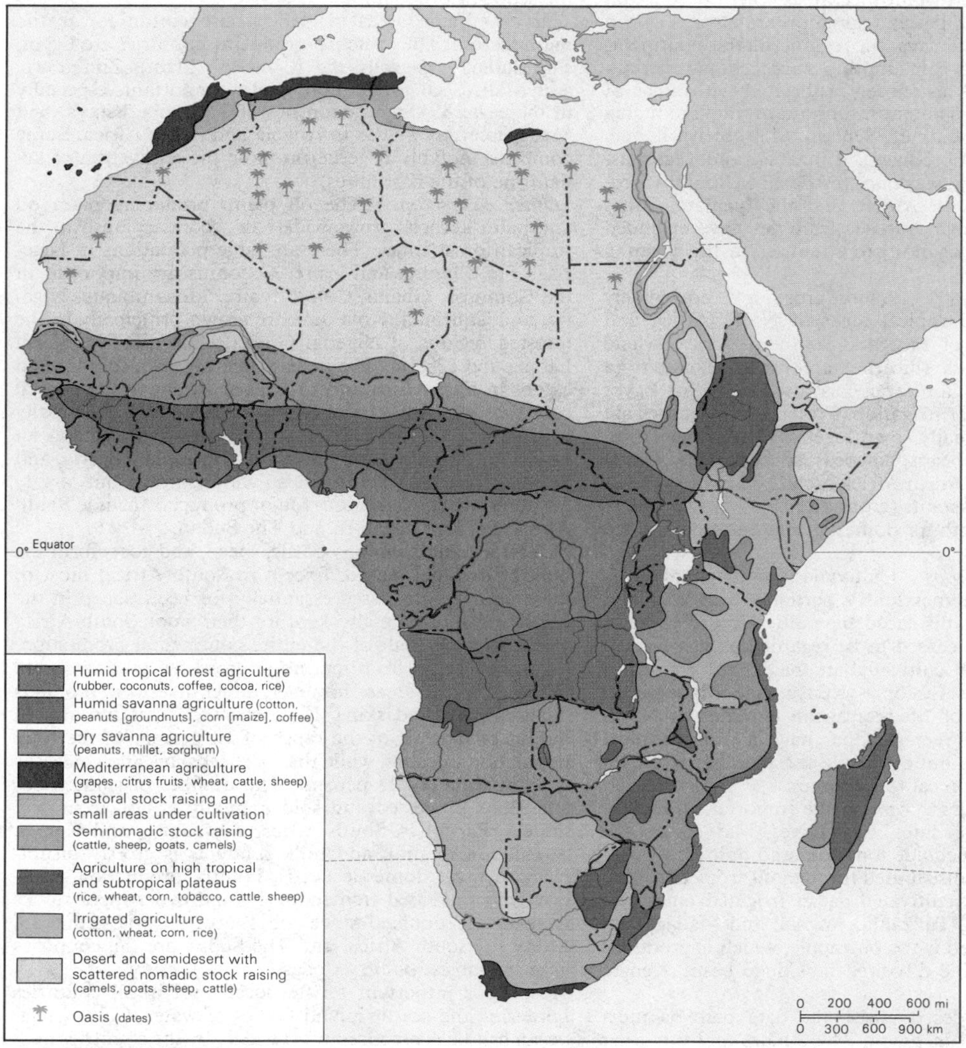

Agricultural regions of Africa.

a lack of integration between crop production and animal husbandry. Traditionally, sedentary cultivators like the Hausa in Nigeria and the Kikuyu in Kenya live apart from their nomadic herdsmen neighbours (the Fulani and Masai, respectively), with the result that over large areas of the continent farmers do not have access to animals for draft power or to manure for fertilizer. The incidence of such insect pests as the tsetse fly also discourages mixed farming in many areas.

The need to sharply increase food production to meet the demands of a rapidly growing population, however, has remained paramount. Intense research at such centres as the International Institute of Tropical Agriculture in Ibadan, Nigeria, has been directed at developing high-performing varieties of crops and designing more appropriate cropping systems. One product of such research is a genetically improved strain of corn (maize). Corn is not in itself a balanced food, being deficient in some amino acids; but a scientific breakthrough in the mid-1960s resulted in an increase of the amino acids lysine and tryptophan in certain new varieties of corn called opaque, or high-lysine, strains. These varieties initially produced low yields, were more prone to disease and vermin, and had a soft texture that was not desirable. Breeding programs, however, have since corrected these defects, and the new strains have begun to improve the nutritional value of diets in Africa (which consist mainly of corn preparations).

Principal crops. *Cereals and grains.* Africa produces all the principal grains—corn, wheat, and rice—in that order of importance. Corn has the widest distribution, being grown in virtually all ecological zones. Highest yields per acre are recorded in Egypt and on the Indian Ocean islands of Réunion and Mauritius, areas where production is under irrigation. Millet and sorghum are also produced but principally in the savanna regions of the continent. Rice production and consumption have become increasingly important and are closely associated with areas of rapid urbanization. The most important rice-producing countries are Egypt, Guinea, Senegal, Mali, Sierra Leone, Liberia, Côte d'Ivoire, Nigeria, Tanzania, and Madagascar. Wheat production was once restricted to South Africa, the countries of North Africa, and the highland zones of Ethiopia and Kenya, but new varieties have extended cultivation (under irrigation) to countries in the savanna region such as Nigeria.

Legumes and fodder. Fodder crops are not widely grown except in subtropical areas of North Africa and the highland zones of East and southern Africa, where pure stands of alfalfa (lucerne) are raised. Berseem (a type of clover used for forage) is also grown in Egypt and The Sudan under irrigation. Protein-rich legumes are produced widely, usually sown together with other crops. They include velvet beans, cowpeas, soybeans, and lablab (hyacinth beans). In North Africa broad beans and vetches are also produced. Peanuts (groundnuts) are grown widely in western Africa, both for domestic consumption and for export.

Cassava cultivation

Tubers and root crops. Cultivation of the hardy cassava has expanded tremendously, particularly in West and central Africa; it has displaced the cultivation of yams in many areas and has ceased to be regarded as just famine reserve. Potatoes are cultivated in the higher elevations of such countries as Ethiopia, Kenya, and Madagascar, as well as in areas of Mediterranean climates in North and South Africa. Sweet potatoes have a more tropical and subtropical distribution, while the plantain is grown extensively in the tropical forest zones.

Fruits and vegetables. Among the important fruits are bananas, pineapples, dates, figs, olives, and citrus; the principal vegetables include tomatoes and onions.

The banana is well distributed throughout tropical Africa, but it is intensively cultivated as an irrigated enterprise in Somalia, Uganda, Tanzania, Angola, and Madagascar. Also widely cultivated is the pineapple, which is produced as a cash crop in Côte d'Ivoire, the Congo basin, Kenya, and South Africa.

A typical tree of desert oases, the date palm is most frequently cultivated in Egypt, The Sudan, and the other countries of North Africa. The fig and olive are limited to North Africa, with about two-thirds of the olive production being processed into olive oil.

The principal orange-growing regions are the southern coast of South Africa and the Mediterranean coast of North Africa, as well as Ghana, Swaziland, Zimbabwe, Zaire, and Madagascar. The largest yields are produced in countries where basin irrigation is practiced. South Africa is the largest producer of grapefruit, followed by The Sudan.

Tomatoes and onions are grown widely, with the largest-producing areas bordering the Mediterranean. Large vegetables, such as cabbages and cauliflowers, are grown in the same region, from where it is possible to export some quantities to southern Europe. Important vegetables of tropical Africa include peppers, okras, eggplants, cucumbers, and watermelons.

Beverage crops. Tea, coffee, cocoa, and grapes are all grown in Africa. Kenya, Tanzania, Malaŵi, Zimbabwe, and Mozambique are the largest producers of tea, while Ethiopia, Uganda, Côte d'Ivoire, Kenya, Cameroon, Zaire, Tanzania, and Madagascar are the major producers of coffee. Cocoa is essentially a tropical forest crop. Its cultivation is concentrated in West Africa, with the principal producers being Côte d'Ivoire, Ghana, Nigeria, and Cameroon. All of these crops are largely grown for export. Sharp price fluctuations have caused African countries to form international cartels with other producing countries in an effort to regulate the market and negotiate better prices. Grapes are produced in northern Africa and in South Africa, essentially for the making of wine for European markets. The agricultural policy within the European Community (EC), however, has had a restraining effect on the scope of production.

Fibres. Large areas of Africa raise cotton for textile manufacture. The principal producing countries are Egypt, The Sudan (especially the Al-Jazīrah Plain), Zimbabwe, and Mali. Sisal production is also important, especially in the eastern African countries of Tanzania, Kenya, and Madagascar, as well as in Angola and South Africa. Some countries, notably Nigeria, promote the cultivation of kenaf (one of the bast fibres).

Oil and coconut palms

Other cash crops. The oil palm, producing palm oil and palm kernels, grows widely in secondary bush in the tropical forest zones. There are large plantations in Nigeria, Côte d'Ivoire, and Zaire. Coconuts are important in the Comoros, Ghana, Côte d'Ivoire, Mozambique, Nigeria, and Tanzania. Kola nuts are grown principally in the forested regions of Nigeria, Ghana, Côte d'Ivoire, Sierra Leone, and Liberia. The cashew tree is grown to a limited extent in East Africa and to a lesser extent in the coastal countries of West Africa. Rubber is produced principally in Nigeria and Liberia. Tobacco is widely cultivated as an export crop in Zimbabwe, Malaŵi, Tanzania, Nigeria, and South Africa. Sugarcane is also widely grown but largely for domestic consumption. Major producers include South Africa, Egypt, Mauritius, and The Sudan.

Livestock and fishing. Cattle, sheep, and goats form the bulk of livestock raised. Except in South Africa, most of these animals are raised essentially for beef. Sheep in the north and south are also kept for their wool; South Africa alone produces half of the entire continental production, much of the clip from merino or crossbred merino sheep. In the tropical areas, however, other livestock products include hides and skins. It is estimated that the annual output of hides is in the range of 10 percent of the total population of cattle, while that of sheepskins and goatskins is approximately 25 percent. The number of game hides and skins processed and sold annually is not accurately known. Except in South Africa, Zimbabwe, and Kenya, production of milk and milk products is grossly insufficient to meet domestic needs. Poultry production, however, has increased tremendously, and everywhere stocks have nearly doubled since the 1960s. Nigeria, Ethiopia, Morocco, South Africa, and The Sudan are the countries with the largest poultry stocks.

Fishing is important on the local level in all countries bordering the sea or inland bodies of water. Commercial ocean fishing is practiced most widely by the countries near the rich fishing grounds of the west coast—South Africa,

Namibia, Angola, Nigeria, Ghana, Senegal, and Morocco. Herring, sardines, and anchovies contribute most to the ocean catch, followed by jack, mullets, sauries, redfish, bass, and conger in tropical waters and cod, hake, haddock, tuna, bonitas, and bullfish in northern and southern waters. Inland countries with well-developed fisheries include Malaŵi, Uganda, Chad, Côte d'Ivoire, and Mali; tilapia and other cichlids constitute the largest catch in inland waters. Some countries, such as Nigeria, have developed both marine and freshwater fishing industries. A number of commissions have been established to monitor and control fishery development on the continent.

INDUSTRY

The countries of North Africa, unlike those of the rest of the continent, have wide-ranging and ancient traditions of manufacture. At the end of the 19th century, however, Africa as a whole was regarded solely as a potential source of raw materials or as a natural market for Europe. In the course of time, limited industrialization tended to converge around the relatively large expatriate settlements, where technical considerations operated in favour of the industrialization of some areas and transport costs constituted the dominant development factor in others. Though World War II led to acceleration in the process of industrial development, by 1950 the total factory output of manufacturing industries (excluding South Africa) still remained small.

Industrial development

After 1950 output rapidly increased. The substantial increase and its range were attributable to such factors as increased demand, the substitution of home-produced for imported goods, the encouragement of manufacturing by individual African administrations, and an influx of development capital and petrodollars. Major weaknesses nevertheless were evident, among them high capital costs; the political division of Africa into more than 50 countries, which inhibited mass production and mass marketing; and a scarcity of skilled personnel.

Despite its expansion since about 1950, the relative significance of manufacturing remains considerably smaller than in the more-advanced countries and smaller also than in continental Asia and in Latin America. Furthermore, the share of manufacturing in the gross domestic product varies widely in different African countries. At the lower end of the spectrum are countries such as Equatorial Guinea, Guinea, Zaire, and Niger; at the upper end of the spectrum are countries such as Egypt, Algeria, South Africa, and Zimbabwe. The total output of manufacturing in South Africa alone, however, is nearly 50 percent of the output in the remainder of the continent.

Manufacturing in Africa tends to concentrate on comparatively simple items and on those where some special advantage is available to the African producer, although the range of products has widened. Industrial production includes electric motors, transport equipment, and tractors, while airplanes are also assembled. The leading heavy industries are chemical and petroleum, coal, rubber, and metal manufacture. Most industrial plants, however, are of the relatively simple kind, being engaged in food processing or in manufacturing textiles, leather products, and cement or other building materials.

The mining industry is an increasingly significant source of national income, foreign exchange, and raw materials for the development of local processing industries. The industry is very unevenly distributed: more than half of mineral earnings came from North Africa alone, and nearly one-fourth from southern Africa.

Except in South Africa, iron and steel are used mostly for construction rather than for engineering. There are integrated iron and steel plants in Algeria, Tunisia, Egypt, Zimbabwe, and South Africa, while smaller production facilities—often based on the transformation of scrap—exist in several other countries.

Petroleum refining

Petroleum-refining capacity is based on domestic crude-oil output in a few cases and on imported crude oil in others. In some countries the development of the petrochemical industry followed the establishment of refineries. In 1965 there were only three major petrochemical complexes in Africa—in Zimbabwe, Egypt, and South Africa; by the late 20th century several more countries had large refinery capacities, including Algeria, Ghana, Kenya, Libya, Morocco, Nigeria, Senegal, The Sudan, and Tunisia.

Most of the textiles are processed in bleaching, dyeing, and printing establishments that form an integral part of composite spinning and weaving units. With the exception of Egypt, producers have concentrated on the home market and on the manufacture of cotton textiles. Although African countries export textiles, their imports are usually larger. Rayon–synthetic and woolen materials are, for the most part, imported. Ready-made clothing, both domestic and imported, has emerged as a major market factor.

Most African countries have cement plants, the leading producers being South Africa and Algeria. The transport costs of cement make its price variable. Prices are lowest on the North African coast, somewhat higher on the west and east coasts, and highest in the inland countries.

By far most of Africa's wood output is used for fuel. Sawmills, however, are distributed throughout the continent. Plants for the manufacture of plywood, particleboard, and fibreboard have a considerable amount of excess capacity. The pulp and paper industry is concentrated in North Africa and in southern Africa, although a number of small paper mills have been established in other parts of the continent. The main products of the paper industry proper comprise newsprint, printing and writing papers, paper and paperboard, and industrial paper. The bulk of the output of all paper products is directed to national markets.

POWER

A spectacular development in the use of electric energy has taken place in the second half of the 20th century, partly because of the growth of the petroleum industry and partly because of the establishment of large hydroelectric plants and some thermoelectric plants. The increased quantity and quality of electric energy have given rise to problems of transmission and distribution. Unlike thermoelectric plants, which may be sited where the consumer demand is greatest, sites of hydroelectric installations are not flexible, and the type of transmission lines in use has therefore changed. Although in the 1950s it was common practice to use lines with transmission voltages of less than 220 kilovolts, transmission lines were later built that could handle higher voltages. In Nigeria, for example, 330-kilovolt lines were strung; similar lines were used in Zimbabwe's system, which feeds Harare and Bulawayo, in Zimbabwe, as well as the Copperbelt, in Zambia. This same system is interconnected in the north with the large Shaba region hydroelectric power stations in Zaire. The construction of high-tension lines to supply power to the Shaba Copperbelt was completed in 1982. Much of the power for Egypt's population centres is supplied by lines from such hydroelectric power stations as that at the Aswan High Dam. Construction of 533-kilovolt lines to transmit power from the Cabora Bassa hydroelectric station in Mozambique to South Africa was completed in 1974. The possibility of supplying landlocked states with energy from the large hydroelectric plants in the coastal states is more likely to be considered in the future.

Steam power stations

A number of steam power stations are located in ports and cities near the coasts. The largest installations of this kind operate in Tunis, Tun.; Casablanca and Oujda, Mor.; Dakar, Senegal; Abidjan, Côte d'Ivoire; and Lagos, Nigeria. Steam power stations using coal are by far the most common, especially in South Africa.

Electric-energy consumption in large urban centres, especially when they are near coastal towns and mining areas where industrial activity has taken shape, has increased considerably. Although some countries have extended networks to the rural areas or have increased the numbers of isolated, low-powered stations and independent networks, progress in rural electrification has not been especially noteworthy.

TRADE

Internal trade. Intra-African trade records frequently understate the amount of trade—partly because of the lack of adequate statistics and partly because of the high rate of smuggling, which allows a substantial amount of traditional border trade to continue unrecorded. Apart from this, commerce between African states has been handicapped by a tendency for trade to remain concentrated within the common-currency areas and trade zones that developed among African countries during the colonial era, by the often inadequate means of transport and communication, by the lack of complementary agricultural or other products, and by the limited development of manufacturing industries.

Much of the intra-African trade consists of consumables—food, drinks, tobacco, sugar, cattle, and meat. The growth of industrialization in some countries, however, has been accompanied by an increase in the trade of durable and nondurable manufactured goods. There has also been a large amount of reexport trade between the coastal and inland states, especially in machinery, transport equipment, and spare parts.

Common-currency and trade zones that have evolved through the granting of preferences or the operation of common currencies inherited from former colonial powers include: the Customs and Economic Union of Central Africa (UDEAC), comprising Cameroon, Gabon, the Central African Republic, Equatorial Guinea, and the Congo, which since 1985 has become part of the larger Economic Community of Central African States (CEEAC) that also includes Burundi, Rwanda, São Tomé and Príncipe, and Zaire; the Economic Community of West African States (ECOWAS), consisting of Benin, Burkina Faso, Cape Verde, Côte d'Ivoire, The Gambia, Ghana, Guinea, Guinea-Bissau, Liberia, Mali, Mauritania, Niger, Nigeria, Senegal, Sierra Leone, and Togo; the Southern African Development Coordination Conference (SADCC), comprising Angola, Botswana, Lesotho, Malaŵi, Mozambique, Swaziland, Tanzania, Zambia, and Zimbabwe; and the Maghrib Permanent Consultative Committee (CPCM), grouping Algeria, Mauritania, Morocco, and Tunisia.

External trade. Since the outbreak of World War II there has been a considerable expansion in Africa's overall external trade. The growth compares favourably with that of the other developing regions, such as Latin America; the value of imports, however, has outweighed exports for some time, resulting in huge trade imbalances for most African countries. The large expansion in African exports is generally attributed to the increase in the demand for primary commodities during World War II and in the immediate postwar reconstruction period. Subsequently, the attainment of independence by a large number of African countries—especially in the early 1960s—followed by a bid for economic development, strengthened the export-expansion drive. Another reason for the rapid growth in African exports was the temporary increase in the price of primary commodities, although subsequently the general trend, except for petroleum, has been toward depressed commodity prices. The persistence of this situation has been part of the reason the economies of many African countries have become crippled by huge foreign debts.

Trade imbalances

Exports. An important factor that has influenced the growth of African exports was the discovery of petroleum in several countries, notably Libya, Algeria, Nigeria, Gabon, Angola, the Congo, and Cameroon, and the dramatic price increases brought about by the Organization of Petroleum Exporting Countries (OPEC) in the 1970s. Other factors include the discovery and the increased exploitation of minerals that are in high demand, such as diamonds—especially in Sierra Leone, the Congo, the Central African Republic, and Zaire—and the exploitation of other minerals, such as uranium ore.

Since achieving independence, many African countries have made attempts to diversify external trade relations. The record of achievement has been poor, however, because Africa's trade patterns have continued to reflect the influence of traditional links with the countries of western Europe. These links have been further consolidated through a series of agreements, collectively called the Lomé Conventions, that have guaranteed preferential access to the European Economic Community (EEC) for various export commodities from African states and that have provided European aid and investment funding. Nonetheless, a significant export trade has developed with the United States and Japan.

In most African states one or two primary commodities dominate the export trade—*e.g.,* petroleum and petroleum products in Libya, Nigeria, Algeria, Egypt, Gabon, the Congo, and Angola; iron ore in Mauritania and Liberia; copper in Zambia and Zaire; cotton in Chad; coffee in Burundi, Uganda, Rwanda, Ethiopia, Madagascar, Kenya, and Côte d'Ivoire; and sugar in Mauritius.

Imports. The tremendous increase of Africa's import trade has meant that the import bill of most African states has exceeded their export earnings; in consequence, many governments have established import restrictions or subsidized many of the required imports. The bulk of imports comes from western Europe, especially the EEC countries, with strong trade ties persisting along former colonial lines. There has, however, been a substantial increase in imports from the United States, Japan, and South Africa. Imports are needed primarily to develop manufacturing industries and are, therefore, confined for the most part to mineral fuels, industrial goods, machinery, transport equipment, and durable consumer goods.

TRANSPORTATION

Although there were highly developed transport networks in many parts of Africa in precolonial times, during the colonial era that followed, these networks were restructured to penetrate into the interior from the seaports and, in the main, to serve the commercial and administrative needs of the colonial powers. Their fragmentation, which led to interregional links being but thinly developed, resulted from the juxtaposition of varied and difficult terrains, the economic artificiality of certain national frontiers, the lack of a developed intra-African trade, and the strong orientation of commodity trade with the administering countries. All of this was further complicated by the existence of vast unpopulated areas lying between the main centres.

The fragmentation of African transport systems

The emergence in the 1960s of independent African governments who recognized the need to lift economies from their generally very low levels and, above all, to develop agriculture and embark on industrialization heralded improvements in economic planning, the development of transport networks, and the introduction of cheaper freight rates. But there remained a serious shortage of qualified African labour to plan and manage transport systems at the national or multinational level and, simultaneously, to keep up with the rapid development of transport technology outside Africa.

Animal transport. There is some evidence that before the arrival of the camel, which was introduced into Africa via Egypt at the time of the Arab conquest, bullocks were used either as pack animals or to draw carts from the northern countries across the Sahara to the gold-producing areas of the ancient Sudan. From the 16th century onward, the Portuguese developed transport inland from the coast at Mozambique, and, from the 17th century, first the Dutch and then British settlers from the Cape trekked northward and northeastward with their wagons. Except in such highland areas as Ethiopia, where pack animals were and still are used, the tsetse fly often prevented the use of animal transport. With the steady progress in the development of transport infrastructure in many African countries, the use of bullocks in southern Africa, donkeys in North and western Africa, horses in northern Nigeria, and camels in western and North Africa and the Horn of Africa has been reduced, but the extent of this reduction cannot be accurately gauged.

Motor transport. The arrival and rapid development of the internal-combustion engine in the 1920s transformed the collection and distribution of goods and personal travel. Roads were built, particularly in North and southern Africa, but also in parts of the west and east. World Bank loans since the 1950s, supplementing contributions to road and highway development from national budgets, have financed the building and improvement of road networks in many African countries.

Rail transport. The early railways were constructed partly to facilitate the administration of interior regions and to bring supplies from ports to central consumption or distribution points and partly—especially in the south—to enable valuable minerals or commodities to reach the coast for export. In Africa, as in Europe and North America, the major period of railway development extended from the end of the 19th century to the end of World War I. This expansion, however, was not coordinated: railways with different gauges of track were built and were operated with rolling stock of different braking and coupling systems. Thus, the colonizing powers left a difficult and costly legacy for independent African countries who wished to link themselves together. As with roads, rail networks have been improved considerably since the 1960s and, as a result, there has been a lowering of transport costs.

Suitability of air transport

Air transport. Air transport is well suited to Africa's geographic vastness, and it has become the primary means of international and sometimes of national travel in Africa. During the late 1940s and the '50s, as great advances were made in the extension and improvement of rail and road services, a new transport factor emerged in the introduction of internal and international scheduled air services. The rapid development of air transport increased the movement of goods and people and began to open up the hitherto largely closed interior of the continent. Transport became much quicker and usually cheaper. Since then, internal air services have steadily increased, and intercontinental air transport, especially of passengers, has developed greatly. The largest international airports are at Casablanca, Mor.; Las Palmas, Canary Islands; Cairo; Dakar, Senegal; Abidjan, Côte d'Ivoire; Lagos, Nigeria; Douala, Cameroon; Addis Ababa, Eth.; Nairobi, Kenya; and Johannesburg, S.Af.

Navigation. Historically, throughout the vast interior between the Sahara and the Zambezi River, people or goods were transported by canoe or boat on the great river systems of the Nile, Sénégal, Niger, Congo, Ubangi, and Zambezi rivers and on the few but very large lakes. Where conditions allowed, engine-powered craft later supplemented or displaced canoes, but further development of water transport has been slight. Also notable were the construction of lake ports and the installation of rail ferries across Lake Victoria.

Meanwhile, on the coasts, artificial harbours have been developed. New berths have been added to established port facilities, and a number of ports have been constructed. In planning new ports, the choice of site, probable costs, and the possibilities of using containers or other unitized loads have been taken into consideration.

(R.K.A.G./A.L.M.)

AFRICAN GEOGRAPHIC FEATURES OF SPECIAL INTEREST

Landforms

ATLAS MOUNTAINS

The Atlas Mountains form the geologic backbone of the countries of the Maghrib (the western region of the Arab world)—Morocco, Algeria, and Tunisia. They extend for more than 1,200 miles (2,000 kilometres), from the Moroccan port of Agadir in the southwest, to the Tunisian capital of Tunis in the northeast. Their thick rim rises to form a high sill separating the Mediterranean basin to the north from the Sahara to the south, thus constituting a barrier that hinders, without completely preventing, communication between the two regions. Across the mountains filter both air masses and human migrations. It is, however, only in the east–west direction that the Atlas Mountains facilitate movement. These are the conditions that create at the same time both the individuality and the homogeneity of the Atlas countries. Although the Saharan region is more likely to be described as the archetypal North African habitat, it is the well-watered mountains north of this vast desert that provide the foundation for the livelihood of most of the peoples of North Africa and a striking green or white background for many North African towns.

Physical features. *Physiography.* The Atlas mountain system takes the shape of an extended oblong, enclosing within its ranges a vast complex of plains and plateaus.

Massifs of the Tell Atlas

The northern section is formed by the Tell Atlas, which receives enough rainfall to bear fine forests. From west to east several massifs (mountainous masses) occur. The first of these is Er-Rif, which forms a half-moon-shaped arc in Morocco between Ceuta and Melilla; its crest line exceeds 5,000 feet (1,500 metres) above sea level at several points, reaching 8,058 feet at Mount Tidirhine. East of the gap formed by the Moulouya River the Algerian ranges begin, among which the rugged bastion of the Ouarsenis Massif (which reaches a height of 6,512 feet), the Great Kabylia, which reaches 7,572 feet at the peak of Lalla Khedidja, and the mountains of Kroumirie in Tunisia are all prominent.

The southern section, which is subject to desert influences, is appropriately called the Saharan Atlas. It includes in the centre a palisade formed by shorter ranges, such as the Ksour and Ouled-Naïl mountains, grouped into massifs between two mighty ranges—the Moroccan High Atlas to the west and the Aurès Mountains to the east. The High Atlas culminates in Mount Toubkal at 13,665 feet (4,165 metres), the highest point in the Atlas Mountains, which is surrounded by high snowcapped peaks; the Aurès Mountains are formed of long parallel folds, which reach a height of 7,638 feet at Mount Chelia.

The Tell Atlas and the Saharan Atlas merge in the west into the long folds of the Middle Atlas and in the east join together in the Tébessa and Medjerda mountains.

Geology. If the relief of the Atlas region is relatively simple, its geology is complex. In essence, the two Atlases comprise two different structural regions.

The Tell Atlas originally arose out of a basin filled with sediment, which was dominated to the north by a marginal rim, of which the massifs of Tizi Ouzou, Collo, and Edough are the remnants. Its elevation took place during a lengthy mountain-building process that was marked by upheavals in the Tertiary Period (which began 66.4 million years ago and ended 1.6 million years ago); over the cluster of folds that were uplifted from the rift valley were spread sheets of flysch (deposits of sandstones and clays), which were carried down from the north over the top of the marginal rim. Thus the Tell Atlas represents an example of a young folded mountain range still in the process of formation, as is shown by the earth tremors to which it is subject.

To the south the Saharan Atlas belongs to another structural grouping, that of the vast plateaus of the African continent, which form part of the ancient base rock largely covered by sediments deposited by shallow seas and by alluvial deposits. The Saharan Atlas is the result either of the mighty folding of the substructure that raised up fragments of the base rock—such as the horst (uplifted block of the Earth's crust), which constitutes the Moroccan High Atlas—or else of the crumpling into folds of the Earth's crust during the Jurassic Period (208 to 144 million years ago) and the Cretaceous Period (144 to 66.4 million years ago).

Drainage. The seasonal character of the rains, which fall in torrents, determines the characteristics of drainage in the Atlas: the runoff feeds streams that are of great erosive capacity and that have cut their way down through the thickness of accumulated layers of sediment to form deep narrow gorges difficult to cross. The pre-Roman fortress of Cirta (now called Constantine) in Algeria stands on a rock sculptured out by one such stream, the winding Rhumel River.

The great Maghribian wadis (French: *oueds;* channels of watercourses that are dry except during periods of rain) issue from the Atlas ranges. Among the more perennial rivers are the Moulouya, which rises from the Middle Atlas, and the Chelif, which rises from the Amour Moun- Wadis tains. Destructive of the soils of their headstreams, they deposit their loads of silt at the foot of the mountain ranges or else leave a long line of conical deposits locally known as *dirs* ("hills").

Soils. Good soil is sparse at higher altitudes in the Atlas region. Most often nothing is to be found but bare rock, debris, and fallen materials incessantly renewed by landslides. Two materials predominate—limestone, which forms ledges that are half-buried in rough debris, and marls (chalky clays) cut by erosion into a maze of ravines and crumbling gullies. The rarer sandstones favour forest growth. The best soils are the alluvia found on the terraced slopes and on the valley bottoms.

Climate. The Atlas Mountains are the meeting place of two different kinds of air masses—the humid and cold polar air masses that come from the north and the hot and dry tropical air masses that move up from the south. To the influences of altitude and latitude must be added that of aspect or exposure.

Rain is more plentiful in the Tell Atlas than in the Saharan Atlas, and more so to the northeast than to the southwest: the highest rainfall is recorded east of the Tell Atlas. ʿAyn ad-Darāhim in the Kroumirie mountains receives 60 inches (1,524 millimetres) a year; nowhere in the Anti-Atlas Mountains, south of the High Atlas, is the total more than 17 inches a year. In a single massif the slopes with a northern exposure receive more rainfall than those with a southern exposure.

With increased altitude the temperature drops rapidly; despite the proximity of the sea, the coastal massifs are cold regions. At 6,575 feet the summits of Mount Babor in the Little Kabylia region are covered with snow for four or five months, while the Moroccan High Atlas retains its snows until the height of summer. Winter in the Atlas is hard, imposing severe conditions upon the inhabitants.

Plant and animal life. Erosion of the soils in the Atlas region is aggravated by the sparseness of the vegetation covering the landscape; only about 39,000 square miles (101,000 square kilometres) of land are forested. On Er-Rif and the Kabylia and Kroumirie ranges, which experience some rainfall, moist forests of cork oaks cover an undergrowth of arbutus (cane apple) and heather shrub, and carpets of rockroses and lavender are found. When the total annual rainfall is less than about 30 inches and limestone is present, green oak and arborvitae (a species of pine tree) cover the soil, forming light, dry forests with a thin and bushy undergrowth. Stands of cedar predominate at higher altitudes. On the dry summits of the Saharan Atlas the vegetation is reduced to scattered stands of green oak and juniper trees.

The clearance of land for agriculture has reduced the forest cover in the Atlas ranges; animal life in the mountains is also in retreat. There remain only a few jackals, some tribes of monkeys (Barbary apes) at higher elevations, and occasional herds of wild boars in the oak woods.

The people. The mountains, with their inhospitable environment, have provided a refuge for the original inhabitants, who have fled successive invasions. Here the Berber people have survived, preserving their own languages, traditions, and beliefs, while at the same time accepting Islām to some extent. Village communities still live according to a code of customary law, known as *kanun,* which deals with all questions of property and persons. The family unit traces its descent from a single ancestor, preserving its cohesion by the sense of solidarity that unites its members; an injury to the honour of one affects the group as a whole and demands vengeance.

Villages high on mountains

The concern of Berber society to preserve its individuality is evident in the choice of habitat. Villages, which are fortified, are generally perched high up on mountain crests. Small in size, such villages are composed of the dwellings, a mosque, a threshing floor, and a place for the assembly of the elders (*jamāʿah,* or *djemaa*), which governs the affairs of each community. Families live, each unit apart, in separate rooms that form a square around a closed interior courtyard.

Despite the fundamental homogeneity of Berber society, there is a considerable diversity in different mountain localities. The Shluh of the High Atlas in Morocco inhabit the river valleys that cut down deeply into the massif. Their villages, with populations of several hundred inhabitants in each, are often located at an altitude of more than 6,500 feet. They consist of terraced houses, crowded one against the other, that are often dominated by a communal fortified threshing floor, or else are grouped around the threshing floor-plus-dwelling of the most powerful family. The mountain slopes in the vicinity are divided up for pasturage and cultivation. In some fields dry (*i.e.,* nonirrigated) farming is practiced for growing cereals. Land that is irrigated by diverting water from wadis yields two crops a year—cereals in winter and vegetables in summer. The Shluh use manure from their cattle as fertilizer. Oxen and

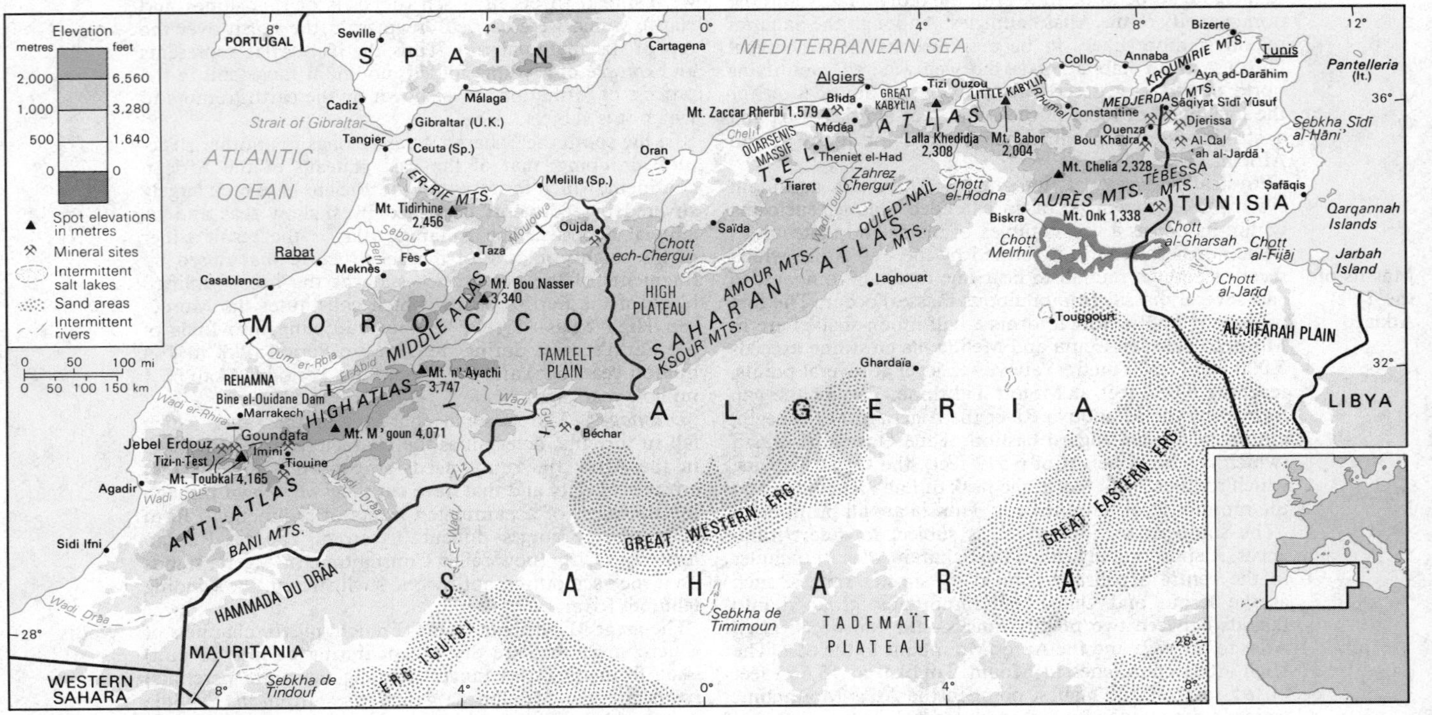

The Atlas Mountains.

Ouzirhlmt valley in the High Atlas, Morocco.
Victor Englebert—Photo Researchers

goats penned together on the ground floor of dwellings graze on stubble and on fallow lands around the villages. Sheepherders follow a pattern of transhumance (seasonal migration), grazing their sheep on low-lying land in winter and on the uplands in summer.

During the period of the French protectorate in Morocco (1912–56), profound changes occurred, transforming the way of life of the Middle Atlas populations. The dominant pattern of transhumance gave way to the practice of sedentary agriculture. The winter descent to the plains (*azarhar*) pasture has become practically a thing of the past, since the land is now under cultivation. The ascent to high pastures in summer, however, still continues. Stock raising in one location is increasingly practiced. Commercial forest products, mainly cork, also bring in an appreciable income.

Where the mountain and the plain meet, the *dir* lands offer rich potentialities, thanks to a light soil and abundant water. Grouped together in large villages, the *diara* populations (*i.e.,* populations who live on the slope of the *dirs*) constitute prosperous agricultural communities.

The Rif of Morocco and the Kabyle of Algeria resemble each other in many ways. Both Berber tribes, they inhabit the same types of wet-mountain slopes covered with oak forests, are similarly attached to a barren soil, and are both inclined to isolationism. In contrast to the way of life of the Berbers of the High and Middle Atlas, stock raising plays only a secondary role in their village life; they are not so much agriculturalists as arboriculturists, although they grow a little sorgo (a sorghum used for fodder), and women grow vegetables in small gardens adjoining their houses. It is, however, the fig and olive trees covering the mountain slopes they inhabit that constitute their principal resources. The Kabyle are also skilled craftsmen, working with wood, silver, and wool. In the past they were also peddlers, selling carpets and jewelry to the people of the plains.

The Aurès Mountains, standing alone in northeastern Algeria, are perhaps the least developed mountain region in the Maghrib. The Shawia (Chaouïa) populations who inhabit them follow a seminomadic style of life, which is partly agricultural and partly pastoral. They live in terraced stone villages in which the houses are built in tiers, one above the other, the whole being dominated by a *guelaa,* or fortified granary. When winter comes, the inhabitants of the high valleys lead their flocks to the lowlands surrounding the massif, where they pitch tents or live in caves. Returning to the uplands in summer, they irrigate the land to grow sorghum and vegetables and maintain apricot and apple orchards, while shepherds take the sheep to pastures on the hilltops.

Despite precarious living conditions, the Atlas Mountains are densely populated—overpopulated even, in certain localities. In the area around Tizi Ouzou in the Great Kabylia, for example, densities reach about 700 persons per square mile (270 per square kilometre). Emigration is a necessity: the mountain regions have become a human reservoir upon which the Maghribian countries draw to obtain the labour force needed for development. Commercial agriculture attracts large numbers of farm workers to the plains either on a seasonal or a permanent basis. The Mitidja Plain of Algeria, for example, has been settled by the Kabyle. In Morocco, the Shluh of the High Atlas have provided labour for the phosphate mines.

Population density

Urban growth has served to increase the volume of the migratory stream that flows down from the mountains; the cities of Algiers, Constantine, Oran, and Casablanca are to a great extent peopled by mountain folk. The shantytowns of Algiers contain numerous Kabyle, and those of Casablanca many Shluh. Many of these urban immigrants find employment as labourers, while others become shopkeepers.

In Algeria the insecurity that became general in most mountain districts during the nationalist uprising that preceded independence led to the departure of large numbers of people. The exodus from the mountains continued after independence, with many mountain dwellers moving into the plains to occupy houses abandoned by departing Europeans. Rural and urban activities, however, still did not provide employment for all, for many emigrants, mostly from Algeria, sought work in France. To a considerable extent the mountain populations subsist on money sent back by these migratory workers.

The economy. *Resources.* Despite their inhospitability and relative inaccessibility, the Atlas Mountains have played an important part in the modern development of the Maghribian countries. The mountain massifs constitute catchment areas with considerable potential. The construction of reservoir dams not only has permitted the storage of enormous amounts of water for irrigating the plains but has also made it possible to generate hydroelectric energy. In Morocco efforts have been made in the last half of the 20th century to exploit the potential of the mountain wadis. In addition to the dams across the Wadi el-Abid and the Wadi el-Rhira on the northern slope of the High Atlas, dams on the southern face have been constructed across the Drâa and Ziz watercourses. In Algeria the Kabylia region has been developed with hydroelectric stations on the Agrioun and Djendjene wadis.

Minerals

The geologic formations of the Atlas are rich in minerals. The Moroccan High Atlas in particular contains important deposits. Among these the most important economically is phosphate, mined principally in the Khouribga area. Other major deposits include lead and zinc from the Middle Atlas and from the Oujda area and copper, silver, and manganese; the output of manganese mining at Imini and Tiounine is transported to Marrakech by overhead cable cars. Anthracite coal is also mined at Oujda. In Algeria iron ore is extracted from the Seba Chioukh Mountains, from Mount Zaccar Rherbi, and from the areas near Ouenza and Bou Khadra, while phosphate is mined at Mount Onk and El Kouif. Lead and zinc have also become important. In Tunisia the High Tell mountains produce phosphate at Al-Qalʿah al-Jardāʾ, iron ore from Mount Djerissa, and lead from Sāqiyat Sīdī Yūsuf. These raw materials are often processed in the coastal towns. The iron ore from Ouenza, for example, supplies the iron-smelting industry of Annaba.

Among forest products, cork is more important than timber; production is centred in the Kabylie region of Algeria, notably on the Collo Massif.

The tourist industry is also being developed, particularly in the High Atlas region of Morocco. In the Middle Atlas, long snow-covered slopes suitable for winter sports are located in the vicinity of major towns. In Algeria the establishment of industry in mountain regions is being encouraged, so that employment for the mountain dwellers can be available. At Constantine, the principal city of the mountain regions, as well as at other larger cities, a number of industries have been established. Despite these efforts, however, contrasts between the life-styles of the mountains and those of the plains and cities of the Maghrib have by no means diminished, nor are they soon likely to do so.

Transportation. The Atlas Mountains have their own internal system of communications. Villages are linked by paths that, avoiding the valley bottoms, follow the crest lines of the hills. Travel is on foot or by mule or local bus.

The massifs constitute an obstacle to traffic; roads and railroads traverse them by means of tunnels and viaducts, which are costly to build. Traffic between Algiers and Constantine, for example, is obliged to cross the Kabylia Massif; the route runs through the Isser River gorges and crosses the mountains at the Portes de Fer Pass. The Chiffa Gorge cuts across the route between Blida and Médéa.

The relative impenetrability of the mountains explains why they have been avoided by the main transportation routes and why, consequently, they constitute strongholds of ancient traditionalism. Obstacles to communication should not, however, be exaggerated; the mountains also offer many natural connecting links, or passes, that facilitate movement. Such topographical accidents localize communication routes: between the desert and the plains, the nomads use synclinal corridors (*i.e.,* corridors formed by folds in the rocks in which the strata dip inward from both sides toward the centre) that separate the ridges of the Saharan Atlas range. The Biskra Gap, situated between the Ouled-Naïl and Aurès ranges, provides a natural conduit for traffic between Constantine on the Rhumel River and Touggourt in the Sahara. Between Algeria and Morocco both the road and the railroad pass through the Atlas along the Taza Pass, which breaks the continuity of the mountain system between Er-Rif and the Middle Atlas. Passes are natural routes across the mountain barriers and thus constitute strategic points. The focal point of communication in the Great Kabylia, for example, is Tizi Ouzou, at the Genêt Pass, which has become in effect the capital of the massif. To surmount the obstacle formed by the Ouarsenis Massif, situated between Chelif Plain and the Sersou Plateau, it is necessary to pass by way of Theniet al-Haad. The passes of the Moroccan High Atlas have also played a decisive role in the history of relations between Morocco and the vast region known as the western Sudan to the south; the ancient caravan route from Marrakech to the Drâa valley used the n'Test Pass, which thus became of great commercial importance.

The mountain passes

Study and exploration. Attempts by European powers to gain control of northwestern Africa began in the 15th century. Portuguese activity was confined to the Strait of Gibraltar and the Atlantic coast of Morocco, where several forts were established. Spanish activity, initiated at the beginning of the 16th century, included the capture of Mediterranean ports and a slow penetration first of the Rif region and after 1860 into other parts of Morocco. French influence was more extensive. Beginning in 1830 with the capture of Algiers, French control expanded eventually to encompass all but the Rifian part of the Atlas region, including a protectorate over most of Morocco (1912–56). Road building to control the mountains and to facilitate the movement of peoples and goods enhanced communication in what had been an isolated and fragmented region, often weakly controlled by government authorities based in lowland areas. No longer the focus of European exploration or exploitation, the Atlas Mountains are a conspicuous feature of the independent states of Morocco, Algeria, and Tunisia. (H.Is./M.W.M.)

EAST AFRICAN MOUNTAINS

The East African mountains of Kenya, Tanzania, Uganda, Zaire, Rwanda, and Burundi are intimately related to the East African Rift System, the fractures of which extend discontinuously between the Zambezi River valley and the Red Sea and are flanked in many areas by highlands. Of the major mountains, all but one—the Ruwenzori (Rwenzori) Range—are of volcanic origin. Rising magnificently from the surrounding plateaus to altitudes of over 16,000 feet (4,900 metres), the highest peaks, despite their proximity to the equator, are ice-capped.

Mount Kenya, the Aberdare Range, and the Mau Escarpment are located wholly within Kenya to the north of Nairobi; Mount Elgon lies astride the Uganda-Kenya border; Kilimanjaro extends along Tanzania's northern boundary with Kenya; and Mount Meru is in northern Tanzania. The Ruwenzori Range stretches between Lakes Edward and Albert on the Uganda-Zaire border, and, farther south, the Virunga Mountains extend along the contiguous borders of Uganda, Rwanda, and Zaire.

Physical features. *Physiography.* The Aberdare Range, of which the highest peak is Mount Lesatima (Satima), reaching a height of 13,120 feet, and the Mau Escarpment rise steeply from the eastern portion of the Eastern (Great) Rift Valley. To the west, beyond the Uasin Gishu Plateau, Mount Elgon emerges gently from a level of about 6,200 feet; but the spectacular cliffs of its western face dominate the lower plains of eastern Uganda, which lie at about 3,600 feet. The rim of Elgon's caldera is approximately five miles (eight kilometres) in diameter and contains several peaks, of which Wagagai, at 14,140 feet, is the highest.

Principal mountain features

The Nyeri-Nanyuki corridor separates the Aberdare Range from Mount Kenya. The second highest mountain in Africa, Mount Kenya has a girth of about 95 miles at 8,000 feet, from which it rises boldly to its restricted summit zone. The craggy twin peaks of Batian (17,057 feet) and Nelion (17,022 feet) are closely followed in height by Lenana (16,355 feet).

Set amid low plateaus, Kilimanjaro is the highest mountain in Africa, rising to 19,340 feet (5,895 metres) at Uhuru peak on the Kibo cone. The generally smooth outlines of the cratered dome of Kibo are in marked contrast with the jagged form of Mawensi, or Mawenzi (17,564 feet); the two summits are connected by a saddle that lies at about 14,500 feet. Mount Meru, about 40 miles southwest of Kilimanjaro, attains an altitude of 14,978 feet.

The Ruwenzori Range runs parallel to the Western Rift Valley, to which it drops steeply. The fall to the uplands of western Uganda, however, is more gradual. At its base the range is some 80 miles long, and its greatest width is about 30 miles. The summit zone contains six distinct mountain massifs, which are separated by well-defined passes and deep river valleys. Mounts Baker and Gessi lie entirely within Uganda, while Mounts Stanley, Speke, Emin, and Luigi di Savoia form part of the Uganda-Zaire

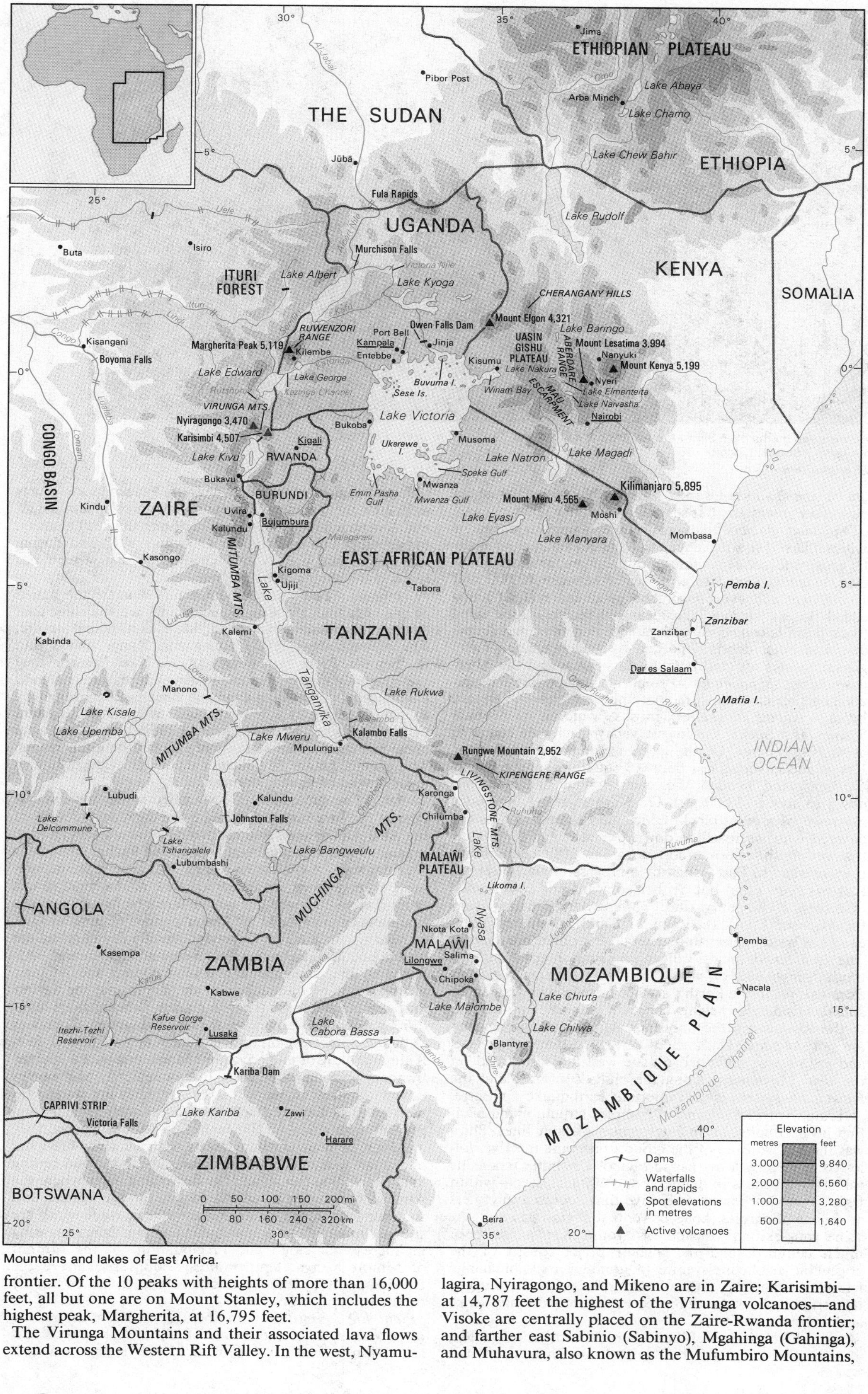

Mountains and lakes of East Africa.

frontier. Of the 10 peaks with heights of more than 16,000 feet, all but one are on Mount Stanley, which includes the highest peak, Margherita, at 16,795 feet.

The Virunga Mountains and their associated lava flows extend across the Western Rift Valley. In the west, Nyamulagira, Nyiragongo, and Mikeno are in Zaire; Karisimbi—at 14,787 feet the highest of the Virunga volcanoes—and Visoke are centrally placed on the Zaire-Rwanda frontier; and farther east Sabinio (Sabinyo), Mgahinga (Gahinga), and Muhavura, also known as the Mufumbiro Mountains,

Acacia trees on the plain below the summits of Kilimanjaro, Tanz. Uhuru peak is at right, Mawensi (Mawenzi) at left.

J.S. Wightman—Ardea London

are on the Rwanda-Uganda frontier. Not all of the cones culminate in craters, but several have crater lakes.

Glaciers

The relict glaciers that occur in the summit zones of Kilimanjaro, Mount Kenya, and the Ruwenzori have little erosive force. Their more powerful predecessors, however, extended down to altitudes of between 12,000 and 10,000 feet and even lower and produced arêtes (sharp-edged ridges), cirques (glacial amphitheatres), rock tarns (rock basin lakes), U-shaped valleys, and moraines (boulders and other debris deposited by glacial action). Early glaciation also affected both Mount Elgon and the Aberdare Range. More than 30 small glaciers on the Ruwenzori together cover a surface of approximately 1.5 square miles (4 square kilometres), most of which is on Mounts Stanley and Speke; the lowest valley glacier descends to about 14,000 feet. Of the glaciers remaining on Mount Kenya and covering less than 0.3 square mile, the largest are Lewis and Tyndall; the lowest tongue of ice reaches down to about 15,000 feet. On Kilimanjaro, Kibo crater is strewn with giant blocks of ice, and the outer rims are covered with ice reaching down to about 16,000 feet on the wet southwestern moorlands. The 20th century has been marked in East Africa by a process of glacial retreat that has been rapid but neither constant nor continuous.

Geology. The peneplain of eastern Africa, dating from the Miocene Epoch (between 23.7 and 5.3 million years ago), has been subject to a general elevational movement. The shoulders of the rift valleys have risen intermittently to produce highlands on which lavas that have been ejected from fissures in the Earth's surface have in some instances added considerable height. The most dramatic uplift is that of the Ruwenzori, the only East African mountains that are not volcanic. The ancient plateau surface of gneisses and schists was upfaulted on the west and upwarped on the east. Movements along the faults continue, and the Ruwenzori system is an important earthquake epicentre.

Kilimanjaro is a volcano of complex structure and alkaline lavas situated at an intersection of fault lines. Shira was the first volcano of the group to become inactive, followed in turn by Mawensi and Kibo. The latter retains its caldera—1.5 miles in diameter and 600 feet deep—within which there are found successive inner cones and craters as well as fumaroles (holes or vents that emit gases).

The long-extinct volcano of Mount Kenya has been much denuded, and the highest peaks consist of the crystalline nepheline-syenite (a granular rock of alkalic feldspar, nepheline, and other minerals), which plugged the former vent. Around this core are gently dipping lavas, agglomerates, and tuffs.

Mount Elgon is part of the Eastern Volcanics in Uganda, which consist of soda-rich lavas and associated fragmental tuffs and agglomerates. The Western Volcanics are represented by the Virunga Mountains, of which Nyamulagira and Nyiragongo have been active during the 20th century. Major eruptions occurred in 1938 and 1948 and during the 1970s, and on several occasions a lava stream has reached the shores of Lake Kivu.

Drainage. The Virunga Mountains separate the basins of the Nile and the Congo rivers and are the only East African mountains to form a divide of continental stature. The entire system of the Ruwenzori Range drains into the Semliki River, a tributary of the Nile. Because they are relatively young, the mountain systems present good examples of consequent drainage (that is, determined by the initial slope of the land) such as the radial system of Mount Elgon, in which streams radiate from a central area, and the parallel streams of the Aberdare dip slopes. The porous nature of volcanic materials often results in areas devoid of surface drainage.

Soils. The succession of soils is from the raw mineral type of the summit area, through the dark peaty loams of the Afro-Alpine zone and the strong brown loams of high organic content in the forest belt, to the ferruginous (iron-bearing) soils of the lower slopes. Volcanic material presents a range from the unaltered rock of the most recent eruptions to the well-developed fertile soils on surfaces that have been exposed for longer periods of time.

Climate. In a region of predominantly dry climate, the mountains are conspicuous as areas of high rainfall. Affected by the convergence of Indian Ocean and Atlantic airstreams, the Ruwenzori as a whole comprise the wettest and the cloudiest of the mountains, where moist conditions penetrate up to the peaks and about 80 inches (2,000 millimetres) of rain annually fall at 15,000 feet. Kilimanjaro, Mount Kenya, and Mount Elgon are affected by their position in relation to southeasterly and northeasterly airstreams. Below 10,000 feet they are wettest on their southeastern and southern sides, with annual total precipitation rising to 100 inches on Mount Kenya; they are driest on their northern flanks, with less than 40 inches of rainfall yearly. Rainfall decreases above a cloud ceiling at about 10,000 feet, especially on Kilimanjaro, where the Afro-Alpine zone is a veritable desert. On the western and southwestern slopes the diverted southeast trade winds are sucked up each of the mountains as westerlies, creating an increase of cloud and precipitation. At the summit of Mount Kenya, temperatures seldom rise above the freezing point, and above 14,500 feet precipitation mainly occurs in the form of snow.

The plant life of Mount Kenya

Plant life. Vegetation in the East African mountains often occurs as a succession of altitudinal zones. This succession is well developed on Mount Kenya, where it emerges from the surrounding savanna (grassland with scattered bushes or trees) and begins on the lower slopes with a crescent of cultivated land. The montane forest extends upward from a lower limit of about 6,000 feet to 10,000 feet and includes giant trees, such as camphor and various figs, cedar, yellowwood, and the East African olive. From about 8,000 feet, the forest consists of montane bamboo, and at its upper limit parkland and low thicket fringe the succeeding zone of giant heather. At 11,000 to 12,000 feet, the heather zone gives way to the Afro-Alpine zone in which tree groundsel and the giant lobelia rise out of a ground vegetation of tussocky grassland and everlastings (composite plants, the flowers of which can be dried without loss of colour or form). Mosses and lichens survive up to about 15,000 feet, but bare rock and ice are exposed above that height.

The montane forest of Kilimanjaro is drier than that of Mount Kenya. Bamboo is virtually absent, although it is abundant on neighbouring Mount Meru, and there is no parkland zone. The heather zone is strongly represented, whereas the Alpine semidesert is poor in flowering plants. Mount Elgon reaches into the Afro-Alpine zone, as do the summits of the Aberdare Range. On the northwest of the Ruwenzori, the lower slopes touch upon the equatorial forest, and the vegetation is moister and more luxuriant than that of the eastern mountains. Above the bamboo forest and the wooded parkland, the Virunga Mountains extend into the heather zone and, in the three highest volcanoes, into the Afro-Alpine zone.

The Afro-Alpine vegetation of the East African mountains is unique. With the increase of temperatures in post-Pleistocene times (since about 10,000 years ago), the cold-loving plants retreated to the mountains, where they have been preserved and somewhat transformed. Despite the enormous distances that separate the mountains, plants in the respective Afro-Alpine zones are closely comparable. There are lobelia and *Alchemilla* (lady's mantle) species common to all the mountains, although the tree groundsel species are limited within neighbouring mountains. The phenomenon of giantism is common, while dwarfism occurs at the highest altitudes.

Animal life. Elephants, rhinoceroses, buffalo, antelope, hyrax, bush pigs, and monkeys, including the black-and-white colobus, are among the main inhabitants of the montane forest. The bongo (forest antelope) and the giant forest hog have not been observed on Kilimanjaro, perhaps because of its lack of bamboo forest and its isolation from the mountains to the north. Mountain gorillas and golden monkeys live in the Virunga Range, and chimpanzees in the Ruwenzori. Trout have been introduced into the streams of the more accessible mountains.

Mammals of the upper forests, including the leopard and antelope such as the duiker and the eland, penetrate into the moorland and Afro-Alpine zones, where the hyrax and the groove-toothed rat are the most obvious inhabitants. Birds include the lammergeier (one of the largest birds of prey, resembling the eagle and vulture), the mountain chat (a songbird), and the scarlet-tufted malachite sunbird (a small, brilliantly coloured songbird). Animal life, like the vegetation, shows resemblances that suggest a retreat of its distribution from the surrounding plateaus to the montane islands of refuge.

The people. Population is confined to the lower slopes, with the upper limit of settlement at about 7,000 feet. Bananas and millet are common subsistence crops, and coffee is an important cash crop. On the southern and eastern slopes of Kilimanjaro the Chaga (Chagga) have long used an effective system of irrigation based on the ridge-and-valley relief of the mountain. High population densities among the Chaga are matched by those among the Kikuyu and related groups on the slopes of the Aberdare Range and around the southern and eastern margins of Mount Kenya. The Gisu have densely settled the western slopes of Mount Elgon below the forest zone.

Population densities

Population density is high on either side of the northern nose of the Ruwenzori; the Konjo hillmen live mainly on the eastern flank of the range. The Pygmy Twa occupy the forests of the Virunga Mountains, the lower slopes of which are cultivated by the far more numerous Hutu.

The economy. *Mining, forestry, and agriculture.* Copper ore was formerly mined at Kilembe, Uganda, on the southeastern flank of the Ruwenzori. Other mineral resources include tin deposits also southeast of the Ruwenzori, tungsten deposits in the Virunga Mountains in Uganda, and diatomite in the Aberdare Range.

The closed forests are mainly under forest reserve and are classed as presently productive of timber. The most important output of sawn wood has come from the more accessible mountains of Kenya and Tanzania, where cedar, podo (or yellowwood), and camphorwood are among the principal timbers; the quantities produced, however, are small. Land cleared for cultivation in the lower part of the forests forms rich agricultural zones in which a considerable variety of crops—including coffee, tea, wheat, pyrethrum (a chrysanthemum used in the production of insecticides), bananas, millet, root crops, and vegetables—may be grown. Cattle are raised on the northern slopes of Mounts Kenya and Elgon and on Kilimanjaro. The narrow agricultural belt could be widened, and there has been a tendency for the extension of cultivation into lower altitudes by the use of irrigation.

Tourism. The mountains are an important tourist attraction. Kilimanjaro National Park covers the mountain from 6,000 feet to the summit, and other parks include Mount Kenya above 10,200 feet, the moorland zone of the Aberdares, and a sector of the Kenya portion of Mount Elgon. In the Uganda section of the Virunga Mountains, the Kigezi Gorilla Game Reserve is situated on the northern slopes of Mounts Muhavura and Mgahinga (Gahinga). In the Rwanda and Zaire portions of the Virunga Mountains, gorillas are protected, respectively, in the Volcanoes National Park and the Virunga National Park.

Transportation. The Ruwenzori form a barrier to east-west transport, and road connections between Uganda and Zaire pass south of the range. The Mau Escarpment and the Aberdare Range deflect the main roads to their northern and southern flanks, but each is crossed by a secondary road. The Nyeri col between the Aberdares and Mount Kenya is used as a gateway to the north. There are circular routes around Mounts Kenya and Elgon, and the bases of all the mountains are reasonably accessible.

Study and exploration. In 1848 the snow-covered summit of Kilimanjaro was observed by the German missionary Johannes Rebmann, and the following year Johann L. Krapf obtained a view of the snows of Mount Kenya. In 1888 the Welsh explorer Henry Morton Stanley glimpsed the Ruwenzori through a break in their cloud cover and equated them with the Mountains of the Moon of Ptolemy.

A number of expeditions on Kilimanjaro preceded that of 1889, in which the German geographer Hans Meyer conquered the summit of Kibo. Partial ascents of Mount Kenya were made before the British geographer Halford John Mackinder reached the summit of Batian in 1899. The Ruwenzori awaited the expedition of Luigi, Duke d'Abruzzi, in 1906 for the conquest of their major peaks, and in 1907–08 Adolf Friedrich, Duke of Mecklenburg, made a comprehensive survey of the Virunga Mountains. The southern side of Elgon was visited in 1883 and the caldera was traversed in 1890; in 1911 Wagagai was climbed. In 1932 a Belgian scientific mission explored the western slopes of the Ruwenzori, climbing several peaks.

Since 1931, aerial photography has assisted in the production of excellent maps of the major mountains and their glaciers. Under the stimulus of the International Geophysical Year of 1957–58, glaciological expeditions were mounted on the Ruwenzori, Mount Kenya, and Kilimanjaro.

Origin of mountain names

Kilimanjaro, Kenya, and Ruwenzori are names of African origin; the first two are of somewhat uncertain meaning, and Ruwenzori may come from Nyoro words meaning "place of rain." Elgonyi was the Masai name for Elgon, but the Gisu name Masaba remains current in the Bantu languages. The names Kibo and Mawensi are of African derivation, and the highest peaks of Mount Kenya were named for Masai chiefs. With one exception, Ensonga, the major mountains and peaks of the Ruwenzori have European names, while Virunga nomenclature is African.

(S.J.K.B.)

ITURI FOREST

The Ituri Forest is an area of dense tropical rain forest that lies on the northeastern lip of the Congo River basin in the central African nation of Zaire. Situated between 0° and 3° N latitude and 27° and 30° E longitude, the precise geographic limits of the Ituri are poorly defined, especially along its southern and western extensions. The Ituri is bounded to the north and northeast by savanna and in the east by the fertile highlands of the Western Rift Valley, while to the south and west it is contiguous with the lowland rain forest, where its rivers drain into the Congo (Zaire) River. The total area of the Ituri Forest is approximately 24,300 square miles (62,900 square kilometres). The forest, which is inhabited by both Bantu-speaking and Pygmy peoples, owes its name to the Ituri River, which flows east-west across the forest into the Aruwimi River and thence to the Congo.

For map coverage of the Ituri Forest, see below *Congo River*.

Physical features. *Physiography.* The magnificence of the tropical rain forest of the Ituri cannot help but inspire the modern-day observer with the same poetic enthusiasm displayed by the famous Welsh explorer Henry Morton Stanley when he described his crossing of the area in 1887–88. The trees of the forest range in size from small saplings just inches in diameter to gigantic hardwoods reaching to heights of 170 feet (52 metres). Like the pillars of a Gothic cathedral, these giant trees are buttressed; roots run down their sides and extend great distances across the forest floor, making the ground a labyrinth of roots that anchor the trees and grab scarce nutrients from the shallow forest soil. In places where the high canopy is nearly continuous, only small, elusive patches of sunlight reach the forest floor. The lack of light at lower levels is accentuated by the darkness of the foliage of the few shrubs and small trees that can grow under such shaded conditions. Where gaps occur in the upper canopy, herbaceous plants with long leaves resembling those of the banana plant take advantage of the available light and grow in dense stands. In many places the forest has been disturbed, either by human activity or by natural treefalls that cut large swathes through the canopy and open up the forest to the strong equatorial sun. There, the vegetation near the ground is a dense tangle of nettles, creepers, and competing species of fast-growing, short-lived trees, which make walking difficult if not impossible. Everywhere on the ground there is a profusion of fallen nuts and fruits, some as large as basketballs and many partially eaten by monkeys, antelope (duikers), and rodents. During certain seasons the air is filled with the nectar of numerous species of flower, including many epiphytes, which cling to the surface of other plants and draw their sustenance from the air. Always there is the sound of myriad insects. Cicadas perch on tree trunks and emit an irritating buzz that seems designed to drive any intruder to madness. Army ants advance in columns, audibly cracking the bodies of their insect prey. Seemingly endless lines of migrating butterflies flutter through the understory and sometimes congregate in colourful displays along streambeds. The buzzing of bees, busily plying the treetops in search of sweet nourishing nectar, is ever present. While magnificent, the forest with its constant high humidity and dark interior may seem oppressive to some. Certainly Joseph Conrad thought so when he referred to the forest as the "heart of darkness." But the overwhelming impression for even the most squeamish visitor is not of darkness, not of oppressive gloom, but of life in its most vibrant and exciting form.

Vegetation in disturbed areas

The Ituri Forest varies in altitude between 2,300 feet (700 metres) in its southern portions to 3,300 feet in the north. The topography is gently undulating in the south, but in the north there are frequent outcroppings of smooth granite that rise several hundred feet above the forest.

Climate and drainage. Steeped in the tannin-rich leaves covering the forest topsoil, the water flowing in the numerous streams that drain the Ituri is the colour of strong tea. Besides the Ituri River itself, there are many broad streams that flow generally from east to west. The most notable are the Nepoko in the north, the Epulu and Nduye in the centre, and the Ibina in the south. None of these rivers is navigable, even by pirogue, for more than a few miles. The streams are fed by rains that are highly variable from month to month and from year to year. Average annual rainfall is 75 inches (1,900 millimetres), and there are approximately 2,000 hours of sunshine per year. Average temperature at lower elevations is 88° F (31° C). There is a dry season that lasts roughly from December through February, when less than 7 inches of rain normally falls. By the end of the dry season humidity within the forest is reduced, and the smaller forest streams become dry. The heaviest rains fall in October and early November; rivers overflow their banks, and large areas of the forest become flooded, making walking through the forest or driving on the few available roads extremely difficult.

Soils. The soils of the Ituri Forest developed from granites, gneisses, and metamorphosed rock of Precambrian age. In most places the soil is sandy clay or sandy clay loam, ranging in colour from reddish brown through ochre to yellowish brown and even white. The soils are acidic, and the layer of humus is thin. If exposed to the strong equatorial sun and high rainfall, as when the forest vegetation is cleared by Bantu farmers, the soil deteriorates rapidly, recovering only if it is again taken over by secondary forest. Traditionally, farmers have shifted their cultivation sites to allow the fragile soils to regenerate.

Plant and animal life. The climax-forest vegetation left undisturbed by human occupation is characterized by three dominant species of tall, hardwood legumes in the subfamily Caesalpinioideae. In the south and west *Gilbertiodendron deweverei* dominates and can constitute 90 percent of the standing vegetation. The regions of the forest dominated by only a few plant species have less abundant and diverse animal life than the other, more botanically mixed areas, such as in the north and east. There, *Cynometra alexandrii* and *Brachystegia laurentii,* which together comprise less than 40 percent of the canopy, are interspersed with numerous other tall species (*e.g., Albizia, Celtis,* and *Ficus*).

Dominant tree species

For many generations, people residing in the Ituri have been practicing a form of agriculture that entails clearing and burning the forest, growing their crops, and then moving after several years to allow the forest to regenerate during a long fallow period. This method of shifting slash-and-burn cultivation has created a patchwork of climax vegetation interspersed with various successional stages of secondary forest on the sites of old gardens and abandoned villages. Some areas are a tangle of lianas and shrubs beneath emerging hardwood trees, while others are in less-advanced stages of succession, with large stands of umbrella trees (*Musanga cecropoides*). These various seral patches—combined with river valleys, swampy waters, rock outcroppings, and the most recent village and garden clearings near the roads—produce a mosaic of diverse habitats that provide cover and food for the greatest abundance of mammals in forested Africa.

Situated near the forest–savanna edge, Ituri fauna include not only species typical of the African equatorial forest but also forms, such as the hyena, that are usually found on the open savanna. The most notable species is the forest giraffe, called okapi, which is endemic to the Ituri. Numerous forest antelopes include five species of duiker, the water chevrotain, and the pygmy antelope. Leopards, genets, and mongooses are the main carnivores. The elephant, buffalo, and bongo (a kind of antelope) are present in forms slightly smaller than their savanna relatives. The Ituri also supports the greatest diversity of primates of any comparable area in the world. The many monkeys include the terrestrial anubis baboon, as well as the leaf-eating imperial black and white colobus and the owl-faced monkey. The only ape is the chimpanzee, which is numerous. Hundreds of species of birds have been recorded, among which the shy Congo peacock, discovered in 1936, is perhaps the most famous.

Efforts to preserve the fauna and flora are largely confined to the Maiko National Park on the southern edge of the Ituri. The park offers some protection for the forest elephant, the okapi, the Congo peacock, the aardvark, and the chimpanzee, but poaching activities and destruction

Efe camp in the Ituri Forest, Zaire.
Robert C. Bailey

of forest habitat seriously threaten these and other species both outside and inside the park boundaries.

The people. Based on their modes of subsistence, there are two principle kinds of inhabitants of the Ituri Forest: the village-living agriculturalists, most of whom are Bantu-speaking, and the nomadic hunting and gathering peoples, often referred to as Pygmies. Neither of these two groups is isolated from the other; in many parts of the Ituri villagers and hunter-gatherers practice a form of mutual interdependence, which includes the sharing of language and many customs.

Four groups of Bambuti

The Pygmies. There are four populations of Pygmies, collectively called the Bambuti, living in the Ituri Forest. Each Pygmy population is associated with a different tribe of Bantu- or Sudanic-speaking agriculturalists. The Sua are associated with the Budu (Babudu) on the western edge of the Ituri, near Wamba; and the Aka, of whom few remain, are found with the Mangbetu in the northwest. The Efe, having the broadest distribution extending across the northern and eastern portions of the Ituri, are associated with the Sudanic-speaking Mamvu and Lese (Walese). The Mbuti live with the Bila (Babila) in the centre of the forest.

The Bambuti hunt and gather forest resources (meat, honey, fruits, nuts, caterpillars, termites, and mushrooms), which they consume themselves or trade to their neighbouring agriculturalists. In return for these forest products, the Bambuti receive agricultural foods, cloth, pots, pans, ax blades, salt, and other material items not available in the forest. In general, the subsistence activities of men consist of hunting mammals and gathering wild honey. Women supply most of the calories by gathering nuts, fruits, and tubers in the forest or by working for the agriculturalists in the gardens and receiving food as payment.

The Bambuti divide themselves into patriclans, each clan numbering between 10 and 100 members and having one area of forest to which it loosely claims exclusive rights. Marriage occurs through "sister exchange," whereby a prospective husband must give a female clan member in marriage to the wife's clan before a marriage is fully recognized.

In order to hunt and gather in the forest effectively, the Bambuti must remain mobile. They live in beehive-shaped huts, which they can construct in a matter of hours, and they move their camps approximately every three weeks to take advantage of the changing position of edible plants and animals. The Bambuti have few material possessions, no inherited offices or wealth, and no institutionalized headmen or chiefs.

Different Bambuti groups use different technologies to hunt in the forest. The Efe hunt monkeys and forest antelope using bows and arrows, and for large game like the buffalo, giant forest hog, and elephant they hunt with spears. The Mbuti use only nets, with which they hunt antelope and other small mammals.

The Bambuti are highly skilled musicians, and singing and dancing are important components of their life. Storytelling is highly developed and widely respected by all members of the society. The forest figures prominently in all Mbuti ritual and myth.

The village-living agriculturalists. People practicing shifting cultivation have been present in the Ituri for 2,000 years or more. Most of these peoples, including the Bila, Budu, and Ndaka, speak one of the numerous Bantu languages spoken throughout sub-Saharan Africa, but others, such as the Mamvu and Lese, speak tonal Central Sudanic dialects. In general, the agriculturalists live in small villages with 10 to 150 residents, all members of the same patriclan. Houses are constructed of saplings plastered with mud and leaf thatch for roofing. When Stanley traversed the Ituri, many villages were fortified and distributed more or less evenly throughout the forest. Disputes that sometimes escalated into armed conflict occurred between clans, and people were afraid to travel any great distance from their own villages. Between 1920 and 1940, the Belgian colonial administration created chiefdoms, imposed peaceful relations, constructed roads, and coerced people to move their villages and gardens to the roadsides, where most remain today.

Staple crops

The staple crops of the agriculturalists are cassava and bananas, but they also raise for their own consumption beans, sweet potatoes, a variety of squashes, oil palms, and tobacco; rice, peanuts, and coffee serve as cash crops. Livestock raising is limited to goats and poultry. The agriculturalists also fish, and during the dry season they may camp in the forest to dam up forest streams. They also hunt using traps and snares, which are usually placed within short walking distance of their clearings.

Villager-Bambuti relations. Each clan of Bambuti is associated with a specific clan of villagers, and individual Bambuti have close economic and ritual ties to individual villagers. Such close dyadic relations are often passed from one generation to another, creating a deep sense of kinship between Mbuti and villager families. While they spend most of their time in the forest, Bambuti rarely reside more than an eight-hour walk from "their" villagers, facilitating trade and social relations. While the Bambuti rely upon the villagers for starchy food crops and a few material possessions, the villagers profit by the Bambuti's skill at supplying highly prized forest resources, namely meat and honey. Bambuti also supply much needed labour around the times of planting and harvest, and they provide ritual and curative functions regarded as crucial by the villagers. (R.C.B.)

The economy. The forest has not played a large part in the Zairian national economy. Only a fraction of its area is exploited for timber because of difficulty of access. A few gold mines operated before the country gained independence, but extraction is now largely restricted to panning by individuals. Cotton growing has all but disappeared. Oil palm cultivation has declined to such an extent that the area is a net importer of palm oil. The larger coffee plantations are being replaced by small independent planters. An illicit ivory trade prospers, despite rapidly declining elephant populations. There are attractions for a tourist industry, but transportation and hotel facilities are poor or absent.

Transportation

Access to the Ituri Forest is extremely difficult. There are no public transportation facilities. Rivers and streams are unnavigable, and the few existing roads are all dirt and often in poor repair. From the southeast, entrance to the forest can be made from Goma, which lies about 125 miles to the south on the northern shore of Lake Kivu, or from Bunia, which is some 60 miles to the east. From the west the best road is from Kisangani through Nia-Nia.

Study and exploration. The Egyptians knew of the existence of the Pygmies; Pepi II Neferkare, last king of the 6th dynasty (*c.* 2325–*c.* 2150 BC), had Pygmies present in his court, and they were depicted on Egyptian pottery some 4,000 years ago. The German botanist Georg Schweinfurth, arriving in the Ituri in 1869 from the north, was the first European to see and write about the Mbuti (*The Heart of Africa;* 1873). Stanley was the first to cross the forest from west to east, following essentially the same route as the present Kisangani to Bunia road. In the 1930s the Jesuit missionary Paul Schebesta performed the first anthropological studies of the people of the Ituri. Since then, many aspects of the behaviour, ecology, and growth and demography of the Bambuti and their villager neighbours have been studied by anthropologists from the United States, Europe, and Japan. (Je.-P.H./R.C.B.)

KALAHARI

The Kalahari is a large, basinlike plain of the interior plateau of southern Africa. It occupies almost all of Botswana, the eastern third of Namibia, and the northernmost part of the Cape of Good Hope province of South Africa. In the southwest it merges with the Namib, the coastal desert of Namibia. The Kalahari's longest north–south extent is roughly 1,000 miles (1,600 kilometres), and its greatest east–west distance is about 600 miles; its area has been estimated at some 360,000 square miles (930,000 square kilometres).

Physical features. *Physiography and geology.* The Kalahari is a featureless, gently undulating, sand-covered plain, which everywhere is 3,000 feet (900 metres) or more above sea level. Bedrock is exposed only in the low but vertical-walled hills, called kopjes, that rarely but conspicuously rise above the general surface. Aside from the kopjes, three surfaces characterize virtually all of the Kalahari: sand sheets, longitudinal dunes, and vleis (pans).

The sand sheets appear to have been formed during the Pleistocene Epoch (1,600,000 to 10,000 years ago), and they have been fixed in place since then. In some areas they appear to have been of fluvial origin, the result of sheet flooding in times of much greater precipitation, but by far the greater part of them were wind-formed. The sheets occupy the eastern part of the Kalahari. Their surface elevation varies only slightly, with relief measured in tens of feet per mile. The depth of the sand there generally exceeds 200 feet. In many areas the sand is red, the result of a thin layer of iron oxide that coats the grains of sand.

The entire western Kalahari is characterized by long chains of dunes, oriented roughly to the north or northwest. The dunes measure at least 1 mile in length, several hundred feet in width, and 20 to 200 feet in height. Each dune is separated from its neighbour by a broad parallel depression locally called a *straat* ("street," or "lane"), because each constitutes the easy way to travel.

Vleis

Vleis, or pans, are the terminal features of desert drainage systems, the "dry lakes" at the end of ephemeral streams. Many are remnant features from an earlier period of greater precipitation. Very little water ever flowed to the sea from the Kalahari. Rather, each stream ended its course in a slightly lower depression from which there was no outlet. There, as the stream dried up, the fine silt particles carried in suspension by the sluggish stream were deposited along with soluble calcium minerals and salts precipitated out of the evaporating water. The results are pans—flat surfaces devoid of vegetation that are gleaming white when dry, hardened by the cementing action of the soluble minerals, and, on occasion, covered by a shallow layer of standing water. Where the salt content is low, pans may become covered with grasses after a rain.

Drainage. In the southern and central parts of the Kalahari, surface water is found only in small, widely scattered waterholes, and surface drainage is nonexistent. Nearly all of the rain that falls disappears immediately into the deep sand. Some is absorbed by the underlying rock strata; some is drawn to the surface by capillary action and evaporated into the air; and some, lifted from the depths by tree roots, is transpired from leaf surfaces. A small amount, landing on nonsandy surfaces, may flow short distances into pans, but this occurs only immediately after the infrequent rains. In some parts of the central and southern Kalahari, extensive ancient drainage systems have been detected—some on the ground and others by way of aerial photographs. None of these operate today, even in the wettest of years.

In the northern Kalahari an extraordinary drainage system prevails. During the summer heavy rains fall on the uplands of central Angola, far to the northwest of the Kalahari. Large amounts of runoff water feed a number of south-flowing streams, which merge to form the Okavango and Cuando (Kwando) rivers. The Okavango flows to the southeast and into the northernmost portion of the Kalahari, eventually breaking up into a number of distributary channels and feeding the vast area of swamps in northern Botswana. After an abnormally wet rainy season in Angola, excess water fills the swamps and overflows, filling Lake Ngami farther to the south, and flows eastward through the Boteti River into Lake Xau and the Makgadikgadi Pans. Similarly, the Cuando River flows south from Angola and partly into a northeastern extension of the same swamps. Thus is created the paradoxical situation of an area with an extensive excess of water in a region chronically short of water.

Soils. Soils in the Kalahari are largely based on sand, are reddish in color, and are low in organic material. Chemically, they are relatively alkaline, and they are extremely dry. In and near the pans, the soils tend to be highly calcareous or saline, and frequently they are toxic to most vegetation.

Climate. Traditionally, an area was classed as desert if it received less than 10 inches (250 millimetres) of rain annually. A more accurate definition of a desert is a region in which the potential evaporation rate is twice as great as the precipitation. Both of these criteria are applicable to the southwestern half of the Kalahari. The northeastern portion, however, receives much more rainfall and, climatically, cannot qualify as a desert; and yet, it is totally lacking in surface water. Rain drains instantly through the deep sands of the area, which creates a situation of edaphic drought (*i.e.,* soil completely devoid of moisture).

Moisture-bearing air is derived from the Indian Ocean, and precipitation is greatest in the northeast (with a mean annual precipitation of more than 20 inches) and declines toward the southwest (less than 5 inches on the southern fringe of the Kalahari). Precipitation, however, is highly variable. Most of the rain comes as summer thunderstorms, with great variation from place to place and from year to year. Winters are extremely dry: humidity is very low, and no rain falls for six to eight months.

Temperatures

Great ranges in both diurnal and seasonal temperatures are the rule, the result of the Kalahari's relatively high altitude and predominantly clear, dry air (allowing strong insolational heating in daytime and great radiational heat loss at night). As a result, shade temperatures often reach 110°–115° F (43°–46° C) on summer days but drop to 70°–80° F (21°–27° C) on the same nights; temperatures on winter nights commonly drop to freezing and may go as low as 10° F (−12° C).

Plant life. The presence of a deep sand cover over most of the area greatly affects the vegetation that grows there. Shallow-rooted plants cannot survive on a perennial basis, although annuals that grow very rapidly after a good rain may be able to sow seeds that will endure until the next good rainy season. Trees with roots deep enough to reach permanently moist sand levels do well.

The southwestern Kalahari, with its very low precipitation, has few trees or large bushes—only scattered xerophytic (drought-tolerant) shrubs and short grasses. The central Kalahari, with more rain, has scattered trees (several species of *Acacia*) and some shrubs and grasses. The northern Kalahari does not have the appearance of a desert at all. It has open woodlands, palm trees growing among thorn brush, and forests of both evergreen and deciduous trees that grow to heights of 50 feet and yield some species suitable for timber; one of the largest and most unusual of these trees is the baobab. The Okavango Swamp supports a dense growth of reeds, papyrus, pond lilies, and other water-loving plants.

Animal life. The animal life of the Kalahari is also richer and more varied in the north than in the south. Yet even in the arid south, many individuals of several species stay for long periods of the year despite the absence of surface water. The principal species found in the south are springbok, gnu (wildebeest), and hartebeest—all of which occasionally are present in great herds—gemsbok (oryx), eland, and many smaller nongregarious species, such as kudu (in areas of denser brush), steenbok, and duiker.

Animals Animals © Anthony Bannister

Springbok in the Kalahari Gemsbok National Park, Cape of Good Hope, S.Af.

The northern Kalahari supports a considerable population of giraffes, zebras, elephants, buffalo, and antelopes (roan, sable, *tsessebe,* and impala); predators such as lions, cheetahs, leopards, wild hunting dogs, and foxes; other large and medium-sized mammals, such as jackals, hyenas, warthogs, baboons, badgers, anteaters, ant bears, hare, and porcupines; and numerous small rodents, several types of snakes and lizards, and a wealth of birdlife. (R.F.Lo.)

The people and the economy. The Kalahari is inhabited primarily by Bantu-speaking Africans and Khoisan-speaking San, with a small number of Europeans.

The Bantu-speaking peoples. The Bantu-speaking peoples—the Tswana, the Kgalagadi, and the Herero—are relative newcomers to the Kalahari. In the late 18th century the Tswana spread west from the Limpopo basin into the northern and eastern Kalahari; the Kgalagadi moved north and west into the southern and western Kalahari; and the Herero refugees from the German colonial wars in South West Africa (Namibia) fled east into the western and northern Kalahari at the beginning of the 20th century.

Those in the remoter parts of the Kalahari who are unaffected by mining or other industry live in villages of between 200 and 5,000 people. Housing is mostly of the traditional type: single-roomed huts with mud walls and thatched roofs. Water is the limiting factor, confining settlement to places situated near wells or boreholes with potable water.

Cattle raising

Cattle, the basis of the economy, are kept on the outskirts of villages, or at distances of up to 50 miles away. Except in the Ghanzi District of Botswana—where most of the livestock raising is done on private ranches, many of them owned by Africans—grazing lands are state-owned, and their use is regulated by local government councils. Wells and boreholes are owned by the councils, syndicates of cattle owners, or private individuals; year-round cattle grazing is limited to their vicinity. In summers of above-average rains, however, pastoralists may trek with their stock to remote pastures, where for a short time water may occur in pools. Cattle and goats feed upon a small range of the available vegetation. Since effective pasture management is little practiced, the grazing of these animals is highly destructive. Pasture loss and subsequent desertification are serious threats to the ecology of the Kalahari. Cattle are prized beyond their economic value, as their ownership is a measure of social status and personal worth. Thus, the desire to possess more cattle puts an increasing load on diminishing pasture, leaving it no chance for recovery. The traditional dangers to livestock—drought, disease, internal parasites, and wild predators—have diminished markedly as more boreholes have been sunk, veterinary care improved, and indigenous fauna have grown scarcer. In addition, wealthier cattle owners have improved their herds by introducing better stock and practicing scientific breeding.

Goats furnish most of the meat and milk for home consumption, and nearly all households cultivate crops of corn (maize), sorghum, and pumpkins. Because of the threat of drought, more crops fail than are successful. Wild food plants and the meat of game animals are important components of diet in the smaller and more remote villages. All villages have trading stores or are visited by hawkers who sell foodstuffs and other commodities.

All but the smallest villages have state-run primary schools, which are attended by the great majority of children, although few proceed to secondary education. State-run health clinics and hospitals in the larger villages supplement the services of herbalists and diviners.

Riding horses and donkeys are the usual means of local travel. Trucks belonging to traders or to the mine labour recruiting agency are used for longer journeys.

Large diamond deposits were discovered in Botswana soon after the country's independence, and the opening of the diamond mine at Orapa in 1971 marked the beginning of the development of mining activities in scattered locations of the Kalahari. In addition, tourism and the sale of handicrafts have become economically important.

San. The San—or Basarwa, as they are called in much of the region—are now either clients of Bantu-speaking pastoralists and work at cattle posts in return for support or they are employees of the cattle ranches of the Ghanzi District or are dependents of such employees. Few San still follow their traditional pattern of hunting and gathering. Many have been resettled by the government of Botswana from their traditional homes in the Central Kalahari Game Reserve to new villages built outside the reserve.

Although all San traditionally were hunter-gatherers, there were significant cultural and social differences between groups. For example, a number of groups had long-standing clientships with Bantu-speaking stockowners, while other groups lived—until the 1970s—solely as autonomous foragers. Of these latter peoples, the Kung (!Kung), !xong, and G/wi tribes (the "!" and "/" representing click sounds) were intensively studied. While each group was distinct, the G/wi of the Central Kalahari Game

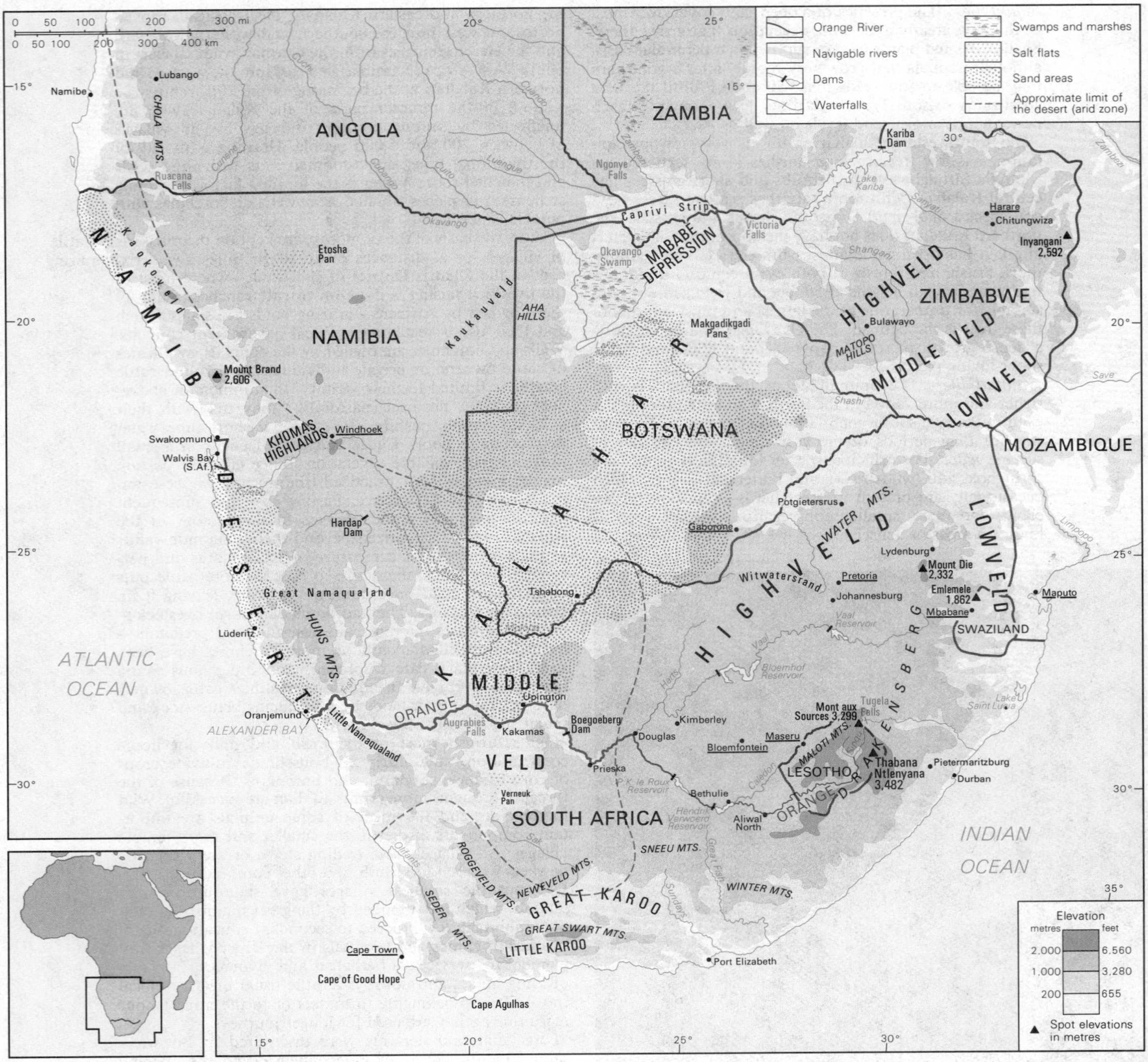

Physical features of southern Africa.

Reserve can be considered an example of the traditional San hunter-gatherer way of life.

The G/wi

The G/wi lived together in bands, each consisting of 5 to 16 households linked by bonds of kinship and friendship. Each band had a recognized territory of 300 to 400 square miles, selected for its resources of food plants (the main part of the diet), wet-season water holes (used during the six to eight weeks when sufficient rainwater gathered in pools), trees (for shade, shelter, firewood, and wood for making artifacts), and areas of grazing to attract and sustain herds of game animals. Subsistence was based on a number of species of edible plants, of which eight were staples in their various seasons. This diet was supplemented by the meat of antelopes and other herbivorous mammals, by tortoises and other reptiles, and by the flesh and eggs of all but raptorial and scavenging birds. Plant-gathering was mostly done by women ranging within five miles of the camp, while men hunted over a much larger area. The main hunting weapon was a light bow shooting flimsy, unfletched, poisoned arrows. The range of these bows was only about 75 feet, and great skill was needed to stalk the quarry within this distance. Antelope leather provided material for clothing, which included cloaks that also served as blankets and carrying bags.

From November to some time between late June and early August—a period when there is sufficient food—the band lived as one community, moving from camp to camp every three or four weeks as the local supply of food plants became exhausted. Blighting frosts depleted the available food plants in winter (May to September), and the band would then split into its constituent households, each retreating to a separate part of the territory. Early-fruiting plants increased the food supply just before the approach of the wet season, allowing the band to reunite at a joint campsite. During dry seasons, shelters were little more than open windbreaks made of branches and grass. In rainy periods, domed structures of branches were thatched and made rainproof.

Europeans. Europeans first entered the Kalahari early in the 19th century as travelers, missionaries, ivory hunters, and traders. The only European settlement was in the Ghanzi District, where a number of families were allowed ranching blocks in the 1890s. Until the 1960s they led a life of isolation and poverty, but since then they have been able to gain ownership of the land and improve their living conditions. Most other whites in the Kalahari are government employees or are engaged in private enterprise. (G.Si.)

Transportation. Because of its sparsely populated expanse, the Kalahari is served by infrequent roads and tracks, the majority of which are passable only by trucks or four-wheel drive vehicles. Maintained roads connect administrative centres, major habitations, and marginal farming areas in the south, southwest, and northwest. Constructed roads now link eastern Botswana with the Okavango Swamp and with mining developments south of the Makgadikgadi Pans.

Study and exploration. The Kalahari's lack of surface water and deep sands constituted a major obstacle to early travelers. The Scottish missionary and explorer David Livingstone, with assistance from local peoples, traversed the Kalahari in 1849 with great effort by utilizing local waterholes. In 1878–79 a party of Boers in the Dorsland ("Thirstland") Trek crossed the Kalahari from the Transvaal to central Angola by a circuitous route, losing along the way about 250 people and 9,000 cattle, largely from thirst. The introduction of motor vehicles in the 20th century greatly improved transport into the Kalahari, but even as late as the 1950s large areas were virtually inaccessible and were never visited by outsiders. By the mid-1970s, however, vehicle mobility had improved to such a degree that the whole of the Kalahari had been opened to study, hunting, and tourist expeditions.

The Dorsland Trek

NAMIB

The Namib is a cool coastal desert extending for 1,200 miles (1,900 kilometres) along the Atlantic coast from Namibe (formerly Moçâmedes) in Angola southward across Namibia to the Olifants River in the Cape Province of South Africa. It reaches inland 80 to 100 miles to the foot of the Great Escarpment. The southern portion merges with the Kalahari on the plateau atop the escarpment. Its name is derived from the Nama language, implying "an area where there is nothing."

The Namib is arid and is almost totally uninhabited, except for several towns. It is important because of the trade routes that cross it, its mineral deposits, the fisheries of the bordering sea, and its increasing utilization for recreational purposes.

For map coverage of the Namib, see above *Kalahari.*

Physical features. The Namib is divided into three successive north–south-trending strips: the very narrow coastal region along the Atlantic, strongly subject to marine influences; the Outer Namib, occupying the rest of the western half of the desert; and the Inner Namib, constituting the eastern portion. The boundaries between them consist of broad transition zones.

Physiography. The desert basically consists of a relatively smooth platform of truncated bedrock of various types and ages. Mica-schist and other metamorphics and granite and similar intrusives predominate. The platform rises gradually from the coast to about 3,000 feet (900 metres) at the foot of the escarpment. Scattered isolated mountains rise steeply and abruptly above the platform, and in the northern half several streams have carved deep, steep-walled gorges into it.

In much of the southern half of the desert the platform is surmounted by a vast expanse of sand—yellow-gray near the coast and brick-red inland—which is derived from the Orange River and from other rivers that flow westward from the escarpment but never reach the sea. The dunes run in lines from north-northwest to south-southeast, with individual dunes having lengths of 10 to 20 miles and reaching heights of 200 to 800 feet. The troughs between these lines of dunes are interrupted by smaller transverse dunes. The extreme southern coastal area consists of wind-scoured bedrock and a few rapidly moving crescent-shaped barchans (*i.e.,* dunes convex to the wind). The northern third—the Kaokoveld region—consists of gravel plains and rock platforms occurring between scattered, rugged mountains, interspersed with a few large dune fields.

Drainage. Being an almost rainless area, the Namib has a poorly developed and fragmentary drainage pattern. Water from the interior plateau flows through or into the desert. In the northern half the larger streams reach the sea, but between the Kuiseb and the Orange rivers, every stream terminates in a vlei (salt pan or mud flat) against or among the dunes.

A portion of the water of major streams seeps through the sands of the streambeds. The underflow of the Kuiseb River has been tapped 25 miles inland to provide water supplies for Walvis Bay and Swakopmund. A pipeline 80 miles long supplies Lüderitz with water from the seepage of the Koichab, a stream that terminates in the dunes. Only the Cunene and the Orange rivers flow permanently on the surface. Other streams have surface flow only after heavy rainfall in the interior plateaus—they normally flow for no more than a few days in several years.

Seepage of stream water

Soils. Large areas of the Namib are completely soilless, with bedrock at the surface. Other areas are covered with shifting sand. Soils that do occur are often highly saline, impregnated with gypsum, or cemented firmly by calcium carbonate, the latter forming a calcrete layer just below the surface. Arable soils in the Namib are limited to floodplains and the terraces of major rivers and are subject to occasional inundation.

Paul Freestone—Robert Harding Picture Library

Sand dunes surrounding Sossusvlei, the termination of the Tsauchab, an intermittent stream in south-central Namib, Namibia.

Climate. The coastal area is almost totally rainless, yet its air is almost always at or near the saturation point. The cold Benguela Current flows northward along the coast, chilling the air above it and thus producing fog. This cool air moves inland as a southwest sea breeze, creating a temperature inversion about 1,000 feet thick, with fog below and hot, dry air above.

At the coast, there is little difference in temperature between day and night or between winter and summer. Temperatures are usually between 50° and 60° F (10° and 16° C). Along the inland margins, summer temperatures normally reach about 88° F (31° C); only in areas sheltered from the cooling sea breeze (lee sides of mountains and bottoms of canyons) do temperatures frequently approach those expected in low-latitude deserts—*i.e.,* in excess of 100° F (38° C). Freezing temperatures occur occasionally along the inner edge of the desert. On a few days each year, usually in fall or spring, berg (or mountain) winds, blowing from the east, bring high temperatures (above 100° F), together with dry air and clouds of dust, across the desert to the coast itself. The rare rains occur usually as short-lived torrential thunderstorms.

Average annual precipitation at the coast is generally about 0.5 inch (13 millimetres), increasing inland, until it reaches 2 inches at the foot of the escarpment. In some years, however, no rain falls at all. Dew, on the other hand, is heavy and for some types of vegetation is more important than the rainfall. In the extreme south, some winter precipitation occurs from frontal storms passing farther south over the Cape region; on rare occasions, snow may fall on the higher southern mountains.

Vegetational regions

Plant life. Six vegetational regions may be identified in the Namib: (1) the coastal region, with highly succulent vegetation, which uses moisture derived from the fog, (2) the almost completely barren Outer Namib, (3) the steppes of the Inner Namib, which in many years are barren but which in wet years are covered with short grasses, both annual and perennial, (4) the dunes of the Inner Namib, which produce a surprisingly rich flora of bushes and tall grasses, (5) the larger river channels, along which large trees, particularly acacias, grow, and (6) the southern winter rainfall area, where a succulent bush growth occurs. A curious Namib plant is the tumboa, or welwitschia (*Welwitschia mirabilis*), whose two gigantic leaves sprawl over the surface of the ground from the crest of its huge root crown.

Animal life. The plains and dunes of the Inner Namib support large numbers of several varieties of antelope, especially gemsbok (oryx) and springbok, as well as ostriches and some zebras. Elephants, rhinoceroses, lions, hyenas, and jackals are found in the northern Namib, especially along the rivers that flow from the interior highlands to the Atlantic. The dunes of the Outer Namib provide habitats for various types of insects and reptiles, especially beetles, geckos, and snakes, but virtually no mammals. The shore area is densely populated by marine birds (notably flamingos, pelicans, and, in the southern part, penguins), as well as a few jackals, some rodents, and a few colonies of seals. Large quantities of guano are scraped annually from the rocks of several offshore islands.

The people and the economy. A few San roamed the Namib until early in the 20th century, gathering whatever was edible along the shore, hunting in the Inner Namib, and often depending for water upon the bitter juices of the tsama (tsamma) melon. A small number of Herero tribesmen continue to herd cattle and goats from waterhole to waterhole in the desert part of the Kaokoveld, living in their traditional manner. A few Topnaar Nama Khoikhoin also graze their sheep and goats on the riverine vegetation along the Kuiseb River. A great part of the Namib is now totally unused and unoccupied, the aboriginal people having left to adopt new homes and new ways of life. A few areas, however, are productive in some way.

The innermost steppes in the southern half of the desert are divided into private "farms" (ranches), which are operated by Europeans using native labour and are devoted to the raising of Karakul sheep; the wavy-haired pelts of newborn lambs of these sheep are used for fur coats in Europe.

Parks and reserves

Much of the central and northern Namib has been set aside for recreation and conservation. The Namib Desert Park in the central area is a desert range for flocks of antelope, zebra, and ostrich. A strip about 130 miles in length along the coast northwest of Swakopmund constitutes the National West Coast Tourist Area; within it is the Cape Cross Seal Reserve, which protects a breeding area. Farther north is the Skeleton Coast National Park, where entry is restricted in order to preserve the fragile desert environment.

A vast area stretching from the Kuiseb River to the Orange River on the South African border and reaching inland some 80 miles constitutes the Sperrgebiet, or "Forbidden Zone," to which all entry is strictly restricted because of the possible presence of diamonds there. Diamonds are extracted from alluvial beds near the coast by large-scale equipment, chiefly in the area near the mouth of the Orange River.

There are four cities on the Namib coast. Swakopmund, the summer capital for Namibia and a popular coastal resort town, still retains much of the atmosphere from the days when South West Africa was a German colony. From mid-December to mid-February many functions of the government are transferred from Windhoek to Swakopmund to escape the heat of the interior. Swakopmund has been greatly changed by the development of a large uranium mine located some 25 miles inland. Walvis Bay, just to the south of Swakopmund, is a coastal enclave belonging to South Africa that is surrounded by Namibia. It is a modern port city with a mixed population of Europeans, Coloureds, and Africans—the Africans consisting partly of Nama families from south-central Namibia but largely of male Ovambo from Angola and the northern part of Namibia, who have found employment at the port. The port serves as a base for fishing fleets that supply both shore canneries and cannery ships on the open sea. It is also the major transhipment port for Namibia. Lüderitz, a small town on a shallow, rock-strewn harbour, has a small trade with Walvis Bay and Cape Town and is the base of a crayfish (lobster) industry. Oranjemund, a company town of the Consolidated Diamond Mines, is a base for large-scale diamond mining in the alluvial gravels along the southern coast.

Transportation

The Namib is crossed by rail lines and tarred roads, both from Walvis Bay-Swakopmund and from Lüderitz, which are integrated with the internal rail and road systems of Namibia and South Africa. Except for roads from Swakopmund north for about 130 miles, between Swakopmund and Walvis Bay, and from Lüderitz to Oranjemund, no improved roads exist along the coast, in the Kaokoveld to the northwest, or in the area between Walvis Bay and Lüderitz.

Study and exploration. Cursory exploratory voyages were made along the coast from the 15th to 17th century, Walvis ("Whale Fish") Bay was used as a base for New England whaling ships in the early 19th century, and there were direct routes for traders and missionaries from Lüderitz and Walvis Bay into the interior. Otherwise, little was known of the Namib until the latter part of the 19th century. After South West Africa was established as a territory of Germany in the early 1890s, the German military began the detailed exploration and mapping of the desert. (R.F.Lo.)

SAHARA

The Sahara is the largest desert in the world. Filling nearly all of northern Africa, it measures approximately 3,000 miles (4,800 kilometres) from east to west and between 800 and 1,200 miles from north to south and has a total area of some 3,320,000 square miles (8,600,000 square kilometres). The Sahara is bordered in the west by the Atlantic Ocean, in the north by the Atlas Mountains and Mediterranean Sea, in the east by the Red Sea, and in the south by a zone of ancient, immobile sand dunes aligned with latitude 16° N.

Physical features. *Physiography.* The principal topographical features of the Sahara include shallow, seasonally inundated basins (chotts and dayas) and large oasis depressions; extensive gravel-covered plains (serirs or regs);

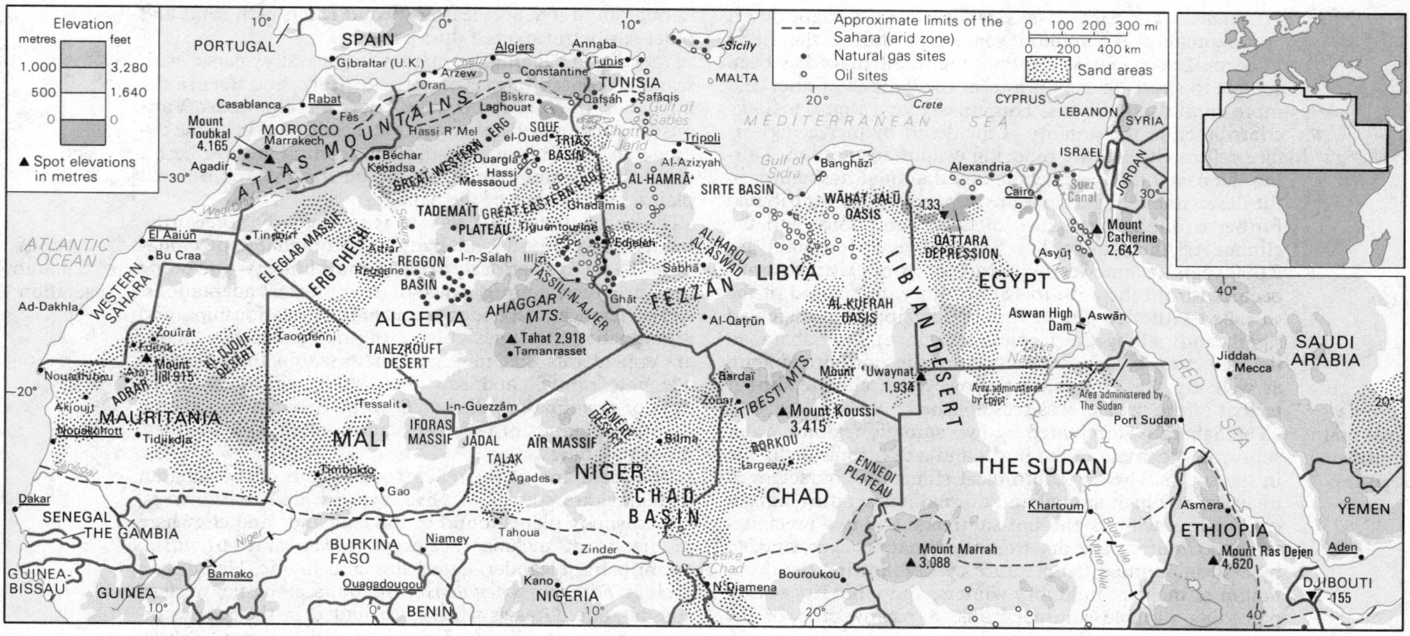

The Sahara.

rock-strewn plateaus (hammadas); abrupt mountains; and sand sheets, dunes, and sand seas (ergs). The highest point in the desert is the 11,204-foot (3,415-metre) summit of Mount Koussi in the Tibesti Mountains in Chad; the lowest, 436 feet (133 metres) below sea level, is in the Qattara Depression of Egypt.

The name Sahara derives from the Arabic noun *ṣaḥrāʾ*, meaning desert, and its plural, *ṣaḥārāʾ*. It is also related to the adjective *aṣḥar,* meaning desertlike and carrying a strong connotation of the reddish colour of the vegetationless plains. There are also indigenous names for particular areas—such as the Tanezrouft region of southwestern Algeria and the Ténéré region of central Niger—which are often of Berber origin.

Geologic framework

The Sahara sits atop the African Shield, which is composed of heavily folded and denuded Precambrian rocks. Because of the stability of the shield, subsequently deposited Paleozoic formations have remained horizontal and relatively unaltered. Over much of the Sahara, these formations were covered by Mesozoic deposits—including the limestones of Algeria, southern Tunisia, and northern Libya, and the Nubian sandstones of the Libyan Desert—and many of the important regional aquifers are identified with them. In the northern Sahara, these formations are also associated with a series of basins and depressions extending from the oases of western Egypt to the chotts of Algeria. In the southern Sahara, downwarping of the African Shield created large basins occupied by Cenozoic lakes and seas, such as the ancient Mega-Chad. The serirs and regs differ in character in various regions of the desert but are believed to represent Cenozoic depositional surfaces. A prominent feature of the plains is the dark patina of ferromanganese compounds, called desert varnish, that forms on the surfaces of weathered rocks. The plateaus of the Sahara, such as the Tademaït Plateau of Algeria, are typically covered with angular, weathered rock. In the central Sahara, the monotony of the plains and plateaus is broken by prominent volcanic massifs—including Mount ʿUwaynat and the Tibesti and Ahaggar mountains. Other noteworthy formations include the Ennedi Plateau of Chad, the Aïr Massif of Niger, the Iforas Massif of Mali, and the outcroppings of the Mauritanian Adrar region.

Sand sheets and dunes cover approximately 25 percent of the Sahara's surface. The principal types of dunes include tied dunes, which form in the lee of hills or other obstacles; parabolic blowout dunes; crescent-shaped barchans and transverse dunes; longitudinal seifs; and the massive, complex forms associated with sand seas. Several pyramidal dunes in the Sahara attain heights of nearly 500 feet, while *draa,* the mountainous sand ridges that dominate the ergs, are said to reach 1,000 feet. An unusual phenomenon associated with desert sands is their "singing" or booming. Various hypotheses have been advanced to explain the phenomenon, such as those based upon the piezoelectric property of crystalline quartz, but the mystery remains unsolved.

Drainage. Several rivers originating outside the Sahara contribute to both the surface water and groundwater regimes of the desert and receive the discharge of its drainage networks. Rivers rising in the tropical highlands to the south are particularly prominent: the main tributaries of the Nile join in the Sahara, and the river flows northward along the desert's eastern margin to the Mediterranean; several rivers discharge into Lake Chad in the southern Sahara, and a significant quantity of water continues northeastward and contributes to the recharge of regional aquifers; and the Niger rises in the Fouta Djallon region of Guinea and flows through the southwestern Sahara before turning southward to the sea. Streams and wadis (ephemeral streams) flowing from the Atlas Mountains and coastal highlands of Libya, Tunisia, Algeria, and Morocco contribute additional water. Prominent among these are the Saoura and Drâa. Many of the smaller wadis discharge into the chotts of the northern Sahara. Within the desert itself, there are extensive networks of wadis: some are seasonally active remnants of systems formed during more humid periods in the past; some, however, have been shaped by the sudden discharge of historically documented storms, such as the flood that destroyed Tamanrasset, Alg., in 1922. Particularly significant are the complex network of wadis, lakes, and pools associated with the Tibesti Mountains and those associated with the Tassili n'Ajjer region and the Ahaggar Mountains, such as Wadi Tamanrasset. The sand dunes of the Sahara store considerable quantities of rainwater, and seeps and springs issue from various escarpments in the desert.

Wadis

Soils. The soils of the Sahara are low in organic matter, exhibit only slightly differentiated horizons (strata), and are often biologically inactive, although nitrogen-fixing bacteria are present in some areas. The soils in depressions are frequently saline. At the margins of the desert are soils containing greater concentrations of organic matter. Weatherable minerals are a prominent constituent of these soils, and chemically active expanding-lattice clays are common. Free carbonates are often present, indicating that little leaching has occurred. Compact and indurated layers, or crusts, are largely restricted to the northwestern section of the desert in association with calcareous bedrock. Fine materials, including deposits of diatomaceous earth, are limited to basins and depressions.

Climate. The Sahara was established as a climatic desert approximately five million years ago, during the Early Pliocene Epoch. Since the Pliocene, the Sahara has been subject to short- to medium-term oscillations of drier and more humid conditions. Human activity seems to have contributed to the stability of the desert by increasing surface reflectivity and by reducing evapotranspiration. During the past 7,000 years cattle-based animal husbandry in the desert and along its margins apparently has contributed further to the maintenance of these conditions, and the climate of the Sahara has been relatively constant for 2,000 years. A noteworthy departure from existing norms occurred from the 16th to 18th century, the period of the so-called Little Ice Age in Europe: precipitation increased significantly along the tropical margin of the Sahara, in the desert itself, and perhaps along the northern margin as well. By the 19th century, however, a climate similar to that of the present was reestablished.

Two main climatic regimes

The Sahara is dominated by two climatic regimes: a dry subtropical climate in the north and a dry tropical climate in the south. The dry subtropical climate is characterized by unusually high annual and diurnal temperature ranges, cold to cool winters and hot summers, and two precipitation maximums. The dry tropical climate is characterized by a strong annual temperature cycle following the declination of the sun; mild, dry winters; and a hot dry season preceding variable summer rains. A narrow strip of the western coastal zone has a relatively cool, uniform temperature reflecting the influence of the cold Canary Current.

The dry subtropical climate of the northern Sahara is caused by stable high-pressure cells centred over the tropic of Cancer. The annual range of average daily temperatures is about 36° F (20° C). Winters are relatively cold in the northern regions and cool in the central Sahara. For the zone as a whole, average monthly temperatures during the cold season are approximately 55° F (13° C). The summers are hot. The highest temperature ever recorded was 136° F (58° C) at Al-ʿAzīzīyah, Libya, on the northern margin of the Sahara. Daily temperature ranges are considerable during both the winter and summer months. Although precipitation is highly variable, it averages about 3 inches (76 millimetres) per year. Most precipitation falls from December through March. Another maximum occurs in August, characterized by thunderstorms. These storms can cause tremendous flash floods that rush into areas where no precipitation has fallen. Little precipitation falls in May and June. Snowfall occurs occasionally over the northern plateaus. Another feature of the dry subtropics are the hot, southerly winds that often carry dust from the interior. Although they occur at various times of the year, they are especially common during the spring. In Egypt they are known as the khamsin, in Libya as the ghibli, and in Tunisia as the chili. The dust-laden haboob winds of The Sudan are of shorter duration, chiefly occur during the summer months, and often usher in heavy rains.

The dry tropical climate to the south is dominated by the same high-pressure cells, but it is regularly influenced by the seasonal interaction of a stable continental subtropical air mass and a southerly, unstable maritime tropical air mass. The annual range in average daily temperatures in the dry tropical regions of the Sahara is approximately 31.5° F (17.5° C). Average temperatures for the coldest months are essentially the same as they are for the subtropical zone to the north, but the diurnal range is more moderate. In the higher elevations of the zone, the lows approximate those of more northerly, subtropical regions. For example, absolute lows of 5° F (−15° C) have been recorded in the Tibesti Mountains. Late spring and early summer are hot; high temperatures of 122° F (50° C) are not unusual. Although the massifs of the dry tropics often receive small quantities of precipitation throughout the year, the lowlands have a single summer maximum. As in the north, much of this rainfall occurs as thunderstorms. Precipitation averages are about five inches per year, occasionally including some snowfall in the central massifs. In the western margin of the desert the cold Canary Current reduces air temperatures, thereby reducing convectional rainfall, but resulting in higher humidity and occasional fogs. In the southern Sahara the winter is the period of the harmattan, a dry northeasterly wind laden with sand and other easily transported dust particles.

Plant life. Saharan vegetation is generally sparse, with scattered concentrations of grasses, shrubs, and trees in the highlands, in oasis depressions, and along the wadis. Various halophytes (salt-tolerant plants) are found in saline depressions. Some heat- and drought-tolerant grasses, herbs, small shrubs, and trees are found on the less well-watered plains and plateaus of the Sahara.

Adaptions of Saharan vegetation

The vegetation of the Sahara is particularly noteworthy for its many unusual adaptations to unreliable precipitation. These are variously seen in morphology—including root structure, a broad range of physiological adaptations, site preferences, dependency and affinity relationships, and reproductive strategies. Many of the herbaceous plants are ephemerals that may germinate within three days of adequate rainfall and sow their seeds within 10 or 15 days of germination. Sheltered in the Saharan massifs are occasional stands of relict vegetation, often with Mediterranean affinities.

Prominent among the relict woody plants of the Saharan highlands are species of olive, cypress, and mastic trees. Other woody plants found in the highlands and elsewhere in the desert include species of *Acacia* and *Artemisia,* doum palm, oleander, date palm, and thyme. Halophytes such as *Tamarix senegalensis* are found along the western coastal zone. Grasses widely distributed in the Sahara include species of *Aristida, Eragrostis,* and *Panicum. Aeluropus littoralis* and other salt-tolerant grasses are found along the Atlantic coast. Various combinations of ephemerals form important seasonal pastures called *acheb.*

Animal life. Relict tropical fauna of the northern Sahara include tropical catfish and chromides found at Biskra, Alg., and in isolated oases of the Sahara; cobras and pygmy crocodiles may still exist in remote drainage basins of the Tibesti Mountains. More subtle has been the progressive loss of well-adapted, more mobile species to the advanced firearms and habitat destruction of humans. The North African elephant became extinct during the Roman period, but the lion, ostrich, and other species were established in the desert's northern margins as late as 1830. The last addax in the northern Sahara was killed in the early 1920s; serious depletion of this antelope has also occurred on the southern margins and in the central massifs.

Mammals

Among the mammal species still found in the Sahara are the gerbil, jerboa, Cape hare, and desert hedgehog; Barbary sheep and scimitar-horned oryx; dorcas gazelle, dama deer, and Nubian wild ass; anubis baboon; spotted hyena, common jackal, and sand fox; and Libyan striped weasel and slender mongoose. Including resident and migratory populations, the birdlife of the Sahara exceeds 300 species. The coastal zones and interior waterways attract many species of water and shore birds. Among the species encountered in the interior regions are ostriches; various raptors; secretary birds, guinea fowl, and Nubian bustards; desert eagle owls and barn owls; sand larks and pale crag martins; and brown-necked and fan-tailed ravens.

Frogs, toads, and crocodiles live in the lakes and pools of the Sahara. Lizards, chameleons, skinks, and cobras are found among the rocks and dunes. The lakes and pools of the Sahara also contain algae and brine shrimp and other crustaceans. The various snails that inhabit the desert are an important source of food for birds and animals. Desert snails survive through aestivation (dormancy), often remaining inactive for several years before being revived by rainfall. (J.A.G.)

The people. Although as large as the United States, the Sahara (excluding the Nile valley) is estimated to contain only some 2.5 million inhabitants—less than 1 person per square mile (0.4 per square kilometre). Huge areas are wholly empty, but wherever meagre vegetation can support grazing animals or reliable water sources occur, scattered clusters of inhabitants have survived in fragile ecological balance with one of the harshest environments on earth.

Early human occupation

Long before recorded history, the Sahara was evidently more widely occupied. Stone artifacts, fossils, and rock art, widely scattered through regions now far too dry for occupation, reveal the former human presence, together with that of game animals, including antelopes, buffalo, giraffe, elephant, rhinoceros, and warthog. Bone harpoons, accumulations of shells, and the remains of fish, crocodiles, and hippopotamuses are associated with prehistoric settlements along the shores of ancient Saharan lakes. Among some groups, hunting and fishing were subordinated to nomadic pastoralism, after domesticated livestock appeared in the Sahara almost 7,000 years ago. The cattle-herding groups of the Ténéré region of Niger are believed to have been either ancestral Berbers or ancestral Zaghawa; sheep and goats were apparently introduced by groups associated with the Capsian culture of northeastern Africa. Direct evidence of agriculture first appears about 6,000 years ago with the cultivation of barley and emmer wheat in Egypt; these appear to have been introduced from Asia. Evidence of the domestication of native African plants is first found in pottery from about 1000 BC discovered in Mauritania. The cultivators have been associated with the Gangara, the ancestors of the modern Soninke.

Archaeological evidence suggests that the Sahara was increasingly inhabited by diverse populations, and plant and animal domestication led to occupational specialization. While the groups lived separately, the proximity of settlements suggests an increasing economic interdependence. External trade also developed. Copper from Mauritania had found its way to the Bronze Age civilizations of the Mediterranean by the 2nd millennium BC. Trade intensified with the emergence of the Iron Age civilizations of the Sahara during the 1st century BC, including the civilization centred in Nubia.

The greater mobility of nomads facilitated their involvement in the trans-Saharan trade. Increasing aridity in the Sahara is documented in the transition from cattle and horses to camels. Although camels were used in Egypt by the 6th century BC, their prominence in the Sahara dates from only the 3rd century AD. Oasis dwellers in the Sahara were increasingly subject to attack by the Sanhaja (a Berber clan) and other camel-mounted nomads—many of whom had entered the desert to avoid the anarchy and warfare of the late Roman period in North Africa. Many of the remaining oasis dwellers, among them the Ḥarāṭīn, were subjugated by the nomads. The expansion of Islām into North Africa between the 7th and 11th centuries prompted additional groups of Berbers, as well as Arab groups wishing to retain traditional beliefs, to move into the Sahara. Islām eventually expanded through the trade routes, becoming the dominant social force in the desert.

Despite considerable cultural diversity, the peoples of the Sahara tend to be categorized as pastoralists, sedentary agriculturalists, or specialists (such as the blacksmiths variously associated with herders and cultivators). Pastoralism, always nomadic to some degree, occurs where sufficient scanty pasturage exists, as in the marginal areas, on the mountain borders, and in the slightly moister west. Cattle appear along the southern borders with the Sahel, but sheep, goats, and camels are the mainstays in the desert. Major pastoral groups include the Regeibat of the northwestern Sahara and the Chaamba of the northern Algerian Sahara. Hierarchical in structure, the larger pastoral groups formerly dominated the desert. Warfare and raids (*ghazw*) were endemic, and in drought periods wide migrations in search of pasture took place, with heavy loss of animals. The Tuareg (who call themselves Kel Tamasheq) were renowned for their warlike qualities and fierce independence. Although they are Islāmic, they retain a matriarchal organization, and the women of the Tuareg have an unusual degree of freedom. The Moorish groups to the west formerly possessed powerful tribal confederations. The Teda, of the Tibesti and its southern borderlands, are chiefly camel herders, renowned for their independence and for their physical endurance.

Pastoral groups

In the desert proper, sedentary occupation is confined to the oases, where irrigation permits limited cultivation of the date palm, pomegranate, and other fruit trees; such cereals as millet, barley, and wheat; vegetables; and such specialty crops as henna. Cultivation is in small "gardens," maintained by a great expenditure of hand labour. Irrigation utilizes ephemeral streams in mountain areas, permanent pools (*gueltas*), foggaras (inclined underground tunnels dug to tap dispersed groundwater in the beds of wadis), springs (*ʿayn*), and wells (*biʾr*). Some shallow groundwaters are artesian, but it is often necessary to use water-lifting devices such as the shadoof (a pivoted pole and bucket) and the animal-driven noria (a Persian wheel with buckets). To a limited extent diesel pumps have replaced these ancient means in more accessible oases. Water availability strictly limits oasis expansion, and, in some, overuse of water has produced a serious fall in the water level, as in the oases of the Adrar region of Mauritania. Salinization of the soil by the fierce evaporation, as well as burial by encroaching sand, are further dangers; the latter, as in the Souf oases of Algeria, necessitates constant hand labour in clearing.

The economy. *Resources.* During the century of colonial dominion over the Sahara, which lasted from the mid-19th to the mid-20th century, there was little fundamental change, except for military pacification; colonial powers were little interested in the economic development of what appeared to be an unpromising region. After World War II, however, the discovery of oil, in particular, attracted international interest and investment. Within a few years major discoveries had been made, particularly in mineral resources.

Metallic minerals are of considerable economic importance. Algeria possesses several major deposits of iron ore, and the reserves at Mount Ijill, in western Mauritania,

Victor Englebert

Kerzaz oasis on Wadi Saoura, western Sahara, Alg.

are substantial; less extensive deposits have been found in Egypt, Tunisia, Morocco, Western Sahara, and Niger. Near Akjoujt, in southwestern Mauritania, lie substantial quantities of copper ore; extensive manganese deposits occur south of Béchar, Alg. Uranium is widely distributed in the Sahara and has been particularly important in Niger. A broad range of other economically significant minerals have been found in the Ahaggar, Aïr, Tibesti, and Eglab regions. Rich phosphate deposits exist in Morocco and Western Sahara, and smaller deposits have been found elsewhere.

Oil and gas reserves

Fuel resources include coal, oil, and natural gas. Sources of coal include anthracite seams in Morocco and bituminous fields near Béchar. Following the discovery of oil near I-n-Salah, Alg., after World War II, major reserves have been found in the Western Desert of Egypt, northeastern Libya, and northeastern Algeria. Minor reserves exist in Tunisia and Morocco, as well as in Chad and Niger in the south. Deposits of oil shale have also been discovered in the Sahara. Major fields of natural gas are exploited in Algeria, and minor fields exist in Egypt, Libya, and Tunisia.

As a result of geologic and oil prospecting, vast underground reserves of water have also been found in a number of sedimentary basins, mainly within sandstone formations. Some recoverable water is also present in surface sand formations.

Economic development of the desert, however, offers enormous difficulties and has not changed the traditional Sahara. Oil and ore extraction have brought modern technology and improved communications to scattered locations, but such activities provide limited opportunities for local employment. Although oil revenues offer the means for desert development, the more immediate and attractive returns possible in inhabited coastal regions tend to take priority. The underground water offers possibilities for major developments in both agriculture and industry; but exploitation on a large scale would be expensive. Heavy exploitation would also result in progressive depletion, and hydrological changes might increase the threat of locust plagues, as locusts congregate into swarms when food supplies are restricted, multiply, and then occupy larger areas when conditions improve.

The desert peoples have benefited little from mineral exploitation—perhaps indeed the reverse. The decline in nomadic pastoralism, started by pacification, has been accelerated by changing economic conditions and official settlement policies (for nomads are administratively inconvenient). Widespread environmental degradation further encourages the drift of nomads to oases and towns, with resultant overcrowding and poverty. High wages in the oil fields attract labour but disrupt traditional life, and the jobs are relatively few and impermanent. Of the traditional desert products—animal skins and wool, surplus fruits, salt—only dates (particularly the *daglet nour* of the northern oases) retain much commercial importance. Salt, although still extracted and sent south to the western Sudan region, now competes with cheap imported salt. Industrial occupations to relieve growing unemployment have as yet made little progress. As manufacturing costs increase in the advanced and overcrowded Western countries, however, the high costs of Saharan development may become more acceptable. It may be possible, for example, to utilize nuclear energy and more efficient solar energy converters to raise deep-seated water (and, if necessary, to remove the salt) for new settlements and to provide power for industries. Tourism has grown considerably since 1950, although the difficulties of transport and of providing accommodations has limited it largely to the Sahara's fringes.

Transportation. Traditionally, travel in the Sahara was by camel caravan and was slow, arduous, and dangerous. To the hazards of losing the way, excessive heat, stifling sandstorms, and death by starvation—or more probably thirst—were added those of attack by raiders. Despite all this, trans-Saharan trade along caravan routes linking oases has persisted from very early times. Most of the principal routes were west of the Tibesti Mountains and tended to shift somewhat over time, although the easternmost of these—which ran northward from Lake Chad to Bilma (now in Niger) and through the Fezzan region to Tripoli—was used continuously through the centuries. East of the Tibesti Mountains oases are few, but the *darb al-arbaʿīn* ("road of the forty [days]"), west of the Nile, was a former slave route. Gold, ivory, slaves, and salt were major items of trade in the earlier days, but today camel caravans have almost ceased, except for a residual trade in salt from Mount Ijill, Bilma, and Taoudenni, Mali. The main routes remain in use, however, by specially equipped motor trucks, often traveling in convoys. Year by year modern highways are extended further along the ancient trade routes into the desert. The French initiated a trans-Saharan bus service, which still operates. Off of the main routes a network of recognized tracks are motorable, with care; but in the open desert four-wheel drive is virtually essential, with at least two vehicles, ample spares, and large emergency supplies of fuel, food, and water—particularly in summer, when special regulations apply to all travelers. In large areas maps are inadequate, and navigational methods may be necessary.

The caravan routes

To supplement ground travel, numerous international air services cross the Sahara on scheduled flights, while local services link the main inhabited centres to one another. Railways, with the abandonment of the "Trans-Saharan" at Abadla (near Béchar, Alg.), have been little developed except for a line built to transport minerals in Mauritania.

Study and exploration. Classical accounts describe the Sahara much as it is today—a vast and formidable barrier. The Egyptians controlled only their neighbouring oases and, occasionally, lands to the south; the Carthaginians apparently continued the commercial relationships with the interior that had been established during the Bronze Age. Herodotus described a desert crossing by an expedition of Berbers during the 5th century BC, and Roman interest in the Sahara is documented in a series of expeditions between 19 BC and AD 86. The descriptions of the Sahara in the works of Strabo, Pliny the Elder, and Ptolemy reflect growing interest in the desert. Geographic exploration, sponsored by the ʿAbbāsids, Fāṭimids, Mamlūks, and other courts in the Middle East, North Africa, and Moorish Spain, was widespread during the medieval period. Descriptions of the Sahara are contained in the works of numerous Arab writers, including al-Yaʿqūbī, ash-Sharīf al-Idrīsī, and Ibn Baṭṭūṭa.

Medieval travelers with religious and commercial motives contributed further to an understanding of the Sahara and its peoples. Abraham Cresque's *Catalan Atlas,* published for Charles V of France in about 1375, renewed European interest in the desert. The atlas contained information based upon the knowledge of Jewish traders active in the Sahara. Its publication was followed by a period of intense Portuguese, Venetian, Genoese, and Florentine activity there. Particularly well documented are the travels of such 15th-century explorers as Alvise Ca' da Mosto, Diogo Gomes, and Pedro de Sintra. Growing interest in the Sahara within northern Europe was reflected in the travels and writings of the 17th-century Dutch geographer Olfert Dapper.

European explorers

Subsequent European exploration of the Sahara, much of it incidental to interest in the major waterways of interior Africa, began in earnest in the 19th century. Attempts to determine the course of the Niger River took the British explorers Joseph Ritchie and George Francis Lyon to the Fezzan area in 1819, and in 1822 the British explorers Dixon Denham, Hugh Clapperton, and Walter Oudney succeeded in crossing the desert and discovering Lake Chad. The Scottish explorer Alexander Gordon Laing crossed the Sahara and reached the fabled city of Timbuktu in 1826, but he was killed there before he could return. The French explorer René Caillié, disguised as an Arab, returned from his visit to Timbuktu by crossing the Sahara from south to north in 1828. Other notable expeditions were undertaken by the German geographer Heinrich Barth (1849–55), the French explorer Henri Duveyrier in 1859–62, and the German explorers Gustav Nachtigal (1869–75) and Gerhard Rohlfs (1862–78).

After the military occupation of the Sahara by the various European colonial powers, more detailed exploration took place; and by the end of the 19th century the main features of the desert were known. Although 20th-century political, commercial, and scientific activities have greatly increased knowledge of the Sahara, vast tracts remained remote, little known, and difficult to reach.

(R.F.Pe./J.A.G.)

VELD

Veld, an Afrikaans word meaning "field" and pronounced "felt," is the name given to various types of open country in southern Africa. To most South African farmers today the "veld" refers to the land they work, much of which has long since ceased to be "natural."

Various types of veld may be discerned, depending upon local characteristics such as elevation, cultivation, and climate. Thus, there is a high veld, a middle veld, a low veld, a bush veld, a thorn veld, and a grass veld. The boundary between these different varieties of veld is frequently vague, and all of them are usually referred to by the general term veld by the local inhabitants. For convenience, its major regions—Highveld, Middle Veld, and Lowveld—are distinguished on the basis of elevation.

For map coverage of the veld, see above *Kalahari*.

Physical features. *Physiography.* The Highveld comprises most of the high-plateau country of southern Africa. Except in Lesotho, where it extends well above 8,200 feet (2,500 metres) and even above 11,000 feet in places, all of it lies between 4,000 and 6,000 feet above sea level. The South African part of the region is bounded on the east and south by the Great Escarpment, which consists of the Drakensberg and Cape ranges, and by the Lesotho Highlands. Its less clearly defined northern and western boundaries coincide roughly with the 4,000-foot contour. Most of it is underlain by sedimentary strata of the Karoo System (or Karoo Super Group), dating from between 345 to 190 million years ago, and to older pre-Karoo material. Among these are coal-bearing strata. These materials have been eroded over a long period of time to produce generally flat plains, dissected occasionally by deeply carved valleys and including relict mountains and scattered steep-sided hills called kopjes, or koppies. The Highveld plains are thought to have been created by pedimentation, in which the areas around resistant rock are eroded away, leaving mountains of low relief and kopjes. Large areas of the western part of the region are also covered by "pans," which are shallow and ephemeral lakes, often with salty crusts; these are found especially in Orange Free State, eastern and western Transvaal, and northwestern Cape Province in South Africa.

Terrain of the Highveld

In Zimbabwe the Highveld coincides roughly with the region lying on either side of the central watershed. Like the Highveld of South Africa, it has a remarkably even surface, broken only by kopjes and low ridges. Throughout the Highveld, soils tend to be thin, poor, and powdery and thus easily carried away by both wind and water erosion.

The Middle Veld is the name given in South Africa to a vast and geologically complex region that lies in the central Transvaal north of Pretoria and Cape Province and in Namibia. Its boundaries are not as well defined as are those for the Highveld, but generally it lies at an altitude between 2,000 and 4,000 feet above sea level. In Zimbabwe to the northeast, the Middle Veld also consists of the land lying roughly between 2,000 and 4,000 feet. Most of the Middle Veld is underlain by Precambrian rocks that have been exposed by erosion. In Transvaal this region is underlain by the unique Bushveld complex, with its wealth of rare minerals. As is the case in the Highveld, the uniformity of the relief is broken by relict mountains and by kopjes. Pans are numerous, especially in the western areas. Middle Veld soils are generally thin and poor.

The Lowveld is the name given to two areas that lie at an altitude of between 500 and 2,000 feet above sea level. One area is in the eastern parts of Transvaal and parts of Swaziland and in northern Natal; and the other is in southeastern Zimbabwe. Both are underlain largely by the soft sediments and basaltic lavas of the Karoo System and by loose gravels. They have been extensively intruded by granites. Other resistant metamorphic rocks also occur; these commonly appear as low ridges or what seem to be archipelagoes of island mountains. The higher western margins of both areas testify to the degree of erosion resulting from the flow of rivers running east or southeast.

The soils of the Lowveld are more varied than those of the other veld regions. Along their higher and wetter western sides, they tend to be deep, leached (percolated by water), acidic, porous, and well drained. In the lower-lying and drier central and eastern portions they tend to be shallow, but they are more fertile and retain moisture better.

Climate. The climate of the veld is highly variable, but its general pattern is mild winters from May to September; hot or very hot summers from November to March, with moderate or considerable variations in daily temperatures; and abundant sunshine. Rainfall mostly occurs in the summer months in the form of high-energy thunderstorms.

Over most of the South African Highveld, the average annual rainfall is between 15 and 30 inches (380 and 760 millimetres), decreasing to about 10 inches near the western border and increasing to nearly 40 inches in some parts of the Lesotho Highlands; the South African Lowveld generally receives more rainfall than the Highveld. Temperature is closely related to altitude. In general, the mean July (winter) temperatures range between 45° F (7° C) in the Lesotho Highlands and 60° F (16° C) in the Lowveld. January (summer) temperatures range between 65° F (18° C) and 80° F (27° C).

Rainfall

In Zimbabwe the rainfall averages around 30 to 35 inches on the Highveld, dropping to less than 15 inches in the

Gerald Cubitt—Bruce Coleman Ltd.

Highveld grassland near Heidelberg, S.Af., southeast of Johannesburg.

lowest areas of the Lowveld. Temperatures are slightly higher than in South Africa.

Over the entire veld, seasonal and annual average rainfall variations of up to 40 percent are common. Damaging drought afflicts at least half of the area about once every three or four years. Everywhere the average number of hours of annual sunshine varies from 60 to 80 percent of the total amount possible.

Plant life. The veld regions support an enormous variety of natural vegetation. No particular species is ubiquitous, and many are highly localized. Grassveld is the characteristic vegetation of the South African Highveld, dominated by species of red grass. Where the red grass grows on well-drained, fertile soils subject to comparatively light rainfall, it tends to be sweeter (and is consequently called sweetveld) than elsewhere, where it is commonly called sourveld. Sweetvelds are more palatable to livestock than sourvelds, the latter being usable as fodder only in winter.

The drier South African Middle Veld favours both red grass and drought-resistant species of grasses. These grasses are less luxuriant and the ground cover less complete than those of the Highveld. As the aridity increases to the west and north, the cover becomes sparser, and grassveld gradually loses ground to thornveld (consisting of such types as thorny acacias and aloes), dwarf, drought-resistant bushes, and desert shrub.

In Zimbabwe the Highveld and Middle Veld consist of open woodland savanna, dominated by leguminous, fire-resistant species of trees belonging to the *Brachystegia* genus. Tall perennial grasses and flowering herbs, which readily catch fire during the dry season, occupy most of the open ground.

The Lowveld everywhere supports a parklike plant cover. In the higher areas the characteristic trees are acacias and marula, an intoxicating plumlike fruit. The open ground is dominated by red grass. In the lower areas, such as the Sabi and Limpopo valleys, tufted finger grasses, euphorbias, and other succulents replace red grass; the acacias increase in number; and the mopane tree, the baobab, and the tall fan palm occur.

Animal life. Mass slaughter, trophy hunting, and the encroachments of farmers and pastoralists have thinned out every major species of mammal and reptile and several species of bird in the veld. The South African and Zimbabwean governments have, however, set aside vast tracts of veld, such as the Kruger National Park in Transvaal, as wildlife reserves. The lion, leopard, cheetah, giraffe, elephant, hippopotamus, oryx, kudu, eland, sable antelope, and roan antelope survive only in or near such protected areas. The smaller mammals, most of the reptiles, and almost all of the birds—except the ostrich, which has virtually been eliminated from the veld—are still found wild.

The people and economy. The veld is believed to be one of the world's oldest regions inhabited by humans and their hominid forebears. Fossil evidence indicates that members of the hominid genus *Australopithecus* occupied the Highveld some three million years ago and that various Stone Age peoples lived there hundreds of thousands of years ago. More recently, the San of the Kalahari inhabited parts of the grassveld until driven from it by Bantu-speaking peoples and the Boers. The generally open character, easy gradients, abundant supply of food, and—in the valleys—water of the Highveld have long attracted migrants as well as settlers. It provided the major routes followed by the Bantu-speaking peoples during their recurrent southward migrations; and in the 1830s the Voortrekkers (pioneer Boer farmers), who moved northward from Cape Colony to escape from the power of the British, made the Highveld their home as well as their highway.

Effects of humans

Until the Voortrekker era the veld remained largely in a natural state. The San, never very populous, lived solely by hunting and gathering. The animal herding and crop raising done by the Bantu-speaking peoples were solely for subsistence. While much of the veld, especially in Zimbabwe, retains its natural cover—modified by the selective grazing habits of oxen, cattle, and other domesticated animals—millions of acres have been brought under the plow. Most of South Africa's corn (maize) crop is now grown on the grassveld in Transvaal and Orange Free State. Most of the Zimbabwean corn crop and almost all of its tobacco crop are grown on the Highveld. The major population centres of these two countries and of Botswana, as well as their major commercial and industrial activities, are also located on the Highveld, which, by virtue of terrain, climate, and mineral and ecological endowment, forms one of the areas most suitable for settlement on the African continent.

Study and exploration. Modern study of the veld has centred on its economic, ecological, and archaeological assets. In the economic area, the emphasis has been on conservation and management of ecosystems, the topics including general geography, vegetation, soils, ecology, geology, and geomorphology. One major focus of investigation has been determining the nutritional potential of various natural vegetation forms in terms of their use in livestock raising and wildlife management.

The discovery of australopithecine fossils on the South African Highveld in the first half of the 20th century sparked great anthropological interest in the region. Since then it has become one of the major centres of hominid exploration and research, and many specimens—including those of other hominid species—have been recovered. In addition, the remains of Stone Age cultures have been found on both the Zimbabwean and the South African velds, and thousands of San rock engravings on the kopjes of the Highveld in Zimbabwe, Transvaal, Lesotho, and Botswana are known. (G.H.T.K./Jo.Co./C.E.F.)

Drainage systems and waterways

LAKE CHAD

Lake Chad (French: Lac Tchad) is a freshwater lake located in the Sahelian zone of west-central Africa at the conjunction of four countries: Chad, Cameroon, Nigeria, and Niger. It is situated in an interior basin formerly occupied by a much larger ancient sea that is sometimes called Mega-Chad. While the surface area of Lake Chad varies greatly, its average area of 6,875 square miles (17,800 square kilometres) ranks it as the fourth largest lake in Africa. The surface of the lake is approximately 922 feet (281 metres) above sea level. The hydrologic contributions and biological diversity of Lake Chad are important regional assets. The region is also noteworthy for important archaeological discoveries, its role in trans-Saharan trade, and its association with historic African kingdoms.

For map coverage of Lake Chad, see below *Niger River.*

Physical features. *Geology and physiography.* The Chad basin is a downwarped section of the Precambrian African Shield. Most of the older crystalline rocks are covered by more recent deposits. The most significant physiographic influence on the basin was the ancient sea. At its maximum extent, the sea was more than 600 feet deep, occupied an area of approximately 154,400 square miles, and drained into the Atlantic Ocean through the Benue River system. It experienced four high stages between 41,000 and 2,300 years ago. The history of the sea is documented in the stratigraphic record, which includes thick layers of diatomaceous earth, lacustrine sands, terraced shorelines, and the remains of modern fish and mollusks in now-arid tracts of the basin. The floor of the basin dips to the northeast of the modern lake, reaching its lowest point in the Djourab Depression, some 300 miles away. Lake Chad occasionally overflows into the generally intermittent El-Ghazal River leading into the depression, but it is usually confined by the dune fields of Kanem.

The ancient sea

Climate. The climate of the Lake Chad region is strongly influenced by the seasonal migration and interaction of the dominant air masses of the region: a dry, subsiding continental air mass and a humid, unstable maritime air mass. The humid air mass moves northward during the summer, wedging beneath the drier air mass. Precipitation occurs when the depth of humid air is sufficiently great. The depth of the air mass varies daily, as well as seasonally, accounting for variation in rainfall. At the end of the summer the dominance of the dry continental air mass is reasserted. Evaporation and transpirational losses from soil and plants increase, and then they decrease as the surface layers of the soil dry and plants lose their leaves.

The dry season is also the period of the harmattan, a dust-laden wind that reduces visibility for days at a time. The increased insolation, reduced humidity, and desiccating winds contribute greatly to water loss in the lake.

Rainfall is greatest from July to September. Annual rainfall averages 22 inches (560 millimetres) at the southern margin of Lake Chad and about 10 inches at the northern margin. Variability during the year is high and increases from south to north; variability from year to year is also high, and droughts are frequent. Temperatures during the rainy season are moderate, with highs of about 90° F (32° C). In October and November, during the transition to the dry season, daily highs rise above 90° F, and diurnal ranges are almost double those of the rainy season. During December and January daytime highs are lower, with nighttime lows sometimes falling to about 47° F (8° C). April is usually the hottest month of the year, with temperatures occasionally exceeding 110° F (43° C).

Hydrology. Lake Chad is a variable body of water, with a surface area that fluctuates from approximately 9,950 square miles in late October or early November to 3,800 square miles in late April or early May. The lake is dotted with numerous islands. The volume of the lake reflects local rainfall and the discharge of its catchment area, balanced against losses through evaporation, transpiration, and seepage. The lake is fed chiefly (more than 90 percent) by the Chari (Shari)–Logone river system. Of the remaining inflow, most is contributed by the Ebeji (El-Béid) and Yedseram rivers. Losses to evaporation and the transpiration of aquatic plants amount to approximately 90 inches each year. It is probable that another 10 inches replenish groundwater supplies in the adjacent Manga and Kanem lowlands and pass as underflow through the El-Ghazal.

Two pools of the lake

The lake is divided into two pools partially separated by a low ridge extending roughly northeast–southwest across the centre of the lake; the ridge was formed during a drought at the beginning of the 20th century. Depths of from 13 to 23 feet are common in the northwestern pool, and depths as great as 33 feet occur among the islands along the eastern margin of the pool. Because of sediment deposition by the Chari River, the southeastern pool is generally shallower—ranging in depth from 10 to 13 feet, but reaching depths of 36 feet along the archipelago. The gentle slope of the lakeshore allows persistent dry-season winds to locally affect water levels for short periods of time. The salt content of Lake Chad is unusually low for a tropical dryland lake with no outlet. As the waters of the lake evaporate during the dry season, the salt content increases, with the highest values recorded along the northeastern shoreline.

Travelers reported high-water levels and overflow into the El-Ghazal during the 13th and 19th centuries. In 1870, for example, Lake Chad covered some 10,800 square miles. At the turn of the 20th century, the lake began to diminish in size, but by the 1920s it had recovered; and in 1956 it again overflowed into the El-Ghazal. During the 1970s and '80s the amplitude of the lake's annual variability was the highest recorded in the 20th century, with average levels falling below long-term norms. The corresponding variability in rainfall appears to have been related to the effects of environmental degradation.

Plant life. The well-drained soils around Lake Chad once supported a relatively dense woodland, including species such as kapok and ebony. Changing patterns of land use and progressive degradation have reduced diversity and resulted in a more open woodland, increasingly composed of species adapted to reduced moisture. They include several acacias, baobab, desert date, palms, African myrrh, and Indian jujube. The periodically inundated lands near the lake are more heavily vegetated. Annual grasses are increasing at the expense of the more economically valuable perennial species. Papyrus, ambatch, water lilies, and reeds dominate aquatic vegetation.

Animal life. Visitors to the medieval kingdom of Kanem in the Lake Chad region described an abundance of wildlife; and until the early 20th century essentially the same faunal assemblages were reported. Since then, however, habitat loss, hunting, and direct competition from livestock have depleted wildlife populations. As with vegetation, the trend is toward decreased diversity and lower levels of biological productivity. Populations of large carnivores, including lions and leopards, have been eliminated in livestock areas; and such game animals as the rhinoceros have been reduced or eliminated. Nocturnal species have been less affected by these changes; and some species, particularly rodents, have benefited from them.

Birdlife of the region

Hundreds of species of birds reside permanently or seasonally in the Lake Chad region. Included are prominent terrestrial birds—such as the ostrich, secretary bird, Nubian bustard, and ground hornbill—and the water and shore birds for which the region is famous—such as garganey, shoveler, fulvous tree duck, Egyptian goose, pink-backed pelican, marabou stork, glossy ibis, and African spoonbill. Included among the amphibians and reptiles are the Nile crocodile, rock python, and spitting cobra. The Chad basin remains an important fishery, with more than 40 species of commercial importance. Also noteworthy are such ancient species as the lungfish and sailfin.

The people and economy. *Settlement history.* The Chad basin contains the earliest evidence of hominid occupation yet found in western Africa, and it appears that the Lake Chad region has been continuously settled since 500 BC. Among the major archaeological discoveries of the region has been the Sao civilization; it is believed that the modern Kotoko, a fishing people on the Chari near Lake Chad, are descendants of the Sao.

During the medieval period (9th to 16th century) the Lake Chad region was both an important refuge and an area in which diverse populations were consolidated by the authority of powerful kingdoms. The modern Kanembu, for example, are composed of several groups consolidated by Kanem in the 9th century; similarly, the modern Kanuri emerged from the imposed authority of Kanem's successor state, Bornu, located southwest of Lake Chad. Some ethnic groups were not assimilated. The metallurgists of Kanem, for example, were apparently the Danoa (Haddad), who currently serve as blacksmiths among the Kanembu. Other groups resisted integration into the medieval kingdoms. The Yedina (Buduma) established themselves among the inaccessible islands and along the marshy northern shore of Lake Chad, and the Kuri did the same in inaccessible areas along the eastern margin of the lake.

Other ethnic groups established themselves on the shores of Lake Chad in the more recent past. Arab settlement dates from the arrival of the Judam tribes in the 16th century. Some ethnic groups, such as Fulani pastoralists, now enter the Lake Chad lowlands on a seasonal basis; and Hausa agricultural communities can often be found along the lake. The economy of these modern peoples of the Lake Chad region is based primarily on fishing, subsistence and commercial agriculture, and animal husbandry—often in combination.

Agriculture and forestry. Subsistence crops include sorghum, corn (maize), African millet, beans, and vegetables. Bottle gourds are grown widely for making utensils. Polders near Bol, used to grow cash crops, are based on traditional agricultural practices. Cultivated by the Kanembu and Yedina, the polders are devoted chiefly to wheat.

The exploitation of such forest products as gum arabic, honey, beeswax, and firewood is of considerable importance in the region. Production of these, however, has been adversely affected by the decline of the forested areas, aggravated by the explosive growth of cattle populations.

Cattle

Livestock and fishing. Cattle are the most important livestock raised. Notable breeds include the Kuri (Chad) and several varieties of zebu (Brahman). Milk is a major component of local diets, and cattle are an important export to the tsetse-infested regions to the south. Large numbers of poultry, goats, sheep, camels, horses, and asses are also kept.

Fishing is the most important economic activity for the peoples of the lake. Much of the catch is dried, salted, or smoked. Dried *Alestes* species, known by the Arabic name *salanga,* and pieces of smoked fish called *banda* are marketed, primarily in Nigeria and Cameroon. In addition, fresh Nile perch are often exported to major African and European cities.

Minerals. Petroleum reserves have been discovered in

Natron being unloaded along the eastern shore of Lake Chad near Baga Sola, Chad.

© Jacques Jangoux—Peter Arnold, Inc.

Chad and Niger. Natron (hydrated sodium carbonate), found in depressions along the northeastern shore of the lake, has long been economically important. Traditionally, it is excavated in blocks and shipped across the lake, where it enters Nigerian commerce.

Transportation. Lake Chad is little used for commercial navigation, although there has been intermittent barge traffic between Bol and N'Djamena since the early 1950s. A variety of watercraft are used in fishing, including the papyrus-reed *kadeï* of the Yedina and the sewn-plank boats of the Kotoko.

Study and exploration. For millennia settlement patterns of peoples of Mediterranean and sub-Saharan origin have overlapped in the Sahara, and there is emerging evidence of a long history of interaction between the Lake Chad region and other regions of northern Africa. There are essentially four periods during which the region was strongly affected by external influences. The first is expressed in hints of Egyptian contact with the region; in the sub-Saharan commerce of Carthage and the Garamantes; and in references in Greek, Roman, and Arabic literature.

The second period was precipitated largely by the expansion of Islām in North Africa during the 7th century AD, when groups of Arabs and Berbers who resisted conversion sought refuge in the dry lands of the south. The third period emerged from trade between Kanem or Bornu and Mediterranean Africa, the penetration of Islām into sub-Saharan Africa, and increased Arab interest in geographic exploration. It is documented in the many Arabic works written in the 9th to 14th centuries and is also reflected in Abraham Cresque's *Catalan Atlas* (*c.* 1375).

The fourth period emerged from growing interest in Africa within European academic and commercial circles and was a prelude to European colonization. Numerous descriptions of the Lake Chad region were written by 19th-century Europeans, and three scientific missions were mounted between 1898 and 1909. (J.A.G.)

CONGO RIVER

The Congo (or Zaire) River, with a length of 2,900 miles (4,700 kilometres), is longer than any other river in Africa except for the Nile. It rises in the highlands of northeastern Zambia between Lakes Tanganyika and Nyasa (Malaŵi) as the Chambeshi River at an altitude of 5,760 feet (1,760 metres) above sea level and at a distance of about 430 miles from the Indian Ocean. Its course then takes the form of a giant counterclockwise arc, flowing to the northwest, west, and southwest before draining into the Atlantic Ocean at Banana (Banane), Zaire. Its drainage basin, covering an area of 1,335,000 square miles (3,457,000 square kilometres), takes in almost the entire territory of Zaire, as well as most of that of the People's Republic of the Congo, the Central African Republic, eastern Zambia, and northern Angola and parts of Cameroon and Tanzania.

With its many tributaries the Congo forms the continent's largest network of navigable waterways. Navigability, however, is limited by an insurmountable obstacle: a series of 32 cataracts over the river's lower course, including the famous Livingstone (Inga) Falls. These cataracts render the Congo unnavigable between the seaport of Matadi, at the head of the Congo estuary, and Malebo (Stanley) Pool, a lakelike expansion of the river. It was on opposite banks of Malebo Pool—which represents the point of departure of inland navigation—that the capitals of the former states of the French Congo and the Belgian Congo were founded: on the left bank, Kinshasa (formerly Léopoldville), now the capital of Zaire, and on the right bank, Brazzaville, now the capital of the Congo.

Comparisons with the Amazon

The Amazon and Congo are the two great rivers of the world that flow out of equatorial zones where heavy rainfall occurs throughout all or almost all of the year. Upstream from Malebo Pool, the Congo basin receives an average of about 60 inches (1,500 millimetres) of rain a year, of which more than one-quarter is discharged into the Atlantic. The drainage basin of the Congo is, however, only about half the size of that of the Amazon; its rate of flow—1,450,000 cubic feet (41,000 cubic metres) per second at its mouth—is considerably less than the Amazon's flow of more than 6,350,000 cubic feet per second.

While the Chambeshi River, as the remotest source, may form the Congo's original main stream in terms of the river's length, it is another tributary—the Lualaba, which rises near Musofi in the Shaba (formerly Katanga) region of Zaire—that carries the greatest quantity of water and thus may be considered as forming the Congo's original main stream in terms of water volume.

When the river first became known to Europeans at the end of the 15th century, they called it the Zaire, a corruption of a word that is variously given as *nzari, nzali, njali, nzaddi,* and *niadi* and that simply means "river" in many African dialects. It was only in the early years of the 18th century that the river was first called the "Rio Congo," a name taken from the kingdom of Kongo that had been situated on the lower part of the river's course. In 1971, when the Democratic Republic of the Congo changed its name to Zaire, the government also renamed the river as the Zaire. As the river, however, has an international status, it continues to be known throughout the world as the Congo. To the literary-minded the river is evocative of the famous 1902 short story "Heart of Darkness" by Joseph Conrad. His book conjured up an atmosphere of foreboding, treachery, greed, and exploitation. Today, however, the Congo appears as the key to the economic development of the central African interior.

Physical features. *Physiography.* The expression Congo basin refers, strictly speaking, to the hydrographic basin. This is not only vast but is also—with the exception of the sandy plateaus in the southwest—covered with a dense and ramified network of tributaries, subtributaries, and small rivers.

The Congo basin is the most clearly distinguished of the various geographic depressions situated between the Sahara to the north, the Atlantic Ocean to the south and west, and the region of the East African lakes to the east. In this basin, a fan-shaped web of tributaries flows downward along concentric slopes that range from 900 to 1,500 feet in altitude and that enclose a central depression. The basin itself stretches for more than 1,200 miles from north to south (from the Congo–Lake Chad watershed to the interior plateaus of Angola) and also measures about 1,200 miles from the Atlantic in the west to the Nile–Congo watershed in the east.

The *cuvette*

The central part of the Congo basin—often called the *cuvette* (literally, "saucer," or "shallow bowl")—is an immense depression containing Quaternary alluvial deposits that rest on thick sediments of continental origin, consisting principally of sands and sandstones. These underlying sediments form outcrops in valley floors at the eastern edge of the *cuvette.* The filling of the *cuvette,* however, began much earlier. Boreholes have revealed that since late Precambrian times (*i.e.,* since at least 570 million years ago) considerable sediment has accumulated, derived from the erosion of formations situated around the periphery of the *cuvette.* The arrangement of surface relief, thick depositional strata, and substratum in amphitheatre-like fashion around the main Congo channel, which has been uniform across time, is evidence of a persistent tendency to subsidence in this part of the continent. This subsidence is accompanied by uplifting on the edges of the *cuvette,* principally on its eastern side—which has also been influenced by the formation of the Western Rift Valley.

From its sources to its mouth, the Congo River system has three contrasting sections—the upper Congo, middle Congo, and lower Congo.

The upper reaches are characterized by three features—confluences, lakes, and waterfalls or rapids. To begin with, several streams of approximately equal size unite to form the river. In a little more than 60 miles, the upper Lualaba joins the Luvua and then the Lukuga. Each stream for part of its course undergoes at least a lacustrine type of expansion, even when it does not form a lake. Thus, Lake Upemba occurs on the upper Lualaba; Lakes Bangweulu and Mweru occur on the Chambeshi–Luapula–Luvua system; and finally Lake Tanganyika, which is fed by the Ruzizi (flowing from Lake Kivu) and by the Malagarasi, itself flows into the Lukuga. Rapids occur not only along the headstreams but also several times along the course of the main stream. Navigation thus is possible only along sections of the upper Congo by vessels of low tonnage; even so, these stretches are in danger of being overgrown by aquatic vegetation, particularly water hyacinths.

Kisangani (formerly Stanleyville)—located just downstream of the Boyoma (Stanley) Falls, a series of seven cataracts—marks the real beginning, upriver, of the navigable Congo. This central part of the river flows steadily for more than 1,000 miles to within 22 miles of Kinshasa. Its course at first is narrow but soon grows wider, after which many islands occur in midstream. This change in the character of the river corresponds to its entry into its alluvial plain. From that point onward, with the exception of a few rare narrow sections, the Congo divides into several arms, separated by strings of islands. It increases from a width of more than three and a half miles downstream from Isangi (where the Lomami enters the Congo) to a width of from five to seven miles and on occasion—for example, at the mouth of the Mongala—to eight miles. Beyond the natural levees (formed by silt deposits) occurring on either bank, some areas are subjected to extensive flooding that increases the river's bounds still further. (It

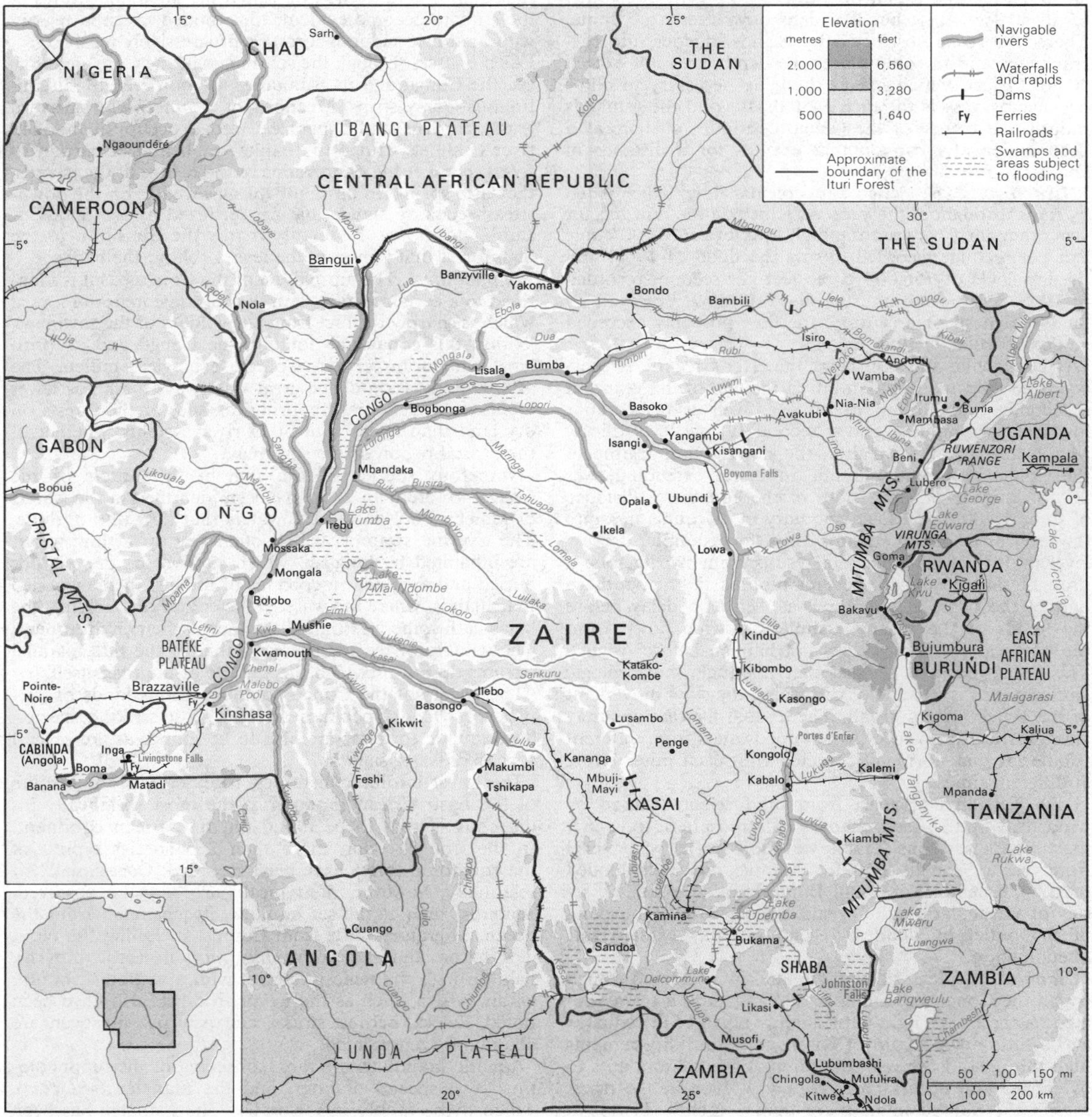

The Congo River basin and its drainage network.

is not always easy to distinguish such areas from the "rain swamps" in regions lying between rivers.) The middle course of the Congo ends in a narrow section called the Chenal (Channel), or Couloir (Corridor). Between banks no more than half a mile to a mile wide, the riverbed deepens, and the current becomes rapid, flowing through a valley that cuts down several hundreds of yards deep into the soft sandstone bedrock of the Batéké Plateau. Along this central reach the Congo receives its principal tributaries, primarily the Ubangi and the Sangha on the right bank and the Kwa on the left bank. An enormous increase in the average rate of flow results, rising from less than 250,000 cubic feet a second at Kisangani to nearly its maximum flow at Kinshasa.

Mouth of the Congo

Upon leaving the Chenal, the Congo divides into two branches, forming Malebo Pool, a vast lacustrine area about 15 miles by 17 miles, which marks the end of the middle Congo. Immediately downstream occur the first waterfalls of the final section of the river's course. Cataracts and rapids are grouped into two series, separated by a fairly calm central reach, in which the altitude drops from a little less than 900 feet to a few yards above sea level. The Congo's estuary begins at Matadi, downstream from the rapids that close off the interior Congo; 83 miles in length, it forms the border between Angola and Zaire. At first the estuary is narrow (less than half a mile to about a mile and a half in width) with a central channel 65 to 80 feet deep, but it widens downstream of Boma. There, the river, obstructed by islands, divides into several arms, and in some places the depth does not exceed 20 to 25 feet, which makes dredging necessary to allow oceangoing vessels to reach Matadi. Beyond the estuary's mouth, the course of the Congo continues offshore as a deep underwater canyon that extends for a distance of about 125 miles.

Hydrology. The Congo has a regular flow, which is fed by rains throughout the year. At Kinshasa the flow has for years remained between the high level of 2,310,000 cubic feet per second, recorded during the flood of 1908, and the low level of 756,000 cubic feet per second, recorded in 1905. During the unusual flood of 1962, however, by far the highest for a century, the flow probably exceeded 2,600,000 cubic feet per second.

At Brazzaville and Kinshasa, the river's regime is characterized by a main maximum at the end of the year and a secondary maximum in May, as well as by a major low level during July and a secondary low level during March and April. In reality, the downstream regime of the Congo represents climatic influence extending over 20° of latitude on both sides of the equator, a distance of some 1,400 miles. Each tributary in its course modifies the level of the main stream. Thus, for example, the low level in July at Malebo Pool results from two factors: a drought that occurs for several months in the southern part of the basin at that time, as well as a delay before the floods of the Ubangi tributary flowing down from the north arrive, which does not happen before August. The Congo basin is so vast that no single meteorologic circumstance is capable of disturbing the slow movement of the waters' rise and fall. The annual fluctuations may alter drastically, however, when floodwaters from different tributaries that normally coincide with each other arrive at different times.

Lake Tanganyika, apart from brief seiches caused by wind drift and sudden changes in atmospheric pressure, may experience considerable variations in its water level from year to year. In 1960, for example, its waters flooded parts of Kalemi, Zaire, and Bujumbura, Burundi. A series of particularly rainy years, followed by a blocking of the outlet by floating vegetation, may explain this phenomenon.

The rainfall pattern

Climate. Typical of the climate in regions through which the Congo flows is that of Yangambi, a town situated on the river's right bank slightly north of the equator and a little downstream of Kisangani. Humidity remains high throughout the year, and annual rainfall amounts to 67 inches and occurs fairly regularly; even in the driest month the rainfall totals more than 3 inches. Temperatures are also uniformly high throughout the year, and there is little diurnal variability. The average temperature at Yangambi is 76° F (24° C).

From the pluviometric equator (an imaginary east–west line indicating the region of heaviest rainfall), which is situated slightly to the north of the geographic equator, the amount of rainfall decreases regularly in proportion to the latitude. The northernmost points of the basin, situated in the Central African Republic, receive only from eight to 16 inches less during the course of a year than points near the equator; the dry season, however, lasts for four or five months, and there is only one annual rainfall maximum, which occurs in summer. In the far southern part of the basin—at a latitude of 12° S, in the Shaba region—the climate becomes definitely Sudanic in character, with marked dry and wet seasons of approximately equal length and with rainfall of about 49 inches a year.

Plant life. The equatorial climate that prevails over a significant part of the Congo basin is coextensive with a dense evergreen forest. The Congolese forest spreads out over the central depression, extending continuously from about 4° N to about 5° S; it is interrupted only by clearings, many of which have a natural origin. The forest region is bordered on either side by belts of savanna (grassy parkland). The forest and savanna often meet imperceptibly, blending together in a mosaic pattern; more rarely, strips of forest invade the grassland. Farther away from the equator, and to the extent that the Sudanic features of the climate become evident, the wooded savanna region, with its thin deciduous forest, is progressively reached.

As it courses through the solid mass of the Congolese forest, the Congo and its tributaries are bordered by discontinuous grassy strips. Meadows of *Echinochloa* (barnyard grass), papyrus, and Cyperaceae (sedge) occupy abandoned river channels, fringe the banks, or, behind a curtain of forest, blanket the depressions in the centre of the islands; they also spring up on sandbanks, as well as on the downstream ends of islands that are fertilized by the floods. A shrub, *Alchornea,* frequently marks the transition to the high forest that grows on the levees behind the banks.

Animal life. The animal life of the Congo basin is identified to a certain extent with that of the equatorial forest, which is sharply distinct from the wildlife of the savannas. Within this equatorial domain, the Congo and its principal tributaries form a separate ecological milieu. The animal population of the great waterways often has fewer affinities with the neighbouring marshes or the forests on dry land than it has with other river systems, whether of the coastal region or the savannas.

Species of fish

Numerous species of fish live in the waters of the Congo—more than 230 have been identified in the waters of Malebo Pool and in the waters that flow into it alone. The riverine swamps, which often dry up at low water, are inhabited by lungfish, which survive the dry periods buried and encysted in cocoons of mucus. In the wooded marshlands, where the water is the colour of black tea, the black catfish there assume the colour of their environment. The wildlife of the marshes and that of the little parallel streams do not mix with the wildlife of the river itself.

The waters of the Congo contain various kinds of reptiles, of which crocodiles are the most striking species. Semiaquatic tortoises are also to be found, as are several species of water snakes.

The forest birdlife constitutes, together with the birdlife of the East African mountains, the most specifically indigenous of that to be found on the African continent. In the Congo region more than 265 species typical of the equatorial forest have been recorded. Occasionally or seasonally, however, nontypical birds may be observed. Seabirds, such as the sea swallow, fly upstream from the ocean. Migratory birds from Europe, including the blongios heron and the *Ixobrychus minutus* (little bittern), pass through the region. Species with a wide distribution within Africa, such as the Egyptian duck, also have been noted. Ducks, herons, storks, and pelicans, however, are abundantly represented.

Aquatic mammals are rare, consisting of the hippopotamus, two species of otter, and the manatee (sea cow), which lives entirely in the water. The manatee has been officially identified only on the Sangha tributary but appears to have given rise to some curious legends on the lower Congo, including its association with a creature called Mami Wata (a kind of siren).

The people and the economy. *Life of the river peoples.* Three types of environment are found, either juxtaposed or in succession, along the river and its tributaries: the narrower sections, bordered by firm ground; the wider stretches, dotted with islands and accompanied by backwaters; and the zones where flooding occurs or where there are extensive marshes.

Almost all the river peoples engage in fishing. Along the narrow sections, where rapids often occur, fishing is only of interest to a small number of villages. The Enya (Wagenia) of Boyoma Falls and the Manyanga living downstream from Malebo Pool attach fish traps to stakes or to dams built in the rapids themselves. Fishing of a very different nature, notably by poison, is conducted in the marshy areas, where the population is more extensive than might be imagined. Among these peoples are the "water people"—the Ngombe—who inhabit the Itimbiri-Ngiri and the triangle formed by the Congo and the Ubangi. Other fisherfolk of the marshes dwell in the lagoons and the drowned forests of the region where the confluence of the Congo and the Alima, Likouala, and Sangha occurs.

Farming

Despite unfavourable conditions, all these peoples are also cultivators. They raise dikes, often of monumental size, to plant cassava on the land thus sheltered from flooding. Other crops, such as sweet potatoes, bananas, and yams, are of little importance. Although the Congo basin has the continent's most important timber resources, the timber industry is still largely undeveloped, mainly because the interior is so inaccessible and because the cost of transporting timber to the coast is so high.

Few modes of existence have undergone such profound changes as a result of contact with the modern world as has that of the river's fisherfolk. The growth of the towns on the banks of Malebo Pool as well as the taste of urban dwellers for river fish have served to stimulate fishing by relating it to a cash economy. It is not just a question of villagers smoking fish that they sell to passing traders. Increasingly numerous fishing crews sail up the Congo, the Ubangi, and the Kasai, well above their confluences, to fish in the shallows.

Transportation. The Congo is the most important navigational system in Africa. Within the territorial limits of Zaire alone, there are some 8,700 miles of navigable waterway. Of this total, 650 miles are accessible at all seasons to barges with capacities of from 800 to 1,100 tons, depending upon the height of the water. The amount of goods transported by water—consisting mainly of agricultural produce, wood, minerals, and fuel—is very modest in comparison to the traffic on European rivers (for example, the commercial traffic from the port of Kinshasa does not reach a million tons), but river transport remains essential for communications with regions that are inaccessible by road, especially in the *cuvette.* The three principal routes, all of which converge on the downstream terminus at Kinshasa on the Malebo Pool, run from Kisangani, from Ilebo (formerly Port-Francqui) on the Kasai, and from Bangui on the Ubangi. River transport, however, falls short of the role it could play in development. It has actually declined since the states of the Congo became independent in 1960 because of serious problems with aging equipment, a lack of maintenance of the infrastructure, and the poor functioning of the public waterway agencies. In Zaire only the section from Ilebo to Kinshasa is still important, because it constitutes the river link (the other link being a railway between Kinshasa and Matadi) by which part of the copper production of Shaba is conveyed to the coast.

This network has fostered economic development in inland areas, far from the coast. Varied activities include the production of palm oil on the banks of the Kwilu, centred on the port of Kikwit, and the establishment of plantations of robusta coffee in the Kisangani area.

Before such developments could be undertaken, however, it was necessary to overcome the barrier to the sea formed by the Congo's lower course. That feat was accomplished in 1898 with the opening of the railway between Matadi and Léopoldville (now Kinshasa) and in 1934 by the completion of the Congo–Ocean rail line on the right bank between Brazzaville and Pointe-Noire.

Railways

While the river system facilitates navigation, it also hinders land transportation. Only a small number of bridges cross the Congo and its tributaries. The Kongolo rail and road bridge over the Lualaba was reconstructed in 1968, and a bridge over the Congo at Matadi was opened in 1983. Numerous projects to improve the situation nevertheless exist, notably a link between Kinshasa and Brazzaville. This project has long been under discussion, although to financial obstacles are added difficulties caused by political dissension. Several times since the two countries gained independence in 1960, such dissensions have interrupted the ferry traffic between the two capitals.

Power. It has been estimated that the hydroelectric potential of the Congo basin amounts to about one-sixth of the known world resources, but only a fraction of this potential has been harnessed. The single site of Inga, just upriver from Matadi, has a power potential estimated at more than 30,000 megawatts. Two hydroelectric projects, called Inga I and Inga II, have been completed there since Zaire's independence. Although the combined installed capacity of Inga is only a small fraction of the total potential, it is greater than the present power consumption of Zaire. Thus, it will be many years before the Congo region's energy needs equal the potential output of the river.

Study and exploration. The problem of the origin of

Superstock

Enya (Wagenia) fishing in the rapids of the Congo River near Kisangani, Zaire.

the Congo confronted European explorers from the time that the Portuguese navigator Diogo Cão discovered the river's mouth in 1482, which he believed to be a strait providing access to the realm of the mythical Prester John, a Christian priest-king. It is virtually certain that, well before the Welsh explorer Henry Morton Stanley arrived in 1877, some 17th-century Capuchin missionaries reached the shores of Malebo Pool. This exploit, however, was not followed up, even by the amply supplied Tuckey expedition, which was sent out by the British admiralty in 1816. The expedition was decimated and had to retrace its footsteps even before it had surmounted the cataracts. Preposterous hypotheses about the river continued to be entertained, connecting, for example, the upper Niger to the Congo or maintaining that the Congo and the Nile both flowed from a single great lake in the heart of Africa.

Even after the discovery of Lake Tanganyika by the British explorers Richard Burton and John Speke (1858), then of the Lualaba (1867) and of Lake Bangweulu (1868) by the Scottish explorer David Livingstone, uncertainty remained—uncertainty that Stanley was to dissipate in the course of his famous expedition in 1876 and 1877 that took him by water over a period of nine months from the Lualaba to the Congo's mouth. In the interior of the Congo basin, and above all on the right bank, the final blank spaces on the map could not be filled in until about 1890, when the exploration of the upper course of the Ubangi was completed. (G.F.S./Ro.Po.)

Stanley's expedition

EAST AFRICAN LAKES

The majority of East African lakes lie within the East African Rift System, which forms a part of a series of gigantic fissures in the Earth's crust extending northward from the Zambezi River valley through eastern and northeastern Africa and the Red Sea to the Jordan River valley in southwestern Asia. In East Africa itself, the southern, eastern, and western branches of the system can be discerned.

For map coverage of the East African lakes, see above *East African mountains.*

Occupying the Southern Rift Valley is Lake Nyasa (Lake Malaŵi), which drains into the Zambezi River. Marking the course of the Western Rift Valley are Lakes Tanganyika, Kivu, Edward, and Albert (also called Mobutu Sese Seko)—the first two of which are situated within the drainage basin of the Congo River, while the other two constitute part of the Nile River drainage system. With the exception of Lake Rudolf (Lake Turkana), the lakes found in the Eastern (Great) Rift Valley are smaller than those of the Western Rift and constitute several independent inland drainage basins.

Located in a shallow downwarping between the Eastern and Western Rift highlands is Lake Victoria, which among the freshwater lakes of the world has a surface area that is second only to that of Lake Superior in North America. On a smaller scale, East Africa also includes some fine examples of crater lakes, and on Mount Kenya and in the Ruwenzori (Rwenzori) Range are found glacial tarns, small lakes each of which occupies a basin, or cirque, scraped out by a mountain glacier.

The eight largest lakes

Of the eight largest lakes—Victoria, 26,828 square miles (69,485 square kilometres) in area; Tanganyika, 12,700; Nyasa, 11,430; Rudolf, 2,473; Albert, 2,160; Kivu, 1,040; Rukwa, 1,000; and Edward, 830—only one, Rukwa, in Tanzania, lies wholly within a single political entity. The northern shore of Kenya's Lake Rudolf is in Ethiopia; Lake Victoria is divided among Uganda, Tanzania, and Kenya. In the west the international boundary between Uganda and Zaire runs through the centre of Lake Albert; the same boundary places two-thirds of Lake Edward in Zaire and the remainder in Uganda. Lake Kivu lies between Rwanda and Zaire; the waters of Lake Tanganyika are shared among Tanzania, Zaire, Burundi, and Zambia. Malaŵi and Mozambique have territorial waters on Lake Nyasa, and, since its independence, Tanzania has also advanced claims to its territorial waters because it also occupies a part of the lakeshore.

Physical features. *Physiography.* The surface levels of the lakes on the irregular floor of the Eastern Rift Valley are of varying heights, rising from Lake Rudolf (1,230 feet [375 metres] above sea level) through Lake Baringo (3,200 feet) to Lake Naivasha (6,180 feet), after which there is a decrease in height to Lake Magadi (1,900 feet). The Omo River from the Ethiopian Plateau is the only perennial affluent of Lake Rudolf, which is the lowest of the major East African lakes. Although it has the typical elongated form of a rift lake, Rudolf is relatively shallow (240 feet at its centre, although it reaches about 400 feet in a small depression at the southern end), as are the other lakes of the Eastern Rift. Its eastern and southern shores are bounded by rocky margins of volcanic origin; the lower western and northern shores are mostly composed of sandy sediments. South of Lake Magadi the splaying continuation of the Eastern Rift into northern Tanzania is indicated by Lakes Natron, Manyara, and Eyasi.

In the Western Rift Valley the northwestern and southeastern shores of Lake Albert are flanked by steep escarpments; wild ravines and fine cascades form a conspicuous feature of these geologically young tectonic (fault-formed) landscapes, the scale being greater on the Zaire than on the Uganda side. There is a considerable lowland area at the northern end of the lake, where, about 20 miles below Murchison (Kabalega) Falls, the Victoria Nile enters Lake Albert, to leave almost immediately as the northward-flowing Albert Nile. The southern end of Lake Albert contains an alluvial flat and a papyrus-choked delta formed by the Semliki River, which both carries the outflow from Lake Edward and provides drainage from the rain-soaked Ruwenzori Range.

Lake Edward, of which the deepest part (367 feet) is in the west under the Congo Escarpment, receives the Rutshuru River as its principal affluent. On the northeast it is connected with Lake George by the 3,000-foot-wide Kazinga Channel. At an altitude of approximately 3,000 feet above sea level, the surfaces of both lakes are nearly 1,000 feet higher than that of Lake Albert.

The Virunga Mountains

Separating the basins of Lake Edward and Lake Kivu are the Virunga Mountains, which thus divide the drainage system of the Nile River from that of the Congo River. With clear water, a broken shoreline, and a mountainous setting, including the relatively recent volcanoes (Nyamulagira and Nyiragongo) of the Virunga Mountains, Lake Kivu possesses outstanding scenic attractions. Its outflow is southward by the turbulent Ruzizi River, which drops more than 2,200 feet on its way to Lake Tanganyika. This latter lake, long and narrow, is second only to the Soviet Union's Lake Baikal in depth, penetrating at its maximum to 4,710 feet, which is more than 2,400 feet below sea level. Typical, too, are the flanking escarpments, which often rise sheer from the lake; the only sizable lowland is the lower Ruzizi valley. The drainage of the Malagarasi River system enters Lake Tanganyika about 25 miles south of Kigoma, Tanz.; at its southern end, on the frontier with Zambia, the 700-foot Kalambo Falls occur where the Kalambo River tumbles over the escarpment. The overflow to the Lualaba River, a tributary of the Congo, is via the shallow and sometimes obstructed Lukuga River outlet on the western side.

Lake Victoria, with its quadrilateral shape, relative shallowness (maximim depth of about 260 feet), and an area that is more than twice as great, is quite different from Lake Tanganyika. Set in a region of erosion surfaces instead of tectonic escarpments, it is bounded by a shoreline of considerable variety: on the west a straight, cliffed coast gives way to papyrus swamp; headlands and deep indentations mark the intricate northern shores; a major inlet, the Winam (formerly Kavirondo) Bay, is located on the east; and on the southern shores the Speke, Mwanza, and Emin Pasha gulfs lie amid rocky, granitic hills. Ukerewe, situated in the southeast, is the largest island in the lake; in the northwest the Sese Islands constitute a major archipelago. At the entrance to the channel leading to Jinja, Uganda, lies Buvuma Island. There are numerous other islands, most being of ironstone formation overlying quartzite and crystalline schists. The Kagera River, largest of the affluents, may be considered as being the most remote headstream of the Nile. The outlet of the lake and the conventional source of the Nile is at Jinja, where after flowing over the now-submerged Ripon Falls, the Victoria Nile begins its journey toward the Mediterranean Sea through the sluices of the dam at Owen Falls.

Lake Rukwa is situated in a northwest- to southeast-trending side rift, parallel with the southern part of the Lake Tanganyika rift and continuing the structural alignment of the northern end of Lake Nyasa. Lying on flat alluvium (soil, gravel, sand, and stone deposited by running water), Rukwa is extremely shallow (20 feet at the greatest depth), and any change of surface level causes great fluctuations in its area. Southeast of Lake Rukwa, beyond the volcanic mass of Rungwe Mountain, Lake Nyasa, third in size among the East African lakes, has the same characteristics as Lake Tanganyika but in less extreme form. It is deepest in the north (2,310 feet), where, on the Tanzanian side, the Livingstone Mountains rise precipitously from the lake surface. In the northwest, however, there is a well-defined alluvial plain. From the east come the waters of the Ruhuhu River, and numerous streams flow across the Malaŵi Plateau to the western shore. In the shallower, southern part there are several lake plains and sandy beaches. The Shire River outlet at the southernmost end has an extremely small gradient in its upper section, but in its middle course the river is interrupted by cataracts before emptying into the Zambezi.

Geology. The East African rifts attained their present form mainly as a result of Pleistocene earth movements from 1,600,000 to 10,000 years ago, and the lakes must have been formed after the landscapes in which they are set. The shallowness of such lakes as Albert (maximum recorded depth 190 feet) and Edward (367 feet) is the result of the thick layers of sediment upon which they rest. In some lakes, too, volcanic activity has played a part in blocking drainage and shaping shorelines. Raised beaches indicate that the lake levels were higher and their surfaces were more extensive during rainy phases of the Pleistocene Epoch. In the Eastern Rift, for instance, Lakes Rudolf and Baringo were formerly part of one lake, from which there was a link via the Sobat River with the White Nile. Subsequent drier conditions caused the eastern lakes gradually to dwindle in size, with many fluctuations, to their present independent status.

Formation of the lakes

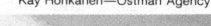

The lakes of the Western Rift have experienced their own geologic changes. Before the geologically recent blocking of the rift by the eruption of the Virunga Mountains, the drainage of Lake Kivu was probably northward into the Nile. The fossil record suggests that the organic content of Lakes Edward and George was considerably reduced during a period of intense volcanic activity around their shores, although several species of fish (*e.g., Tilapia nilotica*) appear to have survived. Toward the end of the Middle Pleistocene (about 100,000 years ago), when the rise in the shoulders of the Western Rift resulted in the reversal of the westward-flowing drainage of such rivers as the Kagera, Katonga, and Kyoga-Kafu, Lakes Victoria and Kyoga were formed by water diverted from the northern section of the rift. Eventually, however, the drainage of most of Uganda returned to the Western Rift and to the Nile. The subsequent reductions in the level of Lake Victoria are indicated by a series of strandlines around its shores.

Climate. Those East African lakes that lie in inland troughs at altitudes of about 2,000 feet or less have a hot, dry climatic environment with a high potential evaporation. In the higher parts of the rift floors, however, climatic conditions approach those of the flanking highlands. In the Western Rift moist air from the Congo basin is a source of the more humid conditions prevailing over Lakes Tanganyika and Kivu. The glacial tarns of Mount Kenya and the Ruwenzori Range are in the frigid zone.

Large lakes tend to create or influence their own climates, and this effect is most marked on the western and northern margins of the immense mass of Lake Victoria. There, in a zone 30 to 50 miles wide, temperatures rarely rise above 80° F (27° C) or fall below 60° F (16° C), and rainfall is well distributed throughout the year. Moreover, annual rainfall is high, being heaviest over the lake and decreasing inland from an average of 50 to 60 inches (1,300 to 1,500 millimetres) at the lake shores. At the northern end of Lake Nyasa, an annual rainfall total of about 120 inches results from similar influences reinforced by air convergence caused by the funnel-shaped relief at the head of the lake. Sudden and dangerous storms are likely to arise over the waters of all the major lakes.

Hydrology. The levels of the East African lakes are perceptibly sensitive to climatic fluctuations. Average seasonal ranges of level are small: no more than a foot on Lake Victoria, 1.3 feet on Lake Albert, and three to four feet on Lake Nyasa. Longer-term fluctuations, with consequential effects on the shorelines, are greater: during the 20th century the extreme range recorded on Lake Victoria has been 10.3 feet, compared with 17.3 feet on Lake Albert and 18.8 feet on Lake Nyasa. In each case the recorded maximum occurred in the early 1960s. The effects of drought are enhanced in small, shallow lakes: Lake Nakuru, in Kenya, dried up completely in 1939–40; at the end of 1949 Lake Rukwa was estimated to be one-fifth its normal size; and Lake Chilwa, in Malaŵi, suffered a drastic reduction of area in 1967–68.

Lake levels

There is a significant correlation between rainfall and variations in the level of Lake Victoria, and Lakes Kyoga and Albert follow—with an appropriate time lag—the conditions of Lake Victoria. In addition to rainfall, other factors affect the longer-term fluctuations of Lakes Tan-

Kay Honkanen—Ostman Agency

Lake Kivu in East Africa between Rwanda and Zaire. The western escarpment of the Western Rift Valley rises on the far side of the lake.

ganyika and Nyasa. The Lukuga River outlet of Lake Tanganyika tends to become blocked intermittently by silting, consolidated by swampy growth. Similarly, in the flat valley of the upper Shire River, periods of erosion alternate with the building of bars of silt and sand reinforced by reeds. As a result, between 1915 and 1935 there was virtually no outflow from Lake Nyasa.

Many of the lakes, especially those in the Eastern Rift, are brackish, but Baringo and Naivasha are exceptions in that they are freshwater lakes and are believed to have subterranean outlets. At the other extreme of salinity, Magadi is a soda lake, in which the continuing source of sodium carbonate (natron) appears to be alkaline waters of deep-seated origin. Lakes Edward and George have the highest salinities among the lakes of the Western Rift, but the alkalinity is not excessive. The problem of the deeper lakes, such as Tanganyika, Nyasa, and Kivu, is that their deeper waters are permanently deoxygenated and thus constitute a biological desert: 75 percent of the volume of Lake Tanganyika and 99 percent of that of Kivu are within this category. Moreover, all three lakes contain lethal amounts of hydrogen sulfide in their deeper waters, and Lake Kivu also contains vast quantities of methane.

Plant life. The vegetation setting of the lakes varies from the semidesert, in which Lake Rudolf is situated, to the patches of closed evergreen forest on the western and northern shores of Lake Victoria. Between the two extremes and in accordance with the position of the individual lakes, bushland and thicket, grassland, savanna, or open woodland occur. The oil palm, which is characteristic of western Africa and of the Congo region, is found on the shores of Lake Tanganyika. Heavily populated and intensively cultivated areas marginal to Lakes Victoria and Nyasa present vegetation types that have been much modified by human activity. The lakeshores may consist of open landscapes of headland or beach or may contain plants associated with swamps, such as the giant sedge, *Cyperus papyrus,* which is the most prevalent.

Fish genera

Animal life. Among the main genera of fish in the East African lakes are the mouthbreeders *Tilapia,* much the most important in number of species and in total quantity; *Haplochromis* (which, like the *Tilapia,* belong to the Cichlidae family), a group of small perchlike fish; *Clarias* (barbel) and *Bagrus* among the catfish; *Hydrocynus* (tiger fish); various carps, including *Labeo, Barilius,* and *Barbus; Protopterus,* a lungfish; *Mormyrus,* a member of the elephant-snout fish family; and *Stolothrissa tanganicae* (*dagaa*), a small sardinelike fish.

The more strongly saline lakes, such as Nakuru, Elmenteita, Manyara, and, above all, Magadi and Natron, have a severely limited fish life. Lake Kivu also has a fish population that is neither varied nor abundant. Although fish are present in enormous quantities in Lake Rukwa, the number of species is not large, and the stock is dominated by the endemic *Tilapia rukwaensis.* Successive droughts such as that of 1949 explain why there are so few species in Lake Rukwa; the years immediately following 1949, on the other hand, provide an excellent example of the amazing recovery powers of tropical fish populations.

The majority of the lakes, though, have a rich and varied fish life, of which a high proportion of species are endemic to the individual lake. The Cichlidae, for example, are especially prone to form new species, and there are between 100 and 200 species of the family in Lakes Victoria and Kyoga.

Lake Albert has a fish life that is related to that of the Nile; it includes Nile perch, tiger fish, and *Polypterus* (bichir). The physical barrier of Murchison Falls, situated near the northern end of Lake Albert, marks the frontier of a separate faunal province formed by Lakes Victoria and Kyoga. Several of the Lake Albert genera are not found in these two lakes, which contain many unique species. Similarly, the rapids on the Semliki River have prevented the introduction of fish species from Lake Albert into Lakes Edward and George, which otherwise are particularly rich in fish. On the other hand, the presence of Nile perch, tiger fish, and bichir in Lake Rudolf serves to indicate its former connection with the Nile. The transplantation of fish by humans, however, has caused a man-made zoogeographic revolution, the full effects of which cannot yet be discerned.

The hippopotamus is ubiquitous around the lakeshores, except those of Lake Kivu; the crocodile is also widespread, although absent from Lakes Edward, George, and Kivu, each of which is sheltered from the spread of this reptile by falls in the outflow river, with cool mountain torrents and sunless forest as additional deterrents. Traditionally there has been an inverse relationship between the density of game and that of human settlement. The establishment of national parks and game reserves, however, has encouraged the increase of game population, although widespread poaching has created serious problems. Among the variety of game to be seen in the neighbourhood of the lakes are elephant, buffalo, and various antelopes.

Waterfowl

Among the resident and migrant birds in evidence, waterfowl are especially noticeable. Several of the Eastern Rift lakes—such as Nakuru, Elmenteita, and Manyara—are famous for their vast congregations of flamingos. Forming the basis of a national park in which the emphasis is on aquatic birds, Lake Nakuru is an ornithologist's paradise; Lake Edward and the Kazinga Channel are also notably rich in birdlife. The fish-eating birds—cormorants, darters, and kingfishers—are also part of the ecology of the lakes.

The people and the economy. Although not all the shores of Lake Victoria are well settled, the lands marginal to the lake are among the most densely populated in Africa. The best-known groups inhabiting these marginal lands are the Ganda, Soga, Luhya, Luo, Sukuma, and Haya, all of whom, except for the Luo (who are Nilo-Saharan speakers), are Bantu-speaking. The eastern margins of Lake Kivu reflect the high population density of Rwanda, and the lowlands at the northern and southern ends of Lake Nyasa are also well populated. In general, though, the shores of the Eastern and Western Rift lakes are sparsely settled.

Resource exploitation. Fish constitute one of the major resources of the East African lakes, but the degree of exploitation varies considerably from lake to lake. Uganda, for example, possesses one of the largest freshwater fishing industries in the world, while production from Kenya is appreciably lower. The potential of Lake Rudolf, well-stocked with Nile perch, has been only partially realized, whereas to the south the waters of the much smaller Lake Baringo have been more strongly exploited. Black bass and several species of *Tilapia,* both of which were introduced, form the basis of the commercial fishery of Lake Naivasha; the lake is also a popular weekend resort for Nairobi residents, many of whom are attracted by the sport fishing. At Lake Magadi, on the other hand, soda ash, which is the leading mineral export of Kenya, is extracted and refined.

The strongly developed Ugandan fishery of Lake Kyoga is largely based on introduced Nile perch; and although Lake Victoria is considered to be essentially a *Tilapia* fishery, there are also important catches of other species, including Nile perch. The fisheries of Lake Victoria are important as a source of protein for the rural and urban population living in the vicinity. The Luo and the Sese Islanders have shown a marked interest in the industry, which is practiced by independent fishermen, typically using planked canoes with outboard motors.

Hydroelectric power

Another important resource at Lake Victoria is the Owen Falls power station at Jinja, which provides electricity for use in Uganda and Kenya. In addition, the dam at the falls enhances the potential of Lake Victoria as a storage reservoir for the Nile River, in the process raising the average level of the lake by three feet. The Lake Victoria region has great potential for economic growth, although greater cooperation among its bordering states is needed to realize this potential.

The varied fish life of Lake Albert includes Nile perch and two genera of tiger fish, of which one, *Alestes,* provides two-thirds of the total weight landed on the Uganda shores of the lake. It is believed, however, that the total catch is below the maximum sustainable yield of the lake. A tourist attraction adjacent to Lake Albert is the Murchison Falls (Kabalega) National Park, which extends down to the narrowing outlet at the northern end of the lake.

Lakes Edward and George support remarkably fertile fisheries. The Zaire shores of Lake Edward are within the Virunga National Park, while the Ugandan portion of the lake lies within the Queen Elizabeth (Ruwenzori) National Park. Close to the northeastern shore of Lake Edward, Lake Katwe, which lies in one of the numerous shallow craters within the Edward–George branch of the Western Rift, is a source of salt.

The fisheries potential of Lake Kivu is more limited than that of the other lakes of the Western Rift, but a large quantity of natural gas is obtained from the lake each year. Tourist attractions are available, and, at the outlet of the lake below Bukavu, Zaire, a hydroelectric station on the Ruzizi River provides power to the Burundi capital of Bujumbura on the northern shores of Lake Tanganyika.

As a whole, the borderlands of Lake Tanganyika are characterized by underdevelopment, although peasant fishermen operate in the northern part of the lake, where fisheries are dominated by the exploitation of *dagaa.* There is a secondary output from other species, but in the absence of shallow, marginal waters *Tilapia* do not form a significant proportion of the catch. Despite the changes in water level to which it is liable and its remoteness from markets, Lake Rukwa is third to Lakes Victoria and Tanganyika among the freshwater fisheries of Tanzania.

In the northern waters of Lake Nyasa the fish caught include catfish and some species of carp, whereas in the southern part of the lake shallow, sheltered waters provide a good habitat for *Tilapia* and for *Labeo mesops* (a species of carp). The majority of the fishermen also practice subsistence agriculture, except on Likoma Island. Commercial fishing, however, has intensified the demand upon the inshore species, resulting in a reduction of the fish population.

Transportation. Most of the East African lakes are reasonably accessible by road and air. Among the major lakes, however, Rudolf remains the least accessible by road. With the exception of Lake Albert, the main lakes of Uganda are well served by surface communications. There are fairly good road communications to Lake Kivu, but considerable stretches of the shores of Lakes Tanganyika and Nyasa have no proper roads. Scheduled inland-waterway services have been developed on Lakes Victoria, Tanganyika, and Nyasa; elsewhere, as on Lake Kivu, there are launch services. Otherwise, canoes and, to a small extent, dhows transport people and goods.

Main ports

Fluctuations of the lake level and changing economic conditions have brought about the closure of a number of ports on Lake Victoria. The main ports in use are Kisumu in Kenya; Musoma, Mwanza, and Bukoba in Tanzania; and Port Bell (serving the Kampala metropolitan area) and Jinja in Uganda. Entebbe, Uganda, which is no longer a lake port, has an international and regional airport; there is also an international airport at Bujumbura, Burundi's port on Lake Tanganyika. Lake services operate on Victoria, including those from rail-ferry terminals at Jinja, Kisumu, and Mwanza; all three have rail connections with the maritime ports. On Lake Tanganyika, a rail line connects Kigoma, Tanz.—terminus of the rail line from the Tanzanian capital of Dar es Salaam—with the Zambian port of Mpulungu. In Zaire a company based at the railway port of Kalemi maintains links with Kigoma, Bujumbura, and Kalundu (for the town of Uvira). Malaŵi's railway system provides services on Lake Nyasa and has rail connections with Beira and Nacala on the coast of Mozambique, and its major ports are Nkhota Kota, Chilumba, and Karonga.

Study and exploration. Following in the track of earlier Arab trading expeditions, the British explorers Sir Richard Burton and John Hanning Speke reached the eastern shore of Lake Tanganyika in 1858. It was there, at Ujiji, that David Livingstone, the Scottish explorer-missionary who had pioneered the Shire River route to Lake Nyasa in 1859, was met by the Welsh explorer Henry Morton Stanley in 1871, after which the two subsequently made a reconnaissance of the northern part of the lake. Then, in 1874, in the course of his east–west traverse of the continent, the English traveler Verney Lovett Cameron explored the Lukuga River outlet on the western shore of Tanganyika.

While Burton remained at Tabora in 1858, Speke journeyed northward and became the first European to view the waters of Lake Victoria. In 1862, after he returned to East Africa with a fellow countryman, James Augustus Grant, Speke stood above the Ripon Falls, which he proclaimed as the source of the Nile. The details of the Lake Victoria shoreline were filled in by Stanley when he circumnavigated the lake in 1875.

Meanwhile another Englishman, Samuel White Baker, and his wife, Florence, had approached the East African lakes from the north, reaching Lake Albert in 1864. In 1888 to 1889 Stanley, in company with Mehmed Emin Paşa (or Pasha), the German explorer, traced the Semliki River to its source in Lake Edward. Finally, in 1894, a German explorer, Adolf von Götzen, became the first European to visit Lake Kivu.

During the 1880s Europeans explored the lakes of the Eastern Rift. Lakes Magadi and Naivasha were visited by a German traveler, Gustav Fischer, in 1883, and in the same year the Scottish explorer Joseph Thomson reached the shores of Lake Baringo. Five years later Count Sámuel Teleki and Ludwig von Höhnel reached Lake Rudolf. Considerable scientific study of the lakes region has been conducted since that time. (S.J.K.B.)

NIGER RIVER

The Niger River, with a length of 2,600 miles (4,200 kilometres), is the principal river of western Africa and the third longest in Africa after the Nile and the Congo. It is believed to have been named by the Greeks. Along its course it is known by several names. These include the Joliba (a Malinke word meaning "great river") in its upper course; the Mayo Balleo and the Isa Eghirren in its central reach; and the Kwarra, Kworra, or Quorra in its lower stretch.

Source of the Niger

Physical features. *Physiography.* The Niger rises in Guinea at 9°05′ N and 10°47′ W on the eastern side of the Fouta Djallon (Guinea) highlands, only 150 miles inland from the Atlantic Ocean. Issuing as the Tembi from a deep ravine 2,800 feet (850 metres) above sea level, it flows due north over the first 100 miles. It then follows a northeasterly direction, during the course of which it receives its upper tributaries—the Mafou, the Niandan, the Milo, and the Sankarani on the right and the Tinkisso on the left—and enters Mali. Just below Bamako, Mali's capital, the Sotuba Dam marks the end of the upper river. From there the Niger once dropped more than 1,000 feet in about 40 miles into a valley formed by tectonic subsidence; but the rapids in this stretch have been submerged by the waters backed up by the Markala Dam, located some 150 miles downstream of the Sotuba Dam near Sansanding. In this stretch, at Koulikoro, the river takes a more east-northeasterly direction, and its bed becomes fairly free from impediments for about 1,000 miles.

At Mopti the Niger is joined by the Bani, its largest tributary on the right, after which it enters a region of lakes, creeks, and backwaters that is often called the "internal delta" of the Niger. These lakes are chiefly on the left bank and are connected to the river by channels that undergo seasonal changes in the direction of flow. At high water most of the lakes become part of a general inundation. Largest of the lakes in this region is Lake Faguibine, which is nearly 75 miles long, 15 miles wide, and more than 160 feet deep in places.

The labyrinth of lakes, creeks, and backwaters comes to an end at Kabara, the port of Timbuktu (Tombouctou). There, the river turns almost due east, passing its most northern point at latitude 17°05′ N. Some 250 miles downstream from Timbuktu, a rocky ridge that obstructs the course of the river is pierced by a defile (narrow gorge) more than a mile long, with an average width of about 800 feet and a depth of more than 100 feet in places. At low water the strong current there endangers navigation. A short way downstream the river turns to the southeast and widens considerably, flowing to Gao across a floodplain three to six miles wide. This most northerly bend of the Niger flows through the southern fringe of the Sahara.

The middle course of the Niger River is navigable to small craft during high water as far downstream as Ansongo—

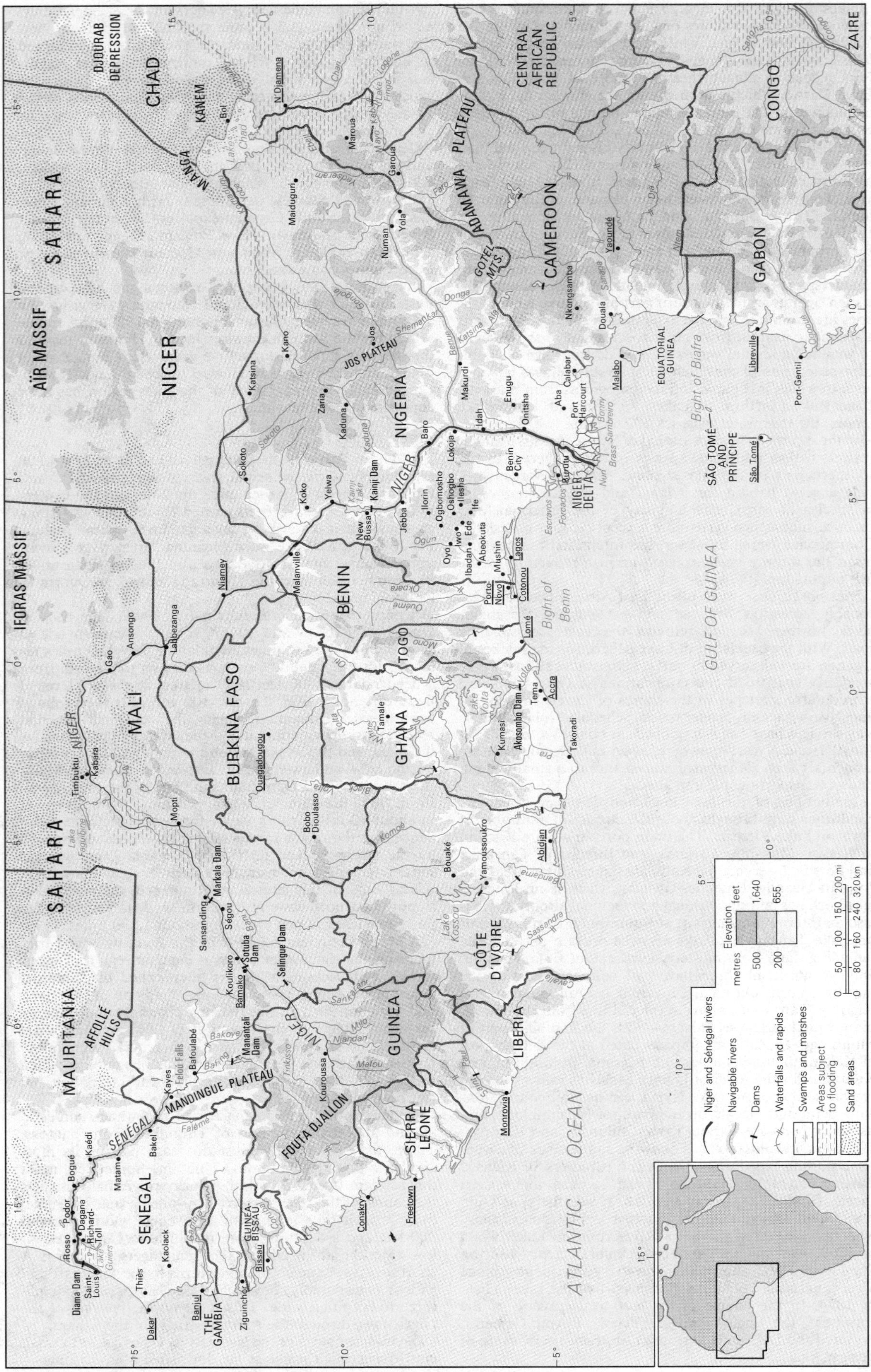

The Niger and Sénégal river basins and the Lake Chad basin and their drainage networks.

The Niger River at Mopti, Mali.

©Brian A. Vikander/West Light

some 1,100 miles in all. Below Ansongo, 430 miles downstream from Timbuktu, navigability is interrupted by a series of defiles and rapids. The river becomes navigable to small vessels again at Labbezanga—from which it flows into Niger—and continues to be navigable to the Atlantic Ocean. Navigation is seasonal, however, because of the fluctuations in the water level in the rainy and dry seasons.

Downstream from Jebba, in Nigeria, the Niger enters its lower course, flowing east-southeast through a broad and shallow valley 5 to 10 miles wide. About 70 miles from Jebba it is joined by the Kaduna River—an important tributary that contributes about 25 percent to the annual discharge of the river below the Niger–Kaduna confluence—and about 25 miles above Lokoja the river turns to the south. At Lokoja the river receives the water of its greatest tributary, the Benue (see below), thereby approximately doubling the volume of its annual discharge. At their confluence the Niger is about three-quarters of a mile wide, and the Benue more than a mile. Together they form a lakelike stretch of water about two miles wide that is dotted with islands and sandbanks. From Lokoja downstream to the town of Idah, the Niger flows in a restricted valley, enclosed by hills and in some places flanked by sandstone cliffs up to 150 feet high. Between Idah and Onitsha the banks are lower and the country flatter. At Onitsha, the largest town on the Niger's banks in Nigeria and the third largest riverine town after Bamako and Niamey (Niger), the valley narrows as the river flows through what is probably a fault in the area's sandstone. It emerges at Aboh, separating into many branches before reaching the Gulf of Guinea via Africa's largest delta.

The Niger delta

The Niger delta, which stretches for nearly 150 miles from north to south and spreads along the coast for about 200 miles, extends over an area of 14,000 square miles (36,000 square kilometres). Within the delta the river breaks up into an intricate network of channels called rivers. The Nun River is regarded as the direct continuation of the river, but some of the other important channels include (from west to east) the Forcados, the Brass, the Sambreiro, and the Bonny. The mouths of these channels are almost all obstructed by sandbars. The Forcados, for instance, which supplanted the Nun as the most traveled channel in the early 20th century, was in turn displaced by the Escravos River in 1964. The delta is being gradually extended seaward by the increments of silt brought down by the river, and mangrove swamps extend beyond its outer edge.

The Benue (meaning "Mother of Water" in the Batta language) rises at 4,400 feet above sea level on the Adamawa (Adamaoua) Plateau in northern Cameroon at about 7°40′ N and 13°15′ E. In its upper course, which extends north-northwest to its confluence with the Mayo Kébi, close to the town of Garoua, it is a mountain torrent, falling more than 2,000 feet over a distance of 110 miles. The river then turns westward into Nigeria and, for the greater part of its course, flows over a broad and fertile floodplain. At Yola, a town 600 feet above sea level and some 850 miles inland, the width of the river in flood is from 1,000 to 1,500 yards (910 to 1,370 metres). Near Numan, some 30 miles downstream from Yola, the Benue is joined on its north bank by its most important tributary, the Gongola. Other important tributaries include the Shemankar, the Faro, the Donga, and the Katsina Ala.

Together with its tributaries, the Niger drains a total area of some 730,000 square miles. The Niger drainage system is bounded in the south by such highlands as the Fouta Djallon, the Banfora Cliffs in Burkina Faso, the Plateau of Yorubaland, and the Cameroon highlands. This southern rampart forms a watershed separating the rivers of the Niger system from others that flow directly southward to the Atlantic Ocean. With the exception of such highlands as the Jos Plateau, the Iforas and Aïr massifs, and the Ahaggar Mountains to the north and east, the northern edge of the Niger basin is, however, less clearly defined than the southern edge.

Climate. Within the Niger basin climate shows great variability. Mean annual rainfall decreases northward from more than 160 inches (4,100 millimetres) in the delta area to less than 10 inches in Timbuktu. Both the upper and the lower stretches of the river, however, drain areas with more than 50 inches of rain per year. The middle Niger is an area where rainfall decreases and is also the sector where the greatest amount of evaporation takes place. It is estimated that in the lake region the Niger loses nearly 65 percent of the annual volume of discharge that flows past Mopti.

The annual floods

Hydrology. Because of climatic variations the annual river flood does not occur at the same time in different parts of the basin. In the upper Niger the high-water discharge occurs in June, and the low-water season is in December. In the middle Niger, a first high-water discharge—the white flood (so called because of the light sediment content of the water)—occurs soon after the rainy season between July and October; a second rise—the black flood (so called because of the greater sediment content)—begins in December with the arrival of floodwaters from upstream. May and June are the low-water months in the middle stretch. On the Benue there is only one high-water season. Because of the Benue's more southerly location, this normally occurs from May to October—earlier than on the middle Niger. The lower Niger below its confluence with the Benue consequently has a high-water period that begins in May or June—about a month earlier than on the middle Niger—and a low-water period that is at least a month shorter, as the rains in the south start earlier. In January a slight rise occurs due to the arrival of floodwaters from the upper Niger. The difference between high and low water often measures as much as 35 feet.

Plant and animal life. Along its course the Niger traverses virtually all the vegetational zones of western Africa. The Fouta Djallon plateau, where the Niger rises, is covered by a type of sedge vegetation consisting of fine, wirelike tufts interspersed with bare rock surfaces. From the Fouta Djallon to well below the Niger's confluence with the Benue, the river flows mainly through savanna grassland country. In the north the grass is short and discontinuous, and thorny shrub and acacia wood occur. In the south of the grassland region, tall, tussocky grass is interspersed with fairly dense wooded vegetation. About the latitude of Onitsha, the river enters the high rain-forest belt, which merges below Aboh with the mangrove swamp vegetation of the delta.

Many varieties of fish are found in the Niger and its tributaries; the chief food species are catfish, carp, and Nile perch. Other Niger fauna include the hippopotamus, at least three different types of crocodile (including the much-feared Nile crocodile), and a variety of lizards. There is a rich collection of birds. Geese are found in the lake region, and heron, egrets, and storks are found both on the river and around the lakes. The striking crown bird is found wherever there is open ground in the grassland zone, and pelicans and flamingos are particularly associated with the upper Benue area. Smaller riverine species include white-headed plover, crocodile bird, sandpiper, curlew, and green-red shank.

The people and the economy. The Niger valley is sparsely settled, although there are population concentrations in the lake region and near the confluence of the Niger and Benue. In medieval times the valley was the heartland of the Mali and Songhai empires, and some of the river towns date from this period. The ethnic pattern along the course of the river includes larger groups—such as the Bambara, the Malinke, the Songhai, and the Zerma (Djerma)—occupying both sides of the river above the Nigerian boundary, below which there are many small ethnic groups.

Fishing

Fishing is an important activity along the length of the river system, especially during the dry season when the deep-sea and coastal fish catch is smallest. River fishing is a specialized occupation for certain peoples, such as the Bozo and Somono in the lake region, the Sorko on the middle Niger, the Kede and the Kakanda between Jebba and Lokoja, and the Wurbo and the Jukun on the Benue. The discovery and exploitation of petroleum in the delta region, however, has seriously disrupted fishing there; oil pollution has killed most of the fish, undermining the economy of the Ijo (Ijaw) people of the region.

Irrigation. The irrigation of the Niger valley—for the purpose of transforming it into a densely populated, agricultural corridor running through the interior of western Africa—has long been a goal of planners. In the 1930s the French colonial administration, for example, began to plan the irrigation of large areas in the lake region; a barrage at Sansanding that raised the level of the Niger was completed in 1947. Feeder canals were constructed, and huge tracts of irrigated land now produce rice, cotton, sugarcane, and vegetables. The British colonial administration also encouraged irrigated rice cultivation in the Bida region. In Nigeria large-scale irrigation schemes have been developed since the 1960s on the Niger and some of its tributaries, notably the Sokoto, Kaduna, and Benue.

The Niger is also a source of hydroelectricity. The largest project is the Kainji Dam in Nigeria, completed in the late 1960s. A 500-square-mile lake has been created upstream, offering opportunities for fishing and irrigation. Other projects include the Sotuba and Markala dams in Mali and dams at Jebba (on the Niger) and Shiroro (on the Kaduna tributary) in Nigeria.

Transportation. Most of the Niger River—more than 75 percent of its total length—is used by commercial shipping. From the Atlantic Ocean to Onitsha the river is navigable by large vessels throughout the year. From Onitsha to the confluence of the Benue and the Niger large vessels can move for 10 months of the year (June–March). Navigation in this stretch is made possible by the influx of water from the Benue River, which is at high level in June. From Lokoja to Jebba the Niger is navigable to all craft only from October to mid-November. Thus, Jebba is in effect the head of navigation of the Niger waterway, although extreme fluctuation in water level at times constitutes a major handicap to vessels plying beyond Lokoja. Above Jebba the Niger is navigable only to smaller craft and is dependent locally on periods when water levels are adequate.

Rail and road routes cross the river at many points. Railway bridges span the river at Kouroussa and Jebba, and another crosses the Benue at Makurdi. There are road bridges over the Niger at Ségou, Malanville, Kainji, Jebba, Lokoja, and Onitsha and over the Benue at Makurdi, Numan, and Yola. Ferries cross the Niger at Bamako, Gao, Niamey, Yelwa, and Idah and cross the Benue at Garoua. The main river ports are Koulikoro, Timbuktu, Baro, Onitsha, Burutu, and Koko.

The coordination of multinational efforts to develop the Niger and its tributaries is the responsibility of the Niger River Commission, formed in 1963. The Commission has sponsored a study of the navigational possibilities of the middle Niger from Gao (Mali) to Yelwa (Nigeria). Moreover, in Nigeria several river basin development authorities have been established to develop more irrigation and fishing projects.

Mungo Park's expedition

Study and exploration. It was not until the late 18th century that Europeans made systematic attempts to find the source, direction, and outlet of the Niger. In 1795 Mungo Park, a Scottish explorer, traveled overland from the Gambia region and reached the Niger near Ségou, where in July 1796 he established that the river flowed eastward. In 1805 Park sailed more than 1,500 miles down the river, seeking to reach its mouth, but he and his party were drowned in the rapids at Bussa (now covered by Lake Kainji). In 1822 another Scottish explorer, Alexander G. Laing, determined but did not visit the source of the river. In 1830 two English explorers, Richard and John Lander, established the lower course of the Niger by canoeing down the river from Yauri (now also covered by Lake Kainji), to the Atlantic Ocean, via the Nun River passage. In the second half of the 19th century two German explorers, Heinrich Barth and Eduard R. Flegel, in separate travels established the course of the Benue from its source to its confluence with the Niger. (A.L.M.)

NILE RIVER

The Nile, the father of African rivers and the longest river in the world, rises south of the equator and flows northward through northeastern Africa to drain into the Mediterranean Sea. It has a length of about 4,132 miles (6,650 kilometres) and drains an area estimated at 1,293,000 square miles (3,349,000 square kilometres). Its basin includes parts of Tanzania, Burundi, Rwanda, Zaire, Kenya, Uganda, and Ethiopia, most of The Sudan, and the cultivated part of Egypt. Its most distant source is the Kagera River in Burundi.

The Nile is formed by three principal streams, the Blue Nile (Arabic: Al-Baḥr al-Azraq; Amharic: Abay) and the Atbara (Arabic: Nahr ʿAṭbarah), which flow from the highlands of Ethiopia, and the White Nile (Arabic: Al-Baḥr al-Abyad), the headstreams of which flow into Lakes Victoria and Albert.

Origin of the name

The name Nile is derived from the Greek Neilos (Latin: Nilus), which probably originated from the Semitic root *naḥal,* meaning a valley or river valley, and hence, by an extension of the meaning, a river. The fact that the Nile—unlike other great rivers known to them—flowed from the south northward and was in flood at the warmest time of the year was an unsolved mystery to the ancient Egyptians and Greeks. The ancient Egyptians called the river Ar or Aur (Coptic: Iaro), or "Black," in allusion to the colour of the sediments carried by the river when it is in flood. Nile mud is black enough to have given the land itself its oldest name, Kem or Kemi, which also means "Black" and signifies darkness. In *The Odyssey,* the epic poem written by the Greek poet Homer (7th century BC), Aigyptos is the name of the Nile (masculine) as well as the country of Egypt (feminine) through which it flows. The Nile in Egypt and the northern Sudan is now called An-Nīl, Al-Baḥr, and Baḥr an-Nīl or Nahr an-Nīl.

Physical features. The Nile River basin, which covers about one-tenth of the area of the continent, served as the stage for the evolution and decay of advanced civilizations in the ancient world. On the banks of the river dwelled people who were among the first to cultivate the arts of agriculture and to use the plow. The basin is bordered on the north by the Mediterranean; on the east by the Red Sea Hills and the Ethiopian Plateau; on the south by the East African Highlands, which include Lake Victoria, a Nile source; and on the west by the less well-defined watershed between the Nile, Chad, and Congo (Zaire) basins, extending northwest to include the Marrah Mountains of The Sudan, the Al-Jilf al-Kabīr Plateau of Egypt, and the Libyan Desert (part of the Sahara).

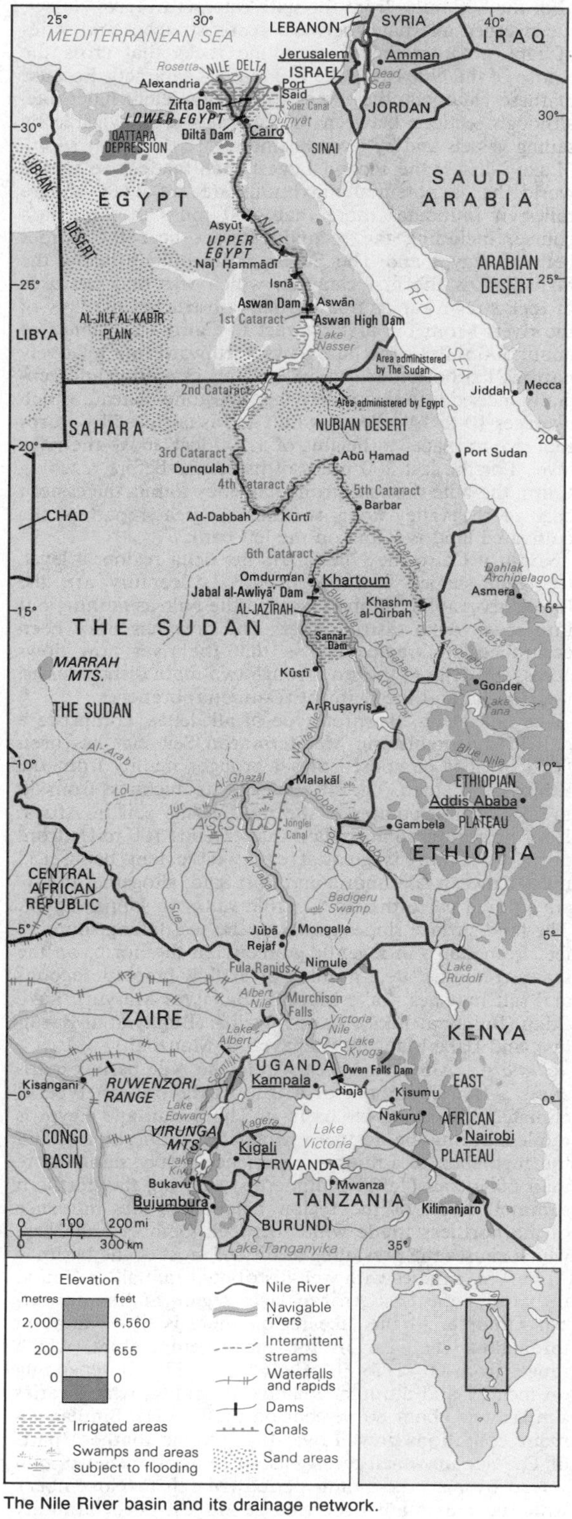

The Nile River basin and its drainage network.

The availability of water from the Nile throughout the year, combined with the area's high temperatures, makes possible intensive cultivation along its banks. Even in some of the regions in which the average rainfall is sufficient for cultivation, such as in The Sudan, marked annual variations in precipitation often make cultivation without irrigation risky. The Nile River is also a vital waterway for transport, especially at times when motor transport is not feasible—*e.g.,* during the flood season. Improvements in air, rail, and highway facilities in the 20th century, however, have greatly reduced dependency on the waterway.

Physiography. It is thought that in the mid-Tertiary Period (approximately 30 million years ago) the early Nile, then a much shorter stream, had its sources about latitude 18° to 20° N. Its main headstream may then have been the present Atbara River. To the south lay the vast enclosed drainage system containing the large Lake Sudd. According to one theory on the evolution of the Nile system, about 25,000 years ago the East African drainage to Lake Victoria developed an outlet to the north, which sent its water into Lake Sudd. With the accumulation of sediments over a long period, the water level of this lake rose gradually; as a result of the overflow, the lake was drained, spilling over to the north. The overflow waters of Lake Sudd, rapidly forming a riverbed, linked the two major parts of the Nile system, thus unifying the drainage from Lake Victoria to the Mediterranean Sea.

The basin of the present-day Nile falls naturally into seven major regions: the Lake Plateau of East Africa, the Al-Jabal (El-Jebel), the White Nile, the Blue Nile, the Atbara, the Nile north of Khartoum in The Sudan and Egypt, and the Nile delta.

Sources of the Nile

The Lake Plateau region of East Africa produces a number of headstreams and lakes that feed the White Nile. It is generally agreed that the Nile has several sources rather than one. The furthest headstream may be regarded as the Kagera River, which rises in the highlands of Burundi near the northern tip of Lake Tanganyika and then flows into Lake Victoria. The Nile proper, however, rises from Lake Victoria, the second largest freshwater lake in the world, which has an area of more than 26,800 square miles and forms a huge but shallow lake. The Nile begins near Jinja, Uganda, on the north shore of the lake, flowing northward over Ripon Falls, which has been submerged since the completion of the Owen Falls Dam in 1954. The northward stretch of the river, known as the Victoria Nile, enters the shallow Lake Kyoga (Kioga) and, passing through its swamp vegetation, flows out in a westerly direction, descending into the East African Rift System over Murchison (Kabalega) Falls before entering the northern end of Lake Albert. Unlike Lake Victoria, Lake Albert is a deep, narrow lake with mountainous sides. There the waters of the Victoria Nile unite with the lake waters, passing northward as the Albert Nile—a portion of the river, somewhat wider and slower, that is fringed with swampy growth and is navigable for steamers.

The Nile enters The Sudan at Nimule, and from there to Jūbā—a distance of some 120 miles—it is called the Al-Jabal River (Mountain Nile). This section of the river descends through narrow gorges and over a series of rapids, including the Fula (Fola) Rapids, and receives additional water from short tributaries on both banks; it is not commercially navigable. Below Jūbā the river flows over a large and very level clay plain, which extends through a narrow valley with hill country on either side, lying some 1,200 to 1,500 feet (370 to 460 metres) above sea level, and through the centre of which flows the mainstream. As the gradient of the Nile there is only 1:13,000, the great volume of additional water that arrives during the rainy season cannot be accommodated by the river, and, as a result, during those months almost the entire plain becomes inundated. This circumstance promotes the growth of enormous quantities of aquatic vegetation—including tall grasses and sedges (notably papyrus)—that collectively is called sudd, literally meaning "barrier," and the region is known as As-Sudd. These great masses of vegetation, the growth of which is exacerbated by the gentle flow of the water, break off and float downstream, effectively choking the mainstream and blocking the navigable channels. Channels have become further choked since the 1950s by the rapid spread of the South American water hyacinth.

This basin receives drainage from numerous other streams. The Al-Ghazāl (Gazelle) River flows in from the southwestern Sudan, joining the Al-Jabal at Lake No, a large lagoon where the mainstream takes an easterly direction. The waters of the Al-Ghazāl undergo extensive loss through evaporation, and only a small proportion of them ever reach the Nile. A short distance above Malakāl the mainstream is joined by the Sobat (Baro in Ethiopia), and downstream from there the river is called the White Nile. The regime of the Sobat is quite different from the steady flowing Al-Jabal, with a maximum flow occurring between July and December; the annual flow of the Sobat is about equal to the water lost through evaporation in the As-Sudd marshes.

The White and Blue Nile rivers

The White Nile, about 500 miles in length, supplies some 15 percent of the total volume entering Lake Nasser (called Lake Nubia in The Sudan) downstream. It begins at Malakāl and joins the Blue Nile at Khartoum, receiving no tributaries of importance. Throughout this stretch the White Nile is a wide, placid stream, often having a narrow fringe of swamps. The valley is wide and shallow, however, thus causing a considerable loss of water by both evaporation and seepage.

The Blue Nile drains from the lofty Ethiopian Plateau, where it descends in a north–northwesterly direction from a height of about 6,000 feet above sea level. Its reputed source is a spring, considered holy by the Ethiopian Orthodox Church, from which a small stream, the Abay, flows down to Lake Tana (T'ana), a fairly shallow lake with an area of about 1,400 square miles. The Abay leaves Lake Tana in a southeasterly direction, flowing through a series of rapids and plunging through a deep gorge. It is estimated that the lake supplies the river with only about 7 percent of its total flow, but this water is important since it is silt-free. The river then flows west and northwest through The Sudan to join the White Nile at Khartoum. In the greater part of its course from Lake Tana down to the Sudanese plains, it runs in a canyon that in places is 4,000 feet below the general level of the plateau. All of its tributaries also run in deep ravines. While the White Nile at Khartoum is a river of almost constant volume, the Blue Nile has a pronounced flood season (late July to October) caused by the summer monsoon rains over the Ethiopian Plateau and the rapid runoff from its numerous tributaries; historically, it was this surge that contributed most to the annual Nile floods in Egypt.

The Atbara River, the last tributary of the Nile, flows into the mainstream nearly 200 miles north of Khartoum. It rises in Ethiopia at heights of 6,000 to 10,000 feet above sea level, not far from Gonder, to the north of Lake Tana. The two principal tributaries that feed the Atbara are the Angereb (Arabic: Baḥr as-Salam) and the Tekezo (Amharic: "Terrible"; Arabic: Nahr Satīt). The Tekezo is the most important of these, having a basin more than double the area of the Atbara itself. It rises among the high peaks of the Ethiopian highlands and flows north through a spectacular gorge to join the Atbara in The Sudan. For most of its course in The Sudan, the Atbara is well below the general level of the plains. Between the plains and the river, the ground is eroded and cut into by gullies formed by water running off the plains after rainfall. The Atbara rises and falls rapidly, like the Blue Nile. In flood it becomes a large, muddy river, and in the dry season it is a string of pools. The Atbara contributes more than 10 percent of the total annual flow of the Nile, but almost all of this comes in the period of July to October.

Along the stretch of the Nile north of Khartoum, which is sometimes called the United Nile, two parts can be distinguished. The first part, which stretches from Khartoum to Lake Nasser, is about 830 miles in length; there the river flows through a desert region where rainfall is negligible, although some irrigation takes place along its banks. The second part includes Lake Nasser—which contains the water held back by the Aswan High Dam in Egypt—and below the dam the irrigated Nile valley and delta region.

The cataracts

Below Khartoum, the Nile flows 50 miles northward until it reaches Sablūkah (Sababka), the site of the sixth and highest cataract. There the river cuts through hills for a distance of eight miles. Flowing northward at Barbar, the river takes an S-bend, in the middle of which, from Abū Ḥamad to Kūrtī and Ad-Dabbah (Debba), the river flows southwestward for about 170 miles; the fourth cataract is in the middle of this stretch. At the end of this bend, at Dunqulah, it again resumes a northerly direction, crossing the third cataract and flowing into Lake Nasser.

For the 800 miles from the sixth cataract to Lake Nasser, the riverbed alternates between gentle stretches and series of rapids. Outcropping crystalline rocks that cross the course of the Nile cause the five famous cataracts. Because of these cataracts, the river is not completely navigable, although sections between the cataracts are navigable by sailing vessels and by river steamers.

Lake Nasser, the second largest man-made lake in the world, has a potential maximum area of 2,600 square miles; it inundates more than 300 miles of the Nile's course, including the second cataract near the border between Egypt and The Sudan. Immediately below the high dam is the first cataract, which was once an area of rock-strewn rapids that partially obstructed the flow of the river. From the first cataract to Cairo—a distance of about 500 miles—the Nile flows northward in a relatively narrow, flat-bottomed groove, sinuous in outline and generally incised into the underlying limestone plateau, which averages 10 to 14 miles in width and is enclosed by scarps that rise in places to heights of 1,500 feet above the river level. For the last 200 miles of its course before reaching Cairo, the Nile shows a strong tendency to hug the eastern edge of the valley floor, so that the greater part of the cultivated land is found on the left bank.

North of Cairo the Nile enters the delta region, a level, triangular-shaped lowland. In the 1st century AD, the Greek geographer Strabo recorded the Nile as fanning out into seven delta distributaries. The flow has since been controlled and redirected, so that the river now flows across the delta to the sea through two main distributaries, the Rosetta and the Dumyāṭ (Damietta) branches.

The Nile delta, the prototype of all deltas, comprises a gulf of the prehistoric Mediterranean Sea that has been filled in; it is composed of silt brought mainly from the Ethiopian Plateau. The silt varies in its thickness from 50 to 75 feet and comprises the most fertile soil in Africa. It forms a monotonous plain that extends 100 miles from north to south, its greatest east–west extent being 155 miles between Alexandria and Port Said; altogether it covers an area twice that of the Nile valley in Upper Egypt. The land surface slopes gently to the sea, falling some 52 feet from Cairo in a gentle gradient. In the north, on the seaward border, are a number of shallow brackish lagoons and salt marshes: Lake Marout (Buḥayrat Maryūṭ), Lake Edku (Buḥayrat Idkū), Lake Burullus (Buḥayrat al-Burullus), and Lake Manzala (Buḥayrat al-Manzilah).

Climate. Almost no area within the Nile basin experiences a true equatorial or a true Mediterranean type of climate. While the Nile basin in The Sudan and Egypt is rainless during the northern winter, its southern parts and the highlands of Ethiopia experience heavy rain—more than 60 inches (1,520 millimetres)—during the northern summer. Most of the region falls under the influence of the northeast trade winds between October and May, which causes the prevailing aridity of most of the basin.

Rainfall

Tropical climates with well-distributed rainfall are found in parts of the East African lakes region and southwestern Ethiopia. In the lake region there is little variation throughout the year in the mean temperature, which ranges from 60° F to 80° F (16° C to 27° C) depending on locality and altitude. Relative humidity, which varies similarly, is about 80 percent on the average. Similar climatic conditions prevail over the extreme southern parts of The Sudan, which receive as much as 50 inches of rain spread over a nine-month period (March to November), with the maximum occurring in August. The humidity reaches its highest at the peak of the rainy season and reaches its low level between January and March. Maximum temperatures are recorded during the dry season (December to February), with the minimums occurring in July and August.

To the north, the rainy season gets shorter, and the amount of rainfall decreases. The rainy season, which occurs in the south from April to October, is confined to July and August in the northern part of the central Sudan, where three seasons may be distinguished. The first of these is the pleasant, cool, dry winter, which occurs from December to February; this is followed by hot and very dry weather from March to June; and this is followed, in turn, by a hot rainy period from July to October. The minimum temperature occurs in January and the maximum in May or June, when it rises to a daily average of 105° F (41° C) in Khartoum. Only about 10 inches of rainfall occurs annually in the Al-Jazīrah area (between the White and Blue Nile rivers), as compared with more than 21 inches at Dakar, Senegal, which is at the same latitude. North of Khartoum less than five inches of rain falls annually, an amount insufficient for permanent settlement. In June and July the central parts of The Sudan are frequently visited by squalls during which strong winds carry large quantities of sand and dust. These storms, which are of three to four hours duration, are called haboobs.

A desert-type climate exists over most of the remainder of the area north to the Mediterranean. The principal characteristics of the northern Sudan and the desert of Egypt are aridity, a dry atmosphere, and a considerable seasonal, as well as diurnal, temperature range in Upper Egypt. Temperatures often surpass 100° F (38° C); in Aswān, for example, the average daily maximum in June is 117° F (47° C). While no low temperatures are recorded anywhere in The Sudan or Egypt, winter temperatures decrease to the north. Thus, only Egypt has what could be called a winter season, which occurs from November to March, when the daily maximum temperature in Cairo is 68° to 75° F (20° to 24° C) and the night minimum is about 50° F (10° C). The rainfall in Egypt is of Mediterranean origin and falls mostly in the winter, with the amount decreasing toward the south. From eight inches on the coast, it falls gradually to a little over an inch in Cairo and to less than an inch in Upper Egypt. During the spring, from March to June, depressions from the Sahara or along the coast travel east, causing dry southerly winds, which sometimes results in a condition called khamsin. These are sandstorms or dust storms during which the atmosphere becomes hazy; on occasion they may persist for three or four days, at the end of which the phenomenon of a "blue" sun may be observed.

Hydrology. The periodic rise of the Nile remained an unsolved mystery until the discovery of the role of the tropical regions in its regime. In effect, there was little detailed knowledge about the hydrology of the Nile before the 20th century, except for early records of the river level that the ancient Egyptians made with the aid of nilometers (gauges formed by graduated scales cut in natural rocks or in stone walls), some of which still remain. Today, however, no other river of comparable size has a regime that is so well known. The discharge of the main stream, as well as the tributaries, is regularly measured.

The Nile flood

The Nile swells in the summer, the floods rising as a result of the heavy tropical rains in Ethiopia. In the southern Sudan the flood begins in April, but the effect is not felt at Aswān, Egypt, until July. The water then starts to rise and continues to do so throughout August and September, with the maximum occurring in mid-September. At Cairo the maximum is delayed until October. The level of the river then falls rapidly through November and December. From March to May the level of the river is at its lowest. Although the flood is a fairly regular phenomenon, it occasionally varies in volume and date. Before it was possible to regulate the river, years of high or low flood—particularly a sequence of such years—resulted in crop failure, famine, and disease.

Following the river from its sources, an estimate can be made of the contribution of the various lakes and tributaries in the Nile flood.

Lake Victoria forms the first great natural reservoir of the Nile system. The heavy rainfall over the lake is nearly balanced by surface evaporation, and the outflow from the lake—some 812 billion cubic feet (23 billion cubic metres)—comes mostly from the rivers draining into it, particularly the Kagera. This water then flows via the Victoria Nile into Lake Kyoga, where there is little net loss of water, and then into Lake Albert. Water lost by evaporation is more than balanced by the rainfall over the lake and the inflow from other smaller streams, notably the Semliki. Thus the annual outflow from Lake Albert to the Al-Jabal River is about 918 billion cubic feet.

In addition to the water it receives from the great lakes, the torrential tributaries of the Al-Jabal supply it with nearly 20 percent of its water. The discharge of the Al-Jabal varies little throughout the year because of the regulatory effect of the large swamps and lagoons of the As-Sudd region. About half of its water is lost in this stage by seepage and evaporation, but the flow of the Sobat River into the main stream just upstream of Malakāl nearly makes up for the loss.

The White Nile provides a regular supply of water throughout the year. During April and May, when the main stream is at its lowest level, more than 80 percent of its water comes from the White Nile. The White Nile obtains its water in roughly equal amounts from two main sources. The first source is the rainfall on the East African Plateau of the previous summer. The second source is the drainage of southwestern Ethiopia through the Sobat (contributed mainly by its two headstreams, the Baro and the Pibor) that enters the main stream below As-Sudd. The annual flood of the Sobat, a consequence of the Ethiopian summer rains, is to a great extent responsible for the variations in the level of the White Nile. The rains that swell its upper valley begin in April and cause widespread inundation over the 200 miles of plains through which the river passes, thus delaying the arrival of the rainwater in its lower reaches until November–December. Relatively small amounts of the mud carried by the Sobat's flood reach the White Nile.

The regime of the Blue Nile

The Blue Nile, the most important of the three great Ethiopian affluents, plays an overwhelming part in bringing the Nile flood to Egypt. It receives two tributaries in The Sudan—the Ar-Rahad and the Ad-Dindar—both of which also originate in Ethiopia. The regime of the Blue Nile is distinguished from that of the White Nile by the more rapid passage of its floodwater into the main stream. The river level begins to rise in June, reaching a maximum level at Khartoum in about the first week in September.

The Atbara River draws its floodwater from the rains on the northern part of the Ethiopian Plateau, as does the Blue Nile. While the floods of the two streams occur at the same time, the Blue Nile is a perennial stream, while the Atbara, as mentioned, shrinks to a series of pools in the dry season.

The swelling of the Blue Nile causes the first floodwaters to reach the central Sudan in May. The maximum is reached in August, after which the level falls again. The rise at Khartoum averages more than 20 feet. When the Blue Nile is in flood it holds back the White Nile water, turning it into an extensive lake and delaying its flow. The Jabal al-Awliyā' Dam south of Khartoum increases this ponding effect.

The peak of the flood does not enter Lake Nasser until late July or August, when the average daily inflow from the Nile rises to some 25.1 billion cubic feet. Out of this amount the Blue Nile accounts for almost 70 percent, the Atbara more than 20 percent, and the White Nile 10 percent. In early May the inflow drops to its minimum; the total discharge of 1.6 billion cubic feet per day comes mainly from the White Nile and the remainder from the Blue Nile. On the average, about 85 percent of the water in Lake Nasser comes from the Ethiopian Plateau, and the rest is contributed by the East African Lake Plateau system. Lake Nasser has an enormous storage capacity—more than 40 cubic miles (about 168 cubic kilometres)—although the content of the reservoir varies with the extent of the annual flood upstream. Because it is situated in a very hot and dry region, however, Lake Nasser can lose up to 10 percent of its volume to evaporation annually when it is full, decreasing to about one-third that amount when it is at minimum capacity.

Plant life. In the areas where no irrigation is practiced, different zones of plant life may be roughly divided according to the amount of rainfall.

Tropical rain forest is found along the Nile–Congo divide, in parts of the Lake Plateau, and in southwestern Ethiopia. Heat and copious rainfall produce thick forests with a great variety of tropical trees and plants, including ebony, banana, rubber, bamboo, and coffee shrub. Mixed woodland and grassland (savanna), characterized by a sparse growth of thinly foliaged trees of medium height and a ground covering of grass and perennial herbs, occurs in large parts of the Lake Plateau, in parts of the Ethiopian Plateau, in the area that fringes the Blue Nile near Ar-Ruṣayriṣ, and in the southern Al-Ghazāl River region.

On the Sudanese plains, a mixture of thin bush, thorny trees, and open grassland prevails. This area is swampy during the rainy season, particularly in the Sudd region of the south-central Sudan, which has an area of nearly 100,000 square miles. The vegetation there includes papyrus, tall bamboolike grasses, reed mace ambatch, or turor, water lettuce, a species of convolvulus, and the South American water hyacinth.

North of latitude 10° N there occurs a belt of thorny savanna or orchard shrub country characterized by small scattered tree stands, thornbush, and—after rain—grass and herbs. North of this, however, rainfall decreases and the vegetation thins out, so that the countryside is dotted with small thorny shrubs, mostly acacias. From Khartoum northward there is true desert, with scanty and irregular rainfall and no permanent vegetation at all except for a few stunted shrubs. Grasses and small herbs may be scattered along drainage lines after rainfall, but these die away in a few weeks. In Egypt the vegetation near the Nile is almost entirely the result of irrigation and cultivation.

Animal life. Many varieties of fish are found in the Nile system. Notable among those found in the lower Nile system are the Nile perch (which may attain a weight of more than 175 pounds), the bolti (a species of *Tilapia*), the barbel, several species of catfish, the elephant-snout fish, and the tiger fish, or water leopard. Most of these species and the sardinelike *Haplochromis,* the lungfish, and mudfish are found as far upstream as Lake Victoria. The common eel penetrates as far south as Khartoum, and the spiny eel is found in Lake Victoria.

Reptiles

The Nile crocodile, found in most parts of the river, has not yet penetrated the lakes of the upper Nile basin. Other reptiles found in the Nile basin include the soft-shelled turtle, three species of monitor lizard, and some 30 species of snakes, of which more than half are venomous. The hippopotamus, once common throughout the Nile system, is now found only in the As-Sudd region and to the south.

Many schools of fish that fed in the waters of the Nile in Egypt during the flood season have been reduced or have disappeared since the construction of the Aswan High Dam. Most of the species of the Nile fish were migrants, and the dam has prevented many from migrating to Lake Nasser. The diminution in the number of anchovies in the eastern Mediterranean has also been attributed to the serious reduction in the outflow of waterborne nutrients due to the dam. Lake Nasser, however, has been developed into a commercial fishery, where the Nile perch and other species thrive.

The people. The Nile flows through regions inhabited by a wide variety of peoples, from the Bantu-speaking populations of the Lake Victoria area to the Arabs of the Sahara and the Nile delta. The wide ethnic and linguistic diversity is mirrored in the numerous ecological relationships between these peoples and the river.

In the southern Sudan are Nilotic-speaking peoples including the Shilluk, Dinka, and Nuer. The Shilluk are sedentary agriculturists whose land is watered by the Nile. The Dinka and Nuer are pastoralists whose movements are dictated by the Nile's seasonal flow. They migrate with their herds from the river's shores during the dry season, to high ground during the wet season, and back to the river when the dry season returns.

Perhaps nowhere is the relationship between people and the river so intense as in the Nile floodplain. The average population density in the cultivated parts of the floodplain south of the delta is more than 3,320 per square mile (1,280 per square kilometre). This great population, composed mostly of peasant farmers (fellahin), can survive only by making the most careful use of the available land and water.

Before the completion of the Aswan High Dam, the large quantities of silt washed down from the rich highlands of Ethiopia were deposited by the floodwaters in Egypt, where the fertility of the riverine lands was maintained over the centuries, despite intensive cultivation. Thus, a vital feature in the life of the Egyptian people was the river's behaviour, since a good harvest followed a good flood, and a poor flood often meant a later food shortage.

The economy. *Irrigation.* As an aid to cultivation, irrigation almost certainly originated in Egypt. A particular phenomenon that makes irrigation from the Nile feasible is the slope of the land from south to north—which amounts to about five inches to the mile—as well as the slightly greater slope downward from the riverbanks to the desert on either side.

The first use of the Nile for irrigation in Egypt began when seeds were sown in the mud left after the annual floodwater had subsided. With the passing of time, these practices were refined until a traditional method emerged, known as basin irrigation. Under this system, the fields on the flat floodplain were divided by earth banks into a series of large basins of varying size but some as large as 50,000 acres (20,000 hectares). During the annual Nile flood, the basins were flooded and the water allowed to remain on the fields for up to six weeks. The water was then permitted to drain away as the river level fell, and a thin deposit of rich Nile silt was left on the land each year. Autumn and winter crops were then sown in the waterlogged soil. Under this system only one crop per year could be grown on the land, and the farmer was always at the mercy of annual fluctuations in the size of the flood.

Basin irrigation

Along the riverbanks and on land above flood level, some perennial irrigation was always possible where water could be lifted directly from the Nile or from irrigation channels by such traditional means as the shadoof (a counterbalanced lever device that uses a long pole); the sakieh, or

Bob Burch/Bruce Coleman Inc.

A stand of sugarcane on the west bank of the Nile River, near Dandarah, Egypt.

Persian waterwheel; or the Archimedean screw. Modern mechanical pumps have begun to replace such human- or animal-operated devices.

Because of the limitations of the basin method of irrigation, perennial irrigation—in which the water is controlled so that it can be made to run into the land at regular intervals throughout the year—has largely replaced it. Perennial irrigation was made possible by the completion of several barrages and waterworks before the end of the 19th century. By the beginning of the 20th century, the canal system had been remodeled and the first dam at Aswān had been completed (see below, *Dams and reservoirs*). Since the completion of the Aswan High Dam, virtually all formerly basin-irrigated land in Upper Egypt has been brought under perennial irrigation.

While the people of The Sudan make use of the waters of the Nile for irrigation, reliance on the river is not absolute, as a fair amount of rainfall occurs in the southern parts. Basin irrigation from the Nile floods is used to a small extent, but it is less satisfactory in these areas because the surface is more uneven, with less deposition of silt; the area inundated also varies from year to year. Since about 1950, these traditional methods of irrigation have been largely displaced by diesel-engined pumps, which are used on large tracts on the banks of either the main Nile, or above Khartoum, the White Nile.

Perennial irrigation in The Sudan began with the completion of the combined dam and barrage near Sannār on the Blue Nile in 1925. This made possible the irrigation of the area of the clay plain called Al-Jazīrah between the two Niles south of Khartoum. The success of this attempt encouraged the construction of more dams and barrages for large-scale irrigation schemes.

Dams and reservoirs. In 1843 it was decided to build a series of diversion dams (barrages or weirs) across the Nile at the head of the delta about 12 miles downstream from Cairo, so as to raise the level of water upstream to supply the irrigation canals and to regulate navigation. This delta barrage scheme was not fully completed until 1861, after which it was extended and improved; it may be regarded as marking the beginning of modern irrigation in the Nile valley. The Zifta Barrage, nearly halfway along the Damietta branch of the deltaic Nile, was added to this system in 1901. In 1902 the Asyūṭ Barrage, more than 200 miles upstream from Cairo, was completed. This was followed in 1909 by the barrage at Isnā (Esna), about 160 miles above Asyūṭ, and in 1930 by the barrage at Najʿ Hammādī, 150 miles above Asyūṭ.

The Aswan High Dam

The first dam at Aswān was constructed between 1899 and 1902; it has a series of four locks to allow navigation. The dam has twice been enlarged—first between 1908 and 1911 and again between 1929 and 1934—thus raising the water level and increasing the dam's capacity. It is also equipped with a hydroelectric plant with an installed power of more than 345 megawatts.

The Aswan High Dam is located about 600 miles upstream from Cairo and 4 miles upstream from the first Aswān Dam. It is built at a place where the river is 1,800 feet wide and has steep banks of granite. The dam is designed to control the Nile water for the expansion of cultivation and for the generation of hydroelectric power and to provide protection downstream for both crops and population against unusually high floods. The work began in 1959 and was completed in 1970. The High Dam is 12,562 feet long at crest level and 3,280 feet wide at the base, with a height of 364 feet above the riverbed. It has a hydroelectric plant with an installed capacity of 2,100 megawatts. Lake Nasser stretches some 310 miles upstream from the dam site, extending 125 miles into The Sudan.

The principal objective behind the construction of the High Dam is to store sufficient water in the reservoir in order to protect Egypt from the dangers of a series of years when the Nile flood is above or below the long-term average and thus to guarantee a steady flow of water from the Nile for both Egypt and The Sudan. An agreement concluded in 1959 between the two countries sets a maximum amount that can be drawn per year and apportions it in a ratio of three to one, with Egypt receiving the larger share. The quantities of water maintained and apportioned are based on the estimated worst possible sequence of flood and drought events over a period of 100 years; and generally, one-fourth of the total capacity of Lake Nasser is reserved as relief storage for the highest anticipated flood during such a period (called "century storage").

The High Dam was a source of considerable controversy during its construction, and since it began operation it has continued to have its critics. Opponents have charged that silt-free water flowing below the dam has caused erosion of the downstream barrages and bridge foundations; that the loss of silt downstream has caused coastal erosion in the delta; that the overall reduction in the flow of the Nile resulting from the construction of the dam has caused the inundation of the lower reaches of the river by saltwater from the Mediterranean Sea, with resulting deposition of salt in the delta soils; and that the creation of Lake Nasser has caused the water table along the river to rise, resulting in waterlogging and an increase in soil salinity in some areas. Already the fish population offshore of the delta has been reduced dramatically by the loss of the nutrient-laden silt. Proponents of the dam have maintained that these harmful effects are worth the security of dependable water and power supplies; and, indeed, Egypt would have suffered a severe water shortage in 1984–88 without the dam.

Dams in The Sudan

In The Sudan the Sannār Dam on the Blue Nile provides water for the Al-Jazīrah plain at the time of year when the water level of the Blue Nile is low. It also produces hydroelectric power. Another dam, at Jabal al-Awliyāʾ on the White Nile, was completed in 1937; it was built to increase the water available to Egypt during the period of low water (January to June) and was not intended to provide irrigation water for The Sudan. Other dams—including one on the Atbara at Khashm al-Qirbah (completed in 1964) and the Ar-Ruṣayriṣ Dam on the Blue Nile (1966)—have enabled The Sudan to take maximum advantage of its allocation of waters from Lake Nasser.

In Uganda, Lake Victoria was made into a reservoir by the completion in 1954 of the Owen Falls Dam; the dam is situated on the Victoria Nile just below the point where the lake waters flow into the river. This permits the storage of surplus water in high-flood years to meet the deficit in years when the waters are low. The fall from the lake is harnessed by a hydroelectric plant that provides power for industries in Uganda and Kenya.

Navigation. As already mentioned, the Nile River is still a vital waterway for the transportation of people and goods, especially in the flood season when motor transport is not feasible; river steamers still provide the only means of transport facilities in most of the area, especially in The Sudan south of latitude 15° N, where motor transport is not usually possible from May to November. Most of the towns in Egypt and The Sudan are situated on or near riverbanks.

In The Sudan steamer service on the Nile and its tributaries extends for about 2,400 miles. Until 1962 the only link between the northern and southern parts of The Sudan was by stern-wheel river steamers of shallow draft. The main service is from Kūstī to Jūbā. There are also seasonal and subsidiary services on the Dunqulah reaches of the main Nile, on the Blue Nile, up the Sobat to Gambela in Ethiopia, and up the Al-Ghazāl River in the high-water season. The Blue Nile is navigable only during the high-water season and then only as far as Ar-Ruṣayriṣ.

Because of the presence of the cataracts north of Khartoum, the river is navigable in The Sudan only in three stretches. The first of these is from the Egyptian border to the south end of Lake Nasser. The second is the stretch between the third and the fourth cataract. The third and most important stretch extends from Khartoum southward to Jūbā.

In Egypt the Nile is navigable by sailing vessels and shallow-draft river steamers as far south as Aswān; thousands of small boats ply the Nile and delta waterways.

Study and exploration. The ancient Egyptians were probably familiar with the Nile as far as Khartoum and with the Blue Nile as far as its source in Lake Tana, but they showed little or no interest in exploring the White Nile. The source of the Nile was unknown to them. The

The Greeks and Romans

Greek historian Herodotus, who visited Egypt in 457 BC, traveled up the Nile as far as the first cataract (Aswān). About the second century BC, the Greek scientific writer Eratosthenes sketched a nearly correct route of the Nile to Khartoum, showing the two Ethiopian affluents, and suggested lakes as the source of the river.

In 25 BC, the Greek geographer Strabo and a Roman governor of Egypt, Aelius Gallus, also explored the Nile as far as the first cataract. A Roman expedition to find the source of the Nile that took place in AD 66, during the reign of the emperor Nero, was impeded by the As-Sudd, and the attempt was therefore abandoned. Ptolemy, the Greek astronomer and geographer who lived in Alexandria, wrote in AD 150 that the White Nile originated in the high snow-covered Mountains of the Moon (since identified with the Ruwenzori Range).

From the 17th century onward, several attempts were made to explore the Nile. In 1613, Pedro Páez, a Spanish Jesuit priest, located the source of the Blue Nile. In 1786, the Scottish explorer James Bruce visited Lake Tana as well as the source of the Blue Nile. (M.M.El.-K./C.G.S.)

Modern exploration of the Nile basin began with the conquest of the northern and central Sudan by the Ottoman viceroy of Egypt, Muḥammad ʿAlī, and his sons from 1821 onward. As a result of this the Blue Nile was known as far as its exit from the Ethiopian foothills, and the White Nile as far as the Sobat mouth. Three expeditions under a Turkish officer, Selim Bimbashi, were made between 1839 and 1842, and two got to the point about 20 miles (32 kilometres) beyond the present port of Jūbā, where the country rises and rapids make navigation very difficult. After these expeditions, traders and missionaries penetrated the country and established stations in the southern Sudan. From an Austrian missionary, Ignaz Knoblecher, in 1850 came reports of lakes farther south. In the 1840s the missionaries Johann Ludwig Krapf, Johannes Rebmann, and Jacob Erhardt, traveling in East Africa, saw the snow-topped mountains Kilimanjaro and Kenya and heard from traders of a great inland sea that might be a lake or lakes.

These reports led to fresh interest in the Nile source and to an expedition by the English explorers Sir Richard Burton and John Hanning Speke, who followed a trade route of the Arabs from the east coast and reached Lake Tanganyika. On the return journey Speke went north and reached the southern end of Lake Victoria, which he thought might be the origin of the Nile. This was followed in 1860 by another expedition by Speke and James A. Grant under the auspices of the Royal Geographical Society. They followed the previous route to Tabora and then turned toward Karagwe, the country west of Lake Victoria. There they saw the Virunga Mountains 100 miles to the west (they thought that they might be the Mountains of the Moon) and discovered the Kagera River. Continuing around the lake, Speke finally reached the Ripon Falls (1862), at which point he wrote, "I saw that old Father Nile without any doubt rises in Victoria Nyanza." Speke then made his way northward with Grant, for part of the way traveling along the Nile, until the two reached Gondokoro, which lies nearly opposite the present Jūbā. They heard rumours on the way of another large lake to the west but were unable to visit it and passed the information on to Samuel White Baker, who met them at Gondokoro, having come up from Cairo. Baker then continued his journey south and discovered Lake Albert. Neither Speke nor Baker had followed the Nile completely from the Ripon Falls to Gondokoro; and Baker, who saw the northern half of Lake Albert, was told that it extended a very long way to the south.

The question of the source of the Nile was finally settled when, between 1874 and 1877, General Charles George Gordon and his officers followed the river and mapped part of it. In particular Lake Albert was mapped, and Charles Chaillé-Long, an American, discovered Lake Kyoga. In 1875 Henry Morton Stanley traveled up from the east coast and circumnavigated Lake Victoria. His attempt to get to Lake Albert was not successful, but he marched to Lake Tanganyika and traveled down the Congo (Zaire) River to the sea. In another memorable journey in 1889, taken in order to relieve the German traveler Mehmed Emin Paşa (Pasha), Stanley traveled up the Congo and across to Lake Albert, where he met Emin and persuaded him to evacuate his Equatorial Province, which had been invaded by the Mahdist forces. They returned to the east coast by way of the Semliki valley and Lake Edward, and Stanley saw the snowy peaks of the Ruwenzori Range for the first time.

Stanley's expeditions

Exploration and mapping has continued over the years: it was not until the 1960s, for example, that a detailed study of the upper gorges of the Blue Nile was completed. (H.E.Ht./C.G.S.)

ORANGE RIVER

The Orange River in southern Africa is one of the longest rivers on the continent and one of the longest south of the tropic of Capricorn. After rising in the Lesotho Highlands, less than 125 miles (200 kilometres) from the Indian Ocean, the river flows to the Atlantic Ocean in a generally westerly direction for some 1,300 miles. The Orange traverses the veld region of South Africa, after which it defines the southern limit of the Kalahari and bisects the southern Namib before draining into the Atlantic at Alexander Bay, S. Af. Along its course the river forms the boundary between two of South Africa's provinces, the Orange Free State and Cape Province, as well as that between Namibia and South Africa.

The Orange River—together with the Vaal, its principal tributary—forms a drainage basin with an area of at least 330,000 square miles (855,000 square kilometres). The western part of the basin is generally dry, flat, and unamenable to cultivation without irrigation. The river itself is of vital economic importance to the region through which it flows. Two projects—the Orange River Project and the Lesotho Highland Project, both in various stages of construction—have been designed to meet the water demand for irrigation, urbanization, and economic development in the central industrial areas of South Africa.

For map coverage of the Orange River, see above *Kalahari*.

Physical features. *Physiography.* The headwaters of the Orange River rise at an altitude of about 10,800 feet (3,300 metres) above sea level on a dissected plateau formed by the Lesotho Highlands that extends from the Drakensberg escarpment in the east to the Maloti (Maluti) Mountains in the west. The main source of the Orange River is officially recognized as the Sinqu (Senqu) River, which rises near the plateau's eastern edge. The Seati (Khubedu) headwater rises near Mont aux Sources to the north. Still farther north is the lesser-known Malibamatso headwater, one site of the Lesotho Highland Project. The Lesotho headwaters flow over the turf soil that covers Drakensberg lava and cut through the lava to expose underlying sedimentary rocks; material eroded from these rocks contributes to heavy silt deposits farther down the river's course.

Headwaters

After entering South Africa southwest of Lesotho, the river flows south and west through more open country, where sandstones, shales, and mudstones appear on the surface and where hard dolerite outcrops form small hills and flat-topped mountains. Near Aliwal North, the river has eroded a broad valley with a width of some 30 miles and a depth of more than 1,000 feet. The river's channel, however, varies greatly in both width and depth because of dolerite outcrops that sometimes narrow it to 3,000 or 4,000 feet. The river receives the Caledon as a tributary at the head of the Hendrik Verwoerd Reservoir.

From the Hendrik Verwoerd Dam the Orange swings to the northwest to its confluence with the Vaal River. The Vaal, which rises in the eastern Transvaal, flows west through the major population and industrial core of South Africa before turning south and joining the Orange near the town of Douglas. From there the Orange turns southwest and flows over calcrete and tillite (glacial clayey deposit). At Prieska it makes another sharp bend to the northwest, and this marks the beginning of its middle course. Quartzites and ironstones form a "barrier zone" through which the river has cut deep gorges. At Upington the river—which by then has turned to the west—spreads out over a granite surface. In this area the Orange splits up into innumerable channels, between which are islands of varying length; and the river attains its greatest width, which may reach nearly four miles in places. About 40 miles downstream from Upington, however, the riverbed is suddenly narrowed to about 2,000 feet.

Some 20 miles below Kakamas the Orange—again flowing in several channels—forms the Augrabies Falls. There, after descending in a series of rapids, the river plunges into a deep pool. The river flows through an almost vertical-sided gorge for about 11 miles, emerging again into more open country. The lower course of the river, from the Augrabies Falls to the sea, is sometimes called the Gorge Tract. Where the rock surface is soft, the river valley is generally open. Where the river traverses harder igneous rock, however, it is confined between almost vertical cliffs more than 1,000 feet high in places. Some of the Orange's most rugged passages are found in the last section of the river, as it flows along the Richtersveld before turning west to the Namib coastal desert.

Mouth of the Orange

The Orange reaches the sea a few miles north of the little inlet known as Alexander Bay. The mouth is less than three miles wide and is nearly closed by sandbars, which are widely breached during high floods. The gap in the southern end of the bars is maintained by the outflow of water from the river mouth during low tides and by the tidal inflow at high tides.

Climate and hydrology. The rainfall patterns in the Orange basin have a direct effect on the river's rate of flow. In Lesotho, above the confluence with the Caledon, the rainfall averages 28 to 32 inches (700 to 800 millimetres) annually; and, combined with the melted winter snows of the highland areas, this small area contributes nearly 60 percent of the Orange River's total annual flow. From the Caledon to the Vaal annual rainfall decreases to about 11 to 16 inches a year, and below the Vaal confluence it decreases from 9 inches to less than 2 inches in the Namib.

The amount of rainfall reaching the river as runoff decreases from about 16 percent in Lesotho to less than one-half of 1 percent in the lower Orange catchment. Conversely, summer maximum temperatures increase from east to west, the high exceeding 86° F (30° C) on an average 5 days per year in Lesotho and 150 days per year in the west. The result of these phenomena is a tremendous increase in the rate of evaporation from east to west. Waters lost to evaporation may amount to 12 times the total precipitation in the lower course of the Orange, and the potential storage capacity of reservoirs in the drier regions may be reduced by up to 60 percent.

Gerard Cubitt—Bruce Coleman Ltd.

The Gorge Tract of the Orange River, near Rosh Pinah, Namibia.

The people and economy. The high valleys of the Orange River's headwaters are uninhabited, though the adjacent plateaus are used by the southern Sotho (Basuto) people for grazing land. Between the Lesotho border and the town of Aliwal North, corn (maize) is cultivated, and this region is also used as pasturage for cattle and sheep. The dry shrub country farther downstream is in general suitable only for grazing. Irrigated sections, however, occur along the river's course; the largest such area is between Upington and the Augrabies Falls, downstream of the Boegoeberg Dam (located midway between Prieska and Upington), where cotton, alfalfa (lucerne), grapes, and dates are grown. While scattered farms stand within reach of the river's freshwater supply, there are no large towns along the riverbank. This situation remains little changed by the Orange River Project (see below): much of the water accumulated by its dams is diverted to the valleys of the Fish and Sundays rivers and to the cities of Port Elizabeth, Bloemfontein, and Kimberley.

Transportation. Navigation is impossible throughout the river's course because of its irregular flow, its constant interruption by falls and rapids, and the silting that occurs in its channels and at the river mouth. Many bridges cross the river along its course between Aliwal North and Oranjemund, the largest being at Upington.

Irrigation. Large irrigation and hydroelectric projects have been hampered on much of the Orange by the enormous amount of waterborne silt that clogs up reservoirs and reduces storage capacity. Efforts to combat this problem have included adding sluice gates to the Boegoeberg Dam (completed in 1931), which allow much of the silt to pass through.

The Orange River Project

In order to obtain comprehensive control of the river, the Orange River Project was located farther upstream, between the Caledon and Vaal confluences. The plan consists of a number of dam and canal projects; work began in 1962. The completed projects include the Hendrik Verwoerd Dam (1972), which has formed the Hendrik Verwoerd Reservoir; the P.K. le Roux Dam (1977), located about 90 miles downstream from the Verwoerd Dam; a tunnel some 50 miles long (1975), which carries water from the Verwoerd Dam to the Great Fish River; and an irrigation canal between the Great Fish and Sundays rivers. Among the projects that were still under construction in the 1990s were the Van der Kloof irrigation canals below the P.K. le Roux Dam.

The two dams have also been equipped to deal with heavy silt accumulation. They have deep dead-storage areas, and their high walls can be raised if necessary to allow for a higher water level. The Verwoerd Dam is the major water-conservation structure of the project. Its main function is to store sufficient water in its reservoir for further distribution via the P.K. le Roux Dam or the Orange–Great Fish tunnel. The maximum height of the dam is 254 feet above the riverbed, it is 3,110 feet long along its crest, and the Verwoerd Reservoir has a maximum surface area of about 140 square miles. The P.K. le Roux Dam has a maximum height of 351 feet, it is 2,510 feet long along its crest, and the reservoir has a maximum surface area of 54 square miles. Both dams have hydroelectric power stations, and their reservoirs provide water-recreation facilities.

Measures to increase the capacity of the Vaal River have also been undertaken. Water has been obtained via the Tugela–Vaal Water Project. More water will be supplied to the Vaal by the Lesotho Highland Project, which, when complete, will consist of several dams and storage reservoirs in the basins of the Sinqu, Malibamatso, and Senqunyane rivers.

Study and exploration. The first white man known to cross the river to the north bank was an Afrikaner elephant hunter, Jacobus Coetsee, who forded the Groot River, as it was then called, near the river mouth in 1760. Later expeditions across the river in the 18th century were led by the Afrikaner explorer Hendrik Hop; Robert Jacob Gordon, a Dutch officer; William Paterson, an English traveler; and the French explorer François Le Vaillant. They explored the river from its middle course to its mouth, and Gordon named it in honour of the Dutch house of Orange. Mission stations were established north of the Orange from the late 18th century. In 1813 John Campbell of the London Missionary Society traced the Harts River and from its junction with the Vaal followed the latter stream to its confluence with the Orange, which he explored as far as the Augrabies Falls. The source of the Orange was first reached by the French Protestant missionaries Thomas Arbousset and François Daumas in 1836.

Throughout the 19th century, the Orange River marked the northern limit of British power in southern Africa. Beginning in the 1830s, the Boers crossed it in search of land and freedom from British rule; they named their first republic—the Orange Free State—for the river.

(J.H.We./P.S.Ha./Jo.Co.)

SÉNÉGAL RIVER

The Sénégal River, 1,020 miles (1,641 kilometres) long, is one of western Africa's longest rivers. Its drainage basin encompasses some 174,000 square miles (450,000 square kilometres). Two of the river's three headstreams rise in the Fouta Djallon highlands in Guinea, after which it flows to the northwest and then to the west to drain into the Atlantic Ocean. For some 515 miles of its course it forms the boundary between Mauritania to the north and Senegal to the south.

For map coverage of the Sénégal River, see above *Niger River*.

Physical features. *Physiography and hydrology.* Of the various headstreams of the river, the Falémé and Bafing rise in the sandstones of the Fouta Djallon plateau in Guinea, while the Bakoye rises in western Mali. The Bafing and Bakoye meet at Bafoulabé in Mali to form the Sénégal, 650 miles from its mouth. The stream is then joined by the Falémé near Bakel, Senegal. From there onward the Senegal–Mauritania boundary lies on the right (northern) bank, so that the river belongs to Senegal; Mauritania, however, generally has been permitted to use the river.

Formation of the Sénégal

From Bakel to Dagana, a distance of 385 miles, the river flows through an alluvial valley as much as 12 miles wide. Floods come in early September at Bakel, reaching Dagana by mid-October. During the flood season the water level rises 12 feet (3.5 metres), the flow is some 300 times greater than in the dry season, and the river occupies the entire valley.

Below Dagana, at Richard-Toll, the Sénégal enters its delta. The river's gradient is extremely slight in the delta, and, until the completion of the Diama Dam near the river's mouth in 1985, salt water was able to flow upstream to Dagana during periods of low water. The mouth of the Sénégal has been deflected southward by the offshore Canary Current and by trade winds blowing from the north; the result has been the formation of a long sandspit, the Barbary Tongue (Langue de Barbarie). Saint-Louis lies in the river's estuary, which extends for about 10 miles to the river's mouth.

Climate. The Bafing and Falémé sources receive about 80 inches (2,000 millimetres) of rainfall annually, mostly from late March to early November; the Bakoye basin receives less. The Sénégal valley proper receives 10 to 30 inches of rain annually, from late May to mid-October, with mean maximum temperatures of about 105° F (41° C) in April, and mean minimum temperatures of about 62° F (17° C) in January. Rainfall diminishes downstream, and the climate of Saint-Louis is similar to that of Dakar, the capital of Senegal, to the south.

Plant and animal life. Typical trees of the Sénégal valley are acacias, notably *Acacia nilotica,* which grows profusely on banks, and *A. senegal,* which provides the gum arabic of commerce and grows on drier slopes. The grass *Vetiveria nigritiana* grows in tufts in wet depressions. In dry areas near the valley sides *A. albida, Balanites aegyptiaca* (a tree with thorny branches), and grasses are common.

The river is overfished, but Nile perch are common. Spoonbills, herons, egrets, and weaverbirds are widespread. Among the animals on the riverbanks hedgehogs, monitor lizards, and warthogs are fairly common.

The people and economy. The Sénégal valley below Dagana is populated by the Wolof; upstream from Dagana to beyond Matam is peopled mainly by the Tukulor (Tokolor), after which Soninke (Serahuli) dominate. Villages average about 300 people except in the delta, which is sparsely settled. Throughout the Sénégal River region small groups of usually nomadic Fulani (Fulbe or Peul) and Mauri (Maure or Moors) are found.

Agriculture and irrigation. The best agricultural land along the Sénégal River is in the alluvial valley between Bakel and Dagana, and this area is the most densely populated part of the valley. As the floods retreat each year, a variety of crops (including millet, rice, and vegetables) are sown, and they grow and mature quickly. Millet is also grown on rain-fed lands. Both areas provide pasture for the livestock of nomads.

Rice cultivation on lands from which floods have retreated has been locally improved by embankments, with sluices constructed mainly on the Senegalese riverbank; diesel pumps have also been used on the Mauritanian bank. At Richard-Toll a large area is irrigated by means of a dam across the Taoué (Taouey), a tributary stream up which Sénégal floods penetrate to Lake Guiers. Rice and, more recently, sugarcane have been grown there by the use of mechanized equipment and paid labour, although rice yields have been lower than expected because of saline soils and the depredations of the quelea bird.

Rice cultivation

In the delta an embankment 50 miles long controls the entry of floodwater to some 120 square miles, part of which has been prepared for cultivation. The Diama Dam, located about 25 miles upstream from Saint-Louis, permits floodwaters to pass through its sluice gates while preventing the encroachment of salt water; it has im-

Owen Franken—Stock, Boston

Boats on the Sénégal River; Kaédi, Mauritania, is on the far shore.

proved considerably the supply of fresh water in the delta region and at the same time has facilitated navigation. The hydroelectric potential of the Sénégal has also been tapped, with hydroelectric stations at Diama and upstream at Manantali in Mali; these projects have been undertaken jointly by Mali, Mauritania, and Senegal.

Transportation. Extension of a railway from Kayes, Mali, to Dakar (completed in 1923) diverted traffic that previously went by river, after which the valley became an economic backwater. Local traffic, however, is carried by shallow-draft boats from Saint-Louis to Podor, Senegal, year-round, and as far as Kayes from early August to mid-October. Most traffic plies between the Mauritanian river ports of Rosso, Bogué, and Kaédi. Minor ferries exist at Rosso and Kayes; there is a dry season causeway across the river at Kayes. Saint-Louis was once a seaport, but because of the dangerous sandbar there it was supplanted by Dakar, 163 miles to the south, after a Dakar–Saint-Louis railway link opened in 1885.

Study and exploration. In medieval times reports of the Sénégal River's existence as the "River of Gold" reached European navigators. From the 16th to the 20th century the river formed a route of advance for French colonial influence. French ships entered the estuary at least as early as 1558. From a French fort established in 1638, reconnaissance parties went 160 miles upriver to Podor. In 1659 a larger fort was erected on N'Dar Island in the estuary and named Saint-Louis-du-Sénégal for the French king Louis IX (St. Louis). This became a base for French exploration of the river and for trade in slaves, gum, gold, skins, ivory, beeswax, and ostrich feathers. André Brüe built a post, Saint-Joseph-de-Galam, 400 miles upstream in 1698, and parties sent by him reached the Félou Falls above Kayes soon after. Some went up the Falémé, where another fort was built. Pierre David penetrated far up that river in 1744. In the 20th century much of the focus of activity has been on the development of the Sénégal's resources. Since the 1970s this has been undertaken co-operatively by Mali, Mauritania, and Senegal under the auspices of the Organization for the Development of the Sénégal River. (R.J.H.-C./Ca.C.)

SUEZ CANAL

The Suez Canal (Qanāt as-Suways in Arabic), a sea-level waterway across the Isthmus of Suez in Egypt connecting the Mediterranean and the Red seas, provides the shortest maritime route between Europe and the lands lying around the Indian and western Pacific oceans. It is one of the world's most heavily used shipping lanes. The

Route of the canal

canal extends 101 miles (163 kilometres) between Port Said (Būr Saʿīd) in the north and Suez in the south, with dredged approach channels north of Port Said into the Mediterranean, and south of Suez. The canal does not take the shortest route across the isthmus, which is only 75 miles, but utilizes several lakes, from north to south, Lake Manzala (Buḥayrat al-Manzilah), Lake Timsah (Buḥayrat at-Timsāḥ), and the Bitter Lakes: Great Bitter Lake (Al-Buḥayrah al-Murrah al-Kubrā) and Little Bitter Lake (Al-Buḥayrah al-Murrah aṣ-Ṣughrā). The Suez Canal is an open cut, without locks, and, though extensive straight lengths occur, there are eight major bends. To the west of the canal is the low-lying delta of the Nile River; to the east is the higher, rugged, and arid Sinai Peninsula. Prior to construction of the canal (completed in 1869), the only important settlement was Suez, which in 1859 had 3,000 to 4,000 inhabitants. The rest of the towns along its banks have grown up since, with the possible exception of Al-Qanṭarah.

Physical features. *Geology.* The Isthmus of Suez, the sole land bridge between the continents of Africa and Asia, is of relatively recent geologic origin. Both continents once formed a single large continental mass, but during Tertiary times (66.4 to 1.6 million years ago) the great fault structures of the Red Sea and Gulf of Aqaba developed, with the opening and subsequent drowning of the Red Sea trough as far as the Gulf of Suez and the Gulf of Aqaba. In the succeeding Quaternary Period, there was considerable oscillation of sea level, leading finally to the emergence of a low-lying isthmus that broadened northward to a low-lying open coastal plain. There, the Nile delta once extended farther east—as a result of periods of abundant rainfall coincident with the Pleistocene Epoch (1,600,000 to 10,000 years ago)—and two river arms, or distributaries, formerly crossed the northern isthmus, one branch reaching the Mediterranean Sea at the narrowest point of the isthmus and the other entering the sea some nine miles east of present Port Said.

Physiography. Topographically, the Isthmus of Suez is not uniform; there are three shallow, water-filled depressions—Lake Manzala and Timsah, and the Bitter Lakes, the last, though distinguished as Great and Little, forming

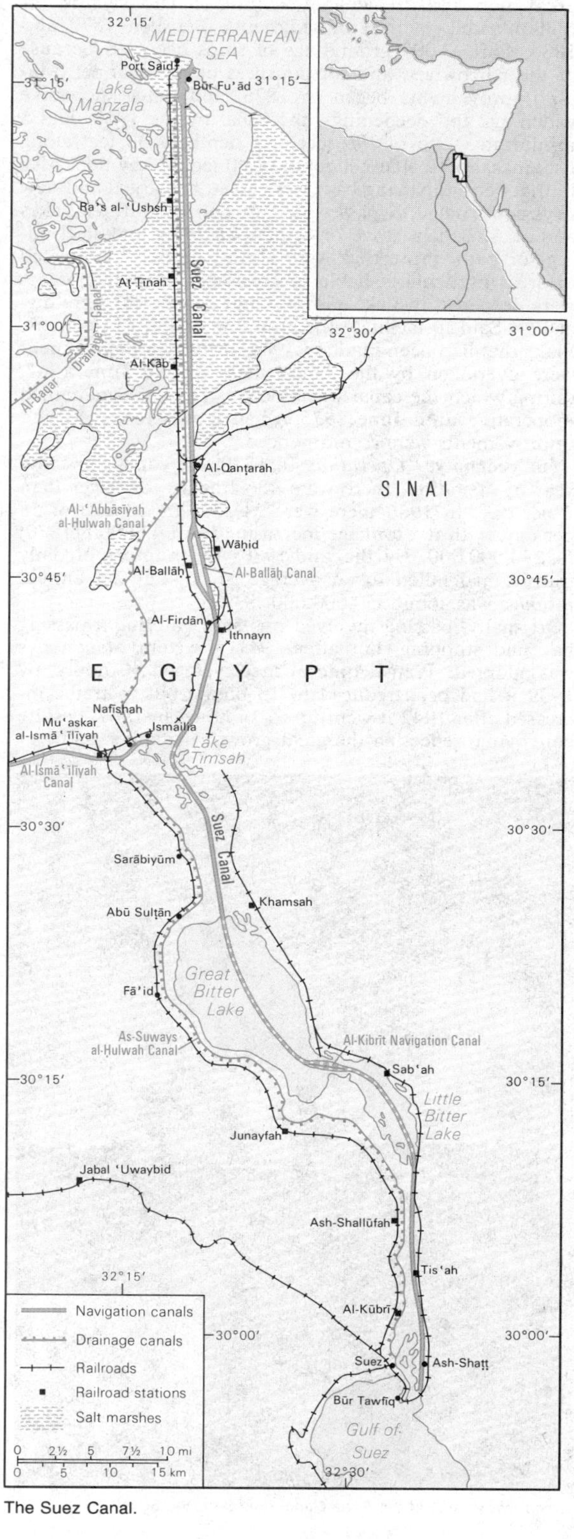

The Suez Canal.

one continuous sheet of water. A number of more resistant bands of limestone and gypsum obtrude in the south of the isthmus, and another significant feature is a narrow valley leading from Lake Timsah southwestward toward the middle Nile delta and Cairo. The isthmus is composed of marine sediments, coarser sands, and gravels deposited in the early periods of abundant rainfall, Nile alluvium (especially to the north), and windblown sands.

Original size of the canal

When first opened in 1869, the canal consisted of a channel barely 26 feet (8 metres) deep, 72 feet wide at the bottom, and 200 to 300 feet wide at the surface. To allow ships to pass each other, passing bays were built every five to six miles. Construction involved the excavation and dredging of 97 million cubic yards (74 million cubic metres) of sediments. Between 1870 and 1884, some 3,000 groundings of ships occurred because of the narrowness and tortuousness of the channel. Major improvements began in 1876, and, after successive widenings and deepenings, the canal by the 1960s had a minimum width of 179 feet at a depth of 33 feet along its banks, and a channel depth of 40 feet at low tide. Also in that period, passing bays were greatly enlarged and new bays constructed, bypasses were made in the Bitter Lakes and at Al-Ballāḥ, stone or cement cladding and steel piling for bank protection were almost entirely completed in areas particularly liable to erosion, tanker anchorages were deepened in Lake Timsah, and new berths were dug at Port Said to facilitate the grouping of ships in convoy. Plans that had been made in 1964 for further enlargement were overtaken by the Arab-Israeli War of June 1967, during which the canal was blocked. The canal remained inoperative until June 1975, when it was reopened and improvements were recommenced.

The economy. *Operation.* In 1870, the canal's first full year of operation, there were 486 transits, or fewer than 2 per day. In 1966 there were 21,250, an average of 58 per day, with net tonnage increasing from 437,000 (1870) to 274,000,000. By the mid-1980s the number of daily transits had fallen to an average of 50, but net annual tonnage was about 350,000,000.

Originally, passing involved one ship entering a passing bay and stopping, but after 1947 a system of convoys was adopted. Transit time at first averaged 40 hours; by 1939 it had been reduced to 13 hours, but as traffic increased after 1942 it went up to 15 hours in 1967, despite convoying, reflecting the great growth in tanker traffic at that time. Convoys leave daily—two southbound and one northbound. Southbound convoys moor at Port Said, Al-Ballāḥ, Lake Timsah, and Al-Kabrīt, where there are bypasses that allow northbound convoys to proceed without stopping. With reduced overall traffic and some enlargement of the canal, transit time since 1975 has been about 14 hours. Upon entering the canal at Port Said or Suez, ships are assessed for tonnage and cargo (passengers have ridden without charge since 1950) and are handled by one pilot (sometimes two) for actual canal transit, which is increasingly controlled by radar.

Hubertus Kauns/Superstock

Soviet cargo ship in the Suez Canal near Ismailia, Egypt.

Nature of canal traffic

The nature of traffic has greatly altered, especially because of the enormous growth in oil shipments from the Persian Gulf since 1950. In 1913, oil in northbound traffic amounted to 291,000 tons; in the peak year of 1966, it amounted to 166,000,000 tons. The closure of the canal from 1967 to 1975 led to the use of large oil tankers on the route around the Cape of Good Hope. Since 1975 the increased size of tankers—the largest of which cannot use the canal—has reduced the canal's importance in the international oil trade. Canal traffic has also been affected by the development of sources of crude oil in Algeria, Libya, Nigeria, the North Sea, and Mexico—all areas outside of the canal route. Competition has also risen from new pipelines to the Mediterranean, including the pipeline from Suez to Alexandria that was opened in 1977.

From an all-time peak in 1945 of 984,000, passenger traffic has declined to negligible numbers because of the competition from aircraft, which also now carry high-value cargoes of small bulk. Further decline in canal traffic resulted from a shift of Australasian trade from Europe to Japan and East Asia. Some movement of oil, however, from refineries in the Soviet Union, southern Europe, and Algeria has continued, chiefly to India, and the shipment of dry cargoes, including grain, ores, and metals, has increased. A more recent feature has been the growth of container (lighter aboard ship, or LASH) and roll-on roll-off traffic through the canal, chiefly destined for the highly congested ports of the Red Sea and Persian Gulf. Asia still receives large quantities of North American wheat, corn (maize), and barley through the canal.

The major northbound cargoes consist of crude petroleum and petroleum products, coal, ores and metals, and fabricated metals, as well as wood, oilseeds and oilseed cake, and cereals. Southbound traffic consists of cement, fertilizers, fabricated metals, and cereals. Much southbound traffic consists of empty oil tankers, for supertankers with a deadweight tonnage of up to 200,000 tons can now transit the canal empty but not laden.

Communications and towns. Construction of the canal led to the growth of settlements in what had been, except for Suez, almost uninhabited arid territory. More than 70,000 acres (28,000 hectares) were brought under cultivation, and about 8 percent of the total population was engaged in agriculture, with approximately 10,000 commercial and industrial activities of various sizes. In 1967 almost all the population was evacuated, and most of the settlements were severely damaged or destroyed during subsequent warfare. With the reopening of the canal in 1975, however, reconstruction of the area was begun, and most of the population had returned by 1978. Port Said was created a customs-free zone in 1975, and tax-free industrial zones have been established along the canal. The major urban centres are Port Said, with its east-bank counterpart, Būr Fuʾād; Ismailia (Al-Ismāʿīlīyah), on the north shore of Lake Timsah; and Suez, with its west-bank outport, Būr Tawfīq. Water for irrigation and for domestic and industrial use is supplied by the Nile via the Al-Ismāʿīlīyah Canal.

Road and railway connections

There are two roads from the pre-1967 period on the west bank. Ferries have largely been replaced by four underpasses: north of Suez, south and north of Lake Timsah, and at Al-Qanṭarah. From this last, a road continues along the east bank to Būr Fuʾād, and another runs eastward through the Sinai to Israel. Newer roads on the east bank run eastward to the Khutmīyah, Giddi, and Mitla passes, which give access to the central Sinai. The railway on the west side of the canal was restored in the 1970s. In 1980, the Ahmad Hamdi road tunnel was opened, connecting

Egypt proper with its governorate (*muḥāfaẓah*) of Shamāl Sīnā'. About one mile of the tunnel passes beneath the canal itself.

History. *Construction.* The first canal in the region seems to have been dug in about 1850 BC, when an irrigation channel navigable at flood period was constructed into the Wadi Tumelat (aṭ-Ṭumaylāt). This channel was extended by the Ptolemies via the Bitter Lakes as far as the Red Sea. From the region of Lake Timsah a northward arm appears to have reached a former branch of the Nile. Extended under the Romans (who called it Trajan's Canal), neglected by the Byzantines, and reopened by the early Arabs, this canal was deliberately filled in by the ʿAbbāsid caliphs for military reasons in AD 775. Throughout, the reason for these changes appears to have been to facilitate trade from the delta lands to the Red Sea rather than to provide a passage to the Mediterranean.

Among the Venetians in the 15th century and the French in the 17th and 18th centuries were writers who speculated upon the possibility of making a canal through the isthmus. A canal there would make it possible for ships of their nations to sail directly from the Mediterranean to the Indian Ocean and so dispute the monopoly of the East Indian trade that had been won first by the Portuguese, then by the Dutch, and finally by the English, all of whom used the route around the Cape of Good Hope. These schemes came to nothing.

It was not until the French occupation of Egypt (1798–1801) that the first survey was made across the isthmus. Napoleon personally investigated the remains of the ancient canal. J.M. Le Père, his chief lines-of-communication engineer, erroneously calculated that the level of the Red Sea was 33 feet above that of the Mediterranean, and, therefore, locks would be needed. Considering the adverse conditions under which the French surveyors worked, and the prevailing belief in the disparity of levels of the two seas, the error was excusable, and Le Père's conclusion was uncritically accepted by a succession of subsequent authors of canal projects. Studies for a canal were made again in 1834 and in 1846. In 1854 Ferdinand de Lesseps received an Act of Concession from the viceroy (khedive) of Egypt, Saʿīd Pasha, to construct a canal; and in 1856 a second act conferred on the Suez Canal Company (Compagnie Universelle du Canal Maritime de Suez) the right to operate a maritime canal for 99 years after completion of the work. Construction began in 1859 and took 10 years instead of the six that had been envisaged; climatic difficulties, a cholera epidemic in 1865, and early labour troubles all slowed down operations. An initial project was the cutting of a small canal (the Al-Ismāʿīlīyah) from the delta along the Wadi Tumelat, with a southern branch (now called the As-Suways al-Ḥulwah Canal; the two canals combined were formerly called the Sweet Water Canal) to Suez and a northern one (Al-ʿAbbāsīyah Canal) to Port Said. This supplied drinking water in an otherwise arid area and was completed in 1863.

The Suez Canal Company

At first, digging was done by hand with picks and baskets, peasants being drafted as forced labour. Later, dredgers and steam shovels operated by European labourers took over, and, as dredging proved cheaper than dry excavation, the terrain was artificially flooded and dredged wherever possible. Other than in the few areas where rock strata were met, the entire canal was driven through sand or alluvium. In August 1869 the waterway was completed, and it was officially opened with an elaborate ceremony in November.

Finance. The Suez Canal Company had been incorporated as an Egyptian joint stock company with its head office in Paris. Despite much early official coolness, even hostility, on the part of Great Britain, de Lesseps was anxious for international participation and offered shares widely. Only the French responded, however, buying 52 percent of the shares; of the remainder, 44 percent was taken up by Saʿīd Pasha. The first board of directors included representatives of 14 countries.

In 1875, financial troubles compelled the new viceroy, Ismāʿīl Pasha, to sell his holding, which (at the instigation of the prime minister, Benjamin Disraeli) was at once bought by the British government. Until that year, the shares had remained below their issue price of 500 francs each. With the British purchase (at 568 francs each), steady appreciation took place, to more than 3,600 francs in 1900.

Originally allocated 15 percent of the net profits, Egypt later relinquished the percentage and, after the sale of Ismāʿīl's 176,602 shares, remained unrepresented on the board of directors until 1949, when it was, in effect, reinstated as a board member and allotted 7 percent of gross profits. In that year, it was also agreed that 90 percent of new clerical jobs and 80 percent of technical appointments would be offered to Egyptians and that the Canal Company would provide hospitals, schools, and other amenities.

In 1956, 13 years before the concession was due to expire, the canal was nationalized by Egyptian president Gamal Abdel Nasser. Since then, the Egyptian government has exercised complete control, though the original company continues in Paris as a conglomerate.

International status. Although the canal was built to serve, and profit from, international trade, its international status remained undefined for many years. In 1888 the major maritime powers at the time (except Great Britain) signed the Convention of Constantinople, which declared that the canal should be open to ships of all nations in times of both peace and war. In addition, the convention forbade acts of hostility in the waters of the canal and the construction of fortifications on its banks. Great Britain did not sign the convention until 1904.

The history of international use of the canal during wartime includes denial of passage to Spanish warships during the Spanish-American War of 1898 and permission of passage by a squadron of the Russian navy during the Russo-Japanese War in 1905 and of Italian vessels during Italy's invasion of Ethiopia in 1935–36. Theoretically, the canal was open to all belligerents during World Wars I and II, but the naval and military superiority of the Allied forces denied effective use of the canal to the shipping of Germany and its allies.

The Suez Crisis

Following the armistice between Israel and its Arab opponents in 1949, Egypt denied use of the canal to Israel and to all ships trading with Israel. The first of two canal closings occurred during the Suez Crisis of 1956–57, after Israel attacked Egyptian forces and French and British troops occupied part of the canal zone. The second closing was a consequence of the Arab-Israeli War of June 1967, during and after which the canal was the scene of much fighting between Egypt and Israel and for several years formed the front line between the two armies. With the reopening of the canal in June 1975 and the signing of a peace treaty between Egypt and Israel in 1979, all ships (including those of Israeli registration) again had access to the waterway. (W.B.Fi./C.G.S.)

ZAMBEZI RIVER

The Zambezi, together with its tributaries, forms the fourth largest river basin of Africa and drains a large portion of the south-central region of the continent. It flows eastward for about 2,200 miles (3,540 kilometres) from its source on the Central African Plateau to empty into the Indian Ocean. With its tributaries, it drains an area of more than 500,000 square miles (1,300,000 square kilometres). The Zambezi (meaning "Great River" in the language of the Tonga people) includes along its course the Victoria Falls, one of the world's greatest natural wonders, and the Kariba and Cabora Bassa dams, two of Africa's largest hydroelectric projects. The river either crosses or forms the boundaries of six countries or territories—Angola, Zambia, Namibia, Botswana, Zimbabwe, and Mozambique—and the use of its waters has been the subject of a series of international agreements.

Physical features. *Physiography.* The Zambezi rises out of a marshy bog near Kalene Hill, Zambia, about 4,800 feet (1,460 metres) above sea level, and flows some 20 miles before entering Angola, through which it runs for more than 175 miles. In this first section of its course, the river is met by more than a dozen tributaries of varying sizes. Shortly after reentering Zambia, the river flows over the Chavuma Falls and enters a broad region of hummocky, sand-covered floodplains, the largest of which is

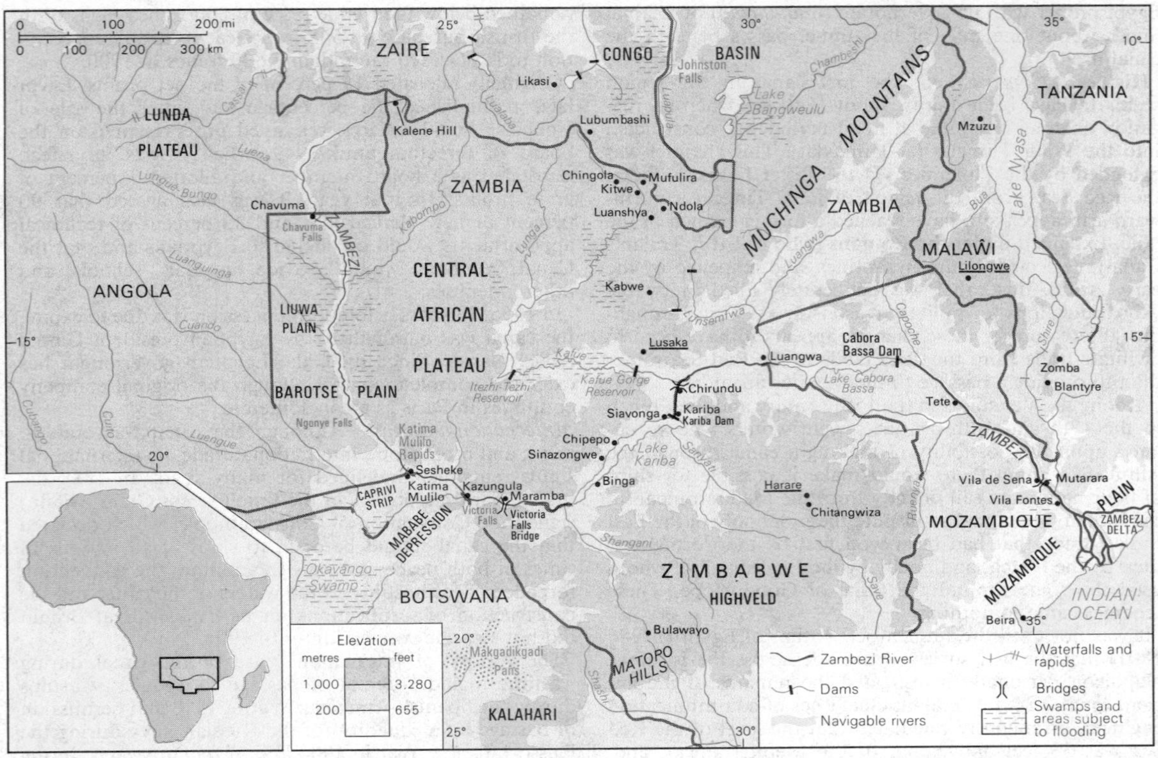

The Zambezi River basin and its drainage network.

the Barotse, or Zambezi, Plain. The region is inundated during the summer floods, when it receives fertile alluvial soils. The main tributaries intersecting the river along the plains are the Kabompo River from the east and the larger Lungué-Bungo (Lungwebungo) River from the west.

The Zambezi then enters a stretch of rapids that extends from Ngonye (Sioma) Falls south to the Katima Mulilo Rapids, after which for about 80 miles it forms the border between Zambia to the north and the eastern Caprivi Strip—an extension of Namibia—to the south. In this stretch the river meanders through the broad grasslands of the Sesheke Plain until it is joined by the Cuando (Kwando) River. Near Kazungula, Zambia, the river, after flowing past Botswana territory to the south, turns almost due east and forms the frontier between Zambia and Zimbabwe. From the Cuando confluence to the Victoria Falls, the Zambezi varies considerably in width, from open reaches with sand islands to stretches of rapids through narrow channels separated by numerous rock islands.

Victoria Falls

The Victoria Falls mark the end of the upper course of the Zambezi, as its waters tumble with a thunderous roar and an enormous cloud of spray. The area around the falls was once covered by a thick layer of lava, which as it cooled formed wide cracks, or joints, that became filled with softer sediments. As the Zambezi cut its present valley it encountered one of these joints, eroded the sediment, and created a trench, eventually forcing a gap at the lower end of the trench that quickly widened into a gorge. The force of the water also created a second gap at the upper end of the trench that gradually diverted the river until the trench itself was left dry. As the river cut backward it repeated the process, scouring eight successive waterfalls in the last half million years.

The Zambezi's middle course extends about 600 miles from Victoria Falls to the eastern end of Lake Cabora Bassa in Mozambique. It continues to form the boundary between Zambia and Zimbabwe until it crosses the Mozambique border at Luangwa. Below the falls a gorge some 60 miles long has been formed by the trench-scouring process, through which the river descends in a series of rapids. Just upstream of Lake Kariba the river valley widens and is contained by escarpments nearly 2,000 feet high. The middle Zambezi is notable for the two man-made lakes, Kariba and Cabora Bassa (see below), that constitute much of this stretch of the river. Between the two lakes the Zambezi trends northeast for nearly 40 miles before it turns east below the confluence with the Kafue River, the Zambezi's largest tributary. In this section, the river rushes through two rocky, narrow gorges, the first just below the Kariba Dam, and the other above the confluence with the Luangwa River.

At the dam at the eastern end of Lake Cabora Bassa, the Zambezi begins its lower course, during which it descends from the Central African Plateau to the coastal plain. At first the hilly country is replaced by flat areas at the head of the Tete Basin, and the river becomes more placid. About 40 miles downstream the river has cut the Lupata Gorge through a range of hills, where it emerges onto the Mozambique Plain and occupies a broad valley that spreads out in places to a width of three to five miles. Near Vila Fontes, the river receives its last great tributary, the Shire River, which drains Lake Nyasa (Malaŵi) some 210 miles to the north.

At its mouth the Zambezi splits into a wide, flat, and marshy delta obstructed by sandbars. There are two main channels, each again divided into two. The wider, eastern channel splits into the Muselo River to the north and the main mouth of the Zambezi to the south. The western channel forms both the Inhamissengo River and the smaller Melambe River. North of the main delta, the Chinde River separates from the Zambezi's main stream to form a navigable channel leading to a shallow harbour.

Hydrology. The Zambezi, according to measurements taken at Maramba (formerly Livingstone), Zambia, experiences its maximum flow in March or April. In October or November the discharge diminishes to less than 10 percent of the maximum. The annual average flow reaches about 247,000 cubic feet (7,000 cubic metres) per second. Measurements taken at Kariba Dam reflect the same seasonal pattern; the highest flood recorded there was in March 1958, when the flow reached 565,000 cubic feet per second.

Climate. The Zambezi River lies within the tropics. The upper and middle course of the river is on an upland plateau, and temperatures, modified by altitude, are relatively mild, generally between 64° and 86° F (18° and 30° C). The winter months (May to July) are cool and dry, with temperatures averaging 68° F (20° C). Between August and October there is a considerable rise in average temperatures, particularly in the river valley itself; just be-

Temperatures

The Victoria Falls Bridge across the Zambezi River, connecting Zambia and Zimbabwe.
© Brian A. Vikander/West Light

fore the rains begin in October temperatures there become excessively hot, often reaching 104° F (40° C). The rainy season lasts from November to April. Rain falls in short, intense thundershowers—the rate sometimes reaching 6 inches (150 millimetres) per hour—with skies clearing between downpours. In these months the upper Zambezi receives nearly all of its total rainfall, and this accounts for the great variation in the flow of the river throughout the year. In all, the upper and middle Zambezi valley receives 22 to 30 inches of rain per year. Studies have suggested that a microclimate in the area of Lake Kariba has created a rise in precipitation, possibly as a result of a lake breeze blocked by the escarpment that produces thunderstorms.

In the lower course of the river in Mozambique the influence of the summer monsoon increases the levels of precipitation and humidity. Temperatures are also higher—determined more by the latitude and less by altitude—as the river descends from the plateau.

Plant life. The vegetation along the upper and middle course of the Zambezi is predominantly savanna, with deciduous trees, grass, and open woodland. Mopane woodland (*Colophospermum mopane*) is predominant on the alluvial flats of the low-lying river valleys and is highly susceptible to fire. Grass, when present, is typically short and sparse. *Baikiaea* forest, found extensively on sandy interfluves between drainage channels, is economically the most important vegetation type in Zambia, for it is the source of the valuable Rhodesian teak (*Baikiaea plurijuga*). Destruction of the *Baikiaea* forest results in a regression from forest to grassland, a slow process involving intermediate stages of scrub vegetation. The river additionally has a distinct fringing vegetation, mainly riverine forest including ebony (*Diospyros mespiliformis*) and small shrubs and ferns (*e.g., Haemanthus*). In the lower course of the Zambezi dense bush and evergreen forest, with palm trees and patches of mangrove swamp, is the typical vegetation.

Animal life. The tiger fish is one of the few species found both above and below the Victoria Falls. Pike is predominant in the upper course of the river, as are yellowfish and barbel. Bream are now common both above and below the falls. Crocodiles abound in the Zambezi, though they generally avoid stretches of fast-running water. Hippopotamuses are also found in the upper and lower stretches of the Zambezi. Elephants are common over much of the river's course, particularly in areas such as the Sesheke Plain and near the Luangwa confluence. Game animals include buffalo, eland, sable, roan, kudu, waterbuck, impala, duiker, bushbuck, reedbuck, bushpig, and warthog. Of the big cats, lions can be found in the Victoria Falls National Park in Zimbabwe and elsewhere along the river's course; cheetahs, although comparatively rare, can be sighted; and leopards, rarely seen by daylight, are common, both in the plains and the river gorges. Baboons and monkeys abound throughout.

The people. The Lozi (Barotse), who dominate much of the upper Zambezi, have taken advantage of the seasonal flooding of the Barotse Plain for centuries and have an agricultural economy that is supplemented by animal husbandry, fishing, and trade. The main groups of the middle Zambezi include the Tonga, Shona, Chewa, and Nsenga peoples, all of whom largely practice subsistence agriculture. In Mozambique the riverine population is varied; many engage in commercial agriculture—the growing of sugarcane and cotton in particular—which was established by the Portuguese.

The Lozi

The economy. *Navigation.* Given its numerous natural barriers—sandbars at the mouth, shallowness, and rapids and cataracts—the Zambezi is of little economic significance as a trade route. About 1,620 miles of the river, however, are navigable by shallow-draft steamers. The longest stretch of unbroken water runs from the river delta about 400 miles upstream to the Cabora Bassa Dam. Above the dam Lake Cabora Bassa is navigable to its confluence with the Luangwa River, where navigation is interrupted again to the Kariba Dam. Lake Kariba is navigable, but the river again becomes impassable from the end of the lake to the Ngonye Falls, some 250 miles upstream. It is again navigable by shallow-draft boats for the 300 miles between the Ngonye and Chavuma falls and then for another 120 miles above Chavuma.

The river has four major crossing points. The Victoria Falls Bridge, the first from the head of the river, carries rail, road, and foot traffic between Zambia and Zimbabwe. The dam wall at Kariba is heavily used by road traffic, and a road bridge at Chirundu, Zimb., also connects the two countries. The fourth major crossing is the rail and road bridge between Mutarara (Dona Ana) and Vila de Sena, Mozambique. There are also a number of motor ferries crossing the river at various points.

Kariba and Cabora Bassa schemes. The Kariba Dam harnesses the Zambezi at Kariba, Zimb., 300 miles below Victoria Falls. A concrete-arch dam with a maximum height of 420 feet and a crest length of 1,900 feet carries a road connecting the Zambian and Zimbabwean banks of the gorge. Six floodgates permit a discharge of some 335,000 cubic feet of water per second. Both Zambia and Zimbabwe obtain most of their electricity from the Kariba Dam. Lake Kariba covers an area of about 2,000 square miles. The flooded land was previously inhabited by about 51,000 Tonga agriculturalists, who had to be resettled. The lake stretches for 175 miles from the dam to Devil's Gorge and is 20 miles across at its widest point. Three townships have been built around lakeshore harbours at Kariba and at Siavonga and Sinazongwe, Zambia. Tourist resorts have also been developed along the lakeshore.

Lake Cabora Bassa was formed by a dam across the Zambezi at the head of Cabora Bassa Gorge, about 80 miles northwest of Tete, Mozambique. The dam, 560 feet high and 1,050 feet wide at its crest, impounds the river for 150 miles to the Mozambique–Zambia border, providing hydroelectric power and water for crop irrigation.

Study and exploration. The first non-Africans to reach the Zambezi were Arab traders, who utilized the river's lower reaches from the 10th century onward. They were followed in the 16th century by the Portuguese, who hoped to use the river to develop a trade in ivory, gold, and slaves. Until the 19th century, the river, then called the Zanbere, was believed to flow south from a vast inland sea that was also thought to be the origin of the Nile River. Accurate mapping of the Zambezi did not take place until the Scottish missionary and explorer David Livingstone charted most of the river's course in the 1850s. Searching for a trade route to the East African coast, he traveled from Sesheke, 150 miles above Victoria Falls, to the Indian Ocean. His map of the river remained the most accurate until the 20th century, when further surveys finally traced the Zambezi to its source. (A.N.L.W./N.J.Mo.)

Mapping of the river by Livingstone

BIBLIOGRAPHY

General works. Overviews of the continent may be found in R. MANSELL PROTHERO (ed.), *A Geography of Africa,* rev. ed. (1973); JOHN I. CLARKE (ed.), *An Advanced Geography of Africa* (1975); WILLIAM A. HANCE, *The Geography of Modern Africa,* 2nd ed. (1975); ALAN C.G. BEST and HARM J. DE BLIJ, *African Survey* (1977); R.J. HARRISON CHURCH *et al., Africa and the Islands,* 4th ed. (1977); A.T. GROVE, *Africa,* 3rd ed. (1978), and *The Changing Geography of Africa* (1989); J.M. PRITCHARD, *Africa,* rev. 3rd ed. (1979, reissued 1986); PHYLLIS M. MARTIN and PATRICK O'MEARA (eds.), *Africa,* 2nd ed. (1986); PAUL BOHANNAN and PHILIP CURTIN, *Africa and the Africans,* 3rd ed. (1988); and ALAN B. MOUNTJOY and DAVID HILLING, *Africa: Geography and Development* (1988). ROLAND OLIVER and MICHAEL CROWDER (eds.), *The Cambridge Encyclopedia of Africa* (1981), is also useful. REGINE VAN CHI-BONNARDEL, *The Atlas of Africa* (1973), presents general physical and thematic maps, as well as maps and text for each country. JOCELYN MURRAY (ed.), *Cultural Atlas of Africa* (1981), includes maps and text on Africa's physical geography, culture, history, language, and social life. General treatments of European exploration in Africa are contained in HEINRICH SCHIFFERS, *The Quest for Africa: Two Thousand Years of Exploration* (1957; originally published in German, 1954); and ROBERT I. ROTBERG (ed.), *Africa and Its Explorers: Motives, Methods, and Impact* (1970). Useful annuals that contain historical overviews of each African country and updated essays on the continent's political, social, and economic developments include *The Middle East and North Africa; Africa South of the Sahara;* and *Africa Contemporary Record.* (D.S.H.W.N./Ed.)

Physical and human geography. *Geologic history:* General discussions of African geology may be found in L. CAHEN and N.J. SNELLING, *The Geochronology and Evolution of Africa* (1984); and ADETOYE FANIRAN, *African Landforms* (1986). Books and essays on specific aspects include BERNARD BESSOLES, *Géologie de l'Afrique: le craton Ouest Africain* (1977); RUSSELL BLACK, "Precambrian of West Africa," *Episodes,* 4:3–8 (1980); M. DEYNOUX, J. SOUGY, and R. TROMPETTE, "Lower Palaeozoic Rocks of West Africa and the Western Part of Central Africa," in C.H. HOLLAND (ed.), *Lower Palaeozoic of North-western and West-central Africa* (1985), pp. 337–495; A. KRÖNER, "The Precambrian Geotectonic Evolution of Africa: Plate Accretion Versus Plate Destruction," *Precambrian Research,* 4(2):163–213; A. KRÖNER *et al.,* "Pan-African Crustal Evolution in the Nubian Segment of Northeast Africa," in A. KRÖNER (ed.), *Proterozoic Lithospheric Evolution* (1987), pp. 235–257; A.J. TANKARD *et al., Crustal Evolution of Southern Africa: 3.8 Billion Years of Earth History* (1982); J.R. VAIL, "Outline of the Geochronology and Tectonic Units of the Basement Complex of Northeast Africa," *Proceedings of the Royal Society of London,* Series A, 350(1660):127–141 (1976); and J.B. WRIGHT (ed.), *Geology and Mineral Resources of West Africa* (1985). (A.K.)

The land: Descriptions of Africa's physical geography can be found in the general works listed above and in M.F. THOMAS and G.W. WHITTINGTON (eds.), *Environment and Land Use in Africa* (1969). WILLIAM G. MCGINNIES, BRAM J. GOLDMAN, and PATRICIA PAYLORE (eds.), *Deserts of the World* (1968), includes detailed appraisals of research on the physiography, hydrology, soils, weather and climate, vegetation, and fauna of the Kalahari, Namib, and Sahara. A comprehensive account of the geomorphology of Africa is given in LESTER C. KING, *The Morphology of the Earth,* 2nd ed. (1967), pp. 241–309. Regional geographies include JEAN DESPOIS and RENÉ RAYNAL, *Géographie de l'Afrique du nord-ouest* (1967, reissued 1975); R.J. HARRISON CHURCH, *West Africa: A Study of the Environment and of Man's Use of It,* 8th ed. (1980); REUBEN K. UDO, *A Comprehensive Geography of West Africa* (1978), and *The Human Geography of Tropical Africa* (1982); JACQUES DENIS, PIERRE VENNETIER, and JULES WILMET, *L'Afrique centrale et orientale* (1971); JOHN H. WELLINGTON, *Southern Africa,* 2 vol. (1955); and A.J. CHRISTOPHER, *Southern Africa* (1976). (Ro.W.St.)

H.L. SHANTZ and C.F. MARBUT, *The Vegetation and Soils of Africa* (1923, reprinted 1971), was the first systematic account of major soil groups. Far more modern and useful is the basic text by ZINAIDA SHOKALSKAIA, *Почвенно географический очерк Африки* (1948), also available in a German translation, *Die Böden Afrikas* (1953). R.P. MOSS (ed.), *The Soil Resources of Tropical Africa* (1968); and PETER M. AHN, *West African Soils* (1970), present discussions of the framework within which tropical soils may be described. B.W. THOMPSON, *The Climate of Africa* (1965), and *Africa: The Climatic Background* (1975), provide general information. GLENN T. TREWARTHA, *The Earth's Problem Climates,* 2nd ed. (1981), gives a more advanced account of the major climatic anomalies in Africa. (K.B.D.)

The undoubted leading survey of African vegetation is F. WHITE, *Vegetation of Africa* (1983), written to explain an accompanying map. The best comprehensive presentation of grasses remains J.M. RATTRAY, *The Grass Cover of Africa* (1960), also with a map. P.W. RICHARDS, *The Tropical Rain Forest: An Ecological Study* (1952, reissued 1979), is a comprehensive classic, with a relevance well beyond its title. BRIAN HOPKINS, *Forest and Savanna* (1965), is a detailed treatment of interactions in western Africa, including the effects of agriculture and pastoralism. MONICA M. COLE, "The Savannas of Africa," part III in her *The Savannas: Biogeography and Geobotany* (1986), pp. 111–290, is also useful. H.L. SHANTZ and B.L. TURNER, *Photographic Documentation of Vegetational Changes in Africa Over a Third of a Century* (1958), presents telling site-by-site comparisons made by two doyens of science in Africa.

Good general treatments of African animal life are to be found in J.L. CLOUDSLEY-THOMPSON, *The Zoology of Tropical Africa* (1969); D.F. OWEN, *Animal Ecology in Tropical Africa,* 2nd ed. (1976); and M.J. DELANY and D.C.D. HAPPOLD, *Ecology of African Mammals* (1979). Two general nature histories, approaching fauna from somewhat different standpoints although complementary to one another, are LESLIE BROWN, *Africa: A Natural History* (1965); and ARCHIE CARR, *The Land and Wildlife of Africa,* rev. ed. (1980), a Time-Life book. Books that provide authoritative surveys of the different forms of animal life include JONATHAN KINGDON, *East African Mammals: An Atlas of Evolution in Africa* (1971–), splendidly artistic and alive in treatment; on hoofed mammals, WALTER LEUTHOLD, *African Ungulates: A Comparative Review of Their Ethology and Behavioral Ecology* (1977); R.E. MOREAU, *The Bird Faunas of Africa and Its Islands* (1966); C.W. MACKWORTH-PRAED and C.H.B. GRANT, *Birds of Eastern and North Eastern Africa,* 2 vol., 2nd ed. (1957–60, reprinted 1980), *Birds of the Southern Third of Africa,* 2 vol. (1962–63, reprinted 1981), and *Birds of West Central and Western Africa,* 2 vol. (1970–73, reprinted 1981); GEOFFREY FRYER and T.D. ILES, *The Cichlid Fishes of the Great Lakes of Africa: Their Biology and Evolution* (1972); MICHAEL HOLDEN and WILLIAM REED, *West African Freshwater Fish* (1972); R.A. JUBB, *Freshwater Fishes of Southern Africa* (1967); VIVIAN F.M. FITZSIMONS, *Snakes of Southern Africa* (1962); and S.H. SKAIFE, *African Insect Life,* new ed. rev. by JOHN LEDGER (1979). JOHN FORD, *The Role of Trypanosomiases in African Ecology* (1971), studies the problems caused by the tsetse fly; and JEFFREY C. STONE (ed.), *The Exploitation of Animals in Africa* (1988), contains several colloquium papers on wildlife, domesticated stock, and conservation. (D.N.McM.)

The people: GEORGE MURDOCK, *Africa: Its Peoples and Their Culture History* (1959), is a standard text on the diverse peoples of Africa. SIMON OTTENBERG and PHOEBE OTTENBERG (eds.), *Cultures and Societies of Africa* (1960); and JAMES L. GIBBS (ed.), *Peoples of Africa* (1965, reissued 1988), contain essays and readings about African peoples. JOHN MIDDLETON (ed.), *Black Africa* (1970), presents readings about the diversity of peoples and cultural change in sub-Saharan Africa. P.C. LLOYD, *Africa in Social Change* (1967), studies social interaction in West Africa between traditional African institutions and those imported from Europe. ALI A. MAZRUI, *The African Condition* (1980), contains a political diagnosis; and MORAG BELL, *Contemporary Africa: Development, Culture, and the State* (1986), examines the links between the political and economic structures and Africa's cultural variety. JOSEPH H. GREENBERG, *The Languages of Africa,* 2nd ed. (1966), is a basic study of language classification; and EDGAR A. GREGERSEN, *Language in Africa: An Introductory Survey* (1977), is also helpful. JOHN S. MBITI, *Introduction to African Religion* (1975), provides a summary; and GEOFFREY PARRINDER, *Africa's Three Religions,* 2nd ed. (1976), discusses Christianity, Islām, and traditional religion. On Islām in particular, RENÉ A. BRAVMAN, *African Islam* (1983); and J. SPENCER TRIMINGHAM, *The Influence of Islam Upon Africa,* 2nd ed. (1980), are general introductions.

ETIENNE VAN DE WALLE, PATRICK O. OHADIKE, and MPEMBELE D. SALA-DIAKANDA (eds.), *The State of African Demography* (1988), reviews the state and dynamics of African populations in the late 1980s. JOHN I. CLARKE and LESZEK A. KOSIŃSKI (eds.), *Redistribution of Population in Africa* (1982), provides overviews of population redistribution as well as national case studies and studies of the impact of settlement schemes and redistribution policies; and JOHN I. CLARKE, MUSTAFA KHOGALI, and LESZEK A. KOSIŃSKI (eds.), *Population and Development Projects in Africa* (1985), examines the general and specific impacts of development projects upon population redistribution, with particular emphasis on The Sudan. ROBERT F. GORMAN, *Coping With Africa's Refugee Burden* (1987), attempts to find solutions to the major problems of refugees in Africa since the mid-20th century. WILLIAM A. HANCE, *Population, Migration, and Urbanization in Africa* (1970), contains a major overview of population and urbanization trends. *Population Growth and Policies in Sub-Saharan Africa* (1986), is a study by the World Bank of the fastest-growing population region in the world.

A.T. GROVE and F.M.G. KLEIN, *Rural Africa* (1979), studies the rural environments in which most Africans live; and KENNETH SWINDELL and DAVID J. SIDDLE, *Rural Change and Development in Tropical Africa* (1990), looks at the nature of rural change and the problems of African rural development. JOSEF GUGLER and WILLIAM G. FLANAGAN, *Urbanization and Social Change in West Africa* (1978), analyzes the process of increasing urbanization in West Africa and the related social changes; and MARGARET PEIL and PIUS O. SADA, *African Urban Society* (1984), views changing urban society in West Africa. ANTHONY O'CONNOR, *The African City* (1983), examines the forms, functions, and patterns of growth of African cities, especially in the postindependence period; as does RICHARD E. STREN and RODNEY R. WHITE, *African Cities in Crisis: Managing Rapid Urban Growth* (1989). (J.I.C.)

The economy: The general economic situation is explored in P. ROBSON and D.A. LURY (eds.), *The Economies of Africa* (1969); MICHAEL HODD, *African Economic Handbook* (1986); MELVILLE J. HERSKOVITZ and MITCHELL HARWITZ (eds.), *Economic Transition in Africa* (1964); A.M. O'CONNOR, *The Geography of Tropical African Development,* 2nd ed. (1978); ANDREW M. KAMARCK, *The Economics of African Development,* rev. ed. (1971); RALPH A. AUSTEN, *African Economic History: Internal Development and External Dependency* (1987); WILFRID KNAPP, *North West Africa: A Political and Economic Survey* (1977); D. HOBART HOUGHTON, *The South African Economy,* 4th ed. (1976); and O. ABOYADE, *Issues in the Development of Tropical Africa* (1976). The problems of regional economic integration are treated by ADEBAYO ADEDEJI and TIMOTHY M. SHAW, *Economic Crisis in Africa* (1985); CAROL LANCASTER and JOHN WILLIAMSON (eds.), *African Debt and Financing* (1986); ARTHUR HAZLEWOOD (ed.), *African Integration and Disintegration: Case Studies in Economic and Political Union* (1967); and B.W.T. MUTHARIKA, *Toward Multinational Economic Cooperation in Africa* (1972). Useful books on mineral resources and industrialization include OYE OGUNBADEJO, *The International Politics of Africa's Strategic Minerals* (1985); and A.F. EWING, *Industry in Africa* (1968). Natural resources and environmental problems are covered by NEVILLE RUBIN and WILLIAM M. WARREN (eds.), *Dams in Africa: An Inter-disciplinary Study of Man-made Lakes in Africa* (1968); D.F. OWEN, *Man in Tropical Africa: The Environmental Predicament* (1973); DAVID DALBY, R.J. HARRISON CHURCH, and FATIMA BEZZAZ (eds.), *Drought in Africa 2,* rev. and expanded ed. (1977); and BONAYA ADHI GODANA, *Africa's Shared Water Resources: Legal and Institutional Aspects of the Nile, Niger, and Senegal River Systems* (1985). Agricultural development and the agrarian crisis are presented by WILLIAM ALLAN, *The African Husbandman* (1965, reprinted 1977); PRABHU PINGALI, YVES BIGOT, and HANS BINSWANGER, *Agricultural Mechanization and the Evolution of Farming Systems in Sub-Saharan Africa* (1987); JOHN W. MELLOR, CHRISTOPHER L. DELGADO, and MALCOLM J. BLACKIE (eds.), *Accelerating Food Production in Sub-Saharan Africa* (1987); PAUL HARRISON, *The Greening of Africa: Breaking Through in the Battle for Land and Food* (1987); STEPHEN K. COMMINS, MICHAEL F. LOFCHIE, and RHYS PAYNE (eds.), *Africa's Agrarian Crisis: The Roots of Famine* (1986); and ROBERT H. BATES and MICHAEL F. LOFCHIE (eds.), *Agricultural Development in Africa: Issues of Public Policy* (1980). (A.L.M.)

Special geographic features. *Landforms:* The best general treatment of the physical and human geography of the Atlas Mountains is JEAN DESPOIS and RENÉ RAYNAL, *Géographie de l'Afrique du nord-ouest* (1967, reissued 1975). A good overview of the region is also offered by J.M. HOUSTON, *The Western Mediterranean World: An Introduction to Its Regional Landscapes* (1964). Information on livelihood and environmental modifications in the Rif Mountains appears in a short work by MARVIN W. MIKESELL, *Northern Morocco: A Cultural Geography* (1961, reprinted 1985). The best one-volume survey of the culture of the peoples of the Atlas region is ERNEST GELLNER and CHARLES MICAUD (eds.), *Arabs and Berbers: From Tribe to Nation in North Africa* (1972). (M.W.M.)

A classic study focused on the East African mountains, including some coverage of Ethiopia, is RENÉ JEANNEL, *Hautes montagnes d'Afrique* (1950). LESLIE BROWN, *East African Mountains and Lakes* (1971); and GUY YEOMAN, *Africa's Mountains of the Moon: A Journey to the Ultimate Sources of the Nile* (1989), are also useful. WILLIAM C. MAHANEY (ed.), *Quaternary and Environmental Research on East African Mountains* (1989), results from more than 20 years of serious scientific research. STEFAN HASTENRATH, *The Glaciers of Equatorial East Africa* (1984), a specialized study of the mountains' glaciers, has a valuable bibliography. DAVID KEITH JONES, *Faces of Kenya* (1977), includes chapters on the mountains. MALCOLM J. COE, *The Ecology of the Alpine Zone of Mount Kenya* (1967), describes the main plant communities and finds them to be more closely related to the mountain's physiography than to altitude. DIAN FOSSEY, *Gorillas in the Mist* (1983), studies the gorillas that inhabit the slopes of the Virunga Mountains. (S.J.K.B.)

An early work on the Ituri Forest is HENRY M. STANLEY, *In Darkest Africa,* 2 vol. (1890, reissued 1913), the tale of his 18-month journey up the Congo (Zaire) River from its mouth, across the Ituri Forest, and across Tanzania to the coast. COLIN M. TURNBULL, *The Forest People* (1961, reissued 1984), contains a beautifully written popular account of the lives and feelings of Mbuti living in the central Ituri Forest, emphasizing the importance of the forest to their subsistence, ritual, and spiritual life. DAVID S. WILKIE, "Hunters and Farmers of the African Forest," in JULIE SLOAN DENSLOW and CHRISTINE PADOCH (eds.), *People of the Tropical Rain Forest* (1988), pp. 111–126, summarizes how agriculturalists and Bambuti have adapted to their tropical forest habitat. ROBERT C. BAILEY, "The Efe: Archers of the Rain Forest," *National Geographic,* 176(5):664–686 (November 1989), is a well-illustrated article by an anthropologist who lived in the region for three and a half years. PAUL SCHEBESTA, *My Pygmy and Negro Hosts* (1936, reprinted 1978; originally published in German, 1934), is one of the first true anthropological studies of Pygmies and their relationship with agriculturalists. ROBERT C. BAILEY and N.R. PEACOCK, "Efe Pygmies of Northeast Zaïre: Subsistence Strategies in the Ituri Forest," in I. DE GARINE and G.A. HARRISON (eds.), *Coping with Uncertainty in Food Supply* (1988), pp. 88–117, studies in detail the diet and subsistence ecology of the Efe and discusses the difficulties of living in the tropical forest and the implications for the health of forest-living peoples. LUIGI LUCA CAVALLI-SFORZA (ed.), *African Pygmies* (1986), contains technical articles on demography, health status, growth patterns, genetic composition, and other biomedical aspects. (R.C.B.)

Early descriptions of the Kalahari and Namib include CHARLES JOHN ANDERSSON, *Lake Ngami* (1856), an account of a four-year exploration; SIEGFRIED PASSARGE, *Die Kalahari* (1904), a thorough study; and HEINRICH VEDDER, *South West Africa in Early Times* (1938, reissued 1966; originally published in German, 1934), a detailed history of the region to 1890. FRANK DEBENHAM, *Kalahari Sand* (1953), reports a modern exploring expedition. NICHOLAS LUARD, *The Last Wilderness: A Journey Across the Great Kalahari Desert* (1981), describes a safari trek and includes observations about the desert's ecological balance and the peoples who live there. KAREN ROSS, *Okavango, Jewel of the Kalahari* (1987), describes this river's wildlife. RICHARD F. LOGAN, *The Central Namib Desert, South West Africa* (1960), thoroughly studies the area's physical and biological geography. B.J. HUNTLEY (ed.), *The Kuiseb Environment: The Development of a Monitoring Baseline* (1985), contains a set of excellent articles covering all phases of the environment of a transdesert river valley. Studies of the peoples of the Kalahari include ROBERT K. HITCHCOCK, *Kalahari Cattle Posts,* 2 vol. (1978), a general review of Bantu-speaking and San (Basarwa) inhabitants of the western Kalahari. RICHARD B. LEE and IRVEN DEVORE (eds.), *Kalahari Hunter-gatherers: Studies of the !Kung San and Their Neighbors* (1976), collects writings on various aspects of San life, mainly in the northwestern Kalahari. RICHARD B. LEE, *The Dobe !Kung* (1984); and LORNA MARSHALL, *The !Kung of Nyae Nyae* (1976), are also informative and engaging accounts. GEORGE B. SILBERBAUER, *Hunter and Habitat in the Central Kalahari Desert* (1981), provides a detailed description of the life and ecology of central Kalahari San when they lived as autonomous hunter-gatherers. (R.F.Lo./G.Si.)

E.-F. GAUTIER, *Sahara: The Great Desert* (1935, reissued 1987; originally published in French, 2nd ed., 1928), provides a wealth of information by an eminent geographer long acquainted with the desert. A more popular introduction to the Sahara, by a naturalist who traveled there extensively, is Jeremy Swift, *The Sahara* (1975), a Time-Life book. Detailed discussions of the geologic past and prehistory of the desert are contained in Martin A.J. Williams and Hugues Faure (eds.), *The Sahara and the Nile* (1980). The most comprehensive climatology available for the desert is Jean Dubief, *Le Climat du Sahara,* 2 vol. (1959–63). An excellent introduction to the vegetation of the desert is P. Quézel, "Analysis of the Flora of Mediterranean and Saharan Africa," *Annals of the Missouri Botanical Garden,* 65:479–534 (1978). Animal life is described in P.-L. Dekeyser and J. Derivot, *La Vie animale au Sahara* (1959). Prehistoric rock art is discussed in Henri Lhote, *The Search for the Tassili Frescoes: The Story of the Prehistoric Rock-paintings,* 2nd ed. (1973; originally published in French, 1973). There are several excellent studies of the peoples of the Sahara: Julio Caro Baroja, *Estudios saharianos* (1955), a detailed description of the little-known peoples of the western desert; Lloyd Cabot Briggs, *Tribes of the Sahara* (1960), a more general study, focusing on the central regions; and Unesco, *Nomades et nomadisme au Sahara* (1963), discussing the nomadic peoples. The most detailed 19th-century travelers' reports are by Henry (Heinrich) Barth, *Travels and Discoveries in North and Central Africa,* 5 vol. (1857–58, reissued in 3 vol., 1965; originally published in German, 1857–58); and Gustav Nachtigal, *Sahara and Sudan,* 4 vol. (1971–83; originally published in German, 3 vol., 1879–89). (J.A.G.)

The geology of the veld is discussed by Lester C. King, *South African Scenery,* 3rd ed. rev. (1963), and *The Natal Monocline: Explaining the Origin and Scenery of Natal, South Africa,* 2nd rev. ed. (1982). The veld environment is explored in J.P.H. Acocks, *Veld Types of South Africa,* 3rd ed. (1988); R.F. Fuggle and M.A. Rabie (eds.), *Environmental Concerns in South Africa* (1983); N.K. Hobson and J.P. Jessop, *Veld Plants of Southern Africa* (1975); J. Stevenson-Hamilton, *The Low-veld: Its Wild Life and Its People,* 2nd ed. (1934); and N.M. Tainton, D.I. Bransby, and P. de V. Booysen, *Common Veld and Pasture Grasses of Natal* (1976). *Veld & Flora* (quarterly) is a useful journal. (Jo.Co./C.E.F.)

Drainage systems and waterways: A general overview of Lake Chad is contained in A.T. Grove, "Lake Chad," *The Geographical Magazine,* 37(7):524–537 (November 1964). Jean Maley, "Histoire de la végétation et du climat de l'Afrique nord-tropicale au Quaternaire récent," *Bothalia,* 14(3–4):377–389 (September 1983), presents a long-term view of climate change in the Chad basin. The annual vegetation of the region is discussed in H. Gillet, "Essai d'évaluation de la biomasse végétale en zone Sahélienne (végétation annuelle)," *Journal d'agriculture tropicale et botanique appliquée,* 14(4-5):123–158 (April–May 1967). J.-P. Carmouze, J.-R. Durand, and C. Lévêque (eds.), *Lake Chad: Ecology and Productivity of a Shallow Tropical Ecosystem* (1983), is a lengthy study of the lake's environment and productivity. The fish of Lake Chad and its tributaries are described in J. Blache and F. Miton, *Les Poissons du bassin du Tchad et du bassin adjacent du Mayo Kebbi* (1964). A particularly useful study of the peoples of the Chad basin is Albert Le Rouvreur, *Sahéliens et Sahariens du Tchad* (1962, reissued 1989). The more recently arrived Arab groups are discussed in J.C. Zeltner, *Les Arabes dans la région du Lac Tchad: problèmes d'origine et de chronologie* (1977). (J.A.G.)

Leslie Brown, *East African Mountains and Lakes* (1971), is a useful introduction to the region's scenery and wildlife. L.C. Beadle, *The Inland Waters of Tropical Africa,* 2nd ed. (1981), has a strong East African section and contains an extensive bibliography. David Keith Jones, *Faces of Kenya* (1977), includes chapters on the lakes. Paul H. Temple, "The Lakes of Uganda," in S.H. Ominde (ed.), *Studies in East African Geography and Development* (1971), pp. 86–98, classifies the lakes in physical terms. M.J. Mann, "Freshwater Fisheries," in W.T.W. Morgan (ed.), *East Africa: Its Peoples and Resources,* 2nd ed. (1972), pp. 229–242, gives a brief account of the fisheries of the individual lakes of Kenya, Uganda, and Tanzania. Victor C.R. Ford, *The Trade of Lake Victoria: A Geographical Study* (1955), describes against a historical background the international trade achieved within this area in the preindependence period. (S.J.K.B.)

Gilles Sautter, *De l'Atlantique au fleuve Congo,* 2 vol. (1966), discusses the Congo basin in general as well as with the river itself, covering hydrology, climate, vegetation, and fishing. G.A. Boulenger, *Les Poissons du bassin du Congo* (1901), is a classic work on ecology. Jan Vansina, *Introduction à l'ethnographie du Congo* (1966), synthesizes available knowledge on the subject, with a section on the relationship between fishing and social organization. André Huybrechts, *Les Transports fluviaux au Congo* (1965), analyzes the evolution and organization of traffic on the middle course of the Congo and its affluents in the period 1925–63. Huybrechts' *Transports et structures de développement au Congo* (1970), studies the role of transportation in the economic transformation of the Congo–Zaire region from 1900 to 1970. Jean-Claude Willame, *Zaïre, l'épopée d'Inga* (1986), critically analyzes the economic and political implications of the Inga Dam. Roland Pourtier, "Transport et développement au Zaïre," *Afrique contemporaine,* 29(153):3–26 (1990), discusses current transportation in Zaire. Henry M. Stanley, *Through the Dark Continent,* 2 vol. (1878, reissued 1988), and *The Congo and the Founding of Its Free State,* 2 vol. (1885, reissued 1970), are classic works on African exploration, describing the author's famous descent of the Congo to Malebo (Stanley) Pool and the two upper Congo expeditions. An introduction to the river's history can be found in Peter Forbath, *The River Congo* (1977). (Ro.Po.)

Accounts of the Niger River environment include Y. Brunet-Monet *et al., Monographie hydrologique du fleuve Niger,* 2 vol. (1986); Jean Gallais, *La Delta intérieur du Niger: étude de géographie régionale,* 2 vol. (1967); and two essays in Bryan R. Davies and Keith F. Walker (eds.), *The Ecology of River Systems* (1986), both by R.L. Welcomme: "The Niger River System," pp. 9–23, and "Fish of the Niger System," pp. 25–48. Christopher Lloyd, *The Search for the Niger* (1973); and Sanche de Gramont (pseud. for Ted Morgan), *The Strong Brown God: The Story of the Niger River* (1975), cover the history of the river's exploration. (A.L.M.)

General works on the Nile River include H.E. Hurst, *The Nile,* rev. ed. (1957); and H.E. Hurst *et al., The Nile Basin* (1931–). Studies of the river's geology and biology can be found in Julian Rzóska (ed.), *The Nile: Biology of an Ancient River* (1976); Rushdi Said, *The Geological Evolution of the River Nile* (1981); and Martin A.J. Williams and Hugues Faure (eds.), *The Sahara and the Nile* (1980), on landforms and human settlement in the region. Hydrology is discussed in A. Azim Abul-Atta, *Egypt and the Nile After the Construction of the High Aswan Dam* (1978); Yusuf A. Shibl, *The Aswan High Dam* (1971); and John Waterbury, *Hydropolitics of the Nile Valley* (1979). Early accounts of the attempts to find the source of the Nile are described by John Hanning Speke, *Journal of the Discovery of the Source of the Nile* (1863, reissued 1971); and Richard F. Burton, *The Nile Basin* (1864, reprinted 1967). Alan Moorehead, *The White Nile,* rev. ed. (1971, reprinted 1983), and *The Blue Nile,* rev. ed. (1972, reprinted 1983), together offer a study of exploration in the 19th century. Other works on the river's history include Karl W. Butzer, *Early Hydraulic Civilization in Egypt: A Study in Cultural Ecology* (1976); and Tom Little, *High Dam at Aswan: The Subjugation of the Nile* (1965). (C.G.S.)

Works on the Orange River include Department of Water Affairs, *Management of the Water Resources of the Republic of South Africa* (1986); and Monica M. Cole, *South Africa,* 2nd ed. (1966). (P.S.Ha./Jo.Co.)

Pierre Michel, *Les Bassins des fleuves Sénégal et Gambie: étude géomorphologique,* 3 vol. (1973), is a fundamental work, providing a detailed description of topography, geology, hydrology, and soils. Louis Papy, "La Valée du Sénégal: agriculture traditionnelle et riziculture mécanisée," *Les Cahiers d'outre-mer,* 4(16):277–324 (October/December 1951), covers hydrology, human exploitation, landscape, cultural traditions, and navigation, with excellent illustrations. *Études sénégalaises,* no. 9, *Connaissance du Sénégal,* fascicle 2, *Hydrographie,* by Félix Brigaud (1961), also studies the river's hydrology. Colette Le Blanc, "Un Village de la vallée du Sénégal: Amadi-Ounaré," *Les Cahiers d'outre-mer,* 17(66):117–148 (April/June 1964), describes in detail the environment and daily life of a village on the Sénégal River. (Ca.C.)

Studies of the Suez Canal include R.E.B. Duff, *100 Years of the Suez Canal* (1969); D.A. Farnie, *East and West of Suez: The Suez Canal in History, 1854–1956* (1969), which traces events from the concession to the nationalization of the canal company; Lord Kinross (Patrick Balfour, Baron Kinross), *Between Two Seas: The Creation of the Suez Canal* (1968); John Marlowe, *World Ditch: The Making of the Suez Canal* (also published as *The Making of the Suez Canal,* 1964), a well-documented account from the canal's inception to the British occupation of Egypt in 1882; Hugh J. Schonfield, *The Suez Canal in Peace and War, 1869–1969,* rev. ed. (1969), a brief, general survey; André Siegfried, *Suez and Panama* (1940; originally published in French, 1940); and Arnold T. Wilson, *The Suez Canal: Its Past, Present, and Future* (1933, reprinted 1977), a classic evaluation of the British interest in the canal. (C.G.S.)

Little is written in English specifically on the Zambezi River. Information can be found in B.M. Fagin (ed.), *The Victoria Falls Handbook,* 2nd ed. (1963); R. Mansell Prothero (ed.), *People and Land in Africa South of the Sahara: Readings in Social Geography* (1972); and N.J. Money, *The Geology of Western Zambia* (1972). (N.J.Mo.)

African Arts

African arts usually refers to the works of black, or sub-Saharan, Africa, that part of the continent originally inhabited by Negro peoples who developed cultures quite distinct from those of Caucasian North Africa. Within this huge geographic area are regions of radically different topography, climate, and natural resources. The economies of these regions, therefore, also differ radically from one another, as do the customs, religions, languages, and artistic expressions of their peoples. There is startling diversity within each of the regions as well. It is common to divide sub-Saharan Africa into the following geographic regions: the open grasslands of the Sudan stretching across the continent just south of the Sahara, the woodlands and forests of West Africa, the basin of the Congo River in Central Africa, the East African savannas, and the savannas and deserts of southern Africa. None of these regions has a uniform culture. The western Sudan, for example, is rich in sculptural styles and production, while sculpture has been little developed in the eastern part, where artistic expression is richest in music and oral literature.

The European powers further divided the cultures of black Africa by creating colonies with boundaries that had little regard for traditional ethnic or linguistic groupings. The contemporary literatures of English-, French-, and Portuguese-speaking Africa, therefore, have a uniformity of theme and language that corresponds not to geographic regions or to ethnic affinities but instead to the rather arbitrary manner in which the colonial powers divided the continent. Colonization also introduced European religion, technology, and politics, which, together with the European languages, created a historical division in the development of black African arts that may be deeper than its regional divisions. Since the 19th century some cultural traditions of precolonial origin have disappeared, and, while others survive and indeed flourish, there has been every possible compromise with the cultural forms of the West.

Despite its variety, African arts can be discussed as a whole for several reasons. One reason is that, while the artworks of different peoples may differ in form, the traditional roles of art and of the artist in the cultural life of the people are quite similar throughout the continent—and quite different from their roles in non-African cultures. Another reason is that the borders of modern African nations do not necessarily correspond to cultural borders, so that it is often necessary to discuss the arts not of one country but of an entire region. In addition, all black African arts, no matter how diverse, went through a common process of adapting to foreign cultures. It is a mistake to think of the subcontinent as having been isolated from the rest of the world until only recently. Trade across the Sahara is probably as ancient as the current stage of desiccation, which began in the 3rd millennium BC. Through this trade, Islām was introduced into and spread throughout much of West Africa, while the trade networks of the Indian Ocean had a comparable effect in East Africa. Coastal trade with Europe, resulting almost immediately in the transatlantic slave trade, began in the late 15th century. This long history of contact means that all discussion of African arts must address a common subject of outside influence.

This article discusses the literature, music, dance, and visual art of black Africa, both in their traditional forms and in their adaptation to modern Western ways of life. Non-African forms of recent adoption are not discussed. For example, this article discusses the thousand-year-old influences of Islām in the literature and architecture of East and West Africa and of Christianity in the painting of Ethiopia, but it does not discuss Christian musical or modernist sculptural forms adopted since the colonial era. For a discussion of North African arts, see the article ISLĀMIC ARTS. For a discussion of white South African writers, see the *Micropædia,* SOUTH AFRICAN LITERATURE. For information on the geographic, economic, and historical background of African arts, see the article SOUTH AFRICA and the articles on the major regions of the continent (*e.g.,* CENTRAL AFRICA, SOUTHERN AFRICA).

For coverage of related topics in the *Macropædia* and *Micropædia,* see the *Propædia,* sections 613, 621, and 624–629, and the *Index.* (J.Pi./Ed.)

The article is divided into the following sections:

General characteristics 122
- Style, tribe, and ethnic identity 122
- African arts in the 20th century 123

Literature and theatre 123
- Oral traditions 123
  - Myths
  - Poetry
  - Folktales
  - Proverbs and riddles
  - Survival of oral tradition
- Modern literatures in European languages 125
  - French
  - Portuguese
  - English
- Literatures in African languages 127
  - West Africa
  - East Africa
  - Southern Africa
- African theatre 129
  - West Africa
  - East Africa
  - Southern Africa

Music 131
- History 131
- Musical instruments 132
  - Idiophones
  - Membranophones
  - Chordophones
  - Aerophones
- Musical structure 135
  - Timing
  - Tone systems and multipart patterns
  - Multipart singing

Dance 139
- The cultural position of dance 139
  - The religious context
  - Masquerade dancers
  - The social context
  - Division between the sexes
  - Work dances
  - Dance as recreation
- Dance style 142
  - Dance formations
  - Dance posture
  - Rhythm
  - Change and tradition

Architecture 144
- Geographic influences 144
  - Nomads and pastoralists
  - Savanna kraals and compounds
  - Forest dwellings
- Palaces and shrines 146
- Influences of Islām and Christianity 148
- Change in the 20th century 149

Sculpture and associated arts 149
- West Africa 149
  - Western Sudan
  - Guinea Coast
  - Nigeria
- Central Africa 155
  - Cameroon grasslands
  - Gabon

Zaire and Congo
East Africa 158
Southern Republic of The Sudan
Horn of Africa
Regions of Lakes Victoria and Tanganyika
Coastal East Africa
Southern Africa 159
Makonde
Mbunda and others
Southern Bantu
Other visual arts 160
Pottery 160
Textiles 160
Weaving the yarn
Embellishing the woven cloth
Other fabrics
Personal decoration 161
Painting 162
The Sahara
Southern Africa
Bibliography 164

General characteristics

It is difficult to give a useful summary of the main characteristics of the arts of sub-Saharan Africa. The variety of forms and practices is so great that the attempt to do so results in a series of statements that turn out to be just as true, for example, of Western art. Thus, some African arts are found to have value as entertainment; some have political or ideological significance; some are instrumental in a ritual context; and some have aesthetic value in themselves. More often than not, a work of African art combines several or all of these elements. Similarly, there are full-time and part-time artists; there are artists who figure in the political establishment and those who are ostracized and despised; and some art forms can be made by anyone, while others demand the devotion of an expert. Claims of an underlying pan-African aesthetic must be viewed as highly contentious.

Fine art or craft

Some further general points can be made, however, in regard to the status of precolonial sub-Saharan art. The first is that, in any African language, a concept of art as meaning something other than skill would be the exception rather than the rule. This is not because of any inherent limitation of African culture but because of the historical conditions under which European cultures arrived at their concept of art. The Western separation of fine art from the lowlier craft (*i.e.,* useful skill) came out of a sequence of social, economic, and intellectual changes in Europe that did not occur in Africa prior to the colonial period at the very earliest. This separation, therefore, cannot be applied without qualification to African traditions of precolonial origin. Philosophers of art in the West might agree that works of art are simply artifacts made with the intention of possessing aesthetic value, and in that sense art, which would include craft work as well as works of fine art, would indeed be found in all parts of Africa (as indeed it is throughout human culture), but even in this case African art must be understood through the investigation and understanding of local aesthetic values rather than through the imposition of categories of external origin. It may be a field of well-hoed yam heaps (as, for example, among the Tiv people of Nigeria) or a display ox castrated in order to enhance its visual effect (as among the Nuer and Dinka pastoralists of the southern Sudan), rather than a sculpted figure, that constitutes the significant work of art in a given area of Africa.

The popular notion of African art in the West, however, is very different, for it is thought to comprise sculpture and very little else—except, perhaps, "local colour." This misconception has been caused by the previously mentioned European concept of fine art, but it was also caused by a dependence, during the first period of Western interest in African arts, upon collectible artifacts—some of which (pieces of sculpture, for instance) fitted neatly into the category of fine art, while others (such as textiles and pottery) were dismissed as craft work. Painting in Africa was long presumed not to exist to any significant extent, largely because it was to be found on the skins of human bodies, on the walls of houses, and on rock faces—none of which were collectible items. Clearly, the aesthetic field in Africa is not so limited.

Another misapprehension is that in the West art is created for art's sake, whereas in precolonial Africa art was solely functional. But the motive for the creation of any work of art is inevitably complex, in Africa as elsewhere, and the fact that most of the sculpted artifacts known from Africa were made with some practical use in mind (whether for ritual or other purposes) does not mean that they could not simultaneously be valued as sources of aesthetic pleasure.

It is also often assumed that the African artist is constrained by tradition in a way contrasting with the freedom given to the Western artist. But, although there are traditions of art in which the expectations of patrons demand repetition of a set form in African art, there are also traditions of precolonial origin that demand a high level of inventive originality—for example, Ashanti silk weaving and Kuba raffia embroidery. There are other traditions in which a standard form can be embellished as elaborately as the artist or patron wishes. The important point is that particular traditions encourage creativity.

STYLE, TRIBE, AND ETHNIC IDENTITY

A commonplace of African art criticism has been to identify particular styles, whether in the performing or visual arts, according to supposedly tribal names—for example, Ashanti, Kuba, or Nuba. The concept of tribe is problematic, however, and has generally been discarded. "Tribal" names, in fact, sometimes refer to the language spoken, sometimes to political entities, and sometimes to other kinds of groupings; yet the boundaries between peoples speaking different languages or acknowledging different chiefs do not necessarily coincide with their respective tribal boundaries. Moreover, the very idea of tribe is an attempt to impose identity from the outside. That this happened is understandable, given the demands of colonial administration, but this historical contingency cannot help in understanding the dynamic of stylistic variation in Africa. The sense of identity that individuals and groups

Figure 1: Benin ivory regalia mask, Nigeria. In the Metropolitan Museum of Art, New York City. Height 23.8 cm.

undoubtedly have with others, which was misunderstood as "tribe" but which is better referred to as "ethnic identity," is something that derives from the relationship built up through many different networks: whom one can marry, one's language and religious affiliations, the chief whose authority one acknowledges, who one's ancestors are, the kind of work one does, and so forth. Sometimes African art plays a part in this, as when a religious cult or a chief or a guild employs distinctive artifacts as a mark of uniqueness. Sometimes boundaries are based on linguistic differences, but this may be coincidental.

Identifying regional styles

As to differences of style, regularities of form and tradition do occur such that it is possible to attribute particular African art objects to particular places, regions, or periods. There seem to be four distinct variables making this kind of stylistic identification possible. The first is geography, in that, all other things being equal, people in different places tend to make or do things in different ways. The second is technology, in that in some areas differences of style depend on the material employed. The third is individuality, in that an expert can identify the works of individual artists, inability to do so usually deriving from lack of familiarity. The fourth is institution, in that the creation of works of art takes place under the influence of the social and cultural institutions characteristic of any given location. But artifacts can be traded and then copied; artists themselves can travel; institutions, complete with associated artifacts, can move or spread from one area to another, sometimes because they are copied by a neighbouring people, sometimes because they are purchased, sometimes as a result of conquest. The end result is a stylistic complexity in African art that defies easy classification. The names previously understood as referring to tribes can continue to be used, however, as convenient shorthand as long as it is realized that they all do not represent equivalent categories. One tribal name may refer to a group numbering no more than a few thousand; another may refer to the language spoken in a given area; yet another may describe an empire comprising peoples of distinct historical identities.

AFRICAN ARTS IN THE 20TH CENTURY

African cultures have never been closed to the rest of the world, but the radical developments forced on the continent as a result of colonialism have made the 20th century a period of unusually rapid change. The majority of known "traditional" works are, in fact, products of the colonial period; thus, it is impossible to maintain a rigid distinction between traditional and modern art forms. It is better to think of the 20th century as a period in which the range of options available to the artist has increased as new cultural and social institutions have developed. This process is better understood for literature than it is for the visual arts.

Nevertheless, the continuing development of artistic traditions of precolonial origin is far more widespread in Africa than is commonly realized. In addition, there are roughly three kinds of development in which African artists have drawn on and adapted European forms. The first is when European forms are copied by illiterate or semiliterate artists, or at any rate mediated via the marketplace, as in popular sign painting or the kind of pamphlet writing typified by the Onitsha market literature of Nigeria. The second is when the medium of transmitting Western artistic practice is the university or some other institution of higher education, as is the case with contemporary African sculpture and painting or with African writers using European languages. The third is when traditional forms are revamped, or pseudotraditional forms invented, for the benefit of foreign tourists and other visitors (for example, some of the finest ivory sculptures of West Africa were produced in what is now Sierra Leone by Sherbro artists and in the kingdom of Benin for Portuguese traders in the early 16th century). Although the forms and materials employed in these developments are of external derivation, the subject matter and style are manifestly African. It is the artists working under these influences who are forming the arts distinctive of the particular nation-states of modern-day Africa. (J.Pi.)

Literature and theatre

The term African literatures covers traditional oral and written literatures together with the mainly 20th-century literature written mostly in European languages but also to an increasing extent in the many languages of the sub-Saharan region. Traditional written literature is limited to a smaller geographic area than is oral literature; indeed it is most characteristic of those sub-Saharan cultures that have participated in the cultures of the Mediterranean. In particular, there is literature in both Hausa and Arabic from the scholars of what is now northern Nigeria; the literature of the likewise Muslim Somali people; and literature in Ge'ez (or Ethiopic) and Amharic of Ethiopia, the one part of Africa where Christianity has been practiced long enough to be considered traditional.

The relationship between oral and written traditions and in particular between oral and modern written literatures is one of great complexity and not a matter of simple evolution. Modern African literatures were born in the educational systems imposed by colonialism, with models drawn from Europe rather than existing African traditions. The modern African writer thus uses tradition as subject matter rather than as a means of effecting a continuity with past cultural practice.

ORAL TRADITIONS

The poetic and narrative forms of oral tradition among those peoples living south of the Sahara are immensely rich and varied. They include myths (in the sense of symbolic accounts of the origins of things, whether the world, particular cultures, lineages, political structures, or gods), praise songs, epic poetry, folktales, riddles, proverbs, and magical spells. The content of this material also varies considerably and includes children's rhymes and oral history, as well as symbolic texts of profound intellectual significance.

Relation of poetry to music

An important feature of African oral traditions is their close link with music. Poetry exists almost exclusively in chanted form or as song, and, among West African peoples with tonal languages (for example, the Akan and the Yoruba), much poetry is recited in musical form rather than spoken or sung.

Myths. African creation stories are as varied and imaginative as elsewhere in the world. The Kono of Guinea believe that the original force in the world was Death, who existed before God; the Lozi of Zambia see God as retreating helplessly from the cruelty of man; for the Ijo peoples of the Niger Delta, God (there regarded as female) allows a person to choose his own fate before birth. The Pangwa of Tanzania have a fantastic vision of the world as having been created from the excrement of ants. The Yoruba of Nigeria tell of a creator who got drunk on palm wine and so created cripples and albinos. The most detailed cosmology known, requiring seven days for its recitation, is that of the Dogon of Mali. An unusually attractive creation myth is that of the Fulani of Mali, a pastoral, cattle-herding people whose mythology centres on milk.

At the beginning there was a huge drop of milk.
Then Doondari came and created the stone.
Then the stone created iron;
And iron created fire;
And fire created water;
And water created air.
Then Doondari descended the second time. And he took the five elements
And he shaped them into man.
But man was proud.
Then Doondari created blindness and blindness defeated man.
But when blindness became too proud,
Doondari created sleep, and sleep defeated blindness;
But when sleep became too proud,
Doondari created worry, and worry defeated sleep;
But when worry became too proud,
Doondari created death, and death defeated worry.
But when death became too proud,
Doondari descended for the third time.
And he came as Gueno, the eternal one,
And Gueno defeated death.

(Eng. trans. by Ulli Beier in *The Origin of Life and Death,* 1966)

According to nearly all African mythologies, God first agreed to give man eternal life, but his message was perverted through the stupidity or malice of the messenger. Several hundred African variants of the myth of the perverted message are known.

The most elaborate pantheons of gods are probably those found among the Yoruba of Nigeria and the Fon of Benin. These deities (*orisha* or *vodun*) are often seen simultaneously as legendary kings and founders of cities, and as supernatural spirits and controllers of the elements. Here the story of a god must often be gleaned from cryptic references embedded in his praise names (*oriki*, or *mlen-mlen*). These are curious mixtures of praise, description, joking abuse, and prayer; and, although the phrases have been handed down for centuries, the singer is free to add new ones. Thus, Shango (the Yoruba god of thunder and lightning) is compared to the power and rumbling noise of the railway.

The most widely used poetic form

Poetry. The praise name is probably the most widely used poetic form in Africa. It is applied not only to gods but to men, animals, plants, and towns. Most important in many African communities are the praise names of chiefs and war leaders, as, for example, those of the great Zulu chieftain Shaka:

He is Shaka the unshakeable,
Thunderer-while-sitting, son of Menzi.
He is the bird that preys on other birds,
The battle-axe that excels over other battle-axes.
(Eng. trans. by Ezekiel Mphahlele)

There are numerous other poetic forms. The Yoruba, for example, distinguish between praise names (*oriki*), the poetry of lineages and towns (*orile*), oracle verse (*ese*), hunters' songs (*ijala*), the poetry of masqueraders (*iwi*), incantations (*ofo*), songs (*orin*), and improvisations (*rara*). Incantations play an important part in all African traditions. The Igbo diviner, for example, invokes truth before consulting his oracular bones or other apparatus.

A common poetic form is the magic formula, in which the meaning of the words is often obscure. These formulas are sacred combinations of words the correct repetition of which, accompanied by the proper ritual, is believed to be effective both in curing and cursing.

Probably the most elaborate body of poetry is that of the Ifa oracle among the Yoruba. Even the most learned priest is not expected to know it all, and the recital of the most important parts takes a whole night. The poems are accompanied by stories that constitute the mythological or historical precedents by which the diviner judges his client's case.

Every situation in African life is accompanied by poetry and song. The herdsman praises his bull ("My bull is dark like the rain cloud in a storm" [Dinka]); the young warrior sings of his bride ("Neither her heel nor her palm are rough, but sweet to the touch like liver" [Fulani]); children invent a song to comment on an important event ("Europeans are little children, at the riverbank they shot an elephant, its blood became a canoe and it sank" [Nyasa, Malaŵi]); the widower mourns the death of his wife ("What are your wares that they sold out so quickly?" [Akan, Guinea Coast]).

Animal-trickster tales

Folktales. The best-known type of African folktale is the animal-trickster tale. In Bantu Africa (East, Central, and southern Africa) and the western Sudan, the trickster is the hare; in West Africa, the spider (Ghana, Liberia, Sierra Leone) or the tortoise (Benin, Nigeria). The Yoruba consciously poke fun at their own faults when they tell stories of the tortoise-trickster. Sometimes the tortoise's cunning defeats itself, as, for example, in the tale in which the tortoise steals from the gods a calabash that contains all the wisdom in the world. He hangs it around his neck and is so eager to get home with it that, when he comes to a tree trunk lying across the road, he is unable to cross it because the calabash gets in his way; in his anxiety he fails to think of putting it on his back. Frustrated, the tortoise smashes the calabash, and so, ever since that day, wisdom has been scattered all over the world in tiny pieces. Anansi (the spider-trickster, of whom stories are told among the Akan and, as Anancy, in Jamaica) often appears as a mythological figure, the fiendish opponent of the sky god, who steals the sky god's stories or tricks him into allowing disease to enter the world. In this function he shows some similarity with the Yoruba trickster god, Eshu, who consistently opposes the other gods and thwarts their intentions. There are a number of African peoples who also have story cycles about human tricksters—for example, the stories of Yo in Benin, the Lay cycle of the Iraqw in Tanzania, and the Zulu Uhlakanyana stories.

A variant of the trickster tale is the escape story, in which the hero extricates himself from an impossible task by imposing an impossible condition. One such story tells how a cruel king of Benin ordered his subjects on pain of death to build a new palace but to start at the top and build downward. All were in despair until one wise old man went to the King and said that they were now ready to begin and asked him, according to tradition, to lay the foundation stone.

Dilemma tales

Stories of another kind, told for entertainment, usually on moonlit nights, are dilemma tales, in which the audience is invited to supply the ending or solution. An example of a dilemma tale told among the Wolof (Senegal, The Gambia) is as follows. Three brothers journey to a strange land and are all married to the same girl, with whom they sleep in turn. One night she is murdered by a robber, and the eldest brother, with whom she is sleeping, is condemned to death on suspicion. He begs leave to visit his father before he dies. When he is late in returning, the second brother offers to die in place of him. As he is about to be executed, the third brother steps forward and "confesses" that he is the murderer. But, at that moment, the eldest brother rides in, just in time to embrace his fate. Which of the brothers (the listeners are asked) is the most noble?

In another group of tales, prominent features of animals are explained (*e.g.*, " . . . so that is why the tortoise has a broken back").

Proverbs and riddles. "Proverbs are the palm oil with which words are eaten," an Igbo proverb says. The art of conversation and argument depends, in fact, on their use. By them the speaker shows his learning. Use of proverbs also enables the speaker to attack an opponent obliquely, without mentioning his name or the subject of the dispute. Proverbs express not only a people's inherited wisdom and code of behaviour ("If a child washes his hands, he will eat with kings" [Igbo]) but also imagination and sense of humour ("If the earthworm does not dance in front of the cock, he will still be eaten, but at least the cock cannot say that he was provoked" [Yoruba]). The largest collection of African proverbs, made by a Swiss Lutheran missionary, J.G. Christaller, and published at Basel in 1879, contains 3,600 in the Twi language of Ghana.

Riddles used as metaphors

Riddles usually take the form of a statement, not a question. In the riddle "People run away from her when she is pregnant, but they rejoice when she has delivered" (the answer is a gun), the question "What is it?" is understood. Often the riddle is an exercise in metaphorical speech, intended to display the questioner's imagination rather than to test the cleverness of the audience (*e.g.*, the Yoruba "We tie a horse in the house, but its mane flies above the roof," to which is answered "fire" and "smoke").

Survival of oral tradition. Many oral traditions, particularly those associated with traditional ritual, are disappearing, and poetic forms are gaining new content and application (*e.g.*, praise names, applied to politicians; songs of abuse during elections, often taking the form of incantations). Nationalism and higher education tend to make Africans more conscious of their cultural heritage, and the collection and conservation of oral traditions is no longer left to foreign anthropologists. Some of the best collections are by African writers and scholars, and many universities in Africa are engaged in recording and interpolating this material.

African folklore has come most powerfully alive in modern writing in the works of Amos Tutuola. *The Palm-Wine Drinkard* (1952) and *My Life in the Bush of Ghosts* (1954) are inspired re-creations of the world of Yoruba folklore. Tutuola, whose long rambling tales are improvisations on traditional themes, is a born storyteller. Better than any exact translation, his books convey the rich inventiveness of traditional Yoruba folktales, the rather grim humour of which is often mingled with fear, pain, and other extremes of sense or impression.

MODERN LITERATURES IN EUROPEAN LANGUAGES

Though the written literatures in African languages antedate in origin those in European languages, they are discussed after the more widespread modern literatures in French, Portuguese, and English—the so-called metropolitan languages of Africa.

The body of published African literature written in European languages is sufficient to be studied in its own right. Critical opinion within Africa remains divided about how authentically African experience can be rendered in a language of European origin, but, despite the growth of indigenous language publications, there is no serious threat to the survival of literatures in the metropolitan languages.

French. The first contemporary literature was born as a protest against French rule and the policy of assimilation. Its leading figure was Léopold Senghor, who in 1960 was elected first president of the Republic of Senegal. In Paris during the 1930s he met Negro writers from the French Caribbean, such as the poets Aimé Césaire of Martinique and Léon Damas of French Guiana. Together, they began an examination of Western values and a reassessment of African culture, and in 1947 they founded *Présence Africaine,* Africa's leading literary journal. Senghor's *Anthologie de la nouvelle poésie nègre et malgache* (1948; "Anthology of the New Negro and Madagascan Poetry") was an important influence in the formation of the idea of a Negritude (a term first used by Césaire) that should include poets outside Africa—in the French Caribbean territories and in Madagascar, for example. Senghor's poems are sometimes regarded as examples of 20th-century French poetry in the manner of Paul Claudel or St. John Perse, but they are, in fact, essentially African: his love poetry, in particular, is intensely so in structure and tempo. Senghor's themes are those of Negritude: he attacks what he sees as the soullessness of Western civilization ("no mother's breast, but only nylon legs") and proclaims that African culture alone has preserved the mystic warmth of a life that could still revive "the world that has died of machines and cannons." This culture, says Senghor, gains strength from its closeness to nature and constant contact with "the ancestors"; Western culture is out of step with the world's natural and ancient rhythm. Therefore, he proclaims, "[We are] the leaven that the white flour needs." In his long rhapsodic lines he tries to make the French language swing and dance in the rhythms of his native Serer language.

Negritude

Another Senegalese, Birago Diop, has similarly explored the mystique of African life in a volume of poems, *Leurres et lueurs* (1960). His fellow countryman David Diop wrote the most violent and full-blooded protest poetry to be produced by the Negritude movement: "When civilization kicked us in the face, when holy water slapped our cringing brows. . . . "

Two of the most important Francophone novelists are the Cameroonians Mongo Beti (pseudonym of Alexandre Biyidi), who wrote *Le Pauvre Christ de Bomba* (1956; *The Poor Christ of Bomba*), and Ferdinand Oyono, author of *Une Vie de boy* (1956; *Houseboy*) and *Le Vieux Nègre et la médaille* (1956; *The Old Man and the Medal*). All three novels aim to explode the French colonial myth of France Outre-Mer: that the French West African possessions were not really colonies and that educated Africans are thus simply "black Frenchmen."

The second generation of French African writers was less concerned with the public rhetoric of Negritude. Thus, though the Congolese poet Tchicaya U Tam'si sometimes speaks of his people's sufferings ("My race remembers the taste of bronze drunk hot"), he does not claim to be the spokesman of his race. In *Le Mauvais Sang* (1955; "Bad Blood"), *Feu de brousse* (1957; *Brush-Fire*), *À tricheceur* (1960; "A Game of Cheat-Heart"), *Épitomé* (1962), and *Le Ventre* (1964; "The Belly"), he explores his personal agonies in Surrealist poems in the dense texture of which mythological, Christian, and sexual imagery are juxtaposed.

Camara Laye became famous with his romantic autobiography *L'Enfant noir* (1953; *The Dark Child*), which draws a poetic, idyllic picture of life in a traditional African town. His most important work, however, is the novel *Le Regard du roi* (1954; *The Radiance of the King*), which describes a white man's quest for personal salvation in the mysterious atmosphere of the West African jungle. It is regarded as among the most imaginative novels to have come from Africa. In a third novel, *Dramouss* (1966; *A Dream of Africa*), Laye, who in 1965 became a political refugee in Senegal, attacks the harsh methods of Guinea's ruling party. Among Africa's Socialist intellectuals, Senegal's Sembène Ousmane is best known as a film director, but his *Les Bouts de bois de Dieu* (1960; *God's Bits of Wood*) is a classic novel about the poor.

In the 1960s there was an important development of the philosophical novel in French-speaking Africa, notably by Sheikh Hamidou Kane in *L'Aventure ambiguë* (1961; *Ambiguous Adventure*) and by Yambo Ouologuem in *Le Devoir de violence* (1968; *Bound to Violence*). Both writers belong to the Islāmic western Sudan and present their novels partly in the form of "dialogues," either between Islām and Western materialism or between traditional autocracy and Christian compassion. Remarkable as women writers in a hitherto male world were Mariama Bâ, recipient of the first Noma Award for publishing in Africa for *Une Si Longue Lettre* (1980; *So Long a Letter*), and Aminata Sow Fall, a fellow Senegalese, who earned praise for *La Grève des battu ou les déchets humains* (1979; *The Beggar's Strike*), an ironic novella of great skill.

Later philosophical novelists

Portuguese. The 20th-century poetry of former Portuguese Africa, first widely known through the Angolan Mário de Andrade's *Antologia da Poesia Negra de Expressão Portuguesa* (1958), is mainly extremely militant. Both Andrade and the more important Agostinho Neto became actively engaged in the Angolan liberation movement, Neto serving as the first president of the People's Republic of Angola from 1975 until his death in 1979.

The Mozambican José Craveirinha, an *assimilado* (*i.e.,* assimilated to Portuguese culture and Roman Catholicism), like all the African writers who have published work in former Portuguese Africa, is yet deeply concerned with problems of race and discrimination. Mozambique's capital of Maputo (Lourenço Marques), the centre of a considerable literary and artistic activity, has also produced Luís Bernardo Honwana, one of Africa's outstanding short-story writers. In 1980 an Angolan writer of stature emerged, Pepetela (Artur Carlos Mauricio Pestana dos Santos), whose novel *Mayombe* is regarded as the major work of African fiction to have derived from guerrilla experience.

English. Although a genuine African literature in English did not emerge until the 1950s, writing in English by Africans goes back to the 18th century. Perhaps the most remarkable of the works published in England by West Africans sold into or born in slavery and later freed is *The Interesting Narrative of the Life and Adventures of Olaudah Equiano or Gustavus Vassa, the African* (1789; 3rd ed., enlarged, 1790), the first known English account by an African of his native country. In the 19th century, with the spread of missionary schools, several Africans published prose works in English, among them Samuel Adjai Crowther (who in 1844 translated part of the Gospel According to Luke), Africanus Horton, and Edward Blyden. In the early 20th century, the Ghanaian minister of religion the Reverend Carl Christian Reindorf wrote one of the first works by an African to make use of oral traditions, *The History of the Gold Coast and Asante* (*c.* 1911); and Joseph E. Casely-Hayford, also a Ghanaian, wrote *Ethiopia Unbound* (1911), a mixture of novel, autobiography, and pamphlet that is a forerunner of Negritude.

18th- and 19th-century English writings

In the 1940s the popular novelettes of the Onitsha market literature, named after the famous market where they were sold, began to be written, and a number of pioneer writers—among them Michael Dei-Anang and Raphael Armattoe of Ghana, Dennis Osadebay of Nigeria, and Edwin Barclay of Liberia—began to publish poems that, technically often crude and somewhat didactic in theme, prepared the way for later poets.

Literary activity in Nigeria

The institution in 1948 of university colleges at Accra, Ghana, and Ibadan, Nigeria, gave impetus to poetry, the novel, and drama in the 1950s and '60s. The most intense activity was in Nigeria, the Igbo proving particularly prolific. Cyprian Ekwensi, who began as an Onitsha pamphleteer, enjoyed great popularity with *Jagua Nana* (1961), the story of a prostitute. Onuora Nzekwu explored the relationship of the educated Igbo to his traditional culture in *Wand of Noble Wood* (1961), *Blade Among the Boys* (1962), and *Highlife for Lizards* (1965). Nkem Nwankwo created the comic figure of *Danda* (1964), the irreverent antihero of a novel perhaps inspired by trickster tales. The outstanding Igbo novelist was Chinua Achebe. All his novels present the conflict of emergent Africa: in *Things Fall Apart* (1958) he showed the impact of British rule on Igbo village life; in *No Longer at Ease* (1960) he analyzed the conflict in the mind of an African civil servant in Lagos who is torn between the social pressures of upper-class urban life and the demands of his village union; in *Arrow of God* (1964) he explored the breakup of traditional values and the struggle for political power in an Igbo village. *A Man of the People* (1966) is a bitter, disillusioned story of political corruption and intimidation in independent Nigeria. The same themes emerge in *Anthills of the Savannah* (1987).

The development of Nigerian literature owed much to two related centres in Ibadan. The journal *Black Orpheus,* founded in 1957 with Ulli Beier and Janheinz Jahn as its first coeditors, took its name from Jean-Paul Sartre's famous "Orphée noir" (1948), the introduction to Senghor's anthology (see above), and from Jahn's anthology, *Schwarzer Orpheus* (1954). Inspired by *Présence Africaine* and the First Congress of African Writers (Paris, 1956), *Black Orpheus* published the earliest efforts of African writers in English to find a literary mode of expression. A second influence on the establishment of an independent Nigerian culture was the foundation (1961) of the Mbari Club (also called the Mbari Mbayo Club), a meeting place for new writers and artists that also published the work of many poets and playwrights.

Among poets published by Mbari was Christopher Okigbo, who, until his early death in 1967 while fighting for Biafran independence, was the most polished and prolific Nigerian poet. In *Heavensgate* (1962) and *Limits* (1964) he developed a sensuous verse using styles borrowed from African and Western sources.

Like Okigbo, John Pepper Clark was graduated from the University of Ibadan. His passionate *Poems* (1962) and *Song of a Goat* (1961) were first published by Mbari. Clark is the most urgent and immediate of the Nigerian poets. Less reflective than Wole Soyinka, less meticulous than Okigbo, he works out each poem on the impetus of a single lyrical impulse. He has also written successful plays: *Song of a Goat* (performed in London at the 1965 Commonwealth Festival) is the tragedy of a childless woman. *The Ozidi of Atazi* (performed in the early 1960s; published, 1966) is a stage version of a traditional Ijo ritual play.

One of Nigeria's most sensitive poets is Gabriel Okara, whose novel *The Voice* (1964) is a fascinating linguistic experiment. Okara forces English into the straitjacket of Ijo syntax, producing an extraordinary and archaic effect that is often as beautiful as it is bizarre.

Africa's most famous playwright is the Nigerian Wole Soyinka (see below *African theatre*). Apart from his plays, Soyinka's tragic view of life is also expressed in his novel *The Interpreters* (1965). Publication in 1967 of *Idanre and Other Poems,* his first anthology, established him as a poet of distinction. Here, too, he explored his tragic sense of the difficulties and cost of human progress. Soyinka's autobiography of childhood, *Aké* (1981), was masterly in its tender recollections of his early years.

Nigerian writing in the 1970s lost some of its momentum. While many writers were coming to terms with the effects of the civil war of 1967–70, new writers emerged dealing with other preoccupations. These included Buchi Emecheta, who documented the position of women in Nigeria and Britain; Festus Iyayi and Ben Okri, who showed the stresses within urban African society; and playwrights such as Zulu Sofola.

Writers outside Nigeria

Among the most important poets outside Nigeria in the late 1960s were a Gambian, Lenrie Peters, and a Ghanaian, George Awoonor Williams (later known as Kofi Awoonor). The early work of both was published by Mbari: Peters' *Poems* and Awoonor Williams' *Rediscovery and Other Poems* (both 1964). Peters brings an unusual scientific intelligence to bear in his poetry, while Awoonor is deeply concerned with his native Ewe poetic tradition and the means of extending this in English.

In 1968 the Ghanaian Ayi Kwei Armah's novel *The Beautyful Ones Are Not Yet Born* was published. On the surface it deals with the dying days of Kwame Nkrumah's government, but, on a more universal level, it sums up the drift and despair of many African writers in the years after the stilling of the drums that celebrated independence. Armah's later work included *The Healers* (1978), a novel set in the 19th century that, like those of many other writers, uses the past as a key to understanding the present.

In East Africa in the 1960s, written literature was only just coming to birth; and the literary review *Transition* (Kampala, Uganda, 1961–68) played an important part in encouraging young writers. In the late 1960s the most original talent in East Africa was that of a Ugandan, Okot p'Bitek, whose long poem *Song of Lawino* (1966) treats the conflict of cultures with freshness and imagination, using the device of a lament by an illiterate woman. Already, however, Ngugi wa Thiong'o of Kenya had emerged as East Africa's leading novelist, with two novels—*Weep Not, Child* (1964) and *The River Between* (1965)—in which he tried to do for his native people, the Kikuyu, what Achebe had done for the Igbo. In a third novel, *A Grain of Wheat* (1967), he reflected profoundly on the meaning of heroism and of national independence. His *Petals of Blood* (1977) is complex in its narrative technique and explicit in its call for popular rebellion against the injustices of external domination. Ngugi's plays in particular were sufficiently outspoken to result in his spending a year in detention. He turned to writing in Kikuyu as well as in English, notably in his novel *Devil on the Cross* (1982), a scathing satirical fantasy.

Literature by South Africans

The emergent work of African and Coloured writers born in, though often living in exile from, the Republic of South Africa has been dominated by the political fact of apartheid. Many found the short story the best medium of protest, among the most successful writers being Bloke Modisane; Todd Matshikiza; Ezekiel Mphahlele; Richard Rive; a Coloured writer, Alex La Guma; a journalist, Can Themba; and Arthur Maimane. In the late 1950s *Drum* magazine provided an important forum for these writers.

Autobiographies are among the most moving and significant works by black South Africans. Mphahlele's *Down Second Avenue* (1959) has become a South African classic; and Alfred Hutchinson's *Road to Ghana* (1960) and Bloke Modisane's *Blame Me on History* (1963) are passionate documents in which the authors try to overcome the humiliation of their experience as blacks living in white-dominated South Africa.

The outstanding nonwhite novelist in South Africa in the 1960s was Alex La Guma. His superb eye for detail makes it possible for him to let the horror of a situation speak for itself, so that he never becomes sentimental, prolix, or overemotional in describing it. His short novels, including *A Walk in the Night* (1962), *And a Threefold Cord* (1964), *The Stone-Country* (1965), and *Time of the Butcherbird* (1979), are tense works of protest. The subtlest treatment of the recurrent theme of race relations, however, was perhaps that by Lewis Nkosi in his extraordinary play *The Rhythm of Violence* (1964).

The leading South African poets of the 1960s were Mazisi Kunene, K.A. Noortje, and Dennis Brutus. Many writers went into exile, but the country continued to produce, as a main focus of opposition to apartheid, some of the outstanding black writers on the continent. Prominent prose writers in the 1980s included Njabulo Ndebele and Mbulelo Mzamane; poets included Sipho Sepamla, Oswald Mtshali, and Mongane Serote. A notable playwright was Maishe Maponya.

The 1980s saw the emergence of Zimbabwean fiction (represented notably by Dambudzo Marechera and Charles

Mungoshi), at least one major Malaŵian poet (Jack Mapanje), the Botswanan (formerly South African) novelist and short-story writer Bessie Head, and a brilliant Somali novelist, Nuruddin Farah. The last two were perhaps Africa's most profound interpreters of women.

(U.Be./Ge.Mo./A.N.R.N.)

LITERATURES IN AFRICAN LANGUAGES

Evidence of the indigenous written literatures of Africa is in some regions ancient and in others comparatively recent. The earliest written African language known is the now-dead language of Geʿez, from Ethiopia (see below). The Latin and Arabic alphabets have had marked influence on developments in written African literature. Arabic was brought to the continent in the 7th century, when the Arabs conquered North Africa, while the Latin alphabet was introduced by Christian missionaries largely in the 19th century.

In West Africa the beginnings of indigenous written literature are linked to the campaigns in the early 1800s of the Fulani reformer Shaykh Usman dan Fodio; in East Africa the earliest extant Swahili text dates from 1652. In southern Africa the history of the earliest written literature, Xhosa, is linked to the printing press of the Lovedale Missionary Institution set up by the Glasgow mission in the 1820s.

Reluctance to accept indigenous literature

There was a great development in both quantity and quality of literary output after World War II, but in many cases, because they saw their own career advancement as being in English and French and perhaps because they regarded those languages as more advanced than their own, African elites tended to be indifferent to indigenous literatures. Indeed, it is only since the 1970s that the dominance of literatures in the metropolitan languages has been challenged and that writers such as Ngugi wa Thiong'o have begun to write in African languages, with translations into English, Swahili, and other languages following publication in the mother tongue. There is in the literary, political, and educational circles of some African countries a growing sense that the fostering of literature in indigenous African languages is important, especially in the drive to create new national models closer to the culture and history of the people.

The success of such a venture depends greatly on government policy. Somalia is a striking example of a country in which such a policy has been successfully applied. The role of publishers is also crucial; in spite of the severe financial constraints that operate in most African countries, some—such as Nigeria, Ghana, Tanzania, and Zimbabwe—now have indigenous publishing houses serving local readers. In some cases international publishing houses with African interests also participate in publishing African-language texts. The rate of illiteracy in Africa is still high, which limits the potential readership for texts in African as well as other languages. However, the huge popularity of stage and radio dramas in a number of countries (for instance, Nigeria, South Africa, Kenya, Somalia, and Tanzania) makes clear the great popular interest in forms of verbal art that both entertain and comment on contemporary life.

The dominant theme in much of the literature in African languages is the conflict between traditional cultures and modernization. In the novel and the short story, although the influence of modern European literary forms is clear, so too is that of the oral narrative. Sharp political comment on corruption and inefficiency is also prevalent. In general the role of public comment on national problems, and on wider topics such as African unity and racism, is a highly developed and important one, just as it is in the metropolitan languages.

Influence of myths and folktales

West Africa. *Yoruba.* The rich oral literature of the Yoruba, who live mainly in Nigeria and Benin, consists of myths, legends, folktales, and song. It is still flourishing, particularly in the rural areas, and has exerted a considerable influence on the written literature. Yoruba orthography was standardized in 1875 by the Church Missionary Society, in Lagos. The Bible was translated in 1900 and was widely used in Yorubaland. It was followed in 1911 by a translation of John Bunyan's *The Pilgrim's Progress,* which has probably exerted more influence on African-language writers than any other English work. The first written poetry, *Iwe Ekini Sobo* ("Sobo's First Book"), came in 1905 from the pen of the prolific and popular J. Sobowole Sowande. Sowande wrote several more collections (the last in 1934), publishing most of them himself. The first Yoruba novel did not appear until 1938, although a few novelettes appeared before then. Daniel Olorunfemi Fagunwa's allegorical novel *Ogboju Ode Ninu Igbo Irunmale* (1950; *The Forest of a Thousand Daemons*) was widely read and enjoyed. It uses the traditional Yoruba themes of virtue, courage, and perseverance and focuses on the vices of cruelty and greed. Fagunwa's first novel was *Igbo Olodumare* (1947; "The Forest of God"). Two others in a similar style followed, but his fifth and last novel, published in 1961, was considerably more realistic. Fagunwa's allegorical and fantastic adventure tales, full of folkloric elements—spirits, monsters, transformation flights, gods, magic, and witchcraft—provided a model for other writers.

A literary competition held at the time of Nigerian independence in 1960 was won by Femi Jeboda's realistic novel *Olowolaiyemo* ("Mr. People-Rally-Only-Around-the-Well-To-Do"), which deals with the hardships of urban life in Yorubaland. The trend of contemporary realism continued with Afolabi Olabimtan's novels. His first, *Kekere Ekun* (1967; "[Lad Nicknamed] Leopard Cub"), depicts the intrigues of a typically polygamous Yoruba home and the role of the church and school in a rural community. His second novel, *Ayanmo* (1973; "Predestination"), follows a village schoolmaster who studies hard to become a medical doctor. Various tempting and sophisticated women almost prevent him from achieving his ambition, but in the end he marries a girl from his hometown. Another successful writer was Akinwunmi Isola. His popular novel, *O Le Ku* (1974; "Heart-Rending Incidents Occurred"), depicts love and tragedy in a contemporary context.

Hausa. There has been a tradition of Arabic writing in Hausaland (northern Nigeria and Niger) since the end of the 15th century. The Hausa language has been written in the Arabic alphabet since the early 19th century and in the Roman alphabet since the early 20th century. Islāmic influence is still strong. A key feature of Hausa literature is the interaction of the oral and written traditions, and the emphasis (as in other literatures, such as Somali) is on recitation. Comment on religious, political, and social life has always been central to Hausa poetry. Its importance as a vehicle for comment is fostered by radio, the press, and television.

A key role in the history of Hausa poetry was played in the late 18th and early 19th centuries by the Islāmic warrior and reformer Shaykh Usman dan Fodio. He wrote poetry in both Arabic and Hausa, using it to exhort the Hausa to follow Islām. Early religious poetry included the mystical writings of the Islāmic Ṣūfī brotherhoods. Of political and religious importance were the praise poems to Muḥammad and to secular leaders and the chronicles of the city-states, such as Sokoto and Kano. One of the best known of early 20th-century poets is Alhaji Umaru. His *Zuwan Nasara* (1903; "Arrival of the Christians") describes the chaos caused to traditional life by the British occupation. The tradition of religious poetry has continued through the custom of public recitations, often by blind beggars who learn by heart the texts of manuscript poems.

Influence of Islām on secular literature

Secular poetry flourished after World War II. It remained deeply influenced by Islām, but poets tended to be drawn from a wider range of occupations, and poetry became far less the preserve of Muslim functionaries. A number of well-known poems were composed by the political leader Sa'adu Zungur; among the best known is *Wakar maraba da soja* (1957; "Song of Welcome to the Soldiers [on Their Return from Burma and India]"). Other eminent poets who followed the tradition of commenting on contemporary life are Mudi Sipikin and Hamisa Yadudu Funtuwa. The latter wrote poems on social evils such as drink. In his *Wakar uwar mugu* (1957; "Song of the Mother of Evil") he wrote on the attraction of prostitution as an emancipated alternative for women facing the tedium and constriction of polygamous marriage. International political relations have also been the subject of poetry, as in

Garba Gwandu's "Julius Nyerere" (1971). Akilu Aliyu, like many of his fellow poets, wrote and recited poetry on the Nigerian civil war and on contemporary politics.

Novel writing in Hausa is more recent than the tradition of written poetry. The first clutch of novels was published as the result of a competition held in 1933. Dominant interests were heroic figures of the past and aspects of traditional life. As in Fagunwa's fiction, much use was made of fantastic figures and allegorical elements from oral narrative. Interest in social comment has been less marked in fiction than in poetry, but it is still present. A theme that occurs often is that of childlessness in marriage and its disastrous effects on those involved. Trenchant comment on political corruption is featured in Sulaiman Ibrahim Katsina's *Turmin Danya* (1983; "Hog-Plum Mortar"). Science fiction is particularly popular with youth; an example is *Tauraruwa maiwutsiya* (1969; "The Comet"), by Umaru Dembo.

Travel writing and biography have also featured in Hausa prose. An interesting comment on the individualism of European society viewed through African eyes is provided by the playwright and biographer Aminu Kano, whose *Motsi ya fizama* (1955; "Moving Is Better than Sitting") is an account of his visit to Europe in 1946.

East Africa. *Ethiopian languages.* The oldest literary language in Ethiopia, Geʻez, which is related to classical Arabic, was first used for the writing of Christian texts in the 4th century AD. It was the literary language of Ethiopia until the 19th century and was used for recording the lives of saints (hagiography) and for writing royal chronicles. A great deal of religious poetry was also written in Geʻez.

Amharic

In Amharic, the official language of Ethiopia, one of the founders of modern literature was Blattengeta Hiruy Walda Sillāse. His two novels, addressed to a new generation educated in European-style schools, criticized outmoded social customs and dubious religious practices. Thus, he focused on child marriage and on the venality of some of the lower clergy. Hiruy argued for the adoption of Western technology and for a return to uncorrupted Christian ethics. Equally important as a founder of modern writing was Āfawarq Gabra Iyasus, author of the first Ethiopian novel, *Libb Wallad Tārīk* (1908; "Imaginative Story").

The critical thrust of the new Ethiopian literary trend was disrupted by the Italian conquest of 1936. However, a novel in the same critical vein, *Arʼāyā,* was published in 1948–49 by Girmācchaw Takla Hāwāryāt. The Western-educated hero of this work is thwarted by intrigues in court and government circles when he returns home and tries to put his newly learned Western skills at the service of his people. Historical fiction, based mainly on the complex and commanding figure of the 19th-century emperor Tewodros II, is also well represented, particularly in *And Lannātu* (1967; "His Mother's Only Child"), by Ābbe Gubaññā, and *Ya-Tewodros Inbā* (1966; "The Tears of Theodore"), by Birhānu Zarīhun. Didactic and socially committed writing is common: some touches on social issues such as prostitution, as in the short story "Abbonas," by Tāddasa Lībān, in his collection *Lelāw Mangad* (1959; "Another Way"). A novel that sympathetically examines the dilemma of a woman faced with the challenge of survival is *Setiññā Ādārī* (1963; "Fallen Woman"), by Innānu Āggonāfir (pseudonym of Nagāsh Gabra Māryām). Hāddis Ālamāyyahu's novel *Wanjalaññāw Dāññā* (1974; "The Crooked Judge") depicts corruption in the government of Emperor Haile Selassie I, while *Fiqir Iska Maqābir* (1958; "Love unto the Grave") is a love story of two people from different social backgrounds.

The conflict between old and new and the antagonisms in Ethiopian society are explored by writers such as playwright Mangistu Lammā (see below *African theatre).* Acculturation and alienation are explored in Tāddasa Lībān's short story "Yatabaṭṭasa Fire" ("The Seed of the Sundering") in his collection *Maskaram* (1956). Writing since the proclamation of socialist Ethiopia is best represented by Birhanu Zarīhun's trilogy, *Māʼibal* (1979–82; "Storm"), which describes the revolution and its effects. Political problems such as apartheid, Pan-Africanism, and the conflict between Somalia and Ethiopia have also been featured.

Somali. Besides the centuries-old practice of composing religious verse in Arabic, Somalia has a very old and rich tradition of oral literature in Somali, which still flourishes and influences the modern written forms. Written Somali literature really did not begin until after World War II—and even then did not flourish until after 1973, when the government introduced a standard orthography based on the Roman alphabet. Two periodicals, *Sahan* ("Reconnaissance") and *Horseed* ("Vanguard"), fostered Somali writing in the 1960s. The first poet to commit his poems to writing was Cali Xuseen Xirsi. Two of his poems appeared in *Sahan* and *Horseed,* although most reached the public in oral form. Cali wrote often on public themes; one of his poems, for instance, commented on the political plight of Somalis in the late 1950s, and another, composed in 1962, protested the importation of foreign automobiles when the mass of the people were still living in poverty. The emphasis on oral performance and transmission has continued in the era of print and amid a strong campaign for adult literacy under the socialist government established by the military in 1969. Poems may now be written down, but they are subsequently recited on the radio or at public or private recitals, or they are circulated on audiocassettes. Cabdulqaadir Xirsi "Yamyam" became one of the leading poets of socialist Somalia. The themes of his and of his contemporaries' poems tend to be public, stressing, for example, dedication to the country and its new order and support for the feminist stance of the government.

Recital of written literature

In prose, the fiction of Faarax M.I. Cawl, which incorporates oral historical narratives and poems, marks a transition from oral to written form. His novel *Aqoondarro waa u nacab jacayl* (1974) is highly didactic, exhorting the virtue of literacy. It is about an illiterate Dervish warrior who is unable to read a vital love letter from a young girl, and so the love affair ends tragically—hence the title of the novel, translated as *Ignorance Is the Enemy of Love.*

Swahili. Written poetry in Swahili—which drew inspiration from the Islāmic literatures in Arabic, Persian, and Urdu taken to the east coast of Africa by Oriental traders and scribes—goes back at least to the mid-17th century. Until the mid-19th century, Arabic script was used, but thereafter Latin script became more common and is now standard. The oldest extant epic is the *Hamziya* (1749), a court poem written by Sayyid Aidarusi, who was assigned the task by Bwana Mkuw II, ruler of the island of Pate off the coast in what is now Kenya. It was written in Arabic script in the old Kingozi dialect of Swahili.

Possibly because of the didactic thrust of Islāmic poetry, Swahili poetry has a strong tradition of public and religious commentary. The first well-known poet writing in this didactic vein was Mwana Kupona binti Msham, from Lamu Island, Kenya. His *Utendi wa Mwana Kupona* ("Poem of Mwana Kupona") dates from 1858. Another poet of the 19th century is Muyaka bin Haji al-Ghassany, from Mombasa, Kenya. Using a variety of styles—including lyrical, satiric, and panegyric—his poems presented a social and political commentary on urban life.

Didactic origin of Swahili poetry

The acknowledged father of contemporary Swahili literature is Shaaban Robert, a Tanganyikan, best known as a poet (*e.g.,* for *Almazi za Afrika* [1960; "African Diamonds"]) but also as a novelist and essayist. Robert's later style moved away from fantasy to the realistic portrayal of contemporary problems in novels such as *Siku ya Watenzi Wote* (1968; "The Day of Reckoning") and *Utubora Mkulima* (1968; "Utubora the Farmer"). The next generation of poets, among whom the best known are the Kenyans Ahmad Nassir and Abdillatif Abdalla, continued to focus on public themes.

Social change and the confusion caused by the clash of tradition with modernity feature strongly in the contemporary novel. The Tanzanian Euphrase Kezilahabi's third novel, *Dunia Uwanja wa Fujo* (1975; "The World Is a Chaotic Place"), exemplifies this preoccupation. The general mood of contemporary novels is pessimistic. Heroes are often unsympathetic characters whose decline and fall reflect the difficulties of maintaining a moral stance in modern urban society.

Like other African-language literatures, Swahili suffers from a publishing and book famine. Poems on a wide range of topical subjects appear regularly in the local Swahili-language newspapers, but the publication of novels is hindered by the lack of strong indigenous publishing houses, despite a large potential readership.

Southern Africa. *Shona.* Writing in Shona, the major African language group of Zimbabwe, is fairly recent, little of note appearing before the 1950s. In the novel a dominant trend has been the imaginative exploration of a heroic past. An example is Solomon Mutswairo's popular novel *Feso* (1956; English translation 1974). Patrick Chakaipa's *Pfumo reropa* (1961; *The Spear of Blood*) also explores the workings of Shona society before the appearance of whites, while his *Rudo ibofu* (1962; "Love Is Blind") and *Garan dichanya* (1963; "I Shall Return") treat the conflict between values of the two cultures. Other writers have focused on the harmful effects of urban life and the alienation that Western education may cause. John Marangwanda's *Kumazi vandadzoke* (1959; "Who Goes to a Place Perhaps Never Comes Back") and Mutswairo's novel *Murambiwa Goredema* (1959; "Murambiwa, Son of Goredema") focus on this urban theme.

Zulu. Early Zulu writing at the beginning of the 20th century comprised mostly historical and religious works. Magema Fuze's reconstruction of the Zulu past, *Abantu abamnyama lapha bavela ngakhona* ("The Black People and Whence They Came") was published in 1922. The Zulu-language newspaper, *Ilanga lase Natal* ("The Natal Sun"), founded in Durban, S.Af., in 1903 by John L. Dube, helped shape the Zulu readership. One of the paper's later editors, R.R.R. Dhlomo, wrote a series of novels on the Zulu kings of the 19th and early 20th centuries: *UShaka* (1936), *UDingane* (1936), *UMpande* (1938), *UCetshwayo* (1952), and *UDinuzulu* (1968). Dube wrote *Insila kaShaka* (1933; *Jeqe, the Bodyservant of King Shaka*), a historical novel on the powerful theme of Zulu royalty, and *UShembe* (1936), a biography of the charismatic Zulu prophet Isaiah Shembe. Fascination with the heroic Zulu past continued in works by later writers—for example, Leonard Mncwango's *Ngenzeni?* (1959; "What Have I Done?"). Muntu Xulu's *Simpofu* (1969; "We Are Poor") focuses on the struggle between the Zulu king Cetshwayo and the white Natal politician Theophilus Shepstone.

Historical fiction

The question of how to accept westernization without abandoning tradition has always been a dominant theme in Zulu fiction. Dhlomo's novel *Indlela yababi* (1946; "The Way of the Wicked") shows the disastrous effects of urban life on people from the village. J.K. Ngubane's *Uvalo lwezinhlonzi* (1957; "The Fear of Authority") touches on the same theme, and C.L.S. Nyembezi's masterly *Inkinsela yaseMgungundlovu* (1961; "The Wealthy Man from Pietermaritzburg") portrays the wiles of a city man set against the upright morality of country people. Nyembezi's earlier *Mntanami! Mntanami!* (1950; "My Child! My Child!") depicts a boy caught in the crime of the city who finally returns to his mourning family. A variety of themes covering the Zulu past, the clash between tradition and modernity, and the benefits and dangers of education feature in the short story collections *Uthingo lwenkosazana* (1971; "The Rainbow"), by D.B.Z. Ntuli, and *Amawisa* (1982; "Fighting Sticks"), by D.B.Z. and C.S.Z. Ntuli.

The finest Zulu poet to date is B.W. Vilakazi, who wrote passionately about nature, the Zulu past, and the injustice and degradation of apartheid in South Africa (see, for example, his famous poem "Ezinkomponi" ["In the Mines"]). Vilakazi's two volumes of poetry, *Inkondlo kaZulu* (1935) and *Amal'ezulu* (1945), are translated together as *Zulu Horizons.* In some instances the traditional praise poem has been effectively used to express contemporary experience, as in J.C. Dlamini's collection *Inzululwane* (1959; "Giddiness") and Phumasilwe Myeni's *Hayani maZulu* (1969; " Sing Zulus!"). A poet who uses traditional and modern styles, covering both public and private themes, is N.J. Makhaye in his collection *Isoka lakwaZulu* (1972; "The Popular Young Man of Zululand").

Xhosa. As in Zulu literature, the themes of the heroic past and of the opposition between beneficent tradition and harsh modernity are much in evidence. The question of how best to come to terms with change is also central in Xhosa literature. Much important early writing, expressing Xhosa aspirations and views on Christianity and tradition, appeared in the Xhosa-language newspapers and journals of the mid- and late 19th century: *Ikhwezi* ("The Morning Star"), *Isigidimi samaXhosa* ("The Xhosa Messenger"), *Imvo zabantsundu* ("Opinions of the Black People") and *Izwi labantu* ("Voice of the People"). Xhosa writers were also concerned with contemporary political themes, particularly the struggle against the loss of their land and power and their economic subjugation by the white South Africans.

The earliest exponents of written poetry were Samuel E.K. Mqhayi and J.J.R. Jolobe. While Mqhayi modeled his verse on traditional praise poetry, Jolobe experimented with such European-inspired forms as rhyme and descriptions of nature, thereby laying the foundations of modern Xhosa poetry. Mqhayi's important novel, *Ityala lamawele* (1914; "The Lawsuit of the Twins") demonstrated how native justice had operated quite successfully before whites arrived. It was, however, A.C. Jordan's *Ingqumbo Yeminyanya* (1940; *The Wrath of the Ancestors*) that set the principal theme of later Xhosa prose: how to retain the strengths of tradition in the face of inevitable change. Some writers, such as Z.S. Qangule and K.S. Bongela, set the rural-versus-urban conflict in stark polarities. Qangule's *Izagweba* (1972; "Weapons") depicts the conflict between uncompromising traditionalists and westernized, urbanized individuals. Bongela's *Alishoni lingenandaba* (1971; "The Sun Does Not Set Without News") deals with the squalor and corruption of life in the black townships surrounding the affluent white cities of South Africa. Some works look critically at tradition—particularly at the custom of the bride-price; others, such as Godfrey Mzamane's *Izinto zodidi* (1959; "Things of Value") suggest that synthesis can be achieved. In Mzamane's novel a strong and clever son succeeds in the new urban world, whereas his less well-prepared father has been corrupted by it and forced to return home. (E.A.W.G.)

The theme of changing traditions

AFRICAN THEATRE

The content and style of urban African theatre are influenced by both African dramatic traditions and Western theatre. The influence of Western styles is the result of a colonial presence, education in European languages, and the training of artists abroad. The degree and manner of foreign influence differ greatly from country to country, however. Such influence has hindered the development of African theatre in Zimbabwe, for example, where a minority continues to produce predominantly commercial Western theatre. The accent on Negritude in the theatre of French-speaking West Africa in the 1960s, on the other hand, was a reaction to the control of French directors, who clearly left their mark on production styles, *e.g.,* in the Daniel Surano Theatre in Senegal, where the works of Aimé Césaire and other leading playwrights are staged. The plays of Bernard Dadié of Côte d'Ivoire reflect French comic traditions, and Jean Pliya of Benin is one of a number of playwrights obsessed by colonial history. The texts of Western-educated writers have built a literary style of theatre, appealing to an elite audience, in which dance and music play, if anything, a subsidiary role.

Western influence

On the other hand, at a popular level, village theatre throughout Africa is based on the traditions of music, song, dance, and spectacle and has offered a rich platform for the development of contemporary urban theatre. Theatre innovators built onto village traditions of storytelling, some borrowing production styles from the colonial music-hall entertainment staged in West African cities in the 1920s and '30s. Concert parties toured Togo and Ghana, and in the 1950s the Ghanaian "Trios" emerged, with Bob Cole and his company delighting audiences in Accra with comic dramatizations of local events.

West Africa. The first professional theatres in Nigeria were companies created by actor-managers. The three most successful—Hubert Ogunde, Kola Ogunmola, and Duro Ladipo—were all Yoruba, and all started work as teachers involved in dramatizing Bible stories in African Christian churches. Ogunde's first production was *The Garden of Eden* (1944), staged in the Church of the Lord in Lagos. It was followed in 1945 by a secular satire, *Strike and*

Hunger, inspired by a clash between Nigerian workers and their colonial bosses. Ogunde's success led him to form the Ogunde Concert Party, which, in a style borrowed from the current British concert parties, staged domestic comedies and astute political satires between opening and closing "glees" of song and dance unrelated to the plot.

The euphoria of Nigerian independence in 1960 brought with it an explosion of creativity in the urban arts oriented toward new African forms and a rejection of colonial influences. This resulted in a creative confidence in literary and popular theatre that was to be influential throughout Africa.

Yoruba Opera

Traveling theatres, loosely known as Yoruba Opera companies, took to the road. Duro Ladipo created spectacular productions dramatizing themes from Yoruba mythology and history. His trilogy on the history of the Kingdom of Oyo, published in 1964 as *Three Yoruba Plays* (*Oba Koso* ["The King Did Not Hang"], *Oba Moro* ["The King of Ghosts"], and *Oba Waja* ["The King Is Dead"]), has the power and serenity of ancient Greek tragedy.

Kola Ogunmola specialized in domestic comedies featuring himself as a brilliant actor and mime. He refined Ogunde's techniques, replacing saxophones with Yoruba drums and writing tightly constructed yet gentle social satires. His most typical play is *Ife Owo* (*c.* 1950; *Love of Money*), but his greatest success was with *Omuti Apa Kini* (1963), an adaptation of Amos Tutuola's *The Palm-Wine Drinkard.* Though Ogunmola and Ladipo died in the early 1970s, their influence continued through the next decade as decorated trucks carried Yoruba Opera companies to one-night stands in towns and villages. The Yoruba music-drama *Obaluaye* (1970), by the composer Akin Euba, added a theatrical sophistication to their idiom, and they had a profound influence on the work of literary playwrights, particularly Wole Soyinka and Ola Rotimi. Soyinka and Rotimi spent years as university playwright-directors, and their skills at staging their own works gave them a theatrical viability lacking in the more poetic work of John Pepper Clark.

Wole Soyinka

Wole Soyinka, a brilliant critic and satirist who in 1986 was the first African to win the Nobel Prize for Literature, is regarded as Africa's leading writer. His work reflects the complexities facing an African playwright writing in English, moving from naturalistic treatment of his subjects to a profoundly Yoruba view of universal themes. His early comic satires *The Lion and the Jewel* (first performed at Ibadan in 1959; published 1963) and *The Trials of Brother Jero* (1960) are popular with all levels of English-speaking audiences, but the verbal and philosophical complexities of his later works are for an intellectual elite. *The Strong Breed* (1963) and *Death and the King's Horseman* (1975) are powerful statements of cultural conflict, while Soyinka's political satires, such as *Kongi's Harvest* (1965), are both savage and entertaining. *The Road* (1965) and *A Dance of the Forests* (1963) delve into the dramatic contrasts of life in Africa through the complexities of Yoruba mythology. In the latter, written for and performed to celebrate Nigerian independence in October 1960, Soyinka criticized the myth of the glorious African past, rejecting the Negritude concept that the revival of African culture must be inspired by African cultural heritage alone. His drama became increasingly pessimistic—as well as more obscure—after the Nigerian civil war, notably in *Madmen and Specialists* (1970). He also turned to past events—for example, in *Death and the King's Horseman*—and to new versions of old plays. His version of the *Bacchae* of Euripides was staged by the National Theatre in London in 1973, and *Opera Wonyosi,* a version of John Gay's *The Beggar's Opera,* appeared at the University of Ife in 1977.

Ola Rotimi evolved a theatrical English enriched by African proverbs and idioms. His style of directing made brilliant use of dramatic movement and drew an enthusiastic response from both university and popular audiences. Rotimi excelled at historical tragedies: *Kurunmi* (1969) deals with the Yoruba wars and *Ovonramwen Nogbaisi* (1971) with the sack of Benin. He also had a flair for satirical comedy, as shown in *Our Husband Is Gone Mad Again* (1966). As directors, both Soyinka and Rotimi made creative use of music and dance.

In Ghana, intercultural exchange had mixed results. In the 1960s Saka Acquaye's *The Lost Fisherman,* a musical based on "highlife" (see below *Dance*), was a popular success, as was Efua Sutherland's traveling theatre, for which she created productions based on village storytelling and local themes. Her plays in English use Greek models, as do those of Joe de Graaft. Ama Ata Aidoo was the most successful Ghanaian playwright after the 1960s. Her *The Dilemma of a Ghost* (1964) explores the complex cultural conflict arising in a Ghanaian village when a young man returns from his studies abroad with an Afro-American wife. *Anowa* (1970) deals with African involvement in the slave trade and the subservience of women.

African language drama

Hausa drama generally has a popular appeal and owes much to the dramatic style of traditional storytelling; it has focused on social problems, particularly those involving the Hausa family, with its tradition of polygamy. This practice has been criticized in many plays—for example, *Tabarmar Kunya* (1969; "Matter of Shame") by Adamu dan Gogo and Dauda Kano. Some plays satirize the dependence of uneducated people on Muslim scholars, and some—for example, Umaru Balarme Ahmed's *Buleke* (1970)—depict characters who lead a hectic modern life but are nevertheless still rooted in tradition. Plays are performed often in schools and are featured frequently on radio and television.

East Africa. An important Ethiopian playwright is Kabbada Mīkael, whose historical play *Hannibal* was performed at the Festival of Arts in Dakar, Senegal, in 1966. The best-known work of Mangistu Lammā is *Yalaccha Gabbiccha* ("Marriage of Unequals"), which deals with social inequality; it was staged for the first time in Addis Ababa in 1964. A play depicting a family in transition from old rural ways to the bleak uncertainty of city life is the Pinteresque *Yakarmo-saw* (1958; "The Origin of Man-made Taboo"), by Saggāye Gabra Madhin.

Somali theatre has been firmly established since the 1950s and is very popular; many scripts still remain to be published, however. *Shabeelnagood* (*Leopard Among the Women*), by Xasan Sheikh Mumin, a play depicting a heartless, wily trickster who marries naive young women, was published in Somali with an English translation in 1974; it was first performed in Mogadishu in 1968 and also had a long provincial tour and radio serialization. Somali theatre has been compared to that of the Elizabethan era in England in its combination of popular entertainment with high art and its ability to excite the interest of a broad cross section of society.

Swahili drama is particularly popular with school and college students, especially when it explores the conflicting pressures of traditional and modern values. Penina O. Mlama's popular play *Pambo* (1975; "Decoration"), depicting this conflict, ends with the central character's reluctant rejection of self-seeking careerism in the interest of his family and community.

Southern Africa. Zulu drama is most successful in serialized radio plays, which are immensely popular and have huge audiences. One of the best-known examples, which has been published, is D.B.Z. Ntuli's *Indandatho-yesithembiso* (1971; "The Engagement Ring").

Protest theatre in South Africa

Protest theatre in South Africa emerged under inventive and dedicated directors—Athol Fugard working through improvisation with John Kani and Winston Ntshona; Barny Simons, the artist behind the Market Theatre for Black Artists in Johannesburg; and Maishe Maponya and his versatile Soweto company. The works of these directors have no sophisticated sets and may be staged in any venue. They speak of the tragedy of South Africa, with twists of humour touching on the most dire of situations—a quality found throughout Africa in village and urban drama. A stark contrast is provided by the officially sponsored vapid extravaganza of the musical *Ipi-Tombi.* An unofficial musical was *Poppie Nongena,* starring Thuli Dumakude in successful seasons in London and New York City in 1984.

In Zimbabwe the most effective theatre was in the hands of small semiprofessional companies such as The People's Theatre, directed by Ben Sibenke in Harare. In Zambia Stephen Chifunyise toured villages with his company, setting up a dramatic dialogue with his audiences.

(E.A.W.G./P.H.)

Music

The term African music refers to the musical practices of all indigenous peoples of Africa, including the Berber in the Sahara and the San (Bushmen) and Khoikhoin (Hottentot) in southern Africa. Not included is the music of European settler communities or that of Arab North Africa.

HISTORY

It is widely acknowledged that African music has undergone frequent and decisive changes throughout the centuries. What is termed traditional music today is probably very different from African music in former times. Nor has African music in the past been rigidly linked to specific ethnic groups. The individual musician, his style and creativity, have always played an important role.

The material sources for the study of African music history include archaeological and other objects; pictorial sources (rock paintings, petroglyphs, book illustrations, drawings, paintings); oral historical sources; written sources (travelers' accounts, field notes, inscriptions in Arabic and in African and European languages); musical notations; sound recordings; photographs and motion pictures; and videotape.

Neolithic origins

In ancient times the musical cultures of sub-Saharan Africa extended into North Africa. Between *c.* 8000 and 3000 BC, climatic changes in the Sahara, with a marked wet trend, extended the flora and fauna of the savanna into the southern Sahara and its central highlands. During this period human occupation of the Sahara greatly increased, and along rivers and small lakes Neolithic, or New Stone Age, cultures with a so-called aquatic life-style extended from the western Sahara into the Nile Valley region. The aquatic cultures began to break up gradually between 5000 and 3000 BC, once the peak of the wet period had passed. The wet climate became more and more restricted to shrunken lakes and rivers and, to a greater extent, to the region of the Upper Nile. Today remnants survive perhaps in the Lake Chad area and in the Nile swamps.

The cultures of the "Green Sahara" left behind a vast gallery of iconographic documents in the form of rock paintings, among which are some of the earliest internal sources on African music. One is a vivid dance scene discovered in 1956 by the French ethnologist Henri Lhote in the Tassili-n-Ajjer plateau of Algeria. Attributed on stylistic grounds to the Saharan period of the Neolithic hunters (*c.* 6000–4000 BC), this painting is probably one of the oldest extant testimonies to music and dance in Africa (see Figure 2). The body adornment and movement style are reminiscent of dance styles still found in many African societies.

Some of the earliest sources on African music are archaeological. Although musical instruments made of vegetable materials have not survived in the deposits of sub-Saharan climatic zones, archaeological source material on Nigerian music has been supplied by the representations of musical instruments on stone or terra-cotta from Ife, Yorubaland. These representations show considerable agreement with traditional accounts of their origins. From the 10th to the 14th century AD, *Ìgbìn* drums (a set of footed cylindrical drums) seem to have been used. The *dùndún* pressure drum, now associated with Yoruba culture and known in a broad belt across the savanna region, may have been introduced around the 15th century, since it appears in plaques made during that period in the Kingdom of Benin. The Yoruba *dùndún* drums are now used as "talking drums" in accompaniment to *oriki* (praise name) poetry (see above *Literature and theatre: Oral traditions*). The double iron clapperless bell seems to have preceded the talking drum. Pellet bells and tubular bells with clappers were known by the 15th century.

Other archaeological finds relating to music include iron bells excavated in the Shaba region of Zaire and at several sites in Zimbabwe. Benin bronze plaques represent a further, almost inexhaustible source for music history, since musical instruments—such as horns, bells, drums, and even bow lutes—are often depicted on them in ceremonial contexts.

Among the most important written sources (though superficial analytically) are accounts from the 14th-century Arab travelers Ibn Baṭṭūṭah and Ibn Khaldūn and from the European navigators and explorers Vasco da Gama, Jan Huyghen van Linschoten, João dos Santos, François Froger, and Peter Kolbe. Early attempts at notating African music were made by T.E. Bowdich (1819) for Ghana, Karl Mauch (1872) for Zimbabwe, and Brito Capelo and Roberto Ivens (1882) for inner Angola.

Migration of musical styles and instruments

Major and minor migrations of African peoples brought musical styles and instruments to new areas. The single and double iron bells, which probably originated in Kwa-speaking West Africa, spread to western Central Africa with Iron Age Bantu-speaking peoples, and from there to Zimbabwe and the Zambezi River valley. Earlier migrating groups moving eastward from eastern Nigeria and central Cameroon to the East African lakes did not know the iron bells or the time-line patterns associated with them. Consequently, both traits were absent in East African music until the recent introduction of the time-line patterns of Congolese and Zairian electric guitar-based music. With

Jean-Dominique Lajoux

Figure 2: Rock painting of a dance performance, Tassili-n-Ajjer, Alg., attributed to the Saharan period of Neolithic hunters (*c.* 6000–4000 BC).

the intensifying ivory and slave trades during the 19th century, the *zeze* (or *sese*) flatbar zither, a stringed instrument long known along the East African coast, spread into the interior to Zambia, the eastern half of Zaire, and Malaŵi.

Beginning in the 17th and 18th centuries, lamellaphones with iron keys, a prominent feature of ancient Zimbabwe and neighbouring kingdoms and chieftainships, spread from the Zambezi Valley northward to the kingdoms of Kazembe and Lunda and to the Katangan and Angolan cultures. In the course of migration, some models became smaller, because they were used as travel instruments; others were modified and gave rise to the numerous types present in western Central Africa during the first half of the 20th century. (For a description of the lamellaphone, see below *Musical instruments: Idiophones.*)

A small box-resonated lamellaphone, called the *likembe* in Zaire, traveled in the other direction, from the west to the east, northeast, and southeast. It was invented in the Lower Congo region probably not earlier than the mid-19th century, and thereafter it spread upriver with Lingala-speaking porters and colonial servants to the northern Bantu borderland. The Azande, Ngbandi, and Baya, who speak Adamawa-Eastern languages, adopted the *likembe.*

Stylistic traits of *likembe* music linking it to its region of origin were only gradually modified in the new areas to suit local styles. At the beginning of the 20th century the *likembe* distribution area extended farther to the northeast into Uganda, where the Nilotic Alur, Acholi, and Lango adopted it. It was later introduced to southern Uganda by northern Ugandan workers; there the Bantu-speaking Soga and Gwere adopted it and began to construct models entirely from metal, even with a metal resonator. The *likembe* also spread southward from the Lower Congo, penetrating Angola from the Kasai region of Zaire and being adopted as recently as the 1950s by the Khoisan-speaking !Kung of Kwando Kubango Province in southeastern Angola.

As a result of migrations and the exchange of musical fashions both within Africa and with foreign cultures, specific traits of African music often show a puzzling distribution. Extremely distant areas in Africa may have similar, even identical, traits, while adjacent areas may have quite different styles. The multipart singing style in triads within an equiheptatonic tone system of the Baule of Côte d'Ivoire (Ivory Coast) is so close, if not identical, to the part singing style of Ngangela-, Chokwe-, and Luvale-speaking peoples in eastern Angola that the similarity is immediately recognized by informants from both cultures. Why this is so is a riddle. The two areas are separated by several countries with different approaches to multipart singing. Another historical riddle is the presence of practically identical xylophone playing styles and instruments among Makonde- and Makua-speaking peoples of northern Mozambique and among certain peoples of Côte d'Ivoire and Liberia, notably the Baule and the Kru. The *jomolo* of the Baule and the log xylophones of northern Mozambique—for example, the *dimbila* of the Makonde or the *mangwilo* of the Shirima—are virtually identical instruments.

Diffusionist theories of various kinds have been offered to resolve such riddles. The English ethnomusicologist A.M. Jones proposed that Indonesian settlers in certain areas of East, Central, and West Africa during the early centuries AD could have introduced xylophones and certain tonal-harmonic systems (equipentatonic, equiheptatonic, and *pelog* scales) into Africa. Ethnohistorians, on the other hand, have tended to accentuate the importance of coastal navigation (implying the traveling of hired or forced African labour on European ships) as an agent of cultural contact between such areas as Mozambique, Angola and Zaire, and the West African coast.

Existing historical sources on African music and dance are more abundant than might be expected. Sometimes historical data can be obtained indirectly from contemporary observation outside Africa, especially in Latin America. It was a rule rather than an exception that people brought as slaves from Africa to the New World often came from the hinterland of the African coastal areas. Between the European slave traders established on the coast and the hinterland areas were buffer zones inhabited by African "merchant tribes," such as the Ovimbundu of Angola, who are still remembered by eastern Angolan peoples as *vimbali,* or collaborators of the Portuguese. In the 18th and 19th centuries the inland areas of Angola were not directly accessible to Europeans. But the music and dance of these areas became accessible indirectly, as European observers saw African captives playing musical instruments in New World countries. In Brazil the music of the Candomblé religious cult, for example, can be directly linked to 18th- and 19th-century forms of *orisha* worship among the Yoruba. In a similar manner, Umbanda religious ceremonies are an extension of traditional healing sessions still practiced in Angola, and Vodun religious music among the Fon of Benin has extensions in the Voodoo of Haiti and elsewhere in the Carribean. African instruments have also been modified and sometimes further developed in the New World; examples are the Central African friction drum and the lamellaphone (in the Cuban *marimbula*).

Spread to the New World

African music as it is known today was also shaped by changes in the ecology of the continent, which drove people into other lands, thus producing changes in their art. With the drying of the Sahara, for example, populations tended to shift southward. When settled populations accepted the intruders, they often adopted musical styles from them. Thus, the choral singing style of the Masai had a fundamental influence on vocal music of the Gogo of central Tanzania, as is audible in their *nindo* and *msunyunho* chants.

It is only relatively recently that scholarly attention has focused on the various urban popular styles, reflecting a blend of local and foreign ingredients, that have emerged during the last 50 years or so. The best known of these are West African "highlife," Congolese (or Zairian) dance music, *tarabu* of East Africa, and South African styles. With the widespread adoption of Christianity in Africa since the 19th century, many new varieties of African church music have risen and continue to evolve. For example, with altered words, hymns—as well as secular songs—are quite often adapted as protest songs in order to rally opposition to political oppression. (G.K./D.K.R.)

MUSICAL INSTRUMENTS

Outsiders have often overlooked the enormous variety of musical instruments in Africa in the mistaken belief that Africans play only drums. Yet even Hanno the Carthaginian, who recorded a brief visit to the west coast of Africa in the 5th century BC during a naval expedition, noted wind instruments as well as percussion. Of an island within the gulf of "Hesperon Keras" he wrote:

> By day we saw nothing but woods, but by night we saw many fires burning, and heard the sound of flutes and cymbals, and the beating of drums, and an immense shouting. Fear therefore seized on us, and the soothsayers bid us quit the island.

Ensembles fitting this description may be found over a wide area of West Africa today, serving as accompaniment to dancing and merrymaking or as an essential ingredient of ceremonial or cultic activities.

Besides the percussion and wind instruments noted by Hanno, there are also stringed instruments of many kinds, ranging from the simple mouth bow to more complex varieties of zithers, harps, lutes, and lyres. While the aggregate of instrumental resources distributed over the continent is vast, each society tends to specialize in a limited assortment, and there is a wide variety from region to region. In some areas interesting new hybrid varieties emerged in the 20th century in response to outside influence, notably the *endingidi* spike fiddle of Uganda, *malipenga* gourd kazoos of Tanzania and Malaŵi, and chordophones such as the *ramkie* and *segankuru* of South Africa.

Non-musical function of instruments

Musical instruments in African societies serve a variety of roles. Some instruments may be confined to religious or cultic rituals or to social occasions. Among some peoples there may also be restrictions as to the age, sex, or social status of the player. Among the Xhosa, for example, only girls play the imported Jew's harp, a modern replacement for the traditional mouth bow, which was formerly their prerogative.

Besides recreational applications, or as accompaniment for dancing, instruments may serve many other roles. In Lesotho it is claimed that cattle graze more contentedly when entertained by the sound of the *lesiba* mouth bow. Among the Shona in Zimbabwe, a local form of lamellaphone known as *likembe dza vadzimu* serves in rituals of ancestor worship, while in the kingdom of Buganda the royal drums formerly held higher status than the king. In West and Central Africa, pressure drums may serve for the transmission of messages or, together with trumpets, for the declamation of praises, by mimicking the tonal and rhythmic patterns of speech. All sub-Saharan languages (except Swahili) are "tone languages," in the sense that the meaning of words depends on the tone or pitch in which they are said. Consequently, instrumental music—or even natural sounds such as birdsong—often imitates or suggests meaningful phrases of the spoken language. Sometimes this is intentional and sometimes it is merely fortuitous, but in either case it escapes the notice of uninformed outsiders.

Certain instruments are used solely for song accompaniment. Here the interplay between voice and instrument is often intricate and delicately balanced. Zulu solo songs, in earlier times, were often self-accompanied on the *ugubhu* gourd bow. In such bow songs, while the instrumental melody was influenced by the tone requirements of the song's lyrics, the tuning of the bow determined the vocal scale to which the singer conformed. Today, when Zulus use the modern Western guitar, precisely the same antiphonal relationship and mutual interdependence between voice and instrument is maintained.

Of the principal instruments found in sub-Saharan Africa, the following is a brief sampling.

Idiophones. In this class the substance of the instrument itself, owing to its solidity and elasticity, yields sound without requiring strings or stretched membranes. Some are sounded by striking, others by shaking, scraping, plucking, or friction. Idiophones are numerous and widely distributed throughout the continent. On musical grounds they may be divided into instruments used mainly for rhythm and several varieties tuned and used melodically.

Rhythmic idiophones. Among the vast array of nonmelodic, rhythmic idiophones, the most common and widespread are probably rattles, sounded by shaking. One type, the sistrum, which has small metal disks loosely suspended on rods, is important in the Ethiopian church and is also used in Guinea. More widespread are hollow rattles, consisting of a gourd enveloped in a net of shells or beads or of a container such as a calabash with seeds or pebbles inside. Besides hand-held varieties, there are many other kinds of rattles, often strung on cords, which may be attached to the limbs or other parts of the body and shaken while dancing or playing another instrument, or which may be fastened onto another instrument, such as the lamellaphone, to serve as a supplementary jingling device. In Zimbabwe, bottle tops, instead of the traditional snail shells, serve this purpose on the *likembe dza vadzimu* of the Shona.

Clappers and bells

Struck and concussion-sounded idiophones are found everywhere. These include stone clappers and multiple rock gongs (in Nigeria); wooden clappers and percussion beams; and implements such as hoe blades, weapons, and shields (in fact, all kinds of domestic items serve as temporary idiophones when required). Further examples are metal or wooden bells, either with internal pellets or clappers or externally struck; inverted half calabashes; bottles; and clay pots, partially water-filled, which in West Africa are struck with fanlike beaters. Stamping sticks are also used in West and Central Africa, as are stamping tubes made from bamboo or from long, open-ended gourds. In Ghana and Nigeria the latter are used for accompanying certain women's songs. Scraped and friction idiophones are quite widely distributed, the most common form being a notched stick or piece of bamboo that is scraped by another stick.

Slit drums. Falling between rhythmic and melodic instruments, the largest and most distinctive member of the African struck-idiophone family is the slit drum, made from a hollowed log. By careful thinning of the flanks at certain places, the instrument may be tuned so as to yield as many as four distinct pitches. Besides their use for transmitting messages, West and Central African slit drums are often played in combination with membrane drums and other instruments.

Xylophones. Two markedly different species of xylophone are distinguishable in Africa: one has free, unattached keys, and the other has fixed keys. With free-key xylophones, found in parts of West and East Africa, loose slabs may be laid across the player's outstretched legs or supported on logs or straw bundles, sometimes above a resonating pit. In Uganda and Zaire, from two to six players may perform together on the same instrument.

Fixed-key xylophones are more elaborate. Mounted below each key, there is usually an individually tuned calabash resonator, often with a mirliton (a vibrating membrane) attached to add a buzzing quality to the sound. A mid-14th-century account mentions a calabash-resonated xylophone in the West African kingdom of Mali, and similar instruments were reported on the east coast in the 16th century. Xylophone ensembles are common in some areas, notably among the Chopi of Mozambique, where *timbila* orchestras of up to 40 xylophones, of six different sizes, have been reported.

Lamellaphones. These "thumb pianos" are plucked idiophones unique to Africa and widely distributed throughout the continent. In construction they consist basically of a set of tuned metal or bamboo tongues of varying length fitted to a board, box, or calabash resonator, their free ends being twanged by the player's thumbs and fingers. Supplementary rattling or buzzing devices are often added, and board-mounted varieties are often played inside a half calabash or bowl to enhance the resonance. They serve mainly for song accompaniment. Some common names for regional varieties of the instrument are *likembe, mbira,* and *timbrh* (see Figure 3).

G. Kubik

Figure 3: *Timbrh* lamellaphones of the Vute people of central Cameroon.

Membranophones. All African drums except the slit drum fall within this class, sharing the basic feature of having a stretched animal skin as their sounding medium. The mirliton, or small "singing membrane," is often added to the bodies of drums and xylophone resonators as a supplementary buzzing device. It is an essential component of the *malipenga* gourd kazoos used in Tanzania and Malaŵi to simulate military band music.

Variety of drums

Africa has a wide variety of drums, which may serve in a number of different roles, some of them not primarily musical. Their manufacture is often steeped in ritual and symbolism, and their use may be restricted to specific contexts. In many societies only men may play them; in others, certain drums are used only by women (as among the Venda, Sotho, and Tswana of southern

Africa). Playing techniques differ widely: some drums are beaten with the bare hands, others with straight or curved sticks. Friction drums are also occasionally found, such as the ingungu used in Zulu girls' nubility rites. Except in the extreme south, drums of contrasting pitch and timbre are frequently played in ensembles, with or without other instruments, to accompany dancing. Though the role of drums is usually rhythmic, the *entenga* drum chime in Uganda, comprising a set of tuned drums, plays vocally derived melodies.

The body of a drum may be either bowl-shaped, tubular, or shallow-framed. Bowl-shaped drums include those made from gourds and pots as well as the small and large kettledrums found in and around Uganda. Tubular and frame drums may have either one skin or two, which are either pegged, pinned, glued, or laced onto the body. Tubular drums come in many sizes and shapes, such as cylindrical, conical, barrel-shaped, goblet-shaped, footed, and hourglass-shaped. The *atumpan* talking drums of the Ashanti are barrel-shaped with a narrow, cylindrical, open foot at the base. East African hourglass drums are single-skinned. In West Africa double-skinned hourglass drums are held under one arm, their pitch rapidly and continually changed by as much as an octave by squeezing the lacing that joins the two heads. In some areas wax may be applied to the centre of the drum skin, and a mirliton, shells, or jingles may be attached to the body to modify the tone.

Chordophones. This class, comprising instruments that produce sound from strings stretched between fixed points, is well represented in Africa. There is an abundance of specimens in the form of zithers, lutes, and harps.

Musical bows. These consist of a string stretched between the two ends of a flexible stave. There are three types: bows with a separate resonator; bows with attached resonators; and mouth bows, which use the player's mouth for resonance. Though it is conjectural whether all varieties evolved from the shooting bow, the San of the Kalahari often convert their hunting bows to musical use. Sometimes it is held against the mouth, yielding a range of mouth-resonated harmonics, as with the Jew's harp, or it is pressed against a hollow container. Apart from adapted shooting bows, more specialized types of musical bows are widespread. Most are sounded by plucking or striking the string, but the Xhosa *umrubhe* is bowed with a friction stick, the *xizambi* of the Tsonga has serrations along the stave that are scraped with a rattle stick, and the Sotho *lesiba* (like the *gora* of the Khoikhoin) is sounded by exhaling and inhaling across a piece of quill connecting the string to the stave. Bows with more than one string are rare, but the *tingle apho* of the Kara people in southern Ethiopia has three.

Possible origin in the shooting bow

Besides mouth-resonated bows, the gourd bow, which has an attached gourd resonator, is commonly used in southern, Central, and East Africa for self-accompanied solo singing. The string is struck with a thin stick or grass stem. The Zulu *ugubhu* is a typical example. Harmonic tones are selectively resonated by moving the mouth of the gourd closer to or farther from the player's chest. The fundamental pitch of the string can be altered by finger stopping; with other types, like the Swazi *makhweyane,* a noose or brace divides the string so as to yield two different "open" notes, and resonated harmonics are selected in the same way.

While all the above types of musical bow are simple forms of the zither, the so-called ground bow or earth bow of Equatorial Africa, which has one end planted in the ground, qualifies as a ground harp.

Lutes. Characterized by strings that lie parallel to the neck, the lute is found in Africa in several varieties. The multiple-necked bow lute, or pluriarc, of central and southwestern Africa is the oldest. This has a separate flexible neck for each string and resembles a set of musical bows fixed at one end to a sounding box. West African plucked lutes such as the *konting, khalam,* and the *nkoni* (which was noted by Ibn Baṭṭūṭah in 1353) may have originated in ancient Egypt. The *khalam* is claimed to be the ancestor of the banjo. Another long-necked lute is the *ramkie* of South Africa.

Fiddles. The bowed-lute family is represented by three types of one-string fiddle, as exemplified by the rebeclike *goje* of Nigeria and the spike fiddles *masenqo* of Ethiopia and *endingidi* of Uganda—the last being a 20th-century invention.

Harp lutes. The sophisticated *kora* of the Malinke people of West Africa is classified as a harp lute. Its strings lie in two parallel ranks, rising on either side of a vertical bridge, which has a notch for each string. The long neck passes through a large, hemispherical gourd resonator covered with a leather sounding table.

Lyres. These have been termed yoke lutes, the strings running from a yoke supported by two side arms. Their distribution in Africa is confined to the northeast. In Ethiopia two types occur: the large *beganna,* with eight to 10 strings and a box-shaped body (corresponding to the ancient Greek kithara); and the smaller six-string *krar,* with a bowl-shaped body (resembling the Greek lyra). The latter type, with from four to eight strings and varying in size, is also used in The Sudan, Uganda, and Kenya. The *litungu* is a typical specimen.

Harps. These are confined to a belt, north of the Equator, running from Uganda to Mauritania. All African harps (like those of ancient Egypt) are classed as open harps, as they have a neck and a resonator with a string holder but lack a supporting pillar to complete the triangle. In most cases some form of buzzing device is incorporated. Examples are the *ennanga* (Uganda), *ardin* (Mauritania), *kinde* (Lake Chad region), and *ngombi* (Gabon).

Aerophones. The archaic bull-roarer (a board attached by rope to a stick and whirled about in the air) survives in various localities, notably in southern Africa among the San and neighbouring peoples. Of the wind instruments proper, the three main divisions—flutes, reed pipes, and trumpets—are all well represented, though the second of these is more restricted in distribution than the others.

Flutes. At the southernmost tip of the continent the navigator Vasco da Gama in 1497 encountered a band of Khoi people (Khoikhoin, later called the Hottentots) "playing upon four or five flutes of reed." Ensembles of single-note stopped flutes playing on the hocket principle, with each flute blowing its note in rotation, have been reported from various regions, ranging from southern Africa through eastern Zaire, Uganda, and The Sudan to southern Ethiopia. Panpipe ensembles are less common, but notable examples have been witnessed in Central Africa, and particularly among the Nyungwe of Mozambique. There are many other types of open and stopped flutes—cylindrical and conical; transverse and end-blown; made from bamboo, reed, roots, stems, wood, clay, bone, and horn. Globular flutes made from small spherical gourds or from hard-shelled fruits such as the *Oncoba spinosa* are found in southern Africa, Zaire, Mozambique, Uganda, Guinea, and elsewhere. End-blown notched flutes, with a U- or V-shaped embouchure, either with or without finger holes, are widely distributed across the continent. The long Zulu *umtshingo* has an obliquely cut embouchure; there are no finger holes, but a double range of overblown harmonics is produced by alternately stopping and unstopping the lower end with a finger. Such instruments and many others throughout the continent are played singly, but in many areas flutes are played in pairs or in combination with other instruments.

Playing single-note flutes in ensemble

Reed pipes. Transverse clarinets are used throughout the West African savanna region, from Guinea to Cameroon. These are single-reed pipes made from hollow guinea corn or sorghum stems, the reed being a flap partially cut from the stem near one end. Single and double clarinets are found in The Sudan among the Dinka people. Conical double-reed instruments of the oboe or shawm type have spread around the northeastern and northwestern fringes of Africa wherever Islām has taken root. Despite local variations, they are basically related to the Arab *zūrnā,* having a disk (or pirouette) below the reed that supports the player's lips.

Trumpets. Lip-vibrated aerophones made from a variety of materials are widespread in Africa. Apart from musical uses, some serve for signaling. In West Africa, side-blown ivory or horn instruments may transmit verbal

Figure 4: Hausa musicians at the court of the *amir* of Zaria, northern Nigeria, performing on *ganga* drums, animal horns, and *kakaki* long trumpets.
G. Kubik

praises of chiefs and rulers. Among the Hausa, the long metal *kakaki* and wooden *farai,* both end-blown, fulfill this role in combination with drums (see Figure 4). In East and Central Africa the instruments are often made from gourds, wood, hide, horn, or a combination of these materials. In Buganda, trumpet sets were part of the royal regalia. Throughout Africa, more than one or two notes are seldom produced from a single trumpet, but trumpet ensembles are common, playing in hocket fashion.

(D.K.R.)

MUSICAL STRUCTURE

Complexity of African music

In Africa it is unrealistic to separate music from dance or from bodily movement. In Europe the body tends to be used as a single block, while in African and Afro-American dance it seems to be "polycentric," that is, split into several independent body areas or "centres." Likewise, the playing of African musical instruments involves a whole combination of body movements. This is one reason African music is less amenable to notation than Western music; for analytical purposes, sound filming, rather than just sound recording, is essential.

In Africa music making is very often collective, involving organized collaboration in which performers contribute not identical, but complementary, constituents. Besides polyrhythmic and polymetric procedures, melodic phrases are frequently offset against one another, with different starting and ending points, either in an antiphonal "call-and-response" relationship or in an overlapping relationship that yields polyphony. In addition, melodic phrasing and instrumental accompaniment may be deliberately out of step—a displacement technique described in 1952 by American anthropologist Richard Waterman as "offbeat phrasing of melodic accents." Complementary participation is also evident in drumming and in flute or trumpet ensembles where each player in turn sounds a different, single note. The Ghanaian musicologist J.H. Kwabena Nketia pointed out the function of this African form of hocket technique in "achieving overall effects of continuity, [and] for building up interlocking, and sometimes complex structures, out of relatively simple elements."

Timing. In a great many African music and dance cultures, movement organization rigidly follows certain principles of timing that cannot be equated with Western metrical systems. African systems of timing are generally based on at least four fundamental concepts:

(1) There is an overall presence of a mental background pulsation, or "metronome sense," consisting of equally spaced pulse units continuing ad infinitum and often at great speed. These so-called elementary pulses serve as a basic orientation screen; they are two or three times faster than the beat rate, or gross pulse.

(2) Musical form is organized so that recurring patterns and themes are timed against a regular number of elementary pulses—usually 8, 12, 16, 24, or their multiples (more rarely, 9, 18, or 27). The recurring sequences are called strophes, or cycles; the number of pulses they contain are referred to as their form numbers, or cycle numbers.

(3) Such strophes or cycles are often divisible in more than one way, allowing simultaneous combinations of contradictory metrical units. For example, 12 pulses—12 is the most important form number in African music—can be divided by 2, 3, 4, and 6.

(4) Patterns with the same form number can be shifted out of phase, so that their starting points and main accents do not coincide, resulting in "cross rhythms." In some cases they cross in such a way that they interlock, or fall between one another, with no two notes ever sounding together.

Interlocking. Interlocking techniques are a prominent feature of many instrumental styles in East and southeastern Africa. From regions in Tanzania and Mozambique come the *ng'oma* drumming of Gogo women and such log xylophone styles as the *dimbila* of the Makonde, the *mangwilo* of the Shirima, and the *mangolongondo* of the Yao people. The drumming in the *ngwayi* dance of northeastern Zambia, the *timbrh* lamellaphone music of the Vute people of central Cameroon, and many other traditions also use interlocking techniques.

Difference between interlocking technique and Western ensemble music

A basic characteristic of interlocking is the absence of a common guide pulse to be taken as a reference point by all players. In a Western music ensemble or a jazz band all the players share a "beat," one common metric point of departure. They may even beat their feet to mark it. While there are many traditional African musics in which such a common reference pulse does exist, in several others the musicians in a group relate their parts to individual reference pulses, which can stand in various relations to one another.

In one type of relation the pulse of one performer or group of performers falls exactly in the middle of the other's pulse. This type of interlocking occurs, for example, in the music of the *amadinda* and *embaire* xylophones of southern Uganda. A special type of notation is now used for these xylophones, consisting of numbers and periods. A number indicates that a player strikes a note; the number refers to the note in the scale, as 5, for example, the fifth note of the scale. An underlined number should be read an octave down; in other words, 5 is an octave below 5. A period indicates that no note is struck. Numbers and periods both occupy one elementary pulse.

The following is an example of interlocking as played on the *amadinda.* The melodies are actually played in parallel octaves; that is, each melody is played at the notated pitch and also at the pitch an octave below:

Musician A plays: 4.3.4.1.3.3.4.2.3.4.2.1.4.3., etc.
(in parallel octaves) ↑
Musician B plays: ...5.3.3.5.5.3.5.2.3.5.1.1., etc.
(in parallel octaves)
↑ = place of entrance for musician B

In interlocking music of this type, one musician's positive action of striking a note always coincides with a negative action, or "non-strike," of his fellow musician, who at that moment lifts his beater. The effect is such that both series of equally spaced notes seem to interlock like the teeth of a cogwheel. Each of the two musicians, however, feels his own series of notes as "on beat."

In the very fast *mangwilo* xylophone music, the interlocking technique is exploited further. In some compositions by two virtuoso players, each musician interlocks with the right hand only. The left hands play different rhythm patterns superimposed over the interlocking pattern.

Triple interlocking is another type, used, for instance, in Zambia in drum music and also in southern Uganda in the music of the *akadinda* xylophone. Here a group of three musicians plays a short pattern of equally spaced notes in parallel octaves. Three musicians sitting opposite them interlock with another pattern that fits two equally spaced notes between each note of the first group's pattern. In numerical notation it looks like this:

Three musicians play: 2 . .4. .2. .2. .1. .1. .2. .5. .
(in three octaves) ↑
Three opposite musicians play: . 14.35.14.35.14.35.14.35
(in three octaves)

Interlocking in performance

Interlocking techniques allow African instrumentalists to produce resultant patterns—overall patterns formed by all the players—that are unbelievably rapid. The resultant pattern of the above *akadinda* musical example is: 214435214235114135214535. This series of 24 notes, when played by expert musicians, is at a speed of approximately 600 notes per minute. But each musician, for himself, plays one-third that fast.

Time-line patterns. In certain areas there is yet another principle of timing, known as time-line patterns. These are struck motional patterns that make up a rhythmic ostinato with an asymmetrical inner structure (such as $5 + 7$ or $7 + 9$), against which the melodic and rhythmic phrasing of other performers is juxtaposed. They are percussive patterns, produced either by hand clapping or on some musical instrument of penetrating sound quality, such as a bell, a high-pitched drum, the rim or body of a drum, a bottle, an ax blade, a calabash, a percussion beam, concussion sticks, or a high-pitched xylophone key. Time-line patterns are a regulative element in many kinds of African music, especially dance music along the West African coast, in western Central Africa, and in a broad belt along the Zambezi River Valley from Zambia into Mozambique. Broadly speaking, they are found in those parts of Africa covered by the Kwa and Benue-Congo subgroups of the Niger-Congo group of languages—with the notable exception that they are not found in most areas of East Africa or in South Africa.

A time-line pattern represents the structural core of a musical piece, something like a condensed and extremely concentrated representation of the rhythmic and motional possibilities open to the musicians and dancers. Singers, drummers, and dancers in the group find their bearings by listening to the strokes of the time-line pattern, which is repeated at a steady tempo throughout the performance. The following are some of the most important time-line patterns:

(1) The 12-pulse seven-stroke pattern

Version a (mainly West African)

⑫ [x . x . x x . x . x . x]

Version b (mainly Central African)

⑫ [x . x . x . x x . x . x]

(Distribution: mostly along the West African coast—for example, in the music of the Yoruba, Fon, and Ewe—but also in Zaire, Angola, and Zambia.)

(2) The 12-pulse five-stroke pattern

⑫ [x . x . x . . x . x . .]

(Distribution: Central Africa, especially in the Congo and Zaire; southern Africa, including Zambia and Malaŵi; West Africa—for instance, among the Baule of Côte d'Ivoire.)

(3) A 16-pulse time-line pattern

⑯ [x . x . x . x x . x . x . x x .]

(Distribution: mostly southern Zaire, Angola, and northwestern Zambia; an isolated occurrence in xylophone music on the Kenya coast.)

The longest time-line pattern is found among the Pygmies of the upper Sangha River in the Central African Republic. It is a 24-pulse pattern of the following structure:

㉔ [x . x . x . x . x . x x . x . x . x . x . x x .]

This pattern is struck on a percussion beam, and the dance style accompanying it emphasizes motions of the pelvis.

Origins of time-line patterns

The asymmetrical time-line patterns of African music are, no doubt, an ancient cultural heritage along the Guinea Coast and in western Central Africa. They were most likely invented by peoples who spoke ancestral forms of Niger-Congo languages. It is likely that the area of origin was the Guinea Coast. One explanation for the absence of time-line patterns in the northern half of East Africa is that they were unknown among the first wave of Bantu-language speakers moving eastward from the Cross River area in eastern Nigeria along the fringes of the equatorial forest toward the East African lakes region *c.* 100–400 BC. Another explanation could be the influence in East Africa of Nilotic cultures. The knowledge of time-line patterns might have been brought to western Central Africa with a second migration of Benue-Congo speakers from eastern Nigeria during the Early Iron Age, a time when time-line patterns had already spread eastward across the Niger River. This second migration could have been responsible for the introduction into western Central Africa of a set of cultural traits that include asymmetrical time-line patterns, the single and double bells, masked dancing, secret societies, and certain initiation ceremonies.

With the beginning of the Later Iron Age in Central Africa (*c.* AD 1000), a second nuclear area for time-line patterns apparently developed in southern Zaire; both the 12- and 16-pulse patterns still play an enormous role in the musical traditions of that region. With the third Bantu dispersal, this time from southern Zaire and carrying with it trade connections, the practice of time-line patterns could have reached the Zambezi Valley and the Nyasa–Ruvuma culture area of Tanzania, Malaŵi, and Mozambique—the only areas in the eastern part of the continent where time-line patterns are prominent today.

Inherent note patterns. Closely associated with interlocking techniques but not necessarily depending on them is the composition of inherent note patterns. These are rhythmic and melodic patterns that emerge when series of notes in distinct intervals are played at high speed.

The human ear perceives not isolated particles of sound but a "gestalt." When sequences of many notes are played rapidly, the ear cannot follow each note. As a result, the hearing tends to pick out and regroup the material, forming several melodic-rhythmic patterns that seem independent of one another. Thus, the heard image of the music differs from the pattern of notes actually played. In a series of notes that are large intervals apart, for example, the ear picks out the notes of about the same pitch level and perceives them as a group. This psychological perception of a gestalt—an inherent note pattern—is an important element in listening to and composing some kinds of African instrumental music, particularly in Central and East Africa.

Function of inherent note patterns

Inherent note patterns are not accidental or coincidental; they are recognized and consciously employed by African musicians. In southern Uganda there are even specific terms referring to them. The main function of inherent note patterns is to suggest words—text passages of a song that is outlined by instrumental accompaniment. Thus, in the music of the *ennanga* harp of Uganda, the inherent note patterns suggest certain phrases of the vocal part. In a performance of the traditional harp song "Olutalo olw'e Nsinsi" ("The Battle of the Nsinsi") by the former court musician Evaristo Muyinda, one inherent pattern seemed to speak the words "Batulwanako ab'edda!" ("How They Forget Those Ancients!") long before they were actually sung. Muyinda often introduces a new phrase of text by first accentuating the corresponding inherent rhythm on the *ennanga.* Once the melody is firmly established as a gestalt, it is sung. By slight accentuation or melodic variation during performance, the harpist may bring one or another of the already existing inherent patterns into prominence. This results in a musical development of the song's text.

Tone systems and multipart patterns. Tone systems and multipart patterns have a functional interrelationship in African music. In other words, the kind of multipart pattern occurring in singing or instrumental music is conditional on the type of tone system, and vice versa.

The tonal material used in African musical traditions varies considerably from region to region. Tonal organization, tuning procedures, and intervallic structure depend upon a broad range of human experience. Several factors have determined the shape of tone systems actually in use. One factor mentioned above (see *Musical instruments*) is language, especially with regard to the semantic and grammatical importance of speech tone. Another is the principle of equidistance, the measuring of space or time in equal steps. In addition, in some cross-perceptual associations, such as from aural to visual and vice versa, pitch may be graded in terms of magnitude or altitude. In African music different pitches are not conceptualized as "high" or "low," as they are in English and some other Germanic languages of Europe, but as "small" and "big" or "tiny" and "fat." Consequently, a lamellaphone of middle size, producing middle-range notes, is called *endongo* in Lusoga, a Bantu language spoken in an area of Uganda east of the former Kingdom of Buganda. *Kadongo* (with the diminutive prefix *ka-*) is a high-tuned lamellaphone, while *gadongo* (with the augmentative prefix *ga-*) is a bass instrument. Finally, tonal structure may be influenced by the human experience of sound in nature and the discovery of acoustics.

Broadly speaking, African tone systems may be divided into the following families and subfamilies: (1) equi-tonal systems, based on the principle of equal intervals; (2) monophonic systems, based on octaves, fifths, and fourths; and (3) systems based on the experience of instrumental harmonics.

Equi-tonal systems. Two varieties are found: (1) equi-pentatonic (for example, in southern Uganda); and (2) equi-heptatonic (for example, in the lower Zambezi Valley and in eastern Angola). These tone systems, with either five or seven notes per octave, differ radically from the two Western equal-interval scales, namely the chromatic scale of 12 semitones to the octave (which is equi-dodecatonic) and the whole-tone scale (which is equi-hexatonic). Each step in the whole-tone scale involves an interval of 200 cents (a cent is a measure of frequency, with each semitone in the Western scale equal to 100 cents). In equi-pentatonic systems, on the other hand, the recurrent interval is theoretically 240 cents (*i.e.,* 2.4 semitones of the Western scale), and in equi-heptatonic systems it is 171 cents (or 1.71 semitones).

Difference between African and Western equi-tonal systems

In practice, the intervals in African equi-tonal systems are only approximately equal. For example, there is evidence that the tonal basis of music in southern Uganda, although equi-pentatonic in principle, accommodates a relatively wide deviation from the ideal equidistant interval of 240 cents. The term pen-equidistant has been coined for such a system. The cause of deviation is the presence in the music of that region of certain consonance principles, based on the recognition of simple ratios of fourths and fifths. Thus, the southern Ugandan tone system seems to have two disparate roots, accommodating both the principle of equidistance and the experience of simple ratios. In particular, the natural fourth is the only interval (besides octaves) recognized as consonant; it is therefore used extensively as "harmonic filler" in the interlocking-composition method of that region. No simultaneous fourths occur, and yet the semblance of a fourth-, fifth-, and octave-based "harmony" is established by durational overlapping of the notes struck. Consequently, seconds (240 cents), in contrast to fourths (480 cents), are avoided to a great extent in interlocking composition.

Similarly, in equi-heptatonic systems the desire for harmonic sound may dictate constant adjustments of intonation away from the theoretical interval of 171 cents. One of the most impressive areas in Africa in which a pen-equidistant heptatonic scale is combined with a distinctively harmonic style based on singing in intervals of thirds plus fifths, or thirds plus fourths, is the eastern Angolan culture area. This music is heptatonic and non-modal; *i.e.,* there is no concept of major or minor thirds as distinctive intervals. In principle all the thirds are neutral, but in practice the thirds rendered by the singers often approximate natural major thirds (386 cents), especially at points of rest. In this manner, the principles of equidistance and harmonic euphony are accommodated within one tonal-harmonic system. For the notation of such music, a seven-line stave is most appropriate, with each horizontal line representing one pitch level.

Monophonic systems. These tonal systems, based on octaves, fifths, and fourths (*i.e.,* on the simple ratios 1:2, 2:3, and 3:4), are found in the western Sudanic belt. There are also many pentatonic systems of this kind in the Sahel zone and on the Guinea Coast (such as those of the Fon and Oyo-Yoruba peoples), where no simultaneous sounds occur except octaves.

Systems based on instrumental harmonics. These tone systems may be divided into two subfamilies: (1) that based on the selective use of harmonics from a single fundamental (for example, the system of the Gogo of central Tanzania); and (2) that based on the selective use of harmonics from two or more fundamentals (for example, the systems of the Fang in Gabon and of the !Kung in southwestern Africa, based on harmonics from two fundamentals, and the hexatonic systems of the Lala, Nsenga, Swaka, and Shona in southern and Central Africa, based on more than two fundamentals). All musical cultures employing this type of tone system practice multipart singing. The regions involved are southern Africa, central and southwestern Tanzania, and much of western Central Africa.

Variety of tonal-harmonic systems

The actual shape of the system depends upon whether the tonal material derives from one fundamental or more, upon the conventionalized intervals between these fundamentals (if there is more than one), and upon which section of the natural harmonic series is selected to form the tone system. Depending upon these variables, completely different tonal-harmonic systems may be encountered. The Gogo tone system, illustrated below, is basically tetratonic (within one octave) with a pentatonic extension. It is based on selective use of the sequence of natural harmonics from partials 4 to 9, over a single fundamental.

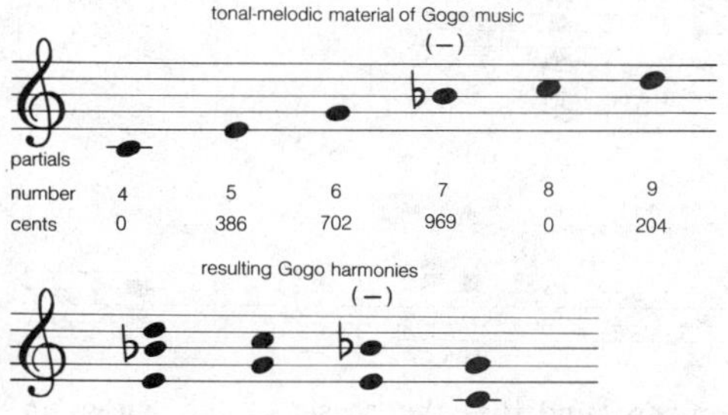

The old tone system (now obsolete) of the Kisi people of Tanzania was hexatonic. It was based on the selective exploitation of the sequence of natural harmonics from partials 6 to 11 over a single fundamental.

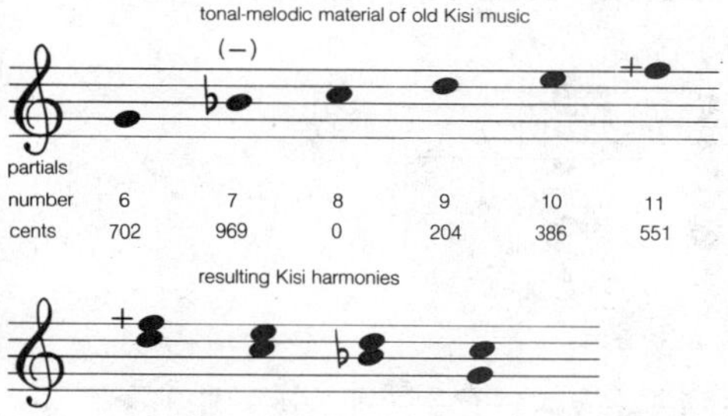

Tone systems based on the use of harmonics from two fundamentals are frequently encountered in areas where the musical bow, particularly the mouth bow in its varieties, is or was an important instrument. Western Central Africa and the whole of southern Africa are the most prominent distribution areas for mouth bows; they are also found in some areas of West Africa.

The tone system of the !Kung people is tetratonic. It may manifest itself, however, in three different versions with different intervals, leading, as in the first of the tunings shown below, to a semitone interval (shown as F–E). Because the melodic and harmonic results of these particular tunings are unique, they provide strong evidence of San heritage in any southern African music in which they occur. In !Kung music the natural harmonic series of each fundamental is not used beyond the fourth partial. This is why fourths, fifths, and octaves are the characteristic simultaneous sounds in !Kung polyphony.

(a) musical-bow tuning at intervals of about 400 cents

(b) musical-bow tuning at intervals of about 300 cents

(c) musical-bow tuning at intervals of about 200 cents

Where, in addition to the second, third, and fourth partials, the fifth partials of each fundamental are also used, hexatonic tone systems arise. The tonal-harmonic system of the Handa-Nkhumbi group in southwestern Angola is one example, based on two fundamentals tuned about 200 cents apart. The resultant chords are thirds and fourths in characteristic positions:

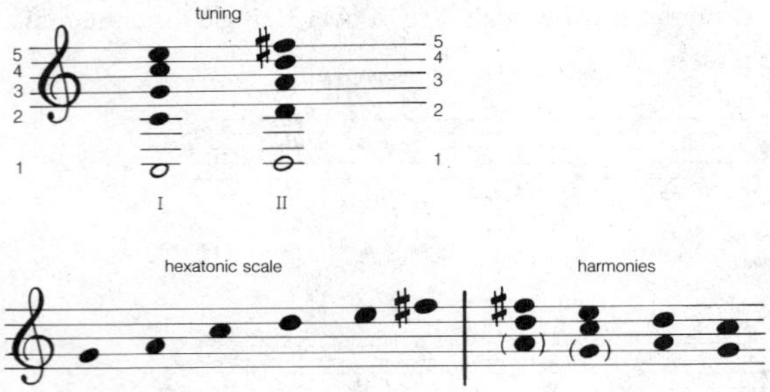

This system also underlies the music of the Xhosa in South Africa. It occurs, too, in some of the music of their neighbours, the Zulu and Swazi, although these latter use a different hexatonic system, based on fundamentals tuned about 100 cents apart. This tuning, used on the Zulu *ugubhu* gourd bow, has three semitone intervals:

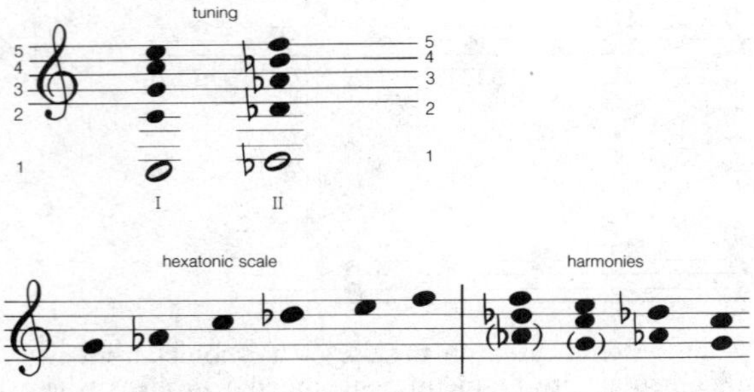

Multipart singing. Multipart singing and harmonic concepts are basic traits of many African musical traditions and have been observed by Western travelers since the earliest periods of contact. Contrary to earlier opinions, "harmony" in African music is now seen to be not a result of acculturation but rather indigenous to many parts of the continent. Polyphonic singing styles were almost certainly used by prehistoric hunters in Central and southern Africa. Among the San, the discovery of the use of the hunting bow as a musical instrument, and with it the discovery of the harmonics of a stretched string, constituted a cluster of traits that were probably interdependent. Questions raised in the 19th and early 20th centuries as to whether the hunting bow or the musical bow was invented first are certainly irrelevant in the culture of southern African prehistoric hunters.

Multipart singing in African music embraces two entirely different approaches, homophonic and polyphonic, with the definition of these words adapted to African cultures.

Homophonic vocal styles. In these styles all melodic lines, though at different pitch levels, are rhythmically the same, and they begin and end together. Individual singers conceive of their voice lines—all carrying the same text—as identical in principle, only sung at different levels. Men sing "with a big voice" (*i.e.,* in low voices), women and children "with small voices" (*i.e.,* high voices). Their voices may stand a third, a fourth, a fifth, or an octave apart, but they are considered to sing the same tune. In practice, though, not only parallel, but also oblique and contrary, motion may occur. To what extent the latter is permitted depends upon the tolerance within the tonality of the particular language. For example, in eastern Angola contrary motion is normal practice. In other cultures movement is strictly parallel within the structure of the tone system concerned.

Homophonic multipart singing is found in particular concentration along the Guinea Coast. It is also found throughout western Central Africa, among most peoples of Angola, Zambia, and Malaŵi, and in many parts of East Africa. In northern Central Africa it is found among the Azande and related peoples. In southwestern parts of the Central African Republic there is three-part harmonic singing with vocal parts shifting chromatically between two roots one semitone apart. Homophonic vocal styles are often linked to a call-and-response (leader–chorus) form.

Polyphonic vocal styles. In these styles the complementary individual lines differ in their rhythm and phrasing and carry different texts or syllables. They may be of different length, and their starting and ending points do not coincide. Such styles are more restricted geographically. The vocal music of the San communities in southwestern Africa is predominantly polyphonic, as are the vocal styles of Pygmy groups in the Ituri Forest and the upper Sangha River area of the Congo and the Central African Republic. (The San and Pygmy peoples, whose polyphonic styles and tone systems are based on different principles, have often mistakenly been lumped together in evolutionist theories.) In other parts of Africa, isolated islands of polyphonic singing occur among or between largely homophonic communities. Thus, the otherwise homophonic Gogo people employ polyphonic techniques in their *saigwa* and *msunyunho* songs, and Nyakyusa children of southwestern Tanzania use yodel and polyphony in a song type called *kibota.*

Geographic distribution

A distinct style of polyphonic singing is found in much of the music of the peoples of the lower Zambezi Valley, in parts of Mozambique, and also in Zimbabwe, as exemplified by the Karanga-Shona threshing song shown here:

This is a diagrammatic transcription showing the relationships between the five male voice parts (here transposed one octave and five semitones higher). In actual performance the voices enter consecutively, each starting from the double bar in his particular line and then repeatedly backtracking to the beginning of the line. The entry point for voices 2 and 3 is one pulse after the commencement of the last note of voice 1. When voice 1 repeats his line, his second syllable signals the entry point for voices 4 and 5. The cycle (which is continually repeated) is 18 pulses long. The harmonic scheme comprises a sequence of bichords in fourths and fifths, characteristic of much Shona music. The roots of these bichords, E A C / E G C, are shown above the top staff. The tone system here is hexatonic.

Polyphony is also prevalent in South Africa and Swaziland. In the dance-songs of the Nguni people (including the Zulu, Xhosa, Swazi, and Ndebele), two or more voice parts, commencing at different points in the cycle, often overlap extensively. At least two parts, solo and chorus, are always regarded as essential. In fact, a solo vocalist singing the entire song usually does not complete a single voice part but instead shifts from one part to another when he arrives at the entry point of each part.

The Zulu bow song transcribed below begins with the bow phrase, which simulates a chorus part. During repetitions of this ostinato, the voices (sung in this transcription by Zulu princess Constance Magogo kaDinuzulu, her son Chief Mangosuthu Gatsha Buthelezi, and several of his young children) enter in turn, each beginning at its double bar: first, voice 1, then, in subsequent repetitions of the 16-pulse cycle, voices 2 and 3. The lines shown below the song may be rendered by additional singers or by voices 2 and 3 as occasional variants.

This song sounds very different indeed from the previous Shona example, mainly on account of its tone system, which has two semitone intervals. A pentatonic variant of the Zulu hexatonic system cited above, it is based on two instrumental roots a semitone apart. The melodic line produced on the *ugubhu* gourd bow employs harmonic partials 3 and 4 of the two fundamentals B and C, these harmonics being selectively resonated by moving the open end of the gourd resonator closer to or farther from the player's chest.

Similar structures underlying different tone systems

Despite the marked tonal dissimilarity between the Shona and Zulu songs, they clearly share an almost identical underlying formal structure, based on the principle of deliberately nonaligned, overlapping voice parts that retain the same relationship to one another through all successive repetitions of the song. The relationships of their parts can be demonstrated by concentric circles, in which clockwise rotation represents a cycle, or strophe, of the song, which is continually repeated.

All the vocal music considered above has as its basis some kind of tone system. Among the Zulu and other Nguni peoples, however, certain non-melodic forms of chanting coexist alongside melodic styles of performance—even among items that fit the same category of "dance-song"—

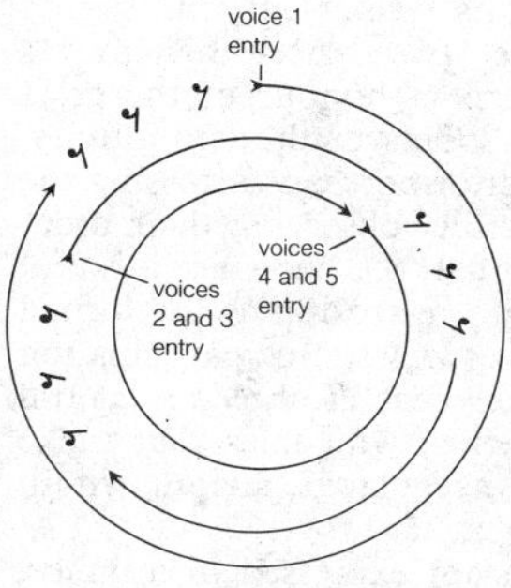

Karanga-Shona threshing song (18-pulse cycle)

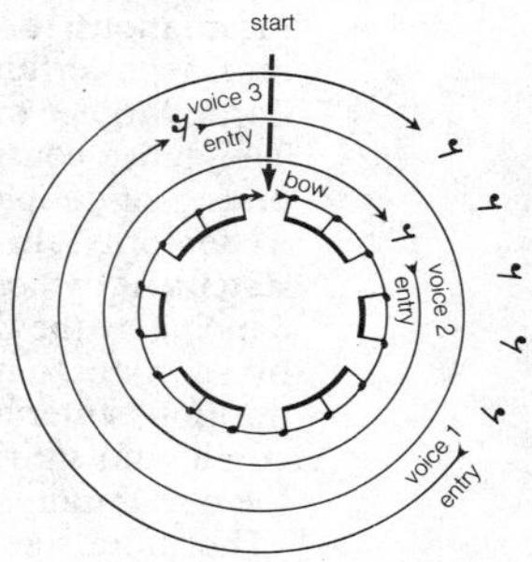

Zulu part-song (16-pulse cycle)

just as some English nursery rhymes are sung while others are recited or chanted. In such cases, fixed musical pitches are absent, and a singsong form of rhythmical recitation is used instead. The close affinity of such pieces with melodic songs is confirmed by their sharing of the same circular, multipart formal structure.

There is indeed evidence from many different parts of Africa of the use of intermediate vocal styles, falling somewhere between the extremes of speech and song. In many African cultures the boundary between the two does not tally exactly with the Western, demonstrating that definitions of music and song are culture-specific.

(G.K./D.K.R.)

Dance

THE CULTURAL POSITION OF DANCE

In African societies, dance serves a complex diversity of social purposes. Within an indigenous dance tradition, each performance usually has a principal as well as a number of subsidiary purposes, which may express or reflect the communal values and social relationships of the people. In order to distinguish between the variety of dance styles, therefore, it is necessary to establish the purpose for which each dance is performed.

Merging of ritual and recreation

Often there is no clear distinction between ritual celebration and social recreation in dance performances; one purpose can merge into the other, as in the appearance of the great Efe mask at the height of the Gelede ritual festival in the Ketu-Yoruba villages of Nigeria and Benin (see Figure 5). At midnight the mask dramatically appears

Frank Speed

Figure 5: A Gelede masquerader dancing in the courtyard of the Ibara palace in Abeokuta, Nigeria.

to the expectant community, its wearer uttering potent incantations to placate witches. The dancer then moves into a powerful stamping dance in honour of the great Earth Mother and the women elders of the community. The dance continues as the performer pauses to sing the praises of people of rank, carefully observing their order of seniority. In this way a ritual act becomes a social statement, which then flows into recreation as the formal dancing by the Gelede team gives way to free participation by spectators until sunrise. The great Efe holds a central position, entertaining his audience with tales that make comic and satiric reference to irregular behaviour within the community over the past year.

The more significant the concept expressed in a dance, the greater the appreciation of the audience and the more insistent their demands for a skillful performance and for movements that fit its purpose. Dance is appreciated as a social occasion but is simultaneously enjoyed as an activity in its own right, entertaining and giving pleasure as an expression of communal life.

The religious context. Thought systems traditional to African cultures are rooted in a world view in which there is continuous interaction between spiritual forces and the community. Spiritual beings may inhabit natural elements or animals and may also take possession of human mediums. This possession of persons is usually temporary and confined to ritual, as when the priest of the Yoruba god Shango dances into a state of deep trance at the annual festival, expressing the wrath of the god of thunder with the lightning speed of his arm gestures and the powerful roll of his shoulders (see Figure 6, top). In Zimbabwe the Mhondora spirit mediums, who relate the Shona people to the guardian spirits of the dead, enter a trance through the music of the *mbira* lamellaphone (or thumb piano), to which they sing while performing simple, repetitive foot patterns. Thus, the dances of priests and mediums confirm their ritual leadership.

Dance is used as therapy by ritual societies in many cultures. Hausa women, for example, find healing through dance and spirit possession in the Bori cult. Among the Jukun of Nigeria, a similar organization is called the Ajun, whose elders deal with hysterical disorders in women by exorcising evil spirits in initiation ceremonies. During a three-month period in a house shrine, the sufferer is taught songs and dances that have a therapeutic function culminating in a ceremony in which the initiate publicly joins the members of the society to perform the Ajun-Kpa dance (see Figure 6, bottom). The female spirit mediums of the Kalabari in the Niger Delta, using dance and song as an essential part of their therapy, are also credited with powers of healing.

Many African religions are based on a bond of continuity between the living and their dead ancestors, who, in some cultures, return as masquerade performers to guide and judge the living. The complex web of human relationships is continuously renewed and restated at ritual festivals through the arts.

Masquerade dancers. Masquerade dancers are a feature of religious societies in many areas. Four main types of masquerader are identified by the roles they play: those who embody deities or nature spirits and to whom sacrifice is made to assure the fertility of land and people, those who embody the ancestral spirits, those who placate the spirits through their dance, and those who perform principally as entertainers.

Animal masks

Animal masks are a common feature of masking societies throughout Africa. In Mali the Tyiwara spirit masqueraders of the Bambara people carry formalized carvings of antelopes and other wild animals, dancing in imitation of their movements to promote the fertility of land and community (see Figure 15). The Isinyaso masked dancers of the Yao and Maku peoples of Tanzania carry elaborate bamboo structures covered with cloth and raffia, which sway rhythmically while their Nteepana mask elongates to great heights as the embodiment of a powerful animal spirit.

The type of mask influences the style of the masquerade dance. The Ikpelweme ancestral masqueraders of the Afemai people of Bendel State, Nigeria, wear richly coloured,

Figure 6: *Ritual dancing in Nigeria.*
(Top) Yoruba performing a dance in honour of the god Shango. (Bottom) Jukun women dancing the Ajun-Kpa, which exorcises evil spirits and heals members of their cult.

Frank Speed

close-fitting costumes with face masks and elaborate headpieces of embroidered cloth, which allow for a dance that accelerates into a climax of rapid, abrupt movement. The Nago and Akakayi ancestral masqueraders of the Gwari wear close-fitting head and body coverings, which permit rapid, staccato movements while dancing at the "second burial" (*i.e.,* the post-burial celebrations) of a leader of the community. The Egungun ancestral masqueraders of Yorubaland appear in a wide variety of loosely flowing cloth or palm-leaf costumes, often with carved headpieces. The heavier the mask, the less freedom for dance. For example, Epa masqueraders of the Ekiti-Yoruba carry carved helmet masks with elaborate superstructures whose weight allows only the type of movement fitting the stately processional dances that confirm the masqueraders' role of ritual leadership. Masked stilt dancers, such as those of the Makonde of Tanzania, are largely restricted to rhythmic strides and gestures; in contrast, the simple cloth costumes of ancestral Egungun Elewe of the Igbomina-Yoruba allow for a dance of acrobatic skill, and the light raffia Igo masks of the neighbouring Edo people enable them to lift their costumes above their heads in a dance of whirling turns.

Secular masqueraders who perform as entertainers have emerged from the ritual societies. The Egungun entertainers of the Oyo-Yoruba, for example, perform at Egungun ancestral festivals, but they may be invited to perform for a fee as entertainers, often traveling to neighbouring towns to earn money (although they are obliged to offer sacrifices to their ancestors before performing). The company members usually start with popular acrobatic dances and then display their magic powers by changing into a series of animal and masked figures. They use an inventive range of mime and dance to praise gods and heroes, to satirize politicians and wrongdoers, and to ridicule strangers,

Figure 7: Mask representing the *mwanapwo*, a mythical figure of a young woman who died. It is one of the prominent figures in masked performances by the Chokwe and related peoples in the eastern Angolan-northwestern Zambian culture area.
G. Kubik

such as visiting Hausa traders or Europeans, with wit and humour. Accompanied by singers and led by a drum ensemble, they present a form of communal or folk theatre.

Masqueraders may play an individual role, as with the circumciser during the initiation rites of the young Nyanga men in eastern Zaire. Initially he dances as a masquerade to send the boys out of the village to their ritual seclusion, where he taunts the initiates before and after the rites of circumcision. As an authoritative figure, he inspires awe in women and children. In some cultures masquerade performance is not allowed to be seen by women, and nocturnal performances are often used to control women and even threaten them into accepting their social role. This is aided by the fact that in many forms of masquerade the body of the carrier is entirely covered in order to hide his identity, and his voice may be distorted by a kazoo (or voice disguiser).

The social context. In all African cultures, dance, music, and song help define the role of the individual and the group within the community. In hierarchical societies a ruler is expected to state his authority in formal dances, and failure to meet the required standard may seriously damage his prestige.

At the crowning of an *oba* (king) in Yorubaland, for example, the ruler leads a procession through the town as he dances with upright carriage and dignified step, his gestures dictated by the nature of his kingly role and the insignia he carries. His wives follow, interpreting the rhythms in a style suitable to their rank, inclining forward from the waist with their attention respectfully directed toward the earth. When the *oba* is seated in state, his war chiefs greet him, each with his appropriate dance rhythm. The hunters then dance to their rapid and complex beat. Palace chiefs and women market chiefs have their own distinctive music, song, and dance to praise the ruler, and girls, young men, and children honour him with dances appropriate to their status.

Children's dances

Dance is also important as an educational tool. Repetitive dances teach children physical control and stress accepted standards of conduct. Children may form their own dance and masquerade groups, join adults at the end of a dance line, or simply have a space allocated to them in a performing area at the time of a festival. In some places, particularly in West Africa, boys have their own masked dances in training for membership in adult societies. Throughout Africa children enjoy dance games, as when Makindu boys of Kenya sing as they play leapfrog to a dance rhythm (see Figure 8, top).

In societies that stress horizontal stratification into age sets, the qualities proper to a particular age are expressed in dances, as in those that keep young men physically fit and teach them the discipline necessary in warfare. The dances of young Zulu and Ndebele men in southern Africa recall the victories of past warriors. Among the Owo-Yoruba the stately Totorigi dance is for senior men and women, while adolescent boys perform the lively Ajabure with ceremonial swords. The transition from one age grade to the next may be marked by rites and festivities. In initiation rites for adolescents, dances may stress sexual fertility as well as customary behaviour between the sexes. In the Otufo initiation rites for girls among the Ga of Ghana, dance is part of their preparation for womanhood and enables them to display their charms to suitors. Young Kaka men of Cameroon perform their Midimu dance after the circumcision rites as a formal precondition of admission into the society of adults.

In some areas dances are designed to be performed during funeral rites, after burial ceremonies, and at anniversaries. Dances may be created for a specific purpose, as in the Igogo dance of the Owo-Yoruba, when young men use stamping movements to pack the earth of the grave into place. In Fulani communities in Cameroon, the corpse is placed in a sitting position in a prominent place, and solo and communal dances are performed in the deceased's honour. In some areas a circle dance surrounds the men performing the required ritual autopsy.

Thus, dance plays a cathartic role during the key transition from one social state to another: a child is welcomed into the community at his naming ceremony; an adolescent is initiated into the responsibilities of adult life; a woman moves from her paternal home to join her husband's family; an elder receives recognition for service in the form of a title; a member leaves the community to join the world of the spirits. The individual is not left alone to bear the emotions that accompany critical change, as members of the community carry him and his family through the crisis with appropriate ceremonies containing the emotions of the moment in music, song, and dance.

Division between the sexes. Within traditions of long standing in many cultures, it is unusual for men and women to dance in direct relation to each other, and they seldom perform the same style of dance—though combination of the sexes is more common in areas where the original dance has been disrupted by non-African forms. Idealized male and female qualities are normally expressed in the movement patterns of their separate dances: for example, Tiv men dance with an attack of rapid, forceful movements expressing masculinity, whereas the women dance with a sustained grace reflecting their femininity. If men and women join a common dance circle, their dance patterns are usually distinct, as with the Kambari of Nigeria: men and women dance to the same musical rhythm, but they hold different postures, with the women singing and using a simpler foot pattern than the men.

Idealized male and female dance styles

Dance occasions for formalized flirtation between the sexes before marriage are common, as in the Sikya dance of the Akan of Ghana. The Bororo of western Cameroon celebrate the coming of the dry season with a dance for young men and women, and couples pair off at the climax of the performance. Among the Nupe of Nigeria ribald songs and joking insults between the sexes have replaced performances allowing for sexual license at harvest festivals. The dances of Ika men and girls (western Igbo, Nigeria) have become openly erotic since the early 1960s, when a master dancer brought the sexes together in a single dance team to entertain visitors to the palace of the *oba* of Agbor in Nigeria. Thus, erotic patterns of dance movement are encouraged in some societies, usually with bawdy humour, whereas the limits of flirtation are clearly defined in others for the sake of social decorum.

Work dances. Men who work together often celebrate a successful project with beer drinking and vigorous dances expressing their occupational skills. In Nigeria, Nupe fishermen are renowned for their net throwing, which they formalize into dance patterns, and young Irigwe farmers on the Jos Plateau leap to encourage the growth of crops at festivals related to the agricultural cycle. Occupational guilds and professional organizations of experts, such as blacksmiths, hunters, or wood-carvers, have their own expressive dances.

Figure 8: *Play and work dances.*
(Top) Wakamba boys playing leapfrog to a dance rhythm, Makindu, Kenya. (Bottom) Tutsi hunters performing the ceremonial lion dance, Kivu, Zaire. The headdress is symbolic of a lion's mane.
(Top) Bill Horman—FPG, (bottom) George Holton—Photo Researchers, Inc./EB Inc.

Hunters may reenact their exploits or mime the movements of animals as a ritual means of controlling wild beasts and allaying their own fears. The Akan of Ghana perform the Abofor dance, a dance-mime staged after the killing of a dangerous animal. This is meant to placate the spirit of the beast and inform the community of the manner in which it was killed. Tutsi hunters in Zaire commemorate a successful hunt in their lion dance (see Figure 8, bottom).

Dance as recreation. Dance is the most popular form of recreation in Africa. In towns, men and women of all ages meet informally in dance clubs to dance to the rhythms of popular musicians. In villages there may be opportunities in the evenings for informal dancing, but relations between the sexes there are more tightly controlled.

Highlife and other westernized dances

Highlife was a style of urban recreational dance popular in West Africa in the 1950s. It originated in Ghana, where musicians adopted Western dance-band instruments at open-air nightclubs to celebrate the exuberant spirit of independence. In Nigeria, local instruments were used as the Yoruba created *juju* rhythms, while the Tiv danced the Swange. Francophone countries elaborated the Latin-American rhythms of the cha-cha, while southern Africans danced to the modern African beats of the *kwela.* Zairian dance bands excelled in the creation of their own popular dance music. These have given way to styles influenced by Caribbean reggae and Western pop music, but they retain a distinctly African character.

DANCE STYLE

Although often similar in social purpose, dances are realized in radically different styles in the multitude of diverse cultures of Africa. Movement patterns vary greatly from one culture to another, depending upon the way in which environmental, historical, and social circumstances have been articulated in working, social, and recreational movements.

People living on dry, spacious farmlands, for example, have different movement habits from those living in swamplands. For farmers of the savanna, the ground is solid and their space open to the far horizon. They place their feet firmly on the sunbaked earth as they follow their team leader on the circular path of their dance, performing simple foot patterns at a steady tempo.

The Ijo people, who live in the mangrove swamps of the Niger Delta, traditionally wrest an uneasy living by fishing creeks and rivers. As they dance, they lean forward from the hips, their torsos almost parallel with the earth as they use a precision of light, rapid foot beats, moving their weight from heel to toe to side of foot in a variety of rhythmic patterns, as though balancing on an unsteady canoe or picking their way through the swamp. Many other riverine peoples mime paddling in their dances.

Manipulating their flowing gowns as an extension of gesture in stately, measured dances, the Kanuri of Maiduguri in northeastern Nigeria conserve energy with economy of movement—a common feature in the dance of desert peoples. By contrast, some forest dwellers dance freely. The southern Yoruba continuously alter their foot patterns and sequence of movements at the dictates of the leading drummer. Their movements suggest finding a way through forest undergrowth, which necessitates reactions ever alert to the unexpected.

Working movements feed into styles of dance. The bend of the knees accompanying the swing of a farmer's machete may be elaborated in a dance pattern. Architecture, furniture, and dress are among features that also influence posture and gesture, producing a distinctive use of energy. The Kambari of Nigeria continuously bend forward to enter their low doors, and their dance posture reflects this habit. The Jukun sit on low stools or on the floor with legs crossed or extended; their flexible knees and strong leg tendons allow for the performance of continuous deep knee bends in their dance movements.

Change and disruption of traditional styles

These cultural influences in the development of dance style have been offset by such historical events as migrations, wars, and slave trading, which have displaced people as refugees over the centuries, changed their habitation patterns, and brought them in touch with new environments. The development of trade routes introduced influences from Arabic and other cultures. Conversion to Christian and Muslim faiths severely disrupted ritual and ceremonial life and thus often disturbed the traditional patterns sustaining music and dance. Colonialism also resulted in the dissipation of cultural homogeneity and the gathering of disparate dance patterns into new styles.

Dance formations. There are four principal African dance formations: a dance team using a formalized floor pattern; a group using a free-flow floor pattern; a group using a formation from which solo dancers emerge to display their individual skills; and the performance of a solo dancer—usually a ruler, ritual specialist, herbalist, or comic entertainer—who may be supported by a group of musicians.

The most common form of dance within the indigenous traditions of Africa is a team dance performed either in a closed circle, with the dancers facing the centre, or in a line following a circular path that is often centred on the musicians. The dancers usually move along the circle line in a counterclockwise direction. In egalitarian societies the circular team dances are a marked expression of the close-knit fraternity within an age grade, as with Tiv men, while Tiv women express their relationship within the extended family through their own circle dance.

Dance teams using straight linear formations are common in cultures with a strong warrior tradition, where a strict spatial discipline is required, as in the Shangani war dances in Zimbabwe. They also are common with people prone to borrow from other cultures, as with the Igbo boys' dances in eastern Nigeria, in which the formation of a number of lines suggests Western patterns of drill. Some migratory cultures favour the line, as do Fulani girls, who form a tightly knit unit with their arms around one another's waists as they perform simple step rhythms from side to side, and the Masai, with their high-jumping dance pattern.

A linear or circular floor pattern is used in cultures

employing a combination of team and soloist. The Olu Kanaanwa dance for unmarried Igbo girls is done in unison in a circular formation, from which each dancer breaks away to perform individually in the centre. Among Ijo women, the dance starts in a loosely knit semicircular line from which virtuoso performers move out toward the spectators. The Urhobo of Nigeria use a loose, linear formation, the soloists dancing toward and away from the musicians. As the tempo of the drumming mounts, individuals dance into an ecstatic trance in which they are caught and controlled by dance organizers. A more ordered line-and-soloist pattern is used by Ashanti women in the Kumasi district of Ghana in their Adua dance, which is notable for elaborating expressive hand movements into a language of gestures.

Dance team organization

The members of dance teams who perform on occasions of social importance are related within an age grade, an extended family, a working guild, a social club, or a ritual society whose elders provide sponsorship, respond to invitations, settle financial arrangements with external bodies, and discipline spectators and dancers at performances. A woman elder is usually the "mother" of the dance, attending to the comfort of the dancers and encouraging them by ululating during the performance. The elders select the team leader on the basis of skill, organizing ability, and creative flair. The leader selects the dancers, arranges and runs rehearsals, and is responsible to the elders for the appropriate dress of the performers. In some cultures the leader may compose songs requiring an elaboration of gesture or new movement patterns, which he or she will then choreograph. In cultures in which the dancers sing either before or during the dance, the leader initiates the singing.

In performance the leader heads the dance line or performs alone in a clearly defined space. The leader responds to the musicians and takes artistic responsibility for the dance interpretation of the music on behalf of the team, which usually follows the leader's movements in unison. In formal team dancing, creative innovations are planned and practiced in rehearsals.

Dance posture. There are three characteristic dance postures. An upright posture with a straight back is used as an expression of authority in the dance of chiefs and priests. In the second posture the dancer inclines forward from the hips, moving his attention and gestures toward the ground. In the third posture the dancer holds the torso nearly parallel to the ground, taking the body weight onto the balls of the feet. Many riverine people use this posture. The downward stress toward the earth does not necessarily imply that the dancer is heavy-footed. In some cultures the dancers use the full foot in stamping out the rhythms, while in others they may leap or perform light foot movements.

Rhythm. African dances are earth-centred. Dancers repeatedly return to the earth as they give themselves to the rhythmic pulses of their dance, interpreting the percussive patterns of the music through their postures, gestures, and steps. They externalize rhythmic patterns in the surrounding space by moving through, rather than to, fixed positions in the space surrounding the body. Thus, the criteria for assessing skill are based on rhythmic rather than spatial precision. Rhythm is provided for the dancer by musicians playing percussive instruments, by singers, or by a combination of music and song. In some cultures the dancers themselves sing or play musical instruments as they perform. Normally the musicians lead the dancers, although there are cultures in which the dancer takes over the initiative and sets up a dialogue of rhythmic exchange.

A dancer is assessed primarily on his ability to follow the percussive musical rhythm, "to play the drums with his feet" or with whatever part of the body articulates the rhythm. Each dance style is immediately identified by its characteristic rhythmic pattern. In some cultures the rhythmic patterns are expressed in foot patterns, in others in contractions of the torso, strong shoulder beats, rapid vibrations or twists of the buttocks, or acrobatic leaps.

A wide variety of rhythmic patterns form the basis of dance in Africa. The most basic is the continuous repetition of a simple beat at a steady tempo for the duration of a dance. This may continue for days, as in the Akbia women's funeral dance in the southern Sudan and the dances of the Mbuti Pygmies of Central Africa.

Instrumental accompaniment

Teams of savanna farmers on the Jos Plateau play instruments as they dance, using simple, repetitive rhythmic phrases. Angas men of West Africa blow 14 large buffalo horns as they perform the repetitive step pattern of the Rumada dance in a circle, following the line or moving in and out of the centre. Neighbouring Chip men perform a light run, playing flutes of four different pitches that combine to form a rhythmic melody. At the end of each phrase the dancers turn toward the centre of their circle to perform a climax of light hopping movements as they play. In many styles of circle dance the music is divided into a number of separate sections, each with its own distinct rhythm and related dance pattern, as in the Lmele le dag Chun dance of the Birom girls of the Jos Plateau.

The Igbo dance to a complex of sophisticated rhythms. In the Ubi-Ogazu dance, a version of the popular Atilogwu performed by a boys' team, the adult leader dances while playing a small flute to lead the rhythm. He is supported by a single-membrane drum, a pot drum, two simple xylophones, and a bamboo gong. The dance has at least 10 variations, each with a distinct rhythm dictating its own movement pattern. As in most African dances, the rhythm gives the name to the dance steps: in the Ikpo Okme, the performers hop from one foot to the other; for Ebenebe, a stamping pattern leads into a cartwheel; Iza requires an upright carriage with high kicks; Nkpopi is a leaping dance; Etukwa requires the torso to be inclined to the earth as the feet drum a staccato beat; Nzaukwu Nabi is a stamping step with sudden pauses.

In the Ubi-Ogazu ("Guinea Fowl"; named for the bird that inspired a hunter to create the dance), the performers hold bird-topped, carved staves for an initial dance in which they execute birdlike hops in a circle. They then drop the staves in favour of horse-tail switches held in both hands as they form two lines facing each other for the main performance. The performers wear brief skirts with girdles of brass bells and seedpod rattles around their ankles to accentuate their movements. The regular introduction of new themes calls for innovation in the dance rhythms. The girls' and women's teams use a more flowing quality of movement that elaborates the intertwining rhythms played by an ensemble or sung by a choir at varying tempos.

While months of practice are required before an Igbo dance team is permitted by the elders to perform on a public occasion, a Yoruba dancer may develop new patterns within the dance style during performance. The Yoruba Apala dance allows individuals to move on a free-flow floor pattern. Each dancer competes with his fellows in the interpretation of the rhythm and in his swift response to change. The leading drummer leaves the ensemble to join an outstanding dancer in a rhythmic exchange in which he praises and urges him into yet greater feats of invention, the drum's tones speaking recognizable proverbs from the tonal Yoruba language. The dancer performs a variety of subtle foot patterns leading into turns, kicks, or small, neat jumps. He flourishes his horse-tail switch and swirls or holds his flowing robe as he continuously alters his tempo at the dictates of the drum.

The Swange is a form of urban recreational dance among the Tiv in which men and women dance together. This dance uses the circle formation familiar in village dances and adapts traditional musical themes to highlife rhythms played on a combination of Tiv and Hausa instruments. The climax of the evening is provided by a solo dancer who improvises freely, using movements from many styles of Tiv dance in a rhythmic dialogue with the lead drummer.

Change and tradition. Scholars studying the emergence of new styles of dance in Africa have distinguished three related forms: traditional, neo-traditional, and contemporary. The last two categories have become increasingly evident as the result of radical social changes since World War II.

Changes in traditional dance styles within a village usually occur gradually, under the creative leadership of master dancers. But major social changes in the community, such as the introduction of formal primary education, radically alter the pattern of life—including children's attitudes toward their dances, which they no longer have time to learn in the inherited manner. Modern transport and communication bring together people of diverse cultures, resulting in cross-cultural influences on dance performance. The spread of transistor radios in villages has caused young people to turn to new styles of dance, with an accent on entertainment. When a master dancer dies, there is often no one to replace him, but the changing patterns of life stimulate creative individuals to build new expressive patterns.

An example of change can be seen in the Sogoni Koun masquerade dancers of the Dogon in Mali, who carry a wide range of carved wooden masks, some surmounted by geometric shapes up to 12 feet high. The masks are so lightly constructed that they do not hamper the vigorous dances of the carriers as they bend to touch the earth, traditionally to honour the dead during funeral rites. According to one theory, the geographic isolation of the Dogon protected the masking societies from changes affecting other Malian cultures, until the introduction of a cash economy forced the young men who carried the masks to migrate to labour markets. They returned with urban tastes and habits, altering the social pattern on which the masking traditions were based. The traditions were further threatened by the spread of Islām.

In the 1930s the establishment of the Malian Tourist Office created a new role for the dancers as entertainers for colonial officers. This later developed into regular paid performances for tourists visiting the villages. Dance leaders tailored performances to run for a limited time, using a performing area unrelated to the funeral rites and therefore necessitating a different pattern of movement and positioning of performers. The dances stressed spectacular movements but lost the social purpose that had infused them with dramatic vitality. The masks are now decorated with commercial paints and the dancers concerned with commercial reward. As members of the Malian National Folk Lore Troupe, they gain prestige as ambassadors for their country at international festivals. Radical changes continue as dancers travel to work in urban centres, where Western forms of entertainment on radio, film, and television have become part of life.

A major catalyst of change is the staging of civic arts festivals organized by government ministries to promote the traditional arts as a means of enhancing national unity. Cultural officers visit villages and hold competitions to select the best dancers to compete against performers of other styles within their own culture. The winners are then taken to urban centres to compete with dancers from other cultures. If successful, they proceed to the capital to compete at the national level for prestigious trophies.

Corruption of traditional dances

When a village dance is taken out of its original context to be performed for an audience whose members regard it purely as entertainment or as a taste of exotic culture, however, the motivation of the dancers changes radically. The dance's original purpose is replaced by the pursuit of financial gain and prestige. Cultural officers rearrange the performances by stipulating their duration and by concentrating spectacular movements from a number of dances into a single performance. Costumes are changed to suit the occasion or express national sentiment. Exits, entrances, and floor patterns are altered to accommodate the design of a modern stage. In this way, the original social purpose of the dance as understood by an acculturated audience is destroyed, and a style of neo-traditional dance emerges.

Ritual dances are usually unsuccessful at national festivals. The performance of a priest, whose dance movements are part of a ritual context, loses the vitality that is dependent on response from members of his own culture. On the other hand, the highly organized dance teams of the Tiv are accustomed to performing on a variety of social occasions within their village tradition. Their well-established discipline of rehearsal makes the transition to a modern stage possible and has had spectacular results.

Thus, some cultures, particularly the more egalitarian, welcome new experiences and can adjust to fresh challenges—though, with continuous repetition for predominantly commercial motives, even spectacular dances like the Igbo Atilogwu or the Zulu war dance can become hackneyed and faded. Other cultures are more conservative toward change, particularly those whose way of life is based on highly structured, hierarchical social and ritual patterns. (P.H.)

Architecture

Compared with the immense literature on African art, particularly sculpture, published since 1920, remarkably little attention has been paid to indigenous African architecture. Of the buildings of the continent south of the Sahara, only the ruins of Great Zimbabwe are widely known. This complex of stone enclosures, particularly those popularly termed the elliptical building and the acropolis, was built on sites established as early as the 3rd century AD. The first Shona phase of building was probably begun six centuries later, continuing until the 15th century when, under the Mwene Matapa, or "Ravager of Nations," in this gold-bearing district, Zimbabwe reached its peak.

Great Zimbabwe

Important though Great Zimbabwe is, in many ways it is not representative of African architecture. First, it is built of stone. As an archaeological site, it has a massive defensive wall and, included in the elliptical building, a conical tower of unknown purpose. It is also monumental in scale, having functioned as a royal citadel, and has become a national symbol. While some of these features can be found in other examples of African building, they are rare, and the emphasis on Zimbabwe has been at the expense of other architectural forms.

Arab and Berber architecture of Egypt and North Africa have had an impact on African architecture south of the Sahara. Similarly, the states of the Persian Gulf and the Red Sea have influenced architectural types in the Sudan, the Horn of Africa, and the coasts of Kenya and Tanzania, where the Muslim presence has also been strong. These influences are discussed below (see *Influences of Islām and Christianity*).

GEOGRAPHIC INFLUENCES

African architectural types reflect the interaction of environmental factors—such as natural resources, climate, and vegetation—with the economies and population densities of the continent's various regions. As the most durable of building materials, stone survives from the past, while other materials have succumbed to rain, rot, or termites. Stone-walled kraals from early Sotho and Tswana settlements (Transvaal; Botswana), and stone-lined pit circles with sunken kraals for pygmy cattle (Zimbabwe), have been the subject of archaeological study. Stone-corbeled shelters and circular huts with thatched roofs have also been recorded in the 20th century among the southern Sotho. Rectangular and circular stone farmhouses, unusual in being two-story, have been built by the Tigre of Ethiopia for centuries, while in Niger the sedentary Tuareg build square houses in stone.

Principal construction materials

Such exceptions apart, the overwhelming majority of Africa's 5,000 peoples build in grasses, wood, and clay. Constructions tend to be light, with much of the material for building transportable. Owing to the impermanence of many of these materials, the dwellings, though based on forms many centuries old, are of relatively recent date. Where vegetation is largely confined to thin grazing, peoples are often nomadic, using animal skins and woven hair for cover. In the veld and less-forested areas, grasses are used as building material as well, being employed widely for thatch and mat roof coverings. Hardwoods in the forest regions are used for building, though bamboo and raffia palm are also often used. Earth and clay constitute a major building resource, the characteristic soils of much of Africa being semidesert chestnut earths and laterites (reddish residuals of rock decay), which are often low in fertility but easily compacted. Earth-sheltered housing is made by the Iraqw of Tanzania, and a number of peoples in Mali and Burkina Faso have partly sunken dwellings. In general, however, Africans do not excavate.

Ecological and demographic factors play an important part in building design. Nomads are in decline, while

Figure 9: Aerial view of the ruins of Great Zimbabwe.
ZEFA

the prevalence of the tsetse fly limits the extent of pastoralism. Past migrations have had a profound effect on the dispersal of house types. Large African populations in cities have developed only in the 20th century, especially after the 1960s. Soil erosion and overgrazing, increasing pressure on land as a result of population growth, and the attractions of the city have all contributed to migratory movements.

Nomads and pastoralists. A hunting and gathering economy obliges the San (Bushmen) of the Kalahari Desert to move camp frequently. Some San *scherms* (shelters) may be little more than a depression in the ground, but groups such as the !Kung build light-framed shelters of sticks and saplings covered with grass. Other hunter-gatherers, such as the Hadza of Tanzania, live amid relative plenty; their dry savanna territory has a wide range of game animals. Their domed huts of tied branches may be given a thick thatch in winter. Some forest dwellers, such as the Mbuti Pygmies of the Ituri Forest, Zaire, are also hunter-gatherers. Their similarly constructed temporary shelters are interlaced with crossed sticks, over which *mongongo* leaves are layered.

Tents of the nomads

Pastoral nomads follow defined routes, which reduces the risk of overgrazing and enables them to contact other nomadic groups. Camel nomads such as the Kababish of the central Sudan use the traditional Bedouin tent, which consists of a rectangular membrane of strips of woven camel hair that is strained on webbing straps and secured with guys over a rectangle of poles. A central row of four poles supporting curved ridge pieces reduces the possibility of damage to the tent. In Niger the Tuareg of the desert use a tent of superficially similar form, though the strips are made of goat skins sewn together. As many as 40 skins are required to complete a tent membrane. Farther south, Tuareg subgroups employ a structure similar to that used by many camel nomads, such as the Afar, from as far away as Ethiopia. Common to these people is the use of the pole frame in the form of a humped dome over which woven mats of grass or palm fronds are secured. Dum palm leaves are split by the Galla of Somalia, the women of which weave strips of coloured cloth into the mat, the patterned side being laid over the frame so as to be visible within the tent, while the shaggy, rough fibres are exposed like thatch on the outside.

The cattle pastoralists of southern and East Africa may settle for some years in one location. The Masai of Kenya and Tanzania construct an oblong, or sometimes square, low-domed hut some six metres long and at shoulder height from closely woven frames of thin *leleshwa* sticks and saplings. Arranged in a circle around the cattle enclosure, or manyatta, the frames are packed with leaves and plastered over with cattle dung, which acts as a deterrent to termites. The huts are aerodynamically proof against high winds, and the manyatta thicket boundary acts as a defensive barrier. A number of other tribes use a similar structure; the Barabaig of Tanzania, for example, build thornbush enclosures in the form of a figure eight, with one loop used as a kraal for the cattle, and the other lined with huts with flat roof frames.

In southern Africa, frame domes are constructed by the Zulu, Swazi, and, in Natal, the Nguni using concentric hoops. Others make a ring of poles inserted into the ground and brought together in a crest, either as a continuous curve (early Xhosa) or to a point (Sotho). These structures are expertly thatched, the Zulu domes, or *indlu,* having finely detailed entrances. Some Nguni types have layers of mats beneath for insulation, the covering thatch being brought to a decorative finial and the whole held down with a grass rope net to withstand strong winds.

Savanna kraals and compounds. Later houses of the Xhosa have tended toward a consistent form, the rondavel, or cylindrical, single-cell house with conical thatched roof. This type is prevalent throughout southern Africa. Variants in the region include a low plinth or curb supporting a domed roof (some Swazi, Zulu), flattened domes or low-pitched cones on head-height cylinders, and high, conical roofs. The methods of construction also vary, though a common method is a wall with a ring of posts and infilling of wattles or basket weave packed and plastered with mud. Rings of posts may have packed earth infilling, and in more wooded regions walls may consist mainly of timber posts. Some southern peoples, including the Venda of the Transvaal and the Tswana of Botswana, build veranda houses, with deep, thatched eaves supported by an outer ring of posts. Traditionally the units are single-cell and undivided and are illuminated only from the doorway. Additional living space may be claimed from the exterior, with a semipublic space to the fore, and a private space, with hard-packed earthen floor, to the rear of the dwelling being used for food preparation, cooking, and domestic occupations. Both spaces are bounded by a low wall. In many areas houses are dispersed, but in others the kraal, with huts ranged around the perimeter of a large cattle enclosure (as among the Ba-Ila of Zambia), serves a defensive function against raiders and predators. In South West Africa/Namibia the kraal of the Ambo people had an outer concentric ring leading to cattle pens, an inner fenced meeting place, and subdivisions for wives', visitors', and headman's quarters.

Cylindrical homes of the savanna

Similar houses are constructed in the East African lakes

region, where the form probably originated. Houses of considerable size are built by some Luo (near Lake Victoria) and Kuria (Tanzania) people, the former making extensive use of papyrus reeds from lake borders, using the thicker stems structurally and the leaves for thatching material. Luo homesteads are frequently ringed with hedges within which cattle are penned; fields extend beyond for the growing of cereals. Most of these Central African peoples construct granaries, often basket-shaped and basket-woven, raised on stilts to keep away rodents, and beneath a thatched roof to keep them dry. Veranda houses are also built, and secondary thatched roof crests permitting ventilation and the escape of smoke are not uncommon.

Cylindrical houses are built by the majority of peoples in the savanna and semidesert regions of the Sudan and West Africa. With less wood available, these are often constructed of mud in a coil pottery technique. It is customary to lay the mud spirally in "lifts" of approximately half a metre, allowing each lift to dry before adding the next. Among the Matakam of Cameroon, conical roofs are covered with thatch or woven mats, often terminating in decorative finials (see Figure 10). Many houses, as among the Sudanese Nuba, have molded doorways shaped to accept the shoulders.

Rene Gardi

Figure 10: Thatch-covered conical roofs of cylindrical houses in a Matakam compound, Cameroon.

Layout of the compound

The characteristic settlement form in West Africa is the compound, a cluster of units linked by walls. Many compounds are circular in plan, but others, conditioned sometimes by the uneven terrain, are more complex. Earthen wall and floor surfaces are plastered smooth and dried to a rocklike hardness. These surfaces are often decorated with coloured clays (as done, for example, by the Bobo in Burkina Faso) and, in some instances, sculpted with ancestral motifs (as the Kassena do in Burkina Faso). Flat roofs with parapets are also built, sometimes in the same compound, supported either independently by a log frame of forked posts and crossmembers or by joists inserted into the clay walls; hollowed half-log gargoyles throw off water during seasonal rains. Dwelling huts, granaries and other stores, and pens for goats and fowl are built within the same compound.

Dwellings of approximately rectangular plan, though often with curved and molded corners, are also found among the cylindrical units, and some peoples, such as the Lobi of Côte d'Ivoire, build compounds with straight walls. Throughout the western savanna region the trend has been toward rectangular-plan houses, largely owing to Islāmic influence from the north (see below *Influences of Islām and Christianity*) and to contact with rain forest peoples from the south.

Forest dwellings. To the south of the savanna is a thinly populated strip, possibly depleted by the slave trade, beyond which lie the rain forests. These regions, especially in Nigeria, are among the most densely populated parts of sub-Saharan Africa and have had contact with European traders since the 16th century. The rectangular-plan houses of the Akan peoples, including those of the Ashanti in Ghana, date from before this, but they may have replaced an earlier savanna form. Until the 20th century Ashanti houses were mainly of pole frames with mud infilling. Frequently they were finely decorated, in mud molded over grass armature, with spiral motifs of a symbolic significance akin to those found on weights used for measuring gold. Today, however, the Ashanti house is constructed of "swish," or *pisé de terre* (earth rammed into a wooden formwork), raised in lifts. The pitched or hipped roof is covered in thatch or, more frequently, with corrugated iron. Though the materials have changed, the basic form remains in the village compounds: four independently constructed, rectangular-plan huts forming the sides of a courtyard. Yoruba compounds in Nigeria are somewhat similar, but the four sides are often under one continuous roof. Rain is collected from the roofs, so that the plan has frequently been compared with the Roman impluvium house. Farther south in Nigeria, the Igbo and related peoples traditionally built rectangular houses, often with open fronts facing a courtyard and surrounded by enclosing mud walls. Similar rectangular buildings with thatched, hipped roofs are used by other rain forest peoples, including some groups of the Fon in Benin and the Baule and Dan of Côte d'Ivoire. But in regions where widely dispersed peoples, such as the Senufo of Côte d'Ivoire, border the savanna, cylinder-and-cone houses with deep thatched eaves are common.

Rectangular homes of the forests

Closer to the coast of West Africa, some peoples build houses raised on stilts; the most notable are those built in the lakeside village of Ganvié in Benin. The buildings are constructed of mangrove poles, a material also used by coastal Swahili-speaking people in Kenya. In some coastal regions, such as that occupied by the Duala in Cameroon, houses are of bamboo, though they are mud-plastered. Bamboo, which grows to heights of over 15 metres in Angola, Congo, and parts of Central Africa, is used by many peoples as a building material. Its straight stalks, used as screen walls, are lashed with thin wood strips to produce crisp, rectangular houses with peaked, thatched roofs, as among the Nyakyusa of Tanzania. Bamboo construction reached its apogee in the tall houses of the Bamileke and other peoples of western Cameroon, who constructed steep, prefabricated pyramidal roofs raised on platforms with verandas; the whole structure frequently reached 10 metres or more, with male and female ancestor figures often flanking the doors (see Figure 11). Tall, conical houses, made of bamboo poles joined at the crest and then leaf-thatched, were built by the Ngelima and the Panga of Zaire.

Widespread use of bamboo

Raffia palm is also used by the Bamileke and the neighbouring Bafut and is an important material among the Kongo of Angola and the Bushongo of Zaire. The most impressive of these structures are the rectangular, pitched-roofed meeting halls of the Mangbetu in Zaire; their houses are of the cylinder-and-cone type, mud-plastered and geometrically decorated. Large meeting houses are found in Nigeria among the Yakö and other peoples. On special occasions pole-frame shelters are constructed with monopitch roofs loosely covered with grass or palm fronds. Awnings are also used, and among the Ashanti immense umbrellas shade dignitaries and members of royal families.

PALACES AND SHRINES

In the 19th century the earth-and-stone palace of the Asantehene (divine king) of the Ashanti empire at the capital city of Kumasi covered some five acres. It had many courtyards with verandas and open screens and more than 60 rooms with steep, thatched roofs. However, little of the palace survived the Ashanti wars and a punitive ex-

Figure 11: Ancestor figures, carved doorframe, and veranda posts on a Bafussam chieftain's house, Bamileke area, Cameroon grasslands.
Photo Hoa-Qui

pedition by the British in 1874. More extensive was the great palace of the *oba* of Benin City, Nigeria. In the 16th and 17th centuries it was as large as a European town, with many courts surrounded by galleried buildings, their pillars encased in bronze plaques. Roofs were shingled, and there were numerous high towers topped with bronze birds. Benin City was burned by the British in 1897. The Yoruba of western Nigeria are also an urban people. Their towns traditionally have as their centre the *afin* (palace) of the *oba,* from which radiate broad roads dividing the town into quarters, each with its compound of a subordinate chief. Some *afin*s in the precolonial era were of great size, encompassing much of the surrounding bush; that at Oyo, the capital of the Oyo empire (17th and 18th centuries), was reported to cover 260 hectares (640 acres). The palace buildings were substantially built, and the open verandas were supported by carved caryatid pillars. Yoruba towns still have *oba*'s palaces; though the architecture of many is Westernized, the traditional courtyards, recreation grounds, and high surrounding walls persist.

The *zimbabwe*s ("stone houses") built in the 17th and 18th centuries by the Rozwi kings of southern Central Africa were royal kraals, an example being the citadel of Chief Changamire at Khami, modern Zimbabwe. Ruins at Regina, Nalatali, and Dhlodhlo (also in Zimbabwe) all display fine mortarless stonemasonry worked with chevron patterns and banded colours. Many African palaces were larger and often better crafted versions of the traditional dwelling type, raised on hillocks or plinths. Such were the palaces of the kabaka (king) of the kingdom of Buganda, including the great barnlike thatched dome with an open reception veranda at Mengo, near present-day Kampala, Uganda. Other palaces were royal compounds, such as that of the *fon* (chief) of Bafut, Cameroon, which within a high fenced enclosure comprised separate quarters for the older and younger wives, dormitories for the adolescent sons, houses for retainers, stores, meeting places, a shrine house and medicine house, burial huts for former chiefs, and huts for secret societies.

While many African peoples have or have had kings, not all have resided in palaces and not all have been divine. Some peoples have no recognized chiefs or leaders at all. Religion, however, plays an essential part in the life of all African societies. Among some, such as the Fali of Cameroon or the Nankani of Burkina Faso, spiritual symbolism informs every part of their dwelling types. Among the most-studied peoples in this respect are the Dogon who live on the rockfall of the Bandiagara escarpment in Mali. The Dogon perceive each dwelling compound anthropomorphically as a man on his side in the act of procreation. The man's head is associated with the hearth, the stores with his arms, the stables with his legs, the central workroom with his belly, and the grinding stones with his genitalia. From the individual parts of the house to the entire village plan, each element has a religiously symbolic association, and totemic sanctuaries with markedly zoomorphic form are built and dedicated to the ancestors of the living.

The Dogon house

Monumental temple architecture is virtually nonexistent in Africa, for in animist religions spirits may reside in trees, carved figures, or small, simple shrines. Cult houses and shrine rooms containing votive objects and dedicated to spirits or ancestors are common, though, like the fetish house of the Ashanti, with its rooms for orchestra and officiating priest, these may be similar to the dwelling compound. A more notable structure is the elaborate *mbari* house of the Owerri Igbo of Nigeria. A large open-sided shelter, square in plan, it houses many life-sized, painted figures sculpted in mud and intended to placate the figure of Ala, the earth goddess, who is supported by other deities of thunder and water. The remaining witty sculptures are of craftsmen, officials, Europeans, animals, and imaginary beasts. Because the process of building is regarded as a sacred act, *mbari* houses, which take years to build, are left to decay, new ones being constructed

(Left) Victor Englebert—EB Inc., (right) Rene Gardi

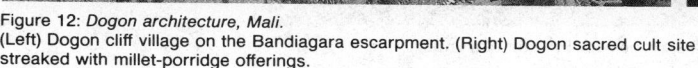

Figure 12: *Dogon architecture, Mali.*
(Left) Dogon cliff village on the Bandiagara escarpment. (Right) Dogon sacred cult site streaked with millet-porridge offerings.

Figure 13: Hausa building with molded low-relief decoration, Zaria, Nigeria.

Frank Willett

rather than old ones maintained. This cycle encourages the continuance of a lively tradition.

INFLUENCES OF ISLĀM AND CHRISTIANITY

Early civilizations in the western Sudan region had strong trading links across the Sahara, and an Islāmic presence south of the desert was established 1,000 years ago. In the 11th century, Kumbi, the capital of the kingdom of Ghana (actually in present-day Mali), was described as having a dozen mosques. Subsequently the kingdoms of Mali and Songhai superseded ancient Ghana, with Timbuktu and Gao on the Niger River becoming major centres of learning and commerce. Excavations have revealed that these towns were large, prosperous, and well constructed. Muslim builders introduced a type of dwelling reflecting their Arab and North African traditions: rectilinear in plan, flat-roofed, and often two stories or more in height, these dwellings were built of sun-dried mud brick or of mud and stone. By the 16th century this form had penetrated the Nigerian savanna with the establishment of the Hausa states. Kano, Katsina, Sokoto, and Zaria today present an appearance probably comparable with that of earlier centuries, but with the former cylindrical huts replaced by those of square plan, reflecting the changing size of families (see Figure 13). New houses are built from *tabali,* or pear-shaped mud bricks, and the large palaces of the *amīr*s (emirs) are often richly decorated within, with spaces spanned by palm ribs.

Replacement of cylindrical with rectangular dwellings

Prominent in many West African towns are the mosques, which frequently display a formal conjunction between Islāmic structure and indigenous conical ancestral pillars and shrines. The earliest surviving of these is probably the ziggurat at Gao, but more typical of the savanna form are the mosques, bristling with wood reinforcement, of Agadez (Niger) and Djénné (Mali) and the great mosque at Mopti (Mali), which was greatly restored under the French administration.

On the east coast of Africa, Islāmic influence began with the establishment of the *dhow* trade, which, relying on the trade winds, linked East Africa with the Arabian and Persian Gulf ports, and with India. Kilwa, an island port that flourished between the 12th and 15th centuries, was built largely of stone, as were Zanzibar (where the mosque at Kizimkazi has a 12th-century inscription), Dar es Salaam, Malindi, Mombasa, and other ports and city-states built by Swahili- and Arabic-speaking traders along the Tanzanian and Kenyan coast. With the coming of the Portuguese at the close of the 15th century, the east coast towns were plundered and burned. Only the northerly island port of Lamu, Kenya, retains the character of the Swahili town. Built of coral rag stone, roofed with mangrove poles, and covered with rag and lime mortar, the houses have fine plasterwork, decorative rows of niches, and deeply carved doors.

Until the late 19th century, Christian influence on African architecture was minimal, with the remarkable exception of the rock churches of Lalibela, Ethiopia. Following the Islāmization of Egypt, the Ethiopian church was isolated for many centuries, but, during the reign of the ascetic Zague king Lalibela in the 13th century, 11 churches were carved out of the red tufa, including the cruciform Church of St. George excavated out of bedrock. Some of the churches, among them St. Mary and St. Mercurius, were richly painted with biblical murals. Throughout the

Ethiopian rock churches

Photo Almasy

Figure 14: Painted house and enclosure walls of a Ndebele village near Pretoria, Transvaal, S.Af.

Tigre region of Ethiopia, there are many other rock-carved and cave churches, such as those at Cherkos, Wik'ro, Abraha Azba, and the great mountain monastery at Debre Damo Debir.

CHANGE IN THE 20TH CENTURY

Churches built by Christian missionaries, sometimes with imported stone, generally followed modified Gothic forms and had no impact on African building, but the growth of colonial towns encouraged the adoption of European styles, including the use of the rectangular-plan house. This trend was reinforced by the infiltration into the hinterland of the indigenous Swahili-style house in East Africa, the rain forest house type in West Africa, and the Islāmic house type of North African origin in the western Sudan—all of which have rectangular plans. Though the effect has been to reduce the variety of house forms and to regimentalize settlement patterns, the trend has not been without interesting hybrids. In particular, the decorated *lapa* (courtyard) walls and facades of the southern African Sotho, Pedi, and Ndebele, with their ziggurat details, have a colourful vitality (see Figure 14). Elsewhere, in Laputo, in Mozambique, and in Johannesburg, owner-built houses and resettlement townships have been erected, extended, or decorated, often with originality, within the limitations of economy and space.

With the westernizing of African cities, much indigenous architecture has been lost, though not necessarily in street life or surface enrichment. Two- and three-story houses and shops have become commonplace with the use of reinforced concrete and steel frame construction. Since World War II, a number of African architects have gained prominence, including Oluwole Olumuyiwa of Nigeria and David Mutiso of Kenya. Their work is immaculately designed and responsive to climate and environment, but it is firmly in the modernist International Style.

Modern African architects

While these and other African architects have shown themselves to be effective designers of major buildings in the urban centres, the greatest challenge to African designers lies in the burgeoning suburbs of African cities. Unserviced, unsanitary, and often in locations subject to disease and flood, the squatter settlements of, for example, Lagos, Nigeria, or Lusaka, Zambia, underline the importance of economical housing that is responsive to the diversity of cultural needs in urban contexts. It is here that the African genius for building unpretentious, functional, and environmentally appropriate housing from indigenous resources can make its most important contribution to the future of its architecture. (P.O.)

Sculpture and associated arts

Although wood is the best-known medium of African sculpture, many others are employed: copper alloys, iron, ivory, pottery, unfired clay, and, infrequently, stone. Unfired clay is and probably always was the most widely used medium in the whole continent, but, partly because it is so fragile and therefore difficult to collect, it has been largely ignored in the literature. Small figurines of fired clay were excavated in a mound at Daima near Lake Chad in levels dating from the 5th century BC or earlier, while others were found in Zimbabwe in deposits of the later part of the 1st millennium AD. These imply an even earlier stage of unfired clay modeling. About the time of these lower levels at Daima (which represent a Neolithic, or New Stone Age, pastoral economy), there was flourishing farther to the west the fully Iron Age Nok culture, producing large, hollow sculptures in well-fired pottery, some of the stylistic features of which imply yet earlier prototypes in wood.

Copper-alloy castings using the cire perdue technique afford evidence of great sculptural achievements from as early as the 9th century AD, when the smiths of Igbo Ukwu, Nigeria, were casting leaded bronze, which is highly ductile, and smithing copper, which is not (see Figure 23). Some three or four centuries later the smiths of Ife, seemingly unaware that unalloyed copper was not suitable for casting (or perhaps wishing to demonstrate their virtuosity), used it to produce masterpieces such as the seated figure in a shrine at Tada and the so-called Obalufon mask in the Ife Museum. In fact, however, zinc brasses were used more than unalloyed copper. The largest corpus of this work is from Benin, where zinc brasses were used almost exclusively. These copper-alloy castings, together with pottery sculptures the traceable history of which goes back even further, are the main evidence for the early history of sculpture in sub-Saharan Africa.

Copper-alloy casting

Wrought-iron sculptures are found in a number of traditions, mostly in West Africa, including the Dogon, Bambara, Fon, and Yoruba peoples.

Stone sculpture occurs in several separate centres, employing both hard and soft rock, but there is usually not much evidence of a development through time in a single place. Ivory is a highly prized medium in many parts of Africa. Its fine texture makes it suitable for delicate sculpture, while its rarity leads to its employment in many societies for items of great prestige.

African wood sculptures are carved with similar tools throughout the continent. An ax may be used to fell the tree, but an adz, with its cutting edge at right angles to the shaft, is used for the substantive work of carving. The skill achieved with this tool is astonishing to the Western observer. Thin shavings can be removed with speed and accuracy, creating a surface (especially when the form is convex) that shows slight facets that catch the light and add to the visual interest. More intricate work is done with knives. A pointed iron rod heated in the fire may be employed to bore holes in a mask for attachment to the costume and to permit the wearer to see. The surface of the sculpture is sometimes polished with the side of a knife or sanded down with rough leaves. Details are commonly picked out by a method involving charring with a red-hot knife (as among the Ibibio of Nigeria), or the carving is immersed in mud to darken its surface before oiling (as among the Dan people of Côte d'Ivoire).

WEST AFRICA

Scholars divide the visual arts of West Africa into three broad areas: the western Sudan, the Guinea Coast, and Nigeria. This is done partly to enable the outsider to comprehend the diversity of styles and traditions within the region, while recognizing that there are themes common to all of the areas.

Western Sudan. This is the name conventionally given to the savanna region of West Africa. It is an area dominated by Islāmic states situated at the southern ends of the trans-Saharan trade routes. The sculpture here is characterized by schematic styles of representation. Some commentators have interpreted these styles as an accommodation to the Islāmic domination of the area, but this is probably not an adequate explanation since Islām in West Africa has either merely tolerated or actually destroyed such traditions while exerting other influences.

Schematic styles of the western savanna

Among the better-known sculptural traditions of the western Sudan are those of the following peoples.

Dogon and Tellem. The Dogon inhabit the Bandiagara escarpment in Mali. Dogon sculpture is intimately linked with the cult of the ancestors. Figures are made to house the spirits of the deceased on the family shrine, and masks are used to drive the spirits away at the end of the mourning period. One type of mask, called *sirige,* has a tall, flat projection above the face (a feature found also in the masks of the neighbouring Mossi and Bobo), which is said to represent a multistory house. The Great Mask, never worn and made anew every 60 years, represents the primordial ancestor who met death while he was in the form of a serpent. Iron staffs topped with human figures are also made, and some personal ornaments are cast in brass.

Also found in Dogon territory are, possibly, the oldest wood sculptures to survive (three have been dated by carbon-14 to the 15th to 17th century AD). They were found in caves in the Bandiagara escarpment. The Dogon attribute them to an earlier population, the Tellem. These figures, usually of simplified and elongated form, often with hands raised, seem to be the prototype of the ancestor figures that the Dogon carve on the doors and locks of their houses and granaries; investigations have confirmed that the Tellem were ethnically a different people from the

Dogon, though the art style appears to have been handed on from one people to the other.

Bambara. The Bambara live in the region around Bamako, the capital of Mali. Their traditions include six male societies, each with its own type of mask. The Ntomo is for young boys before circumcision. Their masks have a line of vertical projections placed transversely over the human face, representing man as God first created him. The Komo is the custodian of tradition and is concerned with all aspects of community life—agriculture, judicial processes, and passage rites. Its masks are of elongated animal form decorated with actual horns of antelope, quills of porcupine, bird skulls, and other objects. Masks of the Kono, which enforces civic morality, are also elongated and encrusted with sacrificial material. The Tyiwara uses a headdress representing, in the form of an antelope, the mythical being who taught men how to farm (see Figure 15). The Kore, concerned with the sky and with the bringing of rain to make the crops grow, employs masks representing the hyena, lion, monkey, antelope, and horse. In addition there are masks of the Nama, which protect against sorcerers. Ancestor figures of the Bambara clearly derive from the same artistic tradition as do many of those of the Dogon; so also do their sculptures in wrought iron. Rectangular intersection of flat planes is a stylistic feature common to Bambara and Dogon sculpture.

Bambara masks

By courtesy of the Ethnographical Department, National Museum, Copenhagen

Figure 15: Bambara dance wood headdress in the form of an antelope, representing the spirit Tyiwara, who introduced agriculture; from Mali. These headdresses, attached to a wickerwork cap, are worn by farmers who, at the time of planting and harvest, dance in imitation of leaping antelope. In the National Museum, Copenhagen. Height 50 cm.

Djénné-Mopti. These are two towns situated on the inland delta of the Niger River, Mali. They are notable as centres of the cloth trade and for their architecture. Moreover, in their immediate vicinity many sculptures in pottery of uncertain age have been found. They may have some association with the empires of Ghana and Mali (7th–13th and 13th–16th centuries, respectively). For all their extensive trade contacts across the Sahara, these medieval empires did not significantly change the basic structure of society in the western Sudan.

Senufo. The Senufo of northern Côte d'Ivoire produce a rich variety of sculptures, mainly associated with the Lo society (known more widely as the Poro), to which all adult men belong and which maintains the continuity of religious and historical traditions, especially through the cult of the ancestors. During initiations, headpieces are worn that have a flat, vertical, round or rectangular board on top, decorated with paint or pierced work. Many wood carvings of male figures depict these headpieces, sometimes on rhythm pounders used by young initiates, who beat the earth to call upon the ancestors to take part in the ceremony and purify the earth. Several types of mask are used. The *kpelie,* a human face with projections all around, is said to remind initiates of human imperfection. Animal-head masks usually combine characteristics of several creatures—hyena, warthog, and antelope. A type of animal mask called *waniugo* has a cup for a magical substance on top; these masks blow sparks from their muzzles in a nighttime ritual protecting the village from sorcerers. Among the Naffara group of the Senufo, masks of similar form but with an interior cavity too small for a human head are carried on the top corner of a rectangular, tent-like costume called *kagba.* This mask is the symbol of the Lo, which only initiates may see. In the Korhogo region, *deguele* masks appear in pairs at funerals. They are of plain helmet shapes topped with figures whose bodies are carved to resemble a pile of rings. Figures of the hornbill are used in initiation, and groups of birds on a pole are trophies for the best farmer. Figures of male and female twins and of horsemen are used in divination. These represent the spirit familiars enabling the divination process. The diviners themselves are women, forming the Sandogo society. Shrine doors and drums are carved in relief, and small figures and ritual rings are cast in bronze. For many years the Senufo have been producing large quantities of carvings for the Western market.

Masks of the Lo society

Guinea Coast. This is the forested region of West Africa, where Islām was not a dominant influence until recent years. Political organizations in the past tended to be small in scale, with government sometimes in the hands of chiefs, sometimes by assemblies of men, sometimes by secret associations manifesting their attributes in masquerade ceremonies. State systems developed toward the eastern end of the region, particularly in areas inhabited by the Ashanti (in present-day Ghana) and Fon (Benin) and in the Yoruba Oyo empire and the Edo kingdom of Benin (Nigeria). These states capitalized on trade both with peoples of the savanna and, from the late 15th century onward, with Europeans.

Guinea Coast sculpture displays a greater tendency to naturalistic styles of representation. Some of the best-known traditions of the area are the following.

Bidyogo. In the Bijagós Islands of Guinea-Bissau, the Bidyogo carve rather simplified human figures seated on stools, bowls supported by human figures with human and animal forms on the lids, and staffs with figures on them. They also carve naturalistic masks of wild bulls, which are carried on the prow of the royal war canoe and also used in dances. Their buildings are round and often painted.

Baga. The Baga, 15th- or 16th-century migrants from the Sudan now occupying the coastal region of Guinea, carve *anok,* or *elek,* bird heads with human features styled in a manner resembling western Sudanic work. They had rich traditions of mask and figure sculpture, many of which were suppressed with the advent of Islām. The best known of these is the massive *dumba* mask (see Figure 16), with its great cantilevered head supported on the upper part of a female torso, carved so as to rest on the shoulders of the wearer, who sees out through a hole between the breasts, his body hidden in raffia fibre. This mask appears at the harvest and threshing of the rice crop. Tall drums supported by a human figure are also carved.

Mende. The Mende of Sierra Leone are best known for smooth, black, helmet-shaped masks (see Figure 17), representing the Sande society, which is responsible for initiating girls into womanhood. This is the only women's society on the continent known to use masks. Because the mask is "found" beside a stream deep in the forest, where the Sande spirit is said to live, and is supposed not to be an artifact at all, the carver in this case is anonymous. Members of the corresponding male society, Poro, also wear masks, although they are of differing form. The women's

Masks of the Sande society

Figure 16: Baga *dumba* mask used in rituals of the Simo society during the harvest and threshing of the rice crop; wood and fibre, Guinea. In the British Museum. Height 1.22 m.

By courtesy of the trustees of the British Museum

Yasse, a divination and healing society, employs slender human figures called *minsere.* Large, ugly *gongoli* masks are also used, but entirely for entertainment. In preparing their rice farms, the Mende often uncover figures carved in soapstone and known as *nomoli,* which they set up in shelters to protect the crop. The figures are similar in style and are thought to be similar in date to ivories carved in the 16th century for Portuguese traders in the adjacent Sherbro area.

Dan-Ngere. The Dan-Ngere complex of styles is named after two extremes of stylistic variation: the smooth, restrained style of the Dan, De, and Diomande; and the grotesque style of the Ngere (or Guere), Wobe, Kran, and Bete, a less extreme form of which is found among the Kru and Grebo, who inhabit adjacent regions of Liberia, Guinea, and Côte d'Ivoire. A single carver will produce masks in both of the extreme modes of the range of style. Miniature, easily portable masks, representing and sharing in the power of the larger masks, protect the owner when he is away from home. The carvers also produce the large anthropomorphic rice ladles used by the mother of the heir apparent at the harvest feast; chiefs' staffs; and female figures that seem to be prestige items, as are small figures cast in brass among the Dan and Kpelle.

Ashanti and Baule. The Ashanti region of southern Ghana is a remnant of the Ashanti empire, which was founded in the early 17th century when, according to legend, a golden stool descended from heaven into the lap of the first king, Osei Tutu. The stool is believed to house the spirit of the Ashanti people in the same way that an individual's stool houses his spirit after death. The Ashanti also carve *akua-ba* (dolls with disk-shaped heads embodying their concept of beauty and carried by women who want to become pregnant) as well as staffs for royal spokesmen, which, like the handles of state swords, are covered in gold foil. The success of the Ashanti empire depended on the trade in gold not only with Europeans at the coast but also with the Muslim north. Gold dust was the currency, weighed against small brass weights that were often geometric or were representations recalling well-known proverbs. Ashanti weavers developed a style of weaving of great technical mastery, incorporating imported silk (see Figure 18). Cast-brass ritual vessels, *kuduo,* used in funeral ceremonies, bear indications of Islāmic inspiration. The Ashanti also cast fine gold jewelry, as do the Baule of Côte d'Ivoire, who separated from them in the mid-18th century.

Goldsmithing among the Ashanti and Baule

Baule gold weights are similar to those of the Ashanti, but the Baule also have types of sculpture that none of the other Akan peoples possess: masks (which, like their low-relief doors, seem to indicate Senufo influence) and standing human figures, apparently sometimes used as ancestor figures. The figures and human masks, the latter reported to be portraits used in commemorating the dead, are elegant—well polished, with elaborate hairdressings and scarification. More roughly finished are the *gbekre* figures, representing minor divinities in human form with animal heads. Masks are made also to represent the spirits of the bush: antelope, bush cow, elephant, monkey, and leopard. Boxes for the mouse oracle (in which sticks are disturbed by a live mouse, to give the augury) are unique to the Baule, whose carvers also produce heddle pulleys, combs, hairpins, and gong mallets.

Fon. The Fon Kingdom of Dahomey, with its capital at Abomey (now in the People's Republic of Benin), was also founded in the early 17th century. The palace is decorated with painted relief panels modeled in clay, representing the different kings and the events of their reigns. The kings are represented also by iron staffs and messengers' staffs with openwork iron symbols on a wooden haft, as well as by a small number of large wooden statues combining human and animal attributes. The thrones of the kings are similar in form to Ashanti stools but are much taller and are preserved as cult objects. Small figures cast in brass, often in groups, are prestige items employed also to decorate the royal tombs. Brightly coloured appliqué cloth is used on state umbrellas and chiefs' caps. A popular art is calabash carving. The greatest achievements of Fon art, however, are the large sculptures for Gun, the god of iron and war, made from sheets of copper or iron (see Figure 19).

Nigeria. The northern and southern parts of Nigeria can be considered part of the western Sudan and Guinea Coast, respectively; but, because of the wealth of evidence for an artistic tradition of some 2,000 years, it is convenient to consider Nigeria separately.

Frank Willett

Figure 17: Mende mask of the Sande (women's initiation) society, wood, Sierra Leone. In the Manchester Museum. Height 38.1 cm.

Figure 18: An Ashanti chief wearing silk cloth and gold jewelry.
Doran H. Ross

Stylized pottery sculpture of the Nok

Nok. The earliest known sculpture of large size in the Sudan is that produced in pottery by the Nok culture, which flourished extensively in northern Nigeria from the 5th century BC into the early centuries AD (see Figure 20). These people were the first known manufacturers of iron in western Africa, furnaces at Taruga having been dated between the 5th and early 3rd centuries BC; they continued, however, to use stone tools. Of well-fired clay, their sculptures represent animals naturalistically; human figures, however, are depicted with heads that are usually tubular, but sometimes conical or spherical, and with simple tubular trunks and limbs. The art of Nok indicates the antiquity of many basic canons of West African sculpture, but the precise relationship between ancient and modern forms is obscure.

By courtesy of the Musee de l'Homme, Paris

Figure 19: Fon iron image of Gun, the god of iron and war, Dahomey. In the Musée de l'Homme, Paris. Height 1.65 m.

Daima and Sao. Not far from the Nok area but very different in style, at Daima near Lake Chad, small, simple clay animal figures were by the 6th century BC being made by a population of Neolithic herdsmen. A little later they began making animals with more extended legs, and sometime after AD 1000 they started to make animals covered with little spikes. The last are similar to examples found on sites of the Sao culture in the Chari Valley, Cameroon, where more elaborate human figure sculptures, thought to represent ancestors and probably spirits, have been found. Carbon-14 dates for these sites range from the 5th century BC to the 18th century AD.

Ife and Yoruba. The Yoruba peoples inhabit a large part of southwestern Nigeria. Their art traditions are of considerable antiquity. Excavations at Ife, in central Yorubaland (the site of the creation of the world in some Yoruba myths), have shown that naturalistic sculpture in brass and pottery was being produced sometime between 1100 and 1450 AD. The sculptures may represent royal figures and their attendants, and life-size portrait heads in brass were perhaps used as part of funerary effigies. During this time, Ife appears to have had widespread importance, and the naturalism of its art seems to have influenced the basic development of Yoruba sculptural style. Throughout Yorubaland, human figures (see Figure 21) are represented in a fundamentally naturalistic way, except for bulging eyes; flat, protruding, and usually parallel lips; and stylized ears. The evolution of these characteristics can be observed in a number of pottery sculptures at Ife, which, on stylistic grounds, are considered to be relatively late.

Frank Willett

Figure 20: Pottery head found at Nok, Nigeria. In the Jos Museum, Nigeria. Height 21 cm.

Within the basic canon of Yoruba sculpture, many local styles can be distinguished, down to the hand of the individual artist. Individual cults, too, have their own characteristic requirements of form and ethnography. Staffs for Shango, the thunder god, bear the symbol of a double ax. On his altars are placed carved mortars, for the pounding of food in a mortar sounds like thunder; on the wall behind hangs his leather bag, with a motif based on the extensive gesture of a Shango dancer. Because Shango was king of Oyo, largest of the Yoruba kingdoms, his cult is mainly restricted to areas that were once under Oyo domination.

Typical of Ekiti is the Epa cult, which is connected with both the ancestors and agriculture. The mask proper,

Figure 21: Brass figure of an *oni* (king) of Ife, Nigeria. In the Museum of Ife Antiquities, Nigeria. Height 46.7 cm.
Frank Willett

Mask of the Epa cult

roughly globular, has highly stylized features that vary little; but the superstructure, which may be four feet (122 centimetres) or more in height, is often of very great complexity—for example, a king on horseback, surrounded by two tiers of attendant warriors and musicians. The most widely distributed cult is of twins, *ibeji,* whose birth among the Yoruba is unusually frequent. Their effigies (Figure 22), made on the instructions of the oracle, are among the most numerous of all classes of African sculpture. Carved doors and house posts are found in shrines and palaces and in the houses of important men. Fulfilling purely secular functions are bowls for kola nuts, offered in welcoming a guest; *ayo* boards for the game, known also as *wari,* played with seeds or pebbles in two rows of cuplike depressions; and stools, spoons, combs, and heddle pulleys.

To the north is Esie, where about 800 sculptures in soapstone were found by the local Yoruba population some centuries ago. Their origin is obscure; they are by no means certainly Yoruba. The city of Owo, to the southeast of Yorubaland near the frontier with the Edo-speaking peoples, developed an art style—indeed, a whole culture—that is a blend of Yoruba and Benin traditions. Ivory carving is especially important, and wooden heads of rams and of humans with rams' horns are used on ancestral altars. Second-burial effigies, life-size and naturalistically carved in wood, have been made during the 20th century but were developed from wickerwork forms such as are still used in Benin and in Igbo towns that were formerly under Benin influence. Excavations in 1971 revealed a large number of pottery sculptures that are clearly related to those of Ife but with some Benin features. The site was dated by carbon-14 to about the 15th century AD.

Edo peoples. According to tradition, the Kingdom of Benin was founded from Ife, whence, in the late 14th century, knowledge of brass casting may have been introduced into Benin City for the manufacture of commemorative heads for royal altars. These heads have been grouped in stylistic sequence from moderate naturalism through increasing stylization. The brasses also include figures in the round, groups on a common base, and plaques. The rectangular shape of the plaques, their narrative content, and in some cases their attempt at perspective have been attributed to the influence of illustrations in books carried by the Portuguese, who were in contact with Benin from the late 15th century. The technique of brass casting, however, had been introduced at least a century earlier. Bronze bars had been imported, probably from the interior, as early as the 13th century, but these were made into bracelets in Benin City only by smithing and chasing techniques, not by casting. There were certain limitations on the use of brass, and also ivory. Cult objects (such as memorial beads) were made of wood when intended for non-royal purposes but of brass for the king. Regalia, if made for the king, were of ivory, but otherwise of brass. The regalia of king and chiefs also included coral beads and red cloth, the colour red signifying a mystical threat to the enemies of the kingdom. Wood was used for staffs commemorating ancestors, and these were placed on their altars. Pottery heads were made for shrines in the brass casters' quarter; and life-size groups of royal figures in mud are still made for the cult of Olokun, divinity of the sea and of wealth.

Brass casting in the Kingdom of Benin

Outside Benin City, the Edo peoples live in villages that have many localized cults of nearby topographical features and founder heroes. The *ekpo* masquerade, occurring to the south and east of Benin, is performed by the warrior age group in ceremonies to purify the village ritually and to maintain health. At Ughoton, to the southwest of Benin, a different type of mask is used, in the cult of the water spirit Igbile. Both the cult and the sculptural style seem to have derived from the Ijo.

A number of bronze castings found in Benin have been classified tentatively as the Lower Niger bronze industries. They include pieces from Tada and Jebba in the region now inhabited by the Nupe people, who regard them as relics associated with their own mythical ancestor, and other pieces from various parts of the delta of the Niger River.

Ijo. The Niger Delta is occupied by Ijo fishermen, whose masks for the cults of the water spirits are made in the form of aquatic animals, especially hippopotamus and crocodile. The western Ijo use *ejiri* figures, in which the head of the household is represented upon a highly schematic quadruped that is said to represent the guardian spirit of the family. Similar objects are made by the Edo-speaking Urhobo, to the north of the Ijo, where they are used in a cult of aggressiveness by the warriors. Among the eastern Ijo, shrines for the water spirits have figures that are often large though frequently kept hidden. They also have masks, similar to those of the western Ijo, worn by men of the Ekine society. In addition, there are shrines that contain sculptures for the village heroes and ancestors. In some Kalabari communities, rectangular screens are fashioned by carpentry into a low-relief frontal group in which a commemorated ancestor is flanked by supporting

Frank Willett

Figure 22: Pair of Yoruba twin figures (*ibeji*), wood, from Efon Alaye, Nigeria. Height 27.6 cm. The starch-resist dyed cloth is also Yoruba. In the Frank Willett Collection.

figures—much like the king in Benin plaques, by which the screens may have been inspired about two centuries ago. All Ijo sculpture exhibits a four-square schematic style that contrasts starkly with the relative naturalism of surrounding styles, such as those of Yorubaland or Benin.

Schematic style of the Ijo

Igbo. On both sides of the Niger, but mainly to the east, live the Igbo. Traditionally, they have lived in small and often isolated settlements scattered through the forest. Only on the northern and western edges of the area, under influence from Igala and Benin, are hereditary rulers found. In Igbo society there is strong social pressure toward individual distinction, and men can move upward through successive grades by demonstrating their achievements and their generosity. One of the traditional representations of this was the *ikenga,* that part of oneself enabling personal achievement, with cult figures representing the attributes of distinction.

The lack of overall centralization among the Igbo-speaking peoples has been conducive to the development of a great variety of art styles and cultural practices. The earliest sculpture known from Igboland is from the village of Igbo Ukwu, where the grave of a man of distinction and a ritual store, dating from the 9th century AD, contained both chased copper objects and elaborate castings of leaded bronze (see Figure 23). The earliest artistic castings from black Africa, these pieces consist of ritual vessels and other ceremonial objects with intricate surface decoration, often small animals and insects represented in the round.

A very great variety of masks is found among the Igbo. The masks, of wood or fabric, are employed in a variety of dramas: social satires, sacred rituals (for ancestors and invocation of the gods), initiation, second burials, and public festivals, which now include Christmas and Independence Day. Some masks appear at only one festival, but the majority appear at many or all. Best known are those of the Northern Igbo Mmo society, which represents the spirits of deceased maidens and their mothers with masks symbolizing beauty. Among the Southern Igbo, the Ekpe society, introduced from the Cross River area, uses contrasting masks to represent the maiden spirit and the elephant spirit, the latter representing ugliness and aggression and the former representing beauty and peacefulness (see Figure 24). A similar contrast is found in their Okorosia masks, which correspond to the Mmo of the Northern Igbo. The Eastern Igbo are best known for masquerades associated with the Iko okochi harvest festival, in which the forms of the masks are determined by tradition, though the content of the play varies from year to year. Stock characters include Mbeke, the European; Mkpi, the he-goat; and Mba, which appear in pairs, one representing a boy dressed as a girl mimicking the behaviour of a girl, the other representing the girl being satirized.

Most impressive are the *ijele* masks of the Northern Igbo, which are 12 feet (366 centimetres) high. Consisting of platforms six feet in diameter, supporting tiers of figures made of coloured cloth and representing everyday scenes, they honour the dead to ensure the continuity and well-being of the community.

Figure 23: Leaded bronze ceremonial object, thought to have been the head of a staff, decorated with coloured beads of glass and stone, 9th century. From Igbo Ukwu, Nigeria. In the Nigerian Museum, Lagos. Height 16.8 cm.
Frank Willett

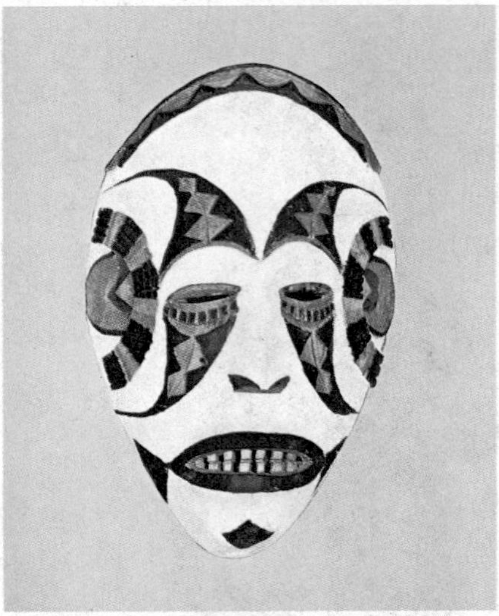

Figure 24: Maiden spirit mask symbolizing beauty and peacefulness, painted wood; Southern Igbo Ekpe society, Nigeria. In the Nigerian Museum, Lagos. Height 21.3 cm.
Frank Willett

Wooden figures are carved for ancestors of both sexes, varying from less than one to more than five feet in height. Those representing founders of the village are kept in a central shrine and sometimes become patrons of the market. A great many other decorative wooden objects are made, including musical instruments, doors, stools, mirror frames, trays for offering kola nuts to guests, dolls, and a variety of small figures used in divination. Shrines called *mbari,* which contain elaborate tableaux of painted, unfired earth, are made in honour of the earth spirit in villages near Owerri in southern Nigeria; and in Igbo communities to the west of the Niger, elaborate pottery groups representing a man and his family are made for the yam cult. There seems to be no tradition of pottery sculpture in other Igbo groups.

Ancestor figures of the 18th century

Ibibio. Among the oldest sculptures of tropical Africa are several hundred ancestor figures, called *ekpu,* of the Ibibio coastal trade centre of Oron, some of which are thought to date from the late 18th century. They are bearded figures, three to four feet high, and are so individual as to suggest portraiture, despite their schematic style. Oron is one group of Ibibio-speaking villages. As with the Igbo, Ibibio is not a single group but several networks of independent communities, with local unity represented by secret associations and their masquerades. The Ekpo society uses black masks, often of naturalistic appearance and with movable jaws, to maintain social order and propitiate the ancestors; some of these masks represent disease and deformity.

Ekoi. The Ekoi-speaking peoples (Anyang, Boki, Ejagham, Keaka, and Yako) are best known for their large, skin-covered masks, which have two or even three faces, and for their smaller headpieces, which represent a head or an entire figure. The headpieces and masks have metal teeth, inlaid eyes, and frequently pegs to represent hair, which, alternatively, may be carved in elaborate coils. They are used by several masking associations. In the northern Ekoi area, around Ikom, are found circles of large stones, *akwanshi,* from one to six feet high, carved in low relief to represent human figures. They are thought to be no earlier than the 16th century.

Fulani. The Fulani are in origin nomadic pastoralists who range from Senegal to the Cameroon grasslands. They are particularly known for their body decoration (see below *Other visual arts: Personal decoration*) and for their engraved milk gourds. In addition, in Mali they have settled groups of artists such as goldsmiths, leatherworkers, blacksmiths, weavers, and potters.

Hausa. Northern Nigeria has long been dominated by the Muslim Hausa who, since the 19th century, have been ruled by Fulani *amīrs* (emirs). For centuries their buildings have been decorated inside with molded and painted low-relief decorations, which have more recently been applied to the exteriors (see Figure 13). Both decorative and of a high technical standard are their crafts: leatherwork for saddles, bags, hilts, and sheaths; gold and silver jewelry; ironwork; pottery; weaving and embroidery.

Nupe. The Nupe have been Muslim for some centuries and are best known for their weaving, embroidery, bead-making, wood carving, and sheet metalwork. They have produced many doors carved in low relief in a blend of decorative designs. Carved and painted masks are made for the *elo,* a purely secular performance intended only to entertain (nowadays on the Prophet's birthday). The *elo* mask has a human face with a motif (sometimes a human figure) rising above it, flanked with stylized horns. The *gugu* masquerader wears a cloth mask decorated with cowrie shells, but sometimes Yoruba masks are used. The *ndako gboya* appears to be indigenous; a spirit that affords protection from witches, it is controlled by a small secret society that cleanses communities by invitation. The mask consists of a tall tube of white cotton supported inside on a bamboo pole about 12 feet long.

Tada and Jebba bronzes

That Nupe art should have been influenced by the Yoruba is not surprising. Yoruba live among the Nupe, and there are bronzes in the Nupe villages of Tada and Jebba—one of them apparently an Ife work, and another in a more recent Yoruba style. Others of this group, which include the largest castings ever made in black Africa, share features with Benin sculpture and have other elements that are widely distributed in time and space on the Lower Niger. Nupe tradition says these sculptures were taken from Idah, the Igala capital, in the early 16th century. Many were probably already ancient, but nothing is known of ancient Igala bronze casting.

Other groups in northern Nigeria. There is a great diversity of sculptural tradition among peoples inhabiting the Niger and Benue valleys, the mountainous regions around the Jos Plateau in the centre of the area, and Adamawa to the east. This is altogether an area of astonishing diversity little understood beyond a confusing list of "tribal" names. Some of the better known traditions include the Igala, Idoma, Afo, Tiv, and Jukun, all of the Benue Valley.

CENTRAL AFRICA

Cameroon grasslands. The Cameroon grasslands area can be divided into three stylistic regions. The Bamileke area is composed of a number of separate chiefdoms, the best known being the Bangwa and the Bacham. Here sculptured human figures are composed of a highly expressive blend of rounded and angular forms. The Bamum kingdom developed roundness of form almost to its extreme, producing figures with big, inflated cheeks. Among the Tikar, Bekom, and Babanki, the forms are rounded but not exaggerated. Throughout the grasslands there have been exchanges of art objects and diffusion of the brass-casting technique, confusing the more detailed stylistic picture. In general, however, all of these societies are hierarchical, with sculpture mainly intended to reflect the power and importance of the king. (F.Wi./J.Pi.)

Gabon. Three major groups live in the equatorial rain forests of Gabon: the Fang and related peoples; the Ogowe (Ogooué) group, including the Ashira and Mpongwe; and the Kota.

Fang masks and figures are characterized by schematic simplicity. Typical of Fang work are *bieri,* boxes containing the skulls and bones of deceased ancestors and carved with figures intended to represent their protective influence (see Figure 26). Fang masks, such as those worn by itinerant troubadours and for hunting and punishing sorcerers, are painted white with facial features outlined in black.

The art of the Ogowe tribes, particularly the Mpongwe, is closely tied to death rituals. Their masks, painted white to symbolize death, represent dead female ancestors, though they are worn by male relatives of the deceased.

Figure 25: Bamum beaded throne of a king, Cameroon grasslands. In the Museum für Völkerkunde, West Berlin. Height 83.2 cm.
Holle Bildarchiv, Baden-Baden, West Germany

The Kota create stylistically unique reliquary figures, called *mbulu-ngulu,* which are covered with a sheet of brass or copper. Like the Fang, the Kota keep the skulls and bones of ancestors in containers, which consist here of a basket surmounted by the carved figure. (P.Wa./J.Pi.)

Zaire and Congo. The region formerly referred to as the "Congo" consists of the modern republics of Zaire and the Congo, which are separated by the Congo River. The area falls into two major geographic divisions: the northern half is an equatorial rain forest inhabited by peoples who hunt, farm, and fish; the southern half is a savanna. It is in the villages of this southern region that the most highly developed political, social, and artistic culture has evolved.

Combination of symbolism and realism

In general, the styles of Zaire and the Congo can be characterized as a combination of symbolism and realism, wherein naturalistic forms—predominantly human and animal figures—are rendered not in precise imitation of nature but in an exaggerated manner. It is this "non-naturalistic reality" that distinguishes the art of this region from West African art.

The sculptural forms are most commonly wood carvings: masks (see Figure 27), ancestor figures, fetishes, bowls, boxes, cups, staffs, pots and lids, pipes, combs, tools, weapons, and musical instruments. Similar objects are also carved in ivory, and in some cases copper, brass, and iron are used. In rare instances, stone figures have been found.

Painting is not utilized greatly as a separate medium, but carved pieces frequently are painted. Masks and other pieces are covered with polychrome (see Figure 28), the colours applied in wide patches and often in planes and angles upon smooth surfaces. In the huts in which rituals take place, wooden figures are hung on brightly painted walls.

Reeds are woven into decorated mats, used for sleeping and for wrapping the dead, and into baskets and boxes, which are used to contain foodstuffs as well as ritual objects. Basketry patterns and sometimes container forms have been imitated by wood carvers; textile weavers, too, use decorative motifs derived from basketry.

Pottery making has depended on four forming techniques: molding, ring building, modeling on a board, and, more recently, throwing on the potter's wheel. Pottery forms are influenced by those of basketry and wood carving as well as by vegetal forms such as the calabash; deco-

Figure 26: Fang wood figure (*bieri*) from a reliquary of ancestor's bones, Gabon. In the Pierre Arman Collection, Paris. Height 47 cm.
By courtesy of Pierre Arman

ration consists of traditional geometric incised or painted patterns. The pots are used for cooking and for carrying and storing food or as ceremonial objects.

Pottery and embroidery are arts practiced by women, whereas sculpture and weaving are male activities.

Stylistic differences within the two major regions of the southern savanna and the northern rain forest can best be seen by subdividing the areas according to the kingdoms that have determined the social, political, and artistic lives of the people. The savanna falls into the Lower Congo, Kuba, and Luba cultural areas; and the rain forest into the northern, northeast, and northwest areas.

Lower Congo (Kongo) cultural area. In the Lower Congo area three sub-styles can be identified: the areas known as the coastal region, the Kwango River area, and the Teke region.

Use of the human figure

Seated mother-and-child figures are found throughout the Lower Congo region. The human figure is used by the peoples of the Lower Congo in the decoration of almost every work—from ceremonial objects and domestic utensils to pieces of furniture and architectural ornament. Although the majority of carved figures are made of wood, many important pieces in metal and ivory have been found. Among them are numerous metal figures clearly influenced by the Portuguese missionaries—statuettes of Christian saints, for example. In addition to the figures, crucifixes were also produced, in brass or bronze (using the lost-wax, or cire perdue, method of casting).

Ancestor figures and fetishes carved by the Kongo and related peoples, who live along the coast and in the Mayombé forest, are more realistically expressive than the figures of other areas. Every detail rendered, the deceased ancestor is portrayed standing, seated, or kneeling, each attitude revealing the dignity and pride with which he is viewed. The fetishes are less realistically portrayed; although the head is treated in great detail, the arms and legs are stylized, appearing to be of equal size, and often the sex of the figure is not indicated. Whereas the ancestor figure typically appears serene, the countenance of the fetish can be protective or malevolent.

The *nkongi,* a group of fetishes characteristic of the coast and the Mayombé forest, consist mainly of human figures, but there are some that combine the forms of a dog and a leopard, sometimes with two heads. The *nkongi* fetish is often completely covered by nails and other sharply pointed metal objects driven into its surface (see Figure 29); these objects mark each appeal made to the spirit embodied in it. All fetishes, whether they represent humans or animals, whether made of wood, horn, ivory, or even calabash, must contain a number of magical substances such as blood along with animal, vegetable, and mineral matter. These ingredients, called *bilongo,* are placed in a cavity, usually in the figure's stomach but sometimes in the back or head. The opening of the cavity is covered by a shell or, in some modern fetishes, by a piece of mirror. The magical substances are believed to invest the fetish figure with power and make it possible for the devotee to establish contact with the spirit (*nkisi*).

Another object common to the Lower Congo area, produced primarily by the coastal peoples, especially the Woyo, is a wooden pot lid carved with pictorial narratives representing proverbs. The pot lid, which covered the meal served by a wife to her husband, illustrates a particular complaint about their marital relationship—a wife's displeasure with her husband, for example; when that lid was used, the husband was obliged to discuss and resolve the problem publicly with the help of mealtime witnesses. This manner of family arbitration was traditional, and each woman was given a variety of carved pot lids on the occasion of her marriage.

Stylized figures of the Kwango River area

The Kwango River area is the home of the Yaka, Suku, Mbala, and Pende, whose masks, figures, and other carved objects show a dynamic stylization. Characterized by geometric patterns formed by the relationship of stylized body parts, Yaka figures lack the organic integration of naturalistic forms produced by the neighbouring Kongo. The turned-up nose is a characteristic of Yaka figures and masks. Large, life-size carved figures stand at the entrances of Yaka initiation huts, the inside walls of which are covered with painted bark panels. *Tudansi* masks, worn by the young men at their initiation into manhood and decorated with polychrome and raffia collars, are topped with animal figures. The dramatically painted *kakungu* mask worn by the leader of the initiation rite represents a gaunt face with exaggerated nose and cheeks. This mask is thought to embody terrific powers and is kept in its own hut. Similar to the Yaka *tudansi* mask is the *hemba* mask of the nearby Suku, which is only slightly less grotesque. Carved Suku figures show more rounded forms than do the Yaka.

Mbala figures have three different types of faces: elongated, wide, and lozenge-shaped. The features (especially the forehead and chin) project forcefully, and the head is surmounted by a crestlike coiffure. Mbala mother-and-

Figure 27: Luba mask, painted wood, Luba cultural area, Congo. In the Cecilia and Irwin Smiley Collection. Height 61 cm.
EB Inc.

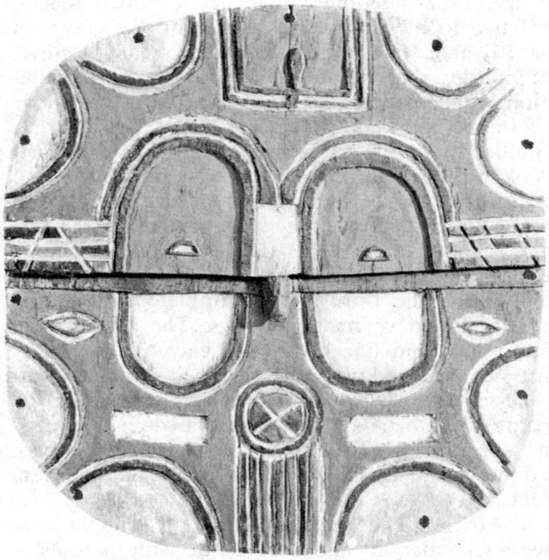

Figure 28: Teke (Bateke) mask, painted wood, Teke tribal region, Lower Congo cultural area. In the Musée de l'Homme, Paris. Diameter 34.9 cm.

By courtesy of the Musee de l'Homme, Paris

child figures are much more powerfully rigid in style than others in the Congo.

Pende masks, made in a realistic style, are among the most dramatic works of all African art. Like the Yaka, small Pende masks fit over the head, helmet style. Representing the mysterious powers to which boys are introduced at initiation, Pende masks are worn in comic entertainments performed during the ceremonies. The masks have facial forms that repeat the angular pattern established by the heavy triangular eyelids, and they are topped by a bushy coif of raffia. Smaller versions of these masks are made as amulets in ivory or wood. The Pende fashion their figures in a style identical to that of their masks. One type of figure, called *tungunlungu,* representing the female ancestry of the tribe, is placed in front of the chief's house.

The Teke live on the banks of the Congo River. They are best known for their fetishes, called *butti,* which serve in the cult of a wide range of supernatural forces sent by the ancestors, who are not worshiped directly. Each figure has its own specific purpose not related directly to its appearance. When a figure is carved for a newborn child, part of the placenta is placed in the stomach cavity of the figure while the rest is buried inside the father's hut (where the family's fetish figures are kept). The figure serves to protect the child until puberty. Figures of identical appearance serve also for success in hunting, trading, and other activities, each figure's specific purpose being known only to the owner. Teke figures are characterized by an angular, geometric form with linear ornamentation. Teke face masks, flat disks painted in bright polychrome, are highly schematic forms bearing no naturalistic associations (see Figure 28).

Artistic achievements of the Kuba

Kuba cultural area. The art of the Kuba is one of the most highly developed of all African traditions, and significant cultural accomplishments are part of their heritage. Mucu Mushanga, their 27th king, was credited with the invention of fire, and he was the first to make clothing out of bark cloth. Shamba Bolongongo (*c.* 1600), the 93rd king, who introduced weaving and textile manufacture to his people, was also the first ruler to have his portrait carved in wood. Shamba Bolongongo's portrait established a tradition of such portraiture among the Kuba people. The kings typically sit facing forward with legs crossed, the left in front of the right; the right hand, with fingers extended, rests on the right knee, and the left hand holds the royal dagger. Geometric patterns cover the stomach and are continued on the back of the figure. The sculptures also include objects significant to each particular king, identifying his own personal accomplishments. Developing from the court style was a popular style, which utilized geometric forms instead of the well-modeled, full-volumed forms of the court figures. Kuba fetishes, emphasizing only essential organs, are highly schematic. The popular style can also be found in the utensils and textiles produced by the Kuba.

The Kuba metalsmith worked with copper, iron, and brass, making weapons and tools to be admired as well as used. In some cases, one metal was inlaid with another. *Mashamboy* and other masks—made of raffia and decorated with shells, beads, and even bells and feathers—were traditionally used to dramatize the founding of the royal dynasty and its matrilineal system of descent (see Figure 30).

Luba cultural area. Although the history of the Luba people (southeast Zaire) is one of violence and warfare, their artistic style is characterized by harmonious integration of organically related forms. Female figures are carved more often than are male figures. Some are freestanding, almost always in a frontal position with their hands on their breasts; others are kneeling, sitting, or standing figures whose upraised hands serve as supports for bowls, seats, and neck rests (see Figure 31). A popular form consists of a kneeling or sitting female figure holding a bowl. Such mendicant figures are used to appeal to spirits for health and aid for pregnant women; neighbours, seeing the figure in front of a woman's hut, will fill it with gifts to help her avoid hardship in pregnancy. The female figures are modeled in rounded forms and have what is called *dodu;* that is, a stylistic tendency toward plumpness.

"Long-face style" of Buli

One well-known Luba sub-style has been called the "long-face style" of Buli. It contrasts strongly with the roundness of other Luba figures. The faces are elongated, with angular, elegant features.

The Songe, who conquered and were conquered by the Luba, created a sculptural style of intense dynamism and vitality. The style of their fetishes, carved from wood or horn and decorated with shells and polychrome, is not as realistic as the classic Luba style, and their integration of non-naturalistic, more geometric forms is impressive. The Songe also produce ceremonial axes, made of iron and copper and decorated with interlaced patterns. One group is known for its *kifwebe* masks, which combine human and animal features painted in red, black, and white.

Louis Loose

Figure 29: Kongo nail fetish, coastal region, Lower Congo cultural area. In the René Vander Straete Collection, Brussels. Height 69.9 cm.

Figure 30: Kuba *mashamboy* mask; fibre, shells, and beads; Kuba cultural area. In the Hampton Institute, Virginia. Height 41 cm.
Frank Willett

In the 19th century the Chokwe and Lunda conquered the Luba kingdom; today these hunters and farmers live in an area that includes part of northern Angola as well as southern Zaire. Their styles are often indistinguishable from one another. The forms they create are monumental and weighty, and both male and female figures are carved in an impressively vigorous style. Also made by these peoples are chairs decorated with figures posed in genre and legendary scenes. Zoomorphic motifs are found on all objects—even utensils such as combs and knives. In ceremonial rites of initiation, men wear painted bark cloth masks and net costumes.

Northern cultural area. The Lega, who inhabit the area between the Luba and the northernmost peoples, have produced figures and masks, mostly carved from ivory in a schematic style (see Figure 32). These objects are used, together with a vast assemblage of artifacts and natural objects, in the initiation to successive grades of the Bwami association.

Northeast cultural area. In the northeast area live the Mangbetu and the Azande. Mangbetu sculpture—in wood, ivory, and pottery—is often characterized by the elongated skull forms produced by binding the heads of young children. Azande sculpture seems largely of Mangbetu derivation.

Northwest cultural area. The Ngbaka and Ngbandi are the peoples whose sculptures are of major significance in the northwest area. There is no single Ngbaka sculptural style: at times the figures are fleshy and rounded; at other times they are considerably more angular. Small animal figures are used as fetishes in hunting. The masks used in circumcision ceremonies are roughly executed. Both the Ngbaka and the Ngbandi make clay images to be used in funeral rituals. The Ngbandi are also known for wooden fetishes and figures. Small carved ivory or wood figures were worn by Ngbandi warriors, who carried shields made of decorated woven fibre. It is often impossible to distinguish the few Ngbandi masks from those of the Ngbaka.

(P.Wa./J.Pi.)

EAST AFRICA

Southern Republic of The Sudan. Agriculture and cattle raising are widespread in this part of The Sudan, though the former is often despised and is engaged in with great reluctance. Among peoples such as the Nuer and Dinka, cattle are a source of aesthetic satisfaction. The prize ox could indeed be regarded as their sculpture.

Schematic wood carving

There is little scope for differentiating local styles of surviving wood carvings, all of which are highly schematic in form. Some of the larger ones, three feet or more in height, are attributed to the Bongo and appear on the graves of important people. The Bongo also made smaller figures, used in murder trials to identify criminals by oracular divination. Other peoples, especially the Bari, also made figures, of uncertain significance.

The Shilluk made life-size representations of their first king, Nyikang; clay figurines of bulls; clay pipe bowls and figurines in hyena form; and masks, typically fashioned of a piece of gourd with applied facial features made of cattle dung and fishbone teeth.

Some peoples decorate their houses with wall paintings and reliefs; the Burun, for example, paint animal murals reminiscent of rock paintings. The Nuba make mural paintings and fine pottery of clay or cow dung, sometimes embellished with finely painted geometric patterns. The southeast Nuba are particularly famous for the body painting of their young men (see Figure 37). Artistic taste appears in weapons, such as throwing knives, and in domestic utensils, elaborate coiffures, and personal ornaments.

Horn of Africa. The Amhara people of Ethiopia have inherited a Christian art and architecture with its roots in Coptic and Byzantine traditions. The Somali, on the other hand, are Muslim, with rich traditions of decorative art.

Wooden tomb posts

The Konso and other peoples of southern Ethiopia carve wooden tomb posts about six feet, six inches high surmounted by carved heads and shoulders, representing deceased nobles or warriors. The Arusi, also of southern Ethiopia, make tombstones of like height, ornamented with engravings filled in with red or black, sometimes showing the deceased in rough relief. Similarly shaped gravestones occur in Somalia, sometimes plain, sometimes adorned with decoration.

The pastoral way of life of the people of this area affects the applied arts; for example, pottery is less used than wood (see Figure 34) or coiled basketry for making containers and dishes for food and liquids. Baskets may be waterproofed and are often patterned in many colours and ornamented with cowrie shells and leather bands. Weaving and leatherwork sometimes reach a high standard; handsome jewelry is made from silver and amber; wooden

Figure 31: Luba chief's stool by the Master of Buli, Buli "long-face style," wood, Luba cultural area. In the Musée Royal de l'Afrique Centrale, Tervuren, Belg. Height 53.3 cm.
By courtesy of the Musee Royal de l'Afrique Centrale, Tervuren, Belg.

Figure 32: Lega carved ivory figure, Zaire. In the Carlo Monzino Collection. Height 14.5 cm.
Mario Carrieri

spoons and combs may be elaborately carved. The Somali have circular shields that are made of antelope hide and have embossed designs; and their swords, daggers, and spears combine utility with artistry.

Region of Lakes Victoria and Tanganyika. A pottery head and torso from Luzira in Uganda (now in the British Museum) is generally regarded as the oldest work of art known from this region, though its age is in fact unknown. Surviving from the treasure of Chief Rumanika of the Karagwe (on the western shore of Lake Victoria), seen by the explorer Henry Morton Stanley in 1876, are wrought-iron figures of two bulls and an eland, a bird of copper foil, and other metal objects that may have formed part of the chief's regalia. Compared to copper and its alloys, iron is little used as an art medium in Africa, and these iron figures are the only such known from East Africa.

The Kerewe of Ukerewe Island in Lake Victoria carved large wooden figures, about three feet high, which appear to have been effigies of deceased chiefs. Other examples of wood sculpture, including figures and masks, are known, some showing possible influences from the Luba of Zaire. In general, however, this is an area in which other artistic mediums clearly dominate.

Decorative arts among the Ganda and Tutsi

The peoples around Lake Victoria, notably the Ganda and Tutsi, have brought the decorative arts to a high peak of excellence. Mats and screens used on house walls are twill plaited or sewn in patterns of black against a pale, straw-coloured ground. Fine baskets, with a variety of motifs in the same colours, come from the same area, as well as fine black pottery burnished to a high lustre. The domestic equipment is made in great variety and is of high artistic merit. Also made are shields, painted or straw-covered and patterned in black or natural colour. Bark cloth robes are printed or painted in black on a rust-red ground colour.

Coastal East Africa. The area of the Eastern Bantu covers Kenya and part of Tanzania, including the Swahili coast. The trade between East Africa, Arabia, and India in the past 1,000 years has had some effect on the decorative art traditions of the region. Swahili art includes wood carving (especially of doors), silversmithing and other metalworking, and finely plaited polychrome mats. Farther inland, direct Arab cultural contact is less obvious. Like the Konso, the Giryama of Kenya produced grave posts surmounted by schematic heads. Notable among the remaining peoples who produce sculpture are the Kamba, who have spontaneously developed a style of wood carving, embellished with coiled-wire jewelry ornament, now sold in gift shops; formerly their art was applied to engraving gourds and inlaying stools with coiled-wire patterns.

Clay figures were made throughout the region for a variety of purposes, including initiation ceremonies at which they had the didactic role of visual aids in traditional education. Murals occur on the mud walls of houses—sometimes decorative, sometimes for ritual and magical purposes. Pottery is normally simple in form and decoration; gourds ornamented with engravings or covered with beadwork are widespread. Stools may be elaborately made, as by the Kamba; shields painted with distinctive polychrome designs occur especially among the Kikuyu and Masai. Traders' beads and coiled brass or iron wire are the raw materials for elaborate personal ornaments in a variety of designs and colour combinations.

SOUTHERN AFRICA

Makonde. The Makonde, living on either side of the Tanzania–Mozambique border, are the most prolific woodcarvers in the area. Masks are more numerous than figures and may be face masks, worn only over the face, or helmet masks, worn over the entire head. Makonde carvers have also developed a new style of spirit-figure carving in ebony (not a wood that is used traditionally).

Mbunda and others. In Zambia the Mbunda, Luvale, and Chokwe make masks; those of the former are made of wood, and those of the latter two are made of painted coarse bark cloth on a wicker frame. Each type is worn with a netted string costume or a fibre skirt. As with the Makonde, the masks may be worn at *makishi* dances (held at the new moon), in initiation ceremonies, or for public entertainments.

Preeminence of the decorative arts in southern Africa

Small figure carvings are made in Zambia, mostly in the west. Decoratively carved food dishes, stools, headrests, *mbira* lamellaphones, and snuff bottles come from Zambia, Malaŵi, and Zimbabwe, together with distinctive baskets and clay pipe bowls carved in animal form, excellent pottery, and fine brass, copper, and aluminum wire intricately wound and plaited to embellish ax handles, hilts and sheaths, and snuff bottles.

Southern Bantu. The Zulu and related peoples of the southern Bantu made wooden figures that are mostly undistinguished and may have been executed under European influence. Attractive small clay models of cattle, made by children, occur here, as they do through much of eastern and southern Africa. Much artistic feeling is revealed in such decorative arts as basketry, pottery, the carving of wooden vessels, stools and headrests, ceremo-

By courtesy of The British Library, London

Figure 33: Full-page illustration of St. George, from a 17th-century Ethiopian manuscript of the Four Gospels. In the British Library, London (Oriental MS. 516, fol. 99v).

Figure 34: Issa wood milk pot, Somali. The vessel was first blackened and then carved in low relief. In the Musée de l'Homme, Paris. Height 50 cm.

By courtesy of the Musee de l'Homme, Paris

nial weapons, spoons, pipes, and personal ornaments consisting of beadwork in great variety. The Ndebele of the Transvaal not only paint the walls of their houses, which is customary, but also decorate their enclosure walls in a variety of coloured geometric patterns (see Figure 14).

(Ma.A.C./J.Pi.)

Other visual arts

POTTERY

Most peoples of sub-Saharan Africa use pottery, many making it themselves. Today, although traditions of pottery-making survive in many rural areas, town dwellers switching from firewood to other sources of fuel are also turning to industrially manufactured wares. The preindustrial traditions involve the molding of fairly coarse-textured clay by hand, either building the clay up in rings or by some variation of the hammer-and-anvil techniques found in preindustrial technologies worldwide. The pots so formed are then fired in open bonfires at a relatively low temperature. The variety of form and design is almost endless.

Pottery techniques are also used in a few places for sculpture, as, for example, in the grave memorials of the Ashanti in Ghana; they are also presumed to have been the means used to form the pottery sculptures of antiquity, such as those of Ife and Nok, in Nigeria, and of Djénné and Mopti, in Mali. In most modern cases, potters are women.

TEXTILES

Demise of traditional cotton spinning and weaving

In both East and West Africa, cloth traditionally was woven of locally grown and hand-spun cotton. In West Africa today most cotton is factory-spun (producing a more regular and easier-to-weave fibre), while in East Africa weaving traditions have virtually disappeared in the face of competition from ready-made fabrics. Woolen yarn is woven in rural Berber areas of North Africa and by Fulani weavers of the inland Niger delta region of West Africa. Silk is also woven in West Africa. Hausa, Nupe, and Yoruba weavers in Nigeria use a locally gathered wild silk; Ashanti and Ewe weavers in southern Ghana use imported silk, a practice begun by Ashanti weavers unraveling imported fabrics in the 17th century. Fibres prepared from the leaves of the raffia palm are woven into cloth principally in Central Africa, especially Zaire, though also in parts of West Africa.

Throughout most of the continent men are the weavers, though in some areas (Nigeria, The Sudan) women also weave. If in any place both sexes weave, each uses a different type of loom. The looms are of two basic types, according to whether one or both sets of warp (the lengths of yarn mounted on the loom) are leashed to a heddle. Each type has more than one version, especially the single-heddle, of which there are various upright and horizontal versions in different regions of Africa.

Textiles are designed either as part of the weaving process—in which case colour, texture, and weave structure are significant—or by a range of techniques employed on the already woven cloth.

Weaving the yarn. The cultures that have developed the greatest skill and creative variety in woven design are undoubtedly the Ashanti and Ewe, with the Fulani and other weavers of the middle Niger, on each side of Timbuktu, following closely in expertise. Three types of woven pattern are common: In the first, yarn of different colours is used for the warp, creating stripes along the length of the cloth. The variety of patterns is almost infinite; most are decorative embellishments of what would otherwise be a plain, naturally coloured textile, but certain patterns can have additional significance, indicating, for example, a corpse, a rich person, or a girl about to be married. This kind of patterning is most developed in West Africa.

In the second type of pattern, the loom is set up in such a way as to allow the weft (the yarn interwoven with the warp) to predominate in the finished cloth, so that the use of different colours gives patterns across the width of the cloth. This type of patterning is typical of North African and of certain types of West African cloth. The third type of patterning employs an extra weft. This second yarn is woven in a different way from the basic weft, using a

By courtesy of the Tropenmuseum, Amsterdam

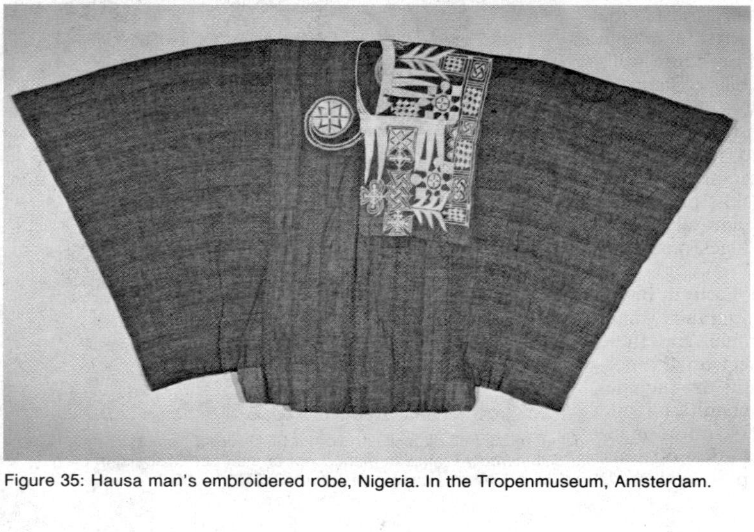

Figure 35: Hausa man's embroidered robe, Nigeria. In the Tropenmuseum, Amsterdam.

Figure 36: *Decorated woven cloth.*
(Left) Fon appliqué banner representing a lion hunt, Dahomey. In the Museum voor Land- en Volkenkunde, Rotterdam. (Right) Kuba raffia pile cloth, Kuba cultural area. In the Hampton Institute, Virginia.
By courtesy of (left) the Museum voor Land- en Volkenkunde, Rotterdam; photograph, Frank Willett

technique known as float weaving. This type of pattern is also common in West Africa.

A further design element is provided by the unusual way in which the double-heddle loom has evolved in West Africa. The construction of the loom is so narrow that it weaves strips of cloth of considerable length; these strips are then sewn together edge to edge to make the finished textile. (The strips range from half an inch in one tradition of Hausa weaving to less than a yard in another: cloth about four inches wide is typical of much of West Africa.) This process can create a repeated pattern of stripes or a juxtaposition of varied patterns.

Dyeing

Embellishing the woven cloth. The most widespread technique of embellishing already woven cloth is dyeing—particularly with indigo but also with other dye colours, all of which are obtained from local vegetable and mineral sources as well as in ready-made, industrially produced form. Another pattern-making technique is known as resist-dyeing, in which parts of the cloth to be embellished are either tied, stitched, or painted with starch to prevent the dye's colouring those parts. Women of the Soninke (Senegal), Guro and Baule (Côte d'Ivoire), and Yoruba peoples have developed contrasting styles in the use of this technique.

Other techniques of embellishing woven cloth are embroidery and appliqué. Embroidery is especially common in two areas. In the first, the savanna stretching across West Africa, male embroiderers give pattern to the wide-sleeved gowns (historically of Saharan origin) typical of that region. The embroidery of the Hausa (see Figure 35) and Nupe are the best-known examples. In the second area, Zaire, women of the Kuba people in particular embroider raffia cloth dyed and woven in complicated geometric motifs (see Figure 36, right). Appliqué, mostly for flags, banners, and tent hangings, is practiced mostly along the Nile and in the savanna region immediately south of the Sahara. It often takes the form of Islāmic texts cut out in cloth of one colour and sewn to cloth of a contrasting colour. An exception to this practice was the Fon Kingdom of Dahomey (present-day Benin), in which banners displayed the attributes of successive kings (see Figure 36, left). In many places appliqué is presently employed in the preparation of masquerade costumes. A related technique is the stitching of glass beads onto a cloth backing, for example, to make royal regalia and sometimes other ceremonial objects. Those practicing this technique are the Yoruba and the Kuba and the various peoples of the Cameroon grasslands.

Other fabrics. Textiles are not traditionally woven throughout sub-Saharan Africa; in some areas other fabrics are used. The stitching of beads to hide is found among some peoples of East and southern Africa—as, for example, in the clothing of Masai women in Kenya. Animal hides are also treated to produce leather, the working of which is an art associated with many of the Islāmic peoples south of the Sahara (for example, the Tuareg and the Hausa), each with its distinctive style. In Uganda bark cloth is prepared by felting and dyeing certain tree barks, which are often then painted or stenciled. The use of vegetable fibres for matting and basketry is universal throughout this region, with particular peoples noted for their styles of pattern and design.

PERSONAL DECORATION

Scarification

The adornment of the human body involves all aspects of the arts as practiced in Africa. The body may be altered in ways that are permanent, especially by scarification, or the cutting of scars. Among the Yoruba, scarification indicates lineage affiliation. Among Nuba women in The Sudan, it is sometimes a mark of physiological status: patterns indicate such stages as the onset of menstruation and the birth of the first child. Sometimes the body is scarified for the aesthetic value of the patterns, as among the Tiv of Nigeria.

The body may be altered in ways that are semipermanent, in the sense that a person is not normally seen in public without certain effects, although they can be removed or adjusted in private. Royal regalia are an example, as are the heavily beaded ornaments worn by Masai women. The body may also be altered in ways that are essentially

James C. Faris

Figure 37: Facial and body design on a young Nuba man, The Sudan.

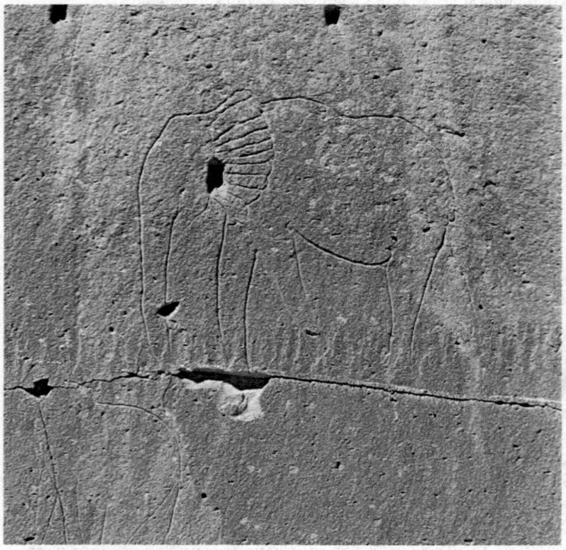

Figure 38: *Rock painting and engraving in the Sahara.*
(Top) Painting of herdsmen and cattle, Sefar; Tassili-n-Ajjer, Algeria; Cattle period. (Left) Engraving of an elephant; Bardaï, Chad; either Bubalus or Cattle period.
Height 20.3 cm.
(Top) J.D. Lajoux, (bottom) Emil Schulthess—Black Star

ephemeral. For example, some young Nuba men celebrate their youthful vigour in extensive body painting (see Figure 37). Hairdressing is done sometimes for its aesthetic value (as among the Yoruba), sometimes to signal age status (East African pastoral peoples such as the Pokot and Samburu). Perhaps the most striking example of body decoration is that of the pastoral Fulani of Nigeria. It reaches its height in the annual *gerewol,* a beauty contest between men whose faces are painted and who wear metal bracelets, bead necklaces, and head ornaments. The women regularly wear elaborate hairstyles (often featuring golden rings around separate locks of hair), together with a profusion of jewelry. The varieties of dress and jewelry found throughout the continent are invariably matters of aesthetic concern whatever social purposes may also be served.

PAINTING

Painting in some form or another is found throughout most of the sub-Saharan region. Besides the paintings and engravings on rock surfaces (see below) and the many traditions of body painting, there are the painting and decorating of houses and other buildings. In any given area numerous art forms may exist, often as completely independent traditions with little obvious relationship to one another in style or content. The purposes fulfilled are equally varied, as seen in personal decoration. Other forms of graphic design are noteworthy as well: the most obvious is calabash (or gourd) decoration, notable traditions of which exist among the Fulani and in Kenya among the Kamba.

There is also the painting of sculpture, whether masks or other forms. Sometimes this is the final stage of the work of the carver, but, as often as not, sculptures are painted and repainted by their owners. For example, mask headpieces among the Kalabari Ijo of Nigeria provide a temporary embodiment of spirits, and the painting of the masks before each performance is part of the ritual by means of which the spirits are summoned.

Paintings and engravings on the surfaces of rocks are found extensively in the Sahara and in southern Africa. The Saharan works were evidently done by successive populations, as is indicated by the different styles and subject matter. Most of the southern African work was probably done by ancestors of the San (Bushmen), the hunter-gatherer peoples of the region. (J.Pi.)

Prehistoric engraving and painting

The Sahara. The earliest known African rock art consists of more than 30,000 engravings and paintings on rocks in the Sahara. At the time most of these works were executed (from about the beginning of the 5th millennium BC into the 2nd), the area was open savanna, supporting animals no longer found in the desert but represented in the art. Representation of the changing fauna makes it possible to divide the art into a succession of periods, the divisions being confirmed by changes in style and in the economy and artifacts possessed by the artists.

The earliest engravings (in southern Oran and in Tassili-n-Ajjer, Algeria, and in Fezzan, Libya) reflect a hunting economy and represent such wild animals as the extinct buffalo *Homoioceras antiquus* (formerly called *Bubalus,* hence the name Bubalus period assigned to these earliest engravings), the elephant, rhinoceros, hippopotamus, giraffe, ostrich, and large antelope (see Figure 38, left). The human figures are armed with clubs, throwing-sticks, axes, and bows.

Carbon-14 dating indicates that there was human occupation (if not drawing) in Tassili-n-Ajjer from the mid-6th millennium BC. Paintings seem to begin a little later than the engravings. These paintings, in which some 30 styles have been distinguished, often represent men and women with globular heads or apparently wearing masks.

There follows, both in painting and in engraving, the Cattle period, in which the depiction of domestic cattle indicates that pastoralism had by then become the basis for human life. The bow is the principal weapon. Bones of domestic cattle and of *Homoioceras* were found together in a deposit dated by carbon-14 to the mid-4th

Figure 39: *San rock painting and engraving in South Africa.*
(Top) Bichrome painting of hunters and animals, near Harrismith, Orange Free State.
(Left) Engraving of a rhinoceros, southwestern Transvaal.

By courtesy of (bottom) A.R. Willcox; photograph, (top) Jean Vertut, France

millennium BC, thus dating this transitional phase of the art. The style of engraving is less naturalistic than in the Bubalus period, the poses stiffer; in contrast, the paintings are more naturalistic, with compositions and a sense of space if not strictly of perspective (see Figure 38, top). The Cattle period ended with the introduction of the horse about 1200 BC.

The Horse period is divided into three sub-periods. The first is the Chariot sub-period, in which the elephant was the only pachyderm still depicted, cattle continued to be represented, and mouflons, or wild sheep, and domesticated dogs appeared. The earliest chariots were carefully rendered with a single shaft and a horse on each side; later chariots consist only of a shaft with two wheels, and human figures are reduced to two isosceles triangles set apex to apex. Spears and shields are introduced and, later, daggers. The distribution of these representations of chariots conforms remarkably to the trans-Saharan trade routes of the more recent past and can be seen as the earliest evidence of them. The Horseman sub-period reflects a change from horse driving to horse riding, though chariots continue. Next, the camel was introduced, possibly as early as 700 BC and certainly by Roman times, producing the Horse and Camel sub-period. Cattle had now become very rare.

Because continuing desiccation led to restricted distribution of the horse (represented mainly in Mauritania), the Camel period reflects only present-day fauna: camel, antelope, oryx, gazelle, mouflon, ostrich, humped cattle, and goat. At first the spear was the only weapon depicted, but later the sword and firearms, weapons that are still in use, were added. The style is highly schematic. The Camel period has continued up to the present time, for their owners, in some cases the nomadic Tuareg, still paint and engrave on rocks, as well as on the occasional truck or airplane, representations of camels in the Sahara.

(F.Wi./J.Pi.)

Rock painting and engraving

Southern Africa. In southern Africa, rock paintings and engravings occur in abundance (see Figure 39). Most surviving paintings were probably made during the last two millennia. The tradition seems to be much older, but no southern African site with either paintings or engravings has been satisfactorily dated to before the time of Christ. The San were still making such paintings in the 19th century, but some of the surviving examples may be the work of Khoikhoin (Hottentots) and Bantu-speakers. The way of life represented is mainly that of Neolithic, or New Stone Age, hunters (which is also more or less the way of life of the San), living off a fauna that has not changed in the area since the middle of the Late Pleistocene Epoch. Many of

By courtesy of the Ethnographical Collection of the University of Zurich

Figure 40: San ostrich-eggshell drinking vessel with incised designs and a necklace of the same material. From Lüderitz, South West Africa/Namibia. In the Ethnographical Collection of the University of Zürich. Height of vessel 14.9 cm.

the paintings depict a peaceful existence; others, perhaps from the 17th century onward, reveal the pressures created by incoming Bantu and Europeans, with scenes of cattle raiding and subsequent fighting between groups (which are recognizable by their stature, dress, and weapons).

The paintings are in three main styles: monochrome, bichrome, and polychrome. The last style has a restricted distribution in the southeast of southern Africa, an area to which the eastern San were confined by incoming Bantu in the early 17th century; yet works in this style are the finest achievements of the art, showing foreshortening and carefully composed groups. Ostrich eggshells (see Figure 40), engraved with linear patterns, are the only recent graphic art form produced by the San, who discontinued rock painting and rock engraving during the 19th century. (F.Wi./Ma.A.C./J.Pi.)

BIBLIOGRAPHY. No attempt has been made in the literature to bring together the arts of Africa as a whole. There is only one journal expressly devoted to all the arts of Africa, *African Arts* (quarterly), and even this concentrates primarily on the visual arts and secondarily on the dramatic context of many visual forms. It is, nevertheless, invaluable as a guide to research, exhibitions, and publications, and it is extremely well illustrated. Otherwise information about the arts has to be culled from a variety of journals concerned either with African studies as a whole—*Africa* (monthly); *Journal of African History* (quarterly); *Odu* (semiannual), mainly Nigerian in content—or with part of the continent only—*Nigeria Magazine* (irregular); *Sudan Notes and Records* (annual)—or from journals devoted to a discipline—*Journal for Ethnomusicology* (3/year); *Yearbook for Traditional Music* (annual); *Objets et Mondes* (quarterly); *Man* (quarterly); and *Research in African Literatures* (quarterly). (J.Pi.)

Literature and theatre: (*Oral traditions*): The single most authoritative work on oral literature is still the full and lucid work by RUTH FINNEGAN, *Oral Literature in Africa* (1970, reissued 1976), covering all the major genres (except epic) and discussing social context, function, and the aesthetic qualities of a wide variety of oral art forms. There are two scholarly bibliographies on oral literatures: VERONIKA GÖRÖG, *Littérature orale d'Afrique noire: Bibliographie analytique* (1981); and HAROLD SCHEUB, *African Oral Narratives, Proverbs, Riddles, Poetry, and Song* (1977). A handbook providing extensive annotated bibliographies on written and (to a lesser extent) oral African literatures is HANS M. ZELL, CAROL BUNDY, and VIRGINIA COULON (eds.), *A New Reader's Guide to African Literature*, 2nd rev. and expanded ed. (1983).

The following works cover and analyze some of the best and most representative collections of oral art forms from many parts of Africa: UCHEGBULAM N. ABALOGU, GARBA ASHIWAJU, and REGINA AMADI-TSHIWALA, *Oral Poetry in Nigeria* (1981), containing articles on a number of different oral genres in contemporary Nigeria; B.W. ANDRZEJEWSKI and I.M. LEWIS, *Somali Poetry: An Introduction* (1964), a detailed and authoritative account of the main genres and their social context by a linguist and a sociologist; ULLI BEIER (comp. and ed.), *Yoruba Poetry: An Anthology of Traditional Poems* (1970), a good introduction to the rich and complex Yoruba oral traditions; JAMES STUART (comp.), *Izibongo: Zulu Praise-Poems* (1968), long poems to kings and chiefs, rich in imagery and allusions, with a discussion of their form, function, and social context; A. COUPEZ and TH. KAMANZI, *Littérature de cour au Rwanda* (1970), analysis and texts of the royal poetry of the kings of Rwanda and accounts of the poets responsible for them; PIERRE SMITH (ed.), *Le Récit populaire au Rwanda* (1975), 30 popular tales from Rwanda that interpret the history of the region in a different way from the royal praises; M. DAMANE and P.B. SANDERS (eds. and trans.), *Lithoko: Sotho Praise-Poems* (1974), an authoritative anthology of praise poems of Basotho chiefs, covering 200 years; FRANCIS MADING DENG, *The Dinka and Their Songs* (1973), a careful account of the performed poetry of the Dinka people of The Sudan; RUTH FINNEGAN (comp. and trans.), *Limba Stories and Story-Telling* (1967, reprinted 1981), stories from the Limba of Sierra Leone, with attention to the creative role of individual narrators; VERONIKA GÖRÖG-KARADY, *Noirs et blancs: Leur Image dans la littérature orale africaine: Étude-anthologie* (1976), an analysis of a large number of tales exploring the different perceptions of the relations between races that the stories reveal; ỌLATUNDE O. ỌLATUNJI, *Features of Yorùbá Oral Poetry* (1984), a full account of the oral genres from the point of view of Yoruba poetics; DENISE PAULME, *La Mère dévorante: Essai sur le morphologie des contes africains* (1976), essays that discuss the social role of the tale and analyze eight archetypal African tales; JEFF OPLAND, *Xhosa Oral Poetry: Aspects of a Black South African Tradition* (1983), an analysis primarily of Xhosa praise poetry and poets, incorporating discussion of the interplay of print, literacy, and orality; and HAROLD SCHEUB, *The Xhosa Ntsomi* (1975), an important collection of Xhosa and Zulu stories with an emphasis on the creative role of the storyteller.

(*Modern literatures in European languages*): The two fullest bibliographies are JANHEINZ JAHN and CLAUS PETER DRESSLER, *Bibliography of Creative African Writing* (1971, reprinted 1975), a list of more than 2,800 books, plays, articles, and anthologies, including works in African languages; and BERNTH LINDFORS, *Black African Literature in English: A Guide to Information Sources* (1979), a list of more than 3,300 critical books and essays on more than 400 African authors, complemented by a 1977–81 supplement (1986), with an additional 2,800 entries. An excellent collection of criticism is ALBERT S. GÉRARD (ed.), *European-Language Writing in Sub-Saharan Africa,* 2 vol. (1986).

Anthologies include CHINUA ACHEBE and C.L. INNES (eds.), *African Short Stories* (1985), stories by major figures such as Ngugi and Ousmane but also containing new writers' work; MARIO DE ANDRADE (ed.), *Antologia da Poesia Negra de Expressão Portuguesa,* prefaced by his essay "Cultura Negro-Africana e Assimilação" (1958, reprinted 1970); GERALD MOORE and ULLI BEIER (eds.), *Modern Poetry from Africa,* rev. ed. (1966, reprinted 1978); JACQUES CHEVRIER (ed.), *Anthologie africaine d'expression française,* vol. 1, *Le Roman et la nouvelle* (1981), prose writing from Francophone Africa, including established and new writers and organized thematically; STEPHEN GRAY (ed.), *The Penguin Book of Southern African Short Stories* (1985, reprinted 1986), a representative selection with translations from Afrikaans and Zulu; MBULELO VIZIKHUNGO MZAMANE (ed.), *Hungry Flames: And Other Black South African Short Stories* (1986), short stories by black South African writers with an introduction by Mzamane; AGOSTINHO NETO, *Sacred Hope* (1974; originally published in Portuguese, 1974), collected poems depicting the struggle for independence; JOHN REED and CLIVE WAKE (comps.), *French African Verse* (1972), poems presented chronologically with parallel French–English texts; K.E. SENANU and T. VINCENT (comps.), *A Selection of African Poetry* (1976), a wide selection, including some oral poetry, with excellent commentary; L.S. SENGHOR (ed.), *Anthologie de la nouvelle poésie nègre et malgache de langue française* (1948, reprinted 1985); *Présence Africaine,* vol. 57 (1966), also called *Nouvelle Somme de poésie du monde noir*, an anthology of poetry by black writers, including Africans; WOLE SOYINKA (ed.), *Poems of Black Africa* (1975), a wide-ranging thematic anthology compiled by one of Africa's major writers; and MICHAEL WOLFERS (comp. and trans.), *Poems from Angola* (1979).

Critical works on writing in French include DOROTHY S. BLAIR, *African Literature in French: A History of Creative Writing in French from West and Equatorial Africa* (1976), an authoritative and thorough coverage of the literature, and *Senegalese Literature: A Critical History* (1984); JACQUES CHEVRIER, *Littérature nègre: Afrique, Antilles, Madagascar,* 3rd ed. rev. and updated (1979, reissued 1984), with chapters on poetry, the novel, and the theatre, and discussing the writers Senghor, Césaire, Jacques Rabemananjara, and Frantz Fanon; MOHAMADOU K. KANE, *Roman africain et traditions* (1982), an examination of the major novelists with attention to social and cultural contexts; LILYAN KESTELOOT, *Black Writers in French: A Literary History of Negritude* (1974; originally published in French, 1963), a detailed account of the major writers of the Negritude school; and LOCHA MATESO, *Littérature africaine et sa critique* (1986), which argues for a critical approach that accepts an African worldview.

Critical works on writings in Portuguese include DONALD BURNESS, *Fire: Six Writers from Angola, Mozambique, and Cape Verde* (1977), a study of Neto, Luandino Vieira, Geraldo Bessa Victor, Mário António, Baltasar Lopes, and Honwana, with frequent comparisons between Lusophone, Francophone, and Anglophone writing, and *Critical Perspectives on Lusophone Literature from Africa* (1981), 22 essays in English and Portuguese on Lusophone African literature; RUSSELL G. HAMILTON, *Voices from an Empire: A History of Afro-Portuguese Literature* (1975); GERALD M. MOSER, *Essays in Portuguese-African Literature* (1969), the first major work in English on Lusophone African writing; and FERNANDO AUGUSTO ALBUQUERQUE MOURÃO, *A Sociedade Angolana Através da Literatura* (1978), on literary life in Luanda over more than a century and on the novelist Castro Soromenho.

Critical works on writings in English include ULLI BEIER (ed.), *Introduction to African Literature: An Anthology of Critical Writing,* new ed. (1979), still an important collection, with seminal essays on Yoruba and Hausa oral literature and on Francophone, Lusophone, and Anglophone writing; MICHAEL CHAPMAN (ed.), *Soweto Poetry* (1982), a collection of reviews, interviews, and critical essays on the black South African poets of the 1970s; DAVID COOK, *African Literature: A Critical View* (1977), which discusses the links and contrasts between English and African literatures, with studies of Achebe and other key African writers; O.R. DATHORNE, *The Black Mind: A History of African Literature* (1974), a broad survey of major contemporary writers and discussion of oral art, early written literature, and work in African languages; GEORG M. GUGELBERGER (ed.), *Marxism and African Literature* (1985), important essays on major writers such as Ngugi and on new developments in African literary criticism; CHRISTOPHER HEYWOOD (ed.), *Aspects of South African Literature* (1976), valuable papers from a critical and historical perspective, including contributions from Nadine Gordimer, Mtshali, and Alan Paton; ABIOLA IRELE, *The African Experience in Literature and Ideology* (1981), critical wide-ranging essays by a distinguished Nigerian critic; and BERNTH LINDFORS (ed.), *Critical Perspectives on Nigerian Literatures* (1976, reissued 1979), essays on oral literatures in the Hausa, Yoruba, and Igbo languages and on the major Nigerian authors. OLADELE TAIWO, *Female Novelists of Modern Africa* (1985); and ELDRED DUROSIMI JONES, *Women in African Literature Today: A Review* (1987), explore a topic largely ignored in earlier criticism. See also G.D. KILLAM (ed.), *The Writing of East and Central Africa* (1984); and BERNTH LINDFORS, *Early Nigerian Literature* (1982).

(*Literatures in African languages*): Two indispensable general references are ALBERT S. GÉRARD, *African Language Literatures: An Introduction to the Literary History of Sub-Saharan Africa* (1981); and B.W. ANDRZEJEWSKI, S. PIŁASZEWICZ, and W. TYLOCH (eds.), *Literatures in African Languages: Theoretical Issues and Sample Surveys* (1985), containing essays on literature in more than 15 different languages, especially Yoruba, Hausa, Amharic, Somali, and Swahili. Also informative is *Review of National Literatures,* vol. 2, no. 2 (Fall 1971), a special issue devoted to black African literatures.

Writings on specific language literatures include ADEBOYE BABALỌLA, "A Survey of Modern Literature in the Yoruba, Efik and Hausa Languages," in BRUCE KING (ed.), *Introduction to Nigerian Literature* (1971), pp. 50–63; PIERRE COMBA, "Le Roman dans la littérature éthiopienne de langue amharique," *Journal of Semitic Studies,* 9(1):173–186 (1964); ALBERT S. GÉRARD, *Four African Literatures: Xhosa, Sotho, Zulu, Amharic* (1971), including a critical study and literary history of Amharic; PAUL E. HUNTSBERGER (comp.), *Highland Mosaic: A Critical Anthology of Ethiopian Literature in English* (1973), extracts from ancient and modern Ethiopian literature with a critical overview; THOMAS LEIPER KANE, *Ethiopian Literature in Amharic* (1975), an indispensable introduction to the literature; MARGARET LAURENCE (comp.), *A Tree for Poverty: Somali Poetry and Prose* (1954, reissued 1970); J.W.T. ALLEN (comp. and trans.), *Tendi: Six Examples of a Swahili Classical Verse Form* (1971); LYNDON HARRIES (ed. and trans.), *Swahili Poetry* (1962), a descriptive survey outlining the themes and forms of early Swahili poetry; JAN KNAPPERT (comp.), *Four Swahili Epics* (1964), and *Four Centuries of Swahili Verse: A Literary History and Anthology* (1979), a scholarly account covering verse in manuscripts and oral traditions; RAJMUND OHLY, *Aggressive Prose: A Case Study in Kiswahili Prose of the Seventies* (1975); G. FORTUNE (ed.), *African Languages in Schools* (1964), containing a number of papers on Shona prose and poetry, and "75 Years of Writing in Shona," *Zambezia,* 1(1):55–67 (January 1969); RUDO GAIDZANWA, *Images of Women in Zimbabwean Literature* (1985), an analysis of women in books in Shona, Ndebele, and English; *Zimbabwe: Prose and Poetry* (1974, reprinted 1979), a collection of Shona prose and poetry in translation, including a translation of the short historical novel *Feso* by Mutswairo; GEORGE P. KAHARI, *Aspects of the Shona Novel and Other Related Genres* (1986), a comprehensive survey of Shona prose writing to date; ABRAHAM KRIEL, *An African Horizon* (1971), a discussion of the ethical and philosophical significance of a number of Shona novels; A.C. JORDAN, *Towards an African Literature: The Emergence of Literary Form in Xhosa* (1973), 12 authoritative essays on oral and written Xhosa literature; and B.W. VILAKAZI, "The Conception and Development of Poetry in Zulu," *Bantu Studies,* 12:105–134 (1938, reprinted 1968), a pioneering critical essay on oral and written Zulu poetry.

(*African theatre*): Studies on contemporary African drama and on theatre in African languages include B.W. ANDRZEJEWSKI, "Modern and Traditional Aspects of Somali Drama," in RICHARD M. DORSON (ed.), *Folklore in the Modern World* (1978), pp. 87–101; MICHAEL ETHERTON, *The Development of African Drama* (1982), which analyzes the literary and traditional roots of African drama from East and West Africa and draws on a wide range of plays; BIODUN JEYIFO, *The Truthful Lie: Essays in a Sociology of African Drama* (1985), a work setting plays by such diverse figures as Soyinka and Fugard in their sociological context and including an essay on the social and dramatic significance of Yoruba popular theatre; ELDRED DUROSIMI JONES, *The Writings of Wole Soyinka,* rev. ed. (1983), a major critical introduction to Soyinka's drama; ROBERT MSHENGU KAVANAGH, *Theatre and Cultural Struggle in South Africa* (1985), a stimulating study of the cultural and political context of South African drama by Gibson Kente and other black South African playwrights and including plays by Fugard, Ntshona, and Kani; OYIN OGUNBA and ABIOLA IRELE (eds.), *Theatre in Africa* (1976, reprinted 1978), a collection of 10 essays on traditional and modern drama in Africa; YENI OGUNBIYI (ed.), *Drama and Theatre in Nigeria: A Critical Source Book* (1981), an excellent survey and overview of Nigerian theatre, both traditional and modern; BAKARY TRAORÉ, *The Black African Theatre and Its Social Functions* (1972; originally published in French, 1958), focusing on a particular variety of theatre in traditional societies in former French colonies and covering the plays of Keita Fodeba; and HAROLD A. WATERS, *Black Theatre in French: A Guide* (1978), including a general introduction and covering the plots of some 150 plays, grouping them thematically.

(E.A.W.G.)

Music: Works dealing with the distribution of style areas and the history of African music include FRANCIS BEBEY, *African Music: A People's Art* (1975; originally published in French, 1969); WOLFGANG BENDER, *Sweet Mother: Moderne Afrikanische Musik* (1985), dealing with highlife and related popular styles; BILLY BERGMAN, *Goodtime Kings: Emerging African Pop* (1985), a discussion of eight styles of popular music; O. BOONE, *Les Xylophones du Congo Belge* (1936); DAVID COPLAN, *In Township Tonight! South Africa's Black City Music and Theatre* (1985), a survey of South African popular music and its history; E.M. VON HORNBOSTEL, "African Negro Music," *Africa,* 1(1):30–62 (January 1928), a pioneer survey in the field; A.M. JONES, *African Music in Northern Rhodesia and Some Other Places,* rev. ed. (1958); GERHARD KUBIK, *The Kachamba Brothers' Band: A Study of Neo-Traditional Music in Malaŵi* (1974; originally published in German, 1972); ALAN P. MERRIAM, "African Music," in WILLIAM R. BASCOM and MELVILLE J. HERSKOVITS (eds.), *Continuity and Change in African Cultures* (1959, reprinted 1970), pp. 49–86, a valuable and concise survey of salient features; PAUL OLIVER, *Savannah Syncopators: African Retentions in the Blues* (1970), which traces African roots of the blues; JOHN STORM ROBERTS, *Black Music of Two Worlds* (1972, reissued 1974), which surveys black popular music in Africa and the Americas; GILBERT ROUGET, "La Musique d'Afrique noire," in ROLAND-MANUEL (ed.), *Histoire de la musique,* vol. 1 (1960), pp. 215–237; KLAUS P. WACHSMANN (ed.), *Essays on Music and History in Africa* (1971); and KLAUS WACHSMANN and PETER COOKE, "Africa," in STANLEY SADIE (ed.), *The New Grove Dictionary of Music and Musicians,* vol. 1 (1981), pp. 144–153. See also L.J.P. GASKIN (comp.), *A Select Bibliography of Music in Africa* (1965), an annotated work useful for locating earlier sources.

The following deal more specifically with musical instruments of Africa: DAVID W. AMES and ANTHONY V. KING, *Glossary of Hausa Music and Its Social Contexts* (1971); JOHN F. CARRINGTON, *Talking Drums of Africa* (1949, reprinted 1969), describing how drums are used to transmit messages in Central Africa; E.M. VON HORNBOSTEL, "The Ethnology of African Sound-Instruments," *Africa,* 6(2):129–157 (April 1933), a survey of types, their distribution, and prehistory; A.M. JONES, "African Drumming: A Study in the Combination of Rhythms in African Music," *Bantu Studies,* 8:1–16 (1934, reprinted 1967), a pioneer study of cross-rhythms in Zambia; PERCIVAL R. KIRBY, *The Musical Instruments of the Native Races of South Africa,* 2nd ed. (1965), the standard work on this subject; GERHARD KUBIK, *Ostafrika* (1982), a well-illustrated survey of East African music and instruments, with a wealth of detailed information; J.S. LAURENTY, *Les Cordophones du Congo Belge et du Ruanda-Urundi* (1960); STANLEY SADIE (ed.), *The New Grove Dictionary of Musical Instruments,* 3 vol. (1984, reprinted 1985), which extensively covers African instruments; HUGH TRACEY, *Chopi Musicians: Their Music, Poetry, and Instruments* (1948, reprinted 1970), about the Chopi of Mozambique, who are famous for their *timbila* xylophone orchestras; MARGARET TROWELL and KLAUS P. WACHSMANN, *Tribal Crafts of Uganda* (1953), including a discussion of musical instruments; KLAUS P. WACHSMANN, "The Primitive Musical Instruments," in ANTHONY BAINES (ed.), *Musical Instruments Through the Ages* (1961, reprinted 1978), pp. 23–54; and ULRICH WEGNER, *Afrikanische Saiteninstrumente* (1984). See also two works in *Essays for a Humanist: An Offering to Klaus Wachsmann* (1977): DAVID K. RYCROFT, "Evidence of Stylistic Continuity in Zulu 'Town' Music," pp. 216–260; and FRANK WILLET, "A Contribution to the History of Musical Instruments Among the Yoruba," pp. 350–389.

Theoretical and practical aspects of African musical structure are to be found in the following: PAUL BERLINER, *The Soul of Mbira: Music and Traditions of the Shona People of Zimbabwe*

(1978, reprinted 1981); A.M. JONES, "African Rhythm," *Africa,* 24(1):26–47 (January 1954), and *Studies in African Music,* 2 vol. (1959, reprinted 1978), based mainly on Ghana and Zambia but also with much general discussion; JOSEPH KYAGAMBIDDWA, *African Music from the Source of the Nile* (1955); J.H. KWABENA NKETIA, *African Music in Ghana: A Survey of Traditional Forms* (1962), *Drumming in Akan Communities of Ghana* (1963), *Folk Songs of Ghana* (1963), and *The Music of Africa* (1974, reprinted 1986), the last a useful survey dealing mainly but not exclusively with West Africa; DAVID RYCROFT, "Nguni Vocal Polyphony," *Journal of the International Folk Music Council,* 19:88–103 (1967), an examination of overlapping antiphonal parts in polyphony among the Zulu and their neighbours; ARTUR SIMON (ed.), *Musik in Afrika* (1983); KWESI YANKAH, "Beyond the Spoken Word: Aural Literature in Africa," *Cross Rhythms,* 2:114–146 (1985); and HUGO ZEMP, *Musique Dan: La Musique dans la pensée et la vie sociale d'une société africaine* (1971), an in-depth study of music and its context among the Dan of Côte d'Ivoire.

The journal *African Music* (irregular), the only periodical devoted solely to African music, has published a great number of valuable and scholarly articles in this field, including, on the history of African music, GERHARD KUBIK, "Harp Music of the Azande and Related Peoples in the Central African Republic," 3(3):37–76 (1964); and ANDREW TRACEY, "The Original African Mbira?" 5(2):85–104 (1972); on musical instruments, K.A. GOURLAY, "Long Trumpets of Northern Nigeria—In History and Today," 6(2):48–72 (1982); DAVID K. RYCROFT, "The Zulu Bow Songs of Princess Magogo," 5(4):41–97 (1975/76), the late princess having been an expert performer and a leading authority on Zulu music and its history; and ANDREW TRACEY, "The Nyanga Panpipe Dance," 5(1):73–89 (1971); and, on theoretical and practical aspects, ROSEMARY JOSEPH, "Zulu Women's Music," 6(3):53–89 (1983); GERHARD KUBIK, "The Structure of Kiganda Xylophone Music," 2(3):6–30 (1960), a detailed analysis of performance and output, "The Phenomenon of Inherent Rhythms in East and Central African Instrumental Music," 3(1):33–42 (1962), and "Composition Techniques in Kiganda Xylophone Music," 4(3):22–72 (1969); and ANDREW TRACEY, "Mbira Music of Jege A. Tapera," 2(4):44–63 (1961), and "The Matepe Mbira Music of Rhodesia," 4(4):37–61 (1970).

(G.K./D.K.R.)

Dance and dance theatre: Among the studies of particular traditions are JAMES W. FERNANDEZ, *Bwiti: An Ethnography of the Religious Imagination in Africa* (1982), concerned with Gabon; W.D. HAMBLY, *Tribal Dancing and Social Development* (1926, reprinted 1974), material on dances of southern, East, and West Africa; PEGGY HARPER, "Dance," in SABURI O. BIOBAKU (ed.), *Living Culture of Nigeria* (1976), pp. 25–32, an analysis of tradition and change in a wide range of Nigerian cultures; ROBIN HORTON, *The Gods as Guests: An Aspect of Kalabari Religious Life* (1960), which describes a cycle of Kalabari ritual festivals in the Niger Delta and the central role played by masquerade dancers; T.O. RANGER, *Dance and Society in Eastern Africa, 1890–1970: The Beni Ngoma* (1975); PAUL SPENCER (ed.), *Society and the Dance: The Social Anthropology of Process and Performance* (1985); ROBERT FARRIS THOMPSON, *African Art in Motion* (1974, reissued 1979), a book on African sculpture that contains interesting writing on mime and dance as features of masquerade performance; HUGH TRACEY, "The Dancers and Dances," ch. 3 in his *Chopi Musicians: Their Music, Poetry, and Instruments* (1948, reprinted 1970), pp. 84–105, an excellent descriptive account, and *African Dances of the Witwatersrand Gold Mines* (1952), an illustrated description of Bantu dances as performed by workers in the gold mines of South Africa; and ARCHIBALD NORMAN TUCKER, *Tribal Music and Dancing in the Southern Sudan (Africa) at Social and Ceremonial Gatherings* (1933), a useful study of music and rhythms in the dance.

Selected articles in the journal *African Arts* (quarterly) include PAULA BEN-AMOS and OSARENREN OMOREGIE, "Ekpo Ritual in Avbiama Village," 2(4):8–13, 79 (Summer 1969), describing the role of masquerades in a ritual festival of the rural Bini of Nigeria; JEAN M. BORGATTI, "Age Grades, Masquerades, and Leadership Among the Northern Edo," 16(1):36–51 (November 1982), on the masquerade ceremonies of the Edo in the Bendel state of Nigeria; PAUL GEBAUER, "Dances of Cameroon," 4(4):8–15 (Summer 1971), a study of the dance traditions of a number of cultures in Cameroon; PEGGY HARPER, "Dance in a Changing Society," 1(1):10–13, 76–77, 79–80 (Autumn 1967), a study of ethnic traditions of dance within Nigerian cultures and the emergence of theatrical forms in urban centres; PASCAL JAMES IMPERATO, "Contemporary Adapted Dances of the Dogon," 5(1):28–33, 68–72 (Autumn 1971), dealing with tradition and change in the masquerade dances of the Dogon, and "Dances of the Tyi Wara," 4(1):8–13, 71–80 (Autumn 1970), a study of the use of animal masks by the Tyi Wara masqueraders of the Bambara; and J.A.R. WEMBAH-RASHID, "Isinyago and Midimu: Masked Dancers of Tanzania and Mozambique," 4(2):38–44 (Winter 1971). Also useful are the following articles: PEGGY HARPER, "Dance in Nigeria," *Ethnomusicology,* 13(2):280–295 (May 1969), on the form and social function of the dance of the Yoruba in Nigeria, "The Kambari People and Their Dances," *Odu,* 7:83–96 (April 1972), a study of dance as an expression of the way of life of rural Kambari in Nigeria, and "The Role of Dance in Gẹ̀lẹ̀dẹ́ Ceremonies of the Village of Ìjìó," *Odu,* 4:67–94 (October 1970), a study of dance and dancing masquerades.

Few works exist on dance drama of Africa as a special study, and most of them are in French. Additional descriptive material can often be found in more general works by anthropologists, cultural historians, and travelers. See especially SAKA ACQUAYE, "Modern Folk Opera in Ghana," *African Arts,* 4(2):60–63 (Winter 1971); KEÏTA GODEBA, "La Danse africaine et la scène," *Présence Africaine,* 14–15:202–209 (June–September 1957), on traditional dance forms; PEGGY HARPER, "African Tradition in Theatre and Liturgy," *Theoria to Theory,* 11(3):185–193 (December 1977); 'BIODUN JEYIFO, *The Yoruba Popular Travelling Theatre of Nigeria* (1984), an excellent account; BAKARY TRAORÉ, *The Black African Theatre and Its Social Functions* (1972; originally published in French, 1958), the standard work; and PIERRE VERGER, *Dieux d'Afrique* (1954), on the nature and forms of ritual and mime.

(P.H./J.Pi.)

Architecture: A general introduction to building in Africa is SUSAN DENYER, *African Traditional Architecture: An Historical and Geographical Perspective* (1978). See also PAUL OLIVER (ed.), *Shelter in Africa* (1971, reissued 1976), case studies, and *Dwellings: The House Across the World* (1987). Early stages of African urbanism are discussed in BASIL DAVIDSON, *The Lost Cities of Africa* (U.K. title, *Old Africa Rediscovered,* 1959, reissued 1970); and RICHARD W. HULL, *African Cities and Towns Before the European Conquest* (1976).

Of the regional studies, the most notable is JAMES WALTON, *African Village* (1956), which deals with southern and East Africa; it is brought up-to-date in FRANCO FRESCURA, *Rural Shelter in Southern Africa: A Survey of the Architecture, House Forms, and Constructional Methods of the Black Rural Peoples of Southern Africa* (1981). Visually impressive, though with less substantial research, is RENÉ GARDI, *Indigenous African Architecture* (1974; originally published in German, 1973), which deals with savanna forms of West Africa; other fine examples are to be found in JEAN-LOUIS BOURGEOIS, *Spectacular Vernacular: A New Appreciation of Traditional Desert Architecture* (1983), with photographs by CAROLLEE PELOS; and JEAN DETHIER, *Down to Earth: Mud Architecture* (1982; originally published in French, 1981).

Of the local studies, the early and influential one by JEAN-PIERRE BÉGUIN *et al., L'Habitat au Cameroun: Présentation des principaux type d'habitat: Essai d'adaptation aux problèmes actuels* (1952), records the styles of former French Cameroun with immaculate drawings and photography. A noteworthy successor, JEAN-PAUL BOURDIER and TRINH T. MINH-HA, *African Spaces: Designs for Living in Upper Volta* (1985), examines comparatively a number of compounds in Burkina Faso. Also important is LABELLE PRUSSIN, *Architecture in Northern Ghana* (1969), in which the forms and functions of six compounds are compared. Four villages in eastern Botswana are discussed in ANITA LARSSON and VIERA LARSSON, *Traditional Tswana Housing* (1984). See also KAJ BLEGVAD ANDERSEN, *African Traditional Architecture: A Study of the Housing and Settlement Patterns of Rural Kenya* (1977).

Perhaps the most exhaustive anthropological study is FRIEDRICH W. SCHWERDTFEGER, *Traditional Housing in African Cities* (1982), comparing the architecture of Zaria and Ibadan, Nigeria, with that of Marrakech, Mor. Hausa mosques and palaces are discussed in J.C. MOUGHTIN, *Hausa Architecture* (1985). The symbolism of built forms is movingly described in MARCEL GRIAULE, *Conversations with Ogotemmêli: An Introduction to Dogon Religious Ideas* (1965, reprinted 1980; originally published in French, 1948). Cult houses or shrines are the subject of MICHAEL SWITHENBANK, *Ashanti Fetish Houses* (1969); while ULLI BEIER, *African Mud Sculpture* (1963), is largely devoted to Igbo *mbari* houses and Yoruba palace reliefs. Studies of palaces include G.J. AFOLABI OJO, *Yoruba Palaces: A Study of the Afins of Yorubaland* (1966); JACOB EGHAREVBA, *A Short History of Benin,* 4th ed. (1968); and JAMES S. KIRKMAN, *Gedi: The Palace* (1963), a study of a number of Arab-Swahili centres. Of these, Lamu survives and is examined in USAM GHAIDAN, *Lamu: A Study of the Swahili Town* (1975). A detailed study of the influence of Islāmic forms on sub-Saharan architecture is to be found in LABELLE PRUSSIN, *Hatumere: Islamic Design in West Africa* (1986). RUTH PLANT, *Architecture of the Tigre, Ethiopia* (1985), surveys the rock-cut Ethiopian Christian cave churches, many dating from the 13th century. Colonial influence on African town form is discussed especially with reference to Lagos in AKIN L. MABOGUNJE, *Urbanization in Nigeria* (1968). Problems in rapid urban growth are the subject of JOSEF GUGLER and WILLIAM G. FLANAGAN, *Urbanization and Social Change in West Africa* (1978); while design by contemporary African architects is included in UDO KULTERMANN, *New Architecture in Africa* (1963; originally published in German, 1963), and *New Directions in African Architecture,* trans. from German (1969). In addition, a number of journals, including *Tribus* (annual), occasionally publish articles on African architecture.

(P.O.)

Visual arts: Recommended general accounts are FRANK WILLET, *African Art: An Introduction* (1971, reprinted 1985); J. VANSINA, *Art History in Africa: An Introduction to Method* (1984); WERNER GILLON, *A Short History of African Art* (1984, reissued 1986); and ROBERT LAYTON, *The Anthropology of Art* (1981), in part about Africa. For a survey of modern developments, see ULLI BEIER, *Contemporary Art in Africa* (1968).

The best account of sculptural traditions is still ELIOT ELISOFON, *The Sculpture of Africa* (1958, reissued 1978), with text by WILLIAM B. FAGG; while for other visual media, see JOHN PICTON and JOHN MACK, *African Textiles: Looms, Weaving and Design* (1979); JOHN PICTON (ed.), *Earthenware in Asia and Africa* (1984); PHILIP ALLISON, *African Stone Sculpture* (1968); MARGARET TROWELL, *African Design,* 3rd ed. (1971); EUGENIA W. HERBERT, *The Red Gold of Africa: Copper in Precolonial History and Culture* (1984); T.J.H. CHAPPEL, *Decorated Gourds in North-Eastern Nigeria* (1977); and ROY SIEBER, *African Textiles and Decorative Arts* (1972), and *African Furniture and Household Objects* (1980).

For studies of particular traditions, see WARREN L. D'AZEVEDO (ed.), *The Traditional Artist in African Societies* (1973); PAULA BEN-AMOS, *The Art of Benin* (1980); DANIEL P. BIEBUYCK, *The Arts of Central Africa: An Annotated Bibliography* (1987), on Zaire, and *Lega Culture: Art, Initiation, and Moral Philosophy Among a Central African People* (1973); R.E. BRADBURY, "Ezomo's *Ikegobo* and the Benin Cult of the Hand," *Man,* 61:129–138 (1961); ROBERT BRAIN and ADAM POLLOCK, *Bangwa Funerary Sculpture* (1971); EUGENE C. BURT, *An Annotated Bibliography of the Visual Arts of East Africa* (1980), concentrating on Kenya, Tanzania, Uganda, and the Makonde; KEVIN CARROLL, *Yoruba Religious Carving: Pagan & Christian Religious Sculpture in Nigeria and Dahomey* (1967); HERBERT M. COLE, *Mbari: Art and Life Among the Owerri Igbo* (1982); HENRY JOHN DREWAL and MARGARET THOMPSON DREWAL, *Gẹlẹdẹ: Art and Female Power Among the Yoruba* (1983); WILLIAM FAGG, *Yoruba, Sculpture of West Africa* (1982); JAMES C. FARIS, *Nuba Personal Art* (1972); EVERHARD FISCHER and HANS HIMMELHEBER, *The Arts of the Dan in West Africa* (1984; originally published in German, 1976); DOUGLAS FRASER and HERBERT M. COLE (eds.), *African Art & Leadership* (1972); ANITA J. GLAZE, *Art and Death in a Senufo Village* (1981); ROBIN HORTON, "The Kalabari *Ekine* Society: A Borderland of Religion and Art," *Africa,* 33(2):94–114 (April 1963), *Kalabari Sculpture* (1965), and "Igbo: An Ordeal for Aristocrats," *Nigeria Magazine,* 90:168–183 (September 1966); KATHERYNE S. LOUGHRAN (ed.), *Somalia in Word and Image* (1986); JOHN MACK, "Bakuba Embroidery Patterns: A Commentary on Their Social and Political Implications," *Textile History,* 11:163–174 (1980), and "Animal Representation in Kuba Art: An Anthropological Interpretation of Sculpture," *Oxford Art Journal,* 4(1):50–56 (November 1981); KATHERYNE S. LOUGHRAN *et al., Somalia in Word and Image* (1986); SIMON OTTENBERG, *Masked Rituals of Afikpo: The Contexts of an African Art* (1975); and SUSAN MULLIN VOGEL, *African Aesthetics* (1986).

For antiquities and rock art, see PETER S. GARLAKE, *Great Zimbabwe* (1973), and *The Kingdoms of Africa* (1978); JEAN-DOMINIQUE LAJOUX, *The Rock Paintings of Tassili* (1963; originally published in French, 1962); J. DAVID LEWIS-WILLIAMS, *The Rock Art of Southern Africa* (1983); HENRI LHOTE, *The Search for the Tassili Frescoes: The Story of the Prehistoric Rock-Paintings of the Sahara,* 2nd ed. (1973); DAVID W. PHILLIPSON, *African Archaeology* (1985); THURSTON SHAW, *Nigeria: Its Archaeology and Early History* (1978), and *Unearthing Igbo-Ukwu: Archaeological Discoveries in Eastern Nigeria* (1977); PATRICIA VINNICOMBE, *People of the Eland: Rock Paintings of the Drakensberg Bushmen as a Reflection of Their Life and Thought* (1976); and A.R. WILLCOX, *The Rock Art of Africa* (1984).

(J.Pi.)

Agricultural Sciences

The agricultural sciences deal with the challenges of food and fibre production and processing. They include the technologies of soil cultivation, crop cultivation and harvesting, animal production, and the processing of plant and animal products for human consumption and use.

Food is the most basic human need. The domestication and cultivation of plants and animals beginning almost 10,000 years ago were aimed at ensuring that this need was met, and then as now these activities also fit with the relentless human drive to understand and control the Earth's biosphere. Over the last century and a half, many of the world's political leaders have recognized what India's Jawaharlal Nehru did, that "Most things except agriculture can wait." Scientific methods have been applied widely, and the results have revolutionized agricultural production. Under the conditions of prescientific agriculture, in a good harvest year, six people can produce barely enough food for themselves and four others. Advanced technologies have made it possible for one farmer in the United States, for example, to produce food for more than 100 people. The farmer has been enabled to increase yields per acre and per animal; reduce losses from diseases, pests, and spoilage; and augment net production by improved processing methods.

Until the 1930s, the benefits of agricultural research derived mostly from labour-saving inventions. Once the yield potentials of the major economic crops were increased through agricultural research, however, crop production per acre increased dramatically. Between 1940 and 1980 in the United States, for example, per-acre yields of corn tripled, those of wheat and soybeans doubled, and farm output per hour of farm work increased almost 10-fold as capital was substituted for labour. New techniques of preserving food products made it possible to transport them over greater distances, in turn facilitating adjustments among locations of production and consumption, with further benefits to production efficiency (*see* FOOD PROCESSING).

From a global perspective, the international flow of agricultural technology allows for the increase of agricultural productivity in developed and developing countries alike. From 1965 to 1985, for example, world trade in grains tripled, as did net exports from the United States. In fact, by the 1980s more than two-fifths of U.S. crop production was exported, making U.S. agriculture heavily dependent upon international markets.

This article is divided into the following sections:

History 168
  Liebig's contribution
  U.S. agricultural education and research
Major divisions 169
  Soil and water sciences
  Plant sciences
  Animal sciences
  Food sciences and other post-harvest technologies
  Agricultural engineering
  Agricultural economics
Other agricultural sciences 171
Emerging agricultural sciences 171
Bibliography 171

HISTORY

Early knowledge of agriculture was a collection of experiences verbally transmitted from farmer to farmer. Some of this ancient lore had been preserved in religious commandments, but the traditional sciences rarely dealt with a subject seemingly considered so commonplace. Although much was written about agriculture during the Middle Ages, the agricultural sciences did not then gain a place in the academic structure. Eventually, a movement began in central Europe to educate farmers in special academies, the earliest of which was established at Keszthely, Hungary, in 1796. Students were still taught only the experiences of farmers, however.

Liebig's contribution. The scientific approach was inaugurated in 1840 by Justus von Liebig of Darmstadt, Germany. His classic work, *Die organische Chemie in ihrer Anwendung auf Agrikulturchemie und Physiologie* (1840; *Organic Chemistry in Its Applications to Agriculture and Physiology*), launched the systematic development of the agricultural sciences. In Europe, a system of agricultural education soon developed that comprised secondary and postsecondary instruction. The old empirical-training centres were replaced by agricultural schools throughout Europe and North America. Under Liebig's continuing influence, academic agriculture came to concentrate on the natural sciences.

U.S. agricultural education and research. Agricultural colleges came into being in the United States during the second half of the 19th century. In 1862 Pres. Abraham Lincoln signed the Morrill Act, under which Congress granted to each state 30,000 acres (12,141 hectares) of land for each representative and senator "for the endowment, support and maintenance of at least one college where the leading object shall be—without excluding other scientific and classical studies and including military tactics—to teach branches of learning as are related to agriculture and mechanic arts." Thus the stage was set for the remarkably successful land-grant system of agricultural education and research in the United States. That same year Iowa became the first state to accept the provisions of the act, and all the other states have followed. Now, land-grant colleges of agriculture offer programs of study leading to both baccalaureate and postgraduate degrees in the various agricultural sciences. These institutions have served as models for colleges established in many nations.

The Morrill Act

In 1887 Congress passed the Hatch Act, which provided for necessary basic and applied agricultural research to be conducted by the state colleges of agriculture in cooperation with the U.S. Department of Agriculture (USDA). Agricultural experiment stations were established in 16 states between 1875 and 1885, and they now exist in all 50 states. These stations, together with USDA research centres around the country, comprise a network of coordinated research installations in the agricultural sciences. Slightly more than half of the agricultural research in the United States, however, is conducted by the private sector.

The Hatch Act

Congress passed the Smith–Lever Act in 1914, providing for, among other things, the teaching of improved agricultural practices to farmers. Thus the agricultural extension service—now recognized as an outstanding example of adult vocational education—was established.

The demand for instruction in agriculture at the secondary level gained momentum around the beginning of the 20th century. Some private agricultural schools had already been founded in the East, and by 1916 agriculture was being taught in more than 3,000 high schools. Federally aided programs of vocational agriculture education began with the passage of the Smith–Hughes Vocational Education Act in 1917. By the second half of the 20th century, an average of 750,000 high-school, young farmer, and adult farmer students were enrolled annually in classes offered by about 10,000 vocational agriculture departments in the United States. Since passage of the Vocational Education Act of 1963, further expansion of agricultural education has occurred in vocational schools and in courses offered at junior and senior colleges.

(G.P./G.F.E./J.R.C./S.E.Cu.)

MAJOR DIVISIONS

The agricultural sciences can be divided into six groups. In all fields, the general pattern of progress toward the solution of specific problems or the realization of opportunities is: (1) research to more accurately define the functional requirements to be served; (2) design and development of products, processes, and other means of better serving these requirements; and (3) extension of this information to introduce improved technologies to the agricultural industries. This has proved to be a tremendously successful approach and is being used the world over.

Soil and water sciences. Soil and water sciences deal with the geological generation of soil, soil and water physics and chemistry, and all other factors relevant to soil fertility. Soil science began with the formulation of the theory of humus in 1809. A generation later, Liebig introduced experimental science, including a theory of the supply of soil with mineral nutrients. In the 20th century, a general theory of soil fertility has developed, embracing soil cultivation, the enrichment of soil with humus and nutrients, and the preparation of soil in accordance with crop demands. Water regulation, principally drainage and irrigation, is also included.

Theory of soil fertility

Soil and water research have made possible the use of all classes of land in more effective ways, while the control of soil erosion and deterioration has made other advances even more striking. Because the amount of water available for plant growth is one of the major limiting factors in crop production, improved tillage and terracing practices have been devised to conserve soil moisture, and soil-management and land-use practices have been developed to increase the infiltration of snow, rain, and irrigation water, thereby reducing losses caused by runoff.

Public and private research into chemical fertilizers and soil management have made it possible for farmers to aid nature in making specific soils more productive. Much has been learned about using crop rotation, legumes, and green manure for replenishing soil humus and nitrogen; determining and supplying the major and minor nutrient needs of crops; and managing soil under irrigation, including salt control. Techniques based on these findings have been put to use on farms to improve soil fertility and increase crop yields. Between 1940 and 1965, for example, farmers in the United States more than tripled their use of chemical fertilizers, resulting in increases of 50 to 150 percent in crop yields.

Scientists have used many sophisticated techniques to unlock a vast storehouse of knowledge about plants. In one case, chemicals tagged with radioactive isotopes were employed to follow the processes by which plants take up soil nutrients to synthesize their fruits, grains, vegetables, nuts, flowers, and fibres.

Plant sciences. The plant sciences include applied plant physiology, nutrition, ecology, breeding and genetics, pathology, and weed science, as well as crop management. They deal primarily with two major types of crops: (1) those that represent direct human food, such as cereals, vegetables, fruits, and nuts; and (2) those that serve as feed and forage for food, companion, laboratory, and recreational animals. Special branches of these sciences have developed to deal with each of the numerous classes of plant crops—*e.g.,* vegetables, small fruits, citrus fruits and other tree fruits, and flowers and other ornamental plants. Other specialties concern the production of raw materials for industry—cotton, hemp, sisal, and silk—although some of these are losing economic importance in the face of competition from synthetic fibres. Branches of the plant sciences that deal with such tropical crops as coffee, tea, cocoa, bananas, coconuts, sugarcane, and pineapples, to the contrary, promise to retain their importance.

Although scientifically based plant production came of age at the end of the 19th century, it started much earlier. Instructions on sowing dates are reported in Egypt by 2000 BC. Throughout the centuries, numerous treatises have included recommendations on how to achieve higher and more efficient yields.

The stimulus for the development of the plant sciences did not come from botany but from agricultural chemistry, the application of which led to the development of plant physiology. Field experiments were started in Rothamsted, England, in 1834, and elsewhere in Europe soon after. Improved methods of experiment design and statistical analysis made possible the comparative study of plants and their cultivation systems.

Cultivation of plants by varieties had already led in the late 18th century to the systematic selection of cereal varieties according to predicted yield. The rediscovery at the start of the 20th century of Gregor Mendel's laws of heredity and later of ways to cause mutations led to modern plant breeding, with momentous results that included the tailoring of crop varieties for regions of climatic extremes. Agronomist Norman E. Borlaug was awarded the Nobel Prize for Peace for 1970 for the development of short-stemmed wheat, a key element in the so-called Green Revolution in developing countries.

Plant breeding

Major advances in the study of plant diseases were recorded in the 19th century, and the science of plant nutrition matured in the second quarter of the 1900s. Serious calamities resulting from the introduction of plant diseases into regions where the indigenous plants had no immunity against them, and the invasion of grapes by insects and of potatoes by fungi, stimulated research efforts. During the 20th century, all diseases have become objects of systematic plant pathology research. Plant pathologists search for chemicals effective against microbial diseases, weeds, and various pests and seek to adjust the biotic balance to reduce losses. That chemical residues have created some problems has led to further scientific activity. Biological control measures may ultimately be less harmful to the environment and more specific and effective in pest and weed management.

Other research has been undertaken because consumers want better fruits and vegetables. New varieties have been developed, methods found to ensure that fresh and processed foods arrive at retail stores in prime condition, and grocers taught to care for these foods so that consumers receive them in the most attractive and nutritious state.

(G.P./B.T.Sh./J.R.C./S.E.Cu.)

Animal sciences. In modern civilizations, people rely on meat, milk, and eggs as major sources of numerous nutrients. To satisfy this demand, sheep, goats, cattle, water buffalo, swine, chickens, ducks, geese, and turkeys are produced on farms all over the world. To understand how agricultural animals convert feedstuffs into the food and other commodities consumers demand, animal scientists have undertaken broad investigations using highly sophisticated techniques. The animal sciences comprise applied animal physiology, nutrition, breeding and genetics, ecology and ethology, and livestock and poultry management. In addition, diseases of food animals are the focus of many veterinary scientists.

Animal nutrition research was well-established in several centres around the world by the turn of the 20th century, and it began to flourish during the second quarter of the 1900s. Many discoveries have been made about animal metabolism and consequent nutrient requirements; the usefulness of hundreds of feedstuffs as sources of essential amino acids, vitamins, and minerals, as well as lipids and carbohydrates; the proper balance of available nutrients in the diet; nutrient supplements and feed-processing technologies; and metabolite-partitioning and growth-promoting compounds. These fundamental findings have been applied widely since 1950, bringing about improved animal feeding. Studies of life processes in farm animals have helped in developing the optimal nutriment for each animal, and human nutrition has benefitted enormously from the knowledge that has come from these investigations.

Animal nutrition

The notion that "like begets like" was already current in biblical times. Long before the science of animal genetics developed, all species of agricultural animals were subjected to selective breeding to some extent. Modifying livestock and poultry to meet consumer demands requires the application of scientific principles to the selection of superior breeding animals and planned matings. For example, consumers have come to prefer more lean tissue and less fat in meat, and so the meat-type hog was developed in two decades of intensive selection and crossbreeding starting in the 1950s. Swine now yield more lean pork, grow faster, and require less feed to reach market weight than before. By the 1980s, a laying hen of any popular genetic strain, if managed properly, could be expected to produce more than 250 eggs annually, while special meat-producing strains of chickens gain body weight at a rate of 1 : 2 in ratio with feed intake. (J.R.C./S.E.Cu.)

Animal breeding and reproduction

Some of the most significant research in animal breeding has been done with dairy cattle and has established the proved sire system, in which bulls are ranked according to the performance of their offspring. The use of sires proved in this way together with artificial insemination has enabled dairymen to improve their herds by greatly expanding the influence of genetically superior bulls. Along with increased emphasis on performance testing, efforts have been made to predict at a young age whether an individual animal will be an efficient meat, milk, or egg producer. Such success has made for earlier culling and for herds and flocks of higher genetic merit. (G.P./B.T.Sh./J.R.C./S.E.Cu.)

Animals represent renewable agricultural resources because they reproduce, and animal scientists have studied animal reproduction assiduously since the 1930s. These investigations began in the United Kingdom but were soon joined by scientists in the United States, where the work blossomed. Basic discoveries have been put to use quickly in the animal industries. Elucidation of reproductive structures and mechanisms made it possible to refine reproductive management in the 1940s, and artificial insemination made possible the widespread use of proved sires in the 1950s. Additional basic knowledge and later technological developments made practical the control of the estrous cycle and of parturition by exogenous hormones and the serial harvesting and transplantation of embryos from donor females of high merit. The result of these changes has been an increase in the reproductive rate and efficiency of all species of farm animals.

Animal ecology and ethology are young branches of the animal sciences. Around the middle of the 20th century, environmental physiologists in the United States and the United Kingdom began to study agricultural animals' relations with their environment, including temperature, air, light, and diet. Interactions among environmental temperature, diet, and the animals' genetic makeup have been characterized, and great strides have been made in improving thermal-environmental management on farms. Lighting management is now essential to profitable poultry production, and the light environment is being controlled in livestock houses as well. Since the 1970s emphasis has shifted to include the behavioral adaptability of animals to their surroundings and the effects of environmental stress on the immune status of livestock and poultry. Farmers have widely adopted intensive systems of animal production, and these systems continue to present opportunities and problems to animal scientists concerned with discovering and accommodating the environmental and ethological needs of food animals.

Animal health science

Animal health is essential to the efficient production of wholesome animal products. An example of the economic effect of animal-disease research conducted by veterinary scientists is the control of Marek's disease, a highly contagious disease affecting the nerves and visceral organs of chickens, which resulted in a loss of more than $200,000,000 annually to the U.S. poultry industry alone. The disease was studied for more than 30 years before it was learned that it is caused by a herpes virus. Within three years of this discovery, a vaccine was developed that reduced the frequency of Marek's disease and the resultant meat condemnations in vaccinated chickens by 90 percent and increased egg production by 4 percent. Veterinary scientists also investigate the chronic infectious diseases associated with high morbidity rates and various metabolic disorders.

Food sciences and other post-harvest technologies. A group of sciences and technologies underlie the processing, storage, distribution, and marketing of agricultural commodities and by-products. Modern post-harvest technology helps provide inexpensive and various food supplies for consumers, meets the demands of a variety of industrial users, and even creates replacements for fossil fuels.

Research having particular significance to post-harvest technology includes genetic engineering techniques that increase the efficiency of various chemical and biological processes and fermentations for converting biomass to feedstock and for use in producing chemicals (including alcohols) that can replace petroleum-based products. Among the expected outcomes are the manufacture of new products from reconstituted ones and the recovery of by-products that would otherwise be considered waste.

Agricultural engineering. Agricultural engineering includes appropriate areas of mechanical, electrical, environmental, and civil engineering, construction technology, hydraulics, and soil mechanics.

The use of mechanized power and machinery on the farm has increased greatly throughout the world, fourfold in the United States since 1930. Research in energy use, fluid power, machinery development, laser and microprocessor control for maintaining grain quality, and farm structures is expected to result in further gains in the efficiency with which food and fibre are produced and processed.

Agricultural production presents many engineering problems and opportunities. Agricultural operations—soil conservation and preparation; crop cultivation and harvesting; animal production; and commodities transportation, processing, packaging, and storage—are precision operations involving large tonnages, heavy power, and critical factors of time and place. Facilities designed to aid farm operations help farm workers to minimize the time and energy requirements of routine jobs. (J.R.C./S.E.Cu.)

Four primary branches have developed within agricultural engineering, based on the problems encountered. Farm power and machinery engineering is concerned with advances in farm mechanization—tractors, field machinery, and other mechanical equipment. Farm structures engineering studies the problems of providing shelter for animals and human beings, crop storage, and other special-purpose facilities. Soil and water control engineering deals with soil drainage, irrigation, conservation, hydrology, and flood control. Electric power and processing engineering is concerned with the distribution of electric power on the farm and its application to a variety of uses, such as lighting to control plant growth and certain animal production operations. (R.A.Pr./J.R.C./S.E.Cu.)

Agricultural economics. The field of agricultural economics includes agricultural finance, policy, marketing, farm and agribusiness management, rural sociology, and agricultural law. The idea that the individual farm enterprise forms a unit—affected by location, production techniques, and market factors—originated during the 19th century. It was later supplemented by the theory of optimum utilization of production factors by the selection of production lines. Further refinement came about through applications of modern accounting methods. Research into farm and agribusiness management led to mathematical planning systems and statistical computation of farm-enterprise data, and interest has been drawn to decision-making behaviour studies of farm managers.

Agricultural policy is concerned with the relations between agriculture, economics, and society. Land ownership and the structure of farm enterprises were traditionally regarded as primarily social problems. The growth of agricultural production in the 20th century, accompanied by a decline in size of the rural population, however, has given impetus to research in agricultural policy. In the capitalist countries, this policy has concentrated on the influence of prices and market mechanisms; in the centrally planned countries, emphasis has been placed on artificially created market structures.

Agricultural marketing

Research in agricultural marketing was originally limited to the problem of supply and demand, but the crises of the Great Depression in the 1930s brought new analytical studies. In Europe, the growth of the cooperative movement—begun in Germany in the 19th century as a response to capital shortage and farm indebtedness—brought satisfactory solutions to problems of distribution of products from farmer to processor. Consequently, little interest in market research developed in Europe until the mid-20th century. Today, agricultural marketing studies focus on statistical computations of past market trends to supply data for forecasting.

Agricultural law concentrates on legal issues of both theoretical and practical significance to agriculture such as land tenure, land tenancy, farm labour, farm management, and taxation. From its beginnings at the University of Illinois in the 1940s, modern agricultural law has evolved to become a distinct field of law practice and scholarship.

Rural sociology, a young discipline, involves a variety of research methods, including behaviour study developed from studies in decision making in farm management.

(G.P./B.T.Sh./J.R.C./S.E.Cu.)

OTHER AGRICULTURAL SCIENCES

Agricultural work science arose in response to the rural social problems experienced in Germany during the Great Depression. The improvement of work procedures, appropriate use of labour, analysis of human capacity for work, and adjustment of mechanized production methods and labour requirements represent the main objects of this branch of ergonomics research. Studies of the influence of mechanization on the worker and of worker training came later. (G.P./J.R.C./S.E.Cu.)

Agricultural meteorology deals with the effects of weather events, and especially the effects of their variations in time and space, on plant and animal agriculture. Atmospheric factors such as cloud type and solar radiation, temperature, vapour pressure, and precipitation are of vital interest to agriculturalists. Agricultural meteorologists use weather and climatic data in enterprise risk analysis as well as in short- and long-range forecasting of crop yields and animal performance.

EMERGING AGRICULTURAL SCIENCES

The agricultural sciences are poised to enter a new era, armed with ever more sophisticated research technologies, such as monoclonal antibodies and gene splicing, in their continuing drive to better harness nature for the ultimate benefit of human beings everywhere. Although broad and deep scientific investigations have been made in the biological, physical, and social realms related to agriculture, the need persists for additional research to close remaining gaps in knowledge, especially in molecular biology and the environmental, social, and economic effects of its fruits.

From results of experiments already conducted, it is clear that molecular biology will influence plant genetics and crop production. Plant genetic engineers are working to improve specific economically important plant varieties by increasing their photosynthetic efficiency, improving their nutritional quality, and transferring to them such favourable properties as the ability to fix atmospheric nitrogen, as do legumes, and to better resist diseases and tolerate herbicides and natural environmental stress.

Animal scientists also are using new research methods in biotechnology, including the micromanipulation of embryos to produce multiple clones. Monoclonal antibodies are used in studies of specific factors in immune mechanisms, and recombinant DNA (deoxyribonucleic acid) technology is used in the genetic engineering of microbes so that they can synthesize specific antigenic proteins useful in vaccine production. The ultimate goal of this research is to improve dramatically the health and productivity of agricultural animals. (J.R.C./S.E.Cu.)

BIBLIOGRAPHY. Development of the agricultural sciences is described in FRIEDRICH AEREBOE, *Beiträge zur Wirtschaftslehre des Landbaues* (1905), a representative publication of Aereboe, who made farm economics and management an independent discipline; GÜNTHER FRANZ (ed.), *Deutsche Agrargeschichte,* 5 vol. (1962–70), a general history of agriculture in Germany and central Europe from the beginning to the middle of the 20th century; THEODOR GOLTZ, *Geschichte der deutschen Landwirtschaft,* vol. 2, *Das 19. Jahrhundert* (1903, reprinted 1963), a comprehensive history of agriculture; DAVID RINDOS, *The Origins of Agriculture: An Evolutionary Perspective* (1984). For education and research, see ALFRED CHARLES TRUE, *A History of Agricultural Education in the United States, 1785–1925* (1929), and *A History of Agricultural Experimentation and Research in the United States, 1607–1925* (1937), reprinted together in one volume of *Alfred True on Agricultural Experimentation and Research* (1980), in the series "Three Centuries of Science in America"; HERBERT M. HAMLIN, *Public School Education in Agriculture* (1962); EDWARD D. EDDY, *Colleges for Our Land and Time* (1957, reprinted 1973); two yearbooks of the UNITED STATES, DEPARTMENT OF AGRICULTURE, *Science in Farming* (1947), and *After a Hundred Years* (1962), and its handbook *The Agricultural Research Center of the United States Department of Agriculture* (1952). Major aspects of the agricultural sciences are explored in J.S. BOYER, "Plant Productivity and Environment," *Science,* 218:443–448 (Oct. 29, 1982), an analysis of the genetic productivity potential of major plants; HENRY PRENTIS ARMSBY, *The Principles of Animal Nutrition* (1903), a representative textbook from an earlier era of the agricultural sciences; JOHN R. CAMPBELL and JOHN F. LASLEY, *The Science of Animals That Serve Humanity,* 3rd ed. (1985), a comprehensive publication on contemporary animal agriculture; STANLEY E. CURTIS, *Environmental Management in Animal Agriculture* (1983). On food technologies, see a technical memorandum of the U.S. CONGRESS, OFFICE OF TECHNOLOGY, *Agricultural Postharvest Technology and Marketing Economic Research* (1983); LENNARD BICKEL, *Facing Starvation: Norman Borlaug and the Fight Against Hunger* (1974), is an account of the Nobel laureate agronomist's life and his experiments that led to the Green Revolution in developing countries; GÜNTHER FRANZ (ed.), *Die Geschichte der Landtechnik in 20. Jahrhundert* (1969), is a publication on the history of agricultural engineering during the 20th century; HENRY C. TAYLOR and ANNE DEWES TAYLOR, *The Story of Agricultural Economics in the United States, 1840–1932* (1952, reprinted 1974), is a history of development of the field. For various agricultural sciences the monthly *Bibliography of Agriculture,* published by the UNITED STATES, DEPARTMENT OF AGRICULTURE, and listing agricultural materials from all over the world, is useful; see also *Agricultural Meteorology: Proceedings of the World Meteorological Organization Seminar on Agricultural Meteorology* (1970); and publications of the FOOD AND AGRICULTURE ORGANIZATION OF THE UNITED NATIONS (FAO), including those in the series *The State of Food and Agriculture; Animal Health Year Book; Plant Protection Bulletin; World Lists of Plant Breeders; World Lists of Genetic Stocks.*

(G.P./J.R.C./S.E.Cu.)

The History of Agriculture

Agriculture, or the practice of cultivating the soil, harvesting crops, and raising livestock, was long believed to have begun in a single centre in the Middle East, about 4000 BC. Modern dating techniques have since disproved this hypothesis; they indicate agriculture already in progress around 7000 BC, and archaeologists have uncovered evidence of animal domestication thousands of years earlier. It has also been shown that some plants were probably cultivated in the New World, which suggests that agricultural development took place simultaneously in many areas and thus did not spread from a single originating centre.

This article discusses developments in crop and stock farming in the ancient societies of the Middle East and Mediterranean; in China and India; in Roman and medieval Europe; and in more recent times, after the introduction of power machinery and scientific farming in the 19th and 20th centuries. For information on the techniques of modern agriculture, see the article FARMING AND AGRICULTURAL TECHNOLOGY. For further treatment of the modern disciplines of agricultural research, engineering, and management, see the article AGRICULTURAL SCIENCES.

The article is divided into the following sections:

Origins of agriculture 172
- Earliest beginnings 172
- Early development 172

Early agricultural societies 173

Agriculture in ancient Asia 175
- China 175
- The Indian subcontinent 177
- Southeast and East Asia 178

Improvements in agriculture in the West: *c.* 200 BC to AD 1600 178
- The Roman epoch 178
- The medieval period: 600–1600 179

Crop-farming changes in western Europe: 1600–1800 181
- The Norfolk four-course system 181
- Improvements in technology 182
- Progress in different countries 182

The 19th-century power revolution on the farm: *c.* 1792–1784 183
- Mechanization 183
- Applying science to farming 184
- Farming outside Europe 185

Scientific agriculture: the 20th century 185
- Developments in power: the internal-combustion engine 185
- New crops and techniques 186
- New strains: genetics 188
- Animal breeding 189
- Electricity in agriculture 190
- Pest and disease control in crops 191
- Economics, politics, and agriculture 192

Bibliography 193

Origins of agriculture

Agriculture has no single, simple origin. At different times and in numerous places, many plants and animals have been domesticated. How many species passed into or out of domestication in prehistory is not known. Cultivation of foxtail millet in America and domestication of the elk in Scandinavia and the gazelle in the Middle East were abandoned long ago. In the 20th century, cultivation of bottle gourds, finger millet, and Galla potatoes is on the decline, while efforts proceed to tame the eland, musk ox, and fox. Cultivation of rice, wheat, barley, potatoes, and corn (maize) met with great success in the favourable climate that followed the last Ice Age, while reindeer husbandry, by contrast, found these climatic changes unfavourable and lost importance.

EARLIEST BEGINNINGS

Nineteenth-century scholars hypothesized four stages in human development: (1) a savage stage in which all people were hunter-gatherers; (2) a herdsman or nomad stage during which man domesticated some animals; (3) a farming stage; and (4) civilization. Researchers have since attempted to determine when and where man first changed from hunter-gatherer to pastoralist or agriculturist.

Effect of domestication on animals

Many authorities have come to think that man's domestication of plants and animals caused changes in their form and that the presence or absence of such changes may indicate whether the animal or plant was domesticated at some time in the past. On the basis of such evidence, some scholars have hypothesized a preliminary agricultural phase of intensive food gathering in the Middle East about 9000–7000 BC, when man passed from hunting and gathering to food producing or agriculture. The Natufians of Palestine, who possessed sickles, lived at this time; whether the grain they harvested was sown or wild is not known. Cattle were probably domesticated during this period or slightly earlier from the wild ox (*Bos taurus*), which stood six to seven feet (1.8 to 2.1 metres) high at the withers (the ridge between the shoulder bones). At Shanidar, in Iraq, it is claimed that sheep, similar to wild varieties in form and structure, were kept in herds. Furthermore, it has been suggested on somewhat speculative grounds that einkorn wheat (*Triticum monococcum*), emmer wheat (*Triticum turgidum*), and wild barley (*Hordeum spontaneum*) were cultivated about 7000 BC at Ali Kosh on the borders of Iraq and Iran.

There seems no compelling reason, however, why these instances should be regarded as the first of their kind. It is possible that domesticated beans (*Phaseolus*), peas (*Pisum*), bottle gourds (*Lagenaria siceraria*), and water chestnuts (*Trapa*) may have been grown at the Spirit Cave in northern Thailand about 9000 BC. In the Americas, pumpkins (*Cucurbita*) and gourds (*Lagenaria*) are known to have existed in domesticated form in northeast Mexico about 7000 BC, and probably beans in the Tehuacán Valley. The bones of a dog, possibly used for hunting about 8500 BC, were discovered in the western United States. In sum, it now seems unlikely that there was either a single or even a very limited number of places of origin of plant and animal domestication and, therefore, of agriculture.

EARLY DEVELOPMENT

The development of agriculture was an intensification by man of his food extractive processes. More food could be obtained from a given area of land by encouraging plant and animal species found useful and discouraging others. This provided for an increased population and gave better opportunity for settled life. Durable houses, as well as tools such as pestles, mortars, and grindstones, all of which had long been known in scattered places, came into more general use. There had even been villages in Stone Age times, among them the hunters' villages at Mezin in the Soviet Union, at Mallaha in Israel, and at Suberde in Turkey. These produced scant archaeological records, however; there exists no satisfactory evidence that they were inhabited by hunter-gatherers.

"Effective" village stage

The Middle East. In the 7th millennium BC, with heightened agricultural development, villages in the Middle East became more numerous. Called the "effective"

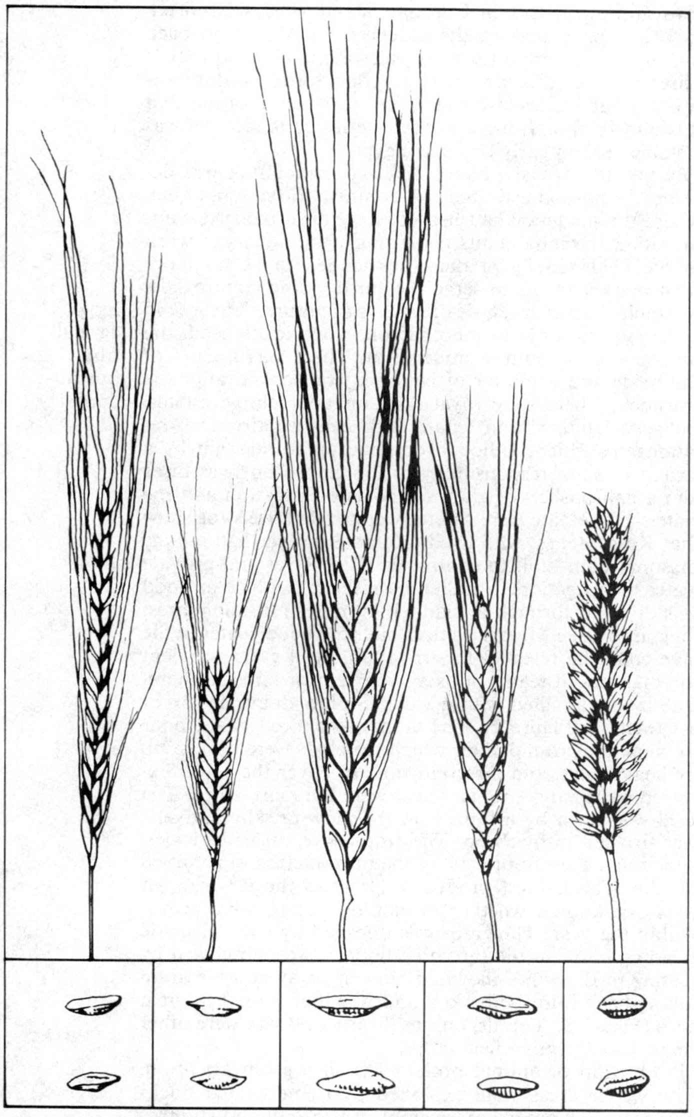

Figure 1: Wild and cultivated wheats. (Left to right) wild einkorn, einkorn, wild emmer, emmer, bread wheat. Scales: Ears, about 1/2; grains, about 9/10.
From E.C. Curwen and G. Hatt, *Plough and Pasture* (copyright 1953); Murnat Publications, Inc.

village stage of development, this period was accompanied by increasingly diversified agriculture, which led to more productive and efficient exploitation of available resources. The earliest known domesticated pigs have been recorded, in association with einkorn, at the village site of Jarmo (Iraq), dated about 6750 BC. The earliest known domesticated cattle date from about 6000 BC, at Argissa and Nea Nikomedeia, in Greece, in association with cultivated einkorn, emmer wheat, and lentils (*Lens culinaris*); and at Knossós on Crete in association with bread wheat (*Triticum aestivum*), emmer, and barley. Hoes or digging sticks were still used to break the ground where necessary. Seeding by treading in with flocks and herds was probably employed at this time. Techniques of food storage, a practice that man shares with many other animals, grew in sophistication; there were pit silos and granaries, sometimes of quite substantial nature. In drier areas, crop irrigation, which greatly increased yield, was developed; and, with the increasing population, more labour was available to carry out wider irrigation projects.

Nitrogen-fixing (fertilizing) crops were also grown; a form of crop rotation came into use either by accident or by design. By this particular means, soil fertility was maintained, and thus additional plant protein was added to the diet.

The Americas. Although domesticates such as peppers, avocados, and amaranths were being grown in the Americas around 7000–5000 BC, villages were not numerous until widespread corn production began about 3500 BC. By then, common beans (*Phaseolus vulgaris*), chili pepper (*Capsicum annuum*), and black and white zapotes were also widely cultivated. An early cereal, the foxtail millet, was probably domesticated around 4000 BC in Tamaulipas, Mex., but was superseded by corn, and its cultivation was abandoned.

China. In China, millet was cultivated by the 5th millennium BC; rice was probably grown by the 4th millennium. Wheat was introduced before 1300 BC, but the arid nature of the uplands made progress slow. In the wetter lowlands, wheat could scarcely compete with already domesticated rice. Barley apparently was not introduced until after 1300 BC, nor was the soybean cultivated until perhaps 1100 BC.

Europe. In Europe, archaeologists have given so much attention to domesticates that are today outstandingly successful, such as wheat, barley, cattle, sheep, and pigs, that other species, possibly of major significance in the past, have largely been ignored.

It is generally assumed—apart from the earliest known incidence in the Old World of the domesticated dog at Star Carr in Yorkshire, England (about 7500 BC), cattle in Greece (about 6000 BC), and a possibility of domesticated pigs in the Crimea at an earlier date—that Europe prior to the introduction of agriculture from the East was inhabited by hunter-gatherers. It has indeed been suggested that the grain called fat hen (*Chenopodium album*) was cultivated at Iron Age settlements in Denmark, as well as Gold of Pleasure (*Camelina sativa*) and curl-topped lady's thumb (*Polygonum lapathifolium*). Since cultivation of these grains is regarded as typifying a late form of agricultural development, it follows that agriculture must have taken about 3,000 years to spread from Greece to Denmark and the British Isles. Furthermore, considerable adaptations to new environments must have taken place in human technology and in the Asian species of sheep, goats, and cereals after their introduction into Europe. The effective village stage appears to have begun as soon as cereals and sheep or goats became important in Europe. In some areas, such as Hungary and Switzerland, many villages for thousands of years continued to rely upon indigenous animals for their animal protein.

Spread of agriculture in Europe

Along the Danube River, the great postglacial European forest was penetrated by slash-and-burn agriculture based on cereals. In the more arid regions along the Mediterranean coast, fewer modifications were necessary. The incorporation of indigenous wild stock, wherever available, into domesticated herds doubtless aided their acclimatization, for this practice continued into historic times, in Hungary until the invasion of the Mongols.

Early agricultural societies

In the Old World, settled life had developed on higher ground from Iran to Anatolia (site of modern Turkey) and the Levant, and in China in the semiarid loess plains, but the earliest civilizations based on complex and productive agriculture developed on the alluviums of the Tigris, Euphrates, and Nile rivers. When the first villages appeared there is not certain. It is known, however, that villages and townships existed in the Euphrates Valley in the latter part of the 5th millennium BC. Soon the population was dispersed over the available area in agricultural units based upon hamlets and villages. Townships provided additional services that the hamlets themselves could not provide. On this basis, Sumerian civilization developed.

Sumer. The Sumerian civilization was marked by an overall increase in wealth rather than by technical or agricultural innovations. The necessary foundations had already been laid. The Early Dynastic Phase began about 3000 BC. In Sumer, barley was the main crop, but wheat, flax, dates, apples, plums, and grapes were also grown. The earliest known white woolly, and therefore carefully bred, sheep and goats were herded and were more numerous than cattle. The sheep were kept mainly for meat and milk; butter and cheese were made. It has been es-

Earliest sheep breeding

timated that at Ur, a large town covering some 50 acres (20 hectares) within a cultivated enclave, there were 10,000 animals confined in sheepfolds and stables, of which 3,000 were slaughtered each year. Ur's population of about 6,000 included a labour force of 2,500 who annually cultivated 3,000 acres of land, leaving 3,000 acres fallow. The work force included storehouse recorders, work foremen, overseers, and harvest supervisors, as well as labourers. Agricultural produce was allocated to temple personnel in return for their services, to important people in the community, and to small farmers.

The land was plowed by teams of oxen pulling light unwheeled plows, and the grain was harvested with sickles in the spring. Wagons had solid wheels with leather tires held in position by copper nails. They were drawn by oxen or the now-extinct Syrian onager (wild ass), harnessed by collars, yokes, and headstalls, and controlled by reins and a ring through the nose or upper lip and a strap under the jaw. As many as four animals, harnessed abreast to a central pole, pulled a wagon. The horse, which was probably domesticated about 2700 BC by pastoral nomads in the Ukraine, did not in fact displace the onager as a draft animal in Mesopotamia until about 2300 BC, when bridles and bits were also introduced. Soon after, written instructions appeared for the grooming, exercising, and medication of horses; presumably for breeding purposes, horses were named and records of sires kept. The upper highland areas continued to be exploited by transhumant nomads.

The Nile Valley. In Egypt, intensified agricultural exploitation apparently did not take place until domesticated animals from the Middle East were introduced. By the first quarter of the 5th millennium BC in al-Fayyūm, there existed villages that kept sheep, goats, and swine and cultivated wheat (emmer), barley, cotton, and flax, which was woven into linen. In this dry climate, village silos consisted of pits lined with coiled basketry; crops were harvested with reaping knives slotted with sharp flints. Elsewhere, at al-Badārī in Upper Egypt, animals were also kept; the fact that domesticated animals were wrapped in linen and buried close to villages perhaps indicates that agriculture was closely associated with some form of religious belief.

By predynastic Amratian times, about 3600 BC, agriculture appears to have begun in the valley alluviums of the Nile. By late predynastic times, about 3100 BC, there is evidence of a considerable growth in wealth consequent upon the earlier agricultural development and accompanied by a more integrated social system.

From depictions on the tombs and other artifacts in dynastic times, it is known that, in addition to present-day domesticates, other animals, such as deer, gazelles, hyenas, and Barbary sheep, were kept either in captivity or under some form of control. Whether or not this man–animal relationship can be regarded as domestication is a matter of semantics, but certainly some aspects of animal husbandry were practiced with these unusual animals. Though it is not known how far back in time such practices existed, some early villages in Egypt were dependent upon gazelles for their source of animal protein, as was the township of Jericho, in Palestine, about 7000 BC. Indeed, such a dependence on the gazelle is known to go back to Upper Paleolithic times in Palestine, and the question arises whether this was due to earlier forms of domestication. Discoveries at Nahal Oren, in Israel, indicate that this may be true. It has also been suggested that millet was a staple crop in early times in Egypt.

By the 4th dynasty, about 3000 BC, agriculture was developed and sophisticated. In contrast to Mesopotamia, where the tendency had been to develop urbanized communities, the inhabitants going out of the towns to work in the fields, in Egypt the cities tended to be no more than market towns to serve the surrounding countryside. A whole bureaucracy dealt with agriculture. The grand vizier, second only to the pharaoh, stood at its head, the ministry of agriculture under him. There was a chief of the fields and a master of largesse, who looked after the livestock. There were royal domains and temple estates. Between landlord and tenant there was a patriarchal relationship, which, although despotic, was underlain by a strong sense of responsibility to the land. Rent was three and a half bushels of grain to the acre. Irrigation and the waters of the Nile were carefully controlled. Records show that King Menes, who lived around 3100 BC, had a large masonry dam built to control the Nile River and provide water for irrigation. A millennium later, the Nile at flood was diverted through a channel, 12 miles (19 kilometres) long, into Lake Moeris, so that, after the flood, water in the lake could be released for irrigation. Seed grain was lent to tenants, and teams of oxen were lent or hired to them. The land was tilled with a wooden plow drawn by ox or ass traction (Figure 2). The land was plowed twice, once to break the ground, after which the clods were broken up by heavy hoes, and a second time to cover the seed. Six-rowed barley and emmer wheat were the main crops. The seed was sown by a funnel on the plow or, alternatively, was trodden in by sheep. The crops were cut with sickles, which had been improved by the introduction of a curved handle. The harvest produced 11 times the sowing, but it is not known whether or not two crops were grown within the year. The grain was threshed by asses or cattle treading on it on the threshing floor. It was winnowed by tossing in the wind, the chaff blowing away and the grain falling back into the basket, and was then stored in great silos (Figure 3). Lentils, onions, beans, and flax were other important Egyptian field crops.

Egypt's agricultural bureaucracy

Production of animal protein was also given attention. The wetter areas were exploited by domesticated ducks and geese. The marshes, swamps, wasteland, and stubbles were grazed by numerous herds of cattle (black, piebald, and white), sheep with kempy (coarse) coats, goats, and pigs. One wealthy landlord in the 6th dynasty owned 1,000 cattle, 760 asses, 2,200 goats, and 1,000 sheep. Animal breeding for specialized purposes was developed; one breed of cattle was kept for meat and another for milk; a Saluki-like hunting dog was bred, as were fat-tailed sheep with tails so heavy they were carried by a small cart drawn behind.

Meso-America and Peru. As far as is known, no ani-

Andre Held

Figure 2: Plowing and sowing in Thebes. Painting from Tomb No. 1, Sennedjem, Thebes, Egypt.

Figure 3: Winnowing grain by the traditional method of tossing it in the wind, Ethiopia.
By courtesy of the United Nations

mals were domesticated in the Americas until a comparatively late date. Available evidence seems to indicate that, in spite of the early domestication of some plants, village life did not begin to develop on any scale until 3500 BC or possibly somewhat earlier in Mexico, following domestication of corn. The process of agricultural development was therefore rather slow, occurring in widely dispersed centres, often in areas of poor fertility, sometimes even in deserts. Cacao (chocolate used to make a beverage), toma-

Domestication of corn

By courtesy of the Kongelige Bibliotek, Copenhagen

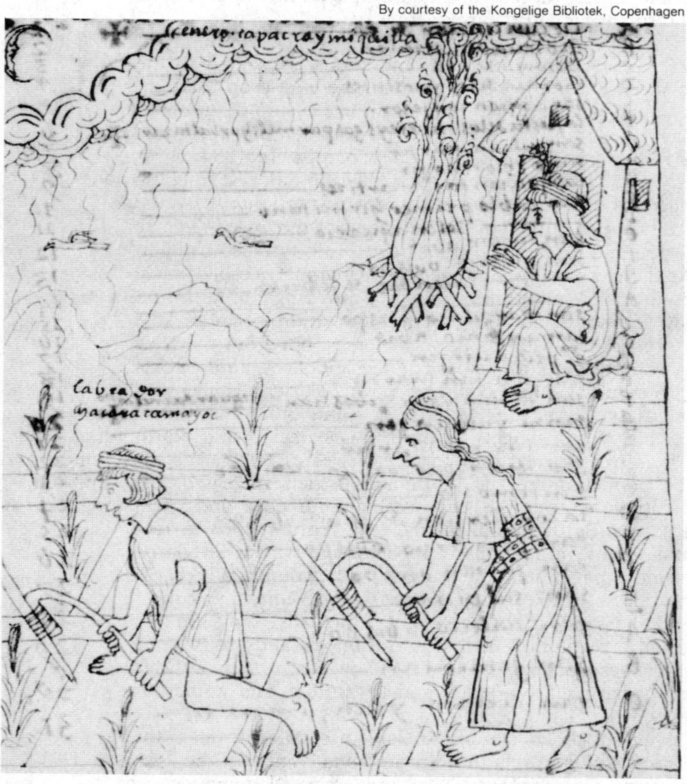

Figure 4: Inca cultivation with fire-hardened digging sticks. Drawing from "Nueva Crónica y Buen Gobierno" by Felipe Guaman Poma de Ayala. In Det Kongelige Bibliotek, Copenhagen.

toes, and avocados were cultivated. Irrigation, terracing, and the construction of islands in lakes increased land usage in drier areas. The land was cleared by chopping and burning, and the seeds were sown with the aid of fire-hardened digging sticks (Figure 4). Crops were stored in pits or granaries. The corn was prepared by boiling in limewater and by wet grinding. Cornmeal paste was then made into tortillas or flat cakes and gruel. Fine textiles were woven of cotton, and paper was made from tree bark. Village life was based on the extended family, composed of parents and their children's families, which provided the labour force. Villages were organized into larger territorial units based on ceremonial centres commonly in the form of flat-topped pyramids. Larger territorial units developed early in the 1st millennium AD.

Agriculture in Peru

Much less is known about the formative stage in Peru. Indeed, a civilization based on agricultural production may have begun there hundreds of years before it did in Meso-America, about the beginning of the Christian Era. Corn did not become important as a main crop in Peru until the 9th century BC, after perhaps 1,000 years of root crop, bean, and cotton agriculture. Corn was not extensively cultivated until irrigation developed; the potato, domesticated since about 2500 BC, was the chief crop in many areas until the 16th century AD.

At some time before the Inca civilization, the guanaco, ancestor of the llama and alpaca, was domesticated. The llama may have been domesticated as early as 2000 BC. Though the llama was essentially a beast of burden, the alpaca's main product was its fine wool. Another animal, raised for food, was the guinea pig. (E.S.H.)

Agriculture in ancient Asia

On his way across the Pamirs in search of Buddhist texts (AD 518) the Chinese pilgrim Sung Yün noted that the crest of the bare, cold, snowy highlands was commonly believed to be "the middle point of heaven and earth":

> The people of this region use the water of the rivers for irrigating their lands; and when they were told that in the middle country (China) the fields were watered by the rain, they laughed and said, "How could heaven provide enough for all?"

Yet, heaven provided. It has long supported more than one-half of humanity on less than a seventh of the Earth's land surface along the continental rim to the south and east of the high interior mass with its festoons of mountains. In the so-called "golden fringe to a beggar's mantle"—from Pakistan through India, Burma, Thailand, Indochina, and eastern China up to the Gulf of Chihli, and the offshore island groups of Japan, Indonesia, the Philippines, and Sri Lanka (formerly Ceylon)—lives the vast majority of the population of Asia. Some 1,800,000,000 people are concentrated in two countries, China and India.

There is no consensus on the origin and progress of plant and animal domestication. The Soviet plant geneticist Nikolay Ivanovich Vavilov postulated several world centres of plant origin, of which,

> an unusual wealth of original genera, species, and varieties of plants is found in India and China, countries which have contributed almost half of our crop plants . . . .

CHINA

Two growing areas of China

Vavilov thought that the mountainous regions of central and western China, together with the adjacent lowlands, constituted the earliest and largest independent centre of the world's agriculture. From earliest times, land use has been divided into two major regions by the Tsinling Mountains, with wheat predominant in the northern realm and rice in the south. At different periods and places, subsidiary crops have included soybean, kaoliang (a grain sorghum), millet, corn, barley, sweet potatoes, peanuts, fruits, and vegetables. Cotton, tobacco, sugarcane, tea, and sericulture (silkworms) have been the important cash crops.

Early history. Archaeological information is comparatively scanty. It does not reveal when and how the first farmers settled down to cultivate food crops. Written records, available from about 1750 BC, are more conclusive.

Tradition accords the honour of inventing agriculture to the legendary emperor Shen Nung, who is said to have carved a piece of wood into a plowshare and bent another piece to make a handle and taught the world the advantages of plowing and weeding. The chronicle *Pai-hu t'ung* relates that he did so out of necessity, because "the ancient people ate meat of animals and birds." At the time of Shen Nung, there were so many people that the wild animals and birds became inadequate for people's wants, and therefore Shen Nung taught the people to cultivate. As for the origin of cultivated plants, the problem was resolved by divinity: "Millet rained from heaven. Shen Nung collected the grains and cultivated them." Pigs are believed to have been domesticated in eastern Asia as early as 2900 BC.

Apparently the "millet from heaven" rained over the North China Plain in the central region of the Yellow River Valley, which is regarded as the birthplace of agriculture-based civilization in China. From there it spread throughout the country, but it failed to penetrate the northern grassland and plateaus. The Great Wall may be taken to demarcate the approximate frontier between the two basically different ways of life—the agrarian to the south and the pastoral nomadic of the steppes and deserts on the other side.

It is thought likely that the practice of irrigation spread to China from Babylonia. The Chinese are known to have had irrigation before 2200 BC. Notable Chinese irrigation works include the Tu-kiang Dam, built about 200 BC, which provided water for about 500,000 acres, and the Grand Canal, built in stages over several centuries and eventually extending for more than 1,000 miles.

The classical-imperial era. In about 335 BC, the Chinese philosopher Mencius wrote that, "If the farmer's seasons are not interfered with, there will be more grain in the land than can be consumed." By the 1st century BC, however, wastelands were being reclaimed for cultivation, and there was a demand for limitation of landholdings. In about AD 9, the first (unsuccessful) attempt was made to "nationalize" the land and distribute it among the peasants. By the end of the 2nd century AD, severe agrarian crises culminating generally in the downfall of the ruling dynasty had become a recurrent theme of history. Through the centuries, Chinese agriculture has been a continual struggle between man and land to raise more food.

Shift in major growing area

By the 4th century AD cultivation was more intensive in China than in Europe or the rest of Asia. The major cereal-producing region and the population, however, were shifting rapidly from the wheat and millet area of the North China Plain to the paddies of the lower Yangtze Valley. By the 8th century the lower Yangtze was exporting enormous quantities of grain into the old Northwest by way of a unified system of canals linking the large rivers.

By about AD 1100 the population of South China had probably tripled, while that of the whole country may have exceeded 100,000,000. Consequently, cultivation became extremely intensive, with a family of 10 crowded, for example, onto a farm of about 14 acres. Again, more new lands were opened to cultivation. Even tanks, ponds, reservoirs, streams, and creeks were reclaimed to be turned into farms. At the same time, complex water-driven machinery came into use for pumping irrigation water onto fields, for draining them, and for threshing and milling grain. A large variety of improved and complicated field implements were also employed; these are described and illustrated in the agricultural literature of the day.

Tools and techniques. The first significant revolution in Chinese agricultural technology had occurred when iron agricultural implements became available to the Chinese peasantry. The earliest iron plow found in northern Honan dates from the Warring States period (475–221 BC) and is a flat V-shaped iron piece that must have been mounted somewhat insecurely on wooden blades and handles to serve as working edges. It was small, and there is no evidence that draft animals were used. Cattle-drawn plows do not appear until the 1st century BC.

Several improvements and innovations, such as the three-shared plow, the *lou-li* (plow-and-sow) implement, and the harrow, were developed subsequently. By the end of the Sung dynasty in 1279, Chinese agricultural engineering had reached a high state of development.

The common farmers continued to use these early medieval techniques into modern times. Their unfenced fields were cultivated by a wooden plow, with or without a cast-iron share and usually drawn by a water buffalo. Harvesting was by sickle or billhook (a cutting tool consisting of a blade with a hooked point fitted with a handle). Sheaves carried from the field were slung at the ends of a pole across an individual's shoulders. The grain was threshed by beating on a frame of slats or by flails on the ground. Winnowing was accomplished by tossing the grain in the wind. Rice was dehusked by hand pounding in a mortar or with a hand-turned mill. Irrigation techniques varied. The most common perhaps was a wooden, square-paddle chain pump with a radial treadle operated by foot. Fields were drained by open ditches and diking. Night soil, oil cakes, and ash fertilized the soil.

Over the past millennium, in fact, the revolution in Chinese agriculture has not been in mechanical or chemical technology but rather in the biological sphere: in crops, cropping systems, and land utilization. Under increasing population pressures, cultivation was forced to become more labour intensive and also to expand into the sandy loams, arid hills, and the upper reaches of lofty mountains. Lacking major technological inventions, the Chinese peasant had to expand the area under cultivation by finding suitable crops for inferior land.

Land use. A "three fields in two years" rotation system for wheat and millet was being practiced by the 6th century AD. Revolutionary changes in land utilization, however, started with the introduction in Fukien Province of an early-maturing and relatively drought-resistant rice from Champa, in central Indochina. In 1012, when there was a drought in the lower Yangtze and Huai Ho regions, 30,000 bushels of Champa seeds were distributed. Usually a summer crop, the native rice plant required 150 days to mature after transplanting. Not only did this make a second crop difficult, but, because of the plant's soil and water requirements, cultivation was confined largely to the deltas, basins, and valleys of the Yangtze. The original Champa rice, on the other hand, ripened in 100 days after transplanting and required less water.

Introduction of Champa rice

The success of Champa rice initiated the development and dissemination of many more varieties suited to the local peculiarities of soil, temperature, and crop rotation. The first new early-ripening strain to develop required 60 days after transplantation. By the 18th century, there was a 50-day Champa and a 40-day Champa. In 1834, a 30-day variety was available—probably the quickest ripening rice ever recorded. The effect was revolutionary. By the 13th century, much of the hilly land of the lower Yangtze region and Fukien had been turned into terraced paddies. At the close of the 16th century, Champa rice had made double, and sometimes triple, rice cropping common.

A second revolution in land utilization began in the 16th century, with adoption of food crops from the New World, such as corn, sweet potatoes, potatoes, and peanuts (groundnuts). These could be grown at drier altitudes and in sandy loams too light for rice and other indigenous cereals. Virgin heights of the Yangtze region and North China were turned into corn and sweet-potato farms. As the population in the mountain districts increased, the potato took over the soils too poor for corn and sweet potatoes. By the middle of the 19th century, even ravines and remote mountains were being cultivated. Similarly, peanuts penetrated the remote and agriculturally backward areas of Kwantung, Kwangsi, and Yunnan provinces and the sandbars of Szechwan. Gradually, they brought about a revolution in the utilization of sandy soils along the lower Yangtze, the lower Yellow River, the southeast coast, particularly Fukien and Kwantung, and numerous inland rivers and streams.

Exploiting remote and unpromising regions

Even so, the revolution in land use failed to alter the basic man–land relationship in China. Again in the 18th century, the emperor Ch'ien-lung rejected demands for limitation of landownership. In an edict (1740), however, he noted that "the population is constantly increasing, while the land does not become any more extensive." He directed his subjects, therefore, to cultivate all and every odd piece of soil,

> on top of the mountains or at the corners of the land. All these soils are suitable either for rice or for miscellaneous crops. . . . no matter how little return the people may receive from cultivation of these lands, it will be always helpful in supplying food provisions for the people.

THE INDIAN SUBCONTINENT

India's most important contribution to world agriculture is rice (*Oryza sativa*), the staple food and crop of most of southern, Southeast, and East Asia. Sugarcane, varieties of legumes, and several kinds of tropical fruit, such as the mango and the muskmelon (*Cucumis melo*), also are native to the Indian subcontinent.

Archaeological records of this region's prehistory are still incomplete and uneven. Evidence of how the transition from pastoralism to crop farming took place is lacking. Toward the close of the 3rd millennium BC, in the alluvial plains of the Indus River in Pakistan, ruins of the twin cities of Mohenjo-daro and Harappā reveal an apparently sudden explosion of an organized, sophisticated urban culture. This society, known as the Indus Valley, or Harappan, Civilization, flourished until around 1750 BC, and was much more extensive than those of Egypt or Babylonia, and earlier than that of northern China. Peculiarly Indian, Harappan society was remarkably homogeneous, thoroughly individual and independent, and technically the peer of China and Egypt. Nothing is known, however, about the farm communities that must have produced a surplus of agricultural products sufficient to sustain the population and fill the granaries of the metropolitan centres. At Harappā, for instance, the granary consisted of two blocks of six chambers each. The floor space of the 12 units covered an area of more than 90,000 square feet (about 8,100 square metres).

Indus Valley Civilization

Barley (*Hordeum vulgare*), a small-seeded, six-rowed variety, and two types of wheat—club wheat (*Triticum aestivum*) and an Indian dwarf variety (*T. sphaerococcum*)—were evidently the main cereal crops, supplemented by dates, sesame, field peas, and lentils. Humped Indian cattle and a humpless breed, goats, sheep, fowl, and the elephant had been domesticated. In addition to the domestication of a great variety of animals, fragments of dyed and woven cotton fabric attest to the antiquity of the cultivation of cotton plants and of the textile industry for which India was to become famous the world over.

No archaeological or pictorial evidence of farm implements has survived, and the Harappan script is yet to be deciphered. It has been surmised, however, that the cereals could have been sown in the fall on inundated land after the annual flooding of the rivers had receded and then harvested in spring. The system is still in use and involves minimal skill, labour, and equipment. The land does not have to be plowed, fertilized, or irrigated.

It was clearly more than a subsistence economy, for there is proof of river and sea traffic. There was a trading post at Lothal on the Gulf of Cambay with a brick dockyard and elaborate channel and spillway. Two-wheeled bullock carts and light, covered wagons—forms of transportation still common—were used for local travel. Caravans of pack oxen were the principal mode of transportation over longer distances.

South India, centre of the later distinctive Tamil culture, constituted a second, initially independent agricultural region. Crops were being raised there during the first half of the 2nd millennium BC. Two varieties of pulses (legumes) and finger millet (also called raggee) were cultivated.

To the north and west of the Deccan Plateau lay a third intermediate area. There, at Lothal and Rangpur, has been found the earliest evidence of rice cultivation, in the later Harappan period. Subsequently, wheat, cotton, flax, and lentils spread into the region from the Indus Valley, and pulses and millets from the south.

In all the three regions the basic cropping pattern of the 2nd millennium BC, except the pattern for rice, has continued into the 20th century.

Early historic period. A fourth agricultural region developed during the 1st millennium BC in the Gangetic Valley. Waves of invading Indo-Aryan tribes presumably destroyed the Harappan cities and penetrated deep into Hindustān proper, the principal seat of the classical Indian civilization. With the Aryans came the horse, coinage, the Brāhmī script, and the whole corpus of Vedic literature. Sources of information henceforth are literary rather than archaeological. The plow, for example, figures in a hymn of the most ancient of the texts, the Rigveda: "Harness the plows, fit on the yokes, now that the womb of the earth is ready to sow the seed therein. . . . "

Gangetic Valley culture

Apparently, rice played an important role in growth of population and new settlements. They had spread eastward to the Ganges Delta by the 7th century BC.

In the later Vedic texts (*c.* 1000–500 BC), there are repeated references to iron. Cultivation of a wide range of cereals, vegetables, and fruits is described. Meat and milk products were part of the diet; animal husbandry was important. The soil was plowed several times. Seeds were broadcast. Fallowing and a certain sequence of cropping were recommended. Cow dung provided the manure. Irrigation was practiced.

A more secular eyewitness account is available from Megasthenes (*c.* 300 BC), a Greek envoy to the court of the Mauryan Empire. In his four-volume *Indica,* he wrote:

> India has many huge mountains which abound in fruit-trees of every kind, and many vast plains of great fertility. . . . The greater part of the soil, moreover, is under irrigation, and consequently bears two crops in the course of the year. . . . In addition to cereals, there grows throughout India much millet . . . and much pulse of different sorts, and rice also, and what is called *bosporum* [Indian millet].

And again,

> Since there is a double rainfall [*i.e.,* the two monsoons] in the course of each year. . . . the inhabitants of India almost always gather in two harvests annually.

Other sources reveal that the soils and seasons had been classified and meteorological observations of rainfall charted for the different regions of the Mauryan Empire, which comprised nearly the whole subcontinent and territory to the northwest.

A special department of the state supervised construction and maintenance of the irrigation system. The best known work of the period is the Sudarshana Lake in Kāthiāwār, created by an artificial dam and furnished with conduits. Roads, too, were the government's responsibility. The swifter horse-drawn chariot provided greater mobility than the bullock cart.

The Mughal century (*c. 1600*). At the climax of the Mughal Empire, with the arrival and presence of the Western powers, a commercial economy based on oceanic trade was evolving. But no technological revolution in cultivating tools or techniques had occurred since roughly the time of the *Upaniṣads* (*c.* 600–300 BC).

The crops were broadly divided into rice zones and wheat and millet zones. Rice predominated in the eastern states, the southwest coast, and in Kashmir. Aside from its original home in Gujarāt, it had spread also to the Punjab and Sind with the aid of irrigation. Wheat grew throughout its "natural" region in north and central India. Millets were cultivated in the wheat areas and in the drier districts of Gujarāt and Khāndesh as well.

Cotton, sugarcane, indigo, and opium were major cash crops; the last two have since passed out of cultivation. Introduced by the Portuguese, cultivation of tobacco spread rapidly. The Malabar coast was the home of spices, especially black pepper, that had stimulated the first European adventures in the East. Coffee had been imported from Abyssinia and became a popular beverage in aristocratic circles by the end of the century. Tea, which was to become the common man's drink and a major export, was yet undiscovered, though it was growing wild in the hills of Assam. Vegetables were cultivated mainly in the vicinity of towns. New species of fruit, such as the pineapple, papaya, and cashew nut, also were introduced by the Portuguese. The quality of mango and citrus fruits was greatly improved.

Spices, coffee, tea, and fruit

Cattle continued to be important for draft and milk. According to a Dutch observer, however, the cows gave far less milk than in his country. Land use never became as intensive as in China and the Far East, although, as noted by Megasthenes, double (and even triple) cropping was fairly common in regions favoured with irrigation or adequate double rainfall. Though the population must have increased many times over since Mauryan times, in the 17th century virgin land was still abundant; peasants were scarce.

Irrigation from wells, tanks, and canals, however, had greatly expanded. Some new water-lifting devices—such as the sakia, or Persian wheel, which consisted of a series of leather buckets on an endless rope yoked to oxen—had been adopted and are still widely used.

Traditional implements

The plow was the principal implement for tillage. Drawn by oxen, the traditional Indian plow has never had a wheel or a moldboard. The part that penetrates the soil is a wedge-shaped block of hardwood. The draft pole projects in front, where it is attached to the neck yoke of the bullocks. A short, upright stilt in the rear serves as a guiding handle. The point of the wedge, to which an iron share may or may not be attached, does not invert the soil. Some plows are so light that the cultivator can carry them daily on his shoulder to and from the fields. Others are heavy, requiring teams of four to six pairs of oxen. Levelers and clod crushers, generally consisting of a rectangular beam of wood drawn by bullocks, are used to smooth the surface before sowing. Among hand tools, the most common is the *kodali,* an iron blade fitted to a wooden handle with which it makes an acute angle.

Drill sowing and dibbling (making small holes in the ground for seeds or plants) are old practices in India. An early 17th-century writer notes that cotton cultivators "push down a pointed peg into the ground, put the seed into the hole, and cover it with earth—it grows better thus." Another simple device was a bamboo tube attached to the plow. The seed was dropped through the tube into the furrow as the plow worked and was covered by the soil in making the next furrow.

Operations of reaping, threshing, and winnowing have continued to be performed almost exactly as described in the Vedic texts. Thus, grain is harvested with a sickle. It is bound in bundles and threshed by bullocks treading on it or by hand pounding. To separate the grain from the chaff, it is either sieved with sieves made of stalks of grass or of bamboo, or it is winnowed by pouring by hand at a height from a *supa* (winnowing scoop). The grain is then measured and stored. The sickle, sieve, and *supa* remain today as they were more than two millennia ago.

SOUTHEAST AND EAST ASIA

The Chinese agrarian system could not conquer the northern steppes and deserts nor could it cultivate the barren heights of the Tibetan plateau to the west. It did reach out, however, to areas with less extreme environmental factors—to the plains of Manchuria, Inner Mongolia, the lower valleys of eastern Tibet, and Chinese Turkistan, wherever conditions were favourable. It encountered no comparable barriers to the east. As a result, crops and cultivation techniques, especially of rice culture, spread to Korea and Japan, where they enjoyed notable success. Japan achieved higher yields per acre of rice than did China and most of the world.

Southeast Asia, on the other hand, constitutes an agricultural subcentre supplementing that of the Indian subcontinent. Though it has a wealth of tropical wild and cultivated flora, rice became the staple and predominantly subsistence crop of the region after its introduction probably by Indian colonists around the middle of the 1st millennium BC. Most of the other key farm products, such as sugar, tea, coffee, cotton, rubber, and corn, also were introduced to this area from the outside by the European colonizers.

Shifting cultivation

Historically, shifting cultivation has been native to all the countries and still survives. As in South Asia, most of the rice is rain fed, and multiple cropping is infrequent, probably because of relatively low population densities in most of the region. With the exception of small pockets, as on the island of Java and in the Red River Delta of northern Vietnam, even wet-rice cultivation techniques have never been as intensive as in South China and Japan, nor have the yields been nearly as high. (K.Na.)

Improvements in agriculture in the West: c. 200 BC to AD 1600

THE ROMAN EPOCH

Crop farming and domestication of animals were well established in western Europe by Roman times. Yields per acre were small by 20th-century standards, and nearly half the annual crop had to be used as seed, but quantities of grain were still exported from Britain to Gaul. Where feasible, Roman farming methods were adopted.

Greek and Roman farming techniques are known from contemporary textbooks that have survived. Methods were dictated to some degree by the Mediterranean climate and by the contours of the area. The majority of the crops cultivated today on the Mediterranean coast, wheat, spelt, barley, some millet, and the legumes (beans, peas, vetches, chick-peas, alfalfa [lucerne], and lupines), were known at that time. The olive, the vine, and fruit trees were grown, as were turnips and radishes.

The farm. Roman holdings were commonly as small as 1¼ acres; the ground was prepared with hand tools, hoes, and mattocks, doubtless edged with bronze or iron. Later, as farming developed, and estates of different sizes came into existence, two writers set out catalogs of the tools, implements, and labour required to exploit a given-size holding. These were Marcus Porcius Cato (234–149 BC) and Marcus Terentius Varro (116–27 BC). Already in Cato's time, emphasis was on production of wine and oil for sale, rather than cultivation of cereal crops, beyond the volume required to feed animals and slaves.

Equipment and labour for an olive grove

For an olive grove of 240 jugers (150 acres), Cato estimated necessary equipment as three large carts, six plows and plowshares, three yokes, six sets of ox harness, one harrow, manure hampers and baskets, three pack saddles, and three pads for the asses. Required tools included eight heavy spades, four smaller spades, shovels, rakes, scythes, axes, and wedges. Some 13 people, including an overseer, a housekeeper, five labourers, three teamsters, a muleteer, a swineherd, and a shepherd responsible for 100 sheep, would do the work. Other livestock included three yokes of oxen, three donkeys to carry manure, and one for the olive-crushing mill. The farm was also to be equipped with oil presses and containers for the oil.

Farm implements. Most Roman-era hand tools were similar in shape to their modern counterparts. The wooden plow was fitted with an iron share and, later, with a coulter (cutter). Though it had no moldboard to turn the soil over, it was sometimes fitted with two small ears that helped to make a more distinct rut. Though it could not turn a furrow, it could invert some of the soil if held sideways. It was usually followed by a man with a mattock who broke up clods and cleared the row so seed would fall into it. Two or three such plowings were given each year to land intended for cereals. Manure was spread only after the second plowing. If spread earlier, it would be buried too deep to do any good. The farm included a compost pit where human and animal excrement were placed along with leaves, weeds, and household waste. Water was added from time to time to rot the mass, and an oak pole was driven into the middle to keep snakes away. Various animal and bird droppings were believed to have different effects on growing plants. Pigeon's dung was valued, but that of aquatic birds was avoided. Marl—earth containing lime, clay, and sand—was used in Gaul and possibly in Britain.

Seeds were sown by hand, broadcast, or dropped. They were covered with a harrow, which may have had iron teeth or may simply have been a thornbush. A more complex plow, fitted with a wheeled forecarriage, may have been used in Cisalpine Gaul (northern Italy) as early as the 1st century AD. Traction normally was supplied by a pair of oxen; the Roman historian Pliny the Elder (AD 23–79) mentions as many as eight being used on heavy land. In light soil, only one was necessary, and sometimes asses were used.

Cropping systems. Olive groves and vineyards were permanent; grain and pulses were annuals. Although it was realized that different soils were better suited to some crops than to others, the same piece of land was used for all crops. A specific crop, however, was grown in alternate years in what is known as the two-field, or crop-and-fallow, system. The fallow land was plowed two or three times during the fallow year to kill the weeds, which typically accumulate where cereal crops are continuously cultivated. Wetland was drained by digging V-shaped trenches, the bottom of which, usually four feet deep, was paved with loose stones, willow branches, or bundles of brushwood placed lengthwise, and covered with the replaced soil. Soil was judged by colour, taste, smell, adhesion to the fingers when rubbed, and whether it filled up a hole from which it had been dug or proved too loose.

Then as now, wheat was mostly sown in autumn, though a species known as *Triticum trimestre* was sometimes planted in spring; it ripened in three months. Barley was a spring-sown crop, as were most others. Though the Romans knew that growing alfalfa and clover was in some way good for the succeeding crop, they did not know why. Similarly, a crop of lupines was sometimes planted for plowing in as green manure, and occasionally a crop of beans was used in the same way.

Harvesting and processing. The harvest was reaped with a curved sickle, a tool that has changed little since Roman times. In some places, the ears of grain were cut and carried in wicker baskets to the threshing floor. The straw was cut and stacked later. In other areas, the plant was cut lower down, and the grain was threshed from the straw. Another set of tools was used, consisting of a short-handled sickle held in the right hand, with the blade at right angles to the handle. A short-handled hooklike implement held in the left hand was used to draw together enough grain to be cut at one stroke. In Gaul, a reaper was used, a cart with an open back pushed by an animal reversed in the shafts. On the edge of the back, a comblike device was fixed to tear off the ears as the vehicle was pushed through the crop. The grain was threshed in the long-established way, by animals treading it on a firm floor, or by an implement known as a *tribulum,* a wooden framework with bits of flint or metal fixed to the underside, hauled over the grain by an animal. Winnowing was still done by tossing in the air from a winnowing basket when there was a favourable wind to blow away the chaff.

The quern

Grain was ground with a quern, a hand implement made of two stones, a concave base with a convex upper stone fitted into it. Some querns turned in a circle, while others merely rubbed up and down on the grain. Though designed before the end of the Roman period, water mills were uncommon.

Some forage crops were necessary to feed the plow animals and the cattle, sheep, and pigs. Grass was cut for hay, and many hours must have been spent in the woods collecting acorns for winterfeed for the swine. Alfalfa was the best fodder; it helped fertility as well. Lupines and a mixed crop of beans, vetch, and chick-peas and another mixture of barley, vetch, and legumes were also employed. Turnips were grown for human and animal consumption in some regions, notably Gaul.

Livestock. Little attempt was made at selective breeding, and little was possible, for most of the animals spent their time at open range or in the woods. Nevertheless, different breeds of cattle were recognized as native to particular places. They were bred between the ages of two and 10 years; two bulls to 60 or 70 cows was the usual proportion. Greek shepherds garbed some of the very fine wooled sheep in skin coats to keep their fleece clean. Ewes were bred at three years old, two if essential. They fed on the stubble after harvest. Transhumance, or seasonal migration in search of pasture, was normal. A supply of clear water near the grazing ground was necessary.

Goats were kept in large herds, with 50 to 100 the optimum. Swine were also important. Very fat animals were preferred, and large numbers of these, whose meat was frequently seen on the Roman table, were kept. Sows were covered (bred) at from 12 to 20 months of age; it was desirable for them to pig in July or August. The best proportion of boars to sows was 10 to 100. Herds of 100 to 150 ranged the woods. The bacon produced in Gaul had a reputation for quality; swine also flourished in northern Italy and eastern Spain.

Swine raising

The methods of the Roman farmer produced only limited yields, and cereals were regularly imported to Italy from lands more naturally favourable to grain growing: Egypt, Sicily, Sardinia, and Gaul. Yet the Roman methods were basically sound and, with the help of modern mechanical aids, remain to a large extent in force today.

THE MEDIEVAL PERIOD: 600–1600

In 1,000 years of medieval history, many details of farming in the Western world changed. The period falls into two divisions: the first, one of development, lasted until the end of the 13th century; the second, a time of recession, was followed by two centuries of recovery.

Agricultural advances. The most important agricultural advances took place in the countries north of the Alps, in spite of the large population changes and warfare that accompanied the great migrations and the later onslaughts of Northmen and Saracens. Agriculture had, of course, been practiced regularly in Gaul and Britain and sporadically elsewhere in Europe both before and during the Roman epoch. The climate and soils and, perhaps, the social organization compelled different arrangements of land division and the use of more complex tools as more and more land was reclaimed from forest, marsh, and heath to meet the needs of a rising population.

Open-field system. The precise origin of the open-field arrangement (Figure 5), which involves long scattered strips of arable land separated from each other by a furrow, balk (ridge of land left after plowing), or mere (boundary), is obscure. The earliest examples of this system date from about 800, the year Charlemagne was crowned emperor of the West. Usually these strips of land, normally about one

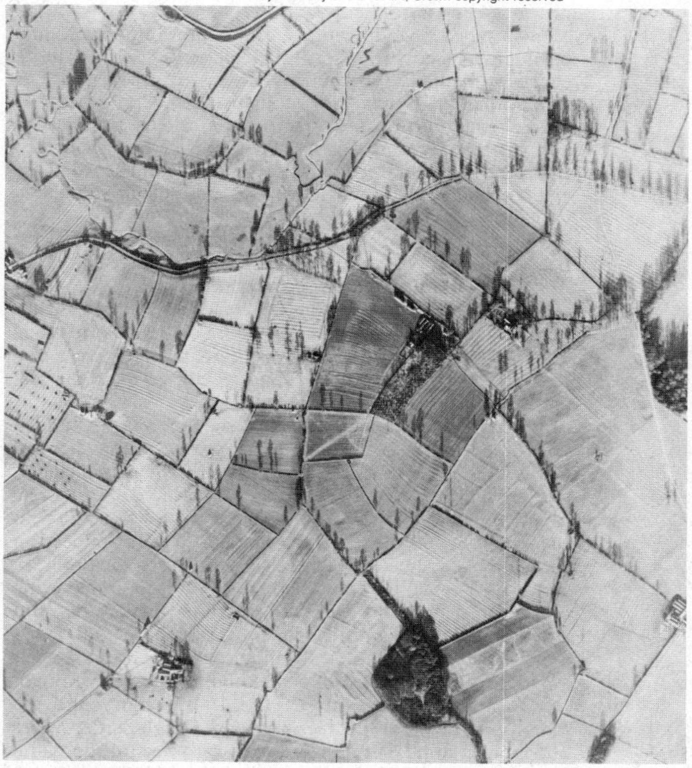

Figure 5: Ridges of the English open-field system as seen today in Leicestershire.

acre in size, were laid out in two or three large fields. Each farmer in the village worked a number of these acres; the units forming his holding were scattered among those of other men. The open-field system continued as more land was reclaimed and lasted for many centuries—longer, of course, in some places than in others. It has been suggested that the length of each strip was determined by the distance a draft animal, usually an ox, could haul a plow before stopping for a rest. The intermingling of the strips was said to have been the result of a jointly owned plow team and plow supplied by a number of farmers working together, each being allotted a strip in turn. A subsequent theory holds that in some places the division of fields, which may have originally been rectangular or square, among a number of heirs led to the creation of long, narrow acres.

In theory each person's holding totaled 30 acres, comprising strips equally divided among the three arable fields. With the passage of time, wide variations in the size of holdings came about; many became very small.

Plows and plowing. Besides the different arrangement of the plowland, there were other changes, some of them important. Though Pliny the Elder claimed a wheeled plow was used in Cisalpine Gaul about the time of Christ, there is a good deal of doubt about this. A wheeled asymmetrical plow was certainly in use in some parts of western Europe by the late 10th century. Illuminations of manuscripts and calendars a little later in date show a plow with two wheels fitted with a rudimentary moldboard and a coulter (Figure 6). This plow could invert the soil and turn a true furrow, thus making a better seedbed. Its use left high ridges on the land, traces of which can still be seen in some places.

The wheeled plow

The horse collar, which replaced the old harness band that pressed upon the animal's windpipe, severely restricting its tractive power, was one of the most important inventions in the history of agriculture. Apparently invented in China, the rigid, padded horse collar allowed the animal to exert its full strength, enabling it to do heavier work, plowing as well as haulage. Many peasants continued to use oxen, however, because horses were more expensive to buy and to keep. Some plowing was done by two oxen as in former times; four, eight, or more were occasionally necessary in very difficult land.

Hand tools. Modifications, slight but important, had been introduced into the design of hand tools. A more effective ax made forest clearance easier and faster. The jointed flail supplanted the straight stick. The scythe was more frequently in use for mowing grass, reaping barley, and performing similar tasks. Wind power was applied to the grinding of grain by the earliest windmills. All these changes and adaptations helped expand the cultivated area and supply food for the growing population.

New lands and crops. Not only were forests cleared and heavy land cultivated but, in the Netherlands, reclamation from marsh and from the sea was extended. In the midst of the marshes, terps, artificially made patches of higher land on which houses and barns could be built, were made at a very early date. Ditches to drain the fens were dug in the 10th century. Polders, land reclaimed from the sea, are first recorded in the 12th century.

In Spain, the Moors had introduced new crops and a new breed of sheep, the Merino, that was to make Spanish wool famous throughout Europe. New crops included sugarcane, rice, cotton, and some subtropical fruits, especially citrus. Grapevines and olive groves flourished in the south, as did the vines the Romans had introduced to the valleys of the Moselle and Rhine rivers. In the 12th century, Venice became a major cotton-manufacturing city, processing cotton from the Mediterranean area into cloth for sale in central Europe; and in the Middle Ages Germany became a cotton-manufacturing centre.

Widespread expansion of farmed land occurred throughout western Europe between the 10th century and the later years of the 13th. German and Dutch settlers were encouraged to take up holdings eastward toward the Baltic countries and south to the Carpathians. In France, new villages were built and new farms carved out of the forest and the waste, while, in England, a great deal of land on the boundaries of the open fields was taken in and cultivated. All this new cultivation was carried out with the same old implements and tools; the same crops were cultivated and animals bred as before. In remote and desolate places, monastic organizations created great estates. These estates were formed to feed growing populations rather than to improve technical skills. A new literature of farming arose, directed to the attention of great lords and ecclesiastical magnates rather than to the illiterate majority of husbandmen. These bright prospects, however, were dimmed in the 14th century by a combination of calamities.

Figure 6: "The Ploughman" behind a two-wheeled plow drawn by horses. Wood engraving from the "Dance of Death" by Hans Holbein, the Younger, *c.* 1540. In the Victoria and Albert Museum, London.

By courtesy of the Victoria and Albert Museum, London

Agricultural recession. What is now called a recession began toward the end of the 13th century. The disasters of the 14th, climatic, pestilent, and military, followed. Famine resulted from excessively bad weather in 1314, 1315, and 1316; a small recovery followed in 1317. Yields, never high (from six to 10 bushels of wheat per acre; a little more for barley, rye, and oats), were reduced to nothing by the weather. Floods wiped out the reclaimed land in the Netherlands. Plague followed famine, bringing suffering to both animals and humans. The Black Death broke out in 1347 and is estimated to have killed approximately one-third of the population of Europe. Renewed outbreaks followed throughout the remainder of the century. The Hundred Years' War desolated much of France; other conflicts, accompanied by similar pillage and destruction, broke out elsewhere. The result of all these misfortunes was to be seen in the landscape throughout western Europe. Much of the arable land could not be cultivated for lack of labourers; in some regions the countryside was inhabited by a few scattered peasants grubbing a scanty living in the grimmest isolation. Many of the newer settlements and some of the established ones were abandoned and became deserted villages.

Effects of the Black Death and Hundred Years' War

The Netherlands. The Netherlands was not as seriously affected as most other countries. The flood destruction was repaired, and a system developed that was to become an example to all Europe. Leguminous and root crops were introduced into the rotation at least as early as the 15th century, and long continuous rotations almost without fallow breaks were employed. Town refuse was added to the supplies of animal manure. The size and milk yield of the Dutch cattle became famous, though possibly exaggerated. Some say that they owed part of their distinction to crosses with animals from Lombardy and Piedmont, which also enjoyed a great reputation. Flemish horses were already renowned for size and strength.

England. In England, when agricultural recovery began in the 15th century, there was no immediate improvement in technique. During this period, England became known as the home of most medium- and long-wooled mutton breeds. The profits of the wool trade and, later, of the woolen manufacture induced landowners to increase the size of their flocks. This led to some difficulties. Not only had some arable land fallen down to rough grazing because of labour scarcity after the diseases and bad seasons of the 14th century, but the profit of wool encouraged enclosure of formerly open fields for grazing; some villages were even destroyed to increase the area of grazing land. Though there was a considerable outcry against enclosure in the 16th and early 17th centuries, the practice was too profitable to halt. At the same time, farmers began exchanging their scattered plots of land in order to consolidate individual holdings. These consolidated plots were then enclosed with a hedge or fence to prevent them from being subjected to the regulations that governed the use of the remaining strips. Land was also acquired by purchase for this purpose. None of these changes, however, involved any technological advances in farming.

Spain. In Spain, the shepherds, whose organization, the Mesta, was a powerful body with great political influence, came into conflict with the farmers. The annual journey of sheep from their northern grazing area to the south carried them along an established route; this route steadily broadened, with the sheep trespassing upon the farmers' lands and consuming crops. At the same time, the Mesta successfully opposed any expansion in the amount of arable land until the mid-16th century.

Italy. In the 14th century the city-states of Italy were devoted to commerce. There was little emphasis on farming, though some attempts at draining marshes were made, and, in spite of the introduction of rice culture in the north, Italian farming on the whole remained much as it had been in Roman times. In the south great flocks were kept and moved up to the mountains for the summer along well-defined paths.

Persistence of Roman farming

France. In the 15th century French farmers made substantial progress toward recovery, but even in France there was little advance in technology. The open-field system was prevalent in the north, and a type of Roman farming suited to the environment was practiced in the south, with alfalfa, clover, lupines, and other legumes grown for fodder and to maintain fertility. A fodder crop called Burgundy grass was grown in Burgundy toward the end of the 16th century.

Germany. Many of the German villages depopulated by the disasters of the 14th century were never resettled. Some of them had been established on marginal land, such as sandy heaths or high in the mountains. By the middle of the 16th century, the advanced farming of the Netherlands penetrated into the north at the mouth of the Rhine and in Schleswig-Holstein. This is clear from one of the earliest printed books on farming, by a German, Conrad Heresbach. Heresbach described and recommended many of the methods used by the Romans, including raising lupines for green manure and rotating fallow-manured, winter-sown rape with wheat, rye, and spring barley. For the preparation of the seedbed, the destruction of weeds, manuring, sowing, and harvesting, implements that derived from the Roman pattern were used.

Heresbach's book followed somewhat the pattern of Crescentius, who wrote in the 13th century, and in that respect was similar to the growing number of agricultural treatises that appeared in Spain and France. These were often encyclopaedias of rural life presumably intended for the landowning public. In the late 16th century, Henry IV of France and his minister, Sully, tried to stimulate interest among the lesser nobility in the management of their estates. In England, translations were made of continental works.

Crop-farming changes in western Europe: 1600–1800

THE NORFOLK FOUR-COURSE SYSTEM

Of the many changes that took place during this period in agricultural history, few were more important than the Norfolk four-course system, characterized by the disappearance of the fallow year and by a new emphasis on fodder crops. The movement toward change was further intensified by the invention of new farm machines, improvements in farm implements, and scientific interest and new biological theories relating to farm and animal life.

In the Norfolk four-course system, wheat was grown in the first year, followed by turnips in the second, then barley, with clover and ryegrass undersown, in the third. The clover and ryegrass were grazed or cut for feed in the fourth year. The turnips were either employed for feeding cattle in open yards during the winter (some covered yards were built) or for feeding sheep confined in folds set up on the ground. This new system was cumulative in effect, for the fodder crops eaten by the livestock produced large supplies of previously scarce animal manure, and that was richer in nature because the animals were better fed. When the sheep grazed the fields, their urine and droppings fertilized the soil, so that heavier cereal yields were obtained in following years.

Increased use of animal manure

Established in Norfolk County, England, and in several other counties before the end of the 17th century, the Norfolk four-course system became fairly general on the newly enclosed farms by 1800, remaining almost standard practice on most British farms for the best part of the following century. The system was used in the Lothians and some other parts of Scotland by about 1800 and, during the first three quarters of the 19th century, was adopted in much of continental Europe.

Enclosure. In order to adopt the Norfolk four-course system, it was first necessary to alter the thousand-year-old layout of the arable fields. It was virtually impossible for an individual farmer to grow fodder crops on his strips of land in open fields, for at certain seasons (after harvest, for example) these fields were opened to grazing by the livestock of the whole community. The improving farmer, who grew clover and ryegrass or other legumes or a root crop, would simply have provided additional feed for his neighbours' as well as his own animals. Such an arrangement was possible, of course, if all the farmers cooperated, a rather unlikely but not absolutely unknown state of affairs. On enclosed land, however, a farmer could cultivate these crops and benefit from his own efforts.

Consequently there was a rapid acceleration of the enclosure movement in England, sometimes by local agreement, by Chancery decree (late 17th century), and by private acts of Parliament in growing numbers (18th century). Some 6,000,000 acres of English fields were enclosed between 1700 and 1845. On the Continent, the change, where it was made, took place slightly later. Some farms are still worked in strips, though communal regulation has vanished.

Livestock. Where new fodder crops were introduced into the rotation, more and better livestock were bred and kept. Animal size increased, and meat development was greater. In cows, milk yield improved. Better breeding increased fleece and flesh production in sheep and improved the size of pigs. Horses, essential to transport, were carefully bred. There were disastrous outbreaks of cattle plague, however, that spread throughout Europe in the second and fourth decades of the 18th century, possibly introduced from eastern Europe by cattle driven to markets in the west. As a result of these calamities, a veterinary school was founded at Lyon, in 1762, and a second at Alfort, Fr., in 1767. Denmark established its first veterinary school in 1773, and England followed in 1791.

Spread of the Merino sheep

An interesting aspect of livestock breeding was the admiration of all Europe for the Spanish Merino sheep, which were forbidden from export for fear of competition. It proved impossible to maintain the prohibition. Merinos were obtained by Louis XVI of France in 1786. Some had been imported into Sweden even earlier, before 1765. Both Prussia and Saxony raised them by midcentury, the Saxon Merino becoming famous. Austria also secured Merinos, and George III of England obtained a few by the end of the century. Merinos were not a success in England, however.

Though a major source of meat since Roman times, pigs had been raised half wild, feeding in the woods under the care of a swineherd and his dogs. Over a large part of western Europe, this system continued, especially where open-field farming prevailed. In England, however, where population doubled during the 18th century from about

5,000,000 to about 10,000,000, more care was taken in breeding productive swine. Several different breeds could already be distinguished; some were crossed with Chinese animals possibly brought from that distant country in vessels carrying spices and tea.

IMPROVEMENTS IN TECHNOLOGY

Plows and farm machinery. Probably of Dutch origin, the Rotherham plow, the main design of which has remained virtually unchanged to this day, was first put into use in the Netherlands, England, and Scotland during the first half of the 18th century. Details of design varied from area to area. Some Rotherham plows were wheeled, and some were not; some were made of timber; others of iron. The first factory for making plows was established in England in 1783.

Though the problem of mechanizing harvest work was not solved until the 19th century, a few fairly simple threshing machines were designed and put in use by 1800. Similarly, a variety of machines for such tasks as preparing animal feed, chopping turnips, and cutting chaff were designed and used.

The English gentleman Jethro Tull made important contributions during this period, among them the horse-drawn hoe and the seed drill. To save expensive hand labour, Tull designed and fabricated horse-drawn hoes that destroyed the weeds and kept the soil between the rows in good crumbly (friable) condition. Tull believed that friable soil would supply all the nutrients a plant required, and he was so convinced of his theory that he planted wheat in rows spaced widely enough to allow for horse hoeing while the plant was growing. Tull also believed that placing the seed into the ground in small holes (drilling) would permit a much lighter rate of seeding than hand broadcast methods and still get high yields. To place the seeds, he designed and used a seed drill.

Tull was not the first man to invent a seed drill. A seed dropper, consisting of a tube attached to a plow through which seed could be dropped by hand at regular intervals, had been attached to an ancient Babylonian plow. A similar system, but with two tubes behind two plowshares set in a rectangular frame, was employed in 17th-century China, and probably at a very much earlier date. An Italian described a modern form of seed drill in the late 16th century. An Austrian, Locatelli, described a *sembrador,* or seed drill attached to a plow, which was either used or proposed for use in Spain. After Tull, inventors were numerous, and, at the end of the 18th century, the drilling of seed, though not commonplace, was accepted. Throughout this period, however, the ordinary farmer continued to prepare his seedbed by plowing three times a year, occasionally more, and broadcasting seed by hand and harrowing it in. All these techniques were thousands of years old.

Water meadows

Irrigation and drainage. Walter Blith, a captain in Cromwell's army, was interested in land drainage and irrigation in the form of water meadows, pieces of low, flat land capable of being kept in fertility by being overflowed from some adjoining stream. During his lifetime considerable drainage work was carried out in eastern England, where it has continued to the present day. At the same time, water meadows were constructed in southwest England. This system was well known and of long standing in Germany. Similarly, there were sporadic attempts to drain wetlands in France and Italy; maintenance of the drainage system was essential to parts of the Netherlands. Colonization of reclaimed lands in eastern England by Dutch settlers also introduced some novel crops to that area, especially rape and cole.

Importance of the New World. The age of exploration that began in the mid-15th century led to discovery of edible plants previously unknown to Europeans. The Arabs had introduced sugarcane and rice to some parts of southern Europe. The voyagers to North America returned with corn (maize), tobacco, and the turkey. South America supplied the potato, cocoa, quinine, and some vegetable drugs, while coffee, tea, and indigo came from the Orient.

Though the tropical plants could not be cultivated in the temperate European climate, corn was rapidly adopted in southern Europe. Imported first to Ireland, the potato came into general use elsewhere by the end of the 18th century.

These novel crops expanded the dietary range in some places, and importation of the new beverages may have helped reduce the very large consumption of alcoholic drinks. Tea drinking was regarded as harmful by some fervent propagandists at the end of the 17th century and later, and, in the 1820s, William Cobbett even condemned the potato. By that time, however, the crop had become the staple food of the Irish rural population and was raised on a moderate scale in Lancashire and Cheshire for consumption by their growing manufacturing population, as it was in some parts of Germany, France, the Low Countries, and Italy.

In the 16th and 17th centuries the introduction of sheep into such New World countries as Argentina, with suitable climate and grazing land, proved highly successful.

Agricultural textbooks and improvement societies. The small number of vernacular farming textbooks printed in Europe during the 16th century increased in the 17th and became much larger in the 18th, indicating a developing interest in commercial farming. Population growth, especially in the urban centres, and the rise of industry opened new opportunities for the enterprising landlord and farmer, even though transport was difficult. English writers on farming were more numerous than those in other countries. The French paid more attention to gardening, and the Thirty Years' War (1618–48) brought a long interruption in agricultural development in Germany and adjacent countries.

Crop rotation in Brabant and Flanders

The Flemish and Dutch produced no agricultural texts, declaring that they were more interested in farming than in writing about it. Indeed, the system of crop rotation in Brabant and Flanders became the pattern for the rest of Europe. In 1645 an Englishman, Sir Richard Weston, wrote the first description of this system, which featured crops such as clover or roots, rotating with industrial crops such as flax, with no fallow break. Adoption in England and other parts of western Europe increased agricultural production between 1600 and 1800.

The problem of educating the ordinary farmer occupied the minds of improving landlords who were the governing class in every European country. Improvement societies formed in Great Britain, and a semiofficial Board of Agriculture, financed in part by a government grant, was established there in 1793. It lasted until 1822. One of the first tasks it undertook was to make and publish a survey of each county in the kingdom in order to make the best local methods known to other districts. A similar plan had been tried in France in 1759. Other countries in western Europe engaged in similar activities. A Royal Society was established in Denmark in 1769 and made practical researches. The Italian Società di Georgofili, founded in 1753, tried to stimulate technical improvement and planned large drainage schemes. The first similar Swiss society was established at Zürich in 1747. Frederick William I of Germany founded an agricultural school at Halle in 1727; and the first agricultural high school was begun, with royal encouragement, at Möglin, near Berlin, in 1806.

PROGRESS IN DIFFERENT COUNTRIES

Italy. Although Italy was the first country where a four-course rotation was advocated, traditional farming persisted there into the 18th century and even later. Italian farmers, however, had accepted corn, potatoes, tomatoes, and tobacco and relied upon these and other subtropical products for subsistence and sale. The vine continued to be important, as did the olive. The north was more advanced than the less fertile south; a wide variety of crops was grown there, often in long rotations with a reduction of the proportion of fallow. An occasional fodder crop of turnips, clover, and ryegrass was cultivated. Shortages of fodder encouraged adoption of the Norfolk four-course system. Plows and other implements, however, remained primitive. The mulberry tree, the leaves of which provided food for silkworms, was important in the Milanese and Piedmont area. Rice was also grown on irrigated land in that area. High-yielding milch cows were also kept. Transhumance was practiced, with sheep on the lower lands in winter and on the mountain pastures in summer.

Spain. Spain remained backward, partly because of its physical and climatic conditions and partly from social pressure. The Merino sheep, fine horses, and mules continued to deserve their high repute. Some subtropical crops were cultivated in the south and east—sugarcane, cotton, grapes, olives, figs, raisins, and oranges—but the arid and stony land of the centre and elsewhere remained substantially unproductive and thinly populated by a poor class of métayers (sharecroppers).

Britain. The Industrial Revolution in Great Britain drew many people from food production; this had happened before in the mercantile and manufacturing Low Countries. Since these people still had to be fed, there existed a strong incentive toward increased farm productivity. These countries could not, however, satisfy local demands, and they sought to import food, especially grain. Thus, industrialization in England stimulated cereal growing in Prussia, Poland, and parts of Russia.

Germany. Increased grain production in Prussia was also stimulated by the personal efforts of Frederick II the Great, who set out to repair some of the damage caused by the Thirty Years' War and generally to improve conditions in his country. He ordered the rearrangement of the open-field farms into separate enclosed holdings and did away with common grazing, doubtless to encourage better animal selection and breeding. He bred horses for the army and gave bulls and rams to favoured landowners. Elsewhere in the German congeries of small states, the princes enforced improvements by royal edicts. Fodder crops were introduced. In addition to keeping the animals indoors in winter, summer stall feeding was introduced in some areas, resulting in preservation of the animal manure formerly dropped on the commons.

Rehabilitation by Frederick the Great

Sugar beets had been grown for feed in Germany, but it was not until 1747 that sugar was successfully extracted and not until 1802 that the first factory for making beet sugar was built. This industry, however, did not really begin to grow until the time of the Napoleonic Wars.

Scandinavia. The countries of Scandinavia were influenced by the spirit of improvement, but less spectacularly. Danish farmers were somewhat hindered in the introduction of novel methods by political restrictions, and it was not until the end of the 19th century that serious advances in technique took place. Sweden had some improvers who imported Merino sheep, English cattle, and Angora goats and who studied plow design. Nevertheless, Swedish farming in general remained almost static until after 1757, when some exchange of strips made enclosed farms possible. Potatoes became a staple.

North America. Changes in farming technique that increased productivity, introduced primarily in Great Britain and the Netherlands before 1800, made British farming the example to the world, even the distant lands of America. That continent, north and south, had indeed supplied Europe with very valuable plants. By the end of the 18th century, the production of North America was sufficient to supply some of the necessities of a warring Europe. The New England settlements, like those of the Southern states, were expanding toward the west, as land was claimed from the forest. Agriculture produced small surpluses for export. The Southern states had, of course, always exported staples like tobacco, cotton, and (Louisiana) sugar; but the processes by which these plants were cultivated remained primitive.

Cattle raising expanded rapidly in the New World. The need for fresh and larger grazing areas drew cattle farming west into Ohio and Kentucky, where corn for fattening purposes could be raised at low cost. Cattle were being driven overland to seaboard markets by 1805.

The 19th-century power revolution on the farm: c. 1792–1914

The development of agriculture between the close of the 18th century and the early years of the 20th century was characterized by the partial mechanization of agriculture in western Europe—especially in Great Britain—and in the previously untapped lands of Australia, New Zealand, and North America, where wild, uncultivated, and virtually unoccupied land was made to yield vast quantities of plant and animal crops.

MECHANIZATION

Though the first steps had been taken earlier, it was not until after 1850 that mechanization took hold in western Europe and the newly settled countries. A variety of machines were slowly coming into use when the French revolutionary wars broke out in the 1790s. An efficient seed drill had been devised but still required demonstration in the 1830s to convince farmers of its value. A few threshing machines were in use before 1800, and they became steadily more popular until, in the 1830s, farm labourers in England rebelled against them because the machine robbed them of their winter employment. The speed with which the thresher was adopted is rather surprising, as there was a surplus rather than a shortage of labour at the time.

The reaper. Yet even an ample supply of labour could not always cope with the harvest by hand methods. Local labour frequently had to be supplemented by traveling

By courtesy of the Library of Congress, Washington, D.C.

Figure 7: The original McCormick reaper, 1831; from R.L. Ardrey, "American Agricultural Implements," 1894.

gangs or by small tradesmen from neighbouring towns. This unsatisfactory situation proved an incentive to invention. Reaping machines had been proposed before, but not until Patrick Bell in Scotland and Cyrus Hall McCormick (Figure 7) in the United States produced their designs did this machine become a practical reality. After the Great Exhibition of London in 1851, the reaper slowly came into general use. About this time an animal-pushed combine harvester, which stripped the grain from the plant like the Gallo-Roman reaper of classical times, was devised. This machine was used successfully in South Australia, where more grain was grown than could be harvested manually by the few labourers available there.

The combine harvester

Plows and plowing. Before harvesting machines could be used, however, the ground had to be prepared, and the fundamental instrument for this purpose was the plow. Though attempts had been made in the 17th and 18th centuries to develop a mathematical theory of plow design, in a less esoteric way practical men had made significant improvements. Prominent among these was the English inventor Robert Ransome, who patented a cast-iron share in 1785 and a self-sharpening share in 1803. Later he designed a plow with standard parts that could be removed and replaced in the field, a double plow (*i.e.,* with two shares), and other patterns.

Plowing the Great Plains

As settlers in the United States moved westward, plowing of the black prairie soils, high in organic matter, posed a special problem to the farmers who had cast-iron and iron-patched plows. The ingenuity of John Deere, an Illinois blacksmith and plow maker of the 1830s, resulted in a new kind of plow that was made entirely of steel except for the braces, beam, and handles. The one-piece share and moldboard of his first steel plow was cut from a mill-saw blade and shaped over a wooden form. This greatly improved implement not only made possible the effective plowing of the black prairie soils but also considerably lessened the animal power needed to turn the soil.

A mole plow, characterized by a cartridge-shaped "mole" attached to the bottom of its wide cutting blade, and intended for plowing a drain in heavy wetland, was successfully fabricated and used in the late 18th century. The plow, pulled by a capstan or team of animals, was a great help in draining wetland. Invention of a method for manufacturing tubular clay pipes also aided and simplified drainage. Use of these pipes spread rapidly beginning about 1850; large areas of land were thus drained all over Europe. Drainage by this method continues today.

Steam-powered equipment. The first attempts at steam-powered plowing took place in the 1830s. Though ingenious, the early apparatus was impractically heavy and cumbersome. A successful steam plow was made in the 1860s, after which steam power was widely adopted, especially on large farms (Figure 8). Supplementary implements helpful to the farmer were also produced about this time. They include hay rakes, hay-loaders, and potato spinners. Barn machinery, housed in especially designed buildings, was driven by a steam engine through a system of belts and pulleys or in more primitive style by horses. Threshing drums and supplementary machines were often hauled about the countryside by steam traction engines and worked on a contract basis by itinerant gangs of agricultural labourers.

Steam power spread rapidly but thinly over Europe. The first steam plow was worked in The Netherlands in 1862. Though milking machines were built, they were not really successful until the end of the century. The cream separator and milk cooler, both little changed since the time of their invention, were introduced in the 1880s.

Progress in mechanization in the second half of the 19th century was not, of course, confined to agriculture. Transport and communications improved enormously. Steamships facilitated the movement of goods and the spread of ideas. Railroads were built throughout the world, making agriculture possible in areas where farmers previously had no way to carry their goods to market. The first shipment of cattle marketed by rail originated in Lexington, Ky., in 1852. These cattle were driven to Cincinnati, Ohio, freighted to Cleveland on Lake Erie, boated to Buffalo, freighted to Albany, N.Y., and then boated down the Hudson River to New York City. By 1860 railroads had extended beyond the Mississippi River, opening the Southwest to range production and the Middle West to cattle feeding.

APPLYING SCIENCE TO FARMING

New fertilizers. Mechanical developments were paralleled by scientific discovery. Research in plant physiology and nutrition, begun in the 18th century, continued and grew in scope. The brilliant English chemist Sir Humphry Davy summarized the current state of agricultural knowledge in a series of lectures, published as *Elements of Agricultural Chemistry* in 1813. Though Davy's lectures probably had little impact on the ordinary farmer, a few enterprising pioneers were soon conducting field experiments with new fertilizers. The beneficial effects of saltpetre (potassium nitrate) had been known since the 17th century. When a firm began to import saltpetre from India in the 1820s, interested farmers bought and used it. Imported Chilean nitrate of soda was more plentiful, however, and more often used. Peruvian guano, an organic fertilizer, was imported and extensively used, even though sellers often diluted it with useless material to increase its bulk. Ground bones and other kinds of waste had been used in the late 18th century for restoring phosphate to pastures in dairy areas. Perhaps it was the use of these bones and their cracking and soaking in sulfuric acid that led to the production of superphosphate of lime in the 1840s. As the 19th century continued, more mineral fertilizers were discovered and marketed. With the development of the chemical industry, other fertilizers were manufactured. Basic slag, a waste product of the iron industry, was applied to grasslands with success. Gypsum was also tried but was later superseded by more effective products.

Peruvian guano

Agricultural research and education. Scientists of the 18th century had established the principles that governed plant life. About 1837 the English agriculturist Sir John Bennet Lawes began to experiment with the effects of manures on plants and crops. In 1842 he patented a process for treating phosphate rock to produce superphosphate and thus initiated the synthetic fertilizer industry. In the following year, Lawes enlisted the services of the English scientist J.H. (later Sir Henry) Gilbert, with whom he worked for more than half a century, performing experiments on crop and animal nutrition. The work of Rothamsted Experimental Station, which Lawes founded and endowed, became world renowned. At the same time similar work was carried out in France, Germany, and the United States.

Though a considerable number of books on agricultural subjects appeared during the 19th century, their effect was perhaps less than that of the measures taken to promote agricultural education in most European countries. Though schools for farmers had been established in some German states in the 18th century, the first professorships of rural agriculture and economy were established at Oxford (1790) and Edinburgh (1797). Though similar events took place in France and Germany in the 19th century, a key date in the history of agricultural research

By courtesy of J I Case Company

Figure 8: Self-propelled steam engines were extensively used during the latter part of the 19th century for operating grain-threshing machines and other stationary farm machines such as corn husker–shredders and shellers.

and education is 1862, when the U.S. Congress set up the Department of Agriculture and provided for colleges of agricultural and mechanical arts in each state.

Disease. An important spur to research was the great prevalence of plant disease, which at intervals became epidemic. Two crops—the potato and the grapevine—were virulently attacked in the 1840s, and irreparable damage resulted. When the potato blight struck Ireland, where the potato was a staple food crop, it caused widespread famine. The vine growers of southern Europe suffered several disastrous epidemics of the vine fungus. Later in the century, infestation by the vine louse grape phylloxera nearly put an end to European viticulture.

FARMING OUTSIDE EUROPE

European colonies. In the 19th century, European colonial expansion and plantation farming spread to many areas of the world. Coffee was grown widely in Ceylon (Sri Lanka) until disease destroyed the plants and they were replaced by tea bushes. Sugarcane was raised on a large scale in the East and West Indies, in the United States, and the Hawaiian Islands. Cocoa was carried from South America to colonies in West Africa, where it prospered. Natural rubber was tapped in the Congo and Brazil and was later cultivated in well-designed plantations in the Malay Peninsula. Palm oil was collected from trees in West Africa and the South Seas. Yet these spectacular developments had little impact on the native agriculture of the underdeveloped regions in general; ancient patterns of cultivation remained largely unchanged.

America and Australia. By 1900 much of the western United States had been settled; great livestock ranches and wheat farms had been established there and in Argentina. A large dairy and sheep industry had grown up in Australia and New Zealand. Imported Merinos were the foundation stock of the vast flocks that grazed the Australian hinterland. Devon cattle were exported from England to South Africa, where sheep were also a significant economic factor.

The Great Plains of the United States, lying between the Mississippi River and the Rocky Mountains, were first used by the open-range cattle industry, the heyday of which lasted from about 1866 to 1886. To improve their lean, lanky longhorn, breeders imported Herefords, Durham Shorthorns, and other fine European cattle. As the range became more and more heavily occupied, and as wheat farmers began to till the soil of the Great Plains, it became necessary to put up fences. This was accomplished with a remarkable invention, barbed wire, a new, cheap, and rapidly erected kind of fencing, used in preference to the post and rail fences or the sod and stone walls that had been common in Europe for centuries.

Barbed wire

Grain farmers rapidly followed the ranchers, and farming spread from Oklahoma north into Canada. Because hand labour was scarce, cultivation and harvesting were rapidly mechanized. A combine harvester hauled by a large team of mules was used in California in the late 1880s. Different from the combine harvester used in South Australia, this was a prototype of today's machine. Iron and steel plows were produced in large numbers, and steam traction engines were used as power units for many mechanized operations such as threshing. Though seed was usually drilled, yields were often low because manure was in short supply. Furthermore, with manure scarce, a three-year rotation was practiced to prevent soil depletion: two crop plantings were followed by a fallow year. In the Southern states, export staples were produced in addition to subsistence crops.

America's prodigious new supplies of meat and grain were generally exported from the wide ranges of the Western states to the more populous Eastern states and to Europe, where they lowered prices paid to European farmers but played an important role in feeding populations in industrial centres. Fresh meat and dairy produce from Argentina and Australia were carried thousands of miles in newly developed refrigerator ships.

The huge quantities of inexpensive food produced by the newly settled countries created a difficult problem for the European farmer. The arable and mixed farming common in most European countries simply could not compete. In Great Britain, much cropland was planted with grass, and farmers began to raise pedigree animals and dairy produce. On the Continent, where many farmers occupied peasant holdings, a kind of subsistence farming continued. Denmark and The Netherlands turned to production of dairy produce and high-quality bacon, feeding pigs on waste dairy materials. (G.E.F.)

Scientific agriculture: the 20th century

Agricultural technology has developed more rapidly in the 20th century than in all previous history. Though the most important developments during the first half of this century took place in the industrial countries, especially the United States, the picture has changed somewhat since the 1950s. With the coming of independence, former colonies in Africa and Asia have initiated large-scale efforts to improve their agriculture. In many cases they have used considerable ingenuity in adapting Western methods to their own climates, soils, and crops (see also FARMING AND AGRICULTURAL TECHNOLOGY).

DEVELOPMENTS IN POWER:
THE INTERNAL-COMBUSTION ENGINE

The internal-combustion engine brought major changes to agriculture in most of the world. In advanced regions it soon became the chief power source for the farm.

The tractor. The first applications to agriculture of the four-stroke-cycle gasoline engine were as stationary engines, at first in Germany, later elsewhere. By the 1890s stationary engines were mounted on wheels to make them portable, and soon a drive was added to make them self-propelled. The first successful gasoline tractor was built in the United States in 1892. Within a few years several companies were manufacturing tractors in Germany, the United Kingdom, and the United States. The number of tractors in the more developed countries increased dramatically during the 20th century, especially in the United States: in 1907 some 600 tractors were in use, but the figure had grown to almost 3,400,000 by 1950.

Design changes

Major changes in tractor design throughout the century have produced a much more efficient and useful machine. Principal among these were the power takeoff, introduced in 1918, in which power from the tractor's engine could be transmitted directly to an implement through the use of a special shaft; the all-purpose, or tricycle-type, tractor (1924), which enabled farmers to cultivate planted crops mechanically; rubber tires (1932), which facilitated faster operating speeds; and the switch to four-wheel drives and diesel power in the 1950s and 1960s, which greatly increased the tractor's pulling power. The last innovations have led to the development of enormous tractors—usually having double tires on each wheel and enclosed, air-conditioned cabs—that can pull several gangs of plows.

Unit machinery. Since World War II, there has been an increase in the use of self-propelled machines in which the motive power and the equipment for performing a particular task form one unit. Though the grain combine is the most important of these single-unit machines, self-propelled units are also in use for spraying, picking cotton, baling hay, picking corn, and harvesting tomatoes, lettuce, sugar beets, and many other crops. These machines are faster, easier to operate, and above all, have lower labour requirements than those that are powered by a separate tractor.

Grain combine. The first successful grain combine, a machine that cuts ripe grain and separates the kernels from the straw, was built in the United States in 1836. Lack of an adequate power unit and the tendency of combined grain to spoil because of excessive moisture limited its development, however. Large combines, powered by as many as 40 horses, were used in California in the latter part of the 19th century. Steam engines replaced horses on some units as a power source, but, about 1912, the gasoline engine began to replace both horses and steam for pulling the combine and operating its mechanism. A one-man combine, powered by a two-plow-sized tractor (*i.e.,* one large enough to pull two plows), was developed in 1935. This was followed by a self-propelled machine in 1938.

Mechanized equipment for corn. Corn, the most important single crop in the United States and extremely important in many other countries, is grown commercially with the aid of equipment operated by tractors or by internal-combustion engines mounted on the machines. Corn pickers came into use in the U.S. Corn Belt after World War I and have been even more widely adopted since World War II. Corn pickers vary in complexity from the snapper-type harvester, which removes the ears from the stalks but does not husk them, to the picker-sheller, which not only removes the husk but shells the grain from the ear. The latter is often used in conjunction with dryers. Modern machines can harvest as many as 12 rows of corn at a time.

The corn picker-sheller

Mechanized equipment for cotton. Mechanization has also reduced substantially the labour needed to grow cotton. Equipment includes tractor, two-row stalk-cutter, disk (to shred the stalks), bedder (to shape the soil into ridges or seedbeds), planter, cultivator, sprayer, and harvester. Cotton fibre is harvested by a stripper-type harvester, developed in the 1920s, or by a picker. The stripper strips the entire plant of both open and unopened bolls and collects many leaves and stems. Though a successful cotton picker that removed the seed cotton from the open bolls and left the burrs on the plant was invented in 1927, it did not come into use until after World War II. Strippers are used mostly in dry regions, while pickers are employed in humid, warm areas. The pickers are either single-row machines mounted on tractors or two-row self-propelled machines.

Where strippers and pickers are used

Tomato-harvesting equipment. The self-propelled mechanical tomato harvester, developed in the early 1960s by engineers working in cooperation with plant breeders, handles virtually all packing tomatoes grown in California. Harvesters using electronic sorters can further reduce labour requirements.

Automobiles, trucks, and airplanes. The automobile and truck have also had a profound effect upon agriculture and farm life. Since their appearance on American farms between 1913 and 1920, trucks have changed patterns of production and marketing of farm products. Trucks deliver such items as fertilizer, feed, and fuels; go into the fields as part of the harvest equipment; and haul the crops to markets, warehouses, or packing and processing plants. Most of the livestock is trucked to market.

The airplane may have been used agriculturally in the United States as early as 1918 to distribute poison dust over cotton fields that were afflicted with the pink bollworm. While records of this experiment are fragmentary, it is known that airplanes were used to locate and map cotton fields in Texas in 1919. In 1921 a widely publicized dusting experiment took place near Dayton, Ohio. Army pilots, working with Ohio entomologists, dusted a six-acre grove of catalpa trees with arsenate of lead to control the sphinx caterpillar. The experiment was successful. It and others encouraged the development of dusting and spraying, mainly to control insects, disease, weeds, and brush. In recognition of the possible long-term harmful effects of some of the chemicals, aerial dusting and spraying have been subject to various controls since the 1960s.

Early experiments with airplanes in agriculture

Airplanes are also used to distribute fertilizer, to reseed forest terrain, and to control forest fires. Many rice growers use planes to seed, fertilize, and spray pesticides, and even to hasten crop ripening by spraying hormones from the air.

During heavy storms, airplanes have dropped baled hay to cattle stranded in snow. Airplanes have also been used to transport valuable breeding stock, particularly in Europe. Valuable and perishable farm products are frequently transported by air. Airplanes are especially valuable in such large agricultural regions as western Canada and Australia, where they provide almost every type of service to isolated farmers.

NEW CROPS AND TECHNIQUES

New crops and techniques are, in reality, modifications of the old. Soybeans, sugar beets, and grain sorghums, for example, all regarded as "new" crops, are new only in the sense that they are now grown in wider areas and have different uses from those of earlier times. Such techniques as terracing, dry farming, and irrigation are nearly as old as the practice of agriculture itself, but their widespread application is still increasing productivity in many parts of the world.

New crops. *The soybean.* This is an outstanding example of an ages-old crop that, because of the development of new processes to make its oil and meal more useful, is widely produced today. In the Orient, where the soybean originated long ago, more than half the crop is used directly for food, and less than a third is pressed for oil. Its high protein and fat content make it a staple in the diet, replacing or supplementing meat for millions of people.

Though first reported grown in America in 1804, the soybean remained a rare garden plant for nearly 100 years. Around the beginning of the 20th century, when three new varieties were introduced from Japan, farmers began growing it for hay, pasture, and green manure. In the early 1930s a soybean oil processing method that eliminated a disagreeable odour from the finished product was developed. World War II brought an increased demand for edible oil. The food industry began using soybean oil for margarine, shortening, salad oil, mayonnaise, and other food products and continues to be its chief user. Manufacturers of paints, varnishes, and other drying oil products are the most important nonfood users.

Development of the solvent process of extracting soybean oil has greatly increased the yield. A 60-pound bushel of soybeans processed by this method yields $10\frac{1}{2}$ pounds of oil and 45 pounds of meal. Soybean meal and cake are used chiefly for livestock feed in the United States. The high protein content of the meal has made it an attractive source of industrial protein, and, with proper processing, it is an excellent source of protein for humans.

Solvent process for soybean oil

Development of new soybean varieties suited for different parts of the world is possible by means of hybridization. This permits isolating types superior in yielding ability, resistance to lodging (breakage of the plant by wind and rain) and shattering (of the bean), adaptation to suit various requirements for maturity, and resistance to disease. Hybridization, however, has not yet led to spectacular gains in yields.

Sorghum. Just as the soybean was used for many centuries in Asia before its introduction into the Western world, so sorghum was a major crop in Africa. Sorghum is fifth in importance among the world's cereals, coming after wheat, rice, corn, and barley. It is called Guinea corn in West Africa, kafir corn in South Africa, durra in The Sudan, and mtama in East Africa. In India it is known as jowar, cholam, and great millet, and it is called kaoliang in China. In America it is often called milo, while the sweet-stemmed varieties are referred to as sweet sorghum, or sorgo.

Sorghum probably had been domesticated in Ethiopia by 3000 BC. From there, it spread to West and East Africa, and then southward. Traders from Africa to the East carried sorghum as provisions on their dhows. It is likely that sorghum thus reached India, where cultivation began between 1500 and 1000 BC. Other traders carried sorghum to China and the Far East. The amber sorghums or sorgos, useful for forage and syrup, may have moved by sea, while the grain sorghums probably moved overland. The movement to the Mediterranean and the Middle East also began through traders.

Sorghum reached the New World through the slave trade. Guinea corn and chicken corn came from West Africa to America as provisions for the slaves. Other types were introduced into the United States by seedsmen and scientists from about 1870 to 1910. Seed was sometimes sold to farmers as a new, highly productive variety of corn. It was not until the 1930s, after the value of the plant as grain, forage, and silage for livestock feeding had been recognized, that acreage began to increase. Yields rose markedly in the late 1950s, after successful hybridization of the crop. Better yields led in turn to increased acreage.

Chinese ambercane was brought from France to the United States in 1854 and was distributed to farmers.

Sorghum sugar

While the cane provided good forage for livestock, promoters of the new crop were most interested in refining sugar from the sorghum molasses, a goal that persisted for many years. While refining technology has been perfected, the present cost of sorghum sugar does not permit it to compete with sugar from other sources.

Large amounts of sorghum grain are eaten every year by people of many countries. If the world population continues to grow as projected, food is likely to be sorghum's most important use. Most of the sorghum is ground into flour, often at home. Some is consumed as a whole-kernel food. Some of the grain is used for brewing beer, particularly in Africa.

The sugar beet. The sugar beet as a crop is much newer than either soybeans or sorghum. Although beets had been a source of sweets among ancient Egyptians, Indians, Chinese, Greeks, and Romans, it was not until 1747 that a German apothecary, Andreas Marggraf, obtained sugar crystals from the beet. Some 50 years later, Franz Karl Achard, son of a French refugee in Prussia and student of Marggraf, improved the Silesian stock beet—probably a mangel-wurzel—as a source of sugar. He erected the first pilot beet-sugar factory at Cunern, Silesia (now Poland), in 1802. Thus began the new use for sugar of a crop traditionally used as animal feed.

When during the Napoleonic Wars continental Europe was cut off from West Indies cane sugar, further experimentation with beet sugar was stimulated. In 1808 a French scientist, Benjamin Delessert, used charcoal in clarification, which insured the technical success of beet sugar. On March 25, 1811, Napoleon issued a decree that set aside 80,000 acres of land for the production of beets, established six special sugar-beet schools to which 100 select students were given scholarships, directed construction of 10 new factories, and appropriated substantial bounties to encourage the peasants to grow beets. By 1814, 40 small factories were in operation in France, Belgium, Germany, and Austria. Although the industry declined sharply after Napoleon's defeat, it was soon revived. For the last third of the 19th century, beets replaced cane as the leading source of sugar.

Napoleonic experimentation with beet sugar

Since World War II, major changes have taken place in sugar-beet production in the United States and, to a lesser extent, in the Soviet Union, Germany, and other nations with a substantial production. These changes may be illustrated by developments in the United States.

In 1931 the California Agricultural Experiment Station and the U.S. Department of Agriculture undertook a cooperative study of the mechanization of sugar-beet growing and harvesting. The goal in harvesting was a combine that would perform all the harvesting operations—lifting from the soil, cutting the tops, and loading—in one trip down the row. By the end of World War II, four different types of harvesters were being manufactured.

The spring and summer operations—planting, blocking (cutting out all plants except for clumps standing 10 or 12 inches [25 or 30 centimetres] apart), thinning, and weeding—did not yield so easily to mechanization, largely because the beet seed, a multigerm seedball, produced several seedlings, resulting in dense, clumpy, and somewhat irregular stands. In 1941 a machine for segmenting the seedball was developed. The problem was solved in 1948, when a plant with a true single-germ seed was discovered in Oregon. Now precision seed drills could be used, and plants could be first blocked and then cultivated mechanically using a cross-cultivating technique; that is, cultivating the rows up and down and then across the field. During World War I, 11.2 hours of labour were required to produce a ton of sugar beets; in 1964, 2.7 hours were needed.

New techniques. As the development of the sugar beet shows, new techniques may bring particular crops into prominence. This discussion, however, is confined to three that, in some forms, are old yet today are transforming agriculture in many parts of the world.

Terracing. Terracing, which is basically grading steep land, such as hillsides, into a series of level benches, was known in antiquity and was practiced thousands of years ago in such divergent areas as the Philippines, Peru, and Central Africa. Today, terracing is of major importance in Japan, Mexico, and parts of the United States, while many other nations, including Israel, Australia, South Africa, Colombia, and Brazil, are increasing productivity through the inauguration of this and other soil-conserving practices.

Colombia provides an example of the modern need for terracing. For many years the steep slopes used for producing the world-renowned Colombian coffee have been slowly eroding. During the 1960s experimental work showed that contour planting and terracing would help preserve the land. Farther south, the Brazilian state of São Paulo created a terracing service in 1938. Since then, the program has become a full conservation service.

Irrigation. The usefulness of a full-scale conservation project is seen in the Snowy Mountains Project of Australia, where three river systems have been diverted to convert hundreds of miles of arid but fertile plains to productive land. Intensive soil conservation methods have been undertaken wherever the natural vegetation and soil surface have been disturbed. Drainage is controlled by stone and steel drains, grassed waterways, absorption and contour terraces, and settling ponds. Steep slopes are stabilized by woven wickerwork fences, brush matting, and bitumen sprays, followed by revegetation with white clover and willow and poplar trees. Grazing is strictly controlled to prevent silting of the reservoirs and damage to slopes. The two main products of the plan are power for new industries and irrigation water for agriculture, with recreation and a tourist industry as important by-products.

Snowy Mountains Project

The Snowy Mountains Project of Australia is a modern successor, so far as irrigation is concerned, to practices that have provided water for crops almost from the beginnings of agriculture. The simplest method of irrigation was to dip water from a well or spring and pour it on the land. Many types of buckets, ropes, and, later, pulleys were employed. The ancient shaduf, which consists of a long pole pivoted from a beam that has a weight at one end to lift a full bucket of water at the other, is still in use. Conduction of water through ditches from streams was practiced widely in the Middle East, in Africa, and in America, where ancient canal systems can be seen. A conduit the Romans built 2,000 years ago to provide a water supply to Tunis is still in use.

Sufficient water at the proper time makes possible the full use of technology in farming—including the proper application of fertilizers, suitable crop rotations, and the use of more productive varieties of crops. Expanding irrigation is an absolute necessity to extend crop acreage in significant amounts; it may be the most productive of possible improvements on present cropland. First, there is the possibility of making wider use of irrigation in districts that already have a high rate of output. Second, there is the possibility of irrigating nonproductive land, especially in arid zones. The greatest immediate economic returns might well come from irrigating productive districts, but irrigation of arid zones has a larger long-range appeal. Most of the arid zones, occupying more than one-third of the landmass of the globe, are in the tropics. Generally, they are rich in solar energy, and their soils are rich in nutrients, but they lack water.

Supplemental irrigation in the United States, used primarily to make up for poor distribution of rainfall during the growing season, has increased substantially since the late 1930s. This irrigation is carried on in the humid areas of the United States almost exclusively with sprinkler systems. The water is conveyed in pipes, usually laid on the surface of the field, and the soil acts as a storage reservoir. The water itself is pumped from a stream, lake, well, or reservoir. American farmers first used sprinkler irrigation in about 1900, but the development of lightweight aluminum pipe with quick couplers meant that the pipe could be moved easily and quickly from one location to another, resulting in a notable increase in the use of sprinklers after World War II.

Irrigation problems

India, where irrigation has been practiced since ancient times, illustrates some of the problems. During the late 20th century, more than 20 percent of the country's cultivated area was under irrigation. Both large dams, with canals to distribute the water, and small tube, or driven, wells, made by driving a pipe into water or water-bearing sand, controlled by individual farmers, have been used. Some have been affected by salinity, however, as water containing dissolved salts has been allowed to evaporate in the field. Tube wells have helped in these instances by lowering the water table and by providing sufficient water to flush away the salts. The other major problem has been to persuade Indian farmers to level their lands and build the small canals needed to carry the water over the farms. In Egypt, impounding of the Nile River with the Aswān High Dam has been a great boon to agriculture, but it has also reduced the flow of silt into the Nile Valley and adversely affected fishing in the Mediterranean Sea. In arid areas such as the U.S. Southwest, tapping subterranean water supplies has resulted in a lowered water table and, in some instances, land subsidence.

Dry farming. The problem of educating farmers to make effective use of irrigation water is found in many areas. An even greater educational effort is required for dry farming; that is, crop production without irrigation where annual precipitation is less than 20 inches.

Dry farming as a system of agriculture was developed in the Great Plains of the United States early in the 20th century. It depended on the efficient storage of the limited moisture in the soil and the selection of crops and growing methods that made best use of this moisture. The system included deep fall plowing, subsurface packing of the soil, thorough cultivation both before and after seeding, light seeding, and alternating-summer fallow, with the land tilled during the season of fallow as well as in crop years. In certain latitudes stubble was left in the fields after harvest to trap snow. Though none of the steps were novel, their systematic combination was new. Systematic dry farming has continued, with substantial modifications, in the Great Plains of Canada and the United States, in Brazil, in South Africa, in Australia, and elsewhere. It is under continuing research by the Food and Agriculture Organization of the United Nations.

The direction of change. While no truly new crop has been developed by modern man, new uses and new methods of cultivation of known plants may be regarded as new crops. For example, subsistence and special-use plants, such as the members of the genus *Atriplex* that are salt-tolerant, have the potential for being developed into new crops. New techniques, too, are the elaboration and systematization of practices from the past.

NEW STRAINS: GENETICS

The use of genetics to develop new strains of plants and animals has brought major changes in agriculture since the 1920s. Genetics as the science dealing with the principles of heredity and variation in plants and animals was established only at the beginning of the 20th century. Its application to practical problems came later.

Early work in genetics. The modern science of genetics and its application to agriculture has a complicated background, built up from the work of many individuals. Nevertheless, Gregor Mendel is generally credited with its founding. Mendel, a monk in Brünn, Moravia (now Brno, Czech.), purposefully crossed garden peas in his monastery garden. He carefully sorted the progeny of his parent plants according to their characteristics and counted the number that had inherited each quality. He discovered that when the qualities he was studying, including flower colour and shape of seeds, were handed on by the parent plants, they were distributed among the offspring in definite mathematical ratios, from which there was never a significant variation. Definite laws of inheritance were thus established for the first time. Though Mendel reported his discoveries in an obscure Austrian journal in 1866, his work was not followed up for a third of a century. Then in 1900, investigators in The Netherlands, Germany, and Austria, all working on inheritance, independently rediscovered Mendel's paper.

Mendel's experiments

By the time Mendel's work was again brought to light, the science of genetics was in its first stages of development. The word genetics comes from "genes," the name given to the minute quantities of living matter that transmit characteristics from parent to offspring. By 1903, scientists in the United States and Germany had concluded that genes are carried in the chromosomes, nuclear structures visible under the microscope. In 1911 a theory that the genes are arranged in a linear file on the chromosomes and that changes in this conformation are reflected in changes in heredity was announced.

Genes are highly stable. During the processes of sexual reproduction, however, means are present for assortment, segregation, and recombination of genetic factors. Thus, tremendous genetic variability is provided within a species. This variability makes possible the changes that man can bring about within a species to adapt it to his specific uses. Occasional mutations (spontaneous changes) of genes also contribute to variability.

Development of new strains of plants and animals did not, of course, await the science of genetics, and some advances were made by empirical methods even after the application of genetic science to agriculture. The U.S. experimenter Luther Burbank, without any formal knowledge of genetic principles, developed the Burbank potato as early as 1873 and continued his plant-breeding research, which produced numerous new varieties of fruits and vegetables. In some instances, both practical experience and scientific knowledge contributed to major technological achievements. An example is the development of hybrid corn (maize).

Corn. Corn originated in America, probably having been first developed by Indians in the highlands of Mexico. It was quickly adopted by the European settlers, Spanish, English, and French. The first English settlers found the northern Indians growing a hard-kerneled, early-maturing flint variety that kept well, though its yield was low. The Indians in the south central area of English settlement grew a soft-kerneled, high-yielding, late-maturing dent corn. There were doubtless many haphazard crosses of the two varieties. In 1812, however, John Lorain, a farmer living near Philipsburg, Pa., consciously mixed the two and demonstrated that certain mixtures would result in a yield much greater than that of the flint, yet with many of the flint's desirable qualities. Other farmers and breeders followed Lorain's example, some aware of his pioneer work, some not. The most widely grown variety of the Corn Belt for many years was Reid's Yellow Dent, which originated from a fortuitous mixture of a dent and a flint variety.

Origins of corn

At the same time, other scientists besides Mendel were conducting experiments and developing theories that were to lead directly to hybrid corn. In 1876 Charles Darwin published the results of experiments on cross- and self-fertilization in plants. Carrying out his work in a small greenhouse in his native England, the man who is best known for his theory of evolution found that inbreeding usually reduced plant vigour and that crossbreeding restored it.

Darwin's work was studied by a young American botanist, William James Beal, who probably made the first controlled crosses between varieties of corn for the sole purpose of increasing yields through hybrid vigour. Beal worked successfully without knowledge of the genetic principle involved. In 1908 George Harrison Shull concluded that self-fertilization tended to separate and purify strains while weakening the plants but that vigour could be restored by crossbreeding the inbred strains. Another scientist found that inbreeding could increase the protein content of corn, but with a marked decline in yield. With knowledge of inbreeding and hybridization at hand, there was yet to be developed a technique whereby hybrid corn with the desired characteristics of the inbred lines and hybrid vigour could be combined in a practical manner. In 1917 Donald F. Jones of the Connecticut Agricultural Experiment Station discovered the answer, the "double cross."

The double cross

The double cross was the basic technique used in developing modern hybrid corn and has been used by commercial firms since. Jones's invention was to use four inbred lines instead of two in crossing. Simply, inbred lines A and B made one cross, lines C and D another. Then AB and CD were crossed, and a double-cross hybrid, ABCD, was the result. This hybrid became the seed that changed much of

American agriculture. Each inbred line was constant both for certain desirable and for certain undesirable traits, but the practical breeder could balance his four or more inbred lines in such a way that the desirable traits outweighed the undesirable. Foundation inbred lines were developed to meet the needs of varying climates, growing seasons, soils, and other factors. The large hybrid seed-corn companies undertook complex applied-research programs, while state experiment stations and the U.S. Department of Agriculture tended to concentrate on basic research.

The first hybrid corn involving inbred lines to be produced commercially was sold by the Connecticut Agricultural Experiment Station in 1921. The second was developed by Henry A. Wallace, a future secretary of agriculture and vice president of the United States. He sold a small quantity in 1924 and, in 1926, organized the first seed company devoted to the commercial production of hybrid corn.

Many Midwestern farmers began growing hybrid corn in the late 1920s and 1930s, but it did not dominate corn production until World War II. In 1933, 1 percent of the total corn acreage was planted with hybrid seed. By 1939 the figure was 15 percent, and in 1946 it rose to 69. The percentage was 96 in 1960. The average per acre yield of corn rose from 23 bushels (2,000 litres per hectare) in 1933, to 83 bushels (7,220 litres per hectare) by 1980.

The techniques used in breeding hybrid corn have been successfully applied to grain sorghum and several other crops. New strains of most major crops are developed through plant introductions, crossbreeding, and selection, however, because hybridization in the sense used with corn and grain sorghums has not been successful.

Wheat. Advances in wheat production during the 20th century include improvements through the introduction of new varieties and strains; careful selection by farmers and seedsmen, as well as by scientists; and crossbreeding to combine desirable characteristics (see Figure 1 for a comparison between wild and cultivated wheat). The adaptability of wheat enables it to be grown in almost every country of the world. In most of the developed nations producing wheat, endeavours of both government and wheat growers have been directed toward scientific wheat breeding.

Canadian Marquis wheat

The development of the world-famous Marquis wheat in Canada, released to farmers in 1900, came about through sustained scientific effort. Sir Charles Saunders, its discoverer, followed five principles of plant breeding: (1) the use of plant introductions; (2) a planned crossbreeding program; (3) the rigid selection of material; (4) evaluation of all characteristics in replicated trials; and (5) testing varieties for local use. Marquis was the result of crossing a wheat long grown in Canada with a variety introduced from India. For 50 years, Marquis and varieties crossbred from Marquis dominated hard red spring wheat growing in the high plains of Canada and the United States and were used in other parts of the world.

In the late 1940s a short-stemmed wheat was introduced from Japan into a more favourable wheat-growing region of the U.S. Pacific Northwest. The potential advantage of the short, heavy-stemmed plant was that it could carry a heavy head of grain, generated by the use of fertilizer, without falling over or "lodging" (being knocked down). Early work with the variety was unsuccessful; it was not adaptable directly into American fields. Finally, by crossing the Japanese wheat with acceptable varieties in the Palouse Valley in Washington, there resulted the first true semidwarf wheat in the United States to be commercially grown under irrigation and heavy applications of fertilizer. This first variety, Gaines, was introduced in 1962, followed by Nugaines in 1966. The varieties now grown in the United States commonly produce 100 bushels per acre (8,700 litres per hectare), and world records of more than 200 bushels per acre have been established.

The Rockefeller Foundation in 1943 entered into a cooperative agricultural research program with the government of Mexico, where wheat yields were well below the world average. By 1956 per acre yield had doubled, mainly because of newly developed varieties sown in the fall instead of spring and the use of fertilizers and irrigation. The short-stemmed varieties developed in the Pacific Northwest from the Japanese strains were then crossed with various Mexican and Colombian wheats. By 1965 the new Mexican wheats were established and were gaining an international reputation.

Improving Mexican wheat

Rice. The success of the wheat program led the Rockefeller and Ford foundations in 1962 to establish the International Rice Research Institute at Los Baños in the Philippines. A research team assembled some 10,000 strains of rice from all parts of the world and began outbreeding. Success came early with the combination of a tall, vigorous variety from Indonesia and a dwarf rice from Taiwan. The strain IR-8 has proved capable of doubling the yield obtained from most local rices in Asia.

The Green Revolution. The introduction into developing countries of new strains of wheat and rice was a major aspect of what became known as the Green Revolution. Given adequate water and ample amounts of the required chemical fertilizers and pesticides, these varieties have resulted in significantly higher yields. Poorer farmers, however, often have not been able to provide the required growing conditions and therefore have obtained even lower yields with "improved" grains than they had gotten with the older strains that were better adapted to local conditions and that had some resistance to pests and diseases. Where chemicals are used, concern has been voiced about their cost—since they generally must be imported—and about their potentially harmful effects on the environment.

Genetic engineering. The application of genetics to agriculture since World War II has resulted in substantial increases in the production of many crops. This has been most notable in hybrid strains of corn and grain sorghum. At the same time, crossbreeding has resulted in much more productive strains of wheat and rice. Called artificial selection, or selective breeding, these techniques have become aspects of a larger field called genetic engineering. Of particular interest to plant breeders has been the development of techniques for deliberately altering the functions of genes by manipulating the recombination of DNA. This has made it possible for researchers to concentrate on creating plants that possess attributes—such as the ability to use free nitrogen or to resist diseases—that they did not have naturally.

ANIMAL BREEDING

The goal of animal breeders in the 20th century has been to develop types of animals that will meet market demands, be productive under adverse climatic conditions, and be efficient in converting feed to animal products. At the same time, producers have increased meat production by improved range management, better feeding practices, and the eradication of diseases and harmful insects. The world production of meat has been increasing steadily since World War II.

While the number of livestock in relation to the human population is not significantly lower in less developed than in more developed regions, there is much lower productivity per animal and thus a much lower percentage of livestock products in diets. Less scientific breeding practices usually prevail in the less developed regions, while great care is given to animal breeding in the more developed regions of North America, Europe, Australia, and New Zealand.

The advances made in developing new, highly productive strains of crops through the application of genetics have not been matched by similar advances in livestock. Except for broiler chickens in the United States, little progress has been made in improving the efficiency with which animals convert feed to animal products. Research on the breeding and nutrition of poultry, for example, makes it possible to produce chickens for market in about 30 percent less time than it took before the research findings were applied.

Hogs. Advances in animal breeding have been made by careful selection and crossbreeding. These techniques are not new. The major breeds of English cattle, for example, were developed in the 18th and early 19th centuries by selection and crossbreeding. The Poland China and Duroc Jersey breeds of swine were developed in the United States in the latter part of the 19th century by the same means.

The hogs developed in the United States in the latter part of the 19th and first part of the 20th century were heavy, fat-producing animals that met the demands for lard. During the 1920s lard became less important as a source of fat because of increasing use of cheaper vegetable oils. Meat-packers then sought hogs yielding more lean meat and less fat, even though market prices moved rather slowly toward making their production profitable.

Breeding leaner hogs

At the same time, Danish, Polish, and other European breeders were crossbreeding swine to obtain lean meat and vigorous animals. An outstanding new breed was the Danish Landrace, which in the 1930s was crossed with several older American breeds, eventually giving rise to several new, mildly inbred lines. These lines produced more lean meat and less fat, as well as larger litters and bigger pigs.

Sheep. Similar crossbreeding, followed by intermating and selection with the crossbreeds, brought major changes in the sheep industries of New Zealand and the United States. The goal in New Zealand was to produce more acceptable meat animals, while that in the United States was to produce animals suited to Western range conditions and acceptable both for wool and mutton.

During the late 19th century, several New Zealand sheep breeders began crossing Lincoln and Leicester rams with Merino ewes. Early in the 20th century, the Corriedale had become established as a breed, carrying approximately 50 percent Australian Merino, with Leicester and Lincoln blood making up the remainder. The Corriedale was successfully introduced into the United States in 1914. Since World War II, a more uniform lamb carcass has been developed in New Zealand by crossing Southdown rams with Romney ewes.

With different objectives in view, breeders in the United States in 1912 made initial crosses between the long-wool mutton breed, the Lincoln, and fine-wool Rambouillets. Subsequent intermating and selection within the crossbreds led to a new breed, the Columbia. Both the Columbia and the Targhee, another breed developed in the same way as the Columbia, have been widely used. They are suited to the Western ranges, and they serve reasonably well both as wool and meat animals.

Beef cattle. Changes in beef cattle, particularly the establishment of new breeds, have resulted from selective linebreeding and from crossbreeding. The Polled Shorthorn and the Polled Hereford breeds were established by locating and breeding the few naturally hornless animals to be found among the horned herds of Shorthorns and Herefords, first established as distinctive breeds in England. It is of particular note that the originator of the Polled Herefords made an effort to locate naturally hornless Herefords and begin linebreeding with them after he had studied Darwin's work on mutations and variations and how they could be made permanent by systematic mating.

New breeds of beef cattle

Three new breeds originating in the United States were developed for parts of the South where the standard breeds lacked resistance to heat and insects and did not thrive on the native grasses. The first of these breeds, the Santa Gertrudis, was developed on the King Ranch in Texas by crossbreeding Shorthorns and Brahmans, a heat- and insect-resistant breed from India. The Santa Gertrudis cattle carry approximately five-eighths Shorthorn blood and three-eighths Brahman. They are heavy beef cattle and thrive in hot climates and have been exported to South and Central America in order to upgrade the native cattle.

The Brangus breed was developed in the 1930s and 1940s by crossing Brahman and Angus cattle. The breed has been standardized with three-eighths Brahman and five-eighths Angus breeding. The Brangus generally have the hardiness of the Brahman for Southern conditions but the improved carcass qualities of the Angus.

The Beefmaster was developed in Texas and Colorado by crossbreeding and careful selection, with the cattle carrying about one-half Brahman blood and about one-fourth each of Hereford and Shorthorn breeding. Emphasis was given to careful selection, major points being disposition, fertility, weight, conformation, hardiness, and milk production.

Artificial breeding. An increase in milk production per cow in the 20th century has come through better nutrition and artificial breeding. Artificial breeding permits the use of proved sires, developed through successive crosses of animals of proved merit. An Italian scientist experimented successfully with artificial insemination in 1780, but its practical usefulness was not demonstrated until the 20th century. The Soviet biologist Ilya Ivanov established the Central Experimental Breeding Station in Moscow in 1919 to continue work that he had begun some 20 years earlier. As early as 1936, more than 6,000,000 cattle and sheep were artificially inseminated in the Soviet Union.

After the Soviets reported their successes, scientists in many nations experimented with artificial breeding. Denmark began with dairy cattle in the 1930s. The first group in the United States began work in 1938. Statistics show that the milk and butterfat production of proved sires' daughters, resulting from artificial breeding, is higher than that of other improved dairy cattle. Furthermore, a single sire can be used to inseminate 2,000 cows a year, as compared with 30 to 50 in natural breeding.

In summary, crossbreeding and careful selection, combined with such techniques as artificial insemination, better feeding, and control of diseases and pests, have made substantial contributions to livestock production in the 20th century. More intensified research, particularly in hybridization, offers promise of help to livestock producers in meeting increasing world demands for their products.
(W.D.R./K.Me.)

ELECTRICITY IN AGRICULTURE

Electric power has had an impact on modern agriculture that has been at least as significant as that of either steam or gasoline, because electricity in its nature is far more versatile than the earlier power sources. Although there had long been scientific interest on the effects electricity had on plant growth, especially after the development of electric lamps, it was the development of the electric motor that really gained the interest of the farming community. Some authorities saw its value to farmers as early as 1870.

Electrical cooperatives. Despite the obvious advantages of the other, more available power sources, progressive farmers in a number of countries were determined to exploit the possibilities of electricity on their farms. To get electricity, farmers formed cooperatives that either bought bulk power from existing facilities or built their own generating stations.

It is believed that the first such cooperatives were formed in Japan in 1900, followed by similar organizations in Germany in 1901. Multiplying at a considerable rate, these farmer cooperatives not only initiated rural electrification as such but provided the basis for its future development.

Rural electrification

From these small beginnings the progress of rural electrification, though necessarily slow, steadily gained impetus until, in the 1920s, public opinion eventually compelled governments to consider the development of rural electrification on a national basis. Today in the most advanced countries virtually all rural premises—domestic, commercial, industrial, and farms—have an adequate supply of electricity.

Early applications of electricity were of necessity restricted to power and some lighting, although the full value of lighting was not completely realized for years. Electric motors were used to drive barn machinery, chaff-cutters and root cutters, cattle cake and grain crushers, and water pumps. Electricity's ease of operation and low maintenance showed savings in time and labour. It was not long before the electric motor began to replace the mobile steam engine on threshing, winnowing, and other crop-processing equipment outside the barn.

In the fields, a number of electrically driven, rope-haulage plowing installations, some of them quite large, came into use in several European countries. These systems, however, did not stand the test of time or competition from the mobile internal-combustion-driven tractor.

Applications of electricity in agriculture did not increase greatly until the 1920s, when economic pressures and the increasing drift of labour from the land brought about a change in the whole structure of agriculture. This change, based on new techniques of intensive crop production resulting from the development of a wide range of mechanical, electrical, and electromechanical equipment, was the start of the evolution of agriculture from a labour-intensive industry to the present capital-intensive industry, and in this electricity played a major part.

Modern applications. Modern applications of electricity in farming range from the comparatively simple to some as complex as those in the manufacturing industries. They include conditioning and storage of grain and grass; preparation and rationing of animal feed; and provision of a controlled environment in stock-rearing houses for intensive pig and poultry rearing and in greenhouses for horticultural crops. Electricity plays an equally important part in the dairy farm for feed rationing, milking, and milk cooling; all these applications are automatically controlled. Computers have increasingly been employed to aid in farm management and to directly control automated equipment.

The engineer and farmer have combined to develop electrically powered equipment for crop conservation and storage to help overcome weather hazards at harvesttime and to reduce labour requirements to a minimum. Grain can now be harvested in a matter of days instead of months and dried to required moisture content for prolonged storage by means of electrically driven fans and, in many installations, gas or electrical heaters. Wilted grass, cut at the stage of maximum feeding value, can be turned into high-quality hay in the barn by means of forced ventilation and with very little risk of spoilage loss from inclement weather.

Controlling storage temperatures

Conditioning and storage of such root crops as potatoes, onions, carrots, and beets, in especially designed stores with forced ventilation and temperature control, and of fruit in refrigerated stores are all electrically based techniques that minimize waste and maintain top quality over longer periods than was possible with traditional methods of storage.

The two most significant changes in the pattern of agricultural development since the end of World War II have been the degree to which specialization has been adopted and the increased scale of farm enterprises. Large numbers of beef cattle are raised in enclosures and fed carefully balanced rations by automatic equipment. Pigs by the thousands and poultry by the tens of thousands are housed in special buildings with controlled environments and are fed automatically with complex rations. Dairy herds of up to 1,000 cows are machine-milked in milking parlours, and the cows are then individually identified and fed appropriate rations by complex electronic equipment. The milk passes directly from the cow into refrigerated bulk milk tanks and is ready for immediate shipment.

(A.W.Gr./K.Me.)

PEST AND DISEASE CONTROL IN CROPS

Beginnings of pest control. Wherever agriculture has been practiced, pests have attacked, destroying part or even all of the crop. In modern usage, the term pest includes animals (mostly insects), fungi, plants, bacteria, and viruses. Man's efforts to control pests have a long history. Even in Neolithic times (about 7000 BC), farmers practiced a crude form of biological pest control involving the more or less unconscious selection of seed from resistant plants. Severe locust attacks in the Nile Valley during the 13th century BC are dramatically described in the Bible, and, in his *Natural History,* the Roman author Pliny the Elder describes picking insects by hand from plants and spraying. The scientific study of pests was not undertaken until the 17th and 18th centuries. The first successful large-scale conquest of a pest by chemical means was the control of the vine powdery mildew (*Unciluna necator*) in Europe in the 1840s. The disease, brought from the New World, was controlled first by spraying with lime sulfur and, subsequently, by sulfur dusting.

First successful chemical pest control

Another serious epidemic was the potato blight that caused famine in Ireland in 1845 and some subsequent years and severe losses in many other parts of Europe and the United States. Insects and fungi from Europe became serious pests in the United States, too. Among these were the European corn borer, the gypsy moth, and the chestnut blight, which practically annihilated that tree.

The first book to deal with pests in a scientific way was John Curtis' *Farm Insects,* published in 1860. Though farmers were well aware that insects caused losses, Curtis was the first writer to call attention to their significant economic impact. The successful battle for control of the Colorado potato beetle (*Leptinotarsa decemlineata*) of the western United States also occurred in the 19th century. When miners and pioneers brought the potato into the Colorado region, the beetle fell upon this crop and became a severe pest, spreading steadily eastward and devastating crops, until it reached the Atlantic. It crossed the ocean and eventually established itself in Europe. But an American entomologist in 1877 found a practical control method consisting of spraying with water-insoluble chemicals such as London Purple, paris green, and calcium and lead arsenates.

Other pesticides that were developed soon thereafter included nicotine, pyrethrum, derris, quassia, and tar oils, first used, albeit unsuccessfully, in 1870 against the winter eggs of the *Phylloxera* plant louse. The Bordeaux mixture fungicide (copper sulfate and lime), discovered accidentally in 1882, was used successfully against vine downy mildew; this compound is still employed to combat it and potato blight. Since many insecticides available in the 19th century were comparatively weak, other pest-control methods were used as well. A species of ladybird beetle, *Rodolia cardinalis,* was imported from Australia to California, where it controlled the cottony-cushion scale then threatening to destroy the citrus industry. A moth introduced into Australia destroyed the prickly pear, which had made millions of acres of pasture useless for grazing. In the 1880s the European grapevine was saved from destruction by grape phylloxera through the simple expedient of grafting it onto certain resistant American rootstocks.

This period of the late 19th and early 20th centuries was thus characterized by increasing awareness of the possibilities of avoiding losses from pests, by the rise of firms specializing in pesticide manufacture, and by development of better application machinery.

Pesticides as a panacea: 1942–62. In 1942 Paul Hermann Müller of Switzerland discovered the insecticidal properties of a synthetic chlorinated organic chemical, dichlorodiphenyltrichloroethane, which was first synthesized in 1874 and subsequently became known as DDT. Müller received the Nobel Prize for Physiology or Medicine in 1948 for his discovery. DDT was far more persistent and effective than any previously known insecticide. Originally a mothproofing agent for clothes, it soon found use among the armies of World War II for killing body lice and fleas. It stopped a typhus epidemic threatening Naples. Müller's work led to discovery of other chlorinated insecticides, including aldrin, introduced in 1948; chlordane (1945); dieldrin (1948); endrin (1951); heptachlor (1948); methoxychlor (1945); and Toxaphene (1948).

Origin of DDT

Research on poison gas in Germany during World War II led to the discovery of another group of yet more powerful insecticides and acaricides (killers of ticks and mites)—the organophosphorus compounds, some of which had systemic properties; that is, the plant absorbed them without harm and became itself toxic to insects. The first systemic was octamethylpyrophosphoramide, trade named Schradan. Other organophosphorus insecticides of enormous power were also made, the most common being diethyl-*p*-nitrophenyl monothiophosphate, named parathion. Though low in cost, these compounds were toxic to humans and other warm-blooded animals. The products could poison by absorption through the skin, as well as through the mouth or lungs, thus, spray operators must wear respirators and special clothing. Systemic insecticides need not be carefully sprayed, however; the compound may be absorbed by watering the plant.

Though the advances made in the fungicide field in the first half of the 20th century were not as spectacular as those made with insecticides and herbicides, certain dithiocarbamates, methylthiuram disulfides, and thaladimides were found to have special uses. It began to seem that almost any pest, disease, or weed problem could be mas-

Figure 9: Low-volume spraying of pesticide on a field of corn.
Grant Heilman

tered by suitable chemical treatment. Farmers foresaw a pest-free millennium. Crop losses were cut sharply; locust attack was reduced to a manageable problem; and the new chemicals, by killing carriers of human disease, saved the lives of millions of people.

Problems appeared in the early 1950s. In cotton crops standard doses of DDT, parathion, and similar pesticides were found ineffective and had to be doubled or trebled. Resistant races of insects had developed. In addition, the powerful insecticides often destroyed natural predators and helpful parasites along with harmful insects. Insects and mites can reproduce at such a rapid rate that often when natural predators were destroyed by a pesticide treatment, a few pest survivors from the treatment, unchecked in breeding, soon produced worse outbreaks of pests than there had been before the treatment; sometimes the result was a population explosion to pest status of previously harmless insects.

At about the same time, concern also began to be expressed about the presence of pesticide residues in food, humans, and wildlife. It was found that many birds and wild mammals retained considerable quantities of DDT in their bodies, accumulated along their natural food chains. The disquiet caused by this discovery was epitomized in 1962 by the publication in the United States of a book entitled *Silent Spring,* whose author, Rachel Carson, attacked the indiscriminate use of pesticides, drew attention to various abuses, and stimulated a reappraisal of pest control. Thus began a new "integrated" approach, which was in effect a return to the use of all methods of control in place of a reliance on chemicals alone.

Integrated control. Some research into biological methods was undertaken by governments, and in many countries plant breeders began to develop and patent new pest-resistant plant varieties.

Biological pest control

One method of biological control involved the breeding and release of males sterilized by means of gamma rays. Though sexually potent, such insects have inactive sperm. Released among the wild population, they mate with the females, who either lay sterile eggs or none at all. The method was used with considerable success against the screwworm, a pest of cattle, in Texas. A second method of biological control employed lethal genes. It is sometimes possible to introduce a lethal or weakening gene into a pest population, leading to the breeding of intersex (effectively neuter) moths or a predominance of males. Various studies have also been made on the chemical identification of substances attracting pests to the opposite sex or to food. With such substances traps can be devised that attract only a specific pest species. Finally, certain chemicals have been fed to insects to sterilize them. Used in connection with a food lure, these can lead to the elimination of a pest from an area. Chemicals tested so far, however, have been considered too dangerous to humans and other mammals for any general use.

Some countries (notably the United States, Sweden, and the United Kingdom) have partly or wholly banned the use of DDT because of its persistence and accumulation in human body fat and its effect on wildlife. New pesticides of lesser human toxicity have been found, one of the most used being mercaptosuccinate, trade named Malathion. A more recent important discovery was the systemic fungicide, absorbed by the plant and transmitted throughout it, making it resistant to certain diseases.

The majority of pesticides are sprayed on crops as solutions or suspensions in water. Spraying machinery has developed from the small hand syringes and "garden engines" of the 18th century to the very powerful "autoblast machines" of the 1950s that were capable of applying up to some 400 gallons per acre (4,000 litres per hectare). Though spraying suspended or dissolved pesticide was effective, it involved moving a great quantity of inert material for only a relatively small amount of active ingredient. Low-volume spraying was invented about 1950, particularly for the application of herbicides, in which 10 or 20 gallons of water, transformed into fine drops, would carry the pesticide. Ultralow-volume spraying has also been introduced; four ounces (about 110 grams) of the active ingredient itself (usually Malathion) are applied to an acre from aircraft. The spray as applied is invisible to the naked eye. (G.O.)

ECONOMICS, POLITICS, AND AGRICULTURE

As the 20th century opened, western Europe was recovering from an economic depression during which most of the nations had turned to protecting agriculture through tariffs. The major exceptions were Great Britain, Denmark, and The Netherlands. In the first decade of the century there was an increasing demand for agricultural products, a result of industrialization and population growth, while agriculture in the United States, France, Germany, and many other nations reached a state of equilibrium in relation to the rest of the economy.

During World War I farmers benefited from high prices, which persisted for a short period after the war because of a shortage of food supplies. European agriculture recovered from wartime losses in land fertility, livestock, and capital and by the early 1920s was fully productive. Elsewhere, production had expanded greatly during the war and afterward continued to rise. After the war prices declined, and, as farmers sought to compensate by expanding their output, the fall in prices was aggravated.

Agricultural tariffs, generally suspended during the war, were gradually reintroduced. The Great Depression of the 1930s brought a new wave of protectionism, leading some industrial nations to look toward self-sufficiency in food supplies. In countries such as France, Germany, and Italy, where agriculture was already protected, the tariff structure was reinforced by new and more drastic measures, while countries such as Britain, Denmark, The Netherlands, and Belgium abandoned free trade and began to support their farmers in a variety of ways. The United States first raised tariffs and then undertook to maintain the prices of farm products. Major exporters of farm products, such as Argentina, Brazil, Australia, Canada, and New Zealand, tried a number of plans to maintain prices.

The milling ratio

One of the most effective of the nontariff measures was the "milling ratio" for wheat or, less often, rye, under which millers were legally obliged to use a certain minimum percentage of domestically produced grain in their grist. This device was first used in Norway in 1927. In 1929 both France and Germany adopted it, and, from 1930 on, it became customary in Europe and in some non-European nations as well. Milling ratios continued in many nations up to World War II and have been reintroduced in several since that time.

Import quotas, although used earlier in a limited way, became a major protective device during the 1930s. Starting with France, by 1939 they had been adopted on a large scale, mainly for agricultural products, by most European and several non-European nations.

The most radical measures were undertaken in Germany under Hitler, where the Nazi government, seeking self-sufficiency in food, fixed farm prices at relatively high levels and maintained complete control over imports.

In the fall of 1931, Great Britain abandoned the free-trade policies followed for nearly a century and turned to protectionism. The new policies emphasized industrial rather than agricultural products. A commodity-by-commodity approach for agriculture through subsidies, marketing schemes, and import restrictions provided help for some farmers. Competition from the Dominions, however, was strong.

In 1932 Great Britain negotiated the Ottawa Agreements with the Dominions, which included comparatively free access of Dominion agricultural products to the British market. The agreement helped considerably to alleviate the difficulties the Dominions faced during the Depression. In addition, export subsidies were adopted by several of the Dominions: for wheat by Canada and Australia; for dairy products by New Zealand; and for several products by South Africa.

In the United States the Agricultural Marketing Act of 1929 established the Federal Farm Board to promote orderly marketing through cooperatives. The Tariff Act of 1930 imposed virtually exclusive tariffs on many products, including those of the farm. These acts, comparatively ineffective in meeting the pressures of the Great Depression, were followed by the Agricultural Adjustment Act of 1933 and subsequent legislation that included restoring the balance between production and consumption, restoration of farm purchasing power, and the attainment of parity, the ratio between prices farmers paid and those they received during the period 1910–14.

Some of the exporting nations adopted extreme measures during the Depression in an attempt to maintain prices for their commodities. Brazil burned surplus coffee stocks, destroying more than 8,000,000,000 pounds of coffee over 10 years beginning in 1931. An Inter-American Coffee Agreement, signed in 1940, assigned export quotas to producer nations for shipment to the United States and other consuming nations and was effective during World War II. Other commodity agreements have met with very limited success.

During World War II, agricultural production declined in most of the European countries, shipping became difficult, and trade channels shifted.

In contrast, agriculture in the United States, undisturbed by military action and with assurance of full demand and relatively high prices, increased productivity. The United States, Great Britain, and Canada cooperated in a combined food board to allocate available supplies. The United Nations Relief and Rehabilitation Administration (UNRRA) was organized in 1943 to administer postwar relief, while the Food and Agriculture Organization (FAO) of the United Nations was established in 1945 to provide education and technical assistance for agricultural development throughout the world.

United Nations activity

By the end of World War II, food production in most of the countries of Europe had fallen below the prewar level. Through assistance given primarily by the United States and the United Nations, recovery was rapid. Western Europe was greatly helped from 1948 on by U.S. aid under the Marshall Plan, administered through the Organisation for European Economic Co-operation (OEEC). In September 1961, this organization was replaced by the Organisation for Economic Co-operation and Development (OECD), with Canada and the United States, and later other non-European developed nations, as full members. Its agricultural programs have dealt, for example, with economic policies, standardization, manpower, and development.

From the 1950s on, agricultural production increased markedly in western Europe, in the United States, and in most of the nations that ordinarily export large quantities of agricultural products. The Soviet Union, which in the 1930s had organized agricultural production into state-run collective farms, has increased its output substantially, in part by opening new lands. It has been hampered, however, by periodic crop failures that have made it necessary to import large quantities of grain. Agricultural production in China, though adversely affected by the social and economic upheavals caused by the policies of the Great Leap Forward (1958–60) and the chaotic atmosphere of the Cultural Revolution (1966–76), has steadily improved, especially since the Cultural Revolution.

Most of the Western nations offer some type of protection to their farmers—price supports, import quotas, and plans for handling surplus production. Notable examples are the agricultural programs run by the U.S. Department of Agriculture and by the European Communities. On the other hand, many of the developing nations have had food deficits, with little in the way of exportable goods to pay for food imports. Several national and international organizations have been established in an effort to deal with the problems of the developing nations, and direct assistance has also been provided by the governments of developed countries.

Individual farmers in the nations where commercial agriculture is important have been forced to make changes to meet the problems of world surpluses and low world prices for farm products. Thus, in many nations, farmers have increased productivity through adopting advanced technology. This has permitted each worker, generally speaking, to farm larger areas and has thus reduced the number of farmers. In some nations, commercialization has led to farming by large-scale corporations. Thus, the world tendency is toward larger farms. The farm operated by a single family, however, is still the dominant unit of production in most of the world. (W.D.R./K.Me.)

BIBLIOGRAPHY

Origins of agriculture and early agriculture societies: SIR JOSEPH HUTCHINSON (ed.), *Essays on Crop Plant Evolution* (1965); and PETER J. UCKO and G.W. DIMBLEBY (eds.), *The Domestication and Exploitation of Plants and Animals* (1969), are collections of papers on the origins of agriculture; E.S. HIGGS (ed.), *Papers in Economic Prehistory* (1972), and *Palaeoeconomy* (1975), contain a reconsideration of theories on the origins of agriculture and some results of modern research; DAVID RINDOS, *The Origins of Agriculture: An Evolutionary Perspective* (1984), concentrates on the history of man's effort to domesticate plants; J. DESMOND CLARK and STEVEN A. BRANDT (eds.), *From Hunters to Farmers: The Causes and Consequences of Food Production in Africa* (1984), analyzes economic changes in prehistoric society; GRAEME BARKER, *Prehistoric Farming in Europe* (1985), gives an account of the evolution of farming after the Ice Age.

Agriculture in ancient Asia: HIUEN TSIANG, *Si-yu-ki: Buddhist Records of the Western World*, 2 vol., trans. by SAMUEL BEAL (1884, reprinted 1981), offers travel accounts of early Chinese

Buddhist pilgrims to India in the 1st millennium, including those of Shih Fa-hian, Sung Yün, and Hiuen Tsiang; MABEL PING-HUA LEE, *The Economic History of China* (1921, reprinted 1969), is a history of Chinese agriculture with emphasis on soil depletion; KWANG-CHIH CHANG, *The Archaeology of Ancient China,* 3rd rev. ed. (1977), is a modern text interpreting prehistoric and protohistoric archaeological evidence in the historical framework of cultural development until 221 BC (illustrated, with bibliography); PING-TI-HO, *Studies on the Population of China, 1368–1953* (1959, reprinted 1967), is a scholarly study of population growth and of interacting variables, such as migrations, land utilization and tenure, and food-production techniques, with extensive data tables, bibliography, and notes; N.I. VAVILOV, *The Origin, Variation, Immunity and Breeding of Cultivated Plants* (1951), presents selected writings of Vavilov, one of the world's outstanding contributors to the theory of genetics, plant breeding, and study of plant variation, systematics, and evolution (illustrated, with selected bibliography); V. GORDON CHILDE, *New Light on the Most Ancient East,* 4th ed. (1952, reprinted 1969), is an excellent introduction to the Indus Valley Civilization in comparison with the prehistories of Egypt and Mesopotamia—from the Nile to the Indus (illustrated, with bibliography); BRIDGET and RAYMOND ALLCHIN, *The Birth of Indian Civilization* (1968), is a useful general history from the Early Stone Age until 550 BC (maps, plates, list of radioactive carbon dates, and bibliography); see also J.W. MCCRINDLE, *McCrindle's Ancient India: As Described by Megasthenes and Arrian* (1877, reissued 1984); IFRAN HABIB, *The Agrarian System of Mughal India (1556–1707)* (1963), is an informative text that covers cultivation techniques, crops, land tenure, village communities, and revenue administration; and ANDREW M. WATSON, *Agricultural Innovation in the Early Islamic World* (1983), a systematic, informative overview.

Agriculture in the West from 200 BC to AD 1900: G.E. FUSSELL, *Farming Technique from Prehistoric to Modern Times* (1966), is a general review of the history of agricultural tools and techniques, with many illustrations and an extensive bibliography; DAVID GRIGG, *The Dynamics of Agricultural Change* (1982), is a survey of historical sources. JEAN PHILIPPE LÉVY, *The Economic Life of the Ancient World* (1967; originally published in French, 1964), describes the various economies of the Greco-Oriental world in the time before Alexander, during the Hellenistic Age, in the early Roman Empire, and also in the later Roman Empire; FRITZ M. HEICHELHEIM, *An Ancient Economic History,* rev. ed., 3 vol. (1958–70; originally published in German, 1938), contains extensive and detailed information on ancient agriculture; see also standard editions of such classical authors as Cato, Columella, Hesiod, Pliny, Varro, and Xenophon. GEORGES DUBY, *Rural Economy and Country Life in the Medieval West* (1968, reprinted 1976; originally published in French, 1962), is a classic work on agriculture from the 9th to 15th centuries; see also ROBERT LATOUCHE, *The Birth of Western Economy,* 2nd ed. (1967, reprinted 1981; originally published in French, 1956); LYNN WHITE, JR., *Medieval Technology and Social Change* (1962, reissued 1980); B.H. SLICHER VAN BATH, *The Agrarian History of Western Europe, A.D. 500–1850* (1963; originally published in Dutch, 1960); WILHELM ABEL, *Geschichte der deutschen Landwirtschaft vom frühen Mittelalter bis zum 19. Jahrhundert,* 3rd rev. ed. (1978); RAYMOND GROMAS, *Histoire agricole de la France* (1947); MARC BLOCH, *French Rural History* (1966; originally published in French, 1952–56); and PAUL LINDEMANS, *Geschiedenis van de Landbouw in België,* 2 vol. (1952). CHRISTABEL S. ORWIN and EDITH H. WHETHAM, *History of British Agriculture, 1846–1914,* 2nd ed. (1971), deals with agricultural policy, social change, and technical and scientific developments during this period in England; LORD ERNLE (ROWLAND D. PROTHERO), *English Farming Past and Present,* 6th ed. (1961), is a classic work describing six centuries of British agriculture; CHRISTOPHER TAYLOR, *Village and Farmstead: A History of Rural Settlement in England* (1983), analyzes the density of population in Britain in the late Iron Age; FREIHERR VON DER GOLTZ, *Geschichte der deutschen Landwirtschaft,* 2 vol. (1902–03), deals with agriculture in Germany. See also ALBERT DEMOLON, *L'Évolution scientifique et l'agriculture française* (1946); MICHEL AUGÉ-LARIBÉ, *La Révolution agricole* (1955); Z.W. SNELLER (ed.), *Geschiedenis van de Nederlandse Landbouw, 1795–1940,* 2nd ed. (1951); HEINZ HAUSHOFER, *Die deutsche Landwirtschaft im technischen Zeitalter,* 2nd ed. (1972); CESARE LONGOBARDI, *Land-Reclamation in Italy,* trans. from the Italian (1936, reprinted 1975); LEWIS CECIL GRAY and ESTHER KATHERINE THOMPSON, *History of Agriculture in the Southern United States to 1860,* 2 vol. (1933, reprinted 1973); PERCY W. BIDWELL and JOHN I. FALCONER, *History of Agriculture in the Northern United States, 1620–1860* (1925, reprinted 1973); NORMAN SCOTT BRIEN GRAS, *A History of Agriculture in Europe and America,* 2nd ed. (1940, reprinted 1968); REYNOLD M. WIK, *Steam Power on the American Farm* (1953); WAYNE D. RASMUSSEN (ed.), *Readings in the History of American Agriculture* (1960); ROBERT LESLIE JONES, *History of Agriculture in Ohio to 1880* (1983); ERIC VAN YOUNG, *Hacienda and Market in Eighteenth-Century Mexico: The Rural Economy of the Guadalajara Region, 1675–1820* (1981); CLARK C. SPENCE, *God Speed the Plow: The Coming of Steam Cultivation to Great Britain* (1960); and RONALD H. CLARK, *The Development of the English Traction Engine* (1960). For broader surveys see JEROME BLUM (ed.), *Our Forgotten Past: Seven Centuries of Life on the Land* (1982), a well-illustrated collection of essays; EMMANUEL LE ROY LADURIE and JOSEPH GOY, *Tithe and Agrarian History from the Fourteenth to the Nineteenth Centuries,* trans. from the French (1982), a comparative description of agricultural production in several countries; and DAVID HOSEASON MORGAN, *Harvesters and Harvesting, 1840–1900: A Study of the Rural Proletariat* (1982), a blend of economic and social history.

The 20th century: ARCHIE A. STONE and HAROLD E. GULVIN, *Machines for Power Farming,* 3rd ed. (1977), is a fine general text describing modern farm machinery, including power sources, tilling equipment, applicators for fertilizer, seeders, pest-control machinery, and harvesting equipment; DANIEL FAUCHER, *Le Paysan et la machine* (1954), is a history of farm machinery; HUBERT MARTIN, *The Scientific Principles of Crop Protection,* 7th ed. (1983), is a classic work by the world's leading authority on pesticides; GEORGE ORDISH, *Untaken Harvest* (1951), describes the economics of plant losses and their control; KENNETH MELLANBY, *Farming and Wildlife* (1981), studies the effects of modern farming on native flora and fauna; and THEODORE SALOUTOS, *The American Farmer and the New Deal* (1982), explores U.S. agricultural policies during the first half of the 20th century.

(E.S.H./G.E.F./K.Na./W.D.R./A.W.Gr./G.O./K.Me.)

Alcohol and Drug Consumption

Human beings have been experimenting for thousands of years with a variety of naturally occurring substances that act on nervous tissues: alcohol to intoxicate a weary mind, belladonna to calm an angry intestine or to poison an adversary, opium to overcome worry and strain. The relief of pain, in particular, is an age-old aim of humankind, and various narcotic and sleep-producing agents were probably used by primitive people. But for many human beings there is another kind of pain—the pain of being—and from time immemorial some people have been trying to expand their vision, enhance their appreciation of their world, change their mood, alter their inner existence, or stupefy their awareness with the use of such drugs as alcohol, opium, and cannabis.

It is written in Genesis (9:20) that Noah planted a vineyard, "and he drank of the wine, and became drunk, and lay uncovered in his tent." Alcohol has been used by many cultures and has been worshipped as a god. Opium has also been used extensively, at least since the time of ancient Greece. Homer tells how some of Odysseus' crew succumbed to forgetfulness in the land of the Lotus-eaters, and the ancient Vedic philosophers of India spoke of soma, a mysterious and probably mythical plant. Coca, coffee, and tobacco have also played their parts in history. (W.G.St./Ed.)

This article treats primarily the psychological and social aspects of alcohol and drug abuse. For further treatment of chemical and physiological aspects, see DRUGS AND DRUG ACTION.

The article is divided into the following sections:

Alcohol 195
- Physiological and psychological effects of alcohol 196
  - What the body does with alcohol
  - Intoxication
    - Effects on the brain
    - Effects on emotional behaviour
    - Direct effects on organs
    - The acute diseases
    - The chronic diseases
    - Fetal alcohol syndrome
- Social conditions of alcohol consumption 199
  - History of the use of alcohol
    - In early societies
    - Among classical peoples
    - Alcohol in complex societies
  - Drinking patterns
    - Kinds and distributions
    - Kinds and customs
- Alcoholism 203
  - Definitions and causal factors of alcoholism
  - Prevalence of alcoholism
  - Treatment of alcoholism
    - Physiological therapies
    - Other therapies
- Contemporary alcohol problems and controls 207
  - Individual and social effects
  - Alcohol control
  - The new scientific orientation

Psychotropic drugs 208
- Characteristics of drug use and abuse 208
  - The functions of psychotropic drugs
  - The nature of drug addiction and dependence
    - Popular misconceptions
    - Physiological effects of addiction
    - Addiction, habituation, and dependence
    - Psychological dependence
  - History of drug control
    - International controls
    - National controls
    - Extent of contemporary drug abuse
- The varieties of psychotropic drugs 212
  - Opium, morphine, heroin, and related synthetics
    - History
    - Physiological effects
    - Types of users
    - Means of administration and their effects
    - Therapy
  - Hallucinogenic drugs
    - Types of hallucinogens
    - History
    - Physiological and psychological effects
    - Types of users
  - Barbiturates, stimulants, and tranquillizers
    - Barbiturates
    - Cocaine
    - Amphetamines
    - Tranquillizers
  - Cannabis
    - Types of cannabis preparations
    - History
    - Physiological and psychological effects
- Social and ethical issues of drug abuse 219
  - Conflicting values in drug use
  - Youth and drugs
- Pharmacological cults 219
  - Types of drugs used by cults
    - Hemp, mushrooms, cacti, and their derivatives
    - Other psychedelic substances
  - Goals of practitioners
    - Ecstasy and union with the divine or sacred
    - Purification, healing, and divination
    - Witchcraft and magic
    - Psychological goals
  - History of drug use in religion

Bibliography 222

ALCOHOL

People do not usually drink pure alcohol but a beverage containing alcohol, specifically ethyl alcohol. This article deals with most aspects of such drinking, from the chemical and the physiological to the medical and social.

Alcoholic beverages include wines, beers, and spirits. Wines are fermented from the sugars in fruits or berries (most commonly grapes), from various plants or their saps, from honey, and even from milk. Beers are fermented from grains after the starch in them is first converted to sugar. Spirits are distilled from wines or beers (see BEVERAGE PRODUCTION). The alcohol in all these beverages is ethyl alcohol, or ethanol (CH_3CH_2OH). Extremely small amounts of other alcohols, such as amyl, butyl, propyl, and methyl alcohol, also occur in alcoholic beverages, along with other so-called congeners that include acids, aldehydes, esters, ketones, phenols, and tannins; there are also numerous inorganic substances, including vitamins and minerals. Some of these ingredients are derived from primary plant materials; some are produced during the fermentation process and may be reduced by purification; and some are introduced during the aging process—for example, by continuous contact with containers such as wooden barrels. The combinations and exact amounts of congeners vary with the type of beverage, ranging from as few as 33 milligrams per litre in vodka, which is purified diluted alcohol, to averages of 500 milligrams per litre in some whiskies and as many as 2,600 milligrams per litre in specially aged whiskies or brandies. Congeners contribute special characteristics of taste, aroma, and colour to the beverages. Some have nutrient and medicinal effects. Some, in spite of their small quantity, slow the rate at which the body disposes of ethyl alcohol and may have toxic effects if very large amounts of alcoholic beverages are consumed. But the main ingredient that characterizes alcoholic beverages and the chief contributor of the effects sought by people who drink them is ethyl alcohol (hereafter referred to simply as alcohol).

In beers the alcohol content varies from about 2 percent in some mild Scandinavian varieties to about 8 percent in especially strong types; most U.S. beers contain between 4 and 5 percent. Natural or unfortified wines (the so-called dry wines, such as burgundy, chianti, and sauterne) usually contain between 8 and 12 percent alcohol, although most U.S. varieties have a somewhat higher content, ranging from 12 to 14 percent. Vermouths and aperitif wines usually contain 18 percent, and dessert, sweet, and cocktail wines (such as sherry, port, and muscatel) contain 20 to 21 percent. These percentages are by volume; *i.e.,* the proportion of alcohol in the fluid volume of an average American beer is 4.5 percent. Since fermentation yields only 14 percent alcohol, the extra strength of fortified wines comes from the addition of alcohol or brandy. Spirits, including vodka, gin, and whiskies (rye, Scotch, bourbon), rum (distilled from sugarcane or molasses), brandies (distilled from fruit wines), and liqueurs (flavoured syrupy spirits) usually contain between 40 and 50 percent alcohol. Cordials, made of flavoured spirits, such as anisette, blackberry, curaçao, maraschino, and sloe gin, usually contain between 25 and 40 percent. The Asiatic beverage kumiss (made from mare's milk) and the Russian kvass rarely contain more than 2 percent alcohol.

Physiological and psychological effects of alcohol

WHAT THE BODY DOES WITH ALCOHOL

Absorption and distribution

When an alcoholic beverage is swallowed, it is diluted by the stomach juices—it may first undergo some dilution in the mouth—and very quickly distributed throughout the body. Alcohol does not require digestion before its absorption into the bloodstream. A small portion is diffused into the bloodstream directly from the stomach wall. Most of the alcohol passes through the pyloric junction into the small intestine, where it is very rapidly absorbed and circulated. The rate of absorption will vary according to the particular beverage and the state of the individual consumer's stomach. A strong alcohol solution, when taken into an empty stomach, may cause a spasm of the pylorus that will impede its passage into the small intestine, resulting in a slower rate of absorption. The presence of food in the stomach, especially some fatty foods, will delay absorption. On the other hand, alcohol taken together with carbonated beverages will ordinarily be absorbed more rapidly. Other factors, such as the emotional state of the drinker, may also affect the rate of absorption. Probably cocktails and highballs, many of which contain carbonated water or other beverage, provide the most rapidly absorbed forms of alcoholic beverage that people consume.

Alcohol is diffused in the body in proportion to the water content of the various tissues and organs, appearing in greater concentration in the blood and brain than in fat or muscle tissue. The absorbed alcohol is greatly diluted by the body fluids. Thus, the alcohol in an ounce (29.57 millilitres) of whiskey at 50 percent strength (100 U.S. proof, 87.6 British proof) will be diluted, in a man of average build, to a concentration of about 2 parts per 10,000 in the blood (0.02 percent). In a larger person the blood alcohol concentration will be proportionately smaller; and, in a smaller person, of course, the concentration will be proportionately greater.

The importance of the rate of absorption, distribution, and dilution of alcohol in the body lies in their relation to the achieved alcohol concentration in various organs, particularly the brain. After rapid intake of a large amount of alcohol that is quickly absorbed, a relatively early "high," or sensation of intoxication will occur. Figure 1 shows a set of probable average curves of blood alcohol concentrations in an average-size man after rapid absorption of various amounts of alcohol. It shows also the average rate of decline of the blood alcohol concentration over time as a result of the disposal of the alcohol by the body through the processes of metabolism (oxidation) and excretion.

The body begins to dispose of alcohol immediately after it has been absorbed. An insignificantly small proportion of alcohol is exhaled through the lungs, and a tiny amount is excreted in sweat. A small proportion is secreted by the kidneys and will be accumulated and retained in the bladder until eliminated in the urine. Only between 2 and 10 percent of the alcohol is eliminated by these means. The remainder, 90 percent or more of the absorbed alco-

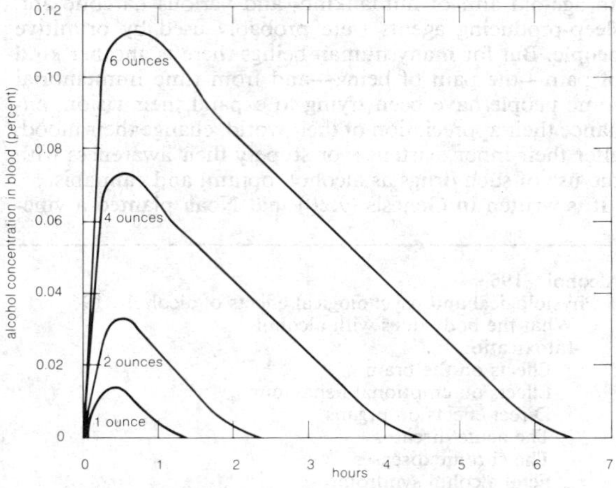

Figure 1: Percent of blood alcohol concentration in an average man at hourly intervals after drinking one, two, four, or six ounces of spirits containing 50 percent alcohol.

hol, is disposed of by metabolic processes, mainly in the liver. Other organs are capable of metabolizing only small amounts of alcohol.

How alcohol is metabolized

As absorbed alcohol is passed through the liver by the circulating blood, it is acted upon by ADH (alcohol dehydrogenase), a zinc-containing enzyme found chiefly in the liver cells. The alcohol molecule is converted by this action to acetaldehyde, itself a highly toxic substance, but this is immediately acted upon by another enzyme, aldehyde dehydrogenase, and converted to acetate, most of which enters the bloodstream and is ultimately oxidized to carbon dioxide and water. Considerable utilizable energy—7.1 calories from each gram of alcohol (about 200 calories per ounce)—is made available to the organism during these processes, and in this sense alcohol serves as a nutrient.

The two enzymatic reactions—that of ADH and aldehyde dehydrogenase—require a co-enzyme, NAD (nicotinamide-adenine dinucleotide), the acceptor of hydrogen from the alcohol molecule, for their effects. The NAD is thus changed to NADH and becomes available again for the same reaction only after its own further oxidation. While adequate ADH seems always present for the first step of alcohol metabolism, the temporary reduction of the available NAD apparently acts as a limit on the rate at which alcohol can be metabolized. That rate is about half an ounce of alcohol (equal to about an ounce of spirits, a 12-ounce bottle of beer, a four-ounce glass of dry wine, or a 2.5-ounce glass of fortified wine) per hour in an average-size man.

The limit on the rate at which the body can dispose of alcohol results in its accumulation in the organism if drinking proceeds at a faster rate than the alcohol is metabolized. The average-size man who drinks and absorbs four ounces of whiskey (at 50 percent alcohol) rapidly will have $1^1/_2$ ounces of alcohol in his body at the end of an hour and a blood alcohol concentration near to 0.07 percent (Figure 1). If he drinks eight ounces within two hours, he will have a blood alcohol concentration of about 0.11 percent. The continued accumulation of alcohol in the organism faster than it can be metabolized leads to increasing degrees of intoxication. This is illustrated in Figure 2, Curve A, which shows what happens if an average man drinks two ounces of spirits each hour for four hours. At the end of the first hour, the blood alcohol concentration has passed its peak and begun to decline, but with the next drink the concentration starts rising again; this is repeated after each drink. Only at the end of four hours—an hour after the last drink—is the highest blood alcohol concentration reached; and, with no more drinking, it declines steadily thereafter. Curve A thus illustrates the combined effects of repeated alcohol absorption and its continuous metabolism. Curve B in Figure 2 shows what the course of blood alcohol concentration would be if the eight ounces of spirits were drunk and absorbed all at once.

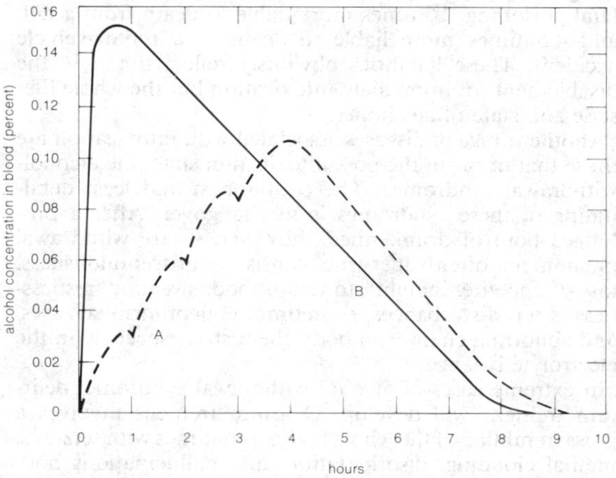

Figure 2: Percent of blood alcohol concentration in an average man at hourly intervals after drinking two ounces of spirits each hour for four hours (curve A) and eight ounces all at once (curve B).

INTOXICATION

General effects of intoxication

The drinking of small amounts of alcohol, even if this is done regularly over a long period of time, does not have any conclusively demonstrated pathological effect. A mild infrequent intoxication produces a variety of temporary biochemical disturbances in the body: the adrenal glands may discharge hormones, sugar may be mobilized from stores in the liver, the electrolyte balance may be slightly upset, the metabolism and equilibrium of the liver may be disturbed. But these changes leave no chronic aftereffects, and the body rapidly returns to normal. A severe intoxication, on the other hand, may produce more serious disturbances, including temporary extensive imbalance in the body chemistry, an acute hepatitis and numerous "hangover" effects: nausea, headache, gastritis, thirst because of the shift of water from cellular to extracellular spaces, and a generalized residual malaise and physical and mental incompetence that may last as long as 24 hours after all the alcohol consumed has been metabolized. Some drinkers are satisfied to suffer the mild and even the severer aftereffects of occasional intoxication for the sake of the temporary dissociation, euphoria, or socialization that the drinking allows. But frequent intoxication, even of moderate degree, imposes a severe and debilitating burden on the organism.

The irritating effects of alcohol, especially in undiluted strong beverages, can result in damage to the tissues of the mouth, esophagus, and stomach, perhaps with increased susceptibility to cancer. The liver is likely to suffer serious damage if it must cope lengthily with the detoxication of large amounts of alcohol. There may also be damage to the heart muscle.

Frequent heavy drinking to severe degrees of intoxication or the prolonged steady maintenance of a high alcohol concentration in the organism has been shown to be linked to many impairments or injuries of many organs. The most common linkage is with diseases caused by defects of nutrition.

Effects on the brain. Alcohol as a drug affecting the central nervous system belongs in a class with the barbiturates, minor tranquillizers, and general anesthetics and is commonly classified as a depressant. Its effect on the brain is rather biphasic: at quite low concentrations it can serve as an excitant or stimulant of some functions, but, as the concentration increases, the effect is constantly more depressant, going on to sedation, stupor, and coma. The excitement phase exhibits the well-known signs of exhilaration, loss of socially expected restraints, loquaciousness, unexpected changes of mood, and occasionally uncontrolled emotional displays. This excitement phase may result from an indirect effect of alcohol in suppressing the function of inhibitory brain centres rather than from a direct stimulation of the manifest behaviour. The physical counterparts of this state of relatively mild intoxication are slurred speech, unsteady gait, disturbed sensory perceptions, and inability to make fine discriminations. These effects are produced not by the direct action of alcohol on the misbehaving muscles and senses but by its effect on the brain centres that control their activity.

Because brain alcohol concentrations can rarely be measured in people, blood alcohol concentrations are used as the standard against which performances are compared. Most people exhibit some degree of functional depression or incapacitation at blood alcohol concentrations of 0.10 percent. Inefficiency in performing some tasks may begin at much lower concentrations, even at 0.03 percent. The majority of drinkers begin to show measurable impairment at just above 0.05 percent, and most people are considered intoxicated at 0.15 percent. In determining the intoxication of automobile drivers, most jurisdictions in Western countries use a blood alcohol concentration of 0.15 percent as the criterion; in some, a presumption of impairment is made at the much lower concentrations of 0.10, 0.08, or 0.05 percent.

The impairments at these concentrations may not be manifested superficially by all individuals, but laboratory tests show diminished alertness, visual acuity, and capacity to distinguish between signals. Reflex responses and the time of reaction to a signal, as well as neuromuscular functions, are slowed. Complex reactions, those that require the brain to process more than one type of incoming information simultaneously, are impaired at blood alcohol concentrations too low to affect simple reflexes and reaction times.

Effects on mental processes

The most important immediate actions of alcohol are on the highest functions of the brain—those of thinking, learning, remembering, and making judgments. The biphasic action of alcohol is evident in its effect on thinking. One group of experiments revealed that at low blood alcohol concentrations, after the equivalent of two drinks (two ounces of spirits), well-trained and highly intelligent young men performed better at solving problems in symbolic logic than they had without alcohol. At medium concentrations, the equivalent of four drinks, their performance was about normal. But, at concentrations equivalent to six drinks, their ability to solve such problems definitely deteriorated. Similar effects were observed in tests of memorizing. More recent experiments indicate the dependence of learning on the state in which it occurs:—*i.e.,* what is learned under the influence of alcohol is better recalled under the influence of alcohol than when sober, but what is learned in the sober state is better recalled when sober. The function of judgment is difficult to define; when evaluated by such a task as willingness to drive a bus through a more or less adequate gateway, judgment progressively deteriorates with increasing blood alcohol concentrations; when evaluated by willingness to take risks, as shown in responses to hypothetical problem situations, the results are similar, although more so in younger than in older people.

As blood alcohol concentrations continue to rise above 0.15 percent, intoxication steadily increases. Well-adapted, very heavy drinkers may continue to function fairly well in some motor and mental tasks even up to concentrations of 0.3 percent, but most people will appear visibly drunk, manifesting the common symptoms of slurred speech, unsteadiness of gait, and confusion of thinking long before this level is reached. At 0.4 percent most people will be anesthetized to the extent that they will be asleep, difficult to arouse, incapable of voluntary activity—indeed, in a state in which they could undergo surgery. At higher blood alcohol levels, deep coma sets in, and, if the intoxicated person is long unattended, death may ensue by accidental stoppage of the breathing passages. Between 0.5 and 1 percent the breathing centre in the brain or the action of the heart may be anesthetized, and then death directly from alcohol intoxication will quickly follow. Ordinarily, the achievement of blood alcohol concentrations above 0.4 percent by drinking is unlikely; in a man of average build it would require the ingestion and absorption, unmetabolized, of almost a fifth of a gallon of spirits (0.757 litre) at 50 percent alcohol.

Effects on emotional behaviour. People ordinarily drink alcohol to obtain effects that they have been taught to expect. Small amounts are drunk in the expectation of reducing feelings of tension, relieving feelings of anxiety, and, conversely, obtaining feelings of gaiety and exhilaration. A sufficient amount of alcohol will usually serve the desired purpose. It is likely, however, that alcohol itself is not solely responsible: the state of expectation combines with the pharmacological action of the drug to produce the desired effect. In favourable circumstances, alcohol will not merely reduce tension and anxiety but suppress them entirely, even allowing a shift of the emotional state to one of indifference or euphoria or elation. The anxiety-suppressing action of alcohol is commonly seen in the gradual removal of social inhibitions. Shy people become outgoing or bold; well-behaved people become disorderly; the sexually repressed become amorous; the fearful become brave; the quiescent or peaceful become verbally or physically aggressive. All these reactions may be the result of the stimulating effect of small amounts of alcohol or the control-anesthetizing (disinhibiting) effects of larger amounts. But they are, in part, also made possible by the social and cultural permissiveness typical of drinking situations. Alcohol is not only a psychoactive but a socioactive drug. These effects apparently occur in most normal drinkers; in alcoholics, the consumption of huge quantities apparently evokes different states of feeling and even an increase of anxiety or tension.

Alcohol and therapeutics

Alcohol is often used for medicinal and therapeutic purposes. Whiskey is popular for treating colds and snakebites, brandy for treating faintness, wine for blood building, beer for lactation, and any alcoholic beverage for treating sleeplessness or overexcitement. Many of these uses survive from folk medicine of many cultures. Alcohol is administered by physicians in hospitals, usually by vein, sometimes for anesthesia before minor surgery; more often it is given for sedation after surgery and as a source of easily absorbed calories when it is desirable to bypass the patient's digestive system. Physicians often prescribe "a drink" for a variety of purposes: to stimulate a sluggish appetite, as a sedative to induce sleep, as an anxiolytic in premenstrual tension in women, as a vasodilator (an agent used to widen the lumen of the blood vessels) in arteriosclerosis, to relieve the vague aches and pains that beset the elderly, and as a supplement in special diets.

Direct effects on organs. After being considerably diluted upon absorption into the bloodstream, alcohol reaches the body organs in extremely small concentrations. A pint (0.473 litre) of whiskey (at 50 percent alcohol), fully absorbed and not metabolized, will produce in a man of average build and weight a concentration of about 0.32 percent in the blood. The concentration in any organ is likely to be less. Concentrations of 1 percent are hardly sufficient to irritate the most delicate tissue. Even with very heavy continuous drinking, a post-absorptive concentration above 0.5 percent in any organ is extremely unlikely. Such small alcohol concentrations cannot be expected to inflict direct damage on the liver, the kidneys, the generative organs, the heart, or the brain, though they may cause temporary derangements of biochemistry and function. A concentration of 0.5 percent in the brain will cause coma and may be lethal. Most of the damage to these and other organs in long-time heavy drinkers consists apparently of side effects related to disturbances of metabolism or to malnutrition and poor hygiene. Some experimental work has suggested that alcohol has a directly adverse effect on the liver and on muscle tissue, and clinical observations have suggested a direct chronic pathological effect on the heart muscle. But the manner in which alcohol produces such direct damages is still unexplained.

The acute diseases. Excessive users of alcohol have been shown to suffer in varying degrees from both acute and chronic diseases. The acute diseases include, first of all, intoxication, with its wide variety of disturbances of neuromuscular and mental functions and of body chemistry. In addition, the intoxicated person is abnormally liable to accidents and injuries. Those who experience severe intoxication chronically, the alcoholics, are said to be seven times as liable to fatal accidents as persons in the general population. They are 30 times more liable to fatal poisoning, 16 times more liable to death from a fall, and 4.5 times more liable to death in a motor-vehicle accident. These liabilities obviously reflect not only the disablements of immediate intoxication but the whole lifestyle and state of alcoholics.

Withdrawal syndromes

Another range of diseases associated with intoxication are those that occur in the post-intoxication state, the alcohol-withdrawal syndromes. The commonest and least debilitating of these syndromes is the hangover. After a prolonged bout of drunkenness, however, severe withdrawal phenomena often supervene, consisting of tremulousness, loss of appetite, inability to retain food, sweating, restlessness, sleep disturbances, sometimes epileptiform seizures, and abnormal changes in body chemistry, especially in the electrolyte balance.

In extreme cases of alcohol withdrawal syndrome, delirium tremens will develop. Delirium tremens involves a gross trembling of the whole body, sometimes with seizures, mental clouding, disorientation, and hallucinations both visual and auditory. Depending on the amount and quality of care and treatment, as well as the possible occurrence of intercurrent diseases, delirium tremens lasts from three to 10 days, with a reported fatality rate ranging from 1 to 20 percent. Acute alcoholic hallucinosis may develop with or without preceding delirium tremens and may last days to weeks. Other brain disorders that may follow a prolonged bout include Wernicke's disease, resulting from an acute complete deficiency of thiamine (vitamin B_1) and marked by clouding of consciousness and paralysis of the optic nerves; the acute form of Korsakoff's syndrome, marked by loss of recent memory, with a tendency to make up for the defect by confabulation; and Jolliffe's encephalopathy, resulting from an acute complete deficiency of nicotinic acid and marked by delirium, together with rigidities of the extremities and sucking and grasping reflexes.

Early signs of polyneuropathy, a degenerative disease of the peripheral nerves, include tenderness of calf muscles, diminished tendon reflexes, and loss of vibratory sensation. Acute hepatitis (inflammation of the liver) is common. Less often seen are severe pancreatitis and Zieve's syndrome, the latter being a combination of jaundice with hemolytic anemia, hyperlipemia, and hepatic tenderness. Numerous other disturbances, for example, severe muscle cramps and defects in nerve conduction, are occasionally observed.

The disorders of the brain and nervous system and possibly many of the symptoms in the other acute consequences of alcoholism are caused largely by dietary deficiencies. Alcohol provides large numbers of calories, but they are empty calories—such as those of refined sugar—devoid of vitamins and other essential microelements of nutrition, including minerals and amino acids. The small amounts of vitamins and minerals present in beers and wines—rarely in spirits—are insufficient for dietary needs. In heavy bouts of drinking, alcoholics neglect normal eating or, because of digestive difficulties, cannot absorb enough of the essential food elements. These nutritional defects are the cause of many of the chronic diseases associated with alcoholism.

Another acute disorder associated with alcohol is sometimes misnamed pathological intoxication in which, after downing a small amount of drink, a person suddenly breaks into a maniacal fury, smashing furniture and attacking people. The seizure ends as suddenly as it began, and the victim usually falls into a stuporous sleep, from which he awakens after some hours—usually without memory of the events. The cause is uncertain; personality factors combined with a temporary deficiency of blood sugar have been suspected.

Degenerative diseases

The chronic diseases. In long-lasting alcoholism, one or more of the chronic nutritional deficiency diseases may develop. The severer effects of vitamin B_1 deficiency are probably commonest—degeneration of the peripheral nerves, with permanent damage in extreme cases, and beriberi heart disease; another common disease is pellagra, due chiefly to deficiency of nicotinic acid. Other diseases include scurvy, resulting from ascorbic acid deficiency; hypochromic microcytic anemia, caused by iron deficiency; and anemia resulting from vitamin B_{12} deficiency. Severe open sores on the skin of alcoholic derelicts whose usual drink is the cheapest form of alcohol—low-quality fortified wines—are sometimes miscalled wine sores, but they result from a combination of multiple nutritional deficiencies and poor hygiene.

The classical disease associated with alcoholism is cirrhosis of the liver (Laënnec's type), frequently preceded by a fatty enlargement of the organ. The exact mechanism by which this cirrhosis develops is still unclear; it appears to involve the consequences both of the metabolism of excessive amounts of alcohol and of defective nutrition. In its severest form, Laënnec's cirrhosis is often fatal; its successful treatment or the retardation of its progress is impossible in an alcoholic who cannot be stopped from drinking.

Besides the mental symptoms that may accompany pellagra, other mental disorders that are more specifically related to the consumption of alcohol include chronic hallucinations and Korsakoff's psychosis, which may last months to years. A relatively uncommon chronic brain disorder is Marchiafava-Bignami's disease; because the symptoms are not specific, this degeneration of the corpus callosum in the brain is usually diagnosed only at autopsy. Other brain damage occasionally reported in alcoholism includes cortical laminar sclerosis, cerebellar degeneration, central pontine myelinolysis, and enlargement of the ventricles as a result of atrophy of brain substance. Alcoholics, especially older ones, frequently show signs of neurological defect and impaired brain function, and these are sometimes blamed on direct damage to the central nervous system by alcohol; it is possible, however, that they are the result of brain damage caused by accidents and blows. Many of those who survive long years of alcoholism show a generalized deterioration involving the brain, muscles, endocrine system, and vital organs, giving an impression of premature old age. Alcoholics die more frequently in all types of accidents and from numerous diseases; their average life span is reduced by about 10 or 12 years.

(M.Ke.)

Fetal alcohol syndrome. The effect that the problem drinker or alcoholic has on others may be generational. There is evidence that habitual or even occasional drinking by an expectant mother can endanger the health of the fetus. Studies have indicated that babies of heavy drinkers may be small in terms of length and weigh less than other babies. The babies may have a high incidence of small heads, defective joints in their hands and feet, cleft palates, and heart abnormalities. Researchers studying such infants have termed their abnormalities "fetal alcohol syndrome." Some babies may be so severely affected that they die after birth; and, when their brains are studied, they are found to be poorly developed; some portions may actually be missing. The infants that survive may show impaired intellectual development as well as decreased ability to use certain muscles. It is believed that fetal alcohol syndrome is not a rare occurrence. It may exist in many degrees of severity, but its most common manifestation is mental impairment.

Opinion is varied in regard to what a pregnant woman should do about the use of alcohol. Some scientists feel that it should be totally avoided because of the possibility that the fetus may be affected by even very low or infrequent doses; others feel that one or two drinks a day may be safe.

(Ed.)

Social conditions of alcohol consumption

HISTORY OF THE USE OF ALCOHOL

In early societies. The origin of alcoholic beverages is lost in the mists of prehistory. Fermentation can occur in any sugar-containing mishmash, such as one of grapes, fruits, berries, or honey, if left exposed in a warm atmosphere. Airborne yeasts will act on the sugar, converting it to alcohol and carbon dioxide. This is the process of fermentation. Alcoholic beverages were thus probably discovered accidentally in the pre-agricultural gathering stage. Early man presumably liked the effects, if not the taste, and proceeded to purposeful production; from merely gathering the wild-growing raw materials, he went on to regular cultivation of the vine and other suitable crops. Few preliterate people did not learn to convert some of the fruit of the earth into alcohol. In the case of starchy vegetation, quite primitive agriculturists learned how to convert the starch to fermentable sugar by providing the necessary zymase from their saliva through such a simple process as preliminary mastication.

Universality of alcohol production

The making of wines and beers has been reported from several hundred preliterate societies. Their importance is evident in the multiplicity of customs and regulations that developed around their production and uses. They often became central in the most valued personal and social ceremonials, especially in the rites of passage, and are ubiquitous in such activities as births, initiations, marriages, compacts, feasts, conclaves, crownings, magic, medicine, worship, hospitality, war making, peace making, and funerals. Alcohol is thus the oldest and still probably the most widely used drug.

The manufacture and sale of alcoholic beverages was already common and commercialized and regulated by government in the earliest civilizations. The oldest known code of laws, that of Hammurabi of Babylonia (*c.* 1770 BC), regulated drinking houses. Sumerian physician-pharmacists prescribed beer (*c.* 2100 BC) in relatively sophisticated pharmacopoeias found on clay tablets. The later Egyptian doctors, in their medical papyri (*c.* 1500 BC), included beer or wine in about 15 percent of their prescriptions. The recently discovered Semitic cuneiform literature of the northern Canaanites, in pre-Biblical Ugarit, contains abundant references to the ubiquitous religious and household uses of the intoxicating fluid.

Early religious uses of alcohol

Water, a precious commodity in the earliest agriculturally dependent civilizations, was probably the original fluid used as offering in worship rites. In time, other fluids—milk, honey, and later wine (in some religions, beer)—were substituted. That alcoholic beverages should have displaced other fluids in early religions, both as offering and drink, is not surprising: its capacity to help the shaman or priest and other participants reach a desired state of ecstasy or frenzy could not long have escaped observation, and its appreciation was naturally attributed to supernatural spirits and gods. The red wine in religious uses was eventually perceived as symbolizing the blood of life and, in this spiritual sense, ultimately passed into the Christian Eucharist. The records of the Egyptian as well as of the Mesopotamian civilizations attest that drinking and drunkenness had passed from the state of religious rite to common practice, often troublesome to government and accompanied by acute and chronic illnesses. There are ample indications that some people so loved drink and were so abandoned to drunkenness that they must be presumed to have been alcoholics.

Among classical peoples. The significance of the classical history of drinking arises from the fact that after about 300 BC the Greek, Hebrew, and Roman cultures became mingled in a mix that was to influence powerfully the development of European culture. The surviving records of ancient Greek and Roman culture, in classic pictorial and plastic art as well as in the literature transmitting prehistoric memories enshrined in myths, reveal the common and copious use of wine by the gods, as well as by people of all classes. The worship of Dionysus, or Bacchus, the wine god, was the most popular; his festival, the Bacchanalia, has given English one of its literary names for a drunken orgy. His female devotees, the Maenads, worshipped him in drunken frenzies. The Greco-Roman classics abound with descriptions of fulsome drinking and often drunkenness. The wine of the ancient Greeks, like that of the Hebrews of the same time, was usually drunk diluted with an equal part or two parts of water, and, thus, the alcohol strength of the beverage was presumably between 4 and 7 percent. But, as a standard drink, diluted wine was apparently more common than plain water, and there were topers who preferred their wine straight.

The literature of the Greeks does not lack warnings of the evil effects of excess in drinking, but in this they are excelled by the classics of the Hebrew Canaanites. The earliest references in the Bible show that abundant wine was regarded as a blessing, on a par with ample milk and honey, grain and fruit. The eyes of the Judaeans were to be bright from wine, which also was known to gladden the heart of man and to bring relief to those who were bitter of heart or ready to perish. In the national religious culture that developed into the Judaism that has survived to the present, drinking was intertwined with all important ceremonial occasions—from the celebration of the eight-day-old boy's circumcision to the toasting of the soul of the departed and, in between, the wedding, the arrival and departure of every Sabbath and festival, and, indeed, any sort of celebration. The purpose of drinking thus became integrated with an attitude of reverence for the sanctity or the importance of the occasion, to the extent that over-drinking, becoming tipsy, would manifestly be inappropriate and disapproved. Drunkenness then became a culturally negative, an alien and rejected behaviour and generally vanished from the Jewish communities. In contemporary terms, drinking was under effective social control, and the result has been the seeming paradox, fascinating to modern students of sociocultural phenomena, that a people with the highest proportion of drinkers exhibit the lowest rates of alcoholism and other alcohol-related problems.

Religious sanctions against drunkenness or drinking

Quite a different kind of religious control was adopted later (in the 7th century) in Islām: the Qur'ān simply condemned wine, and the result was an effective prohibition wherever the devout followers of Muḥammad in Arabia and other lands prevailed. (The same process occurred some 1,000 years later in Europe, after the Reformation, and later still in the United States, when a number of ascetic Christian sects, resting their ideology on the Bible, made abstinence a fundamental tenet.)

Like the early agriculturists of the Near East, the people of the Far East discovered the technology of manufacturing alcoholic beverages in prehistoric times. Barley and rice were the chief crops and the raw materials for producing the drink that, here too, was incorporated into religious ceremonial, both as drink and libation, with festivals featuring divine states of drunkenness. Here too, in time, the sacred drink became secularized, even while its religious uses survived, and evoked public as well as private disorders. The history of China includes several abortive efforts at control or prohibition. But, in the Far East, prohibition was effective only when religiously motivated. The Hindu Ayurvedic texts (*c.* 1000 BC) skillfully describe both the beneficent uses of alcoholic beverages and the consequences of intoxication and the diseases of alcoholism. The devout adherents of Buddhism, however, which arose in India in the 5th and 6th centuries BC and spread over southern and eastern Asia, abstain to this day, as do the members of the Hindu Brahmin caste. But most of the peoples in India, as well as in Ceylon and the Philippines, in China and Japan, have continued, throughout, to ferment a portion of their crops and nourish as well as pleasure themselves with the alcoholic product.

In Africa, maize, millet, bananas, honey, the saps of the palm and the bamboo, and many fruits (including that of the sausage tree) have been used to ferment nutrient beers and wines, the best known being Kaffir beer and palm wines. Most of the peoples of Oceania, on the other hand, seem to have missed the discovery of fermentation. Many of the pre-Columbian Indians of North America are also exceptional in lacking alcoholic beverages until introduced to firewater by Europeans, with explosive and disastrous consequences. But the Papago Indians of the southwestern United States made a cactus wine, and the Tarahumara of northern Mexico made beers from corn and species of agave, while throughout Central and South America the aborigines made chicha and other alcoholic beverages from maize, tubers, fruits, flowers, and saps. For the most part, their drinking appears to have been regulated so as to inhibit individual alcoholism and limit drunkenness to communal fiestas.

Alcohol in complex societies. *Contrasts and similarities between primitive and modern uses.* In primitive societies the uses of alcoholic beverages were multiply motivated. These beverages had important nutritional value. They were the best medicine available for some illnesses and especially in relieving pain (in any case, a patient given a prescription to be taken in beer or wine, with the instruction to drink it liberally, was likely to feel better, regardless of whether the various ingredients affected his disease). They facilitated religious ecstasy and communion with the mystical super-mundane powers thought to control tribal and individual fate. They enabled periodic social festivity and the personal jollification of the participants, thus also serving as the mediator of popular recreation. They helped reduce anxiety, tension, and fears connected with concerns over subsistence, safety, or with the need to engage in aggressive or dangerous activities, such as warfare. They could calm anger or tranquillize hostility so as to allow pacification and reduce suspicion, making possible peaceful associations and commercial or ceremonial relations. And, in individuals with extraordinary responsibilities, such as chiefs, shamans, medicine men, they helped to assuage the personal anxieties and tensions connected with those exceptional roles. In some cases the formalized public binge could serve as the permissive loosener of interpersonal aggressions, allow an interlude of verbal or even physical hostility within the family or clan group, which otherwise the mores of the cohesive small society necessarily forbade. The insults and wounds of the discordant interlude could easily be forgiven by blaming them on the alcohol-induced irresponsibility. Under these circumstances drunkenness could be approved or even mandatory and still serve an integrative social function. In short, the most general effect of alcohol, suggested by its very equivocal uses, appears to be as a facilitator of mood change in any desired direction.

Variety of uses for alcohol

The conditions of primitive or early societies foreshadow the conditions of complex societies, including the contemporary highly industrialized ones. As food, hardly anything but the caloric value of alcohol remains, and this is essentially of no importance in modern dietaries, unless such large amounts are consumed that the value becomes negative, since the carbohydrate calories in modern beverages are deficient in other necessary nutrients, such as vitamins and minerals, provided by other foods. As medicament, alcohol has a limited surviving value in the practice of contemporary physicians equipped with more efficient anesthetics and taught to prescribe more variegated analgesics and tranquillizers. In religion, wine has been relegated to a highly specific, essentially symbolic role, where not completely eliminated. What remains is the satisfaction of personal and group needs that have particular urgency arising out of the very complexity of modern life.

The most distinctive features of the complex technological society, in contrast to the simple primitive type, consist of specialization of functions; membership in limited interest groups (though often with conflicting roles); inequalities of earnings and prestige; social and economic stratification, in addition to religious differentiation; and an irreconcilable disharmony of individualism and interdependence, marked by the fact that individuals command skills and privileges indispensable for the welfare of others (only a baker can produce bread for the supermarket's customers; only a licensed physician can write a prescription), yet the same individuals are totally dependent on others for their own vital needs. All these factors contribute to competitiveness, distrust, insecurity, anxiety, alienation. Those who have abundant goods or positions of power and prestige are not thereby freed of these troubles. The result is, if anything, a more intense need for relief from tension, for relaxation from anxiety, for tranquillization from the effects of competitive effort.

It is not that the ancient uses have been forgotten: a drink is still the symbolic announcer of friendship, peace, agreement, in personal as well as in business or political relations. But in the complex society many people discover that many drinks often help them to suppress the overwhelming inhibitions, shynesses, anxieties, tensions that interfere with urgent needs to function effectively, either socially or economically. In the complex society, characterized by multifarious frustrations of gratifying interpersonal relationships, the capacity of alcohol to serve as socio-activating medicine comes into high value.

Government regulation of alcohol use

Conflicts over drinking. Modern complex societies are troubled by a lack of consensus around many issues of right and wrong or proper and improper behaviour; and drinking, since the latter part of the 18th century, has been a focus of disagreement, sometimes amounting to political warfare among subgroups making up larger national societies. In the United States, the late 18th-century temperance movement became, by the middle of the 19th century, an anti-alcohol movement that culminated in national Prohibition (enacted by constitutional amendment in 1919 and repealed in 1933). Echo movements in other countries had somewhat similar histories. The lack of consensus regarding who may drink how much of what and where and when and with whom is illustrated by the crazy quilt of local regulations extant in the United States. In some localities there is total prohibition or prohibition only of distilled spirits and strong wines; in some, only those over 18 or over 21 years of age may buy drinks; in some, married women under age may buy but not married under-age men; in some, until recently, Indians might not buy; in some, liquor may be sold only by the bottle, not by the drink; in some, drinks may be served only together with food, in others only without food; in some, drinking in public places is permitted only if the drinkers are curtained or only if they are uncurtained or only when they are seated; or men may stand to drink, but women must be seated. Dissonant attitudes toward a custom as common as drinking are believed by many sociologists to account for the inability of the society to establish firm rules inhibiting immoderate behaviour, with a resulting high incidence of damaging use, drunkenness, and many other problems related to alcohol. The Chinese and the Italians, as well as the Jews, are cited as examples of groups having well-developed cultural consensus against drinking to drunkenness, with resulting low rates of alcohol problems. In parallel, France is cited as a country with a consensus favouring steady copious drinking, with a resulting high rate of alcoholism.

The modern conflict over drinking reflects the complex interactions of individual man and small group and larger society. Small groups, formed by common interests in business or occupation or recreation or neighbourhood or politics or ethnicity or religion, use drinking together to facilitate mixing, to engender solidarity, to reduce normal inhibitions against trust in and collaboration with "strangers," to symbolize and ratify accord, to ensure that gatherings for celebration will succeed as festive occasions. Individuals use alcoholic beverages as an agreeable effector of desired mood alteration, such as moderate relief from anxiety or depression or masking of unease and pain, and to enable participation in the various small groups with which they are required to associate. Given favourable contexts, moderate amounts of alcohol apparently function well in fulfilling these purposes. Given consensual practices, moderate amounts of drink function integratively within families and in common-interest groups. This is thought to account for the survival of the drinking custom from early times, in spite of the problems it has engendered and the opposition it has provoked. But individuals and, sometimes, groups, whether formally or informally organized, also indulge in immoderate, self-injurious, and socially damaging drinking. These dysfunctional behaviours account, in part, for the organized societal opposition to any drinking although the antagonism is sometimes based in more fundamental perspectives of the anti-alcohol sentiment: alcohol is, from olden times, the facilitator of pleasurable, morally lax, hedonistic behaviour; as such, it evokes the displeasure and condemnation of those favouring moral strictness and an ascetic way of life.

DRINKING PATTERNS

Places of drinking

The universal and general functions of drinking are displayed in a great variety of ways and customs in different parts of the world and among various subgroups and subcultures within larger societies. The places of drinking vary infinitely: home may be the only place to drink or the one place where it is forbidden. Drinking may be a ceremonial or informal family affair, with or before meals. It may be a lone practice at home, in commercial drinking places, or in private hideaways or a group practice in membership clubs, neighbourhood taverns, beer gardens, sidewalk cafés, or skid-row alleys. The purposes and occasions are infinitely disparate. It may be the benign drunkenness of the men in the quasi-religious fiestas of Central and South American natives, the fiestal abandonment in song and dance—after relatively little drinking—of the members of the Jewish sect of Ḥasidim, the socializing celebrations of fraternal collegians, or the exhibitionistic libationism of business meetings and professional conventions. Or it may be the repeated "killing" of bottles by men or women fixed mindlessly before the television set, or the quick potations of cocktail parties, or the gulping of forbidden liquors by defiant, rebellious youth groups needing to assert their grownupness. Not only an individual's taste, predilection, or psychological need but also his sex, age, residential neighbourhood, education, associations, church and other memberships, and socio-economic status may determine whether, when, what, how much, or with whom he shall drink. In the United States, where nearly one-third of adults are abstainers, the better educated and the economically advantaged are more likely to be drinkers than the poor, though, among the poor who do drink, the proportions of heavy drinkers are higher. By contrast, in France, where abstainers are in a very small minority, they are more likely to be found among the better educated and upwardly mobile. The attitudes toward drinking and abstaining, among or within different countries, are as varied as the practices.

The increasing worldwide consumption

Kinds and distributions. The worldwide pattern of total alcohol consumption on a per capita basis increased generally during the period after 1950. The per capita consumption of distilled spirits, beer, and wine also rose during most of this period, with beer consumption increasing more than spirits or wine. Although the consumption of all alcoholic beverages generally rose during this period, deviations from this general tendency were evident in many countries; countries with traditionally high levels of total alcohol consumption (*e.g.*, France, Italy, Portugal, Spain, and Switzerland) exhibited stable or slightly increased per capita levels; beer consumption in traditionally heavy beer-drinking countries (*e.g.*, West Germany, Belgium, Australia, New Zealand, Ireland, the United Kingdom, and Denmark) did not increase as much as the worldwide pattern; and wine consumption on a per capita basis actually declined in some countries with traditionally high consumption levels (*e.g.*, France and Italy).

Many factors are believed to affect these recent patterns in total alcohol consumption. One factor has been the increased use of alcohol with meals, primarily beer and wine, in part a result of long-term increases in per capita income in many countries and in part a result of fermentation technology that has kept the price of alcoholic beverages relatively low, permitting the purchase of beer and wine more readily for meals. Another factor has been the increased consumption of alcoholic beverages considered to be nontraditional to a specific nation—*e.g.*, increased consumption of wine in traditionally beer- and spirits-drinking countries or vice versa. This increased consumption has followed a pattern in some countries of new nontraditional beverage consumption in addition to the continued consumption of traditional alcoholic beverages. In some other countries with high levels of total alcohol consumption, such as France, Italy, Portugal, and Spain, there has been a substitution pattern: substantial increases in per capita beer consumption have involved concom-

Apparent Consumption of Distilled Spirits, Wine, and Beer*
(in litres per capita of drinking-age population†)

	year	spirits		wine		beer		total
		beverage	absolute alcohol	beverage	absolute alcohol	beverage	absolute alcohol	absolute alcohol
France	1968	7.96	3.97	146.72	15.40	78.26‡	3.25	22.62
Italy	1969	4.23§	2.12	152.51	12.20	14.95	0.67	14.99
Austria	1970	7.14	2.86	54.27	5.70	130.52	5.87	14.43
West Germany	1970	10.21§	3.88	16.00	1.60	182.00	8.01	13.49
Portugal	1970	1.52	0.68	95.78	11.97	17.59	0.79	13.44
Switzerland	1966–69	6.18	2.47	51.90	5.45	111.25‡	5.00	12.98
Spain	1971	7.20§‖	3.24‖	75.15	9.39	4.93	0.22	12.85
Australia	1969	2.55	1.45	11.50	1.96	168.79	8.44	11.85
Hungary	1969	5.95§	2.98	48.73	5.36	68.61	2.75	11.09
Belgium	1967	2.52	1.26	11.89	1.66	159.23‡	7.96	10.88
New Zealand	1967	2.91§	1.66	5.46	0.93	163.25	8.16	10.75
Czechoslovakia	1969	7.29	2.92	17.51	2.20	179.17	5.38	10.50
U.S.	1971	9.92	4.47	7.87	1.25	98.03	4.43	10.15
Denmark	1969	3.40	1.70	6.66	1.00	132.66	5.97	8.67
Canada	1969	7.14§	2.86	4.82	0.77	95.47	4.77	8.40
U.K.	1970	2.14	1.22	4.91	0.83	114.70	5.16	7.21
Sweden	1970	8.40	3.30	8.10	1.00	65.80	2.90	7.20
Ireland	1970	3.71	2.11	4.81	0.51	98.71	4.44	7.06
The Netherlands	1969	5.19	2.59	6.79	1.16	70.90	3.19	6.94
Poland	1970	8.69§	4.35	7.61	1.06	42.66	1.19	6.60
Japan	1968	4.17§	1.32	19.32§¶	3.08	31.13	1.40	5.80
Finland	1969	5.38	2.42	4.97	0.70	60.09	2.64	5.76
Norway	1970	4.83	2.07	3.10	0.44	48.70	2.22	4.73
Iceland	1971	8.52	3.41	2.86	0.41	16.00♀	0.56♀	4.38
Israel	1970	3.44	1.72	5.23	0.63	15.80	0.80	3.15

*The alcohol content of beverages varies among countries. Calculations for this table are based on the best available information from each country. Only countries from which adequate recent statistics on both alcohol and population are available have been included. †Population aged 15 years and over. ‡Includes cider. §These values converted from original reports in different terms. ‖Based on 1970 data. ¶Includes sake. ♀ Estimated from 1966 and 1968 data.
Source: V. Efron, M. Keller, and C. Gurioli, *Selected Statistics on Consumption of Alcohol and on Alcoholism* (1972).

itant declines or stabilizations in wine consumption per capita. While the substitution pattern was exhibited primarily in countries with traditionally high levels of total alcohol consumption, the first pattern of new nontraditional beverage consumption was the more prevalent and was experienced by nations with more moderate levels of alcohol consumption. The countries of Scandinavia, the British Isles, North America, and Oceania, traditionally beer- and spirits-drinking societies, sustained substantial increases in per capita wine consumption but experienced fairly stable or slightly increasing consumption of traditional beverages. In North America, particularly in the United States, the introduction of low-calorie beer and wine in the early 1970s was instrumental in the increased per capita consumption of alcohol in the late 20th century.

During the late 20th century the leading countries in total alcohol consumed per capita were France, Portugal, Spain, Italy, West Germany, and Austria. Except for West Germany, these same countries were also the leading per capita consumers of wine. West Germany and Ireland emerged as the leading consumers of beer per capita, along with the more traditionally heavy beer-drinking countries of Australia, New Zealand, Belgium, and the United Kingdom. The United States, Canada, France, Belgium, and The Netherlands were the leading per capita consumers of distilled spirits.

Drinking in France and Italy

Kinds and customs. In both France and Italy, wine consumption is high, but attitudes as well as patterns and amounts differ in the two countries in many ways. French parents tend to exhibit strong attitudes, either favourable or negative, to their children's drinking; Italian parents typically introduce their children to wine drinking without any emotional overtones. Italian standards of safe limits for drinking are lower than those of the French, and the Italians typically regard getting drunk with disdain, while the French look on it with good humour or even, in men, as a mark of virility; also, as already noted, the French are heavily given to the use of spirits. Although these generalized patterns are not consistent among the various regional populations and socioeconomic groupings of either country, they are thought to be significant in accounting for the much higher mortality and morbidity from alcoholism in France.

Among the Scandinavian countries (including Finland), the alcohol consumption pattern is not one of drinking daily or with meals but rather of telescoped drinking on weekends or special occasions; this is believed to account for the relatively high rate of alcohol-connected problems, such as intoxication, even in a country such as Finland, where the total alcohol consumption is relatively very low. The Scandinavian countries have also had strong anti-alcohol movements, often supported by government funds, and have had abstainer societies with large memberships. It is possible, therefore, that alcohol is consumed by a smaller number of drinkers than is represented by the drinking-age population; in Norway, for example, it is reported that more than 20 percent of men and nearly 40 percent of women are abstainers.

In England and Ireland, the pub has maintained its popularity as a main locus of drinking. In both countries, beer is by far the most popular beverage—in the United Kingdom accounting for more than three-fourths of the total alcohol consumed and in Ireland for two-thirds. The marked preference for beer is seen in other countries overwhelmingly settled and influenced by British populations—Australia, New Zealand, and much of Canada. In these countries, too, the pub tends to dominate the drinking style, apparently allowing an agreeable pattern of prolonged but not necessarily intimate socializing, while preserving the degree of independence that individual drinkers may prefer. Drinking to a moderate grade of intoxication appears to be acceptable and in some of these countries is thought to constitute the permissive societal attitude that partly underlies the development of alcoholism.

Drinking in eastern Europe

The drinking patterns of very few total populations in European countries have been subject to formal examination by social scientists. Studies have been focussed, for the most part, on segments of the population regarded as problem giving, such as alcoholics, traffic offenders, criminals, inmates of mental hospitals, or youths, especially students. Information from eastern European countries tends to be of the same order. There are indications that, in Poland, the shifting of a young population from rural-farm to new urban-industrial centres, with higher cash incomes and few outlets, has resulted in what the authorities regard as an increase in heavy drinking or alcoholism; vodka is the common drink. Somewhat similar reports emanate from Yugoslavia, where old village customs, while permissive of much drinking, nevertheless used to curb gross excesses. In the Soviet Union the growing program of establishing sobering-up stations and treatment clinics in many cities, often with research-oriented staffs, indicates a recognition that alcoholism is a serious problem. Vodka is the national drink, though native wines are increasingly being promoted. But the situation is evidently quite varied in different parts of the country. In the Soviet republic of Georgia, a viticultural region, wine is the favoured drink, and the drinking patterns are much more like the Italian than those of western Russia, with, apparently, a decidedly low rate of problems.

Much of the description of drinking patterns in South and Central America, as in Africa and Oceania, has consisted of anthropologists' observations of small, preliterate groups, with occasional notations on the effects of acculturation. Studies of national patterns do not exist, although, as in Europe, there are occasional reports on special, either local or problem-giving, populations. In Chile, a middle class population is described as similar to some European populations in drinking patterns—moderate consumption, drinking at home with meals, and frowning on drunkenness being typical. The much larger working class customarily drinks outside the home, in male company, on weekends or paydays, seeking intoxication that is valued as signalling both friendship and virility. A third population, identified as Indian, has a pattern such as that of the working class. The favoured drinks are pisco, a strong native brandy, and wine. Drinking accompanies all secular and religious fiestas, as well as the celebrations of births, baptisms, marriages, funerals; women, however, are expected to drink very moderately. Similar patterns have been reported from various areas in Bolivia and Peru.

In Japan, traditional drinking, still practiced in large circles, allowed heavy drinking and drunkenness in well-delimited social situations and was socially integrative. The traditional beverage was sake, often called rice wine but, more properly, a beer, brewed by highly skilled methods up to a strength of at least 14 percent alcohol and possibly up to 16 or 17 percent. A great many drinking customs and rituals involving sake were connected with religious and social occasions. Next to sake the common beverage was a distillate from sake mash, *shōchū,* containing about 25 percent alcohol. There are evidences of heavy drinking and alcoholism and various attempts to impose prohibition, as well as the practice of abstinence by the followers of Buddhism and of some revered Japanese philosophers. Modernization was accompanied in the last quarter of the 19th century by a temperance movement stimulated, in part, by the Woman's Christian Temperance Union and the Salvation Army. Since World War II, the widespread Americanization has included a growing popularity of beer and an increased use of imported beverages, especially whiskey, for which younger people express a preference. Among the young, the development of an ambivalence toward drinking, also characteristic of U.S. attitudes, has been reported.

Drinking in the United States

Drinking patterns and attitudes in the United States have been studied more systematically and completely than those of any other country. The results indicate that there is no pattern or set of attitudes typical of the nation as a whole; instead, there is a variety of patterns, customs, and attitudes. U.S. drinking patterns are a conglomerate of customs brought over by repeated waves of immigrants from different places and of diverse ethnic stocks, modified over time by intermixture, economic circumstances, political developments, and the emergence of some indigenous ways. Nevertheless, certain generalizations are possible. In the post-Prohibition and post-World War II era, several changes in U.S. drinking practices and attitudes have been observed and confirmed by formal systematic studies. The proportion of abstainers has declined, especially among women. In recent years, approximately 77 percent of adult men and 60 percent of adult women are drinkers. Men, however, as is almost the universal custom, drink substantially larger amounts, on average, than women. Among adolescents, about 57 percent of boys and 43 percent of girls are drinkers; these percentages rise with age, and the age class 21–29 contains the highest proportion of drinkers; drinking appears to be associated with separation from home and with courtship behaviour. As they continue to age, apparently many Americans become abstainers, perhaps settling down to living as they were brought up to do by their parents or as they would like to exemplify to their children. Rural populations, those with fewer years of education, lower income, more frequent religious attendance, and membership in fundamentalist Protestant denominations, contain larger proportions of abstainers. Among drinkers, beer tends to be the preferred drink of men and, to a lesser extent, of unskilled and blue-collar workers. Spirits are preferred by middle and upper class drinkers and by women—especially in the form of mixed drinks, such as cocktails. Repeal of Prohibition was advocated with the promise of no return of the saloon. Its successors, the bar, tavern, or cocktail lounge, are a ubiquitous U.S. institution. A good deal of drinking, however, takes place at home—though not, most commonly, with meals—and at parties, especially at the second indigenous U.S. drinking way, the cocktail party, now sometimes a substitute for the vanished frontier drinking style. The popularity of the cocktail party and, more specifically, the cocktail on coming home from work and before the evening meal has been attributed to its function as a separator between the working day and the relaxing evening—a sort of rite of passage, easing the way from one into the other. Whether or not this is the actual reason, the cocktail hour has become increasingly adopted in many countries, like other U.S. customs that are paradoxically sneered at while being assiduously imitated.

Although, in general, styles and customs of drinking are influenced by geographic and ethnic backgrounds, Americans tend to be members of multiple small societies, and, to some extent, they drink differently within each of these societies. People from diverse origins may drink alike when joined in some special association—as fellow collegians, members of a business convention, comrades in one of the armed services, or guests at a special kind of social function. Even then, the expected way and amount of drinking is likely to be at least modified by an individual's background. Even within a situation where drinking—indeed, drunkenness—is institutionalized (that is, on the skid rows), patterned differences are discernible to the systematic observer, giving rise to named classes, such as lushes, bums, winos, and rubby-dubs (habitual drinkers of non-beverage alcohols, such as rubbing alcohol and canned heat), and distinct consequences. The fact that most Americans drink, that drinking rather than abstinence is the norm, does not prevent the paradoxical existence of ambiguous attitudes about the behaviour among the drinkers themselves, many of whom express such views as that which maintains that alcohol, or drinking, is more harmful than beneficent, more wrong than right. These ambivalences account for the massive array of regulations on the sale and distribution of alcohol, most of them intended to interfere with the availability of beverages at certain times, in certain places, or to certain classes of persons.

Alcoholism

The conception of inveterate drunkenness as a disease appears to be rooted in antiquity. The Roman philosopher Seneca classified it as a form of insanity. The term alcoholism, however, appears first in the classical essay "Alcoholismus chronicus" (1849) by the Swedish physician Magnus Huss. The phrase chronic alcoholism rapidly became a medical term for the condition of habitual inebriety conceived as a disease; and the bearer of the disease was called an alcoholic or alcoholist (*e.g.,* Italian *alcoolisto,* French *alcoolique,* German *Alkoholiker,* Spanish *alcohólico,* Swedish *alkoholist*).

DEFINITIONS AND CAUSAL FACTORS OF ALCOHOLISM

Alcoholism consists of a repetitive intake of alcoholic beverages to an extent that causes repeated or continued harm to the drinker. The harm may be physical or mental; it may also be social or economic. Implicit in the conception of alcoholism as a disease is the idea that the person experiencing repeated or long-lasting injury from his drinking would alter his behaviour if he could. His failure to do so shows that he cannot help himself, that he has "lost control over drinking." This conception incorporates the idea of addiction or dependence.

Formal definitions of alcoholism vary according to the point of view of the definer. A simplistic old-fashioned medical definition calls alcoholism a disease caused by chronic excessive drinking. A purely pharmacological–physiological definition of alcoholism classifies it as a drug addiction recognizable by the need for increasing doses to produce desired effects and by the occurrence of a withdrawal syndrome when drinking is stopped. This definition is inadequate, since alcoholism does not resemble other addictions in the need for increased doses. Opium addicts become adapted to and require as much as hundreds of times the normal lethal dose, but the increased amounts to which alcoholics become adapted are well below the normal single lethal dose. Moreover, the withdrawal syndromes in alcoholism occur inconsistently, sometimes failing to appear in the same persons who experienced them previously and apparently never occurring in some persons who cannot be distinguished from confirmed alcoholics.

A comprehensive definition of alcoholism

Behavioral rather than pharmacological–physiological signs are much more consistent and reliable in defining and diagnosing alcoholism. A sophisticated definition representing modern conceptions of comprehensive medicine classifies alcoholism as a disease of unknown cause, without recognizable anatomical signs, manifested by addiction to or dependence on alcohol. A more comprehensive definition incorporating the perspectives of both psychological and physical medicine recognizes that alcoholism may be either a symptom of another underlying, possibly psychological, disorder or a disease itself: alcoholism, in this view, is a chronic and usually progressive disease or a symptom of an underlying psychological or physical disorder, characterized by dependence on alcohol (manifested by loss of control over drinking) for relief from psychological or physical distress or for gratification from alcohol intoxication itself, and characterized also by a consumption of alcoholic beverages sufficiently great and consistent to cause physical or mental or social or economic disability. Here, the conception of disease undoubtedly rests on the evidence of disablement.

The various definitions that rely on the symptom of loss of control over drinking often consider the loss of control to consist of an inability to stop drinking once it is started, implying that the alcoholic can choose not to take the first drink. But the more comprehensive definition sees the alcoholic as starting a drinking episode because he cannot refrain. Nor does the loss of control over drinking hold true all the time. As with symptoms in many diseases, the loss of control is active in most alcoholics only inconsistently. This means that an alcoholic is not always under internal pressure to drink and can sometimes resist drinking, or, if he drinks, he can sometimes drink in a controlled way. The inconsistency of the loss of control is, however, consistent with a definition of alcoholism based on learning psychology: alcoholism, in this definition, is a learned (or conditioned) dependence on (or addiction to) alcohol that irresistibly activates resort to drinking whenever a critical internal or environmental stimulus (or cue) presents itself. This definition leaves room for the conception that alcoholism may start as a symptom of an underlying disorder, which induces the learning of the alcoholismic pattern, and that once the pattern is fixed or conditioned it may become a disease in its own right (that is, an addiction), capable of surviving even the disappearance of the original underlying cause. Some theorists who regard alcoholism as primarily a symptom do not necessarily subscribe to the idea that it is learned, although they recognize that it may progress to the state of a primary disease.

Alcoholism is a multifarious phenomenon requiring more than one definition. Epidemiologists need a definition that will enable them to identify alcoholics within a population not available for individual examination. Such a definition may rely on a quantity-and-frequency measurement of drinking and also on behavioral features, including injurious effects measurable by instrumental indexes, such as a formula resting on the relation of alcoholism to diseases of known frequency among alcoholics or a drinking-history questionnaire or a preoccupation-with-alcohol scale. Sociological–behavioral definitions emphasize deviance from a norm, especially drinking that exceeds customary dietary use or diverges from the social customs of the drinker's community; such a definition may use as a criterion the way a drinker is regarded by those who know him; his arrests, hospitalizations, and clinical diagnoses; or his membership in a self-defining group, such as Alcoholics Anonymous. Legal definitions tend to rest on habitual intemperance that endangers others, injures the public welfare, or threatens the health, welfare, or competence of the person himself.

Causal factors

Many theories of the cause of alcoholism rest on the limited perspectives of specialists in particular disciplines or professions. Thus, alcoholism has been thought to be caused by defects of heredity, nutrition, disorders of endocrine function, latent homosexuality, economic misery or affluence, bad social influences, or sinful gluttony. More discerning definitions and descriptions take into account the complexity of alcoholism, acknowledging that its causes are not yet knowable with certainty. The most comprehensive conceptions recognize that alcoholism may have a genetic or constitutional underlying factor—not a fateful heredity but a predisposition that renders some people more vulnerable to alcoholism than others. Some think the genetic vulnerability is specific not to alcoholism but rather more generally to a neurosis or an affective disorder that may manifest itself as alcoholism; the alcoholism may possibly represent a "choice of symptom" and be for some individuals a useful "sickness." Others think the genetic factor may impose not vulnerability but, on the contrary, immunity to alcoholism, meaning that some people are unable to adapt to drinking on a level sufficient to gain the peculiar rewards that dispose a person to the development of an alcoholismic life pattern.

The comprehensive etiological view suspects that factors in infancy or early childhood, such as lack of parental care and love, overindulgence, or inconsistency in rearing practices, may lay the foundation of a vulnerable personality. On such a foundation, a dependent personality type or one marked by dependence–independence conflict may emerge; in adolescence this may manifest itself in an insecure self-sex image and a need to overcompensate—for example, by defiant exhibitionistic deviance. Such a problem-ridden personality may find exceptionally effective assuagement and reward in alcohol and learn to rely on intoxication as a mechanism for coping with problems. If this learning process is not interrupted and especially if the social surroundings respond encouragingly or permissively or ambivalently to heavy drinking and intoxication, then the vulnerable personality will become conditioned to react to difficulties by resort to intoxication. If the process lasts long enough, the outcome will be addiction to alcohol or a confirmed alcohol dependence. This comprehensive conception takes into account not only the possible genetic, pharmacological, psychological, and social factors but also the sociocultural context. It recognizes that the society defines and labels the phenomenon of alcoholism, that the culture contributes to its development or inhibition, and that behaviour that in one culture matches an adequate rational definition of alcoholism may not constitute alcoholism in another. Thus, periodic intoxication causing sickness for several days and necessitating absence from work may define alcoholism in a modern industrial community, but, in a rural Andean society, periodic drunkenness at appointed communal fiestas, resulting in sickness and suspension of work for several days, is normal behaviour. An essential aspect of the difference is that the drunkenness at fiestas is not individually deviant behaviour.

PREVALENCE OF ALCOHOLISM

Estimates of the prevalence of alcoholism vary greatly, depending on how it is defined as well as on the methods of estimation. In the United States in the late 20th century, according to one sophisticated estimate, there were approximately 5,400,000 alcoholics—about 4,500,000 men and 900,000 women. In percentage terms, 7.3 percent of men and 1.3 percent of women were alcoholics or 4.2 percent of adults aged 20 and over. There were large variations among regions and states, the rates being higher in urban and industrialized areas. There was no objective evidence that the rates of alcoholism had risen since World War II, although the absolute numbers had increased substantially with the growth of the adult population. A widespread impression that alcoholism was increasing among women apparently reflected the greater visibility of female alcoholics caused by changing public and professional attitudes; formerly, there had been more masking of alcoholism in women than in men.

Alcoholics and pre-alcoholics

A constant rate of alcoholism, without any increase in numbers except in proportion to the growth of population, requires an annual incidence of several hundred thousand new cases. The process of becoming an alcoholic usually takes several years. Since in many cases the process is not carried to completion, there must be a population of several million pre-alcoholics (for example, "heavy drinkers" or "heavy-escape" drinkers) from whom the several hundred thousand new cases of alcoholism emerge each year. On the basis of national surveys of U.S. drinking patterns of the last few decades, it is estimated that the size of the "pre-alcoholic" population is about 4,000,000; these, together with the 5,400,000 alcoholics, may be considered the total of problem drinkers. There are indications, however, that among the pre-alcoholics the sex differential is rather smaller than among the alcoholics, probably about four men to one woman. This implies that among women pre-alcoholics a smaller proportion cross the line to become full-fledged alcoholics.

The existence of over 5,000,000 alcoholics in the U.S., plus possibly 4,000,000 other problem drinkers, of whom perhaps between 5 and 10 percent become alcoholics each year, places alcoholism in the front rank of public-health problems. Its gravity is underlined by the higher rates of mortality (2.5 times normal) among alcoholics. Suicide rates are 2.5 times higher; accidental death rates are seven times higher; and there is an enormously higher rate of general morbidity among alcoholics. One study found that among patients in general hospitals, those identifiable as alcoholics range from 13 to 29 percent. Alcoholism-related psychoses account for about 15 percent of the male and roughly 3 to 4 percent of the female admissions to public and private psychiatric hospitals in the U.S. Admissions of alcoholics without psychosis—usually to participate in alcoholism-treatment programs—accounted for another 40 percent of the men and 13 percent of the women admitted to public mental hospitals and for 15 percent of the men and 4 percent of the women admitted to private mental hospitals. These statistics do not include pre-alcoholics and problem drinkers, although, from the viewpoint of preventive public health, they are those most in need of study and help.

Estimates for different countries

Variations in the definition of alcoholism make it difficult to compare U.S. rates with those of other countries. The most comparable statistics are those of Canada, where the rate of alcoholism is much lower than in the U.S., about 2.4 percent, and the ratio of incidence among the sexes is about five men to one woman, as in the U.S. A rate of 3.5 percent has been reported from Sweden and 1.1 percent from Finland, each with a ratio of five men to one woman, and 0.8 percent from Northern Ireland, with a ratio of three men to one woman; other rates include 5.4 percent in Chile and 0.41 percent in Italy, with no indications of sex ratios. In England and Wales different estimators have suggested rates varying from as low as 1.1 percent to as high as 8.8 and 11 percent; and in Switzerland the suggested rates have varied from 2.2 to 13 percent. The rate in France has been estimated at as high as 15 percent of the adult population, but more conservative estimates suggest 9.4 percent.

Although the rate in France is probably higher than in any of the other countries mentioned, the degree of validity that may be attached to these estimates is so uncertain that all comparisons must be considered as unreliable. There is a strong subjective element in statistics of alcoholism. From time to time, professional opinion becomes aroused, a cry of alarm is raised, and the assumption is made that alcoholism is increasing. High estimates are then likely to emerge, based on local and insufficiently refined data. Often, increased admissions to hospitals for alcoholic mental disorders and sometimes increased consumption of alcohol are cited in evidence. But these data invariably fail to take account of changes in availability or use of facilities, changes in admission or diagnostic policies, or changes in the source of beverages—for example, from unrecorded to recorded supplies. In the U.S.S.R. a change in the internal political situation with the death of Stalin resulted in a shift from official denial that any significant problem of alcoholism existed to an outcry that its prevalence was widespread and serious, though no statistics were provided.

TREATMENT OF ALCOHOLISM

The various treatments of alcoholism may be classified as physiological, psychological, and social. Many physiological treatments are given as adjuncts to psychological methods, but sometimes they are applied in "pure" form, without conscious psychotherapeutic intent or even with an effort to avoid it.

Drugs that prevent drinking

Physiological therapies. *Chemical fences.* One of the popular modern drug treatments of alcoholism, initiated in 1948 by Eric Jacobsen of Denmark, uses disulfiram (tetraethylthiuram disulfide). The usual technique is to administer half a gram in tablet form daily for a few days; then, under carefully controlled conditions and with medical supervision, the patient is given a small test drink of an alcoholic beverage. The presence of disulfiram in the drinker's body causes a reaction of hot flushing, nausea, vomiting, a sudden sharp drop of blood pressure, pounding of the heart, and even a feeling of impending death. These symptoms result from an accumulation of the highly toxic first product of alcohol metabolism—acetaldehyde. Normally, as alcohol is converted to acetaldehyde, the latter is rapidly converted, in turn, to other harmless metabolites, but in the presence of disulfiram —itself harmless—the metabolism of acetaldehyde is blocked, with the resulting toxic symptoms. The patient is thus dramatically shown the danger of attempting to drink while under disulfiram medication. A smaller daily dose of disulfiram is then prescribed, and the dread of the consequences of drinking acts as a "chemical fence" to prevent the patient from drinking as long as he continues taking the drug. Most therapists use the period of enforced abstinence to apply psychological and rehabilitative measures that should enable the patient ultimately to refrain from drinking without the chemical crutch. Variations of the technique include group-reaction tests and the substitution of motion pictures or verbal descriptions for the reaction test.

Citrated calcium cyanamide is another drug used with similar effect, preferred by some therapists because the reaction with alcohol is milder, though its protective potency is briefer. In Japan some therapists have reported giving very small doses of the cyanamide compound, thereby allowing the patient to drink very moderately without suffering a severe reaction but provoking the reaction if he attempts to drink immoderately. Other substances that can produce disagreeable reactions with alcohol include animal charcoal, the mushroom *Coprinus atramentarius,* numerous antidiabetic drugs, and the ground pine *Lycopodium selago,* but, except for the latter, which has had some trial in the Soviet Union, they have attracted little clinical interest.

Aversion. The U.S. psychiatrist W.L. Voegtlin developed a method of creating a conditioned reflex of aversion to alcohol by repeatedly giving the patient a precisely timed injection of an emetic drug just before a drink of his favorite beverage, resulting in nausea and vomiting before the alcohol could be absorbed. The consequent association of vomiting with drinking, causing aversion to the taste, smell, and sometimes even sight of alcoholic beverages, does not last indefinitely but may be reinforced periodically. Similar techniques have been tried in several European countries. Other methods of conditioning applied by behaviour therapists and learning psychologists include associating drinking with mild to painful electrical shocks or with temporary interruption of breathing by injection of a paralyzing drug.

Nutrition, hormones, drugs. A genetotrophic theory of disease holds that alcoholism is caused by a genetically determined need for extraordinary amounts of one or more vitamins. Accordingly, alcoholics have been treated with massive doses of multivitamins. Another theory holds that alcoholism is caused by some defect of the endocrine system, the adrenal-hypophyseal axis being most commonly implicated, and, accordingly, alcoholics have been treated by injections of adrenal steroids and adrenocorticotropic hormones. Other physical and drug therapies that have been tried in alcoholics include intravenous injections of alcohol, apomorphine, injections of autoserum and alcoholized serum, brain surgery, carbon-dioxide inhalation, oxygen by injection, nicotinic acid, nicotinamide-adenine dinucleotide, lysergide (LSD, lysergic acid diethylamide), strychnine, antihistaminic agents, and many tranquillizing and energizing drugs. None of these treatments has been shown in controlled studies to be more effective than others. With some treatments, controlled studies are extremely difficult to carry out. In many cases, moreover, the treatments are accompanied by simultaneous measures having potentially psychotherapeutic and socially rehabilitative effects, especially membership in Alcoholics Anonymous. It is possible that the treatment that works best is the one that is most suitable for the particular patient. But it is also possible that the most effective therapy is the one the therapist believes in, and this factor of subjectivity may account for the inferior results achieved when any of them is tested in controlled experiments. In the use of psychoactive drugs such as LSD, the aim often is not directly to affect the alcoholism but to produce changes in the patient's emotional state that will help him respond to other psychosocial measures.

Treatment of psychological factors

Other therapies. *Psychological therapies.* Psychotherapy in alcoholism encompasses the entire range of modalities applied in treating the psychoneuroses and character disorders, including individual and group techniques. The aim varies from eliminating some underlying cause to effecting just enough shift in the patient's emotional state so that he can function at least temporarily without drinking. Psychoanalysis is rarely tried, having shown little success in alcoholism; analytically oriented therapies are more usual, chiefly with supportive aims. The only psychological technique developed specifically for alcoholism consists of gaining the patient's recognition and acceptance of his actual condition, which alcoholics often resist. Such acceptance may then be followed by a therapeutic–rehabilitative regimen. Group therapies are regarded as more effective than individual modalities with alcoholics. These range from instructional lectures and superficial discussions to deep analytic explorations, psychodrama, hypnosis, psychodynamic confrontation, and marathon sessions. Mechanical aids include didactic motion pictures, movies of the patients while intoxicated, and taped records of previous sessions. Some therapists have experimented, as yet without definitive results, with milieus that reward and reinforce socializing behaviour, hoping thereby to extinguish the desocializing drinking behaviour. Many institutional programs rely on "total push," subjecting the patient to a bombardment of methods, including drugs, hypnosis, physiotherapies, group sessions, lectures, Alcoholics Anonymous meetings, and individual psychological and religious counselling, with the hope that each patient will be affected favourably by whatever is most suitable for him. Other institutional programs rely on mere removal from the stressful outside environment, with a period of enforced abstinence. The therapists themselves may be psychoanalysts, psychiatrists, clinical psychologists, pastoral counsellors, social workers, nurses, police or parole officers, or lay counsellors—the latter often former alcoholics with special training.

The places of treatment are as varied as the modalities, ranging from general hospitals to mental hospitals to mental-health outpatient clinics to specialized inpatient sanitariums and specialized alcoholism clinics to jails and penitentiaries to medical and psychiatric private offices, with patients often moving, randomly or systematically, from one milieu to another.

Awareness of the social and environmental elements in alcoholism has led to the development of treatment for spouses and occasionally for whole families, either separately or jointly, in the recognition that "the patient" is not just the alcoholic but the family unit.

A new trend in the United States, partly stimulated by court decisions prohibiting the jailing of alcoholics for public intoxication, is the establishment of detoxication centres that provide first aid along with guidance toward more fundamental treatment. But even if adequate programs and facilities for treating alcoholism were available, it is unlikely that they would solve the problem, given the large number of new cases each year. Only preventive public-health programs can eliminate alcoholism and thus far no likely methods of prevention have been devised.

The effectiveness of Alcoholics Anonymous

Alcoholics Anonymous. The patient-centred self-help fellowship of men and women called Alcoholics Anonymous enables its members to share their common experience and thus to help each other. AA was founded in 1935 by two alcoholics, one of whom had been strongly influenced by the Oxford Movement, and has grown to a worldwide community of hundreds of thousands. The members strive to follow Twelve Steps, a nonsectarian spiritual program the central points of which are reliance on God or a higher power as each individual understands that concept and the value of help to other alcoholics. The fellowship is organized in local groups of indeterminate size, has no dues, and accepts contributions for its expenses only from those attending meetings—where members narrate the stories of their alcoholic careers and their recovery in AA. Affiliation of the society or its groups with churches, politics, organizations, or institutions is barred by the AA Twelve Traditions. AA apparently meets deep-seated needs among its members by enabling them to associate with kindred sufferers who understand them, to accept the disease concept of alcoholism, to admit their powerlessness over alcohol and their need for help, to depend without shame or stigma on others, and to involve themselves in activities within the group and in helping other alcoholics. These seem to provide adequate substitutes for the alcoholismic way of life. AA is thought by many to be the single most successful method yet devised for coping with alcoholism. It has spawned some allied but independent organizations: Al-Anon, for spouses and other close relatives and friends of alcoholics, and Alateen, for their adolescent children, the aim of which is to help the members understand alcoholism, understand themselves better, and learn how to help an alcoholic or, at any event, how to live with one. Professionals in the field tend to think of AA as an inexpensive form of group therapy and a useful ally but recognize, as do the more sophisticated members, that it is not suitable for all types of alcoholics. Most experienced therapists agree that any form of treatment is likely to show a higher rate of success if the patient can be persuaded simultaneously to join Alcoholics Anonymous.

AA groups around the world resemble each other and generally use the ideological literature (including translations) published by the central office in New York, although there are some variations in style and conduct. In some countries the AA groups are sponsored by or affiliated with national temperance societies or accept financial support from government health agencies. There are also clubs for former alcoholics, usually sponsored by a particular institution for its former patients. One Scandinavian group seeks to achieve a stable degree of moderate drinking, rather than total abstinence.

Results of treatment. The success of treatment in behavioral or personality disorders is always difficult to appraise, and this is the case in alcoholism. The effects of new treatments tend to be reported enthusiastically, but critical examination of the results tends to reduce or cast doubt on the rate of apparent success. Controlled studies, when carried out, usually undercut the claims. Follow-up studies of persons treated have usually been too brief to determine whether permanent results had been achieved, and in most cases the investigators failed to locate a substantial proportion of the former patients. Moreover, the measures of "success" are inconsistent. Some investigators regard only total abstinence as a successful outcome; others are satisfied if drinking bouts are curtailed and the patient's life adjustment is improved. Perhaps between 25 and 50 percent of alcoholics who receive some form of treatment either become abstinent or achieve some abatement of the severity of their illness. Alcoholism treatment programs connected with businesses and industries, in which the alcoholic must participate if he wants to keep his job, have reported even higher success rates. Forms of frankly compulsory treatment, even if grudgingly endured by alcoholics, seem to have a high rate of effectiveness. Some investigators have suggested that the older the patient and the longer the duration of his alcoholism, the more frequent is the occurrence of "spontaneous" recovery.

Contemporary alcohol problems and controls

Useful versus detrimental uses of alcohol

Effects of drugs are commonly discussed in terms with negative inference—as if, with drugs, including alcohol, effect and detriment were necessarily synonymous. The personally functional and socially integrative uses of alcohol tend to be overlooked. Alcohol does indeed serve in prophylactic, nutritional, and medicinal roles. The vast majority of drinkers in most of the world are light, occasional, and moderate drinkers—normal drinkers who experience no harm from their own use of alcoholic beverages. Thus, relatively small minorities fall into the class of heavy or excessive or problem drinkers, including alcoholics. Nevertheless, the problem drinkers invoke sufficient troubles for themselves, their families, their employers, their occupational or social associates, and their communities and society generally so that "alcohol problems" are major causes of disorder and suffering, as well as costly focuses of study and responses.

INDIVIDUAL AND SOCIAL EFFECTS

First, in the realm of health, the most serious and detrimental effect is alcoholism. Although drinking itself is hardly ever regarded as the sufficient cause of alcoholism, this disease could not arise without the use of alcohol. Next come the alcoholic diseases—physical and mental disorders that are caused directly or indirectly by alcoholism or heavy drinking. Moreover, alcoholics and heavy drinkers are especially susceptible to the development of some other diseases, not specifically alcoholic, and are then less able to withstand the vicissitudes of ill health. Finally, alcoholics and problem drinkers undoubtedly contribute to the deterioration of the mental health of other members of their families and often to the breakdown of family life. This is seen in the enormously increased rates of divorce and separation in families in which one of the spouses is an alcoholic (four to 12 times higher than in comparable populations) and in the extraordinarily higher rate of alcoholism in the offspring of alcoholics (up to 10 times higher than in comparable samples). This last is now considered to be a social consequence rather than a result of genetic defect.

The social and economic costs of alcoholism and heavy drinking are essentially incalculable. An estimate of $2,000,000,000 as the cost of health and welfare services provided to alcoholics and their families in the United States alone suggests the measure of effects worldwide. Furthermore, the millions of problem drinkers who have jobs and businesses are more frequently absent and often less efficient than their occupational associates. In one study in a very large industry, identified alcoholics accumulated two and a half times as many days absent from work and collected nearly three times as much in sickness payments as matched samples of fellow employees. Crude projections of the annual costs of alcoholism to the national economy of the United States range from $7,000,000,000 to $10,000,000,000.

Crime and motor violations

The role of alcohol in crime has often been gauged by the presence of alcoholics in prisons and jails. It is necessary to discount the self-exculpatory blaming of "drink" by convicts as the cause of their crimes. Moreover, the high proportion of alcoholics among those convicted of serious crimes—estimates range from 22 to 43 percent—may misrepresent the role of alcoholism. It is possible that alcoholics, ineffective in other aspects of life, are also less efficient than nonalcoholic criminals in escaping detection and conviction; this may account for their high frequency in penal institutions. There is no question, however, that a great portion of the work of police departments and costs of local courts and jails is attributable to arrests, prosecutions, and brief incarcerations for public intoxication.

A special offense related to drinking is alcohol-impaired driving of motor vehicles and the resulting high rate of accidents, with fatalities, personal injuries, and property damage. Alcohol, for example, is involved in about one-third of the more than 50,000 annual road traffic fatalities in the United States, in possibly 500,000 injuries to persons, and in more than $1,000,000,000 worth of property damage. Although people with very low alcohol concentrations in their blood—the equivalent of one or two drinks—do not figure in accidents more often than those with no alcohol, the chances of being involved in a traffic accident rise precipitously with increasing blood alcohol concentrations beyond these minimal levels. Laws making specified blood alcohol concentrations prima facie evidence of being drunk, impaired, under the influence of alcohol, or unfit to drive have been passed in most jurisdictions. In some Scandinavian countries the limit is 0.05 percent; in most countries, 0.08 percent; in West Germany, 0.13 percent; in U.S. jurisdictions, from 0.08 to 0.15 percent. Attempts to curb driving while affected by alcohol have taken the form of severe punishments—heavy fines, mandatory jail sentences, and loss of driving licenses for periods ranging from six months to 10 years. Newer ways of coping with this problem are being sought with the consideration that, since drivers and pedestrians involved in accidents after drinking usually have very high blood alcohol concentrations, they are probably alcoholics and should be dealt with under some therapeutic rather than exclusively penal regimen.

ALCOHOL CONTROL

Governmental efforts to control alcoholic beverages go back as far as recorded history. The Code of Hammurabi included regulations of prices, taverns, and sellers. That the laws often failed to produce the desired effects—temperance and good public order and perhaps revenue exceeding the social costs of excess—is inferred from the frequent legislative attempts at total prohibition in numerous lands throughout history, all apparently without lasting success. The most resounding failure was that in the United States from 1920 to 1933. Current prohibitions in parts of India appear to be equally ineffective.

Types of governmental control

Less totalitarian efforts to control the use of alcohol include licensing systems that limit the number and locations of places of sale; restriction of days and hours of sale; prohibitions of sale to the young, with ages varying from 16 in Yugoslavia to 21 in parts of the United States; regulation of the strength of beverages, the size of containers, advertising, prices, or profits. Some governments—for instance, those of Finland and several states of the U.S.—have sought to eliminate the private-profit motive from the sale of alcoholic beverages by reserving a monopoly in the trade to themselves. All Communist countries have government monopolies. But indications that this has made any difference in the kinds, degree, or severity of problems are lacking; apparently problem drinkers do not need to be persuaded by profit seekers. Some governments—for instance, those of Sweden, Finland, and the U.S. state of Ohio—have attempted to control individual drinking by a system of personal ration books for purchases. In Sweden this system was abandoned after 38 years of trial; evidently, those who needed to drink a lot could find supplies—even when their ration books were withdrawn. The most universal regulation of alcoholic beverages takes the form of taxation (or, in government monopolies, an added profit), which is often quite heavy. Usually, however, though the taxing policy may have the ostensible purpose of reducing consumption or controlling licensees, the real object is revenue. In any event, none of the common forms of government control have proved themselves able to promote temperance in those whose need to drink heavily is uncontrollable. The persistence of massive restrictions and regulations, with costly enforcing bureaucracies, reflects the tendency of legislatures to give some satisfaction to the substantial minority of convinced opponents of alcohol and the tendency of segments of the drinking population—and even of some people in the liquor trade—to accept the naïve notions of the anti-alcoholists that these regulations do some good.

Control by temperance movements and religions

Though not significantly influenced by governmental efforts, the rate and severity of alcohol problems have indeed been influenced by nongovernmental movements and agencies. The most obvious example is the success of religious movements, such as Buddhism, Islām, and numerous Christian denominations and sects, in confirming their followers as total abstainers. The Methodist and Baptist denominations, the Quakers, the Mormons, the Christian Scientists, the Seventh-day Adventists, and the Jehovah's Witnesses are examples of Christian churches that have made abstinence a condition of loyal membership, though the Methodist Church has modified its stand in recent times. Other Christian denominations, such as the Congregationalists, have advocated abstinence without making it a requirement. Though not formally allied with these churches, the Woman's Christian Temperance Union (WCTU) and other temperance societies, particularly in the United States, once drew much support from them. In several European countries the abstinence movement also drew some support from the Socialist-influenced labour movement and found some organizational expression in the form of fraternal orders, particularly the Order of Good Templars. The importance of the religious orientation is indicated by the relatively larger proportion of abstainers in the United States than in countries where the ideal was more largely politically motivated. The decline in the numbers of abstainers in recent times may reflect the changing character of religious adherence.

THE NEW SCIENTIFIC ORIENTATION

In the past generation the character and influence of citizen movements have changed markedly. Whereas in former times the personnel, teaching aids, and ideologies of the temperance movement had generally dominated the research and education regarding alcohol, the tendency now is toward deriving objective information from academic and scientific sources. Among the major efforts to bring a scientific orientation to bear on the consideration of alcohol problems has been the founding of a systematic documentation and publication of the biological and social-science knowledge of the entire world; this is now a function of the Center of Alcohol Studies at Rutgers University in New Brunswick, New Jersey. The new trend had its repercussions also on international cooperation.

International concern

The International Bureau Against Alcoholism, founded in 1907, became, in 1964, the International Council on Alcohol and Alcoholism—more recently renamed the International Council on Alcohol and Addictions. The change of name represented a change in aims and policies, from total opposition to any drinking to advocacy of an objective consideration of alcohol problems. This change was manifested also in the character of the international congresses convened by anti-alcohol organizations since 1885 and by the International Bureau since 1925. Formerly devoted essentially to descriptions of the horrible effects and denunciations of the evils of alcohol, beginning with the 26th Congress in 1960 the program has been infiltrated by presentations from the scientific-academic world, and the 28th Congress in Washington, D.C., in 1968 was marked by the total absence of representation from the remnants of the old temperance movement; the papers and lectures offered by representatives of religious organizations and societies were on an equal level of scholarship and objectivity with those from the scientific and academic community.

These developments, in turn, have had repercussions in government activities. In the United States and Canada they have led to the establishment of some 55 state and provincial agencies, some independent, most attached to departments of health or mental health, with missions chiefly to provide treatment for alcoholics but often also to participate in education and occasionally to engage in research. A few county and city agencies have also been created. On the federal level in the United States, a National Institute on Alcohol Abuse and Alcoholism has been established, and the Department of Transportation is engaged in a program aimed to reduce the alcohol-and-traffic problem. Other governments have shown recognition of the potential of newer, science-oriented approaches and have supported research and education as well as therapeutic activities, sometimes through special institutions such as the Canadian Addiction Research Foundation, supported by the province of Ontario; the Finnish Foundation for Alcohol Studies; the Norwegian National Institute for Alcohol Research; and the Northern Committee for Alcohol Research, with membership from all the Scandinavian countries. The new ferment discernible in the late 20th century in the field of alcohol problems is thus far stimulated mainly by concern over the human and economic costs of existing problems and the aim to alleviate them. The idea that only the prevention of alcohol problems or that only the reduction of the numbers of persons who become newly involved in alcohol problems can effect permanent gains is universally given lip service but rarely is the object of direct effort. This is owing to two facts: those who have been chiefly involved in bringing about the new ferment have been inspired mainly by the humanitarian and economic motive to bring relief to those who are already suffering from the consequences of alcohol problems, and practical new methods of prevention, going beyond scattershot education, have yet to be invented.

(M.Ke.)

PSYCHOTROPIC DRUGS

Characteristics of drug use and abuse

THE FUNCTIONS OF PSYCHOTROPIC DRUGS

To consider drugs only as medicinal agents or to insist that drugs be confined to prescribed medical practice is to fail to understand man. The remarks of the American sociologist Bernard Barber are poignant in this regard:

> Not only can nearly anything be called a "drug," but things so called turn out to have an enormous variety of psychological and social functions—not only religious and therapeutic and "addictive," but political and aesthetic and ideological and aphrodisiac and so on. Indeed, this has been the case since the beginning of human society. It seems that always and everywhere drugs have been involved in just about every psychological and social function there is, just as they are involved in every physiological function.

The enhancement of aesthetic experience is regarded by many as a noble pursuit of human beings. Although there is no general agreement on either the nature or the substance of aesthetics, certain kinds of experience have been highly valued for their aesthetic quality. To Schopenhauer (*The World as Will and Representation*), contemplation was the one requisite of aesthetic experience; a kind of contemplation that enables one to become so absorbed in the quality of what is being presented to the senses that the "Will" becomes still and all needs of the body silent. Drugs reportedly foster this kind of Nirvana and are so used by many today. For Nietzsche (*Birth of Tragedy*), man is able to lose his futile individuality in the mystic ecstasy of universal life under the Dionysiac spell of music, rhythm, and dance. The American Indians with their peyote and modern jazz musicians with their marijuana have discovered this kind of Dionysian ecstasy without formal knowledge of aesthetics.

Anesthetic and hallucinogenic functions

Love is a highly valued human emotion. Thus, not surprisingly, there has been a great deal of preoccupation with the feeling of love and with those conditions believed to enhance the attainment of love. Little is known concerning the aphrodisiac action of certain foods and drugs, but both have been associated in people's minds with the increased capacity for love. Though the physiological effects may be doubtful, the ultimate effect in terms of one's feeling of love is probably a potent incentive for the repetition of the experience and for those conditions believed to have produced the experience. Hallucinogenic substances such as LSD are said by many to induce a feeling of lovingness. But what the drug user regards as love and what persons around him regard as love in terms of the customary visible signs and proofs often do not coincide. Even so, it is plausible that the dissipation of tensions, the blurring of the sense of competition, the subsidence of hostility and overt acts of aggression—all have their concomitant effect on the balance between the positive and negative forces within the individual, and, if nothing else, the ability of drugs to remove some of the hindrances to loving is valued by the user.

Native societies of the Western Hemisphere have utilized, apparently for thousands of years, plants containing hallucinogenic substances. The sacred mushrooms of Mexico were called "God's flesh" by the Aztecs. During the 19th century, the Mescalero Apaches of the southwestern United States practiced a peyote rite that was adopted by many of the Plains tribes. Psychedelic drugs have the unusual ability to evoke at least one kind of a mystical-religious experience, and positive change in religious feeling is a common finding in studies of the use of these drugs. Whether they are also capable of producing religious lives is an open question. Their supporters argue that the drugs appear to enhance personal security and that from self-trust may spring trust of others and that this may be the psychological soil for trust in God. In the words of Aldous Huxley (*The Doors of Perception*): "When, for whatever reason, men and women fail to transcend themselves by means of worship, good works and spiritual exercise, they are apt to resort to religion's chemical surrogates."

Stress-reducing and supportive functions

William James (*The Varieties of Religious Experience*) observed at the turn of the century that "Our normal waking consciousness, rational consciousness as we call it, is but one special type of consciousness, whilst all about it, parted from it by the filmiest of screens, there lie potential forms of consciousness entirely different." Some people deliberately seek this other consciousness through the use of drugs; others come upon them by accident while on drugs. Only certain people ever have such a consciousness-expanding (psychedelic) experience in its fullest meaning, and the question of its value to the individual must be entirely subjective. For many people, the search for the psychedelic experience is less a noble aim and more the simple need of a psychic jolt or lift. Human conduct is a paradox of sorts. Although people go to great lengths to produce order and stability in their lives, they also go to great lengths to disrupt their sense of equanimity, sometimes briefly, sometimes for extended periods of time. It has been asserted that there are moments in everyone's life when uncertainty and a lack of structure are a source of threat and discomfort, and moments when things are so structured and certain that unexpectedness can be a welcome relief. Whatever the reason, people everywhere and throughout history have deliberately disrupted their own consciousness, the functioning of their own ego. Alcohol is and has been a favourite tool for this purpose. With the rediscovery of some old drugs and the discovery of some new ones, people now have a wider variety of means for achieving this end.

Many persons face situations with which, for one reason or another, they cannot cope successfully, and in the pressure of which they cannot function effectively. Either the stresses are greater than usual or the individual's adaptive abilities are less than sufficient. In either instance, there are a variety of tranquillizing and energizing drugs that can provide psychological support. This is not chemotherapy in its more ideal sense, but it does enable large numbers of persons to face problems that they might not have otherwise been able to face. Some situations or stresses are beyond the control of the individual, and some individuals simply find themselves far more human and productive with drugs than without drugs. An enormous amount of drug support goes on by way of such familiar home remedies as the aspirin bottle, the luncheon cocktail, and the customary evening drink without anyone calling it that. There is no clear dividing line between drug support and drug therapy. It is all therapy of sorts, but deliberate drug manipulation is a cut different from drug buffering, and much of the psychological support function is just that—taking the "raw edge" off of stress and stabilizing responses.

Therapeutic functions

The therapeutic use of drugs is so obvious as to require little explanation. Many of the chemical agents that affect living protoplasm are not capable of acting on the brain, but some of those that do are important in medical therapeutics. Examples are alcohol, the general anesthetics, the analgesic (pain-killing) opiates, and the hypnotics, which produce sleep—all classified as central-nervous-system depressants. Certain other drugs, such as strychnine, nicotine, picrotoxin, caffeine, cocaine, and the amphetamines, stimulate the nervous system. Most drugs truly useful in the treatment of mental illness, however, were unknown to science until the middle of the 20th century. With the discovery of reserpine and chlorpromazine, some of the major forms of mental illness, especially the schizophrenias, became amenable to chemotherapeutic treatment. These tranquillizing drugs seem to reduce the incidence of certain kinds of behaviour, particularly hyperactivity and agitation. A second group of drugs has achieved popularity in the management of milder psychiatric conditions, particularly those in which patients manifest anxiety. This group includes drugs that have a mild calming or sedative effect and that are also useful in inducing sleep. Not all drugs in psychiatric use have a tranquillizing action. The management of depression requires a different pharmacological effect, and the drugs of choice have been described as being euphorizing, mood-elevating, or antidepressant, depending on their particularly pharmacological properties. There are also drugs useful in overactive states such as epilepsy and Parkinsonism. The so-called psychedelic drugs also may have therapeutic uses.

Drugs have other functions that are not so intimately related to individual use. Several important early studies in physiology were directed toward understanding the site and mode of action of some of these agents. Such studies have proved indispensable to the understanding of basic physiology, and drugs continue to be a powerful research tool of the physiologist. The ability of drugs to alter mental processes and behaviour affords the scientist the unique opportunity to manipulate mental states or behaviour in a controlled fashion. The use of LSD to investigate psychosis and the use of scopolamine to study the retention of learning are examples. The use of drugs as potential instruments of chemical and biological warfare has received wide public attention and scorn, yet it has been studied and pursued by many nations and powers. The political use of drugs is a frightening possibility. Whether as a "truth serum," a "brainwashing" technique, a way of destroying certain stable elements of culture, or a way of reducing entire societies to a tranquil slavery, this aspect of drug use should be viewed with alarm because all such uses are obviously possible.

THE NATURE OF DRUG ADDICTION AND DEPENDENCE

If opium were the only drug of abuse, and the only kind of abuse were one of habitual, compulsive use, discussion of addiction might be a simple matter. But opium is not the only drug of abuse, and there are probably as many kinds of abuse as there are drugs to abuse, or, indeed, as maybe there are persons who abuse. Various substances are used in so many different ways by so many different people for so many different purposes that no one view or one definition could possibly embrace all the medical, psychiatric, psychological, sociological, cultural, economic, religious, ethical, and legal considerations that have an important bearing on addiction. Prejudice and ignorance have led to the labelling of all use of nonsanctioned drugs as addiction and of all drugs, when misused, as narcotics. The continued practice of treating addiction as a single entity is dictated by custom and law, not by the facts of addiction.

Confusion of drug abuse and narcotic addiction

The tradition of equating drug abuse with narcotic addiction originally had some basis in fact. Until recent times, questions of addiction centred on the misuse of opiates, the various concoctions prepared from powdered opium. Then various alkaloids of opium, such as morphine and heroin, were isolated and introduced into use. Being the more active principles of opium, their addictions were simply more severe. More recently, new drugs such as methadone and Demerol were synthesized but their effects were still sufficiently similar to those of opium and its derivatives to be included in the older concept of addiction. With the introduction of various barbiturates in the form of sedatives and sleeping pills, the homogeneity of addictions began to break down. Then came various tranquillizers, stimulants, new and old hallucinogens, and the various combinations of each. At this point, the unitary consideration of addiction became untenable. Legal attempts at control often forced the inclusion of some nonaddicting drugs into old, established categories—such as the practice of calling marijuana a narcotic. Problems also arose in attempting to broaden addiction to include habituation and, finally, drug dependence. Unitary conceptions cannot embrace the diverse and heterogeneous drugs currently in use.

Popular misconceptions. The bewilderment that the public manifests whenever a serious attempt is made to differentiate states of addiction or degrees of abuse probably stems from two all-too-common misconceptions concerning drug addiction. The first involves the stereotype that a drug user is a socially unacceptable criminal. The carry-over of this conception from olden times is easy to understand but not very easy to accept today. Ironically, the so-called dope fiend, if indeed one does exist, is likely to be a person who is not using an opiate. The depressant action of opium and its derivatives is simply not consistent with the stereotype. The second misconception involves the naïve belief that there is something magically druglike about a drug, which makes a drug a drug. Many substances are capable of acting on a biological system, and whether a particular substance comes to be considered a drug depends, in large measure, upon whether it is capable of eliciting a "druglike" effect that is valued by the user. There is nothing intrinsic to the substances themselves that sets one active substance apart from other active substances; its attribute as a drug is imparted to it by use. Caffeine, nicotine, and alcohol are clearly drugs, and the habitual, excessive use of coffee, tobacco, or an alcoholic drink is clearly drug dependence if not addiction. The same could be extended to cover tea, chocolates, or powdered sugar, if society wished to use and consider them that way. The task of defining addiction, then, is the task of being able to distinguish between opium and powdered sugar while at the same time being able to embrace the fact that both can be subject to abuse. This requires a frame of reference that recognizes that almost any substance can be considered a drug, that almost any drug is capable of abuse, that one kind of abuse may differ appreciably from another kind of abuse, and that the effect valued by the user will differ from one individual to the next for a particular drug, or from one drug to the next drug for a particular individual. This kind of reference would still leave unanswered various questions of availability, public sanction, and other considerations that lead people to value and abuse one kind of effect rather than another at a particular moment in history, but it does at least acknowledge that drug addiction is not a unitary condition.

Physiological effects of addiction. Certain physiological effects are so closely associated with the heavy use of opium and its derivatives that they have come to be considered characteristic of addictions in general. Some understanding of these physiological effects is necessary in order to appreciate the difficulties that are encountered in trying to include all drugs under a unitary definition that takes as its model opium.

Characteristics of the development of tolerance

Tolerance is a physiological phenomenon that requires the individual to use more and more of the drug in repeated efforts to achieve the same effect. At a cellular level this is characterized by a diminishing response to a foreign substance (drug) as a result of adaptation. Although opiates are the prototype, a wide variety of drugs elicit the phenomenon of tolerance, and drugs vary greatly in their ability to develop tolerance. Opium derivatives rapidly produce a high level of tolerance; alcohol and the barbiturates a very low level of tolerance. Tolerance is characteristic for morphine and heroin and, consequently, is considered a cardinal characteristic of narcotic addiction. In the first stage of tolerance, the duration of the effects shrinks, requiring the individual to take the drug either more often or in greater amounts to achieve the effect desired. This stage is soon followed by a loss of effects, both desired and undesired. Each new level quickly reduces effects until the individual arrives at a very high level of drug with a correspondingly high level of tolerance. Man can become almost completely tolerant to 5,000 milligrams of morphine per day, even though a "normal," clinically effective dosage for the relief of pain would fall in the 5 to 20 milligram range. An addict can achieve a daily level that is nearly 200 times the dose that would be dangerous for a normal, pain-free adult.

Physical dependence

Tolerance for a drug may be completely independent of the drug's ability to produce *physical dependence.* There is no wholly acceptable explanation for physical dependence. It is thought to be associated with central-nervous-system depressants, although the distinction between depressants and stimulants is not as clear as it was once thought to be. Physical dependence manifests itself by the signs and symptoms of abstinence when the drug is withdrawn. All levels of the central nervous system appear to be involved, but a classic feature of physical dependence is the "abstinence" or "withdrawal" syndrome. If the addict is abruptly deprived of a drug upon which the body has physical dependence, there will ensue a set of reactions, the intensity of which will depend on the amount and length of time that the drug has been used. If the addiction is to morphine or heroin, the reaction will begin within a few hours of the last dose and will reach its peak in one to two days. Initially, there is yawning, tears, a running nose, and perspiration. The addict lapses into a restless, fitful sleep and, upon awakening, experiences a contraction of pupils, gooseflesh, hot and cold flashes, severe leg pains, generalized body aches and constant movement. The addict then experiences severe insomnia, nausea, vomiting, and diarrhea. At this time he has a fever, mild high blood pressure, loss of appetite, dehydration, and a considerable loss of body weight. These symptoms continue through the third day and then decline over the period of the next week. There are variations in the withdrawal reaction for other drugs; in the case of the barbiturates, minor tranquillizers, and alcohol, withdrawal may be more dangerous and severe. During withdrawal, drug tolerance is lost rapidly. The withdrawal syndrome may be terminated at any time by an appropriate dose of the addicting drug.

Distinctions between addiction and habituation

Addiction, habituation, and dependence. The traditional distinction between "addiction" and "habituation" centres on the ability of a drug to produce tolerance and physical dependence. The opiates clearly possess the potential to massively challenge the body's resources, and, if so challenged, the body will make the corresponding biochemical, physiological, and psychological readjustment to the stress. At this point, the cellular response has so altered itself as to require the continued presence of the foreign substance (drug) to maintain normal function. When the substance is abruptly withdrawn or blocked, the cellular response becomes abnormal for a time until a new readjustment is made. The key to this kind of conception is the massive challenge that requires radical adaptation. Some drugs challenge easily, but it is not so much whether a drug can challenge easily as it is whether the drug was actually taken in such a way as to present the challenge. Drugs such as caffeine, nicotine, bromide, the salicylates, cocaine, amphetamine and other stimulants, certain tranquillizers and sedatives are normally not taken in sufficient amounts to present the challenge. They typically but not necessarily induce a strong need or craving emotionally or psychologically without producing the physical dependence that is associated with "hard" addiction. Consequently, their propensity for potential danger is judged to be less, so that continued use would lead one to expect habituation but not addiction. The key word here is *expect*. These drugs, in fact, are used excessively on occasion and, when so used, do produce tolerance and withdrawal signs. Morphine, heroin, other synthetic opiates, and to a lesser extent codeine, alcohol, and the barbiturates, all carry a high propensity for potential danger in that all are easily capable of presenting a bodily challenge. Consequently, they are judged to be addicting under *continued* use. The ultimate effect of a particular drug, in any event, depends as much or more on the setting, the expectation of the user, his personality, and the social forces that play upon him, as it does on the pharmacological properties of the drug itself.

Enormous difficulties have been encountered in trying to apply these definitions of *addiction* and *habituation* because of the wide variations in the pattern of use. (The one common denominator in drug use is variability.) As a result, in 1964 the World Health Organization recommended a new standard that replaces both the term drug addiction and the term drug habituation with the term drug dependence. Drug dependence is defined as a state arising from the repeated administration of a drug on a periodic or continual basis. Its characteristics will vary with the agent involved, and this must be made clear by designating drug dependence as being of a particular type—that is, drug dependence of morphine type, of cannabis type, of barbiturate type, and so forth. As an example, drug dependence of a cannabis (marijuana) type is described as a state involving repeated administration, either periodic or continual. Its characteristics include (1) a desire or need for repetition of the drug for its subjective effects and the feeling of enhancement of one's capabilities that it effects, (2) little or no tendency to increase the dose since there is little or no tolerance development, (3) a psychic dependence on the effects of the drug related to subjective and individual appreciation of those effects, and (4) absence of physical dependence so that there is no definite and characteristic abstinence syndrome when the drug is discontinued.

Drug dependence

Considerations of tolerance and physical dependence are not prominent in this new definition, although they are still conspicuously present. Instead, the emphasis tends to be shifted in the direction of the psychological or psychiatric makeup of the individual and the pattern of use of the individual and his subculture. Several considerations are involved here. There is the concept of psychological reliance in terms of both a sense of well-being and a permanent or semipermanent pattern of behaviour. There is also the concept of gratification by chemical means that has been substituted for other means of gratification. In brief, the drug has been substituted for adaptive behaviour. Terms such as hunger, need, craving, emotional dependence, habituation or psychological dependence tend to connote a reliance on a drug as a substitute gratification in the place of adaptive behaviour.

Psychological dependence. Several explanations have been advanced to account for the psychological dependence on drugs, but as there is no one entity called addiction, so there is no one picture of the drug user. The great majority of addicts display "defects" in personality. Several legitimate motives of man can be fulfilled by the use of drugs. There is the relief of anxiety, the seeking of elation, the avoidance of depression, and the relief of pain. For these purposes, the several potent drugs are equivalent, but they do differ in the complications that ensue. Should the user develop physical dependence, euphoric effects become difficult to attain, and the continued use of the drug is apt to be aimed primarily at preventing withdrawal symptoms.

Predispositions to drug use

It has been suggested that drug use can represent a primitive search for euphoria, an expression of prohibited infantile cravings, or the release of hostility and of contempt; the measure of self-destruction that follows can constitute punishment and the act of expiation. This type of psychodynamic explanation assumes that the individual is predisposed to this type of psychological adjustment prior to any actual experience with drugs. It has also been suggested that the type of drug used will be strongly influenced by the individual's characteristic way of relating to the world. The detached type of person might be expected to choose the "hard" narcotics to facilitate indifference and withdrawal from the world. Passive and ambivalent types might be expected to select sedatives to assure a serene dependency. Passive types of persons who value independence might be expected to enlarge their world without social involvement through the use of hallucinogenic drugs, whereas the dependent type of person who is geared to activity might seek stimulants. Various types of persons might experiment with drugs simply in order to play along with the group that uses drugs; such group identification may be joined with youthful rebellion against society as a whole. Obviously, the above descriptions are highly speculative because of the paucity of controlled clinical studies. The quest of the addict may be the quest to feel full, sexually satisfied, without aggressive strivings, and free of pain and anxiety. Utopia would be to feel normal, and this is about the best that the narcotic addict can achieve by way of drugs.

Although many societies associate addiction with criminality, most civilized countries regard addiction as a medical problem to be dealt with in appropriate therapeutic ways. Furthermore, narcotics fulfill several socially useful functions in those countries that do not prohibit or necessarily censure the possession of narcotics. An old League of Nations report said: "The social and hygienic conditions under which a great part of the working classes in the Far East live are of so low a standard that these classes of people strive to find some form of diversion permitting them to forget at least for some moments the hardships of life." In addition to relieving mental or physical pain, opiates have been used medicinally in tropical countries where large segments of the population suffer from dysentery and fever.

HISTORY OF DRUG CONTROL

The first major national efforts to control the distribution of narcotic and other dangerous drugs were the efforts of the Chinese in the 19th century. Commerce in poppy (opium) and coca leaf (cocaine) developed on an organized basis during the 1700s. The Manchus of China attempted to discourage opium importation and use, but the English East India Company, which maintained an official monopoly over British trade in China, was engaged in the profitable export of opium from India to China. This monopoly of the China trade was eventually abolished in 1839–42, and friction increased between the British and the Chinese over the importation of opium. Foreign merchants, including those from France and the United States, were bringing in ever-increasing quantities of opium. Finally, the Manchu government required all foreign merchants to surrender their stocks of opium for destruction. The British objected, and the Opium War (1839–42) between the Chinese and the British followed. The Chinese lost and were forced into a series of treaties with England and other countries that took advantage of the British victory. In 1858 the importation of opium into China was legalized by the Treaty of Tientsin, which fixed a tariff rate for opium importation. Further difficulties followed. An illegal opium trade carried on by smugglers in south China encouraged gangsterism and piracy, and the activity eventually became linked with powerful secret societies in the south of China.

Chinese opium traffic

International controls. Throughout the 1800s, the Chinese government considered opium an important moral and economic question, but obviously China needed international help. In 1909, U.S. President Theodore Roosevelt proposed an international investigation of the opium problem; a meeting of 13 nations held in Shanghai in the same year resulted in recommendations that formed the basis of the first opium convention held at The Hague in 1912. Ratification of the Hague Convention occurred during the meetings of 1913 and 1914. Although further regulatory activity was suspended during the course of World War I, ratification of the Versailles peace treaties of 1919–20 also constituted a ratification of the Hague Convention of 1912. The League of Nations was then given respon-

League of Nations and United Nations efforts

sibility to supervise agreements with regard to the traffic in opium and other dangerous drugs. A further important development in drug control was the convention of 1925, which placed further restrictions on the production and manufacture of narcotics. Six more international conventions and agreements were concluded between 1912 and 1936.

Under a Protocol on Narcotic Drugs of December 1946 the functions of the League of Nations and of the Office International d'Hygiène Publique were transferred to the United Nations and to the World Health Organization. In 1948 a protocol extended the control system to synthetic and natural drugs outside the scope of the earlier conventions. In 1953 a further protocol was adopted to limit and regulate the cultivation of the poppy plant and the production of, or international and wholesale trade in, and use of opium. Before the protocol became operative in 1963 the international control organs found a need for codifying and strengthening the existing treaties, and a Single Convention on Narcotic Drugs was drawn up in New York in 1961. This Convention drew into one comprehensive control regime all the earlier agreements, limited the use of coca leaves and cannabis to medical and scientific needs, and paved the way for the International Narcotics Control Board. The Convention came into force in 1964, and the new board began duty in 1968.

National controls. The United States is perhaps the nation most preoccupied with drug control, and it is largely the "Americanized" countries that have made narcotics regulation a matter of public policy with the consequent network of laws, criminal detection agencies, and derived social effects. The principal U.S. legislation has been the Harrison Narcotics Act of 1914, the Opium Poppy Control Act of 1942, and the Narcotic Drug Control Act of 1956; the Drug Abuse Control Amendment of 1965 added controls over depressant, stimulant, and hallucinogenic drugs not covered under the other narcotic control acts. Manufacturers and distributors are required to register with the U.S. Food and Drug Administration, retail dealers are required to keep inventories, and physicians are required to limit the period of prescription and the number of refills permitted. Heroin manufacture was prohibited in the United States in 1924, and by 1956 all heroin legally held in the United States was surrendered to the government. The *legal* use of heroin is practically nonexistent today anywhere in the world—largely because of the action of the League of Nations.

Great Britain controls the manufacture, distribution, and sale of narcotics through the Dangerous Drug Act of 1920. The British system, however, is based on a public policy position different from that of the United States, and narcotic addiction has remained a minor social problem. In 1967, England placed the prescription of narcotics under the control of the National Health Service and its associated clinics. Canada and Japan attempt to control narcotics in much the same manner as the United States with much the same consequence in terms of high rates of addiction. Opium traffic appears to still flourish in Asia, but the East has offically gone through a period of regulation, governmental monopoly over cultivation, and finally prohibition of use.

Problems in measuring distribution and use

Extent of contemporary drug abuse. Complete and reliable data on the extent of drug abuse in recent years is simply not available. To specify the size and extent of the drug problem, accurate information as to manufacture, distribution, and sale of drugs would be needed. Complete evaluation would also require knowledge of the incidence of habituation and addiction in the general population, the number of persons admitted to hospitals because of drug intoxication, and the number of arrests for drug sales that do not conform to the law. This kind of determination is not possible under existing laws even for the legitimate sources of drugs. Unfortunately, much of the drug traffic is from uncontrolled, illicit sources, and here there is an almost total absence of reliable information. Black market diversion of drugs may occur at any point from the manufacture of basic chemicals used to synthesize the drugs, through the process of actually preparing the drug, to the distribution of the final drug form, to the retail drugstore, or even the physician. This is a complex chain involving chemical brokers, exporters, and dealers in addition to those who have more direct involvement with the drug process. Finally, there is the problem of currentness. Time is involved in reporting at each level of information, and the final data may be no more recent than three to five years, and a basic source or reference work may contain figures that have suffered a decade of delay from the actual occurrence of the drug abuse. Drug abuse patterns change over a relatively short time. In the 1960s, the youthful drug abuser tended to use a drug that increased the level of consciousness. In contrast, it had been only a short time earlier that youthful drug abuse involved only the hypnotics and alcohol, which depress consciousness and blunt experience.

The U.S. Federal Bureau of Narcotics maintains a register of so-called active addicts who in the early 1970s numbered approximately 60,000 persons; the actual number of narcotic addicts in the United States was probably closer to 120,000 persons. With the exception of Germany, other European countries have relatively small numbers of narcotic addicts. In the Middle and Far East, the highest rates are found in Egypt, India, and Iran, with lesser rates for Borneo, Burma, China, Japan, and Korea. Opium cultivation has been declining in each of the last several years and is found chiefly in Asia. India, the U.S.S.R., and Turkey accounted for almost the total output of opium as reported to the United Nations. Bolivia and Peru are the chief producers of coca leaf (for cocaine).

The extent of problems involving other drugs can only be guessed from certain superficial indicators. It is probable that about half the production of amphetamines is diverted into illegal channels. Barbiturates are the leading mode of suicide in the U.S., accounting for over several thousand deaths each year.

The varieties of psychotropic drugs

OPIUM, MORPHINE, HEROIN, AND RELATED SYNTHETICS

Types of opiates and related synthetics

The opiates are unrivalled in their ability to relieve pain. Opium is the dried milky exudate obtained from the unripe seed pods of the poppy plant (*Papaver somniferum*), which grows naturally throughout most of Asia Minor. Of the 20 or more alkaloids found in opium, only a few are pharmacologically active. The important constituents of opium are morphine (10 percent), papaverine (1 percent), codeine (0.5 percent), and thebaine (0.2 percent). (Papaverine is pharmacologically distinct from the narcotic agents and is essentially devoid of effects on the central nervous system.) In 1803 a young German apothecary's assistant named Sertürner isolated crystalline morphine as the active analgesic principle of opium. Codeine is considerably less potent ($^1/_6$) and is obtained from morphine. Diacetylmorphine—or heroin—was developed from morphine by the Bayer Company of Germany in 1898 and is five to 10 times as potent as morphine itself. Opiates are not medically ideal. Tolerance is developed quite rapidly and completely in the more important members of the group, morphine and heroin, and they are highly addictive. In addition, they produce respiratory depression and frequently cause nausea and emesis. As a result, there has been a constant search for synthetic substitutes: meperidine (Demerol), first synthesized in Germany in 1939, is a significant addition to the group of analgesics, being one-tenth as potent as morphine; alphaprodine (Nisentil) is one-fifth as potent as morphine but is rapid-acting; methadone, synthesized in Germany during World War II, is comparable to morphine in potency; levorphanol (Levo-Dromoran) is an important synthetic with five times the potency of morphine. These synthetics exhibit a more favourable tolerance factor than the more potent of the opiates, but they fall short of an ideal analgesic in being addictive. Of this entire series, codeine has the least addiction potential and heroin has the greatest (see also DRUGS AND DRUG ACTION: *Narcotic*).

History. The narcotic and sleep-producing qualities of the poppy have been known to humankind throughout recorded history. Sumerian records from the time of Mesopotamia (5000 to 4000 BC) refer to the poppy, and medicinal reference to opium is contained in Assyrian medical tablets. Homer's writings indicate Greek usage of the substance at least by 900 BC; Hippocrates (*c.* 400 BC) made extensive use of medicinal herbs including opium. The Romans probably learned of opium during their conquest of the eastern Mediterranean; Galen (AD 130–200) was an enthusiastic advocate of the virtues of opium, and his books became the supreme authority on the subject for hundreds of years. The art of medicinals was preserved by the Islāmic civilization following the decline of the Roman Empire; opium was introduced by the Arabs to Persia, China, and India. Paracelsus (1493–1541), professor at the University of Basel, introduced laudanum, the modern tincture of opium. Le Mort, a professor of chemistry at the University of Leyden (1702–18), discovered paregoric, useful for the control of diarrhea, by combining camphor with tincture of opium.

19th-century medical uses of opiates

There is no adequate comprehensive history of the addictive aspects of opium use in spite of the fact that it has been known since antiquity. Because there were few alternative therapeutics or painkillers until the 19th century, opium was somewhat of a medical panacea. Thus, although at least one account in 1701, by a London physician named Jones, spoke of an excessive use of opium, there appears to have been no real history of concern until recent times, and opiates were easily available in the West in the 19th century, for instance, in a variety of patent medicines. Physicians prescribed them freely, they were easy to obtain without prescription, and they were used by all social classes. At one time, the extensive use of these medicines for various gynecological difficulties probably accounted for the high addiction rate among women (three times the rate among men). Today, in the United States, only one addict out of six is a woman. The invention of the hypodermic needle in the mid-19th century, and its subsequent use to administer opiates during wartime produced large numbers of addicted soldiers (about 400,000 during the U.S. Civil War alone); it was thought mistakenly that if opiates were administered by vein, no hunger or addiction would develop, since the narcotic did not reach the stomach. Toward the end of the 19th century, various "undesirables" such as gamblers and prostitutes began to be associated with the use of opiates, and narcotics became identified more with the so-called criminal element than with medical therapy. By the turn of the 20th century, narcotic use had become a worldwide problem, and various national and international regulatory bodies sought to control traffic in opium from the Near and Far East.

20th-century patterns of use

In the 20th century, until recently, narcotic use was largely associated with metropolitan slums, principally among poor and culturally deprived. Currently, narcotic use has begun to spread to middle class youth, and, interestingly, there is evidence that the middle class is now beginning to look at narcotic addiction as a mental health problem. When it was confined to the slums, it was considered a police problem.

Physiological effects. The various opiates and related synthetics all produce about the same physiological effects. All are qualitatively similar to morphine in action and differ from each other mainly in degree. The most long-lasting and conspicuous physiological responses are obtained from the central nervous system and the smooth muscle of the gastrointestinal tract. These effects, while restricted, are complex and vary with the dosage and the route of administration (intravenous, subcutaneous, oral). Both depressant and stimulant effects are elicited. The depressant action involves the cerebral cortex, with a consequent narcosis, general depression, and reduction in pain perception; it also involves the hypothalamus and brain stem, inducing sedation, the medulla, with associated effects on respiration, the cough reflex, and the vomiting centre (late effect). The stimulant action involves the spinal cord and its reflexes, the vomiting centre (early effect), the tenth cranial nerve with a consequent slowing of the heart, and the third cranial nerve resulting in pupil constriction. Associated effects of these various actions include nausea, vomiting, constipation, itchiness of the facial region, yawning, sweating, flushing of skin, a warm sensation in the stomach, fall in body temperature, diminished respiration, and heaviness in the limbs.

Opiates as analgesics and depressants

The most outstanding effect of the opiates is one of analgesia. All types of pain perception are affected, but the best analgesic response is obtained in relieving dull pain. The analgesic effects increase with increasing doses until a limit is reached beyond which no further improvement is obtained. This point may fall just short of complete relief.

Depression of cortical function results in a euphoric response involving a reduction of fear and apprehension, a lessening of inhibitions, an expansion of ego, and an elevation of mood that combine to enhance the general sense of well-being. Occasionally in pain-free individuals, the opposite effect, dysphoria, occurs and there is anxiety, fear, and some depression. In addition to analgesia and associated euphoria, there is drowsiness, mental and physical impairment, a clouding of consciousness, poor concentration and attention, reduced hunger or sex drives, and sometimes apathy.

Apart from their addiction liability, respiratory depression leading to respiratory failure and death is the chief hazard of these drugs. All of the more potent opiates and synthetics produce rapid tolerance, and tolerance to one member of this group always is associated with tolerance to the other members of the group (cross-tolerance). The more potent members of the group have a very great addiction liability with the associated physical dependence and abstinence syndrome.

Types of users. There is no single narcotic addict personality type: addiction is not a unitary phenomenon occurring in a single type. The great variation in addiction rates and classes of addicts in various countries caution against placing too great an emphasis on personality variables as major causative factors. Even within the United States, there is great danger in generalizing from the cases of the patients found at the public health service hospitals in Lexington, Kentucky, and in Fort Worth, Texas. These inmates are a highly select group of adults who have spent previous time in correctional institutions. They are not representative of the adolescent addict or the adult addict who has not had continual difficulty with the law. The United States has recently experienced a new type of slum-dwelling addict who is a member of a closely knit adolescent gang. This subculture is highly tolerant of drug abuse, and the members have ready access to narcotic drugs. They do not actively seek the opportunity to try heroin; neither are they deliberately "hooked" on heroin by adult drug peddlers. They are initiated to narcotic use by friends, gang members, or neighbourhood acquaintances, and the opportunity for such use is almost always casual but ever present. This "kicks" user is apt to abandon narcotics when gang membership is abandoned. The chronic user is more likely to be the immature adolescent at the periphery of gang activities who uses narcotics for their adjustive value in terms of his deep-seated personality problems. He does not abandon drug use for the more conventional pursuits when he enters adulthood. Instead, old ties are severed; interest in previous friendships is withdrawn; athletic and scholastic strivings are abandoned; competitive, sexual, and aggressive behaviour becomes markedly reduced, and he retreats further into his drug-induced state. Identification is now with the addict group: a special culture with a special language. The addict's world revolves around obtaining drugs.

Emotional and physical feelings of heroin use

Means of administration and their effects. Most persistent users follow a classic progression from sniffing (similar to the oral route), to "skin popping" (subcutaneous route), to "mainlining" (intravenous route)—each step bringing more intense experience, a higher addiction liability. With mainlining, the initial "thrill" is more immediate. Within seconds, a warm, glowing sensation spreads over the body, most intense in the stomach and intestines, comparable to sexual release. This intense "rush" is then followed by a deep sense of relaxation and contentment. The user is "high" and momentarily free. It is this initial state of intense pleasure that presumably brings the novice to repeat the experience, and it is this mode of administration that hastens him on the way to drug tolerance and physical dependence. Soon he finds that the effects are not quite there. Instead, his body is beginning to experience new miseries. At this juncture, he "shoots" to avoid discomfort. The euphoria is gone. He now spends every waking moment in obtaining further supplies to prevent the inevitable withdrawal symptoms should he fail. Habits are expensive. If indigent, the addict must spend all his time "hustling" for drugs—which means that he must steal or raise money by other means such as prostitution, procuring, or small-time narcotics peddling. An addict is judged by his success in supporting his habit. The addict always faces the danger of withdrawal, the danger of arrest, the danger of loss of available supply, the danger of infection, of collapsed veins, or of death from overdosage. Very few individuals are still addicted by the age of 40. They have either died, somehow freed themselves from their addiction, or sought treatment.

Therapy. Drug dependence can be viewed as an ethical problem: Is it right and permissible to need a narcotic agent? How one answers this question dictates the position one will take in regard to addiction therapy. In general, the addict can be given his drug, he can be placed on a substitute drug, or drugs can be barred from him. Narcotic maintenance, which gives the addict his drug, is the system employed in the management of opiate dependence in England. Methadone treatment is a drug substitution therapy that replaces opiate addiction with methadone addiction in order that the addict might become a socially useful citizen. Some drug therapy groups involve an intensive program of family-like resocialization, with total abstinence as the goal. Psychological approaches to total abstinence through reeducation involve psychotherapy, hypnosis, and various conditioning techniques that attempt to attach unpleasant or aversive associations to the thoughts and actions accompanying drug use. Each of these approaches has had successes and has limitations.

Narcotic maintenance

Great Britain began to control the use of narcotics in 1950 but, unlike the United States, has embraced the principle of drug maintenance. Supporters of the approach have insisted that, at least until recently, narcotic addiction in Great Britain remained a very minor problem because addiction is considered an illness rather than a crime. (In recent years, however, addiction has apparently become more widespread, for uncertain reasons.) The British physician was earlier allowed to prescribe maintenance doses of a narcotic if, in his professional judgment, the addict was unable to lead a useful life without the drug. But in 1967 the British government took the right to prescribe for maintenance addiction away from the general practitioner and placed it in the hands of drug-treatment clinics. Although some addicts must obtain legal supplies from the clinic, others are allowed to obtain supplies from a neighbourhood pharmacy and medicate themselves. These clinics also provide social and re-educative services such as psychotherapy for the addict. The general experience among these clinics has been that a large proportion of the addicts are becoming productive, socially useful members of the community.

There are two major drawbacks to the maintenance use of narcotic drugs such as employed by the British. Both the physical and the social health of the user remains unsatisfactory. A high incidence of hepatitis, bacterial endocarditis, abcesses, and, on occasion, fatal overdosage accompanies the self-administration of opiates. Socially, the addict on self-administration also tends to remain less productive than his peers—the reason apparently being that the individual on narcotic maintenance is still very preoccupied with certain aspects of narcotic use. Narcotic addiction is a two-faceted problem: the yearning for the "high" and the felt sense of not being physiologically normal. The addict on narcotic maintenance often attempts to obtain or retain both drug effects: frequent intravenous use prevents the feeling of drug hunger and maximizes his attempt to experience euphoria.

Methadone therapy

Methadone therapy aims to block the abnormal reactions associated with narcotic addiction while permitting the addict to live a normal, useful life as a fully participating member of the community. Methadone provides a "narcotic blockade" in that it is possible to increase methadone medication to a point at which large oral doses will induce a state of cross-tolerance in which the euphoric effects of other narcotics cannot be felt even in very high doses. Additionally methadone has the ability to allay the feeling of not being right physically, which the addict finds he can correct only by repeated narcotic use. Methadone treatment, then, rests on these two pharmacological actions: the blockade of euphoric effects and the relief of "narcotic hunger." Methadone is not successful in every case (10–15 percent failure), but results, to date, have been dramatic. In various studies conducted on addicts who entered a methadone treatment program, most remained in the program, and virtually none returned to daily use of heroin. The majority either accepted employment or started school, and previous patterns of antisocial behaviour were either eliminated or significantly reduced. Methadone is a drug of addiction in its own right, but it does not have some of the more serious undesirable consequences associated with heroin.

There are various types of drug counseling units that advocate complete abstinence from drug dependency. Such drug therapy, usually involving a group of addicts, tries to promote personal growth and teach self-reliance. Individual counseling and psychotherapy may or may not be provided for the members of the group, but generally it is believed that moral support is derived from the experiences of fellow addicts and former addicts who have or are trying to become chemically independent. Success rates for various drug therapy groups vary widely.

In such countries as the United States, where the addict is treated as a criminal, physicians are prevented from administering opiates for the maintenance of addiction. Acceptable treatment includes enforced institutionalization for about four months, strict regulation against ambulatory care until the person is drug free, and the total prohibition of self-administration of drugs even under a physician's care. Estimates of cures based upon decades of these government-regulated procedures range from 1 to 15 percent.

HALLUCINOGENIC DRUGS

Problems of terminology and definition in hallucinogens

It is difficult to find a suitable generic name for a class of drugs having as many diverse effects as have been reported for "hallucinogens." Abnormal behaviour as profound as the swings in mood, disturbances in thinking, perceptual distortions, delusions, and feelings of strangeness that sometimes occur with these drugs is usually indicative of a major mental disorder; consequently these substances are often called psychotomimetic to indicate that their effects mimic the symptoms of a naturally occurring psychosis. There are indeed points of similarity between the drug states and the natural psychoses, but there are also many dissimilarities—so many as to make the resemblance quite superficial. Such substances as the bromides, heavy metals, belladonna alkaloids, and intoxicants can, however, cause abnormal behaviour to a degree sometimes described as psychotic, and if the list is extended to include the drugs being discussed here, then the objection—that the term psychotomimetic should refer only to the mimicking of a natural psychosis—is no longer valid. Taking this point of view, some investigators prefer the term psychotogenic ("psychosis causing"). One of the most conspicuous features of this kind of drug experience is the occurrence of the distinctive change in perception called hallucination. For this reason the term hallucinogenic is sometimes used. Most people are aware, however, even while under the influence of the drug, that their unusual perceptions have no basis in reality; so this is not a very accurate use of the term. Strictly speaking, very few people truly hallucinate as a result of taking a hallucinogen.

All these terms are borrowed from medicine and are closely identified with pathology. In this sense, all are negative. It has been suggested that these drugs be called psychedelic ("mind manifesting"). This term shifts the emphasis to that aspect of the drug experience that involves an increased awareness of one's surroundings and also of one's own bodily processes—in brief, an expansion of consciousness. The term also shifts emphasis from the medical or therapeutic aspect to the educational or mystical-religious aspect of drug experience. Only certain people, however, ever have a psychedelic experience in its fullest meaning, and the question of its value to the individual is entirely subjective. The possibility of dangerous consequences, too, may be masked by such a benign term. None of these terms, then, is entirely satisfactory, and one or two are distinctly misleading. (These terms are used interchangeably henceforth with no particular intent other than to indicate membership in the LSD-type family of drugs.)

LSD, mescaline, and psilocybin

Types of hallucinogens. The psychoactive substances that have aroused widespread interest and bitter controversy are the LSD-type drugs that produce marked aberrations of behaviour. The most important of these are (1) d-lysergic acid diethylamide, commonly known as LSD-25, which originally was derived from ergot (*Claviceps purpurea*), a fungus on rye and wheat; (2) mescaline, the active principle of the peyote cactus (*Lophophora williamsii*), which grows in the southwestern United States and Mexico; and (3) psilocybin and psilocin, which come from Mexican mushrooms (notably *Psilocybe mexicana* and *Stropharia cubensis*). Bufotenine, originally isolated from the skin of toads, is the alleged hallucinogenic agent contained in banana peels. It has also been isolated in the plant *Piptadenia peregrina,* the mushroom *Amanita muscaria,* and is thought to be the active principle of the hallucinogenic snuff called cohoba and yopo and used by the Indians of Trinidad and by the Otamac Indians of the Orinoco Valley. Harmine is an alkaloid found in the seed coats of a plant (*Peganum harmala*) of the Mediterranean region and the Near East and also in a South American vine (*Banisteriopsis caapi*). There are some amides of lysergic acid contained in the seeds of the morning glory (*Rivea corymbosa*), which the Aztecs call *ololiuqui.* Synthetic compounds of interest are DMT (dimethyltryptamine) and STP (dimethoxyphenylethylamine; DOM). Cannabis (discussed separately below) is not usually included in this group of hallucinogenic drugs, but there is no particular justification for its exclusion. It is a resin obtained from the leaves and tops of the hemp plant (*Cannabis sativa;* see also DRUGS AND DRUG ACTION: *Hallucinogen*).

During the late 1970s phencyclidine (PCP), or "angel dust," emerged as a leading street hallucinogen. Developed in 1956 as an anesthetic, PCP was discontinued for human use because of its severe and unpredictable side effects, the psychological effects sometimes persisting for as long as a month. PCP, in liquid or crystal form, can be injected, inhaled, or ingested; most commonly it is sprinkled on marijuana or tobacco and smoked.

History. Native societies of the Western Hemisphere have for 2,000 years utilized various naturally occurring materials such as the "sacred" mushroom of Mexico and the peyote cactus of the southwestern United States. Scientific interest in the hallucinogenic drugs developed slowly. A neurologist wrote about his experience with peyote before the turn of the 20th century, and his account attracted the serious attention of two distinguished psychologists, Havelock Ellis and William James. Mescaline was isolated as the active principle of peyote in 1896, and its structural resemblance to the adrenal hormone epinephrine was recognized by 1919. There followed some interest in model psychoses (that is, drug-induced simulations of abnormal behaviour patterns), but it was not until 1943, when a Swiss chemist accidentally ingested a synthetic preparation of lysergic acid diethylamide and experienced its psychedelic effects, that the search for a natural substance responsible for schizophrenia became widespread. An American mycologist called attention to the powers of the Mexican mushroom in 1953, and the active principle was quickly found to be psilocybin.

Physiological and psychological effects. The psychedelics are capable of producing a wide range of subjective and objective effects; however, there is apparently no reaction that is distinctive for a particular drug. Subjects are unable to distinguish among LSD, mescaline, and psilocybin when they have no prior knowledge of the identity of the drug ingested. These drugs induce a physiological response that is consistent with the type of effect expected of a central-nervous-system stimulant. Usually there is elevation of the systolic blood pressure, dilatation of the pupils, some facilitation of the spinal reflexes, and excitation of the sympathetic nervous system and the brain.

There is considerable difference in the potency of these drugs. A grown man requires about 500 milligrams of mescaline or 20 milligrams of psilocybin or only 0.1 milligram of LSD for full clinical effects when the substances are ingested orally. The active principle in the seeds of the morning glory is about one-tenth as potent as LSD. There are also differences in the time of onset and the duration of effects. Psilocybin acts within 20 to 30 minutes, and the effects last about five to six hours. LSD acts within 30 to 60 minutes, and the effects usually last for eight to 10 hours, although occasionally some effects persist for several days. Mescaline requires two to three hours for onset, but the effects last for more than 12 hours. All psychedelics presumably are lethal if taken in large enough quantities, but the effective dose is so low as compared to the lethal dose that death has not been a factor in experimental studies. Physiological tolerance for these drugs develops quite rapidly in man—fastest for LSD, somewhat more slowly and less completely for psilocybin and mescaline. The effects for a particular dose level of LSD are lost within three days of repeated administration, but the original sensitivity is quickly regained if several days are allowed to intervene. Cross-tolerance has been demonstrated for LSD, mescaline, psilocybin, and certain of the lysergic acid derivatives. Tolerance to one of the drugs reduces the effectiveness of an equivalent dose of a second drug, thus suggesting a common mode of action for the group.

Subjective experiences under the influence of hallucinogens

Most persons regard the experience with one of these drugs as something totally removed from anything they have ever encountered in normal, everyday experience. The subjective effects vary greatly among individuals and, for a particular person, even from one drug session to the next. The variations seem to reflect such factors as the mood and personality of the subject, the setting in which the drug is administered, the user's expectation of a certain kind of experience, the meaning for the individual of the act of taking the drug, and his interpretation of the motives of the person who is administering the drug to him. Nevertheless, certain invariant reactions seem to stand out. The one most easily described by users is the effect of being "flooded" with visual experience, as much when the eyes are closed as when they are open. Light is greatly intensified; colours are vivid and seem to glow; images are numerous and persistent, yielding a wide range of illusions and hallucinations; details are sharp; perception of space is enhanced; and music may evoke visual impressions, or light may give the impression of sounds. A second important aspect, which people have more difficulty in describing, involves a change in the feelings and the awareness of the self. The sense of personal identity is altered. There may be a fusion of subject and object; legs may seem to shrink or become extended, and the body to float; space may become boundless and the passage of time very slow; and the person may feel completely empty inside, or he may believe that he is the universe. This type of reaction has been called depersonalization, detachment, or dissociation. Increased suspiciousness of the intentions and motives of others may also become a factor. At times the mood shifts. Descriptions of rapture, ecstasy, and an enhanced sense of beauty are readily elicited; but there can also be a "hellish" terror, gloom, and the feeling of complete isolation. For some people the experience is so disturbing that psychiatric hospitalization is required. Studies of performance on standardized tests show some reduction in reasoning and memory, but the motivation of the subject probably accounts for much of the performance decrement, since many people are uncooperative in this type of structured setting while under the influence of a drug.

Interest in these drugs was routinely scientific for the first few years following the discovery of LSD, but in the 1950s some professional groups began to explore the use of the psychedelics as adjuncts to psychotherapy and also for certain purposes of creativity. It was at this juncture, when the drugs were employed to "change" people, that they became a centre of controversy. LSD is not an approved drug in most countries; consequently its therapeutic applications can only be regarded as experimental. In the 1960s, LSD was proposed as an aid in the treatment of neurosis with special interest in cases recalcitrant to the more conventional psychotherapeutic procedures. LSD also was being given serious trial in the treatment of alcoholism, particularly in Canada, where experimentation is not heavily restricted. LSD has also been employed to reduce the suffering of terminally ill cancer patients. The drug was also under study as an adjunct in the treatment of narcotic addiction, of autistic children, and of the so-called psychopathic personality; and the use of various hallucinogens continue to be advocated in the experimental study of abnormal behaviour because of the degree of control that they offer.

Undesirable or dangerous effects

LSD can be dangerous when used improperly. Swings of mood, time and space distortion, "hallucinations," and impulsive behaviour are complications especially hazardous to the individual when he is alone. Driving while under the influence of one of these drugs is particularly dangerous. Acts of aggression are rare but do occur. The recorded suicide rate was not high in the various investigational (legal use) groups, but the rate of serious untoward psychological effects requiring psychiatric attention climbed steadily. These drugs do induce psychotic reactions that may last several months or longer. Negative reactions, sometimes called bad trips, are most apt to occur in unstable persons or in other persons taking very large amounts of a drug or taking it under strange conditions or in unfamiliar settings. So far as is known, these drugs are nontoxic, and there are no permanent physical effects associated with their use. There is no physical dependence or withdrawal symptom associated with long-term use, but certain individuals may become psychologically dependent on the drug, become deeply preoccupied with its use, and radically change their life-style with continued use.

A new dimension was added to the LSD controversy when laboratory studies began to appear in the scientific literature that linked LSD to chromosomal and genetic damage, thus intimating that future generations of the LSD user might be subject to the fearful issue of malformation and genetic illness. Unfortunately, there remains only the poorest understanding of exactly what has been found, to date, in such studies. The findings are neither clear nor conclusive, and moreover they involve not only LSD but also several classes of drugs in rather common use, such as aspirin, caffeine, tranquillizers, and antibiotics. The LSD chromosome story, then, is the story not just of LSD-induced changes but also of possible chromosomal and genetic damage that might be induced by wide classes of drugs in general use. If the gene pool of the LSD user is in jeopardy, as these studies suggest, then, the gene pool of the whole population is also in jeopardy, as these studies also suggest. The danger of drugs is the excessive reliance on drugs; the culprit is everywhere present.

The several types of research upon which these chromosomal and genetic findings are based are wrought with difficulties. Genetic studies that attempt to produce structural malformation use, of necessity, the experimental animal; and there is thus the basic problem of evaluating the extent to which these findings can be generalized to the human. The conditions of the experiments in general do not sufficiently parallel the conditions of natural LSD use to render the data very meaningful. The chromosomal studies present equal difficulties—trying to infer from the behaviour of a cell in the test tube how a mass of cells that are part of a living organism will act.

Proselytization among LSD users

Types of users. Prior to the mid-1960s, LSD-type drugs were taken by several different types of persons including many who were respected, successful, and well-established socially. Intellectuals, educators, medical and mental health professionals, volunteer research subjects, psychiatric patients, theological students, and participants in special drug-centre communities were some of the first users of these hallucinogenic substances. Beginning in 1966, experimentation in most countries was severely restricted, and subsequent use has been almost entirely of a black market type. LSD use is markedly on the decline, being replaced by cannabis and the amphetamines. Currently, most users tend to be of the middle class—either young, college-educated persons or those who have drifted to the fringe of society. Drug initiation is typically by way of a personal friend or acquaintance. Employers or teachers also have a powerful influence over subordinates and students in terms of drug acceptance. The user of LSD seems often to have an almost fanatic need to proselytize others to drug use. Those who have taken a hallucinogenic substance generally have had experience with other drugs prior to the LSD experience, and there is also a tendency on the part of those who take these drugs to repeat the drug experience and to experiment with other drugs. The special language, method of proselytizing, and psychological dependence surrounding the use of psychedelics bear striking resemblance to the context of narcotics addiction. The chronic LSD user tends to be introverted and passive. Motives for LSD use are many: psychological insight; expansion of consciousness; the desire to become more loving, more creative, open, religious; a desire for new experience, profound personality change, and simple "kicks."

BARBITURATES, STIMULANTS, AND TRANQUILLIZERS

There are many sanctioned uses for drugs that exert an effect on the central nervous system. Consequently, there are several classes of nonnarcotic drugs that have come into extensive use as sleeping aids, sedatives, hypnotics, energizers, mood elevators, stimulants, and tranquillizers.

Sedatives and hypnotics differ from general anesthetics only in degree. All are capable of producing central-nervous-system depression, loss of consciousness, and death (see also DRUGS AND DRUG ACTION: *Sedative-Hypnotic Drugs*).

The barbiturates, bromides, chloral hydrate, and paraldehyde are well-known drugs—with the barbiturates being of greatest interest because of the increasing number of middle and upper class individuals who have come to rely on them for immediate relaxation, mild euphoria, and an improved sense of well-being. But alcohol has been and continues to be the drug of choice for these same effects (see also DRUGS AND DRUG ACTION: *Sedative-Hypnotic Drugs*).

Of the drugs that excite the nervous system, nicotine, caffeine, the amphetamines, and the potentially addicting cocaine are well known. The use of stimulants to facilitate attention, sustain wakefulness, and mask fatigue has made the amphetamines an increasingly popular drug by students and those who engage in mental work. Originally the drug of truck drivers, amphetamine is now a common cause of arrest among teenagers and young adults who commit drug offenses. Cocaine has always been a potentially dangerous drug, and it has become especially popular among the middle and upper classes. Stimulants do not create energy, and the energy mobilized by these drugs is eventually depleted with serious consequences (see also DRUGS AND DRUG ACTION: *Stimulant*).

The tranquillizers are a heterogeneous group, as are the behaviours that they are employed to alter. In general, tranquillizing drugs reduce hyperactivity, agitation, and anxiety, which tend to cause a loss of behavioral control. Tranquillizing drugs do not characteristically produce general anesthesia, no matter what the dose; this attribute tends to distinguish tranquillizing drugs from the barbiturates (see also DRUGS AND DRUG ACTION: *Tranquillizers*).

Dangers of barbiturates, stimulants, and tranquillizers

All the barbiturates, stimulants, and tranquillizers are widely prescribed by physicians, and all these drugs are available through nonmedical (illegal) sources. Most of these drugs are classified as "habit-forming." The minor tranquillizers are commonly associated with habituation and may induce physical dependence and severe withdrawal symptoms. The amphetamines and cocaine intoxicate at high dosages, and both are capable of inducing serious toxic and psychotic reactions under heavy use. The barbiturates are the leading cause of death by suicide. They are judged to be a danger to health by both the World Health Organization Expert Committee and the United Nations Commission on Narcotic Drugs, which have recommended strict control on their production, distribution, and use. The nonnarcotic drugs in widespread use among middle and upper class citizenry manifest considerable untoward consequences for the individual and for society when abused—thus placing their problem in a different perspective than that normally associated with the opiates, LSD, and marijuana.

Barbiturates. The barbiturates relieve tension and anxiety at low dose levels without causing drowsiness, although some tendency toward drowsiness may be an initial reaction for the first few days on the drug. These drugs exert a selective action in small amounts on higher cortical (brain) centres, particularly those centres that are involved in the inhibitory or restraining mechanisms of behaviour. As a consequence, there is an increase in uninhibitedness such as talkativeness and unrestricted social interaction following the taking of the drug. There is also an impairment of function at low dose levels. All the barbiturates are capable of inducing sleep when given in sufficient amounts. They do not affect the perception of pain as do the analgesics, but they do alter the individual's response to pain (*e.g.,* decreasing his anxiety) and are useful in this regard. Infrequently, the barbiturates produce undesirable reactions ranging from simple nervousness, anxiety, nausea, and diarrhea to mental confusion, euphoria, and delirium. Some tolerance is developed to these drugs, but no physical dependence occurs in the drug range (100 to 200 milligrams) normally employed clinically. Prolonged use may lead to drug habituation and psychic dependence. When the drug is used chronically in higher amounts (400 milligrams per day), physical dependence may develop. Sudden withdrawal of a barbiturate following chronic use is frequently associated with withdrawal symptoms that are more severe than those produced by the opiates. A barbiturate should never be withdrawn abruptly following long continued use. The barbiturate addict shows many of the symptoms associated with chronic alcoholism, including blackouts, irrationality, slurred speech, poor motor coordination, emotional deterioration, mood swings, and psychosis.

Cocaine. Cocaine is an alkaloid derived from the leaves of the coca plant (*Erythroxylon coca*), a bush that is natural to Bolivia, Chile, and Peru along the western slopes of the Andes Mountains. Cocaine has a pronounced excitant action on the central nervous system and, in small doses, produces a pleasurable state of well-being associated with relief from fatigue, increased mental alertness, physical strength, and a reduction of hunger. In greater amounts, cocaine is an intoxicant that produces excitement, mental confusion, and convulsions. The Incas were acquainted with the ability of cocaine to produce euphoria, hyperexcitability, and hallucinations; the practice of chewing the coca leaf as part of religious ceremonials was an established custom at the time of the Spanish conquest in the 16th century. The natives who now work the mines high in the Andes chew coca leaves for increased strength and endurance. Coca plants are under cultivation in Sri Lanka (formerly Ceylon), India, and Java. The alkaloid, tropacocaine, is chemically related to cocaine and is obtained from the Java coca plant.

Mild excitation or intoxication

Cocaine is habit forming and may also be physically addicting in some individuals, but not to the extent of the opiates. Only certain persons display abstinence symptoms on withdrawal. Significant physiological tolerance does not develop. Chronic use is associated with severe personality disturbances, inability to sleep, loss of appetite, emaciation, an increased tendency to violence, and antisocial acts. When a toxic psychosis develops, it is characteristically accompanied by paranoid delusions. Hallucinations are prominent with continued use of cocaine, particularly the tactile hallucinations that give the impression that bugs are under the skin. The drug is a white crystalline powder in pure form and the practice of "snuffing" cocaine was common in Europe at the turn of the 20th century. It is less potent when taken by mouth. When injected by vein, a favourite method in the United States, the effects are rapid in onset, intense, but of short duration. This is followed by a correspondingly deep depression that prompts the user to repeat the dose to restore the sense of well-being. Cocaine is sometimes mixed with heroin to dampen any extreme excitability produced by the cocaine. The great number of undesired effects that come on continued use frequently prompts the cocaine user to turn to other drugs.

Amphetamines. These stimulants are of three types having closely related actions on the nervous system: amphetamine proper (Benzedrine), one of its isomers (Dexedrine), and methamphetamine (Methedrine). The amphetamines have been used to alleviate depression, fatigue, the hyperkinetic behaviour disturbances of children, postencephalitic Parkinsonism, enuresis, nausea of pregnancy, and obesity. More recently, the amphetamines have been used in combination with one of the barbiturates, such as amobarbital or phenobarbital, to produce mood elevating effects. It is the effects of the amphetamines on mood that have led to their widespread abuse. A toxic psychosis with hallucinations and paranoid delusions may be produced by a single dose as low as 50 milligrams if no drug tolerance is present. Although the normal lethal dose for adult humans is estimated to be around 900 milligrams, habitual use may increase adult tolerance up to 1,000 milligrams per day.

Mood elevation and induced psychosis

The ability of amphetamine to produce a psychosis having paranoid features was first reported in 1938, shortly after its introduction as a central stimulant. Sporadic reports of psychosis followed, and in 1958, a monograph on the subject of amphetamine psychosis included these statements:

> Psychosis associated with amphetamine usage is much more frequent than would be expected from the reports in the literature. . . . The clinical picture is primarily a paranoid psychosis with ideas of reference, delusions of persecution, auditory and visual hallucinations in a setting of clear consciousness. . . . The mental picture may be indistinguishable from acute or chronic paranoid schizophrenia. . . . Patients with amphetamine psychosis recover within a week unless there is demonstrable cause for continuance of symptoms; *e.g.,* continued excretion of the drug or hysterical prolongation of symptoms.

There have been subsequent attempts to distinguish between amphetamine psychosis and paranoid schizophrenia. Whatever the outcome, amphetamine induces a psychosis that comes closer to mimicking schizophrenia than any of the other drugs of abuse, including LSD. Some behavioral symptoms such as loss of initiative, apathy, and emotional blunting may persist long after the patient stops taking the drug. Methamphetamine was used extensively by the Japanese during World War II, and by 1953 the habitual users of the drug in Japan numbered about 500,000 persons. This large-scale usage created such a serious social problem that the amphetamines were placed under governmental control in Japan in 1954. This Japanese experience has provided the opportunity for systematic studies on chronic methamphetamine intoxication. One group of 492 addicts who had been institutionalized showed a 14 percent rate of chronic psychosis with evidence of permanent organic brain damage. In the language of the street, "Meth is death." The amphetamines produce habituation, drug dependency, physiological tolerance, and toxic effects, but no physical addiction.

Tranquillizers. Serendipity has played a major role in the discovery of tranquillizers (as it has in all facets of medicine). Tranquillizers were unknown to medical science until the middle of the 20th century when the therapeutic value of reserpine and chlorpromazine in psychiatry was discovered by chance. Reserpine was originally derived in the 1930s from *Rauwolfia serpentina,* a woody plant that grows in the tropical areas of the world, but it has since been synthesized. Because this drug has many undesirable side effects such as low blood pressure, ulcers, weakness, nightmares, nasal congestion, and depression, however, it has been largely replaced in psychiatric practice by chlorpromazine (Thorazine) and a number of other phenothiazine derivatives synthesized in the 1950s. These phenothiazines are inexpensive, easily available, produce little immediate pleasurable effects, can usually be taken in large amounts without harm, and are not physically addicting. They are used extensively in the treatment of various hyperactive and agitated states, and as antipsychotic agents. These drugs, however, may produce jaundice, dermatitis, or, infrequently, convulsive seizures, and they do not combine well with the drinking of alcohol. Chlorpromazine is effective in reversing "bad trips" such as an LSD-induced panic reaction, but it tends to strengthen rather than reverse the powerful hallucinogenic effects of STP (DOM). There is a second group of drugs, inappropriately termed minor tranquillizers, which have achieved popularity in the management of milder psychiatric conditions, particularly anxiety and tension. The major form is meprobamate (Miltown, Equanil). Although these minor tranquillizers are considered to be entirely safe in terms of side effects, they do produce serious complications, for they are commonly associated with habituation and psychic dependence. Heavy, prolonged use may result in physical dependence and severe withdrawal symptoms including insomnia, tremors, hallucinations, and convulsions.

CANNABIS

Marijuana, hashish, ghanja, and bhang

Cannabis is the general term applied internationally to the Indian hemp plant, *Cannabis sativa,* when the plant is used for its pleasure-giving effects. The plant may grow to a height of 16 feet, but the strains used for drug-producing effects are typically short stemmed and extremely branched. The resinous exudate is the most valued part of the plant because it contains the highest concentration of tetrahydrocannabinol (THC), an active hallucinogenic principle associated with the plant's potency. The term cannabis also encompasses the use of the flowering tops, fruit, seeds, leaves, stems, and bark of the hemp plant even though the potency of these plant parts is considerably less than that of the pure resin itself. Hemp grows freely throughout the temperate zones of the world, but the content of the resin in the plant differs appreciably according to the geographic origin of the plant and the climate of the region in which the plant is grown. A hot, dry, upland climate is considered most favourable in terms of the potency of the plant. Careful cultivation is also considered to be an important factor in resin production. The prevention of pollination and the trimming of top leaves to produce dwarfing enhances the content of resin at plant maturity.

Types of cannabis preparations. Marijuana, hashish, charas, ghanja, bhang, kef, and dagga are names that have been applied to various varieties and preparations of the hemp plant. Hashish, named after the Persian founder of the Assassins of the 11th century (Ḥasan-e Ṣabbāḥ), is the most potent of the cannabis preparations, being about eight times as strong as the marijuana used in the United States. Very few geographic areas are capable of producing a plant rich enough in resins to produce hashish. Unless sifted and powdered, hashish appears in a hardened, brownish form with the degree of darkness indicating strength. The North African either eats it in a confection or smokes it, the water pipe often being used to cool the smoke. The effects are more difficult to regulate when hashish is either ingested as a confection or drunk. In India, this resinous preparation of cannabis is called charas.

Ghanja is a less active form of cannabis. Whereas hashish and charas are made from the pure resin, ghanja is prepared from the flowering tops, stems, leaves, and twigs, which have less resin and thus less potency. Ghanja is nevertheless one of the more potent forms of cannabis. It is prepared from specially cultivated plants in India, and the flowering tops have a relatively generous resinous exudate. Ghanja is consumed much in the manner of charas.

Bhang is the least potent of the cannabis preparations used in India. It does not contain the flowering tops found in ghanja. As a result, bhang contains only a small amount of resin (5 percent). It is either drunk or smoked. When drunk, the leaves are reduced to a fine powder, brewed, and then filtered for use. Bhang is also drunk in Hindu religious ceremonials.

Marijuana is the variety of cannabis grown in the Western Hemisphere. Considered mild in comparison to other forms of cannabis, it is similar in potency to the bhang used in India. Typically, it is smoked, but occasionally it is brewed as a tea or baked into cakes. Marijuana varies considerably in potency.

History. Cannabis is an ancient plant in terms of use, having been known in central Asia and China as early as 3000 BC and in India and the Near East shortly thereafter. Its introduction to Europe and the Western Hemisphere was probably by way of Africa. Historically, cannabis has been regarded as having medicinal value, and it was used as a folk medicine prior to the 1900s. Reportedly, it was considered valuable as an analgesic, topical anesthetic, antispasmodic, antidepressant, appetite stimulant, antiasthmatic, and antibiotic. In the 20th century the pattern of pleasure-giving use spread from the lower classes to the middle classes in the West, particularly among intellectuals. From the 1960s it spread throughout various student populations from universities and colleges to secondary schools, finally reaching the elementary schools. This spread to "fad" proportions almost totally obscured the historic use of cannabis as a medicine. Marijuana has been used for victims of glaucoma, and cannabis generally may prove to be of some value in the treatment of depression, loss of appetite, high blood pressure, anxiety, migraine, and various gynecological and menstrual problems.

Antiquity of cannabis use

Physiological and psychological effects. The effects of cannabis are difficult to specify because of the wide variations in the potency of the various preparations of the hemp plant. Hashish or charas would be expected to produce a greater degree of intoxication than marijuana or bhang. It would also make a difference whether the drug is smoked, drunk, eaten, or received as an administration of synthetic tetrahydrocannabinol (THC). In general, hashish produces effects similar to those of mescaline or, in sufficient quantity, to those of LSD—extreme intoxication being more typical when the substance is swallowed. Marijuana, on the other hand, is more apt to produce effects at the opposite or mild end of the continuum from those of LSD. When smoked, physiological manifestations are apparent within minutes. These include dizziness, lightheadedness, disturbances in coordination and movement, a heavy sensation in the arms and legs, dryness of mouth and throat, redness and irritation of the eyes, blurred vision, quickened heartbeat, tightness around the chest, and peculiarities in the sense of hearing such as ringing, buzzing, a feeling of pressure in the ears, or altered sounds. Occasionally drug use is accompanied by nausea and an urge to urinate or defecate. There is also a feeling of hunger that may be associated with a craving for sweets. Toxic manifestations are rare and include motor restlessness, tremor, ataxia, congestion of the conjunctivae of the eye, abnormal dilation of the pupil, visual hallucinations, and unpleasant delusions. Marijuana is not a drug of addiction. Use does not lead to physical dependence, and there are no withrawal symptoms when the drug is discontinued. Psychological dependence does occur among certain types of users. Infrequently, a "cannabis psychosis" may occur, but generally this type of psychiatric reaction is associated only with heavy, long-term use of hashish, such as in India and Morocco. Other effects of chronic hashish use are a debilitation of the will and mental deterioration.

Psychological manifestations are even more variable in response to cannabis. Alterations in mood may include giggling, hilarity, and euphoria. Perceptual distortions may also occur, involving space, time, sense of distance, and sense of the organization of one's own body image. Thought processes may also become disorganized, with fragmentation, disturbances of memory, and frequent shifts of attention acting to disrupt the orderly flow of ideas. One may also experience some loss of reality contact in terms of not feeling involved in what one is doing; this may lead to considerable detachment and depersonalization. On the more positive side, there may be an enhancement in the sense of personal worth and increased sociability. Undesired subjective experiences include fear, anxiety, or panic. These effects vary considerably with practice and with the setting in which the drug is taken.

Inconclusive data on effects of cannabis

Many articles have been written on the subject of cannabis, but there is precious little worthwhile data to support any kind of a conclusion with regard to its use. One carefully controlled study on marijuana suggests that it is a very mild substance that requires considerable practice before its full (desired) effects are achieved. Alcohol clearly appears more potent and far more deleterious.

From the point of view of those who favour the legalization of marijuana, the drug is a mild hallucinogen that bears no similarity to the narcotics. They feel that the evidence clearly indicates that marijuana is not a stepping stone to heroin and that its use is not associated with major crimes. As a means of reducing tension and achieving a sense of well-being, they believe that it is probably more beneficial and considerably safer than alcohol. The current hysteria over the use of marijuana and the harsh penalties that are imposed are perceived by users as a greater threat to society than would be a more rational and realistic approach to drug use.

Social and ethical issues of drug abuse

CONFLICTING VALUES IN DRUG USE

Modern industrialized societies are certainly not neutral with regard to the voluntary nonmedical use of psychotropic drugs. Whether one simply takes the position of psychologist Erich Fromm that people are brought up to desire and value the kinds of behaviour required by their economic and social system or whether one goes further and speaks of the Protestant ethic in the sense that Max Weber used it to delineate the industrialist's quest for salvation through worldly work alone, it is simply judged not "right," "good," or "proper" for people to achieve pleasure or salvation chemically. It is accepted that the only legitimate earthly rewards are those that have been "earned" through striving, hard work, personal sacrifice, and an overriding sense of duty to one's country, the existing social order, and family. This orientation is believed to be fairly coincident with the requirements of industrialization as it has been known up to the middle of the 20th century. But the social and economic requirements of modern society may have undergone a radical change in the last few decades, even though the inertia of the existing social character, its desires and its values, will be felt for some time to come. In one major sense, current drug controversies are a reflection of this cultural lag with all of the consequent conflict of wishes and values that result from the lack of good correspondence between traditional teachings and the view of the world as it is now being perceived by large numbers within society. Modern society is in a state of rapid transition, and this transition is not without its untoward consequences in terms of stability.

Cultural transitions notwithstanding, the dominant social order has strong negative feelings about any nonsanctioned use of drugs that contradicts its existing value system. Can society succeed if individuals are allowed unrestrained self-indulgence? Is it right to dwell in one's inner experience and glorify it at the expense of the necessary ordinary daily pursuits? Is it bad to rely on something so much that one cannot exist without it? Is it legitimate to take drugs if one is not sick? Does one have the right to decide for oneself what one needs? Does society have the right to punish someone if he has done no harm to himself or to others? These are difficult questions that do not admit to ready answers. One can guess what the answers would be to the nonsanctioned use of drugs. The traditional ethic dictates harsh responses to conduct that is "self-indulgent" or "abusive of pleasure." But how does one account for the quantities of the drugs being manufactured and consumed today by the general public? It is one thing to talk of the few hundred thousand or so "hard" narcotic users who are principally addicted to the opiates. One might still feel comfortable in disparaging the widespread illicit use of hallucinogenic substances; these are still the "other guys." But the sedatives, tranquillizers, sleeping remedies, stimulants, alcohol, coffee, tea, and tobacco are complications that trap the advocate in some glaring inconsistencies. It may be asked by partisans whether the cosmetic use of stimulants for weight control is any more legitimate than the use of stimulants to "get with it?"; whether the conflict-ridden businessman or the conflict-ridden housewife is any more entitled to relax chemically (alcohol, tranquillizers, sleeping aids, sedatives) than the conflict-ridden adolescent?; whether physical pain is any less bearable than mental pain or anguish? Billions of pills and capsules of a nonnarcotic type are manufactured yearly.

Massive public use of psychotropic drugs

Sedatives and tranquillizers account for somewhere around 12 to 20 percent of all doctor's prescriptions. In addition there are about 150 different sleeping aids that are available for sale without a prescription. The alcoholic beverage industry produces countless millions of gallons of wine and spirits and countless millions of barrels of beer each year. One might conclude that there is a whole drug culture; that the problem is not confined to the young, the poor, the disadvantaged, or even to the criminal; that existing attitudes are at least inconsistent, possibly hypocritical. One always justifies one's own drug use, but one tends to view the other fellow who uses the same drugs as an abuser who is weak and undesirable. It must be recognized that the social consensus in regard to drug use and abuse is limited, conflict ridden, and often glaringly inconsistent. The problem is not one of insufficient facts but one of multiple objectives that at the present moment appear unreconcilable.

YOUTH AND DRUGS

Young people seem to find great solace in the fact that the "establishment" is a drug user. One cannot deny that many countries today are drug-oriented societies, but the implications of drug use are not necessarily the same for the adult as they are for the adolescent. The adult has already acquired some sense of identity and purpose in life; he has come to grips with the problems of love and sex; he has some degree of economic and social skill; and he has been integrated or at least assimilated into some dominant social order. Whereas the adult may turn to drugs and alcohol for many of the same reasons as the adolescent, drug use does not prevent the adult from remaining productive, discharging his obligations, maintaining his emotional and occupational ties, acknowledging the rights and authority of others, accepting restrictions, and planning for the future. The adolescent, in contrast, is apt to become ethnocentric and egocentric with drug usage. He withdraws within his narrow drug culture and within himself. Drug usage for many adolescents becomes a preposterous "cop-out" at a time when more important developmental experiences are required. To quote one observer:

Escapism in drug use

> It all seemed really quite benign in an earlier time of more moderate drug use, except for the three percent who became crazy and the ten percent we described as socially disabled. Since then, however, more and more disturbed kids have been attracted to the drug world, resulting in more unhappy and dangerous behavior. Increasingly younger kids have come into the scene. Individuals who, in psychoanalytic terms, are simply lesser people, with less structure, less ego, less integration, and hence, are less likely to be able to cope with the drugs. Adolescents are at a crisis period in their lives, and when you intrude regularly at this point with powerful chemicals, the potential to solve these problems of growing up by living them through, working them out, is stopped.

But it would appear that the "establishment" is a drug user, and this has important implications in terms of the expectations, roles, values, and rewards of the social order; but the "establishment" does not "cop-out" on drugs, and this is a fact of fundamental importance in terms of youth. Drugs may be physiologically "safe," but the drug experience can be very nonproductive and costly in terms of the individual's chances of becoming a fully participating adult.

(W.G.St./Ed.)

Pharmacological cults

Though the idea is strange to most modern worshippers, drugs have played an important role in the history of religions. The ceremonial use of wine and incense in contemporary ritual is probably a relic of a time when the psychological effects of these substances were designed to bring the worshipper into closer touch with supernatural forces. Modern studies of the hallucinogenic drugs have indicated that such drugs, in certain persons under certain conditions, release or bring about what those persons claim to be profound mystical and transcendental experiences, involving an immediate, subjective experience of ultimate reality, or the divine, resulting from the stirring of deeply buried unconscious and largely nonrational

The claim that drugs induce religious experience

reactions. Modern students of pharmacological cults who have participated in cultic drug ceremonies and used the drugs themselves have been astonished at the depth of such experiences. R. Gordon Wasson has suggested that the religious impulse itself may have had its origin in the amazement felt by primitives on accidentally finding and ingesting plants with hallucinogenic properties while foraging for food; this view is not held by most scholars of religion.

Whatever the psychological origins of such reactions, they are viewed as religious in nature and have been structured and channelled through cultic forms. Through cultic leaders—such as shamans, witch doctors, and medicine men—as well as through tradition, pharmacological cults have specified not only how the cultic drugs should be assimilated but also how they should be gathered and prepared; generally also there are specifications for participants' behaviour outside the ceremonies, in the practical affairs of living. Western observers of primitive cultures, such as missionaries, colonial administrators, and travellers, have often regarded such practices as demonstrating superstition and folly. Anthropologists and other scientific observers who have attempted to participate sympathetically in tribal rituals, however, not only have reported the useful aspects of such practices in primitive society but also have collected information that is of use to science, medicine, religion, and social theory.

Drugs usually encountered in cultic ceremonies are generally classifiable as narcotic. Few of these are true narcotics, however, in the sense of being numbing or producing sleep. They are called hallucinogens when they produce changes in perception. A hallucinogenic drug may lead to experiences that resemble psychoses, in which case it is called psychotomimetic; under other circumstances it may cause a quasi-mystical, or psychedelic, experience. Most psychedelic drugs tend to stimulate rather than numb the mind, whereas some true narcotics, such as alcohol and opium, in turn stimulate and stupefy the mind at different stages of their physical effect. Most cultic drugs come from plants, though Western cults more recently formed have made use of the active principles of natural drugs in synthetic form and of synthetic analogs of naturally occurring compounds.

TYPES OF DRUGS USED BY CULTS

There are more than 100 plants known to have properties that affect the mind, with more being discovered every year, hence only a few of the major drugs used by cults will be referred to here. Though these drugs vary greatly in composition, their effects on the user tend to be similar. Such factors as the personality, mood, and expectation of the participant, the setting, the nature of those in charge, and the interpretation of the experience may have a more significant determining effect on the experience than the specific properties of the drug.

At one time or another, such common substances as alcohol, tobacco, coffee, and tea have been used in religious cults, but such use is not common today.

Hemp, mushrooms, cacti, and their derivatives. Probably the most widespread plant having psychedelic properties and used in cults is Indian hemp, *Cannabis sativa,* which grows all over the world except in very cold climates. It is used in religious practices in India and Africa (and probably elsewhere) and is also sometimes used illicitly in the United States and Europe.

Certain mushrooms are used by cultists among the Indians in Latin America, especially in the state of Oaxaca in southern Mexico. The chief species is *Psilocybe mexicana,* of which the active principle is psilocybin and its derivative psilocin, in their chemical composition and activity not unlike LSD (D-lysergic acid diethylamide); the latter is synthesized from the alkaloids (principally ergotamine and ergonovine) that are constituents of ergot, a growth present in grasses affected by the disease also called ergot. *Amanita muscaria* (fly agaric) is another mushroom having hallucinogenic properties that has not been thoroughly studied. It may be extremely important, since it may have been the natural source of the ritual *soma* drink of the ancient Hindus and the comparable *haoma* used by the Zoroastrians (see below *History of drug use in religion*). Fly agaric, which is extremely toxic, is said to have, in addition to its hallucinogenic properties, the ability to increase strength and endurance; it is said also to be a soporific.

Peyote

Indians of Mexico discovered other plants with somewhat similar properties. The tops of the peyote cactus, *Lophophora williamsii,* may be dried to form the so-called mescal buttons (to be distinguished from the mescal bean, another mind-expanding but highly poisonous plant found in the same area), which are ingested by widely distributed groups of Indians in Mexico, the United States, and Canada during night-long ceremonies that have been described and studied by a number of anthropologists. The chief active principle of peyote is an alkaloid called mescaline. Like psilocin and psilocybin, mescaline is reputed to produce visions and other evidences of a mystical nature. Despite claims of missionaries and some government agents that peyote—from the Nahuatl word *peyotl* ("divine messenger")—is a degenerative and dangerous drug, there appears to be no evidence of this among the members of the Native American Church, a North American Indian cult that uses peyote in its chief religious ceremony (see below). Peyote, like most other hallucinogenic drugs, is not considered to be addictive and, far from being a destructive influence, is reputed by cultists and some observers to promote morality and ethical behaviour among the Indians who use it ritually.

Other psychedelic substances. Spanish missionaries to Mexico in the 16th century described, primarily in derogatory language, another psychedelic substance, called by the Indians ololiuqui and venerated highly. Ololiuqui has been identified as the seeds of the morning glory, mainly *Rivea corymbosa* and *Ipomoea violacea.* Since the active principles are the alkaloids D-lysergic and D-isolysergic acids, its properties are very similar to those of LSD, producing visions and mystical experiences.

Psychedelic snuffs and drinks

Columbus described the ceremonial sniffing of a powder encountered during one of his voyages to the West Indies. Of the many kinds of snuff, the chief variety was called *yopo, paricá,* or cohoba, a powerful hallucinogen derived from parts of a tree, *Piptadenia peregrina.* This narcotic snuff may be confused with others, as yet not clearly differentiated.

Another substance used in South America, especially in the Amazon basin, is a drink called *ayahuasca, caapi,* or *yajé,* which is produced from the stem bark of the vines *Banisteriopsis caapi* and *B. inebrians.* Indians who use it claim that its virtues include healing powers and the power to induce clairvoyance, among others. This drink has been certified by investigators to produce remarkable effects, often involving the sensation of flying. The effects are thought to be attributable to the action of harmine, a very stable indole (structurally related to LSD) that is the active principle in the plant.

Other cultic drugs may be mentioned in passing. The kava drink, prepared from the roots of *Piper methysticum,* a species of pepper, and seemingly more of a hypnotic–narcotic than a hallucinogen, is used both socially and ritually in the South Pacific, especially in Polynesia. Iboga, or ibogaine, a powerful stimulant and hallucinogen derived from the root of the African shrub *Tabernanthe iboga* (and, like psilocybin and harmine, a chemical relative of LSD), is used by the Bwiti cult in Central Africa. Coca, source of cocaine, has had both ritual and social use chiefly in Peru. *Datura,* one species of which is the jimsonweed, is used by native peoples in North and South America; the active principle, however, is highly toxic and dangerous. A drink prepared from the shrub *Mimosa hostilis* that is said to produce glorious visions in warriors before battle, is used ritually in the *ajuca* ceremony of the Jurema cult in eastern Brazil.

GOALS OF PRACTITIONERS

The drugs used by cults for their hallucinogenic effects were adopted for explicit and implicit religious functions and purposes. The drugs were and are reported to enhance religious experience. Controlled laboratory investigations of the effects of such drugs, performed outside a culturally determined cultic framework, help to make the cults more understandable.

Ecstasy and union with the divine or sacred. The loftiest aim of the cultic use of drugs is the pure delight in what is described as a direct experience of God, ultimate reality, the spirits that preside over one's destiny, or whatever the worshipper may conceive as his object of worship. As a consequence of such worship experience there may ensue a feeling of self-transcendence, sometimes through a melting away of the ego boundaries (with consequent loss of sense of self) and even through the terror of death, resulting in a psychological rebirth that gives a feeling of power and freedom and releases creative energies. Drugs have been used ritually to enhance the puberty ordeal through which, among many peoples, a youth is ushered out of childhood and is certified an adult. The functions of the drugs as teachers, leading participants through experiences of spiritual growth, are attested by many members of contemporary drug cults.

Drugs as sacraments

As a means of appropriating such experiences, the rites surrounding the assimilation of the drugs become types of sacraments in which the qualities and the gifts of the gods are appropriated. The visions, self-knowledge, energy, power, and direction reported to be secured from the rite confirm the feeling of the worshipper that he has been in the presence of God or has assimilated some of God's powers. Other specific skills and benefits—either real or the products of fancy—may be extrapolated from this alleged encounter with the gods, such as sexual attractiveness, skill and luck in hunting, protection in war, or even the ability to transcend war and to love one's enemies.

Purification, healing, and divination. Along with the sacramental function of the drug cults is the concept of purification through drug use. This may take the form of certain ritualistic preparations for the ceremony or the observing of certain taboos for days before it, or may be a part of the ceremony itself. Many psychedelic drugs produce nausea, and the consequent vomiting may be looked on as a purging of faults. In more advanced cults the purification may be seen as the pure and ethical living that should both precede and follow the ceremony. Closely related to the latter may be the devotional function, viewed in the most primitive drug cults as acts of propitiation of the gods for expected favours and in the more developed cults as acts directed toward the needs and wishes of the god through the cultic experience. Ritual drug taking may also be viewed as an act of devotion in itself.

In some of the more primitive cults the ordinary participant is relegated to a secondary role, for the priest or shaman may be the one who principally ingests the drug and mediates benefits, real or supposed, to the worshipper or suppliant. Such is the case when healing is the chief function, when the drug is dangerous, or when it is reserved for those persons having the most prestige. Mediation is also likely to occur when divination of the answers to important questions is involved; *e.g.,* whether to set out on a journey or where to find lost property.

Witchcraft and magic. Some pharmacological cults do not rise much above the level of witchcraft, with ceremonies expressing the participants' insecurities, anxieties, and hostilities. This is particularly true of cults operating among a marginal, competitive people, as in the Peruvian cult that uses *ayahuasca* (*Banisteriopsis caapi*). This is a syncretistic cult in which primitive magical beliefs are interwoven with minimal Roman Catholic features. Bad luck is looked on as the result of the curse of an envious neighbour, and the witch doctor is sought to dispel the curse and, if possible, to turn it onto its originator. At other times illness may be interpreted as the result of possession by evil spirits, and the purpose of the ceremony may be exorcism. In all of these cases the visions produced by the drugs, influenced by the assumptions and desires of the participants, will be interpreted according to the hopes and fears, prejudices, and suspicions of those participants.

Psychological goals. The literal meaning of the term psychedelic ("mind-manifesting") suggests the vast amount of material (feelings, images, etc.) released by these drugs from the unconscious. This material, related as it is to the psychological needs and history of the person, is viewed as both uplifting and creative and, on the other hand, frightening and destructive. Though these drugs are regarded as dangerous by industrially advanced societies and their medical advisers, cults using such drugs have exhibited durability, and in the societies that harbour them there is apparently little or no abuse of the drugs, despite open access to them. Perhaps these cults are so structured that they meet basic psychological needs fairly well, and the resulting cultural expressions are mainly creative and constructive. Hostilities and anxieties expressed in ritual are sublimated and, therefore, less likely to be acted out. Persons who have taken the drugs maintain that they can engender a closeness of feeling among cultic participants that may satisfy the need for comradeship that is one of man's most basic desires, while the excitement of the experience may rescue participants from one of mankind's most pervasive enemies, boredom.

HISTORY OF DRUG USE IN RELIGION

References to the ritual use of drugs are scattered through the history of religions, and there is no doubt that the practice is ancient, its origins lost in prehistory. Presumed ceremonial use of *Cannabis* among the Scythians in the 5th to 2nd century BC is suggested by the censers for burning hemp seeds found in the frozen tombs at Pazyryk in the Altai Mountains. The ancient Greeks used wine in Dionysian rites, and circumstantial evidence points to the use of a hallucinogenic substance in the most solemn moments of the Eleusinian Mysteries of ancient Greece: the drinking of *kykeōn,* a thick gruel of unknown composition. Both the secular and the cultic use of the *Amanita muscaria* mushroom in Siberia probably go back more than 6,000 years, and cultic use has spread beyond the cool temperate climates where the mushroom grows. Evidence of the cultic use of opium in the eastern Mediterranean islands, in Greece, and among the Sumerians points to dates as early as 3000 BC, though some of this evidence is disputed.

Soma and *haoma*

One of the pharmacological mysteries is the nature of the Zoroastrian *haoma* and the early Hindu *soma,* both sacred drinks made from plants. Their source may have been the *Amanita muscaria* mushroom, the mind-affecting chemicals of which pass into the urine with their properties very little diminished; there are scriptural references to sacred urine drunk as the source of divine insights. Allusions to the twigs and branches of *haoma,* however, suggest other plants, perhaps hemp. The mushroom, which does not grow in hot countries, may have been introduced to India by Aryan invaders from the north; subsequently, other plants may have been substituted until their identity was confused and lost.

There is less evidence for the historical use of drugs in Buddhism or Taoism, though it is mentioned occasionally. In Islām, which prohibits use of alcohol, there has been much more general use of *Cannabis.* The fanatical sect known as the Assassins, founded in the 11th century, used hashish; their name is derived from an Arabic word denoting a consumer of hashish. Sensational and fanciful stories, told by Marco Polo and others, of the use of hashish to heighten the undoubted homicidal proclivities of the sect, may, however, be untrue.

The use of kava was reported by travellers to the Pacific Islands, notably Fiji, in the 18th century, though its use must go back much farther. The same may be said for the cultic use of drugs like iboga, in equatorial Africa, where the discovery of such usage is very recent and where historical records are meagre. Doubtless much remains to be discovered in both of these areas.

More is known of the history and practices of pharmacological cults, as well as of the varieties of botanical sources of the drugs, in the New World than in the Old. The finding of many little images sculptured in the form of mushrooms in Guatemala almost certainly indicates a mushroom cult in the Mayan culture of Central America. Columbus reported the use of snuffs, as referred to above. The Spanish priest-historian Bernardino de Sahagún reported with disapproval the cultic use of mushrooms in Mexico in the 16th century, and there were reports of the widespread use of psychotropic mushrooms during the coronation of the Aztec emperor Montezuma in 1502. Suppressed by the Spaniards, the remnants of these once proud cults remain in the backcountry of Mexico, particularly in the state of Oaxaca. In 1955 R. Gordon Wasson and his companions were the first non-Indians invited to eat the sacred mushroom at one of the night ceremonies. Consequent publicity led to an influx of visitors seeking mushrooms and also attracted the attention of Mexican federal police. Despite this attention, the mushroom religion is still alive, though the ceremonies are now carried on less openly.

Spanish reports of about the same era as those dealing with Mexico allude to cultic use of drugs in North America. Sahagún also mentioned in his reports the cultic use of ololiuqui and peyote.

Partly because of the rise of interest in psychedelic drugs, as well as the increased accessibility, the peyote religion has been studied more thoroughly than any other pharmacological cult, mainly by American anthropologists, who have written full and extensive reports of its practices. The peyote cult was harassed by missionaries and government agents alike until, toward the end of the 19th century, Indian cults began to come together in an international body composed of Canadian, American, and Mexican Indians. This federation was finally incorporated in the state of Oklahoma in 1918 as the Native American Church. Despite many laws against the use of peyote, these members of the Native American Church have steadfastly maintained their right to worship in their own way. They have suffered imprisonment and have fought in the courts, which, for the most part, have upheld this right.

The Native American Church

The Native American Church has developed into a syncretistic religion, differing from tribe to tribe in minor details and in the degree to which ancient practices have assimilated Christian elements. The ritual surrounding ingestion of peyote is a highly symbolic night-long ceremony in the charge of an experienced Indian. Whites privileged to attend the service invariably speak of its dignity and impressiveness. Peyote itself is highly venerated and spoken of sometimes as a gift of God, sometimes personified as the Peyote Spirit. It is looked on partly as the possessor of magical qualities of protection and healing and the revealer of hidden knowledge, and partly as a guide that motivates and strengthens the worshipper. There is as much controversy among the Indians themselves over peyote as there is over LSD among whites. But the cult seems to be spreading. Contrary to the assertions of Christian missionaries, who find them hard to convert, the peyote Indians, doubtless influenced by the religions of whites around them, are reported to be superior to the nonpeyote Indians in achieving their aims of brotherly love, hard work and self-reliance, family responsibility, and abstinence from alcohol.

Because hallucinogenic drugs, both natural and synthetic, tend to evoke an experience spontaneously recognized by many as religious and therefore of supreme value to the user, small communities of seekers have grown up wherever the drugs are generally used, most recently among whites in large centres of population. Because of what they consider to be harassment by unsympathetic elements in the cities, many such communities have moved to rural or wilderness areas. Emphasis on spontaneity leads to poor organization, and consequently the histories of most of these communities are short. (W.H.C./Ed.)

BIBLIOGRAPHY

Alcohol: The prime sources for scientific, scholarly, and professional information and documentation on all aspects of the human use of beverage alcohol and its effects are the Rutgers University Center of Alcohol Studies, *Quarterly Journal of Studies on Alcohol:* Part A, *Originals,* Part B, *Documentation* (1940–), and its *Classified Abstract Archive of the Alcohol Literature* (CAAAL), a cumulative indexed collection of world scientific literature, on edge-notched finding cards (1939–). A key to the meanings of both technical and popular terms relating to alcohol is provided by MARK KELLER and MAIRI MCCORMICK, *A Dictionary of Words About Alcohol* (1968). The most complete critical reviews of the acute and chronic pharmacological, physiological, and psychological effects of alcohol intake are in HENRIK WALLGREN and HERBERT BARRY III (eds.), *Actions of Alcohol,* vol. 1, *Biochemical, Physiological and Psychological Aspects,* vol. 2, *Chronic and Clinical Aspects* (1970); H. KALANT, "The Pharmacology of Alcohol Intoxication," *Q. Jl. Stud. Alcohol,* suppl. no. 1, pp. 1–23 (1961); and H. CAPPELL and C.P. HERMAN, "Alcohol and Tension Reduction: A Review," *ibid.,* 33:33–64 (1972). BERTON ROUECHE, *The Neutral Spirit: A Portrait of Alcohol* (1960), is a well-researched, popular account of the history and the beneficent as well as harmful effects of alcoholic beverages. R.G. MCCARTHY (ed.), *Drinking and Intoxication* (1959), is a rich collection of informative writings from the sociological as well as biological fields on every aspect of its title; while D.J. PITTMAN and C.R. SNYDER (eds.), *Society, Culture, and Drinking Patterns* (1962), brings together the best essays on social and cultural factors associated with drinking patterns in many kinds of communities and groups.

Anthropological studies of the drinking practices of early societies, as well as their survival and transmission to and significance for modern man, are described in E.M. LOEB, "Primitive Intoxicants," *Q. Jl. Stud. Alcohol,* 4:387–398 (1943); CHANDLER WASHBURNE, *Primitive Drinking: A Study of the Uses and Functions of Alcohol in Preliterate Societies* (1961); and M.K. BACON *et al.,* "A Cross-Cultural Study of Drinking," *Q. Jl. Stud. Alcohol,* suppl. no. 3 (1965). The prevalence of drinking and abstaining and the distribution and demographic interrelations of alcohol problems and alcoholism in the United States and other countries are dealt with in DON CAHALAN, IRA H. CISIN, and HELEN M. CROSSLEY, *American Drinking Practices: A National Study of Drinking Behavior and Attitudes* (1969); and K. BRUUN *et al.,* "Surveys of Drinking and Abstaining: Urban, Suburban and National Studies," *Q. Jl. Stud. Alcohol,* suppl. no. 6 (1972); while VERA EFRON, MARK KELLER, and CAROL GURIOLI, *Statistics on Consumption of Alcohol and on Alcoholism* (1972), provides comparisons of alcohol consumption in many countries and presents estimates of alcoholism and statistics on alcoholic psychoses and mortality in the United States. CLIFFORD F. GASTINEAU, WILLIAM J. DARBY, and THOMAS B. TURNER (eds.), *Fermented Food Beverages in Nutrition* (1979), discusses the hazardous aspects of alcohol consumption and the often disregarded nutritional aspects, in a collection of papers; JAMES E. ROYCE, *Alcohol Problems and Alcoholism* (1981), is a useful introduction to alcohol use and abuse and alcohol prevention and treatment; PHIL DAVIES, *Alcohol Problems and Alcohol Control in Europe* (1983); ORIANNA J. KALANT, *Alcohol and Drug Problems in Women* (1980); DWIGHT B. HEATH, *Alcohol Use and World Cultures: A Comprehensive Bibliography of Anthropological Sources* (1981), is a thorough listing of more than 1,200 alcohol-use sources on particular topics, regions, and ethnic groups; GRACE M. BARNES, *Alcohol and the Elderly: A Comprehensive Bibliography* (1980), contains more than 1,200 citations dealing with biological and social problems facing elderly persons involved in alcohol abuse; JACK O. WADDELL and MICHAEL W. EVERETT (eds.), *Drinking Behaviour Among Southwestern Indians* (1980); a good companion source is JOHN HAMER (ed.), *Alcohol and Native Peoples of the North* (1980), a collection dealing with the cultural meanings and attachments to alcohol among Arctic and subarctic American Indians.

The NATIONAL INSTITUTE ON ALCOHOL ABUSE AND ALCOHOLISM (U.S.) has published several useful works, including: *Alcohol Consumption and Related Problems* (1982), essays dealing with attitudes toward alcohol among adults and young people, epidemiological problems of alcohol use and abuse, international trends in alcohol consumption and related pathologies, alcohol and family violence, and genetic influences on alcohol-related behaviour; *Biomedical Processes and Consequences of Alcohol Use* (1982), a discussion of the effect of alcohol on membranes, protein synthesis, liver damage, the cardiovascular system, and other topics in several papers; *Prevention, Intervention, and Treatment: Concerns and Models* (1982), a discussion of current research on alcoholism, the problems of drinking and driving, the diagnosis of alcoholism, methods of intervention, treatment, and evaluation; and *Special Population Issues* (1983), problems related to alcohol use among different population groups.

The nature and causes of alcoholism and descriptions of its symptomatology are dealt with in MARK KELLER, *Some Views on the Nature of Addiction* (1969); DAVID LESTER, "Self-Selection of Alcohol by Animals, Human Variation, and the Etiology of Alcoholism," *Q. Jl. Stud. Alcohol,* 27:395–438 (1966); E.M. JELLINEK, *The Disease Concept of Alcoholism* (1960), and "Phases of Alcohol Addiction," *Q. Jl. Stud. Alcohol,* 13:673–684 (1952). Treatments of alcoholism are described in M.J. HILL and H.T. BLANE, "Evaluation of Psychotherapy with Alcoholics: A Critical Review," *Q. Jl. Stud. Alcohol,* 28:76–104 (1967); and MORRIS E. CHAFETZ, HOWARD T. BLANE, and MARJORIE J. HILL (eds.), *Frontiers of Alcoholism* (1970), while the ideology and role of the leading self-help fellowship are detailed in *Alcoholics Anonymous: The Story of How Many Thousands of Men and Women Have Recovered from Alcoholism* (1955); and BARRY LEACH *et al.,* "Dimensions of Alcoholics Anonymous," *Int. J. Addict.,* 4:507–541 (1969). Analyses of classic as well as contemporary attempts to cope with alcohol problems are outlined in the NEW YORK STATE MORELAND COMMISSION ON THE ALCOHOLIC BEVERAGE CONTROL LAW, *Study Paper No. 1: The Relationship of the Alcoholic Beverage Control Law and the Problems of Alcohol* (1963); and S.D. BACONS, "The Classic Temperance Movement in the U.S.A.: Impact Today on Attitudes, Action and Research," *Br. J. Addict. Alcohol,* 62:5 18 (1967). Broad data and perspectives on alcohol-related health and social problems are presented in THOMAS F.A. PLAUT, *Alcohol Problems: A Report to the Nation, by the Cooperative Commission on the Study of Alcoholism* (1967); and the NATIONAL INSTITUTE ON ALCOHOL ABUSE AND ALCOHOLISM, *Alcohol and Health, 1st Special Report . . . from the Secretary of Health, Education, and Welfare* (1972).

Psychotropic Drugs: BERNARD BARBER, *Drugs and Society* (1967), provides an excellent introduction to the general topic of drugs, especially ch. 1, 5, and 6. MADELINE H. ENGEL, *The Drug Scene* (1974), is a brief sociological treatment; ALFRED R. LINDESMITH, *The Addict and the Law* (1965), offers a broad analysis of the narcotic problem; ROBERT W. FERGUSON, *Drug Abuse Control* (1975), reports on agencies of control and rehabilitation in many countries; DAVID SOLOMON (ed.), *LSD: The Consciousness-Expanding Drug* (1964), provides the reader with some of the history, rationale, subjective accounts, and mystique that launched the drug movement. More specialized works of general interest include BRIAN WELLS, *Psychedelic Drugs: Psychological, Medical and Social Issues* (1973); DONALD R. WESSON and DAVID E. SMITH, *Barbiturates: Their Use, Misuse and Abuse* (1977); and SAMUEL S. EPSTEIN *et al.* (eds.), *Drugs of Abuse: Their Genetic and Other Chronic Nonpsychiatric Hazards* (1971). RICHARD R. LINGEMAN, *Drugs from A to Z: A Dictionary,* 2nd ed. (1974), offers an impressive array of general information on almost all aspects of drug use. Technical works covering the same broad scope are J.R. DIPALMA (ed.), *Drill's Pharmacology in Medicine,* 4th ed. (1971); and L.S. GOODMAN and A.Z. GILMAN (eds.), *The Pharmacological Basis of Therapeutics,* 6th ed. (1980). A useful summary of psychological and psychiatric views may be found in JAMES C. COLEMAN, *Abnormal Psychology and Modern Life,* 6th ed. (1980); THEODORE MILLON, *Modern Psychopathology* (1969); and SILVANO ARIETI (ed.), *American Handbook of Psychiatry,* 6 vol. (1974–75). For additional references, see THEODORA ANDREWS, *A Bibliography of Drug Abuse, Including Alcohol and Tobacco* (1977), an annotated guide; and *Drug Abuse and Alcoholism Review* (bimonthly), abstracts of current periodical literature.

Pharmacological cults: D.H. EFRON, B. HOLMSTEDT, and N.S. KLINE (eds.), *Ethnopharmacologic Search for Psychoactive Drugs* (1967), a review by international experts, including material on cults; W. LA BARRE, *The Peyote Cult,* enlarged ed. (1969), and J.S. SLOTKIN, *The Peyote Religion* (1956), detailed and thorough references on the peyote cult; W.T. STACE, *Mysticism and Philosophy* (1960), a very clear account of mysticism that alludes to drugs; V.P. and R.G. WASSON, *Mushrooms, Russia, and History,* 2 vol. (1957), and R.G. WASSON, *Soma: Divine Mushroom of Immortality* (1968), required readings for those who wish to be thoroughly informed on mushroom cults; R.C. ZAEHNER, *Mysticism, Sacred and Profane* (1957), mainly a criticism of the views of Aldous Huxley on drugs, and *Drugs, Mysticism and Make-Believe* (1972; also published as *Zen, Drugs, and Mysticism,* 1973). *Psychedelic Religion?,* ed. by Paul H. Ballard (1972), a collection of papers from a colloquium; FERNANDO BENITEZ, *En la tierra mágica del peyote* (1968; *In the Magic Land of Peyote,* 1975), and *Los hongos alucinantes* (1964), both by an authority on the use of hallucinogens among the Indians of Mexico; and Peter T. Furst (ed.), *Flesh of the Gods: The Ritual Use of Hallucinogens* (1972), based on a lecture series in 1970.

(M.Ke./W.G.St./W.H.C./Ed.)

Alexander the Great

Alexander the Great (Alexander III), king of Macedonia, overthrew the Persian Empire, carried Macedonian arms to India, and laid the foundations for the Hellenistic world of territorial kingdoms. Already in his lifetime the subject of fabulous stories, he later became the hero of a full-scale legend bearing only the sketchiest resemblance to his historical career.

LIFE

He was born in 356 BC at Pella in Macedonia, the son of Philip II and Olympias (daughter of King Neoptolemus of Epirus). From age 13 to 16 he was taught by Aristotle, who inspired him with an interest in philosophy, medicine, and scientific investigation; but he was later to advance beyond his teacher's narrow precept that non-Greeks should be treated as slaves. Left in charge of Macedonia in 340 during Philip's attack on Byzantium, Alexander defeated the Maedi, a Thracian people; two years later he commanded the left wing at the Battle of Chaeronea, in which Philip defeated the allied Greek states, and displayed personal courage in breaking the Sacred Band of Thebes. A year later Philip divorced Olympias; and, after a quarrel at a feast held to celebrate his father's new marriage, Alexander and his mother fled to Epirus, and Alexander later went to Illyria. Shortly afterward, father and son were reconciled and Alexander returned; but his position as heir was jeopardized.

Alexander the Great, portrait head on a coin of Lysimachus (355–281 BC). In the British Museum.

By courtesy of the trustees of the British Museum; photograph, J.R. Freeman & Co. Ltd.

Alexander succeeds Philip

In 336, however, on Philip's assassination, Alexander, acclaimed by the army, succeeded without opposition. He at once executed the princes of Lyncestis, alleged to be behind Philip's murder, along with all possible rivals and the whole of the faction opposed to him. He then marched south, recovered a wavering Thessaly, and at an assembly of the Greek League at Corinth was appointed generalissimo for the forthcoming invasion of Asia, already planned and initiated by Philip. Returning to Macedonia by way of Delphi (where the Pythian priestess acclaimed him "invincible"), he advanced into Thrace in spring 335 and, after forcing the Shipka Pass and crushing the Triballi, crossed the Danube to disperse the Getae; turning west, he then defeated and shattered a coalition of Illyrians who had invaded Macedonia. Meanwhile, a rumour of his death had precipitated a revolt of Theban democrats; other Greek states favoured Thebes, and the Athenians, urged on by Demosthenes, voted help. In 14 days Alexander marched 240 miles from Pelion (near modern Korçë, Albania) in Illyria to Thebes. When the Thebans refused to surrender, he made an entry and razed their city to the ground, sparing only temples and Pindar's house; 6,000 were killed and all survivors sold into slavery. The other Greek states were cowed by this severity, and Alexander could afford to treat Athens leniently. Macedonian garrisons were left in Corinth, Chalcis, and the Cadmea (the citadel of Thebes).

Beginnings of the Persian expedition. From his accession Alexander had set his mind on the Persian expedition. He had grown up to the idea. Moreover, he needed the wealth of Persia if he was to maintain the army built by Philip and pay off the 500 talents he owed. The exploits of the Ten Thousand, Greek soldiers of fortune, and of Agesilaus of Sparta, in successfully campaigning in Persian territory had revealed the vulnerability of the Persian Empire. With a good cavalry force Alexander could expect to defeat any Persian army. In spring 334 he crossed the Dardanelles, leaving Antipater, who had already faithfully served his father, as his deputy in Europe with over 13,000 men; he himself commanded about 30,000 foot and over 5,000 cavalry, of whom nearly 14,000 were Macedonians and about 7,000 allies sent by the Greek League. This army was to prove remarkable for its balanced combination of arms. Much work fell on the lightarmed Cretan and Macedonian archers, Thracians, and the Agrianian javelin men. But in pitched battle the striking force was the cavalry, and the core of the army, should the issue still remain undecided after the cavalry charge, was the infantry phalanx, 9,000 strong, armed with 13-foot spears and shields, and the 3,000 men of the royal battalions, the hypaspists. Alexander's second in command was Parmenio, who had secured a foothold in Asia Minor during Philip's lifetime; many of his family and supporters were entrenched in positions of responsibility. The army was accompanied by surveyors, engineers, architects, scientists, court officials, and historians; from the outset Alexander seems to have envisaged an unlimited operation.

Exploits of the Ten Thousand

After visiting Ilium (Troy), a romantic gesture inspired by Homer, he confronted his first Persian army, led by three satraps, at the Granicus (modern Kocabaş) River, near the Sea of Marmara (May/June 334). The Persian plan to tempt Alexander across the river and kill him in the melee almost succeeded; but the Persian line broke, and Alexander's victory was complete. Darius' Greek mercenaries were largely massacred, but 2,000 survivors were sent back to Macedonia in chains. This victory exposed western Asia Minor to the Macedonians, and most cities hastened to open their gates. The tyrants were expelled and (in contrast to Macedonian policy in Greece) democracies were installed. Alexander thus underlined his Panhellenic policy, already symbolized in the sending of 300 panoplies (sets of armour) taken at the Granicus as an offering dedicated to Athena at Athens by "Alexander son of Philip and the Greeks (except the Spartans) from the barbarians who inhabit Asia." (This formula, cited by the Greek historian Arrian in his history of Alexander's campaigns, is noteworthy for its omission of any reference to Macedonia.) But the cities remained de facto under Alexander, and his appointment of Calas as satrap of Hellespontine Phrygia reflected his claim to succeed the Great King of Persia. When Miletus, encouraged by the proximity of the Persian fleet, resisted, Alexander took it by assault; but, refusing a naval battle, he disbanded his own costly navy and announced that he would "defeat the Persian fleet on land," by occupying the coastal cities. In Caria, Halicarnassus resisted and was stormed; but Ada, the widow and sister of the satrap Idrieus, adopted Alexander as her son and, after expelling her brother Pixodarus, Alexander restored her to her satrapy. Some parts of Caria held out, however, until 332.

Asia Minor and the Battle of Issus. In winter 334–333 Alexander conquered western Asia Minor, subduing the hill tribes of Lycia and Pisidia; and in spring 333 he advanced along the coastal road to Perga, passing the cliffs of Mt. Climax, thanks to a fortunate change of wind.

The fall in the level of the sea was interpreted as a mark of divine favour by Alexander's flatterers, including the historian Callisthenes. At Gordium in Phrygia, tradition records his cutting of the Gordian knot, which could only be loosed by the man who was to rule Asia; but this story may be apocryphal or at least distorted. At this point Alexander benefitted from the sudden death of Memnon, the competent Greek commander of the Persian fleet. From Gordium he pushed on to Ancyra (modern Ankara) and thence south through Cappadocia and the Cilician Gates (modern Külek Boğazi); a fever held him up for a time in Cilicia. Meanwhile, Darius with his Grand Army had advanced northward on the eastern side of Mt. Amanus. Intelligence on both sides was faulty, and Alexander was already encamped by Myriandrus (near modern Iskenderun, Turkey) when he learned that Darius was astride his line of communications at Issus, north of Alexander's position (autumn 333). Turning, Alexander found Darius drawn up along the Pinarus River. In the battle that followed, Alexander won a decisive victory. The struggle turned into a Persian rout and Darius fled, leaving his family in Alexander's hands; the women were treated with chivalrous care.

The Gordian knot

Conquest of the Mediterranean coast and Egypt. From Issus Alexander marched south into Syria and Phoenicia, his object being to isolate the Persian fleet from its bases and so to destroy it as an effective fighting force. The Phoenician cities Marathus and Aradus came over quietly, and Parmenio was sent ahead to secure Damascus and its rich booty, including Darius' war chest. In reply to a letter from Darius offering peace, Alexander replied arrogantly, recapitulating the historic wrongs of Greece and demanding unconditional surrender to himself as lord of Asia. After taking Byblos (modern Jubayl) and Sidon (Arabic Ṣaydā), he met with a check at Tyre, where he was refused entry into the island city. He thereupon prepared to use all methods of siegecraft to take it, but the Tyrians resisted, holding out for seven months. In the meantime (winter 333–332) the Persians had counterattacked by land in Asia Minor—where they were defeated by Antigonus, the satrap of Greater Phrygia—and by sea, recapturing a number of cities and islands.

While the siege of Tyre was in progress, Darius sent a new offer: he would pay a huge ransom of 10,000 talents for his family and cede all his lands west of the Euphrates. "I would accept," Parmenio is reported to have said, "were I Alexander"; "I too," was the famous retort, "were I Parmenio." The storming of Tyre in July 332 was Alexander's greatest military achievement; it was attended with great carnage and the sale of the women and children into slavery. Leaving Parmenio in Syria, Alexander advanced south without opposition until he reached Gaza on its high mound; there bitter resistance halted him for two months, and he sustained a serious shoulder wound during a sortie. There is no basis for the tradition that he turned aside to visit Jerusalem.

The siege of Tyre

In November 332 he reached Egypt. The people welcomed him as their deliverer, and the Persian satrap Mazaces wisely surrendered. At Memphis Alexander sacrificed to Apis, the Greek term for Hapi, the sacred Egyptian bull, and was crowned with the traditional double crown of the pharaohs; the native priests were placated and their religion encouraged. He spent the winter organizing Egypt, where he employed Egyptian governors, keeping the army under a separate Macedonian command. He founded the city of Alexandria near the western arm of the Nile on a fine site between the sea and Lake Mareotis, protected by the island of Pharos, and had it laid out by the Rhodian architect Deinocrates. He is also said to have sent an expedition to discover the causes of the flooding of the Nile. From Alexandria he marched along the coast to Paraetonium and from there inland to visit the celebrated oracle of the god Amon (at Sīwah); the difficult journey was later embroidered with flattering legends. On his reaching the oracle in its oasis, the priest gave him the traditional salutation of a pharaoh, as son of Amon; Alexander consulted the god on the success of his expedition but revealed the reply to no one. Later the incident was to contribute to the story that he was the son of Zeus and, thus, to his "deification." In spring 331 he returned to Tyre, appointed a Macedonian satrap for Syria, and prepared to advance into Mesopotamia. His conquest of Egypt had completed his control of the whole eastern Mediterranean coast.

In July 331 Alexander was at Thapsacus on the Euphrates. Instead of taking the direct route down the river to Babylon, he made across northern Mesopotamia toward the Tigris, and Darius, learning of this move from an advance force sent under Mazaeus to the Euphrates crossing, marched up the Tigris to oppose him. The decisive battle of the war was fought on the plain of Gaugamela between Nineveh and Arbela. Alexander pursued the defeated Persian forces for 35 miles to Arbela, but Darius escaped with his Bactrian cavalry and Greek mercenaries into Media.

Battle of Gaugamela

Alexander now occupied Babylon, city and province; Mazaeus, who surrendered it, was confirmed as satrap in conjunction with a Macedonian troop commander, and quite exceptionally was granted the right to coin. As in Egypt, the local priesthood was encouraged. Susa, the capital, also surrendered, releasing huge treasures amounting to 50,000 gold talents; here Alexander established Darius' family in comfort. Crushing the mountain tribe of the Ouxians, he now pressed on over the Zagros range into Persia proper and, successfully turning the Pass of the Persian Gates, held by the satrap Ariobarzanes, he entered Persepolis and Pasargadae. At Persepolis he ceremonially burned down the palace of Xerxes, as a symbol that the Panhellenic war of revenge was at an end; for such seems the probable significance of an act that tradition later explained as a drunken frolic inspired by Thaïs, an Athenian courtesan. In spring 330 Alexander marched north into Media and occupied its capital Ecbatana. The Thessalians and Greek allies were sent home; henceforward he was waging a purely personal war.

As Mazaeus' appointment indicated, Alexander's views on the empire were changing. He had come to envisage a joint ruling people consisting of Macedonians and Persians, and this served to augment the misunderstanding that now arose between him and his people. Before continuing his pursuit of Darius, who had retreated into Bactria, he assembled all the Persian treasure and entrusted it to Harpalus, who was to hold it at Ecbatana as chief treasurer. Parmenio was also left behind in Media to control communications; the presence of this older man had perhaps become irksome.

In midsummer 330 Alexander set out for the eastern provinces at a high speed via Rhagae (modern Rayy, near Tehrān) and the Caspian Gates, where he learned that Bessus, the satrap of Bactria, had deposed Darius. After a skirmish near modern Shāhrūd, the usurper had Darius stabbed and left him to die. Alexander sent his body for burial with due honours in the royal tombs at Persepolis.

Death of Darius

Campaign eastward, to Central Asia. Darius' death left no obstacle to Alexander's claim to be Great King, and a Rhodian inscription of this year (330) calls him "lord of Asia"—*i.e.,* of the Persian Empire; soon afterward his Asian coins carry the title of king. Crossing the Elburz Mountains to the Caspian, he seized Zadracarta in Hyrcania and received the submission of a group of satraps and Persian notables, some of whom he confirmed in their offices; in a diversion westward, perhaps to modern Āmol, he reduced the Mardi, a mountain people who inhabited the Elburz Mountains. He also accepted the surrender of Darius' Greek mercenaries. His advance eastward was now rapid. In Aria he reduced Satibarzanes, who had offered submission only to revolt, and he founded Alexandria of the Arians (modern Herāt). At Phrada in Drangiana (either near modern Nad-e ʿAli in Seistan or farther north at Farah), he at last took steps to destroy Parmenio and his family. Philotas, Parmenio's son, commander of the elite Companion cavalry, was implicated in an alleged plot against Alexander's life, condemned by the army, and executed; and a secret message was sent to Cleander, Parmenio's second in command, who obediently assassinated him. This ruthless action excited widespread horror but strengthened Alexander's position relative to his critics and those whom he regarded as his father's men. All Parmenio's adherents were now eliminated and men close to Alexander promoted. The Companion cavalry was reorganized in two sections, each containing four squadrons (now known as hipparchies); one group was commanded by Alexander's oldest friend, Hephaestion, the other by Cleitus, an older man. From Phrada, Alexander pressed on during the winter of 330–329 up the valley of the Helmand River, through Arachosia, and over the mountains past the site of modern Kābul into the country of the Paropamisadae, where he founded Alexandria by the Caucasus.

Revolt in Bactria and Sogdiana

Bessus was now in Bactria raising a national revolt in the eastern satrapies with the usurped title of Great King. Crossing the Hindu Kush northward over the Khawak Pass (11,650 feet), Alexander brought his army, despite food shortages, to Drapsaca (sometimes identified with modern Banu [Andarab], probably farther north at Qunduz); outflanked, Bessus fled beyond the Oxus (modern Amu Darya), and Alexander, marching west to Bactra-Zariaspa (modern Balkh [Wazirabad] in Afghanistan), appointed loyal satraps in Bactria and Aria. Crossing the Oxus, he sent his general Ptolemy in pursuit of Bessus, who had meanwhile been overthrown by the Sogdian Spitamenes. Bessus was captured, flogged, and sent to Bactra, where he was later mutilated after the Persian manner (losing his nose and ears); in due course he was publicly executed at Ecbatana.

From Maracanda (modern Samarkand) Alexander advanced by way of Cyropolis to the Jaxartes (modern Syrdarya), the boundary of the Persian Empire. There he broke the opposition of the Scythian nomads by his use of catapults and, after defeating them in a battle on the north bank of the river, pursued them into the interior. On the site of modern Leninabad (Khojent) on the Jaxartes, he founded a city, Alexandria Eschate, "the farthest." Meanwhile, Spitamenes had raised all Sogdiana in revolt behind him, bringing in the Massagetai, a people of the Śaka confederacy. It took Alexander until the autumn of 328 to crush the most determined opponent he encountered in his campaigns. Later in the same year he attacked Oxyartes and the remaining barons who held out in the hills of Paraetacene (modern Tadzhikistan); volunteers seized the crag on which Oxyartes had his stronghold, and among the captives was his daughter, Roxana. In reconciliation Alexander married her, and the rest of his opponents were either won over or crushed.

An incident that occurred at Maracanda widened the breach between Alexander and many of his Macedonians. He murdered Cleitus, one of his most trusted commanders, in a drunken quarrel; but his excessive display of remorse led the army to pass a decree convicting Cleitus posthumously of treason. The event marked a step in Alexander's progress toward Eastern absolutism, and this growing attitude found its outward expression in his use of Persian royal dress. Shortly afterward, at Bactra, he attempted to impose the Persian court ceremonial, involving prostration (*proskynesis*), on the Greeks and Macedonians too; but to them this custom, habitual for Persians entering the king's presence, implied an act of worship and was intolerable before a man. Even Callisthenes, historian and nephew of Aristotle, whose ostentatious flattery had perhaps encouraged Alexander to see himself in the role of a god, refused to abase himself. Macedonian laughter caused the experiment to founder, and Alexander abandoned it. Shortly afterward, however, Callisthenes was held to be privy to a conspiracy among the royal pages and was executed (or died in prison; accounts vary); resentment of this action alienated sympathy from Alexander within the Peripatetic school of philosophers, with which Callisthenes had close connections.

Progress toward absolutism

Invasion of India. In early summer 327 Alexander left Bactria with a reinforced army under a reorganized command. If Plutarch's figure of 120,000 men has any reality, however, it must include all kinds of auxiliary services, together with muleteers, camel drivers, medical corps, peddlers, entertainers, women, and children; the fighting strength perhaps stood at about 35,000. Recrossing the Hindu Kush, probably by Bamian and the Ghorband Valley, Alexander divided his forces. Half the army with the baggage under Hephaestion and Perdiccas, both cavalry commanders, was sent through the Khyber Pass, while he himself led the rest, together with his siege train, through the hills to the north. His advance through Swāt and Gandhāra was marked by the storming of the almost impregnable pinnacle of Aornos, the modern Pir-Sar, a few miles west of the Indus and north of the Buner River, an impressive feat of siegecraft. In spring 326, crossing the Indus near Attock, Alexander entered Taxila, whose ruler, Taxiles, furnished elephants and troops in return for aid against his rival Porus, who ruled the lands between the Hydaspes (modern Jhelum) and the Acesines (modern Chenāb). In June Alexander fought his last great battle on the left bank of the Hydaspes. He founded two cities there, Alexandria Nicaea (to celebrate his victory) and Bucephala (named after his horse Bucephalus, which died there); and Porus became his ally.

Battle of the Hydaspes

How much Alexander knew of India beyond the Hyphasis (probably the modern Beas) is uncertain; there is no conclusive proof that he had heard of the Ganges. But he was anxious to press on farther, and he had advanced to the Hyphasis when his army mutinied, refusing to go farther in the tropical rain; they were weary in body and spirit, and Coenus, one of Alexander's four chief marshals, acted as their spokesman. On finding the army adamant, Alexander agreed to turn back.

On the Hyphasis he erected 12 altars to the 12 Olympian gods, and on the Hydaspes he built a fleet of 800 to 1,000 ships. Leaving Porus, he then proceeded down the river and into the Indus, with half his forces on shipboard and half marching in three columns down the two banks. The fleet was commanded by Nearchus, and Alexander's own captain was Onesicritus; both later wrote accounts of the campaign. The march was attended with much fighting and heavy, pitiless slaughter; at the storming of one town of the Malli near the Hydraotes (Ravi) River, Alexander received a severe wound which left him weakened.

Return from India

On reaching Patala, located at the head of the Indus delta, he built a harbour and docks and explored both arms of the Indus, which probably then ran into the Rann of Kutch. He planned to lead part of his forces back by land, while the rest in perhaps 100 to 150 ships under the command of Nearchus, a Cretan with naval experience, made a voyage of exploration along the Persian Gulf. Local opposition led Nearchus to set sail in September (325), and he was held up for three weeks until he could pick up the northeast monsoon in late October. In September Alexander too set out along the coast through Gedrosia (modern Baluchistan), but he was soon compelled by mountainous country to turn inland, thus failing in his project to establish food depots for the fleet. Craterus, a high-ranking officer, already had been sent off with the baggage and siege train, the elephants, and the sick and wounded, together with three battalions of the phalanx, by way of the Mulla Pass, Quetta, and Kandahar into the Helmand Valley; from there he was to march through Drangiana to rejoin the main army on the Amanis (modern Minab) River in Carmania. Alexander's march through Gedrosia proved disastrous; waterless desert and shortage of food and fuel caused great suffering, and many, especially women and children, perished in a sudden monsoon flood while encamped in a wadi. At length, at the Amanis, he was rejoined by Nearchus and the fleet, which also had suffered losses.

Consolidation of the empire. Alexander now proceeded farther with the policy of replacing senior officials and executing defaulting governors on which he had already embarked before leaving India. Between 326 and 324 over a third of his satraps were superseded and six were put to death, including the Persian satraps of Persis, Susiana, Carmania, and Paraetacene; three generals in Media, including Cleander, the brother of Coenus (who had died a little earlier), were accused of extortion and summoned to Carmania, where they were arrested, tried, and executed. How far the rigour that from now onward Alexander displayed against his governors represents exemplary punishment for gross maladministration during his absence and how far the elimination of men he had come to distrust (as in the case of Philotas and Parmenio) is debatable; but the ancient sources generally favourable to him comment adversely on his severity.

In spring 324 he was back in Susa, capital of Elam and administrative centre of the Persian Empire; the story of his journey through Carmania in a drunken revel, dressed as Dionysus, is embroidered, if not wholly apocryphal. He found that his treasurer, Harpalus, evidently fearing punishment for peculation, had absconded with 6,000 mercenaries and 5,000 talents to Greece; arrested in Athens, he escaped and later was murdered in Crete. At Susa Alexander held a feast to celebrate the seizure of the Persian Empire, at which, in furtherance of his policy of fusing Macedonians and Persians into one master race, he and 80 of his officers took Persian wives; he and Hephaestion married Darius' daughters Barsine (also called Stateira) and Drypetis, respectively, and 10,000 of his soldiers with native wives were given generous dowries.

Attempt at creating a master race

This policy of racial fusion brought increasing friction to Alexander's relations with his Macedonians, who had no sympathy for his changed concept of the empire. His determination to incorporate Persians on equal terms in the army and the administration of the provinces was bitterly resented. This discontent was now fanned by the arrival of 30,000 native youths who had received a Macedonian military training and by the introduction of Orientals from Bactria, Sogdiana, Arachosia, and other parts of the empire into the Companion cavalry; whether Orientals had previously served with the Companions is uncertain, but if so they must have formed separate squadrons. In addition, Persian nobles had been accepted into the royal cavalry bodyguard. Peucestas, the new governor of Persis, gave this policy full support to flatter Alexander; but most Macedonians saw it as a threat to their own privileged position.

The issue came to a head at Opis (324), when Alexander's decision to send home Macedonian veterans under Craterus was interpreted as a move toward transferring the seat of power to Asia. There was an open mutiny involving all but the royal bodyguard; but when Alexander dismissed his whole army and enrolled Persians instead, the opposition broke down. An emotional scene of reconciliation was followed by a vast banquet with 9,000 guests to celebrate the ending of the misunderstanding and the partnership in government of Macedonians and Persians—but not, as has been argued, the incorporation of all the subject peoples as partners in the commonwealth. Ten thousand veterans were now sent back to Macedonia with gifts, and the crisis was surmounted.

In summer 324 Alexander attempted to solve another problem, that of the wandering mercenaries, of whom there were thousands in Asia and Greece, many of them political exiles from their own cities. A decree brought by Nicanor to Europe and proclaimed at Olympia (September 324) required the Greek cities of the Greek League to receive back all exiles and their families (except the Thebans), a measure that implied some modification of the oligarchic regimes maintained in the Greek cities by Alexander's governor Antipater. Alexander now planned to recall Antipater and supersede him by Craterus; but he was to die before this could be done.

Last year and death

In autumn 324 Hephaestion died in Ecbatana, and Alexander indulged in extravagant mourning for his closest friend; he was given a royal funeral in Babylon with a pyre costing 10,000 talents. His post of chiliarch (grand vizier) was left unfilled. It was probably in connection with a general order now sent out to the Greeks to honour Hephaestion as a hero that Alexander linked the demand that he himself should be accorded divine honours. For a long time his mind had dwelt on ideas of godhead. Greek thought drew no very decided line of demarcation between god and man, for legend offered more than one example of men who, by their achievements, acquired divine status. Alexander had on several occasions encouraged favourable comparison of his own accomplishments with those of Dionysus or Heracles. He now seems to have become convinced of the reality of his own divinity and to have required its acceptance by others. There is no reason to assume that his demand had any political background (divine status gave its possessor no particular rights in a Greek city); it was rather a symptom of growing megalomania and emotional instability. The cities perforce complied, but often ironically: the Spartan decree read, "Since Alexander wishes to be a god, let him be a god."

In the winter of 324 Alexander carried out a savage punitive expedition against the Cossaeans in the hills of Luristan. The following spring at Babylon he received complimentary embassies from the Libyans and from the Bruttians, Etruscans, and Lucanians of Italy; but the story that embassies also came from more distant peoples, such as Carthaginians, Celts, Iberians, and even Romans, is a later invention. Representatives of the cities of Greece also came, garlanded as befitted Alexander's divine status. Following up Nearchus' voyage, he now founded an Alexandria at the mouth of the Tigris and made plans to develop sea communications with India, for which an expedition along the Arabian coast was to be a preliminary. He also dispatched Heracleides, an officer, to explore the Hyrcanian (*i.e.,* Caspian) Sea. Suddenly, in Babylon, while busy with plans to improve the irrigation of the Euphrates and to settle the coast of the Persian Gulf, Alexander was taken ill after a prolonged banquet and drinking bout; 10 days later, on June 13, 323, he died in his 33rd year; he had reigned for 12 years and eight months. His body, diverted to Egypt by Ptolemy, the later king, was eventually placed in a golden coffin in Alexandria. Both in Egypt and elsewhere in the Greek cities he received divine honours.

No heir had been appointed to the throne, and his generals adopted Philip II's half-witted illegitimate son, Philip Arrhidaeus, and Alexander's posthumous son by Roxana, Alexander IV, as kings, sharing out the satrapies among themselves, after much bargaining. The empire could hardly survive Alexander's death as a unit. Both kings were murdered, Arrhidaeus in 317 and Alexander in 310/309. The provinces became independent kingdoms, and the generals, following Antigonus' lead in 306, took the title of king.

EVALUATION

Of Alexander's plans little reliable information survives. The far-reaching schemes for the conquest of the western Mediterranean and the setting up of a universal monarchy, recorded by Diodorus, a 1st-century Greek historian, are probably based on a later forgery; if not, they were at once jettisoned by his successors and the army. Had he lived, he would no doubt have completed the conquest of Asia Minor, where Paphlagonia, Cappadocia, and Armenia still maintained an effective independence. But in his later years Alexander's aims seem to have been directed toward exploration, in particular of Arabia and the Caspian.

Achievement

In the organization of his empire, Alexander had been content in many spheres to improvise and adapt what he found. His financial policy is an exception; though the details cannot be wholly recovered, it is clear that he set up a central organization with collectors perhaps independent of the local satraps. That this proved a failure was partly due to weaknesses in the character of Harpalus, his chief treasurer. But the establishment of a new coinage with a silver standard based on that of Athens in place of the old bimetallic system current both in Macedonia and in Persia helped trade everywhere and, combined with the release of vast amounts of bullion from the Persian treasuries, gave a much-needed fillip to the economy of the whole Mediterranean area.

Alexander's foundation of new cities—Plutarch speaks of over 70—initiated a new chapter in Greek expansion. No doubt many of the colonists, by no means volunteers, deserted these cities, and marriages with native women led to some dilution of Greek ways; but the Greek (rather than Macedonian) influence remained strong in most of them, and since the process was carried further by Alexander's Seleucid successors, the spread of Hellenic thought and customs over much of Asia as far as Bactria and India was one of the more striking effects of Alexander's conquests.

His plans for racial fusion, on the other hand, were a failure. The Iranian satraps were perhaps not efficient, for out of 18, ten were removed or executed—with what justice it is no longer possible to say. But, more important, the Macedonians, leaders and men alike, rejected the idea, and in the later Seleucid Empire the Greek and Macedonian element was to be clearly dominant.

How far Alexander would have succeeded in the difficult task of coordinating his vast dominions, had he lived, is hard to determine. The only link between the many units that went to make up an empire more disparate than that of the Habsburgs, and far larger, was his own person; and his death came before he could tackle this problem.

What had so far held it all together was his own dynamic personality. He combined an iron will and ability to drive himself and his men to the utmost with a supple and flexible mind; he knew when to draw back and change his policy, though he did this reluctantly. He was imaginative and not without romantic impulses; figures like Achilles, Heracles, and Dionysus were often in his mind, and the salutation at the oracle of Amon clearly influenced his thoughts and ambitions ever afterward. He was swift in anger, and under the strain of his long campaigns this side of his character grew more pronounced. Ruthless and self-willed, he had increasing recourse to terror, showing no hesitation in eliminating men whom he had ceased to trust, either with or without the pretense of a fair trial. Years after his death, Cassander, son of Antipater, a regent of the Macedonian Empire under Alexander, could not pass his statue at Delphi without shuddering. Yet he maintained the loyalty of his men, who followed him to the Hyphasis without complaining and continued to believe in him throughout all hardships. Only when his whim would have taken them still farther into unknown India did he fail to get his way.

Generalship

As a general Alexander is among the greatest the world has known. He showed unusual versatility both in the combination of different arms and in adapting his tactics to the challenge of enemies who commanded novel forms of warfare—the Śaka nomads, the Indian hill tribes, or Porus with his elephants. His strategy was skillful and imaginative, and he knew how to exploit the chances that arise in every battle and may be decisive for victory or defeat; he also drew the last advantage from victory by relentless pursuit. His use of cavalry was so effective that he rarely had to fall back upon his infantry to deliver the crushing blow.

Alexander's short reign marks a decisive moment in the history of Europe and Asia. His expedition and his own personal interest in scientific investigation brought many advances in the knowledge of geography and natural history. His career led to the moving of the great centres of civilization eastward and initiated the new age of the Greek territorial monarchies; it spread Hellenism in a vast colonizing wave throughout the Near East and created, if not politically, at least economically and culturally, a single world stretching from Gibraltar to the Punjab, open to trade and social intercourse and with a considerable overlay of common civilization and the Greek *koinē* as a lingua franca. It is not untrue to say that the Roman Empire, the spread of Christianity as a world religion, and the long centuries of Byzantium were all in some degree the fruits of Alexander's achievement.

BIBLIOGRAPHY. PETER GREEN, *Alexander the Great* (1970), a complete biography, with genealogy and an annotated bibliography; MARY RENAULT, *The Nature of Alexander* (1975), a popular, illustrated biography; WILLIAM W. TARN, *Alexander the Great,* 2 vol. (1948, reissued in 1 vol., 1981), a survey of ancient sources and a favourable portrait of Alexander; E. BADIAN, *Studies in Greek and Roman History* (1964, reprinted 1968), a scholarly collection that includes criticism of Alexander; J.R. HAMILTON, *Alexander the Great* (1974), a historical study that treats Alexander as an efficient politician; ANDREW R. BURN, *Alexander the Great and the Middle East* (1947, reissued 1963), a biographical study that is both scholarly and popular. Controversial issues are discussed in GUY T. GRIFFITH (ed.), *Alexander the Great: The Main Problems* (1966), in the series "Views and Controversies About Classical Antiquity." The original sources for Alexander are lost; among secondary authorities are: DIODORUS, bk. XVII; QUINTUS CURTIUS RUFUS; PLUTARCH, *Life of Alexander;* JUSTINUS' abridgement of TROGUS; ARRIAN, *Anabasis and Indica,* especially in the edition FLAVIUS ARRIANUS, *Arrian* (1976–), a revised text and translation with introduction, notes, and appendixes by P.A. BRUNT, in the "Loeb Classical Library" edition. See also LIONEL I.C. PEARSON, *The Lost Histories of Alexander the Great* (1960); and J.R. HAMILTON, *Plutarch: Alexander; a Commentary* (1969). For Alexander as a military leader, see JOHN F.C. FULLER, *The Generalship of Alexander the Great* (1960, reprinted 1981); ERIC W. MARSDEN, *The Campaign of Gaugamela* (1964); R.D. MILNS, *Alexander the Great* (1969); DONALD W. ENGELS, *Alexander the Great and the Logistics of the Macedonian Army* (1978); and N.G.L. HAMMOND, *Alexander the Great: King, Commander, and Statesman* (1981). ROBIN LANE FOX, *The Search for Alexander* (1980), a biography drawn from newer research on Alexander, coincides with the exhibit of the same title, described in NATIONAL GALLERY OF ART. WASHINGTON, D.C., *The Search for Alexander: An Exhibition* (1980), a catalog with essays on Alexander and on Macedonian history and art. PSEUDO-CALLISTHENES, *The Romance of Alexander the Great,* trans. by ALBERT M. WOLOHOJIAN (1969), is the first English translation of a 5th-century Armenian version of the *Historia Alexandri Magni,* composed in Greek, probably in the 4th century AD, by an unknown poet and falsely ascribed to Callisthenes. See also NANCY J. BURICH, *Alexander the Great* (1970), an annotated bibliography.

(F.W.W./Ed.)

Alexandria

Alexandria (Arabic al-Iskandarīyah), once the greatest city of the ancient world, was the capital of Egypt from its founding by Alexander the Great in 332 BC to AD 642, when it was subdued by the Arabs. It is the second largest city, an urban governorate (*muḥāfaẓah*), and the chief seaport of Egypt. It lies on the Mediterranean Sea at the western edge of the Nile Delta, about 114 air miles (183 kilometres) northwest of Cairo.

Alexandria has always occupied a special place in the popular imagination by virtue of its association with Alexander and with Mark Antony and Cleopatra, immortalized by Shakespeare. Alexandria also played a key role in passing on Hellenic culture to Rome and in the theological disputes over the nature of Christ's divinity that divided the early church. The legendary reputation of ancient Alexandria grew through a thousand years of serious decline following the Arab conquests, during which time virtually all traces of the Greco-Roman city disappeared. By the time Napoleon invaded Egypt in 1798, Alexandria had been reduced to a fishing village. The modern city and port that flourished on the back of the cotton boom in the 19th century has, therefore, little in common with the Alexandria of the past.

The free port status granted Alexandria by the Ottoman Turks accentuated the cultural ambivalence inherent in the city's location—extended along a spit of land with its back to Egypt and its face to the Mediterranean. This idea of a free city, open to all manner of men and ideas, was something the new Alexandria had in common with the old. It was a theme the Greek Constantine Cavafy, drawing heavily on its legendary past, developed in his poems of the city. This idea of Alexandria was taken further by the English writer Lawrence Durrell in his four-part novel, *The Alexandria Quartet.*

Since the 1952 coup in Egypt most of Alexandria's foreign community has departed. Nevertheless, the city remains a thriving commercial community, an important industrial centre, and Egypt's principal holiday resort.

This article is divided into the following sections:

Physical and human geography 229
- The landscape 229
  - The city site
  - Climate
  - The city plan
- The people 230
- The economy 230
  - Industry and commerce
  - The port
  - Transportation
- Administration and social conditions 231
  - Government
  - Services
  - Education
- Cultural life 231

History 231
- Foundation and medieval growth 231
  - The Greek period
  - The Roman period
  - The Islāmic period
- Evolution of the modern city 232

Bibliography 233

Physical and human geography

THE LANDSCAPE

The city site. The modern city extends 25 miles east to west along a limestone ridge, one to two miles wide, that separates the salt lake of Maryūṭ, or Mareotis, now partly drained and cultivated, from the Egyptian mainland. An hourglass-shaped promontory formed by the silting up of a mole (the Heptastadium), which was built soon after Alexandria's founding, links the island of Pharos with the city centre on the mainland. Its two steeply curving bays now form the basins for the Eastern Harbour and the Western Harbour.

Climate. The prevailing north wind, blowing across the Mediterranean, gives Alexandria a markedly different climate from that of the desert hinterland. The summers are relatively temperate, although humidity can build up in July and in August, the hottest month, when the average temperature reaches 87° F (31° C). Winters are cool and invariably marked by a series of violent storms, which can bring torrential rain and even hail. The mean daily temperature in January, which is the coldest month, is 64° F (18° C).

The city plan. Designed by Alexander's personal architect, Dinocrates, the city incorporated the best in Hellenic planning and architecture. Within a century of its founding, its splendours rivaled anything known in the ancient world. Pride of ancient Alexandria and one of the Seven Wonders of the World was the great lighthouse, the Pharos of Alexandria, which stood on the eastern tip of the island of Pharos. Reputed to be more than 440 feet (135 metres) high, it was still standing in the 12th century. In 1477, however, the sultan Qāʾit Bāy used stones from the dilapidated structure to build a fort (named for him), which stands near the original site of the Pharos.

The Pharos

The Canopic Way (now al-Ḥurrīyah Avenue) was the principal thoroughfare of the Greek city, running east and west through its centre. Most of the Ptolemaic and, later, Roman monuments stood nearby. The Canopic Way was intersected at its western end by the Street of the Soma (now an-Nabī Dānyāl Street), along which is the legendary site of Alexander's tomb, thought to lie under the mosque an-Nabī Dānyāl. Close to this intersection was the Mouseion (museum), the city's academy of arts and sciences, which included the great Library of Alexandria. At the seaward end of the Street of the Soma were the two obelisks known as Cleopatra's Needles, which were given in the 19th century to the cities of London and New York.

Between al-Ḥurrīyah Avenue and the railway station is the Roman Theatre, which was uncovered in 1959 at the Kawm al-Dikkah archaeological site. At the southwestern extremity of the ancient city are the Kawm ash-Shuqāfah burial grounds, with their remarkable Hadrianic catacombs dating from the 2nd century AD. Nearby, on the site of the ancient fort of Rakotis, is one of the few classical monuments still standing: the 88-foot-high marble column known as Pompey's Pillar (actually dedicated to Diocletian soon after 297). Parts of the Arab wall, encompassing a much smaller area than the Greco-Roman city, survive on al-Ḥurrīyah Avenue, but the city contracted still further in Ottoman times to the stem of the promontory, now the Turkish Quarter. It is the oldest surviving section of the city, housing its finest mosques and worst slums.

Pompey's Pillar

The modern city only exceeded the size of the old Greek one at the turn of the 19th century, after which it expanded dramatically. Mīdān at-Taḥrīr ("Liberation Square") used to be the commercial centre, close to the Cotton Exchange and the Bourse. The commercial centre has moved eastward to Saʿd Zaghlūl Square, where the Cecil Hotel and the regional headquarters of the World Health Organization are situated, and inland toward the railway station. Blocked to the west by the port and the industrial area, urban development moved eastward along the Corniche, a seaside promenade officially called al-Jaysh Street, and then inland. Today the Corniche is a ribbon of beach huts, bathing clubs, and cafés faced across the road by a continuous wall of hotels and holiday/apartment blocks.

Corniche beach resorts

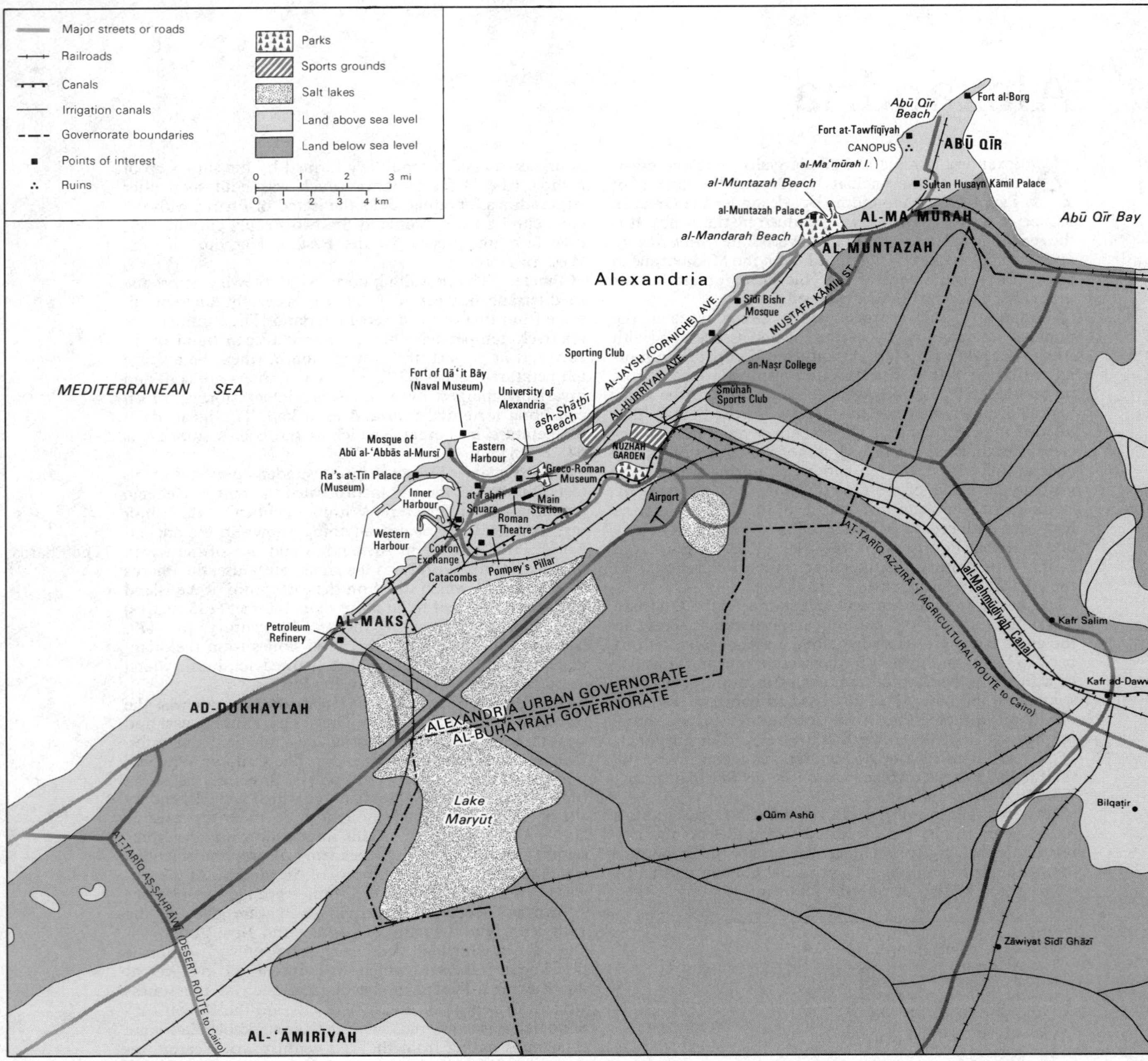

Alexandria.

THE PEOPLE

From the late 19th century to the 1980s the population grew tenfold—the result of high birthrates and migration from the countryside. At the 1976 census the population stood at more than 2,000,000, with half the people under 20 years of age. Projections show that the city will have more than twice that number of people by the year 2000. The once sizable foreign community, which in 1947 still formed one-tenth of the population, has shrunk to insignificant numbers, largely in reaction to the nationalization program and the Israeli-Egyptian conflict. Most Alexandrians belong to one of two main religious groups, the Egyptian Muslims and the Christian Egyptian Copts.

International community depletion

THE ECONOMY

Industry and commerce. Alexandria's chief economic activities, banking, shipping, warehousing, and textile manufacturing, reflect the importance of the port and the cotton trade. The city has become an important industrial centre, accounting for about one-third of Egypt's industrial output. Most industrial development has taken place in the western approaches to the city around the more modern Western Harbour and along its southern flank. Industry is now the city's chief employment sector.

Industrial expansion

The area around the port known as Mīnā' al-Baṣal contains the warehouses and the Cotton Exchange. West across the al-Maḥmūdīyah Canal is al-Qabbārī neighbourhood, site of the asphalt works and rice and paper mills. Farther to the west is al-Maks with its salt and tanning industries. There, also, are Alexandria's principal oil refinery, a cement works, and, farther on, the limestone quarries. Other industrial development is taking place still farther west in ad-Dukhaylah, to the south in al-ʿĀmirīyah, and south of Lake Maryūṭ. Lighter industry is concentrated on the banks of the al-Maḥmūdīyah Canal.

Agriculture is an important economic activity in the hinterland, and land reclamation has been attempted with some success.

The port. The major portion of Egypt's foreign trade passes through Alexandria's two main harbours, of which the Western Harbour is by far the more important. All of the country's cotton and a large part of its oil are exported through the port, as are traditional items such as fruits, vegetables, perfumes, and some finished goods. By

Sa'd Zaghlūl Square on the Mediterranean coast of Alexandria.
Carl Frank

far the largest import is grain. The port handles considerably more than its rated capacity, but improvements are being implemented to relieve congestion, which can be severe. A container terminal was added, and a container port across the bay at ad-Dukhaylah is expected to double Alexandria's port capacity. Egypt's dependence on the port of Alexandria will gradually diminish as the port at Damietta develops.

Congested port conditions

Transportation. Alexandria is linked to other Egyptian urban centres by railway, roads, and air services. It also is connected by canal with the Nile. The main rail link to Cairo has been upgraded, and Alexandria is also the terminus for the rail line that runs to as-Sallūm on the Libyan border. The desert route to Cairo has been improved, thus relieving pressure on the agricultural route through the delta region. Another main road links the city to Libya. Twice-daily air services operate to Cairo, but plans to introduce scheduled international services have not developed. Given the severe limitations on expanding the existing airport at Nuzhah, built on land reclaimed from Lake Maryūṭ, al-ʿĀmirīyah was selected as the site of the new airport.

ADMINISTRATION AND SOCIAL CONDITIONS

Government. In 1895 Alexandria became the first fully constituted municipality in Egypt. Based upon an earlier organization formed by the foreign merchants, it had a high degree of autonomy in financing the city government. After the 1952 revolution the municipality lost its money-raising powers and underwent other changes. In 1960, in accordance with the national government's decentralization policy, the city and its hinterland were incorporated into a *muḥāfaẓah* (governorate). An appointed governor and mostly elected council administer the *muḥāfaẓah* and are responsible to the Ministry of Local Affairs.

Administered as a *muḥāfaẓah*

Services. In city services Alexandria is on a par with other urban *muḥāfaẓāt* of Egypt, providing electricity and pure drinking water to all but a small percentage of homes. Less than half of the city is provided with sewerage, however, and pollution of the beaches is becoming a major health hazard. A new sewerage system is under development, part of an overall plan of city improvements.

Education. In Alexandria, the great learning centre of the ancient world, the state supervises education, as is the rule throughout Egypt. The state system is divided into primary, preparatory, secondary, and technical schools and is the path taken by the vast majority of Egyptians. A few private schools survive from before the 1952 revolution. The University of Alexandria, founded as a state university in 1942 and accommodating about 100,000 students, lies just east of the city centre. Its library is among the largest in Egypt.

CULTURAL LIFE

Alexandria's most important museum, the Greco-Roman Museum, situated behind the Municipality Building on al-Ḥurrīyah Avenue, is noted for its collection of antiquity, most of which comes from finds within the city. Renewed interest in the classical period has revived archaeological exploration, which is focusing on Kawm ad-Dikkah, the underwater site of the Pharos lighthouse, and the search for Alexander's tomb. The Museum of Fine Art, located across the railway line from the city's stadium, presents exhibitions of modern and local art. In addition, two of the royal palaces, Ra's at-Tīn Palace on Pharos island and al-Muntazah Palace at the eastern end of al-Jaysh Avenue are open to the public. Alexandria is well endowed with outdoor recreational establishments. The most popular is the Shallālāt Gardens surrounding the remnants of the Arab walls. The Sporting Club and the Smūhah Sports Club provide a variety of sporting facilities. There are also fine botanical gardens and popular weekend beach resorts.

Archaeological interests

History

FOUNDATION AND MEDIEVAL GROWTH

The Greek period. Alexander the Great founded the city in 332 BC after the start of his Persian campaign; it was to be the capital of his new Egyptian dominion and a naval base that would control the Mediterranean. The choice of the site that included the ancient settlement of Rakotis (which dates back to 1500 BC) was determined by the abundance of water from Lake Maryūṭ, then a spur of the Canopic Nile, and the good anchorage provided offshore by the island of Pharos.

After Alexander left Egypt his viceroy, Cleomenes, continued the creation of Alexandria. With the breakup of the empire on Alexander's death in 323, control of the city passed to his viceroy, Ptolemy I Soter, who founded the dynasty that took his name. The early Ptolemies successfully blended the religions of ancient Greece and Egypt in the cult of Sarapis and presided over Alexandria's golden age. Alexandria profited from the demise of Phoenician power after Alexander sacked Tyre (332 BC) and from Europe's growing trade with the East via the Nile and the canal that then linked it with the Red Sea. Indeed, Alexandria became, within a century of its founding, the greatest city in the world and a centre of Greek scholarship and science. Such scholars as Euclid, Archimedes, Plotinus the philosopher, and Ptolemy and Eratosthenes the geographers studied at the Mouseion, the great research institute founded by the Ptolemies. Alexandria also was a centre of Jewish learning; and, according to tradition, the Septuagint translation of the Old Testament from Hebrew to Greek was produced there.

The Roman period. The decline of the Ptolemies in the 2nd and 1st centuries BC was matched by the rise of Rome. Alexandria played a major part in the intrigues that led to the establishment of imperial Rome.

It was at Alexandria that Cleopatra, the last of the Ptolemies, courted Julius Caesar and claimed to have borne him a son. Her attempts at restoring the fortunes of the Ptolemaic dynasty, however, were thwarted by Caesar's assassination and her unsuccessful support of Mark Antony against Caesar's great-nephew Octavian. In 30 BC Octavian (later the emperor Augustus) formally brought Alexandria and Egypt under Roman rule. To punish the city for not supporting him, he abolished the Alexandrian Senate and built his own city at what was then the suburb of ar-Raml. Alexandria, however, could not be ignored, since it held the key to the Egyptian granary on which Rome increasingly came to rely; and the city soon regained its independence.

In AD 45 St. Mark, the traditional author of the second Synoptic Gospel, is said to have made his first convert to Christianity in Alexandria. Thenceforth, the city's growing Christian and Jewish communities united against Rome's attempts to impose official paganism. Periodic persecutions by various early emperors, especially by Diocletian beginning in 303, failed to subdue these communities; and, after the empire had formally adopted Christianity under Constantine I, the stage was set for schisms within the church.

The first conflict that split the early church was between two Alexandrian prelates, Athanasius and Arius, over the nature of Christ's divinity. It was settled in 325 by the adoption of the Creed of Nicaea, which affirmed Christ's spiritual divinity and branded Arianism—the belief that Christ was lower than God—as heresy. Arianism, however, had many imperial champions, and this sharpened the conflict between the Alexandrian church and the state. In 391 Christians destroyed the Sarapeum, sanctum of the Ptolemaic cult and what Cleopatra had saved of the great Mouseion library. In 415 a Christian faction killed the Neoplatonist philosopher Hypatia, and Greek culture in Alexandria quickly declined.

After the ascendancy of the patriarchate of Constantinople—to which the see of Alexandria answered after the division of the Roman Empire in 364—the local church adopted Monophysitism (belief in the single nature and therefore physical divinity of Christ) as a way of asserting its independence. Although Monophysitism was rejected by the Council of Chalcedon (451), the Alexandrian church resisted Constantinople's attempts to bring it into line. An underground church developed to oppose the established one and became a focus of Egyptian loyalties. Disaffection with Byzantine rule created the conditions in which Alexandria fell first to the Persians, in 616, and then, in 642, to the Arabs.

Acceptance of Monophysitism

The Islāmic period. The Arabs occupied Alexandria without resistance. Thenceforth, apart from an interlude in 645 when the city was briefly taken by the Byzantine fleet, Alexandria's fortunes were tied to the new faith and culture emanating from the Arabian Desert. Alexandria soon was eclipsed politically by the new Arab capital at al-Fusṭāṭ (which later was absorbed into the modern capital, Cairo), and this city became the strategic prize for those wanting to control Egypt. Nevertheless, Alexandria continued to flourish as a trading centre, principally for textiles and luxury goods, as Arab influence expanded westward through North Africa and then into Europe. The city also was important as a naval base, especially under the Fāṭimids and the Mamlūks, but already it was contracting in size in line with its new, more modest status. The Arab walls (rebuilt in the 13th and 14th centuries and torn down in 1811) encompassed less than half the area of the Greco-Roman city.

Alexandria survived the early Crusades relatively unscathed, and the city came into its own again with the development of the East–West spice trade, which Egypt monopolized. The loss of this trade—which came about after the discovery of the sea route to India in 1498 and the Turkish conquest of Egypt in 1517—was the final blow to the city's fortunes. Under Turkish rule the canal linking Alexandria to the Rosetta branch of the Nile was allowed to silt up, strangling the city's commercial lifeline. Alexandria had been reduced to a small fishing village when Napoleon invaded Egypt in 1798.

EVOLUTION OF THE MODERN CITY

Alexandria's rebirth began when Muḥammad ʿAlī was appointed Ottoman viceroy and pasha of Egypt in 1805. Hoping to modernize Egypt, he reopened Alexandria's access to the Nile by building the 45-mile-long al-Maḥmūdīyah Canal (completed between 1818 and 1820), new docks, and an arsenal (1828–33), where he located industry. Foreign traders were encouraged by the Capitulations, which gave them certain legal rights and privileges (for instance, to be tried in their own courts), and they began to settle in and develop the city. Cotton was introduced into Egypt in the 1820s, and by the 1840s Europe's growing appetite for the commodity was making Alexandria rich. The city became an increasingly important banking and commercial centre. The opening of the Cairo railway in 1856, the cotton boom created by the American Civil War in the early 1860s, and the opening of the Suez Canal in 1869, which reestablished Egypt as the principal staging post to India, led to another cycle of rapid growth.

The British bombardment of the city in 1882 to put down a local nationalist revolt led directly to the British occupation that lasted until 1922. The city nevertheless continued to prosper and expand, retaining its position as the second (summer) capital of Egypt. Under British patronage the foreign community—some 100,000 strong—continued to flourish.

During World War I, Alexandria was the chief Allied naval base of the eastern Mediterranean. The city was much more actively involved in World War II, as it came perilously close to being captured by Axis armies and was repeatedly bombarded. British forces left the city in 1946.

Alexandria meanwhile played its part in the nationalist struggle between and after the world wars. In 1952 it was the point of departure from Egyptian soil for King Farouk after he was deposed in the revolution led by Gamal Abdel Nasser. In 1956 the failure of the tripartite British, French, and Israeli invasion, following President Nasser's nationalization of the Suez Canal, discouraged continued residence of the foreign community. The sequestrations that followed Suez and the subsequent nationalizations in the early 1960s drove many more foreigners out.

During the 1960s, Alexandria was thoroughly Egyptianized and brought firmly under the control of the national government. It benefited, however, from Nasser's industrialization program; this boon was felt especially in the food-processing and textile-manufacturing industries, which had been expanded considerably between the wars. The city was adversely affected by Egypt's devastating defeat by Israel in the Six-Day War (June 1967), by the dislocation created when the Suez Canal was closed as a result of the war, and by the Egyptian evacuation of the Canal Zone. Alexandria's port became swamped by trade diverted from Port Said, and it had not fully recovered when in 1974 the Egyptian government introduced an open-door trade policy that led to a flood of imports.

Liberalization, coupled with tentative moves at decentralization under Pres. Anwar el-Sādāt, Nasser's successor, revived calls by the merchant community for greater financial autonomy. These in turn created a new sense of civic identity and pride. The discovery in 1976 of natural gas reserves offshore at Abū Qīr Bay and onshore at Abū Māḍī farther along the Nile Delta has spurred industrial development; the principal beneficiary has been ad-Dukhaylah, which has become a major iron and steel centre. Refinery facilities also were upgraded, especially after the completion (1977) of a crude-oil pipeline from the city of Suez to the Mediterranean near Alexandria and of another pipeline linking Musturud (north of Cairo) with Alexandria; Egypt's petrochemical industry has been established at al-ʿĀmirīyah.

Economic growth

Alexandria's access to the outside world also has been promoted to encourage the development of light industry. A free zone has been established in al-ʿĀmirīyah. Although Alexandria's stock and cotton exchanges were closed in the 1960s, the stock exchange subsequently has been allowed to reopen. The city has launched a master plan designed to bring massive civic improvements in the late 20th century.

BIBLIOGRAPHY. ANTHONY DE COSSON, *Mareotis* (1935), is an authoritative, well-written history and description of the Maryūṭ district; and PERCIVAL G. ELGOOD, *The Ptolemies of Egypt* (1938), is a scholarly but lively history of the Ptolemies, from Ptolemy I (died 283 BC) to Cleopatra (died 30 BC). MARY ROWLATT, *A Family in Egypt* (1956), based on family letters, includes descriptions of 19th- and 20th-century European life in Alexandria. The same author's *Founders of Modern Egypt* (1962) is a detailed account of Egyptian events of the 1870s and 1880s that culminated in Alexandria. JACQUES BERQUE, *Egypt: Imperialism and Revolution* (1972; originally published in French, 1967), is a monumental history of Egypt under British rule; it contains vivid firsthand accounts of late 19th- and early 20th-century Alexandria. LAWRENCE DURRELL, *The Alexandria Quartet: Justine, Balthazar, Mountolive, Clea,* 4 vol. (1957–60; reissued 1970 in 1 vol.), is a group of four novels set in Alexandria between the world wars; perhaps the best-known piece of modern literature on Alexandria, it is widely attributed with having revived interest in the city. E.M. FORSTER, *Alexandria: A History and a Guide,* new ed. (1982), is a revision of the classic guide to the city, which describes it, quarter by quarter, as it was in the 1920s and includes notes on how the same places look half a century later; included is a detailed account of the Greco-Roman Museum. C.P. CAVAFY, *Collected Poems,* trans. by EDMUND KEELEY and PHILIP SHERRARD, ed. by GEORGE SAVIDIS (1975), is the first English publication of the poems of the city's most illustrious modern poet writing in Greek.

(Ma.R./J.A.Ma.)

Algae

Algae (singular alga) are a group of predominantly aquatic, photosynthetic organisms that defy precise definition. They range in size from the tiny flagellate *Micromonas* that is 1 micrometre (0.00004 inch) in diameter to giant kelp that reach 60 metres (200 feet) in length. Algae provide much of the Earth's oxygen, they are the food base for almost all aquatic life, they are an original source of petroleum products, and they provide foods and industrial products for humans. The algae have many types of life cycles, from simple to complex. Their photosynthetic pigments are more varied than those of plants, and their cells have features not found among plants and animals. Some algae are ancient, while other groups have evolved more recently. The taxonomy of algae is changing rapidly because so much new information is being discovered. The study of algae is termed phycology, and one who studies algae is known as a phycologist.

The algae as treated in this article do not include the prokaryotic (nucleus-lacking) blue-green algae (cyanobacteria) and prochlorophyte algae. Beginning in the 1970s, some scientists suggested that the study of the prokaryotic algae should be incorporated into the study of bacteria because of shared cellular features. Other scientists consider the oxygen-producing photosynthetic capability of blue-green and prochlorophyte algae to be as significant as cell structure, and they continue to classify them as algae.

In this article the algae are defined as eukaryotic (nucleus-bearing) organisms that photosynthesize but lack the specialized reproductive structures of plants. Plants always have multicellular reproductive structures where the fertile, gamete-producing cells are surrounded by sterile cells; this never occurs in algae. Algae lack true roots, stems, and leaves, but they share this feature with the plant division Bryophyta (*e.g.,* mosses and liverworts).

Beginning in the 1830s, algae were classified into major groups based on colour. The red, brown, and green seaweeds are well known to those who have walked along a rocky seashore. The colours are a reflection of the chloroplast pigment molecules—*i.e.,* the chlorophylls, carotenoids, and phycobiliproteins. Many more than three groups are now recognized, and each class of algae shares a common set of pigment types that is distinct from those of all other groups.

The algae are not closely related in an evolutionary sense. Specific groups of algae share enough features with protozoa and fungi that it is difficult to distinguish them from certain protozoa or fungi without using the presence of chloroplasts and photosynthesis as delimiting features. Thus, some algae have a closer evolutionary relationship with the protozoa or fungi than they do with other algae, and the converse is also true—some protozoa or fungi are more closely related to algae than to other protozoa or fungi. In fact, if the algae are united into one evolutionary group with a common ancestor, then that evolutionary group will include animals, fungi, plants, and protozoa as well.

Knowledge and use of algae are perhaps as old as mankind (*Homo sapiens*), and possibly earlier species such as *H. erectus* also knew of, and used, algae. Seaweeds are still eaten by coastal societies, and algae are considered acceptable foods in many restaurants. Anyone who has slipped on a "slimy" rock (covered with diatoms) while crossing a stream has had firsthand experience with algae. Others know algae as green sheens on pools and ponds. The algae are the base of the food chain for all marine organisms since most plants do not live in the oceans. Because the oceans occupy about 71 percent of the Earth's surface area, the role of algae in supporting aquatic life is essential.

This article discusses the algae in general terms. For a discussion of the related protists, see the articles PROTOZOA and PROTISTS. For a more complete discussion of photosynthesis, see the articles PHOTOSYNTHESIS and PLANTS.

For coverage of related topics in the *Macropædia* and *Micropædia,* see the *Propædia,* section 313, and the *Index.*

The article is divided into the following sections:

General features 234
Size range and diversity of structure
Distribution and abundance
Importance
Form and function 237
The algal cell
Flagella
Mitosis
Cellular respiration
Photosynthesis
The effects of water on light
Reproduction and life histories
Evolution and paleontology 241
Classification 242
Diagnostic features
Annotated classification
Bibliography 243

GENERAL FEATURES

Size range and diversity of structure. Algae span seven orders of magnitude in size. Many algae consist of only one cell, others have two or more cells, and the largest have millions of cells. In large, macroscopic algae, groups of cells are specialized for specific functions, such as anchorage, transport, photosynthesis, and reproduction. Specialization involving thousands of cells is sometimes interpreted as a measure of complexity and evolutionary advancement. An alga that can accomplish the same functions using only one cell, however, should not be interpreted as a "simple" alga.

Types of structure

The algae are artificially divided into several types based on the morphology of their vegetative, or growing, state (Figures 1–3). Filamentous forms have cells arranged in chains and an overall appearance like strings or filaments. Some filaments (like *Spirogyra,* Figure 1) are unbranched, while others, like *Stigeoclonium,* are branched and appear bushlike. In many red algae—for example, *Palmaria*—numerous adjacent filaments lie together and create the gross morphological form of the alga. Parenchymatous (tissuelike) forms, such as the giant kelp *Macrocystis,* can become very large. Other algae grow to large sizes without forming distinct cells (*i.e.,* the protoplasm flows together as a large living mass); the green seaweed *Codium,* commonly known as dead-man's-fingers, is an example. Some algae have flagella and swim through the water. These flagellates (Figure 1) range from single cells, as in *Ochromonas,* to colonial organisms with thousands of cells. Coccoid and capsoid algae (Figure 1) are unicellular or multicellular. Coccoid organisms, such as *Scenedesmus,* have an exact number of cells, and that number is produced by a series of rapid cell divisions when the organism is first formed; once the exact cell number is obtained, the organism grows in size but not in cell number. Capsoid organisms, such as *Chrysocapsa,* have variable numbers of cells; the cell number increases gradually, and the cells are embedded in a copious gel.

Distribution and abundance. Algae are ubiquitous, although they are most common in aquatic habitats. Algae

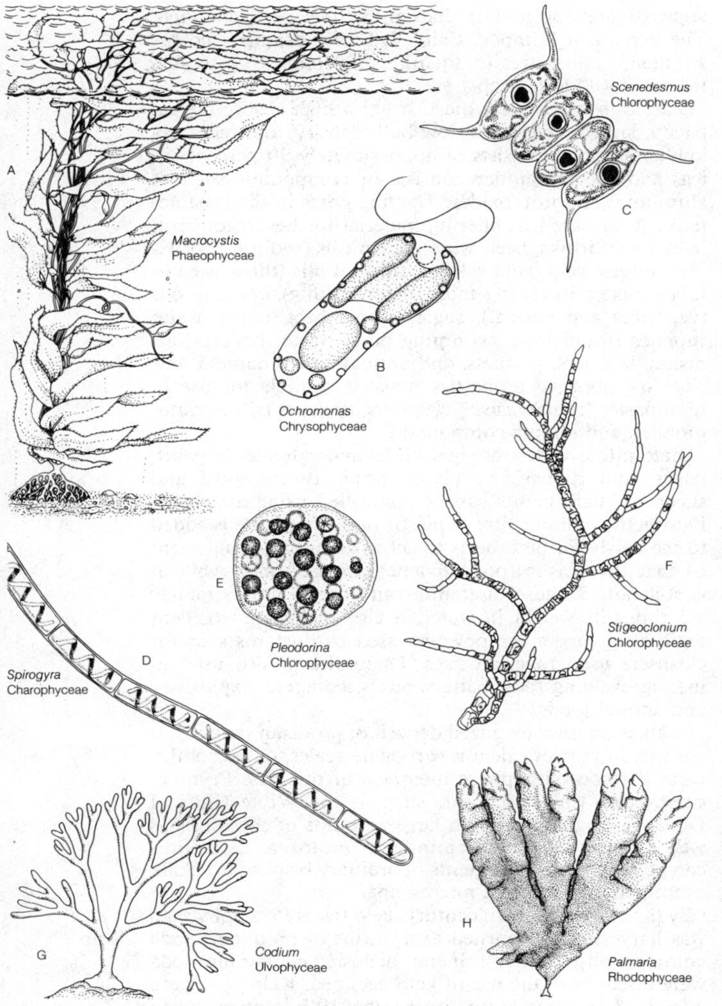

Figure 1. *Representative algae.*
(A) *Macrocystis*, a parenchymatous alga. (B) *Ochromonas*, a single-celled flagellate. (C) *Scenedesmus*, a coccoid alga. (D) *Spirogyra*, an unbranched filamentous alga. (E) *Pleodorina*, a colonial flagellate. (F) *Stigeoclonium*, a branched filamentous alga. (G) *Codium* (or dead-man's-fingers), a large branching alga that is not subdivided by cell walls. (H) *Palmaria*, a complex filamentous alga.

After (A,F,G) R.F. Scagel *et al.*, *Nonvascular Plants: An Evolutionary Survey*, © 1982 Wadsworth Publishing Company, Inc. Adapted by permission of the publisher; (B) R.A. Andersen, *Phycologia*, vol. 21 (3) © 1982 Blackwell Scientific Publishers; (D) H.J. Walter in C.M. Palmer, *Algae in Water Supplies of the United States*, U.S. Department of Health, Education, and Welfare, 1960; (H) G. South and A. Whitick, *Introduction to Phycology*, © 1987 Blackwell Scientific Publications. From photographs (C) by courtesy of J. Pickett-Heaps; (E) by courtesy of R.C. Starr

Categorization by habitat

are often categorized ecologically by their habitat. Planktonic algae are suspended in the water, while neustonic algae grow on the water surface. Cryophilic algae grow in snow and ice, while thermophilic algae live in hot springs. Epidaphic algae live on soil, and endedaphic algae live in soil. Algae can live attached to other organisms: epizoic algae grow on animals such as turtles, polar bears, and tree sloths; epiphytic algae grow on fungi, plants, or other algae. Algae can be classified even more specifically. For example, corticolous algae grow on the bark of trees. Epilithic algae live on rocks, endolithic algae live in rocks, and chasmolithic algae grow in rock fissures. Some algae live inside other organisms, and in a general sense these are called endosymbionts. Specifically, endozoic endosymbionts live in protozoa or animals, while endophytic endosymbionts live in fungi, plants, or other algae. Algae also live in the atmosphere, moving with air currents and receiving moisture and nutrients from clouds.

Algal abundance and diversity varies from one environment to the next, just as plant abundance and diversity varies from tropical rain forests to deserts. Terrestrial vegetation (plants and algae) is influenced most by precipitation and temperature, while aquatic vegetation (primarily algae) is influenced most by light and nutrients. When nutrients are abundant, as occurs in some polluted waters, algal cell numbers can become great enough to produce obvious patches of algae. These patches are called "blooms" or "red tides." The number of organisms necessary for a bloom varies with the size of the organism and the concentration of cells. Blooms are usually linked to favourable growing conditions, including an abundance of nutrients, but blooms do not occur every time favourable conditions exist, and therefore it is difficult to explain or predict their occurrence.

Ecological importance

Importance. Algae use photosynthesis to form organic food molecules from carbon dioxide and water. Like plants, algae are located at the base of the food web, and nonphotosynthetic organisms depend upon this photosynthetic food base for their existence. Nearly three-fourths of Earth is covered by water, and plants are virtually absent from the major water sources, the oceans. Marine life—including whales, seals, fish, turtles, shrimps, lobsters, clams, octopuses, starfish, and worms—ultimately depends upon algae for its existence.

In addition to making organic molecules, algae produce oxygen as a by-product of photosynthesis. Algae produce an estimated 30 to 50 percent of the net global oxygen. This oxygen is available to humans and other terrestrial animals for respiration, and it is consumed when coal, wood, or oil is burned. Although terrestrial ecosystems also produce large amounts of oxygen, the organisms living in these ecosystems consume it relatively rapidly on a geologic time scale, so that the net oxygen production by rain forests over time is low.

Crude oil and natural gas are the remnants of the photosynthetic products of ancient algae, which were subsequently modified by bacteria. The North Sea oil deposits were formed from coccolithophore algae (class Prymnesiophyceae), and the Colorado oil shales were produced by an alga similar to *Botryococcus.* Today, *Botryococcus* (a green alga) produces blooms in Lake Baikal, in the Soviet Union, and produces large amounts of oil. The oil is so abundant on the surface of the lake that it is collected with a special skimming apparatus. Several companies have grown oil-producing algae in high-salinity ponds and have extracted the oil as an alternative to fossil fuels.

Commercial value

Algae, as processed and unprocessed food, have a commercial value of several billion dollars annually. Approximately 500 species are eaten by humans, and some 160 are commercially important. In addition to the use of algal extracts in prepared foods (see below), algae are eaten directly in many parts of the world. Algae are a significant food item in the diets of East Asian and Pacific Island societies, and unprocessed algae are eaten by South Americans, North Americans, and northern Europeans. Hawaiians have the most diverse diet of algae. In the 1800s at least 75 species were eaten by Hawaiians, and in the 1980s more than 50 species of algae were still being consumed.

The red alga *Porphyra* is the most important commercial food alga. In Japan alone approximately 100,000 hectares (247,000 acres) of shallow bays and seas are farmed. *Porphyra* has two major stages in its life cycle, the *Conchocelis* stage and the *Porphyra* stage. The *Conchocelis* stage is a small, shell-boring stage that is artificially propagated on oyster shells. The mature *Conchocelis* produces conchospores that germinate and grow into the large *Porphyra* stage. Either the oyster shells are tied to ropes or nets, or the conchospores are seeded directly onto the ropes or nets. The large, mature *Porphyra* blades are removed from the nets and washed, chopped, and pressed into sheets to dry.

Palmaria palmata, another red alga, is eaten in the north Atlantic region. Known as dulse in Canada and the United States, as dillisk in Ireland, and as *söl* in Iceland, it is harvested by hand from intertidal rocks during low tide. *Laminaria* species (brown algae) are also harvested from wild beds along rocky shores, particularly in Japan. *Laminaria* is eaten with meat or fish and in soups. The green algae *Monostroma* and *Ulva* look like lettuce leaves (their common name is sea lettuce), and they are eaten as salads or in soups, relishes, and meat or fish dishes.

The microscopic, freshwater green alga *Chlorella* is cultivated and eaten in Taiwan, Japan, Malaysia, and the Philippines. It has a high protein content (53–65 percent) and has been considered as a possible food source during extended space travel.

The cell walls of many seaweeds contain phycocolloids that have received increasing use in prepared foods. The term phycocolloid means "algal colloid" and is based upon the colloidal substances that are extracted from cell walls. The usefulness of these compounds is based on the colloidal property of alternating between sol (fluid) and gel (solid) states. The three major phycocolloids are alginates, agars, and carrageenans. Alginates are extracted primarily from brown seaweeds, and agar and carrageenan are extracted from red seaweeds. These phycocolloids are cell-wall polysaccharides that are formed by the polymerization of chemically modified galactose sugar molecules (agars and carrageenans) or of organic acids, such as mannuronic acid and glucuronic acid (alginates). Phycocolloids are safely consumed by humans and other animals and are therefore used in a wide variety of prepared foods, such as "ready-mix" cakes, "instant" puddings and pie fillings, and artificial dairy toppings.

Alginates

Alginates, or alginic acids, are commercially extracted from brown seaweeds, especially the kelp *Macrocystis, Laminaria,* and *Ascophyllum.* Alginates are used in ice creams to limit ice crystal formation, thereby producing a smooth texture, and are also used as emulsifiers and thickeners in syrups and as fillers in candy bars and salad dressings.

Agars are extracted primarily from species of the red alga *Gelidium,* but they are also obtained from other red algae, especially *Gracilaria, Pterocladia, Acanthopeltis,* and *Ahnfeltia.* Agars are used in instant pie fillings, canned meats or fish, and bakery icings. Agar is also used as a clarifying agent in beer and wine.

Carrageenans, from the Irish word "carraigin" (meaning Irish moss), are extracted from various red algae: *Eucheuma* in the Philippines, *Chondrus crispus* in the United States and the Canadian Maritime Provinces, and *Iridaea* in Chile. Carrageenans are widely used in food products, and it is estimated that the average human consumption of carrageenans in the United States is 250 milligrams (0.01 ounce) a day. Carrageenans are used as thickening and stabilizing agents in dairy products, imitation creams, puddings, syrups, and canned pet foods.

Industrial uses

The diatoms have played an important role in industrial development during the 20th century. The frustules, or cell walls, of diatoms (class Bacillariophyceae) are made of opaline silica and contain many fine pores. Occasionally, large quantities of frustules are deposited in ocean sediments, and the fossilized remains are called diatomite. When geologic uplifting brings these deposits above sea level, the diatomite is easily mined. Diatomite contains approximately 50 million diatom frustules per cubic inch. The deposit at Lompoc, Calif., U.S., for example, covers 13 square kilometres (5 square miles) and is up to 425 metres (1,400 feet) deep.

Diatomite is relatively inert. It has a high absorptive capacity, large surface area, low bulk density, and relatively low abrasion. It consists of approximately 90 percent silica, and the remainder consists of compounds such as aluminum and iron oxides. The fine pores in the frustules make it an excellent filtering material for beverages (fruit juices, soft drinks, beer, wine), chemicals (sodium hydroxide, sulfuric acid, gold salts), industrial oils (those used as lubricants or in rolling mills or for cutting), cooking oils (vegetable and animal), sugars (cane, beet, corn), water supplies (municipal, swimming pool, waste, boiler), varnishes, lacquers, jet fuels, and antibiotics, to name a few. The low abrasive properties make it suitable for use in toothpaste, "nonabrasive" cleansers, polishes (silver, automobile), and buffing compounds.

Diatomite is widely used as a filler and extender in paint, paper, and rubber and plastic products; the gloss and sheen of "flat" paints can be controlled using diatomite. During the manufacture of plastic bags, diatomite is added to the newly formed sheets to act as an antiblocking agent so that the plastic (polyethylene) can be rolled while it is still hot. Because diatomite can absorb approximately 2.5 times its weight in water, it also makes an excellent anticaking carrier for powders used to dust roses or for cleansers used to clean rugs. Diatomite is also used in making welding rods, battery boxes, concrete, explosives, and animal foods.

Chalk is another fossilized deposit of protistan remains. It consists in part of calcium carbonate scales, or coccoliths, from the coccolithophore members of the class Prymnesiophyceae. Chalk deposits, such as the White Cliffs of Dover in England, contain large amounts of coccoliths as well as the shells of foraminiferan protozoa. Coccoliths can be observed in fragments of ordinary blackboard chalk examined under a light microscope.

Kelp

By the end of the 18th century, kelp (class Phaeophyceae) was harvested and burned as a means of producing soda commercially. When mineral deposits containing soda were discovered, the use of kelp declined. Kelp was again harvested in abundance during the 19th century when salts and iodine were extracted for commercial use. Once again, however, newly discovered mineral deposits, this time of salt and iodides, led to a demise of the kelp industry. During the 20th century the kelp industry again flourished. During World War I the United States used kelp as a source of potash and acetone.

Seaweeds have been used as agricultural fertilizers for centuries in many parts of the world. Coastal farmers cut seaweeds that were spread over the soil. Kelp is now used

By courtesy of Robert A. Andersen

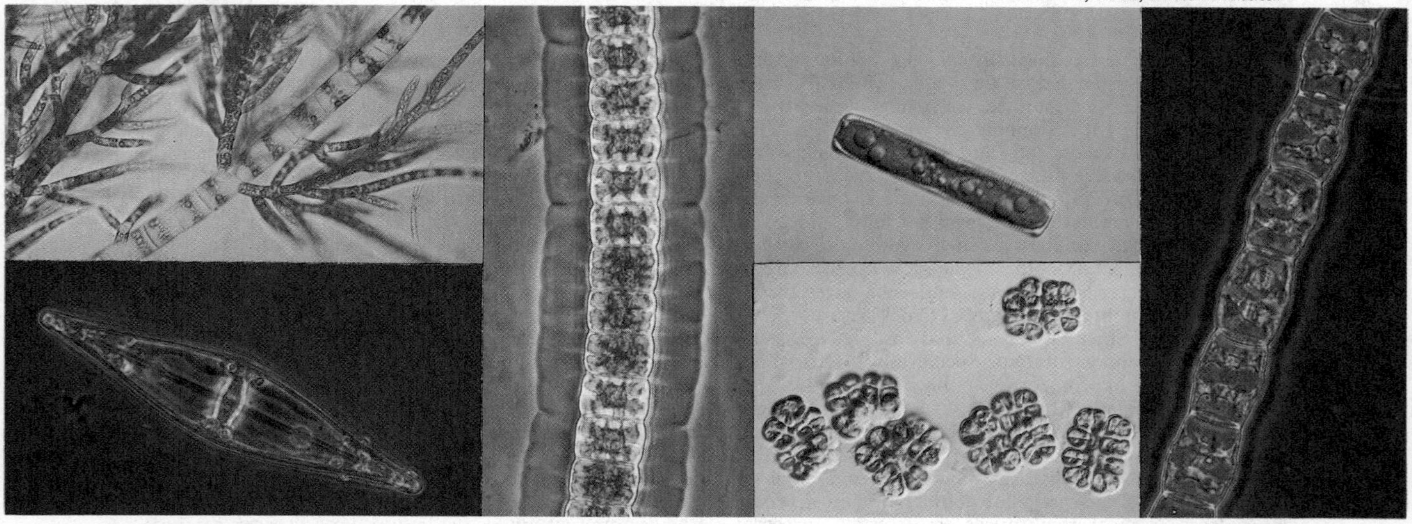

Figure 2: *Unicellular and colonial algae.*
(Top left) *Drapomaldia.* (Bottom left) *Stauroneis.* (Centre left) *Hyalotheca.* (Centre top) *Diatom.*
(Centre bottom) *Phaeoplaca.* (Right) *Bambosina.*

to extract macronutrients and micronutrients for specialized plant fertilizers and animal feed supplements. Dried kelp is almost 50 percent mineral matter; *Ascophyllum nodosum,* for example, contains 55 trace elements. Commercial extracts used as plant fertilizers contain a mixture of macronutrients, micronutrients, and trace elements that provide robust plant growth. The metal and other trace elements are chelated (bound) to organic sugars so that the concentration of free metals, which can be toxic to plants and animals, is very low. The equilibrium between chelated and free forms provides a gradual release of nutrients from the extract (fertilizer) as plants use the free forms.

Phycocolloids have industrial uses in addition to their important roles in food products. Because they are relatively inert and have good gelling properties, they are used as creams and gels for carrying minute amounts of active additives, as in medical drugs or insecticides. Agar is used extensively as a bacteriologic culturing substrate in medical and research facilities and is also used as a substrate for eukaryotic cell and tissue culture, including the culture of algae themselves. Carrageenans are used in the manufacture of shampoos, cosmetics, and medicines.

The green unicellular flagellate *Dunaliella* is cultivated in saline ponds. The culture conditions are manipulated so that carotene or glycerol are produced in large amounts. These compounds are extracted and sold commercially.

Toxic algae

Algae can be harmful to humans. Some algae produce toxins that become concentrated in shellfish and finfish. Although they have little effect on shellfish and finfish, the toxins accumulate in the seafood flesh, making it unsafe or poisonous for human consumption. The dinoflagellates (class Dinophyceae) are the most notorious producers of toxins. Paralytic shellfish poisoning is caused by saxitoxin or any of at least 12 related compounds. Saxitoxin is probably the most toxic compound known and is 100,000 times more toxic than cocaine. Saxitoxin and saxitoxin-like compounds are nerve toxins that interfere with neuromuscular junctions. *Alexandrium tamarense* and *Gymnodinium catenatum* are the two species most often associated with paralytic shellfish poisoning. Diarrheic shellfish poisoning is caused by okadaic acids that are produced by several algae, especially species of *Dinophysis.* Neurotoxic shellfish poisoning is caused by toxins produced in *Gymnodinium breve,* a red tide organism. This alga is notorious for fish kills and shellfish poisoning along the coast of Florida, U.S. When the red tide blooms are blown to shore, wind-sprayed toxic cells can cause health problems for animals that breathe the air.

Ciguatera is a disease of humans caused by consumption of tropical fish infected with the algae *Gambierdiscus* or *Ostreopsis.* Unlike many other dinoflagellate toxins, ciguatoxin and maitotoxin are concentrated in fish rather than shellfish. Levels as low as one part per billion in fish are sufficient to cause human intoxications.

Not all shellfish poisons are produced by dinoflagellates. Amnesiac shellfish poisoning is caused by domoic acid, which is produced by diatoms (Bacillariophyceae) such as *Nitzschia pungens* f. *multiseries,* and *Nitzschia pseudodelicatissima.* Symptoms of this poisoning in humans progress from abdominal cramps to vomiting to memory loss to disorientation and finally to death.

Several algae produce toxins that are lethal to fish. *Prymnesium parvum* (class Prymnesiophyceae) has caused massive die-offs in ponds where fish are cultured, and *Chrysochromulina polylepis* (class Prymnesiophyceae) has caused major fish kills along the coasts of the Scandinavian countries. Other algae, such as *Heterosigma* (class Raphidophyceae) and *Dictyocha* (class Dictyochophyceae), are suspected fish killers as well.

Algae in medicine

Algae can cause human diseases by directly attacking human tissues, although the frequency is rare. Protothecosis is caused by a chloroplast-lacking green alga, *Prototheca.* The alga infects skin lesions, grows subcutaneously, and can eventually spread to the lymph glands. *Prototheca* is also believed to cause ulcerative dermatitis in the Australian platypus. Similar infections, in humans and cattle, are caused by chloroplast-bearing species of *Chlorella* of the class Chlorophyceae.

Some seaweeds contain high concentrations of arsenic and when eaten cause arsenic poisoning. For example, the brown alga *Hizikia* has sufficient arsenic that it was used as a rat poison in Asian countries.

Diatoms have been used in forensic medicine. Where death by drowning is suspected, lung tissue is examined. The presence of silica diatom cell walls can verify death by drowning; in mysterious cases, the diatom species can be used to pinpoint the exact location of death because the species are characteristic for a given lake, bog, or bay. Diatomite used in the manufacture of car polishes, paints, and matches, for example, is used in solving crimes as well.

FORM AND FUNCTION

The algal cell. Eukaryotic algal cells contain three types of double-membrane-bound organelles: the nucleus, the chloroplast, and the mitochondrion. The nucleus contains most of the genetic material of the cell, and the DNA (deoxyribonucleic acid) molecules exist as linear strands. The DNA is condensed into obvious chromosomes only at the time of nuclear division (mitosis) in most algae; however, the nuclear DNA of the classes Dinophyceae and Euglenophyceae is always condensed. The two mem-

(Top left, bottom left, and bottom centre) Heather Angel; (top centre) Richard H. Chesher; (top right) Douglas P. Wilson; (bottom right) Raniero Maltini and Piero Solaini—SCALA from Art Resource/EB Inc.

Figure 3: *Diversity among macroscopic algae.*
(Top left) *Hormosira banksii.* (Top centre) *Caulerpa.* (Top centre) *Halimeda discoidea.* (Bottom left) *Laminaria digitata.* (Bottom centre) *Fucus serratus.* (Bottom right) *Acetabularia.*

branes surrounding the nucleus are referred to as the nuclear envelope, which typically has specialized nuclear pores that regulate the movement of molecules into and out of the nucleus.

The chloroplast is the site of photosynthesis, the complex set of biochemical reactions that convert light energy, carbon dioxide, and water into sugars. The chloroplast contains flattened, membranous sacs, called thylakoids, that contain the photosynthetic light-harvesting pigments, the chlorophylls, carotenoids, or phycobiliproteins (see below *Photosynthesis*).

The mitochondrion is the site where food molecules are broken down and carbon dioxide, water, and chemical bond energy are released, a process called cellular respiration (see below *Cellular respiration*). Photosynthesis and respiration are approximately opposite processes, the former building sugar molecules and the latter breaking them down. The inner membrane of the mitochondrion is infolded to a great extent, and this provides the surface area necessary for respiration. The infoldings, called cristae, have three morphologies: (1) flattened or sheetlike, (2) fingerlike or tubular, and (3) paddlelike. Plants and animals, by comparison, have only flattened cristae.

Chloroplasts and mitochondria also have their own DNA. This DNA is not like nuclear DNA, however, because it is circular rather than linear, and therefore it resembles the DNA of prokaryotes. The similarity of chloroplastic and mitochondrial DNA to prokaryotic DNA has led many scientists to accept the hypothesis that these organelles resulted from a long and successful symbiosis of prokaryote cells inside eukaryote host cells. These symbioses have been used in defining the endosymbiosis hypothesis, which states that eukaryotic cells are formed in part by incorporating prokaryotes as specialized organelles.

Cell organelles

Algae have several single-membrane-bound organelles, including the endoplasmic reticulum, Golgi apparatus, lysosome, peroxisome, vacuole, contractile vacuole, and ejectile organelles. The endoplasmic recticulum is a complex membranous system that forms intracellular compartments, acts as a transport system within the cell, and serves as a site for synthesizing fats, oils, and proteins. The Golgi apparatus is a series of membranous sacs that are stacked like pancakes. The Golgi apparatus performs four distinct functions: it sorts many molecules synthesized elsewhere in the cell; it produces carbohydrates like cellulose or sugars, and sometimes it attaches the sugars to other molecules; it packages molecules in small vesicles; and it marks the vesicles so that they are routed to the proper destination. The lysosome is a specialized vacuole that contains digestive enzymes used to break down old organelles, cells or cellular components during certain developmental stages, and particulate matter that is ingested by species that engulf food. Peroxisomes specialize in metabolically breaking down certain organic molecules and in destroying dangerous peroxide compounds, such as hydrogen peroxide, that are produced during some biochemical reactions. Vacuoles are membranous sacs that store many different substances depending upon the organism and its metabolic state. The contractile vacuole is not involved in long-term storage; rather, it is a highly specialized organelle that regulates the water content of cells. When too much water enters the cells, the contractile vacuole "squirts" it out. Some algae have special ejectile organelles that apparently act as protective structures. The Dinophyceae has trichocysts—harpoonlike structures that lie beneath the cell surface and explode from the disturbed or irritated cell. Ejectosomes, of analogous structure, are found in the class Cryptophyceae. Several classes of algae in the division Chromophyta have mucous organelles. *Gonyostomum semen,* a freshwater member of the class Raphidophyceae, has numerous mucocysts, and when it is collected in a plankton net the mucocysts discharge, giving the net and sample a mucous consistency.

The nonmembrane-bound organelles include the ribosomes, pyrenoids, microtubules, and microfilaments. The ribosome serves as the "workbench" during protein synthesis. It provides the site where genetic information, as messenger RNA, is translated into proteins. The ribosome carefully interprets the genetic code of the DNA so that the protein is made exactly to the genetic specifications. The pyrenoid, a dense structure that occurs within or beside chloroplasts of algae, has a concentration of ribulose biphosphate carboxylase, the enzyme necessary in photosynthesis for carbon fixation and thus sugar formation (see below *Photosynthesis*). Starch, the storage form of sugar, is often found around pyrenoids.

Microtubules

The microtubules are tubelike structures formed from tubulin proteins. Some microtubules are almost always present in the cell, but others appear suddenly when needed and then disassemble after use. Microtubules provide a rigid structure, or cytoskeleton, in the cell that helps determine the shape of the cell, and in species without cell walls the cytoskeleton maintains the cell shape. Microtubules also provide a "rail" system along which vesicles are transported. The spindle apparatus, which separates the chromosomes when the nucleus divides, consists of microtubules. Finally, microtubules also form the basic structure, or axoneme, of the flagellum, and they are a major component of the flagellar root system that anchors the flagellum in the cell. Microfilaments are formed by the polymerization of proteins such as actin. Actin microfilaments contract and relax, and they function as tiny muscles inside the cell.

Flagella. A flagellum, when present, is structurally complex and contains more than 250 types of proteins. Each flagellum consists of an axoneme, or cylinder, with nine outer pairs of microtubules surrounding two central microtubules. The whole cylinder is surrounded by a membrane. Each of the nine pairs of microtubules has an *a* tubule and a *b* tubule. The *a* tubule has numerous molecules of the protein dynein attached along its length. Dynein is involved in converting the chemical energy of adenosine triphosphate (ATP) into the mechanical energy that permits flagellar movement. The scales and hairs apparently aid in swimming. The swellings and para-axonemal structures (crystalline rods and noncrystalline rods and sheets) are often involved in photoreception, providing the swimming cell with a means for detecting light, toward or from which it may swim. The flagellum bends as the dynein arms on one side of the axoneme move up the microtubules during the power stroke. These dynein molecules are then inactivated, and those on the opposite side slide up, causing the flagellum to bend in the opposite direction during the recovery stroke. The result is the whiplike movement characteristic of eukaryotic flagella.

The flagellum membrane is also complex. It contains special chemoreceptors that aid the algal cell in recognizing cues ranging from environmental changes to mating partners. Often, scales, hairs, swellings, and para-axonemal structures cover the flagellum surface. The scales and hairs apparently aid in swimming. The swellings and para-axonemal structures (crystalline rods and noncrystalline rods and sheets) are often involved in photoreception, providing the swimming cell with a means for detecting light, toward or from which it may swim. The flagellum membrane flows into the plasma (cell) membrane, where the nine pairs of axonemal microtubules enter the main body of the cell. Each pair is joined by an additional microtubule, forming nine triplets. The cylinder of nine triplets, called the basal body, anchors the flagellum. Musclelike fibres and special microtubules (called microtubular roots) extend from the basal body and provide a greater anchorage base. Most flagellate cells have two flagella, and therefore two basal bodies. Typically, each basal body gives rise to two sets of microtubular roots. The orientation of the flagella and the arrangement of the microtubular roots and musclelike fibres are used to classify algae.

Mitosis. Mitosis, or the division of the nucleus, is relatively similar among plants and animals, but the algae have a wide diversity of mitotic features. The nuclear envelope breaks apart in some algal groups but remains intact in others. The spindle microtubules remain outside the nucleus in some algae, they enter the nucleus through holes in the nuclear envelope in other algae, and they form inside the nucleus and nuclear envelope in still other algae. The diversity and complexity of algal mitosis has been studied in detail, and it provides a better understanding of how mitosis operates in plants and animals.

Cellular respiration. Cellular respiration is the process by which food molecules are "burned" to obtain chemical energy for the cell. Algae, like all organisms, sustain life by using the engery from the chemical bonds of food molecules. Most algae are aerobic (*i.e.,* they live in the presence of oxygen), although certain Euglenophyceae live anaerobically in environments without oxygen. The biochemical pathways for respiration in algae are similar to those of other eukaroytes; the initial breakdown of food molecules (sugars, fatty acids, and proteins) occurs in the cytoplasm, but the final high-energy-releasing steps occur inside the mitochondria.

Photosynthesis. Photosynthesis is the process by which light energy is converted to chemical energy as carbon dioxide and water are converted into organic molecules. The process occurs in almost all algae, and in fact much of the knowledge of photosynthesis was first discovered by studying the green alga *Chlorella.*

Photosynthesis is divided into the light reactions and the dark reactions (or Calvin-Benson cycle). During the dark reactions, carbon dioxide is bound to ribulose bisphosphate, a 5-carbon sugar with two attached phosphate groups, by the enzyme ribulose bisphosphate carboxylase. This is the initial step of a complex process leading to the formation of sugars. During the light reactions, light energy is converted into chemical energy that is used in the dark reactions.

The light reactions of many algae differ from those of plants because these algae use different pigments to harvest light. Chlorophylls absorb primarily blue and red light, whereas carotenoids absorb primarily blue and green light, and phycobiliproteins absorb primarily blue or red light. Since the amount of light absorbed depends upon the pigment composition and concentration found in the alga, some algae absorb more light at a given wavelength, and therefore, potentially, those algae can convert more light energy of that wavelength to chemical energy via photosynthesis. All algae use chlorophyll *a* to collect photosynthetically active light. Green algae and euglenophytes also use chlorophyll *b.* In addition to chlorophyll *a,* the remaining algae also use various combinations of other chlorophylls, chlorophyllides, carotenoids, and phycobiliproteins to collect additional light from wavelengths of the spectrum not absorbed by chlorophyll *a* or *b.* The chromophyte algae, dinoflagellates, cryptomonads (class Cryptophyceae), and the class Micromonadophyceae, for example, also use chlorophyllides. (Chlorophyllides, often incorrectly called chlorophylls, differ from true chlorophylls in lacking a long, fat-soluble phytol tail.) Some green algae use carotenoids for harvesting photosynthetically active light, but the Dinophyceae and chromophyte algae almost always use carotenoids. Phycobiliproteins, which appear either blue (phycocyanins) or red (phycoerythrins), are found in red algae and cryptomonads.

Chlorophyll and other pigments

The effects of water on light. Red wavelengths are absorbed in the first few metres of water. Blue wavelengths are readily absorbed if the water contains average or abundant amounts of organic material. Thus, green wavelengths are often the most common light in deep water.

Chlorophylls absorb red and blue wavelengths much more strongly than they absorb green wavelengths, which is why chlorophyll-bearing plants appear green. The carotenoids and phycobiliproteins, on the other hand, strongly absorb green wavelengths. Algae with large amounts of carotenoid appear yellow to brown, those with large amounts of phycocyanin appear blue, and those with large amounts of phycoerythrin appear red.

At one time it was believed that algae with specialized green-absorbing accessory pigments outcompeted green algae and plants in deeper water. Some green algae, however, grow as well as other algae in deep water, and the deepest attached algae include green algae. The explanation of this paradox is that the cell structure of the deep-water green algae is designed to capture virtually all light, green or otherwise. Thus, while green-absorbing pigments are advantageous in deeper waters, evolutionary changes in cell structure can compensate for the absence of these pigments.

Not all algae have chloroplasts and photosynthesize. The "colourless" algae obtain their energy from organic molecules, which they absorb from the environment or digest from engulfed particles. They are classified as algae, rather than fungi or protozoa, because in all other features they resemble algae.

Storage products

As in plants, the major carbohydrate storage product of the green algae is usually starch in the form of amylose starch or amylopectin. (These starches are polysaccharides in which the monomer, or fundamental unit, is the sugar glucose.) In green algae, starch consists of more than 1,000 sugar molecules and is stored as a solid grain inside the chloroplast. The individual sugar molecules are bound together, primarily or entirely, with an alpha linkage between the number 1 and 4 carbons. The cell walls of many, but not all, algae contain cellulose. (Cellulose is formed from the same glucose molecules but with a beta linkage between the number 1 and 4 carbons. Although all animals can digest starch, no animals can by themselves digest cellulose. The beta linkage in cellulose causes alternating sugar molecules to be upside down, and this "flip-flop" configuration requires a special enzyme to link or unlink the sugar molecules. The enzyme is absent in animals, although cows, beavers, and other cellulose-eaters harbour intestinal bacteria that have the cellulose-digesting enzyme.)

The Cryptophyceae also store amylose and amylopectin starch. It is stored outside the chloroplast but within the surrounding membranes of the chloroplast endoplasmic recticulum. The Dinophyceae make starch that stains blue-black with iodine (the standard test for amylose starch), but the chemical nature has not been studied in detail. Dinophycean starch is stored outside the chloroplast, often as a cap over a bulging pyrenoid. The major carbohydrate storage product of red algae is a type of starch (Floridean starch) that is more highly branched than amylopectin. Floridean starch is stored as grains outside the chloroplast.

The major carbohydrate storage product of the chromophyte algae and Euglenophyceae is formed from glucose molecules interconnected with beta linkages between the number 1 and 3 carbons. These polysaccharide compounds are distinctly different from starch (and cellulose), and they are always stored outside the chloroplast. The number of glucose units in each storage product varies among the algal classes. Each type is given a special name—*i.e.,* chrysolaminarin in diatoms, laminarin in brown algae, leucosin in chrysophytes, and paramylon in euglenophytes. The exact chemical constituency of the major polysaccharide storage products is unknown for the classes Bicosoecophyceae, Dictyochophyceae, Eustigmatophyceae, Raphidophyceae, Synurophyceae, and Xanthophyceae. In the chromophyte algae, the molecule is usually small (16–40 units of sugar) and is stored in a vacuole; the paramylon of euglenophytes is larger (approximately 150 units of sugar) and is stored as a grain.

The algae also produce many sugars and sugar alcohols, such as rhamnose, trehalose, and xylose. While they are not polysaccharides in that the monomer is not glucose, various algae store energy using these small carbohydrate molecules.

Reproduction and life histories. Algae are formed by either sexual reproduction involving male and female gametes or asexual reproduction; many algae can reproduce in both ways (Figure 4).

Asexual reproduction is the production of progeny without the union of cells or nuclear material. Algae, especially small algae, can reproduce asexually by ordinary cell division or by fragmentation, while others, especially large algae, reproduce via spores. Some red algae produce monospores (walled, nonflagellate, spherical cells) that are carried by water currents and upon germination produce a new organism. The same type of spore is called an aplanospore in the green algae. In contrast, zoospores lack true cell walls and bear one or more flagella. Zoospores are motile and can swim to a favourable environment, whereas monospores and aplanospores rely on water currents for transport.

Asexual reproduction

Sexual reproduction occurs by the union of cells, nuclei, and chromosomes and genes through the process of meiosis. It can complement or replace asexual reproduction, depending upon the organism. Sexual reproduction is usu-

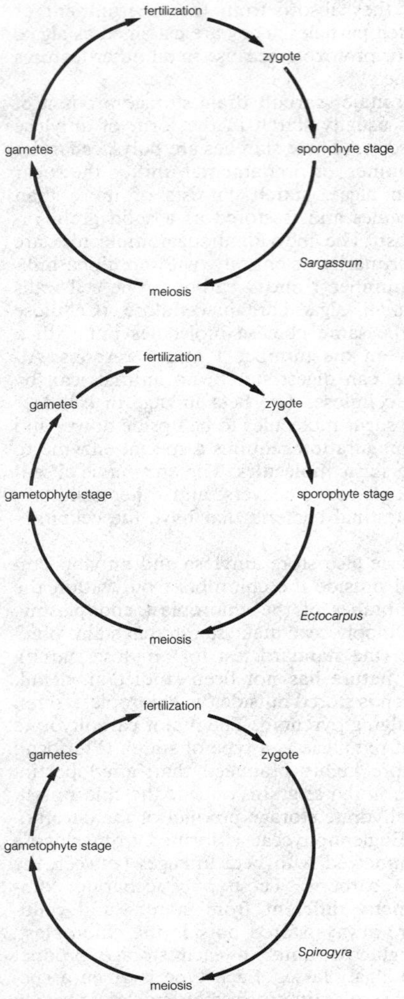

Figure 4: Three types of life cycles found in algae.

ally regulated by environmental events. For example, when temperature, salinity, inorganic nutrients (phosphorus, nitrogen, magnesium), or day length become unfavourable, sexual reproduction is induced. A sexually reproducing organism has two phases in its life cycle. One stage has a single set of chromosomes (or half that of the parent) and is called haploid, whereas the second stage has two sets of chromosomes (or the same as that of the parent) and is called diploid. When one haploid gamete (sex cell) fuses with another haploid gamete during fertilization, the resulting combination has two sets of chromosomes and is called a zygote. Either immediately or at some later time, a diploid cell undergoes a special reductive cell division process called meiosis. During meiosis the chromosome number is halved, and the resulting daughter cells are haploid. At some time, immediately or later, haploid cells act as gametes. In algae, as in plants, a haploid vegetative stage is called the gametophyte stage because it is the gamete-producing stage. Similarly, a diploid vegetative stage is called a sporophyte stage because it is the spore-producing stage (via meiosis).

The life cycles of sexually reproducing algae vary; in some, the dominant stage is the sporophyte, in others it is the gametophyte (Figure 4). For example, *Sargassum* (class Phaeophyceae) has a diploid (sporophyte) body, and the haploid phase is represented by gametes. *Ectocarpus* (class Phaeophyceae) has alternating diploid and haploid vegetative stages, while *Spirogyra* (class Charophyceae) has a haploid vegetative stage, and the zygote is the only diploid cell.

Zygospores

In freshwater organisms especially, the fertilized egg, or zygote, often passes into a dormant state called a zygospore. The zygospore has a large store of food reserves and a thick, resistant cell wall. Following the appropriate environmental stimulus (often changes in light, temperature, or nutrients), the zygospore germinates and starts another period of growth.

Most algae live for days, weeks, or months. Often, small algae are found in abundance during a short period of the year; for the remainder of the year, some remain dormant in resistant cysts and others remain in the vegetative state but at very low population numbers. Some large, attached species are true perennials. They may lose the main body at the end of the growing season, but the attachment site, or holdfast, then produces new growth at the beginning of the next growing season.

The red algae, as exemplified by *Polysiphonia* (Figure 5), have some of the most complex life cycles known for living organisms. Following meiosis, a haploid tetraspore, one of four spores produced following meiosis, is produced. The tetraspore germinates to produce either a male or female gametophyte. When mature, the male gametophyte produces special spermatangial branches that bear structures, called spermatangia, which contain spermatia, the male gametes. The female gametophyte produces special carpogonial branches that bear carpogonia, the female gametes. Fertilization occurs when the male spermatium, carried by water currents, "bumps into" the extended portion of the female carpogonium and the two gametes fuse. The fertilized carpogonium (the zygote) and the female gametophyte tissue around the carpogonium develop into a basketlike or pustulelike structure, the carposporophyte. The carposporophyte produces and releases diploid carpospores that develop into tetrasporophytes. Certain cells of the tetrasporophyte undergo meiosis to produce tetraspores, and the cycle continues. In the life cycle of *Polysiphonia,* and many other red algae, there are separate male and female gametophytes, a carposporophyte growth on the female gametophyte, and a separate tetrasporophyte.

Diatom life cycle

The life cycle of diatoms is unique as well. Diatom walls, or frustules, are composed of two overlapping parts (the valves). During cell division, two new valves form in the middle of the cell and partition the protoplasm into two parts. Consequently, the new valves are slightly smaller than the originals. Over many successive generations, most of the cells in the growing population become smaller.

Adapted from R.E. Lee, *Phycology*, © Cambridge University Press, 1980

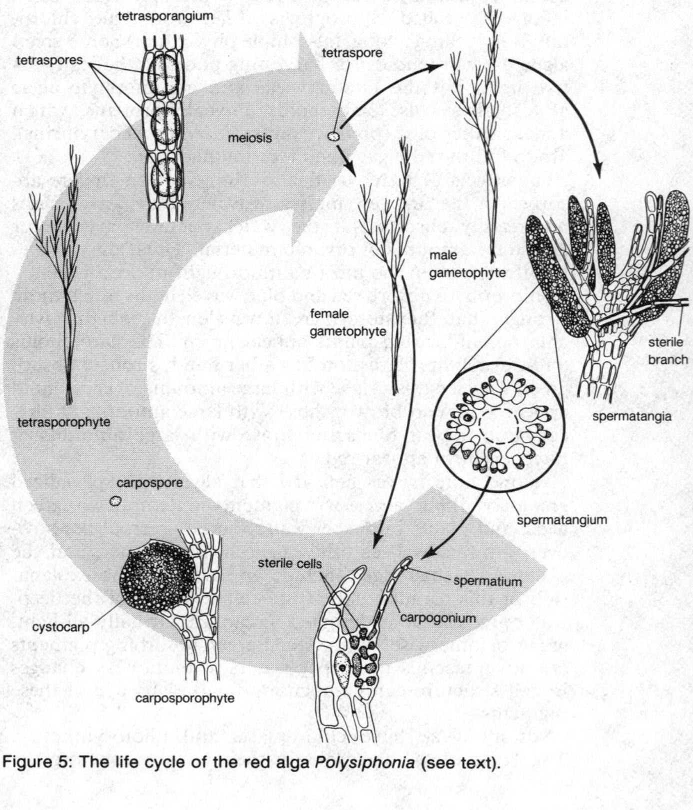

Figure 5: The life cycle of the red alga *Polysiphonia* (see text).

When the diatoms reach a critically small size, sexual reproduction is stimulated. The small diploid cells undergo meiosis, and the resulting gametes form and fuse into a zygote, which grows quite large and forms a special cell, the auxospore. The auxospore divides, forming two large, vegetative cells. In this manner, the larger size is renewed.

EVOLUTION AND PALEONTOLOGY

The evolutionary relationships of algae (Figure 4) are not well understood. Modern ultrastructural and molecular studies have added so much new and important information that the evolution of algae is being reassessed. The poor fossil record for some groups of algae also hinders evolutionary studies. Finally, the realization that some algae are more closely related to protozoa or fungi than they are to other algae came late, producing confusion in evolutionary thought and delays in understanding the evolution of the algae.

Alternative relationships

The Euglenophyceae are believed to be on an ancient lineage that includes some zooflagellate protozoa, which is supported by ultrastructural and molecular data. Most scientists consider the colourless euglenophytes to be an older group and believe that the chloroplasts were added more recently.

Some scientists consider the red algae to be very primitive eukaryotes that evolved from the prokaryotic blue-green algae. Evidence in support of this view are the nearly identical photosynthetic pigments and the very similar starches. Many scientists, however, attribute the similarity to an endosymbiotic origin of the red algal chloroplast from a blue-green algal symbiont. Other scientists suggest that the red algae evolved from the Cryptophyceae with the loss of flagella. It is difficult to imagine, however, the evolutionary selection of a nonflagellate stage for an aquatic organism. Still other scientists suggest that the red algae evolved from the fungi by obtaining a chloroplast. Evidence in support of this view are similarities in mitosis and in cell wall plugs, special structures inserted in a cell wall hole that interconnects two cells. Some evidence suggests that the plug regulates movement between the two cells. Ribosomal gene sequence data from studies in molecular biology suggest that the red algae arose suddenly along with the animal, fungal, and plant (as green algae) lineages. Whatever the origin of the red algae, they bear little resemblance to any other living group.

The green algal classes are evolutionarily related, but their origin is unclear. Most consider the classes Micromonadophyceae to be the most ancient group, and fossil data support this view. The class Ulvophyceae is also ancient, whereas the classes Charophyceae and Chlorophyceae are more recent.

The class Dinophyceae is also of uncertain origin. During the 1960s and '70s the unusual structure and chemical composition of the nuclear DNA was interpreted as a very primitive feature. Some scientists considered the Dinophyceae to be mesokaryotes (an intermediate between the prokaryotes and the eukaryotes). That view is no longer accepted by most scientists, and the peculiar structure is considered simply an evolutionary divergence. Some scientists consider the Dinophyceae to be distantly related to the chromophyte algae. Ribosomal gene sequence data suggest that their closest living relatives are the ciliates, a large, complex group of protozoa.

As in the case of the other algae, the origin of the chromophyte algae is unknown. Ultrastructural and molecular data suggest that they are on a protistan lineage which diverged a long time ago. That lineage, however, apparently remained one of protozoa and later aquatic fungi until about 300 to 400 million years ago. At that time a chloroplast was added (originally as a symbiont), and since then the many chromophyte groups have been evolving. Fossil, ultrastructural, and ribosomal gene sequence data support this hypothesis.

The Cryptophyceae are truly an enigma. They have no fossil record, and other data are conflicting. Although some workers align them near the red algae, because both groups possess phycobiliproteins in their chloroplasts, most scientists suggest that independent symbiotic origins for their chloroplasts could explain the similarity. Cryptophytes have flagellar hairs and other flagellar features that resemble those of the chromophyte algae; however, the mitochondrial structure and other ultrastructural features are distinct and argue against such a relationship. Much like the platypus, the cryptophytes appear as though they were constructed by an administrative committee.

Fossil record

The fossil record for the algae is not nearly as complete as it is for plants and animals (Figure 6). Red algal fossils are the oldest known algal fossils. Microscopic spherical algae (*Eosphaera* and *Huroniospora*) resembling the living genus *Porphyridium* are known from the Gunflint Iron Formation of North America (1.9 billion years ago). Fossils that resemble modern tetraspores are known from the Amelia Dolomites of Australia (1.5 billion years ago). The best fossils are the coralline red algae that are represented in fossil beds since the Precambrian era.

Some of the green algal classes are also very old. Organic cysts resembling modern Micromonadophyceae cysts date from about 1.2 billion years ago. *Tasmanites* formed the Permian "white coal," or tasmanite, deposits of Tasmania and accumulated to a depth of several feet in deposits that extend for miles. Similar deposits in Alaska produce up to 150 gallons of oil per ton of sediment. The Ulvophyceae fossils date from about 1 billion years ago and are abundant in Paleozoic rocks. Some deposit calcium carbonate along their cell walls, and these algae produced some limestone formations. The Charophyceae, as represented by the large stoneworts (order Charales), date from about 400 million years ago. The oospore, the fertilized female egg, has spirals on its surface, a result of pressing

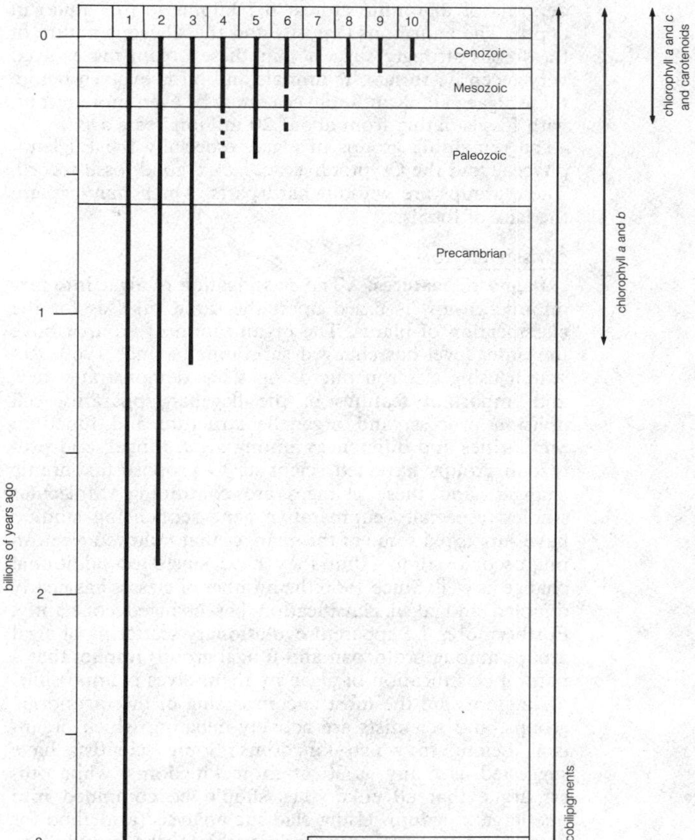

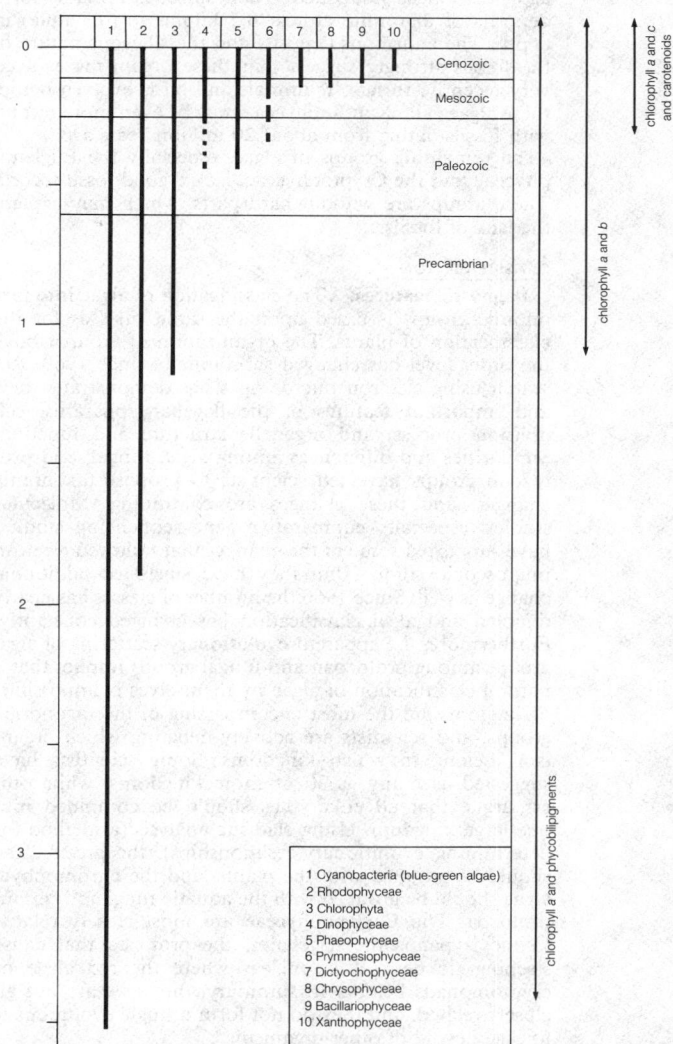

Figure 6: *The fossil record for algae.*
The origin of major photosynthetic systems is shown at the bottom.

against the spiraling protective cells that surround the oospore. Oospores before about 225 million years ago had right-handed spirals, while those formed since that time have had left-handed spirals. The reason for the switch remains a mystery.

Fossil Dinophyceae date from the Silurian period (430 million years ago). Some workers consider at least a portion of the acritarchs, a group of cystlike fossils of unknown affinity, to be Dinophyceae, but most scientists do not agree with that view. The acritarchs occurred as early as 700 million years ago.

The chromophytes

The Chromophyta have the shortest fossil history of the major algal groups. Some believe that the group is ancient, but there are no fossils. Others point out that there is a lack of data to support this view and suggest that the group evolved recently, as indicated by fossil and molecular data. The oldest chromophyte fossils, a putative brown alga, are approximately 400 million years old. Coccolithophores, coccolith-bearing members of the Prymnesiophyceae, date from the late Triassic epoch (230 to 208 million years ago), with one reported from approximately 280 million years ago. Coccolithophores were extremely abundant during the Mesozoic era, contributing to deep deposits such as the White Cliffs of Dover. Most species became extinct at the end of the Cretaceous period (66.4 million years ago), along with the dinosaurs, and there are more extinct species of coccolithophores than there are living species. The Chrysophyceae, Bacillariophyceae, and Dictyochophyceae date from about 100 million years ago, and following the mass extinctions 66.4 million years ago, these algae flourished. Their siliceous remains form deposits of diatomite almost 0.5 kilometre (0.3 mile) in depth. The enormous deposits and the siliceous nature of the fossils strongly suggest that these organisms evolved very recently. In fact, mammals and birds evolved before these algae. The Xanthophyceae may be even more recent, with fossils dating from about 20 million years ago.

The remaining groups of algae, especially the Euglenophyceae and the Cryptophyceae, lack a good fossil record. These groups are without hard parts, which may explain the lack of fossils.

CLASSIFICATION

Diagnostic features. The classification of algae into taxonomic groups is based upon the same rules as for the classification of plants. The organization of groups above the order level has changed substantially since 1960. Research using electron microscopes has demonstrated new and important features of the flagellar apparatus, cell division process, and organelle structure and function. Similarities and differences among algal, fungal, and protozoan groups have led scientists to propose taxonomic changes, and these changes are continuing. Molecular studies, especially comparative gene sequencing studies, have supported some of the changes that followed electron microscopic studies, but they have suggested additional change as well. Since 1960 the number of classes has nearly doubled and algal classification has changed constantly. Furthermore, the apparent evolutionary scattering of algal groups among protozoan and fungal groups implies that a natural classification of algae by themselves is impossible.

Kingdoms are the most encompassing of the taxonomic groups, and scientists are actively debating which organisms belong in which kingdoms. Some scientists have suggested as many as 30 or more kingdoms, while others argue that all eukaryotes should be combined into one large kingdom. Using cladistic analysis (a method for determining evolutionary relationships), the green algae should be grouped with the plants, and the chromophyte algae should be grouped with the aquatic fungi and certain protozoa. The Euglenophyceae are most closely related to the trypanosome flagellates, the protozoa that cause sleeping sickness. It is unclear where the red algae or cryptomonads belong. In summary, the algae are not all closely related, and they do not form a single evolutionary lineage devoid of other organisms.

Division-level classification, like kingdom-level classification, is tenuous for algae. For example, some phycologists place the classes Bacillariophyceae, Phaeophyceae, and Xanthophyceae in the division Chromophyta, while others place each class in separate divisions: Bacillariophyta, Phaeophyta, Xanthophyta. Yet, almost all phycologists agree on the definition of the classes Bacillariophyceae, Phaeophyceae, and Xanthophyceae. In another example, the number of classes of green algae (Chlorophyta), and the algae placed in those classes, has varied greatly since 1960. The five classes given below are accepted by a large number of phycologists, but at least an equal number of phycologists would suggest one of many alternative classification schemes. The classes are distinguished by the structure (scales, angle of insertion, microtubular roots, striated roots) of flagellate cells, the nuclear division process (mitosis), the cytoplasmic division process (cytokinesis), and the cell covering. Many scientists combine the Micromonadophyceae with the Pleurastrophyceae and name the group the Prasinophyceae.

Because classes are better defined and more accepted than divisions, taxonomic discussions of algae are usually conducted at the class level. The divisions provided below are commonly used, but they are by no means accepted by all phycologists.

"Phylum" and "division" represent the same level of organization; the former is the zoological term, the latter is the botanical term. The classification of protists continues to be debated, and a standard outline of the kingdom has not been established. The differences between the classification presented below and that in the article PROTISTS reflect the taxonomic variations that arise from individual interpretations.

Annotated classification.

DIVISION CHLOROPHYTA (green algae)
Chlorophylls *a* and *b;* starch stored inside chloroplast; mitochondria with flattened cristae; flagella, when present, lack tubular hairs (mastigonemes); unmineralized scales on cells or flagella of flagellates and zoospores; conservatively, between 9,000 and 12,000 species.

Class Chlorophyceae
Primarily freshwater; includes *Chlamydomonas, Chlorella,* and *Oedogonium.*

Class Charophyceae
Includes the macroscopic pondweed *Chara,* filamentous *Spirogyra,* and desmids.

Class Micromonadophyceae
Primarily marine; includes the smallest eukaryotic alga, *Micromonas.*

Class Pleurastrophyceae
Freshwater and marine; includes marine flagellate *Tetraselmis.*

Class Ulvophyceae
Primarily marine; includes sea lettuce *Ulva.*

DIVISION CHROMOPHYTA
Most with chlorophyll *a;* one or two with chlorophyllide *c;* carotenoids present; storage product β-1,3-linked polysaccharide outside chloroplast; mitochondria with tubular cristae; biflagellate cells and zoospores usually with tubular hairs on one flagellum; mucous organelles common.

Class Bacillariophyceae (diatoms)
Silica cell walls, or frustules; centric diatoms commonly planktonic and valves radially symmetrical; pennate diatoms found attached to substrate and valves bilaterally symmetrical; primarily in freshwater, marine, and soil environments; at least 12,000 to 15,000 living species; tens of thousands more species described from fossil diatomite deposits; *Cyclotella* and *Thalassiosira* (centrics) and *Navicula* and *Nitzschia* (pennates).

Class Bicosoecophyceae
May be included in the Chrysophyceae or in the protozoan group Zoomastigophora; colourless flagellates found in vase-shaped loricas (wall-like coverings); cell attached to lorica using flagellum as a stalk; lorica attaches to plants, algae, animals, or water surface; in freshwater and marine; fewer than 50 species described; *Bicosoeca.*

Class Chrysophyceae (golden algae)
Many unicellular or colonial flagellates; also capsoid, coccoid, amoeboid, filamentous, parenchymatous, or plasmodial; many produce silica cysts (statospores); predominantly freshwater; approximately 1,200 species; *Chrysamoeba, Chrysocapsa,* and *Ochromonas.*

Class Dictyochophyceae
Predominantly marine flagellates, including silicoflagellates, which are common in diatomite deposits; fewer than 25 described species.

Order Pedinellales

When pigmented, has 6 chloroplasts in a radial arrangement; flagella bases attach almost directly to nucleus.

Order Dictyochales (silicoflagellates)

Typically forms siliceous skeleton that appears as spiny basket in which cell sits; flagella bases attach almost directly to nucleus; silicoflagellate skeletons common in diatomite deposits; *Dictyocha, Pedinella,* and *Pseudopedinella.*

Class Eustigmatophyceae

Newly described, with probably more to be discovered; mostly small, pale green, and spherical; fewer than 15 species; *Eustigmatos* and *Nannochloropsis.*

Class Phaeophyceae (brown algae or brown seaweeds)

Microscopic forms to large kelp more than 60 metres long; more than 1,500 species, almost entirely marine; *Ectocarpus, Macrocystis,* and *Sargassum.*

Class Prymnesiophyceae (Haptophyceae)

Many with haptonema, a hairlike appendage between two flagella; no tubular hairs; many with organic scales; some deposit calcium carbonate on scales to form coccoliths; coccolithophorids may play a role in global warming because they can remove large amounts of carbon from the ocean water; predominantly marine and planktonic species; approximately 300 species; more fossil coccolithophores known; *Chrysochromulina, Emiliania,* and *Prymnesium.*

Class Raphidophyceae (Chloromonadophyceae)

Flagellates; mucocysts (mucilage-releasing bodies) commonly found in freshwater forms; sharply divided between freshwater and marine environments; fewer than 50 species; *Heterosigma, Vacuolaria,* and *Olisthodiscus.*

Class Synurophyceae

Previously placed in Chrysophyceae; silica-scaled; unicellular or colonial flagellates sometimes alternating with capsoid benthic stage; cells covered with elaborately structured silica scales; approximately 250 species, with approximately 10 new described each year since 1970; *Mallomonas, Synura,* and *Tesselaria.*

Class Xanthophyceae (yellow-green algae)

Primarily coccoid, capsoid, or filamentous; mostly freshwater environments; about 600 species; *Bumilleriopsis, Tribonema,* and *Vaucheria.*

DIVISION CRYPTOPHYTA

Unicellular flagellates.

Class Cryptophyceae

Chlorophyll *a,* chlorophyllide c_2, and phycobiliproteins; starch stored outside of chloroplast; mitochondria with flattened cristae; tubular hairs on 1 or both flagella; special ejectosomes lie in a furrow or gullet near the flagella; cell covered with periplast, often elaborately decorated sheet or scale covering; nucleomorph may represent reduced nucleus of symbiotic organism; approximately 200 described species; *Chilomonas, Cryptomonas, Falcomonas,* and *Rhinomonas.*

DIVISION PYRRHOPHYTA (DINOFLAGELLATA)

Predominantly unicellular flagellates; approximately half of the species are heterotrophic rather than photosynthetic; photosynthetic forms with chlorophyll *a,* 1 or more chlorophyllide *c* types, and peridinin or fucoxanthin; mitochondria with tubular cristae and flagella without tubular hairs; ejectile trichocysts below surface in many members; many with cellulosic plates that form an armour around cell; some bioluminescent, some containing symbionts; nucleus contains permanently condensed chromosomes; several produce toxins that either kill fish or accumulate in shellfish and cause sickness or death in humans when ingested; more than 1,200 species described, most in the class Dinophyceae; *Alexandrium, Dinophysis, Peridinium,* and *Polykrikos.*

DIVISION EUGLENOPHYTA

Primarily unicellular flagellates; both photosynthetic and heterotrophic.

Class Euglenophyceae

Chlorophylls *a* and *b;* paramylon stored outside chloroplasts; mitochondria with paddle-shaped cristae; flagella lack tubular hairs, but some with hairlike scales; unusual pellicle covering of sliding sheets allows organisms to change shape easily; approximately 1,000 described species; *Colacium, Euglena,* and *Eutreptiella.*

DIVISION RHODOPHYTA (red algae or red seaweeds)

Predominantly filamentous; mostly photosynthetic but almost one-third parasitic; photosynthetic species with chlorophyll *a;* chlorophyll *d* present in some species; phycobiliproteins (phycocyanin and phycoerythrin) organized into descrete structures (phycobilisomes); starch occurs outside chloroplast; mitochondria with flattened cristae; flagella completely absent; coralline red algae contribute to coral reefs and coral sands; predominantly marine; approximately 4,100 described species; *Bangia, Palmaria, Polysiphonia,* and *Porphyra.*

BIBLIOGRAPHY. General works include E. YALE DAWSON, *Marine Botany* (1966); JOHN MCNEILL SIEBURTH, *Sea Microbes* (1979); F.E. ROUND, *The Ecology of Algae* (1981); G. ROBIN SOUTH and ALAN WHITTICK, *Introduction to Phycology* (1987); and ROBERT EDWARD LEE, *Phycology,* 2nd ed. (1989). Various groups are studied in greater detail in J.C. GREEN, B.S.C. LEADBEATER, and W.L. DIVER (eds.), *The Chromophyte Algae: Problems and Perspectives* (1989); JØRGEN KRISTIANSEN and ROBERT A. ANDERSEN (eds.), *Chrysophytes: Aspects and Problems* (1986); JØRGEN KRISTIANSEN, G. CRONBERG, and U. GEISSLER (eds.), *Chrysophytes: Developments and Perspectives* (1989); ALAN J. BROOK, *The Biology of Desmids* (1981); DIETRICH WERNER (ed.), *The Biology of Diatoms* (1977); F.J.R. TAYLOR (ed.), *The Biology of Dinoflagellates* (1987); DONALD M. ANDERSON, ALAN W. WHITE, and DANIEL G. BADEN (eds.), *Toxic Dinoflagellates* (1985); ELENOR R. COX (ed.), *Phytoflagellates* (1980); CHRISTOPHER S. LOBBAN and MICHAEL J. WYNNE (eds.), *The Biology of Seaweeds* (1981); and GILBERT M. SMITH, *The Fresh-Water Algae of the United States,* 2nd ed. (1950). The effects of algae on the environment are discussed in DANIEL F. JACKSON (ed.), *Algae and Man* (1964); M.B. SAFFO, "New Light on Seaweeds," *BioScience* 37(9):654–664 (October 1987); and ARTHUR C. MATHIESON, "Seaweed Cultivation: A Review," pp. 25–66 in C.J. SINDERMANN (ed.), *Proceedings of the Sixth U.S.-Japan Meeting on Aquaculture* (1982).

The morphology and physiology of algae are examined in HAROLD C. BOLD and MICHAEL J. WYNNE, *Introduction to the Algae: Structure and Reproduction,* 2nd ed. (1985); CHRISTOPHER S. LOBBAN, PAUL J. HARRISON, and MARY JO DUNCAN, *The Physiological Ecology of Seaweeds* (1985); W.D.P. STEWART (ed.), *Algal Physiology and Biochemistry* (1974); JEREMY D. PICKETT-HEAPS, *Green Algae: Structure, Reproduction, and Evolution in Selected Genera* (1975); CRAIG D. SANDGREN (ed.), *Growth and Reproductive Strategies of Freshwater Phytoplankton* (1988); RALPH A. LEWIN (ed.), *The Genetics of Algae* (1976); GRETA A. FRYXELL (ed.), *Survival Strategies of the Algae* (1983); ANNETTE W. COLEMAN, LYNDA J. GOFF, and JANET R. STEIN-TAYLOR (eds.), *Algae as Experimental Systems* (1989); BARRY S.C. LEADBEATER and ROBERT RIDING (eds.), *Biomineralization in Lower Plants and Animals* (1986); E.G. PRINGSHEIM, *Pure Cultures of Algae: Their Preparation & Maintenance* (1946, reprinted 1972); and TRACY L. SIMPSON and BENJAMIN E. VOLCANI (eds.), *Silicon and Siliceous Structures in Biological Systems* (1981). Analyses of algal evolution are found in MARK A. RAGAN and DAVID J. CHAPMAN, *A Biochemical Phylogeny of the Protists* (1978); and HELEN TAPPAN, *The Paleobiology of Plant Protists* (1980). For classification, see D.E.G. IRVINE and D.M. JOHN (eds.), *Systematics of the Green Algae* (1984). (R.A.An.)

Algebra

Algebra may be described as a generalization and extension of arithmetic. Elementary arithmetic is concerned primarily with the effect of certain operations, such as addition or multiplication, on specified numbers, hence, for instance, the multiplication tables; elementary algebra is concerned with properties of arbitrary numbers. For instance, the fact that 2 added to 3 gives the same result as 3 added to 2 is one of arithmetic; the formula $a+b=b+a$ for all numbers a, b is one of algebra.

The particular operations of arithmetic that came to be extended and generalized to provide the materials of algebra emerged only slowly. The earliest writings on the subject dealt with many topics that are not now regarded as part of algebra. (For a treatment of the evolution of algebra as a well-defined branch of mathematics, see MATHEMATICS, THE HISTORY OF.) The earliest extant work with any claim to be regarded as a treatise on algebra is by the Greek philosopher Diophantus of Alexandria (*c.* AD 250). This work is devoted mainly to problems in the solution of equations. For this purpose a suitable notation had to be invented, and Diophantus gave rules for generating powers of a number and for the multiplication and division of simple quantities. Of great significance is his statement of the laws governing the use of the minus sign, which did not, however, imply any idea of negative quantities.

During the 6th century the ideas of Diophantus were improved on by Hindu mathematicians, and many deficiencies in the Greek symbolism were remedied. The development of symbolic algebra by the use of general symbols to denote numbers is due to a 16th-century French mathematician, François Viète, a usage that led to the idea of algebra as generalized arithmetic. Sir Isaac Newton gave it the name Universal Arithmetic in 1707.

The main step in the modern development of algebra was the evolution of a correct understanding of negative quantities, contributed in 1629 by a French mathematician, Albert Girard, whose work was later overshadowed by that of his contemporary, René Descartes. While it is convenient to view Descartes's work as the starting point of modern algebra, for the sake of clarity notations and terminology will be used that were developed later.

Algebra is concerned with certain operations on numbers, and it is necessary to be precise about what a number is. The numbers dealt with are either the natural numbers, 0, 1, 2, 3, 4, · · · (some authors exclude 0); rational numbers, which have the form p/q, in which p and q are integers (natural numbers and their negatives), with $q \neq 0$; real numbers, which correspond to all the points on a line; or complex numbers, which are constructed from the real numbers together with a number i, the square of which is -1. The essential property that these numbers have is that they can be added and multiplied by well-established rules. Arithmetic becomes algebra when general rules are stated regarding these operations, as, for example, the commutative law of addition (see below). First the basic algebraic properties of such numbers are considered.

Linear algebra is the branch of algebra that deals primarily with linear problems, that is to say, problems that depend for the most part on the solution of linear equations. An equation in two or more variables, or "unknowns," is linear if it contains no terms of the second degree or greater; that is, if it contains no products or powers of the variables. The term linear derives from the fact that the graph of a linear equation in x and y is a straight line in the Cartesian xy-plane. Thus a linear equation represents a linear relationship between the variables x and y in a geometric sense. Similarly, a linear equation in three variables x, y, z represents a plane in three-dimensional space, and two such equations considered simultaneously represent the line of intersection of the two planes, provided they are not parallel. When the number of variables is greater than three, there is no longer a simple geometric interpretation because physical space is limited to three dimensions. Nevertheless, it is customary to continue the geometric analogy and to think of the solutions of a linear equation in four variables as constituting a "hyperplane" in a four-dimensional space, and similarly for any finite higher dimension.

The theoretical investigation and solution of general systems of linear equations are facilitated by the introduction of entities called vectors and matrices. Vectors were originally introduced in order to interpret mathematically a physical quantity such as a velocity or force that has both a magnitude and an associated direction. A matrix is a rectangular array of numbers in a definite order, such as the array of coefficients of the unknowns in a system of linear equations. Rules of computation with vectors, which stem from their original physical interpretation, lead to closed systems of vectors called vector spaces, and matrices can be identified with special functions on these vector spaces called linear transformations. The theory of linear transformations of finite-dimensional vector spaces, which embraces the theory of matrices and that of systems of linear equations, constitutes the subject matter of linear algebra. Vectors are more fully treated in the article ANALYSIS: *Vector and tensor analysis;* matrices are covered in the article MATRIX THEORY.

Out of the developments of elementary algebra evolved the abstract algebra used today and the idea of an algebraic structure. Elementary algebra was originally concerned with a set of elements, the numbers used in arithmetic. Together with these elements there were two operations, addition and multiplication (subtraction and division being the inverse of these). It became recognized that there was also a collection of basic rules that constitute an axiomatic structure. The axiomatic structure describes even today the assumptions made in elementary algebra and arithmetic. Certain entities, however, do not follow these rules. Abstract algebra is concerned with the formulation and properties of quite general axiomatic abstract systems of this type. These systems are sets of elements with general operations and with a number of axioms. Just as new self-consistent geometries can be based on axioms other than those of Euclid, new algebras can be based on axioms that differ from those of elementary algebra. These new algebras may describe mathematical objects other than numbers. (Ed.)

This article is divided into the following sections:

Elementary and multivariate algebra 245
Basic theory 245
Elementary operations
Complex numbers and root extraction
Geometric representation of numbers
Quaternions and hypercomplex numbers
Polynomials and rational functions 247
Polynomials
Rational functions
Elementary properties of polynomials and rational functions
Symmetric polynomials
Solution of equations 250
Existence of solutions
Extraction of the roots of a polynomial
Common roots of two polynomials
Two simultaneous equations
Linear systems
Linear and multilinear algebra 253
Linear algebra 253
Historical and conceptual introduction
Vector spaces

Linear transformations
Linear functionals
Inner products
Linear operators in an inner product space
Multilinear algebra 258
The tensor product of vector spaces
The tensor algebra of a vector space
The exterior algebra of a vector space
Lattice theory 260
Definitions and examples 261
Partial orderings
Universal bounds
Formal definition
Examples of lattices
Algebraic definitions
Other examples
Duality
Isotonicity
Power set lattices
Boolean algebra 262
Boolean polynomials
Huntington's theorem
Venn's diagram
Free Boolean algebra
Boole's theorem
Isomorphism; direct product
Binary strings
Logic networks
Distributive lattices 263
Switching circuits
Finite distributive lattices
Some examples
Modular and geometric lattices 264
Modular lattices
Covering properties
Projective geometries
Geometric lattices
Other lattice-ordered structures 265
Relation algebras
Vector lattices
Groups 265
Definition 265
Examples of groups 266
Symmetries of a cube
Symmetries of the regular octahedron
Collineations of the Euclidean plane
Elementary group structure 267
Subgroups 267
Homomorphisms; factor groups 268
Direct products; Abelian groups 269
Automorphisms of groups; semi-direct products 269
Permutation groups 270
Group representation 271
The classical groups; continuous groups 272
Free groups; the word problem; the Burnside problem 272
Simple groups 273
Fields 274
Three familiar fields 274
The rational field
The real field
The complex field
Elementary theory of fields 275
Postulates for a field
Gaussian elimination
Some general concepts 276
Commutative rings; integral domains
Fields of quotients
Ideals and quotient-rings
Morphisms of rings
Subrings and subfields
Characteristic of a ring
Field extensions 277
Simple algebraic extensions
Finite fields
Transcendental extensions
Pythagorean numbers
Fundamental Theorem of Algebra
Applications to coding 278
Binary codes
Optimal binary codes
Galois theory 279
Algebraic number fields
Splitting fields
Galois theory of fields
Ordered fields 280
Positivity
Archimedean fields
Limits and convergence
Completeness
Valuations 281
Underlying ideas
Completing fields
Rings 282
Definition and examples 283
Definition
Examples of rings
Multiplicative groups
Homomorphisms
Algebras 284
Quadratic algebras
Quaternions
Group algebras
Matrices; representations of rings 285
Endomorphisms
Representations
Rings as modules 286
Special classes of rings 286
Domains
Rings of integers
Noetherian rings
Division rings
Categories 288
The notion of a category 288
Functors 289
Natural transformations 289
Universal constructions 290
The duality principle 291
Conclusions 291
Homological algebra 291
Homology groups of groups 292
Derived functors 292
Homology of Lie algebras 293
Applications to algebra 293
The Lie algebra of a Lie group
The topological structure of Lie groups
Other aspects of homological algebra 294
Universal algebra 295
Basic notions of universal algebra 296
The connection with mathematical logic 297
Varieties of algebras 298
Universal algebra and category theory 299
Bibliography 299

Elementary and multivariate algebra

BASIC THEORY

Laws of addition and multiplication

Elementary operations. Addition has the following properties: The order of addition does not affect the result (see Box, equation 1)—that is, addition is commutative. If three numbers are being added, parentheses can be placed around either the first two or the last two, while the terms in the parentheses are added first, and their sum is added to the remaining term. The two results are, however, always equal (see 2). This second property is expressed by saying that addition is associative, and as a result either sum may be expressed as $a+b+c$. There is a number 0 (zero) such that the sum of any number a and zero is a (see 3). Corresponding to each number a there is a number $(-a)$ such that the sum of a and $(-a)$ is zero (see 4). From the second and fourth of these laws it follows that for any two numbers a, b, there is a unique number x such that $a+x=b$, namely, $x=b+(-a)$, more commonly written $x=b-a$. A set of numbers with the law of addition satisfying the above properties is called an additive group.

The result of multiplication of two numbers a, b is usually denoted by ab, but sometimes to avoid confusion $a\times b$ is written.

Multiplication of numbers has the following properties: The order of multiplication does not affect the result (commutativity; see 5) nor does the way the numbers are placed in parentheses (associativity; see 6). The product of a number and the sum of two numbers equals the sum of two appropriate products. This last is known as

$$(1)\quad a+b=b+a$$

$$(2)\quad (a+b)+c=a+(b+c)=a+b+c$$

$$(3)\quad a+0=a$$

$$(4)\quad a+(-a)=0$$

$$(5)\quad ab=ba$$

$$(6)\quad a\times(bc)=(ab)\times c=abc$$

$$(7)\quad a\times(b+c)=ab+ac$$

$$(8)\quad 1\times a=a=a\times 1$$

$$(9)\quad 0a=0, \text{ and if } ab=0, \text{ either } a \text{ or } b \text{ is zero.}$$

the distributive law (see 7). There exists a unique element 1 (unity) such that the product of any number a and 1 is a (see 8).

Any set of elements in mathematics that has two laws of composition, addition and multiplication, such that (1) with addition as the law of combination it forms an additive group, and (2) with multiplication is commutative and associative, and distributive over addition, is called a ring. It is because so much of modern algebra is concerned with groups and rings that it is important to realize that ordinary numbers have these properties. Because the numbers have unity the ring is a ring with unity. One other property of numbers that should be noted is that the product of 0 and a is 0 for all a, and if $ab=0$, either a or b is 0 (see 9). With this last property the ring with unity becomes what is called an integral domain.

All accepted systems of numbers, integers, rational numbers, and real and complex numbers have the above properties (see ARITHMETIC; ANALYSIS: *Real analysis*). If the system has the property that when a is different from zero there is a number x such that $ax=1$ (see 10), then

$$(10)\quad ax=1, \qquad a\neq 0$$

$$(11)\quad \begin{cases}(a+ib)+(c+id)=(a+c)+i(b+d)\\(a+ib)\times(c+id)=(ac-bd)+i(bc+ad)\end{cases}$$

$$(12)\quad \alpha=r(\cos\theta+i\sin\theta), \qquad \beta=\rho(\cos\phi+i\sin\phi)$$

$$(13)\quad \alpha\beta=r\rho[\cos(\theta+\phi)+i\sin(\theta+\phi)]$$

the nonzero numbers of the system form a group in which multiplication is the group operation, and the integral domain is a field. The systems consisting of the rational, real, or complex numbers form a field, but the system of integers does not.

Complex numbers and root extraction. The operations so far considered—namely, addition, subtraction, multiplication, and division—are known as the elementary operations of algebra. In another section the extension of these operations to more complex systems, such as polynomials (see below), will be considered. One other operation on real or complex numbers must be considered here. A theorem states that: If a is any positive real number and n is any positive integer, there exists a unique positive real number x such that $x^n=a$, in which x^n is the product of n factors each equal to x.

It is important to note that if a is an integer (rational number, negative real number) there is, in general, no integer (rational number, real number) such that $x^n=a$. Thus this operation called extracting the nth root is not a satisfactory algebraic operation as it stands. To obtain a satisfactory operation, it is necessary to use complex numbers.

Definition of a complex number

A complex number, symbolized here by the Greek letter alpha, α, is any formal combination $\alpha=a+ib$ of two real numbers a, b, with addition and multiplication defined by certain appropriate rules (see 11). With addition and multiplication so defined, the complex numbers form a field. It should be noted that $i\times i=-1$.

Now, $\alpha=a+ib$ may be considered. Because a^2+b^2 is a positive real number, there exists a unique positive real number r such that $r^2=a^2+b^2$, r being called the amplitude of α. If a, b are not both zero, there is an angle, symbolized by the Greek letter theta, θ, uniquely defined to within a multiple of 2π (Greek letter pi, the ratio of the circumference to the diameter of a circle), such that $a/r=\cos\theta$, $b/r=\sin\theta$, and hence α can be written in terms of r and θ (see 12). Let the Greek letter β stand for any other complex number (see 12). Following the rule for multiplying complex numbers, and again using elementary trigonometry, the product of two complex numbers is given in terms of the product of the amplitudes and the sum of the two angles (see 13).

It is possible to consider the problem of finding a complex number z such that $z^n=\alpha$. From the formula for the product, the amplitude s must satisfy $s^n=r$, and the angle ψ must satisfy $n\psi=\theta$ to within a multiple of 2π; that is, $n\psi-\theta=2t\pi$ for some integer t. Because r is a positive real number, there must be a unique positive real number s satisfying $s^n=r$; ψ must have the form $\psi=(\theta/n)+(2t\pi/n)$, and there are n possible values of ψ (to within a multiple of 2π) satisfying this condition, corresponding to $t=0, 1, 2, \cdots, n-1$, for example. Hence there are n possible numbers z such that $z^n=\alpha$.

Roots of unity

If z_1 is any one of these n numbers, the others can all be written $z_1\omega$, in which ω (omega) is an nth root of unity; that is, $\omega^n=1$. Thus the problem of finding the nth roots of unity is basic in the theory of complex numbers.

It is clear that for any complex number α there are n solutions of $z^n=\alpha$, and this shows one of the advantages of complex numbers over the other kinds of numbers considered. In order to extract roots of integers, or rational numbers or real numbers, one notes that each of these number systems is a subsystem of the succeeding one, and that they are all subsystems of the complex numbers. To find z such that $z^n=a$, when a is, say, a rational number, is to consider a as a complex number that just happens to belong to the subsystem of real numbers, and then to consider the problem for complex numbers. This process is usually referred to as extending the field of rational numbers to the complex field.

Geometric representation of numbers. Numbers may be represented geometrically, and the operations of algebra can be carried out by geometrical methods. The following representation of real numbers (which include the integers and rational numbers) was introduced by Descartes in the 17th century. On a straight line OX point O is fixed, called the origin, and corresponding to each real number a the point A_a is taken, the distance of which from O is equal to a (if a is positive, $-a$ if it is negative), measuring distances to the right when a is positive, to the left when it is negative. One of the postulates of geometry is that there is a one-to-one correspondence between the real numbers and the points of the line established in this way. For convenience another line OY is considered, through O perpendicular to OX, and on it the point B_b is marked corresponding to the real number b, as before. The operations of addition, subtraction, multiplication, and division can then be obtained by simple geometrical constructions. The accompanying diagram (Figure 1) illustrates the geometric constructions necessary for multiplication, division, and the extraction of square roots.

Constructions involving ruler and compass

1. To add a and b the points A_a, A_b are marked. A segment A_aA_d, equal in length and direction to OA_b, is laid off on OX. Then $d=a+b$. By constructing the segment OA_{-b} equal in length to OA_b but in the opposite direction, $-b$ is found. In this way $a-b$ is constructed and geometrical representations of addition and subtraction are obtained.

2. To multiply a and b, A_a is marked on OX and OB_b is marked on OY. B_1 is marked on OY distant one unit from O. A_aB_1 is joined and, through B_b, B_bA_c is drawn parallel to B_1A_a. Then, by the geometry of similar triangles it may

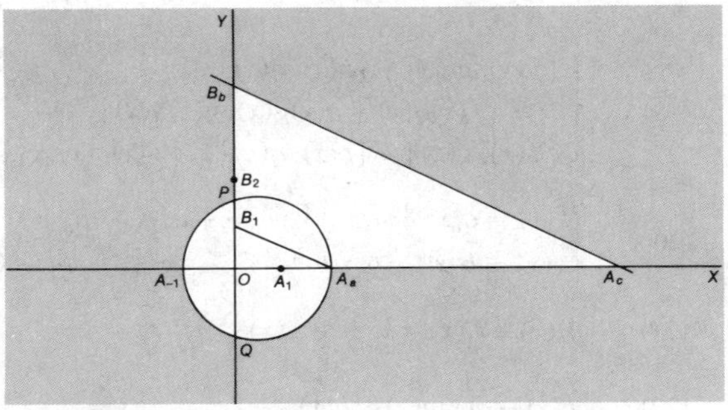

Figure 1: Geometric constructions necessary for the arithmetic operations of multiplication, division, and extraction of square roots (see text).

be shown that $c = ab$. Division by a nonzero number is obtained by a similar process. To construct c/b, when $b \neq 0$, B_b is joined to A_c, and the line through B_1 parallel to it. This meets OX in A_a, where $a = b/c$.

3. Let a be any positive real number, and on $A_{-1}\,A_a$ as diameter construct a circle. This meets OY in P, Q, and Euclidean geometry shows that OP and OQ are of equal length but opposite sign, and $OP \times OQ = OA_{-1} \times OA_a$. P represents a positive real number r on OY such that $r^2 = a$.

The geometrical operations described in 1, 2, 3 can all be carried out using only ruler and compass. It can be shown, on the other hand, that the operation of constructing the nth root of a, when n is not a power of 2, cannot in general be carried out solely by the use of ruler and compass.

Turning next to the representation of complex numbers in the Argand diagram (Figure 2) a number $\alpha = a + ib$ is

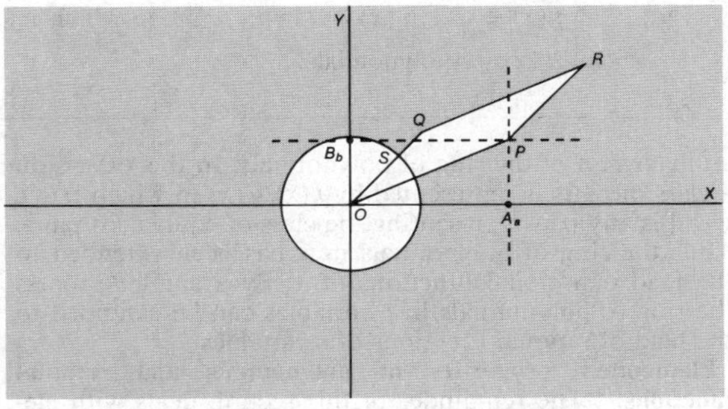

Figure 2: The representation of complex numbers and construction of the representation of the sum of two complex numbers (see text).

The Argand diagram

represented by the point P constructed by constructing A_a on OX as above, B_b on OY similarly. P is then the intersection of the line $A_a\,P$ through A_a parallel to OY, and the line $B_b\,P$ through B_b parallel to OX. To construct $\alpha + \beta$, in which α is represented by P, β by Q, the parallelogram $OPRQ$ is completed. R represents $\alpha + \beta$ (Figure 2). If α has amplitude r and angle θ, r is the length of OP, and θ is the angle XOP. If Q represents β with amplitude ρ and angle φ, then ρ, φ can be interpreted in the same way. To construct the point representing $\alpha\beta$, the procedure adopted in Figure 1 is used to construct the product $r\,\rho$, and the angle $(\theta + \varphi)$ can also be constructed by ruler and compass. It follows that the operations of addition, subtraction, multiplication, and division of complex numbers can be carried out geometrically by means of ruler and compass.

To construct a number z such that $z^n = \alpha$ it is necessary to find z with amplitude s and angle ψ such that $s^n = r$, $n\chi = \theta$ (modulo 2π). It is not possible to construct s by ruler and compass if n is not a power of 2. Nor can an angle be divided into n equal parts using ruler and compass if n is not a power of 2.

The consideration of problems that can be solved by the elementary operations of algebra and the extraction of roots, and by ruler and compass is of great importance in solving equations (see below *Solution of equations*).

Quaternions and hypercomplex numbers. If the properties of order can be sacrificed as well as the commutative law of multiplication, then an interesting further extension of the complex-number system can be made to the so-called quaternion; *i.e.*, o numbers of the form $a + bi + cj + dk$ in which a, b, c, d are real.

Addition and multiplication

The sum $(a + bi + cj + dk) + (a' + b'i + c'j + d'k)$ is defined as $(a + a') + (b + b')i + (c + c')j + (d + d')k$. Multiplication is defined from the equations (generalizing $i^2 = -1$); $i^2 = j^2 = k^2 = -1$, $ij = jk = ki = -ji = -kj = -ik = -1$. Certain laws of arithmetic are satisfied, and subtraction and division (except by zero) are possible. Further, any polynomial equation with quaternion coefficients has a quaternion root.

For many years quaternions were widely used in solving physical problems.

The construction of quaternions can be further generalized. For any set of n^3 real coefficients C_k^{ij}, a linear algebra, or system H of hypercomplex numbers, can be defined as follows. The elements of H are the expressions $a_1\varepsilon_1 + \cdot \cdot \cdot + a_n\varepsilon_n$, in which the units $\varepsilon_1, \cdot \cdot \cdot, \varepsilon_n$ take the place of the special quaternions i, j, and k, and are the same for all elements; $a_1, \cdot \cdot \cdot, a_n$ are arbitrary real numbers. The sum of $a_1\varepsilon_1 + \cdot \cdot \cdot + a_n\varepsilon_n$ and $b_1\varepsilon_1 + \cdot \cdot \cdot + b_n\varepsilon_n$ is defined as $(a_1 + b_1)\varepsilon_1 + \cdot \cdot \cdot + (a_n + b_n)\varepsilon_n$. Their product is defined as the sum $a_1b_1\varepsilon_1^2 + a_1b_2\varepsilon_1\varepsilon_2 + \cdot \cdot \cdot + a_nb_n\varepsilon_n^2$, in which the $\varepsilon_i\varepsilon_j$ are given by $\varepsilon_i\varepsilon_j = C_1^{ij}\varepsilon_1 + C_2^{ij}\varepsilon_2 + \cdot \cdot \cdot + C_n^{ij}\varepsilon_n$.

Although the study of hypercomplex numbers forms an interesting branch of algebra, the complex numbers and quaternions are the only systems of hypercomplex numbers with real coefficients in which multiplication is associative and division is possible.

POLYNOMIALS AND RATIONAL FUNCTIONS

Polynomials. The discussion of polynomials (defined below) begins with the coefficients, which, in elementary algebra, may be natural numbers, or real numbers, or complex numbers. Except when considering some special problems, the reasoning is the same in all three cases, and it is sufficient to speak of the coefficient field (or ring) without being more explicit.

Operations with coefficients and variables

Once the coefficient field is chosen, a new object is introduced, usually denoted by x, and called a variable or an indeterminate, which is not in the coefficient field. Laws are then specified by which to define addition and multiplication in the enlarged set consisting of the elements of the coefficient field and x. The powers of x, x^0, x^1, x^2, x^3, $\cdot \cdot \cdot$, are generated, together with products ax^n, in which a is in the coefficient field. Multiplication of two such products ax^n and bx^m is defined by $ax^n \times bx^m = abx^{n+m}$, and the sum of ax^n and bx^n is defined as $(a + b)\,x^n$; x^0 can be replaced by 1, and ax^0 by a. Moreover, $0x^n = 0$ for all n.

Sums of terms ax^n and bx^m, when $n \neq m$, are defined by introducing compound expressions such as $ax^n + bx^m$. It is finally postulated that multiplication of such expressions is distributive over addition, so that the product of x^n and such an expression is a similar expression with each term multiplied by x^n (see 14).

In this way a system is built up, any element of which can be written uniquely as the sum of terms of the form

(14) $$x^n(ax^p + bx^q) = ax^{p+n} + bx^{q+n}$$

(15) $$f(x) \equiv a_0x^n + a_1x^{n-1} + \cdot \cdot \cdot + a_n$$

(16) $$g(x) \equiv b_0x^m + b_1x^{m-1} + \cdot \cdot \cdot + b_m, \qquad b_0 \neq 0$$

(17) $$a_{mn}x^ny^m + a_{m-1,n}x^ny^{m-1} + \cdot \cdot \cdot + a_{rs}x^sy^r + \cdot \cdot \cdot + a_{00}$$

(18) $$\begin{cases} (a + bx)^n = a^n + c_1a^{n-1}bx + \cdot \cdot \cdot + \\ \qquad + c_ra^{n-r}b^rx^r + \cdot \cdot \cdot + c_nb^nx^n \\ c_r = \dfrac{1}{r!}\,n(n-1) \cdot \cdot \cdot (n-r+1), \qquad c_r = \dbinom{n}{r} \end{cases}$$

$a_r x^{n-i}$, for $i = 0, 1, \cdots, n$ (see 15), in which the coefficients a_i are in the coefficient field, and each expression only involves a finite number of terms $a_r x^{n-r}$. Here, and in what follows, $f(x)$ is an abbreviation for the expression that follows. If $a_0 \neq 0$, $f(x)$ is said to be a polynomial in x of degree n and $a_r x^{n-r}$ is the term of degree $n-r$ in $f(x)$. If $g(x)$ is another polynomial of degree m (see 16), $f(x) + g(x)$ is obtained by adding the terms of like degree, and $f(x) \times g(x)$ is the polynomial of degree $n+m$ obtained by multiplication. With these laws of addition and multiplication, the polynomials in x form a ring. The ring has unity: the polynomial of degree zero written 1. Further, if neither $f(x)$ nor $g(x)$ is zero, their product $f(x) \times g(x)$ is not zero, because its leading term is $a_0 b_0 x^{n+m}$, and $a_0 b_0$ is not zero unless one of a_0, b_0 is zero. Hence the ring of polynomials in x is an integral domain. It is easily seen, however, that it is not a field; for example, there is no polynomial $p(x)$ such that $p(x)(x+1) = 1$.

Degree of polynomial expressions

It is now a straightforward matter to define polynomials in more than one variable. To the polynomials in x a new variable y is adjoined. Products are defined by $ax^p y^q \times bx^r y^s = abx^{p+r} y^{q+s}$, $ax^p y^q + bx^p y^q$ is identified with $(a+b)\, x^p y^q$, and x^0 and y^0 are identified with unity in the coefficient field. In this way the integral domain of polynomials in two variables is built up; a general element is written as a sum of these products (see 17). In a similar way the integral domain of polynomials in r variables may be constructed.

Elementary algebra is rich in identities concerning polynomials. Perhaps the most important is the binomial theorem, which expresses the sum of two terms raised to a power as a sum of products (see 18).

Rational functions. The ring of polynomials in r variables is an integral domain, but not a field. It is possible, however, to embed the ring of polynomials in r variables in a field, the field of rational functions of r variables, just as the integers are embedded in the field of rational numbers. The case of one variable illustrates the general procedure. A rational function is one of the form $f(x)/g(x)$, in which $f(x)$ and $g(x)$ are polynomials; the following discussion makes this idea precise and rigorous. All pairs of polynomials $[f(x), g(x)]$ in which $g(x) \neq 0$, are considered and two pairs $[f(x), g(x)]$, $[F(x), G(x)]$ are defined to be equivalent if $f(x)\, G(x) - g(x)\, F(x) = 0$. This relation has all the necessary and sufficient properties of a true equivalence:

The ring of polynomials

1. $[f(x), g(x)]$ is equivalent to itself (reflexive);
2. if $[f(x), g(x)]$ is equivalent to $[F(x), G(x)]$, then $[F(x), G(x)]$ is equivalent to $[f(x), g(x)]$ (symmetric); and
3. if $[f(x), g(x)]$ is equivalent to $[F(x), G(x)]$, and $[F(x), G(x)]$ is equivalent to $[P(x), Q(x)]$, then $[f(x), g(x)]$ is equivalent to $[P(x), Q(x)]$ (transitive).

As an illustration, this last property is proved. If $f(x)\, G(x) - g(x)\, F(x) = 0$, and $F(x)\, Q(x) - G(x)\, P(x) = 0$, then $Q(x) f(x)\, G(x) = Q(x)\, g(x)\, F(x) = g(x)\, G(x)\, P(x)$ and hence $G(x)\, [f(x)\, Q(x) - g(x)\, P(x)] = 0$. Because the ring of polynomials is an integral domain, and $G(x) \neq 0$, by hypothesis, $f(x)\, Q(x) - g(x)\, P(x) = 0$, which is the condition that $[f(x), g(x)]$ is equivalent to $[P(x), Q(x)]$.

Addition and multiplication of pairs are defined by the appropriate formulas (see 19), which arise from the fact that the pair $[f(x), g(x)]$ is to represent the rational function $f(x)/g(x)$. By methods similar to that used to prove the transitivity of the equivalence relation, it can be shown that if $[f(x), g(x)]$ or $[p(x), q(x)]$ is replaced by an equivalent pair, their sum, or product, is replaced by an equivalent pair. Now consider a new set Σ of elements, one representing each class of equivalent pairs. Addition and multiplication can be defined in Σ and it can be verified that with those operations Σ is an integral domain. The unity of Σ is the class of pairs containing $[1, 1]$: and if $[f(x), g(x)]$ represents a class α that is not zero, $f(x)$ is not zero, and there is a class β represented by $[g(x), f(x)]$. Then $\alpha\beta$ is equal to the unity of Σ, and Σ is a field.

The set Σ contains a subring consisting of elements represented by pairs $[f(x), 1]$. If this class of pairs is identified with $f(x)$, it is seen that addition and multiplication in this subring are consistent with addition and multiplication in the ring of polynomials. Therefore Σ is regarded as

(19)
$$\begin{cases} [f(x), g(x)] + [p(x), q(x)] \\ \quad = [f(x)q(x) + p(x)g(x), g(x)q(x)] \\ [f(x), g(x)] \times [p(x), q(x)] = [f(x)p(x), g(x)q(x)] \end{cases}$$

(20)
$$\begin{cases} f(x) \equiv a_0 x^n + a_1 x^{n-1} + \cdots + a_n, & a_0 \neq 0 \\ g(x) \equiv b_0 x^m + b_1 x^{m-1} + \cdots + b_m, & b_0 \neq 0 \end{cases}$$

(21)
$$f_2(x) = f_1(x) - kx^{n_1 - m} g(x)$$

(22)
$$f(x) = a(x)g(x) + b(x)$$

(23)
$$\begin{cases} f(x) = a_1(x)g(x) + b_1(x) \\ [a(x) - a_1(x)]g(x) = b_1(x) - b(x) \end{cases}$$

(24)
$$g(x) = a_1(x)b(x) + b_1(x)$$

(25)
$$\begin{cases} f(x) = a(x)g(x) + b(x) \\ g(x) = a_1(x)b(x) + b_1(x) \\ b(x) = a_2(x)b_1(x) + b_2(x) \\ \quad \vdots \\ b_{r-2}(x) = a_r(x)\, b_{r-1}(x) + b_r(x) \\ b_{r-1}(x) = a_{r+1}(x)b_r(x) \end{cases}$$

(26)
$$\begin{cases} f(x) = [a(x)a_1(x) + 1]b(x) + a(x)b_1(x), \\ f(x) = c_j(x)b_j(x) + d_j(x)b_{j+1}(x), \text{ in which } c_j(x) \text{ and} \\ d_j(x) \text{ are polynomials.} \end{cases}$$

an extension of the ring of polynomials. In this extension a class of pairs is represented by $f(x)/g(x)$ in which $[f(x), g(x)]$ is any pair representing the class of equivalent pairs. Thus the ring of polynomials in x has been extended to the field of rational functions of x. By a similar process the ring of polynomials in r variables can be extended to the field of rational functions of r variables.

Elementary properties of polynomials and rational functions. The remainder of this section deals with elementary properties of polynomials and rational functions. The division algorithm (procedure) for polynomials in one variable is discussed first. If $f(x)$ and $g(x)$ are two polynomials of degree n and m, respectively (see 20), and if $m \leq n$, then $f(x) - (a_0/b_0)x^{n-m}\, g(x)$ is a polynomial $f_1(x)$ of degree $n_1 (n_1 < n)$. If $n_1 \geq m$, in the same way, a number k in the coefficient field may be found such that a similar expression can be formed in terms of $f_1(x)$ and $g(x)$ (see 21). If $n_2 \geq m$, the process is repeated, and eventually $f(x)$ can be written as the sum of $a(x)\, g(x)$ and $b(x)$ (see 22), in which $a(x)$, $b(x)$ are polynomials [with coefficients in the coefficient field of $f(x)$ and $g(x)$] and the degree of $b(x)$ is less than m. This representation is unique, for if another such expression is formed and subtracted from the first (see 23), the right-hand side will be of degree less than m. Because $g(x)$ is of degree m, the left-hand side is of degree m at least unless $a(x) = a_1(x)$.

Division of polynomials

The equality therefore shows that $a(x) = a_1(x)$, $b(x) = b_1(x)$, and that the representation of $f(x)$ is unique. For use below (see *Solution of equations*) note that if $g(x) = x - a$, $b(x)$ is a polynomial of degree zero equal to $f(a) = a_0 a^n + a_1 a^{n-1} + \cdots + a_n$ (the remainder theorem).

Returning to the case in which $g(x)$ is a polynomial of degree m, suppose that $b(x) \neq 0$. The same process is applied to the polynomials $g(x)$, $b(x)$, leading to a similar formula expressing $g(x)$ as the sum of $a_1(x)\, b(x)$ and $b_1(x)$ (see 24), in which $a_1(x)$, $b_1(x)$ are polynomials the coefficients of which are in the coefficient field of $f(x)$, $g(x)$; and the degree of $b_1(x)$ is less than that of $b(x)$. If $b_1(x)$ is not zero, the process is repeated, until a stage is reached in which the remainder is zero. A set of equations of this form is obtained (see 25) ending when $b_{r+1}(x)=0$.

From the first equation $b(x)=f(x)-a(x)g(x)$; substituting in the second, an expression $b_1(x) = p(x)f(x)+q(x)g(x)$ is obtained, and by successive substitution $b_r(x)=p_r(x)f(x)+q_r(x)g(x)$, in which $p_r(x)$, $q_r(x)$ are polynomials.

Next, starting from $f(x)=a(x)g(x)+b(x)$, one obtains by substitution two expressions for $f(x)$ involving the above quantities and the polynomials $c_i(x)$ and $d_i(x)$ (see 26).

Because $b_{r+1}(x)$ is zero, $f(x)=c_r(x)b_r(x)$. Starting from the second equation of (25), the same procedure gives $g(x)=e_r(x)b_r(x)$, in which $e_r(x)$ is a polynomial.

If $r(x)$ is a polynomial that is a factor of $f(x)$ and $g(x)$, so that $f(x)=l(x)r(x)$, $g(x)=m(x)r(x)$, then $b_r(x)=[p_r(x)l(x)+q_r(x)m(x)]r(x)$; that is, $r(x)$ is a factor of $b_r(x)$. Conversely, if $r(x)$ is a factor of $b_r(x)$, so that $b_r(x) = r(x)s(x)$, then $f(x)=c_r(x)r(x)s(x)$, $g(x)=e_r(x)r(x)s(x)$, so that $r(x)$ is a factor of $f(x)$ and $g(x)$. For this reason $b_r(x)$ is called the highest common factor of $f(x)$ and $g(x)$.

A polynomial $f(x)$ with coefficients in a field K is called reducible if it can be written in the form $f(x)=g(x)h(x)$, in which $g(x)$ and $h(x)$ are polynomials of degree greater than zero; otherwise it is irreducible. If $f(x)$ is reducible it can be written $g(x)h(x)$; if $g(x)$ or $h(x)$ is reducible it can be written as $h(x)=l(x)m(x)$. Thus, after a finite number of steps, one obtains $f(x)=p_1(x)p_2(x)\cdots p_r(x)$, in which each $p_i(x)$ is irreducible.

The unique factorization theorem

This representation of $f(x)$ as a product of irreducible factors is unique, for suppose that $f(x)=q_1(x)q_2(x)\cdots q_s(x)$ is another such representation; $p_1(x)$ is a factor of $q_1(x)q_2(x)\cdots q_s(x)$, and so must be a factor of $q_i(x)$ for some i. This is proved by supposing $p_1(x)$ and $q_1(x)$ are not factors of one another; then their highest common factor is in the coefficient field, and from the above there exist polynomials $a(x)$, $b(x)$ such that $a(x)p_1(x)+b(x)q_1(x)=1$; $b(x)q_1(x)q_2(x)\cdots q_s(x) = b(x)p_1(x)p_2(x)\cdots p_r(x) = [1-a(x)p_1(x)]q_2(x)\cdots q_s(x)$.

Hence $p_1(x)[b(x)p_2(x)\cdots p_r(x)+a(x)q_2(x)\cdots q_s(x)] = q_2(x)\cdots q_s(x)$. Thus $p_1(x)$ is a factor of $q_2(x)\cdots q_s(x)$. The same argument can be repeated to show that if $p_1(x)$ is not a factor of $q_2(x)$, it must be a factor of $q_3(x)\cdots q_s(x)$, and so on, so that $p_1(x)$ must be a factor of $q_i(x)$ for some i. Since $p_1(x)$ and $q_i(x)$ are both irreducible, they can differ only by multiplication by an element of the coefficient field. In this way a pairing is obtained between factors $p_i(x)$ and $q_j(x)$, and the unique factorization theorem is proved.

It is easy to extend the theorem to polynomials in several variables: it is sufficient to demonstrate how it may be done for polynomials in two variables x and y. If $f(x, y)$ be a polynomial in x, y, it may be regarded as a polynomial in y, with coefficients in the field of rational functions of x. Because the unique factorization theorem for one variable is proved by purely rational processes—that is, using only operations of addition and subtraction, and multiplication and division in the coefficients—it follows that $f(x, y)=r_1(x, y)r_2(x, y)\cdots r_k(x, y)$, in which $r_i(x, y)$ is an irreducible polynomial in y with coefficients that are rational functions of x, the k polynomials being uniquely determined save for order and factors that are rational functions of x. Let $b_i(x)$ be a common denominator of the coefficients of y in $r_i(x, y)$, so that each coefficient may be written $a(x)/b_i(x)$, in which $a(x)$ is a polynomial, and let $a_i(x)$ be the highest common factor of the coefficients of y in $b_i(x)r_i(x, y)$. Then $r_i(x, y)=[a_i(x)/b_i(x)]g_i(x, x)$, in which $g_i(x, y)$ is a polynomial in x and y, uniquely determined save for a factor in the field of coefficients. Hence $b_1(x)b_2(x)\cdots b_k(x)f(x, y)=a_1(x)\cdots a_k(x)g_1(x, y)\cdots g_k(x, y)$. Applying the unique factorization for polynomials in one variable to the coefficients of y, $b_i(x)\cdots b_k(x)$ is seen to be a factor of $a_1(x)\cdots a_k(x)$, and so $f(x, y)=c_1(x)\cdots c_8(x)g_1(x, y)\cdots g_k(x, y)$, in which the $c_i(x)$ and $g_j(x, y)$ are irreducible and uniquely determined to within a factor in the coefficient field.

Symmetric polynomials. Polynomials in r variables, $x_1, \cdots, x_r$, which are of importance in many parts of mathematics, for instance in the theory of equations, are the symmetric polynomials. A polynomial $f(x_1, \cdots, x_r)$ is a symmetric polynomial in its arguments $x_1, \cdots, x_r$ if the coefficients are rational numbers and if its value is unchanged whenever the subscripts in the arguments are replaced by any permutation of $(1, \cdots, r)$. For example, (2, 1, 3) is a permutation of (1, 2, 3). Important examples include the elementary symmetric polynomials (see 27), and sums of terms, each of the form x_i^k, for $i=1, 2, \cdots, r$ (see 28).

Operations on symmetrical polynomials

In general (except for a plus or minus sign) the elementary symmetric polynomial γ_k in r variables $x_1, \cdots x_r$ is the coefficient of t^k in $(t-x_1)(t-x_2)\cdots(t-x_r)$ $(k=1, 2, \cdots)$. The principal result concerning symmetric polynomials is that any such polynomial $F(x_1, \cdots, x_r)$ can be obtained by applying the operations of addition and multiplication to the elementary symmetric polynomials $\gamma_1, \gamma_2, \cdots, \gamma_r$, so that F is a polynomial in $\gamma_1, \cdots, \gamma_r$. This may be proved by the process of induction on r. There is, indeed, nothing to prove if $r=1$. To begin the induction, it may be assumed that the theorem is true if applied to symmetric polynomials in $x_1, \cdots, x_{r-1}$. If $\gamma'_1, \gamma'_2, \cdots, \gamma'_{r-1}$ denote the elementary symmetric polynomials in $x_1, \cdots, x_{r-1}$, then $\gamma_1, \cdots, \gamma_r$ can be expressed in terms of $\gamma'_1, \cdots, \gamma'_r$ and x_r (see 29). These equations can be solved for $\gamma'_1 \cdots, \gamma'_r$ (see 30).

Writing $F(x_1, \cdots, x_r)$ as a polynomial in x_r (see 31), with the coefficients a_i being polynomials in $x_1, \cdots, x_{r-1}$, one finds that because $F(x_1, \cdots, x_r)$ is unaltered by any permutation of $x_1, \cdots, x_r$, in particular by any permutation leaving x_r fixed, α_i is a symmetric polynomial in $x_1, \cdots, x_{r-1}$, and can therefore be represented as a polynomial in $\gamma'_1, \cdots, \gamma'_{r-1}$. Replacing γ'_1 by $\gamma_1 - x_r$, γ'_2 by $\gamma_2 - x_r\gamma_1 + x_r^2$, etc., it is possible to write $F(x_1, \cdots, x_r)$ as a polynomial $G(\gamma_1, \cdots, \gamma_{r-1}, x_r)$ in $\gamma_1, \cdots, \gamma_{r-1}, x_r$. Now if $f(z)$ is a product of terms of the form $(z-x_i)$, for $i=1, 2, \cdots, r$ (see 32), then $f(x_r)=0$. Using this, powers of x_r in $G(\gamma_1, \cdots, \gamma_{r-1}, x_r)$

(27) The *elementary symmetric polynomials*:
$$\begin{cases}\gamma_1=x_1+x_2+\cdots+x_r,\\ \gamma_2=x_1x_2+x_1x_3+\cdots+x_2x_3+\cdots+x_{r-1}x_r,\\ \gamma_r=x_1x_2\cdots x_r.\end{cases}$$

(28) The sums of powers: $\rho_k=x_1^k+x_2^k+\cdots+x_r^k$, $k=1, 2, \cdots.$

(29)
$$\begin{cases}\gamma_1=\gamma'_1+x_r, \quad \gamma_2=\gamma'_2+x_r\gamma'_1, \cdots\\ \gamma_r=x_r\gamma'_{r-1}\end{cases}$$

(30) $$\gamma'_1=\gamma_1-x_r, \quad \gamma'_2=\gamma_2-x_2\gamma_1+x_r^2, \cdots$$

(31) $$F(x_1, \cdots, x_r)=\alpha_0x_r^m+\alpha_1x_r^{m-1}+\cdots+\alpha_m$$

(32) $$f(z)=(z-x_1)(z-x_2)\cdots(z-x_r) = z^r-\gamma_1z^{r-1}+\gamma_2z^{r-2}-\cdots\pm\gamma_r$$

(33) $$F(x_1, \cdots, x_r)=\beta_0x_r^{r-1}+\beta_1x_r^{r-2}+\cdots+\beta_{r-1}$$

(34) $$F(x_1, \cdots, x_r)=\beta_0x_i^{r-1}+\beta_1x_i^{r-2}+\cdots+\beta_{r-1} \quad i=1, \cdots, r$$

(35) $$H(z)=\beta_0z^{r-1}+\beta_1z^{r-2}+\cdots+\beta_{r-1}-F(x_1, \cdots, x_r)$$

(36) $$F(x_1, \cdots, x_r)=\beta_{r-1}$$

(37) $$F_i(x_1, x_2, \cdots, x_n)=0, \quad i=1, \cdots, r$$

(38) $$F_i(\alpha_1, \alpha_2, \cdots, \alpha_n)=0, \quad i=1, \cdots, r$$

of degree greater than $r-1$ can be replaced by expressions involving $\gamma_1, \cdots, \gamma_r$ and lower powers of x_r. Finally an equation is reached for $F(x_1, \cdots, x_r)$ as a sum of terms $\beta_{i-1}x_r^{r-i}$ (see 33), in which $\beta_0 \cdots, \beta_{r-1}$ are polynomials in $\gamma_1, \cdots, \gamma_r$—and hence symmetric polynomials in $(x_1, \cdots, x_r)$. Because $F(x_1, \cdots, x_r)$ is symmetric, r similar equations result (see 34).

Now consider the polynomial $H(z)$, formed by subtracting $F(x_1, \cdots, x_r)$ from a similar polynomial in the variable z (see 35), with coefficients in the field of rational functions of $x_1, \cdots, x_r$. $H(z)$ has r zeros, namely $z = a_1, \cdots, a_r$. But (see below *Solution of equations*) a polynomial of degree $r-1$ or less that has r zeros is identically zero. Hence putting $z=0$, $F(x_1, \cdots, x_r)$ equals β_{r-1} (see 36), in which β_{r-1} is a polynomial in the elementary symmetric polynomials $\gamma_1, \cdots, \gamma_r$. So if any polynomial in $r-1$ variables may be expressed as a polynomial in the $r-1$ elementary symmetric polynomials, it follows that any polynomial in r variables may be so expressed. Because the theorem is true for one variable, it is true for any number of variables.

The symmetric polynomials play an important role in the theory of equations (see below). A simple calculation enables expressions to be given for the sums s_r of the rth powers of $(x_1, \cdots, x_r)$ in terms of $\gamma_1, \cdots, \gamma_r$; from these relations it can be shown that $\gamma_1, \cdots, \gamma_r$ are equal to polynomials in $s_1, \cdots, s_r$; hence any symmetric polynomial can be expressed as a polynomial in $s_1 \cdots, s_r$.

SOLUTION OF EQUATIONS

Nature of the problem

One of the principal problems of elementary algebra is the solution of a set of equations in which r polynomials $F_i(x_1, x_2, \cdots, x_n)$, $i = 1, 2, \cdots, r$, with coefficients in a field (rational numbers, real numbers, or complex numbers), are set equal to zero (see 37). By a solution of these equations is meant a set of numbers $(a_1, a_2, \cdots, a_n)$ in the coefficient field, or in some extension of the coefficient field, that, when substituted for $x_1, x_2, \cdots, x_n$, causes the polynomials all to equal zero (see 38).

The problem falls into three parts. (1) Does there exist a solution of the equations, and how can a given set of equations be tested for solvability? This question can be refined by asking whether there exist solutions in the field of the coefficients, or in some prescribed extension of this field. A particular case of this arises when the coefficients are natural numbers, and it is desired to find solutions $(a_1, a_2, \cdots, a_n)$ in which a_i is rational. Such problems really belong to the theory of numbers, though methods of algebraic geometry (see below) play an important role in these investigations. (2) The criteria for determining whether a set of equations has a solution do not, as a rule, give any clue to finding a solution when one is known to exist. One asks whether there exists some algebraic process, involving the elementary operations of addition, subtraction, multiplication, and division, together with the extraction of roots, which, when applied to the coefficients of the equation, will lead to a solution. More precisely, it is of considerable interest to ask whether the solution can be obtained by elementary operations only (the solutions are then said to be rational) or if they can be found by elementary operations together with the extraction of square roots so that the solutions can be constructed geometrically by ruler and compass only (see above). (3) Whether or not it is possible to find the solution of a set of equations explicitly, it may be possible to develop a theory of the aggregate of solutions of a set of equations. This leads to algebraic geometry. In elementary geometry of the plane coordinates (x, y) are introduced consisting of pairs of real numbers x and y, and a one-to-one correspondence is established between all pairs (x, y) and all points of the plane. This notion can be extended in several ways: First the plane may be replaced by the real affine space of n dimensions, in which there is a one-to-one correspondence between the points of the space and all possible sets $(a_1, a_2, \cdots, a_n)$ of real numbers. Again, this notion may be extended to obtain complex affine space, in which the coordinates are sets of n complex numbers. Then each real (complex) solution of the equation defines a unique point in real (complex) affine space of n dimensions. The aggregate of the solutions defines a locus in the affine space, and the geometrical properties of this locus provide important information about the solution of the equations.

Solution as a unique point in affine space

(39) $$y_0^{\pi_i} F_i\left(\frac{y_1}{y_0}, \frac{y_2}{y_0}, \cdots, \frac{y_n}{y_0}\right) \equiv G_i(y_0, y_1, \cdots, y_n)$$

(40) $$G_i(ty_0, ty_1, \cdots, ty_n) = t^{\pi_i} G_i(y_0, y_1, \cdots, y_n)$$

(41) $$G_i(y_0, y_1, \cdots, y_n) = 0, \qquad i = 1, \cdots, r$$

(42) $$f(x) \equiv a_0x^n + a_1x^{n-1} + \cdots + a_n = 0$$

(43) $$f(x) = f_1(x)(x-\alpha) + f(\alpha)$$

(44) $$f_1(x) = (x-\beta)f_2(x), \qquad f(x) = (x-\alpha)(x-\beta)f_2(x)$$

(45) $$f(x) = a_0(x-\alpha_1)(x-\alpha_2)\cdots(x-\alpha_n)$$

(46) $$\alpha_0(\beta-\alpha_1)(\beta-\alpha_2)\cdots(\beta-\alpha_n) = 0$$

(47) $$\begin{cases} a_0x^n + a_1x^{n-1} + \cdots + a_n \\ \quad = a_0(x-\alpha_1)(x-\alpha_2)\cdots(x-\alpha_n) \\ \quad = a_0x^n - a_0(\alpha_1+\alpha_2+\cdots+\alpha_n)x^{n-1} + \cdots \\ \quad = a_0x^n - a_0\delta_1x^{n-1} + a_0\delta_2x^{n-2} - \cdots \end{cases}$$

(48) $$\begin{aligned} x^2 + a_1x + a_2 &= (x+\tfrac{1}{2}a_1)^2 + a_2 - \tfrac{1}{4}a_1^2 \\ &= (x+\tfrac{1}{2}a_1+\alpha)(x+\tfrac{1}{2}a_1-\alpha) \end{aligned}$$

It is familiar that, in the elementary geometry of the plane, simple theorems such as "two (distinct) lines have one point in common" have to be qualified by adding "or else are parallel." This difficulty is overcome by adding to the affine plane a "line at infinity" to make the plane into a projective plane, the points being given by sets of numbers (a, β, γ) not all zero, two sets of numbers which are proportional determining the same point so that (a, β, γ) and $(\lambda a, \lambda\beta, \lambda\gamma)$ represent the same point. The points of the affine plane are identified with the points of the projective plane for which a is not zero. The affine coordinates of the point are $(\beta/a, \gamma/a)$. The same process can be used to extend the real (complex) affine space of n dimensions to a projective space of n dimensions. Now let $(a_1, a_2, \cdots, a_n)$ be any solution of the equations being considered (see 38). This is represented in projective space of n dimensions by the point $(\beta_0, \beta_1, \cdots, \beta_n)$, in which $\beta_0 a_i = \beta_i$, $i = 1, \cdots, r$. In $F_i(x_1, x_2, \cdots, x_n)$ replace x_i by y_i/y_0 and multiply by the lowest power of y_0 that yields a polynomial G_i (see 39). This polynomial is homogeneous (see 40). Now consider the set of homogeneous equations (see 41) in which the G_i are set equal to zero. If $(\beta_0, \beta_1, \cdots, \beta_n)$ is a solution, so is $(\lambda\beta_0, \lambda\beta_1, \cdots, \lambda\beta_n)$ for any λ. If not all β_i are zero, the solution $(\lambda\beta_0, \lambda\beta_1, \cdots, \lambda\beta_n)$ defines a unique point in the projective space of n dimensions. If $\beta_0 \neq 0$, then $(\beta_1/\beta_0, \beta_2/\beta_0, \cdots, \beta_n/\beta_0)$ is a solution of the original equations (see 37). Thus the homogeneous equations (see 41) define a locus in projective space of n dimensions; and the points of this locus not in $y_0 = 0$ can be identified with the points of the affine space from which the projective space was constructed, which corresponds to the solutions of the original equations (see 37).

Just as the use of projective space allows certain difficulties arising in the geometry of affine space to be eliminated, so the restriction to homogeneous equations simplifies some difficulties in algebra, which arise when the solutions of nonhomogeneous equations are considered.

Existence of solutions. As a preliminary to the algebraic study of the equation in r variables, it is necessary to consider the solution of an n-degree polynomial equation in one variable (see 42), in some detail. The fundamental theorem of algebra states that if $n > 0$ and the coefficients are rational, or real, or complex numbers, there exists at least one complex number a such that $f(a) = 0$. The

The fundamental theorem of algebra

number a is called a root of $f(x)$, or a solution of $f(x)=0$. No elementary algebraic proof of this theorem exists, and the result is not proved here. There is an extension of the theorem which states that if the coefficients of $f(x)$ are in any field K, there exists an extension of K in which $f(x)$ has a root. In what follows, however, the coefficients of $f(x)$ are in the complex field: $f(x)$ then has a root in this field.

The remainder theorem proved above (see *Elementary properties of polynomials and rational functions*) can be applied (see 43) to express $f(x)$ as the sum of $f(a)$ and the product $f_1(x)(x-a)$, in which $f_1(x)$ is a polynomial of degree $n-1$. If a is a root of $f(x)$, this implies that $(x-a)$ is a factor of $f(x)$. If $(n-1)>0$, $f_1(x)$ also has a root β, and the process can be continued to express $f(x)$ as a product (see 44 and 45) of terms of the form $(x-a_i)$, for $i=1, 2, \cdots, n$, in which $a_1, a_2, \cdots, a_n$ are complex numbers. Because $f(a_i)=0$, each a_i is a root of $f(x)$. If β is any root of $f(x)$, then this expression equals zero (see 46), and because the complex numbers form a field, one term $(\beta-a_i)$ must be zero. Hence $a_1, a_2, \cdots, a_n$ are the only roots of $f(x)$. So now the polynomial can be written in terms of δ_i (see 47), the result of replacing $x_1, x_2, \cdots, x_n$ by $a_1, a_2, \cdots, a_n$ in the elementary symmetric polynomial γ_i (see 27). A function δ_i is usually called an (elementary) symmetric function of the roots of $f(x)$, and a considerable body of algebra deals with properties of the symmetric functions of the roots of an equation. For example, note that $a_0\delta_i=-a_i$ if i is odd, and that $a_0\delta_i=a_i$ if i is even. Thus the symmetric functions of the roots lie in the coefficient field of $f(x)$, though the individual roots may not.

Finding the roots

Extraction of the roots of a polynomial. Although the fundamental theorem of algebra enables one to show that a polynomial $f(x)$ of degree n has n roots, it gives no clue to finding the roots. In algebra, it is desired to give rules for applying a series of elementary operations, together with the extraction of rth roots (the standard operations of algebra) on the coefficients of $f(x)$ to find the roots. In considering this problem, note that the roots of $f(x)$ are the same as the roots of $bf(x)$ in which b is any nonzero number of the coefficient field; b can be chosen so that $ba_0=1$; this means that without loss of generality a_0 may be set equal to one in $f(x)$; by doing this the notation is greatly simplified.

(I) $n=1$. The equation is $x+a_1=0$, which has the unique solution $-a_1$ in the coefficient field.

(II) $n=2$. Any quadratic expression can be put in the form $x^2+a_1x+a_2$ and then can be factored, giving the solutions $-{}^1\!/\!_2a_1+a$, $-{}^1\!/\!_2a_1-a$ (see 48), in which a, $-a$ are the square roots of ${}^1\!/\!_4a_1{}^2-a_2$. The root a can be constructed by use of ruler and compass, and the roots $-{}^1\!/\!_2a_1+a$, $-{}^1\!/\!_2a_1-a$ are obtained by the standard operations of algebra.

(III) $n=3$. The variable in $f(x)$ is changed by writing $y=x+{}^1\!/\!_3a_1$ giving a cubic equation with no quadratic term (see 49), in which the constants p and q are obtained from a_1, a_2, a_3 by elementary operations. If a root β of $g(y)$ can be found, $\beta-{}^1\!/\!_3a_1$ is a root of $f(x)$. If $p=0$, the roots of $g(y)$ are determined by extracting a cube root, and the solution of $f(x)=0$ is complete.

Consider now $p\neq0$ and make another change of variable determined by $y=z-p/3z$. Then express $g(y)$ in terms of z (see 50), and it is clear that if γ is any root of $h(z)$, $\gamma-p/3\gamma$ is a root of $g(y)$, and so a root of $f(x)$ is obtained. Defining two new quantities ξ and η and using the properties of homogeneous equations (see 40), one can factor $h(z)$ into a product (see 51), with terms of the product constructed by standard processes. By a standard process (but not by ruler and compass) a number a can be constructed such that $a^3=\xi$. If $1, \omega_1, \omega_2$ are the cube roots of unity, the other roots of $z^3-\xi$, one of the factors of $h(z)$, are $a\omega_1, \omega_2$. It can be shown (see 52) that β is a cube root of η. The other cube roots are obtained, similarly, using $a\omega_1, a\omega_2$; they are in fact $\beta\omega_2, \beta\omega_1$, respectively.

If $\gamma_1=a-p/3a$, γ_1 is a root of $g(y)$. Replacing a in this by $a\omega_1$, $a\omega_2$ or β, $\beta\omega_2$, $\beta\omega_1$ the other roots of $g(y)$ are obtained. On account of the relation $\beta=-p/3a$, however, the pairs (a, β), $(a\omega_1, \beta\omega_2)$, $(a\omega_2, \beta\omega_1)$ give the same roots

(49) $$f(x)=g(y)\equiv y^3+py+q$$

(50) $$g(y)=\frac{z^6+qz^3-p^3/27}{z^3}=\frac{h(z)}{z^3}$$

(51) $$\begin{cases} h(z)=(z^3-\xi)(z^3-\eta) \\ \xi=-\tfrac{1}{2}q+\rho, \qquad \eta=-\tfrac{1}{2}q-\rho \end{cases}$$

(52) $$\begin{cases} \beta=\dfrac{-p}{3\alpha} \\ \beta^3=\dfrac{-p^3}{27\xi}=\dfrac{-p^3}{27}\dfrac{1}{-\frac{1}{2}q+\rho}=\dfrac{-p^3}{27}\dfrac{-\frac{1}{2}q-\rho}{\frac{1}{4}q^2-\rho^2}=-\tfrac{1}{2}q-\rho \end{cases}$$

(53) $$x^4+a_1x^3+a_2x^2+a_3x+a_4=0$$

(54) $$y^2+a_1xy+a_2y+a_3x+a_4=0$$

(55) $$y-x^2=0$$

(56) $$F(x, y, \lambda)\equiv\lambda(x^2-y)+y^2+a_1xy+a_2y+a_3x+a_4$$

(57) $$\lambda(\lambda-a_2)^2+a_1a_3(\lambda-a_2)-4a_4\lambda+a_3^2+a_1^2a_4=0$$

(58) $$F(x, y, \lambda_i)=(a_ix+b_iy+c_i)(\alpha_ix+\beta_iy+\gamma_i) \quad i=1, 2, 3$$

(59) $$a_1x+b_1y+c_1=0, \qquad a_2x+b_2y+c_2=0$$

(60) $$a_1x+b_1y+c_1=0, \qquad \alpha_2x+\beta_2y+\gamma_2=0$$

(61) $$f(x)\equiv a_0x^n+a_1x^{n-1}+\cdots+a_n=0$$

(62) $$g(x)\equiv b_0x^m+b_1x^{m-1}+\cdots+b_m=0$$

(63) $$H(f, g)=p(x)f(x)+q(x)g(x)$$

(64) $$f(x)=r(x)H(f, g), \qquad g(x)=s(x)H(f, g)$$

(65) $$\begin{aligned} &a_0^mb_0^n(\alpha_1-\beta_1)(\alpha_1-\beta_2)\cdots(\alpha_n-\beta_m) \\ &=a_0^mg(\alpha_1)g(\alpha_2)\cdots g(\alpha_n) \\ &=\pm b_0^nf(\beta_1)f(\beta_2)\cdots f(\beta_m) \end{aligned}$$

of $g(y)$. Thus three roots of $g(y)$ are obtained by the standard processes of algebra, and hence three roots of $f(x)$.

(IV) $n=4$. It can also be proved that the fourth degree equation (see 53) can be solved by the standard processes of algebra. It is instructive to see how one is led to the solution by simple considerations of geometry in the complex affine plane. In this plane define two conics by equations in x and y (see 54 and 55). A conic in the real plane is formed by the intersection of the plane with a cone. A circle, ellipse, hyperbola, parabola, or pair of intersecting straight lines is a conic. The concept is generalized to the complex plane. If a is any root of the fourth-degree equation (see 53), (a, a^2) is a point common to the conics. Conversely, if (a, β) is any point common to the two conics, $\beta=a^2$ from the second conic, a is a root of the fourth-degree equation (see 53). So it is necessary to find the four points common to the two conics. Define a function $F(x, y, \lambda)$, in which λ is any complex number, from these two conics (see 56). $F(x, y, \lambda)=0$ is the equation of a conic in the plane. It is clear that if λ, μ are different complex numbers, the points common to $F(x, y, \lambda)=0$ and $F(x, y, \mu)=0$ are the points common to the conics (see 54 and 55). Now it is a theorem of geometry that $F(x, y, \lambda)=0$ becomes a pair of lines if λ is a root of a certain cubic polynomial (see 57). By (III), this polynomial in λ has three roots $\lambda_1, \lambda_2, \lambda_3$, which can be found by the standard processes. Then, by solving quadratic equations, as in (II),

$F(x, y, \lambda)$ can be written as a product of two terms, each linear in x and y (see 58). To find the four points common to the conics it is necessary to find the points common to $F(x, y, \lambda_1)=0$ and $F(x, y, \lambda_2)=0$. To find these, four pairs of linear equations (see 59 and 60) must be solved. Because the four points so obtained satisfy the original equation and the second conic (see 37 and 55), the solution of the fourth-degree equation (see 53) is deduced, and can therefore be obtained by the standard processes of algebra.

Equations of degrees higher than four

In the 18th century, much effort was put into attempts to find methods of finding the solution of an equation of degree higher than four by the standard processes of algebra. Early in the 19th century the Norwegian mathematician Niels Henrik Abel proved that the general equation of degree five could not be solved in this way. Before his untimely death in 1832, the French mathematician Évariste Galois extended Abel's result to equations of degree greater than five and developed a general theory of equations that threw much light on the problem (see below *Fields*).

Use of the highest common factor

Common roots of two polynomials. Now let $f(x)$ and $g(x)$ be polynomials of degree n and m, respectively, and let $f(x)=0$ and $g(x)=0$ (see 61 and 62). One may ask if these equations have any common solution, and if so how it is found. It was shown above how to construct the highest common factor of $f(x)$, $g(x)$. This is a polynomial $H(f, g)$, such that there exist polynomials $p(x)$, $q(x)$, $r(x)$, $s(x)$, in terms of which $f(x)$ and $g(x)$ can be written (see 63 and 64). From these equations it follows that any common root of $f(x)$ and $g(x)$ is a root of $H(f, g)$, and any root of $H(f, g)$ is a common root of $f(x)$, $g(x)$. Thus $f(x)$ and $g(x)$ have a common root if and only if the highest common factor is of degree greater than zero. The process described can easily be extended to find the common roots, if any, of any finite set of polynomials $f_i(x)$ $(i=1, \cdots, r)$. The highest common factor $H(f_1, f_2)$ of $f_1(x)$, $f_2(x)$ is constructed; the highest common factor $H(f_1, f_2, f_3)$ of this and $f_3(x)$, and so on. The common roots of $f_i(x)$ are simply the roots of $H(f_1, f_2, \cdots, f_r)$.

If $f(x)$ and $g(x)$ have a common root, then let $\alpha_1, \cdots, \alpha_n$ be the roots of $f(x)$, $\beta_1, \cdots, \beta_m$ the roots of $g(x)$. Consider a product with terms of the form $(\alpha_i-\beta_j)$, for $i=1, 2, \cdots, n$, and $j=1, 2, \cdots, m$ (see 65). The first expression is a symmetric function of the roots of $f(x)$, and hence can be expressed in terms of the elementary symmetric functions of these roots, that is, in terms of $a_0, a_1 \cdots, a_n$. The expression is therefore a polynomial $R(f, g)$ in the coefficients $a_0, \cdots, a_n, b_0, \cdots, b_m$. If, for any given polynomials $f(x)$ and $g(x)$ in which a_0 and b_0 are not zero, $R(f, g)=0$, it follows that the equations have a common solution, and conversely if the equations have a common solution $R(f, g)=0$.

In later developments, the condition of $a_0\neq 0$, $b_0\neq 0$ turns out to be an undesirable restriction. This restriction may be removed to some extent. Suppose that $a_0\neq 0$, $b_0=0$. Because $R(f, g)$ can be written as a product of $a_0{}^m$ and the n terms $g(\alpha_i)$ (see 66), in which $\alpha_1, \cdots, \alpha_n$ are roots of $f(x)$, $R(f, g)=0$ implies $g(\alpha_i)=0$ for some root α_i of $f(x)$. Hence this α_i is a common root of $f(x)$, $g(x)$. If $a_0=0=b_0$, however, this argument breaks down. It can be verified that if a_0 and b_0 both vanish, $R(f, g)=0$, whatever values are given to $a_1, \cdots, a_n, b_1, \cdots, b_m$, and nothing is learned about the roots of $f(x)$, $g(x)$.

To overcome this difficulty a new variable y is introduced in $f(x)$, $g(x)$ by replacing a_i by A_iy^i, b_j by B_jy^j; then three homogeneous polynomials $F(x, y)$, $G(x, y)$ and $R(f, g)$ are obtained (see 67). The polynomial $T(F, G)$ in $A_0, \cdots, A_n, B_0, \cdots, B_m$ is obtained by replacing $a_0, \cdots, a_n, b_0, \cdots, b_m$ by $A_0, \cdots, A_n, B_0, \cdots, B_m$ in $R(f, g)$.

If $F(x, y)$ and $G(x, y)$ both equal to zero (see 68) have a common solution (α, β) in which $\beta\neq 0$, α/β is a common root of $f(x)$, $g(x)$, and hence $T(F, G)=0$. If the homogeneous equations have a common solution $(\alpha, 0)$ in which $\alpha=0$, then A_0, B_0 are zero, and $T(F, G)=0$. Conversely, if $T(F, G)=0$ and A_0, B_0 are not both zero, $F(x, 1)$ and $G(y, 1)$ have a common root α, and $(\alpha, 1)$ is a common solution (see 68). If A_0, B_0 are zero the equations have the common solution $(1, 0)$. Hence $T(F, G)=0$ is a necessary

(66) $$R(f, g)=a_0^m g(\alpha_1)\cdots g(\alpha_n)$$

(67) $$\begin{cases} F(x, y)\equiv A_0x^n+A_1x^{n-1}y+\cdots+A_ny^n \\ G(x, y)\equiv B_0x^m+B_1x^{m-1}y+\cdots+B_my^m \\ R(f, g)=y^{mn}T(F, G) \end{cases}$$

(68) $$F(x, y)=0, \qquad G(x, y)=0$$

(69) $$f(x, y)\equiv a_0x^n+a_1x^{n-1}+\cdots+a_n=0$$

(70) $$g(x, y)=b_0x^m+b_1x^{m-1}+\cdots+b_m=0$$

(71) $$\begin{cases} F(x, y, z)\equiv A_0(y, z)x^N+A_1(y, z)x^{N-1}+ \\ \quad +\cdots+A_N(y, z)=0 \\ G(x, y, z)\equiv B_0(y, z)x^M+R_1(y, z)x^{M-1}+ \\ \quad +\cdots+B_M(y, z)=0 \end{cases}$$

(72) $$\begin{cases} F(x, y, z)=A_0(u, v)x^N+A_1(u, v)tx^{N-1}+ \\ \quad +\cdots+A_N(u, v)t^N \\ G(x, y, z)\equiv B_0(u, v)x^M+B_1(u, v)tx^{M-1}+ \\ \quad +\cdots+B_M(u, v)t^M \end{cases}$$

(73) $$l_i\equiv a_ix+b_iy+c_iz, \qquad i=1, \cdots, r$$

(74) $$b_ic_j-b_jc_i=c_ia_j-c_ja_i=a_ib_j-a_jb_i=0 \quad i, j=1, \cdots, r$$

(75) $$l_i=\rho_il_1$$

(76) $$a_1x+b_1y+c_1z=0$$

(77) $$b_il_j-b_jl_i=(b_ia_j-b_ja_i)x+(b_ic_j-b_jc_i)z=0$$

(78) $$(b_ic_j-b_jc_i)a_k+(c_ia_j-c_ja_i)b_k+(a_ib_j-a_jb_i)c_k=0$$

(79) $$\begin{pmatrix} a_1 & a_2 & \cdots & a_r \\ b_1 & b_2 & \cdots & b_r \\ c_1 & c_2 & \cdots & c_r \end{pmatrix}$$

(80) $$M_i\equiv a_ix+b_iy+c_i=0, \qquad i=1, \cdots, r$$

(81) $$b_iM_j-b_jM_i=0x+b_ic_j-b_jc_i=0$$

and sufficient condition for the homogeneous equations (68) to have a common solution.

The problem of solving equations in two variables (x, y) is now considered. If a simple equation $f(x, y)=0$ is taken, y is given an arbitrary value η in the complex field, and the equation $f(x, \eta)=0$ in one variable remains. If ξ is a root of $f(x, \eta)$, (ξ, η) is a solution for $f(x, y)=0$.

Two simultaneous equations. Now consider two simultaneous nonhomogeneous polynomial equations (see 69 and 70) in which the coefficients a_i, b_j are now polynomials in y. $R(f, g)$ is then a polynomial in y; and it is clear that if (ξ, η) is a common solution of the two equations, then η satisfies $R(f, g)=0$. If, on the other hand, η is a root of $R(f, g)$ and the polynomials a_0, b_0 do not both have η as a root, there exists a common root of $f(x, \eta)$, $g(x, \eta)$ and so a common solution of the two equations (see 69 and 70). If η is a common zero of a_0, b_0, however, the difficulty described above arises. To get over this difficulty, a new variable z is again introduced to make $f(x, y)$, $g(x, y)$ homogeneous, and $F(x, y, z)$ is defined as a sum of $N+1$ terms of the form $A_i(y, z)\,x^{N-i}$, for $i=0, 1, \cdots, N$, and $G(x, y, z)$ as a similar sum of terms of the form $B_j(y, z)x^{M-j}$, for $j=0, 1, \cdots, M$ (see 71), where $A_i(y, z)$ is homogeneous of degree i and $\beta_j(y, z)$ homogeneous of degree j. Then ut is written for y, vt for z (see 72). Regarding these as equations in (x, t), $T(F, G)$ is constructed as before. It is homogeneous in (u, v). If A_0 and B_0 are both zero, the equation $F(x, y, z) = 0$, $G(x, y, z) = 0$ have a common solution (1, 0, 0). If they are not both zero, $F(x, y, z) = 0$ and $G(x, y, z) = 0$ have a common solution (λ, μ, v) if and only if (μ, v) is a solution of $T(F, G) = 0$.

This again illustrates the advantages of studying homogeneous equations and the associated loci in projective space.

Equations in three variables

Linear systems. To conclude, there follows a brief consideration of the solution of a system of linear homogeneous equations in three variables x, y, z, with coefficients a_i, b_i, c_i, respectively, for $i = 1, 2, \cdot \cdot \cdot, r$ (see 73). If each a_i, b_i, c_i, is zero $(i = 1, \cdot \cdot \cdot, r)$, the problem is trivial. Next, suppose, for instance, that a_1, b_1, c_1 are not all zero, and that a certain relation of the coefficients (see 74) holds. Then there is a nonzero number such that l_i equals the product of p_i and l_1 (see 75), and the problem reduces to finding the solution of a single such equation (see 76).

Next, suppose that $b_ic_j - b_jc_i$, $c_ia_j - c_ja_i$, $a_ib_j - a_jb_i$ are not all zero for a particular pair i, j, say $b_ic_j - b_jc_i \neq 0$. Then y can be eliminated yielding a simpler problem (see 77). This equation has a unique solution $[\rho(b_ic_j - b_jc_i), \rho(a_ib_j - a_jb_i)]$ in which $\rho \neq 0$, and substituting in the expressions for l_i, l_j, $l_i = 0 = l_j$ have the unique solution $(b_ic_j - b_jc_i, c_ia_j - c_ja_i, a_ib_j - a_jb_i)$. If equations being considered have any solution, it must be unique and this must be it. This solution, then, substituted into the original system, gives the condition for the existence of a solution (see 78). It must hold for all i, j, k. In the language of linear algebra the equations (73) have an infinity of solutions, a unique solution, or no solution according as the rank of the matrix of coefficients (see 79) is one, two, or three.

It should be noted that if the nonhomogeneous equations (see 80) had been considered, there would have been more possibilities. For instance, suppose that $a_ib_j - a_jb_i = 0$, $b_ic_j - b_jc_i \neq 0$, for given values of i, j. Then a system of equations (see 81) is reached that has no solution, and hence the nonhomogeneous equations have no solution. In this case, the geometrical explanation is that the lines $M_i = 0$, $M_j = 0$ are parallel, but not identical. To obtain an intersection, it is necessary to pass from the affine plane to the projective plane.

Linear and multilinear algebra

LINEAR ALGEBRA

Historical and conceptual introduction. Although the term linear algebra is comparatively recent, the mathematical ideas that it embraces are found in the works of many mathematicians over the past two or three hundred years. The main development of the subject, however, has taken place since 1850. Linear algebra originated in the study of systems of linear equations in several unknowns and in the attempt to find general methods for their solution. This attempt led quite early to the notion of a determinant, in 1693 by the German mathematician Gottfried Wilhelm Leibniz. In 1750 the Swiss physicist Gabriel Cramer gave the rule bearing his name, for expressing the solution of n linear equations in n unknowns in terms of determinants. The French mathematician Joseph-Louis Lagrange noted in 1773 the connection between a third-order determinant and the volume of a tetrahedron. Lagrange and Germany's greatest mathematician, Carl Friedrich Gauss, both observed that if the quadratic form $F = ax^2 + 2bxy + cy^2$ is subjected to a linear transformation (see Box, equations 82), expressed in two linear equations, to obtain the new form $f = a'u^2 + 2b'uv + c'v^2$ in the variables u and v, then the effect (see 83) of the transformation is to multiply the discriminant of the form (a function expressed in terms of the coefficients) by a factor depending on the transformation and not the forming.

Concept of a determinant

The concept of a vector space grew out of the work of Hamilton on the algebra of vectors. An example of a vector space is the set, $\mathfrak{U}_3$, of all ordered triples $[x, y, z]$ in which x, y, z are real numbers. These triples are called vectors with components x, y, z and are added according

(82) $$\begin{cases} x = \alpha u + \beta v \\ y = \gamma u + \delta v \end{cases}$$

(83) $$a'c' - b'^2 = (\alpha\delta - \beta\gamma)^2(ac - b^2)$$

(84) $$[x_1, y_1, z_1] + [x_2, y_2, z_2] = [x_1 + x_2, y_1 + y_2, z_1 + z_2]$$

(85) $$cX = [cx, cy, cz]$$

to the rule (see 84) that respective components of two vectors are added to yield a sum vector. Moreover, if $\mathbf{X} = [x, y, z]$ is a vector and c is a real number, then the product $c\mathbf{X}$, called a scalar multiple of $\mathbf{X}$, is defined (see 85) to be the vector obtained by multiplying each component of $\mathbf{X}$ by c. In this context a real number is called a scalar, as opposed to a triple $[x, y, z]$ that is a vector. The vector $[0, 0, 0]$ is called the null vector or zero vector and is denoted by $\mathbf{0}$.

The vectors of $\mathfrak{U}_3$ have a geometric interpretation. The vector $\mathbf{X} = [x, y, z]$ is represented, relative to a Cartesian coordinate system with origin at O, by the directed line segment $\mathbf{OP}$ with initial point O and terminal point at the point P the coordinates of which are (x, y, z). It is further stipulated that two directed line segments that have the same length and the same direction represent the same vector. Thus, vectors are invariant under translation and hence the vector represented by $\mathbf{AB}$ with initial point $A(x_1, y_1, z_1)$ and terminal point $B(x_2, y_2, z_2)$ is (see Figure 3) the same (see 86) as the vector with initial point at the origin and with terminus at the point with coordinates $(x_2 - x_1, y_2 - y_1, z_2 - z_1)$. If $\mathbf{X}_1$ and $\mathbf{X}_2$ are vectors with geometric representations $\mathbf{OP}$ and $\mathbf{OQ}$, respectively, then $\mathbf{X}_1 + \mathbf{X}_2$ has the geometric representation $\mathbf{OR}$ in which R is the point determined by $\mathbf{PR} = \mathbf{OQ}$. If O, P, and Q are not collinear, then $\mathbf{OR}$ is the diagonal of the parallelogram of which $\mathbf{OP}$ and $\mathbf{OQ}$ are adjacent edges (Figure 4). If c is any scalar, the geometric representation of $c\mathbf{X}$ is a directed segment the length of which is $|c|$ times the length of the segment representing $\mathbf{X}$, and the direction of which is

Geometric interpretation of vectors

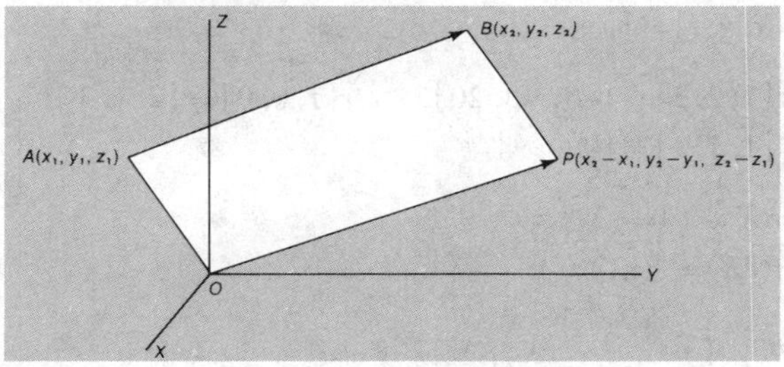

Figure 3: Geometric interpretation of the fact that vectors are invariant under translation. Specifically, the vector represented by the line segment **AB** is the same as the vector represented by **OP**. The coordinates of each point are shown in parentheses (see text).

the same or opposite to that of $\mathbf{X}$ according as $c > 0$ or $c < 0$. If $c = 0$ then $0\mathbf{X} = \mathbf{0}$.

The set $\mathfrak{U}_2$ of all ordered pairs $[x, y]$ of real numbers, with similar definitions of addition and multiplication by scalars, is another example of a vector space. The vectors of $\mathfrak{U}_2$ can be represented geometrically by directed line segments in a Cartesian plane.

A function of mapping τ from $\mathfrak{U}_3$ to $\mathfrak{U}_3$ can be defined by a system of three linear equations (for example, see 87) that give the components u, v, w of the vector $\tau[x, y, z]$ onto which $[x, y, z]$ is mapped by τ (see 88). The vector $[u, v, w]$ is called the image of $[x, y, z]$ under τ and images of particular vectors such as [1, 2, 3] and [1, 0, 0] can be computed from the given equations (see 89). Because the equations defining the mapping are linear, τ has the properties (see 90) that the image of the sum of two vectors is the sum of their images, and the image of a scalar multiple of a vector is the same scalar multiple of its image. A mapping with these properties is called a linear transfor-

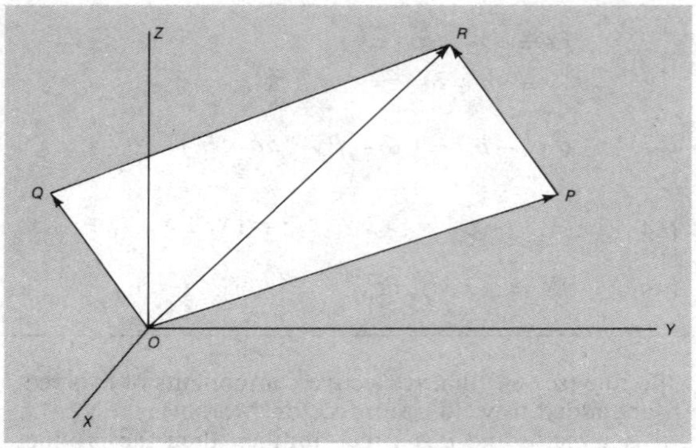

Figure 4: Geometric interpretation of the sum of two vectors. The vectors with representations **OP** and **OQ** add to yield the vector with representation **OR**, which is the diagonal of a parallelogram (see text).

mation, in this case from $\mathfrak{U}_3$ to $\mathfrak{U}_3$. Using Cayley's definition of matrix products, equations (87) defining the mapping τ can be written (see 91) $\mathbf{Y} = A\mathbf{X}$ in which A is the matrix (92) of coefficients of the equations, and **X** and **Y** are the vectors $[x, y, z]$ and $[u, v, w]$ written, for technical reasons, as columns. Thus the matrix A represents the linear transformation τ and operates on the vector **X** to give the vector **Y**. The linearity properties (90) of τ thus become two rules of matrix algebra (see 93). In the same way, a system (see 94) of two equations in three variables determines a linear transformation σ from $\mathfrak{U}_3$ into $\mathfrak{U}_2$ defined (see 95) by specifying the image in $\mathfrak{U}_2$ of each vector in $\mathfrak{U}_3$ under the mapping σ. The equations defining σ can also be written in matrix form (see 96). In general, both matrices and systems of linear equations may be considered as representations of linear transformations.

(86) $$\overrightarrow{AB} = [x_2 - x_1, y_2 - y_1, z_2 - z_1] = \overrightarrow{OP}$$

(87) $$\begin{cases} 2x - 3y + z = u \\ x + y - 2z = v \\ 3x + y + 5z = w \end{cases}$$

(88) $$\tau[x, y, z] = [u, v, w]$$

(89) $$\begin{cases} \tau[1, 2, 3] = [-1, -3, 20], \qquad \tau[1, 0, 0] = [2, 1, 3] \\ \tau[1, 1, 1] = [0, 0, 9] \end{cases}$$

(90) $$\begin{cases} \tau(X + Y) = \tau X + \tau Y \\ \tau(cX) = c(\tau X) \end{cases}$$

(91) $$\begin{bmatrix} u \\ v \\ w \end{bmatrix} = \begin{bmatrix} 2 & -3 & 1 \\ 1 & 1 & -2 \\ 3 & 1 & 5 \end{bmatrix} \begin{bmatrix} x \\ y \\ z \end{bmatrix}$$

(92) $$A = \begin{vmatrix} 2 & -3 & 1 \\ 1 & 1 & -2 \\ 3 & 1 & 5 \end{vmatrix}$$

(93) $$A(X_1 + X_2) = AX_1 + AX_2, \qquad A(cX) = c(AX)$$

(94) $$\begin{cases} 5x - y + 2z = u \\ x + 3y - 4z = v \end{cases}$$

(95) $$\sigma[x, y, z] = [u, v]$$

(96) $$\begin{bmatrix} u \\ v \end{bmatrix} = \begin{bmatrix} 5 & -1 & 2 \\ 1 & 3 & -4 \end{bmatrix} \begin{bmatrix} x \\ y \\ z \end{bmatrix}$$

A subset $\mathfrak{U}$ of $\mathfrak{U}_3$ is called a subspace of $\mathfrak{U}_3$ if it is closed under addition of vectors and multiplication by scalars; that is, if, whenever **X** and **Y** belong to $\mathfrak{S}$, then also $\mathbf{X} + \mathbf{Y}$ and $c\mathbf{X}$ also belong to $\mathfrak{S}$, for all scalars c. The set of all scalar multiples of a fixed vector **X** in $\mathfrak{U}_3$ is a subspace of $\mathfrak{U}_3$ that consists, if $\mathbf{X} \neq \mathbf{0}$, of all vectors with geometric representations **OP** lying in a fixed line through the origin. Similarly, if **X**, **Y** are two vectors the geometric representations of which do not lie in one line (or are not parallel), then the set of all vectors of the form $c_1\mathbf{X} + c_2\mathbf{Y}$ is a subspace consisting of all vectors with geometric representations in the plane through the origin determined by the two vectors **X** and **Y**. Apart from the space $\mathfrak{U}_3$ itself (dimension 3), and the zero subspace consisting of the zero vector only (dimension 0), the subspaces of $\mathfrak{U}_3$ are essentially the straight lines (dimension 1) and the planes (dimension 2) that pass through the origin. Linear transformations always map subspaces onto subspaces, but they may or may not preserve the dimensionality of all subspaces. Subspaces

Vector spaces. In general, a nonempty set $\mathfrak{U}$, the elements of which will be called vectors, is called a vector space, or a linear space, over a field $\mathfrak{F}$ if addition of vectors and multiplication of vectors by elements of $\mathfrak{F}$ are defined and satisfy 10 postulates (see 97).

(97) (1) The sum $V_1 + V_2$ of any two vectors V_1, V_2 is a uniquely defined vector in $\mathfrak{U}$. (2) Addition of vectors is commutative: $V_1 + V_2 = V_2 + V_1$. (3) Addition of vectors is associative: $(V_1 + V_2) + V_3 = V_1 + (V_2 + V_3)$. (4) There is a zero vector O such that $V + O = V$ for all V in $\mathfrak{U}$. (5) Every vector V has a unique negative $-V$ such that $V + (-V) = O$. (6) For any element c of $\mathfrak{F}$ and any vector V in $\mathfrak{U}$ the product cV is a uniquely defined vector in $\mathfrak{U}$. (7) $c(V_1 + V_2) = cV_1 + cV_2$. (8) $(c_1 + c_2)V = c_1V + c_2V$. (9) $c_1(c_2V) = (c_1c_2)V$. (10) $1V = V$.

(98) $$\frac{d^ny}{dx^n} + a_1\frac{d^{n-1}y}{dx^{n-1}} + \cdots + a_ny = 0$$

(99) $$\Sigma c_iV_i$$

Basic concepts. The elements of $\mathfrak{F}$ are called scalars and $\mathfrak{F}$ is called the field of scalars. The field of scalars may be any field (see below *Fields*), but in most applications is either the field $\mathfrak{R}$ of real numbers or the field $\mathfrak{C}$ of complex numbers. The postulates just referred to imply that $0\mathbf{V} = \mathbf{0}$, and $(-1)\mathbf{V} = -\mathbf{V}$. An essential property of a vector space is that if $\mathbf{V}_1, \mathbf{V}_2, \cdots, \mathbf{V}_r$ are vectors in $\mathfrak{U}$ and $c_1, c_2, \cdots, c_r$ are scalars, then the sum $c_1\mathbf{V}_1 + c_2\mathbf{V}_2 + \cdots + c_r\mathbf{V}_r$, called a linear combination of $\mathbf{V}_1, \mathbf{V}_2, \cdots, \mathbf{V}_r$, is a vector in $\mathfrak{U}$.

Examples of a vector space are the spaces $\mathfrak{U}_2$ and $\mathfrak{U}_3$ discussed in the introduction or, more generally, the vector space $\mathfrak{U}^n(\mathfrak{F})$ of all n-tuples $[x_1, x_2, \cdots, x_n]$ in which $x_1, x_2, \cdots, x_n$ belong to $\mathfrak{F}$, and addition and multiplication by scalars are defined as in $\mathfrak{U}_3$. Other examples are the set $\mathfrak{P}$ of all polynomials with coefficients in $\mathfrak{F}$, the set $\mathfrak{P}_n$ of all polynomials of degree $\leq n$ with coefficients in $\mathfrak{F}$. Similarly, the set of all continuous real-valued functions defined on the interval of real numbers between two fixed numbers a and b is a vector space over the field $\mathfrak{R}$ of real numbers. The set of all solutions of a linear differential equation (see 98) with real coefficients is also a vector space over $\mathfrak{R}$.

Subspaces. A subset $\mathfrak{S}$ of a vector space $\mathfrak{U}$ over $\mathfrak{F}$ is called a subspace of $\mathfrak{U}$ if $\mathfrak{S}$ itself is a vector space over $\mathfrak{F}$ under addition and scalar multiplication that it inherits from $\mathfrak{U}$; that is, if, whenever $\mathbf{V}_1$, $\mathbf{V}_2$ belong to $\mathfrak{S}$, $\mathbf{V}_1 + \mathbf{V}_2$ is in $\mathfrak{S}$ and $c\mathbf{V}_1$ is in $\mathfrak{S}$, for every scalar c. The space $\mathfrak{U}$, itself, and the zero space consisting of the zero vector only are included among the subspaces of $\mathfrak{U}$. If $\mathfrak{H}$ is any subset of $\mathfrak{U}$, the set $\mathfrak{S}$ of all linear combinations of vectors in $\mathfrak{H}$ is a subspace of $\mathfrak{U}$, called the subspace spanned by the set $\mathfrak{H}$. It is the smallest subspace of $\mathfrak{U}$ containing all vectors in $\mathfrak{H}$. The set $\mathfrak{H}$ may be finite or infinite, but a linear combination (see 99) must have only a finite number of nonzero terms. If the subspace spanned by the set $\mathfrak{H}$ is $\mathfrak{U}$ itself, then $\mathfrak{H}$ is called a spanning set or generating system of $\mathfrak{U}$. If $\mathfrak{U}$ is spanned by a finite set of vectors, $\mathfrak{U}$ is said to be finitely generated or finite-dimensional. Linear algebra is concerned primarily with finite-dimensional vector spaces. Although many of the theorems of linear algebra can be generalized to infinite-dimensional spaces, in order to do so it is usually necessary to introduce a topology on the space, and the results that are obtained are generally analytic in nature rather than purely algebraic (see ANALYSIS: *Functional analysis*).

Sums and intersections of subspaces

If $\{\mathfrak{S}_\alpha\}$ is any set of subspaces of $\mathfrak{U}$, then their intersection, consisting of all vectors of $\mathfrak{U}$ that belong to each of the subspaces $\mathfrak{S}_\alpha$, is a subspace of $\mathfrak{U}$. For example, the space spanned by the set $\mathfrak{H}$ is the intersection of all subspaces $\mathfrak{S}_\alpha$ that contain all vectors in $\mathfrak{H}$. The sum of the subspaces $\mathfrak{S}_\alpha$ is the space spanned by the set of all vectors $\mathbf{V}$ such that $\mathbf{V}$ belongs to at least one of the subspaces $\mathfrak{S}_\alpha$. The sum of a finite number of subspaces $\mathfrak{S}_1\mathfrak{S}_2, \cdots, \mathfrak{S}_r$ is the set of all vectors $\sum_{i=1}^{r} S_i$, in which S_i belongs to $\mathfrak{S}_i$.

Linear dependence. The vectors $\mathbf{V}_1, \mathbf{V}_2, \cdots, \mathbf{V}_r$ in a vector space $\mathfrak{U}$ over $\mathfrak{F}$ are linearly dependent, or constitute a linearly dependent set, if there exist scalars $c_1, c_2, \cdots, c_r$ in $\mathfrak{F}$, not all zero, such that $c_1\mathbf{V}_1 + c_2\mathbf{V}_2 + \cdots + c_r\mathbf{V}_r = O$. If no such scalars exist, the vectors are linearly independent. For example, the vectors $\mathbf{X} = [2, 5, -1]$, $\mathbf{Y} = [1, 1, 4]$, $\mathbf{Z} = [1, 3, -2]$ in $\mathfrak{U}_3(\mathfrak{R})$ are linearly dependent, because $2\mathbf{X} - 1\mathbf{Y} - 3\mathbf{Z} = O$; but the vectors $\mathbf{V} = [2, 5]$, $\mathbf{W} = [4, 1]$ in $\mathfrak{U}_2(\mathfrak{R})$ are linearly independent because $c_1\mathbf{V} + c_2\mathbf{W} = O$ implies $2c_1 + 4c_2 = 0$, $5c_1 + c_2 = 0$, and the only solution of these two equations is $c_1 = c_2 = 0$. An infinite set of vectors is linearly dependent if it contains a finite subset that is linearly dependent. Linear dependence of two vectors means that one of them is a scalar multiple of the other. Linear dependence of three vectors in $\mathfrak{U}_3(\mathfrak{R})$ means that the three vectors have geometric representations that lie in one plane passing through the origin. In general, a set of vectors in $\mathfrak{U}$ is linearly dependent if, and only if, one of the vectors is in the subspace of $\mathfrak{U}$ spanned by the other vectors of the set.

A basis of the vector space $\mathfrak{U}$ comprises a linearly independent set of vectors that spans $\mathfrak{U}$. Every vector space has a basis. If $\mathfrak{U}$ has a basis containing a finite number of vectors, then every basis of $\mathfrak{U}$ contains the same number of vectors. The number of vectors in a basis of $\mathfrak{U}$ is called the dimension of $\mathfrak{U}$. A finitely generated vector space has finite dimension, because every set of vectors that spans $\mathfrak{U}$ has a maximal linearly independent subset that forms a basis of $\mathfrak{U}$.

The space $\mathfrak{U}_n(\mathfrak{F})$ is n-dimensional, because it is spanned by the n linearly independent vectors $\mathbf{E}_1 = [1, 0, \cdots, 0]$, $\mathbf{E}_2 = [0, 1, 0, \cdots, 0]$, $\mathbf{E}_n = [0, 0, \cdots, 1]$, which therefore form a basis of $\mathfrak{U}_n(\mathfrak{F})$. If $\mathfrak{U}$ has dimension n, then any set of n linearly independent vectors is a basis of $\mathfrak{U}$, and any set of r linearly independent vectors, r less than n, is a subset of a basis.

Basis of a vector space

If $\mathbf{F}_1, \mathbf{F}_2, \cdots, \mathbf{F}_n$, or, more briefly, $(\mathbf{F})$, is a basis of $\mathfrak{U}$, then every vector $\mathbf{V}$ in $\mathfrak{U}$ has a unique representation, namely, $\mathbf{V} = x_1\mathbf{F}_1 + x_2\mathbf{F}_2 + \cdots + x_n\mathbf{F}_n$, as a linear combination of the basis vectors. The vector $\mathbf{X} = [x_1, x_2, \cdots, x_n]$ in $\mathfrak{U}_n(\mathfrak{F})$ is called the coordinate vector of $\mathbf{V}$ relative to the F-basis, and $x_1, x_2, \cdots, x_n$ are called the coordinates of $\mathbf{V}$ relative to this basis. If the coordinate vector $\mathbf{X}$ is denoted by $a(\mathbf{V})$, the mapping a maps the space $\mathfrak{U}$ onto the space $\mathfrak{U}_n(\mathfrak{F})$. This is one-to-one and satisfies the rules that the image of the sum of vectors is the sum of the images and the image of a scalar multiple of a vector is the same scalar multiple of its image. Such a mapping is called an isomorphism and the two spaces $\mathfrak{U}$ and $\mathfrak{U}_n(\mathfrak{F})$ are isomorphic. Every n-dimensional vector space over $\mathfrak{F}$ is isomorphic to $\mathfrak{U}_n(\mathfrak{F})$, and every basis of $\mathfrak{U}$ provides such an isomorphism.

Linear transformations. If $\mathfrak{U}$ and $\mathfrak{W}$ are vector spaces over the same field $\mathfrak{F}$, a mapping σ that associates a unique vector $\sigma\mathbf{V}$ in $\mathfrak{W}$ with each vector $\mathbf{V}$ of $\mathfrak{U}$ is a linear transformation if the image of the sum of any two vectors is the sum of their images and the image of a scalar multiple of any vector is the same scalar multiple of its image (see 100). A linear operator in $\mathfrak{U}$ is a linear transformation of $\mathfrak{U}$ into itself.

Linear operators

(100) $\sigma(V_1 + V_2) = \sigma V_1 + \sigma V_2$ and $\sigma(cV) = c(\sigma V)$

(101) $(\tau f)(x) = \int_0^x f(t)\, dt$

(102) $\tau(O) = O$ and $\tau(c_1V_1 + c_2V_2 + \cdots + c_nV_n) = c_1(\tau V_1) + c_2(\tau V_2) + \cdots + c_n(\tau V_n)$

(103) $\tau(c_1E_1 + c_2E_2 + \cdots + c_nE_n) = c_1F_1 + c_2F_2 + \cdots + c_nF_n$

If A is any $m \times n$ matrix over $\mathfrak{F}$, then the mapping σ from $\mathfrak{U}_n(\mathfrak{F})$ to $\mathfrak{U}_m(\mathfrak{F})$, defined by $\sigma\mathbf{X} = A\mathbf{X}$, is a linear transformation. If $\mathfrak{B}$ is the vector space, over the field $\mathfrak{R}$ of real numbers, of all polynomials in x with real coefficients, and if $\delta[p(x)]$ is the derivative of $p(x)$, then δ is a linear operator in $\mathfrak{B}$. Similarly, the integral (see 101) defines a linear operator τ in the space of continuous functions f from $\mathfrak{R}$ into $\mathfrak{R}$. If τ is any linear transformation that maps a vector space $\mathfrak{U}$ into a vector space $\mathfrak{W}$, then τ maps the zero vector of $\mathfrak{U}$ on the zero vector of $\mathfrak{W}$. Moreover, τ preserves linear combinations (see 102) and maps subspaces of $\mathfrak{U}$ onto subspaces of $\mathfrak{W}$. If $\mathfrak{U}$ is finite-dimensional with basis $(\mathbf{E})$, and if $\mathbf{F}_1, \mathbf{F}_2, \cdots, \mathbf{F}_n$ are arbitrary vectors of $\mathfrak{W}$, there exists a unique linear transformation τ from $\mathfrak{U}$ into $\mathfrak{W}$ such that $\tau\mathbf{E}_i = \mathbf{F}_i$, and hence (see 103) τ is completely determined by its effect on a basis of $\mathfrak{U}$.

The set $\mathfrak{L}(\mathfrak{U}, \mathfrak{W})$ of all linear transformations from $\mathfrak{U}$ to $\mathfrak{W}$ can be given the structure of a vector space. If σ, τ are such linear transformations, then sums and scalar multiples are defined by forming sums and scalar multiples of images (see 104). The zero element of $\mathfrak{L}(\mathfrak{U}, \mathfrak{W})$ is the zero mapping O, defined by $O\mathbf{V} = \mathbf{0}$ for all $\mathbf{V}$, and $(-\sigma)\mathbf{V}$ is defined to be $-(\sigma\mathbf{V})$. If $\mathfrak{U}$ and $\mathfrak{W}$ are finite-dimensional, and σ is a linear transformation that maps $\mathfrak{U}$ into $\mathfrak{W}$, then σ is uniquely determined by equations (105) or by the matrix $A_\sigma^{(E, F)}$ (see 106), called the matrix of σ relative to the $\mathbf{E}$- and $\mathbf{F}$-bases. If a vector $\mathbf{V}$ in $\mathfrak{U}$ has a coordinate vector $\mathbf{X}$ relative to the $\mathbf{E}$-basis, and if $\sigma\mathbf{V}$ has a coordinate vector $\mathbf{Y}$ relative to the $\mathbf{F}$-basis, then $\mathbf{Y} = A_\sigma^{(E, F)}\mathbf{X}$. Because there is an isomorphism of the vector space $\mathfrak{L}(\mathfrak{U}, \mathfrak{W})$ onto the vector space of all $m \times n$ matrices over $\mathfrak{F}$ (see 107), the dimension of $\mathfrak{L}(\mathfrak{U}, \mathfrak{W})$ is mn.

If $\mathfrak{U}$, $\mathfrak{W}$, and $\mathfrak{Z}$ are vector spaces over $\mathfrak{F}$, and if σ and τ are linear transformations that map $\mathfrak{U}$ into $\mathfrak{W}$ and $\mathfrak{W}$ into $\mathfrak{Z}$, respectively, then the composite mapping, or product, $\tau\sigma$ that maps $\mathfrak{U}$ into $\mathfrak{Z}$ is defined by $(\tau\sigma)\mathbf{V} = r(\sigma\mathbf{V})$ and is a linear transformation. Hence, by taking $\mathfrak{Z} = \mathfrak{W} = \mathfrak{U}$, a multiplication is defined (see 108) in the vector space $\mathfrak{L}(\mathfrak{U}, \mathfrak{U})$ that is associative and distributive with respect to addition, and $\mathfrak{L}(\mathfrak{U}, \mathfrak{U})$ becomes a linear associative algebra over $\mathfrak{F}$. In the case of a linear operator σ that maps $\mathfrak{U}$ into $\mathfrak{U}$, the corresponding matrix $A_\sigma^{(E, E)}$ is denoted by $A_\sigma^{(E)}$ and is called the matrix of σ relative to the $\mathbf{E}$-basis of $\mathfrak{U}$. The vector space isomorphism a, which is defined by $a(\sigma) = A_\sigma^{(E)}$, is also an algebra isomorphism of the algebra of linear operators in $\mathfrak{U}$ onto the algebra of $n \times n$ matrices over $\mathfrak{F}$.

The image of a linear transformation

If τ is a linear transformation of $\mathfrak{U}$ into $\mathfrak{W}$, the image of τ, written im τ, is the subspace of $\mathfrak{W}$ consisting of all vectors $\tau\mathbf{V}$ where $\mathbf{V}$ belongs to $\mathfrak{U}$. The rank of τ is the dimension of im τ. The subspace $\mathfrak{N}$ of $\mathfrak{U}$, consisting of all vectors $\mathbf{V}$ such that $\tau\mathbf{V} = \mathbf{0}$, is called the nullspace or kernel of τ. The dimension of $\mathfrak{N}$, written dim $\mathfrak{N}$, is called the nullity

(104) $(\sigma+\tau)V=\sigma V+\tau V$ and $(c\sigma)V=c(\sigma V)$

(105) For basis $E_1, E_2, \cdots, E_n$ of $\mathfrak{V}$ and basis $F_1, F_2, \cdots, F_m$ of $\mathfrak{W}$:

$$\sigma E_1=a_{11}F_1+a_{21}F_2+\cdots+a_{m1}F_m$$
$$\cdots\cdots$$
$$\sigma E_n=a_{1n}F_1+a_{2n}F_2+\cdots+a_{mn}F_m$$

(106) $$A_\sigma^{(E,F)}=\begin{bmatrix} a_{11} & a_{12} & \cdots & a_{1n} \\ a_{21} & a_{22} & \cdots & a_{2n} \\ \cdots & \cdots & \cdots & \cdots \\ a_{m1} & a_{m2} & \cdots & a_{mn} \end{bmatrix}$$

(107) Because $A_{\sigma+\tau}^{(E,F)}=A_\sigma^{(E,F)}+A_\tau^{(E,F)}$ and $A_{c\sigma}^{(E,F)}=cA_\sigma^{(E,F)}$ the mapping $\alpha:\mathfrak{L}(\mathfrak{U},\mathfrak{W})\to[\mathfrak{F}]_{m,n}$ defined by $\alpha(\sigma)=A_\sigma^{(E,F)}$ is an isomorphism.

(108) Also, if (E), (F) and (G) are bases for the three spaces, then $A_{\sigma\tau}^{(E,G)}=A_\sigma^{(E,F)}A_\tau^{(F,G)}$. If σ and τ are both linear operators in $\mathfrak{U}$ then $\tau\sigma$ and $\sigma\tau$ are also linear operators in $\mathfrak{U}$.

(109) The isomorphism $\alpha:\mathfrak{L}(\mathfrak{U},\mathfrak{W})\to[\mathfrak{F}]_{m,n}$ maps im τ onto the column space of $A_\tau^{(E,F)}$ and hence rank $\tau=$ rank $A_\tau^{(E,F)}$. Also α maps the nullspace of τ onto the nullspace of $A_\tau^{(E,F)}$.

(110) $A_\tau^{(F)}=P^{-1}A_\tau^{(E)}P$

of τ. If $\mathfrak{U}$ is finite-dimensional, then for every τ in $\mathfrak{L}(\mathfrak{U}, \mathfrak{W})$, a simple relationship holds between rank, nullity, and dimension, namely: rank $\tau+$ nullity $\tau=$ dim $\mathfrak{U}$. This relationship states, in effect, (see 109) that the solution space of the system of equations $A\mathbf{X}=\mathbf{0}$ has dimension $n-r$, in which n is the number of unknowns and $r=$ rank A. A linear transformation is one-to-one (that is, $\tau\mathbf{V}_1=\tau\mathbf{V}_2$ implies $\mathbf{V}_1=\mathbf{V}_2$) if, and only if, its nullspace is $\mathbf{0}$. If $\mathfrak{U}$ is finite-dimensional and τ belongs to $\mathfrak{L}(\mathfrak{U}, \mathfrak{U})$ then im $\tau=\mathfrak{U}$ only if the nullspace of τ is O. In this case, τ is called a nonsingular or invertible operator, and there exists an inverse mapping τ^{-1}, also a linear operator, such that $\tau^{-1}\tau=\tau\tau^{-1}=I$, in which I is the identity mapping on $\mathfrak{U}$. An operator τ is nonsingular, if and only if the matrix $A_\tau^{(E)}$ is nonsingular; then the matrix of the inverse of τ is the inverse of the matrix of τ relative to the **E**-basis.

If **(E)** and **(F)** are two different bases of $\mathfrak{U}$, and if **X** and **Y** are the coordinate vectors of vector **V** relative to the **E**- and **F**-bases, respectively, then $\mathbf{X}=P\mathbf{Y}$ in which P is a nonsingular $n\times n$ matrix, depending only on the two bases, and is called the transition matrix from the **E**- to the **F**-basis. If τ is a linear operator in $\mathfrak{U}$, then the matrices of τ relative to the two bases are related by equation (110) in which P is the transition matrix from the **E**- to the **F**-basis. $A_\tau^{(F)}$ and $A_\tau^{(E)}$ have the same determinant. Thus det $A_\tau^{(E)}$ is independent of the basis (E) and is called the determinant of the linear operator τ and written det τ. If τ is a linear operator in $\mathfrak{U}_2(\mathfrak{R})$, then the area of the parallelogram with adjacent edges $\tau\mathbf{V}_1$ and $\tau\mathbf{V}_2$ is equal to det τ times the area of the parallelogram with edges $\mathbf{V}_1$ and $\mathbf{V}_2$. Similarly in $\mathfrak{U}_3(\mathfrak{R})$, the parallelepiped with edges $\mathbf{V}_1$, $\mathbf{V}_2$, $\mathbf{V}_3$ is mapped by τ onto the parallelepiped with edges $\tau\mathbf{V}_1$, $\tau\mathbf{V}_2$, $\tau\mathbf{V}_3$ whose volume is det τ times that of the original parallelepiped. If det $\tau=0$, τ is singular and im τ is a proper subspace of $\mathfrak{U}$.

Linear functionals. If $\mathfrak{U}$ is a vector space over $\mathfrak{F}$, then a linear functional on $\mathfrak{U}$ is a mapping τ from $\mathfrak{U}$ into $\mathfrak{F}$ such that the linearity properties (see 111) are satisfied. If $\mathfrak{F}$ itself is considered as a vector space over $\mathfrak{F}$, with field addition as vector addition, and field multiplication as scalar multiplication, then a linear functional on $\mathfrak{U}$ is simply a linear transformation from $\mathfrak{U}$ into $\mathfrak{F}$. If $\mathfrak{U}$ has dimension n and a basis **(E)**, examples (see 112) of linear functionals are easily constructed. In particular, the mapping of each vector **V** onto its ith coordinate, relative to the **E**-basis, is a linear functional. Other examples are the mapping σ that carries $\mathfrak{B}$ into $\mathfrak{F}$ defined by $\sigma f(x)=f(a)$ for a fixed scalar a, in which $\mathfrak{B}$ is the space of all polynomials in x with coefficients in $\mathfrak{F}$, and the mapping φ defined on the space of all continuous real-valued functions on the closed interval of real numbers between a and b in which φ is the integral (see 113) of f over that interval. The set of all linear functionals on $\mathfrak{U}$ can be given the algebraic structure of a vector space by identifying it with $\mathfrak{L}(\mathfrak{U}, \mathfrak{F})$ in which $\mathfrak{F}$ is viewed as a one-dimensional vector space over $\mathfrak{F}$. The vector space $\mathfrak{L}(\mathfrak{U}, \mathfrak{F})$ of linear functionals on $\mathfrak{U}$ is called the dual space of $\mathfrak{U}$ and is denoted by $\mathfrak{U}^*$. Since dim $\mathfrak{F}=1$, if dim $\mathfrak{U}=n$, then $\mathfrak{U}^*$ also has dimension n. If **(E)** is a basis of $\mathfrak{U}$, since $\mathbf{F}_1=1$ is a basis of $\mathfrak{F}$, there is a unique linear functional τ in $\mathfrak{U}^*$ such that, for each i, $\tau\mathbf{E}_i=a_i$ in which the $\{a_i\}$ are n arbitrary scalars. The matrix (see 114) of τ relative to the **E**- and **F**-bases is the vector with components a_i. Thus every linear functional on a finite-dimensional space is defined by a fixed linear homogeneous function of the coordinates relative to the **E**-basis. Corresponding to an **E**-basis of $\mathfrak{U}$, there is a dual τ-basis of $\mathfrak{U}^*$, defined by $\tau_i\mathbf{E}_i=1$ and $\tau_i\mathbf{E}_j=0$ if $j\neq i$. Thus, τ_i is the functional that maps each vector **V** of $\mathfrak{U}$ on its ith coordinate relative to the **E**-basis. The matrix of τ_i, relative to the **E**-basis, is the vector with 1 in the ith place and 0 elsewhere, and every vector **V** of $\mathfrak{U}$ expressed in the **E**-basis has the ith coordinate $\tau_i(\mathbf{V})$ (see 115). The dual space $(\mathfrak{U}^*)^*$ of $\mathfrak{U}^{**}$ is denoted by $\mathfrak{U}^{**}$ and is called the double dual of $\mathfrak{U}$. There is a natural isomorphism a from $\mathfrak{U}$ onto $\mathfrak{U}^{**}$ defined by $a\mathbf{V}=\sigma_\mathbf{V}$ in which $\sigma_\mathbf{V}$ is the linear functional on $\mathfrak{U}^*$, defined by $\sigma_\mathbf{V}\tau=\tau\mathbf{V}$ for all τ in $\mathfrak{U}^*$. The isomorphism a maps the **E**-basis of $\mathfrak{U}$ onto its double dual basis of $\mathfrak{U}^{**}$ (see 116).

Examples of linear functionals

If σ is a linear transformation of $\mathfrak{U}$ into $\mathfrak{W}$, and τ is a linear functional on $\mathfrak{W}$, then the composite $\tau\sigma$ is a linear functional on $\mathfrak{U}$. Thus, σ induces a linear transformation of σ^T of $\mathfrak{W}^*$ into $\mathfrak{U}^*$, defined by $\sigma^T\tau=\tau\sigma$, and called the

(111) $\tau(V_1+V_2)=\tau V_1+\tau V_2$ and $\tau(cV)=c(\tau V)$

(112) $\tau(x_1E_1+x_2E_2+\cdots+x_nE_n)=a_1x_1+a_2x_2+\cdots+a_nx_n$ in which $a_1, a_2, \cdots a_n$ are any fixed scalars

(113) $\phi f=\int_a^b f(x)\,dx$

(114) $A_\tau^{(E,F)}=[a_1, a_2, \cdots, a_n]$

(115) $V=\tau_1(V)E_1+\tau_2(V)E_2+\cdots+\tau_n(V)E_n$

(116) If $\tau_1, \cdots, \tau_n$ is the basis of $\mathfrak{U}^*$ dual to the basis $E_1, \cdots, E_n$ of $\mathfrak{U}$ then the basis of $\mathfrak{U}^{**}$ dual to $\tau_1, \cdots, \tau_n$ is $\alpha E_1, \cdots, \alpha E_n$

(117) $(X, Y)=x_1y_1+x_2y_2+x_3y_3$

(118) $\|X\|=\sqrt{(X, X)}$ $\cos\theta=\dfrac{(X, Y)}{\|X\|\,\|Y\|}$

(119) If $X=[x_1, \cdots, x_n]$ and $Y=[y_1, \cdots, y_n]$, $(X, Y)=x_1y_1+x_2y_2+\cdots+x_ny_n$

(120)
$$\phi(V_1+V_2, W)=\phi(V_1, W)+\phi(V_2, W)$$
$$\phi(V, W_1+W_2)=\phi(V, W_1)+\phi(V, W_2)$$
$$\phi(cV, W)=\phi(V, cW)=c\phi(V, W)$$

transpose of σ. If (**E**) and (**F**) are bases of $\mathfrak{U}$ and $\mathfrak{W}$, and (α) and (β) are the dual bases of $^*\mathfrak{U}$ and $\mathfrak{W}^*$, then the matrix of σ^T, relative to the bases (β) and (α), is the transpose of the matrix $A_\sigma^{(E,F)}$.

Inner products. If **X** and **Y** are any two vectors in $\mathfrak{U}_3(\mathfrak{R})$, then their classical inner product or dot product (see 117) is a scalar-valued function of the pair of vectors **X**, **Y**. Its importance lies in the fact that the length of the vector **X**, denoted by $\|\mathbf{X}\|$, and the angle θ between the directions of **X** and **Y**, can be defined in terms of inner products (see 118). Similarly, if **X** and **Y** are two vectors of $\mathfrak{U}_n(\mathfrak{R})$, their dot product or standard inner product is defined as a sum (see 119) of products of respective components. Because $(\mathbf{X}, \mathbf{X}) > 0$ if $\mathbf{X} \neq \mathbf{0}$, and because the Cauchy-Schwarz inequality ensures that $|(\mathbf{X}, \mathbf{Y})| \leq \sqrt{(\mathbf{X},\mathbf{X})}\sqrt{(\mathbf{Y},\mathbf{Y})}$, the length of a vector and the angle beween vectors can be defined by the same formulas as those used in $\mathfrak{U}_3$. In general, an inner product is used to introduce metric concepts in an abstract vector space over either the real or the complex field.

Inner products and metric concepts

An important property of the dot product in $\mathfrak{U}_n(\mathfrak{R})$ is that the mappings defined by $\sigma_X(\mathbf{Y}) = (\mathbf{X}, \mathbf{Y})$ for a fixed **X**, and $\sigma_Y(\mathbf{X}) = (\mathbf{X}, \mathbf{Y})$ for a fixed **Y**, are both linear functionals on $\mathfrak{U}_n(\mathfrak{R})$. The dot product is therefore an example of a bilinear functional. In general, if $\mathfrak{U} \times \mathfrak{U}$ denotes the set of all ordered pairs (**V**, **W**) in which **V**, **W** are vectors in a vector space $\mathfrak{U}$ over $\mathfrak{F}$, a bilinear functional on $\mathfrak{U}$ is a mapping φ from $\mathfrak{U} \times \mathfrak{U}$ into $\mathfrak{F}$ having linearity properties (see 120) with respect to both members of the pair. A bilinear functional φ is symmetric if $\varphi(\mathbf{V}, \mathbf{W}) = \varphi(\mathbf{W}, \mathbf{V})$, and is positive if $\varphi(\mathbf{V}, \mathbf{V})$ is a real number for every vector **V** and $\varphi(\mathbf{V}, \mathbf{V}) > 0$ whenever $\mathbf{V} \neq \mathbf{0}$.

If $\mathfrak{U}$ is any vector space over $\mathfrak{R}$, an inner product in $\mathfrak{U}$ is a positive symmetric bilinear functional on $\mathfrak{U}$. The dot product in $\mathfrak{U}_n(\mathfrak{R})$ is clearly an inner product under this definition. More generally, if (**E**) is any basis of $\mathfrak{U}$, an inner product in $\mathfrak{U}$ is obtained by defining (**V**, **W**) to be the dot product of the coordinate vectors of **V** and **W**, relative to the **E**-basis. A vector space over $\mathfrak{R}$ in which a fixed inner product is designated is called a real inner product space. A finite-dimensional real inner product space is called a Euclidean vector space. Inner products that lead to a suitable metric can also be defined in a vector space over the complex field $\mathfrak{C}$, but the linearity and symmetry conditions have to be modified. If $\mathfrak{U}$ is a vector space over $\mathfrak{C}$, an inner product on $\mathfrak{U}$ is a function that associates with each ordered pair of vectors **V**, **W** in $\mathfrak{U}$ a scalar (**V**, **W**) such that (see 121) (**V**, **W**) is linear in the first member of the pair, (**V**, **W**) is equal to the complex conjugate of (**W**, **V**), and (**V**, **V**) is real and is positive if $\mathbf{V} \neq \mathbf{0}$.

These postulates can be used to define an inner product on either a real or complex vector space. In the complex case σ_W, defined by $\sigma_W\mathbf{V} = (\mathbf{V}, \mathbf{W})$, is a linear functional on $\mathfrak{U}$ into $\mathfrak{C}$ and, in fact, every linear functional of $\mathfrak{U}$ has this form for some vector **W**. The behaviour of σ_V, defined by $\sigma_V\mathbf{W} = (\mathbf{V}, \mathbf{W})$, is, however, not linear because the functional value of σ_V at $c\mathbf{W}$ is $\bar{c}$ times the value at **W**. An example of an inner product (**X**, **Y**) in the complex case is the standard inner product of $\mathfrak{U}_n\mathfrak{C}$, defined by the sum (see 122) of products of the type $x_i\bar{y}_i$. In general, if $\mathfrak{F}$ is either $\mathfrak{R}$ or $\mathfrak{C}$, and α is the isomorphism that maps each vector **V** on its coordinate vector $\alpha\mathbf{V}$ in $\mathfrak{U}_n\mathfrak{F}$, then $(\mathbf{V}, \mathbf{W})' = (\alpha\mathbf{V}, \alpha\mathbf{W})$, in which (,) denotes the standard inner product in $\mathfrak{U}_n(\mathfrak{F})$, defines an inner product $(\mathbf{V}, \mathbf{W})'$ in $\mathfrak{U}$.

If $\mathfrak{F}$ denotes either the real field $\mathfrak{R}$ or the complex field $\mathfrak{C}$, and $\mathfrak{U}$ is a vector space over $\mathfrak{F}$ with basis (**E**), then an inner product (**V**, **W**) in $\mathfrak{U}$ is completely determined by the n^2 scalars (E_i, E_j). If these scalars are denoted by a_{ij}, then the matrix $A = [a_{ij}]$ has the property $A^* = A$, in which A^* is the transpose of the complex conjugate matrix $\bar{A} = [\bar{a}_{ij}]$. The matrix A^* is called the conjugate of A, and a matrix A for which $A^* = A$ is called a self-conjugate or Hermitian matrix, named for the French mathematician Charles Hermite. If A has real elements, then $A^* = A^T$, and hence a real Hermitian matrix is symmetric in the sense that $A^T = A$. An expression formed from a sum of terms of the type $a_{ij}x_i\bar{y}_j$ in which $a_{ij} = \bar{a}_{ji}$ naturally occurs when taking the inner product of two vectors **V** and **W** with coordinate vectors **X** and **Y** (see 123). Such an expression (see 124) is called a Hermitian bilinear form. It can be written in matrix notation as $\mathbf{X}A\mathbf{Y}^*$, in which **X** and **Y** are the coordinate vectors of **V** and **W**, and $\mathbf{Y}^* = \bar{\mathbf{Y}}^T$.

Hermitian matrices

A Hermitian bilinear form has the property that $\mathbf{X}A\mathbf{X}^*$ is real for all **X**. If in addition $\mathbf{X}A\mathbf{X}^* > 0$ for all nonzero **X**, then the Hermitian form and the Hermitian matrix A are said to be positive. Every inner product in $\mathfrak{U}$ has the form $(\mathbf{V}, \mathbf{W}) = \mathbf{X}A\mathbf{Y}^*$ in which **X**, **Y** are the coordinate vectors of **V**, **W** relative to some basis, and A is a positive Hermitian matrix. Conversely, every positive Hermitian bilinear form in the coordinates of **V** and **W** defines an inner product on $\mathfrak{U}$.

If $\mathfrak{U}$ is an inner product space over $\mathfrak{R}$ or $\mathfrak{C}$, then for any two vectors **V**, **W** the Cauchy-Schwarz inequality holds (see 125). The length of **V** is defined by $\|\mathbf{V}\| = (\mathbf{V}, \mathbf{V})^{1/2}$ and has the three properties (see 126) that are normally associated with length. If $\|\mathbf{V}\| = 1$, then **V** is called a unit vector. Two vectors **V**, **W** are said to be orthogonal if $(\mathbf{V}, \mathbf{W}) = 0$. The zero vector is orthogonal to every vector in $\mathfrak{U}$ and is the only vector with this property. Every n-dimensional inner product space has an orthonormal basis; that is, a basis consisting of n mutually orthogonal unit vectors. If (**E**) is an orthonormal basis of $\mathfrak{U}$, a second basis (**F**) is orthonormal if, and only if, the transition matrix P from the **E**- to the **F**-basis has the property $PP^* = I$. Such a matrix P is called a unitary matrix. The columns (and the rows) of a unitary matrix constitute an orthonormal basis of $\mathfrak{U}_n(\mathfrak{C})$ relative to the standard inner product. If a unitary matrix P has real elements, then $PP^T = I$ and P is called an orthogonal matrix and its columns (and rows) form an orthonormal basis of $\mathfrak{U}_n(\mathfrak{R})$. If $\mathfrak{U}$ is an inner product space with orthonormal basis $\mathbf{E}_1, \mathbf{E}_2, \cdots, \mathbf{E}_n$ and α is the isomorphism that maps each vector **V** on its coordinate vector $\alpha\mathbf{V}$ relative to the **E**-basis, then the inner product (**V**, **W**) in $\mathfrak{U}$ is equal to the standard inner product $(\alpha\mathbf{V}, \alpha\mathbf{W})$ of the coordinate vectors in $\mathfrak{U}_n(\mathfrak{F})$. Hence the standard inner product in $\mathfrak{U}_n(\mathfrak{F})$ is invariant under transformation from one orthonormal basis to another.

Linear operators in an inner product space. If $\mathfrak{U}$ is a finite-dimensional inner product space over $\mathfrak{F}$, in which $\mathfrak{F}$ is either $\mathfrak{R}$ or $\mathfrak{C}$, then for any linear operator τ on $\mathfrak{U}$ there exists a unique linear operator τ^* on $\mathfrak{U}$, called the adjoint of τ, such that $(\tau\mathbf{V}, \mathbf{W}) = (\mathbf{V}, \tau^*\mathbf{W})$ for all vectors **V**, **W** in $\mathfrak{U}$. If A_τ is the matrix of τ relative to an orthonormal basis, then the matrix A_{τ^*} of τ^*, relative to the same basis, is the adjoint matrix A_τ^* of A_τ. If

The adjoint of a linear operator

(72)
$$\begin{cases} (1)\ (V_1+V_2, W) = (V_1, W) + (V_2, W),\ (2)\ (W, V) = \overline{(V, W)}, \text{ in which } \bar{z} \text{ denotes the complex conjugate of } z,\ (3)\ (cV, W) = c(V, W), \text{ and } (4)\ (V, V) \text{ is real and } (V, V) > 0 \text{ if } V \neq 0. \end{cases}$$

(73)
$$(X, Y) = x_1\bar{y}_1 + x_2\bar{y}_2 + \cdots + x_n\bar{y}_n$$

(74)
$$\begin{cases} \text{If } V = x_1E_1 + \cdots + x_nE_n,\ W = y_1E_1 + \cdots + y_nE_n \\ \text{the postulates require that} \\ (V, W) = \sum_{i=1}^{n}\sum_{j=1}^{n} x_i\bar{y}_j(E_i, E_j) = \sum_{i=1}^{n}\sum_{j=1}^{n} a_{ij}x_i\bar{y}_j, \\ \text{in which } A = [a_{ij}] \text{ is Hermitian.} \end{cases}$$

(75)
$$\sum_{i=1}^{n}\sum_{j=1}^{n} a_{ij}x_i\bar{y}_j \quad \text{in which } a_{ij} = \bar{a}_{ji}$$

(76)
$$|(V, W)| \leq (V, V)^{1/2}(W, W)^{1/2}$$

(77)
$$\text{(a) } \|V\| > 0 \text{ if } V \neq 0, \quad \text{(b) } |cV| = |c|\,\|V\| \quad \text{(c) } \|V + W\| \leq \|V\| + \|W\|$$

(78)
$$c_1y_1\bar{y}_1 + c_2y_2\bar{y}_2 + \cdots + c_ny_n\bar{y}_n$$

σ, τ are linear operators on $\mathfrak{U}$, and if c is any scalar, then $(\sigma+\tau)^*=\sigma^*+\tau^*$, $(c\sigma)^*=c\sigma^*$, $(\sigma\tau)^*=\tau^*\sigma^*$, and $(\sigma^*)^*=\sigma$. An operator τ is self-adjoint, or Hermitian, if $\tau^*=\tau$. If τ is Hermitian, then $(\tau\mathbf{V},\mathbf{V})=(\mathbf{V},\tau\mathbf{V})=\overline{(\tau\mathbf{V},\mathbf{V})}$, and hence $(\tau\mathbf{V},\mathbf{V})$ is real for all $\mathbf{V}$. A Hermitian operator τ is positive if $(\tau\mathbf{V},\mathbf{V})>0$ when $\mathbf{V}\neq\mathbf{0}$. If τ is a linear operator in an inner product space with inner product $(\mathbf{V},\mathbf{W})_1$, then the function $(\mathbf{V},\mathbf{W})_2=(\tau\mathbf{V},\mathbf{W})_1$ is an inner product in $\mathfrak{U}$ if, and only if, τ is positive Hermitian. An operator is positive Hermitian if, and only if, its matrix, relative to an orthonormal basis, is positive Hermitian. A Hermitian operator on an n-dimensional inner product space $\mathfrak{U}$ has n real eigenvalues and n mutually orthogonal eigenvectors. Thus, if τ is Hermitian, it is diagonalizable, and $\mathfrak{U}$ is the direct sum of mutually orthogonal one-dimensional subspaces invariant under τ. Applied to the operator τ in $\mathfrak{U}_n(\mathfrak{C})$, defined by $\tau\mathbf{X}=H\mathbf{X}$ in which H is a Hermitian matrix, this implies that H has n mutually orthogonal unit eigenvectors in $\mathfrak{U}_n(\mathfrak{C})$ and, hence, that there exists a unitary matrix U such that $U^{-1}HU=U^*HU$ is a real diagonal matrix whose diagonal elements are the eigenvalues of H. Similarly, in the real case, if A is a real symmetric matrix, there exists a real orthogonal matrix P such that $P^{-1}AP$ is diagonal, and A has n mutually orthogonal eigenvectors in $\mathfrak{U}_n(\mathfrak{R})$. Using this diagonalization procedure, any Hermitian form XHX^* can be reduced by a unitary transformation $X^T=UY^T$ to a canonical form (see 127) in which the coefficients c_i are the eigenvalues of H. It follows that H is positive if, and only if, all its eigenvalues are positive, and the same is true of a positive Hermitian operator.

A unitary operator is a linear operator τ on $\mathfrak{U}$ that preserves lengths, that is, such that for every vector V in $\mathfrak{U}$, $\|\tau V\|=\|V\|$. A necessary and sufficient condition that τ preserves lengths is that for any two vectors V, W in $\mathfrak{U}$, $(\tau V,\tau W)=(V,W)$. Hence, unitary operators preserve orthogonality as well as lengths. Since $(\tau V,\tau W)=(V,\tau^*\tau W)$ it follows that τ is unitary if, and only if, $\tau^*\tau=I$. Thus a unitary operator τ is invertible, with inverse $\tau^{-1}=\tau^*$, and τ^{-1} is also unitary. If σ and τ are unitary, the same is true also of $\sigma\tau$. Thus, the unitary operators on $\mathfrak{U}$ form a group called the unitary group. An operator τ is unitary if, and only if, its matrix A_τ relative to an orthonormal basis, is unitary. The unitary matrices over $\mathfrak{C}$ also form a group under matrix multiplication, and the mapping of τ on A_τ is an isomorphism of the group of unitary operators onto the group of unitary matrices. A unitary operator on a real vector space is called an orthogonal operator. Its matrix relative to an orthonormal basis is orthogonal, and the mapping of τ on A_τ is an isomorphism of the (real) orthogonal group of orthogonal operators onto the group of real orthogonal matrices. Every nonsingular linear operator τ on $\mathfrak{U}$ has a unique polar factorization, $\tau=\rho\sigma$, into the product of a positive Hermitian operator ρ and a unitary operator σ. If τ is singular, it can still be factored in this way, but the Hermitian factor ρ is merely nonnegative (that is, has nonnegative eigenvalues) and the unitary factor σ is not uniquely determined.

Orthogonal operators

An operator τ on $\mathfrak{U}$ is normal if $\tau\tau^*=\tau^*\tau$. Hermitian, unitary, and real orthogonal operators are all normal. In general, an operator is normal if and only if it has n mutually orthogonal eigenvectors with $n=\dim\mathfrak{U}$. Thus, a normal operator is diagonalizable; its matrix, relative to the orthonormal basis of $\mathfrak{U}$, consisting of n mutually orthogonal unit eigenvectors of τ, is a diagonal matrix with the eigenvalues of τ as diagonal elements. An $n\times n$ matrix A over $\mathfrak{C}$ is normal if $AA^*=A^*A$, and an operator is normal if and only if its matrix relative to an orthonormal basis is normal. Just as in the Hermitian case, if A is normal, then there exists a unitary matrix U such that $U^{-1}AU$ is a diagonal matrix. Conversely, every matrix that is unitarily similar to a diagonal matrix, is normal.

If $\mathfrak{U}$ is finite-dimensional, and if $\mathfrak{S}$ is any subspace of $\mathfrak{U}$, then the set $\mathfrak{S}^\perp$ of all vectors of $\mathbf{T}$ in $\mathfrak{U}$ such that $(\mathbf{T},\mathbf{S})=0$ for all $\mathbf{S}$ in $\mathfrak{S}$ is a subspace of $\mathfrak{U}$ called the orthogonal complement of $\mathfrak{S}$. For any subspace $\mathfrak{S}$ of $\mathfrak{U}$, $(\mathfrak{S}^\perp)^\perp=\mathfrak{S}$, and $V=\mathfrak{S}\oplus\mathfrak{S}^\perp$. Thus every vector $\mathbf{V}$ has a unique representation $\mathbf{V}=\mathbf{S}+\mathbf{T}$, in which $\mathbf{S}$ is in $\mathfrak{S}$, and $\mathbf{T}$ is in $\mathfrak{S}$. The mapping π from $\mathfrak{U}$ onto $\mathfrak{S}$ defined by $\pi\mathbf{V}=\mathbf{S}$ is a linear operator called the orthogonal projection of $\mathfrak{U}$ on $\mathfrak{S}$. Since $\pi\mathbf{V}=0$ if and only if $\mathbf{V}$ is in $\mathfrak{S}^\perp$, the nullspace of π is $\mathfrak{S}^\perp$.

If τ is a normal operator on an n-dimensional inner product space $\mathfrak{U}$, $c_1,\cdots,c_r$ are the distinct eigenvalues of τ, and π_i is the orthogonal projection of $\mathfrak{U}$ onto the nullspace of $\tau-c_iI$, then a basic result (see 128) expresses τ as a linear combination of the orthogonal projection π. The result is called the spectral theorem for normal operators.

(128) $$\begin{cases}\tau=c_1\pi_1+c_2\pi_2+\cdots+c_r\pi_r, & \pi_i\pi_j=0 \quad \text{if } i\neq j\\ \text{and} \quad \pi_1+\pi_2+\cdots+\pi_r=I\end{cases}$$

(129) $$\begin{cases}\tau(V_1,\cdots,V_i+V_i',\cdots,V_r)\\ \quad =\tau(V_1,\cdots,V_i,\cdots V_r)+\tau(V_1,\cdots,V_i',\cdots,V_r)\\ \tau(V_1,\cdots,cV_i,\cdots V_r)=c\tau(V_1,\cdots,V_i,\cdots,V_r).\end{cases}$$

(130) $$\begin{cases}(x_1V_1+x_2V_1',V_2)-x_1(V_1,V_2)-x_2(V_1',V_2)\\ \text{or} \quad (V_1,y_1V_2+y_2V_2')-y_1(V_1,V_2)-y_2(V_1,V_2').\end{cases}$$

(131) $$\begin{cases}V_1\otimes(V_2+V_2')=V_1\otimes V_2+V_1\otimes V_2'\\ (V_1+V_1')\otimes V_2=V_1\otimes V_2+V_1'\otimes V_2\\ (cV_1)\otimes V_2=V_1\otimes(cV_2)=c(V_1\otimes V_2)\end{cases}$$

(132) $$\begin{array}{ccc}\mathfrak{U}_1\times\mathfrak{U}_2 & \xrightarrow{\tau} & \mathfrak{A}\\ & \sigma\searrow \quad \swarrow\varphi & \\ & \mathfrak{Z} & \end{array}$$

MULTILINEAR ALGEBRA

The tensor product of vector spaces. If $\mathfrak{U}_1$, $\mathfrak{U}_2$, $\cdots$, $\mathfrak{U}_r$ are vector spaces over a field $\mathfrak{F}$ then, the set of all r-tuples $(\mathbf{V}_1,\mathbf{V}_2,\cdots,\mathbf{V}_r)$ in which $\mathbf{V}_i$ belongs to $\mathfrak{U}_i$, is called the Cartesian product of $\mathfrak{U}_1,\cdots,\mathfrak{U}_r$ and is denoted by $\mathfrak{U}_1\times\mathfrak{U}_2\times\cdots\times\mathfrak{U}_r$. The Cartesian product of r copies of a vector space $\mathfrak{U}$ is called the rth Cartesian power of $\mathfrak{U}$ and is denoted by $\times^r\mathfrak{U}$. If $\mathfrak{W}$ is also a vector space over $\mathfrak{F}$, a mapping τ from $\mathfrak{U}_1\times\mathfrak{U}_2\times\cdots\times\mathfrak{U}_r$ into $\mathfrak{W}$ is multilinear if for each value of i from 1 to r linearity holds (see 129) for the ith variable. A multilinear mapping from $\times^r\mathfrak{U}$ to $\mathfrak{W}$ is called an r-linear mapping. If $\mathfrak{W}$ is the scalar field $\mathfrak{F}$ considered as a vector space, then an r-linear mapping τ from $\times^r\mathfrak{U}$ into $\mathfrak{F}$ is called an r-linear functional on $\mathfrak{U}$.

If $\mathfrak{U}_1$, $\mathfrak{U}_2$ are vector spaces over $\mathfrak{F}$, and if $\mathfrak{M}$ is the free vector space over $\mathfrak{F}$ on the basis set $\mathfrak{U}_1\times\mathfrak{U}_2$, then one may let $\mathfrak{N}$ be the subspace of $\mathfrak{M}$ spanned by the set of all elements having one of the two forms (130). The factor space $\mathfrak{M}/\mathfrak{N}$ consists of elements $\mathbf{Z}+\mathfrak{N}$, $\mathbf{Z}$ in $\mathfrak{M}$, and is a vector space over $\mathfrak{F}$ when addition and scalar multiplication are defined by $(\mathbf{Z}_1+\mathfrak{N})+(\mathbf{Z}_2+\mathfrak{N})=(\mathbf{Z}_1+\mathbf{Z}_2)+\mathfrak{N}$ and $c(\mathbf{Z}+\mathfrak{N})=c\mathbf{Z}+\mathfrak{N}$, respectively. The mapping π from $\mathfrak{M}$ onto $\mathfrak{M}/\mathfrak{N}$ defined by $\pi\mathbf{Z}=\mathbf{Z}+\mathfrak{N}$ is a homomorphism called the canonical projection of $\mathfrak{M}$ onto $\mathfrak{M}/\mathfrak{N}$. The space $\mathfrak{M}/\mathfrak{N}$ is called the tensor product of $\mathfrak{U}_1$ and $\mathfrak{U}_2$ and is denoted by $\mathfrak{U}_1\otimes\mathfrak{U}_2$. If π is the canonical projection, $\pi(\mathbf{V}_1,\mathbf{V}_2)$ is written $\mathbf{V}_1\otimes\mathbf{V}_2$ (read $\mathbf{V}_1$ tensor $\mathbf{V}_2$). The elements $\mathbf{V}_1\otimes\mathbf{V}_2$, with $\mathbf{V}_1$ in $\mathfrak{U}_1$, and $\mathbf{V}_2$ in $\mathfrak{U}_2$, span $\mathfrak{U}_1\otimes\mathfrak{U}_2$, and the operation $\otimes$ satisfies three basic relations (see 131). Thus the mapping τ, defined by $\tau(\mathbf{V}_1,\mathbf{V}_2)=\mathbf{V}_1\otimes\mathbf{V}_2$, is bilinear.

The tensor product

The tensor product $\mathfrak{U}_1\otimes\mathfrak{U}_2$, together with the bilinear mapping τ from $\mathfrak{U}_1\times\mathfrak{U}_2$ into $\mathfrak{U}_1\otimes\mathfrak{U}_2$, has the following "universal property." If σ is any bilinear mapping of $\mathfrak{U}_1\times\mathfrak{U}_2$ into an arbitrary vector space $\mathfrak{Z}$ over $\mathfrak{F}$, then there exists a unique linear transformation φ from $\mathfrak{U}_1\otimes\mathfrak{U}_2$ into $\mathfrak{Z}$, such that $\varphi\tau=\sigma$. Most modern writers use this universal property to define the tensor product. From this point of view, and if $\mathfrak{A}$, $\mathfrak{U}_1$ and $\mathfrak{U}_2$ are vector spaces over $\mathfrak{F}$, and if τ is a bilinear mapping from $\mathfrak{U}_1 \times \mathfrak{U}_2$ into $\mathfrak{A}$, then the pair $(\mathfrak{A}, \tau)$ is a tensor product of the vector spaces $\mathfrak{U}_1$, $\mathfrak{U}_2$, if for every bilinear mapping σ from $\mathfrak{U}_1 \times \mathfrak{U}_2$ into $\mathfrak{Z}$, there exists a unique linear transformation φ from $\mathfrak{A}$ into an arbitrary vector space $\mathfrak{Z}$ over $\mathfrak{F}$, such that $\varphi\tau = \sigma$ (see 132).

The existence of a tensor product, so defined, is proved by showing that $(\mathfrak{M}/\mathfrak{N}, \pi)$ has the required universal property. Moreover, the tensor product $(\mathfrak{A}, \tau)$ is unique in the sense that if $(\mathfrak{A}', \tau')$ is a second tensor product, then there exists an isomorphism α from $\mathfrak{A}$ onto $\mathfrak{A}'$ such that $\alpha\tau = \tau'$. Again, $\tau(\mathbf{V}_1, \mathbf{V}_2)$ is written $\mathbf{V}_1 \otimes \mathbf{V}_2$ and $(\mathfrak{A}, \tau)$ is written $\mathfrak{U}_1 \otimes \mathfrak{U}_2$. The tensor product $\mathfrak{U}_1 \otimes \mathfrak{U}_2$, is spanned by the elements $\mathbf{V}_1 \otimes \mathbf{V}_2$, with $\mathbf{V}_1$ in $\mathfrak{U}_1$, and $\mathbf{V}_2$ in $\mathfrak{U}_2$; and $\mathbf{V}_1 \otimes \mathbf{V}_2 = O$ if and only if $\mathbf{V}_1 = \mathbf{0}$ or $\mathbf{V}_2 = \mathbf{0}$. If $\mathfrak{U}_1 = \mathfrak{S}_1 \oplus \mathfrak{S}_2 \oplus \cdots \oplus \mathfrak{S}_n$ and $\mathfrak{U}_2 = \mathfrak{U}_1 \oplus \mathfrak{U}_2 \oplus \cdots \oplus \mathfrak{A}_m$, then $\mathfrak{U}_1 \otimes \mathfrak{U}_2$ is the direct sum of the nm spaces $\mathfrak{S}_i \otimes \mathfrak{A}_j$. If (**E**) and (**F**) are bases of $\mathfrak{U}_1$ and $\mathfrak{U}_2$, then the elements $\{\mathbf{E}_i \otimes \mathbf{F}_j\}$ form a basis of $\mathfrak{U}_1 \otimes \mathfrak{U}_2$. Thus dim $(\mathfrak{U}_1 \otimes \mathfrak{U}_2) = (\dim \mathfrak{U}_1)$ $(\dim \mathfrak{U}_2)$ if $\mathfrak{U}_1$ and $\mathfrak{U}_2$ are finite-dimensional. If τ and σ are linear transformations from the vector spaces $\mathfrak{U}_1$ and $\mathfrak{W}_1$ to vector spaces $\mathfrak{U}_2$, $\mathfrak{W}_2$, respectively, then the linear transformation ρ, defined by $\rho(\mathbf{V}_1 \otimes \mathbf{W}_1) = \tau\mathbf{V}_1 \otimes \sigma\mathbf{W}_1$, is called the tensor product of τ and σ and is denoted by $\tau \otimes \sigma$. If τ' and σ' are also linear transformations defined on the vector spaces $\mathfrak{U}_2$ and $\mathfrak{W}_2$, the rule for composition is $(\tau' \otimes \sigma')(\tau \otimes \sigma) = \tau'\tau \otimes \sigma'\sigma$, and $1 \otimes 1$ is the identity on $\mathfrak{U}_1 \otimes \mathfrak{W}_1$. The image of the tensor product of two linear transformations is the tensor product of the images. The kernel (nullspace) of a tensor product of linear transformation is given by $\ker(\tau \otimes \sigma) = \ker \tau \otimes \mathfrak{W}_1 + \mathfrak{U}_1 \otimes \ker \sigma$. For a fixed space $\mathfrak{W}$ a linear transformation σ from $\mathfrak{U}_1$ into $\mathfrak{U}_2$ induces a linear transformation σ^* from $\mathfrak{U}_1 \otimes \mathfrak{W}$ into $\mathfrak{U}_2 \otimes \mathfrak{W}$ defined by $\sigma^* = \sigma \otimes 1$; for fixed $\mathfrak{W}$ the mappings $f(\mathfrak{U}) = \mathfrak{U} \otimes \mathfrak{W}$, $f(\sigma) = \sigma^*$ define a covariant functor from the category of vector spaces over $\mathfrak{F}$ to itself. Similarly for a fixed space $\mathfrak{U}$, the mappings $\mathfrak{W} \to \mathfrak{U} \otimes \mathfrak{W}$ and $\tau \to 1 \otimes \tau$ define a covariant functor.

The tensor product of r vector spaces $\mathfrak{U}_1, \mathfrak{U}_2, \cdots, \mathfrak{U}_r$ over $\mathfrak{F}$ is defined similarly. If τ is a multilinear mapping of the set $\mathfrak{U}_1 \times \mathfrak{U}_2 \times \cdots \times \mathfrak{U}_r$ into a vector space $\mathfrak{A}$, then the pair $(\mathfrak{A}, \tau)$ is a tensor product of $\mathfrak{U}_1, \cdots \mathfrak{U}_r$ if, for every multilinear mapping σ from $\mathfrak{U}_1 \times \mathfrak{U}_2 \times \cdots \times \mathfrak{U}_r$ into an arbitrary vector space $\mathfrak{T}$ over $\mathfrak{F}$, there exists a unique linear transformation φ of $\mathfrak{A}$ into $\mathfrak{T}$ such that $\varphi\tau = \sigma$. As before $\tau(\mathbf{V}_1, \mathbf{V}_2, \cdots, \mathbf{V}_r)$ is written as $\mathbf{V}_1 \otimes \mathbf{V}_2 \otimes \cdots \otimes \mathbf{V}_r$ and $(\mathfrak{A}, \tau)$ is denoted by $\mathfrak{U}_1 \otimes \mathfrak{U}_2 \otimes \cdots \otimes \mathfrak{U}_r$. Existence and uniqueness of $\mathfrak{A}$ follow as in the case $r = 2$. There is an isomorphism β of $\mathfrak{U}_1 \otimes \mathfrak{U}_2 \otimes \mathfrak{U}_3$ onto $(\mathfrak{U}_1 \otimes \mathfrak{U}_2) \otimes \mathfrak{U}_3$, such that $\beta(\mathbf{V}_1 \otimes \mathbf{V}_2 \otimes \mathbf{V}_3) = (\mathbf{V}_1 \otimes \mathbf{V}_2) \otimes \mathbf{V}_3$ and similarly for $\mathfrak{U}_1 \otimes (\mathfrak{U}_2 \otimes \mathfrak{U}_3)$. This associativity principle extends to the tensor product of any finite number of vector spaces over $\mathfrak{F}$ (see 133).

$$(133)\quad \begin{cases} \beta: (\mathfrak{U}_1 \otimes \cdots \otimes \mathfrak{U}_r) \otimes (\mathfrak{U}_{r+1} \otimes \cdots \otimes \mathfrak{U}_{r+s}) \\ \quad \to \mathfrak{U}_1 \otimes \cdots \otimes \mathfrak{U}_{r+s} \\ \beta[(\mathfrak{U}_1 \otimes \cdots \otimes \mathfrak{U}_r) \otimes (\mathfrak{U}_{r+1} \otimes \cdots \otimes \mathfrak{U}_{r+s})] \\ \quad = \mathfrak{U}_1 \otimes \cdots \otimes \mathfrak{U}_{r+s} \end{cases}$$

$$(134)\quad T = \sum_{(i)} x_{i_1 \cdots i_r} E_{i_1} \otimes \cdots \otimes E_{i_r}$$

$$(135)\quad \begin{cases} 1(V_1 \otimes V_2 \otimes \cdots \otimes V_n) = (V_1 \otimes V_2 \otimes \cdots \otimes V_n)1 \\ \quad = V_1 \otimes V_2 \otimes \cdots \otimes V_n \\ (V_1 \otimes V_2 \otimes \cdots \otimes V_n)(V_1' \otimes V_2' \otimes \cdots \otimes V_m') \\ \quad = V_1 \otimes V_2 \otimes \cdots \otimes V_n \otimes V_1' \otimes \cdots \otimes V_m' \end{cases}$$

$$(136)\quad \begin{cases} E^{j_1 j_2 \cdots j_n}_{i_1 i_2 \cdots i_n} = E_{i_1} \otimes E_{i_2} \otimes \cdots \otimes E_{i_n} \otimes \\ \quad \otimes E^{j_1} \otimes E^{j_2} \otimes \cdots \otimes E^{j_n} \end{cases}$$

$$(137)\quad \begin{cases} T = \sum x^{i_1 i_2 \cdots i_n}_{j_1 j_2 \cdots j_n} E^{j_1 j_2 \cdots j_n}_{i_1 i_2 \cdots i_n}, \\ \text{the summation extending over each } i \text{ and each } j \end{cases}$$

$$(138)\quad (V_1 \otimes V_2 \otimes \cdots \otimes V_r, W_1 \otimes W_2 \otimes \cdots \otimes W_r) \\ \quad = (V_1, W_1)(W_2, W_2) \cdots (V_r, W_r)$$

$$(139)\quad (T, U) = \Sigma(T_r, U_r)$$

$$(140)\quad G^* = \Sigma(X_i, X_j) X^i \otimes X^j \\ \text{and } G = \Sigma(X^i, X^j) X_i \otimes X_j$$

The tensor algebra of a vector space. If $\mathfrak{U}$ is a vector space over $\mathfrak{F}$, then the tensor product $\mathfrak{U} \otimes \mathfrak{U} \otimes \cdots \otimes \mathfrak{U}$ of r copies of $\mathfrak{U}$ is called the rth tensorial power of $\mathfrak{U}$ and is denoted by $\otimes^r\mathfrak{U}$ or by $\mathfrak{A}_r$. Its elements are called tensors of order r. If $\mathbf{E}_1, \cdots, \mathbf{E}_n$ is a basis of $\mathfrak{U}$, then $\{\mathbf{E}_{i1} \otimes \mathbf{E}_{i2} \otimes \cdots \otimes \mathbf{E}_{ir}\}$ is a basis for $\otimes^r\mathfrak{U}$ and every tensor T of order r can be written in summation form (see 134). The n^r scalars $x_{i1 \ldots ir}$ that appear in this form are called the components of T relative to the **E**-basis of $\mathfrak{U}$.

Tensorial powers

As a notational convenience, $\mathfrak{A}_1$ is identified with $\mathfrak{U}$ and $\mathfrak{A}_0$ with the scalar field $\mathfrak{F}$. The direct sum $\mathfrak{A}(\mathfrak{U}) = \oplus \sum_{r=0}^{\infty} \mathfrak{A}_r$ is a vector space over $\mathfrak{F}$ and each tensorial power $\mathfrak{A}_r$ can be considered a subspace of $\mathfrak{A}(\mathfrak{U})$. Multiplication can be defined formally for the generating elements of $\mathfrak{A}(\mathfrak{U})$ (see 135) and can be extended linearly to arbitrary elements. With this definition of multiplication $\mathfrak{A}(\mathfrak{U})$ becomes an associative algebra over $\mathfrak{F}$, with unity element 1, and is called the tensor algebra of the vector space $\mathfrak{U}$.

The tensor algebra has the following universal mapping property: If τ is the canonical injection of $\mathfrak{U}$ into $\mathfrak{A}(\mathfrak{U})$, and if σ is a linear transformation of $\mathfrak{U}$ into an arbitrary associative algebra **A** over $\mathfrak{F}$ with unity, then there exists a unique algebra homomorphism φ of $\mathfrak{A}(\mathfrak{U})$ into **A** such that $\varphi\tau = \sigma$. This property can be used as the definition of $\mathfrak{A}(\mathfrak{U})$, in which case existence is implied by the construction already given, and uniqueness follows in the same sense as the uniqueness of the tensor product. The universal property of $\mathfrak{A}(\mathfrak{U})$ also implies that every linear transformation σ of $\mathfrak{U}$ into a second vector space $\mathfrak{W}$ over $\mathfrak{F}$ induces a unique algebra homomorphism $T(\sigma)$ of $\mathfrak{A}(\mathfrak{U})$ into $\mathfrak{A}(\mathfrak{W})$ such that $T(\sigma)1 = 1$. Moreover, $T(I) = I$ and if ρ from $\mathfrak{W}$ into $\mathfrak{Z}$ is a second linear transformation $T(\varphi\sigma) = T(\varphi)\,T(\sigma)$. Thus the mappings $\mathfrak{U} \to \mathfrak{A}(\mathfrak{U})$ and $\sigma \to T(\sigma)$ define a covariant functor, from the category of vector spaces over $\mathfrak{F}$ to the category of associative algebras with unit over $\mathfrak{F}$.

If $\mathfrak{U}^*$ is the dual space of $\mathfrak{U}$, the tensor product $\mathfrak{U} \otimes \cdots \otimes \mathfrak{U}^* \otimes \cdots \otimes \mathfrak{U}^*$ of r copies of $\mathfrak{U}$ and s copies of $\mathfrak{U}^*$ is denoted by $\otimes_s{}^r(\mathfrak{U})$. If $s = 0$, $\otimes_0{}^r\mathfrak{U}$ is identified with $\otimes^r\mathfrak{U}$ and its elements are called contravariant tensors of order r. If $r = 0$, then $\otimes^s\mathfrak{U}^0\mathfrak{U} = \otimes^s\mathfrak{U}^*$ and its elements are called covariant tensors of order s. Elements of $\otimes_s{}^r\mathfrak{U}$ are called mixed tensors of contravariant order r and covariant order s. Finally, $\otimes_0{}^1\mathfrak{U}$ is identified with $\mathfrak{U}$, $\otimes_1{}^0\mathfrak{U}$ with $\mathfrak{U}^*$ and $\otimes_0{}^0\mathfrak{U}$ with the scalar field $\mathfrak{F}$. If $\mathbf{E}_1, \mathbf{E}_2, \cdots, \mathbf{E}_n$ is a basis of $\mathfrak{U}$ and $\mathbf{E}^1, \mathbf{E}^2, \cdots, \mathbf{E}^n$ is the dual basis of $\mathfrak{U}^*$, then $n^{(r+s)}$ elements (136) form a basis for $\otimes_s{}^r\mathfrak{U}$. Every tensor T of $\otimes_s{}^r\mathfrak{U}$ can be written in terms of these (see 137). The $n^{(r+s)}$ scalars $x^{i_1 \cdots i_r}_{j_1 \cdots i_s}$ are called the components of T relative to the **E**-basis of $\mathfrak{U}$. By a process analogous to the construction of the tensor algebra $\mathfrak{A}(\mathfrak{U})$, the mixed tensors of all orders can be embedded in a mixed tensor algebra $\mathfrak{A}(\mathfrak{U}, \mathfrak{U}^*)$.

Mixed tensors

If $\mathfrak{U}$ is an inner product space with inner product (,), then an inner product on $\otimes^r\mathfrak{U}$ can be defined (see 138), and $\otimes^r\mathfrak{U}$ is then an inner product space. If (**E**) is an orthonormal basis for $\mathfrak{U}$, then $\{\mathbf{E}_{i1} \otimes \mathbf{E}_{i2} \otimes \cdots \otimes \mathbf{E}_{in}\}$ is an orthonormal basis for $\otimes^r\mathfrak{U}$. Now, if $T = \Sigma T_r$, $U = \Sigma U_r$, T_r, U_r in $\otimes^r\mathfrak{U}$ are any two elements of the tensor algebra $\mathfrak{A}(\mathfrak{U})$, then an inner product (T, U) in $\mathfrak{A}(\mathfrak{U})$ (as a vector space) can also be defined (see 139).

The tensor $G=\sum_{i=1}^{n}\mathbf{E}_i\otimes\mathbf{E}_i$ is independent of the choice of the orthonormal basis (**E**) and is called the contravariant metric tensor of the Euclidean space $\mathfrak{U}$; the covariant metric tensor G^* is defined similarly in terms of the dual basis ($\mathbf{E}^*$) of $\mathfrak{U}^*$. In general if $\mathbf{X}_1, \cdots, \mathbf{X}_n$ and $\mathbf{X}^1, \cdots, \mathbf{X}^r$ are arbitrary dual bases of $\mathfrak{U}$ and $\mathfrak{U}^*$, respectively, then G^* and G can be expressed in terms of these bases (see 140).

The exterior algebra of a vector space. For the following discussion, three definitions are needed. (1) $\mathfrak{U}$ is a vector space over $\mathfrak{F}$; (2) $\mathfrak{A}_r(\mathfrak{U})=\otimes^r\mathfrak{U}$ is the rth tensorial power of $\mathfrak{U}$; (3) $\mathfrak{N}_r(\mathfrak{U})$, $r\geq 2$, is the subspace of $\mathfrak{A}_r(\mathfrak{U})$ spanned by the elements $\mathbf{V}_1\times\mathbf{V}_2\times\cdots\times\mathbf{V}_r$ in which $\mathbf{V}_i=\mathbf{V}_j$ for at least one pair of indices i, j with $i\neq j$. With these definitions, the factor space $\mathfrak{A}_r(\mathfrak{U})/\mathfrak{N}_r(\mathfrak{U})$ is called the rth exterior power of $\mathfrak{U}$ and is denoted by $\mathfrak{U}\wedge\mathfrak{U}\wedge\cdots\wedge\mathfrak{U}$ or $\wedge^r\mathfrak{U}$, and the element $\mathbf{V}_1\otimes\cdots\otimes\mathbf{V}_n+\mathfrak{N}_r(\mathfrak{U})$ is denoted by $\mathbf{V}_1\wedge\mathbf{V}_2\wedge\cdots\wedge\mathbf{V}_n$.

The rth exterior power of a vector space

The rth exterior power can also be defined, like the rth tensorial power, by a universal mapping property. If $\mathfrak{W}$ is a second vector space over $\mathfrak{F}$, then a multilinear mapping τ from $\mathfrak{U}\times\mathfrak{U}\times\cdots\times\mathfrak{U}$ into $\mathfrak{W}$ is said to be skew symmetric if, for every permutation σ of the subscripts, $\tau(\mathbf{V}_1, \mathbf{V}_2, \cdots, \mathbf{V}_r)=\varepsilon(\sigma)\tau(\mathbf{V}_{\sigma(1)}, \mathbf{V}_{\sigma(2)}, \cdots, \mathbf{V}_{\sigma(r)})$, in which $\varepsilon(\sigma)=1$ if σ is an even permutation, and $\varepsilon(\sigma)=-1$ if σ is an odd permutation. A necessary and sufficient condition that τ be skew symmetric is that $\tau(\mathbf{V}_1, \mathbf{V}_2, \cdots, \mathbf{V}_r)=0$ whenever $\mathbf{V}_i=\mathbf{V}_j$ for at least one pair of indices i, j with $i\neq j$. A vector space $\mathfrak{B}_r$ over $\mathfrak{F}$, together with a skew symmetric mapping τ from $\times^r\mathfrak{U}$ into $\mathfrak{B}_r$, is called an rth exterior power of $\mathfrak{U}$ if for every skew symmetric multilinear mapping ρ, from $\times^r\mathfrak{U}$ into an arbitrary vector space $\mathfrak{Z}$ over $\mathfrak{F}$, there exists a unique linear transformation φ from $\mathfrak{B}_r$ into $\mathfrak{Z}$, such that $\varphi\tau=\rho$; that is, the relevant diagram (see 141) is commutative. If $\tau(\mathbf{V}_1, \mathbf{V}_2, \cdots, \mathbf{V}_r)$ is written as $\mathbf{V}_1\wedge\mathbf{V}_2\wedge\cdots\wedge\mathbf{V}_r$, the definition implies that $\mathfrak{B}_r$ is spanned by the elements of the form $\mathbf{V}_1\wedge\mathbf{V}_2\wedge\cdots\wedge\mathbf{V}_r$ and is unique in the sense that, if $(\mathfrak{B}_r, \tau)$ and $(\mathfrak{B}'_r, \tau')$ are two rth exterior powers, then there is an isomorphism a of $\mathfrak{B}_r$ to $\mathfrak{B}'_r$, such that $a\tau=\tau'$. The existence of $\mathfrak{B}_r$ is proved by showing that $\mathfrak{B}_r=\mathfrak{A}_r(\mathfrak{U})/\mathfrak{N}_r(\mathfrak{U})$ has the universal property illustrated in the diagram.

The exterior algebra $\mathfrak{B}(\mathfrak{U})$ of the vector space is constructed from the rth exterior powers by a process analogous to that by which the tensor algebra is constructed from the rth tensorial powers. Defining $\mathfrak{B}_1(\mathfrak{U})$ to be $\mathfrak{U}$, $\mathfrak{B}_0(\mathfrak{U})$ to be $\mathfrak{F}$, the direct sum (see 142) of the $\mathfrak{B}_r(\mathfrak{U})$ can be formed. Each of the spaces $\mathfrak{B}_r(\mathfrak{U})$ is considered as a subspace of $\mathfrak{B}(\mathfrak{U})$. A unique associative multiplication can be defined in $\mathfrak{B}(\mathfrak{U})$ such equations (143) hold. Thus $\mathfrak{B}(\mathfrak{U})$ becomes a linear associative algebra with unity element. It is called the exterior algebra of $\mathfrak{U}$. The product of any two elements $\mathbf{X}$, $\mathbf{Y}$ of $\mathfrak{B}(\mathfrak{U})$ can be written $\mathbf{X}\wedge\mathbf{Y}$ without conflict with the previous use of the symbol $\wedge$.

If $\mathfrak{N}(\mathfrak{U})$ is the direct sum $\oplus\sum_{r=2}^{\infty}\mathfrak{N}_r(\mathfrak{U})$, then $\mathfrak{N}(\mathfrak{U})$ is an ideal in the tensor algebra $\otimes\mathfrak{U}$ and $\mathfrak{B}(\mathfrak{U})$ is isomorphic, as an algebra, to $\otimes\mathfrak{U}/\mathfrak{N}(\mathfrak{U})$. Any elements $\mathbf{X}$ in $\wedge^r\mathfrak{U}$ and $\mathbf{Y}$ in $\wedge^s\mathfrak{U}$ satisfy the commutation rule $\mathbf{X}\wedge\mathbf{Y}=(-1)^{rs}\mathbf{Y}\wedge\mathbf{X}$. In particular, for any vector $\mathbf{V}$ in $\mathfrak{U}$, $\mathbf{V}\wedge\mathbf{V}=0$ or, more precisely, if τ is the canonical projection of $\mathfrak{U}$ into $\mathfrak{B}(\mathfrak{U})$, then $\tau\mathbf{V}=\mathbf{0}$. This property can be used to formulate a universal mapping definition of the exterior algebra: $\mathfrak{U}$ is taken to be a vector space over $\mathfrak{F}$.

The universal mapping definition of the exterior algebra

An associative algebra $\mathfrak{B}$ over $\mathfrak{F}$, with unity element, together with a linear transformation τ, from $\mathfrak{U}$ into $\mathfrak{B}$, will be called an exterior algebra over $\mathfrak{U}$ if (1) for all $\mathbf{V}$ in $\mathfrak{U}$, $(\tau\mathbf{V})^2=0$; and (2) for every associative algebra $\mathfrak{A}$ over $\mathfrak{F}$, with unity, and for every linear transformation σ from $\mathfrak{U}$ into $\mathfrak{A}$ such that $(\sigma\mathbf{V})^2=\mathbf{0}$ for all $\mathbf{V}$ in $\mathfrak{U}$, there exists a unique algebra homomorphism φ from $\mathfrak{B}$ into $\mathfrak{A}$ such that $\varphi\tau=\sigma$. It then follows that $\mathfrak{B}(\mathfrak{U})$, as previously defined, has this universal property and that if $(\mathfrak{B}, \tau)$ and $(\mathfrak{B}', \tau')$ are two exterior algebras over $\mathfrak{U}$, then there is an isomorphism a from $\mathfrak{B}$ to $\mathfrak{B}'$ such that $a\tau=\tau'$.

The universal property for $\mathfrak{B}(\mathfrak{U})$ implies, as in the case of the tensor algebra, that a linear transformation σ from $\mathfrak{U}$ into $\mathfrak{W}$ induces a unique algebra homomorphism $\mathfrak{B}(\sigma)$ from $\mathfrak{B}(\mathfrak{U})$ into $\mathfrak{B}(\mathfrak{W})$ such that the relevant diagram (see 144) is commutative, $\mathfrak{B}(I)=I$, and $\mathfrak{B}(\sigma\rho)=\mathfrak{B}(\sigma)\mathfrak{B}(\rho)$ and hence the mapping of $\mathfrak{U}$ on $\mathfrak{B}(\mathfrak{U})$ and σ on $\mathfrak{B}(\sigma)$ is a functor on the category of vector spaces over $\mathfrak{F}$ to the category of associative algebras over $\mathfrak{F}$.

If $\mathfrak{U}$ is finite-dimensional with basis (**E**), then a basis for the rth exterior power $\wedge^r\mathfrak{U}$ is the set of exterior products $\{\mathbf{E}_{i_1}\wedge\cdots\wedge\mathbf{E}_{i_n}\}$ in which $i_1<i_2<\cdots<i_n$. Thus every vector $\mathbf{U}$ in $\wedge^r\mathfrak{U}$ can be expressed in the form (145) in which scalars $x^{i_1\cdots i_n}$ are called the components of $\mathbf{U}$ with respect to the **E**-basis of $\mathfrak{U}$. If $\dim\mathfrak{U}=n$, then $\dim\wedge^r\mathbf{V}=\binom{n}{r}$ if $r\leq n$. If $r>n$, then $\wedge^r\mathbf{V}=0$, because in that case $\otimes^r\mathfrak{U}$ is a subset of $\mathfrak{N}_r(\mathfrak{U})$. Thus, if $\mathfrak{B}=\wedge\mathfrak{U}$ is the exterior algebra of an n-dimensional space $\mathfrak{U}$, $\dim\mathfrak{B}$ is determined by (146). Finally, if $\mathfrak{U}$ is an inner product space with inner product (,) then an inner product can be defined in $\mathfrak{B}$ (see 147). If (**E**) is an orthonormal basis of $\mathfrak{U}$, then $\{\mathbf{E}_{i1}\wedge\cdots\wedge\mathbf{E}_{ir}\}$, with $i_1<i_2<\cdots<i_r$ is an orthonormal basis of $\mathfrak{B}$. (Ed.)

(141)
$$\begin{array}{ccc} \times^r\mathfrak{U} & \xrightarrow{\tau} & \mathfrak{B}_r \\ & {\scriptstyle\rho}\searrow & \swarrow{\scriptstyle\varphi} \\ & \mathfrak{Z} & \end{array}$$

(142)
$$\mathfrak{B}(\mathfrak{U})=\oplus\sum_{r=0}^{\infty}\mathfrak{B}_r(\mathfrak{U})$$

(143)
$$\begin{cases} 1\cdot V_1\wedge V_2\wedge\cdots\wedge V_r=V_1\wedge V_2\wedge\cdots\wedge V_r\cdot 1 \\ \quad =V_1\wedge V_2\cdots\wedge V_r \\ V_1\wedge V_2\wedge\cdots\wedge V_r\cdot V_{r+1}\wedge V_{r+2}\wedge\cdots\wedge V_{r+s} \\ \quad =V_1\wedge V_2\wedge\cdots\wedge V_{r+s} \end{cases}$$

(144)
$$\begin{array}{ccc} \mathfrak{U} & \xrightarrow{\tau_{\mathfrak{U}}} & \mathfrak{B}(\mathfrak{U}) \\ \sigma\downarrow & & \downarrow\mathfrak{B}(\sigma) \\ \mathfrak{W} & \xrightarrow{\tau_{\mathfrak{W}}} & \mathfrak{B}(\mathfrak{W}) \end{array}$$

(145)
$$U=\Sigma x^{i_1\cdots i_n}E_{i_1}\wedge\cdots\wedge E_{i_n}, \qquad i_1<i_2\cdots<i_n$$

(146)
$$\dim\mathfrak{H}=\sum_{r=0}^{n}\binom{n}{r}=2^n$$

(147)
$$(V_1\wedge V_2\wedge\cdots\wedge V_r, W_1\wedge W_2\wedge\cdots\wedge W_r) =\det[(V_i, W_j)]$$

Lattice theory

Lattice theory is the branch of mathematics that deals in precise mathematical language with the relation of different parts of the same whole to each other. The fundamental concept is that one part x may include (or contain) another part y, a relation written symbolically as $x\geq y$. A lattice, defined in more detail below, is a set of elements related by an inclusion relation such that, for any x and y in the set, there is a largest element, denoted $x\wedge y$, that is contained in both x and y and a smallest element, denoted $x\vee y$, that contains both x and y.

In general, in lattice theory the concepts of order and structure are analyzed from a mathematical standpoint, much as group theory (described later) analyzes the concept of symmetry. Thus, lattice theory considers families of subsets X, Y, $\cdots$ of a given set U under the operation of intersection of sets, denoted $X\cap Y$, in much the same spirit that group theory considers families of symmetry transformations (symbolized by Greek letters alpha, beta, $\cdots$) α, β, $\cdots$ of a given configuration when combined by performing them in succession (*i.e.*, taking their composite $\alpha\circ\beta$). As a generalization of set theory, it forms a fundamental part of higher algebra, geometry, and mathematical logic.

DEFINITIONS AND EXAMPLES

The reflexive law

Partial orderings. In detail, given a selected family S of different parts of the same whole, these parts can be represented symbolically by letters $x, y, \cdots, x \geq y$ signifying that x contains y. The resulting inclusion relation is characterized by the reflexive law, which states that $x \geq x$ for all x; the transitive law, which states that if $x \geq y$ and $y \geq z$, then $x \geq z$; and the antisymmetric law, which states that if $x \geq y$ and $y \geq x$, then $x = y$. In general, any relation having the above properties is called a partial ordering; and a partially ordered set, usually called a poset for short, is just a set S together with a partial ordering of its elements.

The inclusion relation is basic for the study of the subsets of a set (class, or aggregate). The relation of implication in logic has the same formal properties. In logic, $p \supset q$ signifies that the proposition (or statement) p implies the proposition q: that "if p, then q." The reflexive law $p \supset p$ of logic states that any proposition p implies itself; the transitive law, that if p implies q and q implies r, then p implies r; the antisymmetric law, that if p implies q and q implies p, then p and q are logically equivalent. Thus the propositions of any deductive system (*e.g.*, lattice theory or group theory) form a poset when partially ordered by the implication relation.

Mathematics is concerned with many other familiar partial orderings, such as the relation $x \leq y$ of inequality between real numbers, and the relation $a \mid b$ of divisibility (a is said to divide b when $b = na$ for some integer n) between positive integers. That is, if $\mathfrak{R}$ denotes the set of all real numbers and inequality has its usual meaning, then $[\mathfrak{R}, \leq]$ is a partially ordered set or poset. Likewise, if P denotes the set of all positive integers and $a \mid b$ means that $b = na$ for some positive integer n, then $[P, \mid]$ is a poset.

Universal bounds. In a poset P, the identical inequalities relating an element x with an element 0, for all x, and relating an element x with an element I, for all x (see Box, inequalities 148), can be satisfied by at most one element

(1) $0 \leq x$ for all x, $x \leq I$ for all x

0 and by at most one I, respectively. When they exist, 0 is called the null element and I the universal element of the poset, which is said to have universal bounds. In the poset of the subsets $X, Y, \cdots$ of a set U, for example, the empty set, represented by the symbol $\varnothing$, is the null element and U the universal element, because $\varnothing \subset X \subset U$ for any subset X of U. In the poset $[P, \mid]$, 1 is the null element because 1 is a divisor of every positive integer n (in symbols, $1/n$ for all n in P). The poset $[P, \mid]$ has no universal element.

Formal definition. A formal definition of a lattice can now be given. It is in general any abstract system L of elements $x, y, z, \cdots$ having a reflexive, transitive, and antisymmetric relation that satisfies the following lattice condition. For any two elements x and y of L there is a least element including both x and y, denoted by $x \vee y$, and a greatest element included in both x and y, denoted by $x \wedge y$. More precisely, it is required that $x \leq x \vee y$, that $y \leq x \vee y$, and that $x \leq z$ and $y \leq z$ together imply $x \vee y \leq z$. Similarly, it is required that $x \wedge y \leq x$, that $x \wedge y \leq y$, and that $w \leq x$ and $w \leq y$ together imply $w \leq x \wedge y$. Such elements $x \vee y$ and $x \wedge y$ are called the least upper bound (l.u.b.) and greatest lower bound (g.l.b.) of x and y, respectively; when they exist, they are unique.

The preceding examples of posets satisfy this lattice condition. In the case of the subsets $X, Y, \ldots$ of an aggregate U, $X \vee Y$ is the set-union (or sum $X \cup Y$) of X and Y, and $X \wedge Y$ the set of elements common to X and Y (their intersection $X \cap Y$). In logic, $p \wedge q$ is the statement "p and q"; $p \vee q$ means "p or q" (or both p and q); with real numbers, $x \vee y$ is simply the greater and $x \wedge y$ the lesser of x and y. In the example of the positive integers, $m \vee n$ is the least common multiple of m and n and $m \wedge n$ is the greatest common divisor of m and n.

Posets

Examples of lattices. Lattices of various kinds arise in all sorts of mathematical situations. Some of these have very few elements and can be conveniently described by diagrams: any graph with sloping lines defines a poset, the elements of which are the nodes of the graph (the points at which two or more lines meet), and in which $a \geq b$ means that one can go from a to b along a sequence of line segments that slope downward. Figures 5A–5D describe

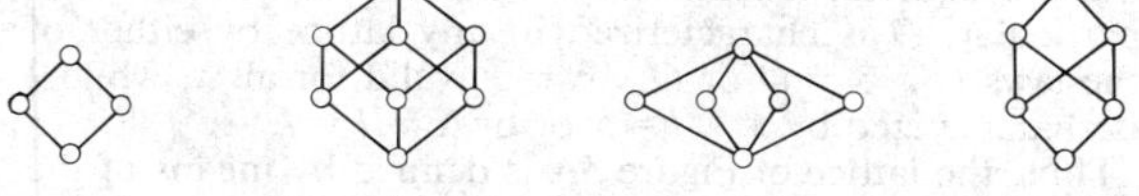

Figure 5: Diagrams of lattices and one non-lattice (see text).

lattices, of which Figure 5A represents the lattice of all subsets of a set of two elements and Figure 5B that of all subsets of a set of three elements. Figure 5C represents the lattice of all subgroups of the group G of all six symmetries of an equilateral triangle. The bottom element represents the (trivial) subgroup consisting of the group identity; the first three elements (nodes) above it the subgroups generated by the reflections in the three altitudes; the fourth the subgroup of rotations of the triangle into itself; and the top element G itself.

Figure 5D represents a poset that is not a lattice: the two elements immediately above the bottom element (the universal lower bound 0) do not have a least upper bound. All four posets of Figures 5A–5D have universal bounds: their bottom and top elements.

Figure 6 represents the partition lattice π_4 of all partitions

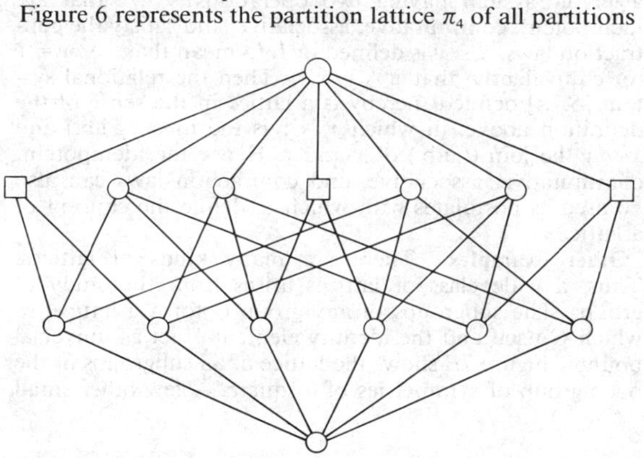

Figure 6: The partition lattice π_4 (see text).

of a set of four elements, in which by a partition of a set is meant a division of its elements into nonoverlapping subsets. In Figure 6, the square nodes represent the three partitions of the set $\{a, b, c, d\}$ into two subsets, each containing two elements, namely: $(ab)(cd)$, $(ac)(bd)$, and $(ad)(bc)$. The circles on the same level represent the four partitions (123)(4), (124)(3), (134)(2), (234)(1) into two subsets, one containing three elements and the other containing one element; and so on.

Algebraic definitions. Lattices can also be defined in terms of the algebraic properties of the two operations $\wedge$ and $\vee$ just defined, without reference to the concept of order. In a general poset P, the l.u.b. $x \vee y$ of two elements x and y (when it exists) is called the join of x and y, and the g.l.b. $x \wedge y$ (when it exists) is called their meet. The relatively colourless words "join" and "meet" are intended to suggest "union" and "intersection" but to refer only to the underlying order abstractly. In any lattice, the join and meet operations are commutative and associative, so that $x \vee y = y \vee x$, $x \wedge y = y \wedge x$, $x \vee (y \vee z) = (x \vee y) \vee z$, and also $x \wedge (y \wedge z) = (x \wedge y) \wedge z$ for all x, y, z. They are idempotent, which means that $x \vee x = x \wedge x = x$ for all x; and they satisfy the law of contraction: $x \wedge (x \vee y) = x \vee (x \wedge y) = x$ for all x, y.

The law of contraction

It is easy to verify the preceding laws in the examples described above; the essential fact is that they can also be deduced formally from the reflexive, transitive, and antisymmetric laws, considered as postulates used to define the abstract concept of a poset.

Conversely, a lattice can be defined as an algebraic system, or algebra, having two commutative, associative, idempotent, and contractive operations. This system can be designated symbolically as $[S, \wedge, \vee]$, in which S stands for the set consisting of all the elements of the lattice, and $\wedge$, $\vee$ for its two operations. The inclusion relation may be defined in terms of either lattice operation, because $x \leq y$ is equivalent either to $x \wedge y = x$ or to $x \vee y = y$. In particular, O is characterized in any lattice by either of the laws $O \wedge x = O$ or $O \vee x = x$, valid for all x; while I is characterized by $x \wedge I = x$ or by $x \vee I = I$.

Thus, the lattice of Figure 5A is defined by means of the tables for combining elements with the operations $\wedge$ and $\vee$ (see 149). From either of these tables, it can be deduced

(149)

$\wedge$	0	a	b	I
0	0	0	0	0
a	0	a	0	a
b	0	0	b	b
I	0	a	b	I

$\vee$	0	a	b	I
0	0	a	b	I
a	a	a	I	I
b	b	I	b	I
I	I	I	I	I

that $0 < a$, $b < I$, and that these are the only proper inclusion relations.

More generally, $L = [S, \wedge, \vee]$ is assumed to be any algebraic system having two operations $\vee$, $\wedge$ that are idempotent, commutative, associative, and satisfy the contraction laws. $x \leq y$ is defined in L to mean that $x \vee y = y$ (or equivalently, that $x \wedge y = x$). Then the relational system $[S, \leq]$ defined thereby is a lattice in the sense of the definition above, in which $x \wedge y$ is the meet (g.l.b.) and $x \vee y$ the join (l.u.b.) of x and y. Hence the idempotent, commutative, associative, and contraction laws can also be used as postulates with which to define the concept of a lattice.

Other examples. There are many kinds of lattices. Thus, a wide class of lattices arises from the study of groups. The subgroups of any group G form a lattice, in which G itself and the identity element 1 act as universal bounds. Figure 7E shows the lattice of all subgroups of the octic group of symmetries of a square. A few other small

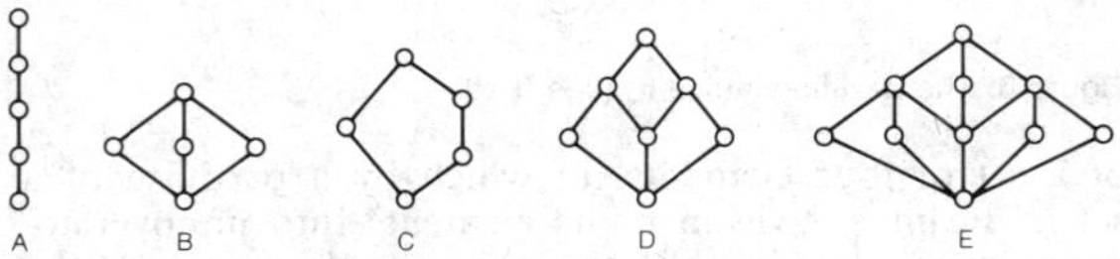

Figure 7: Lattices with special properties (see text).

lattices are depicted in Figures 7A–7D. Thus Figure 7A depicts a chain; *i.e.*, a poset in which for all x, y, either $x \leq y$ or $y \leq x$. Figure 7C depicts the smallest lattice in which not all chains from 0 to I have the same length.

Duality. The concepts of a poset and of a lattice have important duality properties. If $y \leq x$ is defined to mean that $x \geq y$ (by conversion), it is evident that the relation $\leq$ is reflexive, transitive, and antisymmetric if and only if $\geq$ is. Furthermore, if $\geq$ is replaced by $\leq$, $\vee$ and $\wedge$ are simply interchanged in the statement of the lattice condition without affecting the set of postulates as a whole. In other words, the concepts of a poset and of a lattice are self-dual under the duality between greater and less (container and the contained).

In the particular lattice $[P, |\,]$, for instance, the dualization effected by the preceding construction changes greatest common divisors (g.c.d.) into least common multiples (l.c.m.), and vice versa. More generally, it turns the diagram of any finite lattice upside-down.

Isotonicity. Lattices have many general properties. Thus, any lattice with a finite number of elements $x_1, \cdots, x_n$ has the universal bounds $x_1 \wedge \cdots \wedge x_n = 0$ and $x_1 \vee \cdots \vee x_n = I$. More important is the following isotonicity principle, valid in any lattice. This principle is: If for any elements u, u^*, v, and v^*, in a lattice L, $u \geq u^*$ and $v \geq v^*$, then $u \vee v \leq u^* \vee v^*$ and $u \wedge v \geq u^* \wedge v^*$: the lattice operations preserve order.

Power set lattices. The power set lattice $[P(U), \subset]$, defined by the inclusion relation on the power set $P(U)$ of all subsets of a set U, has important special properties not shared by lattices in general. One of these is distributivity (see 150) that holds for any three subsets X, Y, Z of U. In

(150) $$X \cap (Y \cup Z) = (X \cap Y) \cup (X \cap Z)$$
$$X \cup (Y \cap Z) = (X \cup Y) \cap (X \cup Z)$$

(151) $$\begin{cases} x \wedge (y \vee z) = (x \wedge y) \vee (x \wedge z) \\ x \vee (y \wedge z) = (x \vee y) \wedge (x \vee z) \end{cases}$$

(152) $$x \wedge x' = 0, \qquad x \vee x' = I$$

(153) $$(x \wedge y)' = x' \vee y', \qquad (x \vee y)' = x' \wedge y'$$

(154) $$(x \wedge y) \vee (y \wedge z) \vee (z \wedge x) = (x \vee y) \wedge (y \vee z) \wedge (z \vee x)$$

(155) $$x \wedge y = x, \qquad x \vee y = y$$

other words, defining a distributive lattice as a lattice in which this property holds, as expressed with the operations $\wedge$ and $\vee$ (see 151), for all x, y, z, $[P(U), \subset]$ is always a distributive lattice.

Second, every power set lattice $[P(U), \subset]$ has the universal bounds property: the empty set Ø and U itself are universal bounds (in the sense of (1)).

Finally, in the lattice $[P(U), \subset]$ each set X has a complement X', consisting of all elements of U that are not in X. Clearly, two specific properties hold with respect to the complement of a set and the operations $\wedge$ and $\vee$; these are to be expressed in more general form (see 152) in what follows. A poset P may now be defined to be complemented when: (A) it has universal bounds 0 and I satisfying (1), and (B) any x in P has a complement x' in P such that two properties hold (see 152). Summarizing the above, then, it can be said that any power set lattice $[P(U), \subset]$ is a complemented distributive lattice.

BOOLEAN ALGEBRA

Boolean polynomials. Complemented distributive lattices arise in many other contexts besides set theory. They were first studied systematically by the English logician George Boole around 1850, because of their applications to logic, and are called Boolean algebras.

One of the most important concepts of Boolean algebra is that of a Boolean polynomial, by which is meant any symbolic expression built up by repeated application of the two binary lattice operations $\wedge$, $\vee$, and the unary operation $'$, and the special symbols 0 and I. The algebraic manipulations of Boolean polynomials are governed by the laws given below: the idempotent, commutative, associative, contractive, and distributive laws, plus the universal bounds and complementation laws (see 151 and 152). From these many others can be deduced, among which de Morgan's laws (see 153), the law $(x')' = x$, and the curious identity involving three elements combined in pairs with the operations $\wedge$ and $\vee$ (see 154) are especially noteworthy. Also, the inclusion relation $x \leq y$ is equivalent to either $x \wedge y' = 0$ or $x' \vee y = I$ as well as to a pair of inequalities that do not involve 0 and I (see 155).

Laws governing manipulation of Boolean polynomials

Extensive research into the foundations of Boolean algebra has shown that the list of laws given in the preceding paragraph is highly redundant, and that various small subsets taken from this list imply the others. For example, if $[L, \vee, ']$ is an algebraic system that is assumed to have one binary operation $\vee$ and one unary operation $'$, then the following was proved by the U.S. mathematician Edward V. Huntington in 1933.

Huntington's theorem. In an algebraic system $[L, \vee, ']$ define $a \wedge b = (a' \vee b')'$. Suppose $a \vee b = b \vee a$, $a \vee (b \vee c) = (a \vee b) \vee c$, and $(a \wedge b) \vee (a \wedge b') = a$ for all elements a, b, c in L, then $[L, \vee, ']$ is a Boolean algebra.

Venn's diagram. The study of the laws of Boolean algebra, including Huntington's theorem, was motivated by the desire to reduce all of logic and set theory to a purely symbolic calculus. This study is helped by using so-called Venn diagrams, of which two are shown in Figure 8. In

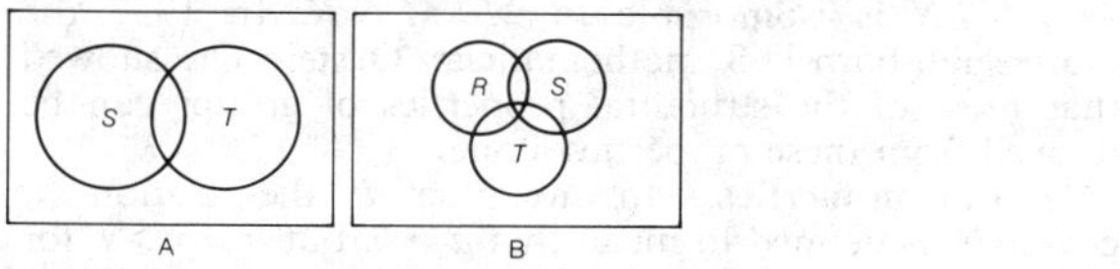

Figure 8: Venn diagrams (see text).

them, U has been taken to be a rectangle. Figure 8A depicts two discs S and T; they are to be imagined as typical subsets of U. Clearly the intersections $S \cap T$, $S \cap T'$, $S' \cap T$ and $S' \cap T'$ divide U into four nonoverlapping parts. If boundaries are neglected, the unions of these parts give precisely $2^4 = 16$ different Boolean combinations of the original sets S, T.

Likewise, John Venn, the British logician for whom the diagram was named, considered three discs R, S, and T as typical subsets of U. The intersections of these discs and their complements divide U into $8 = 2^3$ nonoverlapping regions, the unions of which give $2^8 = 256 = 2^{23} = 16^2$ different Boolean combinations of the original sets S, T.

Free Boolean algebra. These examples suggest the conjecture that, in general, there are exactly 2^{2n} different Boolean polynomials in n symbols $x_1, \cdot \cdot \cdot, x_n$, such that any given polynomial can be reduced to one, and only one, of these by repeated applications of the basic laws listed above. The truth of this conjecture is part of the following basic theorem, essentially due (in another terminology) to Boole himself.

Boole's theorem. A Boolean polynomial $(x_1, \cdot \cdot \cdot, x_n)$ can be reduced to one and only one join $\vee_s p_k$ of meets $p_k = z_1 \wedge \cdot \cdot \cdot \wedge z_n$, in which each z_i is x_i or x'_i (there being 2^n possibilities), depending on k, and S is any subset of the 2^n p_k.

The preceding form, $\vee_s p_k$, is called the disjunctive normal form of the polynomial and provides a systematic way of testing for the equivalence of two Boolean polynomials. Thus it solves the so-called word problem for Boolean algebra in an elementary way.

Isomorphism; direct product. Two general algebraic concepts, which are applicable to groups and rings (for example) as well as to posets, lattices, and Boolean algebras, are those of isomorphism and direct product. They will now be defined in the general context of posets.

An isomorphism between two posets P and Q is, by definition, a pairing of the elements of P with the elements of Q (a so-called bijection $\beta : P \leftrightarrow Q$, the symbol $\leftrightarrow$ denoting bijection) such that $x \leq y$ in P if and only if $\beta(x) \leq \beta(y)$ in Q. If P is a lattice, then the preceding condition implies that Q is also a lattice and that $\beta(x \wedge y) = \beta(x) \wedge \beta(y)$ and $\beta(x \vee y) = \beta(x) \vee \beta(y)$. If P is a Boolean algebra, then so is Q, and in addition $\beta(x') = [\beta(x)]'$: isomorphisms of posets carry complements into complements.

Again, the direct product $P \times Q$ of two posets P and Q is the set of all ordered pairs (x, y) of elements, x from P and y from Q, the inclusion relation $(x, y) \leq (x_1, y_1)$ in $P \times Q$ being defined to mean that $x \leq x_1$ in P and $y \leq y_1$ in Q. If P and Q are both lattices or both Boolean algebras, then the same is true of $P \times Q$; moreover, the combination of pairs is achieved by the operation $\wedge$ (see 156) in $P \times Q$, and dually by the operation $\vee$.

It is easy to show that the direct product of two posets is always a poset and that the formation of direct products is a commutative and associative operation on posets, relative to isomorphism: that $P \times Q \simeq Q \times P$ and $P \times (Q \times R) \simeq (P \times Q) \times R$. For instance, the bijection that pairs $(x, (y, z))$ with $((x, y), z)$ for any x in P, y in Q, and z in R is an isomorphism of $P \times (Q \times R)$ with $(P \times Q) \times R$.

It can therefore be written $P \times P = P^2$,

(156) $(x, y) \wedge (x_1, y_1) = (x \wedge x_1, y \wedge y_1)$

(157)

$\vee$	0	1
0	0	1
1	1	1

$\wedge$	0	1
0	0	0
1	0	1

a	a'
0	1
1	0

(158) $\xi(a_i) = \begin{cases} 1 & \text{if } x \geqslant a_i \\ 0 & \text{otherwise} \end{cases}$

$(P \times P) \times P = P^3$, $\cdot \cdot \cdot$, with the understanding that $P^m \times P^n = P^{m+n}$ for any positive integers m, n; *i.e.*, that the usual laws for powers hold.

Binary strings. The simplest nontrivial Boolean algebra has two elements, 0 and 1, on which its three operations act as is prescribed by certain tables (see 157). Boolean algebra has been called the algebra of 0 and 1, because every Boolean algebra can be built up by combining copies of this simple Boolean algebra, which will be designated by the symbol *2*. Basic elements

Thus, if the set U has n elements, then the power set lattice (Boolean algebra) $P(U)$ is isomorphic with $2^n = 2 \times \cdot \cdot \cdot \times 2$ (n factors). To establish the isomorphism $P(U) = 2^n$, the elements of U must be arranged in some order, as a sequence $p_1, p_2, \cdot \cdot \cdot, p_n$. Each subset A of U is then associated with an n-tuple $a = (a_1, \cdot \cdot \cdot, a_n) = \beta(A)$ of 0's and 1's, by setting $a_j = 1$ when p_j is in A and $a_j = 0$ when it is not. Dropping commas and parentheses, this associates with each A a binary string $a_1 a_2 \cdot \cdot \cdot a_n$.

Logic networks. Boolean algebra is used for designing so-called logic networks for digital computers. Such a network typically has a finite number n of input leads, each of which goes into one of two states when pulsed, which can be designated as 0 and 1. The state of the set of all n leads can therefore be described by a binary string of length n. The problem is to design a circuit that, when it is interposed between these input leads and a specified set of output leads, will put each of the latter in a specified state, 0 or 1, determined by the states of the input leads.

The problem is thus to implement electronically a given Boolean function $f: 2^n \rightarrow 2$ from the set of all binary strings of length n to the set $2 = \{0, 1\}$; but these functions constitute precisely the free Boolean algebra with n generators, namely, the functions $\delta_i: (x_1, \cdot \cdot \cdot, x_n) \rightarrow x_i$ that associate with each string its ith member. Boole showed that every function $f: 2^n \rightarrow 2$ can be represented as a Boolean polynomial in the δ_i (in disjunctive normal form).

The problem of optimal logic network design is to find the Boolean polynomial that does this most economically. Roughly, this corresponds to finding the shortest Boolean polynomial that has a given disjunctive normal form. This problem still lacks a general solution.

DISTRIBUTIVE LATTICES

Switching circuits. The three basic Boolean operations $\wedge$, $\vee$, $'$ (corresponding to "and," "or," and "not" in logic) can be realized electronically by three kinds of simple circuits, called AND-gates, OR-gates, and inverters, respectively. The first general purpose digital computers used, instead of electronic circuits, ordinary relay networks the connections of which could be open or closed. The Boolean operations of "and" and "or" are realized by putting relay networks in series and parallel, respectively. This raises the problem of constructing Boolean functions $f: 2^n \rightarrow 2$ from $\wedge$ and $\vee$ alone without using "not."

Algebraically, this amounts to determining the most general distributive lattice—*i.e.*, the lattice satisfying the distributive laws (see 151)—with n generators. This is also the set of all lattice polynomials in n symbols $\delta_1, \cdot \cdot \cdot, \delta_n$, two polynomials being considered equal when equality follows from the idempotent, commutative, associative, contractive, and distributive laws. This free distributive lattice had been considered by the German mathematician Richard Dedekind in 1900, and in 1912 the Norwegian mathematician Thoralf Albert Skolem showed that it contained precisely those Boolean functions $f: 2^n \rightarrow 2$ that were order-preserving in the following sense. The domain 2^n of the function f may be considered as itself a Boolean algebra, by defining $x \leq y$ for two binary strings $x = (x_1, \cdot \cdot \cdot, x_n)$ and $y = (y_1, \cdot \cdot \cdot, y_n)$ to mean that $x_i \leq y_i$ for all $i = 1, 2, \cdot \cdot \cdot, n$. Then f preserves order (is isotone) when $x \leq y$ implies $f(x) \leq f(y)$.

Generalization of Skolem's theorem

Finite distributive lattices. The most general finite distributive lattice may be constructed by a simple generalization of Skolem's theorem. Namely, L is assumed to be any finite distributive lattice, and A is assumed to be the set of all properly join-irreducible elements of L; that is, the set of all elements $a > 0$ in L with the property that $x \wedge y = a$ implies $x = a$ or $y = a$. The elements of a may be imagined as listed in some order, $a_1, \cdot \cdot \cdot, a_n$. Then each x in L can be associated with the subset $S(x)$ of A, consisting of exactly those elements a_i in A such that $x \geq a_i$. This is clearly order-preserving: $x \geq y$ implies $S(x) \supset S(y)$. Alternatively, each x in L can be associated with the function $\xi: A \rightarrow 2$ defined by assigning the value 1 to $\xi(a_i)$ when $a_i \leq x$, and 0 otherwise (see 158); this function is isotone.

The fundamental theorem on finite distributive lattices asserts that the converse is also true: that every isotone function $f: A \rightarrow 2$ is associated in this way with some x in L.

Some examples. Figures 9A–9D exhibit the diagrams

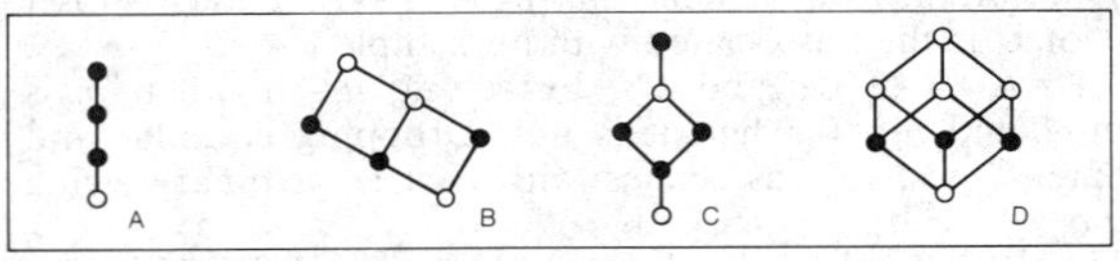

Figure 9: Some distributive lattices (see text).

of four distributive lattices, illustrating the preceding statements. The posets of join-irreducible elements, corresponding to the black circles, have the diagrams respectively.

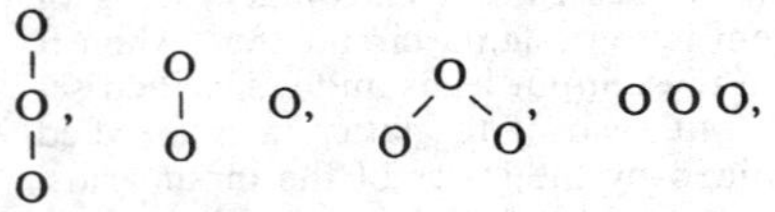

In particular, Figure 9C exhibits similarly the free distributive lattice with two generators: the poset of all isotone functions $f: 2^n \rightarrow 2$; it should be noted that it has four properly join-irreducible elements, which form a poset having the diagram of 2^2, as stated in Skolem's theorem.

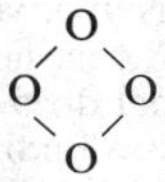

It should also be noted that this distributive lattice has length three, which means that one can ascend from the universal lower bound 0 to the universal upper bound I in four steps. This illustrates the fact that, in general, a distributive lattice of finite length n contains exactly n properly join-irreducible elements, a result that can also be verified (with $n = 3$) in the other examples of Figure 9.

MODULAR AND GEOMETRIC LATTICES

Modular lattices. Although distributive lattices (including especially Boolean algebras) are very important, they are not typical. Most lattices are not distributive and cannot be characterized so simply. The rest of this section will describe properties of nondistributive lattices.

The five-element lattice

The simplest nondistributive lattice is the five-element lattice of Figure 7B. Its elements satisfy the modular law (see 159). This is clearly implied by the distributive law $x \wedge (y \vee z) = (x \wedge y) \vee (x \wedge z)$, because $x \wedge z = z$ when $x \geq z$. It is also self-dual, in the sense of being equivalent to its dual (see above; see 160).

Modular lattices arise in many parts of algebra. Thus the subgroups of any Abelian group form a modular lattice.

(159) If $x \geq z$, then $x \wedge (y \vee z) = (x \wedge y) \vee z$.

(160) If $z \leq x$, then $z \vee (y \wedge x) = (z \vee y) \wedge x$.

More generally, the normal subgroups of any group form a modular lattice, in which, moreover, the quotient-group $M \vee N / N$ is isomorphic to $M / M \wedge N$. In 1937 the Norwegian-born U.S. mathematician Oystein Ore showed that most of the structural properties of groups can be derived from these properties alone.

Covering properties. In any poset P, the relation "a covers b" is defined to mean that $a > b$, but $a > x > b$ for no x. Graphically, "a covers b" means that a is just above b in the diagram of P.

In 1900, Dedekind proved that a lattice of finite length was modular if and only if its covering relation has the following two dual properties:

1. If b and c both cover a, then $b \vee c$ covers both b and c.
2. If a covers both b and c, then b and c both cover $b \wedge c$ (It is understood here that $b \neq c$.)

Projective geometries. If F is any field (see below *Fields*) or division ring, and if $V = V_{n+1}(F)$ is the vector space (see above *Linear and multilinear algebra*) of all vectors $x = (x_0, x_1, \cdot \cdot \cdot, x_n)$ of length $n + 1$ with coordinates x_i in F, then the subspaces of V form a modular lattice under the relation of inclusion, which is called the n-dimensional projective geometry over F, and denoted $PG(F; n)$. (See GEOMETRY.)

In any projective geometry $PG(F; n)$, the universal lower bound 0 is the trivial subspace consisting of the null vector $0 = (0, 0, \cdot \cdot \cdot, 0)$ alone. Geometrically, it is interpreted as the empty set, and the projective points are the elements that cover it. The (projective) lines are the elements that cover points, and every projective line contains at least three points.

Figure 10 exhibits the diagram of the lattice $PG(Z_2; 2)$,

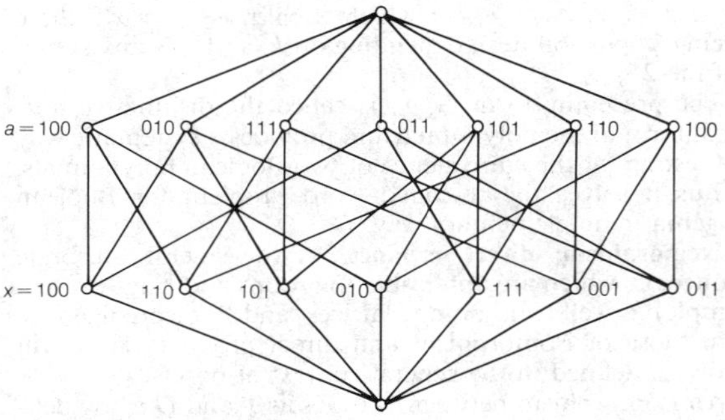

Figure 10: Poset diagram of the Fano plane.

The Fano plane

the so-called Fano plane; it has seven points and seven lines, with exactly three points on each line. Its points are the strings of three binary digits, not all 0: 001, 010, 011, 100, 101, 110, 111; its lines are the sets of points $x_1x_2x_3$ that satisfy an equation of the form $a_1x_1 + a_2x_2 + a_3x_3 \equiv 0$ (mod 2), in which $a_1a_2a_3$ is one of the strings just listed.

Geometric lattices. In any poset with universal lower bound 0, a point (or atom) is an element p that covers 0. That is, it is necessary that $p > 0$ (meaning that $p \geq 0$ but that $p \neq 0$), while $p > x > 0$ for no x. This definition is essentially the same as Euclid's: "a point is that which has no parts." A lattice of finite length is called a geometric lattice when: (1) each of its elements is a join of points, and (2) it satisfies the covering condition (:) under covering properties above. The partition lattice π_4 of Figure 6 and the Fano plane of Figure 10 are (finite) geometric lattices. More generally, any projective geometry is a (modular) geometric lattice, and the lattice of all partitions of any finite set is a geometric, which is not modular if the set contains more than three elements.

Again, if Ω is any map, then the submaps formed from Ω by obliterating boundaries forms a geometric lattice $G(\Omega)$. The number of ways in which Ω can be coloured in λ colours so that no two adjacent regions have the same colour is called the chromatic polynomial of Ω [and of $G(\Omega)$]. This can also be constructed from the Möbius function of $G(\Omega)$, a function that can be defined on any poset and that has many applications to number theory and combinatorial questions.

OTHER LATTICE-ORDERED STRUCTURES

Relation algebras. Ordering relations play an important role in many algebraic structures having operations that, unlike the meet and join operations, cannot be defined purely in terms of order. One such class of structures is defined by binary relations.

Structures defined by binary relations

By a binary relation on a set S is meant a rule ρ that tells for any two elements x and y of S whether x and y are in the given relation or not. If they satisfy the relation, $x\rho y$ is written; if they do not satisfy the relation, $x\rho' y$ is written. The set of all binary relations on S forms a Boolean algebra under the operations $\rho \wedge \sigma$, $\rho \vee \sigma$, and ρ' corresponding to the words "and," "or," and "not." [Thus, $x(\rho \wedge \sigma)y$ means that $x\rho y$ and $x\sigma y$.] In this Boolean algebra, the order relation $\rho \geq \sigma$ defined by the statement that $\rho \wedge \sigma = \sigma$ (ρ and σ is the same as σ) is clearly tantamount to saying that σ "implies" ρ (the statement that $x\rho y$ "adds nothing" to the statement that $x\sigma y$). In logic, this is written $\sigma \supset \rho$.

The algebra of binary relations on a set S involves also the operation of composition. The composite $\rho\sigma = \rho \circ \sigma$ of ρ and σ is defined by the statement:

$x(\rho\sigma)y$ means that, for some z in S, $x\rho z$ and $z\sigma y$.

For functions of a real variable—*i.e.*, when $S = R$, the real field—the definition of composite is equivalent to the usual definition of $\tau = \rho\sigma$, by $\tau(x) = \sigma(\rho(x))$. As another illustration: if the relation ρ (on the set of all people) is defined by "$x\rho y$ if and only if x is a sibling (brother or sister) of y," and σ by "$x\sigma y$ if and only if y is a son of x," then $x(\rho\sigma)y$ means that y is a nephew of x.

The operation of composition is associative: $\rho(\sigma\tau) = (\rho\sigma)\tau$ for any three binary operations on the same set S. The equality relation e (x e y means $x = y$) is an identity for composition: $e\rho = \rho e = \rho$ for all ρ. These facts are summarized in the statement that the algebra $[S^2, {}^\circ]$ defined by the set S^2 of all binary relations on S is a monoid under composition.

Like $\wedge$ and $\vee$, the operation of composition is order-preserving (isotone): if $\rho \geq \rho_1$ and $\sigma \geq \sigma_1$, then $\rho\sigma \geq \rho_1\sigma_1$. Moreover, $\rho(\sigma \vee \tau) = \rho\sigma \vee \rho\tau$ and $(\rho \vee \sigma)\tau = \rho\tau \vee \sigma\tau$, two laws that imply isotonicity. [It is, however, not in general true that $\rho(\sigma \wedge \tau) = \rho\sigma \wedge \rho\tau$ or that $(\rho \wedge \sigma)\tau = \rho\tau \wedge \sigma\tau$.] Lattices that are also monoids and in which the isotonicity relations hold are called lattice-ordered monoids; it has just been shown that the binary relations on any set S form a lattice-ordered monoid.

Vector lattices. Many other kinds of lattice-ordered monoids arise in mathematics, such as the lattice of all ideals of any ring (under the operations of set inclusion and ideal multiplication). One example is provided by the set of all continuous functions f of a real variable x, order being defined (see 161) and the monoid operation being defined as ordinary addition (see 162). Here a previous equation assumes a simpler form (see 163) because addition is commutative.

Another example is provided by the set of all real vectors (see 164), the order relation meaning that $x_j \geq y_j$ for all $j = 1, 2, 3$. In this the positive cone of all $x \geq O = (0, 0, 0)$ consists of the first octant: it is a trihedron with the positive quadrants of the coordinate planes as faces. For any fixed vector c, the set of all $x \geq c$ is obtained by translating the positive cone parallel to the vector c through a distance equal to its length (see 164).

These and other vector lattices are, by definition, (real) vector spaces that are also lattices, in which vector addition and order are related (see 163) and in which if $\lambda > 0$ is any positive scalar and $x > O$ any positive vector, $\lambda x > O$.

The preceding examples should give some idea of the enormous variety of lattices and lattice-ordered algebraic structures; they arise in every branch of mathematics.

(G.Bi.)

(161) $f \geqslant g$ means that $f(x) \geqslant g(x)$ for all x.

(162) $h = f + g$ means that $h(x) = f(x) + g(x)$ for all x.

(163) $f + (g \vee h) = (f + g) \vee (f + h)$

(164)
$$\begin{cases} x = (x_1, x_2, x_3), \qquad x \geqslant y = (y_1, y_2, y_3) \\ \sqrt{c_1^2 + c_2^2 + c_3^2} = \text{length of } c \end{cases}$$

(165)
$$\begin{cases} xu = 1(xu) = (vu(xu)) \\ \quad = ((vu)x)u = (v(ux))u = (v \cdot 1)u = v(1u) = vu = 1 \\ x = 1x = (xu)x = x(ux) = x1 \end{cases}$$

(166)
$$\begin{cases} (x + y) + z = x + (y + z) \quad \text{for all } x, y, z \\ x + y = y + x \text{ for all } x, y \end{cases}$$

Groups

Groups, in mathematics, are systems of elements with a composition satisfying certain laws (these are given below). The elements may be operations; for example, the rotations of a sphere. The symmetries of a geometrical figure are best described as a group. The ornamental wall designs of the ancient Egyptians exhibit all possible combinations of symmetries. Euclid studied the properties of the regular polygons and the five regular solids. Not until the late 18th and 19th centuries, however, were groups recognized as mathematical systems. The French mathematician Joseph-Louis Lagrange was one of the first to consider them. Another French mathematician, Augustin-Louis Cauchy, began a study of permutation groups. In studying the solution of polynomial equations, a Norwegian mathematician, Niels Henrik Abel, showed that in general the equation of fifth degree cannot be solved by radicals. Then the French mathematician Évariste Galois, using groups systematically, showed that the solution of an equation by radicals is possible only if a group associated with the equation has certain specific properties; these groups are now called solvable groups.

Early work on groups

The group concept is now recognized as one of the most fundamental in all of mathematics and in many of its applications. The German mathematician Felix Klein considered geometry to be those properties of a space left unchanged by a certain specific group of transformations. In topology geometric entities are considered equivalent if one can be transformed into another by an element of a continuous group.

DEFINITION

A group, denoted G, is a nonempty set of elements with a composition defined for any ordered pair x, y of its elements. If the composition is written as the product xy, then the following laws hold:

G1. The Associative Law: $(xy)z = x(yz)$ for all x, y, z, of G.
G2. Existence of an identity. There is an identity element 1, such that $1x = x1 = x$ for every x of G.
G3. Existence of an inverse. For every x of G there is an element x^{-1} such that $x^{-1}x = xx^{-1} = 1$, in which 1 is the identity element.

These laws are redundant. Instead of G2 and G3 it is enough to assume the existence of an identity 1 such that $1x = x$ for any x, and that for any x there is a left inverse u such that $ux = 1$. Then let v be the left inverse of u so that $vu = 1$. The desired consequences follow (see 165).

If a group G satisfies the further law:

G4. The Commutative Law. If $yx = xy$ for all x, y of G, then G is called an Abelian group.

The composition of a group may be written as addition, though this is not usually done except for Abelian groups. In this case the laws take the form:

G1. Associative Law (see 166).

G2. Existence of zero. There is a zero element 0 such that its composition with x yields x for every x of g.
G3. Existence of negative. For every x of G there is an element $-x$ such that its composition with x yields 0.
G4. Commutative Law (see 166).

Many of the important applications of groups come from the fact that groups arise naturally from one-to-one mappings (sometimes called bijections). A mapping α of a set S into a set T may be considered a rule (or function) that associates with each element x of S a unique element y of T called the image of x. This mapping may be written $y=(x)\alpha$. Of particular importance is the case in which the set T is the same as the set S. The product $\alpha\beta$ of two mappings α and β of a set S into itself is defined by the rule $(x)\alpha\beta=z$ if $(x)\alpha=y$ and $(y)\beta=z$. This definition of product automatically satisfies the associative law. For if $(x)\alpha=y$, $(y)\beta=z$, $(z)\gamma=w$, then $(x)(\alpha\beta)\gamma=(z)\gamma=w$ and $(x)\alpha(\beta\gamma)=(y)\beta\gamma=w$ so that the two mappings $(\alpha\beta)\gamma$ and $\alpha(\beta\gamma)$ are identical and so $(\alpha\beta)\gamma=\alpha(\beta\gamma)$.

Mappings

A mapping α is said to be a mapping of S onto T (rather than into T) providing that for every y of T there is at least one x of S such that $y=(x)\alpha$. Such a mapping is also called a surjection. If the mapping α also has the property that there is exactly one x of S such that $y=(x)\alpha$ for y in T, then α is called a one-to-one mapping or a one-to-one correspondence, or a bijection.

The one-to-one mappings of a set S onto itself form a group. The identity mapping 1 is naturally defined by the rule $(x)1=x$ for every x of S. And if α is a one-to-one mapping of S onto itself, then an inverse mapping α^{-1} is defined by saying that if $(x)\alpha=y$ then $(y)\alpha^{-1}=x$. For because α is a one-to-one mapping, then given y in S there is exactly one x in S with $(x)\alpha=y$ so that y determines x uniquely. Also $(x)\alpha\alpha^{-1}=x$ for every x and $(y)\alpha^{-1}\alpha=y$ for every y, from which it follows that $\alpha\alpha^{-1}=1$, $\alpha^{-1}\alpha=1$.

A nonempty set H of elements with a composition rule xy satisfying the associative law $(xy)z=x(yz)$ is called a semigroup. As has been shown above, the mappings of a set S into itself form a semigroup. In case S consists of the points of a plane, one mapping is to map all the points onto the points of a single line; for example, by mapping a point onto the foot of the perpendicular to the line through the point. Such a mapping does not have an inverse because a point not on the line is not the image of any point. Semigroups are considerably more general than groups and, by the same token, have fewer properties common to all of them.

Semi-groups

A group G is said to be finite or infinite if the number of distinct elements in it is respectively finite or infinite. Many properties can be proved for finite groups but are false for infinite groups. The number of distinct elements in a group G is called the order of G.

When two groups can be considered as essentially the same group under certain conditions, these conditions require a precise definition as well as a name. The groups are said to be isomorphic. The formal definition is that: Two groups G_1 and G_2 are said to be isomorphic if there is a one-to-one correspondence α between the elements of G_1 and the elements of G_2, such that if $(x_1)\alpha=x_2$ and $(y_1)\alpha=y_2$, then $(x_1y_1)\alpha=x_2y_2$, in which x_1, y_1 are arbitrary elements of G_1, and x_2, y_2 are their images in G_2. From this definition it is easy to see that the identities of the two groups correspond and that if elements correspond, then also their inverses correspond. In particular, any two groups of order 2 are isomorphic because such a group consists of the identity and one further element the square of which must be the identity. A less obvious example of isomorphism is that between the multiplicative group of positive real numbers and the additive group of all real numbers, the logarithmic function log x has the property $\log(xy)=\log x+\log y$, and this gives the isomorphism of these two groups.

Iso-morphic groups

(167) $$\alpha=\begin{pmatrix}1, 2, \cdots, n\\ a_1, a_2, \cdots, a_n\end{pmatrix}$$

(168) $$\begin{cases}\alpha_1=\begin{pmatrix}1,2,3\\1,2,3\end{pmatrix} & \alpha_4=\begin{pmatrix}1,2,3\\1,3,2\end{pmatrix}\\ \alpha_2=\begin{pmatrix}1,2,3\\2,3,1\end{pmatrix} & \alpha_5=\begin{pmatrix}1,2,3\\3,2,1\end{pmatrix}\\ \alpha_3=\begin{pmatrix}1,2,3\\3,1,2\end{pmatrix} & \alpha_6=\begin{pmatrix}1,2,3\\2,1,3\end{pmatrix}\end{cases}$$

(169) $$\alpha=\begin{pmatrix}1,2,3,4,5,6,7,8\\2,3,4,1,6,7,8,5\end{pmatrix}$$

(170) $$\beta=\begin{pmatrix}1,2,3,4,5,6,7,8\\1,4,8,5,2,3,7,6\end{pmatrix}$$

(171) $$\gamma=\begin{pmatrix}1,2,3,4,5,6,7,8\\4,3,2,1,8,7,6,5\end{pmatrix}$$

(172) $$\begin{cases}\alpha=\begin{pmatrix}1,2,3,4,5,6\\1,3,4,5,2,6\end{pmatrix}\\ \beta=\begin{pmatrix}1,2,3,4,5,6\\5,1,4,6,2,3\end{pmatrix}\\ \gamma=\begin{pmatrix}1,2,3,4,5,6\\1,4,3,2,5,6\end{pmatrix}\end{cases}$$

(173) $$(x, y)\alpha=(ax+by+e, cx+dy+f)$$

(174) $$(x, y)\beta=(ax+by, cx+dy), \qquad ad-bc\neq 0$$

(175) $$(x, y)\gamma=((\cos\theta)x+(\sin\theta)y, (-\sin\theta)x+(\cos\theta)y)$$

(176) $$(xy)(zw)=x(y(zw))=x((yz)w)=(x(yz))w=((xy)z)w$$

(177) $$\begin{cases}(x_1x_2\cdots x_n)^{-1}=x_n^{-1}\cdots x_2^{-1}x_1^{-1}\\ x_1x_2\cdots x_nx_n^{-1}\cdots x_2^{-1}x_1^{-1}=0\end{cases}$$

EXAMPLES OF GROUPS

A permutation of a set S is a one-to-one mapping of the elements of S onto themselves. If S consists of the integers $1, 2, \cdots, n$, a permutation α may be written in two rows with a_i below the integer i (see 167) in which this is interpreted to mean that $(i)\alpha=a_i$ for $i=1, 2, \cdots, n$. As has been observed, the permutations of a set form a group. If S is the set 1, 2, 3, there are 3! (=6) permutations (see 168). Here, for example, the product $\alpha_2\alpha_4=\alpha_5$ because for $i=1, 2, 3$ $((i)\alpha_2)\alpha_4=(i)\alpha_5$ (see 168).

Symmetries of a cube. A rotation taking a cube into itself is fully described by the permutation that this yields on the 8 vertices. Here a rotation of 90° about an axis through the midpoints of the top and bottom faces is given by a specific permutation (see 169). A rotation about the axis through the vertex 1 and the opposite vertex 7 is given by a specific permutation that holds the integer 7 fixed (see 170). Combinations of α and β give a total of

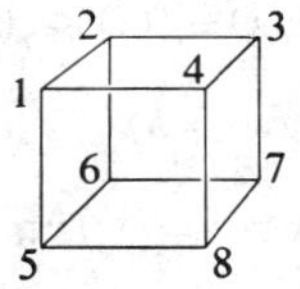

24 rotations (including, of course, the identity rotation). Apart from these rotations that can be achieved by motions in three-dimensional space, there is also a mirror image reflection about a plane through the midpoints of the edges 14, 23, 67, 58 expressed as a permutation of integers that inverts the order of the first four of eight integers and the last four, similarly (see 171). Combining this reflection with the 24 rotations gives the full group of 48 symmetries of the cube.

Symmetries of the regular octahedron. The midpoints of the faces of the cube may be taken as the vertices of the

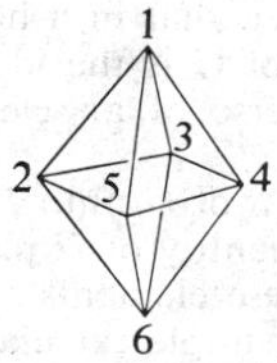

regular octahedron. For this reason, it is intuitively clear that the symmetry group of the octahedron is isomorphic to that of the cube. The corresponding symmetries as they affect the vertices of the octahedron are described by three permutations (see 172).

Collineations of the Euclidean plane. If the points of the plane are given by coordinates (x, y) in which x, y are real numbers, the transformations that transform pairs into pairs of linear combinations (see 173) with coefficients a, b, c, d, e, in which $ad - bc$ is not equal to zero, form a group consisting of the one-to-one mappings of the points onto themselves with the property of taking straight lines into straight lines, and this is called the collineation group. The subsystem of collineations β fixing the origin (0, 0) is also a group (see 174). A subsystem of this consists of rotations γ about the origin. The rotation γ corresponding to an angle θ is also expressible as a transformation on pairs, in which coefficients in the linear combinations after transformation depend on θ (see 175).

ELEMENTARY GROUP STRUCTURE

In a group G the common value of $(xy)z = x(yz)$ can be written xyz. The same principle applies to four factors (see 176), and the common value of these products may be written $xyzw$. It is not difficult to prove that any bracketing of $x_1x_2 \cdot \cdot \cdot x_n$ without changing the order of the factors gives the same product. This fact is known as the generalized associative law. A consequence of it is that the inverse of a product is the corresponding product of inverses taken in reverse order (see 177). Similarly, if both the associative and commutative laws hold, a product $x_1x_2 \ldots x_n$ has the same value as the product of any rearrangement of these factors.

The generalized associative law

A subset H of the elements of a group G that is itself a group under the composition for G is called a subgroup. In many important cases the elements of a group that have certain properties form a subgroup. For example, the one-to-one mappings of the points of the Euclidean plane onto themselves form a group G. Those mappings that take straight lines into straight lines, the group of collineations, form a subgroup G_1 of G. The group G_1 in turn has a subgroup G_2, called the orthogonal group, which consists of the one-to-one mappings that leave distances unchanged.

If $a_1, a_2, \cdot \cdot \cdot, a_r$ are elements of a group G, then all expressions $x_1x_2 \cdot \cdot \cdot x_n$ in which every value of x is one of the a_i or an inverse a_i^{-1} form a subgroup H that is said to be generated by $a_1, a_2, \cdot \cdot \cdot, a_r$, and this is written $H = \langle a_1, a_2, \cdot \cdot \cdot, a_r \rangle$. If H is generated by a single element, $H = \langle a_1 \rangle$, H is called a cyclic group. The product of n factors $a_1a_1 \cdot \cdot \cdot a_1$ can be written $a_1{}^n$ and similarly $a_1{}^{-1}, \cdot \cdot \cdot, a_1{}^{-1} = a_1{}^{-n}$. Then the elements of H are of the form $a_1{}^m$ with m any integer, positive or negative, and the product rule is $a_1{}^r a_1{}^s = a_1{}^{r+s}$. It may happen that all the powers of a_1 are different, in which case H is essentially the additive group of the exponents that are the integers. If two different powers $a_1{}^r$ and $a_1{}^s$ represent the same element, then $a_1{}^{r-s} = 1$. In this case H is finite and there is a positive integer n such that $1, a_1, \cdot \cdot \cdot, a_1{}^{n-1}$ are different and $a_1{}^n = 1$. In this case n is the order of H, and $a_1{}^r = a_1{}^s$ if and only if $r - s$ is some integral multiple of n.

SUBGROUPS

It is not difficult to show that a group G with no subgroup except itself and the identity subgroup must be a finite cyclic group the order of which is a prime number. This describes these groups completely. For a more general group the nature of its subgroups and their interrelations are important in describing the group and its structure.

If H is assumed to be a subgroup of a group G and x some fixed element of G, the set of elements of the form hx with h belonging to H is called a left coset of H and is written Hx. Similarly, the set of elements xh is called a right coset and is written xH. It is easily seen that a left coset Hx contains the same number of elements as the subgroup H because the element hx of Hx can be matched with the element h of H. Similarly a right coset xH has the same number of elements as H. If h_1 and h_2 are any elements of H, and if $x_1 = h_1x$ and $x_2 = xh_2$, then it is easily shown that Hx and Hx_1 are the same set of elements, and also xH and x_2H are the same set of elements. From this it readily follows that any two left (right) cosets of H are identical or disjoint. If $H1 = H$, the subgroup itself and $Hx_2, \cdot \cdot \cdot, Hx_n$ are all the distinct left cosets of H in G, this fact is represented symbolically by $G = H + Hx_2 + \cdot \cdot \cdot + Hx_n$. The plus sign has no arithmetical significance here and the expression means that G is the union of the disjoint cosets. For this reason some writers use a different notation. The number of distinct cosets of H in G is called the index of H in G and is written $[G{:}H]$. The inverses of the elements hx are the elements $x^{-1}h^{-1}$ so that the inverses of the elements in a left coset Hx are precisely the elements of the right coset $x^{-1}H$, because as h runs over all elements of H so also does h^{-1}. Thus even if H is infinite there is a one-to-one correspondence between right and left cosets, and the index $[G{:}H]$ is the same for right cosets as it is for left cosets. If G is a finite group and the subgroup H is taken to be the identity, then each coset consists of a single element so that the index $[G{:}1]$ is the order of G; that is, the number of elements in G. A simple but very important consequence of the fact that distinct cosets of a subgroup are disjoint and have the same number of elements is the theorem of Lagrange. It states that the order of a finite group is the product of the order of a subgroup and the index of the subgroup.

The theorem of Lagrange

The theorem of Lagrange is not true for semigroups, illustrating the sharp differences in the theories of groups and semigroups. For a given semigroup S of order n, it is possible to take one additional element u and define $u^2 = u$, $xu = ux = u$ for every x of S, to obtain a semigroup of order $n + 1$ containing S.

From the theorem of Lagrange, the order of a subgroup H of a finite group G divides the order of G. In particular, if the order of G is a prime number p, then G has no subgroups except itself and the identity. As observed above, G must be a cyclic group. The converse of the theorem of Lagrange is false. If G is a finite group of order n and if m is a divisor of n, there may not be a subgroup of G of order m. As a simple example of this, there is a group of order 12 that does not have a subgroup of order 6.

A partial converse to the theorem of Lagrange was proved by the Norwegian mathematician Ludwig Sylow in 1872. In order to describe this theorem fully it is necessary to introduce the concept of conjugate subgroups. If H is a subgroup of the group G and if x is a fixed element of G, then the elements $x^{-1}hx$ in which h ranges over the elements of H form a subgroup that is designated as $x^{-1}Hx$. It is called the conjugate of H by x. There are three main parts to the Sylow theorem. The first part asserts that if p^r is the highest power of the prime p dividing the order of a finite group G, then there is a subgroup P of order p^r, called a Sylow p-subgroup, and that if P_1 is another Sylow p-subgroup, then for some x of G, $P_1 = x^{-1}Px$. Second, the number of distinct groups of order p^r in G is of the form $1 + kp$ for some integers k and is a divisor of the order of G. A third part of Sylow's theorem says that if p^r is the highest power of the prime p dividing the order of G, then there are subgroups of order $p, p^2, \cdot \cdot \cdot, p^{r-1}$, and each subgroup of order p^i is contained in at least one subgroup of order p^{i+1} for $i = 1, 2, \cdot \cdot \cdot, r - 1$. These Sylow theorems give a great deal of valuable information on the existence of subgroups of prime power order and their interrelations. For example, if G is of order 12, then it has 1 or 4 subgroups of order 3 and has 1 or 3 subgroups of order 4. Also G has subgroups of order 2, each of which is contained in at least one subgroup of order 4. These facts are not independent. It is not possible for a group G of order 12 to have 3 subgroups of order 4 and also 4 subgroups of order 3.

The mapping $(h)\alpha = x^{-1}hx$ from the subgroup H onto the subgroup $x^{-1}Hx$ is an isomorphism because products are preserved (see 178) and also inverses are preserved (see 179). In other words, one of the consequences of the Sylow theorems is that any two Sylow p-subgroups are isomorphic.

(178) $(x^{-1}h_1x)(x^{-1}h_2x) = x^{-1}h_1h_2x$

(179) $(x^{-1}h_1x)^{-1} = x^{-1}h_1^{-1}x$

Of particular importance are those subgroups H of a group G that are conjugate only to themselves; that is, $H = x^{-1}Hx$ for every x of G. This is so important that it is given a special name. A subgroup H of a group G is called a normal subgroup if for every x of G, $H = x^{-1}Hx$. Other names have been used for this property. Normal subgroups have also been called invariant subgroups or self-conjugate subgroups. If the right coset xH contains exactly the same elements as the left coset Hx, then from the equality of the sets $xH = Hx$ it follows that $H = x^{-1}(xH) = x^{-1}Hx$. Conversely, if $H = x^{-1}Hx$, then also $xH = Hx$. Thus H is a normal subgroup of a group G if and only if every right coset xH is also a left coset Hx.

HOMOMORPHISMS; FACTOR GROUPS

It is often possible to map a group G onto a smaller group H, mapping several elements of G onto the same element of H, and to do this so that the product rules are preserved. Such a mapping is called a homomorphism. For example, the real numbers with zero excluded form a group M under multiplication, and mapping every positive number onto $+1$ and every negative number onto -1 gives a homomorphism of M onto the multiplicative group H of the two numbers $+1$ and -1.

A formal definition is: A mapping β of the elements of a group G onto the elements of a group H is called a homomorphism if $(xy)\beta = (x)\beta\,(y)\beta$ for any x, y of G. It should be noted that in this definition, if it should happen that the mapping β is one-to-one, then β is an isomorphism. Thus an isomorphism may be regarded as a special case of a homomorphism.

(180) $\begin{cases} (t_1)\beta = 1, \qquad (t_2)\beta = 1 \\ (t_1t_2)\beta = (t_1)\beta(t_2)\beta = 1 \cdot 1 = 1 \\ (t_1^{-1})\beta = ((t_1)\beta)^{-1} = (1)^{-1} = 1 \end{cases}$

(181) $(x^{-1}tx)\beta = ((x)\beta)^{-1} \cdot 1 \cdot (x)\beta = 1$

(182) $(tx)\beta = (t)\beta(x)\beta = 1 \cdot (x)\beta = (x)\beta$

(183) $G = G_0 \supset G_1 \supset G_2 \cdots G_{r-1} \supset G_r = \{1\}$

(184) $w = b_1v + \cdots + b_m$ with $b_1, \cdots, b_m$

(185) $\begin{cases} (w_1 + w_2)\alpha = (w_1)\alpha + (w_2)\alpha \\ (w_1w_2)\alpha = (w_1)\alpha(w_2)\alpha \end{cases}$

(186) $(x_1, x_2)(y_1, y_2) = (x_1y_1, x_2y_2)$

(187) $(x_1, 1)(1, x_2) = (x_1, y_2) \in G_1 \times G_2$

(188) $(x_1, x_2, \cdots, x_n)(y_1, y_2, \cdots, y_n)$
$= (x_1y_1, x_2y_2, \cdots, x_ny_n)$

(189) $(x_1, x_2, \cdots, x_i, \cdots)(y_1, y_2, \cdots, y_i, \cdots)$
$= (x_1y_1, x_2y_2, \cdots, x_iy_i, \cdots)$

It can be demonstrated that in a homomorphism β the image of the identity of G is the identity of H and that the image of the inverse of an element is the inverse of the image.

In a homomorphism β of G onto H the set of elements t whose image is the identity of H plays a special role. In particular (see 180) these elements t form a subgroup T. Also for any x of G a simple calculation (see 181) shows that $x^{-1}tx$ is in T, and so $x^{-1}Tx = T$ is a normal subgroup of G. T is called the kernel of the homomorphism. As a result of a calculation (see 182) it is seen that elements in the same coset of T in G have the same image in H, and conversely it is true that elements of G with the same image in H are in the same coset of T in G. As T is a normal subgroup of G, $xT = Tx$. Consequently, considered as sets of elements in G, $TxTy = T(Tx)y = TTxy = Txy$, so that the product of two cosets of T is a definite single coset. This property is not true of subgroups in general. If W is a subgroup of G, then usually the set of elements $WxWy$ make up a number of cosets of W.

If T is a normal subgroup of G, and if $G = T + Tx_2 + \cdots + Tx_n$, the cosets Tx_i may be taken as elements of a new system H. Here if x_ix_j belongs to Tx_k, then it is true that $Tx_iTx_j = Tx_k$, considered as sets of elements of G. This new system H is a group, and H is called the factor group of G with respect to T, and this is written $H = G/T$. If the coset Tx_i is the element h_i of H, there is a homomorphism β of G onto H with T as kernel, and $(tx_i)\beta = h_i$. Thus, given a homomorphism β of G onto a group H, the kernel T of the homomorphism is a normal subgroup of G, and conversely any normal subgroup T of G is the kernel of the homomorphism of G onto the factor group G/T. In this way homomorphisms, normal subgroups, and factor groups go hand in hand.

As an example of a homomorphism, the group G of the 48 symmetries of the cube may be considered. Coordinate axes x, y, z are taken joining the midpoints of opposite faces. Then every symmetry of the cube determines a permutation of x, y, z and every one of the six permutations arises, giving a homomorphic image H of order 6. The kernel T of the homomorphism of G onto H is generated by the reflections in the three coordinate planes. Here T is of order 8 and in terms of coordinates consists of transformations $(x, y, z) \rightarrow (\pm x, \pm y, \pm z)$, in which all 8 combinations of the $\pm$ signs arise.

A simple group G is a group that has no proper normal subgroup ("proper" meaning "different from itself or the identity"). The finite cyclic groups of prime order have no proper subgroups and thus are simple groups. There are many other simple groups, the smallest being of order 60. There have been many investigations on simple groups; some of the results will be discussed later.

The notation $G \supset H$ is used to denote that G contains H as a subgroup. A normal chain for a group G is a sequence (see 183) in which each G_i is a normal subgroup of G_{i-1}. If it is not possible to insert a group T between G_{i-1} and G_i so that T is normal in G_{i-1} for any $i = 1, \cdots, r$, then the chain is said to be a maximal normal chain. In a maximal normal chain every factor group G_{i-1}/G_i, $i = 1, 2, \cdots, r$ is a simple group. A celebrated theorem of Jordan–Hölder states that if a group G has two (or more) maximal normal chains, then the chains have the same number of terms, and the simple factor groups G_{j-1}^*/G_j^* in a second chain are isomorphic in some order to the simple factor groups G_{i-1}/G_i of the first. This may be considered an analogue of the fundamental theorem of arithmetic, which asserts that the factorization of a positive integer as a product of primes is unique apart from the order of the factors.

The Jordan–Hölder theorem

A field is a system of elements with both the operations of addition and multiplication such that addition is an Abelian group and multiplication of elements (excluding zero) is an Abelian group. Also the distributive law $(x + y)z = xz + yz$ holds. Of particular interest are fields of numbers, such as $\mathfrak{C}$, the field of all complex numbers. The rational numbers form a field usually designated as Q. The numbers $a + b\sqrt{2}$ in which a and b are rational, however, also form a field. If $f(x)$ is a polynomial of degree n with coefficients from the rational field Q, then

$f(x)$ has n roots $u_1, u_2, \cdots, u_n$; that is, $f(u_i) = 0$, $i = 1, 2, \cdots, n$, which are numbers in the field $\mathfrak{C}$.

Then with $f(x)$ is associated a field K, in which $K = Q(u_1, \cdots, u_n)$ consists of all numbers obtainable from Q and $u_1, u_2, \cdots, u_n$ by adding, subtracting, multiplying, and dividing. It can be shown that there is one irrational number v and an exponent m such that $v^m = a_1 v^{m-1} + \cdots + a_m$ with $a_1, \cdots, a_m$ rational and such that any number w of K has a unique form (see 184) with rational numbers as coefficients of powers of v. Then it is possible to associate with K, and by implication with $f(x)$, a number of mappings $w \rightarrow (w)a$ of K onto itself such that sums map into sums and similarly for products (see 185). These mappings form a group G the order of which turns out to be exactly the number m defined above. G is called the group of the field K or respectively of the polynomial $f(x)$. Galois's great contribution to group theory and to the solution of equations consisted in relating this group G to the matter of the possibility of solving for the roots of $f(x)$ by radicals. In a normal chain for G, $G = G_0 > G_1 > \cdots > G_r = 1$ if every factor group G_{i-1}/G_i is a group of some prime order, then $f(x)$ may be solved by radicals, but not otherwise. For this reason such a group is called a solvable group. For an equation of fifth degree G will in general be of order 120 and will have a normal subgroup of order 60, a simple group. In this situation Abel showed that the equation could not be solved by radicals.

DIRECT PRODUCTS; ABELIAN GROUPS

If any two groups G_1 and G_2 are considered, the ordered pairs (x_1, x_2) with x_1 from G_1 and x_2 from G_2 form a group according to the rule that defines products of pairs (see 186). This group is called the direct product of G_1 and G_2 and is written $G_1 \times G_2$. It is easy to see that $G_1 \times G_2$ and $G_2 \times G_1$ are isomorphic. The ordered pairs $(x_1, 1)$ form a subgroup of $G_1 \times G_2$ isomorphic to G_1 and the ordered pairs $(1, x_2)$ a subgroup isomorphic to G_2, so that in this natural way G_1 and G_2 may be considered as subgroups of $G_1 \times G_2$, and because of a simple relation (see 187) the direct product is generated by G_1 and G_2. In the same way, for any finite integer n, given n groups $G_1, G_2, \cdots, G_n$ the finite sequences $(x_1, x_2, \cdots, x_n)$ with x_i from G_i, $i = 1, 2, \cdots, n$, and the product rule (see 188) form the direct product $G_1 \times G_2 \times \cdots \times G_n$ that contains the G_i as subgroups and is generated by them. If there are infinitely many G_i's, it is still possible to define a group by the rule that is suggested by the finite case (see 189) and the G_i are subgroups of this group G, called the Cartesian product of the G_i. G, however, is no longer generated by the G_i. The subgroup of G generated by the G_i consists of those sequences $(x_1, x_2, \cdots, x_i, \cdots)$ that are the identity in all but a finite number of places, and it is this subgroup that is called the direct product of the G_i. If $G_i = \langle a_i \rangle$ with 2^ith power of a_i equal to 1, $i = 1, 2, \cdots$, then the direct product of the G_i contains only elements of finite order, but the element $a = (a_1, a_2, \cdots, a_i, \cdots)$ is of infinite order in the Cartesian product.

It is easy to see that any relation that holds identically in all groups $G_1, G_2, \cdots$ also holds identically in their direct (or Cartesian) product. In particular, if each of $G_1, G_2, \cdots, G_i, \cdots$ is Abelian and satisfies the identity $yx = xy$, then it is also true that the direct (or Cartesian) product of the G_i is also Abelian.

A fundamental theorem on Abelian groups asserts that a finitely generated Abelian group $G = \langle x_1, \cdots, x_n \rangle$ is the direct product $G = C_1 \times C_2 \times \cdots \times C_m$ of cyclic groups $C_i = \langle c_i \rangle$ in which $m \leq n$. This representation is not unique, because, for example, the cyclic group of order 6 is the direct product of cyclic groups of orders 2 and 3. If the cyclic groups C_i are restricted to be either of infinite order or of finite prime power order p^r, however, then the representation $G = C_1 \times C_2 \times \cdots \times C^m$ is unique apart from the order of the factors. In particular, this result gives a precise description of all finite Abelian groups. This is not to say, however, that all questions of interest are settled with respect to finite Abelian groups.

Infinite Abelian groups

The description of infinite Abelian groups is far from complete. Every subgroup of an Abelian group is normal, but even in an Abelian group the knowledge of a normal subgroup and the factor group does not determine the group. As a very simple example of this, an Abelian group of order p^2 (in which p is a prime) has a normal subgroup of order p and a factor group of order p, but the group may be either the cyclic group of order p^2 or the direct product of two cyclic groups of order p. Infinite Abelian groups are usually written with the group operation as addition and terms are changed accordingly, so that the term direct product is replaced by direct sum.

In an infinite Abelian group G the elements of finite order form a subgroup T that is called the torsion subgroup. Here the factor group G/T contains no elements of finite order except the zero element, and such a group is said to be torsion free. In general it is not possible to express G as the direct sum of the torsion subgroup and a torsion-free subgroup, but most study has been devoted either to torsion groups or torsion-free groups.

An Abelian group D (in additive notation) is said to be divisible if for any y of D and any integer n there is an x of D with $y = nx$. Up to isomorphism there are two basic kinds of divisible groups, first the additive group R^+ of the rational numbers, and $Z(p_\infty)$ the multiplicative group of p^nth roots of 1, in which p is a fixed prime and n ranges over all positive integers. A divisible group D is a direct summand of any Abelian group G containing it, and D is in turn a direct sum of groups each of which is isomorphic to R^+ or some $Z(p_\infty)$.

A primary Abelian group P is a group in which every element has order some power of a fixed prime p. Every torsion group G is the direct sum of its primary subgroups, and this effectively reduces the study of torsion groups to the study of primary groups. Primary groups with at most a countable number of elements have been completely described in terms of certain numerical invariants, but this approach is inadequate for primary groups with more than a countable number of elements. Much less is known on the general theory of torsion-free groups.

AUTOMORPHISMS OF GROUPS; SEMI-DIRECT PRODUCTS

An automorphism a of a group G is a one-to-one mapping of the elements of G onto themselves such that $(g_1 g_2)a = (g_1)a\,(g_2)a$ for any g_1, g_2 of G. This is to say that a is an isomorphism of G with itself. As with any set, the one-to-one mappings form a group, and because the product of two automorphisms is again an automorphism, and the inverse of an automorphism is an automorphism, the automorphisms of G themselves form a group $A(G)$. For a fixed element x of G, the mapping $g \rightarrow x^{-1}gx$ for all g of G is an automorphism called an inner automorphism, which is designated as a_x. It is easy to check that $a_x a_y = a_{xy}$ and that $(a_x)^{-1}$ is the inner automorphism associated with x^{-1}. Here $a_x = 1$ if, and only if, $x^{-1}gx = g$ or $gx = xg$ for every g of G. The elements with this property of commuting with every element of G themselves form a subgroup called the centre $Z(G)$ of G. Clearly $Z(G)$ is an Abelian group and is normal in G. The inner automorphisms form a group $I(G)$ that is isomorphic to $G/Z(G)$. $I(G)$ is a normal subgroup of $A(G)$, and the factor group $A(G)/I(G)$ is called the group of outer automorphisms of G. If G is Abelian, then $Z(G) = G$ and $I(G) = 1$, so that all automorphisms of an Abelian group are outer automorphisms.

(190) $$(h_1k_1)(h_2k_2) = h_1h_2(h_2^{-1}k_1h_2)k_2 = h_1h_2k_1^{h_2}k_2$$

(191) $$(h_1h_2)^{-1}k(h_1h_2) = h_2^{-1}(h_1^{-1}kh_1)h_2$$

(192) $$(h_1k_1)(h_2k_2) = (h_1h_2)(k_1k_2)$$

(193) $$(h_1k_1)(h_2k_2) = (h_1k_2)(k_1^{h_2}k_2)$$

(194) $$H = \langle h \rangle, \qquad K = \langle k \rangle, \qquad h^4 = 1, \qquad k^3 = 1$$

(195) $$h^4 = 1, \qquad k^3 = 1, \qquad h^{-1}kh = k^{-1}$$

(196) $$G = H + Hx_2 + \cdots + Hx_i + \cdots + Hx_n$$

If K is a normal subgroup of a group G, then for any x belonging to G, $x^{-1}Kx=K$, and the mapping $k\rightarrow x^{-1}kx$ for k in K is an automorphism of K. It may happen that in $G=K+x_2K+\cdot\cdot\cdot+x_nK$, it is possible to choose the coset representatives $1, x_2, \cdot\cdot\cdot, x_n$ so that they form a subgroup H. In this case every element h of H is associated with an automorphism $k\rightarrow h^{-1}kh$ of K, and it is convenient to use an exponential notation, writing $h^{-1}kh=k^h$. Then every element x of G has a unique expression in the form $x=hk$ with h from H and k from K. An identity (see 190) gives the product rule for G in terms of the product rule in H, the product rule in K, and the automorphisms of K associated with elements of H. The only requirement on the automorphisms comes from the identity (see 191), which in exponential notation takes a familiar form. This means that the group H is mapped homomorphically onto a group of automorphisms of K. If the automorphism $k\rightarrow k^h$ is always the identity automorphism; *i.e.*, $k^h=k$ in every case, then the multiplication rule takes a form (see 192) so that G is the direct product $H\times K$. In general the product rule (see 193), a slight modification of those considered, and subject to the exponential condition given above, determines a group G known as the semi-direct product of K by H, in which K is a normal subgroup of G, and H is isomorphic to the factor group G/K. This is a useful rule that gives the construction for many groups. An easy example is that in which the fourth power of h and the third power of k are 1 (see 194) and h and h^3 correspond to the automorphism $k\rightarrow k^{-1}$ while 1 and h^2 correspond to the automorphism $k\rightarrow k$. Here $G=HK$ is of order 12 and is fully determined by three particular relations (see 195).

PERMUTATION GROUPS

If G is a permutation group on a set $S=\{1, 2, \cdot\cdot\cdot, n\}$, then G is said to be transitive on S if for every i and j of S there is a permutation x of G for which $(i)x=j$. It is easy to see that if G is transitive, those permutations h that fix 1—*i.e.*, $(1)h=1$—form a subgroup H and that G is analyzed as a sum of terms of the type Hx_i (see 196), in which x_i is a permutation such that $(1)x_i=i$. Thus, in a transitive group G on symbols $1, 2, \cdot\cdot\cdot, n$, each symbol corresponds to a coset of a subgroup. Conversely, given a group G and a subgroup H, in which $G=H+Hx_2+\cdot\cdot\cdot+Hx_n$, there is a mapping of the elements of H onto permutations of $1, 2, \cdot\cdot\cdot, n$ corresponding to the cosets. In general this mapping is a homomorphism and its kernel K is the largest normal subgroup of G contained in H.

If H is the identity subgroup, then each coset consists of a single element and for each element x of G there is a permutation a_x such that $(y)a_x=yx$ for y belonging to G. The correspondence between x and a_x is easily seen to be an isomorphism so that every G is isomorphic to a permutation group of its own elements. Thus every group may be considered to be a permutation group.

Define the polynomial $\Delta(x_1, \cdot\cdot\cdot, x_n)$ in terms of products (see 197), this being the product of all x_i-x_j with i less than j. Every permutation of $x_1, \cdot\cdot\cdot, x_n$ replaces Δ by Δ or $-\Delta$, and the permutation that interchanges x_1 and x_2 and fixes the rest takes Δ into $-\Delta$. Those permutations that take Δ into Δ form a group A_n, called the alternating group. The group of all $n!$ permutations on $x_1, \ldots, x_n$ is called the symmetric group S_n. Here the group A_n consists of half the elements of S_n and is of order $n!/2$.

The permutations that leave an array invariant will form a group. The array of seven triples has the property that every pair of elements occurs in exactly one triple. It can be considered as the set of lines in a finite plane (see 198). Four permutations leave the array invariant (see 199), and they are symbolized by x, y, z, and w.

Because the group G is transitive on $1, \cdot\cdot\cdot, 7$, the subgroup H is of index 7, $[G{:}H]=7$. The subgroup H containing y and z is transitive on $2, \cdot\cdot\cdot, 7$, and so the subgroup T of H that fixes 2 as well as 1 is of index 6 in H, $[H{:}T]=6$. T is generated by z and w and is of order 4, $[T{:}1]$. Hence G is of order 168 as a computation shows (see 200).

Given any two distinct numbers i, j and two other distinct numbers i^*, j^*, there is an element u of G such that $(i)u=i^*$ and $(j)u=j^*$. For this reason G is said to be doubly transitive. In general, a permutation group G is said to be k-ply transitive if given k distinct numbers $i_1, i_2, \cdot\cdot\cdot, i_k$ and another set of k distinct numbers $i_1^*, i_2^*, \cdot\cdot\cdot, i_k^*$, then there is an element u in G such that u post-multiplies each number of the first set to give another in the second (see 201).

The symmetric group S_n is n-ply transitive and the alternating group A_n is n-2-ply transitive. There are many triply transitive permutation groups, but apart from the

(197) $$\Delta=(x_1-x_2)(x_1-x_3)\cdots(x_1-x_n)(x_2-x_3)\cdots(x_{n-1}-x_n)$$

(198) $$\begin{cases} 1, 2, 4\\ 2, 3, 5\\ 3, 4, 6\\ 4, 5, 7\\ 5, 6, 1\\ 6, 7, 2\\ 7, 1, 3 \end{cases}$$

(199) $$\begin{cases} x=\begin{pmatrix}1, 2, 3, 4, 5, 6, 7\\ 2, 3, 4, 5, 6, 7, 1\end{pmatrix}\\ y=\begin{pmatrix}1, 2, 3, 4, 5, 6, 7\\ 1, 3, 5, 7, 2, 4, 6\end{pmatrix}\\ z=\begin{pmatrix}1, 2, 3, 4, 5, 6, 7\\ 1, 2, 5, 4, 3, 7, 6\end{pmatrix}\\ w=\begin{pmatrix}1, 2, 3, 4, 5, 6, 7\\ 1, 2, 6, 4, 7, 3, 5\end{pmatrix} \end{cases}$$

(200) $$[G{:}1]=[G{:}H][H{:}T][T{:}1]=7\cdot 6\cdot 4$$

(201) $$(i_1)u=i_1^*, \qquad \cdots, \qquad (i_k)u=i_k^*$$

(202) $$\begin{cases} ((x, y)\alpha)_1=ax+by\\ ((x, y)\alpha)_2=cx+dy \end{cases}$$

(203) $$\begin{cases} ((x, y)\alpha)_1=y, \quad ((x, y)\beta)_1=y\\ ((x, y)\alpha)_2=-x-y, \quad ((x, y)\beta)_2=x \end{cases}$$

(204) $$\alpha^3=1, \qquad \beta^2=1, \qquad \beta\alpha\beta=\alpha^{-1}$$

(205) $$\begin{cases} ((x)\alpha)_1=a_{11}x_1+a_{12}x_2+\cdots+a_{1j}x_j+\cdots+a_{1n}x_n\\ ((x)\alpha)_2=a_{21}x_1+a_{22}x_2+\cdots+a_{2j}x_j+\cdots+a_{2n}x_n\\ ((x)\alpha)_i=a_{i1}x_1+a_{i2}x_2+\cdots+a_{ij}x_j+\cdots+a_{in}x_n\\ ((x)\alpha)_n=a_{n1}x_1+a_{n2}x_2+\cdots+a_{nj}x_j+\cdots+a_{nn}x_n \end{cases}$$

(206) $$\begin{cases} ((x)\beta)_1=b_{11}x_1+b_{12}x_2+\cdots+b_{1j}x_j+\cdots+b_{1n}x_n\\ ((x)\beta)_2=b_{21}x_1+b_{22}x_2+\cdots+b_{2j}x_j+\cdots+b_{2n}x_n\\ ((x)\beta)_i=b_{i1}x_1+b_{i2}x_2+\cdots+b_{ij}x_j+\cdots+b_{in}x_n\\ ((x)\beta)_n=b_{n1}x_1+b_{n2}x_2+\cdots+b_{nj}x_j+\cdots+b_{nn}x_n \end{cases}$$

(207) $$\begin{cases} ((x)\alpha\beta)_1=c_{11}x_1+c_{12}x_2+\cdots+c_{1j}x_j+\cdots+c_{1n}x_n\\ ((x)\alpha\beta)_2=c_{21}x_1+c_{22}x_2+\cdots+c_{2j}x_j+\cdots+c_{2n}x_n\\ ((x)\alpha\beta)_i=c_{i1}x_1+c_{i2}x_2+\cdots+c_{ij}x_j+\cdots+c_{in}x_n\\ ((x)\alpha\beta)_n=c_{n1}x_1+c_{n2}x_2+\cdots+c_{nj}x_j+\cdots+c_{nn}x_n \end{cases}$$

(208) $$c_{ij}=a_{i1}b_{1j}+a_{i2}b_{2j}+\cdots+a_{in}b_{nj}, \qquad i,j=1, 2, \cdots, n$$

(209) $$A=\begin{bmatrix}a_{11}, a_{12}, \cdots, a_{1n}\\ a_{n1}, a_{n2}, \cdots, a_{nn}\end{bmatrix}=[a_{ij}], \qquad i,j=1, 2, \cdots n$$

groups A_n and S_n, there are only four permutation groups known that are as much as quadruply transitive. These are known as the Mathieu groups after the French mathematician Émile-Léonard Mathieu who discovered them in 1860 and 1873. These groups are M_{11}, of order 7920 quadruply transitive on 11 letters, M_{12} of order 95040 quintuply transitive on 12 letters, M_{23} of order 10,200,960 quadruply transitive on 23 letters, and M_{24} of order 244,922,040 quintuply transitive on 24 letters.

Mathieu groups

GROUP REPRESENTATION

It has been remarked earlier that transformations $(x, y) \rightarrow (ax+by,\ cx+dy)$ in which $ad-bc \neq 0$ form a group. The transformation value $(x, y)a$ is a pair of real numbers which may be called $((x, y)a)_1$ and $((x, y)a)_2$. This transformation may then be written in the form of two equations (see 202). As an example, take transformations α and β in which the corresponding equations are of the above type (see 203). The group $G=\langle \alpha, \beta \rangle$ is a finite group of order 6 in which the basic properties are easily found (see 204).

Linear transformations of n variables that are one-to-one (and so have inverses) will form a group. If the symbol x denotes a sequence $(x_1, \cdots, x_n)$ of numbers, then x_j is the jth term of x. A transformation a taking n-term sequences into n-term sequences can be formed in a fashion similar to the two-term use above. Then $(x)a$ is again a sequence with terms $((x)a)_1, \cdots, ((x)a)_n$. A linear transformation is a transformation a that can be defined by a linear system of equations (see 205). If another transformation β is expressed the same way (see 206), then the product $\alpha\beta$ of these transformations is given by another set of n linear equations (see 207) in which in every case the coefficient c_{ij} is given by the rule that identifies a typical coefficient in the equations of the product transformation with sums of products of coefficients in the equations expressing α and β (see 208).

Matrices

Clearly these transformations are determined by the array of coefficients. The square array that results (see 209) is called a matrix, and a product rule is defined, such that ordinary matrix multiplication (see 210) applies in every instance (see 211). The matrices, six in number, with elements composed of -1, 0, and 1 (see 212) and containing the identity matrix, as well as two matrices of specific structure, correspond to the group of order 6, $G=\langle \alpha, \beta \rangle$ mentioned above, and themselves form an isomorphic group.

A matrix representation, or, more briefly, representation, of a group G is a homomorphism of G onto a subgroup of the group of matrices of dimension n that have inverses. The elements in the matrices may be complex numbers or may be from any field.

As an example of matrix representation, the symmetries of a cube given above should be considered. The vertices may be given coordinates composed of 1 and -1 (see 213) so that the cube is symmetric about the origin. The symmetries α, β, γ take the form of matrices of nine elements each (see 214), composed of the numbers -1, 0, 1.

The determinant of a matrix A, written det A, is a function of the entries of A that can be defined recursively in terms of the dimension n of A. If $n=1$ and $A=[a_{11}]$, then $\det A = a_{11}$. For n greater than one, the det A has an expansion in det A_{1j} (see 215), in which for $j=1, 2, \cdots, n$, A_{1j} is the matrix of dimension $n-1$ obtained from A by deleting the first row and jth column. Thus for $n=2$, $\det A = a_{11}a_{22} - a_{12}a_{21}$. Thus the determinant of a matrix the entries of which are in a field F is an element of that field. The most useful property of determinants is the fact that $\det(AB) = \det A \cdot \det B$. The identity transformation 1, with $(x)1 = x$ for all x, corresponds to the identity matrix I, and if $I=[e_{ij}]$, then $e_{11}=e_{22} \cdots = e_{nn} = 1$ and $e_{ij}=0$ if $i \neq j$. In this $\det(I)=1$, and a matrix A has an inverse if and only if $\det A \neq 0$.

A useful operation on a matrix is called the transpose. If $A=[a_{ij}]$, the transpose A^T is defined as $A^T=[b_{ij}]$, in which $b_{ij}=a_{ji}$.

Matrices may also be added if when A and B are expressed in terms of their elements (see 216) the sum $A+B=C$ is defined by addition of corresponding elements (see 217). If u is an element of the field F, the scalar product uA is defined as the matrix $[ua_{ij}]$. Matrix addition is associative and commutative; matrix multiplication is associative but not commutative ($(AB)C=A(BC)$, but not $BA=AB$). Multiplication is left and right distributive over addition (see 218).

A representation M of a group G is given by matrices $M(x)$ for x in G such that the matrix corresponding to 1 is the identity and the matrix corresponding to a product of elements in the group is a product of corresponding matrices (see 219). If R is any fixed matrix with an inverse R^{-1}, then $R^{-1}M(x)R$ also gives a representation that is considered equivalent to the representation given by $M(x)$. If it happens that for every x of G $M(x)$ is of the form of four blocks, upper left being $M_1(x)$, lower left being $M_{12}(x)$, and lower right being $M_2(x)$ (see 220), with $M_1(x)$ of dimension r, $M_2(x)$ of dimension s, and the block [0] in the upper right corner consisting entirely of zeros, it is said that M is reducible, and if also $M_{12}(x)$ is identically zero it is said that M is the sum of M_1 and M_2. If no representation equivalent to M is reducible, then M is said to be irreducible.

For representations of all finite groups over the complex numbers and certain classes of infinite groups, it is true that, up to equivalence, there are only a finite number of irreducible representations and every represen-

(210) $$\begin{cases} B=[b_{ij}], & i,j=1,2,\cdots,n \\ AB=C=[c_{ij}], & i,j=1,2,\cdots,n \end{cases}$$

(211) $$\begin{cases} c_{ij}=a_{i1}b_{1j}+a_{i2}b_{2j}+\cdots+a_{in}b_{nj} \\ i,j=1,2,\cdots,n \end{cases}$$

(212) $$\begin{cases} 1=\begin{bmatrix}1,0\\0,1\end{bmatrix} \quad A=\begin{bmatrix}0, & 1\\-1, & -1\end{bmatrix} \quad A^2=\begin{bmatrix}-1, & -1\\1, & 0\end{bmatrix} \\ B=\begin{bmatrix}0,1\\1,0\end{bmatrix} \quad AB=\begin{bmatrix}1, & 0\\-1, & -1\end{bmatrix} \quad A^2B=\begin{bmatrix}-1, & -1\\0, & 1\end{bmatrix} \end{cases}$$

(213) $$\begin{cases} 1=(-1,1,-1) & 5=(-1,1,1) \\ 2=(-1,-1,-1) & 6=(-1,-1,1) \\ 3=(1,-1,-1) & 7=(1,-1,1) \\ 4=(1,1,-1) & 8=(1,1,1) \end{cases}$$

(214) $$\alpha=\begin{bmatrix}0, & 1, & 0\\-1, & 0, & 0\\0, & 0, & 1\end{bmatrix} \quad \beta=\begin{bmatrix}0, & -1, & 0\\0, & 0, & -1\\1, & 0, & 0\end{bmatrix} \quad \gamma=\begin{bmatrix}-1, & 0, & 0\\0, & 1, & 0\\0, & 0, & 1\end{bmatrix}$$

(215) $$\det A = a_{11}\det A_{11} - a_{12}\det A_{12} + \cdots + (-1)^{j+1}a_{1j}\det A_{ij} + \cdots + (-1)^{n+1}a_{1n}\det A_{1n}$$

(216) $$A=[a_{ij}], \quad B=[b_{ij}], \quad i,j=1,2,\cdots,n$$

(217) $$c_{ij}=a_{ij}+b_{ij}, \quad i,j=1,\cdots,n$$

(218) $$\begin{cases} A+B=B+A \\ (A+B)+C=A+(B+C) \\ A(B+C)=AB+AC \\ (A+B)C=AC+BC \end{cases}$$

(219) $$M(1)=I \quad \text{and} \quad M(x_1x_2)=M(x_1)M(x_2)$$

(220) $$M(x)=\left[\begin{array}{c|c} M_1(x) & 0 \\ \hline M_{12}(x) & M_2(x) \end{array}\right]$$

(221) $$(AB)^T=B^TA^T \quad \text{and} \quad \det(A^T)=\det A$$

tation is equivalent to the sum of a number of irreducible representations.

If $M(x) = A = [a_{ij}]$, then the quantity $a_{11} + a_{22} + \cdots + a_{nn}$ is called the trace of A, written tr A, and it is known that A and $R^{-1}AR$ have the same trace. If $M(x) = A$, then tr A is called the character of x and may be denoted as $\chi(x)$. Here a representation M of a group G is associated with a character $\chi(x)$. If M is the sum of M_1 and M_2, then obviously $\chi(x) = \chi_1(x) + \chi_2(x)$ for the corresponding traces. From this it follows that, over the complex numbers, the representations of all finite groups (and certain infinite groups) are completely determined by the characters of the irreducible representations. The nature of these characters and the relations on them have been the subject of much investigation, and they have been a very valuable technical tool in the study of groups. Some of these relations are not obviously related to the groups themselves and appear to be a sort of "numerology" or "astrology" of groups.

THE CLASSICAL GROUPS; CONTINUOUS GROUPS

The set of all matrices of dimension n over a field F the determinant of which is not zero forms a group called the general linear group of dimension n and is designated as $GL_n(F)$. Because determinants satisfy det (AB) = det A · det B, it follows that all matrices of determinant unity, det $A = 1$, form a subgroup of $GL_n(F)$ known as the special linear group of dimension n and designated $SL_n(F)$. The transpose operation on matrices has the property that it permutes the order of multiplication when applied to a product and leaves the determinant of a matrix unchanged (see 221). From this it follows easily that matrices X with the property $X^TX = I$, I being the identity matrix, form a group, and this is called the orthogonal group $O_n(F)$. The orthogonal group is also the group of linear transformations that leave $x_1^2 + x_2^2 + \cdots + x_n^2$ invariant. For matrices of even dimension $n = 2t$, the particular matrix composed of four blocks, 0's being on the diagonal, and I_t and its negative being in the other two blocks (see 222),

(222) $A = \left[\begin{array}{c|c} 0 & I_t \\ \hline -I_t & 0 \end{array}\right]$

(223) $x_1\bar{x}_1 + x_2\bar{x}_2 + \cdots + x_n\bar{x}_n$

(224) $F, W^{-1}x^4W, W^{-1}y^3W, W^{-1}x^4yxyW$

(225) $R_1(b_1, \cdots, b_r) = 1, \cdots$

(226) $R_1(a_1, \cdots, a_r), \cdots, R_n(a_1, \cdots, a_r)$

(227) $N(r) = r + r(r-1)/2 + r(r-1)(r-2)/6$

is of importance in which I_t is the t-dimensional identity matrix and 0 stands for a block consisting entirely of zeros. A has the property $A^T = -A$. Those matrices X such that $X^TAX = A$ form a group known as the symplectic group, designated as $Sp_n(F)$ with $n = 2t$.

If the field F is the field $\mathfrak{C}$ of complex numbers, the mapping $a + bi \rightarrow a - bi$ is an automorphism of order 2 and can be written $x \rightarrow x^*$. Here if x is a complex number $a + bi$, then x^* is the conjugate $a - bi$. In general, if a field F has an automorphism $x \rightarrow x^*$ of order 2, those matrices X such that $Y^TX = I$ form a group, in which Y is obtained from X by replacing every entry x_{ij} by its conjugate x^*_{ij}. This group is called the unitary group $U_n(F)$. The unitary group is a generalization of the orthogonal group and may be considered as the group of linear transformations leaving a sum of products of n complex numbers times their conjugates invariant (see 223).

The general linear group, the special linear group, the orthogonal, symplectic, and unitary groups are known as the classical groups.

Only a little will be said here of continuous groups because they are discussed in the article GEOMETRY: *Topological groups* and *Differential topology*. In some groups G it is possible to define a distance between elements of the group. For example, if G consists of the rotations of the surface of a sphere, and if x and y are two of these rotations, the distance between x and y, $d(x, y)$ can be defined as the maximum distance between $(p)x$ and $(p)y$ as p ranges over all points of the sphere. In such a case a neighbourhood of a group element x is defined as the set of all elements y such that $d(x, y) < e$ for some fixed e. Neighbourhoods may also be defined in other ways. The group G is said to be continuous if the product operation xy in G is continuous either in terms of the distance defined or in terms of the neighbourhoods. In some instances continuous groups may be given in terms of continuous parameters (variables that distinguish the elements of the group). For example, the group of orthogonal matrices (an orthogonal matrix is a matrix in which the columns are orthogonal vectors; see above *Linear and multilinear algebra*) over the real field that have determinant one can be parameterized in terms of a number of angles of rotation, and it is a continuous group in terms of these parameters. Continuous groups expressed in terms of parameters are known as Lie groups, after Sophus Lie, who studied them at great length. Lie groups

FREE GROUPS; THE WORD PROBLEM; THE BURNSIDE PROBLEM

If $a_1, a_2, \cdots, a_r$ are elements of a group G, then $H = \langle a_1, a_2, \cdots a_r\rangle$ is said to be the subgroup generated by $a_1, \cdots a_r$ and consists of all finite words, products of the elements $x_1x_2, \cdots x_t$, in which every x_j is some a_i or a_i^{-1}, and also the identity 1 that may be considered the empty word. If x_jx_{j+1} is of the form $a_ia_i^{-1}$ or $a_i^{-1}a_i$, then the same group element is given by $x_1x_2 \cdots x_{j-1}x_{j+2} \cdots x_t$. If no x_jx_{j+1} is of the form $a_ia_i^{-1}$ or $a_i^{-1}a_i$, the word $x_1x_2 \cdots x_t$ is said to be reduced. By deleting consecutive inverses every word is equal to a reduced word, including 1 as a reduced word. It can be shown that the order in which these deletions are carried out does not matter and that in this way every word is equal to a unique reduced word. It can be proved that given generators $a_1, a_2, \cdots, a_r$, there is a unique group in which all the distinct reduced words are distinct elements. This group is called the free group F_r-generated by $a_1, a_2, \cdots, a_r$, and this is written $F_r = \langle a_1, a_2, \cdots, a_r\rangle$.

It is not difficult to show that if G is any group generated by r elements $G = \langle b_1, b_2, \ldots, b_r\rangle$, then G is a homomorphic image of $F_r = \langle a_1, \ldots, a_r\rangle$ under a homomorphism β with $(a_1)\beta = b_1, \ldots, (a_r)\beta = b_r$. The kernel K of this homomorphism consists of those words in the a's that become the identity in G when the a's are replaced by b's. K is, of course, a normal subgroup of F_r and, of course, any normal subgroup of F_r is the kernel of an appropriate homomorphism. Thus every group G is a factor group of a free group F. It is a remarkable fact that every subgroup of a free group is also a free group on an appropriate set of generators.

Free groups give a precise basis for describing defining relations on groups. To say that a group G of order 12 is defined by relations $h^4 = 1$, $k^3 = 1$, and $h^{-1}kh = k^{-1}$, is equivalent to taking the free group $F_2 = \langle x, y\rangle$ and the least normal subgroup K of F containing x^4, y^3 and $x^{-1}yxy$, and defining G as F_2/K, mapping $(x)\beta = h$, $(y)\beta = k$. Here, as W ranges over all words of F, terms of the type $W^{-1}UW$, in which U is one of the three listed elements of K (see 224), are elements of K.

The word problem in groups involves the case in which G is generated by a finite number of elements $b_1, b_2, \cdots, b_r$ and that these satisfy a finite number of relations (see 225) and no other relations not consequences of these. Is it possible to decide whether or not two different words W_1 and W_2 represent the same element of G, or equivalently whether or not $W = W_1W_2^{-1}$ is the identity? In terms of free groups this is the question of deciding whether or not in the free group $F_r = F_1(a_1, \cdots, a_r)$ a word W is contained in the least normal subgroup K of F_r that contains the finite number of functions (see 226) that were used to express the relations.

The word problem is in fact unsolvable. No method can

exist that will in general solve all word problems. This was proved in 1955 by the Soviet mathematician Pyotr Sergeyevich Novikov. In 1959 the U.S. mathematician William W. Boone exhibited a particular set of relations $R_1, \cdots, R_n$ for which the word problem is unsolvable. This unsolvability has been a major difficulty in various natural problems of group theory.

In 1902 the British mathematician William Burnside raised the following question. If a group G is generated by r elements, $G = \langle b_1, \cdots, b_r \rangle$, and if for a fixed n, $x^n = 1$ for every element of G, is G necessarily finite? If $F_r = \langle a_1, \cdots, a_r \rangle$ is the free group with r generators and if $K = K_n$ is the subgroup of F generated by x^n for every x of F, then K is necessarily a normal subgroup of F, and $B(n, r) = F_r/K_n$ is a group with r generators and $x^n = 1$ for every element of $B(n, r)$. Any group such as G is necessarily a homomorphic image of $B(n, r)$, and so for given n and r the question is whether or not the group $B(n, r)$ is finite. If r is 1, then $B(n, r) = B(n, 1)$ is the cyclic group of order n. Burnside showed that for $n = 2$, $B(2, r)$ is of order 2^r and is the direct product of r groups of order 2. He also showed that for $n = 3$ the groups are finite, and that for $n = 4$, $r = 2$, $B(4, 2)$ is of order at most $2^{12} = 4096$. In 1933 the mathematicians F. Levi and B.L. van der Waerden found the exact order and structure of the groups $B(3, r)$. The order of $B(3, r)$ is $3^{N(r)}$, in which the exponent of 3 is a specific algebraic function of r (see 227).

In 1940 I.N. Sanov, a mathematician, showed that the groups $B(4, r)$ are finite. It has been shown that Burnside was right about $B(4, 2)$ and that its order is exactly $2^{12} = 4096$, but for $r = 3$ or greater the order is not known. A mathematician, C. Wright, in 1962 found more reasonable bounds on the order and structure of $B(4, r)$ than Sanov had found, but precise information was still lacking in the 1970s.

In 1958 it was shown by the U.S. mathematician Marshall Hall, Jr., that the groups $B(6, r)$ are finite; and from results of the mathematicians P. Hall and G. Higman, it follows that the order and structure of $B(6, r)$ are fully known. $B(6, r)$ is of order $2^A 3^B$ in which $A = 1 + (r-1)3^{N(r)}$ and with $s = 1 + (r-1)2^r$, $B = N(s)$, in which the exponent of 3 is as above (see 227).

In 1968 it was shown by the mathematicians Novikov and Adjan that $B(n, r)$ is infinite if r is at least 2 and n is odd and at least 4381.

SIMPLE GROUPS

Jordan–Hölder theorem

A simple group is a group that has no normal subgroup except itself and the identity subgroup. The Jordan–Hölder theorem shows that these are the building blocks for all groups. Many important questions about groups in general can easily be reduced to problems on simple groups.

The nature of the simple groups remains a challenging and difficult matter. In one case the answer was found by the French mathematician Élie-Joseph Cartan in 1894. For groups that are continuous in terms of real or complex parameters, the Lie groups, a complete list has been found. The classical groups will in general have a centre Z, consisting of those scalar multiples of the identity that are in the group, and in the case of the orthogonal group there may be a normal subgroup with an Abelian factor group. Such a normal subgroup up to certain identification with its centre (that is, modulo its centre) will be in general a simple group. There are four infinite families, A_t corresponding to the special linear group of dimension $t+1$ modulo its centre, B_t and D_t coming from orthogonal groups respectively of dimensions $2t+1$ and $2t$, and C_t coming from another group of dimension $2t$, called symplectic.

There are also five exceptional groups, G_2, F_4, E_6, E_7, and E_8, which can be expressed with respectively 14, 52, 78, 133, and 248 parameters. The unitary groups are not technically a part of this list because complex conjugation is part of their definition.

For finite simple groups the situation is much more complicated and is currently the subject of intense research effort. To describe the situation it is first necessary to describe finite fields. Let p be a prime number. It is said that integers r and s are congruent modulo p if the difference $r - s$ is a multiple of p, and this is written $r \equiv s \pmod p$. It is also said that r and s are in the same residue class modulo p, and that either r or s is a representative of the residue class. Hence $0, 1, 2, \cdots, p-1$ are representatives of all p residue classes. If $r \equiv s \pmod p$ and $t \equiv u \pmod p$, then $r + t \equiv s + u \pmod p$ and $rt \equiv su \pmod p$. The p residue classes form a field, written $GF(p)$. If $q = p^r$ is a power of the prime p, there is always a unique field with q elements, $GF(q)$, the elements of which are polynomials of a single element with coefficients from $GF(p)$. Thus $GF(4)$ has elements $0, 1, u, u+1$, in which 0, 1 are the residue classes modulo 2. In $GF(4)$, four basic relations hold (see 228, 229) and other relations are consequences of these.

(228, 229)
$$\begin{cases} GF(4),\ 1+1=0, & u+u=0 \\ u^2 = u \div 1, & u(u+1)=1 \end{cases}$$

(230) Mathieu groups:

M_{11}	$2^4 \cdot 3^2 \cdot 5 \cdot 11$
M_{12}	$2^6 \cdot 2^3 \cdot 5 \cdot 11$
M_{22}	$2^7 \cdot 3^2 \cdot 5 \cdot 7 \cdot 11$
M_{23}	$2^7 \cdot 3^2 \cdot 5 \cdot 7 \cdot 11 \cdot 23$
M_{24}	$2^{10} \cdot 3^3 \cdot 5 \cdot 7 \cdot 11 \cdot 23$

(231)

$2^3 \cdot 3 \cdot 5 \cdot 7 \cdot 11 \cdot 19$	Janko
$2^7 \cdot 3^3 \cdot 5^2 \cdot 7$	Hall-Janko
$2^9 \cdot 3^2 \cdot 5^3 \cdot 7 \cdot 11$	Higman-Sims
$2^{13} \cdot 3^7 \cdot 5^2 \cdot 7 \cdot 11 \cdot 13$	Suzuki
$2^7 \cdot 3^6 \cdot 5^3 \cdot 7 \cdot 11$	McLaughlin
$2^7 \cdot 3^5 \cdot 5 \cdot 17 \cdot 19$	Higman-McKay-Janko
$2^{10} \cdot 3^3 \cdot 5^2 \cdot 7^3 \cdot 17$	Held

(232)

$2^{21} \cdot 3^9 \cdot 5^4 \cdot 7^2 \cdot 11 \cdot 13 \cdot 23$	Conway .1
$2^{18} \cdot 3^6 \cdot 5^3 \cdot 7 \cdot 11 \cdot 23$	Conway .2
$2^{10} \cdot 3^7 \cdot 5^3 \cdot 7 \cdot 11 \cdot 23$	Conway .3
$2^{17} \cdot 3^9 \cdot 5^2 \cdot 7 \cdot 11 \cdot 13$	Fischer F_{22}
$2^{18} \cdot 3^{13} \cdot 5^2 \cdot 7 \cdot 11 \cdot 13 \cdot 17 \cdot 23$	Fischer F_{23}
$2^{22} \cdot 3^{16} \cdot 5^2 \cdot 7^3 \cdot 11 \cdot 13 \cdot 17 \cdot 23 \cdot 29$	Fischer F_{24}

(233)

$2^8 \cdot 3^7 \cdot 5^6 \cdot 7 \cdot 11 \cdot 31 \cdot 37 \cdot 67$	Lyons-Sims
$2^{14} \cdot 3^3 \cdot 5^3 \cdot 7 \cdot 13 \cdot 29$	Rudvalis-Conway-Wales

The mathematician Claude Chevalley showed in 1955 that all of the Lie groups have finite analogues if the field of real or complex numbers is replaced by any finite field, and that with a very few exceptions, corresponding to fields with 2 or 3 elements, the analogues of the simple Lie groups are simple. This is also true for the unitary groups. Somewhat like the unitary group, there are several families known as twisted Lie groups corresponding to subgroups of the Lie types fixed by a certain automorphism. For instance, if $q = 2^{2m+1}$ is at least 8, there are simple groups of order $(q^2+1)\, q^2(q-1)$, first discovered by the mathematician M. Suzuki in 1960 in another way. The finite simple groups include the cyclic groups of prime order and the alternating groups A_n in which n is 5 or greater.

The most striking development in the study of finite simple groups was the proof in 1963 by the mathematicians Walter Feit and John Thompson that, apart from the groups of prime order, every finite simple group has even order. Since that time Thompson has determined all minimal simple groups.

Sporadic simple groups

Apart from the families of finite simple groups, there are now known 20 finite simple groups, called sporadic simple groups, that do not belong to the known families. It is not clear whether they belong to families not yet discovered or whether they are truly exceptional, and it is not clear whether further finite simple groups exist.

The designations of the known 20 sporadic groups and their orders in factored form are the Mathieu groups (see 230), the groups, respectively, of Janko, Hall–Janko, Higman–Sims, Suzuki, McLaughlin, Higman–McKay–Janko, and Held (see 231), and the groups identified, respectively, as Conway .1, Conway .2, Conway .3, Fischer F_{22}, Fischer F_{23}, and Fischer F_{24} (see 232).

A 19th group predicted by Lyons was constructed by Sims. The 20th, predicted by Rudvalis, was constructed by Conway and Wales (see 233).

(Ma.H.)

Fields

Broadly speaking, a field is an algebraic system consisting of elements that are commonly called numbers, in which the four familiar operations of addition, subtraction, multiplication, and division are universally defined (except for division by zero) and have all their usual properties. Much of the general theory of vectors and matrices (see above *Linear and multilinear algebra* and MATRIX THEORY) can be developed over an arbitrary field. In particular, this is true of the general theory of simultaneous linear equations and of their solution by a method known as Gaussian elimination (see below). The study of various special fields also explains which geometric constructions, such as angle bisection and angle trisection, can be made with ruler and compass and which cannot. Moreover, finite fields of 2^n elements have been used to construct the best known error-correcting codes.

Although many particular fields—including especially the rational, real, and complex fields, finite fields and algebraic number fields—were intensively studied in the 17th, 18th, and early 19th centuries, the idea of investigating all possible fields seems not to have been conceived until 1910, when the mathematician Steinitz proposed a systematic scheme for classifying them.

Field classification

(234) $$\begin{cases} \dfrac{m}{n} \pm \dfrac{m'}{n'} = \dfrac{mn' \pm nm'}{nn'}, \quad \dfrac{m}{n} \cdot \dfrac{m'}{n'} = \dfrac{mm'}{nn'} \\ \dfrac{m}{n} \div \dfrac{m'}{n'} = \dfrac{mn'}{nm'} \end{cases}$$

(235) $$\frac{m}{n} + 0 = \frac{m}{n}, \quad \frac{m}{n} \cdot 0 = 0 \quad \text{for all } \frac{m}{n}$$

(236) $$1.414214\cdots, 3.14159\cdots, 2.718281828459\cdots$$

(237) $$\frac{5}{7} = 0.714285714285714285\cdots$$

(238) $$\begin{cases} 1.4142 = 14{,}142/10{,}000 \quad \text{or} \\ 3.14159 = 314{,}159/100{,}000 \end{cases}$$

(239) $$\begin{cases} \dfrac{14{,}142}{10{,}000} + \dfrac{314{,}159}{100{,}000} = \dfrac{455{,}579}{100{,}000} \\ \dfrac{14{,}142}{10{,}000} \cdot \dfrac{314{,}159}{100{,}000} = \dfrac{4{,}442{,}836{,}578}{1{,}000{,}000{,}000} \end{cases}$$

(240) $$(x+iy) \pm (x'+iy') = (x \pm x') + i(y \pm y')$$

(241) $$(x+iy)(x'+iy') = (xx'-yy') + i(xy'+yx')$$

(242) $$z = \frac{u+iv}{a+ib} = \frac{(u+iv)(a-ib)}{(a+ib)(a-ib)} = \frac{ua+vb}{a^2+b^2} + i\left(\frac{va-ub}{a^2+b^2}\right)$$

THREE FAMILIAR FIELDS

To illustrate the meaning of the first statement of this section, the three most familiar fields are discussed, namely, the rational field, the real field, and the complex field.

The rational field. The most familiar field of all is the rational field, commonly denoted Q. Its members are the positive rational numbers m/n (in which m and n are positive integers), the negative rational numbers $-m/n$, and 0. Positive rational numbers are added, subtracted, multiplied, and divided by the rules familiar in the manipulation of fractions (see 234). The behaviour of 0 is somewhat exceptional in that, when added to a rational it yields the same rational and when multiplied by a rational it yields 0 (see 235). The rules for adding, subtracting, multiplying, and dividing negative rational numbers (with each other and with positive rational numbers and zero) are very like those for positive rational numbers listed above.

Because $m/n = km/kn$ for any positive integer k, the same rational number can be represented as a quotient of integers in many ways. Of these, only one is in lowest terms; that is, has numerator and denominator without common factors (relatively prime) and a positive denominator.

The real field. Much more sophisticated than the rational field is the real field, commonly designated by $\mathfrak{R}$. Positive real numbers are most easily visualized as unlimited decimals (see 236). There are also negative real numbers such as $-1.4142\cdots$ and zero, designated $0 = 0.0000000\cdots$. Among real numbers, rational numbers can be recognized by the characteristic property that their (unlimited) decimal representation is repeating: from some point on, it consists simply of indefinite repetitions of the same block. Thus $1/24 = 0.041666666\cdots$ (block length one), and $5/7$ has a similar representation with block length 6 (see 237). The fact that every rational number is also a real number (with equivalent addition, multiplication, subtraction, and division rules) can be summarized in the statement that Q is a subfield of the rational field—or in the simple formula $Q \subset R$.

Actually, the rules for adding, subtracting, multiplying, and dividing real numbers are quite sophisticated; they can best be understood in terms of the idea of approximation. Thus, when $\sqrt{2} = 1.4142\cdots$ is written, what is meant is that $14{,}142/10{,}000 \leq \sqrt{2} \leq 14{,}143/10{,}000$. But now it is easy to add or multiply any two decimal fractions (see 238) by applying the rules of addition and multiplication of rationals (see 239). Subtraction is equally easy, although long division is considerably harder (see ARITHMETIC).

To pass from the addition and multiplication of decimal fractions (finite decimals) to that of real numbers (unlimited decimals) is best thought of as a process of successive approximation: arbitrarily close decimal fraction approximations to any two real numbers can be added or multiplied together. Thus an arbitrary close approximation to their sum or product can be obtained.

Real numbers also have a very important and basic geometrical representation as coordinates of points on a straight line. After choosing an origin O and assigning to

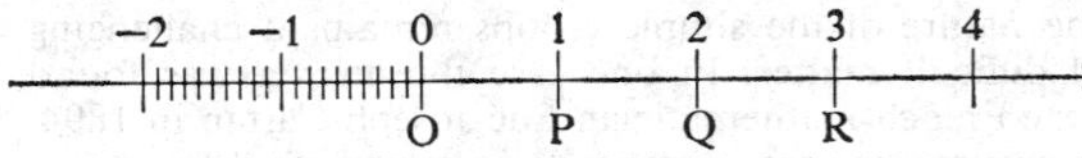

it the coordinate 0 (zero), any other point P can be chosen and the coordinate $1 = 1.000000\cdots$ can be assigned to it. By laying off in the same direction equal segments $\overline{PQ} = \overline{OP}$, etc., infinite sequences of points $P, Q, R, \cdots$ (or $P_1, P_2, P_3, \cdots$) are obtained having positive integral coordinates. The coordinates $-1, -2, -3, \cdots$ can then be assigned to a similar sequence of equally spaced points going in the opposite direction. Each segment can also be divided into 10 equal parts, assigning (for example) to the new points between P and Q the (decimal) coordinates $1.1, 1.2, 1.3, \cdots, 1.9$. By repeated decimal subdivision, in this way points corresponding to all decimal fractions can be obtained and thus arbitrarily close (decimal) approximations to any real point produced. This gives a simple and natural geometrical interpretation of the decimal (fraction) approximations to arbitrary real numbers.

The geometrical representation of real numbers

The complex field. Much more sophisticated even than the real field is the complex field. Indeed, it is doubtful whether this field would ever have been thought of if man had not been curious about polynomial equations, such as $z^2 = -1$ (or, equivalently, $z^2 + 1 = 0$). It is easy to show that no real number z can satisfy this equation, because the square of any two positive or negative real numbers is necessarily positive (see below *Ordered fields*), while $0^2 = 0$. To remedy this deficiency of the real field $\mathfrak{R}$, mathematicians invented a new number $i = \sqrt{-1}$, defined by the properties of the equation $i^2 = -1$.

In order to get a field containing $\sqrt{-1}$ (that is, to be able to carry out addition, subtraction, multiplication, and division subject to the usual rules), all complex numbers of the form $x + yi = x + iy = x + y\sqrt{-1}$ were considered more generally. It was decided to add and subtract these by the rules of adding and subtracting separately the terms not involving i and the terms involving i (see 240). Multiplication followed the rule that the first part of the product was a difference of products not involving i, while the second part included i as a factor and a sum of products, the two parts being added to form a new number in the field (see 241). Finally, division (except by zero) was always possible. Specifically, setting $c = a + ib$, $z = x + iy$, and $w = u + iv$, the solution of the equation $cz = w$ can always be evaluated by setting z equal to a complex number, both summands of which have fractional representation with $a^2 + b^2$ in the denominators (see 242) for $c \neq 0$, $a^2 + b^2 > 0$; hence this quotient always exists as a complex number of the prescribed form.

It is quite straightforward to show that the preceding definitions of addition, multiplication, subtraction, and division of complex numbers are the only ones that are compatible with the usual laws of algebra (see below *Postulates for a field*) and the basic equation $i^2 = -1$ given initially above. It can be proved that, conversely, the above operations do obey all the usual algebraic laws; therefore, it is legitimate to speak of the number system just constructed as the complex field $\mathfrak{C}$.

Just as a real number x can be thought of as the coordinate of a point on an infinite straight line, so each complex number $z = x + iy$ can be thought of as representing a point (x, y) in a plane, the complex plane. The addition and subtraction of two complex numbers $z = x + iy$ and $z' = x' + iy'$ as defined above corresponds to ordinary vector addition and subtraction.

(243) $$z = r[\cos\theta + i\sin\theta]$$

(244) $$zz' = rr'[\cos(\theta + \theta') + i\sin(\theta + \theta')]$$

(245) $$|zz'| = |z| \cdot |z'|, \qquad \arg(zz') = \arg z + \arg z'$$

(246) $$|z^n| = |z|^n \text{ and } \arg z^n = n \arg z$$

(247) $$\begin{cases} b = 0 + b = [(-a) + a] + b = (-a) + [a + b] \\ \quad = (-a) + [a + c] = [(-a) + a] + c = 0 + c = c \end{cases}$$

(248) $$(-1)1 + (-1)(-1) = (-1)[1 + (-1)] = (-1)0 = 0$$

(249) $$(-1)1 + 1 \cdot 1 = [(-1) + 1]1 = 01 = 0$$

(250) $$(-x)(-y) = [(-1)x][(-1)y] = (-1)(-1)(xy) = xy$$

(251) $$ax + by = e, \qquad cx + dy = f$$

(252) $$x = \frac{(ed - bf)}{(ad - bc)}, \qquad y = \frac{(af - ce)}{(ad - bc)}$$

(253) $$a_{i1}x_1 + a_{i2}x_2 + \cdots + a_{in}x_n = k_i, \qquad i = 1, 2, \cdots, n$$

(254) $$\begin{cases} \begin{vmatrix} a & b \\ c & d \end{vmatrix} = ad - bc \\ \begin{vmatrix} a & b & c \\ d & e & f \\ g & h & k \end{vmatrix} = \begin{Bmatrix} aek + dhc + bfg \\ -bdh - ceg - fha \end{Bmatrix} \end{cases}$$

What is more remarkable, the multiplication of two complex numbers also has a simple geometric interpretation, which is most simply explained in terms of polar coordinates. Namely, the vector from the origin $O = 0 + i0$ to $z = x + iy$ has length $r = |z| = \sqrt{x^2 + y^2}$ and makes a certain angle θ with the positive x-axis, called the argument of z. By trigonometry, therefore, $x = r\cos\theta$ and $y = r\sin\theta$, and so z has a representation in terms of r and θ (see 243). If also z' has such a representation, then the multiplication rule (see 241) implies that the product of z and z' is the product of the corresponding r and r' and a complex number whose argument is the sum of corresponding θ and θ' (see 244). In other words, to multiply two complex numbers, multiply their absolute values and add their arguments. These rules can be written in symbols (see 245). As a corollary, it may be stated that for any positive integer n, the absolute value of the nth power of z is the nth power of the absolute value of z, and the argument of the nth power of z is n times the argument of z (see 246). From this, in turn, it follows that any nonzero complex number $c = a + ib$ has exactly n distinct nth roots $c^{1/n}$, all having the same magnitude $|c|^{1/n} = (a^2 + b^2)^{1/2n}$ and having equally spaced arguments $\theta_j = (\arg c)/n + 2\pi j/n$, $j = 0, 1, \ldots, n - 1$. These nth roots are thus the vertices of a regular polygon of n sides, with its centre at the origin.

ELEMENTARY THEORY OF FIELDS

Postulates for a field. The three number systems Q, $\mathfrak{R}$, and $\mathfrak{C}$ defined above have in common a great many properties. In particular, they all admit two binary operations of addition and multiplication, which satisfy the five postulates following:

F1. $a + b = b + a$ and $ab = ba$ for all values of a, b.
F2. $a + (b + c) = (a + b) + c$ and $a(bc) = (ab)c$, for all values of a, b, c.
F3. There exist distinguished elements 0, 1 such that $a + 0 = 0 + a$ and $a1 = 1a = a$ for all values of a.
F4. Given a, there exist elements $-a$ and (if $a \neq 0$) a^{-1} such that $a + (-a) = 0$ and $aa^{-1} = 1$.
F5. $a(b + c) = ab + ac$ and $(a + b)c = ac + bc$, for all values of a, b, c.

Postulate F1 asserts that addition and multiplication are commutative; F2 asserts that they are associative; F3 asserts that any field has identities for addition and multiplication. Postulate F4 asserts that addition and multiplication (except by zero) are invertible operations; the last postulate, F5, is called the distributive law. Fields may now be formally defined.

Formal definition of a field

A field is an algebraic system the members of which, commonly called numbers, can be combined by two universally defined binary operations (addition and multiplication) that satisfy postulates F1–F5 above.

With a little manipulation, it can be shown that (in the presence of F5), F1–F4 can also be summarized in two statements:

1. The numbers of any field form a commutative group (see above *Groups*) under addition.
2. The nonzero numbers of any field form another commutative group under multiplication. This gives a second algebraic characterization of fields.

Many familiar rules of algebra follow directly from postulates F1–F5, which are already redundant. For example, $a + b = a + c$ implies successively several equalities (see 247), which imply the following cancellation law:

In any field, $a + b = a + c$ implies $b = c$.

A similar argument proves a second cancellation law:

In any field, $ab = ac$ implies $b = c$ if $a \neq 0$.

Next, it can be proved that the additive identity 0 is also a zero for multiplication, in the sense that $a0 = 0$ for all values of a. Indeed, $a + 0 = a = a1 = a(1 + 0) = a1 + a0 = a + a0$, from which it follows that $0 = a0$ by the cancellation law. Again, from $1 + (-1) = 0$ there follows $a + (-a) = 0 = 0a = 1 + (-1)a = 1a + (-1)a = a + (-1)a$, from which by cancellation is derived $-a = (-1)a$. Finally, two calculations (see 248 and 249) imply $(-1)(-1) = 1 \cdot 1 = 1$ and a general rule of multiplication of negatives (see 250).

Gaussian elimination. The rules derived above from postulates F1–F5 lie fairly near the surface and would probably be assumed as postulates if they did not follow anyway. A collection of much deeper results concerning simultaneous linear equations is now considered. The study of these leads in turn to the theory of vectors and matrices with components, or entries, in any field F.

The simplest nontrivial case in point concerns two simultaneous linear equations in two unknowns (see 251), the coefficients and constants in which a, b, c, d, e, f are known numbers; the problem is to determine the unknowns x, y. The answer is given, if the coefficients satisfy $ad \neq bc$, by the formulas that, except for a factor common to both x and y, expresses x in terms of the difference $ed - bf$ and y in the terms $af - ce$ (see 252). This answer is easily checked and most easily found by (i) multiplying the first equation by d, the second equation by b, subtracting the results to eliminate y, and then solving for x; and after this (ii) multiplying the second equation by a, the first by c, subtracting the results to eliminate x, and then solving for y.

The above procedure is called Gaussian elimination, and it can be generalized to the case of n simultaneous linear equations (see 253) in n unknowns $x_j (j = 1, 2, \ldots, n)$. The results can also be presented in the compact notation of determinants (see 254). See MATRIX THEORY for details. The main point to be made here is that the entire theory can be developed over an arbitrary field F. In particular, this is true of the properties of the rank and linear dependence of vectors and matrices.

SOME GENERAL CONCEPTS

Commutative rings; integral domains. First of all, it should be realized that, if the part of postulate F4 that asserts the existence of a^{-1} is omitted, a much wider class of algebraic systems is formally defined as follows:

A commutative ring is an algebraic system having two binary operations (addition and multiplication) that satisfy postulates F1, F2, F3, F5, and F4′:

F4′. Every element a has an additive inverse $(-a)$ such that $a + (-a) = 0$.

A commutative ring is an integral domain when postulate F4″ is satisfied:

F4″. If $ab = 0$, then either $a = 0$ or $b = 0$.

The most familiar integral domain consists of the integers $0, \pm 1, \pm 2, \ldots$ under ordinary addition and multiplication; it is commonly designated Z. From the domain Z can be constructed a very important class of modular number systems Z^n, one for each positive integer $n > 1$, as follows. The members of Z^n are the integers $0, 1, \ldots, n-1$, which should be thought of as remainders after division by n. To add two members (numbers) of Z^n, their ordinary sum is taken and then its remainder after division by n (the remainder modulo n) is the answer. Likewise, to multiply two members of Z^n, their ordinary product is taken and again the remainder modulo n is the answer. Thus, in Z_{11}, one has $7 + 9 = 5$, $7 \times 9 = 8$, $5 + 10 = 4$, $5 \times 10 = 6$, and so on.

The proof that every Z^n is a commutative ring is omitted; *i.e.*, that F1–F3, F4′, and F5 hold in Z^n for every integer $n > 1$. When n is a prime number p, multiplication is also invertible and the preceding construction gives a field (*e.g.*, Z_{11} is a field). The modular fields Z^p are the simplest finite fields; others will be constructed later.

When $n = rs$ $(1 < r, s < n)$ is composite, however, it is possible to have $rs = 0$ in Z^n even though $r \neq 0$ and $s \neq 0$. Hence Z^n is not even an integral domain, but only a commutative ring unless n is a prime.

Fields of quotients. There are many integral domains besides Z, however, that are not fields. For example, if J is any integral domain (*e.g.*, if $J = Z$ or if J is a field F), then the domain $J[x]$ of all polynomials over J in the indeterminate x can be formed. Each such polynomial either reduces to 0 or has a canonical form (see 255). (Here and below, the convenient symbol ∈ is used for "belonging to" or "is a member of.") The nonnegative integer m, the highest power of x, is called the degree of the polynomial $a(x)$. Given $a(x)$ and a second polynomial, the sum

(255) $$\begin{cases} a(x) = a_0 + a_1 x + \cdots + a_m x^m \\ \qquad a_m \neq 0, \quad \text{all } a_j \in J^* \\ b(x) = b_0 + b_1 x + \cdots + b_n x^n \end{cases}$$

(256) $$a(x) + b(x) = (a_0 + b_0) + (a_1 + b_1)x + \\ + \cdots + \begin{cases} a_m x^m, & m > n \\ b_n x^n, & n > m \end{cases}$$

(257) $$a(x)\,b(x) = a_0 b_0 + (a_0 b_1 + a_1 b_0)x + \cdots + \\ + \Big(\sum_{j=0}^{k} a_j b_{k-j}\Big)x^k + \cdots + a_m b_n x^{m+n}$$

(258) $$\begin{cases} \dfrac{a}{b} = \dfrac{c}{d} \text{ means } ad = bc \\ \dfrac{a}{b} \pm \dfrac{c}{d} = \dfrac{ad \pm bc}{bd} \\ \dfrac{a}{b} \cdot \dfrac{c}{d} = \dfrac{ac}{bd}, \text{ and } \dfrac{a}{b} \div \dfrac{c}{d} = \dfrac{ad}{bc} \quad \text{if } c \neq 0 \end{cases}$$

(259) $$\begin{cases} [r + (n)] + [r' + (n)] = (r + r') + (n) \\ [r + (n)] \cdot [r' + (n)] = rr' + (n) \end{cases}$$

(260) $$\theta(r \pm r') = \theta(r) \pm \theta(r') \quad \text{and} \quad \theta(rr') = \theta(r)\,\theta(r')$$

(261) $$m1 \pm n1 = (m \pm n)1 \text{ and } (m1)(n1) = (mn)1$$

can be formed [see 256; the case $m = n$ terminates with $(a_m + b_n)x^m$], and the product (see 257), which is always a nonzero polynomial of degree $m + n$ for $a(x)$ nonzero of degree m and $b(x)$ nonzero of degree n. The domain $J[x]$ satisfies postulates F1–F3, F4′, and F5 and therefore is always an integral domain.

From any integral domain J, for example, from the domain $Z[x]$ of all polynomials with integral coefficients or the domain $R[x]$ of all polynomials with real coefficients, a field of quotients $Q(J)$ can be constructed the elements of which are the formal quotients a/b $(a, b \in J$ with $b \neq 0)$, by adopting definitions of equality, sums, differences, and products (see 258). This construction yields from the integral domain Z of all integers the rational field $Q = Q(Z)$, and from the domain $R[x]$ of real polynomials the field $R(x) = Q(R[x])$ of all real rational functions.

Ideals and quotient-rings. It is possible to greatly generalize the construction of the modular fields Z_p and commutative rings Z_n from the familiar integral domain Z of all integers. The key idea of this generalization is contained in the following basic concepts.

In a commutative ring R, an ideal is a nonvoid subset H such that $h, h' \in H$ imply $h \pm h' \in H$, and $h \in H$ and $r \in R$ imply $rh = hr \in H$. A residue class, or additive coset, of the ideal H is a set $H + x$ consisting of all sums $h + x$ of a fixed element $x \in R$ with variable h of H.

The ideals of the integral domain Z consist of the trivial ideals Z and $(0) = \{0\}$, the subset of zero, and the proper ideals (n) of the set of all multiples kn $(k \in Z)$ of a fixed integer $n > 1$. The residue classes $r + (n)$ of any proper ideal (n) are the sets of integers x having a fixed remainder r under division by n, so that $x = qn + r$ for an integer q. Z_n can be regarded as the set of all these residue classes, added and multiplied by specific rules (see 259). When constructed in this way, Z_n is called the quotient-ring $Z/(n)$ of Z by the ideal (n).

Morphisms of rings. The preceding basic construction can also be interpreted in terms of another basic concept, that of morphism. If R and S are any two (commutative) rings, a morphism of rings from R to S is a function $\theta : R \to S$, which assigns to each $r \in R$ a value $s = \theta(r)$ in S, such that $\theta(1) = 1$ and morphisms of sums, differences, and products are sums, differences, and products

Epimorphism

of morphisms of corresponding elements (see 260). Such a morphism is called an epimorphism when it is onto, in the sense that every $s \in S$ is the image $s = \theta(r)$ of some $r \in R$; if it is also one–one, in the sense that $r \neq r'$ in R implies $\theta(r) \neq \theta(r')$ in S, the (epi)morphism is called an isomorphism. Morphisms of rings are related to ideals and quotient rings by the following basic results:

Theorem: If $\theta: R \to S$ is any morphism of rings, then the set $\theta^{-1}(0)$ of all elements $r \in R$ such that $\theta(r) = 0$ in S is an ideal J_θ of R. If θ is an epimorphism, then S is isomorphic to the quotient-ring R/J_θ. Conversely, given any ideal J of a ring R, there exists an epimorphism $\theta: R \to R/J$ under which J is the ideal of all $r \in R$ such that $\theta(r) = 0$ in S.

Subrings and subfields. Here is considered the case in which R is any commutative ring with 1 as its unity element, as postulated in F3. This element is unique because if $1'$ is any other element having the property postulated in F3, then $1' = 11' = 1'1 = 1$. S is a set $S = 0$, ± 1, $\pm(1+1)$, · · · obtained from 1 by repeated addition and subtraction. These elements are not necessarily distinct (for example, in Z_{11}). For any positive integer n, $n1$ (or just n) is used to designate the sum $1 + \cdots + 1$ (with n summands), and $(-n)1$ designates the sum $(-1) + \cdots + (-1)$ (again n summands). A final condition is that $0 \cdot 1 = 0$. Using mathematical induction it is then quite easy to prove from the postulates F1–F3, F4′, and F5 for a commutative ring that, for all $m, n \in Z$ (see 261), the function $\mu: n \to n1$ is a morphism of rings from Z to R. The set $\{n1\}$ of all natural multiples $n1$ of 1 in R is thus closed under the basic ring operations of addition, subtraction, and multiplication, and it includes the unity 1 of R. A subring of a ring R can be defined to be any subset of R with these properties, and the prime subring can be defined to be the subring $\{n1\}$ just constructed; this prime subring is evidently contained in every other subring: it is the least subring of R.

Characteristic of a ring. Using the results about ideals and quotient-rings in Z stated earlier, one can prove quite easily that the prime subring of any ring is isomorphic to Z or to Z_n for some unique integer $n > 1$. (The case $n = 1$ gives the degenerate ring consisting of 0 alone, in which 0 acts as unity, so that $1 = 0$; this is usually excluded from consideration.) This integer n is called the characteristic of the ring; it is the least positive integer n such that $x + \cdots + x = 0$ whenever the number of summands is a multiple of n. Rings the prime subring of which is isomorphic to Z are said to be of characteristic zero (or, more logically, of characteristic infinity, denoted ∞). Rings of characteristic two are quite special; in them, $y = -y$ (because $y + y = 0$), hence $x - y = x + (-y) = x + y$, so that addition is the same as subtraction.

It is easy to show that the characteristic of any field F is a prime p or infinity. In the former case, the prime subring Z_p is already a field (*i.e.*, closed under division). In the latter case the prime subring Z can be (uniquely) extended to its field of quotients Q, which is thus embedded isomorphically in F as its prime subfield; *i.e.*, as a subfield of F contained in every other subfield. To summarize: every field F contains as its smallest prime subfield a copy of Z_p for some prime p (its characteristic), or of Q if of characteristic ∞.

FIELD EXTENSIONS

Simple algebraic extensions. The preceding concepts make possible a far-reaching generalization of the method used to extend the real field $\mathfrak{R}$ to the complex field $\mathfrak{C} = \mathfrak{R}[i]$. Namely, if F is assumed to be any field, and if it is assumed that $p(x)$ is any monic polynomial—*i.e.*, a polynomial with leading coefficient 1 (see 262)—that is irreducible in the sense that it cannot be factored into polynomials of lower degree with coefficients in F, then the multiples of $p(x)$ form an ideal $(p(x))$ in the integral domain $F[x]$ of all polynomials with coefficients in F. Finally, the quotient-ring $F[x]/(p(x))$ the elements of which are the residue classes of this ideal is a field.

Any field constructed in this way is called a simple algebraic extension of F. Each residue class (additive coset) of the ideal $(p(x))$ contains exactly one polynomial of degree less than n, much as each residue class $(p) + n$ of (p) in Z contains exactly one of the remainders $0, 1, \cdots, p-1$ commonly used to represent elements of $Z/(p) = Z_p$. Similarly, the polynomial $r(x)$ (see 263) belonging to any given coset $(p(x)) + f(x)$ can be computed from any member of the coset—*e.g.*, from $f(x)$—as its remainder after polynomial long division by $p(x)$.

(262) $p(x) = x^n + b_1 x^{n-1} + \cdots + b_n$

(263) $r(x) = r_0 + r_1 x + \cdots + r_{n-1} x^{n-1}$

(264) $s(x) = s_0 + s_1 x + \cdots + s_{n-1} x^{n-1}$

(265) $$r(x) + s(x) = (r_0 + s_0) + (r_1 + s_1)x + \cdots + (r_{n-1} + s_{n-1})x^{n-1}$$

(266) $$a + bx + cx^2 = a + b\sqrt[3]{2} + c\sqrt[3]{4}, \qquad x = \sqrt[3]{2}$$

(267) $$\begin{cases} (a + bx + cx^2)(a' + b'x + c'x^2) = (aa' + 2bc' + \\ + 2b'c) + (ab' + ba' + 2cc')x + (ac' + bb' + ca')x^2 \end{cases}$$

(268) $$\begin{cases} x, x^2, x^3, x^4 = x + 1, \quad x^5 = x^2 + x, \quad x^6 = x^3 + x^2 \\ x^7 = x^3 + x + 1, \quad x^8 = x^2 + 1 \\ x^9 = x^3 + x, \quad x^{10} = x^2 + x + 1 \\ x^{11} = x^3 + x^2 + x, \quad x^{12} = x^3 + x^2 + x + 1 \\ x^{13} = x^3 + x^2 + 1 \\ x^{14} = x^3 + 1, \quad x^{15} = x^0 = 1 \end{cases}$$

(269) $GF(16)$: $x, x^2, x^4, x^7, x^8, x^{11}, x^{13}, x^{14}$

(270) $R(x) = p(x)/q(x)$ with $q(x) \neq 0$

Hence the polynomials of degree less than n, such as $r(x)$ (see 263) and (x) (see 264), can be used to represent the elements of $F[x]/(p(x))$ symbolically. They can be added like ordinary polynomials (see 265). To multiply them, their ordinary product is formed (257), then the remainder under division by n is taken. Thus, if $p(x) = x^3 - 2$, the elements of $Q[2^{1/3}] = Q[x]/(x^3 - 2)$ can be taken as all expressions of the form that results (see 266) by replacing x^3 by 2 wherever it occurs; the product (see 267) is obtained in which $2^{1/3}$ could be written for x and $2^{2/3}$ could be written in place of x^2, throughout.

Finite fields. The preceding construction gives all finite fields: any finite field of characteristic p is a simple algebraic extension of its prime subfield Z_p. In more detail, any such field contains p^n elements for some positive integer n and is $Z_p[x]/(p(x))$ for some irreducible monic polynomial of degree n. Moreover, all fields of the same finite order p^n are isomorphic; because they were first constructed by Galois, it is therefore reasonable to speak of the Galois field $GF(p^n)$ of any given prime-power order p^n.

As an example, $GF(16) \cong Z_2[x]/(x^4 + x + 1)$ consists of 0 and the 15 different powers of x (see 268). Under multiplication, the nonzero elements of $GF(16)$ thus form a cyclic group, consisting of the powers of x, or any of the other primitive roots of 1 (see 269) the exponents of which are relatively prime to 15.

The preceding example is typical: in any finite field $GF(p^n)$, the $p^n - 1$ nonzero elements are all powers of some one primitive $(p^n - 1)$th root of unity, which can be taken to be x.

Transcendental extensions. Fields have many extensions besides the simple algebraic extensions discussed above. For example, if F is assumed to be any field, and $F[x]$ is assumed to be the integral domain of all polynomials $p(x)$ in the symbol (indeterminate) x with coefficients in F, then because $F[x]$ is an integral domain, the formal quotients of polynomials (rational forms; see 270) constitute a field $F(x)$ under the definitions (see 258) given earlier for constructing the field of quotients of the domain $F[x]$. An extension E of F that can be constructed from F in this way using a suitable element x of E is called a simple transcendental extension of F. When F is infinite, one can interpret the expressions $R(x)$ (see 270) as rational functions from F to F, defined except for a finite set of values x_i of F in which $q(x_i) = 0$.

By repeating the preceding construction, multiple transcendental extensions of F can be obtained. Thus, for any positive integer n, the field $F(x_1, \cdots, x_n)$ can be constructed of all rational expressions (or forms) in the n indeterminates $x_1, \cdots, x_n$ as the field of (formal) quotients of polynomials in $x_1, \cdots, x_n$ with coefficients in F: the field of quotients of the polynomial ring $F[x_1, \cdots, x_n]$.

Multiple algebraic extensions can be constructed similarly. Before considering the general nature of such multiple algebraic extensions, a special case of multiple quadratic extensions of the rational field Q that has applications to geometry must be considered.

Pythagorean numbers. A real or complex number is called Pythagorean when it can be expressed in terms of rational numbers through a finite number of rational operations and square root extractions; *i.e.*, when it belongs to a multiple quadratic extension of Q. Because the mapping $z \rightarrow z^*$ that carries each complex number $x + iy$ into its conjugate $z^* = x - iy$ is an automorphism of the complex field $\mathfrak{C}$, and $x = (z + z^*)/2$ and $y = (z - z^*)/2$, the real and imaginary parts of any Pythagorean number are themselves Pythagorean. Conversely, $z^2 = c = a + ib$ is equivalent to two simultaneous quadratic equations (see 271). Therefore a complex number $z = x + iy$ is Pythagorean if,

(271) $$\begin{cases} x^2 + y^2 = \sqrt{a^2 + b^2} \quad \text{and} \quad 2xy = b \\ x \pm y = [\sqrt{a^2 + b^2} \pm b]^{\frac{1}{2}} \end{cases}$$

(272) $$x^2 + y^2 + Ax + By = C, \qquad 4C > A^2 + B^2$$

(273) $$C = R[\sqrt{-1}] = \frac{R(x)}{x^2 + 1}$$

(274) $$p(z) = c_0 + c_1 z + c_2 z^2 + \cdots + c_n z^n, \qquad c_n \neq 0$$

(275) $$p(z) = c_n(z - z_1)(z - z_2) \cdots (z - z_n), \quad \text{all } z_k \in C$$

(276) $$(z - z_k)(z - z_k^*) = z^2 - (z_k + z_k^*)z + z_k z_k^*$$

(277) $$\begin{cases} x = 0010 & x^6 = 1100 & x^{11} = 1110 \\ x^2 = 0100 & x^7 = 1011 & x^{12} = 1111 \\ x^3 = 1000 & x^8 = 0101 & x^{13} = 1101 \\ x^4 = 0011 & x^9 = 1010 & x^{14} = 1001 \\ x^5 = 0110 & x^{10} = 0111 & x^{15} = 0001 \end{cases}$$

and only if, x and y (its real and complex parts) are both Pythagorean.

The subfield of all Pythagorean numbers has an interesting relation to ruler-and-compass constructions in plane geometry. In the complex z-plane, a point is called Pythagorean when its coordinate is a Pythagorean number. A straight line that passes through two Pythagorean points is called a Pythagorean line; the angle between two Pythagorean lines, a Pythagorean angle; and a circle that has a Pythagorean centre and a Pythagorean radius, a Pythagorean circle.

It can be proved very easily that a straight line is Pythagorean if and only if its standard equation ($y = ax + b$ or $x = c$) has (real) Pythagorean coefficients. For, any line having such an equation passes through the Pythagorean points $(0, b)$ and $(1, a + b)$, while if $y_i = ax_i + b$ for two Pythagorean points (x_1, y_1) and (x_2, y_2), then $a = (y_2 - y_1)/(x_2 - x_1)$ and $b = y_2 - ax_2$ must be Pythagorean numbers.

A circle is Pythagorean if and only if its equation, written in the customary way as a sum of squares and a linear component (see 272), has coefficients that are (real) Pythagorean numbers. The circle through any three Pythagorean points z_1, z_2, z_3 is Pythagorean; this can be demonstrated by setting $x = x_i$ and $y = y_i$ $(i = 1, 2, 3)$ (see 272) and solving for the unknowns A, B, C.

Likewise, it is easy to show that two Pythagorean lines or circles can only intersect in Pythagorean points. To show this, it suffices to solve for the coordinates (x_i, y_i) of the points of intersection in terms of the (Pythagorean) coefficients of the equations.

From the preceding, it follows that the set of all Pythagorean points, lines, and circles is precisely the set of all points, straight lines, and circles that can be constructed from a given line segment [drawn between (0, 0) and (1, 0)], using a ruler and compass.

Finally, the set of all Pythagorean angles must be determined. Using Galois theory (see below), it can be shown that $1^{1/n}$ is a Pythagorean number if and only if n is the product of a power of two and a Pythagorean prime p_i, such that p_i is one plus a certain power of two. The first few Pythagorean primes are $2 = 2^0 + 1$, $3 = 2^1 + 1$, $5 = 2^2 + 1$, $17 = 2^4 + 1$, and $257 = 2^8 + 1$. It can be shown that they are all of the form $2^{2^x} + 1$, in which $x = 2^n$. Correspondingly, 90°, 72°, 60°, and 45° are Pythagorean angles, but 20° is not.

Fundamental Theorem of Algebra. Now the most remarkable property of the complex field $\mathfrak{C}$ is reached, which can also be characterized as the simple algebraic extension (see 273) of the real field $\mathfrak{R}$. This property will be stated now as a theorem, omitting its proof (which is not algebraic, but depends basically on considerations from analysis). This theorem is called the Fundamental Theorem of Algebra.

For any polynomial of degree $n > 0$ (see 274), with complex coefficients $c_k \in \mathfrak{C}$, there exists a complex number $z_i \in \mathfrak{C}$ such that $p(z_i) = 0$.

A corollary is that the polynomial $p(z)$ (see 274) can always be (uniquely) factored into linear factors (see 275).

As a further corollary, the only polynomials that are irreducible over $\mathfrak{C}$ are linear polynomials, from which it follows that $\mathfrak{C}$ has no proper algebraic extensions.

When the coefficients of $p(z)$ (see 274) are real, its complex roots z_k occur in conjugate pairs, giving real quadratic factors (see 276) with negative discriminant $4x_k^2 - 4(x_k^2 + y_k^2) < 0$. It follows that any real polynomial can be factored into real linear and quadratic factors.

APPLICATIONS TO CODING

Binary codes. Finite fields $GF(2^n)$ of characteristic two are widely used in the design of codes for detecting and correcting errors in the transmission of digital information (see INFORMATION PROCESSING AND INFORMATION SYSTEMS and COMBINATORICS). Such information is commonly transmitted as a sequence of signals of two kinds; for example, dots and dashes, or timed pulses and nonpulses. These can be interpreted as strings of 0's and 1's; the elements of $GF(2^n)$ can also be represented very compactly as strings of binary digits, or bits, 0 and 1. Thus, in $GF(16)$, the x^k, the remainders of which after division by $x^4 + x + 1$ were listed above (see 268) as polynomials, can be expressed in the more compact form of quadruples of binary digits (see 277). Thus, if a message consisting of sequences of binary digits is broken down into segments (words) of length four, each word can be interpreted as an element of $GF(16)$.

Because the transmission of messages consisting of such four-bit (or longer) words is not infallible, it is common practice to add check digits to a given message, so the actual (binary) code word sent is longer than the message word containing the actual information to be transmitted. One speaks of an (m, n)-code $(m < n)$ if the binary code words transmitted all have the same length n, greater than the length m of the message words.

Simple codes

The simplest code consists of one check digit, usually taken to be 1 if the number of digits 1 in the actual message is odd and 0 if it is even. Thus, for the four-bit message words listed above, the code words would be: 00101, 01001, 10001, 00110, 01100, 11000, 10111, 01010, 10100, 01111, 11101, 11110, 11011, 10010, and 00011. The set of all code words clearly consists of just those strings of five 0's and 1's that have an even number of 1's. Note that the set of code words contains with any two code words their sum (all digits being added mod 2); thus 00101 + 10001 = 10100 ($x + x^3 = x^9$).

The preceding code is error-detecting: if there is only one error made in transmitting a given code word, this error can be detected because the received word will have an odd number of 1's. More elaborate codes are error-correcting. A simple error-correcting code would consist in repeating each message word three times, so that $x^8 = 0101$ would be transmitted as 010101010101. If at most one error is made in transmitting each digit of the given message, then the correct message can be decoded by assigning to each near code word the message that gives each digit correctly two or more times. Thus, 011100010100 would still be correctly deciphered as the message 0101, even though it has three errors of transmittal.

Note that in the preceding triple repetition code, the set of all code words is also closed under addition. This is characteristic of the group codes commonly used in practice.

Optimal binary codes. The triple repetition (4, 12)-code just described will correct all single errors, but not all double errors. A much better code for correcting 4-bit messages can be constructed using $GF(8) = Z_2[x]/(x^3 + x + 1)$, as follows. Given a 4-bit message $a_0a_1a_2a_3$, form the product (see 278) of the corresponding binary message polynomial $a(x)$

(278) $$a(x)g(x) = (a_0 + a_1x + a_2x^2 + a_3x^3)(1 + x + x^3)$$

(279) $$a(x)g(x) = b(x) = b_0 + b_1x + b_2x^2 + \cdots + b_6x^6$$

(280) $$a(x)g(x) = (a_0 + a_1x + \cdots + a_6x^6)(1 + x + x^2 + x^4 + x^8)$$

(281) $$g(x) = 1 + x + x^2 + x^4 + x^8 = (1 + x^3 + x^4)(1 + x + x^2 + x^3 + x^4)$$

(282) $$a(x)g(x) = b_0 + b_1x + b_2x^2 + \cdots + b_{14}x^{14}$$

with the fixed encoding polynomial $g(x) = 1 + x + x^3$, and transmit the 7-digit code word $b_0b_1b_2 \cdots b_6$ corresponding to the product in $Z_2[x]$ (see 279). Because the roots of $x^3 + x + 1 = 0$ are primitive 7th roots of unity in $GF(8)$, all code words differ in at least three digits.

Advantages of the (4, 7)-code

Indeed, the (4, 7)-code just constructed is a perfect code in the sense that each 7-digit word not a code word can be corrected to precisely one code word by changing one digit. Because it transmits as much information as the triple repetition (4, 12)-code in less than 60 percent as much time and has roughly the same error-correcting capabilities, it is clearly superior.

Similarly, one can use the field $GF(16)$ to construct a (7, 15) binary code that will correct two errors with certainty and is far superior to the (5, 15) triple repetition code. Namely, given a 7-bit message word $a_0a_1 \cdots a_6$, the product formed (see 280) is of the corresponding binary message polynomial $a(x)$ with the fixed encoding polynomial $g(x)$ (see 281). The product polynomial with typical coefficient b_k (see 282) is transmitted as the 15-digit code word $b_0b_1b_2 \cdots b_{14}$. Because the roots of both of the factors of $g(x)$ above are primitive 15th roots of unity in $GF(16)$, it can be shown that it takes five changes to convert one code word into another, and that each 15-digit word differs in two or fewer letters from at most one nearest code word. That is, the preceding code corrects all double errors. Moreover, it is not far from optimal.

GALOIS THEORY

Algebraic number fields. If E is any extension of a field F—that is, if F is any subfield of the field E—then E can be considered as a vector space over F, which is the field of scalars. A number $x \in E$ is then said to be algebraic over F when it generates with F a finite-dimensional subspace of E. This is the case if, and only if, the powers $1 = x^0$, x, x^2, $\cdots$ of x are linearly dependent over F, so that x satisfies a polynomial equation with coefficients in F.

In particular, a real or complex number z is called algebraic when it is algebraic over the rational field Q, which is, of course, the prime subfield of $\mathfrak{C}$ (and $\mathfrak{R}$). That is, z is algebraic precisely when it satisfies a polynomial equation with rational coefficients, hence an irreducible polynomial equation $p(z) = 0$, so that the extension of Q by z is the simple algebraic extension $Q[z]/(p(z))$. (Actually, every finite-dimensional extension of Q or any Z_p is just such a simple algebraic extension.)

When E itself is a finite-dimensional vector space over F, its dimensionality (over F) is called its degree as an extension of F, and this degree is written symbolically as $[E : F]$. In such cases, every element of E is algebraic over F, and E may properly be called an algebraic extension of F.

More generally, if E is any extension of a field F, the set of all numbers $x \in E$ that are algebraic over F is a subfield. Thus, the set of all algebraic (complex) numbers is a subfield A of $\mathfrak{C}$, which is algebraically complete (or closed) in the sense that any polynomial $p(z)$ of degree $n > 0$ with coefficients in A has a root z_1 in A. This is a proper subfield of $\mathfrak{C}$, because it fails to contain e, π, and other transcendental numbers (a transcendental number is a number that is not the root of a polynomial with integral coefficients).

Still more generally, if F is any field and $p(x)$ any polynomial with coefficients in F, then x will be a root of $p(x) = 0$ in the simple algebraic extension $F[x]/(p(x))$. By repeated extensions, using transfinite induction if necessary, an algebraically complete algebraic extension of F can always be constructed, in which an analogue of the Fundamental Theorem of Algebra holds.

Splitting fields. If F is assumed to be any field, and $p(t)$ any polynomial with coefficients in F, a splitting field of $p(t)$ over F is defined as an extension E of F over which $p(t)$ can be factored into linear factors. To construct a least such splitting field, the following procedure is followed.

First, if it is supposed that $p(t)$ is factored into factors irreducible over F, it is easy to show that such a factorization exists. If the irreducible factors are all linear—that is, of degree one—there is nothing to prove ($E = F$).

Otherwise, $p(t)$ will have an irreducible factor $p_j(t)$ of degree $n > 1$, in which case the simple algebraic extension $E_1 = F[x]/(p_j(x))$ is formed. In E_1, the polynomial p_j, which was written as $p_j(t)$ to avoid confusion between t and the indeterminate x in E_1, will have the root x and hence the linear factor $(t - x)$. Hence $p_j(t)$, and so $p(t)$, can be factored into more factors over E_1.

Repeating this construction at most n times, an extension will be obtained, $E = E_k$ of F over which $p(t)$ can be factored into linear factors. Because E is generated by F and roots $x_1, \cdots, x_k$ of $p(t) = 0$, it is evident that E is a minimal splitting field (it is called the root field of $f(t)$ over F). To prove this rigorously, however, requires a more careful study of isomorphisms and their extensions.

Galois theory of fields. This study, and many other aspects of the deeper algebraic theory of fields (including that of the algebraic solvability of polynomial equations), involves so-called Galois theory, which in turn depends on the concept of a group (see above *Groups*).

Normal field extension

For Galois theory, the concept of a normal field extension is indispensable. An extension E of a field F is called a normal over F when E is a splitting field for every polynomial $p(x)$ that is irreducible over F and has one root in E. Equivalently, the condition is that, if $p(x)$ has one root in E and is irreducible over F, then all its roots are in E. Thus the complex field $\mathfrak{C}$ is a normal extension of the real field $\mathfrak{R}$, and the field $Q[(1 + i)/\sqrt{2}]$ obtained by adjoining the fourth root $\omega = (1 + i)/\sqrt{2}$ of -1 to the rational field Q is a normal extension of Q (it is the root field of $x^4 + 1$ over Q, whose other roots are ω^3, ω^5, ω^7).

If it be assumed that E is a normal extension of a field F, then the Galois group of E over F is defined as the group of those automorphisms γ of the field E that leave every element of F invariant; *i.e.*, satisfy $\gamma(x) = x$ for all $x \in F$.

It is known that if x_1 and x_2 are any two roots in E of a polynomial $p(x)$ that is irreducible over F, then there exists an automorphism in the Galois group of E over F that carries x_1 into x_2. Thus, i and $-i$ are the two roots of $x^2+1=0$ in the normal extension $\mathfrak{C}$ of $\mathfrak{R}$; the automorphism γ: $z \to z^*$ of $\mathfrak{C}$ carries i into $-i$. Likewise, there exist automorphisms of $Q[(1+i)/\sqrt{2}]$ over Q that carry $\omega=(1+i)/\sqrt{2}$ into ω^3, ω^5, and ω^7.

A complex number can be shown to be Pythagorean if and only if the smallest normal extension of Q that contains it has a Galois group (over Q) the order of which is a power of two. (The order of any algebraic system is the cardinal number of its elements.) It follows from this and Lagrange's theorem in group theory that no Pythagorean number can satisfy an irreducible equation the degree of which is not a power of two. On the other hand, using analytic geometry, it can be shown that angle trisection is equivalent to solving a cubic equation that is in general irreducible, as in the case of trisecting an angle of 120° to get an angle of 40°. It follows in general that an angle cannot be trisected by a finite construction with ruler and compass; in particular, an angle of 120° or 60° cannot be so trisected.

One can show that the Galois group of any binomial x^n-a is solvable in a sense defined above in the section *Groups*. More generally, this is true of any normal field extension obtained by successive adjunctions of roots $a^{1/n}$ of constants a already constructed. It follows that if a polynomial equation $p(x)=0$ over a field F can be solved by radicals, in the sense that its roots can be expressed in terms of the elements of F using only rational operations and root extractions, then the Galois group of the root field of $p(x)$ over F is solvable. The converse is also true: if $p(x)$ is a polynomial the root field of which has a solvable group, then the roots of $p(x)=0$ can be expressed in terms of its coefficients using only rational operations and root extractions.

On the other hand, the Galois group of an irreducible polynomial equation of degree n over Q is, in general, the symmetric group of all permutations of its n roots $x_1, \cdots, x_n$. Moreover, this symmetric group is solvable if and only if $n \leq 5$ (the proof of this is quite technical). It follows that any quadratic, cubic, or quartic equation is solvable by radicals, but that quintic and higher degree polynomial equations in general are not.

ORDERED FIELDS

Positivity. To define the real field, to establish the deeper properties of the real and complex fields, and in particular to construct the real field from the rational field, more than the four rational operations of addition, multiplication, subtraction, and division must be considered. For example, these operations fail to distinguish $\sqrt{2}$ from $-\sqrt{2}$: the Galois group of $\mathfrak{C}$ over Q interchanges $\pm\sqrt{2}$.

The simplest and most natural concept with which to construct $\mathfrak{R}$ from Q and to establish its deeper properties (along with those of $\mathfrak{C}$) is the order concept or, equivalently, that of positivity. These concepts are now defined. A field F is said to be ordered when it contains a set P of positive elements having three properties stating that the sum and product of any two elements in P belong to P and that for every x, exactly one of the following is true: $x=0$, x is in P or $-x$ is in P (see 283).

In an ordered field, $x>y$ is defined to mean that $(x-y)\in P$. Then $x\in P$ is equivalent to $x>0$, and the properties of P can be used to prove the transitive property of the order relation, its preservation when elements satisfying it are replaced by their sums or products with appropriate field elements, and the threefold alternative of order between any two elements (see 284). Conversely, in any field F having an order relation satisfying these properties (see 284), the set P of all elements x such that $x>0$ satisfies the definition of an ordered field (see 283), while $u>v$ if, and only if, $(u-v)\in P$; indeed, these results hold more generally in integral domains.

It is a familiar fact that Q and $\mathfrak{R}$ are ordered fields with the usual order. Indeed, in $\mathfrak{R}$, P can be defined as the set of all nonzero a such that $\sqrt{a}$ exists in $\mathfrak{R}$, giving a purely algebraic characterization of the order relation. As a result, there are no nontrivial field automorphisms of $\mathfrak{R}$.

On the other hand, there is no way to make the complex field $\mathfrak{C}$ or any field such as Z_p of finite characteristic into an ordered field. This is because, if x is any nonzero

(283) $$\begin{cases} x\in P \text{ and } y\in P \text{ imply } x+y\in P \\ x\in P \text{ and } y\in P \text{ imply } xy\in P \\ x=0,\ x\in P, \text{ or } -x\in P \end{cases}$$

(284) $$\begin{cases} \text{If } x>y \text{ and } y>z, \text{ then } x>z. \\ \text{If } a\in F \text{ and } x>y, \text{ then } a+x>a+y. \\ \text{If } a>0 \text{ and } x>y, \text{ then } ax>ay. \\ \text{Given } x \text{ and } y, \text{ precisely one of the following} \\ \text{alternatives holds:} \\ x=y, \quad x>y, \quad \text{or} \quad y>x \end{cases}$$

(285) $$x_1^2+x_2^2+\cdots+x_n^2=0 \text{ implies } x_1=x_2=\cdots=x_n=0$$

(286) $$n\delta=\overbrace{\delta+\cdots+\delta}^{n \text{ summands}}>M$$

(287) $$\lim_{n\to\infty}\frac{1}{n}=0$$

(288) $$f(x)=x^r(a_0+a_1x+\cdots+a_nx^n+\cdots)$$

(289) $$\begin{aligned}&[x^r(a_0+a_1x+a_2x^2+\cdots)]\cdot\\ &\cdot[x^s(b_0+b_1x+b_2x^2+\cdots)]\\ &=x^{r+s}[a_0b_0+(a_1b_0+a_0b_1)x+\\ &+(a_2b_0+a_1b_1+a_0b_2)x^2+\cdots]\end{aligned}$$

element of an ordered field, then by the second property of the definition of an ordered field (see 283) $x^2=(-x)^2$ must be positive; hence any sum of squares must be positive. It follows that if a field can be made into an ordered field, then it must satisfy the implication that each of n elements are 0 if the sum of their squares is 0 (see 285). Fields having this property are called formally real; it has been shown that a field cannot be ordered unless it is formally real.

Using the concept of a formally real field, the mathematician Artin solved in 1926 a famous problem of Hilbert, showing that a real polynomial $p(x_1, \cdots, x_n)$ assumes positive values for all real $x_1, \cdots, x_n$ if, and only if, it is a sum of squares of polynomials.

Archimedean fields. As will be shown, there is a vast variety of ordered fields. The familiar ordered fields Q and $\mathfrak{R}$ have a property that sets them apart from many others, the Archimedean property, as follows.

The definition is that an ordered field (or integral domain or even additive group) is called Archimedean when, given $\delta>0$ (no matter how small) and $M>0$ (no matter how large), there exists a positive integer n such that its product with δ, defined in terms of the addition of n summands, is greater than M (see 286). The Archimedean property

In fields, but not necessarily in integral domains, the preceding condition is equivalent to either of the following:

(i) The set $\{n\}$ of all positive integers has no upper bound.
(ii) The set $\{1/n\}$ of all reciprocals of positive integers has greatest lower bound 0.

[Explanation: Condition (i) implies the Archimedean property (see 286), because it allows the choice of $n>M/\delta$; by an upper bound of a set S is meant as usual a number λ such that $\lambda\geq x$ for all $x\in S$.]

Condition (ii) can also be written in the form of a vanishing limit of reciprocals of n as n approaches ∞ (see 287), which means simply that, given $\varepsilon>0$, n can be found such that $n<1/\varepsilon$; in other words, that there is no $\varepsilon>0$ such that $1/n \not< 0$ for all positive integers n. Because 0 is obviously a lower bound to $\{1/n\}$, this is equivalent to saying that it is the greatest lower bound.

An interesting non-Archimedean field is provided by the set consisting of 0 and all extended formal power series, whether convergent or not, expressed with a factor x^r common to all terms and a first coefficient a_0 (see 288), in which r can be any integer, the coefficients c_k belong to a specified ordered field F, and $a_0 \neq 0$. The extended formal power series f (see 288) is called positive if, and only if, $a_0 > 0$, while the sum and product of two such series are defined by the usual formal rules (see 289). It is then straightforward to show that the above construction gives a non-Archimedean ordered field. In this ordered field, the set of all ordinary power series—*i.e.*, extended formal power series (288) with $r \geq 0$—is a subring, hence a non-Archimedean ordered domain.

It is evident that any subfield S of an ordered field F is itself an ordered field (positivity having the same meaning), and that S is an Archimedean ordered field if F is.

Limits and convergence. In any ordered set, whether a field or not, one can speak of limits and convergence. Namely (see 287), if $x_1, x_2, x_3, \cdots$ is any infinite sequence of elements of an ordered set C, it may be said that the sequence $\{x_n\}$ converges to the limit a (see 290) if, and only if, for every $\varepsilon > 0$ there exists an n so large that $a - \varepsilon < x_m < a + \varepsilon$, whenever m is greater than n.

(290) $$\lim_{n\to\infty} x_n = a \quad \text{or simply } x_n \to a$$

(291) $$\begin{cases} \{.3, .33, .333, .3333, .33333, \cdots\} \to \frac{1}{3} \\ \{.7, .67, .667, .6667, .66667, \cdots\} \to \frac{2}{3} \\ \{3, 1, 3.14, 3.141, 3.1415, 3.14159, \cdots\} \to \pi \end{cases}$$

(292) $$\{x_1 \leqslant x_2 \leqslant x_3 \leqslant \cdots \leqslant x_n = \cdots\}$$

(293) $$\{x_n\} = \{y_n\} \text{ means that } \lim_{n\to\infty} (x_n - y_n) = 0$$

(294) $$\begin{cases} |0| = 0, \quad |x| > 0 \quad \text{if } x \neq 0 \\ |a+b| \leqslant |a| + |b| \\ |ab| = |a| \cdot |b| \\ |(|a|)| = |a| \end{cases}$$

(295) $$|z| = \sqrt{x^2 + y^2}, \qquad z = x + iy$$

(296) $$q = (r/s)p^{\nu}$$

(297) $$\begin{cases} \phi_p(0) = 0, \quad \phi_p(q) > 0 \quad \text{if } q \neq 0 \\ \phi_p(a+b) \leqslant \phi_p(a) + \phi_p(b) \\ \phi_p(ab) = \phi_p(a)\, \phi_p(b) \\ \phi_p(a+b) \leqslant \text{Max}\{\phi_p(a), \phi_p(b)\} \end{cases}$$

Mono-tone sequences

The most familiar examples of convergent sequences are provided by the successive lower and upper n-place decimal approximants to a given number. Thus, $1/3$ may be expressed as a limit of decimal fractions composed successively of greater numbers of the digit 3 (see 291) and so on.

The preceding examples are monotone; *i.e.*, increasing or decreasing. Limits of monotone sequences have an especially simple characterization. Thus, if a "less than or equals" relation holds between any pair of elements with adjacent subscripts in a sequence (see 292)—that is, if the sequence is any increasing (or non-decreasing) sequence of numbers from an ordered field F—then $x_n \to a$ if, and only if, a is the least upper bound (l.u.b.) of the set of $\{x_n\}$. By this it is meant that: $a \geq x_n$ for all n, and $b \geq x_n$ for all n implies $b \geq a$. The fact that an increasing sequence $\{x_n\}$ converges to a is often written $x_n \uparrow a$. Likewise, one writes $x_n \downarrow a$ to signify that the sequence $\{x_n\}$ is decreasing (or non-increasing), with greatest lower bound (g.l.b.) a.

Completeness. Now the deepest property of the real field $\mathfrak{R}$ is reached: the property of completeness, which distinguishes it from all other ordered fields. Actually, there are two kinds of completeness, which will be discussed in turn.

Cauchy complete-ness

First, there is sequential, or Cauchy, completeness. If $\{x_n\}$ is any convergent sequence in an ordered field with limit a, then the doubly infinite set of differences $\{x_m - x_n\}$ has the property of being a Cauchy sequence in the following sense.

A sequence $\{x_n\}$ of numbers of an ordered field F is defined to be a Cauchy sequence when, given $\varepsilon > 0$, there exists N so large that $m, n > N$ imply $-\varepsilon < x_m - x_n < \varepsilon$.

In the real field $\mathfrak{R}$, the converse is also true: any Cauchy sequence has a limit to which it converges. This property defines sequential completeness.

An ordered field (or group) F is complete in the sense of Cauchy when every Cauchy sequence converges to some limit.

The real field is complete in the sense of Cauchy. For, choosing $\varepsilon = 10^{-r}$ ($r = 1, 2, 3, \cdots$), from any Cauchy sequence $\{x_n\}$ can be obtained a subsequence $\{x_{n(r)}\}$ of decimal fractions, such that $x_{n(r)}$ differs from all later terms at most in the rth decimal place.

The real field $\mathfrak{R}$ can be constructed from the rational field Q as follows, using the property of Cauchy completeness. The elements of the field $\mathfrak{R}$ can be constructed as the limits of Cauchy sequences of rational numbers with the identification of two such sequences (see 293) meaning that the limit of the difference of corresponding terms is 0.

Second, there is a more powerful, but less constructive, characterization of completeness, which may be expressed as follows.

Dedekind complete-ness

An ordered field (or other set) F is defined to be complete in the sense of Dedekind when every bounded set of its elements has a least upper and a greatest lower bound.

It is easy to show that any ordered field that is complete in the sense of Dedekind is Archimedean, and complete in the sense of Cauchy. Conversely, an ordered field F that is Archimedean and complete in the sense of Cauchy is necessarily complete in the sense of Dedekind. What is even more important, however, the following results are true.

Theorem: An ordered field is Archimedean if and only if it is isomorphic with a subgroup of the real field. An ordered field is isomorphic to the real field if and only if it is complete in the sense of Dedekind.

The deepest questions of all are now reached: those of the existence and uniqueness (up to isomorphism) of complete ordered fields. As will be seen, the notion of an absolute value or valuation plays a central role in discussions of these questions.

VALUATIONS

Underlying ideas. The reader may be familiar with the distinction between the sign $\pm$ and the magnitude of a real number. More generally, in an ordered field, the absolute value $|x|$ of any number x can be defined as having the value x if x is positive or zero and the value $-x$ otherwise. From this definition such standard relations as those that relate to the absolute value of 0 and of sums, products, and absolute values (see 294) can be easily derived.

Even though the complex field cannot be made into an ordered field, the definition of the square root of the sum of squares of components of a complex number (see 295) defines an absolute value function sharing the formal properties (294). The notion of absolute value with this definition (295) is indispensable in complex analysis, the theory of functions of a complex variable.

There are many analogues and generalizations of the preceding absolute-value function. An interesting analogue is defined, on the rational field Q, for any prime number p, by the following observation. Each rational number $q = m/n$ (m, n in lowest terms) is uniquely expressible in the form of a ratio of r and s times a power of p (see 296), in which r and s are relatively prime to each other and to p, and $s > 0$.

Given the decomposition (see 296), the number $\varphi_p(q) = p^{-\nu}$ is called the p-adic valuation of q.

This valuation is counterintuitive (contrary to one's intuitive feeling): for example, $\varphi_2(1024)$ is very small, whereas $\varphi_2(1/1024)$ is a million times as large. Nevertheless, it shares (see 297) the first three formal properties of the more familiar absolute value function (see 295). Only the fourth property fails. By way of compensation, the p-adic valuation of q has a sharper property (see 297) than that of the second property of absolute value, which one can strengthen to an inequality involving the maximum of two p-adic valuations rather than the sum.

There are many other important generalizations of the absolute value concepts to systems other than fields: the absolute value $(x^2 + y^2 + z^2 + t^2)^{1/2}$ of a real quaternion $q = t + xi + yi + zk$; the norm $N(a + b\sqrt{2}) = a^2 - 2b^2$ of a number $c = a + b\sqrt{2}$ in $Q(\sqrt{2})$; the norm of an element of a Banach space; and so on.

Completing fields. The way will now be described by which any valuation having the first three properties of the p-adic valuation (see 297) or their equivalents, the first three properties of absolute value (see 294), can be used to complete a given field. The field extension construction to be described gives the real field $\mathfrak{R}$ from the rational field Q; the complex field $\mathfrak{C}$ from the field $Q(\sqrt{-1})$ of all rational complex numbers $r + s\sqrt{-1}$ $(r, s \in Q)$; and a new family of p-adic number fields from the p-adic valuations of Q. It involves the notion of a Cauchy sequence, which is generalized in the following definition:

Let F be any field with a real valuation φ satisfying the first three properties of the p-adic valuation (see 297). A sequence $\{x_n\} = \{x_1, x_2, x_3, \cdot\cdot\cdot\}$ of elements x_n of F is called a Cauchy sequence (for the valuation φ) when, given $\varepsilon > 0$, there is an integer N such that the value of φ at the difference of two elements with subscripts sufficiently large is less than ε (see 298).

Cauchy sequence

(298) $$\phi(x_m - x_n) < \varepsilon \quad \text{if } m, n > N$$

(299) $$\begin{cases} \{x_n\} + \{y_n\} = \{x_n + y_n\} \\ \{x_n\} \cdot \{y_n\} = \{x_n y_n\} \end{cases}$$

(300) $$\lim_{n \to \infty} \phi(x_n - y_n) = 0$$

(301) $$x = p^{\alpha}(a_0 + a_1 p + a_2 p^2 + a_3 p^3 + \cdot\cdot\cdot)$$

(302) $$u = \cos\frac{2\pi}{n} + i\sin\frac{2\pi}{n}, \qquad u^n = 1$$

(303) $$a_0 + a_1 u + \cdot\cdot\cdot + a_{n-1} u^{n-1}$$

(304) $$x^n = (z - y)(z - uy) \cdot\cdot\cdot (z - u^{n-1} y)$$

(305) $$F_s(x_1, \cdot\cdot\cdot, x_n) = 0, \qquad s = 1, \cdot\cdot\cdot, r$$

The sum and product of two Cauchy sequences can be defined by obvious formulas (see 299). Under these definitions the Cauchy sequences form a commutative ring F_φ (a subring of $F^{(\omega)}$), which is, however, not even an integral domain, let alone a field. To make it into a field, the following equivalence relation must be introduced. (In the language of the theory of commutative rings [see below *Rings*], a maximal ideal M of F_φ must be constructed; the quotient-ring F_φ/M will then be a field.)

Two Cauchy sequences as defined are concurrent when the limit of the valuation φ for differences of corresponding terms in the two sequences is 0 (see 300).

In the construction of the real field $\mathfrak{R}$ from the (ordered) rational field Q, typical Cauchy sequences consist of decimal (or binary) approximations to a given unlimited decimal number; two such Cauchy sequences are concurrent when they ultimately agree to any preassigned number of decimal (or binary) digits, leaving aside decimal numbers such as $0.999999 \cdot\cdot\cdot = 1.000000 \cdot\cdot\cdot$ themselves. In this case, the field constructed is not only complete in the sense of Cauchy, it is also an Archimedean ordered field that is complete in the sense of Dedekind. The positive numbers of F_φ are the Cauchy sequences $\{x_n\}$ the terms of which are ultimately all positive, and that are not null sequences (do not converge to zero, are not concurrent to $\{0, 0, 0, \cdot\cdot\cdot\}$).

To recapitulate, the real field $\mathfrak{R}$ is not only Archimedean and complete in the sense of Cauchy; it is also complete in the sense of Dedekind. Conversely, it can be shown that any field that is complete in the sense of Dedekind is Archimedean and complete in the sense of Cauchy. Moreover, in it, one can reconstruct all numbers as limits of decimal fractions in the usual way and derive the usual laws for adding and multiplying the resulting infinite decimals.

This sequence of arguments shows that any ordered field that is complete in the sense of Dedekind is isomorphic to the real field: up to isomorphism, there is one and only one such field. On the other, the field $\mathfrak{R}[[x]]$ of all extended formal power series with real coefficients is a non-Archimedean ordered field (see 288), which is complete in the sense of Cauchy.

Finally, it may be remarked that for $\varphi = \varphi_p$, the previous field extension by Cauchy sequences (modulo null sequences) gives the so-called p-adic numbers of Hensel. These constitute for each prime p a p-adic field, the nonzero elements of which can be thought of as extended formal series in the symbol p with integral coefficients a_k, first coefficient with subscript 0, and with a factor common to each term of the form p^a (see 301), in which a is an arbitrary integer, every a_k is one of the integers $0, 1, \cdot\cdot\cdot, p-1$, and $a_0 \neq 0$. Though the p-adic fields have characteristic zero, they are not to be thought of as ordered fields, still less as Archimedean ordered fields.

(G.Bi.)

Rings

The notion of a ring has been mentioned at the beginning of this article and used in the preceding section *Fields.* It is a set of elements that can be added, subtracted, and multiplied and in which these three operations obey (more or less) the usual rules. A more formal definition will be given later. In particular, if R is a set of real or complex numbers such that the sum, the difference, and the product of any two elements of R is in R, then R is a ring for the usual operations. It is not required that the division by a nonzero element of a ring be always possible; thus the divisibility problem for elements of a ring is important, as it is for the ordinary integers.

The rings introduced by the German arithmeticians of the 19th century for studying problems involving divisibility and factorization were, in fact, mostly sets of complex numbers (more precisely of algebraic integers) as above. The main impetus came from the intensive study of Fermat's equation $x^n + y^n = z^n$, stated without proof by the French mathematician Pierre de Fermat to have no solution (x, y, z) in integers greater than 1 for exponents n greater than 2.

Fermat's equation

It has been proved that Fermat's statement is true for many exponents n, but the general case is still open. The most fruitful approach to the problem introduces a complex nth root of unity (see 302) and the numbers which are polynomials in such an nth root, coefficients a_i (see 303) being ordinary integers; these numbers form a ring R. Fermat's equation can be written (see 304) in a way that is related with the problem of decomposing x^n in the ring R. If the analogue of the unique decomposition of an integer into prime factors is true in R, then Fermat's statement can be proved. This method (or a variant) works for some values of n (*e.g.*, $n = 3, 5, 14$), but the German mathematicians Peter Gustav Lejeune Dirichlet and Ernst Eduard Kummer noticed that the analogue of the unique decomposition is not true in general. As a remedy, Kummer and Richard Dedekind, introduced the notion of an ideal, which proved to be of fundamental importance for ring theory.

At the end of the 19th century another impetus came from algebraic geometry. Roughly speaking, this branch of mathematics studies the n-tuples $(x_1, \cdot\cdot\cdot, x_n)$ of complex numbers that satisfy a given finite system of polynomial equations (see 305); these n-tuples form what is called an algebraic set, and the polynomial functions on such an algebraic set H form a ring, its coordinate ring, for addition and multiplication in a modified sense, called value-wise addition and multiplication. An important paper of Dedekind and Weber, published in 1882, showed that when this algebraic set H is a curve—*i.e.*, has dimension one—the coordinate ring of H has many properties in common with the rings of algebraic integers studied by the arithmeticians, a striking parallelism between geometry and arithmetic, which has been intensively generalized and fruitfully studied since. In 1893 the German mathematician David Hilbert introduced powerful ideal theoretical methods in the study of general polynomial rings and coordinate rings, proving the important finite basis theorem and the "zeroes theorem." In this theory the substitute for prime decomposition is the primary decomposition of ideals, discovered and studied in 1905 by E. Lasker in Germany and around 1915 by F.S. Macaulay in England. The study of general commutative rings was inaugurated by the German mathematician Emmy Noether around 1925, with a special emphasis on the rings that are now called Noetherian. In the second half of the 20th century the mathematician A. Grothendieck has introduced a far-reaching generalization of both commutative ring theory and algebraic geometry.

Noncommutative rings

Noncommutative rings also exist, the first examples of them coming from elementary geometry. The study of rotations in ordinary 3-space led the Irish mathematician Sir William Rowan Hamilton to discover in 1843 the ring of quaternions, a noncommutative division ring in which every nonzero element has an inverse. At the same time, motivated by the study of linear spaces, the German mathematician Hermann Günther Grassmann introduced what is now called the exterior algebras. The English mathematician Arthur Cayley introduced matrices around 1850 for describing linear transformations, and the fact that the square matrices form a ring was pointed out by the mathematicians B. and C.S. Peirce in 1870. In the second part of the 19th century these rings were studied under the name hypercomplex systems. Around 1930, the tools of the commutative and of the noncommutative theories were unified, giving to the latter one its proper degree of power and generality. Rings of linear transformations in infinite-dimensional spaces and related rings were studied by the Hungarian-born U.S. mathematician John von Neumann and his followers.

DEFINITION AND EXAMPLES

Definition. A ring R is defined to be a set endowed with two binary operations satisfying the axioms that are listed below. The first operation, called addition, associates to every pair x, y of elements of R a well-defined element of R, denoted by $x+y$; this addition satisfies the axioms of associativity, commutativity, the existence of a zero element, and the axiom assuring that for every element there is an opposite (or negative) element:

A1. $x+(y+z)=(x+y)+z$ for all x, y, z in R (associativity).
A2. $x+y=y+x$ for all x, y in R (commutativity).
A3. There exists an element 0 of R such that $0+x=x+0=x$ for every x in R (zero element).
A4. For every x in R, there exists an element (denoted by $-x$) such that $x+(-x)=(-x)+x=0$ (opposite).

In other words, R is a commutative group for the addition.

The second operation, called multiplication, associates to every pair x, y of elements of R a well-defined element of R, denoted by xy or $x \cdot y$; this multiplication satisfies the associativity axiom and two distributive axioms:

(M) $x(yz)=(xy)z$ for all x, z in R.
(D) $x(y+z)=xy+xz$, $(y+z)x=yx+zx$ for all x, y, z in R.

It is easily proved that $x \cdot 0=0 \cdot x=0$ for every x in R. If R contains an element e such that $ex=xe=x$ for every x, R is called unitary; the element e (necessarily unique) is called the unit element of R and is usually denoted by 1. Most rings encountered in mathematics are unitary. A ring R such that $xy=yx$ for all x, y in R is called commutative.

Examples of rings. The set Z of ordinary positive and negative integers $(0, 1, 2, \cdots, -1, -2, \cdots)$ is a unitary commutative ring for the usual addition and multiplication; its zero element is 0, its unit element is 1, so that the general notation for rings coincides with the usual notation for integers.

(306) $0+0=0,\quad 0+1=1+0=1,\quad 1+1=0$

(307) $0 \cdot 0=0 \cdot 1=1 \cdot 0=0,\quad 1 \cdot 1=1$

(308)

addition					multiplication		
0	1	a	b		1	a	b
1	0	b	a		a	b	1
a	b	0	1		b	1	a
b	a	1	0				

(309)

0	1	e	f		1	e	f
1	0	f	e		e	e	0
e	f	0	1		f	0	f
f	e	1	0				

(310)

0	1	2	3		1	2	3
1	2	3	0		2	0	2
2	3	0	1		3	2	1
3	0	1	2				

Another example is the set of two elements, "even" and "odd." This set is made into a ring F_2 by using the following natural definitions of addition and multiplication:

A. even + even = even, even + odd = odd + even = odd, odd + odd = even.
B. even · even = even · odd = odd · even = even, odd · odd = odd.

Here "even" is the zero element and "odd" the unit element. In the general notation for rings, if the digits 0, 1 replace the elements "even" and "odd," the elements of F_2 satisfy other formulas (see 306, 307) instead of (A) and (B).

They have a familiar form, except the strange formula $1+1=0$. Here, it should be remembered that the symbols 0, 1 used here do not stand for the usual numbers. The risks involved with such unusual formulas seem much smaller than the benefit of computing with the symbols 0, 1 according to deeply ingrained habits.

Now three examples of rings with four elements are considered. The elements of the first one are called 0, 1, a, b. Addition and multiplication are given by tables: the value of the sum $x+y$ is obtained by looking, in the addition table, at the element the row of which begins with an x and the column of which begins with a y; similarly for multiplication, except that products of the form $0 \cdot x$ or $y \cdot 0$ are not given, because their values are 0 (see 308). For example, $1+a=b$, $b+a=1$, $b \cdot b=a$.

The elements of the second ring are called 0, 1, e, f, with the tables also used to define addition and multiplication (see 309). For the elements of the third one, the symbols 0, 1, 2, 3 are used, and tables are also used (see 310).

It is easy to verify that the axioms for rings hold. These three rings are commutative and unitary. The additions in two of the examples (308 and 309) are the same, provided a corresponds to e and b to f. Their multiplications, however, are distinct because in the first (308) the product of any two nonzero elements is distinct from 0, whereas in the second (309), $ef=0$; such elements are called zero divisors. Furthermore, in the first, every nonzero element has an inverse; for example, a and b are inverses of one another because $ab=ba=1$. More generally, a unitary ring R in which every element $x \neq 0$ has an inverse—*i.e.*, an element x' such that $xx'=x'x=1$—is called a division ring; if R is commutative, it is called a field.

The additions in two of the examples (309 and 310) are not the same, because $x+x=0$ for every x in one example (309), whereas $3+3=2 \neq 0$ in the other example (310). Also a new feature occurs in one of the multiplications (310): the product $2 \cdot 2$, which can be written as 2^2 with the usual convention for exponents, is equal to zero. An element x of a ring R such that some power x^n of x is equal to 0 is called a nilpotent element of R. So 2 is nilpotent (see 310). The rings in the first two examples (308 and 309), however, have no nilpotent elements except 0.

The fourth example involves polynomials and power series with coefficients a_k in R, a commutative unitary ring. A letter X and formal finite sums of coefficients times integer powers of X are considered. These formal sums, called polynomials over R, are to be added coefficientwise (see 311) and multiplied in such a way that exponents of products of powers are added (see 312).

(311) $$\begin{cases}(a_0+a_1X+\cdots+a_nX^n)+(b_0+b_1X+\cdots+b_nX^n)\\ \quad=(a_0+b_0)+(a_1+b_1)X+\cdots+(a_n+b_n)X^n\end{cases}$$

(312) $$\begin{cases}(a_0+a_1X+\cdots+a_pX^p)(b_0+b_1X+\cdots+b_qX^q)\\ \quad=c_0+c_1X+\cdots+c_{p+q}X^{p+q}\\ c_j=a_0b_j+a_1b_{j-1}+\cdots+a_{j-1}b_1+a_jb_0\end{cases}$$

(313) $$a_0+a_1X+\cdots+a_nX_n+a_{n+1}X^{n+1}+\cdots$$

(314) If $xx''=x''x=1$, then $x'=x'\cdot 1=x'(xx'')$ $=(x'x)x''=1\cdot x''=x''$.

(315) $$\begin{cases}\text{Because } (2+\sqrt{3})^2=7+4\sqrt{3},\\ \text{it follows that } a_2=7, \quad b_2=4 \text{ and}\\ 7^2-3.4^2=49-48=1.\end{cases}$$

(316) $f(x+y)=f(x)+f(y), \qquad f(xy)=f(x)f(y)$ for all x, y in R

A polynomial over R may be viewed as the infinite sequence $(a_0, a_1, \cdots, a_n, 0, 0, \cdots)$ of its coefficients, only a finite number of terms a_i being unequal to 0. These sequences are to be added termwise and multiplied according to the given rule. Then the letter X corresponds to the sequence $(0, 1, 0, 0, \cdots)$.

If the restriction that only a finite number of terms of the sequences be unequal to 0 is removed, the formal power series over R is obtained (see 313).

Either the polynomials or power series over R form a commutative unitary ring for the above defined addition and multiplication; it is denoted by $R[X]$ for polynomials, $R[[X]]$ for power series. By iterating the process, the polynomial and power series rings in several variables over R are obtained. The former kind of ring is important in algebraic geometry, and the latter in analysis.

Multiplicative groups. If one forgets about multiplication in a ring R, its additive group, a commutative one, is obtained. This group is not much more interesting than a general commutative group; for example, the problem of which commutative groups are additive groups of rings is rather trivial.

Much more interesting is the multiplicative group of a unitary ring R. An element x of R for which there is an element x' of R such that $xx'=x'x=1$ is called invertible; such an x' is necessarily unique, as a simple calculation shows (see 314). It is called the inverse of x and denoted by x^{-1}. If x and y are invertible, so is xy because it admits $y^{-1}x^{-1}$ as an inverse. Thus the invertible elements of R form a group for the multiplication, called the multiplicative group of R, and sometimes denoted by R^*.

The multiplicative group of the ring Z of integers is $\{+1, -1\}$. In the example of the set with elements "even" and "odd," and the second and third of the four-element rings above (see 307, 309, and 310), it is reduced to 1. For the first four-element ring above (see 308) it is the 3-elements group $\{1, a, b\}=\{1, a, a^2\}$, with $a^3=1$. If R has no zero divisors, the invertible polynomials over R are the invertible constants—*i.e.*, 1-term polynomials a_0—so that $R[X]^*=R^*$. The invertible power series $a_0+a_1X+\cdots$ is the power series with an invertible constant term a_0. In the ring of numbers $a+b\sqrt{3}$ $(a, b\in Z)$, the invertible elements are the powers $(2+\sqrt{3})^n$ $(n\in Z)$ of $2+\sqrt{3}$, and their negatives (notice that $(2+\sqrt{3})(2-\sqrt{3})=4-3=1$); writing $(2+\sqrt{3})^n=a_n+b_n\sqrt{3}(a_n, b_n\in Z, n\geq 0)$ the pairs (a_n, b_n) provide all the solutions in positive integers of the equation $x^2-3y^2=1$. An example is easily constructed (see 315).

Homomorphisms. Modern mathematics has shown the importance not only of sets endowed with some structures, such as groups, rings, and metric spaces, but also of interesting classes of mappings from one of these sets into another one of the same type. To be interesting, such a mapping must be, in some sense, compatible with the given structures. In algebra, it has to preserve the operations. For example, interesting mappings of a ring R into a ring R' are the homomorphisms; that is, the mappings $f: R\rightarrow R'$ such that sums and products are preserved (see 316). It follows that $f(0)=0$, $f(-x)=-f(x)$. If R and R' are unitary, it is usually also required that a homomorphism f carry the unit element of R to the unit element of R' (*i.e.*, $f(1)=1$). For example, for every integer $x\in Z$, $f(x)$ may be called the remainder of division of x by 4. It is one of the integers 0, 1, 2, 3; *e.g.*, $f(7)=3$, $f(18)=2$, $f(-3)=1$, $f(-12)=0$. Now if R is the set $\{0, 1, 2, 3\}$ endowed with the ring structure defined in the third example of a four-element ring (see 310), it is easily checked that f is a homomorphism of Z into R.

Similarly, for $x\in Z$, $g(x)=$ even, if x is even, and $g(x)=$ odd, if x is odd, may be defined; then g is a homomorphism of Z into the two-elements ring described in the second example given earlier (see 307).

For a ring homomorphism $f: R\rightarrow R'$, the image $f(R)$—*i.e.*, the set of all $f(x)$ with x ranging over R—is a subring of R'; it is a subset of R' stable under sums, differences, and products. The kernel of f, ker f, is the set of all elements x of R such that $f(x)=0$. Given two elements y, z of R, $f(y)=f(z)$ if, and only if, $(y-z)\in$ ker f. The kernel I of f satisfies the conditions: (K.1) If $x, y\in I$, then $(x+y)\in I$, and $-x\in I$; *i.e.*, I is a subgroup of the additive group of R. (K.2) For any $x\in I$ and any $a\in R$, $ax\in I$ and $xa\in I$.

A subset I of a ring R that satisfies conditions (K.1) and (K.2) is called a two-sided ideal of R; such a subset is called simply ideal when R is commutative.

Conversely, any two-sided ideal I of a ring R is the kernel of some homomorphism of R. Namely, the binary relation $(x-y)\in I$ between elements of R is an equivalence relation. Given two elements a and b of R, the equivalence classes of $a+b$ and ab depend only on the equivalence classes of a and b. Thus the set of equivalence classes denoted by R/I is endowed with an addition and a multiplication. It is a simple matter to check that R/I is a ring; it is called the factor ring of R by I. The mapping, which associates to every $x\in R$ its equivalence class, is a homomorphism $R\rightarrow R/I$ of R into R/I, and its kernel is I. Many properties of R, such as commutativity and unit element, are transmitted to R/I. For example, if $n\geq 1$ is an integer, the set Zn of multiples of n in the ring Z of integers is an ideal of Z. The factor ring Z/Zn has n elements, namely, the equivalence classes of $0, 1, 2, \cdots, n-1$. The invertible elements of Z/nZ are the classes of the integers prime to n. Thus Z/nZ is a field if, and only if, n is a prime number.

Another example involves a set X and a commutative ring K, such as the field of real or complex numbers, the mappings of X into K, called functions, forming a commutative ring for value-wise addition and multiplication (in which addition and multiplication of functions are defined by addition and multiplication of corresponding function values). A subring R of this ring can be considered, such as the subring of continuous, or analytic, or polynomial functions, if it makes sense. If X' is a subset of X, the elements $g\in R$ such that $g(X)=0$ for every $x\in X'$ form an ideal I of R. The factor ring R/I may be viewed as a ring of functions on X', namely, the restrictions to X' of the functions $y\in R$.

ALGEBRAS

The hypercomplex systems alluded to earlier will now be defined. Consideration is given to a field K (such as the fields of real numbers $\mathfrak{R}$ or complex numbers $\mathfrak{C}$), an inte-

(317) $$\begin{cases}(\xi_1, \cdots, \xi_n) + (\eta_1, \cdots, \eta_n) = (\xi_1 + \eta_1, \cdots, \xi_n + \eta_n) \\ \alpha(\xi_1, \cdots, \xi_n) = (\alpha\xi_1, \cdots, \alpha\xi_n)\end{cases}$$

(318) $$e_1 = (1, 0, 0, \cdots, 0), \qquad e_2 = (0, 1, 0, \cdots, 0) \qquad e_n = (0, 0, \cdots, 0, 1)$$

(319) $$\alpha(xy) = (\alpha x)y = x(\alpha y), \quad x, y \in K^n, \quad \alpha \in K$$

(320) $$(\xi_1 e_1 + \cdots + \xi_n e_n)(\eta_1 e_1 + \cdots + \eta_n e_n) = \sum_{i,j} \xi_i \eta_j (e_i e_j)$$

(321) $$e_i e_j = \sum_{k=1}^{n} \gamma_{ijk} e_k, \quad \gamma_{ijk} \in K$$

(322) $$\sum_{n=1}^{n} \gamma_{ijp} \gamma_{pkm} = \sum_{p=1}^{n} \gamma_{ipm} \gamma_{jkp}$$

(323) $$\begin{cases}e_1^2 = e_1 \qquad e_1 e_2 = e_2 e_1 = e_2 \\ e_2^2 = \alpha e_1 + \beta e_2, \quad \alpha, \beta \in K\end{cases}$$

(324) $$f^2 = \alpha + \beta f$$

(325) $$(\lambda + \mu i)(\lambda - \mu i) = \lambda^2 + \mu^2$$

(326) $$\begin{cases}i^2 = j^2 = k^2 = -1, \qquad ij = k, \qquad ji = -k \\ jk = i, \qquad kj = -i, \qquad ki = j, \qquad ik = -j\end{cases}$$

(327) $$(\alpha + \beta i + \gamma j + \delta k)(\alpha - \beta i - \gamma j - \delta k) = \alpha^2 + \beta^2 + \gamma^2 + \delta^2$$

(328) $$e_g e_{g'} = e_{gg'}, \quad g, g' \in G$$

(329) $$\begin{cases}\alpha_{11} & \alpha_{12} & \cdots & \alpha_{1n} \\ \alpha_{21} & \alpha_{22} & \cdots & \alpha_{2n} \\ \cdot & \cdot & & \cdot \\ \cdot & \cdot & & \cdot \\ \cdot & \cdot & & \cdot \\ \alpha_{n1} & \alpha_{n2} & & \alpha_{nn}\end{cases}$$

ger $n \geq 0$, and the set K^n of all n-tuples of elements of K. These n-tuples can be added together and multiplied by elements of K, according to the rules that are expressed in terms of addition and multiplication of components (see 317).

The n-tuples form a commutative group for this addition and, furthermore, a vector space over K (see *Linear algebra*). The n-tuples are called a basis that are written with all components 0 except for a single component 1 (see 318). They are expressed as $e_1, e_2, \cdots, e_n$.

Every element $x = (\xi_1, \cdots, \xi_n)$ of K^n can be written in a unique way as $x = \xi_1 e_1 + \cdots + \xi_n \varepsilon_n$ ($\xi_i \in K$). Thus, if a multiplication distributive with respect to addition and satisfying a specific condition of associativity (see 319) is to be defined on K^n, it is sufficient to define the n^2 products $e_i e_j$ ($1 \leq i, j \leq n$), because then products of n-tuples are expressed in terms of products of the basis elements (see 320). Because $e_i e_j$ is an element of K^n, it may be written in a unique way as a linear combination of basis elements (see 321).

These formulas (321) are called a multiplication table and the elements γ_{ijk} the structural constants. Endowed with its addition and with the multiplication defined above (see 320 and 321), K^n is called an algebra, or a hypercomplex system over K. Here this algebra will be denoted by A; as a mathematical object A is distinct from K^n because one of the many possible multiplications in K^n is given in A. All the ring axioms are true in A, except possibly the associativity of multiplication. For this associativity to be true, it is necessary and sufficient that it be true for the basis elements e_i; that is, that $e_i(e_j e_k) = (e_i e_j)e_k$ for all indices i, j, k. This equality can be translated in terms of structural constants (see 322) by means of the multiplication table (321) for all i, j, k, m. If this property (322) holds, A is a ring and is often called an associative algebra over K. It is commutative if, and only if, $\gamma_{ijk} = \gamma_{jik}$ for all indices i, j, k.

It is possible to define various structures of algebras on any vector space, finite- or infinite-dimensional over K, instead of K^n. Some examples are now given.

Quadratic algebras. Here $n = 2$ and e_1 is required to be the unit element of A. Then the multiplication table takes the form of four equations between two elements (see 323). If one writes $e_1 = 1$ and $e_2 = f$, the habits about the use of the symbol 1 make it unnecessary to write the three first equations, and one writes only that the second power of f is linear in f (see 324).

Commutativity and associativity of the multiplication are readily checked on 1 and f. Thus A is an associative and associative algebra, called a quadratic algebra over K.

If for K the field $\mathfrak{R}$ of real numbers is taken and $a = -1$, $\beta = 0$, then $f^2 = -1$. Here f is customarily denoted by i, so that $i^2 = -1$. The algebra A then happens to be a field, and this is the field $\mathfrak{C}$ of complex numbers. The invertibility of any nonzero $z = (\lambda + \mu i) \in \mathfrak{C}$ comes from the formula for the product of z and its conjugate (see 325); in fact, since the real numbers λ and μ are not both zero, $\lambda^2 + \mu^2$ is greater than 0, hence z is invertible in $\mathfrak{C}$. More generally, the quadratic algebra defined over a field K by $f^2 = a + \beta f$ ($a, \beta \in K$) is a field if, and only if, the equation $x^2 = a + \beta x$ has no root x in K.

Quaternions. Here $n = 4$, and 1, i, j, k are the basis elements, the first one being the unit element. The essential part is given in a multiplication table (see 326).

It is an easy, but tedious, exercise to check that this multiplication is associative; it is not commutative in general. The corresponding algebra H is called the algebra of quaternions over K. A simple computation (see 327) proves that if in K a sum of four squares is never 0 unless all its terms vanish, the algebra H is a division ring. This condition is the case if $K = \mathfrak{R}$ and H is then the division ring of quaternions, discovered by Hamilton in 1843.

Group algebras. G denotes a finite group with n elements, multiplicatively written. Instead of indexing the components $\xi_1, \cdots, \xi_n$ of an n-tuple $x \in K^n$ by the integers 1, 2, $\cdots$, n, one can index them by the elements of G, so that such an n-tuple is now written $\{\xi_g\}$. The basic n-tuple corresponding to a given $g \in G$ is thus $e_g = \{\delta_{gh}\}$, in which $\delta_{gg} = 1$, $\delta_{gh} = 0$ for $h \neq g$. Hence, $\{\xi_g\}$ for all $g \in G$ equals $\Sigma \xi_g e_g$ the summation extending over all $g \in G$. The multiplication table is given by definition (see 328) and the associativity follows from the associativity in G. The corresponding algebra is called the group algebra of G over K, and is denoted by $K[G]$. In view of the multiplication table, it is harmless to write g instead of e_g.

MATRICES; REPRESENTATIONS OF RINGS

Endomorphisms. If V is a vector space over a field K, an endomorphism of V is a mapping u of V into V such that $u(x + y) = u(x) + u(y)$ and $u(dx) = du(x)$ for all x, y in V and d in K. If the addition of two endomorphisms u and v is defined value-wise as $(u + v)(x) = u(x) + v(x)$ and their multiplication as the composition of mappings $(uv)(x) = u \circ v(x)$, the set of all endomorphisms of V becomes a ring. In general, it is noncommutative.

Suppose now that a finite basis $(e_1, \cdots, e_n)$ is given on V, then each x in V can be written in a unique way as $x = e_1 a_1 + \cdots + e_n a_n$ ($a_i \in K$). An endomorphism u of V is then uniquely determined by the values $u(e^i)$ ($i = 1, \cdots, n$); if they are written $u(e_i) = \Sigma e_j a_{ji}$, the sum being on j, it can be seen that u is uniquely determined by the n^2 elements a_{ij} of K. It is customary to arrange these elements in a square (see 329).

The ith column is formed by the components of $u(e_i)$. Such an array is called a square $n \times n$ matrix over K. The matrix is called the matrix of u with respect to the basis $(e_1, \cdots, e_n)$, denoted $M(u)$. Any square $n \times n$ matrix over K is the matrix of some endomorphism u.

Because endomorphisms and matrices are in one-to-one correspondence, the addition and multiplication of endomorphisms can be translated in terms of matrices. One finds easily that the sum of the matrices (a_{ij}), (β_{ij}) is the matrix $(a_{ij}+\beta_{ij})$, and that their product [in the order $(a_{ij}) \cdot (\beta_{ij})$] is the matrix (γ_{ij}) in which $\gamma_{ij}=\Sigma a_{ik}\beta_{kj}$ the sum being on k. In this last formula, the row $(a_{i1}, \cdots, a_{in})$ is multiplied by the column $(\beta_{1j}, \cdots, \beta_{nj})$.

The ring of $n \times n$ matrices over K is denoted by $M_n(K)$. It has no two-sided ideal except itself and 0. It may be viewed as an algebra over K, with n^2 basis elements, namely, the matrices $E_{pq}(1 \leq p, q \leq n)$, in which E_{pq} has a 1 at the intersection of the pth row and the qth column, and zeroes elsewhere. In other words, the matrix $M=(a_{ij})$ is $M=\Sigma a_{pq}E_{pq}$, with summation extending over p and q. The multiplication table can be given (see 330).

(330) $$E_{pq}E_{rs}=0 \text{ if } q \neq r, \qquad E_{pq}E_{qs}=E_{ps} \text{ otherwise}$$

(331) $$\begin{cases} (a+b)x=ax+bx \text{ for all } a, b \in R \text{ and } x \in M \\ a(x+y)=ax+ay \text{ for all } a \in R \text{ and } x, y \in M \\ a(bx)=(ab)x \text{ for all } a, b \in R \text{ and } x \in M \end{cases}$$

(332) $$\frac{a}{b}+\frac{a'}{b'}=\frac{ab'+ba'}{bb'}, \qquad \frac{a}{b}\cdot\frac{a'}{b'}=\frac{aa'}{bb'}$$

(333) $$ax=ay, \quad a \neq 0 \quad \text{imply } x=y$$

Representations. Because rings of matrices are rather simple and have a fruitful geometric interpretation, it is important to compare a given ring with rings of matrices. This is the purpose of representation theory. A representation of a ring R is a homomorphism h of R into a ring of matrices $M_n(K)$. Thus, for $x \in R$, $h(x)$ may be viewed as an endomorphism of the vector space K^n. The representation h is called irreducible if no proper subspace of K^n is stable under all the endomorphisms $h(x)$ $(x \in R)$. The irreducible representations of rings, and in particular of K-algebras, have been extensively and fruitfully studied.

Purpose of representation theory

RINGS AS MODULES

In the same way as a group is often considered as acting on a set—that is, as a group of transformations of this set—it is fruitful to make a ring R act on various commutative groups, then called R-modules. This procedure has the advantage of transforming various algebraic problems into linear ones.

More technically, given a ring R, a left R-module (or a left module over R) is a commutative group M (written additively) endowed with a mapping of $R \times M$ into M satisfying axioms to be listed. This mapping associates to every pair (a, x) formed by an element a of R and an element x of M, a well-defined element of M, denoted by $a \cdot x$ or ax. The axioms are three in number (see 331).

If R is unitary, it is usually required that $1 \cdot x=x$ for all $x \in M$; the module M is then called unitary.

A right module is also defined as the element of M associated to the pair (a, x) and is denoted by xa, and the third axiom (see 331) is replaced by $(xb)a=x(ba)$. This is not a simple change of notation; a right module is not in general a left module. The two notions coincide, however, when R is commutative.

If R is a field, the unitary R-modules are the vector spaces. A module over the ring Z of ordinary integers is nothing else than a commutative group G written additively (for $n \in Z$, $n>0$ and $x \in G$, nx is $x+x+\cdots+x$, n times).

If R is a subring of a ring S, S is both a left and a right A-module; for $a \in R$ and $x \in S$, ax (or xa) is defined to be the product of a and x computed in S. In particular, for $S=R$, R is a left module and a right module over itself.

Given a left module M over a ring R, a submodule M' of M is an additive subgroup M' of M such that $a \in R$ and $x \in M'$ imply $ax \in M'$. The submodules of R considered as a left module over itself are called the left ideals of R; similar definition holds for the right ideals. The two-sided ideals defined in *Definition and examples*, above, are the subsets of R that are at the same time left and right ideals.

Given a submodule M' of a left module M over a ring R, the binary relation $(x-y) \in M'$ between elements x, y of M is an equivalence relation called the relation of congruence modulo M'. It is written $x \equiv y \bmod M'$. Given elements a of R and x and y of M, the equivalence classes of ax and of $x+y$ depend only on a and on the equivalence classes of x and y. Thus the set of equivalence classes, denoted by M/M', is endowed with a structure of left R-module and is called the factor module of M by M'. In particular, if I and I' are left ideals of R such that $I' \subset I$, then I/I' is an interesting example of a left R-module. Similar definitions and results hold for right modules.

A representation h of a ring R in a matrix ring $M_n(K)$ endows the space K^n with a structure of left R-module. Thus module theory and representation theory are essentially equivalent.

SPECIAL CLASSES OF RINGS

Domains. It has been shown that a ring may have the unfamiliar feature of zero divisors; that is, nonzero elements a, b such that $ab=0$. It is thus interesting to define a class of rings closer to computing habits. A commutative ring with unit element $1 \neq 0$ and without zero divisors—*i.e.*, $a \neq 0$ and $b \neq 0$ imply $ab \neq 0$—is called an integral domain, or a domain or an entire ring. The ring Z of integers is a domain. A field is a domain; if $a \neq 0$ and if $ab \neq 0$, multiplication by the inverse a^{-1} of a gives $0=a^{-1}ab=1b=b$. If R is a domain, so are the polynomial ring $R[X]$ and the power series ring $R[[X]]$. A subring of a domain, and in particular a subring of a field, is a domain provided it contains the unit element.

Integral domain

Conversely, every domain R is a subring of some field. The elements of this field are constructed in the same way as fractions are constructed from integers. The set of all pairs (a, b) is considered in which a, $b \in R$ and $b \neq 0$. The binary relation $ab'=ba'$ between two such pairs (a, b) and (a', b') is an equivalence relation in this set. The equivalence class of (a, b) is denoted by a/b and called a fraction. The operations of addition and multiplication (see 332) are well defined on the set of fractions and make a field K out of this set; it is called the field of fractions of R. The fractions $a/1$, $a \in R$, form a subring of K, isomorphic with R. The field of fractions of the ring Z of integers is the field Q of rational numbers. In an integral domain R, the cancellation law holds (see 333).

Rings of integers. It was pointed out earlier that ring theory partly originated from arithmetic. It is thus interesting to study the rings in which important properties of the ring Z of integers are valid.

In a domain R, the divisibility relation $x \mid y$ (x divides y, x is a divisor of y, y is a multiple of x) is defined to mean that there exists $z \in R$ such that $y=zx$. The set Rx of multiples of x is clearly an ideal in R; it is called the principal ideal generated by x. The divisibility relation $x \mid y$ is equivalent with the inclusion relation $Rx \supset Ry$. As in Z, an element d of R is said to be a greatest common divisor, GCD, of x and y if it is a divisor of x and of y, and if it is the greatest in the following sense: every common divisor of x and y divides d. Similarly, a least common multiple, LCM, m of x and y is a common multiple of x and y that divides every other common multiple of x and y. Two elements x, y of R such that $x \mid y$ and $y \mid x$ are called associates; this means that there exists an invertible element u of R such that $y=ux$; whenever divisibility is concerned, associates have the same properties. All the GCD's (or LCM's) of two given elements of R, if they exist, are associates. In an arbitrary domain R, LCM's and GCD's need not exist. To say that the elements x and y of R admit an LCM amounts to saying that the ideal $Rx \cap Ry$ is principal. If any two elements x, y of R admit an LCM, say m, they admit a GCD, say d, and conversely; furthermore, xy and md are associates.

An element $p \neq 0$ of a domain R is called irreducible if it is not invertible and if the only divisors of p are either invertible or associates of p. In Z, the irreducible elements are the prime numbers and their negatives. In a domain R in which LCM's exist, an irreducible element p enjoys the following property:

Irreducible elements

(A) If p divides a product ab (a, $b \in R$), it divides one of the factors a, b.

In the ring S formed by the complex numbers including the square root of -5 as a coefficient of one of two elements from Z (see 334), the number 2 is irreducible, but a relation (see 335) shows that (A) does not hold. Thus LCM's do not always exist in S.

(334) $$x+y\sqrt{-5}, \quad x, y \in Z$$

(335) $$(1+\sqrt{-5})(1-\sqrt{-5})=6=2\cdot 3$$

(336) $$\begin{cases} \phi(n)=|n|, \quad n\in Z \\ \phi[P(X)]=1+\text{degree of } P(X) \text{ and } \phi(0)=0 \\ P(X)\in K[X], \quad P(X)\neq 0 \end{cases}$$

(337) $$x^2-x-\frac{d-1}{4}=0$$

(338) $$\phi(x+y\sqrt{d})=|x^2-dy^2|, \quad x, y\in Q$$

In Z the unique decomposition of an integer into prime factors is well known and quite useful. Thus it is interesting to study the domains R in which every element is a product of irreducible ones in an essentially unique way; *i.e.*, unique up to order and invertible factors. The existence of such a decomposition is usually easy to settle: it is implied by the following property (called by algebraists a finiteness condition):

(B) Any strictly increasing sequence $Ra_1 \subset Ra_2 \subset \cdots \subset Ra_n \subset \cdots$ of principal ideals of R (in which equality between adjacent members of the sequence is excluded) is finite.

When existence is proved, essential uniqueness is implied by property (A).

Gaussian domains

The domains in which the essentially unique decomposition into irreducible elements hold are called Gaussian or factorial domains, or unique factorization domains (UFD). Their definition may be restricted as follows: there exists a subset P of R such that every nonzero element x of R can be uniquely written as: $x=up_1^{n(1)}\cdots p_q^{n(q)}$ with $p_1, \cdots, p_q$ distinct elements of P, u invertible and positive integral exponents $n(1), \cdots, n(q)$.

The elements of P are irreducible; more precisely, P contains one, and only one, representative of each class of irreducible associates. In Z, the set of positive prime numbers may be taken for P. The divisibility theory of a factorial domain R closely resembles that of Z; in particular, least common multiples and greatest common denominators exist and can be computed from the decomposition into irreducible factors by the usual rules. The finiteness condition (B) holds. An important theorem, essentially due to Gauss, says that, if a domain R is factorial, so is the polynomial ring R[X]; but the power series ring $R[[X]]$ need not be factorial.

An important subclass of factorial domains is formed by the principal domains, or principal ideal domains, PID; *i.e.*, the domains R in which every ideal is principal. In fact, because the ideals $Rx \cap Ry$ are principal, LCM's exist, and the finiteness condition (B) is easy to prove (consider the union of all Ra_j's, which is an ideal). These PID's are very nice rings: many important facts about their ideals and their modules are known. The ring Z, a polynomial ring $K[X]$ over any field K are PID's, but $Z[X]$ is factorial without being a PID.

These facts about Z and $K[X]$ are usually proved by Euclidean division. More generally, a division algorithm on a domain R is a mapping φ of R into the nonnegative integers such that, given any a, b in R, $b\neq 0$, there exist q and r in R with $a=bq+r$ and $\varphi(r)<\varphi(b)$.

Euclidean domains

If a domain admits a division algorithm, it is called Euclidean. The domains Z and $K[X]$ are Euclidean, the algorithms being easily expressed (see 336). Any Euclidean domain R is a PID: if I is any nonzero ideal in R, take a nonzero element a in I such that $\varphi(a)$ is minimum; then $I=Ra$ is easily proved.

If $d\in Z$ is any squarefree integer (not divisible by the square of any prime) then for $d\equiv 2$ or 3 modulo 4, R_d is defined as the set of complex numbers $a+b\sqrt{d}$ (a, $b\in Z$). For $d\equiv 1$ modulo 4, R_d is defined as the set of numbers $a+b\,\dfrac{1+\sqrt{d}}{2}$ (a, $b\in Z$). In both cases R_d is a domain. An interesting problem is to find out whether R_d is principal or Euclidean. It can be proved that R_d is factorial if, and only if, it is principal. For $d\equiv 1$ modulo 4 the seemingly more natural set R'_d of all $a+b\sqrt{d}$ (a, $b\in Z$), a subring of R_d, is never principal, and less interesting for the purpose (the proof uses the fact that the number $x=\dfrac{1+\sqrt{d}}{2}$ is a root of an equation with integer coefficients (see 337).

The above problem is solved for $d<0$. The domain R_d is Euclidean only for $d=-1$, -2, -3, -7, and -11; the proof is technical but not too hard. It is principal without being Euclidean for $d=-19$, -43, -67, -163, and nonprincipal for all other negative values of d; here the proof is very hard and has been completed only after 1960.

Much less is known for $d>0$. By explicit computations, the values of d for which R_d is principal have been determined at least for $2\leq d\leq 499$. No general theorem, however, indicates whether R_d is principal for finitely many or infinitely many values of d. The ring R_d is Euclidean for the corresponding algorithm (see 338) for only 16 explicitly known values of d. For other values, however, it might perhaps be Euclidean for another algorithm; the problem is open.

At any rate, many nonprincipal domains R_d are known; for example, $d=-5$, $d=-6$, $d=10$, $d=26$. A similar situation arises in the rings of so-called cyclotomic integers connected with Fermat's equation $x^n+y^n=z^n$. This loss of unique factorization led Kummer and Dedekind to introduce the notion of an ideal and to prove that, in a class of domains now called the Dedekind domains that includes the rings R_d and the PID's, every ideal admits a unique decomposition as a product of prime ideals. A well-developed arithmetical theory of Dedekind domains is available.

Noetherian rings. Algebraic geometry motivated the introduction of a larger class of commutative rings, called Noetherian. They are the rings R that satisfy the equivalent conditions:

(N) Every strictly increasing sequence of ideals of R is finite.

(N′) Every nonempty family of ideals of R admits a maximal element (for the inclusion relation).

(N″) Every ideal I of R is finitely generated; that is, there exists a finite number of elements $x_1, \cdots, x_n$ of I such that every element y of I can be written as $y=r_1x_1+\cdots+r_nx_n$ with $r_1, \cdots, r_n\in R$. It is technically useful to introduce also the Noetherian modules: replace ideal by submodule in (N), (N′), (N″). The class of Noetherian rings is rather large. It includes the Dedekind domains, whence the PID's. Furthermore, it is stable by many ring theoretic operations. For example, the celebrated finite basis theorem of Hilbert states that, if R is Noetherian, so is the polynomial ring $R[X]$; the same holds for power series. By induction it can be shown that a polynomial ring in any finite number of variables over a field is Noetherian, whence the importance of Noetherian rings in algebraic geometry. The theory of Noetherian rings is quite extensive.

Division rings. A nonzero ring in which every nonzero element admits an inverse, it may be recalled, is called a division ring; if it is commutative, it is called a field. Division rings are the simplest noncommutative rings, fields the simplest commutative ones: for example, they have no other ideals than the whole ring and the zero ideal; whence their divisibility theory is trivial (see above *Fields*). Here a few words will be said about division rings.

The simplest example of a noncommutative division ring is the ring H of quaternions. It contains a subfield, formed by the quaternions $a\cdot 1+0\cdot i+0\cdot j+0\cdot k$, that is identified with the field $\mathfrak{R}$ of real numbers. For every $a \in \mathfrak{R}$ and every $x \in H$, $ax = xa$.

This introduces the following notion: given a ring S, the set of all elements a of S such that $ax = xa$ for every $x \in S$ is called the centre of S. It contains 0, also 1 if S is unitary, and is a subring of S, necessarily commutative. If S is a division ring, then $a \in Z$, $a \neq 0$ imply $a^{-1} \in Z$, so that the centre Z is a subfield of S. For the ring H of quaternions, the centre is exactly the field of real numbers.

Thus a division ring S is a vector space over its centre Z. The dimension of this vector space may be finite or infinite, the first case being better known than the other. In this case the dimension is the square n^2 of an integer n; *e.g.*, $4 = 2^2$ for the quaternions. Given a field Z, the set of all division rings D (up to isomorphism) admitting Z as centre and finite-dimensional over Z can be organized by a rather technical process into a commutative group Br(Z), called the Brauer group of Z. This group is a powerful instrument for studying the field Z. It is trivial for the field of complex numbers and is a two-elements group for the field of real numbers.

Wedderburn's theorem

A beautiful theorem of the Scottish mathematician Joseph Henry Maclagan Wedderburn says that every finite division ring is commutative; in other words, the Brauer group of a finite field is trivial. Because every element x of a finite division ring D with q elements satisfies $x = x^q$, Wedderburn's theorem is a particular case of the following generalization: if, for every element x of a ring R, there exists an exponent $n(x) \geq 2$ such that $x^{n(x)} = x$, then R is commutative. (P.S.)

Categories

Since the mid-1940s mathematicians have found it valuable to formalize the notions of areas of mathematical discourse and interrelations between such areas; the formalization used is the language of categories and functors.

Theory of categories and functors

A rapidly developing mathematical theory accompanied this formalization so that the theory of categories and functors has become an autonomous part of mathematics. This section deals with the role of this formalization in providing an appropriate language for the expression of mathematical ideas.

The study of mathematics involves certain domains of mathematical discourse, their structural properties, and their interrelations. For example, there is the idea of a set (see SET THEORY) and of functions that are transformations of sets. There is arithmetic, the study of the domain of natural numbers, rational numbers, and integers. Geometry involves subsets of Euclidean space of three dimensions together with the appropriate transformations of such subsets—for example, translations, rotations, and reflections. Algebra is concerned with rational numbers, real numbers, and complex numbers; and abstract algebra involves further mathematical domains such as groups, rings, fields, and lattices. The calculus is again concerned in the first instance with subsets of the real numbers, or of Euclidean space of higher dimension, and with particular transformations of such subsets; *e.g.*, differential operators.

Algebraic topology relates domains of interest in geometry to domains of interest in algebra. Algebraic geometry, on the other hand, goes in the opposite direction, associating, for example, with each commutative ring its spectrum of prime ideals.

Set theory is concerned with a class of objects A, B, C, · · · , called sets, and a class of transformations f, g, h, · · · , called functions. With each function f is associated a domain, which is a set A, and a range or codomain, which is a set B. The notation $f\colon A \to B$, or $A \xrightarrow{f} B$, indicates that f is a function from the domain A to the codomain B. There is a strict distinction between the codomain of the function f and the image of the function f, which is simply the set of values taken by the function f. Thus, in particular, two functions can only be identical if not only their domains but also their codomains coincide. They are then, of course, identical if, and only if, they each take the same value at each element of the domain.

Further, functions may be composed under certain conditions. To be precise, the functions $f\colon A \to B$ and $g\colon B' \to C$ may be composed to yield a function, written gf or $g \circ f$ (see 339), if, and only if, $B = B'$. Further, the law of composition is associative (see 340), provided, of course, that the relevant compositions are defined. With each set A may be associated its identity function 1_A: $A \to A$. This function 1_A has basic properties (see 341) provided the compositions are defined. Thus, 1_A behaves very much like the integer 1 in the ring of integers, a fact that leads to the habit of dropping the subscript A and simply writing $1\colon A \to A$. It is an easy exercise to see that the identity function is entirely characterized by the properties of 1_A (see 341). That is to say, if the function $u\colon A \to A$ also satisfies the conditions $fu = f$, $ug = g$ for all appropriate f, g, then indeed $u = 1_A$.

Of course set theory has more structure than this, but if the ideas described above are abstracted from set theory, a model for the notion of a category is obtained.

(339)	$gf\colon A \to C$
(340)	$h(gf) = (hg)f$
(341)	$f1_A = f, \quad 1_A g = g$
(342)	$\mathfrak{F}(A, B)$
(343)	$\mathfrak{F}(A, B) \times \mathfrak{F}(B, C) \to \mathfrak{F}(A, C)$
(344)	$f1_A = f, \quad 1_A g = g$

THE NOTION OF A CATEGORY

A formal definition can be given in the following way: A category $\mathfrak{F}$ consists of three sets of data:

C1. There is a class of objects A, B, C, · · · .

C2. To each ordered pair of objects A, B in $\mathfrak{F}$, there is associated a set (see 342) called the set of morphisms, or maps or transformations, from A to B in $\mathfrak{F}$.

C3. To each ordered triple of objects A, B, C in $\mathfrak{F}$, there is associated a law of composition, or composition function (see 343), the image of (f, g), $f \in \mathfrak{F}(A, B)$, $g \in \mathfrak{F}(B, C)$, under this law of composition being written gf or $g \circ f$, so that gf is a morphism from A to C.

These data satisfy the following three axioms, of which the first is in the nature of a convention, while the remaining two are more substantial:

C4. $\mathfrak{F}(A_1, B_1)$ and $\mathfrak{F}(A_2, B_2)$ are disjoint unless $A_1 = A_2$, $B_1 = B_2$.

C5. (Associative Law) $h(gf) = (hg)f$, provided the compositions are defined.

C6. (Existence of identities). To each object A of $\mathfrak{F}$ there is associated a morphism $1_A \in \mathfrak{F}(A, A)$ such that two equations hold (see 344) provided the compositions are defined.

Category of sets and functions

As a first example, the category $\mathfrak{C}$ is considered, called the category of sets and functions, or simply the category of sets. Precisely, the objects of $\mathfrak{C}$ are sets A, B, C, · · · . A morphism in $\mathfrak{C}$ from the set A to the set B is merely a function with domain A and codomain (range) B. Thus either of two notations (see 345) can be adopted in an arbitrary category as a convenient representation of the statement $f \in \mathfrak{F}(A, B)$. The law of composition in $\mathfrak{C}$ is simply the familiar composition of functions. The axioms are then certainly satisfied. Moreover, this example serves

(345)	$f\colon A \to B \quad \text{or} \quad A \xrightarrow{f} B$
(346)	$A \xrightarrow{f} B \xrightarrow{g} C$
(347)	$F(fg) = (Ff)(Fg)$
(348)	$F(1_A) = 1_{FA}$

to explain the notation gf for the composition of $f\colon A \to B$ with $g\colon B \to C$. It is usual to write functions on the left of their arguments, so that the image of $a \in A$ under the composite of f and g appears as $g(f(a))$. A less conservative attitude, defying this tradition and leading to a happier notation, would be to write fg for the composite of f and g, especially in view of the natural notational convention (see 346). In this discussion, however, tradition is not defied.

Just as in the special case of the category $\mathfrak{C}$, the equations relating to the identities (344) entirely determine the morphism 1_A in $\mathfrak{I}(A, A)$; 1 is often written for 1_A.

Some further examples of categories follow: finite sets and functions; groups and homomorphisms; Abelian groups and homomorphisms; rings and homomorphisms; subsets of Euclidean space of 3 dimensions and Euclidean movements; subsets of Euclidean space of n dimensions and continuous functions; topological spaces and continuous functions.

The law of composition is not specified explicitly in describing these categories. This is the custom when the objects have underlying set-structure, the morphisms are functions of the underlying sets (transporting the additional structure), and the law of composition is merely ordinary function-composition. Indeed, sometimes even the specification of the morphisms is suppressed if no confusion would arise—thus one speaks of the category of groups.

The examples given suggest a conceptual framework. For example, the concept of group may be regarded as constituting a first-order abstraction or generalization from various concrete, familiar realizations such as the additive group of integers, the multiplicative group of nonzero rationals, groups of permutations, symmetry groups, groups of Euclidean motions, and so on. Then, again, the notion of a category constitutes a second-order abstraction, the concrete realizations of which consist of such first-order abstractions as the category of groups, the category of rings, the category of topological spaces, and so on.

It should not be supposed that, in every category, the objects are sets (probably with additional structure) and that the morphisms are certain preferred functions. One example serves to dispel this misconception. X is a set with a pre-ordering relation $\geq$. Thus the relation $a \geq b$ holds for certain elements a, b of X and the following axioms are satisfied: $a \geq a$; if $a \geq b$, $b \geq c$, then $a \geq c$. For example, the integers may be ordered by size or they may be preordered by the divisibility condition: $a \mid b$ if a is a factor of b. Then if $(X, \geq)$ is a set with a pre-order, a category $\mathfrak{C}_X$ is formed, the objects of which are the elements of X and such that $\mathfrak{C}_X(a, b)$ is the single element $a \to b$ if $a \geq b$ and is empty otherwise. There is evidently a unique law of composition and the category axioms obviously hold.

A morphism $f\colon A \to B$ in the category $\mathfrak{I}$ is said to be invertible, or a unit, or an equivalence, if there is a morphism $g\colon B \to A$ in $\mathfrak{I}$ with $gf = 1_A$, $fg = 1_B$. It is easy to prove that g is then invertible and is determined by f (g is the inverse of f, written $g = f^{-1}$), and that if A is isomorphic to B, there existing an invertible $f\colon A \to B$, then the relation of isomorphism is an equivalence relation on the objects of $\mathfrak{I}$. Thus every category carries automatically with it a notion of the isomorphism of objects, proper to that category. The concept gives a great gain in universality compared with traditional procedures, which involve the definition, as distinct concepts, of one–one correspondence between sets, isomorphism between groups, isomorphism between rings, homeomorphism between topological spaces, bi-continuous isomorphism between topological groups, order type of ordered sets, and so on. It is particularly offensive, from the categorical point of view, to define an isomorphism of groups $\varphi\colon G \to H$ to be a homomorphism that is one–one and onto H; for an isomorphism of groups should be just an invertible morphism of the category of groups. It is a theorem that, in this category, a morphism that is one–one and onto its codomain is an isomorphism. This theorem is false in the category of topological spaces, so that the definition masks the universality of the concept of isomorphism.

FUNCTORS

The notion of category being established as that which gives precision to the concept of domain of mathematical discourse, the formalization of the precise notion corresponding to the intuitive idea of the interrelation or connection between different domains is now considered. Within any particular category not only the objects must be specified but also the morphisms. Furthermore, these morphisms are, in the principal examples, required in some sense to transport the structure characteristic of the objects of the category; *e.g.*, group structure, topological structure. In the same way a functor F from the category $\mathfrak{I}$ to the category $\mathfrak{G}$ is defined as a rule that associates with every object A of $\mathfrak{I}$ an object FA of $\mathfrak{G}$, and with every morphism $f\colon A \to B$ in $\mathfrak{I}$ a morphism $Ff\colon FA \to FB$ in $\mathfrak{G}$, subject to the conditions of transport of structure (see 347, 348).

In expressing the relation (347), there is a tacit assumption that the composition fg is defined. This is standard practice, to avoid unnecessarily complicated statements.

A functor F always sends isomorphisms to isomorphisms, a very crucial property. Otherwise expressed, if Ff is not an isomorphism, then f cannot be an isomorphism. This yields a basic methodological procedure; to demonstrate that A and B, two objects of $\mathfrak{I}$, really are different—*i.e.*, non-isomorphic—it may be possible to find a functor F from $\mathfrak{I}$ to a category $\mathfrak{G}$ in which it is far easier to make the comparison. This procedure may be regarded as a massive generalization of the classical arithmetical test of casting out nines.

Some examples of functors are now given:

Examples of functors

(a) For any group G it is possible to render G commutative by adjoining the relations $xy = yx$ for all x, y in G. The resulting group may be written G_{ab}. If $\varphi\colon G \to H$ is a homomorphism, it is easy to see that φ induces a uniquely determined homomorphism $\varphi_{ab}\colon G_{ab} \to H_{ab}$. Thus there is a functor from the category of groups to the category of Abelian groups. This should be the first functor tried in an attempt to prove two groups nonisomorphic.

(b) For any pointed topological space (X, x)—that is, a topological space X, together with a distinguished point x in X—it is possible to construct the Poincaré fundamental group $\pi(X, x)$. Then π is a functor from the category of pointed topological spaces and pointed continuous functions to the category of groups. Because, for example, the sphere and the torus (a surface in the shape of a doughnut) have non-isomorphic fundamental groups, it follows that they are not homeomorphic.

(c) If X, Y are two pre-ordered sets regarded as categories, as above, then a functor from X to Y is merely an order-preserving function.

Forgetful functors

(d) There are many important functors, called forgetful or underlying functors, that simply forget part of the structure present in the objects and transported by the morphisms. Thus, the objects in the examples in *The notion of a category* all have underlying set structures and the morphisms are all functions; moreover, the law of composition is simply that of functions. Thus, in all these cases, there is an underlying functor to $\mathfrak{S}$. It is also possible to take a ring, forget the multiplication in it, and thereby obtain an Abelian group; this yields an underlying functor. Underlying functors may seem trivial things; actually, they are fundamental to categorical language.

NATURAL TRANSFORMATIONS

One further basic notion in the theory of categories, or, as it may be said, a basic item of categorical language, will now be introduced. This is the notion of a natural transformation of functors from one category to another. Indeed, the whole language and apparatus of categories and functors were developed initially by the U.S. mathematicians Samuel Eilenberg and Saunders MacLane in order to render precise the intuitive concept of naturality. First an example will be given, the example that may be said to have motivated the definition.

Let V be a vector space over some field K, and let V^* be the dual space of V; that is, the space of linear functionals on V. There is then a linear transformation $T\colon V \to V^{**}$ that is given (see 349). There is an intuitive feeling that the linear transformation T is natural because its description only involves the terms v and φ. Now if V is finite-dimensional, then it is known that T is an isomorphism in

$$T(v)(\phi)=\phi(v), \quad v \in V, \quad \phi \in V^* \tag{349}$$

$$e_i^*(e_i)=1, \qquad e_i^*(e_j)=0, \qquad i \neq j \tag{350}$$

$$\begin{array}{ccc} FA & \xrightarrow{T_A} & GA \\ Ff \downarrow & & \downarrow Gf \\ FB & \xrightarrow{T_B} & GB \end{array} \tag{351}$$

$$(T^{-1})_A = T_A^{-1} \tag{352}$$

$$\begin{cases} f^{**}(u^{**})(v^*)=u^{**}(f^*(v^*)) \\ u^{**} \in U^{**}, \quad v^* \in V^* \\ f^*(v^*)(u)=v^*(f(u)), \quad u \in U \end{cases} \tag{353}$$

$$\theta_n\colon \pi_n(X,x) \rightarrow H_n(X,x) \tag{354}$$

the category of vector spaces over K and linear transformations. One way of proving that T is then an isomorphism is to show that V and V^{**} are isomorphic and then to observe that T is one–one. The usual proof that V and V^{**} are isomorphic would be to proceed by establishing an isomorphism between V and V^*, in the case when V is finite-dimensional. Now if a base $(e_1, e_2, \cdots, e_k)$ for V is given, then a basis for V^* may be set up, called the dual basis, by defining e_i^* to be that linear functional on V given by certain rules (see 350). Then the correspondence $e_i \leftrightarrow e_i^*$ sets up an isomorphism between V and V^*.

On the other hand, this isomorphism does not look natural, because it depends on the choice of bases. Of course, the argument above could be generalized to set up a linear transformation from V to V^* even if V is not finite-dimensional over K, but, again, this transformation would not appear to be natural. What is required is a formal and precise expression of the feeling that, for finite-dimensional vector spaces V over the field K, V and V^{**} are naturally isomorphic, while V and V^* are isomorphic in some unnatural way. Eilenberg and MacLane solved this problem in their seminal article, "General Theory of Natural Equivalences," published in 1945, which may be said to have laid the foundation of the theory of categories. The precise definition is:

If $F, G\colon \mathfrak{F} \rightarrow \mathfrak{G}$ are two functors from the category $\mathfrak{F}$ to the category $\mathfrak{G}$, then a natural transformation T, from F to G, is a rule assigning to each object A of $\mathfrak{F}$ a morphism T_A in the set $\mathfrak{G}(FA, GA)$, subject to the condition that a diagram (see 351) should be commutative for every $f\colon A \rightarrow B$ in $\mathfrak{F}$; that is, $Gf[\circ]T_A = T_B[\circ] Ff$. Further, if each T_A is invertible, T is said to be a natural equivalence. It is clear that if T is a natural equivalence from F to G, then T^{-1}, given by an equation (see 352), is a natural equivalence from G to F. Thus the term equivalence used here is fully justified. Indeed, the functors from $\mathfrak{F}$ to $\mathfrak{G}$ may be collected into equivalence classes according to the existence of a natural equivalence between them.

This definition can be tested against the example. There are two functors from $\mathfrak{B}$ to $\mathfrak{B}$, in which $\mathfrak{B}$ is the category of vector spaces over the field K and linear transformations. One functor is the identity functor. The other functor is the double dual functor $^{**}\colon \mathfrak{B} \rightarrow \mathfrak{B}$ that associates with every vector space V its double dual V^{**} and with every linear transformation $f\colon U \rightarrow V$ in $\mathfrak{B}$ the linear transformation $f^{**}\colon U^{**} \rightarrow V^{**}$ (see 353). A linear transformation $T\colon V \rightarrow V^{**}$ was described above. If it is now written as T_V, it is easy to check that T is a natural transformation from the identity functor to the functor **. If the subcategory $\mathfrak{B}_f$ of $\mathfrak{B}$ that consists of finite-dimensional vector spaces over K and their linear transformations is considered, then it turns out that the functor ** transforms $\mathfrak{B}_f$ into itself; and the natural transformation T, restricted to $\mathfrak{B}_f$, is then a natural equivalence. Further examples of natural transformations of functors can be given:

(a) The category $\mathfrak{A}$ of Abelian groups and homomorphisms is considered. With every Abelian group may be associated its torsion subgroup. The torsion subgroup A_t of the Abelian group A consists of those elements of A that are of finite order. A homomorphism from A to B must necessarily send A_t to B_t. Thus a functor F is obtained from $\mathfrak{A}$ to $\mathfrak{A}$ (or to $\mathfrak{A}_t$, the category of torsion Abelian groups and their homomorphisms), by associating with every Abelian group A the Abelian group $FA = A_t$. Now A_t is a subgroup of A. Thus there is always an embedding i_A of A_t in A. It is easy to see that i is a natural transformation from the torsion functor F to the identity functor. Further, the quotient group $A_{fr} = A / A_t$ may be considered. It is a torsion-free Abelian group. This gives a functor G from $\mathfrak{A}$ to $\mathfrak{A}$ (or from $\mathfrak{A}$ to $\mathfrak{A}_{fr}$, the category of torsion-free Abelian groups) by associating with the Abelian group A the Abelian group $GA = A_{fr}$. Then the projection of A onto A_{fr} yields a natural transformation from the identity functor to the torsion-free functor G.

(b) With every group may be associated its commutator subgroup. It is then not difficult to see that the embedding of the commutator subgroup in the group is a natural transformation from the commutator subgroup functor to the identity functor. On the other hand, the centre of every group may be associated with the group. Here, however, there is not a functor because a homomorphism from one group to another does not necessarily map the centre of the first group to the centre of the second. On the other hand, if the category of groups and surjective homomorphisms (a surjective homomorphism is one in which the image coincides with the codomain) is considered, then in this category the centre is a functor. It is a functor, however, from the category of groups and surjective homomorphisms to the category of groups and all homomorphisms, because a surjective homomorphism does not necessarily map the centre surjectively. Then the embedding of the centre of a group in the group may be regarded as a natural transformation from the centre functor to the inclusion functor, both of which are functors from the category of groups and surjective homomorphisms to the category of groups and homomorphisms.

Surjective homomorphisms

(c) In algebraic topology, the singular homology groups and the homotopy groups of a pointed topological space (X, x) are considered. A Hurewicz homomorphism (see 354) exists, from the homotopy groups to the homology groups. Then π_n and H_n, $n \geq 2$, are functors from the category of pointed spaces and pointed continuous functions to the category of Abelian groups, and the Hurewicz homomorphism is a natural transformation of functors.

Hurewicz homomorphism

UNIVERSAL CONSTRUCTIONS

An important procedure that is made possible by the use of categorical language is the relation of apparently distinct concepts in various categories. Here an example is given, but it should be pointed out that the technique described is of extremely broad application.

The Cartesian product

In the category of sets, the notion of Cartesian product is vital. Its description, however, involves mention of the elements of the sets: the Cartesian product of the sets X and Y consists of the ordered pairs (x, y), $x \in X$, $y \in Y$. In a definition of the product of two objects in an arbitrary category, this definition cannot be imitated because, in the definition of a category, it is not required that the objects should be sets with elements. Therefore, a property of the Cartesian product $X \times Y$ must be found that characterizes the Cartesian product and that can be expressed in the language of categories. Such a property must be entirely expressible in terms of the data of a category: in terms of objects, morphisms, and composition of morphisms.

For any given set A and functions $f\colon A \rightarrow X$, $g\colon A \rightarrow Y$, there is a unique function $h\colon A \rightarrow X \times Y$ such that equations involving two projections hold (see 355), in which $p_1\colon X \times Y \rightarrow X$, $p_2\colon X \times Y \rightarrow Y$ are the projections. This is the clue to the generalization. For two objects X and Y of the category $\mathfrak{F}$, the triple $(Z; p_1, p_2)$ is taken to be a product of X and Y if $p_1\colon Z \rightarrow X$ and $p_2\colon Z \rightarrow Y$ are morphisms of $\mathfrak{F}$, and if the universal property holds that, given any object A of $\mathfrak{F}$ and morphisms $f\colon A \rightarrow X$, $g\colon A \rightarrow Y$, there exists a unique morphism $h\colon A \rightarrow Z$ such that certain relations hold (see 355).

$$(355)\quad p_1h = f, \qquad p_2h = g$$

$$(356)\quad p_1'\omega = p_1, \qquad p_2'\omega = p_2$$

$$(357)\quad (X_1 \times X_2) \times X_3 \cong X_1 \times (X_2 \times X_3)$$

$$(358)\quad gcd(gcd(a, b), c) = gcd(a, gcd(b, c))$$

$$(359)\quad \mathfrak{F}^0(A, B) = \mathfrak{F}(B, A)$$

It is easy to prove that the triple $(Z; p_1, p_2)$ is, essentially, uniquely determined by the universal property. This means that if $(Z'; p_1', p_2')$ is also a product, then there exists a unique isomorphism $\omega: Z \rightarrow Z'$ in $\mathfrak{F}$ such that two equalities hold (see 356). Therefore, it is permissible to speak of *the* product of X and Y in $\mathfrak{F}$. Of course, X and Y do not necessarily have a product in $\mathfrak{F}$. If they do have a product in $\mathfrak{F}$, in the sense defined above, however, then that product is unique. Now the product may be sought in various other categories. For example, in the category of Abelian groups the product, as defined, characterizes the direct sum; in the category of topological spaces it characterizes the topological product. In any category corresponding to a pre-ordered set, the product characterizes the greatest lower bound. Thus, in particular, in the category corresponding to the natural numbers ordered by divisibility, the product is precisely the GCD. It is possible to prove that the product in any category in which it exists is associative in the following sense. Given three objects X_1, X_2, and X_3, then there is an equivalence (see 357). This is, of course, a completely familiar—and trivial—fact for sets: in considering the Cartesian product of three sets, the way in which the sets are to be associated is not relevant. If a proof has been given that is valid in any category, however, it is immediately possible to deduce, for example, that the greatest common divisor satisfies associativity. That is, if a, b, c are any three natural numbers, then a relation involving the GCD holds (see 358). Here there are two points to be made. First, there was no apparent connection between this statement (358) and the statement that the Cartesian product of sets is associative. Second, by proving the statement in sufficient generality—*i.e.*, at the categorical level—it is possible to obtain many more instances of the theorem than could have been obtained by simply being confined to the original category in which the definition of product was carried out; that is, the category of sets.

THE DUALITY PRINCIPLE

For any category $\mathfrak{F}$ a new category $\mathfrak{F}^0$ can be formed by interchanging the domains and codomains of the morphisms of $\mathfrak{F}$. More precisely, in the category $\mathfrak{F}^0$ the objects are simply those of $\mathfrak{F}$ and the effect of interchange of domains is expressed in an equation (see 359). Moreover, the composition in $\mathfrak{F}^0$ is simply that of $\mathfrak{F}$, suitably interpreted. $\mathfrak{F}^0$ is called the category opposite to $\mathfrak{F}$; notice that $(\mathfrak{F}^0)^0 = \mathfrak{F}$. This apparently trivial operation leads to highly significant results when specific categories are used. In the general setting it enables any concept in the language of categories to be dualized. For example, the coproduct in $\mathfrak{F}$ is simply the product in $\mathfrak{F}^0$. Any theorem that holds in an arbitrary category has a dual form. For example, the theorem asserting that the product in an arbitrary category is associative may be effectively restated as asserting that the coproduct in an arbitrary category is associative. In the special cases, however, the second statement looks very different from the first. For example, in the category of sets, the coproduct becomes the disjoint union; in the category of groups it is the free product; and in a pre-ordered set regarded as a category, the coproduct is the least upper bound. In particular, for the set of natural numbers, ordered by divisibility, the coproduct is the LCM. Thus, the same universal argument that led to the deduction that the GCD is associative also indicates that the LCM is associative. The duality principle has very wide ramifications indeed. Here it is merely noted that the important concept of a contravariant functor from $\mathfrak{F}$ to $\mathfrak{G}$ may be most simply defined as a functor from $\mathfrak{F}^0$ to $\mathfrak{G}$. Thus the association of the dual vector space V^* with V yields a contravariant functor from $\mathfrak{B}$ to $\mathfrak{B}$.

CONCLUSIONS

Because the concept of a category is so general, it is to be expected that theorems provable for all categories will not usually be very deep. Consequently, many theorems of category theory are stated and proved for particular classes of categories. For example, homological algebra is concerned with Abelian categories, which exhibit features suggested by the category of Abelian groups. In mathematics one seeks generality and depth, but there is a certain conflict between these two aims because the more general the setting, the less likely that the results will be profound. The art of mathematics might be said to be that of finding the best possible compromise between these two aims. Further, a not unimportant purpose of the language of categories and categorical reasoning is to identify within a given argument that part which is trivial and separate it from the part which is deep and proper to the particular context. For example, in the study of the theory of the GCD, the fact that it is essentially unique simply follows from the uniqueness of the product in any category and is thus really trivial. Similarly, as has been demonstrated, the fact that it is associative is trivial. On the other hand, the fact that the GCD of the integers a and b can be expressed as a linear combination of a and b with integer coefficients—$gcd(a, b) = ma + nb$, m, n integers—is a much deeper fact that is special to the particular situation, or, at least, to a highly restricted class of situations.

Homological algebra

Development of homological algebra

The origins of homological algebra are to be found in algebraic topology. The mathematician W. Hurewicz pointed out in 1936 that if X is a connected polyhedron that is aspherical in all dimensions—that is, any map of sphere S^n into X, $n \geq 2$, is contractible—then the homology groups, H_nX, of the space X are entirely determined by $\pi = \pi_1X$, the fundamental group of X. Indeed, the homotopy type of X is determined by π. More generally, consider the Hurewicz homomorphism (354) from the kth homotopy group of X to the kth homology group. If a condition holds (see 360), π entirely determines the quotient of H_nX by the subgroup $\theta_n\pi_nX$, called the subgroup of spherical cycles. The mathematician H. Hopf investigated the nature of this dependence (see 361) and sought a purely algebraic description. In 1941, he was led in his work on the influence of the curvature of a closed Riemannian manifold on its topology to observe that the phenomenon under consideration could be expressed as a connection between π_1X and H_2X, valid for any connected polyhedron X; in fact, he produced a description of $H_2X / \theta_2\pi_2X$. For simplicity it is supposed here that X is aspherical in all dimensions; following Eilenberg–MacLane, one writes $X = K(\pi, 1)$, in which $\pi = \pi_1X$. This notation is justified because the homotopy type of X is determined by π. $K(\pi, 1)$ is called the Eilenberg–MacLane space of type $(\pi, 1)$. Note that a set of conditions holds (see 362). Then Hopf produced a formula for $H_2(K(\pi, 1))$ in terms of a free presentation of the group π. It is presented as the quotient of a free group F by a normal subgroup R; thus $\pi = F / R$. Writing $H_2\pi$ for $H_2(K(\pi, 1))$, the Hopf formula takes a specific form (see 363). Here $[F, F]$ is the commutator subgroup of F; and $[F, R]$ is the (normal) subgroup of F generated by all commutators $f^{-1}r^{-1}fr$, $f \in F$, $r \in R$.

This relation (363) is of considerable intrinsic algebraic interest, apart from the topological significance that it attaches to the group $(R \cap [F, F])/[F, R]$; for it shows that this group actually depends only on π, although it is expressed in terms of an arbitrary free presentation of π. This feature is characteristic of the procedures of homological algebra.

In 1944 Hopf gave his definitive solution of the problem raised by Hurewicz' result. Because World War II had virtually destroyed communication between European

(360) $\pi_k X = 0, \qquad 2 \leqslant k \leqslant n-1$

(361) The dependence of $\dfrac{H_n X}{\theta_n \pi_n X}$ on $\pi = \pi_1 X$

(362) $\pi_1[K(\pi, 1)] = \pi, \qquad \pi_n[K(\pi, 1)] = 0, \qquad n \geqslant 2$

(363) $H_2\pi \cong (R \cap [F, F])/[F, R]$

(364) $H_0 L = Z, \qquad H_n L = 0, \qquad n \geqslant 1$

(365) $\partial(x_0, x_1, \cdots, x_n) = \sum_{i=0}^{n} (-1)^i (x_0, x_1, \cdots, x_i^*, \cdots, x_n)$

(366) $\cdots \to C_n(\pi) \xrightarrow{\partial} C_{n-1}(\pi) \to \cdots \xrightarrow{\partial} C_0(\pi) \xrightarrow{\varepsilon} Z$

(367) $s(x_0, x_1, \cdots, x_{n-1}) = (e, x_0, x_1, \cdots, x_{n-1})$

(368) $H_n K = H_n(C(\pi)_\pi)$

(369) $H_n(K; A) \cong H_n(C(\pi) \otimes_\pi A)$

(370) $H^n(K; B) \cong H^n(\mathrm{Hom}_\pi(C(\pi), B))$

(371) $F(\phi + \psi) = F\phi + F\psi$

(372) $\begin{cases} P: \cdots \to P_n \xrightarrow{\partial} P_{n-1} \xrightarrow{\partial} \cdots \xrightarrow{\partial} P_0 \\ H_0(P) = M, \qquad H_n(P) = 0, \qquad n \geqslant 1 \end{cases}$

(373) $FP: \cdots \to FP_n \to FP_{n-1} \to \cdots \to FP_0$

and American mathematicians, further developments of Hopf's theory, by B. Eckmann and H. Freudenthal in Europe and by Eilenberg and MacLane in the U.S., proceeded quite independently.

HOMOLOGY GROUPS OF GROUPS

Hopf's description of the homology groups of $K = K(\pi, 1)$ was based on a geometrical idea. If L is the universal cover of K, then π acts freely as a permutation group on the simplexes of L lying above a given simplex of K. It follows that, for each n, the chain group $C_n(L)$, with integer coefficients, is a free π-module. Moreover, the boundary homomorphisms are maps of π-modules. Further, because L is contractible, the homology groups of L are given by a set of equations (see 364) in which Z is the group of integers. Thus it may be said that the chain complex $C(L)$ is π-free and acyclic. If $C(L)_\pi$ arises by killing the π-action, then $C(L)_\pi = C(K)$, so that the homology of K, with any coefficients, may be computed from the chain complex $C(L)_\pi$. Hopf observed that if P is any π-free acyclic chain complex, then P_π is chain equivalent to $C(L)_\pi$ and so could be used to calculate the homology of K. He described such a chain complex P purely in terms of the group π itself.

Eilenberg–MacLane space

A particular chain complex $C(\pi)$ will now be described. Let $C_n(\pi)$ be the free Abelian group on $(n+1)$-tuples $(x_0, x_1, \cdot\cdot\cdot, x_n)$ of elements of π. The Abelian group $C_n(\pi)$ can be turned into a π-module by defining $(x_0, x_1, \cdot\cdot\cdot, x_n)x = (x_0x, x_1x, \cdot\cdot\cdot, x_nx)$, and $C_n(\pi)$ is then plainly a free π-module. A differential $\partial: C_n(\pi) \to C_{n-1}(\pi)$ can be defined by the usual simplicial boundary formula (see 365), in which x_i^* indicates that x_i is to be omitted. Obviously ∂ is a module map and $\partial\partial = 0$. An augmentation ε: $C_0(\pi) \to Z$ is defined by $\varepsilon(x) = 1$ and thus is obtained a chain complex of π-modules (see 366).

It can be shown that this chain complex (366) is acyclic by defining a contracting homotopy s: $C_{n-1}(\pi) \to C_n(\pi)$, which is a homomorphism of Abelian groups, by a certain rule (see 367).

Thus $C(\pi)$ may be used to replace $C(L)$, so that the homology groups of K are given (see 368) by an equation in which the group on the right is defined entirely in terms of π.

A little more generally, a local system of coefficients on K may be considered; that is, a π-module A of coefficients. Then $C(L) \otimes_\pi A$, the tensor product over π of the (right) π-complex $C(L)$ and the (left) π-module A, is a chain complex yielding $H_*(K; A)$, the homology of K with local coefficients A; and $C(L) \otimes_\pi A$ is chain equivalent to $C(\pi) \otimes_\pi A$, whence a relation follows (see 369). It is natural to write $H_n(\pi; A)$ for the group on the right of this relation (369), and $H_n(\pi; A)$ is the nth homology group of π with coefficients in the π-module A.

Similarly, as observed by Eckmann and Eilenberg–MacLane, the cochain complex $\mathrm{Hom}_\pi(C(\pi), B)$ may be formed and thus, in cohomology, a similar relation holds (see 370) in which it is natural to write $H^n(\pi; B)$ for the group on the right of (370), so that definitions have been stated for the homology and cohomology groups of the group π (with coefficients in an arbitrary π-module).

It will now be shown how the definitions that have been stated above constitute special cases of the notion of a derived functor, which is basic to homological algebra.

DERIVED FUNCTORS

Let Λ be a fixed unitary ring and consider the category of right Λ-modules, for definiteness. Let F be a functor from this category to the category of Abelian groups that is additive in the sense that, if φ, ψ are Λ-module homomorphisms from the module M_1 to the module M_2, then an equality involving F holds (see 371). For a given module M, let there be given a chain complex of Λ-modules such that each is Λ-free (see 372).

Applying F leads to a chain complex of Abelian groups (see 373), and it may be shown that the homology groups of FP depend only on M and are independent of the choice of P [subject to the conditions described above and in (372)]. P is called a Λ-free resolution of M and a new functor L_nF can be defined because of this independence (see 374). It turns out that L_nF is again an additive functor, called the nth left derived functor of F. For the re-expression of $H_n(FP)$ to be valid, it suffices that each P_n be Λ-projective. This means that if η: $R \to S$ is a surjection of Λ-modules and φ: $P_n \to S$ is a Λ-homomorphism, there is a Λ-homomorphism ψ: $P_n \to R$ that lifts φ; *i.e.*, such

(374) $H_n(FP) = (L_nF)(M)$

(375) $FM = M \otimes_\pi A$

(376) $H_n(\pi; A) = (L_nF)(Z)$

(377) $GM = \mathrm{Hom}_\pi(M, B)$

(378) $H^n(\pi; B) = (R_nG)(Z)$

(379) $\mathrm{Tor}_n^\Lambda(M, N) = (L_nF)(M)$

(380) $FM = M \otimes_\Lambda N$

(381) $\mathrm{Ext}_\Lambda^n(M, N) = (R_nG)(M)$

(382) $GM = \mathrm{Hom}_\Lambda(M, N)$

(383) $\mathrm{Tor}_n^\Lambda(M, N) = (L_n\bar{F})(N), \qquad \bar{F}N = M \otimes_\Lambda N$
$\mathrm{Ext}^n(M, N) = (R_n\bar{G})(N), \qquad \bar{G}N = \mathrm{Hom}_\Lambda(M, N)$

(384) $H_n(\pi; A) = \mathrm{Tor}_n^{Z(\pi)}(Z, A)$

(385) $H^n(\pi; B) = \mathrm{Ext}_{Z(\pi)}^n(Z, B)$

(386) $H_n(g; A) = \mathrm{Tor}_n^{Ug}(K, A), \qquad n \geqslant 0$

(387) $H^n(g; B) = \mathrm{Ext}_{Ug}^n(K, B), \qquad n \geqslant 0$

(388) $A \to E \twoheadrightarrow \pi$

that $n\psi = \varphi$. A Λ-free module is certainly Λ-projective. If each P_n is Λ-projective, P is spoken of as a Λ-projective resolution of M.

The special case of the homology of groups is obtained by taking for Λ the integer group ring, $Z(\pi)$, of π, and for M the additive group of integers regarded as a trivial π-module. Then the functor F, given by the tensor product (see 375) in which A is a π-module, is an additive functor to the category of Abelian groups. The complex $C(\pi)$ is then a π-free resolution of Z, the additive group of integers, so that a relation holds (see 376) in which F is given above (see 375).

There are also right derived functors, obtained by taking Λ-injective resolutions, in which injective is dual, in the categorical sense, to projective; and it is possible to consider contravariant functors. The domain and codomain categories of the additive functor F can also be generalized; the essential requirement is that they be Abelian categories. The cohomology groups of the group π are obtained by taking, for a π-module B, the contravariant functor (see 377); GM is the group of π-homomorphisms from M to B; then, taking right derived fuctors of G, a relation is obtained (see 378).

The homology and cohomology groups of groups thus arise by taking left derived functors of the tensor product functor and right derived functors of the Hom functor. While there is an extensive general theory of derived functors, the theory of derived functors of these particular functors, but for arbitrary unitary rings Λ, is of particular importance. Thus, generalizing the definitions above (see 375 and 377), two sets of derived functors are defined (see 379 and 381) based on certain functors F, G (see 380 and 382), respectively. These are called the Tor and Ext functors, respectively; they are really bifunctors—that is, functors of two variables—and they enjoy the property of being balanced between their two arguments M, N in a sense that two equations express (see 383). Comparing past results (see 376, 379 and see 378, 381), it can be seen that two further relations hold (see 384, 385).

Tor and Ext functors

HOMOLOGY OF LIE ALGEBRAS

Many other homology theories have been found useful in algebra and arise by taking suitable derived functors. Here one will be described in which the derived functors are again Tor and Ext functors.

If g is a Lie algebra over the field K, Ug denotes its universal enveloping algebra. By a g-module, it is understood that A is a K-vector space on which the algebra Ug acts. Definitions are then made (see 386, 387), and these are called the homology groups of g (with coefficients in A) and the cohomology groups of g (with coefficients in B). Just as the (co)homology groups of a group may be interpreted as the (co)homology groups of a suitable space, so may the (co)homology groups of g be interpreted as the (co)homology groups of the underlying topological space of the compact, connected Lie group G the associated Lie algebra of which is g.

APPLICATIONS TO ALGEBRA

The topological significance of the homology theories of groups and Lie algebras has already been explained; these and other homology theories, however, also have important applications in pure algebra. For example, in the homology theory of groups, the group $H^1(\pi; A)$ is isomorphic to the quotient group of the group of derivations from π to A, modulo the inner derivations. The group $H^2(\pi; A)$ is isomorphic to the group $E(\pi; A)$ of equivalence classes of Abelian extensions of the quotient group π by the π-module A; such an extension can be written (see 388) to show that A is embedded in E and E projects onto π with kernel A. Here the group structure in the set $E(\pi; A)$ is by no means obvious, whereas the group structure in $H^2(\pi; A)$ follows immediately as in any homology or cohomology group. Similar interpretations of H^1 and H^2 are available in the homology theory of Lie algebras.

Uses of homological algebra

Many theorems of pure algebra may be proved by homological methods. For example, the homology theory of groups may be used to prove I. Schur's theorem that, if the quotient of a group G by its centre is finite, then the commutator subgroup of G is finite. It may also be used to prove Maschke's theorem that if the order of the finite group G is not divisible by the characteristic of the field K, then the (finite-dimensional) K-representations of G are completely reducible. Similarly, the homology theory of Lie algebras may be used to prove theorems that make no mention of homology; for example, the Levi-Malcev theorem that every (finite-dimensional) Lie algebra g, over a field K, is the split extension of a semisimple Lie algebra by the radical of g. Hilbert's celebrated chain-of-syzygies theorem may also be proved by homological methods—a notable early triumph for homological algebra; and there is the Auslander–Buchsbaum proof (the first given) that a regular local ring is a unique factorization domain. The claim that homological algebra is a useful tool in mathematics is not invalidated by the fact that these theorems can also be proved without the use of homological methods. For the homological methods are extremely systematic and serve to throw into relief the connections between apparently dissimilar areas of mathematics. (P.J.H./Ed.)

The Lie algebra of a Lie group. Consider now a Lie group G. For each g in G, $T(g)$ denotes the left translation map $x \rightarrow gx$ of G onto G. Then T is an analytic operation of G on G. By Lie's first fundamental theorem, the group $T(G)$ has an infinitesimal generator, and by Lie's second fundamental theorem, the infinitesimal generator is a Lie algebra of infinitesimal transformations; this infinitesimal generator is denoted by $\dot{G}$ and is called the Lie algebra of G. It is readily proved that $\dot{G}$ consists of precisely those infinitesimal transformations on G that are left unchanged by the right translations $x \rightarrow xg$ of G into G. It follows at once that each infinitesimal translation in G is uniquely determined by its value at the origin. Thus as a linear space, $\dot{G}$ is equivalent to $\dot{G}_e$, the tangent space of G at the identity element e. If X is an element of $\dot{G}_e$, and $\overline{X}$ is the element of G determined by X, then one defines exp $\overline{X}(e)$. Also, $[X, Y]$ is defined to be the value at e of $[\overline{X}, \overline{Y}]$, in which $\overline{X}$ and $\overline{Y}$ are the elements of G with $\overline{X}(e) = X$ and $\overline{Y}(e) = Y$.

In the special case that G is the group $GL(n)$ of all invertible linear transformations of an n-dimensional linear space V_n over the real numbers, the tangent space to G at the identity element can be identified with the set of all linear transformations of V_n. Then for any $X \in \dot{G}_e$, exp X coincides with the classical exponential of the transformation X; that is, exp $X = \Sigma_i X^i/i!$. For any X and Y in $\dot{G}_e$, $[X, Y] = XY - YX$, in which the multiplication on the right is the usual multiplication of linear transformations.

If the algebraic structure alone is abstracted from $\dot{G}$, it is seen to be an algebra with Poisson brackets as multiplication. This multiplication is nonassociative, but the structure of such algebras is capable of a virtually exhaustive description. On the other hand, there is a very close connection between the algebraic structure of a Lie group and the algebraic structure of its Lie algebra. Indeed, there is a one-to-one correspondence between the subalgebras of the Lie algebra $\dot{G}$ and the connected Lie subgroups of G, the correspondence being: a connected Lie subgroup H corresponds to the subalgebra of $\dot{G}$ that is determined by the tangent subspace H_e to H at the identity. A connected Lie subgroup H is normal in G if, and only if, the corresponding subalgebra $\dot{H}$ is an ideal in G; that is, $[\dot{G}, \dot{H}]$ is contained in $\dot{H}$. To the commutator subgroup of G generated by the elements of the form $xyz^{-1}y^{-1}$, there corresponds the derived subalgebra that is generated by the elements $[X, Y]$ with X and Y in $\dot{G}$. In particular, a connected Lie group G is Abelian if, and only if, $[X, Y] = 0$ for all X and Y in $\dot{G}$.

The most elementary type of Lie algebra is one wherein the multiplication is trivial; *i.e.*, $[G, G] = 0$. Such a Lie algebra is called Abelian. Next in complexity is a Lie algebra wherein the product of some finite number of any elements is zero; *i.e.*, if setting $G^{(1)} = G$, $G^{(n+1)} = [G^{(n)}, G]$, then $G^{(n)} = 0$ for some n. Such a G is called nilpotent. One step more complex are Lie algebras G that have a decreasing sequence of ideals, $G \supset G_1 \supset \cdots \supset G_n \cdots$ with the quotient algebra G_i / G_{i+1} Abelian and $G_n = 0$ for some n; such a Lie algebra is called solvable. The maximum solvable ideal of a Lie algebra is called its radical. If G is a Lie algebra and R denotes its radical, then G/R has no nonzero radical; such a Lie algebra is called semisimple. If a Lie algebra has no nonzero properly smaller ideal, it is called simple. The basic theorems describing the structure of Lie algebras over any field of characteristic zero areas may be stated as follows:

Theorems describing the structure of Lie algebras

Any Lie algebra is a semi-direct sum of its radical and a semisimple subalgebra.

Any semisimple Lie algebra is a direct sum of simple Lie algebras.

Any simple Lie algebra over the field of complex numbers is one of the following type:

A_n: the Lie algebra of the group of all $n+1$ by $n+1$ complex-valued matrices of determinant-1.

B_n: the Lie subalgebra of A_{2n} that annihilates the quadratic form composed of a sum of squares of $\{x_k\}$ (see 389).

C_n: the Lie subalgebra of A_{2n-1} that annihilates the alternating bilinear form (see 390).

D_n: the Lie subalgebra of A_{2n-1} that annihilates the quadratic form composed to a sum of squares of $\{x_k\}$ (see 391).

(389) $x_1^2+x_2^2+\cdots+x_{2n+1}^2$

(390) $x_1y_{n+1}-y_1x_{n+1}+x_2y_{n+2}-y_2x_{n+2}+\cdots+ +x_ny_{2n}-y_nx_{2n}$

(391) $x_1^2+\cdots+x_{2n}^2$

The five exceptional simple Lie algebras G_2, F_4, E_6, E_7, E_8 discovered by the mathematician W. Killing are of dimensions 14, 52, 78, 133, 248, respectively. This remarkable classification is achieved by a study of the so-called root diagram of the Lie algebra.

Although each Lie group has a unique Lie algebra, a Lie algebra in the abstract (*i.e.*, divorced from its presentation as the infinitesimal generator of a Lie group) may arise from inequivalent or nonisomorphic groups. For example, the one-dimension Abelian Lie algebra over the field of real numbers is the Lie algebra of both example G1 and example G2 above. The problem of determining the relation between the various connected Lie groups having abstractly isomorphic Lie algebras was solved by the mathematician Otto Schreier.

The situation may be described in this way: to each abstract Lie algebra g (over the field of real numbers) there corresponds a unique (up to isomorphism) simply connected Lie group G—that is, a connected Lie group in which every closed curve can be deformed continuously to a point; any other Lie group G_1 the Lie algebra of which is isomorphic to g is obtained from G by a homomorphism with a discrete kernel. Thus G_1 is evenly covered by G, and all connected Lie groups the Lie algebras of which are isomorphic to G have the same simply connected covering group. The spin representation of physics provides another example of this phenomenon.

It should be emphasized, however, that in a neighbourhood of the identity, any two Lie groups having isomorphic Lie algebras are isomorphic. This can be seen from the Baker–Campbell–Hausdorff formula (see 392) that identi-

(392) $(\exp X)(\exp Y)=\exp(X+Y-\tfrac{1}{2}[X,Y]+\cdots)$

fies the product of exponentials with the exponential of an algebraic form involving an infinite sum of terms built from X and Y with Poisson brackets. By a process known as complexification it can be proved that the classification of complex simple Lie algebras also applies to compact Lie groups.

Complexification

The topological structure of Lie groups. It has been shown above that to a given abstract Lie algebra there may correspond Lie groups that are not topologically equivalent. Therefore, it cannot be expected that the abstract Lie algebra $\dot{G}$ of a Lie group G will determine the topological structure of G completely. One of the greatest contributions of Cartan to mathematics, however, was his demonstration that the Lie algebra G determines the important topological invariants called Betti numbers of the group G in the very important case that the Lie group G is compact and connected.

Cartan's researches on this problem led him to invent his theory of exterior differential forms and to conjecture the celebrated de Rham theorems, which were proved by his student Georges de Rham.

(G.D.M.)

OTHER ASPECTS OF HOMOLOGICAL ALGEBRA

The scope of homological algebra is extremely broad. Only two homology theories (groups, Lie algebras) have been described from among many. There are also, however, aspects of homological algebra in which homological ideas are further refined and developed or in which homological techniques lead to new algebraic constructs. Two examples are now described.

Attention may be given to the category of Abelian groups that may well be graded by the integers, or even bigraded by pairs of integers. If A is such an Abelian group it is said to be differential if it is equipped with an endomorphism d: $A\rightarrow A$, called the boundary, or differential, such that $d^2=0$. Notice, however, that a chain complex of Abelian groups may be thought of as a differential graded Abelian group, in which d is the boundary homomorphism and so of degree -1; whenever A is (bi)-graded a degree is supposed for d. If A is differential, the group $ZA=\ker d$ may be defined, and ZA is called the cycle group of A; one writes $BA=\text{im } d$, and calls BA the boundary group of A. Because $d^2=0$, it follows that $BA\subset ZA$; HA is written for ZA/BA and HA is called the homology group of A. This is, of course, familiar from topology. A spectral sequence of differential Abelian groups is a sequence $\{E_n, d_n\}$, $n\geq 0$, in which E_n is an Abelian group with differential d_n and $HE_n=E_{n+1}$.

Associated with every spectral sequence there is a limit term, which may be described as follows. If $z\in ZE_n$, then its homology class $\{z\}$ belongs to E_{n+1} and the boundary d_{n+1} may be applied to $\{z\}$. It is convenient to talk of applying d_{n+1} to z itself in this case. Thus one may talk

(393) $E_0^*\rightarrow E_1^*\rightarrow\cdots\rightarrow E_n^*\rightarrow E_{n+1}^*\rightarrow\cdots$

(394) $\cdots\subseteq F_{p-1}G\subseteq F_pG\subseteq\cdots\subseteq G$

(395) $Gr(G)_p=\dfrac{F_pG}{F_{p-1}G}$

(396) $E_2^{pq}=H_p(B;H_q(F;G))$

(397) $E_n^{pq}=E_{n+1}^{pq}=\cdots=E_\infty^{pq}$

(398) $N\rightarrow G\twoheadrightarrow Q$

(399) $E_2^{pq}=H_p(Q;H_q(N;A))$

(400) $L_0G(FP)=GFP, \quad L_nG(FP)=0, \quad n\geqslant 1$

(401) $E_2^{pq}=(L_pG)(L_qF)(A)$

(402) $\mu^*:H^*(M;Q)\rightarrow H^*(M\times M;Q) =H^*(M;Q)\otimes_Q H^*(M;Q)$

(403) $\psi:A\rightarrow A\otimes_Q A$

(404) $(1\otimes\eta)\psi=(\eta\otimes 1)\psi=1: A\rightarrow A$

(405) $(1\otimes\theta)\psi=\psi(1\otimes\theta)=\eta$

of successively applying the differentials $d_n, d_{n+1}, \cdots$ to an element c of E_n, each differential becoming applicable when its predecessor produces the value 0. In particular E^*_n may be defined as the subgroup of E_n consisting of those elements of E_n that are cycles for all d_r, $r \geq n$. Now the passage from cycle to homology class plainly induces a surjection of E^*_n onto E^*_{n+1} and E_∞, the limit of the spectral sequence, is defined to be the direct limit of the resulting sequence (see 393). Thus E_∞ is the quotient of E^*_0 by those cycles that eventually become boundaries; *i.e.*, that go to zero in some E^*_n. It is also said that the spectral sequence converges to E_∞.

Often in applications of spectral sequence theory the terms E_n are graded (or bigraded), and an early term of the spectral sequence is known and the limit term E_∞ is related to an Abelian group to be calculated, or, at least, about which information is sought. The relation of E_∞ to this group is frequently that of the graded group associated to a filtration of that group. A filtration (strictly, an increasing filtration) of the Abelian group G is a sequence of subgroups (see 394) and the associated graded group Gr (G) is the graded group, the pth component of which is given (see 395).

It is plain that if the filtration (see 394) is to be such that Gr (G) yields useful information about G, it must have certain properties. Usually it is asked that $F_pG = 0$ for p less than or equal to some p_0, and that $\cup_p F_pG = G$. Then every nonzero element of G appears as a nonzero element in precisely one component of Gr (G). From the given knowledge of E_2, say, conclusions can be drawn about E_∞ by passing through the spectral sequence and then inferences made about the filtered group G of which E_∞ is the associated graded group; sometimes this procedure is reversed.

The concept of a spectral sequence was invented by the French mathematician Jean Leray. Topologists first became generally aware of its importance, however, when the French mathematician Jean-Pierre Serre applied it to the study of the relations between the homology groups of fibre, total space, and base space in a fibration, in 1951. He was thus able to obtain deep relations between the homology groups and homotopy groups of a space. Precisely, Serre showed the following (his result is not stated here in its fullest generality): If F is the fibre, E the total space, B the base space, all spaces being connected, B simply-connected, and if G is an Abelian coefficient group, then there is a spectral sequence of bigraded Abelian groups $\{E_n, d_n\}$ with specific properties (see 396) and E_∞ is the graded group associated with $H_*(E; G)$, suitably filtered. Moreover, the filtration has the good properties mentioned earlier; and the convergence to the limit is finite in the sense that, given any (p, q), there exists n such that a sequence of equations holds (see 397). The differential d_n on E_n has degree $(-n, n-1)$. Thus knowledge of the homology groups of B and F makes it possible to draw conclusions about the homology groups of E; indeed, knowledge of the homology groups of any two of F, E, B leads to information about the third.

Serre's theorem

Serre's theorem revolutionized homotopy theory; but spectral sequences then began to appear all over algebraic topology and homological algebra. For example, in the homology theory of groups, let a short exact sequence of groups be given (see 398); G is a group with normal subgroup N, such that $G/N \cong Q$. Let A be a G-module. There is then a Lyndon–Hochschild–Serre spectral sequence such that an equation holds (see 399), which converges to the graded group associated with $H_*(G; A)$, suitably filtered. There is a similar sequence in the homology theory of Lie algebras. Indeed, all the sequences described are special cases of a procedure due to the French mathematician Alexandre Grothendieck. Additive functors $F: \mathfrak{A} \to \mathfrak{B}$, $G: \mathfrak{B} \to \mathfrak{C}$ of suitable Abelian categories (for example, categories of modules) may be considered. Suppose that, for every projective object P of $\mathfrak{A}$, FP is (left) G-acyclic, that is to say, the left derived functors of G, evaluated on FP, give a set of equations (see 400). Then, for each A in $\mathfrak{A}$, there is a spectral sequence such that a relation holds (see 401) and it converges to the graded group associated with $L_*(GF)(A)$, suitably filtered. Even this formulation by no means exhausts the scope of useful generalization.

Hopf algebras

Turning now to another topic of homological algebra, namely, that of Hopf algebras, again the source lies in algebraic topology. Suppose there is given a connected Lie group M; for example, the rotation group of Euclidean n-space. The cohomology ring $H^*(M; Q)$ of the underlying space of M with coefficients in the ring Q of rational numbers may then be formed; this is a graded commutative Q-algebra. Moreover, the multiplication map μ: $M \times M \to M$ induces an algebra map (see 402). Further, the fact that there is a two-sided unity for μ shows that if μ^* is followed by either projection onto $H^*(M; Q)$, the composite is the identity. This leads to a study of graded Q-algebras $A = \bigoplus_{n \geq 0} A_n$ admitting a diagonal map ψ, which is a map of Q-algebras (see 403), and a co-unit η: $A \to Q$ such that a consequence follows (see 404). (Note that $A \otimes_Q Q \cong A \cong Q \otimes_Q A$ so that $1 \otimes \eta$ and $\eta \otimes 1$ correspond to the projections mentioned above.) This is now called a graded Hopf algebra. Of course, the example $A = H^*(M; Q)$ has other properties that may qualify the Hopf algebra. It is commutative; it is connected in the sense that $A_0 = Q$ and η is simply the obvious projection onto A_0; it is co-associative in the sense that ψ is associative; and it admits an involution $\theta: A \to A$ such that equations result (see 405).

In a pioneer work published in 1941, Hopf proved that, in the terminology introduced above, if A is a commutative graded connected Hopf algebra over Q, then it is, as an algebra, an exterior algebra on odd-dimensional generators; moreover, if it is co-associative, then these generators are primitive, meaning that $\psi(x) = x \otimes 1 + 1 \otimes x$. Hopf thus explained a phenomenon relating to the four main series of simple Lie groups that had been observed by geometers, algebraists, and topologists in the 1930s. Because Hopf's theorem only required that M admit a continuous multiplication with two-sided unity, it encompassed a broader class of topological space than that defined by the Lie groups. The true breadth of this class is now beginning to be glimpsed, as more and more Hopf manifolds are being discovered.

The study of Hopf algebras is now a part of algebra; moreover, there is a theory of differential Hopf algebras that is securely placed in the domain of homological algebra. Hopf's is seen as the first of many structure theorems that have proved of great value in both algebra and topology. A particularly interesting connection between the theory of Hopf algebras and what has gone before is provided by the group ring, KG, of a (finite) group G, over the field K. The diagonal map Δ: $G \to G \times G$, yields a diagonal map ψ: $KG \to KG \otimes KG$ and so makes of KG a co-associative, co-commutative Hopf algebra over K with involution.

(P.J.H.)

Universal algebra

Historical background

Algebra began as the manipulation of numbers, using the four operations of arithmetic: addition, subtraction, multiplication and division. As the subject developed, the operations have changed very little, if at all, but the notion of number has been progressively enlarged. It was already recognized by the school of Pythagoras that rational numbers do not suffice to describe the diagonal of a unit square (*i.e.*, $\sqrt{2}$). In order to take account of such irrational numbers as $\sqrt{2}$, a geometric theory of proportion was developed during the 4th century BC by Eudoxus of Cnidus; this theory forms the substance of Book V of Euclid's *Elements*.

In the 16th century, when it was found that square roots of negative numbers may be needed to solve cubic equations, even when all their roots are real numbers, complex numbers were introduced. For a long time these numbers were known as impossible or imaginary, and their use was put on a firm basis only at the end of the 18th century, by Gauss.

The 19th century saw a series of discoveries, resulting in the creation of modern function theory. Some extensions of the complex number system were also made. Although these did not rival the complex numbers in importance, they formed a beginning of the more abstract outlook adopted today.

The first of these generalized number systems was Hamilton's quaternions. They were intended to describe points in space just as complex numbers describe points in the plane, and in fact Hamilton had mainly geometric applications in mind. From a somewhat different point of view, Grassmann, in his calculus of extension, treated geometric entities as objects of an algebraic system with addition and multiplication. The ideas of Hamilton and Grassmann gave rise, at the hands of Heaviside and Gibbs, to the modern development of vector analysis, not of concern here, except in so far as both the quaternions and Grassmann algebra may be regarded as an algebraic system with vectors instead of numbers, or a linear associative algebra. A system of quite a different sort, but still formally fitting into the framework of linear associative algebras, was described by Boole, who defined certain operations on statements: If two statements A, B are combined by conjunction (*i.e.*, the new statement "A and B" is formed), disjunction (forming "A or B") and negation (forming "not A"), a system satisfying many of the rules of the ordinary number system is obtained.

Another branch of algebra that began to take shape in the early days of the 19th century was the theory of groups, first as groups of permutations by Abel and Galois and later more generally as groups of transformations by Lie and Klein. The mere existence of all these different types of algebraic systems suggested a comparative study. Such a study was begun by the English mathematician Alfred North Whitehead, who in his 'Universal Algebra' I, described the systems of Boole, Hamilton, and Grassmann, as a preparation to a comparative study, which was to form volume II, but was never written. The name 'Universal Algebra,' according to Whitehead, was taken from a paper by the British mathematician James Joseph Sylvester: "Lectures on the Principles of Universal Algebra," published in the *American Journal of Mathematics,* vol. 6, 1884.

Development of axiomatic foundations

One of the characteristics of 20th-century mathematics has been the development of axiomatic foundations. Instead of referring new developments back to some part of the subject regarded as known, one would base everything on a small set of axioms. The method was used especially in algebra; the whole of group theory could be built up on three or four simple axioms. It also helped to crystallize such general notions as linear associative algebra and ring. Emmy Noether showed how the notion of group with operators allowed a number of different notions, such as group, vector space, representation module, to be treated by the same method. From here it was only a small step to drop the group structure. Universal algebra is nowadays understood to be the study of such general algebraic systems, by methods uniformly applicable to all of them.

BASIC NOTIONS OF UNIVERSAL ALGEBRA

An operation on a set A is a mapping or function defined on A with values in A. For example, if A is mankind, then "mother of x" is an operation in one argument, or a unary operation (here the fact that the mapping is undefined for Adam and Eve is ignored). On the set of integers, the operation of taking the sum of the numbers x and y, written $x + y$, is a binary operation, because it depends on two arguments: x and y. In the plane, the operation of taking the centroid of a triangle ABC is a ternary operation, depending on three arguments, A, B, C. Most operations depend on a finite number of arguments; that is, they are said to be finitary. If an operation depends on n arguments, in which n may be 1, or 2, or any positive integer, then the operation is said to be n-ary, and the number n is called its arity. Occasionally, 0-ary operations are used; such an operation depends on no arguments at all; it simply picks out a particular element of the set. For this reason it is also called a constant operator. For example, in a group the neutral element may be regarded as the value of a 0-ary operation.

Operations that are n-ary

An algebraic structure on a set A consists in specifying a number of operations on A; these operations are not restricted in any way except that the arity of each is usually a preassigned integer. In this way A becomes an algebraic system, or simply an algebra. For example, groups may be regarded as algebras with a binary operation, multiplication: xy; a unary operation, the inverse: x^{-1}; and a 0-ary operation, the neutral: e, together with certain laws (such as the associative law). As an example of an algebra with infinitely many operations, a real vector space is considered. This has the group operations (because it is an additive group) as well as a unary operation for each real number λ: scalar multiplication by λ. To facilitate the comparison of different algebras, a set Ω is usually chosen as operator set; with each member ω of Ω an integer $n(\omega)$ is associated, to indicate the arity of the resulting operation, and an Ω-algebra structure is obtained by prescribing for each ω in Ω an operation $\omega(x_1, \cdots, x_n)$ of arity $n = n(\omega)$.

The notion of a subgroup of a group or a subspace of a vector space is generalized by defining a subalgebra of an algebra A as a subset admitting all the operations of A. The result is an algebraic structure of the same kind as A, just as every subgroup of a group is a group in its own right. To give an example, the complex numbers form a real vector space, with the real numbers as subspace. But the complex numbers may also be regarded as a complex vector space, and now the real numbers do not form a subspace because they do not allow multiplication by $\sqrt{-1}$. This illustrates the need to specify the operations as well as the sets in describing algebras.

If in an algebra A a subset X is taken, it will in general not be a subalgebra; *i.e.*, by applying the algebra operations to elements of X new elements are generally obtained that do not lie in X. $<X>$ denotes the set of all elements obtainable from X by repeated application of the algebra operations. When any of these operations is applied to elements of $<X>$, again an element of $<X>$ is obtained; in other words, $<X>$ admits all the algebra operations and so is a subalgebra of A. It is actually the least subalgebra containing X and is usually called the subalgebra generated by X.

Quotient groups

The notion of a quotient group can be generalized as follows: If an Ω-algebra A is partitioned into classes, it is possible to define an operation ω of A on the set of classes, provided that varying the arguments of ω within a given class does not change the class in which the result lies; that is, if x_1, x'_1 lie in the same class and likewise x_2, x'_2, etc., then $\omega(x_1, \cdots, x_n)$ and $\omega(x'_1, \cdots, x'_n)$ must lie in the same class. When this condition holds for all ω in Ω, the given partition is called a congruence, and denoting it by q say, A/q is written for the set of classes. The above condition ensures that each ω in Ω can be defined unambiguously as an operation on A/q. In this way A/q is turned into an Ω-algebra, called the quotient algebra of A by q. For example, if **Z** is the ring of integers and **Z** is partitioned into classes by putting two numbers in the same class precisely when their difference is divisible by 7, then there are just 7 classes, described by their least remainders after division by 7. If two numbers a, a' leave the same remainder and b, b' do likewise, then so do their respective sums $a + b$ and $a' + b'$; similarly for the other ring operations (subtraction and multiplication), and therefore a congruence is obtained and the residue classes form a quotient ring.

A mapping f from one Ω-algebra, A, to another, B, is called a homomorphism and is written as $f\colon A \rightarrow B$ if it preserves the Ω-algebra structure in the sense that the result of applying f to the value of an operation ω is the same as applying f to the arguments and then taking ω;

$$f(\omega(x_1, \cdots, x_n)) = \omega(f(x_1), \cdots, f(x_n)).$$

For example, if q is a congruence on an algebra A, then there is a natural mapping φ that associates with each element of A the class of q in which it lies; now the condition for q to be a congruence ensures that φ is a homomorphism. A homomorphism from A to B that is a one-one correspondence (bijection) between these algebras is called an isomorphism between A and B, and A is then said to be isomorphic to B.

Given two Ω-algebras A and B, a new Ω-algebra $A \times B$

can be defined, called their direct product, by taking the set of all pairs with the first component a member of A and the second a member of B, and performing the operations of Ω componentwise. More generally, such a direct product can be formed from any collection (even infinite) of Ω-algebras.

These notions of subalgebra, quotient algebra, homomorphism, and direct product arose by generalizing the familiar situation in group theory. There the notion of a quotient group looks simpler than in the general case because the classes of a congruence on a group are just the cosets of a subgroup. For other algebraic systems having no underlying group structure, such as lattices or semigroups, the situation is more involved; nevertheless the notion of congruence has been useful there too, in analyzing homomorphisms. Thus with each homomorphism f: $A \rightarrow B$ between Ω-algebras, there can be associated a quotient algebra A/q of A and a subalgebra B' of B, together with an isomorphism f_1: $A/q \rightarrow B'$ such that the original homomorphism f is obtained by taking in turn the natural mapping $A \rightarrow A/q$, the isomorphism f_1, and the inclusion mapping $B' \rightarrow B$, which leaves each element of B' fixed but considers it as an element of B. The congruence q of A that arises in this way is called the kernel of the mapping f, and it has the following interpretation: two elements of A are mapped to the same element of B by f precisely when they belong to the same class of the kernel of f. The set of values of f, namely B', is also called the image of A under the mapping f, and the above analysis of homomorphisms shows that the images of an algebra under homomorphisms are precisely its quotient algebras. For this reason the quotient algebras of an algebra are also called its homomorphic images.

Now the usual isomorphism theorems of group theory, which allow a comparison of subgroups of quotients, and of quotients of quotients, to be made, can be taken over with hardly any change. One can also prove, under suitable hypotheses, an analogue of the Jordan–Hölder–Schreier theorem, which compares different chains of factor algebras; *i.e.*, quotients of subalgebras. There is a close connection with lattices here: as already observed, the results can be applied to lattices, as particular algebraic systems. At the same time the subalgebras of an algebra form a lattice, as do the congruences on an algebra, and in this way the results of lattice theory can be used in a general analysis of algebraic systems.

THE CONNECTION WITH MATHEMATICAL LOGIC

The results described in the last section are quite general in scope, and apply even to systems with infinitary operations; that is, operations depending on infinitely many arguments. There is, however, another group of results for which finitarity of the operations is essential; these results are often regarded as characteristic of algebraic systems. The basic property is the following algebraicity condition: if A is any algebra and X a subset of A, then an element of A lies in $<X>$, the subalgebra generated by X, precisely when it lies in the subalgebra generated by some finite subset of X. This is so because any member of $<X>$ is obtained by applying the algebra operations repeatedly to elements of X, and, because all operations are finitary, the total number of arguments needed is also finite. This principle forms the basis for the application of Zorn's lemma (an algebraic formulation of the axiom of choice in set theory). It applies not only to algebraic systems—that is, sets with operations—but also to relational systems; that is, sets with operations and relations defined on them, such as ordered groups. It also has a remarkable connection with logic: any mathematical theory may be regarded as an algebraic system the elements of which are the theorems (the provable statements in the theory) and the operations of which are the usual rules of deduction in logic (modus ponens and the rule of substitution); therefore it satisfies the algebraicity condition mentioned earlier. Now a basic theorem of logic due to the logician Gödel, the completeness theorem, states that any theory (composed of statements of the lower predicate calculus) admitting the rules of deduction and not including a contradictory statement has a model. On the other hand one can show, by purely algebraic means, that the theories that have models satisfy the algebraicity condition. The practical consequence is often stated as the compactness theorem: A set of statements within a theory (of the lower predicate calculus) is consistent whenever every finite subset of statements is consistent.

The compactness theorem

A typical application of this result to the algebraic theory of fields states that a sentence holds in every field of characteristic zero, provided that it holds in every field of sufficiently high characteristic. This follows because fields of characteristic greater than a given number n can be defined by the conjunction of the sentences $E_2, E_3, \cdots, E_n$, in which E_2 is: "for each $x \neq 0$, $x+x \neq 0$"; *i.e.*, no nonzero element when added to itself gives zero (to exclude fields of characteristic 2), E_3 is: "for each $x \neq 0$, $x+x+x \neq 0$," and so on, while fields of characteristic zero are defined by the conjunction of all the sentences $E_2, E_3, \cdots$. If a sentence holds for all fields of characteristic exceeding some fixed number N, then it must be consistent with any finite subset of the collection $E_2, E_3, \cdots$, and hence (by the compactness theorem) with all of them; *i.e.*, it holds in characteristic zero.

Besides being a field of application of universal algebra, mathematical logic is also an important tool. Thus to study a particular class of algebraic systems, it is not enough to specify the operations. It is also necessary to lay down which algebras are to be admitted. This is usually done by means of sentences formed from such basic statements as $x+y=z$, in accordance with the rules prescribed by logic; for example, if the system to be specified has a multiplication that is to have an inverse, a sentence is required of the form: For all x, y, there exists u such that $xu=y$. The sentences needed to define a class of algebras can be classified according to logical principles, and conclusions can then be drawn about the class of algebras defined. Thus, if the sentences defining the class of algebras contain only universal quantifiers ("For all . . .") and no existential quantifiers ("There exist . . ."), in other words, if they are universal sentences, then the class of algebras so defined is closed under subalgebras: with an algebra, all its subalgebras belong to the class. This is fairly easy to prove; more difficult (and more interesting) is a result in the opposite direction: A class of algebras that is closed under subalgebras and that is definable by axioms can be defined by universal sentences. The condition of being definable by axioms can also be expressed in terms of explicit conditions on the algebras of the class, but is a little more complicated to state and so is omitted here.

Classes of algebraic systems

As an example, the class of all groups is considered. This can be defined by the following laws: (a) the associative law: $x(yz)=(xy)z$; (b) the law expressing that e is neutral: $xe=ex=x$; and (c) the law expressing that x^{-1} is inverse to x: $xx^{-1}=x^{-1}x=e$. These laws are understood to hold for all group elements x, y, z, and so they are universal sentences, and in fact any subalgebra, within the general sense of the word (that is, any subgroup), of a group is again a group. The same is true if a sentence such as "for all x, $x^3=e$" is added. This picks out the class of groups in which the cube of any element is the neutral element, and any subgroup of such a group has the same property. Next consider the class of periodic groups; *i.e.*, groups in which every element has some power equal to e: $x_n=e$, in which the value of the exponent n depends generally on x. Any subgroup of a periodic group is periodic, but the class of periodic groups cannot be defined by axioms. If one attempts this, one finds oneself having to say that for each x, either $x^2=e$ or $x^3=e$ or $x^4=e$ or $\cdots$, a sentence of infinite length that is not admitted. It might seem as if periodic groups could be defined by the finite sentence: For every x there exists a positive integer n such that $x^n=e$. This is not, however, allowed by the rules of the game, which permit only sentences of the lower predicate calculus, because a quantifier has been applied to an integer (. . . there exists a positive integer n . . .). Next examine the class of all groups that are not periodic; it is easy to find a group that is not periodic but that has a periodic subgroup. So this class cannot be expected to be defined by universal sentences. Finally, the class of aperiodic groups is considered; that is, groups in which no element other than e has any positive power equal to e. This class is closed under subgroups and can in fact be defined by universal sentences, expressing the fact that no power of an element other than e can be e: For all x, if $x \neq e$, then $x^2 \neq e$; for all x, if $x \neq e$, then $x^3 \neq e \cdot \cdot \cdot$. These sentences form the multiplicative analogue of the sentences $E_2, E_3, \cdot \cdot \cdot$ used earlier to define fields of characteristic zero.

VARIETIES OF ALGEBRAS

Many important classes of algebras can be defined entirely by identities; that is, equations that hold for all values of the arguments. Thus groups were defined by the identities expressing the associative law and the properties of neutral and inverse elements. Such a class is called a variety. Groups form a variety, likewise Abelian groups, but not all finite groups, because any law satisfied by all finite groups is also satisfied by all infinite groups. Testing for varieties is facilitated by the following criterion due to Garrett Birkhoff: A class of algebras is a variety if, and only if, it is closed under taking subalgebras, homomorphic images, and direct products. Using this test it is easy to check that finite groups do not form a variety: a direct product of finite groups, with infinitely many factors, is no longer finite. In the same way one finds that periodic groups do not form a variety; nor do the aperiodic groups; the groups satisfying $x^3 = e$, however, do form a variety.

Testing for varieties

Varieties have several properties that make them more amenable to treatment. A useful property, actually characteristic of varieties, is the following: For each integer n, there is an algebra F_n the quotients of which constitute precisely the algebras in the variety that can be generated by n elements; a corresponding algebra exists when n is replaced by an infinite cardinal number. This algebra F_n is called the free algebra of the variety, on n free generators; it is rather like the algebra of polynomials. In elementary algebra a polynomial in n variables $x_1, \cdot \cdot \cdot, x_n$ with real coefficients has the property that any substitution of real numbers for the variables $x_1, \cdot \cdot \cdot, x_n$ gives a real number. Moreover, these polynomials can be added, subtracted and multiplied; *i.e.*, they form a ring, the polynomial ring in the variables $x_1, \cdot \cdot \cdot, x_n$ over the real numbers, and it is not hard to see that any substitution of real numbers for the x's preserves the ring operations; *i.e.*, it is a homomorphism. In the same way group elements can be formed in n variables $x_1, \cdot \cdot \cdot, x_n$, using only the general group laws to simplify the expressions. Thus a variable that is followed or preceded by its formal inverse can always be omitted: $xyy^{-1}z = xz$, $ux^{-1}xu = u^2$, but no other simplification is possible. For example, one may not replace xy by yx because the commutative law $xy = yx$ does not hold in all groups. In this way the free group on $x_1, \cdot \cdot \cdot x_n$ is obtained; its elements are all products in $x_1, \cdot \cdot \cdot, x_n$ and their inverses; that is, all group words in these variables. By the associative law all parentheses can be omitted, and two group words represent the same group element if it is possible to pass from one to the other by inserting or omitting occurrences of a variable together with its inverse. Given any group G, any elements of G can be substituted for the variables in words of the free group. Thus x_1 can be replaced by a_1, x_2 by a_2, etc., taking care to replace x_1^{-1} by a_1^{-1}, etc. In this way each word corresponds to an element of G, and words representing the same element of the free group will certainly correspond to the same element of G. Therefore, a mapping is obtained from the free group into G, and this mapping can easily be shown to be a homomorphism. By taking enough variables (infinitely many if necessary) any group can be expressed in this way as a homomorphic image of a free group. A similar construction applies in any variety of algebras, such as the variety of Abelian groups, or the variety of lattices, or of semigroups with a neutral element.

Defining algebras by means of generators and relations

Algebraic systems often arise in a concrete way; for example, groups may arise as groups of transformations. There is another important method of defining algebras within a given variety, however, which consists in writing down a set of generators and defining relations. This means that a set of symbols is written as the generating set, and a set of relations is written that are to hold between these symbols, such that all other relations can be deduced from them. Such an algebra then consists of all expressions formed from these symbols by the algebraic operations, in which two expressions are to represent the same element whenever it is possible to pass from one to the other using only the given relations and the defining laws of the variety. To give a simple example, the group of complex cube roots of unity has the following presentation: All expressions obtained by applying group operations to a single group variable x are taken; *i.e.*, all group words in x, namely $e, x, x^2, x^3, \cdot \cdot \cdot, x^{-1}, x^{-2}, \cdot \cdot \cdot$. Two of them are declared equal if and only if it is possible to pass from one to the other using the relation expressing that the cube of x is the neutral element: $x^3 = e$. This is abbreviated by writing the group as $gp\{x \mid x^3 = e\}$, called a presentation of the group. In this particular case it is easy to see the structure of the group: two powers of the generator x^m and x^n, say, represent the same element of the group if, and only if, the difference of their exponents $m - n$ is divisible by 3; so there are just three elements, represented by the words e, x, x^2. Of course, few groups have a presentation as simple as this one, and for more complicated presentations it may be quite difficult to decide when two words represent the same group element. This problem is known as the word problem for groups; a given presentation of a group is said to have a soluble word problem if there exists a method enabling one to decide for each pair of words in a finite number of steps whether or not they represent the same element. The word problem has been solved for some simple classes of groups, but more interestingly, it has been shown to be insoluble in general. Group representations have been found that have an insoluble word problem. Similarly, presentations can be obtained for the algebras in any variety, and it will be necessary to solve the word problem. For many algebras encountered in practice, a presentation can be found with soluble word problems, but generally there will also be algebras with insoluble word problems in all but the simplest varieties.

The word problem

The notion of a free algebra is useful in many ways. If it is required to establish a property of groups that is preserved by homomorphisms, the first step is to check whether the free group has it. If so, then the desired conclusion follows because every group is a homomorphic image of a free group; if the free group does not have the property, it is a counter-example. This method is particularly effective for groups (as well as for semigroups and rings) because the word problem for free groups (and semigroups and rings) is rather easy to solve. This means that the elements of free groups can be represented in a very perspicuous form. It is no longer true of such varieties as alternative algebras or Jordan algebras, and as a consequence some apparently quite simple problems—such as the existence of zero-divisors in free Jordan algebras (nonzero elements the product of which is zero)—are still open.

Free algebras

Free algebas (in different varieties) have been the subject of intensive investigation, partly as an end in itself and partly on account of applications. Thus in commutative ring theory, the free algebras are polynomial rings, and the theorem that every commutative ring is the homomorphic image of a free commutative ring is the algebraic counterpart of the geometric fact that every geometric figure lies in n-dimensional space (for a suitable integer n). This accounts for the importance of polynomial rings in the study of algebraic geometry.

A free semigroup in the variables $x_1, \cdot \cdot \cdot, x_n$ may be realized as the set of all finite sequences of letters from $x_1, \cdot \cdot \cdot, x_n$, allowing repetitions; that is, all words in the alphabet $x_1, \cdot \cdot \cdot, x_n$. The study of such words has led to applications in coding theory as well as in the algebraic theory of languages, which has provided much of the impetus for studying free semigroups. As an example, the free semigroup on x, y, z and a set of words is sought such that no spaces or commas are needed to divide any message into its constituent words (this is known as a comma-free code). The set of words x, xy, z, yz clearly will not do, for the expression xyz can be parsed in two ways: as $x \cdot yz$ or $xy \cdot z$. But there is an infinite set of words with the required property: $x, xy, xy^2, xy^3, \cdot \cdot \cdot$. From the algebraic point of view a comma-free code is a set that forms a free generating set for a free subsemigroup, and such sets have been characterized by simple criteria. Another application is to elementary arithmetic: the positive integers may be regarded as the free semigroup on one free generator. Now the basic property, that every mapping of the single free generator defines a unique homomorphism, is just another way of expressing the principle of induction.

Besides applications in algebra itself, free algebras have many uses in algebraic geometry and topology, automata theory, and the statistical theory of queues.

UNIVERSAL ALGEBRA AND CATEGORY THEORY

There are close links between universal algebra and category theory. Although the precise degree of useful interaction is still open to discussion, it is widely agreed that category theory provides a convenient language for stating many of the results of universal algebra. Often there are several ways of expressing the same phenomenon; thus the characteristic property of free algebras is a particular instance of a universal construction, which appears in many different contexts. It may also be described as the left adjoint of the forgetful functor (which passes from an algebra to its underlying set and so forgets the algebra structure).

The definition of an Ω-algebra involved prescribing, for each member of Ω, an operation of the right arity. If n elements of the algebra are taken and m n-ary operations are performed on them, m elements are obtained on which an m-ary operation can be performed. In this way an n-ary operation is obtained by composition. There are also the identity operations, which pick out the first argument, or the second, or any other of the n arguments. Any collection of operations on a set, closed under the composition described above and containing all the identity operations (one unary, two binary ones, three ternary
Clone
ones, etc.) is called a clone, and in studying a particular Ω-algebra the operations corresponding to members of Ω may be replaced by the clone they generate. Now it is possible to define clones abstractly, and to define algebraic systems one may take a particular abstract clone C and define C-algebras as sets on which the clone C is realized by operations. This definition is due to P. Hall, and is very close to the categorical definition, due to Lawvere. The latter defines a theory as a category $\mathfrak{T}$ the objects of which are nonnegative integers, in which the number n is regarded as the coproduct of n copies of the number 1. Any contravariant functor from $\mathfrak{T}$ to the category of sets and mappings, in which coproducts map to products, is called a $\mathfrak{T}$-algebra. If A is the set corresponding to the number 1, then n corresponds to the nth direct power A^n, and the various morphisms in $\mathfrak{T}$ from 1 to n correspond to mappings from A^n to A; *i.e.*, n-ary operations on A. Any morphism in $\mathfrak{T}$ from m to n corresponds to m morphisms from 1 to n; this means that the mappings from A^n to A^m each correspond to m n-ary operations on A. In other words, the $\mathfrak{T}$-algebra structure so defined amounts to picking out a clone of operations on A.

Although many of the results of universal algebra can be proved within the framework of category theory, they can be proved just as easily directly. The most significant progress in universal algebra has been in the areas adjacent to logic, and there category theory has been of little help. On the other hand, in applications to other parts of mathematics (especially in algebraic geometry) category theory has to some extent replaced universal algebra.

(P.M.C.)

BIBLIOGRAPHY

Elementary algebra: For the history of algebra, see ERIC T. BELL, *The Development of Mathematics*, 2nd ed. (1945); and DIRK J. STRUIK, *A Concise History of Mathematics*, 3rd rev. ed., 2 vol. (1967). There are many textbooks on elementary algebra, such as MORRIS S. KNEBELMAN and TRACY Y. THOMAS, *Principles of College Algebra* (1942). Somewhat more advanced are the books on the theory of equations: LEONARD E. DICKSON, *New First Course in the Theory of Equations* (1939); JAMES V. USPENSKY, *Theory of Equations* (1948); and LOIS W. GRIFFITHS, *Introduction to the Theory of Equations*, 2nd ed. (1947). Also more advanced are textbooks on abstract algebra, such as GARRETT BIRKHOFF and SAUNDERS MACLANE, *A Survey of Modern Algebra*, 3rd ed. (1965). See also JOHN R. DURBIN, *College Algebra* (1982); MARSHALL D. HESTENES and RICHARD O. HILL, *College Algebra with Calculators* (1982); JOHN D. LIPSON, *Elements of Algebra and Algebraic Computing* (1981); MUSTAFA A. MUNEM and DAVID J. FOULIS, *Algebra and Trigonometry with Applications* (1982); M.L. KEEDY and MARVIN L. BITTINGER, *Algebra and Trigonometry: A Functional Approach*, 3rd ed. (1982); and ROBERT C. FISHER and ALLEN D. ZIEBUR, *Integrated Algebra, Trigonometry, and Analytic Geometry*, 4th ed. (1982).

(Ed.)

Linear and multilinear algebra: W.H. GREUB, *Linear Algebra*, 3rd ed. (1967), a standard textbook, advanced level; and *Multilinear Algebra* (1967), a standard modern treatment of multilinear algebra that fully exploits universal mapping properties; P.R. HALMOS, *Finite-Dimensional Vector Spaces*, 2nd ed. (1958), a standard textbook, advanced level, which emphasizes methods that can be carried over to infinite-dimensional spaces, particularly to Hilbert space; SIR WILLIAM ROWAN HAMILTON, *Lectures on Quaternions* (1853), mainly of historical interest; K. HOFFMAN and RAY KUNZE, *Linear Algebra*, 2nd ed. (1971), a standard textbook, intermediate level; N. JACOBSON, *Lectures in Abstract Algebra*, vol. 2, *Linear Algebra* (1953), a standard textbook, advanced level; MARVIN MARCUS and HENDRYK MINC, *Introduction to Linear Algebra* (1965), a standard textbook, elementary level; and *A Survey of Matrix Theory and Matrix Inequalities* (1964), a very concise account, omitting standard proofs, of the main facts of matrix algebra, with many references to original sources; DAVID C. MURDOCH, *Linear Algebra* (1970), a standard textbook, elementary level; ROBERT C. THOMPSON and ADIL YAQUB, *Introduction to Linear Algebra* (1970), a standard textbook, at the elementary level. A later, well-motivated work is JAMES W. DANIEL, *Elementary Linear Algebra and Its Applications* (1981).

(Ed.)

Lattice theory: JOHN E. WHITESITT, *Boolean Algebra and Its Applications* (1961), gives a very elementary introduction to Boolean algebra, with some applications to logic and switching circuits; GARRETT BIRKHOFF and THOMAS C. BARTREE, *Modern Applied Algebra* (1970), gives a more comprehensive and more recent discussion from a similar standpoint. JAMES C. ABBOTT, *Sets, Lattices and Boolean Algebras* (1969), is a very readable introductory text on sets and lattices from a purely mathematical standpoint; *Trends in Lattice Theory*, ed. by Abbott (1970), discusses informally some recent trends. GARRETT BIRKHOFF, *Lattice Theory*, 3rd ed. (1967), is the standard treatise on the subject. PAUL R. HALMOS, *Algebraic Logic* (1962), discusses in depth some of the Boolean algebras arising in logic; JOHN B. ROSSER, *Simplified Independence Proofs* (1969), shows how these have been recently applied to prove fundamental theorems in set theory and logic. Relevant later monographs include A.G. HAMILTON, *Numbers, Sets, and Axioms: The Apparatus of Mathematics* (1982); WILLIAM S. HATCHER, *The Logical Foundations of Mathematics* (1982); PETER T. JOHNSTONE, *Stone Spaces* (1983).

Groups: CAMILLE JORDAN, *Traité des substitutions et des équations algébriques* (1870); and WILLIAM BURNSIDE, *Theory of Groups of Finite Order*, 2nd ed. (1911, reprinted 1955), are the great classical works on group theory. For a period the subject was relatively dormant, but in the 1930s a revival began signaled by PHILIP HALL's celebrated paper "A Contribution to the Theory of Groups of Prime Power Orders," *Proc. Lond. Math. Soc.*, Second Series, 36:29–95 (1932). In 1923 there appeared the first edition of ANDREAS SPEISER, *Die Theorie der Gruppen von endlicher Ordnung*, 4th ed. (1956); HANS ZASSENHAUS, *Lehrbuch der Gruppen theorie* (1937; Eng. trans., *The Theory of Groups*, 2nd ed., 1958); B.L. VAN DER WAERDEN, *Gruppen von linearen Transformationen* (1935); and ALEXANDER G. KUROSCH, *The Theory of Groups*, 2 vol. (1955–56; orig. pub. in Russian, 1953), which developed the theory of free groups and free products extensively. IRVING KAPLANSKY, *Infinite Abelian Groups*, rev. ed. (1969), treats a theory that is now a major subject in its own right. The importance of group theory in physics is recognized by VOLKER HEINE, *Group Theory in Quantum Mechanics* (1960); and G.Y. LYUBARSKII, *The Application of Group Theory in Physics* (1960; orig. pub. in Russian, 1957). A turning point was the new approach in the paper by PHILIP HALL and GRAHAM HIGMAN, "On the p-Length of p-Soluble Groups and Reduction Theorems for Burnside's Problem," *Proc. Lond. Math Soc.*, Third Series, 6:1–42 (1956). This more modern approach and the revival of representation theory, omitted by Kurosch and Zassenhaus, is shown in MARSHALL HALL, JR., *The Theory of Groups* (1959); and WILLIAM R. SCOTT, *Group Theory* (1964). GILBERT DE BEAUREGARD ROBINSON, *Representation Theory of the Symmetric Groups* (1961), deals with a special but important topic. WILLIAM MAGNUS, ABRAHAM KARRASS, and DONALD SOLITAR, *Combinatorial Group Theory* (1966), deals mostly with generators and relations. The book-length paper by WALTER FEIT and JOHN THOMPSON, *Solvability of Groups of Odd Order* (1962), brought activity to its present high pitch; and the development and extension of this theory is the subject of the advanced treatise by DANIEL GORENSTEIN, *Finite Groups* (1968). BERTRAM HUPPERT, *Endliche Gruppen I* (1967), is the first volume of an encyclopaedic reference work. DANIEL GORENSTEIN, *Finite Simple Groups: An Introduction to Their Classification* (1982), and *The Classification of Finite Simple Groups: Groups of Noncharacteristic 2 Type* (1983), present detailed outlines of the problem as it stood in the early 1980s; DANIEL SEGAL, *Polycyclic Groups* (1983), illustrates algebraic number theory, algebraic groups, linear groups, and other mathematical areas involved.

Fields: Many works on algebra contain material on fields. Of these, GARRETT BIRKHOFF and SAUNDERS MACLANE, *A Survey of Modern Algebra*, 3rd ed. (1965); SOLOMON FEFERMAN, *The Number Systems: Foundations of Algebra and Analysis* (1964); I.N. HERSTEIN, *Topics in Algebra* (1964); and CYRUS C. MACDUFFEE, *An Introduction to Abstract Algebra*, ch. 1–6, (1940), are four standard undergraduate works.

Rings: Most treatises on algebra have chapters on rings—*e.g.*, BIRKHOFF–MACLANE (*op. cit.*); and SERGE LANG, *Algebra*, ch. 2–6 and 17 (1965). A deeper study of commutative rings may be found in OSCAR ZARISKI and PIERRE SAMUEL, *Commutative Algebra*, 2 vol. (1958–60); MASAYOSHI NAGATA, *Local Rings* (1962); IRVING KAPLANSKY, *Commutative Rings* (1970); and MICHAEL F. ATIYAH and I.G. MACDONALD, *Introduction to Commutative Algebra* (1969). For noncommutative rings, see NATHAN JACOBSON, *The Theory of Rings* (1943, reprinted 1966); and I.N. HERSTEIN, *Noncommuutative Rings* (1968). Applications of ring theory to arithmetic may be found in PIERRE SAMUEL, *Théorie algébriques des nombres* (1967; Eng. trans., *Algebraic Theory of Numbers*, 1970). See also R.B.J.T. ALLENBY, *Rings, Fields, and Groups: An Introduction to Abstract Algebra* (1983); ALEC FISHER, *Formal Number Theory and Computability* (1982); and HAROLD N. SHAPIRO, *Introduction to the Theory of Numbers* (1983).

Categories: Standard texts on the theory of categories include BARRY MITCHELL, *Theory of Categories* (1965); and BODO PAREIGIS, *Categories and Functors* (1970). ION BUCUR and ARISTIDE DELEANU, *Introduction to the Theory of Categories and Functors* (1968), is an excellent account of the theory of categories and functors with special reference to its applications in algebraic topology. SAUNDERS MACLANE, *Categories for the Working Mathematician* (1971), is a recent work in which the author, a distinguished categorist, sets out his view of the material of category theory basic to the professional mathematician. PETER J. FREYD, *Abelian Categories* (1964), is devoted to a special and very important class of categories. The first mention of the notions of category and functor in their explicit form is contained in the paper by SAMUEL EILENBERG and SAUNDERS MACLANE, "General Theory of Natural Equivalences," *Trans. Am. Math. Soc.*, 58:231–294 (1945).

Homological algebra: The classic text in homological algebra is HENRI CARTAN and SAMUEL EILENBERG, *Homological Algebra* (1956). More recent texts are SAUNDERS MACLANE, *Homology* (1963); and PETER J. HILTON and U. STAMMBACH, *A Course in Homological Algebra* (1971)—an abbreviated version of this work may be found in Hilton's *Lectures in Homological Algebra* (1971). A natural context for homological algebra is described in PETER J. FREYD, *Abelian Categories* (1964). The role played by homological algebra in algebraic topology may be inferred from PETER J. HILTON and SHAUN WYLIE, *Homology Theory* (1960); and EDWIN H. SPANIER, *Algebraic Topology* (1966). Particular aspects of homological algebra are to be found in JOHN W. MILNOR and JOHN C. MOORE, "On the Structure of Hopf Algebras," *Ann. Math.*, 81:211–264 (1965); and EDWIN WEISS, *Cohomology of Groups* (1969). The background for the study of homological algebra in the theory of Lie groups and Lie algebras is contained in GERHARD P. HOCHSCHILD, *The Structure of Lie Groups* (1965); and NATHAN JACOBSON, *Lie Algebras* (1962). The pioneer work of Hopf that led to the emergence of homological algebra as a separate discipline is contained in the papers of HEINZ HOPF: "Fundamentalgruppe und zweite Bettische Gruppe," *Comment. math. helvet.*, 14:257–313 (1941–42); and "Über die Bettischen Gruppen die zu einer beliebigen Gruppe gehören," *ibid.*, 17:39–79 (1944–45). His work on Lie groups that led to a Hopf algebra is described in "Über die Topologie der Gruppen-Mannigfaltigkeiten und ihrer Verallgemeinerungen," *Ann. Math.*, 42:22–52 (1941). CZES KOSNIOWSKI, *A First Course in Algebraic Topology* (1980), is a work suitable for independent study.

Universal algebra: Some works on universal algebra are: ALFRED NORTH WHITEHEAD, *A Treatise on Universal Algebra, with Applications*, vol. 1 (1898, reprinted 1960), a description of the algebras of Boole, Hamilton, and Grassmann, with emphasis on geometrical applications; ABRAHAM ROBINSON, *Introduction to Model Theory and the Metamathematics of Algebra* (1963), a treatment of model theory with many applications to algebra; PAUL M. COHN, *Universal Algebra* (1965), a general introduction to the subject, stressing the connections with logic and giving applications to algebra; GEORGE GRATZER, *Universal Algebra* (1968), a comprehensive treatment of the subject, including much current research in the field; J.F.C. KINGMAN, "On the Algebra of Queues," *Methuen's Review Series in Applied Probability*, vol. 6, pp. 1–44 (1966), a description of the algebraic background to the problem of queues (waiting lines) with a single server; GIAN-CARLO ROTA, "Baxter Algebras and Combinatorial Identities I, II," *Bull. Am. Math Soc.*, 75:325–334 (1969), in which an operator identity from probability theory is proved by first solving the word problem for a class of algebras; and GARRETT BIRKHOFF, (*op. cit.*), which has a long chapter on universal algebra. Relevant information can be found in J. CONRAD CROWN and MARVIN L. BITTINGER, *Finite Mathematics: A Modelling Approach*, 2nd ed. (1981), and their *Mathematics: A Modeling Approach* (1982).

(G.Bi./Ma.H./P.S./P.J.H./P.M.C.)

American Literature

Like other national literatures, American literature was shaped by the history of the country that produced it. For almost a century and a half, America was merely a group of colonies scattered along the eastern seaboard of the North American continent—colonies from which a few hardy souls tentatively ventured westward. After a successful rebellion against the motherland, America became the United States, a nation. By the end of the 19th century this nation extended southward to the Gulf of Mexico, northward to the 49th parallel, and westward to the Pacific. By the end of the 19th century, too, it had taken its place among the powers of the world—its fortunes so interrelated with those of other nations that inevitably it became involved in two world wars and, following these conflicts, with the problems of Europe and the Far East. Meanwhile, the rise of science and industry, as well as changes in ways of thinking and feeling, wrought many modifications in people's lives. All these factors in the development of the United States molded the literature of the country.

This article traces the history of American poetry, drama, fiction, and social and literary criticism from the early 17th century to the late 20th century. For information about closely related literary traditions, see ENGLISH LITERATURE and CANADIAN LITERATURE: *English*.

For coverage of related topics in the *Macropædia* and *Micropædia,* see the *Propædia,* section 621, and the *Index*.

This article is divided into the following sections:

The 17th century 301
The 18th century 301
The new nation 302
Notable works of the period 302
Poets and poetry
Drama and the novel
The 19th century 303
Early 19th-century literature 303
American Renaissance 303
New England Brahmins
The Transcendentalists
New England reformers and historians
Hawthorne, Melville, and Whitman
From the Civil War to 1914 304
Literary comedians
Fiction and local colorists
The Naturalists
Henry James
Critics of the gilded age
Henry Adams
Poets of the era
The 20th century 306
Writing from 1914 to 1945 306
Experiments in drama
The new poetry
Fiction
Critics of society
Hemingway, Faulkner, and Steinbeck
Lyric fictionists
Literary criticism
After World War II 308
The novel and short story
Poetry
Drama
Literary and social criticism
Bibliography 311

The 17th century

American literature at first was naturally a colonial literature, by authors who were Englishmen and who thought and wrote as such. John Smith, a soldier of fortune, is credited with initiating American literature. His chief books included *A True Relation of . . . Virginia . . .* (1608) and *The generall Historie of Virginia, New England, and the Summer Isles* (1624). Although these volumes often glorified their author, they were avowedly written to explain colonizing opportunities to Englishmen. In time, each colony was similarly described: Daniel Denton's *Brief Description of New York* (1670), William Penn's *Brief Account of the Province of Pennsylvania* (1682), and Thomas Ashe's *Carolina* (1682) were only a few of many works praising America as a land of economic promise.

Such writers acknowledged British allegiance, but others stressed the differences of opinion that spurred the colonists to leave their homeland. More important, they argued questions of government involving the relationship between church and state. The attitude that most authors attacked was jauntily set forth by Nathaniel Ward of Massachusetts Bay in *The Simple Cobler of Aggawam in America* (1647). Ward amusingly defended the status quo and railed at colonists who sponsored newfangled notions. A variety of counter-arguments to such a conservative view were published. John Winthrop's *Journal* (written 1630–49) told sympathetically of the attempt of Massachusetts Bay Colony to form a theocracy—a state with God at its head and with its laws based upon the Bible. Later defenders of the theocratic ideal were Increase Mather and his son Cotton. William Bradford's *History of Plymouth Plantation* (through 1646) showed how his pilgrim Separatists broke completely with Anglicanism. Even more radical than Bradford was Roger Williams, who, in a series of controversial pamphlets, advocated not only the separation of church and state but also the vesting of power in the people and the tolerance of different religious beliefs.

Theocratic writings

The utilitarian writings of the 17th century included biographies, treatises, accounts of voyages, and sermons. There were few achievements in drama or fiction, since there was a widespread prejudice against these forms. Bad but popular poetry appeared in the *Bay Psalm Book* of 1640 and in Michael Wigglesworth's summary in doggerel verse of Calvinistic belief, *The Day of Doom* (1662). There was some poetry, at least, of a higher order. Anne Bradstreet of Massachusetts wrote some lyrics published in *The Tenth Muse* (1650), which movingly conveyed her feelings concerning religion and her family. Ranked still higher by modern critics is a poet whose works were not discovered and published until 1939: Edward Taylor, an English-born minister and physician who lived in Boston and Westfield, Massachusetts. Less touched by gloom than the typical Puritan, Taylor wrote lyrics that showed his delight in Christian belief and experience.

The poet Edward Taylor

All 17th-century American writings were in the manner of British writings of the same period. John Smith wrote in the tradition of geographical literature, Bradford echoed the cadences of the King James Bible, while the Mathers and Roger Williams wrote bejewelled prose typical of the day. Anne Bradstreet's poetic style derived from a long line of British poets, including Spenser and Sydney, while Taylor was in the tradition of such Metaphysical poets as George Herbert and John Donne. Both the content and form of the literature of this first century in America were thus markedly English.

The 18th century

In America in the early years of the 18th century, some writers, such as Cotton Mather, carried on the older traditions. His huge history and biography of Puritan New England, *Magnalia Christi Americana,* in 1702, and his vigorous *Manuductio ad Ministerium,* or introduction to the ministry, in 1726, were defenses of ancient Puritan convictions. Jonathan Edwards, initiator of the Great Awakening, a religious revival that stirred the eastern seacoast for many years, eloquently defended his burning belief in Calvinistic doctrine—of the concept that man, born totally depraved, could attain virtue and salvation only through God's grace—in his powerful sermons and most notably in the philosophical treatise *Freedom of Will* (1754). He supported his claims by relating them to a complex metaphysical system and by reasoning brilliantly in clear and often beautiful prose.

But Mather and Edwards were defending a doomed cause. Liberal New England ministers such as John Wise and Jonathan Mayhew moved toward a less rigid religion. Samuel Sewall heralded other changes in his amusing *Diary,* covering the years 1673–1729. Though sincerely religious, he showed in daily records how commercial life in New England replaced rigid Puritanism with more worldly attitudes. The *Journal* of Mme Sara Knight comically detailed a journey that lady took to New York in 1704. She wrote vividly of what she saw and commented upon it from the standpoint of an orthodox believer, but a quality of levity in her witty writings showed that she was much less fervent than the Pilgrim founders had been. In the South, William Byrd of Virginia, an aristocratic plantation owner, contrasted sharply with gloomier predecessors. His record of a surveying trip in 1728, *The History of the Dividing Line,* and his account of a visit to his frontier properties in 1733, *A Journey to the Land of Eden,* were his chief works. Years in England, on the Continent, and among the gentry of the South had created gaiety and grace of expression, and, although a devout Anglican, Byrd was as playful as the Restoration wits whose works he clearly admired.

William Byrd's prose

The wrench of the American Revolution emphasized differences that had been growing between American and British political concepts. As the colonists moved to the belief that rebellion was inevitable, fought the bitter war, and worked to found the new nation's government, they were influenced by a number of very effective political writers, such as Samuel Adams and John Dickinson, both of whom favoured the colonists, and Loyalist Joseph Galloway. But two figures loomed above these—Benjamin Franklin and Thomas Paine.

Franklin, born in 1706, had started to publish his writings in his brother's newspaper, the *New England Courant,* as early as 1722. This newspaper championed the cause of the "Leather Apron" man and the farmer and appealed by using easily understood language and practical arguments. The idea that common sense was a good guide was clear in both the popular *Poor Richard's* almanac, which Franklin edited between 1732 and 1757 and filled with prudent and witty aphorisms purportedly written by uneducated but experienced Richard Saunders, and in the author's *Autobiography,* written between 1771 and 1788, a record of his rise from humble circumstances that offered worldly wise suggestions for future success.

Franklin's self-attained culture, deep and wide, gave substance and skill to varied articles, pamphlets, and reports that he wrote concerning the dispute with Great Britain, many of them extremely effective in stating and shaping the colonists' cause.

Thomas Paine went from his native England to Philadelphia and became a magazine editor and then, about 14 months later, the most effective propagandist for the colonial cause. His pamphlet "Common Sense" (January 1776) did much to influence the colonists to declare their independence. "The American Crisis" papers (December 1776–December 1783) spurred Americans to fight on through the blackest years of the war. Based upon Paine's simple Deistic beliefs, they showed the conflict as a stirring melodrama with the angelic colonists against the forces of evil. Such white and black picturings were highly effective propaganda. Another reason for Paine's success was his poetic fervour, which found expression in impassioned words and phrases long to be remembered and quoted.

Thomas Paine's "Common Sense"

THE NEW NATION

In the postwar period some of these eloquent men were no longer able to win a hearing. Thomas Paine and Samuel Adams lacked the constructive ideas that appealed to those interested in forming a new government. Others fared better—for example, Franklin, whose tolerance and sense showed in addresses to the constitutional convention. A different group of authors, however, became leaders in the new period—Thomas Jefferson and the talented writers of *The Federalist* papers, a series of 85 essays published in 1787 and 1788 urging the virtues of the proposed new constitution. They were written by Alexander Hamilton, James Madison, and John Jay. More distinguished for insight into problems of government and cool logic than for eloquence, these works became a classic statement of American governmental, and more generally of republican, theory. At the time they were highly effective in influencing legislators who voted on the new constitution. Hamilton, who wrote perhaps 51 of the *Federalist* papers, became a leader of the Federalist Party and, as first secretary of the treasury (1789–95), wrote messages that were influential in increasing the power of national government at the expense of the state governments.

The Federalist papers

Thomas Jefferson was an influential political writer during and after the war. The merits of his great summary, the Declaration of Independence, consisted, as Madison pointed out, "in a lucid communication of human rights . . . in a style and tone appropriate to the great occasion, and to the spirit of the American people." After the war he formulated the exact tenets of his faith in various papers but most richly in his letters and inaugural addresses, in which he urged individual freedom and local autonomy—a theory of decentralization differing from Hamilton's belief in strong federal government. Though he held that all men are created equal, Jefferson thought that "a natural aristocracy" of "virtues and talents" should hold high governmental positions.

NOTABLE WORKS OF THE PERIOD

Poets and poetry. Poetry became a weapon during the American Revolution, with both Loyalists and Continentals urging their forces on, stating their arguments, and celebrating their heroes in verse and songs such as "Yankee Doodle," "Nathan Hale," and "The Epilogue," mostly set to popular British melodies and in manner resembling other British poems of the period.

Poetry of the American Revolution

The most memorable American poet of the period was Philip Freneau, whose first well-known poems, Revolutionary War satires, served as effective propaganda; later he turned to various aspects of the American scene. Although he wrote much in the stilted manner of the Neoclassicists, such poems as "The Indian Burying Ground," "The Wild Honey Suckle," "To a Caty-did," and "On a Honey Bee" were romantic lyrics of real grace and feeling that were forerunners of a literary movement destined to be important in the 19th century.

Drama and the novel. In the years toward the close of the 18th century, both dramas and novels of some historical importance were produced. Though theatrical groups had long been active in America, the first American comedy presented professionally was Royall Tyler's *Contrast* (1787). This drama was full of echoes of Goldsmith and Sheridan, but it contained a Yankee character (the predecessor of many such in years to follow) who brought something native to the stage.

William Hill Brown wrote the first American novel, *The Power of Sympathy* (1789), which showed authors how to overcome ancient prejudices against this form by following the sentimental novel form invented by Samuel Richardson. A flood of sentimental novels followed to the end of the 19th century. H.H. Brackenridge followed Cervantes' *Don Quixote* and Henry Fielding with some popular success in *Modern Chivalry* (1792–1815), an amusing satire on democracy and an interesting portrayal of frontier life. Gothic thrillers were to some extent nationalized in Charles Brockden Brown's *Wieland* (1798), *Arthur Mervyn,* and *Edgar Huntly* (1799). But all such works were more interesting as beginnings than as outstanding artistic achievements.

The 19th century

EARLY 19TH-CENTURY LITERATURE

After the American Revolution, and increasingly after the War of 1812, American writers were exhorted to produce a literature that was truly native. As if in response, four authors of very respectable stature appeared. William Cullen Bryant, Washington Irving, James Fenimore Cooper, and Edgar Allan Poe initiated a great half century of literary development.

Bryant, a New Englander by birth, attracted attention in his 23rd year when the first version of his poem "Thanatopsis" (1817) appeared. This, as well as some later poems, was written under the influence of English 18th-century poets. Still later, however, under the influence of Wordsworth and other Romantics, he wrote nature lyrics that vividly represented the New England scene. Turning to journalism, he had a long career as a fighting liberal editor of *The Evening Post.* He himself was overshadowed, in renown at least, by a native-born New Yorker, Washington Irving.

Irving and Cooper

Irving, youngest member of a prosperous merchant family, joined with ebullient young men of the town in producing the *Salmagundi* papers (1807–08), which took off the foibles of Manhattan's citizenry. This was followed by *A History of New York* (1809), by "Diedrich Knickerbocker," a burlesque history that mocked pedantic scholarship and sniped at the old Dutch families. Irving's models in these works were obviously Neoclassical English satirists, from whom he had learned to write in a polished, bright style. Later, having met Sir Walter Scott and having become acquainted with imaginative German literature, he introduced a new Romantic note in *The Sketch Book* (1819–20), *Bracebridge Hall* (1822), and other works. He was the first American writer to win the ungrudging (if somewhat surprised) respect of British critics.

James Fenimore Cooper won even wider fame. Following the pattern of Sir Walter Scott's "Waverley" novels, he did his best work in the "Leatherstocking" tales (1823–41), a five-volume series celebrating the career of a great frontiersman named Natty Bumppo. His skill in weaving history into inventive plots and in characterizing his compatriots brought him acclaim not only in America and England but on the continent of Europe as well.

Edgar Allan Poe, reared in the South, lived and worked as an author and editor in Baltimore, Philadelphia, Richmond, and New York City. His work was shaped largely by analytical skill that showed clearly in his role as an editor: time after time he gauged the taste of readers so accurately that circulation figures of magazines under his direction soared impressively. It showed itself in his critical essays, wherein he lucidly explained and logically applied his criteria. His gothic tales of terror were written in accordance with his findings when he studied the most popular magazines of the day. His masterpieces of terror—"The Fall of the House of Usher" (1839), "The Masque of the Red Death" (1842), "The Cask of Amontillado" (1846), and others—were written according to a carefully worked out psychological method. So were his detective stories, such as "The Murders in the Rue Morgue" (1841), which historians credited as the first of the genre. As a poet, he achieved fame with "The Raven" (1845). His work, especially his critical writings and carefully crafted poems, had perhaps a greater influence in France, where they were translated by Charles Baudelaire, than in his own country.

Poe's Gothic tales

Two Southern novelists were also outstanding in the earlier part of the century: John Pendleton Kennedy and William Gilmore Simms. In *Swallow Barn* (1832), Kennedy wrote delightfully of life on the plantations. Simms's forte was the writing of historical novels like those of Scott and Cooper, which treated the history of the frontier and his native South Carolina. *The Yemassee* (1835) and Revolutionary romances show him at his best.

AMERICAN RENAISSANCE

The authors who began to come to prominence in the 1830s and were active until about the end of the Civil War—the humorists, the classic New Englanders, Herman Melville, Walt Whitman, and others—did their work in a new spirit, and their achievements were of a new sort. In part, this was because they were in some way influenced by the broadening democratic concepts that in 1829 triumphed in Andrew Jackson's inauguration as president. In part, it was because, in this Romantic period of emphasis upon native scenes and characters in many literatures, they put much of America into their books.

Jacksonian democracy reflected in humorous writing

Particularly full of vivid touches were the writings of two groups of American humorists whose works appeared between 1830 and 1867. One group created several down-east Yankee characters who used commonsense arguments to comment upon the political and social scene. The most important of this group were Seba Smith, James Russell Lowell, and Benjamin P. Shillaber. These authors caught the talk and character of New England at that time as no one else had done. In the old Southwest, meanwhile, such writers as Davy Crockett, Augustus Baldwin Longstreet, Johnson J. Hooper, Thomas Bangs Thorpe, Joseph G. Baldwin, and George Washington Harris drew lively pictures of the ebullient frontier and showed the interest in the common man that was a part of Jacksonian democracy.

New England Brahmins. Although Lowell for a time was one of these writers of rather earthy humour, his lifelong ties were to a group of New England writers associated with Harvard and Cambridge, Massachusetts—the Brahmins, as they came to be called—at an opposite extreme. Henry Wadsworth Longfellow, Oliver Wendell Holmes, and Lowell were all aristocrats, all steeped in foreign culture, all professors at Harvard. Longfellow adapted European methods of storytelling and versifying to narrative poems dealing with American history, and a few of his less didactic lyrics perfectly married technique and subject matter. Holmes, in occasional poems and his "Breakfast Table" series (1858–91), brought touches of urbanity and jocosity to a perhaps oversober polite literature. Lowell, in poems descriptive of the out-of-doors in America, put much of his homeland into verse. His odes—particularly the "Harvard Commemoration Ode" (1865)—gave fine expression to noble sentiments.

The Transcendentalists. Concord, Massachusetts, a village not far from Cambridge, was the home of leaders of another important New England group. The way for this group had been prepared by the rise of a theological system, Unitarianism, which early in the 19th century had replaced Calvinism as the faith of a large share of the New Englanders. Ralph Waldo Emerson, most famous of the Concord philosophers, started as a Unitarian minister but found even that liberal doctrine too confining for his broad beliefs. He became a Transcendentalist who, like other ancient and modern Platonists, trusted to insights transcending logic and experience for revelations of the deepest truths. His scheme of things ranged from the lowest objects and most practical chores to soaring flights of imagination and inspired beliefs. His *Essays* (1841–44), *Representative Men* (1850), and *English Traits* (1856) were thoughtful and poetic explanations of his beliefs; and his roughhewn lyrics, packed with thought and feeling, were as close to 17th-century Metaphysical poems as any produced in his own time.

An associate of Emerson with a salty personality of his own and an individual way of thinking, Henry David Thoreau, a sometime surveyor, labourer, and naturalist, was closer to the earthy and the practical than even Emerson was. He also was more of a humorist—a dry Yankee commentator with a flair for paradoxical phrases and sentences. Finally, he was a learned man, widely read in Western classics and books of the Orient. These qualities gave distinction to *A Week on the Concord and Merrimack Rivers* (1849) and to *Walden* (1854). The latter was a record of his experiences and ponderings during the time he lived in a hut by Walden Pond—a defense of his belief that modern man should simplify his demands if need be to "suck out all the marrow of life." In his essay "Civil Disobedience" (1849), Thoreau expounded his anarchistic views of government, insisting that if an injustice of government is "of such a nature that it requires injustice to another [you should] break the law [and] let your life be a counter friction to stop the machine."

Thoreau as the great exponent of American individualism

Associated with these two major figures were such minor Transcendentalists as Bronson Alcott, George Ripley, Orestes Brownson, Margaret Fuller, and Jones Very. Fuller edited *The Dial,* the chief Transcendental magazine, and was important in the feminist movement.

New England reformers and historians. A worldwide movement for change that exploded in the revolutions of 1848 naturally attracted numerous Americans. Reform was in the air, particularly in New England. At times even Brahmins and Transcendentalists took part. William Lloyd Garrison, ascetic and fanatical, was a moving spirit in the fight against slavery; his weekly newspaper, *The Liberator* (1831–65), despite a small circulation, was its most influential organ. A contributor to the newspaper—probably the greatest writer associated with the movement—was John Greenleaf Whittier. His simple but emotional poems on behalf of abolition were collected in such volumes as *Poems Written During the Progress of the Abolition Question . . .* (1837), *Voices of Freedom* (1846), and *Songs of Labor, and Other Poems* (1850). The outstanding novelist of the movement—so far as effect was concerned—was Harriet Beecher Stowe. Her *Uncle Tom's Cabin* (1852) combined the elements of contemporary humour and sentimental fiction to dramatize the plight of the Negro.

The New England Historians

One other group of writers—and a great novelist—contributed to the literature of New England in this period of its greatest glory. The group consisted of several historians who combined scholarly methods learned abroad with vivid and dramatic narration. These included George Bancroft, author of *History of the United States* (completed in 12 volumes in 1882), and John Lothrop Motley, who traced the history of the Dutch Republic and the United Netherlands in nine fascinating volumes (1856–74). The leading member of the group was Francis Parkman, who, in a series of books (1851–92), wrote as a historian of the fierce contests between France and England that marked the advance of the American frontier and vividly recorded his own Western travels in *The Oregon Trail* (1849).

Hawthorne, Melville, and Whitman. History also figured in tales and romances of Nathaniel Hawthorne, the leading New England fictionist of the period. Many tales and longer works—for example, his masterpiece, *The Scarlet Letter* (1850)—were set against a background of colonial America with emphasis upon its distance in time from 19th-century New England. Others, such as *The House of the Seven Gables* (1851), dealt with the past as well as the present. Still others, such as *The Marble Faun* (1860), were set in distant countries. Remote though they were at times from what Hawthorne called "the light of common day," they showed deep psychological insight and probed into complex ethical problems.

Another great American fiction writer, for a time a neighbour and associate of Hawthorne, was Herman Melville. After relatively little schooling, Melville went to sea; a whaling ship, as he put it, was his "Yale College and his Harvard." His first books were fiction in the guise of factual writing based upon experiences as a sailor—*Typee* (1846) and *Omoo* (1847); so were such later works as *Redburn* (1849) and *White-Jacket* (1850). Between 1846 and 1851, however, Melville's reading in philosophy and literary classics, as well as in Hawthorne's allegorical and symbolic writings, gave him new interests and aims. The first sign of this interest was *Mardi* (1849), an uneven and disjointed transitional book that used allegory after the model of Rabelais to comment upon ideas afloat in the period—about nations, politics, institutions, literature, and religion. The new techniques came to fruition in *Moby Dick; or, The Whale* (1851), a richly symbolical work, complex but brilliantly integrated. Only in short stories, "Benito Cereno"—a masterpiece of its genre—and others, in the psychological novel *Pierre* (1852), and in the novelette *Billy Budd* (written 1890?) was Melville later to show sporadic flashes of the genius that created *Moby Dick.*

An ardent singer of the praise of Manhattan, Walt Whitman saw less of the dark side of life than Melville did. He was a believer in Jacksonian democracy, in the splendour of the common man. Inspired by the Romantic concept of a poet as prophet and also by the Transcendental philosophy of Emerson, Whitman in 1855 published the first edition of *Leaves of Grass.* As years passed, nine revised and expanded editions of this work were published. This autobiography in verse was intended to show the ideas, beliefs, emotions, and experiences of the common man in a great period of American individualism. Whitman had a hard time winning a following because he was frank and unconventional in his Transcendental thinking, because he used free verse rather than rhymed or regularly metred verse, and because his poems were not conventionally organized. Nevertheless, he steadily gained the approval of critics and in time came to be recognized as one of the great poets of America.

The slow growth of Whitman's reputation

FROM THE CIVIL WAR TO 1914

Like the Revolution and the election of Andrew Jackson, the Civil War was a turning point in U.S. history and a beginning of new ways of living. Industry became increasingly important, factories rose and cities grew, and agrarian pre-eminence declined. The frontier, which before had always been an important factor in the economic scheme, moved steadily westward and toward the end of the 19th century vanished. The rise of modern America was accompanied, naturally, by important mutations in literature.

Literary comedians. Although they continued to employ some devices of the older American humorists, a group of comic writers that rose to prominence was different in important ways from the older group. Charles Farrar Browne, David Ross Locke, Charles Henry Smith, Henry Wheeler Shaw, and Edgar Wilson Nye wrote, respectively, as Artemus Ward, Petroleum V. (for Vesuvius) Nasby, Bill Arp, Josh Billings, and Bill Nye. Appealing to a national audience, these authors forsook the sectional characterizations of earlier humorists and assumed the roles of less individualized literary comedians. The nature of the humour thus shifted from character portrayal to verbal devices such as poor grammar, bad spelling, and slang, incongruously combined with Latinate words and learned allusions. Most that they wrote wore badly, but thousands of Americans in their time and some in later times found these authors vastly amusing.

Fiction and local colorists. The first group of fiction writers to become popular—the local colorists—took over to some extent the task of portraying sectional groups that had been abandoned by writers of the new humour. Bret Harte, first of these writers to achieve wide success, admitted an indebtedness to prewar sectional humorists, as did some others; and all showed resemblances to the earlier group. Within a brief period, books by pioneers in the movement appeared—Harriet Beecher Stowe's *Oldtown Folks* (1869) and *Sam Lawson's Oldtown Fireside Stories* (1871), delightful vignettes of New England; Bret Harte's *Luck of Roaring Camp, and Other Sketches* (1870), humorous and sentimental tales of California mining camp life; and Edward Eggleston's *Hoosier Schoolmaster* (1871), a novel of the early days of the settlement of Indiana. Down into the 20th century, short stories (and a relatively small number of novels) in patterns set by these three continued to appear. In time, practically every corner of the country had been portrayed in local-colour fiction. Additional writings were the depictions of Louisiana Creoles by George W. Cable, of Virginia Negroes by Thomas Nelson Page, of Georgia Negroes by Joel Chandler Harris, of Tennessee mountaineers by Mary Noailles Murfree (Charles Egbert Craddock), of tight-lipped folk of New England by Sarah Orne Jewett and Mary E. Wilkins Freeman, of people of New York City by Henry Cuyler Bunner and William Sydney Porter ("O. Henry"). The avowed aim of some of these writers was to portray realistically the lives of various sections and thus to promote understanding in a united nation. The stories as a rule were only partially realistic, however, since the authors tended nostalgically to revisit the past instead of portraying their own time, to winnow out less glamorous aspects of life, or to develop their stories with sentiment or humour. Touched by romance though they were, these fictional works were transitional to Realism, for they did portray common folk sympathetically; they did concern themselves with dialect and mores; and some at least avoided older sentimental or romantic formulas.

The humour of Mark Twain

Samuel Langhorne Clemens (Mark Twain) was allied with literary comedians and local colorists. As a printer's apprentice, he knew and emulated the prewar sectional humorists. He rose to prominence in days when Artemus Ward, Bret Harte, and their followers were idols of the public. His first books, *The Innocents Abroad* (1869) and *Roughing It* (1872), like several of later periods, were travel books in which affiliations with postwar professional humorists were clearest. *The Adventures of Tom Sawyer* (1876), *Life on the Mississippi* (1883), and *The Adventures of Huckleberry Finn* (1884), his best works, which re-created the life of the Mississippi Valley in the past, were closest to the work of older humorists and local colorists. Even in his best work, however, he succumbed now and then to the temptation to play the buffoon or sink into burlesque. Despite his flaws, he was one of America's greatest writers. He was a very funny man. He had more skill than his teachers in selecting evocative details, and he had a genius for characterization.

Born and raised in Ohio, William Dean Howells was an effective advocate of a new realistic mode of fiction writing. At the start, Howells conceived of Realism as truthful portrayal of ordinary facets of life—with some limitations; he preferred comedy to tragedy, and he tended to be reticent to the point of prudishness. The formula was displayed at its best in *Their Wedding Journey* (1872), *A Modern Instance* (1882), and *The Rise of Silas Lapham* (1885). Howells preferred novels he wrote after he encountered Tolstoy's writings and was persuaded by them, as he said, to "set art forever below humanity." In such later novels as *Annie Kilburn* (1888) and *A Hazard of New Fortunes* (1890), he chose characters not only because they were commonplace but also because the stories he told about them were commentaries upon society, government, and economics.

The Naturalists. Other American writers toward the close of the 19th century moved toward Naturalism, a more advanced stage of Realism. Hamlin Garland's writings exemplified some aspects of this development when he made short stories and novels vehicles for philosophical and social preachments and was franker than Howells in stressing the harsher details of the farmer's struggles and in treating the subject of sex. His *Main-Travelled Roads* (1891) and *Rose of Dutcher's Coolly* (1895) displayed Garland's particular talents. These and a critical manifesto for the new fiction, *Crumbling Idols* (1894), were influential contributions to a developing movement.

The influence of Zola on Dreiser

Other U.S. authors of the same period or slightly later were avowed followers of French Naturalists led by Émile Zola. Theodore Dreiser, for instance, treated subjects that had seemed too daring to earlier Realists and, like other Naturalists, illustrated his own beliefs by his depictions of characters and unfolding of plots. Holding that men's deeds were "chemical compulsions," he showed characters unable to direct their actions. Holding also that "the race was to the swift and the battle to the strong," he showed characters defeated by stronger and more ruthless opponents. His major books included *Sister Carrie* (1900), *Jennie Gerhardt* (1911), *The Financier* (1912), *The Titan* (1914), and—much later—*An American Tragedy* (1925).

Dreiser did not bother with—or did not care for—niceties of style or elaborate symbolism such as were found in French Naturalistic works; but Stephen Crane and Frank Norris were attentive to such matters. In short novels, *Maggie: A Girl of the Streets* (1893) and *The Red Badge of Courage* (1895), and in some of his short stories, Crane was an impressionist who made his details and his setting forth of them embody a conception of man overwhelmed by circumstance and environment. Frank Norris, who admired Crane's "aptitude for making phrases—sparks that cast a momentary gleam upon whole phases of life," himself tried to make phrases, scenes, and whole narratives cast such gleams in *McTeague* (1899), *The Octopus* (1901), and *The Pit* (1903). Both Crane and Norris died young, their full abilities undeveloped but their experiments foreshadowing later achievements in the 20th-century novel.

Henry James. In the books of Henry James, born in New York but later an expatriate in England, fiction took a different pathway. Like Realists and Naturalists of his time, he thought that fiction should reproduce reality. He conceived of reality, however, as twice translated—first, through the author's peculiar experiencing of it, and, second, through his unique depicting of it. Deep insight and thorough experience were no more important, therefore, than the complicated and delicate task of the artist. *The Art of Fiction* (1884), essays on novelists, and brilliant prefaces to his collected works showed him struggling thoroughly and consciously with the problems of his craft. Together, they formed an important body of discussion of fictional artistry.

Formal excellence and psychological insight in Henry James

An excellent short-story writer, James nevertheless was chiefly important for novels in which his doctrines found concrete embodiment. Outstanding were *The American* (1877), *The Portrait of a Lady* (1881), *The Spoils of Poynton* (1897), *What Maisie Knew* (1897), *The Wings of the Dove* (1902), *The Ambassadors* (1903), and *The Golden Bowl* (1904). The earliest of these were international novels wherein conflicts arose from relationships between Americans and Europeans—each group with its own characteristics and morals. As time passed, he became increasingly interested in the psychological processes of his characters and in a subtle rendering of their limited insights, their perceptions, and their emotions.

Critics of the gilded age. Writers of many types of works contributed to a great body of literature that flourished between the Civil War and 1914—literature of social revolt. Novels attacked the growing power of business and the growing corruption of government, and some novelists outlined utopias. Political corruption and inefficiency figured in Henry Adams' novel *Democracy* (1880). Edward Bellamy's *Looking Backward* (1888) was both an indictment of the capitalistic system and an imaginative picturing of a utopia achieved by a collectivist society in the year 2000. Howells' *Traveler from Altruria* (1894) pleaded for an equalitarian state in which the government regimented men's lives. The year 1906 saw the publication of Upton Sinclair's *Jungle,* first of many works by him that criticized U.S. economic and political life and urged Socialism as the remedy.

Two poets embodied criticisms in songs. Edwin Markham's "Man with the Hoe" (1899) was a protest against the exploitation of labour and vaguely threatened revolution; it immediately stimulated nationwide interest. A year later William Vaughn Moody's "Ode in Time of Hesitation" denounced growing U.S. imperialism as a desertion of earlier principles; his "On a Soldier Fallen in the Philippines" (1901) developed the same theme even more effectively.

With the rise of journalistic magazines, a group of journalists became notable as critics of America—the group dubbed "the muckrakers" by Theodore Roosevelt. Ida M. Tarbell's *History of the Standard Oil Company* (1904) and Lincoln Steffens' *Shame of the Cities* (1904) were typical contributions by two members of a large group of journalistic crusaders.

Henry Adams. One of the most devastating and most literate attacks on modern life was an autobiography of a scion of an ancient New England family, the Adamses. Educated at Harvard and abroad, Henry Adams was a great teacher and historian (*History of the United States* [1889–91] and *Mont-Saint-Michel and Chartres* [1904]). *The Education of Henry Adams* (printed privately 1906; published 1918), however, complained that a lifelong hunt for some sort of order in the world, some sort of faith for man, left him completely baffled. The quiet, urbane style served well to underline, in an ironic way, the message of this pessimistic book.

Poets of the era. The latter 19th century and early years of the 20th century were a poor period for American poetry; yet (in addition to William Vaughn Moody) two poets of distinction wrote songs that survived long after scores of minor poets had been forgotten. One was Southern-born Sidney Lanier, a talented musician who utilized the rhythms of music and the thematic developments of symphonies in such fine songs as "Corn" (1875), "The Symphony" (1875), and "The Marshes of Glynn"

(1878). Distressed, like many of his contemporaries, by changes in American life, he wove his doubts, fears, and suggestions into his richest poems.

The other poet was a New Englander, Emily Dickinson. A shy, playful, odd personality, she allowed practically none of her writings to be published during her lifetime. Not until 1890, four years after her death, was the first book of her poems published, to be followed at intervals by other collections. Later poets were to be influenced by her individual techniques—use of imperfect, or eye, rhymes, avoidance of regular rhythms, and a tendency to pack brief stanzas with cryptic meanings. Like Lanier, she rediscovered the value of conceits for setting forth her thought and feeling. Such poems as "The Snake," "I Like to See It Lap the Miles," "The Chariot," "Farther in Summer than the Birds," and "There's a Certain Slant of Light" represented her unusual talent at its best.

The poetic techniques of Emily Dickinson

The 20th century

WRITING FROM 1914 TO 1945

Important movements in drama, poetry, fiction, and criticism took form in the years before, during, and after World War I. The eventful period that followed that war left its imprint upon books of all kinds, for it was a time when writers were much involved with interpreting life about them. Literary forms of the period were extraordinarily varied, and in drama, poetry, and fiction leading authors tended toward radical technical experiments.

Experiments in drama. Although drama in the 19th century had not been a preeminent form, no type of writing embodied wider experimentation than a new drama that arose as a result of rebellion against the glib commercial stage. In the early years of the 20th century, Americans travelling abroad found a vital theatre flourishing in Europe; returning home, some of them became active in founding a Little Theatre movement in every corner of their country. Freed from commercial limitations, playwrights experimented with dramatic forms and methods of production, and in time producers, actors, and dramatists appeared who had been trained in college classrooms and community playhouses. Some Little Theatre groups became commercial producers; for example, the Washington Square Players, founded in 1915, which became the Theatre Guild (first production in 1919). The drama that resulted was marked by a spirit of innovation and by a new seriousness and maturity.

The plays of Eugene O'Neill

Eugene O'Neill, the most admired dramatist of the period, was a product of this movement. He worked with the Provincetown Players before his plays were commercially produced. His dramas are remarkable for their range. *Beyond the Horizon* (first performed 1920), *Anna Christie* (1921), *Desire Under the Elms* (1924), and *The Iceman Cometh* (1946) were Naturalistic works, while *The Emperor Jones* (1920) and *The Hairy Ape* (1922) made use of the Expressionistic techniques developed in German drama in the period 1914–24. He also employed a stream-of-consciousness form in *Strange Interlude* (1928) and produced a work of subtle psychological analysis in *Mourning Becomes Electra* (1931).

No other dramatist was as generally praised as O'Neill, but many others wrote plays of a high order that reflected the growth of a serious and varied drama. Marc Connelly wrote touching fantasy in a Negro folk biblical play, *The Green Pastures* (1930). Like O'Neill, Elmer Rice made use of both Expressionistic techniques (*The Adding Machine* [1923]) and Naturalism (*Street Scene* [1929]). Beginning as a Realist, Maxwell Anderson turned to verse drama in plays such as *Elizabeth the Queen* (1930) and *Winterset* (1935) and then to musical comedy satire in *Knickerbocker Holiday* (1938). Robert Sherwood produced a distinguished body of work, writing comedy (*Reunion in Vienna* [1931]) and tragedy (*There Shall Be No Night* [1940]). Clifford Odets, in *Waiting for Lefty* (1935), a plea for labour unionism, utilized auditorium as well as stage for action and in *Awake and Sing* (1935) wrote in the vein of Naturalism. Thornton Wilder used stylized settings and poetic dialogue in *Our Town* (1938) and turned to fantasy in *The Skin of Our Teeth* (1942).

Robinson and Frost

The new poetry. Poetry ranged between traditional types of verse and experimental writing that departed radically from the established forms of the 19th century. Two New England poets, Edwin Arlington Robinson and Robert Frost, who were not noted for technical experimentation, both won critical as well as popular acclaim in this period. Robinson, whose first book appeared in 1896, found sonnets, ballad stanzas, and blank verse satisfactory to his thought. In the 1920s he won three Pulitzer Prizes—for his *Collected Poems* (published 1921), *The Man Who Died Twice* (1925), and *Tristram* (1927). Like Robinson, Frost used traditional stanzas and blank verse in volumes such as *A Boy's Will* (1913), his first book, and *North of Boston* (1914), *New Hampshire* (1923), *A Further Range* (1936), and *A Masque of Reason* (1945). The best known poet of his generation, Frost, like Robinson, saw and commented upon the tragic aspects of life and the complexities of human existence and was skeptical of pat solutions.

Just as modern U.S. drama had its beginnings in little theatres, modern U.S. poetry took form in little magazines. Particularly important was *Poetry: A Magazine of Verse*, founded by Harriet Monroe in Chicago in 1912. The surrounding region soon became prominent as the home of three poets: Vachel Lindsay, Carl Sandburg, and Edgar Lee Masters. Lindsay's blend of legendary lore and native oratory in irregular odelike forms was well adapted to oral presentation, and his lively readings from his works contributed to the success of such books as *General William Booth Enters into Heaven, and Other Poems* (1913) and *The Congo, and Other Poems* (1914). Sandburg wrote of life on the prairies and in Middle Western cities in Whitmanesque free verse in such volumes as *Chicago Poems* (1916) and *The People, Yes* (1936). Masters' very popular *Spoon River Anthology* (1915) consisted of free-verse monologues by village men and women, most of whom spoke bitterly of their frustrated lives.

Writing traditional sonnets and brief, personal lyrics, Edna St. Vincent Millay and Sara Teasdale were innovative in being unusually frank (according to old standards) for women poets. Three fine Negro poets—James Weldon Johnson, Langston Hughes, and Countee Cullen—also found old molds satisfactory for dealing with new subjects, specifically the problems of their race. In general, however, the range of experimentation was great. While Conrad Aiken experimented with poetical imitations of symphonic forms often mingled with stream-of-consciousness techniques, e.e. cummings used typographical novelties to produce poems that had surprisingly fresh impact. Marianne Moore invented and brilliantly employed a kind of free verse that was to make her one of the most distinguished voices in modern U.S. poetry. Stephen Vincent Benét, in *John Brown's Body* (1928), produced a stirring novel in verse. Robinson Jeffers used violent imagery and modified free or blank verse to express perhaps the most bitter views voiced by a major poet in this period.

Pound, Eliot, and the influence of the 17th-century Metaphysical poets

Except for a period after World War II, when he was confined in St. Elizabeth's Hospital, Washington, D.C., Ezra Pound lived outside the United States after 1908. He had, nevertheless, a profound influence on 20th-century writing in English, both as a practitioner of verse and as a patron and impresario of other writers. His most controversial work remained *The Cantos,* the first installment of which appeared in 1925 and the latest in 1959 (*Thrones: 96–109 de los cantares*).

Like Pound, to whom he was much indebted, T.S. Eliot lived abroad most of his life, becoming a British citizen in 1927. His first volume, *Prufrock and Other Observations,* was published in 1917. In 1922 appeared *The Waste Land,* the poem by which he first became famous. As a poet and critic, Eliot exercised a strong influence, especially in the period between World Wars I and II. In what some critics regard as his finest work, *Four Quartets* (1943), Eliot explored through images of great beauty and haunting power his own past, the past of the human race, and the meaning of human history.

Eliot was the acknowledged master of many members of a varied group of poets whose work was indebted to 17th-century English Metaphysical poets, especially to John Donne. Eliot's influence was clear in the writings of

Archibald MacLeish, whose earlier poems were similar in both manner and thought to *The Waste Land.* In later poems MacLeish voiced a positive belief in social advance that contrasted with the religious attitude advocated by Eliot. A number of Southern poets showed affiliations, though not so clearly—John Crowe Ransom, Donald Davidson, and Allen Tate. Their poems were particularly concerned with the South—its past and its problems. Hart Crane had a similar Metaphysical manner but a subject matter of his own. Other American Metaphysicals having individual qualities of thought and method were Louise Bogan, Léonie Adams, Muriel Rukeyser, Delmore Schwartz, and Karl Shapiro.

The influence of the little magazines

Fiction. The little magazines that helped the growth of the poetry also contributed to a development of the fiction of the era. Not only did they print short stories that diverged from the older patterns, but they also published attacks upon the established writers and stressed the merits of unconventional fiction. The *Dial* (1880–1929), the *Little Review* (1914–29), the *Seven Arts* (1916–17), and others encouraged rebellion. More potent than any of these were two magazines edited by the ferocious but humorous journalist-critic H.L. Mencken—*The Smart Set* (editorship 1914–23) and *American Mercury* (which he coedited between 1924 and 1933). Mencken published short stories in the new manner, attacked established American beliefs and institutions, and praised fiction writers who were unconventional in thought and manner. A powerful influence, he helped launch the new fiction.

The trend was indicated by one of Mencken's favourites, James Branch Cabell. Cabell, who had been writing since 1905, sprang to fame with *Jurgen* (1919), a novel that attacked America's orthodoxies and institutions by telling a cynical story full of Freudian symbolism. Other authors whom Mencken favoured launched "a revolt against the village," an attack on the narrow, frustrated quality of life in rural communities—*e.g.,* Zona Gale and Ruth Suckow. The most distinguished of these village writers was Sherwood Anderson. His *Winesburg, Ohio* (1919) and *Triumph of the Egg* (1921) were collections of short stories that showed villagers suffering from all sorts of phobias and suppressions. Anderson in time wrote several novels of superior quality, the best being *Poor White* (1920), which treated both a frustrated character and the impact of industry upon American living.

In 1920 critics noticed that a new school of fiction had risen to prominence with the success of books such as F. Scott Fitzgerald's *This Side of Paradise* and Sinclair Lewis' *Main Street.* Thereafter, fiction took on new qualities related to the modern period. Writers tended toward Realism and Naturalism—frank portrayals of contemporary life. There was a trend away, however, from completely documented Realism toward the selection of detail. The novelists' portrayal of characters and motives, and even their selection of detail, were consistently much influenced by the psychology of Freud and others.

The novel tended to be particularly concerned with the problems of the day. In the decades that followed, fiction voiced reactions to changing times: novels of the 1920s expressed disillusionment with established institutions and ideologies; some from the 1930s protested against the economic and political system; others advocated remedies of some sort, telling of new-found hope and faith. The drift toward World War II and the war itself led many novelists to see qualities of excellence in American life not before realized, to voice patriotic enthusiasm. Some authors wrote works that fell into one or two of these periods; others ran the gamut from disillusionment to the acquisition of a new faith. The number of competent—even superior—novelists was huge, so large that the following study can discuss only a few of those who generally were felt to be outstanding.

Critics of society. F. Scott Fitzgerald's *This Side of Paradise* (1920) showed the disillusionment and moral disintegration of post-World War I America. The book initiated a career of great promise that found its finest fruition in *The Great Gatsby* (1925), a more poignant and unified development of the same theme. These two books of criticism of American society were destined to be Fitzgerald's best achievements. Like Fitzgerald, Sinclair Lewis was best as social critic. His onslaughts against the "village virus" (*Main Street* [1920]), average businessmen (*Babbitt* [1922]), materialistic scientists (*Arrowsmith* [1925]), and the racially prejudiced (*Kingsblood Royal* [1947]) were satirically sharp and thoroughly documented.

Novels of satire and protest

Similar careful documentation, though little satire, characterized James T. Farrell's Naturalistic *Studs Lonigan* trilogy (1932–35), which indignantly underlined social inequalities. Similar in pattern were Richard Wright's books that protested against the plight of the Negro—*Uncle Tom's Children* (1938) and *Native Son* (1940). A number of authors wrote proletarian novels attacking capitalistic exploitation—*e.g.,* Albert Halper in *The Foundry* (1934) and *The Chute* (1937). Satire directed against some of the aristocratic New England groups featured the rather lighter indictments of J.P. Marquand, *The Late George Apley* (1937) and *Wickford Point* (1939).

Particularly admired as a novelist of protest was John Dos Passos, who first attracted attention with an anti-World War I novel, *Three Soldiers* (1921). His most sweeping indictments of the modern social and economic system, *Manhattan Transfer* (1925) and the *U.S.A.* trilogy (*The 42nd Parallel, 1919,* and *The Big Money* [1930–36]), employed various narrative innovations such as the "camera eye" and "newsreel" to attack society from the left. His later books, attacks on leftists, had less merit.

A bitter vision of an inhuman and brutal world and a black-comedy style distinguished Nathanael West's novels, particularly *Miss Lonelyhearts* (1933) and *The Day of the Locust* (1939).

Hemingway, Faulkner, and Steinbeck. Three authors whose writings showed a shift from disillusionment were Ernest Hemingway, William Faulkner, and John Steinbeck. Hemingway's early short stories and his first novels, *The Sun Also Rises* (1926) and *A Farewell to Arms* (1929), were full of the disillusionment of the "lost generation" expatriates concerning war and peace. The Spanish Civil War, however, led him to believe in the possibility of collective action to solve social problems, and his novels *To Have and Have Not* (1937), *For Whom the Bell Tolls* (1940), and *The Old Man and the Sea* (1952) embodied this new belief. At his best, Hemingway showed a power to select and arrange details and to write simple, hard-hitting prose that critics found most effective.

Less controlled but equally distinctive, at its best, was the prose of William Faulkner. His handling of point of view, his use of stream-of-consciousness techniques, and even some of his descriptions of backgrounds and actions all at times led to the puzzlement of the reader. But such novels as *The Sound and the Fury* (1929), *As I Lay Dying* (1930), *Light in August* (1932), and *The Hamlet* (1940) overcame handicaps of occasional obscurity. Many of his short stories and novels were parts of the unfolding of a history of Yoknapatawpha County, a mythical Mississippi community, which showed his convictions about the decadence of the South. The picture as a whole was grim and dark, but Faulkner had convictions about the solutions to the problem that became increasingly clear. These were set forth most clearly and explicitly in *Intruder in the Dust* (1948) and *The Reivers* (1962).

Steinbeck's career, marked by uneven achievements, began with a historical novel, *Cup of Gold* (1929), wherein he voiced a distrust of society and a glorification of the anarchistic individualist typical of the rebellious 1920s. Later, however, he appeared to move toward a belief in the possibilities of collectivist action as a pathway to man's salvation. Such, at least, was the implication of *In Dubious Battle* (1936) and *The Grapes of Wrath* (1939), generally considered to be his best books. The latter is a narrative, interrupted by prose-poem interludes, of the migration of an Oklahoma Dust Bowl family to California. Their great discovery, symbolically set forth, was the necessity for cooperation among the poor and downtrodden for the betterment of the lot of men.

Lyric fictionists. An interesting development in fiction was a movement toward poetry. An increased tendency to select details and endow them with symbolic meaning, to set down the thought processes and emotions of the characters, and to make use of rhythmical prose gave fiction more of a lyrical quality than it had had. In varied ways, Crane, Norris, Cabell, Dos Passos, Hemingway, Steinbeck, and Faulkner all showed the trend—in passages, in short stories, and even in entire novels. Faulkner showed the trend at its worst in *A Fable* (1954), which, ironically, won a Pulitzer Prize.

Lyricism was especially prominent in the writings of Willa Cather. *O Pioneers!* (1913), *The Song of the Lark* (1915), and *My Ántonia* (1918) contained poetic passages about the disappearing frontier and the creative efforts of frontier folk. *A Lost Lady* (1923) was elegiac in form, and *Death Comes for the Archbishop* (1927) was an exaltation of the past and of spiritual pioneering. Katherine Anne Porter, whose works took the form of novelettes, wrote more in the style of the Metaphysical poets. Her use of the stream-of-consciousness method in *Flowering Judas* (1930) and *Pale Horse, Pale Rider* (1939) had the complexity, the irony, and the symbolic sophistication characteristic of this group.

Another leading poetic fictionist was Thomas Wolfe, the author of four large novels that were in effect a lyrical recording of his life—his strivings, his thoughts, and his feelings turned into fiction. *Look Homeward, Angel* (1929), *Of Time and the River* (1935), *The Web and the Rock* (1939), and *You Can't Go Home Again* (1940) dealt with a figure much like Wolfe—his youth in the South, his young manhood in the North, and his eternal search to fulfill a vision. The memories of the author of details of his past and his contemplations on the significance and meaning of his experiences were set forth in prose reminiscent of Walt Whitman's poetry. The books, despite their chaotic qualities (or perhaps because of them), were essentially lyrical achievements.

Literary criticism. Some historians, looking back over the first half of the 20th century, were inclined to think that it was particularly noteworthy for its achievements in literary criticism. Beyond doubt, it was true that criticism thrived as it had not for several generations, that it was an important influence on the shaping of literature, and that it quickened the perceptions of readers.

The New Humanists and their opponents

The period began with a battle between a group who called themselves the New Humanists—a group that stood for the older values in judging literature—and a group who urged that old standards be overthrown and new ones adopted. The New Humanists, allied in some ways with the earlier Brahmin critics of New England, were led by Irving Babbitt, a Harvard University professor whose scholarly books included *The New Laokoön* (1910), *Rousseau and Romanticism* (1919), *Democracy and Leadership* (1924), and *On Being Creative* (1932). In these books and in vigorous essays Babbitt preached his belief that man has a tendency toward the good, the true, and the beautiful and a contrary tendency toward evil. The application of this scheme was that modern writers, with their tendency toward Naturalism (the base in man's nature), were a vicious influence. Such associates of Babbitt as Paul Elmer More, Norman Foerster, and Stuart Sherman upheld this claim. The leader of the opposition was the pugnacious H.L. Mencken, who doubted that the values of the New Humanists existed and who claimed that regardless, the duty of writers was to present "the unvarnished truth" about life. His magazine articles and reviews gathered in *Prejudices* (1919–27) shouted this claim, as did the writings of his associates, a number of figures of lesser fame. In the end, the results were the liberation of literature from a number of ancient restrictions and the progress of Naturalism.

Socio-literary critics. In this period of social change, it was natural for a number of critics to consider literature in relationship to society and politics. Their study took many forms, but consistently this group judged books as (1) reflections of society or (2) expressions of social truth. Van Wyck Brooks and V.L. Parrington illustrated the two chief approaches. Brooks, who wrote numerous studies that embodied such an interest, in *America's Coming-of-Age* (1915) and *The Ordeal of Mark Twain* (1920) scolded the American public for making it all but impossible for an author to realize his genius fully. Later books by him presented rather different pictures but ones developed from similar interests: *The Flowering of New England* (1936), *New England: Indian Summer* (1940), *The World of Washington Irving* (1944), *The Times of Melville and Whitman* (1947), and *The Confident Years* (1952) showed how in the past many authors expressed their time and their locality. Parrington, in *Main Currents in American Thought* (1927–30), reevaluated American literature in terms of its adherence to the tenets of Jeffersonian democracy.

Marxian critics

The growth of Marxian influence upon thinking in the 1920s and '30s was shown in several books. V.F. Calverton set forth the general principles of Marxian evaluation of literature in *The Newer Spirit* (1925), and in *The Liberation of American Literature* (1932) judged literary figures on the basis of their representation of life and their implementation of the rise of the proletariat. Granville Hicks' *The Great Tradition* (1933) applied similar yardsticks. Many writers for a time followed the same lines of thinking, but beginning in 1939, as enthusiasm for Communism waned, many (including Hicks) renounced the dogmas of the theory. Some critics, however, found that some Marxian suggestions for critical procedures could be adapted and amended so as to be of service. Two outstanding critics in this group were Edmund Wilson and Kenneth Burke.

Moral-aesthetic critics. Wilson and Burke, however, like many critics of the time, were interested in other matters than just the relationships between literature and society; they were interested in both analyzing and evaluating literary creations. In a sense, they, like other moral-aesthetic critics, were eager to see in detail how a literary work was constructed; however, they were equally eager to assess the sensitivity that the literary work embodied. Morton D. Zabel, himself a leading critic and scholar of modern criticism, suggested that Henry James had aptly formulated the aim of this group when he said, "The critic's judgment, being in the best analysis an estimate of the artist's quality of mind, is at once moral and aesthetic." The group was distinguished, as a result, for its close attention to the creative process involved in a work and for care in ranking the work.

As in poetry, T.S. Eliot here proved a leader. In essays and books—*e.g., The Use of Poetry and the Use of Criticism* (1933)—he subjected writings and writers to careful analyses, and he developed the thesis that "the 'greatness' of literature cannot be determined solely by literary standards. Others used various ways of discussing relationships between form and value—R.P. Blackmur in *The Double Agent* (1935), Allen Tate in *Reactionary Essays on Poetry and Ideas* (1936), John Crowe Ransom in *The World's Body* (1938), Yvor Winters in *Maule's Curse* (1938), and Cleanth Brooks in *The Well Wrought Urn* (1947). This school of the New Criticism greatly advanced ways of discussing literary structure; it also distinguished and applied contrasting methods of evaluation. It therefore did much to advance the understanding and appreciation of literature. (Wa.B.)

AFTER WORLD WAR II

The literary historian Malcolm Cowley described the years between the two world wars as a "second flowering" of American writing. Certainly American literature attained a new maturity and a richer diversity in the 1920s and '30s, and significant works by several major figures from those decades were published after 1945. Faulkner, Hemingway, Steinbeck, and Katherine Anne Porter wrote memorable fiction; and Frost, Eliot, Wallace Stevens, Marianne Moore, e.e. cummings, William Carlos Williams, and Gwendolyn Brooks published important poetry. Eugene O'Neill's most distinguished play, *Long Day's Journey into Night,* appeared posthumously in 1956. Before and after World War II, Robert Penn Warren published influential fiction, poetry, and criticism. His *All the King's Men,* one of the best American political novels, won the 1947 Pulitzer Prize. Henry Miller's fiction, influential primarily because of its frank exploration of sexuality, first appeared in the United States in the 1960s. Still, impressive new novelists, poets, and playwrights emerged after the war. There was, in fact, a gradual changing of the guard.

The novel and short story. Two distinct groups of novelists responded to the cultural impact, and especially the technological horror, of World War II. Norman Mailer's *The Naked and the Dead* (1948) and Irwin Shaw's *The Young Lions* (1948) were realistic war novels. Using a Naturalistic technique, James Jones documented the war's tragic legacy in an ambitious trilogy, *From Here to Eternity* (1951), *The Thin Red Line* (1962), and *Whistle* (1978). Younger novelists, profoundly shaken by Hiroshima and the real threat of human annihilation, found the Realistic-Naturalistic tradition inadequate for treating the war's nightmarish implications. Joseph Heller, in *Catch-22* (1961), satirized the military mentality with surrealistic black humour; and Kurt Vonnegut, Jr., in *Slaughterhouse-Five* (1969), described the U.S. firebombing of Dresden, Ger., within a larger context of dark fantasy.

Black humour and absurdist fantasy

In part because of the atomic bomb, American writers of fiction turned increasingly to black humour and absurdist fantasy. According to several influential novelists and critics, the Realistic-Naturalistic tradition was outdated, incapable of communicating the rapid pace and the sheer implausibility of contemporary life. Consequently, a highly self-conscious fiction, which imitated earlier fiction rather than social reality, emerged. Russian-born Vladimir Nabokov and the Argentine writer Jorge Luis Borges were strong influences on this new "metafiction." Nabokov, who became a U.S. citizen in 1945, produced a body of highly sophisticated fiction distinguished by linguistic and formal innovation. His novels *Lolita* (1955), *Pnin* (1957), *Pale Fire* (1962), and *Ada; or, Ardor: A Family Chronicle* (1969) were particularly important. In a major 1967 essay, "The Literature of Exhaustion," John Barth declared himself an American disciple of Nabokov and Borges. After dismissing Realism as a "used up" tradition, Barth described his own work as "novels which imitate the form of the novel, [written] by an author who imitates the role of Author." In fact, Barth's earliest fiction, *The Floating Opera* (1956) and *The End of the Road* (1958), fell within the Realistic tradition, but in later, more ambitious work, he simultaneously imitated and parodied conventional forms—the historical novel in *The Sot-Weed Factor* (1960), Greek and Christian myth in *Giles Goat-Boy* (1966), and the epistolary novel in *Letters* (1979). Similarly, Donald Barthelme mocked the fairy tale in *Snow White* (1967) and Freudian fiction in *The Dead Father* (1975). Barthelme was most successful in his short stories that caricatured contemporary values and institutions.

Thomas Pynchon emerged as the major American practitioner of the absurdist fable. Assuming paranoia to be the only viable reaction to contemporary existence, Pynchon investigated elaborate "conspiracies" in *V* (1963), *The Crying of Lot 49* (1966), and *Gravity's Rainbow* (1973). The underlying assumption of Pynchon's fiction was the inevitability of entropy—the disintegration of physical and moral energy. In *Naked Lunch* (1959) and other novels, William Burroughs, abandoning plot and coherent characterization, used a drug addict's consciousness to depict a hideous modern landscape. Vonnegut, Terry Southern, and John Hawkes were other major practitioners of black humour and the absurdist fable.

Inevitably, such writers as Barth, Barthelme, and Pynchon rejected the novel's traditional function as a mirror reflecting society. If existence was incomprehensible, the novelist could hardly assume the Flaubert-Zola role of social critic. Still, a significant number of contemporary novelists were reluctant to abandon Social Realism. Highly conscious of the contemporary nightmare, 1976 Nobel laureate Saul Bellow nevertheless rejected despair. In such novels as *The Victim* (1947), *The Adventures of Augie March* (1953), *Herzog* (1964), *Mr. Sammler's Planet* (1970), and *Humboldt's Gift* (1975), Bellow proclaimed the necessity of "being human." While few contemporary writers saw the ugliness of urban life more clearly than Bellow, his mystical vision, derived from sources as diverse as Judaism and American Transcendentalism, was affirmative. Three other Jewish writers—Bernard Malamud, Philip Roth, and Isaac Bashevis Singer—treated the human condition with humour and forgiveness. Malamud's gift for comedy was especially evident in his short-story collection *The Magic Barrel* (1958). His novels *The Natural* (1952), *The Assistant* (1957), and *The Fixer* (1966) were also significant works of fiction. While Roth was best known for the outrageously satiric novel *Portnoy's Complaint* (1969), his most lasting achievement was his three-volume account of the misadventures of a controversial Jewish novelist—*The Ghost Writer* (1979), *Zuckerman Unbound* (1981), and *The Anatomy Lesson* (1983). The Polish-born Singer won the Nobel Prize for Literature in 1978 for his stories written originally in Yiddish. The sexual and moral confusion of the American middle class was the focus of John Updike's *Rabbit, Run* (1960), *Couples* (1968), and *Rabbit Redux* (1971), as it was of the fiction of J.D. Salinger. Long associated with *The New Yorker* magazine, John Cheever created in his short stories and novels a gallery of memorable eccentrics. In sharp contrast, Nelson Algren (*The Man with the Golden Arm* [1949]) and Hubert Selby, Jr. (*Last Exit to Brooklyn* [1964]), documented lower-class urban life with brutal frankness. Similarly, John Rechy portrayed America's urban homosexual subculture in *City of Night* (1963).

The Social Realists

Southern writers

Post-World War II Southern writers inherited Faulkner's rich legacy. Three women—Eudora Welty, Flannery O'Connor, and Carson McCullers—further advanced Southern fiction. O'Connor, writing from a deeply religious perspective, provided new directions for Southern Gothicism in her short stories. Always a brilliant stylist, Welty received the 1973 Pulitzer Prize for her novel *The Optimist's Daughter.* Initially known for his lyrical portraits of Southern eccentrics (*Other Voices, Other Rooms* [1948]), Truman Capote published *In Cold Blood,* a classic work of documentary realism, in 1966. William Styron's first novel, *Lie Down in Darkness* (1951), clearly revealed the Faulkner influence. In two ambitious later works, Styron fictionalized the dark side of human history—*The Confessions of Nat Turner* (1967) depicted an antebellum slave revolt, while *Sophie's Choice* (1979) attempted to capture the horror of the Holocaust. *The Moviegoer* (1961) and *The Last Gentleman* (1966) established Walker Percy as an important voice in Southern fiction. Inspired by Faulkner and Mark Twain, William Humphrey wrote two powerful novels set in Texas, *Home from the Hill* (1958) and *The Ordways* (1965).

Postwar black writers found alternatives to the Richard Wright tradition of social protest. In a series of essays, James Baldwin called for a literature that reflected the full complexity of black American life. In *Go Tell It on the Mountain* (1953) and *Just Above My Head* (1979), Baldwin attempted to portray the diversity of the black community. Other writers, however, were more successful in creating a truly complex black fiction. Ralph Ellison combined Afro-American history with Western myth to produce a modern classic, *Invisible Man* (1952). Later, two black women novelists published some of the most important postwar American fiction. In *The Bluest Eye* (1970), *Sula* (1973), and *Song of Solomon* (1977), Toni Morrison created a strikingly original fiction drawing from influences as diverse as Afro-American history, African and Western mythology, the Western fairy tale, and black folk culture. Alice Walker received the 1983 Pulitzer Prize for her black feminist novel *The Color Purple.*

It is impractical to generalize about postwar American fiction. Since reality itself seemed inaccessible, the traditional social role of fiction was constantly challenged and sometimes totally discarded. Writers of novels and short stories therefore were under unprecedented pressure to discover, or invent, new and viable kinds of fiction. A brief discussion of two of the most fascinating contemporary writers, Norman Mailer and Joyce Carol Oates, will perhaps illustrate this search for new directions. In his 1948 World War II novel, *The Naked and the Dead,* Mailer wrote in the Dos Passos tradition of social protest. He subsequently felt the limitations of the Realistic-Naturalistic tradition, however, and turned to his own brand of dark fantasy in *An American Dream* (1965) and *Why Are We in Vietnam?* (1967). Yet, it was only when he turned to "nonfiction fiction" or "fiction as history" in *The Armies of the Night* (1968) that Mailer discovered his truest voice. He further refined this approach in the 1980 Pulitzer Prize

Mailer and Oates

"true life novel" *The Executioner's Song.* Later, Mailer published a long, mystical novel set in ancient Egypt, *Ancient Evenings* (1983). Mailer was hardly the most consistent contemporary novelist, but he may well have been the most fascinating. In her early work, especially *A Garden of Earthly Delights* (1967) and *them* (1969), Joyce Carol Oates worked primarily out of the Naturalistic tradition. Incredibly prolific, she later experimented with Surrealism in *Wonderland* (1971) and Gothic fantasy in *Bellefleur* (1980). While Mailer and Oates refused to surrender the novel's obligation to capture reality, both were compelled to expand new fictional forms in order to fulfill that obligation.

Poetry. As with fiction, new voices emerged in postwar poetry. Robert Lowell, for example, produced distinguished dramatic poetry in *Lord Weary's Castle* (1946) and *For the Union Dead* (1964), while Theodore Roethke revealed a genius for ironic lyricism in *The Lost Son, and Other Poems* (1948). Along with Lowell, Roethke, Gwendolyn Brooks, and Robert Penn Warren, such diverse voices as John Berryman (*77 Dream Songs* [1964]), Randall Jarrell (*Losses* [1948]), Louis Simpson (*At the End of the Open Road, Poems* [1963]), Richard Wilbur (*Things of This World* [1956]), W.D. Snodgrass (*Heart's Needle* [1959]), and W.S. Merwin (*The Carrier of Ladders* [1970]) ultimately formed a new establishment in American poetry.

The poet-critic Yvor Winters inspired a Pacific school of writers of moral focus and plain style, among them his friend J.V. Cunningham and such later poets as N. Scott Momaday and Edgar Bowers. Charles Olson and Robert Creeley were associated with a group inspired by William Carlos Williams and known as the Black Mountain school. The 1950s saw the emergence of the San Francisco "beatniks" (Allen Ginsburg, Lawrence Ferlinghetti, and Gregory Corso). Gary Snyder, in *Turtle Island* (1974), continued the American tradition of nature poetry; while Galway Kinnell's poetry was shaped by a mythic consciousness. Like James Dickey, Kinnell was often fascinated by nature at its most primitive and brutal.

A number of important new women poets appeared. Before her suicide in 1963, Sylvia Plath wrote idiosyncratic, and often painfully introspective, poetry. Adrienne Rich was an important voice in poetry as well as feminist thought. Often as emotional and intimate in subject matter and tone as Plath, Anne Sexton won the 1967 Pulitzer Prize for *Live or Die,* while English-born Denise Levertov published several volumes of poetry after moving to the United States in 1948. Finally, Alice Walker's poetry was often as arresting as her fiction.

Drama. Two post-World War II playwrights established reputations comparable to O'Neill's. In essays, Arthur Miller eloquently defended his belief in a modern, democratic concept of tragedy; *Death of a Salesman* (1949) came close to vindicating this belief. Experimental in form as well as concept, *Salesman* was a distinctly American play. *All My Sons* (1947) and *The Crucible* (1953) were protest plays that reflected Miller's liberal idealism. Though his work was decidedly uneven, Tennessee Williams must be viewed as a more important playwright than Miller. Williams brought a passionate poetry and a tragic Southern vision to such plays as *The Glass Menagerie* (1944), *A Streetcar Named Desire* (1947), *Cat on a Hot Tin Roof* (1955), and *The Night of the Iguana* (1961).

Until the 1960s, Miller and Williams so dominated the postwar theatre that no other playwright emerged to challenge them. Then, in 1962, Edward Albee's reputation was secured by the stunning power of *Who's Afraid of Virginia Woolf?* A master of absurdist theatre, Albee has since emerged as the third major figure in postwar American drama. After the centre of American drama shifted from Broadway to off- and off-off-Broadway, American playwrights were increasingly free to write radical and innovative plays with some realistic hope of seeing them produced. David Rabe's *The Basic Training of Pavlo Hummel* (produced in 1971) and *Sticks and Bones* (1972) satirized America's militaristic nationalism and cultural shallowness. David Mamet won a 1976–77 New York Drama Critics Award for *American Buffalo.* Imamu Amiri Baraka (LeRoi Jones) and Ed Bullins inspired an angry black nationalist theatre. Baraka's *Dutchman* and *The Slave* (1964) communicated anger through experimental techniques, while Bullins' *In the Wine Time* (1968) made use of "street" lyricism. A clear indication of off-Broadway's ascendancy in American drama came in 1979 when Sam Shepard, a prolific and experimental playwright, won the Pulitzer Prize for *Buried Child.* Other important new voices in American drama were Lanford Wilson, the 1980 Pulitzer winner for *Talley's Folly,* and Ntozake Shange, whose "choreopoem," *For Colored Girls Who Have Considered Suicide/When the Rainbow Is Enuf,* moved to Broadway in 1976.

Literary and social criticism. Until his death in 1972, Edmund Wilson solidified his reputation as one of America's most versatile and distinguished men of letters. Later, Gore Vidal emerged as a potential heir to Wilson's legacy. Like Wilson, Vidal wrote important literary criticism, fiction, history, and social commentary. In *A Second Flowering* (1973) and *The Dream of the Golden Mountains* (1980), Malcolm Cowley investigated the effects of social and political change on 20th-century American literature. Alfred Kazin wrote literary history (*Bright Book of Life* [1973]) and autobiography (*New York Jew* [1978]); while Irving Howe produced literary theory and social criticism. The iconoclastic literary criticism of Leslie Fiedler was distinguished by its wit and creativity. Fiedler's *Love and Death in the American Novel* (1960) remains the most important Freudian study of American literature. Lionel Trilling, in *The Liberal Imagination* (1950) and other works, rejected V.L. Parrington's concept of literature as social reportage but insisted on its humanistic role. In *The Way of the New World* (1975), Addison Gayle, Jr., defended his theory that black literature must promote a sense of militant nationalism.

Men of letters

Despite the insistence by Wilson, Cowley, Trilling, and others that literature has a social function, the New Criticism of Robert Penn Warren and Cleanth Brooks remained a dominant influence in postwar literary studies. In addition, scholars published important biographies of several major American novelists. Leon Edel's exhaustive study of Henry James appeared in five volumes: *Henry James: The Untried Years, 1843–1870; The Conquest of London, 1870–1881; The Middle Years, 1882–1895; The Treacherous Years, 1895–1901;* and *The Master, 1901–1916* (1953–72). Mark Schorer's *Sinclair Lewis, An American Life* (1961), Carlos Baker's *Ernest Hemingway: A Life Story* (1969), Michel Fabre's *The Unfinished Quest of Richard Wright* (1973), and Joseph Blotner's *Faulkner: A Biography* (1974) were uniquely perceptive biographies. The impressive *Harvard Guide to Contemporary American Writing,* edited by Daniel Hoffman, appeared in 1979.

One positive result of the accelerating complexity of postwar life was a body of distinguished journalism and social commentary. John Hersey's *Hiroshima* (1946) was a deliberately controlled, unemotional account of atomic holocaust. In *Notes of a Native Son* (1955), *Nobody Knows My Name* (1961), and *The Fire Next Time* (1963), black novelist James Baldwin published a body of the most eloquent essays written in America. Norman Mailer's "new journalism" proved especially effective in capturing the drama of political conventions. Novelist Joan Didion published two collections of incisive social and literary commentary, *Slouching Towards Bethlehem* (1968) and *The White Album* (1979). The title essay of the first collection was the first truly detached and honest investigation of the forces behind, and the implications of, the 1960s counterculture. Robert M. Pirsig's *Zen and the Art of Motorcycle Maintenance* (1974) defied all classification. In it, Pirsig equated the emotional collapse of his central character with the disintegration of American workmanship and cultural values.

The emergence in academic circles of two sharply contrasting critical movements illustrated the complexity of the time. First, the French-inspired school of Structuralism reached the United States. Centred primarily at Yale, the American disciples of Jacques Derrida and Roland Barthes practiced an abstract criticism based on linguistic and philosophic innovation. For them, criticism often

Structuralism and feminist criticism

supplanted literature as the focus of attention. In sharp contrast, feminist literary criticism often emphasized the social, even the political, function of literature. Tillie Olsen's *Silences* (1978) exemplified a feminist criticism stressing androgyny. (J.R.G.)

BIBLIOGRAPHY. ROBERT E. SPILLER *et al.* (eds.), *Literary History of the United States,* 4th ed., 2 vol. (1974), a standard general work; MARCUS CUNLIFFE (ed.), *American Literature to 1900* (1973), and *American Literature Since 1900* (1975); VERNON L. PARRINGTON, *Main Currents in American Thought,* 3 vol. (1927–30; reprinted in 1 vol., 1958), essential background reading; WALTER BLAIR, THEODORE HORNBERGER, and RANDALL STEWART (eds.), *The Literature of the United States,* 3rd ed., 2 vol. (1966; 1-vol. ed., 1970); CLEANTH BROOKS, R.W.B. LEWIS, and ROBERT PENN WARREN (eds.), *American Literature: The Makers and the Making,* 2 vol. (1973); ALFRED KAZIN, *An American Procession* (1984), literary history from Emerson to Fitzgerald.

Studies that focus on specific periods or trends of American literary history include PERRY G. MILLER, *The New England Mind: From Colony to Province* (1953), and *The New England Mind: The Seventeenth Century* (1939, reprinted 1961), two authoritative works; MOSES C. TYLER, *A History of American Literature, 1607–1765,* 2 vol. (1879, reissued 1973), and *The Literary History of the American Revolution, 1763–1783,* 2 vol. (1897, reissued 1970), useful histories of the Colonial Period and early Republic; FRANCIS O. MATTHIESSEN, *American Renaissance* (1941, reissued 1979); JAY MARTIN, *Harvests of Change: American Literature, 1865–1914* (1964), a useful study; ARTHUR H. QUINN, *A History of the American Drama from the Beginning to the Civil War* (1923, reissued 1979), and . . . *From the Civil War to the Present Day* (1936, reissued 1980), the most thorough treatment; ALFRED KAZIN, *On Native Grounds: An Interpretation of Modern American Prose Literature,* rev. ed. (1956, reissued 1982), a readable, useful critical history; MORTON D. ZABEL (ed.), *Literary Opinion in America,* 3rd ed. rev., 2 vol. (1962). Important studies of the pastoral tradition in American literature are R.W.B. LEWIS, *The American Adam* (1955); RICHARD CHASE, *The American Novel and Its Tradition* (1957, reprinted 1978); and LEO MARX, *The Machine in the Garden* (1964, reprinted 1972). Critical studies of post-World War II fiction include IHAB HASSAN, *Radical Innocence* (1961), an Existentialist analysis; TONY TANNER, *City of Words* (1971), useful for understanding contemporary metafiction; JOSEPHINE HENDIN, *Vulnerable People* (1978), a volume of feminist criticism; and DANIEL HOFFMAN (ed.), *Harvard Guide to Contemporary American Writing* (1979), a comprehensive collection of essays by major scholars.

(Wa.B./J.R.G.)

Arts of Native American Peoples

To achieve an understanding of the art of aboriginal Americans—*i.e.,* Native Americans (or American Indians) and Arctic peoples (variously called Eskimos or Inuit)—hereafter generally referred to as "Indian art," requires at the outset a willingness to discard many long-standing preconceptions and judgments based upon an evaluation of Western art. Above all, it is important to recognize that the basic aesthetic tenets and artistic goals of Indian art are different from those of European-derived Western art; and any art critic employing the usual Western criteria in an attempt to comprehend Indian art is bound to be unsuccessful.

At best, it is difficult for non-Indian peoples to evaluate Indian art. Although it is not necessarily true that one must be a Native American to appreciate Indian art—or even, for example, a Navajo to understand the value of that people's earthenware and weaving—it is true that the finer subtleties and depths of significance that are so obvious to the Indian are often lost to the non-Indian observer.

Finally, the cultural interaction of the past five centuries between Europeans and their descendents and the aboriginal peoples of the Western Hemisphere by and large has been one of extreme hostility, fraught with a considerable degree of cultural bias. Most, if not all, of the major commentaries on Indian cultures have been recorded by those who were natural enemies; the best eyewitness accounts of the Aztec, for example, were written by Spanish conquistadores and Roman Catholic missionaries. Even modern white ethnographers and historians, however sympathetic they might be, simply cannot ignore the fact that they are, after all, evaluating the product of cultures that their forebears successfully suppressed and of peoples who in many cases whites exterminated or drove to near extinction. This inevitably introduces emotional and psychological elements into the act of judgment that result in tremendous distortions. Not until the 20th century did Indian art begin to enjoy serious, balanced consideration, and even this has been in meagre terms.

One of the major obstacles to a realistic evaluation and appreciation of Native American art by whites and other non-Indians is the belief held by many that the creators of Indian art are in some way "primitive" artists who occupy a place so close to nature that they somehow are endowed with a privileged status insofar as "natural artistic expression" is concerned. To regard an object or a ceremonial activity as a work of art simply because it was Indian-crafted defies reason. While it is reasonable to state that none of the Native American and Arctic tribes and peoples failed to develop some degree of art—and many were responsible for aesthetic masterworks—it would be misleading to declare that all of these expressions are equally impressive. The quality, beauty, and workmanship of these arts vary widely; for, just as in the Western world, there have been good and bad artists, and the fact that a native craftworker turned his or her hand to a given task in no way guaranteed success.

Another obstacle to a full appreciation of the arts of Native American peoples is a belief held by many sympathetic viewers of aboriginal art: that there are eternal aesthetic truths, expressions of which can be found in all cultures, and that to the truly sensitive eye these aesthetic verities are manifest wholly independent of the particular cultural milieu, the purpose of the artistic expression, or the relative level of cultural development. The position taken in this discussion, therefore, is that, since the literature, music, dance, and visual arts of Native American and Arctic peoples did not evolve in isolation from the sociological, religious, and political milieus of those peoples, an understanding of the latter cannot be divorced from an appreciation of the former. (F.J.D./Ed.)

This article addresses the arts of Native American and North American Arctic peoples, in relation to the culture and subcultures of each of these peoples and in relation to the predominantly European-based Western world. For detailed cultural and historical discussion of Native American peoples, see AMERICAN PEOPLES, NATIVE and PRE-COLUMBIAN CIVILIZATIONS; and, for discussion of Arctic peoples, see ARCTIC, THE.

For coverage of related topics in the *Macropædia* and *Micropædia,* see the *Propædia,* sections 613, 621–622, 624–627, and 629, and the *Index.*

The article is divided into the following sections:

Literature 313
General characteristics 313
Oral literatures 313
North American cultures
Eskimo
Northwest Coast
California
Southwest
Eastern Woodlands
Plains
Middle American cultures
South American and Caribbean cultures
Written literatures 316
Study and evaluation 317
Music 317
Dominant native style 317
Melody and rhythm
The significance of song texts
Musical instruments 318
Drums: membranophones
Rattles: idiophones
The jingler
Shaken rattles of animal origin
Metal rattles
Turtle shells
Gourd rattles
Other varieties of rattles
Wind instruments: aerophones
Stringed instruments: chordophones
Regional customs: North America 320
The Far North
Eskimo music
Far northern tribes
The Eastern Woodlands area
The Algonkian musical renaissance
Traditional Iroquois music
The Great Plains
The West
The tribes of the Northwest
Music of desert and plateau tribes
The Southwest (Arizona and New Mexico)
The Navajo and Apache
Pueblo music and ritual
Regional customs: Mexico and Middle America 321
Northern Mexico
Yaqui music and dance
Other northern Mexican peoples
Middle America
Regional customs: South America 322
Musical traits of Amazon peoples
Andean music
Mestizo music of the coast
Studies and publications 323
Musical transcriptions and analysis
Other fields of American Indian musicology
Dance 323
General characteristics of American Indian dance 323
Extent of dance forms
Patterns of participation
Socially determined roles in dance
Religious expression in dance
Patterns and body movement

Foreign influences
Regional dance styles 326
Eskimo
Eastern Woodlands
The Great Plains
The Northwest Coast
The northern desert and California
The Southwest
Mexico and Middle America
South America
Northern South America
The Andean region
The southern plains
Study and evaluation 330
Visual arts 330
Nature and elements 330
The role of the artist
The function of art
Materials
Regional styles of American Indian visual arts 331
North America
American Southwest
Great Lakes–Midwest
Great Plains
Peripheral North America
Eskimo
Northwest Coast
Mexico and Middle America
West Indies
South America
Colombia
Ecuador
Brazil
Peru and highland Bolivia
Chile and Argentina
Arts of the American Indian peoples in the contemporary world 345
Bibliography 346

Literature

GENERAL CHARACTERISTICS

Folktales have been a part of the social and cultural life of American Indian and Eskimo peoples regardless of whether they were sedentary agriculturists or nomadic hunters. As they gathered around a fire at night, the hard-working Indians could be transported to another world through the talent of a good storyteller. The effect was not only derived from the novelty of the tale itself but also from the imaginative skill of the narrator, who often added gestures and songs and occasionally adapted a particular tale to suit a certain culture.

Use of repetition

One adaptation frequently used by the the storyteller was the repetition of incidents. The description of an incident would be repeated a specific number of times (depending on the ceremonial number in the culture—three, four, five, or seven), with the hero killing that many monsters or that number of brothers who had gone out on the same adventure. This type of repetition was very effective in oral communication, for it firmly inculcated the incident in the minds of the listeners—much in the same manner that repetition is used today in radio and television advertising. In addition, there was an aesthetic value to the rhythm gained from repetition and an even greater dramatic effect, for the listener knew that when the right number of incidents had been told, some supernatural character would come to the aid of the hero, sometimes by singing to him. For this reason, oral literature is often difficult and boring to read. Oral literature also loses effect in transcription because the reader, unlike the listener, is often unacquainted with the worldview, ethics, sociocultural setting, and personality traits of the people in whose culture the story was told and set.

Because the effect of the story depended so much on the narrator, there were many versions of every good tale. Each time a story was told, it varied only within the limits of the tradition established for that plot and according to the cultural background of the narrator and the listeners. While studies have been made of different versions of a tale occurring within a tribe, there is still much to be discovered, for instance, in the telling of the same tale by the same narrator under different circumstances. These gaps in the study of folktales do not indicate lack of interest but rather the difficulty in setting up suitable situations for recordings.

The terms myth and folktale in American Indian oral literature are used interchangeably because in the Indian view the difference between the two is a matter of time rather than of content. If the incidents related happened at a time when the world had not yet assumed its present form, the story may be regarded as a myth; but, even if the same characters appear in the "modern" present, it is considered a folktale. Whereas European fairy tales traditionally begin with the vague allusion "once upon a time," the American Indian myth often starts with "before the people came" or "when Coyote was a man." To the Eskimo, it is insignificant whether an incident occurred yesterday or 50 years ago—it is past. Thus, while the mythology of nonliterate people has a historical development of its own, it cannot be admitted to the present-day classification of historical because it lacks documentation.

Cultural regions

American Indian mythology can be divided into three major cultural regions: North American cultures (from the Eskimos to the Indians of the Mexican border), Central and South American higher civilizations, and the Caribbean and South American simpler cultures. Though each region exhibits a wide range of development, there are recurrent themes along the cultures, and the importance of mythology itself within each culture varies. In North America, for example, stories are not involved with a panoply of divine beings, whereas those of Middle America and South America bear some resemblance to the complicated mythologies of the surrounding higher cultures and are quite confusing with their many hybrid monsters and giants. In North America many mythologies (like the Dreaming of the Australian Aborigines) deal with a period in the distant past in which the world was different and people could not be distinguished from animals. These mythologies are related to the concept that all animals have souls or spirits that give them supernatural power. Because man has subsequently been differentiated from the animals, they come to him in visions, and in the stories they help the hero out of trouble. When there are many tales involving a single character, such as Raven, Coyote, or Manabozho, the transcriptions are linked together today and called cycles. Whether this cyclic presentation of tales is or is not indigenous to the Indian mind remains questionable, but it is used by folklorists who have been accustomed to legendary cycles of medieval European literature, such as the tales of *Beowulf, La Chanson de Roland (The Song of Roland),* or even *The Canterbury Tales.*

The body of American Indian folklore does not include riddles as found in African folklore, for example, nor does it include proverbs, though there are tales with morals attached.

The importance of mythology within a culture is reflected in the status of storytellers, the times assigned to this activity, and the relevance of mythology to ceremonialism. In many instances the relationship between mythology and ceremonialism is very close. The Navajo ceremonials, like the chants, are based entirely on the characters and incidents in the mythology. The dancers make masks under strict ceremonial control, and, when they wear them to represent the gods, they absorb spiritual strength. The Aztec ceremonials and sacrifices placate the gods who are the heroes of the mythology. If, however, the mythology consists primarily of animal tales and stories of personal and social relationships, the actors and characters involved in the stories are also an index to the beliefs and customs of the people.

ORAL LITERATURES

North American cultures. *Eskimo.* Eskimo culture can be divided into two major subgroups: one culture extending from Greenland to the Mackenzie River and another west from the river to the Pacific Ocean. The Eskimo culture embodies simple stories of hunting incidents in which the heroes are sometimes helped through supernatural power. Other stories include themes in which people ascend to the sky to become constellations: maltreated children become animals, and an orphan boy becomes successful. Still others surround the exploits and priestly magic of the shamans. In the region from Greenland to the Mackenzie River, Sedna is the highest spirit and controls the sea mammals; the Moon is a male deity who lives incestuously with his sister, the Sun. When she discovers he is her brother, she seizes a burning faggot and rushes away into the sky, the Moon pursuing her.

There are many stories involving family life and others dealing with the feuds between Eskimos and the Indians south of them.

Stories of the western Eskimos

The western Eskimos along the Pacific and Arctic coasts have the Raven cycle, a series of tales centred around Raven, a protagonist whose role ranges from culture hero to the lowest form of trickster. Many of the same plots and themes also occur in tales of the Northwest Coast culture. Around some coastal villages, a story about a flood that took place in the first days of the Earth is told. Many stories are especially intended for children and stress proper behaviour. They are often told by young girls to younger ones and are illustrated by incising figures in the snow or on the ground with an ivory snow knife. On the lower Yukon, a migration legend is told about a long journey from east to west. The usual incident breaking up this party of travellers is a quarrel, after which they divide into two groups, occupying separate villages, and for years make constant war on each other. Tales of hunting begin as personal adventures but become stylized with supernatural characters and events.

Northwest Coast. There is greater similarity in the mythology of the various tribes along the Northwest Coast than in other regions of North America. Collectors of folktales have gathered a long series of stories told in the region from the mouth of the Columbia River through southeastern Alaska and have gathered them into a Raven cycle. The protagonists of these stories—from south to north, Coyote, Mink, and Raven—again vary from culture hero to trickster. In each subarea the stories elucidate the origin of a village, a clan, or a family and are regarded as the property of these clans or families. Thus, they can only be used by others through permission or, sometimes, purchase. Examples of this type of myth are Bungling Host, Dog Husband, and Star Husband. In Bungling Host, Trickster, after seeing his host produce food in various ways (*e.g.,* letting oil drip from his hands), fails to imitate the magic methods to procure food and barely escapes death. In Dog Husband, a girl has a secret lover who is a dog by day and a man by night. When she gives birth to pups, she is deserted by her tribe. She then destroys her children's dog skins, and they turn human, becoming successful hunters. In some versions parents lose all their sons to a monster, and when a new baby is born, it grows rapidly, kills the monster, and restores the brothers. Star Husband, another widely known myth, relates the story of two girls sleeping outdoors who wish the stars would marry them. They ascend to the sky, marry the stars, and experience a series of remarkable adventures.

Mythology of the Kwakiutl and Salish-speaking tribes

Among the Kwakiutl of Vancouver Island, the mythology is represented in an elaborate series of dances that illustrate characters and incidents with masks, puppets, and other mechanical devices. The principal events during the winter ceremonial season, these ceremonies include initiation into the secret societies, the highest of which is the Cannibal Society. Less elaborate forms of this winter ceremonial are found among the southern tribes who base their activities on the quest for the guardian spirit and on the return of the spirits to those who have seen them in visions. In order to exorcise these spirits, their songs must be sung and their dances performed. The Salish-speaking tribes of southern British Columbia and Washington have less complicated costumes for this ceremonial, but their dancing is very interesting and vigorous. The attitude of the Indians of the Northwest Coast toward animals is expressed in rituals such as the first salmon ceremony and the ceremonial attitude toward the bear. When the first salmon of the spring run is caught, it is ceremonially cleaned and placed on a clean mat or a bed of fern leaves. It is welcomed with an address of thanks and promised good treatment. The entrails are wrapped in a mat and thrown into the river so that they can return to the land in the west where the salmon can tell how well he was treated. The salmon is carried to the house by a selected group—children, women only, or the family of the successful fisherman—and is roasted and eaten, also by the selected group. The bear is never killed wantonly. When seen, it is addressed in terms of kinship, expressing an attitude that is known sporadically from the Ainu of northern Japan to many places in northwestern America.

California. The many small tribes of California exhibit more unity in their mythology than is present in many other features of their culture. In the north central area, the Kuksu cults enact the myths of the creator and culture hero with Coyote and Thunder as the chief characters. In southern California in ceremonies of the Chungichnich cults, contact with the highest god is achieved by smoking datura or jimsonweed, which produces hallucinations of animals. The boys initiated into the cults regard the animals as their guardian spirits. This concept relates the cult activity with the most fundamental feature of American Indian religion, the concept of the individually attained guardian spirit.

In general, the Californian tribes have a very confused mythology, which was disintegrating even before the white man settled in their territory. Though some animal stories and a few themes about vague characters existed, little of it has been recorded and carefully studied.

Southwest. The Indians of New Mexico and Arizona, along with a few small tribes related to them in southern California, have cultural traditions with some features in common. In the folklore of the Southwest, the emergence and migration myths show the Indians emerging from an unpleasant underworld at the time when the Earth is not yet completely formed. They start a long trek southward, some looking for a sacred spot, others looking specifically for the centre of the Earth. In some instances they are led by a pair of culture heroes, the Twins, also called the Little War Gods, who help stabilize the surface of the Earth and teach the Indians many features of their culture, including ceremonials. When the people were weary during the migration, the gods, the kachinas, came and danced for them until someone made fun of their peculiar faces and insulted them. They allowed the people to copy their masks and costumes, and then they returned to their home in the underworld. Since that time the men from the kivas, the ceremonial chambers to which all the men belonged, have made these costumes and masks and have performed the dances necessary to stimulate and protect the harvest, bring rain, and promote the general welfare.

The Twin Gods of the Pueblo villages are a combination of the helpful god and the trickster. They sometimes behave like unruly children and tease their grandmother to death. Coyote, in the Pueblo literature, is not the trickster he often is in the folklore of cultures farther north. Though he does share some of the trickster plots and is always sly, he is often caught in his own wiles. A group of very crude and vulgar tales about him exist, which have been transcribed from Spanish days, surrounding two characters who travel together named Djos and Ley, a corruption of "God" and "King." Certain European tales, such as the Cinderella stories, have been added to the collections of Pueblo folklore.

Ceremonials of the Navajo and Apache

The Athabascan-speaking tribes of the Southwest are the Navajo and Apache. Nowhere in America are mythology and ceremonial more closely associated than among the Navajo, where the myths are poetically expressed through great "chants." The principal characters are the gods of the wind, the rain, the dawn, the Sun, the semiprecious stones, the sacred plants, corn, tobacco, squash, and the bean. The ceremonials are intended to cure sickness, both mental and physical, and to protect people on dangerous missions, rather than to inspire any sense of worship. All the arts are combined in the ceremonies: the story itself, the poetic expression of it, the painting of the masks, the beautiful combinations of feathers in the headdresses, the sand paintings illustrating the story while the chants are sung, and, finally, the dancing of the characters who wear the regalia. This is one of the most inspiring ceremonials devised by the American Indian.

The other Athabascan-speaking people, the Apache, are divided into several groups, of which the Lipan are particularly interesting. The southernmost of North American tribes, they live partly across the Mexican border. They have an emergence myth and share with all southern Athabascans the culture hero known as "Killer-of-enemies" and his younger brother "Child-of-the-Water" (comparable to the Twin War Gods of the Pueblos). One of the monsters in the tales is Big Owl, a destructive cannibal in the form of a large owl. The story of the man seeking spiritual power from the gods who goes down the Colorado River in a hollow log to reach the holy places where the spirits live is almost identical to its Navajo version. There is a Lipan Coyote cycle, but there are no Spanish-derived tales.

The White Mountain Apache tell stories only between dusk and dawn and during cold weather. They have two major cycles, the creation myths, in which something is created out of nothing, and Coyote myths surrounding the trickster par excellence of that name. Two minor cycles centre around Big Owl and Gain, a supernatural being who lives in mountains and caves and underground worlds. The White Mountain Apache learned some European stories from captives in Spanish and Mexican towns in the late 18th and early 19th centuries. The Jicarilla Apache divide their didactic stories into sacred and secular, telling them at night during the winter with a break at midnight for a festive meal. The Jicarilla are seriously absorbed in their mythology, into which they inject objects of modern life such as the telegraph and the automobile. They also have creation stories and the legend of the man who went down the Colorado River in a hollow log. Among the trickster stories, the Coyote cycle is well developed. The Colorado River tribes, which are closely affiliated with the people of southern California, comprise the last division of the Southwest cultures. These tribes were Christianized by missionaries so early that little of their mythology remained to be recorded. It is known that Coyote played an important part in their sacred stories, though he was also portrayed as a deceitful trickster. Like the Pueblo tribes, the Luiseño also migrated, looking for the centre of the world, where their god, Wiyot, had died. His death was the first among the people, and they lost their immortality. Wiyot later returned as the new moon. There are many stories about the stars, which were regarded as the souls of the dead. The Chungichnich cult was also known here but may have come within the mission period.

Eastern Woodlands. The northeastern Algonkins were the first groups of American Indians north of Mexico to have protracted contact with Europeans, so their own ways of living were disrupted at a very early date. Some of their culture traits can still be found among the Central Algonkin to the west, and some of the most elementary stories are known to all groups in this region. This mythology centres around a culture hero known as GlusKap to the Micmac and as GlusKabe among the Algonkin; his consistently altruistic character and human appearance distinguish him from many other culture heroes. He carries out the usual exploits, one of the most popular being the episode in which he kills a Monster Frog who has been impounding the water. Though he revels in the trickster adventures of all American Indian characters, he appears somewhat exempt from the crude buffoonery of other culture heroes.

To the west, the Central Algonkin developed the Midewiwin or the Grand Medicine Society—shared by the Eastern Sioux—whose activities revolved around the quest for a vision that would bring them in direct contact with supernatural beings who instructed them in curing ceremonies. The members of the society were not shamans, had no individual powers, and were only effective when they acted together. In its use of certain mnemonic devices containing a series of symbols used for instructing initiates, the society foreshadowed an approach to writing.

Folklore of the Iroquois

The Iroquois, who developed one of the great confederacies of American Indians, had a strong religious and mythological background for their folklore. In their creation story, which is the basis of their religious beliefs, they acknowledged a supreme being "beyond the conception of man." This "being" sent from heaven is a woman who in her descent fell on a big turtle imbedded in mud. She gave birth to a daughter conceived by the turtle who bore two sons. The good one was born first; the other was born through the mother's side and killed her. The sons grew up and helped their grandmother finish the formation of the Earth. The Iroquois had curing societies similar to the Midewiwin; their members were not shamans, and they cured in a group rather than as individuals.

Many tribes in the Southeast exhibit cultural systems very similar to those of the northeastern tribes; but others, especially in the lower Mississippi Valley, had a more elaborate religion and mythology that divulged a definite relationship to the higher cultures of Meso-America.

Plains. The expansive area of North America between the Mississippi River and the Rocky Mountains, extending from the Gulf of Mexico to the sub-Arctic Indians of Canada, embodied many cultures whose various rites and ceremonies emerged from a common background. Many tribes were seminomadic and depended more on buffalo hunting than on agriculture for their living. The more sedentary groups, the Eastern Siouan, included the Mandan and Hidatsa. Marginal groups, which seem to have continued an older form of Plains culture before the advent of the horse, lined the borders of the Plains area.

The Sioux narrate the following creation story: the Old Man, Waziya, lived beneath the Earth with his wife. Their daughter married the Wind and bore four sons, the winds North, East, South, and West. Together with the Sun and Moon, the winds were the "Controllers" of the universe, and a series of very involved stories tells of their powers. As the world was being formed by the invisible being, Iktoma, the trickster made trouble wherever he could. The usual plots are found in this collection of trickster stories. In order to reach the supernaturals or "Controllers," rituals and ceremonies had to be conducted. The most important ritual was the Sun Dance, because the Sun was one of the principal powers. A medicine man was responsible for the whole ritual, which had to be recited in letter-perfect fashion, because great harm could be inflicted on the whole group if the performance was not exact.

Creation myth of the Crow

In contrast to the Sioux, the Crow are a bit more lighthearted about their approach to the universe. Their culture speaks of a creation myth in which Old Woman's Grandchild, the son of an Indian woman and the Sun, destroys monsters. He then goes to the sky and becomes Morning Star. The genealogy of this character very closely resembles the Navajo myth of Changing Woman, the Sun's mistress who bore the children Monster-slayer and Child-born-of-Water. This concept of change into an astral body is quite widespread in the Plains. In a Cheyenne version of the Dog Husband story, the mother and her children go to the sky and become the Pleiades constellation. The Crow liked to express themselves poetically, and often they recited in song. The military societies have many songs that express their high aims and others that are songs of bravado. In many of their amusing stories, there are plays on words that are often difficult to translate.

The last of the Plains tribes, the Comanche, believe that the Great Spirit created some people, but that there were white people existing before them. A flood washed these white people away, and they turned into white birds and flew away. A secondary spirit was then sent to create the Comanche. But they were not perfect at first; therefore the spirit came a second time, giving them intelligence and showing them how to make everything. There are the usual trickster stories with Old Coyote as the central figure. Since the Comanche were a very aggressive tribe, there are many stories based on war exploits.

Middle American cultures. The cultures of Middle or Central America comprise the highest developments of the New World and have been considered comparable to some of the oldest cultures of the Mediterranean. Included are the Aztecs of Mexico, the Maya of Central America, and the Inca of Peru.

The Maya, who will be mentioned again below, have a

very complicated creation myth relating the several stages at which man did not satisfy his creator. After each stage he was destroyed, and another attempt to create a more perfect being was made. Since Maya culture in its highest form can only be reconstructed from the art and the hieroglyphics, little is known except the mythology that can be derived from the religious ceremonial art (see below *Written language* for details).

Mythological eras of the Toltec period Aztecs

The Aztecs of the Toltec period had four mythological eras: those of (1) the Water Sun, which was destroyed by flood; (2) the Sun of the Earth, which was destroyed by earthquake; (3) the Wind Sun, which was destroyed by a giant and only Quetzalcóatl, the feathered serpent, remaining, prophesying the destruction of the Earth by wind and the evolution of humans into monkeys; and (4) the present Sun of Fire, which will end in a general conflagration. Quetzalcóatl, the survivor of the age of the Wind Sun, brought civilization to the people. This mythology, which was the basis of the ceremonial life, was maintained by the ceremonial priest, but there were also simple folktales that resembled those of North America.

Much more information about the Aztecs exists than about the Maya, because their civilization was still functioning at the time of the Spanish conquest; whereas Maya culture had completely changed, and the old traditions were almost unknown. What is available is the result of painstaking scholarly work in the analysis of the hieroglyphics.

The Inca civilization of Peru has been added to the higher cultures of Meso-America because it resembles them more closely than it does its neighbours, the simpler tribes of South America. As far back as mythological history can be traced, the Incas have worshipped Viracocha, the creator. He was the omnipotent being who took part in every mythological incident. He created man from painted stone dolls, a specific way of saying that man evolved from the living rock. He also had the primitive capacity for infinite self-multiplication, and some of his offspring also became local gods. Another cycle of creation in which Viracocha functions bears some resemblance to the periods listed for the Aztec. The "Origin People" came out from their caves, and the creator organized the process of living for them. They became the ruling class. Then the "Wilderness People" came from other caves and became the common people, who increased rapidly. Many diverse languages and cultures developed. The next cycle produced the "Wartime People," who placed a premium on being ruthless, strong, and cunning. They took whatever they wanted and forced people to move to more unfavourable places; in this way, they spread the population. In all of these myths the flood is present, which requires the recreation of man after each incident.

Since Peruvian mythology covers a large and difficult terrain, local cults developed in many places utilizing the same characters in different incidents. When all the incidents are assembled they seem very confusing and contradictory.

South American and Caribbean cultures. There are so many cultures among the Indians of South America, and so little is known about many of them, that a selection was made of four tribes, some of whose mythology has been published. The Aymara in northern Chile share the culture hero creator Viracocha with the Peruvians. According to the Aymara, he rose from Lake Titicaca, created the Earth, the sky, and man, and then resubmerged. Man was disobedient to him, and he therefore led man to Tiahuanaco and turned him into stone. Viracocha created the Sun, Moon, and stars because man, whom he created again, lived in darkness. Another mythological character of the Aymara culture is Thunnupa, a bearded white man from the north who opposed polygamy and chicha, the national drink. Animal tales are also very common in this culture, some having Aesop-like plots. Fox is the comical character in tales, and, because of this European aspect, it is often postulated that the tales might have been brought in with the Spanish conquest.

The Mapuche culture, also in Chile, relates tales characterized by fairly long narratives about such supernatural characters as Shooting Star, who may also be a cannibal, hybrid monster, winged serpent, ghost, or apparition. Again, the wily Fox is the principal character in the animal stories, though he is often outwitted. Folktales are told at night and are accompanied by mimicry and gestures.

The many folktales of the Cágaba, who inhabit the Sierra Nevada de Santa Marta in Colombia, are religious in nature, having supernatural characters who arrange the world for man and who try to control the demons that plague him.

Finally, the Chibcha, who live in Colombia north of the Orinoco River, have a body of mythology that reflects the lack of organization found also in their culture. The stories are cosmological and ritual but lack all perspective of time. Many are concerned with Bochica, a culture hero who is one of the major gods of the Chibcha pantheon.

Mythology of the Caribbean Indians

Because many islands in the Caribbean were populated by people who came from the northern parts of South America, the scanty information available concerning their folktales and mythology is included in this section. The Arawak were the first Indians encountered in the New World by Columbus at Hispaniola. A typically Caribbean type of Indian who migrated from the tropical forests of South America, they combine the concept of a guardian spirit with fetish worship and fabricate idols representing plants, animals, and human spirits. The Sun and the Moon, who are connected with a myth about human emergence from a cave, together with various astral beings and a culture hero, are typical characters of Arawak mythology.

The Arawak Indians were soon decimated by Spanish invaders in the Caribbean, and by 1535 only about 500 were left at Hispaniola. The Spanish therefore brought blacks and other Indians to work on plantations. This situation also occurred on Puerto Rico and Jamaica, where the Indian cultures were totally changed because of the influx of blacks and the subsequent mingling of the races. One outstanding collection of tales from this region consists of stories about Spider, a culture hero of West African folklore.

WRITTEN LITERATURES

Maya hieroglyphs

One of the great scholars of Maya culture, J. Eric Thompson, has said:

> In the New World only Maya culture extends to us the privilege of sharing its thoughts and its struggles, its triumphs and its failures, for in the glyphs the dead past has left a chart to guide the living present along the corridors of time.

In the 16th century, the area of hieroglyphic writing did not coincide with that of Maya speech. It appears that the hieroglyph originated in such lowland languages as Olmec and Zapotec. Though people may have used hieroglyphs at an early date, they seem to have never passed the rudimentary stages. Maya hieroglyphs on stone and wood are confined to the Classical period (AD 300–900). Inscriptions on monuments record the passage of time, often the close or decline of certain periods, and invoke images of the gods, the "rulers" of each day, to which they could bring fortune or disaster. Written codices comprised books of divination and a mixture of prophecy and history that were similar to the historical codices of Mexico. Three codices remain extant: Dresden Codex, Paris Codex, and Madrid Codex Tro-Cortesianus (in two parts), each named for the cities in whose museums the codices are currently exhibited. Maya hieroglyphic writing manifested a calendric system and also certain religious concepts of the Maya culture that reveal a mythology of surprising richness, demonstrating the independent growth of New World civilization.

The Maya culture is divided by scholars into four periods: first, the Formative or middle culture horizon in the second half of the millennium before Christ. During the latter part, the earliest known carving has been found, dated in terms of the Maya calendar at AD 320. Second, the Classical period, from about AD 300–900, saw the development of the great "cities," architecture, sculpture, and ceramics. At this time a series of sophisticated deities appeared that were no longer directly related to the soil or the elements. The culture became divided into two levels, a theocratic government and priesthood and a lay culture that remained simple and agricultural, with home industries, a simple family organization, and a religion built around the personification of powers of nature, which was served by a nonprofessional priest. Toward the end of this period, influences from Mexico made themselves felt. The third period, or the Early Post-Classic period, from 900 to 1200, followed a transition period when metal appeared. The first gold working area was Panama and Costa Rica. In this period, the Mexicans or the Chontal Maya conquered and settled in several large cities in Yucatán, including Chichén Itzá. Itza, the conqueror of Chichén Itzá, introduced Mexican architecture and religion, including the cult of Quetzalcóatl, the feathered serpent god, as well as militaristic organizations such as the fighting orders of the Eagle and the Jaguar. Influences from Tula also modified Maya culture. According to later records, some mural texts and codices were made during this period, but they no longer exist.

Concurrently with the Classical period of the Maya, the Mexicans were also developing a written language, which was not so highly sophisticated as that of the Maya and could more correctly be called picture writing. The pictographic writing of the Aztecs was too simple to record literature, offering no way of making general statements or expressing abstract ideas. Though there was no alphabet in this writing, a picture of an object or an animal could be combined with another and given a new meaning. This writing was taught by the priests who were entrusted with the education of the young boys.

Development of pictographic writing

Pictographic writing developed in several areas, including the Mixtec-Puebla region and Texcoco. Meanwhile, the Aztecs were becoming more powerful along the outer borders of a highly civilized region, and about 1200 they moved closer to the centre of activity. As the government became more centralized, reports had to be submitted, and pictographic writing provided a satisfactory medium for this task. Even after the Spanish conquest, these reports were still presented in the same manner and form. Even when the writing was scribed by the Spaniards, Indians continued to do the illustrations.

After the conquest, historical accounts were written that reiterated the past history of the principal Aztec regions. Much of what is known today about the early history of the Aztecs is derived from these works. A method of recording Nahuatl, the language of a large portion of Mexico, was combined with Spanish to supplement the graphic records. It is believed that some of the graphic records represent oral traditions possibly learned in chants that were recited on ceremonial occasions.

Historically, the only recognized attempt at writing an Indian language (other than by linguists) was made by Sequoyah, a Cherokee born at Taskigi, Tennessee, about 1760. The son of the mixed-blood daughter of Chief Echota and a German father, he became a trapper and hunter until crippled in an accident. In 1809 he became interested in writing and printing, and in 1821 he gave a syllabary of his language to the chief men of his nation, which they accepted. Two years later he visited the western Cherokee in Arkansas, where he took up residence. In 1824 parts of the Bible were written in his script and others followed in 1828. The *Cherokee Phoenix*, a weekly paper, was published, to which Sequoyah contributed, and he exerted much influence in the reorganization of Indian Territory by the government. He set out to find the origin of his language but died en route to Mexico.

STUDY AND EVALUATION

Many large collections of Indian folktales exist that are historically important, though they lack information necessary for a modern study of the works. To make such a study, the folklorist must have a biography of the raconteur and the circumstances and exact date of the collection. If the study is to encompass literary style as well as theme, the folklorist must know whether the tale was originally told in a European language or, if an interpreter was necessary, his relationship to the raconteur and his experience as an interpreter.

Anthropological and linguistic studies

In the 1920s and 1930s anthropologists experimented with a type of ethnographic recording in certain tribes, which served two purposes: it explained cultural activities and attitudes of a culture and supplied the anthropologists or folklorists with a new vocabulary not found in the transcribed folktales. The folktale has served as a source of study for linguistics scholars, and tales recorded in an accepted phonetic code have always been a great asset to their study also. In order to get more text of this kind, the famous anthropologist Franz Boas taught a Kwakiutl to write phonetic text, which was then translated. Anthropologists also realized that the folktale reflects the culture in which it is told and sometims keeps up with culture changes or, conversely, retains historic patterns of the culture. Again Boas pioneered in a study of Tsimshian mythology, recording the pattern and customs of Tsimshian life as revealed in the myths.

Students of mythology in the 19th century were interested in distributional studies or in following a plot or a group of motifs around the world to discover how myths spread and how plots disintegrate and become motifs in other plots. They concluded that the life of a folktale among preliterate people depended upon how often it was heard and remembered, and that each place it was found it became part of its history.

Studies have been made of personality traits of a culture as expressed in their tales, and scholars search for symbols that articulate human experience in a culture. A raconteur's analysis of the ethical code expressed in a story often reveals the ethics of a particular society. Such studies have been made by Margaret Lantis in "Nunivak Eskimo Personality as Revealed in the Mythology" and by Melville Jacobs in his analyses of the Chinook myths, *The People Are Coming Soon.*

Indians have attempted to collect and publish stories of their own tribes. So far they have not been very successful, however, because they have made too great an effort to conform to the literary style and taste of the non-Indian reader, and hence the tales have lost much of their vitality.

(E.Gu.)

Music

Native musicians of the New World have preserved many traditional songs and, at the same time, have also been receptive to European influence; thus, any examination of their music raises the problem of distinguishing native from hybrid music. This consideration of American Indian music involves an outline of the dominant features of native styles, such as melodic and rhythmic characteristics and the meaning of song texts, and includes a description of the principal musical instruments used. There follows an examination of the stylistic features of various Indian cultures within North America, Central America, and South America.

DOMINANT NATIVE STYLE

The definition of the native American Indian musical style is complicated by variety between tribes and within tribal repertoires. It is feasible to approach the problem by contemplating the songs in prominent native rituals of four different North American tribes—Iroquois midwinter rites, Dakota war (grass) dance ceremonies, Pueblo plaza dances, and Navajo medicine ceremonies.

An evident feature of the music is male dominance. Equally evident is the limitation of music to song, performed without harmonization and with percussion accompaniment. The singing voice is well supported from the diaphragm and has a pulsating quality caused by rhythmic expulsion of the breath. Yet within this basic vocal-tone quality the tribes show considerable variation. The voice of the Dakotas and other Great Plains Indians is shrill, loud, and ornate, compared with the full-toned vocalization of the other three tribes—especially the deep, rich Pueblo quality.

Melody and rhythm. Despite exceptions among other tribes, melodies are sparse, sometimes even monotone. Only rarely do songs expand beyond the notes of the five-tone (pentatonic) scale, for example, c–d–e–g–a–(c'). In Navajo songs there is a preference for the intervals of the triad, that is, for two successive rising or falling thirds (the third is the interval, or distance between notes, encompassed by three notes of a European major or minor scale plus the octave, as in bugle intervals, thus c-e-g-c′). The tones of the melody most commonly spread over the range of an octave (as, from c to c′; eight notes of a Western scale), although special song types may have narrower or wider ranges. Melodies characteristically descend from a high note, frequently by a sequence of repetitions of the theme on ever lower pitch levels. Sometimes they end with the maintone as the lowest note; sometimes they dip below the maintone but conclude on this note.

The melodic themes vary in complexity. They may include syncopations (accents not coinciding with the normal musical beat) and melismata, flourishes with many notes to a syllable of text. The musical metres are almost always in irregular patterns, in contrast with the regular patterns of two, three, or four beats found in most European folk songs. The theme may be repeated or may be varied in pitch level and length, or it may lead to a second theme or a free development.

Drummer and singer coordination

Although some chants flow in free timing, most melodies adjust their accents to the duple beat (alternation of two beats, one strong, one weak) of the accompanying drums or rattles. The melody may lag behind the accompaniment or may syncopate the instrumental beat; but it holds to the same tempo, or basic speed, as the accompaniment, whether speeding up, slowing, or maintaining a steady tempo. This occurs whether the singer himself is the percussionist or whether he follows a separate drummer. If the percussionist uses a tremolo in certain song sections, the singer continues with the basic beat. At all times the musical pulse of the singer reinforces that of the instruments.

This vocal-instrumental pulsation guides the dancers, especially in the self-accompanied Iroquois stomp dances with their bouncy step. At all times the song structure guides the dancers. The structure as a whole may consist of a series of short songs—from six to 100 or more. Perhaps there is an increase in tempo and force, as in the Iroquois bear dance. Perhaps there is a succession of paired songs, slow and fast, as in the Pueblo harvest dance. Perhaps each song is split into two parts, one marked by vibrato, the other by duple beat, with corresponding different dance motions, as in the Iroquois eagle dance and the Pueblo buffalo dance. Since the tunes are set—be they ancient or newly composed—the dancers know exactly how to follow the musicians. In Iroquois rites the dancers often engage in some improvisation within the basic framework, although the singers do not improvise.

Within these four North American groups and among other tribes as well, these definitions would require modification. Some tribes, as in British Columbia, use microtonic scales (*i.e.,* having intervals smaller than a European half step) and complex percussion rhythms. To the south, flutes and other instruments are used. In Latin America hybridization of European and Indian styles presents the challenge of disentangling native elements from imported elements.

The significance of song texts. The language and the meaning of the song texts provide evidence of the extent of European influence. Many texts consist of repeated syllables formalized within each tribe, *e.g.,* Iroquois "yo yowine," Plains "wida weha wehiyo." The meaningful words in native rituals may address the supernaturals, the animal spirits, the deities of the four cardinal points of the compass, or the sacred mountains. Navajo texts are especially rich in symbolic imagery.

European influences on text and tune

European influence manifests itself in various ways. Songs of the Peyote Cult, or Native American Church, may introduce the name of Jesus. Hymns of Great Lakes Christian Indians fit native words to European folk tunes or Wesleyan, harmonized hymn tunes. On a more secular plane, Oklahoma social round dancers sometimes include amourous English texts; yet the tunes are clearly indigenous. By contrast, Mexico's Aztecs have invented Aztec poetry to go with tunes in Spanish style to honour the Virgin Mary or the beloved. As the final stage of de-Indianization, the dance songs of the Zapotecs of Mexico combine love poetry in Spanish with languorous waltz-like tunes.

MUSICAL INSTRUMENTS

Musical instruments may be clearly native, clearly imported, or ambiguous in origin. Percussion instruments—drums and rattles—are the mainstay of New World instrumentation. In Arizona, Sonora (Mexico), and areas farther south, wind instruments, native or imported, add to the tonal richness. Stringed instruments have a tremendous vogue in Latin America. Despite their adaptation to native ceremonies and musical styles, they reveal their Iberian origin.

Drums: membranophones. As in many Asian tribal societies, the single-headed shaman's drum with its narrow, round frame is widely distributed. More unusual are the square drums found in British Columbia in Canada, Veracruz State in Mexico, and Guatemala. Other hide-covered drums are more localized. The Iroquois use a water drum made by stretching hide on a small, wooden keg partly filled with water. The same type of water drum also accompanies the incantations for the Midwestern Midewiwin medicine rite. A similar pottery drum serves the singers for the peyote rites of many tribes. The gentle tone of these drums contrasts with the power of the Great Plains powwow drum, a doubleheaded boomer suspended horizontally from a frame. In the drum society ceremonies, war dance ceremonies, and secular Oklahoma war dances, four men surround the drum and beat it relentlessly as they shout their aggressive tunes. The ceremonial drum of Pueblo dances, played by one drummer, is equally forceful but has a different, vertical shape; four or five drums can produce a volume balancing that of the 70-odd singers. These drums are always struck with a stick rather than by the finger.

Drums peculiar to Middle America

As exceptions, the Aztec upright, wooden, carved drum, the *huehuetl,* and the Maya pottery *kayuum* are finger drums. Skillful manipulation of the head produces various tones. The *huehuetl* is paired with the horizontal, wooden *teponaztli,* which is a slit-drum, a hollowed-out, carved log struck with sticks on various parts of the resonant body. The *teponaztli* is not a membranophone but an idiophone, an instrument whose hard body vibrates to produce sound. Another curious idiophone is the ancient *ayotl,* a turtle shell that was scraped with bone sticks in pre-Hispanic rites of the Olmec and Zapotec peoples of Mexico.

Rattles: idiophones. The forms and materials of rattles, which are classified as idiophones, are derived from the natural resources at the disposal of various cultures as well as from the purpose of the instrument.

The jingler. The jingler, or rattle, attached to a dancer's body or clothing, is probably the oldest form of rattle. Prominent in nomadic and hunting tribes, it frequently consists of animal hoofs or of imitations. Alaskan Eskimo dancers shake mittens with attached puffin beaks and belts with animal teeth. Deer hoofs are fastened to the belts of both the *maso,* or deer dancer, and the *chapayekas* dancers of the Yaqui tribe of Arizona and Sonora, Mexico, and also to bands worn across the shoulders of the peyote (*hikuli*) dancers of the Huichol, a tribe of northern Mexico. From northern Mexico to South America deer hoofs are worn on the girdles and ankles of curing shamans, or medicine men. Deer, peccary, or tapir claws are worn on the legs or ankles among Brazilian tribes such as the Kamakán, Apinayé, and the Amazonian Huitoto. Antelope, elk, goat, ox, or buffalo hoofs may augment or substitute for the deer hoofs, as on Iroquois dancers' knee bands in the knee-rattle dance. Among eastern tribes in the United States, they are used by the Shawnee and Delaware and in the Penobscot and Wabanaki leading dance. In modern times, metal cones in hoof shapes have been fastened onto the dress of the adolescent girl in the Apache puberty rite and onto dresses of women dancers among the Havasupai of the Grand Canyon. Siberian shamans wear iron, cone-shaped jinglers on their drums and kilts and collars, the iron itself conferring power over demons. Aztec dancers fastened gold, copper, or shell bells on ankles or breast. In South America snail shells or nuts are commonly substituted, as among the Brazilian Bororo and Amazonian Jívaro. The Incas of ancient Peru used anklets of fruits shells or gold.

Shaken rattles of animal origin. Deer-hoof rattles in

clusters are shaken by the Yuma Indians of Arizona and by kachina dancers of the Rio Grande Pueblos; by the leader of the California Diegueño *keruk,* or mourning rites; and by Brazilian Kamakán dancers. Bunches of hoofs are fastened to short sticks in the rattles of numerous men's societies of the Great Plains, particularly the dog societies of the Crow, Hidatsa, and Kiowa and the corresponding Oglala and Iowa Mawatani society. Among the Flathead of Montana such a rattle was used in the hysterical cures of the Bluejay shaman's dance and in bison-calling rites. Rattles of hoof clusters spread east to the Sauk, Fox, and Iroquois Indians, west to the California Hupa dancing doctors, and southwest to the shaman-singer of the Apache puberty rite. In California and South America the deer-hoof rattle is commonly associated with girls' puberty ceremonies. Among the Maidu and Karok of California, the girl herself shakes the rattle. Usually, older women surround the girl and thump long, hoof-tipped poles on the ground, as among the California Klamath, Tolowa, Shasta, Achomawi, and Maidu mountain tribes, as well as among the Chaco tribes of South America.

Deer-hoof rattles for girls' puberty rites

Sand-filled butterfly cocoons were fastened on sticks manipulated by the leader of boys' initiation rites of the Yokut, Maidu, Pomo, and Miwok of California. In the rain ceremony of the Arizona Papago tribe, the singer-dancers wear cocoons, along with bells and shells, and the Yaqui native dancers all tie strings of cocoons around their ankles.

Metal rattles. In recent times the Indian has taken with delight to the sleigh bells and metal-pellet bells (jingle bells), as well as to metal rattles introduced by the white man, preferring them to natural materials that are harder to obtain. The dancers and runners of the Hopi and Tiwa Pueblo Indians at Taos, New Mexico, and, generally, Oklahoma festival dancers tie them around their ankles, below their knees, around their waist, and in a strip from belt to knee.

Turtle shells. Another animal source for both worn and shaken rattles is the turtle or tortoise. With attached deer hoofs, a turtle shell is worn behind the right knee of members of Hopi men's societies and Snake societies and commonly by Hopi kachina dancers. Small tortoise shells are worn at the knees of the leading woman in Oklahoma stomp dances. In the eastern United States, Delaware reciters of visions shook a tortoise shell, and (a borrowing from the Cherokee) the Iroquois society of women planters passes such a rattle from singer to singer. In the Great Lakes region Huron shamans are reported to have shaken a tortoise shell, filled with pebbles, near the ears of their patients. Cure motivates the most spectacular use of the turtle rattle, namely by the therapeutic rituals of the Iroquois, Delaware, and Cherokee-Shawnee. The shells are cleaned and filled with cherry pits, and the neck is reinforced by inserting a wooden handle. In the Iroquois False Face Society ceremony, the huge turtles furnish instruments for "doorkeepers," the 10-inch ones for the singers, and the little ones for the False Face beggar boys.

Gourd rattles. Agriculture introduced the gourd rattle, which is always shaken by the dancer or singer, never worn. Its shapes and sizes are as varied as those of the squash and gourd, and it is ornamented with ingenuity. The Arizona Papago shaman, sometimes the Iroquois and Cherokee, leaves the stem on as a handle. Usually a wooden handle is inserted, perhaps decorated with beads or feathers or with carvings. Perhaps the largest ones are the pair used in the *maso,* or deer dance, of the Yaqui of Arizona and Sonora, Mexico. The smallest gourd rattles are the tufted rattles of the Iroquois eagle dancers. In between are the flat Hopi and the egg-shaped Cherokee rattles and the small round *sonaja* rattle common throughout Mexico, particularly in the *Matachini* ritual dance. These are an inheritance from the ancient Aztec *ayacachtli* rattle used, for instance, in the springtime ceremony. The designs of perforations that covered these calabash rattles have spread to northern Brazil and to California and have even been imitated in wood by the Tsimshian of British Columbia. Symbolic painted designs may cover the surface, particularly of the Hopi kachina rattles. Ritualistically, they should be filled with maize kernels, a few squash seeds, and, in the Southeast, grains of wheat. The Iroquois prefer chokecherry seeds. Nowadays unsymbolic materials are inserted: buckshot, pebbles, even macaroni.

Ornamentation of gourd rattles

Other varieties of rattles. Where gourds are not available, other materials are pressed into service. Tribes of the North Pacific Coast have developed a fine art of carving wooden rattles into animal and bird shapes. North American Plains Indians and South American Patagonian tribes make them of hide, in various shapes: spherical, doughnut-shaped, or flat disks attached to drumsticks. The Ojibwa (Chippewa) and Naskapi (Eastern Woodlands tribes) shaman's *cicigwan* resembles a small drum. The Iroquois and Cherokee-Shawnee have introduced cowhorn rattles, and the Ojibwa construct cylinders out of birchbark. The Yaqui *pascola* (clown dancer) shakes a wood-and-metal *sena'asom,* a form of sistrum, an ancient type of rattle consisting of small metal bars hung with copper rings and set loosely in a small, oval, wooden frame. Peruvian pottery and Argentine Araucanian basketry rattles add to the wealth of variety of materials used, but they by no means exhaust the list. For again civilization has introduced harsh substitutes in the tin can, spice box, and almost any old box that is handy: even for the sacrosanct Midewiwin ("medicine ceremony") of the Ojibwa and Menominee of the Great Lakes region.

Wind instruments: aerophones. In North America, flutes are limited to courtship, except for a whistle in an Iroquois medicine rite and in a gens (kinship-group) ceremony of the Meskwaki. In Mexico and southward, wind instruments provide colour and symbolic significance. At least two dances feature a one-man drummer-flutist who holds a flute in his left hand and plays a drum with his right. These are the *pascola,* or clown dance, of the Yaqui (performed with a cane flute and 15-inch [36-centimetre] drum) and the *volador,* or flying acrobat, dance of eastern Mexico. Such flute–drum combinations resemble the pipe and tabor combination found in Europe, raising the question of importation. Yet it is probable that this is a coincidence and that the one-man drummer-flutist of Middle America is native. In contrast, the penetrating, oboe-like *chirimía* of Oaxaca, Mexico, originated in Spain.

Flute–drum combination

Wind instruments have a long history in Arizona, Middle America, and South America. Archaeological repositories have proved that the Aztecs had many kinds of flutes of diverse materials, including double and triple flutes capable of playing harmonies. They also paired trumpets in harmony.

In Bolivia, Peru, and Ecuador the ancient panpipe is still in use. Its harmonized, plaintive, pentatonic melodies provide an enchanting accompaniment to ritual and secular dances. In South America, the long *botuto* horn of Venezuela resembles the alphorn of the Austrian Alps and the gigantic Tibetan trumpet. Among the Araucanians of Argentina the horn appears in two forms, both fashioned of bamboo—the doleful ten-foot *tutruka* and the more melodious, three-foot *llolkin.* Particularly in Central and South America, conch-shell trumpets are important ritual instruments.

Stringed instruments: chordophones. With one exception, stringed instruments used in Indian music are of Spanish origin. Despite their nativistic ideology, even Central Mexico's Indian performers of the *concheros* society manipulate their armadillo-shell lutes in guitar harmonies and with a brushing technique. In the *matachines* dance-dramas of the Pueblos and Yaqui, the accompaniment of fiddle and guitar or fiddle and harp uses tunes resembling those of England's Morris dances—harmonized, four-square, in diatonic (seven-note) major scales. Picturesque stringed instruments include the fiddles of the Tarahumara of northern Mexico. Small ukuleles, called *jaranas,* are plucked by the *viejitos* (little old men) dancers of the western Mexican Tarascan tribe. The only native stringed instrument is the Tarahumara earthbow. Serving as a percussion instrument, it consists of a bow held vertically upon a gourd set over a small hole in the ground. The bowstring is struck with a stick, the gourd and hole acting as a resonator.

The list of instruments gives some idea of their rich variety. Their playing techniques and their materials and forms show tribal and functional variety. So does the relation to melody and dance movement.

REGIONAL CUSTOMS: NORTH AMERICA

North American cultural areas include the Far North, the Eastern Woodlands, the Great Plains, the West, and the Southwest.

Decline of Eskimo's ancient songs

The Far North. *Eskimo music.* The Eskimos are rapidly losing their ancient songs for shamanistic cures and animal dances. They retain a shadow of the creative contests in the "drum dance" exhibits of individual songs with asymmetrical, complex rhythms and narrow-ranged, erratic melodies. All around Hudson Bay, the acculturated tundra dwellers delight in the hymnody of the Catholic and Anglican missions, singing "What a Friend We Have in Jesus" in the Eskimo language.

Far northern tribes. The far northern Indians of Canada—*e.g.,* the Catholic Dogrib near Lac la Martre, Northwest Territories, and the Anglican Cree near Rupert House, Quebec—have also become experts in plainchant and in native versions of "Nearer, My God, to Thee." Among the few native retentions are the Dogrib songs for the Hand Game and for the drum dance and the tea dance, social round dances. These songs are remarkable because they show similarities between these Indians of the Athabascan linguistic group and their linguistic relatives, the Southwestern Navajo and Apache. The Dogrib prefer triad melodies and vocal pulsations, carrying pulsation to extremes of speed and complexity. The few reports on the music of other northern tribes indicate a substitution of hymnody in the native language for native songs, even among the isolated Mistassini Indians.

The Eastern Woodlands area. In the Eastern Woodlands, all along the northern Atlantic Coast and inland to the Great Lakes (even to Lake Winnipeg in Canada), some older people deplore the young people's lack of interest in the Indian hymns, from the 17th-century chants of the Catholic Penobscot of Maine to the vigorous, 19th-century Ojibwa (Chippewa) revival songs, with piano, organ, saxophone, guitar, and male and female vocal harmonies.

The Algonkian musical renaissance. Algonkians old and young, however, manifest a resurgence of racial pride. They usually show their enthusiasm in public programs, in New Brunswick and Maine for St. Anne's Day (July 26); in Cape Cod, Rhode Island, and Long Island at the ancient harvest time, August. Women have played a prominent role in musical resurrections at various locations, on Manitoulin Island, Ontario, and in Michigan.

The Algonkian song-and-dance repertoires contain a few local vestiges of earlier tribal music, besides introductions by visiting Iroquois, Oklahoma, and Pueblo Indians, and some inventions. They always feature corn dances, war dances, calumet (peace pipe) dances, and antiphonal (alternating two groups of singers) stomp dances.

Survivals of antiphonal singing

Collections of surviving music of the Abnaki (Wabanaki) and Penobscot tribes suggest a traditional prevalence of antiphonal singing throughout the Eastern Woodlands as far west as the Mississippi River. This singing style survives among the Cherokee of North Carolina; the Seminole of Florida; and most potently among the Creek and Yuchi tribes, now removed to Oklahoma; and among the Iroquois of New York state and Six Nations Reserve, Ontario.

Traditional Iroquois music. In their scattered reservations, the Iroquois preserve a rich tradition of native, ritually functional music. They provide for individual creativity in the variations between various renderings of ancient songs and in new compositions for women's dance and the social fish dance. But they insist on tradition, admit no European influence on their music, and have been reluctant to accept the pan-Indian songs from Oklahoma.

Their vast and varied repertoire defies categorization. Most of their songs, however, reveal four styles, each with a separate historical origin. Some shamanistic medicine songs and individual men's songs recall Eskimo chants in their wavering, limited melodies, although they use much simpler, repetitive rhythms. Another style, for war and animals, fits into the definition at the beginning of this article, with pentatonic, sequentially descending melodies. These songs have two repeats, contrary to the quadruple repeats common in songs of the Great Plains Indians. In some ceremonies, women pick up the tune and render the second repeat during their dancing. The somewhat similar third style, exemplified by the eagle dance and several other rites, provides the most terse examples of the dual, Iroquois musical structure. Paradoxically, these songs probably emanate from the Central Plains. The moiety system, dividing the tribe into two groups of matrilineal clans, dominates the cast of singers and dancers. Each song has two repeats, within an extended series. Each melody—that is, song half—contains two parts: one with drum vibrato and tremulous movement and the second with a rhythmic beat and dance progression. The song cycle starts with a free, introductory invocation, and it ends with a more complex finale.

The fourth type is the antiphonal, self-accompanied song; it prevails in agricultural rituals. One distinguishing feature is the "rise" in the middle of the song. That is, after several repeats of the antiphonal theme, it reappears on a higher tone, with change also in the dance movements; then it subsides to several repeats on the original level. Thus, there is a three-part, not a dual, pattern. The Iroquois also use a more ancient and primordial type of antiphonal singing. Thus, there are numerous responses sung at the end of certain songs. These responses, primarily monotone with a temporary rise of one step, have in performance an insistent power that unites the song-dance leaders and the chorus of people, who sing the response.

Reciprocal influence from Eastern Woodlands tribes

The Great Plains. The Indians of the Great Plains have spread their influence far and wide—to the Eastern Woodlands Iroquois and the Pueblos of the Southwest. Their influence on the Algonkians of Wisconsin and Minnesota has been so strong that it has drawn them into the Plains rather than the Woodlands area. Thus influences of the Dakota tribe have fashioned the present Algonkian drum society and war dance and have displaced the ancient Great Lakes animal songs with their simple, repetitive themes and imitative dance movements.

Conversely, the Plains tribes of North Dakota, Manitoba, and Saskatchewan have borrowed several Algonkian rituals. In powwows they feature war dances with duple drumbeat and round dances with a triple beat (beats in groups of three: strong-weak-weak), and with a shrill female chorus an octave above the men. Within the dominant song-dance style, the war-grass dance displays such special characteristics as high pitch, wide intervals in the melody, and wide melodic range. The singers vary the intensity. They attack notes with barks, slides, glottal stops, hiccoughs. On a second rendition of a chorus phrase, they shift from the duple beat to four or six strong beats; then they continue softly, tapping the edge of the drum, gradually increasing to the final strong, loud volume. In Oklahoman versions of this type of dance song, the dance responds to the musical changes, but in the Northern Plains there is no corresponding change of step or movement.

The more northwesterly Plains tribes, especially the Salishan Flathead and Algonkian Blackfoot, do not include Algonkian rites. They intensify some musical features of the Dakotas—the pulsation, strident vocal quality, and the wide range of musical scales in war dances. But they also retain some old medicine songs and sun dance songs with a less dramatic style. The Flathead have substituted such Plains traits characteristic of the Dakota for the wavering, more subdued musical qualities of the Salishan tribes.

Complex melodies of British Columbia

The West. *The tribes of the Northwest.* The tribes of British Columbia share the dramatics of trancelike, Eskimo shaman dances, as well as their rhythmic complexity. But the British Columbia tribes have evolved a unique musical style, with elusive tonality, or musical orientation, around the maintone and clearly perceived notes of the scale. Thus, they use semitones, or half steps, and even microtones, with counter-rhythms of song and percussions, erratic musical metres, and complex song structures. Other special features are a drone (sustained note heard against a melody), which provides a rudimentary harmony; occasional use of simple flutes; and an extensive vocabulary of musical patterns and performance techniques, especially among the Nootka and Kwakiutl tribes. Their flamboyance differs from that of the Plains Indians and even more from the other western tribes in the deserts of California and Arizona and the Rocky Mountain Plateaus.

Music of desert and plateau tribes. The tribes of the deserts and plateaus can be grouped together because of the simplicity of their aboriginal cultures and musical styles. Unifying factors are ritualistic preoccupation with visions, cures, and death (as in the elaborate Yuma mortuary rites) and long, mythological ballads. They also share a nonpulsating, relaxed vocal quality, an undulating, narrow-range melodic contour, and simple rhythmic patterns. Variations among tribes include instruments like the Ute scraping stick and the Pima upturned-basket drum.

A special Yuman feature is termed the "rise," a higher pitch level in the middle of a song that recalls a "rise" of the Woodland stomp-dance song but without its antiphonal singing style. These simple people, however, have become very susceptible to Euro-American culture and religion and are losing their traditions and accepting Mormon hymns and jazz dances.

The Southwest (Arizona and New Mexico). Geographically, Arizona tribes such as the Pima, Papago, and Havasupai can be included in the heterogeneous Southwest, but their subdued musical styles differ from the styles of the vigorous nomads—the Navajo and Apache of the Athabascan language group and the richly endowed Pueblo-dwellers, with similar cultures but diverse languages.

The Navajo and Apache. The Navajo and Apache live miles apart and have been subjected to diverse influences, but they retain common qualities in their consistent preference for melodies with "bugle" intervals and their pounding percussion beats. Their social round dance songs and chants of the Peyote Cult are related to the Plains Indians. The Navajo corn-grinding songs and the masked *yeibichai* spirit dance suggest Pueblo influences, although the eerie falsetto voice and light rattling used in the *yeibichai* dance songs are distinctive. The Apache songs for the masked crown dance fit the incisive musical beat to the angular postures and gestures of the four mountain spirits.

Pueblo music and ritual. The Pueblo peoples, from the Arizona Hopi and Zuni to the Tewa of the Rio Grande Valley, have in the course of hundreds of years evolved analogous musical arts with local differences, such as greater complexity in the westernmost villages. The most sacred songs for the appearances of the masked kachina rain gods resemble songs for unmasked, public, summer rain and corn dances. These songs (specifically as studied along the Rio Grande) combine terse, traditional musical forms with elusive tonality and rhythm. In the rain dances and so-called basket dances, the men provide their own rattle-and-song accompaniment. In corn dances they and the female dancers are supported by numerous separate singers and a chorus. The male singers start on a low, growling pitch, sometimes increasing in speed from a slow tempo. In the course of three or four melodic themes, repeats, and interpolated melodic fragments, they raise their voices an octave and a half. Finally, they subside to the growl, marking time all the while with the right foot on the powerful, pulsating accents. While the dominant beat is duple, the metre shifts at times to triple beat or to a slower beat, which they call *t'a,* or "pause," then returns to the earlier pulsation. The rain dances are simple and stationary; the performers of the corn dances move in elaborate designs within an allover pattern of a slow and a fast dance.

Pueblo music in sacred dances

Two-part song structures and elaborate dance patterns govern a dance type that shows influence from the Kiowa and Comanche tribes of the adjacent Plains. The buffalo and game animal dances, eagle dance, and Comanche dance precede the slow-fast parts with an entrance song of evident Kiowa origin. The dance songs resemble the typical American Indian style of pentatonic, descending melodies, in contrast to the pyramiding, rise-and-fall melodies and elusive tonality of the agricultural songs. The fast dances tie in with the Plains Calumet dances and Iroquois eagle dances, having a repeated pattern of a drum tremolo, followed by a section with a regular duple beat. The wintertime animal dances follow diverse Pueblo patterns, with a repeat of the dance in several plazas and with four appearances during the day. These dances require traditional songs for specified occasions and new creations within the frame for other occasions.

In addition, various Pueblo tribes perform an assortment of unclassifiable dance-songs, such as the San Juan Deer Dance with its Apache musical characteristics. For public shows, Pueblo Indians of Taos and other northern communities show their expertness at secular, clearly Kiowa war dances, hoop dances, and round dances. Most Rio Grande Pueblos also display Spanish influences. On saint's day fiestas they hold a Catholic mass, with Roman Catholic chants and hymns in English or Spanish. At Christmas and at other times they perform a *matachina* dance (a ritual dance for men), usually with fiddle and guitar accompaniment. At Santa Clara and Jemez, New Mexico, the accompaniment is with voice and drum, and the dance movement is in native style. The *matachina* dance relates the Pueblos to Mexican peoples—the Yaqui of Arizona and Sonora, Mexico. The polytheistic religion of the Pueblos resembles that of the ancient Aztecs and Maya. But their indigenous styles of music and dance appear very different from the aboriginal and contemporary styles of Latin America, even from those of the adjacent tribes of northern Mexico.

Relation of the Pueblos to Mexican peoples

REGIONAL CUSTOMS: MEXICO AND MIDDLE AMERICA

The cultures in Middle America include both the tribes of northern Mexico and peoples of southern Mexico who are grouped with those of Central American countries such as Guatemala.

Northern Mexico. *Yaqui music and dance.* The Yaqui of Arizona and Sonora have had much contact with Southwestern tribes. They relate to the Pueblos in their ceremonial *matachina* dance, using the same kind of longways formations (two parallel lines of dancers) and instrumentation (fiddle and harp) but without the Pueblo farce of a bull killing.

At Eastertime this dance forms part of a festive complex in church and atrium. A fantastic, Jesuit-Indian Passion Play bypasses the drama on Calvary. It consists of stations-of-the-cross processionals, with plainchant wailing by women; surging groups of black-robed *pilatos* (Pontius Pilates), and wriggling, jumping, masked *chapayekas* clowns to spastic fiddle scratchings. It also features the native dances of the deer and his pursuers, the *pascola* clowns, next to a group of coyote impersonators.

Yaqui Easter ceremonies

For their animal drama the Yaqui have evolved their own native orchestra—for the deer an ensemble with rubbing of mechanically precise notched sticks and with a drum consisting of a half gourd floating in a bowl of water, along with subdued singing of ancient, symbolic deer chants; for the *pascolas,* first a fiddle and harp in jig tunes, then a one-man flute-and-drum in irregular, pentatonic tunes; for the coyotes a low, gurgling chant to drum and the dancers' brushing across a bow that they straddle. The repetitious tunes with their limited scales and the medium-loud production seem to contradict the free and forceful dance style. By their restraint they blend with the subtle sounds of the dancers' rattles, deerhoof belts, gravel-filled cocoons, and bells.

The various passive and active rattles of the deer dance interplay with the musical accompaniment. The cocoons swish with every step. The deer hoofs descend with the knee and foot in thumping steps, but in leaping steps their momentum causes them to syncopate—to work in opposition to the dance movements—to fly apart as the dancer descends and to strike together as he rises. Add to this the circular swish of one gourd and the alternately accented beat of the other. The *pascola* dancer shows a similar complexity, in the syncopated rhythm of the *sena'asom* rattle against the left hand. At times he vibrates it back and forth in front, with a motion of sowing seeds. He is probably replacing a native rattle by this brass-and-ironwood sistrum known in Mesopotamia and ancient Egypt.

Interplay of dancers' rattles and music

The Yaqui have been given much attention because of their accessibility and their extraordinary ceremonial arts. They seem stylistically related to other, less publicized tribes of northern Mexico.

Other northern Mexican peoples. Northern Mexico's

Uto-Aztecan tribes share with the Yaqui a medium-loud, nonpulsating song style, with repetitious, undulating melodies emphasizing the tonic and third in a scale using only the fifth, fourth, third, and tonic notes of a European major scale (as, g-f-e-c). The Seri Indians of coastal Sonora state show their affinity with Arizona's desert tribes in this singing style and also in their long, legendary narrative songs. East of the Sierra Madre Occidental Range, the Cora, Huichol, and Tarahumara have retained some examples of music in this same style. One might expect a link across the United States border in the *hikuli* ("peyote") songs of the Huichol, the alleged originators of the widely diffused Peyote Cult, yet the Huichol songs are quite distinct from peyote songs in the United States.

Middle America. The northern boundary of Middle America is rather vague, lying somewhere in the central Mexican state of Jalisco, where the Indians are largely acculturated to Mexican society. The area from Jalisco to the Panama Canal displays a bewildering network of native musical styles in mountain and jungle, hybrid and modern music, and rural and urban styles. It would be convenient to assign the flute and drum music to native rites and the stringed music to Spanish fiestas, but there are exceptions. Flutes, not stringed instruments, accompany the European-derived dances of *moros y cristianos* ("Moors and Christians") and *conquista* ("conquest") dramas with clearly medieval tunes. These and other dances, such as the *santiaguitos* and the *matachines,* are derived from European ritual dances for small groups of men. Cacaphonous flute ensembles hail the birth, marriage, and death rites of the acculturated Tarascan Indians in Michoacán state. On the other hand, stringed instruments appear in Carnival and Lenten festivals, in the armadillo-shell lutes of the *concheros* dancers, and in the fiddle accompaniments for the *arrieros* ("mule-drivers") dance. The shrill, oboe-like *chirimías,* probably originally from the Mediterranean island of Majorca, accompany fireworks fiestas in Oaxaca. Again, the delightfully sour village bands present clearly Euro-American marches and polkas.

Every fiesta is a conglomerate, with, perhaps, a native *volador* (flying acrobat) performance; a variant of the *santiaguitos–matachines–moros y cristianos* dances; morality plays with chants and fiddles; and, finally, *huapangos,* lively couple dances with fiddles in jig tunes.

To further confuse the issue, contiguous tribal groups manifest contrasting styles. In southern Chiapas state, city dwellers delight in the Indian *chiapanecas* girls' dance and its music. The mountain Tzotzil Indians of Chamula and Zinacantán, Chiapas, have devised their own versions of stringed music, with handmade guitars and harps, and, again, contrapuntal combinations (*i.e.,* with two or more simultaneous melodies) of trumpet, reed flute, and drum. In the nearby swamps, the Lacandón, an isolated branch of the Maya, maintain their ancient, shamanistic chants, their conch-shell trumpets, and prehistoric drums. Again, descendants of the ancient horizontal slit-drums of the Maya survive in the city of Mérida, Yucatán.

A special oddity is the marimba, a wooden xylophone probably derived from Malaya via Africa, with primitive forms extending even into South America. The well-constructed marimbas of Mexico and Guatemala serve various purposes, from Guatemalan religious dances to regional and jazz dancing in plaza socials of cities like Mazatlán, Salina Cruz, Tehuantepec in Oaxaca state, and Zacatecas in Zacatecas state.

Though it would be a vast simplification, it is not impossible to set off the native musical styles retained in mountains, jungles, deserts, and generally in rural settlements as distinctly different from the music encountered at urban political fiestas and tourist attractions.

REGIONAL CUSTOMS: SOUTH AMERICA

The same overgeneralization of rural–urban styles fits South American music, with qualifications. Native music survives among remote tribes of jungle and desert, but the highest Indian musical cultures remain in the Andes. Geographically, the distribution contrasts with that of Mexico, where native survivals surround the centralized cultures of the mestizos. In South America, simpler tribes have occupied the interior. The rural–urban distinction is similar on both continents, with Indian influence stronger in the villages and Iberian secular styles in the cities, especially on the coasts.

Musical traits of Amazon peoples. Amazonian tribes have proved to be fairly tenacious because of their inaccessibility. Some, like the Chaco tribes, have been losing their aboriginal arts. But other Amazonians display complex music for voice, percussion, and flute. The songs of two of the best known tribes—the Motilón of Venezuela and the Jívaro of eastern Ecuador—are medium-fast and generally medium-loud and show a preference for the interval of the third, as in songs of northern Mexico. Some Jívaro songs are pentatonic. The range varies from two tones to an octave. Frequently, the maintone lies in the centre. The rhythms are often complex and irregular, with triplets (three notes where two would normally lie) and dotted notes (two-note figures that either divide the beat into long–short values instead of notes of equal length or divide the beat into a snapped short–long rhythm known as the Scotch snap). The Motilón have some heterophonic songs, that is, songs in which the singers simultaneously vary the same melody in different ways. Such songs serve for amusement rather than for ritual.

Songs of the Motilón and Jívaro tribes

Andean music. Andean tribes, across the mountains from the Jívaro, also favour pentatonic scales, but they evolved a more sophisticated musical style during prehistory and in the period of Spanish colonization. They retain fragments of ancient ceremonial music, such as the invocation to the rain god on the Island of Taquila in Lake Titicaca—a repetitious tune for whistle and drum. The Pampa Hash, a district in Canas Province near Cuzco, Peru, perpetuates an ancient agricultural rite, with the flutes and chants both crossing each other and sounding in unison, or with chant accompanied by a background of two chords played on the *chillador,* a tiny, lutelike instrument. The elaborate, composite fiesta of the *chunchus* and *collas* near Cuzco combines native and hybrid components. A native prologue for side-blown flutes and drum is played on the eve of this continuation of the ancient Inti-raymi, the Inca festival of the solstice on June 24. A drama of *chunchus* ("Spaniards") and *collas* ("Indians") ends with the defeat of the *collas,* as in the Mexican *conquista* dramas. The music combines voices, flutes, conch-shell trumpet, and *chillador.* There is social dancing in the streets, and, finally, the *kacarpari* farewell music, for flutes and drum.

Among social dances, the *wayno* (or *huayno*), is preeminent. This paired longways dance (*i.e.,* in a double line of couples) in duple time sometimes uses a background of *sicuris,* or panpipes, their tuning corresponding to the Western G major scale with F natural. Highland mestizos prefer a combination of the *charango,* a five-stringed ukulele, with harp and other strings, sometimes with shifting metres, from $\frac{6}{4}$ to $\frac{4}{4}$. In either case, the melodies in pentatonic scales shift continually from a tonality suggesting a European major key in the higher register to a cadence, or stopping point, in a tonality suggesting a European minor key. The harmonies change correspondingly.

This uncertain major–minor tonality pervades the Andean music. It appears in the *chinguinada* for church festivals, with a basso ostinato (repeated melodic-rhythmic pattern); in the mestizo *yaraví* serenade and in the mestizo *marinera* couple dance, with its metre alternating $\frac{3}{4}$ and $\frac{6}{8}$ patterns. Other, more urban dances, such as the *vals criollo,* use European major and minor scales. They fall in line with regional couple dances of Venezuela, Colombia, the Pacific coast through Chile, and inland to the pampas.

Uncertain major–minor tonality of Andean music

Mestizo music of the coast. The Creole people of the coast and plains have been replacing the indigenous music of the mountains with their own music, especially with the ubiquitous *cueca,* or *zamacueca,* couple dance. Their string ensembles, analogous to the Mexican mariachi bands, play to fit waltz steps or *zapateados* ("heel strikes"), with syncopations and shifts of metre. At times the instruments provide counter-rhythms with the gay songs in major scales. The lively, popular *pericón* and *firmeza* dances reveal very little black influence in their music, in contrast with dance music of Brazil and coastal

Colombia; but they owe much to the *contradanza,* or longways couple dance, of Spanish colonial times.

Although North America's tribes did not mix native and European styles, the natives and mestizos from Middle America to the tip of South America have created infinitely varied hybrid musical styles.

STUDIES AND PUBLICATIONS

Musical fieldwork, recording, transcription, analysis, and publication in books, articles, and records have been prolific since the turn of the century. The early musical transcriptions taken down by ear were not too accurate and musical scores based on phonograph-cylinder recordings leave much to be desired. The improved quality of disc recordings about 1930 greatly helped fieldworkers and analysts. The tape recorder, especially in its transistorized form, has boosted the studies of tribal repertoires before their extinction and during changes and revivals.

At first the field collector and the musical analyst were frequently different people, anthropologists enlisting musicians to transcribe their field recordings, sometimes with success.

Musical transcriptions and analysis. The techniques of musical transcription and methods of analysis are in flux. Various scholars have employed machines for tonometric and sonometric transcriptions. Such devices, based on sound-wave frequencies, show melodic intervals more precisely than normal musical notation. Nevertheless, most transcribers have found it convenient—and generally easily readable—to use the conventional European musical notation, with various diacritical marks to show divergent pitches and ornaments. Some transcribers have copied the scores to show analogous musical phrases next to each other, for convenient comparison. Usually they include the corresponding texts with translations.

In the realm of musical analysis there have been many experiments. The most useful method for melody analysis is the long-standing system of "weighted scales," according to which the scales used in given melodies are presented in terms of frequently and infrequently used initial and final notes and important intervals. Presentations of music in the form of graphs have been useful in the determination of tribal styles and in the comparisons of tribal and European tonalities.

Other fields of American Indian musicology. One aspect of the study of American Indian music still underexplored is the relationship of musical rhythms and structures to their associated dances, though some workers have included descriptions and diagrams of dances. The process of music and dance coordination is laborious, little used; yet it is important for the future.

Another aspect, the harmonization of native tunes and the composition of Indian ballet music, has been exploited but with questionable success. As in tribal performance of traditional music, modern study and use of Indian elements in contemporary compositions combine a knowledge of traditions with creative imagination.

(G.P.K.)

Dance

The dances of the American Indian peoples are comparable in many ways to the folk dances of Europe. They represent forms passed down over centuries and modified through interaction with foreign and other Indian cultures. The origins are similar, lying in religious rite; in attempts to invoke magic and thus cure illness or assure success in food production, hunting, and warfare; and in such life-passage rites as birth, puberty, and death.

Nowhere among the many diverse Indian cultures is there a sense of dance comparable to that expressed in the staged art dance of the West. A number of influences from European dancing passed into the American Indian dance, but in many places the descendants of the aboriginal inhabitants of the Western Hemisphere have retained the traditional dances.

The treatment of American Indian dance in this article is meant to focus first on certain general features of dance and their manifestation in a number of areas. The diversities existing within this larger framework then become apparent through consideration of the dances of the several cultural regions or tribal groupings. (More detailed comparisons between American Indian dance and the folk dance of European and other peoples will be found in the article FOLK ARTS.)

GENERAL CHARACTERISTICS OF AMERICAN INDIAN DANCE

Among the essential factors in an overall picture of American Indian dance are the diverse kinds of dance, the organization of the dances in terms of participation, and the relations of man and deity expressed in the dances. In addition, a variety of other stylistic considerations are relevant, as are the foreign influences that have been absorbed.

Extent of dance forms. Many themes, typically the celebrations of life crises, developed in the New World during millennia of residence, migration, and exchange. These were most prominent in the marginal cultures of California, Venezuela, and Tierra del Fuego in the most southerly reaches of South America. Mortuary rites were prominent in the northland and the deserts. War and hunt dances have had different degrees of prominence, their greatest development being among the hunters in the Great Plains of North America. So-called animal dances varied according to the local fauna, a tiger mime belonging to tropical peoples and a bear cult reaching across the northern part of the New World and into Siberia.

Religious magic, or shamanism, practiced by societies or individual priests is probably derived from such Siberian tribes as the Tungus and Chukchi. In various forms and used usually for cure, it extends to southeastern Brazil but is most potent and most trance-oriented among the Eskimo. From Mexico, and probably earlier from Peru, agricultural rites fanned out into the southeastern woodlands and the Southwest. More recent than the other rites, their forms show enrichment from Iberian rituals.

Patterns of participation. A distinction between performer and spectator has long existed in American Indian dance, though it is not the artificial separation that characterizes much of Western stage dancing. This latter condition has occurred only with the performance, largely in North America, of dances for tourists and during Indian participation in folk dance festivals or regional "powwow" gatherings.

Dancer-spectator interaction

Spirit impersonations, including maskings and noise, were used in widely separated areas to frighten nondancers. Specific instances of such practice included the puberty rites of the Yaghan and Ona of Tierra del Fuego; and among the Kwakiutl Kusiut of British Columbia in Canada, similar ceremonies were held in dance houses with a definite performing area. Except for a few specialized rites

By courtesy of the Museum of the American Indian, Heye Foundation, New York; photograph, M.R. Harrington

Masked Iroquois dancer of the Cayuga tribe performing False Face Society dance, 1907. A turtle rattle is held in the right hand.

like the eagle and False Face dances, the change of roles among spectators, dancers, and musicians is characteristic of the sacred ceremonies of the Iroquois longhouses in the Eastern Woodlands region of North America. White visitors are welcomed, especially into such dances for the Creator as the great feather and drum dances; and all Indians, from the aged to mothers with babies in arms, are expected to join in.

Among the Pueblos of the U.S. Southwest, the dancers remain separate because they require special rehearsals and ritual blessings. When they emerge from their sanctuaries, or kivas, onto the dancing plaza, they dance to invoke rain, health, and other blessings for the people from the supernatural spirits. After the ceremony the Indians often join in less formal social dances uniting all participants and observers. Though they have religious connotations, as among the Iroquois, these dances are secular, and anyone may enter or drop out at will.

Socially determined roles in dance. Visitors may not perceive the patterns of social organization reflected in the dances. It is clear that men or women alone begin some dances and the other sex may then join in, and that men monopolize some dances, women others. Less clear are the relations, especially complex in the longhouse dances of the Iroquois, between the moieties, the complementary divisions of the tribe based either on kinship or on ceremonial function. In all Iroquois dances, specific traditions decree the nature and degree of male and female participation and whether they dance simultaneously but separately or in various sexual pairs or other combina-

Courtesy of the Denver Art Museum, Colorado

Detail of Ojibwa birchbark scroll showing a moiety pattern ceremonial dance, *c.* 1875. In the Denver Art Museum, Colorado. Detail 46 × 41 cm.

tions. The leader of the dance and song and his helper, however, must be of different moieties, whether they lead from the floor or from the sidelines. When women enter a dance line, singly or with another, they must pair with a moiety opposite, or "cousin."

The Iroquois moiety pattern is crossed by another comprising various public or secret societies whose members are bound together for life, often joining the society during illness or other catastrophe. These societies perform such dances as the False Face curative rites, the female mortuary dances known as *ohgiwe,* and the dances of the sexually integrated Bear and Buffalo medicine societies. Elsewhere, religious dance societies were based on ages, as in the male warrior societies of the northern plains.

Some of these societies crossed local and even tribal boundaries, as in the extremely complex organization of Mexico's *concheros,* whose intertribal hierarchy runs from a *capitán general de la conquista de Tenochtitlán* through various local commanders and military ranks with specific duties to the attendant devil, sorcerers, and mythological figures. The *concheros'* claim to an Aztec heritage is given considerable credence despite some Spanish mixture, but, compared to that of the pre-Columbian Aztec, their ceremonial organization appears to be limited.

Aztec round dance for Quetzalcóatl and Xolotl, detail from a facsimile Codex Borbonicus (folio 26), *c.* 1520. Original in the Chamber of Deputies, Paris. 76 × 20 cm.

By courtesy of the Newberry Library, Chicago

Early Aztec dances

In the organization of, and participation in, dance according to priestly or social status, the earlier Aztec dances were images of the completely theocratic government. A far cry from the democratic customs of the Iroquois, the circumscribed ceremonial roles of Aztec actor-dancers reflected the social structure comprising priests, nobles and warriors, commoners, serfs, and slaves. The priestly and noble-warrior classes took active roles in the many festivals of the Aztec calendar, and the priests trained noble youths for the priesthood or in dancing and singing. Warrior youths performed ceremonial combat, and the warrior orders of the eagle and of the ocelot fought captive slaves during certain festivals. Both commoners and serfs constituted the audiences, the former sometimes doing serpent dances with the nobility, the latter sometimes ceremonially attacked and routed by the priests. There were age roles and sexual roles as well, but the slaves, captives of sacred war with other city-states or purchased in the marketplace, as victims, had a passive role in the ceremonial activities.

Opposites played dramatically against one another in these rites: nobles and commoners, old and young, male and female. The warrior orders symbolized the clash of the sky and light with the earth and darkness, and, as aggressors against poorly armed captives, they enacted the drama of sacrificer and victim. It was the priests and the passive slaves, however, who played the supreme moment of the ritual. The circle of social gradations was closed as the highest and the lowest ranks performed together the most crucial act of the Aztec dance-drama, human sacrifice.

Religious expression in dance. Religious symbolism is significant even in the human interactions of the dance. Men often symbolize phallic, aggressive supernatural beings and rain-bringing deities, whereas women symbolize actual fertility. In Iroquois ceremonies, women represent the "Three Life-giving Sisters"—*i.e.,* the spirits of corn, beans, and squash, with no mimetic representation. Similarly, Pueblo women promote plant and human fertility by their symbolic dancing.

With no mimetic elements, the basket dance of the Tewa Pueblo rites includes invocations for plant growth and for the transmission of the gift of human life. The ceremony symbolizes the woman's central role in sustaining of the life of the pueblo.

Degrees of stylization of animal representations

In the animal realm there are also separate roles for men and women. Ottawa and Winnebago women imitate the winged flight of wild swans and geese, whereas the Iroquois and Pueblo men represent eagles. Both sexes join in the mime of supernatural bears and buffalo in ceremonies of the latter tribes, more realistically in Iroquois dances. In the Southwest, especially in the New Mexican pueblos, male representations of supernatural deer show gradations of stylization ranging from the naturalistic portrayals of Taos pueblo to the semistylization in the Santa Clara, San

Ildefonso, Cochiti, and San Felipe pueblos, in which sticks replace forepaws, to the abstract, upright deer dancers of San Juan pueblo and masked, unreal deer in the kachina dance of the Hopi. The solo deer dancer of the Arizona and Sonora, Mexico, Yaqui, always a man, is relatively realistic, with mime of the hunt and killing.

On the whole, in both Americas agricultural dances tend to be abstract, and animal dances are usually decidedly mimetic. The animal maskers of British Columbia are terrifying portrayals of supernatural beings. In Venezuela,

Miguel Salgado

Yaqui deer dancer from Sonora, Mexico.

masked beasts of the former Maipure puberty dance, *mauari,* threatened a pubescent girl and her cortege and had to be subdued magically.

Here and there the man-deity relationship is expressed in hand gestures. The Kwakiutl of northwest North America evolved codified ceremonial sign languages, as did the Pueblos, Aztecs, and Maya. In the San Juan Pueblo of New Mexico, the appearance of the rain gods is heralded by two ceremonial clowns using traditional gestures. Looking for the rain gods in the clouds, one of the clowns claps from his hands the ashes representing a cloud. He looks upward, shading his eyes to indicate his attempt to see into the distance. This gesture is always used whenever the clown speaks of what he "sees." The clowns repeat this action toward the four points of the compass, continuing to see the approaching rain gods, who bring with them the rain cloud. Similar performers may appear in the pueblo's plaza, outside the kiva, or sanctuary. Dancing, unmasked clowns enact motions of luring rain, of sowing seeds, of digging, and of gathering the plants as they rise from the ground. Clowns also appear in the men's spring dances and in the summer corn dances. After their entrance with a large group of male and female dancers, the corn dance singers station themselves in an arc near the drummers. They fit gestures to tunes and texts that are composed for each occasion but follow a traditional pattern and trend of ideas, beckoning to the rain gods in their cloud homes in the north, west, south, and east.

Invocations to the directions survive in the Great Plains and Great Lakes area, especially in the pipe dance. A single man offers a pipe to the thunderbird in the east, south, west, and north, moving clockwise, then to the deities of the sky and earth. Similar invocations to the directions survive in Middle America as fragments of the rich gestural symbolism of the Aztec and Maya. There, as in New Mexico, counterclockwise patterns emphasize the cardinal points.

Patterns and body movement. This religious, nature-oriented concept of space differs from that of Western man's folk and art dance, which has only geometrical or emotional significance. The geometric ground plans, however, show similarities with Western practices. The circling dances are sunwise in areas of former hunting people and countersunwise, or widdershins, among agriculturalists. Serpentine line dances also prevail among agriculturalists, among the Iroquois, Pueblo, Middle American, and Andean peoples. Among the Iroquois, many round dances are open, with a leader, coincidentally resembling dances of the Balkans of southeastern Europe.

Nature-oriented concepts of space

Aboriginal line dances are quite simple, whether they are single file or double file. Spanish influences are apparent, however, in the elaborations used in the double-file dances of the Southwest and Latin America. Spanish and Austrian influences probably inspired the couple dances of Latin America, for aboriginal dances juxtapose male and female partners only rarely, and never in overt courtship mime.

In body movement, the Indian style differs from that of northwestern Europe but coincidentally resembles the posture and quality of Serbian dancers. Characteristic of Indian dancers is a slightly forward-tilted posture, forward raising of the knee, flat-footed stamp or toe–heel action, and tendencies toward muscular relaxation and restraint in gesture. This basic style of body movement varies not only from area to area or from tribe to tribe but also from dance to dance and even from one individual to another. The agricultural dances generally are performed with an upright posture and an easy manner. Male war dances may include complex gyrations and flexion of the torso, as do animal dances. Vision and clown dances may induce bodily distortion.

Throughout Europe and the Americas, the posture varies with sex. Women tend to be more erect than men, to lift their feet and knees less, and in general to perform in a more restrained manner. Except for the war dances, Indian women use the same steps as the men, within the stylistic restrictions. In the woodlands of eastern North America, everyone proceeds with the stomp step, a flat-footed trot. In the Pueblo area, where men and women use a similar step, the dancers also specialize in a foot lift and solid stamp. In certain dances, especially clown, animal, and war dances and in some social round dances, individuals often invent variants of the basic steps. Sometimes the innovators borrow American ballroom steps such as those of the Charleston, though they adapt them to their own

By courtesy of the Rare Book Division, the New York Public Library, Astor, Lenox and Tilden Foundations

Dancer of the Hidatsa Dog Society, showing style of body movement used by North American Indian dancers. Aquatint by Karl Bodmer, 1834. 38.7 × 53.3 cm.

styles. The steps and formations of the Indian dance, as well as the overall structure of a dance or ceremony, follow the music closely. This connection is covered in more detail in the foregoing section on Indian music.

Foreign influences. Among the influences from the Old World, the dances of northern Europe and the Anglo-American dances have found little acceptance. The Longhouse Iroquois reject all white men's dances. Among the few influences are some Oklahoma jazzlike, war-dance steps, an Indian two-step danced by couples, a waltz in a Pueblo social dance, and numerous couple dances of Latin America.

Iberia, on the other hand, has not only loaned some steps but has metamorphosed the dances of Middle America and western South America to Argentina. The hybrid dances reveal every conceivable shade of stylistic adjustment.

Introduction of Iberian elements

Adaptations of mazurka, waltz, and other European dance steps occur in some ritual dances as well as in such secular couple dances as the Mexican *jarabes.* The European origin, reinforced by the Europeanized music, is obvious despite the subdued manner of performance. The most significant dances are the religious dance dramas taken over from such medieval religious productions as *moros y cristianos* (Moors and Christians) and the *matachina* dances—both for trained male societies.

Black influences on Indian dance are scattered—the *huapango* couple dances of Vera Cruz, Mexico, the carnival dances of the Black Caribs in British Honduras, the *tamborito* of Panama, and couple dances of coastal Colombia. Except for the Indian-influenced *candomblé de caboclo,* a ritual of the *candomblé* sect (a variant of the voodoo cult), the religious dances of Brazil comprise only African and Portuguese elements. Such popular Latin-American ballroom dances as the samba of Brazil contain no Indian elements.

REGIONAL DANCE STYLES

The most distinctive tribal dance customs originated in response to animistic religious beliefs—*i.e.,* that all objects and living things have living souls. The customs changed with prehistoric and historic migrations, with intertribal contact, and, since European contact, with upheavals in the way of life and thought. Although many dances became extinct, some survived European influences; others are amazing hybrids or new creations of the period after European colonization.

To give an accurate understanding of the role of dance in traditional Indian society it is necessary to examine both dances that became extinct as European influences weakened tribal customs, and dances that have survived, with or without European modification.

Eskimo. The traditional shamanistic exhibitions and masked animal rites are being replaced by Western-style square dances among the Eskimo. The most prominent ritual figure was the *angakok,* the shaman who communed with spirits by the rhythm of a single-headed drum and by ecstatic dancing, usually inside an igloo.

Whaling dances of the Eskimo

Formerly Eskimos held elaborate outdoor ceremonies for whale catches and similar events. In Alaska, preliminaries included the rhythmic mime of a successful whale catch, with a woman enacting the whale. A sprinkling of ashes on the ice drove away evil spirits, and there were incantations and songs when leaving shore, when sighting the whale, and before throwing the spear, all of them songs that the "great kashak" sang when he created the whale. As the whale was towed in, Fox Islands men and boys danced naked in wooden masks that reached to their shoulders. At Cape Prince of Wales on the Bering Strait, the whaler's wife came to meet the boat in ceremonial dress, dancing and singing, and boys and girls performed gesture dances on the beach. Then inside a circle of large whale ribs, the whaler's wife and children performed a dance of rejoicing. On the west coast of Hudson Bay in Canada, communal feasting, dancing, singing, games, and shamanistic performances took place within a circle of bones or one of stones. The men's motions consisted of vigorous and angular arm jerking and jumping, the women's of curving gestures and swaying with the torso and arms, in a seated or standing posture.

Eastern Woodlands. In the area from the Atlantic coast to about the Mississippi River and across the Great Lakes and the St. Lawrence River, dream, medicine, plant, war, calumet (ceremonial peace pipe), and animal dances predominate. Among the northern tribes of this area, mortuary and hunting rites are dominant; among southern tribes, corn, bean, and squash rites are most frequent. The recurrent dance pattern is a counterclockwise circling by large groups, with a running step or stomp to antiphonal singing (alternation of two groups or of leader and group). Medicine rites are often exclusively for female or male members of a society, but dances for hunting or agriculture admit men, women, and children. In winter and in war or hunting ceremonies, men are the organizers and leaders; in summer and in agricultural ceremonies, women are featured performers.

Photo Trends

Moros y cristianos dance-drama from Guatemala. The Moor is on the right and the Christian on the left.

Iroquois ceremonial dances

The Iroquois continue to maintain their ancient ceremonies and a large repertory of dances and songs, including rites for crises of life and for animals and plants. They also have acquired steps and dances from other tribes, especially those of formations in two straight lines. The Iroquois bear dance combines former hunting associations both with a clan-origin legend and with a curative society. When the bear spirit is displeased, he causes neurotic spasms in a person and must be appeased in a ritual at midwinter or in private summer ceremonies. The focal personnel consist of the patient and paired conductors, dance leaders, and singers from opposite moieties. Ceremonial songs and ritual offerings are followed by group dancing in which visitors and society members participate.

Although the Cherokee of the Smoky Mountains in North Carolina and Tennessee, a southern Iroquois people, have animal dances, they emphasize corn dance ceremonies. The Creek, Yuchi, Seminole, and other tribes of the southeastern United States greatly emphasize the summer green corn harvest ceremony, or Busk. Before the removal of many of those tribes to reservations in Oklahoma, they acquired few dances outside their own traditions. They carried the stomp circling to its utmost development by winding the line of dancers into a spiral or even into four spirals at the four corners of the dance ground. They differed from the northerners in preferring an outdoor dance setting.

Dance ceremonies of the Algonkian tribes

Among tribes of the large Algonkian family, survivors on the northeastern Atlantic coast of North America have long forgotten their tribal lore. The stomp dances performed until a few decades ago by the Penobscot of Maine and Narraganset of Rhode Island have experienced

Crop fertility dance of an Algonkian tribe in Virginia, detail of an engraving by Theodor de Bry after a watercolour by John White, 1590. In the collection of the Thomas Gilcrease Institute of American History and Art, Tulsa, Oklahoma. 31 × 22 cm.
By courtesy of the Thomas Gilcrease Institute of American History and Art, Tulsa, Oklahoma

a strong revival. Algonkian tribes around the Great Lakes share many of the medicine and animal dance ceremonies known to the Iroquois, and the more southerly groups hold corn dances. The Ojibwa (Chippewa) in the Upper Peninsula of Michigan and the Menominee and Winnebago of Wisconsin have maintained a hunting dance and a special wild-rice ceremonial danced in September when this crop is harvested. These groups show the influence of the adjoining Great Plains tribes in some of the circle dances, men's war dances, and buffalo dances.

The Great Plains. In the area extending from the Mississippi River to the Rocky Mountains and from Texas and Oklahoma into Canada, the dream dance ritual is made part of a visionary cult associated with boys' puberty and with a votive sun dance ceremony. During the one to four days' duration of the sun dance, usually held during the summer solstice, the participants abstained from food and drink. Dancers painted their bodies in symbolic colours and carried an eagle-wing bone whistle in their mouths. To a large drum and special songs, they circled in procession and saluted the sun with lamentation. They danced in place facing the sun, and continued until they fell unconscious or achieved their vision.

By courtesy of the National Collection of Fine Arts, Smithsonian Institution, Washington, D.C.

"Bull Dance of the Mandan Indians," oil painting by George Catlin, 1832. In the National Collection of Fine Arts, Washington, D.C. 70 × 57 cm.

The calumet (peace pipe) or peace dance originated in the tobacco rite of such northern Plains tribes as the Crow, Dakota, and other Sioux tribes. Its most elaborate development, however, was in the central plains ritual of the Pawnee and the neighbouring Omaha, Iowa, Ponca, and Osage. The war dance is organized into male war societies. Women have few such societies, although they perform a scalp dance. Animals are associated as tutelaries, or guardian spirits, both in the vision and war cults. The most spectacular hunting ceremonies, such as the bull dance of the Mandan Indians, developed from the economic significance of the buffalo herds. Buffalo rites merged with sun and war ceremonies and spread to tribes in other areas. The individual warrior, his prowess, and dancing skill were extolled as women progressed clockwise in a closed circle, with a sideward shuffle or bounce unlike the running step of the woodlands Indians.

The Northwest Coast. Indian tribes along the Pacific coasts of Washington and British Columbia developed masked medicine dances and elaborate fishing ceremonies, such as that performed for a bountiful salmon catch. Their two most striking types of ceremonies are the potlatch, a feast and a dance for display and distribution of the host's wealth, and the midwinter initiation ceremony. Lasting several months in a special dance house, this rite initiates young men into a ceremonial society and includes many highly individual masked enactments of totemic spirits.

The northern desert and California. Southerly tribes, such as the Havasupai of the Grand Canyon and the related Yumans, developed agricultural dances. The Yuman Mojave (Mohave) stress cremation processions and ceremonies, but, like the Navajo, they also have curative and animal dances with long song cycles. In this area, the vision quest ceremony is at its peak, and in southern California the Diegueño and Luiseño aided the vision by means of a narcotic, *Datura.* The Northern Plateau tribes, such as the Paiute and the Salishan, individually danced themselves into trances. In this area arose the Ghost Dance, a hypnotic circle dance that spread to the Great Plains in the 19th century. The ceremonies are frequently addressed to the spirits of the dead. There are also many two-line dances, especially among the Ute and southern Paiute. The innumerable small tribes of California shared some of the preoccupations with vision, cure, and death, as well as the seed and root gathering economy of the tribes adjoining them on the east. They specialized in elaborate masked ceremonies for the initiation of boys and less elaborate circle dances for girls' puberty rites. The more northerly groups also stressed exhibition of dexterity and costuming.

The Ghost Dance

The Southwest. The semi-arid desert country from the Rio Grande west to the Mohave Desert of southern California and into northern Mexico and the southern Rocky Mountains is subdivided into three tribal areas: the Pueblo farmers along the Upper Rio Grande, the Zuni of New Mexico, and the Hopi of northern Arizona; the Navajo nomads, now turned shepherds; and the desert tribes that include agriculturists such as the Pima, Papago, Yaqui, and former nomads, such as the Apache. The Pueblo dwellers of New Mexico and Arizona perform medicine rites and many winter animal and fertility dances. But the cycle of summer corn ceremonies and continuous prayers for rain form the core of their ceremonialism. The dances, organized by a male priesthood, are mostly well-drilled collective performances. Summer and winter clan groupings or moieties dominate ceremonies in alternation rather than through interaction as among the Iroquois. The most characteristic step is a stamp followed by a foot lift in a stationary line. This predominates especially in the very sacred dances held in the kivas, or sanctuaries. Semi-sacred dances in the village plaza add other steps and formations such as double lines, circles, and interweavings.

The most spectacular public dances of the Pueblos are the corn dances or *tablita* dances, after the women's tablet crowns with cloud symbols. They recur at various times during the spring and summer, with most pageantry after Easter and on the Pueblo's saint's day. The Indians pay homage to the patron saint in an early morning mass and a procession to the plaza carrying his image, followed in

Masked medicine dance of the Clallam Indians, British Columbia, Canada. Oil painting by Paul Kane (1810–71). In the Royal Ontario Museum, Toronto. 76 × 46 cm.
By courtesy of the Royal Ontario Museum, Toronto

the evening by a recessional to the church. By tradition each performance of the corn dance includes a slow and a fast dance. In the slow dance for entering the plaza, a chorus of seven to 70 older men shuffles across the plaza, singing and invoking the rain gods. A banner bearer leads a double file of 12 to 200 dancers, with a pair of men always ahead of a pair of women. For 10 minutes they trot counterclockwise around the plaza. Following a pause, the singers form an arc, and the dancers line up face to face in two or four long files. They cross over, circle, and interweave in elaborate formations. Clowns meander in and out among the lines. The entire set is repeated at the other end of the plaza, and the group retires. The two moieties make alternate appearances. On the last appearance they combine, the two choruses singing simultaneously.

The Hopi snake-antelope dance

One of the most famous ceremonies is the snake-antelope dance of the Hopi in Arizona, a rite in which snakes are released in the four directions to seek rain. It includes swaying dancing to rattles and guttural chant, circling of the plaza with snakes, and ceremonial sprinkling of corn meal on the principal dancers by women of the snake clan.

Masked dancers are a striking feature of Pueblo ceremonialism. The kachina dancers are sacred and represent the rain gods. Clowns with various names represent an ancient ritual heritage; in their black-and-white striped disguise of paint, they are eerie and also comical. Pueblo masking influenced neighbouring tribal dances such as the curative *yeibichai* of the Navajo. Curative ceremonies, with long song cycles, are emphasized by the Navajo, along with circular social dances, recalling those of the Great Plains tribes. The Apache have developed a spectacular masked dance, called the *gahan,* to obtain cures but chiefly to celebrate a girl's coming of age. They also have rites for vision and divination, sometimes with the aid of a vision-inducing communal drinking ceremony. The male dance style is strong, angular, even acrobatic, while the women's style is subdued.

Courtesy of the Denver Art Museum, Colorado

"Hopi Snake Dance," watercolour by Awa Tsireh, c. 1920. In the Denver Art Museum, Colorado. 62 × 48 cm.

Mexico and Middle America. The triple teams of *pascolas,* or wooden-masked clown dancers, of the Yaqui Indians in Arizona and the Sonora desert in Mexico, descend from prehistoric clown-shamans. They dance without masks in semi-Spanish style, then, with masks, in an aboriginal, mimed deer hunt. By contrast, the *chapayekas* clown society recalls the Pueblo *tsaviyo* clowns in their antinatural behaviour and hide masks. The serious, vowed-membership society of the *matachini* dancers ties in with the semi-Hispanic *matachina* dancers of the Rio Grande tribes and of the northern Mexican mountains. These dances are related to those further south such as the various types of *moriscas.* A fantastically hybrid Passion drama points toward Middle America.

A few indigenous dances survive in the mountains of Mexico. The circular *mitote* remains the ritual dance of the southern Tepehuan and other tribes of the Sierra Madre Occidental, like the Tepecano, Cora, and Huichol. Men and women skip in a counterclockwise circle, five circuits in one direction, then five in the other. A shaman accompanies with native songs, assisted by a musical bow on a gourd resonator. Formerly a deer dance followed the rounds.

The *hikuli,* or peyote dance, held in November, follows Huichol and Tarahumara pilgrimages for peyote. The dance of the Huichol is the more ecstatic. After consuming the trance-inducing peyote, men and women move in a counterclockwise progression, leaping jerkily and twisting their bodies.

The *rutuburi* is the typical ritual dance of the northern Mexican Tarahumara for three agricultural festivals—rain, green corn, and harvest—and for death and memorial rites. After triple invocations by a shaman, the women cross the dance space six times, then circle counterclockwise, holding hands and leaping with a stamp from left to right foot.

The *voladores,* or flying acrobats

Tribes of the Sierra Madre Oriental also engage in native survivals such as the *quetzales,* with great disc headdresses, and *voladores,* or flying acrobats. After ritual preludes to a fiesta, the flyers first dance around the pole with their musician and his flute and tabor. Traditionally there are four dancers, but the Otomí prefer six, including a man-woman, Malinche. They climb up a rope ladder and seat themselves on a small framework near the top, while each in turn dances on a two-foot central platform. During the flight songs they launch themselves into space with ropes tied around their waists and descend head down in 13 ever-widening circles until they reach the ground and land on their feet. The musician often performs special acrobatics, leaning back in an arc as he sits on the platform or jumping or pirouetting as he salutes the four directions. He may slide down one of the ropes amid acclaim.

The numerous clown dancers throughout Middle America are usually associated with various rituals. Some impersonate animals, like the *tecuanes* (tigers) of Guerrero state. Some, like the *viejitos* (little old men) of Michoacán state, combine native and Spanish features. Some, like the *catrines,* wear ragged modern outfits and poke fun at the bourgeoisie. Always connected with the dance dramas held in conjunction with religious fiestas, the clowns are not simply comics but also social satirists.

The semi-urban Indian fiestas of Middle America include three types of European-influenced dance dramas: the *morisca* and its variants, *moros y cristianos, santiagos, matachini,* and related plays; Passion plays; and *posadas, pastorelas,* and Guatemalan *loas.* These are often true dramas, with dance and music. The dialogue may be in Spanish or in an Indian language or a mixture of both.

Moriscas, ritual dances deriving from ancient European ritual dances, abound during carnival (the week before Lent begins) but also occur at Corpus Christi (second

By courtesy of the Museo Nacional de Antropologia, Mexico City

Voladores of Mexico.

Thursday after Pentecost), Santiago (St. James Day, July 25), and on other feasts. In the drama of *moros y cristianos,* two factions mimetically tangle in arguments and battle with the ultimate victory of the Christians and the conversion of the Moors.

Posadas and *pastorelas* are danced episodes of the Christmastime *coloquio de los pastores,* or "Play of the Shepherds." Most popular in southern and central Mexico, New Mexico, and Texas, the *posadas* are generally processions by city boys and girls who go from house to house asking gifts and lodging and singing special hymns. On Christmas Eve, youngsters dance quadrilles of *pastores* and *pastoras* (shepherds and shepherdesses). The Guatemalan *loas* are short religious dramas presented at Christmas, during Holy Week, and on other holy days.

Secular couple dances

In form, the regional, secular dances are distinct from the ritualistic dances. Except for the circular *mitote* types, they are all for couples who do not touch. Among the best known are the *jarana* of Yucatán, the *zandunga* and *llorona* of the Zapotec Indians of Oaxaca state, the *chiapanecas* of Chiapas state, and the *huapangos* (called *fandangos* in some locales) of the east coast. The *jarabe* has many regional variants, as the *jarabe tapatío* (or Mexican Hat Dance) of Guadalajara, the *jarabes* of Tlaxcala and Michoacán states, and the *zarabanda* of Guatemala. Sometimes the theme of flirtation or female coyness blossoms forth in humorous interludes. Contests of improvisations to *la bamba,* widely danced in the Mexican Gulf Coast area, also contribute to the merriment of the Veracruz *huapango.*

These regional couple dances blend European and native steps and styles and use European or European-derived instruments and tunes. Even though they are mestizo dances, Indians enjoy them and give them a native flavour—*e.g.,* in steps or posture. The dances' European origins must usually be deduced from the style—Andalusia for the *zandunga,* the flamenco *fandango* for *huapangos,* and the *jota* of Aragon for *jarabes.*

South America. South American dances resemble those of Middle America. Native dance rituals have their last strongholds in the jungles and highlands of the interior. Iberian dance-dramas show their relationship with those of Middle America. Couple dances are prominent.

Northern South America. In Venezuela several tribes of the Orinoco River held masked puberty rites. For example, among the Maipure and Baniva tribes, Mauari, the spirit of evil, is impersonated by a dancer who is fully covered with red and black body paint, a face-covering of puma or jaguar pelt, and a crown of deer antlers. At the initiation of a youth or girl, he emerges from the forest with maskers representing lions, tigers, deer, bears, and other wild beasts. Their bloodcurdling growls and howls mingle with the groans of the *botutos,* the sacred trumpets, to fill the night with a gruesome din. With wild leaps and contortions, they dance around the neophyte and four shamans.

Ancient puberty ceremonies evidently had wide distribution, with distinctive features, in the Amazon Basin and in the Mato Grosso highlands of Brazil, the Gran Chaco region of Bolivia and Paraguay, and Patagonia and the Tierra del Fuego in Argentina. They formed part of a complex emphasizing shamanistic cures, death rites, and animal dances for the hunt.

Today the most prominent dances of Venezuela are the many versions of the *morisca* on Christian holidays and a dance of medieval devils on Corpus Christi. The *joropo,* a lively couple dance in waltz time, is the national dance of Venezuela.

Profusion of courtship dances in Colombia

Colombia has fewer religious celebrations and a greater profusion of courtship dances. The *joropo* extends into eastern Colombia. On the Caribbean coast the *bullerengue, lumbalu,* and the circular *cumbia* mingle Indian reticence and black ebullience. The Colombian *fandango* derives more from Spanish diversions. The national dance, the *bambuco,* originated in the Andean zone. Male and female partners, waving kerchiefs, enact a courtship mime of pursuing and flirting, combining dignity with sensuousness.

The Andean region. Along the Pacific coast and in Ecuador, Peru, Bolivia, and Chile, native dances have received Spanish influences. On Catholic holidays the northern Andean Indians perform vestiges of aboriginal animal rites for the vicuña, the tiger, and the condor by a solo mime within a large circle. Conveniently, Corpus Christi synchronizes with the Inca solstice ceremony, *intiraymi,* and presents an excuse for the reappearance of the native sun god in a huge, gold disc headdress.

The Araucanians of Chile, who resisted Incan influences, preserve a shamanistic harvest ceremony, the *ñillatun,* a combination of Christian ritual and an indigenous mass dance. During interludes two men mime ostrichlike rheas, with shawls as wings.

The highland fiestas of Andean Indians show more European influences than the *ñillatun.* Generally timed in accordance with Catholic festivals, the dances feature battles of Moors and Christians, clowns, demons in fantastic masks, and European animal characters. Some dramas ridicule the Spanish. The mountain fiestas often conclude with gay couple dances.

The coastal celebrations feature widespread couple dances of mixed Indian-Spanish origin. Only the *cumbia* shows Negro qualities. The mournful *huayno* (or *wayno*), *yaraví,* and *sanjuanito* of Ecuador, Peru, and Bolivia reveal Incan origins in their restrained manner and haunting music. The gay *marinera* of Peru and the headstrong *cueca* are more Spanish. The *fandango* and *pasacalle* are also at home in the urban ballroom.

The southern plains. Argentinians have developed such ritualistic mestizo (Spanish-Indian) dances as *las cintas,* a maypole dance, and the *sumamao* ("beautiful river") celebration. Argentina shares some Andean social dances, as the semi-Indian *carnavalito,* a collective circle dance. The richest repertoire of Argentina and adjoining Uruguay developed among the cowboys, or gauchos, of the Pampas. Their dances reveal more of the Spanish elements than those of the Andean regions. In the *pericón,* the dancers manipulate handkerchiefs; and in the *pericón, chacarera,* and *gato,* couples perform *zapateados* as groups. In the *bailecito, cuando, firmeza,* and *cueca,* they enact courtship mime with emphatic waltz steps. Other dances are urban, as the *milonga* of the lower classes and the sophisticated Spanish-French tango ballroom dance. Andeans and Argentinians have exchanged dances. In fact, the diffusion of dances is much greater in this area of South America than in Middle America.

STUDY AND EVALUATION

The secular pan-Indian dances of North America, such as the Oklahoma dances, the round and war dances of plains tribes, and the stomps of southeastern tribes all have in modern times spread from coast to coast—to the salvation of tribes who lost their heritage but want to perform something Indian, especially in urban gatherings. The most copious and reliable materials on these and other aboriginal dances are strewn through the works of anthropologists, folklorists, and a few musicians. General descriptions are often incorporated into anthropological studies and into notes on earlier observations by colonists, missionaries, and 19th-century scholars. Lacking a major specialist, Middle American Indian dances are in large part unstudied in a scholarly manner. Essential to future studies is an examination of the arts in their cultural context. It is equally important to recognize the dance as an expressive art, to learn and analyze the movements, and to present them in dance notation alongside musical scores. Such presentation facilitates intertribal and intercontinental comparisons. The materials must stem from field work, but they can be supplemented by the many motion pictures in college archives and museums and in repositories such as the Wenner-Gren Foundation and the American Philosophical Society.

(G.P.K.)

Visual arts

NATURE AND ELEMENTS

The role of the artist. The very use of the word art suggests one of the basic differences between Western and American Indian concepts. For not only did few Indian groups allow art to become a major way of life, as in the West, but many Indian languages even lack a term for "art" or "artist." If one wished to refer to a beautiful basket or a well-carved sculpture, it was usually necessary to rely upon such terms as well-done, effective, or perhaps powerful (in the magical sense). And the concept of an artist was largely of a person who was simply better at the job than was another. Generally, artists were accorded special significance only where wealth was a major factor in the culture. Wealthy chiefs, particularly on the Northwest Coast, hired stables of carvers for their personal aggrandizement, giving rise to a class of professional artists. Yet, the fact that the talented artist was in such demand did not set him apart as a person of undue importance; rather, his role was important at the moment his product was in demand—and if he happened also to be a religious, political, or war leader, so much the better.

Although Indian people, unlike Westerners, may not consider artistic skill in terms of a superior individual attribute, the difference between a well-woven basket and a careless piece of work or a particularly well-designed carving and a crudely made example did not go unnoticed. Fine workmanship commanded a premium, even in pre-European times, and with the advent of the dollar system, it was even more highly prized.

Collective versus individual art. The basic role of the American Indian artist is the same as that of the artist in any culture: to arouse an emotional response in his audience. In Indian cultures, the artist's ability to communicate successfully with his own people depended largely upon his recognition of the force of tradition. The social organization of the various tribes allowed less latitude for experimentation than Western cultures and usually compelled him to work in familiar channels. (The frequent failure to communicate with a non-Indian audience does not necessarily mean that the Indian artist has failed as an artist but that many of the cultural, racial, social, and political traditions involved in his work have proved to be almost insuperable barriers to understanding.) Yet, within this rigid framework of tradition, there was sometimes a surprising degree of freedom of expression. There are recorded instances of individuals having made considerable changes in the art (and the economy) of their tribes. Perhaps the most striking have been the careers of Nampeyó (1859?–1942), the famed Hopi potter, and María (1881?–1980) and Julián Martínez (1897–1943), of San Ildefonso pueblo. Through sheer individual talent these people achieved a personal triumph by developing a style that not only was copied by other artists but in time also was regarded as "traditional" in that particular village. Although there is no way of knowing how often this happened in the past, there are suggestions that it occurred at Mimbres, among the Haida slate carvers, and quite possibly in some areas of the so-called Mound Builder cultures of the Southeast.

Role of tradition

Origins of Indian decorative designs

The origins of most Indian decorative designs cannot be traced accurately today; most of them are lost in antiquity. Many obviously came from natural forms, while others are simple developments of geometric or lineal motifs. Some have become so interwoven with alien concepts—Western, after the advent of the European, for example—that it is impossible to completely unravel their sources. There is evidence, however, that some of the original forms were creations of individual artists and were often inspired by what the Indians called a vision. The vision is closely akin to a dream. To the Indian, the dream world was a mysterious, supernatural land, where his soul, which had left his body, participated in many strange activities and saw many strange sights. Since many of the designs or creatures that he saw were regarded as protective forms or beings, sent as signs from the spirit world, he would carefully re-create this dream world during his waking hours. If he were not an artist, he would occasionally describe his dream creature so that the proper individual could record it on hide, in wood, or in stone. But since these supernatural vision designs were extremely personal, they were usually recorded by the individual himself; hence, they vary tremendously in aesthetic quality.

Because art designs were regarded as personal property, an artist could buy a design or receive it as a gift from its creator, but to appropriate and use it for his own purposes was taboo. This custom amounted to quasi-religious and social copyright.

Importance of utilitarian considerations

The function of art. Since the early Indian peoples travelled extensively, their household goods had to have the maximum utility; thus, Indian art objects are basically intended to perform a service—for example, to act as a container or to provide a means of worship. Only in later years could these peoples afford the sophisticated luxury of household possessions that did nothing but "look nice."

The particular utilitarian form that Indian arts take often reflects the social organization of the cultures involved. Political and military societies seem to have found their major art forms in the world of weaponry, pageantry of costume, and panoply. This is most pronounced in the Plains, Aztec, and Inca civilizations, all of which reflect the dominant warrior cult forces active in their arts. Those cultures in which life was heavily governed by religion—the so-called theologies of America—tended toward a greater degree of ceremonial art than those in which life was less ritualized. All of the aesthetic expressions that have come down from the Maya, for example, obviously reflect the considerable weight of theocracy that existed in their world.

Generally, but not necessarily, the best of Indian artwork was applied to those objects intended to please a deity, soothe the angry gods, and placate or frighten the evil spirits. Through such means, the Indian sought to control his environment and the human or supernatural beings that surrounded or threatened him.

Some specific articles were reserved solely for religious uses, and some were for secular needs alone. Decoration does not always provide a clue as to these uses. Some of the most highly revered religious articles are completely devoid of ornamentation—in fact, may be rather ugly—while others are highly embellished. Sometimes plainware bowls were used for food preparation, while other peoples did the same chore in polychrome bowls. Many objects served a dual function: normally, they were used for everyday household purposes, yet under a different set of circumstances they could fulfill a religious function. Beneath the surface, there was a magic at work, and, in initiated hands, a mundane article might release its supernatural power, calling upon unseen forces to aid the owner. This power might be visually evident in the form, shape, or decoration of the object, or might simply be "believed in" no matter what the physical state or appearance of the object might be.

Supernatural powers of art objects

The aim of the Indian artist was not merely to set down realistic records but to create the semi-magical designs so common in primitive art. He quickly realized that he could not draw a tree as perfectly as it could be made by the Creator; so, with common sense, he did not try. Instead, he sought the spirit or essence of the tree and represented this in his design. Carvings, paintings, effigies, or "realistic" portraits are not simply pictures *of* people or objects; they embody the essence of that particular subject as well. In a sense, this can be called a form of witchcraft, since it captures the soul of the object or the person. This semi-magical character of Indian art is difficult for the Western mind to understand. Not infrequently, the non-Indian will ask, "what does that design mean?"—a question that makes little sense to the artist. He might reply, were he so inclined, that it meant what he wanted it to mean. Also confusing to the questioner is the fact that the Indian often attaches names to designs, largely for convenience. When asked, an Indian will frequently call a given design a "leaf," or an "arrowhead," when what he actually means is that the design is "leaflike," or "leaf-shaped," and so on. But the inquirer immediately translates this to mean that the design signifies a leaf or an arrowhead and tries to impart a "story" to the overall visual concept that may have no basis in reality insofar as the original artist is concerned.

Ritual was often interwoven into the very process of creating Indian art. The Westerner, whose attention is devoted primarily to the product and not the process of art, is satisfied to define the Zuni war god Ahayuta as wood sculpture of a religious nature; other details are simply added ethnographic data. To the Zuni, however, it is vitally important that the wood come from a tree that has been struck by lightning and that it be ritually prepared for carving. This is equally important in the making of an Iroquois False Face mask, which must be carved from the trunk of a living tree—hence the term "live mask." The tree is ritually addressed before the carver begins, and the mask and the tree are "fed" tobacco before separating the two. Such prescribed ritual is of equal, if not more, importance than the artistic skill employed in the production of the work. If the ceremonial acts were ignored, the article would lose its efficacy—and might even prove dangerously counteractive. This ritual aspect of Indian art, which permeates most of the ceremonial paraphernalia, is extremely complex and must be considered throughout the creation of the work of art.

Not all Indian art, however, was religious or political. There was also a considerable amount of mundane, humorous, and even profane art produced by most cultures. Although much of the eroticism has disappeared in the Puritan fires that continue to burn the Westerner, sufficient examples remain from prehistoric and recent times to indicate a wholly relaxed freedom of expression reflecting a healthy, naturalistic outlook.

Materials. Working in the materials natural to their respective homelands, the various Indian cultures produced art that reflected their environment. Those peoples living

Wooden figure of the Zuni war god Ahayuta, *c.* 1900. In the Denver Art Museum, Colorado. Height 70 cm.

Courtesy of the Denver Art Museum, Colorado

in heavily forested regions, for example, inevitably became gifted sculptors in wood; those for whom clay was a major resource became skillful potters; and those living in the grasslands became fine basket weavers. There is virtually no medium, however, that has not been explored and mastered by the Indian: jade, turquoise, shell, metals, stone, milkweed fibre, birch bark, porcupine quills, deer hair, llama dung, sea lion whiskers—all were used by the artist to lend colour or texture to the finished product. In many instances, such materials became desired commodities in themselves, to be traded over great distances; for certain objects were not regarded as "official" unless they were manufactured from a prescribed material, and, especially for religious purposes, a substitute could not be tolerated. Often, in such cases, the materials became, in a sense, currency, for they achieved a standard value within the economy, with ready acceptance wherever they were in vogue.

Role of art materials in trade

The relationship between material and design in Indian art was quite different from that in the Western tradition. The Western painter usually imposed a design on the artificially limited surface of a flat, rectangular canvas; and the sculptor, following predetermined spatial arrangements, imposed a shape on his material. On the other hand, the Indian painter and sculptor were less likely to force their materials to conform to a preconceived design. They tended instead to adapt their design to the natural outlines of their materials, which often happened to be a complete and therefore irregular buffalo hide, a tree branch, or a stone. This naturalism is one of the most pleasing aspects of Indian art and often demonstrates the artist's remarkable ability to incorporate the natural form into his composition.

REGIONAL STYLES OF AMERICAN INDIAN VISUAL ARTS

The term "Indian art" covers an extremely broad category, encompassing all art expressions of the original inhabitants of the Americas and their cognate descendants. It thus includes not only varied and completely disparate cultures but also spans great time sequences—from the mid-20th century back to prehistoric times. (Sur-

Diverse natural materials used by North American Indians.
(Left) Iroquois buckskin shoulder-bag decorated with porcupine quills and deer hair, *c.* 1750. In the Linden-Museum für Völkerkunde, Stuttgart, West Germany. Length of pouch 24 cm. (Centre) Karok twined basket, *c.* 1890. Height 15.5 cm. (Right) Woodland Cree birchbark container with scraped-surface motifs, *c.* 1870. Height 19 cm. (Centre and right) In the Denver Art Museum, Colorado.
(Left) By courtesy of the Linden-Museum fur Volkerkunde, Stuttgart, Germany, (centre, right) courtesy of the Denver Art Museum, Colorado

viving artifacts clearly demonstrate that ancient man was already possessed of considerable aesthetic ability; flint, for example, was carefully flaked into attractive, well-balanced forms; and stone carving and pottery were capably handled.)

Although the dissimilarities between the artistic expressions of different cultures and different times are great, there are also similarities; for the borrowing of art forms from distant and occasionally alien peoples was a common practice. Objects in museum collections reveal, for example, that prehistoric merchants travelled thousands of miles seeking and bringing back from other tribes such ornamental materials as feathers, shells, jade, and turquoise. This far-flung trade expanded the limits of tribal styles, for the Indian merchant returned with new ideas as well as materials. In time, new designs and motifs became part of the stylistic concepts and traditions of his own people. Intertribal marriage, too, affected regional styles. While in some tribes marriage within the group was required, in others it was forbidden. In the latter case, the girl—who was often the artist—took her own artistic traditions to the new group, into which they were subsequently incorporated.

It is becoming increasingly evident that there were common forces at work in the art of various groups, even if widespread in time and space. There are certain symbols that are widely encountered, and some would seem to have had similar significance over a wide area. It is likely that trade routes or political hegemony levied the major influences upon this phenomenon, and it may be said that the depth and spread of symbols is relatively equal to the migration of the peoples involved. In Middle America, for example, the so-called Plumed Serpent motif is to be found in one form or another in almost every culture, and this motif extends even into the United States, where it is encountered in visual form as well as in legend. The existence of the feline deity virtually throughout South America, from the south up into the northern Andean region, is another instance of the travel of an idea and a visual element. Certain customs also have enjoyed wide acceptance; for example, the role of trophy heads, the use of masked personations, and winter solstice New Fire ceremonies. And each of these customs was accompanied by related visual art expressions.

Despite the similarities between the art forms of different cultural groups and different times, one cannot speak of Indian art as though it were a single concept. Just as there were several hundred native tongues, dialects, and speech forms, so were there an equal number of tribal styles, motifs, and design forms. In trying to establish a common aesthetic bond, the well-schooled researcher generally finds as many differences as he does similarities.

When two completely different peoples move into a common area, such as occurred with the migration of the Athabascan Navajo into the Pueblo Southwest, the eventual result may be a melding of cultures, the loss of certain ancient individualities—since each contributes to the new expression—and the emergence of new aesthetic qualities. It is not certain just how skilled the Navajo weavers were when they arrived in the Southwest, but the Pueblo people were highly developed in that art. Subsequently, the Navajo not only learned new weaving techniques and designs but in time also improved upon the acquired Pueblo methods, transferred the sex role of the weaver from male to female, and matured as far more sophisticated craftspeople. On the other hand, under the same circumstances, surprising differences can sometimes be found; for example, while the Hopi and Zuni people live almost side by side and under similar cultural conditions, it is quite possible to identify the art products of both groups without great difficulty. This is equally true of cultures in ancient times, such as the Aztec and Mayan, or in another time and another region, the Sioux and the Crow.

It is in those tribes or cultural entities that at one time were part of a whole but have subsequently split off that one most often finds common themes, art elements, and cultural patterns so similar as to be confusing.

To most readily understand some of the artistic impulses active among the Indian tribes of the New World, it is convenient to take them in geographical sequence, north to south.

North America. The aesthetic products of the prehistoric Indian artist in North America are perhaps the least well known to the non-Indian public. This is partly because these early people left few spectacular architectural ruins as compared with their Latin-American cousins. This is not to say that architectural monuments did not exist. Spanish accounts report that great temple mounds were in use in the Southeast at the time of the first European entry, in the mid-16th century. But most of these structures were of perishable wood and have long since disappeared—as have most examples of the great use of colour (in which the ancient folk gloried) and their tremendous range of textiles.

So many Indian materials were perishable that scholars have little by which to judge their arts and must, in effect, evaluate a people by only a small proportion of their achievement.

American Southwest. In the United States, it is only in the Southwest that any major prehistoric architectural sites are to be found. The monumental stone cliff dwellings that remain are eloquent testimony to the culture that existed there. Progressing from a simple pit house through aboveground homes, these people moved out onto the plateau regions of Arizona and New Mexico and built

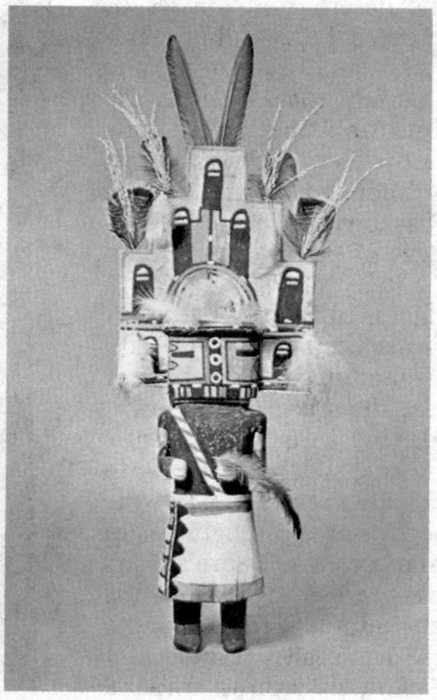

Southwest Indian arts.
(Above) Hopi kachina wooden doll, *c.* 1925. In the Museum of the American Indian, Heye Foundation, New York City. Height 64 cm. (Left) Classic Navajo blanket, *c.* 1855–65. In the Newark Museum, New Jersey. 110 × 156 cm.

(Right) By courtesy of the Museum of the American Indian, Heye Foundation, New York; (left) collection of the Newark Museum, New Jersey

Pueblo Bonito

remarkable multistoried structures, some—such as Pueblo Bonito in New Mexico—sheltering hundreds of families in over 400 rooms.

These apartment houses were well suited for the demands of their environment; their walls were of stone, clay, and sand mixed as an adobe—although true mixed adobe in block form did not come into use until the arrival of the Europeans. The thick stone walls provided excellent insulation, being warm in winter and cool in summer. Heights reached to seven stories, although most villages were of three or four levels.

Major divisions of these early Southwestern Indians, often called by the generic name *Anasazi,* include the Hohokam, of southern Arizona; the true Anasazi, of northern Arizona–New Mexico; and the Mimbres, of southwestern New Mexico. In addition to these groups—each of which produced a style of its own distinct from all others—were dozens of lesser subgroups that archaeologists have been studying for decades in an effort to assemble the pieces of this giant jigsaw puzzle.

The people living in the pueblos produced some of the most successful Indian art work. They were masters of weaving, painting, and particularly of pottery-making. Their weaving techniques long antedated the arrival of Spanish sheep; a native cotton provided ample fibre for intricate weaves coloured with native dyes. Mineral and vegetable pigments provided colourful decorations when applied with a fibre brush to wood, clay, or to white-plastered walls in a fresco technique. Fortunately, abundant kaolin deposits yielded high-quality clay for the creation of excellent pottery forms. Although small stone effigies have been found, sculpture was not a highly developed art form. Pueblo art is essentially linear or geometric in design and reveals a preference for applied decoration. The large underground kivas (rooms used for religious purposes) were decorated with murals executed in brilliant mineral-pigment colours.

Pueblo art became a strongly conventionalized art, held to relatively rigid forms. This characteristic was determined, no doubt, by the closely knit communal nature of a culture that depended upon close cooperation for survival. At its best, early Southwestern art is marked by technical competence and fine control of line and form; but it reflected little experimentation, tending more to rework established patterns in many intricate designs.

Conventionalized forms and technical competence

Because of this conservatism, the culture of the contemporary Pueblo Indian shows striking parallels to that of his ancient ancestors.

In more recent times, the richest variety of art expressions is to be found in the Southwest. Whereas in other regions the arts flourished and waned, here they are still active forces in the lives of the Indian people. Almost all of the crafts practiced in prehistoric times are still practiced today, along with some newly introduced expressions.

Following early trade routes, merchants brought new ideas to the Pueblos, departing with the finished products they had sought. Thus, new creations continued to develop, and new markets strengthened—as continues to be true today. Yet, because of its essential conservatism, Pueblo art remains a closely related continuum of ancient techniques, affected more by the introduction of new tools than of new ideas.

Along the same trade routes came invading tribes from other regions, particularly the Navajo and Apache, who subsequently settled in the Southwest and in time surpassed their teachers in certain arts that they adopted, improved upon, and made their own—notably, silversmithing and weaving. Whereas Pueblo weavers once dominated the textile field, the work of the remarkably inventive Navajo weavers became highly sought after in the late 20th century. Silversmithing, another famed Navajo art, is more recent; it was only in 1853 that the first Navajo smith took up the tools of his craft, but within the next century Navajo jewelry and ornaments acquired a wide appreciation.

As in the prehistoric era, Southwest sculpture has failed to develop as a major art form. The most active sculptural work in the Southwest is reflected in the carved and painted cottonwood kachina dolls of the Hopi and Zuni, which have enjoyed wide popularity as collectors' items. Many variations of these wood carvings are also found in altar and shrine figurines, which are not produced for commercial consumption.

The crafts of basketry and pottery are moderately active. Both face the problems of economic balance: the problem of the time invested as against the economic return of the craft object exacts a serious price. By and large, a craftworker today can enjoy a more stable income from manual labour, or by clerking in a store, than from any creative activity. This is particularly true if one includes the time required to go into the desert, find grasses or pigments, then wash, grind and process them—all preparatory to the tedious hours spent actually forming the products for later sale. It seems certain that, in time, the former will entirely disappear, and only the luxury-scale pottery arts will continue. Even now, very little pottery is made for native use; it is largely intended for the outside market. Although pottery and basketry are produced in much smaller quantity, the work is of better quality than in years past.

Specialization in Southwestern art

Specialization has long been a factor in Southwestern art and has become increasingly so in recent years. Certain tribes produce almost all of the small carved fetishes, or tiny drilled shell and stone beads; the Zuni favour intricately worked silver jewelry with tiny turquoise settings, while the Navajo make use of massive silver castings with heavy turquoise sets. The Navajos also make most of the heavy rugs and textiles, while the Hopi supply lightweight ceremonial kilts, sashes, and similar costume fabrics.

Another art form that may have been brought from the north, but that was more likely adopted from Pueblo culture, is sand painting (more accurately termed dry painting). The use of a variety of finely-ground mineral pigments, which are allowed to trickle through the fingers to form a variety of complicated patterns, has become uniquely Navajo. These designs provide a focus for curing ceremonies.

Great Lakes–Midwest. The existence of rich textile art in the prehistoric Middle West is known, but its range and development are lost in hundreds of years of history from which few examples survive. Examples of basketry and wood are similarly rare. Enough of these perishable items have survived to indicate that these people had mastered the arts, but not enough to enable scholars to judge their aesthetic development. What has survived in profusion is stone, worked skillfully and in many ways. Pottery, too, though not of highest quality, and copper ornaments have been found. Of the relatively perishable substances, finely carved and incised shell is common, which, along with bone, indicates the artistic range of these early peoples. The quantity of objects found is impressive. Numerically significant groups, the peoples of the region were active in the production of materials and implements with which to meet the challenge of their environment. The function of all of the recovered examples of stonework is not known, but it is known that much of the archaeological wealth was ceremonial in nature, indicating a highly organized civilization.

"Effigy mounds"

Ritual structures existed, such as the so-called "effigy mounds"—great piles of earth fashioned in various forms

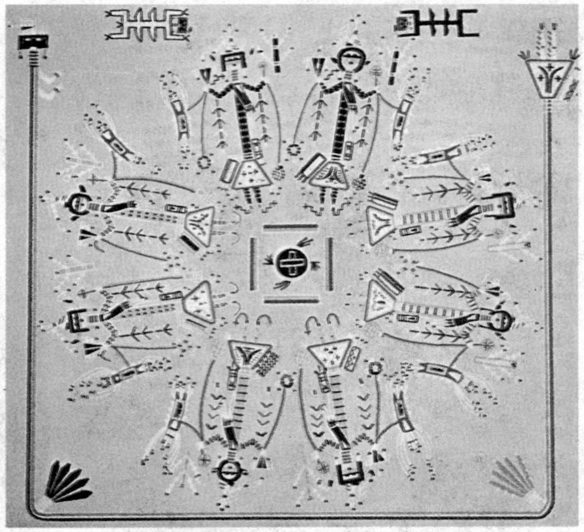

Navajo sand painting, *c.* 1940. In the Denver Art Museum, Colorado. 115 × 111 cm.

Courtesy of the Denver Art Museum, Colorado

to represent animals. The Serpent Mound in Ohio is an example of this custom. Truncated pyramids apparently served as large bases for wooden "temples," now long vanished but still in use when Spanish explorers first entered the region. Cahokia, in Illinois, was the largest such earthwork in existence before it was bulldozed to make way for modern buildings.

Major cultural expressions from this region included the Adena, Hopewell, Oneota, and copper culture peoples; their art was extensive, making great use of sculptured stone pipes, polished ornaments of both stone and copper, and incised shell decorations that may have served as both inlays and clothing accessories.

Great Plains. The later Great Plains region is the area most familiar to the average non-Indian, for this is the world of the "Buffalo Bill" shows, television and movie programs, and fiction. From it came the buckskin and beadwork costume, feathered war bonnets, colourful porcupine quill decoration, and painted shields that personify the American Indian in the minds of most people.

Yet, there was no monolithic culture. The arts of the Great Plains Indian varied from tribe to tribe; some peoples seem to have had superior aesthetic taste, with sensitive and inventive developments in the arts.

Tony Linck

Adena Serpent Mound near Locust Grove, Ohio, *c.* 2nd century BC. Length 405 m, height 1–2 m.

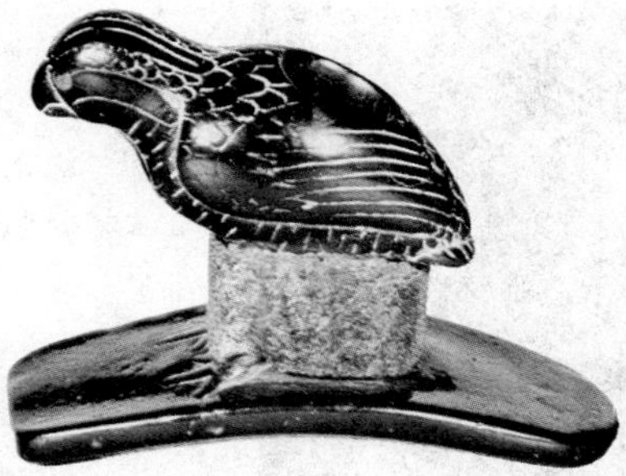

Hopewell pipestone pipe, c. 300 BC–AD 400. In the Museum of the Ohio Historical Society, Columbus. Length 7.5 cm.

By courtesy of the Ohio Historical Society, Columbus

Very little woodcarving was produced here in proportion to the other arts; yet a respectable body of wooden bowls, clubs, effigies, figurines, and similar objects indicates that the Plains artist did not ignore this medium. Even less pottery and basketry was produced, for containers were primarily made from buffalo hide.

A great deal of Plains art served both decorative and spiritual ends. A given design might appear to be primarily a colourful decoration, yet to the initiated it was also the guardian spirit of the owner.

Colour was originally achieved by mineral pigments or vegetable dyes. In time, these were supplanted by commercial dyes and trade colours. Porcupine quilling—the use of small quills of the American porcupine, *Erethizon dorsatus,* which are flattened, dyed, and then applied to the surface of animal hides or textile materials—is an art produced nowhere else in the world. It became outmoded in favour of glass trade beads, which were not only technically similar in their application to quillwork but did not fade and gave a richness of colour unobtainable in any other way.

The art forms themselves range from realistic to extremely abstract and symbolic. Often they are narrative in content, as with the Winter Counts, those painted records that recounted tribal history by means of annual symbols, and the personal history paintings on hide that recount the exploits of the owner.

Not only did the Plains Indian decorate his home but also his person, with carefully coiffured hair, facial painting, and clothing enhancement. And he devoted the same aesthetic attention to his horse as he did to himself, creating beautifully decorated gear for special occasions. Statically displayed in a museum exhibit, much of this ornamentation loses the grace of motion. When worn as intended, the motion of the wearer and the wafting of the plains breeze gives the feathered war bonnet or the fringed buckskin a lively grace and colour.

By courtesy of the Museum of the American Indian, Heye Foundation, New York

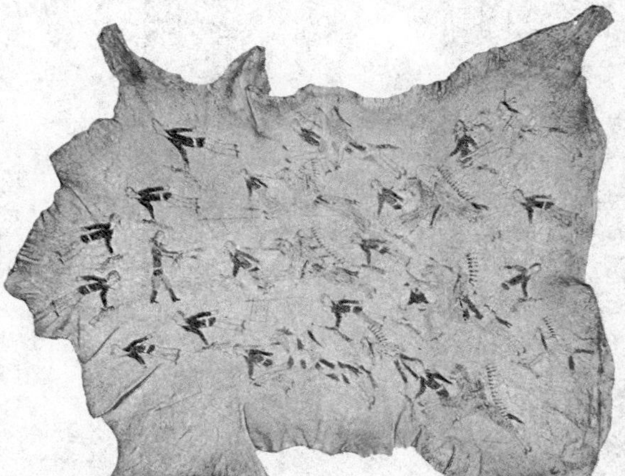

Cheyenne painted buffalo hide, depicting the Battle of the Little Bighorn, c. 1878. In the Museum of the American Indian, Heye Foundation, New York City. 116 × 87 cm.

Peripheral North America. Four other art-producing regions of North America include the far west, northeast, central south, and southeast.

Prehistoric art of central south and southeast North America

In prehistoric times, the central south and southeast were part of the most artistically exciting region of the North American continent. This land of temples, mounds, and monuments was an amazing world, and one can truly understand the legends that grew up around the riches that were evident when the Spanish arrived and that are still found in archaeological excavations. Testifying to the highly developed civilizations that existed are the beautifully carved shells, incised gorgets, and intricately decorated clothing ornaments; the carved stone effigies of ancestor figures or deities, which suggest a strong affinity with ancient Mexico; and the many bird and animal pipes in museums throughout the country. Had the Middle Mississippian culture diorite bowl (Museum of the American Indian, New York City) found at Moundville, Alabama, been the only masterpiece to survive, however, no other proof of the artistic brilliance of these peoples would be required.

By courtesy of the Museum of the American Indian, Heye Foundation, New York

Middle Mississippian diorite bowl in the shape of a crested wood duck, from Moundville, Alabama, c. AD 1500. In the Museum of the American Indian, Heye Foundation, New York City. Length 25.4 cm.

Wood was used in profusion, although little of it has been preserved in anything resembling its original condition. A quantity of textiles, albeit in fragments, has also survived. Other perishables include decorative freshwater pearls, featherwork, bone, and animal hides.

But it is in the claywork that the greatest vitality seems to have been expressed. While much of the clay used was of inferior quality, the results were astonishing. Exuberant forms, delicately traced surface lines, and strong, powerful designs were all executed with a confidence and grace that still attracts contemporary art students. A tremendous assortment of vessel designs was created in the Southeast: floral, geometric, clay appliqué, delicate polished water bottles and huge burial jars, as well as many lovely vessels created to hallow a shrine, decorate a temple, or do homage to a god—all providing evidence of the imagination, skill, and sheer love of clay for its own sake that these early potters must have felt. While much of this pottery art is extremely fragile, enough of the remarkably large output has survived to give an excellent idea of the aesthetic heights that were attained.

With the coming of the white man, this creativity was ended or diverted. Tribes were killed off or dispersed, or their social organization was so disrupted that normal pursuits were destroyed or directed into other, non-Indian channels. While the introduction of new and better tools allowed greater technical proficiency, the pride and dignity that had formerly provided such a strong creative impetus was no longer present. The artist had lost his old market—purchasers who understood what they were buying—and instead served a customer more concerned with external appearance than with the function of the object. The result was what is disparagingly known as tourist art—ostentatious elaboration that had little to do with the integrity of the product.

Today, almost all of the aboriginal arts of the Southeast have been lost or are much less actively pursued. The great stone sculpture for which it was so famous has entirely disappeared, although excellent wood sculpture is a continuing art; pottery is quite different from the earlier styles and far less imaginative. The clays from which contemporary Cherokee and Catawba pottery is produced are better grade, but the range of design is markedly limited. The most active art, and probably the most successful, is basketry, in which the present-day artists are in every way equal to, or better than, their tribal predecessors.

The breakup of the great Cherokee tribe, when a major portion was forced to remove from South Carolina and Georgia to Oklahoma in 1838–39, destroyed the unity of the people. Today, very little Cherokee culture as such is to be found in Oklahoma; it has been kept alive largely by the smaller Eastern band still living in North Carolina. It is this group that is responsible for the pottery, wood sculpture, and basketry referred to above.

Basketry of the California Indians

The great art of the California Indians was basketry; no other people in the world has produced such a wide variety of superb basketry. The Pomo, Hupa, Yurok, and Karok peoples of the north developed basketry to its ultimate with weaves so tightly composed as to provide a watertight container, baskets so small that they measure less than one-eighth inch (three millimetres) in diameter, huge grain-storage baskets, and delicately woven "gift" baskets with the feathers of birds interwoven that provided not only an opportunity for the weaver to demonstrate her mastery of the art, but also a means whereby she could display her affection for the deceased. Elsewhere the Chumash, Mono-Paviosto, Washo, and Koso proved no less skilled.

The Woodlands tribes of the East fall into two divisions: the south-southeast (discussed above), and the Great Lakes and northeast. The Great Lakes group produced various arts, including woodwork, a style of weaving with rush and hemp, and a strong porcupine quill art, later replaced by beadwork. This style of beadwork was popular around the turn of the 19th century, when large quantities of it became available. The art depended upon a weaving frame, which allowed the manufacture of long strips, useful for necklaces, belts, panels, and headbands. Wood art made effective use of burls (hemispherical outgrowths on a tree), from which bowls and containers were fashioned. Pottery was almost nonexistent.

The people of the Northeast, notably the Iroquois, are famous for their False Face Society masks, quillwork and beadwork, wooden bowls and ladles, and the woven wampum belts, which are important historical documents. Some pottery was produced, but not of significant quantity or quality. Woodlands basketry was common, but it was not of the quality found elsewhere. Primarily a splint-weave type, it was rarely ornamented, and when it was, the ornament consisted of stamped or painted vegetable-dye designs.

Eskimo. It may seem unlikely that art would occupy very much of the attention of the inhabitants of the bleak Arctic regions; not only is there little raw material to work with but the ever-present need to secure a food supply would seem to leave little time for craftwork. Yet, from this harsh environment came some of the most imaginative and humorous of Indian carvings. During the long winter nights, the Eskimo had ample time to work the ivory that came from the walrus and whale, much as the Yankee farmer passed the time during the winter whittling on a stick of wood as he sat by the stove.

Art styles of the area favoured carving in the round, decoration by incising, and a modest amount of inlay. Since the basic material was often a tusk or a tooth, these objects partially dictated the form, which was embellished after carving by incising or engraving. Black pigment, from charcoal fires, was rubbed into the lines for emphasis. Such prehistoric wood carving as may have existed has almost entirely disappeared, but enough has survived to indicate that it was a rich and varied art form. Ancient ivory carvings have also been excavated, revealing a sophisticated, formal style. The so-called fossil ivory from which these carvings were made is highly prized even today and, when found, is invariably turned into beautiful carvings that gain value because of the scarce, richly colourful raw material.

Pomo feathered gift basket decorated with shell pendants, *c.* 1890. In the Museum of the American Indian, Heye Foundation, New York City. Diameter 22 cm.

By courtesy of the Museum of the American Indian, Heye Foundation, New York

Humour in Eskimo art

A predominant characteristic of Eskimo art is the warm sense of humour that is so prevalent. Sometimes it is expressed in caricature, sometimes in sequential, "cartoon" form. Its surrealistic expression is probably a reflection of the Eskimo's awareness that, because he lives close to death throughout his life, humour is vital to his psychological health.

Another significant feature of Eskimo art is the remarkable mechanical skill that was often involved in the creative process. Part of the Eskimo's artistry was his ability to neatly piece together small parts to create a whole—and his ability to fashion the tools needed to carry out the operation, many of which were works of art themselves. This skill is evident in the Eskimo's most famous art form: the fantastic wooden masks used for various dances and social affairs. While many tribes made wooden masks

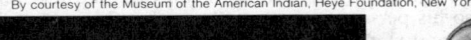

By courtesy of the Museum of the American Indian, Heye Foundation, New York

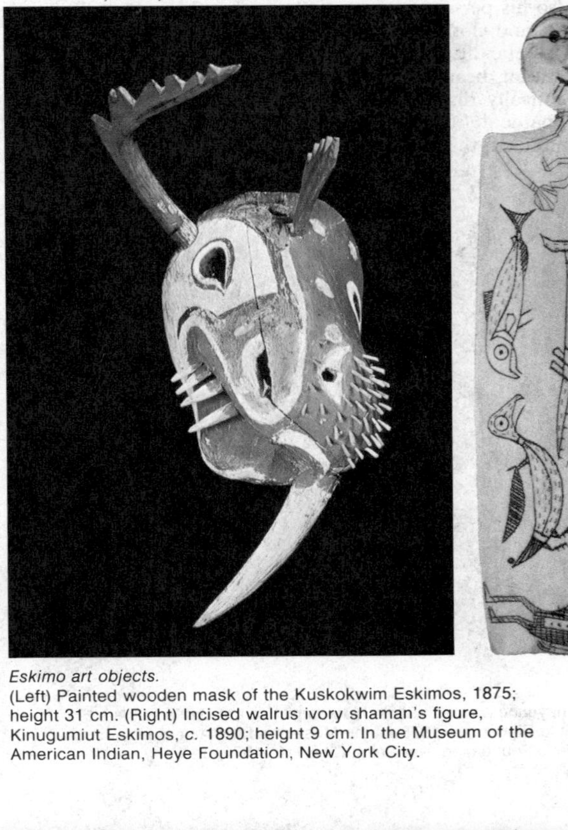

Eskimo art objects.
(Left) Painted wooden mask of the Kuskokwim Eskimos, 1875; height 31 cm. (Right) Incised walrus ivory shaman's figure, Kinugumiut Eskimos, *c.* 1890; height 9 cm. In the Museum of the American Indian, Heye Foundation, New York City.

and decorated them with colourful ingenuity, no North American aboriginal people developed the art of imaginative characterization to such an extreme. Surrealism *par excellence*. These masks demonstrate a combination of realistic, imaginative, and supernatural qualities that is uniquely Eskimo.

In more recent times, with its inception around 1950, a stone art form, utilizing deposits of gray and green soapstone, or steatite, found in the vicinity of Hudson Bay, has become familiar to art collectors. Usually given an artificial colouring, these examples of small-scale sculpture are popular examples of genre art. While they reflect the inherent sculptural skills of the Eskimo, they owe their origin and promotion to non-Indian agencies that have worked closely with several of the crafts groups in the region. A form of graphic art derived from Japanese printmaking techniques has also become popular in this way.

Northwest Coast. It was in this region, richly endowed with tremendous cedar and spruce forests, that the American Indian sculptor achieved his finest expression. It is probably here that the influence of tools upon the artist is best exemplified; for, with the introduction of steel cutting knives, the Northwest Coast artist was free to demonstrate his latent talent in the aesthetically superb sculpture that is rivalled by no other Indian people in North America.

Tall, straight cedar poles furnished the material for the huge totem poles, the smaller wooden figures, the masks, and the other carved objects so loved by the Northwest Coast Indian. Inlaid with *Haliotis,* or abalone shell, and carefully painted, these products took on a quality so distinctive that they are immediately identifiable.

Courtesy of the Denver Art Museum, Colorado

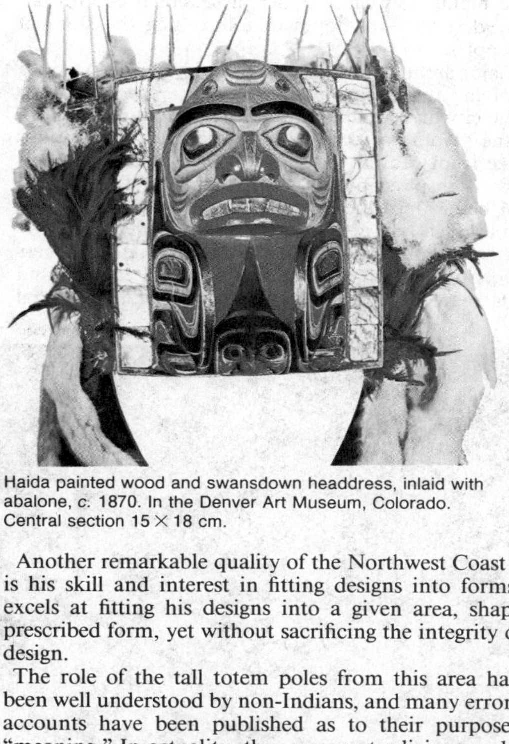

Haida painted wood and swansdown headdress, inlaid with abalone, *c.* 1870. In the Denver Art Museum, Colorado. Central section 15 × 18 cm.

Another remarkable quality of the Northwest Coast artist is his skill and interest in fitting designs into forms. He excels at fitting his designs into a given area, shape, or prescribed form, yet without sacrificing the integrity of the design.

Totem poles

The role of the tall totem poles from this area has not been well understood by non-Indians, and many erroneous accounts have been published as to their purpose and "meaning." In actuality, they were not religious and were never intended to be worshipped. They were historical documents of a sort, recording the social position, wealth, and relative importance of the person who had paid for the pole. Because family lineage, class status, wealth, and other social facts were thus recorded, it was possible to gain an "introduction" to the village chief or house owner by simply examining the tall pole.

The goal of most of this rich art was the exaltation of the individual—more specifically, a wealthy village chief or a great noble, for the society was based on a class system. Part of the insignia of social position was the accumulation of wealth, and *objets d'art* were an important part of that wealth. With the coming of the white man, who coveted the rich furs of the region, the control of the great fishing

Reconstructed Tlingit longhouse with totem poles. In the Totem Bight Totem Pole Park, Ketchikan, Alaska.
Bob and Ira Spring

areas and strategic position of the Northwest Coast tribes enabled them to acquire staggering wealth in an extremely brief space of time. The existence of an Indian purchasing class, with its ever-increasing need for impressive possessions, created a supplier: the professional artist. This was thus one of the very few aboriginal cultures that gave rise to art patrons who hired artists on a commission basis.

The short existence of works of art

More surprising, the works that were commissioned were destined to be destroyed, given away, or otherwise neglected. For the life goal of many of these tribes involved the belief that the greatest value was to give away all of one's possessions. While this may seem paradoxical the logic was simple: the more one gave away, the greater one's prestige.

Combined with the potlatch, this system tended to impoverish groups from time to time, sometimes to the point of enslaving whole villages. The rule was that the wealthy individual hold a feast to which his major rival was invited. The host would give away all of his possessions, and the rival would return the courtesy, giving back more than he had received. To show even greater contempt for material possessions (and one's rival), frequently goods were publicly burned, broken up, or cast into the sea. Slaves were even killed and families sold into slavery. From all of this megalomania came the surviving aesthetic masterpieces that are valued so highly today.

The Northwest Coast tribes were among the first American Indians to master metalcraft. While some copper came from local sources, most came from whaling ships,

By courtesy of the Museum of the American Indian, Heye Foundation, New York

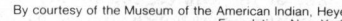

Haida "slate carving" of three bears depicting cesarean birth, argillite *c.* 1890. In the Museum of the American Indian, Haye Foundation, New York City. Height 18 cm.

both as cargo brought in for trade and as scrap peeled from the hulls of wrecked ships. This metal was worked with great skill by Tlingit and Haida artists into fighting knives, masks, overlays for art works, and the great shield-shaped *tinneh* that were so highly prized.

Among the Northwest Coast tribes, the Tlingit people of Alaska seem to have produced the most sensitive and sophisticated sculpture. The Kwakiutl, on the other hand, expressed their feeling for line and form in extremely impressive and powerful painted carvings: the designs are usually outlined in strong colours; there is far less subtlety of form; and the overall feeling is of a potent force at work. Between the two extremes are the Haida carvers, whose work, often less strongly painted than Kwakiutl work, is marked by precision of design, skill in execution, and strength of expression. These are the people who were responsible for the familiar black "slate carvings," which are actually made of argillite, a stone found locally only on Queen Charlotte Islands, in British Columbia.

The work of the neighbouring Northwest Coast peoples, such as the Niska, Kitksan, and Tsimshian, who lived upriver from the Tlingit, is perhaps slightly less well known, due largely to the smaller population and their more remote interior location. It is, however, of equal aesthetic merit, and can stand comparison on any basis with the art of the rest of the peoples of this region.

With the coming of the white man, there was a brief period of economic benefit enjoyed by the Northwest Coast people, but this soon disappeared, and the arts rapidly degenerated to curio-shop products. In time, even these provided so little income that all but a few Indian carvers and basket weavers abandoned the arts. Today, again, there are several crafts products that seem destined to disappear, particularly the famed Chilkat blankets. On the other hand, some crafts objects, especially wooden masks that are often carved and painted replicas of older ones, have enjoyed a revival; but, in essence, this is a copying process, largely mechanical and lacking any of the creativity of the original. Argillite carving is experiencing a modest renaissance, but as yet most of the products are very small, ornamental, accessory forms. In general, the exuberance and power of the earlier forms is yet to be fully realized by these gifted, determined artists of Northwest Coast Indian descent.

Mexico and Middle America. Although Mexico is geographically part of the North American continent, its cultural world is so different that it is more convenient to consider it as part of Middle or Central America. The Indian groups in the region are also somewhat different in that they reflect a strong Spanish influence that was largely absent from most of the North American aboriginal peoples. It is true, however, that a strong intertribal trade existed between Mexican tribes and those of North America in prehistoric times, and this influence must be borne in mind when considering the arts of both regions.

Olmec art

The earliest identifiable art form of major significance in Mexico is that of the Olmec, the mysterious "rubber people," whose culture was flourishing as early as 1000 BC over an area from Guerrero to Veracruz in Mexico, and into Guatemala, Honduras, and El Salvador. These Indians carved the tremendous "colossal heads" that the American anthropologist Matthew W. Stirling found at La Venta; delicate greenstone "baby-face" figures; and figurines with a rounded facial form, thick features, heavy-lidded eyes, and down-turned mouth that are referred to as "were-jaguars" because the image of this mythological or quasi-symbolic, supernatural being is a humanoid type thought by many to combine human aspects with the jaguar concept.

Closely associated with, but somewhat later than, the Olmec culture came the people who inhabited Tlatico, Chupícuaro, and related early sites, which have become well-known for their lovely clay figurines of nude women with fantastic coiffures. At about the time of the slow demise of these civilizations, other peoples had begun to develop their own way of life in western Mexico, notably in Colima, Jalisco, Nayarit, and Michoacán. Far less is known about the cultures of these areas, for relatively little professional archaeological work had been undertaken on the scale that would be needed for accurate investigation. The tremendous amount of looting that took place before the major sites came under professional control has virtually destroyed all hopes of unravelling the story of these peoples.

The major architectural construction in ancient America was evolving at this time and reached its apogee about AD 600. The city of Teotihuacán (outside present-day Mexico City), the "Home of the Gods," exercised a tremendous influence from central Mexico into lower Central America; objects inspired by ideas originating at Teotihuacán are still being unearthed throughout the region. The famous masks, so typical of the style, were made *c.* AD 250–750. Their monumental quality formed by the great mass of stone from which the oval eyes, sensual mouth, and broad face are fashioned, provides a powerful sculptural

Tlingit "Chilkat blanket," mountain goat wool and cedar bark, late 19th century, Alaska. In the Metropolitan Museum of Art, New York City. 167 cm × 134 cm.

By courtesy of the Metropolitan Museum of Art, New York City, The Michael C. Rockefeller Memorial Collection of Primitive Art, bequest of Nelson A. Rockefeller, 1979; photograph, Lisa Little

George Holton—Photo Researchers

Olmec colossal head, basalt, *c.* 1st century BC. In Parque La Venta, Tabasco, Mexico. Height 2.4 m.

Teotihuacán, Valley of Mexico, with the Pyramid of the Sun in the background, *c.* 3rd century BC–8th century AD.
Gianni Tortoli—Photo Researchers

concept. Far too massive to have been worn, it is more likely they were intended as burial offerings, or perhaps facial coverings for wooden effigies.

The Toltecs, Mixtecs, and Zapotecs, widely separated one from the other, have also left their imprint. The former, spreading out from their home area around Tula, eventually travelled as far as the Yucatán Peninsula, leaving evidences of their culture wherever they went. The Zapotec and Mixtec peoples of Puebla and Oaxaca were famed for their unique arts, particularly Mixtec goldwork; these master craftsmen were sought out over great distances for the beautiful jewelry and finely fitted craftworks that are still so highly valued today.

Mixtec goldwork

Along the east coast, in the state of Veracruz, a group of Mayan people called the Huástec had settled by about 250 BC. In time they developed a new cultural expression, which, because they were isolated by Totonac settlers then building up a major centre at El Tajín, remained limited to their own group. Other pre-Totonac folk who were active in Veracruz produced innumerable "smilingface" figurines and related works that give an impression of an exuberant, happy people. Remarkable among these clayworks are the small clay whistles that abound in the area. They are valuable not only as artworks but also as examples of musical instruments popular during that period.

Unique to this region is the use of *chapopote,* a native asphalt commonly applied to clay figurines as a decoration; occasionally, *chapopote* entirely covers the figures, while in other examples, it is used to decorate only the face, mouth, or eyes.

Some puzzling stone carvings also have been discovered in Veracruz. Although these objects have been found throughout Central America from central Mexico to El Salvador, their centre seems to have been in the coastal Veracruz area. One of the objects, the *palma,* or palmate stone (shaped like a hand with extended fingers), was first thought to have had some religious significance. The thin-bladed *hacha,* or "axe," so termed because of its resemblance to that implement, was thought to have a ceremonial function of some sort. The *yugo,* or "yoke," was believed to have been used to hold down the head and neck of a sacrificial victim. Today, none of these theories is accepted. Although scholars are still uncertain as to the use of these objects, the best evidence suggests that the *hacha* had an architectural function, perhaps as a wall fitting, or protruding structural decoration. It is possible that some *hachas* were used with the *yugo;* extant sculptures suggest such a use, along with the *palma,* in connection with the ceremonial ball game, *tlachtli.* These sculptures portray an elaborately costumed individual, wearing what is apparently a *yugo* around his waist. Supported by and protruding from the latter is a *palma,* indicating that the two may somehow have been fastened together, or were used in combination. It is not believed by scholars that the player actually engaged in the game so encumbered. *Tlachtli* was not unlike today's soccer game; the object was to propel a gutta-percha ball through the air without touching it with the hands; if it went through a small hole in the carved stone disk, or hit that circular goal, the game was won. Tremendous exchanges of personal property resulted from such a victory—indeed, often life itself was forfeit in important contests.

As the Zapotec people of Oaxaca yielded in turn to the more warlike Mixtec, whose centre at Cholula was the site of the largest pyramid of the ancient world (it considerably exceeded the size of the pyramid of Giza in Egypt), so the latter in time became secondary to the Aztec. By 1200, these nomads, who came from the northwest, had established themselves in the central valley, which they called México, whence the name Mexico. The world they built gave rise to a powerful—at times brutal—art form, in which stone was a favourite medium. The rounded, muscular figures that they produced were originally brilliantly painted, much like ancient Greek sculptures. The Aztec turned out an astonishing quantity of these figures, which, standing in rows, served as standard bearers along the avenues leading to various buildings. The other arts, such as pottery and goldwork, seem not to have fared so well during Aztec times. Even the examples that have been found were perhaps less products of Aztec craftsmanship than creations of neighbouring peoples that were introduced into the Aztec empire as tribute or as trade objects.

Aztec sculpture

By courtesy of (top left, bottom) The Metropolitan Museum of Art, New York City, The Michael C. Rockefeller Memorial Collection of Primitive Art, bequest of Nelson A. Rockefeller, 1979, (top right) the Asian Art Museum of San Francisco, the Avery Brundage Collection, Adriani Bequest to the California Palace of the Legion of Honor; photographs (top left, bottom) Lisa Little

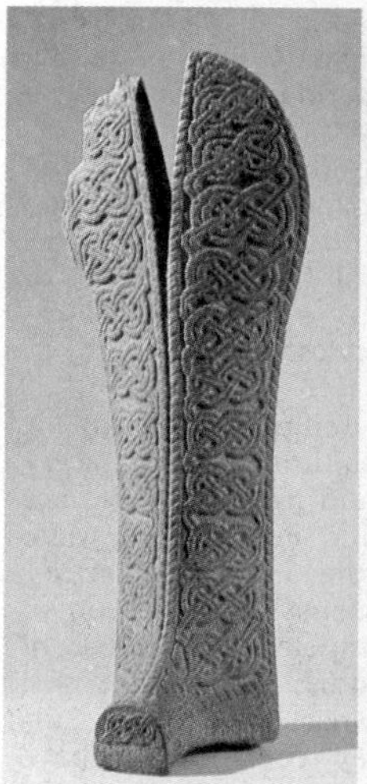

Stone carvings from Veracruz, Mexico, about AD 300–900.
(Top left) *Palma.* In the Metropolitan Museum of Art, New York City. Height 51 cm. (Top right) *Hacha.* In the Asian Art Museum of San Francisco, The Avery Brundage Collection. Height 40 cm. (Bottom) *Yugo.* In the Metropolitan Museum of Art, New York City. Length 41 cm.

Mayan fresco from Bonampak, original *c.* AD 800. Reconstruction by Antonio Tejeda F. In Chiapas, Mexico.
Ygunza—FPG

To the east and south, another completely different world appeared under the name of the Maya. Centring in Guatemala and Honduras, where the twin capitals of Quiriguá and Copán are still well-known sites, the Maya spread out to El Salvador, into what is today British Honduras, and into well over one-half of Mexico. The Yucatán Peninsula and the neighbouring state of Campeche are areas where a large number of Mayan sites have been found; of these, undoubtedly the most famous Mayan architectural monuments are at Uxmal, Labná, Kabah, and Sayil and the most renowned examples of Mayan fresco painting have been found at Bonampak. Chichén Itzá, the famous archaeological area near Mérida, combines both Maya and Toltec influences.

Jaina figurines

Just off the coast of Campeche is the island cemetery of Jaina, from which have come magnificently modelled figurines that are certainly among the finest clay works of antiquity. These sacrificial burial figures, replicas of Mayan personages in ceremonial finery, provide a remarkable insight into the customs, life-styles, and costumes of the classic Mayan people.

Unlike the brutal force of Aztec sculpture, Mayan art forms are relatively delicate. Yet, although light tracery is characteristic of their sculpture and painting, there are also occasional bursts of sheer power. Perhaps they were the most art-conscious people of the ancient Americas; certainly everything they created seems to have been in terms of aesthetics. They were competent in the use of many raw materials—shell, bone, stone of various kinds, wood, fibres, even feathers became part of their art. Surprisingly, with all of their skills, they seem never to have undertaken much metalwork: gold, silver, and copper objects are exceedingly rare from Mayan sites.

From an early beginning, around AD 250, the Mayan civilization had reached its apogee around 750 and had disappeared by 900. Remnant groups kept the cultural thread as a continuum up to about 1200; but by then, except for their language, they could no longer be regarded as cognate with the earlier Mayan.

Farther south, in Nicaragua, Costa Rica, and Panama, the relationships of the various people are less clear, due largely to the paucity of archaeological work that has been undertaken. Moreover, because Panama was something of a crossroads, both east–west and north–south, the variety of influences found there makes conclusive evaluations of the native art almost impossible. But even though far less is known about these peoples, there is no question about the excellent quality of their various kinds of artwork.

The two greatest artistic achievements of the region seem to have been in jade carving and goldsmithing. From the isthmus area come some of the finest gold castings known. Although some delicate, finely wrought goldwork is known, most pieces consist of heavy casting, with lost-wax tracery (interlaced patterns of metal cast in a wax mold) in which animal and bird forms predominate. The polished jadework of Costa Rica is famous throughout the Central American area. The beautiful "ax gods," carved from green jade, must have been as sought after in ancient times as they are today.

Central American jade carving and goldwork

Pottery was not an unknown art, and the brilliantly painted vessels found here are emphatic proof of this fact. Surprisingly, the art has yet to receive the recognition due it on aesthetic grounds. Some of the designs are remarkably intricate, bold in form, and frequently as sophisticated as anything found in the Western Hemisphere. And here and there are intriguing touches of humour—a quality largely absent from Aztec and Mayan arts.

Little has survived of the architectural expressions from this area. Some large stone sculptures from Penonomé, in Chiriquí province, Panama, suggest that the use of stone in large structures was not unknown; but apparently all of these structures were destroyed, in the years after the Spanish Conquest, by people using the stones for building.

Following the Conquest, the eradication of native culture in Central America was more rigorous than in many areas, and the net result is that south of Guatemala, there is almost no truly indigenous culture to be found. There are some remnants in Costa Rica, but they are few, and evidence of their pre-Columbian culture is only marginal. Today, such arts and crafts as are pursued may reflect a continuum of design but they are basically dominated by European influence. The only regions in which considerable prehistoric aesthetic influence survives are Mexico and Guatemala, where the native craftsman has been able to keep his art somewhat alive by recourse to ancient designs and functions.

West Indies. The Caribbean region of the Americas has undoubtedly lost more of its aboriginal character than any other region. The total decimation of the islands shortly after the Conquest and the subsequent populating of the area by black slaves made any carry-over of Indian cultural expressions impossible. And so it is today that residents of those islands rarely feel any sense of relationship to the ancestral inhabitants. Certainly it is true that the average non-Indian has no understanding of the wealth of arts that were to be found there in the past.

The delicate wood carvings, textiles, featherwork, and related perishable objects that are known from references in Spanish accounts to have existed have largely disap-

Jadeite ornament, or "ax god" from Costa Rica, *c.* 500–750. In the Dumbarton Oaks Collection, Washington, D.C. 5.1 × 12.5 cm.
By courtesy of Dumbarton Oaks Research Library and Collection, Washington, D.C.

peared. Only a few wood carvings and a small number of shell and bone carvings are known. The great strength of surviving prehistoric art from the area is in stone; and in this medium there are remarkably sophisticated, powerful works. Small, tripointed carvings, that were often human or zoomorphic in form, represented the spirits (*zemi*) of the land. The Taino culture is famous for these *zemi* carvings, which are found in many of the islands, notably

Wooden effigy figure inlaid with shell teeth that is a variant of the *zemi* form, from Jamaica, *c.* AD 1500. In the Metropolitan Museum of Art, New York City. Height 69 cm.

By courtesy of the Metropolitan Museum of Art, New York City, The Michael C. Rockefeller Memorial Collection of Primitive Art, bequest of Nelson A. Rockefeller, 1979; photograph, Lisa Little

Puerto Rico and Hispaniola. Carved stone pestles, with human and animal designs, are also common, along with strange "stone collars"—oval carvings that may be related to the *yugos* of Mexico and Guatemala. The most prevalent form, however, is the human head, often a death's-head, which suggests a culture preoccupied with mortality. The peoples of this area were also fascinated by odd shapes in stone. Unusual "comma stones," the meaning of which—if they had any—scholars have been unable to discover, have been found scattered throughout the Antilles. Their number and the care and skill with which they are carved suggests that they had an important role in the culture.

Although the Taino are thought to have surpassed the other peoples of the West Indies in aesthetic development, examples of later artistic forms and techniques characteristic of the Arawak, Carib, and related tribes still surviving in neighbouring South America may provide a link between ancient and modern. Since the Taino were a division of the Arawak, so may modern Arawak weaving indicate something of what must have existed among the prehistoric Taino.

The trans-Caribbean sea route from the islands to the mainland obviously carried influences, as well as materials, back and forth; but far too little is known about these influences to be able to determine which area (the islands or the mainland) was most affected. Little more is known about the West Indies civilization, therefore, than that it produced extremely successful sculpture. The civilization disappeared so rapidly and completely that one can admire but not wholly comprehend it.

Role of Inca art

South America. The greatest single problem in assessing the Indian art of this region is the unfortunate historical tendency to lump everything together under the heading Inca, as though no other culture had ever attained significance. In fact, when one examines the continent critically, it is evident that the Incas were among the least aesthetically remarkable of the peoples of South America, almost all of whom attained artistic levels only occasionally equalled by the latecomers. It is probably only in the architectural use of stone and in the textile arts that the Inca held his own in artistic comparison.

Weaving was one of the three arts that were South American strengths, the two others being metalwork and pottery. No other peoples in the Western Hemisphere—and less than a handful elsewhere in the world—came close to equalling the aesthetic and technical accomplishment of the Peruvian weaver. One can imagine the astonishment of the early Spanish explorers when they saw this radiant clothing for the first time, even though they very soon passed it over for the gold they coveted.

Metalwork was at its zenith in Peru, Colombia, and Ecuador, each of which developed major cultures whose arts were equal to the demands of the raw material. Tairona gold, in Colombia, rates very high in design and craftsmanship, as does the work of the Quimbaya, whose skill in creating polished metal flasks is remarkable. Notable also is Sinú casting, which could execute works weighing several pounds. In Ecuador, the goldwork found at La Tolita is legendary and shows a skill in casting and overlay that did not seem to exist elsewhere in the region. In Peru, most surviving goldwork was created by the Chimú and Nazca peoples. Yet, that this was a well-advanced art as early as the Chavín era is demonstrated by major discoveries at Chongoyape; indeed, these pieces seem to be the earliest gold products in America, having been created around 900–500 BC.

Perhaps the art that was most widespread and had the greatest variety of form is pottery. In the exciting range of imaginative forms, exuberant vessels are found side by side with sombre, formal works. The use of brilliant colour is common, and the degree of careful modelling makes of many of these pottery containers veritable sculptural masterpieces.

A popular material, stone was used throughout most of South America for massive forms; the small delicately traced stone carvings found in Central America are rarely encountered south of that region. Architecturally, the Incas surpassed all others in their use of intricately cut, giant-size stone blocks, at the sites of Machu Picchu, Sacsahuamán, and Ollantaytambo. Only in San Agustín, in Colombia, was there a similar monumental use of stone. In Manabí, in Ecuador, blocks of stone were skillfully carved into thrones and huge seats. None of this South American stonework, however, reflects the degree of skill common in Mexico.

Antiquity of Colombian art

Colombia. Colombia is among the first South American regions to have enjoyed settlement. A pre-pottery Indian culture is known to have come into the region around 10,000 BC; and Puerto Hormiga excavations reveal that a pottery-making culture existed as early as 3,000 BC. The more definite cultural expressions, however, are not found in quantity until San Agustín, which came into existence with the advent of the Christian Era. Little pottery has been recovered from the region as yet, but stone carvings are very well known. A later culture north of this site, which has yielded a more generous quantity of art objects, is Calima, known for its goldwork, and Quimbaya, whose gold and pottery are both important cultural indicators.

Since the southern and eastern regions of the country are almost unknown archaeologically, conclusive evidence is absent, but at the moment it does not appear that their prehistory was artistically rich. Early pre-pottery sites have been found, notably at El Jobo, in Falcón, that date to about 14,920 BC. Carved stone was used for such objects as small pendants or fetishes; shell and bone are also known to have been used.

It is certain that this was a contact point with many

of the Antillean peoples and that travel back and forth between the two regions was a regular custom. Columbus reported such trade—which seems to have been a long-time practice—at the time of his arrival.

Ecuador. It is to Ecuador that one must turn for an examination of early art forms. Straddling the Equator, as the name implies, this region—today the smallest republic in South America—is one of the most intriguing on the continent. For decades the region had been ignored by scholars in favour of the more glamorous Peruvian area, but in recent years its tremendous antiquity has begun to be recognized. It now seems that ancient man may have established his first foothold in Ecuador and that the region is also the site of the earliest datable pottery. From perhaps as early as 15,000 BC until about 3200 BC, when pottery was known to exist at Valdivia, there was a long, steady period of development in the region. And the development was not spotty, for the population increase was also constant.

Although the great cities and some of the major cultural activities found farther south were not found in Ecuador, there was, nevertheless, considerable cultural accomplishment. Weaving was done in quantity, as evidenced by Spanish accounts; and, more spectacularly, goldsmithing was a major expression of the artist's skill. Large pieces, such as crowns and breastplates, and tiny miniatures reflecting the sureness of a master's hand have been found. None of these pieces is unique; they are known in sufficient quantity to prove the existence of a long-time craft. Literally hundreds of thousands of tiny gold beads, each cast individually, have been found in the sands of La Tolita; and others, slightly larger, with granulated surfaces indicating the mastery of a complex casting process, have also been recovered. The technique of inlaying had also been mastered, and the use of emeralds and other gemstones as settings was commonplace. Platinum was worked, as in Colombia; not only was it cast but it also was frequently used in combination with other metals. Copper, too, was worked, both in its "pure" form and combined with tin to make bronze; occasionally, it was gilded to create a pseudo-gold finish. Heavy cast copper axes were stock-in-trade, and many smaller objects were turned out in quantity.

Metalwork in Ecuador

The pottery that emerged from the hands of the clay workers was of high quality, beautifully designed, and well finished. Modelling was powerful, and there were touches of humour. Scholars are not sure to what extent colour was used, for time and soil have removed much of it. Modelled clay effigies discovered in 1966 at Bahía de Manta are not only remarkable for their size and quantity but even more for the astonishing amount of original colour that had been preserved.

It seems evident that this was one of South America's major civilizations and that in time much more will be discovered about it.

Brazil. Like the archaeology of Venezuela, little is actually known of the archaeology of the vast region of Brazil. Only around the Amazon area has very much work been done, and there primarily on the Ilha de Marajó. Size has hampered much of the effort to unravel prehistory, but weather conditions and jungle overgrowth have also combined to resist penetration. What is known, however, is tantalizing to the scholar, for at Lagoa Santa, in Minas Gerais, the bones of a human being have been linked with a mammoth slaughtered for food as early as around 10,000 BC; and pottery vessels have been discovered attesting to a remarkably advanced civilization in the Amazon lowlands perhaps as early as AD 1000. But what lies between these two extremes in time is yet to be discovered.

The most aesthetically exciting object excavated in Brazil is a unique pottery form, found on the Ilha de Marajó and called Marajoara, which incorporates modelling and painting with a low relief carving of the surface. Several successful expeditions have recovered modest amounts of material, but the island, which is regularly flooded by the mouth of the Amazon, has resisted complete excavation. An individual style found on the tiny isle of Maracá, and another from Santarém, suggest the existence in this region of a hodgepodge of aesthetic expressions, some related, some alien. Surprisingly, the strong geometric Marajoara style seems not to have influenced any of the cultures around it.

Marajoara pottery

Peru and highland Bolivia. The great civilizations of Peru and highland Bolivia—with their monolithic stone structures, major political organizations, and elaborate material wealth—have long attracted the attention of the outside world. This was the only area where structures of any real magnitude were built in South America; the ruins of Tiahuanaco, Cuzco, Chan Chan, and similar well-developed urban centres attest to the achievement of highly skilled peoples. Pottery has been found in all styles and types, from relatively crude wares to the most highly

Ray Manley—Shostal/EB Inc.

Ruins of the Inca city of Machu Picchu, Peru, *c.* 15th century.

Chavín (1000–400 BC) hammered gold crown, from Chongoyape, Peru, 900–500 BC. In the Museum of the American Indian, Heye Foundation, New York City. 14 × 24 cm.

By courtesy of the Museum of the American Indian, Heye Foundation, New York

painted and polished masterpieces. Whistling vessels are common, and the various forms of musical instruments perhaps exceed those found in other civilizations on the continent. Representations of daily life on the pottery reflect complete, well-rounded civilizations.

Man was definitely active in Peru as early as 10,000 BC, and his pottery making dates to no later than 1200 BC. Slowly, these dates will be pushed back, as scholars unravel more and more of prehistory; for, in view of the advanced stage of some early works, it is certain that they will be found to have been preceded by others.

Art of the Chavín civilization

The great Peruvian ruins around Chavín de Huántar have given the name Chavín to one of the most remarkable civilizations in South America—and one of the earliest, though it is not certain whether it was coeval with the Valdivia of Ecuador (*c.* 3200 BC). Here, remnants, famous throughout the archaeological world, have been found of one of America's earliest cultures. Carved stone objects, fantastic pottery that demonstrates the most advanced skills, evidences of stone construction, and remarkably sophisticated goldwork—all bear witness to a truly magnificent era in ancient history.

A recent discovery has brought to light evidences of a civilization at Ayabaca, in Piura, which was probably coeval with the Chavín. Named Vicús after the valley in which it was uncovered and dating between 250 BC and AD 500, this civilization produced pottery that resembles the ware of nearby Ecuador and goldwork not unlike other early forms. The discovery of this wholly new civilization, unknown until just a few years ago, suggests the existence of others.

By courtesy of the National Archaeological Museum, Lima; photograph, Lee Boltin

Detail of embroidered Paracas mantle, *c.* 300–100 BC. In the Museo Nacional de Antropologia y Arqueologia, Lima.

South of the Chavín region, another high culture developed around the Paracas Peninsula. This civilization produced a famous thin-walled pottery and some of the most extraordinary textiles in existence. Great woven mantles, ponchos, and small tapestries were created between 1000 and 250 BC.

Paracas textiles

Just as elements from the Chavín civilization filtered south to influence the Paracas people, so they influenced a development in the north, around the Virú, Chicama, and Moche valleys from 250 BC to AD 750. Commonly termed Mochica, these people developed a mature art form that includes some of the finest plastic sculpture in the history of pottery. The range of designs makes these objects remarkable not only as art but also as revelations of the civilization from which they come. The extensive number of objects produced suggests that the civilization was an extremely populous one, in which power and wealth were major goals.

Gradually, this civilization gave way to that of invaders, the Chimú, whose capital of Chan Chan was from AD 1000 to 1500 one of the great urban centres of ancient Peru. This huge city, now largely destroyed, once housed 100,000 persons and produced a spectacular array of artistic works: gold jewelry, feather mantles, great textiles, and considerable work in wood and clay. The arid climate has preserved more art from the Chimú region than from many other sections, and Spanish accounts aid scholars in understanding what they find here. Pottery was as skilled as any found elsewhere, although by now something of a paralysis had set in; certainly, many of the designs have a static quality, doubtless due to the extensive use of molds. By now customer demand was so great that the craftsman had to resort to mass production to keep up with his clients.

By courtesy of the Museum of the American Indian, Heye Foundation, New York

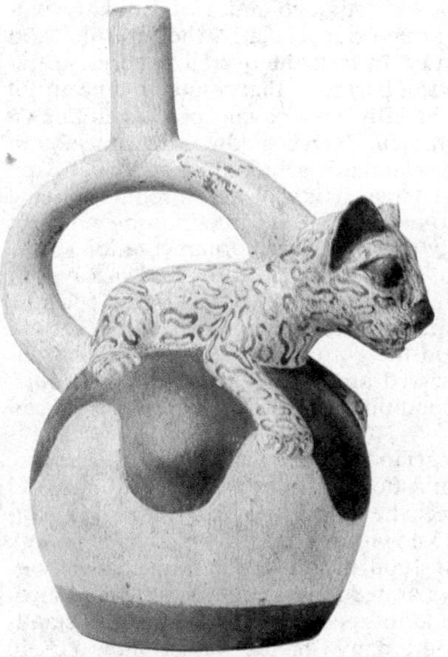

Mochica stirrup-spouted water bottle, *c.* AD 250–500. In the Museum of the American Indian, Heye Foundation, New York City. Height 24 cm.

Chimú and Nazca pottery

In the south, a great pottery talent was at work from *c.* 250 BC to AD 750 around the Nazca Valley. There, perhaps the most technically advanced potters in South America were producing perfectly formed clay vessels, highly fired, brilliantly painted, and often intricately fashioned. Mostly mold-made, they were turned out in great quantities, with the same stiff formality seen in Chimú pottery. The Nazca

Nazca painted clay double-spouted water jar, 1st–2nd century AD. In the American Museum of Natural History, New York City. Height 21 cm.

By courtesy of The American Museum of Natural History, New York

weavers, however, succeeded in defeating the mass market, for their work was devoted to highest quality, and their skill was such that even though miles of similarly patterned cloth were turned out regularly, the repetition did not destroy its beauty. In fact, the overall patterns so frequently seen provide a harmony that results in a beautiful fabric. There was literally no weaving process unknown to the ancient Peruvian. Nazca goldwork seems not to have been up to the standards achieved by other Peruvian metalwork; by and large, it is a listless product, having only the material to recommend it. Thin, hammered sheet gold was commonly used for Nazca ornamentation.

Closely related to, and extending from, the Nazca work is the art of the Ica civilization (AD 1000–1500). These people produced fine textiles, the designs of which were often reproduced on the pottery of the area. The dry climate has also preserved a wealth of wood carving, much of it in such fine condition that the quality of the art can be clearly seen.

In the central Peruvian area, a group of people emerged, built a modest civilization, and developed it into a world that was in existence when the Spanish arrived. The Chancay people are not known for great artworks; their pottery produced from AD 1000 to 1500 is a simple, black-on-white ware, usually painted in soft colours, simply defined, and frequently crude in appearance. Their one outstanding quality is humour; many Chancay vessels show a lively sense of the absurd, almost providing a Peruvian comic strip. Chancay weaving is excellent, and many thousands of surviving examples attest to this technical pre-eminence.

The art of Tiahuanaco

Farther afield, in Bolivia, another major civilization had been developing: the Tiahuanaco world. Its origin and the whole story of its development are not yet fully understood, but it is known that it came to exert a tremendous influence over a wide area of South America from AD 250 to 750. One of its most characteristic qualities was the use of stone—in walled cities, huge doorways with intricately carved panelling, and great paved roads. Tiahuanaco art is a rather angular expression, with repetitive, rather unoriginal motifs. The pottery from this site is equally uninspiring; although strong in colour, it does not show the variety and technical perfection seen in the wares of the nearby Inca and Nazca. Again, the great art is weaving. It seems that in many cultures the attention devoted to the textile arts far overshadowed that devoted to all of the other arts. And so it is with the Tiahuanaco, who produced ponchos, caps, pouches, and other costume pieces that are instantly recognizable wherever seen and challenge the contemporary weaver with their variety, fantastically tight weave, and remarkable richness of colour.

The Inca civilization had begun around AD 1200, but the empire itself was not established until 1438, with the accession of Pachacuti Inca Yupanqui, the greatest of the Inca rulers. With the arrival of the Spanish in 1532, the empire was at its height but was suffering from a schism that proved fatal in the face of the European attack. So savage was the Spanish invasion that the empire, numbering some 6,000,000 individuals at its height, was left without a head, and, within a period of thirty years, its population had dwindled to 1,500,000. Part of this legacy is that less art survives from the Inca culture than from many of the far older Peruvian cultures; there are many more Tiahuanaco ponchos known than those from the Inca period, for example. Enough has survived, however, to enable scholars to characterize Inca art forms. The aryballus (globular bottle for liquids) is known the world over, and stonework was common and of excellent quality. Silver and gold were no mystery to the Inca: religious tribute was claimed in the form of worked metal, treated as a gift to the sun god. Indeed, it was this very practice that proved the Inca's undoing, for the Spanish treasure seekers abandoned all other pursuits in their greed for precious metals.

In due course, the Inca civilization declined to a point where it was little more than a shell, as it is today. While much of the ancient weaving is still an active art, there is no pottery of a quality similar to the old, nor is there the wealth of woodwork, stone carving, or other crafts products. As for goldwork, it can safely be said that this art is completely in the hands of Westerners.

By courtesy of The American Museum of Natural History, New York

Inca silver figurine of an alpaca, Inca period (13th–15th century). In the American Museum of Natural History, New York City. Height 19 cm.

Chile and Argentina. Farther to the south, as he continued on his long journey past the Peruvian and Bolivian highlands, man crossed the great Atacama wasteland into Chile and, in so doing, changed his aesthetic expressions. This journey probably took place not much before 500 BC, when pottery-making people became active in the south. However late man came, he quickly set up civilizations. Wandering back and forth over the Andes, he settled both Chile, where he was known as Diaguita, and northern Argentina, where he was known as Chalchaquí. Very soon the peoples of this region developed their own arts, some of which are unique. They produced fine pottery and strong, colourful textiles. Gold was never a major product, although copper became an important metal, due in part to its prevalence. The people cast huge copper disks and plaques and made special burial urns for their children, even reserving cemetery areas in a touching demonstration of affection. The period of Diaguita settlement covered about 1500 years, or from about AD 1 to 1500.

With the extension of the Inca Empire into the Chilean and Argentine regions, the ubiquitous aryballus form found its way there, as did other, similar Inca expressions. Indeed, the pottery forms give a clue as to the presence or absence of the Inca overlords.

With the arrival of the Europeans all of this changed.

Late Aguada or Early Chalchaquí cast copper plaque from Argentina depicting a man between two felines, *c.* AD 700–1000. In the University Museum of Archaeology and Ethnology, Cambridge. 16 × 14 cm.

By courtesy of the University Museum of Archaeology and Ethnology, Cambridge

Western influence on South American Indian cultures

Of all of the South American Indian civilizations, only in Ecuador, Peru, Bolivia, and Chile is there anything like a continuum of native arts. And even in these the Western influence has been so pervasive as to eradicate all but the most dominant aesthetic characteristics. Weaving retains more of its ancestry than perhaps any other art; pottery has taken on much of the Western aura; woodworking is not at all what it was in pre-Columbian times; and very little metalwork is done in what can be called prehistoric design. Although much of the work done today is of highest quality, it reflects more of the tastes and needs of the white man than the Indian.

ARTS OF THE AMERICAN INDIAN PEOPLES IN THE CONTEMPORARY WORLD

In the contemporary art world, American Indian arts occupy a peripheral role. Until the last few decades, the only strong effort to exhibit this art in galleries or museums was made by those few institutions specializing in ethnological, exotic, or art history subjects, together with the rare specialized museum devoted only to Indian materials or to those of the American West. And in these the usual focus was upon sensational or romantic themes, not upon a carefully balanced understanding of the subject.

The most active interest in American Indian art seems to have been less in products of still-living cultures than in prehistoric arts and less in the arts of prehistoric North American peoples than in "pre-Columbian art," which is generally understood to mean the works of the so-called high civilizations—notably the Maya, Aztec, Inca, and Moche. This is to be regretted, for it not only results in an overemphasis that destroys intellectual balance but it also has relegated to the background some of the more exciting aesthetic accomplishments of the native American. The diorite bowl representing a crested wood duck that has been called by some "the Portland vase of America" is not an isolated instance, for there are other fine sculptures equally deserving of attention.

The reasons for these attitudes are not difficult to discover. With the displacement of the Indian by the Westerner came the rejection of his products, other than as curiosities of a vanquished people. Only in the last few decades has there been a concerted effort to develop an appreciation for art and a concern for the survival of this New World heritage.

More active efforts to preserve Indian art have been made in the United States than elsewhere. The first was in the 1920s, when a group of white artists located in and around Santa Fe, New Mexico, found excitement in the work of the Indians of the Southwest. Together with the so-called Taos Colony of artists, these influential people succeeded in bringing the values of Indian art to the attention of the outside world through publications, exhibitions, and their art works, in which Indian design often figured predominantly. In time, this group saw to the establishment of a School of Indian Art in Santa Fe. Out of this school came many of the most familiar names in Indian art today. Oqwa Pi, Jack Hokeah, Awa Tsireh, Pablita Velarde, Andy Tsinajinnie, Allan Houser, Ben Quintana, Gerónima Cruz Montoya, Eva Mirabal, and Waldo Mootzka are but a very few of the students involved during this exciting period. Following an initial success, the school enjoyed a period of prosperity but then fell victim to the Depression.

Indian Arts and Crafts Board

Another surge of interest came with the enactment of the Indian Reorganization Act of 1934, by means of which the Indian Arts and Crafts Board came into existence. Sparked by John Collier, then commissioner of Indian affairs, this body is one of the few governmental organizations set up specifically to promote, encourage, and revive native arts and crafts. While intended largely as an economic device to increase Indian income, the Board fortunately included members who were knowledgeable about, and sensitive to, the aesthetic and cultural strengths of the Indian. A program of exploration revealed surprising resilience in native crafts, and a core of still-active craftspeople who remembered older techniques was engaged to perpetuate their arts. Out of this program came a renaissance that still continues, even after the Board has become less influential, as the native artist more and more finds himself in his art. What promises to become the major factor influencing Indian art is the Institute of American Indian Arts in Santa Fe, New Mexico, an outgrowth of the early interest of the Indian Arts and Crafts Board in assisting young Indian artists to secure needed training.

Stimulated by these developments, the interest of art museums and collectors in native art brought home to the general public the existence of a remarkable, if overlooked, art form.

Today, a growing interest in Indian cultural expression is found among North American Indians themselves, as

Courtesy of the Denver Art Museum, Colorado

"Herding Sheep," watercolour on paper by Allan Houser, Chiricahua Apache, 1953. In the Denver Art Museum, Colorado. 72 × 46 cm.

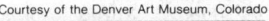

they seek their rightful place in contemporary society. Realizing the values in their heritage, and seeing much of it diminishing, many Indians want to learn what they can of their past and salvage what can be preserved.

Perhaps the greatest positive force to appear in some time are the Indian tribal councils, many of which support the arts in their own areas, not only to augment income but also out of an awareness of the cultural value of those arts. Many of these people, particularly the Navajo, Hopi, Cherokee, and Crow, have set up funds to develop crafts areas, sales centres, and museums to promote the appreciation of their traditional arts and thereby strengthen the fabric of the tribe. Some have set up crafts schools so that the younger people will have access to the necessary training.

Modern painting by North American Indians

With so many years of cultural denial, however, the native artist can no longer draw upon his rich heritage freely but must seek an adjustment with Western-derived motifs that have intruded upon, and in some cases overwhelmed, his world. Among all of the North American tribes, painting is perhaps the one art that has taken a new and positive direction. Many younger Indians of talent are creating remarkable works in acrylic, tempera, oil, and related media, gaining recognition in the fine arts field and showing promise of successful careers in the non-Indian world. Their most serious problem is that of identification. Some prefer to paint in a completely "free" manner, meaning that their work will not necessarily reflect their Indian ancestry. Others remain concerned over the demonstration of the racial or ethnic strain and seek means whereby they can paint in "Indian style" and yet escape the stereotype so prevalent in the minds of most non-Indians.

In other parts of the Western Hemisphere, organizations similar to those in the United States have recently been established to promote native crafts movements. In general, such movements find their greatest support in areas where nationalism is on the rise and pride in one's background is preeminent. The Latin-American nation that has taken the most effective steps in this direction has certainly been Mexico; its Museo Nacional de Arqueología (National Museum of Archeology), built in 1964, is perhaps the finest such structure in the world and stands as a monument to the heritage of that country. Guatemala, Colombia, Peru, and Ecuador also have devoted major architectural attention to their native cultures. (F.J.D.)

BIBLIOGRAPHY

Literature. *North America—United States and Canada:* The place of Native American literature in the body of American literature is analyzed in A. LAVONNE BROWN, *Literatures of the American Indian* (1991); BRIAN SWANN and ARNOLD KRUPAT (eds.), *Recovering the World: Essays on Native American Literature* (1987); and ARNOLD KRUPAT, *The Voice in the Margin: Native American Literature and the Canon* (1989). See also VIRGINIA ARMSTRONG (comp.), *I Have Spoken: American History Through the Voices of the Indians* (1971), a graphic résumé of Indian oratory from the 17th to the 20th century, emphasizing the eloquent speech of the tribes of North America; JOHN BIERHORST (comp.), *In the Trail of the Wind* (1971), a survey of American Indian poetry from many tribes; JESSIE CORNPLANTER, *Legends of the Longhouse* (1938), oral traditions of the Seneca as set down and illustrated by an Iroquois artist-writer; RICHARD ERDOES and ALFONSO ORTIZ (eds.), *American Indian Myths and Legends* (1984), tales from 100 tribes; JOHN BIERHORST, *The Mythology of North America* (1985), a comparative analytical study; GEORGE W. CRONYN (ed.), *The Path of the Rainbow: An Anthology of Songs and Chants from the Indians of North America,* new ed. (1934; reprinted as *American Indian Poetry,* 1970), a volume of Indian poetry from many tribes; A. GROVE DAY, *The Sky Clears: Poetry of the American Indians* (1951), a compilation of American Indian poetry, including more than 200 poems and lyrics from 40 tribes; ABRAHAM CHAPMAN, *Literature of the American Indians: Views and Interpretations: A Gathering of Indian Memories, Symbolic Contexts, and Literary Criticism* (1975), with important treatment of Indian poetry; WALTER DYK, *The Son of Old Man Hat: A Navaho Autobiography* (1938, reprinted 1967), a classic work recounting a Navajo's life story in his own words; HORATIO HALE (ed.), *The Iroquois Book of Rites* (1883, reprinted 1963), ancient ceremonies as revealed by two aboriginal "manuscripts" discovered at Grand River, with insights into Iroquois social and political life; MELVILLE JACOBS, *The Content and Style of an Oral Literature: Clackamas Chinook Myths and Tales* (1959), a discussion of a method by which oral literature can be understood in terms of its own content; LOUIS T. JONES, *Aboriginal American Oratory* (1965), a collection of Indian speeches and orations; GARRICK MALLERY, *Picture-Writing of the American Indians* (1893), an exhaustive consideration of the visual forms of communication adopted by many tribes, particularly strong in Plains Indian research. GUY MARY-ROUSSELIERE, *Beyond the High Hills* (1971), a sensitive collection of poems from the Hudson Bay Eskimo people, illustrated with photographs; KAREN PETERSEN, *Howling Wolf: A Cheyenne Warrior's Graphic Interpretation of His People* (1968), a pictorial history of the Cheyenne Indians, based on a collection of drawings by an artist-historian; PAUL RADIN, *The Road of Life and Death* (1945), a translation of the sacred rituals of the Winnebago, from their origin to their death and reincarnation; LEO W. SIMMONS (ed.), *Sun Chief: The Autobiography of a Hopi Indian* (1942), a revealing life story depicting the contrast of cultures within the experience of a single individual; STANDS IN TIMBER, JOHN and MARGOT LIBERTY, *Cheyenne Memories* (1967), a systematic collection of tribal history recording early Cheyenne life, by an Indian historian; SARAIN STUMP, *There Is My People Sleeping* (1970), a book of poems by a young Cree-Shoshoni artist; STITH THOMPSON (ed.), *Tales of the North American Indians* (1929, reprinted 1966), one of the earlier and more complete studies of American Indian legend; JUDITH C. ULLOM, *Folklore of the North American Indians* (1969), a collection of titles largely of popular versions but including some excellent analysis of folktales, their distribution, and place in the culture, with special attention given to children's literature; W.C. VANDERWERTH (comp.), *Indian Oratory: Famous Speeches by Noted Indian Chieftains* (1971), a collection of orations by 37 individuals, recorded from 1750 to 1910; JAMES WELCH, *Riding the Earthboy 40* (1971), poems by a Blackfoot youth, reflecting sound knowledge of his people, as related in vibrant terms. For literature of the second half of the 20th century, see RAYNA GREEN (ed.), *That's What She Said: Contemporary Poetry and Fiction by Native American Women* (1984); JAMAKE HIGHWATER (ed.), *Words in the Blood: Contemporary Indian Writers of North and South America* (1984); LAURA COLTELLI (comp. and ed.), *Winged Words: American Indian Writers Speak* (1990), a collection of analytical interviews; CHARLES R. LARSON, *American Indian Fiction* (1978), focusing on several novels; and W.H. NEW (ed.), *Native Writers and Canadian Writing* (1990).

Mexico, Central America, and South America: MIGUEL LEON-PORTILLA, *Las literaturas precolombinas de México* (1964; Eng. trans., *Pre-Columbian Literatures of Mexico,* 1969), a selection of myths, hymns, poetry, and prose accounts from Aztec, Maya, Mixtec-Zapotec, and Otomí peoples of Mexico recorded and discussed in depth; ADRIAN RECINOS (trans.), *Popol Vuh: The Sacred Book of the Ancient Quiché Maya* (1950), a complete version of the most important example of Maya literature to survive the conquest; FRANCES GILLMOR, *Flute of the Smoking Mirror: A Portrait of Nezahualcoyotl, Poet-King of the Aztecs* (1949, reprinted 1968), a sensitive portrayal of a major Nahuatl ruler, reflecting the thought processes of the Aztec as expressed through ancient graphic documents; RALPH L. ROYS (trans.), *The Book of Chilam Balam of Chumayel,* new ed. (1967), an account by the prophet of Chumayel village recorded in 1782, rich in Mayan ritual and oral traditions; JOHN BIERHORST, *The Mythology of Mexico and Central America* (1990), and *The Mythology of South America* (1988), comparative studies. (E.Gu./Ed.)

Music. *North America—United States and Canada:* PAUL COLLAER (ed.), *Amerika: Eskimo und indianische Bevölkerung,* 2 vol. (1967; Eng. trans., *Music of the Americas: An Illustrated Ethnology of the Eskimos and American Indian Peoples,* 1971), a magnificently illustrated study of the forms and instruments of the aborigines of the New World; FREDERICK R. BURTON, *American Primitive Music* (1909, reprinted 1969), an important book because of its early exposition of the little-known Garden River Reserve area in Ontario and for its transcriptions of Indian hymnody; WALLACE L. CHAFE, *Seneca Thanksgiving Rituals* (1961), a painstaking transcription of texts and melodies by a musically trained linguist; NATALIE CURTIS-BURLIN (ed.), *The Indians' Book* (1907), a pioneering collection of many tribal tunes, written down by ear and lucidly presented; FRANCES DENSMORE, *The American Indians and Their Music* (1926), one of the first major studies of the subject that combined anthropological knowledge with sound musical training to produce a well-organized ethnomusicology; and *Chippewa Music,* 2 vol. (1910–13), *Teton Sioux Music* (1918), *Menominee Music* (1932), and *Music of Santo Domingo Pueblo, New Mexico* (1938), particularly important books by Densmore, a pioneer who spent a lifetime salvaging the lore of one tribe after another, transcribing tunes from recordings—early cylinders, then discs, of poor fidelity but of inestimable cultural value; GEORGE HER-

ZOG, *Research in Primitive and Folk Music in the United States* (1936), a useful survey by a pioneer musicologist; GERTRUDE P. KURATH, *Iroquois Music and Dance* (1964), transcription and analysis of many Seneca songs, from recordings by William N. Fenton and Martha Huot, with dance diagrams and interpretations from the author's field work; and "Dogrib Choreography and Music," in JUNE HELM MACNEISH and NANCY O. LURIE, "The Dogrib Hand Game," *Bull. Natn. Mus. Can.*, no. 205, pp. 13–28 (1966), transcription, analysis, and choreography; BERNARD S. MASON, *Drums, Tomtoms and Rattles* (1938), a practical book on North American instruments; DAVID P. MCALLESTER, *Peyote Music* (1949), transcription and interpretation of the songs used in this semi-Christian, nativist cult; and *Enemy Way Music* (1954), one of the few books with musical scores of a Navajo curative rite, with valuable material on native aesthetic concepts; ALAN P. MERRIAM, *Ethnomusicology of the Flathead Indians* (1967), an exhaustive study of the music of a Montana tribe, with musical scores, analyses, and historical notes by an anthropologist; BRUNO NETTL, *Music in Primitive Culture* (1956), and *North American Indian Musical Styles* (1954), representative works by a prolific ethnomusicologist with anthropological as well as musical training, including selected musical scores and bibliographies. HELEN H. ROBERTS, *Musical Areas in Aboriginal North America* (1936), one of the earliest attempts to divide American Indian into its geographic subdivisions; and with DIAMOND JENNESS, *Songs of the Copper Eskimos* (1925); and with MORRIS SWADESH, *Songs of the Nootka Indians of Western Vancouver Island* (1955), two painstaking works with detailed musical scores and background notes by collaborators; FRANK G. SPECK, *Ceremonial Songs of the Creek and Yuchi Indians* (1911), and *Penobscot Man* (1940), two reliable books by an anthropologist, with musical scores by JACOB SAPIR (also contains comments on dance). LEANNE HINTON and LUCILLE J. WATAHOMIGIE (eds.), *Spirit Mountain: An Anthology of Yuman Story and Song* (1984), includes translated songs from eight tribes.

Mexico, Central America, and South America: GILBERT CHASE, *A Guide to the Music of Latin America,* 2nd ed. rev. (1962), an indispensable bibliography; RAOUL and M. D'HARCOURT, *La Musique des Incas et ses survivances,* 2 vol. (1925), still one of the most exhaustive studies of the ancient Inca and his music and its present-day place in South America; KARL GUSTAV IZIKOWITZ, *Musical and Other Sound Instruments of the South American Indians* (1935), a remarkable compilation of facts on the forms and functions of instruments; SAMUEL MARTI, *Canto, danza y música precortesianos* (1961), a well-illustrated study of the subject by one of Mexico's foremost ethnomusicologists; and *Instrumentos musicales precortesianos* (1955), a valuable description of native instruments, past and present, with excellent photographs, scales of prehistoric flutes, and notations of native South American and Middle American tunes; CHARLES W. MEAD, *The Musical Instruments of the Inca* (1924), an illustrated examination of various Peruvian examples, largely from the American Museum of Natural History collections; SEGUNDO L. MORENO, *La música de los Incas* (1957), a well-rounded survey, written by an Ecuadorean ethnomusicologist, of the ancient and contemporary Inca musical world; ROBERT STEVENSON, *Music in Aztec and Inca Territory* (1968), a major survey of attitudes toward ancient music, its instrumentation, and social position in the two areas at the time of the conquest.

Dance. *North America—United States and Canada:* JULIA M. BUTTREE-SETON, *The Rhythm of the Red Man* (1930), choreographies, some music; FREDERICK J. DOCKSTADER, *The Kachina and the White Man: A Study of the Influences of White Culture on the Hopi Kachina Cult* (1954), a survey on the origin of Pueblo masked dances and their development among the Hopi people of Arizona; BESSIE and MAY G. EVANS, *American Indian Dance Steps* (1931), descriptions of steps, six choreographies, and music; WILLIAM N. FENTON and GERTRUDE P. KURATH, *The Iroquois Eagle Dance: An Offshoot of the Calumet Dance* (1935), history, choreographies, music, analysis, photographs, and bibliography; ERNA FERGUSSON, *Dancing Gods* (1931), an evaluation of ceremonial dances of the Indians of the Southwest; ALICE C. FLETCHER, *Indian Games and Dances with Native Songs* (1915), a combined study of games, songs, and dances, useful to younger readers; GERTRUDE P. KURATH, *Michigan Indian Festivals* (1966), history, choreography, music, photographs, and bibliography; *Iroquois Music and Dance* (1964), diagrams, choreography, music, analysis, and photographs; and *Music and Dance of the Tewa Pueblos* (1970), background, choreography, music, photographs, and bibliography; BERNARD S. MASON, *Dances and Stories of the American Indian* (1944), almost entirely concerned with North American Indian dance steps, forms, and costumes (well illustrated); VIRGINIA M. ROEDIGER, *Ceremonial Costumes of the Pueblo Indians* (1941), a superbly illustrated volume, dealing with all Pueblo tribes and their ritual dress, including dance costumes; CURT SACHS, *Eine Weltgeschichte des Tanzes* (1933; Eng. trans., *World History of the Dance,* 1937, reprinted 1963), includes several sections on various Indian tribal dance performances; FRANK G. SPECK and LEONARD BROOM, *Cherokee Dance and Drama* (1951), a specialized study of Eastern Cherokee dances and related ritual; JOHN L. SQUIRES and ROBERT E. MCLEAN, *American Indian Dances* (1963), a volume intended primarily for hobbyist readers.

Mexico, Central America, and South America: AUGUSTE GENIN, *Notes on the Dances, Music, and Songs of the Ancient and Modern Mexicans* (1922), a comparison of pre-Columbian with contemporary folk dances; LISA LEKIS, *Folk Dances of Latin America* (1958), exhaustive bibliography, with historical notes and descriptions; SAMUEL MARTI, *Canto, danza y música precortesianos* (1961), thoroughly illustrated, with equal sections given to an examination of musical instruments, songs, and the forms of the dance in pre-Columbian times; and with GERTRUDE P. KURATH, *Dances of Anáhuac: The Choreography and Music of Precortesian Dances* (1964), a thorough and well-illustrated analysis of the subject; ROBERT STEVENSON, *Music in Aztec and Inca Territory* (1968), includes a large amount of valuable material on the dance in pre-Columbian times, although primarily involved with music, singing, and the vocal arts; FRANCES TOOR, *A Treasury of Mexican Folkways* (1947), a volume on folklore, including the dance, by a longtime resident of Mexico; CARLOS VEGA, *Las danzas populares argentinas* (1952), authoritative history, choreography, and some music. (G.P.K.)

Visual and material arts. *General:* FERDINAND ANTON and FREDERICK J. DOCKSTADER, *Das Alte Amerika* (1967; Eng. trans., *Pre-Columbian Art and Later Tribal Arts,* 1968), a popular treatment that covers the Western Hemisphere, extremely valuable for the many illustrations, most of which are in colour; FRANZ BOAS, *Primitive Art* (1927; new ed., 1955), an old-time classic with considerable discussion of the place of native arts in European society—especially helpful for the section on Northwest Coast art; G.H.S. BUSHNELL, *Ancient Arts of the Americas* (1965), a general treatment of the Western Hemisphere, with greater attention given to Latin America; MIGUEL COVARRUBIAS, *The Eagle, the Jaguar and the Serpent* (1954), a splendid volume on the arts of the Americas, with many line drawings and colour plates by the author, a major Mexican artist, and *Indian Art of Mexico and Central America* (1957), a continuation of the above and one of the best single treatments on the formative centuries of ancient Mexican civilization; HANS D. DISSELHOFF and S. LINNE, *Alt-Amerika* (1960; Eng. trans., *The Art of Ancient America,* 1961), a well-illustrated volume that concentrates primarily upon the prehistoric cultures of Central and South America, and largely ignores North American Indian art; FREDERICK J. DOCKSTADER, *Indian Art in America: The Arts and Crafts of the North American Indian,* 3rd ed. (1966), a survey of the native arts of the United States and Canada, *Indian Art in Middle America: The Arts and Crafts of the Indians of Mexico, Central America and the Caribbean* (1964), extending the study to the southern boundary of Panama, with particular emphasis on the lesser-known tribes of the region, and *Indian Art in South America: Pre-Columbian and Contemporary Arts and Crafts* (1967), the final volume in this series, completing a survey of the entire range of aboriginal art of the New World; ALVIN M. JOSEPHY, JR., *The Indian Heritage of America* (1968), one of the few volumes to discuss the Indian from North to South—a sound introduction to the New World native, although written from the historical point of view; PAL KELEMEN, *Art of the Americas, Ancient and Hispanic* (1969), a well-illustrated study of the earlier periods of the Americas, particularly valuable for its inclusion of the colonial influences on Indian aesthetics; and *Medieval American Art,* 3rd rev. ed., 2 vol. (1969), a rich sourcebook of illustrations that includes the entire hemisphere; GORDON R. WILLEY, *An Introduction to American Archaeology,* 2 vol. (1966–71), a profusely illustrated, comprehensive survey of the prehistory of the New World, by one of its leading archaeologists, RALPH T. COE, *Lost and Found Traditions: Native American Art 1965–1985* (1986), a treatment of the contemporary development of the native tradition.

North America—United States and Canada: CHARLES A. AMSDEN, *Navaho Weaving: Its Technic and History* (1934, reprinted 1964); KATE PECK KENT, *Prehistoric Textiles of the Southwest* (1983), and *Pueblo Indian Textiles: A Living Tradition* (1983); MARIUS BARBEAU, *Totem Poles . . .,* 2 vol. (1929–30); ROBERT T. DAVIS, *Native Arts of the Pacific Northwest* (1949); FREDERIC H. DOUGLAS and RENE D'HARNONCOURT, *Indian Art of the United States* (1941, reprinted 1969); DOROTHY DUNN, *American Indian Painting of the Southwest and Plains Areas* (1968); WOLFGANG HABERLAND, *The Art of North America* (1964); CAMPBELL GRANT, *The Rock Art of the North American Indians* (1983); ROBERT B. INVERARITY, *Art of the Northwest Coast Indians* (1950); PETER NABOKOV and ROBERT EASTON, *Native American*

Architecture (1989); WILLIAM C. ORCHARD, *Beads and Beadwork of the North American Indians,* 2nd rev. ed. (1972), the most complete single study of Western Hemisphere bead artistry; CLARA LEE TANNER, *Southwest Indian Craft Arts* (1968); SARAH PEABODY TURNBAUGH and WILLIAM A. TURNBAUGH, *Indian Baskets* (1986), and *Indian Jewelry of the American Southwest* (1988); PATRICK HOULIHAN *et al., Harmony by Hand: Art of the Southwest Indians, Basketry, Weaving, Pottery* (1987); JOHN C. EWERS, *Plains Indian Sculpture: A Traditional Art from America's Heartland* (1986).

Mexico, Central America, and the West Indies: MIGUEL COVARRUBIAS, *Indian Art of Mexico and Central America* (1957); ANDRE EMMERICH, *Art Before Columbus* (1963); JESSE W. FEWKES, *A Prehistoric Island Culture Area of America* (1922); PAL KELEMEN, *Medieval American Art,* 3rd rev. ed., 2 vol. (1969); GEORGE KUBLER, *The Art and Architecture of Ancient America: The Mexican, Maya, and Andean Peoples* (1962); SAMUEL K. LOTHROP, *Pottery of Costa Rica and Nicaragua,* 2 vol. (1926); IGNACIO MARQUINA, *Arquitectura Prehispánica* (1951); SYLVANUS G. MORLEY, *The Ancient Maya,* 3rd ed. (1956); TATIANA PROSKOURIAKOFF, *An Album of Maya Architecture* (1946); HENRI STIERLIN, *Art of the Maya: From the Olmecs to the Toltec-Maya* (1981; originally published in French, 1981); DONALD ROBERTSON, *Mexican Manuscript Painting of the Early Colonial Period* (1959); MARSHALL H. SAVILLE, *The Goldsmith's Art in Ancient Mexico* (1920); HERBERT J. SPINDEN, *A Study of Maya Art* (1913; rev. as *Maya Art and Civilization,* 1957); J. ERIC THOMPSON, *The Rise and Fall of Maya Civilization* (1954); GEORGE C. VAILLANT, *The Aztecs of Mexico,* rev. ed. (1962); HENRI STIERLIN, *Art of the Aztecs and Its Origins* (1982; originally published in French, 1982); HASSO VON WINNING, *Pre-Columbian Art of Mexico and Central America* (1968); KARL TAUBE, *The Albers Collection of Pre-Columbian Art* (1988); MURIEL P. WEAVER, *The Aztecs, Maya, and Their Predecessors* (1972).

South America: WENDELL C. BENNETT, *Ancient Arts of the Andes* (1954); HENRI STIERLIN, *Art of the Incas and Its Origins* (1984; originally published in French, 1983); JUNIUS B. BIRD and LOUISA BELLINGER, *Paracas Fabrics and Nazca Needlework, 3rd Century B.C.–3rd Century A.D.* (1954); G.H.S. BUSHNELL, *Peru,* rev. ed. (1963); RAOUL D'HARCOURT, *Les Textiles anciens du Pérou, et leurs techniques* (1934; Eng. trans., *Textiles of Ancient Peru and Their Techniques,* 1934); FERDINAND ANTON, *Ancient Peruvian Textiles* (1987; originally published in German, 1984); ANDRE EMMERICH, *Sweat of the Sun and Tears of the Moon: Gold and Silver in Pre-Columbian Art* (1965); JAN MITCHELL, *The Art of Precolumbian Gold: The Jan Mitchell Collection,* ed. by JULIE JONES (1985); PAL KELEMEN, *Art of the Americas, Ancient and Hispanic* (1969); SAMUEL K. LOTHROP, *Treasures of Ancient America* (1964); J. ALDEN MASON, *Ancient Civilizations of Peru* (1957); BETTY J. MEGGERS, *Ecuador* (1966); G. REICHEL-DOLMATOFF, *Colombia* (1965); ALAN R. SAWYER, *Ancient Peruvian Ceramics* (1966).

(F.J.D./Ed.)

Native American Peoples

The aboriginal peoples of the Western Hemisphere usually are recognized as constituting two broad groupings. The first and larger group, called Native Americans (or, conventionally, American Indians), is further divided geographically into North American, Middle American, and South American Indian peoples. The second group consists of a number of Arctic peoples, most of whom are variously called Eskimos or Inuit but also including such other groups as Aleuts.

Although all of these peoples had their origins in Asia and have retained some physical affinities with modern Asiatic peoples, they were isolated long enough to have developed into a distinct group, generally called the American Indian geographic race. The distinction between Asiatics and Americans has remained somewhat blurred, however, in extreme northeastern Siberia and northwestern Alaska, where the indigenous peoples of that region have exhibited greater affinities with each other than with their respective geographic races.

The date of the arrival of humans in North America has not been accurately established, but it is known to have occurred during the Pleistocene Epoch (1,600,000 to 10,000 years ago). For some time the earliest human occupation of America was thought to date to the last (Wisconsin) glacial period, or about 35,000 to 20,000 years ago. More recently, however, some authorities have asserted that the first arrivals were much earlier, even up to 60,000 years ago. The site of entry into North America is widely assumed to have been a land bridge—formed as glaciers advanced and sea levels fell—where the Bering Strait now divides Asia and America.

The waves of newcomers to the Americas possessed a series of traits that were relatively ancient and were shared by most peoples of Africa and Eurasia. These included the use of fire and the fire drill; the domesticated dog; stone implements of many kinds; the spear thrower, harpoon, and simple bow; cordage, netting, and basketry; and various rites and healing beliefs and practices. By the time Europeans began arriving in significant numbers at the beginning of the 16th century AD, the descendants of these and later waves of migrants had spread over the Americas and had developed a variety of cultures adjusted to various ecological conditions.

The peoples of the New World developed markedly different cultures from those of the Old World during their many millennia of isolation. Some Old World practices, such as the use of the wheel and the plow and the fashioning of iron implements, did not emerge; others, such as pottery making and urbanization, reached high levels of sophistication in the Americas. Many New World cultures depended on hunting and gathering, although agriculture came to be the economic base of more advanced civilizations. The focus in the New World was on corn (maize), beans, squash, and tubers as the staple crops, as contrasted to the Old World reliance on such cereal grains as wheat, barley, and rice.

The scope of this article is a survey of the Native American peoples and cultures of North, Middle, and South America, with an emphasis on traditional ways of life and the changes wrought by contact with European civilization. The traditional culture of the North American Arctic peoples is treated in the article ARCTIC, THE. Additional cultural and historical information on indigenous American peoples can be found in the articles PRE-COLUMBIAN CIVILIZATIONS and PREHISTORIC PEOPLES AND CULTURES. See also the articles CENTRAL AMERICA and WEST INDIES, THE, and articles on individual countries (*e.g.,* CANADA) for the treatment of modern Native Americans in national contexts. The art forms of Native American and North American Arctic peoples are discussed in the article AMERICAN PEOPLES, ARTS OF NATIVE.

For coverage of related topics in the *Macropædia* and *Micropædia,* see the *Propædia,* section 511, and the *Index.*

The article is divided into the following sections:

North American peoples and cultures 350
- The people
  - Physical types
  - Population and languages
  - Culture areas
- The prehistoric period
  - Early cultures
  - The Archaic cultures
  - Early agriculturalists
  - Mississippi Valley and peripheral woodlands
  - Southwestern village farmers
- Evolution of contemporary cultures
  - Colonial policies
  - United States policy
- American subarctic cultures 359
  - Traditional culture patterns
  - Modern developments
- Northwest Coast Indians 362
  - Traditional culture patterns
  - Modern developments
- Californian Indians 366
  - Traditional culture patterns
  - Modern developments
- North American Plateau Indians 369
  - Traditional culture patterns
  - Modern developments
- North American Great Basin Indians 372
  - Traditional culture patterns
  - Modern developments
- Southwest American Indians 375
  - Traditional culture patterns
  - Modern developments
- North American Plains Indians 379
  - Traditional culture patterns
  - Modern developments
- Eastern Woodlands Indians 383
  - Traditional culture patterns
  - Modern developments
- Southeast American Indians 387
  - Traditional culture patterns
  - Modern developments

Middle American peoples and cultures 391
- The people
- The prehistoric period
- Evolution of contemporary cultures
- North Mexican Indian cultures 394
  - Traditional culture patterns
  - Modern developments
- Meso-American Indian cultures 398
  - Traditional culture patterns
  - Modern developments
- Central American and Northern Andean cultures 400
  - Traditional culture patterns
  - Modern developments

South American peoples and cultures 402
- The people
- The prehistoric period
- Evolution of contemporary cultures
- Andean cultures 406
  - Central Andes—traditional culture patterns
  - Southern Andes—traditional culture patterns
- South American tropical forest cultures 408
  - Traditional culture patterns
  - Modern developments
- South American nomad cultures 412
  - Traditional culture patterns
  - Modern developments

Bibliography 414

NORTH AMERICAN PEOPLES AND CULTURES

The North American continent into which the Asian migrants descended is divided roughly into three major physiographic landforms: the high Cordilleras in the west, the relatively lower Appalachian Highlands and Piedmont in the east, and, between them, the Great Plains, which spearhead from the Arctic Ocean to the Gulf of Mexico in a great triangle. The Western Cordilleras are a series of parallel north–south ranges cutting from Alaska to Central America; in the area of Canada and the United States they enclose, from north to south, a large plateau of grasslands and forests, an even broader, arid plateau known as the Great Basin, and a desert plain and range area of Arizona and New Mexico (as well as northwestern Mexico). The Cordilleras along the Pacific Coast separate a plethora of basins and plateaus from the coastlands. The central Great Plains, in the extreme north, consists of subarctic land that is swampy and coniferous and similar to the taiga and tundra of Siberia; to the south, the great Mississippi drainage system divides the relatively drier high plains to the west from the low, well-watered prairies and rolling hills to the east. The Appalachian Highlands and Piedmont contain, to the north, the great eastern woodlands and, to the south, a series of highlands and foothills descending to lowlands on the coast of the Atlantic and the Gulf of Mexico.

At the time of European contact there were perhaps as many as 240 different tribal entities in North America. Groups of these tribes, however, have been classified by anthropologists into a more convenient limited number of culture areas, determined very much by physiographic or environmental differences: the subarctic, the Northwest Coast, California, the western Plateau, the western Great Basin, the Southwest, the Plains, the Eastern Woodlands, and the Southeast. This section, in dealing with the major culture areas of North America, excludes the Arctic Eskimo and Aleuts. The peoples of Mexico, other parts of Middle America, and the peoples of South America are treated in separate sections below.

THE PEOPLE

Physical types. Although American Indians are fundamentally Mongoloid, considerable variation is found. The generally uniform physical features are these: the hair is usually straight, coarse, and uniformly black; the skin is reddish brown, the eyes dark, and the body hair scant; the cheekbones are prominent; and the facial size is generally large. Such features as cephalic index, nasal form, and stature, however, are extremely variable.

Mongoloid characteristics of American Indians

The uniform features are definitely Mongoloid; the variable features are more difficult to assess. Some scholars believe that the early migrant populations were essentially Mongoloid and that the variations came about through adjustment to American environments. Other scholars argue that the New World was peopled by a variety of physical types, with later mixtures but some marginal survival in isolated regions.

Archaeologically, the earlier populations were generally long headed (dolichocephalic) and showed fewer Mongoloid characteristics. These early peoples were slight in build with well-developed brow ridges, and many represent either a proto-Mongoloid type or an unspecialized early Caucasoid form related to the Ainu of Japan.

Detailed study of the distribution of blood groups among the American Indians may eventually aid in solving the problem of their origins. Thus, for example, it has been found that blood type B is generally absent in the aboriginal population of the Americas (though its incidence is high among Asian Mongoloids), and type A is found mainly in North American Indians.

Modern genetic theory would explain much of the variation found in terms of such factors as mutation, selection, admixture, and random genetic drift. In the small-scale groups involved in the early peopling of the New World, relatively rapid changes were possible and could account for all of the variation found.

Population and languages. Estimates of the aboriginal population are based on information supplied by explorers, traders, missionaries, and other early reporters and are only as good as the reporters' observations were trustworthy. A more serious impediment to an accurate count is that some tribes, by the time they were visited, had already been depopulated by European diseases and weapons. The estimates in the Table, it should be noted, are given an approximate dating.

The American anthropologist Alfred Louis Kroeber submitted a population total for the area north of Mexico almost identical to that given in the Table, since he used the same figures except for California. He subgrouped the material, however, to accord with subsistence areas rather than geographical boundaries. In addition, he ranked the areas according to population densities, expressed in numbers of persons per square kilometre: California area, 43.40; northwest Pacific Coast, 28.30; southwestern United States, 10.70; Columbia–Fraser rivers area, 7.15; eastern area, 6.95; Arctic coast, 4.02; Great Basin, 2.47; and northern area, 1.35. Although agricultural areas of the east and southwest contained the greater population (about 405,000 in all), Kroeber believed that the predominantly fishing economy of the Pacific Coast (Bering Strait to southern California) had greater relative density of population. His estimates were Pacific Coast, 25.2 persons per square kilometre; agricultural areas, 10.1; remaining area north of Mexico, 2.2.

The population of a little over 1,000,000 for North America north of Mexico contrasts with the estimated 5,000,000 for Mexico and Central America and with the estimated 25,000,000 for the Western Hemisphere as a whole. (These uncertifiable estimates must, however, be approached with caution.)

The outstanding characteristic of American Indian languages is their diversity. There were more than 60 language families in North America, comprising over 500 languages, but these have been reduced to a smaller num-

Aboriginal Indian Population North of Mexico

	date	estimated population
North Atlantic		
New England, New York, New Jersey, Pennsylvania	1600	55,600
South Atlantic		
Delaware, Maryland, Virginia, West Virginia, the Carolinas, except Cherokee country	1600	52,200
Gulf States		
Georgia, Florida, Alabama, Mississippi, Louisiana, Arkansas, Tennessee, Cherokee country	1650	114,400
Central States		
Ohio valley from Allegheníes to Mississippi, Chippewa in Canada	1650	75,300
The Plains (Canada to Gulf)		
Northern	1780	100,800
Southern	1690	41,000
Columbia River basin		
Washington, most of Oregon, northern half of Idaho	1780	89,300
California	1769	260,000
Central mountain		
Nevada, Utah, parts of surrounding states	1845	19,300
New Mexico and Arizona	1680	72,000
Subtotal United States (except Alaska)*		849,000
British America		
Eastern Canada, central Canada, British Columbia	1600–1780	190,950
Subtotal British America*		221,000
Alaska	1740	72,600
Greenland	1721	10,000
Total		1,153,450

*From analysis according to modern political divisions as of dates given.
Source: James Mooney, "The Aboriginal Population of America North of Mexico," Smithsonian Miscellaneous Collection, vol. 80, no. 7 (1928).

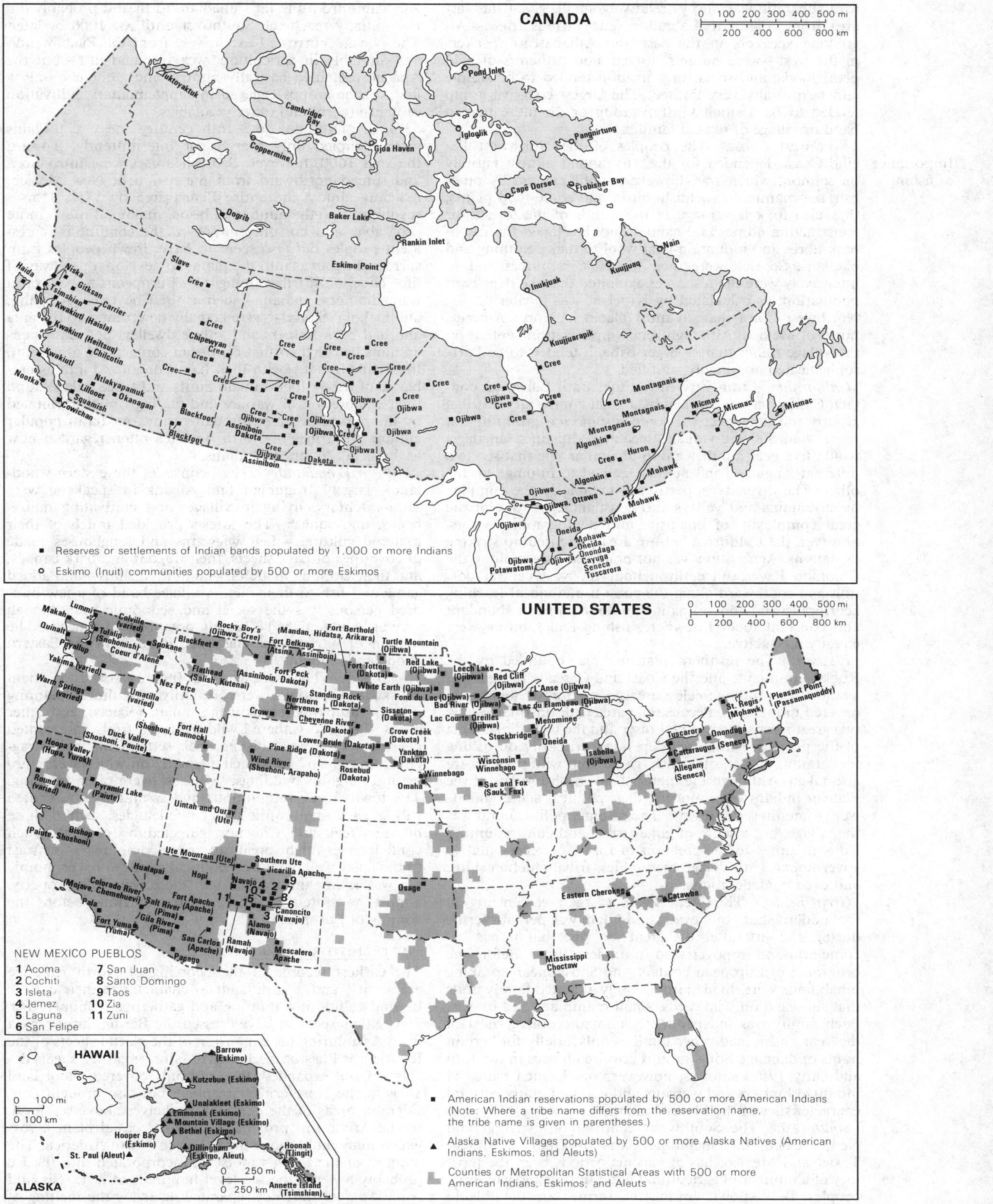

Distribution of North American peoples and cultures (top) in Canada and (bottom) in the United States.

Diversity of languages

ber of superstocks by modern linguists. The American linguist and anthropologist Edward Sapir, for instance, proposed six linguistic groups for North America (including the Arctic): Eskimo-Aleut, Algonkian-Wakashan, Na-Dené, Penutian, Hokan-Siouan, and Aztec-Tanoan (see LANGUAGES OF THE WORLD). No American language has any genetic relationship to any language group in the Old World that has yet been fully demonstrated. It may be concluded from this that the ancestors of the Indians left the Old World so long ago that any relationship was lost through linguistic change.

Culture areas. *Subarctic.* The population of the American subarctic was always relatively small, given the vast area from Alaska to Labrador. The various tribes—Algonkian speakers in the east and Athabascan speakers in the west—were hunters, fishers, and gatherers of wild plant foods; and social organization tended to be simple and territorially very limited. The largest cohesive group tended to be a small kinship group or no more than a band or village of related families.

Northwest Coast. The peoples of the Northwest Pacific Coast depended for their livelihood almost entirely on salmon, which was, however, supplemented by other fish, sea mammals, shellfish, birds, and some food plants; they also took advantage of the woods of the forests for constructing homes and canoes and developed the use of bark fibres and mountain-goat wool to make clothing and blankets. So rich were their available resources and so intensively were the resources exploited that the density of population, as calculated by Kroeber, was greater on the Northwest Coast than in most places in North America north of Mexico. Although social organization centred on the village rather than a larger tribe, it tended to be fairly sophisticated and highly stratified.

Importance of fishing

California. From very early times until European contact, California was marked by a great complexity of tribal groups and languages. In some instances a group of not more than 500 individuals, speaking a distinct language, would live near another group of similar size that spoke a different language, and neither seemed to impinge on the other. The diversity is partly attributable to the complex of mountains and valleys and coastlands. In spite of the great complexity of linguistic and demographic factors, however, the California culture area presented no striking deviations. Agriculture was not practiced except along the Colorado River, since throughout the vast central portion and southward along the coast a method of leaching acorn pulp and converting it into flour supplied abundant and constant food. Elsewhere, fishing and hunting were equally productive.

Plateau. The northern plateau area, bounded by the Rocky Mountains and the Coast and Cascade ranges, was a land of vast rolling treeless areas, dense forests, and snow-covered mountains. Because the area is drained largely by two great river systems, the Fraser and the Columbia, most of the peoples of the area depended primarily on fishing for salmon, though other fish, game, and wild plants were also taken. Although the material accomplishments of the Plateau Indians were modest, their political achievements were sometimes impressive. The primary political unit was the village, but a sense of larger tribal and cultural unities led sometimes to the creation of forms of representative government, with village hierarchies, tribal chieftainships, and even confederations.

Great Basin. The Great Basin, a large area centring on the modern states of Nevada and Utah, was perhaps fertile during and just after the great Ice Age, but it has become arid and impoverished in modern times. Before the beginning of European contact, the Shoshonean-speaking inhabitants were divided into loosely affiliated family units that subsisted on wild seeds, small mammals, and insects. Each family was independently nomadic during most of the year and joined other families only briefly for certain hunts or dancing. Some groups acquired horses in the 18th and early 19th centuries, however, and formed bands of mounted hunters and warriors and adopted many cultural characteristics of the Plains Indians.

Southwest. The Southwest, centring on Arizona and New Mexico, but including parts of Utah, Colorado, Texas, and Mexico, has at various periods been the territory of a number of agricultural and hunting and gathering peoples. Best known among the former are the Pueblo Indians, from the Zuni and Hopi on the west to the Rio Grande groups on the east, who built architecturally remarkable multiple apartment houses of adobe and stone masonry and developed to a high state agriculture, arts, and crafts. Their ancestors occupied the Southwest thousands of years ago, and their high cultural development began during the 1st millennium AD with the arrival of influences from Mexico. Two other major groups, the Athabascan-speaking Navajo and the Apache, undoubtedly came from the far Canadian north and probably did not initially reach the Southwest until AD 1000 or later. The Navajo borrowed extensively from the Pueblo Indians—notably in agriculture, weaving, and arts—but the Apache remained basically hunters and gatherers; only a few Apache groups engaged in supplementary cultivation of maize (corn) and other vegetables.

Plains. Until the late 16th century the Great Plains were occupied only sparsely or intermittently. Toward the year 1600, however, Spanish horses were introduced and spread northward from the region of New Mexico, reaching almost the entire Plains area by 1750. Horses revolutionized the hunting of bison, making it much more profitable, and not only improved the conditions of resident peoples but also seem to have drawn peoples from surrounding areas into the plains to develop a new way of life. Thus, most tribes thought by Europeans to be typical nomadic horse Indians—such as the Cheyenne, Arapaho, and Dakota (Sioux)—were actually newcomers to the area and had been farmers and village dwellers not many generations before their first European contacts. In any event, the Plains Indians, with their bands organized into assemblages of tribes, their buffalo hunts and tepee villages, and their elaboration of warfare and raiding (much facilitated by the horse), became, through various media of popular culture, the tribes of North America often regarded now as "typical" American Indians.

Revolution of the horse

Eastern Woodlands. The peoples of the eastern woodlands, largely Iroquoian and Algonkian speakers, were semi-sedentary, living in villages and cultivating maize, beans, and squash. The forests provided much of their material cultures—their wigwams and longhouses made of coverings of bark sheets, their dugout and bark canoes, and their clothing made of wild animal skins—and added game and fish to their diet. A village band of a few hundred persons was the social and economic unit, though several bands might be loosely organized into tribes. The honour of warfare was engrained in most of the Eastern Woodlands Indians.

Southeast. The southeastern Indians, most of them Muskogean speakers, were primarily agricultural, planting maize, pumpkins, beans, cane millet, tobacco, and other crops; they also gathered wild nuts and fruits and hunted deer or, in the west, bison. Their settlements were straggling; the "town" contained a square, on which were public and religious buildings; "villages" were often outlying. The towns were autonomous and essentially constituted tribes. They might unite into confederacies, such as those of the Creek and Choctaw, directed by councils; such confederacies might break up and recombine. In contrast to the fairly well organized political institutions, economic life was rather unsophisticated; there was little property, almost no stored wealth, and limited trade before the coming of Europeans.

THE PREHISTORIC PERIOD

The earliest records of the peopling of North America are scanty, and it is difficult to characterize their culture beyond calling it a hunting and gathering economy. The first settlers seem to have crossed the Bering Strait region from Asia during the expansion of the glacial sheets of the Ice Age (or Pleistocene Epoch). As the great ice sheets developed and expanded, they not only covered major land areas in the Northern Hemisphere but also brought considerable areas of the continental shelves above sea level. In the Arctic this provided a tundra coastal plain across which man could move from Asia to North America. The amount of the Earth's moisture incorporated into the ice probably lowered the sea level hundreds of feet. Asia and America were thus not separated again by the melting of the glaciers and the consequent gradual rise of the sea until about 9,000 or 10,000 years ago; likely sites of the earliest migrants are now below sea level.

Early migrations from Asia

The Americas were the last major land mass, with the possible exception of Australia, to be occupied by prehistoric man, who, in order to spread over the vast area of the two continents, first had to develop the cultural equipment to exist in the Arctic area. Once this adjustment was made, he was able to move by way of ice-free, open-land routes into the Mackenzie Basin and down into climatically less rigorous and ecologically richer and more accomodating central North America. In addition to the Mackenzie route southward, at a later time the Yukon River valley also offered an ice-free route, and still later (8,000–10,000 years ago) the Liard and Peace river systems were available for intramontane travel. The Pacific Coast slope was probably available for travel at about the same time. Some migrations may also have occurred by way of the Aleutian Islands, but this would have taken place at a considerably later date.

Early cultures. The earliest well-defined cultures in the New World have been placed by radiocarbon dating at about 10,000 to 8000 BC. At this period, two distinct traditions in North America are known: the Paleo-Indian big-game hunters of the West, the Great Plains, and eastern North America; and the Desert culture peoples of the western Basin–Range region.

Paleo-Indian hunting cultures. In spite of regional differences in detail, there was a remarkable similarity in the economic complex of the hunters. They lived in a variety of environments, from mountain passes and valleys in the west to the then better watered grasslands of the Plains and the varied forest and parkland environment of the eastern woodlands. The variety of their bone tools indicates that one of their major food supplies came from animals, the hides of which provided clothing. In the western Plains and the Southwest they hunted such extinct North American animals as the camel, ground sloth, tapir, mammoth, and horse.

In the Great Lakes area of the eastern woodlands they may have hunted mastodon, but other commoner animals, such as the elk and deer, presumably formed the bulk of their meat diet. Some of their bone and wooden tools were probably used for working and ornamentation. These early hunters had temporary shelters and moved about as small bands in search of game. Their physical type is not clearly known, but it was related to that of an eastern Asian Early Stone Age population and is less Mongoloid than many groups of American Indians of the historic period.

Oldest archaeological remains

Archaeologically, the oldest remains of the Paleo-Indian tradition are found on kill sites, where large Pleistocene mammals were killed and butchered. The most distinctive artifact type of this horizon is the Clovis Fluted projectile point (named after the site of first discovery, near Clovis, New Mexico); this was a lance-shaped point of chipped stone that had had one or more longitudinal flakes struck from the base of each flat face. These points are accompanied by side scrapers and, in one instance, by long cylindrical shafts of ivory. They are most frequently associated with mammoth. A second Paleo-Indian horizon, which seems in part to be contemporary with the Clovis material and partially to postdate it, is the Folsom phase of the central High Plains (Folsom, New Mexico, being the site of initial discovery). It is characterized by lance-shaped points of more careful manufacture (including broader fluted surfaces) than Clovis, associated with the remains of extinct *Bison antiquus.* The Lindenmeier site, a Folsom campsite in northeastern Colorado, has yielded a wide variety of end and side scrapers, gravers, and miscellaneous bone artifacts. Clovis sites have been dated at about 9000 BC and Folsom sites at about 500 to 1,000 years later.

The Desert culture. In the western United States, over a region extending from Oregon to northern Mexico and from the Pacific coast to the eastern foothills of the Rocky Mountains, there was a distinctive cultural adaptation to the dry, relatively impoverished upland environment. There, in the relative absence of large game resources, vegetation was exploited to a great extent, with the development of grinding tools and related equipment. The Cochise Desert culture (named from Cochise County in southern Arizona, where it was discovered) ran from about 8000 BC through several stages, persisting down to the historic period in some areas.

Development of seed milling

The Desert culture people lived as small bands of wandering seasonal food gatherers, collectors, and hunters. They ate a wide variety of animal and plant foods and developed techniques for small-seed harvesting and processing; an essential feature of Desert assemblages was the milling stone, for use in grinding wild seeds. Their best known habitations were caves and rock shelters, and they had twined basketry, nets, mats, cordage, fur cloaks, sandals, wooden clubs, and digging sticks. They also had the spear thrower, with darts of pointed hardwood or with points of flint and later of obsidian. Their rough stone implements were shaped by percussion, and consequently many of their choppers and scrapers had an Earlier Stone Age appearance. Their projectile points, however, showed excellent craftsmanship and followed continent-wide styles. The domesticated dog, another migrant from Asia, was known by about 4000 BC in the Desert culture (though by this time the dog was also known elsewhere in North America).

The far west. On the far west coast in California, the marked variety of geographical situations encouraged the development of a number of diverse regional complexes dependent upon intensive exploitation of the local resources. None of these cultures was agricultural. In the southern desert area the people subsisted upon plant seeds and small game and used crude flint tools, grinding stones, and (later) arrowheads. In the mountainous areas and in the better watered central areas, larger game animals such as the elk and deer, supplemented by acorns, fish, and birds, constituted the major items in the food supply. By at least 2000 BC, in this central area, the utilization of the local resources plus cultural intrusions from the north resulted in full adaptation to the area. The coastal groups from north to south depended upon the sea for their food supply, some subsisting mainly on shellfish, some on sea mammals, others on fish, and still others on a mixture of all three.

In the north Pacific part of the United States and in western British Columbia, some of the early sites of the hunters have yielded fluted blades, crude choppers, and cutting tools. Between 9000 and 7000 BC there were varied economic activities but with an emphasis on hunting. By about 8000 BC there was a strong orientation toward salmon fishing, particularly during the salmon runs, and the peoples tended to emphasize the use of bone and antler tools. The burin, a chisel-like bone working tool, has been found in such sites, along with prepared cores and blades. During the postglacial warming period that culminated between 3000 and 2000 BC, the inhabitants of the drier areas without permanent streams took on more of the traits of the Desert culture to the south, while others turned toward riverine fishing and marsh resources or to food from the sea. In the 1st millennium BC, the so-called Marpole complex, a distinctive ground slate complex, was known in the Fraser River area, with basic resemblances to the northwest coast historic culture in maritime emphasis, woodworking, large houses, and substantial villages. The emphasis on ground slate and woodworking tools is like that in the Eastern Woodlands Archaic (see below) and recalls similar emphasis in certain northwestern Siberian cultures. In most of the areas of the Northwest Coast, clear indications of the beginnings of the historic cultures were not known until about AD 1300.

The Archaic cultures. *The Eastern Archaic.* With the retreat of the ice sheets in the north, beginning about 10,000 years ago, the cool, moist climate gradually became hot and dry in the Great Plains and Great Basin regions, with consequent extinction or migration of Pleistocene animal life. The High Plains were largely deserted by man for a considerable period. In the eastern woodlands area, partly as a result of the variety of forest environments, climatic differences, and physiographic features, there developed a series of regional readaptations to changed local food supplies. The change from the primarily hunting economy of the early American hunters was gradual and is clearly seen in the slowly evolving form of the projectile point and other implement changes. The pattern of life became one of mixed hunting and collecting, with some groups developing by 6000 BC a taste for riverine and coastal living in order to exploit abundant fish and mollusk resources to supplement such vegetational products as acorns, seeds, berries, and tubers.

Change from hunting economy

During the long Eastern Archaic, from 8000 to 1500 BC, regional social and economic diversification was developed, and it was during the Archaic that significant early linguistic differentiation also probably occurred and during which varieties of physical types developed.

The typical Archaic house was a small circular structure with wooden posts for the wall and roof supports; the covering was probably bark. Cooking was done in the open by boiling in containers of wood, bark, or hides or by baking in pits or by roasting and grilling. Lists of mammal, fish, and bird bones from Archaic sites read like a listing of the early historic fauna. Game-gathering devices, including nets, traps, and pitfalls, were used along with the spear and dart thrower. Fishhooks, gorges, and net sinkers were known, and in some areas fish weirs were built. River, lake, and ocean mollusks were consumed, and probably a great many native roots, berries, fruits, and tubers known in the early historic period were incorporated into the diet during the Archaic. The extensive lists of plant medicines recorded by the early colonists were probably a part of the primitive Archaic pharmacopoeia.

Developing trade and technology

The large variety of chipped-flint projectiles, knives, scrapers, perforators, drills, and adzes reflect regional styles and changes during the long Archaic period. The late Archaic was distinguished by the gradual development of ground and polished, grooved stone axes, pestles, gouges, adzes, plummets, and forms attached to the spear thrower. This was a reflection of a growing versatility in the technology and economy. Trade and exchange are also known from the distribution of native copper implements from the Michigan–Wisconsin area to as far south as Louisiana and Florida and the finds of southeastern marine shells as far north as the upper Mississippi–Great Lakes area. An extensive system of trails and water routes was probably in existence during the Late Archaic.

The great boreal forest zone of spruce, fir, and pine that now runs from New England and the maritime provinces of Canada westward to the Canadian plains and the Mackenzie Valley gradually acquired its present distribution following the retreat and melting of the Arctic ice cap. Its present distribution was reached by about 2500 BC. The forest cover and climate had a limiting effect on the cultural development and on the general pattern of hunting and fishing. These efforts were supplemented by some use of plant material.

In the upper Great Lakes area there was an Old Copper culture, which has special interest because copper implements and weapons were made from the native copper of the Lake Superior basin. This culture appeared about 3000 BC and lasted about 2,000 years. It was a northern expression of the Late Archaic. Its tools and weapons, particularly in the adzes, gouges, and axes, clearly indicate an adaptation to the forest environment. In the area south of James Bay to the upper St. Lawrence about 2000 BC, there was a regional variant called the Laurentian Boreal Archaic and, in the extreme east, the Maritime Boreal Archaic. In this eastern area, slate was shaped into points and knives of forms similar to those of the copper implements to the west. Trade between the eastern and western areas has been recognized, and this evidence, along with general similarities of the culture, suggests that water transportation by canoe was known at this time.

Along the southern border of the central and eastern boreal forest zone between 1500 and 500 BC, there developed a distinctive burial complex, reflecting an increased attention to burial ceremonialism. These burials, many including cremations, were often accompanied by red ochre, caches of triangular blanks, fire-making kits of iron pyrites and flint strikers, copper needles and awls, and polished stone forms. The triangular points of this complex may have represented the introduction of the bow and arrow from the pre-Eskimo cultures east of Hudson Bay. The earliest Woodland pottery appeared in the Great Lakes area about 1000 BC. It is another of the culture traits derived from northeastern Asia and across northern Alaska to northwestern Canada. The route by which it reached the Great Lakes is not known.

The Plains Archaic. In the western Plains from about 8000 to 3000 BC the fluted blade points were no longer made, and many styles or types were produced that have been identified by such local names as Plainview, Angostura, Milnesand, Agate Basin, and Scottsbluff. These minor varieties of dart and spear point and their primarily hunting culture may be included in the term Plano. The Plano complex or culture type was a direct descendant from the fluted-blade early American hunters. Their primary game animal was the bison, for the larger animals of the preceding period had died out or were exterminated.

Plano culture

The stone complex associated with the Plano hunters was markedly similar from site to site over a considerable period of time during which the climate became increasingly warmer and until the major warm period was reached, about 3000 to 2000 BC. As the climate moderated, peoples of the Late Plano complex moved north into Saskatchewan and Alberta with the grazing game animals and, by 3000 BC, had reached the Arctic tundra zone in the Northwest Territories of Canada at Grant and Dismal lakes and Great Bear River. Important elements of this culture also moved east in the Mississippi valley and western Great Lakes area. Many of the sites of this culture type were kill sites with abundant bison bones that accounted for the number of implements and tools associated with hunting and leatherworking. In the tundra zone the major game animal was the caribou. Choppers, pounders, and milling stones have been found there.

Early agriculturalists. *Early southwestern planters.* Primitive agricultural practices began in Mexico by 6000 to 4000 BC and by approximately 2000 BC were known on the northern fringe of the Middle American culture area. Maize was not the only crop plant, for gourds, squash, peppers, cotton, and varieties of beans were also domesticated. Maize was grown in the southwestern United States by 2000 to 1000 BC, but most of the other domesticates did not arrive until just before and after AD 1. The early introduction of maize in the Southwest had no marked effect on cultural development, and the existence of pottery, storage pits, and domestic houses with semi-subterranean floors and lateral entryways was not known until about AD 1. These houses had wood uprights for walls, central roof supports, radiating beams, and wattle-and-daub plastered walls. The small settlements of the early Puebloan, or Basket Maker, people of the Four Corners area (namely northwestern New Mexico, southwestern Colorado, southeastern Utah, and northeastern Arizona) were among the first village agricultural societies in the Southwest.

Adena and Hopewell cultures

Ohio Valley cultures. In eastern North America one of the Early Woodland phases preceding the introduction of maize agriculture is the Adena culture, which occupied the middle Ohio River Valley by about 500 BC (Adena takes its name from an estate near Chillicothe, Ohio, the site of a large burial mound). The Adena were hunters and gatherers but apparently provided the stimulus that brought about the spectacular Hopewell culture in the Illinois and Ohio valleys. (Hopewell is similarly named after a farmsite in Ohio). The success of the Hopewell peoples, particularly from 100 BC to AD 200, seems to have been due largely to their combining elements of the preceding Archaic cultures with elements of Adena and other Early Woodland cultures, and perhaps with some features of a local cultivating tradition, since some corn and squash has been found. It is evident that the Hopewell culture included a well-organized village-based society in which surplus resources were used in the construction of elaborate earthworks and were concentrated as wealth by a restricted group of individuals. The most outstanding feature of Hopewell culture is a burial complex that called for the deposition of concentrations of wealth in tombs of one or several deceased individuals. The interment procedure was elaborate and involved the construction of a large log tomb, later burned and covered by an earth mound. Artifacts found within these burial mounds indicate that the Hopewell were able to obtain goods from widespread localities in North America. Obsidian and grizzly bear teeth were apparently derived from the Rocky Mountain region; copper from the northern Great Lakes; and conch shells and other exotic objects from the southeast and along the coast of the Gulf of Mexico. Ohio, particularly, served as a distributing centre for ceremonial goods and special products over a wide area in the eastern United States. The ceramics of the Hopewell appear to be based in two major traditions: one derived from an Ohio Valley development which began about 1000 BC, stimulated by the early fibre-tempered pottery of the Southeast, and the other from a pottery with complex decorations, which probably developed in the Illinois area around AD 1. In less favourable areas of eastern North America, a "generalized Woodland" culture paralleled the Hopewell in time, probably based more on collecting than on cultivation for subsistence.

There is a clear evidence of cultural regression between AD 200 and 700 in the north central United States following the Hopewell expansion and florescence. This is attributed to a number of changes in their activities which are not well understood as yet. Although there was concurrent change in the south, this did not take the form of a lowering of the cultural level.

Mississippi Valley and peripheral woodlands. The last major cultural development in the eastern United States is called Mississippian because its primary centre was in the valleys of the Mississippi River and its major tributaries and in the southeast. This predominantly agricultural complex was a marked cultural advance over earlier stages in the east. Its initial growth and expansion was at approximately the same period (AD 700–1200) as that of the southwestern Puebloan complex. The initial growth was along the Mississippi between modern St. Louis and Vicksburg. It was stimulated by the introduction of concepts, religious practices, and improved agricultural procedures from northern Mexico, plus local developments, which resulted in a sedentary societal organization. By AD 1000, large villages were in existence with subsidiary villages and farming communities nearby. Regional specialized production in pottery, projectile points, house types, and other utilitarian products reflected the tribal groupings of the period. An outstanding feature of this culture type was the earthen temple mound, which served as a raised platform on which the major community buildings were placed. These council houses and temples served as the political and ceremonial centres. The platform mounds were placed on the sides of a central plaza that served as a ceremonial centre for the tribal community during important recurrent functions or during times of crisis. The more permanent buildings, both family and community, were of wattle-and-daub construction, usually rectangular in floor plan. In some areas large, circular charnel houses received the remains of the dead, but burial was normally made in large cemeteries or in the floors of dwellings. The size of the ceremonial tribal centres varied from 10 to 100 acres (four to 40 hectares). Important household industries involved the production of mats, baskets, clothing, and a variety of vessel forms for specialized uses. Food surplus was kept in ground storage pits and in storage cribs above the ground.

The Mississippian culture complex

One of the more striking developments was the production of ceremonial costumes and ornaments, for use in the religious ceremonies that were conducted by an organized priesthood with a well-established ritual. The religious symbolism spread throughout the Mississippian complex, and a number of centres of production of specialized ceremonial items are known. Other innovations were walled fortifications with timber palisades and bastions surrounding the village, which reflected an increase in intergroup aggression and a tendency, continuing into the historic period, toward the development of confederacies. The intergroup conflicts apparently were primarily quests for prestige and revenge instead of a means of territorial expansion or economic control.

Spread of Woodland culture

Along the eastern and northern periphery, some tribes, while retaining the older Woodland complex, were somewhat influenced by the Mississippian culture. The extent of this influence seems to have depended on their nearness to the more advanced cultural complex and on their ability to maintain an agricultural economy along with hunting and gathering. There was a spread of Woodland culture from about 200 BC to AD 200 into the eastern part of the Plains from Oklahoma to North Dakota, with some sites, particularly in eastern Kansas, clearly forming a part of the Hopewellian complex. In the Plains there was evidence of corn and bean cultivation during this period, and later there was cultivation of gourds and squash, but between about AD 300–400 and 800 there was little occupation of the western part of the Plains by agricultural people because of the relative aridity.

After 800, however, Late Woodland populations had spread west to the eastern slopes of the Rockies and were in contact with eastward-moving Puebloan people. A favourable agricultural period was indicated by the marked increase in village size and in population density for the next 400 years, during which hospitable areas along major streams were occupied by various interrelated cultural groups collectively known as the Plains Mississippian cultures. Part of this complex was connected to the developing Mississippi complexes to the east by diffusion and, to some degree, by a migration of such groups as the Omaha and Ponca from the St. Louis area by about AD 1000.

Between AD 1500 and 1700 the High Plains from New Mexico to Wyoming and in eastern Oklahoma, Kansas, and Nebraska were pre-empted by horse-using, semi-agricultural peoples of the plains—the Apache and Comanche. Prehistoric village agriculturalists of a plains Mississippi tradition came into the historic period as the Pawnee, Arikara, Mandan, Hidatsa, Crow, and Wichita.

Southwestern village farmers. *Anasazi, Mogollon, and Hohokam cultures.* The southwestern village farmers were distributed from eastern Utah and southern Colorado through most of New Mexico and Arizona. The effective agricultural area varied with fluctuations in climate that profoundly affected the ability of the Indians to occupy marginal regions. Although corn and some other agricultural plants were introduced from Mexico between 2000 BC and AD 1, the first village complexes, with five to 15 pit or surface houses, ceremonial buildings, refuse pits, and pottery, did not appear until shortly before AD 1 in southern Arizona and New Mexico. Two of the major farming complexes began at this time: Mogollon was located in the mountainous belt of west central New Mexico and east central Arizona, while Hohokam was located in the desert area of the Gila basin of southern Arizona. The latter group depended upon irrigation for its crops, whereas Mogollon depended upon rainfall and stream diversion over floodplains. Mogollon became the pattern of agriculture that later was developed in the Anasazi or Puebloan culture, the third major farming complex of the Southwest.

Pre-Pueblo cultures

The geographical expansion, population growth, and striking development of permanent villages with multiroom and multilevel buildings came during the period from AD 700 to 1200, which coincided with a minor climatic period of favourable distribution of rainfall for plant growth over the entire Southwest. For the same climatic reasons, there was an expansion of population and cultural movement from central and western Mexico into northwestern Mexico. Trade and cultural stimuli then moved from northwestern Mexico into the American Southwest at a time when the climate in both areas was most favourable for population and cultural growth. Indicating such cultural movement, cast copper bells, parrots, ball courts, shell trumpets, and pottery vessel shapes and designs have been found; they clearly reflect the transmission of religious beliefs and ceremonies. These southern influences were blended into local and regional complexes.

The Anasazi village agricultural complex had expanded by AD 900 to occupy northeastern Arizona, southwestern Colorado, and northwestern New Mexico. By AD 1100, expansion had taken place into the Virgin River valley of southeastern Nevada, north as far as the Great Salt Lake and northwestern Colorado, to the east into southeastern Colorado and to the Pecos and upper Canadian river valleys of New Mexico. During this period there was probably a development of priestly offices and of rituals and ceremonialism. The increasing population concentration in large pueblos was apparently organized into households according to lineage. Control of the agricultural activities was presumably in the hands of clan leaders, who were also the priests who officiated in the rain-producing ceremonies. During this period some of the larger village populations ranged from 300 to more than 1,000 people.

Primarily because of increasing aridity there was a marked retraction of Anasazi culture between 1100 and 1300. As a result, a concentration of the pueblos took place in northeastern Arizona, along the Rio Grande and its immediate tributaries, and in the present Zuni area of western New Mexico. The Anasazi groups maintained their societies by sand-dune farming with floodwater and some canal irrigation. The increased importance and elaboration of religious rain-producing ceremonies between 1300 and 1540 is deduced from paintings on walls and from symbolic pottery decoration.

Mogollon and Hohokam cultures

The Mogollon complex in its early phases, from 200 BC to AD 700, consisted of relatively small villages of pit houses grouped near a large ceremonial structure. No organization of the village structures into a pattern is apparent, however, and trash disposal was random. Although the initial impetus for sedentary village life appeared early in the Mogollon area, there was a period of apparent cultural quiescence about AD 400 to 600. With the growth and spread of the Anasazi complex in the period after 700, the main flow of culture was from that area, and Mogollon villages from AD 900 to 1100 were a blend of local development strongly influenced from Anasazi. During the climatic deterioration after AD 1200, much of the Mogollon territory in southwestern New Mexico was abandoned.

The Hohokam culture of southeastern Arizona was primarily limited to main river valleys. Agriculture was made possible by extensive irrigation canals that required cooperation between villages. The people lived in villages of scattered pit houses made of brush and mud that were dispersed along the streams and canals. Their main settlements and major culture growth took place also during the period AD 700–1200. Following this for 200 years, there was a blend with Anasazi and Mexican elements and a tendency toward the construction of more compact settlements surrounded by compound walls with a few massive multiroom and two-story buildings. There is relatively little evidence of trade and influences from northwestern Mexico. Such historic groups as the Pima and Papago are descended from the Hohokam people.

Pueblo culture. Best known of the prehistoric and historic southwestern peoples are the Pueblo Indians proper, whose ancestors built great cliff villages now seen in ruins and equally remarkable multiple apartment houses of adobe and stone masonry. Some of the latter are still occupied, and the Pueblo Indian inhabitants speak languages and observe ceremonies that are at least pre-Spanish in origin.

Pueblo culture periods

The beginnings of Pueblo culture, in the 1st millennium AD, are obscure. The traditional type of aboveground, straight-line, or crescent-shaped multiple house continued to be built, two rooms wide; stone masonry, however, began to replace the earlier pole-and-mud and adobe construction. Agriculture, including several varieties of corn, may have been augmented at that time by the cultivation of a native long-staple cotton. Pottery was not much changed, but it included a greater variety of shapes and decoration. Basketry was much less common. These early phases of Pueblo culture are termed Developmental Pueblo.

The great Classic Pueblo period followed in about AD 1050–1300, a period most popularly associated with the term Pueblo. It was the time of the great cliff houses, such as Mesa Verde, and the large apartment-like structures in Chaco Canyon (Pueblo Bonito) and elsewhere. An actual shrinking in area took place as inhabitants of the outer fringes moved in to build the large dwelling units. Also, because a number of outstanding structures were built in quite inaccessible canyons and mesa walls, there is the possibility that hostile strangers had reached the outlying districts. The most notable advance over previous periods was in architecture and pottery. Masonry walls were greatly thickened, dressed stones being used in many localities to bear the greater weight of massive structures. These community structures had from 20 to as many as 1,000 rooms and from one to four stories. Each of the larger houses was in effect a single village. Windows and doors were quite small, and usually no openings were made in the lowest rooms, which were entered by ladder through the roof. Floors were terraced or set back, and the terraces were much used as outdoor living space. Roofs were constructed to carry great weights by laying heavy beams covered with a mat of smaller poles and brush, then laying on a coat of adobe six to eight inches thick. Some semi-subterranean ceremonial chambers, known as kivas, were enlarged to as much as 80 feet (25 metres) in diameter. Craftsmanship in pottery reached a high level, and specialization became so pronounced in the different centres, as in Chaco canyon, Mesa Verde, Kayenta, and a number of others, that the style of each can be recognized easily. To the earlier black-on-white and red-on-white designs were added polychromes of three or more colours applied more lavishly. Cotton cloth, blankets, and bags were woven, and yucca fibre also entered into various articles of clothing and such utility objects as mats. Feather-cloth robes were worn in cold weather.

Abandonment of the cliff houses and large community buildings marked the close of the great Pueblo period. In part this may have resulted from incursion into the northern part of the territory by nomadic Athabascans (Navajo and Apache) and a prolonged drought that occurred in the late 13th century. It is also possible that lack of central leadership led to internal dissensions.

The next period (AD 1300–1700), called Regressive Pueblo, was characterized by a general movement southward and eastward, and new villages, some larger than those of Classic Pueblo, were built on the Little Colorado, Puerco, Verde, San Francisco, Rio Grande, Pecos, upper Gila, and Salt rivers. Pottery showed new developments; geometric patterns were largely replaced by naturalistic representations of birds, animals, insects, and the human figure; glazing was frequently used. The modern Pueblo period is usually dated from the beginning of permanent Spanish settlement at the close of the 17th century. From 1540 on, when the Spaniards first entered the Pueblo country, the number of Pueblo settlements declined considerably, though much of the culture and many of the skills in agriculture and crafts continued down to present times.

EVOLUTION OF CONTEMPORARY CULTURES

The great diversity that marked Indian cultures also persisted into modern times. After the arrival of the Europeans, some tribes disappeared by amalgamation with others or by wars and epidemics, and some languages perished. The process of adaptation to white encroachments and of acculturation to European ways worked at varying rates within the various Indian societies, transforming and devitalizing segments of custom and practice. Nevertheless, many Indian populations north of Mexico continued to manifest an unexpected viability, and Indian attitudes, customs, and values persisted.

Colonial policies. The formulation of public policy toward the Indians was of concern to the major European colonizing powers. The Spanish tried assiduously to Christianize the natives and to remake their living patterns. Orders were issued to congregate scattered Indian villages in orderly, well-placed centres, assuring the Indians at the same time that by moving to such centres they would not lose their outlying lands. This was the first attempt to create Indian reservations. The promise failed to protect Indian land, according to the Franciscan monk and historian of Mexico, Juan Torquemada, who reported about 1599 that there was hardly "a palm of land" that the Spaniards had not taken. Many Indians who did not join the congregations for fear of losing what they owned fled to mountain places and lost their lands anyway.

Early Spanish policies

The Russians never seriously undertook colonization in the New World. When Peter I the Great sent Vitus Jonassen Bering into the northern sea that bears his name, interest was in scientific discovery, not overseas territory. Later, when the problem of protecting and perhaps expanding Russian occupation was placed before Catherine II the Great, she declared (1769):

> It is for traders to traffic where they please. I will furnish neither men, nor ships, nor money, and I renounce forever all lands and possessions in the East Indies and in America.

The Swedish and Dutch attempts at colonization were so brief that neither left a strong imprint on New World practices. The Dutch government, however, was probably the first (1645) of the European powers to enter into a formal treaty with an Indian tribe, the Mohawk. Thus began a relationship, inherited by the British, that contributed to the ascendancy of the English over the French in North America.

France handicapped its colonial venture by transporting to the New World a modified feudal system of land tenure that discouraged permanent settlement. Throughout the period of French occupation, emphasis was on trade rather than on land acquisition and development, and thus French administrators, in dealing with the various tribes, tried primarily only to establish trade relations with them. The French instituted the custom of inviting the headmen of all tribes with which they carried on trade to come once a year to Montreal, where the governor of Canada gave out presents and talked of friendship. The governor of Louisiana met southern Indians at Mobile. The English, reluctantly, found themselves competing on the same basis with annual gifts. Still later, United States peace commissioners were to offer permanent annuities in exchange for tribal concessions of land or other interests.

Early English policies

In contrast to the French, the English were primarily interested in land and permanent settlements; beginning quite early in their occupation, they felt an obligation to bargain with the Indians and to conclude formal agreements with compensation to presumed Indian landowners. The Plymouth settlers, coming without royal sanction, thought it incumbent upon them to make terms with the Massachuset Indians. Cecilius Calvert (the 2nd Baron Baltimore) and William Penn, while possessing royal grants in Maryland and Pennsylvania respectively, nevertheless took pains to purchase occupancy rights from the Indians. It became the practice of most of the colonies to prohibit indiscriminate and unauthorized appropriation of Indian land. The usual requirement was that purchases could be consummated only by agreement with the tribal headman, followed by approval of the governor or other official of the colony. At an early date also, specific areas were set aside for exclusive Indian use. Virginia in 1656 and commissioners for the United Colonies of New England in 1658 agreed to the creation of such reserved areas. Plymouth Colony in 1685 designated for individual Indians separate tracts that could not be alienated without their consent.

In spite of these official efforts to protect Indian lands, unauthorized entry and use caused constant friction through the colonial period. Rivalry with the French, who lost no opportunity to point out to the Indians how their lands were being encroached upon by the English; the activity of land speculators, who succeeded in obtaining large grants beyond the settled frontiers; and, finally, the startling success of the Ottawa chief Pontiac in capturing English strongholds in the old Northwest (the Great Lakes region) as a protest against this westward movement, together prompted King George III's ministers to issue a proclamation (1763) that formalized the concept of Indian land titles for the first time in the history of European colonization in the New World. The document prohibited issuance of patents to any lands claimed by a tribe unless the Indian title had first been extinguished by purchase or treaty. The proclamation reserved for the use of the tribes "all the Lands and Territories lying to the Westward of the sources of the Rivers which fall into the Sea from the West and Northwest." Land west of the Appalachians might not be purchased or entered upon by private persons, but purchases might be made in the name of the king or one of the colonies at a council meeting of the Indians.

This policy continued up to the termination of British rule and was adopted by the United States. The Appalachian barrier was soon passed—thousands of settlers crossed the mountains during the American Revolution—but both the Articles of Confederation and the federal Constitution reserved either to the president or to Congress sole authority in Indian affairs, including authority to extinguish Indian title by treaty. When French dominion in Canada capitulated in 1760, the English announced that "the Savages or Indian Allies of his most Christian Majesty, shall be maintained in the lands they inhabit, if they choose to remain there." Thereafter, the proclamation of 1763 applied in Canada and was embodied in the practices of the dominion government. (The British North America Act of 1867, which created modern Canada, provided that the parliament of Canada should have exclusive legislative authority with respect to "Indians, and lands reserved for the Indians." Thus, both North American countries made control over Indian matters a national concern.)

United States policy. The first full declaration of U.S. policy was embodied in the Northwest Ordinance (1787):

> The utmost good faith shall always be observed toward the Indians, their lands and property shall never be taken from them without their consent; and in their property, rights, and liberty, they shall never be invaded or disturbed, unless in just and lawful wars authorized by congress; but laws founded in justice and humanity shall from time to time be made, for preventing wrongs being done to them, and for preserving peace and friendship with them.

This doctrine was embodied in the act of August 7, 1789, as one of the first declarations of the U.S. Congress under the Constitution.

The final shaping of the legal and political rights of the Indian tribes is found in the opinions of Chief Justice John Marshall, notably in decision in the case of *Worcester* v. *Georgia:*

> The Indian nations had always been considered as distinct, independent, political communities, retaining their original natural rights, as the undisputed possessors of the land, from time immemorial. . . . The settled doctrine of the law of nations is, that a weaker power does not surrender its independence—its right to self-government—by associating with a stronger, and taking its protection. A weak state, in order to provide for its safety, may place itself under the protection of one more powerful, without stripping itself of the right of government, and ceasing to be a state.

Indian Removal Act of 1830

The first major departure from the policy of respecting Indian rights came with the Indian Removal Act of 1830. For the first time the United States resorted to coercion, particularly in the cases of the Cherokee and Seminole tribes, as a means of securing compliance. The Removal Act was not in itself coercive, since it authorized the president only to negotiate with tribes east of the Mississippi on a basis of payment for their lands; it called for improvements in the east and a grant of land west of the river, to which perpetual title would be attached. In carrying out the law, however, resistance was met with military force. In the decade following, almost the entire population of perhaps 100,000 Indians was moved westward. The episode moved Alexis de Tocqueville to remark in 1831:

> The Europeans continued to surround [the Indians] on every side, and to confine them within narrower limits . . . and the Indians have been ruined by a competition which they had not the means of sustaining. They were isolated in their own country, and their race only constituted a little colony of troublesome strangers in the midst of a numerous and dominant people.

Indian wars

The territory west of the Mississippi, it turned out, was not so remote as had been supposed. The discovery of gold in California (1848) started a new sequence of treaties, designed to extinguish Indian title to lands lying in the path of the overland routes to the Pacific. The sudden surge of thousands of wagon trains through the last of the Indian country and the consequent slaughtering of prairie and mountain game that provided subsistence for the Indians brought on the most serious Indian wars the country had experienced. For three decades, beginning in the 1850s, raids and sporadic pitched fighting took place up and down the western Plains, highlighted by such incidents as the Custer massacre by Sioux and Cheyenne Indians (1876), the Nez Percé chief Joseph's running battle in 1877 against superior U.S. army forces, and the Chiricahua Geronimo's long duel with authorities in the Southwest, resulting in his capture and imprisonment in 1886.

Toward the close of that period, the Ghost Dance religion, arising out of the dream revelations of a young Paiute Indian, Wovoka, promised the Indians a return to the old life and reunion with their departed kinsmen. The songs and ceremonies born of this revelation swept across the northern Plains. The movement came to an abrupt end December 29, 1890, at Wounded Knee Creek, South

Dakota. Believing that the Ghost Dance was disturbing an uneasy peace, government agents moved to arrest ringleaders. Sitting Bull was killed (December 15) while being taken into custody, and two weeks later units of the U.S. 7th Cavalry at Wounded Knee shot down more than 200 men, women, and children who had already agreed to return to their homes.

A further major shift of policy had occurred in 1871 after congressional discussions lasting several years. U.S. presidents, with the advice and consent of the Senate, had continued to make treaties with the Indian tribes and to commit the United States to the payment of sums of money. The House of Representatives protested, since a number of congressmen had come to the view that treaties with Indian tribes were an absurdity (a view earlier held by Andrew Jackson). The Senate yielded, and the act of March 3, 1871, declared that "hereafter no Indian nation or tribe" would be recognized "as an independent power with whom the United States may contract by treaty." Indian affairs were brought under the legislative control of the Congress to an extent that had not been attempted previously. Tribal authority with respect to criminal offenses committed by members within the tribe was reduced to the extent that murder and other major crimes were placed under the jurisdiction of the federal courts.

Radical land allotment legislation

The most radical undertaking of the new legislative policy was the Dawes General Allotment Act of 1887. By that time the Indian tribes had been moved out of the mainstreams of traffic and were settled on lands that they had chosen out of the larger areas that they had formerly occupied. Their choice in most cases had been confirmed by treaty, agreement, act of Congress, or executive order of the president. The tribes that lived by hunting over wide areas found reservation confinement a threat to their existence. Generally, they had insisted on annuity payments or rations, or both, and the U.S. peace commissioners had been willing to offer such a price in return for important land cessions. In time the view came to be held that reservation life fostered indolence and perpetuated customs and attitudes that held Indians back from assimilation. The strategy offered by proponents of this theory was the Allotment Act authorizing the president to divide the reservations into individual parcels and to give every Indian, whether he wanted it or not, a particular piece of the tribally owned land. In order not to make the transition too abrupt, the land would be held in trust for a period of 25 years, after which ownership would devolve upon the individual. With it would go all the rights and duties of citizenship. Reservation land remaining after all living members of the tribes had been provided with allotments was declared surplus, and the president was authorized to open it for entry by non-Indian homesteaders, the Indians being paid the homestead price.

A total of 118 reservations was allotted in this manner, but the result was not what had been anticipated. Through the alienation of surplus lands (making no allowance for children yet unborn) and through patenting of individual holdings, the Indians lost 86,000,000 acres (35,000,000 hectares), or 62 percent, of a total of 138,000,000 acres in Indian ownership prior to 1887. A generation of landless Indians resulted, with no vocational training to relieve them of dependence upon land. The strategy also failed in that ownership of land did not effect an automatic acculturation in those Indians who received individual parcels. Through scattering of individuals and families, moreover, social cohesiveness tended to break down. The result was a weakening of native institutions and cultural practices with nothing offered in substitution. What was intended as transition proved to be a blind alley.

Indian population had been dwindling through the decades after mid-19th century. The California Indians alone, it was estimated, dropped from 100,000 in 1853 to not more than 30,000 in 1864 and 19,000 in 1906. Cholera in the central Plains in 1849 struck the Pawnee. As late as 1870–71 an epidemic of smallpox brought disaster to the Blackfeet, Assiniboin, and Cree. These events gave currency to the concept of the Indian as "the vanishing American." The decision of 1871 to discontinue treaty making and the passage of the Allotment Act of 1887 were both founded in the belief that the Indians would not survive, and hence it did not much matter whether their views were sought in advance of legislation or whether lands were provided for coming generations. When it became obvious after about 1920 that the Indians, whose numbers had remained static for several years, were surely increasing, the United States was without a policy for advancing the interests of a living people.

Indian Reorganization Act of 1934

A survey in 1926 brought into clear focus the failings of the previous 40 years. The investigators found most Indians "extremely poor," in bad health, without education, and lacking adjustment to the dominant culture around them. Under the impetus of these findings and other pressures for reform, Congress adopted the Indian Reorganization Act of 1934, which contemplated an orderly decrease of federal control and a concomitant increase of Indian self-government and responsibility. The essentials of the new law were as follows: (1) allotment of tribal lands was prohibited in the future, but tribes might assign use rights to individuals; (2) so-called surplus lands not pre-empted by homesteaders might be returned to the tribes; (3) tribes might adopt written constitutions and charters of incorporation embodying their continuing inherent powers to manage internal affairs; and (4) funds were authorized for the establishment of a revolving credit program, for land purchases, for educational assistance, and for aiding the tribes in forming organizations. Moreover, the act could be rejected on any reservation by referendum.

The response to the 1934 act was indicative of the Indians' ability to rise above adversity. About 160 tribes, bands, and Alaska villages adopted written constitutions, some of which combined traditional practices with modern parliamentary methods. The revolving credit fund helped Indians build up their herds and improve their economic position in other ways. Borrowers from the fund were tribal corporations, credit associations, and cooperatives that loaned to individual Indians and to group enterprises on a multimillion-dollar scale. Educational and health services were also improved through federal aid.

Originally, the United States exercised no guardianship over the person of the Indian; after 1871, when internal tribal matters became the subject of national legislation, the number and variety of regulatory measures multiplied rapidly. In the same year that the Indian Reorganization Act was passed, Congress significantly repealed 12 statutes that had made it possible to hold Indians virtual prisoners on their reservations. Indians were then able to come and go as freely as all other persons. The Snyder Act of 1924, extending citizenship to all Indians born in the United States, opened the door to full participation. Few Indians took advantage of the law, and because of their lack of interest a number of states excluded Indians from the franchise. Organization of tribal governments following the Reorganization Act, however, seemed to awaken an interest in civic affairs beyond tribal boundaries, and when Indians asked for the franchise, they were generally able to secure it eventually, though not until 1948 in Arizona and New Mexico, after a lengthy court action.

The federal courts consistently upheld the treaties made with Indian tribes and also held that property may not be taken from Indians, whether or not a treaty exists, "except in fair trade." The latter contention was offered by the Hualapai Indians against the Sante Fe Railway. The company was required by the courts in 1944 to relinquish about 500,000 acres it thought had been granted to it by the U.S. The lands had been occupied since prehistory by the Indians, without benefit of treaty recognition, and the Supreme Court held that, if the occupancy could be proved, as it subsequently was, the Indians were entitled to have their lands restored. In 1950 the Ute Indians were awarded a judgment against the United States of $31,750,000 for lands taken without adequate compensation. A special Indian Claims Commission, created by act of Congress on August 13, 1946, received many petitions for land claims against the United States and awarded, for example, about $14,789,000 to the Cherokee nation, $10,242,000 to the Crow tribe, $3,650,000 to the Snake-Paiute of Oregon, $3,000,000 to the Nez Percé, and $12,300,000 to the Seminole.

Search for new policies

The period from the early 1950s to the 1970s was one of increasing federal attempts to seek new policies regarding the Indians, and it was also a period in which Indians themselves became increasingly vocal in their quest for a better measure of human rights and the correction of past wrongs. The first major shift in policy came in 1954, when the Department of the Interior began terminating federal control over those Indians and reservations deemed able to look after their own affairs. From 1954 to 1960, support to 61 tribes and other Indian groups was ended by the withdrawal of federal services or trust supervision. The results, however, were unhappy. Some Indian groups, in extreme poverty, lost more acreage in deals for the private exploitation of Indian land and water resources. Indians in certain states became subject exclusively to state laws that were less liberal or sympathetic than federal laws. Finally, the protests of Indians, anthropologists, and other interested groups became so insistent that the program was decelerated in 1960. In 1961 a trained anthropologist was sworn in as commissioner of Indian Affairs, the first anthropologist ever to hold that position. Federal aid expanded greatly, and in the ensuing decade Indians were specifically brought into various federal programs for equal economic opportunity. Indian unemployment remained severe, however.

American Indians came more and more into public attention in the 1970s and 1980s as they sought (along with other minorities) to achieve a better life. Following the example set by black civil-rights activists of the 1960s, Indian groups drew attention to their cause through mass demonstrations and protests. Perhaps the most publicized of these actions were the 19-month seizure (1970–71) of Alcatraz (California) by members of the militant American Indian Movement (AIM) and the February 1973 occupation of a settlement at the Oglala Sioux Pine Ridge (South Dakota) reservation, the latter incident becoming known as the second Battle of Wounded Knee. Representing an attempt to gain a more traditional political power base was the establishment in 1971 of the National Tribal Chairman's Association, which eventually grew to include more than 100 tribes.

Indian leaders also expanded their sphere of influence into the courts; fishing, mineral, forest, and other rights involving tribal lands became the subject of litigation by the Puyallup (Washington state), the Northern Cheyenne (Montana), and the Penobscot and the Passamaquoddy (Maine), among others. Although control of economic resources was the focus of most such cases, some groups sought to regain sovereignty over ancient tribal lands of primarily ceremonial and religious significance. (Ed.)

American subarctic cultures

Resources and populations

The subarctic, or the physiographic zone called the taiga, is a land of coniferous forest covered with sphagnum moss and traversed by many waterways. Its main natural resources utilized by the Indians include wood, of which spruce, tamarack, and alder have been especially important for manufactures; game animals, such as moose, caribou, and beaver, whose meat is used for food and whose skins are used for blankets and clothing; berries; fish, usually the most abundant and therefore the staple food; and coloured earths converted into paints. Cold winters, when the ground is covered with snow and the waterways are frozen, are reflected in many technological adaptations, including the use of fur garments, toboggans, ice chisels, and snowshoes.

Since the 17th century, traders have been attracted to the region by its wealth in fur-bearing animals. Together with missionaries, they decisively influenced the native Indians' history. Many old beliefs, hunting customs, kinship relations, and so on, however, persisted throughout the fur-trade years in this marginal area and are only now beginning to vanish.

The subarctic contains two relatively distinct culture areas. The eastern subarctic is inhabited by Algonkian-speaking Indians, including the Naskapi of northern Quebec; the far-flung Cree; and an intrusive wedge of Ojibwa, who, after the beginning of the fur trade, displaced the Cree from west central Ontario and eastern Manitoba. The western subarctic belongs largely to Athabascan speakers, who extend from Canada into Alaska. Cultural differences among the Athabascans justify the delineation of two subareas. The first subarea, drained mostly by the northward-flowing Mackenzie River system, is inhabited by Chipewyan, Beaver, Slave, and Kaska Indians. Their

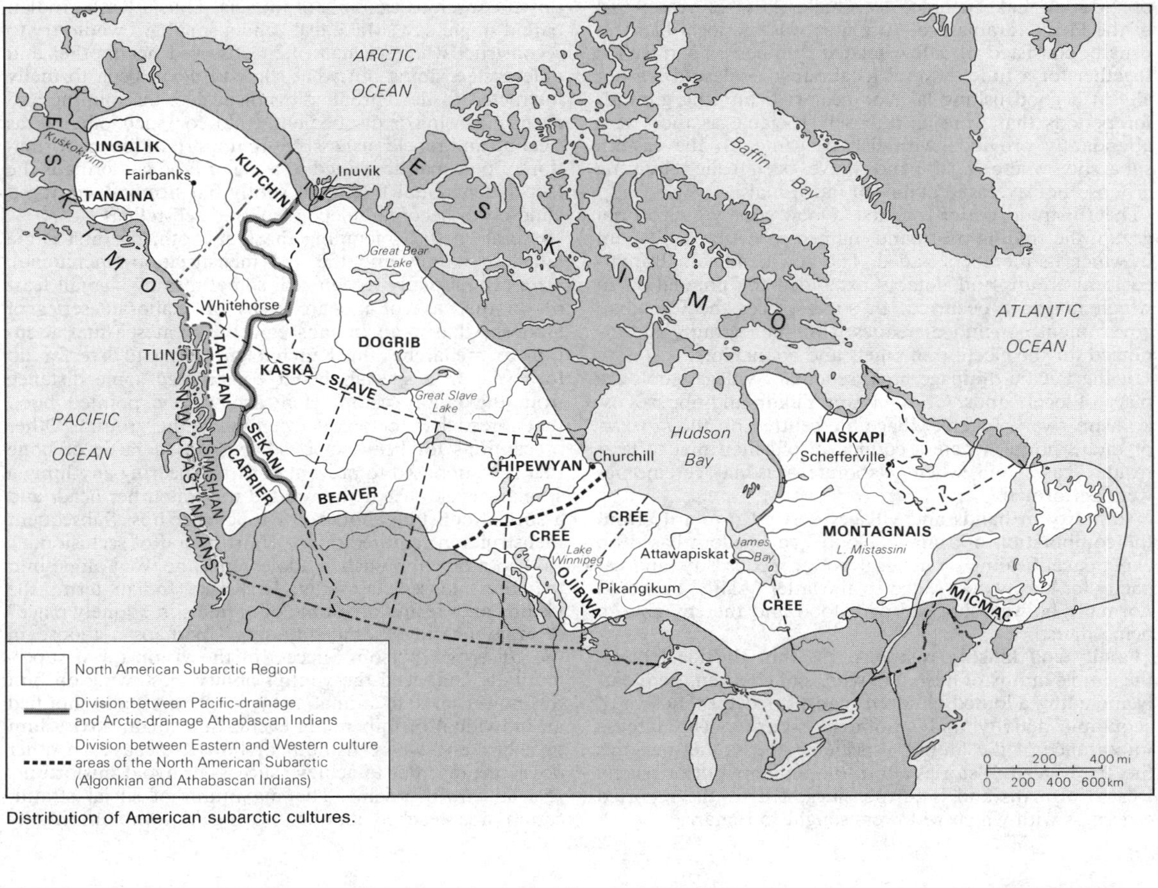

Distribution of American subarctic cultures.

culture was generally simpler and less sedentary than that of the second subarea, whose salmon streams drain into the Pacific Ocean. Its groups include the Carrier, part of the Kutchin, the Tanaina, and Ingalik Indians.

Northward the Algonkians and Athabascans border on the Eskimo; to the west the Canadian Athabascans encounter the Tlingit, Tsimshian, and other Northwest Coast tribes, while the Alaskan groups again abut on the Eskimo. (For a discussion of the cultures of the Northwest Coast, see below. Eskimo groups are treated in the article ARCTIC.)

TRADITIONAL CULTURE PATTERNS

Ethos. In most of the region east of Alaska, the uncomplex nature of subsistence and manufacturing technology is reflected in the Indians' elemental social structure, based on the family and the small local band, and in their individualistic relationship to the supernatural. Both features of the culture pattern are linked in turn with characteristic personality features, such as the high value placed on personal autonomy; the generalized conception of the world as dangerous; the emphasis on concrete, current realities rather than on future possibilities; and self-reliance, manifested, for example, in bearing up stoically to deprivation. Psychological homogeneity in the subarctic extends to other personal traits such as reticence, nondemonstrative emotionality, deference to other people, and strong individual control of aggressive impulses. Hostility is not absent, but it is only indirectly revealed through such outlets as sorcery, fear of sorcery, or malicious gossip.

Territorial organization. At the time of first white contact with the Indians, social structure tended to be extremely simple. The Indians had no stable, territorial political systems, no special offices charged with the task of coordinating groups, no formal social stratification, and no occupational specialization except as related to age and sex. Temporary leadership emerged when one group raided another or fought with the Eskimo or when there were other tasks requiring cooperation beyond the family.

Bands and villages

The Indians were territorially grouped in informal regional bands without chiefs. These units took their identity from some geographical feature of the land that members exploited—hence such appellations as "mountain people," or "Marten Lake people." A smaller kind of group east of the Pacific drainage culture area was the local band. It usually consisted of a few related families who travelled together for a time. Several local bands coalesced seasonally at a good fishing lake or near rich hunting grounds for periods that were as intensely sociable as they were abundantly provided with fish or game. In the eastern subarctic, where local bands have been called hunting groups, they averaged about 20 individuals.

The fur-trade period created a new type of territorial group: the trading-post band, named from the settlement in which its members traded. The new bands amalgamated local groups and notably expanded the population in which marriage occurred. In some places the Canadian government concluded treaties with such groups and arranged for the election of chiefs and councillors.

In the Pacific drainage area, sedentary villages took the place of local bands. On the lower Yukon and upper Kuskokwim rivers, Ingalik village life centred on the *kashim,* or men's house, where a council of old men met to hear trouble cases and where elaborate seasonal ceremonies were performed.

Authority in bands and villages derived primarily from the combination of a man's eloquence, wisdom based on experience, healing or magical power, generosity, and capacity for hard work. Aided by the latter quality, he would normally be well supplied with food and thereby able to help others.

Family and kinship relations. Within the local band, the simple family of husband, wife, and children, frequently including adopted children, constituted the nucleus of economic activity and emotional security. The intense importance of the family, especially in a young person's life, is revealed in stories about the unhappy lot of cruelly treated orphans and is further suggested by the reported eagerness with which widowers sought to remarry.

Marriage, friendship, and avoidance

The prevailing modes of obtaining a wife required bride service rendered to the wife's father or transfer of a sister of the groom in exchange for a bride. Although households were primarily monogamous, a man occasionally had two wives. This could happen, for example, when by custom a man espoused his dead brother's widow. Cross-cousin marriage (that is, a man's marriage with his mother's brother's daughter or his father's sister's daughter) is known to have been practiced, perhaps by preference, among some groups. Elsewhere it can be inferred from several features in kinship terminology. For example, a man uses the same term for his female cross-cousins and for his wife's sister. The custom declined when it was opposed by missionaries, who condemned it as incest, and when marriageable populations expanded around trading posts and missions.

Kin relations among the Kaska included teasing between grandparents and grandchildren, initiated by the youngsters. Siblings of the opposite sex who had reached puberty conducted themselves circumspectly in each other's presence and even tended to practice polite avoidance, as a father and a grown daughter also did. Parallel cousins (mother's sisters' children and father's brothers' children) were treated as siblings, both being called by the same kinship term. Ceremonial avoidance also governed the relationship of a man and his mother-in-law, contrasting with the camaraderie linking brothers-in-law, which was one of the warmest of all relationships between grown men. A Kaska man could joke freely with his wife's sister and brother's wife, sexual ribaldry not being barred from their conversation.

Socialization of children. Pregnancy taboos and postnatal observances served to ensure the well-being of mother and child. Birth took place in the dwelling, in a special birth hut, or, according to early travellers among the eastern seaboard Micmac, in the woods. One or more knowledgeable women assisted the mother in giving birth and in caring for the delivered child. Swaddled babies were diapered with moss and carried on the mother's back in an ornamented skin bag or a cradleboard.

Education and initiation

Family members and other relatives played the major role in the informal process of childhood education. A child had considerable scope to learn through copying the unself-conscious example of models. Thus a Kaska Indian parent might say "Make tea!" and a small girl would try to reconstruct what she had often observed her mother and older sisters doing but what she had never been formally instructed to do. Parents did not neglect disciplining and even chastising a disobedient child for such offenses as stealing and rebelliousness. More important for the formation of personalities suited to a life of food gathering is the fact that parental treatment subtly but firmly encouraged children to become independent and self-reliant.

Several "firsts," including the first tooth, the first game killed by a boy, and the first menstruation (menarche), were ceremonially recognized, sometimes by a small feast or, in the case of menarche, by an elaborate series of taboos. Athabascan Indians paid the greatest ritual attention to menarche, the Kutchin girl going to live for up to a year in a special shelter constructed some distance from the family camp. Here she wore a pointed hood that forced her to look down toward the ground. Other precautions for her own good included a rattle of bone that was supposed to prevent her from hearing anything; a special stick to use if she wanted to scratch her head, and a special cup that should not touch her lips. Subsequent menstruation required only a short period of seclusion.

When a boy approached adolescence, he went alone into the forest to seek a vision. In Kaska Indian terms the vision came from "dreaming of animals in a lonely place" or from hearing "somebody sing," perhaps a moose in the guise of a person. Success in the vision quest supernaturally enhanced the youth's ability, bestowing on him the power of the animal helpers. Dreams also notified an individual of impending events and might advise him on when and where to hunt or how to behave on other occasions in order to achieve success or avoid misfortune.

Social stratification. The maximum of social stratification was reached among the Ingalik, who informally recognized three classes of families. Three-quarters of the village comprised common people. Rich families, so called because they accumulated surplus food thanks to members' industry or superior hunting and fishing abilities, constituted about 5 percent of the community. They took the lead in the community's ceremonial life. The rest of the people did "nothing" and lived off the others; consequently, they enjoyed so little respect that they had a hard time finding spouses.

Seasonal migration

Settlement and housing. In pursuit of a livelihood, families and local bands shifted their location as the seasons changed. In northwest Canada groups scattered in early winter to hunt caribou in the mountains; elsewhere, autumn drew people to shorelines of lakes and bays where large numbers of ducks and geese could be taken for the winter larder. At other times people gathered around fish lakes. Ingalik Indians in late winter quit the village and headed for spring camps, as much for a change as for the good fishing. As dependence on fur trapping became heavier, the Cree, Slave, Kaska, and many other Indians adopted a two-part annual cycle. In winter the family lived on its trapline. Then, with summer, it brought its furs to the trading post where people camped until fall, enjoying a rest from work and abundant sociability. The warm months with their long daylight became a time for dances (the steps and fiddle music being copied from early European types), for marriages, and for visits of the Anglican or Roman Catholic bishop.

Despite much movement, shelters were not always portable. The Ingalik spent winters in houses excavated in the soil, roofed with beams and poles, hung with mats, and provided with an entry. Other groups, such as the Cree and Ojibwa, built conical winter lodges durably roofed with boughs, earth, and snow. On the trail, however, people put up skin or brush shelters, sometimes only a simple lean-to, or camped in the open facing a fire.

Production and technology. Everywhere in the subarctic, fish and game, augmented by berries and a slight quantity of other vegetable products, provided the food supply. Meat was boiled with the aid of hot stones in containers of bark or woven spruce roots. A large, varied set of weapons, traps, and other ingenious appliances played a vital role in providing subsistence. Important devices included the bow and arrow, with stone or bone tips for different kinds of game; lances; the spear thrower and spear; weirs and basket traps for fish; nets of willow bark and of other substances; snares for such small game as rabbits; deadfalls (traps with logs or other weights that fall on game and kill them); pit traps; and decoys for birds. No less vital for people who depended heavily on mobility for survival were vehicles, such as bark canoes or snow toboggans of hardwood, and travel aids, such as large sinew-netted snowshoes to run down large game, a smaller variety to break trail for the toboggan, and snow goggles to use against the glare of the spring sun. Dogs large or numerous enough to pull toboggans were unavailable until the fur-trade period.

Techniques and skills

In addition to the Indians' technical resourcefulness and skill, magic and divination aided hunting. A noteworthy form of divination used in locating game required heating a large animal's shoulder blade over fire until it cracked. Hunters then went in the direction of the crack. The random element in the method increased the chances that they would go to a fresh, relatively undisturbed piece of ground.

An idea of the extent to which people depended on game and of the labour involved in food getting can be gained from food-consumption figures obtained in the mid-20th century. In the relatively poor country west of James Bay, 400 Cree men, women, and children in the course of a fall, winter, and spring (nine months) consumed about 128,000 pounds (58,000 kilograms) of meat and fish in addition to staples from the store, especially flour, lard, and sugar.

Across the subarctic, people preserved meat by drying and pounding it together with fat and berries to make pemmican. The Pacific-drainage Athabascans also preserved salmon by smoking. Other widely distributed, basic technical skills included complicated chemical processes, using animal brains or human urine, to tan caribou and moose skins; these were then sewn into garments with the help of bone needles and animal sinew. Women also plaited rabbit skins into ropes and wove roots to form watertight baskets.

Property. Land and water, the sources of food, were not considered to be either individual or group property, yet nobody would usurp the privilege of a group that was currently exploiting a berry patch, beaver creek, or hunting range. Clothing, the contents of food caches, and other portable goods had individual owners. Legally inalienable family trapping territories came into being with the fur trade and in many places have been registered by the government. Sharing game was always important economically, while gifts other than food were bestowed primarily ceremoniously.

Religious beliefs. Two important concepts of the Naskapi and other Algonkian groups were Manitou and the "big man." Manitou represents a pervasive power in the world that individuals can learn to use in their own behalf. The term Great Manitou, designating a personal god, probably represents a missionary-inspired adaptation of the Indians' older idea. Among the Naskapi and Rupert House Cree, a person's big man is a spirit intimately associated with him. It confers wisdom, competence, skill, and strength in the food quest as well as in other areas of life, including magic. Maintaining this spirit requires ethically good conduct. Spirit "bosses" who control the supply of caribou, fish, and other creatures are another traditional belief shared by Algonkian and certain Athabascan groups.

Among many subarctic Indians, success in the vision quest augmented personal competence by allying the individual with animal helpers. There was also a widespread belief that if one wanted to continue to hunt game successfully, the dead animals and their remains must be treated with reverence. This required disposing of their bones carefully so that dogs could not chew them. Respect was particularly evident in the use of polite circumlocutions to refer to bears. Quebec Indians undertook several ceremonial observances in bear hunting, including a purifying sweat bath before departing on the hunt and an offer of tobacco to a bear that had been killed. Afterward the people feasted and danced in its honour.

Folklore, magic, and spirit relations

Three of the most popular characters in Algonkian folklore are Wiitiko (Windigo), a terrifying cannibalistic giant apt to be encountered in the forest; Tcikapis, a kindly, powerful young hero and the subject of many myths; and Wiskijan, an amusing, prankful trickster. Wiitiko psychosis refers to a condition in which an Indian would be seized by the obsessive idea that he was turning into a cannibal with a compulsive craving for human flesh.

The shaman, the sole religious functionary, served subarctic people as a part-time specialist curer and diviner. Occasionally he also behaved malignantly. Shamanistic ability came to an individual from dreaming of animals who taught the dreamer to work with their aid; such ability had to be validated through successful performance.

The Ingalik conceived of man as comprising body, soul, and "speech," the latter an element surviving after death but not, like the soul, reincarnated. Hazards to life came from the soul always being menaced by various supernatural figures that were the primary enemies of human survival, and by the souls of powerful evil shamans acting on behalf of these supernatural figures. The animal and berry people supported life. Animal "songs" and amulets created good relations with helpful animal people; and elaborate ceremonies in the men's house, to which animals were invited, protected the food supply.

MODERN DEVELOPMENTS

One view of culture change in the subarctic is that, during the fur-trade and missionary period, the Indians lost vital cultural traits faster than satisfactory replacements were absorbed. An opposite view holds that the fur-trapping era enriched Indian culture. Life came to be organized around the trading post; an emotionally satisfying belief system came to be centred in the Christian Church; and trapping offered new opportunities for prestige. Formal education and modern health care began during fur-trade times, the churches choosing a few localities to institute boarding schools and hospitals that in time received government subsidies.

After World War II the fur-trade era was succeeded by a new period characterized by planned social change, incipient urbanization, and intensified modernization. The growing unprofitability of trapping, chronic illness (especially tuberculosis), and high infant-mortality rates aroused the conscience of Canada and introduced the welfare state into the Canadian subarctic. Local schools and health stations replaced distant boarding schools and hospitals. Other government-sponsored programs brought about modern housing, large-scale fur farming, and vocational training. The fishing industry in Alaska, military and other construction, and iron mining in Quebec gave Indians the opportunity to work for wages in place of trapping. A slow trend of migration began to draw native families to established northern cities, such as Fairbanks (Alaska), Whitehorse (Yukon Territory), and Churchill (Manitoba), as well as to new towns, such as Schefferville (Quebec) and Inuvik (Northwest Territories). At the same time expanding jobs in health care, education, mining, defense, and administration stimulated an influx of white families from southern Canada to the north who settled in the northern towns.

Town life

Town life for some Indian migrants means a squatter's cabin, welfare, and occasional odd jobs; but many men and women have regular employment at open-pit mining, as janitors and hospital aides, in construction and domestic service, or as equipment operators. Indian townsmen restrict hunting and fishing, of which they are still very fond, to holidays and weekends. If the coming of the fur trade and missions widened the intellectual horizons beyond what they were in aboriginal times, then town life with its grade school, high school, library, movies, television, church groups, civic groups, and other associations increases awareness much more and provides many added chances to enact new, modern roles. Subarctic Indians of all ages are adapting successfully to urban economic and social opportunities, but the ease with which people take to jobs and adjust to new conditions varies in the same town, and some families are experiencing difficulties. Indians are not modernizing as rapidly as Eskimos, who live under similar conditions and sometimes in the same town.

Many Indians remain attached to small, isolated trading-post settlements and to a way of life that revolves around the forest, at least for the men. Even among the non-townspeople, one perceives a heightened awareness of native identity, together with growing objectivity about their "traditional" Indian cultural heritage. Their awareness is believed to stem from the knowledge that a different identity and way of life are possible. For the time being, however, they prefer to be cautious about changing the life that they know for one fraught with new challenges.

(J.J.Ho./Ed.)

Northwest Coast Indians

The most sharply delimited culture area of native North America was the Northwest Coast. It covered a long narrow arc of Pacific coast and offshore islands from Yakutat Bay in the northeast Gulf of Alaska south to Cape Mendocino in modern California. Its eastern limits were the crest of the Coast Ranges from the north down to Puget Sound, the Cascades south to the Columbia, and the coastal hills of Oregon and northwest California. The Kuroshio (Pacific Ocean current) offshore warms the coast and deluges it with rain. The northern Coast Range, cresting at heights of 5,000 feet and more, rises steeply from the sea and is cut by a myriad of narrow channels and fjords. The shores of Puget Sound, southwest Washington, and the Oregon coast hills are lower and less rugged.

Physical aspects of the Northwest Coast

Coastal forests are dense and predominantly coniferous with spruces, Douglas fir, hemlock, red and yellow cedar, and, in the south, coast redwood. These forests support an abundant fauna. Most important from the cultural point of view was the aquatic fauna, for it was on this that the areal culture depended primarily. Five species of salmon; herring; oil-rich "candlefish," or eulachon; smelt; cod; halibut; and mollusks abounded.

The peoples of the Northwest Coast linguistically consisted of a series of units related to widespread "stocks" of native North America (see LANGUAGES OF THE WORLD). From north to south the following linguistic divisions occurred: Tlingit; Haida; Tsimshian; northern Kwakiutl, or Heiltsuq; Bella Coola; southern Kwakiutl; Nootka; Coast Salish; Quileute-Chimakum; Kwalhioqua; Chinook. Then along the Oregon Coast and northwest California a series of small divisions occurred: Tillamook, Alsea, Siuslaw, Umpqua, Coos, Tututni-Tolowa, Yurok, Wiyot, Karok, and Hupa.

Major Indian groups

Culturally, Northwest Coast groups can be classified into four subareal units, or "provinces": the northern one, including speakers of Tlingit, Haida, Tsimshian, and the Tsimshian-influenced Haisla (northernmost Heiltsuq or Kwakiutl); the Wakashan province, including all other Kwakiutl, the Bella Coola, and the Nootka; the Coast Salish–Chinook province, which included various enclaves of other speech down to the central coast of Oregon; and the northwest California province plus the Athabascan-speaking Tututni-Tolowa.

The Northwest Coast was densely populated. Estimates of density in terms of persons per square mile mean little in a region where long stretches of coast consisted of uninhabitable cliffs rising from the sea. But early historic sources indicate that many villages had hundreds of inhabitants. One conservative population estimate of 129,000 persons on the coast at the dawn of the historic period must represent nearly the maximum that the area could support without improvement of the already complex technology.

TRADITIONAL CULTURE PATTERNS

Social structure. The Northwest Coast was the outstand-

From H. Driver *et al.*, *Indiana University Publications in Anthropology and Linguistics* (1953)

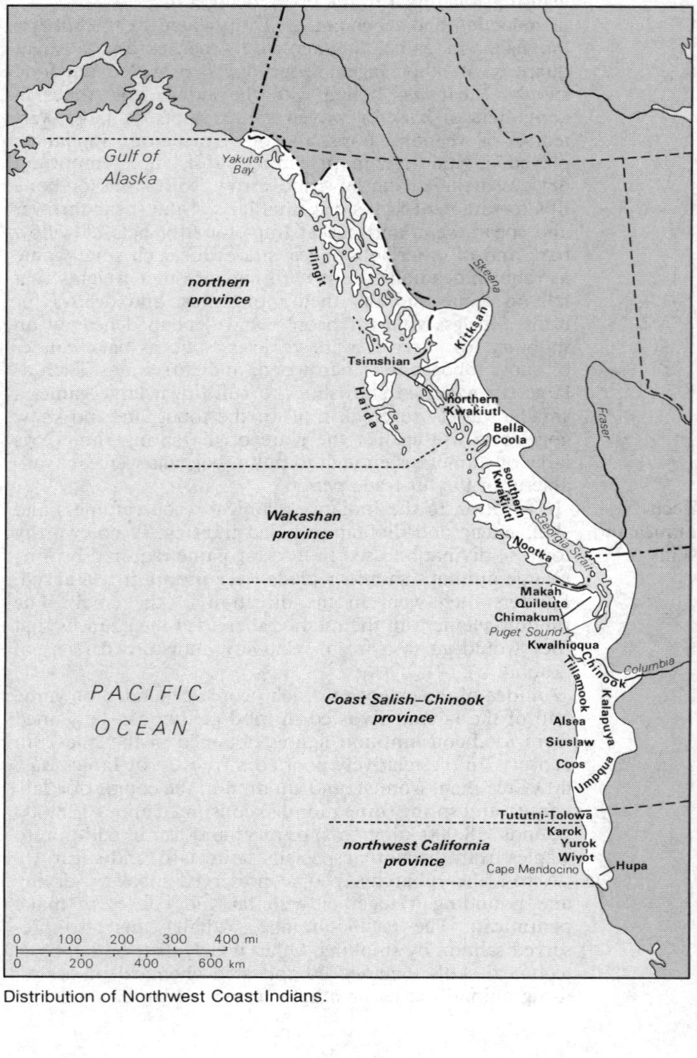

Distribution of Northwest Coast Indians.

ing exception to the anthropological truism that "hunting-and-gathering" (in this case "fishing-and-gathering") cultures are characterized by simple technologies, sparse possessions, and egalitarian, loosely organized societies consisting of small bands comprising small total populations. In this area, complex patterns of culture were the rule.

Familial and group organization

The nuclear family—a man, his wife or wives, their children or, in the northern provinces, the man's sisters' sons—was the basic production unit. In the native view, the significant social unit was the local group—that is, a group of men who considered themselves related and who formed a corporate entity holding title to fishing places, berry-picking and hunting grounds, habitation sites, and a host of incorporeal rights, such as names, songs, dances, and, especially in the north, totemic representations called "crests." Members of each group were graded in an integrated sequence from high to low, according to closeness to the direct line of descent from the group ancestor. The highest in rank, invariably holder of a special title that in each language translated into English as "chief," was administrator of the group's properties. It was he who set the time for the move to the salmon-fishing station, decided when the weirs and traps should be built, when the first catch should be made and the rite propitiating the first salmon of the season celebrated, when other groups should be invited to feasts, and so on. He had many prerogatives and sumptuary privileges, but he was expected to administer efficiently and to tend to social and ritual affairs for the general welfare of his group.

From Tlingit country in the north at least as far south as Puget Sound and perhaps farther, several such local groups assembled at a site in some sheltered cove protected from winter winds to pass the winter. Food-gathering activities were limited by weather but were unimportant; the stores of salmon dried in the fall were adequate. Practice of arts and crafts, jollity, and feasts and ceremonials were the order of the day. These assemblages of several local groups at winter village sites are often called "tribes," but it must be noted that such units were not politically integrated, for each of the component local groups retained its economic and political autonomy. For ceremonial purposes, though, the local groups were ranked in series from highest to next highest, and so on.

Individual social ranking

Stratification. A signal feature of Northwest Coast society was the emphasis on each individual's hereditary social rank. His position within his local group depended on his genealogical closeness to the legendary group ancestor. When several groups assembled at a common winter site to form a "tribe," the relative rank of the individual's group also was another factor important for ranking purposes.

Indian informants tend to oversimplify the situation in casual conversation, describing their former society as a class-structured one with a class of "chiefs," a class of commoners, and below these two a class of slaves. It is true that slaves (*i.e.,* war captives) formed a special social division, but the division into two great classes of "chiefs" and "commoners" is an inadequate explanation. The fact is that each person had his particular hereditarily acquired status, which placed him within his group as though he stood on a step of a long staircase of statuses, with the eldest of the senior line on the highest step, the most remotely related at the bottom. Strictly speaking, each person was in a class by himself.

Nominally, those of high rank were said to have had vast authoritarian powers, and group members of low degree have been described as serflike. In actual fact, mature persons of the latter sort voiced their opinions on group affairs, for they held interest in group properties. The chief refrained from abusing them because they were his kin and also because he was aware that he needed their assistance. Many strong arms and sturdy backs were needed to obtain, assemble, and position the heavy materials needed to build or repair a house, to construct fish weirs and traps, and to launch and paddle the chief's huge dugout canoe. Many singers, dancers, and attendants were necessary to stage an important ceremonial properly. Many bold warriors were needed to defend the group's wealth against foemen. There was enough flexibility in the social structure so that those of low rank could abandon an abusive chief and reside with kindred elsewhere who would welcome them.

Slaves usually were persons captured in childhood and taken or traded so far from their original homes that they had little hope of finding their way back. They were mere chattels, who might be treated well or ill, traded off, slain, or freed at their owner's whim.

Potlatch

The statuses of group members were hereditary, but they were not automatically assumed at birth. They had to be formally and publicly assumed at a "potlatch," a performance given by all coast groups north of the Columbia River. The term comes from a widespread trade jargon and means "to give." A potlatch always involved invitation of another group or groups, who were received as guests with great formality; they served as witnesses to the announcements by the host chief at the assumption or bestowal of prerogatives, such as noble titles, crests, or ceremonial rights, and then were given gifts. The previously assumed statuses of the guests were recognized in the gift-giving, for distribution was made in the order of their rank sequence, and the more splendid gifts were given to guests of highest status. Not only were titles and other honours announced for the host chief or his heir and for his close kin of high position but children of low-rank group members were awarded names from the group stock and, at times, minor prerogatives. Participation of all members in major or minor roles in the proceedings also served to identify them with the social unit. There were some regional variations: in the northern province, a major potlatch was part of the cycle of mortuary observances after the death of a chief, at which his heir formally assumed his rights; in the Wakashan and Salish regions a chief gave such affairs to bestow rights on an heir apparent before his own demise.

Some early anthropologists, and a few modern ones, considered potlatch to be an economic enterprise in which the giver expected to recover a profit on the goods he distributed when his various guests potlatched in their turn. This actually was an impossibility because only a few guests of highest rank would ever stage such affairs and invite their former hosts; those of intermediate and low rank never did so, yet the total amount of gifts bestowed on them was considerable. Indeed, before white traders came and made great quantities of trade goods available, potlatches were few, whereas feasts, though also formal but not occasions for bestowing titles and gifts, were very frequent.

Early training of youth

Socialization and education. An interesting aspect of Northwest Coast culture was the emphasis on teaching children etiquette, moral standards, and other traditions of social import. Every society has processes by which children are taught the behaviour proper to their future roles, but often such teaching is not overtly a deliberate process. On the Northwest Coast, particularly northward of the Columbia, children were instructed formally. This instruction began at an age when modern educators would consider children too young to learn effectively—while they were still in their cradles. Children born to high statuses were given formal instruction throughout childhood and adolescence. They had to learn not only routine etiquette but also the lengthy traditions by which the rank and privileges of their particular group were validated and many rituals including songs and formulaic prayers. It was not only the parents (or, in some groups, the mother's brother) who taught children. All elder relatives, particularly grandparents, participated. The educative procedure did not consist of dry, barebones moral lectures. Some of it was given in the form of folktales, amusing and entertaining but with pointed morals: the troubles of the anti-hero, Raven, in the tales were obviously the result of his dissolute way of life, his laziness, his gormandizing, and his lechery.

Other socialization processes, those that involved public recognition of the attainment of new status, were usual among Northwest Coast groups. One variety included ritual observances considered necessary at each critical stage in a person's lifetime. At the birth of an infant, at a girl's attainment of puberty (there were no boys' puberty rites in the area), and at death, it was considered that persons involved might be in danger or might be dangerous to the society at large. A newborn infant was believed to be in danger from supernatural causes; the infant's parents were both in danger and dangerous. A girl at puberty was similarly viewed, as were the close kin of a deceased person and those who actually participated in preparing and disposing of the body. Such perils were avoided by isolating the persons involved, either within a boarded-off cubicle in the house or in a makeshift hut out in the woods, and by limiting his or her diet to old dried fish and water. At the conclusion of the isolation period some sort of formal ritual purification was carried out, such as ceremonial bathing. The intensity of the restrictions varied considerably, not only in different parts of the coast but within individual groups. Often the pubescent daughter of a chief, for example, was secluded for many months, whereas her low-ranking kinswoman might have to observe only a few days of confinement.

Over most of the coast there was a very great fear of the dead. A body was removed from the house through some makeshift aperture other than the door, to be disposed of as rapidly as possible. Only in the northern region were bodies of chiefs set up in state for several days while the clan dirges were sung. Disposal of the dead varied. In the northern province cremation was practiced (anciently, interment was customary). In the Wakashan and part of the Coast Salish areas large wooden boxes suspended from branches of tall trees or placed in rock shelters served as coffins. Other Coast Salish deposited their dead in canoes set up on stakes. In southwest Oregon and northwest California interment in the ground was preferred.

Economic systems. Of the various distinctive attributes of Northwest Coast culture, one of the most important was the highly efficient exploitation of natural resources. The resources, particularly the fisheries, were very bountiful; but they were scattered and not equally easy to exploit. Certain species of salmon, for example, ran in certain rivers at various times of the year. The important species for preservation for winter stores were the pink and the chum salmon. Because these species ceased to feed for some time before entering freshwater and their flesh thus had less fat content, they could be smoked and dried and kept for a long period of time. Other species, such as sockeye, coho, and the flavorsome chinook or king salmon, could be utilized immediately or dried and kept for a short period but could not be preserved the whole winter through. Therefore, the principal fishing sites were those along rivers and streams in which pink or chum salmon ran in the fall. In the spring of the year other sorts of fish became available in tremendous schools: herring, which came in to spawn in coves; "candlefish" (eulachon), which entered certain rivers; and, farther south, "smelt," which spawned on sandy beaches in summer. Elsewhere, in the summer months, bottom fishing for such species as halibut was a profitable enterprise on shallow offshore banks.

Reliance on fishing

To exploit the total resources of the region it was most efficient for the people to have various bases of operation. In the winter months when storm winds blew and heavy seas slammed against the coasts, shelter behind some point of land that broke the force of the sea was highly desirable. The Northwest Coast adaptation to this pattern was shifting residence. The people moved from one site to another, according to the season and according to the resources about to become available. This was not nomadism. The Indians moved systematically in certain seasons from one fixed site to another for convenient access to seasonal resources. Typically at these seasonal stations there were either permanent houses or permanent houseframes that could be covered over with planks brought along for the purpose. Occasionally, when the weather permitted or only a short stay was planned, makeshift shelters were erected.

Patterns of production and technology

Aboriginal Northwest Coast economy may be viewed as a system comprised of several mutually supporting subsystems. The first of these subsystems is the efficient techniques for taking fish and other marine resources and for preserving them. The second subsystem consisted in the construction of large rectangular plank houses that made possible the smoking and drying of fish during the torrential rains of autumn. Such houses also provided storage space for the bulky preserved foods. The third subsystem consisted of the water-transport complex. Canoes, both large and small, provided access to fishing grounds and the means of transporting preserved foodstuffs to other habitation areas. It was the combination of these subsystems that made the exploitation of local resources so efficient that the people were able to live with a wide margin of plenty.

Northwest Coast houses shared a few significant traits. All were rectangular in floor plan with plank walls and plank roof, and all but those of northwestern California were large structures designed for multifamily use. At the northern and southern extremes of the area deep central pits were dug within the house. In the north, houses were built on a nearly square plan—averaging about 50 feet wide by 55 feet long—and had gabled roofs; walls and framework were intermeshed to form a permanent structural unit. In the Wakashan province, on the other hand, the houses were rectangular—40 feet by 60 to 100 feet. Huge cedar posts with side beams and ridgepoles comprised the permanent framework, and to these were attached wall planks and roof planks that could be taken down, loaded onto canoes, and transported from one site to another. Some Coast Salish similarly built houses of permanent frameworks with detachable siding and roofing; their houses, however, had "shed-roofs," that is, a roof with only one slope instead of the two of the Wakashan house. Some Coast Salish houses were tremendously long, housing many people. Along the lower Columbia the typical house had a deep large rectangular pit, lined with planks, capped with a gabled roof. Only roof and gable ends showed above ground. The northwestern California house type was designed for single family only. Each house had low side walls of redwood planks and a three-pitch roof. Living space was the plank-lined central pit. Northwestern California also added a specialized structure: the men's combined clubhouse and sweat house, a common native Californian institution.

Water transport was highly important in the area. All groups made efficient dugout canoes. Northern groups, as well as the Kwakiutl and Salish down to Puget Sound, made dugouts with projecting bow and stern pieces, vertical "cutwaters," rounded sterns, and rounded hulls. The Nootka and some of their neighbours made vessels with projecting bow pieces, curving cutwaters, vertical sterns, and angular flat bottoms. Northwest Californian dugouts had upturned rounded ends, rounded hull, a carved seat and foot braces for the steersman. All types were made in different proportions for different purposes: large, beamy ones for moving people and cargo; shorter, narrow ones with racy lines for sea mammal hunting, and so on.

Crafts

Northwest Coast woodworking was facilitated by the natural abundance of easily worked timbers, especially the red cedar and the redwood. Trunks of these trees could be split into planks or they could be hollowed out into canoes, containers, or other useful objects. Along the Northwest Coast as far south as the Columbia, wooden boxes were made of red-cedar boards that were "kerffed"—cut nearly through transversely. The wood was steamed at these points until it was flexible enough to bend into the form of a box. Dishes often were hollowed out of pieces of wood, sometimes plain, sometimes in the form of animals and monsters. Also of wood were spoons and ladles (some were of horn), canoe bailers, trinket boxes, chamber pots, and masks used in ceremonials and rattles for musical accompaniment. A special character of Northwest Coast woodworking was the emphasis on symmetry, neatness of finish, and frequent decoration of the surfaces, with relief carving or with relief carving and painting. All of this woodworking was accomplished with rather limited tools, the principal ones being the adz, mauls and wedges, chisels, drills, curved knives, abrasive stones and sharkskin for polishing. Mountain-goat horn, mountain-sheep horn traded from the interior, and, in the south, elk horn were carved by essentially the same methods as wood.

Another highly developed craft was weaving. The inner bark of red cedar was stripped long and ribbonlike to be woven into mats and baskets in a checkerwork technique. The same bark was shredded into finely divided flexible hanks, which were twined together to make a slip-on rain cape shaped like a truncated cone. The softer inner bark of yellow cedar was made into robes. Persons of high status wore such robes edged with strips of sea-otter fur and a few strands of yarn made of mountain-goat wool. Salish of the Georgia Strait wove robes of mountain-goat wool and also of wool from a special breed of shaggy little dog. The Chilkat, a Tlingit group, wove robes of mountain-goat wool that was twilled like basketry. Chilkat blankets bore representations of crests in blue, yellow, black, and white.

Twined basketry made from long, flexible splints split from spruce roots was made with great technical skill in several regions. Baskets so tightly woven as to be waterproof were made for cooking in the northern and northwestern Californian regions. Storage containers, receptacles for valuables large and small, and rain hats (Californians' hats were snug and caplike, worn only by women) also were woven. The Coast Salish specialty was coiled basketry.

Clothes

Dress patterns of the area were simple. Only the northernmost Tlingit and the Kitksan of the upper Skeena wore tailored buckskin clothing: breechclouts, leggings, and shirts for men; long gowns for women. Elsewhere, men wore robes of yellow cedar bark or of crudely tanned pelts in cold weather, rain capes in downpours, and nothing but ornaments on the infrequent bright sunny days. Ornaments, such as necklaces, earrings, bracelets, and anklets, were made of various materials, mostly shells, copper, wood, and fur. Some groups practiced tattooing.

Head-flattening was considered a beautifying process from the northern Kwakiutl region to the central Oregon coast. A newborn infant in its cradle had its head bound in such a way as to produce a long subconical form, a strong slope from the eyebrows back, or a distinctive wedge shape in which the back of the skull was flattened.

Belief and the aesthetic systems. *Religion.* Among no group or groups on the Northwest Coast did religion consist of an organized coherent body of beliefs in and attitudes toward the supernatural. Rather, there were several quite unrelated concepts that provided the widespread bases for various kinds of religious activity.

Fish spirits

One concept was that salmon were supernatural beings who voluntarily assumed piscine form to sacrifice themselves annually for the benefit of mankind. On being taken, the spirits of the fish returned to their home beneath the sea, where they were reincarnated if their bones were returned to the water. If offended, however, the salmon-beings would refuse to return to the river. Hence, there were numerous specific prohibitions on acts believed to offend them and observances designed to propitiate them, chief of which was the first salmon ceremony. This rite varied in detail along the coast but invariably involved honouring the first salmon of the main fishing season by sprinkling them with eagle down, red ocher, or some other sacred substance, welcoming them in a formal speech, cooking them and distributing their flesh, or morsels of it, communion-fashion, to all the members of the local group and any guests. The maximal elaboration of this rite was found in northwestern California, combined there with first fruits observances, and dances in which lineage wealth was displayed, in what have been called world-renewal ceremonies. Elsewhere the first salmon rituals were less elaborate but still important (except among the Tlingit, who did not perform them).

Another concept was that of acquiring personal power by seeking contact with a spirit—as through prayer and a vision. Among Coast Salish all success in life—whether hunting, woodworking, accumulating wealth, military ventures, or magic—was bestowed by spirits encountered in the spirit quest. From his spirit or spirits each person acquired songs, special regalia, and dances. Collectively, the dances comprised the major ceremonials of these people; known as the Spirit Dances, they were performed during the winter months. In the Wakashan province and the northern one it was believed that remote ancestors on spirit quests had been rewarded with totemic symbols called "crests." Displaying these hereditary crests and recounting their traditional acquisition formed an important part of the potlatches. In the Wakashan area certain ceremonial cycles called for the dramatization of the whole tale of the supernatural encounter, including the spirit's possession of the seeker and the eventual exorcism of the spirit; such dramas were performed by what were called "dancing societies."

Shamanism differed from other acquisitions of supernatural power only in the nature of the power obtained—that is, power to heal the sick through extraction of disease objects or recovery of a strayed soul. It was commonly believed that some shamans, or medicine men, had power to cause these infirmities as well as to cure them. Witchcraft, to kill or make ill, was also believed to be carried out by malicious persons who knew secret rituals for that purpose.

Art. The Northwest Coast is noted for its art styles. In the northern province, low-relief carving accented by painting was essentially an applied art. The motifs were the hereditary crests of the clans or parts of the crests, applied to the magnificent memorial poles and interior house-posts, painted on house-fronts and screens, wrapped around carved wooden boxes and dishes, painted on basketry hats, woven into Chilkat robes, and carved on the handles of ladles and spoons, on halibut hooks, and even on the triggers of animal traps. There were differences within this style. Haida art tended to be massive, of highly conventionalized balanced elements, and slightly static. In Tsimshian carving and painting there was an effort to leave no open space in or between the conventionalized motifs: filler elements such as eye-designs and miniature figures were used intensively. Tlingit art was slightly less conventionalized, more vigorous by modern standards, with relatively little use of filler elements.

Wakashan representative art was more frankly sculptural than applied, and it was impressionistic and bold. There was a limited amount of simple geometric design on such things as whalebone clubs and whaling harpoon barbs. Their Coast Salish neighbours used some, but less, representative art, similar if cruder in style. On Puget Sound there was little if any representative art; the formless painted designs on the canoe boards were unlike anything else on the Coast. All that is known of Chinook art is represented by a few angular figures incised on mountain sheephorn bowls. In northwestern California, art was limited to geometric patterns incised on elkhorn objects and shells. (See also AMERICAN PEOPLES, ARTS OF NATIVE.)

MODERN DEVELOPMENTS

The impact of white man's culture on that of the Northwest Coast varied at different periods and in different regions. Maritime traders, searching for precious sea-otter pelts, purveyed Euro-American manufactures to the Indians; but the material objects affected native culture only slightly. The Indians picked and chose the articles that had meaning to them—those that could fit well into their existing culture patterns. They acquired steel blades, for example, that could be fitted to their adzes to cut more efficiently than the aboriginal stone or shell blades; they spurned axe and hatchet blades that required a drastic change in motor habits and coordination patterns. In other words, the Indians accepted what they wanted; they were under no compulsion to change their way of life. Contagious diseases—smallpox, venereal infections, and the rest, introduced incidentally—had more effect on native society. The abnormal rate of deaths forced unusual distributions of roles and status positions, involving frequent adoptions, allocation of various titles to the same person, and other makeshift compromises to maintain the social system despite rapid population decline.

The establishment of white trading posts had somewhat more effect; and the great pressures started when white settlers began streaming into western Washington, Oregon, Vancouver Island, and the lower Fraser River Valley about the middle of the 19th century. This foreign occupation was accompanied by removal of the Indians to small reservations in Washington and Oregon under the provisions of formal treaties. In the area that became British Columbia there were no treaties extinguishing Indian title to the land; land transfers were private affairs.

Economic problems

In the closing decades of the 19th century, the Indians were in dire straits. Divested of most of their lands and at the same time more and more dependent upon white

American and British-Canadian manufactured goods, the Indians had to develop new economic patterns. The fur trade was inconsequential; logging and mining were still underdeveloped, requiring skills that the Indians did not have. Northwest Coast concepts of wealth differed from the Euro-American ones, but there were enough general similarities so that the Indians could perceive and accept certain equivalences. Northwest Coast Indians thus came to be more disposed to enter the new economic system, working for wages in a dull day-after-day routine, something that most other North American Indians refused to do. There was at first, however, little hired work available—guiding prospectors, back-packing cargo over mountain passes, cutting cordwood for coastal steamers—until the canned salmon industry developed, principally from the Fraser River northward. It was this industry that most effectively deprived the Indians of their fishing economy by monopolizing salmon streams, while at the same time offering them entrée into the new economy. Indian labour was cheaper than Oriental because it did not have to be imported.

The Indians also knew more about the habits of the salmon than anyone else. Of great importance was the fact that the commercial salmon fishery began with a very simple technology. The Indians themselves had long used canoes, spears, and weirs and other trapping devices. As motive power changed from paddles and oars to two-cycle gasoline engines, to high-speed gasoline engines, to diesel engines; as harvesting changed from gill nets and crude "beach seines" to huge purse seines handled with power gear; and as navigation changed from eyeball piloting to navigation using tide tables, compasses, and charts, the Indians could learn the new skills along with white and Oriental fishermen. The problem now is that the Indians are largely committed to a short-season industry, which ties up capital in expensive boats and nets. When the salmon run is over, there is no significant source of income until the next year.

Effective missionary activity began in various parts of the coast at about the same time that administrative controls were established. Missionaries on the Northwest Coast as elsewhere have been very successful at directed culture change, teaching not only Christian precepts but also etiquette, values of work and sobriety, household hygiene, and a host of other things that the Indian needed to know in order to participate in modern culture. Formal schooling of Indian children was in the hands of missionaries on much of the coast for many decades.

The aggressive and warlike Northwest Coast Indians never mounted a major war against the whites. There were only a few isolated local conflicts. This pacific pattern was not due to cowardice but to a realistic appraisal of the vulnerability of their coastal villages to naval gunfire.

There were some nativistic movements—that is, attempts to preserve or resuscitate former valued concepts or activities: for instance, the southern Kwakiutl tried to revive potlatch on a splendid scale, despite administrative prohibitions; and the Canadian Coast Salish tried to continue their Spirit Dances. But there is a distinction between these limited efforts of the Northwest Coast Indians and the "revitalization" movements of the Great Plains Indians, who, with their Ghost Dance, sought by supernatural means to evict the oppressor culture and return completely to the "good old days."

In southeast Alaska and later on in coastal British Columbia a different type of organization was created, the "Native Brotherhoods," whose purpose is to foster cultural change. The accomplishments of the Alaska Native Brotherhood have surpassed those of the Canadian organization, but both have been effective in creating a sense of Indian unity and community of interest. The organizations also provide valuable training in modern political processes and negotiations. The Alaskan organization has been partially superseded by the Tlingit-Haida Association, which handles matters related to the successfully prosecuted land claims of those people. Leaders of the British Columbia Brotherhood also have been effective in legal suits for compensation for lands.

(P.Dr.)

Californian Indians

Native peoples found in California were only generally circumscribed by the present state boundaries. Some of the peoples within these boundaries were culturally intimate with other areas neighbouring California. The Colorado River groups, such as the Mojave (Mohave) and Yuma, shared traditions with both the Southwest (Arizona and New Mexico) and southern California, whereas the peoples of the Sierra Nevada, such as the Washo, shared traditions with the Great Basin peoples. In northern California were to be found native traditions of the Northwest Coast; the remaining native groups occupied the greater part of California, and they represented indigenous cultural developments.

A conservative estimate of the pre-Spanish population of California is 275,000, making it one of the most populous culture areas of native North America. Various ecologic features—seacoasts, tidelands, river and lake areas, valleys, deserts, and foothills—and various historical traditions contributed to great cultural diversity. Thus there existed a seemingly endless variety of local environmental niches, each contributing advantages and disadvantages to human adaptation.

The peoples of California were politically stable, sedentary, and conservative and less in conflict with one another than was usually the case in other areas of North America; and neighbouring groups often developed elaborate systems of economic exchange of goods and services. The Californian Indians reached peaks of cultural attainment rarely seen among peoples depending almost wholly for subsistence on hunting, fishing, and the gathering of wild plant foods.

TRADITIONAL CULTURE PATTERNS

Local and territorial organization. California was occupied by a large number of cultural groups that have been described as ethnic nationalities—that is, groups of

From H. Driver *et al.*, *Indiana University Publications in Anthropology and Linguistics* (1953)

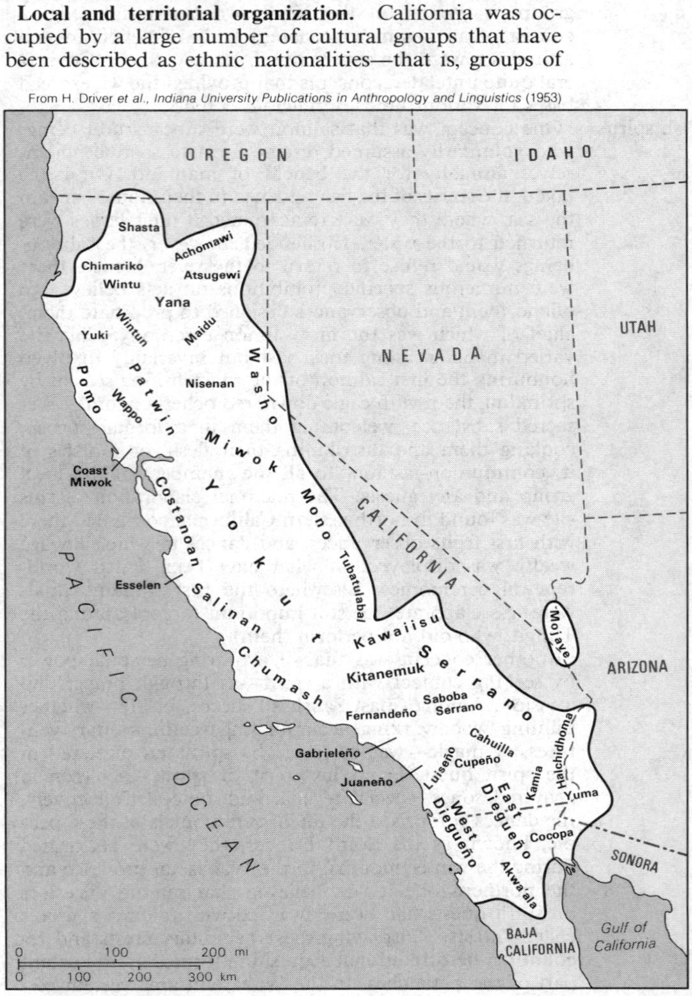

Distribution of Californian Indians.

people sharing common linguistic, social, and cultural traditions and recognizing themselves as part of a single culture distinct from that of other groups. Except for the Colorado River peoples (Mojave and Yuma) and perhaps some Chumash groups, these ethnic nationalities had no centralized governmental structures; instead, each group comprised independent territorial and political units that may be termed tribelets, tightly organized polities that were smaller than the average groupings in most other parts of North America. Populations in these tribelets ranged from a hundred to a few thousand people, depending on the richness of locally available resources; tribelet territories ranged in size from about 50 to 1,000 square miles (150 to 3,000 square kilometres).

"Tribelet" organization

Within each tribelet there might be only one principal village in which all the people lived and from which some of them ranged for short periods of time to collect food, hunt, or visit other tribelets for ritual or economic purposes. In some tribelets there was a principal village surrounded by settlements of people who came to the principal village for ritual, social, economic, and political occasions. In other tribelets there were two or more villages, each having various satellite settlements and one serving as a "capital" or central village. Here a principal chief would usually reside, and major rituals and political and economic affairs would be held.

Community organization of tribelet villages was varied, but basic patterns are discernible. Among the Miwok and the peoples south of them, village ownership was usually based on clan arrangements, whereas in northern California land ownership was based more on territorial principles than on kinship ties. Bilateral or nonlineal descent organization usually occurred where village land ownership was not clan based, as in the case of the southeastern desert-dwelling peoples, although exceptions to this occurred in the far northern part of the state.

Kinship and status patterns. Marriage was almost always a matter arranged by the families because it created long-range economic and social bonds between families. Generally the families exchanged goods at the time of the marriage, the bulk of goods coming from the husband's family. In most cases the wife resided with the husband's family and was taught the ways of the husband's group by the mother-in-law. Levirate (widow marriage to the brother of the deceased) and sororate (widower marriage to the sister of the deceased) were widely observed, maintaining relationships between already connected families and stabilizing child-care conditions. Men could often have more than one wife; this was particularly true of chiefs and shamans (medicine men) because heavy social responsibilities were required of their offices and because political ties between groups could thereby be established.

The aged served as the teachers and advisers. Young adults were active in subsistence, and the elders prepared the children for adulthood. The aged made most of the decisions concerning legal disputes and economic crises.

Role of the chief

The role of chief was generally an inherited position providing political stability to the group (though in northern California no formal chief appears to have existed). Women in some groups, such as the Pomo, were chosen as chiefs or "little chiefs." The chief was an economic administrator whose instructions to his people ranged from general admonitions to specific directions for particular tasks, such as indicating where food was available and how many people it would require to collect it. He redistributed the economic resources of his community and, through donations from village members, maintained resources from which emergency needs of individuals could be met. He was the major decision maker and the final authority in most villages, but he had the aid of a council consisting of such persons as heads of extended families, ritualists, assistant chiefs, and shamans. In some areas the chief functioned as a priest, maintaining the ceremonial house and ritual artifacts. The chief was generally a conspicuous person, wealthier, more elaborately dressed, and often displaying the symbols of his office. He was treated with great respect. Chiefs' families formed a superstratum of the community elites, especially in areas in which lineage development was present.

Shamans and ritualists

Shamans served not only as physical and mental healers and diviners but also as artists and poets. They defined and described the world of the sacred and regulated the fortune of souls before and after death, thereby serving as mediators between the profane and sacred worlds. Most tribelets in California had one or more shamans, usually men. Shamans were active in political life, working with other leaders and placing their powers at the disposal of the community.

Alongside chiefs and shamans in native California there were ritualists—dancers, singers, fire tenders—who were carefully trained in their crafts, and they functioned intimately within the political, economic, and religious spheres of their communities. They were men or women who acquired considerable respect and often wealth because of their skills and placement in the social structure. In effect, they were members of the power elite. When performing, ritualists were usually costumed in headdresses, dance skirts, wands, jewelry, and other items.

Socialization and education. Formal learning was a continuous process in native California life. Older persons instructed children through elaborate tales containing lessons concerning behaviour and values. Constant supervision—provided by adults, older siblings, or other relatives—instructed and reminded the child about how things should be done.

Rites of passage

The dramatic time of the educational process occurred during rites of passage, when individuals attained new status and responsibility. The girls' puberty ceremony, for example, generally consisted of a time of isolation because the female was considered dangerous (or especially empowered) at menarche. During this time, which varied from several days to several weeks, an older woman would care for the girl and instruct her in her role as an adult. Ceremonies for boys' initiation were less common and, when carried out, were usually less formal, involving instruction in manly occupations and behaviour and prediction of the boys' future religious, economic, or political careers.

Sometimes education was quite institutionalized. Young Chumash men, for instance, purchased positions from guildlike associations of specialists in order to receive apprenticeship as professional artisans of some kind, while young Pomo men were charged a fee to be trained as apprentices by recognized professional craftsmen.

Leaders and specialists continued their training on a less formal level throughout their lifetimes. A man destined to become chief received his learning from others (such as ritualists and shamans) and continued to receive such instruction even after assumption of office.

Economic systems. *Settlement patterns.* In most of California the villages were occupied the year round, with small groups moving out only for short periods of time to hunt or collect food. In areas poor in economic resources, people moved more frequently, only temporarily gathering together in large groups for such activities as antelope drives and piñon-nut harvests. Riverine and coastal peoples as a rule enjoyed more stable settlements than those living in the desert and foothills.

Housing

House types varied throughout California from permanent, carefully constructed houses occupied for a lifetime or more to the most temporary type of structure, such as a brush shelter, as dictated by circumstances. Types of houses ranged from wood-framed (northern California), earth-covered (various areas), semi-subterranean (Sacramento area), and brush (desert areas) to thatched palm (southern California). Communal and ceremonial houses were found throughout the region and were often large enough to hold several hundred people for rituals or festivals. Domestic houses ranged in size from five or six feet (almost two metres) in diameter to apartment-style houses in which several families lived together in adjoining units. Another common type of housing consisted of the sweathouses, earth-covered permanent structures that were used by most Californians (the Colorado River groups and the northern Paiute, on the margins of California, were exceptions); sweating was usually a daily activity for men.

Patterns of production and technology. Food production in native California centred on hunting, fishing, and collecting wild plant foods. Men usually hunted and fished while women collected plant foods and small game. Hunting and fishing equipment such as bows and arrows, throwing sticks, fishing gear, snares, and traps were made by men; women manufactured clothing, nets, baskets, pots, and other cooking utensils. Older people commonly made the productive equipment used in the harder labours of production by younger adults.

For coastal Californians, shellfish, deep-sea fish, surf fish, acorns, and game were the main subsistence staples; peoples in the riverine and lake areas relied on fish, acorns, tule, game, and waterfowl. Native groups of the foothills, valleys, and plains depended on acorns, tule, game, and fish; and those living in the desert regions sought piñon nuts, mesquite, and game (especially antelope and rabbit) and practiced some marginal agriculture.

Special technologies

There were also various special technological devices. The Chumash of southern coastal California made large seagoing plank canoes, which allowed them to hunt large sea mammals. Peoples living on the bays and lakes used tule balsas or rafts, while riverine groups had flat-bottom dugouts (canoes made by hollowing out large logs). Techniques of food preservation included drying, hermetic sealing, and leaching of some foods high in acid content. Milling and grinding equipment was common.

Property and exchange systems. Concepts of property tended to vary in degree rather than kind throughout California. Everywhere, property was owned by individuals, family groups, lineages, communities, or larger political groups such as clans. In general, socially defined groups (such as clans and villages) owned the land and protected it against infringement from other groups. Individuals, lineages, or extended families usually owned exclusive rights only to certain food-collecting, fishing, and hunting areas. Such resources as obsidian mines or areas where medicinal plants grew might be owned by either groups or individuals. Individual articles could be acquired by manufacture, inheritance, purchase, or gift.

Goods and foodstuffs were distributed through two main institutions—reciprocal exchange between kin and "trade fairs," often ritualized. Both operated similarly in that they served as a redistribution and banking system for spoilable foodstuffs; a group with a surplus of foods, that is, would bring it to another group and exchange it for goods (such as shells), which could be used in the future to acquire foodstuffs in return.

There were professional traders in most California groups who travelled long distances among many ethnic nationalities. Goods from as far away as Arizona and New Mexico were exchanged by coastal peoples. Generally, shells from the coastal areas were valued and exchanged for products of the inland areas, such as obsidian or food. Medicines, manufactured goods such as baskets, and other objects were also commonly exchanged in these systems.

Religion. Throughout native California religious institutions were intensely and intimately associated with all other institutions—political, economic, social, and legal. In all the groups there were shamans, religious leaders who served as intermediaries between the supernatural world and the world of man. Priests and other ritualists were common in many groups.

Kuksu and Toloache religions

Two religious systems—the Kuksu and the Toloache—were associated with social organizations into which initiates were formally indoctrinated. In the Kuksu religion common to northern California (as among the Pomo, Yuki, Maidu, Wintun), members "impersonated" spiritual beings and engaged in colourful and dramatic rituals requiring special costumes and equipment; these events usually were conducted in large public communal houses. Within the Toloache religion of southern California (as among the Luiseño and Diegueño), initiates performed while drinking a hallucinogenic decoction made of the plant *Datura meteloides*, which put them in a trance and provided them with supernatural knowledge about their future life and role as members of the sacred societies. In both religions special instruction was a significant factor in the recruitment of members into the ritual society. Members exercised considerable economic, political, and social influence.

Religions on the Colorado River differed slightly because they were not concerned with developing formal organizations and recruitment procedures. Individuals received religious information through dreams; and members recited long narrative texts, explaining the creation of the world, the travel of culture heroes, and the adventures of historic figures.

In the northwest there was another informally structured religious system. It was associated with rituals concerned with world renewal (as in the white-deerskin dance), in which privately owned myths were recited. One communal need served by these ceremonies was that of restructuring relationships in societies lacking the rigid social ordering found in many other native California groups. The display of costumes and valuable possessions (such as white deerskins or delicately chipped obsidian blades) reaffirmed social ranking, and the success of the ritual reaffirmed the orderly relationship of man to the supernatural.

Use of magic

The use of supernatural power to control events or transform reality was basic to every California group. Generally, magic was used in attempts to control the weather, increase the harvest of crops, and foretell the future. Magic was deemed not only the cause of sickness and death but also the principal means of curing many diseases. Magic was considered also as an agent to protect oneself, to punish wrongdoers, or to satisfy personal ends.

Arts and crafts. Oral literature was the art form for which native California was most renowned—especially esoteric and elaborate creation tales and epic poems. There were also songs with accompanying narratives, tales of victory, recollections of recent events or daily activities, and airs of love. Songs were usually short but could, in narrative form, last for days. Singing was accompanied by rattles, whistles, or drums.

Visual art forms ranged from decoration on items of daily use (such as baskets and tools) to elaborate rock paintings and rock engravings. California natives are generally most remembered for their exquisite basketwork, though pottery in the eastern desert was shaped and decorated handsomely. Costuming, particularly in relation to the Kuksu religion, involved the creation of elaborate headdresses, skirts, feathered costumes, and so on, which were often symbolic of supernatural beings. Body painting was also popular.

Incising or pecking designs into rock was practiced in various parts of the area, and rock paintings were widespread. They were associated probably with individual and group rituals and hunting and gathering activities on the one hand and served as simple trail markers or indicators of food or water on the other.

MODERN DEVELOPMENTS

Contemporary native Californians are rural peoples residing mainly on reservations or rancherias. There is, however, a long-established pattern of individuals moving to urban areas to find work when necessary but considering their reservation or rancheria as "home," as a place where they will be welcomed upon return. In this manner many native Californians may live away from their lands for the better part of a lifetime and yet come back at last to a way of life compatible with their cultural ideals and involving their family and friends. Many individuals come and go sporadically, depending upon economic conditions; some live only seasonally on the reservations. Native Californians move from depressed areas to towns, villages, and cities, however, not only to find employment but also to arrange for schooling for their children and to find the amenities of life that are often totally lacking in the more remote Indian lands.

Depressed economic conditions in many areas

In the late 20th century, as industries moved into some rural areas, the nearby reservations became more attractive, offering some prospects of local employment. In many areas, the permanent populations of reservations were expanding, particularly with more young people with children. In other more remote rural areas, the economic situation remained bleak.

Since the United States government withdrew most federal responsibility for native Californians in 1955, reservations have become relatively autonomous. Each reservation or rancheria has an elected body of officials, known variously as a business committee or tribal council, which acts as a liaison between the people and such outside interests as the U.S. Bureau of Indian Affairs, business corporations desiring the purchase or lease of reservation lands, public utilities concerned with seeking rights-of-way across lands, and individuals having some form of business with the group. The council acts with the advice and consent of the people in dispersing tribally owned assets such as the lands or funds, and it also acts as the receiving agent for grants from various economic-development or relief organizations of the government. It is often involved in litigation with the government or other agencies concerning tribal grievances, and today it almost invariably participates directly in planning economic and social development programs for the future protection of the group's assets.

Generally speaking, native Californians have adopted much of the ways of contemporary society. In clothing, housing, transportation, education, and often religion, they are not significantly distinguishable from other people residing in California. In more subtle ways, however, native culture, attitudes, ritual, and psychology are still viable throughout the state from north to south. Wherever there are native populations, one finds ceremonial houses, ritual, and the continued use and manufacture of ritual materials, as well as occasional use of native foods. Many arts and crafts, especially basket weaving, have been maintained. The Indian languages, though spoken less and less as first languages, are being maintained and revived for cultural and nostalgic reasons. On some reservations there are cultural centres and museums helping to preserve the culture and languages, and on other reservations and in some local school districts classes in native languages and culture are being offered to both children and adults. Various organizations of native Californians, such as the American Indian Historical Society and the California Indian Education Association, are aggressively examining, criticizing, and providing new teaching materials for schoolteachers who deal with native Californians in the classrooms.

Attempts to preserve the cultural heritages

On the other hand, few if any traces of traditional cultures remain in some areas of California. These areas generally coincide with what have become the major population centres of California, from San Francisco and Oakland south to San Diego. A new form of native American cultural development is under way, however, as Indians from all over the United States, not only from rural California but also from reservations in the central great plains of the United States and the Southwest, gravitate to these major urban areas, bringing with them diverse tribal and cultural backgrounds that add up to a new measure of cultural diversity in urban life. Many of these people came in large numbers during World War II, often to work in defense industries, while others came in large numbers after the war as part of the aggressive planning and development of the Bureau of Indian Affairs in the 1950s. These moves led to serious problems among some of the relocatees because Bureau of Indian Affairs coordination was ineptly carried out, with the result that many native American groups have had to develop their own self-help organizations to care for their people in the cities. A pattern of replicating the institutions of the cultural groups they came from is apparent throughout the state. Recreational groups as well as educational and political groups have developed generally along lines of cultural similarity.

(Lo.J.B.)

North American Plateau Indians

The North American Plateau is both a complex physiographic unit and a native cultural area. It is bounded on the west by the Canadian Coast Mountains and the Cascade Range, on the south by the Blue Mountains and the Salmon River (excepting a narrow corridor to California), on the east by the Rocky Mountains and the Lewis Range, and on the north by low extensions of the Rocky Mountains, such as the Cariboo Mountains. It may be defined as the drainage territory of the Columbia and Fraser rivers and as the high plateau between the main range of the Rocky Mountains and the coastal mountain system. In the south the natural area of the Plateau gradually merges with the Great Basin natural area: the boundaries between the corresponding culture areas are indeed also very imprecise. Previously, anthropologists included both culture areas as one, the Plateau.

The climate is a harsh, continental type. Temperatures range from −30° F (−34° C) in winter to 100° F (38° C) in summer. Precipitation is low, except in the mountainous areas, and forms a snow cover during the winter. There are three different provinces of vegetation, which correspond to three subcultures: the Middle Columbia area, a steppe of sagebrush and bunchgrass fringed by yellow pine on higher levels, is the territory of the Sahaptin groups and some Salish; the Upper Columbia area, a mainly wooded area with grassland in river valleys, is the home country of such Salish groups as the Okanagon and Flathead, and of the Kutenai; and the Fraser area, with a semi-open coniferous forest interspersed with dry grassland and a partly maritime flora, is the tribal ground of the northern Salish groups. The fauna is not rich, but there are deer and elk in the mountains and salmon and trout in the rivers.

From H. Driver *et al.*, *Indiana University Publications in Anthropology and Linguistics* (1953)

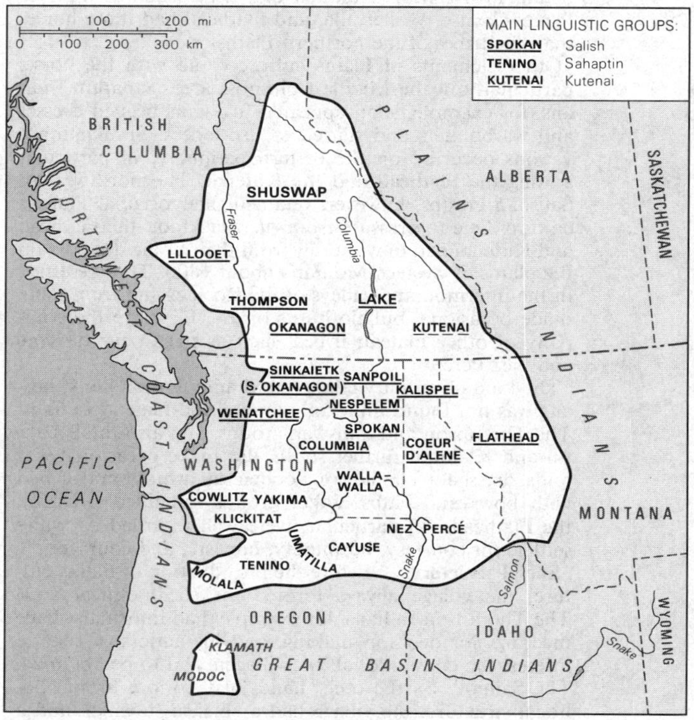

Distribution of North American Plateau Indians.

Peoples and languages

The Indians of the Plateau belong mainly to four linguistic families: Salish, Kutenai, Sahaptin, and Klamath-Modoc (Lutuami). The majority of Plateau groups speak Salishan and Sahaptian. The Salish may be conveniently divided into Northern Plateau and Interior Salish (there are also Coast Salish on the Northwest Coast). To the Northern Plateau group belong the Shuswap, Lillooet, and Thompson (Ntlakyapamuk) Indians; to the Interior group belong (mostly in the Upper Columbia area) the Okanagon (with Sinkaietk), the Lake (Senijextee), the Wenatchee, Sanpoil and Nespelem, the Spokan, Kalispel (with Pend d'Oreille), Coeur d'Alene, and Flathead. Some early works term all Salish "Flathead." The Sahaptin may be subdivided into three main groups: the Nez Percé, the Cayuse-Molala, and the Central Sahaptin (Umatilla, Yakima, Wallawalla, Tenino, and others).

TRADITIONAL CULTURE PATTERNS

The main characteristics of the Plateau cultures are best discernible against a historical background, for the Plateau cultural pattern was not stable. Opinion is divided as to whether its origins lay with the "desert culture" of arid Western North America, a primitive, seed-gathering culture, or with the "old Cordilleran culture" of the Plateau and North Pacific Coast, a culture with hunting, fishing, and gathering activities. It is certain, however, that the latter subsistence pattern predominated after 1500–1000 BC. By AD 1200–1300 the "classic" Plateau culture, characterized by permanent winter villages with semi-subterranean earth lodges along the main rivers and by summer camps with mat-covered conical lodges on the meadows, had emerged. There is evidence that the Plateau culture expanded as far south as the Snake River, including for some time Shoshoni groups in Idaho. During the centuries that followed, the Plateau area was influenced by cultural elements from the highly specialized Northwest Coast culture. Thus, mat and plank houses, carving in wood and bone with animal motifs, and cremation and scaffold burial appeared. Part of this diffusion was possibly brought about by a Chinook group, the Wishram, who migrated from the coast into the Cascade Mountains.

"Classic" Plateau culture

During the 18th century there were influences from the east. The Shoshoni had acquired horses by this time and furnished their closest neighbours on the Plains and the Plateau with horses. White traders, from the beginning of the 19th century, testified that tribes such as the Nez Percé, Cayuse, Wallawalla, and Flathead had more horses than the tribes of the northern Plains.

Other elements of Plains culture came with the horse, particularly in the Middle Columbia area. Sahaptin Indians, for example, soon appeared in Plains beaded dresses and warbonnets and started to use tepees. Similar innovations occurred on the eastern periphery, in particular among the Flathead and the Kutenai. The northwestern Salishan groups, however, retained their original Plateau culture. Due to pressure from the Blackfoot, the Flathead and Kutenai had to withdraw from their home quarters on the plains of western Montana about 1800. They resettled in the intermontane valleys of the Rockies and from there made occasional buffalo hunts on the Plains in the company of other Plateau tribes, such as the Coeur d'Alene and Nez Percé.

The kind of military ethos found among the Plains Indians was not found uniformly among the Plateau Indians. The Thompson and Shuswap groups, and also the Sahaptin and Klamath further south, did make occasional war raids, dressed in elk hide or wooden slat armour and armed with bows and clubs. Other groups remained peaceful; the Flatheads, in particular, were well regarded by white settlers for courtesy, hospitality, honesty, and courage.

Social structures. Before the introduction of Plains culture, the village always formed the sociopolitical unit. The Thompson Indians, for example, had informal village meetings for decision making, and in matters of general interest the consent of all the villagers had to be obtained. The Sanpoil, on the other hand, had a more formal political structure: the village had a chief, a subchief, and a general assembly in which every adult had a vote (except for young men who were not married). The Nez Percé had a similar organization until the buffalo hunts on the Plains started. Each village had a chief whose office was hereditary, except in the case of poorly qualified sons. Sometimes groups from several villages came together at certain fishing sites or camas (edible lily) meadows, and on these occasions the leading men of the villages constituted an informal council. Early in the 19th century this organization was overruled when families from different villages joined to form bands for the autumn hunts on the Plains. The authority of the village chiefs lapsed as good hunters and fighters became band chiefs. As a result of pressure from missionary and governmental agencies, a tribal head chief was appointed in the 1840s, but he was unable to win any influence over the people. A truly tribal political organization existed among the Flathead, who had a head chief of great power and band chiefs under him. The head chief decided on matters of peace and war and was not bound by the recommendations of his council.

In many Plateau societies chiefs played a more prominent role than in Plains Indian culture, and they were also to a greater extent hereditary. But, although Sahaptin chiefs could exert their authority through whipping (perhaps a Spanish trait), social control was as a rule achieved through social pressure and public opinion. Nobody was coerced into following the advice of a chief or the decisions of a council meeting, and those who did not want to conform could move to another village or another band.

Kinship patterns

The simple, bilateral-descent system prevailed in typical Plateau groups. The average Plateau kin group consisted of the nuclear family and the closest relatives on the father's as well as the mother's side. This is the case among, for instance, the Tenino. Their kinship terminology reveals the close connection between family relatives of the same generation on both paternal and maternal sides, so that all female cousins are called by the same terms as those used for sisters. Marriages do not occur among first cousins (in distinction to the custom in clan-organized societies), and newly wedded couples may put up their residence with the father's or the mother's group. The Tenino also show a patterned kinship behaviour that has possibly existed in other Plateau groups, such as a "joking relationship" between a father's sister's husband and his wife's brother's child, and permitted sexual license between a man and his sister-in-law. All over the Plateau, marriages between one man and several wives (polygyny) were practiced, although they were not common.

It has been observed that kin term distinctions and ranked status distinctions tend to counteract each other: the Coast Salish have a ranked society with reduction of kinship terminology, whereas the majority of Plateau Salish have prevalence of descriptive kin terms and few status distinctions. Among the Sinkaietk or Southern Okanagon, chiefs were hereditary and the most important persons in the tribe in regard to moral influence, for the chief and his family were supposed to exemplify the virtues of the group. He was, on the other hand, not necessarily the wealthiest man in his group, although he was economically supported by his people. The chief had a female relative among his advisers. Such highly respected women also existed in other groups, such as the Coeur d'Alene, and bear witness of the independence of women in Plateau society (excepting the Plains-influenced Kutenai and Flathead). Although marked off as hereditary in his office, the Plateau chief did not separate himself from his group. The general spirit was one of equality and personal autonomy, particularly among the Interior Salish. The Northern Plateau Salish, however, and several other groups kept slaves, as did the Indians on the Northwest Coast, and traded them between each other. The tribes on the eastern fringe who shared the Plains values had a rank of honoured warriors and war chiefs.

The life cycle of the individual was marked by fixed ritual acts that opened the gateway to the different social roles he had to enact. One could say that it started before birth. Among the Sinkaietk, for example, a pregnant woman was not supposed to give birth to her child in her regular home but in a menstrual lodge or another separate lodge. The newborn baby spent its day strapped in a cradle of the flat board type. At the age of one the child was ceremonially conferred a name from the wealth of names in the family. The training of the child was left to the mother and grandmother, but even as a small boy a Sinkaietk could accompany his father on fishing and small-game hunting trips, while the little girls helped their mothers about the house and gathered roots in the fields. Grandparents saw to it that the child was hardened by such practices as bathing in cold streams. Disobedience was rare but could sometimes result in the child being whipped.

Puberty rites

At puberty the boy was sent out to spend some days fasting on a mountain top and probably to receive a blessing vision from some spirit. Upon returning to the community, he took his place among the adult men. The girl who had her first menstruation was secluded in a menstrual lodge some distance from the village. Her hair was bound up in rolls, and she was only allowed to touch it with a small comb. Her face was painted red or yellow, and she wore undecorated clothing. She was not allowed to drink directly from a well but had to use a drinking tube, and she cleansed herself after the flow in a sweathouse. After a time—one or several months—she finished her seclusion with prayers in the evening on a hill. Then she returned to the village, a full-grown woman.

Marriage was an entirely informal affair, as was divorce; a woman who was tired of her husband or had been expelled by him returned to her parents if they were alive. She could then remarry if she wished.

Two forms of burial predominated in the Plateau area, pit burials and rockslide burials. The pit burials took place in sand or gravel near the river banks and were often marked with piles of boulders. The rockslide burials were also located close to the river flats, with a cedar stake as a marker. Some cremation burials occurred in the Yakima Valley and at The Dalles and also in the Lillooet-Thompson area. The bereaved had to observe certain taboos, and a widow was supposed to dress poorly and wail at the grave, sometimes for as long a period as a year. There are reports that the house where the death occurred was torn down so that the dead person would not reappear there.

Economic life. The Plateau villages were generally located on waterways and particularly at rapids and other places where fish were abundant during the winter season. Each village had an upland for hunting; in contradistinction to the fishing localities, these uplands were mostly open for people from other villages as well. There were also permanent or semipermanent summer camps for hunting and root gathering in mountain valleys. River villages were permanent winter quarters and could at least temporarily lodge several hundred people. A Kalispel village, for example, numbered 300–400 and a Yakima village as many as 2,000.

Winter dwellings were of two main types, the semi-subterranean earth lodge and the mat-covered surface house. The latter was apparently more recent and existed only in the southern Plateau, where it had replaced an older earth lodge. It was replaced in its turn by the Plains Indian tepee. The average earth lodge was circular, with a pit 4–6 feet (1–2 metres) deep and a diameter of 10–40 feet (3–12 metres). The roof was conical or flat and was supported by leaning poles fastened to some central posts. The smoke hole in the top was also the entrance, the floor being reached by an inside ladder or notched log. The other type of dwelling was formed of two walls of varying length leaning together and covered with tule mats. It was a "longhouse" with a series of hearths in the middle, each one of them shared by two families, one on each side. During the summer people housed in conical mat lodges of small size or in simple windbreaks.

Food-gathering techniques

Fishing was the most important source of food. The Plateau Indians used one- or three-pronged fish spears, traps, and nets when taking their staple fish—eels, suckers, trout, and especially salmon. Large quantities of fish were dried on elevated wooden racks or kept in storage pits and preserved for winter consumption. Roots were dug with digging sticks provided with cross handles of antler or wood. The main root was the camas bulb (*Camassia esculenta*), but bitterroot, onions, wild carrots, and parsnips were also gathered. They were then cooked in earth ovens heated by hot stones. Berries—serviceberries, huckleberries, blueberries—were harvested as well. Hunting occasionally played an important role, even in the winter. Equipped with bow and arrows and perhaps a short spear, the Indian hunted deer first of all but also bear and caribou. In the winter he wore long and narrow snowshoes to track animals; in the summer he could use a canoe—a dugout in the southern Plateau, a dugout or a bark canoe in the northern Plateau.

In historical times all Plateau peoples used tailored skin garments of the type well-known from the Plains. In prehistoric days both sexes wore a bark breechclout or apron and a twined bark poncho falling a little below the waist. During the cold season men wrapped their legs with fur, and women had leggings of hemp. Rabbit-fur robes or other skin robes were worn in winter. Sahaptin women had twined basket hats, whereas men everywhere had headbands; caps of fur and feathered headdresses appeared with the Plains influences. Both sexes braided their hair. The Chinook practiced flattening of the infant's head as sign of free birth. Curiously, the Flathead never shared this custom.

The village community owned the land, in particular the fishing sites. Household tools, weapons, traps and snares, and similar items were the property of individuals, except for larger weirs that were communal property. Food resources were in most places distributed according to needs. A more restricted system prevailed on the northern Plateau, where gift-giving ceremonies occurred, reminiscent of the potlatches of the Northwest Coast Indians: after some days of games and contests, gifts were distributed to the guests, who in their turn reciprocally handed over presents to their hosts. Although possessions were valued in many parts of the Plateau, the Klamath paid greater attention to them than any other group and held wealthy persons in great esteem. This value orientation, most probably derived from the Northwest Coast, contrasted with the general Plateau pattern of equality and sharing of necessities.

Belief and aesthetic systems. Religion was, like the rest of the culture, closely intertwined with Plateau ecology. In many ways religious beliefs echoed North American religions in general: there was a "great spirit," among the Okanagon conceived of as a bearded white man, and there were spirits of the atmosphere (winds, thunder, etc.) and a host of zoomorphic lesser spirits serving as personal guardian spirits.

Religious rituals

The main rituals were the guardian-spirit quest, the firstling rites, and the winter dance. The guardian-spirit quest was compulsory for boys and recommended for girls and was usually performed in connection with the puberty ceremony. The spirits who granted their blessings in lonely places were very specialized. Some made their clients into hunters, others into warriors or medicine men (shamans). Both boys and girls, but preferably the former, could become medicine men. Medicine men were much feared and sometimes very wealthy. They cured diseases by extracting the bad spirit that had entered the patient's body, and on the Northern Plateau they brought back souls that had been stolen by the dead, describing their feats in a dramatic pantomime.

The firstling rites concentrated on the first salmon or berries (roots, fruits) that had been caught or gathered during the summer season. The first salmon ceremony celebrated the arrival of the salmon run with the ritual cutting and eating of the first fish and the ritual throwing of the bones back into the water, in this way ensuring a good return next year. Some Salish had a "salmon chief" who surveyed the rituals. The Okanagon, Thompson, and Lillooet had similar rites for the first berries, which were eaten ceremonially, whereas they lacked the salmon ritual.

The winter or spirit dance, finally, was a ceremonial meeting at which participants personified their respective guardian spirits. The dramatic performances and the songs were, among the Nez Percé, thought to bring warm weather, plentiful game, and successful hunts.

Plateau mythology and folklore revolved around the culture hero and transformer, mostly the Coyote but in some places the Bluejay or another mythical personage. He is a beloved character in the stories, creator and trickster at the same time. The Coyote cycle is well-known from adjacent areas as well.

There is nothing distinctive about Plateau art. On the contrary, most art historians divide it into a western branch, peripheral to the Northwest Coast, and an eastern branch, peripheral to the Plains. Plastic art is on the whole very rare, except in the vicinity of the Northwest Coast. Decorative art consisted of pictographic designs with a symbolic content, referring to supernatural beings and cosmic things. The same division between east and west characterizes musical styles.

MODERN DEVELOPMENTS

The preceding description of traditional Plateau culture demonstrates that the culture was neither static nor unitary but changed with time and place. The most dynamic development was introduced when the first impulses from white civilization penetrated the area: the coming of the horse in the beginning of the 18th century, the appearance of epidemics from 1780 onward, and the arrival of eschatological ideas, adapted in the Prophet Dance from perhaps the same time. The latter, which was the origin of the famous Ghost Dance, was a mixture of aboriginal and Christian elements: by dancing like the dead in the other world the Indians thought they could hasten the renewal of the world and the return of the dead. The Prophet Dance seems to have been a reaction against the increasing disruption of traditional culture through the new influences.

Early in the 19th century the fur trade brought Indian and white trappers from the east into the country, particularly to the northern Plateau. Roman Catholic Iroquois trappers propagated Christian ideas among the Flathead, who thereafter visited St. Louis to call on missionaries. The great invasion of white settlers and gold seekers in the 1850s and 1860s and the ensuing Indian wars (of which the Nez Percé War of 1877 is the most famous) resulted in the reduction of Indian territories, the creation of a series of small reservations, and the isolation and deprivation of the Indians in "white" surroundings.

In the 20th century, the blending of aboriginal and white cultures accelerated continuously and produced a variety of mixed cultures on the reservations, some more conservative, others more Europeanized. The Kutenai, for instance, have turned into ranchers or ranch hands during the warm season but use their fishing traps during the winter, a seasonal pattern that in a way conforms with the old culture. The Nez Percé, on the other hand, have at least partly become farmers. Their cultural assimilation has been furthered by political and religious factionalism. Summarily, it may be said that the Plateau Indians have retained their group feelings, part of their old economics, and in places much of their religion, whereas technology and material culture have long been characteristic of white poverty levels. (A.G.B.H.)

North American Great Basin Indians

The Great Basin Indians in aboriginal times occupied a 398,000-square-mile (1,031,000-square-kilometre) area of interior western North America. Aboriginal population density was sparse, ranging from 0.8 to 11.7 persons per 100 square miles. The area includes the physiographic Great Basin—the interior mountain and basin region of present-day southeastern California, Nevada, southeastern Oregon, and western Utah—and the Snake River Plain of Idaho, the mountains to the northeast, the Bridger Basin of southwestern Wyoming, the Colorado Plateau area of Utah and Colorado, and the mountains of central and southern Colorado. The entire region is arid to semi-arid, annual average precipitation being four inches in the lowlands to 20–25 inches in the mountains. The precipitation falls primarily in the form of winter snow. Ecologically, the area is characterized by a vertical succession of life zones, each with a dominant xerophytic (desert-type) flora and related fauna.

Peoples and languages

The languages spoken by the Indians are of two widely divergent language families. The Washo, whose territory centred on Lake Tahoe, speak a Hokan language related to languages spoken in parts of California, Arizona, and Baja California. The remainder of the Great Basin culture area was occupied by speakers of Numic languages. Numic, formerly called Plateau Shoshonean, is a division of the Uto-Aztecan language family, a group of related languages widely distributed in the western United States and Mexico. Linguists distinguish three Numic branches, Western, Central, and Southern, each branch having a pair of languages. Western Numic languages are Mono, spoken by the Eastern Mono and Owens Valley Paiute of California, and Northern Paiute, spoken by the several

From H. Driver et al., *Indiana University Publications in Anthropology and Linguistics* (1953)

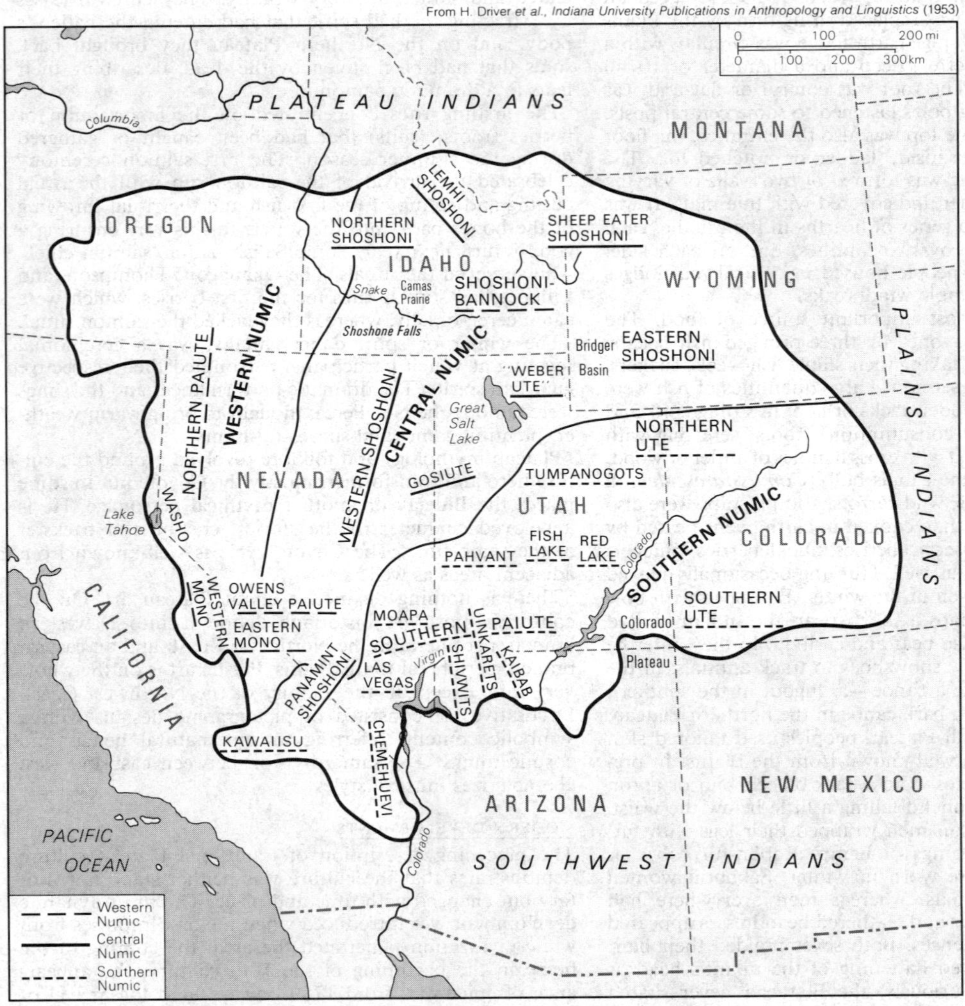

Distribution of Numic languages and major groups of Great Basin area Indians.

Northern Paiute groups of northeastern California, western Nevada (Paviotso), and southern Oregon and by the Bannock of southern Idaho. Central Numic languages are Panamint, spoken by the Koso, or Panamint Shoshoni, near Death Valley, California; and Shoshone, spoken by the Western Shoshoni of Nevada, the Gosiute of western Utah, the now extinct "Weber Ute" of northern Utah, the Northern Shoshoni of Idaho, the Lemhi and Sheep Eater (Tukuarika) Shoshoni of the northeastern Idaho mountains, the Eastern (or Wind River) Shoshoni of western Wyoming, and the Comanche of the southern Plains. The Comanche separated from the Eastern Shoshoni in late prehistoric times, moved southward through the Rocky Mountains, and became Plains Indians culturally.

Southern Numic languages are Kawaiisu, spoken by the Kawaiisu band of southern California, and Ute, spoken by the several Southern Paiute bands, including the Chemehuevi of southeastern California and the Las Vegas, Moapa, Kaibab, Shivwits, and Uinkarets bands of southern Nevada, southern Utah, and northern Arizona. Ute is also spoken by the several Ute bands, the Fish Lake, Red Lake, Pahvant, and Tumpanogots of central Utah, the various Northern Ute bands of eastern Utah and the several Southern Ute bands of southern Colorado. The distinction between Southern Paiute and Ute is cultural rather than linguistic: Ute speakers who had horses in the early historic period are regarded as Ute; those without horses were Southern Paiute. The Numic peoples called themselves "Numa" or "Numu," meaning "people" or "human beings." The Washo called themselves "Washoe," meaning "Washo people" as distinguished from people of other tribes.

Linguistic and archaeological evidence indicates that the Washo had long been separated from other California Hokan-speaking groups, possibly for several millennia. Similar evidence indicates that the Numic-speaking peoples spread across the Great Basin from southeastern California sometime after the year 1000.

TRADITIONAL CULTURE PATTERNS

Social and cultural patterns. Great Basin Indians of the early historic period (1800–50) were divided into horse-using and non-horse-using groups. Horse-using groups generally occupied the northern and eastern sections of the Great Basin culture area. The Southern Ute and Eastern Shoshoni were among the first Indians north of the Spanish settlements of New Mexico to obtain horses, perhaps as early as 1680. There is some evidence that these bands acted as middlemen in the transmission of horses and horse culture from New Mexico to the northern Plains in the 1700s. As the Northern Shoshoni of Idaho obtained horses in the 18th century, they were joined by Northern Paiute speakers from eastern Oregon and northern Nevada to form the Shoshoni-Bannock bands of historic times. By 1800, the Southern and Northern Ute, the Ute of central Utah, the Eastern Shoshoni, the Lemhi Shoshoni, and the Shoshoni-Bannock were well equipped with horses, lived in skin tepees, and were oriented toward the Great Plains, the pursuit of bison, and warfare with other tribes. To the south and west in the Great Basin proper and on the western Colorado Plateau, the people did not take up the use of horses until 1850–60. The Washo did not use horses prior to white settlement, and rarely used them thereafter.

Basic social organization

The basic Great Basin social and cultural patterns were those of the nonhorse bands. The people were closely adapted to their arid environment. Small family bands moved through an annual cycle, exploiting available food resources in the various ecological zones of a particular valley and adjacent mountains. The exigencies of the food quest structured Great Basin society and culture. Food supplies were seldom adequate to permit groups of any size to remain together for more than a few days. Consequently, social organization was fluid and atomistic. For most of the year the people lived in small local groups, coming together into larger aggregates only for certain brief periods—during rabbit drives or when fish were spawning, as the Washo did at Lake Tahoe in the spring, or during the piñon nut season in the autumn. But despite periodic gatherings, there was no sustained sense of political cohesion or "tribalness," as that term is understood for other American Indian groups.

The same fluidity of social organization was characteristic of the horse-using bands. Possession of horses permitted larger numbers of people to remain together for much of the year, but such aggregation did not lead to the development of formal tribal organizations. Among both horse- and non-horse-using groups, a particular leader was followed as long as he was successful in leading people to food, or in war. If he failed, people would leave to join other bands, or to form their own bands.

Kinship, marriage, and rites. The basic local social unit usually was one or more "kin cliques," consisting of a nuclear family (parents and their dependent children) or two brothers and their families, in addition to assorted other individuals related by blood or by marriage to someone in the core group.

Kin ties were reckoned bilaterally through both the mother's and the father's sides and were widely extended to distant relatives. Such extension permitted people to invoke kin ties and move from one group to another if circumstances warranted.

Marriage practices varied, with a tendency among some groups to marry true cross-cousins (mother's brother's or father's sister's child), or pseudo cross-cousins (mother's brother's or father's sister's stepchild). Both the sororate (compulsory marriage of a man to his dead wife's sister) and the levirate (compulsory marriage of a widow to her dead husband's brother), were practiced, as were their logical extensions, sororal polygyny and fraternal polyandry. Usually the latter was not formalized, consisting only of a man extending sex privileges with his wife to a brother for a time. Marriages were brittle and divorce frequent. Yet to survive, it was necessary to be married, as most men and women were throughout their adult lives. There was no set pattern of postmarital residence. A newly married couple might live with the bride's family for the first few years until children were born, but the availability of food supplies was the determining residence factor.

Children began to learn about and participate in the food quest as soon as they were old enough. There was little emphasis on puberty rites except among the Washo, who held a special dance and put a girl through various tests at the time of menarche.

Death rites were minimal. An individual was buried with his possessions or they were destroyed. The Washo abandoned or burned a dwelling in which a death occurred. Occasionally, old people who could not keep up with the group or who could no longer produce their share of the food supply were abandoned.

Technology and economy. The Numic people and the Washo built two types of shelters; semicircular brush windbreaks in the summers, and domed brush, bark-slab, grass, or reed-mat dwellings in the winter. The horse-using groups used Plains-style tepees but sometimes built grass or brush houses. Winter villages were sited along the edge of valley floors, near water, food caches, and firewood. Summer encampments were near food areas and were shifted as necessary. Horse-using groups camped along wooded stream bottoms near firewood and forage areas for their horses.

Tools and food-gathering

Tools were simple and portable: the bow and arrow, stone knife, rabbit stick, digging stick, several types of baskets and nets, and flat seed-grinding slab and handstone. Some Western Shoshoni and Southern Paiute groups made a coarse brown-ware pottery; some Northern Shoshoni made steatite jars and cups. In fishing areas, lines and hooks, harpoons, nets, and willow fish weirs were used. The Northern Paiute used duck decoys made of tule reeds covered with duck skins. Rodents were taken with snares and traps or pulled from burrows with long, hooked sticks. Rabbits were driven into nets and clubbed, or they were shot with bow and arrows. Antelope were driven into corrals and traps. Waterfowl were netted, trapped, or shot with bunt arrows (arrows with rounded heads, intended simply to stun). Deer, elk, and mountain sheep were taken by individual hunters with bow and arrows.

The people followed an annual round, exploiting plant and animal resources as they became available in the several ecological zones. Well over 70 percent of the food supply was vegetal. Over 200 species of plants were named and used, principally seed and root plants. Piñon pine groves were found in upland areas of Nevada and central Utah, and large quantities of piñon nuts were collected in the autumn and cached for winter use. Rabbit drives were also held in the autumn. The drives provided an occasion for larger numbers of people to come together for gambling, dancing, and courting. Winter was spent in small villages, living on cached foods and such game as might be taken. Early spring was a poor time; stored resources were often exhausted, and the people were forced to seek early greens and roots for food. Late spring and summer were devoted to collecting seeds, roots, insects, fishing where possible, and continued hunting.

Some Southern Paiute bands practiced limited horticulture along the Colorado and Virgin rivers. Some bands of Mono and Northern Paiute reportedly irrigated patches of wild seed plants to increase the yield.

The horse-using groups also followed an annual round but ranged over a much larger area. In some years, they ventured onto the Northern Plains for bison in the autumn, returning to the Bridger Basin, the Snake River area, or the Colorado Mountains for the winter. In the spring and summer, Shoshoni and Shoshoni-Bannock obtained roots from the Camas Prairie in Idaho and salmon from the Snake River, below Shoshone Falls. Deer, elk, and mountain sheep were taken when possible. Seed and root foods were collected as they became available.

Clothing consisted of sage bark aprons and breechclouts and rabbit-skin robes in the winter. The horse-using peoples wore Plains-style, tailored skin garments. Artwork was largely confined to basketry decoration. Among the horse-using bands, quill and beadwork decorated clothing and rawhide shields, and bags and containers were painted.

Trade was minimal among western Great Basin groups, although there is some evidence of the use of strings of shells as a medium of exchange in aboriginal times. Horse-using groups were more active, trading among themselves and with other tribes. The Eastern Shoshoni and some Ute bands participated in the fur trade between 1810 and 1840. Between about 1800 and 1850, mounted Ute and Navaho bands preyed on Southern Paiute, Western Shoshoni, and Gosiute bands for slaves, capturing and sometimes trading women and children to be sold in the Spanish settlements of New Mexico and southern California.

Religious concepts. Religious concepts derived from a mythical cosmogony, beliefs in "power" beings, and a belief in a dualistic soul. Mythology provided a cosmogony and cosmography of the world. Mythical animals, notably wolf, coyote, rabbit, bear, and mountain lion, were believed to be the progenitors of the modern animals. They lived prior to Indian life but were anthropomorphic, speaking and acting as people do in the present world. They created the world and were responsible for present-day topography, ecology, food resources, seasons of the year, and the distribution of Indian tribes. They set the nature of social relations—that is, defined how various classes of kinsmen should behave toward each other—and set the customs surrounding birth, marriage, puberty and death. Their actions in the mythic realm set moral and ethical precepts and determined the physical and behavioral characteristics of the modern animals. Most of the motifs and tale plots of Great Basin mythology are found widely throughout North America.

Power beings were animals, birds, or natural phenomena, each attributed with a specific natural power according to an observed characteristic. Some such beings were thought to be benevolent, or at least neutral, toward men. Others, such as Water Babies—small, long-haired creatures who lured men to their deaths in springs or lakes and who ate children—were malevolent and feared. There were conceptions of various other vague beings, such as the Southern Paiute *unupits,* mischievous spirits who caused illness.

Shamanism

Shamans, or curers, were prominent in all Great Basin groups. Both men and women might become shamans. Shamans received their powers to cure disease, foretell the future, and, sometimes, to practice sorcery from a power being who came unsought to a prospective shaman. It was considered dangerous to resist being given a shaman's power, for those who did sometimes died. The being became a tutelary spirit, instructing an individual in curing and sources of power. Some shamans had several tutelary spirits, each providing instruction for specific types of treatment. Among Northern Paiute and Washo and probably elsewhere, a man who had received power apprenticed himself to an older, practicing shaman and from him learned rituals, cures, and feats of legerdemain associated with curing performances. Curing ceremonies were performed with family members and others present and might last several days. The widespread American Indian practice of sucking an object said to cause the disease from the patient's body was often employed. Shamans who lost too many patients were sometimes killed.

In the western Basin, some men had powers to charm antelope and led communal antelope drives. Beliefs that some men were arrow-proof (and after the introduction of guns, bulletproof) are reported for the Northern Paiute and Gosiute but were probably general throughout the area.

Among the Eastern Shoshoni, young men sought power beings through a visionary experience. The active seeking of power beings through visions is a practice the Eastern Shoshoni probably learned from their Plains neighbours, although the characteristics of the beings sought were those common to Great Basin beliefs.

There was a concept of soul-dualism among most, if not all, Numic groups. One soul, or soul aspect, represented vitality or life; the other was the individual as he was in a dream or vision state. During dreams or visions, the latter soul left the body and moved in the spirit realm. At death, both souls left the body.

MODERN DEVELOPMENTS

Contact with white civilization drastically altered Great Basin societies and cultures. The Southern Ute were in sustained contact with the Spanish in New Mexico as early as the 1600s, but other Great Basin groups had no direct or continued contact with whites until after 1800. The fur trade, between 1810 and 1840, brought new tools and implements to the eastern bands. Settlement began in the 1840s, as did the surge of emigrants through the area on their way to Oregon and California. Mining, ranching, and farming activities destroyed or closed off traditional Indian food-gathering areas. Piñon groves were cut for firewood, fence posts, and mining timbers. The Indians attempted to resist white encroachment. Mounted bands of Ute, Shoshoni, Shoshoni-Bannock, and Northern Paiute preyed on ranches and wagon trains and tried to drive the intruders away. The struggle culminated in several local "wars" and "massacres" in the 1850s and 1860s. After 1870, Indians were forced onto reservations or into small groups on the edges of white settlements, thus reducing their land base to a small fraction of its former size. This forced the abandonment of aboriginal subsistence patterns in favour of limited agriculture or stock raising, where possible, and wage work, especially as farm and ranch hands.

In 1870 and again in 1890, so-called Ghost Dance movements started among the Northern Paiute of western Nevada. The dances were millenarian in character. Prophets foretold that if the Indians danced and prayed, the whites would go away and the "old days" would be restored. The 1870 dance, led by a man named Wodziwob, centred in Nevada and California. The 1890 dance, led by Wovoka, or Jack Wilson, of Smith Valley, Nevada, spread to many Indian tribes in the western United States.

A Peyote Cult was introduced to the Ute and Eastern Shoshoni in the early 1900s by Oklahoma Indians. It later spread to other Great Basin peoples. Most peyote groups became members of the Native American Church, a nationally recognized organization. Great Basin peyote rituals are a mixture of aboriginal and Christian elements. Ceremonies are led by "road chiefs"; that is, those who lead believers down the Peyote Road or Way. A ceremony, which lasts all night, includes singing, praying, and eating peyote buttons or drinking a concoction made therefrom, producing a mild hallucinogenic experience. The tenets of the Native American Church stress moral and ethical precepts and behaviour.

In postreservation times, the Eastern Shoshoni and Ute adopted the sun dance from the Plains Indians. The four-day dance is performed yearly to achieve health and valour for the participants, and partly as a tourist attraction.

The Indian Reorganization Act of 1934 led to the establishment of local elected "tribal councils" for the various reservations and colonies. Councils have sought to develop various economic activities including ranching, light industry, and tourism.

Indian children were sent to federal day schools and boarding schools beginning in the 1880s. These federal schools were phased out and Indian children began to attend local schools and universities.

Great Basin Indian peoples have retained some of their traditional culture in crafts, dances, and visiting patterns. Older people speak the native languages, but many of the younger people have neither learned nor used them. Many people remain on the reservations, but others have moved to towns and cities.

(D.D.F./C.S.F.)

Southwest American Indians

More than one-third of the rapidly growing population of American Indians live in the southwestern United States, mainly in or bordering Arizona and New Mexico. In this predominantly arid and climatically unstable region, located between the Rocky Mountains and the Mexican Sierra Madre, the Continental Divide separates the watersheds of two great river systems: the Colorado–Gila–San Juan, in the west, and the Rio Grande–Pecos, in the east.

Environment of the area

From the viewpoint of human habitation, the region's main geographic features are the two river systems, cyclical droughts, and arid lands, some low and hot, others high and cold. The hot deserts have sparse and irregularly occurring rainfall. Their long growing season supports a great variety of plant and animal communities adapted to desert conditions—creosote, sage, tarbush, and numerous cactus species, as well as such small, nocturnal, burrowing animals as the kangaroo rat. Along the river flood plains grow cottonwood, willow, mesquite, and sycamore. Basin and range landscape, from about 1,000 to 4,000 feet (300 to 1,200 metres) in elevation, predominates.

Despite its low moisture content, coarse texture, and occasional salty patches, the soil of most of the Southwest is relatively fertile.

The cold semideserts include the Colorado and other plateaus of northern Arizona. The frost-free growing season is relatively short. Much of this plateau area is covered with scrub or with piñon–juniper woodland, where rattlesnakes, rabbits, coyote, bobcat, and mule deer are found. Antelope, American elk, and mountain sheep were once plentiful. Bordering the plateau country are sheer cliffs, deep canyons, and forested mountains. Ponderosa pine, Douglas fir, blue spruce, and alpine meadows shelter weasel, deer mouse, porcupine, squirrel, and chipmunk, as well as the larger animals of the region.

In the past century most of the wild mammals have disappeared from the region. Domesticated species brought to America from Europe by the Spaniards during the 16th and 17th centuries, such as cattle, sheep, goats, horses, and burros, have multiplied and destroyed delicate ecological balances, critically accelerating natural erosion processes, especially on the Colorado Plateau and in the basin and range country.

The peoples

The Indian tribes that have gained a foothold in the Southwest are highly diversified culturally, linguistically, and psychologically. From a comparative viewpoint, however, they fall roughly into four groupings, each of which is characterized by living patterns designed to cope with the practical problems of communities attempting to survive and prosper in the diverse geographical zones of the region.

The ancient Yuman tribes inhabit the floodplains on both sides of the Lower Colorado River (Yuma, Mojave [Mohave]) and the Middle Colorado highlands (Havasupai, Hualapai [Walapai]), as well as the lower Gila (Cocopa, Maricopa) and the Rio Verde (Yavapai). The Pima and Papago, constituting the second group, live along the middle Gila River and in the basin and range country west of the Santa Cruz River, as well as in Sonora across the Mexican border.

The Colorado Plateau and the Middle Rio Grande, with its tributaries, have long been the home of the third group, the Pueblo (village-dwelling) Indians, who, although highly diverse linguistically, share many basic cultural traits. These form three subgroups: the western Pueblos (Hopi, Hano, Zuni, Acoma, and Laguna); the central Pueblos (Jemez, Santa Ana, Zia, Cochiti, Santo Domingo, and San Felipe); and the eastern Pueblos (San Juan, Santa Clara, San Ildefonso, Nambe, Tesuque, Taos, Picuris, Isleta, and Sandia).

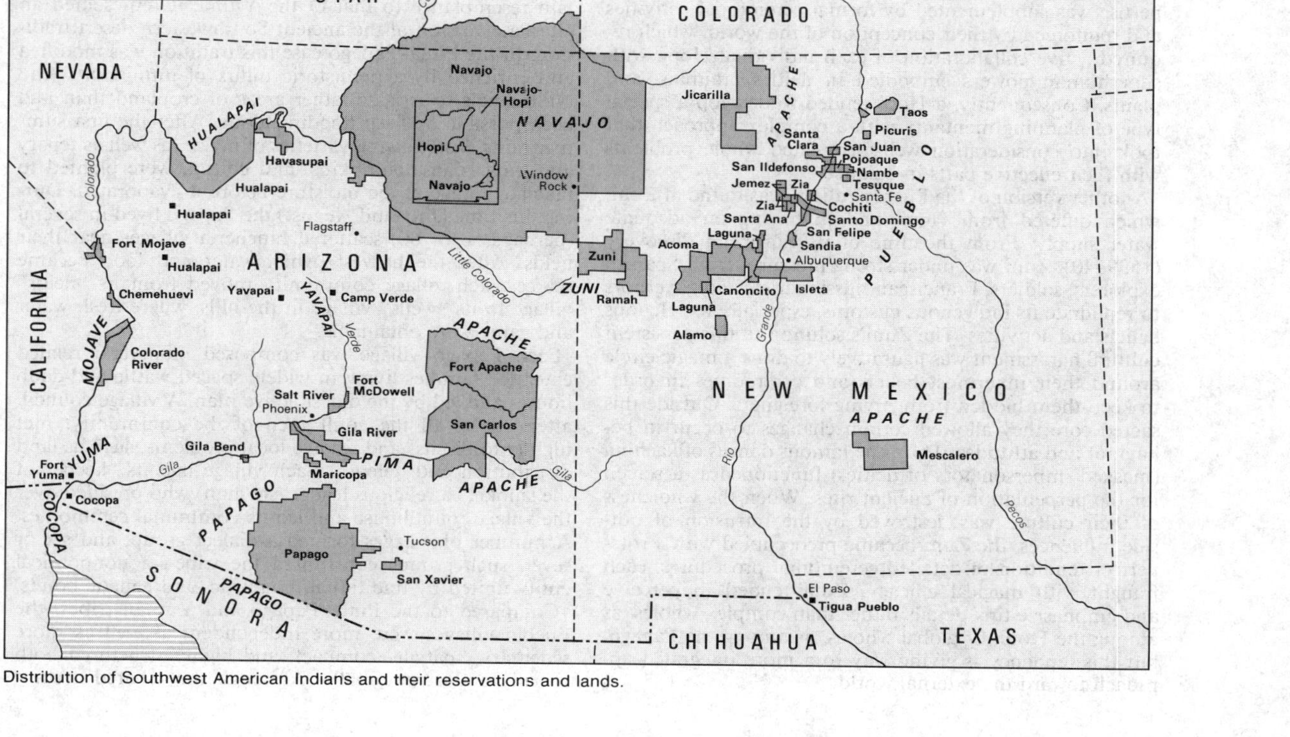

Distribution of Southwest American Indians and their reservations and lands.

Finally, also on the Colorado Plateau, completely surrounding the Hopi villages and Hano and separating them from the other Pueblos, dwell the fast-growing Navajo, a branch of the Athabascan-speaking Apache who are relative late comers to the Southwest. Their nearest linguistic relatives are found in parts of California, Canada, and Alaska. The Apache, inhabiting the mountains of the plateau rim, form a wedge between ancient Pueblo inhabitants of the region and the Pima–Papago. The major Apache tribes are the Western Apache, the Chiricahua, the Mescalero, the Jicarilla, the Lipan, and the Kiowa Apache.

TRADITIONAL CULTURE PATTERNS

Differences among the four native groupings

General characteristics: ethos. Even though the four native groupings share some patterns of behaviour, they also evidence considerable variety in the ways in which they adapt to life and perceive life. Moreover, all of the distinctively Indian points of view differ radically from Euro-American patterns of thought. For example, River Yuman tribes, who combined collecting edible fruits and seeds with farming rich bottomland, were relatively free of the food anxiety common to most desert dwellers. Yuma tended to focus attention on the acquisition of supernatural power by means of singing songs acquired through dreaming and illustrative of myth sequences. The individual's success in life, including leadership in warfare and curing rites, was considered to be entirely dependent on this unusual form of solitary dreaming.

On the other hand, the desert-dwelling Papago tempered their reliance on magical power achieved through singing, vision seeking, and intoxication, with concentration on such practical living problems as the defense of village communities dependent on flood farming, hunting, and collecting wild foods. Their wary approach toward any sort of personal commitment and their preference for perceiving the world in terms of flexible wholes and a continuous range of inductions, rather than the two-sided options characteristic of Euro-Americans, directly reflected a long-range, successful adjustment to an exceptionally inhospitable environment.

The Hopi Indians expressed an extreme variation of Pueblo culture developed in response to their unusually dry niche of the high, semiarid Colorado Plateau. The Hopi tribe's solution to the well-nigh insoluble living problem of village farmers without a permanent water supply was embodied in a flexibly balanced social system that stressed not only group self-defense, sobriety, and peaceful relations but also dry and arroyo flood-farming techniques developed to a high degree of skill. Their technological expertise was supplemented by formal ceremonial activities and reinforced by their conception of the world, which required active collaboration of each individual Hopi, with superhuman powers embodied in deities, animals, and plants. Consequently, a Hopi tended to develop a special type of planning mentality with a complex approach that took into consideration well-formulated whole problems with their effective parts in balance.

Another version of the Pueblo culture was found at Zuni, which differed from Hopi land in having an adequate water supply. From the time of its European discovery (1539–40), Zuni was under strong pressures from Spanish explorers, soldiers, Franciscan missionaries, and governors to repudiate its indigenous customs, especially its religious beliefs and activities. The Zuni's solution to this persistent cultural harassment was figuratively to draw a magic circle around their innermost beliefs and ceremonies in order to keep them hidden from prying foreigners. Outside this sacred core they allowed certain changes to occur in behaviour and attitudes. Thus, the famous dances of kachina (masked impersonators of deities) functioned as a screen for the perpetuation of ancient rites. When the wholeness of their culture was destroyed by the intrusion of outside influences, the Zuni became preoccupied with a rote-perfect rendition of detailed ceremonial procedures, each fraught with magical efficacy. Zuni tended to perceive and emphasize tiny details rather than complex wholes, as among the Hopi, or global wholes, as among the Papago, but this tendency is giving way to a more integrated approach toward the external world.

In contrast to the Pueblos, the Navajo, who entered the southwestern region more recently than other Indian tribes and settled there by expropriating crops, herds, and rangelands, expressed an aggressive, mobile way of life. Their culture pattern, bolstered by an animistic conception of the world, fostered in the individual a matter-of-fact mental approach that singled out for attention large, discrete details with little interest in relationships between them. Such an approach relied both on adjusting to new situations by adapting segments from other cultures and on avoiding long-range planning. The Navajo were well able to make and carry out complex planning projects, however, if they believed such activities would enhance their welfare.

Social structures and economic systems. The most favourable habitation sites of the region, from the indigenous viewpoint, were probably the basins of permanent rivers, especially the floodplains of the Lower Colorado. Toward the end of the 18th century, the most desirable patches of bottomland were densely settled by village-dwelling Yuma Indians. Each village comprised a relatively stable and autonomous band composed of a number of large families living in brush shelters or rectangular, sand-covered houses. The male head of each family participated in an informal village council that settled disputes (often over land ownership) and made decisions on community problems. The wisest, ablest, and most powerful senior member of the band was its acknowledged leader. A number of bands constituted the loosely organized but strongly identified tribe, which fostered friendly relations and trade with neighbouring tribes (Mojave, Yavapai, Papago) and maintained a state of hostility or open warfare with others (Cocopa, Maricopa).

Yuma social and economic patterns

Unlike most other southwestern tribes, the Yuma did not suffer from a water problem, despite a minimum of rainfall and a hot desert climate. Although they collected edible fruits and seeds, fished, and hunted small game, the river was their lifeline. In small, irregular fields that were flooded and silted in spring when the Colorado overflowed its banks, they cultivated, with simple hand tools, several varieties of rapidly maturing maize, as well as beans, pumpkins, melons, and grasses (later, wheat and cowpeas acquired from the Spaniards). Such fields were privately owned and were inherited in the male line. Abundant harvests, supplemented by gathering and storage of food in large baskets, coupled with a simple inventory of material possessions, allowed the Yuma to concentrate on a rich world of dream and fantasy.

Pima–Papago social and economic patterns

Although the culture of the Pima–Papago showed a certain resemblance to that of the Yuma, it represented an alternate version of the ancient Southwestern desert tradition. In the Pima–Papago case this tradition was modified and enriched by a prehistoric influx of immigrants who built canals to irrigate larger areas of cropland than had been possible by flash flooding alone. After the first summer rains, fast-growing varieties of maize, as well as tepary and lima beans, pumpkins, and cotton, were planted to take advantage of the moisture before it evaporated. During this time (July and August) the Papago lived in several (perhaps 50 or 60) scattered rancheria villages near their fields. After the harvest, when water and food became scarce, each village community moved from its "fields" village to its "wells" village in the hills, where fresh water and game were obtainable.

Each Papago village was composed of several related extended families living in widely spaced wattle-and-daub houses and led by the oldest active man. A village council, attended by all the adult men of the community, met nightly to discuss and resolve local problems, such as land distribution and defense. Each village had its "keeper of the smoke," a religious leader (shaman) who presided over the village roundhouse and led its communal ceremonies. A number of villages formed a dialect group, and six or seven such groups constituted the tribe—a nonpolitical entity united by traditional, linguistic, and genetic bonds.

Compared to the Pima–Papago and Yuman tribes, the Pueblo villages were more independent as well as more sedentary, spatially compact, and highly structured both socially and ceremonially. Although they shared a com-

Western Pueblo social and economic patterns

mon theocratic life-style based on complex interweaving ties between kinship and religious groups and also a similar pattern of perceiving the world of nature, they differed considerably both in language and in the way the members of each village organized themselves to cope with the vicissitudes of their particular environment. Life for the western group of Pueblo farmers on the high, semiarid Colorado Plateau was particularly hazardous and nowhere more so than on the mesas of the Hopi lands. Here the well-being, even the survival, of whole communities long depended on what seemed to the casual observer to be minute, even insignificant variations in climate and topography—especially in the amount and seasonal rhythm of precipitation, the configuration of floodplains and erosion of ephemeral stream beds, the presence and flow of freshwater springs, even the piling of sand into fixed dunes that conserved moisture.

In all of the western Pueblos the key social grouping was the maternal family line, or lineage. This was a kinship group centred in a core of blood-related women but conceived as timeless, extending backwards into the remote past and forward through generations yet unborn. Several related lineages formed a corporate clan with descent through the female line.

Among the Hopi, sets of linked clans, considered to be ceremonial "partners," formed what have been called phratries. Under this system a person was not allowed to marry into the lineage of his mother, his father, his mother's father, or into his own phratry or set of clans. The Hopi clan owned croplands and ritual paraphernalia, and its oldest active woman functioned as its "real" head, while her brother assumed the responsibilities of ceremonial leader. Although the ceremonial leader supervised the annual reenactment of various ceremonies, the performance of a major ceremony was the responsibility not of a single clan but rather of a voluntary secret society that drew its predominantly male initiates from the entire pueblo. In each pueblo were several such societies. Their elaborate ritual activities were centred in a number of kivas (underground ceremonial chambers).

The kinship system was extended symbolically beyond the human community into the world of nature, linking clans with certain kinds of animals and plants as well as with other classes of natural and supernatural phenomena into a supersociety that included all aspects of the Pueblo world considered important to its well-being.

The basic local unit in the social organization of the western Pueblos was the extended family. This was a female-centred group occupying a common household of two or more adjoining rooms in a three-storied terraced communal structure. It was built of stone, faced the sun, and partially surrounded a central dance plaza. A household normally consisted of a core of women related through the female line, together with their husbands and unmarried sons (and unattached male relatives of the women), as well as their daughters, sons-in-law, and maternal grandchildren. Among the Hopi the women of the household cared for the children, cultivated spring-irrigated gardens, produced baskets and pottery, and had charge of the cooking and storage of food as well as of certain clan fetishes. On the other hand, the men of the household raised field and dune crops of corn, squash, beans, and cotton (later apricots and peaches) and wove clothing. They were also the sheep herders. They "belonged ceremonially" to their mothers' households, however, to which they returned frequently to fulfill religious responsibilities.

The Hopi fired their painted clay pots and warmed their ceremonial chambers and homes with soft coal, which they mined by hand methods from open veins near their villages. Coal mining (the Hopi were the only American Indians to have discovered it) helped to create favourable wintertime conditions for building a surplus of skillfully fabricated craft goods—baskets, pottery, cloth woven of cotton (later of wool), and ceremonial paraphernalia. Such goods formed the basis of a trade network that supplied food and other necessities to the mesas.

Except for Acoma and Laguna, the Keresan-speaking central Pueblos are located on the banks of the Rio Grande and its tributaries, with a permanent and dependable water supply that is used for household purposes and irrigation. In contrast to the pueblos in the west, the Keresans and their eastern-Pueblo neighbours inhabited adobe, rather than stone, houses and built circular, rather than rectangular, kivas. These villages also cooperated in inter-pueblo ceremonies, but each formed an economic unit engaged in agriculture, gathering, and hunting.

Central and eastern Pueblo social and economic patterns

Except for the Tewa, knowledge of the social structure of the central and eastern Pueblos is incomplete and often conflicting, partly because, in reaction to the Spanish system of administration, they tended to disguise their native rites and beliefs (while still holding on to them strongly). It is known, however, that the Tewa-speaking eastern Pueblos exhibited a unique type of dual organization of social and ceremonial life—one division associated with summer and the other with winter and each, on the basis of solar observations, regulating various seasonal activities and interpersonal village rivalries. In general, they divided communal responsibilities.

The most aggressive Southwestern tribes were its most recent (about the 11th century) Indian settlers—the Athabascan-speaking Apache and Navajo. (The Navajo are generally believed to be descendants of a band of hunters and gatherers closely related to the Apache.) By the beginning of the 17th century the Navajo on the Colorado Plateau achieved a relatively settled way of life. From the neighbouring Pueblos, they had learned to grow corn, to weave, and to care for livestock. Toward the end of the 17th century, however, when the Spaniards and Pueblo Indians attempted to reestablish themselves in the area, the Navajo developed their propensity to spread into and prey upon settled communities to acquire food, sheep, horses, and cattle. The movement of Navajo groups westward into and around Hopi lands seriously threatened the precarious economic situation of that tribe.

Navajo and Apache social and economic patterns

The basic socioeconomic unit of the Navajo was the extended family, which consisted of one or more related women, their husbands and unmarried sons, their daughters, sons-in-law, and grandchildren. Certain other unattached relatives might also reside with the group. Each "nuclear" family of husband, wife, and children—or each wife and her children, if a man had more than one wife—occupied a separate hogan (circular, earth-covered lodge), but the entire extended family cooperated in activities such as farming, sheepherding, and family ceremonies. Navajo extended families were grouped into about 60 clans, with descent reckoned through the female line; and marriage within one's clan was considered incestuous. Neighbouring extended families cooperated in solving land-use problems, such as range management, farmland development, and water use, under the direction of a noncoercive type of headman chosen for his leadership qualities. Such a community (which might occupy 12,000–80,000 acres [5,000–30,000 hectares]) was called an outfit. All the outfits together constituted the Navajo tribe, which was not a political unit but was unified by traditional, linguistic, and cultural bonds.

The Apache were probably the least understood of Southwestern Indians. Their culture ranged from that of the Western Apache group, who resembled Pueblos and Navajo in the practice of agriculture, in clan organization, and in the elaboration of mythology, to that of the Chiricahua Apache, who retained their mobile, war-geared organization and their hunting economy until the late 19th century. The Chiricahua consisted of three bands, which were associated respectively with the northern, central, and southern parts of their vast semiarid tribal territory ranging from the Rio Grande to southwestern Arizona and from northern Mexico to Zuni and Acoma. Within each band's hunting grounds, sites favourable for defense, hunting, and food collecting were used as temporary encampments and rallying points for smaller local groups the members of which cooperated in such undertakings as war and important ceremonies. Each local group consisted of a number of widely scattered extended families similar to the families of the Navajo, except that descent was reckoned through both parents. The Chiricahua family, however, was more mobile than that of the Navajo.

As among the Navajo, the family in all the Apache groups

was centred in related women who cared for the children; gathered and processed edible seeds and other wild plants, such as yucca fruit and mescal; collected firewood and water; produced buckskin clothing, baskets, and pottery; and constructed the dome-shaped, branch-covered shelters that housed the group. The men of the family, on the other hand, hunted, fought, raided, and made weapons, such as arrows, slings, and shields. The most persuasive, strong, and successful family heads became Apache leaders whose authority depended primarily on their personal charisma and success in warfare.

Socialization and education. In all the Southwestern tribes, child training was a serious adult responsibility. The Indians were conscious of a maturation process, which was regarded in several tribes as a "path" along which the individual made his "journey through life."

Without exception in these tribes, a child was treated with warmth and permissiveness during the period of infancy (which might last from one to three or four years). He was given the breast whenever he cried. Weaning was gradual, and training in cleanliness was delayed until a child could walk or even longer. Care was taken not to agitate him unduly, and he was protected from harm (often by means of magical prophylactics) and accepted as an integral part of the family. In some tribes the infant spent much of his time laced onto a cradle board which, among the Navajo at least, was hung up in the hogan so that his head was level with the other members of a seated family circle. The effect of this treatment was apparently to augment the child's physical safety and to enhance his feeling of security. Among the Hopi the use of the cradle was viewed as an early conditioning to the restrictions of the difficult Hopi way.

After the infancy period, tribal socialization patterns began to diverge. From the beginning of childhood there was a strict sexual division of labour. Little boys were given chores appropriate to developing strength, such as collecting firewood or tending animals, while little girls early began to learn food processing and child care. But the child soon learned that every individual in the group was expected to pull his own weight, at every age grade, according to his sex, strength, and capacities.

Adolescence

When they were between five and seven years old, the boys in all the tribes began to associate almost exclusively with the men of their households, who from then on directed their education into masculine tasks and lore, while the girls remained with their mothers and aunts, taking on increasing responsibilities for the exacting tasks of the household. Among the warrior tribes the physical strength, stoicism, and skill needed for the warpath were stressed, and warrior training intensified as the youth grew to young manhood. Even among the peace-oriented Pueblos, however, boys learned agility, endurance, and speed in running. Racing was important ceremonially because it was considered to possess magical efficacy in helping plants, animals, and human beings to grow.

Among the Papago–Pima a child early learned the fundamental principles of family life: the precedence of males over females; seniority and respect for age, regardless of sex; solidarity among all family members under the leadership of the oldest active male; and respect for the role, function, and opinion of every member of the group. Within these limitations the Papago child, male or female, was allowed more freedom of action than was customary elsewhere among the Southwestern tribes.

By contrast, the Pueblo child, after infancy, was probably the most restricted, the degree of harshness in his training apparently depending on the severity of the living problem that the particular Pueblo community had to resolve. The transition from each phase of the Pueblo life cycle to the succeeding one was marked with a major ceremony. Any child who failed to move along the path of life at the culturally designated pace was pulled or pushed in formalized ways to meet the standard. For example, during the secret kachina ceremony, which marked the initiation of all Hopi children into the tribe at about seven years of age and their introduction to the Hopi gods (impersonated as masked dancers), it is reported that all the novices were ceremonially whipped to exorcise evil influences. "Bad" boys, however, were whipped more severely than the others.

Whereas the Pueblos stressed life-crisis ceremonies that offered symbolic solutions to the major problems faced by the entire community of humans, animals, and plants, the warrior groups in this region emphasized rites by which an individual might ward off sickness and acquire magical power for personal success in war and the hunt. In still another manner, the Papago youth was expected to go alone into the desert in quest of a power-giving vision to help him through life.

Belief and aesthetic systems. The life-crisis rites reflected the religious belief systems of the several tribal groups. The spectacular, communally centred Pueblo ceremonies for rain and growth reflected a conception of the universe in which every person, animal, plant, and supernatural being considered significant to the Pueblo lifestyle had its place and role. Without the active participation of every individual in the group, it was believed that the life-giving sun would not return from his "winter house" after the solstice; the rain would not fall nor could the crops grow. In fact, without human help in an annual cycle of ceremonies, the cosmic order would be in danger of breaking down.

Importance of rites and ceremonies

To the Yuma, on the other hand, the universe was pervaded by a single animating principle that was the source of all supernatural power. There was only one medium, namely dreaming, for the personal acquisition of power that was considered necessary for success in life. Sequences of traditional myths acquired through dreaming were converted into songs and acted out in ceremonies. So great was Yuman interest in this kind of dreaming and the power that it could bring to an individual religious or war leader that all other activities—farming, food collecting, and even hunting—were of secondary concern.

The religion of the Papago seems to reflect their position between the Yuman tribes and the Pueblos. Not only did they "sing for power" and go on individual vision quests, but they also held regular communal ceremonies to "bring down the clouds" and keep the world in order.

By contrast, the Apache conceived of the universe as composed of a great many different kinds of power entities, such as animals, plants, witches, superhuman beings, rocks, and mountains. Each power source could exert force in the world for good or ill, and each had to be separately propitiated. Each was personalized, talked to, sung to, scolded, or praised. Apache ceremonies were concerned mainly with the magical coercion of these power entities for the curing of disease and the acquisition of personal success in hunting and warfare.

Navajo ceremonial was apparently based on an elaboration of a similarly animistic view of the universe, with the power sources both diffused and specified. Power was localized in a great many autonomous personal beings who were dangerous and unpredictable. These were of two classes: Earth Surface People (human beings, ghosts, and witches) and Holy People (supernaturals who could aid or harm Earth Surface People by sending sickness).

With the acquisition of techniques of farming, herding, weaving, and silversmithing, and the abandonment of hunting and warfare, the Navajo turned their attention to elaborate and colourful ceremonies (called "sings") that aimed, by means of compulsive magic, to cure sickness and bring an individual into harmony with his family group, nature, and the supernatural.

MODERN DEVELOPMENTS

Heritage of integrating and disintegrating factors. Each local community tried to maintain a delicate balance between population and natural resources. If the population outgrew the capacities of its base within the limitations of the group's technology, a segment or faction might split off and form a colony in a favourable habitat resembling that of its parent group. Under normal conditions the daughter colony was so constituted to reproduce as far as possible the parent culture even in its most esoteric aspects. If prolonged drought (as in 1272–99) dried up springs needed by Hopi villages for drinking water, an entire community might migrate.

Traditional adaptations to change

By contrast, human pressures from without, such as raids by marauding bands or aggressive missionary activity, caused some pueblos to consolidate or to move to less vulnerable mesa sites. In 1680, for instance, all the Pueblos united to kill or drive out the Spaniards (who, however, eventually reestablished Roman Catholic missions in all the pueblos except those of the Hopi). Papago settlements consolidated into large compact villages for defense against the Apache, but they spread out again after the raids ceased.

Religious reactions

Constant or intermittent efforts by missionaries, educators, and administrators to undermine native ceremonies and to change indigenous beliefs were resisted in various ways. The mobile Navajo–Apache tribes rejected all efforts of the Spaniards to reduce or convert them. The more accessible sedentary Pueblos employed various devices, under cover of practicing the outer forms of Catholicism, to hide their sacred religious paraphernalia and to perpetuate their essential beliefs and ceremonies. The Papago produced their own Christian sect, a blend of native and mission practices known as Sonoran Catholicism.

Unless totally destroyed, a pueblo of the western type, which was relatively decentralized, did not surrender structurally to foreign control. In fact, pueblo organization was characterized by a permanence and continuity that would not accommodate externally imposed social change. Alterations in sociopolitical or ceremonial patterns due to foreign intervention occurred only at superficial levels, while basic religious beliefs and practices tended to persist (even to the present day).

By contrast, pueblos of the eastern type, with more centralized control, proved more vulnerable to attack at both the sociopolitical and the ceremonial levels. If not utterly destroyed, most of them incorporated aspects of the foreign system into their own structures so that the result was a blend of the two.

The Navajo and the Western Apache adapted their mobile hunting cultures by borrowing from the Pueblos whole complexes of traits, such as agriculture, herding, weaving, and sand painting, and later from their industrialized neighbours, such traits as lumbering, mining, and commercial enterprises.

In virtually all the Southwestern tribes, however, the native languages are still spoken in the family groups, which continue to organize themselves according to traditional principles and values. Native ceremonies are still practiced, often secretly, in all the tribal groups, even those considered to be at least nominally Christian.

Effects of modernization

Current cultural conditions. Although the seeds of "modernization" probably were sown earlier, the process did not get under way until the end of the 19th century and the beginning of the 20th. The isolation of many of the tribes, the vastness, aridity, and poor natural endowment of many of their lands, and, of course, the ferocity of the Athabascans all played a part in delaying modernization of the Southwestern tribes. Indeed, military defeat, the loss of traditional lands, and missionary efforts to change their religious beliefs and practices left a heritage of rejection and bitterness among these Indians.

Under the administration of the United States, many changes have been made on the reservations in the interests of Indian welfare. Tribal government has been developed and empowered with legal authority. Schools and hospitals have been constructed. Irrigation systems have been built and crops increased in quantity and quality. Roads and highways have been improved and communications by telephone and radio, bus and airplane inaugurated.

Indian incomes, however, remain generally low compared to those of the rest of the American population, especially among the Papago, Hopi, Fort Apache, and some of the highland Yuman tribes. Unemployment is high among Indians both on and off the reservations.

Biculturalism

In the opinion of some authorities, however, the Indian problem in this region is not poverty or lack of industriousness or even apathy. The primary problem rather is biculturalism. In the late 20th century the tribal reservations served as the physical and spiritual homes of the several Indian groups, although some 50 percent of the members resided outside their boundaries. All except a few who have identified with the surrounding American culture periodically returned to their family households on the reservations for ceremonies and for deep religious and social nourishment.

(L.Th./Ed.)

North American Plains Indians

The Indians of the North American Plains are popularly regarded as the typical American Indians. They were essentially big-game hunters, the buffalo being a primary source of food and equally important as a source of materials for clothing, shelter, and tools. Until supplanted by the white man from the 16th century onward, they occupied the area between the Mississippi River and the Rocky Mountains, which includes portions of both the United States and Canada. It is a vast grassland stretching from northern Alberta and Saskatchewan in Canada to the Rio Grande border of Texas.

The climate is in general a continental one, with a wide seasonal range. Temperatures in winter may go below 0° F (−18° C) and in summer as high as 110° F (43° C). The plant cover varies with the amount of moisture, the tall grass of the prairies in the east giving way at about the 100th meridian to the shorter grass of the High Plains in the west. The area is drained principally by the Missouri–Mississippi river system.

Peoples and languages

The peoples of the Plains are designated by the languages they speak. It is permissible to call them "tribes" or "nations," bearing in mind, however, that in some cases, for example the Dakota (popularly known as Sioux), the designation covers several completely autonomous political divisions. The northern and southern divisions of the Cheyenne retained their unity as a tribe, while the Pawnee on the other hand comprised at least four independent groups. Many of the tribes of the Plains, such as the Cheyenne, migrated into them from the prairies and woodlands of the east. In addition, some of the tribes to the west of the area—the Ute and Jicarilla Apache, for instance—were influenced to a degree by the Plains culture and can be regarded as marginal to the area.

Six distinct language families or stocks were represented in the Plains area, although none of them was confined to it. The speakers of the several languages within a stock might or might not be geographically contiguous. Some of the languages, moreover, were more closely related to each other than to others within the same stock. Thus languages belonging to the Algonkian stock included the Blackfoot (Piegan–Blood–Northern Blackfoot), Arapaho–Atsina (Gros Ventre), Plains Cree, and Plains Ojibwa, all in the Northern Plains, while Cheyenne, also an Algonkian language, was in the central part of the area. The Siouan language stock embraced Mandan, Hidatsa, Crow, Dakota–Assiniboin, Omaha–Ponca–Osage–Kansa, and Iowa–Oto–Missouri. The Pawnee–Arikara and Wichita were Caddoan languages, whereas Wind River Shoshoni and Comanche were of the Uto-Aztecan stock. The Athabascan (Na-Dené) stock was represented by the Sarcee (Sarsi) in the northern part of the area and by the Kiowa–Apache in the southern. Finally the Kiowa–Tanoan stock was represented in the area by one language, Kiowa.

Sign language provided a common, if limited, means of communication among tribes speaking different languages. This was a system of fixed hand and finger positions symbolizing ideas, the meanings of which were known to the majority of the tribes of the area.

TRADITIONAL CULTURE PATTERNS

General cultural characteristics

In aboriginal times the only domestic animal was the dog, which served some tribes for food but was in general use as a pack animal. Dogs were also made to draw the travois, a vehicle consisting of two poles in the shape of a V, the point of the V dragging on the ground; the ends were attached to the animal, and a platform was put across to carry the burden. The Spaniards introduced the horse in the 16th century, in the southwest, and its use gradually spread northward. By the middle of the 18th century or earlier, all of the Plains Indians were equestrian. There was also a flowering of what one authority has termed luxury developments—"showy clothing, embroidered footgear, medicine-bundle purchases, elaborate rituals [culminating in the sun dance], [and especially] gratuitous and time-consuming warfare." The fighting seldom involved major tribal forces; it was carried out mainly by raiding parties of a few warriors, to avenge a death, to steal horses, and especially to gain glory. Touching an enemy's body was considered among many groups of greater moment than killing or scalping him.

In many of its aspects, Plains culture emphasized intense individualism and aggression, placing a high valuation on violent experience. Rivalry and hostility between men were part of the pattern, so much so that military organizations had to be established to maintain order at tribal assemblies. Nevertheless, a man who became eminent in war could enhance his status by showing generosity to the poor, sharing his goods with relatives, engaging in lavish hospitality, and behaving cooperatively with others.

The tribes who were marginal to the Plains generally borrowed only the external traits of Plains culture and not the religious, ceremonial, or social customs. On the other hand, the southern tribes of the Siouan language family, along with the Pawnee, Mandan, Hidatsa, and Arikara, while possessing most of the typical Plains Indian cultural traits, had a number of others, such as horticulture, pottery, and residence in fixed villages for part of the year; they may be said to constitute a subculture within the Plains Indians.

Social organization. *Local and territorial units.* Among the nomadic tribes the local units were bands—*i.e.*, groups of people wandering together in search of food. The size and composition of the bands varied. Comanche bands were loosely organized, each centring its activities in a vaguely defined area within the tribal territory. Only the larger bands received permanent recognition and a name. The bands did not fight one another, but neither did they act in concert as a tribe. The Teton Dakota tribe comprised seven independent bands, the largest being the Oglala. The Cheyenne, however, were more highly organized than the Teton; their ten bands sent representatives to a council of 44 peace chiefs, whose decrees were binding on all the bands. Only in late spring and summer, as a rule, did the nomadic band or tribe come together as a unit on the open Plains, when they engaged in the communal hunt and held major ceremonies. During the remainder of the year, the members dispersed in small groups to more sheltered areas.

From H. Driver et al., *Indiana University Publications in Anthropology and Linguistics* (1953)

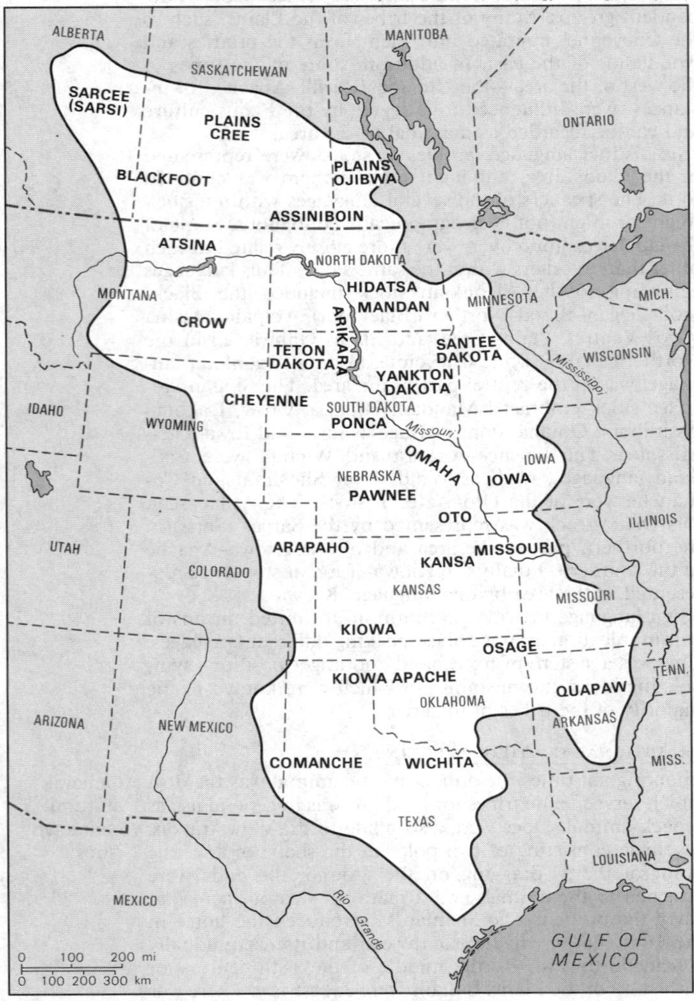

Distribution of North American Plains Indians.

Villagers

The semi-sedentary prairie dwellers lived in villages. The three Hidatsa villages were each independent of the others, whereas the Skidi Pawnee villages were united. The seasonal round of the village peoples may be illustrated by the Arikara, who spent the period between planting their crops and harvesting them on the summer hunt living as nomads. After the harvest small groups went to the Plains for another hunt, returning not to their permanent villages but to protected areas in the bottomlands, going back to the permanent villages to plant their crops in the spring.

Family and kinship units. Each local band or village was composed of families and wider kinship units. Every group had regulations governing the mating of kin. Some, such as the Atsina and Blackfoot, did not tolerate marriage between consanguineal relatives, no matter how distant the tie, and others proscribed marriage within varying degrees of relationship. On the other hand, marriage between those who were already relatives by marriage was often prescribed or preferred; the custom of a man marrying the widow of his deceased brother was widespread, as was also the replacement of a deceased wife by her sister. Most marriages were monogamous, but a man might have several wives, sisters being preferred.

Ideally, marriages were arranged between the families of the bride and groom, the latter usually paying a bride-price; sometimes, as among the Mandan, each side provided exactly equivalent gifts. Virginity was highly prized among most of the tribes, particularly the Cheyenne. Among the Blackfoot, women known to be chaste were selected for roles in important ceremonies. The double standard prevailed, however, and men in all of the tribes were expected to make sexual conquests. A husband who had evidence of his wife's infidelity might disfigure her by cutting off her nose or demand compensation from her lover. Romantic love and elopement were not unknown, but attitudes varied; the Teton tolerated the couple on their return, while the Cheyenne considered the girl disgraced forever.

Most Plains tribes had definite rules governing conduct between in-laws, such as the widespread "mother-in-law taboo" in which a man and his wife's mother showed their mutual respect by not speaking to, or in some cases not even looking at, each other. In some tribes, as among the Arapaho, the taboo was extended to include a woman and her father-in-law. The Atsina and a few other tribes required brothers-in-law to be very circumspect in their speech, avoiding any reference to sex no matter how indirect. Yet many of the tribes adhering strictly to this respect taboo permitted the greatest freedom between a man and his sister-in-law. Among the Crow they were expected to romp with each other and to talk to each other in vile language; the Atsina encouraged mutual practical joking and teasing; the Blackfoot allowed the same freedom as between man and wife. It is notable that, according to marriage rules on the Plains, the parties to this joking relationship were potential mates.

Family lines

While some of the Plains societies reckoned descent bilaterally—that is, equally in both the male and female lines—others reckoned descent exclusively in either the male or female line. This did not mean that there was no recognition of the other parent and his or her relatives. The Hidatsa had a matrilineal clan system (*i.e.*, they traced their descent through females back to a common ancestress), yet there were important relationships to the father and his clansmen; they were always treated with respect and often presented with gifts; before battle a man would ask his clan father to paint his face; the clan father would give personal names to a clansman's son; and ceremonially the father's clan folk played an important part in performances such as the sun dance.

The Mandan and Crow also had matrilineal clan systems. The Oto and Missouri are reported to have had them as well, but there is little information on these groups. The patrilineal clan system was characteristic of the Iowa, Kansa, Omaha, Osage, and Ponca. There is some question as to whether or not the Blackfoot and Atsina had clans, since there was a tendency for the child to be a member of his father's subdivision, and marriage within this subdivision was frowned upon. The organization of the eastern Dakota and the Assiniboin is likewise in doubt.

Among some groups certain clans regarded themselves as more closely related to each other than to other clans. Among the Kansa the 16 clans were grouped into seven larger units. Often the larger units, or phratries, had no important function, although presumably in some cases they regulated marriage. Occasionally there was a further, higher grouping of phratries into two complementary units, or "moieties," as anthropologists call them. The Ponca moieties were composed of two phratries, each consisting of two clans. A similar dual division also existed among societies lacking clans and phratries. The Pawnee, for instance, were divided into the Summer People and the Winter People.

Social rank and warfare. There were no hereditary social classes, but there was ranking of individuals. A poor man, with the help of supernatural power, could win wealth and standing, mainly through prowess at war; but the son of a wealthy family would have an advantage over an orphan.

Most tribes ranked war exploits, but they did not all evaluate particular deeds alike. The taking of scalps was common, but many tribes considered scalping of lesser merit than counting coups—touching one's enemy. Stealing a valuable horse that had been picketed at its owner's lodge was considered a feat.

Most tribes had a number of clubs or associations, religious and secular. Among the latter were the military societies that often functioned as police for the tribal hunt. Some organizations were rivals. Among the Crow, for example, there were two outstanding societies, the Lumpwoods and the Foxes, that were of equal rank but competed violently in feats of war. The Arapaho, Atsina, Blackfoot, Mandan, and Hidatsa differed from the other Plains tribes in that their military societies were ranked in an ordered series. Distinctive regalia and membership privileges in each society were purchased collectively by one group of roughly the same age from an older group. Then the sellers as a group bought from the next older group, the exchange continuing until the oldest group sold out completely and retired from the system. The number of societies varied. The Hidatsa at one time had as many as ten military societies.

Women participated in many of the associations, often playing important roles. Among the Mandan and Hidatsa, women's societies existed similar to the men's graded societies.

Child rearing

Socialization and education. Training began early for Plains children, as part of their play. A very small boy would be given a bow and blunt arrows; as he grew stronger, he would receive larger, heavier bows and be shown how to stalk small game and to hit moving targets. Groups of boys engaged in shooting matches and sham battles, the winners receiving acclaim from their elders; the losers were praised if they had fought bravely. Competition marked almost all of the boys' games.

Girls were taught domestic skills. A father might make toy scraping tools for a girl, which her mother would teach her to use. She would learn to sew by making clothes for her doll and be given a toy tepee to put up while her mother was erecting the big one. In general the line between work and play was not sharply drawn.

The young were encouraged to behave in desired ways by praise and reward, special attention being given in many of the tribes to the first success. Thus an Oto father publicly gave away property to honour his son when the boy first walked, when he brought in his first small game, when he killed his first deer, and when he returned from his first war party. When a Crow boy killed his first big game animal, he was given public recognition; a song celebrating the achievement was sung at a ceremony similar to that which would mark his return from a first war party. Progress toward maturity was generally rewarded by removing restrictions and granting special privileges. Blackfoot boys who won shooting matches were allowed to wear feathers in their hair. As soon as he went on his first war party, the Cheyenne boy was relieved from the duty of herding horses and also from the necessity of listening to long lectures on proper behaviour.

Relatives helped to train children. Grandparents were often consultants and advisers. In a number of tribes, the mother's brother and the father's sister played important roles as mentors and disciplinarians. Among the matrilineal Hidatsa, the maternal uncle was responsible for the direction and supervision of his nephews; he guided them and punished them, but also praised them. Arapaho parents relied on the father's sister to instruct a girl in proper behaviour and to reprimand her when necessary. Physical punishment was seldom employed. Praise and reward for achievement seem to have been generally emphasized more than ridicule and admonishment for failure.

Though the quest for supernatural power through a vision or dream was important among all of the Plains tribes, the experience was not sought primarily at puberty, as was the case in other areas. Again, while fear of menstrual blood was universal, only a few tribes, including the Cree, marked the occurrence of the girl's first menses with an adolescent rite.

Housing

Economic systems. The nomadic tribes lived throughout the year in portable dwellings, while the semi-sedentary peoples used them only seasonally. The tent, or tepee, was conical in shape, the foundation being either three or four poles with other poles placed around them to form a circular base. The cover was made from dressed buffalo skins carefully fitted and sewn together. Since the fireplace was in the centre, a smoke hole was left at the top that could be closed in bad weather.

When the whole tribe assembled, a camp circle was usually formed, leaving the space in the centre for ceremonial structures. Among some peoples, such as the Cheyenne and Atsina, each subgroup had a defined place in the circle. Among many tribes, too, the orientation of the lodges and the opening of the circle was toward the rising sun.

The earth lodge of the semi-sedentary peoples was a permanent structure much larger than a tepee; it was dome shaped, roofed with earth, and entered by a covered passage. The Pawnee, the Mandan, and some other tribes excavated the floor so that their dwellings were partly subterranean. The Osage and Wichita houses differed from those of the other horticultural tribes; the dwellings of the Osage were oval in ground plan, composed of upright poles arched over on top, interlaced with horizontal withes, and covered with mats or skins, while the Wichita houses were conical in shape and thatched with grass.

Technology

The nomads depended for subsistence primarily on big game: buffalo, antelope, deer, and elk. These were also important in the diet of the semi-sedentary tribes. While the animals could be hunted by individuals, the usual methods involved the whole tribe in driving the game down a cliff or into a corral or encircling it by fire. The introduction of the horse increased hunting efficiency, allowing larger numbers of game animals to be killed more quickly. The mounted hunter continued to prefer the bow and arrow over guns.

The semi-sedentary tribes practicing horticulture raised principally maize (corn), but also beans, squashes, and sunflowers. The plots were cultivated by the women, using only a rake, a digging stick, and a hoe made from the shoulder blade of an elk or a buffalo.

Animal skins were used for clothing. On the Northern Plains, men wore a shirt, leggings reaching to the hips, moccasins, and a buffalo robe—the role being painted to depict the war deeds of the owner. Women's clothing consisted of a long dress, leggings to the knee, and moccasins.

Among the villagers and some southern nomads, men traditionally left the upper part of the body bare. Clothes were decorated with porcupine-quill embroidery, fringe, and, in later times, beadwork. Ordinarily the head was not covered, the feathered warbonnet and other elaborate headgear being reserved for ceremonial occasions.

Receptacles of various kinds were made from rawhide and leather. Traditional tools were of bone, horn, antler, and stone—before the introduction of metal by Europeans. Pipes were usually of stone. Basketry and pottery were characteristic products of the villagers; some of the nomads, including the Cheyenne, Comanche, and Arapaho, were said to have made flat coiled gambling trays, while the Atsina, Blackfoot, and Cree, among others, had traditions of having once made earthenware.

Property and exchange

Some anthropologists have argued that Indians could not have lived on the Plains before the introduction of the horse. Others, pointing to the fact that Francisco Vázquez de Coronado's expedition in 1541 encountered fully nomadic buffalo-hunting tribes on the Southern Plains who lacked horses and depended on dogs for transport, claim that the acquisition of the horse produced only minor changes. One consequence of the horse was the creation of great differences in wealth. Horse stealing became a major motive for warfare. The man who had horses to give away or to offer as bride-price was at a distinct advantage in social prestige.

There was very little intratribal trade in material goods, although there was much exchange of intangibles. The transfer of war medicine and of curing rites brought high prices in horses and other goods among practically all of the tribes. For the spiritual benefit believed to accrue from viewing the contents of a sacred pipe bundle (*i.e.*, a pack containing various sacred objects) of the Mandan, the individual had to pay, in the 1830s, the equivalent of what was then $100. Among the Hidatsa a person wishing to learn to chip flint and make arrows had to buy the rights and receive the instructions from those with ceremonial rights who possessed bundles carrying arrow-making songs.

Intertribal trade was fairly common, one form being that between nomads and villagers; *e.g.*, the exchange of skin robes for grain. The Cheyenne were middlemen in the trade of horses between the Indians of the Southern Plains and those of the north central Plains. Guns and other materials such as blankets, beads, cloth, and kettles, introduced into the northeast by the British and French, were highly valued by the Comanche, Kiowa, and other groups, who were willing to give horses in exchange for them.

Communication with spirits

Belief systems. The Plains Indians did not distinguish sharply between the sacred and the secular nor between religion and magic. They attached much importance to visions. Success in life was believed to depend in large measure on the intervention of friendly spirits. The usual procedure for obtaining spirit help was to go to some lonely spot to fast, mortify the flesh, and beg for aid. If the suppliant was successful, the spirit would appear to him or be audible to him and would give him detailed instructions to follow to win immunity in battle, ability to cure illness, or various other kinds of power. The spirit might assume the form of an animal or a bird. Not everyone was successful in this quest, and, among the Crow and some other tribes, those with power were permitted to transfer it to others less fortunate. Among the Atsina and Teton Dakota, women might be vouchsafed visions, although they did not usually seek the experience.

All of the tribes had medicine men, or shamans, who had received supernatural powers. Arapaho, Atsina, and Cheyenne medicine men would walk on fire as a proof of their powers. More important was the ability of the shaman to cure illness. While, in most of the groups, ordinary illnesses such as dysentery or headaches would be treated with herbal remedies, a shaman was called in to diagnose and treat more serious illnesses. It was widely believed that illness was caused by intrusion of a foreign substance in the body and that the medicine man could cure the patient by extracting the object. If the medicine man failed, the reason was that there had been some unwitting infraction of the rules as laid down by his supernatural sponsor. He was not required to take every case; among the Teton Dakota he could refuse after examining a patient. Other services a medicine man might render included locating enemies and game animals and even finding lost objects.

In some tribes it is difficult to distinguish the role of medicine man, who had direct contact with the supernatural, from that of the priest who obtained his knowledge from other practitioners. The Cheyenne medicine man is thought to have been more of a priest than a shaman, since his main road to supernatural power was through acquisition of ritual knowledge from one who was already a priest, although some did seek power through visions. The same individual may have acted in some situations as a shaman and in others as a priest.

Among the tribes having a clear belief in a spirit superior to all other spirits were the Cheyenne, the Atsina, and the Pawnee. The Cheyenne, for instance, held that "the Wise One above" knew better than all other creatures; long ago he had left the Earth and retired to the sky. In smoking ceremonies the first offering of the pipe was always made to him. Some of the other tribes, such as the Crow, are not known to have believed in such a supreme deity.

Ceremonial and ritual were well developed on the Plains. They ranged from very simple rites to complicated proceedings requiring weeks of preparation, the final performance lasting for days. A number of common ritual elements were used alone or combined in various ways by the several tribes. Medicine bundles figured prominently in rituals throughout the area. In some cases the bundle was a personal one, the contents of which had been suggested to the individual by a supernatural sponsor, while in others it was a tribal property originating in the mythological past. It was handled reverently and opened according to definite rules. The opening of the Cheyenne sacred arrow bundle, for instance, was the focus of an elaborate tribal rite extending over four days.

The sacred number for most tribes was four, entering into the rituals in many ways. A less common number was seven. Many rituals centred on a kind of altar, a specially prepared space in a ceremonial structure for arranging sacred objects or smoking them with incense. The dimensions of the altar and the symbols that were used varied with the ceremony. Ritual purification in a sweat lodge was a widespread practice, required in connection with many ceremonies.

The sun dance

One important ceremony found among about 20 tribes is known inaccurately in English as the sun dance. The native terms varied: the Cheyenne phrase may be translated as "New Life Lodge"; the Atsina term means "Sacrifice Lodge." While the central features were the same among all the tribes, there were many differences in detail. The sun dance was always held in summer, when the whole tribe gathered, and was usually performed in fulfillment of a vow by someone who had promised it if he were relieved of some grave difficulty. The ceremony was an annual event among the Teton Dakota but occurred at quite irregular intervals among the Crow. The pledger was instructed by a priest or medicine man, and some weeks were needed for gathering food and other preparations. A ceremonial structure was built in the centre of the camp circle, and, before it was erected, offerings were placed in the fork of the central log. Within the structure was an altar upon which buffalo skulls were laid. The pledger and other participants fasted and danced for several days, praying for power. A widespread, though not universal, feature of the ceremony was self-torture by some of the participants. The skin of the breast or back was pierced, and a wooden skewer inserted. One end of a rope was tied to the skewer, the other end being attached to the centre pole. The dancer leaned back until the line was taut and he strained until he tore himself loose. The Teton elaborated on this torture by dragging around buffalo skulls attached to skewers on the dancers' legs.

MODERN DEVELOPMENTS

Cultural changes

With the coming of the white man, the Plains Indians began to acquire manufactured articles such as guns, metal utensils, axes, knives, blankets, and cloth. This led to a decline of the native arts and crafts. Paradoxically, however, some aspects of social life were intensified as a result of the fur trade. Since women dressed the hides, the successful hunters secured more and more wives to do the dressing for them, and therefore polygyny increased on the Northern Plains. Religion was affected insofar as wealth brought by the fur trade encouraged more frequent transfer of medicine bundles, at higher prices.

With the coming of immigrant wagons, the building of railroads across the Plains, and the encroachment of white settlements, warfare became a unifying force. During the latter half of the 19th century, tribes that had formerly been hostile to one another often united against the intruders. Not infrequently the Indians were successful, although in the end they were overwhelmed. Eventually the buffalo disappeared, the system of status and rank collapsed, and the tribes were placed on reservations. The culture of the Indians was radically changed.

The United States government hoped to make the Indians into literate farmers, but the agents sent to teach them encountered many obstacles. The nomadic groups were loath to settle down, looking upon cattle as a poor substitute for buffalo. The reservation land was often unsuitable for agriculture. The semi-settled village peoples, among whom digging-stick cultivation was traditionally considered women's work, resisted the change in division of labour brought by the plow. Much confusion resulted when officials insisted on listing families by surnames, which Indians did not possess. Many misunderstandings arose among the matrilineal tribes when inheritance rules were changed so that land passed from father to son.

Schools were established on and off the reservation. Boarding schools had the advantage of facilitating the learning of the white man's language and customs. While some individual Indians adapted to the new conditions and were able to make their way among whites, those who returned from school to the reservations often found themselves in a difficult and marginal position.

Many Indians were Christianized. A new religious movement known as peyotism, combining pagan and Christian elements, spread among the Plains Indians in the latter part of the 19th century. It centred on a species of cactus that when eaten or imbibed caused hallucinations. Since it was considered dangerous by the government as well as by the missionaries, efforts were made to suppress it. But groups practicing the peyote religion were incorporated in 1918 as the Native American Church. (R.F.-He.)

Eastern Woodlands Indians

At the time of the European discovery of North America, the area stretching from Lake Superior to the Atlantic coast was occupied by many different Indian groups speaking languages that belong to three distinct language families: Iroquoian, Algonkian, and Siouan. The major speakers of northern Iroquoian languages include the Iroquois confederacy (Mohawk, Oneida, Onondaga, Cayuga, Seneca, and, later, Tuscarora), the Huron confederacy, Tionontati (Petun or Tobacco Nation), Wyandot (a group of Hurons and Tionontati), Neutral, Wenrohronon, Erie, Susquehanna (Conestoga), and Laurentian Iroquois. The major speakers of Algonkian languages include the Passamaquoddy, Malecite, Abnaki, Penobscot, Pennacook, Massachuset, Nauset, Wampanoag, Narraganset, Niantic, Pequot, Mohegan, Nipmuc, Pocomtuc, Mahican, Wappinger, Montauk, Delaware (Lenni Lenape), Powhatan, Ojibwa (Chippewa), Menominee, Sauk (Sac), Kickapoo, Miami, and Illinois. The Winnebago, who also lived in the eastern woodlands, spoke a Siouan language.

Although the area generally was a wooded one, it was in the open spaces in the forests that many of the best natural resources were to be found. In consequence, the heaviest population concentrations were near or along the seacoast, lakes, ponds, marshes, creeks, and rivers. There animals could be hunted, fish caught, birds taken, leaves, seeds, and roots of wild plants gathered, shellfish collected, and crops grown. Certain areas were favoured with resources not found elsewhere in the region. In certain parts of the upper Great Lakes area, wild rice (*Zizania aquatica*) grew in abundance, and the Menominee especially depended on it. Buffalo (bison) roamed the plains–prairie area, and such groups as the Sauk, Fox, Illinois, and Miami, who lived near the prairie, hunted them. On

Forest resources

Adapted from *International Journal of American Linguistics* (1953)

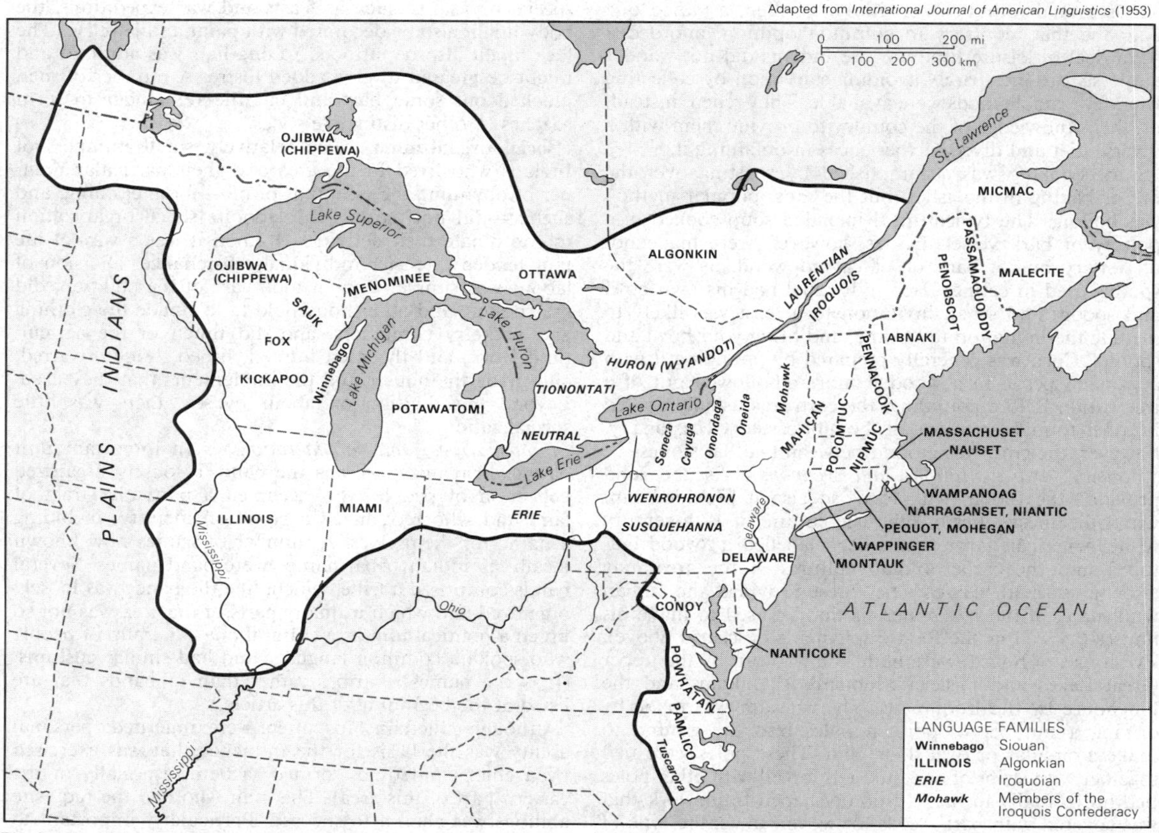

Distribution of Eastern Woodlands Indians.

the Atlantic coast, shellfish were plentiful and played an important part in the diet.

TRADITIONAL CULTURE PATTERNS

Economic systems. *Food production and consumption.* Except in the northern part of the upper Great Lakes area and the northern part of the Eastern Seaboard—areas that do not have a growing season long enough for corn (maize) to mature—some agriculture was practiced. The three principal plants cultivated were corn, beans, and squash, plants the Iroquois termed the three sisters because they were to be found like sisters together in the fields. Generally, it was the women who cultivated the fields, planting the seed, weeding, and harvesting the crops. Men, however, usually aided in clearing the land preparatory to planting. The type of agriculture practiced is often termed horticulture, as domesticated draft animals were not used. The implements used in planting were the hoe and the digging stick (dibble stick), a wooden stick pointed at one end that was used to make a hole in the ground into which the seeds could be dropped and then covered.

Of all the groups in the area, the Iroquoian tribes were probably the most dependent on agriculture, but even they did not rely wholly on it. The population of the area was never great enough to have exhausted the supply of wild plants and animals, and as a result the Indians living there did not have to expend the time and effort necessary for intensive agriculture. They also could avoid a dull and monotonous, though balanced, diet confined to corn, beans, and squash and could enjoy a rich and varied diet merely by travelling to the proper places at the proper times of the year to collect food. Leaves of wild plants were gathered in the spring and cooked as greens. Later in the year, berries and other seeds were gathered. Fish were caught in the spring, summer, and fall—different species being plentiful at different times of the year. Birds were taken, and in certain areas the spring roosting places of pigeon provided virtually unlimited amounts of squab. In early spring, the maple trees were tapped for their sap. Fall was the best time for hunting, and numbers of families went into the forests at this season of the year to hunt. The seasonal round of activities was, then, a varied one and one that, contrary to common opinion, afforded a great deal of leisure time, for the Indians did not wander aimlessly around, barely avoiding starvation by collecting what few eatable foods were available. They relied, instead, on their knowledge of the country to provide them with a diverse diet and diverse experiences in obtaining it.

Some cooking was accomplished by roasting over the fire or baking in the ashes, but the most popular method was boiling. The typical meal included soup cooked in a pottery or bark vessel. Dishes, however, were made not of pottery but of bark or of carved wood, as were the spoons used in eating. Each individual had his own bowl and spoon, and so an invitation to a feast was likely to include the invitation to "Come, and bring your bowl and spoon." Corn was generally prepared by pounding it with a wooden pestle in a wooden mortar hollowed out of a tree trunk. Before pounding, the corn was usually soaked in ashes to make removal of the hull easier. Occasionally, however, the corn was ground between two flat stones.

Housing, transportation, and weapons. As the land provided the Indian with food, so also it provided him with other necessities of life. The culture of 19th-century white American farmers has been labelled a "wood culture," and the earlier Indian cultures of the area may also be so characterized: the forest provided the Indian with many of the raw materials that he used to make his houses (as well as the food implements described above). Two types of houses were built: the wigwam by the upper Great Lakes and Eastern Seaboard Algonkians and the longhouse by the Iroquoians. The wigwam was made by driving a number of pointed poles into the ground to make a circular or oval floor plan. These poles were tied together with strips of bark and reinforced with other poles tied horizontally to make a dome-shaped framework that was covered with bark, reeds, or woven mats, the type of covering depending on the availability of materials in the area. A fire in the centre provided heat for cooking and for warmth. Although the Iroquoian longhouse, like the wigwam, was made of a framework of poles covered with bark sheets, it was arbor-shaped rather than dome-shaped, having straight sides and an arched roof. After European contact, the roof shape often was of the gable type. Rather than being circular or oval, the longhouse was rectangular in floor plan and had a door at either end. A longhouse was approximately 20 feet wide and ranged from less than 50 feet to more than 200 feet in length, depending on the number of families living in it. Down the middle of the house were the fires, two families on either side sharing the fire in the middle. The average longhouse probably had five fires and ten families.

Wigwams and longhouses

The forest also provided materials for the dugouts and bark canoes commonly used for transport in this area of many lakes and streams, the birchbark of the northern portions of the area making the best canoes. The forest also provided materials for the frames of the snowshoes, which made travel in the winter easier and which were essential in the north (a man on snowshoes could outrun a moose or other large animal in the snow and take him with an ease that was not possible in more clement seasons). The bows and arrows and the spears used in hunting and warring were also made of wood provided by the forest. Points for the arrows and spears were chipped from flint or other suitable stone, as were the knives and other sharp-edged implements.

Clothing. Animals of the forest provided the skins from which the women made clothing. The basic item of men's dress was the breechclout, a strip of skin drawn between the legs and held in place by looping it over a belt at the waist. For protection from the cold or while travelling in the forest, leggings (basically, two tubes of skin also attached to the waist belt) were added. A cape or robe of skin or fur was also worn in cold weather. The basic item of women's dress was a skirt, to which might be added leggings tied at the knee and a cape or robe. Both men and women wore moccasins, the soft-soled and heelless shoe adapted, among other things, for use with the snowshoe. The clothing of both sexes might be decorated with painting, porcupine-quill embroidery, shells, or shell beads. For special occasions, such as feasts and war expeditions, the body might also be decorated with paint and jewelry. (The face might also be tattooed.) Long hair was admired and might be greased to give added lustre. A number of men plucked out some hair and cut the remainder to form roaches or other distinctive styles.

Social organization. The relatively small numbers of Indians who lived in the area and their particular manner of obtaining the essentials of life—food, clothing, and shelter—did not require an elaborate social organization to coordinate their activities. Rather, it was a way of life that tended to foster individual self-reliance. Division of labour was simple: women took care of the children, did the cooking and other household tasks, made the clothing and basketry containers, and did much of the agricultural work; and the men hunted, fished, traded, warred, and made the houses and the implements that they used. Beyond this division of labour by sex, there was little specialization.

Bands, tribes, and confederations. An important unit of social organization was the band, a loosely organized collection of people who occupied a particular tract of land and who recognized a common identity, including a name for themselves. A number of names now known locally as Indian tribal names were band names. Several bands comprised a tribe, which, like the band, was loosely organized and which in many parts of the area was not so much a political unit as a cultural one—a group of people who spoke a common language and had similar customs. (It is the names of tribes rather than of bands that are listed at the beginning of this article.)

Leaders and councils

Although chieftainships often were inherited, personal ability was the basis for the influence that was exercised by a chief (sometimes termed sachem, especially in the eastern part of this area). The man who had the requisite abilities was chosen to succeed. Particularly important to a chief was his ability to persuade. As one result, oratory was highly valued and developed into a fine art; even in English, the power of Indian oratory is evident. Typically, the councils of the Indians involved the making of speeches, but the intent of this oratory was not to impress others with mere rhetoric but to find a solution to the issue at hand that all could agree to. If unanimity was not achieved, no action could be taken. The dissidents would either continue to express their opposition or withdraw; in either case, the effectiveness of the group would be weakened. Speech making, then, served as a means of ascertaining the diversity of opinion within the group and the manner in which consensus could be reached, for commonly each speaker summarized the opinions previously expressed before offering his own. Councils often were lengthy affairs.

Councils (including some religious councils—the Indians typically did not draw a sharp distinction between sacred and secular affairs) normally opened with the smoking of a pipe. In the Midwest, this practice was elaborated into the calumet ceremony used to greet foreigners and on other occasions. It is from this custom that the phrase "smoke the peace pipe" is derived.

League of the Iroquois

The most elaborate and powerful political organization developed in this area was that of the League of the Iroquois, but even this league rested on the political principles to be found elsewhere. Unanimity was required (the failure to achieve this unanimity being one of the reasons for the Iroquois defeat at the hands of the Revolutionists during the Revolutionary War), and oratory was highly regarded. Tradition has it that the league was formed as a result of the efforts of Dekanawida and Hiawatha probably sometime in the 15th or 16th century. The intent of the league was to establish peace among the five tribes of the Iroquois (the sixth member of the league, the Tuscarora, was to join it in the early part of the 18th century); and thus one of the most important parts of the constitution of the league established the price for murder: ten strings of wampum (shell beads) for the life of a man and 20 strings of wampum for the life of a woman, to be paid to the kinsmen of the murdered person. (If a man murdered another man, the total paid by the relatives of the murderer was 20 strings of wampum—ten for the murdered man's life and ten for the murderer's life, which had been forfeited by the act of murder; the total for murder of a woman by a man was 30 strings of wampum, and so on.) Before the establishment of the league, tribes might go to war if the compensation was not considered just, a common custom in the area. (Witchcraft, not murder, was the most serious crime among Indians and evoked capital punishment.) The fixing of the price prevented war from occurring between members of the league, although not between members of the league and other tribes.

If the League of the Iroquois was a league of peace to its members, it was not to other Indian groups. In the 17th century, beaver had become scarce in Iroquois territory. They began a series of wars with their neighbours, defeating and dispersing the Hurons and Tionontati in 1649–50 (a number of Hurons and Tionontati were to join forces to become the Wyandot), the Neutrals in 1651, the Erie in 1656, and the Susquehanna in 1675. Earlier, about 1638, the Wenrohronons had joined the Hurons in consequence of Iroquois attacks on them. The Iroquois then took on still more distant Indian peoples.

The founding of the League of the Iroquois has been dated variously from about 1460 to about 1600, but, regardless of whether the date is pre- or post-Columbian, it seems likely that its strength and effectiveness increased as a consequence of European influence on the continent. Somewhat similarly, loose confederacies of various Indian bands were established along the Eastern Seaboard after European contact, in part to counter the force of the whites. Later, diverse groups of Indians living in the upper Great Lakes area banded together in a like manner, under the leadership of particularly influential chiefs, in order to affect events in that region.

Warfare

It seems likely that warfare among Indians increased in the years following European settlement and the establishment of trading posts. War parties were, typically, groups of men gotten together for the purpose of raiding for loot or for captives. For example, if compensation for murder had not been agreed on, a war party might be raised to avenge the murder and might include the taking of a captive to replace the murdered person. Before setting out, there might be a ceremony in which the men would boast of previous exploits, both to gain recruits and to rouse feelings to the proper pitch.

Among the Iroquoian, captives taken during war might be killed or brought back to the village, where they were either tortured to death or adopted into the tribe. If the captive was taken to compensate for a previous murder, he was often given to the family of the murdered person, and that family decided whether the captive was to be tortured to death or adopted as a member of the family. If the decision was for torture, members of the community tried to excel each other in the invention of tortures. The captive tried to accept these tortures without crying out—a practice that has contributed to the white stereotype of the stoic Indian. A captive who was killed might be scalped. Scalping may have been introduced by the Europeans, but the evidence is not conclusive. It may have been merely an elaboration of the old Indian custom to take a piece of hair or clothing of the killed person as a trophy of the event.

Clans. An important kind of social group in the area, particularly in the more southerly parts, where agriculture was relatively more important and population density higher, was the clan (sometimes now termed sib). The division of a tribe into clans served both to divide the community into smaller cooperating units and to provide a means of uniting it with others. Members of the same clan had certain obligations toward one another, regardless of tribal or community affiliations. They were expected to provide hospitality to visitors of the same clan, for example. Loyalty to clan often overshadowed that to the nuclear family, but the marriage tie among Indians often was a relatively unstable one and frequently was marked by little or no ceremony. In contrast, clan affiliation continued for life. On occasion, clan membership was as important as tribal, band, or village membership.

Names and relationships

Clans often have names that refer to an animal. The Seneca clans, for example, are Turtle, Bear, Beaver, Wolf, Snipe, Hawk, Deer, and Heron. The animal, or totem (a word adopted into English from the Algonkian word meaning "kinsmen"), had a special relationship to the clan. Members of a clan considered themselves to be related, whether an actual genealogical relationship could be traced or not. Partly because of this view, the members of a clan were not permitted to marry within the clan (that is, clans were exogamous).

Among the Iroquoians and the Delawares, a child automatically belonged to the clan of his mother (that is, the clans were matrilineal). Among the Winnebago and many other upper Great Lakes (Central) Algonkians, a child belonged to the clan of his father (that is, the clans were patrilineal—such patrilineal clans sometimes being termed gentes; singular, gens). Thus, for example, an Iroquois child of a father who belonged to the Wolf clan and a mother who belonged to the Turtle clan was a member of the Turtle clan, the clan of his mother. Further, he could not marry (without being accused of committing incest) a girl who also belonged to the Turtle clan. And if he married a girl, say, of the Bear clan, she did not become a member of the Turtle clan but remained a member of her own clan, the Bear clan, because clan membership was for life. (In a few instances, an individual might be adopted into another clan, but this had nothing to do with marriage.) In tribes that had clans, everyone in the tribe belonged to a clan; and, if a captive or other person was adopted into the tribe, he was also adopted into a clan of that tribe.

Commonly in this area, each clan owned a number of names, and a newborn child was given one of the clan's names that was not currently in use (that is, a name belonging to someone then deceased or a name that had been given up for a new name by someone still living). Certain names carried special responsibilities, such as those belonging to the 50 chiefs of the Iroquois League. When a chief died, the women of his clan decided on a successor, who was a member of the same clan. If the successor was approved by the other chiefs, he was given the name of the deceased chief in the condolence ceremony, in which the chief was "raised up" and resuscitated by giving his name to his successor.

Among many upper Great Lakes tribes, the clan owned a bundle of sacred objects, with which there was associated a ritual that was performed periodically by members of the clan. At least in recent times, the Iroquois had no comparable clan ceremonies; rather, a significant part of their ritual life centred on ceremonies in recognition of foods as they matured. These rituals included the maple, strawberry, bean, green corn, and harvest festivals, as well as the midwinter ceremony.

In some groups, such as the Winnebago and the Iroquois, the clans were grouped into two sides or moieties ("halves"), which had reciprocal obligations. Among the Iroquois, for example, members of a moiety buried the dead of the opposite moiety. Traditionally, the moieties were exogamous, and thus, in a sense, they provided wives for each other.

Medicine societies. Also often important in Indian religion are the medicine societies, so termed because one of their important functions was curing and because their membership consisted of individuals who had undergone such cures. The most famous medicine society among the upper Great Lakes Indians was the Mide Society (Midewiwin, or Grand Medicine Society), a society that held elaborate annual or semi-annual meetings during which various magical feats were performed. Of the various Iroquois medicine societies, the False Face Society is most familiar to whites because the carved wooden masks worn by members of this society during their rituals often are to be found exhibited in museums and pictured in books on Indian art.

Belief systems. Not all curing was performed by members of medicine societies. Certain individuals (often termed medicine men or shamans in anthropological literatures or powwows in the literature on New England Indians) had the power to cure, a power that was often indicated in a vision or dream. Dreams were especially important, because, generally among the people of this area, dreams indicated not only the causes of illness and an individual's power to cure but also the means of maintaining good fortune in various aspects of life. So much attention was paid to dreams that, among some Indians, a mother customarily asked her children in the morning if they had dreamed, for dreams were to be cultivated and attended to. Dreams could also influence the decisions of councils; as some early writers said, "The dream is the God of the country." Although the vision had some importance and although boys in the various tribes might seek a vision experience (particularly about the time of puberty), the vision quest (and the concomitant acquisition of a guardian spirit) was not as important in the area as a whole as it was among the Plains Indians.

Dreams and visions

The reliance on dreams, on the other hand, should not be interpreted as meaning that these Indians lived in a fantasy world. In these societies in which great emphasis was placed on self-reliance and on individual competence, attention to the content of dreams provided a means of understanding oneself and of bringing to consciousness knowledge stored in the unconscious, including knowledge as to where one's greatest abilities lay; for dreams and visions might indicate whether one had special ability in warfare, hunting, and the like.

Indians, moreover, did not lack real knowledge of herbal medicine. Indeed, it was the reputed success of their medicine that added credibility to the value of bottles of "Indian oil" and other medicines sold by the touring "Indian shows." Certain other practices, such as the sweat baths taken in small structures built for the purpose, also were beneficial in the treatment of others. The Indian practice of soliciting the aid of medicine societies and shamans to cure illnesses not cured by "natural" means is not unlike the modern-day treatment of psychosomatic illnesses.

More difficult for a member of Western civilization to comprehend is the "spirit world" of the Indian, for it appears to the outsider as if the Indian world was populated by a number of spirits, including spirits of such natural objects as the sun, the moon, thunder, and the trees. Some anthropologists have interpreted these beliefs as meaning that the Indians believed in pure supernatural power—that is, a force in the universe that, like electricity, could attach itself to certain persons and things. The Algonkian word *manito,* the Siouan word *wakan,* and the Iroquoian word *orenda* have been interpreted as referring to such supernatural power. There is some recent evidence, however, suggesting that this difference between Western and Indian thought rests on a different classification of the animate and inanimate worlds. The Indians classed as animate such things as the sun and the moon. And even those things that they regarded as inanimate they treated as "beings"—to be feasted as human beings are, to be called by kinship terms as human beings are, and in general to be paid attention to. Their exploits, like those of human beings, are reported in tales and myths.

MODERN DEVELOPMENTS

When the whites arrived on the North American continent, they brought manufactured goods that the Indians wanted and new diseases that they did not. Certain of the new diseases proved particularly virulent among Indians because they did not have the immunity that the whites had developed through centuries of exposure. At one time or another, all the Indian tribes were decimated by epidemics. In one notable instance, an epidemic swept over New England, killing many Indians in 1616–17, just a few years before the Pilgrims landed at Plymouth, a catastrophe that the Pilgrims saw as a sign of God's favour. (One reason that the Indian Squanto was so friendly to the Pilgrims was that he had been taken as a captive to Europe, spent some time in England, and had returned after the epidemic.)

Trade

The extensive trade that developed between the Indians and the Europeans (French, English, and Dutch) rested on the European desire for furs, particularly for beaver fur (beaver fur makes a fine felt, and beaver hats were the rage in Europe), and on the Indian desire for European-manufactured objects, particularly guns, kettles, needles, fishhooks, other metallic objects, and beads.

The Europeans soon discovered the Indians' desire for wampum (tubular beads made of shell) and thus established "wampum factories" in New Jersey and on Long Island. The Indians used wampum for jewelry and for gifts or signs to mark significant occasions. Important messages, for instance, were accompanied by strings of wampum; the making of treaties involved the exchange of wampum belts to confirm the sincerity of the parties and to serve as reminders of the agreement. They also were used on other political and religious occasions and kept as reminders of the occasions. Because it was valuable, wampum became a medium of exchange not only between Indians and white traders but also among the colonists. Because the coinage in common use in the colonies was already various, including Spanish, Portuguese, French, and Dutch coins as well as English ones, the adoption of wampum as another medium of exchange was an easy matter. Wampum, however, was not used as money before European contact.

Indian resistance to the settlers

The initial European settlement clung to the Atlantic coast—the sea providing the lifeline to the European homeland that the colonists needed—and thus the Eastern Seaboard Indians were first affected by the newcomers' desire for land. They were ill equipped to counter the invasion. Not only were their numbers relatively small and made even smaller by the epidemics, but their political organization was not of the kind that easily led to unified action of numbers of men. Friction between Indians and colonists did occasionally erupt, however, as in the Pequot War (1637) and King Philip's War (1675–76). Such resistance could not be maintained long, and these eastern Indians, as other Indians after them, began to adopt European ways as a means of survival. Such adoption often involved the acceptance and practice of Christianity as well as other features of European life. Some missionaries were especially influential. John Eliot, for example, accomplished the monumental task of translating the Bible into Algonkian and publishing it. There remain in New

England and on Long Island some few reservations on which the Indians still are to be found. Further south, however, the Delawares gradually sold their land in the 18th century and began to drift west, becoming involved in the affairs of the country there.

The Iroquois fared somewhat better than the coastal Algonkians. In the 17th century and in the 18th century, they lived too far inland for European settlement, and only parts of their eastern territory were settled by whites. Also, the Europeans wished to maintain their trading relations with them and, through them, with Indians living farther west. The Iroquois themselves took advantage of this situation, engaging in war and diplomacy to maintain their position of power in the Northeast. Their power was finally broken in the American Revolution when George Washington, aware of the alliance of a number of Iroquois with the British, sent a punitive expedition into what is now upstate New York. After the Revolution, a number of Iroquois moved to Canada, though many remained in New York state. With the exception of many Oneida who moved to Wisconsin, those who remained in New York successfully resisted 19th-century efforts to move them (along with other eastern Indians) west of the Mississippi, and a number of them still live on the six Iroquois reservations in the state.

Like the Indians farther east, those of the upper Great Lakes area were greatly affected by the fur trade. The French established a series of trading posts, and the English challenged them for control of the area. Indians from the east, such as the Delawares, Wyandots, Ottawas, and Shawnee, drifted into the area seeking furs and land. The result was a series of wars and skirmishes between the English and the French and the Indians. Among the Indians, there emerged a series of prophets who attempted to revitalize Indian society and a series of chiefs who attempted to unite the Indians for the purposes of war. Notable among these were the Delaware Prophet, the Ottawa Pontiac, the Miami Little Turtle, the Shawnee Tecumseh and his half brother, the Shawnee Prophet (Tenskwatawa), and the Sauk Keokuk and Black Hawk. The upper Great Lakes Indians responded to various pressures put on them by whites, and many of them moved west. They are now to be found on reservations and other settlements of the more western states, though some still live in the upper Great Lakes area.

If there is any single thread that runs through the complex history of Indian–white relations, it is probably that of ambivalence. The Indians had certain resources that the whites wanted, and the whites had certain items that the Indians wanted. At times, these interests could be pursued to the benefit of all involved, but too often the interests of the various groups were in conflict. Emotionally, too, the attitudes have often been those of ambivalence: the Indians both wanting acceptance by whites and wanting their own separate identity and the whites both wanting to be rid of the Indians and admiring them. This ambivalence is likely to continue, for their histories and cultures are now so entwined that it is impossible to separate them.

(E.To.)

Southeast American Indians

The Southeastern American culture area is bounded on the east and south by the Atlantic Ocean and the Gulf of Mexico (though some scholars would place the southern portion of aboriginal Florida within the orbit of the circum-Caribbean culture area). To the west, the Southeastern area merges with the southern Plains and the extreme easternmost part of the Southwestern culture area. To the north, the Southeast blends into the northeastern woodlands area with no discernible break in cultural tradition (see also above *North American Plains Indians* and *Eastern Woodlands Indians*.)

Physiographically, the Southeast is characterized first by a coastal lowland belt broadly encompassing the subtropical zone of southern Florida; the scrub forest, sandy soil, and savannah grassland of the Atlantic and Gulf coastal plains; and the alluvial floodplains of the Mississippi drainage. Second, there is the piedmont of the midland interior, where the landscape changes to rolling hills, crisscrossed by several major river systems and covered predominantly with oak-hickory forest. Third, there is the southern Appalachian Mountains area of eastern Tennessee and the western Carolinas, a land of high peaks and deeply etched valleys, containing hardwood forests and, at high elevations, flora and fauna typical of more northerly regions.

Populations of the Southeast

The Southeast was one of the more densely populated areas of native North America, having an aboriginal population conservatively estimated at 120,000. The bulk of this population resided inland, where advantage could be taken of extensive game resources, wild plant foods, and an abundance of arable land. Only the non-horticultural peoples of south Florida appear to have satisfactorily adjusted to a basically maritime way of life.

Population was distributed among a large number of separate groups—independent villages, autonomous village clusters, and "tribelets." Most of those tribelets disappeared soon after white contact and left only faint traces in recorded history. They perished through the lethal combination of newly introduced diseases, removal into slavery, and direct warfare with white invaders or intertribal conflicts generated by white pressure. The survivors, if any, were assimilated into such larger, more powerful tribes as the Choctaw and Cherokee and various member tribes of the Creek Confederacy. These latter tribes persist to the present as distinctive peoples possessing a rich history and viable cultural heritage. Other intermediate-sized groups, such as the Houma, Catawba, and Chickasaw, survive as marginal enclaves but have lost much of their historic Indian identity. Such groups as the Seminoles (a branch of the Creek that migrated to Florida in the 18th century) and the Lumbee (a large group of Indians in Robeson County, North Carolina, whose precise Indian ancestry is unknown) appear to be entering an active phase of retribalization in which their Indian identification is being reasserted.

Languages of the Southeast

Muskogean-speaking peoples constituted the major linguistic family in the aboriginal Southeast. The Muskogean family included the following five main subdivisions: (1) Choctaw and Chickasaw, two different dialects of a single language, found in Mississippi and western Tennessee; (2) Apalachee, a long extinct language of northwestern Florida; (3) Alabama and Koasati, two closely related languages spoken in the central Southeast; (4) Hitchiti and Mikasuki, two related dialects, formerly spoken in Georgia; and (5) Creek and Seminole, also closely related dialects, spoken in eastern Georgia and later in Florida.

Four Lower Mississippi Valley languages, namely Natchez, Tunica, Chitimacha, and Atakapa, are thought to have distant affinity to Muskogean, but they show sufficient divergence both from the main Muskogean languages and from each other to warrant semi-independent status as linguistic isolates. Timucua, the major language of aboriginal north Florida, was once thought to be related to Muskogean, but its present status is problematic. One linguist believes it may be related to a language spoken in Venezuela, while others feel it may bear ultimate relationship to Siouan.

There are four definite representatives of the Siouan family in the Southeast: Tutelo, Biloxi, Ofo (Mosopelea), and Catawba. These tribes were widely scattered and, with the exception of Biloxi and Ofo, show little relationship to one another and probably represent different prehistoric penetrations of Siouan speakers into the Southeast. Yuchi, the language of a major tribal group once residing in eastern Tennessee and later in Georgia, also demonstrates distant affinities to Siouan but is sufficiently distinctive to be classified as an isolate. Many small piedmont tribes were probably Siouan speaking, but surviving data are insufficient to make definite identifications.

The Cherokee represent the sole member of the Iroquoian family in the presently demarcated Southeast, though the Iroquoian-speaking Tuscarora, Nottaway, and Meherrin, residing on the margin of the area, are included in the Southeast in some culture area maps. The Caddoan speakers on the western boundary of the Southeast belong to a distinctive language family that shows distant relationships to the Siouan and Iroquoian families. The

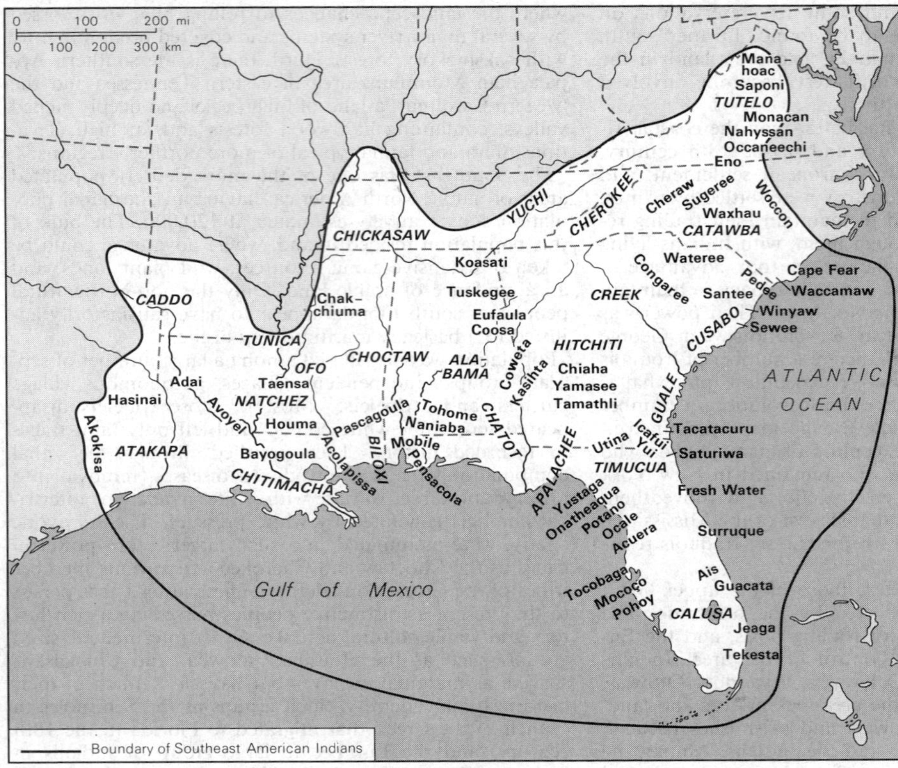

Distribution of Southeastern American Indian cultures.
From H. Driver *et al., Indiana University Publications in Anthropology and Linguistics* (1953)

affiliations of many of the smaller coastal and piedmont tribes are unknown. Mention should also be made of Mobilian, an important trade language containing many Choctaw components, which served as a lingua franca in the Mississippi Valley.

TRADITIONAL CULTURE PATTERNS

It is difficult to describe the Southeast in terms of a total cultural pattern or dominant ethos. The environment provided possibilities for such different ecological adaptations as the dependence on maritime resources and the wild zamia root by the Calusa of south Florida and the seasonal buffalo hunts of the horticultural Caddoan tribes. Besides the internal diversity, the external relations of the Southeast are also complex. The lack of geographic barriers to the north and west allowed significant cultural interchange between the Southeast and adjacent areas. There is evidence of overseas cultural connections with the Antilles; however, the dominant thrust of this diffusion seems to have been from the mainland to the islands. Such individual culture traits as the cane blowgun, double-weave basketry, fibre-tempered pottery, and miscellaneous musical, ritual, and mythological details suggest at least limited contact with northern South America. More definite is prehistoric cultural contact with Meso-America. Not only did such basic cultivated plants as maize, beans, and squash ultimately derive from Meso-America, but numerous symbolic motifs in Southeast religious art have close analogues in ancient Mexico.

The picture of the Southeast that emerges at the time of first European contact is one of intensive cultural change. One senses a period of cultural levelling marked by considerable population movement, warfare, and the formation of confederacies, all of which was accompanied by large-scale technological and ideological diffusion. A distinctive Southeastern cultural tradition or style was in the process of being forged, but this fusion was far from complete on the eve of European contact.

The village or town

Social organization. *Settlement patterns.* The basic political unit for most Southeastern tribes was the local village or town. This basic unit varied in size and configuration depending on differences in local ecological potential and cultural preference. Some towns attained populations of over 1,000 individuals, but the more typical Southeastern village numbered less than 500 people. Settlement patterns conformed to two basic types: (1) dispersed hamlets, with households strung out for several miles, usually following valley bottoms or streams, and (2) tightly nucleated settlements often surrounded with protective timber palisades. The heart of the local town was a ceremonial centre consisting of a central council house or temple, which in the interior region might be semisubterranean or located on a pre-existing mound; a central plaza or square, which, among the Muskogean-speakers, was usually surrounded by three or four benches or arbours oriented in the cardinal directions; a ball pole or scalp post sometimes culminating in a carved animal emblem; the residences of the chief and other important local dignitaries; and sometimes storage structures for communal produce.

Considerable variation in house types existed. In much of the area, the Indians constructed circular, conical-roofed winter "hot houses," sealed tight, except for an entryway and smoke hole. Summer dwellings tended to be rectangular, gabled structures made from a framework of upright poles, lashed together and covered with lath, grass, cane matting, or bark and plastered with clay. To the south, housing tended to be more flimsy, with raised floors, palmetto thatched roofs, and, often, open sides. To the west, the Caddoans lived in domed "grass houses." A homestead might contain auxiliary storage buildings and a special cookhouse.

Each town or village was fairly autonomous. Superordinate control at the tribal level tended to be weakly developed, although pressure for tribal consolidation and even the formation of intertribal confederacies was greatly increased with the coming of Europeans. A village might be linked to other villages in the same area by ties of kinship, language, and shared cultural traditions; nevertheless, each village claimed sovereignty over its local area and was governed by its own chiefs and war leaders.

Chiefs and other leaders

Stratification. Over most of the Southeast, chieftainship tended to be hereditary within certain lineages. The degree of chiefly power and authority varied, however, from the almost divine kingship of the Great Sun among the theocratic Natchez to the self-effacing status of the peace-making, consensus-seeking *micos* and *ukus* among the more egalitarian Choctaws, Creeks, and Cherokees. War leaders normally achieved their positions on the basis of past accomplishment. War chiefs tended to be active and assertive personalities and younger, by about a generation, than the peace chiefs.

The alternation between peace and war or the occurrence of such competitive activities between alien groups as ball games, communal hunts, and trading expeditions helped to imbue much of Southeastern social structure with a characteristic dualism. The peace chief held sway in the domestic village, whereas the war chief was ascendant in areas external to the village, except when the village was under threat of imminent attack. Young men in the village alternately adjusted to roles appropriate to war and peace, often symbolically represented as red and white activities, and these transformations were usually effected through extensive ritual. This dualistic emphasis was also frequently expressed in the organization of clans, subtribes, and villages into complementary social divisions.

Social stratification was highly developed in some parts of the Southeast, while its significance in other subareas was minimal. Although much has been written about the supposed caste systems among the tribes of the Lower Mississippi, the Chitimacha appear to have been the only society to have possessed true castes in the sense of ranked groups that practiced strict endogamy (marriage within the group).

Social ranking among the Natchez

The elaborate rank system of the Natchez consisted of four groups: three upper classes, composed hierarchically of the suns, the nobles, and the honoured people, and a lower class of commoners (or stinkards, as they are referred to in the early French sources). Upper class individuals were required to marry into the lower class of commoners, and many commoners also married other commoners. Offspring of males in the upper classes would assume a rank one step below that of their fathers (thus, the child of a sun father and commoner mother would become a member of the noble class). The progeny of upper class females, however, would retain the rank of their mothers rather than descend to a lower station. The system, as described, would be unstable, since the supply of available commoner women would soon be depleted after several generations. Many explanations have been advanced to explain this so-called "Natchez paradox," but the difficulties probably reside in the inaccuracies or incompleteness of the original French sources.

Social stratification also was highly elaborated among the aboriginal inhabitants of Florida. Among the Timucua, for instance, the "king" enjoyed an elevated status considerably above that of his followers and was sometimes carried about in a litter. In many other Southeastern societies there was a trend toward the ranking of towns or clans. Member towns of the Creek Confederacy were sometimes ranked in terms of their tribal affiliations or on the basis of outcomes of inter-town ballgames. The Caddo were said to have ranked their clans on the basis of the reputed strength of the totemic animal ancestor in a kind of natural "pecking order." In other tribes, such as the Cherokee, stratification was only weakly developed, though certain clans might possess special ceremonial prerogatives and recruitment to certain offices might be determined on the basis of clan.

Kinship and marriage. In the Southeast, descent was almost universally reckoned in the female line, though not all societies possessed matrilineal clans. Clans, where they existed, were apparently not restricted to nor localized within specific villages. The resulting dispersal of clan members throughout a tribe or nation thus served as a kind of social adhesive binding together the larger body politic. Certain ceremonial knowledge and privileges might also be passed down along clan lines, and clans were also important as mechanisms of social control, since vengeance for serious crimes was frequently a clan responsibility.

Marital customs

Marriage was often marked by a symbolic ceremonial exchange whereby the groom presented his bride with game and the bride reciprocated with vegetable food. Because residence after marriage normally found the man moving into the wife's natal household, the husband was expected to contribute to the economic maintenance of his wife's family, as a form of bride service. After a few years the couple might leave to form their own household. Most Southeastern tribes permitted and some even encouraged pre-marital sexuality. After marriage, however, adultery—especially on the part of the wife—was often severely punished. Nevertheless, divorce seems to have been a frequent and, often, almost casual event. Polygamy was permitted in most groups, although a man usually had to gain the assent of his first wife before taking on a second spouse. The levirate, a custom by which a widow was remarried to her deceased husband's brother, was fairly common, particularly as male mortality increased during the wars of the European period.

Socialization. During a woman's late pregnancy, both she and the father were often subjected to various dietary taboos and restrictions on their activities. Children were nursed until they tired of the breast or until the mother again became pregnant. Responsibility for the child's early education was vested in the mother. Later, a young boy received instruction in male skills from his father and his mother's brother; in many systems the mother's brother, as the senior male in the matrilineage, assumed considerable importance as a disciplinarian, tutor, and sponsor for his sister's son. Young girls remained at their mother's side and were trained in various duties associated with the domestic household. Behaviour considered proper was reinforced with praise and encouragement, as when a boy killed his first deer or a young girl manufactured her first basket; behaviour considered improper might be greeted with mild rebuke, ridicule, or shame. Children were rarely subjected to physical punishment. In those few instances in which punishment was deemed necessary, it was generally meted out by someone other than the parents. A popular method of chastisement throughout the Southeast was raking the skin with briars or a special pointed scratching instrument, but, even here, such action was regarded as strengthening or toughening the youth, rather than as delivering direct retribution for misdeeds. Young boys enjoyed considerable permissiveness. They spent much time with their peers in wrestling, playing games imitative of adult activities, and stalking rabbits, squirrels, and birds with blowguns and scaled-down bows and arrows. The freedom and wide behavioral space permitted the young boy contrasted markedly with the restricted sphere, close surveillance, and early responsibility training that characterized the daily routine of his sister.

Rites of passage

Puberty rituals were either absent or only weakly developed in the Southeast. Girls were secluded during their first menstruation, but this event occasioned no public celebration. (Menstrual blood, though, was regarded as a potent and polluting substance, and women either absented themselves from the household during their periods or were subjected to restrictive taboos.) Similarly, no special rituals attended the transition from boyhood to manhood. A boy might receive instructions from tribal elders in esoteric lore or in preparation for special ritual offices, but graduation from such training seldom was marked by a formal commencement. A young man's first participation in a war party and the achievement of military honours were, however, given public recognition. Probably the clearest marker of the passage from adolescence to adulthood was marriage.

Economic systems. As already implied, the primary division of labour was by sex. Women were responsible for cultivating the fields, gathering wild-plant food, cooking and preserving food, rearing the young children, and manufacturing such basic domestic items as cordage, baskets, pottery, and clothing. Men assumed the primary roles of warriors and hunters, occupations that often took them away from the village for extended periods of time. Men also cleared the fields by girdling trees, assisted in the harvest, constructed houses and public buildings, and manufactured ceremonial objects and implements for personal use.

Except for the marginal groups on the western Gulf Coast, villages were semipermanent and located near rich alluvial soil or, in the Lower Mississippi region, near natural levees. Such land was easily tilled, possessed adequate drainage, and enjoyed enduring productivity. Fertility was enhanced by the custom of annually burning off the brush. The length of the growing season in most regions of the Southeast allowed multiple crops. Planting was done in spring, and some produce was available by mid-summer. The major harvest time, however, was late summer and early fall, a time of plenty when most of the major ceremonies were celebrated. Many villages became deserted, except for older people, during the winter months, when families took to the woods in search of game. Men also departed for a shorter hunt in late spring and early summer, after the crops had been planted.

Cultivation of maize

Principal foods and goods. The economic mainstay of the Southeast was maize, the cultivation of which was well established in most areas by the time of first European contact in the mid-16th century. Several varieties of maize were grown, including "little corn" (related to popcorn); flint, or hominy, corn; and flour, or dent, corn. Early corn was baked as roasting ears; later corn was pounded into hominy or cornmeal in wooden mortars made of large, upright, partly hollowed logs. Associated in the maize complex were varieties of beans and squash. Fields were prepared with mattocks and hoes and planted by punching holes in the ground with dibbles (digging sticks), inserting seed, and covering the holes with earth to form a small mound. Cornfields belonged to individual households, but among some tribes communal fields were also cultivated, with the produce going to the chiefs for support of the civil–religious hierarchy or for redistribution to the needy.

The importance of maize cultivation to the way of life of the southern Indians cannot be overemphasized. Not only did maize provide a high yield of nutritious food with a minimal expenditure of labour, but maize, beans, and squash could be easily dried and stored for later consumption. This reliable food base enabled men to spend much time away from their villages on hunting, trading, and war expeditions. It was not fortuitous that the standard war ration was parched corn.

Other important plants and animals

Secondary cultivated plants included the sunflower (processed for its oil), chenopodium or orache (spinach-like greens), and tobacco. Many additional plants, such as species of wild grapes, plums, and perhaps walnut and pecan trees, can be regarded as being in a condition of incipient domestication, since there is evidence to suggest that Indians exerted some effect on selection. Important wild-plant foods were various types of berries, nuts and acorns, wild potatoes and amaranths, smilax, zamia root, and maple sugar or honey locust sap. The economic botany of the Southeastern Indians can be expanded to encompass the vast array of plants utilized for cordage, clothing, dyes, fish poisons, medicines, building materials, and various tools and utensils. Perhaps mention should be made of the distinctive Southeastern use of two species of holly (*Ilex cassine* and *Ilex vomitoria*) as ingredients in a special decoction, the "black drink," to induce sweating and vomiting in ceremonial and medical contexts.

The only native domesticated animal in the Southeast was the dog, which was used to a minor extent in hunting and was probably more important as a sentinel to warn of the approach of strangers. In accounts of the Hernando De Soto expedition (1539–43), there are several references to small, fat, barkless dogs that were served to the Spanish visitors by their Indian hosts. Spanish trail hogs, brought by De Soto to feed his troops, became wild and were ancestral to the modern mongrel razorback hog. Horses were introduced later, mostly through the intermediacy of tribes to the west.

The aboriginal Southeast also teemed with wild game: deer, black bears, bison, elks, beavers, squirrels, rabbit, otters, and raccoon—some of which were used for their hides, bone, or fat as well as for food. In Florida, turtles and alligators played an important part in subsistence. Among birds, wild turkeys were the principal quarry, but partridges, quails, and seasonal flights of pigeons, ducks, and geese also contributed to the larder. The feathers of eagles, hawks, swans, and cranes were highly valued for ornamentation, and in some tribes a special status was reserved for an eagle hunter.

Both on the coast and on inland rivers, streams, and lakes, a wide variety of fish were taken in weirs, fish traps, and dip nets and dragnets and by hooks and lines, bows and arrows, and spears. In the interior, poison was administered in ponds and sluggish or dammed streams to gather a rich harvest of stunned fish. Coastal groups gathered oysters, clams, mussels, cockles, and crabs. Interior groups found freshwater mussels and crawfish.

Economic organization and ecology. In the well-endowed Southeastern area, each household group was fairly self-sufficient. The economic specializations and trade networks that did develop tended to centre on subsidiary and luxury items. Salt deposits were unequally distributed and formed one basis for trade. There also was regular trade between the coast and interior, with shells, which were used for beads, pendants, and horns, exchanged for soapstone, flint, furs, and other inland resources. The presence in the Southeast of artifacts made of imported copper and certain types of red clay suggests important trade connections with the western Great Lakes tribes.

Indians are popularly viewed as living in a primeval or virginal territory. Such was not the case in the Southeast. Indians maintained a delicate balance with their environment, and their presence was a vital link in a complex ecological chain. By tillage, controlled use of fire, and hunting, they altered the landscape significantly. Large areas of secondary re-growth favoured certain types of berry bushes and groundnuts. The presence of this secondary-growth flora was, in turn, essential for supporting large populations of browsing deer, squirrels, rabbit, and wild turkeys on which man depended for a large measure of his sustenance. In this process and in combination with hunting, the decline of other animals, such as the wood bison, was probably accelerated. In areas where intensive maize cultivation had already taken hold, such as in the Lower Mississippi, game animals had become scarce in historical time. In the central Southeast, however, the very diversity of plant and animal resources and the highly generalized adaptation of the Indian in exploiting these resources seems to have resulted in maintenance of an equilibrated balance between man and nature.

Belief systems. *World views.* The delicate man–nature relationship is well expressed in what is known of Southeastern religion and world view. The world was perceived as animated by a proliferation of ghosts, witches, and spiritual essences of animals, plants, and natural objects or phenomena. As can be inferred from the frequent elaboration of funerary practices, most groups professed belief in an afterlife. The location of the resting place for deceased souls was either in the direction of the western setting sun or up above in a celestial firmament. It was generally thought that the souls of the recently deceased would hover around the community and try to induce close friends and relatives to join them in their journey to eternity. The elaborate funerary rites and the extensive taboos associated with death were as much a protection for the living as a commemoration of the dead. Death was nowhere considered a natural event but always the result of malevolent animal spirits or witches or the deadly machinations of sorcerers. If death was thought to be caused by human agents, the soul of the deceased would never rest until vengeance had been secured by living relatives.

Death and afterlife

It was also believed that animals possessed souls. Slain animals sought vengeance against man through the agency of their species "chief," a mythological animal with great supernatural power. Hunting thus became a sacred act, much imbued with taboos, ritual, and sacrifice. Most disease was attributed to failure to placate the souls of slain animals.

The plant world was considered friendly to mankind, and the Cherokees thought that every animal-sent disease could be cured by a plant antidote. The economic significance of maize was memorialized by the near universality of the Green Corn, or Busk, ceremonies throughout the Southeast. This major ceremonial was suffused with an ethos of annual renewal in which the sacred fire was rekindled; old debts and grudges were forgotten; and a sense of community was regenerated.

Spiritual power might also reside in physical objects. Medicine men possessed sacred stones, quartz crystals, and other mystically endowed paraphernalia. Other objects were consecrated to symbolize the collective solidarity of the group. The Cherokees made use of a palanquin or litter within which were placed revered objects; the Tukabahchee Creeks possessed sacred embossed copper plates; the temples of several Lower Mississippi tribes contained an assortment of idols and icons. Natural objects could be infused with sacred power in a variety of ways: contact with thunder, as in lightning-struck wood; immersion in a rapidly flowing stream; exposure to the smoke of the sacred fire or of ritually prepared tobacco.

Mythology

Remnants of a formal theology can be reconstructed from early accounts of some of the stratified societies and of tribes who survived the immediate ravages of European contact. Most groups possessed origin myths, often involving a primal deluge into which prototypical beings from on high plunged to secure a portion of mud that magically expanded to create the Earth island. The subsequent course of mythological history is frequently related in terms of a cosmic struggle between good and bad culture heroes, one of whom bestows boons on mankind, the other serving as the source of the fatality and misfortune inherent in the human condition. Southeastern myths and folktales are populated by an incredible host of nature spirits, monsters, tricksters, giants, and little people.

Among many tribes, evidence survives that suggests belief in a supreme being, or master of breath. This ultimate divinity was frequently associated with the sun and its earthly aspect, fire. In addition, the world was viewed as divided into four quarters defined by the cardinal directions; each section had a presiding deity and appropriate colour symbolism. Concern with the remote supreme being seems to have rested more with the priesthood than with the everyday activities of the average man. The life of the latter was more intimately tied up with more proximal spiritual beings who were felt to intervene more directly into human affairs.

Priests and diviners. In some of the wealthier stratified societies, priests were given specialized training and became full-time religious practitioners responsible for the spiritual health of the community and assuming responsibilities for conducting the major collective religious rituals that punctuated the annual cycle.

Complementary to the priesthood were various individual magico-medical practitioners, such as sorcerers, conjurors, diviners, and medicine men, who were generally only part-time specialists and catered to individual needs and crises, especially the treatment of illness. Medical therapy was intricately enmeshed in the magical view of the world but might include such practical procedures as isolation, sweating, bathing, bloodletting, sucking, vomiting, and the internal and external application of herbal medicines.

MODERN DEVELOPMENTS

The complex history of the Southeastern Indians after contact with Europeans can be outlined here only briefly. The 16th century witnessed European exploration of the Southeast, though without permanent settlement. During the 17th century, settlement was begun on the coastal fringes, and the deerskin trade made the Indians increasingly dependent on whites for firearms, metal tools, and luxury items. By the 18th century the Southeastern Indians became counters in the struggle between France, Spain, England, and the nascent United States for control of North America. With the ascendance of the United States, the military threat of the Indians became gradually neutralized, and Indians ceded large tracts of their land in an attempt to placate the insatiable appetite of land-hungry frontiersmen and the ensuing waves of white settlers.

Removal to Indian Territory

A short-lived Indian renaissance occurred during the first third of the 19th century, when the major surviving Southeastern groups became known as the Five Civilized Tribes. Unabated pressure for Indian land continued, however, and federal policy eventually culminated in the 1830s in the removal of the Cherokees, Choctaws, Creeks, Chickasaws, and Seminoles to the Indian Territory west of the Mississippi. Allotment of tribal lands to individual Indians, which paved the way for Oklahoma statehood, began in the 1890s; some of the land was also opened to white homesteaders, held in trust by the federal government, or allotted to freed slaves. It was originally agreed that tribal governments would be dissolved in 1906, but they continue to exist in a limited form.

Most of the surviving Southeastern Indian population resides in Oklahoma. Although this population reflects a full spectrum of assimilation—from oil company executives to culturally conservative "full bloods"—the increasingly numerous segment of people occupying the culturally conservative end of the continuum exists in poverty. Small contingents of Cherokee, Seminole, and Choctaw who managed to escape the general removal of the 1830s live on tribal landholdings in their traditional homelands. In addition, several remnant groups, such as the Catawba, Lumbee, and Houma, remain in the Southeast, though much of their cultural distinctiveness has disappeared.

(R.D.Fo.)

MIDDLE AMERICAN PEOPLES AND CULTURES

The physical spine of Middle America is the broad mountain chain extending from the southern end of the Rockies to the northern tip of the Andes, with Middle America in the area from northern Mexico to Nicaragua. The mountain chain marks off the area into four major regions. The heartland of Middle America is the central valley of Mexico. A second region is the highlands along the southern Pacific slope of Mexico. Beyond the Isthmus of Tehuantepec are the southeastern highlands in the Mexican state of Chiapas and in Guatemala. The arid region in the northwest of Mexico is a fourth region.

Within these four major geophysical regions there is tremendous variety in ecology, climate, soil, and the possibilities of human life. The mountains crumple the face of the land into a multitude of valleys and microenvironments; the result is a mosaic of crops, peoples, and settlements about which it is difficult to generalize. The high valleys of central Mexico, Oaxaca, Jalisco, and Guatemala have been the most densely settled parts of Middle America. But the lower slopes of mountains near the seacoasts have also carried substantial populations. The steamy tropics of the Isthmus of Tehuantepec and the hot limestone thumb of Yucatán have also been heavily populated.

The Indians of Middle America live almost everywhere in the region. The basic requirement for human settlement is water. The major river systems and the high valley lakes have been the primary settlement sites since prehistoric times.

THE PEOPLE

The Indians of Middle America are all descended from Asiatic forebears who crossed the Bering Strait and moved southward. They tend, except in the Isthmus of Tehuantepec, to be small in stature (155–160 centimetres or a little over five feet on the average), with brown to coppery skin, straight black hair, and dark-brown eyes often set above high cheek bones, sometimes with epicanthic folds. The Maya facial features are particularly distinctive, being flatter than those of the other groups; the Maya also have more prominent noses, and a tendency to rounder heads. Mexico is basically a mixed (*mestizo*) nation; there has long been extensive interbreeding between Indians and non-Indians. In Guatemala there has been much less interbreeding. But the term "Indian" is not a biological designation so much as a social, cultural, economic, and linguistic summary of the differences between some rural ways of life and the dominant national culture. Race in and of itself is not socially as important as it is in other parts of the world. The usual census definition of "Indian" is based on linguistic criteria, and the population figures for Indians must therefore be read as figures for speakers of Indian languages.

Cultural areas. While the social heritage of Middle America is highly complex, within the broad historical flow five separate cultural areas can be distinguished. They are regional configurations of the basic Middle American cultural patterns. One cultural area is that of the Maya. The southern, highland Maya were and are concentrated in western Guatemala and the state of Chiapas in Mexico. The northern Maya inhabited the Yucatán Peninsula of Mexico and the jungle of Petén in Guatemala. The Maya of these two regions form a continuous territorial and historical entity. (There are also contemporary Maya people in Veracruz and San Luis Potosí in Mexico, known as the Huastec.) The monumental ruins left by the pre-Columbian Maya are one of the puzzles of anthropology; theirs is the only civilization known to have flourished in a tropical rain forest.

The Mayan cultural area

The southern Mexican highlands and the adjacent coastal regions form a second cultural area within the basic Middle American pattern. This region covers most of the present Mexican states of Guerrero and Oaxaca, the southeastern part of Veracruz, and parts of Puebla and Morelos. Its highland people developed the traditions of the Mixtec and Zapotec, whose ruins survive at Mitla and Monte Albán, whereas the coastal people seem to have been somewhat isolated from them.

A third cultural area is the central Mexican highlands, including the valleys of Puebla, Toluca, and Morelos, along with the eastern slopes of the Mesa Central and parts of the Balsas River Basin. This area was the centre of the Aztec Empire. Mexico City is built on the ruins of the Aztec capital of Tenochtitlán, and descendants of the Aztecs still live in the area.

The mountain chain around the high lake of Pátzcuaro, in present-day Michoacán, forms another cultural area. The relative isolation created by the mountains permitted the Tarascans to work out their own cultural variant. They reached a level of social and political organization comparable to that of the Aztec and the Maya.

A fifth cultural area is northwest Mexico. This region is not historically or culturally a single unit; it exhibits three major types of ecology and three major types of human adaptation. The high mountains provided possibilities for simple agriculture without irrigation, whereas the desert required settlements around valley bottoms dependent on floodwaters in the rainy season. In the west the abundant shellfish were the basis for a coastal culture. The historical forces at work in the northwest area were different from those in the four other cultural areas. The population was taken over by the Jesuits, who built mission communities. The relative isolation of the region following the collapse of Spanish power, together with the weakness of the succeeding Mexican governments, permitted the survival of a blend of Spanish–Indian culture.

Language groups. Hundreds of languages were spoken in Middle America. Some linguists have grouped them in a number of phyla, or superfamilies, each phylum being at the same classificatory level as, say, Indo-European. The Hokaltecan superfamily includes the Yuman family (four surviving languages, two extinct); the Serian family (one surviving language, four extinct); the Coahuiltecan family (four extinct languages); the Tequistlatecan family, with one living language; the Supanecan family (one surviving language, two extinct); and the Jicaquean family, with one living language. A second phylum, Uto-Aztecan, comprises the Piman family (four surviving languages, eight extinct); the Taracahitian family (two surviving languages, 39 extinct); and the Aztecoidan family (three surviving languages, 18 extinct).

Attempts have been made in the past to associate the large family of Mayan languages (about 27 living languages) with several other Meso-American Indian languages (the Mixe-Zoque and Totonacan families, primarily) as the Macro-Mayan or Macro-Penutian languages; the latter term supposes an association also between the Mayan languages and the Penutian phylum of North American Indian languages. These groupings are not generally accepted by modern linguists.

The Oto-Manguean phylum includes the Oto-Pamean family (six surviving languages, one extinct); the Chinantecan family (one living language); the Zapotecan family (two surviving languages, one of which, Zapotec, is so diversified that its many dialects constitute mutually unintelligible languages); the Mixtecan family (three living languages); the Popolocan family (four surviving languages, one extinct); the Chorotegan family (eight extinct languages); and the Amuzgo family (one living language).

In addition to the four phyla there are the Tarascan family of one living language; the Huavean family of one living language; and the Xinca-Lenca languages spoken in small enclaves in the southern part of the region. Finally, there are also 39 extinct languages that linguists have not been able to relate to each other or to any other (see LANGUAGES OF THE WORLD).

Characteristics of Indian cultures. This linguistic variety shows how diverse were the aboriginal cultures. Even though it is possible to generalize broadly about cultural resemblances or patterns, the actual cultural unit was local or regional. This is true despite the existence of larger political units, such as the Quiché of classical Guatemala, or the Aztec Empire. The broad characteristics of the Indians of Middle America may nevertheless be sketched in profile, with the caveat that the profile is everywhere varied by local circumstance. When the Spaniards conquered the Indians, they removed the indigenous ruling class and placed themselves at the apex of society. They also brought Roman Catholicism, horses, cattle, wheels, iron, and new forms of political and economic organization. The Indian culture of today is a blend of indigenous elements, the culture of the Spanish, and the historical precipitate of the 500 years since the conquest.

Middle American cultures exist in located, named communities, each of which has a physical centre housing the patron saint of the community. The basis of subsistence is maize (corn), cultivated in small plots; but there is a myriad of crafts and artisans, and communities tend to be economically specialized. The family is the basic social unit, each living in a separate structure. Males and females wear distinctive costumes; where they have adopted modern dress, it is chiefly among the men rather than the women. Men do the heavy agricultural tasks and women the domestic chores. Men are in charge of the indigenous cults; women are more prominent in the Catholic aspects of religion. There is little restriction on any economic activity, and no taboos hedge occupational choice; but modern economic organization is little developed. The marketplace is the focus of economic life.

Families are internally hierarchical, with males and elders dominating. Both the father's and the mother's kin are recognized in tracing relatives, but there is a patrilineal emphasis in the transmitting of names and of some real property. Marriages are arranged for sons and daughters by their elders, who negotiate among themselves through a series of fixed visits and gift exchanges. Often the groom must perform service for his in-laws; during this period he may reside with them, later to set up his own abode. Marriages are easily dissolved in the absence of children, and a man may have a succession of wives; when children arrive, however, they stabilize a marriage.

The community's political organization is housed in a central building, usually opening upon a plaza. The personnel of the political organization form a hierarchy, with its top members recognized as spokesmen or representatives of the Indian community by the national government. The political offices are closely interwoven with a similar hierarchy, whose personnel serve the local church and the religious brotherhoods (*cofradías*), and plan the annual festal cycle. The personnel of the two hierarchies tend to alternate their periods of service between the civil and the religious wings. All adult men serve in this civil–religious hierarchy; in small communities they eventually reach the top posts and retire to become respected elders (*principales*). The annual change of personnel is accompanied by ritual.

Community political organization

There are no social classes in the Indian communities, but there are considerable differences in prestige, wealth, and individual achievement. There is an age hierarchy, especially among males, largely based on previous public service in the civil–religious hierarchy.

In the life cycle of these Indians, the important events are baptism and marriage. There are no puberty rites; and death is accepted matter-of-factly, followed by a Catholic wake. The concepts of sickness and disease are various. Illness is often thought to be caused by invasions of wind (*aires*) into the body or by disturbed emotional states, or it is thought to be most likely to strike during certain periods. Foods and natural substances are thought to be hot and cold, strong and weak; these conceptions are used both in diagnosis and in curing. Those who cure are specialists or semispecialists, frequently believed to perform witchcraft or other noxious magic.

In the realm of the sacred there are a large number of supernatural beings and places. The deities are arranged in a vague hierarchy, sometimes with the Christian God at the apex. Christian saints are the chief focus of worship, but with them are associated various pagan attributes and forces, including the natural forces of wind, rain, and lightning. Some saints have strong cults, their effigies being housed in a cult house or special temple and cared for on a daily basis. Liquor is consumed during sacred ceremonies and in that context is itself sacred.

The annual cycle is regulated by the European calendar. There is a series of religiously derived festivals, the chief of which are All Saints' Day, All Souls' Day, Easter week, and the Day of the Cross (in September). At least 82 different Indian communities still use the old pre-Conquest calendars in some agricultural rituals and for purposes of divination.

The prevalence of animism

The world view is animistic in the sense that the Indians see the world as peopled by spirits, souls, ghosts, and witches capable of inflicting harm if the proper ritual precautions are not taken. Omens, dreams, and talismans are of great importance. People are also believed to transform themselves into animals and mystically eat the life from a victim. Some communities execute witches. In religious practice, ritual conformity is more important than inner piety; if a person does not hold a ritual office, he engages in very little daily religious activity.

Slander, gossip, and envy are strongly condemned, although they are an important means of influencing social behaviour. In general, however, the rule of law, as expressed in the formal organization of the civil–religious hierarchy, is much more important than personal leadership. Great ambition is discouraged, but industry and diligence are much lauded.

This generalized profile of Middle American cultures fits most closely the areas of the former high cultures—the Aztec, Maya, Zapotec, Tarascan, and Mixtec areas. It needs modification for the northwest culture area, where the communities have less economic specialization and interdependence. It also does not fit some coastal Indians who have become part of the export economy, such as the vanilla-growing Totonac of Veracruz, or the Indians who work on the sisal plantations of Yucatán, where many approach the status of a rural proletariat.

THE PREHISTORIC PERIOD

The earliest inhabitants

More than 10,000 years ago, the Middle American Indians were hunters who roamed the country in bands of four to ten persons. Their quarry were mammoths, llamas, bison, and wild horses, as can be seen from the remains found at Tequixquiac, north of the central valley of Mexico. Some also hunted small game and gathered the seeds of wild plants. The seed gatherers and the big-game hunters coexisted for thousands of years, until a climatic shift around 7500 BC favoured the seed gatherers.

About 4500 BC, cultivated squash and gourds became part of the subsistence of the Indians, and they adopted a seasonal nomadic pattern. Around 3500 BC the basic crops were domesticated: maize, beans, and squash have been found in remains at Tehuacán. The Neolithic Period was beginning. By 2500 BC farming supplied about 10 percent of the food intake of the people, and by 2000 BC the first permanent settlements based on farming had been established, apparently villages of fewer than 100 persons. After 2000 BC farming became of major importance, and in the main areas the people were fully sedentary. They now produced forms of pottery.

From 1500 BC to the beginning of the Christian Era (often called the Formative period), the basic techniques of intensive agriculture were worked out, the full range of cultivated plants was developed, the pottery and art styles were formed, and the transition from small villages to ceremonial towns of 5,000 inhabitants was completed. The archaeological evidence of this may be seen in the central valley of Mexico at El Arbolillo, Zacatenco, Tlatilco, and, finally, Ticoman. The same developmental sequence occurred in the Formative period of highland Guatemala, as shown in the excavations at Kaminaljuyú near Guatemala City.

From the beginning of the Christian Era to about AD 1000 the cultures of Middle America passed through their Classic, or Florescent, period. In the Pyramids at Teotihuacán and at Cholula, in the Oaxaca valley at Monte Albán, in the ruins at Tikal and Uaxactún in Petén, and at Copán and Piedras Negras, there is monumental testimony to the rise of theocratic civilizations. The differentiation between the earthbound peasants and the class of priests is marked by the spread of the hieratic art called by archaeologists the Olmec style, the greatest example being at La Venta in Tabasco, Mexico. Olmec art made much use of carved jade and the symbol of the jaguar. In the symbolic vocabulary of Middle America, the jaguar is associated with Tlaloc, the god of rain and fertility, and therefore represents the forces of nature that make the crops grow. Tlaloc also dwells in caves from which lightning is thought to come; caves mean towns and settlements, so the jaguar probably represents the control of society as well as of nature. Jaguars are carved on axes, pots, and human likenesses; men wear jaguar skins; and human faces are depicted with jaguar-like mouths.

Mayan theocratic societies

This symbolism fitted well the new theocratic societies of the Maya—the Nahuatl, the Zapotec, and the Mixtec. Large raised pyramids were built for the public enactment of religious rites by the ruling priestly class. These structures were ceremonial centres where priests and specialists lived, and where the populace assembled for periodic rituals. The priests were important in the agricultural cycle, for which the ancient calendars were first devised. These calendars evolved into precise instruments for the measurement of time and came to express the philosophical ideas of the priestly intellectuals. The full poetry of Middle American calendrics is expressed in the Maya calendar "long counts," for which stone pillars were erected.

The ceremonial centres of the Classic period produced many luxury items made from imported goods such as seashells, feathers, obsidian, fine flint, jade, cotton, and cocoa beans. The centres paid for these imports by exporting finished ceremonial objects to the peripheries. The economy of the city-states of this period depended on the intensive cultivation of maize and on huge drafts of peasant labour for the building of the temple complexes. The building was done with a rather simple technology for beasts of burden, a functional wheel, and metal tools were lacking. The major achievements of the Classic period were its calendrics and its religious thought, which represented the efforts of the priestly class to systematize the universe and make it predictable.

Around the end of the Classic period a warrior group came into power. With the coming of the warriors a period of militarism began. War gods replaced the rain gods, and the jaguar symbolism gave way to the eagle complex in iconography. Human sacrifice, an occasional thing in the Classic period, became a mass phenomenon under the warlords of the Toltec and Aztec empires. The Toltecs, and later the Aztecs, were expansionist. When the Spaniards arrived, the Aztec Empire extended over most of Middle America, from the central valley to Yucatán, with garrisons, frontier fortifications, and foreign colonies. With the fall of the Aztec capital in 1519, the Guatemala conquest of 1524, and the long-drawn-out battles with the Indians of the northwest region, the Spaniards ended the isolation of Middle America.

EVOLUTION OF CONTEMPORARY CULTURES

The Conquest and its effects. The Spaniards overthrew the urbanized, class-structured high civilization of the

Aztecs and established a system of alliances with the tributary states. The conquerors decapitated native society, substituting the Spanish for the Indian nobility. They introduced a host of new agricultural techniques and crops, along with steel, horses and cattle, mines, European crafts, and new forms of social organization. They also created dichotomies between ethnic and racial groups, giving them different rights and obligations.

From the colonial period to independence

In the early colonial period following the conquest, a small minority of Spaniards administered and controlled vast Indian populations. The religion of the conquerors spread rapidly, as did many of their domesticated plants and animals. In this period the Indians were grouped into villages modelled on the grid plan, with a central plaza on which stood the church and town hall. The basic economic institutions were the encomienda and the religious reservation: the encomienda was an allotment of land and labour to a Spanish overlord, used in the densely peopled areas of the former high civilizations; the religious reservation was established by the Jesuits in the northwest.

The later colonial period saw the abolition of the encomienda and the secularization of the religious reservation. Where previously the upper strata of the Indian population had intermarried with the Spanish, the later colonial period brought a more rigid separation of the Spanish and the Indians. Although the encomienda was legally dead, its economic consequences persisted: the colonial-plantation economy developed, along with the cattle ranch and the mining complex. Indian lands were taken over at an increasing rate, and the Indians gave up whatever illusion they may have had as to the benefits to be gained from the white man's culture.

Mexico and Guatemala became independent of Spain in 1821. The early republican period involved the Indians only marginally. As the native Spanish and mestizos threw off European domination with the slogans and banners of the French Revolution, they neither considered the Indians nor involved them in their struggles. For the Indians it was a time of cultural and social consolidation, spent in the building of defenses against land encroachment and in the erection of communication barriers to protect their cultural heritage.

The later republican period was for Mexico and Guatemala a time of nation building, of moderate industrialization, and of commercial agriculture. The Indian was seen as anachronistic, an obstacle to the march of triumphant nationalism. For the Indian, the consequences were drastic. The national and international economy led him to develop a social structure and cultural pattern that would keep the Indian community intact, even at a low economic level. The strong corporate Indian community reached its most definitive form under the pressures of land-grabbing and anti-Indian social policies.

The 20th century. In the Mexican revolution that began in 1910, the Indians won a place in the political structure. The official policy became pro-Indian. This policy exalts the Indian heritage and makes it the root of the national heritage. In its economic and political aspects it aims at "incorporation" of the Indian into national society on terms set by the Indians themselves. It also provides special services to Indians, as demonstrated in the many programs of the Instituto Nacional Indigenista de Mexico in health, road building, agriculture, and literacy. It employs themes from Indian culture, as in the murals of the Mexican neo-Realists and the music of modern Mexican composers. In Guatemala a similar policy had a brief vogue, but it was reversed following the counterrevolution of 1954.

But the forces shaping contemporary Indian life lie largely outside these official policies. Population increase, the expansion of physical and cultural communication, industrialization, urbanization, and the power struggle between factions of the left and right are the basic forces that influence the lives of the Indians of Middle America.

(Ma.N.)

North Mexican Indian cultures

The generally accepted ethnographic definition of northern Mexico includes that portion of the country roughly north of a convex line extending from the Río Grande de Santiago on the Pacific coast to the Río Soto la Marina on the Gulf of Mexico. This southern boundary coincides in a general way with the northern margins of pre-Columbian Meso-America. Northern Mexico is more arid and less favourable for human habitation than central Mexico, and its native Indian peoples have always been fewer in numbers and far simpler in culture than those of Meso-America. Today, the native peoples are extinct over all of northeastern Mexico; the only Indians present in that area are a group of Kickapoo who immigrated to Coahuila from the United States in the 19th century. In the west the Sierra Madre Occidental, a region of high plateaus that break off toward the Pacific into a series of rugged *barrancas,* or gorges, has served as a refuge area for the Indian groups of the northwest, as have the deserts of Sonora. At present only the northwestern states of Baja California, Sonora, Sinaloa, Nayarit, Jalisco, Chihuahua, and Durango have Indian populations.

Although accurate population data is lacking in parts of this region, estimates place the total population that is still Indian in language and culture at approximately 130,000, a tiny minority among the several million non-Indians of northwest Mexico.

The people

Surviving Indian peoples of northern Mexico today fall easily into two divisions. By far the greater number are members of the first type, the ten groups which speak some language of the Uto-Aztecan linguistic stock and are traditionally agriculturists. The second type is now reduced to four groups—the descendants of nomadic bands who resided in Baja California and coastal Sonora and lived by hunting and gathering wild foods. The second type spoke various languages not related to Uto-Aztecan.

Uto-Aztecan peoples of northern Mexico have been divided into three branches—Taracahitian, Piman, and Aztecoidan. The Taracahitian branch consists of the Tarahumara of the southwestern Chihuahua; the Varohío, a small group which borders the Tarahumara on the northwest and are closely related to them; the Yaqui, in the Río Yaqui valley of Sonora and in scattered colonies in towns of that state and in Arizona; and finally the Mayo of southern Sonora and northern Sinaloa. Another Taracahitian group, the once prominent Opata, have lost their own language and no longer maintain a separate identity. The Piman branch consists of three groups: the Pima Bajo of the Sierra Madre border of Sonora–Chihuahua; the Papago of northwest Sonora, identical with a much larger portion of the same tribe in Arizona; and the Tepehuán, one enclave of which is located in southern Chihuahua and another in the sierras of southern Durango and Nayarit. The third branch of Uto-Aztecan is the Aztecoidan family, including the Cora located on the plateau and gorges of the Sierra Madre of Nayarit and the Huichol in similar country of northern Jalisco and Nayarit. A final member of this branch, locally called the Mexicanero, includes speakers of Nahuatl, remnants of central Mexican Indians introduced into the area by the Spaniards. The Mexicanero number only a few hundred and live in the mountains of Nayarit and southern Durango.

Baja Californian and coastal Sonoran peoples

The remnants of the Baja California Indians—the Tipai (Diegueño), Akwa'ala (Paipai), and Kiliwa—live in ranch clusters and other tiny settlements in the mountains near the American border. Speaking Yuman languages of Hokan stock, they are little different today from their relatives in American California. A small number of Cocopa in the Colorado Delta in like manner represent a southward extension of Colorado River Yumans from the American Southwest. The remaining Seri are found along the desert coast of north central Sonora. This famous group also speaks a language of Hokan origin and is probably related to now extinct peoples who lived across the gulf in Baja California two hundred years ago.

Missions and isolation helped to preserve the several surviving Indian groups of northwest Mexico through the colonial period (1530–1810), but all underwent considerable alteration under the influence of European patterns. Nearly all the agricultural tribes adopted some form of Roman Catholicism and much Spanish material culture. It was at this time that the traditional cultures of northern

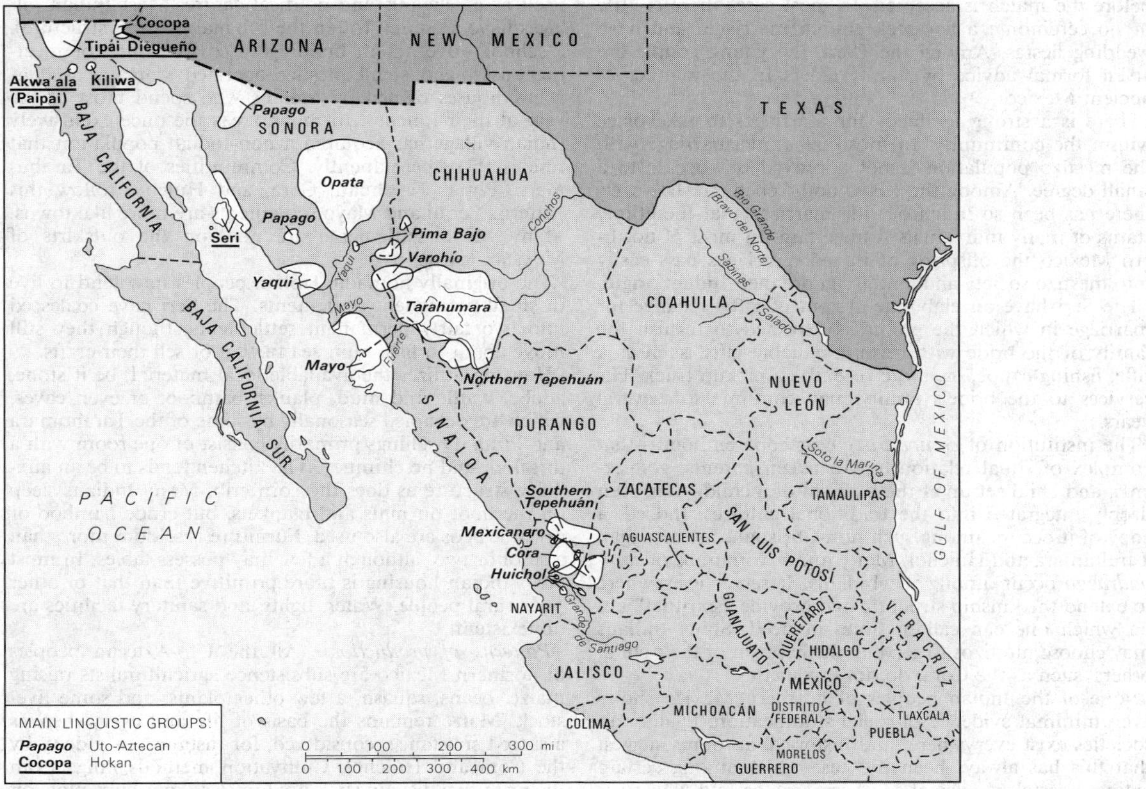

Distribution of north Mexican Indians.

Mexico were formed, the basic patterns continuing until the present. Many groups faded away—gradually losing their languages and identities in the emerging mestizo, or mixed-blooded European and Indian population, the predominant people of present-day Mexico. Only the Huichol, Seri, and Tarahumara remained primarily aboriginal cultures, but even these groups adopted many items and ideas from the Spanish invaders.

Today, all these peoples exist as ethnic enclaves surrounded by, and in most cases sharing their lands with, non-Indians and manifesting some of the characteristics of ethnic minorities everywhere. There is competition for lands with mestizo ranchers and, in most groups, a conscious desire for survival as distinct cultural entities.

TRADITIONAL CULTURE PATTERNS

Basic orientation in life

Although in some aspects of culture the Indian groups share much with other rural Mexicans, psychologically they tend to be very distinct. The basic orientation of life of the traditional Indian cultures is primarily religious in that they look to the supernatural to solve their problems and tend to see their own lives as requiring continuous service to the deities. This is in strong contrast to the practical and materialistic orientation of other northern Mexicans. The average Uto-Aztecan Indian in this area is reserved toward outsiders, especially non-Indians, and prefers not to be too much in evidence. The ideal person is industrious, carries out his religious obligations, and does not seek change in his traditional lifeways. In contrast, the Seri and Yuman groups, being of another tradition, are less inclined to secrecy and more aggressive toward outsiders.

Social structures. The social structure of the Uto-Aztecan peoples of northwest Mexico are variations of one basic type, while those of the Seri and Baja California remnants follow other forms.

The Uto-Aztecan agriculturalists of modern times possess only two real social units, the family and the Indian village community. No real tribal organizations exist, and only among the Cora and Yaqui are there strong feelings of tribal solidarity. For all these peoples the community is the society, and there is little movement in or out—or even interaction with other communities of the same "tribe."

The typical Indian community

The traditional Indian community is largely the result of colonial missionary efforts to concentrate the scattered rancherias, or hamlets, of aboriginal times into Spanish-type villages in which the natives could be more easily administrated. Usually furnished with land grants, these communities survived the close of the mission period and remained viable social units. The modern Indian community is built around a political and religious structure having its origin in the village organization set up by early missionaries to carry out church fiestas. It consists of a series of *cargos,* or civil and religious offices, in which most males of the village participate, the higher offices being achieved with age and experience. Some version of this structure or copy of it is or was present among all these groups. Today, among most groups it is still the backbone of the community, serving to produce the village fiestas as well as settle disputes among the people. While serious crimes or major issues are now handled by the Mexican government, in most situations the Indian *gobernador* (governor) and elders are consulted as well.

Kinship patterns. The family is of one type for all the agricultural peoples. Kinship is based largely on descent from both parents, though with some orientation toward the authority of the father. The judgment of the elder males is highly respected, and in most groups the advice and permission of family elders is sought on all important occasions—to produce a ceremony, sell a cow, contract a marriage. Everywhere, however, the role of women is more nearly equal to that of men than is the case among the heavily male-dominated rural mestizo families. Needless to say, there is little of the famous Mexican *machismo* (cult of the male) among the aboriginal peoples of northern Mexico. The normal system of Spanish Christian and family names is present in all these groups.

Marriage customs

Marriage is primarily monogamous, though some informal polygyny occurs. Polygyny is most common among the Huichol (constituting about 5 percent of the marriages), which suggests that it was more common in northern Mexico in aboriginal times. Marriage tends to be brittle, and many unions are not permanent. Parents commonly arrange a match, though the custom is not uniform over the area. Among the Cora and Huichol, the boy's parents must make a series of ritual requests before the match is accepted. In most cases there is little or no ceremony; a few seek church marriages and have wedding fiestas. Among the Cora, the young couple are given formal advice by family elders in the manner of ancient Mexico.

There is a strong tendency for marriages to take place within the community. In most areas intermarriage with the mestizo population is not approved but occurs to a small degree. Among the Mayo and Tepehuán, however, there has been so much outside marriage that the ethnic status of many individuals is uncertain. In most of northern Mexico the offspring of mixed marriages pass easily into mestizo society and tend to ignore their Indian origin.

The Seri have an elaborate system of gift exchange for marriage in which the groom is expected to furnish the family of the bride with certain valuable gifts, such as a rifle, fishing canoe, or, more recently, a pickup truck. His services to the bride's family may continue for several years.

The institution of *compadrazgo,* or coparenthood—that complex of ritual relationships between parents, godparents, and child set up at the baptism of a child—has been deeply integrated into the traditional cultures. Indeed, a copy of it occurs among such non-Christians as the pagan Tarahumara and Huichol. Many minor variations of *compadrazgo* occur among the Indians. It serves everywhere to extend the kinship structure and provide "spiritual" kin on which one can call in times of need. Some Indians may choose mestizos to serve at the baptism of their child; others, such as the Cora, do not favour this.

Egalitarianism

None of the Indian peoples of northern Mexico shows even minimal evidence of social stratification. Egalitarian societies exist everywhere, and historical accounts suggest that this has always been the case. Only among certain extinct coastal peoples of southern Sinaloa and Nayarit is there found some mention of stratification on the Meso-American pattern. Prestige accrues to wealth and ceremonial knowledge, but this seldom passes to the children.

Socialization and education. Socialization and native education follow traditional patterns. A child is given little formal training, but is often admonished by his elders as to proper behaviour. Training in household tasks for the girls and men's work for the boys is through observation and gradually increasing participation until the techniques of maintaining oneself and family are mastered. Both boys and girls are expected to contribute their work as soon as possible. At an early age, children haul water, gather wood, or herd sheep. Small Seri boys spear crabs with miniature turtle harpoons as training for their adult pursuit of the sea turtle. Among the farming peoples all ages take part in the work during critical periods, such as periods of weeding and harvesting.

Rites of passage survive for children among several of the least Hispanicized groups. Cora, Huichol, and Tepehuán have rites in which a newborn is introduced to the gods. The Cora have a ceremony in which children are symbolically introduced to the use of alcoholic drinks.

Today, all Mexican Indian groups have access to schools, usually federal rural schools, and most attend to some degree, though the remote areas in which most Indians live and their lack of interest in education designed for the mestizo world does not make for the most effective program. In some areas native Indians have been trained as teachers with somewhat better results. The Kickapoo have steadfastly refused schools, seeing in them a strong threat to their cherished way of life.

Economic systems. *Settlement patterns and housing.* The aboriginal settlement pattern of the agricultural Indians centred on the rancheria, which consisted of a number of household units clustered in spots convenient to cultivation sites or water. When colonial missionaries incorporated these into larger villages, the lowland peoples, such as the Yaqui, Mayo, and Opata, accepted this arrangement. They continue to live in concentrated settlements today. In the Sierra Madre, subsistence patterns did not lend themselves to such towns, and the Indians returned to their rancherias when the missionaries withdrew.

Villages and rancherias

As a result, all contemporary Indians of the mountain regions live in scattered ranch clusters using the village itself as a religious and political centre. Most Indian villages have a church (often the original mission structure), a school, government buildings used for courts or meetinghouses, and small mestizo-operated stores as well as a few houses owned by Indians who spend most of the year at their ranches. In many areas the once exclusively Indian village has acquired a non-Indian population that resides there permanently. Communities of the Tarahumara, Pima, Tepehuán, Cora, and Huichol follow this pattern. Yaqui and Mayo settlements are more like towns. Many Mayo settlements are now on the outskirts of Mexican towns.

The originally nomadic Hokan peoples now tend to live in small permanent settlements. The Seri have coalesced into two fairly permanent settlements, though they still move about to fish, hunt sea turtles, or sell their crafts.

Housing utilizes the available local material, be it stone, adobe, wattle and mud, planks, bamboo, or even caves, which are occupied seasonally by some of the Tarahumara and Pima. Dwellings primarily consist of one room with a dirt floor and no chimney. The kitchen tends to be an auxiliary structure as does the corn crib. Many Indians sleep on the floor on mats and blankets, but crude bamboo or rawhide beds are also used. Furniture is seldom more than a stool or two, although a few may possess tables. In most areas Indian housing is more primitive than that of other poor rural people. Water, lights, and sanitary facilities are nonexistent.

Subsistence agriculture

Patterns of production. All the Uto-Aztecan peoples of northern Mexico are subsistence agriculturalists raising maize, beans, squash, a few other plants, and some livestock. Maize remains the basis of life and everywhere is a sacred substance, considered, for instance, as a deity by the Cora and Huichol. Cultivation methods range from the primitive digging stick used in slash-and-burn plots on hillsides and ox-plow agriculture in level fields, to some mechanized agriculture among the Yaqui. Characteristically, farm technology is primitive and of low yield. Few of the Indians have any considerable amount of good productive land, and there is competition with mestizos for even the poor mountainside plots of the Sierra Madre Occidental. The corn supply seldom lasts out the year, and in many areas it is significantly supplemented by gathering wild plants, cactus fruits, wild greens, maguey, and the usually abundant seedpods of mesquite, guamuchil, and other treelike legumes. The cash needed for outside items comes from the occasional sale of a young bull or from sporadic wage work in which many Indians engage. Deer and other game once abundant both in the sierra and in the desert are now rare. All the Uto-Aztecan tribes still hunt, but scarcity of game makes hunting relatively unimportant. The rivers yield a few fish and crayfish, which are much esteemed. Among the Seri, hunting of deer and sea turtles as well as fishing is still common but, even so, is of decreasing importance.

Wage labour

For centuries individuals from all these groups have worked for wages first in Spanish and then in Mexican mines and fields. The great silver mines at Hidalgo del Parral, Chihuahua, in colonial times made use of Tarahumara, Pima, Opata, and Yaqui labour. Yaqui and Mayo have long laboured on ranches and railroads and in mines away from their own country, even in the United States. Today, wage work is a factor in every Indian community in northern Mexico with some members of every group working for wages in the new agricultural areas of the Mexican west coast. The typical pattern is for young men or whole families to go to the coast for a few weeks to pick cotton or harvest corn or tobacco, returning to their own homesteads to plant and care for their maize. Some Tarahumara and Tepehuán work in lumber camps. No matter how important wages are as supplementary income, these peoples all prefer their own agriculture in their own communities, and few are drawn away permanently. It is rare indeed for sierra Indians to live and work in cities. This is not as true for the Yaqui, who have permanent settlements in several large Sonora towns.

About 1930 the Seri adopted commercial fishing and developed a mixed economy that included traditional hunting and gathering. Since 1965, however, a new industry has grown up in which the Indians have learned to carve animal figurines from the dense wood of the palo fierro, a desert tree. A large number of Seri families turned to production of the figurines for sale to tourists and appeared to be abandoning gathering and fishing as primary means of livelihood.

Property and personal customs. The Indian market system of central Mexico does not exist in northern Mexico. All Indian areas are served by small rural stores almost entirely owned by non-Indians. Here the few but important necessities such as cloth, metal tools, soap, salt, tin cups, and matches are purchased. Money, in use everywhere, is completely a part of modern Indian culture.

Clothing and grooming

Clothing combines the older styles of rural Mexico with modern lower class dress. Only the Tarahumara, some communities of whom still wear a type of loincloth, and the Huichol, with a colourful embroidered costume, have retained forms that stand out as distinct. Some, like the Cora and Tepehuán men, favour the pajama-like muslin garments of two generations ago and today consider them Indian dress. All others wear modern clothing with few reminders of earlier attire. Huaraches (sandals) are generally worn, as are homemade or commercial hats, usually made of palm; people near the United States border, however, prefer modern shoes and cowboy hats. Women's dress throughout tends toward a skirt and blouse with a rebozo, or head scarf.

Long hair is worn by males in some Tarahumara and Huichol communities and by many adult Seri. Elsewhere, short hair is the custom. Women wear the hair loose or, among the more Mexicanized, in braids.

Food is largely vegetable and consists of local varieties of the rural Mexican staples—tortillas, tamales, beans, and cheese. Indians, however, make much use of *atole* (corn mush) and pinole (ground parched corn) both of which were aboriginal favourites and are not as popular with the mestizos.

Crafts, nearly everywhere disappearing, are very largely limited to household necessities and are seldom made primarily for sale. Wool blankets are produced by the Mayo, Tarahumara, and Cora and woven shoulder bags by the Cora and Huichol. Utilitarian pottery and twilled containers and mats are still made in most groups, using native Indian techniques. The only objects produced for the tourist market are copies and elaborations of colourful ceremonial material by some Huichol and the figurines and shell beads produced by the Seri.

Other technology differs but little from that of other rural Mexicans of the northwest. Ranch tools and the paraphernalia used in handling livestock are identical. None of the sierra Indians possess automobiles. Some individuals in the other groups, including the Kickapoo, have acquired motor vehicles.

Religion. The northern Mexican tribes, like all Mexican Indians, have had contact with Christian missionaries for centuries, and all the agricultural Indians of northern Mexico are nominal Roman Catholics except for a few communities of pagan Tarahumaras, called "gentiles," and the majority of the Huichol. Even pagan groups, however, have incorporated Christian ideas and ritual practices. It can be generally stated that all the Uto-Aztecan speakers of northern Mexico today practice some form of Roman Catholicism blended with native religion. The extent of aboriginal retentions varies from group to group, with the Huichol approximating pre-Columbian patterns to the greatest degree, keeping their gods, pilgrimages to sacred places, and native religious concepts almost intact. Others like the Cora have fused these, retaining native gods but equating them with Christian personages. The Yaqui and Mayo, both with a strong religious orientation to their culture, have an even more homogenous mixture. It is doubtful, though, whether any of the groups have absorbed Christian philosophy or belief systems to any great degree. Religion retains its aboriginal functions of protecting one's health, bringing the rains, and insuring the abundance of agriculture, rather than as a means to a glorious afterlife.

Blend of Roman Catholicism and native religion

The relationship of many of these peoples to the modern Roman Catholic Church is tenuous. Modern priests tend to discourage folk observances such as the fiestas; the Indians, by and large, produce them without help of a priest. In the southern Sierra Madre, among the Cora, Huichol, and Tepehuán, there are modern Franciscan missionaries, while in the Tarahumara area there are Jesuits. Among all the Uto-Aztecans, religion remains central to the traditional culture, and it is an area in which there is great resistance to outside pressure for change.

Protestants have been active among the Seri and Yumans, achieving their greatest success with the Seri, who in the 1950s were all converted by an evangelical sect and largely abandoned their non-Christian practices. The Kickapoo, though also contacted by Protestants, remain, for the most part, followers of their aboriginal religion.

Shamans, or *curanderos*

The shaman, or medicine man, still exists in most of these groups. Called a *curandero* in Spanish, he uses supernatural means to cure illnesses, to insure the success of crops, or to assist in other situations requiring divine aid. He is very distinct from the mestizo *curandero,* who utilizes European folk medicine. Huichol medicine men, or *marakame,* are especially famous among the tribes of the Sierra Madre for their knowledge and power. Belief in witchcraft still exists among all these peoples. A shaman himself may be accused of being a witch.

MODERN DEVELOPMENTS

The traditional Indian cultures of northern Mexico that emerged from the Spanish colonial world remained remarkably stable throughout the 19th century. Combinations of isolation, poverty, and conservatism resulted in what were essentially static societies. There were sporadically some uprisings, but it was not until the Mexican Revolution of 1911 and after that most Indian cultures were significantly affected by changes taking place elsewhere in Mexico. All these peoples took part in the revolutionary conflicts, and some disorganization took place everywhere. Thousands of individual Indians followed the armies, many never to return. The aftermath of the revolution marked the beginning of governmental concern with the Indians. The Instituto Nacional Indigenista was established and took upon itself the task of raising living standards and gradually integrating the Indians into the national life. Some groups benefitted significantly by the revolution and its results. Many Yaqui and Mayo escaped from hacienda peonage, and the Yaqui had a large portion of their ancestral lands restored to them.

Developments since World War II

It has been only since World War II that real changes have been taking place in the cultures themselves. There are multiple reasons for increased pressures from the outside world, but the primary cause is simply the development of modern transportation and a corresponding loss of centuries-long isolation. A major factor has been the construction of dams in the rivers flowing out of the Sierra Madre and the development of major irrigation projects and large modern cities on the coastal plain. There is now greater interest in the resources of the mountain hinterlands on the part of non-Indians, and there are opportunities for the mountain and desert peoples to engage in migrant farm labour.

Opening of the Mexican west coast highway brought major changes in the whole area. The desert lands of the Papago, the Sonoran seacoast of the Seri, and the thorn forests of the Yaqui and Mayo were penetrated by paved roads. A railroad across the Sierra Madre from the city of Chihuahua to Los Mochis on the Pacific bisects the Tarahumara country, and roads have made numerous villages of this tribe accessible to truck traffic. Truck roads are approaching even the gorges of the Cora and the Huichol. Many parts of the Sierra Madre previously accessible only by animals or by foot are served by local airlines that fly small planes hauling freight and passengers to most of the mountain communities. It is a common sight at the airport in Tepic, Nayarit, to see rural mestizos, Cora, and Huichol Indians waiting to board a plane for airstrips near their remote homes. Although there are still vast areas in these mountain regions not reached by modern transportation, the outside world has become more accessible, and all of these peoples have been affected to some extent.

Development of modern transportation has greatly increased the possibility that many Indian communities in time will cease to exist. There is growing competition for lands in all areas as non-Indian cattlemen, lumbermen, and farmers exploit these regions more intensely. Almost everywhere Indians find themselves being pushed or crowded out of ancestral lands by more sophisticated forces who have use for their resources. The Instituto Nacional Indigenista has come to the aid of some, such as the Tarahumara and Huichol, and given them legal assistance in securing land titles. In most areas, though, Indians, having no legal knowledge and lacking sophisticated leadership, are severely handicapped in dealing with these problems. Without a land base it is doubtful that communally oriented societies such as these can long survive.

The basic strength of the Indian groups in the late 20th century is found in their village organization and associated ceremonial structures that effectively preserve ethnic boundaries. Those retaining the strongest organized communities—the Tarahumara, Yaqui, Cora, and Huichol—while threatened, appear to be in no immediate danger of cultural disintegration. Others, few in number (such as the Pima) or lacking well preserved independent village structures (such as the Mayo), appear less likely to survive the impact of modernization.

Fear of alienation of lands and ultimate loss of ethnic identity has led to avoidance of innovations in many cases. Most still continue to resist social and religious change and avoid too close contact with non-Indians. There is, it is true, less reluctance to adopt material objects. The spread of modern communications media, even to the depths of the Sierra Madre, has resulted, among other things, in the increased learning of Spanish. The cast-iron corn mill is now used to grind *masa* (tortilla dough), saving hours of kneeling at a *metate,* or millstone, grinding by hand. Pedal sewing machines and metal containers are common. Nevertheless, most northern Mexican Indians express concern that their lifeways are dying. They fear that loss of community lands and the cultural seduction of their youth will mean that their days as separate peoples are indeed numbered.

(T.B.H.)

Meso-American Indian cultures

Indigenous to Mexico and Central America (roughly between latitudes 14° N and 22° N), Meso-American Indian cultures had a common origin in the pre-Hispanic civilizations of the area. Most Meso-American peoples belong to one of three linguistic groups: the Macro-Mayan (or Mayan), the Oto-Manguean, or the Uto-Aztecan. Macro-Mayan peoples, with the exception of a northeastern enclave, the Huastecs, live at the southeastern extremity of Meso-America. Oto-Mangueans are to be found in a wide area of Meso-America between Uto-Aztecan peoples to the north and east and Mayan and other peoples to the south. Oto-Manguean languages (now extinct) were spoken south of the Mayan area along the Pacific coasts of El Salvador, Honduras, and Nicaragua; and one Oto-Manguean language, North Pame, spoken in the central desert of highland Mexico, is outside Meso-America to the north. The main branches of the Oto-Manguean family are Oto-Pamean, Amuzgoan, Popolocan, Chinantecan, Mixtecan, Zapotecan, Manguean, and perhaps Huave and Tlapanec. The Tlapanec and Chontal languages of Oaxaca, spoken on the Pacific coast of Mexico, are held by some scholars to be related to the Hokan Coahuiltecan (sometimes termed the Hokaltecan) languages farther north. As a result of the expansion of the Aztec Empire centred in the valley of Mexico, Uto-Aztecan enclaves are found throughout the area. Tarascan, a language the filiation of which is still in doubt, is spoken in the highlands of Michoacán, Mexico. (See also LANGUAGES OF THE WORLD.)

Main linguistic groups

TRADITIONAL CULTURE PATTERNS

Settlement patterns. The territorial unit that has prime importance for most Meso-American peoples is the *municipio,* a unit roughly corresponding to a county in Great Britain or the United States. Each *municipio* has a municipal centre where most civic, religious, and marketing activities take place. In the modern pattern, this centre is the largest settlement in the area. The usual elements, which vary according to the size and importance of the community, are laid out according to the standard pattern imposed by early Spanish administrators throughout New Spain: a plaza surrounded by public edifices (church or chapel, curacy, jail, perhaps a school, and a meeting place for civil authorities). Houses nearest the plaza are those of the principal persons. Larger communities are often divided into sociopolitical enclaves called barrios.

An older pattern, still found in some areas (as among some Mayan peoples of the south and among the Huichol of the north), is for the *municipio* centre to be an empty town, occupied continuously only by civil and religious authorities and perhaps a few merchants. The bulk of the population resides in hamlets or on individual farms most of the year, moving to town residences only for short periods either to transact business or to participate in a religious festival.

Social, political, and religious institutions. The basic social and economic unit of Meso-America is the extended family of from two to four generations. There is a strong tendency for the extended family to fragment into individual nuclear families, each consisting of one couple and their children. Kinship is reckoned bilaterally, no distinction being made between kinsmen related through males and those related through females. Such distinctions are made in a few Mayan and Zoque communities, and they are common immediately north of Meso-America. These and other facts have led some anthropologists to suggest that small preconquest communities were patrilineal clans or lineages. Named clans and lineages have actually been reported in a few present-day Tzeltal (Mayan) communities.

Throughout Meso-America generally, newly married couples tend to locate near the groom's family in a slight majority of cases. Inheritance also generally favours the male line, including family names, which are almost invariably inherited from males. Inherited names are now most commonly of Spanish origin, but native surnames are known among some Mayan groups. In certain Mixtec (Oto-Manguean) communities, a man's first name becomes the surname of his offspring.

Marriage, traditionally an alliance between two families, is initiated by the groom's parents and arranged by them directly or through the services of a go-between. A period of bride service by the groom, often involving at least temporary residence with the bride's family, is not uncommon. Polygyny is known and socially acceptable but is not common.

Political and religious institutions are traditionally bound together into a complex of hierarchically arranged year-long offices through which adult males may attain status and power in the community. All males must serve in the lower ranked offices at one time or another, but only the most successful attain the highest positions.

Progress through the ranks typically involves an alternation between civil and religious offices. Successful passage to the highest ranks results in election to the position of elder. Elders form a more or less informal group of senior men to whom the community looks for experienced guidance in policy matters and in times of crisis.

Meso-American religion, called Christo-pagan by anthropologists, is a complex syncretism of indigenous beliefs and the Christianity of early Roman Catholic missionaries. A hierarchy of indigenous supernatural beings (some benign, others not) have been reinterpreted as Christian deities and saints. Mountain and water spirits are appeased at special altars in sacred places by gift or animal sacrifice. Individuals have companion spirits in the form of animals or natural phenomena, such as lightning or shooting stars. Disease is associated with witchcraft or failure to appease malevolent spirits.

Economic institutions. The cultivation of Indian corn, as well as of a number of secondary crops, provides basic subsistence for all Meso-America. Secondary crops include the bean, the squash or pumpkin, the chili pepper for seasoning, and tomatoes of both cooking and eating varieties. Additional foods with a limited distribution because of differing climates and terrain are the pineapple, sweet

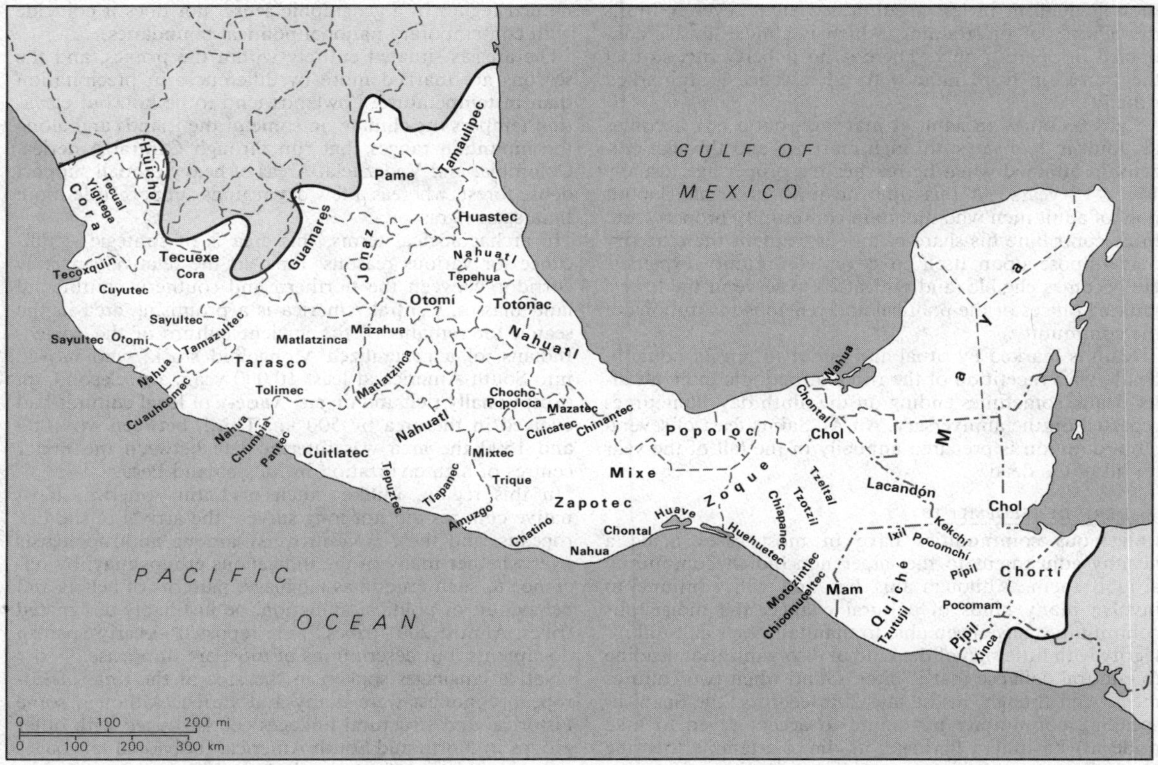

Distribution of Meso-American Indians.
From H. Driver *et al.*, *Indiana University Publications in Anthropology and Linguistics* (1953)

potato, cassava (manioc), chayote, vanilla, maguey, nopal, mesquite, cherimoya, papaya, and avocado. Pre-Hispanic commercial plants included cotton, tobacco, henequen for its fibre, and cocoa beans, which served as a medium of exchange. Important commercial crops that have been introduced since European contact include Old World cereals (wheat, barley, oats), bananas, coffee, sugarcane, sesame, and the peanut.

Agricultural methods

Traditional slash-and-burn agriculture persists in the most isolated areas, but plow agriculture has replaced it in many places. *Chinampa* agriculture is limited to the valley of Mexico: small artificial islands are built up about one foot above the level of shallow waters of a freshwater lake, formed from the mud and vegetation of the lake floor. After settling, this serves as a rich bed for mixed-crop rotation, nurseries, and seed plots.

All Meso-American communities are tied to national and international markets, but the extent of this relationship varies considerably. The Lacandón of the Chiapas lowland jungles bordering Guatemala lie at one extreme. If the machete, ax, rifle, matches, and similar items from the outside became unavailable to the Lacandón through some catastrophe, they, of all Meso-Americans, would have perhaps the least difficulty in adjusting to the challenge of their ecological situation. Living members of the community still retain personal knowledge of such traditional skills as working flint and stone and the making of fire, cloth, and pottery.

A larger segment of Indian populations is tied to the outside cash economy by one or more products, such as coffee, citrus, vanilla, livestock, or manufactured goods. Specialization is not the norm, but from pre-Hispanic times certain communities have developed products and skills that depend upon trade relations. An entire community may be known for its pottery, weaving, or basketry.

Markets are typically organized into a network in which each of several towns hosts the market in its central plaza, a different town each day of the week. The network may or may not include a central market that is held every day of the week. Such a market consists of a core of local merchants the ranks of which are swollen once a week by merchants from the outlying hamlets of the area. All of the merchants, whether from the central market or from outlying markets, tend to be organized in single household units.

Arts and crafts

Craft specializations that figure in marketing operations are also widely practiced to meet family needs only. Before the appearance of inexpensive commercial cloth, it was the norm throughout Meso-America for every young girl to learn to weave cotton cloth and, as a married woman, to provide clothing materials for her family. This skill is declining in the face of easy access to materials of cotton, wool, silk, and synthetic materials and blends. The introduction of the treadle loom by the Spaniards brought men into the weaving industry, especially as a commercial operation.

Both men and women are hat and basket weavers. Commercial products are produced from grasses, reeds, and palms, and lowland peoples also produce baskets of vine for local use.

A variety of pottery-making techniques is known in Meso-America. Before Hispanization, female potters made most ware, forming vessels by hand modelling, by building with coils, or by using a wooden paddle or molds. The Spaniards introduced the potter's wheel. Present-day techniques are a synthesis of indigenous and Spanish methods.

A lacquering art, now an integral part of the tourist trade, was practiced at the time of the conquest. A variety of gourd vessels of many sizes and shapes are artistically painted, using local materials and techniques. The beautifully decorated vessels serve a range of purposes, from simple utilitarian items, such as dippers, to elaborate ceremonial bowls.

The life cycle. Christian baptism is the first major event in the life of an individual. Indeed, among Chinantecs, a child is not considered fully human until the rite has been performed. If an unbaptized infant dies, the body is buried immediately without the usual ritual observances—ringing of the church bells, burning of incense, and reading and singing of prayers in the home, at the church, and at the graveside.

Formal education

Nursing may continue for as long as three or four years, and childhood is a period of little discipline except for the responsibility placed on older children to care for their younger siblings while the parents work. Formal schooling is now available in most areas for at least a few years, but monolingualism in less acculturated areas severely limits the efficacy of the training, which is almost always conducted in Spanish only. There is no puberty rite, so that the transition from infancy to adolescence is unmarked ritually.

A girl becomes an adult at marriage, but a boy becomes an adult in two ways: through marriage and through citizenship attained when he reaches the proper age, usually 14 or 15 years. At this time he must enter the labour pool of adult men who maintain community property and must contribute his share of any assessment the citizenry may impose upon itself to cover community expenses. He becomes eligible (and obligated) to serve in the lowest ranking offices of the political and religious institutions of the community.

Death is marked by ritual and burial within 24 hours of death, with repetition of the ritual at periodic intervals after death, sometimes ending on the ninth day, sometimes repeated on the anniversary. An All Saints feast of several days' duration is prepared annually in the fall of the year for all of the dead.

MODERN DEVELOPMENTS

Indigenous communities have in most cases made a healthy adjustment to the larger non-Indian community around them. Although this has and will continue to involve many kinds of cultural change, the indigenous communities have been able to maintain their cultural integrity with little sign of the kind of disorganization leading to cultural collapse that is often found when two cultures meet. And though, in the late 20th century, the Spanish-speaking community has come to accept (even to take pride in) its Indian heritage, its direct attempts to bring the Indian way of life more in line with that of its own have met with much resistance. While it has been possible to introduce technological changes that have improved the economic position of Indian communities, attempts to change those parts of the culture that have symbolic value—political and religious ideologies that tend to preserve indigenous social systems—have met with less success.

(Ed.)

Central American and Northern Andean cultures

The Central American and Northern Andean culture area comprises most of Central America (south from Guatemala) and the northern coast of South America (including the northern drainage of the Orinoco River); the West Indies are also customarily included. Although the area has meaning in terms of the distribution of indigenous cultures and languages, it does not coincide with any named region in a geographic sense, nor does it coincide with contemporary national political boundaries.

The area is situated entirely within the tropics, and the seasons are marked more by differences in precipitation than in temperature. Lowlands tend to be hot, but elevation tempers the climate on some of the islands and along the mountain ranges that run through Central America, Colombia, and Venezuela. Areas of heavy rainfall support dense forest, whereas a few dry regions support little more than sparse grass.

In archaeological terms, this area is of strategic significance for various reasons. First, as the relatively narrow corridor between the northern and southern continental land masses, Central America is a promising area in the search for remains of the ancient culture of the palaeo-Indians, of a generalized Mongoloid stock, who moved into South America at least 10,000 years ago. Second, an exceptionally rich and diverse variety of local cultures had evolved in the area by 500 BC. Third, between AD 1000 and 1500 the area was intermediate between the major centres of high civilization in Mexico and Peru. The people

In this region, unlike much of Latin America, most native cultures did not long survive the arrival of the Europeans, and there is controversy among anthropologists over whether many of the indigenous groups may, by reference to such criteria as language, patterns of beliefs and behaviour, or political affiliation, be justifiably designated tribes. Almost 200 "tribes" were reported in early Spanish documents, but descriptions of most are imprecise.

Native languages spoken in the area at the time of European conquest were many and varied. Although some historical and structural linkages can be traced with other groups in North and South America, individual languages reflect millennia of relative isolation (see LANGUAGES OF THE WORLD).

TRADITIONAL CULTURE PATTERNS

Accounts of the indigenous cultures are fragmentary and based largely on occasional reports by missionaries, explorers, and soldiers. In some instances, widespread and apparently important cultures are represented by little more than archaeological evidence, but it is possible to note a series of characteristic patterns and variations on those patterns that recur in the area.

With respect to basic subsistence, for example, intensive horticulture by the slash-and-burn (swidden) method was general. A variety of crops, including manioc, maize, sweet potato, bean, and others, were staples in various regions. Numerous other vegetables, as well as tropical fruits and sometimes cotton, were also grown in some areas. This form of horticulture was far more efficient than is popularly believed and produced abundant food Economic practices

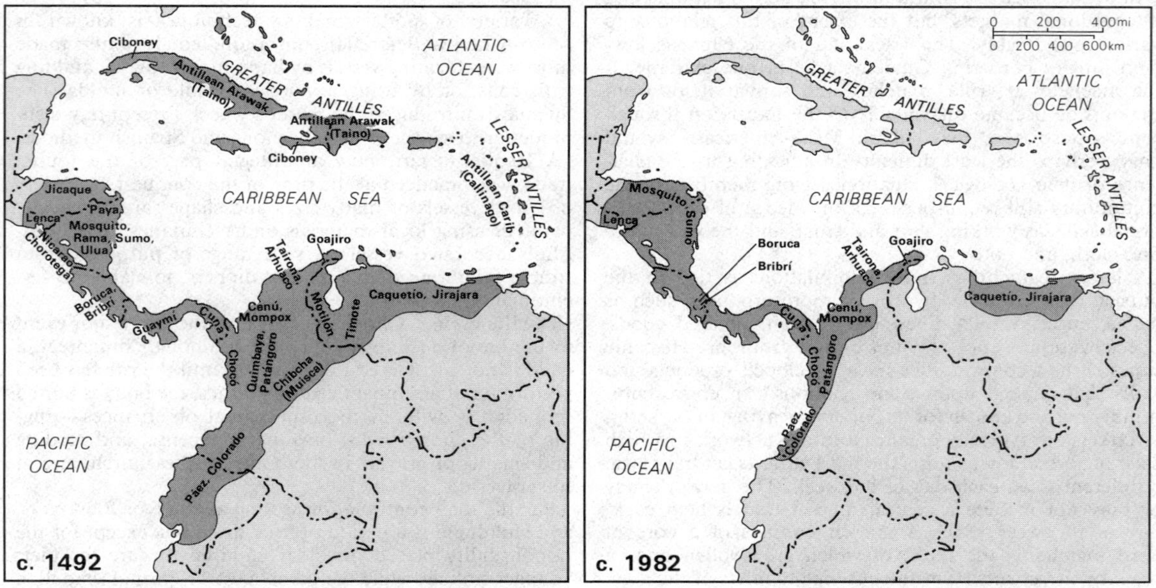

Distribution of Central American and Northern Andean cultures.

without enormous or constant effort. In the cultures of this region, unlike many of those in the Amazon Basin, such intensive farming was usually done by the men. Improvements on the basic slash-and-burn pattern have been rare throughout the world, but in this area they included irrigation, and even occasional terracing, by the Antillean Arawak, Arhuaco, Chibcha, Jirajara, Páez, and Timote, all of whom showed evidence of other cultural elaborations as well. In contrast with such highly developed groups, a few cultures in the area were based more on hunting or fishing than on even simple farming; among those were the Antillean Carib, Chocó, Ciboney, and Motilón.

The form and scale of communities tended to be closely linked to economic activities. Those groups, for example, whose subsistence base was fishing or gathering, had the smallest houses and most dispersed settlement patterns in the area. Similarly, the largest and most permanent buildings, as well as the most densely populated villages, occurred among those tribes that had the most intensive and varied food production, including some with highly developed agriculture. The warring expansionist groups, such as the Chibcha and Guaymí, even built palisades around their larger towns, many of which included palaces and temples. Ball courts and large ceremonial plazas were constructed only among the Antillean Arawak, who were unusual in having communities with as many as 3,000 people.

Arts and crafts

The high degree of regional variation in crafts is probably related to the small scale of political organization, in which regional chiefdoms predominated. The hammock apparently originated in this area and was widespread; little other furniture was used. Houses varied considerably in size and shape, although virtually all had palm-thatched roofs and walls of thatch or adobe. A wide variety of baskets was made, usually by women; bark cloth was made in those few regions where loom weaving was unknown. Clothing was simple, usually comprising no more than a breechclout for men and a short skirt for women, and few remains of textiles have survived. Most of the Indians adorned their bodies richly, however, with painted designs, tattooing, and a wide variety of jewelry and feathered ornaments.

Nearly all of the peoples in the area made at least some pottery, and a few of the mainland groups produced exceptionally abundant, fine, and varied ceramics. Excellent in their own right, some of these wares reflect styles, media, and techniques from both the Andean and the Mexican centres of high civilization. The same few groups—notably the Chibcha, Chorotega, Guaymí, and Nicarao—carved jade and other stones and worked copper, gold, and several alloys with an unusual combination of technical skill, imagination, and aesthetic sensitivity. Abundant ornaments were made of metal and of precious and semiprecious stones, both for adornment and for interment in the graves of distinguished men, but few utilitarian tools are known.

Overland transportation was by foot, and widespread trade was carried on throughout much of the area without the benefit of either draft or pack animals. Dugout canoes, often of considerable size, provided transportation from island to island and along rivers.

Outposts of the sophisticated and warlike Aztec Empire extended as far south as the region inhabited by the Nicarao, where military and commercial operations linked what is now Costa Rica with Mexico. In the south the Colorado and Páez peoples of the northern Andes similarly faced the frontier of an empire—that of the Incas—and carried on trade with the centre of high civilization in what is now Peru. The Chibcha proper (also called Muisca) comprised several feudal states, among whom war and tribute were commonplace, and their fine manufactures of gold, copper, and pottery became widespread through extensive trade. Not only were there regular markets but in some regions even a standard of exchange (namely cacao) was recognized.

The majority of the cultures of this region, however, were small chiefdoms, in which a single village or a small group of nearby communities was led by a chief whose semidivine position was inherited through the maternal line of descent. Such men were powerful within limited regions, but widespread confederations of such chiefdoms were rare, and warfare among them was typical in some areas. The Antillean Caribs, for example, had been encroaching on the peaceful Antillean Arawaks just prior to the arrival of the Europeans, taking both territory and captives. In general, it was the cultures with more highly developed agriculture that had the greatest degree of political integration, whereas those with the simplest subsistence economies rarely had any organization beyond the local community.

Religious practices

The practice of shamanism for curing and sorcery, as well as the popular worship of natural phenomena, was widespread. In areas of relatively dense population there were full-time religious practitioners who maintained temples dedicated to idols at ceremonial centres. The elaborate and bloody state religion of the Aztec Empire extended as far south as the Nicarao region; the Chibcha practiced large-scale human sacrifice; and the cannibalism of the Antillean Caribs also apparently had some religious significance. A trait distinctive of the Antillean Arawaks was the *zemi,* a triangular carved stone that represented the hierarchically ranked individual guardian deities of each household in the society.

Social stratification varied in much the same way as political organization. It ranged from virtually absent among the nonagricultural Ciboney to fairly complex among the warring tribes that had highly developed agriculture. At most, four classes were differentiated: semidivine chiefs (whose Arawakan name, *cacique,* has come through Spanish into English), who usually enjoyed considerable power and luxury; nobles (usually by descent but sometimes on the basis of wealth or military exploits), whose prestige and perquisites included little political authority; commoners; and often slaves. The meaning of slavery in this context is somewhat different from the Western tradition of using human beings as chattel. In many instances, women taken in warfare were kept as low status wives or concubines, their children not being slaves. Captive men were usually slain in religious sacrifice, as human trophies, or for cannibalism.

The idea that a man should have many wives was widespread, especially among chiefs and nobles, and descent was often reckoned through the maternal line, but there is no firm basis for popular accounts of female-dominated societies that were given by some early writers. An unusual outcome of the pattern of marriage with prisoners was the use of Arawak as "the language of women" in Carib society, illustrating how a vanquished people can change the customs of their conquerors.

MODERN DEVELOPMENTS

The coming of Europeans resulted in the downfall of most of the cultures of the Central American and Northern Andean region. Few of the chiefdoms survived beyond the 17th century, and none exists in similar form today. Many of the cultures summarily described above are now extinct, including all of those in the West Indies and most of those in Central America. Vestiges of some cultures remain, significantly transformed, in a few areas remote from cities and roads.

Although this was the area first explored by the Spaniards, it was soon surpassed in importance by Mexico and Peru, both of which were rich in minerals and had large native populations accustomed to paying tribute in wealth and labour. Shallow sources of gold in the Antilles were quickly exhausted, and neither Central America nor the northern coast of South America offered much of interest to the conquistadors. None of the peoples of the region worked effectively under the Spaniards.

Disintegration of indigenous cultures

One striking feature that characterizes the history of contact with European culture in virtually every one of these instances is the disintegration or impoverishment of the indigenous culture. Whereas many observers might have expected new and increasing elaborations in those cultures that survived, the opposite has occurred. Agriculture is less varied and less productive; pottery and weaving are practiced less and are less sophisticated, and metallurgy has disappeared. Communities are generally smaller now than they were four centuries ago, and even regional political integration is lacking. The temples, warfare, and class stratification characteristic of many chiefdoms are gone, and, with few exceptions, the contemporary peoples try to avoid contact with others.

Although there had been warfare, trade, and other kinds of intercultural contact in pre-Columbian times, the impact of the Spanish conquest was different in kind as well as in scale, involving as it did not only unprecedented military power but also a wholly new economic system and a deliberate policy of reshaping Indian life to conform to European ideals.

One need not believe literally in the "black legend" about Spanish cruelty toward the Indians to understand the rapid depopulation of the West Indies. Newly introduced diseases took a heavy toll among the natives during the early years of contact, as did forced labour at unaccustomed tasks. Survivors often fled to the forested mainland coasts that were scorned as useless by the Europeans. Others quickly lost their cultural and racial identity as a result of mixture with blacks who had been imported from Africa as slaves. Some of the mixed populations remained in the islands while others sought refuge from the Europeans on the coasts. Noteworthy among this latter group are the Black Caribs (descendants of Carib Indians and Africans, also called Bush Negroes), who went to British Honduras and Guyana.

There are, however, a few exceptions to the general pattern of extinction or isolation. The Cuna of Panama, for example, became largely Hispanicized, although their colourful dress made them an asset in terms of the tourist trade, unlike the similarly acculturated Lenca of Honduras. As early as 1550, the Goajiro of northeastern Colombia had virtually abandoned their pre-Columbian slash-and-burn horticulture in favour of an economic pattern previously unknown in the New World—the herding of goats and cattle. Small nomadic bands, based on ties of kinship, travel constantly to find pasturage within their limited and arid territories, which are the subject of frequent feuds. The hot, humid Mosquito Coast of eastern Honduras and Nicaragua was long used as a base by English loggers, buccaneers, and others who sought to undercut Spain's commercial and political dominance throughout the Caribbean, and the Jicaque, Misquito (Mosquito), Paya, and Sumo Indians, as well as many free and runaway blacks, collaborated with them. These peoples, however, have again been relegated to an economically and politically marginal position.

During the 20th century the remaining cultures resisted modernization to a degree unusual among Indians of the Americas. As pressures on their refuge areas mounted however, it was not clear whether they would adapt or become extinct.

(D.B.H.)

SOUTH AMERICAN PEOPLES AND CULTURES

The customs and social systems of South American peoples are closely and naturally related to the environments in which they live. These environmental relationships are mediated by the systems of technology that the people use to exploit their resources.

Four basic types of social and cultural organization of South American peoples emerge from the archaeological and historical records: (1) central Andean irrigation civilizations, (2) chiefdoms of the northern Andes and the circum-Caribbean, (3) tropical-forest farming villages, and (4) nomadic hunters and gatherers. Each type developed in its own fashion during thousands of years, and since the 16th century each has made a distinctive adjustment to the impact of European civilization.

Early men, hunters and gatherers with no knowledge of agriculture, gradually worked their way across the Bering Strait in pursuit of food and meandered over North and South America in small, migratory bands for thousands of years. They reached Tierra del Fuego in approximately 6000 BC, after passing through the bottleneck of Central America, dispersing in the rugged terrain of the northern Andes, following the resource-laden Caribbean coastline eastward, and filtering southward through the tropical lowlands now making up part of Venezuela, the Guianas, and Brazil. They also hunted game through the highland basins of the central Andes and hunted and fished along the west coast of South America until they reached land's end.

THE PEOPLE

In South America, native language families encompassed large blocks of territory and numerous societies. They cut across different cultural and social types and are found represented in different geographical and environmental surroundings. Languages may be grouped in many ways, but the major language groupings or families of South America may be conveniently divided into the Macro-Chibchan, Andean-Equatorial (including Tupian), Ge-Pano-Carib, and Hokan. This is the most simplified classification of South American Indian languages (see also LANGUAGES OF THE WORLD).

Racially, the Indians of North and South America belong to a Mongoloid subtype known as Amerind. They show certain diagnostic physical traits of Mongolian peoples, among which are the shovel-shaped incisor tooth pattern, the distinctive fold of the eyelid, and the darkening of the lower back known as Mongolian spot. Such traits were scattered in South America. Hair form is generally straight and hair colour black, but there are instances of brownish, reddish brown, curly, and even frizzy hair.

Great physical variation is to be expected in so large a population dispersed over an entire continent. Wide differences are apparent in body form, height, skin colour, and head shape. Of the more than 100 societies for which there are physical data of reliable value, height ranges greatly between means of about 57 inches (145 centimetres) and about 69 inches (175 centimetres). The peoples of smaller stature are found in the northwestern part of South America (for example, the Chocó and the Cuna) and continue southeastward in a broad band that extends into south central Brazil. They overlap considerably, however, with peoples whose mean height falls between 60 and 64 inches (152 and 163 centimetres). These peoples of moderate height extend farther south, down into Chile as far as the Isla de Chiloé, where there is again overlap with a very short people, the Chono. The next tallest groups of peoples comprise a narrow band from northern Brazil to southern Argentina. The tallest peoples in South America were the hunters and gatherers of the southern plains and Tierra del Fuego—the Puelche, Tehuelche, and Ona.

Population densities in the 16th century

In the 1500s, the central Andes, the area of greatest population density in South America (about 10 persons per square mile), was sparsely populated compared to centres of Old World civilization. Yet its population of approximately 3,500,000, crowded into narrow coastal valleys and small highland basins on approximately 1 percent of Peru's total land area, constituted a much higher density than could be found in any other part of South America. The chiefdoms of the northern Andes, northern Venezuela, and the Antilles had an estimated total population of 1,900,000, with densities ranging from 6.6 to 1.1 persons per square mile (2.5 to 0.4 persons per square kilometre). The southern Andes was inhabited by the Atacama, Diaguita, and Araucanians, whose combined population was possibly 1,131,000, with a density range of 0.38 to seven persons per square mile. Tropical-forest peoples numbered about 2,200,000 and had a density of 0.6 per square mile. Hunting and gathering peoples of the Chilean archipelago, Patagonia, the Gran Chaco, and eastern Brazilian uplands had a combined population of less than 800,000 and a density range of 0.2 (Chilean archipelago) to 1.1 (western Chaco).

The population density of the central Andes was about 200 times greater than that of the hunters and gatherers,

20 times greater than that of the tropical-forest farmers, and 30 to 40 percent greater than that of the Araucanians and the chiefdoms of the northern Andes and the circum-Caribbean.

THE PREHISTORIC PERIOD

Human life forms did not evolve in the New World, despite certain claims to the contrary which have never been taken seriously by most scholars. Man migrated from Siberia to Alaska, probably some 20,000 to 35,000 years ago, when there was a land and ice bridge between the two continents. He seems to have remained locked in the northwestern sector of North America for eons, held back by impenetrable glacial formations. When the glacial cap retreated and valleys opened up, a full-blown *Homo sapiens* (then existing as a hunter and gatherer) began to follow the southward progression of game animals, fanning out over North America and wedging through Central America into South America, again a process occupying thousands of years. Archaeological discoveries have unearthed man's skeletal remains in association with now-extinct species of animals and in geological deposits of the last phases of the Ice Age.

Early man. Archaeological evidence demonstrates that South America was occupied by early man at least 10,000 years ago, ample time for high civilizations to have evolved in the central Andes and for ecological adjustments to have been worked out elsewhere on the continent. Scientific dating techniques establish that agriculture was practiced along the Peruvian coast at least as early as 2300 BC. By 1000 BC agricultural societies flourished. This does not mean that all of South America had reached this stage of development nor that it was densely populated by farming communities. On the contrary, the continent was spottily inhabited by simply organized hunters and gatherers who then occupied the most favourable regions. As knowledge diffused from the central Andes to other parts of South America and as agriculture and other techniques were adopted by those peoples living in favourable environments, farming communities took form, and populations among them began to increase. Thus, on the foundation of early hunting and gathering societies, the more complex social and cultural systems gradually were built in those areas where agriculture developed; cultural growth and social complexity followed apace. Hunters and gatherers were pushed out of the farming regions to agriculturally marginal areas, where some of them are found today.

The original migrants to the New World had no knowledge of the domestication of plants or animals, with the exception of dogs, which were used in hunting. Recent discoveries in Mexico indicate that agriculture was independently discovered in the New World in roughly the same era that it was in the Near East (about 7000–8000 BC) and that New World civilizations were built on an indigenous agricultural base.

Independent American development

It is known archaeologically that cultural influences from Asia, as well as latter day migrations of people such as the Eskimo, continued to impinge on parts of the New World over the millennia, but New World cultural developments that culminated in the formation of high civilizations in Mexico and Peru were overwhelmingly the product of native, independent invention in almost all spheres of cultural and social life. Sporadic influences probably reached Peru and the western parts of the tropical forests from across the Pacific Ocean, but their effect on the course of cultural development in this hemisphere was negligible. Native America constituted a separate cultural unit, compared with the Old World.

The development of civilizations. The archaeological record for the central Andes shows a step-by-step development of cultural and social forms from a pre-agricultural, hunting and gathering baseline some 10,000 years ago to the Inca Empire in the 15th century AD. The record does not show any significant cultural influence on this development from transpacific contacts.

The evidence on early hunting and gathering peoples in Peru is still sparse. It is not yet possible to reconstruct social patterns, since most of the remains consist only of shellfish middens and small, widely scattered campsites along the coast. It was a period of thousands of years' duration, however, toward the end of which some knowledge of plant domestication reached the Peruvian coast.

The next major era is set off by incipient agriculture and is also characterized by the remains of small, hamlet-type communities along the Pacific Ocean near river mouths, where the alluvial soil was able to support crops. Technology remained simple, irrigation was not practiced, and population remained small.

After the passage of 1,000 years or so, marked developments appear in the archaeological record. These include many new crops, irrigation ditches that extended the arable area and controlled the supply of water, more and larger communities that attest to a growing population, and important temple mounds that formed the symbolic centres of theocratic government controlled by a priestly class. The formative era saw the development of the basic technologies and life-styles that were to become elaborated into even more complex cultural forms and state institutions. The emergence of city-states and empires in the central Andes is the result of local cultural-ecological adjustments of this sort, based on an irrigation agriculture that supported growing populations and necessitated controls in the hands of priests and nobles, with a warrior class subservient to the state.

Around 500 BC strong regional styles began to appear in the manufacture of utilitarian and luxury goods and public buildings. An abundance of large temple mounds, more extensive and intricate irrigation networks, cities, roads, bridges, reservoirs, and other works calling for mass labour and tight controls characterize this cultural florescence. It was capped by the crystallization of class-organized societies, supported by masses of farm families and conscript labour, defended by well-organized and well-disciplined troops, catered to by a large number of master craftsmen, and ruled and regulated by a class of priests and nobles.

Imperial expansion in the central Andes

During the last phase of the prehistoric era in the central Andes, which began around AD 1000, regional states came to be absorbed into vast empires, the best known of which was the Inca Empire. The Inca began their expansion in 1438 and completed it in 1532, by which time the Spaniards landed on the northern coast of Peru at what is now the seaport of Paita. The Inca spread their imperial bureaucracy from Ecuador to central Chile and implanted their religious beliefs and practices, as well as much of their culture and the Quechua language, in the process of empire building. Their achievement was cut short by the Spanish Conquest under Pizarro, at a time when the Inca Empire seemed on the verge of civil war.

Traditional ways of life. *Hunters and gatherers.* Peoples who led a nomadic hunting and gathering life inhabited the agriculturally marginal areas of South America and were peripheral to the centres of great cultural development. All of Argentina and the archipelagic zone of southern Chile comprised the habitat of such hunting and gathering peoples as the Chono, Alacaluf, and Yâmana (Yaghan) of Chile, the Ona of the island of Tierra del Fuego, and the Tehuelche, Puelche (Guennakin), Charrúa, and Querandí of mainland Argentina. In the Gran Chaco region were the Guaycuruan-speaking Indians, the Abipón, Mataco, Vilela, and others, who were migratory peoples roaming the grassy plains of their small territories in search of rhea, guanaco, peccary, and jaguar. In the tropical rain forests of Brazil and neighbouring countries, societies that are off the mainstreams of diffusion of ideas and technologies have remained at a hunting and gathering subsistence level. Many such peoples became extinct shortly after contact with Europeans, through warfare, enslavement, and disease. Others, such as the Guaraní Indians of Paraguay, made prolonged adjustments to European colonization and gradually mixed with the conquerors biologically and culturally.

In the tropical forests were the Jívaro, Yaruro, Makú, and many other small societies eking out a livelihood mainly by hunting, fishing, and gathering wild plants. They kept a wary eye on their more powerful neighbours, the village agriculturalists, who coursed the main rivers and their tributaries in canoes, searching for food and sometimes human heads.

Distribution of aboriginal South American and circum-Caribbean cultural groups.

Social behaviour of hunters and gatherers

The hunting and gathering peoples of aboriginal South America were organized into small social units made up of a single kin group or of several loosely linked groups of relatives. Members of these societies were differentiated almost entirely on the basis of their sex and age rather than on status characteristics of an economic, military, political, or religious nature, as in more complexly organized social systems. Behaviour was sanctioned by tribal customs that involved kinship rights and obligations and constituted the basis of morality. These peoples had very similar rites throughout the South American continent and similar beliefs in cures and magic. Their technology and material culture, though not homogeneous from one society to another, was always rudimentary and generally lacked agriculture, well-developed building arts, and manufacturing processes found among other South American Indians. They lived in marginal areas, exploiting the limited natural resources with elementary techniques. This kept their social units small, widely scattered, and simply organized.

Tropical-forest farming villages. The agricultural villagers of the tropical forests had more developed exploitative techniques than the hunters and gatherers. Farming, food storage, and canoe transportation along rivers made for greater economic sufficiency and the ability to live in larger and more stable units. The forest-dwelling agriculturalists included the bulk of the Arawakan-, Cariban-, and Tupian-speaking peoples, such as the coastal Arawak proper and those of the Greater Antilles, the Achagua, Guahibo, Palicur, and many other societies; the Carib of the Guianas, such as the Barama River Carib, the Taulipang, and the Makushí (Macushí); the Tupians of the coast of Brazil, such as the Tupinambá; and inland groups among whom were the Mundurukú, Kawaíb (Parintintín), and their neighbours.

Tropical-forest farming villagers, like hunters and gather-

Society and economy of the tropical forest

ers, had sociocultural units consisting mainly of kin-based populations which were structured along lines of age and sex, without much in the way of economic, political, or religious grounds for social-status differentiation. Social controls were largely based on kinship rights and obligations of a moral nature, except in cases of certain military activities that were often under the temporary leadership of special chiefs. Their richer technology and production of agricultural surpluses enabled villages to remain in the same place for many years, even though the depletion of soils necessitated the periodic reestablishment of new villages and the abandonment of older ones. Populations were larger and, of course, more concentrated. They were supported by a more adequate and dependable food supply, which included maize (corn), beans, squash, manioc, and tropical vegetables and fruits, as well as the riches of the rivers on which these peoples lived, such as turtles and the thousands of turtle eggs harvested annually and abundant fish and game. Hunting was important but subsidiary to agriculture. The rites of these peoples—those surrounding birth, puberty, initiation into men's secret societies, marriage, and death, and the shamanistic practices involved in the supernatural curing of illness—tended to be similar throughout the tropical-forest region. Many of the rites were similar to those of the simpler hunting and gathering peoples.

Chiefdoms of the northern Andes and the circum-Caribbean. In this extensive and geographically varied region there existed many peoples who lay in the main path of the Spanish conquistadores and who were overwhelmed by them. The Spaniards were attracted by the abundance of gold ornaments and religious objects displayed in the native villages and were excessive in their search for even greater wealth.

Among the chiefdoms were the Chibcha of highland Ecuador (the greatest chiefdom of them all) and the Coconuco, Pijao, Páez, Puruhá, Cana, and Palta of the northern Andes; the Jirajara and their neighbours, the Caquetío, Palenque, and Cumanagoto of northern Venezuela; and the Arawakan Taino of the Greater Antilles.

Though having a technology similar to that of the tropical-forest farming villages and sharing a basic material culture with them, the chiefdoms of the northern Andes and the circum-Caribbean areas had a still more productive food complex, which supported much denser populations in quite large and permanent villages and towns. Natural resources were more varied and abundant in the regions that they inhabited, and farming was more productive.

Social and political life of the chiefdoms

Villages were composed of multikinship groups organized on the basis of social strata which had attributed statuses, rather than merely on the basis of kinship considerations such as age, sex, and the moral obligations these incurred. Some social ranks were hereditary, such as chieftainship and ritual office. Warfare was of great importance in many societies of this type. Participation in military activities insured upward social mobility for individuals and families and the eventual achievement of membership in the topmost strata of the village. War captives were taken as drudge servants and for sacrificial victims in religious rites. There was a foreshadowing of state institutions in the offices of priest, chief, military leaders, and nobles and captive slaves. In the chiefdoms, however, these institutions had not crystallized as they eventually did in the Andean kingdoms and empires. A major diagnostic feature of chiefdoms was their priest–temple–idol complex, a ritual organization of a different order of complexity from the supernatural beliefs and practices of the tropical-forest villagers and the hunters and gatherers.

Central Andean irrigation civilizations. First occupied by small groups of hunting and gathering peoples who filtered southward along the Pacific coast and through the highland basins thousands of years ago, the central Andes eventually became the seat of the highest form of civilization developed in native South America. The earliest archaeological evidence of agriculture in this region has a date of 2300 BC, which is probably much later than the first domestication of plants. With the spread of agricultural knowledge throughout the central Andes, populations increased in size and attained more settled and larger communities. A thousand years before the Spanish Conquest, the central Andes had the most developed agricultural and irrigational system in all of South America, the densest population south of Mexico, and the most efficient system of overland transportation in the Western Hemisphere. The combination of these features permitted the growth of true urban centres, an intricate class system, a strongly entrenched bureaucracy, and the extension of social controls over vast areas by means of political, religious, and military institutions.

Two of the most famous early kingdoms in the central Andes were the Tiahuanaco and the Chimú; the former spread its culture from what is today highland Bolivia northward to the vicinity of Lima and beyond. In the north of Peru arose the Chimú kingdom, which expanded southward and overlapped the northern extension of the Tiahuanaco culture, as the latter's influence had begun to decline. Following these two great cultural spreads and military conquests came the expansion of the Inca state. When Inca civilization reached imperial proportions it controlled the area occupied today by Peru, Ecuador, Bolivia, and the northern half of Chile. The expansion of the Inca Empire preceded the Spanish Conquest by slightly less than 100 years.

Irrigation, agriculture, and bureaucracy in Andean civilizations

All of these imperial states, as well as other smaller ones before them, shared a number of characteristics that set them apart from the chiefdoms and other peoples. They were based on state-controlled irrigation works, which made the production of huge agricultural surpluses possible. These surplus crops were controlled by the emperor and apportioned among the state, the church, and the populace according to a standard formula. As a result of an abundant food supply and surpluses that could be stored against adverse times, population steadily increased. There developed a rigidly hereditary class system—with the agricultural masses at the bottom and the Inca royal family at the top, with ranks of nobles, chiefs, lesser administrators, artisans, and others in between. The state waged war for territorial conquest and taxed the defeated peoples. It imposed the Inca religion, with its emperor-god and hierarchy of deities, its shrines and temples attended by priests and sacred virgins, and its ceremonial calendar. The Inca were masters of bureaucratic regimentation who ruled the lives of the commoners through political controls enforced by state machinery and statute law rather than by customary sanctions. Inca institutions overshadowed and to some extent replaced the traditional behaviour patterns of the thousands of farming communities that made up the empire.

Central Andean technology differed little from that of surrounding areas, except in metallurgical skills and in the building arts, but it was outstanding in the quality, variety, and excellence of its products, the most outstanding of which were produced for the state and the nobility by highly skilled artisans.

EVOLUTION OF CONTEMPORARY CULTURES

The European conquest. A full appreciation of the force and nature of the European conquest of South America must take into consideration postcontact population trends among the indigenous societies. Today, there are at least as many people of overwhelmingly Indian ancestry as there were just prior to the European conquest, but the vast majority of these, approximately 7,000,000, live in the central Andes and represent a resurgence after a marked population decline following the conquest. Elsewhere in South America, Indian populations declined rapidly after contact with Europeans and, for the most part, have not increased appreciably since. This loss of Indian populations is related directly to the intensity of European exploitation and the density of the native populations in question, two principal factors in adjustments during the colonial period.

Population decline was heaviest along the South American coastlines and major rivers, where Indian concentrations were greatest. Along the coasts of Brazil, the Guianas, Venezuela, Colombia, and Ecuador, where Europeans came in great force, the Indians were killed in large numbers, died in the course of enslavement, succumbed to new diseases, or fled into the hinterlands in depleted numbers. Conditions were similar along the great river systems, where native populations declined sharply in the first decades after coming into contact with Europeans, their places being filled in the labour pools of colonial society by African slaves, who have made a great contribution to South America's mixed population.

Spanish influences

Indians who survived European intrusions are those small communities in the marginal, unattractive areas scarcely touched by soldiers and settlers. South of the tropical-forest area, in Argentina and Uruguay, where Indian populations were small and scattered, the coastal groups were again the first to succumb to conquest. In the Gran Chaco, resistance to Spanish settlement was fierce and temporarily successful, but, in time, these Indians were nearly wiped out by disease in mission centres and elsewhere, and the survivors were absorbed into the gaucho population that developed along with Argentine cattle raising. In Chile, the Atacama and Diaguita Indians were rapidly suppressed and absorbed, as were the northern Araucanians (Picunche). The southern Araucanians (Mapuche and Huilliche) held out against white subjugation and developed a military organization to defend their heartland until the latter decades of the 19th century. The southernmost groups—the Puelche, Tehuelche, Ona, Yaghan, and Alacaluf—have become virtually extinct.

In contrast to the rest of South America, the highland populations of the Andes are today larger than at the time of conquest. They have maintained great cultural stability, have survived epidemics, and continue to live in small farming and pastoral communities established centuries ago. Their population is steadily and rapidly increasing, and there is great population pressure on arable land, which constitutes a national problem in Bolivia and Peru.

Effects of colonialism. The kinds of changes induced by European conquest varied according to the intensity of settlement and exploitation, the density and organization of Indian populations, and the ecological adjustments made by the conquerors. Three examples of these variables may serve to indicate general trends.

Peru. Inca culture and society were deeply affected by the Spanish Conquest and the intensive settlement that followed. Spanish patterns of bureaucratic government replaced those of the Inca Empire, land use and ownership changed radically, tribute and forced labour threatened the agricultural base of the old society, ancient deities succumbed to Roman Catholicism, and community and domestic life were geared to the demands of the new colonial regime.

Economic and religious effects of European influences

Inca agriculture underwent great change through the introduction of European crops demanded by Spanish overlords. Indians were parcelled out among the settlers as tribute producers, menial labourers, and house servants. The abuses of exploitation were so great that very quickly most of the land was alienated from the Indians, who became a large, landless, and rootless population available for conscript labour in service of the colony.

The Spaniards imposed the Roman Catholic religion and tried to stamp out native beliefs and practices, a work of long duration that has not been wholly successful. Although the Inca state religion was totally suppressed with relative ease, an almost incalculable number of cults of lesser deities persisted in the villages.

The Inca upper classes were most readily assimilated into Spanish colonial society, whereas the agricultural masses retained much of their traditional culture. The native nobles entered the administrative ranks of colonial society and adopted Spanish dress and other customs. Artisans, servants, and others in direct contact with the settlers also became rapidly acculturated to a colonial way of life. Where native communities remained outside the main force of the colonial economy and where communal land was retained, the traditional culture was preserved somewhat intact, with customs of land use, ownership, family organization, marriage practices, and some home industries surviving into the 20th century. Villages have economic links with the cities through the production of marketable crops and may now be considered as peasant communities in a national economy.

Chile. The Spaniards conquered the northern half of Chile several years after having become established in Peru. They brought the Picunche under their control with relative ease by 1544 and used them to placer mine gold in the rivers, perform agricultural labour on settlers' farms, and build and provide services in colonial towns, cities, and military outposts.

In response to the colonists' demands for more Indian labour, Spanish troops attempted to conquer the southern Araucanians, the Mapuche and Huilliche. These Indians rebelled against harsh treatment at the hands of the Spaniards and succeeded in burning all their outposts and settlements and driving them north again. The history of northern Chile, after that, is one of peaceful colonization and the assimilation of the Indian population into a colonial labour force. Mapuche-Huilliche territory, however, remained a frontier zone for centuries. The Mapuche and Huilliche were placed on reservations after they sued for peace in 1884.

Panama. The Chocó Indians of the tropical forests of Provincia de Darién and nearby Colombia survived the Spanish intrusion because they had nothing of value to the Europeans and were bypassed. In turn, the Chocó were not especially warlike and avoided the dangers of contact.

The Chocó retained many of their traditional values and ways of life into the 20th century. They emphasize magical curing, observe age-old marriage practices, and live in pole and thatch houses built on pilings along rivers, where they have small groves of plantains and also grow manioc, cacao, and other tropical crops in jungle clearings. Most Chocó have no knowledge of Spanish. They are by no means integrated into national life and prefer to live apart in the densely forested areas. (L.C.F.)

Andean cultures

Although the Andes mountain chain extends from Venezuela to the southern tip of the continent, it is conventional to call "Andean" only the people who were once part of Tawantinsuyu, the Inca Empire in the Central Andes, or those considerably influenced by it. Even so, Andean is very wide. It encompasses the peoples of Ecuador, including those of the humid coast, many of whose contacts were as frequently with maritime peoples, to both north and south, as with the peoples of the highlands. Most of the populations and civilizations of Bolivia and Peru are Andean in a central, nuclear way, and here again are included the kingdoms of the irrigated desert coast. The peoples who for the past four and a half centuries have occupied the northern highlands of Chile and Argentina also must be included. (For a description of northern Andean peoples, see above *Central American and Northern Andean cultures.*)

CENTRAL ANDES—TRADITIONAL CULTURE PATTERNS

There is a stereotyped image of the Andes showing poverty against a background of bleak, unproductive mountains, where millions insist, against all apparent logic, on living at 10,000 feet (3,000 metres) or more above sea level. Nowhere else have people lived for so many thousands of years in such visibly vulnerable circumstances.

Yet, somehow this perception of the Andean peoples coexists with another, based on the breathtaking stage setting of such archaeological sites as Machu Picchu, the majesty of Inca stone palaces at Cuzco or Huánuco Pampa and such Chimú mud-walled cities as Chan Chan, the beauty of Andean textiles or ceramics in museums the world over, the reported concern of the Inca kings for the welfare of their subjects, and the mostly abandoned large-scale irrigation works or terraces constructed by these peoples.

These two visions of Andean peoples and their accomplishments can be reconciled only if it is recognized that what the resources and ecologic potential of an area and a people may be depends on what part of these resources the people use or are allowed to use by their masters. The Andean region was once rich and produced high civilizations because, over millennia, its people developed an agriculture, technologies, and social systems uniquely adapted to the very specialized if not unique ecologic conditions in which they lived.

Economic systems. Since 1532, under European rule, extractive activities, such as silver, tin, and copper mining, for foreign markets have been favoured to the point to which Andean agriculture and the ecologic wisdom in handling productively the extremely high altitudes have been gradually devalued and mostly forgotten. The population of the Central Andes is both less dense and less urban today than it was in 1500. The coastal cities of South America, from Guayaquil to Buenos Aires, are filling with highlanders who have been convinced by four and a half centuries of colonial rule that cultivating at 12,000 feet is too strenuous.

Although human occupation began over 20,000 years ago, the beginnings of agriculture and population growth are much more recent. Within the last 8,000 years a specialized desert-and-highland agriculture was developed. There are two significant achievements in the Andean agricultural endeavour. First, given the wide range of geographic circumstances—very high mountains in equatorial and tropical latitudes, a 3,000-mile coastal desert, the Amazon rain forest to the east—there were thousands of quite different ecologic pockets, each with its own microenvironment to be understood and exploited. Dozens of crops, with literally thousands of varieties, were domesticated; most of them remain unknown outside the Andean area. Only the potato has acquired a following elsewhere; and only maize (corn) and possibly cotton were known in the Andean region as well as in the rest of the Americas. It is this multiplicity of minutely adapted crops and the domestication of the alpaca and the llama that made the mountains habitable to millions (the bulk of the population in the Central Andes has always lived between 8,000 and 13,000 feet).

Andean agriculture

Second, no matter how specialized Andean plants or herds may become, the leap from bare survival to dense populations and civilizations requires something more. The high altitude, with its 200, 250, even 300 frost-threatened nights a year, represents a challenge to any agricultural system. On the high, cold plains, known in the Andes as puna, there are only two seasons: summer every day and winter every night. By alternately using the freezing temperatures of the nocturnal winter and the hot sunshine of the daily tropical summer, Andean peoples developed preserves of freeze-dried meat, fish, and mealy tubers (*charki, chuñu*) that kept indefinitely and weighed much less than the original food. The giant warehouses that lined the Inca highways could be filled with these preserves and used to feed the engineers planning cities and irrigation canals, the bureaucracy, and the army, not to mention the royal court, with its thousands of male and female retainers.

Political systems. Even these two technological developments, however, are not enough to characterize and explain the emergence of Andean civilizations. From the intimate knowledge of their environmental conditions, the people developed a set of values that may have started from a desire to minimize risks but that soon was elaborated into an economic and political ideal. Every Andean society—be it a tiny, local ethnic group of 20 to 30 villages in a single valley or a large kingdom of 150,000 souls, such as the Lupaca—tried to control simultaneously a wide variety of ecologic stories up and down the mountainsides; some of them were many days' march from the political core of the nation. If the society was small, the outliers (herders or salt winners above the core; maize, cotton, or coca-leaf cultivators in the warm country below) would be only three or four days away. When the political unit grew large and could mobilize and maintain several hundred young men as colonists, the outliers could be 10 or even 15 days' walk away from the core.

The colonies were permanent, not seasonal establishments. Since more than one highland kingdom or principality would have maize or coca-leaf oases in a given coastal or upland Amazonian valley, there would be not only competition for their control but also coexistence for long periods of time in a single environment of outlying colonies sent out by quite different core societies.

The Inca state, or Tawantinsuyu as it was known to its own citizens, was perhaps the largest political or military enterprise of all. It reached from Carchi in northern Ecuador to at least Mendoza in Argentina and Santiago in Chile. Its scouts roamed even wider, as recent Chilean archaeology has shown. The Incas expanded and projected on earlier, pre-Incan solutions and adaptations; in the process, many tactics that had worked well on a smaller scale became inoperative; others were reformulated in such ways that their original outline was barely recognizable. For example, they kept an old Andean method of creating revenues for their princes, which involved setting aside acreage for regional authorities and demanding from the conquered peasantry not tribute in kind but rather labour on the field thus set aside. In this way the granary of the peasant household was left untouched; the authority took the risk of hail, frost, or drought decreasing its own revenues.

Inca expansion

The Inca state at its zenith did not breach this tradition overtly; the local ethnic groups continued to work the state's acreage and owed nothing from their own larders. But since the needs of kings kept growing, revenues produced on state lands were soon inadequate; acreage could be and was expanded through such public works as irrigation and terracing. A more tangible way was to increase the amount of energy available for state purposes. For some reasons, still insufficiently understood, the kings did not increase productivity by introducing tribute; they preferred to magnify on an imperial scale the patterns of reciprocal obligations and land use familiar to everyone from earlier times.

Beyond the strategic colonies set up on an expanded model, the Incas did not interfere too much with life of the many local groups that they had incorporated into Tawantinsuyu. Most of the cultures that existed in Ecuador, Peru, Bolivia, Argentina, and Chile before the Inca expansion can be identified. In fact, because the European invasion beginning in 1532 was mostly concerned with breaking the resistance of the Inca overlords, frequently more is known about the pre-Inca occupants than about Cuzco rule. Inca power was broken and decapitated within 40 years of 1532. The ethnic groups, many of which (like the Wanka or the Cañari) sided with Europeans against the Inca, were still easy to locate and identify in the 18th century. In isolated parts of Ecuador (Saraguro, Otavalo) and Bolivia (Chipaya, Macha) this can still be done today. (J.V.M.)

SOUTHERN ANDES—TRADITIONAL CULTURE PATTERNS

The area commonly referred to as the Southern Andes is separated from the Central Andes by a broad band of desert covering extreme southern Peru and northern Chile and Argentina. The Southern Andes includes those peoples occupying the mountain regions of northeastern Argentina and northern and central Chile south to Isla Grande de Chiloé. (Tribes farther south are discussed below; see *South American nomad cultures.*) Generally, it is an area of moderate to extreme aridity, with a temperate climate. Agriculture has been an important feature of village life and, in many places, has been sustained by irrigation techniques; however, the agricultural potential—limited by the availability of moisture—has always been much less than that of Peru.

Prior to the advent of farming, the peoples of the area followed a life pattern based on hunting, collecting, or fishing, depending upon their geographical location. Cultivation of plants, including corn, was introduced at some time after 500 BC, almost certainly diffused to the Southern Andes from Peru; and Inca influence finally appeared in the latter part of the 15th century AD. It is known from ethnohistoric sources, as well as from the presence of Inca-style fortifications and way stations, that the Cuzco government had established its authority over these peoples of the south. These southern tribesmen—the Atacama of northern Chile, the Diaguita of northwestern Argentina, and others—lived in small, compact towns or villages and practiced irrigation farming and llama and alpaca herding. In general, the cultures of the area may be said to show a marginal and somewhat delayed expression of Andean civilization. These primary influences were also blended with influences from Amazonian cultures by way of the Bolivian lowlands. Socially, for instance, the people were organized into autonomous villages of related kinship groups, much like the tropical forest village farmers and not at all like the highly class-stratified imperial Incas; war was conventionally waged for human trophies, not for territorial conquest. (Ed.)

South American tropical forest cultures

Problems of generalization

The tribal cultures of South America are so various that they cannot be adequately summarized in a brief space. The mosaic is baffling in its complexity: the cultures have interpenetrated one another as a result of constant migratory movements and through intertribal relations, leading to the obliteration of formerly significant differences, and to new cultural systems made up of elements of heterogeneous origin. Hundreds of languages, in very irregular geographic distribution, with innumerable dialects, are or have been spoken in the tropical area of South America. Thus, only the broadest generalizations can be made; one can mention certain cultural manifestations that are present in a great number of groups, even though varying in their actual expression, and illustrate them with specific examples—but always with the qualification that in a neighbouring tribe or group a distinctly contrasting idea or institution may exist.

The people

The innumerable native peoples differ in their patterns of adaptation to their natural environment. Whether they live in the rain forest, in the gallery forests lining the rivers, in the arid savannas, or in the swamps, however, they share a common cultural background; they often combine fishing and hunting with rudimentary farming. Most are relatively sedentary, but some are nomadic or semi-nomadic. Greater differences are sometimes found among neighbouring groups living in the same forest than between some forest and savanna peoples. And some tribes, when migrating to open areas, maintain to a great extent the forest characteristics of their culture.

On the banks of the great rivers but also in zones between the forest and the savanna live tribes who gain their subsistence from farming and fishing. Hunters and gatherers, almost all of whom also practice some farming, have settled near the heads of rivers, in open land, or in gallery forests.

Tribes speaking related languages are scattered over a large part of the continent. The tribes of the Arawak and the Carib linguistic families are most numerous in the Guianas (French Guiana, Guyana, Suriname, and the adjacent regions of Venezuela and Brazil) as well as in other parts of the northern Amazon, but the former have representatives as far south as the Chaco and the latter as far south as the upper Xingu. The Tupí tribes extend to the south of the Amazon valley.

The Ge family includes groups most of which are located in the semi-arid lands of central Brazil. In the extreme northwest of Brazil and in the jungles of eastern Peru and Bolivia live the Pano tribes. The Jívaro of Ecuador are famous headhunters. They cut off the enemy's head, separate the soft part from the skull, and, with the help of hot sand, reduce it to the size of a fist without altering the physiognomy. They attribute great magical power to these trophies, or *tsantsa.*

TRADITIONAL CULTURE PATTERNS

A characteristic feature of the tropical forest cultures is their combination of farming with hunting, fishing, and gathering. Before the arrival of the white man, the Indians of the tropical forest had no domestic animals except the dog. These people did not write or erect stone buildings as did the Indians of Middle America. They did not form states with centralized political organizations. They had no castes of warriors or priests. Their utensils and instruments were almost all of vegetable or animal origin, since in large sections of the area stones for making axes, arrowheads, and other objects were quite scarce. One finds evidence of metalwork only in the regions near the Andean civilizations, although objects of copper and other metals occasionally found their way across the continent, through channels of trade.

Social organization. In almost all of the tropical forest area the population density was low, averaging probably less than one person per square mile.

Populous centres existed only along the coast and the main rivers, particularly the Amazon; the latter, according to reports by early white explorers, was fringed with Indian villages. For the most part, however, the Indians were dispersed throughout the vast territory in innumerable tribes and tribelets. This is why a classification by languages and cultures gives only a vague idea of the complex picture of the forest populations. Peoples having the same dialect and culture might exist as separate groups, even as enemies. While some Indians considered themselves primarily members of their local group, others, like the Xerente (Sherenté), gave greater value to a common language and culture than to village divisions. But differences in dialect and culture often imposed obstacles to the recognition of tribal solidarity.

There were no permanent political associations or confederations encompassing tribes of different languages and cultures. At most, some tribes might form ephemeral confederations for warfare against a common enemy. Certain close relations sometimes existed between groups of diverse origin, especially through tribal intermarriage. The best known examples are along the Río Negro in northwest Brazil, where numerous populations, mostly Arawak and Tucano, are united in a vast network of interethnic relations. At the headwaters of the Xingu, a complex system of intertribal institutions also exists among formerly autonomous groups.

Marriage customs

Few tropical forest tribes are strictly monogamous. Marriage with two or more women is usually restricted, however, to chiefs and other men of prestige. Polygyny is perhaps most accentuated among the Jívaro, where headhunting has killed off many of the men; it frequently takes the form of marriage with two or more sisters. Examples of polyandry are rare.

The choice of a partner is sometimes limited by the division of the tribe into clans and segments to which an individual belongs by heredity and within which marriage is prohibited. In some cases, for example in the Guianas and in the Río Negro region, the individual must find a mate outside his village or even outside his tribe (exogamy). The Terena of the southern Mato Grosso divide themselves into endogamous groups: the man and wife must come from the same group, called by ethnologists a moiety. Marriage between cross cousins, that is, between children of siblings of different sex, is considered ideal in many tribes; that of parallel cousins, children of siblings of the same sex, is frequently prohibited.

Kinship groups and household communities are based predominantly on the principle of lineage, that is, on relation through either the male or female line. Communities of extended patrilineal families were typical of the Tupí-Guaraní. In many Amazon tribes and in others farther north, the lineages or groups of lineages are patrilineal exogamous clans. Tribes with matrilineal clans, although less numerous, can be found throughout South America. In some tribes the clans number 40 or more, as among the Mundurukú; they are generally organized into two groups so that the whole tribe comprises two exogamous moieties. The dual divisions of the Ge Indians, often not related to kinship and marriage, are mainly ceremonial.

The tropical forest cultures do not exhibit much social stratification. When there is a servile element, it is normally made up of ethnic outsiders who do not constitute a class as such. War captives may be reduced to slavery, as among the northern Carib and Arawak, the Huitoto, and the Mundurukú. Among the extinct Tupí of the Brazilian coast, slavery was the fate of those destined for ritual sacrifice. In many cases, chiefly among the northern Carib, slavery has primarily an economic function: the captives form a servile group known as *peito*—the same term that is applied to a fiancé during the period in which he is obliged to work for his future father-in-law. The Rucuyen, a Carib tribe of French Guiana, for some time maintained in servitude a great number of the Oyampī, their Tupí neighbours. In the northwest Amazon valley, Arawak and Tucano tribes hunt and enslave Makú men, who are forced to work in their gardens; the Makú women and children are used as domestic servants.

A tendency to form a class of nobility has been found in many Arawak groups, who not uncommonly impose themselves over other tribes by means of intermarriage, especially among families of chiefs. In some regions, relatives of chiefs constitute a kind of nobility. In tribes divided into clans, it is common to attribute superior status to a certain clan or even to scale them in hierarchic order. Nevertheless, the local or tribal community is essentially egalitarian.

Education and socialization

The children learn through play and imitation. Boys acquire skill in the use of weapons by practicing with small bows or blowguns made by their fathers. Girls learn to cook in little clay pots and to weave on small looms; they help their mothers in the preparation of manioc flour. The young also participate in the general religious life. The transmission of moral standards is rarely of a formal nature, and there is little punishment or repression.

The institution of the couvade is found throughout the forest culture. The father of a newborn infant must observe a rigorous diet for a week or so after the infant's birth. It is based on the idea of a mystical relation between the father and the child.

Puberty rites are often quite elaborate. In many tribes, such as the Guaraní, the symbol of masculine maturity is the labret, an ornament worn in a perforation of the lip; the ritual is preceded by an instruction period during which the boys, isolated from the community, learn the religious chants and dances, and it culminates with the perforation of their lower lips. Initiation rites may be limited to boys or to girls or may be for both sexes. The initiation of the boys is generally done collectively for those who have reached the eve of sexual maturity, while that of the girls is normally held individually on the occasion of the first menstruation.

In many of the Indian cultures these rites take a central position among other important ceremonies such as funerals and fertility rites. In the Guianas and the northwest Amazon region, the initiation of the boys is very complex. The Yurupary celebration inducts the boys into the secret society of mature men. Special rites are revealed to them; they are shown the sacred trumpets or the masks representing ancestral spirits. They are subjected to violent whippings, which they must tolerate without the least expression of pain. In the Guianas, the ritual torture consists of the stings of hornets or the bites of poisonous ants. The girls' initiation, generally more developed in the Amazon area near the Andes, is also frequently accompanied by difficult tests. Among the Tikuna (Tucuna) and other Amazonian groups, all the hair of the girl is pulled out; its regrowth symbolizes the emergence of a new adult personality.

The initiation of the boys assumes great importance in the social structure of some Ge groups of central Brazil, whose complex of rites begins at ten years of age and continues in cycles until 20. In one such tribe, the Xerente, candidates spend three years isolated from community life preparing themselves for manhood. In these Ge groups, those who have been initiated together form a distinct set of persons who feel united the rest of their lives.

Economic systems. Most of the tropical forest Indians are neither entirely sedentary nor entirely nomadic. Some wandering bands do not remain in the same place for more than a few days. Some farming populations are more or less attached to the earth. But even the latter make seasonal moves, especially those in semi-arid regions. The semi-nomadic tribes live in villages during the rainy season and go hunting in dry spells—*e.g.,* the Xavante and other Ge—or break up into little bands for gathering, as do the Nambikwara (Nambicuara). The Karajá (Carajá) of the Araguaia build their villages in rows of houses on high ground near the river, but in the dry season they move down to the long beaches. Most of the villages of the tropical forest farmers are not permanent; after some years they have to move because of soil exhaustion.

Housing

While the bands of gatherers rarely exceed a few dozen individuals, the farmers' villages have been known to include as many as 2,000. As a rule they are much smaller, dividing whenever the population becomes too large. A characteristic arrangement is the circular village of houses placed around a central plaza. This is found, for example, in the upper Xingu, in various Ge tribes, and among the Bororo of the Mato Grosso. The plan of the Bororo village, like that of the Ge, is a real map of the social structure. Each household represents a particular segment of the local group, such as an extended family or a patrilineal or matrilineal clan. The centre of the plaza is often occupied by the men's house, where the men spend the night and the greater part of the day, and which is at times the locus of ceremonial activities.

The house reflects the economic organization and social structure. Designs range from the simple shelter of the Guayakí and the wind screens of the Nambikwara up to large communal houses containing 200 or more individuals, even the entire tribe. The latter, known as *malocas,* have been found in the Guianas, northwestern Amazonia, and in some regions farther to the south in the area of the Purus and the Guaporé rivers. The Tupinamba houses are reported to have measured up to 20 metres in length. Houses on piles are found in marshy and swampy locations, for example among the Warao (Warrau) and other Indians of Venezuela but sometimes also among tribes that inhabit dry lands and savannas. The Mura, who live on the Madeira and Purus rivers, and the Guató of the upper Paraguay River, who spend a good part of the year on rivers and lagoons, fishing and hunting aquatic animals, have made their canoes into dwellings. At other times they live in small shacks at the water's edge.

Most houses are made of rough wood, covered with palm leaves or grass. The great circular *malocas* with conical roofs in southeastern Venezuela merit special attention for their size and solidity. Although there are no walls in the *malocas,* the space is customarily divided according to social distinctions, giving a specific place to each family and sometimes even to each of its members. The furniture is very rudimentary. Some Indians sleep on mats or on platform beds, but more of them use hammocks which are found throughout the tropical region.

A great variety of economic systems is found in the tropical forest. The tribes cannot accurately be classified as hunters and gatherers on the one hand or as farmers on the other. The differences lie in the emphasis given to agriculture rather than in the presence or lack of it. The Guayakí of the forests of eastern Paraguay are one of the few tribes without any agriculture; they feed on wild honey and larvae, catch fish with arrows, and hunt jaguars and armadillos. The Sirionó of Bolivia and most of the Makú (a denomination that comprises rather heterogeneous Amazonian groups) are nomads who hunt, fish, and gather. A few Makú groups, however, influenced by their neighbours, have become more or less sedentary farmers. The same holds for the Shirianá and Waica of the Orinoco–Amazon headwaters.

Production and technology

The crops are chiefly bitter manioc as well as other tubers and roots, and, in the western regions, maize (corn). Some Ge tribes grow mainly sweet potatoes and yams. The forest is cleared by felling the trees (the stone axe has now been everywhere replaced by the iron axe) and, when the underbrush is dry, setting fire to it. The same plot is used for several (but never more than six) consecutive crops and then left fallow for several years until it is covered by new vegetation. The group must therefore move periodically. The slash-and-burn system does not, except in the more fertile lowlands, permit the growth of dense populations. It does, however, provide a seasonal food surplus that might in many cases, considering the available techniques, be increased. But the Indian has no incentive to store up goods in a generally egalitarian society, since goods are not a source of prestige.

The tropical forest Indians are highly inventive. They have developed many types of harpoons, arrows, traps, snares, and blowguns. In fishing they employ a variety of drugs that stun or kill the fish without making them inedible. The bow and arrow are today known everywhere; in some Amazon regions they have replaced the spear thrower, a device still in use in certain western tribes. The bow and arrow are the principal weapons of warfare, although some groups fight with clubs and lances.

The techniques of basketry have a wealth of variations, mainly in the Guianas, the northwest Amazon region, and among the Ge peoples. Along with many kinds of baskets and hampers, these folk plait sifters, traps, fans, mats, and other household articles out of palm leaves and shafts of *taquara,* or bamboo.

The potter's wheel was traditionally unknown, but coiled ceramics reached a high degree of development, particularly among the Arawak and Pano tribes. Among nomadic groups pottery is either nonexistent or very rudimentary; instead, the nomads use gourds, calabashes, baskets, and fibre pouches.

Spinning and weaving, though well-known, remain at an elementary level since most tropical forest Indians, instead of dressing, prefer to paint the body and to embellish it with all sorts of adornments. From cotton, growing wild or planted, they make tunics, as well as belts of various types, skirts, and particularly hammocks. They use simple spindles, which they whirl like tops. The most common loom is the heddle loom: the threads of the weft, separated by heddles, are wound around a vertical frame. In regions close to the Andes, especially in eastern Bolivia, the Indians make cloth of beaten bark.

The roots of the manioc or cassava plant is a staple of the Indian diet, and its processing requires a number of implements including baskets and sifters, graters made of planks with little stones embedded in them, the *tipiti* (a plaited cylinder used to squeeze the prussic acid from the grated pulp), great clay pots for preparing the flour, and earthen fryers for making flat cakes.

Land is generally owned by the group occupying or exploiting it—a band, a village, or a clan—and parcelled out to families or other small units for hunting, fishing, or planting. Collective tribal land or territory exists only in rare cases, when the solidarity between the various groups of a people is particularly strong. There are rigorous norms for the distribution of game among the hunter's family and among other families to which he is associated by certain ties; the hunter himself may receive a rather small share. Cleared land almost always belongs to the family using it, but when necessary others may have access to its products. Generosity is greatly valued: the generous person is good, the miser bad. This also holds for intertribal relations, when gifts are exchanged on the occasion of visits or celebrations.

Weapons and household utensils are the property of individual men and women, but canoes and other objects used collectively are not. Body adornments generally belong to the wearer. Intangible property may belong to the clan or other social unit, but it may also be individually owned, as in the case of the name or ritual functions among Ge tribes, and magical–religious chants among the Guaraní.

Brisk trade among tribes is carried on in parts of the Guianas, in northwest Amazonia, and in upper Xingu. Indians of the upper Orinoco export *urucu,* a red dye, to groups living downriver. The Arawak frequently trade ceramic wares produced by their women; they also supply blowguns in exchange for poisonous curare and barter manioc graters. Carib tribes often trade cotton products. Some groups specialize in the manufacture of canoes, which are much in demand by neighbouring groups. The most complex trading system is that of the upper Xingu; it includes a dozen tribes, each with its own products. Commerce contributes significantly toward reducing cultural differences among the tribes, the more so because it is accompanied at times by ceremonial activities through which religious ideas and practices, as well as elements of social organization, are transmitted.

Belief and aesthetic systems. The jungle Indians believe that their well-being depends on being able to control innumerable supernatural powers, which in personal or impersonal form permeate or inhabit objects, living beings, and nature in general. Through shamanistic rites or collective ceremonies, man must encourage and maintain his harmonious integration in the universe, controlling the forces that govern it; their beneficial or harmful effects are largely determined by human action. In most of the cultures, magical measures and precautions are more important than the religious cult as such. The strength and health of the body, the normal growth of children, the capacity to procreate, and even psychic qualities are obtained by magical means. For the individual these means may include the perforation of the lips, nasal septum, or ear lobes, the painting of the body, and the use of various adornments. A little stick passed through the nasal septum, such as that used by the Pawumwa of the Guaporé River, prevents sickness. The hunter or fisherman, in order to be successful and not to be *panema* (unlucky), as they say in many Amazonian regions, takes precautions such as scarring his arms or abstaining from certain foods. The magical devices of the hunter, the fisherman, and the warrior are considered much more important than their ability. Arrows must be treated by rubbing with a certain drug, since their magical attributes are believed to be more effective than their technical properties.

Magic

Stimulants and narcotics are of great importance in the magic and religious practices of most tropical forest Indians. Secular use of drugs is much rarer. Tobacco is known by almost all tribes. The Tupinamba shaman fumigates his rattle with tobacco, which he believes contains an animating principle that confers on the rattle the faculty of "speaking," that is, of revealing the future. Alcoholic beverages, consumed mainly in religious festivals, are obtained by fermentation of manioc, corn, and other plants. They are unknown among the Ge, in the upper Xingu, and in some regions of Bolivia and Ecuador. Coca leaves are chewed, especially in the sub-Andean regions. Infusion of maté is taken in the Paraguay area, as well as by the Jívaro and other groups of Ecuador. Hallucinogens are used mainly in the Amazon–Orinoco area; they include species of *Banisteriopsis* (a tropical liana), from which is made a potion that produces visions. In certain tribes the use of this drug is restricted to shamanistic practices; in others, as in the Uaupés River area, it is an essential element in religious festivals in which the community revives its mythic tradition. Other narcotics in ritual use, among them the *yopo,* or *paricá* (*Piptadenia*), known among many northern groups, are often breathed in the form of snuff, which partners blow into one another's nostrils; the Omagua of the upper Amazon used it as an enema.

Some magical practices are reserved for the shaman, who acquires his status by natural endowment, by inspiration, by apprenticeship, or by painful initiation. The shaman may practice medicine, perform magic rites, and lead religious ceremonies. Rarely, however, is he a priest in the usual sense of the term. In many groups his influence is superior to that of the political chief; in some, as among the Guaraní, the two roles may coincide. Not uncommonly, his influence continues even after his death: in the Guianas and elsewhere, his soul becomes an auxiliary spirit of his living colleagues, helping them in their curing practices and in the control of harmful spirits; among the Rucuyen, the bodies of common individuals were cremated, while that of the shaman was kept in a special place so that his soul might live on.

The shaman as healer

In curing the sick, the shaman must remove the object causing the sickness: a small stone, a leaf, an insect, any substance that has been sent through the black magic of an evildoer. The cure consists of massages, suction, blowing, and fumigation. If the illness comes from loss of the soul, the shaman must search for and recover it. If it comes from a bad spirit, he tries to overcome the evil influence with the help of one or more auxiliary spirits.

The soul has its seat in the bones, the heart, the wrist, or in other parts of the body. Some Indians believe that two or more souls are responsible for various vital functions. One finds also the idea of a purely spiritual soul. The Guaraní believe that man has an animal soul governing his temperament and his instinctive reactions but that he also has a second, spiritual one, sent by a divinity at the moment of conception. Thanks to his second soul, man thinks, speaks, and is capable of noble sentiments. After death this second soul returns to live among the gods, while the other soul wanders the Earth as a ghost menacing the living.

Nature is believed to be peopled by demons and spirits that are beneficial or malevolent, depending on man's behaviour. Besides the soul that gives life to every living thing, many plants and animals have a "mother" or "master," as do manioc, maize, and game animals.

The mythology of almost all tribes includes a creator of the universe and of man. This creator seldom sustains interest in his handiwork, and thus there is usually no cult attached to him. Social institutions, customs, knowledge, techniques, and cultivated plants are deeds or gifts of a culture hero or a pair of them, sometimes twin brothers who may represent the Sun and Moon. A number of myths are told about these figures; sometimes the pair consists of a hero and a trickster who opposes him.

Ceremonial practices vary, depending on the tribe and its way of life. Some great collective ceremonies have been associated with war, as among the northern Carib and the coastal Tupí, both famous for cannibalism, and the headhunting Mundurukú and Jívaro. Ceremonies are often believed to be indispensable for regulating the course of the Sun and the Moon, the sequence of the seasons, the fertility of plants, the procreation of animals, and the very continuity of human life. Their objective may also be to commune with the dead or with mythical ancestors; when they are connected with the disposal of the dead, they are at the same time passage rites, by means of which the spirits of the dead are made harmless. Among the Guaraní, most religious ceremonies mean profound spiritual communion with the gods.

Corpses are commonly disposed of by ground burial within or without the house. Urn burial has also been known, especially among Tupí groups; some groups have been known to unearth bones, clean them, and then rebury them. The Tarariu (Tarairiu) of northeastern Brazil and some Pano broiled the flesh of their dead and mixed the pulverized bones and hair with water or with a manioc-base beverage that they drank. Tribes of the Caribbean coast, after drying the body by fire, allowed it to decompose and later added the powder to a drink. In other northern regions, one still finds the custom of cremating the cadaver and consuming the charred and crushed bones in a banana mush.

Aesthetic expression

Artistic efforts are most commonly applied to decoration, whether of the human body, objects of practical or ritual use, or even houses. The most common body adornments are paint and feather ornaments. Tattooing has also been practiced, especially among the Mundurukú and many Arawak tribes. Magical and religious ideas are usually expressed in these adornments. The Carib tribes of the Guianas and some Tupí were outstanding in featherwork. The plumed mantles of the Tupinamba, the delicate and elaborate adornments of the Caapor of Maranhão state, and the rich and varied ones of the Mundurukú are much celebrated.

The design of ornaments is almost always geometrical, with characteristic patterns for particular tribes; the styles vary with the cultural areas.

Masks, generally used in ceremonial dances, are restricted to the tribes of certain areas: the Cágaba of northern Colombia, the Tikuna and others of the northwestern Amazon, the Tucuna and their neighbours of the upper Amazon, the Guartegaya and Amniapé (Amniepe) of the upper Madeira, the tribes of the upper Xingu, the Karajá and the Tapirapé of the Araguáia River area, some Ge of central Brazil, and the Chiriguano of southern Bolivia. The masks represent the spirits of plants, fish, and other animals, as well as mythical heroes and divinities. They are highly stylized in form but, on occasion, naturalistic in expression.

The Waurá women of the upper Xingu are famous for their pots and animal-shaped bowls. Of the historic tribes, the Tapajó of the Amazon had the richest style in ceramics, excelled only by the archaeological remains of the Ilha de Marajó. Among some groups in the Guianas and western Amazonia, artistic activity includes wood carving.

MODERN DEVELOPMENTS

The great majority of the Indian groups are closed societies, despite intense intertribal relations in certain areas. They lack institutions that would enable them to become part of a larger, all-embracing, and technologically superior society. Their relations with the whites have placed them in a situation of dependency that usually ends with their breaking up. The white man's prohibition of warfare, headhunting, cannibalism, polygamy, and other institutions that have profound meaning in tribal life sets in motion a process of social disorganization. In addition, numerous tribes have been extinguished by violent destruction, slavery, the loss of lands required for subsistence, epidemics, and by marriage with whites and blacks. Innovations introduced by the whites often have harmful effects: *e.g.,* iron utensils, which not only subject the Indians to those who supply them but also change the traditional division of labour in tribal society, and clothing, which alters personal hygiene and makes its wearers susceptible to new diseases.

Disruption and crisis

Contact with the white man creates a profound crisis for the tribal leadership. Either the chief of the group is deprived of his authority, since the conditions for realizing the values essential to tribal life no longer exist, or he becomes despotic and a tool of the whites, using his power to benefit himself at the expense of his community.

Agricultural tribes are sometimes able to adapt to the new conditions for a time by trading their products, especially manioc flour. The sale of products such as fur skins, babassu nuts, copaiva oils, and carnauba wax helps in certain cases, as with the Tenetehara of Maranhão state, to maintain economic stability without breaking up the community organization. This is impossible, however, when the Indian undertakes to collect rubber for commercial firms, since this obliges the tribe to split into family units and to spread over vast areas; the result is an enormous cultural impoverishment. The transformation of the Indian into a labourer has generally led to the rupture of tribal bonds, much misery, and the disappearance of the tribes as ethnic entities.

There have been cases in which the Indian successfully integrated into the regional economic system as a paid worker or even as an independent producer. The Terena, an Arawak group of southern Mato Grosso, work on cattle breeding farms, an activity they learned long ago while vassals of the Guaycurú, who had become horse breeders after the Spanish conquest. The Goajiro of Colombia, another Arawak group, own great herds of cattle.

The disruption and crisis that follow inevitably upon contact with the whites are, however, less serious when the Indian has had earlier contact with a hybrid population carrying a cultural system that already incorporates many of the elements of civilization. These mixed cultures, such as those on the Brazilian–Paraguayan frontier and in some parts of Maranhão state, act as a kind of sieve between the system of tribal life and that of the white invader. In the past such cultures took numerous solutions, especially of an adaptive kind, from the Indian culture, helping to give the Indian a feeling of worth when facing the invader. Today he no longer has this privilege, since the hybrid cultures already possess whatever Indian elements they can use.

Messianic movements

The cultural crisis the Indians undergo in contact with the whites has brought about sporadic messianic outbreaks. Since the Indians face a problem for which there often seems to be no solution, they may appeal to the supernatural and wait for a miracle to happen. They hope for a return to the "lost paradise," that is, to the old life without the white man, whose expulsion or destruction may be part of the miracle. At the same time they want to avail themselves of some of the advantages of civilized life. Insofar as civilization seems an ideal impossible to realize without recourse to supernatural aid, because of the Indian's economic and social inferiority, the messianic miracle in many cases takes the form of a social and cultural revolution: in the new era the Indian will dominate over the white man and will have all those things in the civilized world that to him symbolize superior status.

In certain regions of the tropical forest these movements appear from time to time. Along the Río Negro in northwest Brazil, there have been several messiahs since the end of the 19th century. These leaders combined elements of their tribal religion with teachings and rites of Christian origin, although the predominant note was always hostility to the whites. Such movements have also occurred among the Tikuna of the upper Amazon; in one in 1956 the leaders proclaimed, among other things, that a city would appear suddenly in the middle of the forest, lighted by electricity and providing all the comforts of modern civilization. In 1963 the Canela, a Ge tribe of Maranhão state, had a messianic movement announcing that, when the new day came, the civilized people would be obliged to live in the forest or in the savanna, hunting with bow and arrow, while the Indians would become rich farmers. In this, as in other cases, the miracle was to be brought about by the great hero of tribal myth. The Guaraní of Paraguay and adjacent Brazilian regions are most famous for their frequent messianic movements, the fundamental myth of which is that a cataclysm will destroy the world and the Indian will find salvation in a distant paradise called the Land Without Evils. Probably the messianic tradition of the Guaraní dates from before the coming of the whites, but it seems to have undergone great expansion since then.

(Eg.S.)

South American nomad cultures

In the past, South American nomadic hunters, gatherers, and fishers could be found all the way from Cape Horn to the Orinoco River in northern South America. The most variable groups were found in the southern half of the continent, occupying a variety of habitats and exploiting differing resources. With the technology known to them, food production was low, the population sparse, the social organization simple. Constant movement within prescribed territories prevented large permanent villages or the accumulation of material wealth.

TRADITIONAL CULTURE PATTERNS

Types of South American nomads. *Shellfish gatherers.* In the south, the Chono, Alacaluf, and Yaghan Indians occupied the whole Chilean archipelago down to Cape Horn. This is a rugged terrain of islands and fjords with heavy rainfall, an average winter temperature of 32° F (0° C), and an average summer temperature of 50° F (10° C). The dense forests make land travel extremely difficult and horticulture impracticable. The area is poor in game, fish, and edible plants. The archipelagic tribes thus depended on shellfish and seals or whales that had been stranded on the beaches. Travel was almost entirely by canoe.

Hunters and gatherers of the steppes and plains. The large area of the steppes and plains extends from Tierra del Fuego, in the south, through Patagonia, to the Pampas of northern Argentina and Uruguay. The Ona occupied the islands of Tierra del Fuego. The brush-covered, semi-arid Patagonian plateau was the home of the Tehuelche, while the Puelche and Querandí inhabited the flat grassy Pampas. The Charrúa lived in the grasslands north of the Río de la Plata. In aboriginal times, these people practiced no agriculture and had no domesticated animals, with the possible exception of the dog. Throughout the region the tribal groups depended on hunting guanaco, rhea (the South American ostrich), and smaller animals and on gathering some roots and herbs. The population was one of the sparsest in South America.

Hunters, gatherers, and fishermen of the Gran Chaco. The Gran Chaco extends northward from the grasslands of the Pampas to Paraguay and southern Mato Grosso in Brazil. It is an arid region covered with drought-resisting vegetation. The area is drained by the Paraguay River and its western tributaries, such as the Pilcomayo, Bermejo, and Salado rivers, that originate in the Andean foothills. During the summer months the Chaco experiences the highest temperatures in South America.

The people subsisted on plant food, supplemented near the rivers by fish at certain times of the year. The plant foods were supplied by such pod-bearing thorny bushes as the algarrobo and by many local trees. Some wild rice was also available. Honey and larvae were also eaten. In the southeastern part, guanaco and rhea were hunted. On the whole, however, the people depended primarily on plant foods, in contrast to the nomads to the south, who were essentially hunters.

In aboriginal times all the nomadic peoples of the Chaco travelled on foot or, in some cases, in canoes. The horse was introduced into the Chaco after the Spanish conquest, and its adoption by some tribes had far-reaching consequences in the area. It is convenient to separate the Chaco tribes of historic times into foot Indians and horsemen. Among the foot Indians were such groupings as the Zamuco, of the northeast, and the Mataco, of the central Chaco. Each such grouping consisted of a number of tribes. The mounted bands, who spoke Guaycuruan, consisted of such groups as the Abipón, Mocoví, and Caduveo (Mbayá, or Guaycurú).

Forest hunters and gatherers. North of the Chaco, the country merges gradually into the tropical forest zone, particularly in the western section of Bolivia. In Brazil the forest zone comprises columns of forests on both banks of the major rivers. There are also island forests—large patches of forest standing on a plain or plateau, evidently supplied by springs that flow the year round. Typical nomadic tribes in this area were the Sirionó of eastern Bolivia and the Nambikwara (Nambicuara) of Mato Grosso, Brazil, and the Guayakí of eastern Paraguay.

Aquatic nomads. In the marshes of the upper Paraguay River in Brazil an unusual tribe of Indians, called the Guató, lived most of their lives in canoes, fishing and hunting cayman and other aquatic animals. They built temporary shelters on small islands that stood slightly above flood level. There are also other aquatic nomads in the north of South America and in the Caribbean.

Economic system. Because of their nomadic habits, all the hunters and gatherers had very little in the way of such material equipment as weapons, textiles, clothing, ornaments, and buildings. Their technical processes were very simple and appear to have been invented long ago.

Housing

Shelter was provided by caves if available. In the colder climate of the south, the archipelagic tribes of Chile and the nomads of the Chaco made domed huts of bent poles covered with bark, skins, or brush. When the people moved on they left the frame for others to use, taking only the skin coverings with them. The Patagonians made a skin-covered hut known as the *toldo.* The Yaghan used a conical tepee-like shelter or a double lean-to. The Nambikwara used a lean-to in the dry season or camped under trees, sleeping on fire-warmed ground. During the rainy season a larger double lean-to was used. There were no permanent settlements, although people sometimes gathered together to perform ceremonies and to feast when food was plentiful.

The forest hunters, such as the Sirionó and Nambikwara, wore no clothing. The southern nomads wore skin robes and crude moccasins. There was no sewn clothing. Earplugs, nose plugs, and lip plugs were widely used, except by the archipelagic people. Featherwork, armbands and leg bands, necklaces, and body painting were common in many areas. Some of these ornaments were used to distinguish bands or lineages and other groupings, but they were not used as status symbols.

Finger weaving of yarn spun from native cotton and palm frond fibres was practiced in the Chaco and among the Sirionó and Guató. The heddle loom, a later development, was known among the Sirionó, Nambikwara, and Chono. Long strips of fabric were woven for making armbands and leg bands and other decorations. Netting was used for making fishnets and bags for the transportation of goods, particularly in the Chaco.

Pottery was known to some of the nomads but was little used because pots were difficult to transport. Coiled basketry was widely used by the nomads. In the Chaco, twilled baskets made from palm fronds were used at campsites and abandoned when the people moved on. The Patagonian and Pampean hunters used containers made of skins.

Two methods of making fire were widespread. The first involved a spark with flint on iron pyrite. A later technique involved twirling a hardwood pointed stick in a socket in softer wood: dried pith was then placed around the drill, and by gently blowing on the spark the pith ignited. Meat and fish were cooked by placing them directly on coals or putting them into earth ovens, lined with heated stones and covered with earth and coals. The Chono boiled food by placing heated stones in tightly woven baskets. The hunting and fishing people used no salt, but the Chaco tribes, who depended primarily on plant food, traded for salt with the highland people. Some of the forest nomads used ashes in place of salt.

Weapons

Bows and arrows were used by all the nomads. Among the Patagonian and Pampean hunters, however, there is archaeological evidence to suggest that the bow and arrow was preceded by the bola. Before the introduction of the horse, guanaco and rhea were hunted by stalking, the hunter throwing the bolas around the neck or legs of the game. Bolas were made by attaching stone weights to two or three short cords that, in turn, were fastened to a longer lasso. With the coming of the horse after the Spanish conquest, the bolas became very important, for from horseback they could be easily swung to ensnare guanaco, rhea, wild cattle, and other large game. Among the Patagonians, Pampeans, and inhabitants of parts of the Chaco, it became the principal hunting device. Spears and the *atlatl,* or spear thrower, were used to some extent.

Among the forest nomads, such as the Sirionó and Nambikwara, the principal weapon for hunting and fishing was the longbow, which was six feet in length. The barbed arrows were from five to eight feet long. Because they had no canoes, both shot fish from the banks of a stream.

Among the archipelagic tribes of southern Chile it was predominantly the women who gathered shellfish on the beaches at low tide and who, from bark canoes, dived with a shell blade and a basket held in their teeth. The shellfish gatherers were careful not to exhaust the supply in one area. These people also always carried a fire on a clay platform in their canoes, both for warmth and for roasting shellfish over the coals. The men hunted cormorants, penguins, steamer ducks, petrels, and other marine birds at night with torches while they roosted, and clubbed them to death. Ducks and geese were lured by decoys, then captured with pole snares.

Seals and sea lions were harpooned in the water or clubbed on shore. Porpoises and sick whales were harpooned. Whale hunting was a cooperative enterprise involving many men, who risked their lives in flimsy bark canoes. Fish were sometimes found in shallows or in pools at low tide and, with the help of dogs, were driven into nets. Because the Indians had no knowledge of food preservation, they had to be constantly on the move to provide for their food supply.

Social organization. The typical organization among nomadic hunters, gatherers, and fishers was the band, which, depending on the resources, could be large or very small. Low productivity and the lack of developed transportation prevented the accumulation of a surplus to maintain permanent communities. There were no social or occupational specialists; every family produced its own equipment. Despite these general similarities there was wide diversity in social structure depending on the methods of obtaining food.

Among the Chono, Alacaluf, and Yaghan of the Chilean archipelago, the natives were dispersed in elementary family units of father, mother, and children with perhaps an elder or two. These small family bands, if they can be so called, moved from one beach to another. There were no permanent territorial claims to shellfish beds, although individual families repelled others while they were using a particular shellfish bed. Sometimes close relatives or friends would move together briefly; and at times a number of families would gather together to feast on a stranded whale or join in hunting seals or seal lions. The family was also the economic unit among the Guató and, during the dry season, among the Nambikwara. This, of course, does not mean that the people did not visit relatives when circumstances permitted or when certain religious and ceremonial activities demanded.

Multifamily bands. The hunting of guanaco and rhea among the eastern Yaghan and Ona and among the Patagonian and Pampean tribes was more productive when carried out cooperatively by a number of families banded together. Such bands numbered from 40 to 100 persons and had defined hunting territories, which the men defended against trespass. Chieftainship does not appear to have been hereditary but was ceded to a leader able in settling both internal disputes and conflicts between bands.

Composite bands. With the introduction of horses and cattle, a great change took place in the band organization. Horse nomadism permitted greater mobility, new techniques of hunting, and much larger bands. The former foot hunters joined into bands ranging from 500 to 1,000 persons. They roamed over ill-defined areas hunting wild cattle and raiding Spanish settlements and other Indians lacking horses. Each of these bands consisted of a number of lineages under a leader of proven ability; a strong leader might attract a huge following, including members drawn away from other bands. Warfare between bands increased because of uncertainties over rights to territory.

The southern hunters of Patagonia and the Pampas were patrilineal (descent was reckoned in the male line) and patrilocal (a wife resided with her husband's lineage and band).

Forest nomads, such as the Guayakí and Sirionó, on the other hand, were matrilineal and matrilocal; that is, an individual traced his ancestry through his mother's lineage, and a man went to live with his wife's band. Matrilineal descent and matrilocal residence were associated with the importance of women in collecting wild plant foods.

Chaco tribes

Although little is known about the social structure of the Chaco tribes in aboriginal times, there appears to have been a contrast between the peoples of the dry western area and the wetter eastern area. Because the people in the west depended on water holes, they were forced to shift camp frequently as holes dried up. The groups nevertheless seem to have claimed territorial rights to gathering, fishing, and hunting areas. With the arrival of the Spaniards and an increase in warfare, the authority of the chiefs was strengthened, although chieftainship was rarely hereditary. In the eastern Chaco, on the other hand, the presence of fish runs in the larger rivers and the practice of fairly productive cultivation permitted the settlements to be larger and less mobile. After acquiring the horse from the Spanish, however, the Caduveo and other Guaycuruan-speaking peoples gave up what little horticulture they practiced and became predatory nomads raiding Spanish settlements, taking cattle, and capturing slaves from more sedentary tribes. Other Chaco tribes, such as the Abipón, Mocoví, Toba, and Lengua, also became horsemen and raiders. These tribes continued to move their camps in search of pasture for their herds of horses and cattle. Incipient class differences based on war honours and wealth appeared.

Caduveo raiders

The Caduveo were outstanding raiders in the Chaco. Although roaming over great areas, the warrior bands always returned to their base settlements, where they had permanent houses and kept their slaves and livestock. The Caduveo also exhibited the clearest form of social stratification, which, although pre-Spanish, crystallized with the coming of the horse and the intensification of warfare. Caduveo society became stratified into nobles, warriors, serfs, and slaves. The nobles were divided into those who inherited their titles and those upon whom titles were bestowed for lifetime only. The warrior class was basically hereditary, but other men demonstrating greatness in war could become members, thereby establishing new hereditary lines. The serfs, who served only the members of the noble class, were from subjugated peoples. The lower class was made up of captured and purchased slaves, who included not only Indians from neighbouring tribes but also mestizos from the Spanish settlements. Slaves could gain their freedom by marrying into the warrior class.

Family and kinship. Marriage among most nomadic tribes was consensual, similar to common-law marriage. It was easily entered into and easily dissolved, although there were strong forces supporting its continuance, especially whenever women played an important role as food gatherers. Noble classes, where they existed, as among the Caduveo, were practically endogamous; virtually all men, that is, married within their own class.

Marriage customs

Marriage among the shellfish gatherers of the Chilean

archipelago, on the other hand, was a stronger institution. Postmarital fidelity was demanded. The family formed a strong autonomous unit that performed nearly all cultural activities on its own and cooperated with other families only briefly during sea hunts and initiation ceremonies. Marriage between known relatives was forbidden, but in practice this meant merely that first cousins and closer kin could not marry. A widow, however, could marry the brother of her deceased husband; and a widower could marry the sister of his deceased wife; these practices of levirate and sororate helped to maintain family alliances, when almost everything else tended to draw families apart.

The larger nomadic bands in South America practiced band exogamy; that is, a person in one band could marry only someone in another band. These marriages were not made at random, however, for (as among the Nambikwara) cross-cousin marriage was preferred; in a matrilineal society a man married his mother's brother's daughter; in a patrilineal society he married his father's sister's daughter.

Rites of passage. Birth ceremonies were simple family affairs. After the birth, both parents fasted for a few days and observed food taboos. Couvade was practiced; that is, the father stayed in the hut several days, mimicking labour, while relatives and friends provided essential needs.

Among the Sirionó a child was born openly in the communal house; and after birth the parents walked in the forest scattering ashes as a purification rite and then lit a new fire that signified new life.

Before the age of puberty, boys and girls learned by imitating older children and adults. Among the shellfish gatherers, children by the age of four began to gather shellfish and spear sea urchins close to shore, returning to camp to roast them and eat them. From an early age children thus took care of their food needs as far as shellfish were concerned. Boys and girls were separated after the age of seven. The boys played with bows and arrows. The girls learned to swim and dive. Males did not learn to swim or dive, since diving for shellfish was women's work. Corporal punishment was rare, but children were lectured by elders on manners and morals.

Socialization was formalized especially in the initiation rite, which marked the passage from youth to adulthood for both sexes. There was usually no fixed date, the time depending upon the number of neophytes and the opportunity to amass a supply of food for the feast.

Initiation rites

The initiation ceremonies began with the men preparing sealing clubs and shellfish poles in a special hut in which they painted their faces and participated in singing, dancing, and mummery. The men then went out to hunt seals on the coastal rookeries, and the women went for shellfish. The men then built a large hut, where they sang, danced, and instructed the young men in proper vocational and moral behaviour. Later, women joined in the ceremony instructing girls in the proper behaviour for women. Then followed a mock battle between the sexes. After a feast, the assembly disbanded.

Among the Patagonian and Pampean tribes, a special hut known as the pretty house was erected for initiation ceremonies (as well as for some other rites, such as first menses). Medicine men bled themselves and smeared the novices with blood. There was dancing by the men and singing by the women. Horses were killed and roasted, and horsemeat was passed out to the guests.

In the Chaco there was considerable variation in the details of the initiation rites, but the underlying purpose of education and socialization was the same as among the shellfish gatherers and the Patagonian and Pampean guanaco hunters. Boys went through several rites, and when blood was drawn from their genitals they were considered mature warriors. On the Bermejo and Pilcomayo rivers, girls' puberty rites were attended with singing and dancing designed to protect the girls from evil spirits. A girl was kept in isolation and observed a special diet. After the rites pubescent girls were allowed sexual liberty and often took the initiative in love affairs.

Among none of the nomadic peoples did marriages involve any special ceremonies; gifts, though, were exchanged between the bride's and the groom's parents. Death rites were more complex. Mourners painted their faces black, beat on the outside of the dead person's hut, fasted, and lamented. They also directed their anger at the supreme deity. In the Chilean archipelago, the dead person and his effects were either buried or cremated. Among the Patagonian and Pampean tribes, the corpse was left on a hilltop or placed in a cave; some belongings were placed near the body.

Religion. Among the Yaghan shellfish gatherers there was a belief in a Supreme Being who was not a creator but a ruler. He was one who gave life to men and who gave humans animal and plant foods. People prayed to this being for success in fishing and hunting. Among the Patagonian and Pampean tribes there was a belief in a supreme being who, after creating the world, did not enter further into human affairs. There was a belief in good and evil bush spirits.

The Chaco groups did not believe in a supreme being. Although celestial bodies sometimes were thought to affect human beings, they were not objects of worship. The Chaco people had great fear of the ghosts of the dead and disposed of the corpse as quickly as possible. The body was buried in a cemetery, and food offerings were made. The house and property of the deceased were burned.

Forest nomad ceremonies

Among such forest nomads as the Sirionó and Nambikwara, rituals and ceremonies were much less developed than in the Chaco. This no doubt was due to incessant search for food and the inability to accumulate surpluses for large-scale feasts. Although the Sirionó did not believe in a supreme being, they did consider the Moon to be a culture hero who gave them maize and manioc and other features of their culture. They also feared the ghosts of the dead and bush spirits.

Shamans, or medicine men, who were thought to receive their curative powers through the ghosts of dead shamans and special guardian spirits, were important among all the tribal groups. Among the Chaco groups shamanism was very highly developed, both for curing illnesses and in working for the general welfare of the tribe. Sickness was caused, it was thought, by one of two means: mysterious foreign objects would magically penetrate the body, causing disease, or a person's soul would leave the body, leaving him ill. In the former instance, the shaman would suck out the foreign object; in the latter, he would go out at night and bring the wandering soul back.

MODERN DEVELOPMENTS

The existing nomadic hunters and gatherers are marginal survivors who retain many archaic culture traits and share very few of the more recent inventions. In areas in which they have not been disturbed by the whites or in which they have had opportunity to withdraw into refuge areas, they have been able to maintain much of their original culture. In areas in which they have come into permanent contact with the whites, some have become rudimentary agriculturalists, building permanent houses, making pottery, and weaving. In the late 20th century, the conversion of the nomadic habitat into large-scale agricultural projects seemed to be bringing many of these tribal peoples to the verge of extinction. (K.Ob./Ed.)

BIBLIOGRAPHY

North American peoples and cultures. Some of the more notable general surveys of the American Indians are ALICE B. KEHOE, *North American Indians, A Comprehensive Account* (1981); ROBERT F. SPENCER and JESSE D. JENNINGS *et al.*, *The Native Americans,* 2nd ed. (1977); CLARK WISSLER, *Indians of the United States,* rev. ed. (1966), and *The American Indian: An Introduction to the Anthropology of the New World,* 3rd ed. (1938); H.E. DRIVER, *Indians of North America,* 2nd ed. rev. (1969); A.L. KROEBER, *Cultural and Natural Areas of Native North America* (1939); RUTH M. UNDERHILL, *Red Man's America* (1953); PAUL S. MARTIN, GEORGE I. QUIMBY, and DONALD COLLIER, *Indians Before Columbus* (1947); FRED EGGAN (ed.), *Social Anthropology of North American Tribes,* 2nd ed. (1955); and E.B. LEACOCK and N.O. LURIE (eds.), *North American Indians in Historical Perspective* (1971). An extensive listing of books and articles on particular Indian groups is given in GEORGE P. MURDOCK, *Ethnographic Bibliography of North America,* 3rd ed. (1960). Names, locations, and historical events are summarized in FREDERICK WEBB HODGE (ed.), *Handbook of American Indians North of Mexico,* 2 vol. (1912, reprinted 1968). An encyclopaedic summary of current knowledge, literature, and research is provided by WILLIAM C. STURTEVANT (ed.), *Handbook of North American Indians* (1978–); when complete the work will comprise 20 volumes summarizing knowledge about 11 principal cultural regions north of Mexico, as well as cross-cultural themes such as race relations, technology, languages, biography, and the place of these peoples in contemporary society. An older, but still useful summary is provided by JOHN R. SWANTON, *The Indian Tribes of North America* (1952).

For archaeology and prehistory some useful introductory works are JESSE D. JENNINGS, *Prehistory of North America,* 2nd ed. (1974); DIAMOND JENNESS (ed.), *The American Aborigines* (1933); KENNETH MACGOWAN and J.A. HESTER, JR., *Early Man in the New World* (1962); and H.M. WORMINGTON, *Ancient Man in North America,* 4th ed. (1957). For physical anthropology some important surveys are W.S. LAUGHLIN (ed.), *Papers on the Physical Anthropology of the American Indian* (1951); T.D. STEWART, "A Physical Anthropologist's View of the Peopling of the New World," *SWest. J. Anthrop.* 16:259–273 (1960); and T.D. STEWART and M.T. NEWMAN, "An Historical Résumé of the Concept of Differences in Indian Types," *Am. Anthrop.,* 53:19–26 (1951).

American subarctic cultures. Major ethnographic accounts of the pre-fur-trade period include, for the eastern or Algonkian area, FRANK G. SPECK, *Naskapi: The Savage Hunters of the Labrador Peninsula* (1935; reprinted 1977), an account of beliefs, many of which survive into the present; and JOHN J. HONIGMANN, "The Attawapiskat Swampy Cree: An Ethnographic Reconstruction," *Anthrop. Pap. Univ. Alaska,* 5:23–82 (1956). EDWARD S. ROGERS has written fully on pre- and post-contact culture of the Round Lake (Ontario) Ojibwa; see especially *The Round Lake Ojibwa* (1962). For the western or Athabascan area, JOHN J. HONIGMANN has done an ethnographic reconstruction of *The Kaska Indians* (1954); and CORNELIUS OSGOOD, the leading authority on the Athabascans, reports exhaustively on *Ingalik Material Culture, Ingalik Social Culture,* and *Ingalik Mental Culture* (1940, 1958, and 1959). *Man in Northeastern North America,* ed. by FREDERICK JOHNSON (1946), brings together authoritative papers on geography, physical anthropology, linguistics, mythology, psychological characteristics, and culture in general. A study of a northern town, Inuvik, where Indians live, is JOHN J. and IRMA HONIGMANN, *Arctic Townsmen* (1970).

Northwest Coast Indians. There are few books that treat Northwest Coast culture on an area-wide basis; among the principal ones are: P. DRUCKER, *Indians of the Northwest Coast* (1963), and *Cultures of the North Pacific Coast* (1965). The former emphasizes material culture, technology, and art; the second, social and ceremonial organization. There are many good descriptions of individual Northwest Coast divisions: A. KRAUSE, *Die Tlinkit-Indianer* (1885; Eng. trans., *The Tlingit Indians,* 1956); V.E. GARFIELD and PAUL S. WINGERT, *The Tsimshian Indians and Their Arts* (1967); T.F. MCILWRAITH, *The Bella Coola Indians,* 2 vol. (1948); FRANZ BOAS, *Kwakiutl Ethnography,* ed. by H. CODERE (1966); P. DRUCKER, *The Northern and Central Nootkan Tribes* (1951); H.G. BARNETT, *The Coast Salish of British Columbia* (1955); and A.L. KROEBER, chapters on Yurok, Karok, and Hupa in *Handbook of the Indians of California,* 2nd ed. (1953).

Californian Indians. A.L. KROEBER, *Handbook of the Indians of California,* 2nd ed. (1953); ROBERT F. HEIZER and M.A. WHIPPLE (eds.), *California Indians: A Source Book,* 2nd ed. (1971); and EDWARD S. CURTIS, *The North American Indian,* vol. 15–16 (1907, reprinted 1970), provide the most general summaries of native California cultures, although each source is not wholly representative of the latest thoughts. More recent accounts appear in various publications of the University of California, such as *Anthropological Records, University of California Publications in American Archaeology and Ethnology,* and the *Reports of the University of California Archaeological Research Facility.* Many new interpretations of native California cultures are also contained in the *Annual Reports of the Archaeological Survey of the University of California at Los Angeles.* Several books of interest are RAYMOND C. WHITE, *Luiseño Social Organization* (1963); LOWELL JOHN BEAN, *Mukat's People* (1972); JACK D. FORBES, *Native Americans of California and Nevada* (1968); and ROBERT F. HEIZER and ALAN ALMQUIST, *The Other Californians* (1971). Books recently prepared for the nonspecialist, which are very readable, are THEODORA KROEBER, *Ishi i två världar* (1963; Eng. trans., *Ishi in Two Worlds,* 1964); and ROBERT F. HEIZER and THEODORA KROEBER, *Almost Ancestors* (1968). B.W. and E.G. AGINSKY, *Deep Valley* (1967), provides a readable fictional account of the Pomo Indians.

North American Plateau Indians. The archaeological background has been described by E.H. SWANSON, *The Emergence of Plateau Culture* (1962); and B.R. BUTLER, *The Old Cordilleran Culture in the Pacific Northwest* (1961). A noteworthy paper is R.D. DAUGHERTY, *Archaeology of the Lind Coulee Site, Washington* (1956). General ethnological perspectives have been presented in two papers by V.F. RAY, *Cultural Relations in the Plateau of Northwestern America* (1939) and *Culture Element Distributions,* pt. 22, *Plateau* (1942). There are several good monographs on single tribes: J.A. TEIT, *The Thompson Indians of British Columbia* (1900); H.J. SPINDEN, *The Nez Percé Indians* (1908); LESLIE SPIER, *Klamath Ethnography* (1930); V.F. RAY, *The Sanpoil and Nespelem: Salishan Peoples of Northeastern Washington* (1932); and the work edited by LESLIE SPIER, *The Sinkaietk or Southern Okanagon of Washington* (1938). Demographic, linguistic, and sociopolitical analyses may be found in V.F. RAY, "Native Villages and Groupings of the Columbia Basin," *Pacif. NW. Q.,* 27:99–152 (1936); T.R. GARTH, "Early Nineteenth Century Tribal Relations in the Columbia Plateau," *SWest. J. Anthrop.,* 20:43–57 (1964); and W.W. ELMENDORF, "Linguistic and Geographic Relations in the Northern Plateau Area," *ibid.,* 21:63–78 (1965). Kinship systems are discussed in M. JACOBS, "Northern Sahaptin Kinship Terms," *Am. Anthrop.,* 34:688–693 (1932); and W.W. ELMENDORF, "System Change in Salish Kinship Terminologies," *SWest. J. Anthrop.,* 17:365–382 (1961). LESLIE SPIER, *The Prophet Dance of the Northwest and Its Derivatives: The Source of the Ghost Dance* (1935), has become a classic, but must now be checked against D.E. WALKER, JR., "New Light on the Prophet Dance Controversy," *Ethnohistory,* 16:245–256 (1969). Modern culture contact problems are dealt with in a skilful way in D.E. WALKER, *Conflict and Schism in Nez Percé Acculturation* (1968).

North American Great Basin Indians. There is no general monograph on all Great Basin Indians. CATHERINE S. FOWLER, *Great Basin Anthropology: A Bibliography* (1970), lists some 6,500 sources on the area. Summary articles on various aspects of Great Basin anthropology are contained in W.L. D'AZEVEDO *et al.* (eds.), *The Current Status of Anthropological Research in the Great Basin: 1964* (1966); and in E.H. SWANSON, JR. (ed.), *Languages and Cultures of Western North America* (1970). The earliest systematic study of Great Basin Indians was by JOHN WESLEY POWELL; see D.D. and C.S. FOWLER (eds.), *Anthropology of the Numa: John Wesley Powell's Manuscripts on the Numic Peoples of Western North America, 1868–1880* (1971). Modern ethnographic studies include J.H. STEWARD, *Basin-Plateau Aboriginal Sociopolitical Groups* (1938); R.H. LOWIE, *Notes on Shoshonean Ethnography* (1924); R.F. and Y. MURPHY, *Shoshone-Bannock Subsistence and Society* (1960); V.C. TRENHOLM and M. CARLEY, *The Shoshonis: Sentinals of the Rockies* (1964); JAMES F. DOWNS, *The Two Worlds of the Washo, an Indian Tribe of California and Nevada* (1966); and I.T. KELLY, *Southern Paiute Ethnography* (1964). Religious beliefs are treated by W.Z. PARK, *Shamanism in Western North America* (1938); and B.B. WHITING, *Paiute Sorcery* (1950). Important linguistic studies include E. SAPIR, *Southern Paiute Texts and Dictionary* (1930–31); W.H. JACOBSEN, JR., "Washo Linguistic Studies," and W.R. MILLER, "Anthropological Linguistics in the Great Basin," both in W.L. D'AZEVEDO (*op. cit.*). Great Basin prehistory is summarized in J.D. JENNINGS, "The Desert West" in J.D. JENNINGS and E. NORBECK (eds.), *Prehistoric Man in the New World,* pp. 149–174 (1964).

Southwest American Indians. EDWARD H. SPICER, *Cycles of Conquest: The Impact of Spain, Mexico, and the United States on the Indians of the Southwest, 1533–1960* (1962); and FRED EGGAN, *The American Indian,* ch. 5 (1966), are the most comprehensive, authoritative accounts. Among other significant studies of the region as a whole are: EMIL W. HAURY (ed.), "The Southwest Issue," *Am. Anthrop.,* 56:529–731 (1954); JOHN COLLIER, *Patterns and Ceremonials of the Indians of the Southwest* (1949); RUTH M. UNDERHILL, *Ceremonial Patterns in the Greater Southwest* (1948); ELSIE CLEWS PARSONS, *Pueblo Indian Religion* (1939); RUTH BENEDICT, "Psychological Types in the Cultures of the Southwest," in the *Proceedings of the Twenty-Third International Congress of Americanists,* pp. 572–581 (1930); and GEORGE FRANCIS CARTER, *Plant Geography and Culture History in the American Southwest* (1945). Recommended tribal studies are: for the Yumans, C. DARYLL FORDE, *Ethnography of the Yuma Indians* (1931); and LESLIE SPIER, *Yuman Tribes of the Gila River* (1933, reprinted 1970); for the Pima-Papago, WILLIAM H. KELLY, *The Papago Indians of Arizona* (1963); RUTH M. UNDERHILL, *Singing for Power* (1938, reprinted 1968); and ALICE JOSEPH, R.B. SPICER, and J. CHESKY, *The Desert People* (1949); for the Pueblos, FRED EGGAN, *Social Organization of the Western Pueblos* (1950); EDWARD P. DOZIER, *The Pueblos of the Southwestern United States* (1960); ALFONSO ORTIZ, *The Tewa World* (1969); CHARLES H. LANGE, *Cochití* (1960); DOROTHEA C. LEIGHTON and J. ADAIR, *People of the Middle Place: A Study of the Zuni Indians* (1963); and LAURA THOMPSON and ALICE JOSEPH, *The Hopi Way* (1944, reprinted 1965). Other viewpoints regarding Pueblo personality development are found in ESTHER S. GOLDFRANK, "Socialization, Personality, and the Structure of Pueblo Society (with Particular Reference to Hopi and Zuni)," *Am. Anthrop.,* 47:516–539 (1945); and DOROTHY EGGAN, "General Problem of Hopi Adjustment," *Am. Anthrop.*, 45:357–373 (1943). Recommended for the Navajo are CLYDE KLUCKHOHN and DOROTHEA LEIGHTON, *The Navaho* (1946); DOROTHEA LEIGHTON and CLYDE KLUCKHOHN, *Children of the People* (1947, reprinted 1969); for the Apache, MORRIS OPLER, *An Apache Life-Way* (1941).

North American Plains Indians. ROBERT H. LOWIE, *Indians of the Plains* (1963), is a short but authoritative general work. Accounts of particular tribes include: Lowie's *The Crow Indians* (1935); ALFRED W. BOWERS, *Mandan Social and Ceremonial Organization* (1950) and *Hidatsa Social and Ceremonial Organization* (1965); ALICE C. FLETCHER and FRANCIS LAFLESCHE, *The Omaha Tribe* (1911); JOHN C. EWERS, *The Blackfeet* (1958); GEORGE B. GRINNELL, *The Cheyenne Indians*, 2 vol. (1923); and E. WALLACE and E.A. HOEBEL, *The Comanches* (1952). GEORGE P. MURDOCK, *Ethnographic Bibliography of North America* (1960), covers the Plains in general and each tribe specifically. Records by early observers include JEAN LOUIS BERLANDIER, *The Indians of Texas in 1830*, ed. by JOHN C. EWERS (1969); and GEORGE CATLIN, *North American Indians*, 2 vol. (1926). GORDON MACGREGOR, *Warriors Without Weapons* (1946), is a study of the society and personality of the Teton Dakota under reservation conditions.

Eastern Woodlands Indians. Names, locations, and historical events are summarized in FREDERICK WEBB HODGE (ed.), *Handbook of American Indians, North of Mexico*, 2 vol. (1907–10); and JOHN R. SWANTON, *The Indian Tribes of North America* (1952). Indian cultures of the area are summarized in ROBERT E. and PAT RITZENTHALER, *The Woodland Indians of the Western Great Lakes* (1970); W. VERNON KINIETZ, *The Indians of the Western Great Lakes, 1615–1760* (1940); and in general surveys of North American Indians as listed above. Descriptions of particular cultures include: FRANK G. SPECK, *Penobscot Man: The Life History of a Forest Tribe in Maine* (1940); W.D. and R.S. WALLIS, *The Micmac Indians of Eastern Canada* (1955); ROGER WILLIAMS, *A Key into the Language of America* (1643, reprinted 1971), despite its formidable title a delightful book and the best description of a southern New England Indian people; ALDEN T. VAUGHAN, *New England Frontier: Puritans and Indians, 1620–1675* (1965); WILLIAM W. NEWCOMB, JR., *The Culture and Acculturation of the Delaware Indians* (1956); LEWIS H. MORGAN, *League of the Ho-de-no-sau-nee, or Iroquois* (1851, reprinted 1966); GEORGE T. HUNT, *The Wars of the Iroquois* (1940); ANTHONY F.C. WALLACE, *The Death and Rebirth of the Seneca* (1970); ELISABETH TOOKER, *An Ethnography of the Huron Indians, 1615–1649* (1964); BRUCE G. TRIGGER, *The Huron Farmers of the North* (1969); PAUL RADIN, *The Winnebago Tribe* (1923); WALTER JAMES HOFFMAN, *The Menomini Indians* (1896); RUTH LANDES, *Ojibwa Sociology* (1937, reprinted 1969); WILLIAM T. HAGAN, *The Sac and Fox Indians* (1958); and BERT ANSON, *The Miami Indians* (1970). Modern reservation life is described in EDMUND WILSON, *Apologies to the Iroquois* (1960); and FREDERICK O. GEARING, *The Face of the Fox* (1970).

Southeast American Indians. JOHN R. SWANTON, *The Indians of the Southeastern United States* (1946), is the standard starting point for information on the traditional cultures of the Southeast. Other indispensable works by Swanton are *Indian Tribes of the Lower Mississippi Valley and Adjacent Coast of the Gulf of Mexico* (1911), *Early History of the Creek Indians and Their Neighbors* (1922, reprinted 1970), *Social Organization and Social Usages of the Indians of the Creek Confederacy* (1928), *Religious Beliefs and Medical Practices of the Creek Indians* (1928), *Social and Religious Beliefs and Usages of the Chickasaw Indians* (1928), *Myths and Tales of the Southeastern Indians* (1929), *Source Material for the Social and Ceremonial Life of the Choctaw Indians* (1931), and *Source Material on the History and Ethnology of the Caddo Indians* (1942). A later summary is provided by CHARLES HUDSON, *The Southeastern Indians* (1976). Also valuable are various works by FRANK G. SPECK, including, *The Creek Indians of Taskigi Town* (1907), *Ethnology of the Yuchi Indians* (1909), and, with LEONARD BROOM, *Cherokee Dance and Drama* (1951). JAMES MOONEY, *Myths of the Cherokee* (1900), remains the basic source on the Cherokee and may be usefully supplemented by WILLIAM H. GILBERT, *The Eastern Cherokees* (1943). For the Seminoles, CLAY MACCAULEY, *The Seminole Indians of Florida* (1887); ALEXANDER SPOEHR, *Camp, Clan and Kin Among the Cow Creek Seminole of Florida* (1941), and *The Florida Seminole Camp* (1944); and various articles by WILLIAM C. STURTEVANT, referred to in his essay "Creek into Seminole" in E.B. LEACOCK and N.O. LURIE (eds.), *North American Indians in Historical Perspective* (1971), provide basic background. For the piedmont tribes, see JAMES MOONEY, *The Siouan Tribes of the East* (1894); and recent works by DOUGLAS S. BROWN, *The Catawba Indians* (1966); and CHARLES M. HUDSON, *The Catawba Nation* (1970).

On more specialized topics, MARY R. HAAS, "Southeastern Indian Linguistics," in C.M. HUDSON (ed.), *Red, White, and Black* (1971), is an important review of linguistic relations; WILLIAM C. STURTEVANT, *The Significance of Ethnological Similarities Between Southeastern North America and the Antilles* (1960), clears up some difficult issues; EMMA L. FUNDABURK and MARY D.F. FOREMAN, *Sun Circles and Human Hands* (1957), provides fine illustrations and commentary on prehistoric and historic Southeastern art; JOHN WITTHOFT, *Green Corn Ceremonialism in the Eastern Woodlands* (1949), is an important contribution to Southeastern religion; as is JAMES H. HOWARD, *The Southeastern Ceremonial Complex and Its Interpretation* (1968). Many detailed scholarly works exist on the post-contact history of the Southeastern Indians, among which might be mentioned GRANT FOREMAN, *The Five Civilized Tribes* (1934, reprinted 1971), and *Indian Removal* (1932); ANGIE DEBO, *And Still the Waters Run* (1940, reprinted 1966), and *The Rise and Fall of the Choctaw Republic* (1934); ROBERT S. COTTERILL, *The Southern Indians* (1954); VERNER CRANE, *The Southern Frontier, 1670–1732* (1929); DAVID H. CORKRAN, *The Cherokee Frontier* (1962), and *The Creek Frontier* (1967); and THURMAN WILKINS, *Cherokee Tragedy* (1970).

Middle American peoples and cultures. The most authoritative work on Middle America is the monumental *Handbook of Middle American Indians*, ed. by ROBERT WAUCHOPE, 16 vol. (1964–76). These volumes cover all aspects of the area from physical geography, linguistics, archaeology, physical anthropology, and ethnology to social anthropology. ERIC WOLF, *Sons of the Shaking Earth* (1959), is the best single book on Middle America. SOL TAX (ed.), *Heritage of Conquest* (1952), is a professional anthropological estimate of the content of Middle American Indian culture. *The Maya and Their Neighbors* (1940) is an introduction to the archaeological and historical problems of the region and contains the basic essay on Indian history by OLIVER LA FARGE. S.G. MORLEY, *The Ancient Maya*, 3rd rev. ed. (1956); J. ERIC THOMPSON, *The Rise and Fall of Maya Civilization*, 2nd ed. (1970); and MICHAEL D. COE, *The Maya* (1966), give views on that civilization. G.C. VAILLANT, *The Aztecs of Mexico*, rev. ed. (1956), is a basic book; and H.J. SPINDEN, *Ancient Civilizations of Mexico and Central America*, 3rd rev. ed. (1968), is important for its calendrical correlations. For an understanding of the colonial period, the works of BERNARDINO DE SAHAGUN, trans. by A.J.O. ANDERSON and C.E. DIBBLE, *The Florentine Codex*, pt. 9–10 (1959); and A.M. TOZZER's annotated translation of Landa's *Relación de las cosas de Yucatán* (1941), is essential. For historical accounts, see R.N. ADAMS, *Crucifixion by Power: Essays on Guatemalan National Social Structures, 1944–1966* (1970). GEORGE M. MCBRIDE, *The Land Systems of Mexico* (1923, reprinted 1971); FRANCOIS CHEVALIER, *La Formation des grands domaines au Mexique* (1952; Eng. trans., *Land and Society in Colonial Mexico: The Great Hacienda*, 1963); and NATHAN L. WHETTEN, *Rural Mexico* (1948), give an adequate picture. The modern studies in Middle American communities are listed in HOWARD CLINE, "Mexican Community Studies," *Hispanic American Historical Review*, 32:212–242 (1952); and in R.H. EWALD, *Bibliografía comentada sobre antropología social guatemalteca, 1900–1955* (1956). Modern developments are described in J.L. ARRIOLA (ed.), *Integración social en Guatemala* (1956); W.E. MOORE, *Industrialization and Labor* (1951); and by R.N. ADAMS in *Political Changes in Guatemalan Indian Communities* (1957).

North Mexican Indian cultures. CARL LUMHOLTZ, *Unknown Mexico*, 2 vol. (1902), gives the first modern account of North Mexican groups and is still a major source. Another excellent source is EVON Z. VOGT (ed.), *Handbook of Middle American Indians*, vol. 8 (1969), which contains articles covering each of the groups. A basic source on the history, cultural geography, and ethnography are the following bulletins of the *Ibero-Americana* series that cover western Mexico in depth: RALPH L. BEALS, *Comparative Ethnology of Northern Mexico Before 1750* (1932), *Acaxee: A Mountain Tribe of Durango and Sinaloa* (1933), and *Aboriginal Culture of the Cáhita Indians* (1943); CARL O. SAUER, *Distribution of Aboriginal Tribes and Languages in Northwestern Mexico* (1934), and *Aboriginal Population of Northwestern Mexico* (1935); ALFRED L. KROEBER, *Uto-Aztecan Languages of Mexico* (1934). EDWARD SPICER, *Cycles of Conquest: The Impact of Spain, Mexico, and the United States on the Indians of the Southwest, 1533–1960* (1962), presents the only overview of change since colonial times. CAMPBELL W. PENNINGTON, *The Tarahumara of Mexico* (1963), and *Tepehuan of Chihuahua* (1969), are very good for material culture and ethnogeography of the northern sierra. CARL LUMHOLTZ, *Symbolism of the Huichol Indians* (1900), furnishes much on Huichol gods and belief, as does R.M. ZINGG, *The Huichol: Primitive Artists* (1938). A definitive work on Cora religion is found in K.T. PREUSS, *Die Nayarit-Expedition* (1912), in German.

Meso-American Indian cultures. SOL TAX (ed.), *Heritage of Conquest: The Ethnology of Middle America* (1952, reprinted 1968), includes Paul Kirchhoff's ground-breaking article "Mesoamerica" and is the best early synthesis of ethnographic information on the area. A comprehensive statement on all aspects of the subject is found in ROBERTWAUCHOPE (ed.), *Handbook of Middle American Indians*, 16 vol. (1964–76). Volumes 4 and 11 of THOMAS A. SEBEOK (ed.), *Current Trends in Linguistics* (1968 and 1972), provide the latest syntheses of linguistic relationships. Ethnographic material includes: RALPH L. BEALS, *The Ethnology of the Western Mixe* (1945); GEORGE M. FOSTER, *Empire's Children: The People of Tzintzuntzan* (1948); ROBERT REDFIELD, *A Village That Chose Progress: Chan Kom Revisited* (1950, paperback 1962); WILLIAM MADSEN, *The Virgin's Children: Life in an Aztec Village Today* (1960); OSCAR LEWIS, *Life in a Mexican Village: Tepoztlán Restudied* (1963); EVON Z. VOGT, *Zinacantan: A Maya Community in the Highlands of Chiapas* (1969); and PHILLIP BAER and WILLIAM R. MERRIFIELD, *Two Studies on the Lacandones of Mexico* (1971). Linguistic descriptions include: RICHARD S. PITTMAN, *A Grammar of Tetelcingo (Morelos) Nahuatl* (1954); VELMA B. PICKETT, *The Grammatical Hierarchy of Isthmus Zapotec* (1960); JOSEPH E. GRIMES, *Huichol Syntax* (1964); MARVIN K. MAYERS (ed.), *Languages of Guatemala* (1966); H. HARWOOD HESS, *The Syntactic Structure of Mezquital Otomi* (1968); WILLIAM R. MERRIFIELD, *Palantla Chinantec Grammar* (1968); and MARION M. COWAN, *Tzotzil Grammar* (1969).

Central American and Northern Andean cultures. A comprehensive work is JULIAN H. STEWARD (ed.), *Handbook of South American Indians*, vol. 4, *The Circum-Caribbean Tribes* (1948). JULIAN H. STEWARD and LOUIS C. FARON, *Native Peoples of South America* (1959), provides a convenient summary and relates the peoples of the area to their neighbours. On the prehistoric and early historic periods, useful articles appear in GORDON F. EKHOLM and GORDON R. WILLEY (eds.), *Handbook of Middle American Indians*, vol. 4, *Archaeological Frontiers and External Connections* (1966).

South American peoples and cultures. JULIAN H. STEWARD (ed.), *Handbook of South American Indians*, 7 vol. (1946–59), is a monumental compilation of articles on South American ethnography, archaeology, physical anthropology, and languages. JULIAN H. STEWARD and LOUIS C. FARON, *Native Peoples of South America* (1959), is a synthesis and updating of the *Handbook* written in a consistent theoretical framework. LOUIS C. FARON, *Mapuche Social Structure* (1961), is a study of the reintegration of these people of Chile since the time of conquest.

Andean cultures. The best account of Andean cultures as they appeared to an eyewitness of the early years (16th century) of European rule is PEDRO DE CIEZA DE LEON, *Crónica del Perú* (Eng. trans., *The Incas*, 1959). The earliest periods of human occupation are covered by R.S. MACNEISH, "Early Man in the Andes," *Scient. Am.*, 224:36–55 (1971). For an introduction to Andean archaeology, see JOHN HOWLAND ROWE and DOROTHY MENZEL (eds.), *Peruvian Archaeology* (1967), with selections mainly by American scholars. The role of irrigation in the cultural and political elaboration of coastal kingdoms is well illustrated in PAUL KOSOK, *Life, Land, and Water in Ancient Peru* (1965). Special regional problems are introduced in BETTY MEGGER, *Ecuador* (1966); and DONALD LATHRAP, *The Upper Amazon* (1970). Information on the Southern Andes is included in JULIAN H. STEWARD and LOUIS C. FARON, *Native Peoples of South America*, ch. 10 (1959); and in LOUIS C. FARON, *Hawks of the Sun* (1964).

South American tropical forest cultures. JULIAN H. STEWARD (ed.), *Handbook of South American Indians*, 7 vol. (1946-59), includes description and interpretation of the native cultures of the tropical forest; an abridged version is JULIAN H. STEWARD and LOUIS C. FARON, *Native Peoples of South America* (1959). JANICE H. HOPPER (ed.), *Indians of Brazil in the Twentieth Century* (1967), is a collection of essays by American and Brazilian specialists. BETTY J. MEGGERS, *Amazonia: Man and Culture in a Counterfeit Paradise* (1971), is a comparative study of Amazonian tribes and their adaptation to the natural environment. More specialized works include GERARDO REICHELDOLMATOFF, *Desana: simbolismo de los indios tukano del Vaupés* (1968; Eng. trans., *Amazonian Cosmos: The Sexual and Religious Symbolism of the Tukano Indians*, 1971); IRVING GOLDMAN, *The Cubeo: Indians of the Northwest Amazon* (1963); and ALLAN R. HOLMBERG, *Nomads of the Long Bow: The Sirionó of Eastern Bolivia* (1950). The complex social organization of the Ge tribes is studied in CURT NIMUENDAJU, *The Apinayé* (1939, reprinted 1967), *The šerente* (1942), and *The Eastern Timbira* (1946); and in DAVID MAYBURY-LEWIS, *Akwẽ-Shavante Society* (1967). A general view of the religious ideas of indigenous peoples may be found in RAFAEL KARSTEN, *Studies in the Religion of the South-American Indians East of the Andes* (1964). Acculturation among tribes in contact with whites is discussed in CHARLES WAGLEY and EDUARDO GALVAO, *The Tenetehara Indians of Brazil: A Culture in Transition* (1949, reprinted 1969); ROBERT F. MURPHY, *Mundurucú Religion* (1958), and *Headhunter's Heritage: Social and Economic Change Among the Mundurucú Indians* (1960); and JAMES B. WATSON, *Cayuá Culture Change: A Study in Acculturation and Methodology* (1952).

South American nomad cultures. JULIAN H. STEWARD (ed.), *Handbook of South American Indians*, vol. 1, *The Marginal Tribes* (1946), is the outstanding authoritative work. JULIAN H. STEWARD and LOUIS C. FARON, *Native Peoples of South America* (1959), is a one-volume work summarizing the material in the handbook for the lay reader. ALLAN R. HOLMBERG, *Nomads of the Long Bow: The Sirionó of Eastern Bolivia* (1950; paperback ed., 1969), is the best work on these people, a good example of the forest nomads. KALERVO OBERG, *The Terena and Caduveo of Southern Mato Grosso, Brazil* (1949), is a Smithsonian Institution monograph that includes an account of the Caduveo, a sub-tribe of the once powerful Mbayá. OBERG, *Indian Tribes of Northern Mato Grosso, Brazil* (1953), includes a short account of the Nambikwara.

Amphibians

The class Amphibia of vertebrate animals occupies an intermediate position in both the evolutionary series and life history between the fishes and the reptiles. Extant amphibians include the frogs and toads, the salamanders and sirens, and the caecilians. They occupy fresh waters or the border zones between fresh water and land. The importance of the amphibians lies in their evolutionary development: amphibians represent the point in the history of animal radiation when a group of aquatic vertebrates developed the ability to live on land for extended periods of time.

Amphibians are ectotherms—that is, their body temperature is about the same as that of the ambient temperature. Unlike fishes and higher vertebrates (reptiles, birds, and mammals), amphibians have no epidermal coverings, such as scales, hairs, and feathers, although some caecilians have rudimentary dermal scales. Adults have lost the dependence on gills characteristic of the fishes and have evolved more vascularized lungs and other internal and external respiratory surfaces. The amphibians have glandular skin, which secretes a mucous coating that keeps the skin moist, preventing desiccation and aiding in respiration. A three-chambered heart regulates the more complex circulatory system. Two pairs of strong, muscular limbs, which have been completely lost in caecilians, have developed from the lateral fins of the fish ancestor. Amphibians have paired nostrils and eyes, the latter usually covered by a lid in terrestrial species to prevent dessication, and a mouth, often with teeth and/or a protrusible tongue. The skull contains two occipital condyles (bone prominences on the occipital lobes).

Apart from the epidermal characteristics that distinguish amphibians from reptiles, certain reproductive strategies also help to define the amphibians. Unlike eggs in reptiles, which are protected by a shell and amnion, the eggs of amphibians lack a protective shell and membrane and so must be laid in fresh water or in a moist area on land to avoid desiccation. Further, amphibians often include a larval form in their life history, which metamorphoses into an adult.

Perhaps the most important adaptation amphibians developed to survive their move to a terrestrial habitat is the prevention of desiccation. Structural changes, such as the development of internal organs for gas exchange, smaller body size, and glandular skin and an absence of epidermal structures (for example, hairs, feathers, and scales), as well as behavioral adaptations such as nocturnal activity, were effective in conserving internal water levels. The successful dispersion of these animals has been limited by their dependence on respiration through a moist integument, the absence of a mechanism to concentrate urine as in more advanced vertebrates, and their anamniotic eggs.

For coverage of related topics in the *Macropædia* and *Micropædia,* see the *Propædia,* section 313, and the *Index.*

The article is divided into the following sections:

Amphibians: class Amphibia 418
- General features 418
  - Distribution and abundance
  - Size range and diversity of structure
  - Economic importance
- Natural history 419
  - Life history
  - Reproduction
  - Metamorphosis
  - Parental care
  - Adaptations
  - Food and feeding
  - Defense
- Form and function 421
  - General features
  - Major groups
- Evolution 423
- Classification 424
  - Distinguishing taxonomic features
  - Annotated classification
  - Critical appraisal

Major amphibian groups 426
- Urodela (salamanders and sirens) 426
- Anura (frogs and toads) 429

Bibliography 435

AMPHIBIANS: CLASS AMPHIBIA

GENERAL FEATURES

Distribution and abundance. Although amphibians are found on all continents except Antarctica, they are concentrated in the tropics, and some families and many genera are confined to these regions. Their general structure, physiology, and reproductive strategies overall are adapted to a warm, humid or freshwater habitat, although some species, especially among the salamanders, have adapted to arid desert regions.

Salamanders are primarily animals of the north temperate zone, a geographic region between the Tropic of Cancer (latitude 23.5° N) and the Arctic Circle, although the range of one family extends into Central America and northern South America, where it has evolved a large number of species.

Anurans (frogs and toads) are distributed throughout the world, except for extreme latitudes in the Arctic and Antarctica and very arid regions of the world. They are most diverse in the tropics. Frogs of the family Hylidae range as far north as the swamplands of northwestern Canada. Some members of *Rana,* a genus in the family of true frogs, Ranidae, live north of the Arctic Circle; in fact, the family is found on all major landmasses except Antarctica, southern and western Australia, New Zealand, Greenland, southern South America, the West Indies, and many oceanic islands.

The caecilians occur throughout the tropics, and the sirens only in the southeastern United States and northeastern Mexico.

Amphibians, for the most part, are found as isolated individuals; but many of the frogs, particularly in the temperate zones, assemble in large breeding choruses during spring and summer.

Size range and diversity of structure. Among the caecilians, some species of the South American genus *Caecilia* grow to at least 1 metre (3 feet); one of the largest caecilians is *C. thompsoni,* with a length of 1.5 metres. The genus *Andrias* contains examples of the largest salamanders, such as *A. davidianus* and *A. japonicus,* which reach up to 1.5 metres long. Other large amphibians include *Amphiuma tridactylum* and *Siren lacertina. Conrana goliath* (sometimes called *Gigantorana goliath*) is one of the largest of the anurans in West Africa and is followed by *Bufo blombergi* and *B. marinus.*

Some of the smallest caecilians are the West African *Idiocranium russeli* and the Seychellean *Grandisonia bre-*

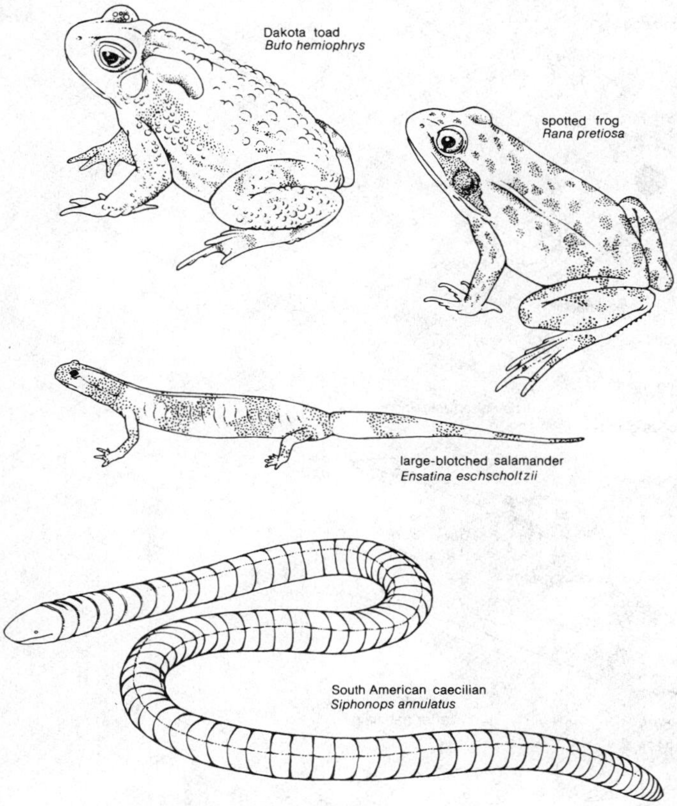

Representative amphibians.
Drawing by S. Jones

vis, which are smaller than 115 millimetres (4.5 inches). Among the salamanders the genus *Thorius* contains some of the smallest members, reaching only 26.9 millimetres in length. One of the smallest anurans is found in the Brazilian genus *Psyllophryne; P. didactyla* attains a length of only 9.8 millimetres. *Sminthilus limbatus* reaches only 11.5 millimetres.

The frogs and toads are short and broad-bodied. They lack a tail except in the larval form, the head and trunk are joined, the forelimbs are much shorter than the long hindlimbs, and the eardrums are exposed. The salamanders are long-bodied animals with a long tail and usually short limbs. They have a distinct head and neck. The caecilians are long wormlike animals that lack limbs. Their dermis may house small scales.

Economic importance. The amphibians are of little direct economic importance to humans. Because they are important predators of insects, the toad *Bufo marinus* was introduced into the West Indies, Puerto Rico, the Philippines, and Hawaii during the 19th century to help control pests in sugarcane fields. About 1935 they were released into cane fields in Queensland, Australia, for the same purpose, where they thrived and spread to other areas of the country. The absence of any natural predators and their prodigious spawning ability put them at risk of upsetting the balance of nature that exists among the indigenous species of the country.

Some species of the Dendrobatidae family of frogs, especially *Phyllobates aurotaenia, P. bicolor,* and *P. terribilis,* secrete poisons, which some tribes of the Chocó Indians of western Colombia use on the tips of darts.

Frogs continue to be a popular terrarium pet throughout the world, although emphasis has been placed increasingly on breeding them in captivity rather than collecting them in the wild. Amphibians in general, but frogs in particular (especially *Rana temporaria* and *R. pipiens*), have been used as dissection models in courses on comparative physiology and anatomy.

Frogs are eaten as a delicacy in Europe, especially *R. esculenta,* and Asia, especially *R. tigrina, R. crancivara,* and *R. macrodon.* Usually only the legs are consumed.

Frogs figure prominently in the folklore of a number of ancient civilizations. In some Chinese and Indian cultures, for example, the world was believed to rest on the back of a giant frog, and any movement of the animal caused earthquakes or tremors.

NATURAL HISTORY

Life history. The reproductive cycles in amphibians are under the immediate control of hormones. These hormones are released by the body in response to climate, developmental size, mode of reproduction, and amount of parental care. Ultimately, therefore, the life cycle is at least in part determined by the environment.

Environmental influences

Seasonal variations in habitat are among the most important factors controlling the reproductive cycle. Because the life history usually involves both land and water, most amphibians have behavioral patterns built around a seasonal movement between breeding sites and other places. The breeding site for the caecilians, sirens, and some salamanders is probably essentially the same as the nonbreeding site. Other salamanders undertake annual journeys, perhaps from a relatively dry hillside to some pond or stream in a valley. Evidence indicates that they are guided on such journeys by chemical stimuli as well as by physical characteristics of the land (*e.g.,* slope). In frogs and toads that have voices, the calls of the males that have located a suitable breeding site attract other males and females, often from up to about 800 metres (0.5 mile) away. Some amphibians are able to use celestial bodies for orientation.

Changes in temperature and rainfall contribute substantially to regulating gametogenesis (the development of eggs and sperm), fertilization, and oviposition (egg laying) or larval development. (Ed.)

Reproduction. In the more primitive salamanders, reproduction involves laying eggs in water, external fertilization, and free-swimming larvae. The male salamander deposits his sperm in a gelatinous structure (spermatophore) consisting of a stalk on which rests a little cap containing the sperm. The female maneuvers the cap into her cloaca, where the gelatinous material dissolves, and the sperm are freed to fertilize the eggs as they descend through her reproductive tubes. More advanced species undergo internal fertilization and release their young in various ways. They may lay their eggs in the water, where they develop into aquatic larvae, or lay their eggs on land, where they become terrestrial hatchlings, or bear live young. Sirens and many salamanders lay eggs in water. Other salamanders lay them on land, in burrows in rotten logs, or under debris where they will remain moist. It is not yet known whether fertilization is internal or external in the sirens.

With few exceptions, the frogs and toads (anurans) have external fertilization. The male clasps the female and releases sperm over the eggs as the female extrudes them. The anurans show a number of adaptations toward the terrestrial habitat. Eggs can be deposited on vegetation above the water, and the larvae then develop in the water; or the eggs can be deposited on land, and developing larvae or froglets are carried by the adult. Some anurans bear live young. Frogs have various means of caring for the eggs after they are deposited. In the north temperate regions, most species abandon their eggs in a pool or stream; many tropical species have developed other, sometimes bizarre, techniques of egg care. Some lay eggs in a hole on land; after the eggs hatch into tadpoles, the male transports them on his back to the water. In other species, the mother has a special pouch on her back in which she carries the eggs until they hatch.

In caecilians, fertilization is external, and sperm are introduced into the female's body by means of a protrusible portion of the male's cloaca (the lower part of the digestive tract), which is modified to form a copulatory organ. Most caecilians deposit their eggs on land; the aquatic forms bear live young. The eggs are laid in moist areas. The larvae have external gills, as do other amphibians, but they are usually lost before birth or hatching, and some aquatic species retain open gill slits.

Adaptations in egg-laying

Because the eggs of amphibians lack a shell and amniotic fluid, they are susceptible to drying out. The fertilized eggs must be deposited in water or in a moist area, such

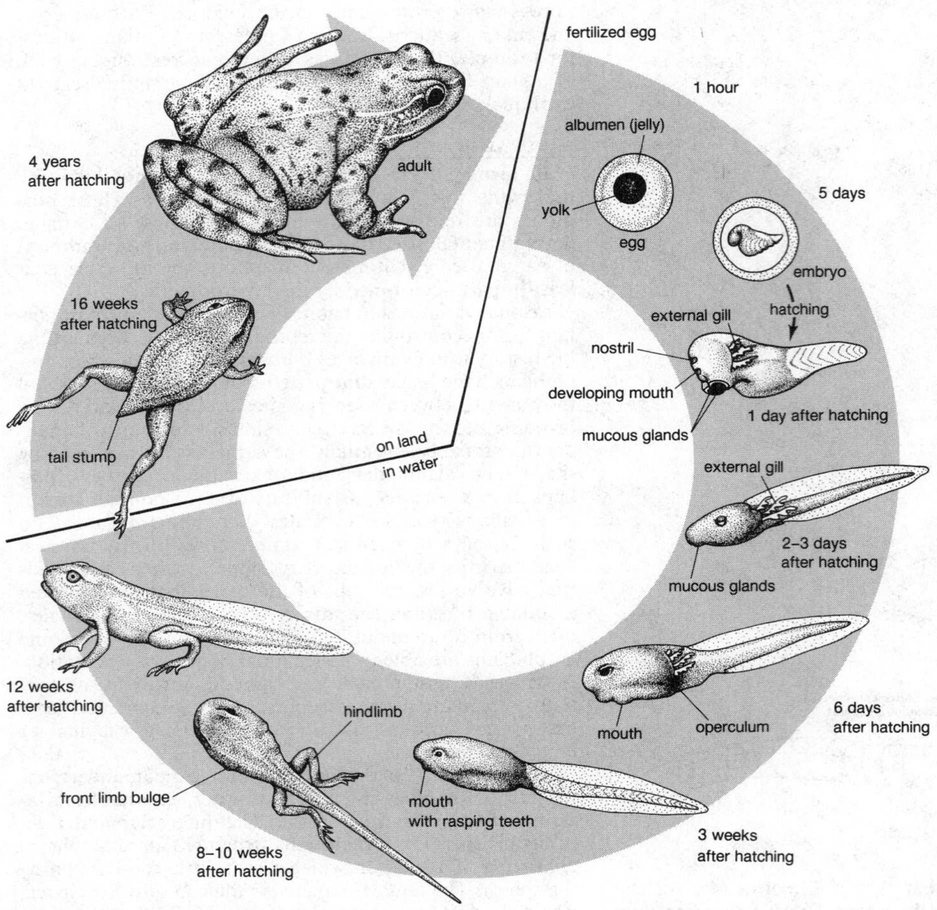

Figure 1: *Life cycle of the European common frog.*
Within hours of spawning, the fertilized egg begins embryonic development, and, about five days after fertilization, the embryo is ready to hatch. Upon hatching, the tadpole absorbs oxygen through the skin and attaches to weeds by the mucous glands. Within three days, the mouth opens, the external gills become functional, and the larva begins to swim and feed. Within six days, the external gills begin to shrivel and the operculum (skin fold) covers the gills. By three weeks after hatching, the external gills are gone and the tadpole breathes using internal gills. Within 10 weeks, the hindlimbs are well formed, the forelimbs begin to bulge, the lungs have appeared, and the tadpole begins to breathe surface air. By 12 weeks, the forelimbs appear, the tail shortens, and the eyes and mouth become more prominent. After 16 weeks, the young frog leaves the water for short periods but remains near it. After about four years, the frog has matured enough to breed.
After T.R. Halliday and K. Adler (eds.), *The Encyclopedia of Reptiles and Amphibians* (1986), Equinox Ltd., Oxford

as soil, rotting wood, or the skin of the parent's back. Many salamanders and frogs and all egg-laying caecilians deposit their eggs away from open water. Some species lack an aqueous larval stage. The larvae have gills and, when aquatic, are free-swimming. The larval stage is often absent in terrestrial species. (C.J.G./Ed.)

Metamorphosis. Metamorphosis is a postembryonic change in structure, physiology, biochemistry, and behaviour as the larva transforms into an adult. Three types of change may take place during metamorphosis: regression of larval structure or functions, transformation to a form suitable for adult survival, or development of new adult structures that were not previously present in the larva. All the events of metamorphosis are controlled ultimately by hormones. Absence of food, desiccation of the aqueous habitat, or alterations in the temperature and climate of the habitat also may play a role in encouraging the larva to metamorphose into the adult form.

Parental care. Parental care is a behaviour found commonly among the higher vertebrates, but it is also found to some extent in many of the higher amphibians. Parental care can be considered to be any parental behaviour that increases the chances of survival for the egg or larva. These forms of behaviour might include simply attending the eggs (*e.g.,* aerating aquatic eggs, moistening terrestrial eggs, protecting the eggs, or removing dead eggs), transporting the eggs or larvae, or even feeding the larvae.

Parental behaviour is generally found among amphibians that concentrate their eggs in one place rather than scattering them. It is thus a behaviour that is more common among terrestrial amphibians, usually salamanders but also some anurans. Parental behaviour is rare in caecilians.

Adaptations. Although amphibians can be found in almost any habitat, from the Arctic tundra to deserts to elevations of 5,000 metres (16,400 feet) above sea level, most are found in moist areas with moderate to warm temperatures. Because amphibians are particularly susceptible to environmental fluctuations, they have developed various morphological, physiological, or behavioral adaptations to maintain homeostasis.

One of the most important adaptations evolved by amphibians is the regulation of water loss. Aquatic and semiaquatic amphibians, which are constantly bathed in water, have little difficulty regulating the amount of water intake. In terrestrial amphibians, however, water is lost through the skin, as well as during excretion and respiration. In general, the behavioral and physiological mechanisms developed by amphibians tend to increase the amount of water taken in, regulate the amount of water lost through the skin and kidneys, and increase the amount of water stored in vesicles, tissues, and the urinary bladder.

Regulation of water loss

One behavioral adaptation to minimize water loss is for the amphibian to assume a nocturnal habit, thereby avoiding the higher temperatures and lower atmospheric humidity of the daylight hours. Such amphibians tend to occupy daytime retreats that have a high moisture content, such as logs, shaded crevices, and burrows, permitting them to absorb water in anticipation of nocturnal activity. There are amphibians that are active during the daytime, although their habitats tend to be humid or located near water.

Another behavioral adaptation on the part of some amphibians is the ability to selectively limit the amount of surface area exposed to the air, thus decreasing evaporation. For example, some amphibians curl into a tight ball, and others aggregate into closely packed clusters of individuals.

Morphological adaptations to terrestrial habitats are usually found in the skin or urinary bladder and lymph sacs. The integument of the amphibians lacks scales (except dermal scales in many caecilians), feathers, hairs, or other such structures found in the other vertebrate classes. The skin is extremely permeable in the amphibians, which makes it an important respiratory surface but also puts the amphibian at risk of desiccation. An animal capable of increasing the surface area exposed to the substrate is more prone to increasing the amount of water absorbed. Terrestrial amphibians generally have a granular skin surface, which provides more surface area for water absorption. Aquatic amphibians, however, tend to have smooth skin surfaces, since they are continually bathed in water.

Water storage

The urinary bladder is an important water-storage organ, especially in terrestrial amphibians. When distended with water, an amphibian's size in relation to body weight is related to whether the animal is primarily terrestrial or aquatic. Aquatic amphibians have a bladder that is extremely small (perhaps 1 percent) in relation to the total body weight, whereas in *Bufo cognatus,* a terrestrial frog, the water-storage capacity of the urinary bladder is up to 30 percent of body weight and in the desert burrowing frog *Notaden nicholsi* the bladder may be almost 50 percent of body weight.

Every species has certain physiological adaptations to water conservation, although generally the rate of rehydration depends on the structure and absorptive properties of the skin. Terrestrial species have a higher rate of rehydration than do the aquatic species, but the latter can survive longer periods without rehydration.

Waterproofing is generally concerned with cutaneous secretions that dramatically retard water loss. Some species, such as the subterranean burrowing salamander *Siren intermidia,* which lives in dry areas, encase the entire body, except for the mouth, in a cocoon, in which the animal remains dormant. Some members of the tree frog genus *Phyllomedusa* are able to sit exposed on the limbs of trees because of the impermeable lipid secretion that protects them from dehydration.

The body temperature of amphibians is about the same as that of their environment (ectothermy). Amphibians, however, do operate in well-defined temperature ranges that are specific for every species. As a result, drastic changes in the ambient temperature create a number of problems for amphibians. They tend to lose or gain heat from the atmosphere by convection. They are also subject to heat conducted to and from the substrate, as well as to thermal radiation and evaporative heat loss.

Amphibians, however, are capable of responding to prolonged changes in the ambient temperature by adjusting their thermal tolerances (acclimatization), thereby establishing newer "normal" temperature ranges. The ability of the amphibian to increase its body temperature allows the body to increase the rate of digestion and maximize the growth rate of the juvenile as well as to increase the fat deposits in anticipation of a dormant period.

The mechanisms of gas exchange with the environment, or respiration, are dependent on the habitat. Gills are used by aquatic adults and larvae, and the lungs, skin, and buccopharyngeal tissues are used by terrestrial species. Any or all may be used in species that alternate terrestrial and aquatic habitats in their reproductive life cycles.

Larvae use gills, the lungless salamanders (family Plethodontidae) use only the skin and buccopharyngeal tissues, and most adult amphibians make use of a combination of lungs, skin, and buccopharyngeal tissues, depending on environmental conditions. If, for example, a semi-aquatic amphibian returns to the water from land, blood vessels feeding the lungs, which were used in respiring on land, constrict and those vessels feeding the skin and gills open while the animal is underwater. In addition, respiratory rates change with changes in such environmental variables as temperature, oxygen, moisture, and light. Generally, larger amphibians require more oxygen, and pulmonary oxygen intake increases with temperature, although the rates of increase vary; the greatest rates are usually those of temperate amphibians, followed by tropical anurans, plethodontids, and aquatic salamanders.

Food and feeding. Although most adult amphibians are carnivores, feeding on insects and other invertebrates, some, including anuran larvae and the salamanders of the genus *Siren,* can be herbivores. Their choice of prey is influenced by the abundance of food, the competitors that are present, and their ability to capture the prey.

Capturing prey

Two basic strategies are involved in capturing the prey, and these are often characteristic of an order and dependent on the morphological constraints of the animal. A sit-and-wait technique is typical of the anurans, and an active foraging technique is common among the salamanders and caecilians.

Amphibians are able to locate their prey visually—a tactic common among those amphibians (most anurans and salamanders) that sit and wait for the prey to come to them—through chemosensory stimulation using specialized chemoreceptors, or through auditory stimulation from the sounds of the prey.

Almost all terrestrial amphibians except caecilians use the tongue to capture prey. The differences in the method by which this is achieved, however, are reflected in the structures and support of the tongue. Furthermore, the amphibian tongue has a sticky secretion that adheres the prey to its surface. Advanced anurans are able to protrude the tongue so that the posterodorsal surface of the retracted tongue becomes the anteroventral surface of the extended tongue. Caecilians, however, do not have an extrusible tongue. They capture prey by biting; many have fanglike teeth that hold the struggling prey.

Defense. Although the amphibians may appear to be quite vulnerable, they have evolved a number of mechanisms to thwart or escape attacks by potential predators. Terrestrial caecilians, when alarmed, are able to burrow into the soil quite quickly, and anurans are able to jump distances, thereby interrupting any chemosensory trail that might be followed by a predator. Some amphibians have developed coloration or camouflage patterns that match the substrate or disrupt the body's outline, thereby confusing a predator. If encountered, some amphibians, especially anurans, feign death, while others enlarge or change their body outline, as when an anuran inflates its lungs and puffs up its body. Many have warning coloration. Some salamanders, for example, elevate the chin and tail, showing bright ventral colours. They also secrete toxic substances from dorsal glands. Large caecilians have been known to bite.

Many amphibians have two types of glands: mucous glands, which are distributed throughout the skin, providing a moist coat for cutaneous respiration; and granular, or poison, glands that are evenly or locally distributed and secrete noxious or toxic chemicals, making the animal unpalatable to predators.

FORM AND FUNCTION

Musculoskeletal system

General features. The amphibian musculoskeletal system is divisible into three regions, the cranium and hypobranchial apparatus, the axial skeleton, and the appendicular skeleton. The skull and hypobranchium are diverse within the amphibians. The skull is the seat of the central nervous system in amphibians, as in other vertebrates, and is the principal site of the sense organs or sight, olfaction, hearing, and equilibrium.

The hypobranchial apparatus is situated on the floor of the mouth between the pectoral girdle and the mandible and is the attachment site for the muscles of the mandible, branchial arches, and tongue. It thus forms the basis of the mechanical system for ventilation and for securing, manipulating, and ingesting food. The cranium, middle ear, and miscellaneous bones of the head are ossified cartilage, whereas the roof and floor of the skull and many of the supporting bones are bony tissues. Voluntary and involuntary muscles invest the skull.

The axial skeletal system is a flexible, rigid, longitudinal brace for the head and visceral support. From it is suspended the appendicular system; it also acts as a conduit for the spinal cord. In addition, the axial system supports a tail, if present. The musculature of the system is innervated by the spinal nerves. The individual muscle segments (myotomes) are divided into dorsal and ventral halves, the former forming the epaxial musculature and the latter comprising the hypaxial musculature. Epaxial musculature consists of one continuous sheet with many deeper fibre tracts spanning two or more successive vertebrae; it facilitates the angular movements that permit lateral undulations (a characteristic retained from fish ancestors), except in frogs. The hypaxial system is arranged in a series of three muscle types, imparting flexible support for the spine and providing support for the viscera and ventral flexibility for the vertebral column.

The appendicular system comprises the pectoral and pelvic girdles and the associated limbs. The girdles are suspended from the axial system. The pectoral girdle forms no solid attachment to the vertebral column; rather, it is suspended by muscles from the ribs and/or transverse processes and skull. The pelvic girdle, on the other hand, forms strong fibrous attachments to the axial column so that the attached muscles are used for movement rather than for support. The pectoral girdle lies behind the head, and the pelvic girdle lies at the end of the trunk.

Limbs

The five segments of the tetrapod limb are, from the region closest to the trunk to the region farthest from the trunk, the propodium (humerus, or forelimb, and femur, or hindlimb), epipodium (radius and ulna or tibia and fibula), mesopodium (wrist and ankle and several small bones), metapodium (palm and sole), and phalanges (digits).

The skin (integument) is a water-permeable organ important in respiration, osmoregulation, and thermoregulation. The colour and patterns of the skin are the result of chromatophores (pigment-bearing cells), and its texture stems from integumentary modifications. Except in the caecilians, which have fishlike scales quite similar to those of ancient and extinct animals, the skin is not covered by scales, feathers, or hairs.

The outer layer of skin, the epidermis, is divisible into two parts. The outermost layer, the stratum corneum, is keratinized in most adult amphibians, especially terrestrial ones. Periodic shedding, or molting, is controlled by hormones of the pituitary and thyroid glands. The innermost layer, the stratum germinativum, is the source of new cells for the stratum corneum.

A basement membrane of collagen fibres forms the intermediate area between the epidermis and the innermost region of the skin, the dermis. The dermis is rich in capillaries, nerve fibres, and smooth muscle cells. The outer layer, the stratum spongiosum, contains areolar cells, fibres, and chromatophores, as well as mucous and granular glands and the basal portion of scales in the caecilians. The inner stratum compactum contains collagen fibres.

Mucous glands

All amphibians have both granular and mucous glands in the integument. The numbers vary generally; however, the mucous glands are widely distributed along the ventral surface, and the granular glands are aggregated in specific regions. Mucopolysaccharides are continuously secreted to keep the skin moist; granular glands, however, usually secrete their fluids only after nervous or humoral (hormonal) stimulation.

The texture of the skin is the result of epidermal or dermal modifications or both. Warts (verrucae) or coni (pointed projections) are covered by keratin at the apex. The epidermis varies in thickness. Structures of the integument are associated with an increase in cutaneous vascularity and therefore with an increase in the amount of water taken up in terrestrial amphibians and an increase in the surface area exposed for respiration in aquatic species. Disruptive outlines for concealment, such as small irregular ridges, are common. Keratinized digit tips can be clawlike. Webbing in between the fingers and toes of anurans increases surface area for swimming. Toe pads in arboreal frogs provide adhesive toes that, together with mucous secretions, create a surface tension that allows them to adhere to surfaces.

Chromatophores are found in the dermis or the epidermis. Melanophores, the predominant type of epidermal chromatophore, secrete the pigment eumelanin. Dermal chromatophores are of three types, which together form a unit: xanthophores are responsible for yellow, red, and orange colours; iridophores, white or silvery cells, are responsible for reflecting light of certain wavelengths and, together with xanthophores, are capable of showing bright colours; and melanophores secrete eumelanin. The intensity of the green colour of most frogs results from the kind and quantity of yellow pigments in the xanthophores, and the shade, or tone, results from the arrangement of the iridophores.

The dermal chromatophore unit responds to changes in physiology by changing colour—that is, lightening or darkening the skin colour. Rapid changes in colour result from hormonal stimulation and are caused by the intracellular mobilization of pigment-bearing organelles. The changes are rapid but short-lived. Slow changes in colour are morphological changes and are caused by sustained stimulation or destimulation of the pigment cells, resulting in a synthesis or destruction, respectively, of pigment. The change is long-lived, lasting up to many months in some species.

Lateral line system

The lateral line system is a series of epidermal sense organs found on the head and body of aquatic larvae and some adult aquatic amphibians. It consists of mechanoreceptors that sense changes in water current and probably pressure and transmit information about these changes to the brain. They are located on the lateral or dorsal surface of the body. Three additional sensory receptor systems in amphibians are for vision (eyes), olfaction (nares), and acoustics and vibraton (ears). The pineal gland also is a photoreceptor organ.

The nervous system, though generally more advanced than that of fish, is still primitive in that it has nerve cell bodies around the ventricles in the brain. Invagination of the hemispheres in the brain is advanced. The same is true of the two meninges (the pia mater, which is attached to the brain and spinal cord, and the tough outer dura mater). However, innervation pathways are relatively simple and limited.

The amphibian has diverse respiratory modes: pulmonary, branchial, and buccopharyngeal. This requires different vascular systems to effectively transport oxygen from, and carbon dioxide to, the respiratory surfaces. The pulmonary (oxygenated) and systemic (unoxygenated) circulatory systems were separated for the first time in evolutionary development of the amphibians. The three-chambered heart, with two atria and one ventricle (although some salamanders have a septum that divides the ventricle into two parts), accommodates the two separate systems. The larvae have gills and cutaneous respiration, and the adults have lungs (usually paired) and buccopharyngeal (mouth and pharynx, both highly vascularized) and cutaneous respiration. (Ed.)

Kidneys

The kidneys are paired and on either side of the dorsal aorta and are characteristic of each of the three orders. They are highly vascularized with capillaries clustered in the Bowman's capsule, which constitutes a filtration device. The bladder is a ventral outgrowth of the cloaca. The permeable skin in amphibians presents special problems involving the maintenance of internal water balance and the removal of the nitrogenous wastes that are the by-products of metabolism. Amphibians take in water through the skin and excrete it together with the nitrogenous wastes, through the kidneys.

Most larval amphibians and permanently aquatic adults live in fresh water, which flows constantly into the body and removes nitrogenous wastes in the form of ammonia. The kidneys produce copious amounts of very dilute urine, thereby eliminating both excess water and waste products. Terrestrial forms, lacking an unlimited supply of water, cannot excrete such dilute urine; instead, they convert their nitrogenous wastes into urea, which, because it is less toxic than ammonia, can be excreted in a much more concentrated form.

A physiological mechanism also controls urine production in relation to temperature. As temperature rises, water flows more rapidly through the skin, and urine flow increases; conversely, water flow and urine production decrease with a decline in temperature. In experiments with the green frog (*Rana clamitans*), it has been found that no urine was formed at 2.5° C (36.5° F), although some water moved into the body.

Variations in form

Major groups. The major groups of living amphibians differ markedly from one another in structure. Caecilians are slender, wormlike animals without limbs or limb girdles, with practically no tail, and with a simple intestine. The minute eyes are buried in the smooth skin, and there are no eyelids. Because caecilians use their heads to burrow in the soil of the forest floor and in the mud along riverbanks, the skull is compact. The cloaca of the male is modified into a protrusible copulatory organ. The body is segmented into circular folds, called annuli, separated by shallow grooves. The more primitive species have tiny scales embedded in the dermis. Some aquatic forms have a dorsal fin fold. All caecilians have tentacles, small sensory structures that lie buried in pits near each eye and are protrusible in many species. Several series of teeth are arranged on different bones around the jaws.

The sirens, or trachystomes, which lack hindlimbs and pelvic girdles, are elongated, aquatic animals with an anterior pectoral girdle to which the upper bones of the front legs are attached. The tiny front legs have three or four toes on each foot. Gills are present. Sirens also breathe by gulping the surface air. The eyes are lidless and are buried in the smooth glandular skin, which is lacking in scales and annuli, although so-called costal folds are present along each side of the body. A horny claw caps each toe, and a horny sheath covers part of each jaw. Except for the tiny splenial bones, the bones of the jaws lack teeth, but teeth are present on the bones forming the roof of the mouth. The well-developed tail has dorsal and ventral fin folds. Sinuous body motions and the tail fins are used for locomotion.

In most cases, the salamanders have forelegs and hindlegs of approximately the same size, although the hindlimbs may be absent in some species. The tail is retained throughout the entire life of the animal. A distinct neck is present between the head and body. The smooth skin lacks scales, and the eyes of terrestrial forms have lids. Teeth are present on the jaws and roof of the mouth. Although fertilization is internal in most species, the male lacks a copulatory organ, sperm transfer occurring via spermatophores (sperm capsules). Some species never metamorphose but remain in the water as permanent larvae, retaining gills throughout their life.

Leg bones of frogs and toads

The largest group of amphibians are the frogs and toads. The one characteristic that clearly distinguishes this group from others is the presence in the hindleg of a segment formed by two elongated tarsal bones, the astragalus and calcaneum. In salamanders these bones are small, merely forming part of the ankle. The elongated hindleg of frogs and toads is an adaptation for hopping or swimming. The body is shorter and broader than that of a salamander, and the adults lack a tail. Teeth, although usually found on the upper jaw, are (except in one tropical species) absent from the lower jaw. The tympanic membranes, used for hearing, are on the sides of the head, behind the eyes. Males of species with well-developed voices have resonating pouches, called vocal sacs, in the throat region. The glandular skin, which lacks scales, is usually smooth and soft; in some terrestrial forms, however, it is rather dry and rough.

EVOLUTION

The amphibians evolved from the lobe-finned fishes (Crossopterygii), which were abundant and diversified during the Devonian Period (408 to 360 million years ago). The crossopterygian skull was divided transversely into front and back parts that were slightly movable on each other. Early crossopterygians had teeth with an infolding of the enamel surface. (Similar teeth were also present in the primitive amphibians.) These fishes had muscular fins supported by bony elements comparable to the bones of amphibian limbs; functional lungs; and, in certain species, passages leading from the nasal sacs to openings (internal nares) in the roof of the mouth, an arrangement characteristic of all terrestrial vertebrates.

Amphibian ancestor

Fossil remains of the earliest known amphibians have been discovered in freshwater beds of the Early Devonian Period (approximately 370 million years ago). The amphibian ancestor was able to take air into the mouth and lungs through the nasal passages and internal nostrils when the mouth was closed and only the external nostrils were above water.

From J.Z. Young, *The Life of Vertebrates*, 2nd ed. (1962); the Clarendon Press, Oxford

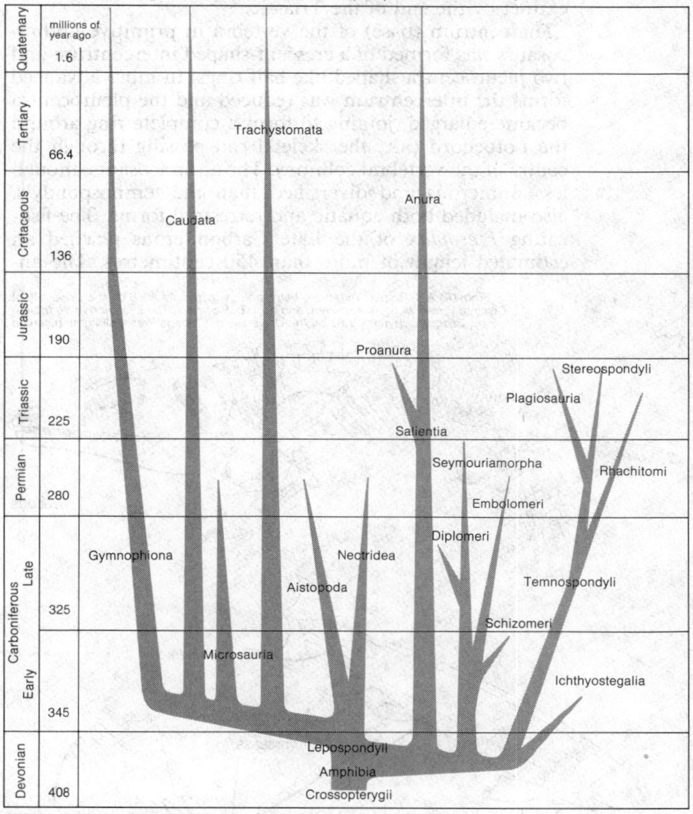

Figure 2: Dendrogram of Amphibia. The fossil record of many forms is incomplete, particularly during the Carboniferous Period.

The earliest amphibians of the Early Devonian are the ichthyostegalians. The best-known member of the group, *Ichthyostega* from freshwater beds of Greenland, was a fairly large animal with a skull 150 millimetres or more in length. Instead of fins it had short, stubby limbs with five toes; its tail was something like that of a modern lungfish, with a caudal, or tail, fin supported by fin rays. Small, bony scales were present on the belly and tail. The vertebrae were like those of crossopterygians, the skull more amphibian-like. *Ichthyostega* probably spent most of its time in water, but the well-developed limbs indicate that it must have been capable of walking on land. In many ways the ichthyostegalians were intermediate between the crossopterygians and the later amphibians, but they had some specializations that suggest they represent a sideline rather than the main stock from which the later amphibians evolved. One of the bones of the skull, the intertemporal, which is present in many fossil amphibians, had been lost by the ichthyostegalians.

Fossil remains of amphibians are rare in deposits of the Early Carboniferous Period (360 to 320 million years ago), but during the Late Carboniferous (320 to 286 million years ago) amphibians were abundant and diversified. They were divided into three major stocks: temnospondyls, anthracosaurs, and lepospondyls. The earliest temnospondyls were probably aquatic, but some later members of the group were well adapted to life on land. They were a widespread and flourishing stock, showing considerable morphological diversity. Almost all the large amphibians of the Permian Period (roughly 286 to 245 million years ago) belonged to this group. *Eryops* of the Early Permian (about 286 to 258 million years ago) was about 150 centimetres long. As the reptiles spread over the land during the late Paleozoic Era (about 360 to 245 million years ago), the terrestrial amphibians declined. The temnospondyls of the Triassic Period (about 245 to 208 million years ago) were aquatic animals with reduced limbs. Some were very large. *Mastodonsaurus,* with a skull length of more than 90 centimetres (about three feet), was the largest known amphibian. The temnospondyls were extinct by the end of the Triassic.

The centrum (base) of the vertebra in primitive anthracosaurs was formed of a crescent-shaped intercentrum and two pleurocentra shaped like half rings. In more advanced forms the intercentrum was reduced and the pleurocentra became enlarged, joining to form a complete ring around the notochord (*i.e.,* the skeletal rod passing through the centre of the vertebral column). The anthracosaurs, though less numerous and diversified than the temnospondyls, also included both aquatic and terrestrial forms. The fish-eating *Pteroplax* of the Late Carboniferous reached an estimated length of more than 450 centimetres. The anthracosaurs are of interest because the reptiles evolved from them. They became extinct during the Permian.

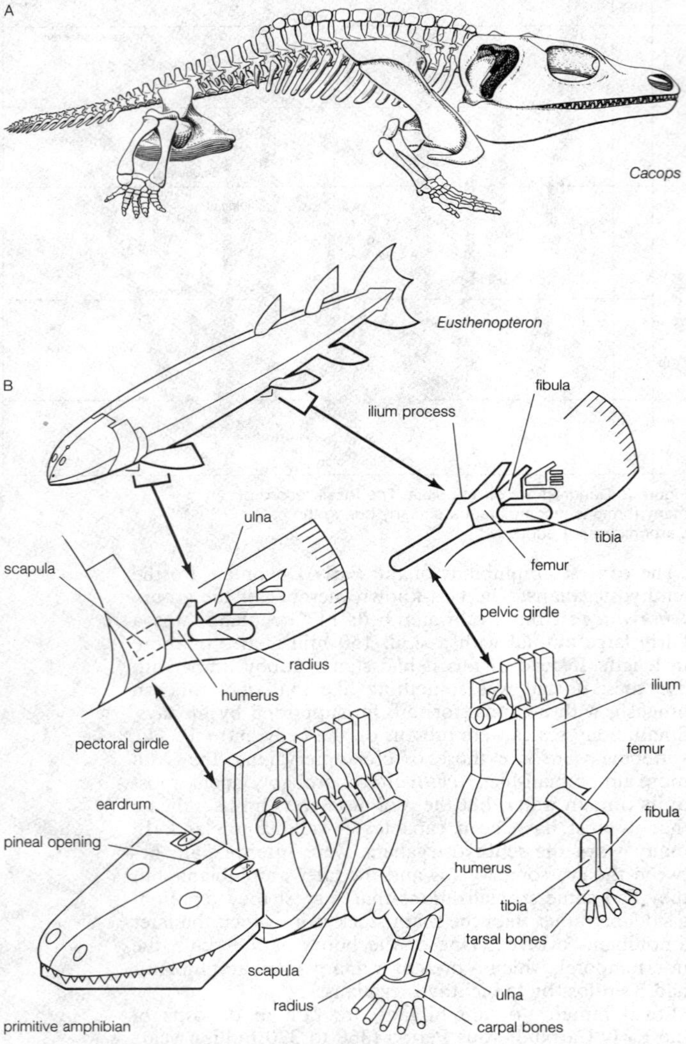

Figure 3: *Primitive amphibians and an ancestor.*
(A) *Cacops,* a primitive amphibian. (B, top) *Eustehnopteron,* a crossopterygian fish, and (bottom) an early labyrinthodont amphibian, showing the modifications of the pectoral and pelvic girdles and the associated appendages.

Lepospondyls of the Paleozoic were of modest size; many were eellike or snakelike in appearance and had lost their limbs. They were aquatic or semi-aquatic; a few may have been fossorial—that is to say, burrowing forms. They were present in the Early Carboniferous, flourished during the Late Carboniferous, and disappeared in the Early Permian.

Origin of modern orders

The modern orders of amphibians cannot be positively traced to any of the Paleozoic groups. No fossil caecilians are known. The trachystomes have been found in the Cretaceous Period (about 144 to 66.4 million years ago), and the salamanders in the Jurassic Period (roughly 208 to 144 million years ago). Both groups seem to have evolved in the Northern Hemisphere; in fact, only recently have members of one family of salamanders (Plethodontidae) radiated to the Southern Hemisphere in South America. The earliest remains of frogs, on the other hand, have all been found in the southern landmasses. It has been suggested that certain footprints in the Permian of South Africa may have been made by a form ancestral to the frogs. *Triadobatrachus* of the Early Triassic Period (about 245 to 240 million years ago) of Madagascar had a skull similar to that of a frog, elongated hindlegs, and a short tail. Frogs were undoubtedly present in the Early Jurassic (approximately 208 to 187 million years ago) in the southern part of South America.

Evolutionary adaptations

The radiation of the earliest amphibians meant both subtle and dramatic modifications in their anatomy. The large fins of the ancestor fishes became the powerful limbs, and the pelvic and pectoral girdles were strengthened to support the body on land. The attachment between the pectoral girdle and head in the ancestor fishes was lost, allowing the head to move independently of the body. Further, the hindlimbs were connected to the vertebral column, permitting the hindlimbs and tail, when present, to give a propulsive thrust. The massive muscles attached to the pectoral and pelvic girdles imparted greater strength and mobility to the animal. The vertebral column also became strengthened to support the viscera and to prevent the body from excessive twisting along the axis.

The earliest ancestors of the amphibians also had lungs, which were used as respiratory organs. Therefore, the lungs were not new with the amphibians, but rather the lungs became more vascularized and developed as a more important respiratory organ in the adult, which lost the gills. The lungs also solved the problem of desiccation since they were internal structures from which water did not evaporate as easily.

The question of why the ancestral amphibian moved from an aquatic environment to a terrestrial one has been much debated. One theory is that during a drought these animals would have been able to heave themselves out of the drying pools with their muscular fins and well-developed lungs and travel overland in search of other bodies of water. It has also been proposed that the migration to a land habitat was the result of competition between populations in the water. Since the crossopterygians were carnivorous, they probably preyed on the young of various species, including their own. Small individuals may have remained in shallow water inaccessible to larger fish or they may have fled to the land in order to escape a predator. Perhaps they later spent more time on shore, especially at night when the humidity was high, returning to the water only to feed during the day; gradually, they could have supplemented their diet with primitive terrestrial arthropods, and so become less dependent on water except to breed.

CLASSIFICATION

Distinguishing taxonomic features. The method of formation of the vertebral centrum (*i.e.,* the heavy ventral, or bottom, part that connects with the adjacent vertebra) is important in the classification of the amphibians, particularly of fossil forms. The recent orders are distinguished by general body structure and by the presence or absence of limbs and tail. The structure of the sound-transmitting mechanism of the ear is also an important clue to identification. Adult frogs have an otic notch on either side of the skull that houses the tympanic membrane, or eardrum. Salamanders, caecilians, and sirens lack the otic notch, eardrum, and middle-ear cavity. Sound transmission in salamanders is by way of the forelimb and shoulder blade to a muscle (opercularis) that passes from the shoulder blade to the operculum, a bone in the ear. Some fossil amphibians have the otic notch; presumably, many also possessed an eardrum and middle-ear cavity. Others lack the otic notch.

Annotated classification. The classification of the amphibians has not yet been satisfactorily established. The lack of critical fossil material prevents the establishment of clear-cut relationships between the major groups. The arrangement below is based on that of A.S. Romer (1966) and Coleman J. and Olive B. Goin (1971). Differences between classifications represented here and in the following sections reflect the variations that arise from individual interpretations. Groups indicated by a dagger (†) are extinct and known only from fossils.

CLASS AMPHIBIA
Vertebrate animals without hair, feathers, or horny scales of epidermal origin (epidermis is the outer cell layer of the integument); small bony scales of dermal origin (dermis is the inner cell layer of the integument) occasionally present; skin soft and glandular; ectothermic (*i.e.*, dependent on external sources for body heat); fertilization external or internal; eggs usually laid in water; typically an aquatic larval stage; about 2,400 living species.

†Superorder Ichthyostegalia
Fossils only; Late Devonian to Early Carboniferous; Europe, North America, Greenland; with limbs and fishlike tail; otic notch present; size to about 90 cm; probably largely aquatic.

†Superorder Temnospondyli
Fossils only; centrum primitively formed of wedge-shaped blocks; otic notch present; no more than 4 toes on front feet.

Order Rhachitomi
Early Carboniferous through Early Triassic; worldwide distribution; intercentrum (crescent-shaped structure of centrum) not forming a complete ring, pleurocentra (semicircular structures of centrum) bony; size to 150 cm; aquatic and terrestrial.

Order Stereospondyli
Middle Permian to Late Triassic; worldwide distribution; intercentra sometimes forming complete disks, pleurocentra reduced or absent; includes largest known amphibian, *Mastodonsaurus;* all forms aquatic.

Order Plagiosauria
Late Permian to Late Triassic; Europe and Africa; centrum closed cylinder; body broad and flat; scales present; size to about 90 cm; aquatic.

Superorder Lepospondyli
Centrum a bony cylinder around notochord; body more or less elongated; otic notch usually absent; limbs frequently reduced or absent.

†Order Aistopoda
Fossils only; Early Carboniferous to Early Permian; North America and Europe; elongated body form, limbs absent; ribs attached to vertebrae by one head; length about 75 cm; possibly fossorial (burrowing).

†Order Nectridea
Fossils only; Early Carboniferous to Early Permian; Europe and North America; body elongated or broad and flat; limbs reduced or absent; caudal vertebrae with expanded fan-shaped neural (dorsal) spines and hemal (ventral) spines; otic notch sometimes present, though small; some with cranium extended into posterior "horns"; length to about 60 cm; aquatic, some possibly fossorial.

Order Trachystomata (sirens)
Early Cretaceous to Recent; North America; eellike forms, hindlimbs absent, forelimbs minute; expanded spines on caudal vertebrae; ribs 2-headed; length to 90 cm; aquatic; 3 living species.

†Order Microsauria
All fossil; Early Carboniferous to Early Permian; Europe and North America; body somewhat elongated, limbs rather small; caudal vertebrae without expanded spines; ribs 2-headed; small forms, probably most were semi-aquatic.

Order Gymnophiona (caecilians)
Recent; worldwide in tropics; wormlike burrowing forms without limbs or limb girdles; eyes reduced; fertilization internal, with copulation; length to approximately 135 cm but most considerably smaller; burrowing or aquatic; about 160 living species.

Order Urodela (*Caudata;* salamanders)
Jurassic to Recent; worldwide in Northern Hemisphere, 1 family widely distributed in northern South America; vertebral centrum develops by direct development of bone tissue around notochord; ribs 2-headed; fertilization external or internal by means of spermatophore; size to 160 cm but most substantially smaller; terrestrial or aquatic; approximately 300 living species.

Superorder Salientia (frogs and toads and their possible Triassic predecessor)

†Order Proanura
One fossil form from Triassic of Madagascar; skull like that of a frog; tail short; hindlegs elongated.

Order Anura (frogs and toads)
Jurassic to Recent; worldwide; hindlegs elongated, body short and stout, tail absent; centrum preformed in cartilage; otic notch present; fertilization usually external, no spermatophore; body length to 30 cm; terrestrial or aquatic; about 1,900 living species.

†Superorder Anthracosauria
Fossils only; elements of centrum primitively crescent-shaped, pleurocentra later fuse to form main body of centrum, intercentrum reduced; otic notch present; 5 toes on front feet.

Order Schizomeri
Early Carboniferous; Europe; pleurocentra paired half rings, intercentrum large and crescent-shaped; trunk elongated, limbs reduced; length to approximately 120 cm; most likely aquatic.

Order Embolomeri
Late Carboniferous to Early Permian; Europe and North America; intercentrum and pleurocentrum complete disks, body elongated, tail powerful, limbs reduced; length to more than 450 cm; probably aquatic eaters of fish.

Order Seymouriamorpha
Late Carboniferous to Late Permian; North America, Europe, Australia; intercentrum reduced and crescent-shaped, pleurocentrum ring-shaped; limbs well developed, body stout; otic notch very large; length to 300 cm; terrestrial.

Order Diplomeri
Late Carboniferous; Europe and North America; intercentrum large and crescentic, pleurocentrum disk-shaped; limbs well developed; otic notch present, skull otherwise like that of a primitive reptile; presumably represents stock from which reptiles evolved; body length (without tail) approximately 10 cm; terrestrial.

Critical appraisal. There is no agreement among herpetologists that the amphibians evolved from a single stock. It has been suggested that the fossil lepospondyls and the salamanders are derived from one group of crossopterygians (porolepiforms) and that the ichthyostegids, temnospondyls, anthracosaurs, and frogs are derived from another (osteolepiforms). For alternate classification of Caudata (salamanders), see the *Annotated classification* in *Urodela* that follows.

A.S. Romer and others divide the amphibians into three subclasses: Labyrinthodontia for the ichthyostegalians, temnospondyls, and anthracosaurs; Lepospondyli for the fossil orders of lepospondyls; and Lissamphibia for the modern amphibians. The labyrinthodonts include those extinct forms whose teeth were covered by a series of surface folds (labyrinthine folds); most species superficially resembled salamanders, with weak limbs and a well-developed tail. The lepospondyls had teeth lacking folds; these extinct species were either four-legged (resembling salamanders) or legless (resembling snakes). The combination of ichthyostegalians, temnospondyls, and anthracosaurs into one subclass is based in large part on the assumption that the three-part centrum found in primitive members of the last two groups is derived from the crossopterygian-type centrum of *Ichthyostega.* It has been suggested that this assumption is false and that the divided centrum of the temnospondyls and anthracosaurs represents a new, tetrapod structure.

Whether the modern amphibians should be placed in one suborder is another much-debated question, which will probably not be answered unless and until sufficient fossil material is found to allow the modern orders to be traced to their Paleozoic ancestors. (C.J.G./Ed.)

MAJOR AMPHIBIAN GROUPS

The following sections of this article consist of a detailed discussion of two important orders of living amphibians, the salamanders and sirens (Urodela) and the frogs and toads (Anura). The remaining living members of the class Amphibia, such as the caecilians (Gymnophiona), are treated individually in the *Micropædia*. Additional information about extinct groups (designated in the *Annotated classification* by a dagger [†]) is contained in the *Macropædia* article FOSSIL RECORD.

Urodela (salamanders and sirens)

Salamanders and sirens, constituting the order Urodela (Caudata), together with frogs (order Anura) and caecilians (order Gymnophiona) are major living groups of the class Amphibia. The relatively small and inconspicuous salamanders are important members of north temperate and some tropical animal communities. They are important as subjects of experimental studies in embryology, developmental biology, physiology, anatomy, biochemistry, genetics, and behaviour. Convenient size, low food requirements, low metabolic rate, and hardiness make them good laboratory animals.

GENERAL FEATURES

Size range and diversity of structure. The most typical salamanders are short-bodied, four-legged, moist-skinned vertebrates about 100 to 150 millimetres (about four to six inches) long. The tail is usually about as long as the body. There is much variation in size, and terrestrial salamanders range from 40 to nearly 350 millimetres (about 1.6 to 14 inches) in length. Some live in moist places on land but must go to water to breed. Others are completely terrestrial. Wholly aquatic salamanders attain larger sizes than do terrestrial ones, the former reaching a maximum of 180 centimetres (about six feet). Salamanders may retain gills throughout life, lose the gills but retain a spiracle (breathing pore) or gill slit, or completely metamorphose (*i.e.,* alter radically in structure and appearance) and lose both gills and gill slits. Many aquatic species resemble their terrestrial relatives in body form, but aquatic genera such as *Siren* and *Pseudobranchus* lack hindlimbs, and *Amphiuma* has an extremely elongated body, short tail, and diminutive legs; several cave-dwelling forms (*Proteus, Haideotriton, Typhlomolge*) are blind and almost without pigment.

Distribution and abundance. Salamanders are classic examples of animals with a Holarctic distribution (*i.e.,* in the north-temperate regions of both the Eastern and Western hemispheres); eight of the nine families (see below *Annotated classification*) are found almost entirely in northern regions that lie outside the tropics. Typically, they occur in moist, forested habitats, where they are often common in aquatic and terrestrial communities. Members of the family Salamandridae extend south to extreme northern Africa, the southern foothills of the Himalayas, northern Vietnam, and the island of Okinawa. Some ambystomatids reach the southern margins of the Mexican Plateau, but only the lungless salamanders (plethodontids) have truly entered the tropics. One group of plethodontids, which occupies a wide variety of tropical habitats in the New World—from northern Mexico to southern Brazil and central Bolivia—contains nearly half of all recognized species of salamanders, an indication that the plethodontids have been highly successful in the tropical environment. Other areas in which salamanders have been successful include temperate North America (Appalachian and Ozark uplands; Pacific coast areas with a moist habitat), western Europe, Japan, and China.

NATURAL HISTORY

Life cycle and reproduction. Most salamanders are terrestrial or semiterrestrial as adults, but many return to aquatic habitats to breed. Courtship, which is simple or nonexistent in hynobiids and cryptobranchids, is increasingly elaborate and prolonged in the more highly evolved families. In primitive species comprising the suborder Cryptobranchoidea, fertilization of the egg is external. The females deposit sacs or strings of eggs that may be grasped by the male, who then sheds milt (which contains the sperm) over them. Nothing is known of courtship in sirens, but they, too, may have external fertilization, for the males lack the cloacal glands that produce the spermatophore, or sperm case, in species with internal fertilization, and the females lack spermathecae—chambers inside the cloaca used for sperm storage. All other species of salamanders have more complex courtship behaviour—often differing in details between species—and internal fertilization. The male deposits from one to many spermatophores on the ground or other surface. These consist of a gelatinous base, which is produced by cloacal glands, and a so-called sperm cap at the tip. The female moves by herself or is led by the male onto the spermatophore, and she takes the sperm mass into her cloaca. Breeding often occurs in ponds, but some salamandrids and most plethodontids breed on land. Egg deposition may take place shortly after mating but in many plethodontids may be delayed for several months, the eggs being fertilized by stored sperm. Eggs are laid in masses in streams or ponds, often in the shallows near shore. In most plethodontids and in some species of other families, eggs are laid singly, in short strings, or in small groups in terrestrial sites—*e.g.,* under surface objects, in rotting logs, or underground. Some species deposit eggs in tree cavities, and tropical species may deposit them in bromeliad plants, the leaves of which are arranged so that they often hold water. Frequently, the female stays with the eggs until they hatch, a period of several weeks. The number of eggs varies greatly and is correlated with adult size. Aquatic forms deposit as many as 400 eggs; terrestrial forms, as few as five or six.

Fertilization

Typical salamanders undergo an aquatic larval stage that lasts for a period ranging from a few days to several years. A short period of metamorphosis usually occurs before the terrestrial phase of the life cycle begins. The newly metamorphosed salamander is usually very small, and from one to several years elapse before it achieves sexual maturity.

Some salamander species never metamorphose and thus retain most of their larval characteristics. In other species, individuals or populations may occasionally fail to metamorphose. Still other species undergo partial metamorphosis. This phenomenon, known as paedomorphosis—*i.e.,* retention of larval or juvenile features by adults—characterizes all salamanders to a degree but is particularly evident in species such as *Necturus maculosus* (mud puppy) and *Ambystoma mexicanum* (axolotl), which retain gills and other larval structures throughout life. These animals breed in what is essentially a larval state. This extreme condition, which characterizes the Proteidae, Necturidae, and Sirenidae, is also found in several species of the Plethodontidae and Ambystomatidae. In most species the permanent larval state is determined by heredity, but in some it is induced by environmental factors, such as unfavourable terrestrial conditions resulting from drought or cold. The most complete metamorphosis is found in the families Hynobiidae, Salamandridae, Ambystomatidae, and Plethodontidae.

Paedomorphosis

Most species of the family Plethodontidae develop entirely on land, with no aquatic larval stage. The hatchling has either rudimentary gills that soon disappear or none at all and, in virtually all respects, is a miniature of the adult.

Females of the genus *Salamandra* (Salamandridae) may retain the fertilized eggs in the reproductive tract for a varying time. The fire salamander (*Salamandra salamandra*) deposits a relatively advanced larva in the water. In the Alpine salamander (*Salamandra atra*) and some other *Salamandra* species, fully metamorphosed individuals are born. One individual develops from the first egg in each oviduct, the tube leading from the ovary to the outside. Initially, the young salamander lives on its own yolk sup-

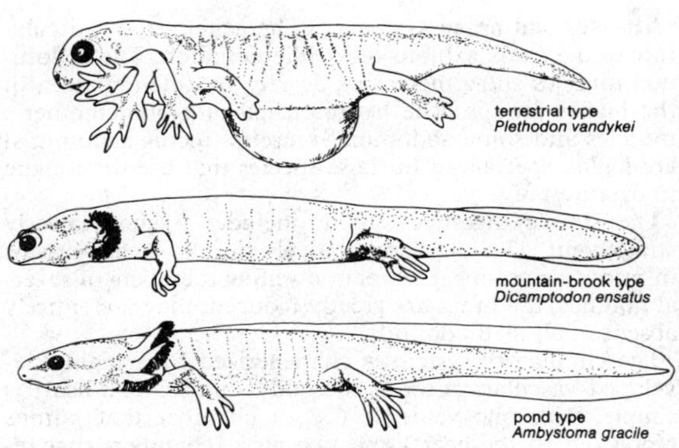

Figure 4: Principal types of urodele larvae.

Adapted from G.K. Noble, *The Biology of the Amphibia*, copyright 1931; used with permission of McGraw-Hill Book Co.

ply; later it eats the yolk of the other eggs, and finally it develops enlarged gills that form an intimate association with the walls of the oviduct to convey nutrients to itself. The gills are lost shortly before birth. Such salamanders are the only live-bearing members of the order.

Larval salamanders are exclusively aquatic. They may occur in a variety of habitats, from temporary ponds to permanent swamps, rivers, slow-moving streams, mountain brooks, springs, and subterranean waters. In all habitats they are exclusively carnivorous, feeding primarily on aquatic invertebrates. In most salamander larvae, feeding is accomplished by a "gape and suck" method, in which the throat is expanded, or gaped, to produce a suction that draws water and prey into the opened mouth. Skin flaps around the mouth direct the water movement. The larvae are well equipped with teeth, which aid in holding and shredding prey. Pond larvae have a high fin on the upper side of the tail that extends far anteriorly (toward the head) and large gills. Limbs are rather slow to develop. By contrast, stream larvae have a low, short tail fin, small gills, and limbs that develop early.

Larval feeding habits

Metamorphosis, although a period of major reorganization, is not so dramatic as that in frogs. In the final stages, metamorphosis is usually a rapid process; it is mediated by several hormones (*i.e.*, chemical substances that serve to regulate the function of various organs) produced by the thyroid and pituitary glands. The following typically occur during metamorphosis: loss of the gills; closure of the gill slits; appearance of a tongue pad and reorganization of the gill skeleton and musculature to produce a tongue; enlargement of the mouth and eyes; development of eyelids; and major changes in the structure of the skull and skin.

Locomotion. Locomotion is by means of limbs and by sinuous body movements. Some very elongated species of the genera *Phaeognathus, Batrachoseps, Oedipina,* and *Lineatriton* have reduced limbs and rely mainly on body movements for rapid locomotion. Species of the genus *Aneides* have arboreal (*i.e.*, tree-climbing) tendencies, and their long legs and digits, expanded toe tips, and prehensile (grasping) tails make them effective climbers. Some salamanders of the genera *Pseudoeurycea* and *Chiropterotriton,* found in the New World tropics, are similarly adapted. Others, members of the genus *Bolitoglossa,* have extensively webbed forefeet and hindfeet with indistinct digits, allowing them to move across moist leaves and other smooth surfaces.

Behaviour and ecology. Adult salamanders are nearly all nocturnal (*i.e.*, active mainly at night) animals. They may be highly seasonal, remaining hidden underground until the breeding season, or they may emerge from hiding places on any evening when moisture and temperature are at the proper levels. Fallen logs, rocks, crevices in soil, and surface litter commonly provide daytime refuge. Home ranges of salamanders are small, often less than three or four square metres (30 to 40 square feet), and, in favourable areas, some of the smaller species can be very abundant, occasionally numbering thousands per acre.

Insects are by far the most important food of salamanders. Primitive salamanders seize their prey by a combination of jaw and tongue movements. Some members of the Salamandridae and Plethodontidae, however, have evolved highly specialized tongue protrusion mechanisms. These are especially well developed in the tropical plethodontids, many of which are arboreal. The tongue can be extended from the mouth for a considerable distance and retracted almost instantaneously, with the prey attached to the sticky tongue pad.

Habitat

Most terrestrial species live near the surface of the ground, often in thick leaf litter and rock piles. Some enter subterranean retreats, sometimes by way of burrows made by mammals and invertebrates. Caves are often occupied during cold or dry periods. Climbing species live on rock faces and in crevices, in trees, on broad-leaved herbs and shrubs, and in bromeliads. Many species are semi-aquatic, frequenting streamside and spring habitats throughout their lives. The terrestrial species that have direct development have been able to free themselves entirely from reliance on standing or flowing water. Among one group of plethodontids, species are found in habitats ranging from true deserts and frigid Alpine areas to tropical rain forests and from sea level to elevations of more than 4,000 metres (13,000 feet).

FORM AND FUNCTION

Skin and external features. The most distinctive and important feature of amphibians in general and salamanders in particular is their smooth, moist skin. This organ consists of an epidermis, or surface tissue, that is several layers thick and a rather thick dermis containing mucus and poison glands as well as pigment cells. The integument, or skin, is highly vascular and serves a major respiratory function. The poison glands of some species produce some of the most virulent toxins known. The fleshy tongue pad contains many mucus-secreting glands.

Most species are drab gray or brown; but many species, especially the more poisonous ones, are spectacularly coloured, with bright spots, blotches, or streaks on a

From *The Life of Vertebrates* by J.Z. Young, 1st ed. 1950, 3rd ed. © J.Z. Young 1981; published by Oxford University Press

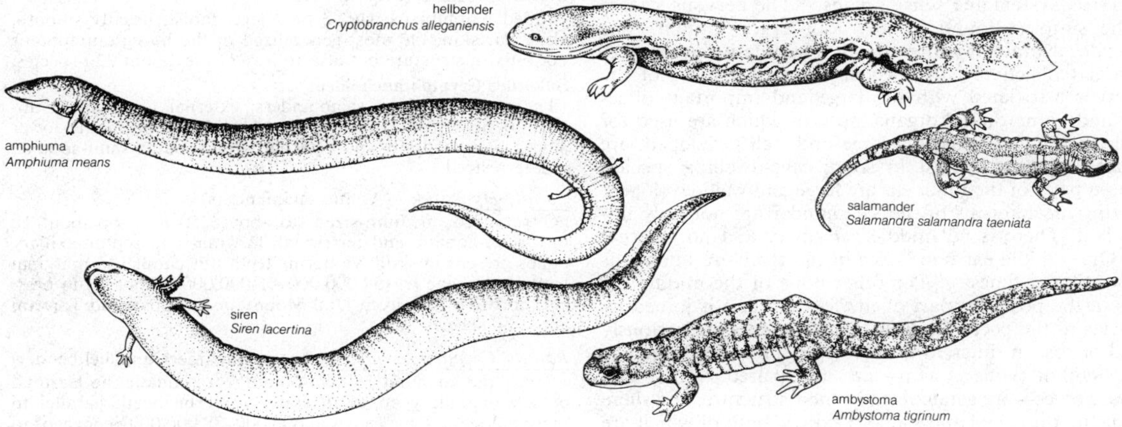

Figure 5: Representative urodeles.

contrasting dark background. The few integumentary specializations include keratinized (*i.e.,* infused with a tough, horny material: keratin) skins of the terrestrial stages of many salamandrids; keratinized claws in stream-dwelling hynobiids; and so-called hedonic glands (believed to stimulate sexual activity of the opposite sex) that are variously distributed in many species. Cryptobranchids have large, lateral folds of skin that serve respiratory functions.

Bones and cartilage. The rather weak skull of adults is comprised of various paired bones. These bones may fuse or be lost in different groups, and their presence and arrangement are important in classification. Much of the fusion and loss of skull bones is frequently associated with a trend toward tongue feeding. Small, double-cusped teeth line the margins of the jaw and spread over parts of the palate. They are important in holding but not chewing the prey.

Cartilage plays an important role in the urodele head, especially in supportive structures in the throat region. These are ossified (bony) to different degrees, with more cartilage in the more highly evolved groups. Species that display tongue protrusion often have flexible, cartilaginous tongue skeletons. In larvae and permanently gilled species the tongue is not developed.

The vertebrae comprising the spinal column are generalized with centrums (*i.e.,* ventral, or lower, sections connecting with the adjacent vertebrae) that are rather poorly developed. The notochord (*i.e.,* a resilient, flexible cord of specialized cells passing through the vertebral column) is usually persistent in adults. An intervertebral cartilage forms the articulation between vertebrae. If it remains cartilaginous, the vertebrae are said to be amphicoelous (biconcave, or depressed on both the anterior and posterior sides), but, if it mineralizes or ossifies, the vertebrae are termed opisthocoelous (bulged on the anterior side and depressed on the posterior side). There is one cervical vertebra with a characteristic projection called the odontoid process and two large facets for articulation with the skull. There may be from 11 (*Ambystoma talpoideum*) to 60 (*Amphiuma*) dorsal, or trunk, vertebrae, all but the last one or two usually bearing ribs. Most salamanders have from 14 to 20 trunk vertebrae. One sacral vertebra, two to four caudosacral vertebrae, and from about 20 to over 100 (*Oedipina*) caudal, or tail, vertebrae complete the column. Many plethodontids are capable of autotomizing, or dropping off, the tail, a valuable defense mechanism in the event that the tail is grasped or bitten by a predator. These salamanders have various specialized features associated with the last caudosacral and the first caudal vertebrae, between which the break usually occurs.

The limbs and girdles are similar to those of generalized vertebrates. The pectoral, or chest, girdle, supporting the forelimbs, is relatively reduced; all elements are fused and remain largely in a cartilaginous condition. An ypsiloid cartilage, used in exhalation, is present in several groups, especially ambystomatids and salamandrids. Digits and digital bones have been lost in many different groups. There are never more than four fingers, but nearly all species have five toes.

Fingers and toes

Nervous system and sense organs. The nervous system is the simplest found in any four-legged animal. The generalized brain is rather small. The relatively large cerebrum (collectively, the two large anterior lobes of the brain) is associated with the large and important olfactory and vomeronasal organs, both of which are used for smelling. The eyes, usually large and well developed, are reduced and nearly lost in some cave-dwelling species. Certain parts of the inner ear are large and well developed. Hearing mechanisms of the salamander are not fully understood. There is no middle ear cavity and no external ear. One middle ear bone rests in the structure known as the vestibular fenestra. The other bone of the middle ear rests in the posterior part of the fenestra and is joined by muscles to the pectoral girdle. The elements are variously fused or lost in different groups. The spinal cord and the peripheral nervous system—*i.e.,* the paired cranial and spinal nerves—are generalized in their structure, and there are distinct brachial and sacral plexuses, both of which are important nerve networks supplying the limbs.

Muscles and organ systems. The generalized musculature of the trunk exhibits little differentiation. The abdominal muscles show increasing degrees of differentiation in the higher groups. The hyobranchial and branchiomeric muscles and some abdominal muscles (rectus abdominis) are highly specialized in those species that use the tongue to capture prey.

The simple digestive system includes a short, nearly straight gut. The lungs are relatively simple, saclike organs in primitive groups. In stream-dwelling members of several families, the lungs are greatly reduced; they are entirely absent in all plethodontids.

The circulatory system is characterized by a highly developed vascularization of the body surface. The heart is simple, with one ventricle (*i.e.,* a chamber that pumps blood out of the heart) and two atria (chambers that receive blood from the rest of the body); separation between the two atria is not distinct in lungless forms.

The urogenital system consists of an elongated kidney with a distinct sexual segment and a posterior concentration of large renal units, which filter urine from the blood. Testes, the male sex glands, are small and compact, increasing in size with age. Ovaries of females are thin sacs. The cloaca is relatively complex in highly evolved groups with a spermatheca in females and several sets of cloacal glands in both sexes.

Gonads

EVOLUTION AND CLASSIFICATION

Paleontology. Fossils have contributed little, as yet, to the understanding of salamander evolution. The earliest definitive salamander is one of unknown affinities from the Jurassic Period (about 136,000,000 to 190,000,000 years ago). Several ambystomatoid families (Prosirenidae, Scapherpetonidae, Batrachosauroididae) are known only from fossils. The relationships of urodeles to other living and fossil amphibians are unclear, but recent workers consider the three living groups to form the subclass Lissamphibia.

Distinguishing taxonomic features. The features used to establish the limits of the order and of the groups within it include: general body size and organization—*e.g.,* presence or absence of external gills, numbers and relative proportions of limbs and digits, number and arrangement of skull bones; organization of the hyobranchial apparatus (cartilage in the throat region); structure and distribution of the teeth; structure of the vertebrae and intervertebral articulations; numbers of vertebrae; number and organization of the hand and foot elements; anatomy of the pelvic girdle; anatomy of external structures, such as hedonic (sex-attractant) glands, body and tail fins, webbing of hands and feet, and cloacal glands. Distinctive also is the general way of life, whether permanently aquatic, semiaquatic, or terrestrial.

Annotated classification. The classification below is based on that of A.H. Brame, Jr. (1967). There is as yet no widely accepted scheme for classification below the order level. The plethodontids of the New World tropics remain poorly known, taxonomically.

ORDER URODELA (OR CAUDATA)

Tailed amphibians with 2 or 4 legs; moist, usually smooth, glandular skin; the most generalized of the living amphibians not only in structure but also in way of life; about 320 species.

Suborder Cryptobranchoidea

The most primitive salamanders; external fertilization; angular bone separate from the prearticular bone in the lower jaw; 2 pairs of limbs; no external gills; aquatic, semi-aquatic, and terrestrial.

Family Hynobiidae (Asiatic salamanders)

Generalized, medium-sized (to about 250 mm, or about 10 in.), semi-aquatic and terrestrial; lacrimal and septomaxillary bones present in skull; vomerine teeth not parallel to marginal teeth; Paleocene (?) (54,000,000–65,000,000 years ago) to present; northern Asia from Ural Mountains to Japan and Taiwan; about 30 species.

Family Cryptobranchidae (giant salamanders and hellbender)

Very large, to about 180 cm (about 6 ft), aquatic; no lacrimal or septomaxillary bones in skull; vomerine teeth parallel to marginal teeth; Oligocene (26,000,000–38,000,000 years ago) to present; Japan, China, and eastern United States; 3 species.

Suborder Sirenoidea
Mode of fertilization unknown; angular bone fused with prearticular bone in lower jaw; only anterior pair of limbs present; external gills; aquatic.

Family Sirenidae (sirens and dwarf sirens)
Small to very large, to about 100 cm (about 40 in.), predators; inhabitants of lowland waters; Late Cretaceous (65,000,000–90,000,000 years ago) to present; southeastern United States from South Carolina to Tamaulipas, Mexico; 3 species.

Suborder Salamandroidea
Fertilization internal; angular bone fused with prearticular bone in lower jaw; no septomaxillary bones in skull; tooth replacement of vomerine teeth from medial side in metamorphosed forms; 2 pairs of limbs; external gills in a few species; aquatic, semi-aquatic, and terrestrial.

Family Proteidae (olms)
Blind; lacking pigment, cave-dwelling; elongated body, length to 30 cm (about 1 ft), and slender limbs (3 fingers, 2 toes); external gills present; Pliocene (2,500,000–7,000,000 years ago) to present; 1 species, native to Yugoslavia.

Family Necturidae (mud puppies)
Small to moderately large, to 45 cm (about 1½ ft), permanently aquatic, lake and stream dwellers; eyes and skin pigmentation present; 4 fingers and 4 toes; external gills present; no fossil record; eastern North America; 5 species, of genus *Necturus.*

Family Amphiumidae (congo eels)
Large, to over 100 cm (about 40 in.); very elongated, aquatic to semi-aquatic; predaceous, with powerful jaws and teeth; limbs diminutive, 1 to 3 fingers and toes; external gills absent, but spiracle open; Late Cretaceous to present; eastern North America; 3 species, of genus *Amphiuma.*

Family Salamandridae (salamanders and newts)
Generalized form and habit; moderate size, to 32 cm (about 13 in.); limbs with 4 fingers, 4 to 5 toes; usually no external gills or spiracle; Upper Cretaceous (?) to present; Europe, North Africa; Middle East; Afghanistan to Japan, China, and northern Vietnam; eastern and western North America; about 42 species.

Suborder Ambystomatoidea
Fertilization internal; angular bone fused with prearticular bone in lower jaw; septomaxillary bones present primitively in skull; tooth replacement of vomerine teeth from posterior or lateral direction; 2 pairs of limbs; external gills in some species; aquatic, semi-aquatic, or terrestrial.

Family Ambystomatidae (mole salamanders and others)
Small to moderate size, to 35 cm (about 14 in.); usually with well developed lungs; no nasolabial grooves; ypsiloid cartilage present; Paleocene to present; North America; about 33 species, including *Ambystoma.*

Family Plethodontidae (lungless salamanders)
Very small to moderate size, 4 to about 30 cm (about 1.6 to 12 in.); includes the most specialized and most terrestrial salamanders, and the only truly tropical species; lungless; nasolabial grooves present; no ypsiloid cartilage; Pliocene to present; North America, Central America, and most of South America; 2 species in Europe (Sardinia, southern France, and north central Italy); more than 200 species.

Critical appraisal. Some controversy exists concerning the classification of salamanders below the ordinal level. Some authorities place the sirenids in a separate order, Trachystomata, while others separate the Necturidae from the Proteidae, but neither scheme has been widely accepted. Chromosomal evidence of proteidnecturid similarity has recently been presented. Close association of Ambystomatidae and Plethodontidae is now accepted, but placement of Amphiumidae remains controversial.

Anura (frogs and toads)

Frogs and toads comprise the order Anura (Salientia of some authors) of the vertebrate class Amphibia and because of their wide distribution are known by most people around the world. The name frog is commonly applied to those forms with long legs and smooth, mucus-covered skins, toad being used for a variety of robust, short-legged anurans, especially those with rough skins. The name toad is applied so unevenly that one member of a family may be called a toad and a closely related member a frog. The familiar members of the family Bufonidae may be distinguished as "true toads." In this article, "frog" is applied generally to members of the Anura and "toad" to those for which it has traditionally been used. Many school children catch and keep frogs as pets and obtain one of their first biology lessons by rearing the larvae, known as tadpoles or pollywogs, in science classes. College students become familiar with frog anatomy and embryology in biology courses. People in various parts of the world eat frog legs, and some kinds of toads are used in insect control. Certain South American Indians use the poisonous secretions of some kinds of frogs for poison arrows, and now biochemists are studying the possible medical uses of the constituents of the poison. The biologist interested in evolution finds a vast array of interesting, and often perplexing, problems in the study of frogs, a highly specialized group of amphibians.

GENERAL FEATURES

Size range and diversity of structure. Although all frogs are readily recognizable, there are great varieties of sizes and of structural modifications. Many frogs are tiny animals; the smallest is the Cuban *Sminthillus limbatus,* adults of which do not exceed 12 millimetres (½ inch) in body length (with legs drawn in), whereas the African giant frog, *Conrana goliath,* has a body length of nearly 300 millimetres (slightly less than one foot). Many anurans have smooth, moist skins. Toads of the genus *Bufo* are familiar as "warty" amphibians, the skin being highly glandular and covered with tubercles. Frogs of many other families have rough, tubercular skins, usually an adaptation for life in the less humid environments. The opposite extreme is found in the small arboreal frogs of the tropical American family Centrolenidae, in which the skin on the under side is thin and transparent, and the heart and viscera can be seen through the skin.

Most frogs move by leaping. The long and powerful hind limbs are straightened rapidly from the crouching position, propelling the frog through the air into water or to a distant place on the ground. Many arboreal frogs, especially members of the family Hylidae, have adhesive discs on the ends of the fingers and toes and leap from branch to branch or from leaf to leaf. Members of the families Bufonidae, Rhinophrynidae, and Microhylidae and certain burrowing species in other families have relatively short hindlimbs and move forward by series of short hops. Some bufonids actually walk instead of hopping. Highly modified members of the hylid subfamily Phyllomedusinae have opposable digits on the hands and feet and walk slowly along branches, deliberately grasping the branch in the manner of tiny lemurs. Many kinds of frogs have membranous webbing between the fingers and toes; in the aquatic species the webbing on the feet aids in swimming. The extreme in this specialization is seen in the aquatic family Pipidae. Members of that family normally never leave the water. In regions of the earth subjected to long dry periods, frogs must seek cover in order to avoid desiccation and have behavioral and structural adaptations to conserve water.

Although many frogs are unimpressively coloured, some species are brilliantly marked. The most common colours are brown, gray, green, and yellow. Uniformly coloured frogs are the exception rather than the rule. The markings of a frog may seem bold when observed out of the natural habitat, but they usually are concealing or disruptive when the frog is in its environment.

Distribution and abundance. Because of their morphological and physiological adaptations, frogs are able to inhabit most regions of the world except the extremely cold land masses at high latitudes and some oceanic islands that they have been unable to colonize due to the barriers provided by saltwater. Frogs live in desert regions below sea level and in montane areas up to elevations above 4,560 metres (15,000 feet). Some members of the genus *Rana* live north of the Arctic Circle. Although widely distributed on the earth, frogs are most diverse and abundant in the tropics, and 7 of the 17 families are restricted to the tropics. In most temperate areas of the world, the number of species of frogs at any one locality is usually less than ten; but in the tropics, especially in rain forests, the number of species is much greater. At one locality in the upper Amazon Basin in eastern Ecuador, 83 species are known to occur, about the same number as is known for all of the United States.

In a complex environment, such as the tropical rain forest, the large number of species of frogs partition the environmental resources in a variety of ways. In the humid tropics, frogs can be active throughout the year, but many species are seasonal in their breeding activity. Various kinds of sites and different seasons are used for calling and egg laying; such temporal and spatial separation avoids interspecific competition. Frogs feed mostly on insects and other invertebrates, and the abundance of food in tropical rain forests probably places no competitive restrictions on this aspect of environmental resources. Some large species eat vertebrates, including small rodents and other frogs.

NATURAL HISTORY

Breeding behaviour. The breeding behaviour is one of the most distinctive attributes of the Anura. Since the eggs can develop only under moist conditions, most frogs place their eggs in bodies of fresh water. Many species congregate in large numbers at temporary pools for short breeding seasons. Mating calls serve to attract males and females to breeding sites. Other frogs breed along the mountain streams where they live year round. In the

Mating calls

H.V. Lacey—Annan Photo Features

Figure 6: Frogs (*Rana*) in copulatory embrace.

latter species and in those that breed on the land, there is no great concentration of breeding individuals at one place. In all cases, the mating call produced by the male attracts the females. It has been observed in the field and experimentally in the laboratory that the females can discriminate between mating calls of their own species and those of other species. At a communal breeding site, such as a pond, swamp, or stream, differences in specific calling sites of the males help the frogs to maintain their identities. Differences in mating calls, however, constitute the principal premating isolating mechanism preventing hybridization of closely related species living in the same area and breeding at the same time and place. Frogs have rather simple vocal cords, in most species a pair of slits in the floor of the mouth opening into a vocal pouch. Air is forced from the lungs over the vocal cords, causing them to vibrate and thus produce sound of a given pitch and pulsation. The air passes into the vocal pouch, which, when inflated, acts as a resonating chamber emphasizing the same frequency or one of its harmonics. In this manner, different kinds of frogs produce different calls.

Females move toward and locate calling males. Once the male clasps the female, a copulatory embrace called amplexus, she selects the site for depositing the eggs. In the primitive frogs (superfamilies Discoglossoidea, Pipoidea, and Pelobatoidea), the male grasps the female from above and around the waist (inguinal amplexus); whereas in the advanced frogs (superfamilies Bufonoidea and Ranoidea), the position is shifted anteriorly to the armpits (axillary amplexus). The latter position brings the cloacae of the amplectic pair into closer proximity and presumably insures more efficient fertilization.

Most frogs deposit their eggs in quiet water as clumps, surface films, strings, or as individual eggs. The eggs may be freely suspended in the water or attached to sticks or submergent vegetation. Some frogs lay their eggs in streams, characteristically firmly attached to the lee sides or under sides of rocks where they are not subject to the current. The large pond-breeding frogs of the genus *Rana* and toads of the genus *Bufo* apparently produce more eggs than any other frogs. More than 10,000 eggs have been estimated in one clutch of the North American bullfrog, *Rana catesbeiana.* The habit of spreading the eggs as a film on the surface of the water apparently is an adaptation for oviposition in shallow temporary pools and allows the eggs to develop in the most highly oxygenated part of the pool. This type of egg deposition is characteristic of several groups of tree frogs, family Hylidae, in the American tropics, one of which, *Smilisca baudinii,* is known to lay more than 3,000 eggs. Frogs breeding in cascading mountain streams lay far fewer eggs, usually no more than 200.

The problem of fertilization of eggs in rapidly flowing water has been overcome by various modifications. Some stream-breeding hylids have long cloacal tubes so that the semen can be directed onto the eggs as they emerge. Some other hylids have huge testes, which apparently produce vast quantities of sperm, helping to insure fertilization. Males of the North American tailed frog, *Ascaphus truei,* have an extension of the cloaca that functions as a copulatory organ (the "tail") to introduce sperm into the female's cloaca.

Aggressive behaviour

Most frogs are considered to be placid animals, but recent observations have shown that some species exhibit aggressive tendencies, especially at breeding time. Male bullfrogs (*Rana catesbeiana*) and green frogs (*Rana clamitans*) defend calling territories against intrusion by other males by kicking, bumping, and biting. The South American nest-building hylid, *Hyla faber,* has a long, sharp spine on the thumb with which males wound each other when wrestling. The small Central American *Dendrobates pumilio* calls from leaves of herbaceous plants. Intrusion into a territory of one calling male by another results in a wrestling match that terminates only after one male has been thrown off the leaf. Males of the Central American dendrobatid *Colostethus inguinalis* have calling sites on boulders in streams. The intrusion by another male results in the resident uttering a territorial call, and if the intruder does not leave, the resident charges him, attempting to butt him off the boulder. Females of the Venezuelan *Colostethus trinitatus* wrestle in defense of territories in a stream bed.

Males of at least three South American species of *Hyla* build basin-like nests, 25–30 centimetres (10–12 inches) wide and 2–5 centimetres (1–2 inches) deep, in the mud of riverbanks. Water seeps into the basin providing a medium for the eggs and young. Calling, mating, and oviposition take place in the nest, and the tadpoles undergo their development in the nests.

Some frogs in the families Leptodactylidae, Ranidae, and Microhylidae build froth nests. The small toadlike leptodactylids of the genus *Physalaemus* breed in small, shallow pools. Amplexus is axillary, and the pair floats on the water; as the female exudes the eggs, the male emits semen and kicks vigorously with his hind legs. The result is a frothy mixture of water, air, eggs, and semen, which floats on the water. This meringue-like nest is about 7.5–10.0 centimetres (3–4 inches) in diameter and about 5 centimetres (2 inches) deep. The outer surfaces exposed to the air harden and form a crust covering the moist interior, in which the eggs are randomly distributed. Upon hatching, the tadpoles wriggle down through the decaying froth into the water.

Metamorphosis

Most frogs have an aquatic, free-swimming larval stage (tadpole). After a period of growth, the tadpole undergoes a striking change (metamorphosis) in which the tail is lost and limbs appear. These are only two of the most obvious changes that take place. Tadpoles have a cartilaginous skeleton, thin nonglandular skin, and a long, coiled intestine;

they lack jaws, lungs, and eyelids. Among the first changes that take place is the appearance of hindlimb buds, which grow and develop into differentiated hindlimbs, complete with toes, webbing, and tubercles. Much later, the front limbs emerge through the skin; in contrast to the hindlimbs, the forelimbs develop before they emerge. At the time of emergence of the forelimbs, the tail begins to shrink, being absorbed by the body. The tadpole mouth begins to change; as the horny denticles and papillae, if present, disappear, the jaws and true teeth develop. The eyelids develop, and mucous glands form in the skin. The vertebral column and limb bones ossify, and the adult digestive system differentiates as the long, coiled intestine shrinks to the short, thick-walled, folded intestine of the adult. These radical changes are equalled in the animal kingdom only by the metamorphosis found in insects.

Just how and where the changes from larva to adult take place is highly varied and is one of the most fascinating aspects of the study of frogs. The differences in modes of life history reflect varied environmental conditions. In various evolutionary lines in frogs, there is a strong tendency toward an escape from the ties that bind the less advanced frogs to the water for breeding.

The tadpoles of the pond breeders characteristically have rather large bodies and deep caudal (tail) fins, which in some have a terminal extension, as do the familiar swordtail fishes. The mouths are relatively small, either at the end of the snout or on the underside, and usually contain rather weak denticles (small toothlike projections). These tadpoles swim easily in the quiet water and feed on attached and free-floating vegetation, including algae. In contrast, the stream tadpoles have depressed bodies, long muscular tails, and shallow caudal fins. The mouth is relatively large and usually contains many rows of strong denticles. In highly modified stream tadpoles, the mouth is ventral and modified as an oral sucker, with which the tadpole anchors itself to stones in the stream. Such tadpoles move slowly across stones, gnawing off moss or algae as they move. It is conceivable that a tadpole can complete its larval life on a single large stone.

Drawing by Linda Trueb

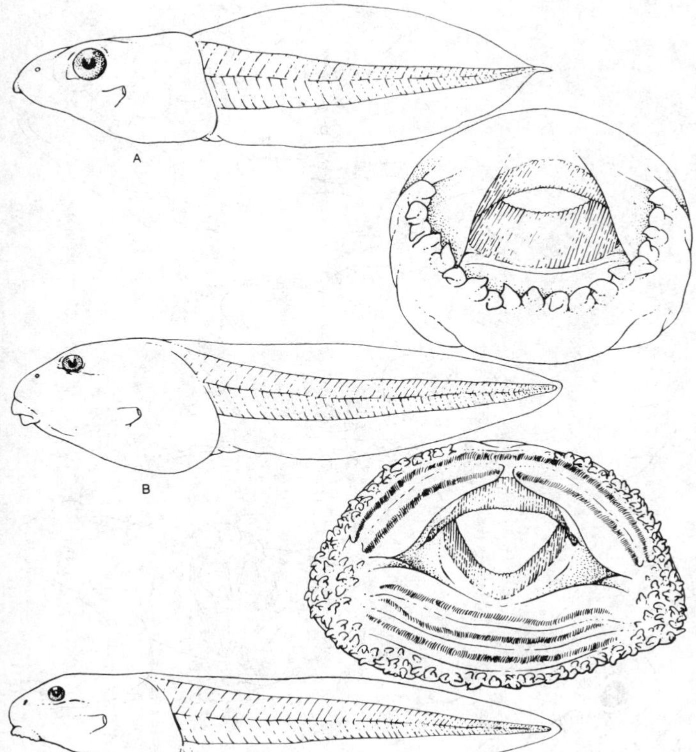

Figure 7: *Specializations of tail (left) and mouth (right) in tadpoles.*
(A) For pelagic life in ponds. (B) For bottom life in ponds. (C) For life in running water.

Most tadpoles complete their development in two or three months, but there are notable exceptions. Tadpoles of spadefoot toads, genus *Scaphiopus,* develop in temporary rain pools in arid parts of North America, where it is imperative for the tadpoles to complete their development before the pools dry up. Some *Scaphiopus* tadpoles metamorphose about two weeks after hatching. In the northern part of its range in North America, the tadpoles of the bullfrog *Rana catesbeiana* require three years to undergo their development.

Some tree frogs of the family Hylidae deposit their eggs in water in trees. Several tropical species of *Hyla* lay their eggs in the water held in the overlapping bases of leaves of epiphytic bromeliads high in trees. Their tadpoles, which are slender with long muscular tails, develop in small quantities of water high above the ground. The Mexican hylid, *Anotheca spinosa,* lays its eggs in bromeliads or water-filled cavities in trees. The small tadpoles, like those of *Hyla,* feed on aquatic insect larvae, such as mosquitoes, but the larger tadpoles of *Anotheca* apparently feed only on the eggs of frogs.

A modification of the basic behaviour of aquatic eggs and aquatic tadpoles is the habit of depositing eggs on vegetation above water; this pattern occurs in some arboreal hylids and ranids and in all species in the family Centrolenidae. *Hyla ebraccata,* a small Central American tree frog, deposits its eggs in a single layer on the upper surfaces of horizontal leaves just a few inches above the pond. Upon hatching, the tadpoles wriggle to the edge of the leaf and drop into the water. The Mexican *Hyla thorectes* suspends 10–14 eggs on ferns overhanging cascading mountain streams. The phyllomedusine hylids in the American tropics suspend clutches of eggs from leaves or stems above ponds. Males call from trees; once a female has been attracted and amplexus takes place, the male placidly hangs onto the back of the female as she descends to the pond and absorbs water. This accomplished, she climbs into a tree, selects an oviposition site, and deposits eggs until her water supply is depleted. She again descends to the pond and repeats the performance at a different site until the entire complement of eggs is deposited. Upon hatching, the tadpoles drop into the pond below. Most of the tree frogs of the family Centrolenidae are less than one inch long. Males call from leaves of trees or bushes over cascading mountain streams in the American tropics. Individuals return to the same leaf night after night. Attracted females are clasped on the leaf, and egg deposition takes place there immediately. A highly successful male may have three or four egg clutches on his leaf, each consisting of only about two dozen eggs. Upon hatching, the tadpoles drop into the stream bed; and if the tadpole lands on a stone, it flips about vigorously until it falls into the water, where it hides in the loose gravel on the bottom of the stream.

Parental care

Many kinds of frogs lay their eggs on land and subsequently transport the tadpoles to water. The ranid genus *Sooglossus* of the Seychelle Islands and all members of the family Dendrobatidae in the American tropics have terrestrial eggs. Upon hatching, the tadpoles adhere to the backs of adults, usually males. The exact means of attachment is not known. The frogs carry the tadpoles to streams, bromeliads, or pools of water in logs or stumps, where the tadpoles complete their development. The most unusual example of tadpole care known is that exhibited by the mouth-breeding frog, or Darwin's toad, *Rhinoderma darwinii,* in southern South America. An amplectic pair deposits 20–30 eggs on moist ground. Several males gather around the eggs, and when the eggs are about ready to hatch, with the embryos moving, each male picks up some eggs with his tongue. The eggs pass through the vocal slits in the floor of the mouth and into the vocal sac. The eggs hatch, and the larvae complete their development in the large vocal sac. Upon metamorphosis, the young frogs emerge from the male's mouth.

The European midwife toad, *Alytes obstetricans,* displays a peculiar breeding habit. Inguinal amplexus takes place on land; at the time of oviposition the female extends her legs to form a receptacle for the string of 20–60 eggs. After fertilizing the eggs, the male moves forward on the back of the female and pushes his legs into the string of eggs until they are wound around his waist and legs. Then the female departs. The male carries the eggs with him on land until they are ready to hatch, at which time he moves to a pond, where the eggs hatch and complete their development.

The hylid *Gastrotheca marsupiata* lives in the high Andes of South America, one of several so-called marsupial frogs, so named because of a brood pouch in the back of the female. In amplexus the male exudes a quantity of semen, which flows into the pouch. The female extrudes eggs, a few at a time; these are pushed into the pouch by the male who uses the hindfeet to catch and push the eggs. The eggs are fertilized in the pouch, where they hatch and the tadpoles begin their development. Subsequently, the female moves to a pond, where the tadpoles emerge from the pouch and complete their development in the water.

In each of the above instances of parental care, there is a trend away from the aquatic environment. Far fewer eggs (less than 50) are laid in comparison with those species depositing eggs in the water. The bonds with the aquatic environment have been partially broken, for, although the tadpoles must develop there, the eggs are effectively terrestrial, but not truly so, lacking the necessary embryonic membranes (allantois and amnion) to maintain physiological balance and lacking a shell. Consequently, if they are to survive and develop, the eggs must be maintained in moist places, such as damp soil or a part of the parental body. Water and waste products are transported through the membranes by osmosis.

The next evolutionary step in mode of life history is the elimination of the larval stage, thereby completely severing the ties with the aquatic environment. Direct development of the egg, in which the larvae undergo their development within the egg membranes and emerge as tiny froglets, occurs in many species, scattered in seven families (Leiopelmatidae, Pipidae, Leptodactylidae, Bufonidae, Brachycephalidae, Hylidae, and Microhylidae). Typical direct development of terrestrial eggs occurs in the many species of the leptodactylid genus *Eleutherodactylus* of Central and South America and the West Indies. During axillary amplexus, the female deposits a clutch of eggs in a moist place (beneath a log or stone, amidst leaf litter, in a rotting stump, in moss, or in a bromeliad). The parents depart, leaving the eggs to develop and subsequently hatch. In some *Eleutherodactylus* and in the New Zealand leiopelmatid *Leiopelma hochstetteri,* the hatching froglet still has a tail. In *Leiopelma,* at least, vigorous thrusts of the tail are used to rupture the egg membranes. Soon after hatching, the tail is completely absorbed.

Brooding of terrestrial eggs is known in a few species. Females of two species of *Eleutherodactylus* that lay their eggs on leaves of bushes or trees sit on the eggs. Apparently this brooding serves to prevent desiccation of the eggs by dry winds. Females of the Papuan microhylid *Sphenophryne* lay their few eggs beneath stones or logs and sit on top of them until they hatch.

Marsupial frogs

Direct development occurs in several genera of hylid marsupial frogs (*Gastrotheca* and *Amphignathodon*) living in mountain rain forests in northwestern South America. In these frogs, amplexus is axillary, and the female raises her cloaca so that the eggs, which are extruded one at a time, roll forward on her back and into the pouch. There the eggs develop into frogs. Large, external, gill-like structures envelop the developing embryo. These structures, which are attached to the throat of the embryo by a pair of cords, apparently function in respiration. These frogs live high in trees and complete their life cycle without descending to the ground. Thus they are rare in collections, and their biology is poorly known.

Some other South American genera of Hylidae also exhibit the phenomenon of direct development of eggs carried on the backs of the females. In *Flectonotus* and *Fritziana,* the eggs are contained in one large basin-like depression in the back, whereas in others each egg occupies its own individual depression. In *Hemiphractus,* gill-like structures and cords similar to those in *Gastrotheca* are present. At hatching, the expanded gill adheres to the

Drawing by Linda Trueb

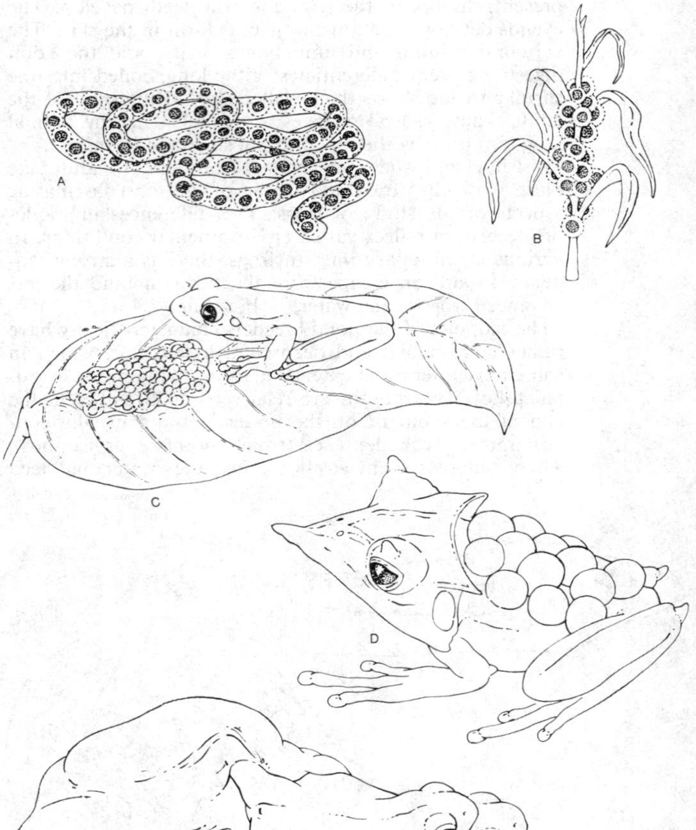

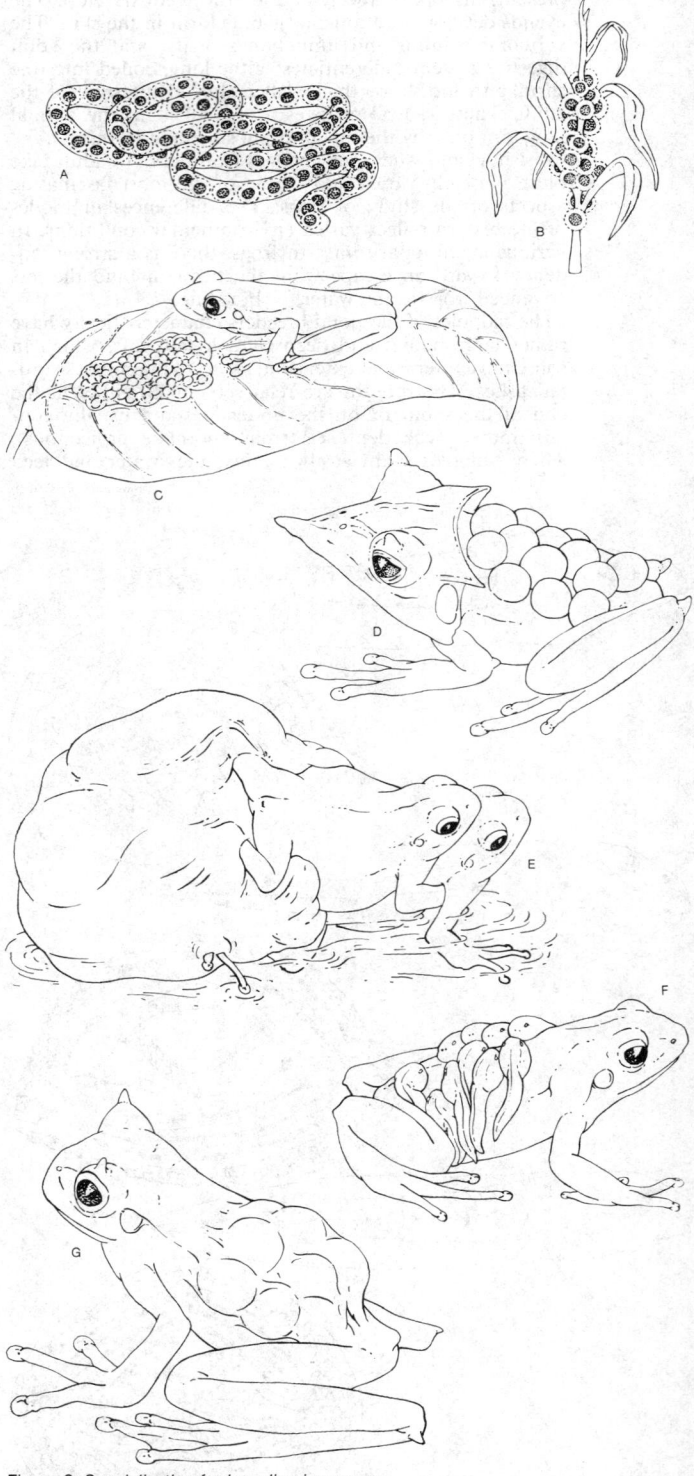

Figure 8: *Specialization for breeding in anurans.*
(A) Aquatic eggs free-floating in a string. (B) Aquatic eggs attached to submerged vegetation. (C) Eggs of *Phyllomedusa* on leaf above water. (D) *Hemiphractus* with eggs on its back. (E) Meringne-like nest made by amplectic pair of *Physalaemus.* (F) Tadpoles on the back of a male *Colostethus.* (G) Marsupial frog (*Gastrotheca*) with eggs in pouch.

modified skin of the maternal depression and is attached to the young by the pair of cords. The female carries the young until they are sufficiently well developed to care for themselves. The manner of detachment of gill from female and young is unknown.

The strictly aquatic Surinam toad *Pipa pipa* of northern South America also has direct development, in this case in the water. Eggs are carried in individual depressions in the back of the female. Amplexus is inguinal, and the pair rests on the bottom of the pond. The female initiates vertical circular turnovers, at the height of which she extrudes a few eggs. These are fertilized, fall against the belly of the then upside down male, and are pushed forward onto the female's back, where they adhere and subsequently become enclosed in tissue. Upon completion of development, the young frogs emerge from the skin of the female's back.

The most advanced form of reproduction known in frogs takes place in the small African bufonids of the genus *Nectophrynoides.* By some unknown means, fertilization is internal, and the young are born alive. It is noteworthy that the evolution of live birth has taken place independently in all three living orders of amphibians, for this phenomenon also occurs in salamanders and caecilians.

Feeding habits. The great majority of frogs feed on insects, other small arthropods, or worms, but some larger species eat vertebrates. The South American leptodactylid *Ceratophrys varia* and the large bufonid *Bufo marinus* eat other frogs and small rodents. The superficially similar Solomon Island ranid, *Ceratobatrachus guentheri,* and the South American hylids, *Hemiphractus,* eat other frogs. Large North American bullfrogs, *Rana catesbeiana,* have been reported to consume other frogs, mice, small snakes, and even small turtles.

FORM AND FUNCTION

Adult anurans are easily recognized, by layman and specialist alike, by the short body and elongated hindlimbs, the absence of a visible neck, and the absence of a tail. The compact body has been attained by a reduction of the number of trunk vertebrae and the fusion of tail vertebrae into a single rodlike bone, the coccyx or urastyle. The lengthening of the hindlimbs has been attained, in part, by the elongation of two bones (astragalus and calcaneum) in the foot. Considering the variety of habitats occupied by anurans, there is remarkably little gross variation in body plan. The female is usually larger than the male. In most frogs the tympanic membrane (eardrum) is visible as a prominent disc on each side of the head. Correlated with a sound-oriented existence, the larynx is also well developed, often accompanied by single or paired inflatable resonating sacs.

Poisons

All frogs have poison glands in the skin, well developed in many diverse groups. In the Dendrobatidae, the skin secretions are especially toxic. *Dendrobates* and *Phyllobates* are small, diurnal frogs living in Central and South America, brilliantly coloured, solid red, yellow, or orange, or patterned with bold stripes or cross bars. These bright patterns are believed to act as warning colours to ward off predators. One nonpoisonous South American leptodactylid, *Lithodytes lineatus,* mimics the dendrobatid *Phyllobates femoralis,* thus gaining protection from predation (see also MIMICRY).

The biochemical properties of amphibian skin toxins are highly varied, most being complex nitrogenous compounds. The toxically active ingredients are of various types, from local irritants to convulsants, hallucinogens, neurotoxins (nerve poisons), and vasoconstrictors (acting to narrow blood vessels). The medical importance of these ingredients is now being investigated. Although these skin secretions irritate human skin and mucous membranes, they do not cause warts.

The skin toxins of most frogs do not provide security from predators; in fact, frogs are a basic food for many snakes, birds, and mammals. Edible anurans rely on modifications of shape, skin texture, and colour, supplemented by behaviour, to escape detection. These modifications may reach remarkable extremes. Hylids of the South American genus *Hemiphractus* live on the forest floor among leaf litter and have flattened bodies that enable them to blend well with dead leaves. Several tree frogs, rough skinned and greenish-gray, resemble lichens when flattened out on tree trunks.

Coloration

The coloration of many frogs changes from night to day. In most species the colour is darker and the pattern more distinct by day than by night, but the reverse is true for some tree frogs inhabiting semi-arid regions. Colour change is brought about through the stimuli of light and moisture, which create a physiological change and result in contraction or expansion of the melanophores (pigment cells) in the skin.

More difficult to comprehend is the striking array of colours on the hidden surfaces of frogs. Many frogs that are rather dull or uniformly coloured when in a resting position have bright colours or patterns on the flanks, groin, posterior surfaces of the thighs, and belly. For example, the South and Central American hylid, *Agalychnis calcarifer,* when observed sleeping by day, is nothing more than a green bump on a leaf. The eyes are closed, the hindlimbs drawn in close to the body, and the hands folded beneath the chin. Upon moving, the frog creates a striking appearance, previously hidden surfaces showing a deep golden orange, interrupted by vertical black bars on the flanks and thighs. These so-called flash colours are common in frogs and are thought to serve in species recognition or in confusing predators. Some colour patterns obviously do confuse predators. The South American leptodactylids of the genus *Eupsophus* have a pair of brightly coloured "eyespots" on the rump. When approached by a potential predator, the frog lowers its head and elevates the rump, thus confronting the predator with a seemingly much larger head.

Structural modifications allow certain specialized frogs to survive dry periods. Some arboreal frogs hide in bromeliad plants (various genera of the family Bromeliaceae), which hold water in the axils of their leaves. Among the Hylidae are genera that have the head modified into a bony casque ("helmet") and the skin co-ossified with the underlying bone. The head is used by some species to plug the constricted base of the bromeliads and by others to plug up holes in trees, the frogs surviving the dry season by utilizing what little moisture is trapped in the cavity.

Most toads of the genus *Bufo* and many genera in the families Rhinophrynidae, Pelobatidae, Myobatrachidae, Leptodactylidae, Hylidae, Ranidae, and Microhylidae burrow in sand, soil, or mud. Many of these species have the tubercles on the middle (metatarsal) part of each foot modified into a spade-shaped digging organ. The animals are highly resistant to desiccation and conserve water in the body by the mucous skin secretions that tend to make the skin impermeable. This modification is carried to the extreme in some Australian myobatrachids, which secrete a cocoon formed of hardened mucus.

CLASSIFICATION

Distinguishing taxonomic features. The superfamilies and families of the Anura are based on anatomical, developmental, and behavioral characteristics. Important anatomical features include: the type of vertebrate present, especially with respect to the articulating surfaces, which may be concave on the anterior end of each vertebra (procoelus), on the posterior side (opisthocoelus), or concave on both ends (amphicoelus); the presence or absence of intercalary cartilages (between the terminal and penultimate bones of the digits); whether the pectoral girdle is firmisternal (*i.e.,* with the cartilages of the two epicoracoid bones fused together) or arciferal (with these cartilages separate and overlapping); the presence or absence of an anterior projection, the omosternum, on the pectoral girdle; the presence or absence of teeth on the maxillary bone; and the presence or absence of Bidder's organ (a rudimentary ovary) in the male. The type of egg and anatomy of the tadpole are often important. The key behavioral characteristics are primarily those involved with reproduction, such as the type of amplexus and method of egg deposition.

Annotated classification. The classification presented here is an amalgamation of recent views by various specialists, none of whom has surveyed the entire order. A scanty record of meaningful fossils and inadequate knowledge of the morphology and mode of life history of many kinds of frogs result in inconclusive evidence for any classification of the families; consequently, the following classification must be considered to be tentative.

ORDER ANURA

Amphibians lacking a tail in the adult stage; 6 to 9 presacral vertebrae; postsacral vertebrae (posterior to the pelvis) fused into a bony coccyx; hindlimbs elongated, modified for jumping; fertilization normally external; eggs laid in water or not; an aquatic larval stage (tadpole) present in most; males usually with vocal cords, vocal sac (resonating chamber), and a voice. About 2,660 species.

Superfamily Discoglossoidea

Vertebrae amphicoelous with labile centra (*i.e.,* joined by rings of cartilage); pectoral girdle arciferal; ribs present on anterior vertebrae; amplexus inguinal; larvae with single median spiracle (respiratory opening) and complex mouthparts or with direct development (froglet hatching directly from the egg).

Family Leiopelmatidae

No fossil record. Nine presacral vertebrae (*i.e.,* anterior to the pelvic girdle); parahyoid and caudalipuboischiotibialis ("tail-wagging") muscles present; direct development (*Liopelma*) or stream-adapted tadpoles (*Ascaphus*). New Zealand and northwestern North America; 2 genera, 4 species. Adult length about 5 cm.

Family Discoglossidae (fire-bellied and midwife toads)

Eocene to present. Usually 8 presacral vertebrae; parahyoid tongue muscle and caudalipuboischiotibialis muscle absent. Still-water tadpoles. Eurasia, North Africa, and Philippine Islands; 4 genera, 8 species. Adult length to about 10 cm.

Superfamily Pipoidea

Vertebrae opisthocoelous; pectoral girdle arciferal; ribs absent or fused to transverse processes of vertebrae; amplexus inguinal; larvae with paired spiracles and simple mouthparts or with direct development.

Family Rhinophrynidae (burrowing toad)

Oligocene to present. Eight presacral vertebrae; ribs absent; coccyx free, with 2 articulating surfaces; tongue free and protrusible; body robust; burrowing; aquatic larvae present. Mexico and Central America, 1 species; adult length to about 7 cm.

Family Pipidae (tongueless frogs)

Cretaceous to present; 5 to 8 presacral vertebrae; ribs present and free in larvae, but fused to transverse processes of vertebrae in adults; coccyx fused to sacrum or free and monocondylar (*i.e.,* with 1 articulation); tongue absent; body flattened. Aquatic, direct development or aquatic larvae present. Africa south of Sahara and tropical South America, east of Andes; 6 genera, 14 species; adult length 5–20 cm.

Superfamily Pelobatoidea

Vertebrae procoelous with labile centra; pectoral girdle arciferal; ribs absent; amplexus inguinal; larvae with single spiracle on the left, and complex mouthparts.

Family Pelobatidea (spadefoots)

Eocene to present. Eight presacral vertebrae; coccyx fused to sacrum or free and monocondylar. Ten genera, 59 species; adult length 4 to about 15 cm. Three subfamilies: Megophryinae (Southeast Asia, Indo-Australian Archipelago, Philippine Islands), Pelodytinae (southwestern Europe and southwestern Asia), Pelobatinae (Europe and North America).

Family Myobatrachidae

Eocene to present. Eight presacral vertebrae; coccyx free, bicondylar. Eighteen genera, 76 species; adult length to about 10 cm. Three subfamilies: Myobatrachinae (New Guinea and Australia), Cycloraninae (New Guinea and Australia), Heleophryninae (South Africa).

Superfamily Bufonoidea

Vertebrae procoelous; pectoral girdle arciferal (in some, secondarily firmisternal); ribs absent; amplexus axillary; larvae usually with single spiracle, on the left, and complex mouthparts, or with direct development.

Family Rhinodermatidae (mouth-breeding frog)

No fossil record. Eight presacral vertebrae, 1st and 2nd fused; pectoral girdle partly firmisternal; maxillary teeth, intercalary cartilages, and Bidder's organ absent; omosternum cartilaginous. Southern South America; 1 species; adult length 2.5 cm.

Family Leptodactylidae

Ecocene to present. Eight presacral vertebrae; pectoral girdle arciferal; maxillary teeth present; Bidder's organ and intercalary cartilages absent; omosternum cartilaginous or ossified. Thirty-nine genera, about 625 species; adult length 2 to about 20 cm. Four subfamilies: Ceratophryinae (South America), Telmatobiinae (South and Central America, West Indies), Elosiinae (South America), Leptodactylinae (South and Central America).

Family Bufonidae (true toads)

Oligocene to present. Five to 8 presacral vertebrae; pectoral girdle arciferal, or partly or even completely firmisternal; intercalary cartilages and omosternum absent; Bidder's organ present; maxillary teeth present or absent; aquatic larvae, direct development, or live birth (*Nectophrynoides* only). Worldwide, except eastern part of Indo-Australian Archipelago, Polynesia, Madagascar; *Bufo marinus* introduced into Australia and some Pacific islands; 13 genera, about 234 species; adult size 2 to about 25 cm.

Family Brachycephalidae

No fossil record. Seven presacral vertebrae, pectoral girdle partly firmisternal; intercalary cartilages and omosternum absent; Bidder's organ present; maxillary teeth present; direct development. Southeastern Brazil; 1 species; adult length 2 cm.

Family Dendrobatidae (arrow-poison frogs)

No fossil record. Eight presacral vertebrae; pectoral girdle completely firmisternal; intercalary cartilages absent; omosternum present; Bidder's organ absent; maxillary teeth present or absent. Larvae carried on backs of adults. Central and South America; 3 genera, about 70 species; adult length 1.5–5 cm.

Family Pseudidae

No fossil record; 8 presacral vertebrae; sacral diapophyses round; pectoral girdle arciferal; intercalary cartilages present, ossified; omosternum present; Bidder's organ absent; maxillary teeth present; aquatic larvae (which grow to a much larger size than the adult). South America east of Andes; 2 genera, 5 species; adult length 2–5 cm, larval length to 25 cm.

Family Centrolenidae

No fossil record; 8 presacral vertebrae; pectoral girdle arciferal; intercalary cartilages present; omosternum absent; Bidder's organ absent; maxillary teeth present; terminal phalanges T-shaped; astragalus and calcaneum bones of the foot fused. Stream-adapted larvae. Central and South America; 2 genera, about 45 species; adult length 2–6 cm.

Family Hylidae (tree frogs)

Miocene to present; 8 presacral vertebrae; pectoral girdle arciferal; intercalary cartilages present; omosternum absent; Bidder's organ absent; maxillary teeth usually present; terminal phalanges claw-shaped; astragalus and calcaneum not fused; aquatic larvae or direct development; adult length 1.3 to about 12 cm. Four subfamilies: Phyllomedusinae (Central and South America), Hemiphractinae (Central and South America), Amphignathodontinae (Central and South America), Hylinae (North and South America, Europe, Asia except Indian subregion, Africa north of Sahara and Australasia).

Superfamily Ranoidea

Pectoral girdle firmisternal; ribs absent; amplexus axillary; larvae with single sinistral spiracle and complex mouthparts, single median spiracle and simple mouthparts, lacking spiracle or undergoing direct development.

Family Ranidae (true frogs)

Miocene to present. Vertebral column diplasiocoelous (mixed amphicoelous and procoelous); intercalary cartilages present or absent; larvae with single spiracle, on left, and complex mouthparts. About 55 genera and 842 species, adult length about 2–25 cm. Nine subfamilies: Raninae (worldwide except for southern South America, southern and central Australia, New Zealand, and eastern Polynesia), Astylosterninae (Africa), Scaphiophryninae (Madagascar), Rhacophorinae (Africa, Madagascar, southeastern Asia, Indo-Australian Archipelago), Arthroleptinae (Africa), Cacosterninae (Africa), Hyperoliinae (Africa, Madagascar, Seychelles), Hemisinae (Africa), Petropedatinae (Africa).

Family Sooglossidae

No fossil record. Vertebrae procoelous; sacral diapophyses dilated; intercalary cartilages absent; larvae lacking spiracle. Seychelle Islands; 2 genera, 3 species; length about 4 cm.

Family Microhylidae

No fossil record. Vertebrae procoelous or diplasiocoelous; intercalary cartilages usually absent; larvae with single median spiracle and simple mouthparts, or undergoing direct development. Eight subfamilies: Cophylinae (Madagascar), Dyscophinae (Malay Peninsula, western Indo-Australian Archipelago, Madagascar), Asterophryninae (New Guinea and Sulu Islands), Sphenophryninae (Philippine Islands, eastern Indo-Australian Archipelago, New Guinea, northern Australia), Brevicipitinae (Africa), Microhylinae (North and South America, Southeast Asia, Sri Lanka, western Indo-Australian Archipelago, Philippine and Riu Kiu Islands), Melanobatrachinae (east-central Africa, India), Phrynomerinae (Africa).

Critical appraisal. Modern authorities do not agree on all aspects of anuran classification, and further study is needed to clarify the relationships of certain groups. The most widely used classification above the family level is that established by G.K. Noble in 1931, in which five suborders were recognized, based on vertebral characteristics. The superfamilies given above are not exactly equivalent to the suborders of Noble, the following modifications being most noteworthy: (1) The names Ascaphidae and Leiopelmatidae are interchangeable, the first being used by most American authorities, the latter by most others. (2) The family Myobatrachidae includes what were formerly recognized as Old World members of the Leptodactylidae, a family now considered restricted to the New World. (3) The Brachycephalidae, as recognized by Noble, included the dendrobatids and the peculiar mouth-breeding frog (*Rhinoderma*), now considered distinct families, as well as several genera (*e.g., Atelopus*) currently placed in the Bufonidae. Most authorities now restrict the family Brachycephalidae to the single genus *Brachycephalus.* (4) The family Atelopodidae (sometimes spelled Atelopidae) of many authors is now relegated to the Bufonidae. (5) *Rhinoderma,* which other authors have placed in the Atelopodidae, Leptodactylidae, and Bufonidae, is now given family status. (6) The relationships of the Microhylidae are uncertain, and their placement in the suborder Ranoidea must be considered tentative. This family may have had an evolutionary history entirely independent from the ranoids. (W.E.D.)

BIBLIOGRAPHY

Amphibia: FERNAND ANGEL, *Vie et moeurs des amphibiens* (1947), a popular account in French; DORIS M. COCHRAN, *Living Amphibians of the World* (1961), a lively and beautifully illustrated popular account; E.T.B. FRANCIS, *The Anatomy of the Salamander* (1934), the only complete account of salamander anatomy; HANS GADOW, *Amphibia and Reptiles* (1901, reprinted 1958), an English classic, old but still worth reading; E. GAUPP, *Ecker and Wiedersheims' Anatomy of the Frog* (1904), the standard work on this topic; COLEMAN J. and OLIVE B. GOIN, *Introduction to Herpetology,* 2nd ed. (1971), a college-level textbook; ROBERT MERTENS, *La Vie des amphibiens et reptiles* (1959; Eng. trans., *World of Amphibians and Reptiles,* 1960), a beautifully written and illustrated popular book; JOHN A. MOORE (ed.), *Physiology of the Amphibia* (1964), technical but with much useful information; G.K. NOBLE, *Biology of the Amphibia* (1931, reprinted 1954), the standard English work on amphibians, already a classic; JAMES A. PETERS, *Dictionary of Herpetology* (1964), a useful guide, especially for nonspecialists, to an understanding of the technical terms used by herpetologists; A.S. ROMER, *Vertebrate Paleontology,* 3rd ed. (1966), a standard text; EDWARD H. TAYLOR, *The Caecilians of the World* (1968), the only comprehensive account of the order; J.Z. YOUNG, *The Life of Vertebrates,* 2nd ed. (1962), an evolutionary approach that contains much more than the usual anatomical accounts.

Urodela: S.C. BISHOP, *Handbook of Salamanders* (1943), the only account of all the salamanders of the United States, now badly out-of-date; A.H. BRAME, JR., "A List of the World's Recent and Fossil Salamanders," *Herpeton,* 2:1–26 (1967), a taxonomic checklist of all recognized species to 1967; R. CONANT, *A Field Guide to Reptiles and Amphibians of the United States and Canada East of the 100th Meridian* (1958), identifying characteristics, illustrations, and maps; E.R. DUNN, *The Salamanders of the Family Plethodontidae* (1926), a classic that retains value; R. ESTES, "Fossil Salamanders and Salamander Origins," *Am. Zool.,* 5:319–334 (1965), the most recent account in a rapidly changing area; E.T.B. FRANCIS, *The Anatomy of the Salamander* (1934), the only detailed anatomical treatment, restricted to *Salamandra;* C.J. and O.B. GOIN, *Introduction to Herpetology* (1962), an elementary textbook; G.K. NOBLE, *The Biology of the Amphibia* (1931), a classic that is out-of-date but still very useful; S.N. SALTHE, "Courtship Patterns and the Phylogeny of the Urodeles," *Copeia,* pp. 100–117 (1967), a recent summary; I.I. SCHMALHAUSEN, *The Origin of Terrestrial Vertebrates* (1968; orig. pub. in Russian, 1964), a detailed consideration of salamander morphology and evolution from an unorthodox viewpoint; R.C. STEBBINS, *A Field Guide to Western Reptiles and Amphibians* (1966), an exceptionally well illustrated guide, with maps and identifying characteristics; R. THORN, *Les Salamandres d'Europe, d'Asie et d'Afrique du Nord* (1968), an excellent, recent treatment of Old World salamanders, with maps and illustrations; V.C. TWITTY, *Of Scientists and Salamanders* (1966), a superb treatment of the life of an outstanding scientist, and of the scientific value of urodeles; D.B. WAKE, "Comparative Osteology and Evolution of the Lungless Salamanders, Family Plethodontidae," *Mem. So. Calif. Acad. Sci.,* 4:1–111 (1966), a recent account of the largest family of salamanders, with comments on other groups.

Anura: W.E. DUELLMAN, *The Hylid Frogs of Middle America,* 2 vol. (1970), a detailed study of the taxonomy, distribution, life history, and ecology of the tree frogs of Mexico and Central America; C.M. BOGERT, "The Influence of Sound on the Behavior of Amphibians and Reptiles," in W.E. LANYON and W.N. TAVOLGA, *Animal Sounds and Communication,* pp. 137–320 (1960), a thorough account of the calling behaviour of frogs; H.W. PARKER, *A Monograph of the Frogs of the Family Microhylidae* (1934), a thorough account of one of the most interesting families of frogs; R. RUGH, *The Frog: Its Reproduction and Development* (1953), a good account of larval development; R.M. SAVAGE, *The Ecology and Life History of the Common Frog* (1961), a well-documented study of the biology of *Rana temporaria* in England; R.C. STEBBINS, *A Field Guide to Western Reptiles and Amphibians* (1966), an excellent identification manual for frogs in the western United States, illustrated in colour and in black and white; A.H. and A.A. WRIGHT, *Handbook of Frogs and Toads of the United States and Canada,* 3rd ed. (1949), a well-documented account of North American frogs and toads with many black-and-white photographs.

Amsterdam

To the scores of tourists who visit each year, Amsterdam is known for its historical attractions, for its collections of great art, and for the distinctive colour and flavour of its old sections, which have been so well preserved. The visitor to the city, which celebrated its 700th anniversary in 1975, also sees an overcrowded metropolis beset by the familiar urban afflictions of environmental pollution, traffic congestion, and housing shortages. It is easy to describe Amsterdam as a living museum of a bygone age and to praise the eternal beauty of the centuries-old canals, the ancient patrician houses, and the atmosphere of freedom and tolerance, but the modern city has yet to work out its own solutions to the pressing urban problems that confront it.

Amsterdam is the nominal capital of The Netherlands but not the seat of government, which is at The Hague. The royal family, for example, is only occasionally in residence at the Royal Palace on the Dam square in Amsterdam. The city lacks the monumental architecture found in other capitals. There are no wide squares suitable for big parades, nor are there triumphal arches or imposing statues. Amsterdam's intimate character is best reflected in the narrow, bustling streets of the old town, where much of the population still goes about its business. There are reminders of the glorious past—the gabled houses, the noble brick facades clad with sandstone, the richly decorated cornices, the towers and churches, and the music of carillons and barrel organs—but the realities of life in the modern city often belie this romantic image.

The inner city is divided by its network of canals into some 90 "islands," and the municipality contains approximately 1,300 bridges and viaducts. Amsterdam is the main wholesale, retail, and industrial centre of The Netherlands. Nevertheless, tradition persists alongside innovation. Although the first part of a new rapid transit system opened in 1977, about 20 percent of the work force still rely on the time-honoured bicycle for transportation. The city continues to be famous for its countless Chinese and Indonesian restaurants and the hundreds of houseboats that line its canals. Since the mid-1960s the city, now sometimes called "Swinging Amsterdam," has been known for a permissive atmosphere, attracting numerous persons seeking an alternative life-style.

This article is divided into the following sections:

Physical and human geography 436
- The landscape 436
  - The city layout
  - City planning
- The people 438
- The economy 438
  - Finance
  - Trade
  - Industry
  - Tourism
- Administration 439
- Cultural life 439

History 439
- Early settlement and growth 439
- The modern city 440

Bibliography 440

Physical and human geography

THE LANDSCAPE

The city layout. Amsterdam is situated at the mouth and on the south side of the IJ, an inland arm of the former Zuiderzee, now IJsselmeer, and connected by canal with the North Sea. It is divided by the canalized Amstel River into two main sections.

The old town

The medieval town lies on either side of the Amstel at the city's centre, enclosed by the semicircular Singel (ditch or moat). Outside the Singel are the three main canals dating from the 17th century: the Herengracht (Heren Canal), Keizersgracht, and Prinsengracht. Within this area smaller canals run north and south. One tower (the Schreierstoren) of the old fortifications still stands.

The old part of Amsterdam has many ancient buildings, among which the Old Church (Oude Kerk), built in the 13th century, and the New Church (Nieuwe Kerk), begun in the 15th century, are outstanding. Next to the New Church is the 17th-century town hall, now the Royal Palace, built in classical Palladian style. Other notable buildings include the Mint Tower (Munttoren), with a 17th-century upper part superimposed on a medieval gate; the South Church (Zuiderkerk, 1611); the West Church (Westerkerk, 1631), where Rembrandt is buried; the Trippenhuis, housing the Royal Netherlands Academy of Arts and Sciences; and the Old Man's House Gate (Oudemanhuispoort), now the entrance to one of the University of Amsterdam's main buildings. The Sint Nicolaas Church (1886), the Central Station (1889), the Beurs (the bourse, or Commercial Exchange Building, 1903), and the Shipping House (1916) are more modern in style. The former Jewish quarter, in the east of the old town, is the location of the Portuguese Synagogue (1670) and the Rembrandt House (Rembrandthuis), which is now a museum. The old town's three main squares are the Dam, the Leidseplein (Leidse Square), and the Rembrandtsplein. Fine 17th- and 18th-century patrician houses line the canals.

In the 17th century the Buitensingel (Outer Moat), today called the Singelgracht (Singel Canal), enclosed the three main canals. Along it now run three quays: the Nassaukade (Nassau Quay), Stadhouderskade, and Mauritskade. Buildings outside the Singelgracht date from the late 19th century onward and include the Rijksmuseum (State Museum, 1876–85); the Concertgebouw, or Concert Hall (home of the Concertgebouw Orchestra); the Stedelijk, or Municipal, Museum (1895); the Olympic Stadium (1928); and the Amstel Station (1939).

The General Extension Plan

City planning. A development plan, called the General Extension Plan, was realized after World War II when the urgent need for houses was an incentive to build as quickly as possible. Simultaneously, a further detail of the master plan was realized: Forest Park, in the southwestern part of the city, situated more than 13 feet (four metres) below sea level, was developed into a recreation centre.

Soon after World War II certain developments made it necessary to revise the General Extension Plan: it became obvious that the existing residential areas were inadequate. Further space, moreover, was required for traffic and parking as well as for schools, service industries, and recreation. In addition, the urban renewal of the old city, including the 19th-century residential areas, required much replacement space in the outer areas for dwellings and businesses that were razed in the inner areas.

Amsterdam's planning problems differ little from those of any major city in the world; the particular problem has been that the city, with many areas more than 300 years old, must integrate its growth with the existing features of the area. The streets are narrow, for example, and the great concentration of employment in the city produces heavy radial traffic flows. Public transportation carries a large part of the passenger load and private cars only a relatively small part. As the metropolitan area has grown, and because large radial highways from the outer areas

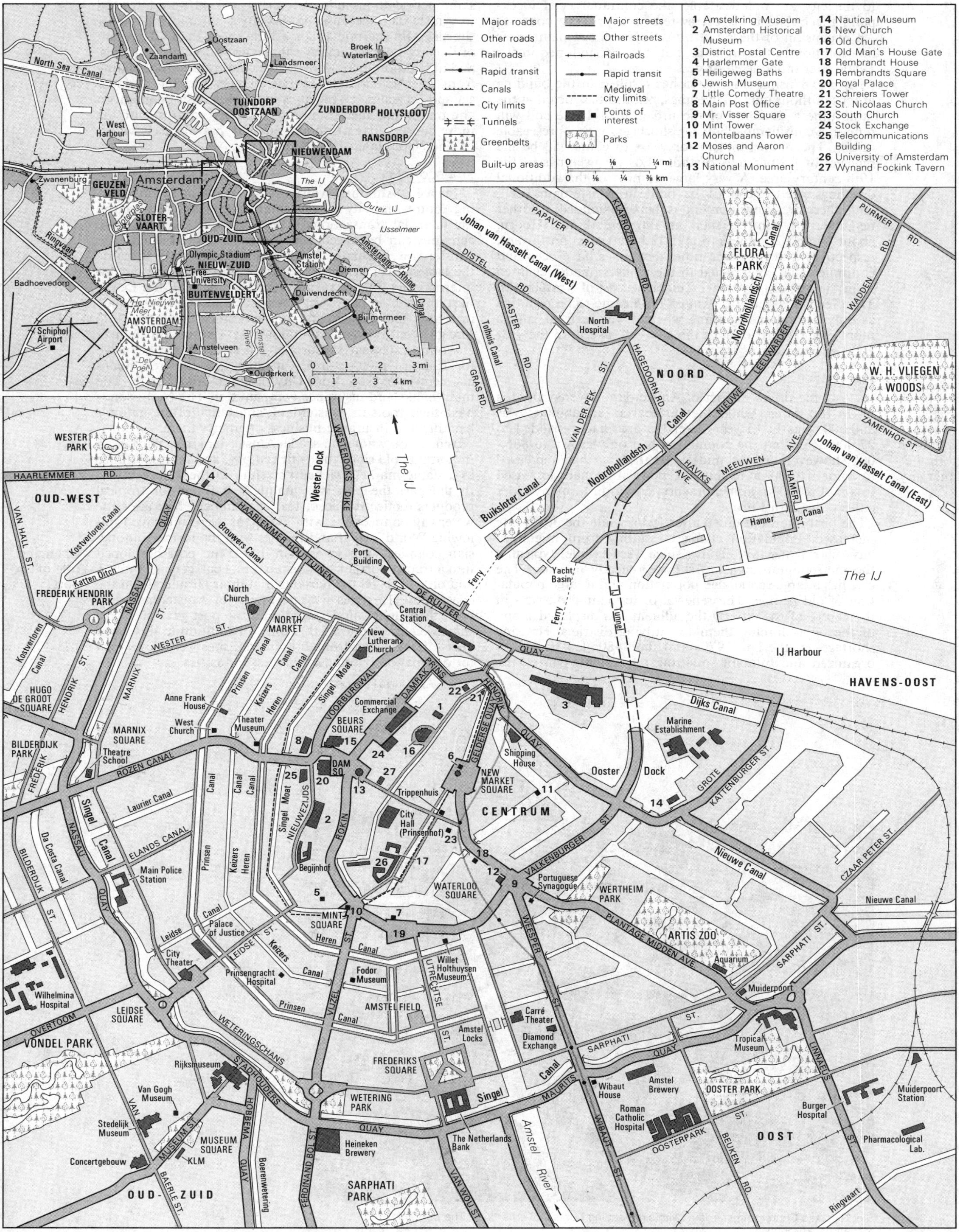

Central Amsterdam and (inset) its metropolitan area.

to the city are not desirable, the continual need to expand the public transport system is a primary concern. An expansion of the rapid transit system was planned as one solution to the problem, but it was abandoned in the 1980s after much local protest.

Town expansion since 1945 has resulted in the building of tens of thousands of dwellings, but this has meant at the same time a doubling of the urban area. There still will remain a considerable housing shortage for the foreseeable future. The main problem for years to come will be the renewal of further tens of thousands of dwellings in the 19th-century area. A very large number of the additional dwellings needed cannot be built in Amsterdam itself, and, therefore, development is being extended to other neighbouring centres, such as Purmerend and Hoorn, about 10 and 20 miles (16 and 32 kilometres) northward, respectively. At the same time, new cities have been and continue to be constructed in the polders (land reclaimed from the sea) of the former Zuiderzee, east of Amsterdam. The General Extension Plan of 1935 came to be regarded as only a modest beginning when it was realized, and a more complete renewal of the city will take until the year 2000 or beyond.

THE PEOPLE

In 1947 the urban district of Amsterdam covered an area of 14,100 acres, while the number of inhabitants was 800,000. Nearly 18 years later the area had expanded to 27,000 acres, but the population had only grown to 866,000; however, by the mid-1980s the area had increased to some 41,000 acres and the population had decreased to about 675,000, a phenomenon common to many older cities of western Europe.

Migration from the inner city

The birthrate went down after 1946, while the death rate increased. Population changes resulting from migration have shown negative figures since 1951, while, typically, the metropolitan area has shown a steady increase. The city has a large school-age population and a large population of old people. The renewal of residential districts in the centre of the city by the affluent has displaced many of the poor, forcing them to outlying districts. Housing shortages in the late 1970s and the 1980s led to a well-organized and militant squatting movement. During the same period thousands of foreign workers were attracted to Amsterdam because of the city's chronic manpower shortage. By the mid-1980s a little more than 12 percent of the city's population was made up of foreign nationals, and in addition there were sizable communities originating from The Netherlands' former colonies (notably Indonesia and Suriname). The city's increasing cosmopolitanism and traditional liberalism present a sharp contrast with the more conservative attitudes generally prevalent elsewhere in The Netherlands.

THE ECONOMY

Finance. Although Amsterdam is a major manufacturing centre, the city is even more important as a centre for financial transactions. The origins of most of these activities can be traced back several hundred years. The Amsterdam Exchange Bank, founded in 1609, became the largest clearinghouse in Europe and made the city an international financial centre. Earlier, in 1602, the Dutch East India Company was founded, and the lively trade in shares laid the basis for modern stock dealings. More foreign securities are now quoted in Amsterdam than in any other exchange in Europe; and as the home exchange for leading Dutch securities, it ranks with the great financial centres of New York City, London, and Zürich. The main banks and insurance companies in The Netherlands have their roots in Amsterdam, and much of the nation's banking and insurance business originates there.

Trade. In wholesale trade Amsterdam has played an important role since the 14th century, and its importance as a staple market reached its zenith in the 17th century. In the past the port was mainly a harbour for tropical products (coffee, tobacco, tea, and rubber), but, after the waterway connections with Germany were improved following World War II and the ties with the former Indonesian colonies were severed in 1949, the port developed into a transit port for bulk cargo (ore, coal, cereals, timber, and oil). By 1968 the harbour mouth at IJmuiden (on the coast some 15 miles west-northwest of Amsterdam) had been thoroughly modernized, and the port gave access to ships weighing up to 85,000 tons. In addition to this, large areas of deepwater-fronted industrial sites were developed for occupation by modern process industries.

Changing role of the port

Louis Goldman—Rapho Photo Researchers

Sint Nicolaas Church, Amsterdam, with sight-seeing boats in the harbour. The port is in the left background.

In civil aviation Amsterdam occupies a prominent place because of the importance and proximity of Schiphol Airport (linked by a five-mile railway to the city centre) and because of KLM Royal Dutch Airlines' large share of international air transport. Schiphol, which began operation in 1967, now ranks among the top European airports in volume of passenger and freight traffic.

Industry. Amsterdam is the largest industrial city in The Netherlands. The city accounts for an important part of the production value of the printing and publishing business, of the chemical and petrochemical industries, of textile manufacturing, of metal goods and mechanical engineering, and of the conveyance industry. A special attraction for tourists is the diamond industry, introduced to Amsterdam in the 1570s when refugees from Antwerp settled there. Two thousand diamond workers of Jewish origin were deported and murdered during World War II by the Germans, and large quantities of precious stones disappeared during the occupation. With foreign assistance and government support, the industry was rebuilt, and now there are several diamond factories. Most (by weight) of the total world production of industrial diamonds is processed there.

Tourism. The tourist trade is one of Amsterdam's most important sources of employment and revenue and is served by the city's numerous hotels and its many boardinghouses, youth hostels, restaurants, and retail businesses. The principal attractions for tourists include the Rijksmuseum, the Artis Zoo, and sight-seeing trips on the canals. Amsterdam is also an important centre for international conferences and exhibitions.

ADMINISTRATION

According to the constitution, every municipality in The Netherlands is headed by a council, the size of which depends on the number of inhabitants. The Amsterdam City Council has 45 members, who are elected for a four-year period. The Executive Committee consists of the burgomaster and nine elected aldermen. The burgomaster is not an elected official: he is appointed by the crown for a period of six years, and, though he presides at the meetings of the council, he is not a member of this institution. The council has no say in his appointment, but he usually represents the largest political group in the council. Since the end of World War II, the Socialists have dominated the council, and the burgomasters have been members of the Socialist Party. The council, however, is made up of members of many different political persuasions, including the Communists.

Methods of political appointment

The aldermen are chosen by and from the members of the council. They, too, have a four-year period of office and receive an income, in contrast to the council members, who get only an attendance fee.

As a rule the council meetings are open to the public. The meeting place has been the old city hall—the Prinsenhof, formerly the Admiralty Court. In the 15th century this was a convent, but after alteration in 1578 it was converted into a suitable "inn for Princes and High Personages." From 1655 to 1808 the seat of the council was at the Dam square, where the medieval town hall was replaced by a new building designed by Jacob van Campen. When Louis Bonaparte, the French king of Holland, chose this as his residence in 1808 and converted it into what is now the Royal Palace, the council moved to the Prinsenhof. In the mid-1980s a new city hall and opera house were built on the north bank of the Amstel. In 1926 Herengracht 502, which was built for a director of the Dutch East India Company in 1672, became the burgomaster's official residence.

The various tasks of the municipality cover a wide range of activities. These include public transport, public works (including acquisition and allocation of grounds and buildings), public health, housing, electricity and gas, the port, markets, police, fire brigade, cleaning, social services, waterworks, education, old people's welfare work, and churchyards. The city has its own clearing bank, credit bank, advertising department, printing shop, swimming pools, theatre, archive department, museums, slaughterhouse, and orphanage.

CULTURAL LIFE

Museums

As a centre of art, Amsterdam has much to offer. The Rijksmuseum is famous for its collection of 17th-century Dutch masterpieces. The museum has about 1,100,000 art objects, including some 7,000 paintings, displayed in more than 150 rooms. The Stedelijk Museum is a leading international centre of modern art, representing such artists as the Spanish Pablo Picasso, the Russian-born Marc Chagall, the French Henri Matisse, the Dutch Karel Appel, the Dutch-American Willem de Kooning, and the American Robert Rauschenberg. The Van Gogh Museum, opened in 1972, is dedicated to the work of Vincent van Gogh and his contemporaries. Among the many other museums is the notable Amsterdam Historical Museum, located in the former Sint Lucien Convent built around 1420.

The city's Concertgebouw Orchestra has an international reputation, and Amsterdam is also a home for hundreds of painters, sculptors, authors, musicians, and actors. There are scores of curio and antique shops. Institutions of higher learning include the University of Amsterdam (founded 1632) and the Free (Vrije) University (founded 1880).

The city is situated in a region with many opportunities for recreation. In addition to the Amsterdam Woods, outdoor recreation, including water sports, is offered at the seaside resort of Zandvoort to the west, Sloter Lake (Sloterplas) in the heart of the western suburbs, the neighbourhood of the former Zuiderzee, and many smaller lakes to the south and the north of the city.

History

EARLY SETTLEMENT AND GROWTH

Although modern historians do not exclude the possibility that during the Roman period some form of settlement existed at the mouth of the Amstel River, evidence of such has never been found. So far as is known, Amsterdam originated as a small fishing village in the 13th century AD. To protect themselves from floods, the early inhabitants had to build dikes on both sides of the river, and in about 1270 they built a dam between these dikes.

Early dike building

Even then, merchant ships from Amsterdam sailed as far as the Baltic Sea and laid the foundation of the future trade centre, acting as a link between northern countries and Flanders (roughly modern Belgium). The city was under the jurisdiction of the counts of Holland, one of whom, Count Floris V, granted the *homines manentes apud Amestelledamme* ("the people living near the Amsteldam") a toll privilege in 1275. In this document the name Amsterdam is mentioned for the first time, though a full charter was not granted until 1306. The city rapidly extended its business, and in 1489, as a sign of gratitude for the support given by the city to the Burgundian-Austrian monarchs, Emperor Maximilian I allowed Amsterdam to adorn its armorial bearings with the imperial crown. By then Holland's greatest commercial town and port, as well as the granary of the northern Netherlands, Amsterdam had become a centre of wealth and influence in Europe.

In the 16th century there was religious and political resistance in the Netherlands against Spanish oppression. Amsterdam hesitated to accept the leadership of William I the Silent, prince of Orange, but in 1578 there was a bloodless revolution. The magistrates, together with the majority of Roman Catholic priests, were deported, the religious communities were secularized, and the Roman Catholic Church underwent reform.

Development as a trading centre

Amsterdam was still a small town with no more than about 30,000 inhabitants, but things changed quickly, especially when, in 1585, Antwerp (in modern Belgium) was recaptured by Spanish troops, and the Scheldt (Schelde) River was closed. Antwerp's fall led to a wholesale influx of mainly Protestant refugees into the towns of the northern Netherlands, principal among them Amsterdam. Their arrival enriched the city's intellectual, cultural, and commercial life. Banking and shipbuilding especially flourished. Much of the trade formerly concentrated in Antwerp then moved to Amsterdam, and with the Flemish merchantmen soon came hundreds of Jews expelled from Portugal, followed by their coreligionists from the area of modern Germany and eastern Europe. The city soon became a trading metropolis, whose population more than trebled between 1565 and 1618; merchant ships from Amsterdam not only sailed to the Baltic and the Mediterranean but also plied the long sea route to the East Indies and established colonies in South America and southern Africa.

At this time, the still outwardly medieval town developed into a big city, and in 1612 the City Council decided upon a new extension—the Three Canals Plan. Furthermore, the city needed a new and stately town hall, and the architect Jacob van Campen was commissioned to build one in the Dam square in the shadow of the New Church. In 1632 the Athenaeum Illustre (which became the University of Amsterdam in the 19th century) was erected. When, in 1648, the Treaty of Münster ended the Eighty Years' War (1568–1648) with Spain, Amsterdam was the financial, trading, and cultural centre of the world, lending money to foreign kings and emperors and thus exerting political influence internationally.

Conflict between the City Council and other political forces in the Dutch Republic was inevitable because the country was effectively no longer ruled by the States General in The Hague but by a small elite of burgomasters and merchants in Amsterdam. This situation led to political difficulties with William II, prince of Orange, who in 1650 planned to besiege the city. Amsterdam, nevertheless, maintained its dominant position for many years. Decline gradually came in the 18th century; London and Hamburg surpassed Amsterdam as trade centres, but the city remained the financial heart of Europe. Amsterdam was occupied in 1787 by the Prussians who backed the policy of William V, prince of Orange. The French, welcomed as liberators in 1795, brought freedom, but within a few years trade and shipping nearly stopped because of Napoleon's embargo on trade with Britain. In 1806 Napoleon proclaimed the Netherlands a kingdom, with Amsterdam as its capital, but by 1810 the country was incorporated into the French Empire. Russian Cossacks entered the town in 1813, and, on March 30, 1814, William VI, prince of Orange, was inaugurated as William I, king of The Netherlands, in Amsterdam's New Church.

The Napoleonic era

THE MODERN CITY

Several attempts to restore prosperity to the city failed outwardly because of the harbour's disastrous condition. Economic rehabilitation came only after the digging of the North Sea Canal from 1865 to 1876. The population expanded rapidly (to 500,000 by 1900), with the East Indian trade remaining the backbone of its economic activities. A sudden end to prosperity came in 1940, when the German Army occupied the country. Allied bombers attacked industrial areas several times during World War II, but the city's severest loss was the deportation of about 70,000 Jewish inhabitants. In May 1945 Amsterdam was liberated by Canadian troops, and, on March 29, 1946, Queen Wilhelmina granted the town the right to add to its armorial bearings the device "Heroic, Resolute, Compassionate," in recognition of the citizens' attitude during the German occupation. In the latter part of the 20th century the city's traditional individualism and resistive attitude found an outlet in movements that called attention to issues such as nuclear disarmament, world peace, and the environment.

BIBLIOGRAPHY. One of the earliest descriptions of Amsterdam may be found in LODOVICO GUICCIARDINI, *The Description of the Low Countreys and of the Provinces Thereof* (1593, reprinted 1976; originally published in Italian, 2nd ed., 1581). More exact details are in JOHANNES PONTANUS, *Historische beschrijvinghe der seer wijt beroemde coop-stadt Amsterdam* (1614; originally published in Latin, 1611); PHILIPP VON ZESEN, *Filips von Zesen Beschreibung der Stadt Amsterdam* (1664); and in JAN WAGENAAR, *Amsterdam, in zyne opkomst, aanwas, geschiedenissen, voorregten, koophandel, gebouwen, kerkenstaat, schoolen, schutterye, gilden en regeeringe,* 23 vol. (1760–1801). See also JOHN J. MURRAY, *Amsterdam in the Age of Rembrandt* (1967, reissued 1972). A modern history of the city was written by HAJO BRUGMANS, *De geschiedenis van Amsterdam van den oorsprong af tot heden,* 8 vol. in 4 (1930–33). The rise of the city during the Netherlands' Golden Age is covered by VIOLET BARBOUR, *Capitalism in Amsterdam in the Seventeenth Century* (1950, reissued 1963). Many details of cultural life in the 17th century are presented by PIERRE DESCARGUES in *Rembrandt et Saskia à Amsterdam* (1965). Works dealing with specific aspects are A. VAN DER HEYDEN and BEN KROON, *The Glory of Amsterdam: An Explorer's Guide* (1975; originally published in Dutch, 1975); and IDS HAAGSMA *et al., Amsterdamse gebouwen, 1880–1980* (1981), on architecture; J.J. VAN DER VELDE, *Stadsontwikkeling van Amsterdam 1939–1967,* also with an English summary (1968); AMSTERDAM. TOWN PLANNING SECTION, *Amsterdam, Planning and Development: Rise, Spatial Development, Structure, and Design* (1975), on town planning in modern times; and G.H. KNAP, *The Port of Amsterdam* (1970; originally published in Dutch, 1969). The best guides for tourists are HENDRIK F. WIJNMAN, *Historische gids van Amsterdam* (1971); BRYCE ATTWELL, *Amsterdam* (1968), with parallel English, Dutch, German, and French texts; GEOFFREY COTTERELL, *Amsterdam: The Life of a City* (1972); and *Baedeker's Amsterdam* (1982), a guide in English.

(Ev.W./P.F.V.)

Analysis (in Mathematics)

Analysis is one of the main divisions of mathematics, the others being history and foundations, algebra, combinatorics and number theory, geometry, topology, and applied mathematics. In extent, analysis is the largest of these, comprising subdivisions that are nearly autonomous and easier to describe than the division as a whole. Analysis may be defined as that part of mathematics concerned with smooth abstract objects such as sets of numbers, sets of geometric points, or sets of functions that map numbers into numbers or points into points and with the processes, called limit processes, that depend on a measure of closeness between numbers, points, or functions. Analysis developed initially out of ad hoc arguments in which curves, geometric bodies, and physical motions were analyzed by an informal process of decomposition into infinitesimal parts.

Limit and approximation processes, the usefulness of which was discovered during this early period of development, came to be used systematically in the 17th and 18th centuries in the differential and integral calculus of Sir Isaac Newton and Gottfried Wilhelm Leibniz. Limit processes were applied by their followers and by 19th-century French and German schools of analysts to sequences of values of a single function. Differential and integral calculus, ordinary differential equations, and the calculus of variations have thus arisen from mechanics; so-called Fourier series from acoustics and thermodynamics; complex analysis from optics, hydrodynamics, and electricity; and partial differential equations from elasticity, hydrodynamics, and electrodynamics. Even mathematical probability, although born from problems of gambling and human chance, drew much of its syllogistic strength in the 19th century from statistical theories of mechanics and thermodynamics. (Ed.)

For coverage of related topics in the *Macropædia* and *Micropædia*, see the *Propædia*, sections 10/21 and 10/22, and the *Index*.

This article is organized into the following sections:

Real analysis 441
Origins and concepts of analysis 441
Early stages of development
From calculus to analysis
The basic number systems 443
Functions and differential calculus 444
Functions
Differential calculus
Measure and integral calculus 447
Historical development
Integral calculus
Infinite series 451
Vector and tensor analysis 454
Vector algebra and analysis
Tensor analysis
Measure theory 460
Complex analysis 462
Theory of analytic functions of one complex variable 462
Foundations
The Cauchy theory
Entire and meromorphic functions
Elliptic functions
Theory of analytic functions of several complex variables 465
Development of complex analysis
Holomorphic functions of several complex variables
Conformal maps
Differential equations 466
Ordinary differential equations 468
Historical background
Types of problems solvable with this discipline
Types of solutions
Existence and uniqueness of solutions
Forms of solutions
First-order equations
Linear differential equations
Boundary value problems
Systems of differential equations
Stability
Partial differential equations 480
Partial differential equations of special interest
Classification of partial differential equations
Initial value and boundary value problems
Systems of partial differential equations
Techniques of solution of partial differential equations
Existence and uniqueness of solutions to partial differential equations
Generalized theory of partial differential equations
Dynamical systems on manifolds 488
Nonlinear differential equations and dynamical systems
Examples of state spaces
Manifolds
Dynamical systems as vector fields on manifolds
Examples of dynamical systems
Hamiltonian mechanics
Potential theory 492
Historical survey of problems and concepts
Basic concepts and results of classical potential theory
Special functions 496
Fourier analysis 498
Fourier series
Harmonic analysis and integral transforms
Representations of groups and algebras
Calculus of variations 512
Mathematical formulation of variational problems
Euler's equation
Some questions involving arcs
Multiple-integral problems
Morse's theory of critical points
Functional analysis 514
A broad view of functional analysis 514
Early development
Linear functional analysis; theory of distributions
Geometric principles; analysis of linear operators
Hilbert space; spectral analysis
Linearization as a method; ergodic theory, classical and generalized harmonic analysis
Functional algebra
Nonlinear functional analysis
Generalized functions, or theory of distributions 519
Bibliography 520

REAL ANALYSIS

Origins and concepts of analysis

EARLY STAGES OF DEVELOPMENT

The concept of number. The concept "number" has changed its meaning repeatedly throughout history, as new demands on mathematics have required a broader view of the nature of numbers. The main number systems used in analysis are those of the real numbers and the complex numbers, for it is in these systems, that ideas of continuity and limiting processes can be given rigorous meaning.

The simplest number system comprises the natural numbers (0, 1, 2, 3, . . . ; some mathematicians exclude 0) and is used for counting. The incorporation of negative numbers (−1, −2, −3, . . .) leads to the integers. The system

Number systems

that includes all fractions p/q in which p and q are integers and q is not zero comprises the rational numbers. However, the ancient Greeks discovered that some naturally occurring geometric lengths, such as the diagonal of a unit square, cannot be expressed as rational numbers. This discovery led eventually to the notion of irrational numbers (numbers that cannot be expressed as a ratio of integers) and real numbers, which include both rational and irrational numbers and can most simply be defined as numbers whose decimal expansion may not terminate—for example, the number π, whose decimal expansion 3.14159 . . . goes on forever. The final step in this series of extensions of the number concept was the invention of the complex number system, in which there exists a number i whose square is -1 (or $i=\sqrt{-1}$). Problems now recognized as being part of the prehistory of analysis have played a major role in the evolution of today's main number systems.

Irrational numbers. In the 5th and 4th centuries BC the Greeks gave the first known satisfactory solution to a problem in analysis. In a square the side of which has length equal to 1, the diagonal has a length equal to $\sqrt{2}$. The decimal expansion of $\sqrt{2}$ is a nonterminating quantity, 1.4142 . . . , so that the value $\sqrt{2}$ is determined as the sum of an infinite series (see Box, sum 1), each term of which is an integer times a (nonpositive) power of 10. The Greeks proved that $\sqrt{2}$ is not a rational number—that is, not a quotient p/q of any integers p and q. But they apparently found for $\sqrt{2}$ an approximate representation by certain rational numbers, or rather they found for the diagonal of the square approximations by line segments that are commensurate with the side of the square. The approximate numbers were later called the partial sums of the continued fraction for $\sqrt{2}$, and apparently from the study of this problem there evolved the so-called Euclidean algorithm, a chain of operations (indicated by equations) for finding the largest integer that divides two given integers.

(1) $$1+\frac{4}{10}+\frac{1}{100}+\frac{4}{1{,}000}+\frac{2}{10{,}000}+\cdots$$

(2) $$\frac{1}{2}+\frac{1}{4}+\frac{1}{8}+\frac{1}{16}+\cdots+\frac{1}{2^n}+\cdots$$

General theory of irrational numbers

The most profound achievement in this entire context was the development of a general theory of irrational numbers, or of incommensurate ratios of certain types of "magnitudes" and of proportions between ratios. This achievement was the work of Eudoxus of Cnidus of the 4th century BC but was recorded by Euclid.

Areas and volumes. The Greeks also investigated the number $\pi=3.14159\ldots$, which is the area of a circle the radius of which is 1, and the problem of squaring the circle that was widely known to the Athenian public. Computations of other areas and volumes and of centres of masses are known from the works of Archimedes, and these results taken cumulatively can be viewed as a precursor to the 17th-century theory of integration. But these "direct" Greek calculations of many particular areas and volumes by circumscribed and inscribed approximating figures, when compared with the procedures of the integral calculus proper, are rather awkward and tedious.

Limit processes. The Greeks were also puzzled by the fact that the ordinary number 1 is the sum of the geometric series (see 2) composed of the numbers $^1/_2$, the square of $^1/_2$, the cube of $^1/_2$, and so forth, and this was for them part of a range of problems relating to the concepts "infinitely small" and "infinitely large." The preoccupation with such problems is reflected in the paradox of Achilles and the Turtle put forward by Zeno of Elea and in the distinction between potential and actual infinite as proposed by Aristotle.

FROM CALCULUS TO ANALYSIS

Analytic geometry. The Greek achievements in analysis were but a prelude. A notable step was taken in the 14th century by the French bishop Nicole d'Oresme, who discovered the logical equivalence between tabulation and graphing, more or less, and, in a way, proposed the use of a graph for plotting a variable magnitude the value of which depends on that of another.

The systematic theoretical basis for this possibility, however, evolved only later from the work of a leading French philosopher and mathematician, René Descartes, who in 1637 laid the foundation for analytic geometry—that is, a geometry in which everything is reduced to numbers. In this geometry a point is defined as a set of numbers called its coordinates. A figure is viewed as an aggregate of points, but it is usually described by formulas, equations, and inequalities. This approach to geometry is the basis for the maps, graphs, and charts that have penetrated into all walks of life and for the mathematical concept of a function or rule of correspondence identifying with each value of x at most one value of y, which, first intended only for analysis, eventually penetrated into all corners of mathematics and into all areas of rational thinking as well.

Later in the 17th century the culminating event took place simultaneously in England and Germany when Sir Isaac Newton and Gottfried Wilhelm Leibniz introduced derivatives and laid the foundation for calculus and mechanics. Archimedes had been groping for the concept of a derivative but hit upon it only dimly in his book on spirals. Archimedes' methods, comparable to those of the 16th and 17th centuries, were in fact analytical in the modern sense of the term. The 17th and 18th centuries produced much mathematics in all directions, but analysis was the underlying theme.

The concept of the derivative. Greek mathematics was largely geometric. It initiated some durable topics of analysis, but the organized creation of analysis began only around 1600. Geometry deals with spaces and configurations; topology with spatial deformations; algebra with the general nature of the basic operations of addition, subtraction, multiplication, and division; and arithmetic with additive and multiplicative properties of general integers—that is, natural numbers and negative forms of these. Analysis also deals with specific operations, namely with differentiation and integration. It is more appropriate to say, however, that it deals with the mathematical infinite in many of its aspects, such as those of an infinite multitude, the infinitely large, infinitely small, infinitely near, and infinitely subdivisible. Its first objects and concepts, introductory and basic, are infinite sequence; infinite series; a function such as $y=f(x)$; continuity of a function, which is a property of a function in an infinitely small neighbourhood of a point; derivative of a function such as $y'=df/dx$; and integral of a function, both of which can be defined in terms of infinite limits. The derivative is a master concept, one of the most creative in analysis as well as in all of human cognition. Without it there would be no proper expression of such fundamental properties in physics as velocity, acceleration, density, gradient, and potential. The wave equation would not exist, and, indeed, physics as a discipline would be vastly different if the concept were unavailable. The formal textbook definition of the derivative took more than 150 years to evolve, and it is rewarding to begin with Newton's own description of it under the name of "ultimate ratio":

Concern of analysis for the infinite

> For those ultimate ratios with which quantities vanish are not truly the ratios of ultimate quantities, but [they are] limits towards which the ratios of quantities, decreasing without a limit, do always converge: and to which they approach nearer than by any given difference, but never go beyond, nor in effect attain to, until the quantities have diminished *in infinitum*.

Newton's generation was able to listen to a recondite mathematical definition, all in words, without symbols; and the Marquise du Châtelet, woman of the world, could undertake to translate Newton's formidable *Principia* from Latin into French, ultimate ratios and all.

The introduction of rigour. The techniques introduced by Newton and Leibniz revolve around various "limiting" processes, involving quantities that are infinitely small or infinitely large. As George Berkeley pointed out with some force in 1734, there was then no adequate logical basis for the use of such quantities. However, Newton's ideas of 1704 are very close to the modern view: "I consider mathematical quantities not as consisting of very small parts, but as described by a continual motion." In his *Cours d'analyse de l'École Royale Polytechnique* of 1821, the French mathematician Baron Augustin-Louis Cauchy based all of analysis on the notion of a limit and defined it thus: "When the successive values attributed to a variable approach indefinitely a fixed value so as to end by differing from it by as little as one wishes, this last is called the limit of all the others." This definition is not totally satisfactory because the words "end" and "last" suggest that the limit has to be reached. Newton was in some ways nearer to the modern view because he realized that the limit need only be approached indefinitely closer.

The notion of limit was finally provided with a firm logical basis in the mid-19th century by Bernhard Bolzano of Prague and, definitively, by the German Karl Weierstrass. In effect, Weierstrass made Cauchy's definition quantitative by assigning two real numbers, ε and δ, to measure how closely the dependent and independent variables differ from their limits. In his definition a function $f(x)$ tends to the limit l as x tends to some value a if, given any positive number ε, there always exists a positive number δ such that, whenever the difference between x and a is less than δ, the difference between $f(x)$ and l is less than ε. This rather cumbersome "epsilon-delta" style of reasoning became the cornerstone of analysis and remains the accepted approach.

In 1961, however, the logician Abraham Robinson discovered a new extension of the number concept in which infinitesimals and infinite quantities exist and can be subjected to rigorous calculations. This idea provides an alternative foundation for analysis, and the approach is generally known as nonstandard analysis. It has useful applications for research mathematicians and is in many respects simpler than the epsilon-delta approach, but it has not yet become established as a standard technique.

The basic number systems

Number as quantity. Mankind was early led to the concept of a real number by the need for symbols to represent such geometric quantities as length, area, and volume and such physical quantities as weight and (more recently) electric charge.

Characteristics of geometric quantities

The characteristic features of such quantities are that (1) two quantities of the same kind can be added by some obvious geometric or physical operation (such as laying two segments next to each other on a straight line) and (2) any quantity can be divided into parts. The second feature, of infinite divisibility, is the crudest way of expressing the principle that the real-number system is continuous and not discrete like the system of positive integers.

The laws of addition are frequently intuitively obvious from the physical definition of this operation. In the case of lengths, it is obvious that $a + (b + c) = (a + b) + c$ because both represent the sum of three segments of lengths a, b, and c in order on a line (see Figure 1). It is also obvious that $a + b = b + a$ because the segment $a + b$ can be transformed into the segment $b + a$ by rotating the segment through 180°.

In representing geometric or physical quantities by numbers, it is usually necessary to choose first an arbitrary unit, such as a foot, a square inch, or a pound. This unit of quantity is assigned arbitrarily the numerical value 1, and exact multiples of this quantity (*i.e.,* sums of an integral number of unit quantities) are assigned corresponding

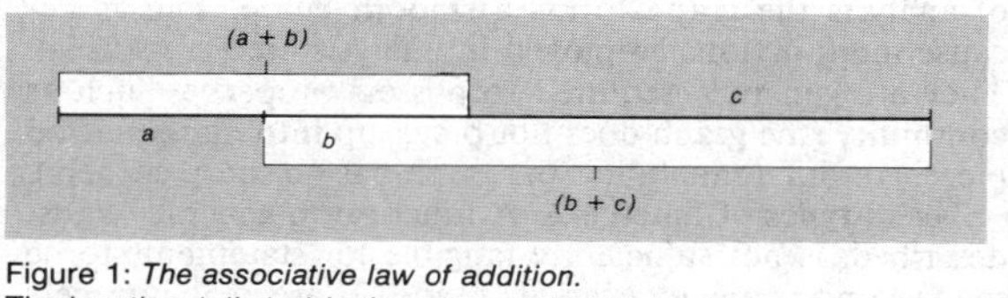

Figure 1: *The associative law of addition.*
The length $a + (b + c)$ is the same as $(a + b) + c$ because both represent the sum of three segments of lengths a, b, c in order on a line.

integral values. Because the entire addition table for positive integers can be constructed from the law for positive integers, which states that the sum of an integer a and an integer $(b + 1)$ is the same as the sum of the integers $(a + b)$ and 1, the sum of two such quantities must be represented by the sum of the corresponding positive integers.

Multiplication; number as ratio. A simple definition of the product of two quantities is not always possible. If the product of two lengths a and b is defined as the area of the rectangle with sides a and b, it may logically be objected that this is a quantity of a different kind.

To get around this logical difficulty, the Greeks suggested that a number should be considered as representing the ratio between a certain quantity and the unit quantity and never as representing the quantity itself. Thus, 160 pounds is a weight; the number 160 is the ratio of this weight to the weight of a pound.

Numbers as dimensionless ratios

This idea that numbers are dimensionless ratios has wide applicability: it leads to plausible "proofs" of the laws of multiplication. For example, the hypothesis that $a \times (b \times c) = (a \times b) \times c$ for all real numbers is given substantial support by the fact that both quantities may be regarded as representing the volume of a box of sides a, b, and c. These laws $a \times b = b \times a$ and $a \times (b + c) = (a \times b) + (a \times c)$ can be given similar plausible geometric interpretations in terms of areas. But these plausible arguments are not proofs in any rigorous sense. They depend not only on postulates for geometry but also on definitions of area and volume.

The only known way of getting rid of these difficulties is to define real numbers abstractly in terms of the system of positive integers, deducing all properties of real numbers by pure logic from these definitions and properties of the positive integers and using geometric and physical concepts only to suggest possible postulates and definitions. In this way the properties of real numbers may be made to depend on pure logic and the concept of a class alone (see MATHEMATICS, THE FOUNDATIONS OF). This abstract procedure will be followed henceforth.

Rational numbers. If it be assumed that division (except by zero) and subtraction are always possible, the system of positive integers then leads to a system of rational numbers (positive and negative fractions and integers, as well as zero). For the fundamental laws of arithmetic, see ARITHMETIC. The assumption that every equation $by = a$ in which a and b are positive integral coefficients has a solution corresponds to the idea that a quantity, a, can be divided into any positive whole number, b, of equal parts. The fundamental laws of arithmetic and the cancellation law for multiplication, which states that, if $a \times m = a \times n$, then $m = n$, can all be preserved.

By the cancellation law for multiplication, $by = a$ can have only one solution, which is written a/b. It may be shown that the usual rules for adding and multiplying fractions must hold. For example, if $by = a$ and $dz = c$, then $bdy = ad$, $bdz = bc$; and so $bd(y + z) = bdy + bdz = ad + bc$, which proves the rule for adding fractions having different denominators. It can also be proved that division by fractions as well as by integers is possible in the new system.

Conversely, it can be proved that the rules for adding and multiplying fractions do give a system in which the laws of arithmetic, as well as the cancellation law for multiplication and certain other basic laws, are valid.

A more thorough study would reveal that a considerable reduction in the number of postulates (fundamental laws needed to imply the others) is possible. All the laws for positive fractions thus can be deduced from the associative law for addition; the distributive laws, $a \times (b + c) = (a \times b) + (a \times c)$ and $(a + b) \times c = (a \times c) + (b \times c)$; and the unit laws, $a \times 1 = 1 \times a = a$ and $1 + 1 \neq 1$.

Irrational numbers. Fractions were used as early as 1700 BC by the ancient Egyptians, but it was not until Pythagoras (530 BC) that the need for other numbers, such as $\sqrt{2}$, was discovered. The need for such irrational numbers is corroborated in modern mathematical analysis, in which they play a fundamental role in the integral calculus, trigonometry, and other fields. Pythagoras showed

Pythagorean theorem

that the ratio x of the diagonal of an isosceles right triangle to the length of a side must satisfy the equation $x^2 = 2$ (Pythagorean theorem). No fraction m/n, however, can satisfy $(m/n)^2 = 2$; that is, $m^2 = 2n^2$ has no solution among the integers, because 2 divides m^2 an even number of times, and it divides $2n^2$ an odd number of times.

Eudoxus of Cnidus pointed out in about 367 BC that, although $\sqrt{2}$ could not be represented exactly by any one fraction, it could be represented as a limit of a sequence of fractions. Thus, $\sqrt{2}$ can be represented in the form of an infinite decimal: $\sqrt{2} = 1.4142\ldots$; this amounts to specifying $\sqrt{2}$ as the limit of the sequence of decimal fractions.

The clear exposition of these ideas from the modern point of view is due to Georg Cantor (1871). Real numbers, including both rational and irrational numbers, are defined by Cantor as infinite sequences, $x = (x_1, x_2, x_3, \ldots)$, $y = (y_1, y_2, y_3, \ldots), \ldots$, of fractions $x_n, y_n, \ldots$, that converge in the sense that $(x_m - x_n), (y_m - y_n), \ldots$, approach zero as m and n increase indefinitely. Here x is regarded as the limit of the sequence $(x_1, x_2, x_3, \ldots)$.

Real numbers. Equality is defined by making $x = y$ mean that $(x_n - y_n)$ approaches zero as n increases indefinitely. Addition and multiplication are defined by adding and multiplying corresponding terms (see 3). Laws valid for rational numbers can be extended to all real numbers by the principle of continuity. Each approximating term $(x + y)_n = x_n + y_n$ of $x + y$, for example, is equal to the corresponding approximation $(y + x)_n = y_n + x_n$ of $y + x$; hence, $(x + y)_n - (y + x)_n = 0$ for all n, and $x + y = y + x$ by definition of equality. In general, the principle of continuity holds that laws involving continuously varying functions like $x + y$ and $x \times y$ that are valid for arbitrarily good approximations $x_n, y_n, \ldots$ of $x, y, \ldots$ must be valid also for the limit values $x, y, \ldots$.

The Dedekind cut

Another interesting definition of real numbers was made by the 19th-century German mathematician Richard Dedekind: by a section in the class R of fractions is meant a division of all fractions into two classes L and U, such that $x \leq y$ for every x in L and every y in U. Each fraction (rational number) determines a section: L consists of the $x \leq a$ and U of the $y \geq a$. The other sections define the irrational numbers; thus, the section dividing the fractions into the $x < \sqrt{2}$ and the $y > \sqrt{2}$ (more precisely, the positive y with $y^2 > 2$) may be regarded as defining $\sqrt{2}$. Dedekind's definition is in fact equivalent to Cantor's.

The real numbers defined by this process have so far been found adequate for the mathematical treatment of most geometric and physical quantities such as length, area, weight, electric charge, and the like. Not only are the fundamental laws of arithmetic, the cancellation laws, and the order properties true, but division (except by zero) and subtraction are always possible. Finally, there is the property of any increasing sequence $x_1 < x_2 < x_3 \cdots$ the terms of which are all bounded above by a fixed constant c tending to a limit.

$$(3) \quad \begin{cases} x + y = (x_1 + y_1, x_2 + y_2, x_3 + y_3, \ldots) \\ x \times y = (x_1 \times y_1, x_2 \times y_2, x_3 \times y_3, \ldots) \end{cases}$$

$$(4) \quad \begin{cases} (a + bi) + (c + di) = a + c + bi + di \\ \qquad = (a + c) + (b + d)i \\ (a + bi) \times (c + di) = ac + (ad + bc)i + bdi^2 \\ \qquad = (ac - bd) + (ad + bc)i \end{cases}$$

$$(5) \quad z = \frac{a + bi}{c + di} = \frac{ac + bd}{c^2 + d^2} + \frac{bc - ad}{c^2 + d^2} i$$

$$(6) \quad \frac{(-B \pm \sqrt{B^2 - 4AC})}{2A}$$

$$(7) \quad \frac{(-B \pm i\sqrt{D})}{2A}$$

Complex numbers. The equation $x^2 = -1$ can have no real solution because the square of any real quantity is either positive or zero. But $i = \sqrt{-1}$ can be introduced as an imaginary number, and those laws of addition and multiplication that do not involve the relation $a \geq b$ may thus be preserved. To do this, all combinations $a + bi = a + b \times \sqrt{-1}$ must be introduced; these are the so-called complex numbers. If addition and multiplication of complex numbers are defined appropriately (see 4), the basic laws familiar from the properties of real numbers will be satisfied. It can be verified by substitution, for example, that the equation $(c + di)z = (a + bi)$ has a solution (see 5). Furthermore, any quadratic equation $Ax^2 + Bx + C = 0$ with real coefficients has complex roots (see 6), because, even if $B^2 - 4AC = -D$ is negative, the roots (see 7) can be found as complex numbers.

This is a special case of a fundamental theorem of algebra that asserts that any polynomial equation $x^n + a_1x^{n-1} + \cdots + a_n = 0$ with real or complex coefficients has a complex root. From a strictly algebraic standpoint, no further generalization is called for.

Although the theory of algebraic equations is greatly simplified by the use of complex numbers, it is necessary to sacrifice the properties of order. That is, if $z_1, z_2, \ldots, z_n$ are a collection of n distinct complex numbers, it is generally not possible to order these such that, say, $z_1 < z_2 < \cdots < z_n$. This is in contrast to the corresponding case of a collection of n distinct real numbers, for which such an ordering is always possible.

Complex numbers are useful not only in pure mathematics (theory of equations and function theory) but also throughout the physical sciences. (Ed.)

Functions and differential calculus

FUNCTIONS

The concept of a function. A concept central to analysis is that of a function. Mathematics contains numerous instances of a variable y depending in some fixed manner on another variable x. For example, y may be the square of x, the reciprocal, the cube, the sine, the inverse hyperbolic tangent, or some more complicated expression that can be calculated if the value of x is known. In this case y is said to be a function of x. In the traditional terminology x is the independent variable and y is the dependent variable.

Classically, the notion of function was mixed up with that of continuity, and both were confused with representation as a formula. For example, there was considerable debate on whether the absolute value $|x|$, which is x when x is positive but $-x$ when x is negative, is "really" a function, because it cannot be defined by a single formula and because its slope changes abruptly from -1 to 1 at the origin.

Current notion of function

The current notion of function is extremely general. Given two sets X and Y, a function f is a well-defined rule that assigns to each element x of X a unique element $y = f(x)$ of Y. Thus, X might be the set of all circles, Y the real numbers, and $f(x)$ the radius of the circle x. The geometric concept of radius becomes a function entirely analogous to square or sine. There is a more technical definition that replaces the word rule by a mathematical construction in set theory.

If both variables are real numbers, as is often the case in analysis, then a function may be represented geometrically by its graph. This is a collection of points in a plane, formed by plotting the dependent variable on the vertical axis against the independent variable on the horizontal axis. The graph of a general function may appear extremely complicated, but for the traditional functions of analysis the graph forms a smooth curve. This is because the functions employed in analysis are very special. They are generally required to possess properties such as continuity (the graph does not break up into disconnected pieces) or differentiability (the graph has no sharp corners).

Special types of function. A function in general, as just described, is not sufficiently tangible for statements to be made concerning it, even if X and Y are real numbers (except if one of them is a finite set). Rather, in order to start, it is necessary to impose on the functions some restrictions or qualifications—that is, to single out classes of functions with some particular features that may be analyzed. Together with the general notion of function, certain overall descriptive properties also began to emerge by means of which classes of functions could be characterized: continuity, differentiability, integrability, bounded variation, and others. Earlier, however, especially in the 17th century, it had been taken for granted, expressly or not, that a function is a "formula" or "expression" that is a tangible prescription for finding y if x is given. Certain functions, then familiar, were taken as being basic, as it were—for instance, $x, x^2, \ldots, \sin x, \tan x, \arctan x, e^x, \log x$—and a formula arose by taking one or several such functions and performing a finite number of "natural" operations, primarily the four arithmetical basic operations but including also extraction of roots and, what is important, the substitution of one function into another.

There soon appeared in these manipulations, however, certain expressions involving an infinite, or unending, succession of operations: certain infinite series, infinite products, and infinite continued fractions. Of these, the infinite series proved the most important by far, and two types of such series have advanced into positions of leadership and command that no phase of development has seriously impaired since, although there have been cases of evasion from authority, half in mathematical sport and a little in earnest. These two are the power series and the Fourier series (named after the 19th-century French mathematician and Egyptologist Jean-Baptiste-Joseph Fourier).

Infinite series

DIFFERENTIAL CALCULUS

The derivative. The derivative of a function represents the rate at which the dependent variable changes relative to the independent variable. Graphically, it is the slope of the tangent to the graph. Rates of change are highly important in science; for example, velocity is the rate of change of position, and acceleration is the rate of change of velocity. The idea of rate of change is given mathematical precision as follows.

If $f(x)$ is a real-valued function of a real variable and x_0 a real number, consider the difference quotient constructed by taking the ratio of the difference $f(x_0+h)-f(x_0)$ to h, in which h is any real number except zero. If this difference quotient approaches a number as h approaches zero, this number is called the derivative of the function $f(x)$ at the point x_0. If $f(x)=x^2$ and $x_0=1$, for example, the difference quotient is, by a direct calculation (see 8), seen to be $2+h$. As h approaches zero, the difference quotient approaches the number 2. The function thus has for its derivative the value 2 at the point 1.

The difference quotient

(8) $$\frac{f(1+h)-f(1)}{h}=\frac{(1+h)^2-1^2}{h}=\frac{2h+h^2}{h}=2+h$$

(9) $$\frac{f(0+h)-f(0)}{h}=\frac{h-0}{h}=1$$

(10) $$\frac{f(0+h)-f(0)}{h}=\frac{-h-0}{h}=-1$$

On the other hand, there exist functions that fail to have a derivative at some given point. A simple example is the following: Let $f(x)=x$ if x is positive or zero and $f(x)=-x$ if x is negative (that is, $f(x)=|x|$, the absolute value of x) and choose x_0 to be 0. It follows that, if h is positive, the difference quotient is the number 1, as shown by calculation (see 9); whereas, if h is negative, the quotient is -1 (see 10). Thus, $f(x)$ does not have a derivative at $x_0=0$ because, arbitrarily close to 0, the difference quotient assumes the values 1 and -1; *i.e.,* this difference quotient does not approach one unique number as h approaches zero.

The derivative of $f(x)$ at x_0 (if it exists) is usually denoted by the symbol $f'(x_0)$ or $(df/dx)(x_0)$.

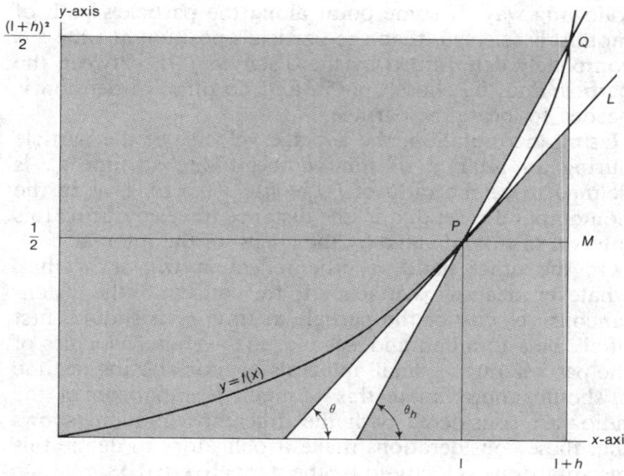

Figure 2: Geometric representation of the concept of the derivative (see text).

Geometric interpretation. Perhaps the quickest way to obtain some insight into the concept of the derivative is to consider its geometric interpretation. For example, if $f(x)=x^2/2$ and $x_0=1$, then inspection of the graph of this function near the point $P=[x_0, f(x_0)]=(1, \frac{1}{2})$ shows that the difference quotient, the ratio of $f(x_0+h)-f(x_0)$ to h, is equal to the ratio QM/PM (see Figure 2). But, as is well known from analytic geometry, this ratio is the slope of the line passing through the two points P and Q; that is, it is the trigonometric tangent of the angle, symbolized by the Greek letter theta followed by an inferior h, θ_h, made by this line and the x-axis. Now, if L be the line tangent to the graph of $f(x)$ at the point P, then, as h approaches zero, the point Q moves along the graph of $f(x)$ toward the point P, and the angle θ_h approaches the angle θ made by the line L and the x-axis. Consequently, the trigonometric tangent of θ_h approaches the trigonometric tangent of θ. The latter, by definition, is the slope of the line L. On the other hand, by the definition of the derivative, this slope must also be the derivative of $f(x)$ at x_0. The derivative of $f(x)$ at x_0, therefore, is the slope of the line tangent to the graph of $f(x)$ at the point $[x_0, f(x_0)]$.

This geometric interpretation and the argument justifying it extend equally well to other functions, provided that their graphs are sufficiently smooth—*i.e.,* smooth enough to guarantee the existence of a unique tangent line passing through the point in question. Conversely, if the graph of $f(x)$ fails to satisfy this condition at a point, then the derivative fails to exist; it has already been shown that the function $f(x)=|x|$ fails to have a derivative at $x_0=0$. This is reflected geometrically by the fact that the graph of $f(x)$ has a "corner" at the point $[x_0, f(x_0)]=(0, 0)$ (see Figure 3).

Non-existence of a derivative

Instantaneous velocity. An important physical application of the derivative is embodied in the concept of instantaneous velocity. In fact, a precise definition of the velocity of a moving particle at a given time, t, involves exactly the same limiting process that occurred in the definition of the derivative, as will now be shown.

If, for simplicity, a particle is considered to be moving along a straight line and in a fixed direction, then its position as a function of time can be represented in the

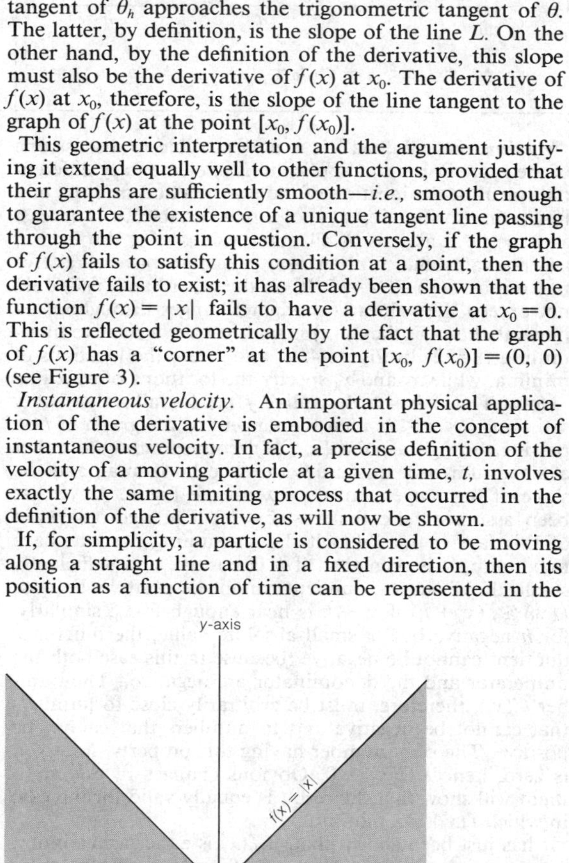

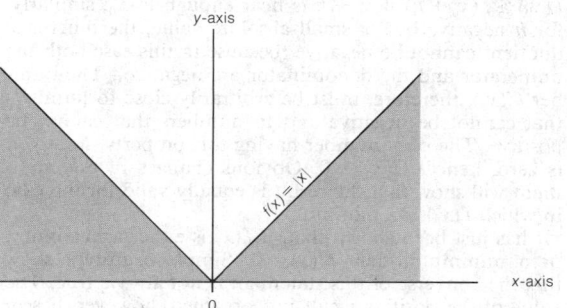

Figure 3: Graph of $f(x)=|x|$ showing the absence of a derivative for the function at $x_0=0$.

following way. If some point along the particle's path of motion is selected, then the particle's position at time t is completely determined by the distance, $f(t)$, between the particle and the chosen point, and no other dimension is needed to locate the particle.

Particle velocity and freely falling bodies

Using this notation, the average velocity of the particle during an interval of time h, beginning at time t_0, is defined to be the ratio of $f(t_0 + h) - f(t_0)$ to h, as in the nontemporal case; that is, the distance traveled during this interval of time divided by the length of the interval.

On the other hand, a little reflection will show that, whatever meaning is attached to the concept of the instantaneous velocity of the particle at time t_0, it should, first of all, be a number, and, second, the average velocities of the particle during small intervals of time starting at time t_0 should approximate this number. Comparison of the ratio just considered with the difference quotient shows that these considerations make it obligatory to define this instantaneous velocity to be the derivative $f'(t_0)$.

An important example of this situation is given by a freely falling body. It is an experimentally established law that, if a body is allowed to fall from rest, it will traverse, in time t, a distance that is proportional to t^2 (provided the medium through which it falls offers no resistance). This law can also be expressed by asserting that the distance traveled by the body is a function of time, the expression having the form $f(t) = ct^2$ (in which the constant c depends on the units used in measuring distance and time). Thus, the average velocity of the body during an interval of time h, beginning at time t_0, is by calculation (see 11) found to be $c(2t_0 + h)$. The limiting value of this ratio, as h approaches zero, is $2ct_0$. Thus, the instantaneous velocity of the freely falling body at time t_0 is $2ct_0$ and also $f'(t_0) = 2ct_0$.

$$(11)\quad \frac{f(t_0+h)-f(t_0)}{h} = \frac{c(t_0+h)^2 - ct_0^2}{h} = \frac{2ct_0h + ch^2}{h} = c(2t_0 + h)$$

Maxima and minima. It is now possible to discuss one of the more important applications of elementary differential calculus: the location of the maxima and minima of a function. If a function $f(x)$ of a real variable, x, is at least as large at $\bar{x}$ as it is at all other values of x throughout an interval about $\bar{x}$, then $f(x)$ is said to have a relative maximum, $f(\bar{x})$, at $x = \bar{x}$. If, on the other hand, $f(\bar{x})$ does not exceed the values $f(x)$ when x ranges throughout an interval about $\bar{x}$, then $f(x)$ is said to have a relative minimum at $x = \bar{x}$. In Figure 4, x_1 and x_3 are the locations of minima, while x_2 and x_4 specify the locations of maxima.

Now, if $f(x)$ has a derivative $f'(x)$ for all values of x satisfying $a < x < b$, then the tangent to the graph of $f(x)$ passing through a point $[x, f(\bar{x})]$ corresponding to either a maximum or a minimum must be horizontal, and the slope of the tangent must be zero (see Figure 4). (It has been assumed here that $a < \bar{x} < b$.) The rigorous proof of this fact is not difficult: For, assuming $f(x_0)$ to be a maximum, it is seen that, if h is positive and sufficiently small, the difference quotient cannot be positive, because $f(x_0) \geq f(x_0 + h)$ if $x_0 + h$ is near enough to x_0; similarly, for h negative but of small absolute value, the difference quotient cannot be negative (because in this case both the numerator and the denominator are negative). The number $f'(x_0)$, therefore, must be arbitrarily close to numbers that cannot be negative and to numbers that cannot be positive. The only number having this property, however, is zero; hence, $f'(x_0) = 0$. Obvious changes in this argument will show that the result is equally valid for the case in which $f(x_0)$ is a minimum.

Meaning of zero derivative

It has just been shown that, if $f(x)$ is either a maximum or a minimum, then $f'(x) = 0$. Simple examples show that the converse of this statement is not always true. The value of the positive result just obtained, however, lies in the fact that, if it is desired to locate a maximum or a minimum of a function $f(x)$, it is necessary only to determine those numbers x for which $f'(x) = 0$. In general, this greatly simplifies the task.

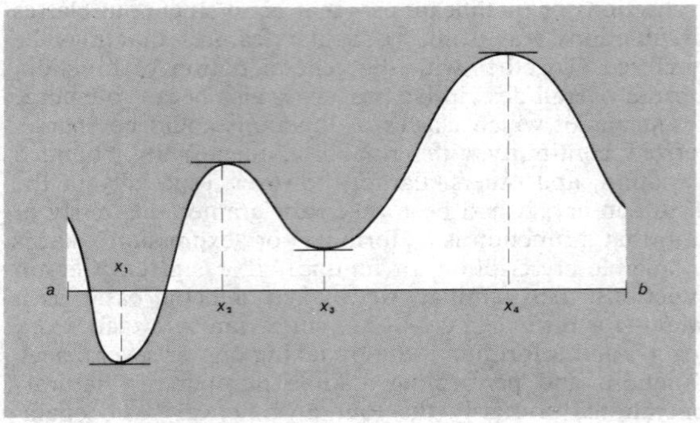

Figure 4: Maxima and minima of a function.

Consider a simple but illuminating example. Suppose that 100 feet of fence is available to enclose a rectangular pasture. What dimensions should the pasture have in order to contain the maximum possible area? If x denotes one length of the rectangle, then $50 - x$ must be the other length. Thus, the area of the pasture is $(50 - x)x = 50x - x^2$. The problem, then, reduces to finding the largest value (hence, a maximum) of the function $f(x) = 50x - x^2$, $0 \leq x \leq 50$. It is found by calculation (see 12) that the difference quotient is $50 - 2x - h$; therefore $f'(x) = 50 - 2x$. A maximum must satisfy, thus, the equation $f'(x) = 50 - 2x = 0$; therefore, $x = 25$. The area is largest when $x = 25$; that is, when the rectangle is a square of side 25 feet.

Computation of derivatives. It has already been shown that, if $f(x) = x^2$, then $f'(x) = 2x$. This is just a special case of one of several formulas for differentiation that are obtained in elementary calculus. It follows from the definition of the derivative that, if $n = 1, 2, 3, \ldots$ is any positive integer and $f(x) = x^n$, then $f'(x) = nx^{n-1}$.

In fact, by means of an appropriate limiting process, it can be shown that, for each real number n, the expression x^n for positive x has a natural definition as a real number (for example, $n = 1/2$ gives the familiar square root function: $x^{1/2} = \sqrt{x}$). The formula for differentiation extends to include all functions of the form $f(x) = x^n$.

Many other well-known functions have simple expressions for their derivatives. The trigonometric functions, for example, have derivatives that are expressible in terms of other trigonometric functions (see 13).

In addition to such specific formulas, several general rules for differentiation are derived from the definition of

$$(12)\quad \frac{f(x+h)-f(x)}{h} = \frac{50h - 2xh - h^2}{h} = 50 - 2x - h$$

$$(13)\quad \begin{cases} (\sin x)' = \cos x \\ (\cos x)' = -\sin x \\ (\tan x)' = \sec^2 x \\ (\cot x)' = -\csc^2 x \end{cases}$$

$$(14)\quad [af(x) + bg(x)]' = af'(x) + bg'(x)$$

$$(15)\quad [f(x)g(x)]' = f(x)g'(x) + f'(x)g(x) \quad \text{(Leibniz' rule)}$$

$$(16)\quad \left[\frac{f(x)}{g(x)}\right]' = \frac{f'(x)g(x) - f(x)g'(x)}{[g(x)]^2}$$

$$(17)\quad h'(x) = f'[g(x)] \cdot g'(x)$$

$$(18)\quad p(x) = a_0 + a_1x + \cdots + a_kx^k$$

$$(19)\quad p'(x) = a_1 + 2a_2x + \cdots + ka_kx^{k-1}$$

the derivative. The four most basic of these rules will now be referred to.

Suppose that $f(x)$ and $g(x)$ are two functions and a and b are two constants. Whenever $f'(x)$ and $g'(x)$ exist, rules can be derived for the derivative of the sum (see 14), or linear combination, of $f(x)$ and $g(x)$, for the product (see 15), and for the ratio (see 16) of $f(x)$ to $g(x)$, provided $g(x) \neq 0$.

The chain rule

The fourth basic rule, the chain rule, may be stated in the following way. Suppose that, for each real number x for which $g(x)$ is defined, the number $g(x)$ is such that $f[g(x)]$ is defined. The composite function $h(x) = f[g(x)]$ can then be formed. The chain rule asserts that, if both $g'(x)$ and $f'[g(x)]$ exist, then $h'(x)$ exists and equals (see 17) the product of the former two derivatives.

These four rules, together with formulas for the derivatives of the powers of x and the basic trigonometric functions of x, permit the computation of the derivatives of a large class of functions. These include the derivative of the most general polynomial (see 18 and 19).

In addition, a formula for the derivative of the most general rational function (*i.e.*, the quotient of two polynomials) can be obtained.

Measure and integral calculus

HISTORICAL DEVELOPMENT

The abstract concepts of measure and of integration are best understood in the light of the historical evolution and growth of the problem of measure. This problem always has been present in everyday life as well as in science. It pertains to measures of such properties as the length of a curve (rectification), area of a surface (quadrature), volume of a solid (cubature), mass or weight or electric charge of a body, probability of a random event, and so on. Yet the abstract concept of measure, of which the preceding measures are but particular concrete cases, was not isolated until the 20th century. The corresponding evolution may be loosely divided into several periods, each characterized by its particular attitude toward the problem of measure.

The empirical period. The purely empirical period began with prehistory and lasted until the 6th century BC. The most advanced organized knowledge of this era was that of the ancient Babylonians and Egyptians, providing precise and correct rules for finding areas and volumes of such geometric figures as the triangle, trapezoid, and circle. For the Babylonians, π equaled 3 (this value of π is also found in the Old Testament), and for the Egyptians π equaled 256/81 (= 3.160 . . .). They also had correct rules for the volumes of the parallelepiped, prism, pyramid, and circular cylinder, thought of in concrete terms—mainly as storage containers for grain. The ancient Egyptians even had a correct rule for measuring the frustum of a square pyramid—*i.e.*, the part next to the base and formed by cutting off the top by a plane parallel to the base.

Babylonian and Egyptian knowledge

Apparently these rules were discovered empirically. To become proved mathematical propositions, deduced from a set of definitions and postulates, they had to await the "Greek miracle": the emergence of organized abstract thinking in Greece, which includes the earliest known treatment of mathematics as a deductive discipline. Available information prompts some historians to attribute the birth of abstract mathematics to Thales of Miletus (6th century BC), one of the Seven Wise Men of ancient Greece.

The Greek period. This period began with Thales of Miletus and lasted until about 200 BC. By the 5th century BC, problems of quadrature and cubature were so popular that Aristophanes in his satiric comedy *The Birds* alludes to the quadrature of circles, and the problem of duplication of cubes is attributed to the Delphic oracle. The first abstract proofs of rules for finding some areas and volumes are said to have been developed by Eudoxus of Cnidus in about 367 BC. About a century later, his method of approximation was developed and exploited by Archimedes, called the greatest mathematician of antiquity. This procedure, called the method of exhaustion in the 17th century AD, was at the root of all further developments of the mathematical problem of measure. The method culminated in the 19th-century isolation of the concept of Riemann integration, defined by means of approximating Riemann sums (which, in all justice, could be called Eudoxus or Archimedes sums or, as will be seen below, Cauchy sums).

In modern terms, the method of exhaustion applied to surfaces, for example, may be stated as follows: if S is a surface of unknown area s, then one may choose another surface of known area s' contained in S, and yet another surface S'' of known area s'' containing S; thus $s' < s < s''$. The approximating surfaces S' and S'' are polygons or sums of slices, mainly trapezoidal or rectangular, selected by Eudoxus and by Archimedes according to the particular figure S. In fact, sums of rectangular slices (the areas of which are particularly simple to compute) were to become predominant from the 16th century AD on. To complete the proof, Archimedes used the following proposition: if a known area a is such that for every positive ε there exist surfaces S' and S'' with $s' < a < s''$ and $s'' - s' \leq \varepsilon$, then $s = a$. Archimedes did not isolate this proposition. He proved it, in concrete geometric terms for every particular figure that he considered, by a double reductio ad absurdum (double, because negative numbers were not available to him): If $s < a$, then $\varepsilon < a - s$ is taken; but, if $s > a$, then the choice $\varepsilon < s - a$ is made. In either case, a contradiction is reached, so that $s = a$. The method does not specify how the value of a is to be found.

The period of indivisibles. This period extended from 1615 to about 1670, heavily influenced by Archimedes, whose works had become available in 1544 in Greek and in Latin. The concept of integration (see below *Integral calculus*) gradually emerged, but neither in Archimedean nor in modern dress—especially in England; there, integration became for a time not a primary operation but the inverse of differentiation.

After the efforts of the Dutch mathematician and physicist Simon Stevin and other followers of Archimedes came the pioneering work of the German astronomer Johannes Kepler, *Nova Stereometria Doliorum Vinariorum* (1615; "Solid Geometry of a Wine Barrel"). From then on and until the 19th century, Archimedean rigour was abandoned in favour of an intuitive "infinitesimal" reasoning. For Kepler, the circle consisted of an "infinity" of infinitesimal triangles with a common vertex at the centre, the sphere consisted of an "infinity" of pyramids, and so on. Nevertheless, he obtained more than 80 new results for certain areas and volumes. The language of infinitesimals, or method of indivisibles, was then codified by the Italian mathematician Bonaventura Cavalieri in 1635, in his *Geometria Indivisibilibus Continuorum Nova Quadam Ratione Promota* ("A Certain Method for the Development of a New Geometry of Continuous Indivisibles"). For the first time in the history of the problem of measure, instead of measures of specific geometric figures, general principles for quadratures and cubatures were announced. While not proved rigorously, the principles were at least justified in the language of infinitesimals.

Pioneering work of Kepler

During this period, the method of indivisibles yielded a very large number of special integrals as quadratures, cubatures, and centres of gravity. Most were formulated geometrically. Yet more abstract algebraic formulations were already apparent: Pierre de Fermat of France and Cavalieri integrated x^n for rational values of $n \neq -1$; the French mathematician Grégoire de Saint-Vincent integrated it for $n = -1$ in a geometric form that is readily recognized as the logarithmic function; and Pascal integrated cos x. Fermat, Pascal, and the Scottish mathematician James Gregory geometrically manipulated changes of variables and integrations by parts. In fact, geometric methods, formulations, and results were gradually made analytic. Pascal first discussed the types of sums that he would need and then only computed them in the concrete geometric case under consideration. The English mathematician John Wallis in *Arithmetica Infinitorum* (1655; "Infinitesimal Algebra") started straight from algebraic grounds, introducing infinite series and infinite products, and Nicolaus Mercator, a German mathematician, discovered the series expansion of $\log(1 + x)$.

The birth of analytic geometry

The impetus and the tools for abstraction were provided by the growth of algebra, the birth of analytic geometry with René Descartes's *Géométrie* (1637), Fermat's *Isagoge* (written before 1636), and the birth and growth of kinematics, the consideration of motion leaving aside considerations of mass and force. Consideration of time as a concept in kinematics, and the notion of abscissa (the horizontal coordinate of a point in a plane Cartesian coordinate system), led to a gradual emergence of the idea of independent variable. Velocities and slopes of tangents led to the concept of differentiation. Performance of rectifications, such as that of parabolic arcs, forged a first link between differentiation and integration, because the rectification of curves $y = f(x)$ was reduced to the quadrature of $\sqrt{1 + [f'(x)]^2}$, where $f'(x)$ is the derivative of $f(x)$. In fact, integration lost its predominant role in favour of differentiation. The basic link was provided by the recognition that differentiation and integration are inverse operations, to be found in the English mathematician Isaac Barrow's *Lectiones Geometricae* of 1670. Although a crowning of the period of indivisibles, Barrow's work also represented the dying spirit of that period. He began with kinematic considerations that seemed to lead at once to the basic link. The relation between differentiation and integration, however, was given only much later in two widely spaced propositions and in geometric terms: the derivative in terms of slopes of tangents, and the integral in terms of areas.

Development by Newton and Leibniz

The calculus period. This period extended from about 1670 to the beginning of the 19th century, beginning with the creation of the calculus by Leibniz and Newton.

Newton, influenced by his teacher Barrow and his preoccupation with dynamics—dealing with forces and their relation, primarily to motion—used a universal independent variable conceived primarily as time; thus, he had no concept of functions of several variables and hence none of partial derivatives. The primary concept was that of fluxion (derivative) and arose from kinematic considerations. The concept of integral was not isolated, and no symbol for integration was introduced. His first basic problem was to find fluxions. Integration was treated in a geometric form as a search for fluents (antiderivatives, primitives, indefinite integrals), functions the fluxions of which are given.

Newton depended mainly on the fact that the derivative of a variable area $F(x)$ under a curve is the ordinate $f(x)$ of this curve. For Newton, moreover, integration was only a particular case of his second basic problem: given an equality containing fluxions, find the corresponding relation for fluents (solve ordinary differential equations). He solved this problem formally by means of series.

Leibniz, influenced by Pascal, conceived the derivative as the slope of a tangent and the integral as *summa omnium linae* ("the sum of all lines"). The main purpose of his activity was to devise a universal language—that is, a general formalism for the acquisition and organization of knowledge. He largely succeeded in the creation of such a formalism for the calculus, and the present formalism is still essentially and properly his, including the integral symbol (a stylized form of the letter S standing for *summa omnium*). His also are the terms constant, variable, parameter, and (with the help of the Swiss mathematician Johann Bernoulli) function and integral.

The heroic years of the calculus at the end of the 17th century saw the constant flow of new results from Leibniz and his school, as embodied in the work of Jakob Bernoulli, Johann Bernoulli, and G.F.A. de l'Hospital. During the 18th century, the Scottish mathematician Colin Maclaurin pursued and developed Newton's ideas and attempted to clarify them in his *Treatise of Fluxions* (1742), while the Swiss mathematician Leonhard Euler pursued further the ideas of Leibniz and his school in his *Introductio in Analysin Infinitorum* of 1748 and attempted to found the calculus upon an obscure passage to the limit, starting with the calculus of differences.

Mathematicians of the 18th century devoted little effort to the shaky foundations of the calculus, apparently happy with the powerful tools at their disposal, the fecundity of the methods, the beauty and consistency of the results. Discussions about the metaphysics of calculus were left to philosophers and theologians, among whom the Irish-born Anglican Bishop George Berkeley figured prominently. The whole subject of metaphysics of calculus vanished into thin air, however, with the French mathematician Jean Le Rond d'Alembert's two articles on "Limite" and "Différentielle" in the *Encyclopédie* (1751–65). At last the concept of limit was isolated, a concept that had run as an almost invisible thread in the fabric of infinitesimals as woven since Stevin and others at the turn of the 17th century. The concept of differentiation, too, was finally defined rigorously in terms of limits. (Yet, after d'Alembert, Lagrange still tried to define integration in terms of Newton's conception of a function as a power series.)

The concept of limit as a basis

The analysis period. A new era opened in France with Augustin-Louis Cauchy's *Résumé des leçons sur le calcul infinitésimal* (1823), the basis of which was the concept of limit. Differentiation was defined by a passage to the limit. At last, the integral was defined directly and in purely analytic terms by returning to the very essence of the method of exhaustion as follows: Given a bounded function $f(x)$ defined for $a \leq x \leq b$, the interval $[a, b]$ may be divided into n subintervals by means of points $a = x_0 < x_1 < \cdots < x_n = b$, and the Eudoxus-Archimedes-Cauchy sums (see 20; nowadays called Riemann sums) may be formed by adding n terms, each composed of a product of a value of f and the length of a subinterval, with f evaluated at an intermediate point of the subinterval. The limit of these sums, as the largest length of the subintervals converges to zero, is, by definition, the integral of the function f on $[a, b]$, provided that this limit exists and is independent of the choice of the t_k, the intermediate point in the subinterval at which f is evaluated.

$$(20) \qquad \sum_{k=0}^{n-1} f(t_k)(x_{k+1} - x_k), \qquad x_k \leq t_k \leq x_{k+1}$$

$$(21) \qquad \sum_{k=0}^{n-1} M_k(x_{k+1} - x_k), \quad \sum_{k=0}^{n-1} m_k(x_{k+1} - x_k)$$

A new way of thinking was thus born; existence of integrals as well as of derivatives was no longer a question of faith but a problem to be studied. Cauchy gave an incomplete proof of the existence of integrals of continuous functions, a proof that was completed only in 1875 by the French mathematician Gaston Darboux. Meanwhile, Riemann in 1854 (published in 1867) gave necessary and sufficient conditions for the existence of the integral called the Riemann integral and showed that continuous and piecewise monotone functions satisfy these conditions. Instead of Riemann sums, Darboux introduced the upper and lower Darboux sums (see 21), replacing the value of f at an intermediate point in an interval by M_k and m_k, which, respectively, denote the least upper and the greatest lower bounds of $f(x)$, as x varies between x_k and x_{k+1}. The passage to the limit yields the upper and lower Darboux integrals. These two integrals coincide if and only if the bounded function f is Riemann-integrable on $[a, b]$.

INTEGRAL CALCULUS

Geometric aspects of the integral

The definite integral. As mentioned earlier in this article, the integral is a limit concept. The geometric aspects of this concept will now be explored. First, consider two real numbers, a and b, and a function $f(x)$ defined for all x satisfying $a \leq x \leq b$. For the sake of simplicity it will be further supposed, for the moment, that the values $f(x)$ are never negative. The basic problem of integral calculus can then be stated, based on Figure 5, as follows: What is the meaning (and numerical value) of the area of the region below the graph of $f(x)$ and above the interval (a, b) on the x-axis?

Other basic assumptions are that it is known what is meant by "area" in case the region is a rectangle and also that, if a region can be subdivided into a finite number of nonoverlapping rectangles, then its area is the sum of the areas of these rectangles. Having made these assumptions,

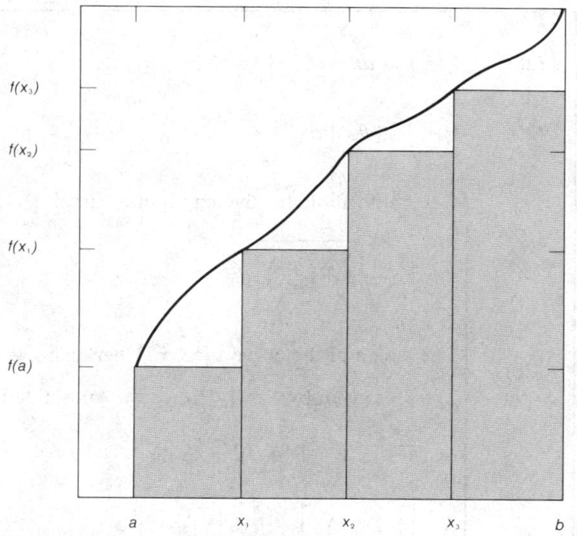

Figure 5: Representation of the area under a curve that underestimates the integral value.

the question raised may be answered using the following.

Estimation of the integral value

First, the interval (a, b) is to be subdivided into n subintervals by choosing consecutive points $a = x_0, x_1, x_2, \ldots, x_n = b$. In each of the subintervals $I_i = (x_{i-1}, x_i)$, a point ζ_i $(i = 1, 2, \ldots, n)$ is chosen such that the value $f(\zeta_i)$ is smallest among the values assumed by the function in I_i (if such a point ζ_i exists). The rectangle with base I_i and height $f(\zeta_i)$ (see Figure 5, in which $n = 4$ and $\zeta_i = x_{i-1}$) then lies below the graph of $f(x)$. It is reasonable to assume, therefore, that the area in question should be a number exceeding the sum of the areas of the rectangles that have been constructed (that is, the area of the shaded region in Figure 5). This can be expressed algebraically (see 22) in terms of A, in which A denotes the area below the graph of $f(x)$ and above the interval (a, b).

$$(22) \quad A \geq f(\zeta_1)(x_1 - x_0) + f(\zeta_2)(x_2 - x_1) + \cdots + f(\zeta_n)(x_n - x_{n-1})$$

$$(23) \quad A \leq f(\mu_1)(x_1 - x_0) + f(\mu_2)(x_2 - x_1) + \cdots + f(\mu_n)(x_n - x_{n-1})$$

Next, using a similar construction, instead of choosing the point ζ_i in the subinterval I_i, a point μ_i (if it exists) may be chosen such that the value $f(\mu_i)$ is the largest among the values assumed by the function in I_i (see Figure 6, in which $\mu_i = x_i$ and, again, $n = 4$). An inequality between the area A and a sum of rectangles can, again, be expressed algebraically (see 23).

A sum of the type in which the smallest value of $f(x)$ in each subinterval I_i is used is called a lower sum (with respect to the given subdivision); a sum of the type in which the largest value of $f(x)$ in each subinterval is used is called an upper sum. The area in question should be a number, A, less than or equal to any upper sum and greater than or equal to any lower sum. If the notion of area as used here is to have a unique meaning, however, there should exist only one number with this property.

It will be noted that the restriction $f(x) \geq 0$, which was made only in order to obtain a better grasp of the geometric aspects of the construction, can be dropped without necessitating any change in the above definition. Dropping the restriction, however, implies that regions below the x-axis and above the graph of a negative-valued function will have negative areas.

The Riemann integral

The area that has just been defined is usually called the Riemann integral (or the definite integral, for reasons that will be shown) of the function $f(x)$ over the interval (a, b).

Integrable and nonintegrable functions. It is natural, at this point, to attempt to determine what classes of functions have a Riemann integral. It can be shown that, if $f(x)$ is continuous—roughly speaking, this means that, whenever x_1 and x_2 are close, then $f(x_1)$ and $f(x_2)$ are close—then it is (Riemann) integrable. In fact, this restriction is not only sufficient but comes close to being also a necessary condition for this type of integrability.

Two simple examples of functions that are not integrable are the following: Suppose $a = 0$ and $b = 1$. Let $f(x) = 1/x$ for $0 < x \leq 1$, and let $f(0) = 0$. Then it can be seen that the upper sums of this function are not defined (for, in the first interval, I_1, of any subdivision, there is no number μ_1 such that the value $f[\mu_1]$ is the largest among the values that may be assumed by the function in I_1).

In the second case, again, let $a = 0$ and $b = 1$, and suppose $f(x) = 0$ if x is rational, but $f(x) = 1$ if x is irrational. It is then easy to check that each upper sum is 1 and each lower sum is 0. In this case there does not exist a unique number less than or equal to any upper sum but greater than or equal to any lower sum.

Fundamental theorem of calculus. The connection between the two basic concepts, the derivative and the integral, is perhaps the most important feature of calculus. This connection can be summarized roughly by saying that integration and differentiation are inverse operations; if first one of these operations and then the other is applied to a function, the original function is obtained (this is analogous to the operation of addition, and then subtraction, with a given number).

In order to describe this more precisely, the concept of the indefinite integral must be introduced. Suppose that $f(x)$ is continuous (hence, integrable) in some interval I, and let a and y be two points of this interval. If the number a is fixed, then a function of y, $F(y)$, can be formed by letting $F(y)$ be the integral of f from a to y; if $y < a$, $F(y)$ is equal to the negative of the integral from y to a. The function $F(y)$ is called an indefinite integral of the function $f(x)$.

The connection between differentiation and integration can then be stated in the following way: the function $F(y)$ (as defined above) is differentiable, and $F'(y) = f(y)$; furthermore, if $G(y)$ is any other differentiable function satisfying $G'(y) = f(y)$ for all y in I, then the difference $F(y) - G(y)$ is constant. This statement is known as the fundamental theorem of the integral calculus.

The antiderivative

A function such as $G(y)$, satisfying $G'(y) = f(y)$, is called an antiderivative of $f(y)$. If a constant is added to an antiderivative of $f(y)$, another antiderivative of the same $f(y)$ is obtained (because the derivative of a constant is zero). The fundamental theorem of the integral calculus can then be paraphrased by saying that the most general antiderivative of $f(y)$ can be obtained by adding a constant function to an indefinite integral of $f(y)$.

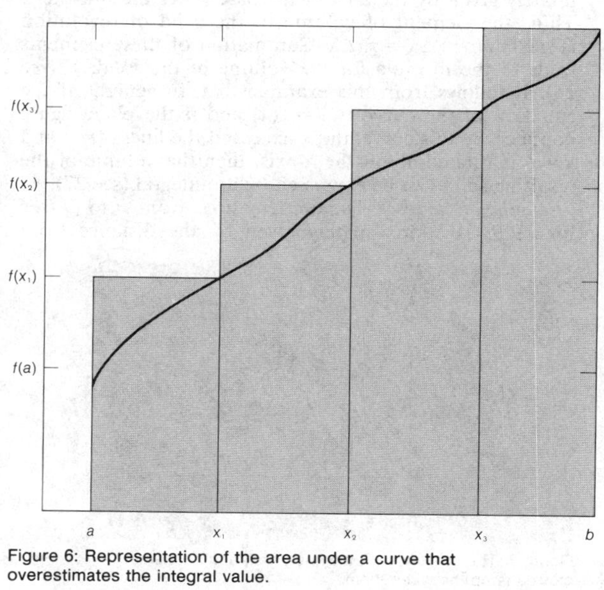

Figure 6: Representation of the area under a curve that overestimates the integral value.

One of the immediate, and most important, consequences of the fundamental theorem is that the integrals of a large class of functions can be obtained merely by inverting the formulas already developed for differentiation. For example, it can be found that sin x is an antiderivative of cos x. Thus, $F(y)$ is the integral from 0 to y of the cosine function and must differ from sin y by a constant; that is, $F(y) = \sin y + C$. The constant C is easily determined, because it follows from the definition of the integral that $F(0) = 0$. Hence, $0 = F(0) = \sin 0 + C = C$. It has been shown, therefore, that the sine is the indefinite integral of the cosine, for all y (see 24).

(24) $$\sin y = \int_0^y \cos x \, dx$$

(25) $$A = \left[\frac{x^2}{2} - \frac{x^3}{3}\right]_0^1 = \frac{1}{2} - \frac{1}{3} = \frac{1}{6}$$

The power of the fundamental theorem can be appreciated once it is realized that explicit formulas for integration, such as the formula for the integral of the cosine, are by no means easy to obtain by working directly from the definition of the integral. Unlike the case of differentiation, however, there are many functions that can be expressed by simple formulas but that do not have simple expressions for their antiderivatives.

Applications. *Areas.* The method of computing areas under curves has already been indicated in the formal definition of integral. As a further illustration, the area bounded by the curve $y = x^2$ and by the line $y = x$ will be found (see Figure 7). The points of intersection of the curve and the line are (0, 0) and (1, 1). The strip of width Δx and height $x - x^2$ has an area approximated by the product $(x - x^2)\Delta x$. This is the element of area ΔA. Summation of these elements, and subsequent passage to the limit by letting Δx approach zero, leads to the formula for the area as the integral of $x - x^2$. An antiderivative of $x - x^2$ is the function $x^2/2 - x^3/3$. Hence, the integral becomes 1/6 (see 25).

Elements of area

Volumes of solids of revolution. If a plane region is rotated about a line in the plane, the resulting figure is called a solid of revolution. The volume of this solid is readily represented in the form of an integral. As an example, the volume generated by revolving the plane region bounded by the curve $y = \sqrt{x}$, the x-axis, and the lines $x = 0$ and $x = 5$ will be calculated (see Figure 8). When this plane figure is rotated about the x-axis, the strip of width Δx and height $\sqrt{x}$ generates a thin disk (or cylinder) of radius $\sqrt{x}$ and thickness Δx. The volume of this cylinder is approximately given by the area of the base times the thickness. Thus, the element of volume of the solid of revolution is $\Delta V = \pi(\sqrt{x})^2\Delta x = \pi x \Delta x$. Summation of these elements leads to the formula for the volume of the solid: V (see 26). It follows from this example that, in general, if the equation of the curve is $y = f(x)$ and if the plane figure bounded by this curve, the x-axis, and the lines $x = a$ and $x = b$ is rotated about the x-axis, then the volume of the resulting solid can be expressed by an integral (see 27).

Lengths of curves. The arc length Δs from P to Q (see Figure 9) is approximately given by the distance from

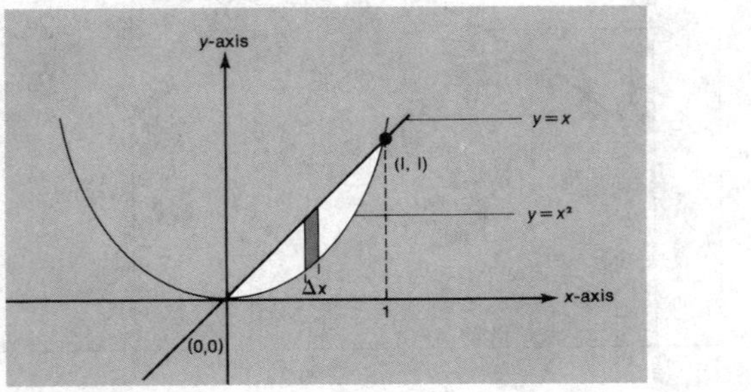

Figure 7: The curve $y = x^2$, the line $y = x$, and an element of area (strip) between them.

(26) $$V = \int \pi x \, dx = \pi\left[\frac{x^2}{2}\right]_0^5 = 12.5\pi$$

(27) $$V = \int_a^b \pi[f(x)]^2 dx$$

(28) General formula for the length of a curve:

$$S = \int_a^b \sqrt{1 + \left(\frac{dy}{dx}\right)^2} \, dx$$

The length of the curve $y = \frac{2}{3}x^{3/2}$, between $x = 0$ and $x = 3$, is given by $S = \int_0^3 \sqrt{1 + x} \, dx$. An antiderivative of $\sqrt{1 + x}$ is $\frac{2}{3}(1 + x)^{3/2}$, so that

$$S = \left[\frac{2}{3}(1 + x)^{3/2}\right]_0^3 = \frac{2}{3}(8 - 1) = \frac{14}{3}.$$

(29) $$S = \int_a^b 2\pi y \sqrt{1 + \left(\frac{dy}{dx}\right)^2} \, dx$$

(30) $$S = \int_0^3 4\pi\sqrt{x} \sqrt{1 + \left(\frac{1}{x}\right)} \, dx$$

$$= 4\pi\int_0^3 \sqrt{1 + x} \, dx = \frac{56\pi}{3}$$

(31) $$W = \int_0^2 100x \, dx = 100\left[\frac{x^2}{2}\right]_0^2 = 200 \text{ lb-in.}$$

(32) $$M_x = \int \int y \, dx \, dy$$

(33) $$\int_{\frac{1}{2}(y^2-1)}^{y+1} y \, dx = y \int dx$$

$$= y\Big[x\Big]_{\frac{1}{2}(y^2-1)}^{y+1} = [(y + 1) - \tfrac{1}{2}(y^2 - 1)]$$

(34) $$M_x = \int_{-1}^3 y[(y + 1) - \tfrac{1}{2}(y^2 - 1)]dy$$

P to Q if these two points are sufficiently close to each other. Thus, the element of arc length Δs is approximately $\sqrt{(\Delta x)^2 + (\Delta y)^2}$, which can also be written in a form with the common factor Δx. Summation of these arc lengths, and passage to the limit, yields the formula for the length of the curve between the points A, B (see 28), in which a and b are the abscissas of the points A, B. The length of a specific curve has therefore been obtained by calculation (see 28).

Areas of solids of revolution. If the plane region of Figure 9 is rotated about the x-axis, the lateral area of the thin slab bounded by the segment PQ is given by the circumference of the cross section times the slant height, or $2\pi y$ times length of PQ. Since the arc length from P to Q is approximated by the length of the segment from P to Q, the element of surface area of the solid of revolution is given by $\Delta S = 2\pi y \Delta s$. With Δs approximated by $\sqrt{(\Delta x)^2 + (\Delta y)^2}$, subsequent passage to the limit gives the surface area (see 29). For example, if $y = 2\sqrt{x}$, $a = 0$, and $b = 3$, then $s = 56\pi/3$ (see 30).

Work done by a force. If a constant force F is directed along the x-axis and acts on a particle, displacing it through a distance x, then the work done by the force is given

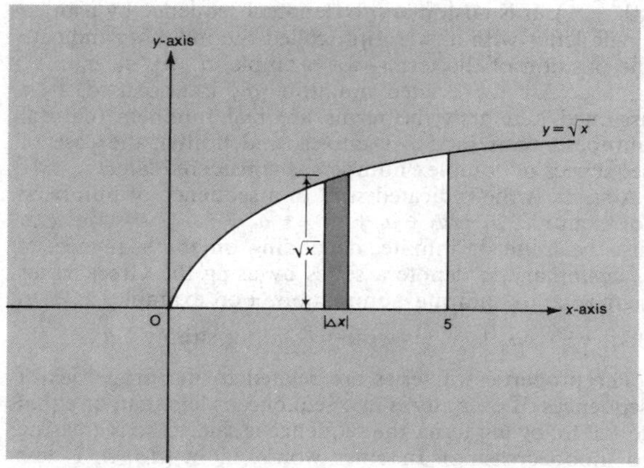

Figure 8: The plane region bounded by the curve $y = \sqrt{x}$, the x axis, and the lines $x = 0$ and $x = 5$; when the plane figure is rotated about the x-axis to generate a solid of revolution, the strip of width Δx and height $\sqrt{x}$ generates a thin disk of radius $\sqrt{x}$ and thickness Δx, which is an element of volume.

by the product of the force and the distance: $W = Fx$. If the force is not constant, the formula for the work done is represented by an integral. The element of work ΔW is given by $F(x)\Delta x$, in which $F(x)$ is the value of the force at x, and Δx is a small displacement from x to $(x + \Delta x)$. Summation of the elements of work, followed by passage to the limit, leads to the formula in which W equals the integral from a to b of $F(x)$.

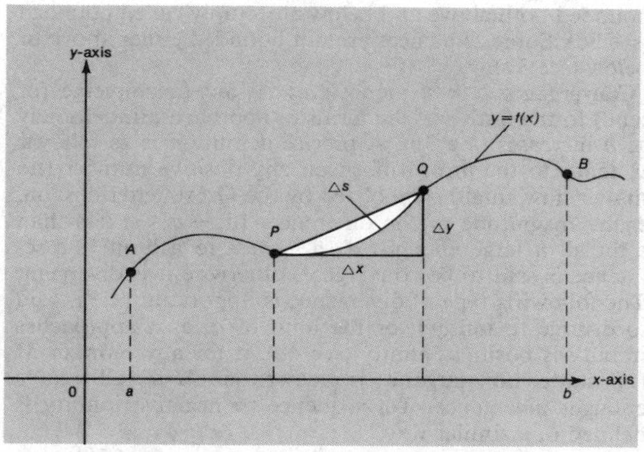

Figure 9: The arc length Δs from P to Q is approximated by the distance from P to Q if these two points are sufficiently close together.

Work required to stretch a spring

For example, the force required to stretch a spring is proportional to the amount of stretch: $F(x) = kx$ (see Figure 10). For a certain spring it is found that a force of 50 pounds is required to extend it by 0.5 inch. The constant of proportionality k, therefore, has the value 100, and $F(x) = 100x$. If the unstretched length of the spring is 10 inches, the work required to stretch the spring to a length of 12 inches is $W = 200$ lb-in. (see 31). If the upper limit of integration (that is, 2) is replaced by 0.5, the same formula (31) indicates that the work required to extend the spring by 0.5 inch is only 12.5 lb-in.

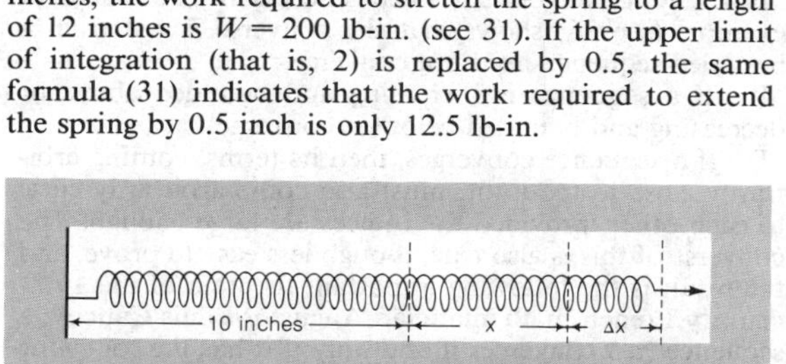

Figure 10: A 10-inch spring displaced to length $10 + x + \Delta x$.

Moments and centroids. The moment of an element of area about an axis (perpendicular to the plane of the area) is defined as the product of the element of area by its distance from the axis. In particular, the moment of ΔA about the x-axis is $y\Delta A$, and the moment about the y-axis is $x\Delta A$ (see Figure 11). Summation of these elements over the whole area and a passage to the limit lead to formulas for the moment of the plane area A expressed as double integrals: the moment about the x-axis is the double integral of y with respect to A; the moment about the y-axis is the double integral of x with respect to A.

The evaluation of these integrals is achieved by the computation of successive single integrals whose limits are determined by the boundary of the region. The centroid of the plane area A is defined as the point (x, y) at which $\bar{x} = M_y/A$, $\bar{y} = M_x/A$. For example, if the area is bounded by the curve $y^2 = 2x + 1$ and the line $y = x - 1$ (see Figure 12), the points of intersection are $(0, -1)$ and $(4, 3)$. Using the methods previously discussed, the area is

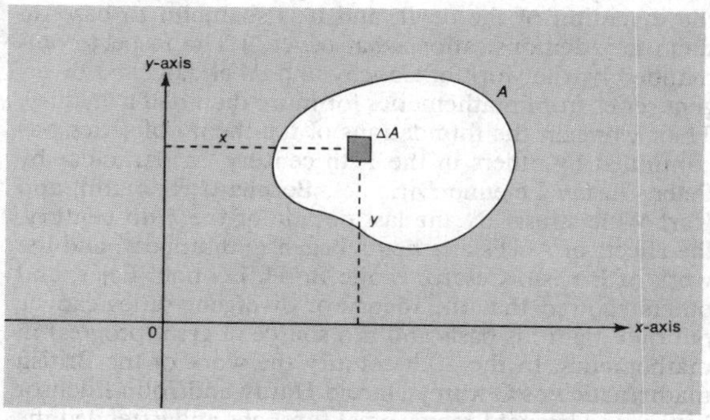

Figure 11: For a plane area A, the moment of an element of area ΔA about the x-axis is $y\Delta A$, and the moment about the y-axis is $x\Delta A$.

found to be $A = 16/3$. With the element of area written as $\Delta x\Delta y$, the moment about the x-axis can be written (see 32, in which the inner integral is taken with respect to x, keeping y fixed). From the diagram it is seen that the lower and upper limits of integration for this integral are $x = \frac{1}{2}(y^2 - 1)$, and $x = y + 1$. Thus, the inner integral is calculable (see 33). The moment is also obtainable (see 34, in which the limits are determined by the points of intersection of the curve and straight line). Evaluation of the integral yields $M_x = 16/3$.

A similar evaluation for the moment about the y-axis gives $M_y = 129/20$. The centroid is therefore located at $(387/320, 1)$. (Hy.K./Ed.)

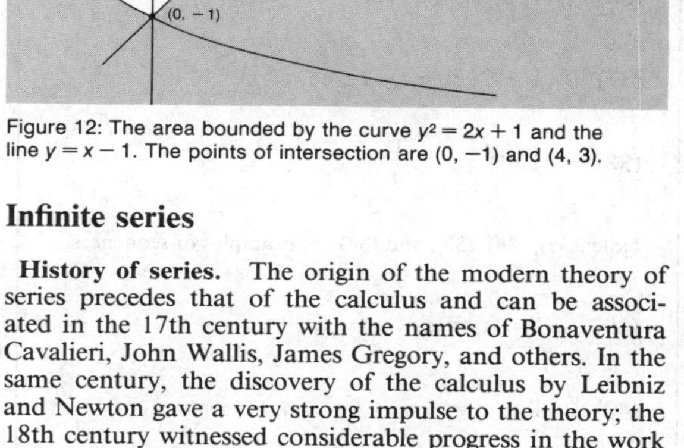

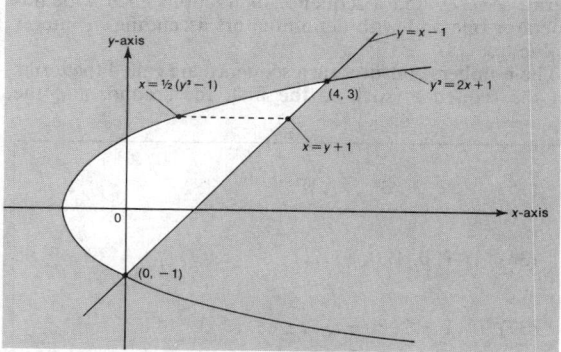

Figure 12: The area bounded by the curve $y^2 = 2x + 1$ and the line $y = x - 1$. The points of intersection are $(0, -1)$ and $(4, 3)$.

Infinite series

Origin and development of the theory

History of series. The origin of the modern theory of series precedes that of the calculus and can be associated in the 17th century with the names of Bonaventura Cavalieri, John Wallis, James Gregory, and others. In the same century, the discovery of the calculus by Leibniz and Newton gave a very strong impulse to the theory; the 18th century witnessed considerable progress in the work of Jakob and Daniel Bernoulli, Jean Le Rond d'Alembert, Leonhard Euler, and others. Much of this work was of purely formal character, and mathematical rigour was not the primary concern of the investigators.

Though Newton and Leibniz avoided divergent series, formal and uninhibited use of them brought such mathematical rewards that the temptation was too much to withstand, and divergent series became—mostly through the work of Euler—an accepted tool of investigation. Mathematical instinct of the great mathematicians of the 18th century prevented them, however, from making mistakes, and their results, properly interpreted, can now be proved rigorously. Rigorous foundations for the theory of infinite series were laid in the first half of the 19th century by the French mathematician Augustin-Louis Cauchy and Norwegian mathematician Niels Henrik Abel; their definitions and proved results can be found in all textbooks of calculus. Their attitude toward divergent series, however, was purely negative. (Abel wrote in 1828: "Divergent series are the invention of the devil, and it is shameful to base on them any demonstration whatsoever.") The respect commanded by the work of Cauchy and Abel banished divergent series from mathematics for more than half a century. Their work on the foundations of the theory of series was continued by others in the 19th century, in particular by Peter Gustav Lejeune Dirichlet, Bernhard Riemann, and Karl Weierstrass. By the last decade of the 19th century, the effects of Abel's anathema began to disappear, and the work of Ernesto Cesàro, Émile Borel, Leopold Fejér, and others showed that the theory of divergent series can be put on a rigorous basis and is a source of great progress in mathematics. In the 20th century the work of the British mathematicians Godfrey Harold Hardy and John Edensor Littlewood brought major breakthroughs and extended the field in depth. Important progress in Tauberian theorems (of the Slovak mathematician Alfred Tauber) was made by Norbert Wiener.

Sequences and series. The notion of a series has a close connection with that of a sequence, a set of numbers arranged in order. The simplest example of a sequence is that of the positive integers 1, 2, 3, . . . , n, ... A sequence may be finite or infinite, depending on whether the number of terms is limited or unlimited. An infinite sequence of numbers exists if every positive integer 1, 2, 3, . . . , n, . . . is assigned a number; in what follows, the expression "sequence" means an infinite sequence of numbers.

Examples of sequences

Some examples of sequences are as follows: a sequence of squares of positive integers (see sequence 35), an alternating sequence of the integers one and zero (see 36), an alternating sequence of integers (alternating means that the sign of each term is opposite to that of the preceding term; see 37), and a sequence of fractions each with numerator one and with denominators ascending in integer value (see 38).

The numbers constituting a sequence are called the terms of the sequence (such as the first, the second, . . . , the nth, . . .). It is customary to denote a sequence by using a single letter with a subscript (called the index) to indicate the position of the term—for example, a_1, a_2, a_3, a_4, . . . , a_n, ... An abbreviated notation $\{a_n\}$ is also used. It is assumed here that the terms are real numbers (natural numbers, their ratios, negatives, and limits); the case of sequences of complex numbers is considered later.

A series is the indicated sum of a sequence of numbers; for example, $a_1 + a_2 + a_3 + \cdots + a_n + \cdots$. A series can also be finite or infinite, depending on the sequence. It is customary to denote a series by using the Greek letter sigma Σ, to indicate summation. For example, $a_1 + a_2 + a_3 + \cdots a_n + \cdots$ is written $\sum_{n=1}^{\infty} a_n$, or simply Σa_n.

The properties of series are related to the properties of sequences. If every term in a sequence is less than or equal to the following term, the sequence is said to be increasing (or nondecreasing). In other words, if, in $\{a_n\}$, a_n is less than or equal to a_{n+1} for every n, then $\{a_n\}$ is increasing. If each term is less than the following one (that is, if $a_n < a_{n+1}$), the sequence is strictly increasing. On the other hand, if, for a sequence $\{a_n\}$, a_n is greater than or equal to a_{n+1}, the sequence is decreasing (or nonincreasing); if $a_n > a_{n+1}$, it is strictly decreasing.

Sequences that are either increasing or decreasing are called monotone (monotonically increasing or monotonically decreasing, as the case may be; see 35 and 38). Some sequences are not monotone (see 36 and 37). If all the terms of the sequence a_n are less than a given number M (in symbols, $a_n < M$ for some M and all n), the sequence is said to be bounded above. If all a_n exceed a certain number, $\{a_n\}$ is said to be bounded below (see 35). Sequences bounded both above and below are simply called bounded (see 36). Some sequences are not bounded either above or below (see 37).

Convergence and divergence

Convergence. A sequence $\{a_n\}$ is said to converge (or tend) to the limit a if the terms a_n approach a indefinitely as n increases (see 39). A precise definition is as follows: a_n tends to the limit a if, given any positive number (no matter how small) symbolized by the Greek letter epsilon, ε, the magnitude of the difference, $|a_n - a|$, is less than ε for all n large enough. If $\{a_n\}$ tends to a limit, the sequence is said to be convergent; otherwise it is divergent. The following type of divergence is important: $\{a_n\}$ is said to diverge to infinity, or the limit of a_n as n approaches infinity is positive infinity (see 40), if for any number M (no matter how large) a_n is greater than M for all n large enough; divergence of a sequence to negative infinity is defined in a similar way.

Of the sequences mentioned above, one (see 38) converges to the limit 0; others (see 35 and 36) diverge. Whether a given sequence converges and, if so, toward what limit is not always easy to decide. The following facts, however, can be helpful.

I. If $a_n \to a$ and $b_n \to b$, then the limit of the sum, the product, and the ratio of a_n and b_n is the sum, the product, and the ratio of a and b, respectively (see 41), the last relation requiring, however, the additional assumption that b is not equal to ($\neq$) 0.

II. Every convergent sequence is necessarily bounded; an example (see 36) shows that the converse is not true: a bounded sequence need not converge.

III. If a sequence is increasing and bounded above or decreasing and bounded below, it converges.

IV. If a sequence converges, then its terms, coming arbitrarily close to the limit, must also come arbitrarily close to each other, provided the indices are large enough. The converse of this is also true, though less easy to prove, and the result is the following important theorem of the 19th-century French mathematician Augustin-Louis Cauchy: a sequence $\{a_n\}$ converges if and only if it has the following property: for any positive number ε (no matter how small) $|a_m - a_n| < \varepsilon$ for all m and n large enough.

Starting with a sequence a_1, a_2, . . . , a_n, . . . , a new sequence s_1, s_2, . . . , s_n, . . . is formed by the following rule: a sequence of partial sums is generally labeled s_n and defined as a sum of the first n of its terms (see 42). If $\{s_n\}$ converges to limit s, then it is said that the infinite series, an infinite sum of a_k (see 43), converges to sum s.

(35) $1^2, 2^2, 3^2, \ldots, n^2, \ldots$

(36) $1, 0, 1, 0, 1, \ldots$

(37) $1, -2, 3, -4, 5, -6, \ldots$

(38) $1, \frac{1}{2}, \frac{1}{3}, \ldots \frac{1}{n}, \ldots$

Note: (35), (36), (37), and (38) are examples of sequences.

(39) $\lim_{n\to\infty} a_n = a,$ or $a_n \to a$

(40) $\lim_{n\to\infty} a_n = +\infty,$ or $a_n \to +\infty$

(41) $a_n + b_n \to a + b, \quad a_n b_n \to ab, \quad \frac{a_n}{b_n} \to \frac{a}{b}$

The numbers s_n are called the partial sums of the series Σa_n, and the relation $s_n \to s$ is also written $\Sigma a_n = s$. The numbers a_n are the terms of the series Σa_n.

For any sequence $b_1, b_2, \ldots, b_n, \ldots$, there is always an associated series that is a sum of differences constructed of b_k and with typical term b_n minus b_{n-1} (see 44), the partial sums of which are $b_1, b_2, b_3, \ldots, b_n, \ldots$. Hence, every series is represented by a sequence (that of its partial sums) and, conversely, every sequence by a series. It follows that every statement about series can be given in a form bearing on sequences, and conversely (but usually, in individual cases, one form may be preferable to the other). For example, Cauchy's theorem stated above and pertaining to sequences assumes, in the case of series, the following form:

V. A series Σa_n converges if, and only if, given any positive number ε, $|a_{m+1} + a_{m+2} + \cdots + a_n| < \varepsilon$ for all m large enough and any n greater than m. In particular (taking $n = m + 1$), the terms of a convergent series must necessarily tend to 0.

Tests for convergence

For example, if a is any number and q is any number of absolute value less than 1, the series $a + aq + aq^2 + \cdots + aq^{n-1} + \cdots = \Sigma aq^{n-1}$ (called a geometric series) converges, and its sum is $a/(1 - q)$.

The series $\Sigma 1/n = 1 + 1/2 + 1/3 + \cdots$, called the harmonic series, diverges.

If the terms of a series are positive numbers, the series is called positive. The partial sums of a positive series form a strictly increasing sequence and, in view of proposition III, a positive series converges if its partial sums are bounded above. If the partial sums of a positive series are not bounded above, the series diverges to $+\infty$. Proposition III also shows the following:

VI. If Σa_n and Σb_n are positive series and if $a_n \geq b_n$ for all n, then the convergence of Σa_n implies convergence of Σb_n and, equivalently, the divergence of Σb_n implies that of Σa_n. This result, which is usually called the comparison test, is very useful because the knowledge of convergence or divergence of some positive series can be used to obtain information about other series.

For example, from the fact that the geometric series Σaq^{n-1} converges if a is positive and q is positive and less than 1, it is possible to deduce the following corollaries for positive series.

VII. If $a_{n+1}/a_n \to l$, then, if $l < 1$, the series Σa_n converges; if $l > 1$, the series diverges. This is known as the ratio test.

VIII. If $a_n^{1/n} \to l$ and if $l < 1$, the series Σa_n converges; if $l > 1$, the series diverges. This is known as the root test.

If the limit l in VII or VIII exists but is equal to 1, the test fails (the case $l = 1$ can occur for both convergent and divergent series) and other tests are sought. There are many of them, but the most useful is the following one based on the notion of the integral.

IX. If $f(x)$ is a function defined for x positive, itself positive and steadily decreasing to 0 as x increases indefinitely, then the series $\Sigma f(n) = f(1) + f(2) + f(3) + \cdots$ converges or diverges according as the $\int_1^\infty f(x)dx$ is finite or not. This is known as the integral test.

When applied to the function $f(x) = x^{-k}$, in which k is a fixed positive constant, the test shows that the series that is a sum of reciprocals of kth powers of positive integers (see 45) converges if $k > 1$ and diverges in all other cases. The result is not deducible from either the ratio or root test, because, for the series $\sum_{n=1}^{\infty} n^{-k}$, l is equal to 1 both in VII and VIII.

Of interest among series that are not positive is a type called alternating series; this name is given to series $a_1 - a_2 + a_3 - a_4 + \cdots$ in which the numbers a_n themselves are of constant sign. It can be shown that such a series converges if $\{a_n\}$ decreases monotonically to 0. For example, the series $1 - 1/2 + 1/3 - 1/4 + \cdots$ converges.

Absolute convergence

A series Σa_n is said to converge absolutely if $\Sigma |a_k|$ converges. Cauchy's theorem for series shows that, if a series converges absolutely, then it converges in the ordinary sense; but the example of the convergent alternating series $1 - 1/2 + 1/3 - \cdots$ shows that a series may converge without converging absolutely. It follows that absolutely convergent series form a special class among all convergent series. Because series $\Sigma |a_k|$ have positive or zero terms, the problem of whether a given series converges absolutely can be solved by applying one of the tests for the convergence of positive series. In many cases the simplest way of proving that a certain series converges is by showing that the series converges absolutely, and this shows the importance of positive series for the general theory of series. Absolutely convergent series have a number of properties that are not shared by all convergent series. The most important of these properties is the fact that if a series converges absolutely, then arbitrary changes in the order of the terms of the series affect neither the convergence nor the sum of the series.

The situation is completely different for series that converge but do not do so absolutely (such series are called conditionally convergent); by a suitable change of the order of the terms, such a series can be made to converge to any prescribed sum or can even be made divergent. This is a theorem of the 19th-century German mathematician Bernhard Riemann. Hence, unlike the case of absolutely convergent series, a conditionally convergent series has no intrinsic sum and everything depends on the order of the terms.

The number of important series that occur in mathematics is enormous. A few basic convergent series are given in five examples of series the sums of which are known and are expressed in terms of the natural logarithm and the numbers π and e (see 46).

Series of functions. If $\Sigma u_n(x)$ is a series the terms $u_1(x), u_2(x), \ldots, u_n(x), \ldots$ of which are functions defined in an interval of the real variable x and if $\Sigma u_n(x)$ converges at each point of the interval, then the series is said to converge pointwise in the interval; $f(x)$ denotes the sum, and $S_n(x)$ the partial sums, of the series. Pointwise convergence means that for any positive ε there is an index n_0, depending in general on ε and x, in symbols $n_0 = n_0(\varepsilon, x)$, such that $|f(x) - S_n(x)| < \varepsilon$ for $n > n_0$. If for each $\varepsilon > 0$ an n_0 can be found independent of x, the series is said to converge uniformly in the interval considered; geometrically this means that for each $n > n_0$ the graph of the curve $y = s_n(x)$ and that of the curve $y = f(x)$ differ by less than ε in the whole interval under consideration. Pointwise convergence in general does not preserve properties of the terms of the series. For example, if the functions $u_n(x)$ are continuous and $\Sigma u_n(x)$ converges pointwise, the sum $\Sigma u_n(x)$ need not be continuous. A simple example is provided by the series $(1 - x) + x(1 - x) + x^2(1 - x) + \cdots$, which converges at each point of the interval $0 \leq x \leq 1$ and the sum of which is equal to 0 for $x = 1$ and equal to 1 at the remaining points of the interval. Similarly,

(42) $$\begin{cases} s_1 = a_1, \quad s_2 = a_1 + a_2, \quad s_3 = a_1 + a_2 + a_3, \quad \ldots \\ s_n = a_1 + a_2 + \cdots + a_n, \cdots \end{cases}$$

(43) $$a_1 + a_2 + a_3 + \cdots + a_n + \cdots$$

(44) $$b_1 + (b_2 - b_1) + (b_3 - b_2) + \cdots + (b_n - b_{n-1}) + \cdots$$

(45) $$1^{-k} + 2^{-k} + 3^{-k} + \cdots + n^{-k} + \cdots = \sum_{n=1}^{\infty} n^{-k}$$

(46) $$\begin{cases} 1 - \frac{1}{2} + \frac{1}{3} - \frac{1}{4} + \frac{1}{5} - \cdots = \ln 2 \\ 1 - \frac{1}{3} + \frac{1}{5} - \frac{1}{7} + \frac{1}{9} - \cdots = \frac{1}{4}\pi \text{ (Leibniz' series)} \\ 1 + \frac{1}{2^2} + \frac{1}{3^2} + \frac{1}{4^2} + \frac{1}{5^2} + \cdots = \frac{1}{6}\pi^2 \\ 1 + \frac{1}{3^2} + \frac{1}{5^2} + \frac{1}{7^2} + \frac{1}{9^2} + \cdots = \frac{1}{8}\pi^2 \\ 1 + \frac{1}{1} + \frac{1}{1 \times 2} + \frac{1}{1 \times 2 \times 3} + \frac{1}{1 \times 2 \times 3 \times 4} + \cdots \\ \quad = e = 2.7182818\ldots \end{cases}$$

These series converge to known values as shown.

if the $u_n(x)$ are integrable over an interval and the series $\Sigma u_n(x)$ converges pointwise, the sum of $\Sigma u_n(x)$ need not be integrable. The significance of the notion of uniform convergence is that the sum of a uniformly convergent series of functions inherits many important properties of the terms—in particular their continuity and integrability. Not all properties, however, are preserved by uniform convergence; for example, the sum of a uniformly convergent series of differentiable functions need not be differentiable. As a matter of fact, examples of continuous and nowhere differentiable functions are usually given as sums of uniformly convergent series of differentiable functions. The three theorems that now follow about uniformly convergent series are particularly useful.

X. If the functions $u_n(x)$ are continuous in an interval and if the series $\Sigma u_n(x)$ converges uniformly in the interval, the sum of the series is continuous in the interval.

XI. If the $u_n(x)$ are integrable over a finite interval (a, b) and if $\Sigma u_n(x)$ converges uniformly in (a, b), then the sum $f(x)$ of $\Sigma u_n(x)$ is integrable over (a, b) and a definite integral of the function f is written as a sum of integrals of functions u_n (see 47).

XII. If each term of the series $\Sigma u_n(x)$ has a continuous derivative in a finite interval (a, b), if the series $\Sigma u'_n(x)$ of derivatives converges uniformly in (a, b), and if the series $\Sigma u_n(c)$ converges for one point c in (a, b), then the series $\Sigma u_n(x)$ also converges uniformly in (a, b), its sum $f(x)$ is differentiable, and $f'(x) = \Sigma u'_n(x)$.

There are no special tests for the pointwise convergence of series because pointwise convergence simply means ordinary convergence at each point x separately. There are tests for the uniform convergence of a series of functions, among which the following, usually called Weierstrass' M-test, is particularly useful.

Uniformly convergent series; Weierstrass' M-test

XIII. If there are positive constants $M_1, M_2, \ldots, M_n, \ldots$ such that the series ΣM_n converges and if $|u_n(x)| \leq M_n$ for each n and all x of an interval, then the series $\Sigma u_n(x)$ converges uniformly in the interval.

Only the uniform convergence of series has been considered. There are parallel definitions and results for the uniform convergence of sequences. One can also consider the uniform convergence of double series and sequences. Special types of series of functions are particularly important for various branches of analysis (as in the Fourier series described later). The convergence of series $\Sigma u_n(z)$ the terms of which depend on a complex variable $z = x + iy$ may be considered. The most important among them is the case of power series.

Power series. Power series are of the form with coefficients a_n (see 48), in which the a_n are constants (in general, complex) and $z = x + iy$ is a complex variable; in the symbol $\Sigma a_n z^n$ the index n ranges through the values $0, 1, 2, \ldots, n, \ldots$. Each power series has a circle of convergence; this is a circle (disk) with the centre at the point $z = 0$ and the following properties: the series converges at each point interior to the circle and diverges at each point exterior to the circle. As to the behaviour on the circumference of the circle of convergence, $\Sigma a_n z^n$ may converge at some points, diverge at others. The intersection of the circle of convergence with the real axis is an interval $(-R, R)$; and the series $\Sigma a_n x^n$, a power series of the real variable x, converges in the interior of this interval and diverges in the exterior. The radius R of the circle of convergence is called the radius of convergence of the power series. The circle of convergence can degenerate to a point; each power series $\Sigma a_n z^n$ necessarily converges at the point $z = 0$ but may converge at no other point: the series $\Sigma n! z^n$ is an example of this ($n!$—factorial n—is the product $n(n-1)(n-2) \cdots 1$). The circle of convergence may also cover the whole complex plane, as in the series $\Sigma z^n/n!$. Finally, the radius of convergence may have any prescribed positive value R because the radius of convergence of the geometric series $\Sigma (z/R)^n$ is precisely R.

Circle of convergence of power series

At each point interior to the circle of convergence, the power series not only converges but converges absolutely. What is very important is that, in each circle concentric with the circle of convergence but of smaller radius, the power series converges uniformly. Series of the form $a_0 + a_1(z-b) + a_2(z-b)^2 + \cdots = \Sigma a_n(z-b)^n$, in which b is a fixed complex number, are called power series with centre b. Their study does not require the introduction of new concepts because by replacing $z - b$ with a new variable Z the series is reduced to the previously discussed case $\Sigma a_n Z^n$. It follows that $\Sigma a_n(z-b)^n$ also has its circle of convergence, but this time the circle has its centre at the point b. Functions representable by power series have very important properties. Listed above are a few basic power series, considering for simplicity only real values of z (see 49).

(A.Zy./C.L.F./Ed.)

(47) $$\int_a^b f(x)dx = \sum \int_a^b u_n(x)dx$$

(48) $$a_0 + a_1 z + a_2 z^2 + \cdots + a_n z^n + \cdots = \Sigma a_n z^n$$

(49)
$$(1+x)^a = 1 + ax + \frac{a(a-1)}{1 \times 2}x^2 + \frac{a(a-1)(a-2)}{1 \times 2 \times 3}x^3 + \cdots \quad \text{(Newton's binomial series; R = 1)}$$

$$\ln(1+x) = x - \frac{1}{2}x^2 + \frac{1}{3}x^3 - \cdots \quad (R = 1)$$

$$\arctan x = x - \frac{1}{3}x^3 + \frac{1}{5}x^5 - \cdots \quad (R = 1)$$

$$e^x = 1 + \frac{x}{1} + \frac{x^2}{1 \times 2} + \frac{x^3}{1 \times 2 \times 3} + \cdots \quad (R = \infty)$$

$$\cos x = 1 - \frac{x^2}{1 \times 2} + \frac{x^4}{1 \times 2 \times 3 \times 4} - \frac{x^6}{1 \times 2 \times 3 \times 4 \times 5 \times 6} + \cdots \quad (R = \infty)$$

$$\sin x = x - \frac{x^3}{1 \times 2 \times 3} + \frac{x^5}{1 \times 2 \times 3 \times 4 \times 5} - \cdots \quad (R = \infty)$$

Vector and tensor analysis

Many physical quantities, such as temperature, pressure, and mass, have only magnitude. The numbers representing them are called scalars and obey the simple rules of arithmetic. On the other hand, quantities such as velocity, force, or position in two or more dimensions relative to a fixed point have both magnitude and direction and can be represented mathematically by two or more numbers that constitute what is called a vector. Geometrically, a vector is drawn as a line in a specific direction with a length equal to its magnitude (Figure 13).

Resolution of forces by vector parallelogram

The earliest knowledge of how to manipulate vector quantities dates from the time of Galileo, who in the course of his studies in the 17th century first formulated the simple parallelogram law for combining forces. If two forces act on a body, their resultant force can be obtained from a parallelogram in which two adjacent sides have lengths and directions representing the forces. The two forces acting together are equivalent to a single force represented, in magnitude and direction, by the diagonal of the parallelogram. This is equivalent to the rule that two or more vectors can be added by putting their geometric representations end to end, so to speak.

A vector can be multiplied by a positive number by simply multiplying its magnitude by that number (it has the same direction). To multiply a vector by a negative number, its direction is reversed and its magnitude multiplied. The process of multiplication by numbers is called scalar multiplication. An example of its application to physical quantities is the process of multiplying the mass of a body by its velocity to give its momentum. The momentum of a body is, thus, a vector quantity having the same direction as the velocity and a magnitude equal to the product of the magnitudes of its mass and its velocity.

Expression of vectors in three-dimensional space

Vectors in three dimensions may be expressed in the following way. A set of three mutually perpendicular vectors each of unit length is chosen, and any vector may be represented uniquely as a combination of these. If these vectors are written ***i***, ***j***, and ***k*** (it should be noted that vectors in physical applications are often printed in boldface type), then any vector can be represented by $a_1\boldsymbol{i} + a_2\boldsymbol{j} + a_3\boldsymbol{k}$. The numbers a_1, a_2, and a_3 are called the components of the vector. By Pythagoras' theorem, the length of $a_1\boldsymbol{i} + a_2\boldsymbol{j} + a_3\boldsymbol{k}$ is the square root of the sum of the squares of the components. The magnitude of an arbitrary vector $\boldsymbol{v}$ is written $\|\boldsymbol{v}\|$.

Vectors may be multiplied together in two ways. The scalar product of two vectors (also called the dot product) is, in two dimensions only, defined to be the product of their lengths multiplied by the cosine of the angle between their directions. A physical example concerns the work done if a force $\boldsymbol{F}$ moves in a straight line that has magnitude and direction $\boldsymbol{d}$. If the force moves along the direction of $\boldsymbol{d}$, the work is $\|\boldsymbol{F}\|\ \|\boldsymbol{d}\|$; if it acts at an angle θ to that direction, it is $\|\boldsymbol{F}\|\ \|\boldsymbol{d}\| \cos\theta$. If the force acts at right angles to the direction, the work done is zero.

In three dimensions, two vectors can be multiplied to give a third. The vector product of $\boldsymbol{a}$ and $\boldsymbol{b}$ is written as $\boldsymbol{a} \times \boldsymbol{b}$ and is also called the cross product. It is a vector perpendicular to $\boldsymbol{a}$ and $\boldsymbol{b}$ with length $\|\boldsymbol{a}\|\ \|\boldsymbol{b}\| \sin\theta$, θ being the angle between them. When an electric charge moves in a magnetic field, for example, it experiences a force that is mutually perpendicular to the field and the direction of motion, hence the principle from which it is inferred that the wire moving in the magnetic field of a generator will carry electrical current.

Many physical quantities take the form of mappings (or correspondences) from one collection of vectors to another. For example, the stress at a point in a fluid is the relation between two vectors. The stress is an example of a tensor, which has a general mathematical definition that will be presented below. It will be seen that the tensor concept depends upon ideas involving more than one vector—in fact, collections of vectors that are called vector spaces. The idea of vectors and tensors was suggested by particular needs in problems of mathematical physics.

Once the concepts of vector and tensor are known from the study of particular physical or mathematical questions, it becomes natural, by the route of mathematical reasoning, to express individual vectors or tensors as members of an appropriate space. By doing so, a setting of generality is established and the properties of these entities can be studied without reference to particular representatives that might have been encountered first historically or that might have been important in special cases. Therefore, with the advantage of historical maturity, discussion will begin here with the treatment of a vector space. (Ed.)

VECTOR ALGEBRA AND ANALYSIS

Vector space: history and basic ideas. The germinal idea of an abstract vector space that is not limited to applications grew out of investigations of the mathematicians Sir William Rowan Hamilton and Hermann Günther Grassmann during the early 1840s. In that era mathematicians still regarded complex numbers that involve the square root of -1 with a mixture of mysticism and suspicion, although by 1800 Caspar Wessel had suggested representing the complex number $a_1 + ia_2$, in which i is the square root of -1, concretely by a point in a plane (specifically, by the point $[a_1, a_2]$ so that a_1 and a_2 become distances to the point measured along straight lines parallel to two rectilinear axes). In 1831 Carl Friedrich Gauss showed that complex numbers can be regarded as ordered pairs of real numbers for which the operations of addition and multiplication are defined (see equations 50) in terms of the component parts of the pairs. The resulting algebra of pairs is a perfect replica of the algebra of complex numbers, without any reference to complex numbers or to the symbol i. This algebra proved to be useful in describing rotations in the plane.

Unaware of Gauss's work, Hamilton discovered the same device six years later and continued to search for a comparable algebraic description of rotations in three-dimensional space. His early efforts were thwarted, however, by an algebraic dogma that insisted on certain familiar properties of addition, subtraction, and multiplication growing out of centuries of exclusive concern with familiar numbers. Each of the number systems known was an example

$$(50)\quad \begin{cases}(a_1, a_2) + (b_1, b_2) = (a_1 + b_1, a_2 + b_2)\\ (a_1, a_2) \cdot (b_1, b_2) = (a_1b_1 - a_2b_2, a_1b_2 + a_2b_1)\end{cases}$$

$$(51)\quad (a_1, a_2, \ldots, a_n) + (b_1, b_2, \ldots, b_n) = (a_1 + b_1, a_2 + b_2, \ldots, a_n + b_n)$$

$$(52)\quad c(a_1, a_2, \ldots, a_n) = (ca_1, ca_2, \ldots, ca_n)$$

of an algebraic system that in today's terminology is called a field. Formally, a field is a set of elements and two operations, called addition and multiplication, satisfying well-defined postulates, as discussed fully in the article ALGEBRA: *Fields*.

Hamilton's modification of the field postulates

Hamilton's eventual success came from his willingness to discard the notion that any useful and consistent algebraic system must satisfy all of the field postulates. His new algebra provided a means of describing rotations in three-dimensional space by an algebraic system that satisfies all the field postulates except the commutative law for multiplication, which identifies the products $a \cdot b$ and $b \cdot a$ as equal. In Hamilton's algebra $a \cdot b = -b \cdot a$. Thus, Hamilton provided the first example of a noncommutative field, which is now called a division ring. The elements of his algebra were called quaternions.

The realization that useful algebraic systems could be constructed by replacing some traditional postulates proved to be as liberating to algebra as the corresponding discovery had been to geometry only a few years before, when the parallel postulate of Euclidean geometry had been replaced by Gauss and the Hungarian and Russian discoverers of non-Euclidean geometry, János Bolyai and Nikolay Ivanovich Lobachevsky. Mathematical heresy apparently was in the air in those days. In 1844 Grassmann independently developed a theory that was far more imaginative and comprehensive than Hamilton's, providing an algebraic mechanism for n-dimensional space and allowing for various definitions of multiplication. At the same time in England, Arthur Cayley invented matrix algebra, which includes the quaternions invented by Hamilton as a very special case.

The contemporary concept of a vector is a natural or closely related abstraction and extension of the observation that an ordered pair of real (not complex) numbers (a_1, a_2) represents a unique point in the Cartesian plane (that for which pairs of numbers are identified with numbers as described above); similarly, an ordered triple of numbers (a_1, a_2, a_3) represents a point in three-dimensional Cartesian space (Figure 13), and an ordered n-tuple of numbers $(a_1, a_2, \ldots, a_n)$ represents a point in Cartesian n-dimensional space.

Addition of two n-tuples is defined by the parallelogram law, which states (see 51) that components of the n-tuples are added to form components of a new n-tuple called the sum. Multiplication of an n-tuple by a number is defined by extending the multiplication (by the number) to each

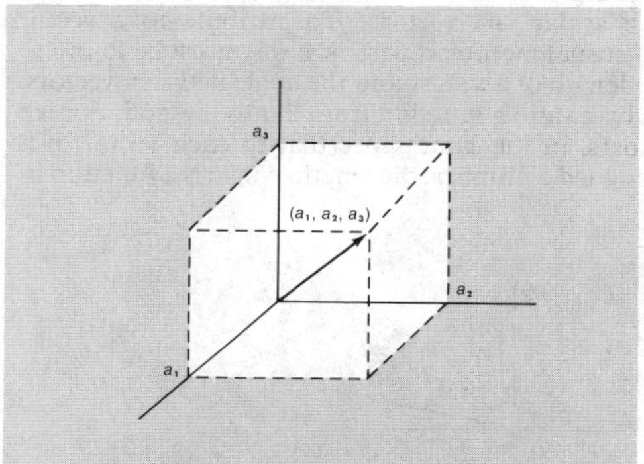

Figure 13: A vector regarded geometrically as a directed line segment (or arrow) from the origin to a point with coordinates a_1, a_2, a_3 (see text).

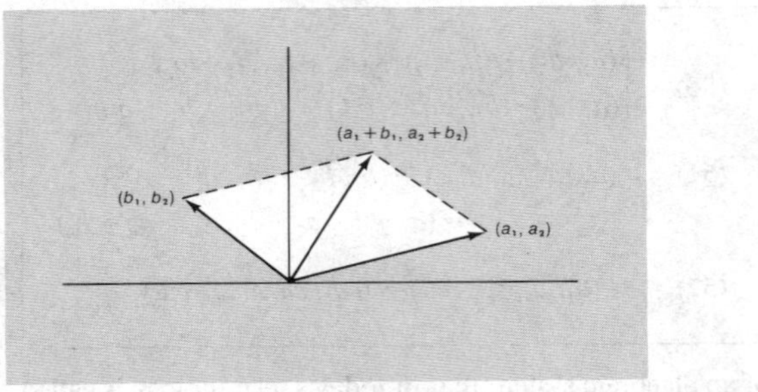

Figure 14: Addition of two n-tuples (see text).

component (see 52). The laws of addition and multiplication are illustrated in Figures 14 and 15.

The resulting algebraic system is a particular example of a vector space, and the example is general enough to suggest an axiomatic formulation of the concept of a vector space. To begin with, observe that two types of objects are involved in this example: numbers (which are called scalars and will be denoted here by lower case letters) and n-tuples of numbers (which are called vectors and will be denoted here by capital letters). Normally the set of scalars is assumed to be a field, although a comparable theory of vector spaces exists for the case in which the scalars form only a division ring. It need not be assumed that a vector is an n-tuple of scalars; in general, the set V of vectors can be any set of objects that can be combined according to specific laws. Because the laws make specific references to a field of scalars, the term vector space over a field is used. Two of the most important fields that appear in this context are the field $\mathfrak{R}$ of real numbers and the field $\mathfrak{C}$ of complex numbers.

In the familiar notation used for many years for vectors in three-dimensional real space $\mathfrak{R}^3$, the vectors along the three mutually perpendicular axes are denoted $\boldsymbol{i}$, $\boldsymbol{j}$, and $\boldsymbol{k}$.

The standard basis for $\mathfrak{R}^3$

Then an arbitrary vector $\boldsymbol{v}$ is written $\boldsymbol{v} = x\boldsymbol{i} + y\boldsymbol{j} + z\boldsymbol{k}$, thus designating the point (x, y, z) in $\mathfrak{R}^3$. This particular basis is called the standard basis for $\mathfrak{R}^3$, and much of the late-19th-century work in vector analysis and vector calculus, developed by the American physicist J. Willard Gibbs and the English physicist Oliver Heaviside, was expressed in this form. One of the great advantages of the abstract approach to vector space algebra is that it emphasizes coordinate-free methods and thereby avoids long arithmetic computations for properties that are intrinsic, and therefore it is independent of the choice of coordinates.

It is important to observe that the definition of a vector space describes only the algebraic operations of vector sum and scalar multiple of a vector. Special types of vector spaces can be obtained by superimposing additional operations on a vector space. The most glaring omission up to this point concerns metric concepts or concepts that define distance. In itself a vector space provides no means for measuring distance, or angle, or area, or any of the usual concepts needed for geometry and most applications. Therefore, in particular, the reference in the previous paragraph to mutually perpendicular axes was intuitive and premature.

Products: scalar and vector. To attribute to a vector space $\mathfrak{L}$ the usual metric properties, a way must be found to define the length of a vector and the angle between vectors. Length is by nature a function from $\mathfrak{L}$ into the nonnegative real numbers, in the same sense that to each vector in $\mathfrak{L}$ there is assigned a number, the length. Angle is a function in a similar sense from the space of all ordered pairs of vectors into the real numbers between 0 and π. Therefore, the real numbers are needed for such computations; for simplicity the scalar field can be chosen to be the complex numbers $\mathfrak{C}$, which include the real scalar field as a special case. Accordingly, the complex conjugate $\bar{z}$ of a complex number $z = x + iy$ is defined by $\bar{z} = x - iy$. It follows that $\overline{z_1 + z_2} = \bar{z}_1 + \bar{z}_2$, and $\overline{z_1 z_2} = \bar{z}_1 \bar{z}_2$. The magnitude $|z|$ of z is defined by $|z| = \sqrt{x^2 + y^2}$.

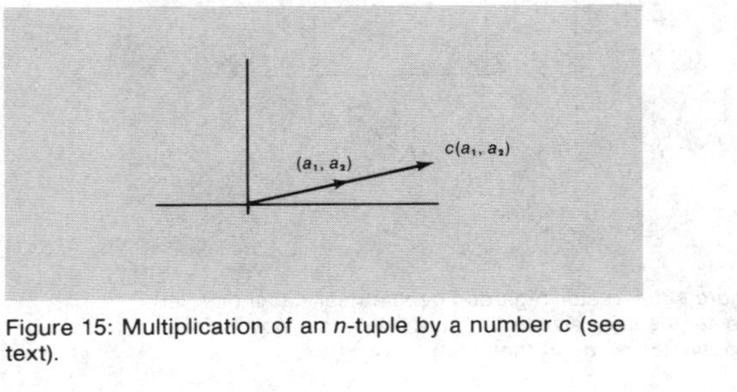

Figure 15: Multiplication of an n-tuple by a number c (see text).

$$(53)\quad \begin{cases} \text{For all } \boldsymbol{A}, \boldsymbol{B} \text{ in } \mathfrak{L} \text{ and all } c_1, c_2 \text{ in } \mathfrak{C}: \\ p(c_1\boldsymbol{A}_1 + c_2\boldsymbol{A}_2, \boldsymbol{B}) = c_1 p(\boldsymbol{A}_1, \boldsymbol{B}) + c_2 p(\boldsymbol{A}_2, \boldsymbol{B}), \\ p(\boldsymbol{B}, \boldsymbol{A}) = \overline{p(\boldsymbol{A}, \boldsymbol{B})}, \\ p(\boldsymbol{A}, \boldsymbol{A}) \text{ is a positive real number if } \boldsymbol{A} \neq 0. \end{cases}$$

$$(54)\quad p((a_1, \ldots, a_n), (b_1, \ldots, b_n)) = a_1\bar{b}_1 + \cdots + a_n\bar{b}_n$$

$$(55)\quad p((a_1, \ldots, a_n), (b_1, \ldots, b_n)) = a_1 b_1 + \cdots + a_n b_n$$

$$(56)\quad p(f, g) = \int_a^b f(x)\overline{g(x)}\,dx$$

$$(57)\quad |p(\boldsymbol{A}, \boldsymbol{B})|^2 \leq p(\boldsymbol{A}, \boldsymbol{A})p(\boldsymbol{B}, \boldsymbol{B})$$

$$(58)\quad \|\boldsymbol{A}\| = \sqrt{p(\boldsymbol{A}, \boldsymbol{A})}$$

$$(59)\quad \begin{cases} \|c\boldsymbol{A}\| = |c|\,\|\boldsymbol{A}\| \\ \|\boldsymbol{A}\| > 0 \text{ if } \boldsymbol{A} \neq 0 \\ \|\boldsymbol{A} + \boldsymbol{B}\| \leq \|\boldsymbol{A}\| + \|\boldsymbol{B}\| \end{cases}$$

$$(60)\quad d(\boldsymbol{A}, \boldsymbol{B}) = \|\boldsymbol{A} - \boldsymbol{B}\|$$

$$(61)\quad d(\boldsymbol{A}, \boldsymbol{B}) \leq d(\boldsymbol{A}, \boldsymbol{C}) + d(\boldsymbol{C}, \boldsymbol{B})$$

$$(62)\quad \frac{|p(\boldsymbol{A}, \boldsymbol{B})|}{\|\boldsymbol{A}\|\,\|\boldsymbol{B}\|} \leq 1 \text{ if } \boldsymbol{A} \neq 0 \neq \boldsymbol{B}$$

$$(63)\quad \cos\{\psi(\boldsymbol{A}, \boldsymbol{B})\} = \frac{p(\boldsymbol{A}, \boldsymbol{B})}{\|\boldsymbol{A}\|\|\boldsymbol{B}\|} \text{ for } 0 \leq \psi(\boldsymbol{A}, \boldsymbol{B}) \leq \pi$$

$$(64)\quad \begin{cases} \|\boldsymbol{A}\| = \sqrt{a_1^2 + \cdots + a_n^2} \\ d(\boldsymbol{A}, \boldsymbol{B}) = \sqrt{(a_1 - b_1)^2 + \cdots + (a_n - b_n)^2} \\ \boldsymbol{A} \cdot \boldsymbol{B} = \|\boldsymbol{A}\|\,\|\boldsymbol{B}\| \cos\{\psi(\boldsymbol{A}, \boldsymbol{B})\} \end{cases}$$

$$(65)\quad (a_1, a_2, a_3) \times (b_1, b_2, b_3) = (a_2b_3 - a_3b_2, a_3b_1 - a_1b_3, a_1b_2 - a_2b_1)$$

$$(66)\quad \begin{cases} \boldsymbol{A} \times \boldsymbol{B} = -\boldsymbol{B} \times \boldsymbol{A} \\ (\boldsymbol{A} + \boldsymbol{B}) \times \boldsymbol{C} = (\boldsymbol{A} \times \boldsymbol{C}) + (\boldsymbol{B} \times \boldsymbol{C}) \\ (c\boldsymbol{A}) \times \boldsymbol{B} = c(\boldsymbol{A} \times \boldsymbol{B}) \\ \boldsymbol{A} \cdot (\boldsymbol{A} \times \boldsymbol{B}) = 0 \\ \|\boldsymbol{A} \times \boldsymbol{B}\|^2 = \|\boldsymbol{A}\|^2\,\|\boldsymbol{B}\|^2 - (\boldsymbol{A} \cdot \boldsymbol{B})^2 \end{cases}$$

If a vector space $\mathfrak{L}$ is defined so that vectors multiply with members of the field $\mathfrak{C}$ of complex numbers, a scalar product (or inner product) on $\mathfrak{L}$ is a function p with certain properties that maps pairs of vectors into complex numbers. The properties of the function p are those that define the inner product (see 53).

Examples of inner products

Examples of inner products are the following: First, on the space of n-tuples of complex numbers (see 54), p maps the pair $(a_1, \ldots, a_n)$, $(b_1, \ldots, b_n)$ into $a_1\bar{b}_1 + \cdots + a_n\bar{b}_n$. Second, on the space of n-tuples of real numbers (see 55), the value of the function at $(a_1, \ldots, a_n)$, $(b_1, \ldots, b_n)$ becomes $a_1b_1 + \cdots + a_nb_n$. Third, on the infinite-dimensional space of complex valued functions continuous on the interval of real numbers between a and b (see 56), the pair of functions (f, g), is mapped into the limit of a sum, namely, the value of an integral.

The central fact about any scalar product is expressed in the Schwarz inequality, first employed by the German mathematician Hermann Amandus Schwarz (see 57). The length $\|A\|$ of a vector A is defined (see 58) in terms of inner product, and it has the usual properties of Euclidean length (see 59). Distance between points (vectors) A and B is then defined in terms of length (see 60). Distance is symmetric—that is, independent of the order of the vectors in the pair (A, B)—positive if $A \neq B$ and satisfies the triangle inequality (see 61).

In the case of the space of all real n-tuples with the inner product defined as in the examples above, these concepts of length and distance coincide with the usual Euclidean distance. Hence, any real inner product space is called a Euclidean space. Any complex inner product space is called a unitary space.

A major distinction between Euclidean and unitary spaces occurs in the definition of angle. In either case the Schwarz inequality assumes the same form (see 62). In the Euclidean case there is precisely one number $\psi(A, B)$ the cosine of which corresponds to the intuitive notion of the cosine between two directed line segments (see 63). Thus $\psi(A, B)$ is defined to be the angle between vectors A and B. In a unitary space $p(A, B)$ is a complex number, in general, and so the real definition of angle cannot apply. The important case of perpendicularity (orthogonality) of A and B, however, can be defined by $p(A, B) = 0$ in a unitary space, just as in a Euclidean space.

The standard basis in terms of which all other vectors can be expressed for n-dimensional Euclidean or unitary space is a set of n vectors, each of unit length and each pair orthogonal. Such a basis is called orthonormal. Relative to an orthonormal basis, any inner product on an n-dimensional space assumes the first form given in the examples above (54). This form is also called the dot product because of the notation frequently used, $A \cdot B = p(A, B)$, in which $A = (a_1, \ldots, a_n)$ and $B = (b_1, \ldots, b_n)$ are expressed relative to an orthonormal basis for n-dimensional unitary space. The same form is valid in the Euclidean case, because $\bar{b} = b$ whenever b is real. The metric concepts assume familiar forms (see 64).

Quite a different form of product of vectors is used extensively in studying the geometry of Euclidean three-dimensional space and its physical applications. As contrasted with the scalar (or dot) product $A \cdot B$, which is a scalar, the vector (or cross) product $A \times B$ is a vector. Geometrically, $A \times B$ is the vector that, first, is perpendicular to both A and B; second, that is of length $\|A\|\ \|B\|$ sin $\psi(A, B)$, which numerically equals the area of the parallelogram having A and B as adjacent sides; and, third, that extends from the origin in the direction of travel of a right-hand screw when it is rotated from A to B through ψ, which is the smaller of the two possible angles.

Geometric meaning of vector cross product

An expression for $A \times B$ in terms of components is essential for computations and precise reasoning (see 65). The basic algebraic properties satisfied by $A \times B$ are important to compare with those of the inner product (see 66). The first of these properties shows that a cross product is anticommutative (or alternating), as first described by Hamilton for quaternions. The last of these properties relates $A \times B$ to the Schwarz inequality.

Unlike the concept of scalar product, the existence of a vector product having the properties listed above depends critically upon the dimension n of the vector space on which it is defined. Except for the trivial cases ($n = 0$ and $n = 1$), such a vector product exists only for $n = 3$ and $n = 7$. This odd fact is closely related to long-standing problems in algebra, originating in the work of Hamilton and Cayley but only fully solved in the 1960s. (D.T.F.)

Field theory. A particle moving in three-dimensional space can be located at each instance of time t by a position vector r drawn from some fixed reference point O. Because the position of the terminal point of r depends on time, r is a vector function of t. Its components in the directions of Cartesian axes, introduced at O, are the coefficients of i, j, and k in the representation that identifies these three vectors with vectors of unit length

(67) $$\boldsymbol{r} = x(t)\boldsymbol{i} + y(t)\boldsymbol{j} + z(t)\boldsymbol{k}$$

(68) $$\frac{d\boldsymbol{r}}{dt} = \frac{dx}{dt}\boldsymbol{i} + \frac{dy}{dt}\boldsymbol{j} + \frac{dz}{dt}\boldsymbol{k} = \boldsymbol{v}$$

(69) $$\frac{d^2\boldsymbol{r}}{dt^2} = \frac{d^2x}{dt^2}\boldsymbol{i} + \frac{d^2y}{dt^2}\boldsymbol{j} + \frac{d^2z}{dt^2}\boldsymbol{k} = \boldsymbol{a}$$

(70) $$\overrightarrow{PP'} = \Delta \boldsymbol{r}$$

(71) $$\frac{u(P') - u(P)}{|\Delta \boldsymbol{r}|}$$

(72) $$\nabla u = \boldsymbol{i}\frac{\partial u}{\partial x} + \boldsymbol{j}\frac{\partial u}{\partial y} + \boldsymbol{k}\frac{\partial u}{\partial z}$$

(73) $$\frac{\int_S \boldsymbol{v} \cdot \boldsymbol{n} d_\sigma}{\tau}$$

(74) $$\text{div } \boldsymbol{v} = \frac{\partial v_1}{\partial x} + \frac{\partial v_2}{\partial y} + \frac{\partial v_3}{\partial z}$$

(75) $$\boldsymbol{v} = \boldsymbol{i}v_1 + \boldsymbol{j}v_2 + \boldsymbol{k}v_3$$

(76) $$\text{curl } \boldsymbol{v}(P) = \lim_{\tau \to 0} \frac{\int_S \boldsymbol{n} \times \boldsymbol{v} d\sigma}{\tau}$$

(77) $$\text{curl } \boldsymbol{v} = \boldsymbol{i}\left(\frac{\partial v_3}{\partial y} - \frac{\partial v_2}{\partial z}\right) + \boldsymbol{j}\left(\frac{\partial v_1}{\partial z} - \frac{\partial v_3}{\partial x}\right) + \boldsymbol{k}\left(\frac{\partial v_2}{\partial y} - \frac{\partial v_1}{\partial x}\right)$$

along the three mutually perpendicular axes (see 67). If the components are differentiable functions, the derivative of r with respect to t is defined by a formula (see 68) that represents the velocity v of the particle. The Cartesian components of v appear as coefficients of i, j, and k. If these components are also differentiable, the acceleration $a = dv/dt$ is obtained by differentiation (see 69). It may also be verified that the rules for differentiating products of scalar functions remain valid for derivatives of the dot and cross products of vector functions, and suitable definitions of integrals of vector functions allow the construction of the calculus of vectors. Such calculus has become a basic analytic tool in physical sciences and technology.

Applications of vector calculus to problems of continuum mechanics (*e.g.*, fluid mechanics, aerodynamics) call for a consideration of scalar and vector functions specified at each point of some region. A region of space with each point of which a scalar function is associated is called a scalar field, while a region in which a vector function is determined is a vector field. Examples of scalar fields are regions at each point of which the temperature or density of a body can be determined. A region in the vicinity of a charged body in which the electric-intensity vector is determined is an example of a vector field. A scalar function $u(P)$ determined at each point P of a scalar field is called a scalar point-function, while a vector function $v(P)$ specified in a vector field is a vector point-function.

Examples of scalar fields

Gradient of a scalar field. If there is a scalar point-function $u(P)$ at a point P and another scalar point-function $u(P')$ at a nearby point P', the vector from P to P' being expressed as Δr (see 70), then the ratio (see 71) of the difference between u at P and u at P' relative to Δr represents the average space rate of change of $u(P)$ in the direction of Δr. The limit of this ratio as $|\Delta r| \to 0$, when this limit exists, represents the space rate of change of $u(P)$ in the direction of Δr. The vector in that direction for which the space rate of change of $u(P)$ is a maximum is called the gradient of $u(P)$ and is denoted by grad u or ∇u. It can be shown that in Cartesian coordinates the vector components of the gradient are partial derivatives of u—that is, derivatives of u, obtained by holding all but one variable fixed and differentiating with respect to the unrestricted variable (see 72). Thus, with each point of a scalar field, in which ∇u exists, there can be associated a vector field. If $u(P)$ is the temperature, then ∇u gives the direction of the heat-flow vector in the field.

Divergence of a vector field. On the other hand, two important fields can be associated with each continuously differentiable vector point-function $\boldsymbol{v}(P)$: one is a scalar field and the other a vector field. If $\boldsymbol{v}(P)$ is defined in some region T bounded by a sufficiently smooth surface S, then the component of $\boldsymbol{v}(P)$ (which for the sake of concreteness can be thought to represent velocity $\boldsymbol{v}$ of fluid particles moving in T) in the direction of the unit vector $\boldsymbol{n}$ that is exterior (directed away from) and normal to the surface S is $\boldsymbol{v}\cdot\boldsymbol{n}$. The amount of fluid issuing from S then is given by $\int \boldsymbol{v}\cdot\boldsymbol{n}d\sigma$, in which the integration symbol represents the summation of $\boldsymbol{v}\cdot\boldsymbol{n}$ over the elements of area $d\sigma$ of the surface S.

The flux of fluid per unit volume is thus equal to a ratio of the integral referred to, relative to τ, in which τ is the volume of T (see 73). The limit of this ratio as $\tau \to 0$, so that S shrinks toward some point P in T, is an important scalar called the divergence of $\boldsymbol{v}(P)$. Thus, the divergence of $\boldsymbol{v}(P)$, written div $\boldsymbol{v}(P)$, represents the rate of fluid flow from P. If div $\boldsymbol{v}(P)$ is positive at P, then P is a source of fluid; if it is negative, then P is a sink. If div $\boldsymbol{v}(P) = 0$, then no fluid issues from P.

Divergence in Cartesian coordinates

In Cartesian coordinates div $\boldsymbol{v}(P)$ is given by a formula (see 74) that is the sum of partial derivatives of vector components of the velocity vector $\boldsymbol{v}$ (see 75).

Curl of a vector field. Associated with $\boldsymbol{v}(P)$ is an important vector field in which the vector called curl of $\boldsymbol{v}(P)$ is defined by a formula that expresses, in the limit of small volume, the ratio of $\int \boldsymbol{n}\times\boldsymbol{v}d\tau$ relative to that volume, in which the integral is calculated over the surface S (see 76). This vector provides a measure of the angular velocity of the fluid at any point P in the field. In Cartesian coordinates curl $\boldsymbol{v}$ is given by an especially convenient formula in which the vector components are differences of partial derivatives (see 77). When curl $\boldsymbol{v} = 0$ at every point of the region, the field is said to be irrotational, and, when $\boldsymbol{v}(P)$ is such that div $\boldsymbol{v} = 0$, the field is solenoidal. The importance of these two special fields stems from the fact that every continuously differentiable vector function $\boldsymbol{v}(P)$ defined in a region τ (subject to mild restrictions) can be expressed as a sum of two vector functions $\boldsymbol{f}(P)$ and $\boldsymbol{g}(P)$ such that $\boldsymbol{f}(P)$ is solenoidal and $\boldsymbol{g}(P)$ is irrotational. The possibility of such decomposition greatly simplifies the study of many velocity and force fields occurring in physics.

TENSOR ANALYSIS

Tensors, or generalizations of vectors, as characterized at the beginning of this article, were invented to express geometric entities arising in the study of manifolds—that is, spaces that resemble Euclidean space in small regions but which may be curved in an arbitrary manner. Originally these small regions were used to define coordinate systems on the manifold, and tensors were expressed in terms of functions involving many indices that obey certain transformation laws when the coordinate system is changed. Subsequently, a global study of manifolds resulted in an invariant treatment of tensors and their algebraic rules of combination. This is the subject of tensor or multilinear algebra.

The concept of tensors and the knowledge of some of their properties can be traced back to the work of Gauss and to the work of his younger countrymen Bernhard Riemann and Elwin Bruno Christoffel as well. Their algebra and analysis eventually were shaped into a systematic method by the Italians Gregorio Ricci-Curbastro and Tullio Levi-Civita, who coined for this powerful branch of mathematics the name absolute differential calculus. It is now known as tensor analysis. The chief aim of tensor analysis is to construct and discuss relations of laws that are generally covariant—that is, laws that remain valid in passing from one to any other system of coordinates. Thus, the method of tensor analysis is of prime importance for differential geometry. It became the object of widespread interest after the advent of general relativity theory, in which a principal requirement is precisely such unrestricted covariance of physical laws. There are many useful applications of tensor analysis—both finite and infinite dimensional—to classical mechanics, quantum mechanics, fluid mechanics, and other fields.

Consider a continuous n-dimensional manifold or space S_n (see GEOMETRY: *Topological groups* and *Differential topology*), the element or point $P(x_\iota)$ of which is determined by assigning the values of n real independent variables or coordinates x_ι. Let $Q(x_\iota + dx_\iota)$ be another point of S_n. Then the ordered point-pair P, Q or the set of differentials dx_ι is a vector. To begin with, the idea of size or length is foreign to this concept, as S_n thus far is a nonmetrical manifold.

Tensor transformation and rank

If the x_ι be transformed into any other system of n coordinates x'_ι, the former being continuous functions of the latter with continuous derivatives $\partial x_\iota/\partial x'_\kappa$ and nonvanishing, finite Jacobian $J = \partial x_\iota/\partial x'_\kappa$; then dx_ι are transformed into differentials dx'_ι by a linear transformation in which the coefficients are partial derivatives (see 78). (The convention will be adopted that every term in which an index occurs twice is to be summed over all its values.) Any set of n magnitudes A^ι, functions of the x_ι, that are transformed by this rule, that is, by the rule of transformation that governs differentials (see 79), forms a contravariant tensor of rank 1, the A^ι being its n components. For contravariant tensors upper indices are used, except for dx_ι, the prototype of all such tensors. Next, any n magnitudes A_ι that are transformed as the differentiators $\partial/\partial x_\iota$, which are arrived at by formally inverting the partial derivatives that constitute the coefficients (see 80), form a covariant tensor of rank 1; lower indices are used for such tensors. These two kinds of tensors, or rank 1, are also termed vectors—*e.g.*, three-vectors, four-vectors (such as the relativistic four-velocity or four-potential, in space-time, S_4) and so on, according as $n = 3, 4, \ldots$. Similarly, any n^2 magnitudes $A_{\iota\kappa}$ transformable by a natural generalization of the rank 1 covariant tensor transformation (see 81) form a covariant, and any A^ι transformable by a natural generalization of the rank 1 contravariant tensor transformation (see 82) form a contravariant tensor of rank 2. Again, n^2 magnitudes A_ι^κ transformable by a linear transformation in which coefficients are products of coefficients from rank 1 covariant and contravariant tensor transformations (see 83) are said to form a mixed tensor of rank 2, covariant in ι and contravariant in κ.

(78) $$dx'_\iota = \frac{\partial x'_\iota}{\partial x_a} dx_a$$

(79) $$A'_\iota = \frac{\partial x'_\iota}{\partial x_a} A^a$$

(80) $$A'_\iota = \frac{\partial x_a}{\partial x'_\iota} A_a$$

(81) $$A'_{\iota\kappa} = \frac{\partial x_a}{\partial x'_\iota} \frac{\partial x_\beta}{\partial x'_\kappa} A_{a\beta}$$

(82) $$A'^{\iota\kappa} = \frac{\partial x'_\iota}{\partial x_a} \frac{\partial x'_\kappa}{\partial x_\beta} A_{a\beta}$$

(83) $$A'^{\kappa}_{\iota} = \frac{\partial x_a}{\partial x'_\iota} \frac{\partial x'_\kappa}{\partial x_\beta} A^\beta_a$$

(84) $$\left(A^{ik\cdots}_{\iota\kappa\cdots}\right)' = \frac{\partial x_a}{\partial x'_\iota} \frac{\partial x_\beta}{\partial x'_\kappa} \cdots \frac{\partial x'_\iota}{\partial x_a} \frac{\partial x'_\kappa}{\partial x_b} \cdots A^{ab\cdots}_{a\beta\cdots}$$

The extension to any rank is obvious. Any $n^{r_1+r_2}$ magnitudes $A_{\iota\kappa\ldots}^{ik\ldots}$, with r_1 lower and r_2 upper indices, which are transformed according to a generalized rule (see 84), form a mixed tensor of rank $r=r_1+r_2$. This is the most general concept of a tensor. A tensor of rank zero, called also a scalar, is a single function of the x_ι, invariant with respect to any transformations of coordinates, $f'=f$. $\boldsymbol{A}_{\iota\kappa}$ is symmetrical if $\boldsymbol{A}_{\iota\kappa}=\boldsymbol{A}_{\kappa\iota}$ and is antisymmetrical or a skew tensor if $\boldsymbol{A}_{\iota\kappa}=-\boldsymbol{A}_{\kappa\iota}$, implying $\boldsymbol{A}_{\iota\iota}=0$. Similarly for $\boldsymbol{A}^{\iota\kappa}$. Analogous definitions hold for mixed tensors and for higher ranks. Symmetry and antisymmetry are invariant properties.

Differentiation. The differentiation of tensors with respect to the coordinates yields, in certain circumstances, further tensors. If f is a scalar function of the x_ι or scalar field, $\partial f/\partial x_\iota=f_\iota$ is a covariant vector, the gradient of f (but $\partial^2 f/\partial x_\iota \partial x_\kappa$ is not a tensor; again, if du is an invariant, dx_ι/du is, but d^2x_ι/du^2 is not a vector). Further, if $\boldsymbol{A}_\iota$ is a vector, $\mathbf{B}_{\iota\kappa}=\partial \boldsymbol{A}_\iota/\partial x_\kappa-\partial \boldsymbol{A}_\kappa/\partial x_\iota$ is a skew tensor, the rotation of $\boldsymbol{A}_\iota$. Finally, if $\boldsymbol{A}_{\iota\kappa}$ is antisymmetric, $\boldsymbol{B}_{\iota\kappa\lambda}=\partial \boldsymbol{A}_{\iota\kappa}/\partial x_\lambda+\partial \boldsymbol{A}_{\lambda\kappa}/\partial x_\iota+\partial \boldsymbol{A}_{\lambda\iota}/\partial x_\kappa$ is again such a tensor, the expansion of $\boldsymbol{A}_{\iota\kappa}$.

In what precedes only such properties of tensors were treated as are independent of any metrical considerations; the space S_n thus far is a nonmetrical, amorphous manifold. Its metrics may now be fixed by laying down the line element, a quadratic differential form (see 85) to be considered as invariant and to serve as the measure of the (squared) size or length of the vector $\boldsymbol{dx}_\iota$. In the differential form there are coefficients $g_{\iota\kappa}=g_{\kappa\iota}$ that are prescribed functions of x. It follows that, because $\boldsymbol{dx}_\iota$ is contravariant, $\mathbf{g}_{\iota\kappa}$ is covariant. Equivalently, it may be said that a certain symmetrical tensor $\mathbf{g}_{\iota\kappa}$ is impressed upon S_n as the fundamental or metrical tensor, converting it into a metrical manifold called a Riemannian space.

The minors $g^{\iota\kappa}$ of $g=|\boldsymbol{g}_{\iota\kappa}|$, divided by g, form again a symmetrical tensor, the contravariant metrical tensor, to be used along with $\boldsymbol{g}_{\iota\kappa}$. The outer product and contraction can be used in raising and lowering tensor indices. Thus, $\boldsymbol{g}^{\iota\kappa}\boldsymbol{A}_\kappa=\boldsymbol{A}^\iota$ and $\boldsymbol{g}_{\iota\kappa}\boldsymbol{B}^\kappa=\boldsymbol{B}_\iota$.

The angle θ between two (copunctal) vectors $\boldsymbol{A}^\iota$ and $\boldsymbol{B}^\iota$ is defined by the invariant $\cos\theta=\mathbf{g}_{\iota\kappa}A^\iota B^\kappa/AB$, where A, B defines their sizes. The unit vector $\dot{x}_\iota=dx_\iota/ds$ determines, locally, a direction in S_n. The angle between two directions $\dot{x}_\iota$, $\dot{y}_\iota$ is given by $\cos\theta=\dot{g}_{\iota\kappa}\,\dot{x}_\iota\,\dot{y}_\kappa$.

Integrals. The integral $\int dx_1,\ldots, dx_n$, briefly $\int dx$, extended over a region of S_n, is transformed into $\int Jdx'$, and the determinant g into $g'=J^2g$. Consequently, $\int\sqrt{g}dx$ is an invariant metrically impressed upon that region's size or volume (area, if $n=2$). This concept is readily extended to any submanifold of S_n characterized by x_ι as functions of $m<n$ parameters p_a, the role of metrical tensor is taken over by a linear transformation of it (see 86). If, by a proper choice of the coordinate system, all components $\boldsymbol{g}_{ik}$ are reducible to constants, the metric space S_n is Euclidean or homaloidal (flat). This is but a very special case of Riemannian space. In general, such a reduction is not possible, and S_n is non-Euclidean.

Differentiation of tensors by metrics

Differentiation of tensors, aided by metrics, yields an unlimited number of new tensors. The oldest of such is Riemann's set of four-index symbols of 1861. The simplest metrically differential tensor, however, was discovered in 1869 by Christoffel. This is the covariant derivative of a vector $\boldsymbol{A}_\iota$ (see 87) in which certain terms $[\iota\kappa, \mu]$ are Christoffel's symbols (not forming a tensor) (see 87). Again, the generalization of this is a mixed tensor (see 88). Detailed symbolism is necessary to express the covariant derivatives of $\mathbf{C}^{\iota\kappa}$ and $\mathbf{C}_{\iota\kappa}$ (see 89, 90). The covariant derivative of $\boldsymbol{g}_{\iota\kappa}$ itself vanishes identically. Noteworthy for their applications are the vector divergence of a skew $\boldsymbol{A}^{\iota\kappa}$ and the scalar divergence of A^κ (see 91); *e.g.*, one group of the 19th-century Scottish physicist James Clerk Maxwell's equations is represented by div $(\mathbf{F}^{\iota\kappa})=\mathbf{C}^\iota$, where $\mathbf{C}^\iota$ is the four-current and $\mathbf{F}^{\iota\kappa}$ the electromagnetic skew tensor (six vector); the second group is expressed by equating to zero the expansion of $\mathbf{F}_{\iota\kappa}=g_{\iota a}g_{\kappa\beta}\mathbf{F}^{a\beta}$.

Geodesics, null lines. The most characteristic curves of the metric S_n are its null or minimal lines, $ds=0$, and shortest curves or geodesics defined by $\delta\int ds=0$, with fixed terminals. The equations of a geodesic are second-order differential equations expressed in terms of Christoffel symbols and $\dot{x}$, in which $\dot{x}=dx/ds$ (see 92). They determine—*e.g.*, in the case of space-time—the motion of a free particle in the metric, and gravitational, field $g_{\iota\kappa}$. The null lines are imaginary or real, depending on whether the form (85) expressing the square of the differential of the line element is a definite or nondefinite form. The definite form holds in the case of spaces proper as contemplated by the pure geometer, and the nondefinite form characterizes space-time with one positive and three negative $g_{\kappa\kappa}$. The null lines of space-time represent light propagation. The definiteness or nondefiniteness of the quadratic form and its index of inertia (number of negative $g_{\kappa\kappa}$ terms) are invariant properties.

Levi-Civita's concept

Parallel displacement of vectors. A fruitful contribution to tensor analysis due to Levi-Civita is the concept of parallel displacement of a vector with respect to a curve. The metric S_n can in general be imagined as imbedded locally in a Euclidean space E of $\frac{1}{2}(n+1)$ dimensions. Levi-Civita defined parallel displacement in S_n as a consequence of a parallel displacement in E. In spite of the ultraspatial construction, parallelism is intrinsic, expressible by the S_n metrics alone.

If $x_\iota=f_\iota(s)$ are the parametric equations of any chosen curve C, then there are differential equations along C that with the initial vector $\boldsymbol{A}^\iota(S_0)=\boldsymbol{A}_0{}^\iota$ determine uniquely a contravariant vector $\boldsymbol{A}^\iota$ at each point of the curve (see 93). The vector $\boldsymbol{A}^\iota$ at the point corresponding to $s=s$ is said to be obtained by a parallel displacement of the vector $\boldsymbol{A}_0{}^\iota$ with respect to the given curve C and is said to be parallel to $\boldsymbol{A}_0{}^\iota$. Any two vectors generated as above, one at each point, are parallel with respect to C. If it be required to construct a curve the tangents of which follow from each other by parallel displacement along the curve itself, the result will be the equations of a geodesic (92), so that the curve is a geodesic. The latter is thus throughout parallel to itself. Accordingly, a vector transferred along a geodesic remains equally inclined to it.

(85) $$ds^2=g_{\iota\kappa}dx_\iota dx_\kappa$$

(86) $$h_{ab}=g_{\iota\kappa}\left(\frac{\partial x_\iota}{\partial p_a}\right)\left(\frac{\partial x_\kappa}{\partial p_b}\right)$$

(87) $$\begin{cases} \boldsymbol{A}_{\iota,\kappa}=\dfrac{\partial \boldsymbol{A}_\iota}{\partial x_\kappa}-\{\iota\kappa,\lambda\}\boldsymbol{A}_\lambda \\ \{\iota\kappa,\lambda\}=g^{\lambda\mu}[\iota\kappa,\mu]=\{\kappa\iota,\lambda\} \\ [\iota\kappa,\mu]=\dfrac{1}{2}\left(\dfrac{\partial g_{\mu\iota}}{\partial x_\kappa}+\dfrac{\partial g_{\kappa\mu}}{\partial x_\iota}-\dfrac{\partial g_{\iota\kappa}}{\partial x_\mu}\right) \end{cases}$$

(88) $$\mathbf{B}_{\iota\kappa}^{\lambda}=\frac{\partial \mathbf{B}^\iota}{\partial x_\kappa}+\{a\kappa,\iota\}\,\mathbf{B}^a$$

(89) $$\mathbf{C}_{\lambda}^{\iota\kappa}=\frac{\partial \mathbf{C}^{\iota\kappa}}{\partial x\lambda}+\{\lambda a,\iota\}\mathbf{C}^{a\kappa}+\{\lambda a,\kappa\}\mathbf{C}^{\iota a}$$

(90) $$\mathbf{C}_{\iota\kappa,\lambda}=\frac{\partial \mathbf{C}_{\iota\kappa}}{\partial x^\lambda}-\{\iota,a\}\mathbf{C}_{a\kappa}-\{\kappa\lambda,a\}\mathbf{C}_{\iota a}$$

(91) $$\begin{cases} \boldsymbol{A}^\iota=\mathrm{div}(\boldsymbol{A}^{\iota\kappa})\equiv\dfrac{1}{\sqrt{g}}\dfrac{\partial}{\partial x_\kappa}(\sqrt{g}\,\boldsymbol{A}^{\iota\kappa}) \\ \mathrm{div}(\boldsymbol{A}^\kappa)\equiv\dfrac{1}{\sqrt{g}}\dfrac{\partial}{\partial x_\kappa}(\sqrt{g}\,\boldsymbol{A}^\kappa) \end{cases}$$

(92) $$\ddot{x}_\iota+\{a\beta,\iota\}\dot{x}_a\,\dot{x}_\beta=0$$

(93) $$\frac{d\boldsymbol{A}^\iota}{ds}+\{a\beta,\iota\}\boldsymbol{A}^a\dot{x}^\beta=0$$

If a vector X^ι be carried by a parallel displacement along two different paths a, b from O to O', the two vectors at O', equal in size, generally differ in direction. One is parallel to X^ι via a, the other via b. In short, parallelism depends on the route of transfer or is nonintegrable (unless S_n is essentially Euclidean). Thus also, if the vector is carried around a circuit, it returns at O with its direction changed.

The covariant derivative of the vector is the tensor $\mathbf{X}_{,\iota\alpha}$. Its covariant derivative $\mathbf{X}_{,\iota,\alpha,\beta}$ is not symmetric in α and β. A straightforward calculation shows that the difference of the two forms of this covariant derivative involves the important tensor $\mathbf{R}^{\kappa}_{\iota\alpha\beta}$ (see 94). This latter tensor is the Riemann-Christoffel, or curvature, tensor (see 95) the vanishing of which is the necessary and sufficient condition for the reducibility of $\mathbf{g}_{\iota\kappa}$ to a constant tensor, or the criterion of a homaloidal space.

The Riemann-Christoffel curvature tensor

Riemann's four-index symbols and curvature. Riemann's own set of four-index symbols is the covariant tensor $(\iota\mu, \lambda\kappa) \equiv \mathbf{R}_{\iota\mu\lambda\kappa} = g_{\mu a}\, \mathbf{R}_{\iota\kappa\lambda}{}^{a}$. Conversely, $\mathbf{R}_{\iota\kappa\lambda}{}^{a} = g^{\mu a}$ $(\iota\mu, \lambda\kappa)$. Like equation (95), the symbols are antisymmetric in κ, λ. Three more linear relations hold between them. This reduces the number of independent symbols to $n^2(n^2-1)/12$—*e.g.*, six for a three-space, 20 for an S_4, and but one for a surface, say (12, 12). This symbol divided by g is a scalar of the surface, its Gaussian curvature K. If a vector undergoes parallel displacement around a circuit on a surface, it returns with its direction changed by an amount equal to $\int K d\sigma$, the Gaussian curvature of the surface integrated over the surface area enclosed by the circuit. As a consequence, the excess (over π) of the angle sum in any geodesic triangle is $\int K d\sigma$, a theorem proved by Gauss.

When there are three or more dimensions, the curvature properties can no longer be expressed by a single magnitude but require for their description the knowledge of the whole curvature tensor or the associated Riemann symbols. The concept of Gaussian curvature is now replaced by that of Riemannian curvature—*i.e.*, at any point $O(x)$ of S_n, the set of Gaussian curvatures K of geodesic surfaces of all possible orientations laid through O. If $h_{\alpha\beta}$ be the metric tensor of such a surface as submanifold, $K = 1/h(12, 12)_k$, the symbol is calculated with $h_{\alpha\beta}$. This and the determinant h can be expressed in terms of the tensor $\mathbf{g}_{\iota\kappa}$ of the manifold and the vector pair, ξ^ι, η^ι, fixing the orientation (see 96).

$$(94) \qquad \mathbf{X}_{,\iota,\beta,\alpha} - \mathbf{X}_{,\iota,\alpha,\beta} = \mathbf{R}^{\kappa}_{\iota\alpha\beta}\mathbf{X}_{\kappa}$$

$$(95) \qquad \mathbf{R}^{\kappa}_{\iota\alpha\beta} = \frac{\partial}{\partial x_\alpha}\{\iota\beta, \kappa\} - \frac{\partial}{\partial x_\beta}\{\iota\alpha, \kappa\} + \{\alpha\gamma, \kappa\}\{\iota\beta, \gamma\} - \{\beta\gamma, \kappa\}\{\iota\alpha, \gamma\}$$

$$(96) \qquad K = \frac{(\iota\kappa, \lambda\mu)\xi^\iota\eta^\kappa\xi^\lambda\eta^\mu}{(g_{\iota\lambda}g_{\kappa\mu} - g_{\iota\mu}g_{\kappa\lambda})\xi^\iota\eta^\kappa\xi^\lambda\eta^\mu}$$

In general, K will depend on position and on orientation. In other words, with regard to curvature, S_n may be nonhomogeneous and anisotropic (*e.g.*, space-time within or around matter); but, if K is everywhere isotropic, it is also constant throughout S_n (Schur's theorem). By the expression (96) for K in terms of the tensor $\mathbf{g}_{\iota\kappa}$ and the vector pair, ξ^ι, η^ι, the necessary and sufficient condition for isotropy of Riemannian curvature becomes $(\iota\lambda, \kappa\mu) = K(\mathbf{g}_{\iota\kappa}\, g_{\lambda\mu} - g_{\iota\mu}\, g_{\lambda\mu})$ or $\mathbf{R}_{\iota\kappa\lambda}{}^{a} = K(\delta_\kappa{}^a g_{\iota\lambda} - \delta_\lambda{}^a \mathbf{g}_{\iota\kappa})$ with constant K. (D.T.F./Ed.)

Measure theory

The classical integral calculus is founded on the concept of the Riemann integral. However, this is not an entirely satisfactory basis. Certain functions that "ought to be" integrable fail to possess a well-defined Riemann integral. Functions that are limits of sequences of Riemann integrable functions may not themselves be Riemann integrable. The search for a more general and better behaved notion of integral led to the subject of measure theory, which among other things has provided the long-sought foundations for the concept of probability.

Beyond the Riemann integral. The general concept of a real-valued function of a real variable that had appeared in a more or less vague or restrictive form throughout the calculus period was finally isolated by Dirichlet in 1829. Dirichlet examined the problem of convergence of Fourier series. Since the coefficients of these series are given by integrals, the knowledge of Fourier series expanded with the evolution of the concepts of integration and of function. From the time of Dirichlet and Riemann on, the knowledge of trigonometric series and, more generally, of harmonic analysis thus gained in depth and in extension.

Modern set theory

In fact, modern set theory, which changed the whole outlook on measure and integration, began in 1872 with Cantor's investigation of the structure of some exceptional sets of trigonometric series: sets S such that, if a trigonometric series (see 97) converges to zero except at the points of S, then each coefficient $c_n = 0$. The evolution of set theory between 1872 and 1890, due primarily to Cantor's genius, together with the parallel investigation of the system of reals and of functions of reals by such mathematicians as Richard Dedekind, Karl Weierstrass, and Paul du Bois-Reymond, all of Germany, as well as Ulisse Dini of Italy, brought on the "great mathematical revolution" at the turn of the 20th century.

$$(97) \qquad \sum_{n=-\infty}^{+\infty} c_n e^{inx}$$

Measure and content. The problem of foundations was revived but was applied to the tremendous wealth of accumulated knowledge at a level of abstraction far beyond that known to the ancient Greeks. In particular, the problem of measure was no longer confined to a few special sets—the geometric figures available to Eudoxus or Pascal. Moreover, the very nature of the problem was different.

Eudoxus' or Pascal's problem was to find the measure (area, volume) of some specific geometric figure. The existence of this measure was a question of faith, and it was approximated by sums of measures of simple figures. The new problem was to define a measure for as large a class of sets as possible by means of such approximations. The first attempts were made in 1884–85 by the German mathematicians Carl Gustav Axel Harnack, Otto Stolz, and Cantor. They did not succeed because they used only approximations from above; they assigned to any set S the greatest lower bound of sums of ordinary measures of simple sets—intervals, rectangles, parallelepipeds, the finite unions of which cover S.

The outer content so defined does not correspond to the intuitive idea of measure, for it is not additive: in everyday experience as well as in experimental science, the "measure" of a union of two disjoint sets is the sum of their "measures." For example, the volume (or mass) of two disjoint bodies is understood as the sum of their volumes (or masses). This requirement was recognized in Italy and France by Giuseppe Peano and Camille Jordan, who introduced approximations both from above and from below. To a set S, contained in a bounded interval I, they assigned also its inner content (the difference between the ordinary measure of I and the outer content of S). If the inner and outer contents of S are the same, then their common value defines the content of S. This content measure is additive. The most important types of sets encountered in analysis, however, such as the set of all rationals or general open sets, have no content. The content measure is thus of limited use.

Borel measure. The extension (or theory of measure) period began in 1898 with Émile Borel, the modern French Eudoxus. It is characterized by the extension of the idea of measure to wider and more abstract classes of sets and by the parallel extension of the idea of integration to wider and more abstract families of functions until both ideas coalesce. It was stimulated by and intricately interwoven with the explosive growth of general topology following Maurice Fréchet's thesis in France in 1902.

The Borel sets and measure

At the root of the theory of measure lie a few crucial remarks by Borel in his *Leçons sur la théorie des fonctions* (1898). While studying series of functions, Borel found the need for a measure such that sets whose measure is not zero are not countable. He therefore introduced the Borel measure on the Borel field, prototypes of all measures and all σ-fields considered below.

In the present discussion, the following terminology will be used. Unions of disjoint sets will be called sums, and the symbol $\cup$ for union will be replaced by the Greek letter sigma, Σ. "Countable" will mean finite or denumerable. Countable (or finite) set operations are complementations taking countable (or finite) unions and intersections. A σ-field (or field) of sets is a class of sets closed under countable (or finite) set operations.

Borel began by extending the ordinary measure on intervals to a measure on open sets, as follows. As Cantor had shown that every open set G of reals is a countable sum of open intervals I_j, Borel realized that the "natural" extension consists in assigning to G the sum of ordinary measures of its constituent intervals I_j. Hence, if G is not bounded, this sum may be infinite, but it always exists. By indefinite iteration of countable set operations and using the same extension procedure, he then extended the class of open sets and their measure to the class of Borel sets and their Borel measure. This class is a σ-field (the smallest σ-field containing the class of open sets), and this measure is σ-additive; the measure of a countable sum of sets is the sum of their measures. From then on, the Borel field of Borel sets in any topological space will be the smallest σ-field containing the topology; that is, the class of open sets in the space. (In fact, some authors use the term Borel field as a synonym for σ-field.)

The "Archimedes of France"

Lebesgue measure and integration. The Archimedes of the extension period in France was Henri-Léon Lebesgue. He took the decisive step in his thesis *Intégrale, aire, volume* (1902), which he immediately applied to trigonometric series (1903), and pursued further in *Sur l'intégration des fonctions discontinuous* (1910). Lebesgue combined the ideas of his immediate predecessors, Jordan and Borel, and created and exploited the powerful tools of modern measure and integration. The evolution of his ideas, methods, and results consisted primarily in the gradual shedding of their extraneous coverings.

The Lebesgue measure is defined by extending the ordinary measure on intervals by means of outer and inner Lebesgue measures, exactly as the Jordan content was defined, except that coverings by countable unions of intervals replace coverings by finite unions. The intervals are one-dimensional or N-dimensional, and the same method applies. Thus, the Lebesgue integral of a function $f \geq 0$, defined on a set, becomes simply the Lebesgue measure of the ordinate set of the function, provided this set is Lebesgue-measurable. As may be expected, every Riemann-integrable function is Lebesgue-integrable, but the converse is not true. Riemann's integrability condition for bounded functions f becomes: the discontinuity set of f is of Lebesgue measure 0. Thus, the famous Dirichlet function $f(x) = 0$ or 1 (according as x is irrational or not), which is Lebesgue-integrable on every bounded interval, is not Riemann-integrable.

Lebesgue's main contribution, however, does not lie in the above concepts. The Lebesgue measure, for example, is simply the completed Borel measure; that is, a Lebesgue-measurable set is a Borel-measurable set up to a subset of a set of Borel-measure 0. What really mattered were Lebesgue's discovery and use of the properties of his concepts of measure and of integration.

Using the Lebesgue approach, the problem of finding a process of integration that includes both that of Leibniz (*summa omnium*) and that of Newton (primitive) was solved by Arnaud Denjoy of France (1912) and also by Oskar Perron of Germany (1914).

The cleaning up of Lebesgue's ideas was essentially achieved in the 15 years or so that followed the publication of his thesis. It yielded a general answer to the problem of measure for areas, masses, probabilities, and the like and finally isolated its conceptual substance. The answer and the substance, however, were to be formulated in terms far removed from the everyday experience. The steps in the cleaning-up process included the generalization that stemmed from Thomas Jan Stieltjes of France and was due to Johann Radon of Germany and the abstraction that began with Fréchet in 1915 and with Constantin Carathéodory of Germany in 1918.

Conditions for existence of the Riemann integral. The question may now be raised: if a function f is bounded on an interval $a \leq x \leq b$, can a criterion be found that will ensure the integrability, or nonintegrability, of f? (A function f is bounded on $a \leq x \leq b$ if there exists a number M such that $|f(x)| \leq M$ for all x in the interval. Boundedness, in effect, prevents the function from assuming arbitrarily large values at any points of the interval.)

This question can be concisely answered in terms of the concept of a set of points of measure zero. A set of points is of measure zero if the points can be covered by intervals the sum of whose lengths can be made arbitrarily small. For example, the set of points $x_0, x_1, x_2, \ldots, x_k, \ldots$, in which $x_0 = 0$, $x_k = 1/k$ $(k = 1, 2, 3, \ldots)$, is of measure zero because for any positive number ε (no matter how small) x_0 can be covered by an interval of length $\varepsilon/2$; x_1 by an interval of length $\varepsilon/2^2, \ldots$; x_k by an interval of length $\varepsilon/2^{k+1}$; and by the theory of infinite series it can be shown that the sum of these lengths is precisely ε. It should be noted, for the sake of clarity, that any finite set of points is of measure zero.

Sets of discontinuity of measure zero

The following criterion provides a necessary and sufficient condition for Riemann integrability: If a function f is bounded on an interval $a \leq x \leq b$, then the Riemann integral of f on the interval exists if and only if the set of discontinuities of f is of measure zero. The result for piecewise-continuous functions is a special case of this theorem.

The function $f(x) = \sin[1/\sin(\pi/x)]$, for example, is not defined at the points 0, 1, $1/2$, $1/3$, ... At these points the function can be assigned any values. The resulting function is bounded on the interval $0 \leq x \leq 1$, however, and its only discontinuities in this interval are the above points, which form a set of measure zero. Hence, the integral of f from 0 to 1 exists.

A property that holds at all points of a given set, except for a subset of measure zero, is said to hold almost everywhere on the set. The above theorem therefore states, in effect, that, for the Riemann integral to exist, the function f must be continuous almost everywhere on the specific interval. The extension of the concept of an integral to the Lebesgue integral is designed to cover cases that are not so restricted.

Probability theory. The basic setup of the history of measure also yields the foundations of probability theory. Deserving mention is the concept of stochastic independence, which was, and to a great extent still is, essential to the evolution of probability theory since its inception in 1654 by Blaise Pascal and Pierre de Fermat. It, too, became measure-theoretic with the creation and abstraction of finite and infinite product measures by Lebesgue and by the American mathematician P.J. Daniell.

Recent developments. Since about 1930, when integrals of functions with values in a Banach space were introduced by the Polish-born mathematician Salomon Bochner, a further abstraction began. Measures and functions (hence, integrals) take values in more and more abstract spaces instead of taking numerical values as above, and various types of convergence are used. Of particular importance are the various stochastic integrals. In fact, the foregoing indications concerning the theory of measure and integration have many variants, even in the numerical case. In the final analysis, their conceptual substance is the same, but it is seen from different points of view in various settings, from Eudoxus and Archimedes, through Leibniz and Riemann, to Lebesgue and the present day. The most important fact is the ever-spreading use of the powerful tools that these concepts provide for such areas as differentiation theory, boundary problems, ergodic theory, probability theory, group theory, potential theory, and harmonic analysis.

(Hy.K./Ed.)

COMPLEX ANALYSIS

Complex analysis arose from studies of analytic functions of complex variables. A function $f(z)$ is said to be analytic in a two-dimensional region if, at each point of the region, the derivative $f'(z)$ exists. Analytic functions are also called holomorphic, monogenic, regular, or regular-analytic functions. Historical usage and the many varieties of context recommend the different terms for the same concept, as will be seen below.

Cauchy's contribution

The theory of analytic functions was created by the French mathematician Augustin-Louis Cauchy, who in 1814 began the task of integrating between complex limits (see *Real analysis* above). His results were first made known in 1825. He used his new ideas to lay the foundation for a theory of ordinary and partial differential equations, including applications to mathematical physics. In 1851 Bernhard Riemann of Germany outlined a theory in which the analytic function is defined by a pair of harmonic functions (functions that satisfy Laplace's equation; see *Differential equations: Partial differential equations* below) joined by the Cauchy-Riemann equations. The values of the function form a geometric entity that is called a Riemann surface. In the same paper the idea of conformal mapping (see below) was introduced.

His contemporary Karl Weierstrass took the view that analytic functions are defined by power series (in which each term is a constant multiplied by the independent variable to some power; see *Infinite series* above) that are linked by a method of analytic continuation.

Theory of analytic functions of one complex variable

FOUNDATIONS

Complex numbers and the complex plane. Complex numbers are numbers of the form $a+bi$, in which a and b are real numbers and i is the square root of -1. They can be written also as ordered pairs of real numbers (a, b). The complex numbers form a field. The elements of this field are ordered pairs of real numbers (a, b) for which equality, addition, multiplication, and scalar multiplication are defined by well-specified rules involving ordered pairs (see Box, equations 98). The associative, commutative, and distributive laws (see ALGEBRA: *Elementary and multivariate algebra*) hold; $(0, 0)$ acts as zero, $(1, 0)$ as unity. From one of these laws the result that an arbitrary ordered pair can be written as a linear combination of two fixed ordered pairs each having components one or zero in some order (see 99) is obtained, using the classical notation. The numbers $(a, 0)$ are identified with the real numbers a so that the equalities $(1, 0)=1$ and $(0, 1)=i$ may be written.

The notation (a, b) suggests the geometric representation of the complex number $a+bi$ by the point (a, b) in an ordinary Euclidean plane. The x-axis is then called the real axis, and the y-axis the imaginary one. An alternate representation is by the vector (see *Vector and tensor analysis* above) joining $(0, 0)$ with (a, b). The length r of this vector is called the absolute value of the complex number $c=a+bi$ and is written $|c|=r$. The angle, symbolized here by the Greek letter theta, θ, that the vector makes with the positive real axis is called the argument, $\theta=\arg c$ (see Figure 16). Thus, an arbitrary complex number can be written in trigonometric or exponential form (see 100). The point $a-bi=\bar{c}$ is called the conjugate of c. In the geometric representation of complex numbers, addition becomes vector addition. The absolute value of a product is the product of the absolute values, and the argument is congruent to the sum of the arguments, modulo 2π.

The plane used for this representation is known as the complex plane. The complex variable is usually denoted by $z=x+iy$. There is an extensive geometry of the complex numbers based on this representation. In its trigonometric form z can be expressed by $z=r(\cos\theta+i\sin\theta)$. Given another complex number z', it can be shown that the product $z\cdot z'$ accords with the general relationship $z^n=r^n(\cos n\theta+i\sin n\theta)$, which is known as de Moivre's formula (devised in the 18th century by Abraham de Moivre). It holds for any real number n and can be used to compute the nth roots of a complex number. For the following discussion it is important to realize that the equation $|z-c|=r$ represents a circle with centre at c and radius r and that the inequality, the absolute value of $z-c$ less than r (that is, $|z-c|<r$) defines the interior of the circle, often called a disk.

The idea of correspondence

Functions. The idea underlying the function concept is that of a correspondence, or of a mapping of one set of objects D, called the domain, upon another set of objects R, called the range. If there is a unique definite object Q of R corresponding to every object P of D, then Q is said to be a function of P and is written $Q=f(P)$. If R and D are sets of real numbers, then the function is a function Q of a real variable.

For functions of complex variables, D and R are sets of complex numbers, and D is usually required to be a domain in a narrower sense, namely, an open connected set. This means that for every point of D there is a small

$$(98)\quad \begin{cases}(a, b)=(c, d) \text{ if and only if } a=c,\ b=d\\ (a, b)+(c, d)=(a+c,\ b+d)\\ (a, b)\cdot(c, d)=(ac-bd,\ ad+bc)\\ c\cdot(a, b)=(ac,\ bc)\end{cases}$$

$$(99)\quad (a, b)=a\cdot(1, 0)+b\cdot(0, 1)=a+bi$$

$$(100)\quad c=r(\cos\theta+i\sin\theta)=re^{i\theta}$$

$$(101)\quad \frac{f(z)-f(z_0)}{z-z_0}$$

$$(102)\quad U_x=V_y,\qquad U_y=-V_x$$

$$(103)\quad F_{xx}+F_{yy}=0$$

$$(104)\quad \sum_{n=0}^{\infty} a_n(z-a)_n$$

$$(105)\quad \frac{1}{R}=\lim\sup|a_n|^{1/n}$$

$$(106)\quad F(z)=\sum_{k=0}^{\infty}\frac{F^{(k)}(b)(z-b)^k}{k!}$$

$$(107)\quad \int_C f(z)dz=\int_0^1 f[g(t)]\,dg(t)$$

$$(108)\quad \int_C f(z)dz=0$$

$$(109)\quad f(z)=\frac{1}{2\pi i}\int_C\frac{f(t)dt}{t-z}$$

$$(110)\quad f^{(n)}(z)=\frac{n!}{2\pi i}\int_C\frac{f(t)dt}{(t-z)^{n+1}}$$

$$(111)\quad \begin{cases}f(z)=\sum_{-\infty}^{\infty}a_n(z-b)^n\\ a_n=(2\pi i)^{-1}\int_C f(t)(t-b)^{-n-1}dt\end{cases}$$

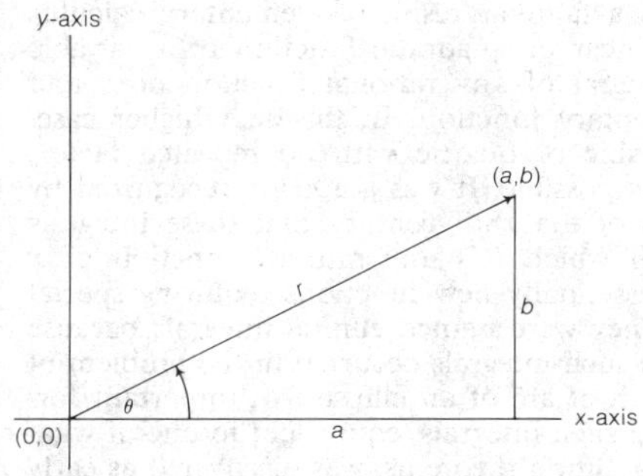

Figure 16: Geometric representation of a complex number $a + bi$ by the vector of length r that joins the origin (0, 0) and the point (a, b) in the x, y plane, making an angle θ with the x-axis. As indicated by the relations shown, $r = \sqrt{a^2 + b^2}$ and $\theta = \arctan b/a$.

neighbourhood that is also in D and that any two points of D may be connected by an unbroken line in D.

A function $f(z)$ defined in D may be continuous there. This means that if z is near to z_0 in D, then $f(z)$ is near to $f(z_0)$ in R. The differentiable functions form a subclass of the continuous functions. In the present case $f(z)$ is said to be differentiable at a point z_0 in D if the ratio (see 101) of the difference of the function evaluated at two points to the difference of the two points approaches a finite limit when z approaches z_0, the limit being independent of how z approaches z_0. This limit is known as the derivative of $f(z)$ at $z = z_0$ and is denoted by $f'(z_0)$ (see *Real analysis* above). If $f'(z)$ exists everywhere in D, the function $f(z)$ is said to be holomorphic or analytic in D. The term analytic, however, will be used below in a more general sense.

Holomorphic functions

The formal rules of the calculus apply to complex-valued functions. Thus, sums and products of functions holomorphic in D are also holomorphic in D, although in the case of a quotient the points at which the denominator is zero must be excepted. If n is a positive integer, z^n is holomorphic in the finite plane; this implies that every polynomial is a holomorphic function and that rational functions are holomorphic except at the zeros of the denominators.

If $f(z) = U(x, y) + iV(x, y)$ is holomorphic in D, then the real-valued functions U and V have partial derivatives with respect to x and y that satisfy the Cauchy-Riemann equations relating these partial derivatives (see 102, in which subscripts indicate differentiation with respect to x and y). Conversely, if a pair of real-valued functions has continuous partials in D that satisfy the Cauchy-Riemann equations, then $f = U + iV$ is holomorphic in D. The functions U and V are known as conjugate harmonic or logarithmic potential functions. They satisfy Laplace's equation in which the sum of two second partial derivatives is restricted to equal zero (see 103). This is the two-dimensional analogue of the equation satisfied by the Newtonian potential.

Power series. The basic class of holomorphic functions is formed by the power series (see 104). Such a series converges for a given z if the sequence of partial sums converges to a finite limit. This may happen only for $z = a$ or, at the other extreme, for all values of z. In general, there exists a positive number R, known as the radius of convergence of the series, such that it converges (even absolutely) for $|z - a| < R$ and diverges for every z outside the circle $|z - a| = R$, known as the circle of convergence. The value of R is given by a limiting form for its reciprocal (see 105).

The sum of the series in $|z - a| < R$ is a holomorphic function $F(z)$, the derivative of which can be obtained by termwise differentiation of the power series. The resulting power series has the same radius of convergence and may be differentiated as often as desired. Thus $F(z)$ has derivatives of all orders. According to Weierstrass, the power series defines an element of an analytic function. Further elements can be obtained by elementary rearrangements of the power series (see 104).

If $|b - a| < R$, $z - a = (z - b) + (b - a)$ can be written, and the nth power of this expression can be expanded by the binomial theorem, multiplied by a_n and added. Collection of terms results in Taylor's series (named after the 17th–18th-century English mathematician Brook Taylor); that is, the result of such collection is a power series for f in which the coefficients are constructed from values of derivatives of f (see 106) and that converges at least for $|z - b| < R - |a - b|$. If the radius of convergence exceeds this value, then the new series defines a holomorphic function in a disk that overlaps the old one. In the intersection of the two disks the functions coincide; outside, each function defines the analytic continuation of the other. The new element (see 106) can be rearranged in the same manner and gives rise to further new elements. The totality of such elements (with some adjunctions; see below) constitutes the analytic function defined by the first power series (104). In this process, it is possible to get back to the starting point with an element distinct from this series (104). The number of distinct elements having the same centre $z = a$ is at most countable.

Taylor's series

It may happen that the power series (104) cannot be continued outside its circle of convergence, which in this case is said to be the natural boundary of the function $F(z)$. In a certain sense this is the rule rather than the exception; the phenomenon is apt to present itself if the coefficients exhibit recurrent nonperiodic irregularities, such as very long gaps between terms, or if the coefficients have only a finite number of distinct values that do not recur periodically.

THE CAUCHY THEORY

Cauchy's integral theorem. A rectifiable curve C is given by $z = g(t)$, for t greater than or equal to zero and less than or equal to unity; that is, $0 \leq t \leq 1$, in which $g(t)$ is continuous and of bounded variation. If $f(z)$ is continuous on C, then the Riemann-Stieltjes integral of $f[g(t)]$ with respect to $g(t)$ (see 107) exists. If D is a simply connected domain with $f(z)$ holomorphic in D and, further, if C is a simple, closed, rectifiable curve in D, then the integral of the function around the curve is zero (see 108).

This basic theorem, announced by Cauchy in 1825, is the source of most of the results in analytic-function theory. First, it gives a representation of $f(z)$ in terms of its boundary values on C. If z is interior to C, then the function evaluated at that point has a representation in terms of an integral extended around the boundary (see 109). The integral can be differentiated with respect to z under the sign of integration as often as desired (see 110). Thus, the existence of a first derivative implies the existence of derivatives of all orders.

Representation theorems. Cauchy's formula (see 109) can also be used to obtain expansions of $f(z)$ in infinite series. The Cauchy kernel $(t - z)^{-1}$ is expanded in a series of the desired type; multiplication by $f(t)$ and termwise integration then gives the corresponding series for $f(z)$. In this manner, for instance, Taylor's series (106), with F replaced by f, which converges in the largest circle with centre at b in which $f(z)$ is holomorphic, is obtained. Laurent's series, named for the French mathematician Pierre Alphonse Laurent, is obtained in an analogous manner (see 111). It is valid in the largest annulus (a ring-shaped region) $0 \leq R_1 < |z - b| < R_2 \leq \infty$ in which $f(z)$ is holomorphic. Various expansions of holomorphic functions in so-called interpolation series are obtainable by the same method.

The Cauchy kernel

If in the Laurent series (111) $R_1 = 0$, the point $z = b$ is an isolated singularity of $f(z)$. This singularity is removable if $a_n = 0$ for $n < 0$. It is a pole of order m if $a_{-m} \neq 0$ but a_{-k} is identically equal to zero—that is, $a_{-k} \equiv 0$, for $k > m$; it is an essential singularity in the remaining case. The coefficient a_{-1} is known as the residue of $f(z)$ at $z = b$. In the case of a pole, $|f(z)|$ is uniformly large in the neighbourhood of $z = b$. The function $f(z)$ is assigned the value ∞ (infinity) at $z = b$, and the expansion (111) is adjoined to the elements that define the analytic function.

At an essential singularity no value can be assigned to the function; in fact, $f(z)$ assumes every value infinitely often, with at most one exception, in every neighbourhood of $z = b$ (which was proved by Charles Émile Picard, a French mathematician, in 1879).

Residue theorem. Cauchy's theorem (see 108) must be modified if $f(z)$ is not holomorphic inside C. If the only singularities are isolated and none lies on C, then the integral of the function around the curve is expressed in terms of a sum (see 112), in which the summation extends over the residues of the integrand inside C. This residue theorem of Cauchy also has a large number of applications. Cauchy used it to evaluate definite integrals—a problem of considerable practical importance in electrical engineering, physics, and other fields. He also used his residue theorem for the first rigorous discussion of series expansions arising in boundary value problems of mathematical physics, and this is still a valuable method. The residue theorem also plays a central role in the theory of elliptic functions.

Applications

(112) $$\int_C f(z)dz = 2\pi i \,\Sigma a_{-1,k}$$

(113) $$\begin{cases} \displaystyle\int \frac{dx}{\sqrt{(1-x^2)(1-k^2x^2)}} \\ \displaystyle\int \sqrt{\frac{1-k^2x^2}{1-x^2}}\,dx \\ \displaystyle\int \frac{dx}{(1+nx^2)\sqrt{(1-x^2)(1-k^2x^2)}} \end{cases}$$

(114) $$u = \int_0^x \frac{ds}{\sqrt{(1-s^2)(1-k^2s^2)}}$$

Another important application of the residue theorem is the principle of the argument. Suppose that inside C there are no singularities other than poles of $f(z)$ and that no pole or zero lies on C. If the residue theorem is applied to the logarithmic derivative of $f(z)$, it is found that the change in the argument of $f(z)$ as z describes C in the positive sense equals 2π times the difference in the number of zeros and poles of $f(z)$ inside C.

ENTIRE AND MEROMORPHIC FUNCTIONS

A function $f(z)$ is entire (integral in British terminology) if it is holomorphic in the finite plane. It is transcendental if it does not reduce to a polynomial. In 1876 Weierstrass showed how to construct an entire function of given zeros. An entire function without zeros is of the form exp $[g(z)]$, where $g(z)$ is also entire. Entire functions are classified according to a quantity called their order, which is closely related to the asymptotic behaviour of the coefficients of the defining power series and imposes an upper bound on the frequency of the zeros.

An entire function takes on every value infinitely often, with at most one exception. This theorem, proved by Picard in 1879 by use of the elliptic modular function, has been in the centre of attention ever since. Elementary proofs have been found by the French mathematician Émile Borel and by the German mathematician Edmund Landau, and the theorem also follows from a mapping theorem due to André Bloch, proved in 1924. It is now a simple consequence of an elaborate theory of the distribution of the values assumed by an entire or meromorphic function developed by Frithiof Nevanlinna and Rolf Nevanlinna of Finland starting in 1924.

A function having only polar singularities is said to be meromorphic. The representation of such a function by partial fractions was given by the Swedish mathematician Magnus Gösta Mittag-Leffler in 1877. (Ed.)

ELLIPTIC FUNCTIONS

One example of analytic functions is the class of functions known as elliptic functions. They have many applications in algebraic geometry, topology, the algebraic theory of numbers, and other fields of mathematics. Also, they have influenced the development of the general theory of functions of complex variables.

Origins. It is a familiar result of elementary calculus that if R is a linear or quadratic function of a variable x, then the integral of any rational function of x and $\sqrt{R}$ is an elementary function. In the next higher case, when R is a cubic or quartic with no repeated factor, no such result is possible. It was gradually recognized by mathematicians of the 18th century that these integrals $\int f(x, \sqrt{R})dx$, in which f is any rational function of x and $\sqrt{R}$, were essentially new functions requiring special investigation. They were named elliptic integrals because a special case of such integrals occurred in the problem of finding the length of arc of an ellipse. An important formula connecting such integrals, equivalent to one of what are now called addition theorems, was discovered as early as 1761 by Leonhard Euler of Switzerland. The first systematic treatment of the new integrals, however, is a legacy of Adrien-Marie Legendre, a French mathematician, who proved, among other results, that any elliptic integral can be reduced to the sum of an elementary function and of constant multiples of integrals in three standard forms (see 113) involving the variable x as well as k and n, in which k and n are constants called the modulus and the parameter, respectively. These three integrals are called Legendre's standard (or normal) elliptic integrals of the first, second, and third kinds, respectively.

Abel's work

But before Legendre finished his *Traité des fonctions elliptiques et des intégrales Eulériennes* in 1826, Niels Henrik Abel of Norway, in competition with Karl Gustav Jacob Jacobi of Germany, revolutionized the subject. If a variable u is expressible as an indefinite integral of one of the three standard forms in which k appears (see 114) and if the parameter k is 0 in this integral, then $u = \sin^{-1}x$ or $x = \sin u$. In 1825 Abel recognized this fact and inverted the relation between u and x (for k not necessarily 0) by treating x as a function of u instead of following Legendre in treating the integral u as a function of x. The function x obtained in this manner is denoted by sn u or, more precisely, by sn (u, k). Two more functions, cn u and dn u, are defined similarly; together with sn u they are called Jacobi's elliptic functions, as distinguished from Legendre's elliptic integrals, which, however, Legendre himself called *fonctions elliptiques*. From the analogy with trigonometric functions, Abel and Jacobi immediately obtained important properties of the new functions: their double periodicity (see below *Properties*) and the addition theorems that express sn $(u + v)$, etc., as rational functions of sn u, cn u, dn u, and sn v, cn v, dn v. It is now known that many of the fundamental results of Abel and Jacobi had been anticipated, but not published, by Carl Friedrich Gauss, a German mathematician.

Properties. Jacobi's sn u, cn u, dn u are simple cases of a more general class of functions having the same or similar properties, namely, elliptic functions. Let ω_1, ω_2 be any complex numbers such that $\omega_2/\omega_1 = \tau$ is not real. A function $f(u)$ of a complex variable u is said to be doubly periodic in ω_1, ω_2 if $f(u + \omega_1) = f(u + \omega_2) = f(u)$. An elliptic function is a single-valued doubly periodic analytic function $f(u)$ that has no singularities other than poles for any finite value of u. To obtain the properties of such a function, it is convenient to use the geometric representation of complex numbers by points in a plane (the Argand diagram, named for the Swiss mathematician Jean-Robert Argand). Any parallelogram with vertices at a, $a + \omega_1$, $a + \omega_1 + \omega_2$, $a + \omega_2$ (a arbitrary) is called a parallelogram of the periods; if the properties of $f(u)$ are known throughout any one parallelogram, then from the periodicity its properties are known everywhere, so that it suffices to study one parallelogram. The function $f(u)$ may also be considered as an analytic function on the torus obtained by identifying opposite sides of a parallelogram of periods. This interpretation of elliptic functions as functions on tori is the starting point of the modern analytic approach to the theory.

Theta functions. To study the properties of his elliptic functions, Jacobi introduced four allied functions $\theta_j(u, \tau)$, $j = 1, 2, 3, 4$, called theta functions. Jacobi could express his elliptic functions as quotients of θ's and obtain most of the fundamental properties of elliptic functions by using theta functions.

$$(115)\quad p(u) = \frac{1}{u^2} + \sum{}' \left(\frac{1}{(u-\omega)^2} - \frac{1}{\omega^2} \right)$$

$$(116)\quad p'^2(u) = 4p^3(u) - g_2 p(u) - g_3$$

$$(117)\quad u = \int_{\infty}^{x} \frac{ds}{\sqrt{4s^3 - g_2 s - g_3}}$$

The Weierstrass theory. Weierstrass founded his theory of elliptic functions on a function $p(u)$ defined by (115) in which the sum is taken over all numbers $\omega \neq 0$ of the form $m\omega_1 + n\omega_2$, m, $n = 0, \pm 1, \pm 2, \ldots$, ω_1 and ω_2 being any given complex numbers such that ω_2/ω_1 is not real. The function $p(u)$ is an elliptic function with periods ω_1, ω_2; it has poles of order 2 at the points ω and at 0, is regular elsewhere, and satisfies a differential equation that is quadratic in the derivative of the function and cubic in the function itself, coefficients being g_2 and g_3 as well as the constant 4 (see 116), where g_2, g_3 are constants depending only on the periods. Thus, $p(u)$ is the inverse function of the elliptic integral that involves the cubic just mentioned (see 117).

Letting $x = p(u)$, $y = p'(u)$, then $u \leftrightarrow (x, y)$ defines a one-to-one correspondence between points u in a parallelogram of periods and points (x, y) on the plane algebraic curve defined by $y^2 = 4x^3 - g_2x - g_3$, and the elliptic functions with the given periods may be considered as rational functions on this curve. This observation enabled mathematicians to develop the theory of elliptic functions entirely within the realms of algebra and algebraic geometry without recourse to the theory of functions of a complex variable. Thus, the scope of the theory of elliptic functions can be broadened considerably. (K.Iw./Ed.)

Theory of analytic functions of several complex variables

DEVELOPMENT OF COMPLEX ANALYSIS

Complex analysis arose from the study of analytic functions of one or several complex variables. Beginning with Riemann's fundamental discoveries in the middle of the 19th century, there was a gradual but continual shift of emphasis toward the investigation of global properties of analytic functions by topological (see GEOMETRY: *General topology*) and algebro-geometrical methods, with the result that complex analysis became rather intricately interwoven with the other principal mathematical disciplines and could be viewed only against the background of mathematical development as a whole, which is characterized in the 20th century by a remarkable synthesis of ideas.

Functions of one complex variable

Analysis of the properties of functions of one complex variable (complex analysis in one dimension) had a remarkable growth during the second half of the 19th century as a result of the brilliant research of Riemann and others. Shortly after 1900 the general principle of uniformization, conceived by Felix Klein of Germany and Henri Poincaré of France, was established by Paul Koebe. These developments were presented as a unified theory in 1913 by Claus Hugo Hermann Weyl, a German-born mathematician who emigrated to the United States in 1933.

During the latter part of the 19th and the beginning of the 20th century, the theory of functions of several complex variables made its appearance, as did algebraic geometry, especially the theory of algebraic surfaces founded by Max Noether of Germany, Charles Émile Picard, Henri Poincaré, and, last but not least, the Italian geometers Guido Castelnuovo, Federigo Enriques, and, somewhat later, Francesco Severi. In 1895 Pierre Cousin investigated certain global properties of analytic functions on domains in complex n-space and brought to the attention of mathematicians two problems that were later to bear his name; the study of these and related problems led to some of the most important developments of complex analysis during the first half of the 20th century.

In the years following the publication of Weyl's book, the geometric concepts, first introduced into complex analysis by Riemann, were studied for their own sake and vastly generalized as a result of the growth of topology as a branch of mathematics. Solomon Lefschetz, a Russian-born American mathematician, made a profound study of the topological properties of algebraic surfaces in a tract that exerted considerable influence on the later development of complex analysis, topology, and algebraic geometry. Élie-Joseph Cartan, a French mathematician, developed and applied systematically the theory of exterior differential forms that merged with topology in the fundamental theorem proved by the Swiss mathematician Georges de Rham in 1932 and helped give birth to the concept of cohomology in algebraic topology (see ALGEBRA). Stefan Bergman discovered an important type of Hermitian metric on subdomains of complex n-space that was subsequently generalized by Erich Ernst Kähler of Germany and became known as a Kähler metric.

Harmonic differential forms

Beginning about 1932, the British mathematician Sir William Vallance Douglas Hodge generalized the theory of harmonic functions on Riemann surfaces to harmonic differential forms on higher dimensional compact Riemannian manifolds, and on complex manifolds that possess Kähler metrics. Hodge's theory was developed and perfected during the 1940s by the Japanese mathematician Kodaira Kunihiko, who also generalized the theory to open manifolds and introduced systematically the method of orthogonal projection in Hilbert space (named after David Hilbert, a German mathematician).

Simultaneous with the development of the theory of harmonic differential forms, an intensive investigation of questions related to the Cousin problems was made by Oka Kiyoshi of Japan, Heinrich Adolf Louis Behnke and Karl Stein of Germany, Henri Cartan of France, and others. Although the methods used by these investigators differed somewhat from those of Hodge, Kodaira, and de Rham, the time was becoming ripe for a remarkable confluence of ideas, and this took place shortly after 1950 with the introduction into complex analysis of new notions from algebraic topology, namely, fibre bundles and cohomology with coefficients in sheaves (see GEOMETRY: *Algebraic topology*).

The idea of a fibre bundle was first recognized during the period 1935–40, while the notion of a sheaf was introduced into topology a few years later by the French mathematician Jean Leray (similar concepts, never precisely defined, had occurred earlier in various special contexts). The introduction of these concepts had an explosive effect on the development of complex analysis during the following years.

A third advance of great importance in complex analysis, which took place during the period 1935–50, was the development, principally by the German mathematician Carl Ludwig Siegel, of the theory of automorphic functions of several complex variables.

HOLOMORPHIC FUNCTIONS OF SEVERAL COMPLEX VARIABLES

If C denotes the set of all complex numbers, C^n is used to denote the set of n-tuples $z = (z_1, \ldots, z_n)$. Here n is an integer and each of $z_1, \ldots, z_n$ is a complex number. For any z in C^n, $|z|$ denotes the positive square root of a sum of absolute values of components (see 118); here $z = (z_1, \ldots, z_n)$, and $|z_j|$ is the absolute value of the complex number z_j for $j = 1, \ldots, n$.

Now, if Ω is a subset of C^n, it is called an open set if, for any point a in Ω, all points of C^n sufficiently close to a actually lie in Ω (that is, there is a positive number ρ such that any z in C^n with $|z - a| < \rho$ belongs to Ω).

$$(118)\quad (|z_1|^2 + \cdots + |z_n|^2)^{1/2}$$

$$(119)\quad \sum_{k_1, \ldots, k_n} c_{k_1 \ldots k_n} (z_1 - a_1)^{k_1} \ldots (z_n - a_n)^{k_n}$$

$$(120)\quad f(z) = (f_1(z), \ldots, f_m(z))$$

An open set Ω is called a domain if it is connected—that is, if any two points of Ω can be joined by an arc lying entirely in Ω.

If a complex-valued function f is defined on the open set Ω [f associates to any point z in Ω a complex number $f(z)$], f is said to be holomorphic on Ω if the following holds:

For any point $a = (a_1, \ldots, a_n)$ in Ω, there is a family $\{c_{k_1 \ldots k_n}\}$ of complex numbers, one for each n-tuple $(k_1, \ldots, k_n)$ of nonnegative integers, such that, for each z in C^n sufficiently near a, the series of generalized power series type with coefficients from the family of complex numbers (see 119) converges to the value $f(z)$ of the function f at z.

Some basic properties of holomorphic functions are the following:

1. A holomorphic function is continuous; it possesses partial derivatives of any order; and each partial derivative is again a holomorphic function.

2. If f and g are two holomorphic functions on the domain Ω (Ω is open and connected) and if $f(z) = g(z)$ for all z in some neighbourhood of a point of Ω, then f and g are identical.

3. In the maximum principle, f is taken to be holomorphic on Ω, in which Ω is a domain in C^n. Furthermore, there is a point a in Ω such that $|f(a)| \geq |f(z)|$ for any z in Ω. It follows that f is a constant ($f(z)$ is independent of z).

For later use, the following notation is introduced. Ω is an open set in C^n, and $f: \Omega \rightarrow C^m$ is a map of Ω into C^m (n and m are positive integers). For each z in Ω, the value $f(z)$ is a point in C^m, hence is an m-tuple (see 120). This defines m functions $f_1, \ldots, f_m$ on Ω. The map $f: \Omega \rightarrow C^m$ is said to be holomorphic if each of $f_1, \ldots, f_m$ is a holomorphic function on Ω.

Another basic fact concerning holomorphic functions can be stated as follows:

4. Ω is taken to be open in C^n, and $f: \Omega \rightarrow C^m$ is a holomorphic map. Furthermore, Ω' is taken to be an open set in C^m containing all the points $f(z)$ as z runs over Ω. Finally, φ is a holomorphic function on Ω'. Then the function $\varphi \circ f$ defined on Ω' by $\varphi \circ f(z) = \varphi[f(z)]$ is holomorphic on Ω'.

Topological space

A topological space is a set on which the notion of open set is given. Hence, on a topological space, the notion of a continuous function is defined. A map of one topological space onto another is said to be bicontinuous, or to be a homeomorphism, if it is one-one, continuous, and the inverse map is also continuous. Two topological spaces are said to be homeomorphic if they are connected by a homeomorphism. Homeomorphic spaces are topologically equivalent; *i.e.*, their intrinsic topological properties are the same.

A map of one open set of C^n onto another is said to be biholomorphic if it is one-one and holomorphic (which implies that the inverse is also holomorphic). The ball of C^n cannot be mapped biholomorphically onto the polycylinder of C^n if $n > 1$. Thus, topologically equivalent domains are not generally holomorphically equivalent, except under certain circumstances in the case when n is equal to 1.

CONFORMAL MAPS

The study of conformal maps arose from the necessity of constructing geographic maps. Because the surface of the Earth is approximately a sphere, it is readily seen that it cannot be represented on a flat surface with preservation of the proportion of all distances. The next best property to be preserved is the relative shape of configurations in the neighbourhood of each point; this, in a more precise mathematical formulation, amounts to preservation of the magnitude and sense of angles at each point. Such a map is called conformal. Examples of conformal maps include the familiar Mercator (which was named after Gerardus Mercator, a Flemish mathematician and geographer of the 16th century) and stereographic projections. In a conformal map of one open set of the plane onto another, it is possible to verify that the map is given locally by a biholomorphic transformation of one complex variable.

On the other hand, a biholomorphic map of one open set of C^n onto another is not generally conformal if $n > 1$. Throughout this section it will be supposed that $n = 1$.

The preceding local characterization of a conformal map disposes only of the most trivial aspect of the map because the characterization gives no information concerning the existence of a conformal map of one given plane domain onto another. Because it is impossible, except in the most trivial cases, to construct conformal maps explicitly, attention has centred mainly on the problems of proving their existence and of determining their properties.

A necessary condition in order that there should exist a biholomorphic (one-one conformal) map of one plane domain onto another is that there should exist a bicontinuous map (homeomorphism) of the one domain onto the other, and it is a remarkable fact that this necessary condition is in some cases sufficient.

Riemann mapping theorem

If D is a domain of C that is not the whole of C, and D is homeomorphic to the unit disk $|z| < 1$, then there exists a unique biholomorphic (one-one conformal) map of D onto the unit disk $|z| < 1$. It has the property that a prescribed point Z_0 of D goes into the centre of the disk, and a given direction at Z_0 transforms into the direction of the positive real axis.

Although the whole plane C is homeomorphic to the unit disk, it is impossible to map it conformally onto the unit disk; this is a consequence of a classical theorem of the 19th-century French mathematician Joseph Liouville.

The symbol S is used to denote the class of functions f of the complex variable z that are holomorphic in the unit disk, that map it one-one conformally onto domains of C, and that are normalized by the condition that their power series in z, convergent for $|z| < 1$, are of the form with lowest power z being 1 and with coefficient of z being 1 (see 121). In his proof of the general uniformization principle (of which the Riemann mapping theorem is a special case), Koebe introduced the class S and studied some of its properties. If the class S is suitably topologized, then, for each integer $n > 1$, the map $F^n: S \rightarrow C^n$, which sends the function f of S into the point $(a_2, a_3, \ldots, a_{n+1})$ of C^n, determined by the n coefficients $a_2, a_3, \ldots, a_{n+1}$ in the power series development of f, is continuous. If the image of S under the map F is denoted by B^n, then the set B^n, homeomorphic to the closed unit ball $|w^1|^2 + |w^2|^2 + \cdots + |w^n|^2 \leq 1$ of C^n, is called the nth coefficient region of S. The structure of the class S is completely determined by a knowledge of these coefficient regions and the maps F^n.

$$f(z) = z + a_2 z^2 + a_3 z^3 + a_4 z^4 + \cdots + a_n z^n + \cdots \qquad (121)$$

In 1916 the German mathematician Ludwig Georg Elias Moses Bieberbach proved that B^1 is the region $|a_2| \leq 2$ and, soon thereafter, posed the problem of investigating the regions B^n for all n. He further conjectured that $|a_n| \leq n$ for all n (the Bieberbach conjecture). This problem and conjecture were later followed by an intensive study of the class S. The Bieberbach conjecture was eventually proved in 1984 by Louis de Branges. (R.Na./Ed.)

DIFFERENTIAL EQUATIONS

Extensive use in science and technology

Differential equations are equations that relate a function f to its derivatives. This type of equation finds widespread application in science and technology because it can be used to express natural laws that describe the behaviour of rates of change of quantities. A well-known example in physics concerns radioactivity. A radioactive element changes spontaneously into a stable element, a process that is known as radioactive decay or disintegration. The law describing this behaviour states that the rate of decay with time—that is, the amount of a substance changing per second, say—is proportional to the amount of substance present. Initially, when the material is a pure radioactive element, this rate of decay is high. As the radioactive element changes into a stable element, however, the rate of change falls because there is less radioactive material. Therefore, the rate of decay decreases continuously with time.

In this process the quantity of interest is the amount of substance (n) remaining after a given time—*i.e.*, the number of atoms or the mass. Clearly this quantity will depend in some way on the time that has elapsed; in other words, it is a mathematical function of time and can be denoted by $n(t)$.

A formulation of the law is that dn/dt equals the product of $-\lambda$ and n (see Box, law 122). In this case n represents the amount of radioactive material, λ is a constant, and dn/dt is a notation for the rate at which n increases with time. The minus sign is required because n is decreasing with time and not increasing. The expression dn/dt is known as the derivative of n with respect to t. An idea of the nature of a derivative can be obtained by considering the behaviour of a specific function of x, say x^2. If x has the value a (a real number), this function has the value a^2. If this value now changes to $(a+h)$, the value of the function becomes $(a+h)^2$. The change in the value of the function is $(a+h)^2-a^2$, and this change has occurred as a result of x changing by h. Thus, the rate at which x^2 has changed with respect to the change in x is given by the quotient $\frac{(a+h)^2-a^2}{h}$. This gives an average rate of change over the value h. If h now becomes smaller and tends to zero, the quotient tends to the value $2a$, because, when the $(a+h)^2$-term is expanded and the a^2-term subtracted from it, the division yields $2a+h$ (see 123). $2a$ is the rate of change of x^2 with x at the point a and is known as the derivative of the function. If a is allowed to vary—*i.e.*, to take any values—a new function $2x$ is obtained that for a given value of x expresses the rate of growth of x^2 with x at that value. In general, a function of a single real variable x can be denoted by $u(x)$ and its derivative by $du(x)/dx$ or by $u'(x)$. This process can be repeated: the derivative of $u'(x)$ can be formed and denoted by $u''(x)$ or by $d^2u(x)/dx^2$, and similarly for higher derivatives $u^{(n)}(x)$.

(122) $$\frac{dn}{dt}=-\lambda n$$

(123) $$\frac{(a+h)^2-a^2}{h}=\frac{a^2+2ah+h^2-a^2}{h}=2a+h$$

(124) $$a\frac{d^2\theta}{dt^2}=-g\sin\theta$$

(125) $$\frac{d^2x}{dt^2}=0,\qquad \frac{d^2y}{dt^2}=-g$$

(126) $$\kappa=\left[1+\left(\frac{dy}{dx}\right)^2\right]^{-3/2}\frac{d^2y}{dx^2}$$

(127) $$\left[1+\left(\frac{dy}{dx}\right)^2\right]\frac{d^3y}{dx^3}-3\frac{dy}{dx}\left(\frac{d^2y}{dx^2}\right)^2=\left[1+\left(\frac{dy}{dx}\right)^2\right]^{5/2}\psi(x)$$

(128) $$y'=\frac{dy}{dx},\qquad y''=\frac{d^2y}{dx^2},\qquad y'''=\frac{d^3y}{dx^3},\qquad \ldots$$

(129) $$[1+(y')^2]y'''-3y'(y'')^2=[1+(y')^2]^{5/2}\psi(x)$$

(130) $$[1+(y')^2]y'''=3y'(y'')^2$$

(131) $$c^2\frac{\partial^2y}{\partial x^2}=\frac{\partial^2y}{\partial t^2}$$

When the independent variable is time and the dependent variable distance, the first derivative is velocity, the rate at which distance changes with time. The second derivative is acceleration, the rate at which velocity changes.

Returning to the example of radioactive decay, the equation involves a derivative and is one example of a differential equation. The solution of this differential equation is the function $n(t)$, which shows how n depends on t. The problem of solving it is that of finding the function of t the derivative of which is $-\lambda n(t)$.

Motion of a pendulum

A common example of a differential equation that involves a second derivative is the equation describing the motion of a simple pendulum under the influence of gravity. The second derivative of the angular displacement from the vertical θ is proportional to the sine of the angular displacement (see 124). The equation involves the length a of the pendulum and g, the acceleration of a falling body under the influence of gravity, called the acceleration of free fall. The equation may be expressed in words as follows. The rate of increase with time of the rate of increase of angular displacement with time (the angular acceleration) is directed toward the vertical position and is inversely proportional to the length of the pendulum and directly proportional to the sine of the angular displacement. This rather complicated verbalization illustrates the economy and precision of the mathematical formulation.

Most physical situations are too complicated to be expressed simply by one variable depending on another. For example, the position of a body in a vertical plane is given by two coordinates x and y, indicating the distances from a vertical and horizontal axis respectively. The motion of a body moving in this plane can be expressed by an equation involving these two coordinates (x, y), each of which depends on the time t.

In particular, if air resistance is neglected, a particle moving under the influence of gravity is described by a pair of differential equations expressed in terms of second derivatives (see 125), in which g denotes the acceleration caused by gravity. There is no acceleration in the horizontal direction because there is no force in this direction.

A further example is provided by geometry. It is shown in calculus that the curvature κ of a curve the equation of which in Cartesian coordinates is $y=y(x)$ is defined in terms of the second derivative of y (see 126). A curve with the property that the rate of change with respect to x of its curvature is a prescribed function $\psi(x)$ therefore has an equation that satisfies the equation $d\kappa/dx=\psi(x)$, which is equivalent to an equation involving a third derivative (see 127). By using the alternative notation of primes denoting differentiation (see 128), it is also possible to write this equation in a more simple form (see 129). For example, a circle has constant curvature so that it has $\psi(x)\equiv 0$; hence, all circles are symbolized by the same differential equation with the term involving $\psi(x)$ set equal to zero (see 130).

The preceding examples are all equations that involve functions of a single variable. Derivatives of such functions are called ordinary derivatives, and, therefore, equations of this type are called ordinary differential equations. The pair of equations involves simultaneously the derivatives of two independent variables x and y and is an example of a pair of ordinary simultaneous differential equations.

The transverse displacement of a vibrating string is determined by an equation of a totally different kind. If the string is at rest stretched to a tension T between points $x=0$ and $x=a$ of the x-axis, then, if the string is set vibrating, the displacement, y, of a point that originally had a coordinate x will depend not only on x but also on the time t. In other words, y is a function of two independent variables, x and t. Its variation is governed by the fact that the second partial derivative with respect to x is proportional to the second partial derivative with respect to t (see 131), the proportionality constant $c=\sqrt{T/\sigma}$, σ being the mass per unit length of the string. The derivatives in this equation are partial derivatives, and the equation is an example of a partial differential equation. The theory of such equations is markedly different from the theory of ordinary differential equations, and it will be considered later in this article.

Ordinary differential equations

Equations of the first order and first degree

An ordinary differential equation is a relation connecting the function y of an independent variable x and its derivatives $y', y'', \ldots, y^{(n)}$ (see 132). If the derivative of the highest order occurring in the equation is $y^{(n)} = d^ny/dx^n$, the equation is said to be of order n. For example, equation (122) is a first-order equation, and equations (124) and (125) have an order of two. The power to which the highest derivative occurs is called the degree of the equation. Equations (122), (124), and (125) are of the first degree; a second-order differential equation involving $(y'')^2$ and no higher of y' (see 133), however, is of the second degree because the highest derivative occurs to the power 2. If the equation is of a form (see 134) in which the function y and its derivatives occur linearly and in which the coefficients $a_n(x), \ldots, a_1(x), a_0(x)$ depend only on x and not on y or any of its derivatives, the equation is said to be linear. If $\psi(x) \equiv 0$ (equal for all values of x), the equation is said to be homogeneous; and, if $\psi(x)$ is not equal to zero for all values of x, it is said to be nonhomogeneous. Equation (122) is linear and homogeneous, but equation (124) is nonlinear.

(132) $f(x, y, y', \ldots y^{(n)}) = 0$

(133) $(y'')^2 + (y')^3 + y^4 = 0$

(134) $a_n(x)y^{(n)} + \cdot \cdot \cdot + a_1(x)y' + a_0(x)y = \psi(x)$

(135) $(b^2y - a^3)^{1/2}y' = a$

(136) $(1 - x^4)^{1/2}y' + (1 - y^4)^{1/2} = 0$

HISTORICAL BACKGROUND

The study of differential equations is almost as old as that of the calculus itself. Newton discovered a method of infinite series and the calculus in 1665–66. In 1671 he wrote an account of his theory of "fluxions," a fluxion being a derivative of a "fluent," the name Newton gave to his dependent variables. Newton discussed "fluxional equations," or, as they are now called, differential equations. These he divided into three categories. In modern notation, the first category is that in which dy/dx is a function of x alone or of y alone; the second consists of ordinary differential equations of the first order of the form $dy/dx = f(x, y)$; and the third is made up of partial differential equations of the first order. Newton derived solutions of differential equations by a method using power series with indeterminate coefficients, which he claimed to be universally effective. Though written in 1671 in Latin, his work, entitled *The Method of Fluxions and Infinite Series,* was not published until 1736. As a result it had little or no influence on the development of the theory of differential equations.

Leibniz and his followers

A greater impact was made by the work of the German mathematician and philosopher Gottfried Wilhelm Leibniz. Although his investigations were not begun until 1673, Leibniz became known through the publication of his results in 1684 in the *Acta Eruditorum* ("Deeds of Distinguished Men"), a scientific journal that had been established only two years earlier.

Foremost among the devoted followers of Leibniz were the Swiss mathematicians, the brothers Jakob and Johann Bernoulli. With others of their family, they played a notable part in the development of the theory of differential equations and of the use of such equations in the solution of physical problems.

In May 1690 in a paper in the *Acta Eruditorum,* Jakob Bernoulli showed that the problem of determining the isochrone—*i.e.,* the curve in a vertical plane such that a particle will slide from any point to the bottom in exactly the same time, no matter what the starting point—is equivalent to that of solving a first-order nonlinear differential equation (see 135). He then solved the equation by what is now called the method of separation of variables; the general method was enunciated by Leibniz in the following year. Jakob Bernoulli's paper of 1690 is a milestone in the history of calculus, for in it the term integral occurs in the literature for the first time.

In 1692 Leibniz discovered the method of solving first-order equations of homogeneous type and still later that of solving linear equations of the first order. The problem of finding the general solution of what is now called Bernoulli's equation was proposed by Bernoulli in 1695 and solved by Leibniz and Johann Bernoulli by different methods. Thus, within a few years of the birth of the infinitesimal calculus, most of the known methods of solving first-order ordinary differential equations had been developed.

Early applications

Numerous applications of the use of differential equations in deriving the solutions of geometric problems were made before 1720. Among these may be mentioned the problem of determining a plane curve the curvature of which is a prescribed function of position and that of finding the orthogonal trajectories of a given family of plane curves. Some of the differential equations formulated in this way were of the second or higher order. Second-order equations of the form $F(y, y', y'') = 0$, in which the independent variable x does not appear explicitly, were discussed as early as 1712 by an Italian mathematician, Count Iacopo Francesco Riccati, although, in fact, Jakob Bernoulli had earlier studied the special case $y' = x^2 + y^2$. Some of the younger members of the Bernoulli family, particularly Daniel, contributed to studies of such equations. Important work on first-order equations of exact type and of first-order equations of degree higher than the first was done in the 1730s by Alexis-Claude Clairaut, a Frenchman who was one of the most precocious mathematicians of all time.

The second period in the history of differential equations was dominated by Leonhard Euler, the Swiss mathematician who made many contributions to the theory, starting in 1728. He introduced several methods of lowering the order of an equation, the concept of an integrating factor, the theory of linear equations of arbitrary order, the development of the use of series solutions, and the discovery that a first-order nonlinear differential equation with square roots of quartics as coefficients (see 136) has an algebraic solution. This last result, which is a special case of Abel's theorem, led to the theory of elliptic functions created in the 1820s by Niels Henrik Abel and Karl Gustav Jacob Jacobi.

Much of the early work on differential equations was concerned with the discussion of basic questions about what is meant by a function or by the solution of a differential equation. Such questions continued to be raised because the answers found satisfactory by one generation of mathematicians were challenged by their successors. The first attempt to establish a rigorous theory of functions was made by Abel and Augustin-Louis Cauchy in the 1820s. Cauchy's work in real analysis gave an entirely new direction to the theory of ordinary differential equations, steering it away from the investigating of techniques of solution into the asking of general questions about the existence and uniqueness of solutions. Cauchy himself proved the first existence theorem and gave methods of deriving solutions through limiting processes. The theory of analytic functions, also due to Cauchy, led to the creation of the theory of differential equations in the complex domain and, in turn, to the study of functions of several complex variables.

Recent work

Much recent work in ordinary differential equations is of a basic nature, concerned with the conditions that guarantee the existence of a solution of a given equation; the theory is more concerned with establishing that a solution exists than with trying to derive a closed form for it. Such an attitude is essential when many of the practical problems involving differential equations are solved by the use of electronic computers; the validity of numerical processes must be thoroughly investigated. The study of differential equations continues to contribute to the solution of practical problems in control theory, in orbital mechanics, and in many other branches of science and technology, and also to ask challenging questions of pure mathematicians working in such apparently abstract subjects as functional analysis and the theory of differentiable manifolds.

TYPES OF PROBLEMS SOLVABLE WITH THIS DISCIPLINE

Some simple examples of how differential equations may arise in the analysis of problems in physics and geometry have already been given. In such problems the unknown quantity has to satisfy not only a differential equation but also some other conditions. For example, the quantity $n(t)$ may have to satisfy the condition that at $t=0$ it takes a prescribed value N. Some other problems that can be solved with the help of differential equations are listed below.

Problems in mechanics. *The catenary.* If a cable of uniformly distributed mass m per unit length is suspended between two points A and B, the curve formed by the cable is called a catenary. If a coordinate system is chosen with an origin vertically below the lowest point of the curve, and with a y-axis that is vertically upward, the shape of the curve is determined by a second-order nonlinear differential equation (see 137), involving a constant a (with the dimensions of length). The constant is expressed in terms of T, the vertical tension acting on the cable at its lowest point, and g, the acceleration caused by gravity, by the formula $a = T/(mg)$. If the distance of the origin below the lowest point of the cable is taken to be a, the required solution must satisfy the conditions $y(0) = a$, $y'(0) = 0$.

Motion in a line under known forces. The motion of a particle of mass m projected vertically upward in a straight line with velocity v is described by a differential equation relating the time derivative of mv to g (see 138) and the resistance of the medium $R(v)$, the function R being known. If the mass m is constant, the left side of the equation reduces to the time derivative of the velocity (see 139). If m is a prescribed function of v, the left side can be attacked by the rule for differentiating a product (see 140).

(137) $$a\frac{d^2y}{dx^2} = \left[1 + \left(\frac{dy}{dx}\right)^2\right]^{1/2}$$

(138) $$\frac{1}{m}\frac{d}{dt}(mv) = -g - R(v)$$

(139) $$\frac{dv}{dt} = -g - R(v)$$

(140) $$\left[1 + \frac{vm'(v)}{m(v)}\right]\frac{dv}{dt} = -g - R(v)$$

(141) $$\frac{d^2r}{dt^2} = -g\left(\frac{R}{r}\right)^2$$

(142) $$r = R, \qquad \frac{dr}{dt} = V, \quad \text{when } t = 0$$

(143) $$\frac{d^2x}{dt^2} + g\left(1 + \frac{x}{R}\right)^{-2} = \frac{V_e f}{m_0 - ft}$$

(144) $$\begin{cases} \dfrac{d^2\rho}{dt^2} - \rho\left(\dfrac{d\varphi}{dt}\right)^2 = -c\rho^2 \\ \dfrac{d}{dt}\left(\rho^2\dfrac{d\varphi}{dt}\right) = 0 \end{cases}$$

(145) $$\begin{cases} L\dfrac{dx}{dt} + Rx + \dfrac{q}{C} = E(t) \\ L\dfrac{d^2q}{dt^2} + R\dfrac{dq}{dt} + \dfrac{q}{C} = E(t) \end{cases}$$

(146) $$\begin{cases} L_1\dfrac{dx}{dt} + R_1x + \dfrac{q}{C} + M\dfrac{dy}{dt} = E(t) \\ M\dfrac{dx}{dt} + L_2\dfrac{dy}{dt} + R_2y = 0, \quad \text{with } x = \dfrac{dq}{dt} \end{cases}$$

Escape velocity from the Earth. If the acceleration caused by gravity at the Earth's surface is g, then, at time t, the distance r from the Earth's centre of a particle moving vertically upward is determined by a differential equation which states that the second derivative of v is proportional to $(R/r)^2$ (see 141), in which R is the radius of the Earth. If the initial velocity of projection is V, then the initial conditions are the position and velocity at $t = 0$ (see 142). The motion at any point in the upward trajectory is determined by the solution of this initial value problem. If the particle is to escape from the Earth's gravitational field, $(dr/dt)^2$ must exceed zero for all values of r. It turns out that this condition is satisfied only if V^2 is greater than or equal to $2gR$. For this reason $\sqrt{(2gR)}$ is called the escape velocity from the Earth.

Vertical motion of a rocket. A problem of interest is that of a rocket ascending in a straight line under the influence of gravity with a thrust that is constant both in magnitude and direction.

The thrust of the rocket is produced by the ejection of mass at a constant rate f with exhaust velocity V_e, which when measured relative to the rocket is constant. The height x above the Earth's surface at a time t while the rocket is still firing is determined by the nonlinear differential equation (see 143) relating the second derivative of x to an expression of the form $(1 + x/R)^2$ and involving g, the acceleration caused by gravity at the Earth's surface; R, the radius of the Earth; and m_0, the initial mass of the rocket. The initial conditions in this case are that $x = 0$, $dx/dt = V$ when $t = 0$.

Motion of a planet under an inverse square law. If a planet is moving in a plane under an inverse square law, then its motion can be described by the plane polar coordinates r, θ, the origin of which is situated at the centre of force.

The inverse square law relates the radial force on the planet to the inverse of the square of the distance from the origin. The motion is described by a pair of second-order differential equations derived from Newton's second law (see 144) involving a constant c.

Problems in other areas of physics. *Electrical circuits.* The electrical current x in a simple circuit containing a resistance R, a self-inductance L, and a capacitance C when a voltage $E(t)$ is applied is determined by a simple differential equation (compare Figure 17A). The drops in voltage across the ends of the resistance and the inductance are, respectively, Rx and $L(dx/dt)$. The drop across the capacitance is q/C, in which q is the charge on the condenser. The current is given by $x = dq/dt$, and the voltage $E(t)$ must equal the sum of the voltage drops. The charge is therefore determined by the differential equation obtained by substituting $x = dq/dt$ (see 145).

Similarly, for the coupled circuits shown in Figure 17B, the currents x and y are determined by a pair of similar linear second-order differential equations (see 146).

Self-oscillatory problems. Certain electrical circuits, such as feedback circuits controlled by thermionic values, have the property that a source of power increases with the amplitude of the oscillation. To exhibit the main features of the behaviour of such systems, the 20th-century Dutch mathematician Balthasar van der Pol took as his mathematical model a second-order equation (see 147), which is now called van der Pol's equation. This equation is typical of the models describing a series of self-oscillatory problems. For example, the equation for the oscillations of a valve generator with a cubic valve characteristic can be reduced to van der Pol's equation; van der Pol himself used this equation in the theory of the oscillations in a symmetric multivibrator, in which there is an inductance.

The equations of van der Pol and Laplace

Potential theory. In many branches of physics, such as electrostatics, magnetostatics, irrotational motion of perfect fluids, and others, an equation of interest is the partial differential equation named after Pierre-Simon Laplace, the 18th-century French mathematician. This equation

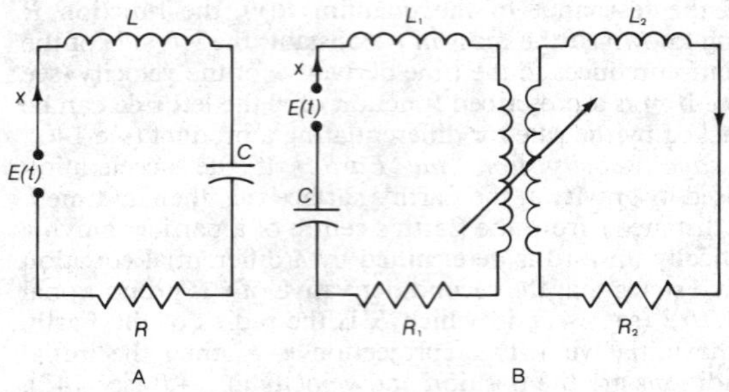

Figure 17: *Electrical circuits.*
(A) Simple circuit containing a resistance R, a self-inductance L, and a capacitance C. (B) Coupled circuits in which the currents x and y are determined by a set of differential equations.

(see 148) relates second partial derivatives of the potential u. The equation can be expressed in cylindrical coordinates (ρ, φ, z) (see 149). If there are solutions of this equation in the form of a product of $\exp(-\xi z)$, $\cos(\nu\varphi)$ and some function of ρ, $R(\rho)$ (see 150), then R must be a solution of a second-order linear ordinary differential equation with variable coefficients so that $R(\rho) = \omega(\xi\rho)$ in which $\omega(t)$ is a solution of a second-order linear equation with variable coefficients (see 151) known as Bessel's equation of order ν, so named after Friedrich Wilhelm Bessel, the 19th-century German mathematician and astronomer.

Similarly, Laplace's equation can be expressed in spherical coordinates (see 152). For axisymmetric solutions of the form $v(r, \theta) = r^n\Theta(\theta)$ (*i.e.*, solutions that do not depend on the azimuthal angle φ) Θ must be a solution of another linear ordinary differential equation with variable coefficients (see 153). Changing the independent variable in this equation from θ to $\mu = \cos\theta$ gives solutions of the desired form if $\Theta(\theta) = w(\cos\theta)$, in which $w(\mu)$ is any solution of the ordinary differential equation (see 153) called Legendre's equation of order n, named after Adrien-Marie Legendre. (See *Potential theory* below.)

Legendre's equation

Stellar structure. An interesting ordinary differential equation arises in the discussion of the theory of stellar structure. If the gravitational equilibrium of a mass of gas is considered, it is found that its pressure p varies with the distance r from the centre of the mass according to a second-order differential equation involving G, the gravitational constant, and ρ, the density (see 154). The density is related to the pressure through the physical law $\log p = \log k + (1 + 1/\mu) \log \rho$ in which K and μ are constants. If $\log \rho = \log \rho_c + \mu \log \theta$, in which ρ_c is the central density, and a new independent variable $\xi = kr$ is introduced, in which k is defined in terms of ρ_c and constants (see 155), the Lane-Emden equation and initial conditions for it are obtained (see 156). (The equation was named for the astronomers Jonathan Homer Lane of the United States and Robert Emden of Switzerland.) Unless μ is 0 or 1, the equation is nonlinear.

The harmonic oscillator in wave mechanics. One problem in wave mechanics is that of determining the wave function ψ of a particle of mass m moving on the x-axis under the action of a force $-kx$. The wave function ψ for a particle has the physical significance that $|\psi(x, y, z)|^2\, d\tau$ is the probability of finding the particle in a small element of volume $d\tau$ centred at the point with coordinates (x, y, z). In this problem the equation describing the particle is a particular case of a more general second-order differential equation named after a 20th-century Austrian physicist, Erwin Schrödinger (see 157), involving E, the total energy of the particle, and h, Planck's constant. The problem here is not so much to solve this ordinary differential equation as to find the possible values of E that ensure $|\psi| \to 0$ as $|x| \to \infty$. (For an understanding of convergence to the real number "infinity," see *Real analysis* above.) If the variables are changed to $x = (h^2/4\pi^2mk)^a z$, $a = 1/4$, and $\lambda = (4\pi E/h)(m/k)^{1/2}$, an equation relating $d^2\psi/dz^2$ and $(\lambda - z^2)\psi$ (see 158) is obtained. The problem is to find the set of allowed values of λ ensuring the existence of solutions such that $|\psi| \to 0$ as $|z| \to \infty$. Such a problem is called a Sturm-Liouville problem (named after the 19th-century French mathematicians Charles-François Sturm and Joseph Liouville).

Control theory. A different kind of problem involving differential equations arises in optimal control theory. In control theory attention is first of all focused on a process—that is, some action changing with time and usually described by a differential equation or a system of differential equations. In parallel with the concept of process, controls are considered for influencing the particular process being discussed, and the objective is the result achieved by the process through a properly applied control strategy. If, with respect to some criterion of performance, the strategy that is best is sought, the problem is called an optimal control problem.

A simple problem of this kind is that of driving a railroad locomotive from one station to another on the assumption that the same force is available for both starting and stopping—*e.g.*, two rocket motors pointed in opposite directions and each capable of a maximum thrust P. If the locomotive is treated as a particle of mass m and the

Typical control theory problem

(147) $$\frac{d^2x}{dt^2} - \mu(1 - x^2)\frac{dx}{dt} + w^2x = 0$$

(148) $$\frac{\partial^2 u}{\partial x^2} + \frac{\partial^2 u}{\partial y^2} + \frac{\partial^2 u}{\partial z^2} = 0$$

(149) $$\frac{\partial^2 u}{\partial \rho^2} + \frac{1}{\rho}\frac{\partial u}{\partial \rho} + \frac{1}{\rho^2}\frac{\partial^2 u}{\partial \varphi^2} + \frac{\partial^2 u}{\partial z^2} = 0$$

(150) $$u(\rho, \varphi, z) = e^{-\xi z}\cos(\nu\varphi)\, R(\rho)$$

(151) $$\begin{cases} \dfrac{d^2R}{d\rho^2} + \dfrac{1}{\rho}\dfrac{dR}{d\rho} + \left(\xi^2 - \dfrac{\nu^2}{\rho^2}\right)R = 0 \\[2ex] \dfrac{d^2w}{dt^2} + \dfrac{1}{t}\dfrac{dw}{dt} + \left(1 - \dfrac{\nu^2}{t^2}\right)w = 0 \end{cases}$$

(152) $$\frac{\partial^2 v}{\partial r^2} + \frac{2}{r}\frac{\partial v}{\partial r} + \frac{1}{r^2 \sin\theta}\frac{\partial}{\partial\theta}\left(\sin\theta\,\frac{\partial v}{\partial\theta}\right) + \frac{1}{r^2\sin^2\theta}\frac{\partial^2 v}{\partial\theta^2} = 0$$

(153) $$\begin{cases} \dfrac{1}{\sin\theta}\left[\dfrac{d}{d\theta}\sin\theta\,\dfrac{d\Theta}{d\theta}\right] + n(n+1)\Theta = 0 \\[2ex] (1 - \mu^2)\dfrac{d^2w}{d\mu^2} - 2\mu\dfrac{dw}{d\mu} + n(n+1)w = 0 \end{cases}$$

(154) $$\frac{1}{r^2}\frac{d}{dr}\frac{r^2}{\rho}\frac{dp}{dr} + 4\pi G\rho = 0$$

(155) $$k^2 = \frac{4\pi G\rho_c^{1-1/\mu}}{[K(1+\mu)]}$$

(156) $$\begin{cases} \dfrac{d^2\theta}{d\xi^2} + \dfrac{2}{\xi}\cdot\dfrac{d\theta}{d\xi} + \theta^\mu = 0 \\[2ex] \theta = 1,\quad \dfrac{d\theta}{d\xi} = 0,\quad \xi = 0 \end{cases}$$

(157) $$\frac{d^2\psi}{dx^2} + \frac{8\pi^2 m}{h^2}\left(E - \frac{1}{2}kx^2\right)\psi = 0$$

(158) $$\frac{d^2\psi}{dz^2} + (\lambda - z^2)\psi = 0$$

(159) $$m\frac{d^2x}{dt^2} = f$$

decreases in m caused by loss of fuel and all resistance phenomena are neglected, the product of m and the second derivative of x equals f (see 159), in which x is the distance traveled by the locomotive from its starting point and f is the force applied by the rocket motors. The control is defined by the inequality $|f| \leq P$. As an objective, one of the following conditions could be taken:

1. The journey must be accomplished in the minimum time.
2. To avoid excessive wear on components, the journey must be accomplished with the minimum expenditure of energy.
3. The amount of rocket fuel used should be kept to a minimum.

Once one of these criteria has been decided upon, the optimal control problem consists of designing a scheme for applying f in such a way as to achieve the desired result—*i.e.*, of selecting from the set of solutions of the differential equations corresponding to all permissible forms of f the one that is best.

Chemical kinetics. Simple chemical reactions can be described by first-order ordinary differential equations. A simple first-order reaction such as the decomposition of nitrogen pentoxide may be considered first. If c is the concentration of nitrogen pentoxide at time t, then the derivative of c is equal to the product of a constant k, which is called the rate constant for the reaction, and $-c$ (see 160).

Similarly, in a second-order reaction of the type $A + B \rightarrow A' + B'$ in which a and b are the initial concentrations of A and B, respectively, and x is the change in the concentration of either A or B that has occurred at time t, the derivative of x is proportional to the product of $(a - x)$ and $(b - x)$ (see 161).

Reversible reactions can also be described by differential equations. For example, consider a simple reaction of the type $A \underset{k_2}{\overset{k_1}{\rightleftharpoons}} B$, such as the interconversion of *a-d-*glucose (A) and *β-d-*glucose (B) in which a and b are the initial concentrations of A and B and $a - x$ and $b + x$ their values at time t. (If $dx/dt = 0$ the reaction is at equilibrium.) The derivative of x is proportional to the difference of $k_1(a - x)$ and $k_2(b + x)$, in which k_1 and k_2 are constants (see 162).

A catalytic reaction is one in which some substance, known as a catalyst, changes the reaction rate without itself going through any permanent change. In an autocatalytic reaction a substance A is transformed to another substance B, which then acts as a catalyst for the reaction. If x is the concentration of B at time t and N is its final value, then such a process can be described by a differential equation in which dx/dt is proportional to the product of x and $(N - x)$ (see 163).

Growth of populations. To illustrate how ordinary differential equations arise in biology, an equation arising in a simple study of the growth of populations is considered. The expression $p(t)$ denotes the number of inhabitants of a given area at time t, and it is assumed that, in the time interval t to $t + h$, (i) the number of individuals born is Nph, (ii) the number of individuals dying is Mph, (iii) the number of individuals entering the area is Ih, and (iv) the number of individuals leaving the area is Eh, in which N, M, I, and E will, in general, be functions of both p and t. The function $p(t)$ is then determined by the fact that its first derivative is proportional to the obvious combination of these quantities (see 164).

In one population model it is assumed that I and E are constants and that $N = n - \nu p$, $M = m + \mu p$ in which m, n, μ, and ν are constants. If these forms are substituted into the above population equation and $n - m = \varepsilon$ and $\mu + \nu = k$, a nonlinear differential equation known as Verhulst's equation is obtained (see 165), the constant ε being called the coefficient of increase and k being called the limiting coefficient.

If the population is isolated (*i.e.*, if there is neither immigration nor emigration), $I = E = 0$, and the equation reduces to a simpler form in which dp/dt equals the product of p and $\varepsilon - kp$ (see 166).

Physiology. *Regulation of carbon dioxide in the body.* An example of the occurrence of a pair of ordinary simultaneous equations in physiology is provided by a simple model of the regulation of carbon dioxide (CO_2) in the human body. In this model it is assumed that the carbon dioxide is distributed between two compartments corresponding to the lungs and the remaining tissue and that respiration is a function of CO_2 only. With further simplifying assumptions it can be shown that during respiration C_A, the alveolar (lung) CO_2 concentration, and C_T, the concentration of CO_2 in the tissue, are determined by the pair of simultaneous equations that relate dC_A/dt and dC_T/dt each to C_A and C_T (see 167), in which V_A and V_T are the respective volumes of the alveolar and tissue compartments; C_I is the concentration of inspired carbon dioxide; a_1, a_2, a_3, b_1, b_2 are constants; and R is the rate at which carbon dioxide is formed by metabolism.

Distribution of creatinine in the human body. Another example taken from physiology arises in the analysis of a two-compartment model for the distribution of creatinine in the human body. The first compartment is the blood plasma; the second is not clearly identified, but there is evidence that such a compartment exists. If Q_1, Q_2 denote, respectively, the quantities of creatinine in the first and second compartments, their variation is determined by a pair of linear first-order differential equations relating dQ_1/dt and dQ_2/dt to Q_1 and Q_2 (see 168), with rate constants k_1, k_2, and k_3.

TYPES OF SOLUTIONS

A relation $y = \varphi(x)$ is said to be a solution or integral of the differential equation $f(x, y, y', \ldots, y^{(n)}) = 0$ in the range $a \leq x \leq b$ if, when substituted into the equation, it gives a result that is identically zero in that range (see 169). It is frequently difficult or undesirable to express a solution y explicitly as a function of x, but instead to have an implicit relation $F(x, y) = 0$ between the solution y and the independent variable x. Such a relation is a solution if, when solved explicitly for y in terms of x, it yields a

(160) $$\frac{dc}{dt} = -kc$$

(161) $$\frac{dx}{dt} = k(a - x)(b - x)$$

(162) $$\frac{dx}{dt} = k_1(a - x) - k_2(b + x)$$

(163) $$\frac{dx}{dt} = kx(N - x)$$

(164) $$\frac{dp}{dt} = (N - M)p + (I - E)$$

(165) $$\frac{dp}{dt} = \varepsilon p - kp^2 + (I - E)$$

(166) $$\frac{dp}{dt} = p(\varepsilon - kp)$$

(167) $$\begin{cases} \dfrac{dC_A}{dt} = \dfrac{1}{V_A}[a_1C_T - a_2C_A - a_3 + (b_1C_T - b_2)(C_T - C_A)] \\ \dfrac{dC_T}{dt} = \dfrac{1}{V_T}[R - a_1C_T + a_2C_A + a_3] \end{cases}$$

(168) $$\begin{cases} \dfrac{dQ_1}{dt} = k_2Q_2 - (k_1 + k_3)Q_1 \\ \dfrac{dQ_2}{dt} = k_1Q_1 - k_2Q_2 \end{cases}$$

(169) $$f\{x, \varphi(x), \varphi'(x), \ldots, \varphi^{(n)}(x)\} \equiv 0, \quad a \leq x \leq b$$

solution in the way described above. For example, if both sides of a polynomial equation in x and y are differentiated with respect to x, then the function $y(x)$ determined by this implicit relation will be a solution of the differential equation thereby obtained (see 170). The simplest of all ordinary differential equations is $y' = g(x)$, in which g is an elementary function. An example is $g(x) = 2x$. The problem of solving this differential equation is equivalent to finding a function $y(x)$ the derivative of which is $2x$; this leads to the solution $y = x^2 + c$ in which c is an arbitrary constant. The process of integration has led to the occurrence of an arbitrary constant in the solution. It can be seen intuitively (and it can be proved rigorously) that finding the solution of a differential equation of the nth order will somehow be equivalent to performing n integrations and that the final solution $y(x)$ will contain n arbitrary constants of integration.

Occurrence of arbitrary constants

$$(170)\quad \begin{cases} x^3 + y^3 + 3xy = 1 \\ (x + y^2)y' + x^2 + y = 0 \end{cases}$$

$$(171)\quad (y')^2 + xy' - y = 0$$

$$(172)\quad y = cx + c^2$$

$$(173)\quad y = x + 1$$

$$(174)\quad y(x) = -\frac{1}{4}x^2$$

$$(175)\quad 2(y')^3 = 3y$$

$$(176)\quad 9y^2 = 4(x - c)^3$$

$$(177)\quad \frac{d^2y}{dx^2} + \omega^2 y = 0$$

$$(178)\quad y(x) = c_1 \cos(\omega x) + c_2 \sin(\omega x)$$

$$(179)\quad y(a) = y_0, \qquad y'(a) = v_0$$

Any solution of an nth order equation of the form $y = \varphi(x, c_1, c_2, \ldots, c_n)$ in which $c_1, \ldots, c_n$ are arbitrary constants is called a general solution of the equation. Any solution that may be obtained from the general solution of an equation by assigning particular values to the constants is called a particular solution of that equation. It sometimes happens that a nonlinear differential equation has a solution that cannot be obtained by assigning specific values to the arbitrary constants in the general solution. Such a solution is called a singular solution of the differential equation.

For example, a particular nonlinear differential equation (see 171) has a general solution that is linear in the independent variable (see 172) with an arbitrary constant c. A particular solution may be obtained from (172) by taking $c = 1$ (see 173). On the other hand, a function proportional to x^2 (see 174) also satisfies the differential equation. Because this solution cannot be obtained from the general solution by assigning a particular value to c, it is a singular solution of the differential equation (171). In this instance the graphs of the functions defined by (172) are straight lines, and the graph of the function defined by (174) is a parabola that is the envelope of that family of straight lines (cf. Figure 18).

Similarly, a nonlinear equation with the cube of the derivative proportional to y (see 175) has a general solution with y^2 proportional to $(x - c)^3$ (see 176) and the singular solution $y = 0$. Here the general solution is represented by a family of semicubical parabolas, and the singular solution is the line that passes through the cusp of each member of the family (cf. Figure 19). Such a line is called a cusp locus.

It has been pointed out above that the solution of problems in physics or engineering is equivalent to that of finding solutions of differential equations satisfying certain additional conditions. To illustrate the kind of problem arising in this way, the following equation may be considered: with the product of a constant, ω^2, and the function y being added to the second derivative of y to give a result of zero (see 177). Its general solution is found to

Boundary value problems

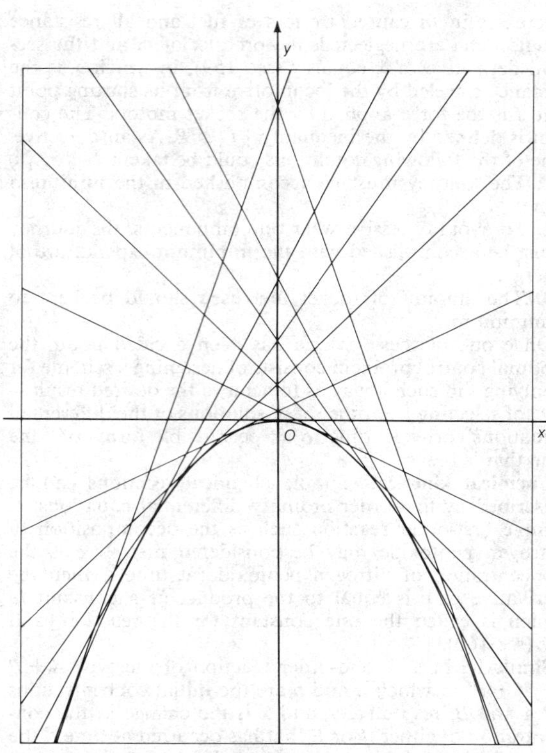

Figure 18: Graphs of functions defined by straight lines and a parabola that is the envelope of that family of straight lines (see text).

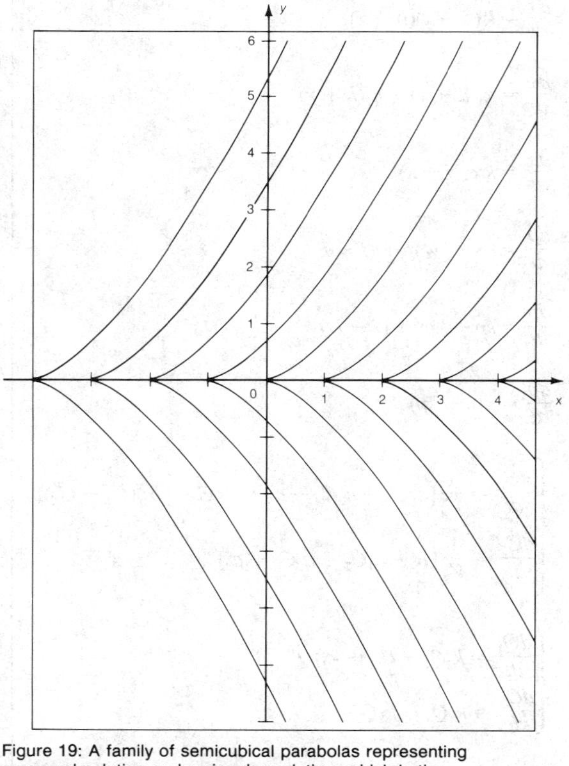

Figure 19: A family of semicubical parabolas representing a general solution and a singular solution, which is the line that passes through the cusp of each member of the family (see text).

be the product of a constant, c_1, and a cosine, added to the product of another constant, c_2, and a sine (see 178). The solution corresponding to the conditions of y and its derivative at some point a being set equal to y_0 and v_0, respectively (see 179), in which a, y_0, v_0 are prescribed real numbers, is obtained by choosing c_1 and c_2 to satisfy the linear algebraic equations obtained by setting the general solution at a equal to y_0 while its derivative is set equal to v_0 (see 180). The solution corresponding to the conditions of y at two different points a and b being set equal to constants y_0 and y_1, respectively (see 181), is obtained by choosing c_1 and c_2 to satisfy the linear equations obtained by setting the general solution at a and b equal to y_0 and y_1, respectively (see 182).

Problems of this kind are called boundary value problems; the problem posed by equations (177) and (179) is called a one-point boundary value problem or an initial value problem, while that posed by equations (177) and (181) is called a two-point boundary value problem.

Another kind of problem can be exemplified by reference to equation (177). It may be stated as a question: Do there exist real values of ω such that the equation (177) has nonzero solutions satisfying the boundary conditions $y(0) = y(a) = 0$? That there are real values of ω follows immediately from the fact that, if n is an integer, then the function $y = \sin(n\pi x/a)$ satisfies these boundary conditions and the differential equation considered above, with $\omega = n\pi/a$ (see 183). Hence, $\pm n\pi/a$, $n = 1, 2, 3, \ldots$, are possible values of ω. A problem of this kind is called an eigenvalue problem or a Sturm-Liouville problem.

(180) $$\begin{cases} c_1 \cos(\omega a) + c_2 \sin(\omega a) = b \\ -c_1 \sin(\omega a) + c_2 \cos(\omega a) = v_0 \end{cases}$$

(181) $$y(a) = y_0, \qquad y(b) = y_1$$

(182) $$\begin{cases} c_1 \cos(\omega a) + c_2 \sin(\omega a) = y_0 \\ c_1 \cos(\omega b) + c_2 \sin(\omega b) = y_1 \end{cases}$$

(183) $$\frac{d^2y}{dx^2} + \frac{n^2\pi^2}{a^2} y = 0$$

(184) $$\frac{dy}{dx} = f(x, y), \qquad y(a) = y_0$$

(185) $$y(x) = y_0 + \int_a^x f(t, y(t))dt$$

(186) $$|f(x, y_1) - f(x, y_2)| \le K\,|y_1 - y_2|$$

(187) $$\frac{dz}{dx} = Az, \qquad z(a) = z_0$$

(188) $$z = \begin{bmatrix} y \\ y' \end{bmatrix}, \quad A = \begin{bmatrix} 0 & 1 \\ -\omega^2 & 0 \end{bmatrix}, \quad z_0 = \begin{bmatrix} y_0 \\ v_0 \end{bmatrix}$$

(189) $$n = n_0 e^{-\lambda t}$$

(190) $$x = c_1 + c_2 t, \qquad y = c_3 + c_4 t - \frac{1}{2} g t^2$$

(191) $$y = a \cosh(x/a)$$

(192) $$\sum_{r=0}^{\infty} \frac{(-1)^r \left(\frac{1}{2}x\right)^{2r+v}}{r!(v+1)_r}$$

(193) $$\sum_{r=0}^{\infty} \frac{\left(\frac{1}{2}n + \frac{1}{2}\right)_r \left(\frac{1}{2}n + 1\right)_r}{r!\left(n + \frac{3}{2}\right)_r} x^{-2r-n-1}$$

(194) $$\sum_{r=0}^{[\frac{1}{2}n]} \frac{\left(\frac{1}{2} - \frac{1}{2}n\right)_r \left(-\frac{1}{2}n\right)_r}{r!\left(\frac{1}{2} - n\right)_r} x^{n-2r}$$

(195) $$\sum_{r=0}^{\infty} \frac{(-n)_r (n+1)_r}{r!r!} \left(\frac{1-x}{2}\right)^r$$

EXISTENCE AND UNIQUENESS OF SOLUTIONS

From the geometric interpretation of the derivative of a function, it is tempting to assume that the initial value problem consisting of a differential equation and the value y_0 of the function y at some point a (see 184) has a unique solution through each point (a, y_0) of the xy-plane. It is a simple matter, however, to construct differential equations that do not have a solution at all at a specific point and others that have more than one solution—often an infinite number—at a point. For this reason it is necessary to study sufficient conditions for the existence and uniqueness of solutions of the initial value problem (see 184). The proof of the classic theorem in this area depends on the fact that any solution of the initial value problem (184) satisfies the integral equation given by formally integrating both sides of the differential equation, the constant of integration being y_0 (see 185). Conversely, any solution of this integral equation is a solution of the initial value problem (184).

The Lipschitz condition

To state the fundamental result, the following concept is required: a function $f(x, y)$ is said to satisfy a Lipschitz condition with respect to y in a region D of the xy-plane if there exists a constant K such that the magnitude of the difference between $f(x, y_1)$ and $f(x, y_2)$ is less than or equal to K times the magnitude of the difference between y_1 and y_2 (see 186), for every pair of points $(x; y_1)$, (x, y_2) belonging to D. The condition is named after a 19th-century German mathematician, Rudolf Lipschitz.

The basic theorem states that, if $f(x, y)$ is continuous and satisfies a Lipschitz condition with respect to y in some region D of the xy-plane and if (a, y_0) is any point in this region, then the initial value problem (184) has a unique solution.

It turns out that continuity of f is sufficient to guarantee existence and that it is the Lipschitz condition on f that ensures uniqueness.

By generalizing the Lipschitz condition (see 186) to the case in which both f and y are n-vectors and D is a region of the xy-space (of dimension $n+1$), the theorem can be established for a vector differential equation (see 184). Now any differential equation of order n can be written as a first-order equation for an n-vector. For example, the initial value problem posed by equations (177) and (179) can be written in the form of an initial value problem for a first-order equation (see 187), but in this case z, A, z_0 denote matrices (see 188). The existence theorem for an nth-order equation can therefore be deduced from that for a first-order equation in which the independent variable is an n-vector.

FORMS OF SOLUTIONS

Closed-form solutions. In many cases it is possible to express the solution of a differential equation by a simple formula. For example, if the derivative of n is proportional to $-n$, then the general solution is an arbitrary constant n_0 times a negative exponential (see 189). The pair of equations describing motion in a gravitational field has as the general solution for x a linear function and for y a quadratic (see 190), with arbitrary constants c_1, c_2, c_3, and c_4. Similarly, the solution of the equation for a catenary satisfying the initial conditions $y = a$, $dy/dx = 0$ at $x = 0$ is a hyperbolic cosine (see 191).

Series solutions. Often when it is not possible to find a closed-form solution, it is a simple matter to find a solution in the form of an infinite series. This form of solution is particularly appropriate to the solution of second-order linear equations. For example, Bessel's equation has a series solution in powers of $x/2$ (see 192), in which the symbol $(v+1)_r$ denotes the product $(v+1)(v+2)\cdots(v+r)$. Similarly, Legendre's equation has a solution in the form of descending powers of x that is valid only if $|x|>1$ (see 193). The same equation has a power series solution valid if $|x|<1$ (see 194), and a series solution in powers of $(1-x)/2$ that is valid for $-1<x<3$ (see 195). It will be noted that in the case in which n is a positive integer,

Power series

(196) $$\int_\theta^a \frac{d\varphi}{\sqrt{(\cos\varphi-\cos a)}}=\frac{2g}{a}t$$

(197) $$\int_1^\infty \frac{e^{-zt}dt}{\sqrt{(t^2-1)}}$$

(198) $$y_{r+1}(x)=y_0+\int_a^x f\{t,\, y_r(t)\}dt, \qquad y_0(x)=y_0$$

(199) $$\frac{dy}{dx}=1+x^2y^2, \qquad y(0)=0$$

(200) $$x, \qquad x+\frac{1}{5}x^5, \qquad x+\frac{1}{5}x^5+\frac{2}{45}x^9+\frac{1}{325}x^{13}, \qquad \ldots$$

(201) $$y''=f(x,\, y,\, y'), \qquad y(a)=y_0, \qquad y'(a)=y_1$$

(202) $$y'''=\frac{\partial f}{\partial x}+\frac{\partial f}{\partial y}y'+\frac{\partial f}{\partial y'}y''$$

(203) $$y(a+h)=y_0+y_1+\frac{1}{2}y''(a)h+\cdots+\frac{1}{n!}y^{(n)}(a)h^n$$

(204) $$y(a+h)=y(a)+h\sum_{k=0}^{p}a_k f(a+b_kh,\, y_0+c_kh)$$

(205) $$y(a+h)=y(a)+(1-c)hf(a,\, y_0)+chf\left(a+\frac{h}{2c},\, y_0+\frac{k_0}{2c}\right)$$

(206) $$y_{r+1}=y_r+(1-c)k_r+cm_r$$

(207) $$\frac{dy}{dx}=f(x,\, y)$$

(208) $$\frac{dy}{dx}=f(x)g(y)$$

(209) $$y\frac{dy}{dx}=xy+x$$

(210) $$\int\frac{dy}{g(y)}=\int f(x)dx+c$$

(211) $$\int\frac{ydy}{y+1}=\int xdx+c$$

(212) $$\frac{dy}{dx}=g\left(\frac{y}{x}\right)$$

(213) $$x\frac{dv}{dx}+v=g(v)$$

each of the last two series reduces to a polynomial of degree n in x.

Integral forms. In a similar way, the solution of a differential equation can be expressed in the form of an integral that cannot be expressed in terms of elementary functions. For example, the solution of equation (124) satisfying the initial conditions $\theta=a$, $d\theta/dt=0$ when $t=0$ may be expressed by an equation involving an integral of a linear combination of a cosine to the $-1/2$ power (see 196). The integral on the left side of this equation cannot be expressed in terms of elementary functions. Similarly, Bessel's equation of order 0 has the solution as the integral of an expression involving exponentials and square roots (see 197).

Approximations. In many cases it is not possible to derive the solution of a differential equation in any of the above forms, and recourse has to be made to approximate methods.

Iteration method. In dealing with initial value problems, one of the simplest ways of obtaining an approximate solution is to solve the integral equation discussed earlier (see 185) by iteration—*i.e.*, to construct a sequence of approximations $y_1(x)$, $y_2(x)$, . . . , $y_n(x)$ by the scheme of substituting an approximation for y into the integral equation and obtaining as the result a better approximation and repeating the process (see 198). It can be proved that, if the conditions of the existence-uniqueness theorem are satisfied, this sequence will converge to the correct solution. By taking the nth iterate, an approximate solution of the initial value problem is obtained.

Approximate methods

For example, for the initial value problem for a certain first-order nonlinear differential equation (see 199), a sequence of approximations that are partial sums of a power series (see 200) is given.

Taylor series method. In theory this method is applicable to an equation of any order. As an example, the initial value problem for a second-order differential equation (see 201) is considered. First $y''(a)=f(a,\, y_0,\, y_1)$ is calculated. The given equation is differentiated with respect to x (see 202). This is evaluated at a to yield the value of $y'''(a)$. By successive differentiation $y^n(a)$ can be found for $n=3, 4, 5, \ldots$, and an approximation to the value of $y(a+h)$ can be found from the truncated Taylor series (see 203). The process is then repeated at the point $x=a+h$, and so on.

The Runge-Kutta methods. To indicate the methods devised by the German mathematicians Carl David Tolmé Runge (1895) and Martin Wilhelm Kutta (1901), the initial value problem (184) is considered. In these methods the Taylor expansion is used indirectly: $y(a+h)$ is calculated (see 204) in terms of $y(a)$, the function $f(x,\, y)$, and constants $a_0, \ldots, a_p$, $b_0, \ldots, b_p$, $c_0, \ldots, c_p$, which are chosen in such a way that, when the expression is expanded for $y(a+h)$ in ascending powers of h, the coefficients agree with those of the Taylor expansion for $y(a+h)$.

For example, if $p=1$ is taken, a formula involving two values of $f(x,\, y)$ is obtained (see 205). In this formula $k_0=hf(a,\, y_0)$, and c is any nonzero real number. The numerical solution of the initial value problem (184) can be generated by repeated applications of this relationship. If $x_r=a+rh$, $y_r=y(a+rh)$, $k_r=hf(x_r,\, y_r)$, and $m_r=hf(x_r+h/2c,\, y_r+k_r/2c)$, $(c\neq 0)$, then y_{r+1} can be calculated from y_r, k_r, m_r, and c (see 206). This is known as the Runge-Kutta second-order process. More elaborate schemes can, of course, be derived by taking a higher value of p. (I.N.S.)

Runge-Kutta second-order process

FIRST-ORDER EQUATIONS

When first-order equations of the first degree are solved for the derivative, they are of a form in which the derivative y' equals $f(x,\, y)$, an explicit function of x and y (see 207). There are certain distinguishable types of such equations that may be easily solved and that are now discussed briefly.

Equations with separable variables. If the derivative can be expressed as the product of $f(x)$ and $g(y)$ (see 208), in which $f(x)$ is a function of x alone and $g(y)$ is a function of y alone, it is said to have its variables separable. For example, the nonlinear equation in which the product of

$$(214)\quad \frac{dy}{dx} = \frac{2y^2 + x^2}{xy} = \frac{2\left(\frac{y}{x}\right)^2 + 1}{\frac{y}{x}}$$

$$(215)\quad x\frac{dv}{dx} + v = \frac{2v^2 + 1}{v}$$

$$(216)\quad \int \frac{v dv}{v^2 + 1} = \int \frac{dx}{x} + k$$

$$(217)\quad \log(v^2 + 1) = 2 \log x + \log c$$

$$(218)\quad v^2 + 1 = cx^2$$

$$(219)\quad x^2 + y^2 = cx^4$$

$$(220)\quad \frac{\partial \psi}{\partial x} = P(x, y), \qquad \frac{\partial \psi}{\partial y} = Q(x, y)$$

$$(221)\quad P(x, y) + Q(x, y)y' = 0$$

$$(222)\quad \psi(x, y) = c$$

$$(223)\quad \frac{\partial \psi}{\partial x} + \frac{\partial \psi}{\partial y}\, y' = 0$$

$$(224)\quad \frac{\partial P}{\partial y} = \frac{\partial Q}{\partial x}$$

$$(225)\quad 2e^x yy' + y^2 e^x - 1 = 0$$

$$(226)\quad \frac{\partial}{\partial y}(y^2 e^x - 1) = \frac{\partial}{\partial x}(2e^x y)$$

$$(227)\quad y^2 e^x - x = c$$

$$(228)\quad 2xy' + 3y = 0$$

$$(229)\quad 2yy'x^3 + y^2 \cdot 3x^2 = 0$$

$$(230)\quad \frac{\partial}{\partial y}(\mu P) = \frac{\partial}{\partial x}(\mu Q)$$

$$(231)\quad \frac{1}{Q}\left(\frac{\partial P}{\partial y} - \frac{\partial Q}{\partial x}\right) = g(x)$$

$$(232)\quad \frac{\mu'(x)}{\mu(x)} = g(x)$$

$$(233)\quad \mu(x) = \exp\{\textstyle\int g(x)dx\}$$

$$(234)\quad y' + a(x)y = b(x)$$

$$(235)\quad \mu(x) = \exp\{\textstyle\int a(x)dx\}$$

$$(236)\quad \begin{cases} xy' + (x^2 + 1)y = x \\ a(x) = x + x^{-1} \end{cases}$$

$$(237)\quad \begin{cases} \mu = \exp[\int (x + x^{-1})dx] \\ \quad = \exp\left[\frac{1}{2}x^2 + \log x\right] = xe^{(1/2)x^2} \end{cases}$$

$$(238)\quad \frac{d}{dx}[xe^{(1/2)x^2}y] = xe^{(1/2)x^2}$$

$$(239)\quad y = x^{-1} + cx^{-1}e^{(-1/2)x^2}$$

y and its derivative equals the sum of xy and x (see 209) has its variables separable. The general solution of such an equation is obtained by moving the expressions involving x to one side of the equation and those involving y to the other, and then integrating both sides (see 210), involving c, as arbitrary constant. For example, the equation just considered (see 209) has general solution in terms of an integral of y divided by $y + 1$ and an integral of x (see 211). These integrals can be evaluated, giving the result that $y - \log(y + 1) = x^2/2 + c$.

Homogeneous equations. A differential equation in which the derivative dy/dx equals $g(y/x)$, in which g is a function of y/x alone (see 212), is said to be homogeneous. Such an equation is reduced to separable form (see 213) by the substitution $y = xv$. For example, the equation in which dy/dx equals $2y^2 + x^2$ divided by xy (see 214) is homogeneous; the substitution $y = xv$ reduces it to the separable form as a differential equation with v as the dependent variable (see 215). It is possible to obtain the solution of this differential equation by certain integrations (see 216), in which k is an arbitrary constant. Performing the integrations, the general solution is obtained in terms of logarithms (see 217), in which c is an arbitrary constant; ($2k = \log c$)—*i.e.*, the sum of v^2 and 1 equals cx^2 (see 218). Returning to the original variables, the sum of x^2 and y^2 equals cx^4 (see 219), which is the general solution of equation (214).

Exact equations. If there exists a function $\psi(x, y)$ such that the partial derivative of ψ with respect to x equals $P(x, y)$, and the partial derivative of ψ with respect to y equals $Q(x, y)$ (see 220), the differential equation formed by the sum of $P(x, y)$ and the product of $Q(x, y)$ and y' being equal to zero (see 221) is said to be exact. The reason for this is that the function $y(x)$ defined by $\psi(x, y)$ being equal to an arbitrary constant c (see 222) has a derivative y' that satisfies the equation obtained by differentiating $\psi(x, y)$ with respect to x by the chain rule (see 223). Hence, because of these relations (see 220), the differential equation (221) follows. It is obvious from equations (220) that a necessary condition for the equation (221) to be exact is that the partial derivative of $P(x, y)$ with respect to y equals the partial derivative $Q(x, y)$ with respect to x (see 224); it can also be shown that this condition is sufficient. For example, a nonlinear differential equation with exponential coefficients (see 225) is exact because the partial derivative with respect to x of the coefficient of y' equals the partial derivative with respect to y of the rest of the equation (see 226). It has the general solution in implicit form with an arbitrary constant (see 227). Instead of saying that the equation (221) is exact, $P(x, y)dx + Q(x, y)dy$ is sometimes termed an exact differential.

Integrating factors. Although a differential equation may not be exact in the form in which it is encountered, it has been proved that it may be made exact by multiplication by a suitable factor. Such a multiplier is called an integrating factor. For example, the equation formed by the sum of $2xy'$ and $3y$ being equal to zero (see 228) is not exact, but multiplying throughout by x^2y gives an equation (see 229) that is exact and has a general solution $y^2x^3 = c$.

If both sides of equation (221) are multiplied by $\mu(x, y)$ and the exactness condition (224) is used, then μ will be an integrating factor of the equation if, and only if, it satisfies the condition that the partial derivative of μP with respect to y equals the partial derivative of μQ with respect to x (see 230). For example, the general first-order differential equation being considered (221) will possess an integrating factor $\mu(x)$ if, and only if, the difference of the partial derivative of P with respect to y and that of Q with respect to x, divided by Q, equals $g(x)$, a function of x alone (see 231), and then μ may be taken to be any solution of the equation given by $g(x)$ being equal to $\mu'(x)$ divided by $\mu(x)$ (see 232); *i.e.*, $\mu(x)$ is an exponential (see 233).

Linear equations. If the above procedure is applied to the linear first-order equation with the coefficient of y being $a(x)$ and the inhomogeneous term being $b(x)$ (see 234), it is found to have an integrating factor $\mu(x)$ equal to an exponential with the integral of $a(x)$ in the exponent (see 235).

$$(240)\quad P_n(x)y^{(n)} + P_{n-1}(x)y^{(n-1)} + \cdots + P_1(x)y' + P_0(x)y = f(x)$$

$$(241)\quad P_n(x)D^n + P_{n-1}(x)D^{n-1} + \cdots + P_1(x)D + P_0(x)$$

$$(242)\quad a_1y_1(x) + a_2y_2(x) + \cdots + a_ny_n(x) = 0$$

$$(243)\quad y(x) = c_1y_1(x) + \cdots + c_ny_n(x) + Y(x)$$

$$(244)\quad W(y_1, \ldots, y_n) = \begin{vmatrix} y_1(x) & \ldots & y_n(x) \\ y_1'(x) & \ldots & y_n'(x) \\ & \vdots & \\ y_1^{(n-1)}(x) & \ldots & y_n^{(n-1)}(x) \end{vmatrix}$$

$$(245)\quad \Pi_n(D)y = f(x)$$

$$(246)\quad \Pi_n(t) = p_nt^n + p_{n-1}t^{n-1} + \cdots + p_1t + p_0, \qquad (p_n \neq 0)$$

$$(247)\quad c_1e^{\lambda_1x} + c_2e^{\lambda_2x} + \cdots + c_ne^{\lambda_nx}$$

For example, if the sum of xy' and $(x^2 + 1)y$ equals x (see 236), then $\mu(x)$ is equal to the product of x and an exponential with exponent $x^2/2$ (see 237). The equation can be written as the derivative of the product of $\mu(x)$ and y being equal to $\mu(x)$ (see 238). Integrating and dividing by $x\exp(x^2/2)$ yields the general solution in terms of x^{-1}, an exponential, and an arbitrary constant c (see 239).

LINEAR DIFFERENTIAL EQUATIONS

Equations of *n*th order. A linear differential equation of order n is an equation involving y and its derivatives linearly, the coefficient of y^j being P_j, and the nonhomogeneous term being $f(x)$ (see 240), in which $P_n, \ldots, P_0, f$ are given functions of x, and $P_n(x)$ does not vanish identically. The linear differential equation obtained from equation (240) by replacing $f(x)$ by 0 is called the homogeneous equation, corresponding to the nonhomogeneous equation (240). For example, Bessel's equation and Legendre's equation are linear equations of the second order and of homogeneous type.

Homogeneous and nonhomogeneous equations

If the differential operator d/dx is denoted by D and if $\mathbf{L}$ is written for the operator formed by the sum of terms of the form P_jD^j (see 241), then equation (240) may be written in the form $\mathbf{L}y = f(x)$ and the corresponding homogeneous equation in the form $\mathbf{L}y = 0$.

Functions $y_1(x), \ldots, y_n(x)$ are said to be linearly independent solutions of the homogeneous equation $\mathbf{L}y = 0$ if $\mathbf{L}y_r(x) = 0$, $r = 1, 2, \ldots, n$ and if the functions are such that there does not exist a set of constants $a_1, a_2, \ldots, a_n$, not all of which are zero, such that, for all values of x, the sum of the terms $a_jy_j(x)$ is equal to zero (see 242).

The basic result in the theory of linear differential equations is that, if $y_1, y_2, \ldots, y_n$ are n linearly independent solutions of $\mathbf{L}y = 0$ and if $Y(x)$ is any solution of equation (240), then the general solution of (240) is $Y(x)$ added to a sum of terms of the form $c_jy_j(x)$ (see 243), in which $c_1, \ldots, c_n$ are arbitrary constants.

The general solution of a linear differential equation is therefore the sum of two parts: $c_1y_1(x) + \cdots + c_ny_n(x)$, which is called the complementary function, and $Y(x)$, which is called a particular integral. To determine whether a set of functions is linearly independent, the following criterion must be used: a necessary and sufficient condition that $y_1(x), \ldots, y_n(x)$ are linearly independent is that the Wronskian W, defined by the 19th-century Polish mathematician Hoëné Wronski as the determinant of the matrix formed by the n linearly independent solutions and their first $n - 1$ derivatives (see 244), is not identically zero.

Equations with constant coefficients. There is a simple theory of linear equations of the type (240) in which $P_r(x) = p_r$, a constant, $(r = 0, 1, \ldots, n)$. Such equations can be written in the form of an expression $\Pi_n(D)y$ set equal to $f(x)$ (see 245), in which $\Pi_n(t)$ denotes the polynomial defined as the sum of terms of the form p_jt^j (see 246).

The form of the complementary function depends on the zeros of the polynomial Π_n. If $\Pi_n(t)$ has n distinct zeros $\lambda_1, \lambda_2, \ldots, \lambda_n$, then the complementary function of the equation (245) is in the form of a sum of terms $c_j\exp(\lambda_jx)$ (see 247) in which, as before, $c_1, c_2, \ldots, c_n$ denote arbitrary constants. Some of the zeros may, of course, be complex, but if the coefficients $p_n, \ldots, p_0$ are real, then complex zeros when they do occur will occur in complex pairs.

For example, if $\lambda_1 = \mu_1 + i\omega_1$, then there will be another zero, which may be labeled λ_2, of the form $\lambda_2 = \mu_1 - i\omega_1$; the linearly independent solutions $\exp(\lambda_1x)\exp(\lambda_2x)$ may be replaced by $\exp(\mu_1x)\cos(\omega_1x)\exp(\mu_1x)\sin(\omega_1x)$. Putting this another way, it can be said that, if $\Pi_n(t)$ contains the simple quadratic factor $(t - \mu_1)^2 + \omega_1^2$, then the complementary function contains the corresponding terms that are products of the exponential $\exp(\mu_1x)$ and a linear combination of the sine and cosine of ω_1x (see 248).

On the other hand, if λ_1 is a multiple root, of order m, say—*i.e.*, if $\Pi_n(t)$ has a factor $(t - \lambda_1)^m$—the complementary function contains the terms $(c_1x + c_2x^2 + \cdots + c_mx^{m-1})\exp(\lambda_1x)$. Similarly, if $\Pi_n(t)$ has a factor of the form $[(t - \mu_1)^2 + \omega_1^2]^m$, there are $2m$ terms of the analogous form involving $\exp(\mu_1x)\cos(\omega_1x)$ and $\exp(\mu_1x)\sin(\omega_1x)$ (see 249) in the complementary function.

In many practical cases it is possible to obtain a particular integral $Y(x)$ by inspection. When this cannot be done, the Laplace transform is used. Because for $Y(x)$ any solution (see 245) may be taken, it is only necessary to find the solution $Y(x)$ of that equation satisfying the conditions of $Y(x)$ and its first $n - 1$ derivatives at $x = 0$ being equal to zero (see 250). If a function $\varphi(x)$ is defined for all positive real values of x, its Laplace transform is defined as the result of multiplying the function by e^{-px} and integrating from $x = 0$ to infinity (see 251). When $\mathfrak{L}[\varphi(p)]$ is the Laplace transform of $\varphi(x)$, $\varphi(x)$ is said to be the inverse Laplace transform of $\mathfrak{L}[\varphi(p)]$ and $\varphi(x) = \mathfrak{L}^{-1}[\varphi(p); x]$.

Use of the Laplace transform

To apply the Laplace transform to the solution of equations of the type (245), a formula is used expressing the Laplace transform of the derivative of a function in terms of the Laplace transform of the function itself. Suppose that the function $Y(x)$ satisfies the conditions (250). Let $\mathfrak{L}[Y(p)]$ denote the Laplace transform of $Y(x)$. For $m = 1, 2, \ldots, n$ the Laplace transform of the mth derivative of $Y(x)$ is the product of p^m and $\mathfrak{L}[Y(p)]$ (see 252). Taking the Laplace transform of both sides of equation (245), it is found that $\mathfrak{L}[Y(p)]$ satisfies the simple al-

$$(248)\quad e^{\mu_1x}(c_1\cos\omega_1x + c_2\sin\omega_1x)$$

$$(249)\quad (c_1 + \cdots + c_mx^{m-1})e^{\mu_1x}\cos(\omega_1x) + (c_{m+1} + \cdots + c_{2m}x^{m-1})e^{\mu_1x}\sin(\omega_1x)$$

$$(250)\quad Y(0) = Y'(0) = \cdots = Y^{(n-1)}(0) = 0$$

$$(251)\quad \bar{\varphi}(p) \equiv \mathfrak{L}[\varphi(x); p] = \int_0^\infty \varphi(x)e^{-px}dx$$

$$(252)\quad \mathfrak{L}[Y^{(m)}(x); p] = p^m\bar{Y}(p)$$

$$(253)\quad Y(x) = \mathfrak{L}^{-1}\left[\frac{\bar{f}(p)}{\Pi_n(p)}; x\right]$$

$$(254)\quad p(x)y' + s(x)y = c_1$$

$$(255)\quad \mathbf{L}^*z = (pz)'' - (qz)' + r$$

$$(256)\quad y_2(x) = y_1(x)\int_a^x \frac{dt}{p(t)[y_1(t)]^2}$$

$$(257)\quad \sum_{r=0}^\infty a_rx^{r+\rho}, \qquad a_0 \neq 0$$

gebraic equation $\Pi_n(p)\mathfrak{L}[Y(p)] = \mathfrak{L}[f(p)]$ in which $\mathfrak{L}[f(p)]$ denotes the Laplace transform of $f(x)$. For the particular integral, this equation may be solved for $Y(p)$ and the inverse Laplace transform (see 253) may be taken.

Linear equations of the second order. The general theory of linear differential equations will be illustrated by examples of equations of the second order $\mathbf{L}y = f(x)$, in which $\mathbf{L}$ denotes the operator $p(x)D^2 + q(x)D + r(x)$. A homogeneous equation $\mathbf{L}y = 0$ is said to be exact if it can be written in the form $D\mathbf{M}y = 0$, in which $\mathbf{M}$ is a first-order linear differential operator of the form $p(x)D + s(x)$. The equation $\mathbf{L}y = 0$ can be integrated once to give a first-order linear equation in which $\mathbf{M}y$ is equal to an arbitrary constant c_1 (see 254), which can in turn be integrated by the method described above for the solution of equation (234); this will, of course, involve a second arbitrary constant c_2. This equation (254) is called a first integral of the original second-order equation. The equation $py'' + qy' + ry = 0$ is exact if, and only if, $p'' - q' + r = 0$ for all values of x, in which case $s(x) = q(x) - p'(x)$.

If the equation $\mathbf{L}y = 0$ is not exact but there exists a function $z(x)$ such that $z\mathbf{L}y = 0$ is exact, then z is said to be an integrating factor of $\mathbf{L}y = 0$. From the condition for a second-order equation to be exact, it is easily deduced that z is an integrating factor if it is a solution of the equation $\mathbf{L}^*z = 0$, in which the operator $\mathbf{L}^*$ is defined in terms of differentiation (see 255) and is called the adjoint of $\mathbf{L}$. If $\mathbf{L}^* = \mathbf{L}$, the operator $\mathbf{L}$ is said to be self-adjoint; the condition for this is that $q(x) = p'(x)$.

The two standard methods of solution

The two standard methods of solving a second-order equation are based on writing the solution in the form $y = uv$, in which u is a prescribed function of x and v is the new dependent variable.

If u is chosen to be any solution of the first-order equation $2pu' + qu = 0$, the resulting equation for v is of the form $v'' + P(x)v = 0$, and the general solution of this equation may be known. This procedure is known as reducing the equation to normal form, or as removing the first derivative.

The second method consists in finding a particular solution of the equation by inspection and taking this solution to be u. The resulting second-order equation for v is, in effect, a first-order linear equation for $w = v'$. This can easily be solved and v obtained by a further integration. This method is particularly useful in the case of a self-adjoint equation $(py')' + ry = 0$; if $y_1(x)$ is any solution of this equation, then the general solution is $c_1y_1(x) + c_2\,y_2(x)$, in which $y_2(x)$ is defined in terms of $y_1(x)$ and an integral (see 256), the lower limit of integration a being chosen to ensure that the integral exists.

Another method of solving a linear second-order equation is to derive a solution in the form of a power series (see 257) by substituting a series in the equation. If the coefficient of the lowest power of x is equated to zero, a quadratic equation is obtained; either of the roots of this equation gives a possible value of ρ. If the coefficient of x to the power $r + \rho$ is equated to zero, a recurrence relation is obtained for the coefficients a_r of this series.

(I.N.S./Ed.)

BOUNDARY VALUE PROBLEMS

When differential equations occur in the discussion of a physical problem, it usually happens that the solution of interest is not the general solution but the particular solution that satisfies certain additional conditions. For instance, to solve the problem of the catenary does not require the general solution of the second-order differential equation (137) but the particular solution $y(x)$ that satisfies the additional geometric conditions $y(0) = a$, $y'(0) = 0$.

To illustrate the ideas involved, equations of the second order will be discussed; they are easily generalized to equations of the nth order.

Initial value problems. The problem of finding a function $y(x)$ in the interval $a < x < b$ satisfying a second-order differential equation $F(x, y, y', y'') = 0$ and the conditions $y(a) = y_0$, $y'(a) = y_1$, in which y_0, y_1 are prescribed real numbers, is called the initial value problem for the differential equation. The values y_0, y_1 are called the initial values of the required solution. The adjective "initial"

(258) $$y'' + \alpha(x)y' + \beta(x)y = f(x), \qquad a < x < b$$

(259) $$y(x) = c_1y_1(x) + c_2y_2(x) + Y(x)$$

(260) $$\begin{cases} c_1y_1(a) + c_2y_2(a) = y_0 - Y(a) \\ c_1y'_1(a) + c_2y'_2(a) = y_1 - Y'(a) \end{cases}$$

(261) $$c_1 = \frac{y_0y'_2(a) - y_1y_2(a)}{W(y_1,\, y_2;\, a)}, \qquad c_2 = \frac{y_1y_1(a) - y_0y'_1(a)}{W(y_1,\, y_2;\, a)}$$

(262) $$\begin{cases} \dfrac{\partial^2 G}{\partial x^2} + \alpha(x)\dfrac{\partial G}{\partial x} + \beta(x)G = 0, \qquad G(a,\, \xi) = 0 \\[2ex] \dfrac{\partial G(a,\, \xi)}{\partial x} = 0, \qquad G(\xi,\, \xi) = 0, \qquad \dfrac{\partial G(\xi,\, \xi)}{\partial x} = 1 \\[2ex] Y(x) = \displaystyle\int_a^x G(x,\, \xi)f(\xi)d\xi \end{cases}$$

is appropriate because in a dynamical problem (as in the problem of determining the escape velocity from the Earth, discussed above) the conditions of this type specify the initial state and initial rate of change of the system the subsequent history of which is described by the differential equation itself. Initial value problems are also known as one-point boundary value problems.

Linear equations. The linear second-order differential equation with x between a and b—in which $\alpha(x)$, the coefficient of y', $\beta(x)$, the coefficient of y, and $f(x)$, the inhomogeneous term, are prescribed functions (see 258)—may now be considered with the initial values prescribed as above.

If $y_1(x)$ and $y_2(x)$ are linearly dependent solutions of the homogeneous form of the equation and $Y(x)$ is a particular solution of the nonhomogeneous equation (258), then the solution of the initial value problem for the differential equation is the sum of $Y(x)$ and a linear combination, with constants c_1 and c_2 of $y_1(x)$ and $y_2(x)$ (see 259).

The constants c_1 and c_2 are chosen to satisfy the simultaneous linear equation arising from setting the solution and its derivative equal to y_0 and y_1, respectively (see 260). If the particular solution $Y(x)$ is chosen in such a way that $Y(a) = Y'(a) = 0$, the equations for c_1 and c_2 reduce to a simple pair the solution of which can be found by Cramer's rule (see 261), named for the 18th-century Swiss mathematician Gabriel Cramer. This solution involves $W(y_1, y_2; a)$, the Wronskian $y_1(a)y_2'(a) - y_2(a)y_1'(a)$, which is nonzero because the solutions y_1 and y_2 are linearly independent. The solution of the initial value problem is given by equations (259) and (261).

Cramer's rule

Green's function for a linear initial value problem. There is a simple formula for the determination of the particular integral $Y(x)$ of the linear differential equation of second order (see 258) satisfying the initial condition $Y(a) = Y'(a) = 0$. If $G(x, \xi)$ is a function of the two variables x and ξ such that G and its partial derivatives with respect to x satisfy the homogeneous equation, conditions at $x = \xi$ and at $x = a$, then $Y(x)$ can be expressed as an integral of the product $G(x, \xi)f(\xi)$ (see 262). The function $G(x, \xi)$ is called Green's function of the problem (named after George Green, a 19th-century English mathematician). It can be shown that Green's function can be expressed in terms of y_1, y_2, and the Wronskian $W(y_1;\, y_2;\, \xi)$ (see 263) in which $y_1(x)$ and $y_2(x)$ have the same meanings as before.

For example, for the initial value problem in which the sum of the second derivative y'' and ω^2y equals $f(x)$ with y and its first derivative equaling y_0 and y_1, respectively, at $x = 0$ (see 264), the functions $y_1(x) = \cos(\omega x)$ and $y_2(x) = \sin(\omega x)$ may be taken to obtain the formula $G(x, \xi) = \omega^{-1}\sin\{\omega(x - \xi)\}$ from equation (263). Therefore, it is possible to express the solution as the sum of a linear

(263) $$G(x, \xi) = \frac{y_1(\xi)y_2(x) - y_1(x)y_2(\xi)}{W(y_1, y_2; \xi)}$$

(264) $$\begin{cases} \dfrac{d^2y}{dx^2} + \omega^2 y = f(x), & x > 0 \\ y(0) = y_0, & y'(0) = y_1 \end{cases}$$

(265) $$y_0(x) = y_0 \cos(\omega x) + \frac{y_1}{\omega}\sin(\omega x) + \frac{1}{\omega}\int_0^x f(\xi)\sin\{\omega(x-\xi)\}\,d\xi$$

(266) $$y''' = \frac{\partial g(x, y, y')}{\partial x} + \frac{\partial g(x, y, y')}{\partial y}y' + \frac{\partial g(x, y, y')}{\partial y'}y''$$

(267) $$\begin{cases} y(a) = y_0, \quad y'(a) = y_1, \quad y''(a) = g(a, y_0, y_1) \\ y'''(a) = g_x(a, y_0, y_1 + y_1 g_y(a, y_0, y_1) \\ \qquad + g(a, y_0, y_1)g_{y'}(a, y_0, y_1) \end{cases}$$

(268) $$y(x) = y(a) + \frac{(x-a)}{1!}y'(a) + \frac{(x-a)^2}{2!}y''(a) + \frac{(x-a)^3}{3!}y'''(a) + \cdots$$

(269) $$\lambda_1 y(a) + \mu_1 y'(a) = y_0 \lambda_2 y(b) + \mu_2 y'(b) = y_1$$

(270) $$y(x) = y_0\frac{y_2(x)}{y_2(a)} + y_1\frac{y_1(x)}{y_1(b)} + \eta(x)$$

(271) $$\eta(x) = y_2(x)\int_a^x \frac{y_1(\xi)f(\xi)d\xi}{W(y_1, y_2; \xi)} + y_1(x)\int_x^b \frac{y_2(\xi)f(\xi)d\xi}{W(y_1, y_2; \xi)}, \quad a < x < b$$

(272) $$G(x, \xi) = \begin{cases} \dfrac{y_1(\xi)y_2(x)}{W(y_1, y_2; \xi)}, & a < \xi < x \\ \dfrac{y_1(x)y_2(\xi)}{W(y_1, y_2; \xi)}, & x < \xi < b \end{cases}$$

(273) $$y(x) = \frac{y_0 y_2(x)}{y_2(a)} + \frac{y_1 y_1(x)}{y_1(b)} + \int_a^b G(x, \xi)f(\xi)d\xi$$

(274) $$y_1(a) = 0, \quad y_2(b) = 0$$

(275) $$\begin{cases} \dot{x} = a_{11}x + a_{12}y \\ \dot{y} = a_{21}x + a_{22}y \end{cases}$$

(276) $$\begin{cases} (a_{11} - \lambda)A + a_{12}B = 0 \\ a_{21}A + (a_{22} - \lambda)B = 0 \end{cases}$$

(277) $$\begin{vmatrix} a_{11} - \lambda & a_{12} \\ a_{21} & a_{22} - \lambda \end{vmatrix} = 0$$

combination of $\cos(\omega x)$ and $\sin(\omega x)$ and the integral of the product of $f(\xi)$ and Green's function (see 265).

Nonlinear equations. The solution of the initial value problem for a nonlinear equation is a much more difficult problem except in those rare cases in which it is possible to find a general solution of the differential equation. The particular values of the arbitrary constants c_1 and c_2 are then found by fitting the values of $y(a)$ and $y'(a)$.

For equations of the type $y'' = g(x, y, y')$, a solution can be generated in the following manner. Differentiation of both sides of the equation by the chain rule produces an expression for the third derivative y''' (see 266), and it is possible to obtain higher derivatives by repeated differentiation.

Substitution of the initial values, the expressions for $y''(a)$, $y'''(a)$, and higher derivatives at $x = a$ (see 267) in the Taylor expansion about $x = a$ (see 268) leads to a series expansion for the solution of the initial value problem.

Two-point boundary value problems. The problem of finding a function $y(x)$ in the interval $a < x < b$ satisfying a second-order differential equation $F(x, y, y', y'') = 0$ and the conditions $y(a) = y_0$, $y(b) = y_1$ in which y_0, y_1 are prescribed real numbers is called the two-point boundary value problem for the differential equation. This problem can be generalized to cover the boundary conditions expressed by setting linear combinations of y and y' at each point equal to prescribed constants (see 269); only the simple case is treated here.

Two-point boundary value problem

Linear equations. The two-point boundary value problem for a second-order linear equation (see 258) is considered: $y_1(x)$ and $y_2(x)$ are taken to be linearly independent solutions satisfying the conditions $y_1(a) = 0$, $y_2(b) = 0$, and $\eta(x)$ is taken as the particular solution of the equation (258) satisfying the conditions $\eta(a) = \eta(b) = 0$. The solution of the two-point boundary value problem is then the sum of a linear combination of $y_1(x)$ and $y_2(x)$ and a function $\eta(x)$ (see 270).

Green's function for a linear two-point boundary value problem. It can be shown that the function $\eta(x)$ can be expressed in terms of $y_1(x)$, $y_2(x)$, and integrals involving $f(\xi)$ (see 271), which gives the required particular integral. The function $G(x, \xi)$ defined in terms of the functions and their Wronskian (see 272) is called Green's function of the two-point boundary value problem. In terms of it the solution of the problem may be written as the sum of an integral of $G(x, \xi)f(\xi)$ and a linear combination of $y_1(x)$ and $y_2(x)$ (see 273). In the use of this formula it is necessary to remember that $y_1(x)$, $y_2(x)$ are not completely arbitrary linearly independent solutions of the homogeneous form of (258) but must satisfy the boundary conditions (see 274).

Nonlinear equations. When the general solution of a second-order nonlinear equation is not known, the solution of a two-point boundary value problem is obtained by solving the initial value problem for $y(a) = y_0$, $y'(a) = \gamma$, and (usually by a method of trial and error) finding the value of γ that leads to a solution for which $y(b) = y_1$.

SYSTEMS OF DIFFERENTIAL EQUATIONS

Two simultaneous differential equations in two variables. Two simultaneous equations in two variables will now be considered. They can be solved if they are linear and of first order.

Linear systems. A pair of homogeneous linear equations of the first order with dependent variables x and y and independent variable t can be solved for dx/dt and dy/dt formally written as dotted letters. In other words, the system is reduced to a pair of equations expressing the derivative with respect to t each in terms of a linear combination of x and y (see 275). The functions $x(t) = Ae^{\lambda t}$, $y(t) = Be^{\lambda t}$ satisfy these equations if the linear algebraic equations obtained by substituting these expressions for $x(t)$ and $y(t)$ into the original system are satisfied (see 276).

Regarded as equations for A and B, these equations have a nontrivial solution only if λ is a root of the equation that arises from the requirement that the determinant of the matrix of a system of homogeneous linear algebraic equations be zero (see 277), in which case A and B may be expressed in terms of an arbitrary constant c (see 278).

Nontrivial solution of equations

(278) $A = a_{12}c, \quad B = (\lambda - a_{11})c$

(279) $$\begin{cases} x(t) = a_{12}c_1e^{\lambda_1 t} + a_{12}c_2e^{\lambda_2 t} \\ y(t) = (\lambda_1 - a_{11})c_1e^{\lambda_1 t} + (\lambda_2 - a_{11})c_2e^{\lambda_2 t} \end{cases}$$

(280) $$\begin{cases} \dot{x} + 4x + y = 0, & \dot{y} - 6x - y = 0 \\ a_{11} = -4, \quad a_{12} = -1, & a_{21} = 6 \\ a_{22} = 1, \quad \lambda_1 = -1, & \lambda_2 = -2 \end{cases}$$

(281) $x(t) = -c_1e^{-t} - c_2e^{-2t}, \quad y(t) = 3c_1e^{-t} + 2c_2e^{-2t}$

(282) $-c_1 - c_2 = x_0, \quad 3c_1 + 2c_2 = y_0$

(283) $$\begin{cases} x(t) = (3e^{-2t} - 2e^{-t})x_0 + (e^{-2t} - e^{-t})y_0 \\ y(t) = 6(e^{-t} - e^{-2t})x_0 + (3e^{-t} - 2e^{-2t})y_0 \end{cases}$$

(284) $\mathfrak{L}[\dot{x}(t); p] = p\bar{x}(p) - x_0, \quad \mathfrak{L}[\dot{y}(t); p] = p\bar{y}(p) - y_0$

(285) $$\begin{cases} (a_{11} - p)\bar{x}(p) + a_{12}\bar{y}(p) + x_0 = 0 \\ a_{21}\bar{x}(p) + (a_{22} - p)\bar{y}(p) + y_0 = 0 \end{cases}$$

(286) $(p+4)\bar{x}(p) + \bar{y}(p) = x_0, \quad -6\bar{x}(p) + (p-1)\bar{y}(p) = y_0$

(287) $\bar{x}(p) = \dfrac{(p-1)x_0 - y_0}{(p+1)(p+2)}, \quad \bar{y}(p) = \dfrac{6x_0 + (p+4)y_0}{(p+1)(p+2)}$

(288) $$\begin{cases} \bar{x}(p) = \dfrac{3x_0 + y_0}{p+2} - \dfrac{2x_0 + y_0}{p+1} \\ \bar{y}(p) = \dfrac{6x_0 + 3y_0}{p+1} - \dfrac{6x_0 + 2y_0}{p+2} \end{cases}$$

(289) $$\begin{bmatrix} \dot{x} \\ \dot{y} \end{bmatrix} = \begin{bmatrix} a_{11} & a_{12} \\ a_{21} & a_{22} \end{bmatrix} \begin{bmatrix} x \\ y \end{bmatrix}$$

(290) $$z = \begin{bmatrix} x \\ y \end{bmatrix}, \quad A = \begin{bmatrix} a_{11} & a_{12} \\ a_{21} & a_{22} \end{bmatrix}$$

(291) $\dot{z} = Az$

(292) $\dfrac{d^2x}{dt^2} + p(t)\dfrac{dx}{dt} + q(t)x = f(t)$

(293) $\dfrac{dx}{dt} - y = 0, \quad \dfrac{dy}{dt} + p(t)y + q(t)x = f(t)$

(294) $$z = \begin{bmatrix} x \\ y \end{bmatrix}, \quad A(t) = \begin{bmatrix} 0 & -1 \\ q(t) & p(t) \end{bmatrix}, \quad \varphi = \begin{bmatrix} 0 \\ f(t) \end{bmatrix}$$

(295) $\dot{z} + A(t)z = \varphi(t)$

(296) $$\begin{cases} \dot{x}_1 = a_{11}x_1 + a_{12}x_2 + \cdots + a_{1n}x_n \\ \dot{x}_2 = a_{21}x_1 + a_{22}x_2 + \cdots + a_{2n}x_n \\ \vdots \\ \dot{x}_n = a_{n1}x_1 + a_{n2}x_2 + \cdots + a_{nn}x_n \end{cases}$$

(297) $\dot{z} = Az$

If the roots λ_1, λ_2 of the quadratic equation (277) are distinct, there are two linearly independent solutions, and the general solution of the pair of equations (275) may be written as linear combinations of these two solutions involving the a_{ij} and two arbitrary constants, c_1 and c_2 (see 279). For example, if the sum of the derivative of x with respect to t, ax, and y equals zero and the derivative of y with respect to t equals the sum of $6x$ and y, then λ_1 must equal -1, λ_2 must equal -2, and the a_{ij} are determined (see 280) so that the general solution is a linear combination of e^{-t} and e^{-2t} involving arbitrary constants c_1 and c_2 (see 281). In order to obtain the solution for which $x(0) = x_0$, $y(0) = y_0$, it is necessary to choose the constants c_1 and c_2 in such a way that the solution satisfies these conditions at $t = 0$ (see 282). These equations are solved for c_1 and c_2 to give the particular solution desired (see 283).

Use of the Laplace transform. To obtain the solution of the pair of first-order linear differential equations (275), the formulas expressing the result of using the Laplace transform (often formally written as a bar over the expression transformed) on a derivative (see 284) are used to obtain simultaneous linear algebraic equations (see 285) for the Laplace transforms $\mathfrak{L}[x(p)]$, $\mathfrak{L}[y(p)]$ of the unknown functions $x(t)$, $y(t)$. For instance, the pair (280) considered above can be attacked in this way (see 286) with the solution giving the Laplace transforms $\mathfrak{L}[x(p)]$ and $\mathfrak{L}[y(p)]$ in terms of p, x_0, and y_0 (see 287). If these equations are appropriately rewritten (see 288) and the Laplace transforms are inverted, the solution (283) is obtained.

Matrix form of the pair of equations. The pair of equations (275) may be written in matrix form (see 289) if matrices $\boldsymbol{z}$, with elements x and y, and $\boldsymbol{A}$, with elements a_{11}, a_{12}, a_{21}, and a_{22} (see 290), are introduced. This last equation can be written in a matrix form similar to the form of a single first-order equation (see 291).

Second-order equations. The general second-order linear differential equation (see 292) can be written as a pair of simultaneous equations by defining a new variable y as equal to the first derivative dx/dt (see 293). In terms of matrices (see 294) similar to those in the previous example, this pair can, in turn, be written in matrix form (see 295).

A system of *n* simultaneous equations in *n* variables. The system (275) can be generalized to the set of linear differential equations in n variables (see 296), which can be written in matrix form by writing the derivative of $\boldsymbol{z}$ with respect to t as equal to the matrix product $\boldsymbol{Az}$ (see 297), in which $\boldsymbol{z}$ is an n-component column vector and A is an $n \times n$ matrix of coefficients (see 298). If $\boldsymbol{z}$ equals a constant vector $\boldsymbol{c}$ times an exponential $e^{\lambda t}$ (see 299) and if I is the unit $n \times n$ matrix, then the matrix product Ac must equal λIc (see 300) for $\boldsymbol{z}$ to be a solution of the system.

In order for $\boldsymbol{c}$ to be a non-null vector, it is necessary that $\det(A - \lambda I) = 0$; *i.e.*, the vector (299) is a solution of equation (297) only if λ is an eigenvalue (see ALGEBRA: *Linear and multilinear algebra*) of the matrix A. This is illustrated by equation (277) in the case $n = 2$.

The main result is that the general solution of the system of equations (297) is the product of a constant vector z_0 and an exponential e^{tA} (see 301), the exponential with matrix exponent being defined by the Maclaurin series expansion of the exponential (see 302) (named after the 17th-century Scottish mathematician Colin Maclaurin).

(I.N.S.)

STABILITY

There are very few differential equations the general solution of which can be derived, and so mathematicians have studied the qualitative properties of solutions of differential equations without solving the equations explicitly. One qualitative phenomenon of great practical interest is the concept of stability of a certain solution of a system of differential equations.

Suppose, for the sake of illustration, that a physical system is represented by a differential equation in which the derivative of an n-vector $\boldsymbol{x}$ equals a function of $\boldsymbol{x}$ and t, $f(\boldsymbol{x}, t)$, which is also an n-vector (see 303), and that $\boldsymbol{x} = u(t)$ is a special solution of this equation describing a special regime of the system. Any physical system will be subject to small disturbances so that the regime $u(t)$ will not maintain itself, and a disturbed motion $\boldsymbol{x} = w(t)$ results. As time goes on, either $w(t) \to u(t)$, in which

$$(298)\quad \boldsymbol{z}=\begin{bmatrix}x_1\\x_2\\\cdot\\\cdot\\\cdot\\x_n\end{bmatrix},\quad \boldsymbol{A}=\begin{bmatrix}a_{11} & a_{12} & \cdots & a_{1n}\\ a_{21} & a_{22} & \cdots & a_{2n}\\ \cdot & \cdot & & \cdot\\ \cdot & \cdot & & \cdot\\ \cdot & \cdot & & \cdot\\ a_{n1} & a_{n2} & & a_{nn}\end{bmatrix}$$

$$(299)\quad \boldsymbol{z}=\boldsymbol{c}e^{\lambda t}$$

$$(300)\quad (A-\lambda I)\boldsymbol{c}=0$$

$$(301)\quad \boldsymbol{z}(t)=e^{tA}\boldsymbol{z}_0$$

$$(302)\quad e^{tA}=1+\frac{tA}{1!}+\frac{t^2A^2}{2!}+\cdots\frac{t^nA^n}{n!}+\cdots$$

$$(303)\quad \dot{\boldsymbol{x}}=\boldsymbol{f}(\boldsymbol{x},t)$$

$$(304)\quad \dot{\boldsymbol{z}}=\boldsymbol{g}(\boldsymbol{z},t)$$

case stability occurs, or $w(t)$ deviates from $u(t)$ and instability results.

Lyapunov's equation

From $w(t)=u(t)+z(t)$, a 19th–20th-century Soviet mathematician, Aleksandr Lyapunov, obtained an equation in which $\boldsymbol{z}$ and $\boldsymbol{g}$ are n-vectors, the derivative of $\boldsymbol{z}$ with respect to t equals $\boldsymbol{g}(\boldsymbol{z}, t)$ (see 304), and $\boldsymbol{g}(0, t)=0$ for $t>0$. To the regime $u(t)$ of the first equation (see 303) there corresponds the regime $\boldsymbol{z}=\boldsymbol{0}$ of the second equation (see 304). The origin $\boldsymbol{z}=\boldsymbol{0}$ is now considered as the basic motion and a solution $\boldsymbol{z}(t)$ of (304) is thought of as a disturbed motion. The terms stability of the undisturbed motion or simply the stability of the origin are used in this case.

The property $\boldsymbol{g}(0, t)=\boldsymbol{0}$ for a suitable range of t characterizes the origin as a critical point of (304). It is assumed that this critical point is isolated and also that $\boldsymbol{g}$ is continuous and satisfies conditions for the uniqueness of solutions of Lyapunov's equation (304) in a certain region Ω specified by $\|\boldsymbol{x}\|<A$, $t>0$, in which $\|\boldsymbol{x}\|$ denotes the length of the vector $\boldsymbol{x}$ and A denotes a positive constant. Stability is characterized by Lyapunov as follows: if for any prescribed ε, $0<\varepsilon<A$, there exists $\delta>0$ such that every trajectory originating within the sphere $\|\boldsymbol{x}\|=\delta$ always remains within the sphere $\|\boldsymbol{x}\|=\varepsilon$, the origin is stable (cf. Figure 20, in which these spheres are denoted by $S(\delta)$ and $S(\varepsilon)$, respectively). If every trajectory originating within $S(\delta)$ tends to 0 the origin is said to be asymptotically stable. If, however, no matter what δ is chosen, some trajectory originating from a point within $S(\delta)$ eventually reaches $S(\varepsilon)$, the origin is unstable.

Lyapunov attacked the stability problem by applying two distinct methods. The first, applicable only to some analytical systems, consists essentially in finding explicit series solutions convergent near the origin and considering the behaviour of this series as $t\to\infty$. The second method he used does not require the construction of explicit solutions, and for this reason that method has a greater range of validity than the first; it rests on the construction of a scalar function $V(\boldsymbol{x}, t)$.

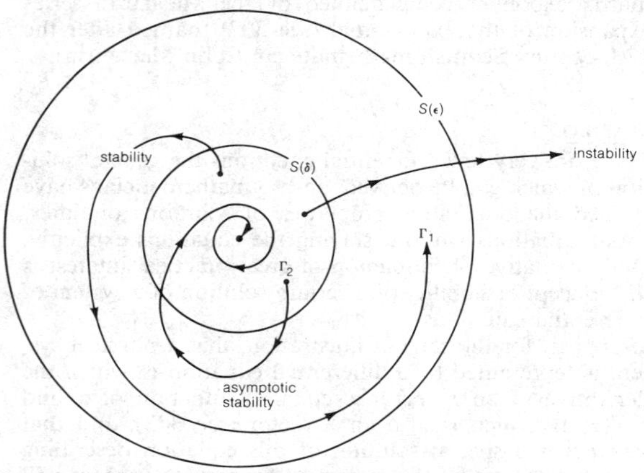

Figure 20: Three types of trajectories, stable as represented by Γ_1, asymptotically stable as represented by Γ_2, and unstable, drawn in relation to an origin and two spheres denoted by $S(\delta)$ and $S(\varepsilon)$.

For example, Lyapunov's stability states that if there can be found a positive definite function $V(\boldsymbol{x}, t)$ the time derivative of which taken along all the trajectories in Ω is negative or zero, then the origin is stable. Of four such theorems of Lyapunov, two refer to stability and two to instability; the latter may be replaced by a more comprehensive theorem of Četaev.

Partial differential equations

In most physical problems any dependent variable is likely to be a function of more than one independent variable. The example of a vibrating string has already been given. Another example is in the study of thermal effects in a solid body in which the temperature u may vary from point to point in the solid as well as from time to time. As a consequence, the function $u(x, y, z, t)$ is written to denote that u depends on (x, y, z), the coordinates of a typical point, and on the time t.

Thermal effects in a solid body

If for such a function, the difference quotient, the difference between $u(a+h, b, c, \tau)$ and $u(a, b, c, \tau)$, divided by h (see 305), tends to a finite number as h tends to zero, that number is denoted by $u_x(a, b, c, \tau)$, or by $\partial u(a, b, c, \tau)/\partial x$, and is called the partial derivative with respect to x of the function $u(x, y, z, t)$ at the point (a, b, c, τ). It measures the rate of change at that point of the function u with respect to x, the other variables remaining fixed. As the point (a, b, c, τ) varies, a new function $u_x(x, y, z, t)$ or $\partial u/\partial x$ is generated that expresses the rate of growth with x of the function u. The process can be repeated: the partial derivative of $\partial u/\partial x$ with respect to x is denoted by $\partial^2u/\partial x^2$. Similarly the consideration of the variation of u with respect to the other variables leads to the definition of the other partial derivatives, the partial derivatives with respect to y, z, and t (see 306); and the partial derivatives with respect to x of these yield in turn the mixed derivatives of the second order in which u is differentiated twice, once with respect to each of two different variables (see 307).

When the laws of physics are applied to a situation involving a function of this kind, a relation involving the function u and its partial derivatives is often obtained. Such a relation is called a partial differential equation. For example, if $u(x, y, z, t)$ were the temperature at time t at the point (x, y, z) in a homogeneous isotropic solid, the variation of u is specified by the heat conduction equation, in which the sum of the second partial derivatives with respect to x, y, and z is proportional to the first partial derivative with respect to t (see 308). The expression on the left side of this equation arises so frequently that it is given a special name and a special symbol; it is called the Laplacian of u and is now denoted by Δ_3u.

As in the theory of ordinary differential equations, the order of a partial differential equation is defined to be the order of the derivative of highest order occurring in the equation. For example, the heat equation (see 308) is a second-order equation in four variables, an equation stating that the sum of the cube of the partial derivative of u with respect to x and the partial derivative of u with respect to y equals zero (see 309) is a first-order equation in two variables while an equation involving first partial derivatives with respect to x, y, and t with variable coefficients (see 310) is a first-order equation in three variables.

Early work on partial differential equations

The study of partial differential equations began with the study of continuum mechanics and physics. Although there were some earlier investigations, the first proper studies of these types of equations began in the 18th century with the studies of Leonhard Euler and Jean Le Rond d'Alembert on wave motion, Pierre-Simon Laplace on potential theory, Jean-Baptiste-Joseph Fourier on the conduction of heat, and Carl Friedrich Gauss on potential

$$(305)\quad \frac{u(a+h,\,b,\,c,\,\tau)-u(a,\,b,\,c,\,\tau)}{h}$$

$$(306)\quad \frac{\partial u}{\partial y},\ \frac{\partial u}{\partial z},\ \frac{\partial u}{\partial t}$$

$$(307)\quad \frac{\partial^2 u}{\partial x\partial y},\ \frac{\partial^2 u}{\partial x\partial z},\ \frac{\partial^2 u}{\partial x\partial t}$$

$$(308)\quad \frac{\partial^2 u}{\partial x^2}+\frac{\partial^2 u}{\partial y^2}+\frac{\partial^2 u}{\partial z^2}=\frac{1}{\kappa}\frac{\partial u}{\partial t}$$

$$(309)\quad \left(\frac{\partial u}{\partial x}\right)^3+\frac{\partial u}{\partial y}=0$$

$$(310)\quad x\frac{\partial u}{\partial x}+y\frac{\partial u}{\partial y}+\frac{\partial u}{\partial t}=0$$

$$(311)\quad \frac{\partial u}{\partial \xi}=0$$

$$(312)\quad u=f(\eta)$$

$$(313)\quad \frac{\partial^2 u}{\partial \xi\partial \eta}=0$$

$$(314)\quad u=f(\xi)+g(\eta)$$

$$(315)\quad \frac{\partial E_x}{\partial x}+\frac{\partial E_y}{\partial y}+\frac{\partial E_z}{\partial z}=4\pi\sigma(x,\,y,\,z)$$

theory and electromagnetic theory. The theory of partial differential equations has always gone hand-in-hand with developments in mathematical physics and has drawn much of its strength from the association, as is seen even in the more theoretical works of pure mathematicians of distinction such as Augustin-Louis Cauchy, Bernhard Riemann, and Sofya Kovalevskaya. The growth of abstract analysis has had important repercussions on the theory of partial differential equations, and this influence has in turn suggested fruitful problems to workers in both abstract and numerical analysis.

Probably the simplest partial differential equation involving a function $u(\xi,\,\eta)$ of two independent variables is the one that may be verbalized as follows: the first partial derivative with respect to one of the variables equals zero (see 311), which may readily be seen to have the general solution of an arbitrary function $f(y)$ of the other variable only (see 312). A comparison with the case of ordinary differential equations in which the equation $u'(x)=0$ has solution $u(x)=c$ illustrates the point that the role played by arbitrary constants in the theory of ordinary differential equations is taken over by arbitrary functions in the theory of partial differential equations.

Similarly, if the second mixed partial derivative of u with respect to ξ and η equals zero (see 313), then the general solution is the sum of $f(\xi)$ and $g(\eta)$, in which the functions f and g are arbitrary and are each functions of only one variable (see 314).

This statement can be extended to a general partial differential equation of order n for a function of k independent variables. Subject to a variety of restrictions that must be imposed, the general solution of such an equation depends on n arbitrary functions of $k-1$ independent variables.

PARTIAL DIFFERENTIAL EQUATIONS OF SPECIAL INTEREST

Some partial differential equations have arisen so frequently in the study of physics that they have been studied intensively. Collectively, they are known as the equations of mathematical physics, and have throughout the development of the theory of partial differential equations provided the motivation for many studies of theoretical, as well as practical, interest.

Equations of mathematical physics

Poisson's equation. A simple linear partial differential equation of the second order is named after the 19th-century French physicist Baron Siméon-Denis Poisson. It arises in the mathematical treatment of electrostatics. Gauss's law of electrostatics states that the flux of the electric vector $(E_x,\,E_y,\,E_z)$ out of a surface is equal to 4π times the charge contained within that surface; this leads to the relation that the sum of $\partial E_x/\partial x$, $\partial E_y/\partial y$, and $\partial E_z/\partial z$ is proportional to $\sigma(x,\,y,\,z)$ (see 315), in which σ, the density of electric charge, is assumed to be known. It is also known physically that the electrostatic field is characterized by the fact that the electric vector can be derived from a potential function u; *i.e.*, that there exists a function u such that each component of the electric vector equals minus the partial derivative of u with respect to that variable (see 316). The insertion of these expressions into the previous equation leads to the relation that the sum of $\Delta_3 u$ and $4\pi\sigma(x,\,y,\,z)$ equals zero (see 317), in which Δ_3 is the Laplacian operator introduced above. Poisson's equation arises also in the theory of the gravitational potential.

Laplace's equation. In the absence of electric charges the function σ of equation (317) reduces to the simpler form in which the Laplacian of u equals zero (see 318). This is called Laplace's equation. It arises also in the analysis of the irrotational motion of a perfect fluid and in the steady-state conduction of heat (see below *The diffusion equation*).

In the cylindrical coordinates $(\rho,\,\varphi,\,z)$ Laplace's equation assumes a form that can be derived by the chain rule (see 319) in which it is more suitable for the discussion of problems involving regions bounded by cylinders. In a similar manner, in spherical polar coordinates $(r,\,\theta,\,\varphi)$, which are used in the analysis of problems concerning regions that are bounded by spheres or cones, Laplace's equation is transformed to an expression involving partial derivatives with respect to these variables (see 320).

The wave equation. *Sound waves in space.* If, because of the passage of a sound wave, the gas at a point $(x,\,y,\,z)$ at time t has velocity $(u,\,v,\,w)$ and pressure p and density ρ, then for small oscillations $\rho=\rho_0(1+s)$, $p=p_0+c^2\rho_0 s$, in which s is the condensation of the gas and $c^2=(dp/d\rho)_0$, and ρ_0, p_0 are the equilibrium values of p and ρ. The equations of (small) motions are that the partial derivative of each component of the velocity with respect to time equals the product of c^2 and the appropriate partial derivative of s (see 321); and the equation of continuity is to the same approximation that the sum of $\partial u/\partial x$, $\partial v/\partial y$, $\partial w/\partial z$, and $\partial s/\partial t$ equals zero (see 322). For irrotational motion there exists a function ψ with the property that each component of the velocity equals minus the appropriate partial derivative of ψ (see 323).

The above equations (see 321 and 323) are therefore equivalent to the equation that the partial derivative of $\partial\psi/\partial t-c^2 s$ with respect to each of x, y, and z is zero (see 324). The equation of continuity (322) is equivalent to the restriction that the partial derivative of s with respect to t equals the Laplacian of ψ (see 325) so that the function ψ satisfies the relation that the second partial derivative of ψ with respect to t is proportional to the Laplacian of ψ (see 326). This equation is called the three-dimensional wave equation.

It can also be shown that in the absences of charges or currents the scalar potential and each component of the vector potential of an electromagnetic field satisfy the three-dimensional wave equation with c the velocity of light.

Transverse vibrations of a membrane. If a thin elastic membrane of uniform areal density σ is stretched to a uniform tension T and if, in the equilibrium position, the membrane coincides with the xy-plane, then the small transverse vibration $u(x,\,y,\,t)$ of the point $(x,\,y)$ of the membrane satisfies an equation in which the two-dimensional Laplacian of u (see 327) is proportional to the second partial derivative with respect to t (see 328), and the wave velocity c is defined by the equation $c^2=T/\sigma$. Equation (328) is called the two-dimensional wave equation.

Transverse vibrations of a string. If a string of uniform linear density σ is stretched to a uniform tension T, and if, in the equilibrium position, the string coincides with

$$(316)\quad E_x = -\frac{\partial u}{\partial x}, \quad E_y = -\frac{\partial u}{\partial y}, \quad E_z = -\frac{\partial u}{\partial z}$$

$$(317)\quad \Delta_3 u + 4\pi\sigma(x, y, z) = 0$$

$$(318)\quad \Delta_3 u = 0$$

$$(319)\quad \frac{\partial^2 u}{\partial \rho^2} + \frac{1}{p}\frac{\partial u}{\partial \rho} + \frac{1}{\rho^2}\frac{\partial^2 u}{\partial \varphi^2} + \frac{\partial^2 u}{\partial z^2} = 0$$

$$(320)\quad \frac{\partial^2 u}{\partial r^2} + \frac{2}{r}\frac{\partial u}{\partial r} + \frac{1}{r^2 \sin\theta}\left(\frac{\partial}{\partial \theta}\sin\theta\frac{\partial u}{\partial \theta}\right) + \frac{1}{r^2 \sin^2\theta}\frac{\partial^2 u}{\partial \varphi^2} = 0$$

$$(321)\quad \frac{\partial u}{\partial t} = -c^2\frac{\partial s}{\partial x}, \quad \frac{\partial v}{\partial t} = -c^2\frac{\partial s}{\partial y}, \quad \frac{\partial w}{\partial t} = -c^2\frac{\partial s}{\partial z}$$

$$(322)\quad \frac{\partial s}{\partial t} + \frac{\partial u}{\partial x} + \frac{\partial v}{\partial y} + \frac{\partial w}{\partial z} = 0$$

$$(323)\quad u = -\frac{\partial \psi}{\partial x}, \quad v = -\frac{\partial \psi}{\partial y}, \quad w = -\frac{\partial \psi}{\partial z}$$

$$(324)\quad \begin{cases} \dfrac{\partial}{\partial x}\left(\dfrac{\partial \psi}{\partial t} - c^2 s\right) = 0, \quad \dfrac{\partial}{\partial y}\left(\dfrac{\partial \psi}{\partial t} - c^2 s\right) = 0 \\ \dfrac{\partial}{\partial z}\left(\dfrac{\partial \psi}{\partial t} - c^2 s\right) = 0 \end{cases}$$

$$(325)\quad \frac{\partial s}{\partial t} = \Delta_3 \psi$$

$$(326)\quad \frac{1}{c^2}\frac{\partial^2 \psi}{\partial t^2} = \Delta_3 \psi$$

$$(327)\quad \Delta_2 u = \frac{\partial^2 u}{\partial x^2} + \frac{\partial^2 u}{\partial y^2}$$

$$(328)\quad \Delta_2 u = \frac{1}{c^2}\frac{\partial^2 u}{\partial t^2}$$

$$(329)\quad \frac{\partial^2 u}{\partial x^2} = \frac{1}{c^2}\frac{\partial^2 u}{\partial t^2}$$

$$(330)\quad c_x = -\kappa\frac{\partial u}{\partial x}, \quad c_y = -\kappa\frac{\partial u}{\partial y}, \quad c_z = -\kappa\frac{\partial u}{\partial z}$$

$$(331)\quad \frac{\partial u}{\partial t} + \frac{\partial c_x}{\partial x} + \frac{\partial c_y}{\partial y} + \frac{\partial c_z}{\partial z} = 0$$

$$(332)\quad \frac{\partial u}{\partial t} = \frac{\partial}{\partial x}\left(\kappa\frac{\partial u}{\partial x}\right) + \frac{\partial}{\partial y}\left(\kappa\frac{\partial u}{\partial y}\right) + \frac{\partial}{\partial z}\left(\kappa\frac{\partial u}{\partial z}\right)$$

the x-axis, then when the string is disturbed slightly from its equilibrium position, the transverse displacement $u(x, t)$ satisfies an equation in which the second partial derivative of u with respect to x is proportional to the second partial derivative with respect to t (see 329), with constant of proportionality $c^2 = T/\sigma$. This equation is known as the one-dimensional wave equation.

The diffusion equation. Another interesting partial differential equation arises in the analysis of the diffusion process in physical chemistry. This is a process leading to the equalization of concentrations within a single phase, and it is governed by laws relating the rate of flow of the diffusing substance with the concentration gradient causing the flow. If u is the concentration of the diffusing substance, then the diffusion current vector (c_x, c_y, c_z) is defined by the equations in which each component of the diffusion current vector equals a quantity $-\kappa$ times the appropriate first partial derivative of u (see 330). This is known as Fick's law, named after a 19th-century German physiologist, Adolf Fick, in which κ is the diffusion coefficient for the substance under consideration. Fick's law

The continuity for the diffusion substance takes a form (see 331) that is similar to the usual continuity equation so that the concentration $u(x, y, z, t)$ satisfies the diffusion equation (see 332) obtained by substituting Fick's law into the equation of continuity. In the most general case, the quantity κ is a function of x, y, z and of the concentration u, but if κ does happen to be a constant, the diffusion equation (332) reduces to the form of the heat conduction equation (308).

The diffusion equation (332) is satisfied also by the temperature u in a solid conducting heat; for that reason this equation is sometimes known as the heat conduction equation. In the steady-state case in which κ is constant, it follows from equation (308) with $\partial u/\partial t \equiv 0$ that u satisfies Laplace's equation (318).

The form (308) of the diffusion equation is also satisfied by the vorticity in a viscous fluid started into motion from rest and by the electric field vector in the propagation of long waves in a good conductor.

If u depends only on one space coordinate x and the time t, the heat conduction equation (308) reduces to a form in which the second partial derivative of u with respect to x is proportional to the first partial derivative of u with respect to t (see 333); this is called the one-dimensional diffusion equation.

The Fokker-Planck equation. An equation very similar to the diffusion equation (333) is the Fokker-Planck equation (named for Adriaan Fokker and Max Planck), linearly relating a quantity P and its first and second derivatives with respect to x with its first derivative with respect to t (see 334), which reduces in the case that the coefficient D of the second derivative is equal to zero to a first-order equation with a variable coefficient of $\partial P/\partial x$ (see 335). The physical interpretation is that P is the probability that a random variable has the value x at time t. For instance, P might be the probability distribution of the deflection x of an electrical noise trace at time t.

Birth-and-death equations. Equations similar to the Fokker-Planck equation arise in the theory of birth and death processes in bacterial populations. If it is assumed that the probability of the birth or death of a bacterium is proportional to the number present, and if $P_n(t)$ is the probability of there being n bacteria in the population at time t, the probability generating function $u(z, t)$ defined by a power series in z with the nth term having coefficient $P_n(t)$ (see 336) satisfies a partial differential equation in which $\partial u/\partial t$ equals a quadratic in z, with constants λ and μ, times $\partial u/\partial z$ (see 337).

Similar equations arise in birth-and-death problems in which different physical assumptions are made and in discussions of the probability distribution of telephone conversations carried on over a certain number of telephone lines.

Schrödinger's equation. In wave mechanics the wave function ψ of a single particle such as an electron has the physical interpretation that $|\psi(x, y, z)|^2 d\tau$ is the probability that the electron will be found in a small element of volume $d\tau$ the centre of which is at the point with coordinates (x, y, z). In the steady-state case the variation of ψ throughout a field the potential energy of which is $V(x, y, z)$ is described by Schrödinger's equation involving m, the mass of the particle, h, Planck's constant, and E, the total energy of the particle and linearly relating the Laplacian of ψ and the quantity $(E - V)\psi$ (see 338).

Higher-order equations in physics. The above equations are—with the exception of one or two first-order equations—all of the second order. It is therefore important to notice that not all physical problems can be formulated in terms of partial differential equations of the second order.

For instance, a state of plane strain in a two-dimensional solid free from body forces can be specified by three stress components σ_{xx}, σ_{xy}, and σ_{yy} that satisfy equilibrium conditions that can be stated as first-order linear partial differ-

(333) $$\frac{\partial^2 u}{\partial x^2} = \frac{1}{\kappa}\frac{\partial u}{\partial t}$$

(334) $$\frac{\partial P}{\partial t} = \beta\frac{\partial}{\partial x}(xP) + D\frac{\partial^2 P}{\partial x^2}$$

(335) $$\frac{\partial P}{\partial t} = \beta P + \beta x\frac{\partial P}{\partial x}$$

(336) $$u(z, t) = \sum_{n=0}^{\infty} P_n(t)z^n$$

(337) $$\frac{\partial u}{\partial t} = (z-1)(\lambda z - \mu)\frac{\partial u}{\partial z}$$

(338) $$\Delta_3\psi + \frac{8\pi^2 m}{h^2}(E - V)\psi = 0$$

(339) $$\frac{\partial \sigma_{xx}}{\partial x} + \frac{\partial \sigma_{xy}}{\partial y} = 0, \quad \frac{\partial \sigma_{xy}}{\partial x} + \frac{\partial \sigma_{yy}}{\partial y} = 0$$

(340) $$\sigma_{xx} = \frac{\partial^2\psi}{\partial y^2}, \quad \sigma_{xy} = -\frac{\partial^2\psi}{\partial x\partial y}, \quad \sigma_{yy} = \frac{\partial^2\psi}{\partial x^2}$$

(341) $$\frac{\partial^2}{\partial y^2}\{\sigma_{xx} - \eta(\sigma_{xx} + \sigma_{yy})\} + \frac{\partial^2}{\partial x^2}\{\sigma_{yy} - \eta(\sigma_{xx} + \sigma_{yy})\} = 2\frac{\partial^2\sigma_{xy}}{\partial x\partial y}$$

(342) $$\frac{\partial^4\psi}{\partial x^4} + 2\frac{\partial^4\psi}{\partial x^2\partial y^2} + \frac{\partial^4\psi}{\partial y^4} = 0$$

(343) $$\left(\frac{1}{2}\sigma_{xx} - \frac{1}{2}\sigma_{yy}\right)^2 + \sigma_{xy}^2 = k^2$$

(344) $$\left(\frac{\partial^2\psi}{\partial x^2} - \frac{\partial^2\psi}{\partial y^2}\right)^2 + 4\frac{\partial^4\psi}{\partial x^2\partial y^2} = 4k^2$$

ential equations (see 339). If σ_{xx}, σ_{xy}, and σ_{zz} are equal to the appropriate second partial derivatives of any arbitrary function ψ, then they satisfy the equilibrium conditions (see 340) and ψ is called an Airy stress function (after the 19th-century British astronomer George Biddell Airy).

The Airy stress function

If the body is elastic, the components of stress satisfy compatibility equations involving the second partial derivatives of σ_{xx}, σ_{xy}, and σ_{yy} (see 341), from which it follows that $\psi(x, y)$ satisfies a fourth-order linear equation that can be written $\Delta_2\Delta_2\psi = 0$ and is called the two-dimensional biharmonic equation (see 342). (The reason for this is that Laplace's equation is sometimes referred to as the harmonic equation.)

If, instead of being elastic, the body is perfectly plastic, then the stress components satisfy the quadratic condition; this quadratic condition is known as the Hercky-Mises condition (see 343). Hence, the Airy stress function satisfies a fourth-order nonlinear partial differential equation (see 344). (I.N.S./Ed.)

CLASSIFICATION OF PARTIAL DIFFERENTIAL EQUATIONS

In classification, a partial differential equation governing a dependent variable u is said to be linear if u and its partial derivatives occur only to the first power. For example, if second-order equations in two independent variables x and y are considered, then a linear equation involves a sum of u and its first and second derivatives, with coefficients a, b, c, f, g, h, and k that are functions of x and y only (see 345).

The solution of a nonlinear equation is considerably more difficult to obtain than is the solution of a linear equation; general methods of solution have been devised, however, for two special types of nonlinearity. A nonlinear equation in which the partial derivatives of u occur linearly—but in which u itself does not do so (see 346)—is said to be quasi-linear, whereas, on the other hand, an equation that is linear in only the highest order derivatives (see 347) is said to be semilinear.

First-order equations. There is a particular kind of nonlinear equation of the first order in which the product a and $\partial u/\partial x$ is added to the product of b and $\partial u/\partial y$ to yield c (see 348), in which a, b, and c are functions not only of x and y but of u also. This type of equation has been investigated by the 18th-century French mathematician Joseph-Louis Lagrange.

The general solution of this equation is $F(\xi, \eta) = 0$, in which F is an arbitrary function of two variables and $\xi(x, y, u) = C_1$ and $\eta(x, y, u) = C_2$ form a solution of the simultaneous ordinary differential equations expressed by equating the ratios of dx to a, dy to b, and du to c (see 349). For example, because a system of equations of this form with x^2 for a, y^2 for b, and $(x + y)u$ for c (see 350) has solution $xy/u = c_1$, $(x - y)/u = c_2$, it follows that the general solution of the equation with these terms for a, b, and c (see 351) is $F(xy/u, (x - y)/u) = 0$, in which the function F is arbitrary.

Classes of integrals in first-order equations

The problem of solving a general nonlinear equation of the first order $f(x, y, u, u_x, u_y) = 0$ in which the function f is not linear in u_x and u_y is more difficult. It turns out that there are three classes of integrals of an equation of this type:

1. The first class involves two-parameter systems of surfaces $F(x, y, u, a, b) = 0$; such an integral is called a complete integral.

(345) $$a\frac{\partial^2 u}{\partial x^2} + 2b\frac{\partial^2 u}{\partial x\partial y} + c\frac{\partial^2 u}{\partial y^2} + f\frac{\partial u}{\partial x} + g\frac{\partial u}{\partial y} + hu = k$$

(346) $$a\frac{\partial^2 u}{\partial x^2} + 2b\frac{\partial^2 u}{\partial x\partial y} + c\frac{\partial^2 u}{\partial x\partial y} + f\frac{\partial u}{\partial x} + g\frac{\partial u}{\partial y} + h(x, y, u)$$

(347) $$a\frac{\partial^2 u}{\partial x^2} + 2b\frac{\partial^2 u}{\partial x\partial y} + c\frac{\partial^2 u}{\partial y^2} = f\left(x, y, u, \frac{\partial u}{\partial x}, \frac{\partial u}{\partial y}\right)$$

(348) $$a\frac{\partial u}{\partial x} + b\frac{\partial u}{\partial y} = c$$

(349) $$\frac{dx}{a} = \frac{dy}{b} = \frac{du}{c}$$

(350) $$\frac{dx}{x^2} = \frac{dy}{y^2} = \frac{du}{(x + y)u}$$

(351) $$x^2\frac{\partial u}{\partial x} + y^2\frac{\partial u}{\partial y} = (x + y)u$$

(352) $$u^2(1 + u_x^2 + u_y^2) = 1$$

(353) $$\begin{cases} F(D, D')z = f(x, y) \\ F(D, D') = \sum_r\sum_s c_{rs}D^r D'^s, \quad D = \dfrac{\partial}{\partial x}, \quad D' = \dfrac{\partial}{\partial y} \end{cases}$$

(354) $$\sum_{s=1}^{n} x^{s-1}\varphi_s(ax - y)e^{-bx}$$

(355) $$F(D, D')e^{ax+by} = F(a, b)e^{ax+by}$$

(356) $$\sum_{n=0}^{\infty} c_n\cos(nx + \varepsilon_n)e^{-\kappa n^2 t}$$

2. If any one-parameter subsystem $F(x, y, u, a, \varphi(a))=0$ is taken and its envelope is formed (by eliminating a from the equations $F=0$, $F_a=0$), a general integral is obtained.
3. If the envelope of the complete integral in (1) (obtained by eliminating a, b from the equations $F=0$, $F_a=0$, $F_b=0$) exists, a singular integral of the equation is obtained.

For example, there is the equation in which the sum of 1, u_x^2, and u_y^2, which, when multiplied by u^2 (see 352), has the complete integral $(x-a)^2+(y-b)^2+u^2=1$. If $b=a$ and if the envelope of the resulting subsystem of spheres is written, then the general integral $(x-y)^2+2u^2=2$ is obtained; moreover, because the envelope of the complete integral consists of the planes $u=\pm1$, then it follows that $u=1$ and $u=-1$ are both singular integrals of the equation.

Solutions of nonlinear first-order equations are usually obtained by a method known as Charpit's method, which is too complicated to be described here. The solutions of some special types are, however, easily derived.

If the equation is of the type $f(u_x, u_y)=0$—*i.e.*, if it involves only the derivatives u_x, u_y—the complete integral is $u=ax+Q(a)y+b$, in which a and b are arbitrary constants and $q=Q(a)$ is the solution of the algebraic equation $f(a, q)=0$.

If the equation is of the type $f(u, u_x, u_y)=0$, u_x and u_y are found by solving the equations $f(u, u_x, u_y)=0$, $u_x=au_y$ and then determining $u(x, y)$ from the equation $du=u_x dx+u_y dy$.

A separable equation $f(x, u_x)=g(y, u_y)$ is solved by determining u_x and u_{xy} from the equations $f(x, u_x)=a$ and $g(y, u_y)=a$, respectively, and finding u as in the last case.

Clairaut equations

And, finally, there are Clairaut equations, $u=xu_x+yu_y+f(u_x, u_y)$, which have complete integrals $u=ax+by+f(a, b)$.

Linear equations with constant coefficients. Linear partial differentials with constant coefficients can be solved simply. Such an equation can be written in the form of an equality between a linear combination of derivatives $F(D, D')z$ and $f(x, y)$, a function of x and y (see 353). Any solution of the equation is called a particular integral and the most general solution of the corresponding homogeneous equation $F(D, D')z=0$ is called the complementary function of the equation; if z_1 is a particular integral and u is the complementary function, the general solution is $u+z_1$. It follows from the linearity of the operator F that, if $u_1, u_2, \ldots, u_n$ are solutions of $Fz=0$, then $\sum_{r=1}^{n} c_r u_r$, in which the c's are arbitrary constants, is also a solution.

The operators $F(D, D')$ are classified into two main types: $F(D, D')$ is reducible if it can be written as the product of linear factors of the form $D+aD'+b$ with a, b constants; if it cannot be written in such a form, then $F(D, D')$ is said to be irreducible.

The form of the complementary function in the reducible case follows from the fact that, if $(D+aD'+b)^n$ is a factor of (D, D') and if the functions $\varphi_1, \varphi_2, \ldots, \varphi_n$ are arbitrary, then a sum involving these functions and an exponential (see 354) is a solution of $F(D, D')=0$. When F is irreducible it is not always possible to find a solution with the full number of arbitrary functions, but it is possible to construct solutions that contain as many arbitrary constants as are required. The method of deriving such solutions depends on the result of differentiating an exponential (see equation 355) so that e^{ax+by} is a solution of $F(D, D')=0$, provided that a and b are connected through the equation $F(a, b)=0$. In this manner it is possible to construct a solution of the homogeneous equation that contains as many arbitrary constants as may be required.

For example, the one-dimensional diffusion equation (see 333) has a solution $\exp(ax+bt)$ only if $b=a^2\kappa$, and this relation is satisfied if $a=\pm in$ and $b=-\kappa n^2$ are taken. In this way solutions of the diffusion equation can be constructed as the sum of terms each of which is the product of a cosine and an exponential and involving constants c_n and ε_n (see 356).

Semilinear equations of the second order with variable coefficients. Next in order of complexity to an equation with constant coefficients is a semilinear second-order equation (see 347). This equation is reduced to canonical form by changing the independent variables from x, y to ξ, η. The choice of ξ and η is dictated by the nature of the roots $\lambda_1(x, y)$, $\lambda_2(x, y)$ of the quadratic equation $a\lambda^2+2b\lambda+c=0$. There are three cases to be considered, depending on the sign of the discriminant Δ defined by the equation $\Delta=b^2-ac$:

The three types of semilinear second-order equations

(i) $\Delta>0$: If for every (x, y) in a region Ω of the xy-plane, $\Delta>0$, the roots λ_1, λ_2 are real and distinct. If ξ and η are now chosen to be such that $\xi(x, y)=c_1$ and $\eta(x, y)=c_2$ are, respectively, the integral curves of the ordinary differential equations $y'+\lambda_1(x, y)=0$ and $y'+\lambda_2(x, y)=0$, the equation is transformed to the canonical form in which the second mixed partial derivative equals some function of ξ, η, u and the first partial derivatives of u (see 357). In this case the equation is said to be hyperbolic in the region Ω. The curves $\xi(x, y)=c_1$, $\eta(x, y)=c_2$ are called the characteristic curves of the equation, or, more simply, the characteristics of the equation. An equation that is hyperbolic in a region Ω, therefore, has two families of characteristics in that region.

For example, an equation in which the coefficient of $\partial u/\partial x$ is $1/x$ and the coefficient of $\partial^2u/\partial y^2$ is x^2 (see 358) is hyperbolic at all points in the xy-plane, has the two families of characteristics $x^2/2+y=$ constant and canonical form with the second mixed partial equal to zero (see 359). On the basis of past equations, it becomes apparent that this equation has the general solution $u=f(\xi)+g(\eta)$, and thus the original equation has the general solution

(357) $$\frac{\partial^2 u}{\partial\xi\partial\eta}=h\left(\xi,\eta,u,\frac{\partial u}{\partial\xi},\frac{\partial u}{\partial\eta}\right)$$

(358) $$\frac{\partial^2 u}{\partial x^2}-\frac{1}{x}\frac{\partial u}{\partial x}=x^2\frac{\partial^2 u}{\partial y^2}$$

(359) $$\frac{\partial^2 u}{\partial\xi\partial\eta}=0$$

(360) $$\frac{\partial^2 u}{\partial\eta^2}=h\left(\xi,\eta,u,\frac{\partial u}{\partial\xi},\frac{\partial u}{\partial\eta}\right)$$

(361) $$\frac{\partial^2 u}{\partial x^2}+2\frac{\partial^2 u}{\partial x\partial y}+\frac{\partial^2 u}{\partial y^2}=0$$

(362) $$\frac{\partial^2 u}{\partial\eta^2}=0$$

(363) $$u=(x+y)f(x-y)+g(x-y)$$

(364) $$\alpha=\frac{1}{2}(\xi+\eta),\qquad \beta=\frac{1}{2}i(\eta-\xi)$$

(365) $$\frac{\partial^2 u}{\partial\alpha^2}+\frac{\partial^2 u}{\partial\beta^2}=k\left(\alpha,\beta,u,\frac{\partial u}{\partial\alpha},\frac{\partial u}{\partial\beta}\right)$$

(366) $$\frac{\partial^2 u}{\partial x^2}+x^2\frac{\partial^2 u}{\partial y^2}=0$$

(367) $$\frac{\partial^2 u}{\partial\alpha^2}+\frac{\partial^2 u}{\partial\beta^2}+\frac{1}{2\alpha}\frac{\partial u}{\partial\alpha}=0$$

(368) $$u(0,t)=0,\qquad u(a,t)=0,\qquad t>0$$

(369) $$u(x,0)=f(x),\qquad u_t(x,0)=g(x),\qquad 0<x<a$$

(370) $$u_{xy}=f(x,y,u,u_x,u_y)$$

$u = f(x^2/2 + y) + g(x^2/2 - y)$, in which the functions f and g are arbitrary.

(ii) $\Delta = 0$: The function ξ is defined in precisely the same way as in case (i), and η is taken to be any function of x and y that is independent of ξ. The canonical form of the equation in this case has the second partial derivative with respect to η equal to a function of ξ, η, u and the first partial derivatives of u (see 360). An equation of this type is said to be parabolic.

For example, an equation in which twice the second mixed partial derivatives is added to the other two second partial derivatives to give a result of zero (see 361) is parabolic. If $\xi = x - y$ and $\eta = x + y$, it is found that it reduces to the canonical form in which the second partial derivative with respect to η equals zero (see 362), with solution $u = \eta f(\xi) + g(\xi)$, in which f and g are arbitrary functions. The solution of the original equation is therefore obtained by substituting the appropriate quantities for η and ξ in this expression (see 363).

(iii) $\Delta < 0$: In this case the roots λ_1 and λ_2 are complex conjugates so that if ξ and η are chosen as in case (i) they will be complex-valued functions of the real variables x and y. In terms of this pair of functions ξ, η another pair α, β are defined as a linear combination of ξ and η involving complex numbers (see 364). When transformed to the new independent variables, the equation takes the canonical form in which the second partial derivative with respect to α, when added to the second partial derivative with respect to β, equals some function of α, β, u, and the first partial derivatives of u (see 365). Such an equation is said to be of elliptic type.

For example, an equation in which the second partial derivative with respect to x, when added to the product of x^2 and the second partial derivative with respect to y, gives zero (see 366) is elliptic throughout the whole xy-plane. If the method in (i) is used, then it is found that $\xi = x^2/2 + iy$ and $\eta = x^2/2 - iy$ may be taken, and hence $\alpha = x^2/2$, $\beta = y$. Transforming to these new variables, the equation has the canonical form with the function being the product of $-1/(2\alpha)$ and the first partial derivative with respect to α (see 367).

INITIAL VALUE AND BOUNDARY VALUE PROBLEMS

In applications of partial differential equations, the concern is not so much with determining the general solution of an equation as with finding the solution that satisfies some other prescribed conditions. Problems involving the solution of a partial differential equation and the fulfillment of additional conditions have been classified into the following types. Only second-order equations in two independent variables will be considered.

Transverse oscillations of a stretched string

Initial value problems. The classic case of an initial value problem arises in the discussion of the transverse oscillations of a stretched string. The transverse displacement $u(x, t)$ satisfies the partial differential equation (329) for $0 < x < a$, $t > 0$, in which a denotes the length of the string. Because the string is assumed to be fixed at its ends, $u(0, t)$ and $u(a, t)$ must both equal zero for all positive values of t (see 368), and if the problem is that of determining the subsequent shape of the string when its initial shape and velocity are prescribed, the function u must satisfy equations in which $u(x, 0)$ and $u_t(x, 0)$ equal prescribed functions $f(x)$ and $g(x)$ (see 369).

These particular equations—that is, (329), (368), and (369)—describe a problem that is analogous to an initial value problem in the theory of differential equations. Arguing from this fact and also from physical intuition, one would expect to realize the existence of a unique solution $u(x, t)$. Because u satisfies the boundary conditions (368) as well as the initial conditions (369), the present problem is said to be a mixed initial and boundary value problem.

A different example is provided by solutions of the heat conduction equation (see 333). Here, on physical grounds, it would be expected that a unique function $u(x, t)$ would be determined by the boundary conditions (see 368) and the single initial condition $u(x) = f(x)$, $0 < x < a$.

Cauchy problems. A generalization of the initial value problems considered above is Cauchy's problem. This is best described for a hyperbolic equation in canonical form with independent variables x and y (see 370). The Cauchy problem for this equation consists of finding a solution u with the property that prescribed values $u = u(s)$, $u_x = p(s)$, $u_y = q(s)$ are assumed along a given curve with parametric equations $x = x(s)$, $y = y(s)$. Because u, p, q must satisfy the compatibility equation found by the chain rule (see 371), p and q cannot be assigned independently. The values of u and its normal derivative $\partial u/\partial n$ on the curve are in fact sufficient for the specification of u, p, and q. These quantities are referred to as the Cauchy data.

Dirichlet problems. The first boundary value problem, also called the Dirichlet problem, consists of finding a solution $u(x, y)$ of an elliptic equation in a region Ω of the xy-plane that takes on prescribed values on the boundary of Ω.

Neumann problems. The second boundary value problem for an elliptic partial differential equation in a region Ω consists in finding a solution that possesses a prescribed normal derivative $\partial u/\partial n = f$ on the boundary B of Ω.

(371) $$\frac{du}{ds} = p(s)\frac{dx}{ds} + q(s)\frac{dy}{ds}$$

(372) $$\int_B f ds = 0$$

(373) $$\frac{\partial u}{\partial n} + \alpha u = f$$

(374) $$\begin{cases} \dfrac{\partial u}{\partial x} + a_{11}\dfrac{\partial u}{\partial y} + a_{12}\dfrac{\partial v}{\partial y} = b_1 \\ \dfrac{\partial v}{\partial x} + a_{21}\dfrac{\partial u}{\partial y} + a_{22}\dfrac{\partial v}{\partial y} = b_2 \end{cases}$$

(375) $$(a_{11} - \lambda)(a_{22} - \lambda) - a_{21}a_{12} = 0$$

(376) $$\begin{cases} D_1 u + (\lambda_1 - a_{11})D_1 v = b_1 + (\lambda_1 - a_{11})b_2 \\ D_2 u + (\lambda_2 - a_{11})\, D_2 v = b_1 + (\lambda_2 - a_{11})b_2 \end{cases}$$

(377) $$D_j = \frac{\partial}{\partial x} + \lambda_j \frac{\partial}{\partial y}, \qquad j = 1, 2$$

(378) $$\frac{dy}{dx} = \lambda_j(x, y), \qquad j = 1, 2$$

(379) $$U = \begin{bmatrix} u \\ v \end{bmatrix}, \qquad A = \begin{bmatrix} a_{11} & a_{12} \\ a_{21} & a_{22} \end{bmatrix}, \qquad B = \begin{bmatrix} b_1 \\ b_2 \end{bmatrix}$$

(380) $$U_x + AU_y = B$$

(381) $$\det(A - \lambda I) = 0$$

(382) $$\sum_{k=1}^{m} c_{jk} D_j U_k + \sum_{k=1}^{m} c_{jk} b_k = 0, \qquad j = 1, 2, \ldots, m$$

(383) $$U_x = AU_y$$

(384) $$u(x, y, \ldots, t) = X(x)Y(y) \ldots T(t)$$

(385) $$c^2 X''(x)/X(x) = T''(t)/T(t)$$

(386) $$X''(x) + \lambda X(x) = 0, \qquad T''(t) + c^2 \lambda T(t) = 0$$

It is often called a Neumann problem. It turns out the Neumann problem cannot be solved for Laplace's equation $u_{xx} + u_{yy} = 0$ unless the prescribed function f satisfies the condition that the integral of f around the boundary equals zero (see 372).

Robin problems. The third boundary value problem, or Robin problem (Gustave Robin, 1855–97), for an elliptic partial differential equation in a region Ω consists of finding a solution u of the equation satisfying the condition that the sum of au and the normal derivative of u equal f (see 373) at all points of the boundary of Ω, a and f being prescribed.

SYSTEMS OF PARTIAL DIFFERENTIAL EQUATIONS

In many applications it is necessary to consider a pair of first-order equations, each involving one partial derivative with respect to x and two partial derivatives with respect to y (see 374) with coefficients of the partial derivatives with respect to y being a_{11}, a_{12}, a_{21}, a_{22}, which are functions of x and y and b_1, b_2 are functions of x, y, u. The first stage in solving equations of this type is to transform the system into one in which each equation involves differentiations in one direction only.

If a certain quadratic equation in λ formed from a_{11}, a_{22}, a_{12}, and a_{21} (see 375) has two real distinct roots $\lambda_1(x, y)$, $\lambda_2(x, y)$, the system can be transformed to a pair of equations, each involving only one differentiation operator D_j (see 376), in which D_j is the operator of differentiation consisting of differentiation with respect to x added to the product of λ_j and differentiation with respect to y (see 377) in the direction defined by an ordinary differential equation in which the derivative of y equals λ_j (see 378). It should be emphasized that this reduction is possible if, and only if, the equation (375) has two distinct real roots. When this is the case, the system is said to be of hyperbolic type. On the other hand, if the roots of (375) are complex, the system is of elliptic type. The two families of curves in the xy-plane defined by the ordinary differential equations (378) are called the characteristics of the system.

Hyperbolic type and elliptic type

If the column vector U, with elements u and v, the column vector B, with elements b_1 and b_2, and the square matrix A, with elements a_{11}, a_{12}, a_{21}, and a_{22} (see 379), are introduced, the system may be written as a matrix equation relating the partial derivatives U_x and U_y (see 380) and the equation in λ (see 375) as an equation stating that the determinant of $A - \lambda I$ is zero (see 381). It is now an easy matter to generalize the system being considered (see 380) by taking U, B to be column vectors with m components and A is a matrix with m rows and m columns. The determinant equation (381) now has m roots. If these roots are real and distinct the system can be transformed to m equations, each involving only one differentiation operator D_j (see 382). The only change in the interpretation is that the equations defining D_j (377 and 378) now hold for $j = 1, 2, \ldots, m$. Again the system (380) is hyperbolic.

A quasi-linear second-order partial differential equation can be replaced by a system of the type in which the partial derivative of U with respect to x equals the matrix product of A and the partial derivative of U with respect to y (see 383), in which U has eight components and A is an 8×8 matrix.

TECHNIQUES OF SOLUTION OF PARTIAL DIFFERENTIAL EQUATIONS

Separation of variables. One of the oldest techniques for the solution of a linear partial differential equation for a function u of the independent variables $x, y, \ldots, t$ is to assume a solution that is a product of $X(x), Y(y), \ldots, T(t)$ of functions of one variable (see 384) and by substituting in the original equation to obtain ordinary differential equations for the functions $X, Y, \ldots, T$.

For example, if u satisfies the one-dimensional wave equation (see 329), the equation has solutions of the type $u(x, t) = X(x)T(t)$ if X and T can be chosen such that the ratio of $X''(x)$ to $X(x)$ is proportional to the ratio of $T''(t)$ to $T(t)$ (see 385). Because the left side of this equation is a function of x alone and the right side is a function of t alone, the two can be equal for all values of x and t if, and only if, each is equal to a constant $-\lambda c^2$, say; *i.e.*, it is necessary that X and T satisfy second-order linear differential equations with constant coefficients (see 386).

The value of λ is determined by the boundary conditions. For example, if the boundary conditions are that $u(0, t) = u(a, t) = 0$ for all values of $t > 0$, they are satisfied if $X(0) = X(a) = 0$. This is possible only if $\lambda = n^2\pi^2/a^2$, $n = 1, 2, \ldots,$ when $X(x) = \sin(n\pi x/a)$. If in addition $u_t(x, 0) = 0$, then $T'(0) = 0$ also; *i.e.*, $T(t) = \cos(n\pi ct/a)$; thus a solution of the equation (329) in the form of a function $u_n(x, t)$ equaling the product of a cosine and a sine, involving t and x respectively (see 387), is obtained. This technique is called separation of variables.

Quite complicated solutions can be constructed by combining this method with the principle of linear superposition. For example, an infinite linear combination of the $u_n(x, t)$, with coefficients c_n (see 388) with u_n given above (see 387), will be a solution of the wave equation (see 329) for $0 \le x \le a$, $t \ge 0$, satisfying the boundary conditions $u(0, t) = u(a, t) = 0$ and the initial conditions

Principle of linear superposition

(387) $$u_n(x, t) = \cos\left(\frac{n\pi ct}{a}\right)\sin\left(\frac{n\pi x}{a}\right)$$

(388) $$u(x, t) = \sum_{n=1}^{\infty} c_n u_n(x, t)$$

(389) $$f(x) = \sum_{n=1}^{\infty} c_n \sin\left(\frac{n\pi x}{a}\right)$$

(390) $$u_{xx} + u_{yy} = 0$$

(391) $$u(x, y) = \int_0^\infty F(\xi)\frac{\sinh(\xi y)}{\sinh(\xi a)}\sin(\xi x)d\xi$$

(392) $$f(x) = \int_0^\infty F(\xi)\sin(\xi x)d\xi$$

(393) $$\begin{cases} \mathfrak{L}[u(x, p)] = \int_0^\infty u(x, t)e^{-pt}dt \\ \mathfrak{L}[f(p)] = \int_0^\infty f(t)e^{-pt}dt \end{cases}$$

(394) $$I(u) = \int_V F(x, y, z, u, u_x, u_y, u_z)\, d\tau$$

(395) $$\frac{\partial F}{\partial u} = \frac{\partial}{\partial x}\left(\frac{\partial F}{\partial u_x}\right) + \frac{\partial}{\partial y}\left(\frac{\partial F}{\partial u_y}\right) + \frac{\partial}{\partial z}\left(\frac{\partial F}{\partial u_z}\right)$$

(396) $$I(u) = \int_V [u_x^2 + u_y^2 + u_z^2]\, d\tau$$

(397) $$\begin{cases} u_{xx} + u_{yy} + u_{zz} = 0 & \text{within } V \\ u = f, & \text{on } S \end{cases}$$

(398) $$\frac{\partial^2 u}{\partial x^2} - \varepsilon\frac{\partial^4 u}{\partial x^4} = \frac{1}{c^2}\frac{\partial^2 u}{\partial t^2}$$

(399) $$X''(x) - \varepsilon X^{(iv)}(x) + \lambda X(x) = 0$$

(400) $$\mathbf{L}(\varepsilon) = \mathbf{L}(0) + \varepsilon\mathbf{L}^{(1)} + \varepsilon^2\mathbf{L}^{(2)} + \cdots$$

(401) $$\begin{cases} X_n = X_n^{(0)}(x) + \varepsilon X_n^{(1)}(x) + \varepsilon^2 X_n^{(2)}(x) + \cdots \\ \lambda_n = \lambda_n^{(0)} + \varepsilon\lambda_n^{(1)} + \varepsilon^2\lambda_n^{(2)} + \cdots \end{cases}$$

$u(x, 0) = f(x)$, $u_t(x, 0) = 0$ if an infinite sequence of constants $c_1, c_2, \ldots$ can be found such that $f(x)$ can be written as an infinite series with terms $c_n \sin(n\pi x/a)$ (see 389). This leads to a consideration of the theory of Fourier series (see below *Fourier analysis*). It should also be observed that the values $\lambda_n = n^2\pi^2/a^2$, $n = 1, 2, \ldots$, are called the eigenvalues of the stated problem.

Integral transform solutions. Closely related to the method of separation of variables is the method of integral transforms. To illustrate the method, the solution of Laplace's equation in two dimensions (see 390) is considered in the semi-infinite strip $x \geq 0$, $0 \leq y \leq a$, when u satisfies the boundary conditions $u(0, y) = 0$, $u(x, y) \to 0$ as $x \to \infty$, $0 \leq y \leq a$ and $u(x, 0) = 0$, $u(x, a) = f(x)$.

The method of separation of variables then gives a solution of the form $\sin(\xi x) \sinh(\xi y)$, in which ξ is any constant. By the superposition principle such a solution, when multiplied by $F(\xi)/\sinh(\xi a)$ and integrated from zero to infinity (see 391), will be the required solution if a function F can be found with the property that for all $x > 0$, $f(x)$ equals the integral from zero to infinity of $F(\xi)\sin(\xi x)$ (see 392). This leads to a consideration of the theory of Fourier integrals. The Fourier sine transform of $f(x)$ is $F(\xi)$.

Probably the best-known example of an integral transform is the Laplace transform, which was considered earlier. To illustrate its use, the solution of the one-dimensional diffusion equation (see 333) is considered in the range $x \geq 0$, $t \geq 0$, and satisfying the conditions $u(x, 0) = 0$, $u(0, t) = f(t)$, $u(x, t) \to 0$ as $x \to \infty$. If the Laplace transforms $\mathfrak{L}[u(x, p)]$ of $u(x, t)$ and $\mathfrak{L}[f(p)]$ of $f(t)$ (see 393) are introduced, then it is easily shown that $\mathfrak{L}[u(x, p)] = \mathfrak{L}[f(p)]\exp[-x\sqrt{(p/k)}]$; thus the required solution is the function the Laplace transform of which is $\mathfrak{L}[f(p)]\exp[-x\sqrt{(p/k)}]$. The solution can be found by means of the inversion theorem, which gives a method of finding a function the Laplace transform of which is prescribed.

Variational methods. Approximate solutions of partial differential equations can often be obtained by using the fact that the function u that makes a certain integral an extremum satisfies a partial differential equation.

To illustrate the procedure, the function $u(x, y, z)$ is considered that makes the volume integral $I(u)$ of a function $F(x, y, z, u, u_x, u_y, u_z)$ of the coordinates, u, and its first partial derivatives (see 394), an extremum with respect to twice-differentiable functions that assume prescribed values at all points of the boundary S of V. This must satisfy the Euler-Lagrange equation (see 395). Hence, the solution of the Dirichlet problem for the Euler-Lagrange equation (395) is the function u that takes prescribed values on S and makes $I(u)$ an extremum. The value of this observation lies in the fact that in certain cases direct methods may produce a solution of the extremal problem.

Dirichlet's principle

For example, from among the functions that have continuous second derivatives in V and on S and take on the prescribed values f on S, that function which makes the integral of the squares of the first derivatives (see 396) an extremum is the solution of the Dirichlet problem for Laplace's equation (see 397). This is known as Dirichlet's principle.

Perturbation methods. Perturbation theory was created by a British physicist, Lord Rayleigh (John William Strutt), in the 19th century. He gave a formula for computing the natural frequencies and modes of a vibrating system the physical characteristics of which differ slightly from those of a simpler system the behaviour of which is completely known. In terms of the method of separation of variables, a differential equation of the form $[\mathbf{L}(\varepsilon) + \lambda]X = 0$ has to be solved, subject to certain boundary conditions, $\mathbf{L}(\varepsilon)$ being a differential operator containing a small numerical parameter ε, when the eigenvalues and eigenfunctions of $[\mathbf{L}(0) + \lambda]X = 0$ with the same boundary conditions, are known.

For example, the method of separation of variables applied to the one-dimensional wave equation with an additional term of the product of ε and the fourth partial derivative of u with respect to x (see 398) leads to the perturbed form of the first of the separated equations (386), a fourth-order linear ordinary differential equation (see 399).

The perturbation method consists essentially in expanding $\mathbf{L}(\varepsilon)$ in powers of ε with coefficients $\mathbf{L}^1, \mathbf{L}^2, \ldots$, which are differential operators (see 400) and assuming that X_n and λ_n can also be expanded in powers of ε, in which $X_n^{(0)}(x)$ is the eigenfunction corresponding to the eigenvalue $\lambda_n^{(0)}$ of the unperturbed problem (see 401).

Approximate solutions. One of the most frequently used methods of obtaining approximate solutions of partial differential equations is the method of finite differences, which consists essentially in replacing each partial derivative by a difference quotient. To be specific, the case of a function $u(x, t)$ of two independent variables x and t is considered. If the value of u were known at each point (rh, sk) in which r and s are integers and h and k are small positive quantities, an approximation could be made to the partial derivative $\partial u/\partial x$ at the point (rh, sk) by the difference quotient formed by taking the difference between $u_{r+1,\,s}$ and $u_{r,\,s}$ and dividing by h (see 402) in which $u_{r,\,s} \equiv u(rh, sk)$, and the second derivative $\partial^2u/\partial x^2$ by applying the process again to the difference quotient just obtained (see 403). By applying the same process (see 404), it is possible to find suitable approximations for $\partial u/\partial t$ and $\partial^2u/\partial t^2$.

One possible finite-difference approximation to the one-dimensional diffusion equation (see 333) is therefore found by replacing the derivatives by the appropriate difference quotients (see 405), and the equation can be solved for $u_{r,\,s+1}$, with $p = k/h^2$. This gives a formula by means of which the unknown $u_{r,\,s+1}$ might be determined at the $(r, s+1)$ mesh point in terms of the known functions along the sth row. In this way the unknown values of u can be calculated along the first row, $t = k$, in terms of the known boundary values along $t = 0$. The values along

(402) $$\frac{u_{r+1,\,s} - u_{r,\,s}}{h}$$

(403) $$\frac{u_{r+1,\,s} - 2u_{r,\,s} + u_{r-1,\,s}}{h^2}$$

(404) $$\begin{cases} \dfrac{u_{r,\,s+1} - u_{r,\,s}}{k} \\[2ex] \dfrac{u_{r,\,s+1} - 2u_{r,\,s} + u_{r,\,s-1}}{k^2} \end{cases}$$

(405) $$\begin{cases} \dfrac{u_{r,\,s+1} - u_{r,\,s}}{k} = \kappa\dfrac{u_{r+1,\,s} - 2u_{r,\,s} + u_{r-1,\,s}}{h^2} \\[2ex] u_{r,\,s+1} = u_{r,\,s} + \kappa p(u_{r-1,\,s} - 2u_{r,\,s} + u_{r+1,\,s}) \end{cases}$$

(406) $$u_x = A(u)u_y \qquad u(0, y) = h(y)$$

(407) $$\int_\Phi f(x, y)\frac{\partial^{r+s}\varphi}{\partial x^r \partial x^s}\,dx\,dy = (-1)^{r+s}\int_\Phi g(x, y)\Phi(x, y)\,dx\,dy$$

(408) $$\begin{cases} u_{xx} + u_{yy} = f(x, y) \text{ in } \Omega \\ u = g(x, y) \text{ on } \partial\Omega \end{cases}$$

(409) $$\begin{cases} B(\varphi, u) = -\displaystyle\int_\Omega (D_{1,\,0}\varphi D_{1,\,0}u + D_{0,\,1}\varphi D_{0,\,1}u)\,dx\,dy \\[2ex] B(\varphi, u) = \displaystyle\int_\Omega \varphi f\,dx\,dy \end{cases}$$

(410) $$\int_\Omega \varphi(u_{xx} + u_{yy})\,dx\,dy = -\int_\Omega (\varphi_x u_x + \varphi_y u_y)\,dx\,dy$$

the second row, $t = 2k$, can be obtained in terms of the calculated values along the first row, and the operation may be repeated as many times as necessary to obtain the values along successive rows in terms of previously calculated values.

If u is the exact solution of the one-dimensional diffusion equation (see 333) and U the exact solution of the difference equation (see 405), then if $U \rightarrow u$ as both h and k tend to zero, the finite difference equations are said to be convergent. At first sight it appears as though the mesh lengths h and k can be chosen arbitrarily, but this is not always so; for example, for the particular case of the difference equation (see 405) convergence occurs only if $\rho \leq 1/2$. In the case of hyperbolic equations, it is possible to combine the use of characteristics with that of finite differences to obtain numerical solutions with a high degree of accuracy.

In order to obtain approximate solutions of boundary value problems for elliptic equations, students of the subject have found that it is sometimes possible to reformulate the problem as an integral equation and then to obtain approximate solutions of it.

EXISTENCE AND UNIQUENESS OF SOLUTIONS TO PARTIAL DIFFERENTIAL EQUATIONS

The Cauchy-Kovalevskaya theorem

The basic existence and uniqueness theorem of the theory of partial differential equations is the Cauchy-Kovalevskaya theorem, which in its simplest form relates to a system in two independent variables x, y in which u_x equals the product of $A(u)$ and u_y, $u(0, y)$ being equal to $h(y)$ (see 406), u and h being column vectors with m components, the vector h being prescribed, and A is an $m \times m$ matrix.

To state the result it is necessary to use the fact that a function is said to be analytic at a point if it has a Taylor expansion at that point.

The Cauchy-Kovalevskaya theorem then states that about any point at which the components of the given matrix A and of the given vector h are analytic, a neighbourhood can be found in which there exists a unique vector u, with analytic coefficients, that is a solution of the initial value problem (see 406).

Although it has the appearance of great generality, this theorem has the severe limitation that it is restricted to problems involving only analytic functions. What it does show is that within the class of analytic solutions of equations with analytic coefficients, the number of arbitrary functions required for a general solution is equal to the order of the equation. When k independent variables are involved, a generalization of the theorem shows that each such arbitrary function is a function of $k - 1$ variables.

GENERALIZED THEORY OF PARTIAL DIFFERENTIAL EQUATIONS

The generalized theory of partial differential equations depends on generalizing the concept of a derivative. In order to do this it is necessary to introduce the idea of a test function.

Again the treatment is restricted to two dimensions. The function $\varphi(x, y)$ is said to be a test function if it vanishes outside a bounded region Φ of the xy-plane and if it is infinitely differentiable in that region. If f is locally integrable in a region Ω and if there exists a locally integrable function g such that for all test functions φ, the integral of $f(x, y)\partial^{r+s}\varphi/\partial x^r \partial y^s$ over Φ equals the integral of $(-1)^{r+s} g(x, y)\, \varphi(x, y)$ over Φ (see 407), g is called a generalized derivative of f and $g = D_{r,s} f$ is written.

Now the Dirichlet problem for Laplace's equation in two dimensions may be considered (see 408); in this instance, $\partial\Omega$ denotes the boundary of Ω. A generalized solution of the Dirichlet problem is defined by introducing a bilinear function $B(\varphi, u)$, and $B(\varphi, u)$ is defined for all test functions φ (see 409).

A function u is said to be a generalized solution of the stated Dirichlet problem if, and only if, $u = g$ on $\partial\Omega$ and if for every test function φ, $B(\varphi, u)$ equals the integral of φf over Ω (see 409). On the other hand, a classical solution is a twice-differentiable function that assumes the correct boundary values; therefore, from Green's theorem (see 410), it follows that, if a classical solution to the stated Dirichlet problem exists, then it is also a generalized solution.

The theory of generalized solutions of partial differential equations forms what is known as the abstract theory of partial differential equations. (I.N.S.)

Dynamical systems on manifolds

NONLINEAR DIFFERENTIAL EQUATIONS AND DYNAMICAL SYSTEMS

The differential equations described so far in this section are mainly linear—that is, the superposition of two solutions is again a solution. However, nonlinear differential equations are also extremely important, but until recently their theory existed only in rudimentary form because their analysis is extremely difficult and requires an entirely new approach. Apart from a few classical tricks of limited interest, nonlinear differential equations can seldom be solved by an explicit formula. Instead, they are studied by approximate methods of numerical analysis, by local analytic methods that apply only in small regions, and by qualitative methods of geometry and topology.

Henri Poincaré

The qualitative theory of differential equations was founded by Henri Poincaré around 1900 and has grown into an extensive and vigorous field. With the rise of interest in nonlinear systems and new phenomena such as "chaos"—the occurrence of random behaviour in deterministic systems—it has become vital to many areas of application and has developed into an extensive subject known as dynamical systems theory.

The natural geometric setting for this theory is that of a manifold, the multidimensional analogue of a curved surface. A dynamical system is a system of first-order ordinary differential equations defined on a manifold. The manifold is called the state space or phase space of the system. It is necessary to use manifolds rather than ordinary Euclidean space because in many applications the natural phase space is "curved." For example, the state space determining the possible positions of a pendulum is a circle.

Dynamical systems theory is the study, especially from a geometric or topological point of view, of the qualitative properties of solutions of differential equations on manifolds or their discrete-time analogues. Nowadays the term also covers quantitative studies carried out by numerical methods, provided these are based upon a geometric understanding of the nature of the flow. Because the equations for most dynamical systems are nonlinear, the computer plays an important role in the mathematics, both as an experimental tool to suggest rigorous theorems and as an aid to practical applications.

A central concept is that of structural stability, which arose from attempts to describe the "typical" behaviour of a dynamical system—behaviour that persists when the system itself is perturbed. It must be distinguished from the stability of an individual solution—behaviour that persists when the initial conditions of a fixed system are perturbed. Structural stability is a formal way to capture the idea of behaviour that is not destroyed by small changes to the system. It was originally hoped that it would be a generic property—that is, be possessed by almost all dynamical systems. While that hope turned out to be misplaced, the concept remains important.

Another important idea is that of an attractor. An attractor is a region of state space that captures the long-term behaviour of the system. It is now known that structurally stable systems can possess attractors on which the systems behave in an apparently random manner. The equations that define a dynamical system are fully deterministic; that is, given initial conditions lead to uniquely specified behaviour. The sense in which a deterministic model can produce random effects is a major discovery of the last few decades, giving rise to a central branch of dynamical systems theory known as chaotic dynamics. The word chaos—more accurately, deterministic chaos—refers to any instance of such behaviour. The associated attractors are said to be strange or chaotic. Dynamical systems theory provides a major source of understanding for the phenomenon of chaos.

A dynamical system is a way of describing the passage in time of all points of a given space $\mathfrak{S}$. $\mathfrak{S}$ can be thought of, for example, as the space of states of some physical system. Then if x is in $\mathfrak{S}$, one unit in time later x will have moved to a point denoted by x_1. At time zero x is at x or x_0. Two units after time zero x will have moved to x_2. One unit before time zero x was at x_{-1}. If this procedure is extrapolated to fill up the real numbers R, the trajectory x_t is obtained, for all time t, a real number. Thus, for each x, x_t is a curve in $\mathfrak{S}$ and represents the life history of x as t goes from $-\infty$ to ∞. If x_t is also assumed to be differentiable in (t, x), then $x \rightarrow x_t$ can be regarded as a transformation, or diffeomorphism, from $\mathfrak{S}$ onto $\mathfrak{S}$ for each t. In this case $(\mathfrak{S}, x_t)$ defines a dynamical system.

Definition of a state of a system

In applications of dynamical systems to fields outside of mathematics, the first goal is to explicate the manifold of states $\mathfrak{S}$. A state of a system is information characterizing the situation at a given moment. The first step in this explication process is to define the state in the most obvious unrestricted way. This will give a space that is possibly too large, and natural constraints on physical laws will cut down the unrestricted states to a subset of attainable or physical states. A physical state is one that has an actual possibility of occurring. These physical states form the final manifold of states. A number of examples in the following section will explain the process given in the previous sentences.

EXAMPLES OF STATE SPACES

Pure exchange economy

Example from economics. In the pure exchange economy of theoretical economics, a model is used with n different commodities, each measured in quantity by a positive real number (fixing a unit of measurement). Thus commodity space P will be the set of points of real Cartesian space $\mathfrak{R}^n$ with each coordinate positive. A point of P represents a bundle of commodities possessed, for example, by a certain consumer in the economy.

It is assumed that there are a finite number of consumers, say m, with the possessions of the ith consumer denoted by x_i in P. An unrestricted state of the economy is a point $x = (x_1, \ldots, x_m)$ in which each x_i is in P. The space of all these states is denoted by P^m, the Cartesian product of P with itself m times. Thus, an unrestricted state of the economy simply gives the possessions of the consumers of that economy.

Now, it is supposed that the total resources in this economic model are fixed, say, at a point w in P. Thus, the space of attainable states is a subset W of P^m described by the following condition: $(x_1, \ldots, x_m)$ is in W if the sum of the x_i is w.

Examples from classical mechanics. *Particle in Euclidean space* E^3. Ordinary three-dimensional Euclidean space is denoted by E^3. A particle in E^3 has its state characterized by its position x, a point in E^3, and its velocity $\boldsymbol{v}$, a vector (or point) in E^3. Thus, $\boldsymbol{v}$ gives the direction in which the particle is moving together with its speed, the length of $\boldsymbol{v}$. The vector $\boldsymbol{v}$ can be thought of as being based at x. The states of this system are then all pairs $(x, \boldsymbol{v})$, x, $\boldsymbol{v}$ each in E^3. This space is denoted by $E^3 \times E^3$, the Cartesian product of E^3 with E^3.

Particle on a sphere. D^3 is a unit ball in E^3, so that D^3 consists of all points whose distance from the origin is less than or equal to one. The 2-sphere S^2 is its boundary, or points of unit distance, from the origin of E^3. The space of states for the physical system of a particle on S^2 will then be a certain subset of $E^3 \times E^3$ of the first example.

There are two constraints: the first is that x must be in S^2; the second is that $\boldsymbol{v}$ must be perpendicular to x. The first constraint follows by definition, and the second constraint follows because, if the velocity were not perpendicular to x, then x would have to leave the 2-sphere. The set of points $(x, \boldsymbol{v})$ that satisfies these two constraints is the state space $\mathfrak{S}$ for this problem. $\mathfrak{S}$ can also be thought of in the following way. If $T_x(S^2)$ is the tangent space to S^2 at x, so $T_x(S^2)$ is the set of all vectors $\boldsymbol{v}$ in E^3 based at x with $\boldsymbol{v}$ tangent to the surface S^2 (or perpendicular to x), then $\mathfrak{S}$ is the union of all these $T_x(S^2)$ as x varies over S^2. In other words, $\mathfrak{S}$ is the tangent bundle of S^2, $T(S^2)$ or the set of all $(x, \boldsymbol{v})$ in $S^2 \times E^2$ in which $\boldsymbol{v}$ is in $T_x(S^2)$.

Plane rigid body. A point x_0 and a directed line n_0 are fixed in B through x_0. Then the position of B in the plane E^2 is characterized by the position of x_0 in E^2 and the angle between n_0 and a fixed directed reference line n in E^2. (For simplicity it is assumed that B has only one possibility for its orientation in E^2.) Therefore, the space of positions or configurations of B is a three-dimensional space or manifold, the Cartesian product of E^2 and the circle S^1, $E^2 \times S^1$. In this instance, the fact that there is a correspondence between angles and points on the circle is used. $M = E^2 \times S^1$ is sometimes called the space of generalized coordinates for the configuration of B. If (x, θ) is in $E^2 \times S^1$, then (x, θ) stands for the configuration of B, in which x_0 is located at x and θ is the angle between n_0 and n.

The possible velocities for B at (x, θ) are vectors $(\boldsymbol{v}_1, \boldsymbol{v}_2)$ in $E^2 \times \mathfrak{R}$ (or E^3), in which $\boldsymbol{v}_1$ is the ordinary velocity of x in E^2 and $\boldsymbol{v}_2$ is angular velocity. Therefore, for this mechanical system, the state space $\mathfrak{S}$ is the product $(E^2 \times S^1) \times (E^2 \times \mathfrak{R})$ of configuration and velocity space.

A circuit with three electrical components. A series connection between a resistor, an inductance, and a capacitor, wired to form a closed loop, may now be considered. To form the space of states, each of these three components is oriented. A state of the circuit consists of the current through each component and the voltage across each component. If i_ρ, v_ρ stand for the current and voltage, respectively, in the resistor, then i_λ, v_λ stand for current and voltage in the inductance and i_γ, v_γ for current and voltage in the capacitor. For historical reasons the capacitor is conventionally oriented in the opposite direction from the other two components. The Kirchhoff laws (from the 19th-century physicist Gustav Robert Kirchhoff) imply the following relations on the currents and voltages. The Kirchhoff current law (KCL) asserts that $i_\lambda = i_\rho = -i_\gamma$ or that the current that flows into a junction between two components is equal to the current that is flowing out. The Kirchhoff voltage law (KVL) asserts that $v_\lambda + v_\rho = -v_\gamma$, or that the voltages around a loop of components sum to zero.

The Kirchhoff laws and Ohm's law

The set of states in $\mathfrak{R}^6$ satisfying these Kirchhoff laws forms a three-dimensional linear subspace K of $\mathfrak{R}^6$. Any physical state has to lie in K. To obtain the precise set of physical states, another step is needed, in order to bring in the implications of the resistors on (i_ρ, v_ρ).

The most common type of resistor is linear in that it obeys Ohm's law (named for the German physicist Georg Simon Ohm); *i.e.*, $v_\rho = R_\rho i_\rho$, in which R_ρ is some positive constant. For a physical state, Ohm's law must be satisfied as well as Kirchhoff's laws. This cuts down the space of physical states to a two-dimensional linear subspace $\mathfrak{S}$ for $\mathfrak{R}^6$.

More generally, any resistor, linear or nonlinear, is defined by its characteristic Λ_ρ, which is a curve in the two-dimensional (i_ρ, v_ρ)-plane. Then a generalized version of Ohm's law stipulates that, for a physical state in $\mathfrak{R}^6$, the components (i_ρ, v_ρ) lie in Λ_ρ. It can be proved in the general case that these constraints force the physical states to lie in a two-dimensional manifold Σ of $\mathfrak{R}^6$.

Suppose, for example, that the resistor is current controlled so that the characteristic Λ_ρ is the graph in $\mathfrak{R}^2$ of some smooth real function f. Thus, $v_\rho = f(i_\rho)$. In this case it is convenient to take as a representation of Σ the Cartesian (i_λ, v_γ)-plane $\mathfrak{R}^2$ identifying $\mathfrak{R}^2$ and Σ under the diffeomorphism $\mathfrak{R}^2 \rightarrow \Sigma \subset \mathfrak{R}^6$, which sends (i_λ, v_γ) into a state in $\mathfrak{R}^6$ that is completely determined by i_λ and v_γ (see 411). Then the space of states for this circuit is equivalent to $\mathfrak{R}^2$ or (i_λ, v_γ)-space.

Simple electrical circuits. This example just given can be generalized to what could be called simple electrical circuits. A simple electrical circuit consists of components and nodes. The components are circuit elements that are either resistors, inductances, or capacitors, each with two terminals. In the circuit, groups of terminals meet at the different nodes. It is assumed that the components have a given orientation so that the current flowing in one direction is given by a positive real number, and the current flowing is given by a negative number if it flows in the opposite direction.

$$(411)\quad (i_\lambda, i_\lambda, -i_\lambda, f(i_\lambda), v_\gamma - f(i_\lambda), v_\gamma) = (i_\rho, i_\lambda, i_\gamma, v_\rho, v_\lambda, v_\gamma)$$

$$(412)\quad \left.\frac{d\varphi_t(x)}{dt}\right]_{t=0} = X(x)$$

$$(413)\quad \frac{d}{dt}\varphi_t(x) = X(x)$$

The unrestricted states of the current have as components the currents through each component and the voltages across each component. So if there are N components, the space of unrestricted states $\mathfrak{S}$ is $2N$-dimensional Cartesian space $\Re^{2N}$.

Physical constraints

The laws of physics impose constraints on these states. First of all, Kirchhoff laws assert that a physical state must be in a linear subspace K of $\Re^{2N}$ with dimension K equal N. In formal terms Kirchhoff's current law says that for each node, the sum of the currents entering the node equals the sum of the currents issuing from the node. Kirchhoff's voltage law then requires that the voltages across each component of a closed cycle add to zero. It follows that the set of states in $\Re^{2N}$ satisfying Kirchhoff's current law and Kirchhoff's voltage law forms a linear subspace of dimension N.

The final physical constraint is given by a generalization of Ohm's law. A resistor component ρ is allowed to have as characteristic any nonsingular curve—*i.e.*, one-dimensional submanifold—Λ_ρ in the (i_ρ, v_ρ)-plane. This means that a physical state in K must have i_ρ, v_ρ components satisfying the condition that (i_ρ, v_ρ) is in Λ_ρ. If the ρth resistor is linear, then Λ_P is a line through the origin with positive slope. Thus the physical states finally satisfy these further conditions, one for each resistor. The final subspace Σ of $\mathfrak{S}$ defined by these conditions and Kirchhoff conditions will be a submanifold in the general case whose dimension is equal to the number of inductor components plus the number of capacitor components.

MANIFOLDS

In each case of the examples, the state space is a manifold. A manifold can often be thought of as a domain (or open set) in Euclidean space of some dimension. More generally, a manifold is defined by glueing together such open sets; thus, for example, while the 2-sphere is a two-dimensional manifold, it is not equivalent to an open set of the plane. It can be obtained though as the union of two, two-dimensional disks that overlap in a ring. Every k-dimensional manifold can be represented by a k-dimensional surface in Euclidean space of some higher dimension. It is most reasonable to take a manifold—*i.e.*, differentiable manifold—as the basic space of a dynamical system.

If U is an open set in Euclidean space E and x is in U, then a tangent vector of U at x is simply a vector in E, which can be thought of as being based at x. The tangent bundle $T(U)$ is the product $U \times E$, and a point $(x, \mathbf{v})$ in $U \times E$ consists of base point x, vector $\mathbf{v}$.

More generally if x is a point in a manifold M, in which M is represented as a k-dimensional surface in some Euclidean space E, then a tangent vector of M at x is simply a vector in E based at x and tangent to M. The space of all tangent vectors to M at x is the tangent space $T_x(M)$ of M at x. Then $T(M)$, the tangent bundle of M, is the (disjoint) union of all these $T_x(M)$ as x varies over M and is a manifold itself in a natural way.

In all the examples of mechanical systems, the initial step was to take the manifold M of positions or configurations. Then the space of states was the tangent bundle $T(M)$ of M. A state in all of these examples consists of a configuration together with a (generalized) velocity based at that configuration. This persists in much more general examples of mechanical systems.

DYNAMICAL SYSTEMS AS VECTOR FIELDS ON MANIFOLDS

On manifolds (*e.g.*, open sets of Euclidean space) differentiation makes sense, and a differentiable map (*i.e.*, transformation) from a manifold to itself with a differentiable inverse is called a diffeomorphism. In these terms the definition of a dynamical system can be restated as assigning to each time t (a real number), a diffeomorphism φ_t: $M \to M$ with φ_0 the identity, $\varphi_{t+s} = \varphi_t \circ \varphi_s$, and so that $\varphi_t(x)$ is differentiable in (t, x). Thus for each x in the manifold, the trajectory $\varphi_t(x) = x_t$ is a curve through x. The derivative of this curve $t \to \varphi_t(x)$ at $t=0$ can be taken, letting $X(x)$ be the derivative of $\varphi_t(x)$ (see 412) to obtain the velocity or the tangent vector of the curve at x. Thus $X(x)$ is in the tangent space $T_x(M)$. The association $x \to X(x)$ is a vector field on M (or tangent vector field on M). More generally, a vector field on M is any differentiable map $X{:}M \to T(M)$ with $X(x)$ in $T_x(M)$. For example, if M is an open set in Euclidean space E, then $T(M) = M \times E$ and a vector field $Y{:}M \to M \times E$ must be of the form $Y(x) = (x, X(x))$ for some map $X{:}M \to E$. In this case, by a slight abuse of language, X is called a vector field, so that a vector field can be thought of as assigning to each point x, in M, a vector in E based at x.

Diffeo-morphisms

The notion of vector field on a manifold is of basic importance because among other things a dynamical system is characterized by its associated vector field. A converse to this statement is roughly true, and the converse could be regarded as the fundamental theorem of ordinary differential equations. More precisely, if $x \to X(x)$ is a vector field on a manifold M, the ordinary differential equation can be considered for $\varphi_t(x)$, given by the derivative of $\varphi_t(x)$ being equal to $X(x)$ (see 413).

This equation has a solution, at least for all t satisfying $t^-(x) < t < t^+(x)$ in which t^-, t^+ are real functions on M defining some (perhaps maximal) open set Q in $R \times M$ containing $O \times M$. This solution $\varphi_t(x)$, defined for (t, x) in Q, then has the properties of a dynamical system except that it may not be defined for all t going to $\pm\infty$. This system of trajectories is still called a dynamical system (or flow), and in this sense vector fields on manifolds are equivalent to dynamical systems.

EXAMPLES OF DYNAMICAL SYSTEMS

Particle in E^3 in a force field. Consider the example of a particle in three-dimensional Euclidean space. It is supposed now that there is a certain vector field, a force field defined on E^3, say $x \to F(x)$, $E^3 \to E^3$. Thus, if the particle is at x in E^3, the force exerted on it is $F(x)$, and Newton's law reads $ma = F(x)$. Here m is a constant positive real number, the mass of the particle, and $a = x''(t)$ (or the second derivative of x with respect to t) is the acceleration with $t \to x(t)$ a curve in E^3 that represents the passage of the particle in time. For an actual or physical path, Newton's equation is satisfied, or $mx''(t) = F(x(t))$ for all t.

Newton's equation is seen to be equivalent to the pair of equations (see 414) relating the derivatives of position and velocity to the velocity and the force, respectively. In this last form, the map $(x, \mathbf{v}) \to (\mathbf{v}, F(x)/m)$ is a vector field on the state space for this mechanical system $T(E^3)$. This is the form of a vector field on the state space determining the passage in time of the space. The initial conditions are $(x, \mathbf{v})$, the position and velocity of the particle.

The force field $x \to F(x)$ is called conservative if it is of the form $F(x) = -\operatorname{grad} V(x)$ in which V is some real function on E^3. Grad $V(x)$ is defined as the vector in which the ith component is $\partial v/\partial x_i$, for $i = 1, 2, 3$ (see 415), in terms of Cartesian coordinates. V is called the potential for the system. The classical example of a force field is that of gravitational force. If the source of this force is the point located at the centre of E^3, then (see 416) the force is inversely proportional to the square of the distance, involving the Euclidean norm on E^3 (see 417) in Cartesian coordinates. In this case, $F(x)$ is a conservative force field because a potential can be chosen (see 418) that is inversely proportional to the distance. This gives what is sometimes called the Kepler problem because the solution curves lead to the elliptical orbits of the Earth about the Sun first announced in the 17th century by the German astronomer Johannes Kepler. Strictly speaking, in the Kepler problem configuration space is $E^3 - 0$, because the vector field describing the dynamics is not defined at 0.

Conservative force fields

Van der Pol equation. The particular example of an

electrical circuit given earlier is now considered. Physical laws of the inductor and capacitor give the differential equations for motion directly in terms of the representation of the state space found there. More precisely (see 419) the derivative of i_λ is proportional to v_λ and the derivative of v_γ is proportional to i_γ (see 419), in which *L*, the inductance, and *C*, the conductance, are constants of proportionality. For simplicity, *L* and *C* are taken as constants equal to unity. Here $v_\lambda = v_\gamma - f(i_\lambda)$ and $i_\gamma = -i_\gamma$ by Kirchhoff's laws and the resistor characteristic. The differential equations then become appropriately changed (see 420). The corresponding vector field on $\mathfrak{R}^2$ at the point (i_λ, v_γ) is $(v_\gamma - f(i_\lambda), -i_\lambda)$.

In the case in which f is linear, of the form $v_p = R_p i_p$, $R_p > 0$, then it can be deduced that all solution curves of this dynamical system tend toward the origin. The origin is a steady state and an attractor. This means that a solution at the origin stays at the origin for all time or that the vector field is zero at the origin (steady state). That the origin is an attractor means that nearby solutions tend to the origin as $t \to \infty$. Steady-state attractors play a central role in applications of dynamical systems.

On the other hand, if a highly nonlinear characteristic is considered, say the derivative $f'(0) < 0$, then the unique zero $(0, f(0))$ of the vector field can be shown to be a source. This means that orbits tend to $(0, f(0))$ as $t \to -\infty$. If the characteristic $(i_\lambda, f(i_\lambda))$ stays well inside the first and third quadrants for large $|i_\lambda|$ (a natural assumption even for nonlinear resistors), then as $t \to \infty$ all orbits tend toward some bounded region in $\mathfrak{R}^2$. This follows from a general energy theorem. From these facts, the Poincaré-Bendixson theorem (with I.O. Bendixson) implies the existence of a periodic orbit, and one will be an attractor in the general case. A periodic orbit, period $w > 0$ is an orbit where $\varphi_{t+w}(x) = \varphi_t(x)$ for all t. This amounts to an oscillatory behaviour of the physical variables. That it is an attractor means that all nearby solutions tend toward it and thus will also oscillate, at least to a high degree of approximation. Periodic attractors are of basic importance in applications of dynamical systems.

The Poincaré-Bendixson theorem

The characteristic defined (see 421) by $f(i_l)$ being equal to $\mu(i_\lambda{}^3 - i_\lambda)$ satisfies the conditions of the previous paragraph. Here there is a unique periodic attractor; the differential equation is called van der Pol's equation.

Volterra-Lotka equations. The equations describing how the populations of rabbits and foxes vary in time are called the Volterra-Lotka equations and are (see 422) a pair of coupled first-order equations with positive constants α, β, λ, μ. For example, $dr/dt = ar$ governs how the number of rabbits increases eating grass, without taking into account the foxes that eat them. The Volterra-Lotka equation can be interpreted as giving a vector field on the positive quadrant in $\mathfrak{S}^2$; its solution curves are in fact periodic so that the populations are expected to change in cycles under these conditions. (S.Sm./Ed.)

HAMILTONIAN MECHANICS

Hamiltonian mechanics as developed on manifolds has the virtue of including quite general mechanical systems and shows basic principles most simply. To define gradients, the inner product on Euclidean space *E* was of central importance. Hamiltonians are developed similarly with the bilinear form *B*, or inner product, replaced by a symplectic bilinear form Ω on *E*. $B(x, \mathfrak{L}[x])$ is a sum of terms $x_i(\mathfrak{L}x_i)$ (see 423) for Cartesian coordinates $(x_1, \ldots, x_n) = x$ on *E*. *E* is taken to have even dimension $2n$ and a bilinear form Ω on *E* is defined (see 424). Not only is it seen that Ω is bilinear, but it is also clearly antisymmetric, $\Omega(x, \mathfrak{L}[x]) = -\Omega(x, \mathfrak{L}[x])$. It can also be seen that Ω is nondegenerate or that the map $\varphi_\Omega = E \to E^*$ is an isomorphism with $\varphi_\Omega(x)(\mathfrak{L}[x]) = \Omega(x, \mathfrak{L}[x])$. In fact, any nondegenerate, antisymmetric bilinear form Ω can be used in the following, and such an Ω is called a symplectic structure on *E*. Ω can be used to define Hamiltonian dynamical systems.

Open sets of E^{2n}. If *U* is an open set of *E* in which *E* has a symplectic structure (and so has even dimension) and $H{:}U \to \mathfrak{R}$ is any differentiable function, called a Hamiltonian in this context, then the derivative $DH{:}U \to E^*$ is a 1-form on *U*, and $X_H = \varphi_\Omega{}^{-1}DH$ is a vector field (or ordinary differential equation) on *U*. Thus X_H is a map from *U* to *E*, and $\Omega(X_H(x), Y)$ equals $DH(x)(Y)$ for all *x* in *U* and *Y* in *E*. Note that X_H is defined as grad *H* except that *B* has been replaced by Ω.

In terms of the Cartesian coordinates on *E* in which $\Omega(x, \mathfrak{L}[x])$ has a specific form (see 425), X_H has for its first *n* coordinates $\partial H/\partial x_{n+i}$ and for its second *n* coordinates

(414) $\dot{x} = v, \quad \dot{v} = \frac{1}{m}F \quad \text{on} \quad E^3 \times E^3 = T(E^3)$

(415) $\left(\frac{\partial V}{\partial x_1}, \frac{\partial V}{\partial x_2}, \frac{\partial V}{\partial x_3}\right)$

(416) $F(x) = -\frac{x}{\|x\|^3}$

(417) $(\|x\|) = (\Sigma x_i^2)^{1/2}$

(418) $V(x) = -\frac{1}{\|x\|}$

(419) $L\frac{di_\lambda}{dt} = v_\lambda, \quad C\frac{dv_\gamma}{dt} = i_\gamma$

(420) $\begin{cases} \frac{di_\lambda}{dt} = v_\gamma - f(i_\lambda) \\ \frac{dv_\gamma}{dt} = -i_\lambda \end{cases}$

(421) $f(i_\lambda) = \mu(i_\lambda^3 - i_\lambda), \quad \mu > 0$

(422) $\frac{dr}{dt} = ar - \lambda rf, \quad \frac{df}{dt} = -\beta f + \mu rf$

(423) $B(x, \mathfrak{L}[x]) = \sum_{i=1}^{n} x_i\, \mathfrak{L}(x_i)$

(424) $\Omega\,(x, \mathfrak{L}[x]) = \sum_{i=1}^{n} x_i\, \mathfrak{L}(x_{i+n}) - \sum_{i=1}^{n} x_{i+n}\, \mathfrak{L}(x_i)$

(425) $\begin{cases} \Omega(x, \mathfrak{L}[x]) = \sum_{i=1}^{n} x_i\, \mathfrak{L}(x_{i+n}) - \sum_{i=1}^{n} x_{n+i}\, \mathfrak{L}(x_i) \\ X_H = \left(\frac{\partial H}{\partial x_{n+1}}, \ldots, \frac{\partial H}{\partial x_{2n}}, -\frac{\partial H}{\partial x_1}, \ldots, -\frac{\partial H}{\partial x_n}\right) \end{cases}$

(426) $\frac{dx_i}{dt} = \frac{\partial H}{\partial y_i}, \quad \frac{dy_i}{dt} = -\frac{\partial H}{\partial x_i}, \quad i = 1, \ldots, n$

(427) $(y_1, y_2, y_3),\ y_i = mv_i$

(428) $H(x, y) = \frac{1}{2m}\sum y_i^2 + V(x)$

(429) $\frac{dx_i}{dt} = v_i, \quad \frac{mdv_i}{dt} = \frac{\partial V}{\partial x_i}$

(430) $\frac{1}{2m}\sum y_i^2, \quad \frac{1}{2}m\sum v_i^2$

(431) $X_H(x) = \varphi_{\Omega x}^{-1}\, DH(x)$

(432) $(DH(x))(X_H(x)) = \Omega_x(X_H(x), X_H(x))$

$-\partial H/\partial x_i$ (see 425). If $y_i = x_{n+i}$, $i = 1, \ldots, n$ the ordinary differential equations represented by X_H are the classical Hamilton's equations in which the derivative of x_i equals $\partial H/\partial y_i$ and the derivative of y_i equals $-\partial H/\partial x_i$ (see 426).

Particle in E^3. A special case of the foregoing is the earlier mechanical system of a particle of mass m moving in 3-space under a conservative force field $F(x) = -\text{grad } V(x)$ with $V{:}E^3 \to \mathfrak{R}$, (potential) function. Then on the state space $E^3 \times E^3$ coordinates are chosen (x_1, x_2, x_3) for the configuration and y_i is proportional to $\boldsymbol{v}_i$ (see 427) for the second factor (or momentum coordinates). If Ω is taken as above and $H{:}E^3 \times E^3 \to \mathfrak{R}$ defined in terms of a sum of the y_i^2 and $V(x)$ (see 428), then Hamilton's equations coincide with Newton's equations (see 429). The term involving the y_i^2 (see 430) is called the kinetic energy, and V is the potential energy of this mechanical system; the sum $K + V$ is the total energy or simply energy.

Manifolds. The concept of symplectic structure can be generalized easily to manifolds. If W is an even-dimensional manifold and x is a point of W, then a symplectic structure Ω at x is simply a nondegenerate, antisymmetric bilinear from Ω_x on the tangent space $T_x(W)$. A manifold W with such Ω_x given for each x, Ω_x varying differentially with x, is called a symplectic manifold. As before, for each x, $\varphi_{\Omega_x}{:}T_x(W) \to T_x^*(W)$ is an isomorphism from the tangent space to its dual, the cotangent space at x. Given a Hamiltonian $H{:}W \to \mathfrak{R}$, then for each x, the derivative $DH(x)$ is in $T_x^*(W)$, and the above isomorphism converts the 1-form DH to a vector field X_H (see 431). The vector field X_H is then the Hamiltonian vector field (or ordinary differential equation) corresponding to the Hamiltonian H. As a Riemannian manifold is required to define gradient vector fields, a symplectic manifold is required in order to define Hamiltonian vector fields.

Symplectic manifold

Conservation laws. Various physical principles can be derived in this setting. For example, conservation of energy amounts to the function H being constant on trajectories of X_H. This is the same thing as the assertion that for each x, $DH(x)$ evaluated at $X_H(x)$ is zero. But another condition holds (see 432) from the definition of X_H, and the last is zero since Ω_x is antisymmetric.

Liouville's theorem asserts that Hamiltonian systems preserve volume. In this context, that volume on the abstract manifold W is the n-fold wedge product of Ω with itself. Without pursuing the technical definition of wedge product, it can be said that if Ω is defined as above on E in coordinate, then the Liouville volume is just ordinary volume on E. It can be first checked that Ω itself is invariant under a Hamiltonian flow X_H, and then it naturally follows that the wedge product, the Liouville volume is preserved. This can be contrasted with the gradient case. For example, neighbourhoods of a local maximum of a gradient flow are shrunk into smaller subsets by the dynamics. Volume is strictly decreased.

Simple mechanical systems. A simple mechanical system (M, K, V) has a manifold M that is the configuration space of the system. $V{:}M \to \mathfrak{R}$ is a function, the potential energy, and kinetic energy K is considered to be given by some Riemannian metric on M. Thus for each x in M there is an inner product K_x on $T_x(M)$ and $K(v) = K_x(v, v)$ for v in $T_x(M)$. This can be compared with the earlier mechanical system of a particle constrained to move on the 2-sphere in E^3. In this case, K_x on $T_x(S^2)$ is the restriction of inner product on E^3 times half the mass. Together these sum to give the energy $E{:}T(M) \to R$ as a real function on the tangent bundle of M as defined by $E(v) = K(v) + V(x)$ for v in $T_x(M)$.

To put this into the symplectic perspective, it is convenient to consider the cotangent bundle $T^*(M)$. There is a canonically defined symplectic structure Ω defined on $T^*(M)$, which extends the earlier example of Ω on $E^3 \times E^3$. Furthermore, the energy E can be transferred to $T^*(M)$ by a map called the Legendre transformation $L{:}T(M) \to T^*(M)$. More precisely, if $v \in T_x(M)$, then $L(v) = \varphi_{K_x}(v)$ in which φ_{K_x} is the usual linear map induced by a bilinear form. Then the Hamiltonian $H{:}T^*(M) \to \mathfrak{R}$ is defined by $H = E \circ L^{-1}$. The corresponding Hamiltonian vector field X_H on $T^*(M) = W$ gives the dynamics for this mechanical system. The inverse of the Legendre transformation takes trajectories of X_H back to solutions of the Euler-Lagrange equations on $T(M)$. (S.Sm.)

Potential theory

HISTORICAL SURVEY OF PROBLEMS AND CONCEPTS

Until around 1800, potential theory was actually that part of theoretical physics basically concerned with electrostatics (see the article ELECTRICITY AND MAGNETISM) and Newtonian attraction between masses. The potential of a unit mass concentrated at a point X is equal at any other point x to the inverse $\dfrac{1}{|X-x|}$ of the distance $|X-x|$ to X. It is a harmonic function of x $(x \neq X)$; that is, it is equal at x to its mean value on any ball centred at x and not containing X, or, equivalently, it satisfies Laplace's equation (see 433), a second-order partial differential equation. The potential of a general distribution of masses is then defined by multiplication and summation (actually by an operation of integration) and it is harmonic outside of the masses. Thus, physical problems became mathematical ones.

Important results due to the mathematicians Siméon-Denis Poisson and George Green were followed in 1840 by a fundamental work of Carl Friedrich Gauss, amazingly deep and rich, in which he solved for Euclidean space three connected problems that remain essential subject to various adaptations.

Work of Carl Friedrich Gauss

The first one is the problem of equilibrium; this is the determination of a distribution of a given mass on a conductor for which the potential is constant on it; this corresponds to minimizing the (potential) energy.

Given masses inside a closed conductor, the second problem asks how they can be distributed on the conductor so as to give the same potential outside. This is solved physically by the phenomenon of influence that creates on the conductor (on which one makes the potential zero) a distribution of masses such that the total potential is zero outside. Similar problems arise by commuting (interchanging) interior and exterior. This operation was later called *balayage* (sweeping-out process) by Poincaré.

The third problem is the determination in a domain of a harmonic function the limiting values of which agree on the boundary with a given function (first supposed to be finite continuous). As noted earlier, this standard boundary value problem was called the Dirichlet problem by Riemann.

For lack of sufficient mathematical tools, the solutions given by Gauss were not rigorous and the results not quite correct or precise; actually they needed some restrictions. Because of these difficulties, the first two problems were put aside for a long time, but the Dirichlet problem, more important, was studied by different methods, which at first were not rigorous either. For example, an important method was based on the minimizing of a so-called Dirichlet integral (Dirichlet principle). This was made rigorous by David Hilbert of Germany only around 1900. If so many great mathematicians gave different solutions, it is perhaps also because the restrictions on the boundary seemed unnecessary; actually they were necessary, as S. Zaremba of Poland and Henri-Léon Lebesgue of France noted after 1900.

Some other questions considered in this period include the analytic character of harmonic functions (expansion as power series), other types of boundary value problems (such as the Neumann problem, named for Karl Gottfried Neumann of Germany, for given normal derivatives), the connections of harmonic functions with functions of a complex variable, conformal mapping, Fourier series, similar developments for equations more general

(433) $$\Delta u = \sum_{i=1}^{3} \frac{\partial^2 u}{\partial u_i^2}$$

(434) $$\int N(x, y)\, d\mu(y)$$

than the Laplace one, polyharmonic functions or more precisely harmonic functions of order p, satisfying to $\Delta^p u = \Delta(\ldots \Delta u) = 0$ with $p|\Delta$-operators.

A second period of the development of potential theory was characterized chiefly by the introduction, in the study of potential theory, of wider notions of measure and integral (those of Lebesgue and Radon), and of capacity, a notion inspired by electrostatics, first clearly defined and discussed by Norbert Wiener of the United States and Charles-Jean de la Vallée Poussin of Belgium, and greatly generalized much later by the French mathematician Gustave Choquet.

The use of integrals allowed a new development of the subject, chiefly by means of a larger definition of the potential of a general distribution of masses—*i.e.*, a measure μ. This potential is defined by the integral of a function N integrated with respect to y and to a measure μ (see 434) in which $N(x, y)$, called a kernel, is $\dfrac{1}{|x-y|^{n-2}}$ in the space $\Re^n$ with $n \geq 3$ (Newtonian kernel) and is $\log \dfrac{1}{|x-y|}$ in $\Re^2$ (logarithmic kernel).

A new setting and a generalized solution of the Dirichlet problem appeared (resulting from a remark of Lebesgue and results of Wiener), avoiding any restriction on the boundary; the boundary behaviour of the new solution and its relation with the previous one were made clear later by O.D. Kellogg and Griffith C. Evans of the United States, thanks to the notion of capacity, and a more general problem with discontinuous boundary data was solved by Marcel-Émile Brelot of France.

Sub-harmonic and super-harmonic functions

New important tools, the concepts of subharmonic and superharmonic functions, were introduced by Frigyes Riesz, a Hungarian mathematician. These functions stand in relation to harmonic functions as arcs of convex and concave curves, respectively, do to their chords. They are locally equal modulo harmonic functions to potentials of negative and positive masses, respectively, in the general new sense.

A rigorous and more precise development of the ideas of Gauss was made in the famous thesis of the Swedish mathematician Otto Frostman (1935). A definitive convergence theorem on decreasing potentials of positive masses, given by the French mathematicians Marcel-Émile Brelot and Henri Cartan, was an essential tool for all refinements in potential theory. The sets of (outer) capacity zero emerged as the standard exceptional sets in potential theory and in its application to the functions of a complex variable.

The third period from about 1940 to 1955 was marked by the role of topology in potential theory.

The notion of energy in Euclidean space was used more deeply by Cartan. The measures were considered as points of a space, with the distance to the origin equal to the square root of the energy corresponding to the measure: in such a space the well-known methods of Hilbert space theory (geometry in a space with infinitely many coordinates) were applied, and a striking and powerful theory was developed. Later Jacques Deny continued this theory of finite energy, using, instead of measures, the more general distributions of the French mathematician Laurent Schwartz, but preserving the essential ideas.

Another example of the role of topology is the introduction of the notion of a thin set and equivalently of the fine topology in which all classical potentials become continuous. This notion due to Brelot and Cartan is adapted to the study of discontinuous potentials and nonsmooth boundaries and gives rise to new problems.

Martin boundary

The most striking example is the introduction of the Martin boundary. The solution of the Dirichlet problem in a ball had led to the (integral) representation of a positive harmonic function in the ball by means of a positive measure on the boundary. A similar problem for a general Euclidean domain remained unsolved until 1941 when Martin introduced a quite new boundary and its useful minimal part. This work later inspired Choquet's profound study of extreme points of a compact convex set, which is one of the great discoveries in analysis after the mid-20th century.

This period also marks the introduction in potential theory of spaces much more general than Euclidean spaces or certain manifolds and of more general kernels N than the Newtonian or logarithmic ones, N a suitable function of two variables (and even of more general concepts). Around 1940 certain basic properties of the classical theory were introduced as axioms in suitably chosen topological spaces and a discussion began of various generalizations and interactions between different axioms or principles.

Since about 1955 topological refinements and new axiomatizations have been made and the role of probability introduced. Fine topology was extended to the Martin boundary, and it became an essential tool for the study of the boundary behaviour of functions connected with potential theory.

Rather than speaking about the further developments with kernels $N(x, y)$, an axiomatic theory is sketched that is not based on such kernels. Given real-valued continuous functions are used, called harmonic functions, defined on every domain of a suitable topological space and satisfying some well-known properties of the classical theory that are considered as axioms. It was found possible to imitate the classical developments. In this direction, after some attempts, Joseph Leo Doob of the United States constructed a better base of an axiomatic theory but for probabilistic purposes. This inspired a detailed potential theory by Brelot and followers, such as the French mathematician Rose-Marie Hervé. The solutions of partial differential equations of elliptic type more general than that of the Laplace equation satisfy the basic axioms under some restrictions. But the theory is not applicable to equations of a more general type like the classical heat equation. In order to include such equations, Heinz Bauer of West Germany and others extended the previous theory by weakening the axioms. Later the systematic search for all theories satisfying such local axioms was partly solved by Jean-Michel Bony.

On the other hand, the concepts of energy and Dirichlet integral led Deny and the Swedish-born American mathematician Arne Carl-August Beurling to another axiomatic theory of global character, called the theory of Dirichlet spaces (for complex functions). Problems similar to those of equilibrium and balayage were studied.

Gilbert Hunt

These axiomatic theories, including interesting cases of the last one, are actually contained in a fundamental probabilistic theory developed by Gilbert Hunt between 1957 and 1958. A function of a point x and of a set e, called a kernel $V(x, e)$, which transforms a nonnegative function f into a nonnegative function Vf, is considered. Under certain conditions, this V may be expressed by means of similar kernels of a certain family $\{P_t\}_{t \geq 0}$ by means of which the so-called excessive functions can be defined. These majorize their P_t-transforms. This $\{P_t\}$ has an essential probabilistic interpretation in terms of "Markov processes," named for the Russian mathematician Andrey Andreyevich Markov, of which the Brownian motion of physics is a particular case.

It was shown by Paul-André Meyer and others that, given any of the above local axiomatic theories, it is possible to find a V for which the excessive functions of the corresponding $\{P_t\}$ are precisely the nonnegative hyperharmonic functions.

Various probabilistic notions like trajectories (of a particle) or martingales led to probabilistic interpretations of concepts and results of the above classical or axiomatic theories. The relations between probability and potential theory, known for a long time as "folklore" in the classical theory, deeply studied by Doob then Hunt and many others, have now produced a new and rich chapter in analysis. The latest researches are also concerned with a converse problem: given a family of functions, under what conditions can one interpret them as potentials or superharmonic functions in the above local axiomatics or excessive functions in a global extension of Hunt theory?

BASIC CONCEPTS AND RESULTS OF CLASSICAL POTENTIAL THEORY

Using more advanced mathematical tools, the most important points of classical theory will now be outlined. A

Euclidean space $\mathfrak{R}(n \geq 2)$ will be considered first, the case $n = 1$ being rather trivial.

Harmonic functions. A real finite continuous function u on an open set ω is said to be harmonic, if it is equal at each point x to its mean value on any ball (that is, a disc in $\mathfrak{R}^2$) B_x^r (centre x, radius r), or equivalently (using the corresponding Lebesgue measure), on the boundary $\partial B_x^r (\bar{B}_x^r \subset \omega)$. This implies that u is C^∞ (infinitely differentiable) and, further, is equivalent to saying that $\Delta u = 0$ (local condition). Also, $\Delta u = 0$ in the sense of Schwartz is equivalent to saying that u is a function equal almost everywhere to a harmonic function.

The definition implies that a harmonic function that attains its maximum (or minimum) at a point x_0 is constant on a neighbourhood. This maximum or minimum principle is a key tool. A form that will be valid later in more general theories may be stated in the following manner. If at any boundary point (which may be the Aleksandrov point [named for the Soviet mathematician Aleksandr Danilovich Aleksandrov] at infinity) lim inf $u \geq 0$, then $u \geq 0$.

This implies that for a finite boundary function f the Dirichlet problem possesses at most one solution. The question of existence is more difficult. For a ball $B = B_0^R$ and a finite continuous function f, the solution is given by the Poisson integral (see 435) integrated with respect to the measure σ (σ being the normalized measure on ∂B proportional to angle or solid angle). For any f, $\bar{I}_f$ will denote the upper-integral which is $+\infty$, $-\infty$, or harmonic. Note that by changing $f\,d\sigma$ into any Radon measure $d\mu$ on ∂B, the corresponding $I_\mu(y)$ (called a Poisson-Stieltjes integral) is harmonic in B and represents in the general case the difference of two nonnegative harmonic functions.

Poisson integral

The Poisson integral I_f implies many properties: a local criterion (by considering in the definition for any x only those ∂B_x^r with $0 < r < r(x)$ an arbitary function); analyticity (and various power series); the Harnack inequalities: u harmonic > 0 in B_0^R implies upper and lower bounds for the ratio of u at y to u at zero (see 436), which in turn implies the equicontinuity at any point of any family of positive-bounded harmonic functions.

It should be emphasized that uniform convergence preserves harmonicity and implies local uniform convergence for any derivative, that in a domain (connected open set) an increasing sequence u_n of harmonic functions tends to $+\infty$ or to a harmonic function (uniformly locally in an obvious sense), and that there is an extension to an increasing directed family.

(435) $$I_f^B(y) = \int \frac{R^2 - |y|^2}{|x-y|^n} R^{n-2} f(x)\, d\sigma(x)$$

(436) $$R^{n-2}\frac{R - |y|}{(R + |y|)^{n-1}} \leq \frac{u(y)}{u(0)} \leq R^{n-2}\frac{R + |y|}{(R - |y|)^{n-1}}$$

(437) $$u(y) = H_1(y) + |y|^2 H_2(y) + \cdots + |y|^{2p-2} H_p(y)$$

(438) $$\bar{B}_x^r(w), \qquad u \geq \bar{I}_u^{B_x^r}$$

(439) $$h_x(y) - I_{h_x}^B(y) = G(x, y)$$

(440) $$\int G(x, y)\, d\mu(x), \qquad \mu \geq 0$$

(441) $$\int G(x, y)\, d\mu(x) + u^*(y)$$

(442) $$G(x, y) = |x - y|^{2-n}$$

(443) $$\int G(x, y)\, d\mu(x)$$

Polyharmonic functions. Definitions, by iteration of Δ, were previously given. Extensions were made systematically of many properties of harmonic and subharmonic functions. The old development of Almansi is mentioned for a function of ε^{2p} type, harmonic of order p in a domain containing 0, by means of harmonic functions H_i (see 437).

Sub- and superharmonic functions. In an open set ω, u is said to be hyperharmonic if (i) u is lower semicontinuous; (ii) $u > -\infty$; (iii) for each ball contained in an open set, u has a specific lower bound (see 438; equivalently, only at x and for sufficiently small r; a local definition). In a domain, such a function is either identically $+\infty$ or finite on a dense set and in the first case is called superharmonic ($-u$ is called hypoharmonic and subharmonic, respectively).

The previous minimum-principle is still valid. Any set of superharmonic functions ≥ 0 has a greatest harmonic minorant. The set of the harmonic functions ≥ 0 is a complete lattice for the natural order. The set of the superharmonic functions ≥ 0 is a complete upper semi-lattice for the natural order and also for the specific order defined by setting $u > \omega$ if $u = \omega + a$ nonnegative superharmonic function.

Riesz representation. Any superharmonic function u is locally equal to $\int h(|x-y|)d\mu(x)$ plus a harmonic function, for a suitable measure $\mu \geq 0$.

For a ball B a specific function symmetric in x and y (see 439) is called Green's function. An integral of Green's function integrated with respect to x and μ (see 440), in which nonnegative μ is a Radon measure on B, is superharmonic or $+\infty$. Any superharmonic function u on B with a harmonic minorant is equal to such an integral plus a function u^* (see 441) in which u^* is the greatest harmonic minorant of u on B. (Unique in both local and global representations, μ is called the associated measure.) In $\mathfrak{R}^n$ ($n \geq 3$), the same result is valid in the whole $\mathfrak{R}^n$ by taking a specific form of Green's function (see 442).

If u is an e^2 function the result is easy to show; the general case is less easy unless Schwartz distributions are used. It is also possible, for the global form, to use a Choquet theorem on extreme elements.

The fact that $u^* = 0$ means that u is a Green potential (see 443).

Reduced function. On a fixed open set ω, a real function $\varphi \geq 0$ and a set e are considered. The reduced function of φ relative to e (denoted R_φ^e) is defined to be the lower envelope of all hyperharmonic nonnegative functions on ω majorizing φ on e. If $\hat{R}_\varphi^e(x)$ is the lim inf at x of R_φ^e, then $\hat{R}_\varphi^e$ is hyperharmonic.

When φ is superharmonic, $\hat{R}_\varphi^e$ is superharmonic and is called the "swept-out" or "balayaged" function of φ relative to e.

Polar sets and capacity. A set e in an open set ω is called polar in ω if there exists a nonnegative superharmonic function in ω equal to $+\infty$ on e. When there exists a superharmonic $u > 0$ on ω, e is polar if $R_v^e \equiv 0$.

Note that, if a set is locally polar, then it is polar in $\mathfrak{R}^n (n \geq 3)$ or in any domain where there exists a nonconstant superharmonic function ≥ 0.

A superharmonic function $u \geq 0$ on $\omega - e$ where e is closed and locally polar has a unique continuation to ω as a superharmonic function. If u is bounded and harmonic, the continuation is harmonic.

A real-valued function ζ (finite or not) defined on the class of all subsets of a Hausdorff space E is called a general capacity if (*a*) ζ is an increasing function; (*b*) for any increasing sequence $\{e_n\}$ of subsets of E, $\zeta(e_n) \to \zeta(Ue_n)$; and (*c*) for any decreasing sequence of compact sets K_n, a similar convergent holds expressed in terms of intersection (see 444).

A K-analytic set of E is one that is the continuous image of $K_{\sigma\delta}$ set (countable intersection of K_σ sets; that is, of countable unions of compact sets) contained in a compact space, as, for example, the ordinary-Borel sets (named for the French mathematician Émile Borel) in a space like $\mathfrak{R}^n$. The celebrated Choquet capacitability theorem asserts that any K-analytic set e contained in a K_σ set is "ζ-capacitable" (K compact $\subset e$; see 445).

Choquet capacitability theorem

An example is where E is a ball on $\mathfrak{R}^n$ ($n \geq 3$).

(444) $\zeta(K_n) \to \zeta(\cap K_n)$

(445) $\zeta(e) = \sup_K \zeta(K)$

(446) $C_*(K) = \sup\{C(K) \mid K \subset e, \text{ compact}\}$

(447) $C^*(e) = \inf\{C_*(\omega) \mid e \subset \omega, \text{ open}\}$

(448) $u(x_0) < \liminf_{x \in e,\, x \to x_0} u(x)$

(449) $\lim_{r \to 0} \sigma_r (e \cap \partial B^r_{x_0}) = 0$

$C(K)$ denotes the supremum of $\{\mu(K), \mu \geq 0$, a measure on K whose Green potential is $\leq 1\}$.

It equals the infimum of $\{\nu(E) \mid \nu \geq 0$, a measure on E whose Green potential is ≥ 1 on $K\}$. Letting $C_*(K)$ be an innercapacity (see 446) and $C^*(e)$ be an outercapacity (see 447) then C^* is a general capacity, $C^*(e) = C_*(e)$ for any Borel set e; and for any relatively compact set e, $C_*(e)$ is the total mass of the measure associated to $\hat{R}_1^e$ in E (which is even a potential). As a consequence of this, in the space E, the sets of outercapacity 0 are thus the polar sets.

Thin sets and fine topology. A set e is thin at $x_0 \notin e$ if $x_0 \notin \bar{e}$ or if there exists a superharmonic function u in the neighbourhood of x_0 such that at x_0 it is strictly less than its inferior limit (see 448). The family of complements of sets thin at x form the family of neighbourhoods of x in the so-called "fine topology" which is the coarsest one, making all superharmonic functions continuous. It is finer than the Euclidean one. In $\mathfrak{R}^n$ the definition is extended by saying that e is thin at $x_0 \in e$ if $e - \{x_0\}$ is thin at x_0.

Thinness of e at x_0 is much stronger than the condition in which σ_r is the surface measure (see 449).

Locally polar sets are characterized as thin at every point, or sets of "fine isolated" points. In $\mathfrak{R}^2$, for a set thin at x_0, there exist arbitrarily small circles centred at x_0 and not intersecting the set.

As an example of application: if u is a nonnegative superharmonic function on an open set ω, with a boundary point x_0 such that $C\omega$ is thin at x_0, then it has a fine limit at x_0, and this coincides with the Euclidean limit on $\omega \backslash e$ where e is a suitable thin set.

Dirichlet problem. ω is taken to be a bounded open set of $\mathfrak{R}^n$ and f is a given extended real-valued function on $\partial\omega$. All hyperharmonic functions v on ω are considered, satisfying $\liminf v \geq f(x)$ and also $<-\infty$, for $y \in \omega$, $y \to x$ every $x \in \partial\omega$. The lower envelope is a function H_f that, in every component of ω, is $+\infty$, $-\infty$, or harmonic. The similar envelope $H_f = -\overline{H}_f$ is $\leq \overline{H}_f$. In case both are equal and finite, the common value is denoted by H_f (solution) and f is said to be resolutive. This happens when f is continuous. Then $H_f(y)$ has, for a fixed y, a linear form $\int f d\rho_y^\omega$ with a measure ρ_y^ω called harmonic measure. For a domain ω, resolutivity of any f is equivalent to its ρ_y^ω-integrability (independent of y in ω).

A boundary point x is said to be regular if, for any finite continuous f, $H_f(y)$ tends to $f(x)$ at x. This is equivalent to saying that ω is not thin at x_0. It will be shown later that the irregular points form a locally polar set, as a consequence of a powerful convergence theorem.

Green's function; Green space. It is possible to define on the space $\overline{\mathfrak{R}}^n$ (compactified from $\mathfrak{R}^n$ with an Aleksandrov point $\mathfrak{U}$ at infinity) harmonic, hyper-, or superharmonic functions (even in the neighbourhoods of $\mathfrak{U}$) by a suitable mean value property, so as to preserve the minimum principle. The Newtonian and logarithmic kernels may be adapted and the local Riesz representation is preserved with a unique associated measure.

Hausdorff space

A $\mathfrak{G}$-space is defined to be a Hausdorff space with, for each point x, a homeomorphism of an open neighbourhood V of x onto an open set of $\overline{\mathfrak{R}}^n$, such that for any two such neighbourhoods say V' and V'' the images of $V' \cap V''$ under the different homeomorphisms are isometric or also if $n = 2$ in conformal (but not necessarily orientation-preserving) correspondence. Examples are $\mathfrak{R}^n$ and the classical Riemann surfaces.

This gives, on a $\mathfrak{G}$-space, local notions of harmonic, hyper-, or superharmonic functions. When there exists a nonconstant superharmonic function greater than 0, one says that $\mathfrak{G}$ is a Green space. Examples are $\mathfrak{R}^n$ $(n \geq 3)$ or any bounded domain of $\mathfrak{R}^n$. Then there exists a smallest superharmonic function ≥ 0 whose associated measure contains the unit mass at a point x. It is a generalization $G(x, y)$, still symmetric, of the Green's function of a ball. Green's potential $\int G(x, y) d\mu(x)$ $(\mu \geq 0$ on $\Omega)$, when not everywhere $+\infty$, is superharmonic with the greatest harmonic minorant equal to 0. The previous theory may be extended. Here it is only noted that a point at infinity (that is, one whose local image is $\mathfrak{U}$) is nonpolar for $n > 2$ and that it is suitable to define the thinness of $e \in x_0$ at x_0 with the supplementary condition that x_0 is polar. On a Green space, locally polar is equivalent to polar; one says "quasi-everywhere" for "except on a locally polar set."

The general classical convergence theorem. Given on an open set ω (in a $\mathfrak{G}$-space) a family of locally lower-bounded superharmonic functions u_i, $\inf u_i$ (which is at every point the lim inf of $\inf u_i$) is superharmonic and differs from $\inf u_i$ on a locally polar set.

Applications in a Green space Ω: (*a*) A superharmonic function $u \geq 0$ is considered. Then $\hat{R}_u^e$ is equal to u quasi-everywhere on e, and harmonic outside of $\bar{e}$. If u is a potential or e is relatively compact, $\hat{R}_u^e$ is a potential. In $\mathfrak{R}^3$, for example, for a nonpolar compact set e, $\hat{R}_1^e$ is the Newtonian potential of a measure ≥ 0 on e, with value 1, quasi-everywhere on e. This gives a solution of the equilibrium problem of Gauss but with a constant value only quasi-everywhere on e, and it is unique when the potential is bounded.

(*b*) The set of points where a set e is thin is polar. As an example, the set of irregular points of a Dirichlet problem for a relatively compact open set ω is polar.

(*c*) In treating a general form of the balayage, if a measure $\mu \geq 0$ with Green's potential V is given, the balayaged potential $\hat{R}_V^e$ is characterized by the following properties:

i. This potential is equal to V quasi-everywhere on e;

ii. The associated measure b_μ is supported by the "base" B_e of e, which is the set of points where e is not thin $(b_\mu(CB_e) = 0)$.

Dirichlet principle. Consider first a bounded open set ω of $\mathfrak{R}^n$ and a C^∞-function f on ω, with a finite Dirichlet norm (see 450) and possessing a finite continuous extension on $\partial\omega$. Then there exists a harmonic function u on ω, unique up to a constant, such that $\|u - f\|$ is minimum; and it is H_f^ω.

This can be generalized by considering a $\mathfrak{G}$-space Ω without any points at infinity, a domain ω relatively compact in Ω and a (BLD) function f on Ω that is a function which is a limit at every point, and also a limit according to the Dirichlet norm, of a Cauchy sequence of C^∞-functions with finite norms. Let f_ω be the restriction on ω. Then the minimizing function u is the projection of f_ω in the Hilbert space of the (BLD) functions on ω defined by the scalar product $\int(\text{grad } u, \text{grad } v)\, dx$, on the complete subspace of the harmonic (BLD) functions on ω; u is, in addition, the

(450) $\|f\| = \sqrt{\int \text{grad}^2 f\, dx}$

(451) $(\mu, \nu) = \int U^\mu d\nu$

(452) $\int (U^{\mu_1} - U^{\mu_2})(d\nu_1 - d\nu_2)$

(453) $G(x, y),\ K(x, y) = \dfrac{G(x, y)}{G(x, y_0)}$

(454) $\int K(X, y)\, d\mu_u(X)$

(455) $R^e_{K(X, y)} \neq K(X, y)$

unique harmonic function the continuation of which by f is (BLD) in Ω.

Energy. First $\mathfrak{R}^n$ ($n \geq 3$) or a ball of $\mathfrak{R}^n$ is considered. Inspired by the kernels $|x-y|^{-\alpha}$, of Marcel Riesz, Cartan introduced with the classical potential U^r the mutual energy of positive measures (see 451), the energy (μ, μ), and then the same notions for differences of measures of finite energy using for such differences a formal development of an integral (see 452). Then the energy is ≥ 0 and is zero only when $\mu_1 - \mu_2 \equiv 0$ (the principle of energy). The space $\mathfrak{G}$ of these signed measures of finite energy with mutual energy as scalar product is pre-Hilbert, and the subset $\mathfrak{G}^+$ of the nonnegative measures is complete. As an application, the balayage of a measure μ in $\mathfrak{G}^+$ relative to a compact K is given by the projection in $\mathfrak{G}$ of μ on the set of measures of $\mathfrak{G}^+$ supported by K. It is now known that a polar set has μ-measure 0 for (μ, μ) finite; the previous definitions can be directly extended to the case of a Green space and Green's potentials. The principle of energy with its consequences holds. Note that such potentials are BLD functions and also that the energy-norm and the Dirichlet norm are proportional. Other extensions are possible. Deny even developed a similar theory in $\mathfrak{R}^n$ with Schwartz distributions, a fixed one as kernel N, a variable one T, and the convolution as potential.

Martin boundary. In a Green space Ω, Green's function G and its ratio to the functional value obtained by setting the Green's function argument y equal to a fixed point y_0 (see 453) may be considered. Here there exists a compact space $\hat{\Omega}$ (Martin space) unique up to homeomorphism, in which Ω is dense and such that all functions $K(x, y)$ of x have continuous continuations $K(X, y)$ separating the (Martin) boundary $\Delta = \hat{\Omega} - \Omega$. It is identical to the Euclidean closure when Ω is a ball or a sufficiently regular domain, but generally is quite different. A harmonic function $u > 0$ is called minimal if any other similar but smaller function must be proportional to it. The minimal functions are proportional to certain of the functions of y $K(X, y)$ (where X is in Δ) and the corresponding points are called minimal and form a part Δ_1 of Δ.

Any harmonic function $u \geq 0$ has a unique representation as an integral of K integrated with respect to the measure μ_u (see 454) where μ_u is a Radon measure ≥ 0 on Δ supported by Δ_1. A Dirichlet problem may be studied with this boundary and any finite continuous function is resolutive. A set e is said to be thin at $X \in \Delta_1$ if a condition involving K holds (see 455). The fine topology on Ω may be extended to $\Omega \cup \Delta_1$, in a unique way such that the neighbourhoods of any $X \in \Delta_1$ intersect Ω in sets that are the complements of sets in Ω thin at X.

Among many applications of this new tool, Doob's result is important—that for any superharmonic $u > 0$ and any harmonic $h > 0$, u/h has a fine limit at the points of Δ_1 except on a set of u_h measure 0. This implies old results, as, for example, the famous result of Pierre Fatou that a harmonic function $u > 0$ in a ball has a nontangential limit almost everywhere on the boundary. (Ed.)

SPECIAL FUNCTIONS

Certain special functions are often used in mathematics and in physics, chemistry, engineering, and other branches of science and technology. It is possible to classify these into elementary functions and higher transcendental functions. The elementary functions include the exponential, logarithmic, trigonometric, and related functions. Frequently the term special functions is only applied to high transcendental functions. Some of the more important ones arising in differential equations will now be described.

The gamma and beta functions. The gamma function arose from attempts to extend the factorial function, $n! \equiv n(n-1)(n-2) \cdot \cdot \cdot 1$, to nonintegral values of n. This function is defined by $\Gamma(x)$ being equal to the integral from $t=0$ to infinity of $e^{-t}t^{(x-1)}$ (see 456), for values of x greater than zero. The function has the property that $\Gamma(x+1)$ equals the product of x and $\Gamma(x)$.

It follows that, if n is a positive integer, then $\Gamma(n+1)$ equals $n!$. Furthermore, $\Gamma(^1/_2)$ equals the square root of π (see 457).

The function was first defined by Euler and is widely used in mathematics, physics, engineering, and especially in probability theory and statistics. It arises in the series solutions of many differential equations.

Some useful related functions are:

(i) The incomplete gamma functions, which are defined by letting the upper or the lower limit of integration be a variable (see 458).

(ii) The beta function $\beta(p, q)$, which is defined as being equal to the integral from zero to one of the products of t^{p-1} and $(1-t)^{q-1}$ (see 459) for positive values of p and q. It is related to the gamma function because $\beta(p, q)$ equals the product of $\Gamma(p)$ and $\Gamma(q)$ divided by $\Gamma(p+q)$ (see 460).

Hypergeometric function. The hypergeometric function is the function $F(a, b; c; x)$ defined by the so-called hypergeometric series (see 461). It gets its name from the fact that it is a generalization of the geometric series $(1+x+x^2+\cdot\cdot\cdot)$ and reduces to this series when $a=1$ and $b=c$. It satisfies the hypergeometric equation, a second-order linear differential equation with variable coefficients (see 462). Twenty-four solutions of this equation can be expressed in terms of hypergeometric equations.

Hyper-geometric function

The hypergeometric equation occurs in problems in fluid flow and other branches of physics and engineering. The hypergeometric function is important in mathematics because many other special functions are related to it.

Legendre polynomials. Legendre polynomials arise as particular solutions of Laplace's equation: $\Delta_3 u = 0$. If R is the distance between a point with Cartesian coordinates (x, y, z) and the point $(0, 0, 1)$, then the reciprocal distance, $1/R$, is a solution of Laplace's equation. If spherical polar coordinates are used for the point (r, θ, φ), this solution is $1-2r\cos\theta+r^2$ to the $-^1/_2$ power. It is axisymmetric because it is independent of φ, the azimuthal angle.

If $\cos\theta$ is replaced by μ the solution is $(1-2r\mu-r^2)^{-1/2}$, and it can be expanded to give a power series in r with the coefficients being polynomials in μ. Thus it can be written in the form of an infinite series with terms of the form $r^nP_n(\mu)$ for r less than 1 (see 463).

The coefficients P_n are called the Legendre polynomials of degree n.

The polynomials are solutions of Legendre's equation (see 319), a particular case of Laplace's equation expressed in spherical polar coordinates for axisymmetric solutions. They can be produced from the generating function $(1-2r\mu-r^2)^{1/2}$ and are explicitly given by Rodrigues' formula (see 464), which is named after a 19th-century French mathematician, Olinde Rodrigues.

Associated Legendre functions. These are functions satisfying the associated Legendre differential equation, a second-order linear equation with variable coefficients (see 465). This reduces to Legendre's equation when $m=0$. Its solutions are associated Legendre functions (or polynomials). They are denoted by P_n^m and can be expressed in terms of the Legendre polynomials (see 466).

Spherical harmonics. The Legendre polynomials and associated Legendre functions are particular solutions of Laplace's equation. In general, functions satisfying this equation are known as harmonic functions; solutions that are homogeneous in x, y, and z are called spherical solid harmonics. If polar coordinates (r, θ, φ) are used, a spherical solid harmonic of degree n, R_n, can be written as the product of r^n and $S_n(\theta, \varphi)$ (see 467), a function of θ and φ satisfying a second-order linear partial differential equation that is found by substituting R_n into Laplace's equation and separating the variables (see 468). It is called a spherical surface harmonic. If $R_n(x, y, z)$ is a polynomial of degree n (n a positive integer), then S_n is a polynomial in $\cos\theta$, $\sin\theta$, $\cos\varphi$, and $\sin\varphi$.

Zonal, sectoral, and tesseral harmonics. A polynomial spherical harmonic of degree n can be represented uniquely

$$\Gamma(x)=\int_0^\infty e^{-t}\,t^{x-1}dt \tag{456}$$

$$\begin{cases}\Gamma(x+1)=x\Gamma(x)\\ \Gamma(n+1)=n!\\ \Gamma(\tfrac{1}{2})=\sqrt{\pi}\end{cases} \tag{457}$$

$$\begin{cases}\gamma(x,\,y)=\displaystyle\int_0^z e^{-t}t^{x-1}dt\\ \Gamma(x,\,z)=\displaystyle\int_z^\infty e^{-t}t^{x-1}dt\end{cases} \tag{458}$$

$$\beta(p,\,q)=\int_0^1 t^{p-1}(1-t)^{q-1}dt \tag{459}$$

$$\beta(p,\,q)=\frac{\Gamma(p)\Gamma(q)}{\Gamma(p+q)} \tag{460}$$

$$\begin{cases}1+\dfrac{abx}{c\cdot 1}+\dfrac{a(a+1)b(b+1)x^2}{c(c+1)+2!}\\ \quad+\dfrac{a(a+1)(a+2)b(b+1)(b+2)x^3}{c(c+1)(c+2)3!}+\cdots\end{cases} \tag{461}$$

$$x(1-x)\frac{d^2y}{dx^2}+[c-(a+b+1)x]\frac{dy}{dx}-aby=0 \tag{462}$$

$$\begin{cases}\dfrac{1}{\sqrt{1-2r\cos\theta+r^2}}=1+r\mu+\tfrac{1}{2}r^2(3\mu^2+1)+\cdots\\ \qquad=\displaystyle\sum_0^\infty r^nP_n(\mu)\end{cases} \tag{463}$$

$$P_n(\mu)=\frac{1}{2^nn!}\frac{d^n}{d\mu^n}(\mu^2-1)^n \tag{464}$$

$$(1-\mu^2)\frac{d^2\omega}{d\mu^2}-2\mu\frac{d\omega}{d\mu}+\left\{(n+1)-\frac{m^2}{1-\mu^2}\right\}\omega=0 \tag{465}$$

$$P_n^m(\mu)=(-1)^m(1-\mu^2)^{m/2}\frac{d^m}{d\mu^m}P_n(\mu) \tag{466}$$

$$R_n(x,\,y,\,z)=r^nS_n(\theta,\,\varphi) \tag{467}$$

$$\frac{\partial^2S}{\partial\theta^2}+\cot\theta\frac{\partial S}{\partial\theta}+\csc^3\theta\frac{\partial^2S}{\partial\varphi^2}+n(n+1)S=0 \tag{468}$$

$$C_n\frac{r^{2n+1}\,\partial^n}{\partial h_1\partial h_2\cdots\partial h_n}\frac{1}{r} \tag{469}$$

by the product C_nr^{2n+1}, in which C_n is a constant, times n differentiations $\partial/\partial h_1$, $\partial/\partial h_2$, . . . , $\partial/\partial h_n$ of $1/r$, in which (see 469) h_1, h_2, . . . , h_n are n directions in space, and $\partial/\partial h$ denotes differentiation in a direction h. If the n directions coincide, then, on a unit sphere about the origin, there are n circles of latitude on which the spherical surface (or solid) harmonic vanishes. These divide the sphere into zones, and the spherical harmonic is known as a zonal harmonic. The curves on the unit sphere on which the surface harmonic vanishes are called nodal lines. If the n directions are situated on a plane and are at angles of π/n to each other, the nodal lines are n circles of longitude. These divide the sphere into sectors, the spherical harmonic being known as a sectoral harmonic. If $(n-m)$ directions coincide in one particular direction and the remaining m directions lie in a plane at right angles to this direction and are at angles π/m, then there are m circles of longitude and $(n-m)$ circles of latitude. These divide the unit sphere into rectangles, the spherical harmonic being a tesseral harmonic.

Nodal lines

It can be proved that spherical surface harmonics can be represented by the product $S_n^m(\theta,\,\varphi)$ of the associated Legendre function $P_n^m(\cos\theta)$ and the complex exponential exp $[im\varphi]$ (see 470). Laplace's equation is satisfied by a linear combination of terms $R_n^m(x,\,y,\,z)$, which are products of r^n, exp $[im\varphi]$, and $P_n^m(\cos\theta)$ (see 471).

$P_n{}^m(\cos\theta)$ is an associated Legendre polynomial. If $m=n$, the harmonic is a sectoral harmonic. If $1\le m\le n\le 1$, it is a tesseral harmonic. If $m=0$, it is a zonal harmonic; the Legendre polynomial $P_n(\cos\theta)$ is a zonal harmonic of degree n.

Spherical harmonics and surface harmonics arise in a variety of physical applications of Laplace's equation. Surface harmonics also arise in connection with Poisson's equation (see 317), the wave equation (see 326), the diffusion equation (see 332), Schrödinger's equation (see 338), and other partial differential equations.

Bessel functions. Just as the Laplace equations expressed in spherical polar coordinates lead to the Legendre equation and Legendre polynomials, its expression in cylindrical polar coordinates leads to the equation known as Bessel's equation. Bessel's equation of order ν is a second-order differential equation with variable coefficients (see 472) and is satisfied by the Bessel function (or Bessel function of the first kind), which can be expressed as a power series in powers of $t/2$ (see 473). $J_\nu(t)$ is the Bessel function of order ν. Such functions were used by the German astronomer Friedrich Wilhelm Bessel in the 19th century

$$S_n^m(\theta,\,\varphi)=e^{im\varphi}P_n^m(\cos\theta) \tag{470}$$

$$R_n^m(x,\,y,\,z)=r^ne^{im\varphi}P_n^m(\cos\theta) \tag{471}$$

$$\frac{d^2\omega}{dt^2}+\frac{1}{t}\frac{d\omega}{dt}+\left(1-\frac{\nu^2}{t^2}\right)\omega=0 \tag{472}$$

$$J_\nu(t)=\sum_{n=0}^\infty\frac{(-1)^n}{n!\,\Gamma(\nu+n+1)}\left(\frac{t}{2}\right)^{\nu+2n} \tag{473}$$

$$Y_\nu=\frac{J_\nu(t)\cos(\nu\pi)-J_{-\nu}(t)}{\sin(\nu\pi)} \tag{474}$$

$$Y_p(t)=\lim_{\nu\to p}\frac{J_\nu(t)\cos(\nu\pi)-J_{-\nu}(t)}{\sin(\nu\pi)} \tag{475}$$

$$\begin{cases}H_\nu^1(t)=J_\nu(t)+iY_\nu(t)\\ H_\nu^2(t)=J_\nu(t)-iY_\nu(t)\end{cases} \tag{476}$$

$$\begin{cases}I_\nu(t)=(i)^{-\nu}J_\nu(it)\\ K_\nu(t)=\dfrac{1}{2}\pi(\sin\nu\pi)^{-1}[I_{-\nu}(t)-I_\nu(t)]\end{cases} \tag{477}$$

$$H_n(x)=(-1)^ne^{x^2}\frac{d^ne^{-x^2}}{dx^n} \tag{478}$$

$$\frac{d^2y}{dx^2}-2x\frac{dy}{dx}+2ny=0 \tag{479}$$

$$\int_a^b P_n(x)P_m(x)W(x)dx=0,\qquad m\neq n \tag{480}$$

$$\int_a^b [P_n(x)]^2W(x)dx=1 \tag{481}$$

$$L_n(x)=e^x\frac{d^n}{dx^n}(x^ne^{-x}) \tag{482}$$

$$x\frac{d^2y}{dx^2}+(1-x)\frac{dy}{dx}+nx=0 \tag{483}$$

in problems in astronomy; they had been used earlier by Bernoulli and Euler.

A second solution of the equation, if v is not an integer, is $J_{-v}(t)$, leading to the general solution $AJ_v(t) + BJ_{-v}(t)$, A and B being constants.

If v is an integer, p, the second solution is denoted by $Y_p(t)$, and a general solution is $AJ_v(t) + BY_v(t)$. For nonintegral and zero values of v, $Y_v(t)$ can be expressed as the difference of $J_v(t)\cos(v\pi)$ and $J_{-v}(t)$, divided by $\sin(v\pi)$ (see 474), and is called a Bessel function of the second kind. It can be shown that if v tends to an integer p (or to zero) in the limit, the expression gives $Y_P(t)$ (or $Y_0(t)$; see 475). Thus $AJ_v(t) + BY_v(t)$ is a general solution for all values of v. Bessel functions of the second kind are sometimes called Neumann functions. The functions $H_v^1(t)$, defined as the sum of $J_v(t)$ and $iY_v(t)$, and $H_v^2(t)$, defined as their difference (see 476) are called Hankel functions, after the 19th-century German mathematician and historian Hermann Hankel, or Bessel functions of the third kind.

Neumann functions

If t is replaced by it (in which $i = \sqrt{-1}$), the differential equation is the modified Bessel equation and its solutions are modified Bessel functions (of the first and second kind) of which $I_v(t)$, the modified Bessel function of the first kind, is the product of $(i)^{-v}$ and $J_v(it)$, and $K_v(t)$, the modified Bessel function of the second kind, is defined in terms of $I_v(t)$ and $(\sin v\pi)^{-1}$ (see 477). If v is an integer p, $K_p(t)$ is the limit of the expression.

Bessel functions are widely used in physics, especially in problems in potential theory and diffusion. They frequently arise in problems involving cylindrical boundaries and are sometimes called cylinder functions.

Hermite polynomials. Hermite polynomials are defined in terms of the derivatives of $\exp(-x^2)$ for nonnegative integers n (see 478). They are solutions of Hermite's equation, named after the 19th-century French mathematician Charles Hermite. This is a reduced form of Schrödinger's equations and is used in wave mechanics, especially in the theory of wave functions of the harmonic oscillator. Hermite's equation, also, is a second-order differential equation, with the coefficient of the first derivative being $-2x$ (see 479).

Orthogonal polynomials. Hermite polynomials are examples of orthogonal polynomials. A system of polynomials P_n is orthogonal on the interval (a, b) with respect to a weight function $w(x)$ if the integral over the interval of the product of two elements of the system, $P_n(x)$ and $P_m(x)$ and the weight $w(x)$, equals zero whenever m and n are not equal (see 480). The system is orthonormal if it is orthogonal and normalized by the integral over the interval of the product of the square of $P_n(x)$ and $w(x)$ being equal to unity (see 481).

Hermite polynomials are orthogonal on the interval $(-\infty, \infty)$ with a weighting function of $\exp(-x^2)$. Other systems of orthogonal polynomials exist. For example, Legendre polynomials are orthogonal in the interval $(-1, 1)$ with a weighting factor of 1. The Laguerre polynomials (named after the 19th-century French mathematician Edmond Laguerre), the nth of which is defined as the product of e^x and the nth derivative of $x^n e^{-x}$ (see 482), are orthogonal over the interval $(0, \infty)$ with a weighting factor of e^{-x} (in some cases more general functions with a weighting factor of $x^n e^{-x}$ are called Laguerre polynomials). These polynomials are solutions of Laguerre's equation (see 483). This, like Hermite's equation, is used in wave mechanics. The associated Laguerre polynomials $L_n^m(x)$ are defined by $L_n^m(x)$ being equal to the mth derivative of the nth Laguerre polynomial (see 484), and they, in turn, satisfy the associated Laguerre equation (see 485). (Ed.)

(484) $$L_n^m(x) = \frac{d^m}{dx^m} L_n(x)$$

(485) $$x\frac{d^2y}{dx^2} + (m + 1 - x)\frac{dy}{dx} + (n - m)y = 0$$

FOURIER ANALYSIS

Fourier analysis, one of the most important tools of mathematics and mathematical physics, arose originally from problems involving vibrating cords as studied by Leonhard Euler and Daniel Bernoulli in the 18th century. The subject was named for Jean-Baptiste-Joseph Fourier, whose work on the representation of mathematical functions as sums of trigonometric functions was published in his *Théorie analytique de la chaleur* (*The Analytical Theory of Heat*) in 1822.

FOURIER SERIES

Fourier series are a particular case of the general class of series of functions discussed in the section *Infinite series* above.

An infinite series of trigonometric functions

An infinite series of the form of a sum composed of a constant term and weighted trigonometric functions with angles x, $2x$, and so forth (see 486) is called a trigonometric series. The quantities $a_0, a_1, b_1, a_2, b_2, \ldots$ are constants and x takes values between $-\infty$ and $+\infty$. If the series converges for all values of x, and $f(x)$ denotes the sum of the series, then $f(x)$ is periodic with a period 2π, because replacing x by $x + 2\pi$ does not change the series. If both sides of $f(x) = \frac{1}{2}a_0 + (a_1 \cos x + b_1 \sin x) + \cdots$ are multiplied by $\cos nx$ or $\sin nx$ and the result is integrated over the interval $(0, 2\pi)$, then two integral expressions for the a_n and b_n involving the function f and a trigonometric function are obtained (see 487); this argument is purely formal (it is justified if the series converges uniformly, or even in some more general case). It suggests, however, an interesting problem. If for any periodic function $f(x)$ with period 2π the numbers a_n, b_n are computed by means of the integral formulas to form a series (see 486), does the series so defined represent the function $f(x)$? The numbers obtained from the formulas (487) are called the Fourier coefficients of $f(x)$ and the series (486) is the Fourier series of $f(x)$. The fact that, subject to suitable conditions on $f(x)$, this problem admits of an affirmative answer is one of the main achievements of the theory.

(486) $$\frac{1}{2}a_0 + (a_1 \cos x + b_1 \sin x) + (a_2 \cos 2x + b_2 \sin 2x) + \cdots$$

Historical development of Fourier series

Although Fourier series originated in mathematical physics, their influence upon the development of analysis has been almost as great. Very often they appear there in a more general form, as orthogonal series (see below), and provide a unifying link in such mathematical theories as differential and integral equations and analytic functions. Especially important are trigonometric (and, in particular, Fourier) series for the theory of analytic functions because for $z = e^{ix}$ the real part of the power series, which is a power series in z with complex coefficients (see 488), is the series already obtained (see 486). Thus trigonometric series are real parts of power series, and so form a bridge between real and complex functions. Aside from the value of trigonometric series as a method of investigation, they have played a great role in the historic development and clarification of various mathematical concepts, some of them quite abstract. A few examples may suffice.

Already in the days of its inception in the 18th century, the theory of Fourier series stirred controversies in connection with the notion of mathematical function. The general attitude at that time was to call $f(x)$ a function if $f(x)$ could be represented by a single analytic expression such as a polynomial, a power series, or a trigonometric series. If the graph of $f(x)$ were arbitrary—*e.g.*, a polygonal line—$f(x)$ would not have been accepted as a

$$(487)\quad \begin{cases} a_n = \dfrac{1}{\pi}\displaystyle\int_0^{2\pi} f(x)\cos nx\,dx \\ b_n = \dfrac{1}{\pi}\displaystyle\int_0^{2\pi} f(x)\sin nx\,dx \end{cases}$$

$$(488)\quad \frac{1}{2}a_0 + (a_1 - ib_1)z + (a_2 - ib_2)z^2 + \cdots$$

$$(489)\quad s_n(x) = \frac{1}{\pi}\int_0^{2\pi} f(x+t)\frac{\sin(n+\frac{1}{2})t}{2\sin\frac{1}{2}t}\,dt$$

$$(490)\quad \int_0^{\pi}\frac{|f(x+t)+f(x-t)-2f(x)|}{t}\,dt$$

function. So it came as a shock to many when the discovery of Fourier series showed that many such arbitrary graphs could be represented by trigonometric series and so should be treated as functions. It took a long time before the matter was clarified, and it was not merely a coincidence that the now universally adopted definition was first formulated in 1837 in a memoir of Dirichlet, devoted to the theory of Fourier series. (Incidentally, this memoir contains the first rigorous proofs of the representation of functions by their Fourier series. The work of Fourier himself and of his predecessors was rather formal.) Another instance of application of trigonometric series to the theory of functions is due to Weierstrass, who in 1861 gave the first example of a continuous function without a derivative at any point. Weierstrass' function was given in the form of a trigonometric series, and it exemplified the general fact that trigonometric series are particularly useful in the construction of functions with various peculiarities. Another much more important example of the influence of Fourier series may be found in the history of the notion of integral. On account of previous formulas (see 487), this notion is a prerequisite to that of Fourier series. It is therefore interesting that the classical definition of integral due to Riemann (usually given in textbooks of calculus) was for the first time expounded in 1854 in his fundamental paper *Über die Darstellbarkeit einer Funktion durch eine trigonometrische Reihe* ("Concerning the Representation of Functions by Trigonometric Series"). The ideas contained in that paper influenced the work of Georg Cantor concerning the uniqueness of the representation of a function by a trigonometric series. Cantor had to consider various sets of points that would not interfere with the uniqueness of representation. Starting from simplest cases he tried to master the structure of such sets—sets of uniqueness (see below *Uniqueness of representation by trigonometric series*). He was not completely successful, but his investigations led him to the general theory of sets, and in particular of point sets, one of the greatest mathematical discoveries of the 19th century. His results have permeated and changed the aspect of many mathematical theories. The theories of measure and of integral developed later by Émile Borel and Henri-Léon Lebesgue, so fundamental in mathematical analysis, are based on Cantor's work on the theory of sets.

Cantor's contribution

Particularly important is the work of Lebesgue, who put Fourier series on a new basis through his theory of integral. Though more general definitions of integral are possible, and though some of them are of interest for Fourier series, Lebesgue's definition is the most appropriate and is almost universally adopted in research. In this connection a French mathematician, Arnaud Denjoy, showed with a definition of integral more general than that of Lebesgue that an everywhere-convergent trigonometric series is always the Fourier series of its sum. Important for Lebesgue's theory is the notion of set of measure zero. A point set S situated, for example, on a straight line is said to be of measure zero if S can be covered by a finite or infinite system of intervals of total length arbitrarily small. In Lebesque's theory, sets of measure zero are considered as negligible, and if a certain property holds for all points except those forming a set of measure zero, that property is said to hold almost everywhere.

Convergence and divergence of Fourier series. If $s_n(x)$ denotes the sum of the first $n+1$ terms of the Fourier series (486), using the integral formulas (487), s_n as a function of x is a definite integral from zero to 2π with integrand formed with the function f and certain sine function expressions (see 489), a formula basic for Fourier series. It may be proved that as n increases indefinitely $s_n(x)$ tends to $f(x)$, provided the function $f(x)$ satisfies certain conditions. For example, if the graph of the function $f(x)$ in the interval $0 \leq x \leq 2\pi$ has only a finite number of maxima and minima (Dirichlet's condition), the Fourier series of $f(x)$ converges to $f(x)$ at every point of continuity of the function. At points x at which such a function is discontinuous, the Fourier series also converges, its sum being $[f(x+0)+f(x-0)]/2$ in which $f(x+0)$ represents the limit of the function at the point x from the right, and $f(x-0)$ a similar limit from the left. Another condition ensuring the convergence of the Fourier series to sum $f(x)$ is the convergence of a definite integral from zero to π with integrand formed in terms of the function f and variable x (the Dini condition; see 490). It certainly is satisfied at every point at which the function $f(x)$ is differentiable. These and all other known conditions for convergence are sufficient conditions only. Conditions that would be both necessary and sufficient (and would not be trivial tautologies) are not known. That mere continuity of the function is not sufficient to ensure the convergence of the Fourier series was shown by the German Paul David Gustave du Bois-Reymond in 1873. He constructed a continuous function for which the Fourier series diverges at some points. Whether the Fourier series of a continuous function must converge at least almost everywhere, that is, everywhere except possibly for a set of points of measure zero, was for a long time an unsolved and tantalizing problem. In 1966 it was shown by the Swedish mathematician Lennart Axel Edvard Carleson that it is actually so, a major achievement of mathematical analysis. More generally, Carleson showed that the Fourier series of any integrable (in the Lebesgue sense) function $f(x)$ the square $f^2(x)$ of which is also integrable must necessarily converge almost everywhere. Using his method, the American mathematician Richard Hunt proved in 1967 that the same conclusion holds if $|f(x)|^p$ is integrable for some p strictly greater than 1. That the result fails for $p=1$ was shown in 1926 by the Soviet mathematician Andrey Nikolayevich Kolmogorov, who constructed an integrable function the Fourier series of which diverges at each point. These results basically settle the problem of convergence almost everywhere of Fourier series.

Conditions for convergence

Summability of Fourier series. The fact that Fourier series of continuous functions need not converge everywhere endangered the whole theory of the representation of functions by their Fourier series. The situation was salvaged by the Hungarian mathematician Leopold Fejér in 1900, who showed that the Fourier series of a continuous function $f(x)$ is summable to $f(x)$ by the method of the arithmetic mean. More precisely, if $s_n(x)$ has the same meaning as above, the expression in which σ_n as a function of x is an arithmetic average of terms expressed as $s_n(x)$ (see 491) tends to $f(x)$ at every point of continuity of the function. Following this, Lebesgue proved that for every integrable function $f(x)$ the expression $\sigma_n(x)$ tends to $f(x)$ almost everywhere. This again put the theory on a firm basis, and at the same time showed that summability rather than convergence is important for Fourier series. Using formulas already given (see 489, 491) leads to an expression in which σ_n as a function of x is an integral from zero to 2π with integrand expressed in terms of f and certain sine functions (see 492), but there is one essential difference. The factor $\sin^2 \frac{1}{2}(n+1)t/2(n+1)\sin^2 \frac{1}{2}t$, called Fejér's kernel, is nonnegative, whereas the factor $\sin (n+\frac{1}{2})t/2 \sin\frac{1}{2}t$, Dirichlet's kernel, is of variable sign. This positive character of Fejér's kernel is responsible for many properties of the expressions $\sigma_n(x)$, and in particular for the fact that they represent $f(x)$ better than the $s_n(x)$ do.

Fejér's, Dirichlet's kernels

Besides the method of the arithmetic mean, many other

(491) $$\sigma_n(x) = \frac{s_0(x) + s_1(x) + \cdots + s_n(x)}{n+1}$$

(492) $$\sigma_n(x) = \frac{1}{\pi(n+1)} \int_0^{2\pi} f(x+t) \frac{\sin^2 \frac{1}{2}(n+1)t}{2 \sin^2 \frac{1}{2} t} dt$$

(493) $$\frac{1}{2} a_0 + (a_1 \cos x + b_1 \sin x) r + (a_2 \cos 2x + b_2 \sin 2x) r^2 + \cdots$$

(494) $$\frac{1}{2\pi} \int_0^{2\pi} f(x+t) \frac{1 - r^2}{1 - 2r \cos t + r^2} dt$$

(495) $$(a_1 \sin x - b_1 \cos x) + (a_2 \sin 2x - b_2 \cos 2x) + \cdots$$

(496) $$-\frac{1}{\pi} \int_0^{\pi} \frac{f(x+t) - f(x-t)}{2 \tan \frac{1}{2} t} dt, \text{ defined as } \lim_{\epsilon \to 0} \left\{ -\frac{1}{\pi} \int_{\epsilon}^{\pi} \right\}$$

(497) $$\frac{1}{\pi} \int_0^{2\pi} f^2(x) dx = \frac{1}{2} a_0^2 + (a_1^2 + b_1^2) + (a_2^2 + b_2^2) + \cdots$$

Abel's method

methods of summability have been applied to Fourier series. The most important of them is the method of Abel that defines the sum of Fourier series (see 486) as the limit of the expression that is a power series in r with typical coefficient expressed in terms of cosine and sine (see 493), in which r tends to 1 through values less than 1. The last expression may be written as a definite integral from zero to 2π with integrand composed of the function f and a function involving cosine and the variable r (see 494) and is called the Poisson integral of $f(x)$. As r approaches 1, it tends to $f(x)$ at every point of continuity of the function (or almost everywhere, if $f(x)$ is merely integrable).

Conjugate series and functions. For $z = e^{ix}$ the real part of a power series (see 488) is the trigonometric series (see 486). The imaginary part is a trigonometric series, a sum of terms with typical member composed of the sine and the cosine (see 495), called the conjugate of the series (486). Suppose that there is the Fourier series of a function $f(x)$ (see 486); the conjugate series is then almost everywhere summable by the method of the arithmetic mean, or by the method of Abel, the generalized sum being equal to the definite integral from zero to π with integrand constructed of the function f and the tangent (see 496).

This integral is called the function conjugate to $f(x)$ and will be denoted by $f(x)$. The fact that for every integrable function $f(x)$ the integral (see 496) exists almost everywhere is a very remarkable property that is far from obvious even in the case in which $f(x)$ is continuous. Even in this special case, the integral (496) need not exist everywhere; it is a curious fact that continuous functions may have certain metric properties almost everywhere, without having them everywhere. Conjugate series are a link between trigonometric series and power series. They are also of importance for the theory of Fourier series because there seems to be a close relation between the behaviour of the partial sums of Fourier series and the behaviour of certain conjugate functions. As a matter of fact, the proofs of the theorems of Carleson and Hunt (see above) strongly use refined results on conjugate functions. The function conjugate to an integrable function $f(x)$ need not be integrable. Thus the series conjugate to the Fourier series of $f(x)$ need not be a Fourier series.

Parseval's formula. Suppose that one has the Fourier series of $f(x)$ (see 486). If in the formula $f(x) = {}^1\!/_2 a_0 + (a_1 \cos x + b_1 \sin x) + \cdots$ both sides are squared and the result is integrated over the interval $0 \leq x \leq 2\pi$, then a definite integral from zero to 2π of the square of the function f is equal to an infinite sum with typical term composed of the square of a_k plus the square of b_k (see 497), called Parseval's formula after Marc Antoine Parseval (1755–1836). The above argument was formal, but rigorous proofs are available to show that the formula is valid for any function $f(x)$ such that $f^2(x)$ is integrable. Thus the Fourier coefficients a_0, a_1, b_1, . . . of any such function have the property that $\Sigma(a_n{}^2 + b_n{}^2)$ is finite. That the converse is true was proved by the mathematicians Frigyes Riesz and Ernst Sigismund Fischer in 1907. The Riesz-Fischer theorem, which is one of the great achievements of the Lebesgue theory of integration, asserts that, given any sequence of numbers a_0, a_1, b_1, a_2, b_2, . . . such that the series $\Sigma(a_n{}^2 + b_n{}^2)$ converges, there is always a function $f(x)$ having the numbers a_0, a_1, b_1, . . . as Fourier coefficients and such that $f^2(x)$ is integrable. This function is unique. Thus, the theorems of Parseval and of Riesz-Fischer give a very simple characterization of functions with integrable squares in terms of their Fourier coefficients. There is no other class of function that has a characterization of comparable simplicity and completeness.

The Riesz-Fischer theorem

Uniqueness of representation by trigonometric series. Can a function be represented by two different and everywhere-convergent trigonometric series? By taking the difference of two such series, the problem may be restated as follows. Can a trigonometric series not identically zero (*i.e.*, a series the coefficients a_n, b_n of which are not all zero) converge everywhere to zero? That this is impossible was proved by Cantor. His result is the simplest theorem on the uniqueness of the representation of a function by a trigonometric series. A point set S situated in the interval $0 \leq x \leq 2\pi$ is called a set of uniqueness (set U, for brevity) if every trigonometric series convergent to zero outside S is identically zero. Otherwise, the set S will be called a set of multiplicity (set M), and there will be trigonometric series convergent to zero outside S, but not identically zero. Generalizing the result just stated, Cantor proved that every set S consisting of a finite number of points, and even certain infinite sets, are sets U. It may be shown that every set U must be of measure zero, but it is remarkable that among sets of measure zero are found sets U as well as sets M. The problem of characterizing sets U and M in structural terms was still unsolved in the mid-1970s. One of its implications is that from the point of view of trigonometric series the notion of set of measure zero is too general, and that special classes of such sets may be of particular importance.

Trigonometric polynomials

Trigonometric interpolation. A finite sum, a sum from $k = 1$ to n of weighted trigonometric terms (see 498), is called a trigonometric polynomial of order n (or less, if both a_n and b_n are zero). A trigonometric polynomial of order n has $2n + 1$ coefficients a_0, a_1, b_1, . . . , a_n, b_n, and it can be shown that if $2n + 1$ distinct points (see 499) are fixed in the interval $0 \leq x < 2\pi$, there is always a trigonometric polynomial of order n or less that takes prescribed values at these points; moreover, this polynomial is unique. Consider now a function $f(x)$ defined on the interval $(0, 2\pi)$ and take the trigonometric polynomial $T(x)$ of order n that coincides with $f(x)$ at certain points (see 499). Such a polynomial is called an interpolating polynomial for $f(x)$. Suppose now that n increases indefinitely; does the polynomial $T(x)$ approach the function $f(x)$ at all points? This must depend on the geometric configuration of the points (see 499) and the answer is not known in full generality. If, however, the points (see 499) are assumed distributed equally to form an arithmetic progression with difference $2\pi/(2n + 1)$, and if the function $f(x)$ satisfies some smoothness conditions (*e.g.*, is differentiable), then the answer is affirmative, and the whole problem has points in common with the theory of Fourier series.

Orthogonal series. Fourier series as defined above are a special class of more general series. Suppose that in an interval $a \leq x \leq b$ there is a fixed set of functions $\varphi_1(x)$, $\varphi_2(x)$, . . . with the integrals involving the product of the functions $\varphi_m\varphi_n$, being zero if m is not equal to n and being a constant, λ_n, if m equals n (see 500) for all m and n. Such sets of functions are called orthogonal. If a function $f(x)$ has a representation $f(x) = c_1\varphi_1(x) + c_2\varphi_2(x) + \cdots$, then, multiplying both sides by $\varphi_n(x)$, integrating over x in the interval (a, b), and using orthogonality (see 500) formally leads to the equation in which c_n is a definite integral from a to b involving the function f and the function φ_n (see 501) for all n. Conversely, given any function $f(x)$, the latter formulas may be used to construct the series $c_1\varphi_1(x) + c_2\varphi_2(x) + \cdots$, and it may be asked whether this

(498) $T(x)=\frac{1}{2}a_0+\sum_{k=1}^{n}(a_k \cos kx + b_k \sin kx)$

(499) $x_0, x_1, x_2, \ldots x_{2n}$

(500) $\int_a^b \varphi_m \varphi_n dx = 0, \text{ if } m \neq n; \quad \int_a^b \varphi_n{}^2 dx = \lambda_n > 0$

(501) $c_n = \frac{1}{\lambda_n}\int_a^b f(x)\varphi_n(x)dx$

(502) $\int_a^b \varphi_m \bar{\varphi}_n dx = 0, \text{ if } m \neq n, \quad \int_a^b |\varphi_n|^2 dx = \lambda_n > 0$

(503) $c_n = \frac{1}{\lambda_n}\int_a^b f(x)\bar{\varphi}_n(x)dx$

(504) $\sum_{n=-\infty}^{+\infty} c_n e^{inx}$, in which $c_n = \frac{1}{2\pi}\int_0^{2\pi} f(x)e^{-inx}dx$

(505) $c_0 + \sum_{n=1}^{\infty}(c_n e^{inx} + c_{-n} e^{-inx})$

(506) $\int_0^{\infty} \{a(u) \cos ux + b(u) \sin ux\}\, du$

(507) $\begin{cases} a(u) = \frac{1}{\pi}\int_{-\infty}^{+\infty} f(t) \cos ut\, dt \\ b(u) = \frac{1}{\pi}\int_{-\infty}^{+\infty} f(t) \sin ut\, dt \end{cases}$

(508) $\sum_{m=1}^{\infty}\sum_{n=1}^{\infty} c_{m,n}\varphi_m(x)\psi_n(y)$

series actually represents $f(x)$. This last series is called the Fourier series of $f(x)$ with respect to the orthogonal system $\varphi_1, \varphi_2, \ldots$. Trigonometric Fourier series are obtained if for $\varphi_1, \varphi_2, \ldots$ the system 1, cos x, sin x, cos $2x$, sin $2x, \ldots$ is taken, and for (a, b) the interval $(0, 2\pi)$. Many other orthogonal systems are of considerable importance for mathematics.

In the definition of orthogonality (see 500), it was tacitly assumed that the functions were real-valued. If the functions $\varphi_1, \varphi_2, \ldots$ are complex-valued, the definition (500) must be slightly modified, and certain requirements must be met concerning two integrals involving φ_m and $\bar{\varphi}_n$ (see 502), in which $\bar{\varphi}_n$ is the conjugate (in the sense of complex numbers) to φ_n. The Fourier series is, as before, $c_1\varphi_1(x) + c_2\varphi_2(x) + \cdots$, but now the Fourier coefficients are c_n as a definite integral from a to b of the function f and a weighted term composed of $\bar{\varphi}_n$ (see 503). The most important special case is that of the system $e^{inx}(n = 0, \pm1, \pm2, \ldots)$ that is readily seen to be orthogonal over $(0, 2\pi)$, with all $\lambda_n = 2\pi$. This system is called the complex trigonometric system. The Fourier series of a function $f(x)$ defined in the interval $(0, 2\pi)$ is a sum with integer index ranging from minus infinity to plus infinity with summand of exponential type and coefficient c_n, the coefficient determined by an integral (see 504). The latter series is called the complex Fourier series of $f(x)$ and is meant as a sum including a constant term and terms of exponential type and negative exponential type (see 505). It can be shown that this series is nothing else but the Fourier series (486) with coefficients given by the familiar formula (487). Hence, except for notation, complex Fourier series are the same as ordinary trigonometric Fourier series, but the complex form sometimes simplifies proofs.

The complex Fourier series

Fourier integrals. Fourier series are used for the representation of periodic functions. For the study of a nonperiodic function $f(x)$, the Fourier integral of $f(x)$ is used. It has the form of an integral from zero to infinity with integrand composed of functions a and b and functions cosine and sine (see 506), in which $a(u)$ and $b(u)$ are defined by the formulas in which a as a function of u is expressed as an integral involving f and the cosine, b as a function of u is expressed as an integral involving f and the sine (see 507). The integral (506) is analogous to the series (486), the only difference being that instead of summation there is integration. The functions $a(u)$ and $b(u)$ are analogues of Fourier coefficients and are called the Fourier transforms of $f(x)$. Under very general conditions, the integral (506) actually represents $f(x)$, the proofs being similar to the corresponding proofs in the case of Fourier series.

Multiple Fourier series. If $\varphi_1(x), \varphi_2(x), \ldots$ is an orthogonal system over an interval $a \leq x \leq b$, and if $\psi_1(y), \psi_2(y), \ldots$ is another orthogonal system over an interval $c \leq y \leq d$, then it may be shown that the double system $\varphi_m(x)\psi_n(y)$ (in which $m, n = 1, 2, \ldots$) is orthogonal over the rectangle $a \leq x \leq b, c \leq y \leq d$ of the plane, and a function $f(x, y)$ defined in this rectangle can be developed into a double Fourier series, a double sum with summand composed of a product of a constant, the function φ_m, and the function ψ_n, two variables x and y being involved (see 508). The most interesting case occurs when both systems φ_m and ψ_n are complex trigonometric systems. The Fourier series is then a double sum with summand composed of a coefficient with double index and exponential with complex argument depending upon x and y (see 509). Similarly, triple Fourier series can be considered, and so on. The problems concerning the behaviour of multiple Fourier series are usually much more difficult than those of ordinary Fourier series.

The integral (506) can also be written in the form of a definite integral from minus infinity to plus infinity with integrand of exponential complex type and coefficient determined by an integral again of exponential type (see 510), which is an analogue of a complex Fourier series. Multiple Fourier integrals are also considered (analogues of multiple Fourier series) and have become a very important tool in various branches of analysis.

(509) $\sum_{m=-\infty}^{+\infty}\sum_{n=-\infty}^{+\infty} c_{m,n}\, e^{i(mx+ny)}$

(510) $\int_{-\infty}^{+\infty} c(u)e^{ixu}du$, in which $c(u) = \frac{1}{2\pi}\int_{-\infty}^{+\infty} f(t)e^{iut}dt$

(511) $F(x) = \int_a^x f(y)dy$

(512) $F(x) = \int_a^x h(y)f(y)\,dy$

(513) $\Phi(x) = \int_a^b K(x, y)f(y)\,dy, \qquad c \leq x \leq d$

(514) $F(x) = \int_a^x f(y)\,dy$

(515) $K(x, y) = k(x - y)$

(516) $\Phi(x) = \int_{-\infty}^{\infty} k(x - y)\, f(y)\,dy$

(517) $\Phi = k * f$

(518) $\hat{f}(x) = (2\pi)^{-1/2}\int_{-\infty}^{\infty} e^{-ixy}f(y)dy$

(519) $K(x, y) = (2\pi)^{-1/2}e^{-ixy}$

(520) $|e^{-ixy}| = 1$

HARMONIC ANALYSIS AND INTEGRAL TRANSFORMS

It usually happens in mathematical analysis that certain given functions are to be operated on, and other functions or numbers are thus obtained. Often, the operations used involve integration, and here is found a very general class of operators, the so-called integral transforms. The simplest integral transform is the operation of integrating. If f is a function defined on the interval $[a, b]$, a new function F on $[a, b]$ can be defined (see 511). A somewhat more general example arises if f is multiplied by another function $h(y)$ before integrating: F is expressed as a definite integral from a to b with integrand f multiplied by h, each being functions of the variable of integration (see 512).

The following situation already embraces quite a number of important integral transforms: if the function $f(y)$ is given in the interval $a \leq y \leq b$, and $K(x, y)$ is a function of two variables, defined when $a \leq y \leq b$ and $c \leq x \leq d$, then Φ as a function of x is an integral from a to b with integrand a product of terms including K with two arguments and the function f with a single argument (see 513). This is an integral transform of $f(y)$ by means of the function K, which is called the kernel. [Here K is regarded as fixed, and the integral transform (513) is regarded as an operation that can be performed on any one of a large class of functions f, yielding for each appropriate f a new function Φ.] The operation F as a function of f equal to an indefinite integral of the function f (see 514) is merely a special case of the integral transform (513), in which $K(x, y) = 1$ if $y \leq x$ and $K(x, y) = 0$ if $y > x$. By considering a variety of kernels K, a number of important classical integral transforms are obtained, some of which will be discussed below.

Function *K*, the kernel

The definitions given above may be generalized in various ways, one of which is to use functions f of several variables (see below). In many important special cases of the integral transform (513), the intervals $[a, b]$ and $[c, d]$ are replaced by the whole real line $(-\infty, \infty)$, or a half-line, such as $[a, \infty)$.

At this stage in the discussion, two technical points should be mentioned. First of all, there may be a restriction to real-valued functions $f(y)$ and $K(x, y)$, or more generally to functions $f(y)$ taking complex values, $f(x) = u(x) + iv(x)$, and likewise for the kernel K. It is preferable to adopt the latter point of view, especially because operations performed on real-valued functions often lead to complex-valued functions anyway. A more delicate point is the notion of integral to be employed. In many cases, especially in practical applications, it is enough to deal with the classical Riemann integral, or with the improper Riemann integral, for example, when functions are integrated over infinite intervals. In most instances, however, coherence and generality are best achieved by introducing the notion of integral due to Lebesgue (see above *Real analysis: Measure and integral calculus*). To help the reader not familiar with Lebesgue's theory, this point will not be stressed, and only in the cases in which the mathematical results depend most strongly on Lebesgue measure or integration will the fact be indicated.

Convolution. Before passing to various special cases, one very important type of integral transform will be indicated. If $f(y)$ is a function defined in $(-\infty, \infty)$, and $k(x)$ is another (fixed) function defined in $(-\infty, \infty)$, then the kernel K as a function of x and y equal to a function of the difference of the arguments (see 515) may be considered. In this case the transform (513) takes the form in which Φ as a function of x is a definite integral over the entire real line of the product of the function k and the function f (see 516). This integral (assuming it converges) is called the convolution of the functions f and k (see 517). The centred asterisk symbol for convolution resembles that of the centred dot for multiplication; and there is actually a close connection between the two notions, as will be indicated below. The convolution is an integral transform occurring often in analysis. Usually, after fixing the kernel k, a class of functions f is considered, and the effect of the transform investigated, in order to determine which properties of functions f are preserved and which properties changed, and in what way. Below are considered a number of important special cases.

The Fourier transform. As a second example of an integral transform, the Fourier transform is now introduced, initially of a function of a single variable. If $f(y)$ is a given function defined in the interval $(-\infty, \infty)$, $\hat{f}$ is a definite integral over the entire real line in which the integrand is composed of a product of a negative complex exponential and the function f (see 518), in which x is a real variable and $\hat{f}$ is called the Fourier transform of f. The Fourier transform is an integral transform of the form already discussed (see 513), with kernel of the form in which K as a function of two variables is of exponential type with negative complex unit multiplied by the product of the variables in the argument (see 519). In view of the fact that the absolute value of the negative complex exponential is unity (see 520), the integral defining $\hat{f}(x)$ converges for all values of x and represents a continuous function of x, provided f is absolutely integrable over $(-\infty, \infty)$. In this case it can also be shown that $\hat{f}(x)$ tends to zero as x tends to $\pm\infty$. The Fourier transform also exists in some cases in which f is not necessarily absolutely integrable on $(-\infty, \infty)$. Thus $\hat{f}$ is an integral transform that makes sense for a large class of functions f; the study of this transform and its generalizations is called harmonic analysis. It should be added that certain variants of the definition (518) are sometimes useful and frequently occur in the literature. Thus the Fourier transform is sometimes defined by the equation in which $\hat{f}$ is a definite integral extended from minus to plus infinity of the complex negative exponential in which the variables appear as products (see 521), or by omission of the minus sign in the exponent. But adherence here is to the definition (518).

The main questions to be studied are: What are the properties of $\hat{f}$ in terms of those of f, or of f in terms of $\hat{f}$; and also, can f be found if $\hat{f}$ is known (the problem of inversion of the Fourier transform)? Typical properties of interest are the size and the smoothness of a function. The former question is considered first.

Fourier transforms and inversions

The simplest way of measuring the size of a function is by giving its bounds, $A \leq f(x) \leq B$. (Upper and lower bounds may be given if f is real-valued; bounds for $|f|$ may also be considered if f is complex-valued.) Other estimates, however, especially in the case of unbounded functions, can also be used. If p is a fixed positive number, $L^p[a, b]$ represents the class of functions f on $[a, b]$ for which the definite integral from a to b of the pth power of

(521) $$\hat{f}(x) = \int_{-\infty}^{+\infty} e^{-2\pi ixy} dy$$

(522) $$\int_a^b |f(x)|^p \, dx < \infty$$

(523) $$\left(\int_a^b |f(x)|^p \, dx\right)^{1/p}$$

(524) $$\|f - g\|_p \leq \|f - h\|_p + \|h - g\|_p$$

(525) $L^p[a, b]$, the set of functions such that $\|f\|_p < \infty$

(526) $$\int_0^1 |f(x)|^p dx \leq \int_0^1 M^p dx = M^p < \infty$$

(527) $$L^2[a, b] : \|f - g\|_2 = \left(\int_a^b |f(x) - g(x)|^2 \, dx\right)^{1/2}$$

(528) $X = (x_1, x_2, \ldots, x_n)$ and $Y = (y_1, y_2, \ldots, y_n)$

(529) $$\hat{f}_M(x) = (2\pi)^{-1/2} \int_{-M}^{M} e^{-ixy} f(y) dy$$

(530) $$\int_{-\infty}^{\infty} |\hat{f}(x)|^2 \, dx = \int_{-\infty}^{\infty} |f(x)|^2 \, dx$$

the absolute value of f is finite (see 522). In this case, the pth root of the integral from a to b of the pth power of the absolute value of f (see 523) may serve as a measure of the size of f. It will be called the pth norm, or L^p-norm, of f, denoted by $\|f\|_p$. (For the sake of economy, $[a, b]$ are not displayed in the symbol for the norm of f.) The functions f and g may be considered close to each other if $\|f-g\|_p$ is small. If $\|f-g\|_p$ is regarded as a measure of the distance from f to g, it is natural to expect that the pth norm of the difference between f and g is less than or equal to the sum of two such norms involving a third function h (the triangle inequality; see 524) for any three functions f, g, and h. Indeed, this inequality holds, provided $p \geq 1$. In the vast majority of uses of L^p in analysis, it is customary to consider only the case $p \geq 1$; this will be the assumption below.

It would probably be beneficial to acquaint the reader further with $L^p[a, b]$ (see 525) by means of some simple examples. On a finite interval, say $0<x<1$, every bounded function f belongs automatically to L^p, because the integral from 0 to 1 of the pth absolute value of f is less than or equal to a constant, which is less than infinity (see 526), if M is an upper bound for $|f|$. In addition, certain unbounded functions also belong to L^p. If $f_\delta(x)=x^{-\delta}$, with $0<x<1$, and $\delta>0$ fixed, then each f_δ is unbounded; as x tends to zero, $f_\delta(x)$ tends to infinity. If $f_{\delta 1}$ is compared with f_{δ_2} where say $\delta_1>\delta_2$, however, then it is found that $f_{\delta_1}(x)$ goes to infinity as x tends to zero more rapidly than does $f_{\delta_2}(x)$. Now it may be shown that f_δ belongs to L^p for $p<1/\delta$, but not for $p\geq 1/\delta$. Thus, an unbounded function may belong to L^p, but, if so, it may not tend to infinity too rapidly. As p increases, more and more functions are ruled out as being too large for L^p, so that fewer functions belong to L^p.

Use of L^2 functions

Having considered the L^p-classes in general, an important special case can now be mentioned, namely, $p=2$. The class L^2 is of fundamental importance in analysis. To understand the special significance of L^2, it is possible to begin with the formula for the distance between two functions f and g in the L^2 sense for the range a to b, the squared norm identified with the difference of two functions expressed as a square root of the integral of the square of the function (see 527). This equation is very similar to the Pythagoras formula

$$\|X-Y\|=\Big(\sum_{j=1}^{n}|x_j-y_j|^2\Big)^{1/2}$$

for the distance between two points (see 528) in n-dimensional Euclidean space. This similarity suggests a way of understanding $L^2[a, b]$: functions f, g, etc., may be regarded as points that lie in a space $H=L^2[a, b]$, and the geometrical properties of H may be studied almost as if H were merely Euclidean space. Because of the similarity of the distance formulas noted above, virtually all of classical Euclidean and coordinate (analytic) geometry can be carried out in the setting of $L^2[a, b]$. Furthermore, the geometric insights thus gained into the structure of L^2 can be applied to numerous concrete problems throughout analysis. For other L^p-classes ($p\neq 2$), the present state of geometrical understanding is relatively crude, and consequently many simple theorems on L^2 functions become more difficult when generalized to L^p. As a result, it is preferable to use L^2 as much as possible.

In the above, the notion of the Fourier transform was introduced. For which functions f does the definition (518) of f make sense? A great deal of work has been done on this problem, and a few highlights can be mentioned briefly. Suppose f belongs to $L^p(-\infty, \infty)$. If $p=1$, the integral in the definition of f (see 518) exists as an absolutely convergent integral for each point x. The situation is somewhat different if p is greater than 1. Restriction may be made initially to $p=2$, which is in many ways the central case of the theory.

To define the Fourier transform of an L^2 function, consider the partial integral in which $\hat{f}_M$ as a function of x is a definite integral from minus to plus M in which the integrand is a product of a negative exponential and the function f (see 529). (This integral is absolutely convergent for all finite M.) It can be shown that $\hat{f}_M$ belongs to $L^2(-\infty, \infty)$ for each fixed M, and that as M tends to infinity, the $\hat{f}_M$ tend to a limit in an appropriate sense. One way to express precisely the convergence of the $\hat{f}_M$ to a limit is as follows: There is one (and only one) function $\hat{f}$ in $L^2(-\infty, \infty)$ for which the distance $\|\hat{f}_M-\hat{f}\|_2$ tends to zero as M tends to infinity; the function $\hat{f}$ is called the Fourier transform of f. Thus, the Fourier transform makes sense for all L^2 functions.

The action of the Fourier transform on $L^2(-\infty, \infty)$ has been exhaustively studied by making use of the geometric properties of $L^2(-\infty, \infty)$ already alluded to above. The main point of the L^2-theory is Michel Plancherel's celebrated formula, which may be stated thus: a function f in $L^2(-\infty, \infty)$ is considered. By what has been said above, $\hat{f}$ also belongs to L^2. By means of the Plancherel formula, it is possible to predict exactly the size of $\hat{f}$ in terms of that of f. The formula states that two integrals are identified, each extended over the entire real line and each with integrands of the type absolute value of a function squared, one function being $\hat{f}$ and the other f (see 530). Thus f and $\hat{f}$ have the same L^2-norms. A closely related theorem asserts that an arbitrary function g in $L^2(-\infty, \infty)$ can be written as the Fourier transform of some function f in L^2, $\hat{f}=g$, and that there is only one f that serves. It will be explained presently how to calculate f for any given g. These results determine completely the behaviour of the Fourier transform on $L^2(-\infty, \infty)$.

Plancherel formula

The solution to the problem of inversion of the Fourier transform will now be stated; *i.e.*, an explicit formula will be given for a function f in terms of its Fourier transform $\hat{f}$. Define the function $\check{g}(x)$ such that $\check{g}$ is definite integral from minus infinity to plus infinity of a product of a complex exponential and the function g (see 531). This operation differs from the Fourier transform only in the negative sign in the exponential and is called the inverse Fourier transform. Just as for the Fourier transform, the integral in the definition of $\check{g}$ (see 531) is absolutely convergent if g is absolutely integrable, while if g belongs to $L^2(-\infty, \infty)$ partial integrals (see 532) may be formed and the limit obtained in the sense described above in connection with $\hat{f}_M$. Just as was seen above, the inverse Fourier transform sends L^2 functions to L^2 functions and satisfies an equation in which two integrals are equal, each extended over the entire real line, each having as integrand an absolute value of a function squared, one function being g and the other $\check{g}$ (see 533).

The connection between g and the problem of inverting the Fourier transform is as follows: Every function f in $L^2(-\infty, \infty)$ is the inverse Fourier transform of its Fourier transform $\hat{f}$. In other words, written formally, $\hat{f}$ as a function of x is a definite integral extended over the entire real line of a product in which factors are a complex exponential and the function f (see 534), in which the nonabsolutely convergent integral is defined by the procedure explained above. This formula, which is called the Fourier inversion formula, solves the problem of inverting the Fourier transform and thus completes

(531) $\check{g}(x)=(2\pi)^{-1/2}\int_{-\infty}^{\infty} e^{ixy}g(y)dy$

(532) $\check{g}_M(x)=(2\pi)^{-1/2}\int_{-M}^{M} e^{ixy}g(y)dy$

(533) $\int_{-\infty}^{\infty}|\check{g}(x)|^2dx=\int_{-\infty}^{\infty}|g(x)|^2dx$

(534) $f(x)=(2\pi)^{-1/2}\int_{-\infty}^{\infty} e^{ixy}\hat{f}(y)dy$

(535) $x=(x_1, x_2, \ldots, x_n)$

(536) $y=(y_1, y_2, \ldots, y_n)$

coverage of the relationship between an L^2 function and its Fourier transform.

Harmonic oscillations

For each y, the expression $e^{ixy} = \cos(xy) + i \sin(xy)$ represents a harmonic oscillation in x. Hence, for each y, the integrand in the inverse Fourier transform (see 534) is a harmonic oscillation in x, and so the formula for the inverse (534) gives a decomposition of f into a sum of harmonic oscillations. For this reason the theory of Fourier transforms is often called harmonic analysis.

The notion of Fourier transform that was initially considered for functions of a single variable can be extended to functions of several variables. If x denotes a point in the n-dimensional Euclidean space R^n, then x can be treated as an n-tuple of real numbers (the coordinates of x; see 535). Correspondingly, $f(x)$ may be written for a function of n real variables $f(x_1, \ldots, x_n)$. Similarly, the vector y has n components y_k (see 536) for another point of Euclidean space. It should be noted that in the context of n-dimensional space, x_j y_k, etc., will represent real numbers, while x, y, etc. (without indices), will denote points of Euclidean space; $x + y$ is defined as the n-tuple in which a vector has n components, each of which is a sum of two terms x_k and y_k (see 537), and ax as the n-tuple in which a vector has n components, each of which has as a factor a (see 538), which is a real number; $x \cdot y$ will be used for the expression that is a sum of products of components, a typical summand being $x_k y_k$ (see 539), and $|x|$ for the square root of the sum of squares of components equal to the square root of the scalar product of the vector x by itself (see 540). (In geometric terms, $|x|$ is simply the distance from the point x to the origin.) Given a function $f(y)$ defined in R^n, the Fourier transform of f will be called the function in which the transform of f as a function of x is an integral over n-dimensional Euclidean space with complex exponential in the integrand involving a scalar product and with integrand including as a factor $f(y)$ (see 541), with dy representing $dy_1 dy_2 \cdots dy_n$. For $n = 1$, this definition coincides with that previously given. Just as in the one-variable case, the integral (541), suitably interpreted, is well defined, and the Fourier transform has all the various properties mentioned above for $n = 1$. In particular, the Plancherel formula holds and the Fourier inversion formula is obtained, in which $f(x)$ is an integral over n-dimensional Euclidean space with the integrand containing as factors the transform of f and the complex exponential involving a scalar product (see 542).

A key equation shows that the transform of the partial derivative of f with respect to one of the variables is equal to a product of i times the variable times the transform of f (see 543), which will later be applied to partial differential equations.

(537) $(x_1 + y_1, x_2 + y_2, \ldots, x_n + y_n)$

(538) $(ax_1, ax_2, \ldots, ax_n)$

(539) $x_1y_1 + x_2y_2 + \cdots + x_ny_n$

(540) $(x_1^2 + x_2^2 + \cdots + x_n^2)^{1/2} + (x \cdot x)^{1/2}$

(541) $\hat{f}(x) = (2\pi)^{-n/2} \int_{R^n} e^{-ix \cdot y} f(y)dy$

(542) $f(x) = (2\pi)^{-n/2} \int_{R^n} e^{ix \cdot y} \hat{f}(y)dy$

(543) $\widehat{\frac{\partial}{\partial x_j}} f(x) = ix_j \hat{f}(x)$

(544) $\hat{f}(x) = (2\pi)^{-1/2} (ix)^{-1} [e^{ibx} - e^{iax}]$

(545) $\hat{f}(x) = (2\pi)^{-1/2}\, 2x^{-2} e^{icx} \left[\left(\cos \frac{d}{2}\, x\right) - 1\right]$

(546) $f(x) = e^{-x^2/2}$

(547) $\hat{f}(x) = \exp(-\frac{1}{2}x^2) = f(x)$

(548) $f_\delta(x) = \delta^{-1} \exp\left(-\frac{1}{2}\frac{x^2}{\delta^2}\right)$

(549) $\hat{f}_\delta(x) = \exp\left(-\frac{1}{2}\delta^2 x^2\right)$

(550) $f(x) = (1 - x)^{a - 1/2}$

(551) $J_a(x) = c_a x^a \hat{f}(x)$

(552) $k(x) = |x|^{a-n}$

(553) $|x| = (x_1^2 + \cdots + x_n^2)^{1/2}$

(554) $\mathfrak{L} f(x) = \int_0^\infty e^{-xy} f(y)\, dy$

(555) $\hat{f}(x) = (2\pi)^{-1/2}\, \mathfrak{L}(ix)$

Examples of Fourier transforms. A few examples of Fourier transforms will be given, largely restricted to the one-variable case. (1) If $f(x) = 1$ for x belonging to a finite interval $[a, b]$ and $f(x) = 0$ for x outside this interval, then the transform of f is proportional to a difference of exponentials times the reciprocal of i times x (see 544). (2) The function $f(x)$ is called a triangular function if $f = 0$ outside an interval $[a, b]$, $f = 1$ at the centre point $c = 1/2(a + b)$, and is linear in the intervals $[a, c]$ and $[c, b]$. Then the transform of f is proportional to a product of three functions of x, one being algebraic, one being exponential, and one being trigonometric (see 545), in which $d = b - a$ is the length of $[a, b]$. (3) The expression in which f as a function of x is a negative exponential with the square of x over 2 appearing in the argument (see 546) is a function basic in the calculus of probability (see PROBABILITY THEORY). Then the transform of f is the same as f, namely, the negative exponential with the square of x over 2 in the argument (see 547), and so f is its own Fourier transform. Slightly more generally, by setting f_δ as a function of x proportional to a negative exponential in which the reciprocal of the square of δ appears in the argument and in which the reciprocal of δ is the proportionality factor (see 548), then the transform of f_δ is a negative exponential in which the square of δ is a factor with the square of x in the argument (see 549); here can be seen an instance of an important general principle: As f becomes more concentrated, $\hat{f}$ spreads out. In the present example, the graph of f_δ is a bell-shaped curve of width δ, while the graph of $\hat{f}_\delta$ has width $1/\delta$. (4) By selecting suitable f, a large number of functions important in analysis are obtained as $\hat{f}$. Consider only one example. Set f as a function of x equal to the difference of 1 and x raised to the $a - 1/2$ power (see 550) if $-1 < x < 1$, and $f(x) = 0$ otherwise. Then J_a as a function of x includes the transform of f as a factor and x raised to the a power as a factor (see 551), which is called the Bessel function of order a. (Here c_a is a constant the value of which is of no present concern.) This function occurs often in mathematical physics and elsewhere. (5) Finally, one example in higher dimensions will be given. If $k(x)$ is defined on R^n by an equation such that $k(x)$ is the absolute value of x raised to the $a - n$ power (see 552), in which $0 < a < n$, and the length of x equals the square root of the sum of squares of the components (see 553), then $\hat{k}(x) = c_a |x|^{-a}$, in which c_a is a certain positive constant. Use will be made of the example later.

Variants of the Fourier transform. In addition to the Fourier transform, harmonic analysis deals with other closely related integral transforms. It is sufficient here to list only a few. (1) The Laplace transform: If $f(y)$ is a

The Laplace transform

function defined on the interval $(0, \infty)$, the Laplace transform of f, denoted by $\mathfrak{L}f$, is given by an equation such that the Laplace transform of f as a function of x is a definite integral from zero to infinity in which the negative exponential appears as a factor in the integrand and the product of x and y constitutes the argument in the exponential, f being the remaining factor in the integrand (see 554), for all real or complex values of x for which the defining integral converges. It may be observed that extension of the domain of f to the whole real line by setting $f(x) = 0$ for $x < 0$ gives formally the equation in which the transform of f is proportional to the Laplace transform of i times x (see 555), for all real values of x. Thus, the Laplace transform is a natural extension of the Fourier transform, and for this reason the former is sometimes called the Fourier-Laplace transform. This integral transform is rather useful in studying ordinary differential equations and also in the theory of analytic functions (see above *Differential equations: Linear differential equations;* and below *Functional analysis*). (2) The Hankel transform of a function f defined in the interval $(0, \infty)$ is given by $H_a f(x) = \int_0^\infty J_a(xy) \cdot (xy)^{1/2} f(y)dy$, in which J denotes the Bessel function defined in the last section. This transform occurs in the study of those functions and equations in Euclidean space that depend only on the distance from the origin. (3) The Mellin transform of a function on $(0, \infty)$ is defined as $Mf(x) = \int_0^\infty x^{it} f(t)dt$ for all real values of x. As seen below, the Mellin transform, first expressed by Robert Hjalmar Mellin (1854–1933), arises from the multiplicative structure of the real line just as the Fourier transform comes from the additive structure.

Convolution and the Fourier transform. The notion of convolution is now extended to functions of n real variables. If $x = (x_1, x_2, \ldots, x_n)$ is an n-tuple of real numbers and $f(x)$, $g(x)$ are functions of x, then $f * g$ as a function of x is an integral over the n-dimensional Euclidean space of a product of f and g, arguments $x - y$ and y appearing in the functions of the integrand (see 556), in which $dy = dy_1, dy_2 \ldots dy_n$; such an expression is called the convolution of f and g. When $n = 1$ this reduces to the previous definition. By making a change of variable $z = x - y$, $dz = dy$, this integral may be written in the form of an integral over n-dimensional Euclidean space of the product of f and g, the variables z and $x - z$ serving as arguments, respectively (see 557), so that $f * g = g * f$.

It is easily shown that a linear combination of functions f_1 and f_2 convoluted with g equals a linear combination of convolutions (see 558). The connection between convolutions and Fourier transforms lies deeper. If f and g both have Fourier transforms $\hat{f}$ and $\hat{g}$, respectively, then a simple formal argument shows that a transform of the convolution is the product of the transforms (see 559), so that in terms of the Fourier transform, convolution corresponds to multiplication. In view of the analogy between Fourier transform and inverse Fourier transform, the result could also be interpreted as follows: to multiplication of functions corresponds the convolution of their Fourier transforms. And so, convolution actually is a kind of multiplication. Clearly, the properties of $f * g$ depend on those of both f and g. The theory of convolutions shows that the "good" properties of both f and g (integrability over R^n, boundedness, continuity, differentiability, etc.) are inherited by their convolution. For instance, the formula in which a general differential operator composed of powers of partial derivatives operating upon a convolution is equal to a convolution in which one function remains unmodified and the other is modified with the equivalent differential operation (see 560) holds for differentiation. Now if f belongs to L^p, in which $p > 1$, and g belongs to L^q, then it can be shown that $h = f * g$ belongs to L^r in which r is defined by a relationship in terms of equality between reciprocals r, p, and q (see 561; provided r is positive), and hence r is greater than q, and the inequality in which the rth norm of h is less than or equal to the product of the pth norm of f and the qth norm of g (see 562) holds.

"Good" functions

Convolutions are useful in giving approximations to general functions by good functions. This approximation is based on the following idea: For any kernel

(556) $$(f * g)(x) = \int_{R^n} f(x - y)g(y)dy$$

(557) $$\int_{R^n} f(z)g(x - z)dz$$

(558) $$(af_1 + \beta f_2) * g = a(f_1 * g) + \beta(f_2 * g)$$

(559) $$\widehat{f * g} = \hat{f} \cdot \hat{g}$$

(560) $$\left(\frac{\partial}{\partial x_1}\right)^{a_1}\left(\frac{\partial}{\partial x_2}\right)^{a_2} \cdots \left(\frac{\partial}{\partial x_n}\right)^{a_n}(f * g)$$
$$= \left[\left(\frac{\partial}{\partial x_1}\right)^{a_1}\left(\frac{\partial}{\partial x_2}\right)^{a_2} \cdots \left(\frac{\partial}{\partial x_n}\right)^{a_n} f\right] * g$$
$$= f * \left[\left(\frac{\partial}{\partial x_1}\right)^{a_1}\left(\frac{\partial}{\partial x_2}\right)^{a_2} \cdots \left(\frac{\partial}{\partial x_n}\right)^{a_n} g\right]$$

(561) $$\frac{1}{r} = \frac{1}{p} + \frac{1}{q} - 1$$

(562) $$\|h\|_r \leq \|f\|_p \|g\|_q$$

(563) $$\int_{R^n} k(x)dx = 1$$

(564) $$k_\varepsilon(x) = \varepsilon^{-n} k\left(\frac{x}{\varepsilon}\right) = \varepsilon^{-n} k\left(\frac{x_1}{\varepsilon}, \frac{x_2}{\varepsilon}, \ldots, \frac{x_n}{\varepsilon}\right)$$

(565) $$\int_{R^n} k_\varepsilon(x)dx = \int_{R^n} k(x)dx = 1$$

(566) $$\frac{\partial^2 u}{\partial x_1^2} + \frac{\partial^2 u}{\partial x_2^2} + \cdots + \frac{\partial^2 u}{\partial x_n^2} = -f$$

$k(x) = k(x_1, x_2, \ldots, x_n)$ of, say, a total integral over n-dimensional Euclidean space of k equal to 1 (see 563), and given any positive number ε, a new kernel $k_\varepsilon(x)$ can be formed by the equation in which k_ε as a function of x is a product of the negative nth power of ε and k as a function of n arguments, the typical one being x_k divided by ε (see 564). For any f, the convolution of f with k_ε can also be defined. The graph of $k_\varepsilon(x)$ is that of $k(x)$, contracted horizontally by the ratio ε, and expanded vertically by the ratio ε^{-n}, so that the integral over n-dimensional Euclidean space of k_ε is 1 (see 565) for all ε. It is assumed for the moment that $k(x) = 0$ outside the sphere of radius 1 centred at the origin. Then $k_\varepsilon(x) = 0$ outside the sphere of radius ε centred at the origin. On the other hand, if f happens to be continuous at the point x_0, then $f(x)$ is practically constant on a ball of radius ε centred at x_0, and so it is not difficult to see that $f_\varepsilon(x_0)$ tends to $f(x_0)$ as ε tends to zero. For this reason, $f\varepsilon = k\varepsilon * f$ is called an approximate identity. The functions f_ε provide good approximations to f under very general circumstances. For example, if k is absolutely integrable and f is in L^p, then likewise f_ε is in L^p, and $\|f - f_\varepsilon\|_p$ tends to zero as ε tends to zero; if f is uniformly continuous, then f_ε tends uniformly to f as ε tends to zero. It may be noted that if k is a good function—say a times differentiable—then k_ε is likewise good, and so f_ε is good. Thus the convolution $k_\varepsilon * f$ gives an approximation to f by good functions.

Applications to partial differential equations. The applications of convolutions and Fourier transforms will now be illustrated with an example from partial differential equations and potential theory. If a distribution of electrical charges throughout Euclidean space $R^n (n \geq 3)$ has a density of charge at the point x given by a function $f(x)$, it can be shown that the electrical potential $u(x)$ arising from the charge distribution f satisfies an expression in which the sum of second-order partial derivatives of u taken with respect to each of the n arguments is equal to the negative value of f (see 566).

Traditionally, the left-hand side (see 566) is called the Laplacian of u and denoted by Δu or $\nabla^2 u$. The equation $\Delta u = 0$ is called Laplace's equation and its solutions are called harmonic functions. The inhomogeneous Laplace equation (566) is sometimes called Poisson's equation.

The inhomogeneous Laplace equation

Now given any f (subject to some technical conditions that are not specified) the equation (566) can be solved by using the Fourier transform. To do so, the effect of the Fourier transform on Δu must be examined. From two consecutive applications of an earlier formula (543), it can be seen that the transform of the second-order partial derivative of u with respect to one variable all considered as a function of x is a product of the negative square of the variable times the transform of f (see 567), and therefore the transform of Δu as a function of x is the negative of the squared absolute value of x times the transform of u (see 568). Consequently, the Fourier transform changes (566) to the equation in which the absolute square of x times the transform of u as a function of x is equal to the transform of f as a function of x (see 569), which has the solution that the transform of u as a function of x is equal to the square of the reciprocal of the absolute value of x multiplied by the transform of f considered as a function of x (see 570). In principle, this formula (570) solves the problem completely. For, given any well-behaved function f, the function $\hat f$ may be computed from its definition (see 541), $\hat u$ found from the above formula (570), and then passage from $\hat u$ back to u made by means of the Fourier inversion formula. This procedure, however, is cumbersome in practice, and in order to solve the problem (566) more explicitly, the solution (570) will be combined with a formula involving convolution. If k as a function of x is equal to a constant times the $2-n$ power of the absolute value of x (see 571), in which c is a constant the exact value of which is not of concern here, $k(x)$ is called the Newtonian potential. Some calculations show that the transform of k as a function of x is the -2 power of the absolute value of x (see 572; see above *Examples of Fourier transforms*). It can be seen that the transform of the convolution of k and f is by calculation the transform of u (see 573) by virtue of the formula (570) for $\hat u$. Consequently, $u = k * f$; that is, u as a function of x is proportional to an integral over n-dimensional Euclidean space in which the integrand includes as a factor f and as a factor the reciprocal of the absolute difference between x and y raised to the $n-2$ power (see 574).

Thus an explicit solution has just been found to the inhomogeneous Laplace equation.

Certain formulas (see 570 and 574) form the starting point for many further investigations in harmonic analysis. Some formulas (see 570, 574) may be generalized to define an interesting family of integral transforms, the fractional integrals. If a is any positive number, the transform of $I^a f$ as a function of x is a product, one term of which is the negative a power of the absolute value of x, one term of which is the transform of f, considered as a function of x (see 575), or, what is in fact the same thing, the product $I^a f$ considered as a function of x is equal to a constant times an integral over n-dimensional Euclidean space in which the integrand contains as a factor f and as a factor the reciprocal of the $n-a$ power of the absolute difference between x and y (see 576). It follows that $\widehat{(I^a f)}$ tends to zero at infinity more rapidly than f. Because rapid decrease of a Fourier transform $\hat g$ corresponds (more or less) to smoothness of the function g, it can be seen that I^a transforms rough functions f to smooth functions $I^a f$. It may be said that a function g on R^n belongs to the class $L_a^p(R^n)$ if g arises by applying I^a to an L^p function f: $I^a f = g$. The classes $L_a^p(R^n)$, called Sobolev spaces (after Sergey L'vovich Sobolev), are a powerful tool to measure the smoothness of functions, occuring often in harmonic analysis and partial differential equations. In the special case in which $n = 1$, $1 < p < \infty$ and $a =$ integer k, a function f belongs to L_a^p if, and only if, its kth derivative $f^{(k)}$ is in L^p. When a is not an integer, the Sobolev spaces give meaning to such statements as "the function f is 3½ times differentiable."

Sobolev spaces

(567) $$\widehat{\frac{\partial^2 u}{\partial x_j^2}}(x) = -x_j^2\, \hat f(x) \quad \text{for } j = 1, 2, \ldots, n$$

(568) $$\widehat{\Delta u}(x) = -(x_1^2 + x_2^2 + \cdots + x_n^2)\hat u(x) = -|x|^2\, \hat u(x)$$

(569) $$|x|^2\, \hat u(x) = \hat f(x)$$

(570) $$\hat u(x) = |x|^{-2} \hat f(x)$$

(571) $$k(x) = c|x|^{2-n}$$

(572) $$\hat k(x) = |x|^{-2}$$

(573) $$\widehat{k * f}(x) = |x|^{-2} \hat f(x) = \hat u(x)$$

(574) $$u(x) = c \int_{R^n} \frac{f(y)}{|x-y|^{n-2}}\, dy$$

(575) $$\widehat{I^a f}(x) = |x|^{-a} \hat f(x) \text{ for all } x \text{ in } R^n$$

(576) $$I^a f(x) = c_a \int_{R^n} \frac{f(y)}{|x-y|^{n-a}}\, dy \text{ for all } x$$

In addition to the inhomogeneous Laplace equation, there are a number of other partial differential equations arising from mathematical analysis and physics that can be solved by methods that are similar to those outlined above.

Generalizations of the Fourier transform. Much of the highly developed theory of Fourier integrals, which has just been sketched in the setting of Euclidean space, can actually be carried out in a wider context. The theory of various generalizations of the Fourier transform is known as abstract harmonic analysis. In addition to providing new mathematical results, abstract harmonic analysis sharpens an understanding of classical Fourier analysis by elucidating the essential unity that exists among the many classical integral transforms: Fourier integrals, Fourier series, Mellin transforms, and expansions in spherical harmonics, to cite a few examples. The present exposition of abstract harmonic analysis will concentrate on the part of the subject that is easiest to understand, namely the study of Fourier transforms on Abelian groups (see below), and attention will now be turned to this topic. It is best to begin by viewing the classical theory from a proper perspective.

Abstract harmonic analysis

From its very definition (see 541) it can be seen that the

(577) $$\chi_x(y) = e^{ix \cdot y}$$

(578) $$\hat f(x) = (2\pi)^{-n/2} \int_{R^n} \chi_x(y)\, f(y)\,dy$$

(579) $$\chi_x(y_1 + y_2) = \chi_x(y_1) \cdot \chi_x(y_2)$$

(580) $$(x + y) + z = x + (y + z)$$

for any three elements x, y, and z in G

(581) $$\chi(y_1 + y_2) = \chi(y_1) \cdot \chi(y_2)$$

(582) $$(x_1, x_2, \ldots, x_n) + (y_1, y_2, \ldots, y_n) = (x_1 + y_1, x_2 + y_2, \ldots, x_n + y_n)$$

(583) $$-(x_1, x_2, \ldots, x_n) \text{ is } (-x_1, -x_2, \ldots, -x_n)$$

Fourier transform on R^n is built up from the functions of such a form as χ as a function of y equal to a complex exponential containing a vector product of x and y in the product (see 577). (Here x is thought of as a fixed point in R^n and $\chi_x(y)$ regarded as a function of y.) Indeed, the Fourier transform (541) may be rewritten in a form such that the transform of f as a function of x is an integral over n-dimensional Euclidean space of a product of χ_x and f (see 578). The essential property of χ_x that is used in harmonic analysis is the multiplicative law of the exponential: χ_x operating upon the sum of y_1 and y_2 is a product of terms, χ operating upon y_1 and y_2, respectively (see 579). Now if G is any set on which there is defined some notion of the sum $y_1 + y_2$ of two elements y_1 and y_2 of G, and also some notion of integral, then the key formulas (578) and (579) are valid for complex-valued functions χ_x and f defined on G, and thus harmonic analysis can be carried out on G. More precisely, the following definitions can be made:

Abelian groups

An Abelian group is a set G, together with an operation $+$, that combines any two elements x and y of G into a third element $x+y$ of G, and that satisfies axioms 1–4:

1. $(x+y)+z=x+(y+z)$ for any three elements x, y, and z in G (the associative law; see 580).
2. $x+y=y+x$ for any two elements x and y in G (the commutative law).
3. There is an element called 0 in G, with the property that $x+0=x$ for every element x of G (existence of an identity element).
4. Corresponding to any given element x in G, there is an element called $(-x)$ in G, which satisfies the equation $x+(-x)=0$ (existence of an inverse element).

A locally compact Abelian group is an Abelian group in which, very roughly, statements such as "x is close to y" or "f is a continuous function," or various similar remarks involving the limit concept can be made. (The precise definition is omitted, because it is technical and requires some background in general topology. All the Abelian groups considered in this article, however, will be locally compact.) If G is a locally compact Abelian group, a character χ of G is a continuous complex-valued function defined on G, which has the properties: (*a*) $\chi(y)$ has modulus one for every element y of G; (*b*) χ operating upon $y_1 + y_2$ is equal to the product of χ operating upon y_1 and χ operating upon y_2 (see 581) for every two elements y_1 and y_2 of G.

A significant portion of harmonic analysis can be carried out in the setting of locally compact Abelian groups. Three classical examples that will be used later are now considered. (1) $G=R^n$ is an Abelian group under the sum between two n component vectors that is a vector of n components, a typical one being x_k+y_k (see 582), with identity element (0, 0, . . . , 0); the inverse of the vector composed of n components is the vector composed of n negatives of the same components (see 583). The characters of R^n are seen to be precisely the functions $\chi_x(y)=\exp(ix\cdot y)$. Thus, characters play a basic role in harmonic analysis on R^n. (2) $G=R^+$, the set of all positive real numbers is not an Abelian group under ordinary addition. (For instance, axiom 3 is violated, for the only number a with the property that $x+a=x$ for all x in R^+ is zero, and zero does not belong to R^+.) If the symbol $+$ is allowed to stand for multiplication of real numbers, however, then R^+ becomes a locally compact Abelian group. (For instance, the identity element demanded by axiom 3 is one, and the inverse of a given element x of R^+ is $1/x$.) The characters of R^+ are functions $\chi_t(x)=x^{it}$, in which t is any fixed real number. It should be possible to do harmonic analysis on R^+ in terms of the functions $\chi_t(x)$, and as will be seen below, this is the case. (3) The circle, denoted by S^1, may be made into a group by regarding it as the set of all complex numbers z of modulus $|z|=1$, with the operation $+$ as ordinary multiplication of complex numbers. Then S^1 becomes a locally compact Abelian group. Via the correspondence $z=e^{i\theta}$, the circle S^1 may also be thought of as consisting of all angles θ in the interval $[0, 2\pi]$. The characters on S^1 are precisely the functions in which χ_n as a function of θ is a complex exponential with the product $n\theta$ in the argument, n being any integer (see 584). According to the classical theory of Fourier series (see above *Fourier series*), any integrable function $f(\theta)$ defined on $[0, 2\pi]$ may be expanded in an infinite series of a form such that f as a function of θ is an infinite sum with indices extending from minus infinity to plus infinity and summands having factors a_n and either a factor of exponential form or of the form χ_n, arguments being θ (see 585), in which a_n being a transform of n is an integral from zero to 2π of the product of f with either a negative exponential or the complex conjugate of χ (see 586). Here again, characters appear as the fundamentals of harmonic analysis on the group $G=S^1$.

Returning to the general theory of Abelian groups: If χ_1 and χ_2 are two characters of a locally compact Abelian group G, a new character, denoted $\chi_1+\chi_2$, may be defined by the formula $(\chi_1+\chi_2)(y)=\chi_1(y)\cdot\chi_2(y)$ for every element y in G. Under this "addition" operation, the set $\hat{G}$ of all the characters of G becomes a locally compact Abelian group, called the dual group or character group of G with $\chi_0(x)$ identically equal to 1 as the identity element, and $(-\chi)(y)=1/\chi(y)$ as the inverse to a given character χ. For the three classical examples above, the dual groups G are as follows: R^n is its own dual group, R^1 is the dual group of R^+, and the set Z of integers $0, +1, +2, \ldots$ with the operation of addition is the dual group of S^1. In each case, the Fourier transform $\hat{f}$ of a function f on G is a function on the dual group G.

In order to define the Fourier transform and study harmonic analysis on a generally locally compact Abelian group G, it is desirable to have a notion of the integral of a real- or complex-valued function defined on G. Initially only continuous functions f that are equal to zero outside of some bounded—*i.e.*, compact—subset of G will be considered. The class of all such functions is denoted by $C_c(G)$. In the known case, $G=R^n$, $I(f)$ equal to an integral over n-dimensional Euclidean space of f (see 587), defined for functions in $C_c(G)$, has the following key properties: (*a*) I as a function of a linear combination of f and g is a linear combination of I as a function of f and I as a

(584) $$\chi_n(\theta)=e^{in\theta}, \quad \text{in which } n=0, \pm1, \pm2, \ldots$$

(585) $$f(\theta)\sim\sum_{n=-\infty}^{\infty} a_n e^{in\theta}=\sum_{-\infty}^{\infty} a_n\chi_n(\theta)$$

(586) $$a_n=\hat{f}(n)=(2\pi)^{-1}\int_0^{2\pi} e^{-in\theta} f(\theta)d(\theta)$$
$$=(2\pi)^{-1}\int_0^{2\pi} \overline{\chi_n(\theta)}\, f(\theta)d(\theta)$$

(587) $$I(f)=\int_{R^n} f(x)dx$$

(588) $$I(af+bg)=aI(f)+bI(g)$$

(589) $$f_{x_0}(x)=f(x+x_0)$$

(590) $$I(f)=k\int_{R^n} f(x)dx$$

(591) $$I(f)=\int_{R^n} f(x)dx$$

(592) $$I(f)=\int_0^{2\pi} f(\theta)d\theta$$

(593) $$I(f)=\int_0^{\infty} f(t)\frac{dt}{t}$$

(594) $$\hat{f}(\chi)=c\int_G \chi(y)f(y) \quad \text{for all } \chi \text{ in } G$$

function of g (see 588) for any functions f and g in $C_c(R^n)$ and any two numbers a and b. (*b*) If $f(x) \geq 0$ for all x, then $I(f) \geq 0$; in fact, $I(f) > 0$ unless $f(x)$ is identically zero. (*c*) For a given function f and an element x_0 of G, the translate f_{x_0} of f by x_0 is defined by the equation in which f_{x_0} as a function of x is equal to f as a function of the sum x and x_0 (see 589) (thus on R^n, the graph of f_{x_0} is obtained from that of f simply by sliding horizontally)—then for arbitrary f and x_0, the equation is $I(f_{x_0}) = I(f)$ (translation-invariance of the integral).

Moreover, it is not hard to prove that the only way of associating a number $I(f)$ to each f in $C_c(R^n)$ in such a way that (*a*), (*b*), and (*c*) are satisfied is to set $I(f)$ equal to a constant times an integral over n-dimensional Euclidean space of f (see 590) for some positive constant k. Thus, except for an insignificant constant factor, properties (*a*), (*b*), and (*c*) uniquely characterize the Riemann integral on R^n. In the general case of a locally compact Abelian group G, a method of associating a number $I(f)$ to each function f in $C_c(G)$ is an integral if properties (*a*), (*b*), and (*c*) hold. It can be shown that on any locally compact Abelian group G, there is one and (essentially) only one integral on G; it is called the Haar integral on G, and $I(f)$ is written $\int_G f$, by analogy with the case $G = R^n$. Once the Haar integral is defined for functions in $C_c(G)$, it may be extended to a large class of (possibly discontinuous) functions on G. (See *Real analysis: Measure and integral calculus.*) Thus, in particular, L^p classes are definable on any locally compact Abelian group.

The Haar integral

Haar measure can be illustrated by considering the same three classical examples. On $G = R^n$, the Haar integral is just $I(f)$ equal to an integral over n-dimensional Euclidean space of the function f (see 591), as was seen above. On $G = S^1 = [0, 2\pi]$, the Haar integral is given by $I(f)$ as an integral from zero to 2π of f (see 592). Finally, on $G = R^+$, the Haar integral is I as a function of f equal to an integral over the positive real line of f divided by its argument (see 593).

The basic notions of the character group and Haar integral having been defined, the basic results of harmonic analysis on a locally compact Abelian group G can be stated. For any absolutely integrable function f on G, the Fourier transform $\hat{f}$ of f is defined to be the following function on the character group $\hat{G}$: the transform of f as a function of χ is a constant times the integral over G of the product of χ and f (see 594). If f is a square-integrable function on G, then the integral (594) need not converge absolutely, but can be interpreted by a procedure analogous to that used above to define (541) in the case $G = R^n$. Moreover, several of the major results of harmonic analysis on R^n are also valid on G. For example, there is the Plancherel formula: two integrals are equal, one extended over G, one over $\hat{G}$, the integrand of the first being the absolute squared of f, the integrand of the second being the absolute squared of $\hat{f}$ (see 595), and there is the Fourier inversion formula: f as a function of x is a constant times the integral over $\hat{G}$ of a product of terms, one being the complex conjugate of χ, the other being $\hat{f}$ (see 596); both hold for suitable functions f on G. (Integration over $\hat{G}$ in formulas [595] and [596] makes sense, because $\hat{G}$ is a locally compact Abelian group, and thus has its own Haar integral. The bar over $\chi(x)$ [see 596] denotes complex conjugation.) Convolutions and approximate identities can be defined on G, and their relationship to the Fourier transform is much the same as in the Euclidean case $G = R^n$. On a general locally compact Abelian group, however, there is no notion of differentiation, so that the rich interplay between harmonic analysis and partial differential equations in the Euclidean case is lost.

Fourier transform and inversion

The meaning of the Fourier transform (594) and inverse Fourier transform (596) may be illustrated by the three classical examples $G = R^n$, $G = R^+$, and $G = [0, 2\pi]$. On R^n, the Fourier transform and inverse Fourier transform are precisely the usual expressions (see 541 and 542). The Fourier transform (594) on R^+ is given by an expression in which f is an integral extended over the positive real axis with integrand composed of three terms, one of which is x to a complex exponent, one of which is f, one of which

(595) $$\int_G |f(x)|^2 = \int_{\hat{G}} |\hat{f}(\chi)|^2$$

(596) $$f(x) = c\int_{\hat{G}} \overline{\chi(x)}\hat{f}(\chi)$$

(597) $$\hat{f}(t) = \int_0^\infty x^{it} f(x)\frac{dx}{x}$$

(598) $$\text{for } R^+,\quad f(x) = c\int_{-\infty}^{\infty} x^{it}\hat{f}(t)dt$$

(599) $$\hat{f}(n) = (2\pi)^{-1}\int_0^{2\pi} e^{inx} f(x)dx$$

(600) $$f(x) = \sum_{n=-\infty}^{\infty} \hat{f}(n)e^{-inx}$$

(601) $$(2\pi)^{-1}\int_0^{2\pi} |f(x)|^2\, dx = \sum_{n=-\infty}^{\infty} |\hat{f}(n)|^2$$

is the reciprocal of x (see 597), and thus is none other than the Mellin transform defined earlier. The inversion formula (596) becomes an expression in which f as a function of x is a constant times an integral extended over the entire real line, one factor in the integrand being x raised to a complex exponent, the other factor being f (see 598; the Mellin inversion formula). Finally, on $G = [0, 2\pi]$, the Fourier transform becomes an expression in which f as a function of n is proportional to the integral from zero to 2π of the product of an exponential times f, nx being the argument in the exponential (see 599). In other words, the Fourier transform on G simply associates to every function f on $[0, 2\pi]$ its sequence of Fourier coefficients. The inversion formula (596) asserts that f as a function of x is a sum extending over integers from minus infinity to plus infinity with summand composed of the product f times an exponential, nx appearing in the exponential (see 600), and the Plancherel formula (see 595) specializes to Parseval's relation, the expression in which an integral and a sum are equal, the integral extending from zero to 2π and applying to the integrand absolute square of f, the sum extending over integers from minus infinity to plus infinity with summand being the absolute square of f (see 601). Thus the basic elementary results in the classical theories of Fourier series and integrals are part of the larger whole of harmonic analysis on locally compact Abelian groups.

Finally, it is noted that highly significant results are known about Fourier analysis on non-Abelian groups—*i.e.*, roughly, mathematical structures satisfying axioms 1, 3, and 4 above but not axiom 2.

REPRESENTATIONS OF GROUPS AND ALGEBRAS

Since their formal introduction in the early 19th century, groups have been one of the principal objects of mathematical attention (see ALGEBRA: *Groups*). Their widespread and profound applications to such physical subjects as crystallography, quantum mechanics, and hydrodynamics and to such other mathematical regimes as number theory, harmonic analysis, and geometry have demonstrated their importance.

The main general technique for studying groups is the method of group representation. Technically, a representation of a group is a homomorphism of it into another group, most commonly into the group of invertible linear transformations (or matrices) on some linear space. Less technically, this method amounts to comparing the given group with better known examples of groups. Representation theory plays a significant part in all branches of mathematics in various ways; it also is important in theoretical physics, particularly in quantum theory.

Historical development. The general representation theory for finite groups was developed by the mathematicians Ferdinand Georg Frobenius, Issai Schur, and William

Origin

Burnside at the end of the 19th and the beginning of the 20th century. Nothing of the deeper theory of finite groups developed by such later workers as Emil Artin and Richard Brauer has been discussed here. The extension of the finite group theory to compact groups is due in part to Schur, who developed the representation theory of the rotation group in those terms. The general extension to compact groups of the completeness and orthogonality of the finite-dimensional irreducible unitary representations is known as the Peter-Weyl theorem (published in 1927). Lie groups are named after Sophus Lie, a Norwegian mathematician who discovered their fundamental properties in the last decades of the 19th century. A deeper analysis of their properties and, in particular, the classification of the semisimple groups were carried out by Élie-Joseph Cartan in the early part of the 20th century. The general finite-dimensional representation theory for semisimple Lie groups was developed principally by Weyl in the mid-1920s, as were the connections between group theory and quantum mechanics. The general representation theory for topological groups started with the discovery by Alfred Haar in the early 1930s of an invariant measure on locally compact groups. The existence of a separating family of irreducible unitary representations for locally compact groups was established by the Soviet mathematicians Izrail M. Gel'fand and Dmitry A. Raikov in the early 1940s. The decomposition of unitary representations of locally compact groups into irreducible and factor unitary representations was carried out by Friederich I. Mautner at the end of the 1940s. This decomposition was based on the powerful theory of operator algebras developed by John von Neumann in collaboration with Francis Joseph Murray in the 1930s and early 1940s. In particular, the theory of factors is their creation. A general duality and function transform theory based on the Murray-von Neumann operator algebras was developed by Irving E. Segal in the early 1950s. George W. Mackey created a forceful technique for the analysis of representations of groups with type I representations by generalizing the Frobenius theory of induced representations. The detailed analysis of the infinite-dimensional representations of the semisimple Lie groups is the work of Gel'fand, Mark Aronovich Naimark, and Harish-Chandra. The fact that these groups have type I representations is a consequence of Harish-Chandra's results. Jacques Dixmier established this same fact for the so-called nilpotent Lie groups. Examples of Lie groups with representations not of type I are known.

Groups. To sketch briefly, a group is a set on which a multiplication satisfying certain specific properties is defined. Corresponding to each pair of elements a, b (in a given order) is another element (written ab), and this law of combination has the properties: (1) $a(bc) = (ab)c$; (2) there is an element e, called the group identity element, such that $ae = ea = a$; and (3) for each a there is an element a^{-1}, called the inverse of a such that $aa^{-1} = a^{-1}a = e$. If in addition $ab = ba$ for each a and b, the group is said to be Abelian (also commutative). A homomorphism is a mapping (function, correspondence) f of one group G into another group H such that $f(ab) = f(a)f(b)$ for each a and b in G; that is, f preserves multiplication. The positive and negative integers with their usual addition provide an example of an infinite Abelian group (here, addition plays the role of group multiplication, 0 is the group identity and, for example, -5 is the group inverse to 5). The two integers 0 and 1 with the usual addition as group multiplication (except that 1 is to combine with 1 to give 0) provide an example of a finite Abelian group, as does the set of two integers $+1$ and -1 with the usual multiplication of integers. The mapping of an integer into 0 if it is even and into 1 if it is odd provides an example of a homomorphism of the group of integers onto the first two-element group. The function which assigns 0 to $+1$ and 1 to -1 is an example of an isomorphism (*i.e.*, one-to-one homomorphism) of the second two-element group onto the first. Structurally, as far as group theoretical properties are concerned, the existence of this isomorphism indicates that both two-element groups are the same—they are different (isomorphic) representations of the same abstract group, so to speak.

Isomorphism

Group representations. The process of group representation may be likened to measuring some physical object with a ruler. By comparing the object to be studied with the known object (the ruler), special information is obtained. Spreading the object out completely along the ruler might be thought of as an isomorphic representation, but such a procedure may not be possible. For example, a polyhedron would have to be studied by applying a series of partial measurements and combining them (corresponding to combining information from homomorphic representations). It would be hoped that sufficiently many measurements could be made to give detailed information—corresponding to the case of sufficiently many (a separating family of) representations so that each pair of distinct elements is carried into a pair of distinct elements by at least one of the representations. An instance of combining information is afforded by the simple fact that a group with a separating family of representations in Abelian groups is itself Abelian (ab and ba are identified by all such representations). It would help little to make measurements with an unmarked straightedge; in the same way, the representations would be expected to take place in groups with some discernible structure. On the other hand, if the ruler is too specialized, for example, circular, it is available for only a limited type of measurement; by analogy, the class of groups in which the representations take place should remain broad enough to have general application. The so-called linear groups, groups of invertible linear transformations on a linear vector space, are well suited to this task. Representations in such groups often are referred to as linear representations, or simply as representations if confusion is unlikely. In particular, representations by unitary operators on Hilbert spaces, called unitary representations, and representations by operators on finite-dimensional linear spaces, called finite-dimensional representations, have proved very useful.

Group algebra

In applying the technique of representations to the study of groups, the allied method of associating an algebra, the so-called group algebra, with the group has a key function. (An algebra is a linear space with a multiplication satisfying certain specific conditions.) For finite groups and the complex group algebra, this amounts to associating with the group sums of formal complex multiples of the group elements and multiplying two such sums by distributing products in the usual way, commuting numbers past group elements, and multiplying group elements by means of the group multiplication.

A linear representation of the group can be extended to the group algebra by assigning to each sum of multiples of group elements the same sum of multiples of the operators (matrices) corresponding to those group elements under the given representation. This extension is a representation of the group algebra, a mapping into the algebra of operators on the representation space that preserves both products and sums. The analysis of the algebra representation is somewhat simpler than that of the group representation and yields much information about the group representation. The process of extension can be reversed, for the group elements are found in a natural way among those of the group algebra; a representation of the group algebra gives rise to a representation of the group.

There are several ways of constructing new representations from one or more given representations. The first, restriction of a representation, starts with a representation f of a group G (or algebra) and a subspace V of the representation space that is mapped into itself by each of the representing operators, a so-called reducing or invariant subspace. The restricted representation assigns to each g in G the operator $f_V(g)$ on V that is $f(g)$ restricted (in its action) to V. If V is not 0 or the full space, the representation f is said to be reducible. If no such proper invariant subspace exists, the representation is said to be irreducible. (In the case of representations on Hilbert spaces, subspace is understood to mean closed subspace.) Representations of finite groups enjoy the important property of complete reducibility. If V is a reducing subspace, there is a complementary space V' that is also invariant; V and V' have only 0 in common and each vector in the representation space is the sum of one from V and one from V'.

The representation f is said to be the direct sum of f_V and $f_{V'}$. This description of direct sum from an internal viewpoint has an external counterpart. If f and f' are representations of G on spaces V and V', respectively, a representation $f \oplus f'$, called the direct sum of f and f', on the direct sum $V \oplus V'$ of V and V' (*i.e.*, the linear space of pairs of elements, one from V and one from V') is defined by assigning to each group element g the operator on $V \oplus V'$ that transforms a pair (v, v') into the pair $([f(g)](v), [f'(g)](v'))$. In the case of reducing complementary spaces V and V' for a representation f, it is an easy matter to see that $f_V \oplus f_{V'}$ is f when the full space is viewed as $V \oplus V'$. In a similar manner, direct sums of more than two representations can be defined. For finite groups, the process of decomposition of a representation may be continued on each of the restricted representations until a full reduction into irreducible representations is effected; the representation is a direct sum of irreducible representations and such a decomposition is unique.

The tensor product

A more complicated procedure for constructing representations from families of representations, the tensor product, stems from the tensor product of linear spaces (the space of sums of multiples of formal products of basis elements one from each space in a given order—the dimension is the product of the dimensions of the individual spaces as contrasted with that of the direct sum which is the sum of the dimensions). If f and f' are representations of G on spaces V and V', respectively, then $f \otimes f'$, their tensor product, assigns to each g in G the operator $f(g) \otimes f'(g)$ that transforms one of the generating elements $v \otimes v'$ of the tensor product $V \otimes V'$ of V and V' into $[f(g)](v) \otimes [f'(g)](v')$. In particular, the square of a representation consists of tensoring it with itself (similarly for higher powers).

Irreducible representations. A problem of some importance and difficulty is that of describing the irreducible representations that appear in the decomposition of the higher powers of irreducible representations of specific groups, because these are the basic representations not only of the general theory but also of the fundamental physical situation to which the theory applies. Concerning the possible occurrence of a representation that is reducible in the description of a general scheme for quantum mechanics, Claus Hugo Hermann Weyl, who was one of the founders of modern representation theory, wrote, "Nature could hardly be expected to indulge in such a superfluous luxury."

In dealing with representations of a given group, there is clearly no additional information to be obtained by passing from one representation to a second the space of which can be identified with that of the first in such a way that the operators corresponding to each group element under both representations act in the same way on the spaces (relative to the identification). In this case, the representations are said to be equivalent. (Technically, if f and f' are the equivalent representations of G on spaces V and V', there is a linear isomorphism P of V onto V' such that $Pf(g)P^{-1} = f'(g)$ for each g in G.) When a representation f of a group is expressed as the direct sum of irreducible representations and precisely n of these are equivalent to a given irreducible representation f', then f' is said to occur in f with multiplicity n. If the group G has m elements the set of complex-valued functions on G is a linear space of dimension m (addition and scalar multiplication performed pointwise). A natural representation of G on this space is available—to the function a is assigned the function a_g the value of which at g' is $a(g^{-1}g')$, and $f(g)$ is taken to be the transformation of the function space so defined. Then f is a representation of G, called the left regular representation of G. In a similar manner, there is the reflected situation of the right regular representation of G. The crucial property of the regular representations is that each contains every irreducible representation of G in its direct sum decomposition (with multiplicity equal to the dimension of the representation space—as a consequence of the reflection situation of the right and left regular representations). The regular representation is an isomorphic one, from which it is concluded that the group G has a separating family of irreducible representations.

If f is a representation of the finite group G as operators on a Hilbert space, then the function that assigns to a pair of vectors x, y in the space the number $\Sigma_g(f(g)x, f(g)y)$ is again an inner product equivalent to the original one and relative to which each $f(g)$ is a unitary operator (orthogonal transformation, in the real case), so that each such representation of G is equivalent to a unitary representation of G. If f and f' are a pair of inequivalent (irreducible) unitary representations of G, then the sum over g of a product of inner products is zero, one of the inner products being composed of f', x', and y' (see 602), in which x, y, and x', y' are orthonormal pairs of vectors in their respective spaces (the same holds when $f' = f$ and x', y', x, y is an orthonormal set such that not both $x = x'$ and $y = y'$); while $\Sigma_g|(f(g)x, y)|^2$ is the number of elements in G, called the order of G, divided by the dimension of the representation. These are the so-called orthogonality relations. The sum of the diagonal entries of the matrix corresponding to an operator on and a basis for some finite-dimensional space is called the trace of the operator. It is independent of the basis chosen. If f is a representation of the finite group G on a finite-dimensional space, the function that assigns to each element of G the trace of its representing operator is called the character of f. A critical result of the theory states that two such representations are equivalent if, and only if, their characters are identical; the study of such representations is reduced to the study of the characters of G. The character of a direct sum of representations is the sum of their characters and that of a tensor product is their product. The character of the n-dimensional identity representation, which assigns the identity operator on n-dimensional space to each group element, has the constant function n as its character, and that of the regular representation is 0 at each group element except the identity in which it takes the value equal to the order of the group; this equality value is easily checked on the basis consisting of functions that are 1 at some group element and 0 at all others. The characters of the irreducible representations are precisely those characters k such that $\Sigma_g|k(g)|^2$ is the order of G.

Schur's lemma

Schur's lemma, which states that the only operators commuting with a unitary irreducible representation are the scalar multiples of the identity operator, is a key result in the development of representation theory. (Because each representation of a finite group is equivalent to a unitary representation, Schur's lemma covers all such representations.) Applying this fact to Abelian groups, it follows that each irreducible unitary representation of such a group is one-dimensional; each group element is mapped into a complex multiple (having absolute value 1) of the identity operator. The function on the group that assigns to each element its corresponding complex number is the character of the representation. There is, of course, no need to distinguish between the representation and its character in this situation. The complex conjugate of such a character is again a character as is the product of two such characters. With this multiplication, the characters form a group—the character or dual group (to the original group). If G is an Abelian group and G' its dual, then each g in G gives rise to a character of G' that assigns to an element of G' its value at g. The duality theorem for Abelian groups states that the mapping of G just described is an isomorphism of G onto the character group of G'; roughly speaking, G is the dual group of its dual group. A function a on G may be viewed as the element $\Sigma_g a(g)g$ in the group algebra of G, and each character g' of G has the extension to this group algebra that assigns to $\Sigma a(g)g$ the number $\Sigma a(g)g'(g)$. Denoting this number by $a'(g')$, the transformation that maps a onto a' is an isomorphism of the group algebra of G onto the function algebra of G', the linear space of functions on G' with pointwise multiplication. For finite Abelian groups, this function mapping is the counterpart of the Fourier transform, which is so important in mathematical analysis (see above *Harmonic analysis and integral transforms*).

(602) $$\Sigma_g(f(g)x, y)(f'(g^{-1})x', y') = 0$$

Topological groups and Lie groups. The applications of the theory of group representations to mathematical analysis and to physics entail, for the most part, the description of the representations of infinite groups that have a topological structure related to their group structure—the so-called topological groups. (The topological structure is a mathematical formulation of the concepts of nearness. The topological groups are those in which nearness is so defined that the product of an element and the inverse of another element is near to the group identity, provided both elements are themselves near the identity.)

The most important and the most intensively studied of these groups are the Lie groups. These are the topological groups in which the topology near each point is like that of n-dimensional Euclidean space for some fixed n. A more general class of topological groups, the locally compact groups, have received some attention. These include the discrete groups (those in which no group element is infinitely near the others—every group can be given such a topology), the Lie groups, and those that can be constructed from these two classes by certain group-theoretic processes. The various Euclidean spaces with vector addition as group multiplication and the complex numbers of modulus 1 (the circle group) with the usual multiplication of complex numbers each with its usual notion of nearness are examples of Abelian Lie groups. The invertible operators on n-dimensional Euclidean space form a non-Abelian Lie group, the general linear group of dimension n. Here group multiplication is the multiplication of operators, and two operators are near each other if the images of a specific vector under those operators are near each other.

Haar measure of locally compact groups

The crucial property of locally compact groups is the existence of a measure on them, Haar measure (a notion of volume for subsets), which assigns the same number (measure) to a subset of the group and to the subset obtained from it by left multiplying each element of the subset by a fixed group element (each left translate of the set). Those groups with finite total measure constitute an especially important subclass, the compact groups. The circle group and the subgroup of the general linear group consisting of those operators that preserve the lengths of vectors, the orthogonal group (unitary group in the complex case), are examples of compact Lie groups. The finite groups are compact (discrete) groups.

The most satisfactory aspects of this general theory are to be found in its application to the classes of compact groups and of Abelian (locally compact) groups. The theory of representations developed for finite groups is valid for continuous representations of compact groups on Hilbert spaces, once summation over the finite group (divided by the group order) is replaced by integration with respect to Haar measure (normalized so that the group has measure 1). The equivalence of such representations with unitary ones, the character theory, direct sum decomposition into irreducible representations, the orthogonality relations, and the existence of a separating family of (finite-dimensional) irreducible unitary representations are valid for compact groups. The critical new fact that must be established in the general case is the finite dimensionality of each irreducible representation. The duality theory for finite Abelian groups carries over intact to the general case. The dual (character) group of a compact Abelian group is discrete (and that of a discrete group is compact). In particular, the character group of the circle is the additive group of integers—the correspondence between (L_2) functions on the circle and those on the integers (described for finite Abelian groups) is the Fourier series expansion of periodic functions. The additive group of real numbers is its own dual, and the function mapping, in this case, is the important Fourier transform.

The representations of the three-dimensional rotation group, R_3, supply an excellent and physically significant illustration of the theory for compact groups. The group R_3 consists of linear transformations of (real) three-dimensional space that preserve the lengths of vectors and have determinant 1. The rotations preserve area on the unit sphere about the origin (best described in terms of three-dimensional polar coordinates), so that each such rotation induces a unitary transformation on the Hilbert space of square integrable functions over the sphere. The resulting unitary representation decomposes into a direct sum of irreducible, finite-dimensional unitary representations. From a direct analytical study this representation can be shown to decompose into a direct sum of spaces of odd dimension, one for each odd number. This decomposition is effected by means of the spherical harmonic functions on 3-space and their associated surface harmonics on the sphere. The orthogonality relations for the surface harmonics establish the fact that this decomposition yields all the irreducible representations of R_3.

For general locally compact groups it is still possible to establish the existence of a separating family of strongly continuous irreducible unitary representations, and it is still possible to decompose reducible representations into a direct integral of irreducible representations; but much of the value of this fact is lost in the observation that the decomposition can often be performed in many totally distinct ways, so that no irreducible component of one decomposition is equivalent to any component of the others. These developments have given rise to the opinion that the appropriate process is not decomposition into irreducible representations but rather into factor representations. (A unitary representation is said to be a factor representation when the weak closure of the sums of multiples of the representing unitary operators has only multiples of the identity operator in its centre. Such an algebra of operators is said to be a factor.) The factors have been broadly classified into types depending on the nature of a dimension function on the projections in the factor (its discreteness or nondiscreteness, its finiteness or infiniteness). The so-called factors of type I are the most manageable type from the point of view of group representations. These are the factors isomorphic with the algebra of all bounded operators on some Hilbert space. The (direct integral) decomposition of a group representation into factor representations is essentially unique. When the resulting factors are of type I the decomposition of the representation into irreducible components is also essentially unique. The problem of the types of factor representations a specific group has (the so-called type problem) is central to the general theory. In particular, establishing that specific classes of groups have only type I representations is of vital importance to the general theory.

Lie algebra of a group

The detailed investigation of a Lie group and its representations proceeds via the study of its associated Lie algebra. If the Lie group with its associated topology is thought of as a surface in three-dimensional space (or, more generally, a manifold in n-dimensional space), each vector in the tangent plane (space) at the group identity determines a unique vector at each group element by means of (left) translation by that group element. Relative to (*i.e.,* in the direction of) the invariant vector field so obtained, (differentiable) functions can be differentiated to give another function on the group. If two such vector fields are involved, differentiation is performed with respect to each successively in both orders, and the result of one is subtracted from that of the other; the mapping on functions obtained by this process is the same as that due to differentiation with respect to some third invariant vector field. This third vector field is said to be the Lie product or bracket of the other two. These vector fields, or—what amounts to the same thing because each is determined by a tangent vector at the group identity e—the tangent space at e, with the Lie product is the Lie algebra of the group (it is a nonassociative algebra). Because differentiation is a local process, depending only on the points near a point at which it takes place, the Lie algebra of a group is in reality a construct associated only with that portion of the group near the identity—the so-called local Lie group. Several Lie groups that are distinct globally may have the same local structure and hence the same Lie algebra; for example, the circle group and the group of real numbers both have the real line with the Lie product of each pair of elements 0 as their Lie algebra.

The distinction between Lie groups that have the same Lie algebra is a (global) topological one. Loosely speaking, they differ in the number and relation of the holes in them. A particular one of them covers the other; that is, maps homomorphically onto the other by a mapping that is an isomorphism near the identity. For example, the circle has a hole, the real line does not, and the real line may be wrapped homomorphically around the circle. In the family of Lie groups with a given Lie algebra, there is one that covers all the others—the so-called universal covering group of the others (also called simply connected covering group—the one that has no holes). The group of reals is the universal covering group of the circle. The rotation groups in dimensions 3 and higher are not themselves simply connected but have a twofold universal covering group; each point in the rotation group is the image of precisely two points in this covering group. These are the spinor groups (Spin(n) for the n-dimensional rotation group R_n).

Spinor groups

The Lie algebra of a Lie group may be thought of as a linear approximation to the local Lie group in the same sense that a tangent plane to a surface is the best planar approximation in the neighbourhood of the point of tangency. The multiplicative nature of the local group is made linear (additive) by the transition to the Lie algebra in much the same way that the logarithm converts multiplicative numerical problems into additive ones. In fact, there is a generalized logarithmic mapping (which preserves differentiability) carrying the local Lie group onto a neighbourhood of the origin in the Lie algebra—or, technically more manageable, an exponential mapping of the entire Lie algebra into the group. By means of this mapping, (local) questions about the group can be transferred to questions about the Lie algebra, which are more easily handled because of the added linearity.

The deeper analysis of the representation theory for Lie groups, the finite-dimensional representations of which are completely reducible (the semisimple Lie groups), involves the undertaking of a profound analysis of the semisimple Lie algebras and the so-called theory of weights that is associated with their representations. It has been established for such groups that their unitary representations on Hilbert spaces are of type I. (A.Zy./C.L.F./Ed.)

CALCULUS OF VARIATIONS

The calculus of variations is an old subject; some of its problems were considered and partially solved by the ancient Greeks. Leonhard Euler in the mid-18th century deduced the first general rules for dealing with the subject, while much of the terminology was introduced soon after by Joseph-Louis Lagrange.

When two points, A and B, are given in a plane, as shown in Figure 21, there is an infinity of arcs joining them. A simple problem of the calculus of variations is that of finding in this group of arcs (such as E and E') one that has the shortest length, the solution of the problem being a straight line segment. It may also be desired, however, to find in the group of arcs joining A with B one down which a particle, started with a given initial velocity, will fall from A to B in the shortest time; or which one of these arcs, when rotated about the x-axis, will generate a surface of revolution of minimal area.

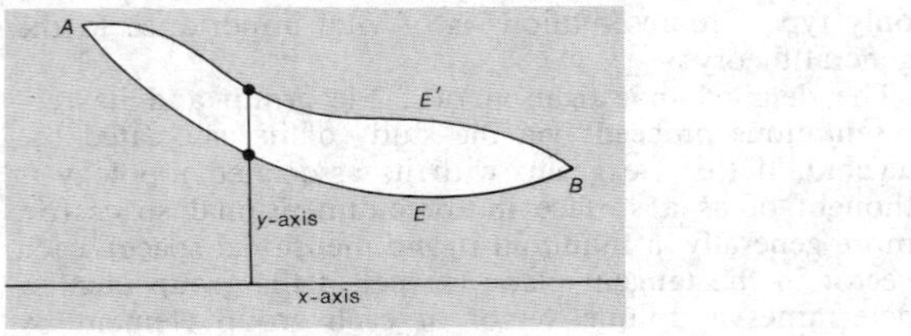

Figure 21: Simple problem of arc length (see text).

These examples are typical problems of the calculus of variations of the so-called simplest type.

These problems illustrate the usual situation in the calculus of variations, in which mathematicians seek to find that arc from some given class for which some quantity, whose value depends on the entire arc (its length, etc.), is a minimum or a maximum. The calculus of variations also deals with problems involving surfaces or functions of several variables. For example, if a circular wire is bent in any way, dipped in a soap solution, and then withdrawn, the soap film spanning the wire will assume the shape of the surface of least area bounded by the wire.

The calculus of variations has been useful as a unifying principle in mechanics and as a guide for the determination of new laws of physics.

Albert Einstein's theory of general relativity, for example, utilizes the calculus of variations extensively. One of the most widely applicable variational statements of classical mechanics is known as Hamilton's principle (after the 19th-century Irish mathematician William Rowan Hamilton); it states that the trajectories of many dynamical systems are the solutions of some variational problem involving an energy integral.

Hamilton's principle

The introduction of the calculus gave great impetus to the study and to the solution of variational problems. After a number of special problems had been solved, Euler in 1744 deduced the first general rule, now known as Euler's differential equation, for the characterization of the maximizing or minimizing arcs.

MATHEMATICAL FORMULATION OF VARIATIONAL PROBLEMS

All the problems mentioned in the first paragraph of this section reduce to the determination of that differentiable arc $y = y(x)$ joining the two points (x_1, y_1) and (x_2, y_2) that minimizes an integral extended over a segment of the x-axis and having its argument a function of x, of y, and of the derivative of y (see 603). The length of the arc and the area of the surface of revolution obtained by revolving it around the x-axis are found from elementary calculus to be given respectively by the integrals of the general type described above in which the function in the integrand involves the square root of one plus the square of the derivative of y (see 604). In the case of the curve of steepest descent, the time required for a bead to descend along a wire in the shape of an arc from the point (x_1, y_1) to the point (x_2, y_2) under the action of gravity is given by the integral of the above type with a special form in the integrand that accounts for the special type of problem involved (see 605) if friction is neglected; here the term a in the integrand is of the form $v_1{}^2$ divided by twice g (see 606), in which v_1 is the initial velocity of the bead and g is the acceleration of gravity.

It is the case in the preceding examples that the function $f(x, y, p)$ occurring in the minimizing integral (see 603) has one of several forms, each involving the square root of one plus p^2 (see 607). The integrals arising from Hamilton's principle are of the type in formula (603), in which x is replaced by the time t (this usually does not appear in the function f in such applications) and the single variables y and p are replaced by several variables $y_1, \ldots, y_n$, and $p_1, \ldots, p_n$, the p_i standing for the derivatives dy_i/dt.

EULER'S EQUATION

Euler's differential equation for the determination of a minimizing arc is derived as follows: Suppose that $y = y(x)$ is a minimizing arc that passes through the two points, and assume that the second derivative y'' and the second partial derivatives of f are all continuous. If $\eta(x)$ is any differentiable function which vanishes at the end points x_1 and x_2 (see 608), then for any λ the arc obtained by adding to the function y the function λ times η (see 609) is another arc joining the two given points. Forming an integral for this new arc gives a function $I(\lambda)$ in the form of a definite integral in which λ appears as a parameter (see 610) which is differentiable and must have a minimum for $\lambda = 0$.

Determination of a minimizing arc

From elementary calculus, it follows that the integral in-

(603) $$\int_{x_1}^{x_2} f[x, y(x), y'(x)]dx, \quad y' = \frac{dy}{dx}$$

(604) $$\begin{cases} \int_{x_1}^{x_2} \sqrt{1+\left(\frac{dy}{dx}\right)^2}\, dx, \text{ length of arc} \\ \int_{x_1}^{x_2} 2\pi y(x) \sqrt{1+\left(\frac{dy}{dx}\right)^2}\, dx, \text{ area of surface} \end{cases}$$

(605) $$\int_{x_1}^{x_2} (a-y)^{-1/2} \sqrt{1+\left(\frac{dy}{dx}\right)^2}\, dx$$

(606) $$a = y_1 + \frac{v_1^2}{2g}$$

(607) $$\sqrt{1+p^2}, \quad 2\pi y\sqrt{1+p^2}, \quad \sqrt{1+p^2}/\sqrt{a-y}$$

(608) $$\eta(x_1) = \eta(x_2) = 0$$

(609) $$y = y(x) + \lambda\eta(x)$$

(610) $$I(\lambda) = \int_{x_1}^{x_2} f[x, y(x) + \lambda\eta(x), y'(x) + \lambda\eta'(x)]dx$$

(611) $$I'(0) = \int_{x_1}^{x_2} \{\eta(x) f_y [x, y(x), y'(x)] + \eta'(x) f_p [x, y(x), y'(x)]\}dx = 0$$

(612) $$\int_{x_1}^{x_2} \eta(x)\left\{f_y - \frac{d}{dx} f_p\right\} dx = 0$$

(613) $$\frac{d}{dx} f_p = f_y$$

(614) $$f_{pp}\frac{d^2y}{dx^2} + f_{py}\frac{dy}{dx} + f_{px} = f_y$$

volving λ can be differentiated with respect to the parameter λ. A necessary condition for a minimum is that this derivative should be equal to 0 (see 611). The integral that results is called the first variation of the original integral (see 603); this corresponds roughly to the total differential of a function of several variables, the function $\eta(x)$ corresponding to the set of differentials of the variables. Now, using the differentiability assumptions, the term involving $\eta'(x)$ in the first variation (see 611) may be eliminated by integrating by parts to obtain an integral of which the integrand includes η as a factor, the total integral being equal to 0 (see 612).

Because the last integral expression (see 612) holds for every function $\eta(x)$ allowed above, it follows from a well-known theorem in analysis that the first derivative of f_p is restricted to equal f_y (see 613), which is Euler's differential equation; it is understood in the derivation that the values x, $y(x)$ and $y'(x)$ are to be inserted in the expressions for f_p and f_y.

If Euler's equation (see 613) is written out in more detail, the rules of differentiation yield an equation in which the second derivative of y appears (see 614), which shows that Euler's equation is of the second order. Euler's equation becomes singular, however, if $f_{pp} = 0$. Therefore, regular variational problems are those for which f_{pp} never vanishes; in that case, it is assumed that $f_{pp} > 0$, which makes minimum problems more natural than maximum problems.

SOME QUESTIONS INVOLVING ARCS

The analysis leading to Euler's equation applies just as well to a maximizing arc as to a minimizing one. The first attempt to find a condition that would single out a minimizing arc was to consider the second variation, which is obtained, for any given $\eta(x)$, by finding $I''(0)$, $I(\lambda)$ being defined by (610).

Clearly $I''(0) \geq 0$ for every $\eta(x)$ if $y(x)$ is a minimizing arc, but the condition that $I''(0) \geq 0$ for every $\eta(x)$ is not sufficient to ensure that $y(x)$ is minimizing. The attempt to find conditions that would ensure a given arc being a relative minimum led to a variety of rather interesting discoveries and also raised a number of new questions.

After Weierstrass' famous example of a continuous function that does not possess a derivative at any point (thereby showing that a function with a continuous first derivative does not necessarily have to have a continuous second derivative), the question then was raised as to why a minimizing arc, or, more generally, why any arc for which the first variation is zero for every η, should possess a continuous second derivative, as is required in the derivation of Euler's equation. By the end of the 19th century, the problem of the existence of a minimizing arc had been raised, and the existence had been proved by Hilbert under certain hypotheses. Leonida Tonelli developed the so-called direct methods of the calculus of variations in order to simplify and amplify the results of Hilbert concerning the existence of minimizing arcs. Tonelli's methods

These results were applied to general situations by the metric geometry methods of Karl Menger and Herbert Busemann. Most of the remaining problems involving arcs were solved between 1910 and 1940 by such mathematicians as Oskar Bolza, Gilbert Ames Bliss, and Edward James McShane.

The fact that not every minimum problem has a solution is seen by studying a definite integral extending from 0 to 1 symbolized by I in which the integrand includes the derivative of y (see 615). In this case $0 < I < 1$ for every $y(x)$. Setting $y(x) = x^n$, $n = 1, 2 \ldots$ shows that I may be made arbitrarily close to 1. By taking $y(x)$ to be equal to x plus a sinusoidal function (see 616), it is seen that I may be made arbitrarily close to zero. There is, however, no $y(x)$ for which I is equal to zero or one.

MULTIPLE-INTEGRAL PROBLEMS

Meanwhile interest had developed in problems involving functions of two or more variables, and the derivation of Euler's equation had been extended to integrals of a more complicated form (see 617). Replacing z by $z + \lambda\zeta$, in which ζ has a role similar to that of η in the preceding problem, $\zeta = 0$ on the boundary of the region G, and proceeding as in the derivation of Euler's equation (see 610–612) results in the equation known as Euler's equation (see 618) for the multiple integral (see 617).

Early in the 19th century Carl Friedrich Gauss and William Thomson, Lord Kelvin, had observed that Laplace's equation was the Euler equation for a particular integral (see 619), as is seen by setting $f(x, y, z, p, q) = (p^2 + q^2)/2$ in the derivation of Euler's equation for the multiple integral (see 617, 618).

This fact is the formal basis for what is now known as Dirichlet's principle, which states that (subject to certain hypotheses) there is a unique function z that minimizes the integral of the sum of squares of z_x and z_y (see 619) among all differentiable functions having given boundary values and that that unique function is the solution of Laplace's equation with those boundary values.

This principle has proved to be of great importance not only in potential theory and in the theory of partial differential equations, but also in the theory of functions of a complex variable and in conformal mapping. The applications to these fields was begun by Bernhard Riemann around 1850 and important advances have been made in them since 1935 by such mathematicians as Richard Courant, Lars V. Ahlfors, Donald Clayton Spencer, Menahem Max Schiffer, Paul Roesel Garabedian and others. Bernard Riemann
Riemann simply assumed the principle but, of course, the objections that were raised concerning problems involving arcs applied to the Dirichlet principle with even greater force; the first proof of the principle was given by Hilbert in 1900.

The almost simultaneous solutions by Jesse Douglas and

$$(615)\quad \begin{cases} I=\int_0^1 \{1+[y'(x)]^2\}^{-1}\,dx \\ y(0)=0, \quad y(1)=1 \end{cases}$$

$$(616)\quad y(x)=x+n\sin n\pi x, \qquad n=1,2,\ldots$$

$$(617)\quad \begin{cases} I=\iint_G f[x,y,z(x,y),z_x(x,y),z_y(x,y)]\,dx\,dy \\ z_x=\dfrac{\partial z}{\partial x}, \quad z_y=\dfrac{\partial z}{\partial y} \end{cases}$$

$$(618)\quad \frac{\partial}{\partial x}(f_p)+\frac{\partial}{\partial y}(f_q)=f_z, \qquad p=z_x, \qquad q=z_y$$

$$(619)\quad \frac{1}{2}\iint_G (z_x^2+z_y^2)\,dx\,dy$$

$$(620)\quad f(x_1+\eta_1,\ldots,x_n+\eta_n)-f(x_1,\ldots,x_n) = \frac{1}{2}\sum_{i,j=1}^{n} a_{ij}\,\eta_i\,\eta_j+R$$

$$(621)\quad a_{ij}=\frac{\partial^2 f}{\partial x_i\,\partial x_j}$$

$$(622)\quad -\xi_1^2-\cdots-\xi_r^2+\xi_{r+1}^2+\cdots+\xi_s^2$$

Tibor Radó in 1930 of the problem of the Belgian physicist Joseph Antoine Ferdinand Plateau, *i.e.*, the proof of the existence of a minimal surface (surface of least area) bounded by a simple closed curve in space, aroused a renewed interest in variational problems for surfaces. The Plateau problem was solved for surfaces bounded by several curves and for more complicated surfaces by Douglas, Courant, and others. More general variational problems for surfaces were solved by Tonelli, McShane, Charles B. Morrey, Jr., Lamberto Cesari, A.G. Sigalov, and others between 1930 and 1957 by extending the direct methods of Tonelli; these involve considering the surfaces as points in a space in which limits are defined and using the general theorem in functional analysis that a function that is lower-semicontinuous on a compact set attains its minimum on that set. In order to apply this theorem it was found expedient to enlarge the classes of arcs or surfaces, etc., within which the minimum is sought. Unfortunately, the enlarged classes usually contain surfaces that do not possess the properties of differentiability required in the derivation of Euler's equation.

The Plateau problem

In the case of the Plateau problem the differentiability of the solutions follows from the Dirichlet principle. The differentiability of the generalized solutions of certain other problems for surfaces was proved by Morrey, and some of his results were extended in 1957 to problems in higher-dimensional spaces by Ennio De Giorgi and John Nash, Jr.

An interesting attack on problems for surfaces has been made by L.C. Young, Wendell Helms Fleming, and others through their introduction of generalized surfaces.

MORSE'S THEORY OF CRITICAL POINTS

If a function $f(P)$ is defined on an n-dimensional manifold, its behaviour near a particular point may be studied by introducing coordinates, in which case f becomes just a function of n coordinates $x_1, \ldots, x_n$. A point (*i.e.*, set of numbers $x_1, \ldots, x_n$) is a critical point of f if all its partial derivatives are zero there. If $x_1, \ldots, x_n$ is such a point, then a formal finite difference constructed with the function f equals the summation of terms plus a final term symbolized by R (see 620), in which R consists of the higher order terms; here the coefficients in the summation of terms are obtained from the second-order partial derivatives (see 621) evaluated at the point. It is known that linear combinations $\xi_1, \ldots, \xi_n$ of the η_i can be chosen so that the double sum becomes expressed in terms of the squares of the ξ_i, the indices ranging from one through r to s (in which r is zero if there are no negative terms, etc.; see 622). Moreover, the numbers r and s are independent of the coordinate system and the way the ξ_i are chosen as long as the given quadratic form (see 622) is obtained. If $s=n$, the critical point is said to be nondegenerate, in which case r is called the index.

Harold Marston Morse, a 20th-century American topologist, first proved certain inequalities between the number of critical points of a given index of a (nondegenerate) function on a manifold and the so-called Betti numbers (after the 19th-century Italian mathematician Enrico Betti) of the manifold. His greatest contribution was to generalize the notion of a nondegenerate critical point and his inequality results to situations in which the functions and spaces were too general for differentiability to be defined. Morse applied his theory to spaces the elements of which were arcs or closed curves on a manifold or surfaces in space. He was able to prove the existence of unstable minimal surfaces (*i.e.*, surfaces furnishing some critical value other than a minimum to the area) and to prove such theorems as that there exist at least three closed shortest paths on a sphere. His theory has been applied to variational problems for arcs with great success. Stephen Smale and others have found a way to apply the Morse theory to multiple integral problems. (C.B.My.)

FUNCTIONAL ANALYSIS

A broad view of functional analysis

EARLY DEVELOPMENT

The development of analysis in the 19th century led eventually to the realization that limit processes originally developed for sequences of values of a single function could usefully be applied to whole sequences of functions and, further, that individual functions of interest could be studied to advantage using an indirect technique that established the properties of such a function by considering appropriate sequences of other, and generally simpler, functions that converged to it. This approach was pioneered by Jean-Baptiste-Joseph Fourier, a French mathematician who died in 1830, and it was developed subsequently by many other mathematicians, who improved and generalized the theory of Fourier series, which Fourier's work initiated. Studies of functions using this same method of approximation also played a central role in the theory of functions of a complex variable, the systematic work of Karl Weierstrass in the 19th century being especially notable in this connection. Out of repeated applications of the technique of functional approximation there grew the gradual realization that individual functions ought to be looked at as members of broader collections or spaces of functions. By focusing attention not on a single function f in isolation but rather on an appropriate collection of functions containing f, and on the special position or defining property of f within this collection, important properties of a particular function f could in many cases be established in a more ready and transparent fashion than was otherwise possible; old proofs could be simplified, and new proofs could be attained. In such studies it was often useful to make use of expressions assigning a value to each member of a space of functions; such expressions were dubbed functionals, this term being coined in analogy with the word function, which designates a rule assigning a value to each member of a collection of numbers. The body of mathematical work growing out of the viewpoint outlined above, in which functions are studied collectively, and in which the older methods of analysis

Fourier's contribution

are applied to whole collections of functions, consequently became known as functional analysis.

At the turn of the 20th century, the work of Vito Volterra and Erik Ivar Fredholm began to underscore the utility of the functional approach and to make use of this approach in an explicit way. At about the same time, studies undertaken by David Hilbert, Erhald Schmidt, Frigyes Riesz, and others served to make plain the analogies between analytic and classical algebraic principles that emerged when collections of functions were regarded as abstract global totalities, and the value of regarding a function as a point in a space of functions became plain. This was recognized clearly by Schmidt, for example, in a 1908 study of systems containing infinitely many equations; Schmidt introduced various geometric notations and terms, which are still in use, for describing spaces of functions. At approximately the same time the foundations of modern point-set topology, originally the study of geometric properties that remain unchanged under continuous maps, were being laid by Maurice-René Fréchet, Felix Hausdorff, and Riesz. These topological studies gave an abstract and extremely general form to the basic notions of continuity and differentiability that played a central role in the older analysis, thus allowing these notions to be carried over to spaces of functions. General definitions of the type of space of functions in which the new functional methods could be applied were offered a few years later by Norbert Wiener and Stefan Banach. In 1932 Banach's *Théorie des opérations linéaires* summarized much of the most interesting work in functional analysis up to that time and inspired much of the work in functional analysis through succeeding decades. The important general class of Banach spaces take their name from him. At about the same time John von Neumann began a brilliant series of investigations into the functional analysis of Hilbert space (see below *Hilbert space; spectral analysis*), which is that particular space of functions bearing the closest geometric analogy with ordinary Euclidean space. This work, which gave an abstract, transparent, and greatly generalized form to older analyses of integral equations by Hilbert and Schmidt, soon made contact with other broad areas of algebra and classical analysis, and has led to rich subsequent developments. Von Neumann's work had also a particularly close relation to, and influence on, the mathematical apparatus of quantum physics.

LINEAR FUNCTIONAL ANALYSIS; THEORY OF DISTRIBUTIONS

Linear properties

Many important spaces of functions are linear. A collection of functions possesses this property if the sum of any two functions belongs to the same collection and if an arbitrary constant multiple of a function in the collection still belongs to the collection. For example, the sum of two continuous functions is continuous, the sum of two bounded functions is bounded, the sum of two smooth functions is smooth, etc., so that continuous functions constitute a linear space of functions, smooth functions another, bounded functions a third, etc. When a space of functions is linear, useful analogies exist between its elements and the vectors of ordinary two- and three-dimensional space. These analogies suggest many useful geometric lines of investigation, and the availability of addition and multiplication operations makes it possible to adapt many of the powerful algebraic procedures of conventional vector algebra or linear algebra to the study of function spaces. To emphasize this analogy, one often speaks of a collection of functions having the property of linearity as a linear space of functions, and of its elements as points or vectors.

Many significant methods of functional analysis grow out of this analogy. Using terminology adapted from vector algebra, a function f which is the sum of terms of the type $a_k f_k$ (see equation 623), in which $a_1, \ldots, a_n$ are numbers and $f_1, \ldots, f_n$ are functions belonging to the same space as f, is spoken of as a linear combination of $f_1, \ldots, f_n$; the expression $a_1 f_1 + \cdots + a_n f_n$ may be called the expansion of f in terms of $f_1, \ldots, f_n$. The same terms are also used in connection with infinite sums of the form $a_1 f_1 + a_2 f_2 + \cdots$, provided that these sums are convergent (*i.e.*, approach a limit) in an appropriate sense. In studying a problem set within some particular function space, it is often useful to find some particularly simple collection of functions $f_1, f_2, \ldots$ in terms of which every function may be expanded. The observation that such expansions could be useful for analysis goes back to Daniel Bernoulli and Leonhard Euler in the 18th century, who, in studying the motions of a vibrating string, found it useful to expand certain functions in terms of simpler ones. The British engineer Oliver Heaviside and many other 19th-century mathematicians showed that other similar series expansions were useful for treating a wide range of specific problems. Modern functional analysis affords a comprehensive generalization of all these earlier investigations and makes plain the relatively simple algebraic-geometric basis on which they rest.

Expansion of functions

$$(623) \qquad f = a_1 f_1 + \cdots + a_n f_n$$

$$(624) \qquad F(a_1 f_1 + a_2 f_2) = a_1 F(f_1) + a_2 F(f_2)$$

Many techniques related to the linear combination of functions are used within functional analysis. Certain important function-associated operations have the property that when applied to the sum of two functions they give a value that is the sum of the values obtained by applying the same operation to the two functions individually. Designating such an operation by the symbol F, this general property may be represented by an algebraic formula (see 624). An operation or functional having this property is said to be linear. Many of the central operations of classical analysis—as, for example, differentiation and integration—are linear: the integral of the sum of two functions in the sum of their integrals, etc. Taking an abstract and general view, functional analysis sees in the collection of all operations satisfying the condition (624) another space of objects, related in a natural way to an initial collection X of functions f. If the operations F in (624) are restricted to have numerical values, one speaks of F as a linear functional on the collection X; if the operations F have values that are themselves functions, one calls F a linear operator on X; if the values of F lie in X, F is called a linear operator in X. The collection of all linear functionals on X, the collection of all linear operators on X, and the collection of all linear operators in X, all form spaces associated with the space X in a natural way. The collection of all linear functionals on X is often called the conjugate space or dual space of X, and it is conventionally designated by the symbol X^*. The conjugate space X^* is important in functional analysis for a variety of reasons. Many operations that are defined for the elements of X carry over in a natural way to the elements of X^*. The study of X^*, and of various detailed relationships between X and X^*, can yield important information concerning X. Moreover, consideration of the dual space X^* of an artfully chosen collection X may provide the key to the solution of a problem in which X itself plays only a subsidiary role.

Schwartz's theory of distribution

The theory of distributions, introduced in the late 1940s by Laurent Schwartz, gives a famous example of the systematic use of this last observation. Schwartz begins by considering the space of all extremely smooth functions f of a real variable y that are zero for sufficiently large values of the variable y. This collection X_0 of functions is one of the smallest (*i.e.*, most restricted) yet still quite general classes of functions that can be defined. Analytically important operations, such as differentiation and integration, are easily defined for the elements of X_0; the relationship between X_0 and X_0^* allows these operations to be carried over to the very much larger space X_0^*. The elements of X_0^* are called distributions by Schwartz. Because X_0 can be regarded as a subspace of X_0^*, the elements of X_0^* have a natural interpretation as generalized functions. Schwartz's construction makes differentiation, etc., available over a wide range of nonconventional mathematical objects, and in a manner preserving all the formal properties of these operations that are central to traditional analysis. There results a considerable broadening of the differential and integral calculus, including and generalizing many of the formal extensions of calculus developed on *ad hoc* lines for specific application, notably by Heaviside and the British physicist P.A.M. Dirac. Until Schwartz's development of the theory of distributions, most of these schemes of formal calculation lacked rigorous justification and were regarded as slightly illegitimate curiosities. Distribution theory has brought these and even more powerful tools for calculation into general mathematical currency (see below *Generalized functions, or theory of distributions*).

GEOMETRIC PRINCIPLES; ANALYSIS OF LINEAR OPERATORS

As already noted, linear functional analysis aims to exploit the formal similarity that exists between addition of functions and addition of vectors in two, three, and more dimensions and, accordingly, tends to consider any collection of functions having the necessary property of linearity as an infinite-dimensional analogue of the familiar Euclidean spaces. In accordance with this fundamental point of view, a systematic attempt is made to carry as many useful geometric notions as possible over from two- and three-dimensional Euclidean space to arbitrary linear collections of functions. One notion of this kind, which has been quite successfully exploited in functional analysis, is that of convexity. A body B in two- or three-dimensional Euclidean space is convex if, and only if, the entire straight-line segment S between any two of its points belongs to the body; if B is closed, this will be the case if, and only if, the midpoint of each such segment S belongs to the body. Phrased in terms of vector algebra, this last condition amounts merely to the demand that the midpoint $(f+g)/2$ of S belongs to B whenever the endpoints f and g of S are both points of B; in this formulation, the notion of convexity generalizes immediately to any linear space of functions. This last observation suggests that many of the properties of convex bodies in two and three dimensions can be carried over to convex collections of functions within a linear space of functions; and such is indeed the case. Thus, for example, if one is given a convex body B in three-dimensional space and a point p not belonging to the body, one can always draw a plane with the point on one side of the plane and the body on the other side. If the equation of the plane is written $F(x) = c$, it follows that $F(p)$ is smaller than c, but that $F(x)$ is larger than c for each point x of the body B. This simple but basic geometric fact generalizes at once to convex collections B in linear spaces of functions, giving the so-called Hahn-Banach theorem, a theorem possessing many applications. This case will serve to illustrate the more general remark that functional analysis contains generalizations of much of the rich geometric theory of convex bodies, in which corners, shortest paths, inscribed and circumscribed bodies, cones, and so forth, are all studied to advantage. Many of the most useful inequalities belonging to the older analysis of single functions turn out to have simple geometric interpretations when they are reformulated in functional-analytic terms.

Linear operators

As has already been noted, an operation F on functions with values $F(f)$ that are themselves functions satisfying the algebraic condition (see 624) is called a linear operator. Such a linear operator may be regarded as the natural generalization, to linear spaces of functions, of the rectangular matrices of conventional finite-dimensional vector algebra. If F is a linear mapping in a space X—*i.e.*, if the values $F(f)$ of F belong to the same space X as do the functions f for which F is defined—then F is analogous not merely to a rectangular but to a square matrix; *i.e.*, to a matrix having equally many rows and columns. Matrices of this type may freely be added and multiplied; the study of their particularly interesting algebraic relationships, which in the finite dimensional case was initiated in the 19th century by Arthur Cayley of Great Britain, generalizes at once to linear operators. Given that F is a linear operator in a linear space X, the "square" of F, for example, may be defined as the transformation G specified by the formula $G(f) = F(F(f))$, and higher powers of F may be defined in analogous fashion. The elementary infinite series that expresses the nonnegative reciprocal of $1 - x$ as a sum of all integer powers of x (see 625) then generalizes in a straightforward way to linear operators,

(625) $$\frac{1}{1-x} = 1 + x + x^2 + x^3 + \cdots$$

(626) $$e^x = 1 + x + \frac{1}{2}x^2 + \frac{1}{6}x^3 + \cdots$$

(627) $$e^F = I + F + \frac{1}{2}F^2 + \frac{1}{6}F^3 + \cdots$$

(628) $$a^{t_1} a^{t_2} = a^{t_1 + t_2}$$

(629) $$e(t_1)e(t_2) = e(t_1 + t_2)$$

its generalization proving to be the key to many of those results of the early-20th-century theory of linear integral equations from which the historic development of modern functional analysis began. Other power series can also be used to define functions of a linear operator F, provided always that F acts *in* a single linear space X of functions; *i.e.*, that F is defined for each f in X and that each value $F(f)$ of F belongs to X. For example, the exponential function e^x has the power series expansion, with coefficients formed of reciprocals of factorials (see 626), which suggests the possibility of defining an operator exponential by writing a formal power series for the linear operator f with coefficients as before (see 627); here I denotes the unit, or identity, linear operator specified by the equation $I(f) = f$. This definition of an exponential function for linear operators is in fact quite useful and provides the key to several important calculations and theorems. Further extension of this same technique yields a systematic calculus of functions of linear operators.

Other analogies between collections of operators and ordinary algebra have been quite fruitful for functional analysis. To give a further example, the exponential function a^t has the property that the product of two function values evaluated at distinct points is equal to the function value evaluated at the sum of the two corresponding points (see 628). Moreover, any continuous numerical function $e(t)$ having this multiplicative property—*i.e.*, any function satisfying the condition that the product of two function values for distinct points is equivalent to the function value for the sum of the distinct points (see 629)—is necessarily expressible as an exponential function; *i.e.*, $e(t) = a^t$. This fact suggests the study of families $E(t)$ of linear operators depending on a real parameter t and satisfying the algebraic condition that is defined by the formula given as (630), namely: $E(t_1)E(t_2) = E(t_1 + t_2)$. Operator families satisfying this condition are called semigroups of linear operators; they arise in a variety of physical, mathematical, and probabilistic settings. Naturally enough, their study centres upon techniques for defining fractional powers A^t of a linear operator A and around attempts to find conditions guaranteeing that a particular semigroup $E(t)$ of linear operators must have the exponential form $E(t) = A^t$.

HILBERT SPACE; SPECTRAL ANALYSIS

In the preceding paragraphs it was stressed that many of the most fruitful ideas of functional analysis arise in analogy with algebraic and geometric notions belonging to the vector analysis and the geometry of two- and three-dimensional Euclidean space. These analogies become most compelling if there is imposed upon the spaces of functions a condition that plays a fundamental role in

(630) $$E(t_1)E(t_2) = E(t_1 + t_2)$$

(631) $$|f+g|^2 = |f|^2 + |g|^2 - 2|f|\,|g| \cos\theta$$

(632) $$[F(f), g] = [f, F(g)]$$

(633) $$g(x) = \frac{1}{\sqrt{2\pi}} \int_{-\infty}^{+\infty} f(y) e^{ixy}\, dy$$

Euclidean geometry: namely, the relation contained in Pythagoras' theorem. For easy generalization it is useful to state Pythagoras' relationship in the following slightly unconventional way: the sum of the squares of the lengths of the diagonals of a parallelogram is equal to twice the sum of the squares of the length of its sides. A linear space of functions in which every parallelogram has this property is called a Hilbert space, in honour of Hilbert, whose penetrating investigations of integral equations in certain particular spaces of this kind influenced the subsequent development of formal functional analysis in a particularly profound way. For such spaces it may be shown that the Pythagoras principle allows many other familiar geometric facts to be derived. For example, one can define a notion of the angle between two vectors in such a way as to preserve all the ordinary geometric properties of angles. This is done by analogy with the law of cosines of Euclidean trigonometry, according to which the square of the length of the vector sum of two functions is equal to the sum of the squares of the lengths of the two vectors taken separately minus a term equal to twice the product of the lengths of the vectors multiplied by the cosine of the angle θ between them (see 631). The geometrically significant expression $|f|\,|g|\cos\theta$, which has particularly simple algebraic properties, and which plays a fundamental role in geometric investigations of Hilbert space, is then called the inner product of the vectors f and g and is often designated by the symbol (f, g).

Relation of Pythagoras' theorem to Hilbert space

In analogy with ordinary geometry, a linear transformation R in a Hilbert space is called a rotation if it preserves lengths; *i.e.*, if the length of the vector $R(f)$ is in every case the same as the length of the vector f. In Hilbert space, rotations and other related basic geometric transformations continue to have many of the familiar properties possessed by similar transformations in ordinary Euclidean two- and three-dimensional space. Orthogonal (mutually perpendicular) sequences $f_1, f_2, f_3, \ldots$ of functions in Hilbert space—that is, sequences of functions for which the inner product (f_i, f_j) is equal to zero whenever the indices i and j are different—appear as the geometric analogue of sets of mutually perpendicular axes in ordinary Euclidean space. The process of expanding a function as a linear combination of such vectors is then seen to be closely analogous to the geometric decomposition of a vector into components directed along several mutually orthogonal axes; this gives a transparent geometric meaning to the expansion into sines and cosines introduced by Fourier.

In Hilbert space it is possible to distinguish a class of linear operators, the study of which constitutes one of the most successful branches of the whole of functional analysis. A linear operator F in Hilbert space is said to be self-adjoint if it satisfies the simple algebraic condition that identifies two inner products, one with the left-hand element being the effect of the linear operator x operating upon a vector and one being an inner product in which a right-hand number is the effect of the linear operator f operating upon a second vector (see 632).

Self-adjoint linear operators

Given a bounded function $m(x)$, the mapping, which sends each function $f(x)$ into the product function $m(x)f(x)$, is linear; a mapping M of this particularly simple kind is called a multiplication operator. Multiplication operators are the simplest general type of linear operator, self-adjoint (see 632). The fundamental spectral theorem of Hilbert and von Neumann asserts that, given any self-adjoint linear operator in Hilbert space, one can always find a rotation R of the Hilbert space and a multiplication operator M such that $R(F(f)) = M(R(f))$ for each vector f of the Hilbert space; this means that in the rotated axes defined by the rotation, R, F is expressed, in the simplest possible way, as an operation of multiplication. Many other useful properties of self-adjoint linear operators in Hilbert space follow from this basic theorem, and, generally speaking, the spectral theorem tends to reduce the study of a particular self-adjoint operator F to the problem of finding the rotation R that allows F to be expressed as a multiplication. Many of the most interesting linear transformations of classical analysis turn out to be rotations of this type. This observation covers not only Fourier's initial sine-cosine series expansion and all the Sturm-Liouville generalizations of this expansion, but also many related integral expansions, of which the most famous is the Fourier integral, which expresses a rotated version $g = R(f)$ of an initially given function f by the formula that expresses g as a definite integral extended over the entire real line, the integrand being the product of f and an exponential function, multiplied by an appropriate normalizing factor (see 633).

Linear operators satisfying the self-adjointness condition (see 632) are of common occurrence in classical mathematical physics, wherein the self-adjointness condition is often a consequence of some underlying law of energy conservation. They also are of fundamental importance in quantum theory, in which the self-adjointness condition appears as an assumption basic to the physical interpretation of the theory.

The spectacular conceptual and computational simplifications afforded in the study of self-adjoint operators by the spectral theorem has led to a long series of efforts to generalize this theorem to linear operators F not satisfying the basic condition of self-adjointness (see 632). Unfortunately, these efforts, in which the works of Nelson Dunford and Ciprian Foiaş have featured prominently, have been successful only in part. The fact is that general linear operators are more complex than self-adjoint operators, even if attention is restricted to operators acting in Hilbert space. Moreover, phenomena appear in the study of general operators in Hilbert space that have no analogue in the more elementary algebraic theory of finite square matrices acting in spaces of vectors. In spite of this, it has been possible to find classes of non-self-adjoint operators having many properties in common with multiplication operators and with other special classes of linear operators of simple structure for which calculation is easy.

LINEARIZATION AS A METHOD; ERGODIC THEORY, CLASSICAL AND GENERALIZED HARMONIC ANALYSIS

As has been noted, linear functional analysis makes systematic use of the possibility of expressing one function as a linear combination of others, thereby attaining great simplifications in the problems that it studies. Problems for which this is not possible—*i.e.*, cases in which it is necessary to deal with sets of points or of functions within which an operation of addition is not available in any useful way—are normally much more complicated. When problems of this kind are attacked, it is generally necessary to have recourse to the elaborate tools of global (or algebraic) topology, and, even so, the attack may be unsuccessful. Global topological methods began to be used extensively in functional analysis around 1960, though work in the 1930s by the mathematicians Juliusz Schauder and Jean Leray and by the topologist Marston Morse introduced some basic techniques.

The use of global topological methods in combination with more conventional techniques of functional analysis defines what has come to be called nonlinear functional analysis (see below). The relative simplicity of linear spaces suggests, however, that whenever it is possible to relate a linear space to an object to be studied, even if this object is initially nonlinear, analysis of the linear space may allow interesting properties of the original object to be established. This technique, which may be called linearization, has been applied successfully in a great variety of rather important investigations. Ergodic theory, which grew originally out of statistical mechanics (that is, out of the statistical analysis of physical systems containing a large number of particles of interest), constitutes an important instance of this general remark.

Ergodic theory

If at a given instant one records the momentary position and velocity of each particle in a system of particles, one obtains a multidimensional vector υ; υ is called the momentary state of the system, and the collection of all relevant vectors υ is called the system's phase space. It follows from the laws of Newtonian mechanics that after t seconds have elapsed a system initially in a state υ will find itself in a state $\varphi_t(\upsilon)$, in which the mapping φ_t is determined by the details of the forces that each particle exerts on all the others. The Newtonian law of energy conservation implies that even if the time parameter t is allowed to vary, all the states $\varphi_t(v)$ will lie on some single energy surface. Given this fact, detailed investigation of the overall motion of a system will naturally focus on one single such surface and on the transformations $\varphi_t(v)$, all of which map each point of such a surface to some other point of the same surface. These energy surfaces are, however, described by complicated equations and are in consequence highly curved, nonlinear objects. This characteristic makes direct study of the transformations φ_t difficult. Using the technique of linearization described above, some of these difficulties may be alleviated, as follows.

An appropriate linear space of functions $f(v)$, defined for all the points v of an energy space, is set up, and the nonlinear maps φ_t are used to define linear maps F_t in this space of functions; F_t is defined simply by specifying that $F_t(f)$ is to be the function g given by the formula in which the value of g at v is equal to the function f evaluated at a nonlinear map of the argument v (see 634). A suitable choice of functions f will yield a Hilbert space within which the maps F_t turn out to have properties that allow them to be studied using the Hilbert space spectral theorem mentioned in the preceding section. This makes it possible to establish a number of interesting facts concerning the nonlinear maps φ_t. The method sketched above has been used in a series of investigations stretching from the 1930s to the present day, in which the names von Neumann, Birkhoff, Hopf, Kolmogorov, Sinai, Arnold, and Ohrenstein feature prominently. These investigations have elucidated many properties of nonlinear mappings significant for mechanics, probability theory, and geometry.

A closely related method has played a central role in the elucidation of important algebraic problems. In abstract algebra, a group is a collection of elements x, y, etc., any two of which may be multiplied to give a product xy, any one of which has an inverse x^{-1} satisfying $x^{-1}(xy)=y$ and $(yx)x^{-1}=y$. If a group is given, the linear space of all functions f on the group may be considered, and for each group element x a linear mapping F_x can be defined by requiring that $F_x(f)$ be the function g specified by the simple formula identifying the function value of g with the function value of f, the argument of the former being y, the argument of the latter being the group product yx (see 635). If appropriate conditions are imposed upon the functions f, a Hilbert space of functions will result; each of the mappings F_x will then be a linear transformation to which the spectral theorem can be seen to apply. This theorem then implies that one can find functions called group characters and irreducible representation coefficients, related to the mappings F_x in particularly simple ways. The line of reasoning just described was initiated by Ferdinand Georg Frobenius and Issai Schur, who analyzed the properties of finite groups using this method. The gradual development of functional analytic technique subsequently made it possible to extend Schur's techniques to important groups containing infinitely many elements, including the groups of three-dimensional and of higher-dimensional rotations, and of the Lorentz group, which is important in all relativistic physical theories. In this connection the work of Claus Hugo Hermann Weyl, I.M. Gel'fand, M.A. Naimark, and Harish-Chandra has been particularly important.

Because of the close correspondence (see 635) between the mappings F_x and the fundamental group multiplication operation yx, group characters and irreducible representation coefficients are most useful for analyzing the algebraic structure of a group. They inevitably play a central role in the understanding of any system of functions having a given group of symmetries. Such function systems occur in crystallography, in the study of sound and electromagnetic waves, and in the quantum theory of nuclear, atomic, and molecular energy levels and scattering processes.

(634) $g(v)=f[\varphi_t(v)]$

(635) $g(y)=f(yx)$

(636) $S(f)=F(f)+G(f)$

(637) $P(f)=F[G(f)]$

(638) $$\begin{cases}(F+G)+H=F+(G+H)\\ F(GH)=(FG)H\\ F(G+H)=FG+FH\end{cases}$$

FUNCTIONAL ALGEBRA

If a linear space of functions is given, and if F and G are both linear operators acting in this space, then F and G can be added and can be multiplied together. The sum of F and G is the linear operator S defined by the formula $S(f)=F(f)+G(f)$ (636). The product of F and G is the linear operator P defined by the formula $P(f)=F[G(f)]$ (637). The sum of F and G is customarily designated by $F+G$, and the product of F and G by FG.

The algebraic combinations of linear operators (see 636, 637) have many of the formal properties that are familiar from ordinary algebra; for example, the identities known as the laws of associativity for addition and multiplication as well as the distributive law (see 638) all hold. This observation suggests that the methods of algebra can fruitfully be applied to the study of collections of linear operators. This is indeed the case; the subject area that arises when algebraic techniques are combined with the methods of functional analysis is called functional algebra.

Gel'fand's contribution

Functional algebra began to develop rapidly after 1941, in which year a famous paper of Gel'fand demonstrated that important earlier work of Wiener on Fourier series could be conceptually simplified by reformulating it in algebraic terms, and that some of the methods of functional analysis could be fruitfully combined with abstract algebraic arguments and with reasonings adapted from the classical theory of functions of a complex variable. The theory initiated by Gel'fand subsequently achieved many points of contact with profound questions in classical analysis.

A brilliant series of papers by von Neumann and F.J. Murray led at about the same time to the development of yet another major branch of functional algebra. Von Neumann and Murray considered algebras of operators in Hilbert space; that is, sets V of linear operators having the property that $F+G$, FG, and cF all belong to V whenever F and G belong to G (c is an arbitrary numerical constant). A linear operator F in Hilbert space can always be written as $F=H_1+iH_2$, in which H_1 and H_2 are self-adjoint and i is the square root of -1; the operator F^*, which is called the adjoint of F, is then related to F in much the same way that the complex conjugate $\bar{z}$ of a complex number z is related to z.

It had been known for some time that *-closed algebras V of finite square matrices—that is, algebras having the property that F^* is a member of V whenever F is a member of V—had a particularly simple structure, and von Neumann and Murray set out to generalize this structural fact to *-closed algebras of operators in Hilbert space. The class of algebras that these two studied are currently known either as W^*-algebras or as von Neumann algebras.

In the von Neumann-Murray theory, a far-reaching generalization of the Hilbert space spectral theorem may be established, according to which a general W^*-algebra is decomposable into a family of simpler W^*-algebras, which were called factors by von Neumann and Murray. The simplest factors are finite or infinite matrix algebras. More complex factors also exist, and these are related in various interesting ways to algebraic structures such as infinite discrete groups, the decomposition of a general W^*-algebra into factors providing a quite useful tool for the treatment of a number of the main properties of group characters and irreducible representation coefficients.

NONLINEAR FUNCTIONAL ANALYSIS

As has been noted above, nonlinear functional analysis attempts to combine the global methods of topology with the approximation techniques used in linear functional analysis, thereby making it possible to study systems of functions in which the simplifications afforded by linearity are not available. This part of functional analysis was initiated in the late 1920s by Schauder, who showed that the Brouwer fixed-point theorem of topology could be generalized to linear functional spaces. Subsequent work extended other basic theorems of topology to linear functional spaces and applied these principles to the study of various interesting classes of partial differential equations, including the equations of fluid flow. This work revealed the topological basis underlying several subtle existence theorems of classical analysis.

At about the same time Morse established some important results concerning the behaviour of smooth functions on curved surfaces, showing that the number of critical points of such a function (*i.e.,* the number of points at which the rate of change of the function in every direction is zero) is closely related to certain topological properties of the surface. Morse himself extended his results from finite-dimensional surfaces to spaces of curves; the suggestion, implicit in this pioneering work, that the topology of curved functional spaces ought to be studied, lay dormant for 20 years, probably because adequate study tools were not available. In the late 1950s, however, the leads left by Morse began to be pursued. Subsequently, the area of contact between global topology and functional analysis has broadened significantly, topology having contributed to the solution of nonlinear analytic problems, and the study of certain linear and nonlinear functional spaces having provided keys to questions in pure topology. (J.T.Sc.)

Generalized functions, or theory of distributions

In the second half of the 19th century mathematical analysts had raised their sights beyond the relatively orderly world of analytic functions—that is, functions with convergent Taylor expansions (after the English mathematician Brook Taylor)—and had begun to study and handle nonanalytic and even nondifferentiable functions. This led to the discovery of various kinds of pathological behaviour, or behaviour that was unfamiliar to the classically trained intuition. The complexity of the picture, in the theory of functions of real variables, was further compounded with the appearance of the integration theory formulated by Henri-Léon Lebesgue, one of the great events in the history of mathematics. Standard ingredients of Lebesgue's theory are measurable and integrable functions and sets, which can exhibit irregularities of a degree and of a nature unknown until then. The Lebesgue theory had a strong influence on the investigation of integral equations. The space $\mathfrak{L}^2$—the space of (Lebesgue) square integrable functions—was recognized by Hilbert to be the right framework for the study of many problems in the calculus of variations. What is now called its Hilbert space structure was described and exploited, notably by Hilbert and by Riesz, to unify and reinterpret earlier results on integral equations, among them the pioneering work of Fredholm, in which ideas from finite-dimensional linear algebra had been transposed with unexpected success.

Lebesgue's integration theory

In 1894, quite off the mainstream of research in pure mathematics, Heaviside introduced his symbolic calculus to help solve the ordinary differential equations that arise in the theory of electrical circuits. His suggestion was simple and daring: replace the differentiation operator d/dx by the variable p, which amounts to replacing the differential equation under study, namely, an nth order linear inhomogeneous equation (see 639), by a multiplicative equation (see 640). Solve the latter for $\hat{y}(p)$ by division and revert, possibly with the help of appropriate tables of correspondences, from the symbolic solution $\hat{y}(p)$ to the actual solution $y(x)$. Although highly successful from the pragmatic viewpoint, Heaviside's calculus remained unexplained for several decades. Among other features it entailed the differentiation of nondifferentiable functions, such as the so-called Heaviside function $Y(x)$ with a unit step at the origin (see 641).

The need to extend the operation of differentiation beyond its classical limitations is also strongly felt in pure mathematics, particularly in the theory of partial differential equations. One of the fundamental concepts of functional analysis, that of duality and of linear functionals, led, around 1930, to the introduction of weak derivatives. Two functions f and φ are considered with real or complex values, defined and continuously differentiable on the real line $\mathfrak{R}$. Furthermore, it is assumed that φ vanishes identically outside some finite interval. The classical formula of integration by parts leads to an equality in integrals involving the functions f and φ and their derivatives (see 642). It is clear that the right-hand side of this equality makes sense even when f is not differentiable, for instance when f is the Heaviside function (see 641). When $f = Y$ the value of the right-hand side is $\varphi(0)$, whereas the left-hand side makes no sense at all: if the derivative of Y is to have a reasonable meaning, it must vanish for all $x \neq 0$. But then integration over the set consisting of a single point, $x = 0$, if understood in Lebesgue's sense, can only yield zero, not $\varphi(0)$. In order to resolve this apparent paradox and to extend the concept of derivative, the expressions that continue to make sense when applied to nondifferentiable functions (in the classical sense), such as the right-hand side in the integration by parts (see 642), are retained. The latter is viewed as a linear functional in φ, which varies in the class C_c^1 of once continuously differentiable functions on the real line, vanishing outside a finite interval. It is precisely this functional that is called the weak derivative of f. Now, if f happens to be continuously differentiable (in the classical sense), its weak derivative will coincide with the integration of $\varphi f'$, in other words, with the integration of φ with respect to the density $f'(x)dx$, a functional of φ that, from now on, shall be identified to the concept of f' itself, the classical derivative of f. As for integration by parts (see 642), it becomes a special identity, valid when f' is continuous or, more generally, locally integrable.

Weak derivatives

(639) $$y^{(n)} + a_1 y^{(n-1)} + \cdots + a_n y = f(x)$$

(640) $$(p^n + a_1 p^{n-1} + \cdots + a_n)\,\hat{y}(p) = \hat{f}(p)$$

(641) $$Y(x) = 1 \text{ for } x > 0, \qquad Y(x) = 0 \text{ for } x \leq 0$$

(642) $$\int_{-\infty}^{+\infty} f'(x)\varphi(x)dx = -\int_{-\infty}^{+\infty} f(x)\varphi'(x)dx$$

(643) $$\int_{-\infty}^{+\infty} \varphi(x)\delta(x)dx = \int_{-\infty}^{+\infty} \varphi(0)\delta(x)dx = \varphi(0)$$

(644) $$\varphi(0) = \int_{-\infty}^{+\infty} \varphi(x)\delta(x)dx = \int_{-\infty}^{+\infty} Y'(x)\varphi(x)dx$$

(645) $$\int \delta'(x)\varphi(x)dx = -\int \delta(x)\varphi'(x)dx = -\varphi'(0)$$

(646) $$\delta = \lim_{y\to+0} \frac{1}{2\pi i}\left\{\frac{1}{x-iy} - \frac{1}{x+iy}\right\}$$

It is not possible here to give an account of all the currents and crosscurrents that eventually culminated in the present-day formulation of the theory of generalized functions, from the work of Jacques Hadamard on the Cauchy problem (see above), which goes back to World War I, to that of Torsten Carleman, Arne Beurling, and especially of Salomon Bochner, just before and after World War II. A contribution particularly relevant to the present discussion, however, is that of the physicists, foremost among them Dirac, in their efforts to create the mathematical tools required by the development of quantum field theory. Dirac introduced in 1925, and systematically used thereafter, the mathematical object that was soon to be called Dirac's function and to be defined as a function $\delta(x)$ equal to 0 for all points $x \neq 0$ and to $+\infty$ at $x = 0$, the integral of which, moreover, is equal to +1. Though such a definition is unacceptable, that of the associated functional, which to every continuous function φ assigns

Dirac's function

the number $\varphi(0)$ (see 643), is unobjectionable. As a matter of fact, δ turns out to be an object that rigorous mathematicians had been using for quite a while, for instance in the theory of summation of Fourier series, as the limit of sequences of true functions, the limit of which was never explicitly written down. Dirac's δ also entered into Heaviside's symbolic calculus: it is the function having a symbolic transform equal to the constant one. And returning to the earlier consideration of the weak derivative of Heaviside's function, and momentarily adopting the physicist's notation (see 644), it is seen that $Y' = \delta$: the weak derivative of Heaviside's function is Dirac's function or, rather, as it is now called, Dirac's distribution.

There is no reason not to repeat the procedure of weak differentiation and apply it to δ itself. Again in physicists' notation, an integral identity can be obtained (see 645). In mathematical language this simply means that δ' is the functional that, to every continuously differentiable function φ, assigns the number $-\varphi'(0)$. If one wishes to iterate this procedure and define the mth derivative of δ for any $m = 1, 2, \ldots$, one must evaluate the relevant functionals on functions φ, the degree of differentiability of which accordingly increases. Finally, it is convenient to use, as test-functions, the infinitely differentiable (or C^∞) functions. Thus, $\delta^{(m)}$ will be the functional that to every $\varphi \in C^\infty$ assigns the value $(-1)^{(m)}\varphi^{(m)}(0)$.

Laurent Schwartz's idea (in 1947) was to give a unified interpretation of all the generalized functions that had infiltrated analysis as (continuous) linear functionals on the space C_c^∞ of infinitely differentiable functions vanishing outside compact sets. He provided a systematic and rigorous description, entirely based on abstract functional analysis and on duality. It is noteworthy that such an approach had a precedent, in the presentation by André Weil of the integration of locally compact groups: there, Radon measures on the group G are introduced and handled as continuous linear functionals on the space $C_c^0(G)$ of the continuous functions in G that vanish outside some compact subset. Because of the demands of differentiability in distribution theory, the spaces of test-functions and their duals are somewhat more complicated. This has led to extensive studies of topological vector spaces beyond the familiar categories of Hilbert and Banach spaces, studies that, in turn, have provided useful new insights in some areas of analysis proper, such as partial differential equations or functions of several complex variables. Schwartz's ideas can be applied to many other spaces of test-functions beside C_c^∞, as he himself and others have shown; numerous examples can be found.

The Schwartz procedure is rather unsatisfactory if the analytic functions (on real space) are to be taken as test-functions, an action desirable in order to increase the pool of generalized functions: because analytic functions are fewer than C^∞ functions, the linear functionals on the space of the former are more numerous than those on C_c^∞. Such an increase of the pool is permitted when the functions intervening in the problem under consideration, for example the coefficients of a partial differential equation, are analytic. It was noted some time ago (in particular, by theoretical physicists) that many important distributions could be regarded as jumps across the real line of holomorphic functions of nonreal z. The simplest example is Dirac's δ expressed in terms of a limit (see 646), which means that the integration of the function under the limit sign, with respect to $\varphi(x)dx$ with arbitrary $\varphi \in C_c^\infty$, converges to $\varphi(0)$. Observations such as these were developed and systematized by Mikio Sato and others, resulting in the theory of hyperfunctions, which is based not on functional analysis but on cohomology of sheaves and which appears to be the right framework for the treatment of differential problems within the (real) analytic category. The term sheaf involves the notion of functions or distributions defined only locally, while cohomology involves patching local distributions together to create a genuine distribution of the type described above. (F.Tr.)

Theory of hyperfunctions

BIBLIOGRAPHY

Real analysis: The history of the calculus is well covered in OTTO TOEPLITZ, *The Calculus: A Genetic Approach* (1963; originally published in German, 1949); and CARL B. BOYER, *The Concepts of the Calculus* (1949, reprinted as *The History of the Calculus and Its Conceptual Development* (1959). Good introductions may be found in RICHARD COURANT and HERBERT ROBBINS, *What Is Mathematics?* (1941, reissued 1980); and IAN STEWART, *The Problems of Mathematics* (1987). Many excellent texts at all levels of difficulty are available. Two interesting examples are SHERMAN K. STEIN, *Calculus in the First Three Dimensions* (1967); and MORRIS KLINE, *Calculus: An Intuitive and Physical Approach,* 2nd ed. (1977). For modern theories of measure and integration, the following may be consulted: STANISŁAW SAKS, *Theory of the Integral,* trans. from Polish, 2nd rev. ed. (1937, reprinted 1964); ANGUS E. TAYLOR, *General Theory of Functions and Integration* (1965, reprinted 1985); and EDGAR ASPLUND and LUTZ BUNGART, *A First Course in Integration* (1966). These all require a good foundation in calculus. Additional references include A.N. KOLMOGOROV and S.V. FOMIN, *Introductory Real Analysis,* rev. ed. (1970; originally published in Russian, 2 vol., 1954–60); M.E. MUNROE, *Calculus* (1970), and *Introductory Real Analysis* (1965); H.L. ROYDEN, *Real Analysis,* 3rd ed. (1988); WALTER RUDIN, *Principles of Mathematical Analysis,* 3rd ed. (1976); G.H. HARDY, *A Course of Pure Mathematics,* 10th ed. (1952, reprinted 1975); and ANGUS E. TAYLOR and W. ROBERT MANN, *Advanced Calculus,* 3rd ed. (1983).

General references to the elements of the theory of convergent series may be found in any book of calculus. More advanced texts include TOMLINSON FORT, *Infinite Series* (1930); THOMAS J. I'A. BROMWICH, *An Introduction to the Theory of Infinite Series,* 2nd ed. rev. (1926, reprinted 1965); KONRAD KNOPP, *Theory and Application of Infinite Series,* 2nd ed. (1951, reissued 1971; originally published in German, 2nd enlarged ed., 1924), containing a wealth of material; and I.I. HIRSCHMAN, *Infinite Series* (1962, reprinted 1978). Also useful are GODFREY H. HARDY, *Divergent Series* (1949, reprinted 1973); H.R. PITT, *Tauberian Theorems* (1958); and, for summability of integrals and related topics, K. CHANDRASEKHARAN and S. MINAKSHISUNDARAM, *Typical Means* (1952).

The following works concern vector and tensor analysis. Textbooks on the algebra of vectors include, in approximate order from elementary to advanced, DANIEL ZELINSKY, *A First Course in Linear Algebra,* 2nd ed. (1973); DANIEL T. FINKBEINER II, *Introduction to Matrices and Linear Transformations,* 3rd ed. (1978); KENNETH HOFFMAN and RAY KUNZE, *Linear Algebra,* 2nd ed. (1971); PAUL R. HALMOS, *Finite-Dimensional Vector Spaces,* 2nd ed. (1958, reprinted 1974); and NATHAN JACOBSON, *Lectures in Abstract Algebra,* vol. 2, *Linear Algebra* (1953, reprinted 1975). Vector analysis is examined by LOUIS BRAND, *Vector and Tensor Analysis* (1947); HARRY LASS, *Vector and Tensor Analysis* (1950); I.S. SOKOLNIKOFF and R.M. REDHEFFER, *Mathematics of Physics and Modern Engineering,* 2nd ed. (1966); and S. SIMONS, *Vector Analysis for Mathematicians, Scientists, and Engineers,* 2nd ed. (1970). CLAUDE CHEVALLEY, *The Construction and Study of Certain Important Algebras* (1955); and A.I. BORISENKO and I.E. TARAPOV, *Vector and Tensor Analysis with Applications,* rev. ed. (1968, reissued 1979; originally published in Russian, 3rd ed., 1966), are works that may be consulted by the reader interested in tensor algebra. References on tensor analysis and its applications include HENRY D. BLOCK, *Introduction to Tensor Analysis* (1962); D.F. LAWDEN, *An Introduction to Tensor Calculus, Relativity, and Cosmology,* 3rd ed. (1982); I.S. SOKOLNIKOFF, *Tensor Analysis: Theory and Applications to Geometry and Mechanics of Continua,* 2nd ed. (1964); and LÉON BRILLOUIN, *Tensors in Mechanics and Elasticity* (1964; originally published in French, 1938). See also JERROLD E. MARSDEN and ANTHONY J. TROMBA, *Vector Calculus,* 3rd ed. (1988). (Hy.K./A.Zy./C.L.F./D.T.F./Ed.)

Complex analysis: The reader interested in the foundations of the subject and the Cauchy theory may consult LARS V. AHLFORS, *Complex Analysis,* 3rd ed. (1979); E.T. COPSON, *An Introduction to the Theory of Functions of a Complex Variable* (1935, reprinted 1972); EINAR HILLE, *Analytic Function Theory,* 2 vol. (1959–62, reprinted 1977–82); KONRAD KNOPP, *Theory of Functions,* 2 vol. (1945–47; originally published in German, vol. 1, 5th ed., 1937, and vol. 2, 4th ed., 1931); ZEEV NEHARI, *Conformal Mapping* (1952, reissued 1975); E.C. TITCHMARSH, *The Theory of Functions,* 2nd ed. (1939, reissued 1975); and E.T. WHITTAKER and G.N. WATSON, *A Course of Modern Analysis,* 4th ed. (1927, reissued 1979).

Elliptic functions and related topics are discussed in FRANK BOWMAN, *Introduction to Elliptic Functions, with Applications* (1953, reissued 1961); PAUL F. BYRD and MORRIS D. FRIEDMAN, *Handbook of Elliptic Integrals for Engineers and Scientists,* 2nd ed., rev. (1971); and A. FLETCHER *et al., An Index of Mathematical Tables,* 2nd ed. (1962).

Classic works dealing with the theory of functions of several complex variables and related subjects include ROBERT C. GUNNING and HUGO ROSSI, *Analytic Functions of Several Complex*

Variables (1965), containing an extensive bibliography; LARS HÖRMANDER, *An Introduction to Complex Analysis in Several Variables,* 2nd ed. (1979); RAGHAVAN NARASIMHAN, *Introduction to the Theory of Analytic Spaces* (1966); and KIYOSHI OKA, *Collected Papers,* rev. ed. edited by R. REMMERT (1984; originally published in French, 1961). (K.Iw./R.Na./Ed.)

Differential equations: A good elementary introduction to the theory of ordinary differential equations is WALTER LEIGHTON, *A First Course in Ordinary Differential Equations,* 5th ed. (1981). The best accounts of the classical theory are contained in EARL A. CODDINGTON and NORMAN LEVINSON, *Theory of Ordinary Differential Equations* (1955, reprinted 1984); PHILIP HARTMAN, *Ordinary Differential Equations* (1964, reprinted 1982); and EINAR HILLE, *Lectures on Ordinary Differential Equations* (1968). The qualitative theory is discussed in V.V. NEMYTSKII and V.V. STEPANOV, *Qualitative Theory of Differential Equations* (1960, reprinted 1989; originally published in Russian, 1949). The theory of differential equations in Banach spaces is treated in HENRI CARTAN, *Differential Calculus* (1971; originally published in French, 1967). See also ROGER C. MCCANN, *Introduction to Ordinary Differential Equations* (1982).

Elementary accounts of partial differential equations, especially of the equations of mathematical physics, and of techniques of solving them may be found in ARNOLD SOMMERFELD, *Partial Differential Equations in Physics* (1949, reissued 1967; originally published in German, 2nd ed., 1947); and IAN N. SNEDDON, *Elements of Partial Differential Equations* (1957). The classical theory is treated fully in I.G. PETROVSKY, *Lectures on Partial Differential Equations* (1954, reissued 1966; originally published in Russian, 1950); BERNARD EPSTEIN, *Partial Differential Equations: An Introduction* (1962, reprinted 1975); and PAUL R. GARABEDIAN, *Partial Differential Equations,* 2nd ed. (1986). Finite-difference methods of obtaining approximate solutions are contained in GEORGE E. FORSYTHE and WOLFGANG R. WASOW, *Finite-Difference Methods for Partial Differential Equations* (1960). DOROTHY L. BERNSTEIN, *Existence Theorems in Partial Differential Equations* (1950, reissued 1965), gives a complete account of existence and uniqueness theorems. For an introduction to the abstract theory, see AVNER FRIEDMAN, *Partial Differential Equations* (1969, reprinted 1976); and ROBERT W. CARROLL, *Abstract Methods in Partial Differential Equations* (1969).

The reader interested in dynamical systems on manifolds can obtain additional background on manifolds from SHLOMO STERNBERG, *Lectures on Differential Geometry,* 2nd ed. (1983); SERGE LANG, *Differential Manifolds* (1972, reissued 1985), a very basic book; and MICHAEL SPIVAK, *Calculus on Manifolds: A Modern Approach to Classical Theorems of Advanced Calculus* (1965), an especially readable elementary work. Works on the mathematics of chaos include JAMES GLEICK, *Chaos: Making a New Science* (1987); and IAN STEWART, *Does God Play Dice?* (1989). For more information on ordinary differential equations, in addition to the works mentioned above, see WITOLD HUREWICZ, *Lectures on Ordinary Differential Equations* (1958, reissued 1970), a highly recommended and less-imposing book than most on this subject; and SOLOMON LEFSHETZ, *Differential Equations: Geometric Theory,* 2nd ed. (1963, reprinted 1977), which discusses structural stability and the van der Pol equation. For the mathematics of electrical circuits, see CHARLES A. DESOER and ERNEST S. KUH, *Basic Circuit Theory* (1969). GERARD DEBREU, *Theory of Value* (1959, reissued 1979), gives a good background in mathematical economics. An excellent standard text with a traditional view is HERBERT GOLDSTEIN, *Classical Mechanics,* 2nd ed. (1980). Other approaches are found in LYNN H. LOOMIS and SHLOMO STERNBERG, *Advanced Calculus,* rev. ed. (1990); RALPH ABRAHAM and JERROLD E. MARSDEN, *Foundations of Mechanics,* 2nd ed. rev. and enlarged (1978, reprinted 1987); and V.I. ARNOLD and A. AVEZ, *Ergodic Problems of Classical Mechanics* (1968, reprinted 1988; originally published in French, 1967).

Classical potential theory is examined in a number of works. WOLFGANG J. STERNBERG and TURNER L. SMITH, *The Theory of Potential and Spherical Harmonics,* 2nd ed. (1946), is an elementary work. OLIVER DIMON KELLOGG, *Foundations of Potential Theory* (1929, reprinted 1970), is more advanced. GRIFFITH CONRAD EVANS, *The Logarithmic Potential, Discontinuous Dirichlet and Neumann Problems* (1927); and L.L. HELMS, *Introduction to Potential Theory* (1969, reprinted 1975), use modern integration theory. MASATSUGU TSUJI, *Potential Theory in Modern Function Theory,* 2nd ed. (1975), deals with applications. For modern developments in potential theory, see MARCEL BRELOT, *Lectures on Potential Theory,* expanded ed. (1967), and *On Topologies and Boundaries in Potential Theory* (1971); PAUL A. MEYER, *Probability and Potentials* (1966; originally published in French, 1966); R.M. BLUMENTHAL and R.K. GETOOR, *Markov Processes and Potential Theory* (1968); and JOHN WERMER, *Potential Theory,* 2nd ed. (1981). (I.N.S./S.Sm./Ed.)

Special functions: In addition to the many works on various aspects of analysis that contain discussions of special functions, there are also works devoted entirely to special functions. MILTON ABRAMOWITZ and IRENE A. STEGUN (eds.), *Handbook of Mathematical Functions, with Formulas, Graphs, and Mathematical Tables* (1964, reissued 1972), is a large handbook covering many special functions, statements of mathematical properties, bibliographies, and other information. A very extensive treatise is BATEMAN MANUSCRIPT PROJECT, *Higher Transcendental Functions,* ed. by ARTHUR ERDÉLY, 3 vol. (1953–55, reprinted 1981). IAN N. SNEDDON, *Special Functions of Mathematical Physics and Chemistry,* 3rd ed. (1980), contains a good treatment of special functions. For spherical harmonic functions, see T.M. MACROBERT, *Spherical Harmonics,* 3rd ed. rev. (1967). There are also many works entirely devoted to one or another particular special function. (Ed.)

Fourier analysis: Fourier series and related topics are discussed in G.H. HARDY and W.W. ROGOSINSKI, *Fourier Series,* 3rd ed. (1956, reissued 1965); ANTONI ZYGMUND, *Trigonometric Series,* 2nd ed., 2 vol. (1959, reissued 1988); SALOMON BOCHNER, *Harmonic Analysis and the Theory of Probability* (1955); E.C. TITCHMARSH, *Introduction to the Theory of Fourier Integrals,* 3rd ed. (1986); NORBERT WIENER, *The Fourier Integral and Certain of Its Applications* (1933, reissued 1988); GABOR SZEGŐ, *Orthogonal Polynomials,* 4th ed. (1975); M.J. LIGHTHILL, *Introduction to Fourier Analysis and Generalised Functions* (1958, reissued 1970); RICHARD R. GOLDBERG, *Fourier Transforms* (1961); R.E. EDWARDS, *Fourier Series,* 2 vol. (1967); and YITZHAK KATZNELSON, *An Introduction to Harmonic Analysis,* 2nd corrected ed. (1976). H.S. CARSLAW, *Introduction to the Theory of Fourier's Series and Integrals,* 3rd ed. rev. and enlarged (1930, reissued 1950); and DUNHAM JACKSON, *Fourier Series and Orthogonal Polynomials* (1941, reissued 1961), contain elementary theory based on Riemann integration.

In addition to the references on Fourier series, the reader interested in harmonic analysis and integral transforms may wish to consult MICHAEL B. MARCUS and GILLES PISIER, *Random Fourier Series with Applications to Harmonic Analysis* (1981); N.K. BARY (BARI), *A Treatise on Trigonometric Series,* 2 vol. (1964; originally published in Russian, 1961), which deals with the classical theory of Fourier series and integrals; ELIAS M. STEIN and GUIDO WEISS, *Introduction to Fourier Analysis on Euclidean Spaces* (1971), which treats the *n*-dimensional theory extensively and systematically and also has a systematic treatment of convolutions; and I.I. HIRSCHMAN and D.V. WIDDER, *The Convolution Transform* (1955), another good reference on convolutions. For variants of the Fourier transform (such as Hänkel or Mellin transforms), see GEORGE N. WATSON, *A Treatise on the Theory of Bessel Functions,* 2nd ed. (1944, reprinted 1966); D.V. WIDDER, *The Laplace Transform* (1941); and BATEMAN MANUSCRIPT PROJECT, *Tables of Integral Transforms,* ed. by ARTHUR ERDÉLYI, 2 vol. (1954). The topic of singular integrals is treated in ELIAS M. STEIN, *Singular Integrals and Differentiability Properties of Functions* (1970, reissued 1986). An exposition of abstract harmonic analysis may be found in WALTER RUDIN, *Fourier Analysis on Groups* (1962). LYNN H. LOOMIS, *An Introduction to Abstract Harmonic Analysis* (1953); and HERMANN WEYL, *The Classical Groups: Their Invariants and Representations,* 2nd ed. (1946, reissued 1966), deal with both abstract harmonic analysis and representations of groups and algebras. Some additional references on representations of groups and algebras are CLAUDE CHEVALLEY, *Theory of Lie Groups* (1946); FRANCIS D. MURNAGHAN, *The Theory of Group Representations* (1938, reprinted 1963); L.S. PONTRYAGIN, *Topological Groups,* 3rd ed. (1986; originally published in Russian, 1938); HERMANN WEYL, *The Theory of Groups and Quantum Mechanics* (1931, reissued 1949); and G. DE B. ROBINSON, *Representation Theory of the Symmetric Group* (1961). (A.Zy./C.L.F./Ed.)

Calculus of variations: There are many works available on the calculus of variations. For an introduction to the theory for problems involving arcs only, see GILBERT A. BLISS, *Calculus of Variations* (1925, reprinted 1962), and *Lectures on the Calculus of Variations* (1946, reprinted 1980). For problems involving multiple integrals, see CHARLES B. MORREY, *Multiple Integrals in the Calculus of Variations* (1966). For expositions of Morse's theory of critical points, see MARSTON MORSE, *The Calculus of Variations in the Large* (1934). (C.B.My.)

Functional analysis: A comprehensive account of a large part of linear functional analysis is found in NELSON DUNFORD and JACOB T. SCHWARTZ, *Linear Operators,* 3 vol. (1958–71). The first volume covers the general theory of linear operators and the second the theory of self-adjoint operators in Hilbert space. This work includes a bibliography of several thousand items and gives historical accounts of many of the topics that it discusses. A systematic study of semigroups of linear operators, together with more general background material on functional analysis, is contained in EINAR HILLE and RALPH S. PHILLIPS, *Functional*

Analysis and Semi-groups, rev. ed. (1957). For an account of the application of Hilbert space spectral theory to the analysis of differential equations, see M.A. NAIMARK, *Linear Differential Operators* (1967; originally published in Russian, 1954); and ch. 13 in vol. 2 of the work by Dunford and Schwartz cited above. For further developments in the application of functional analysis to differential equations, see TOSIO KATO, *Perturbation Theory for Linear Operators,* 2nd ed. (1976, reprinted 1984); and PETER D. LAX and RALPH S. PHILLIPS, *Scattering Theory,* rev. ed. (1989). The spectral analysis of non-self-adjoint operators is reviewed in vol. 3 of Dunford and Schwartz cited above. ION COLOJOARA and CIPRIAN FOIAȘ, *Theory of Generalized Spectral Operators* (1968), contains additional material concerning this developing area. PATRICK BILLINGSLEY, *Ergodic Theory and Information* (1965, reprinted 1978), gives an elegant short account of many of the main theorems of ergodic theory; see also WILLIAM PARRY, *Entropy and Generators in Ergodic Theory* (1969). Harmonic analysis is treated in many works; in particular, see EDWIN HEWITT and KENNETH A. ROSS, *Abstract Harmonic Analysis,* vol. 1, *Structure of Topological Groups, Integration Theory, Group Representations,* 2nd ed. (1979), which gives a useful picture of this area. GERALD M. LEIBOWITZ, *Lectures on Complex Function Algebras* (1970), gives an account of some of the deeper issues in classical harmonic analysis. The generalized Fourier integral theory central to harmonic analysis is closely related to some of the principal theorems of group representation theory and of functional algebra. MARTIN BURROW, *Representation Theory of Finite Groups* (1965), contains an account of the representation theory of finite groups. The final chapter of SIGURDUR HELGASON, *Differential Geometry and Symmetric Spaces* (1962), contains the representation theory of noncompact continuous groups. M.A. NAIMARK, *Normed Rings,* rev. ed. (1970; originally published in Russian, 1956), covers many results of functional algebra. A more specialized discussion, devoted to the theory of von Neumann or W^*-algebras, can be found in J.T. SCHWARTZ, *W^*- Algebras* (1967). For a general account of the use of global topological methods in functional analysis, see Schwartz's *Nonlinear Functional Analysis* (1965). The reader interested in the present state of this rapidly developing field should consult the current journal literature.

The most used text on generalized functions is I.M. GEL'FAND *et al., Generalized Functions,* 5 vol., trans. from Russian (1964–68), a very clearly written work, with numerous applications to partial differential equations, mathematical physics, and harmonic analysis. See also D.S. JONES, *The Theory of Generalized Functions,* 2nd ed. (1982).

For a discussion on the general theory of locally convex spaces, see ALEX P. ROBERTSON and WENDY ROBERTSON, *Topological Vector Spaces,* 2nd ed. (1973), which is very clear and very short. FRANÇOIS TRÈVES, *Topological Vector Spaces, Distributions, and Kernels* (1967), is another reference on distributions. HANS BREMERMANN, *Distributions, Complex Variables, and Fourier Transforms* (1965), is a short and well-written book, with a slant toward applications to physics and to electrical circuits, emphasizing the boundary values of analytic functions. KŌSAKU YOSIDA (YOSHIDA), *Functional Analysis,* 6th ed. (1980), is a wide-ranging presentation of functional analysis, from the theory of linear operators in Hilbert spaces to Banach algebras, ergodic theorems, and diffusion equations. (J.T.Sc./F.Tr.)

Physical and Chemical Analysis and Measurement

Scientific and technological disciplines rely on measurements of physical and chemical properties. Such measurements are central to, for example, analytical chemistry, that branch of chemistry concerned with determining the identity of a substance (qualitative analysis) or with calculating the amount of a substance whose identity is known (quantitative analysis). This article includes a description of the techniques and measurements that are most often used by scientists, engineers, and laboratory technicians to identify a substance, separate it into its components, remove impurities, or determine a specific chemical or physical property. Various methods of analysis are discussed, including classical wet techniques such as precipitations and titrations and instrumental methods such as chromatography, mass spectrometry, spectroscopy, and electroanalysis. Many methods of analysis and measurement involve the interaction of radiation with matter. Accordingly, the sources, interactions, detection, and measurement of various types of ionizing radiations are discussed in some detail, as are significant applications of radiation detection and measurement in science and industry. The behaviour of materials—*e.g.,* certain metals, ceramics, and plastics—under various conditions is an important factor in determining their suitability for specific applications. Measuring the behaviours and characteristics of materials is the concern of materials testing. Several test methods, along with the properties that they measure, are discussed here.

For coverage of related topics in the *Macropædia* and *Micropædia,* see the *Propædia,* sections 111, 112, 122, 128, and the *Index.*

This article is divided into the following sections:

Chemical analysis 523
General considerations 523
Major categories of analysis
Development of chemical analytical methods
Principal stages 524
Sampling
Sample preparation
Evaluation of results
Preliminary laboratory methods 525
Density measurements
Specific gravity measurements
Viscosity measurements
pH determinations
Interference removal 526
Classical methods 527
Classical qualitative analysis
Classical quantitative analysis
Instrumental methods 528
Spectral methods
Electroanalysis
Separatory methods
Chemical separations and purifications 535
Basic concepts of separations 536
Principles of specific methods 538
Chromatography 542
History
Methods
Sample recovery
Methods of detection
Efficiency and resolution
Theoretical considerations
Applications
Mass spectrometry 548
History
General principles
Important technical adjuncts
Applications
Accelerator mass spectrometry
Spectroscopy 556
Survey of optical spectroscopy 557
General principles
Practical considerations
Foundations of atomic spectra 563
Basic atomic structure
Hydrogen atom states
The periodic table
Atomic transitions
Perturbations of levels
Molecular spectroscopy 567
General principles
Theory of molecular spectra
Experimental methods
Fields of molecular spectroscopy
X-ray and radio-frequency spectroscopy 575
X-ray spectroscopy
Radio-frequency spectroscopy
Resonance-ionization spectroscopy 579
Ionization processes
Atom counting
Resonance-ionization mass spectrometry
RIS atomization methods
Additional applications of RIS
Radiation measurement 582
Radiation interactions in matter
Passive detectors
Active detectors
Materials testing 597
Mechanical testing
Measurement of thermal properties
Measurement of electrical properties
Testing for corrosion, radiation, and biological deterioration
Nondestructive testing
Bibliography 600

CHEMICAL ANALYSIS

General considerations

MAJOR CATEGORIES OF ANALYSIS

Chemical analysis, which relies on the use of measurements, is divided into two categories depending on the manner in which the assays are performed. Classical analysis, also termed wet chemical analysis, consists of those analytical techniques that use no mechanical or electronic instruments other than a balance. The method usually relies on chemical reactions between the material being analyzed (the analyte) and a reagent that is added to the analyte. Wet techniques often depend on the formation of a product of the chemical reaction that is easily detected and measured. For example, the product could be coloured or could be a solid that precipitates from a solution.

Most chemical analysis falls into the second category, which is instrumental analysis. It involves the use of an instrument, other than a balance, to perform the analysis. A wide assortment of instrumentation is available to the analyst. In some cases, the instrument is used to characterize a chemical reaction between the analyte and an added reagent; in others, it is used to measure a property of the analyte. Instrumental analysis is subdivided into categories on the basis of the type of instrumentation employed.

Both classical and instrumental quantitative analyses can be divided into gravimetric and volumetric analyses. Gravimetric analysis relies on a critical mass measurement. As an example, solutions containing chloride ions can be assayed by adding an excess of silver nitrate. The reaction product, a silver chloride precipitate, is filtered from the solution, dried, and weighed. Because the product was formed by an exhaustive chemical reaction with the analyte (*i.e.,* virtually all of the analyte was precipitated), the mass of the precipitate can be used to calculate the amount of analyte initially present.

Gravimetric analysis

Volumetric analysis relies on a critical volume measurement. Usually a liquid solution of a chemical reagent (a titrant) of known concentration is placed in a buret, which is a glass tube with calibrated volume graduations (see Figure 1). The titrant is added gradually, in a procedure termed a titration, to the analyte until the chemical reaction is completed. The added titrant volume that is just sufficient to react with all of the analyte is the equivalence point and can be used to calculate the amount or concentration of the analyte that was originally present.

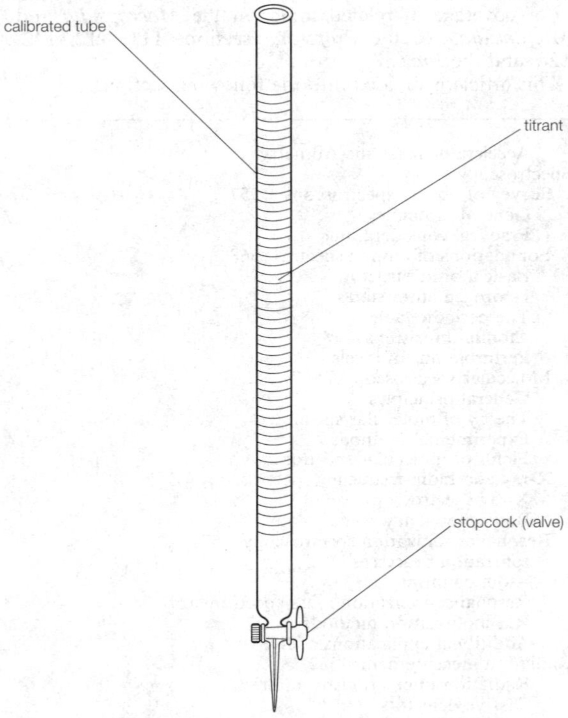

Figure 1: A conventional buret used in volumetric analysis.

DEVELOPMENT OF CHEMICAL ANALYTICAL METHODS

Since the advent of chemistry, investigators have needed to know the identity and quantity of the materials with which they are working. Consequently, the development of chemical analysis parallels the development of chemistry. The 18th-century Swedish scientist Torbern Bergman is usually regarded as the founder of inorganic qualitative and quantitative chemical analysis. Prior to the 20th century nearly all assays were performed by classical methods. Although simple instruments (such as photometers and electrogravimetric analysis apparatus) were available at the end of the 19th century, instrumental analysis did not flourish until well into the 20th century. The development of electronics during World War II and the subsequent widespread availability of digital computers have hastened the change from classical to instrumental analysis in most laboratories. Although most assays currently are performed instrumentally, there remains a need for some classical analyses.

Principal stages

The main steps that are performed during a chemical analysis are the following: (1) sampling, (2) field sample pretreatment, (3) laboratory treatment, (4) laboratory assay, (5) calculations, and (6) results presentation. Each must be executed correctly in order for the analytical result to be accurate. Some analytical chemists distinguish between an analysis, which involves all the steps, and an assay, which is the laboratory portion of the analysis.

SAMPLING

During this initial step of analysis, a portion of a bulk material is removed in order to be assayed. The portion should be chosen so that it is representative of the bulk material. To assist in this, statistics is used as a guide to determine the sample size and the number of samples. When selecting a sampling program, it is important that the analyst has a detailed description of the information required from the analysis, an estimate of the accuracy to be achieved, and an estimate of the amount of time and money that can be spent on sampling. It is worthwhile to discuss with the users of the analytical results the type of data that is desired. Results may provide needless or insufficient information if the sampling procedure is either excessive or inadequate.

Generally the accuracy of an analysis is increased by obtaining multiple samples at varying locations (and times) within the bulk material. As an example, analysis of a lake for a chemical pollutant will likely yield inaccurate results if the lake is sampled only in the centre and at the surface. It is preferable to sample the lake at several locations around its periphery as well as at several depths near its centre. The homogeneity of the bulk material influences the number of samples needed. If the material is homogeneous, only a single sample is required. More samples are needed to obtain an accurate analytical result when the bulk material is heterogeneous. The disadvantages of taking a larger number of samples are the added time and expense. Few laboratories can afford massive sampling programs.

SAMPLE PREPARATION

After the sample has been collected, it may be necessary to chemically or physically treat it at the sampling site. Normally this treatment is done immediately after the sample has been collected. The nature of the treatment is dependent on the sample and the substances for which it is being analyzed. For example, natural water samples that are assayed for dissolved oxygen generally are placed in containers that are sealed, stored, and transported in a refrigerated compartment. Sealing prevents a change in oxygen concentration owing to exposure to the atmosphere, and refrigeration slows changes in oxygen levels caused by microscopic organisms within the sample. Similarly, samples that are to be assayed for trace levels of metallic pollutants are pretreated in order to prevent a decrease in the concentration of the pollutant that is caused by adsorption on the walls of the sample vessel. Metallic adsorption can be minimized by adding nitric acid to the sample and by washing the walls of the vessel with the acid.

Field pretreatment

After the samples arrive at the laboratory, additional operations might be required prior to performing the assay. In some cases, multiple samples simply are combined into a composite sample which is made homogeneous and then assayed. This process eliminates the need to assay each of the individual specimens. In other instances, the sample must be chemically or physically treated in order to place it in a form that can be assayed. For example, ore samples normally must be first dissolved in acidic solutions. Sometimes it is necessary to change the concentration of the analyte prior to performing the assay so that it will fall within the range of the analytical method. Once the specimen is prepared, enough laboratory assays are completed to allow the analyst to estimate the amount of random error. Typically a minimum of three assays are performed on each sample.

EVALUATION OF RESULTS

After the assays have been completed, quantitative results are mathematically manipulated, and both qualitative and quantitative results are presented in a meaningful manner.

In most cases, two values are reported for quantitative analyses. The first value is an estimate of the correct value for the analysis, and the second value indicates the amount of random error in the analysis. The most common way of reporting the best value is to give the mean (average) of the results of the laboratory assays. In specific cases, however, it is better to report either the median (central value when the results are arranged in order of size) or the mode (the value obtained most often).

Accuracy is the degree of agreement between the experimental result and the true value. Precision is the degree of agreement among a series of measurements of the same quantity; it is a measure of the reproducibility of results rather than their correctness. Errors may be either systematic (determinant) or random (indeterminant). Systematic errors cause the results to vary from the correct value in a predictable manner and can often be identified and corrected. An example of a systematic error is improper calibration of an instrument. Random errors are the small fluctuations introduced in nearly all analyses. These errors can be minimized but not eliminated. They can be treated, however, using statistical methods. Statistics is used to estimate the random error that occurs during each step of an analysis, and, upon completion of the analysis, the estimates for the individual steps can be combined to obtain an estimate of the total experimental error.

Statistical methods

The most frequently reported error estimate is the standard deviation of the results; however, other values, such as the variance, the range, the average deviation, or confidence limits at a specified probability level are sometimes reported. For the relatively small number of replicate samples that are used during chemical assays, the standard deviation (s) is calculated by using equation (1) where Σ represents summation, x_i represents each of the individual analytical results, a is the average of the results, and N is the number of replicate assays.

$$s = \left(\frac{\Sigma(x_i - a)^2}{N-1}\right)^{1/2} \tag{1}$$

The standard deviation is a popular estimate of the error in an analysis because it has statistical significance whenever the results are normally distributed. Most analytical results exhibit normal (Gaussian) behaviour, following the characteristic bell-shaped curve. If the results are normally distributed, 68.3 percent of the results can be expected to fall within the range of plus or minus one standard deviation of the mean as a result of random error. The units of standard deviation are identical to those of the individual analytical results.

The variance (V) is the square of the standard deviation and is useful because, in many cases, it is additive throughout the several steps of the chemical analysis. Consequently, an estimate of the total random error in the analysis can be obtained by adding the variances for each of the individual steps in the analysis. The standard deviation for the overall analysis can then be calculated by taking the square root of the sum of the variances.

A simple measure of variability is the range, given as the difference between the largest and the smallest results. It has no statistical significance, however, for small data sets. Another statistical term, the average deviation, is calculated by adding the differences, while ignoring the sign, between each result and the average of all the results, and then dividing the sum by the number of results. Confidence limits at a given probability level are values greater than and less than the average, between which the results are statistically expected to fall a given percentage of the time.

Preliminary laboratory methods

A summary, though not comprehensive, of the common laboratory measurements that can be performed to supplement information obtained by another analytical procedure is provided in this section. Many of the methods can be used in the field or in process control apparatus as well as in the laboratory.

Some physical measurements that do not require instrumentation other than an accurate balance can be useful in selected circumstances. Density, specific gravity, viscosity, and pH measurements are among the more useful measurements in this category.

DENSITY MEASUREMENTS

This property is defined as the ratio of mass to volume of a substance. Generally the mass is measured in grams and the volume in millilitres or cubic centimetres. Density measurements of liquids are straightforward and sometimes can aid in identifying pure substances or mixtures that contain two or three known components; they are most useful in assays of simple mixtures whose components differ significantly in their individual densities. Densities can be used, for example, as an aid in the quantitative analysis of aqueous sugar solutions. Liquid densities usually are measured by using a calibrated glass vessel called a pycnometer, which typically has a volume of about 10 millilitres. The vessel is weighed by using an analytical balance with an accuracy of at least 0.0001 gram and is subsequently filled to the calibration mark with the liquid. After the filled vessel has been weighed, the mass of the liquid is determined by subtracting the mass of the empty vessel. The density is calculated by dividing the mass of the liquid by the volume of the pycnometer.

Pycnometer

SPECIFIC GRAVITY MEASUREMENTS

Specific gravity is a related quantity that is defined as the ratio of the density of the analyte to the density of water at a specified temperature. The procedure used to measure specific gravity is similar to that used to measure density, although it does not require accurate knowledge of the volume of the vessel that contains the liquid. After the weight of the vessel when empty has been obtained, the vessel is filled to the calibration mark with distilled water at a specified temperature (often 4°, 20°, or 25° C [39°, 68°, or 77° F, respectively]) and weighed. From the difference between the weights, the mass of the water is determined. The vessel is emptied and then filled with the analyte and reweighed. The mass of the analyte is determined as during density measurements (*i.e.*, by subtracting the mass of the empty vessel), and the ratio of the analyte mass to the water mass is calculated. The resultant ratio is the specific gravity of the analyte. It is not necessary to know accurately the volume of the container, because it and the volume of the analyte cancel one another while the ratio of the densities is obtained. Density and specific gravity measurements rarely provide sufficient information to qualitatively identify a pure analyte. They can be used as supporting evidence, however, when an assay is performed by another procedure.

VISCOSITY MEASUREMENTS

Measurements of this kind also provide limited analytical information. Viscosity is a measure of the resistance of a substance to change of shape. Often it is defined as the resistance to flow of a fluid. It is measured in units of poises (dyne-seconds per square centimetre) or a subdivision of poises. For liquids viscosity is measured in a calibrated glass vessel known as a viscometer. There are various types of viscometers; a typical apparatus is shown in Figure 2. After inversion, the upper glass bulb is filled to the lower calibration mark by applying suction with a rubber bulb and drawing the liquid analyte into the apparatus. The device is stoppered at the end near the lower bulb, inverted to its upright position, and placed in a constant-temperature bath. After temperature equilibrium has been established, the stopper is removed. The time required for the volume of liquid between the two marks to drain from the bulb is measured. The time elapsed is used in conjunction with a table supplied by the manufacturer of the bulb to determine the viscosity. The tube at the lower end of the upper bulb has a fixed length and radius that is used along with the pressure differential between the upper and lower ends of the apparatus to measure the viscosity. Viscosity measurements are common in industries that produce oils or other relatively slow-flowing liquids. They often are employed in oil refineries to determine the viscosities of refined oils.

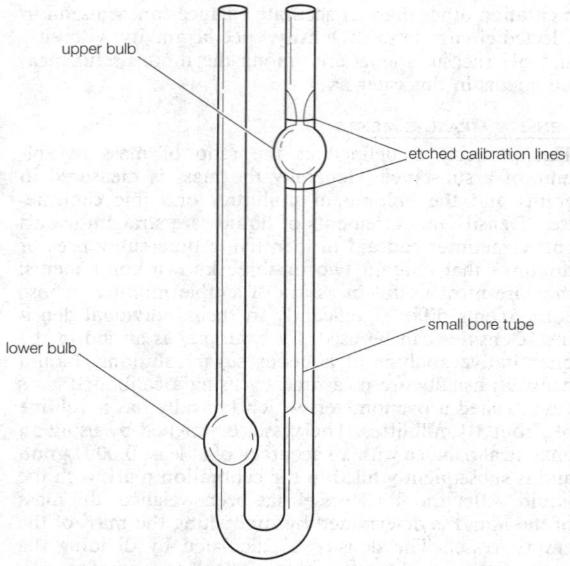

Figure 2: A typical viscometer used for measuring the viscosity of liquids.

PH DETERMINATIONS

The pH of a solution is the negative logarithm (base 10) of the activity (the product of the molar concentration and the activity coefficient) of the hydrogen ions (H^+) in the solution. In solutions of low ionic strength, pH can be defined as the negative logarithm of the molar concentration of the hydrogen ions because activity and concentration are nearly identical in these solutions. One method for determining pH is by use of a chemical acid-base indicator, which consists of a dye that is either a weak acid or a weak base. The dye has one colour in its acidic form and a second colour in its basic form. Because different dyes change from the acidic to the basic form at different pH values, it is possible to use a series of dyes to determine the pH of a solution. A small portion of the dye or dye mixture is added to the analyte, or a portion of the analyte is added to the dye mixture (often on a piece of paper that is permeated with the indicator). By comparing the colour of the indicator or indicator mixture that is in contact with the sample to the colours of the dyes in their acidic and basic forms, it is possible to determine the pH of the solution. Although this method is rapid and inexpensive, it rarely is used to determine pH with an accuracy greater than about 0.5 pH units. More accurate measurements are performed instrumentally as described below (see *Instrumental methods: Electroanalysis: Potentiometry*).

Acid-base indicators

Interference removal

Regardless of whether a classical or instrumental method is used, it may be necessary to remove interferences from an analyte prior to an assay. An interference is a substance, other than the assayed material, that can be measured by the chosen analytical method or that can prevent the assayed material from being measured. Interferences cause erroneous analytical results. Several methods have been devised to enable their removal. The most popular of such separatory methods include distillation, selective precipitation, filtration, complexation, osmosis, reverse osmosis, extraction, electrogravimetry, and chromatography. Some of these methods can be used not only to remove interferences but also to perform the assay.

Distillation. During distillation a mixture of either liquid or liquid and solid components is placed in a glass vessel, called a pot (or boiling flask), and heated. The more volatile components—*i.e.,* those with the lower boiling points—are converted to a gaseous state and exit the pot through a cooling tube, called a condenser, that is located above the pot. The condensed liquids, termed the distillate, are collected in a receiving flask and thereby separated from the less volatile components. Separation is based on relative boiling points of the components. Normally the efficiency of the separation is increased by inserting a column between the pot and the condenser. A distillation column is a tube that provides surfaces on which condensations and vaporizations can occur before the gas enters the condenser in order to concentrate the more volatile liquid in the first fractions and the less volatile components in the later fractions. The analyte typically goes through several vaporization-condensation steps prior to arriving at the condenser. A sketch of a typical simple distillation apparatus is shown in Figure 3; see also the discussion of distillation below in *Chemical separation and purification: Equilibrium separations.*

Selective precipitation. In some cases, selective precipitation can be used to remove interferences from a mixture. A chemical reagent is added to the solution, and it selectively reacts with the interference to form a precipitate. The precipitate can then be physically separated from the mixture by filtration or centrifugation. The use of precipitation in gravimetric analysis is described below (see *Classical methods: Classical quantitative analysis*).

Filtration. This operation can be used to separate particles according to their dimensions. One application is the removal of the precipitate after selective precipitation. Such solid-liquid laboratory filtrations are performed through various grades of filter paper (*i.e.,* those differing in pore size). The mixture is poured either onto a filter paper that rests in a funnel or onto another filtering device. The liquid passes through the filter while the precipitate is trapped. When the filter has a small pore size, the normal filtration rate is slow but can be increased by filtering into a flask that is maintained under a partial vacuum. In that instance, fritted glass or glass fibre filters often are used in place of paper filters. Solid-gas filtrations are carried out in the laboratory as well.

Vacuum filtration

Complexation. This is another method used to prevent a substance from interfering with an assay. A chemical complexing agent is added to the analyte mixture for the purpose of selectively forming a complex with the interference. A complex is a combination of the two substances and normally remains dissolved. Because the chemical nature of the complex is different from that of the original interference, the complex does not interfere with the assay.

Osmosis. This is a separation technique in which a semipermeable membrane is placed between two solutions containing the same solvent. The membrane allows passage of small solution components (usually the solvent) while preventing passage of larger molecules. The natural

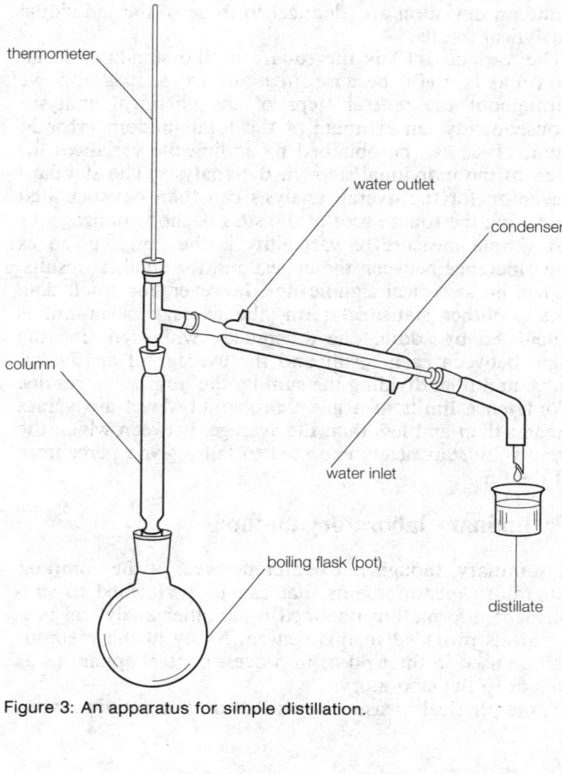

Figure 3: An apparatus for simple distillation.

tendency is for the solvent to flow from the side where its concentration is higher to the side where its concentration is lower. Reverse osmosis occurs when pressure is applied to the solution on the side of the membrane that contains the lower solvent concentration. The pressure forces the solvent to flow from a region of low concentration to one of high concentration. Reverse osmosis often is used for water purification. Osmosis or reverse osmosis can be utilized in certain instances to perform separations prior to a chemical assay.

Extraction. Extraction takes advantage of the relative solubilities of solutes in immiscible solvents. If the solutes are in an aqueous solution, an organic solvent that is immiscible with water is added. The solutes will dissolve either in the water or in the organic solvent. If the relative solubilities of the solutes differ in the two solvents, a partial separation occurs. The upper, less dense solvent layer is physically separated from the lower layer. The separation is enhanced if the process is repeated on each of the separated layers. It is possible to perform the extractions in a continuous procedure, called counter current extraction, as well as in the batch process described here.

Electrogravimetry. This method employs an electric current to deposit a solid on an electrode from a solution. Normally the deposit is a metallic plate that has formed from the corresponding metallic ions in the solution; however, other electrode coatings also can be formed. The use of electrogravimetry as an instrumental analytical method is described below (see *Instrumental methods: Electroanalysis: Electrogravimetry*).

Chromatography. Chromatography consists of a large group of separatory methods in which the components of a mixture are separated by the relative attraction of the components for a stationary phase (a solid or liquid) as a mobile phase (a liquid or gas) passes over the stationary phase. Chromatography usually is divided into two categories depending on the type of mobile phase that is used. If the mobile phase is a liquid, the technique is liquid chromatography; if it is a gas, the technique is gas chromatography.

A sketch of a simple liquid chromatographic apparatus is shown in Figure 4. The stationary phase is held in place either in a column or on a plane (such as a plate of glass, metal, or plastic or a sheet of paper). For the simple

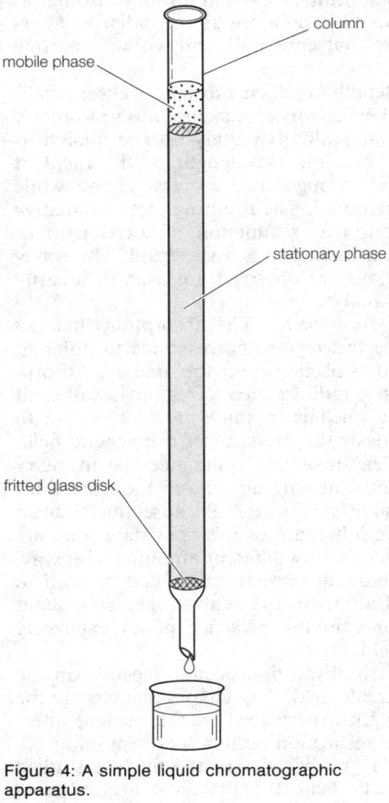

Figure 4: A simple liquid chromatographic apparatus.

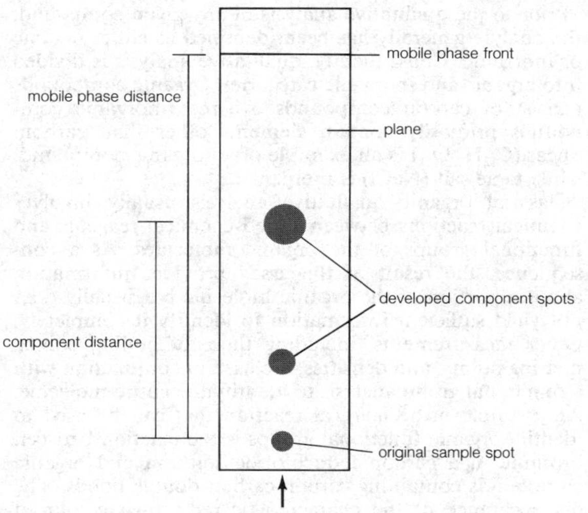

Figure 5: A developed plane chromatographic plate.

apparatus shown in the figure, the column is a glass tube that is loosely plugged at the lower end with glass wool or a sintered glass disk. Prior to the separation, the column is filled with the mobile phase to a level that is slightly above the level of the stationary phase. The mixture to be separated is added to the top of the column and is allowed to drain onto the stationary phase.

In the most common form of chromatography, known as elution chromatography, the mobile phase is continuously added to the top of the column as solution flows from the bottom. The stationary phase must be continuously immersed in the mobile phase to prevent air bubbles from entering the column and impeding the mobile-phase flow. As the components of the mixture are flushed through the column, they are partitioned between the two phases depending on their attractions to the stationary phase. Because different mixture components have different attractions for the stationary phase, a separation occurs. The components that are more attracted to the stationary phase remain in the column longer, while those components that are less attracted are flushed more rapidly from the column. The separated components are collected as they exit the column.

Elution chromatography

A similar process occurs during separations that are performed on a plane. In such a case, however, the separations occur in space after a fixed time period rather than in time at a fixed location as was described for column chromatography. The separated components appear as spots on the plane. A sketch of a developed chromatographic plate is shown in Figure 5.

Classical methods

The majority of the classical analytical methods rely on chemical reactions to perform an analysis. In contrast, instrumental methods typically depend on the measurement of a physical property of the analyte.

CLASSICAL QUALITATIVE ANALYSIS

Classical qualitative analysis is performed by adding one or a series of chemical reagents to the analyte. By observing the chemical reactions and their products, one can deduce the identity of the analyte. The added reagents are chosen so that they selectively react with one or a single class of chemical compounds to form a distinctive reaction product. Normally the reaction product is a precipitate or a gas, or it is coloured. Take for example copper(II), which reacts with ammonia to form a copper-ammonia complex that is characteristically deep blue. Similarly, dissolved lead(II) reacts with solutions containing chromate to form a yellow lead chromate precipitate. Negative ions (anions) as well as positive ions (cations) can be qualitatively analyzed using the same approach. The reaction between carbonates and strong acids to form bubbles of carbon dioxide gas is a typical example.

Prior to the qualitative analysis of any given compound, the analyte generally has been identified as either organic or inorganic. Consequently, qualitative analysis is divided into organic and inorganic categories. Organic compounds consist of carbon compounds, whereas inorganic compounds primarily contain elements other than carbon. Sugar ($C_{12}H_{22}O_{11}$) is an example of an organic compound, while table salt (NaCl) is inorganic.

Functional group analysis

Classical organic qualitative analysis usually involves chemical reactions between added chemical reagents and functional groups of the organic molecules. As a consequence, the result of the assay provides information about a portion of the organic molecule but usually does not yield sufficient information to identify it completely. Other measurements, including those of boiling points, melting points, and densities, are used in conjunction with a functional group analysis to identify the entire molecule. An example of a chemical reaction that can be used to identify organic functional groups is the reaction between bromine in a carbon tetrachloride solution and organic compounds containing carbon-carbon double bonds. The disappearance of the characteristic red-brown colour of bromine, due to the addition of bromine across the double bonds, is a positive test for the presence of a carbon-carbon double bond. Similarly, the reaction between silver nitrate and certain organic halides (those compounds containing chlorine, bromine, or iodine) results in the formation of a silver halide precipitate as a positive test for organic halides.

Classical qualitative analyses can be complex owing to the large number of possible chemical species in the mixture. Fortunately, analytical schemes have been carefully worked out for all the common inorganic ions and organic functional groups. Detailed information about inorganic and organic qualitative analysis can be found in some of the texts listed in the *Bibliography* at the end of this article.

CLASSICAL QUANTITATIVE ANALYSIS

Classical quantitative analysis can be divided into gravimetric analysis and volumetric analysis. Both methods utilize exhaustive chemical reactions between the analyte and added reagents. As discussed above, during gravimetric analysis an excess of added reagent reacts with the analyte to form a precipitate. The precipitate is filtered, dried, and weighed. Its mass is used to calculate the concentration or amount of the assayed substance in the analyte.

Volumetric analysis is also known as titrimetric analysis. The reagent (the titrant) is added gradually or stepwise to the analyte from a buret. The key to performing a successful titrimetric analysis is to recognize the equivalence point of the titration (the point at which the quantities of the two reacting species are equivalent), typically observed as a colour change. If no spontaneous colour change occurs during the titration, a small amount of a chemical indicator is added to the analyte prior to the titration. Chemical indicators are available that change colour at or near the equivalence point of acid-base, oxidation-reduction, complexation, and precipitation titrations. The volume of added titrant corresponding to the indicator colour change is the end point of the titration. The end point is used as an approximation of the equivalence point and is employed, with the known concentration of the titrant, to calculate the amount or concentration of the analyte.

Instrumental methods

The instrumental methods of chemical analysis are divided into categories according to the property of the analyte that is to be measured. Many of the methods can be used for both qualitative and quantitative analysis. The major categories of instrumental methods are the spectral, electroanalytical, and separatory.

SPECTRAL METHODS

Spectral methods measure the electromagnetic radiation that is absorbed, scattered, or emitted by the analyte. Because the types of radiation that can be monitored are multitudinous and the manner in which the radiation is measured can significantly vary from one method to another, the spectral methods constitute the largest category of instrumental methods. Since a detailed description of the spectral methods of analysis is included in a later section, only an introduction is provided here.

Absorptiometry. In the most often used spectral method, the electromagnetic radiation that is provided by the instrument is absorbed by the analyte, and the amount of the absorption is measured. Absorption occurs when a quantum of electromagnetic radiation, known as a photon, strikes a molecule and raises it to some excited (high-energy) state. The intensity (*i.e.*, the energy, in the form of electromagnetic radiation, transferred across a unit area per unit time) of the incident radiation decreases as it passes through the sample. The techniques that measure absorption in order to perform an assay are absorptiometry or absorption spectrophotometry.

Types of absorptiometry

Normally absorptiometry is subdivided into categories depending on the energy or wavelength region of the incident radiation. In order of increasingly energetic radiation, the types of absorptiometry are radiowave absorptiometry (called nuclear magnetic resonance spectrometry), microwave absorptiometry (including electron spin resonance spectrometry), thermal absorptiometry (thermal analysis), infrared absorptiometry, ultraviolet-visible absorptiometry, and X-ray absorptiometry. The instruments that provide and measure the radiation vary from one spectral region to another, but their operating principles are the same. Each instrument consists of at least three essential components: (1) a source of electromagnetic radiation in the proper energy region, (2) a cell that is transparent to the radiation and that can contain the sample, and (3) a detector that can accurately measure the intensity of the radiation after it has passed through the cell, and the sample.

Essentially, the amount of absorbed radiation increases with the concentration of the analyte and with the distance through the analyte that the radiation must travel (the cell path length). As radiation is absorbed in the sample, the intensity of the radiative beam decreases. By measuring the decreased intensity through a fixed-path-length cell containing the sample, it is possible to determine the concentration of the sample. Because different substances absorb at different wavelengths (or energies), the instruments must be capable of controlling the wavelength of the incident electromagnetic radiation. In most instruments, this is accomplished with a monochromator. In other instruments, it is done by use of radiative filters or by use of sources that emit radiation within a narrow wavelength band.

Because the wavelength at which substances absorb radiation depends on their chemical makeup, absorptiometry can also be used for qualitative analysis. The analyte is placed in the cell, and the wavelength of the incident radiation is scanned throughout a spectral region while the absorption is measured. The resulting plot of radiative intensity or absorption as a function of wavelength or energy of the incident radiation is a spectrum. The wavelengths at which peaks are observed are used to identify components of the analyte.

Nuclear magnetic resonance. The absorption that occurs in different spectral regions corresponds to different physical processes that occur within the analyte. Absorption of energy in the radiofrequency region is sufficient to cause a spinning nucleus in some atoms to move to a different spin state in the presence of a magnetic field. Consequently, nuclear magnetic resonance spectrometry is useful for examining atomic nuclei and the transitions between their possible spin states. Because nuclei from different atoms have different possible spin states that are separated from each other by different amounts of energy, nuclear magnetic resonance spectrometry can be used to identify the type of atoms in the analyte. The spin states can be observed only in the presence of an externally applied magnetic field.

The energy at which absorption occurs depends on the strength of the magnetic field. Any factors that change the magnetic field strength experienced by the nucleus affect the energy at which absorption occurs. Since spinning nuclei of other atoms in the vicinity of the nucleus studied can affect the magnetic field strength, those neighbouring nuclei cause the absorption to be shifted to slightly different energies. As a result, nuclear magnetic resonance spectrometry can be used to deduce the number and types of different nuclei of the groups attached to the atom containing the nucleus studied. It is particularly useful for qualitative analysis of organic compounds.

Microwave absorptiometry. In a manner that is similar to that described for nuclear magnetic resonance spectrometry, electron spin resonance spectrometry is used to study spinning electrons. The absorbed radiation falls in the microwave spectral region and induces transitions in the spin states of the electrons. An externally applied magnetic field is required. The technique is effective for studying structures and reactions of materials that contain unpaired electrons.

Electron spin resonance

Absorbed microwave radiation can cause changes in rotational energy levels within molecules, making it useful for other purposes. The rotational energy levels within a molecule correspond to the different possible ways in which a portion of a molecule can revolve around the chemical bond that binds it to the remainder of the molecule. Because the permitted rotational levels depend on the natures of the bonded atoms (*e.g.,* their masses), microwave radiation can be used for qualitative analysis of some organic molecules.

Thermal analysis. During thermal analysis heat is added to an analyte while some property of the analyte is measured. Often the temperature of the sample is monitored during the addition of heat. The manner in which the temperature changes is compared to the way in which the temperature of a completely inert material changes while being exposed to the same heating program. The results are employed for qualitative and quantitative analysis and for determining decomposition mechanisms of the analyte. For example, compounds that contain water exhibit a constant temperature region as the water is stripped from the compound even though heat is continuously added. If the manner in which a compound responds to a heating program is known, the technique can be used for quantitative analysis by measuring the time necessary for a particular change within the analyte to occur.

Infrared spectrophotometry. Absorbed infrared radiation causes rotational changes in molecules, as described for microwave absorption above, and also causes vibrational changes. The vibrational energy levels within a molecule correspond to the ways in which the individual atoms or groups of atoms vibrate relative to the remainder of the molecule. Because vibrational energy levels are dependent on the types of atoms and functional groups, infrared absorption spectrophotometry is primarily used for organic qualitative analysis. It can be used for quantitative analysis, however, by monitoring the amount of absorbed radiation at a given energy corresponding to one of the peaks in the spectrum of the molecule.

Ultraviolet-visible spectrophotometry. Absorption in the ultraviolet-visible region of the spectrum causes electrons in the outermost occupied orbital of an atom or molecule to be moved to a higher (*i.e.,* farther from the nucleus) unoccupied orbital. Ultraviolet-visible absorptiometry is principally used for quantitative analysis of atoms or molecules. It is a useful method in this respect because the height of the absorption peaks in the ultraviolet-visible region of the spectra of many organic and inorganic compounds is large in comparison to the peak heights observed in other spectral regions. Small analyte concentrations can be more easily measured when the peaks are high. If the analyte consists of discrete atoms (which exist only in the gaseous state), the method is termed atomic absorption spectrophotometry.

Atomic absorption spectrophotometry

Some ions and molecules do not absorb strongly in the ultraviolet-visible spectral region. Methods have been developed to apply ultraviolet-visible absorptiometry to those substances. Normally a chemical reagent is added that reacts with the analyte to form a reaction product that strongly absorbs. The absorption of the product of the chemical reaction is measured and related to the concentration of the nonabsorbing analyte. When a nonabsorbing metallic ion is assayed, the added reagent generally is a complexing agent. For example, 1,10-phenanthroline is added to solutions that are assayed for iron(II). The complex that forms between the iron and the reagent is red and is suitable for determining even very small amounts of iron. When a chemical reagent is used in a spectrophotometric assay, the procedure is called a spectrochemical analysis.

Spectrophotometric titrations are another example of spectrochemical analyses. The titrant (reagent) is placed in a buret and is added stepwise to the assayed substance. After each addition, the absorption of the solution in the reaction vessel is measured. A titration curve is prepared by plotting the amount of absorption as a function of the volume of added reagent. The shape of the titration curve depends on the absorbances of the titrant, analyte, and reaction product; from the shape of the curve, it is possible to determine the end point. The end-point volume is used with the concentration of the reagent and the initial volume of the sample solution to calculate the concentration of the analyte.

The detectors that are used in ultraviolet-visible spectrophotometry measure photons. If these photon detectors are replaced by a detector that measures pressure waves, the technique is known as photoacoustic, or optoacoustic, spectrometry. Photoacoustic spectrometers typically employ microphones or piezoelectric transducers as detectors. Pressure waves result when the analyte expands and contracts as it absorbs chopped electromagnetic radiation.

Photoacoustic spectrometry

X-ray absorption. Absorbed X rays cause excitation of electrons from inner orbitals (those near the nucleus) to unoccupied outer orbitals. In some cases, the energy of the incident X ray is sufficient to ionize the analyte by completely removing the electron from the atom or molecule. The energy required to excite the electron from an inner orbital is greater than that which is available in the ultraviolet-visible region. Because the inner shell electrons that are excited during X-ray absorption are associated with atoms in molecules rather than with the molecule as a whole, the information that is provided from a study of X-ray absorption spectra relates to the atoms within a molecule rather than to the entire molecule. X-ray absorption is used for qualitative analysis by comparing the spectrum of the analyte to spectra of known substances. Quantitative analysis also is performed in a manner similar to that used in other spectral regions. X-ray absorption spectra differ in shape from those observed in other regions, but the same measurement principles are applied during the assays.

Scattered radiation. Radiative scattering is utilized in the second major spectral method of analysis. In this technique some radiation that passes through a sample strikes particles of the analyte and is scattered in a different direction. A detector is used to measure either the intensity of the scattered radiation or the decreased intensity of the incident radiation. Depending on the scattering mechanism, the method can be employed for either qualitative or quantitative analysis. If the intensity of the scattered radiation is measured, quantitative analysis is performed by preparing a working curve of intensity as a function of concentration of a series of standard solutions (*i.e.,* solutions containing known concentrations of the component being analyzed). Working curves also are used with other analytical methods, including absorptiometry. The intensity of the scattered radiation in the analyte is measured and compared to the working curve. The concentration of the analyte corresponds to the concentration on the curve that has an intensity identical to that of the analyte.

For chemical analysis three forms of radiative scattering are important—namely, Tyndall, Raman, and Rayleigh scattering. Tyndall scattering occurs when the dimensions of the particles that are causing the scattering are larger than the wavelength of the scattered radiation. It is caused by reflection of the incident radiation from the surfaces of the particles, reflection from the interior walls of the particles, and refraction and diffraction of the radiation as it passes through the particles.

Tyndall, Raman, and Rayleigh scattering

Raman and Rayleigh scattering occur when the dimensions of the scattering particles are less than 5 percent of the wavelength of the incident radiation. Both Rayleigh and Raman scattering are caused by the effect on the analyte of the fluctuating electromagnetic field that is associated with the passing incident radiation. The fluctuating field induces an electric dipole (separation of charges equal in size but opposite in sign) within the scattering particles that oscillates at the same frequency as the incident radiation. The oscillating dipole behaves as a point source of emitted radiation.

Turbidimetry and nephelometry. Scattered radiation can be used to perform quantitative analysis in either of two ways. If the apparatus is designed so that the detector is aligned with the cell and the radiative source, the detector responds to the decreased intensity of the incident radiation that is caused by scattering in the cell. Measurements of the decreased intensity are turbidimetric measurements; the technique is called turbidimetry. The measurements are completely analogous to absorption measurements. The only difference is in the phenomenon that causes the decreased radiative intensity. As with absorption measurements, the decreased intensity is related to the concentration of the scattering species in the cell at a constant wavelength. In both Tyndall scattering and Rayleigh scattering, the wavelength of the scattered radiation is identical to that of the incident radiation. Consequently, neither type provides information that is useful for qualitative analysis.

If the intensity of the scattered radiation is measured, rather than the decrease in intensity of the incident radiation, the method is known as nephelometry. The apparatus used for nephelometric measurements differs from that used for turbidimetric measurements in the placement of the detector. In nephelometry the detector is not aligned with the radiation source and the cell; normally it is placed perpendicular to the path of the incident radiation. Placing the detector out of the path of the incident radiation eliminates the possibility of measuring its intensity. Both nephelometry and turbidimetry are used with Tyndall scattering to quantitatively assay turbid solutions.

As mentioned above, Raman and Rayleigh scattering are caused by induced dipoles that are formed as the electromagnetic radiation passes the scattering particles. Raman scattering differs from Rayleigh scattering in that in the former the induced dipole relaxes to a different vibrational level than it originally had. Accordingly, the wavelength of the scattered radiation differs from the wavelength of the incident radiation by an amount corresponding to the difference between the particle's original and final vibrational levels. Shifts between the wavelengths of the incident radiation and the scattered radiation correspond to differences in vibrational levels within the scattering molecule and therefore can be used for qualitative analysis in much the same way that infrared spectrophotometry is used.

Refractometry. Another category of spectral analysis in which the incident radiation changes direction is refractometry. The refractive index of a substance is defined as the ratio of the velocity of electromagnetic radiation in a vacuum to its velocity in the medium of interest. Because it is difficult to accurately measure velocities as large as those of electromagnetic radiation, the refractive index is determined from the extent to which the radiation changes direction, owing to the decrease in velocity, as it passes from one medium into another. This phenomenon is refraction. Measurements of refractive index are used to qualitatively analyze pure substances because each substance has a constant and unique refractive index that can be determined with great accuracy. Quantitative analysis of simple mixtures containing known components is possible because the refractive index changes with the composition of the mixture.

Refractive index

Emitted radiation. The spectroanalytical methods in the final major category utilize measurements of emitted radiation. Except for a few radionuclides that spontaneously emit radiation, emission occurs only after initial excitation of the analyte by an external source of energy.

Luminescence. In the most common case excitation occurs after the absorption of electromagnetic radiation. The absorption process is identical to that which occurs during absorptiometric measurements. After ultraviolet-visible absorption, an electron in the analyte molecule or atom resides in an upper electron orbital with one or more vacant orbitals nearer to the nucleus. Emission occurs when the excited electron returns to a lower electron orbital. The emitted radiation is termed luminescence. Luminescence is observed at energies that are equal to or less than the energy corresponding to the absorbed radiation.

After initial absorption, emission can occur by either of two mechanisms. In the most common form of luminescence, the excited electron returns to the lower electron orbital without inverting its spin—*i.e.,* without changing the direction in which the electron rotates in the presence of a magnetic field. This phenomenon, known as fluorescence, occurs immediately after absorption. When absorption ceases, fluorescence also immediately ceases.

Although it occurs with low probability, the excited electron sometimes returns to a lower electron orbital by a path in which the electron first inverts its spin while moving to a slightly lower energy state and then inverts the spin again while returning to the original spin state in the unexcited electron orbital. Emission of ultraviolet-visible radiation occurs during the transition from the excited, inverted spin state to the unexcited electron orbital. Because inversion of the spinning electron during the last transition can require a relatively long time, the emission does not immediately cease when the absorption ceases. The resulting luminescence is called phosphorescence. Both fluorescence and phosphorescence can be used for analysis. Fluorescence can be distinguished from phosphorescence by the time delay in emission that occurs during the latter. If the luminescence immediately stops when the exciting radiation is cut off, it is fluorescence; if the luminescence continues, it is phosphorescence.

Fluorescence and phosphorescence

Owing to the arrangement of electron orbitals in molecules and atoms, phosphorescence is observed only in polyatomic species, whereas fluorescence can be observed in atoms as well as in polyatomic species. When fluorescence is observed in discrete, gaseous atoms, it is termed atomic fluorescence.

The apparatus used to make fluorescent and phosphorescent measurements is similar to that used to make measurements of scattered radiation. The detector is usually placed perpendicular to the path of the incident radiation in order to eliminate the possibility of monitoring the incident radiation. Devices that are used to measure fluorescence are fluorometers, and those that are employed to measure phosphorescence are phosphorimeters. Phosphorimeters differ from fluorometers in that they monitor luminescent intensity while the exciting radiation is not striking the cell.

At dilute concentrations, the intensity of the luminesced radiation is directly proportional to the concentration of the emitting species. As with other spectral methods, qualitative analysis is performed by comparing the spectrum of the analyte (a plot of the intensity of emitted radiation as a function of wavelength) with spectra of known substances. A sketch of the essential components of a fluorometer is shown in Figure 6.

Luminescence can be initiated by a process other than

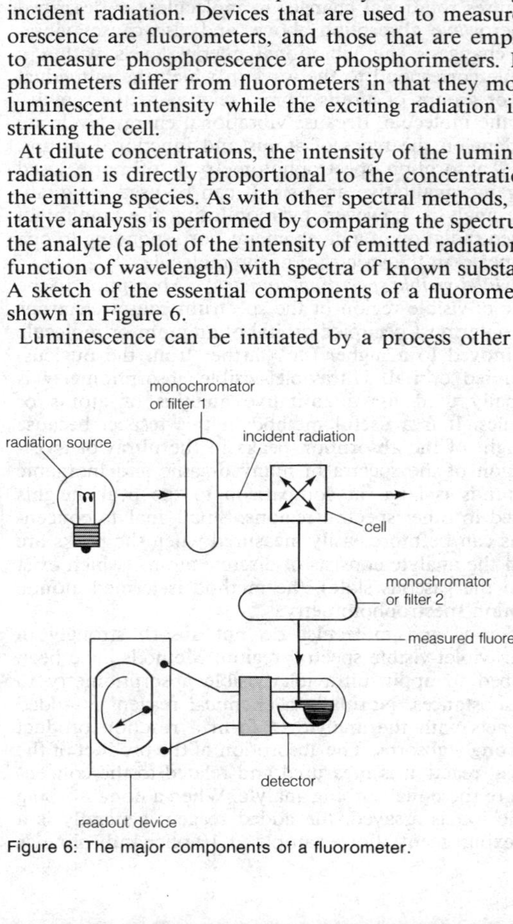

Figure 6: The major components of a fluorometer.

absorption of electromagnetic radiation. Some atoms can be sufficiently excited to emit radiation when exposed to the heat in a flame. The analytical technique that measures the wavelength and/or the intensity of emitted radiation from a flame is flame emission spectrometry. If electrical energy in the form of a spark or an arc is used to excite the analyte prior to measuring the intensity of emitted radiation, the method is atomic emission spectrometry. If a chemical reaction is used to initiate the luminescence, the technique is chemiluminescence; if an electrochemical reaction causes the luminescence, it is electrochemiluminescence.

Flame and atomic emission spectrometry

X-ray emission. X-ray emission spectrometry is the group of analytical methods in which emitted X-ray radiation is monitored. X rays are emitted when an electron in an outer orbital falls into a vacancy in an inner orbital. The vacancy is created by bombarding the atom with electrons, protons, alpha particles, or another type of particles. The vacancy also can be created by absorption of X-ray radiation or by nuclear capture of an inner-shell electron as it approaches the nucleus. Often the bombardment is sufficiently energetic to cause the inner orbital electron to be completely removed from the atom, thereby forming an ion with a vacant inner orbital.

Emitted X rays are used for qualitative and quantitative analysis in much the same way that emitted ultraviolet-visible radiation is employed in fluorometry. X-ray fluorescence is used more often for chemical analysis than the other X-ray methods. The diffraction pattern of X rays that are passed through solid crystalline materials is useful for determining the crystalline structure of solids. The analytical method that measures the diffraction patterns for the purpose of determining structure is termed X-ray diffraction analysis.

Several methods of surface analysis utilize X rays. Particle-induced X-ray emission (PIXE) is the method in which a small area on the surface of a sample is bombarded with accelerated particles and the resulting fluoresced X rays are monitored. If the bombarding particles are protons and the analytical technique is used to obtain an elemental map of a surface, the apparatus utilized is a proton microprobe. An electron microprobe functions in much the same manner. The scanning electron microscope utilizes electrons to bombard a surface, but the intensity of either backscattered (deflected through angles greater than 90°) or transmitted electrons is measured rather than the intensity of X rays. Electron microscopes are often used in conjunction with X-ray spectrometers to obtain information about surfaces.

Electron spectroscopy. Electron spectroscopy comprises a group of analytical methods that measure the kinetic energy of expelled electrons after initial bombardment of the analyte with X rays, ultraviolet radiation, ions, or electrons. When X rays are used for the bombardment, the analytical method is called either electron spectroscopy for chemical analysis (ESCA) or X-ray photoelectron spectroscopy (XPS). If the incident radiation is ultraviolet radiation, the method is termed ultraviolet photoelectron spectroscopy (UPS) or photoelectron spectroscopy (PES). When the bombarding particles are electrons and different emitted electrons are monitored, the method is Auger electron spectroscopy (AES). Other forms of less frequently used electron spectroscopy are available as well.

Auger spectroscopy

Radiochemical methods. During use of the radiochemical methods, spontaneous emissions of particles or electromagnetic radiation from unstable atomic nuclei are monitored. The intensity of the emitted particles or electromagnetic radiation is used for quantitative analysis, and the energy of the emissions is used for qualitative analysis. Emissions of alpha particles, electrons (negatrons and positrons), neutrons, protons, and gamma rays can be useful. Gamma rays are energetically identical to X rays; however, they are emitted as a result of nuclear transformations rather than electron orbital transitions.

A radioisotope is an isotope of an element that spontaneously emits particles or radiation. Radioisotopes can be assayed using a radioanalytical method. In other cases, it is possible to bombard a nonradioactive sample with a particle or with radiation in order to transform temporarily all or part of the sample into a radioactive material that can be assayed. Sometimes it is possible to dilute a sample with a radioactive isotope of the assayed element. If the amount of the dilution can be deduced, the intensity of the emissions from the added radioisotope can be used to assay the nonradioactive analyte. This method is called isotopic dilution analysis.

ELECTROANALYSIS

The second major category of instrumental analysis is electroanalysis. The electroanalytical methods use electrically conductive probes, called electrodes, to make electrical contact with the analyte solution. The electrodes are used in conjunction with electric or electronic devices to which they are attached to measure an electrical parameter of the solution. The measured parameter is related to the identity of the analyte or to the quantity of the analyte in the solution.

The electroanalytical methods are divided into categories according to the electric parameters that are measured. The major electroanalytical methods include potentiometry, amperometry, conductometry, electrogravimetry, voltammetry (and polarography), and coulometry. The names of the methods reflect the measured electric property or its units. Potentiometry measures electric potential (or voltage) while maintaining a constant (normally nearly zero) electric current between the electrodes. Amperometry monitors electric current (amperes) while keeping the potential constant. Conductometry measures conductance (the ability of a solution to carry an electric current) while a constant alternating-current (AC) potential is maintained between the electrodes. Electrogravimetry is a gravimetric technique similar to the classical gravimetric methods that were described above, in which the solid that is weighed is deposited on one of the electrodes. Voltammetry is a technique in which the potential is varied in a regular manner while the current is monitored. Polarography is a subtype of voltammetry that utilizes a liquid metal electrode. Coulometry is a method that monitors the quantity of electricity (coulombs) that are consumed during an electrochemical reaction involving the analyte.

Most of the electroanalytical methods rely on the flow of electrons between one or more of the electrodes and the analyte. The analyte must be capable of either accepting one or more electrons (known as reduction) from the electrode or donating one or more electrons (oxidation) to the electrode. As an example, ferric iron (Fe^{3+}) can be assayed because it can undergo a reduction to ferrous iron (Fe^{2+}) by accepting an electron from the electrode as shown in the following reaction:

Oxidation and reduction

$$Fe^{3+} + e^- \text{ (from the electrode)} \rightarrow Fe^{2+}$$

Conductometry. This is the method in which the capability of the analyte to conduct an electrical current is monitored. From Ohm's law ($E = IR$) it is apparent that the electric current (I) is inversely proportional to the resistance (R), where E represents potential difference. The inverse of the resistance is the conductance ($G = 1/R$). As the conductance of a solution increases, its ability to conduct an electric current increases.

In liquid solutions current is conducted between the electrodes by dissolved ions. The conductance of a solution depends on the number and types of ions in the solution. Generally small ions and highly charged ions conduct current better than large ions and ions with a small charge. The size of the ions is important because it determines the speed with which the ions can travel through the solution. Small ions can move more rapidly than larger ones. The charge is significant because it determines the amount of electrostatic attraction between the electrode and the ions.

Because conductometric measurements require the presence of ions, conductometry is not useful for the analysis of undissociated molecules. The measured conductance is the total conductance of all the ions in the solution. Since all ions contribute to the conductivity of a solution, the method is not particularly useful for qualitative analysis—*i.e.,* the method is not selective. The two major uses of conductometry are to monitor the total conductance of a solution and to determine the end points of titrations that involve ions. Conductivity meters are used in conjunction with water purification systems, such as stills or deionizers, to indicate the presence or absence of ion-free water.

Conductometric titration curves are prepared by plotting the conductance as a function of the volume of added titrant. The curves consist of linear regions prior to and after the end point. The two linear portions are extrapolated to their point of intersection at the end point. As in other titrations, the end-point volume is used to calculate the amount or concentration of analyte that was originally present.

Voltammetry. Voltammetry can be used for both qualitative and quantitative analysis of a wide variety of molecular and ionic materials. In this method, a set of two or three electrodes is dipped into the analyte solution, and a regularly varying potential is applied to the indicator electrode relative to the reference electrode. The analyte electrochemically reacts at the indicator electrode. The reference electrode is constructed so that its potential is constant regardless of the solution into which it is dipped. Usually a third electrode (an auxiliary or counter electrode) is placed in the solution for the purpose of carrying most of the current. The potential is controlled between the indicator electrode and the reference electrode, but the current flows between the auxiliary electrode and the indicator electrode.

The several forms of voltammetry differ in the type of varying potential that is applied to the indicator electrode. Polarography is voltammetry in which the indicator electrode is made of mercury or, rarely, another liquid metal. In classic polarography, mercury drops from a capillary tube. The surface of the mercury drop is the site of the electrochemical reaction with the analyte. The manner in which the direct-current (DC) potential of the indicator electrode varies with time is a potential (or voltage) ramp. In the most common case, the potential varies linearly with time, and the analytical method is known as linear sweep voltammetry (LSV).

Polarography

Typically the potential is initially adjusted to a value at which no electrochemical reaction occurs at the indicator electrode. The potential is scanned in a direction that makes an electrochemical reaction more favourable. If reduction reactions are studied, the electrode is made more cathodic (negative); if oxidations are studied, the electrode is made more anodic (positive). Initially the current that is measured, before the electrochemical reaction begins, is small. As the electrode potential is changed, however, sufficient energy is applied to the indicator electrode to cause the reaction to take place. As the reaction occurs, electrons are withdrawn from the electrode (for electrochemical reductions) or donated to the electrode (for oxidations), and a current flows in the external electrical circuit. A voltammogram is a plot of the current as a function of the applied potential. The shape of a voltammogram depends on the type of indicator electrode and the potential ramp

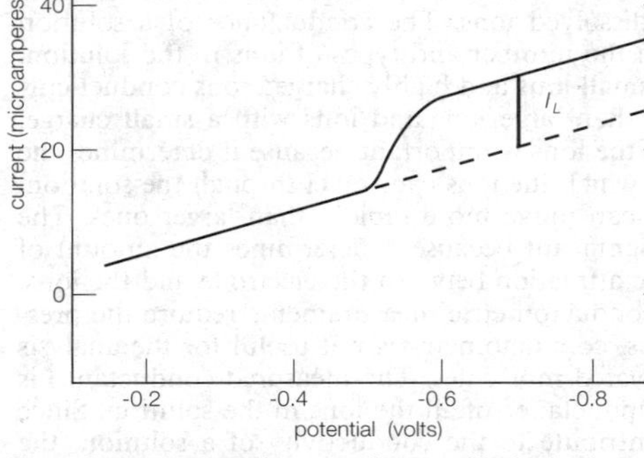

Figure 7: A voltammetric wave of copper(II) obtained by using a rotating platinum indicator electrode. The limiting current (I_L) is the height of the wave measured from the extrapolated linear portion of the current and is proportional to concentration.

that are used. In nearly all cases, the voltammogram has a current wave as shown in Figure 7 or a current peak as shown in Figure 8.

This technique can be used for qualitative analysis because substances exhibit characteristic peaks or waves at different potentials. The height (current) of the wave or the peak, as measured by extrapolating the linear portion of the curve prior to the wave or peak and taking the difference between this extrapolated line and the current peak or plateau, is directly proportional to the concentration of the analyte and can be used for quantitative analysis. Normally the concentration corresponding to the peak or wave height of the analyte is determined from a working curve.

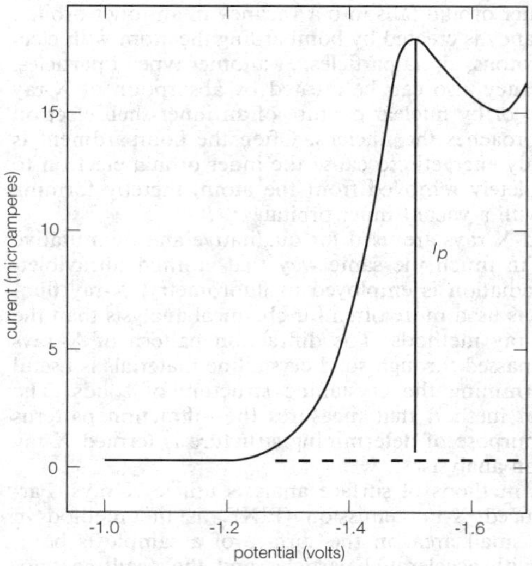

Figure 8: A voltammetric peak of gossypol ($C_{30}H_{30}O_8$) dissolved in methanol. The peak current (I_p) is proportional to concentration.

Triangular wave voltammetry (TWV) is a method in which the potential is linearly scanned to a value past the potential at which an electrochemical reaction occurs and is then immediately scanned back to its original potential. A triangular wave voltammogram usually has a current peak on the forward scan and a second, inverted peak on the reverse scan representing the opposite reaction (oxidation or reduction) to that observed on the forward scan. Cyclic voltammetry is identical to TWV except in having more than one cycle of forward and reverse scans successively completed.

During AC voltammetry an alternating potential is added to the DC potential ramp used for LSV. Only the AC portion of the total current is measured and plotted as a function of the DC potential portion of the potential ramp. Because flow of an alternating current requires the electrochemical reaction to occur in the forward and reverse directions, AC voltammetry is particularly useful for studying the extent to which electrochemical reactions are reversible.

Differential pulse voltammetry adds a periodically applied potential pulse (temporary increase in potential) to the voltage ramp used for LSV. The current is measured just prior to application of the pulse and at the end of the applied pulse. The difference between the two currents is plotted as a function of the LSV ramp potential. Pulse voltammetry utilizes a regularly increasing pulse height that is applied at periodic intervals. In pulse and differential pulse polarography the pulses are applied just before the mercury drop falls from the electrode. Typically the pulse is applied for about 50–60 milliseconds; and the current is measured during the last 17 milliseconds of each pulse. The voltammogram is a plot of the measured current as a function of the potential of the pulse. Many other variations of voltammetry also are available but are not as commonly used. Sketches showing the various potential ramps that are applied to the indicator electrode during the various types of polarography, along with the

Pulse voltammetry

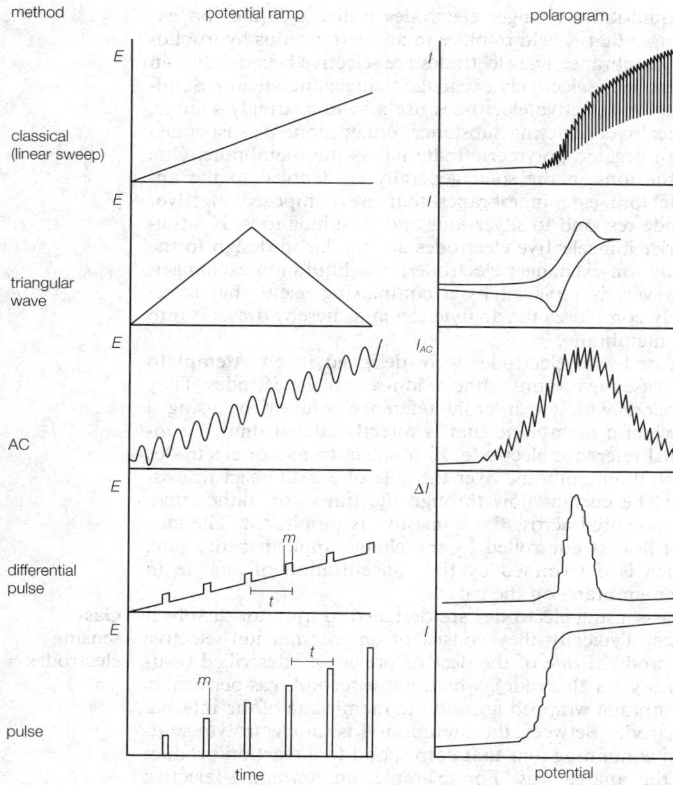

Figure 9: The potential ramps applied to the indicator electrode during selected forms of polarography and the corresponding polarograms. *E* is the potential; *I*, the current; Δ*I*, the current difference; I_{AC}, the AC current; *t*, the mercury electrode drop time; and m, the points at which measurements are made.

typical corresponding polarograms, are shown in Figure 9.

Electrogravimetry. Electrogravimetry was briefly described above as an interference removal technique. This method employs two or three electrodes, just as in voltammetry. Either a constant current or a constant potential is applied to the preweighed working electrode. The working electrode corresponds to the indicator electrode in voltammetry and most other electroanalytical methods. A solid product of the electrochemical reaction of the analyte coats the electrode during application of the electric current or potential. After the assayed substance has been completely removed from the solution by the electrochemical reaction, the working electrode is removed, rinsed, dried, and weighed. The increased mass of the electrode due to the presence of the reaction product is used to calculate the initial concentration of the analyte.

Assays done by using constant-current electrogravimetry can be completed more rapidly (typically 30 minutes per assay) than assays done by using constant-potential electrogravimetry (typically one hour per assay), but the constant-current assays are subject to more interferences. If only one component in the solution can react to form a deposit on the electrode, constant-current electrogravimetry is the preferred method. In constant-potential electrogravimetry the potential at the working electrode is controlled so that only a single electrochemical reaction can occur. The applied potential corresponds to the potential on the plateau of a voltammetric wave of the assayed material.

Coulometry. This technique is similar to electrogravimetry in that it can be used in the constant-current or in the constant-potential modes. It differs from electrogravimetry, however, in that the total quantity of electricity (coulombs) required to cause the analyte to completely react is measured rather than the mass of the electrochemical reaction product. It is not necessary for the reaction product to deposit on the electrode in order to perform a coulometric assay; however, it is necessary that the current that flows through the electrode be ultimately used for a single electrochemical reaction. This requirement can be met in constant-current coulometry by using the current to perform a coulometric titration. In a coulometric titration, the current generates a titrant that chemically reacts with the analyte. By keeping the precursor to the titrant in excess, it is possible to ensure that all of the current is used to form the chemical reactant. Because the electrochemically formed titrant reacts completely with the analyte, it is possible to perform a quantitative analysis. Constant-potential coulometry is not subject to the effects of interferences, because the potential of the working electrode is controlled at a value at which only a single electrochemical reaction can occur.

Amperometry. During amperometric assays the potential of the indicator electrode is adjusted to a value on the plateau of the voltammetric wave, as during controlled-potential electrogravimetry and coulometry (see above). The current that flows between the indicator electrode and a second electrode in the solution is measured and related to the concentration of the analyte. Amperometry is commonly employed in two ways, both of which take advantage of the linear variation in current at constant potential with the concentration of an electroactive species. A working curve of current as a function of concentration of a series of standard solutions is prepared, and the concentration of the analyte is determined from the curve, or amperometry is used to locate the end point in an amperometric titration. An amperometric titration curve is a plot of current as a function of titrant volume. The shape of the curve varies depending on which chemical species (the titrant, the analyte, or the product of the reaction) is electroactive. In each case the curve consists of linear regions before and after the end point that are extrapolated to intersection at the end point.

Amperometric titrations

Potentiometry. This is the method in which the potential between two electrodes is measured while the electric current (usually nearly zero) between the electrodes is controlled. In the most common forms of potentiometry, two different types of electrodes are used. The potential of the indicator electrode varies, depending on the concentration of the analyte, while the potential of the reference electrode is constant. Potentiometry is probably the most frequently used electroanalytical method. It can be divided into two categories on the basis of the nature of the indicator electrode. If the electrode is a metal or other conductive material that is chemically and physically inert when placed in the analyte, it reflects the potential of the bulk solution into which it is dipped. Electrode materials that are commonly used for this type of potentiometry include platinum, gold, silver, graphite, and glassy carbon.

Inert-indicator-electrode potentiometry utilizes oxidation-reduction reactions. The potential of a solution that contains an oxidation-reduction couple (*e.g.*, Fe^{3+} and Fe^{2+}) is dependent on the identity of the couple and on the activities of the oxidized and reduced chemical species in the couple. For a general reduction half reaction of the form $Ox + ne^- \rightarrow Red$, where Ox is the oxidized form of the chemical species, Red is the reduced form, and n is the number of electrons (e^-) transferred during the reaction, the potential can be calculated by using the Nernst equation (equation 2). In the Nernst equation E is the potential at the indicator electrode, E° is the standard potential of the electrochemical reduction (a value that changes as the chemical identity of the couple changes), R is the gas law constant, T is the absolute temperature of the solution, n is the number of electrons transferred in the reduction (the value in the half reaction), F is the faraday constant, and the a_{Ox} and a_{Red} terms are the activities of the oxidized and reduced chemical species, respectively, in the solution. The activities can be replaced by concentrations of the ionic species if the solution is sufficiently dilute.

$$E = E^\circ - \frac{RT}{nF} \ln \frac{a_{Red}}{a_{Ox}} \qquad (2)$$

The most common use for potentiometry with inert-indicator electrodes is determining the end points of oxidation-reduction titrations. A potentiometric titration curve is a plot of potential as a function of the volume of added titrant. The curves have an "S" or backward "S"

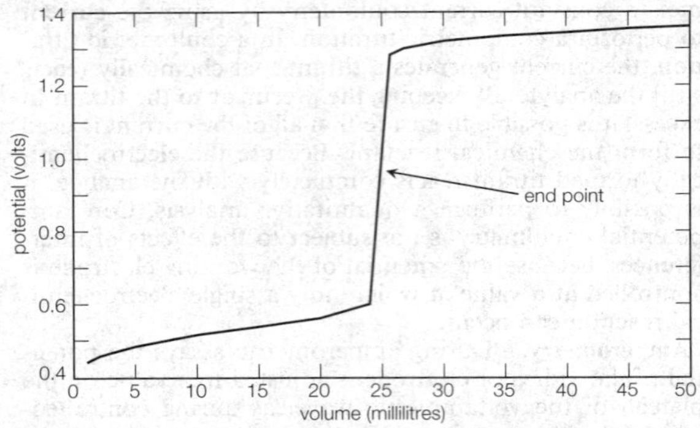

Figure 10: The potentiometric titration curve for the titration of 0.01 molar iron(II) with 0.01 molar cerium(IV).

shape, where the end point of the titration corresponds to the inflection point. A typical potentiometric titration curve is shown in Figure 10.

Ion-selective electrodes

The second category of potentiometric indicator electrodes is the ion-selective electrode. Ion-selective electrodes preferentially respond to a single chemical species. The potential between the indicator electrode and the reference electrode varies as the concentration or activity of that particular species varies. Unlike the inert indicator electrodes, ion-selective electrodes do not respond to all species in the solution. The electrodes usually are constructed as illustrated in Figure 11. An internal reference electrode dips into a reference solution containing the assayed species and constant concentrations of the species to which the internal electrode responds. The internal reference electrode and reference solution are separated from the analyte solution by a membrane that is chosen to respond to the analyte. As usual, a second external reference electrode is also dipped into the analyte solution.

The selectivity of the ion-selective electrodes results from the selective interaction between the membrane and the analyte. The electrodes are categorized according to the nature of the membrane. The most common types of ion-selective electrodes are the glass, liquid-ion-exchanger, solid-state, neutral-carrier, coated-wire, field-effect transistor, gas-sensing, and biomembrane electrodes. The glass membranes in glass electrodes are designed to allow partial penetration by the analyte ion. They are most often used for pH measurements, where the hydrogen ion is the measured species.

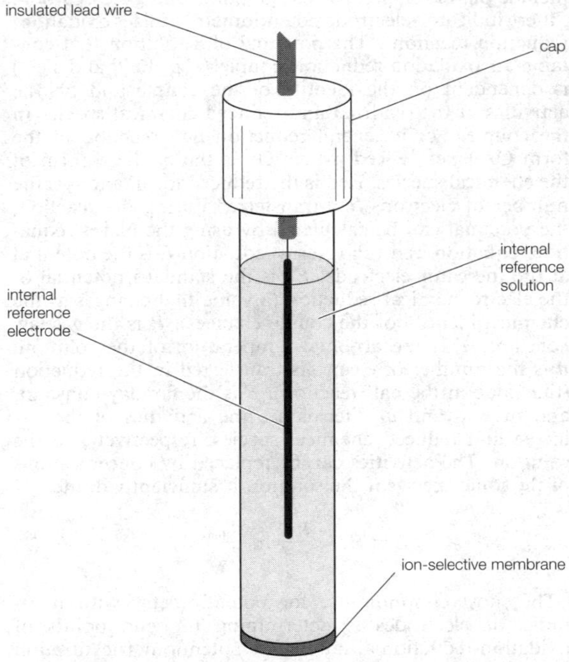

Figure 11: An ion-selective electrode for use in potentiometric measurements.

Liquid-ion-exchanger electrodes utilize a liquid ion exchanger that is held in place in an inert, porous hydrophobic membrane. The electrodes are selective because the ion exchangers selectively exchange a single analyte ion. Solid-state ion-selective electrodes use a solid sparingly soluble, ionically conducting substance, either alone or suspended in an organic polymeric material, as the membrane. One of the ions in the solid generally is identical to the analyte ion; *e.g.,* membranes that are composed of silver sulfide respond to silver ions and to sulfide ions. Neutral-carrier ion-selective electrodes are similar in design to the liquid-ion-exchanger electrodes. The liquid ion exchanger, however, is replaced by a complexing agent that selectively complexes the analyte ion and thereby draws it into the membrane.

Coated-wire electrodes were designed in an attempt to decrease the response time of ion-selective electrodes. They dispense with the internal reference solution by using a polymeric membrane that is directly coated onto the internal reference electrode. Field-effect transistor electrodes place the membrane over the gate of a field-effect transistor. The current flow through the transistor, rather than the potential across the transistor, is monitored. The current flow is controlled by the charge applied to the gate, which is determined by the concentration of analyte in the membrane on the gate.

Gas-sensing electrodes

Gas-sensing electrodes are designed to monitor dissolved gases. Typically they consist of an internal ion-selective electrode of one of the designs previously described (usually a glass electrode), which has a second, gas-permeable membrane wrapped around the membrane of the internal electrode. Between the membranes is an electrolyte solution containing ions that correspond to a reaction product of the analyte gas. For example, an ammonia-selective electrode can be constructed by using an internal glass pH electrode and an ammonium chloride solution between the membranes. The ammonia from the sample diffuses into the ammonium chloride solution between the membranes and partially dissociates in the aqueous solution to form ammonium ions and hydroxide ions. The internal pH electrode responds to the altered pH of the solution caused by the formation of hydroxide ions.

Biomembrane electrodes are similar in design to gas-sensing electrodes. The outer permeable membrane is used to hold a gel between the two membranes. The gel contains an enzyme that selectively catalyzes the reaction of the analyte. The internal ion-selective electrode is chosen to respond to one of the products of the catalyzed reaction. Internal pH electrodes are commonly used.

In the absence of electrode interferences from other ions, ion-selective electrodes usually obey equation (3), where E is the potential measured between the electrode and a reference electrode, z is the charge on the analyte ion, a_i is the activity of the ion, and the other terms represent the same terms as given above for the Nernst equation.

$$E = \text{constant} + \frac{RT}{zF}\ln a_i \tag{3}$$

Quantitative analysis of all ions except hydrogen generally is performed by using the working curve method. A working curve is prepared by plotting the potential of a series of standard solutions as a function of the logarithm or natural logarithm (ln) of the activities or concentrations of the solutions. The activity or concentration of the analyte is determined from the curve.

pH meter

Normally pH measurements are performed with a modified voltmeter called a pH meter. Buffer solutions of known pH are used to standardize the instrument. After standardization, the electrodes are dipped into the analyte and the pH of the solution is displayed. A similar approach can be used in place of the working curve method to determine the concentration of ions other than the hydrogen ion by using standard solutions to adjust the meter.

SEPARATORY METHODS

The final major category of instrumental methods is the separatory methods. Chromatography and mass spectrometry are two such methods that are particularly important for chemical analysis. Because both are described in detail below, they are only introduced in this section.

Chromatography. Chromatography was described earlier as a method for removing interferences prior to an analysis. Both gas and liquid chromatographic methods can be used for chemical analysis.

Gas chromatography. In gas chromatography the stationary phase is contained in a column. The column generally is a coiled metallic or glass tube. An injector near the entrance to the column is used to add the analyte. The mobile phase gas usually is contained in a high pressure gas cylinder that is attached by metallic tubing to the injector and the column. A detector, placed at the exit from the column, responds to the separated components of the analyte. The detector is electrically attached to a recorder or other readout device (*e.g.*, a computer) that displays the detector response as a function of time. The plot of the detector response as a function of time is a chromatogram. Each separated component of the analyte appears as a peak on the chromatogram.

Qualitative analysis is performed by comparing the time required for the component to pass through the column with the corresponding times for known substances. The interval between the instant of injection and the detection of the component is known as the retention time. Because retention times vary with the identity of the component, they are utilized for qualitative analysis. Quantitative analysis is performed by preparing a working curve, at a specific retention time, by plotting the peak height or peak area of a series of standards as a function of the concentration of the component being assayed. The concentration of the component in the analyte is determined from the chromatographic peak height or area of the component and the working curve.

Retention time

Liquid chromatography. This procedure can be performed either in a column or on a plane. Columnar liquid chromatography is used for qualitative and quantitative analysis in a manner similar to the way in which gas chromatography is employed. Sometimes retention volumes, rather than retention times, are used for qualitative analysis. For chemical analysis the most popular category of columnar liquid chromatography is high-performance liquid chromatography (HPLC). The method uses a pump to force one or more mobile phase solvents through high-efficiency, tightly packed columns. As with gas chromatography, an injection system is used to insert the sample into the entrance to the column, and a detector at the end of the column monitors the separated analyte components.

The stationary phase that is used for plane chromatography is physically held in place in or on a plane. Typically the stationary phase is attached to a plastic, metallic, or glass plate. Occasionally, a sheet of high-quality filter paper is used as the stationary phase. The sample is added as a spot or a thin strip at one end of the plane. The mobile phase flows over the spot by capillary action during ascending development or as a result of the force of gravity during descending development. During ascending development, the end of the plane near and below the sample spot is dipped into the mobile phase, and the mobile phase moves up and through the spot. During descending development, the mobile phase is added to the top of the plane and flows downward through the spot.

Qualitative analysis is performed by comparing the retardation factor (R_f) of the analyte components with the retardation factors of known substances. The retardation factor is defined as the distance from the original sample spot that the component has moved divided by the distance that the mobile phase front has moved and is constant for a solute in a given solvent. A sketch of a developed plane chromatogram is shown in Figure 5. Quantitative analysis is performed by measuring the sizes of the developed spots, by measuring some physical property of the spots (such as fluorescence), or by removing the spots from the plane and assaying them by another procedure.

Mass spectrometry. This is the analytical method in which ions or ionic fragments of an analyte are separated based on mass-to-charge ratios (m/z). Most mass spectrometers have four major components: an inlet system, an ion source, a mass analyzer, and a detector. The inlet system is used to introduce the analyte and to convert it to a gas at reduced pressure. The gaseous analyte flows from the inlet system into the ionic source of the instrument where the analyte is converted to ions or ionic fragments. That is often accomplished by bombarding the analyte with electrons or by allowing the analyte to undergo collisions with other ions.

The ions that are formed in the ionic source are accelerated into the mass analyzer by a system of electrostatic slits. In the analyzer the ions are subjected to an electric or magnetic field that is used to alter their paths. In the most common mass analyzers the ions are separated in space according to their mass-to-charge ratios. In time-of-flight mass analyzers, however, no electric or magnetic field is employed, and the time required for ions of varying m/z that are accelerated to the same kinetic energy to pass through a flight tube is measured. The detector is placed at the end of the mass analyzer and measures the intensity of the ionic beam. A mass spectrum is a plot of the ionic beam intensity as a function of the mass-to-charge ratio of the ionic fragment.

Mass analyzer

Mass spectrometry is used for quantitative analysis by relating the height of a specific mass spectrometric peak to the concentration of the analyte. The peak heights vary linearly with concentration. Qualitative analysis is performed by using the entire spectrum. Generally the major peak with the largest m/z is the molecular ion peak that has a charge of +1, corresponding to the loss of a single electron. Consequently, the m/z of the peak corresponds to the molecular weight of the analyte. The spacing between peaks is used to deduce the manner in which the analyte has fragmented in the ionic source. By carefully examining the fragmentation pattern, it is possible to deduce the structure of the analyte molecule. Computerized comparisons of analyte mass spectra with mass spectra of known materials is commonly used to identify an analyte. (R.D.Br.)

CHEMICAL SEPARATIONS AND PURIFICATIONS

Since ancient times, people have used methods of separating and purifying chemical substances for improving the quality of life. The extraction of metals from ores and of medicines from plants is older than recorded history. In the Middle Ages the alchemists' search for the philosophers' stone (a means of changing base metals into gold) and the elixir of life (a substance that would perpetuate youth) depended on separations. In the industrial and technological revolutions, separations and purifications have assumed major importance. During World War II, for example, one of the main problems of the Manhattan Project, the U.S. government research project that led to the first atomic bombs, was the separation of uranium-235 from uranium-238. Many industries now find separations indispensable: the petroleum industry separates crude oil into products used as fuels, lubricants, and chemical raw materials; the pharmaceutical industry separates and purifies natural and synthetic drugs to meet health needs; and the mining industry is based on the separation and purification of metals.

Industrial and military importance

Separations and purifications also find their places in medicine and the sciences. In the life sciences, many advances can be directly traced to the development of each new separation method. The first step in understanding the chemical reactions of life is to learn what substances are present in samples obtained from biological sources. As an example of the challenge and power of such separations, Figure 12 shows the two-dimensional gel electrophoretic separation of sulfur-35 methionine-labeled polypeptides, or proteins, from transformed epithelial amnion cells (AMA). A total of 1,244 polypeptides have been observed, many of whose functions are currently unknown.

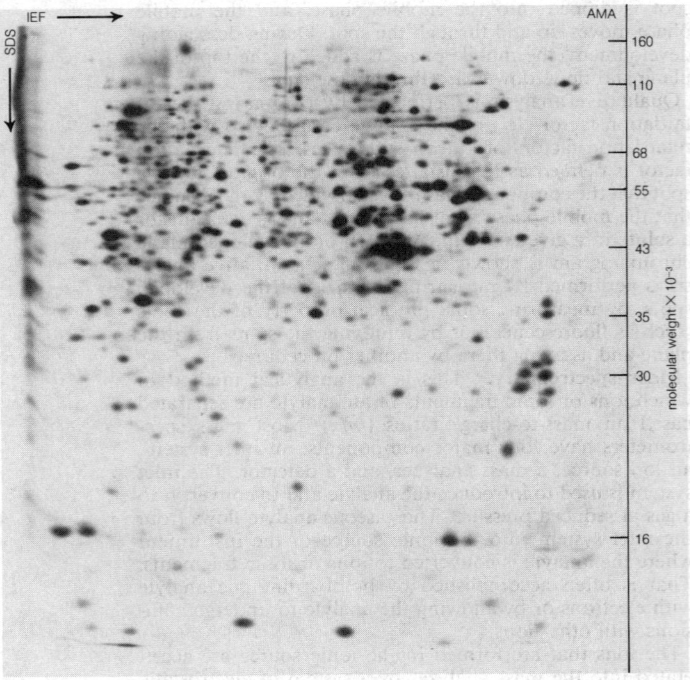

Figure 12: *Two-dimensional gel electrophoretic separation.* Separations based on charge—isoelectric focusing (IEF)—and size—sodium dodecyl sulfate (SDS) protein complexes—are combined in two-dimensional gel electrophoresis, as in this separation of sulfur-35 methionine-labeled proteins from transformed epithelial amnion cells (AMA). Each spot represents one or more proteins.

J.E. Celis, Danish Centre for Human Genome Research

Basic concepts of separations

This section is concerned with separations of the smallest subdivisions of matter, such as atoms, molecules, and minute particles (sand, minerals, bacteria, etc.). Such processes start with a sample in a mixed state (composed of more than one substance) and transform it into new samples, each of which—in the ideal case—consists of a single substance. Separation methods, then, can be defined as processes that change the relative amounts of substances in a mixture. In chemical methods, one may start with a completely homogeneous mixture (a solution) or a heterogeneous sample (*e.g.,* solid plus liquid); in the act of separation, some particles are either partially or totally removed from the sample.

Reasons for making separations. There are two general reasons for performing separations on mixtures. First, the mixture may contain some substance that should be isolated from the rest of the mixture: this process of isolating and thus removing substances considered to be contaminants is called purification. For example, in the manufacture of synthetic drugs, mixtures containing variable proportions of several compounds usually arise. The removal of the desired drug from the rest of the mixture is important if the product is to have uniform potency and is to be free of other components that may be dangerous to the body.

The second reason for performing separations is to alter the composition of a sample so that one or more of the components can be analyzed. For example, the analysis of air pollutants to assess the quality of the air is of great interest, yet many of the pollutants are at a concentration too low for direct analysis, even with the most sensitive devices. Pollutants can be collected by passing samples of air through a tube containing an adsorbent material. By this process the pollutants are concentrated to a level such that straightforward analysis and monitoring can take place. In a second example, several impurities in a sample may interfere with the analysis of the substance of primary interest. Thus, in the analysis of trace concentrations of metals in rivers, organic substances can cause erroneous results. These interferences must be removed prior to the analysis. Several techniques for removing interferences are discussed above in *Chemical analysis: Interference removal.*

Interference removal

Classification of separations. There are a variety of criteria by which separations can be classified. One is based on the quantity of material to be processed. Some methods of separation (*e.g.,* chromatography) work best with a small amount of sample, while others (*e.g.,* distillation) are more suited to large-scale operations.

Classification may also be based on the physical or chemical phenomena utilized to effect the separation. These phenomena can be divided into two broad categories: equilibrium and rate (kinetic) processes. Table 1 lists some separation methods based on equilibria, and Table 2 indicates those methods based on rate phenomena.

Separations based on equilibria. All equilibrium methods considered in this section involve the distribution of substances between two phases that are insoluble in one another. As an example, consider the two immiscible liquids benzene and water. If a coloured compound is placed in the water and the two phases are mixed, colour appears in the benzene phase, and the intensity of the colour in the water phase decreases. These colour changes continue to occur for a certain time, beyond which no macroscopic changes take place, no matter how long or vigorously the two phases are mixed. Because the dye is soluble in the benzene as well as in the water, the dye is extracted into the benzene at the start of the mixing. But, just as the dye tends to move into the benzene phase, so it also tends to be dissolved in the aqueous phase. Thus dye molecules move back and forth across the liquid-liquid interface. Eventually, a condition is reached such that the tendencies of the dye to pass from benzene to water and from water to benzene are equal, and the concentration of the dye (as measured by the intensity of its colour) is constant in the two phases. This is the condition of equilibrium. Note that this is static from a macroscopic point of view. On a molecular level it is a dynamic process, however, for many molecules continue to pass through the liquid-liquid interface (although of equal number in both directions).

The condition of equilibrium in this example can be described in terms of the distribution coefficient, K, by the equation

Distribution coefficient

$$K = \frac{\text{concentration of dye in the benzene phase}}{\text{concentration of dye in the water phase}},$$

in which the concentrations in the equilibrium state are considered. For $K = 1$, there are equal concentrations of the dye in the two phases; for $K > 1$, more dye would be found in the benzene phase at equilibrium. At $K = 100$, 99.01 percent is in the benzene, and only 0.99 percent is in the water (assuming equal volumes of the two liquids). For certain purposes, this condition might be considered to represent essentially complete removal of the dye from the water, but more often $K = 1{,}000$ is selected (*i.e.,* 99.9 percent removal). Depending on the phases and conditions, it is often possible to achieve a K value of 1,000 or more.

Table 1: Separations Based on Phase Equilibria

gas-liquid	gas-solid	liquid-solid	liquid-liquid	supercritical fluid-solid	supercritical fluid-liquid
distillation gas-liquid chromatography foam fractionation	adsorption sublimation	precipitation zone melting crystallization ion exchange adsorption exclusion clathration	extraction partition chromatography	supercritical-fluid chromatography	supercritical-fluid extraction

Separation results when the distribution coefficient values for two substances (*e.g.,* two dyes) differ from one another. Consider a case in which $K = 100$ for one substance and $K = 0.01$ for a second substance: then, upon reaching equilibrium, 99 percent of the former substance will be found in the benzene phase, and 99 percent of the latter substance will be found in the aqueous phase. It is clear that this sample is rather easily separated by liquid-liquid distribution. The ease of the separation thus depends on the ratio of the two distribution coefficients, α (sometimes called the separation factor):

$$\alpha = \frac{K_2}{K_1},$$

in which K_1 and K_2 are the respective distribution coefficients of components 1 and 2. In the above example, $\alpha = 10{,}000$. In many other cases, α can be extremely small, close to unity (α is defined such that it is always unity or greater): then separation is difficult, requiring very efficient methods. Part of the art of separations is finding conditions that produce large separation factors of pairs of substances.

In Table 1 most of the important chemical equilibrium separation methods are subdivided in terms of the two insoluble phases (gas, liquid, or solid). A supercritical fluid is a phase that occurs for a gas at a specific temperature and pressure such that the gas will no longer condense to a liquid regardless of how high the pressure is raised. It is a state intermediate between a gas and a liquid. The example previously cited involved extraction (liquid-liquid). The other methods are described below.

Separations based on rates. Rate separation processes are based on differences in the kinetic properties of the components of a mixture, such as the velocity of migration in a medium or of diffusion through semipermeable barriers.

The separation of mixtures of proteins is often difficult because of the similarity of the properties of such molecules. When proteins are dissolved in water, they ionize (form electrically charged particles). Both positive and negative electrical charges can occur on various parts of the complex molecule, and, depending on the pH of the solution, a protein molecule as a whole will be either net positively or negatively charged. For a given set of solution conditions, the net charges on different proteins usually are unequal.

Electrophoresis

Electrophoresis takes advantage of these charge differences to effect a separation. In this method, two electrodes are positioned at opposite ends of a paper, starch gel, column, or other appropriate supporting medium. A salt solution is used to moisten the medium and to connect the electrodes electrically. The mixture to be separated is placed in the centre of the supporting medium, and an electrical potential is applied. The positively charged proteins move toward the negatively charged electrode (cathode), while the negatively charged proteins migrate toward the positively charged electrode (anode). The migration velocity in each direction depends not only on the charge on the proteins but also on their size: thus proteins with the same charge can be separated.

This example demonstrates the separation of charged species on the basis of differences in migration velocity in an electric field. The extent of such a separation (based on the rate of a process) is time-dependent, a feature that distinguishes such separations from those based upon equilibria.

The velocity can be either positive or negative, depending on direction. It depends not only on the size and electrical charge of the molecule but also on the conditions of the experiment (*e.g.,* voltage between the two electrodes). In analogy to equilibrium methods, the separation factor can be defined as the ratio of migration velocities for two proteins:

$$\alpha = \frac{\nu_2}{\nu_1}.$$

The extent of separation (*i.e.,* how far one protein is removed from another) depends on the different distances traversed by the two proteins:

$$\text{extent} = \nu_2 t - \nu_1 t,$$

where t is the time allowed for migration. Thus the extent of separation is directly proportional to the time of migration in the electric field.

Diffusion through membranes

Another major category of rate separation methods is based on the diffusion of molecules through semipermeable barriers. Besides differing in charge, proteins also differ in size, and this latter property can be used as the basis of separation. If a vessel is divided in half by a porous membrane, and a solution of different proteins is placed in one section and pure water in the other, some of the proteins will be able to diffuse freely through the membrane, while others will be too large to fit through the holes or pores. Still others will be able to just squeeze through the pores and so will diffuse more slowly through the membrane. The extent of separation will thus be dependent on the time allowed for diffusion to take place.

Table 2: Separations Based on Rate Phenomena

barrier separations	field separations
membrane filtration dialysis ultrafiltration electrodialysis reverse osmosis	electrophoresis ultracentrifugation electrolysis field-flow fractionation

Table 2 lists the various barrier separation methods discussed in this article. The differences in the methods involve the type of substances diffusing through the semipermeable barrier and whether an external field or pressure is applied across the membrane.

Particle separations. Up to this point, only separations at the molecular level have been discussed. Separations of particles are also important in both industry and research. Particle separations are performed for one of two purposes: (1) to remove particles from gases or liquids, or (2) to separate particles of different sizes or properties. The first reason underlies many important applications. The electronics industry requires dust-free "clean rooms" for assembly of very small components. The second purpose deals with the classification of particles from samples containing particles of many different sizes. Many technical processes using finely divided materials require that the particle size be as uniform as possible. In addition, the separation of cells is important in the biotechnology industry. The more important particle separation methods are filtration, sedimentation, elutriation, centrifugation, particle electrophoresis, electrostatic precipitation, flotation, and screening, which are described in a later section.

Single-stage versus multistage processes. As shown earlier, ease of separation in equilibrium methods is based on the value of the separation factor, α. When this value is large, separation is easy, requiring little input of work. Thus, if α lies between 100 and 1,000, a single equilibration in liquid-liquid extraction is sufficient to separate at the level of 90 percent or higher. This type of process is called a single-stage process.

The multistage process

If the separation factor is smaller, separation is more difficult: more work must be done on the system to achieve the desired separation. This result can be accomplished by repeating the equilibration process many times, such a method being called a multistage process.

Consider a liquid-liquid extraction experiment in which the volumes of the two liquid phases (A and B) are equal and in which equal amounts of two components, 1 and 2, are present in one of the phases (say A). If $K_1 = 0.5$ and $K_2 = 2.5$, then $\alpha = 5$, according to the previous definition. After equilibration, 66.7 percent of component 1 and 28.5 percent of component 2 remain in the original liquid phase (A), because $K_1 = 0.5 = 33.3/66.7$ and $K_2 = 2.5 = 71.5/28.5$; so that the concentration ratio in this phase has gone from unity to 66.7/28.5, or 2.3. If the extracting liquid phase (B) is removed and replaced with an equal portion of fresh liquid (B) containing none of components 1 and 2, and a second extraction is performed, 44.4 percent of component 1 and 8.1 percent of component 2 are left in the original phase (A). The concentration ratio has increased from 2.3 to 5.5; however, note that there is less of components 1 and 2 in the original phase. If the equilibration is carried out again with fresh solvent (B), the original phase contains 29.6 percent of component 1 and only 2.3 percent of component 2, a concentration ratio of approximately 13. Thus the purity of component 1 is increased by repeating the process of equilibration.

Before examining multistage separations in more detail, consider an alternate procedure by which component 2 (with $K = 2.5$) could be removed from the original liquid phase. Three consecutive extractions with fresh solvent result in the removal of $100 - 2.3 = 97.7$ percent of the component. Suppose one extraction is performed instead, using the same volume of liquid B employed in the three consecutive extractions. It can be calculated that only 88 percent of component 2 would be extracted in this case. Thus, repeated equilibrations with a small amount of solvent remove more material than a single extraction with a large amount.

Returning to the separation of two components, the experiments described are quite wasteful of material. While the concentration ratio is 13, only 30 percent of the concentrated component remains in the original phase. It seems clear that the extracted phase should not be discarded. The separation can be performed without loss of either component by employing a sequence of extractions: each vessel in a series is half filled with a pure portion of the denser, or lower, liquid phase (*i.e.*, without components 1 and 2). The mixture is added to the lower phase (A in the above example) of the first vessel, and fresh upper phase (B) is added in the correct amount; after shaking to achieve equilibration, the upper phase is transferred to the second vessel, and fresh upper phase is added to vessel 1. Vessels 1 and 2 are both equilibrated, and the upper phases are moved along the train, one vessel at a time.

In this experiment, component 2 (with $K = 2.5$) will move more quickly down the train of vessels than component 1. After a large number of transfers, the different migration velocities of the two components will result in complete separation. The number of transfers required to achieve complete separation is dependent on the value of the separation factor (α) of the two components; the smaller the value is, the larger must be the number of tubes.

Countercurrent extraction

This discontinuous, multistage, liquid-liquid extraction scheme has been highly refined: a specially designed apparatus is used to permit automatic operation. In the past, this method played an important role in biochemistry for preparing purified materials. Because flow of the two solvents occurs in both directions, this mode of operation is called countercurrent.

Today chromatography has for the most part superseded automated liquid-liquid extraction procedures. Chromatography is closely related to the above countercurrent process, with one phase being stationary and the other mobile. In essence, chromatography can be envisioned as repeating the equilibration or distribution process many times as the sample components travel through the chromatographic system. The power of this technique can thus be appreciated.

Principles of specific methods

Equilibrium separations. *Distillation.* Distillation (as discussed above in *Chemical analysis: Interference removal*), is a method of separation based on differences in the boiling points of substances. It has been known for centuries. The essential operation in distillation is the boiling of a liquid; after being converted to a vapour, the substance is then condensed to a liquid that is collected separately rather than allowed to flow back into the original liquid.

Above the surface of any pure liquid (or solid) substance, a definite amount of its vapour is present. The concentration of the vapour and, therefore, the pressure that it exerts increase as the temperature is raised. When the pressure of the vapour equals the pressure of the surroundings (one atmosphere in an open vessel at sea level), the substance boils: bubbles of vapour form within the liquid and rise to the surface. Above the surface of a mixture, the vapour contains all the substances present in the mixture, each making a contribution to the total pressure exerted by the vapour. The boiling point of the mixture is the temperature at which the total vapour pressure equals the pressure of the surroundings. In general, the composition of the vapour above a liquid mixture differs from that of the liquid: the vapour contains a larger proportion of the substance having the lower boiling point. This difference in composition of the two phases is the basis of separations effected by distillation.

Liquid-vapour equilibrium

Separation by distillation thus is based on gas-liquid equilibrium, differing from the previously cited example of liquid-liquid extraction in that the phases are constituted from the components themselves. The ease of separation is based on the differences in the boiling points of the substances; because boiling point is related, to a first approximation, to the molecular weight of the substance, distillation separates on the basis of weight (or size) of molecules. If the boiling points are close together, a multistage operation, which can most conveniently be achieved by placing a column above the boiling liquid solution, is required. This glass column contains some loosely packed material (*e.g.*, glass beads), and the hot vapours from the boiling solution partially condense on the surfaces. The condensed liquid flows back toward the solution until it meets rising hot vapours, whereupon the more volatile portion of the returning liquid revaporizes, and the less volatile part of the rising vapour condenses. Thus in the column there occurs a multistage operation, the outcome of which is that the component of lower boiling point concentrates at the upper part of the column and that of higher boiling point in the lower part. Condensation of the vapour at the top of the column provides material much richer in the component having the lowest boiling point.

Applications

Distillation finds its greatest application in the large-scale separation of liquid mixtures, as in petroleum-refining plants, where crude oil is distilled into fractions having various boiling points, such as gasoline, kerosene, and lubricating oils. The large towers in refineries are efficient distillation columns that effect sharp separation of the fractions. Distillation is a procedure essential to the chemist, who uses it to purify synthetic products. In general, however, because of its inability to handle small quantities of material or to separate closely related compounds, the current use of distillation for difficult separations is limited.

Chromatography. Chromatography, as noted above, is a separation process involving two phases, one stationary and the other mobile. Typically, the stationary phase is a porous solid (*e.g.*, glass, silica, or alumina) that is packed into a glass or metal tube or that constitutes the walls of an open-tube capillary. The mobile phase flows through the packed bed or column. The sample to be separated is injected at the beginning of the column and is transported through the system by the mobile phase. In their travel through the column, the different substances distribute themselves according to their relative affinity for the two phases. The rate of travel is dependent on the values of the distribution coefficients, the components interacting more strongly with the stationary phase requiring longer time periods for elution (complete removal from the column). Thus, separation is based on differences in distribution behaviour reflected in different migration times through the column. As in repetitive extraction, the larger that the separation factor is for a pair of components, the shorter will be the column necessary to resolve them. Chromatography is thus analogous to multistage extraction, except that in chromatography there are no discontinuous steps but rather a continuous flow. At the present time, chromatography is the most significant method for separation of organic substances and, along with electrophoresis, is most widely used for biological substances.

The various chromatographic methods are characterized in terms of the mobile phase—gas: gas chromatography (GC); liquid: liquid chromatography (LC); supercritical fluid: supercritical-fluid chromatography (SFC). The methods are then further subdivided in terms of the stationary phase; thus, if the stationary phase is a solid adsorbent, there are methods such as gas-solid chromatography (GSC) and liquid-solid chromatography (LSC). Chromatography is conducted with computer-controlled instrumentation for high precision and unattended operation. In addition, a detector is frequently placed on-line after the column for either structure analysis or quantitation or both. One of the most powerful approaches of analysis now available is the on-line coupling of chromatography to mass spectrometry (see below *Mass spectroscopy*).

Gas chromatography

Gas chromatography is an important method owing to its speed, resolving power, and detector sensitivity. Since it depends on vaporization, this technique is best suited to compounds that can be vaporized without suffering decomposition. Many substances that normally do not easily vaporize can be chemically derivatized for successful volatilization separation by gas chromatography.

In addition to chromatography, gas-solid distribution is also widely employed for purification, using special adsorbents called molecular sieves. These materials contain pores of approximately the same dimensions as small molecules. This property can be exploited in the separation of molecules having linear structures from those having bulky structures. The former can readily enter the pores, but the latter are unable to penetrate. This is an example of an exclusion mechanism of separation (based on shape differences). Molecular sieves also play an important role in the drying of gases: water, a polar substance (*i.e.*, its net positive and negative electrical charges are unevenly distributed within the molecule), is readily adsorbed on the particles, but less polar gases are not retained.

In sublimation, another method of gas-solid distribution, a solid evaporates without passing through the liquid state. Sublimation is somewhat analogous to distillation in that, like the latter, it involves evaporation. Since not all substances sublime, the applicability of the method is limited.

Liquid chromatography

Since the early 1970s, liquid chromatography has developed as the premier separation method for organic substances. Because the mobile phase is a liquid, the requirement for vaporization is eliminated, and therefore LC can separate a much broader range of substances than GC. Species that have been successfully resolved include inorganic ions, amino acids, drugs, sugars, oligonucleotides, and proteins. Both analytical-scale liquid chromatography with samples at the microgram to milligram level and preparative-scale liquid chromatography at the tens of gram level have been developed. In biotechnology, preparative-scale liquid chromatography is especially important for purification of proteins and peptide hormones made by recombinant technology.

One important method is liquid-solid chromatography in which the porous adsorbent is polar and separation is based on the properties of classes of compounds—*e.g.*, amines (alkaline) from alcohols (neutral) and esters (neutral) from acids.

Liquid-solid chromatography is the oldest of the chromatographic methods. Until the mid-20th century, the experimental procedure had not changed much from its original form. After significant improvements, liquid-solid chromatography now is conducted with porous particles as small as 3–5 micrometres (0.00012–0.00020 inch) in diameter, and liquid pumps are used to drive the liquid through the particle-filled column. High resolution and fast separations are achieved since the small particles allow good efficiency with fast mobile phase velocities (one centimetre per second or higher). This technique is also important in purification, and separated substances can be automatically collected after the column using a fraction collector.

Reverse-phase chromatography

A significant liquid-solid chromatography procedure is reverse-phase chromatography, in which the liquid mobile phase is water combined with an organic solvent such as methanol or acetonitrile and the stationary phase surface is nonpolar or hydrocarbon-like. In contrast to normal-phase chromatography, where the adsorbent surface is polar, in reverse-phase chromatography the elution of substances from the column is in the order of increasing polarity. In addition, separation is based on the nonpolar aspects of the substances. The separation of a series of peptides from human growth hormone, a recombinantly made drug, is shown in Figure 13. An enzyme, trypsin, is used to break peptide bonds containing the basic amino acids—arganine and lysine—to yield a specific fingerprint of the protein. Peptide mapping, as illustrated in Figure 13, is a critical method for evaluating the purity of complex substances such as proteins. For example, the only difference in the top and bottom chromatograms is the addition of amino acid methionine at the *N*-terminal amino acid in the top separation.

From R.L. Garnick, N.J. Solli, and P.A. Papa, *Analytical Chemistry*, 60, 2546 (1988)

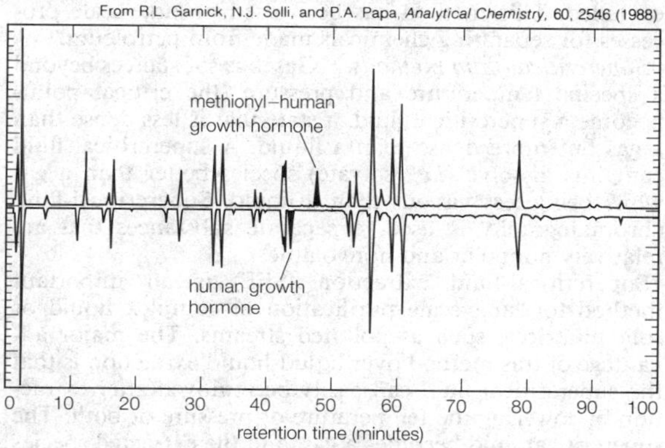

Figure 13: *Tryptic map chromatograms of methionyl-human growth hormone and human growth hormone.*
Peptide mapping can distinguish these two substances, which differ only in the presence of amino acid methionine at the *N*-terminal peptide in the top protein. The slight differences in retention times of the peaks early in the chromatogram result from high-performance liquid chromatography problems with shallow gradients.

Ion-exchange chromatography

Ion-exchange chromatography (IEC) is a subdivision of liquid-solid chromatography, but its importance is such that it deserves special mention. As the name implies, the process separates ions; the basis of the separation is the varying attraction of different ions in a solution to oppositely charged sites on a finely divided, insoluble substance (the ion exchanger, usually a synthetic resin). In a cation-exchange resin all the sites are negatively charged, so that only positive ions can be separated; an anion-exchange resin has positively charged sites. Ion-exchange chromatography has become one of the most important methods for separating proteins and small oligonucleotides.

An important application of ion exchange is the removal of dissolved iron, calcium, and magnesium ions from hard water. The negative sites on a cation exchanger are first neutralized with sodium ions by exposure to a strong solution of common salt (sodium chloride); when the hard water is passed through the resin, the undesirable ions in the water are replaced by sodium ions.

Liquid-solid adsorption chromatography also can be performed on thin, flat plates (thin-layer chromatography, or TLC). TLC is inexpensive and rapid but not as sensitive or efficient as column chromatography. In practice, the adsorbent is spread on a glass plate and dried. The sample is applied as a spot near one end of the plate, which is placed (vertically) in a shallow reservoir containing the mobile phase. As the mobile phase travels up the plate by capillary action, the sample dissolves in the liquid, and its components are transported up the plate to new positions at varying distances from the starting point. (For further discussion, see the section *Chromatography* below.)

Exclusion and clathration. Differences in the sizes of molecules can also be the basis for separations. An example of these techniques is the use of molecular sieves in gas-solid chromatography.

Size-exclusion chromatography

Size-exclusion chromatography (SEC) has proved effective for the separation and analysis of mixtures of polymers. In this method the largest molecules emerge from the chromatographic column first, because they are unable to penetrate the porous matrix of the support. Smaller molecules appear later, because they can traverse the entire porous matrix. A column can be calibrated with polymer samples of known molecular weight so that the time required for emergence of the unknown mixture can be used to deduce the molecular weights of the components of the sample as well as their proportions; such molecular weight distributions are very important characteristics of polymers. Exclusion chromatography also finds use in the separation of mixtures of proteins, which are natural polymers.

In clathration, separation also is based on fitting molecules into sites of specific dimensions. Upon crystallizing from solution, certain compounds form cages (on the molecular scale) of definite size. If other substances are present in the liquid solution and they are small enough, then they will be entrapped in the cage; larger components will be excluded. This method has been used in large-scale processes for separating chemicals made from petroleum.

Supercritical-fluid methods. Gaseous substances beyond a specific temperature and pressure (the critical point) become a supercritical fluid, a state that is less dense than a gas but more dense than a liquid. A supercritical fluid can thus dissolve (*i.e.,* solvate) species better than a gas while being less viscous than a liquid. Supercritical-fluid chromatography is used to separate substances that are relatively nonpolar and nonvolatile.

Supercritical-fluid extraction (SFE) is an important method for large-scale purification of complex liquid or solid matrices, such as polluted streams. The major advantage of this method over liquid-liquid extraction is that the supercritical fluid can easily be removed after extraction by lowering the temperature or pressure or both. The supercritical fluid becomes a gas, and the extracted species condense into a liquid or solid. The problem of removing the extracting liquid is eliminated. An example of the SFE method is the removal of caffeine from coffee.

Crystallization and precipitation. Crystallization is a technique that has long been used in the purification of substances. Often, when a solid substance (single compound) is placed in a liquid, it dissolves. Upon adding more of the solid, a point eventually is reached beyond which no further solid dissolves, and the solution is said to be saturated with the solid compound. The concentration of the saturated solution depends on the temperature, in most cases a higher temperature resulting in a higher concentration.

These phenomena can be employed as a means of effecting separation and purification. Thus, if a solution saturated at some temperature is cooled, the dissolved component begins to separate from the solution and continues to do so until the solution again becomes saturated at the lower temperature. Because the solubilities of two solid compounds in a particular solvent generally differ, it often is possible to find conditions such that the solution is saturated with only one of the components of a mixture. When such a solution cools, part of the less soluble substance crystallizes alone, while the more soluble components remain dissolved.

Crystallization, the process of solidifying from solution, is highly complex. Seed particles, or nuclei, form in the solution, and other molecules then deposit on these solid surfaces. The particles eventually become large enough to fall to the bottom of the container. In order to achieve a high purity in the crystallized solid, it is necessary that this precipitation take place slowly. If solidification is rapid, impurities can be entrapped in the solid matrix. Entrapment of foreign material can be minimized if the individual crystals are kept small. It is sometimes necessary to add a seed crystal to the solution in order to begin the crystallization process: the seed crystal provides a solid surface on which further crystallization can take place.

Chemical precipitation

The term precipitation sometimes is differentiated from crystallization by restricting it to processes in which an insoluble compound is formed in the solution by a chemical reaction. It often happens that several substances are precipitated by a given reaction. To achieve separation in such cases, it is necessary to control the concentration of the precipitating agent, so that the solubility of only one substance is exceeded. Alternatively, a second agent can be added to the solution to form stable, soluble products with one or more components in order to suppress their participation in the precipitation reaction. Such compounds, often used in the separation of metal ions, are called masking agents.

Precipitation was used for many years as a standard method for separation and analysis of metals. It has now been replaced, however, by selective and sensitive instrumental methods that directly analyze many metals in aqueous solutions.

Zone melting. Another separation procedure based on liquid-solid equilibria is zone melting, which has found its greatest use in the purification of metals. Purities as high as 99.999 percent often are obtained by application of this technique. Samples are usually in a state of moderate purity before zone melting is performed.

The zone-melting process is easy to visualize. Typically, the sample is made into the form of a thin rod, from 60 centimetres to 3 metres (2 to 10 feet) or more in length. The rod, confined within a tube, is suspended either horizontally or vertically, and a narrow ring that can be heated is positioned around it. The temperature of this ring is held several degrees above the melting point of the solid, and the ring is made to travel very slowly (a few centimetres per hour) along the rod. Thus, in effect, a melted zone travels through the rod: liquid forms on the front side of this zone, and solid crystallizes on the rear side. Because the freezing point of a substance is depressed by the presence of impurities, the last portion of a liquefied sample to freeze is enriched in the impurities. As the molten zone moves along, therefore, it becomes more and more concentrated with impurities. At the end of the operation, the impurities are found solidified at the end of the rod, and the impure section can be removed simply by cutting it off. Ultrahigh purities can be achieved through multistage operation, either by recycling the ring several times or by using several rings in succession.

Rate separations. *Field separations.* Electrophoresis, described in an earlier section of this article, is an important method in the separation of biopolymers—namely, deoxyribonucleic acid (DNA) molecules and proteins. Electrophoresis is conventionally conducted on plates or slabs as in thin-layer chromatography. To maintain the ionic buffer solution on the plate, some anticonvective medium or gel is necessary, and the method is thus called slab-gel electrophoresis. Polyacrylamide or agarose is typically used as the gel material.

Slab-gel electrophoresis

As noted earlier, electrophoresis separates on the basis of charge. Size separation or sieving can also be important applications of gels; in this case the pore dimensions of the gel are comparable to the dimensions of the biopolymers. The gel matrix then becomes a resistance to the migration of the substances in the electric field, and separation is based on the size of the molecules, with the smallest migrating the fastest. This principle is essential for the separation of DNA molecules, since these species cannot be electrophoretically separated without the porous gel matrix. An important application of this method is DNA sequencing in which the order of the four nucleotides (adenine, cytidine, guanine, and thymidine) in an oligonucleotide molecule must be determined. The method thus aids in the sequencing of the human genome.

Proteins can also be electrophoretically separated by gel sieving. In this technique, the protein is denatured (*i.e.,* its higher structural features are destroyed) and combined with an excess of detergent, such as sodium dodecyl sulfate (SDS). The resulting SDS-protein complexes have the same charge density and shape and are therefore resolved according to size in a gel matrix. This method is useful in characterizing proteins and evaluating their purity.

In addition to being separated by size, proteins can also be separated according to their specific charge residues. A particularly useful method based on this principle is isoelectric focusing (IEF). At a given pH of a solution, a specific protein will have equal positive and negative charges and will therefore not migrate in an electric field. This pH value is called the isoelectric point. A slab gel (or column) can be filled with a complex mixture of buffers (known as ampholytes) that, under the influence of an applied field, migrate to the position of their respective isoelectric points and then remain fixed. A pH gradient is established, which then allows focusing of proteins at their respective isoelectric points.

Charge (IEF) and size (SDS-protein complex) separations can be combined in a two-dimensional approach as shown in Figure 12. Two-dimensional gel electrophoresis is one of the most powerful resolving methods now available.

Electrophoresis can also be used in a preparative mode. In continuous-flow paper electrophoresis, the sample is continuously fed (with a salt solution) at the top centre of a vertically mounted sheet of paper. As the sample flows down the paper, it is subjected to an electrical potential at right angles to the direction of flow. The various species disperse across the paper, depending on their charge and mobility, and drop from the coarsely serrated bottom edge of the paper into receivers.

Another field-separation technique, ultracentrifugation, involves separation on the basis of the centrifugal force created by very rapid rotation (50,000 revolutions per minute or more). Different species, depending on their masses, will settle at different speeds under these conditions. Ultracentrifugation finds its greatest use in the separation of polymeric materials, such as proteins and nucleic acids.

Field-flow fractionation

Field-flow fractionation consists of a series of methods based on a field applied perpendicular to a flow stream in a narrow channel. Because of friction at the channel walls, the velocity of the liquid will be faster in the centre than at the walls. In sedimentation field-flow fractionation, for example, the channel is spun and the applied perpendicular field is a centrifugal force (gravity). Particles sediment toward the channel walls and reach a steady-state position. Since the flow velocity is nonuniform across the channel, the rate of migration will vary for different substances, resulting in separation. The applied force can be centrifugal, electrical, or thermal. Field-flow fractionation is best suited to particle- or colloid-size substances. An example is the separation of latex particles used in paints. Other methods of particle separation are discussed below.

Electrolytic separations and purifications are effected by taking advantage of the different voltages required to convert ions to neutral substances. A particularly important example of this method is the refining of copper. Copper ores typically contain minor amounts of other metals that are not removed by the initial processes that reduce the ores to the metal. A slab of the impure copper and a sheet of pure copper are placed in a vessel containing a solution of sulfuric acid in water, and the two pieces of copper are connected to a source of direct electric current, so that the pure copper becomes the cathode and the impure copper becomes the anode. The anode dissolves, the metal atoms becoming positive ions that migrate through the solution to the cathode. The voltage between the electrodes is regulated so that, as the metal ions arrive at the cathode, only the copper ions are reduced to metal atoms, which deposit on the cathode. Some of the original impurities, such as zinc and nickel, remain as their ions in the solution, because their conversion back to neutral metal atoms requires a higher voltage than that of the system; other impurities, such as silver and gold, never dissolve at all, but, as the atoms around them dissolve, they fall to the bottom of the vessel as a slime from which they can be recovered by other processes.

Barrier separations. Several separation methods depend on penetration of molecules through semipermeable membranes. Membrane filtration involves simple migration resulting from a concentration difference on the two sides of the membrane. In ultrafiltration, this diffusion through the membrane is accelerated by means of a pressure difference. In electrodialysis, an electrical field accelerates the migration.

Unrestricted migration of the individual components of a solution results in equalization of the concentration of each component throughout the solution. All the components take part in this process: there is just as much tendency for the solvent to diffuse from regions where its concentration is high (and the solution is therefore dilute) to regions where its concentration is low (and the solution is concentrated) as there is for the dissolved substance to diffuse from regions where it is concentrated to those where it is dilute. In many separations, attention is focused on the tendency of the dissolved particles to migrate, while the corresponding tendency of the solvent particles to migrate is largely ignored. Osmosis, however, is a phenomenon in which only the solvent is free to migrate through a membrane that separates two regions of different composition. The solvent, driven by its tendency to move from the region where its concentration is higher, passes from the dilute solution into the concentrated one and would continue to do so indefinitely if the liquid levels on the two sides of the membrane remained the same. But, as the solvent passes through the membrane, the amounts of the two solutions become unequal, and the resulting difference in pressure eventually brings the migration to a stop. This pressure difference is called the osmotic pressure of the solution.

Osmosis

In a separation technique called reverse osmosis, a pressure is applied opposite to and in excess of the osmotic pressure to force the solvent through a membrane against its concentration gradient. This method is an effective means of concentrating impurities, recovering contaminated solvents, cleaning up polluted streams, and desalinizing seawater. Dialysis, a technique frequently used in biochemistry, is a membrane-separation method used for removing dissolved salts from solutions of proteins or other large molecules.

Particle separations. *Sedimentation.* Particles such as viruses, colloids, bacteria, and small fragments of silica and alumina may be separated into different fractions of various sizes and densities. Suspensions of relatively massive particles settle under the influence of gravity, and the different rates can be exploited to effect separations. To separate viruses and the like, it is necessary to employ much more powerful force fields, such as those produced in an ultracentrifuge.

Filtration and screening. In filtration, a porous material is used to separate particles of different sizes. If the pore sizes are highly uniform, separation can be fairly sensitive to the size of the particles, but the method is most commonly used to effect gross separations, as of liquids from suspended crystals or other solids. To accelerate filtration, pressure usually is applied. A series of sieves is stacked, with the screen of largest hole size at the top. The mixture of particles is placed at the top, and the assembly is agitated to facilitate the passage of the particles through successive screens. At the end of the operation, the particles are distributed among the sieves in accordance with their particle diameters.

Elutriation. In this method, the particles are placed in a vertical tube in which water (or another fluid) is flowing slowly upward. The particles fall through the water at speeds that vary with their size and density. If the flow rate of the water is slowly increased, the most slowly sinking particles will be swept upward with the fluid flow and removed from the tube. Intermediate particles will remain stationary, and the largest or densest particles will continue to migrate downward. The flow can again be increased to remove the next smallest size of particles. Thus, by careful control of flow through the tube, particles can be separated according to size.

Particle electrophoresis and electrostatic precipitation. As the name implies, particle electrophoresis involves the separation of charged particles under the influence of an electric field; this method is used especially for the separation of viruses and bacteria. Electrostatic precipitation is a method for the precipitation of fogs (suspensions of particles in the atmosphere or in other gases): a high voltage is applied across the gas phase to produce electrical charges on the particles. These charges cause the particles to be attracted to the oppositely charged walls of the separator, where they give up their charges and fall into collectors.

Foam fractionation and flotation. There are a few methods that employ foams to achieve separations. In these, the principle of separation is adsorption on gas bubbles or at the gas-liquid interface. Two of these methods are foam fractionation, for the separation of molecular species, and flotation, for the separation of particles. When dissolved in water, a soap or detergent forms a foam if gas is bubbled through the solution. Collection of the foam is a means of concentrating the soap. Flotation is a process in which particles are carried out of a suspension by a foam. In this case, a soap or other chemical agent first adsorbs on the surface of the particle to increase its ability to adhere to small air bubbles. The clinging bubbles make the particle light enough to float to the surface, where it

Use of foams

can be removed. This method is extremely important in concentrating the valuable constituents of minerals before chemical processing to recover the metals present. (B.L.K.)

Chromatography

Chromatography is a technique for separating the components, or solutes, of a mixture on the basis of the relative amounts of each solute distributed between a moving fluid stream, called the mobile phase, and a contiguous stationary phase. The mobile phase may be either a liquid or a gas, while the stationary phase is either a solid or a liquid. Kinetic molecular motion continuously exchanges solute molecules between the two phases. If, for a particular solute, the distribution favours the moving fluid, the molecules will spend most of their time migrating with the stream and will be transported away from other species whose molecules are retained longer by the stationary phase. For a given species, the ratio of the times spent in the moving and stationary regions is equal to the ratio of its concentrations in these regions, known as the partition coefficient. (The term adsorption isotherm is often used when a solid phase is involved.) A mixture of solutes is introduced into the system in a confined region or narrow zone (the origin), whereupon the different species are transported at different rates in the direction of fluid flow. The driving force for solute migration is the moving fluid, and the resistive force is the solute affinity for the stationary phase; the combination of these forces, as manipulated by the analyst, produces the separation. Chromatography is one of several separation techniques defined as differential migration from a narrow initial zone. Electrophoresis is another member of this group. In this case, the driving force is an electric field, which exerts different forces on solutes of different ionic charge. The resistive force is the viscosity of the nonflowing solvent. The combination of these forces yields ion mobilities peculiar to each solute.

Partition coefficient

Chromatography has numerous applications in biological and chemical fields. It is widely used in biochemical research for the separation and identification of chemical compounds of biological origin. In the petroleum industry the technique is employed to analyze complex mixtures of hydrocarbons. (Ro.A.K.)

As a separation method, chromatography has a number of advantages over older techniques—crystallization, solvent extraction, and distillation, for example. It is capable of separating all the components of a multicomponent chemical mixture without requiring an extensive foreknowledge of the identity, number, or relative amounts of the substances present. It is versatile in that it can deal with molecular species ranging in size from viruses composed of millions of atoms to the smallest of all molecules—hydrogen—which contains only two; furthermore, it can be used with large or small amounts of material. Some forms of chromatography can detect substances present at the picogram (10^{-12} gram) level, thus making the method a superb trace analytical technique extensively used in the detection of chlorinated pesticides in biological materials and the environment, in forensic science, and in the detection of both therapeutic and abused drugs. Its resolving power is unequaled among separation methods.

HISTORY

The first purely pragmatic application of chromatography was that of the early dye chemists, who tested their dye mixtures by dipping strings or pieces of cloth or filter paper into a dye vat. The dye solution migrated up the inserted material by capillary action, and the dye components produced bands of different colour. In the 19th century, several German chemists carried out deliberate experiments to explore the phenomenon. They observed, for example, the development of concentric, coloured rings by dropping solutions of inorganic compounds onto the centre of a piece of filter paper; a treatise was published in 1861 describing the method and giving it the name "capillary analysis."

The discovery of chromatography, however, is generally attributed to the Russian botanist Mikhail S. Tsvet (also spelled Tswett), because he recognized the physicochemical basis of the separation and applied it in a rational and organized way to the separation of plant pigments, particularly the carotenoids and the chlorophylls. Tsvet's book, published in 1910, described a technique that is used today in essentially the same form. He packed a vertical glass column with an adsorptive material, such as alumina, silica, or powdered sugar, added a solution of the plant pigments to the top of the column, and washed the pigments through the column with an organic solvent. The pigments separated into a series of discrete coloured bands on the column, divided by regions entirely free of pigments. Because Tsvet worked with coloured substances, he called the method chromatography (from Greek words meaning colour writing). Tsvet's development of chromatographic procedures was generally unknown to chemists in the Western world because he published either in German botanical journals or in Russian works. In 1931 chromatography emerged from its relative obscurity when the German chemist Richard Kuhn and his student, the French chemist Edgar Lederer, reported the use of this method in the resolution of a number of biologically important materials. In 1941 two British chemists, Archer J.P. Martin and Richard L.M. Synge, began a study of the amino acid composition of wool. Their initial efforts, in which they used a technique called liquid-liquid countercurrent distribution, failed to give them adequate separation; they conceived, therefore, of an alternative method, in which one liquid was firmly bound to a finely granulated solid packed in a glass tube and a second liquid, immiscible with the first, was percolated through it. Silica gel served as the granular solid, and Martin and Synge pictured the gel as composed of water tightly bonded to the crystals of silica; the mobile phase was chloroform. Their work with this technique was remarkably successful. Although their method was mechanically identical with Tsvet's approach, it was innovative in that it involved the concept of a stationary liquid (water) supported on an inert solid (silica), with the result that the solute molecules partitioned between the stationary liquid and a separate mobile liquid phase (chloroform). The technique came to be called partition chromatography. At that time, Martin and Synge suggested that the moving phase could well be a gas. It is a historical oddity that this idea was overlooked for nearly a decade, possibly because of the war, until Martin in collaboration with the British chemist Anthony T. James initiated studies of gas-liquid partition chromatography. In 1952 Martin and Synge were awarded the Nobel Prize for their work, perhaps not so much for the newness of the technique but for a model that suggested other systems, a mathematical theory, and an applicability to amino acid and peptide separations with far-reaching impact on biochemical studies.

Discovery of chromatography

Contributions of Martin and Synge

The initial partition-chromatography system presented difficulties because of lack of reproducibility in the properties of the silica gel and lack of uniformity in the packing of columns. Partly for this reason, Martin and his coworkers worked out a new procedure in which the stationary medium was a sheet of filter paper. The paper was thought of as water bonded to cellulose, providing another partition method. The technique gave the desired reproducibility, and beginning in the 1940s paper chromatography found wide application in the analysis of biologically important compounds, such as amino acids, steroids, carbohydrates, and bile pigments. In this field it replaced, to a large extent, the column technique initiated by Tsvet.

Motivated probably by the same drawbacks to column chromatography, two Soviet pharmacists, Nikolay A. Izmaylov and Maria S. Shrayber, distributed the support material as a thin film on a glass plate. The plate and support material could then be manipulated in a fashion similar to that of paper chromatography. The results of the Soviet studies were reported in 1938, but the potential of the method was not widely realized until 1956, when the German chemist Egon Stahl began intensive research on its application. This system became known as thin-layer chromatography.

Still another chromatographic technique, gas chromatography, was first carried out in Austria in 1944 by the

Discovery of gas chromatography

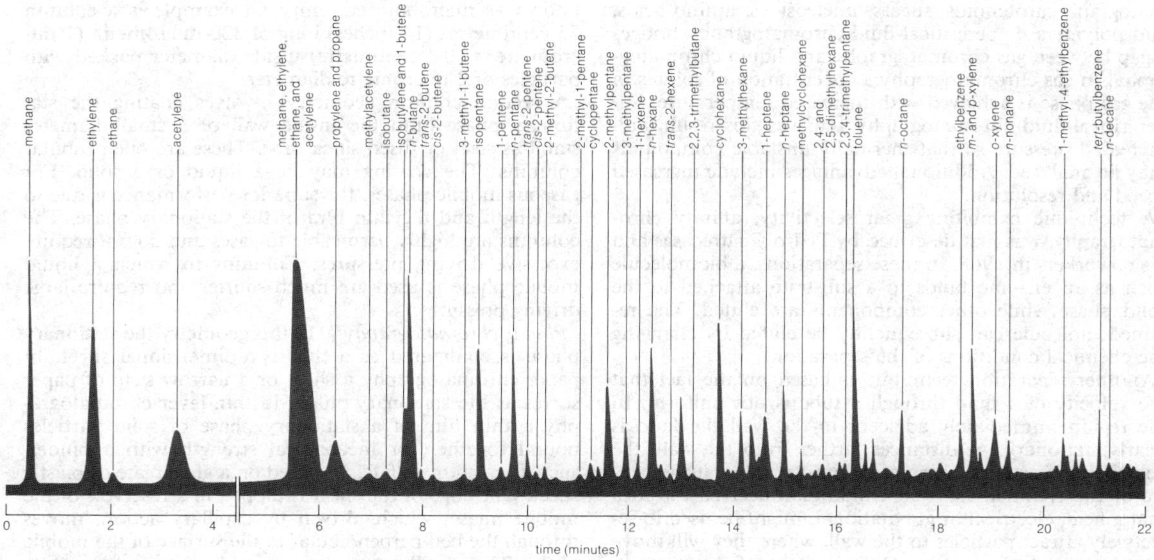

Figure 14: Composite of two gas chromatograms of hydrocarbon auto-exhaust pollutants.
From J. Giddings and R. Keller (eds.), *Advances in Chromatography*, vol. 8, p. 338; Marcel Dekker, Inc., N.Y. (1969)

chemist Erika Cremer, who used a solid stationary phase. The first extensive exploitation of the method was made by Martin and James in 1952, when they reported the elution gas chromatography of organic acids and amines. In this work, small particles of support material were coated with a nonvolatile liquid and packed into a heated glass tube. Mixtures injected into the inlet of the tube and driven through by compressed gas appeared in well-separated zones. This development was immediately recognized by petroleum chemists as a simple and rapid method of analysis of the complex hydrocarbon mixtures encountered in petroleum products. British Petroleum Co. and Shell Oil Co. laboratories immediately began basic research in their own laboratories. Instrument companies, sensing an extensive market, also made major contributions.

(J.C.Gi./Ro.A.K.)

In 1957, while doing a theoretical study of gas chromatographic columns, Marcel J.E. Golay, as a consultant for the Perkin-Elmer Corporation, concluded that a very long column (90 to 180 metres [300 to 600 feet]) of narrow-diameter tubing (internal diameter of 0.25 millimetres [0.0098 inch]) with its wall coated with a thin film of liquid would yield superior separations. Fortunately, at about this same time, detectors with extremely low limits of detection became available, which could sense the small sample sizes required by these new columns. These capillary, or Golay, columns, now called open-tubular columns and characterized by their open design and an internal diameter of less than one millimetre, had an explosive impact on chromatographic methodology. It is now possible to separate hundreds of components of a mixture in a single chromatographic experiment (see Figure 14).

Molecular sieves are porous substances that trap a mobile-phase gas. Large molecules cannot enter the pores, and so they flow largely unimpeded through the system. Small molecules are interrupted in their migration as they meander in and out of the pores by diffusion. Molecules of intermediate sizes show different rates of migration, depending on their size. In 1959 Per Flodin and Jerker Porath in Sweden developed cellulose polymeric materials that acted as molecular sieves for substances dispersed in liquids. This extended the molecular weight range of chromatography to polypeptides, proteins, and high-molecular-weight polymers. The generic term for such separations is size-exclusion chromatography.

In 1964 the American chemist J. Calvin Giddings, referring to a theory largely worked out for gas chromatography, summarized the necessary conditions that would give liquid chromatography the resolving power achievable in gas chromatography—that is, very small particles with a thin film of stationary phase in small-diameter columns. The development of the technique now termed high-performance liquid chromatography (HPLC) depended on (1) the development of pumps that would deliver a steady stream of liquid at high pressure to the column to force the liquid through the narrow interstitial channels of the packed columns at reasonable rates, and (2) detectors that would sense the small sample sizes mandated. At first, only adsorptive solids were used as the stationary phase, because liquid coatings were swept away by the mobile phase. Previously gas chromatography had employed chemical bonding of an organic stationary phase to solids to reduce adsorptive activity; István Halász of Germany exploited these reactions to cause a separation based on liquid solution effects in the bonded molecular layers. These and similar reactions were employed to give firmly attached molecules that acted as a thin film of solvent in liquid systems. These bonded phases gave high-performance liquid chromatography such scope and versatility that the technique is now the dominant method for separations.

Ion exchangers are natural substances—for example, certain clays—or deliberately synthesized resins containing positive ions (cation exchangers) or negative ions (anion exchangers) that exchange with those ions in solution having a greater affinity for the exchanger. This selective affinity of the solid is called ion, or ion-exchange, chromatography. The first such chromatographic separations were reported in 1938 by T.I. Taylor and Harold C. Urey, who used a zeolite. The method received much attention in 1942 during the Manhattan Project as a means of separating the rare earths and transuranium elements, fission products of uranium, and other elements produced by thermonuclear explosions. Ion-exchange chromatography can be applied to organic ion separations and has particular importance for the separation of amino and nucleic acids.

Ion-exchange chromatography

As early as 1879, the solubility of solids in gases at high pressure had been observed. In 1958 the British scientist James Lovelock suggested that gases above their critical temperature (*i.e.,* the temperature above which the appearance of a liquid phase cannot be produced by increasing the pressure) might be used at high pressure as mobile phases. A substance in this state is termed a supercritical fluid. At very high pressure, the density of the fluid can be 90 percent or more of the liquid density. The German chemist Ernst Klesper and his colleagues working at Johns Hopkins University were the first to report separation of the porphyrins with dense gases in 1962. Carbon dioxide at 400 atmospheres is a typical supercritical-fluid mobile phase. (One atmosphere equals 760 millimetres, or 29.92 inches, of mercury; standard sea-level pressure is one atmosphere.) In an extreme case, Giddings and his group used gases at pressures of up to 2,000 atmospheres to chromatograph carotenoids, sugars, nucleosides, amino acids, and polymers. Supercritical-fluid chromatography bridges a gap between gas chromatography and liquid chromatography. In gas chromatography, concentration of solutes in the gas phase is achieved with increased temperature. Supercritical-fluid chromatography achieves this result with increased pressure so that thermally unstable compounds may be analyzed. Additional advantages include increased speed and resolution.

A technique exhibiting great selectivity, affinity chromatography, was first described by Pedro Cuatrecasas and his coworkers in 1968. In these separations, a biomolecule such as an enzyme binds to a substrate attached to the solid phase while other components are eluted. The retained molecule can subsequently be eluted by changing the chemical conditions of the separation.

Another separation technique is based on the fact that the velocity of a fluid through a tube is not uniform. In the region immediately adjacent to the wall the fluid is nearly stationary. At distances farther from the wall, the velocity increases, reaching a maximum value at the centre of the channel. In 1966 Giddings conceived the idea that a field, electrical or gravitational, might be used to selectively attract particles to the wall, where they will move slowly through the system. Diffusion away from the high concentrations at the wall into faster inner streams would enhance migration. The net effect would yield differential migration. A thermal gradient between two walls has also been used. This recently developed technique is called field-flow fractionation. It has been termed one-phase chromatography because there is no stationary phase. Its main applications are to polymers and particulate matter. The method has been used to separate biological cells, subcellular particles, viruses, liposomes, protein aggregates, fly ash, colloids, and pigments. (See also above *Principles of selected methods: Rate separations: Field separations.*)

Field-flow fractionation

The battery of chromatographic techniques, along with field-flow fractionation, provides separations from the level of hydrogen molecules to particulates, encompassing a 10^{15}-fold mass range. An analogous mass range is one of grains of sand to boulders.

METHODS

Chromatographic methods are classified according to the following criteria: (1) geometry of the system, (2) mode of operation, (3) retention mechanism, and (4) phases involved.

Geometry. *Column chromatography.* The mobile and stationary phases of chromatographic systems are arranged in such a way that migration is along a coordinate much longer than its width. There are two basic geometries: columnar and planar. In column chromatography the stationary phase is contained in a tube called the column. A packed column contains particles that either constitute or support the stationary phase, and the mobile phase flows through the channels of the interstitial spaces. Theory has shown that performance is enhanced if very small particles are used, which simultaneously ensures the additional desired feature that these channels be very narrow. The effect of mobile-phase mass transfer on band (peak) broadening will then be reduced (see discussions of mass transfer and peak broadening in *Efficiency and resolution* and *Theoretical considerations* below). Constructing the stationary phase as a thin layer or film will reduce band broadening due to stationary-phase mass transfer. Porous particles, either as adsorbents or as supports for liquids, may have deep pores, with some extending through the entire particle. This contributes to band broadening. Use of microparticles alleviates this because the channels are shortened. An alternate packing method is to coat impermeable macroparticles, such as glass beads, with a thin layer of microparticles. These are the porous-layer, superficially porous, or pellicular packings. As the particle size is reduced, however, the diameter of the column must also be decreased. As a result, the amount of stationary phase is less and the sample size must be reduced. Detection methods must therefore respond to very small amounts of solutes, and large pressures are required to force the mobile phase through the column. The extreme cases are known as microbore columns; an example is a column 35 centimetres (14 inches) long of 320-micrometre (1 micrometre = 10^{-4} centimetre) inside diameter packed with particles of 2-micrometre diameter.

A second column geometry involves coating the stationary phase onto the inside wall of a small-diameter stainless steel or fused silica tube. These are open tubular columns. The coating may be a liquid or a solid. For gaseous mobile phases, the superior performance is due to the length and the thin film of the stationary phase. The columns are highly permeable to gases and do not require excessive driving pressures. Columns in which a liquid mobile phase is used are much shorter and require large driving pressures.

Planar chromatography. In this geometry the stationary phase is configured as a thin two-dimensional sheet. In paper chromatography a sheet or a narrow strip of paper serves as the stationary phase. In thin-layer chromatography a thin film of a stationary phase of solid particles bound together for mechanical strength with a binder, such as calcium sulfate, is coated on a glass plate or plastic sheet. One edge of the sheet is dipped in a reservoir of the mobile phase, which, driven by capillary action, moves through the bed perpendicular to the surface of the mobile phase. This capillary motion is rapid compared to solute diffusion in the mobile phase at right angles to the migration path, and so the solute is confined to a narrow path.

Thin-layer chromatography

Mode of operation. *Development chromatography.* In terms of operation, in development chromatography the mobile phase flow is stopped before solutes reach the end of the bed of stationary phase. The mobile phase is called the developer, and the movement of the liquid along the bed is referred to as development. With glass columns of diameter in the centimetre range and large samples (cubic-centimetre range), the bed is extruded from the column, the solute zones carved out, and solutes recovered by solvent extraction. Although this is easily done with coloured solutes, colourless solutes require some manner of detection, such as ultraviolet light absorption or fluorescence or the streaking of the column with a reagent that reacts with the solute to form a coloured product.

Planar systems involve placing the samples (in the 10^{-3} cubic-centimetre range) as spots at an edge of the stationary bed parallel to the developer. Solute zones are located by light irradiation or by spraying the bed with a colour-producing reagent. Migration is reported in terms of the R_f value, the distance moved by the centre of the zone relative to the distance moved by the mobile phase front, where both are measured from the origin. Use of the solvent front as a reference point is frequently inconvenient. A standard solute is often included, and the migration of the solutes relative to the standard reported as the relative R value. If larger samples are required for subsequent manipulation, either simultaneous separations are performed or the sample is applied as a streak across the stationary phase. The final spot or band is carved or cut from the chromatogram. In one type of planar chromatography, the mixture is placed at one corner of a square bed, plate, or sheet and developed, the mobile phase is evaporated, and the plate is rotated 90° so that the spots become the origins for a second development with a different developer. This is termed two-dimensional planar chromatography.

R_f value

Elution chromatography. This method, employed with columns, involves solute migration through the entire system and solute detection as it emerges from the column. The detector continuously monitors the amount of solute in the emerging mobile-phase stream—the eluate—and transduces the signal, most often to a voltage, which is registered as a peak on a strip-chart recorder. The recorder trace where solute is absent is the baseline (see Figure 15). A plot of the solute concentration along the migration coordinate of development chromatograms yields a similar solute peak. Collectively the plots are the concentration profiles; ideally they are Gaussian (normal, bell, or error curves). The signal intensity may also be digitized and stored in a computer memory for recall later. Solute behaviour is reported in terms of the retention time, which is the time required for a solute to migrate, or elute, from the column, measured from the instant the sample

Retention time

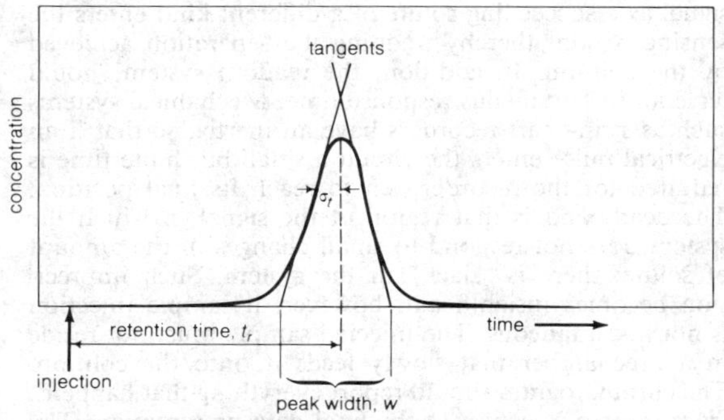

Figure 15: Peak shape, peak width, and plate height parameters in elution chromatography.

is injected into the mobile phase stream to the point at which the peak maximum occurs. The adjusted retention time is measured from the appearance of an unretained solute at the outlet. The dependence of these times on flow rate is removed by reporting the retention volumes, which are calculated as the retention times multiplied by the volumetric flow rate of the mobile phase.

The spots on the developed planar bed, the series of peaks on the paper produced by the recorder, or the printout of the computer data are various forms of chromatograms.

Retention mechanism. Classification in terms of the retention mechanism is approximate, because the retention actually is a mixture of mechanisms. If the partition coefficient is constant as the amount of solute is varied, the separation is referred to as linear chromatography. This condition is highly desirable because solute zones approach symmetrical Gaussian distributions. If the system is nonlinear, solute zones are asymmetrical. In the most common asymmetrical case, a zone "tails" into a following solute zone to contaminate it.

In adsorption chromatography solute molecules bond directly to the surface of the stationary phase. Stationary phases may contain a variety of adsorption sites differing in the tenacity with which they bind the molecules and in their relative abundance. The net effect determines the adsorbent activity. Partition chromatography utilizes a support material coated with a stationary-phase liquid. Examples are (1) water held by cellulose, paper, or silica, or (2) a thin film coated or bonded to a solid. The solid support ideally is inactive in the retention of solutes, but it actually is not; retention is mostly due to solute solution in the stationary liquid phase.

As mentioned above, the stationary phase in size-exclusion chromatography consists of molecules of the mobile phase trapped in the porous structure of a solid. Solute molecules are retained when they diffuse into and out of these pores. The time they remain in the pores is a function of their size, which determines the depth of penetration. There is a certain molecular size that represents the "just excluded" case. Molecules of this size and larger are excluded from the pores and are not separated. They appear first in elution chromatography. At the other end of the size spectrum, there is a certain size for which all molecules of this magnitude and smaller penetrate all the pores. These molecules also are not separated; they elute last. Gel-filtration chromatography refers to size-exclusion methods employing water as the mobile phase; gel-permeation chromatography makes use of an organic mobile phase.

Very specific intermolecular interactions, "lock and key," are known in biochemistry. Examples include enzyme-protein, antigen-antibody, and hormone-receptor binding. A structural feature of an enzyme will attach to a specific structural feature of a protein. Affinity chromatography exploits this feature by binding a ligand with the desired interactive capability to a support such as a gel used in gel-filtration chromatography. The ligand retards a solute with the compatible structural feature and passes all other solutes in the mixture. The solute is then eluted by a mobile-phase change such as incorporating a competing solute, changing the acidity, or changing the ionic strength of the eluent.

Affinity chromatography

There is no stationary phase in field-flow fractionation; the different-velocity streams or layers of the mobile phase with the solute distributed between them produce the separation.

Phases. *Gas chromatography.* Classification by phases gives the physical state of the mobile phase followed by the state of the stationary phase. Gas chromatography employing a gaseous fluid as the mobile phase, called the carrier gas, is subdivided into gas-solid chromatography and gas-liquid chromatography. The carrier gases used, such as helium, hydrogen, and nitrogen, have very weak intermolecular interactions with solutes. Molecular sieves are used in gas size-exclusion chromatography applied to gases of low molecular weight. Adsorption on solids tends to give nonlinear systems. Gas-liquid chromatography employs a liquid stationary phase where solution forces provide retention. At ordinary pressures the solutes in the gas phase behave as a mixture of ideal gases. All interactions responsible for selective retention occur in the stationary phase. Thus a wide variety of liquid stationary phases have been employed; more than 300 have been reported.

A basic rule in organic chemistry is that "like dissolves like." Thus the polar solvent water dissolves the polar solute ethanol but not the hydrocarbon octane. The nonpolar solvent benzene will dissolve octane but not ethanol. Polar stationary phases will retain polar solutes and pass those that are nonpolar. The order of emergence is reversed with nonpolar stationary phases. Lutz Rohrschneider of Germany initiated studies that led to a standard set of solute species, solvent probes, which helped order stationary phases in terms of polarity and intermolecular interactions present.

In gas chromatography the retention of solutes is most often referred to the behaviour of the straight-chain hydrocarbons; *i.e.,* relative retention volumes are used. On a logarithmic scale this becomes the retention index (RI) introduced by the Swiss chemist Ervin sz. Kováts. The RI values of the solvent probes serve as the basis for the classification method introduced by Rohrschneider. Similar schemes have been suggested for liquid systems.

Gas-phase intermolecular interactions occur and are exploited in supercritical-fluid chromatography. Examples of interactive gases used at high pressure are carbon dioxide, nitrous oxide, ammonia, hydrocarbons, sulfur hexafluoride, and halogenated methanes.

Mixtures of solutes that have a wide boiling point or polarity range or have a large variety of functional groups pose a particular problem. At low column-operating temperatures, the solutes with high volatility (or, more precisely, solutes with a large numerical value for the liquid solution activity coefficient) appear early on the chromatogram as well-resolved peaks. Solutes with low volatility progress slowly through the column, with ample opportunity for the peak broadening. These solutes appear as very low, broad peaks that may be overlooked. An increase in column temperature increases the concentration of the solutes in the gas phase. The solutes of high volatility, however, now spending most of their time in the mobile-gas phase, migrate rapidly through the column to appear as unresolved peaks. The succeeding solutes are adequately resolved. This is termed the general elution problem. A simple solution is to increase the column temperature during the course of the separation. The well-resolved, highly volatile solutes are removed from the column at the lower temperatures before the low-volatility solutes leave the origin at the column inlet. This technique is termed temperature-programmed gas chromatography.

Temperature programming

Liquid chromatography. This form of chromatography employs a liquid mobile phase. Liquid-solid chromatography utilizes a solid stationary phase, and the major mechanism of retention is adsorption. Popular adsorbents are silica and alumina, which both retain polar compounds. If a polar mobile phase is used, the solutes are rapidly swept from the bed. Thus the preferred mobile phase is a nonpolar or slightly polar solvent. The American chemist Lloyd R. Snyder arranged solvents in an eluotropic strength scale based on the chromatographic behaviour of selected solutes on silica. Normal-phase chromatography involves a polar stationary phase and a less polar mobile phase.

Liquid-liquid chromatography employs liquid mobile and stationary phases. High-performance liquid chromatography uses small particles with molecules bonded to their surface to give a thin film that has liquidlike properties. A number of bonding agents are available. A nonpolar molecule can be bonded to the solid and a polar mobile phase used. This method is termed reverse-phase liquid chromatography. The partition coefficient depends on the identity of both mobile and stationary phases. In this case, however, the number of stationary phases is limited, while there is a large number of liquids and combinations of them used for the mobile phase. Mobile phases of constant composition are called isocratic.

The general elution problem encountered in liquid chromatography involves samples that contain both weakly and strongly retained solvents. This is handled in a manner analogous to the temperature programming used in gas chromatography. In a process termed gradient elution, the concentration of well-retained solutes in the mobile phase is increased by constantly changing the composition, and hence the polarity, of the mobile phase during the separation.

SAMPLE RECOVERY

Sample recovery from development chromatograms has been described—that is, detection followed by carving zones from an extruded column or carving or cutting zones from the planar stationary-phase bed. In elution chromatography successive samples of the effluent are collected in tubes held in a mechanically driven rotating tray called a fraction collector. Analogous arrangements exist to condense and trap solutes from effluent gas streams. Large samples can be used to prepare relatively large amounts of pure solutes for further manipulation; this is the realm of preparative-scale chromatography.

METHODS OF DETECTION

High-resolution gas or liquid elution chromatography of multicomponent samples deals with small amounts of solutes emerging from the column where they are to be detected. Refinement of chromatographic methods is inseparable from refinement of detectors that accurately sense solutes in the presence of the mobile phase. Detectors may be classified as general detectors in which all solutes are sensed regardless of their identity, or as specific detectors, which sense a limited number of solutes—for example, those containing halogens or nitrogen. Detectors may be nondestructive, whereby sensing does not alter the nature of the solutes, as in the case of light absorption, so they may be collected for further use. Destructive detectors, on the other hand, destroy the solutes. Detectors include not only the component that senses the solutes but also those that perform the associated transduction, electronic amplification, and final readout.

Detector characteristics

There are three essential detector characteristics. The first is the lower limit of detection, the smallest amount of solute measured in terms of moles (mass-sensitive detectors) or moles per litre (concentration-sensitive detectors) that can be detected; this entails distinguishing a signal from the random noise inherent in all electronic systems. A second is the sensitivity, which is the change in signal intensity per unit change in the amount of solute. The third is the linear range—*i.e.,* the range of solute amount where the signal intensity is directly proportional to the amount of solute; doubling the amount doubles the signal intensity. Solutes may respond differently to a detector. For example, if equal amounts of methane (containing one carbon) and ethane (two carbons) enter a flame-ionization detector, the peak for ethane will be twice the size of that for methane. The detector acts as a "carbon counter." A response factor may be determined for each solute to accommodate this. The perfect detector ideally has "zero volume"; that is, only an infinitesimal amount of solute enters the sensing region, produces a signal, and exits before the next infinitesimal amount enters the detector chamber. In the worst case, a solute enters the detector chamber and remains there producing a signal while the next portion of the solute enters behind it. This invites the possibility of a solute still being present and producing a signal as a succeeding solute of a different kind enters the sensing region, thereby undoing the separation achieved by the column. In addition, the readout system should have an instantaneous response time. Mechanical systems such as strip-chart recorders have an inertia, so that if an electrical pulse enters the circuit a small but finite time is required for the recorder pen to reach its final position. The dead-band is that region of the signal in which the system does not respond to small changes in the amount of solute; there is "slack" in the system. Such imprecision becomes insignificant, however, if sample injection is not instantaneous. The injected sample must not reside in a prechamber that slowly feeds it onto the column. The chromatogram should report everything that happens, from sample injection to the final data presentation. The most challenging detection problem is a sample containing a wide variety of solutes that covers a large range of concentrations and produces very closely spaced, narrow peaks (see Figure 14).

Gas chromatographic detectors

Gas chromatographic detectors sense the solute vapours in the mobile phase as they emerge from the column. Thermal-conductivity detectors compare the heat-conducting ability of the exit gas stream to that of a reference stream of pure carrier gas. To accomplish this, the gas streams are passed over heated filaments in thermal-conductivity cells. Measured changes in filament resistance of the cells reflect temperature changes caused by increments in thermal conductivity. This resistance change is monitored and registered continuously on a recorder. An alternate type of detector is the flame-ionization detector, in which the gas stream is mixed with hydrogen and burned. Positive ions and electrons are produced in the flame when organic substances are present. The ions are collected at electrodes and produce a small, measurable current. The flame-ionization detector is highly sensitive to hydrocarbons, but it will not detect carrier gases, such as nitrogen, or highly oxidized materials, such as carbon dioxide, carbon monoxide, sulfur dioxide, and water. In another device, the electron-capture detector, a stream of electrons from a radioactive source is produced in a potential field. Materials in the gas stream containing atoms of certain types capture electrons from the stream and measurably reduce the current. The most important of the capturing atoms are the halogens—fluorine, chlorine, bromine, and iodine. This type of detector, therefore, is particularly useful with chlorinated pesticides. Certain elements will emit light of distinctive wavelength when excited in a flame. The flame photometric detector measures the intensity of light with a photometric circuit. Solute species containing halogens, sulfur, or phosphorus can be burned to produce ionic species containing these elements and the ions sensed by electrochemical means.

Liquid chromatographic detectors suitable for high-performance columns require clever technology. If the solutes contain structural features that absorb light at certain wavelengths, the decrease in the intensity of the transmitted beam of light compared to the intensity of the incident beam can be used to monitor the effluent stream. In order for the solute to be detected, it must contain light-absorbing groups, the excitation source must contain light of a wavelength peculiar to this group, and the photoelectric sensor must respond to this wavelength. Also, the mobile phase must be transparent at this wavelength. The scope of solute species detected can be enlarged by reacting a light-insensitive solute with a reagent that contains a light-sensitive group and passing the product through the detector. Solutes may contain groups that absorb light at one wavelength and reemit light of a different wavelength. The fluorescence detector responds to these substances. Light bends or refracts on passing through an interface between air and a liquid or liquid solution. The degree of refraction depends on the nature of the liquid or the composition of the solution. The refractive index detector compares the refraction of the pure mobile phase with that of the column effluent.

The mass spectrometer is an analytical instrument that bombards molecules with a stream of electrons in a chamber at extremely low pressure to produce a stream of charged fragments that differ in mass (see below *Mass spec-*

trometry). The population of the fragments and the ratio of mass to charge is characteristic of the target molecule. Each fragment is deflected differently in a magnetic field to produce a pattern, the mass spectrum, which can be used to identify the target. The system is a very specific identifying detector when coupled with chromatography. The spectrum can be stored in a computer and compared with entries in a mass spectrum library. For some time the problem with gaseous effluents had been to match the column effluent at one atmosphere pressure to the high-vacuum inlet of the mass spectrometer, while the problem with liquid chromatography had been the large amount of mobile phase entering the ionization chamber of the spectrometer. These incompatibility problems have finally been overcome, and the mass spectrometer is now used in both gas and liquid chromatography. The technology of mass spectrometry is as great, if not greater, than that of chromatography.

If mass spectral data are lacking, solutes in a sample are identified by comparing their behaviour with that of known compounds. In gas chromatography this is best done by determining the retention index of the unknown solute and comparing it with the tabulated data for known compounds on the stationary phase used. Methods exist for estimating the effect of temperature and temperature programming on the retention index.

Quantitative measurements

The area enclosed by a peak, suitably adjusted for the detector response factor for that solute, is proportional to the amount of solute producing the peak. The area is frequently approximated from the peak width and height. Modern electronic integrators will, when properly instructed, ignore electronic noise, compensate for baseline drift, start integration when a peak appears, integrate, and stop the process when the peak exits the detector. Integration, a process of summation, is accomplished by opening and closing a narrow electronic window, registering the signal intensity, repeating the process, and then summing the stored signals to produce a number proportional to the area. The integrator will also sense the peak maximum. The chromatogram is a printed tape with the retention times and peak areas. Programs exist that will incorporate the response factor and calculate the relative peak areas, which give the percentage composition of the sample. Stored mass spectral data may be manipulated to produce the same data. Peak heights are used as quantitative measures for narrow peaks for which the area is difficult to determine accurately. (Ro.A.K.)

EFFICIENCY AND RESOLUTION

There are two features of the concentration profile important in determining the efficiency of a column and its subsequent ability to separate or resolve solute zones. Peak maximum, the first, refers to the location of the maximum concentration of a peak. To achieve satisfactory resolution, the maxima of two adjacent peaks must be disengaged. Such disengagement depends on the identity of the solute and the selectivity of the stationary and mobile phases.

The second feature important to efficiency and resolution is the width of the peak. Peaks in which the maxima are widely disengaged still may be so broad that the solutes are incompletely resolved. For this reason, peak width is of major concern in chromatography.

Column efficiency. The efficiency of a column is reported as the number of theoretical plates (plate number), N, a concept Martin borrowed from his experience with fractional distillation:

$$N = 16\left(\frac{t_r}{w}\right)^2,$$

where t_r is the retention time measured from the instant of injection and w is the peak width obtained by drawing tangents to the sides of the Gaussian curve at the inflection points and extrapolating the tangents to intercept the baseline. The distance between the intercepts is the peak width (see Figure 15). If the peak is a Gaussian distribution, statistical methods show that its width may be determined from the standard deviation, σ, by the formula $w = 4\sigma$. Poor chromatograms are those with early peaks (small t_r) that are broad (large w), hence giving small N values, while excellent chromatograms are those with late-appearing peaks (large t_r) that are still very narrow (small w), thereby producing a large N. The number of theoretical plates is a measure of the "goodness" of the column. Plate numbers may range from 100 to 10^6. The peak width determined from the chromatogram includes contributions from the sample-injection technique, extraneous tubing, and the detector. These are extra column contributions to peak broadening. Although very important, they are not part of the chromatographic process and will be ignored here. The plate number depends on the length of the column. The extreme value of 10^6 plates was obtained with an open tubular gas chromatographic column 1.6 kilometres (1 mile) long. A more appropriate parameter for measuring efficiency is the height equivalent to a theoretical plate (or plate height), HETP (or h), which is L/N, L being the length of the column. Efficient columns have small h values (see below *Theoretical considerations: Plate height*).

Plate number

Resolution. In general, resolution is the ability to separate two signals. In terms of chromatography, this is the ability to separate two peaks. Resolution, R, is given by

$$R = \frac{(t_{r2} - t_{r1})}{\frac{1}{2}(w_1 + w_2)},$$

where t_{r1} and t_{r2} and w_1 and w_2 are the times and widths, respectively, of the two immediately adjacent peaks. If the peaks are sufficiently close, which is the pertinent problem, w is nearly the same for both peaks and resolution may be expressed as

$$R = \frac{(t_{r2} - t_{r1})}{4\sigma}.$$

If the distance between the peaks is 4σ, then R is 1 and 2.5 percent of the area of the first peak overlaps 2.5 percent of the area of the second peak. A resolution of unity is minimal for quantitative analysis using peak areas.

THEORETICAL CONSIDERATIONS

Retention. The rates of migration of substances in chromatographic procedures depend on the relative affinity of the substances for the stationary and the mobile phases. Those solutes attracted more strongly to the stationary phase are held back relative to those solutes attracted more strongly to the mobile phase. The forces of attraction are usually selective—that is to say, stronger for one solute than another. At least one of the two phases must exert a selective effect, and very often both phases are selective, as in liquid and supercritical-fluid chromatography. In gas chromatography, the mobile phase is ordinarily a gas that exerts essentially no attractive force on the solutes at all. In this case, the mobile phase is entirely nonselective.

The forces attracting solutes to the two phases are the normal forces existing between molecules—intermolecular forces. There are five major classes of these forces: (1) the universal, but weak, interaction between all electrons in neighbouring atoms and molecules, called dispersion forces, (2) the induction effect, by which polar molecules (those having an asymmetrical distribution of electrons) bring about a charge asymmetry in other molecules, (3) an orientation effect, caused by the mutual attraction of polar molecules resulting from alignment of dipoles (positive charges separated from negative charges), (4) hydrogen bonding between dipolar molecules bearing electron-pair-accepting hydrogen atoms, and (5) acid-base interactions in the Lewis acid-base sense—*i.e.*, the affinity of electron-accepting species (Lewis acids) to electron donors (Lewis bases). The interplay of these forces and temperature are reflected in the partition coefficient and determine the order on polarity and eluotropic strength scales. In the special case of ions, a strong electrostatic force exists in addition to the other forces; this electrostatic force attracts each ion to ions of opposite charge. This is an important element of ion-exchange chromatography.

Forces affecting solute molecules

Plate height. In chromatography, peak width increases in proportion to the square root of the distance that the peak has migrated. Mathematically, this is equivalent to saying that the square of the standard deviation is equal to a constant times the distance traveled. The height equivalent to a theoretical plate, as discussed above, is defined as the proportionality constant relating the standard deviation and the distance traveled. Thus, the defining equation of the height equivalent to a theoretical plate is as follows: HETP $= \sigma^2/L$, in which σ is the standard deviation and L the distance traveled. The use of the plate height is superior to the use of peak width in evaluating various chromatographic systems, because it is constant for the chromatographic run, and it is nearly constant from solute to solute.

In elution chromatography, in which the peak develops on a time scale, an equivalent form of the above equation is HETP $= L\,\sigma_t^2/t_r^2$, in which L is now the column length, t_r the time of retention of the peak by the column, and σ_t the standard deviation of the peak measured in units of time; this form is another expression of the equation HETP $= L/N$ given above (see *Efficiency and resolution: Column efficiency*).

Processes contributing to plate heights

During a chromatographic separation, three basic processes contribute to plate height (HETP): (1) Molecular diffusion, in which solute molecules diffuse outward from the centre of the zone. This effect is inversely proportional to the average linear flow velocity, u, because rapid flow reduces the time for diffusion. Mathematically, the contribution to plate height of this factor is expressed as B/u, in which B is a constant. (2) Eddy diffusion, in which solute is carried at unequal rates through the tortuous pathways of the granular bed of the packing particles. The contribution to plate height is a constant factor, A, independent of velocity. (3) Nonequilibrium or mass transfer, in which the slowness of diffusion in and out of the stationary and mobile phases causes fluctuations in the times of residence of the solute in the two phases and a consequent peak broadening. The effect is proportional to velocity and is expressed as $C_s u$ and $C_m u$, in which C_s and C_m are constants relating to the stationary and mobile phases, respectively.

A function of chromatographic theory has been twofold: (1) to evaluate B, A, C_m, and C_s, in terms of underlying diffusivity and flow processes, and (2) to assemble them into a total plate height equation.

The general equation used is HETP $= A + B/u + C_s u$. This is inadequate at high velocities, however, and is replaced by the equation

$$\text{HETP} = \left(\frac{1}{A} + \frac{1}{C_m u}\right)^{-1} + \frac{B}{u} + C_s u.$$

Knowledge of the component terms in such equations allows one to optimize chromatographic operating conditions. (J.C.Gi./Ro.A.K.)

APPLICATIONS

Chromatographic methods will separate ionic species, inorganic or organic, and molecular species ranging in size from the lightest and smallest, helium and hydrogen, to particulate matter such as single cells. No single configuration will accomplish this, however. Little preknowledge of the constituents of a mixture is required. At its best, chromatography will separate several hundreds of components of unknown identity and unknown concentrations, leaving the components unchanged. Amounts in the picogram or parts per billion range can be detected with some detectors. The solutes can range from polar to nonpolar—*i.e.*, water-soluble to hydrocarbon-soluble.

Substances of low critical temperature or low molecular weight, such as the gases at laboratory conditions showing dispersive or London intermolecular forces only, are separated with molecular sieves or gas-solid techniques. Gas-liquid chromatography is applicable to species with high critical temperatures and normal boiling points as high as 400° C. Substances that are solids at normal laboratory conditions with molecular weights below 1,000 are best separated with liquid-solid or liquid-liquid systems. Lower members of the molecular weight scale range are amenable to supercritical-fluid separations. Size-exclusion methods are involved at molecular weights above 1,000. Field-flow fractionation extends the size range to colloids and microscopic particles.

Separations are fast, ranging from analysis times of a few minutes to several hours. The prechromatographic world would have considered a time of several hours to separate multicomponent mixtures to be miraculously fast. Now several hours is considered excessive, and there is much emphasis on increasing speed. (Ro.A.K.)

MASS SPECTROMETRY

Mass spectroscopy denotes that field of physics in which the motion of ions in electric and magnetic fields is used to sort ions according to their mass-to-charge ratios. The instruments used in these studies are called mass spectrometers and mass spectrographs, and they operate on the principle that moving ions may be deflected by electric and magnetic fields. The two instruments differ only in the way in which the sorted charged particles are detected. In the mass spectrometer they are detected electrically, in the mass spectrograph by photographic or other nonelectrical means; the term mass spectroscope is used to include both kinds of devices. Since electrical detectors are now most commonly used, the field is typically referred to as mass spectrometry.

Mass spectroscopes consist of five basic parts: a high vacuum system; a sample handling system, through which the sample to be investigated can be introduced; an ion source, in which a beam of charged particles characteristic of the sample can be produced; an analyzer, in which the beam can be separated into its components; and a detector or receiver by means of which the separated ion beams can be observed or collected.

Applications

Many investigations have been conducted with the help of mass spectrometry. These include the identification of the isotopes of the chemical elements and determination of their precise masses and relative abundances, the dating of geologic samples, the analysis of inorganic and organic chemicals especially for small amounts of impurities, structural formula determination of complex organic substances, the strengths of chemical bonds and energies necessary to produce particular ions, the identification of products of ion decomposition, and the analysis of unknown materials, such as lunar samples, for their chemical and isotopic constituents. Mass spectroscopes also are employed to separate isotopes and to measure the abundance of concentrated isotopes when used as tracers in chemistry, biology, and medicine.

HISTORY

The foundation of mass spectroscopy was laid in 1898, when Wilhelm Wien, a German physicist, discovered that beams of charged particles could be deflected by a magnetic field. In more refined experiments carried out between 1907 and 1913, the British physicist J.J. Thomson, who had already discovered the electron and observed its deflection by an electric field, passed a beam of positively charged ions through a combined electrostatic and magnetic field. The two fields in Thomson's tube were situated so that the ions were deflected through small angles in two perpendicular directions. The net result was that the ions produced a series of parabolic curves on a photographic plate placed in their paths. Each parabola corresponded to ions of a particular mass-to-charge ratio with the specific position of each ion dependent on its velocity; the lengths of the parabolic curves provided a measure of the range of ion energies contained in the beam. Later, in an attempt to estimate the relative abundances of the various ion species present, Thomson replaced the photographic plate with a metal sheet in which was cut a parabolic slit. By varying the magnetic field, he was able to scan through a mass spectrum and measure a current corresponding to each separated ion species. Thus he may be credited with the construction of the first mass spectrograph and the first mass spectrometer.

The most noteworthy observation made with the parabola spectrography was the spectrum of rare gases present in the atmosphere. In addition to lines due to helium (mass 4), neon (mass 20), and argon (mass 40), there was a line corresponding to an ion of mass 22 that could not be attributed to any known gas. The existence of forms of the same element with different masses had been suspected since it had been found that many pairs of radioactive materials could not be separated by chemical means. The name isotope (from the Greek for "same place") was suggested by the British chemist Frederick Soddy in 1913 for these different radioactive forms of the same chemical species, because they could be classified in the same place in the periodic table of the elements. The ion of mass 22 was, in fact, a stable heavy isotope of neon.

Focusing spectroscopes. The spectroscopes discussed so far are analogous to the pinhole camera in optics, because no focusing of the ion beams is involved. The introduction of focusing types of mass spectroscopes came in the years 1918–19 and was due to the British chemist and physicist Francis W. Aston and to the American physicist Arthur J. Dempster.

In Aston's version, successive electric and magnetic fields were arranged in such a way that all perfectly collimated ions of one mass were brought to a focus independent of their velocity, thus giving rise to what is known as velocity focusing. Aston's design was the basis of his later instruments with which he systematically and accurately measured the masses of the isotopes of many of the elements. He chose ^{16}O (the isotope of oxygen of mass 16) as his standard of mass.

Dempster's spectrometer utilized only a magnetic field, which deflected the ion beam through an arc of 180°. In Dempster's machine, an ion beam homogeneous in mass and energy but diverging from a slit could be brought to a direction focus. This spectrometer was employed by Dempster to make accurate determinations of the abundances of the isotopes of magnesium, lithium, potassium, calcium, and zinc, laying the foundation for similar measurements of the isotopes of all the elements.

Resolving power

The resolving power, or resolution, of a mass spectroscope is a measure of its ability to separate adjacent masses that are displayed as peaks on the detector. If two peaks due to mass m and $(m + \Delta m)$ can just be separated, the resolving power is $m/\Delta m$. The early machines had resolving powers of only a few hundred. In 1935 and 1936, Dempster, Kenneth T. Bainbridge, both working in the United States, and Josef Mattauch, in Germany, independently developed instruments with electric and magnetic fields arranged in tandem in such a way that ion beams that emerged from the source slits in divergent directions and with different velocities were refocused. Such focusing is termed double focusing. It was thus possible to achieve a resolving power of about 60,000.

Ion-velocity spectrometers. The energy of an ion is proportional to the square of its velocity, so ions of constant energy can be separated through the use of fields that vary with time. In the United States William R. Smythe first proposed such a device in 1926 based on electrodes to which radio-frequency voltages are applied and which are arranged so that ions of a given velocity pass undeflected. He built a working model a few years later in collaboration with Mattauch. The method did not prove to be particularly useful and did not see further development. Following World War II the techniques of manipulating very short electrical pulses allowed the construction of the time-of-flight mass spectrometer, in which a short emission of ions is released from the source and their arrival times recorded after having traversed a distance sufficiently long to sort out the different speeds.

In 1953 the West German physicists Wolfgang Paul and Helmut Steinwedel described the development of a quadrupole mass spectrometer. The application of superimposed radio frequency and constant potentials between four parallel rods can be shown to act as a mass separator in which only ions within a particular mass range will perform oscillations of constant amplitude and be collected at the far end of the analyzer. This device has the advantage of high transmission.

GENERAL PRINCIPLES

The evolution of mass spectrometry has been marked by an ever-increasing number of applications in science and technology. New applications and new developments have gone hand in hand to create a complex array of instruments, but all may be understood by tracing the ions through three basic elements: an ion source, a method of analyzing the ion beams according to their mass-to-charge ratio, and detectors capable of measuring or recording the currents of the beams. These elements exist in many forms and are combined to produce spectrometers with specialized characteristics. The needs of users vary, as do the chemical form and the amount of sample available for analysis, which may be in submicrogram quantities. The result is a great variety of design.

Ion sources. *Direct-current arc.* Historically this was the first way of producing a beam of ions and came quite naturally out of the 19th-century experiments for observing the passage of electricity in gases at low pressure. Two planar electrodes oriented perpendicular to the axis of the electric field can, with a few hundred-volt potential difference, form a plasma discharge. (Plasma refers to an ionized gas containing an approximately equal number of positive ions and electrons.) Electrons attracted to the anode collide with molecules of the gas to form ions and free more electrons; the positive ions contribute in turn to further ionization by their collisions. A hole in the cathode allows positive ions to emerge collimated into a beam. Such sources are found with many electrode configurations, including electron-emitting filaments, and operate with wide ranges of pressures and voltages. Sources with magnetic fields parallel to the electric fields can yield beams greater than one milliampere. Direct-current sources were widely used during the first decades of mass spectrography. They served well for gases and liquids introduced as vapours and for many solids as well, because these could be transformed into gaseous atoms and incorporated into the plasma through impact by the ions, a process called sputtering. One disadvantage of this kind of ionization is the wide band of energies attained by the ions, ranging from the maximum electrode potential to almost zero. Such a distribution of energies was the cause of Thomson's parabolas, but accurate work requires a narrow energy range, which in this case must be achieved in the analyzer section of the instrument.

Sputtering

Electron bombardment. Electrons extracted from a glowing filament may be used to ionize gases. This is the basis for the electron bombardment ion source (see Figure 16). A satisfactory electrode arrangement enables the production of a beam of ions much more nearly homogeneous in energy than with the arc, greatly simplifying the ensuing analyzing method. Electron impact has remained the most widely used method of ionization in mass spec-

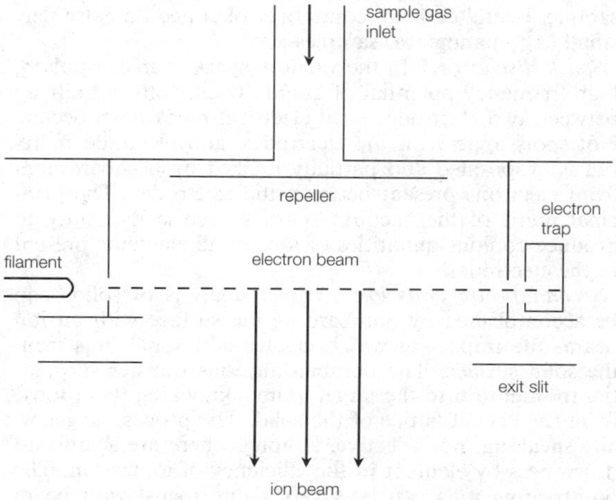

Figure 16: *An electron bombardment ion source in cross section.*
An electron beam is drawn from the filament and accelerated across the region in which the ions are formed and toward the electron trap. An electric field produced by the repeller forces the ion beam from the source through the exit slit.

trometry. It is subject to problems common to the arc: an almost total lack of selectivity as to the chemical element ionized and, to a lesser extent, the production of ions with degrees of ionization greater than one. Electron impact is utilized extensively in fields of study in which the sample is gaseous or prepared in gaseous form. Isotopic studies of carbon, nitrogen, oxygen, sulfur, and the noble gases make up a large field of endeavour. Electron impact is useful for studying organic compounds. Organic molecules are ionized not only as ions of the whole molecule but in a range of fragments as well. This property, which may at first seem disadvantageous, is actually quite valuable in organic identifications because the resulting mass spectrum allows the identification of the source molecule as uniquely as fingerprints are used in human identification. This forms the basis of a powerful method of organic analysis. If the fragmentation of the molecule is harmful to the objectives of the experiment, another method of ionization can be employed that produces few fragments. In this technique a reagent such as methane (CH_4) is mixed with the sample gas and subjected to electron bombardment. The ionized methane (CH_4^+) reacts to form CH_5^+, which in turn reacts to ionize the sample gas by proton or charge transfer. This process is called chemical ionization, and in some cases it increases the mass of the ion formed by one unit.

Chemical ionization

Thermal ionization. Atoms with low ionization potentials can be ionized by contact with the heated surface of a metal, generally a filament, having a high work function (the energy required to remove an electron from its surface) in a process called thermal, or surface, ionization. This can be a highly efficient method and has the experimental advantage of producing ions with a small energy spread characteristic of the filament temperature, typically a few tenths of an electron volt, as compared with beam energies of thousands of electron volts. The filaments, generally made of platinum, rhenium, tungsten, or tantalum, are heated by current. Surface ionization requires a nearby source of atoms, often another filament operating at lower temperatures. Samples can also be loaded directly on the filament, a widely used and successful technique and one that has resulted in many interesting chemical treatments of the sample when it is deposited on the filament. One such application changed lead from a difficult to an easy element to analyze, enabling important geochronological and environmental measurements. A disadvantage of thermal ionization is the possible change in isotopic composition during the measurement. This effect is caused by Rayleigh distillation, wherein light isotopes evaporate faster than heavy ones. Studies done on isotopes that come from radioactive decay, such as those used in determining the ages of rocks, encounter this problem, but it is correctable using the measured values of the isotopes that are not radiogenic. With few exceptions the use of a thermal source requires the chemical separation of the sample. Useful data are commonly obtained on extremely small (*e.g.,* nanogram) samples.

Spark discharge. In the vacuum spark source, a pulsed, high-frequency potential of about 50 kilovolts is built up between two electrodes until electrical breakdown occurs. Hot spots appear on the electrodes, and electrode material is evaporated and partially ionized by bombardment from electrons present between the electrodes. The principal merit of the vacuum spark source is its ability to produce copious quantities of ions of all elements present in the electrodes.

Secondary-ion emission. Direct analysis of solids can be accomplished by bombarding the surface with an ion beam, the impact of which creates additional ions from the solid surface. The bombarding ions transfer substantial momentum to the target atoms, knocking them loose from the crystal lattice of the solid. The process is, generally speaking, not selective, although there are significant differences by element in the efficiency of ionization. The bombarding ions can be given a fine focus, with beam diameters of a few micrometres attainable. This allows the observer to select specific regions of the solid surface for analysis through the use of an auxiliary microscope and micrometre values for sample motion. Ion bombardment eats away the surface with time, allowing the solid to be analyzed for depth as well. This method is the basis for the ion microprobe.

Field ionization. Intense fields, of the order of 10^8 volts per centimetre, can be generated in the neighbourhood of sharp points and edges of electrodes, and these have been used as field ionization, or field emission, sources. This source is becoming popular in the study of organic compounds, which can be introduced as vapours and ionized in the intense fields. The ions are formed with very little excitation energy, so that there is little fragmentation of the molecular ions, making molecular formulas easier to determine.

High-frequency-produced plasma. An oscillator can create an electrodeless discharge in gas at low pressure within a glass tube. The plasma so produced is now a commonly used source for mass spectrometers but was first used in plasma-emission spectrometry (optical and near optical). Samples are introduced by means of a carrier gas, typically argon, and ions result as from the direct-current arc but with very few molecular ions and with the absence of impurities introduced by source electrodes. Such discharges are generally coupled by a coil to an oscillator having a frequency of about 20 megahertz and are called inductively coupled. Discharges can also be produced for specialized experiments in a device called a waveguide that is connected to a cavity magnetron, which has a frequency more than 100 times higher and significantly greater power. This is the basis for the inductively coupled mass spectrometer.

Inductively coupled mass spectrometer

Photoionization. Instead of electrons, photons in the far ultraviolet region may be used, as they have sufficient energy to produce positive ions in a sample gas or vapour to be analyzed. A discharge in a capillary tube through which is passed a suitable gas, such as helium, is a good source for such radiation. Photoionization sources usually produce fewer ions than electron-bombardment sources but have advantages when the ionization chamber must be held at low temperature.

Resonance photoionization. All of the methods of ionization described above suffer from a lack of selectivity as to which element is ionized and depend either on the mass spectrometer for differentiation or on careful sample chemistry. A technique that achieves higher elemental selectivity is resonance ionization. In this scheme, a laser with adjustable wavelength irradiates the volume of gas from which the ions are to be extracted, exciting a transition from an atom's ground state to one of its excited (high-energy) states. This strong excitation enables an equilibrium to be established between the two states, while at the same time other radiation—or sometimes the same radiation—takes atoms from the well-populated excited state to ionization. A slight change in the irradiating wavelength stops the equilibration and leaves the excited state unpopulated, which cuts off the ionization. The intense levels of radiation required are produced by pulsed lasers with very short duty cycles, however, making efficient sample use difficult. (The duty cycle is the ratio of the number of atoms irradiated in a given volume to the total number of atoms entering that volume.) For further discussion, see below *Spectroscopy: Resonance-ionization spectroscopy.*

Negative ions. Discussions of the above methods have assumed that the ionization process removes one or more electrons from the atom or molecule to produce a positive ion. Negative ions are formed by many of these same methods as well and can be useful in mass spectrometry. The accelerating voltages of the source and the direction of analyzing fields must be reversed, but the detectors respond equally well, with the exception of the Daly detector (see below *Ion beam detection: Daly detector*). Arc discharges and electron impact produce negative ions, although at rates varying widely according to the construction and mode of operation. Negative ions can be formed in a two-stage process wherein positive ions are accelerated into a gas from which they capture two electrons, a technique infrequently used in mass spectrometry. Negative ions can result from thermal ionization, with those of the halogens easily formed. The elements rhenium, iridium, platinum, and gold are efficiently ionized as molecular

Cesium sputter source

negative ions for important applications in geochemistry. The cesium sputter source produces copious quantities of negative ions and is used exclusively for accelerator mass spectrometry. In this source the low ionization potential of cesium is utilized in two ways: (1) surface ionization provides a beam of positive cesium ions that bombard a sample having a thin layer of cesium condensed on it; and (2) the atoms or molecules dislodged by the bombarding beam capture an electron from this layer. In addition to providing beams for accelerator mass spectrometry, this source completely changed the manner in which tandem Van de Graaff accelerators are employed in nuclear physics (see below *Accelerator mass spectrometry*). Roy Middleton of the United States invented and developed the cesium sputter source.

Sample introduction. The wide use of mass spectrometers as analytical instruments is accompanied by a correspondingly wide range of forms that the sample can take. Gases for which electron impact is a suitable ionization method are introduced into the vacuum of the source through a fine valve from the sample reservoir, although in some cases the gas may be devolved from a solid by heating in the source. Liquids invariably have vapour pressures high enough for them to be handled as gases. Organic chemistry often furnishes mixtures of gas and liquid in need of analysis. As mentioned above, electron bombardment not only ionizes these molecules but fragments them as well with distributions by which they can be identified. By comparison with a catalog of mass spectra, one can even identify limited mixtures. In 1952 the invention of the gas chromatograph by A.T. James and A.J.P. Martin provided chemists with a method of separating mixtures of volatile substances into their component fractions. In this technique the substance to be analyzed is introduced into a stream of gas, usually helium or nitrogen, and carried by it through a capillary containing or coated with an absorbing substance. The various fractions move with different speeds, and the arrival of each at the end of the column is signaled by a suitable detector. In 1957 a mass spectrometer was first employed as the detector, and an important instrument for organic analysis found its place in the modern laboratory, the gas chromatograph–mass spectrometer. The chromatograph causes the fractions of the sample mixture to arrive at the ion source in succession. Mass analyses of the fractions then allow determinations of high reliability. Liquid chromatography may be combined with mass spectrometry as well (see above *Chromatography: Methods of detection*).

Chromatography-spectrometry combinations

Ion-beam analysis. *General objectives.* The separation of ions according to their mass is accomplished with static magnetic fields, time-varying electric fields, or methods that clock the speeds of ions having the same energies—the time-of-flight method. Static electric fields cannot separate ions by their mass but do separate them by their energy and so provide an important design element by functioning as an energy filter; they are described here along with magnetic fields.

Magnetic field analysis. Ions of mass m and charge z moving in vacuo with a velocity v in a direction perpendicular to a magnetic field B will follow a circular path with radius r given by

$$r = \frac{mv}{Bz}.$$

Therefore, all ions with the same charge and momentum entering the magnetic field from a common point will move in the same radius r and will come to a first-order focus after 180°, as shown in Figure 17, regardless of their masses. Hence, the mass spectrometer used by Dempster can be referred to as a "momentum spectrometer." If all ions of charge z enter the magnetic field with an identical kinetic energy zV, owing to their acceleration through a voltage drop V, a definite velocity v will be associated with each mass, and the radius will depend on the mass. Since $zV = \frac{1}{2}mv^2$, substitution in the previous equation will give $m/z = B^2r^2/2V$. This formula shows that the radius of curvature r for ions in this spectrometer depends only on the ratio of the ions' mass to charge, as long as their kinetic energy is the same. Thus, a magnetic field can be used to separate a monoenergetic ion beam into

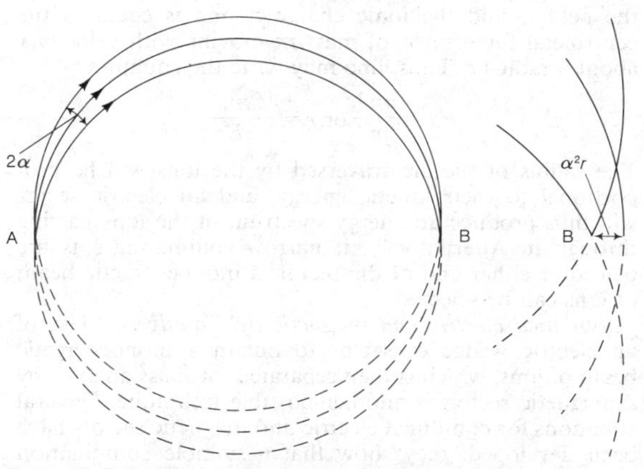

Figure 17: Paths of monoenergetic ions moving in a plane perpendicular to a magnetic field, passing through focal point B after originating at point A (see text).

its various mass components. A magnetic field will also exert a focusing action on a monoenergetic beam of ions of mass m as is shown in Figure 17. In this figure an ion beam emerges from a point A with a spread in direction 2α and comes to an approximate focus at B after traversing 180°. When a molecular ion of mass m_1 carries a single positive charge, it may decompose in front of the magnetic sector to form a fragment ion of mass m_2 and a neutral fragment. If there is no kinetic energy of separation of the fragments, the ion m_2, and also the neutral fragment, will continue along the direction of motion of m_1 with unchanged velocity. The equation of motion for the ion m_2 entering the magnetic sector can now be written from a previous relationship, $r = m_2v/Bz$. In this equation v is the initial velocity appropriate to m_1 and given by $\sqrt{2zV/m_1}$. Multiplying both sides of the equation $v = \sqrt{2zV/m_1}$ by m_2, one obtains $m_2v = \sqrt{2zV(m_2^2/m_1)}$. Since the general momentum equation for any mass m can be written $mv = \sqrt{2zVm}$, it is apparent from the former equation that the momentum m_2v is appropriate to an ion of mass m_2^2/m_1. Thus, the decomposition of the metastable ion will give rise to a peak at an apparent mass $m^* = m_2^2/m_1$, not necessarily an integral number. This peak is known as a metastable peak. Generally, metastable peaks occur at nonintegral mass numbers, and, because there usually is a kinetic energy of separation during fragmentation of the polyatomic ion, they tend to be more diffuse than the normal mass peaks and thus are recognized easily. For any value of m^* a pair of integers m_1 and m_2 can be found such that $m^* = m_2^2/m_1$. Thus, the action of the magnetic field on the charged metastable-ion decomposition product can be used to give information on the individual fragmentation processes taking place in a mass spectrometer.

Metastable peaks

Electrostatic field analysis. An electrostatic field that attracts ions toward a common centre—*i.e.,* a radial field—will also exert a focusing action on a divergent beam of ions as shown in Figure 18. The radial force on the ions due to the electrostatic field will be Ez, the product of

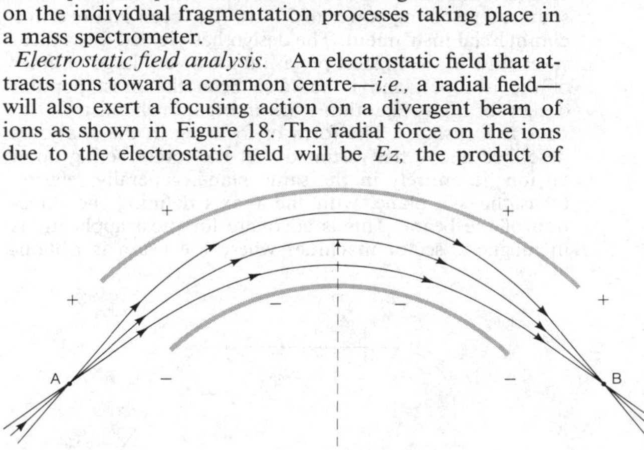

Figure 18: Focusing action of a radial electrostatic field produced by two semicylindrical charged electrodes on a monoenergetic beam of ions. The ions diverging from point A are brought to a focus at point B.

the field E and the ionic charge z, and is equal to the centripetal force mv^2r, of mass m moving with velocity v about a radius r. Thus, one may write the equation

$$Ez = \frac{mv^2}{r} \text{ or } r = \frac{\frac{1}{2}mv^2}{\frac{1}{2}Ez}.$$

The radius of the arc traversed by the ions will be proportional to their kinetic energy, and an electric sector will thus produce an energy spectrum of the ions passing through it. Alternatively, if narrow collimating slits are placed at either end of the sector, a monoenergetic beam of ions can be selected.

Combined electric and magnetic field analysis. Use of an electric wedge or sector to obtain a monoenergetic beam of ions, which is then separated for mass analysis by a magnetic sector, is another possible technique. General equations for combined electric and magnetic sectors have been developed; they show that a suitable combination of fields will give direction focusing for an ion beam of given mass-to-charge ratio, even though the beam may be heterogeneous in energy. The term double focusing is used for those combinations in which the angular and velocity aberrations effectively cancel.

Double focusing

Two of the best examples of double-focusing mass spectroscopes, both of which have been used in a variety of commercial instruments, were built by Mattauch and Richard Herzog in West Germany and by the American physicist Alfred O. Nier and his collaborators. The Mattauch-Herzog geometry is shown in Figure 19. Ions of all masses focus along a line that coincides with the second magnetic field boundary. Many versions of this design have been used when high resolution (up to 10^5) is desired for accurate mass and abundance measurements and general analytical work. It can give good spectra, even for a spread of 5 percent in energy of the ion beam, and can be used with virtually any ion source. The resolved ion beams can be recorded electrically or with a photographic plate.

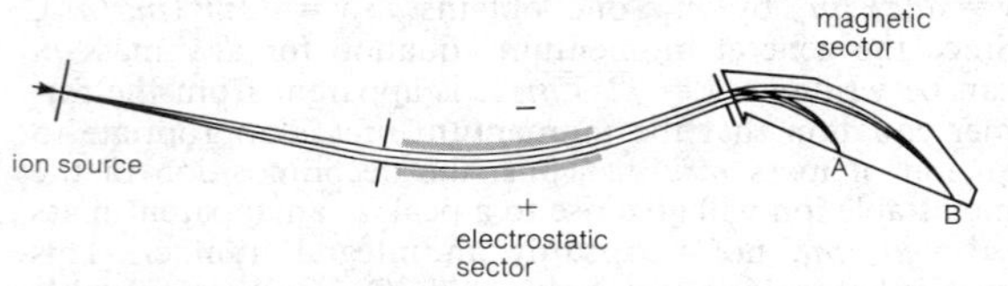

Figure 19: *Arrangement of the electrostatic and magnetic sectors in the Mattauch-Herzog double-focusing mass spectrometer.*
The ions are deflected in opposite directions in the electrostatic and magnetic fields. The divergent monoenergetic beam contains two ion species of different mass-to-charge ratio. All ions are brought to a focus along the plane AB.

Nier's efforts

Nier's design is illustrated in Figure 20. In this instrument, Nier was able to achieve high sensitivity as well as high resolution. Using an electron-bombardment ion source, a resolving power of 2×10^5 has been attained in a commercial instrument. The design has yielded mass measurements of the highest precision for a very large number of the isotopes, and it has also been the most popular design for high-resolution work in organic chemistry.

z-axis focusing. The form of focusing in the analyzers described above has assumed that the forces acting upon an ion lie entirely in the same plane, generally referred to as the x-y plane, with the y axis defining the direction of the beam. This is adequate for most applications in magnetic sector machines where the beam is ribbon-shaped and where slight deviations in velocity in the z direction, which is perpendicular to the principal plane, cause negligible beam loss. At the entrance and exit of a trajectory passing through a field produced by a magnet, the field is not parallel but rather is bowed out. As a consequence, an ion encounters a small, but not negligible, field component parallel to the x-y plane, which generates a correspondingly small force in the z direction. Magnets have been constructed that take advantage of such forces to focus the beam in the z direction. It is possible to make the x focus and z focus coincident. Focusing in the z direction is often accomplished electrostatically by a suitably arranged pair of electrodes in the ion source.

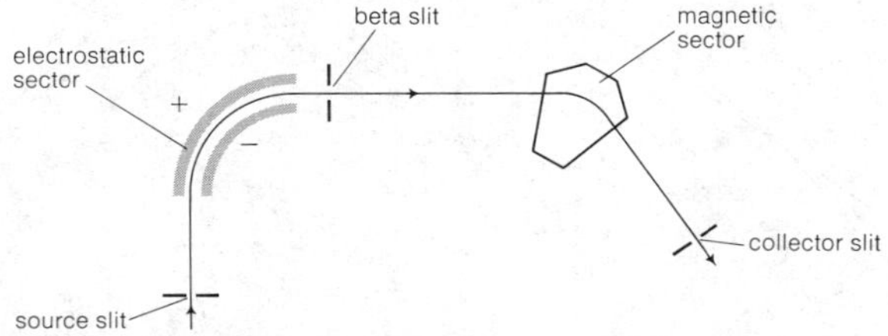

Figure 20: *Arrangement of the electrostatic and magnetic sectors in the Nier double-focusing mass spectrometer.*
The angle of the electrostatic sector is 90° and that of the magnetic sector 60°. The direction of deflection of the ion beam is the same in both sectors.

Time of flight. The simplest form of mass analysis that does not use magnetic fields depends on the differing speeds of ions with the same energy but different masses. The ion source is generally of the electron-impact type and has one or more electrodes modulated so as to extract ions for a time that is brief compared with the time it takes them to reach the detector. The ion velocities, as given above by $v = \sqrt{2zV/m}$, and the distance between source and detector allow the mass to be calculated directly. In practice, the response of the detector is displayed on a cathode-ray oscillograph and recorded by a computer. This method has two advantages: it is fast and, if desired, can display the entire mass spectrum. Its deficiencies are poor resolution, poor accuracy of signal, and poor efficiency, due to the short period during which ions are extracted from the source.

Ion-trap methods. It is possible to configure electric and magnetic fields so that ions can be held in stable orbits for a period of time long enough to perform useful measurements on them. Two forms of mass spectrometers are derived from this idea, the omegatron and the Fourier-transform spectrometer. Both make use of the cyclotron principle (see PARTICLE ACCELERATORS: *Cyclotrons*), in which positive ions produced by a beam of electrons flowing along the axis of a uniform magnetic field follow circular trajectories with a radius proportional to momentum, $r = mv/zB$, and a frequency of rotation inversely proportional to mass, $\omega = v/r = zB/m$. In the omegatron the frequency of an oscillator is varied so as to bring ions of various masses in tune and by so doing increase their momenta until they reach a radius at which a detector is located. Mass can be directly calculated from frequency. Resolution can be remarkably high if a sufficient magnetic field is provided, but this analyzer is most frequently operated with less than ideal resolution as a device for analyzing the residual gas of a vacuum, information that can be extremely valuable in diagnosing the problems that often befall such systems.

Fourier-transform spectrometer

In the Fourier-transform method, the frequency of the oscillator is swept through the range corresponding to the mass range of interest. Each ion is placed into a circular orbit of approximately constant radius but well-defined frequency. The oscillator is turned off, and an electrode picks up radio-frequency radiation from the moving ions. The amplified output can be recorded either directly or after having been mixed with the frequency of a local oscillator, a standard radio technique. This yields a complex time-varying signal that follows the amplitude of the various ion radiators. The signal is converted to digital form and stored in a computer memory. The computer converts this periodic signal to its frequency spectrum by the mathematical technique known as the Fourier transform, with mass being inversely proportional to frequency. The process is repeated many times in order to enhance accuracy. These devices are capable of resolutions exceeding one million. In order to have orbital radii of convenient size, very high magnetic fields are required, generally provided by superconductors.

Tandem spectrometry. The combination of two analytical techniques, such as resulted in the gas chromatograph–mass spectrometer, has been followed by the combination of two mass spectrometers, which has proved helpful in determining the structure of complicated molecules. A beam from the first spectrometer is passed into a gas cell (maintained in the vacuum system by differential pumping), where it is dissociated by collisions, and these fragments are passed on to a second mass analyzer, which generally discloses a more easily identified spectrum.

Quadrupole spectrometer. Positive ions incident along an axis parallel to four cylindrical electrodes, as shown in Figure 21, experience for the static potentials indicated a focusing force along the x axis and a defocusing one in the z direction. If one superimposes a radio frequency voltage onto the static voltage, oscillatory ion trajectories can be found that allow ions of a given mass to pass through the quadrupole with other masses being defocused and lost from the beam. A knowledge of the potentials and frequency specifies the mass. This device is widely used where speed of data acquisition and high transmission are important. It is compact and lightweight and can trade off sensitivity for resolution by simple adjustment of electrical parameters. It is the common analyzing element of gas chromatograph–mass spectrometers.

Advantages of the quadrupole analyzer

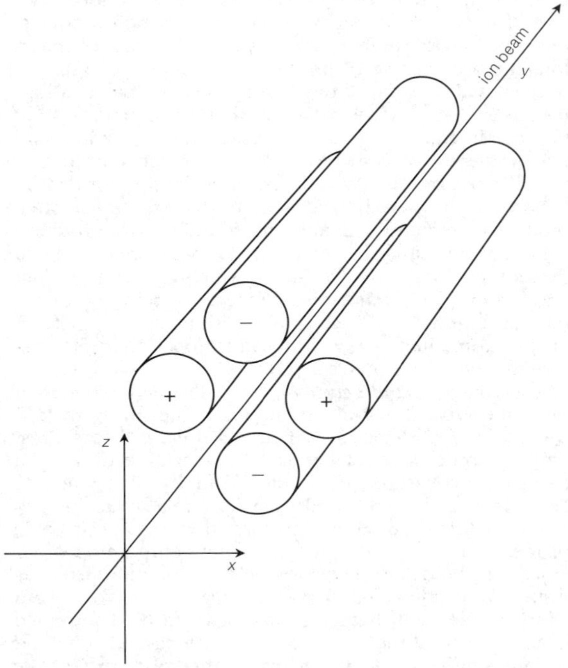

Figure 21: *Schematic diagram of a quadrupole mass spectrometer.*
The pairs of opposing electrodes are electrically connected to a balanced voltage source having a radio frequency component superimposed on a constant potential. Combinations of values for the amplitude and frequency exist that allow ions of a given mass from a beam of constant energy to emerge undeflected.

Ion beam detection. *Photographic plates.* Especially sensitive photographic plates are employed to compensate for the low penetrating power of the ions. It has proved possible with these to detect an element over a sensitivity range of one part in one billion. In addition to the sensitivity, a major advantage of the photographic plate arises when it is used in a double-focusing mass spectroscope in which the whole or a major part of the mass spectrum is focused in a plane (see the design of Mattauch and Herzog shown in Figure 19 and described above). In this case, one can make use of the integrating action of the plate and compare the densities of lines due to different elements.

Faraday cup. The direct measurement of ion currents collected by a shielded electrode, called a Faraday cup, became possible in the 1930s with the introduction of electrometer tubes capable of measuring currents below a nanoampere, although sensitive galvanometers had been used for larger currents. The introduction of feedback led to greater stability and accuracy and faster response time, but it was the introduction of the vibrating-reed electrometer that allowed isotopic ratios to be routinely measured to a few parts in a hundred thousand. For more than three decades, these electrometers functioned unsurpassed as laboratory workhorses and were only slightly modified in design. They can now be equaled and in some respects surpassed in performance by the feedback electrometer, which uses a metal-oxide silicon field-effect transistor instead of a tube to measure extremely small currents.

Electron multipliers. The development of electronic techniques for television during the 1930s yielded a device of extraordinary sensitivity for measuring small electron beams—namely, the secondary electron multiplier. Although originally invented for the amplification of the tiny currents from a photocathode, it soon proved to be an excellent detector for ion beams with a sensitivity sufficient to record the arrival of single ions. The fundamental principle of the multiplier is, as the name suggests, a multiplication of the number of electrons emerging from an electrode as compared with the number incident upon it. Electrodes, called dynodes, are so arranged that each succeeding generation of electrons is attracted to the next dynode. For example, if 4 electrons are released at the first dynode, then 16 will emerge from the second and so forth. Gains of as much as one million are easily attained; the noise is limited to the currents originating from the few electrons leaving the first dynode as a result of thermal electron emission. Multipliers were originally constructed with discrete dynodes, a form still in wide use. Continuous dynode multipliers, which use a semiconducting glass to provide the distribution of electrostatic potential, are smaller and perform equally well in most applications. A multiplier can be employed in an analog mode, in which the output current is measured with an electrometer as is any small current, or in a pulse-counting mode, in which individual ions are counted.

Types of dynodes

The mass spectrum of osmium (Os), obtained using an electron multiplier detector, is shown in Figure 22. It is a recorder trace of the electrometer output from an electron multiplier detecting OsO_3^- taken as the field of the analyzing magnet was steadily increased. Owing to their small sizes, the leftmost and two rightmost peaks were recorded with an electrometer gain 100 times what was used for the other peaks; the change in gain is marked by a change in the position of the baseline. The osmium isotopes observed, from left to right, are 184, 186, 187, 188, 189, 190, and 192. The oxygen (O) in the ions results in very small satellite peaks caused by the low abundance isotopes ^{17}O and ^{18}O; the satellite peaks of ^{192}Os are at the right. This trace is typical of machines used in geochronology, where flat-topped peaks are desired rather than high resolution. The irregular signal of the three weak isotopes results from the low rate at which these ions are detected.

Daly detector. In 1960 N.R. Daly introduced a form of detector with properties superior to the electron multipliers described above. In this design the incident ions are attracted to a rounded electrode of a few centimetres in dimension that is held at 10,000 to 20,000 volts negative. The ions strike the "door knob" and release a few secondary electrons for each incident ion; these electrons are then accelerated from the high negative potential to a scintillation crystal mounted on a photomultiplier at ground potential. The electrons generate a light signal in the scintillation crystal that is amplified by the photomultiplier. The output is then treated just as the output of an elec-

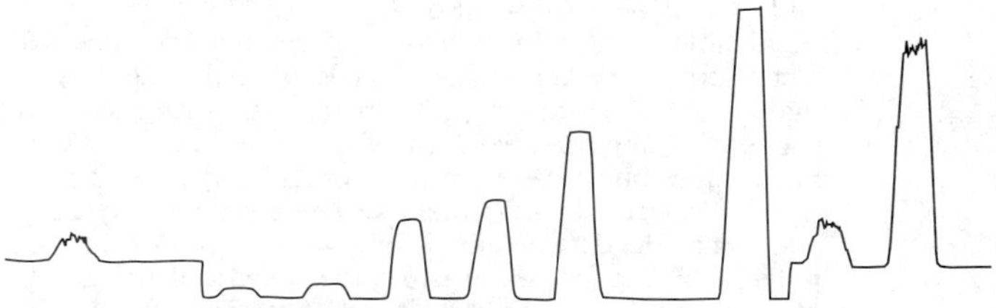

Figure 22: *The mass spectrum of osmium.*
This recorder trace was obtained with an electron multiplier detecting OsO_3^-. The leftmost and rightmost peaks were recorded with the detector gain set at a value 100 times that used for the rest of the spectrum; this change is marked by the change in the baseline position. The small satellite peaks to the left are those of the low abundance oxygen isotopes ^{17}O and ^{18}O; the osmium isotopes are, from left to right, ^{184}Os, ^{186}Os, ^{187}Os, ^{188}Os, ^{189}Os, ^{190}Os, and the satellite peaks of ^{192}Os.

Independence of signal size and beam position

tron multiplier. The advantage of this more complicated device is an almost complete independence of the signal size with the position of the ion beam in the defining slit that precedes the detector. This is an important property for accurate measurement of isotopic ratios because the invariable instability of the analyzing magnet and the ion-source voltage cause the beam to drift within the limits set by the slit, and so a nonuniform response gives rise to errors in the measured ratios. Electron multipliers require various adjustments, not always satisfactory, to produce a signal size independent of beam position. The Daly detector cannot be used with negative ions.

Multiple detectors. In instances in which the ratio of two or more isotopes is the experimental goal with a magnetic sector analyzer, there are advantages in measuring the currents of the beams simultaneously in multiple detectors rather than switching the magnetic field. This is relatively simple for light elements that have widely spaced beams at the detector location and is often employed in such cases. For heavy elements the small spacing necessitates more difficult techniques that came into routine use only in the 1980s.

IMPORTANT TECHNICAL ADJUNCTS

Vacuum. In the devices heretofore described, the presence of a good vacuum system has been assumed. Mass spectroscopy originated at about the time that high vacuum was first attained in the laboratory. High vacuum refers to a pressure low enough that the mean free path (the distance traveled between collisions) of molecules in the residual gas is greater than the dimensions of the vacuum vessel. Mass spectroscopists invariably seek conditions of improved vacuum. The properties that render low pressures desirable include a reduction in the scattering of the beam in the analyzer, which causes interfering background effects and a reduction in the production of spurious beams out of the residual gases, particularly from the organic compounds that are present. The history of vacuum techniques is varied and great and has provided present mass spectrometrists with pressures that are routinely four to five orders of magnitude lower than those first used by Thomson, Aston, and Dempster. The invention of the diffusion pump by the German physicist Wolfgang Gaede in 1915, with important improvements by the American chemist Irving Langmuir shortly thereafter, freed mass spectroscopy from the severe limitations of poor vacuum. During the 1960s diffusion pumps began to be replaced by ion-getter pumps, with turbomolecular pumps becoming common in the 1980s.

Vacuum pumps

Electronics. The operation of a mass spectrometer depends on elaborate electronic equipment: ion sources require extremely stable power supplies, magnets need instruments for measuring the magnetic field and controlling the current supply for the coils, detectors use a variety of power supplies and amplifiers, and general operation requires electronic auxiliary equipment. The rapid increase in the use of mass spectrometers following World War II can likely be attributed in part to the large number of physicists who had gained electronic training during the war, many of whom had utilized mass spectroscopy during that conflict to monitor uranium isotope separation and to analyze aviation gasoline.

Computers. The introduction of small computers for laboratory work during the 1960s altered entirely the manner in which mass spectrometry was performed and widened its applications to an extraordinary degree. Computers were interfaced with spectrometers, making it possible to repeat a measurement schedule on a steady basis and record the data acquired. In organic analysis the computer was programmed to store the spectra of thousands of compounds, allowing rapid identification of the substance under study. Users soon devised ways by which the answers to their questions came within minutes after the conclusion of the analysis.

APPLICATIONS

Atomic. *Atomic masses.* The discovery of isotopes with the first mass spectrograph answered the question about the integer value of atoms only to a crude level of accuracy and made all too clear the need for more accurate mass determinations. These were first undertaken by Aston and repeated with increasing precision by succeeding generations. The first data showed slight deviations from an integer law but also showed a quasi-systematic variation as a function of atomic number. In the early 1930s these data explained the energies of nuclear reactions then being observed through the mass-energy relation that had been given two decades earlier by the special theory of relativity. Since that time mass spectroscopy and nuclear physics have combined to determine isotopic masses to a high degree of accuracy. The mass unit now used is defined so that the mass of the carbon-12 isotope is exactly 12 atomic mass units (amu). Nuclear theory is continually tested in its ability to reproduce the observed values. Indeed, these masses provide an early and critical test of nuclear models. Mass spectrometry has been closely associated with nuclear physics since its beginning. A mass spectrometer is frequently found in some form as a part of nuclear experiments to identify reaction products. Large mass spectrometers are employed as isotope separators and are capable of producing weighable amounts of selected stable isotopes that have valuable analytical applications. They are used for labeling compounds so that they can be traced through various chemical, physical, and environmental processes without the problems created by radioisotope tracers. Analysis is, of course, performed by mass spectrometer. In addition, nuclear reactions often produce extremely small amounts of radioactive products, which cannot easily be manipulated by normal chemical procedures. In such cases, stable isotopes of the product are added to the radioactive element, thereby increasing the concentration so that it falls within the range of the analytical method. These enriched isotopes are indispensable for research in nuclear physics.

Relationship to nuclear physics

Geochronology and geochemistry. The early studies of the radioactive decay of uranium and thorium into lead caused the British physicist Ernest Rutherford to suggest that this process could be used to determine the age of rocks and consequently of the Earth by observing the amount of helium retained by a rock relative to its uranium and thorium contents. Mass spectrometers capable of measuring isotopic ratios allow the composition of elements to be determined in which one or more isotopes result from radioactive decay. The age of the rock from which the element has been obtained can be determined if the amount of the parent element can be measured and certain requirements on the environmental history of the rock are met (see GEOCHRONOLOGY: *Relative and absolute dating: Absolute dating*).

The Earth's crust is generally richer in oxygen-18 (^{18}O) than is the mantle, as a result of the reaction of these upper-layer rocks with the hydrosphere and atmosphere. This fact allows oxygen-18 to be used to assess the degree to which ascending magmas have incorporated crustal rocks as they rise to the surface. The use of isotopes has proved especially valuable in understanding the origin and nature of the solar system. A great body of evidence now suggests that meteorites are objects that solidified very early in the history of the solar system. Extinct radioactivities of elements with various half-lives have been identified that set limits on the time between the synthesis of the elements and their condensation. (Extinct radioactivities are nuclides that have nearly completely decayed into their daughter elements.) An example is the excess of magnesium-26 (^{26}Mg) found in primitive meteorites that resulted from the decay of aluminum-26 (^{26}Al), which has a 720,000-year half-life.

Hydrogen, carbon, nitrogen, oxygen, and sulfur in nature. These elements, each of which has two or more stable isotopes, are vital to life. All show measurable variation in isotope composition as a result of natural and, in particular, metabolic processes. It was observed as early as 1939 that living matter preferentially incorporates the light isotope of carbon at rates differing according to species and environment. Knowledge of this is valuable in understanding the early biochemical evolution of the Earth. The evaporation of seawater causes a lower ratio of ^{18}O to ^{16}O in fresh water during times of high average tem-

Variation in isotopic composition

perature than in times of low temperatures. Examination of the oxygen preserved in polar ice and calcareous fossil shells has revealed the climatic evolution of the recent geologic past.

Trace element analysis. Mass spectrometry may be used to measure with high sensitivity trace amounts of an element through the technique of isotope dilution. A small, measured amount of an isotopically enriched sample, called a spike, is added to the original material, thoroughly mixed with it, and extracted with that element. The mass spectrum of this mixture will be a combination of the natural spectrum of the element plus the unnatural one of the spike. By knowing the amount of the spike added, one may calculate the amount of the unknown. Rigorous measures must be undertaken to ensure that the reagents and vessels used do not themselves supply the element, but this is easily controlled by chemically processing a known amount of the spike alone and determining the amount of the element picked up.

Molecular. *Ion-molecule reactions.* Owing to the poor vacuums available prior to the contributions of Gaede and Langmuir (see above), this subject was forced on the attention of early experimenters. They observed masses of 3 and 19, which could not have been produced by simple ionization and which arise from the following reactions, respectively:

$$H_2^+ + H_2 \rightarrow H_3^+ + H$$
$$H_2^+ + H_2O \rightarrow H_3O^+ + H.$$

These "problems" disappeared with improved vacuum. Ion-molecule reactions are important in understanding the chemistry of flames, of electrical discharges, of the upper atmosphere, and of samples subject to radiation. The mass spectrometer is the instrument of choice for such investigations.

Organic chemistry. Mass spectrometry has a critical role in organic chemistry. Its utility in chemical analysis was discussed earlier when describing appropriate experimental techniques. The same techniques can be used in determining the structure of complicated molecules, but perhaps of even greater value for such work are high-resolution measurements.

With a high-resolution mass spectrometer it is possible to carry out mass measurements on the molecular ion (or any other ion in the spectrum) to an accuracy of approximately one part in one million. This mass provides the best index for determining ionic formulas. The accurate masses of the ions $C_6H_{12}^+$ and $C_4H_4O_2^+$ are, for example, 84.0939 and 84.0211, respectively, and these ions can easily be distinguished solely on the basis of their masses. Once the molecular formula is known it is possible to deduce the total of rings and double bonds making up the molecular structure and to begin to speculate on possible

Structural formulas

structural formulas. In order to deduce structural formulas from molecular formulas, it is essential to study the fragment ions in the mass spectrum. It is still not possible to predict definitively the fragmentation patterns for organic molecules, but many semi-empirical rules of fragmentation are known, and it is usually possible to pick out peaks in the spectrum that are characteristic of particular chemical groups. The technique is valuable in that it is generally not necessary to know any details of the composition of the unknown compound in order to deduce a complete or partial structure. Only a small quantity of compound, a hundred micrograms or less, is necessary for an analysis. A low-resolution mass spectrum of methyl benzoate ($C_6H_5COOCH_3$) produced with a quadrupole mass spectrometer is shown in Figure 23. The parent ion at mass 136 results from an intact molecule that has had one electron removed. The ions at masses 105, 77, and 51 result from fragments that have been dissociated by the impact. Mass 105 results from the loss of a methoxy group (OCH_3) from the parent, mass 77 from the intact benzene ring, and mass 51 from the fragmentation of the benzene ring. The smaller lines are caused by more complicated dissociation and chemical ionization.

Using a computer coupled to a high-resolution mass spectrometer, about 1,000 mass peaks per minute can be plotted at a resolving power of up to 20,000, accurate measurements can be made on each peak, and peak heights and ion compositions can be printed out in the form of an "element map" to aid in the interpretation of the spectrum. It is also possible for the computer to carry out many of the logical steps in reducing the data that lead to structural elucidation.

Analysis of reaction intermediates

Continuous sampling of the materials contained in a reaction vessel, followed by analysis with a mass spectrometer, has been used to identify and measure the quantity of intermediate species formed during a reaction as a function of time. This kind of analysis is important, both in suggesting the mechanism by which the overall reaction takes place and in enabling the detailed kinetics of reactions to be resolved.

Isotopic labeling is widely used in such studies. It can indicate which particular atoms are involved in the reaction; in rearrangement reactions it can show whether an intramolecular or intermolecular process is involved; in exchange reactions it can show that particular atoms of, for example, hydrogen are exchanging between the reacting species. Labeling is also widely used in mass-spectrometric research to give information about the fragmentation reactions occurring in the mass spectrometer.

Fields of investigation that employ mass spectrometry include studies of protein structure, drug metabolism, flavour and smell, petroleum and petrochemicals, organic fossils, inherited metabolic diseases, atmospheres and respiratory gases, and many other highly specialized subjects.

Space probes. Future space exploration, addressing the question of whether life exists elsewhere in the solar system, will rely on the mass spectrometer to produce spectra of those molecules characteristic of life. An unmanned spacecraft equipped with a mass spectrometer has already revealed much about the surface and atmosphere of Mars and set limits on the amount of organic matter present.

Leak detection. A widely used commercial device designed to locate leaks in vacuum systems consists of a small mass spectrometer with an electron-bombardment ion source that is connected to the troubled system. The mass spectrometer is set to detect helium, and the gas is played onto suspected parts through a capillary. A signal develops when the helium enters through the leak, and the exact location can be determined by adept manipulation of the capillary.

ACCELERATOR MASS SPECTROMETRY

The particle accelerators used in nuclear physics can be viewed as mass spectrometers of rather distorted forms, but the three principal elements—the ion source, analyzer, and detector—are always present. L.W. Alvarez and Robert Cornog of the United States first used an accelerator as a mass spectrometer in 1939 when they employed a cyclotron to demonstrate that helium-3 (^3He) was stable rather than hydrogen-3 (^3H), an important question in nuclear physics at the time. They also showed that helium-3 was a constituent of natural helium. Their method was the same as that described above for the omegatron except

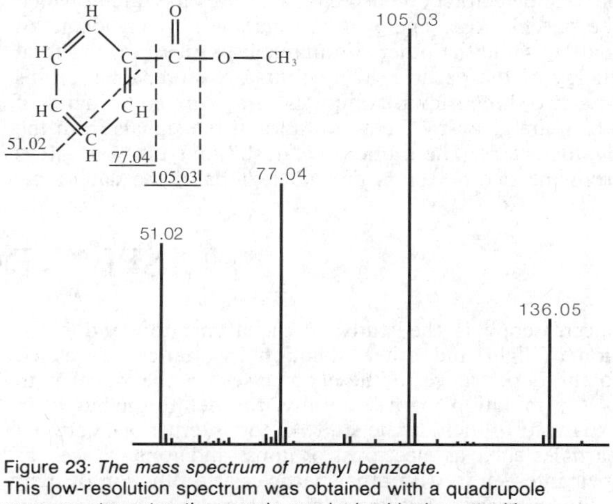

Figure 23: *The mass spectrum of methyl benzoate.*
This low-resolution spectrum was obtained with a quadrupole mass spectrometer; the sample was ionized by impact with a 70-electron volt electron beam (see text).

that a full-sized cyclotron was used, and it easily distinguished the two isotopes. The method was not employed again for nearly 40 years; however, it has found application in measuring cosmogenic isotopes, the radioisotopes produced by cosmic rays incident on the Earth or planetary objects. These isotopes are exceedingly rare, having abundances on the order of one million millionth of the corresponding terrestrial element, which is an isotopic ratio far beyond the capabilities of normal mass spectrometers. If the half-life of a cosmogenic isotope is relatively short, such as beryllium-7 (^{7}Be; 53 days) or carbon-14 (^{14}C; 5,730 years), its concentration in a sample can be determined by radioactive counting; but if the half-life is long, such as beryllium-10 (^{10}Be; 1.5 million years) or chlorine-36 (^{36}Cl; 0.3 million years), such a course is ineffective. The advantage of the large, high-energy accelerator mass spectrometer is the great detector selectivity that results from ions having 1,000 times more energy than any previously available machine could provide. Conventional mass spectrometers have difficulty measuring abundances less than one hundred-thousandth of the reference isotope, because interfering ions are scattered into the analyzer location where the low-abundance isotope is to be sought. Extremes of high vacuum and antiscattering precautions can improve this by a factor of 10 but not the factor of 100 million that is required. An accelerator suffers from this defect to an even greater degree, and large quantities of "trash" ions are found at the expected analyzer location of the cosmogenic isotope. The ability of certain kinds of nuclear particle detectors to identify the relevant ion unambiguously enables the accelerator mass spectrometer to overcome this shortcoming and function as a powerful analytical tool.

Measurement of cosmogenic isotopes

Tandem electrostatic accelerator

The tandem electrostatic accelerator (see PARTICLE ACCELERATORS) quickly displaced all other machines for this purpose, primarily because its ion source, the cesium sputter source described above, is located near ground potential and is easily accessible for changing samples. The ions must be negative, but this does not prove to be a handicap as they are easily and efficiently produced. Before entering the high-voltage tube, the ions are mass-analyzed so that only the beam emerging at the mass location of the cosmogenic isotope enters the accelerator; the intense reference isotope beam is often measured at this location without entering the accelerator at all. The cosmogenic isotope beam is attracted to the high-voltage terminal of the machine where collisions with gas or a thin carbon foil or both strip various numbers of electrons, thereby leaving the subject isotope with a distribution of multiple positive charge states that are repelled by the positively charged terminal. All molecular ions are broken up. The emerging beam then passes through analyzing fields of which a high dispersion magnet is the principal part. Upon leaving the analyzer, the beam enters the detector. Each ion is examined individually in a manner that allows its identity to be established. The most common way of doing this is by using a combination of two particle detectors: one detector measures the rate at which the particle loses energy when passing a given length of matter, while the other simultaneously measures the total energy of the particle. The counts are stored in the bins of a two-dimensional computer array, the coordinates of which are given by the amplitudes of the signals from the two detectors. The numerous "trash" ions take on values from the two detectors that fill regions of the data array but generally do not overlap the well-defined region occupied by the subject ion. Each kind of isotope requires a specially designed detector system with various additional analyzing fields and, in some cases, even the use of time-of-flight techniques. A schematic diagram of an accelerator mass spectrometer is shown in Figure 24.

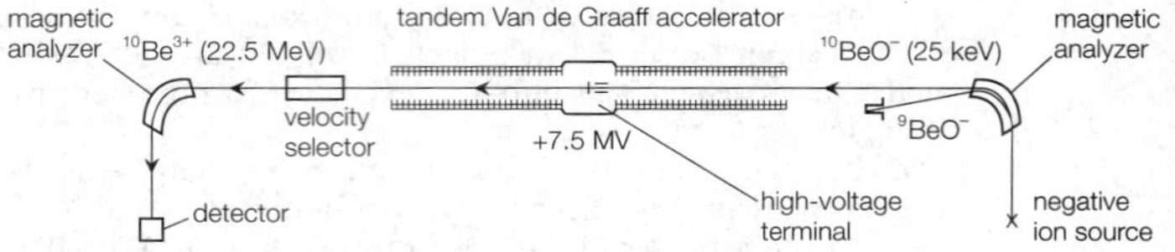

Figure 24: *Schematic diagram showing the ion trajectories in an accelerator mass spectrometer with application to ^{10}Be.*
Negative ions of BeO leave the source and are mass analyzed with $^{10}BeO^{-}$ directed into the accelerator and $^{9}BeO^{-}$ into a Faraday cup. The molecular ions are broken up by gas and a thin carbon foil in the high-voltage terminal with much of the ^{10}Be ionized to the 3+ charge state. The emerging ions pass through a velocity selector, are again analyzed for mass, and pass to the detector. Velocity selection is attained by a magnetic field and an electric field that are orthogonal to one another and to the beam direction; they are adjusted so that no deflection takes place for ions of the desired velocity.

The accelerator method has opened lines of investigation that had previously been inaccessible. A strong motivation for the inventors was the improvement of radiocarbon dating. Scientists are now able to make age determinations from much smaller samples and to make them much more rapidly than by radioactive counting, but carbon-14 proved to be a considerably more difficult problem for instrumental development than the other cosmogenic isotopes. The method was applied almost immediately to analyses involving beryllium-10 and chlorine-36, with aluminum-26 (^{26}Al), calcium-41 (^{41}Ca), and iodine-129 (^{129}I) following soon after; notable achievements resulted from all five. Cosmic rays striking the atmosphere are a strong source of beryllium-10, carbon-14, and chlorine-36, which are deposited in rain and snow, whence their migration may be followed. A question concerning the origin of the lavas of island-arc volcanoes, which had been disputed since the general acceptance of the plate tectonic theory of the Earth's structure, was settled from the observation of beryllium-10 in these lavas. The presence of beryllium-10 proved that deep-ocean sediment, rich in the isotope, had been subducted (*i.e.,* carried on the surface of a descending tectonic plate beneath another such plate) and some of the sediment incorporated into the magma. The first application of chlorine-36 was the study of the migration of ancient groundwater. Later improvements in instrumental techniques added iodine-129 as a needed tracer for this challenging problem. Nuclear bomb tests at oceanic sites produced huge amounts of chlorine-36 that were injected into the atmosphere. For a few years rain contained this isotope at a level up to 1,000 times higher than the cosmogenic level. This yielded a tracer with a well-defined time of origin that will be useful long into the future for following the course of such water in soils and aquifers (water-bearing layers of rock). The four lightest of these isotopes have proved useful in determining the ages and irradiation histories of meteorites and lunar samples. There have been extensive studies of beryllium-10 in cores of polar ice and ocean sediments that give unique information about the intensity of cosmic rays over the past few million years. (J.H.Be./L.Br.)

Radioactive tracing

SPECTROSCOPY

Spectroscopy is the study of the absorption and emission of light and other radiation by matter, as related to the dependence of these processes on the wavelength of the radiation. More recently, the definition has been expanded to include the study of the interactions between particles such as electrons, protons, and ions, as well as their interaction with other particles as a function of their collision energy. Spectroscopic analysis has been crucial in the development of the most fundamental theories in physics, including quantum mechanics, the special and general theories of relativity, and quantum electrodynamics. Spectroscopy, as applied to high-energy collisions, has been a key tool in developing scientific understanding not only of the electromagnetic force but also of the strong and weak nuclear forces.

Applications in science and technology

Spectroscopic techniques have been applied in virtually all technical fields of science and technology. Radio-frequency spectroscopy of nuclei in a magnetic field has been employed in a medical technique called magnetic resonance imaging (MRI) to visualize the internal soft tissue of the body with unprecedented resolution. Microwave spectroscopy was used to discover the so-called three-degree blackbody radiation, the remnant of the big bang (*i.e.,* the primeval explosion) from which the universe is thought to have originated (see below *Survey of optical spectroscopy: General principles: Applications*). The internal structure of the proton and neutron and the state of the early universe up to the first thousandth of a second of its existence is being unraveled with spectroscopic techniques utilizing high-energy particle accelerators. The constituents of distant stars, intergalactic molecules, and even the primordial abundance of the elements before the formation of the first stars can be determined by optical, radio, and X-ray spectroscopy. Optical spectroscopy is used routinely to identify the chemical composition of matter and to determine its physical structure.

Spectroscopic techniques are extremely sensitive. Single atoms and even different isotopes of the same atom can be detected among 10^{20} or more atoms of a different species. (Isotopes are all atoms of an element that have unequal mass but the same atomic number. Isotopes of the same element are virtually identical chemically.) Trace amounts of pollutants or contaminants are often detected most effectively by spectroscopic techniques. Certain types of microwave, optical, and gamma-ray spectroscopy are capable of measuring infinitesimal frequency shifts in narrow spectroscopic lines. Frequency shifts as small as one part in 10^{15} of the frequency being measured can be observed with ultrahigh resolution laser techniques. Because of this sensitivity, the most accurate physical measurements have been frequency measurements.

Spectroscopy now covers a sizable fraction of the electromagnetic spectrum. Table 3 summarizes the electromagnetic spectrum over a frequency range of 16 orders of magnitude. Spectroscopic techniques are not confined to electromagnetic radiation, however. Because the energy E of a photon (a quantum of light) is related to its frequency ν by the relation $E = h\nu$, where h is Planck's constant, spectroscopy is actually the measure of the interaction of photons with matter as a function of the photon energy. In instances where the probe particle is not a photon, spectroscopy refers to the measurement of how the particle interacts with the test particle or material as a function of the energy of the probe particle.

Table 3: Electromagnetic Phenomena

	approximate wavelength range (metres)	approximate frequency range (hertz)
Radio waves	10–1,000	3×10^5–3×10^7
Television waves	1–10	3×10^7–3×10
Microwaves, radar	1×10^{-3}–1	3×10^8–3×10^{11}
Infrared	8×10^{-7}–1×10^{-3}	3×10^{11}–4×10^{14}
Visible light	4×10^{-7}–7×10^{-7}	4×10^{14}–7×10^{14}
Ultraviolet	1×10^{-8}–4×10^{-7}	7×10^{14}–3×10^{16}
X rays	5×10^{-12}–1×10^{-8}	3×10^{16}–6×10^{19}
Gamma rays (γ rays)	1×10^{-13}–5×10^{-12}	6×10^{19}–3×10^{21}
Cosmic rays	less than 1×10^{-13}	greater than 3×10^{21}

Particle spectroscopy

An example of particle spectroscopy is a surface analysis technique known as electron energy loss spectroscopy (EELS) that measures the energy lost when low-energy electrons (typically 5–10 electron volts) collide with a surface. Occasionally, the colliding electron loses energy by exciting the surface; by measuring the electron's energy loss, vibrational excitations associated with the surface can be measured. On the other end of the energy spectrum, if an electron collides with another particle at exceedingly high energies, a wealth of subatomic particles is produced. Most of what is known in particle physics (the study of subatomic particles) has been gained by analyzing the total particle production or the production of certain particles as a function of the incident energies of electrons and protons.

The following sections focus on the methods of electromagnetic spectroscopy, particularly optical spectroscopy. Although most of the other forms of spectroscopy are not covered in detail, they have the same common heritage as optical spectroscopy. Thus, many of the basic principles used in other spectroscopies share many of the general features of optical spectroscopy.

Survey of optical spectroscopy

GENERAL PRINCIPLES

Basic features of electromagnetic radiation. Electromagnetic radiation is composed of oscillating electric and magnetic fields that have the ability to transfer energy through space. The energy propagates as a wave, such that the crests and troughs of the wave move in vacuum at the speed of 299,792,458 metres per second. The many forms of electromagnetic radiation appear different to an observer; light is visible to the human eye, while X rays and radio waves are not.

The distance between successive crests in a wave is called its wavelength. The various forms of electromagnetic radiation differ in wavelength. For example, the visible portion of the electromagnetic spectrum lies between 4×10^{-7} and 8×10^{-7} metre (1.6×10^{-5} and 3.1×10^{-5} inch): red light has a longer wavelength than green light, which in turn has a longer wavelength than blue light. Radio waves can have wavelengths longer than 1,000 metres, while those of high-energy gamma rays can be shorter than 10^{-16} metre, which is one-millionth of the diameter of an atom. Visible light and X rays are often described in units of angstroms or in nanometres. One angstrom (abbreviated by the symbol Å) is 10^{-10} metre, which is also the typical diameter of an atom. One nanometre (nm) is 10^{-9} metre. The micrometre (μm), which equals 10^{-6} metres, is often used to describe infrared radiation.

Units of measurement

The decomposition of electromagnetic radiation into its component wavelengths is fundamental to spectroscopy. Evolving from the first crude prism spectrographs that separated sunlight into its constituent colours, modern spectrometers have provided ever-increasing wavelength resolution. Large-grating spectrometers (see below *Practical considerations: Methods of dispersing spectra*) are capable of resolving wavelengths as close as 10^{-3} nanometre, while modern laser techniques can resolve optical wavelengths separated by less than 10^{-10} nanometre.

The frequency with which the electromagnetic wave oscillates is also used to characterize the radiation. The product of the frequency (ν) and the wavelength (λ) is equal to the speed of light (c); i.e., $\nu\lambda = c$. The frequency is often expressed as the number of oscillations per second, and the unit of frequency is hertz (Hz), where one hertz is one cycle per second. Since the electromagnetic spectrum spans many orders of magnitude, frequency units are usually accompanied by a Latin prefix to set the scale of the frequency range. (See MEASUREMENT SYSTEMS: *The metric system of measurement: The International System of Units* for a table of the prefixes commonly used to denote these scales.)

Basic properties of atoms. An isolated atom can be described in terms of certain discrete states called quantum states. Each quantum state has a definite energy associated with it, but several quantum states can have the same energy. These quantum states and their energy levels are calculated from the basic principles of quantum mechanics. For the simplest atom, hydrogen, which consists of a single proton and a single electron, the energy levels have been calculated and tested to an uncertainty of better than one part in 10^{11}, but for atoms with many electrons, the accuracy of the calculations may not be much better than a few percent of the energy of the levels.

Atomic energy levels are typically measured by observing transitions between two levels. For example, an atom in its lowest possible energy state (called the ground state) can be excited to a higher state only if energy is added by an amount that is equal to the difference between the two levels. Thus, by measuring the energy of the radiation that has been absorbed by the atom, the difference in its energy levels can be determined. The energy levels are identical for atoms of the same type; allowed energies of a particular atom of silver are equal to those for any other atom of the same isotope of silver.

Energy-level transitions

Other isolated systems, including molecules, ions (charged atoms or molecules), and atomic nuclei, have discrete allowed energies. The analysis of these simple systems is carried out with techniques that are analogous to those that were first applied to simple atomic spectra. More complex structures, such as clusters of atoms, and bulk condensed matter, such as solids and liquids, also have energy levels describable by quantum mechanics. The energy levels in these complex systems, however, are so closely spaced that they smear into a continuous band of energies. Transitions between these bands allow researchers to discern many important properties of a given material. The location and properties of the energy states are often referred to as the electronic structure of the material. By comparing spectroscopic measurements to quantum mechanical calculations based on an assumed model of the material, one can use knowledge of a material's electronic structure to determine its physical structure.

If an atom in its ground state is given some amount of energy so that it is promoted to an excited state, the atom will release that extra energy spontaneously as it moves back into lower states, eventually returning to the ground state. For an isolated atom, the energy is emitted as electromagnetic radiation. The emitted energy E equals the upper-state energy minus the lower-state energy; this energy is usually carried by a single quantum of light (a photon) having a frequency ν in which photon energy (E) is equal to a constant times the frequency, $E = h\nu$, where h, Planck's constant, equals 6.626×10^{-34} joule second. This relationship determines the frequencies (and wavelengths, because $\lambda = c/\nu$) of light emitted by atoms if the energies of the states are known. Conversely, the relationship allows the energy states of an atom to be determined from measurements of its frequency or wavelength spectrum. The analysis of the discrete wavelengths emitted or absorbed by an atom or molecule was historically carried out using prism or grating spectrometers; because of the appearance of the separated light in these instruments, these discrete wavelengths are sometimes called spectral lines (see Figure 25).

Historical survey. The basis for analytical spectroscopy is the discovery, made in 1859 by the German physicist Gustav R. Kirchhoff, that each pure substance has its own characteristic spectrum. Another German physicist, Joseph von Fraunhofer, repeating more carefully an earlier experiment by a British scientist, William Wollaston, had shown in 1814 that the spectrum of the Sun's electromagnetic radiation does not grade smoothly from one colour to the next but has many dark lines, indicating that light is missing at certain wavelengths because of absorption (see Figure 25). These dark lines, sometimes called Fraunhofer lines, are also collectively referred to as an absorption spectrum. The spectra of materials that were heated in flames or placed in electric-gas discharges were studied by many scientists during the 18th and 19th centuries. These spectra were composed of numerous bright discrete lines, indicating that only certain wavelengths were present in the emitted light. They are called brightline, or emission, spectra.

Fraunhofer lines

Although the possibility that each chemical element has a unique characteristic spectrum had been considered by numerous investigators, the early studies were hampered by the difficulty of obtaining relatively pure substances. Any sample could contain impurities that would result in the simultaneous production of many spectra. By using carefully purified substances, Kirchhoff demonstrated characteristic spectra and initiated the technique of spectroscopic analysis of the chemical composition of matter. The technique was applied by Kirchhoff and his colleague the German chemist Robert Bunsen in 1861 to the

By courtesy of John O. Stoner, Jr.

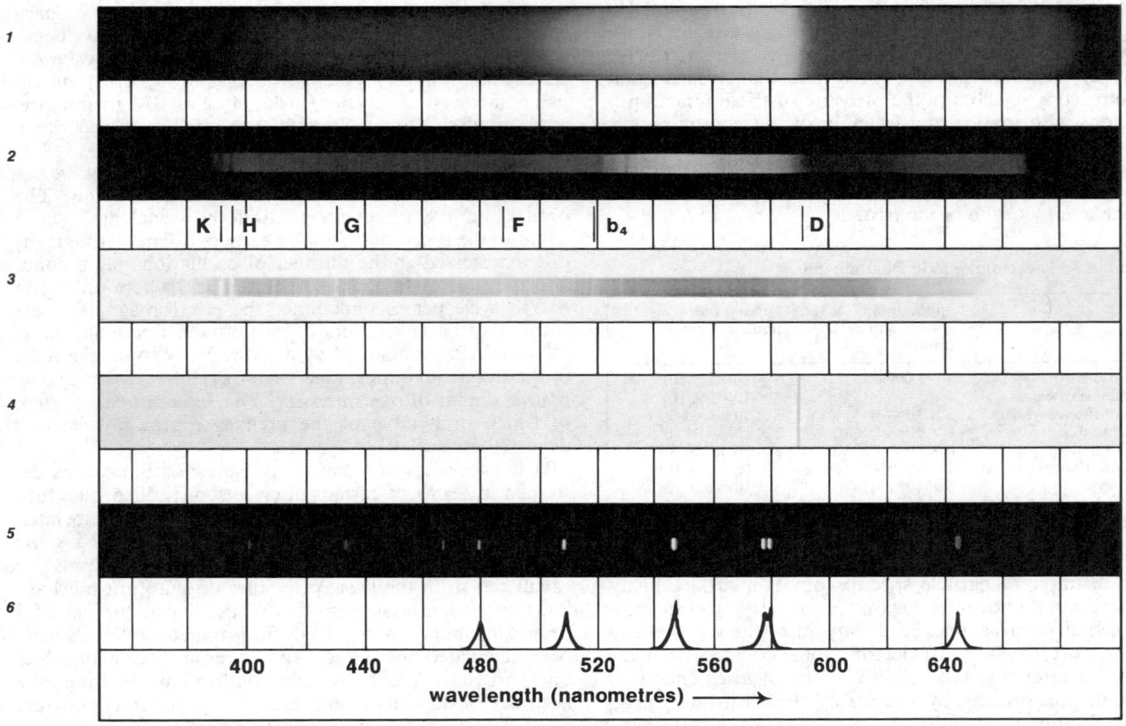

Figure 25: *Emission and absorption spectra of various light sources.*
(1) Continuous-emission spectrum from an ordinary incandescent lamp. (2,3) Spectrum of the Sun showing an absorption (dark-line) spectrum characteristic of the cooler outer layers of the Sun superimposed upon the continuous-emission spectrum of the hotter inner layers. The Fraunhofer lines (marked by letters) are characteristic of sodium (D), iron and magnesium (b_4), hydrogen (F), iron and calcium (G), and calcium (H,K). On the negative film (3), the film is darker where it has been more exposed; hence an absorption line appears white.
(4) Emission-line spectrum of sodium showing a closely spaced pair of lines in the yellow. Other lines in this spectrum are much weaker than these and hence do not appear. (5,6) Emission-line spectrum of a discharge lamp containing mercury and cadmium as registered on colour positive film (5) and schematically as registered by a scanning spectrometer in which the height of the curve at any particular wavelength is the line intensity at that wavelength (6).

analysis of the Sun's electromagnetic spectrum and the identification of the chemical elements in the Sun.

Before the 20th century, there was no theory that could satisfactorily explain the origin of the spectra of the elements or the reason why different elements have different spectra. The quantitative understanding of the elemental spectra needed the development of a fundamentally new physical theory, and the spectra of the simplest atoms played the key role in the development of this theory. Many of the major developments in 20th-century physics were motivated by an ever-increasing accuracy in the measurement of the spectra of the hydrogen atom; highlights include the discovery in 1885 by the Swiss scientist Johann J. Balmer that the frequency spectrum of hydrogen followed a simple numerical pattern, later revised by the Swedish physicist Johannes R. Rydberg and given in modern notation as $1/\lambda = R_H\,(1/2^2 - 1/n^2)$, where R_H is the so-called Rydberg constant for hydrogen (see Figure 26.) In 1913 the Danish physicist Niels Bohr presented the first theoretical model that could give quantized energy levels that were in quantitative agreement with measurements of the hydrogen spectrum.

Arthur L. Schawlow, Stanford University, and Theodore W. Hansch, Max Planck Institute for Quantum Optics

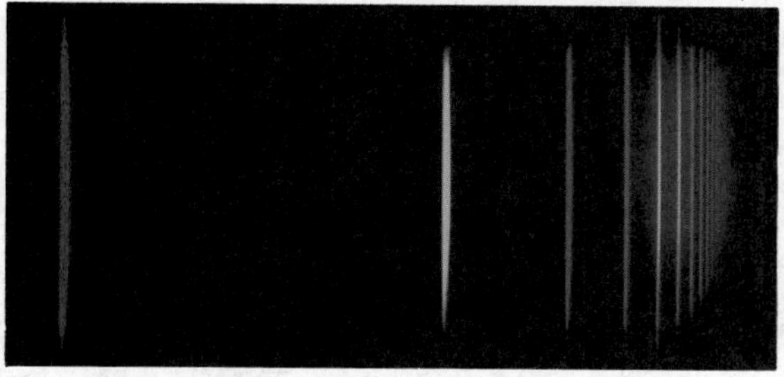

Figure 26: The Balmer series of hydrogen as seen by a low-resolution spectrometer.

Despite the success of the Bohr theory in describing the hydrogen spectrum, the theory failed badly when applied to the next simplest atom, helium, which contains two electrons. It was also incapable of predicting the likelihood of transitions between energy levels. In 1925–26 a new theory that could explain the discrete, quantum nature of the spectra was developed by the German physicists Werner Heisenberg and Erwin Schrödinger. This theory, known as quantum mechanics, was extended by the Austrian-born Swiss physicist Wolfgang Pauli, the German physicist Max Born, and others. It has been remarkably successful in describing the spectra of complex atoms, ions, simple molecules, and solids.

As the spectral lines of the hydrogen atom were measured with increased accuracy, greater demands were placed on the theoretical understanding of atomic spectra. The British physicist Paul A.M. Dirac combined quantum mechanics with the special theory of relativity in 1928 to describe particles moving close to the speed of light. His formulation of relativistic quantum mechanics provided an explanation for the so-called fine structure of the hydrogen spectrum (see below *Foundations of atomic spectra: Hydrogen atom states: Fine and hyperfine structure of spectra*). At still higher resolution, two energy levels of the hydrogen atom in the first excited state were predicted by Dirac's theory to be exactly the same. In 1947, the American physicists Willis Lamb and Robert Retherford discovered that the levels actually differ by roughly 10^9 hertz (see below *X-ray and radio-frequency spectroscopy: Radio-frequency spectroscopy: Methods*). In contrast, the transition frequency between the ground state and the first excited states was calculated as approximately 2.5×10^{15} hertz. Two American physicists, Richard Feynman and Julian Schwinger, and a Japanese physicist, Shinichirō Tomonaga, developed yet another refinement to quantum mechanics to explain this measurement. The theory, known as quantum electrodynamics (QED), had its foundations in the discoveries of Dirac, Heisenberg, and Pauli. It is a complete description of the interaction of radiation with matter and has been used to calculate the energy levels of the hydrogen atom to an accuracy of better than 1 part in 10^{11}. No other physical theory has the ability to predict a measurable quantity with such precision, and, as a result of the successes of quantum electrodynamics, the theory has become the paradigm of physical theories at the microscopic level.

Quantum electrodynamics

Applications. Spectroscopy is used as a tool for studying the structures of atoms and molecules. The large number of wavelengths emitted by these systems makes it possible to investigate their structures in detail, including the electron configurations of ground and various excited states.

Spectroscopy also provides a precise analytical method for finding the constituents in material having unknown chemical composition. In a typical spectroscopic analysis, a concentration of a few parts per million of a trace element in a material can be detected through its emission spectrum.

In astronomy the study of the spectral emission lines of distant galaxies led to the discovery that the universe is expanding rapidly and isotopically (independent of direction). The finding was based on the observation of a Doppler shift of spectral lines. The Doppler shift is an effect that occurs when a source of radiation such as a star moves relative to an observer. The frequency will be shifted in much the same way that an observer on a moving train hears a shift in the frequency of the pitch of a ringing bell at a railroad crossing. The pitch of the bell sounds higher if the train is approaching the crossing and lower if it is moving away. Similarly, light frequencies will be Doppler-shifted up or down depending on whether the light source is approaching or receding from the observer. During the 1920s, the American astronomer Edwin Hubble identified the diffuse elliptical and spiral objects that had been observed as galaxies. He went on to discover and measure a roughly linear relationship between the distance of these galaxies from the Earth and their Doppler shift. In any direction one looks, the farther the galaxy appears, the faster it is receding from the Earth.

Doppler shift

Spectroscopic evidence that the universe was expanding was followed by the discovery in 1965 of a low level of isotropic microwave radiation by the American scientists Arno A. Penzias and Robert W. Wilson. The measured spectrum is identical to the radiation distribution expected from a blackbody, a surface that can absorb all the radiation incident on it. This radiation, which is currently at a temperature of 2.73 kelvin (K), is identified as a relic of the big bang that marks the birth of the universe and the beginning of its rapid expansion.

PRACTICAL CONSIDERATIONS

General methods of spectroscopy. Production and analysis of a spectrum usually require the following: (1) a source of light (or other electromagnetic radiation), (2) a disperser to separate the light into its component wavelengths, and (3) a detector to sense the presence of light after dispersion. The apparatus used to accept light, separate it into its component wavelengths, and detect the spectrum is called a spectrometer. Spectra can be obtained either in the form of emission spectra, which show one or more bright lines or bands on a dark background, or absorption spectra, which have a continuously bright background except for one or more dark lines (see Figure 25 above).

Absorption spectroscopy measures the loss of electromagnetic energy after it illuminates the sample under study. For example, if a light source with a broad band of wavelengths is directed at a vapour of atoms, ions, or molecules, the particles will absorb those wavelengths that can excite them from one quantum state to another. As a result, the absorbed wavelengths will be missing from the original light spectrum after it has passed through the sample. Since most atoms and many molecules have unique and identifiable energy levels, a measurement of the missing absorption lines allows identification of the absorbing species. Absorption within a continuous band of wavelengths is also possible. This is particularly common when there is a high density of absorption lines that have been broadened by strong perturbations by surrounding atoms (*e.g.,* collisions in a high-pressure gas or the effects of near neighbours in a solid or liquid).

Absorption spectroscopy

In the laboratory environment, transparent chambers or containers with windows at both ends serve as absorption cells for the production of absorption spectra. Light with a continuous distribution of wavelength is passed through the cell. When a gas or vapour is introduced, the change in the transmitted spectrum gives the absorption spectrum of the gas. Often, absorption cells are enclosed in ovens because many materials of spectroscopic interest vaporize significantly only at high temperatures. In other cases, the sample to be studied need not be contained at all. For example, interstellar molecules can be detected by studying the absorption of the radiation from a background star.

The transmission properties of the Earth's atmosphere determine which parts of the electromagnetic spectrum of the Sun and other astronomical sources of radiation are able to penetrate the atmosphere. The absorption of ultraviolet and X-ray radiation by the upper atmosphere prevents this harmful portion of the electromagnetic spectrum from irradiating the inhabitants of the Earth. The fact that water vapour, carbon dioxide, and other gases reflect infrared radiation is important in determining how much heat from the Earth is radiated into space. This phenomenon is known as the greenhouse effect since it works in much the same way as the glass panes of a greenhouse; that is to say, energy in the form of visible light is allowed to pass through the glass, while heat in the form of infrared radiation is absorbed and reflected back by it, thus keeping the greenhouse warm. Similarly, the transmission characteristics of the atmosphere are important factors in determining the global temperature of the Earth.

Emission spectroscopy

The second main type of spectroscopy, emission spectroscopy, uses some means to excite the sample of interest. After the atoms or molecules are excited, they will relax to lower energy levels, emitting radiation corresponding to the energy differences, $\Delta E = h\nu = hc/\lambda$, between the various energy levels of the quantum system. In its use as an analytical tool, this fluorescence radiation is the complement of the missing wavelengths in absorption spectroscopy. Thus, the emission lines will have a characteristic "fingerprint" that can be associated with a unique atom, ion, or molecule. Early excitation methods included placing the sample in a flame or an electric-arc discharge. The atoms or molecules were excited by collisions with electrons, the broadband light in the excitation source, or collisions with energetic atoms. The analysis of the emission lines is done with the same types of spectrometer as used in absorption spectroscopy.

Types of electromagnetic-radiation sources. *Broadband-light sources.* Although flames and discharges provide a convenient method of excitation, the environment can strongly perturb the sample being studied. Excitation based on broadband-light sources in which the generation of the light is separated from the sample to be investigated provides a less perturbing means of excitation. Higher energy excitation corresponds to shorter wavelengths, but unfortunately, there are not many intense sources of ultraviolet and vacuum-ultraviolet radiation, and so excitation in an electron discharge remains a common method for this portion of the spectrum. (The term vacuum ultraviolet refers to the short-wavelength portion of the electromagnetic spectrum where the photons are energetic enough to excite a typical atom from the ground state to ionization. Under these conditions, the light is strongly absorbed by air and most other substances.)

A typical broadband-light source that can be used for either emission or absorption spectroscopy is a metal filament heated to a high temperature. A typical example is a tungsten light bulb. Because the atoms in the metal are packed closely together, their individual energy levels merge together; the emitted lines then overlap and form a continuous—*i.e.,* nondiscrete—spectrum. Similar phenomena occur in high-pressure arc lamps, in which broadening of spectral lines occurs owing to high collision rates.

An arc lamp consists of a transparent tube of gases that are excited by an electric discharge. Energetic electrons bombard the atoms, exciting them to either high-energy atomic states or to an ionized state in which the outermost electron is removed from the atom. The radiation that is emitted in this environment is usually a mixture of discrete atomic lines that come from the relaxation of the atoms to lower energy states and continuum radiation resulting from closely spaced lines that have been broadened by collisions with other atoms and the electrons. If the pressure of the gas in the arc lamp is sufficiently high, a large fraction of the light is emitted in the form of continuum radiation.

Line sources. Light sources that are capable of primarily emitting radiation with discrete, well-defined frequencies are also widely used in spectroscopy (see Figure 27). The early sources of spectral emission lines were simply arc lamps or some other form of electrical discharge in a sealed tube of gas in which the pressure is kept low enough so that a significant portion of the radiation is emitted in the form of discrete lines. The Geissler discharge tube, such as the neon lamp commonly used in advertising signs, is an example of such a source. Other examples are hollow cathode lamps and electrodeless lamps driven by microwave radiation. If specific atomic lines are desired, a small amount of the desired element is introduced in the discharge.

Geissler discharge tube

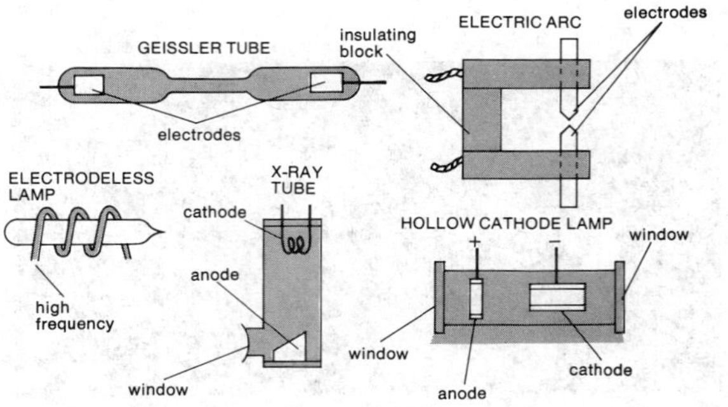

Figure 27: *Sources of laboratory spectra.*
All these sources, except for the X-ray tube, generate visible and ultraviolet light.

Laser sources. Lasers are line sources that emit high-intensity radiation over a very narrow frequency range. The invention of the laser by the American physicists Arthur Schawlow and Charles Townes in 1958, the demonstration of the first practical laser by the American physicist Theodore Maiman in 1960, and the subsequent development of laser spectroscopy techniques by a number of researchers revolutionized a field that had previously seen most of its conceptual developments before the 20th century. Intense, tunable (adjustable-wavelength) light sources now span most of the visible, near-infrared, and near-ultraviolet portions of the spectrum. Lasers have been used for selected wavelength bands in the infrared to submillimetre range, and on the opposite end of the spectrum, for wavelengths as short as the soft X-ray region (that of lower energies).

Typically, light from a tunable laser (examples include dye lasers, semiconductor diode lasers, or free-electron lasers) is directed into the sample to be studied just as the more traditional light sources are used in absorption or emission spectroscopy. For example, in emission (fluorescence) spectroscopy, the amount of light scattered by the sample is measured as the frequency of the laser light is varied. There are advantages to using a laser light source:

Advantages of laser sources

(1) The light from lasers can be made highly monochromatic (light of essentially one "colour"—*i.e.,* composed of a very narrow range of frequencies). As the light is tuned across the frequency range of interest and the absorption or fluorescence is recorded, extremely narrow spectral features can be measured. Modern tunable lasers can easily resolve spectral features less than 10^6 hertz wide, while the highest-resolution grating spectrometers have resolutions that are hundreds of times lower. Atomic lines as narrow as 30 hertz out of a transition frequency of 6×10^{14} hertz have been observed with laser spectroscopy. (2) Because the laser light in a given narrow frequency band is much more intense than virtually all broadband sources of light used in spectroscopy, the amount of fluorescent light emitted by the sample can be greatly increased. Laser spectroscopy is sufficiently sensitive to observe fluorescence

from a single atom in the presence of 10^{20} different atoms.

A potential limitation to the resolution of the spectroscopy of gases is due to the motion of the atoms or molecules relative to the observer. The Doppler shifts that result from the motion of the atoms will broaden any sharp spectral features. A cell containing a gas of atoms will have atoms moving both toward and away from the light source, so that the absorbing frequencies of some of the atoms will be shifted up while others will be shifted down. The spectra of an absorption line in the hydrogen atom as measured by normal fluorescence spectroscopy is shown in Figure 28A. The width of the spectral features is due to the Doppler broadening on the atoms.

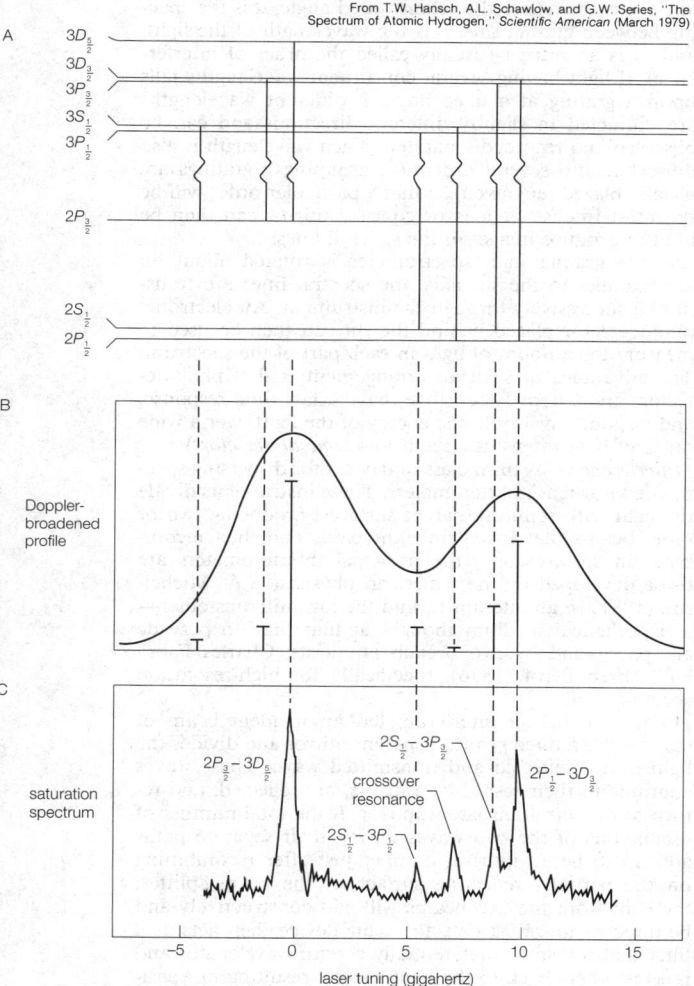

From T.W. Hansch, A.L. Schawlow, and G.W. Series, "The Spectrum of Atomic Hydrogen," *Scientific American* (March 1979)

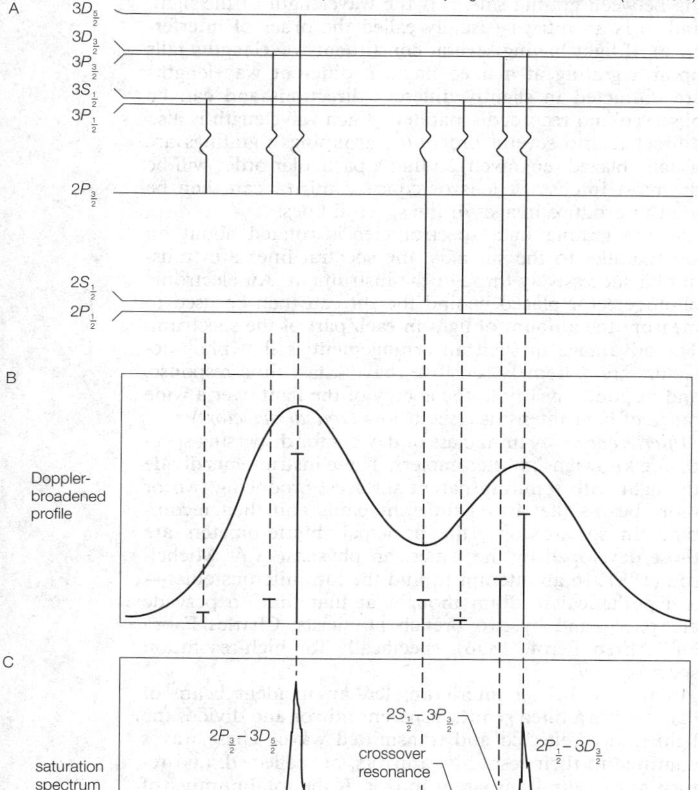

Figure 28: *Balmer-alpha line absorption spectra.*
(A) The seven allowed transitions between the $n = 2$ and $n = 3$ energy levels of hydrogen. (B) The Doppler-broadened profile of the absorption spectra. Only two components can be distinguished. (C) An early example of Doppler-free spectra. Peaks resulting from four of the seven transitions can be resolved; the fifth peak marked as a crossover resonance is not significant. The frequency scale on this data is relative to an arbitrary starting point, but subsequent measurements have determined the frequency ν of these transitions to an uncertainty $\Delta\nu/\nu$ of less than one part in one billion.

Saturation spectroscopy

The high intensity of lasers allows the measurement of Doppler-free spectra. One method for making such measurements, invented by Theodore Hänsch of Germany and Christian Borde of France, is known as saturation spectroscopy (see Figure 29). Here, an intense, monochromatic beam of light is directed into the sample gas cell. If the frequency spread of the light is much less than the Doppler-broadened absorption line, only those atoms with a narrow velocity spread will be excited, since the other atoms will be Doppler-shifted out of resonance. Laser light is intense enough that a significant fraction of the atoms resonant with the light will be in the excited state. With this high excitation, the atoms are said to be saturated, and atoms in a saturated state absorb less light.

If a weaker probe laser beam is directed into the sample along the opposite direction, it will interact with those atoms that have the appropriate Doppler shift to be resonant with the light. In general, these two frequencies will be different so that the probe beam will experience an absorption that is unaffected by the stronger saturating beam. If the laser frequency is tuned to be resonant with both beams (this can only happen when the velocity relative to the direction of the two beams is zero), the intense beam saturates the same atoms that would normally absorb the probe beam. When the frequency of the laser is tuned to the frequency of the atoms moving with zero velocity relative to the laser source, the transmission of the probe beam increases. Thus, the absorption resonance of the atoms, without broadening from the Doppler effect, can be observed. Figure 28B shows the same hydrogen spectra taken with saturation spectroscopy.

In addition to saturation spectroscopy, there are a number of other techniques that are capable of obtaining Doppler-free spectra. An important example is two-photon spectroscopy, another form of spectroscopy that was made possible by the high intensities available with lasers. All these techniques rely on the relative Doppler shift of counterpropagating beams to identify the correct resonance frequency and have been used to measure spectra with extremely high accuracy. These techniques, however, cannot eliminate another type of Doppler shift.

Time dilation effect

This other type of frequency shift is understood as a time dilation effect in the special theory of relativity. A clock moving with respect to an observer appears to run slower than an identical clock at rest with respect to the observer. Since the frequency associated with an atomic transition is a measure of time (an atomic clock), a moving atom will appear to have a slightly lower frequency relative to the frame of reference of the observer. The time dilation can be minimized if the atom's velocity is reduced substantially. In 1985 an American physicist, Steven Chu, and his colleagues demonstrated that it is possible to cool free atoms in a vapour to a temperature of a quarter of a thousandth of a degree above absolute zero (absolute zero = 0 K, or −273.15° C), the random atomic velocities are about 50,000 times less than their velocity at room temperature. At these temperatures the time dilation effect is reduced by a factor of 10^8, and the Doppler effect broadening is reduced by a factor of 10^3. Since then, temperatures of less than 10^{-6} K have been achieved with laser cooling.

Not only have lasers increased the frequency resolution and sensitivity of spectroscopic techniques, they have greatly extended the ability to measure transient phenomena. Pulsed, so-called mode-locked, lasers are capable of generating a continuous train of pulses where each pulse may be as short as 10^{-14} second. In a typical experiment, a short pulse of light is used to excite or otherwise perturb the system, and another pulse of light, delayed with respect to the first pulse, is used to probe the system's response. The delayed pulse can be generated by simply diverting a

From T.W. Hansch, A.L. Schawlow, and G.W. Series, "The Spectrum of Atomic Hydrogen," *Scientific American* (March 1979)

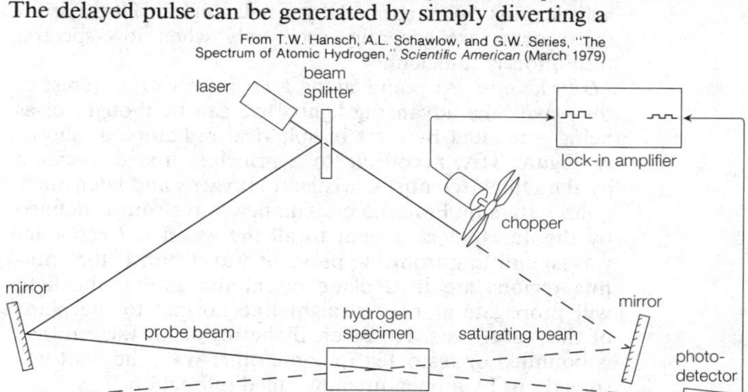

Figure 29: *Experimental configuration used in saturation spectroscopy.*
The transmission of the weak probe beam is modulated by the high-intensity saturating beam if the atoms that are excited by the saturating beam and those that are addressed by the probe beam are not Doppler-shifted relative to either of the beams.

portion of the light pulse with a partially reflecting mirror (called a beam splitter). The two separate pulses can then be directed onto the sample under study where the path taken by the first excitation pulse is slightly shorter than the path taken by the second probe pulse. The relative time delay between the two pulses is controlled by slightly varying the path length difference of the two pulses. The distance corresponding to a 10^{-14}-second delay (the speed of light multiplied by the time difference) is three micrometres (1.2×10^{-4} inch).

Methods of dispersing spectra. A spectrometer, as mentioned above, is an instrument used to analyze the transmitted light in the case of absorption spectroscopy or the emitted light in the case of emission spectroscopy. It consists of a disperser that breaks the light into its component wavelengths and a means of recording the relative intensities of each of the component wavelengths. The main methods for dispersing radiation are discussed here.

Refraction. Historically glass prisms were first used to break up or disperse light into its component colours. The path of a light ray bends (refracts) when it passes from one transparent medium to another—*e.g.,* from air to glass. Different colours (wavelengths) of light are bent through different angles; hence a ray leaves a prism in a direction depending on its colour (see Figure 30). The degree to which a ray bends at each interface can be calculated from Snell's law, which states that if n_1 and n_2 are the refractive indices of the medium outside the prism and of the prism itself, respectively, and the angles i and r are the angles that the ray of a given wavelength makes with a line at right angles to the prism face as shown in Figure 30, then the equation $n_1 \sin i = n_2 \sin r$ is obtained for all rays. The refractive index of a medium, indicated by the symbol n, is defined as the ratio of the speed of light in a vacuum to the speed of light in the medium. Typical values for n range from 1.0003 for air at 0° C and atmospheric pressure, to 1.5–1.6 for typical glasses, to 4 for germanium in the infrared portion of the spectrum.

Snell's law

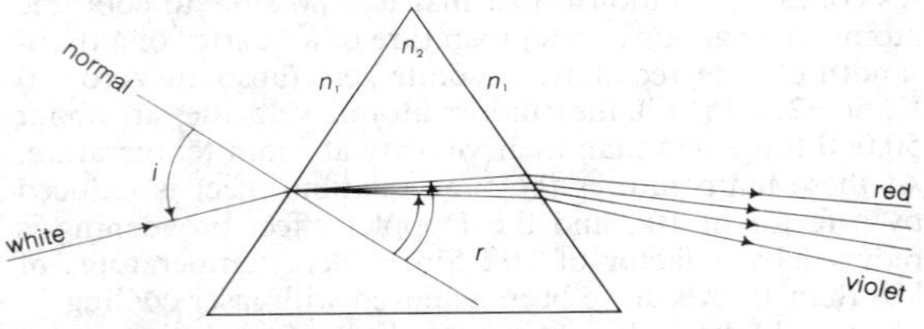

Figure 30: Refraction of light by a prism having index n_2 immersed in a medium having refractive index n_1. The angles i and r that the rays make with the normal are the angles of incidence and refraction. Because n_2 depends upon wavelength, the incident white ray separates into its constituent colours upon refraction, with deviation of the red ray the least and the violet ray the most.

Since the index of refraction of optical glasses varies by only a few percent across the visible spectrum, different wavelengths are separated by small angles. Thus, prism instruments are generally used only when low spectral resolution is sufficient.

Diffraction. At points along a given wavefront (crest of the wave), the advancing light wave can be thought of as being generated by a set of spherical radiators, as shown in Figure 31A, according to a principle first enunciated by the Dutch scientist Christiaan Huygens and later made quantitative by Fraunhofer. The new wavefront is defined by the line that is tangent to all the wavelets (secondary waves) emitting from the previous wavefront. If the emitting regions are in a plane of infinite extent, the light will propagate along a straight line normal to the plane of the wavefronts. However, if the region of the emitters is bounded or restricted in some other way, the light will spread out by a phenomenon called diffraction.

Diffraction gratings are composed of closely spaced transmitting slits on a flat surface (transmission gratings) or alternate reflecting grooves on a flat or curved surface (reflection gratings).

If collimated light falls upon a transmission grating, the wavefronts successively pass through and spread out as secondary waves from the transparent parts of the grating. Most of these secondary waves, when they meet along a common path, interfere with each other destructively, so that light does not leave the grating at all angles. At some exit angles, however, secondary waves from adjacent slits of the grating are delayed by exactly one wavelength, and these waves reinforce each other when they meet—*i.e.,* the crests of one fall on top of the other. In this case, constructive interference takes place, and light is emitted in directions where the spacing between the adjacent radiators is delayed by one wavelength (see Figure 31B). Constructive interference also occurs for delays of integral numbers of wavelengths. The light diffracts according to the formula $m\lambda = d(\sin i - \sin r)$, where i is the incident angle, r is the reflected or transmitted angle, d is the spacing between grating slits, λ is the wavelength of the light, and m is an integer (usually called the order of interference). If light having several constituent wavelengths falls upon a grating at a fixed angle i, different wavelengths are diffracted in slightly different directions and can be observed and recorded separately. Each wavelength is also diffracted into several orders (or groupings); gratings are usually blazed (engraved) so that a particular order will be the most intense. A lens or concave mirror can then be used to produce images of the spectral lines.

Constructive interference

As the grating in a spectrometer is rotated about an axis parallel to the slit axis, the spectral lines are transmitted successively through the instrument. An electronic photodetector placed behind the slit can then be used to measure the amount of light in each part of the spectrum. The advantage of such an arrangement is that photodetectors are extremely sensitive, have a fast time response, and respond linearly to the energy of the light over a wide range of light intensities (see below *Optical detectors*).

Interference. A third class of devices for dispersing spectra are known as interferometers. These instruments divide the light with semitransparent surfaces, producing two or more beams that travel different paths and then recombine. In spectroscopy, the principal interferometers are those developed by the American physicist A.A. Michelson (1881) in an attempt to find the luminiferous ether—a hypothetical medium thought at that time to pervade all space—and by two French physicists, Charles Fabry and Alfred Pérot (1896), specifically for high-resolution spectroscopy.

In the Michelson interferometer, an incident beam of light strikes a tilted semitransparent mirror and divides the light into a reflected and transmitted wave. These waves continue to their respective mirrors, are reflected, and return to the semitransparent mirror. If the total number of oscillations of the two waves during their separate paths add up to be an integral number just after recombining on the partially reflecting surface of the beam splitter, the light from the two beams will add constructively and be directed toward a detector. This device then acts as a filter that transmits preferentially certain wavelengths and reflects others back to the light source, resulting in a visible interference pattern. A common use of the Michelson interferometer has one mirror mounted upon a carriage so that length of the light path in that branch can be varied. A spectrum is obtained by recording photoelectrically the light intensity of the interference pattern as the carriage is moved when an absorption cell is placed in one of the arms of the interferometer. The resulting signals contain information about many wavelengths simultaneously. A mathematical operation, called a Fourier transform, converts the recorded modulation in the light intensity at the detector into the usual frequency domain of the absorption spectrum (see ANALYSIS: *Fourier analysis*). The principal advantage of this method is that the entire spectrum is recorded simultaneously with one detector.

Fourier-transform spectrometer

The Fabry-Pérot interferometer consists of two reflecting mirrors that can be either curved or flat. Only certain wavelengths of light will resonate in the cavity: the light is in resonance with the interferometer if $m(\lambda/2) = L$, where L is the distance between the two mirrors, m is an integer, and λ is the wavelength of the light inside the cavity. When this condition is fulfilled, light at these specific wavelengths will build up inside the cavity and be transmitted out the back end for specific wavelengths. By

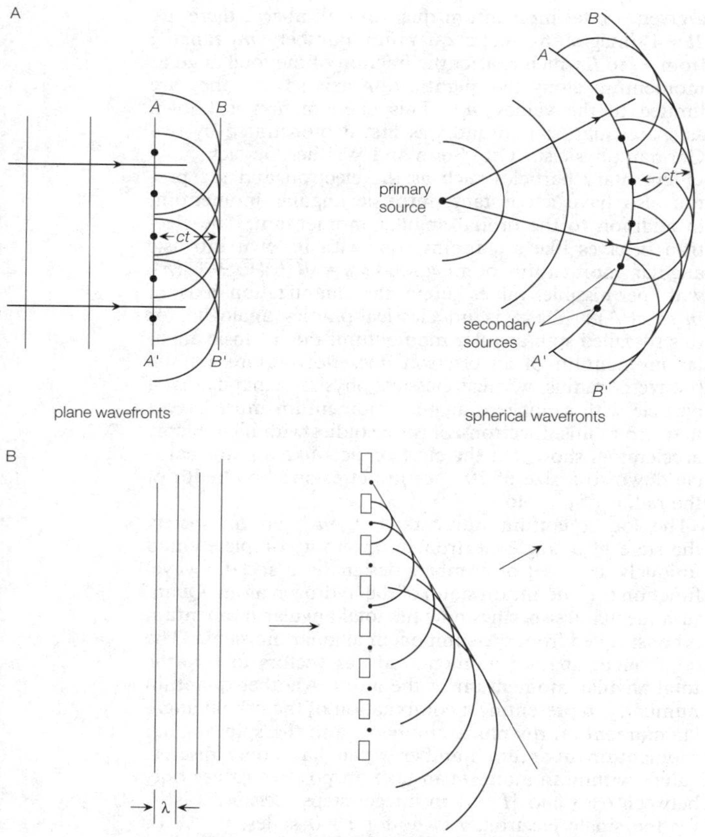

Figure 31: (A) Huygens' principle applied to both plane and spherical waves. Each point on the wave front *AA'* can be thought of as a radiator of a spherical wave that expands out with velocity *c*, traveling a distance *ct* after time *t*. A secondary wave front *BB'* is formed from the addition of all the wave amplitudes from the wave front *AA'*. (B) Huygens' construction of a diffracted wave from a transmission grating. The wave front is constructed by adding spherical waves from each slit of the grating. The wave emitted at a given slit is delayed by one full cycle with respect to the wave from an adjacent slit.

From (A) A. Hudson and R. Nelson, *University Physics* (1990), Saunders College Publishing, Philadelphia

adjusting the spacing between the two mirrors, the instrument can be scanned over the spectral range of interest.

Optical detectors. The principal detection methods used in optical spectroscopy are photographic (*e.g.,* film), photoemissive (photomultipliers), and photoconductive (semiconductor). Prior to about 1940, most spectra were recorded with photographic plates or film, in which the film is placed at the image point of a grating or prism spectrometer. An advantage of this technique is that the entire spectrum of interest can be obtained simultaneously, and low-intensity spectra can be easily taken with sensitive film.

Photoemissive detectors have replaced photographic plates in most applications. When a photon with sufficient energy strikes a surface, it can cause the ejection of an electron from the surface into a vacuum. A photoemissive diode consists of a surface (photocathode) appropriately treated to permit the ejection of electrons by low-energy photons and a separate electrode (the anode) on which electrons are collected, both sealed within an evacuated glass envelope. A photomultiplier tube has a cathode, a series of electrodes (dynodes), and an anode sealed within a common evacuated envelope. Appropriate voltages applied to the cathode, dynodes, and anode cause electrons ejected from the cathode to collide with the dynodes in succession. Each electron collision produces several more electrons; after a dozen or more dynodes, a single electron ejected by one photon can be converted into a fast pulse (with a duration of less than 10^{-8} second) of as many as 10^7 electrons at the anode. In this way, individual photons can be counted with good time resolution.

Other photodetectors include imaging tubes (*e.g.,* television cameras), which can measure a spatial variation of the light across the surface of the photocathode, and microchannel plates, which combine the spatial resolution of an imaging tube with the light sensitivity of a photomultiplier. A night vision device consists of a microchannel plate multiplier in which the electrons at the output are directed onto a phosphor screen and can then be read out with an imaging tube.

Solid-state detectors

Solid-state detectors such as semiconductor photodiodes detect light by causing photons to excite electrons from immobile, bound states of the semiconductor (the valence band) to a state where the electrons are mobile (the conduction band). The mobile electrons in the conduction band and the vacancies, or "holes," in the valence band can be moved through the solid with externally applied electric fields, collected onto a metal electrode, and sensed as a photoinduced current. Microfabrication techniques developed for the integrated-circuit semiconductor industry are used to construct large arrays of individual photodiodes closely spaced together. The device, called a charge-coupled device (CCD), permits the charges that are collected by the individual diodes to be read out separately and displayed as an image.

Foundations of atomic spectra

BASIC ATOMIC STRUCTURE

The emission and absorption spectra of the elements depend on the electronic structure of the atom. An atom consists of a number of negatively charged electrons bound to a nucleus containing an equal number of positively charged protons. The nucleus contains a certain number (Z) of protons and a generally different number (N) of neutrons. The diameter of a nucleus depends on the number of protons and neutrons and is typically 10^{-14} to 10^{-15} centimetre (3.9×10^{-15} to 3.9×10^{-16} inch). The distribution of electrons around the nuclear core is described by quantum mechanics.

Nucleus

The chemical and spectroscopic properties of atoms and ions are primarily determined by their electronic structure—*i.e.,* by the number and arrangement of electrons surrounding their nucleus. Typical energies of electrons within an atom range from a few electron volts to a few thousand electron volts. Chemical reactions and other processes occurring in spectroscopic sources usually involve energy exchanges on this order of magnitude. Processes that occur within nuclei (*e.g.,* electromagnetic transitions between energy states of the nucleus, beta decay, alpha decay, and electron capture) typically involve energies ranging from thousands to millions of electron volts; hence the internal state of nuclei are nearly unaffected by the usual processes occurring in chemical reactions, light absorption, and light sources. On the other hand, nuclear magnetic moments can be oriented by light through their coupling to the atom's electrons. A process known as optical pumping, in which the atom is excited with circularly polarized light, is used to orient the spin of the nucleus.

The forces holding an atom together are primarily the electrostatic attractive forces between the positive charges in the nucleus and the negative charge of each electron. Because like charges repel one another, there is a significant amount of electrical repulsion of each electron by the others. Calculation of the properties of the atom first require the determination of the total internal energy of the atom consisting of the kinetic energy of the electrons and the electrostatic and magnetic energies between the electrons and between the electrons and the nucleus.

The size scale of the atom is determined by the combination of the fact that the atom prefers to be in a state of minimum energy and the Heisenberg uncertainty principle. The Heisenberg uncertainty principle states that the uncertainty in the simultaneous determination of the position and the momentum (mass times velocity) of a particle along any direction must be greater than Planck's constant. If an electron is bound close to the nucleus, the electrostatic energy decreases inversely with the average distance between the electron and the proton. Lower electrostatic energy corresponds to a more compact atom and, hence, smaller uncertainty in the position of the electron.

Minimization of energy

On the other hand, if the electron is to have low kinetic energy, its momentum and its uncertainty in momentum must be small. According to the Heisenberg principle, if the uncertainty in momentum is small, its uncertainty in position must be large, thus increasing the electrostatic energy. The actual structure of the atom provides a compromise of moderate kinetic and electrostatic energies in which the average distance between the electron and the nucleus is the distance that minimizes the total energy of the atom.

Going beyond this qualitative argument, the quantitative properties of atoms are calculated by solving the Schrödinger wave equation, which provides the quantum mechanical description of an atom. The solution of this equation for a specified number of electrons and protons is called a wavefunction and yields a set of corresponding eigenstates. These eigenstates are analogous to the frequency modes of a vibrating violin string (*e.g.*, the fundamental note and the overtones), and they form the set of allowed energy states of the atom. These states of the electronic structure of an atom will be described here in terms of the simplest atom, the hydrogen atom.

HYDROGEN ATOM STATES

The hydrogen atom is composed of a single proton and a single electron. The solutions to the Schrödinger equation are catalogued in terms of certain quantum numbers of the particular electron state. The principal quantum number is an integer n that corresponds to the gross energy states of the atom. For the hydrogen atom, the energy state E_n is equal to $-(me^4)/(2\hbar^2n^2 = hcR_H/n^2$, where m is the mass of the electron, e is the charge of the electron, c is the speed of light, h is Planck's constant, and $\hbar = h/2\pi$, and R_H is the Rydberg constant. The energy scale of the atom, hcR_H, is equal to 13.6 electron volts. The energy is negative, indicating that the electron is bound to the nucleus where zero energy is equal to the infinite separation of the electron and proton. When an atom makes a transition between an eigenstate of energy E_m to an eigenstate of lower energy E_n, where m and n are two integers, the transition is accompanied by the emission of a quantum of light whose frequency is given by $\nu = |E_m - E_n|/h = hcR_H(1/n_n^2 - 1/n_m^2)$. Alternatively, the atom can absorb a photon of the same frequency ν and be promoted from the quantum state of energy E_n to a higher energy state with energy E_m. The Balmer series, discovered in 1885, was the first series of lines whose mathematical pattern was found empirically. The series corresponds to the set of spectral lines where the transitions are from excited states with $m = 3,4,5, \ldots$ to the specific state with $n = 2$. In 1890 Rydberg found that the alkali atoms had a hydrogen-like spectrum that could be fitted by series formulas that are a slight modification of Balmer's formula: $E = h\nu = hcR_H[1/(n_n - a)^2 - 1/(n_m - b)^2]$, where a and b are nearly constant numbers called quantum defects.

Principal quantum number

Angular momentum quantum numbers. There are a set of angular momentum quantum numbers associated with the energy states of the atom. In terms of classical physics, angular momentum is a property of a body that is in orbit or is rotating about its own axis. It depends on the angular velocity and distribution of mass around the axis of revolution or rotation and is a vector quantity with the direction of the angular momentum along the rotation axis. In contrast to classical physics, where an electron's orbit can assume a continuous set of values, the quantum mechanical angular momentum is quantized. Furthermore, it cannot be specified exactly along all three axes simultaneously. Usually, the angular momentum is specified along an axis known as the quantization axis, and the angular momentum of the atom along this axis is limited to the quantum values $\sqrt{l(l+1)}\,(\hbar)$, in which l is an integer. The number l, called the orbital quantum number, must be less than the principal quantum number n, which corresponds to a "shell" of electrons. Thus, l divides each shell into n subshells consisting of all electrons of the same principal and orbital quantum numbers.

Quantization axis

There is a magnetic quantum number also associated with the angular momentum of the quantum state. For a given orbital momentum quantum number l, there are $2l+1$ integral magnetic quantum numbers m_l ranging from $-l$ to l, which restrict the fraction of the total angular momentum along the quantization axis so that they are limited to the values $m_l\hbar$. This phenomenon is known as space quantization and was first demonstrated by two German physicists, Otto Stern and Walther Gerlach.

Elementary particles such as the electron and the proton also have a constant, intrinsic angular momentum in addition to the orbital angular momentum. The electron behaves like a spinning top, with its own intrinsic angular momentum of magnitude $s = \sqrt{(1/2)(1/2 + 1)}\,(\hbar)$, with permissible values along the quantization axis of $m_s = \pm(1/2)\hbar$. There is no classical-physics analogue for this so-called spin-angular momentum: the intrinsic angular momentum of an electron does not require a finite (nonzero) radius, whereas classical physics demands that a particle with a nonzero angular momentum must have a nonzero radius. Electron-collision studies with high-energy accelerators show that the electron acts like a point particle down to a size of 10^{-15} centimetre, one hundredth of the radius of a proton.

The four quantum numbers n, l, m_l, and m_s specify the state of a single electron in an atom completely and uniquely; each set of numbers designates a specific wavefunction (*i.e.*, quantum state) of the hydrogen atom. Quantum mechanics specifies how the total angular momentum is constructed from the component angular momenta. The component angular momenta add as vectors to give the total angular momentum of the atom. Another quantum number, j, representing a combination of the orbital angular momentum quantum number l, and the spin angular momentum quantum number s can have only discrete values within an atom: j can take on positive values only between $l + s$ and $|l - s|$ in integer steps. Because s is $1/2$ for the single electron, j is $1/2$ for $l = 0$ states, $j = 1/2$ or $3/2$ for $l = 1$ states, $j = 3/2$ or $5/2$ for $l = 2$ states, and so on. The magnitude of the total angular momentum of the atom can be expressed in the same form as for the orbital and spin momenta: $\sqrt{j(j+1)}\,(\hbar)$ gives the magnitude of the total angular momentum; the component of angular momentum along the quantization axis is $m_j\hbar$, where m_j can have any value between $+j$ and $-j$ in integer steps. An alternative description of the quantum state can be given in terms of the quantum numbers n, l, j, and m_j.

The electron distribution of the atom is described as the square of the absolute value of the wavefunction. The probability of finding an electron at a given point in space for several of the lower energy states of the hydrogen atom is shown in Figure 32. It is important to note that the electron density plots should not be thought of as the time-averaged locations of a well-localized (point) particle orbiting about the nucleus. Quantum mechanics describes the electron with a continuous wavefunction in which the location of the electron should be considered as spread out in space in a quantum "fuzz ball" as depicted in Figure 32.

Electron probability distribution

Fine and hyperfine structure of spectra. Although the gross energies of the electron in hydrogen are fixed by the mutual electrostatic attraction of the electron and the nucleus, there are significant magnetic effects on the energies. An electron has an intrinsic magnetic dipole moment and behaves like a tiny bar magnet aligned along its spin axis. Also, because of its orbital motion within the atom, the electron creates a magnetic field in its vicinity. The interaction of the electron's magnetic moment with the magnetic field created by its motion (the spin-orbit interaction) modifies its energy and is proportional to the combination of the orbital angular momentum and the spin angular momentum. Small differences in energies of levels arising from the spin-orbit interaction sometimes cause complexities in spectral lines that are known as the fine structure. Typically, the fine structure is on the order of one-millionth of the energy difference between the energy levels given by the principal quantum numbers.

The hyperfine structure is the result of two effects: (1) the magnetic interactions between the total (orbital plus spin) magnetic moment of the electron and the magnetic moment of the nucleus and (2) the electrostatic interaction between the electric quadrupole moment of the nucleus

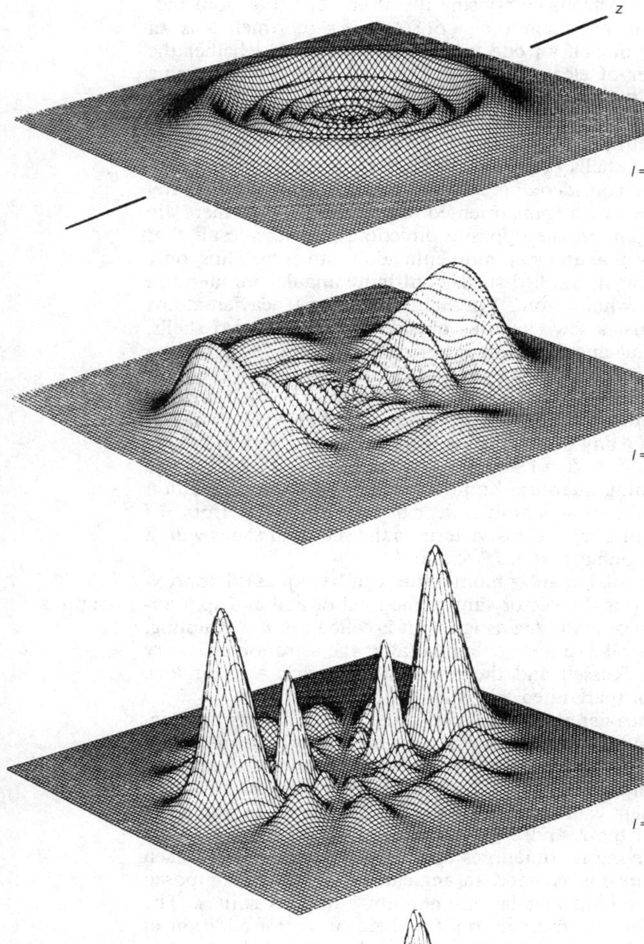

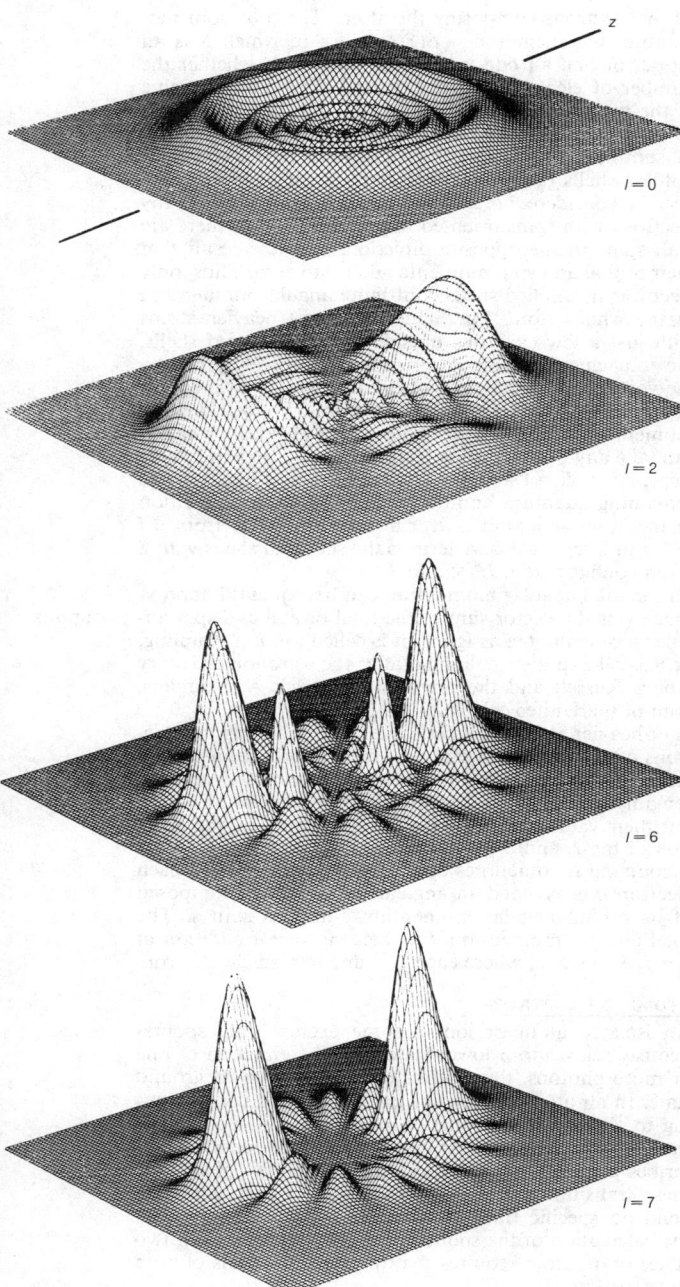

Figure 32: *Electron density functions of a few hydrogen atom states.*
The hydrogen atomic states for the $n = 8$, $m_l = 0$, $l = 0$, 2, 6, and 7 are shown projected onto the x–y plane. The z axis gives the projected three-dimensional electron density. For example, the $l = 0$ state should be visualized as a spherically symmetric standing wave, and the $l = 7$ state as having the electron density localized into two blobs near the two poles of the atom.
Daniel Kleppner and William P. Spencer, Massachusetts Institute of Technology

and the electron (see also below *X-ray and radio-frequency spectroscopy: Radio-frequency spectroscopy*).

THE PERIODIC TABLE

In any atom, no two electrons are found to have the same set of quantum numbers. This is an example of the Pauli exclusion principle; for a class of particles called fermions (named after Enrico Fermi, the Italian physicist), no two identical fermions can occupy the same quantum state. Electrons, protons, and neutrons are examples of fermions; fermions have intrinsic spin values of $\pm 1/2$, $\pm 3/2$, $\pm 5/2$, etc.

There is another class of particles called bosons, named after the Indian physicist S.N. Bose, who with Einstein worked out the quantum statistical properties for these particles. Bosons all have integral intrinsic angular momentum—*i.e.,* $s = 0$, 1, 2, 3, 4, etc. While fermions do not occupy one another's quantum space, bosons not only can but prefer to occupy identical quantum states. Examples of bosons include photons that mediate the electromagnetic force, the Z and W particles that mediate the weak nuclear force, and gluons that mediate the strong nuclear force (see SUBATOMIC PARTICLES).

This astounding relationship between a particle's spin and its quantum behaviour can be proved mathematically using the assumptions of quantum field theory. Composite particles such as helium-4 (^{4}He) atoms (an isotope of helium with two protons and two neutrons) act as bosons, whereas helium-3 (^{3}He) atoms (two protons and one neutron) act as fermions at low energies. Chemically, the atoms behave nearly identically, but at very low temperatures their properties are remarkably different.

Fermions and bosons

Since electrons are fermions, they must occupy different quantum states of the atom. This fact has a profound effect on the way complex atoms are structured. The periodic table of the elements, first developed independently by two chemists, Dmitri Ivanovich Mendeleyev of Russia and Lothar Meyer of Germany, can be explained crudely by the sequential filling of hydrogen-like eigenstates. This table lists the elements in rows in order of increasing atomic number; the elements in the same column have similar chemical properties (see Figure 33). For an understanding of how elements fit into the periodic table, it is helpful to start with a hydrogen atom, consisting of a singly charged atomic nucleus and one electron. The hydrogen atom in its ground state occupies the $n = 1$, $l = 0$, $m_l = 0$, and either the $m_s = +1/2$ or $-1/2$ state; these numbers specify the resulting configuration, or arrangement, of electrons of a hydrogen atom in its ground state. If a positive charge is added to the nucleus along with a second external electron, the second electron will occupy the lowest energy state, again $n = 1$, $l = 0$, $m_l = 0$, but with m_s opposite from that of the first electron (otherwise both electrons would have the same set of quantum numbers, and this would violate the Pauli exclusion principle). The resulting configuration is that of helium in its ground state. If both states are occupied by electrons, the $n = 1$ shell is filled or closed. This closed shell is relatively stable and difficult to excite or ionize; helium is the first of the inert, or noble, gases. If a third electron and proton pair is added to make a lithium atom, the electron cannot occupy the $n = 1$ shell. The lowest allowed energy state for the third electron is the $n = 2$ state. For this value of n, the orbital quantum number l can be either 0 or 1, but the state for $l = 0$ has slightly lower energy. The quantum numbers of the third electron are then $n = 2$, $l = 0$, $m_l = 0$, $m_s = \pm 1/2$. The inner $n = 1$ shell is relatively stable and remains inert in chemical processes while the chemical and spectroscopic

	group Ia	IIa	IIIb	IVb	Vb	VIb	VIIb	VIII	VIII	VIII	Ib	IIb	IIIa	IVa	Va	VIa	VIIa	0
1*s*	1 H																1 H	2 He
2*s*, 2*p*	3 Li	4 Be											5 B	6 C	7 N	8 O	9 F	10 Ne
3*s*, 3*p*	11 Na	12 Mg											13 Al	14 Si	15 P	16 S	17 Cl	18 Ar
4*s* 3*d*, 4*p*	19 K	20 Ca	21 Sc	22 Ti	23 V	24 Cr	25 Mn	26 Fe	27 Co	28 Ni	29 Cu	30 Zn	31 Ga	32 Ge	33 As	34 Se	35 Br	36 Kr
5*s* 4*d*, 5*p*	37 Rb	38 Sr	39 Y	40 Zr	41 Nb	42 Mo	43 Tc	44 Ru	45 Rh	46 Pd	47 Ag	48 Cd	49 In	50 Sn	51 Sb	52 Te	53 I	54 Xe
6*s*, 4*f* 5*d*, 6*p*	55 Cs	56 Ba	57 La *	72 Hf	73 Ta	74 W	75 Re	76 Os	77 Ir	78 Pt	79 Au	80 Hg	81 Tl	82 Pb	83 Bi	84 Po	85 At	86 Rn
7*s* 6*d*, 5*f*	87 Fr	88 Ra	89 Ac **	104 *Rf*	105 *Ha*													

* 4*f*, 5*d*	58 Ce	59 Pr	60 Nd	61 Pm	62 Sm	63 Eu	64 Gd	65 Tb	66 Dy	67 Ho	68 Er	69 Tm	70 Yb	71 Lu
** 5*f*, 6*d*	90 Th	91 Pa	92 U	93 Np	94 Pu	95 Am	96 Cm	97 Bk	98 Cf	99 Es	100 Fm	101 Md	102 No	103 Lr

Figure 33: *Periodic table of the elements.*
Left column indicates the subshells that are being filled as atomic number Z increases. The body of the table shows element symbols and Z. Elements with equal numbers of valence electrons—and hence similar spectroscopic and chemical behaviour—lie in columns. In the interior of the table, where different subshells have nearly the same energies and hence compete for electrons, similarities often extend laterally as well as vertically.

behaviour of this atom is similar in many ways to that of hydrogen, since lithium has one outer electron around a closed, tightly bound shell.

Addition of the next electron and proton to produce a beryllium atom completes the subshell with $n=2$, $l=0$. The beryllium atom is analogous to helium in that both atoms have two outer electrons, but the atom is not chemically similar to helium. The reason is that the $n=2$ shell is not filled because an electron with $n=2$ can also have $l=1$. Outside the inner shell $n=1$, there are six possible electron states with $l=1$ because an electron can have any combination of $m_l=1$, 0, or -1, and $m_s=+1/2$ or $-1/2$. As successive electrons are added to yield boron, carbon, nitrogen, oxygen, fluorine, and neon, the electrons take quantum numbers $n=2$, $l=1$, and all possible different combinations of m_l and m_s, until a total of six have been added. This completes the $n=2$ shell, containing a total of eight electrons in its two subshells. The resulting atom neon, the second of the noble gases, is also chemically stable and similar to helium since the electrons' shells are complete. Increasingly complex atoms are built up in the same manner; chemical similarities exist when the same number of electrons occupy the last partially or completely filled shell, as shown in Table 4.

Table 4: The Shell Structure of the Light Elements*

		shells and subshells								
		K	*L*		*M*			*N*		
element	atomic number	1*s*	2*s*	2*p*	3*s*	3*p*	3*d*	4*s*	4*p*	4*d*
H	1	1								
He	2	2								
Li	3	2	1							
Be	4	2	2							
B	5	2	2	1						
C	6	2	2	2						
N	7	2	2	3						
O	8	2	2	4						
F	9	2	2	5						
Ne	10	2	2	6						
Na	11	2	2	6	1					
Mg	12	2	2	6	2					
Al	13	2	2	6	2	1				
Si	14	2	2	6	2	2				
P	15	2	2	6	2	3				
S	16	2	2	6	2	4				
Cl	17	2	2	6	2	5				
A	18	2	2	6	2	6				
K	19	2	2	6	2	6		1		
Ca	20	2	2	6	2	6		2		
Sc	21	2	2	6	2	6	1	2		
Ti	22	2	2	6	2	6	2	2		

*The main shells and the subshells within each main shell are filled sequentially for the light elements up to potassium (K). For the heavier elements, a higher shell may become occupied before the preceding shell is filled. The observed filling sequence can be calculated by quantum mechanics.

Source: Adapted from E.H. Wichmann, *Berkeley Physics Course,* vol. 4, *Quantum Physics,* copyright © 1971 by McGraw-Hill, Inc.; used with permission of McGraw-Hill, Inc.

Electron configurations

As a shorthand method of indicating the electron configurations of atoms and ions, the letters *s, p, d, f, g, h,* . . . are used to denote electrons having, respectively, $l=0$, 1, 2, 3, 4, 5, ... A number prefixed to the letters gives the value for *n,* and a superscript to the right of each letter indicates the number of electrons with those values of *n* and *l.* For example, the configuration $2s^1$ represents a single electron with $n=2$, $l=0$. The configuration $1s^22s^22p^3$ represents two electrons with $n=1$, $l=0$, two electrons with $n=2$, $l=0$, and three electrons with $n=2$, $l=1$. The ground state configurations of the first portion of the periodic table is given in Table 4.

For atoms in the first three rows and those in the first two columns of the periodic table, the atom can be described in terms of quantum numbers giving the total orbital angular momentum and total spin angular momentum of a given state. The total orbital angular momentum is the sum of the orbital angular momenta from each of the electrons; it has magnitude $\sqrt{L(L+1)}\,(\hbar)$, in which *L* is an integer. The possible values of *L* depend on the individual *l* values and the orientations of their orbits for all the electrons composing the atom. The total spin momentum has magnitude $\sqrt{S(S+1)}\,(\hbar)$, in which *S* is an integer or half an odd integer, depending on whether the number of electrons is even or odd. The possible value of the total spin angular momentum can be found from all the possible orientations of electrons within the atom. In summing the *L* and *S* values, only the electrons in unfilled shells (typically the outermost, or valence, shell) need be considered: in a closed subshell, there are as many electrons with spins oriented in one direction as there are with spins in the opposite direction, with the result that their orbital and spin momenta add up to zero. Thus, only electrons in unfilled shells contribute angular momentum to the whole atom. For light atoms and heavier atoms with just a few electrons outside the inner closed shells, the total angular momentum is approximately given by the vector sum of the total of orbital angular momentum and the total spin angular momentum. The total angular momentum has the magnitude $\sqrt{J(J+1)}\,(\hbar)$, in which *J* can take any positive value from $L+S$ to $L-S$ in integer steps; *i.e.,* if $L=1$ and $S=3/2$, *J* can be $5/2$, $3/2$, or $1/2$. The remaining quantum number, m_J, specifies the orientation of the atom as a whole; m_J can take any value from $+J$ to $-J$ in integer steps. A term is the set of all states with a given configuration: *L, S,* and *J.*

L-S coupling

If the total angular momentum can be expressed approximately as the vector sum of the total orbital and spin angular momenta, the assignment is called the *L-S* coupling, or Russell-Saunders coupling (after the astronomer Henry Norris Russell and the physicist Frederick A. Saunders, both of the United States).

For heavier atoms, magnetic interactions among the electrons often contrive to make *L* and *S* poorly defined. The total angular momentum quantum numbers *J* and m_J remain constant quantities for a given state of an atom, but their values can no longer be generated by the addition of the *L* and *S* values. A coupling scheme known as *jj* coupling is sometimes applicable. In this scheme, each electron *n* is assigned an angular momentum *j* composed of its orbital angular momentum *l* and its spin *s.* The total angular momentum *J* is then the vector addition of $j_1+j_2+j_3+\ldots$, where each j_n is due to a single electron.

ATOMIC TRANSITIONS

An isolated atom or ion in some excited state spontaneously relaxes to a lower state with the emission of one or more photons, thus ultimately returning to its ground state. In an atomic spectrum, each transition corresponding to absorption or emission of energy will account for the presence of a spectral line. Quantum mechanics prescribes a means of calculating the probability of making these transitions. The lifetimes of the excited states depend on specific transitions of the particular atom, and the calculation of the spontaneous transition between two states of an atom requires that the wavefunctions of both states be known.

The possible radiative transitions are classified as either allowed or forbidden, depending on the probability of their occurrence. In some instances, as, for example, when both the initial and final states have a total angular momentum equal to zero, there can be no single photon transition between states of any kind. The allowed transitions obey certain restrictions, known as selection rules: the *J* value of the atom can change by unity or zero, and if *L* and *S* are well defined within the atom, the change in *L* is also restricted to 0 or ±1 while *S* cannot change at all. The time required for an allowed transition varies as the cube of the frequency of the photon; for a transition in which a photon of visible light (wavelength of approximately 500 nanometres), a characteristic emission time is 1–10 nanoseconds (10^{-9} second).

Forbidden transitions proceed slowly compared to the allowed transitions, and the resulting spectral emission lines are relatively weak. For atoms in about the first third of the periodic table, the *L* and *S* selection rules provide useful criteria for the classification of unknown spectral lines. In heavier atoms, greater magnetic interactions among electrons cause *L* and *S* to be poorly defined, and these selection rules are less applicable. Occasionally, excited states are found that have lifetimes much longer than the average because all the possible transitions to lower energy states are forbidden transitions. Such states are called metastable and can have lifetimes in excess of minutes.

PERTURBATIONS OF LEVELS

The energies of atomic levels are affected by external magnetic and electric fields in which atoms may be situated. A magnetic field causes an atomic level to split into its states of different m_J, each with slightly different energy; this effect is known as the Zeeman effect (after Pieter Zeeman, a Dutch physicist). The result is that each spectral line separates into several closely spaced lines. The number and spacing of such lines depend on the J values for the levels involved; hence the Zeeman effect is often used to identify the J values of levels in complex spectra. The corresponding effect of line splitting caused by the application of a strong electric field is known as the Stark effect.

Zeeman effect

Small modifications to electronic energy levels arise because of the finite mass, nonzero volume of the atomic nucleus and the distribution of charges and currents within the nucleus. The resulting small energy changes, called hyperfine structure, are used to obtain information about the properties of nuclei and the distribution of the electron clouds near nuclei. Systematic changes in level positions are seen as the number of neutrons in a nucleus is increased. These effects are known as isotope shifts and form the basis for laser isotope separation. For light atoms, the isotope shift is primarily due to differences in the finite mass of the nucleus. For heavier atoms, the main contribution comes from the fact that the volume of the nucleus increases as the number of neutrons increases. The nucleus may behave as a small magnet because of internal circulating currents; the magnetic fields produced in this way may affect the levels slightly. If the electric field outside the nucleus differs from that which would exist if the nucleus were concentrated at a point, this difference also can affect the energy levels of the surrounding electrons (see below *X-ray and radio-frequency spectroscopy: Radio-frequency spectroscopy*). (St.C.)

Molecular spectroscopy

GENERAL PRINCIPLES

A molecule is a collection of positively charged atomic nuclei surrounded by a cloud of negatively charged electrons. Its stability results from a balance among the attractive and repulsive forces of the nuclei and electrons. A molecule is characterized by the total energy resulting from these interacting forces. As is the case with atoms, the allowed energy states of a molecule are quantized (see above *Basic properties of atoms*).

Molecular spectra result from either the absorption or the emission of electromagnetic radiation as molecules undergo changes from one quantized energy state to another. The mechanisms involved are similar to those observed for atoms but are more complicated. The additional complexities are due to interactions of the various nuclei with each other and with the electrons, phenomena which do not exist in single atoms. In order to analyze molecular spectra it is necessary to consider simultaneously the effects of all the contributions from the different types of molecular motions and energies. However, to develop a basic understanding it is best to first consider the various factors separately.

Molecular interactions

There are two primary sets of interactions that contribute to observed molecular spectra. The first involves the internal motions of the nuclear framework of the molecule and the attractive and repulsive forces among the nuclei and electrons. The other encompasses the interactions of nuclear magnetic and electrostatic moments with the electrons and with each other.

The first set of interactions can be divided into the three categories given here in decreasing order of magnitude: electronic, vibrational, and rotational. The electrons in a molecule possess kinetic energy due to their motions and potential energy arising from their attraction by the positive nuclei and their mutual repulsion. These two energy factors, along with the potential energy due to the mutual electrostatic repulsion of the positive nuclei, constitute the electronic energy of a molecule. Molecules are not rigid structures, and the motion of the nuclei within the molecular framework gives rise to vibrational energy levels. In the gas phase, where they are widely separated relative to their size, molecules can undergo free rotation and as a result possess quantized amounts of rotational energy. In theory, the translational energy of molecules through space is also quantized, but in practice the quantum effects are so small that they are not observable, and the motion appears continuous. The interaction of electromagnetic radiation with these molecular energy levels constitutes the basis for electron spectroscopy, visible, infrared (IR) and ultraviolet (UV) spectroscopies, Raman spectroscopy, and gas-phase microwave spectroscopy.

The second set of molecular interactions form the basis for nuclear magnetic resonance (NMR) spectroscopy, electron spin resonance (ESR) spectroscopy, and nuclear quadrupole resonance (NQR) spectroscopy. The first two arise, respectively, from the interaction of the magnetic moment of a nucleus or an electron with an external magnetic field. The nature of this interaction is highly dependent on the molecular environment in which the nucleus or electron is located. The latter is due to the interaction of a nuclear electric quadrupole moment with the electric field generated by the surrounding electrons; they will not be discussed in this article.

Observation of molecular spectra

Molecular spectra are observed when a molecule undergoes the absorption or emission of electromagnetic radiation with a resulting increase or decrease in energy. There are limitations, imposed by the laws of quantum mechanics, as to which pairs of energy levels can participate in energy changes and as to the extent of the radiation absorbed or emitted. The first condition for the absorption of electromagnetic radiation by a molecule undergoing a transition from a lower energy state, E_{lo}, to a higher energy state, E_{hi}, is that the frequency of the absorbed radiation must be related to the change in energy by $E_{hi} - E_{lo} = h\nu$, where ν is radiation frequency and h is Planck's constant. Conversely, the application of electromagnetic radiation of frequency ν to a molecule in energy state E_{hi} can result in the emission of additional radiation of frequency ν as the molecule undergoes a transition to state E_{lo}. These two phenomena are referred to as induced absorption and induced emission, respectively. Also a molecule in an excited (high) energy state can spontaneously emit electromagnetic radiation, returning to some lower energy level without the presence of inducing radiation.

THEORY OF MOLECULAR SPECTRA

Unlike atoms in which the quantization of energy results only from the interaction of the electrons with the nucleus and with other electrons, the quantization of molecular energy levels and the resulting absorption or emission of radiation involving these energy levels encompasses several mechanisms. In theory there is no clear separation of the different mechanisms, but in practice their differences in magnitude allow their characterization to be examined independently. Using the diatomic molecule as a model, each category of energy will be examined.

Rotational energy states. In the gas phase, molecules are relatively far apart compared to their size and are free to undergo rotation around their axes. If a diatomic molecule is assumed to be rigid (*i.e.,* internal vibrations are not considered) and composed of two atoms of masses m_1 and m_2 separated by a distance r, it can be characterized by a moment of inertia $I = \mu r^2$, where μ, the reduced mass, is given as $\mu = m_1 m_2/(m_1 + m_2)$. Application of the laws of quantum mechanics to the rotational motion of the diatomic molecule shows that the rotational energy is quantized and is given by $E_J = J(J+1)(h^2/8\pi^2 I)$, where h is Planck's constant and $J = 0, 1, 2, \ldots$ is the rotational quantum number. Molecular rotational spectra originate when a molecule undergoes a transition from one rotational level to another, subject to quantum mechanical selection rules. Selection rules are stated in terms of the allowed changes in the quantum numbers that characterize the energy states. For a transition to occur between two

Selection rules

rotational energy levels of a diatomic molecule, it must possess a permanent dipole moment (this requires that the two atoms be different), the frequency of the radiation incident on the molecule must satisfy the quantum condition $E_{J'} - E_J = h\nu$, and the selection rule $\Delta J = \pm 1$ must be obeyed. For a transition from the energy level denoted by J to that denoted by $J + 1$, the energy change is given by $h\nu = E_{J+1} - E_J = 2(J + 1)(h^2/8\pi^2 I)$ or $\nu = 2B(J + 1)$, where $B = h/8\pi^2 I$ is the rotational constant of the molecule.

Vibrational energy states. The rotational motion of a diatomic molecule can adequately be discussed by use of a rigid-rotor model. Real molecules are not rigid; however, the two nuclei are in a constant vibrational motion relative to one another. For such a nonrigid system, if the vibrational motion is approximated as being harmonic in nature, the vibrational energy, E_v, equals $(V + \frac{1}{2})h\nu_0$, where $v = 0, 1, 2, \ldots$ is the vibrational quantum number, $\nu_0 = (\frac{1}{2\pi})(k/\mu)^{1/2}$, and k is the force constant of the bond, characteristic of the particular molecule. The necessary conditions for the observation of a vibrational spectrum for a diatomic molecule are the occurrence of a change in the dipole moment of the molecule as it undergoes vibration (nomonuclear diatomic molecules are thus inactive), conformance to the selection rule $\Delta v = \pm 1$, and the frequency of the radiation being given by $\nu = (E_{v+1} - E_v)/h$.

Electronic energy states. Unlike the atom where the system is centrosymmetric (see above *Foundations of atomic spectra: Basic atomic structure*), the energy relationships among the nuclei and electrons in a diatomic molecule are more complex and are difficult to characterize in an exact manner. One commonly used method for consideration of the electronic energy states of a diatomic molecule is the molecular orbital (MO) approach.

Molecular orbital theory

In this description the electronic wavefunctions of the individual atoms constituting the molecule, called the atomic orbitals (AOs), are combined, subject to appropriate quantum mechanical and symmetry considerations, to form a set of molecular orbitals whose domain extends over the entire nuclear framework of the molecule rather than being centred about a single atom. Molecular electronic transitions, and the resulting spectra, can then be described in terms of electron transfer between two MOs. Since the nuclear framework is not rigid but is constantly undergoing vibrational motion, a convenient method of quantitatively characterizing the electronic energy of a particular MO involves the use of a potential-energy diagram whereby the potential energy of an electron in a particular MO is plotted relative to the internuclear separation in the molecule (see Figure 34). Molecular electronic spectra arise from the transition of an electron from one MO to another.

Energy states of real diatomic molecules. For any real molecule, absolute separation of the different motions is seldom encountered since molecules are simultaneously undergoing rotation and vibration. The rigid-rotor, harmonic oscillator model exhibits a combined rotational-vibrational energy level satisfying $E_{vJ} = (v + \frac{1}{2})h\nu_0 + BJ(J + 1)$. Chemical bonds are neither rigid nor perfect harmonic oscillators, however, and all molecules in a given collection do not possess identical rotational, vibrational, and electronic energies but will be distributed among the available energy states in accordance with the principle known as the Boltzmann distribution.

Oscillation of bond length

As a molecule undergoes vibrational motion, the bond length will oscillate about an average internuclear separation. If the oscillation is harmonic, this average value will not change as the vibrational state of the molecule changes; however, for real molecules the oscillations are anharmonic. The potential for the oscillation of a molecule is the electronic energy plotted as a function of internuclear separation (Figure 34A). Owing to the fact that this curve is nonparabolic, the oscillations are anharmonic and the energy levels are perturbed. This results in a decreasing energy level separation with increasing v and a modification of the vibrational selection rules to allow $\Delta v = \pm 2, \pm 3, \ldots$.

Since the moment of inertia depends on the internuclear separation by the relationship $I = \mu r^2$, each different vibrational state will possess a different value of I and therefore will exhibit a different rotational spectrum. The

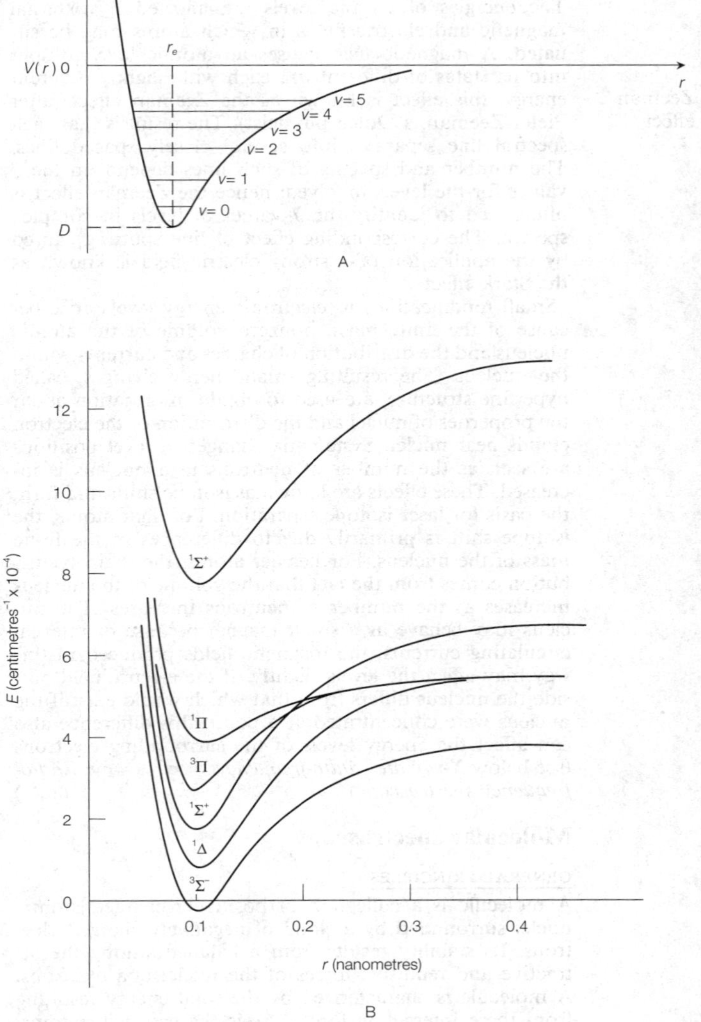

Figure 34: *Potential energy curves.*
(A) Potential energy, $V(r)$, as a function of the internuclear separation r for a typical diatomic molecule. The equilibrium bond length, r_e, is the internuclear distance corresponding to the depth of the potential minimum (D) of the molecule. Horizontal lines represent vibrational energy levels. (B) The energy of the nitrogen hydride (NH) molecule in six different electronic states as a function of the internuclear separation r. The curves are labeled with the standard term symbol notation for the corresponding state.
From J.D. Graybeal, *Molecular Spectroscopy* (1988), McGraw-Hill Book Co., New York City

nonrigidity of the chemical bond in the molecule as it goes to higher rotational states leads to centrifugal distortion; in diatomic molecules this results in the stretching of the bonds, which increases the moment of inertia. The total of these effects can be expressed in the form of an expanded energy expression for the rotational-vibrational energy of the diatomic molecule; for further discussion, see the texts listed in the *Bibliography*.

A molecule in a given electronic state will simultaneously possess discrete amounts of rotational and vibrational energies. For a collection of molecules they will be spread out into a large number of rotational and vibrational energy states so any electronic state change (electronic transition) will be accompanied by changes in both rotational and vibrational energies in accordance with the proper selection rules. Thus any observed electronic transition will consist of a large number of closely spaced members owing to the vibrational and rotational energy changes.

EXPERIMENTAL METHODS

Spectrometers

There are three basic types of spectrometer systems that are commonly used for molecular spectroscopy: emission, monochromatic radiation absorption, and Fourier transform. Each of these methods involves a source of radiation, a sample, and a device for detecting and analyzing radiation.

Emission spectrographs have some suitable means of exciting molecules to higher energy states. The radiation emitted when the molecules decay back to the original energy states is then analyzed by means of a monochromator and a suitable detector. This system is used extensively for the observation of electronic spectra. The electrons are excited to higher levels by means of an energy source such as an electric discharge or a microwave plasma. The emitted radiation generally lies in the visible or ultraviolet region. Absorption spectrometers employ as sources either broadband radiation emitters followed by a monochromator to provide a signal of very narrow frequency content or a generator that will produce a tunable single frequency. The tunable monochromatic source signal then passes through a sample contained in a suitable cell and onto a detector designed to sense the source frequency being used. The resulting spectrum is a plot of intensity of absorption versus frequency.

A Fourier-transform spectrometer provides a conventional absorption spectrometer-type spectrum but has greater speed, resolution, and sensitivity (see Figure 35). In this spectrometer the sample is subjected to a broadband source of radiation, resulting in the production of an interferogram due to the absorption of specific components of the radiation. This interferogram (a function of signal intensity versus time) is normally digitized, stored in computer memory, and converted to an absorption spectrum by means of a Fourier transform (see also ANALYSIS: *Fourier analysis*). Fourier-transform spectrometers can be designed to cover all spectral regions from the radiofrequency to the ultraviolet.

Spectrometers allow the study of a large variety of samples over a wide range of frequencies. Materials can be studied in the solid, liquid, or gas phase either in a pure form or in mixtures. Various designs allow the study of spectra as a function of temperature, pressure, and external magnetic and electric fields. Spectra of molecular fragments obtained by radiation of materials and of short-lived reaction intermediates are routinely observed. Two useful methods for the observation of spectra of short-lived species at low (4 K) temperature is to trap them in a rare gas matrix or to produce them in a pulsed adiabatic nozzle.

FIELDS OF MOLECULAR SPECTROSCOPY

Microwave spectroscopy. For diatomic molecules the rotational constants for all but the very lightest ones lie in the range of 1–200 gigahertz (GH_2). The frequency of a rotational transition is given approximately by $\nu = 2B(J + 1)$, and so molecular rotational spectra will exhibit absorption lines in the 2–800-gigahertz region. For polyatomic molecules three moments of inertia are required to describe the rotational motion. They produce much more complex spectra, but basic relationships, analogous to those for a diatomic molecule, exist between their moments and the observed absorption lines. The 1–1,000-gigahertz range is referred to as the microwave region (airport and police radar operate in this region) of the electromagnetic spectrum. Microwave radiation is generated by one of two methods: (1) special electronic tubes such as klystrons or backward-wave oscillators and solid-state oscillators such as Gunn diodes, which can be stabilized to produce highly monochromatic radiation and are tunable over specific regions, and (2) frequency synthesizers, whose output is produced by the successive multiplication and addition of highly monochromatic, low-frequency signals and consists of a series of discrete frequencies with small separations that effectively provide a continuous wave signal (*e.g.,* 6 hertz separations at 25 gigahertz).

Generation of microwave radiation

There are two types of microwave spectrometer in use. In the conventional Stark-modulated spectrometer, the sample is contained in a long (1- to 3-metre, or 3.3- to 9.8-foot) section of a rectangular waveguide, sealed at each end with a microwave transmitting window (*e.g.,* mica or Mylar), and connected to a vacuum line for evacuation and sample introduction. The radiation from the source passes through a gaseous sample and is detected by a crystal diode detector that is followed by an amplifier and display system (chart recorder). In order to increase the sensitivity of the instrument, signal modulation by application of a high-voltage square wave across the sample is used. The second type is the Fourier-transform spectrometer, in which the radiation is confined in an evacuated cavity between a pair of spherical mirrors and the sample is introduced by a pulsed nozzle that lowers the temperature of the sample to less than 10 K. The sample is subjected to rotational energy excitation by application of a pulsed microwave signal, and the resulting emission signal is detected and Fourier-transformed to an absorption versus frequency spectrum. In both instruments the energy absorbed or emitted as the molecules undergo transitions from one quantized rotational state to another is observed. The Fourier-transform instrument has the advantage of providing higher resolution (1 kilohertz [kHz] relative to 30 kHz) and of exhibiting a much simpler spectrum due to the low sample temperature that insures that the majority of the molecules are in the few lowest energy states.

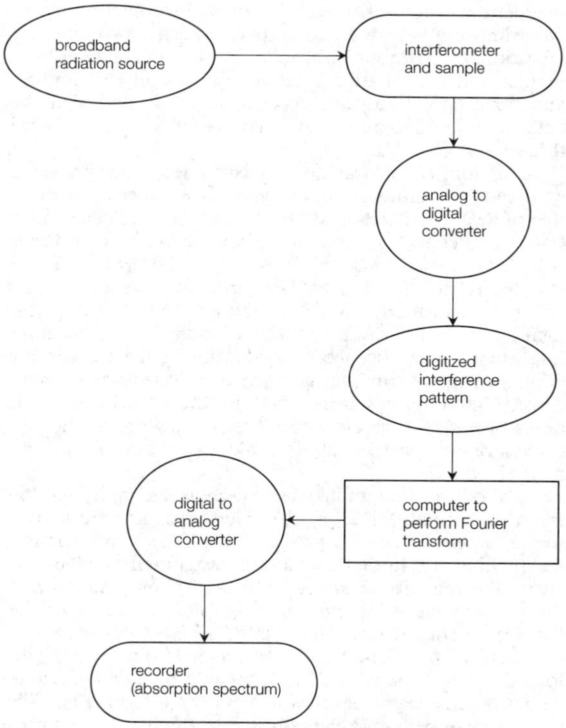

Figure 35: The operation of a Fourier-transform spectrometer.
From J.D. Graybeal, *Molecular Spectroscopy* (1988), McGraw-Hill Book Co., New York City

For observation of its rotational spectrum, a molecule must possess a permanent electric dipole moment and have a vapour pressure such that it can be introduced into a sample cell at extremely low pressures (5–50 millitorr; one millitorr equals 1×10^{-3} millimetre of mercury or 1.93×10^{-5} pound per square inch). The spectra of molecules with structures containing up to 15 atoms can be routinely analyzed, but the density and overlapping of spectral lines in the spectra of larger molecules severely restricts analysis.

Molecular applications

The relationship between the observed microwave transition frequency and the rotational constant of a diatomic molecule can provide a value for the internuclear distance. The quantitative geometric structures of molecules can also be obtained from the measured transitions in its microwave spectrum. In addition to geometric structures, other properties related to molecular structure can be investigated, including electric dipole moments, energy barriers to internal rotation, centrifugal distortion parameters, magnetic moments, nuclear electric quadrupole moments, vibration-rotation interaction parameters, low-frequency vibrational transitions, molecular electric quadrupole moments, and information relative to electron distribution and bonding. Microwave spectroscopy has provided the detailed structure and associated parameters for several thousand molecules.

The use of Fourier-transform spectrometers has provided a method for studying many short-lived species such as free radicals (*i.e.*, OH, CN, NO, CF, CCH), molecular ions (*i.e.*, CO^+, HCO^+, HCS^+), and Van der Waals complexes (*i.e.*, $C_6H_6{-}HCl$, $H_2O{-}H_2O$, Kr—HF, $SO_2{-}SO_2$). There is a special relationship between microwave spectroscopy and radio astronomy. Much of the impetus for the investigation of the microwave spectra of radical and molecular ions stems from the need for identifying the microwave emission signals emanating from extraterrestrial sources. This collaboration has resulted in the identification in outer space of several dozen species, including the hydroxyl radical, methanol, formaldehyde, ammonia, and methyl cyanide.

For a polyatomic molecule, which is characterized by three moments of inertia, the microwave spectrum of a single molecular species provides insufficient information for making a complete structure assignment and calculating the magnitude of all bond angles and interatomic distances in the molecule. For example, the values of the three moments of inertia of the $^{12}CH_2{}^{81}Br^{12}C^{14}N$ molecule will depend on eight bond parameters (four angles and four distances), hence it is not possible to obtain discrete values of these eight unknowns from three moments. This problem can be circumvented by introducing the assumption that the structure of the molecule will not significantly change if one or more atoms are substituted with a different isotopic species. The three moments of an isotopically substituted molecule are then derived from its microwave spectrum and, since they depend on the same set of molecular parameters, provide three additional pieces of data from which to obtain the eight bond parameters. By determining the moments of inertia of a sufficient number of isotopically substituted species, it is possible to obtain sufficient data from which to completely determine the structure. The best structural information is obtained when an isotopic species resulting from substitution at each atom site in the molecule can be studied.

Structure determination

Infrared spectroscopy. This technique covers the region of the electromagnetic spectrum between the visible (wavelength of 800 nanometres) and the short-wavelength microwave (0.3 millimetre). The spectra observed in this region are primarily associated with the internal vibrational motion of molecules, but a few light molecules will have rotational transitions lying in the region. For the infrared region, the wavenumber ($\tilde{\nu}$, the reciprocal of the wavelength) is commonly used to measure energy. Infrared spectroscopy historically has been divided into three regions, the near infrared (4,000–12,500 inverse centimetres [cm^{-1}]), the mid-infrared (400–4,000 cm^{-1}) and the far infrared (10–400 cm^{-1}). With the development of Fourier-transform spectrometers, this distinction of areas has blurred and the more sophisticated instruments can cover from 10 to 25,000 cm^{-1} by an interchange of source, beam splitter, detector, and sample cell.

For the near-infrared region a tungsten-filament lamp (6,000–25,000 cm^{-1}) serves as a source. In the middle region the standard source is a Globar (50–6,000 cm^{-1}), a silicon carbide cylinder that is electrically heated to function as a blackbody radiator. Radiation from a mercury-arc lamp (10–70 cm^{-1}) is employed in the far-infrared region. In a grating-monochromator type instrument, the full range of the source-detector combination is scanned by mechanically changing the grating position. In a Fourier-transform instrument, the range available for a single scan is generally limited by the beam-splitter characteristics. The beam splitter functions to divide the source signal into two parts for the formation of an interference pattern. In the near-infrared region either a quartz plate or silicon deposited on a quartz plate is used. In the mid-infrared region a variety of optical-grade crystals, such as calcium flouride (CaF_2), zinc selenide (ZnSe), cesium iodide (CsI), or potassium bromide (KBr), coated with silicon or germanium are employed. Below 200 cm^{-1} Mylar films of varying thickness are used to cover narrow portions of the region. Thermal detection of infrared radiation is based on the conversion of a temperature change, resulting from such radiation falling on a suitable material, into a measurable signal. A Golay detector employs the reflection of light from a thermally distortable reflecting film onto a photoelectric cell, while a bolometer exhibits a change in electrical resistance with a change in temperature. In both cases the device must respond to very small and very rapid changes. In the Fourier-transform spectrometers, the entire optical path can be evacuated to prevent interference from extraneous materials such as water and carbon dioxide in the air.

Detectors

A large variety of samples can be examined by use of infrared spectroscopy. Normal transmission can be used for liquids, thin films of solids, and gases. The containment of liquid and gas samples must be in a cell that has infrared-transmitting windows such as sodium chloride, potassium bromide, or cesium iodide. Solids, films, and coatings can be examined by means of several techniques that employ the reflection of radiation from the sample.

The development of solid-state diode lasers, F-centre lasers, and spin-flip Raman lasers is providing new sources for infrared spectrometers. These sources in general are not broadband but have high intensity and are useful for the construction of instruments that are designed for specific applications in narrow frequency regions.

The absorption of infrared radiation is due to the vibrational motion of a molecule. For a diatomic molecule the analysis of this motion is relatively straightforward because there is only one mode of vibration, the stretching of the bond. For polyatomic molecules the situation is compounded by the simultaneous motion of many nuclei. The mechanical model employed to analyze this complex motion is one wherein the nuclei are considered to be point masses and the interatomic chemical bonds are viewed as massless springs. Although the vibrations in a molecule obey the laws of quantum mechanics, molecular systems can be analyzed using classical mechanics to ascertain the nature of the vibrational motion. Analysis shows that such a system will display a set of resonant frequencies, each of which is associated with a different combination of nuclear motions. The number of such resonances that occur is $3N-5$ for a linear molecule and $3N-6$ for a nonlinear one, where N is the number of atoms in the molecule. The motions of the individual nuclei are such that during the displacements the centre of mass of the system does not change. The frequencies at which infrared radiation is absorbed correspond to the frequencies of the normal modes of vibration or can be considered as transitions between quantized energy levels, each of which corresponds to excited states of a normal mode. An analysis of all the normal-mode frequencies of a molecule can provide a set of force constants that are related to the individual bond-stretching and bond-bending motions within the molecule.

Resonant frequencies

When examined using a high-resolution instrument and with the samples in the gas phase, the individual normal-mode absorption lines of polyatomic molecules will be separated into a series of closely spaced sharp lines. The analysis of this vibrational structure can provide the same type of information as can be obtained from rotational spectra, but even the highest resolution infrared instruments (0.0001 cm^{-1}) cannot approach that of a Fourier-transform microwave spectrometer (10 kilohertz), and so the results are not nearly as accurate.

Owing to the anharmonicity of the molecular vibrations, transitions corresponding to multiples ($2\nu_i$, $3\nu_i$, etc, known as overtones) and combinations ($\nu_1+\nu_2$, $2\nu_3+\nu_4$, etc.) of the fundamental frequencies will occur.

The normal-mode frequencies will tend to be associated with intramolecular motions of specific molecular entities and will be found to have values lying in a relatively narrow frequency range for all molecules containing that entity. For example, all molecules containing a carboxyl group (C=O) will have a normal vibrational mode that involves the stretching of the carbon-oxygen double bond.

Its particular frequency will vary, depending on the nature of the atoms or groups of atoms attached to the carbon atom but will generally occur in the region of 1,650–1,750 cm^{-1}. This same type of behaviour is observed for other entities such as the oxygen-hydrogen (O—H) stretching motion in the hydroxyl group and the C═C stretching motion in molecules with carbon-carbon double bonds (see Figure 36). This predictable behaviour has led to the development of spectral correlation charts that can be compared with observed infrared spectra to aid in ascertaining the presence or absence of particular molecular entities and in determining the structure of newly synthesized or unknown species. The infrared spectrum of any individual molecule is a unique fingerprint for that molecule and can serve as a reliable form of identification.

Correlation charts

From L. Bellamy, *The Infrared Spectra of Complex Molecules*, 2nd ed. (1958); Barnes & Noble Publishers, New York, and Methuen & Co. Ltd.

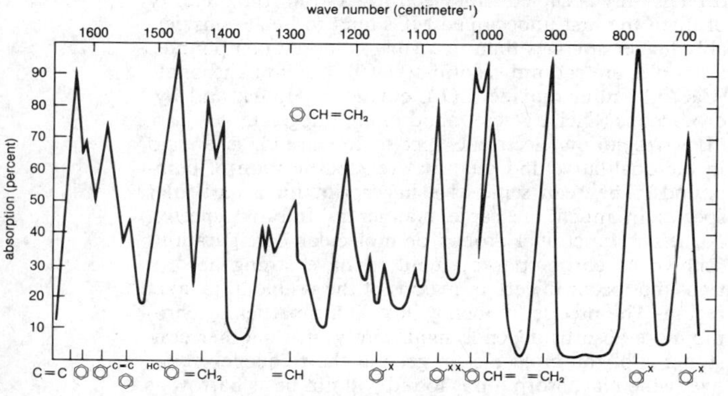

Figure 36: Vibrational infrared spectrum of styrene. The individual peaks are characteristic of the various structural features of the styrene molecule shown along the bottom edge of the figure. The hexagons represent the benzene ring of six carbon atoms present in the structure; X represents the entire group of carbon and hydrogen atoms attached to the benzene ring.

Raman spectroscopy. Raman spectroscopy is based on the absorption of photons of a specific frequency followed by scattering at a higher or lower frequency. The modification of the scattered photons results from the incident photons either gaining energy from or losing energy to the vibrational and rotational motion of the molecule. Quantitatively, a sample (solid, liquid, or gas) is irradiated with a source frequency ν_0 and the scattered radiation will be of frequency $\nu_0 \pm \nu_i$, where ν_i is the frequency corresponding to a vibrational or rotational transition in the molecule. Since molecules exist in a number of different rotational and vibrational states (depending on the temperature), many different values of ν_i are possible. Consequently, the Raman spectra will consist of a large number of scattered lines.

Most incident photons are scattered by the sample with no change in frequency in a process known as Rayleigh scattering. To enhance the observation of the radiation at $\nu_0 \pm \nu_i$, the scattered radiation is observed perpendicular to the incident beam. To provide high-intensity incident radiation and to enable the observation of lines where ν_i is small (as when due to rotational changes), the source in a Raman spectrometer is a monochromatic visible laser. The scattered radiation can then be analyzed by use of a scanning optical monochromator with a phototube as a detector.

Raman spectrometer

The observation of the vibrational Raman spectrum of a molecule depends on a change in the molecules polarizability (ability to be distorted by an electric field) rather than its dipole moment during the vibration of the atoms. As a result, infrared and Raman spectra provide complementary information, and between the two techniques all vibrational transitions can be observed. This combination of techniques is essential for the measurement of all the vibrational frequencies of molecules of high symmetry that do not have permanent dipole moments. Analogously, there will be a rotational Raman spectra for molecules with no permanent dipole moment that consequently have no pure rotational spectra. The rotational Raman spectrum of such a molecule, diatomic oxygen (O_2), which is Raman-active and infrared-inactive, is shown in Figure 37.

Visible and ultraviolet spectroscopy. Colours as perceived by the sense of vision are simply a human observation of the inverse of a visible absorption spectrum. The underlying phenomenon is that of an electron being raised from a low-energy molecular orbital (MO) to one of higher energy, where the energy difference is given as $\Delta E = h\nu$. For a collection of molecules that are in a particular MO or electronic state, there will be a distribution among the accessible vibrational and rotational states. Any electronic transition will then be accompanied by simultaneous changes in vibrational and rotational energy states. This will result in an absorption spectrum which, when recorded under high-resolution conditions, will exhibit considerable fine structure of many closely spaced lines. Under low-resolution conditions, however, the spectrum will show the absorption of a broad band of frequencies. When the energy change is sufficiently large that the associated absorption frequency lies above 7.5×10^{14} hertz the material will be transparent to visible light and will absorb in the ultraviolet region.

The concept of MOs can be extended successfully to molecules. For electronic transitions in the visible and ultraviolet regions only the outer (valence shell) MOs are involved. The ordering of MO energy levels as formed from the atomic orbitals (AOs) of the constituent atoms is shown in Figure 38. In compliance with the Pauli exclusion principle each MO can be occupied by a pair of electrons having opposite electron spins. The energy of each electron in a molecule will be influenced by the

MO energy levels

By courtesy of the Pennsylvania State University, University Park

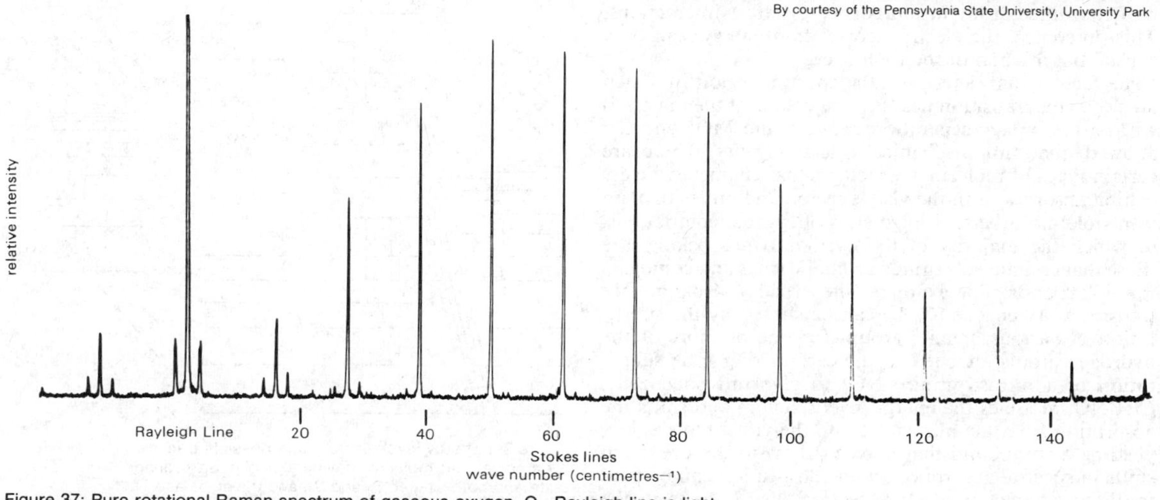

Figure 37: Pure rotational Raman spectrum of gaseous oxygen, O_2. Rayleigh line is light scattered without change of rotational or vibrational energy. Stokes lines involve an increase in rotational energy of the molecules.

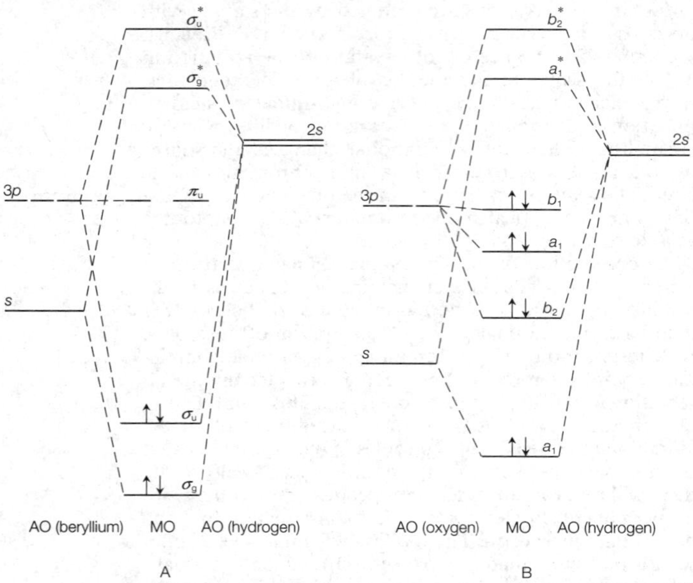

Figure 38: Molecular orbital energy-level diagrams for (A) beryllium hydride, BeH_2, with linear shape, and (B) water, H_2O, with bent shape. The molecular orbitals (MOs) are labeled to reflect the atomic orbitals (AOs) from which they are composed as well as their symmetry properties.

Adapted from J.D. Graybeal, *Molecular Spectroscopy* (1988), McGraw-Hill Book Co., New York City

motion of all the other electrons. So that a reasonable treatment of electron energies may be developed, each electron is considered to move in an average field created by all the other electrons. Thus the energy of an electron in a particular MO is assigned. As a first approximation, the total electronic energy of the molecule is the sum of the energies of the individual electrons in the various MOs. The electronic configuration that has the lowest total energy (*i.e.,* the ground state) will be the one with the electrons (shown as short arrows in Figure 38) placed doubly in the combination of orbitals having the lowest total energy. Any configuration in which an electron has been promoted to a higher energy MO is referred to as an excited state. Lying above the electron-containing MOs will be a series of MOs of increasing energy that are unoccupied. Electronic absorption transitions occur when an electron is promoted from a filled MO to one of the higher unfilled ones.

Although the previous description of electron behaviour in molecules provides the basis for a qualitative understanding of molecular electronic spectra, it is not always quantitatively accurate. The energy calculated based on an average electric field is not equivalent to that which would be determined from instantaneous electron interactions. This difference, the electron correlation energy, can be a substantial fraction of the total energy.

Factors determining colour

The factors that determine the spectral region in which an electronic transition lies (*i.e.,* the colour of the material) will be the energy separation between the MOs and the allowed quantum mechanical selection rules. There are certain types of molecular structures that characteristically exhibit absorptions in the visible region and others that are ultraviolet absorbers. A large class of organic compounds, to which the majority of the dyes and inks belong, are those that contain substituted aromatic rings and conjugate multiple bonds. For example, the broad 254-nanometre transition in benzene (C_6H_6) can be shifted by the substitution of various organic groups for one or more of the hydrogen atoms attached to the carbon ring. The substitution of a nitroso group (NO) to give nitrosobenzene, C_6H_5NO, modifies the energy level spacings and shifts the absorption from the ultraviolet into the violet-blue region, yielding a compound that is pale yellow to the eye. Such shifts in spectral absorptions with substitution can be used to aid in characterizing the electron distributions in the bonds of a molecule.

Coordination compounds

A second class of highly coloured compounds that have distinctive visible absorption are coordination compounds of the transition elements (see CHEMICAL COMPOUNDS: *Coordination compounds*). The MOs involved in the spectral transitions for these compounds are essentially unmodified (except in energy) *d*-level atomic orbitals on the transition-metal atoms. An example of such a compound is the titanium (III) hydrated ion, $Ti(H_2O)_6^{3+}$, which absorbs at about 530 nanometres and appears purple to the eye.

A large number of compounds are white solids or colourless liquids and have electronic absorption spectra only in the ultraviolet region. Inorganic salts of this type are those that contain nontransition metals and do not have any atomic *d*-electrons available. Covalently bonded molecules consisting of nonmetal atoms and carbon compounds with no aromatic rings or conjugated chains have all their inner orbitals fully occupied with electrons, and for the majority of them the first unoccupied MOs tend to lie at considerably higher energies than in visibly coloured compounds. Examples are sodium chloride (NaCl), calcium carbonate ($CaCO_3$), sulfur dioxide (SO_2), ethanol C_2H_5OH, and hydrocarbons (C_nH_m, where n and m are integers).

Low-resolution electronic spectra are useful as an aid in the qualitative and quantitative identification of compounds. They can serve as a fingerprint for a particular species in much the same manner as infrared spectra. Particular functional groups or molecular configurations (known as chromophores) tend to have strong absorptions that occur in certain regions of the visible-ultraviolet region. The precise frequency at which a particular chromophore absorbs depends significantly on the other constituents of the molecule, in general the frequency range over which its absorption is found will not be as narrow as the range of the infrared vibrational frequency associated with a specific structural entity. A strong electronic absorption band, especially in the visible region, can be used to make quantitative measurements of the concentration of the absorbing species.

Both rotational and vibrational energies superimpose on an electronic state. This results in a very dense spectrum. The analysis of spectra of this type can provide rotational constants and vibrational frequencies for molecules not only in the ground state but also in excited states. Although the resolution is not as high as for pure rotational and vibrational spectra, it is possible to examine electronic and vibrational states whose populations are too low to be observed by these methods. Improvements in resolution

From J.D. Graybeal, *Molecular Spectroscopy* (1988), McGraw-Hill Book Co., New York City

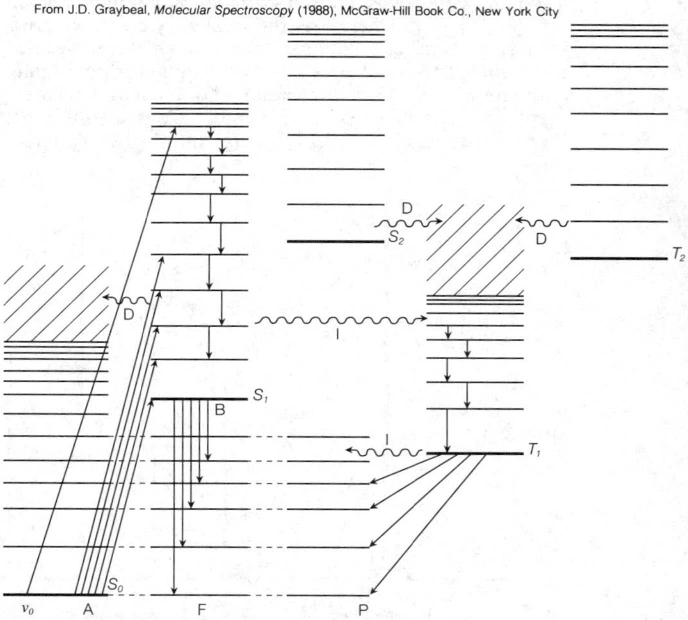

Figure 39: Energy-level diagram and possible transitions for a polyatomic molecule having a singlet, S_0, ground state and both singlet, S_1 and S_2, and triplet, T_1 and T_2, excited states. A = absorption, B = vibrational deactivation, F = fluorescence, I = intersystem crossing, D = dissociation, and P = phosphorescence. Rotational levels are not shown.

of electronic spectra can be achieved by the use of laser sources (see below *Laser spectroscopy*).

Fluorescence and phosphorescence. These phenomena are closely related to electronic absorption spectra and can be used as a tool for analysis and structure determination. Both involve the absorption of radiation via an electronic transition, a loss of energy through either vibrational energy decay or nonradiative processes, and the subsequent emission of radiation of a lower frequency than that absorbed.

Electrons possess intrinsic magnetic moments that are related to their spin angular momenta. The spin quantum number is $s = 1/2$, so in the presence of a magnetic field an electron can have one of two orientations corresponding to magnetic spin quantum number $m_s = \pm 1/2$. The Pauli exclusion principle requires that no two electrons in an atom have the same identical set of quantum numbers; hence when two electrons reside in a single AO or MO they must have different m_s values (*i.e.,* they are antiparallel, or spin paired). This results in a cancellation of their magnetic moments, producing a so-called singlet state. Nearly all molecules that contain an even number of electrons have singlet ground states and have no net magnetic moment (such species are called diamagnetic). When an electron absorbs energy and is excited to a higher energy level, there exists the possibility of (1) retaining its antiparallel configuration relative to the other electron in the orbital from which it was promoted so that the molecule retains its singlet characteristic, or (2) changing to a configuration in which its magnetic moment is parallel to that of its original paired electron. In the latter case, the molecule will possess a net magnetic moment (becoming paramagnetic) and is said to be in a triplet state. For each excited electronic state, either electron spin configuration is possible so that there will be two sets of energy levels (see Figure 39). The normal selection rules forbid transitions between singlet (S_i) and triplet (T_i) states; hence there will be two sets of electronic transitions, each associated with one of the two sets of energy levels.

Singlet and triplet states

Fluorescence is the process whereby a molecule in the lower of two electronic states (generally the ground state) is excited to a higher electronic state by radiation whose energy corresponds to an allowed absorption transition, followed by the emission of radiation as the system decays back to the original state. The decay process can follow several pathways. If the decay is back to the original lower state, the process is called resonance fluorescence and occurs rapidly, in about one nanosecond (see Figure 39). Resonance fluorescence is generally observed for monatomic gases and for many organic molecules, in particular aromatic systems that absorb in the visible and near-ultraviolet regions. For many molecules, especially aromatic compounds whose electronic absorption spectra lie predominately in the shorter-wavelength ultraviolet region (below 400 nanometres), the lifetime of the excited electronic state is sufficiently long that prior to the emission of radiation the molecule can (1) undergo a series of vibrational state decays, (2) lose energy through interstate transfer (intersystem crossing), or (3) lose vibrational energy via molecular collisions.

In the first case, the system will emit radiation in the infrared region as the vibrational energy of the excited state decays back to the lowest vibrational level. The molecule then undergoes an electronic state decay back to one of the vibrational states associated with the lower electronic state. The resulting emission spectrum will then be centred at a frequency lower than the absorption frequency and will appear to be a near mirror image of the absorption spectrum. The second mechanism can be illustrated by reference to the potential energy curves for nitrogen hydride (NH) shown in Figure 34B. The curves for the $^1\Sigma^+$ and $^1\Pi$ states intersect at a radius value of 0.2 nanometre. If a molecule in the $^1\Pi$ excited electronic state is in a vibrational level corresponding to the energy value of this intersection point, it can cross over to the $^1\Sigma^+$ state without emission or absorption of radiation. Subsequently it can undergo vibrational energy loss to end up in the lowest vibrational state of the $^1\Sigma^+$ electronic state. This can then be followed by an electronic transition back to the lower $^1\Delta$ state. Thus the absorption of energy corresponding to an original $^1\Delta \rightarrow {}^1\Pi$ transition results in the emission of fluorescence radiation corresponding to the lower frequency $^1\Sigma^+ \rightarrow {}^1\Delta$ transition. In the third case, when two molecules collide there exists the possibility for energy transfer between them. Upon colliding, a molecule can thus be transformed into a different electronic state whose energy minimum may lie lower or higher than its previous electronic state.

Intersystem crossing

The lifetimes of the excited singlet electronic states, although long enough to allow vibrational relaxation or intersystem crossing, are quite short, so that fluorescence occurs on a time scale of milliseconds to microseconds following irradiation of a material. The most common mode of observation of fluorescence is that of using ultraviolet radiation (invisible to the human eye) as an exciting source and observing the emission of visible radiation. In addition to its use as a tool for analysis and structural determination of molecules, there are many applications outside the laboratory. For example, postage stamps may be tagged with a visually transparent coating of a fluorescing agent to prevent counterfeiting, and the addition of a fluorescing agent with emissions in the blue region of the spectrum to detergents will impart to cloth a whiter appearance in the sunlight.

Phosphorescence is related to fluorescence in terms of its general mechanism but involves a slower decay. It occurs when a molecule whose normal ground state is a singlet is excited to a higher singlet state, goes to a vibrationally excited triplet state via either an intersystem crossing or a molecular collision, and subsequently, following vibrational relaxation, decays back to the singlet ground state by means of a forbidden transition. The result is the occurrence of a long lifetime for the excited triplet state; several seconds up to several hours are not uncommon. These long lifetimes can be related to interactions between the intrinsic (spin) magnetic moments of the electrons and magnetic moments resulting from the orbital motion of the electrons.

Molecules in singlet and triplet states react chemically in different manners. It is possible to affect chemical reactions by the transfer of electronic energy from one molecule to another in the reacting system. Thus the study of fluorescence and phosphorescence provides information related to chemical reactivity.

Photoelectron spectroscopy. Photoelectron spectroscopy is an extension of the photoelectric effect (see RADIATION), first explained by Einstein in 1905, to atoms and molecules in all energy states. The technique involves the bombardment of a sample with radiation from a high-energy monochromatic source and the subsequent determination of the kinetic energies of the ejected electrons. The source energy, $h\nu$, is related to the energy of the ejected electrons, $(1/2)m_e v^2$, where m_e is the electron mass and v is the electron velocity, by $h\nu = (1/2)m_e v^2 + \Phi$, where Φ is the ionization energy of the electron in a particular AO or MO. When the energy of the bombarding radiation exceeds the ionization energy, the excess energy will be imparted to the ejected electron in the form of kinetic energy. By knowing the source frequency and measuring the kinetic energies of the ejected electrons, the ionization energy of an electron in each of the AOs or MOs of a system can be determined. This method serves to complement the data obtained from electronic absorption spectra and in some cases provides information that cannot be obtained from electronic spectroscopy because of selection rules.

Determination of ionization energy

Laser spectroscopy. As mentioned above, the invention and subsequent development of the laser opened many new areas of spectroscopy. Although the basic processes investigated remain those of rotational, vibrational, and electronic spectroscopies, this tool has provided many new ways to investigate such phenomena and has allowed the acquisition of data previously unavailable. At least two dozen new types of experiments using lasers have been developed. To illustrate the nature and utility of lasers in spectroscopy a limited number will be reviewed.

Lasers by their nature provide an output that consists of a relatively small number of very narrow-banded transitions. While these high-intensity sources can provide radiation useful for certain limited types of spectroscopic studies, a high-intensity tunable narrow-band source is needed for conventional high-resolution spectroscopic studies. This type of source is provided by the dye laser, in which laser emissions arise from the decay of dye molecules that have been excited into a multitude of closely spaced rovibronic (rotational-vibrational-electronic) levels by the application of an intense secondary laser signal (a process known as pumping). Dye lasers can provide radiation over a limited region within the range of 330 to 1,250 nanometres. The region covered by the radiation can be varied by changing the dye and pump source. Thus there exist essentially continuously tunable sources in the region where electronic spectra are normally observed. Although lasers with continuous tunability over all spectral ranges of interest are not available, it is possible to observe transitions between molecular energy levels by using a fixed-frequency laser and shifting the energy levels by application of electric or magnetic fields to the sample. Other techniques such as the observation of fluorescence, dissociation, multiple photon absorption, and double resonance are used to enhance sensitivity and circumvent the lack of tunability. While the use of conventional spectroscopic methods generally employs established designs of spectrometers and techniques, the use of lasers often requires the development of new and ingenious experimental methods to extract desired spectroscopic information.

Tunability

Doppler-limited spectroscopy. With the exception of specially designed molecular-beam spectrometers, the line width of a molecular absorption transition is limited by the Doppler effect. The resolution of conventional spectrometers, with the exception of a few very expensive Fourier-transform instruments, is generally limited to a level such that observed line widths are well in excess of the Doppler width. Tunable laser sources with extremely narrow bandwidths and high intensity routinely achieve a resolution on the order of the Doppler line width (0.001–0.05 nanometre). The design of a laser absorption spectrometer (Figure 40) is advantageous in that no monochromator is needed since the absorption coefficient of a transition can be measured directly from the difference in the photodiode current generated by the radiation beam passing through the sample (I_1) and the current generated by a reference beam (I_2). In addition, the high power available from laser sources, concurrent with their frequency and intensity stabilization, eliminates problems with detector noise. Since the sensitivity of detecting spectral transitions increases with resolution, laser spectrometers are inherently more sensitive than conventional broadband source types. The extremely narrow nature of a laser beam permits it to undergo multiple reflections through a sample without spatial spreading and interference, thus providing long absorption path lengths. Lasers can be highly frequency-stabilized and accurately measured, one part in 10^8 being routinely achieved. A small fraction of the source signal can be diverted to an interferometer and a series of frequency markers generated and placed on the recording of the spectral absorption lines. Lasers can be tuned over a range of several wavenumbers in a time scale of microseconds, making laser spectrometers ideal instruments for detecting and characterizing short-lived intermediate species in chemical reactions. Laser spectrometers offer two distinct advantages for the study of fluorescence and phosphorescence. The high source intensity enables the generation of larger upper-state populations in the fluorescencing species. The narrow frequency band of the source provides for greater energy selectivity of the upper state that is being populated.

High sensitivity of lasers

Coherent anti-Stokes Raman spectroscopy (CARS). This technique involves the phenomenon of wave mixing, takes advantage of the high intensity of stimulated Raman scattering, and has the applicability of conventional Raman spectroscopy. In the CARS method two strong collinear laser beams at frequencies ν_1 and ν_2 ($\nu_1 > \nu_2$) irradiate a sample. If the frequency difference, $\nu_1 - \nu_2$, is equal to the frequency of a Raman-active rotational or vibrational transition ν_R, then the efficiency of wave mixing is enhanced and signals at $\nu_A = 2\nu_1 - \nu_2$ (anti-Stokes) and $\nu_S = 2\nu_2 - \nu_1$ (Stokes) are produced by wave mixing due to the nonlinear polarization of the medium. While either output signal may be detected, the anti-Stokes frequency is well above ν_1 and has the advantage of being readily separated by optical filtering from the incident beams and fluorescence that may be simultaneously generated in the sample. Although the same spectroscopic transitions, namely, those with frequencies ν_R, are determined from both conventional Raman spectroscopy and CARS, the latter produces signals that have intensities 10^4–10^5 times as great. This enhanced signal level can greatly reduce the time necessary to record a spectrum. Owing to the coherence of the generated signals, the divergence of the output beam is small, and good spatial discrimination against background signals is obtained. Such noise may occur in the examination of molecules undergoing chemiluminescence or existing in either flames or electric discharges. Since the generation of the anti-Stokes signal occurs in a small volume where the two incident beams are focused, sample size does not have to be large. Microlitre-size liquid samples and gases at millitorr pressures can be used. Another advantage of the spatial discrimination available is the ability to examine different regions within a sample. For example, CARS can be used to determine the composition and local temperatures in flames and plasmas. Owing to the near collinearity of the exciting and observing signals, the Doppler effect is minimized and resolution of 0.001 cm^{-1} can be achieved. The primary disadvantage of the technique is the need for laser sources with excellent intensity stabilization.

Anti-Stokes frequencies

Laser magnetic resonance and Stark spectroscopies. Because of the nature of laser-signal generation, most lasers are not tunable over an appreciable frequency range and even those that can be tuned, such as dye lasers, must be driven by a pump laser and for a given dye have a limited tuning range. This limitation can be overcome for molecules that possess permanent magnetic moments or electric dipole moments by using external magnetic or electric fields to bring the energy spacing between levels into coincidence with the frequency of the laser.

Laser magnetic resonance

Molecules that have one or more unpaired electrons will possess permanent magnetic moments. Examples of such paramagnetic systems are free radicals such as NO, OH, and CH_2 and transition-metal ions like $Fe(H_2O)_6^{3+}$ and $Cr(CN)_6^{4-}$. A hypothetical electronic energy-level diagram for a radical having a single unpaired electron and two energy levels, a ground state having zero orbital angular momentum ($L = 0$), and an excited state with $L = 1$

From W. Demtroder, *Laser Spectroscopy* (1981), Springer-Verlag, New York City

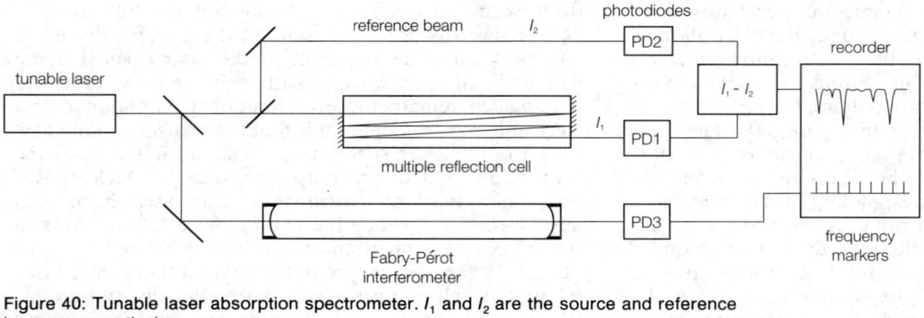

Figure 40: Tunable laser absorption spectrometer. I_1 and I_2 are the source and reference beams, respectively.

is shown in Figure 41. When the magnetic field is increased, the separation of the Zeeman components will shift, and each allowed transition ($\Delta M = 0$ or ± 1, where $M = L + M_S$ [spin angular momentum]) will progressively come into coincidence with the laser frequency and a change in signal intensity will be observed. To enhance the sensitivity of this technique, the sample is often placed inside the laser cavity, and the magnetic field is modulated. By making the laser cavity part of a reacting flow system, the presence of paramagnetic reaction intermediates can be detected and their spectra recorded. Concentrations of paramagnetic species as low as 10^9 molecules per cubic centimetre have been observed. This method has made it possible to identify radicals observed in interstellar space and to provide spectral detail for them.

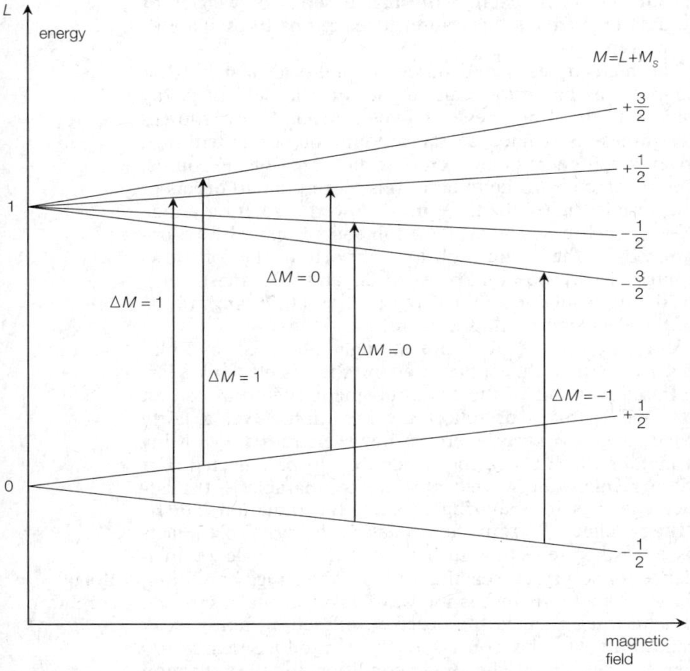

Figure 41: Electronic energy-level diagram for a radical species with one unpaired electron (see text).

An analogous method, called Stark spectroscopy, involves the use of a strong variable electric field to split and vary the spacing of the energy levels of molecules that possess a permanent electric dipole moment. The general principle is embodied in Figure 41, with the substitution of an electric field for the magnetic field. Since very high fields (1,000–5,000 volts per centimetre) are required, the sample must be located between closely spaced metal plates. This precludes the inclusion of the sample inside the laser cavity. Sensitivity is enhanced by modulating the electric field. Although the frequency of the laser can be stabilized and measured to within 20–40 kilohertz, the determination of molecular parameters is limited to the accuracy inherent in the measurement of the electric field—namely, one part in 10^4. This method is useful for the determination of the dipole moment and structure of species whose rotational transitions fall above the microwave region. (J.D.G.)

X-ray and radio-frequency spectroscopy

X-RAY SPECTROSCOPY

A penetrating, electrically uncharged radiation was discovered in 1895 by the German physicist Wilhelm Conrad Röntgen and was named X-radiation because its origin was unknown. This radiation is produced when electrons (cathode rays) strike glass or metal surfaces in high-voltage evacuated tubes and is detected by the fluorescent glow of coated screens and by the exposure of photographic plates and films. The medical applications of such radiation that can penetrate flesh more easily than bone were recognized immediately, and X rays were being used for medical purposes in Vienna within three months of their discovery. Over the next several years, a number of researchers determined that the rays carried no electric charge, traveled in straight trajectories, and had a transverse nature (could be polarized) by scattering from certain materials. These properties suggested that the rays were another form of electromagnetic radiation, a possibility that was postulated earlier by the British physicist J.J. Thomson. He noted that the electrons that hit the glass wall of the tube would undergo violent accelerations as they slowed down, and, according to classical electromagnetism, these accelerations would cause electromagnetic radiation to be produced.

Diffraction of X rays

The first clear demonstration of the wave nature of X rays was provided in 1912 when they were diffracted by the closely spaced atomic planes in a crystal of zinc sulfide. Because the details of the diffraction patterns depended on the wavelength of the radiation, these experiments formed the basis for the spectroscopy of X rays. The first spectrographs for this radiation were devised in 1912–13 by two British physicists—father and son—William Henry and Lawrence Bragg, who showed that there existed not only continuum X-ray spectra, to be expected from processes involving the stopping of charged particles in motion, but also discrete characteristic spectra (each line resulting from the emission of a definite energy), indicating that some X-ray properties are determined by atomic structure. The systematic increase of characteristic X-ray energies with atomic number was shown by the British physicist Henry G.J. Moseley in 1913 to be explainable on the basis of the Bohr theory of atomic structure, but more quantitative agreement between experiment and theory had to await the development of quantum mechanics. Wavelengths for X rays range from about 0.1 to 200 angstroms, with the range 20 to 200 angstroms known as soft X rays.

Relation to atomic structure. X rays can be produced by isolated atoms and ions by two related processes. If two or more electrons are removed from an atom, the remaining outer electrons are more tightly bound to the nucleus by its unbalanced charge, and transitions of these electrons from one level to another can result in the emission of high-energy photons with wavelengths of 100 angstroms or less. An alternate process occurs when an electron in a neutral atom is removed from an inner shell. This removal can be accomplished by bombarding the atom with electrons, protons, or other particles at sufficiently high energy and also by irradiation of the atom by sufficiently energetic X rays. The remaining electrons in the atom readjust very quickly, making transitions to fill the vacancy left by the removed electron, and X-ray photons are emitted in these transitions. The latter process occurs in an ordinary X-ray tube, and the resultant series of X-ray lines, the characteristic spectrum, is superimposed on a spectrum of continuous radiation resulting from accelerated electrons.

The shells in an atom, designated as $n = 1, 2, 3, 4, 5$ by optical spectroscopists, are labeled $K, L, M, N, O \ldots$ by X-ray spectroscopists. If an electron is removed from a particular shell, electrons from all the higher-energy shells can fill that vacancy, resulting in a series that appears inverted as compared with the hydrogen series. Also, the different angular momentum states for a given shell cause energy sublevels within each shell; these subshells are labeled by Roman numerals according to their energies.

The X-ray fluorescence radiation of materials is of considerable practical interest. Atoms irradiated by X rays having sufficient energies, either characteristic or continuous rays, lose electrons and as a result emit X rays characteristic of their own structures. Such methods are used in the analyses of mixtures of unknown composition.

Auger emission

Sometimes an electron with a definite energy is emitted by the atom instead of an X-ray photon when electrons in the outer shells cascade to lower energy states. This process is known as Auger emission. Auger spectroscopy, the analysis of the energy of the emitted electrons when a surface is bombarded by electrons at a few kilovolt energies, is commonly used in surface science to identify the elemental composition of the surface.

If the continuous spectrum from an X-ray source is passed through an absorbing material, it is found that the absorption coefficient changes sharply at X-ray wavelengths corresponding to the energy just required to remove an electron from a specific inner shell to form an ion. The sudden increase of the absorption coefficient as the wavelength is reduced past the shell energy is called an absorption edge; there is an absorption edge associated with each of the inner shells. They are due to the fact that an electron in a particular shell can be excited above the ionization energy of the atom. The X-ray absorption cross section for photon energies capable of ionizing the inner-shell electrons of lead is shown in Figure 42. X-ray absorption edges are useful for determining the elemental composition of solids or liquids (see below *Applications*).

From R.M. Eisberg, *Fundamentals of Modern Physics* (1961), reprinted with permission of John Wiley & Sons, New York City

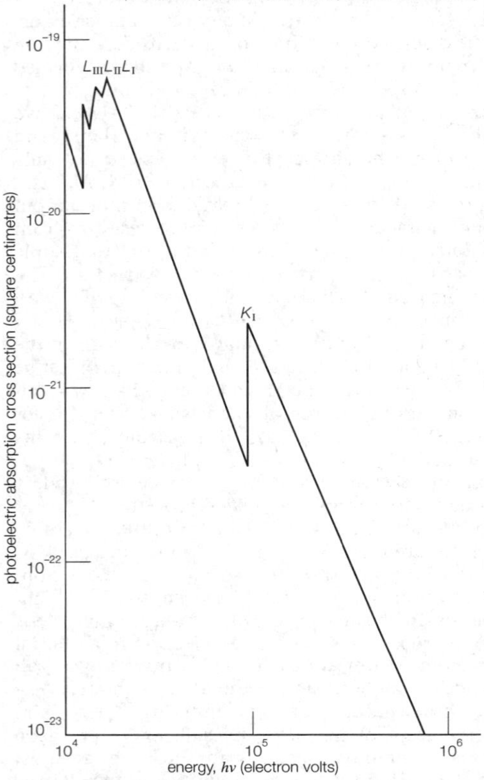

Figure 42: The photoelectric absorption cross section for lead, showing the absorption edges for the innermost shells K_I, L_I, L_{II}, L_{III}.

Production methods. *X-ray tubes.* The traditional method of producing X rays is based on the bombardment of high-energy electrons on a metal target in a vacuum tube. A typical X-ray tube consists of a cathode (a source of electrons, usually a heated filament) and an anode, which are mounted within an evacuated chamber or envelope. A potential difference of 10–100 kilovolts is maintained between cathode (the negative electrode) and anode (the positive electrode). The X-ray spectrum emitted by the anode consists of line emission and a continuous spectrum of radiation called bremsstrahlung radiation. The continuous spectrum results from the violent deceleration of charges (the sudden "braking") of the electrons as they hit the anode. The line emission is due to outer shell electrons falling into inner shell vacancies and hence is determined by the material used to construct the anode. The shortest discrete wavelengths are produced by materials having the highest atomic numbers.

Synchrotron sources. Electromagnetic radiation is emitted by all accelerating charged particles. For electrons moving fairly slowly in a circular orbit, the emission occurs in a dipole radiation pattern highly peaked at the orbiting frequency. If the electrons are made to circulate at highly relativistic speeds (*i.e.*, those near the speed of light, where the kinetic energy of each electron is much higher than the electron rest mass energy), the radiation pattern collapses into a forward beam directed tangent to the orbit and in the direction of the moving electrons. This so-called synchrotron radiation, named after the type of accelerator where this type of radiation was first observed, is continuous and depends on the energy and radius of curvature of the ring; the higher the acceleration, the higher is the energy spectrum.

Synchrotron radiation

The typical synchrotron source consists of a linear electron accelerator that injects high-energy electrons into a storage ring (see PARTICLE ACCELERATORS: *Synchrotrons*). Since the intensity of the synchrotron radiation is proportional to the circulating current, many electron pulses from the injecting accelerator are packed into a single high-current bunch of electrons, and many separate bunches can be made to circulate simultaneously in the storage ring. The radiation can be made even more intense by passing the high-energy electrons (typically a few billion electron volts in energy) through a series of wiggler or undulator magnets that cause the electrons to oscillate or spiral rapidly.

The high intensity and broad tunability of synchrotron sources has had enormous impact on the field of X-ray physics. The brightness of synchrotron X-ray sources (brightness is defined as the amount of power within a given small energy band, cross section area of the source, and divergence of the radiation) is more than 10 orders of magnitude higher than the most powerful rotating anode X-ray machines. The synchrotron sources can also be optimized for the vacuum-ultraviolet portion, the soft (low-energy) X-ray portion (between 20 and 200 angstroms), or the hard (high-energy) X-ray portion (1–20 angstroms) of the electromagnetic spectrum.

X-ray optics. X rays are strongly absorbed by solid matter so that the optics used in the visible and near-infrared portions of the electromagnetic spectrum cannot be used to focus or reflect the radiation. Over a fairly wide range of X-ray energies, however, radiation hitting a metal surface at grazing incidence can be reflected. For X rays where the wavelengths are comparable to the lattice spacings in analyzing crystals, the radiation can be "Bragg reflected" from the crystal: each crystal plane acts as a weakly reflecting surface, but if the angle of incidence θ and crystal spacing d satisfy the Bragg condition, $2d \sin \theta = n\lambda$, where λ is the wavelength of the X ray and n is an integer called the order of diffraction, many weak reflections can add constructively to produce nearly 100 percent reflection. The Bragg condition for the reflection of X rays is similar to the condition for optical reflection from a diffraction grating. Constructive interference occurs when the path difference between successive crystal planes is equal to an integral number of wavelengths of the electromagnetic radiation.

Bragg condition

X-ray monochromators are analogous to grating monochromators and spectrometers in the visible portion of the spectrum. If the lattice spacing for a crystal is accurately known, the observed angles of diffraction can be used to measure and identify unknown X-ray wavelengths. Because of the sensitive wavelength dependence of Bragg reflection exhibited by materials such as silicon, a small portion of a continuous spectrum of radiation can be isolated. Bent single crystals used in X-ray spectroscopy are analogous to the curved line gratings used in optical spectroscopy. The bandwidth of the radiation after it has passed through a high-resolution monochromator can be as narrow as $\Delta\lambda/\lambda = 10^{-4}$, and, by tilting a pair of crystals with respect to the incident radiation, the wavelength of the diffracted radiation can be continuously tuned without changing the direction of the selected light.

For X-ray wavelengths significantly longer than the lattice spacings of crystals, "superlattices" consisting of alternating layers of atoms with high and low atomic numbers can be made to reflect the softer X rays. It is possible to construct these materials where each layer thickness (a layer may consist of hundreds of atoms to a single atom) can be controlled with great precision. Normal-incidence mirrors with more than 40 percent efficiency in the soft X-ray portion of the spectrum have been made using this technology.

Superlattices

X-ray detectors. The first X-ray detector used was photographic film; it was found that silver halide crystallites would darken when exposed to X-ray radiation. Alkali halide crystals such as sodium iodide combined with about 0.1 percent thallium have been found to emit light when X rays are absorbed in the material. These devices are known as scintillators, and when used in conjunction with a photomultiplier tube they can easily detect the burst of light from a single X-ray photon. Furthermore, the amount of light emitted is proportional to the energy of the photon, so that the detector can also be used as a crude X-ray spectrometer. The energy resolution of sodium iodide is on the order of 10 percent of the total energy deposited in the crystal. X-ray photons are readily absorbed by the material; the mean distance that a 0.5-million electron volt (MeV) photon will travel before being absorbed is three centimetres.

Semiconductor crystals such as silicon or germanium are used as X-ray detectors in the range from 1,000 electron volts (1 keV) to more than 1 MeV. An X-ray photon absorbed by the material excites a number of electrons from its valence band to the conduction band. The electrons in the conduction band and the holes in the valence band are collected and measured, with the amount of charge collected being proportional to the energy of the X-ray photon. Extremely pure germanium crystals have an energy resolution of 1 keV and an X-ray energy of 1 MeV.

Low-temperature bolometers are also used as high-resolution X-ray detectors. X rays absorbed in semiconductors and cooled to very low temperatures (approximately 0.1 K or less) deposit a small amount of heat. Because the material has a low heat capacity at those temperatures, there is a measurable rise in temperature. Energy resolution as high as 1 eV out of 10 keV X rays have been obtained.

Ionization chamber

X rays also can be detected by an ionization chamber consisting of a gas-filled container with an anode and a cathode. When an X-ray photon enters the chamber through a thin window, it ionizes the gas inside, and an ion current is established between the two electrodes. The gas is chosen to absorb strongly in the desired wavelength region. With increased voltage applied across the electrodes, the ionization chamber becomes a proportional counter, which produces an amplified electrical pulse when an X-ray photon is absorbed within it. At still higher voltages, absorption of an X-ray photon with consequent ionization of many atoms in the gas initiates a discharge breakdown of the gas and causes a large electric pulse output. This device is known as a Geiger-Müller tube, and it forms the basis for radiation detectors known as Geiger counters (see below *Radiation measurement: Active detectors*).

Edward Rubenstein, Stanford University School of Medicine

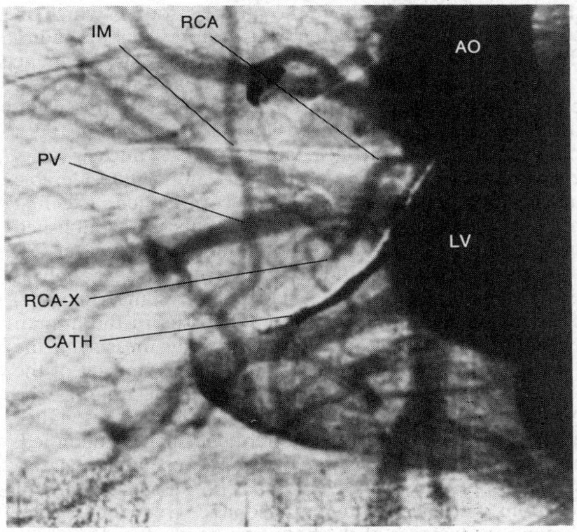

Figure 43: A synchrotron X-ray image of the coronary artery circulation of a human subject taken after an intravenous injection of an iodine-based contrasting agent. The angiogram was taken at the National Synchrotron Light Source (NSLS) at Brookhaven National Laboratory, New York, U.S. A complete blockage of the right coronary artery (RCA) is seen at the position RCA-X. Other structures visualized are the aorta (AO), the left ventricle (LV), a catheter in the right atrium (CATH), pulmonary veins (PV), and the right internal mammary artery (IM).

Applications. The earliest application of X rays was medical: high-density objects such as bones would cast shadows on film that measured the transmission of the X rays through the human body. With the injection of a contrast fluid that contains heavy atoms such as iodine, soft tissue also can be brought into contrast. Synchronized flash X-ray photography, made possible with the intense X rays from a synchrotron source, is shown in Figure 43. The photograph has captured the image of pulsing arteries of the human heart that would have given a blurred image with a conventional X-ray exposure.

A source of X rays of known wavelength also can be used to find the lattice spacing, crystal orientation, and crystal structure of an unknown crystalline material. The crystalline material is placed in a well-collimated beam of X rays, and the angles of diffraction are recorded as a series of spots on photographic film. This method, known as the Laue method (after the German physicist Max Theodor Felix von Laue), has been used to determine and accurately measure the physical structure of many materials, including metals and semiconductors. For more complex structures such as biological molecules, thousands of diffraction spots can be observed, and it is a nontrivial task to unravel the physical structure from the diffraction patterns. The atomic structures of deoxyribonucleic acid (DNA) and hemoglobin were determined through X-ray crystallography. X-ray scattering is also employed to determine near-neighbour distances of atoms in liquids and amorphous solids.

X-ray fluorescence and location of absorption edges can be used to identify quantitatively the elements present in a sample. The innermost core-electron energy levels are not strongly perturbed by the chemical environment of the atom since the electric fields acting on these electrons are completely dominated by the nuclear charge. Thus, regardless of the atom's environment, the X-ray spectra of these electrons have nearly the same energy levels as they would if the atom were in a dilute gas; their atomic energy level fingerprint is not perturbed by the more complex environment. The elemental abundance of a particular element can be determined by measuring the difference in the X-ray absorption just above and just below an absorption edge of that element. Furthermore, if optics are used to focus the X rays onto a small spot on the sample, the spatial location of a particular element can be obtained.

EXAFS

Just above the absorption edge of an element, small oscillations in the absorption coefficient are observed when the incident X-ray energy is varied. In extended X-ray absorption fine structure spectroscopy (EXAFS), interference effects generated by near neighbours of an atom that has absorbed an X ray, and the resulting oscillation frequencies, are analyzed so that distances to the near-neighbour atoms can be accurately determined. The technique is sensitive enough to measure the distance between a single layer of atoms adsorbed on a surface and the underlying substrate.

Emission of X rays from high-temperature laboratory plasmas is used to probe the conditions within them; X-ray spectral measurements show both the composition and temperature of a source. X-ray and gamma-ray astrophysics is also an active area of research. X-ray sources include stars and galactic centres. The most intense astronomical X-ray sources are extremely dense gravitational objects such as neutron stars and black holes. Matter falling toward these objects is heated to temperatures as high as 10^{10} K, resulting in X-ray and soft gamma-ray emissions. Because X rays are absorbed by the Earth's atmosphere, such measurements are made above the atmosphere by apparatus carried by balloons, rockets, or orbiting satellites.

RADIO-FREQUENCY SPECTROSCOPY

The energy states of atoms, ions, molecules, and other particles are determined primarily by the mutual attraction of the electrons and the nucleus and by the mutual repulsion of the electrons. Electrons and nuclei have magnetic properties in addition to these electrostatic properties. The spin-orbit interaction has been discussed above (see *Foun-*

dations of atomic spectra: Hydrogen atom states). Other, usually weaker, magnetic interactions within the atom exist between the magnetic moments of different electrons and between the magnetic moment of each electron and the orbital motions of others. Energy differences between levels having different energies owing to magnetic interactions vary from less than 10^7 hertz to more than 10^{13} hertz, being generally greater for heavy atoms.

Origins. Nuclei of atoms often have intrinsic angular momentum (spin) and magnetic moments because of the motions and intrinsic magnetic moments of their constituents, and the interactions of nuclei with the magnetic fields of the circulating electrons affect the electron energy states. As a result, an atomic level that consists of several states having the same energy when the nucleus is nonmagnetic may be split into several closely spaced levels when the nucleus has a magnetic moment. The levels will have different energies, depending on the relative orientation of the nucleus and the magnetic field produced by the surrounding electrons. This additional structure of an atom's levels or of spectral lines caused by the magnetic properties of its nucleus is called magnetic hyperfine structure. Separations between levels differing only in the relative orientation of the magnetic field of the nucleus and electron range typically from 10^6 hertz to 10^{10} hertz.

Magnetic hyperfine structure

Atoms, ions, and molecules can make transitions from one state to another state that differs in energy because of one or more of these magnetic effects. Molecules also undergo transitions between rotational and vibrational states. Such transitions either can be spontaneous or can be induced by the application of appropriate external electromagnetic fields at the resonant frequencies. Transitions also can occur in atoms, molecules, and ions between high-energy electronic states near the ionization limit. The resulting spectra are known as radio-frequency (rf) spectra, or microwave spectra; they are observed typically in the frequency range from 10^6 to 10^{11} hertz.

The spontaneous transition rate as an atom goes from an excited level to a lower one varies roughly as the cube of the frequency of the transition. Thus, radio-frequency and microwave transitions occur spontaneously much less rapidly than do transitions at visible and ultraviolet frequencies. As a result, most radio-frequency and microwave spectroscopy is done by forcing a sample of atoms to absorb radiation instead of waiting for it to emit radiation spontaneously. These methods are facilitated by the availability of powerful electronic oscillators throughout this frequency range. The principal exception occurs in the field of radio astronomy; the number of atoms or ions in an astronomical source is large enough so that spontaneous emission spectra may be collected by large antennas and then amplified and detected by cooled, low-noise electronic devices.

Methods. The first measurements of the absorption spectra of molecules for the purpose of finding magnetic moments were made in the late 1930s by an American physicist, Isidor Rabi, and his collaborators, using molecular and atomic beams. A beam focused by magnets in the absence of a radio-frequency field was defocused and lost when atoms were induced to make transitions to other states. The radio-frequency or microwave spectrum was taken by measuring the number of atoms that remained focused in the apparatus while the frequency was varied. One of the most famous laboratory experiments with radio-frequency spectra was performed in 1947 by two American physicists, Willis Lamb and Robert Retherford. Their experiment measured the energy difference between two nearly coincident levels in hydrogen, designated as $2^2S_{1/2}$ and $2^2P_{1/2}$. Although optical measurements had indicated that these levels might differ in energy, the measurements were complex and were open to alternative interpretations. Atomic theory at the time predicted that those levels should have identical energies. Lamb and Retherford showed that the energy levels were in fact separated by about 1,058 megahertz; hence the theory was incomplete. This energy separation in hydrogen, known as the Lamb shift, contributed to the development of quantum electrodynamics.

The Lamb shift

Radio-frequency measurements of energy intervals in ground levels and excited levels of atoms can be made by placing a sample of atoms (usually a vapour in a glass cell) within the coil of an oscillator and tuning the device until a change is seen in the absorption of energy from the oscillator by the atoms. In the method known as optical double resonance, optical radiation corresponding to a transition in the atom of interest is passed through the cell. If radio-frequency radiation is absorbed by the atoms in either of the levels involved, the intensity, polarization, or direction of the fluorescent light may be changed. In this way a sensitive optical measurement indicates whether or not a radio-frequency interval in the atom matches the frequency applied by the oscillator.

Microwave amplification by stimulated emission of radiation (the maser) was invented by an American physicist, Charles Townes, and two Russian physicists, Nikolai Basov and Alexandr Prokhorov, in 1951 and 1952, and stimulated the invention of the laser. If atoms are placed in a cavity tuned to the transition between two atomic levels such that there are more atoms in the excited state than in the ground state, they can be induced to transfer their excess energy into the electromagnetic radiation resonant in the cavity. This radiation, in turn, stimulates more atoms in the excited state to emit radiation. Thus an oscillator is formed that resonates at the atomic frequency.

Microwave frequencies between atomic states can be measured with extraordinary precision. The energy difference between the hyperfine levels of the ground state in the cesium atom is currently the standard time interval. One atomic second is defined as the time it takes for the cesium frequency to oscillate 9,192,631,770 times. Such atomic clocks have a longer-term uncertainty in their frequency that is less than one part in 10^{13}. Measurement of time intervals based on the cesium atom's oscillations are more accurate than those based on Earth rotation since friction caused by the tides and the atmosphere is slowing down the rotation rate (*i.e.,* our days and nights are becoming slightly longer). Since an international time scale based on an atomic-clock time standard has been established, "leap seconds" must be periodically introduced to the scale known as Coordinated Universal Time (UTC) to keep the "days" in synchronism with the more accurate atomic clocks.

Measurement of time intervals

In those atoms in which the nucleus has a magnetic moment, the energies of the electrons depend slightly on the orientation of the nucleus relative to the magnetic field produced by the electrons near the centre of the atom. The magnetic field at the nucleus depends somewhat on the environment in which the atom is found, which in turn depends on the neighbouring atoms. Thus the radio-frequency spectrum of a substance's nuclear magnetic moments reflects both the constituents and the forms of chemical binding in the substance. Spectra resulting when the orientation of the nucleus is made to oscillate by a time-varying magnetic field are known as nuclear magnetic-resonance (NMR) spectra and are of considerable utility in identification of organic compounds. The first nuclear magnetic resonance experiments were published independently in 1946 by two American physicists, Edward Purcell and Felix Bloch. A powerful medical application of NMR spectroscopy, magnetic resonance imaging, is used to allow visualization of soft tissue in the human body. This technique is accomplished by measuring the NMR signal in a magnetic field that varies in each of the three dimensions. Through the use of pulse techniques, the NMR signal strength of the proton (hydrogen) resonance as a function of the resonance frequency can be obtained, and a three-dimensional image of the proton-resonance signal can be constructed. Because body tissue at different locations will have a different resonance frequency, three-dimensional images of the body can be produced.

Magnetic resonance imaging

Radio-frequency transitions have been observed in astronomy. Observation of the 21-centimetre (1,420-megahertz) transition between the hyperfine levels in the ground level of hydrogen have provided much information about the temperature and density of hydrogen clouds in the Sun's galaxy, the Milky Way Galaxy. Charged particles spiraling in galactic magnetic fields emit synchrotron radiation in the radio and microwave regions. Intergalactic molecules and radicals have been identified in radio-astronomy spectroscopy, and naturally occurring masers have been observed. The three-degree blackbody spectrum that is the remnant of the big bang creation of the universe (see above) covers the microwave and far-infrared portion of the electromagnetic spectrum. Rotating neutron stars that emit a narrow beam of radio-frequency radiation (much like the rotating beam of a lighthouse) are observed through the reception of highly periodic pulses of radio-frequency radiation. These pulsars have been used as galactic clocks to study other phenomena. By studying the spin-down rate of a pulsar in close orbit with a companion star, Joseph Taylor, an American astrophysicist, was able to show that a significant amount of the rotational energy lost was due to the emission of gravitational radiation. The existence of gravitational radiation is predicted by Einstein's general theory of relativity but has not yet been seen directly.

(J.O.S./St.C.)

Resonance-ionization spectroscopy

Resonance-ionization spectroscopy (RIS) is an extremely sensitive and highly selective analytical measurement method. It employs lasers to eject electrons from selected types of atoms or molecules, splitting the neutral species into a positive ion and a free electron with a negative charge. Those ions or electrons are then detected and counted by various means to identify elements or compounds and determine their concentration in a sample.

Advantages of RIS

The RIS method was originated in the 1970s and is now used in a growing number of applications to advance knowledge in physics, chemistry, and biology. It is applied in a wide variety of practical measurement systems because it offers the combined advantages of high selectivity between different types of atoms and sensitivity at the one-atom level.

Applications of a simple atom counter include physical and chemical studies of defined populations of atoms. More advanced systems incorporate various forms of mass spectrometers, which offer the additional feature of isotopic selectivity. These more elaborate RIS systems can be used, for instance, to date lunar materials and meteorites, study old groundwater and ice caps, measure the neutrino output of the Sun, determine trace elements in electronic-grade materials, search for resources such as oil, gold, and platinum, study the role of trace elements in medicine and biology, determine DNA structure, and address a number of environmental problems.

IONIZATION PROCESSES

Basic energy considerations. A basic understanding of atomic structure is necessary for the study of resonance ionization (see above *Foundations of atomic spectra: Basic atomic structure*). Unless an atom is subjected to some external influence, it will be in the state of lowest energy (ground state) in which the electrons systematically fill all the orbits from those nearest the nucleus outward to some larger orbit containing the outermost (valence) electrons. A valence electron can be promoted to an orbit even farther from the nucleus if it absorbs a photon.

Photon absorption

To initiate the excitation, the photon must have an energy that lies within a very narrow range, as the energies of all the orbits surrounding the nucleus, including the unfilled ones, are rigorously prescribed by quantum mechanics. Each element has its own unique set of energy levels, which is the foundation for both emission spectroscopy and absorption spectroscopy. Ionization of an atom occurs when an electron is completely stripped from the atom and ejected into the ionization continuum. The gap between energy possessed by an atom in its ground state and the energy level at the edge of the ionization continuum is the ionization potential.

The photon energies used in the resonance (stepwise) ionization of an atom (or molecule) are too low to ionize the atom directly from its ground state; thus at least two steps are used. The first absorption is a resonance process as illustrated in the examples in Figure 44, and this assures that the ionization will not be observed unless the laser is tuned to the atom—*i.e.,* operating at the appropriate wavelength. Quantum mechanics does not restrict the energy of free electrons in the continuum, and so a photon of any minimum energy can be absorbed to complete the resonance-ionization process.

With certain pulsed lasers, the two-photon RIS process can be saturated so that one electron is removed from each atom of the selected type. Furthermore, ionization detectors can be used to sense a single electron or positive ion. Therefore, individual atoms can be counted. By taking advantage of tunable laser technology to implement a variety of RIS schemes, it is feasible to detect almost every atom in the periodic table. The combined features of selectivity, sensitivity, and generality make RIS suitable for a wide variety of applications.

RIS schemes. A simple scheme in which two photons from the same laser cause resonance ionization of an atom is illustrated in Figure 44. A single wavelength must be chosen to excite the atom from its ground state to an excited state, while the second photon completes the ionization process. For example, to achieve resonance ionization in the cesium atom that has an ionization potential of only 3.9 electron volts, the scheme of Figure 44A works well with a single-colour laser at the wavelength of 459.3 nanometres, or a photon energy of about 2.7 electron volts. (Photon energies and atomic energy levels are given in units of electron volts [eV], or in wavelength units of nanometres [nm]. A useful and approximate relationship between the two is easy to remember since eV = 1,234/nm.) Similar schemes have been used for other alkali atoms because these atoms also have low ionization potentials.

For most atoms, more elaborate resonance-ionization schemes than the simple two-step process shown in Figure 44A are required. The higher the ionization potential of the atom, the more complex is the process. For example, the inert element krypton has an ionization potential of 14.0 electron volts and requires a more elaborate RIS scheme of the type shown in Figure 44B. The first step is a resonance transition at the wavelength of 116.5 nanometres, followed by a second resonance step at 558.1 nanometres. Subsequent ionization of this second excited state is accomplished with a long wavelength, such as 1,064 nanometres. Generation of the 116.5-nanometre radiation requires a complex laser scheme. Another useful type of RIS scheme is shown in Figure 44C. In this method the atom is excited to a level very near the ionization continuum and exists in a so-called Rydberg state.

Rydberg states

In such a state the electron has been promoted to an orbit that is so far from the nucleus that it is scarcely bound. Even an electric field of moderate strength can be pulsed to remove the electron and complete the resonance-ionization process. With the schemes discussed above and reasonable variations of them, all the elements in nature can

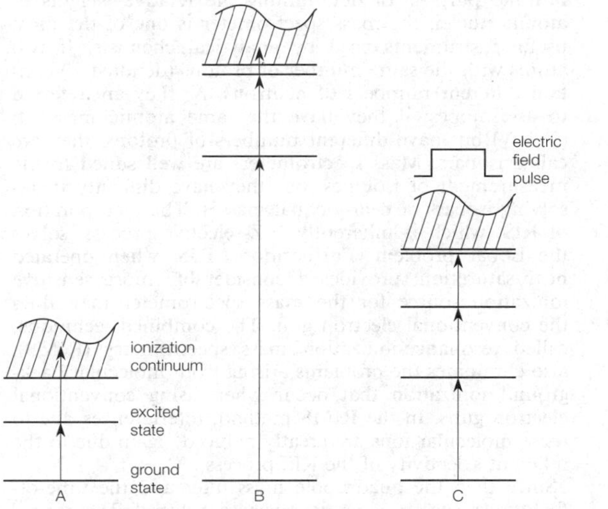

Figure 44: *Resonance-ionization schemes.*
Photons from lasers are tuned so that their frequencies, hence energies, just match allowable transition energies for electrons in a selected atom (see text).

be detected with RIS except for two of the inert gases—helium and neon.

Lasers for RIS. The essential components of RIS methods are tunable lasers, which can be of either the pulsed or the continuous-wave variety. Pulsed lasers are more frequently used since they can add time resolution to a measurement system. In addition, pulsed lasers produce high peak power, permitting the efficient use of nonlinear optics to generate short-wavelength radiations. For example, in frequency doubling, photons of frequency ω_1 incident to a crystal will emerge from the crystal with frequencies ω_1 and $2\omega_1$, where the component $2\omega_1$ can have a large fraction of the intensity of ω_1. Nonlinear processes are efficient when laser beams are intense, a condition that favours pulsed lasers but that does not exclude the use of certain types of continuous-wave lasers. For each atom, the volume that can be saturated in the RIS process depends on the laser energy per pulse and other aspects of the laser.

Practical information on a wide variety of useful lasers can be obtained by consulting references listed in the *Bibliography.*

ATOM COUNTING

The concept of the atom is an ancient one; the Greek philosopher Democritus (*c.* 460–*c.* 370 BC) proposed a form of "atomism" that contained the essential features of the chemical atom later introduced by the British chemist John Dalton in 1810. The British physicist Ernest Rutherford spoke of counting the atoms and in 1908, with the German physicist Hans Geiger, disclosed the first electrical detector for ionizing radiations. The development of wavelength-tunable lasers has made it possible to carry out Rutherford's concept of counting atoms. As stated above, RIS can be used to remove one electron from each of the atoms of a selected type, and the modern version of the electrical detector, known as the proportional counter, can even be made to count a single electron. Thus, all that is required for the most elementary form of atom counting is to pulse the proper laser beam through a proportional counter.

Detection of cesium atoms

Experimental demonstrations of atom counting can be performed by introducing low concentrations of cesium vapour into proportional counters, commonly used for nuclear radiation detection, that contain a "counting" gas composed of a mixture of argon and methane. Pulsed laser beams used to implement the RIS scheme of Figure 44A can be directed through a proportional counter, as shown in Figure 45, to detect individual atoms of cesium without interference from the much larger number of argon atoms and methane molecules.

RESONANCE-IONIZATION MASS SPECTROMETRY

For the purpose of determining the relative weights of atomic nuclei, the mass spectrometer is one of the most useful instruments used by analytical chemists. If two atoms with the same number of protons (denoted Z) contain different numbers of neutrons, N, they are referred to as isotopes; if they have the same atomic mass, A, $(Z+N)$ but have different numbers of protons, they are called isobars. Mass spectrometers are well suited to the measurement of isotopes, but they have difficulty in resolving isobars of nearly equal masses. The incorporation of RIS, which is inherently a Z-selective process, solves the isobar problem. Furthermore, RIS, when operated near saturation, provides a considerably more sensitive ionization source for the mass spectrometer than does the conventional electron gun. The combined technique, called resonance-ionization mass spectrometry (RIMS), also eliminates the problems arising from molecular background ionization that occur when using conventional electron guns. In the RIMS method, interferences due to these molecular ions are greatly reduced, again due to the inherent selectivity of the RIS process.

Since then the quadrupole mass filter and the time-of-flight mass spectrometer have been developed. These three types have been built into RIMS systems (see above *Mass spectrometry*).

As discussed above, RIS can be applied to the inert, or

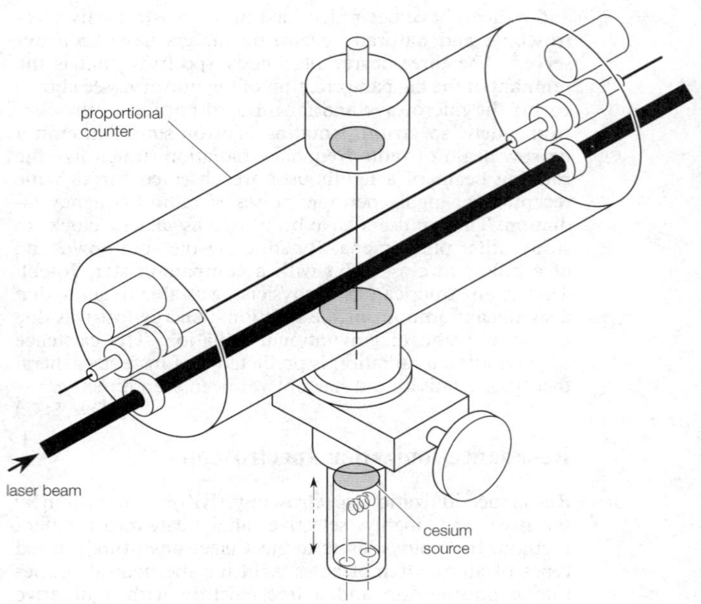

Figure 45: *Apparatus for atom counting.*
By directing a pulsed laser through a proportional counter, the few cesium atoms introduced can be counted individually.

By permission of Oak Ridge National Laboratory, managed by Martin Marietta Energy Systems, Inc., for the U.S. Department of Energy under Contract No. DE-AC05-840R21400

Noble gas detection

noble, gases only with great difficulty due to the short wavelength required for the first excitation step. The detection of specific isotopes of the noble gases, such as krypton-81 (^{81}Kr), is quite important. Consequently, the system shown in Figure 46 was developed to demonstrate that RIS can be used for counting small numbers of krypton-81 atoms. The purpose of this apparatus is essentially to carry out the concept of the sorting demon introduced by the Scottish physicist James Clerk Maxwell, which was of considerable interest to physicists in the late 1800s in connection with the second law of thermodynamics, or the entropy principle. Thus, the experimental objective is to detect all the krypton-81 atoms and count them individually, even when mixed with enormously larger numbers of krypton-82 atoms, other isotopes of krypton, and many other types of atoms or molecules. The scheme involves first achieving Z-selectivity using RIS to sort krypton, followed with A-selectivity using the quadrupole mass filter. It is necessary to include an "atom buncher" to increase the chance that a krypton atom will be in the laser beam when the beam is pulsed through the apparatus. The atom buncher consists of a surface held near the temperature of liquid helium to condense the krypton atoms and another pulsed laser to heat the surface just prior to the application of the RIS laser pulse. Following resonance ionization, the inert atoms are implanted into the detector, which removes them from the vacuum portion of the apparatus where they were initially confined. As each ion is implanted, a small number of electrons are emitted, and these pulses are counted to determine the number of implanted atoms. The process is continued until nearly all the krypton-81 atoms are counted. Variations of the design of this apparatus have included implementing a time-of-flight mass spectrometer for the selection of krypton-81 or another isotope.

Atom buncher

Because of the long radioactive-decay half-life (210,000 years) of krypton-81, it is impossible to determine small numbers of these atoms by decay counting. Because the RIS method can count the small numbers of krypton-81 atoms, it can be used for dating polar ice to obtain histories of the climate to about one million years ago and also for studying the history of glaciers. Dating of groundwater up to one million years old is an important application for the study of hydrology and for knowledge on the safe deposition of nuclear wastes. Also, analysis of krypton-81, along with at least one of the stable isotopes of krypton, provides a method for obtaining the cosmic-ray exposure ages of lunar materials and meteorites.

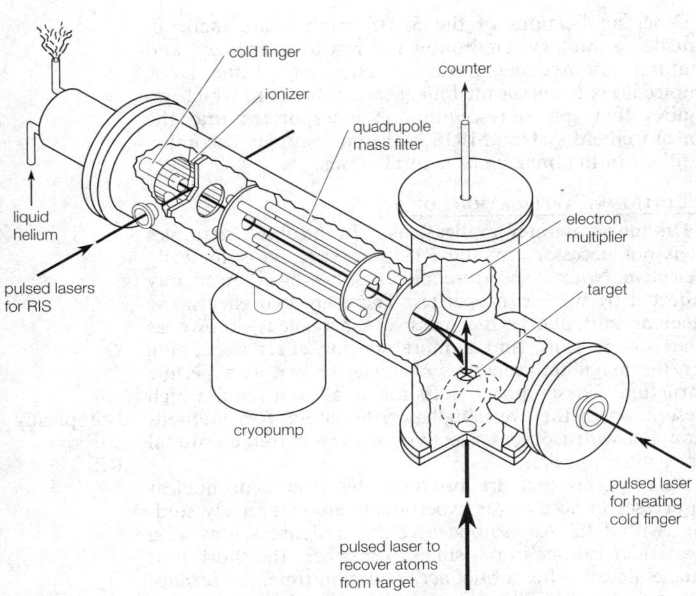

Figure 46: *Resonance-ionization mass spectroscopy system.* The selectivity and sensitivity of RIS make it possible to sort out and count a small number of noble gas atoms, such as krypton-81, in this device that works much like the sorting demon visualized by James Clerk Maxwell (see text).

By permission of Oak Ridge National Laboratory, managed by Martin Marietta Energy Systems, Inc., for the U.S. Department of Energy under Contract No. DE-AC05-840R21400

Radiochemical experiments, conducted deep beneath the Earth's surface to shield out cosmic rays, have revealed much new information about the Sun and about the properties of neutrinos (electrically neutral, virtually massless particles) emitted from its active core. In large vats filled with solutions rich in chlorine atoms, the flux from the boron-8 (^{8}B) source of solar neutrinos can convert a few of the chlorine-37 (^{37}Cl) atoms to argon-37 (^{37}Ar) atoms with a half-life of 35 days. These atoms can then be detected by nuclear decay counting to determine the flux of the high-energy neutrinos striking the Earth. A similar experiment for detecting the much larger flux of the beryllium-7 (^{7}Be) neutrinos of lower energy can now be done because of the ability to count a small number of krypton-81 atoms produced by neutrino capture in bromine-81 (^{81}Br). Since the atoms are counted directly without waiting for radioactive decay, the 210,000-year half-life of krypton-81 is not an impediment.

Neutrino detection

RIS ATOMIZATION METHODS

Thermal atomization. Because the RIS technique is limited to the study of free atoms or molecules in the gas phase, the analysis of solids and liquids requires a means for releasing atoms from the bulk material. A simple and effective system in which samples are atomized with a graphite oven is illustrated in Figure 47. A small solid or liquid sample is placed into the graphite oven, which is electrically heated to more than 2,000° C. As the sample evaporates, it dissociates into a plume containing free atoms, some of which are ionized with pulsed RIS. In the illustration of Figure 47, a RIS scheme similar to that of Figure 44C is used, in which the final stage in the ionization process is accomplished by pulsing an electric field onto the atoms in a high Rydberg state. Following ion extraction, mass analysis is performed with a time-of-flight technique to eliminate isobars and unwanted molecular ion fragments.

Substantial work is accomplished with thermal atomization methods. With detection limits of less than one part per trillion, the graphite furnace version can be installed aboard ships to explore the ocean for noble metals such as gold, platinum, and rhodium. In another important application to the Earth sciences, the furnace technique is used to study the rhodium content of geologic samples associated with the great Mesozoic extinction of 65 million years ago. Correlation of the concentrations of rhodium and iridium, the latter determined by neutron-activation analysis (see below *Radiation measurement*), has provided much support to the theory that the high concentration of iridium found in the Cretaceous-Tertiary boundary was caused by a large body of cosmic origin falling on the Earth. Analysis of samples taken from this boundary show that the ratio of iridium to rhodium is about the same as the ratio found in meteorites, and this strengthens the theory that a cosmic body striking the Earth caused mass extinction of the biological species associated with the Mesozoic Era, including the dinosaurs.

Filamentary heating methods also are utilized for important geologic research. For instance, the age of rocks is determined by measuring the amounts of isotopes of rhenium and osmium. The isotope rhenium-187 (^{187}Re) decays to osmium-187 (^{187}Os) having a half-life of 43 billion years; hence, the Re-Os system can be used to determine when geologic materials were solidified in the Earth.

Thermal techniques are producing significant practical results in the exploration of natural resources, medical research and treatment, and environmental research. An especially impressive example of exploration is taking place in China, where RIS is used to sample gold, platinum, and other precious metals in water streams to locate ore deposits. Since the average concentration of gold in fresh water is only 0.03 parts per billion, the analytical methods employed must be extremely sensitive and selective against other species in the sample.

Exploration of natural resources

Sputter atomization. When energetic particles (such as 20-keV [thousand electron volts] argon ions) strike the surface of a solid, neutral atoms and secondary charged particles are ejected from the target in a process called sputtering. In the secondary ion mass spectrometry (SIMS) method, these secondary ions are used to gain information about the target material (see above *Mass spectrometry: General principles: Ion sources*). In contrast, the sputter-initiated RIS (SIRIS) method takes advantage of the much more numerous neutral atoms emitted in the sputtering process. In SIRIS devices the secondary ions are rejected because the yield of these ions can be greatly affected by the composition of the host material (known as the matrix effect). Ion sputtering, in contrast to thermal atomization, can be turned on or off in short pulses; for this reason, good temporal overlap with the RIS beams is achievable. This feature allows better utilization of small samples.

Analysis of high-purity semiconducting materials for the electronics industry is one of the principal applications of the SIRIS method. The method can detect, for example, indium in silicon at the one part per trillion level. The high efficiency of the pulsed sputtering method makes it possible to record one count due to indium at the de-

Applications of SIRIS

By permission of the Institute of Spectroscopy of the Russian Academy of Sciences

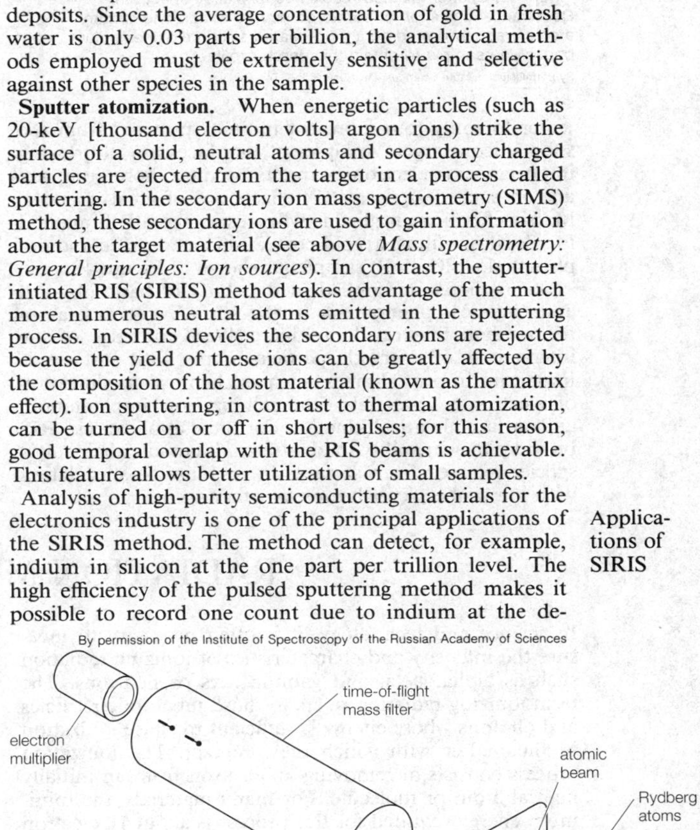

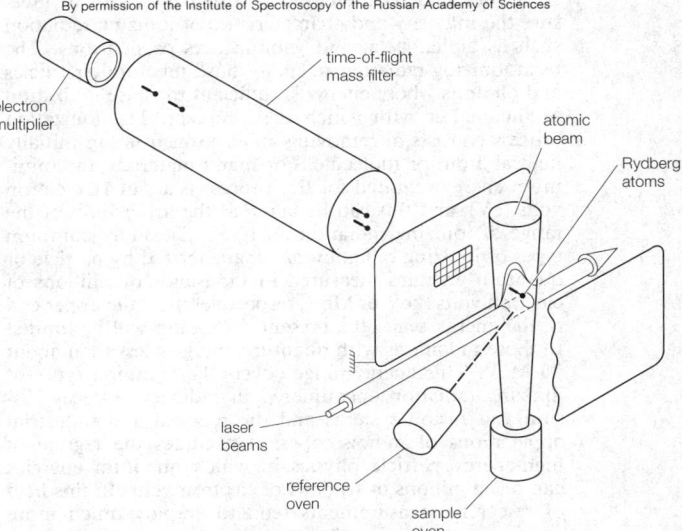

Figure 47: *RIS system using thermal atomization.* A graphite oven, such as the one incorporated in this system, is an effective apparatus for atomizing liquid or solid samples that are to undergo RIS analysis. The low-detection limits enable analysis of low-concentration levels of most of the elements.

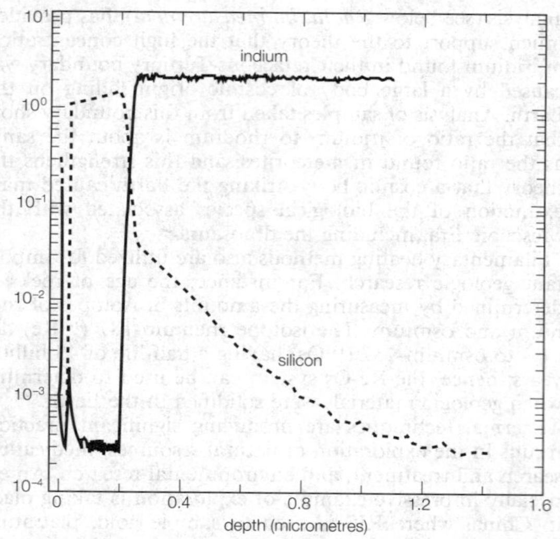

Figure 48: Sputter-initiated resonance-ionization spectrum. Resonance ionization of sputtered neutral silicon and indium atoms was performed on a gold-coated silicon dioxide–indium phosphide sample to obtain this depth profile.

By permission of Atom Sciences, Inc., Oak Ridge, Tenn.

tector for only four atoms of indium sputtered from the solid silicon target. Analyses of interfaces are of growing importance as electronic circuits become more compact, and in such designs matrix effects are of great concern. Matrix effects are negligible when using the SIRIS method for depth-profiling a gold-coated silicon dioxide–indium phosphide (SiO_2/InP) sample, as shown in Figure 48.

RIS methods are applied in the study of basic physical and chemical phenomena in the surface sciences, as in the method illustrated in Figure 49. Knowledge of the interactions of energetic particle beams with surfaces is important in several areas, such as chemical modification of electronics materials, ion etching, ion implantation, and surface chemical kinetics. For these applications, RIS provides the capability to identify and measure the neutral species released from surfaces in response to stimulation with ion probes, laser beams, or other agents.

Other applications of the SIRIS method are made in medicine, biology, environmental research, geology, and natural resource exploration. Sequencing of the DNA molecule is a significant biological application, which requires that spatial resolution be incorporated into the measurement system. SIRIS is also increasingly becoming utilized in the imaging of neutral atoms.

ADDITIONAL APPLICATIONS OF RIS

On-line accelerator applications. In the above examples it is not necessary for the RIS process to be isotopically selective. Normal spectroscopic lines, however, are slightly affected by nuclear properties. There are two effects: the general shift due to the mass of the nucleus, known as the isotope shift, and a more specific effect depending on the magnetic properties of nuclei known as hyperfine structure. These optical shifts are small and require high resolution in the wavelengths of the lasers. RIS methods coupled with isotopic selectivity can be extremely useful in nuclear physics.

Isotopically selective RIS

Rare species that are produced by atomic or nuclear processes in accelerator experiments are extensively studied with RIS. An isotope accelerator delivers ions of a particular isotope into a small oven where the short-lived nuclei decay. After a brief accumulation time, the furnace creates an atomic beam containing the decay products. These decay products are then subjected to the RIS process followed by time-of-flight analysis of the ions. Analysis of the optical shifts leads to information on magnetic moments of nuclei and on the mean square radii of the nuclear charges. Such measurements have been performed on several hundred rare species, and these studies continue at various laboratories principally in Europe, the United States, and Japan.

Molecular applications. While most applications of RIS have been made with free atoms, molecular studies are increasingly important. With simple diatomic molecules such as carbon monoxide (CO) or nitric oxide (NO), the RIS schemes are not fundamentally different from their atomic counterparts, except that molecular spectroscopy is more complex and must be understood in detail for routine RIS applications. On the other hand, RIS itself is a powerful tool for the study of molecular spectroscopy, even for the study of complex organic molecules of biological importance. (G.S.Hu.)

RADIATION MEASUREMENT

In science and technology, it is often necessary to measure the intensity and characteristics of ionizing radiation such as alpha, beta, and gamma rays or neutrons. The term ionizing radiation refers to those subatomic particles and photons whose energy is sufficient to cause ionization in the matter with which they interact. The ionization process consists of removing an electron from an initially neutral atom or molecule. For many materials, the minimum energy required for this process is about 10 electron volts (eV), and this can be taken as the lower limit of the range of ionizing radiation energies. The more common types of ionizing radiation are characterized by particle or quantum energies measured in thousands or millions of electron volts (keV or MeV, respectively). At the upper end of the energy scale, the present discussion will be limited to those radiations with quantum energies less than about 20 MeV. This energy range covers the common types of ionizing radiation encountered in radioactive decay, fission and fusion systems and the medical and industrial applications of radioisotopes. It excludes the regime of high-energy particle physics in which quantum energies can reach billions or trillions of electron volts. In this field of research, measurements tend to employ much more massive and specialized detectors than those in common use for the lower-energy radiations.

RADIATION INTERACTIONS IN MATTER

For the purposes of this discussion, it is convenient to divide the various types of ionizing radiation into two major categories: those that carry an electric charge and those that do not. In the first group are the radiations that are normally viewed as individual subatomic charged particles. Such radiation appears, for example, as the alpha particles that are spontaneously emitted in the decay of certain unstable heavy nuclei. These alpha particles consist of two protons and two neutrons and carry a positive electrical charge of two units. Another example is the beta-minus radiation also emitted in the decay of some radioactive nuclei. In this case, each nuclear decay produces a fast electron that carries a negative charge of one unit. In contrast, there are other types of ionizing radiation that carry no electrical charge. Common examples are gamma rays, which can be represented as high-frequency electromagnetic photons, and neutrons, which are classically pictured as subatomic particles carrying no electrical charge. In the discussions below, the term quantum will generally be used to represent a single particle or photon, regardless of its type.

Alpha particles

Only charged radiations interact continuously with matter, and they are therefore the only types of radiation that are directly detectable in the devices described here. In contrast, uncharged quanta must first undergo a major interaction that transforms all or part of their energy into secondary charged radiations. Properties of the original uncharged radiations can then be inferred by studying the charged particles that are produced. These major interactions occur only rarely, so it is not unusual for an uncharged radiation to travel distances of many centime-

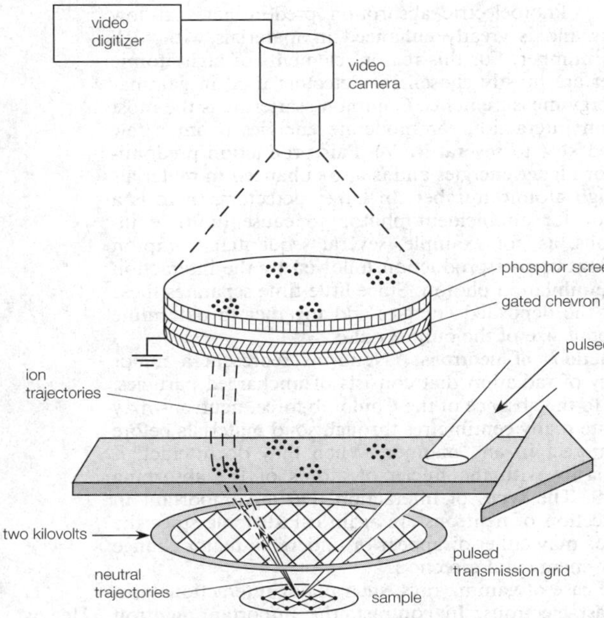

Figure 49: *RIS apparatus for basic studies of surface physics and chemistry.*
A multichannel plate (MCP) is used to measure angular distributions of energy-selected neutral atoms emitted from surfaces irradiated with argon ions (Ar^+).
By permission of Pennsylvania State University

tres through solid materials before such an interaction occurs. Instruments that are designed for the efficient detection of these uncharged quanta therefore tend to have relatively large thicknesses to increase the probability of observing the results of such an interaction within the detector volume.

Interactions of heavy charged particles. The term heavy charged particle refers to those energetic particles whose mass is one atomic mass unit or greater. This category includes alpha particles, together with protons, deuterons, fission fragments, and other energetic heavy particles often produced in accelerators. These particles carry at least one electronic charge, and they interact with matter primarily through the Coulomb force that exists between the positive charge on the particle and the negative charge on electrons that are part of the absorber material. In this case, the force is an attractive one between the two opposite charges. As a charged particle passes near an electron in the absorber, it transfers a small fraction of its momentum to the electron. As a result, the charged particle slows down slightly, and the electron (which originally was nearly at rest) picks up some of its kinetic energy. At any given time, the charged particle is simultaneously interacting with many electrons in the absorber material, and the net result of all the Coulomb forces acts like a viscous drag on the particle. From the instant it enters the absorber, the particle slows down continuously until it is brought to a stop. Because the charged particle is thousands of times more massive than the electrons with which it is interacting, it is deflected relatively little from a straight-line path as it comes to rest. The time that elapses before the particle is stopped ranges from a few picoseconds (1×10^{-12} second) in solids or liquids to a few nanoseconds (1×10^{-9} second) in gases. These times are short enough that the stopping time can be considered to be instantaneous for many purposes, and this approximation is assumed in the following sections that describe the response of radiation detectors.

Stopping time

Several characteristics of the particle-deceleration process are important in understanding the behaviour of radiation detectors. First, the average distance traveled by the particle before it stops is called its mean range. For a given material, the mean range increases with increasing initial kinetic energy of the charged particle. Typical values for charged particles with initial energies of a few MeV are tens or hundreds of micrometres in solids or liquids and a few centimetres in gases at ordinary temperature and pressure. A second property is the specific energy loss at a given point along the particle track (path). This quantity measures the differential energy deposited per unit path-length (dE/dx) in the material; it is also a function of the particle energy. In general, as the particle slows down and loses energy, the dE/dx value tends to increase. Thus, the density with which energy is being deposited in the absorber along the particle's track tends to increase as it slows down. The average dE/dx value for charged particles is relatively large because of their short range, and they are often referred to as high dE/dx radiations.

Interactions of fast electrons. Energetic electrons (such as beta-minus particles), since they carry an electric charge, also interact with electrons in the absorber material through the Coulomb force. In this case, the force is a repulsive rather than an attractive one, but the net results are similar to those observed for heavy charged particles. The fast electron experiences the cumulative effect of many simultaneous Coulomb forces, and undergoes a continuous deceleration until it is stopped. As compared with a heavy charged particle, the distance traveled by the fast electron is many times greater for an equivalent initial energy. For example, a beta particle with an initial energy of 1 MeV travels one or two millimetres in typical solids and several metres in gases at standard conditions. Also, since a fast electron has a much smaller mass than a heavy charged particle, it is much more easily deflected along its path. A typical fast-electron track deviates considerably from a straight line, and deflections through large angles are not uncommon. Because a fast electron will travel perhaps 100 times as far in a given material as a heavy charged particle with the same initial energy, its energy is much less densely deposited along its track. For this reason, fast electrons are often referred to as low dE/dx radiations.

There is one other significant difference in the energy loss of fast electrons as compared with that of heavy charged particles. While undergoing large-angle deflections, fast electrons can radiate part of their energy in the form of electromagnetic radiation known as bremsstrahlung, or braking radiation. This form of radiation normally falls within the X-ray region of the spectrum. The fraction of the fast-electron energy lost in the form of bremsstrahlung is less than 1 percent for low-energy electrons in light materials but becomes a much larger fraction for high-energy electrons in materials with high atomic numbers.

Bremsstrahlung

Interactions of gamma rays and X rays. Ionizing radiation also can take the form of electromagnetic rays. When emitted by excited atoms, they are given the name X rays and have quantum energies typically measured from 1 to 100 keV. When emitted by excited nuclei, they are called gamma rays, and characteristic energies can be as high as several MeV. In both cases, the radiation takes the form of photons of electromagnetic energy. Since the photon is uncharged, it does not interact through the Coulomb force and therefore can pass through large distances in matter without significant interaction. The average distance traveled between interactions is called the mean free path and in solid materials ranges from a few millimetres for low-energy X rays through tens of centimetres for high-energy gamma rays. When an interaction does occur, however, it is catastrophic in the sense that a single interaction can profoundly affect the energy and direction of the photon or can make it disappear entirely. In such an interaction, all or part of the photon energy is transferred to one or more electrons in the absorber material. Because the secondary electrons thus produced are energetic and charged, they interact in much the same way as described earlier for primary fast electrons. The fact that an original X ray or gamma ray was present is indicated by the appearance of secondary electrons. Information on the energy carried by the incident photons can be inferred by measuring the energy of these electrons. The three major types of such interactions are discussed below.

Creation of secondary electrons

Photoelectric absorption. In this process, the incident X-ray or gamma-ray photon interacts with an atom of the absorbing material, and the photon completely disappears; its energy is transferred to one of the orbital electrons of the atom. Because this energy in general far exceeds the binding energy of the electron in the host atom, the electron is ejected at high velocity. The kinetic energy of this secondary electron is equal to the incoming energy of the photon minus the binding energy of the electron in the original atomic shell. The process leaves the atom with a vacancy in one of the normally filled electron shells, which is then refilled after a short period of time by a nearby free electron. This filling process again liberates the binding energy in the form of a characteristic X-ray photon, which then typically interacts with electrons from less tightly bound shells in nearby atoms, producing additional fast electrons. The overall effect is therefore the complete conversion of the photon energy into the energy carried by fast electrons. Since the fast electrons are now detectable through their Coulomb interactions, they can serve as the basis to indicate the presence of the original gamma-ray or X-ray photon, and a measurement of their energy is tantamount to measuring the energy of the incoming photon. Because the photoelectric process results in complete conversion of the photon energy to electron energy, it is in some sense an ideal conversion step. The task of measuring the gamma-ray energy is then reduced to simply measuring the equivalent energy deposited by the fast electrons. Unfortunately, two other types of gamma-ray interactions also take place that complicate this interpretation step.

Compton scattering. An incoming gamma-ray photon can interact with a single free electron in the absorber through the process of Compton scattering. In this process, the photon abruptly changes direction and transfers a portion of its original energy to the electron from which it scattered, producing an energetic recoil electron. The fraction of the photon energy that is transferred depends on the scattering angle. When the incoming photon is deflected only slightly, little energy is transferred to the electron. Maximum energy transfer occurs when the incoming photon is backscattered from the electron and its original direction is reversed. Since in general all angles of scattering will occur, the recoil electrons are produced with a continuum of energies ranging from near zero to a maximum represented by the backscattering extreme. This maximum energy can be predicted from the conservation of momentum and energy in the photon-electron interaction and is about 0.25 MeV below the incoming photon energy for high-energy gamma rays. After the interaction, the scattered photon has an energy that has decreased by an amount equal to the energy transferred to the recoil electron. It may subsequently interact again at some other location or simply escape from the detector.

Recoil electrons

Pair production. A third gamma-ray interaction process is possible when the incoming photon energy is above 1.02 MeV. In the field of a nucleus of the absorber material, the photon may disappear and be replaced by the formation of an electron-positron pair. The minimum energy required to create this pair of particles is their combined rest-mass energy of 1.02 MeV. Therefore, pair production cannot occur for incoming photon energies below this threshold. When the photon energy exceeds this value, the excess energy appears as initial kinetic energy shared by the positron and electron that are formed. The positron is a positively charged particle with the mass of a normal negative electron. It slows down and deposits its energy over an average distance that is nearly the same as that for a negative electron of equivalent energy. Therefore both particles transfer their kinetic energy over a distance of no more than a few millimetres in typical solids. The magnitude of the deposited energy is given by the original photon energy minus 1.02 MeV. When the positron member of the pair reaches the end of its track, it combines with a normal negative electron from the absorber in a process known as annihilation. In this step both particles disappear and are replaced by two annihilation photons, each with an energy of 0.511 MeV. Annihilation photons are similar to gamma rays in their ability to penetrate large distances of matter without interacting. They may undergo Compton or photoelectric interactions elsewhere or may escape from detectors of small size.

Annihilation photons

Role of energy and atomic number. The probability for each of these three interaction mechanisms to occur varies with the gamma-ray energy and the atomic number of the absorber. Photoelectric absorption predominates at low energies and is greatly enhanced in materials with high atomic number. For this reason, elements of high atomic number are mostly chosen for detectors used in gamma-ray energy measurements. Compton scattering is the most common interaction for moderate energies (from a few hundred keV to several MeV). Pair production predominates for higher energies and is also enhanced in materials with high atomic number. In larger detectors, there is a tendency for an incident photon to cause multiple interactions, as, for example, several sequential Compton scatterings or pair production followed by the interaction of an annihilation photon. Since little time separates these events, the deposited energies add together to determine the overall size of the output pulse.

Interactions of neutrons. Neutrons represent a major category of radiation that consists of uncharged particles. Owing to the absence of the Coulomb force, neutrons may penetrate many centimetres through solid materials before they interact in any manner. When they do interact, it is primarily with the nuclei of atoms of the absorbing material. The types of interaction that are important in the detection of neutrons are again catastrophic since the neutrons may either disappear or undergo a major change in their energy and direction.

In the case of gamma rays, such major interactions produce fast electrons. In contrast, the important neutron interactions result in the formation of energetic heavy charged particles. The task of detecting the uncharged neutron is thus transformed into one of measuring the directly observable results of the energy deposited in the detector by the secondary charged particles. Because the types of interaction that are useful in neutron detection are different for neutrons of different energies, it is convenient to subdivide the discussion into slow-neutron and fast-neutron interaction mechanisms.

Heavy charged particle formation

Slow neutrons. These are conventionally defined as neutrons whose kinetic energy is below about 1 eV. Slow neutrons frequently undergo elastic scattering interactions with nuclei and may in the process transfer a fraction of their energy to the interacting nucleus. Because the kinetic energy of a neutron is so low, however, the resulting recoil nucleus does not have enough energy to be classified as an ionizing particle. Instead, the important interactions for the detection of slow neutrons involve nuclear reactions in which a neutron is absorbed by the nucleus and charged particles are formed. All the reactions of interest in slow neutron detectors are exoenergetic, meaning that an amount of energy (called the *Q*-value) is released in the reaction. The charged particles are produced with a large amount of kinetic energy supplied by the nuclear reaction. Therefore, the products of these reactions are ionizing particles, and they interact in much the same way as previously described for direct radiations consisting of heavy charged particles. Some specific examples of nuclear reactions of interest in slow-neutron detection are given below in the section *Active detectors: Neutron detectors.*

Q-value

Fast neutrons. Neutrons whose kinetic energy is above about 1 keV are generally classified as fast neutrons. The neutron-induced reactions commonly employed for detecting slow neutrons have a low probability of occurrence once the neutron energy is high. Detectors that are based on these reactions may be quite efficient for slow neutrons, but they are inefficient for detecting fast neutrons.

Instead, fast neutron detectors are most commonly based on the elastic scattering of neutrons from nuclei. They exploit the fact that a significant fraction of a neutron's kinetic energy can be transferred to the nucleus that it strikes, producing an energetic recoil nucleus. This recoil nucleus behaves in much the same way as any other heavy charged particle as it slows down and loses its energy in the absorber. The amount of energy transferred varies from nearly zero for a grazing angle scattering to a maximum for the case of a head-on collision. Hydrogen is a common choice for the target nucleus, and the resulting recoil protons (or recoiling hydrogen nuclei) serve as the basis for many types of fast-neutron detectors. Hydrogen provides a unique advantage in this application since a fast neutron can transfer up to its full energy in a single scattering interaction with a hydrogen nucleus. For all other elements, the heavier nucleus limits the maximum energy transfer in a single scattering to only a fraction of the neutron energy. In any elastic-scattering interaction, the energy that is not transferred to the recoil nucleus is retained by the scattered neutron which, depending on the dimensions of the detector, may interact again or simply escape from the detector volume.

Applications of radiation interactions in detectors. A number of physical or chemical effects caused by the deposition of energy along the track of a charged particle are listed in the first column of Table 5. Each of these effects can serve as the basis of instruments designed to detect radiation, and examples of specific devices based on each effect are given in the second column.

One category of radiation-measurement devices indicates the presence of ionizing radiation only after the exposure has occurred. A physical or chemical change is induced by the radiation that is later measured through some type of processing. These so-called passive detectors are widely applied in the routine monitoring of occupational exposures to ionizing radiation. In contrast, in active detectors a signal is produced in real time to indicate the presence of radiation. This distinction is indicated for the examples in Table 5. The normal mode of operation of each detector type is also noted. These include pulse mode, current mode, and integrating mode as defined below (see *Active detectors: Modes of operation*). An indication is also given as to whether the detector is normally capable of responding to a single particle or quantum of radiation or whether the cumulative effect of many quanta is needed for a measurable output.

In the descriptions that follow, emphasis is placed on the behaviour of devices for the measurement of those forms of ionizing radiation consisting of heavy charged particles, fast electrons, X rays, and gamma rays. Techniques and devices of primary interest for the measurement of neutrons are discussed separately in a later section because they differ substantially in operation or composition or both. The detection methods that are included also are limited to those that are relatively sensitive to low levels of radiation. There are a number of other physical effects resulting from exposure to intense radiation that can also serve as the basis for measurements, many of which are important in the field of radiation dosimetry (the measurement of radiation doses). They include chemical changes in ionic solutions, changes in the colour or other optical properties of transparent materials, and calorimetric measurement of the heat deposited by intense fluxes of radiation.

Effects of intense radiation

PASSIVE DETECTORS

Photographic emulsions. The use of photographic techniques to record ionizing radiations dates back to the discovery of X rays by Röntgen in the late 1800s, but similar techniques remain important today in some applications. A photographic emulsion consists of a suspension of silver halide grains in an inert gelatin matrix and supported by a backing of plastic film or another material. If a charged particle or fast electron passes through the emulsion, interactions with silver halide molecules produce a similar effect as seen with exposure to visible light. Some molecules are excited and will remain in this state for an indefinite period of time. After the exposure is completed, this latent record of the accumulated exposure can be made visible through the chemical development process. Each grain containing an excited molecule is converted to metallic silver, greatly amplifying the number of affected molecules to the point that the developed grain is visible. Photographic emulsions used for radiation detection purposes can be classified into two main subgroups: radiographic films and nuclear emulsions. Radiographic films register the results of exposure to radiation as a general darkening of the film due to the cumulative effect of many radiation interactions in a given area of the emulsion. Nuclear emulsions are intended to record individual tracks of a single charged particle.

Radiographic films. Radiographic films are most familiar in their application in medical X-ray imaging. Their properties do not differ drastically from those of normal photographic film used to record visible light, except for an unusually high silver halide concentration. Thickness of the emulsion ranges from 10 to 20 micrometres, and they contain silver halide grains up to 1 micrometre in diameter. The probability that a typical incident X ray will interact in the emulsion is only a few percent, and so methods are often applied to increase the sensitivity so as to reduce the intensity of the X rays needed to produce a visible image. One such technique is to apply emulsion to both sides of the film base. Another is to sandwich the photographic emulsion between intensifier screens that consist of thin layers of light-emitting phosphors of high atomic number, such as calcium tungstate, cesium iodide, or rare earth phosphors. If an X ray interacts in the screen, the light that is produced darkens the film in the immediate vicinity through the normal photographic process. Because of the high atomic number of the screens, they are more likely to cause an X ray to interact than the emulsion itself, and the X-ray flux needed to achieve a given degree of darkening of the emulsion can be decreased by as much as an order of magnitude. The light is produced in the normal scintillation process (see below *Active detectors: Scintillation and Čerenkov detectors*) and travels in all directions from the point of the X-ray interaction. This spreading causes some loss of spatial resolution in X-ray images, especially for thicker screens, and the screen thickness must therefore be chosen to reach a compromise between resolution and sensitivity.

Intensifier screens

Nuclear emulsions. In order to enable visualization of single particle tracks, nuclear emulsions are generally made much thicker than ordinary photographic emulsions (up to 500 micrometres) and they have an even higher silver halide content. Special development procedures can reveal the tracks of individual charged particles or fast electrons as a nearly continuous trail of developed silver grains that is visible under a microscope. If the particle is stopped in the emulsion, the length of its track can be measured to give its range and therefore an estimate of its initial energy.

Table 5: Applications of Radiation Interactions in Detectors

results of interaction of incident radiation	detector category	active or passive	single quantum sensitivity	mode type (for active detectors)
Sensitized silver halide grains in photographic emulsion	radiographic film	passive	no	
	nuclear emulsion	passive	yes	
Trapped charges in crystalline materials	thermoluminescent dosimeter	passive	no	
	memory phosphor	passive	no	
Damaged track in dielectric materials	track-etch film	passive	yes	
Radioactivity induced by neutrons	activation foil	passive	no	
Vaporized superheated liquid drop	bubble chamber	active and passive	yes	pulse
Ion pairs in a gas	ion chamber pocket dosimeter	(integrating)	no	
	current-mode ion chamber	active	no	current
	proportional tube	active	yes	pulse
	Geiger-Müller tube	active	yes	pulse
Mobile electron-hole pairs in semiconductor	silicon diode	active	yes	current and pulse
	coaxial germanium detector	active	yes	pulse
Prompt fluorescence in transparent materials	scintillation detector	active	yes	current and pulse
Čerenkov radiation	Čerenkov detector	active	yes	pulse

The density of the grains along the track is proportional to the dE/dx of the particle, and therefore some distinction can be made between particles of different type.

Film badge dosimeters. Small packets of photographic emulsions are routinely used by workers to monitor radiation exposure. The density of the developed film can be compared with that of an identical film exposed to a known radiation dose. In this way, variations that result from differences in film properties or development procedures are canceled out. When used to monitor exposure to low-energy radiation such as X rays or gamma rays, emulsions tend to overrespond owing to the rapid rise of the photoelectric cross section of silver at these energies. To reduce this deviation, the film is often wrapped in a thin metallic foil to absorb some of the low-energy photons before they reach the emulsion.

One of the drawbacks of photographic film is the limited dynamic range between underexposure and overexposure. In order to extend this range, the holder that contains the film badge often is fitted with a set of small metallic filters that cover selected regions of the film. By making the filters of differing thickness, the linear region under each filter corresponds to a different range of exposure, and the effective dynamic range of the film is extended. The filters also help to separate exposures to weakly penetrating radiations (such as beta particles) from those due to more penetrating radiations (such as gamma rays).

Thermoluminescent materials. Another technique commonly applied in personnel monitoring is the use of thermoluminescent dosimeters (TLDs). This technique is based on the use of crystalline materials in which ionizing radiation creates electron-hole pairs (see below *Active detectors: Semiconductor detectors*). In this case, however, traps for these charges are intentionally created through the addition of a dopant (impurity) or the special processing of the material. The object is to create conditions in which many of the electrons and holes formed by the incident radiation are quickly captured and immobilized. During the period of exposure to the radiation, a growing population of trapped charges accumulates in the material. The trap depth is the minimum energy that is required to free a charge from the trap. It is chosen to be large enough so that the rate of detrapping is very low at room temperature. Thus, if the exposure is carried out at ordinary temperatures, the trapped charge is more or less permanently stored.

Trapping of charges

After the exposure, the amount of trapped charge is quantified by measuring the amount of light that is emitted while the temperature of the crystal is raised. The applied thermal energy causes rapid release of the charges. A liberated electron can then recombine with a remaining trapped hole, emitting energy in the process. In TLD materials, this energy appears as a photon in the visible part of the electromagnetic spectrum. Alternatively, a liberated hole can recombine with a remaining trapped electron to generate a similar photon. The total intensity of emitted light can be measured using a photomultiplier tube and is proportional to the original population of trapped charges. This is in turn proportional to the radiation dose accumulated over the exposure period.

The readout process effectively empties all the traps, and the charges thus are erased from the material so that it can be recycled for repeated use. One of the commonly used TLD materials is lithium fluoride, in which the traps are sufficiently deep to prevent fading, or loss of the trapped charge over extended periods of time. The elemental composition of lithium fluoride is of similar atomic number to that of tissue, so that energy absorbed from gamma rays matches that of tissue over wide energy ranges.

Memory phosphors. A memory phosphor consists of a thin layer of material with properties that resemble those of TLD crystals in the sense that charges created by incident radiation remain trapped for an indefinite period of time. The material is formed as a screen covering a substantial area so that it can be applied as an X-ray image detector. These screens can then be used as an alternative to radiographic films in X-ray radiography.

The incident X rays build up a pattern of trapped charges over the surface of the screen during the exposure period. As in a TLD, the screen is then read out through the light that is generated by liberating these charges. The energy needed to detrap the stored charges is supplied in this case by stimulating the crystal with intense light from a laser beam rather than by heating. The luminescence from the memory phosphor can be distinguished from the laser light by its different wavelength. If the amount of this luminescence is measured as the laser beam scans across the surface of the screen, the spatial pattern of the trapped charges is thereby recorded. This pattern corresponds to the X-ray image recorded during the exposure. Like TLDs, memory phosphors have the advantage that the trapped charges are erased during readout, and the screen can be reused many times.

Use as an X-ray image detector

Track-etch detectors. When a charged particle slows down and stops in a solid, the energy that it deposits along its track can cause permanent damage in the material. It is difficult to observe direct evidence of this local damage, even under careful microscopic examination. In certain dielectric materials, however, the presence of the damaged track can be revealed through chemical etching (erosion) of the material surface using an acid or base solution. If charged particles have irradiated the surface at some time in the past, then each leaves a trail of damaged material that begins at the surface and extends to a depth equal to the range of the particle. In the materials of choice, the chemical etching rate along this track is higher than the rate of etching of the undamaged surface. Therefore, as the etching progresses, a pit is formed at the position of each track. Within a few hours, these pits can become large enough so that they can be seen directly under a low-power microscope. A measurement of the number of these pits per unit area is then a measure of the particle flux to which the surface has been exposed.

There is a minimum density of damage along the track that is required before the etching rate is sufficient to create a pit. Because the density of damage correlates with the dE/dx of the particle, it is highest for the heaviest charged particles. In any given material, a certain minimum value for dE/dx is required before pits will develop. For example, in the mineral mica, pits are observed only from energetic heavy ions whose mass is 10 or 20 atomic mass units or greater. Many common plastic materials are more sensitive and will develop etch pits for low-mass ions such as helium (alpha particles). Some particularly sensitive plastics such as cellulose nitrate will develop pits even for protons, which are the least damaging of the heavy charged particles. No materials have been found that will produce pits for the low dE/dx tracks of fast electrons. This threshold behaviour makes such detectors completely insensitive to beta particles and gamma rays. This immunity can be exploited in some applications where weak fluxes of heavy charged particles are to be registered in the presence of a more intense background of gamma rays. For example, many environmental measurements of the alpha particles produced by the decay of radon gas and its daughter products are made using plastic track-etch film. The background to omnipresent gamma rays would dominate the response of many other types of detectors under these circumstances. In some materials the damage track has been shown to remain in the material for indefinite periods of time, and pits can be etched many years after the exposure. Etching properties are, however, potentially affected by exposure to light and high temperatures, so some caution must be exercised in the prolonged storage of exposed samples to prevent fading of the damage tracks.

Thresholds for pit development

Automated methods have been developed to measure the etch pit density using microscope stages coupled to computers with appropriate optical-analysis software. These systems are capable of some degree of discrimination against "artifacts" such as scratches on the sample surface and can provide a reasonably accurate measurement of the number of tracks per unit area. Another technique incorporates relatively thin plastic films, in which the tracks are etched completely through the film to form small holes. These holes can then be automatically counted by passing the film slowly between a set of high-voltage electrodes and electronically counting sparks that occur as a hole passes.

Measurement of etched tracks

Neutron-activation foils. For radiation energies of several MeV and lower, charged particles and fast electrons do not induce nuclear reactions in absorber materials. Gamma rays with energy below a few MeV also do not readily induce reactions with nuclei. Therefore, when nearly any material is bombarded by these forms of radiation, the nuclei remain unaffected and no radioactivity is induced in the irradiated material.

Among the common forms of radiation, neutrons are an exception to this general behaviour. Because they carry no charge, neutrons of even low energy can readily interact with nuclei and induce a wide selection of nuclear reactions. Many of these reactions lead to radioactive products whose presence can later be measured using conventional detectors to sense the radiations emitted in their decay. For example, many types of nuclei will absorb a neutron to produce a radioactive nucleus. During the time that a sample of this material is exposed to neutrons, a population of radioactive nuclei accumulates. When the sample is removed from the neutron exposure, the population will decay with a given half-life. Some type of radiation is almost always emitted in this decay, often beta particles or gamma rays or both, which can then be counted using one of the active detection methods described below. Because it can be related to the level of the induced radioactivity, the intensity of the neutron flux to which the sample has been exposed can be deduced from this radioactivity measurement. In order to induce enough radioactivity to permit reasonably accurate measurement, relatively intense neutron fluxes are required. Therefore, activation foils are frequently used as a technique to measure neutron fields around reactors, accelerators, or other intense sources of neutrons.

Materials such as silver, indium, and gold are commonly used for the measurement of slow neutrons, whereas iron, magnesium, and aluminum are possible choices for fast-neutron measurements. In these cases, the half-life of the induced activity is in the range of a few minutes through a few days. In order to build up a population of radioactive nuclei that approaches the maximum possible, the half-life of the induced radioactivity should be shorter than the time of exposure to the neutron flux. At the same time, the half-life must be long enough to allow for convenient counting of the radioactivity once the sample has been removed from the neutron field.

Bubble detector. A relatively recent technique that has been introduced for the measurement of neutron exposures involves a device known as a superheated drop, or bubble detector. Its operation is based on a suspension of many small droplets of a liquid (such as Freon [trademark]) in an inert matrix consisting of a polymer or gel. The sample is held in a sealed vial or other transparent container, and the pressure on the sample is adjusted to create conditions in which the liquid droplets are superheated; *i.e.,* they are heated above their boiling point yet remain in the liquid state. The transformation to the vapour state must be triggered by the creation of some type of nucleation centre.

Super-heating

This stimulus can be provided by the energy deposited from the recoil nucleus created by the scattering of an incident neutron. When such an event occurs, the droplet suddenly vaporizes and creates a bubble that remains suspended within the matrix. Over the course of the neutron exposure, additional bubbles are formed, and a count of their total number is related to the incident neutron intensity. The bubble detector is insensitive to gamma rays because the fast electrons created in gamma-ray interactions have too low a value of dE/dx to serve as a nucleation centre. Bubble detectors have found application in monitoring the exposure of radiation personnel to ionizing radiation because of their good sensitivity to low levels of neutron fluxes and their immunity to gamma-ray backgrounds. Some types can be recycled and used repeatedly by collapsing the bubbles back to droplets through recompression. The same type of device can be made into an active detector by attaching a piezoelectric sensor. The pulse of acoustic energy emitted when the droplet vaporizes into a bubble is converted into an electrical pulse by the sensor and can then be counted electronically in real time.

ACTIVE DETECTORS

In many applications it is important to produce a signal that indicates the presence of ionizing radiation in real time. Such devices are classified as active detectors. Many types of active detectors can produce an observable signal for an individual quantum of radiation (such as a single alpha particle or an X-ray photon). Others may provide a signal that corresponds to the collective effect of many quanta interacting in the detector within its response time.

Modes of operation. In many types of detectors, a single particle or quantum of radiation liberates a certain amount of charge Q as a result of depositing its energy in the detector material. For example, in a gas, Q represents the total positive charge carried by the many positive ions that are produced along the track of the particle. (An equal charge of opposite sign is carried by the free electrons that are also generated.) This charge is created over a very short time, typically less than a nanosecond, as the particle slows down and stops; it is then collected over a much longer period of time, ranging from a few nanoseconds to several microseconds. In a gas or a semiconductor, the charge is collected through the motion of individual charge carriers in the electric field that is established within the detector. As these moving charges represent an electric current, detector response to a single quantum of radiation can then be modeled as a momentary burst of current that begins with the stopping of the charged particle and ends once all the charge carriers have been collected. If the detector is undergoing continuous irradiation, a sequence of these current bursts will be produced, one for each interacting quantum. In most applications the time of arrival of each quantum of radiation is randomly distributed. For purposes of this discussion, it is assumed that the average time between events in the detector is long compared with the charge collection time. Each burst of current is then distinct, and the integral or area under the current versus time profile for each burst is the charge Q formed for that event. Because the amount of energy deposited may be different for individual events, each of these current pulses may represent a different total charge Q. Furthermore, the charge collection time may also be variable, so the length of each of these current bursts may be different.

Detector current

Current mode. One way to provide an electrical signal from such a detector is to connect its output to an ammeter circuit with a slow response time. If this response time is long compared with the average time spacing between current bursts, then the ammeter will measure a current that is given by the mean rate of charge formation averaged over many individual radiation quanta. This mode of operation is called current mode, and many of the common detector types can be operated in this way. The measured current represents the product of the rate at which quanta are interacting in the detector multiplied by the average charge Q created by a single quantum of radiation. For a given source of radiation, doubling its intensity will double the observed current. However, different currents will result from radiations that have equal interaction rates but deposit a different average energy per interaction.

Integrating mode. There are circumstances in which the current from the detector is simply integrated during the time of exposure, and the accumulated total charge is measured at its completion. This integration mode of operation produces information that is related to the total exposure, but it cannot provide detail on possible variation of the intensity during the exposure time. In that sense, it is similar to the operation of passive detectors. Portable ion chambers are sometimes used in this manner; the total ionization charge is measured by noting the drop in voltage across the chamber after it has been initially charged using a reference voltage source. The integration mode can be useful when a direct measurement of small signal currents may be difficult or impractical.

Pulse mode. In many applications information is sought about the properties of individual quanta of radiation. In such cases, a mode of detector operation known as the pulse mode is employed, in which a separate electrical pulse is generated for each individual radiation quantum that interacts in the detector. The detector output may be connected to a measuring circuit as indicated in Figure

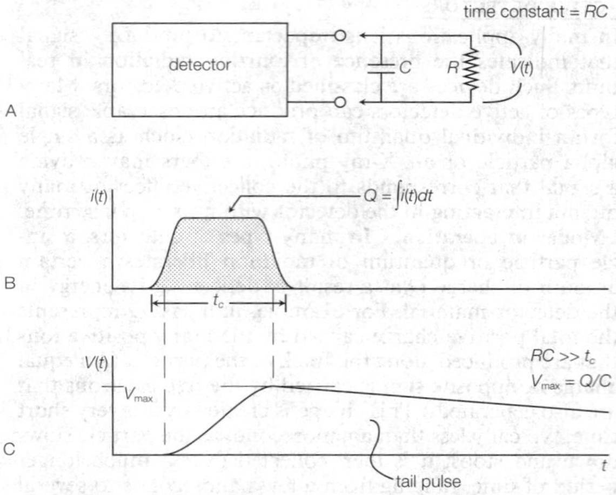

Figure 50: (A) A simple equivalent circuit for the development of a voltage pulse at the output of a detector. *R* represents the resistance and *C* the capacitance of the circuit; *V*(*t*) is the time (*t*)-dependent voltage produced. (B) A representative current pulse due to the interaction of a single quantum in the detector. The total charge *Q* is obtained by integrating the area of the current, *i*(*t*), over the collection time, t_c. (C) The resulting voltage pulse that is developed across the circuit of (A) for the case of a long circuit time constant. The amplitude (V_{max}) of the pulse is equal to the charge *Q* divided by the capacitance *C*.

Adapted from G.F. Knoll, *Radiation Detection and Measurement*, 2nd ed. (1989), reprinted with permission of John Wiley and Sons, Inc., New York City

50. This circuit could represent, for example, the input stage of a preamplifier unit. The basic signal is the voltage observed across the circuit consisting of a load resistance (R) and capacitance (C). This type of configuration has an associated time constant given by the product of the resistance and capacitance values (RC). For simplicity, it will be assumed that this time constant is long compared with the charge collection time in the detector but small relative to the average time between interactions of individual quanta in the detector.

Time constant

Under these circumstances each interacting quantum gives rise to a voltage pulse of the form sketched in Figure 50C. The voltage pulse rises over the charge collection time, reaches its maximum when all the charge has been collected, and then exponentially decays back to zero with a characteristic time set by the time constant of the measuring circuit. This type of signal pulse is called a tail pulse, and it is observed from the preamplifier used with many kinds of common radiation detectors.

The most important property of the tail pulse is its maximum size, or amplitude. Under the conditions described, the amplitude is given by $V_{max} = Q/C$, where Q is the charge produced by the individual quantum in the detector and C is the capacitance of the measuring circuit. Under typical conditions tail pulses are then amplified and shaped in a second unit known as a linear amplifier in a manner that preserves the proportionality of the pulse amplitude to the charge Q produced in the detector.

Amplitude of tail pulses

Counting and spectroscopy systems. Detector systems operating in pulse mode can be further subdivided into two types: simple counting systems and more complex spectroscopy systems. The basic elements of both types of pulse-processing systems are shown in Figure 51.

Counting systems. In simple counting systems, the objective is to record the number of pulses that occur over a given measurement time, or alternatively, to indicate the rate at which these pulses are occurring. Some preselection may be applied to the pulses before they are recorded. A common method is to employ an electronic unit known as an integral discriminator to count only those pulses that are larger than a preset amplitude. This approach can eliminate small amplitude pulses that may be of no interest in the application. Alternatively, a differential discriminator (also known as a single-channel analyzer) will select only those pulses whose amplitudes lie within a preset window between a given minimum and maximum value. In this way, the accepted pulses can be restricted to those in which the charge Q from the detector is within a specific range. When the number of pulses meeting these criteria are accumulated in a digital register over the measurement time, the measurement consists of reporting the total number of accepted events over the time period.

One property that must be considered in counting systems is the concept known as dead time. Following each event in a detector, there is a period of time in which the measurement system is processing that event and is insensitive to other events. Because radiation events typically occur randomly distributed in time, there is always some chance that a true event will occur so soon after a previous event that it is lost. This behaviour is often accounted for by assigning a standard dead time to the counting system. It is assumed that each accepted event is followed by a fixed time period during which any additional true event will be ignored. As a result, the measured number of counts (or the counting rate) is always somewhat below the true value. The discrepancy can become significant at high radiation rates when the dead time is a significant fraction of the average spacing between true events in the detector. Corrections for dead-time losses can be made assuming that the behaviour of the counting system and length of its dead time are known.

Dead time

As an alternative to simply registering the total number of accepted pulses over the counting time, the rate at which the accepted events are occurring in real time can be indicated electronically using a rate meter. This unit provides an output signal that is proportional to the rate at which accepted pulses are occurring averaged over a response time that is normally adjustable by the user. Long response times minimize the fluctuations in the output signal due to the random nature of the interaction times in the detector, but they also slow the response of the rate meter to abrupt changes in the radiation intensity.

Spectroscopy systems. The pulse-mode counting systems described above provide no detailed information on the amplitude of the pulses that are accepted. In many types of detectors, the charge Q and thus the amplitude of the signal pulse is proportional to the energy deposited by the incident radiation. Therefore, an important set of measurement systems are based on recording not only the

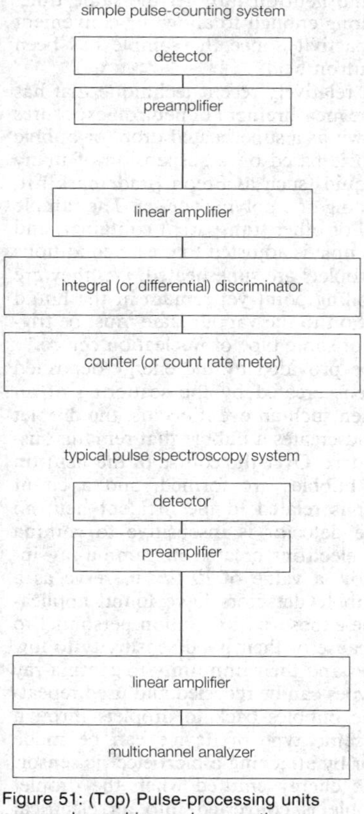

Figure 51: (Top) Pulse-processing units commonly used in a pulse-counting system. (Bottom) The units constituting spectroscopy system.

number of pulses but also their distribution in amplitude. They are known as spectroscopy systems, and their main application is to determine the energy distribution of the radiation that is incident on the detector.

Pulse-height spectra

In spectroscopy systems the objective is to sort each pulse according to its amplitude. Every pulse from the linear amplifier is sorted into one of a large number of bins or channels. Each channel corresponds to signal pulses of a specific narrow amplitude range. As the pulses are sorted into the channels matching their amplitude, a pulse-height spectrum is accumulated that, after a given measurement time, might resemble the example given in Figure 52. In this spectrum, peaks correspond to those pulse amplitudes around which many events occur. Because pulse amplitude is related to deposited energy, such peaks often correspond to radiation of a fixed energy recorded by the detector. By noting the position and intensity of peaks recorded in the pulse-height spectrum, it is often possible to interpret spectroscopy measurements in terms of the energy and intensity of the incident radiation.

This pulse-height spectrum is recorded by sending the pulses to a multichannel analyzer, where the pulses are electronically sorted out according to their amplitude to produce the type of spectrum illustrated in Figure 52. Ideally, every incoming pulse is sorted into one of the channels of the multichannel analyzer. Therefore, when the measurement is completed, the sum of all the counts that have been recorded in the channels equals the total number of pulses produced by the detector over the measurement period. In order to maintain this correspondence at high counting rates, corrections must be applied to account for the dead time of the recording system or the pileup of two pulses spaced so closely in time that they appear to be only one pulse to the multichannel analyzer.

One important property of spectroscopy systems is the energy resolution. This concept is most easily illustrated by assuming that the detector is exposed to radiation quanta of a single fixed energy. (A radioisotope emitting a single gamma-ray energy in its decay comes very close to this ideal.) Many radiation quanta then deposit the same energy in the detector and ideally should produce exactly the same charge Q. Therefore, a number of pulses of precisely the same amplitude should be presented to the multichannel analyzer, and they all should be stored in a single channel. In actual systems, however, some fluctuations are observed in the amplitude of these pulses, and they are actually spread out over a number of channels in the spectrum, as illustrated in Figure 53. A formal definition of energy resolution is shown in the figure, expressed as the ratio of the full-width-at-half-maximum (FWHM) of the peak divided by the centroid position of the peak. This ratio is normally expressed as a percentage, and small values correspond to narrow peaks and good energy resolution. If the incident radiation consists of multiple discreet energies, good energy resolution will help in separating the resulting peaks in the recorded pulse-height spectrum.

Adapted from G.F. Knoll, *Radiation Detection and Measurement*, 2nd ed. (1989), reprinted with permission of John Wiley and Sons, Inc., New York City, after J.C. Philippot, *IEEE Transactions on Nuclear Science* NS-17(3), 446, © 1970 IEEE

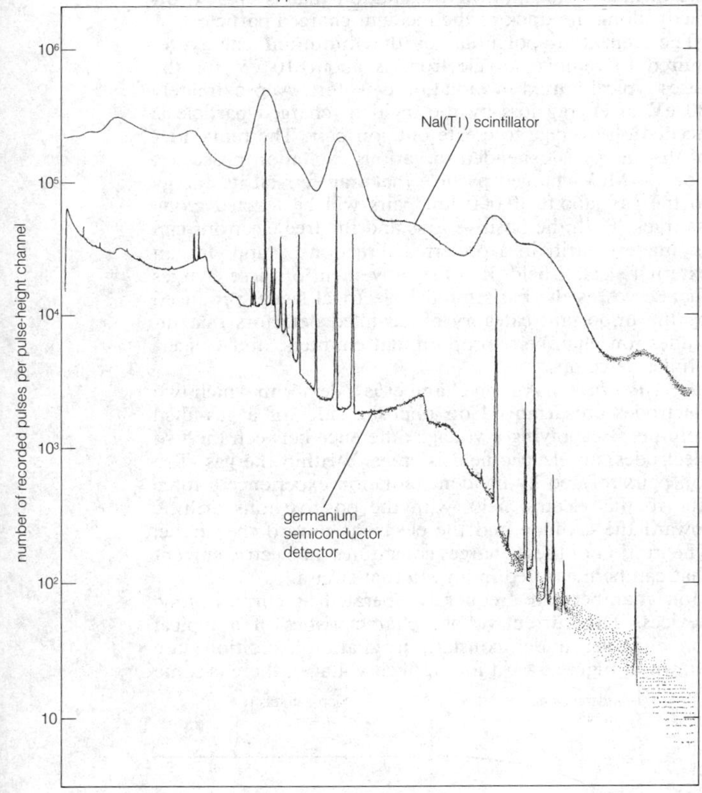

Figure 52: *Representative pulse-height spectra for a source emitting gamma rays of many different energies.* The top spectrum is from a scintillation detector, and the bottom is from a germanium semiconductor detector. The superior energy resolution of the germanium is evident from the much narrower peaks, allowing separation of gamma-ray energies that are unresolved in the scintillator spectrum.

Causes of peak broadening

Some potential causes of fluctuations that broaden the peaks include drifts in the detector-operating parameters over the course of the measurement, random fluctuations introduced by the noise in the pulse-processing electronics, and statistical fluctuations due to the fact that the charge Q consists of a finite number of charge carriers. This latter statistical limit is in some ways the most fundamental determinant in energy resolution since, as opposed to the other sources of fluctuation, it cannot be reduced by more careful experimental procedures. Poisson statistics predicts that the fractional standard deviation that characterizes these fluctuations about the average number of charge carriers N should scale as $1/\sqrt{N}$. Therefore, detectors that produce the largest number of carriers per pulse show the best energy resolution. For example, the charge Q from a scintillation detector normally consists of photoelectrons in a photomultiplier tube. The average number produced by a 1-MeV particle is normally no more than a few thousand, and the observed energy resolution is typically 5–10 percent. In contrast, the same particle would produce several hundred thousand electron-hole pairs in a semiconductor, and the energy resolution is improved to a few tenths of a percent.

Detection efficiency. The intrinsic detection efficiency of any device operated in pulse mode is defined as the probability that a quantum of radiation incident on the detector will produce a recorded pulse. Especially for radiations of low intensity, a high detection efficiency is important to minimize the total time needed to record enough pulses for good statistical accuracy in the measurement. Detection efficiency is further subdivided into two types: total efficiency and peak efficiency. The total efficiency gives the probability that an incident quantum of radiation produces a pulse, regardless of size, from the detector. The peak efficiency is defined as the probability that the quantum will deposit all its initial energy in the detector. Since there are almost always ways in which the quantum may deposit only part of its energy and then escape from the detector, the total efficiency is generally larger than the peak efficiency.

Types of detection efficiency

For a given detector, efficiency values depend on the type and energy of the incident radiation. For incident charged particles such as alpha particles or beta particles, many detectors have a total efficiency that is close to 100 percent. Since these particles begin to deposit energy immediately upon entering the detector volume, a pulse of some amplitude is inevitably produced if the particle reaches the active volume of the device. Very often, any departure from 100 percent efficiency in these cases is due to absorption or scattering of the incident particle before it reaches the active volume. Furthermore, if the detector is thick compared with the range of the incident particle, most particles are fully stopped in the active volume and deposit all their energy. Under these circumstances, the peak efficiency also will be near 100 percent.

For incident gamma rays, the situation is quite different. Except for low-energy photons, it is quite possible for an incident gamma-ray photon to pass completely through

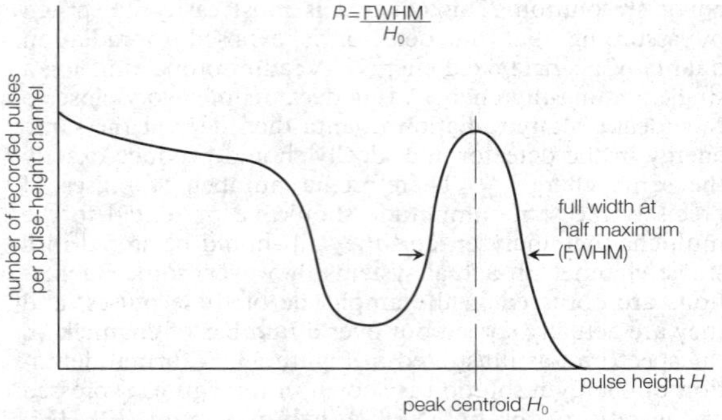

Figure 53: A simple pulse-height spectrum (such a spectrum might be recorded from a scintillator for a single energy gamma-ray source) showing the definition of energy resolution *R*.

the detector without interacting. In such cases, the total efficiency will then be substantially less than 100 percent. Furthermore, many of the gamma-rays may deposit only a fraction of their energy in the detector. These events do not contribute to the peak efficiency so, although they produce pulses, their amplitude does not indicate the initial energy of the incident gamma ray. Thus the peak efficiency values incorporate only those gamma-ray photons that interact one or more times in the detector and eventually deposit all their energy. The total efficiency for gamma rays may be enhanced by increasing the detector thickness in the direction of the incident gamma-ray flux. For a given thickness, the peak efficiency is enhanced by choosing a detector material with a high atomic number to increase the probability that all the energy of the original photon will eventually be photoelectrically absorbed. Full energy absorption could take place in a single photoelectric interaction but, more likely, it happens after the incident photon has Compton-scattered one or more times elsewhere in the detector. Alternatively, full absorption is also observed if pair production is followed by subsequent full absorption of both annihilation photons. Since these multiple interactions are enhanced in detectors of large volume, the peak efficiency for gamma-ray detectors improves significantly with increasing size.

Factors that enhance efficiency

Timing characteristics. One of the added benefits of pulse-mode operation is the fact that the arrival time of an individual quantum of radiation is closely related to the time of appearance of a pulse at the detector output. In many nuclear measurements, it is advantageous to be able to determine that two quanta are emitted in the same nuclear process and therefore may be sensed by two separate detectors in virtual time coincidence. Another example of the application of timing information is in the determination of the velocity or energy of a particle by measuring its flight time between its point of origin and a distant detector.

The timing information is carried by the leading edge or rising portion of the detector output pulse. The precision of timing measurements is enhanced in detectors that produce a prompt output pulse with a fast rise time. The time characteristics of the leading edge are related to the charge collection time from the detector, and the best timing performance is generally obtained from detectors in which the charges are collected most rapidly. For example, timing precision of less than one nanosecond can be obtained using organic scintillators for which the light (that is subsequently converted to charge in a photomultiplier tube) is emitted within a period of several nanoseconds following the deposition of the particle energy. On the other hand, timing measurements from gas-filled detectors may have an imprecision of up to one microsecond or more owing to the relatively long and sometimes variable charge-collection time of these devices.

Gas-filled detectors. The passage of a charged particle through a gas results in the transfer of energy from the particle to electrons that are part of the normal atomic structure of the gas. If the charged particle passes close enough to a given atom, the energy transfer may be sufficient to result in its excitation or ionization. In the excitation process, an electron is elevated from its original state to a less tightly bound state. Energy levels in typical gas atoms are only spaced a few electron volts apart, so that the energy needed for excitation is a small fraction of the kinetic energy of typical radiation quanta. The excited state exists for a specific lifetime before the atom decays back to the original ground energy state. Typical mean lifetimes for excited atomic states in gases are normally only a few nanoseconds. When the atom spontaneously returns to the ground state, the excitation energy is liberated, generally in the form of an electromagnetic photon. The wavelength of electromagnetic radiation for typical gases is in the ultraviolet region of the spectrum. Thus, for every excited gas atom that is formed, the observable result is the appearance of an ultraviolet photon. As a typical charged particle will create thousands of excited atoms along its track, a resulting flash of ultraviolet photons appears, originating along the track of the particle. Some detectors, based on directly sensing this ultraviolet light and known as gas scintillators, are described below (see *Scintillation and Čerenkov detectors*). Similar ultraviolet photons also play an important part in the generation of a pulse from a Geiger-Müller tube.

Release of ultraviolet radiation

For close encounters between an incident charged particle and a gas atom, enough energy may be transferred to totally remove an electron. This is the process of ionization, and it results in the creation of an ion pair. Because the ionized atom is electron-deficient, it carries a net positive electric charge and is called a positive ion. The other member of the ion pair is the electron that is no longer bound to a specific atom and is known as a free electron. Most free electrons are formed with low kinetic energy, and they simply diffuse through the gas, taking part in the random thermal motion of all the atoms. Some free electrons are formed with enough kinetic energy to cause additional excitation and ionization. These are called delta rays, and their motion follows short branches away from the primary ionization and excitation that is created directly along the track of the incident charged particle.

The ionization potential, or the minimum energy required to remove an electron, is about 10 eV for the gases typically used in radiation detectors. Approximately 30 eV of energy loss by the incident charged particle is needed on average to create one ion pair. The remainder of the energy is expended in various excitation processes. For a 1-MeV charged particle that transfers all its energy to the gas, about 30,000 ion pairs will be formed along its track. Both the positive ions and the free electrons can be made to drift in a preferred direction by applying an external electric field. It is the movement of these charges that serves as the basis for the electrical signal produced by the important category of gas-filled detectors that includes ion chambers, proportional counters, and Geiger-Müller detectors.

Ion chambers. An ion chamber is a device in which two electrodes are arranged on opposite sides of a gas-filled volume. By applying a voltage difference between the two electrodes, an electric field is created within the gas. The ion pairs formed by incident radiation experience a force due to this electric field, with the positive ions drifting toward the cathode and the electrons toward the anode. The motion of these charges constitutes an electric current that can be measured in an external circuit.

Ion chambers are frequently operated as current-mode devices. The current-voltage characteristics of a typical ion chamber under constant irradiation conditions are shown in Figure 54. At low applied voltages, there is some

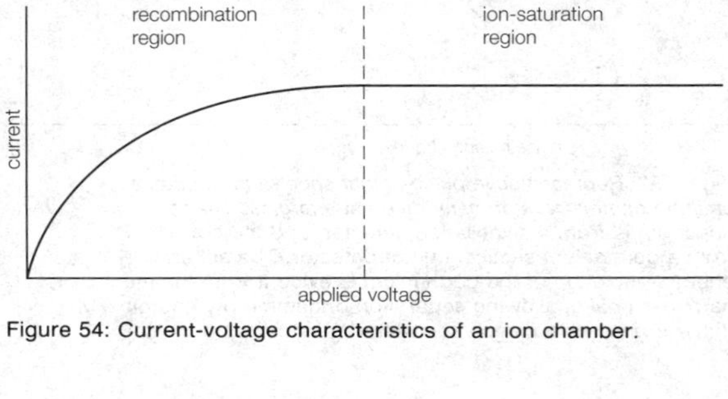

Figure 54: Current-voltage characteristics of an ion chamber.

tendency for the positive and negative charges to collide and recombine, thereby neutralizing them and preventing their contribution to the measured current. As the voltage is raised, the stronger electric field separates the charges more quickly, and recombination is eventually made negligible at a sufficient applied voltage. This point marks the onset of the ion-saturation region, where the current no longer depends on applied voltage; this is the region of operation normally chosen for ion chambers. Under these conditions the current measured in the external circuit is simply equal to the rate of formation of charges in the gas by the incident radiation.

Ion saturation

Air-filled ion chambers operated in current mode are a common type of portable survey meter used to monitor potential personnel exposure to gamma rays. One reason is that the historical unit of gamma-ray exposure, the roentgen (*R*), is defined in terms of the amount of ionization charge created per unit mass of air. Because of the close connection of the signal produced in an ion chamber with this definition, a measurement of the ion current under proper conditions can give an accurate measure of gamma-ray exposure rate over a wide range of incident gamma-ray energies.

The magnitude of the current observed from a typical ion chamber for a modest gamma-ray exposure rate is quite small. For example, at a gamma-ray exposure rate of 10^{-3} roentgen per hour (a small but significant level for personnel monitoring purposes), the expected ion current from a one-litre ion chamber at atmospheric pressure is about 0.1 picoampere (pA). These low currents require the use of sensitive electrometers for their accurate measurement.

Ion chambers are sometimes operated in a manner similar to passive detectors in integration mode. In this case, the ion chamber is first connected to a constant voltage source V_0. The chamber has an inherent capacitance C, and this initial charging step has the effect of storing an electrical charge on it equal to CV_0. The chamber is then disconnected from the voltage source and exposed to the radiation. During the exposure period, ion pairs are formed in the gas and are swept to their corresponding electrodes by the electric field created by the voltage on the chamber. At the end of the exposure period, the voltage on the chamber will have dropped, as the ionization charge that is collected serves to partially discharge the stored charge CV_0. The chamber is then read out by recording the voltage drop ΔV that has occurred. If there are no other losses (such as leakage current across insulators), the amount of ionization charge created during the exposure is simply given by $C\Delta V$. Small pocket chambers of this type are frequently used to monitor exposure of personnel at radiation-producing facilities.

Ion chambers are rarely operated in pulse mode, and this mode of operation is only considered for high-dE/dx particles that can deposit large amounts of energy in the gas. The main problem is the small size of the voltage pulse that is produced by the interaction of a single quantum of radiation. The deposition of 1 MeV of energy in an ion chamber with a typical capacitance of 100 picofarads (pF) results in a voltage pulse with amplitude of only about 50 microvolts (μV). While it is possible to work with signals of such low level using careful techniques, it is much more common to use gas-filled detectors in pulse mode in the form of proportional or Geiger-Müller counters.

Proportional counters. The small pulse amplitude encountered in ion chambers can be remedied by using gas-filled detectors in a different manner. A proportional counter utilizes the phenomenon of gas multiplication to increase the pulse size by factors of hundreds or thousands. As a result, proportional-counter pulses are in the millivolt rather than microvolt range and therefore can be processed much more easily.

Gas multiplication

Gas multiplication is a consequence of the motion of a free electron in a strong electric-field. When the strength of the field is above about 10^4 volts per centimetre, an electron can gain enough energy between collisions to cause secondary ionization in the gas. After such an ionizing collision, two free electrons exist in place of the original one. In a uniform electric field under these conditions, the number of electrons will grow exponentially as they are drawn in a direction opposite to that of the applied electric field. The growth of the population of electrons is terminated only when they reach the anode. The production of such a shower of electrons is called a Townsend avalanche and is triggered by a single free electron. The total number of electrons produced in the avalanche can easily reach 1,000 or more, and the amount of charge generated in the gas is also multiplied by the same factor. The Townsend avalanche takes place in a time span of less than one microsecond under the typical conditions present in a proportional counter. Therefore, this additional charge normally contributes to the pulse that is observed from the interaction of a single incident quantum.

In a proportional counter, the objective is to have each original free electron that is formed along the track of the particle create its own individual Townsend avalanche. Thus, many avalanches are formed for each incident charged particle. One of the design objectives is to keep each avalanche the same size so that the final total charge that is created remains proportional to the number of original ion pairs formed along the particle track. The proportionality between the size of the output pulse and the amount of energy lost by the incident radiation in the gas is the basis of the term proportional counter.

Virtually all proportional counters are constructed using a wire anode of small diameter placed inside a larger, typically cylindrical, cathode that also serves to enclose the gas. Under these conditions, the electric-field strength is nonuniform and reaches large values in the immediate vicinity of the wire surface. Almost all of the volume of the gas is located outside this high-field region, and electrons formed at a random position in the gas by the incident radiation drift toward the wire without creating secondary ionization. As they are drawn closer to the wire, they are subjected to the continually increasing electric field, and eventually its value becomes high enough to cause the initiation of a Townsend avalanche. The avalanche then grows until all the electrons reach the wire surface. As nearly all avalanches are formed under identical electric-field conditions regardless of the position in the gas where the free electron was originally formed, the condition that their intensities be the same is met. Furthermore, the high electric-field strength needed for avalanche formation can be obtained using applied voltages between the anode and cathode of no more than a few thousand volts. Near the wire surface, the electric-field strength varies inversely with the distance from the wire centre, and so extremely high field values exist near the surface if the wire diameter is kept small. The size of the output pulse increases with the voltage applied to the proportional tube, since each avalanche is more vigorous as the electric-field strength increases. This behaviour is illustrated in Figure 55.

Electric-field strength

In order to sustain a Townsend avalanche, the negative charges formed in ionization must remain as free electrons. In some gases there is a tendency for neutral gas molecules to pick up an extra electron, thereby forming a negative ion. Because the mass of a negative ion is thousands of times larger than the mass of a free electron, it cannot gain sufficient energy between collisions to cause secondary ionization. Electrons do not readily attach to noble gas molecules, and argon is one of the common choices for the fill gas in proportional counters. Many other gas species also are suitable. Oxygen readily attaches to electrons, however, so air cannot be used as a proportional fill gas under normal circumstances. Proportional counters must therefore either be sealed against air leakage or operated as continuous gas-flow detectors in which any air contamination is swept out of the detector by continuously flowing the fill gas through the active volume.

For proportional counters of normal size, only heavy charged particles or other weakly penetrating radiations can be fully stopped in the gas. Therefore, they can be used for energy measurements of alpha particles but not for longer-range beta particles or other fast electrons. Low-energy electrons produced by X-ray interactions in the gas may also be fully stopped, and proportional counters find application as X-ray spectrometers as well. Even though fast electrons do not deposit all of their energy, the gas-multiplication process results in a pulse that is generally

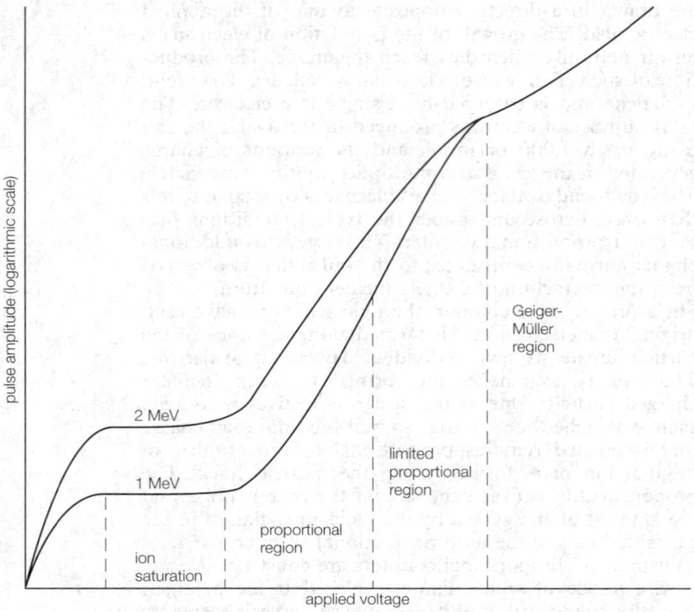

Figure 55: *Regions of operation of gas-filled detectors.* The two curves represent the observed pulse height for quanta depositing two different amounts of energy in the gas.

Adapted from G.F. Knoll, *Radiation Detection and Measurement*, 2nd ed. (1989) reprinted with permission of John Wiley and Sons, Inc., New York City

large enough to record, and therefore proportional counters can be used in simple counting systems for beta particles or gamma rays.

Geiger-Müller counters. In a Townsend avalanche there are many excited molecules formed in addition to the secondary ions. Within a few nanoseconds, many of these excited molecules return to their ground state by emitting an ultraviolet photon. This light may travel centimetres through the gas before being reabsorbed, either in a photoelectric interaction involving a less tightly bound shell of a gas atom or at a solid surface. If a free electron is liberated in this absorption process, it will begin to drift toward the anode wire and can produce its own avalanche. By this mechanism, one avalanche can breed another, spreading throughout the entire volume of the gas-multiplication region around the anode wire. This uncontrolled spread of avalanches throughout the entire detector is known as a Geiger discharge.

Geiger discharge

In a proportional counter the spread of avalanches is inhibited through the addition of a small amount of a second gas (for example, methane) that absorbs the ultraviolet photons without producing free electrons. In a Geiger-Müller counter, conditions are such that each avalanche creates more than one additional avalanche, and their number grows rapidly in time. The propagation of avalanches is eventually terminated by the buildup of a cloud of positive charge around the anode wire that consists of the positive ions that were also formed during the avalanches. Ions move thousands of times more slowly than free electrons in the same electric field, and in the short span of a few microseconds needed to propagate the avalanches, their movement is minimal. Because most avalanches are clustered around the anode wire, this positive space charge reduces the electric field in the critical multiplication region below the strength required for additional avalanches to form, and the Geiger discharge ceases. In the process a huge number of ion pairs have been formed, and pulses as large as one volt are produced by the Geiger-Müller tube. Because the pulse is so large, little demand is placed on the pulse-processing electronics, and Geiger counting systems can be extremely simple.

Gas-filled detectors can be operated in several regimes, as illustrated in Figure 55. At low applied voltage, no gas multiplication takes place, and the detector functions as an ion chamber. At some minimum voltage, avalanches begin to form, marking the start of the proportional-counter region, and they become more vigorous as the voltage increases. Finally, at high voltages a transition to the Geiger-Müller mode of operation takes place as the large avalanches inevitably result in their uncontrolled spread. Because the Geiger discharge is self-limiting, radiation that creates only a single ion pair in the gas will result in an output pulse as large as that produced by a particle that deposits a great deal of energy and creates many ion pairs. Therefore, the amplitude of the output pulse carries no energy information, and Geiger tubes are useful only in pulse-counting systems. They will produce a pulse for virtually every charged particle that reaches the fill gas, and many Geiger tubes are fitted with a thin entrance window to allow weakly penetrating radiations such as alpha particles to enter the gas.

Gamma-ray detection efficiency

As with all gas-filled detectors, the detection efficiency for gamma rays is low, only a few percent. Almost no gamma-ray photons interact directly in the gas. A pulse can be produced if the gamma ray interacts in the solid wall of the tube and the secondary electron that is formed subsequently enters the gas before losing all its energy. As typical secondary electrons travel no more than one or two millimetres in solids, only the inner layer of the wall closest to the gas will contribute any secondary electrons. The probability that the incoming gamma ray interacts in this thin layer is small, leading to the low value of detection efficiency.

Nonetheless, Geiger tubes make useful instruments to check for the presence of alpha, beta, or gamma radiation. Despite the fact that the gamma detection efficiency is low, a Geiger tube will respond to single gamma-ray photons and thus can indicate lower levels of gamma radiation than is possible from an ion chamber operated in less sensitive current mode. The output of a portable Geiger survey meter may be displayed using a rate meter to indicate the average rate of pulse production from the tube or through the generation of an audible sound on a loudspeaker for each detected pulse. This is the origin of the stereotypical clicking of the Geiger counter that is often associated with radiation detectors.

Semiconductor detectors. When a charged particle loses its energy in a solid rather than a gas, processes similar to ionization and excitation also take place. In most solids or liquids, however, the resulting electrical charges cannot be transported over appreciable distances and thus cannot serve as the basis of an electrical signal. There is one category of solids that are an exception. These are semiconductor materials, of which silicon and germanium are the predominant examples. In these materials, charges created by radiation can be collected efficiently over distances of many centimetres.

The electronic structure of semiconductors is such that, at ordinary temperatures, nearly all electrons are tied to specific sites in the crystalline lattice and are said to have an energy in the valence band. At any given time, a few electrons will have gained sufficient thermal energy to have broken loose from localized sites and are called conduction electrons; their energy lies in a higher conduction band. Since some energy must be expended in freeing an electron from its normal place in the covalent lattice of a crystal, there is a band gap that separates bound valence electrons from free conduction electrons. In pure crystals no electrons can have an energy within this gap. In silicon the band gap is about 1.1 eV, and in germanium it is about 0.7 eV. In perfect materials held at absolute zero temperature, all electrons would theoretically be bound to specific lattice sites, so that the valance band would be completely filled and the conduction band empty. The thermal energy available at ordinary temperatures allows some electrons to be freed from specific sites and be elevated across the band gap to the conduction band. Therefore, for each conduction electron that exists, an electron is missing from a normally occupied valence site. This electron vacancy is called a hole, and in many ways it behaves as though it were a point positive charge. If an electron jumps from a nearby bond to fill the vacancy, the hole can be thought of as moving in the opposite direction. Both electrons in the conduction band and holes in the valence band can be made to drift in a preferred direction under the influence of an electric field.

The passage of an energetic charged particle through a semiconductor transfers energy to electrons, the vast majority of which are bound electrons in the valence band. Sufficient energy may be transferred to promote a valence electron into the conduction band, resulting in an electron-hole pair. In semiconductor detectors, an electric field is present throughout the active volume. The subsequent drift of the electrons and holes toward electrodes on the surface of the semiconductor material generates a current pulse in much the same manner as the motion of ion pairs in a gas-filled ion chamber.

Electron-hole pair

The minimum energy transfer required for creation of an electron-hole pair is the band-gap energy of about 1 eV. Experimental measurements show that, as in the production of an ion pair in a gas, about three times the minimum energy is required on the average to form an electron-hole pair. Thus, a 1-MeV charged particle losing all its energy in a semiconductor will create about 300,000 electron-hole pairs. This number is about 10 times larger than the number of ion pairs that would be formed by the same particle in a gas. As one consequence, the charge packet for equivalent energy loss by the incident particle is therefore 10 times larger, improving the signal-to-noise ratio as compared with a pulse-type ion chamber. More significant is the improvement in energy resolution. The statistical fluctuations in the number of charge carriers per pulse (that often limit energy resolution) become a smaller fraction as the total number of carriers increases. Thus semiconductor detectors offer the best energy resolution provided by common detectors, and values of a few tenths of a percent are not uncommon.

Another benefit derives from the fact that the detection medium is a solid rather than a gas. In solids, the range of heavy charged particles such as alphas is only tens or hundreds of micrometres, as opposed to a few centimetres in atmospheric pressure gases. Therefore, the full energy of the particle can be absorbed in a relatively thin detector. More importantly, it is practical to fully absorb fast electrons such as beta particles. As opposed to ranges of metres in gases, fast electrons travel only a few millimetres in solids, and semiconductor detectors can be fabricated that are thicker than this range. Therefore, spectroscopic methods can be employed to measure the energies of fast electron radiations.

Silicon detectors. Silicon detectors with diameters of up to several centimetres and thicknesses of several hundred micrometres are common choices for heavy charged particle detectors. They are fabricated from extremely pure or highly resistive silicon that is mildly *n*- or *p*-type owing to residual dopants. (Doping is the process in which an impurity, called a dopant, is added to a semiconductor to enhance its conductivity. If excess positive holes are formed as a result of the doping, the semiconductor is a *p*-type; if excess free electrons are formed, it is an *n*-type semiconductor.) A thin layer of the oppositely doped silicon is created on one surface, forming a rectifying junction—*i.e.,* one that allows current to flow freely in only one direction. If voltage is now applied to reverse-bias this diode so that the free electrons and positive holes flow away from the junction, a depletion region is formed in the vicinity of the junction. In the depletion region, an electric field exists that quickly sweeps out electron-hole pairs that may be thermally generated and reduces the equilibrium concentration of the charge carriers to exceedingly low levels. Under these circumstances the additional electron-hole pairs suddenly created by the energy deposited by a charged particle now become detectable as a pulse of current produced from the detector. Raising the applied voltage increases the thickness of the depletion layer, and fully depleted configurations are commercially available in which the depletion region extends from the front to back surfaces of the silicon wafer. The entire volume of silicon then becomes the active volume of the detector. Silicon diode detectors with thicknesses of less than a millimetre are generally small enough in volume so that the thermally generated carriers can be tolerated, allowing operation of these detectors at room temperature.

Depletion region

These simple silicon diode detectors are presently limited to depletion depths of about one millimetre or less. In order to create thicker detectors, a process known as lithium-ion drifting can be employed. This process produces a compensated material in which electron donors and acceptors are perfectly balanced and that behaves electrically much like a pure semiconductor. By fabricating *n*- and *p*-type contacts onto the opposite surface of a lithium-drifted material and applying an external voltage, depletion thicknesses of many millimetres can be formed. These relatively thick lithium-drifted silicon detectors are widely used for X-ray spectroscopy and for the measurement of fast-electron energies. Operationally, they are normally cooled to the temperature of liquid nitrogen to minimize the number of thermally generated carriers that are spontaneously produced in the thick active volume so as to control the associated leakage current and consequent loss of energy resolution.

Germanium detectors. Semiconductor detectors also can be used in gamma-ray spectroscopy. In this case, however, it is advantageous to choose germanium rather than silicon as the detector material. With an atomic number of 32, germanium has a much higher photoelectric cross section than silicon (atomic number, *Z,* of 14), as the probability of photoelectron absorption varies approximately as $Z^{4.5}$. Therefore, it is far more probable for an incident gamma ray to lose all its energy in germanium than in silicon, and the intrinsic peak efficiency for germanium will be many times larger. In gamma-ray spectroscopy, there is an advantage in using detectors with a large active volume. The depletion region in germanium can be made several centimetres thick if ultrapure material is used. Advances in germanium purification processes in the 1970s have led to the commercial availability of material in which the residual impurity concentration is about one part in 10^{12}.

Germanium coaxial configuration

The most common type of germanium gamma-ray spectrometer consists of a high-purity (mildly *p*-type) crystal fitted with electrodes in the coaxial configuration shown in Figure 56. Normal sizes correspond to germanium volumes of several hundred cubic centimetres. Because of their excellent energy resolution of a few tenths of a percent, germanium coaxial detectors have become the workhorse of modern-day high-resolution gamma-ray spectroscopy. The band gap in germanium is smaller than that in silicon, so thermally generated charge carriers are even more of a potential problem. As a result, virtually all germanium detectors, even those with relatively small volume, are cooled to liquid-nitrogen temperature during their use. Typically, the germanium crystal is sealed inside a vacuum enclosure, or cryostat, that provides thermal contact with a storage dewar of liquid nitrogen. Mechanical refrigerators are also available to cool the detector for use in remote locations where a supply of liquid nitrogen may not be available.

Although semiconductor detectors can be operated in current mode, the vast majority of applications are best served by operating the device in pulse mode to take advantage of its excellent energy resolution. The time required to collect the electrons and holes formed along a particle track is typically tens to hundreds of nanoseconds,

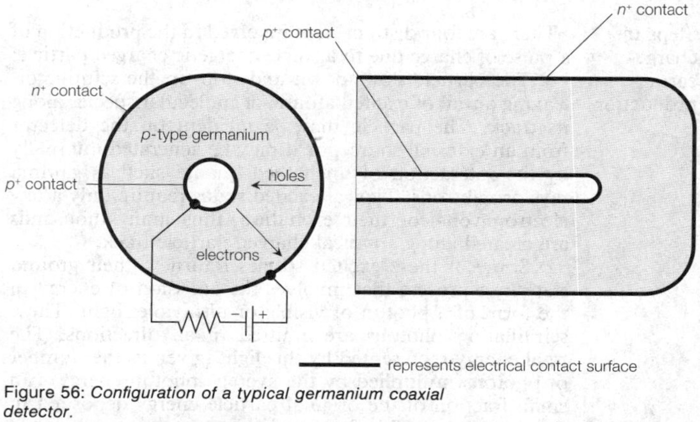

Figure 56: *Configuration of a typical germanium coaxial detector.*
Cross sections oriented (left) perpendicular to and (right) along the cylindrical axis.

depending on detector thickness. The rise time of the output pulse is therefore of the same order, and relatively precise timing measurements are possible, especially for thin detectors.

Scintillation and Čerenkov detectors. One of the overworked images of radiation in popular perception is the idea that radioactive materials glow, emitting some form of eerie light. Most materials when irradiated do not emit light; however, low-intensity visible and ultraviolet light can be detected from some transparent materials owing to the energy deposited by interacting charged particles. The intensity of this light is far too small to be seen with the naked eye under ordinary circumstances, and visible glowing requires radiation fields of extraordinary intensity. One example is the blue luminescence that can be seen in the water surrounding the core of some types of research reactors. This light originates from the Čerenkov radiations (see below) from secondary electrons produced by the extremely intense gamma-ray flux emerging from the reactor core.

Scintillators. In certain types of transparent materials, the energy deposited by an energetic particle can create excited atomic or molecular states that quickly decay through the emission of visible or ultraviolet light, a process sometimes called prompt fluorescence. Such materials are known as scintillators and are commonly exploited in scintillation detectors. The amount of light generated from a single charged particle of a few MeV kinetic energy is very weak and cannot be seen with the unaided eye. However, some early historic experiments by the British physicist Ernest Rutherford on alpha-particle scattering were carried out by manually counting scintillation flashes from individual alpha particles interacting in a zinc sulfide screen and viewed through a microscope. Modern scintillation detectors eliminate the need for manual counting by converting the light into an electrical pulse in a photomultiplier tube or photodiode (see below). A typical scintillator-photomultiplier assembly is illustrated in Figure 57.

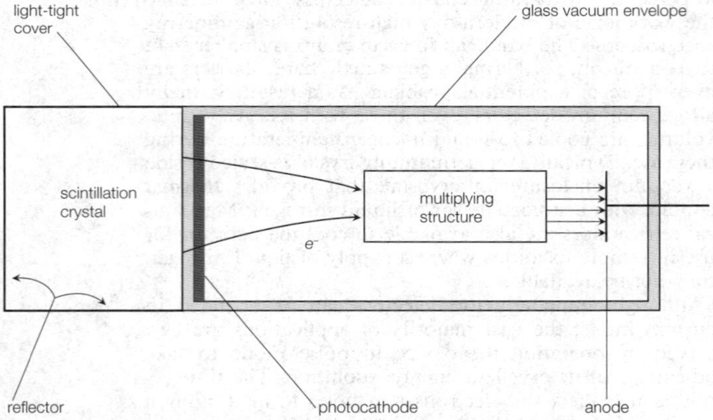

Figure 57: Scintillation detector consisting of a scintillator mounted in optical contact with a photomultiplier tube.

Steps in charge-carrier production

There are four distinct steps involved in the production of a pulse of charge due to a single energetic charged particle:

1. The particle slows down and stops in the scintillator, leaving a trail of excited atomic or molecular species along its track. The particle may be incident on the detector from an external source, or it may be generated internally by the interaction of uncharged quanta such as gamma rays or neutrons. Typical excited states require only a few electron volts for their excitation; thus many thousands are created along a typical charged particle track.

2. Some of these excited species return to their ground state in a process that involves the emission of energy in the form of a photon of visible or ultraviolet light. These scintillation photons are emitted in all directions. The total energy represented by this light (given as the number of photons multiplied by the average photon energy) is a small fraction of the original particle energy deposited in the scintillator. This fraction is given the name scintillation efficiency and ranges from about 3 to 15 percent for common scintillation materials. The photon energy (or the wavelength of the light) is distributed over an emission spectrum that is characteristic of the particular scintillation material.

The excited species have a characteristic mean lifetime, and their population decays exponentially. The decay time determines the rate at which the light is emitted following the excitation and is also characteristic of the particular scintillation material. Decay times range from less than one nanosecond to several microseconds and generally represent the slowest process in the several steps involved in generating a pulse from the detector. There is often a preference for collecting the light quickly to form a fast-rising output signal pulse, and short decay times are therefore highly desirable in some applications.

3. Some fraction of the light leaves the scintillator through an exit window provided on one of its surfaces. The remaining surfaces of the scintillator are provided with an optically reflecting coating so that the light that is originally directed away from the exit window has a high probability of being reflected from the surfaces and collected. As much as 90 percent of the light can be collected under favourable conditions.

4. A fraction of the emerging light photons are converted to charge in a light sensor normally mounted in optical contact with the exit window. This fraction is known as the quantum efficiency of the light sensor. In a silicon photodiode, as many as 80 to 90 percent of the light photons are converted to electron-hole pairs, but in a photomultiplier tube, only about 25 percent of the photons are converted to photoelectrons at the wavelength of maximum response of its photocathode (see below).

Quantum efficiency

The net result of this sequence of steps, each with its own inefficiency, is the creation of a relatively limited number of charge carriers in the light sensor. A typical pulse will correspond to at most a few thousand charge carriers. This figure is a small fraction of the number of electron-hole pairs that would be produced directly in a semiconductor detector by the same energy deposition. One consequence is that the energy resolution of scintillators is rather poor owing to the statistical fluctuations in the number of carriers actually obtained. For example, the best energy resolution from a scintillator for 0.662 MeV gamma rays (a common standard) is about 5 to 6 percent. By comparison, the energy resolution for the same gamma-ray energy in a germanium detector may be about 0.2 percent. In many applications, the disadvantage of poor energy resolution is offset by other favourable properties, for example, high gamma-ray detection efficiency.

There are many characteristics that are desirable in a scintillator, including high scintillation efficiency, short decay time, linear dependence of the amount of light generated on deposited energy, good optical quality, and availability in large sizes at modest cost. No known material meets all these criteria, and therefore many different materials are in common use, each with attributes that are best suited for certain applications. These materials are commonly classified into two broad categories: inorganic and organic scintillators.

Most inorganic scintillators consist of transparent single crystals, whose dimensions range from a few millimetres to many centimetres. Some inorganics, such as silver-activated zinc sulfide, are good scintillators but cannot be grown in the form of optical-quality large crystals. As a result, their use is limited to thin polycrystalline layers known as phosphor screens.

The inorganic materials that produce the highest light output unfortunately have relatively long decay times. The most common inorganic scintillator is sodium iodide activated with a trace amount of thallium [NaI(Tl)], which has an unusually large light yield corresponding to a scintillation efficiency of about 13 percent. Its decay time is 0.23 microsecond, acceptable for many applications but uncomfortably long when extremely high counting rates or fast timing measurements are involved. The emission spectrum of NaI(Tl) is peaked at a wavelength corresponding to the blue region of the electromagnetic spectrum and is well matched to the spectral response of photomultiplier tubes. Thallium-activated cesium iodide [CsI(Tl)] also produces excellent light yield but has two relatively long decay components with decay times of 0.68 and 3.3 microseconds. Its emission spectrum is shifted toward the longer-wavelength end of the visible spectrum and is a better match to the spectral response of photodiodes. Both NaI(Tl) and CsI(Tl) have iodine, with an atomic number of 53, as a major constituent. Therefore the photoelectric cross section in these materials is large enough to make them attractive in gamma-ray spectroscopy. They are available economically in large sizes so that the corresponding gamma-ray intrinsic peak efficiency can be many times greater than that for the largest available germanium detector. Other inorganic scintillation materials are listed in Table 6. Included are some recently developed materials with much shorter decay times but, unfortunately, also lower light yields. These materials are useful for timing measurements but will have poorer energy resolution compared with the brighter materials.

Organic scintillators

A number of organic molecules with a so-called π-orbital electron structure exhibit prompt fluorescence following their excitation by the energy deposited by an ionizing particle. The basic mechanism of light emission does not depend on the physical state of the molecule; consequently, organic scintillators take many different forms. The earliest were pure crystals of anthracene or stilbene. More recently, organics are used primarily in the form of liquid solutions of an organic fluor (fluorescent molecule) in a solvent such as toluene, or as a plastic, in which the fluor is dissolved in a monomer that is subsequently polymerized. Frequently, a third component is added to liquid or plastic scintillators to act as a wave shifter, which absorbs the primary light from the organic fluor and reradiates the energy at a longer wavelength more suitable for matching the response of photomultiplier tubes or photodiodes. Plastic scintillators are commercially available in sheets or cylinders with dimensions of several centimetres or as small-diameter scintillating fibres.

One of the most useful attributes of organic scintillators is their fast decay time. Many commercially available liquids or plastics have decay times of two to three nanoseconds, allowing their use in precise timing measurements. Organics tend to show a somewhat nonlinear yield of light as the deposited energy increases, and the light yield per unit energy deposited is significantly higher for low dE/dx particles such as electrons than for high dE/dx heavy charged particles. Even for electrons, however, the light yield is two to three times smaller than that of the best inorganic materials.

Because liquids and plastics can be made into detectors of flexible size and shape, they find many applications in the direct detection of charged particle radiations. They are seldom used to detect gamma rays because the low average atomic number of these materials inhibits the full energy absorption needed for spectroscopy. The average atomic number is not greatly different from that of tissue, however, and plastic scintillators have consequently found some useful applications in the measurement of gamma-ray doses. A unique application of liquid scintillators is in the counting of radioisotopes that emit low-energy beta particles, such as hydrogen-3 (^3H) or carbon-14 (^{14}C). As these low-energy beta particles have rather short ranges, they can be easily absorbed before reaching the active volume of a detector. This attenuation problem is completely avoided if the sample is dissolved directly in the liquid scintillator. In this case, the beta particles find themselves in the scintillator immediately after being emitted.

Čerenkov light

Čerenkov detectors. Čerenkov light is a consequence of the motion of a charged particle with a speed that is greater than the speed of light in the same medium. No particle can exceed the speed of light in a vacuum (c), but in materials with an index of refraction represented by n, the particle velocity v will be greater than the velocity of light if $v > c/n$. For materials with an index of refraction in the common range between 1.3 and 1.8, this velocity requirement corresponds to a minimum kinetic energy of many hundreds of MeV for heavy charged particles. Fast electrons with relatively small kinetic energy can reach this minimum velocity, however, and the application of the Čerenkov process to radiations with energy below 20 MeV is restricted to primary or secondary fast electrons. Čerenkov light is emitted only during the time in which the particle is slowing down and therefore has very fast time characteristics. In contrast with the isotropically emitted scintillation light, Čerenkov light is emitted along the surface of a forward-directed cone centred on the particle velocity vector. The wavelength of the light is preferentially shifted toward the short-wavelength (blue) end of the spectrum. The total intensity of the Čerenkov light is much weaker than the light emitted from equivalent energy loss in a good scintillator and may be only a few hundred photons or less for a 1-MeV electron. Čerenkov detectors are normally used with the same type of light sensors employed in scintillation detectors.

Conversion of light to charge. There are two major types of devices used to form an electrical signal from scintillation or Čerenkov light: the photomultiplier tube and the photodiode. Photomultiplier tubes are vacuum tubes in which the first major component is a photocathode. A light photon may interact in the photocathode to eject a low-energy electron into the vacuum. The quantum efficiency of the photocathode is defined as the probability for this conversion to occur. It is a strong function of wavelength of the incident light, and an effort is made to match the spectral response of the photocathode to the emission spectrum of the scintillator in use. The average quantum efficiency over the emission spectrum of a typical scintillator is about 15 to 20 percent.

The result of sensing a flash of light is therefore the production of a corresponding pulse of electrons from the photocathode. Their number at this point is typically a few thousand or less, so that the total charge packet is too small to be conveniently measured. Instead, the photomultiplier tube has a second component that multiplies the number of electrons by a factor of typically 10^5 or

Table 6: Some Properties of Inorganic Scintillators

material	specific gravity	wavelength of maximum emission (nm)	principal decay constant (μs)	total light yield (photons/MeV)	relative gamma-ray pulse height with Bialkali photomultiplier tube
NaI(Tl)	3.67	415	0.23	38,000	1.00
CsI(Tl)	4.51	560	0.68	65,000	0.49
CsI(Na)	4.51	420	0.63	39,000	1.11
LiI(Eu)	4.08	470	1.4	11,000	0.23
BGO	7.13	505	0.30	8,200	0.13
BaF_2 slow component	4.89	310	0.62	10,000	0.13
BaF_2 fast component	4.89	220	0.0006	—	0.03*
ZnS(Ag) (polycrystalline)	4.09	450	0.2	—	1.30†
CaF_2(Eu)	3.19	435	0.9	24,000	0.78
CsF	4.11	390	0.004	—	0.05
Li glass‡	2.5	395	0.075	—	0.10
For comparison, a typical organic (plastic) scintillator:					
NE 102A	1.03	423	0.002	10,000	0.25

*Using an ultraviolet-sensitive photomultiplier tube. †For alpha particles. ‡Properties vary with exact formulation.

Source: Adapted from G.F. Knoll, *Radiation Detection and Measurement,* 2nd ed., copyright © 1989 by John Wiley & Sons, Inc. Reprinted by permission of John Wiley & Sons, Inc.

10^6. The electron multiplication takes place along a series of electrodes called dynodes that have the property of emitting more than one electron when struck by a single electron that has been accelerated from a previous dynode. After the multiplication process, the amplified pulse of electrons is collected at an anode that provides the tube's output. The amplitude of this charge is an indicator of the intensity of the original light flash in the scintillator.

Photodiodes

Alternatively, the light can be measured using a solid-state device known as a photodiode. A device of this type consists of a thin semiconductor wafer that converts the incident light photons into electron-hole pairs. As many as 80 or 90 percent of the light photons will undergo this process, and so the equivalent quantum efficiency is considerably higher than in a photomultiplier tube. There is no amplification of this charge, however, so the output pulse is much smaller. When the photodiode is operated in pulse mode, many sources of electronic noise are large enough to degrade the quality of the signal, and for a given scintillator a poorer energy resolution is usually observed with a photodiode than with a photomultiplier tube. However, the photodiode is a much more compact and rugged device, operates at low voltage, and offers corresponding advantages in certain applications. Scintillators coupled to photodiodes can also be conveniently used in current mode, especially for intense radiation fluxes. The current of electron-hole pairs induced by the scintillation light can be large enough to make noise contributions less important.

Neutron detectors. The general principle of detecting neutrons involves a two-step process. First, the neutron must interact in the detector to form charged particles. Second, the detector must then produce an output signal based on the energy deposited by these charged particles. Many of the major detector types that have already been discussed for other radiations can be adapted to neutron measurements by incorporating a material that will serve as a neutron-to-charged-particle converter.

Slow-neutron detectors. For slow neutrons, the principal conversion methods involve one of the nuclear reactions shown in Table 7. In each case, the reaction is characterized by a positive Q-value, meaning that this amount of energy is released in the reaction. Since the incoming slow neutron has a low kinetic energy and the target nucleus is essentially at rest, the reactants have little total kinetic energy. Consequently, the reaction products are formed with a total kinetic energy essentially equal to the Q-value. When one of these reactions is induced by a slow neutron, the directly measurable charged particles appear with the same characteristic total kinetic energy. Since the neutron contributes nothing to the kinetic energy of the reaction products, these reactions cannot be used to measure the energy of slow neutrons; they may only be applied as the basis for counters that simply record the number of neutrons that interact in the detector.

Table 7: Some Reactions Useful for Slow-Neutron Detection

reaction*	Q-value (MeV)	cross section (in barns) for thermal (0.025 eV) neutrons
$^{10}B + n \rightarrow {}^{7}Li + \alpha$	2.31	3,840
$^{6}Li + n \rightarrow {}^{3}H + \alpha$	4.78	940
$^{3}He + n \rightarrow {}^{3}H + p$	0.764	5,330
$^{235}U + n \rightarrow X + Y$ (fission fragments)	~200	575

*n represents a neutron, p a proton, and α an alpha particle.

In the lithium-6 (^{6}Li) and boron-10 (^{10}B) reactions, the isotopes of interest are present only in limited percentage in the naturally occurring element. To enhance the conversion efficiency of lithium or boron, samples that are enriched in the desired isotope are often used in the fabrication of detectors. Helium-3 (^{3}He) is a rare stable isotope of helium and is commercially available in isotopically separated form.

Boron trifluoride proportional tube

One of the common detectors for slow neutrons is a proportional tube filled with boron trifluoride (BF_3) gas. Some incident neutrons interact with the boron-10 in the gas, producing two charged particles with a combined energy of 2.3 MeV. These particles leave a trail of ion pairs in the gas, and a pulse develops in the normal manner as in any proportional counter. Boron trifluoride performs as an acceptable proportional gas only at pressures of less than one atmosphere, and the detection efficiency is therefore limited by the corresponding low density of boron nuclei at such pressures. Alternatively, a conventional proportional gas can be used, and the boron can be present in the form of a solid layer deposited in the inner surface of the tube.

Proportional counters filled with helium-3 also are based on a neutron interaction in the gas that produces charged particles. In this case, the Q-value of 0.76 MeV imparts this energy to the particles formed in the reaction. Helium works well as a proportional gas even at high pressure; thus helium-3 proportional tubes filled to 20 atmospheres or more provide neutron detection with relatively high intrinsic efficiency.

Also common are slow-neutron detectors in the form of scintillators in which either boron or lithium is incorporated as a constituent of the scintillation material. Europium-activated lithium iodide is one example of a crystalline scintillator of this type, and boron-loaded plastic scintillators are also available.

The fission reaction is often used as a neutron converter in conjunction with ion chambers. The enormous energy released in a fission reaction appears primarily as the kinetic energy of the two fission products. These fission fragments are highly ionizing charged particles, and they result in an unusually large energy deposition in the detector. Uranium-lined ion chambers (fission chambers) are common neutron sensors employed to monitor nuclear reactors and other intense sources of neutrons.

Fast-neutron detectors. The probability of inducing one of the reactions listed in Table 7 is expressed as the magnitude of its neutron cross section. These values are relatively large for slow neutrons but decrease by several orders of magnitude for fast neutrons. Therefore, slow-neutron detectors such as the boron trifluoride tube become inefficient for the direct detection of fast neutrons. One method used to increase this efficiency is to surround the detector with a material that effectively moderates or slows down the fast neutrons. For example, a polyethylene layer with a thickness of 20 to 30 centimetres will cause some incident fast neutrons to scatter many times from the hydrogen nuclei that are present, giving up energy in the process. A fraction of these moderated neutrons may then diffuse to the detector as slow neutrons with a high interaction probability. Since the moderation process obscures any information on the original energy of the fast neutron, these devices are useful only in simple neutron-counting systems.

Fast-neutron elastic scattering

The preferred conversion reaction for the direct detection of fast neutrons tends to be the elastic-scattering interaction. The resulting recoil nuclei can absorb a significant fraction of the original neutron energy in a single scattering and then deposit that energy in a manner similar to that of any other charged particle. The scattered neutron, now with a lower energy, may either escape from the detector or possibly interact again elsewhere in its volume. The most common scattering target is hydrogen, and a fast neutron can transfer up to all its energy in a single collision with a hydrogen nucleus. The amount of energy transferred varies with the scattering angle, which in hydrogen covers a continuum from zero (corresponding to grazing-angle scattering) up to the full neutron energy (corresponding to a head-on collision). Thus, when monoenergetic fast neutrons strike a material containing hydrogen, a spectrum of recoil protons is produced that ranges in energy between these limits. Some information about the original energy of the neutrons can be deduced by recording the pulse height-spectrum from a hydrogen-containing detector. This process generally involves applying a computer-based deconvolution code to the measured spectrum and is one of the few methods generally available to experimentally measure fast-neutron energy spectra.

The result of a fast-neutron scattering from hydrogen is a recoiling energetic hydrogen nucleus, or recoil proton. One type of detector based on these recoil protons is a proportional counter containing a hydrogenous gas. Pure hydrogen can be used, but a more common choice is a heavier hydrocarbon such as methane in which the range of the resulting recoil protons typically is short enough to be fully stopped in the gas. Recoil protons also can be generated and detected in organic liquid or plastic scintillators. In instances such as these, many more hydrogen nuclei are present per unit volume than in a gas, so that the detection efficiency for fast neutrons can be many times larger than in a proportional counter.

(G.F.K.)

MATERIALS TESTING

Materials testing involves measuring the characteristics and behaviour of such substances as certain metals, ceramics, or plastics under various conditions. The data thus obtained can be used in specifying the suitability of materials for various applications—*e.g.,* building or aircraft construction, machinery, or packaging. A full- or small-scale model of a proposed machine or structure may be tested. Alternatively, investigators may construct mathematical models that utilize known material characteristics and behaviour to predict capabilities of the structure.

Use of mathematical models

Materials testing breaks down into five major categories: mechanical testing; testing for thermal properties; testing for electrical properties; testing for resistance to corrosion, radiation, and biological deterioration; and nondestructive testing. Standard test methods have been established by such national and international bodies as the International Organization for Standardization (ISO), with headquarters in Geneva, and the American Society for Testing and Materials (ASTM), Philadelphia.

MECHANICAL TESTING

Structures and machines, or their components, fail because of fracture or excessive deformation. In attempting to prevent such failure, the designer estimates how much stress (load per unit area) can be anticipated, and specifies materials that can withstand expected stresses. A stress analysis, accomplished either experimentally or by means of a mathematical model, indicates expected areas of high stress in a machine or structure. Mechanical property tests, carried out experimentally, indicate which materials may safely be employed.

Static tension and compression tests. When subjected to tension (pulling apart), a material elongates and eventually breaks. A simple static tension test determines the breaking point of the material and its elongation, designated as strain (change in length per unit length). If a 100-millimetre steel bar elongates 1 millimetre under a given load, for example, strain is $(101-100)/100 = 1/100 = 1$ percent.

Elements of a static tension test

A static tension test requires (1) a test piece, usually cylindrical, or with a middle section of smaller diameter than the ends; (2) a test machine that applies, measures, and records various loads; and (3) an appropriate set of grips to grasp the test piece. In the static tension test, the test machine uniformly stretches a small part (the test section) of the test piece. The length of the test section (called the gauge length) is measured at different loads with a device called an extensometer; these measurements are used to compute strain.

Conventional testing machines are of the constant load, constant load-rate, and constant displacement-rate types (see Figure 58). Constant load types employ weights directly both to apply load and to measure it. Constant load-rate test machines employ separate load and measurement units; loads are generally applied by means of a hydraulic ram into which oil is pumped at a constant rate. Constant displacement-rate testing machines are generally driven by gear-screws.

Test machine grips are designed to transfer load smoothly into the test piece without producing local stress concentrations. The ends of the test piece are often slightly enlarged so that if slight concentrations of stress are present these will be directed to the gauge section, and failures will occur only where measurements are being taken. Clamps, pins, threading, or bonding are employed to hold the test piece. Eccentric (nonuniform) loading causes bending of the sample in addition to tension, which means that stress in the sample will not be uniform. To avoid this, most gripping devices incorporate one or two swivel joints in the linkage that carries the load to the test piece. Air bearings help to correct horizontal misalignment, which can be troublesome with such brittle materials as ceramics.

Static compression tests determine a material's response to crushing, or support-type loading (such as in the beams of a house). Testing machines and extensometers for compression tests resemble those used for tension tests. Specimens are generally simpler, however, because gripping is not usually a problem. Furthermore, specimens may have a constant cross-sectional area throughout their full length. The gauge length of a sample in a compression test is its full length. A serious problem in compression testing is the possibility that the sample or load chain may buckle (form bulges or bend) prior to material failure. To prevent this, specimens are kept short and stubby.

Static shear and bending tests. Inplane shear tests indicate the deformation response of a material to forces applied tangentially. These tests are applied primarily to thin sheet materials, either metals or composites, such as fibreglass reinforced plastic.

A homogeneous material such as untreated steel casting reacts in a different way under stress than does a grained material such as wood or an adhesively bonded joint. These anisotropic materials are said to have preferential planes of weakness; they resist stress better in some planes than in others, and consequently must undergo a different type of shear test.

Shear strength of rivets and other fasteners also can be measured. Though the state of stress of such items is generally quite complicated, a simple shear test, providing only limited information, is adequate for most purposes.

Tensile testing of brittle materials

Tensile testing is difficult to perform directly upon certain brittle materials such as glass and ceramics. In such cases, a measure of the tensile strength of the material may

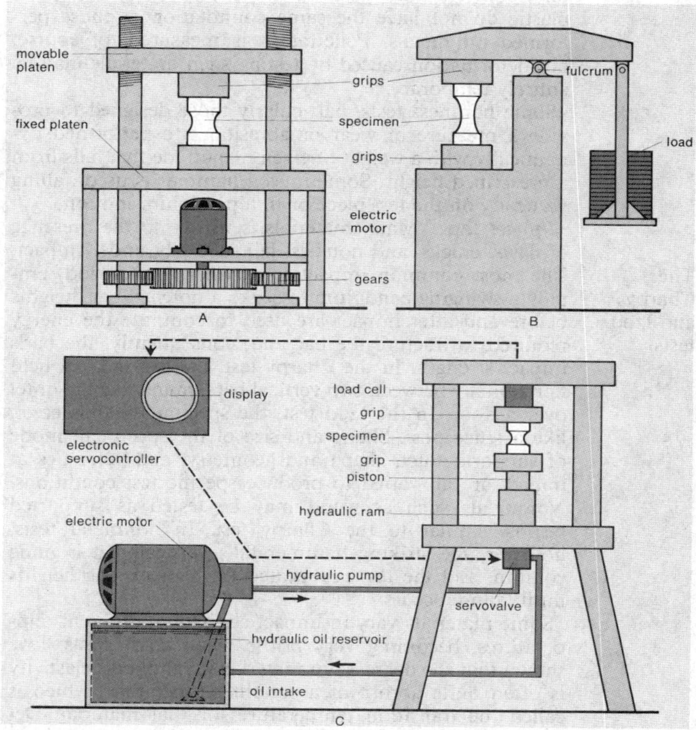

Figure 58: *Testing machines:*
(A) constant displacement-rate type; (B) constant load type;
(C) constant load-rate type.

be obtained by performing a bend test, in which tensile (stretching) stresses develop on one side of the bent member and corresponding compressive stresses develop on the opposite side. If the material is substantially stronger in compression than tension, failure initiates on the tensile side of the member and, hence, provides the required information on the material tensile strength. Because it is necessary to know the exact magnitude of the tensile stress at failure in order to establish the strength of the material, however, the bending test method is applicable to only a very restricted class of materials and conditions.

Measures of ductility. Ductility is the capacity of a material to deform permanently in response to stress. Most common steels, for example, are quite ductile and hence can accommodate local stress concentrations. Brittle materials, such as glass, cannot accommodate concentrations of stress because they lack ductility; they, therefore, fracture rather easily.

When a material specimen is stressed, it deforms elastically (*i.e.,* recoverably) at first; thereafter, deformation becomes permanent. A cylinder of steel, for example, may "neck" (assume an hourglass shape) in response to stress. If the material is ductile, this local deformation is permanent, and the test piece does not assume its former shape if the stress is removed. With sufficiently high stress, fracture occurs.

Ductility can be expressed as strain, reduction in area, or toughness. Strain, or change in length per unit length, was explained earlier. Reduction in area (change in area per unit area) may be measured, for example, in the test section of a steel bar that necks when stressed. Toughness measures the amount of energy required to deform a piece of material permanently. Toughness is a desirable material property in that it permits a component to deform plastically, rather than crack and perhaps fracture.

Hardness testing. Based on the idea that a material's response to a load placed at one small point is related to its ability to deform permanently (yield), the hardness test is performed by pressing a hardened steel ball (Brinell test) or a steel or diamond cone (Rockwell test) into the surface of the test piece. Most hardness tests are performed on commercial machines that register arbitrary values in inverse relation to the depth of penetration of the ball or cone. Similar indentation tests are performed on wood. Hardness tests of materials such as rubber or plastic do not have the same connotation as those performed on metals. Penetration is measured, of course, but deformation caused by testing such materials may be entirely temporary.

Some hardness tests, particularly those designed to provide a measure of wear or abrasion, are performed dynamically with a weight of given magnitude that falls from a prescribed height. Sometimes a hammer is used, falling vertically on the test piece or in a pendulum motion.

Impact test. Many materials, sensitive to the presence of flaws, cracks, and notches, fail suddenly under impact. The most common impact tests (Charpy and Izod) employ a swinging pendulum to strike a notched bar; heights before and after impact are used to compute the energy required to fracture the bar and, consequently, the bar's impact strength. In the Charpy test, the test piece is held horizontally between two vertical bars, much like the lintel over a door. In the Izod test, the specimen stands erect, like a fence post. Shape and size of the specimen, mode of support, notch shape and geometry, and velocities at impact are all varied to produce specific test conditions. Nonmetals such as wood may be tested as supported beams, similar to the Charpy test. In nonmetal tests, however, the striking hammer falls vertically in a guide column, and the test is repeated from increasing heights until failure occurs.

The Charpy and Izod tests

Some materials vary in impact strength at different temperatures, becoming very brittle when cold. Tests have shown that the decrease in material strength and elasticity is often quite abrupt at a certain temperature, which is called the transition temperature for that material. Designers always specify a material that possesses a transition temperature well below the range of heat and cold to which the structure or machine is exposed. Thus, even a building in the tropics, which will doubtless never be exposed to freezing weather, employs materials with transition temperatures slightly below freezing.

Fracture toughness tests. The stringent materials-reliability requirements of the space programs undertaken since the early 1960s brought about substantial changes in design philosophy. Designers asked materials engineers to devise quantitative tests capable of measuring the propensity of a material to propagate a crack. Conventional methods of stress analysis and materials-property tests were retained, but interpretation of results changed. The criterion for failure became sudden propagation of a crack rather than fracture (see Figure 59). Tests have shown that cracks occur by opening, when two pieces of material part in vertical plane, one piece going up, the other down; by edge sliding, where the material splits in horizontal plane, one piece moving left, the other right; and by tearing, where the material splits with one piece moving diagonally upward to the left, the other moving diagonally downward to the right.

By courtesy of K.E. Hofer, IIT Research Institute

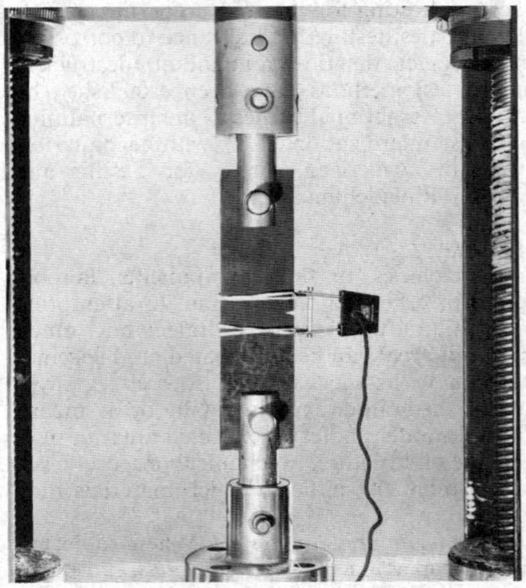

Figure 59: Typical fracture toughness test. The clip-on extensometer output signal is monitored to recognize the stress level at which the crack suddenly propagates because the extensometer will sense a sudden increase in strain without a corresponding increase in load.

Creep test. Creep is the slow change in the dimensions of a material due to prolonged stress; most common metals exhibit creep behaviour. In the creep test, loads below those necessary to cause instantaneous fracture are applied to the material, and the deformation over a period of time (creep strain) under constant load is measured, usually with an extensometer or strain gauge. In the same test, time to failure is also measured against level of stress; the resulting curve is called stress rupture or creep rupture. Once creep strain versus time is plotted, a variety of mathematical techniques is available for extrapolating creep behaviour of materials beyond the test times so that designers can utilize thousand-hour test data, for example, to predict ten-thousand-hour behaviour.

A material that yields continually under stress and then returns to its original shape when the stress is released is said to be viscoelastic; this type of response is measured by the stress-relaxation test. A prescribed displacement or strain is induced in the specimen and the load drop-off as a function of time is measured. Various viscoelastic theories are available that permit the translation of stress-relaxation test data into predictions about the creep behaviour of the material.

Fatigue. Materials that survive a single application of stress frequently fail when stressed repeatedly. This phenomenon, known as fatigue, is measured by mechanical tests that involve repeated application of different stresses varying in a regular cycle from maximum to minimum value. Most fatigue-testing machines employ a rotating eccentric weight to produce this cyclically varying load. A material is generally considered to suffer from low-cycle fatigue if it fails in 10,000 cycles or less.

The stresses acting upon a material in the real world are usually random in nature rather than cyclic. Consequently, several cumulative fatigue-damage theories have been developed to enable investigators to extrapolate from cyclic test data a prediction of material behaviour under random stresses. Because these theories are not applicable to most materials, a relatively new technique, which involves mechanical application of random fatigue stresses, statistically matched to real-life conditions, is now employed in most materials test laboratories.

Factors in material fatigue

Material fatigue involves a number of phenomena, among which are atomic slip (in which the upper plane of a metal crystal moves or slips in relation to the lower plane, in response to a shearing stress), crack initiation, and crack propagation. Thus, a fatigue test may measure the number of cycles required to initiate a crack, as well as the number of cycles to failure.

A cautious designer always bears the statistical nature of fatigue in mind, for the lives of material specimens tested at a common stress level always range above and below some average value. Statistical theory tells the designer how many samples of a material must be tested in order to provide adequate data; it is not uncommon to test several hundred specimens before drawing firm conclusions.

MEASUREMENT OF THERMAL PROPERTIES

Thermal conductivity. Heat, which passes through a solid body by physical transfer of free electrons and by vibration of atoms and molecules, stops flowing when the temperature is equal at all points in the solid body and equals the temperature in the surrounding environment. In the process of attaining equilibrium, there is a gross heat flow through the body, which depends upon the temperature difference between different points in the body and upon the magnitudes of the temperatures involved. Thermal conductivity is experimentally measured by determining temperatures as a function of time along the length of a bar or across the surface of flat plates while simultaneously controlling the external input and output of heat from the surfaces of the bar or the edges of the plate.

Specific heat. Specific heat of solid materials (defined as heat absorbed per unit mass per degree change in temperature) is generally measured by the drop method, which involves adding a known mass of the material at a known elevated temperature to a known mass of water at a known low temperature and determining the equilibrium temperature of the mixture that results. Specific heat is then computed by measuring the heat absorbed by the water and container, which is equivalent to the heat given up by the hot material.

Thermal expansion. Expansion due to heat is usually measured in linear fashion as the change in a unit length of a material caused by a one-degree change in temperature. Because many materials expand less than a micrometre with a one-degree increase in temperature, measurements are made by means of microscopes.

MEASUREMENT OF ELECTRICAL PROPERTIES

An understanding of electrical properties and testing methods requires a brief explanation of the free electron gas theory of electrical conduction. This simple theory is convenient for purposes of exposition, even though solid-state physics has advanced beyond it.

Electrical conductivity involves a flow or current of free electrons through a solid body. Some materials, such as metals, are good conductors of electricity; these possess free or valence electrons that do not remain permanently associated with the atoms of a solid but instead form an electron "cloud" or gas around the peripheries of the atoms and are free to move through the solid at a rapid rate. In other materials, such as plastics, the valence electrons are far more restricted in their movements and do not form a free-electron cloud. Such materials act as insulators against the flow of electricity.

The effect of heat upon the electrical conductivity of a material varies for good and poor conductors. In good conductors, thermal agitation interferes with the flow of electrons, decreasing conductivity, while, as insulators increase in temperature, the number of free electrons grows, and conductivity increases. Normally, good and poor conductors are enormously far apart in basic conductivity, and relatively small changes in temperature do not change these properties significantly.

Effect of heat upon conductivity

In certain materials, however, such as silicon, germanium, and carbon, heat produces a large increase in the number of free electrons; such materials are called semiconductors. Acting as insulators at absolute zero, semiconductors possess significant conductivity at room and elevated temperatures. Impurities also can change the conductivity of a semiconductor dramatically by providing more free electrons. Heat-caused conductivity is called intrinsic, while that attributable to extra electrons from impurity atoms is called extrinsic.

Conductivity of a material is generally measured by passing a known current at constant voltage through a known volume of the material and determining resistance in ohms. The total conductivity is then calculated by simply taking the reciprocal of the total resistivity.

TESTING FOR CORROSION, RADIATION, AND BIOLOGICAL DETERIORATION

Testing for breakdown or deterioration of materials under exposure to a particular type of environment has greatly increased in recent years. Mechanical, thermal, or electrical property tests often are performed on a material before, during, and after its exposure to some controlled environment. Property changes are then recorded as a function of exposure time. Environments may include heat, moisture, chemicals, radiation, electricity, biological substances, or some combination thereof. Thus, the tensile strength of a material may fall after exposure to heat, moisture, or salt spray or may be increased by radiation or electrical current. Strength of organic materials may be lessened by certain classes of fungus and mold.

Corrosion. Corrosion testing is generally performed to evaluate materials for a specific environment or to evaluate means for protecting a material from environmental attack. A chemical reaction, corrosion involves removal of metallic electrons from metals and formation of more stable compounds such as iron oxide (rust), in which the free electrons are usually less numerous. In nature, only rather chemically inactive metals such as gold and platinum are found in pure or nearly pure form; most others are mined as ores that must be refined to obtain the metal. Corrosion simply reverses the refining process, returning the metal to its natural state. Corrosion compounds form on the surface of a solid material. If the compounds are hard and impenetrable, and if they adhere well to the parent material, the progress of corrosion is arrested. If the compound is loose and porous, however, corrosion may proceed swiftly and continuously.

Analogy of the galvanic cell battery

If two different metals are placed together in a solution (electrolyte), one metal will give up ions to the solution more readily than the other; this difference in behaviour will bring about a difference in electrical voltage between the two metals. If the metals are in electrical contact with each other, electricity will flow between them and they will corrode; this is the principle of the galvanic cell or battery. Though useful in a battery, this reaction causes problems in a structure; for example, steel bolts in an aluminum framework may, in the presence of rain or fog, form multiple galvanic cells at the point of contact between the two metals, corroding the aluminum.

Corrosion testing is performed to ascertain the performance of metals and other materials in the presence of various electrolytes. Testing may involve total immersion, as would be encountered in seawater, or exposure to salt fog, as is encountered in chemical-industry processing operations or near the oceans where seawater may occur in fogs. Materials are generally immersed in a 5 percent or 20 percent solution of sodium chloride or calcium chloride in water, or the solution may be sprayed into a chamber where the specimens are freely suspended. In suspension testing, care is taken to prevent condensate from dripping from one specimen onto another. The specimens are exposed to the hostile environment for some time, then removed and examined for visible evidence of corrosion. In many cases, mechanical tests after corrosion exposure are performed quantitatively to ascertain mechanical degradation of the material. In other tests, materials are stressed while in the corrosive environment. Still other test procedures have been developed to measure corrosion of metals by flue or stack gases.

Radiation. Materials may be tested for their reactions to such electromagnetic radiation as X rays, gamma rays, and radio-frequency waves, or atomic radiation, which might include the neutrons emitted by uranium or some other radioactive substance. Most affected by these forms of radiation are polymers, such organic compounds as plastic or synthetic rubber, with long, repeated chains of similar chemical units.

Radiation tests are performed by exposing the materials to a known source of radiation for a specific period of time. Test materials may be exposed by robot control to nuclear fuels in a remote chamber, then tested by conventional methods to ascertain changes in their properties as a function of exposure time. In the field, paint samples may be exposed to electromagnetic radiation (such as sunlight) for prolonged periods and then checked for fading or cracking.

Exposure to radiation is usually, but not always, detrimental to strength; for example, exposure of polyethylene plastic for short periods of time increases its tensile strength. Longer exposures, however, decrease tensile strength. Tensile and yield strength of a type of carbon-silicon steel increase with exposure to neutron radiation, although elongation, reduction in area, and probably fracture toughness apparently decrease with exposure. Certain wood/polymeric composite materials are even prepared by a process that employs radiation. The wood is first impregnated with liquid organic resin by high pressure. Next, the wood and resin combination is exposed to radiation, causing a chemical change in the form of the resin that produces a strengthened material.

Biological deterioration. In recent years there has been considerable activity in the new field of formulating tests to ascertain the resistance of organic materials to fungi, bacteria, and algae. Paints, wrappers, and coatings of buried pipelines, structures, and storage tanks are typical materials exposed to biological deterioration.

When biological composition of the soil in a given area is unknown, colonies or cultures of its various fungi, bacteria, or algae are isolated and incubated by standard laboratory techniques. These are then used to test materials for biological degradation or to test the effectiveness of a fungicide or bactericide. In testing for algae resistance, for example, treated and untreated strips of vinyl film—such as might be used to line a swimming pool—are immersed in growing tanks along with seed cultures of algae plants. Within three days, luxuriant algae growths appear on untreated samples.

NONDESTRUCTIVE TESTING

The tensile-strength test is inherently destructive; in the process of gathering data, the sample is destroyed. Though this is acceptable when a plentiful supply of the material exists, nondestructive tests are desirable for materials that are costly or difficult to fabricate or that have been formed into finished or semifinished products.

Liquids. One common nondestructive technique, used to locate surface cracks and flaws in metals, employs a penetrating liquid, either brightly dyed or fluorescent. After being smeared on the surface of the material and allowed to soak into any tiny cracks, the liquid is wiped off, leaving readily visible cracks and flaws. An analogous technique, applicable to nonmetals, employs an electrically charged liquid smeared on the material surface. After excess liquid is removed, a dry powder of opposite charge is sprayed on the material and attracted to the cracks. Neither of these methods, however, can detect internal flaws.

Radiation. Internal as well as external flaws can be detected by X-ray or gamma-ray techniques in which the radiation passes through the material and impinges on a suitable photographic film. Under some circumstances, it is possible to focus the X rays to a particular plane within the material, permitting a three-dimensional description of the flaw geometry as well as its location.

Sound. Ultrasonic inspection of parts involves transmission of sound waves above human hearing range through the material. In the reflection technique, a sound wave is transmitted from one side of the sample, reflected off the far side, and returned to a receiver located at the starting point. Upon impinging on a flaw or crack in the material, the signal is reflected and its traveling time altered. The actual delay becomes a measure of the flaw's location; a map of the material can be generated to illustrate the location and geometry of the flaws. In the through-transmission method, the transmitter and receiver are located on opposite sides of the material; interruptions in the passage of sound waves are used to locate and measure flaws. Usually a water medium is employed in which transmitter, sample, and receiver are immersed.

Ultrasonic method

Magnetism. As the magnetic characteristics of a material are strongly influenced by its overall structure, magnetic techniques can be used to characterize the location and relative size of voids and cracks. For magnetic testing, an apparatus is used that contains a large coil of wire through which flows a steady alternating current (primary coil). Nested inside this primary coil is a shorter coil (the secondary coil), to which is attached an electrical measuring device. The steady current in the primary coil causes current to flow in the secondary coil through the process of induction. If an iron bar is inserted into the secondary coil, sharp changes in the secondary current can indicate defects in the bar. This method only detects differences between zones along the length of a bar and cannot detect long or continuous defects very readily. An analogous technique, employing eddy currents induced by a primary coil, also can be used to detect flaws and cracks. A steady current is induced in the test material. Flaws that lie across the path of the current alter resistance of the test material; this change may be measured by suitable equipment.

Infrared. Infrared techniques also have been employed to detect material continuity in complex structural situations. In testing the quality of adhesive bonds between the sandwich core and facing sheets in a typical sandwich construction material such as plywood, for example, heat is applied to the surface of the sandwich skin material. Where bond lines are continuous, the core materials provide a heat sink for the surface material, and the local temperatures of the skin will fall evenly along these bond lines. Where the bond line is inadequate, missing, or faulty, however, temperature will not fall. Infrared photography of the surface will then indicate the location and shape of the defective adhesive. A variation of this method employs thermal coatings that change colour upon reaching a specific temperature.

Finally, nondestructive test methods also are being sought to permit a total determination of the mechanical properties of a test material. Ultrasonics and thermal methods appear most promising in this regard. (K.E.H.)

BIBLIOGRAPHY

Chemical analysis. HERBERT A. LAITINEN and GALEN W. EWING (eds.), *A History of Analytical Chemistry* (1977), provides a historical overview. General works on analytical chemistry are LARRY G. HARGIS, *Analytical Chemistry: Principles and Techniques* (1988); DOUGLAS A. SKOOG, DONALD M. WEST, and F. JAMES HOLLER, *Fundamentals of Analytical Chemistry,* 5th ed. (1988), also available in an abbreviated version, *Analytical Chemistry: An Introduction,* 5th ed. (1990); KENNETH A. RUBINSON, *Chemical Analysis* (1987); DANIEL C. HARRIS, *Quantitative Chemical Analysis,* 3rd ed. (1991); JOHN H. KENNEDY, *Analytical Chemistry: Principles,* 2nd ed. (1990); and STANLEY E. MANAHAN, *Quantitative Chemical Analysis* (1986). *Analytical Chemistry* (semimonthly); and *Analytical Biochemistry* (16/yr.), are useful periodicals.

The following are useful texts on qualitative analysis: DANIEL J. PASTO and CARL R. JOHNSTON, *Organic Structure Determination* (1969); RALPH L. SHRINER *et al., The Systematic Identification of Organic Compounds,* 6th ed. (1980), a laboratory manual; JOHN W. LEHMAN, *Operational Organic Chemistry: A Laboratory Course,* 2nd ed. (1988); and J.J. LAGOWSKI and C.H. SORUM, *Introduction to Semimicro Qualitative Analysis,* 7th ed. (1991).

Instrumental analysis is the focus of ROBERT D. BRAUN, *Introduction to Instrumental Analysis* (1987); HOBART H. WILLARD *et al., Instrumental Methods of Analysis,* 7th ed. (1988); GARY D. CHRISTIAN and JAMES E. O'REILLY (eds.), *Instrumental Analysis,* 2nd ed. (1986); J.D. WINEFORDNER (ed.), *Spectrochemical Methods of Analysis* (1971); JOSEPH B. LAMBERT *et al., Organic Structural Analysis* (1976); JAMES D. INGLE, JR. and STANLEY R. CROUCH, *Spectrochemical Analysis* (1988); ALLEN J. BARD and LARRY R. FAULKNER, *Electrochemical Methods* (1980); E.P. SERJEANT, *Potentiometry and Potentiometric Titrations* (1984); A.M. BOND, *Modern Polarographic Methods in Analytical Chemistry* (1980); and R. BELCHER (ed.), *Instrumental Organic Elemental Analysis* (1977). (R.D.Br.)

Chemical separations and purifications. Broad coverage of the field is provided in BARRY L. KARGER, LLOYD R. SNYDER, and CSABA HORVÁTH, *An Introduction to Separation Science* (1973), a modern treatment of theory and practice, with emphasis on small-scale operation; J. CALVIN GIDDINGS, *Unified Separation Science* (1991), a fundamental text on the principles of separation methods; and C. JUDSON KING, *Separation Processes,* 2nd ed. (1980), a fundamental text dealing with large-scale engineering and separation procedures. ANTHONY T. ANDREWS, *Electrophoresis: Theory, Techniques, and Biochemical and Clinical Applications,* 2nd ed. (1986), introduces this method. *Advances in Electrophoresis* (annual) reviews the literature. Useful journals include *Separation Science and Technology* (monthly); and *Electrophoresis* (monthly).

Chromatography in particular is introduced in COLIN F. POOLE and SHEILA A. SCHUETTE, *Contemporary Practice of Chromatography* (1984); and E. HEFTMANN (ed.), *Chromatography: Fundamentals and Applications of Chromatographic and Electrophoretic Methods,* 2 vol. (1983). The history of chromatography is chronicled in L.S. ETTRE, "Evolution of Liquid Chromatography," in CSABA HORVÁTH (ed.), *High-performance Liquid Chromatography,* vol. 1 (1980), pp. 1–74; and L.S. ETTRE and A. ZLATKIS (eds.), *75 Years of Chromatography: A Historical Dialogue* (1979). Discussions of specific methods of chromatography include ROBERT L. GROB (ed.), *Modern Practice of Gas Chromatography,* 2nd ed. (1985); MILTON L. LEE, FRANK J. YANG, and KEITH D. BARTLE, *Open Tubular Column Gas Chromatography* (1984); ROGER M. SMITH, *Gas and Liquid Chromatography in Analytical Chemistry* (1988); L.R. SNYDER and J.J. KIRKLAND, *Introduction to Modern Liquid Chromatography,* 2nd ed. (1979); R.P.W. SCOTT, *Liquid Chromatography Detectors,* 2nd rev. ed. (1986); BERNARD FRIED and JOSEPH SHERMA, *Thin-layer Chromatography,* 2nd ed. rev. and expanded (1986); JOSEPH C. TOUCHSTONE and MURREL F. DOBBINS, *Practice of Thin Layer Chromatography,* 3rd ed. (1992); FRANK J. YANG (ed.), *Microbore Column Chromatography: A Unified Approach to Chromatography* (1989); MILOS V. NOVOTNY and DAIDO ISHII (eds.), *Microcolumn Separations: Columns, Instrumentation, and Ancillary Techniques* (1985); W.W. YAU, J.J. KIRKLAND, and D.D. BLY, *Modern Size-exclusion Liquid Chromatography: Practice of Gel Permeation and Gel Filtration Chromatography* (1979); HAMISH SMALL, *Ion Chromatography* (1989); ROGER M. SMITH (ed.), *Supercritical Fluid Chromatography* (1989); A.F. BERGOLD *et al.,* "High Performance Affinity Chromatography," in CSABA HORVÁTH (ed.), *High-performance Liquid Chromatography,* vol. 5 (1988), pp. 95–209; and JOSEF JANČA, *Field-flow Fractionation,* trans. from Czech (1988). *Advances in Chromatography* (1965–), is a multivolume series on various topics of chromatography. Periodicals include *Journal of Chromatography* (irregular); *Chromatographia* (monthly); *Preparative Chromatography* (quarterly); and *LC GC: Magazine of Liquid and Gas Chromatography* (monthly). (B.L.K./Ro.A.K.)

Mass spectrometry. F.W. ASTON, *Mass-spectra and Isotopes,* 2nd ed. (1942), is a comprehensive account of the early work that laid the foundations of accurate mass and isotopic abundance measurements. H.E. DUCKWORTH, R.C. BARBER, and V.S. VENKATASUBRAMANIAN, *Mass Spectroscopy,* 2nd ed. (1986), provides good general coverage of techniques and applications. IAN HOWE, DUDLEY H. WILLIAMS, and RICHARD D. BOWEN, *Mass Spectrometry: Principles and Applications,* 2nd ed. (1981), emphasizes applications to molecular reactions. F. ADAMS, R. GIJBELS, and R. VAN GRIEKEN (eds.), *Inorganic Mass Spectrometry* (1988), surveys the most recent experimental developments. J.R. CHAPMAN, *Practical Organic Mass Spectrometry* (1985), is a simple, up-to-date text. GORDON M. MESSAGE, *Practical Aspects of Gas Chromatography/Mass Spectrometry* (1984), contains a general treatment of practice and application. PETER H. DAWSON (ed.), *Quadrupole Mass Spectrometry and Its Applications* (1976), gives an extensive treatment of theory. ALAN G. MARSHALL and FRANCIS R. VERDUN, *Fourier Transforms in NMR, Optical, and Mass Spectrometry* (1990), very lucidly explains this technique. DAVID ELMORE and FRED M. PHILLIPS, "Accelerator Mass Spectrometry for Measurement of Long-lived Radioisotopes," *Science,* 236(4801):543–550 (May 1, 1987), surveys this method. (L.Br.)

Spectroscopy. J. MICHAEL HOLLAS, *Modern Spectroscopy* (1987), is a broad introductory-level presentation. Optical data, X-ray data, samples of optical spectra of some materials, tabulation of wavelengths, and details of methods of radiation detection may be found in DWIGHT E. GRAY (ed.), *American Institute of Physics Handbook,* 2nd ed. (1963). J.W. ROBINSON, *Practical Handbook of Spectroscopy* (1991), lists a range of spectroscopic data covering X-ray and neutron spectroscopy, photoelectron spectroscopy, ultraviolet, optical, and infrared spectroscopy.

WOLFGANG DEMTRÖDER, *Laser Spectroscopy* (1981); and STIG STENHOLM, *Foundations of Laser Spectroscopy* (1984), discuss many of the basic concepts and instrumentation of laser spectroscopy. Y.R. SHEN, *The Principles of Nonlinear Optics* (1984), focuses on nonlinear spectroscopic techniques made available with lasers. MURRAY SARGENT III, MARLAN O. SCULLY, and WILLIS E. LAMB, JR., *Laser Physics* (1974), is a reference text on the theory of the laser. ANTHONY E. SIEGMAN, *Lasers* (1986), provides an updated and extensive discussion of laser physics, optical beams and resonators, Q-switching, and mode-locking.

Principles of atomic spectroscopy are related in HANS A. BETHE and EDWIN E. SALPETER, *Quantum Mechanics of One- and Two-electron Atoms* (1957, reissued 1977), an authoritative account of the basic quantum mechanics of hydrogen- and helium-like atoms; and IGOR I. SOBELMAN, *Atomic Spectra and Radiative Transitions,* 2nd ed. (1992), a more modern version. ALAN CORNEY, *Atomic and Laser Spectroscopy* (1977), covers the foundations of atomic physics and the interactions of electromagnetic radiation with atoms plus applications at the advanced undergraduate level. Extensive tabulations of wavelengths of the elements are in CHARLOTTE E. MOORE, *Atomic Energy Levels as Derived from the Analysis of Optical Spectra,* 3 vols. (1949–58, reprinted 1971). Tabulations of the lifetimes of excited states of the elements are listed in W.L. WIESE, M.W. SMITH, and B.M. GLENNON, *Atomic Transition Probabilities* (1966–).

Introductions to molecular spectroscopy are provided in the books by Demtröder and by Stenholm, cited earlier; and by JACK D. GRAYBEAL, *Molecular Spectroscopy* (1988), which concentrates on the development of fundamental relationships; MARLIN D. HARMONY, *Introduction to Molecular Energies and Spectra* (1972), an intermediate-level introduction to the primary areas of spectroscopy; JEFFREY I. STEINFELD, *Molecules and Radiation: An Introduction to Modern Molecular Spectroscopy,* 2nd ed. (1985), an intermediate-level introduction to general principles and selected areas; E. BRIGHT WILSON, JR., J.C. DECIUS, and PAUL C. CROSS, *Molecular Vibrations: The Theory of Infrared and Raman Vibrational Spectra* (1955, reprinted 1980), the definitive treatment of the fundamentals; and GERHARD HERZBERG, *Molecular Spectra and Molecular Structure,* 4 vol. (1939–79), with a 2nd ed. of vol. 1 (1950), comprising the most comprehensive and advanced-level treatment of basic concepts. Advanced-level treatments include HARRY C. ALLEN, JR., and PAUL C. CROSS, *Molecular Vib-rotors* (1963), on rotation and vibration; WALTER GORDY and ROBERT L. COOK, *Microwave Molecular Spectra,* 3rd ed. (1984), a comprehensive treatment; and J. MICHAEL HOLLAS, *High Resolution Spectroscopy* (1982), a review of all areas with a minimum of mathematical development.

Studies of X-ray and radio-frequency spectroscopy include ARNE ELD SANDSTRÖM, "Experimental Methods of X-ray Spectroscopy: Ordinary Wavelengths" in *Handbuch der Physik,* vol. 30 (1957), pp. 78–245, a survey of X-ray spectroscopy; and B.E. WARREN, *X-ray Diffraction* (1969, reprinted 1990), an authoritative treatment. HERMAN WINICK and S. DONIACH (eds.), *Synchrotron Radiation Research* (1980), covers many X-ray spectroscopy techniques made possible with synchrotron sources. (St.C./J.D.G.)

Two textbooks deal exclusively with resonance-ionization spectroscopy: VLADILEN S. LETOKHOV, *Laser Photoionization Spectroscopy* (1987), reviews the general subject with considerable detail on laser schemes and applications, including an excellent account of the early work in the Academy of Sciences of the U.S.S.R.; and G.S. HURST and M.G. PAYNE, *Principles and Applications of Resonance Ionisation Spectroscopy* (1988), covers the early experiments and relevant theory on resonance ionization. International symposia on RIS have convened on approximately a two-year cycle since 1981, and the more recent proceedings from them are published with the title *Resonance Ionization Spectroscopy, e.g., Resonance Ionization Spectroscopy 1990,* ed. by J.E. PARKS AND N. OMENETTO (1991). (G.S.Hu.)

Radiation measurement. General works on radiation detection and measurement include RALPH E. LAPP and HOWARD L. ANDREWS, *Nuclear Radiation Physics,* 4th ed. (1972), a good fundamental coverage of sources, interactions, and other aspects of ionizing radiation; NICHOLAS TSOULFANIDIS, *Measurement and Detection of Radiation* (1983), a good general coverage of the field intended for an undergraduate reader, including a detailed treatment of methods of data analysis; NATIONAL COUNCIL ON RADIATION PROTECTION AND MEASUREMENTS, *A Handbook of Radioactivity Measurements Procedures* (1985), an extensive report and an excellent textbook-like coverage of many of the important procedures in radionuclide measurements; W.B. MANN, A. RYTZ, and A. SPERNOL, "Radioactivity Measurements: Principles and Practice," *International Journal of Radiation Applications and Instrumentation,* part A, *Applied Radiation and Isotopes,* 39(8):717–937 (1988), a thorough coverage of topics of particular interest in radionuclide metrology; and GLENN F. KNOLL, *Radiation Detection and Measurement,* 2nd ed. (1989), a widely used comprehensive textbook. E. FENYVES and O. HAIMAN, *The Physical Principles of Nuclear Radiation Measurements* (1969; originally published in German, 1965), is a rigorous treatment of the theory of various detection processes, with less emphasis on specific devices. FRANK H. ATTIX, WILLIAM C. ROESCH, and EUGENE TOCHILIN (eds.), *Radiation Dosimetry,* 2nd ed., 3 vol. (1966–69); and KENNETH R. KASE, BENGT BJÄRNGARD, and FRANK H. ATTIX (eds.), *The Dosimetry of Ionizing Radiation,* 3 vol. (1985–90), are comprehensive collections of chapters by various authors on all aspects of radiation dosimetry and instrumentation for dose measurement.

General discussion of radiation detectors is found in JACK SHARPE, *Nuclear Radiation Detectors,* 2nd ed. rev. (1964), a short monograph emphasizing basic detector mechanisms, with good coverage of gas-filled detectors; GEOFFREY G. EICHHOLZ and JOHN W. POSTON, *Principles of Nuclear Radiation Detection* (1979, reissued 1985), general coverage at the undergraduate level; and P.N. COOPER, *Introduction to Nuclear Radiation Detectors* (1986), an introductory-level short monograph with brief descriptions of the major instruments used in radiation measurements and dosimetry.

Several detectors are examined in the following works: scintillation detectors in J.B. BIRKS, *The Theory and Practice of Scintillation Counting* (1964), very detailed coverage of all aspects of scintillation counting, from the basic scintillation mechanisms to practical aspects of counters; E. SCHRAM, *Organic Scintillation Detectors: Counting of Low-energy Beta Emitters* (1963), a short specialized coverage of organic scintillation mechanisms and specific devices; and STEPHEN M. SHAFROTH (ed.), *Scintillation Spectroscopy of Gamma Radiation* (1967), a collection of individual articles on various aspects of practical scintillation spectroscopy; ionization detectors in BRUNO B. ROSSI and HANS H. STAUB, *Ionization Chambers and Counters* (1949), a classic text that is still a useful source of detailed analysis; and DENYS HAIGH WILKINSON, *Ionization Chambers and Counters* (1950, reissued 1970), still a valuable reference; and semiconductor detectors in G. DEARNALEY and D.C. NORTHROP, *Semiconductor Counters for Nuclear Radiations,* 2nd ed., rev. and enlarged (1966), a specialized treatment; and KLAUS DEBERTIN and RICHARD G. HELMER, *Gamma- and X-ray Spectrometry with Semiconductor Detectors* (1988), a thorough monograph on all aspects of high-resolution photon spectroscopy, with an excellent collection of reference data. Other specific detector types are discussed by ROBERT L. FLEISCHER, P. BUFORD PRICE, and ROBERT M. WALKER, *Nuclear Tracks in Solids* (1975), a thorough description of techniques useful in track-etch detectors; R.H. HERZ, *The Photographic Action of Ionizing Radiations in Dosimetry and Medical, Neutron, Auto-, and Microradiography* (1969), a thorough description of radiographic techniques for various types of ionizing radiation; and KONRAD KLEINKNECHT, *Detectors for Particle Radiation* (1986), an excellent specialized coverage of the gas-filled and position-sensitive devices of primary interest in high-energy particle physics. (G.F.K.)

Materials testing. ZBIGNIEW D. JASTRZEBSKI, *The Nature and Properties of Engineering Materials,* 3rd ed. (1987), describes the qualitative mechanical behaviour of materials. W.D. KINGERY, H.K. BOWEN, and D.R. UHLMANN, *Introduction to Ceramics,* 2nd ed. (1976), illustrates the utilization of ceramic materials. HARMER E. DAVIS, GEORGE EARL TROXELL, and GEORGE F.W. HAUCK, *The Testing of Engineering Materials,* 4th ed. (1982), is a highly comprehensive and easily understood work offering detailed information on the various testing methods for use in the training of materials testing personnel. Discussions of testing techniques for various materials include three volumes in the *Metals Handbook,* 9th ed., prepared under the direction of the ASM INTERNATIONAL HANDBOOK COMMITTEE: vol. 8, *Mechanical Testing* (1985), vol. 13, *Corrosion* (1987), and vol. 17, *Nondestructive Evaluation and Quality Control* (1989); ROBERT BABOIAN and SHELDON W. DEAN (eds.), *Corrosion Testing and Evaluation* (1990); R.S. SHARPE, *Research Techniques in Nondestructive Testing* (1970–); DON E. BRAY and RODERICK K. STANLEY, *Nondestructive Evaluation: A Tool for Design, Manufacturing, and Service* (1989), examining the theory and practice of ultrasonic techniques, magnetic flux leakage techniques, radiographic methods, penetrant inspection, and eddy current concepts, with an extensive bibliography and examples of actual applications; JOSEF KRAUTKRÄMER and HERBERT KRAUTKRÄMER, *Ultrasonic Testing of Materials,* 4th fully rev. ed. (1990), a classic text treating the use of ultrasonic waves to detect such defects as strength variations, nonbonding, and cavities; and *International Advances in Nondestructive Testing* (annual), addressing methods that currently have applications in various industries and new techniques for possible future applications. (K.E.H./Ed.)

Angiosperms

Angiosperms, also known as the flowering plants, are the largest and most diverse group within the kingdom Plantae. They represent approximately 80 percent of all the known green plants now living. The angiosperms are vascular seed plants in which the ovule (egg) is fertilized and develops into a seed in an enclosed hollow ovary. The ovary itself is usually enclosed in a flower, that part of the angiospermous plant that contains the male or female reproductive organs or both. Fruits are derived from the maturing floral organs of the angiospermous plant and are therefore characteristic of angiosperms. By contrast, in gymnosperms (*e.g.,* conifers), the other large group of vascular seed plants, the seeds do not develop enclosed within an ovary but are usually borne exposed on the surfaces of reproductive structures, such as cones, that originally produced the spores.

Unlike such nonvascular plants as the bryophytes, in which all cells in the plant body participate in every function necessary to support, nourish, and extend the plant body (*e.g.,* nutrition, photosynthesis, and cell division), angiosperms have evolved specialized cells and tissues that carry out these functions and have further evolved specialized vascular tissues that translocate the water and nutrients to all areas of the plant body. The specialization of the plant body, which has evolved as an adaptation to a principally terrestrial habitat, includes extensive root systems that anchor the plant and absorb water and minerals from the soil; a stem that supports the growing plant body; and leaves, which are the principal sites of photosynthesis for most angiospermous plants. Another significant evolutionary advancement over the nonvascular and the more primitive vascular plants is the presence of localized regions for plant growth, called meristems and cambia, which extend the length and width of the plant body, respectively. Except under certain conditions, these regions are the only areas in which cell division takes place in the plant body, although cell differentiation continues to occur over the life of the plant.

The angiosperms as a group contain more than 250,000 species and dominate the Earth's surface and vegetation in more environments, particularly terrestrial habitats, than any other group of plants. As a result, angiosperms are the most important ultimate source of food for birds and mammals, including humans. In addition, the flowering plants are the most economically important group of green plants, serving as a source of pharmaceuticals, fibre products, timber, ornamentals, and other commercial products.

Although in the past the taxonomy of the angiosperms was somewhat controversial, a consensus began to develop among plant taxonomists toward the end of the 20th century. The angiosperms came to be considered a group at the division level (comparable to the phylum level in animal classification systems) called Magnoliophyta.

Throughout this article the orders or families are given, usually parenthetically, following the vernacular or scientific name of a plant. Following taxonomic conventions, genera and species are italicized. The higher taxa are readily identified by their suffixes: families end in -aceae, orders in -ales, subclasses in -idae, and classes in -opsida.

For a comparison of angiosperms with the other major groups of plants, see PLANTS, BRYOPHYTES, FERNS AND OTHER LOWER VASCULAR PLANTS, and GYMNOSPERMS.

For coverage of related topics in the *Macropædia* and *Micropædia,* see the *Propædia,* section 313, and the *Index.*

The article is divided into the following sections:

Angiosperms: division Magnoliophyta 604
- General features 604
- Structure and function 609
  - Vegetative structures
  - Tissue systems
  - Plant organs
  - Reproductive structures
- Reproduction 625
  - General features
  - Pollination
  - Fertilization and embryogenesis
  - Seedlings
- Paleobotany and evolution 628
- Classification 629
  - Diagnostic classification
  - Annotated classification
  - Critical appraisal

Class Magnoliopsida: the dicotyledons 634
- Subclass Magnoliidae 634
  - General features
  - Natural history
  - Form and function
  - Evolution
  - Representative groups
    - Magnoliales
    - Laurales
    - Ranunculales
- Subclass Hamamelidae 648
  - General features
  - Natural history
  - Form and function
  - Evolution
  - Representative groups
    - Urticales
    - Fagales
- Subclass Caryophyllidae 661
  - Polygonales and Plumbaginales
  - Caryophyllales
- Subclass Dilleniidae 665
  - General features
  - Natural history
  - Form and function
  - Evolution
  - Representative groups
    - Violales
    - Capparales
    - Theales
    - Ericales
    - Malvales
- Subclass Rosidae 685
  - General features
  - Representative groups
    - Fabales
    - Myrtales
    - Euphorbiales
    - Rosales
    - Sapindales
- Subclass Asteridae 707
  - General features
  - Representative groups
  - Asterales
  - Scrophulariales
  - Solanales

Class Liliopsida: the monocotyledons 721
- Subclass Alismatidae 723
  - General features
  - Natural history
  - Form and function
  - Evolution
- Subclass Arecidae 728
  - General features
  - Natural history
  - Form and function
  - Evolution
  - Representative group
    - Palmae
- Subclass Commelinidae 736
  - General features
  - Representative groups
    - Cyperaceae

Poaceae
Subclass Zingiberidae 745
Zingiberales
Bromeliales
Subclass Liliidae 752
General features
Form and function
Natural history
Classification and evolution
Representative groups
Liliales
Orchidales
Bibliography 762

ANGIOSPERMS: DIVISION MAGNOLIOPHYTA

General features

The variety of forms found among angiosperms is greater than that of any other plant group. The size range alone is quite remarkable, from probably the smallest individual flowering plant, the watermeal (*Wolffia;* Arales), at less than 2 millimetres (0.08 inch) to one of the tallest angiosperms, Australia's mountain ash tree (*Eucalyptus regnans;* Myrtales) at about 100 metres (330 feet). Between these two extremes lie angiosperms of almost every size and shape. Examples of this variability include the succulent cacti (Cactaceae), the fragile orchids (Orchidales), the baobab (*Adansonia digitata;* Malvales), vines, rosette plants such as dandelion, and carnivorous plants such as sundews (*Drosera;* Nepenthales) and Venus' flytrap (*Dionaea muscipula;* Nepenthales). To understand this vast array of forms, it is necessary to consider the basic structural plan of the angiosperms.

From E.M. Gifford and A.S. Foster, *Morphology and Evolution of Vascular Plants,* 3rd ed. (1989); W.H. Freeman and Co., New York City, redrawn from W. Troll, *Vergleichende Morphologie der hoheren Pflanzen* (1935), Gebruder Borntraeger, Berlin

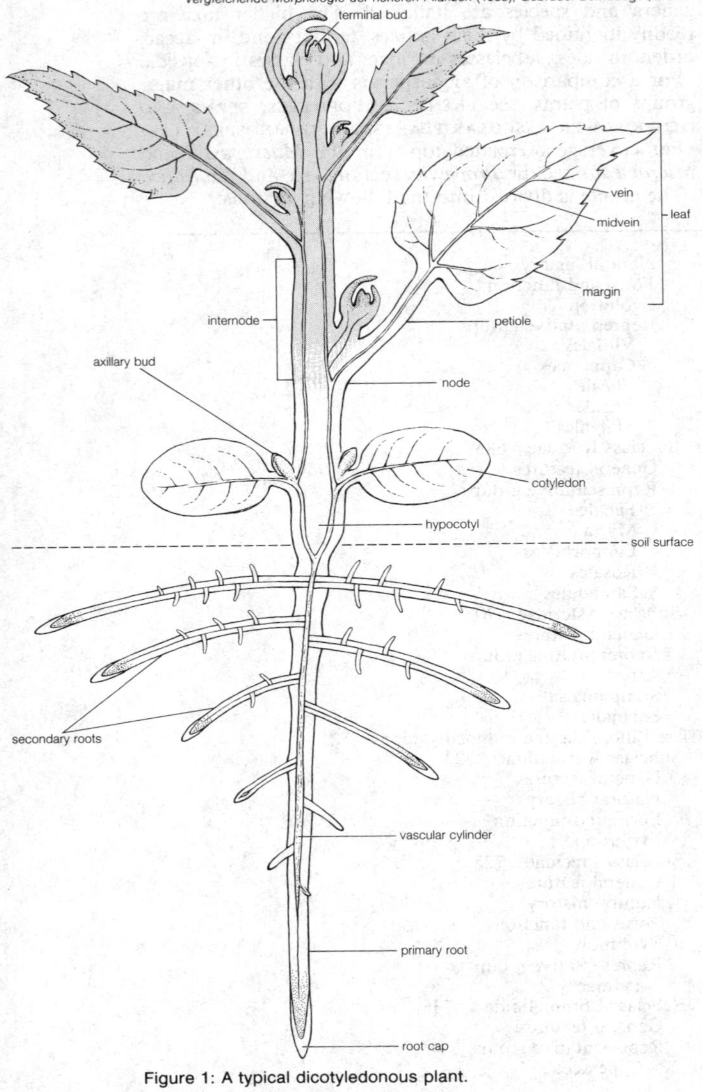

Figure 1: A typical dicotyledonous plant.

The basic angiosperm form is woody or herbaceous. Woody forms (generally trees and shrubs) are rich in secondary tissues, while herbaceous forms (herbs) rarely have any. Annuals are herbs that complete their growing cycle (growth, flowering, and death) within the same season. Examples of annuals can be found among cultivated garden plants, such as beans (*Phaseolus;* Fabales), corn (maize; *Zea mays;* Cyperales), and squashes (*Cucurbita;* Violales), as well as among the wildflowers, such as some buttercups (*Ranunculus*) and larkspurs (*Delphinium*). Biennials are also herbs, but, unlike annuals, their growing cycle spans two years: the vegetative (nonreproductive) plant growth takes place from seed during the first year, and flowers and fruit develop during the second. The beet (*Beta vulgaris;* Caryophyllales) and wild carrot (*Daucus carota;* Apiales) are well-known biennials.

A perennial grows for many years and often flowers annually. In temperate areas the aerial parts of a perennial die back to the ground at the end of each growing season and new shoots are produced the following season from such subterranean parts as bulbs, rhizomes, corms, tubers, and stolons.

The basic angiosperm body has three parts: roots, stems, and leaves (Figure 1). These primary organs constitute the vegetative (nonreproductive) plant body. Together, the stem and its attached leaves constitute the shoot. Collectively, the roots of an individual plant make up the root system and the shoots the shoot system.

Root systems

The roots anchor a plant, absorb water and minerals, and provide a storage area for food. The two basic types of root systems are a primary root system and an adventitious root system. The most common type, the primary system, consists of a taproot (primary root) that grows vertically downward (positive geotropism). From the taproot are produced smaller lateral roots (secondary roots) that grow horizontally or diagonally. These secondary roots further produce their own smaller lateral roots (tertiary roots). Thus, many orders of roots of descending size are produced from a single prominent root, the taproot. Most dicotyledons produce taproots, as, for example, the dandelion (*Taraxacum officinale*).

In some cases, the taproot system is modified into a fibrous, or diffuse, system, in which the initial secondary roots soon equal or exceed the primary root in size. The result is several large, positively geotropic roots that produce higher-order roots, which may also grow to the same size. Thus, in fibrous root systems there is no well-defined single taproot. In general, fibrous root systems are shallower than taproot systems.

The second type of root system, the adventitious root system, differs from the primary variety in that the primary root is short-lived and is replaced within a short time by many roots that form from the stem. Most monocotyledons (class Liliopsida) have adventitious roots; examples include orchids, bromeliads, and many other epiphytic plants in the tropics. Grasses (family Poaceae) and many other monocotyledons produce fibrous root systems with the development of adventitious roots.

Root adaptations

Many primary root and adventitious root systems have become modified for special functions, the most common being the formation of tuberous (fleshy) roots for food storage. For example, carrots and beets are tuberous roots that are modified from taproots, and cassava (manioc) is a tuberous root that is modified from an adventitious root. (Tubers, on the other hand, are modified, fleshy, underground stems and will be discussed below.)

Adventitious roots, when modified for aerial support,

are called prop roots, as in corn or some figs (*Ficus;* Urticales). In many tropical rain forest trees, large woody prop roots develop from adventitious roots on horizontal branches and provide additional anchorage and support. Many bulbous plants have contractile adventitious roots that pull the bulb deeper into the ground as it grows. Climbing plants often grip their supports with specialized adventitious roots. Some lateral roots of mangroves become specialized as pneumatophores in saline mud flats; pneumatophores are lateral roots that grow upward (negative geotropism) for varying distances and function as the site of oxygen intake for the submerged primary root system. The plants mentioned above are only a few examples of root diversity in angiosperms, a condition that is unparalleled in any other vascular plant group.

The stem is an aerial axis of the plant that bears leaves and flowers and conducts water and minerals from the roots and food from the site of synthesis to areas where it is to be used. The main stem of a plant is continuous with the root system through a transition region called the hypocotyl. In the developing embryo, the hypocotyl is the embryonic axis that bears the seedling leaves (cotyledons).

Stems and branching

In a maturing stem, the area where a leaf attaches to the stem is called a node, and the region between successive nodes is called an internode. Stems bear leafy shoots (branches) at the nodes, which arise from buds (dormant shoots). Lateral branches develop either from axillary, or lateral, buds found in the angle between the leaf and the stem or from terminal buds at the end of the shoot. In temperate-climate plants these buds have extended periods of dormancy, whereas in tropical plants the period of dormancy is either very short or nonexistent.

The precise positional relationship of stem, leaf, and axillary bud is important to understanding the diversity of the shoot system in angiosperms. Understanding this relationship makes it possible to identify organs such as leaves that are so highly modified they no longer look like leaves, or stems that are so modified that they resemble leaves.

Branching in angiosperms may be dichotomous or axillary. In dichotomous branching, the branches form as a result of an equal division of a terminal bud (*i.e.,* a bud formed at the apex of a stem) into two equal branches that are not derived from axillary buds, although axillary buds are present elsewhere on the plant body. The few examples of dichotomous branching among angiosperms are found only in some cacti, palms, and bird-of-paradise plants.

The two modes of axillary branching in angiosperms are monopodial and sympodial. Monopodial branching occurs when the terminal bud continues to grow as a central leader shoot and the lateral branches remain subordinate—*e.g.,* beech trees (*Fagus*). Sympodial branching occurs when the terminal bud ceases to grow (usually because a terminal flower has formed) and an axillary bud or buds become new leader shoots, called renewal shoots—*e.g.,* the Joshua tree (*Yucca brevifolia*). Plants with monopodial growth are usually pyramidal in overall shape, while those with sympodial growth often resemble a candelabra.

By combining monopodial and sympodial branching in one plant, many different tree architectures have evolved. A simple example is found in dogwoods (*Cornus*), where the main axis is monopodial and the lateral branches are sympodial.

Very different plant forms result from simply changing the lengths of the internodes. Extreme shortening of the internodes results in rosette plants, such as lettuce, *Lactuca sativa* (Asterales; Asteridae), in which the leaves develop but the internodes between them do not elongate. Extreme lengthening of the internodes often results in twining vines, as in the yam, *Dioscorea esculenta* (Liliales; Liliidae).

Variations in leaf structure

The basic angiosperm leaf is composed of a leaf base, two stipules, a petiole, and a blade (lamina). The leaf base is the slightly expanded area where the leaf attaches to the stem. The paired stipules, when present, are located on each side of the leaf base and may resemble scales,

From (arrangement, margins, shape) K.B. Sandved and G.T. Prance, *Leaves* (1985); Crown Publishers, Inc.; (venation, arrangement on the stem) N.A. Campbell, *Biology* (1987); the Benjamin/Cummings Pub. Co., Inc.

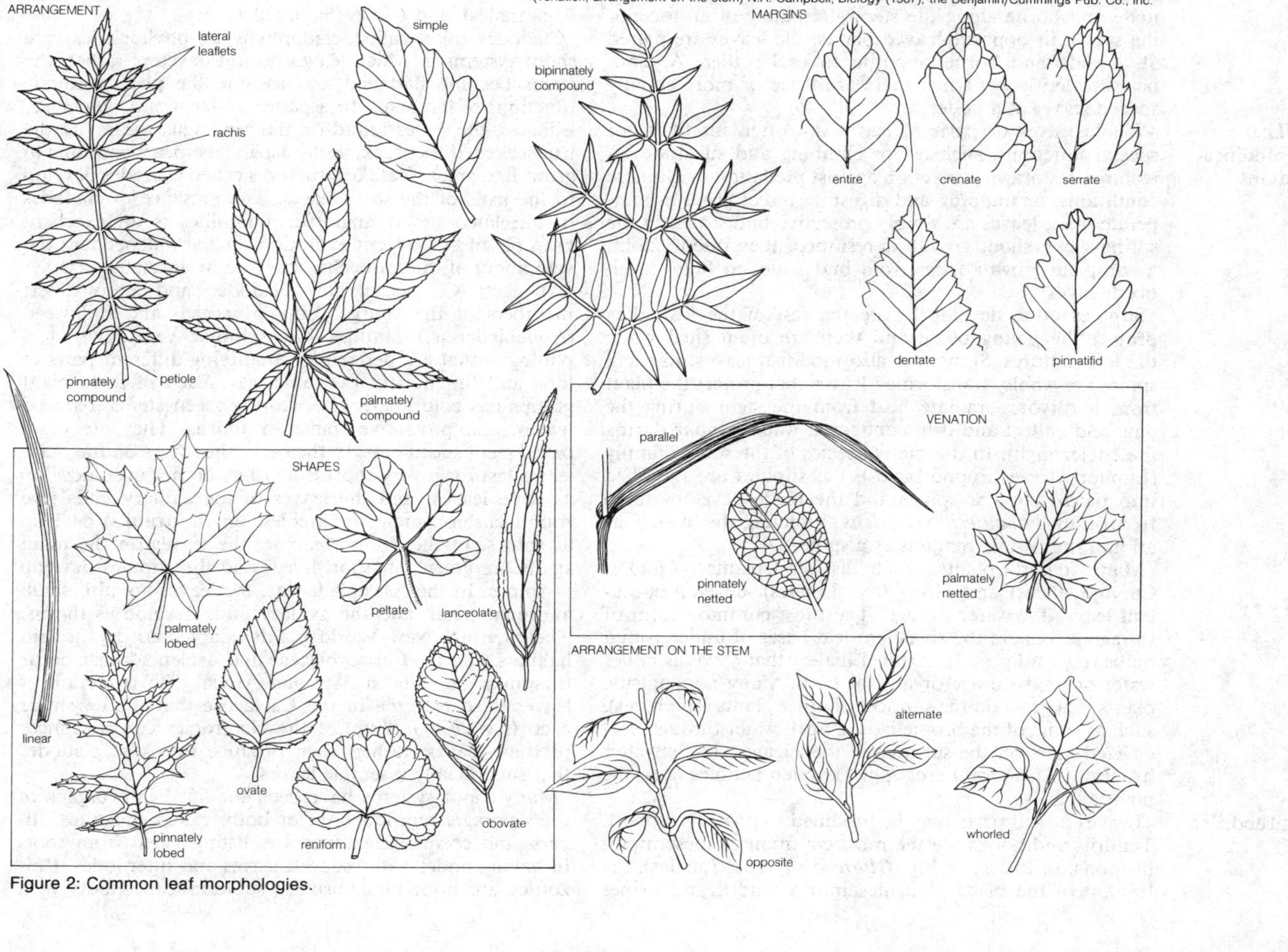

Figure 2: Common leaf morphologies.

spines, glands, or leaflike structures. The petiole is a stalk that connects the blade with the leaf base. The blade is the major photosynthetic surface of the plant and appears green and flattened in a plane perpendicular to the stem.

When only a single blade is inserted directly on the petiole, the leaf is called simple (Figure 2). Simple leaves may be variously lobed along their margins. The margins of simple leaves may be entire and smooth or they may be lobed in various ways. The coarse teeth of dentate margins project at right angles, while those of serrate margins point toward the leaf apex. Crenulate margins have rounded teeth or scalloped margins. Leaf margins of simple leaves may be lobed in one of two patterns, pinnate or palmate. In pinnately lobed margins the leaf blade (lamina) is indented equally deep along each side of the midrib (as in the white oak, *Quercus alba*), and in palmately lobed margins the lamina is indented along several major veins (as in the red maple, *Acer rubrum*). A great variety of base and apex shapes also are found.

Many leaves contain only some of these leaf parts; for example, many leaves lack a petiole and so are attached directly to the stem (sessile), and others lack stipules (exstipulate). In compound leaves (Figure 2), a blade has two or more subunits called leaflets: in palmately compound leaves, the leaflets radiate from a single point at the distal end of the petiole; in pinnately compound leaves, a row of leaflets forms on either side of an extension of the petiole called the rachis. Some pinnately compound leaves branch again, developing a second set of pinnately compound leaflets (bipinnately compound). The many degrees of compoundness in highly elaborated leaves, such as bipinnately or tripinnately compound, cause these leaves to often appear to be shoot systems. It is always possible to distinguish them, however, because axillary buds are found in the angle between the stem and the petiole (axil) of pinnately or palmately compound leaves but not in the axils of leaflets.

The three patterns of leaf arrangement on stems in angiosperms are alternate, opposite (paired), and whorled. In alternate-leaved plants, the leaves are single at each node and borne along the stem alternately in an ascending spiral. In opposite-leaved plants, the leaves are paired at a node and borne opposite to each other. A plant has whorled leaves when there are three or more equally spaced leaves at a node.

Leaf modifications

Whole leaves or parts of leaves are often modified for special functions, such as for climbing and substrate attachment, storage, protection against predation or climatic conditions, or trapping and digesting insect prey. In temperate trees, leaves are simply protective bud scales; in the spring when shoot growth is resumed, they often exhibit a complete growth series from bud scales to fully developed leaves.

Stipules often develop before the rest of the leaf; they protect the young blade and then are often shed when the leaf matures. Spines are also modified leaves. In cacti, spines are wholly transformed leaves that protect the plant from herbivores, radiate heat from the stem during the day, and collect and drip condensed water vapour during the cooler night. In the many species of the spurge family (Euphorbiaceae; Euphorbiales), the stipules are modified into paired stipular spines and the blade develops fully. In ocotillo (*Fouquieria splendens;* Violales), the blade falls off and the petiole remains as a spine.

Many desert plants, such as stoneplants (*Lithops;* Caryophyllales) and aloe (*Aloe;* Liliales), develop succulent leaves for water storage. The most common form of storage leaves are the succulent leaf bases of underground bulbs (*e.g.,* tulip and *Crocus;* Liliales) that serve as either water or food storage organs, or both. Many nonparasitic plants that grow on the surfaces of other plants (epiphytes), such as some of the bromeliads, absorb water through specialized hairs on the surfaces of their leaves. In the water hyacinth (*Eichhornia crassipes*), swollen petioles keep the plant afloat.

Tendrils

Leaves or leaf parts may be modified to provide support. Tendrils and hooks are the most common of these modifications. In the flame lily (*Gloriosa superba;* Liliales), the leaf tip of the blade elongates into a tendril and twines around other plants for support. In the garden pea (*Pisum sativum;* Fabales), the terminal leaflet of the compound leaf develops as a tendril. In nasturtium (*Tropaeolum majus;* Geraniales) and *Clematis* (Ranunculales), the petioles coil around other plants for support. In catbrier (*Smilax;* Liliales), the stipules function as tendrils. In certain vining angiosperms with compound leaves, some of the leaflets have modified into grapnellike hooks—*e.g., Tecoma radicans.* Many monocotyledons have sheathing leaf bases that are concentrically arranged and form a pseudotrunk, as in banana (*Musa*). In many epiphytic bromeliads, the pseudotrunk also functions as a water reservoir.

Insectivorous (carnivorous) plants use their leaves to attract and trap insects. Glands in the leaves secrete enzymes that digest the captured insects, and the leaves then absorb the nitrogenous compounds (amino acids) and other products of digestion. Plants that use insects as a nitrogen source tend to grow in nitrogen-deficient soils.

Entire shoot systems are often modified for such special functions as climbing, protection, adaptation to arid habitats, and water or food storage. The modifications generally involve structural and shape changes to the stem and the reduction of the leaves to small scales. Many of the modifications parallel those previously described for leaves. In the passion flower (*Passiflora;* Violales) and grape (*Vitis vinifera;* Rhamnales), axillary buds develop as tendrils with reduced leaves and suppressed axillary buds. In the grape these axillary tendrils are actually modified and reduced inflorescences. In the plant from which strychnine is obtained (*Strychnos nux-vomica*), the axillary buds develop into hooks for climbing. The tendrils of ivy (*Hedera helix;* Apiales) produce enlarged cuplike holdfasts.

Thorns and cladodes

Thorns represent the modification of an axillary shoot system in which the leaves are reduced and die quickly and the stems are heavily sclerified and grow for only a limited time (determinate growth). Thorns appear to protect the plant against herbivores. Examples are found in the *Bougainvillea* (Caryophyllales), where the thorn is a modified inflorescence, the honey locust (*Gleditsia triacanthos;* Fabales), the anchor plant (*Colletia paradoxa;* Rhamnales), and *Citrus* (Sapindales).

Cladodes (also called cladophylls or phylloclades) are shoot systems in which leaves do not develop; rather, the stems become flattened and assume the photosynthetic functions of the plant. In asparagus (*Asparagus officinalis;* Liliales), the scales found on the asparagus spears are the true leaves. If the thick, fleshy asparagus spears continue to grow, flat, green, leaflike structures called cladodes develop in the axils of the scale leaves. The presence of cladodes in unrelated desert angiosperm families is an excellent example of convergent evolution, or the independent development of the same characteristic in unrelated taxa.

All cacti (Cactaceae) have cladodes, and many desert members of the spurge (Euphorbiaceae) and milkweed (Asclepiadaceae) families have similar vegetative morphologies that are derived by modifying different parts to look and function in the same way. Each of these plant groups has columnar, water-storing green stems, reduced leaves, and protective spines or thorns. They are often called stem succulents. In the cacti, the leaves on the main stems last for a very short time (they do not even develop as scale leaves) and the leaves of the axillary buds (the round cushion areas, or areoles, on the trunks) develop as spines. In the Euphorbiaceae, the leaves on the main stems are green but short-lived, and the stipules develop as spines. In the Asclepiadaceae, the leaves are also small and ephemeral, and the axillary buds develop as thorns. The cacti are New World plants adapted to dry or arid habitats, and the Euphorbiaceae and Asclepiadaceae occur in similar habitats in Asia and Africa. The reduction of leaves is so extreme in the Cactaceae that the epiphytic cacti (*e.g., Epiphyllum*) of the Neotropics can no longer produce leaves; rather, they produce thin, flat cladodes that superficially resemble leaves.

Rhizomes, tubers, and corms

Many shoot systems have been modified into organs of food storage, reproduction, or both, called rhizomes, tubers, and corms. Rhizomes are distinguished from roots in having nodes with reduced leaves and internodes. Rhizomes are horizontal, usually subterranean shoots with scale leaves and adventitious roots on the underside. Their chief functions are vegetative reproduction and food storage; food stored in the rhizomes allows these plants to survive drought and extended winters. Most rhizomes are perennial, sending up new shoots from the nodes and spreading the colony. Often the terminal bud of a rhizome becomes upright and then flowers, with a rhizome axillary bud becoming a renewal shoot. Many economically important plants, such as banana, and almost all grasses, including bamboo, and sugarcane, have rhizomes. Such plants are propagated primarily by fragmentation of the rhizome. In some plants, the growing tips of rhizomes become much enlarged food storage organs called tubers. The common potato (*Solanum tuberosum*) forms such tubers. The much-reduced scale leaves and their associated axillary buds form the eyes of the potato. Tubers should not be confused with tuberous roots. Tubers are modified shoots, whereas tuberous roots are modified roots. The common feature, and hence the similar names, derives from the fleshy nature of both organs. Tubers and tuberous roots function in water and food storage, but only tubers are involved in vegetative (nonsexual) reproduction. Tuberous roots develop from taproots in carrots and from adventitious roots in dahlias (*Dahlia;* Asterales).

Another distinctive modification for food storage is the corm, a short, upright shoot system with a thick, hard stem covered with thin membranous scale leaves as in jack-in-the-pulpit (*Arisaema triphyllum;* Arales) and gladiolus (*Gladiolus;* Liliales). Corms are usually hard and fibrous and function for overwintering and drought resistance.

Slender creeping stems that grow above the soil surface are called stolons, or runners. Stolons have scale leaves and can develop roots and, therefore, new plants, either terminally or at a node. In the strawberry (*Fragaria*), the stolons are used for propagation; buds appear at nodes along the stolons and develop into new strawberry plants.

The diversity of form within the angiosperms has contributed to their successful colonization of more habitats than any other group of land plants. Gymnosperms (the nonflowering seed plants) are only woody plants with a few woody twining vines. There are few herbaceous or aquatic gymnosperms; most gymnosperms do not occur in mangrove (swampy) vegetation or marine habitats. With the exception of cycads, gymnosperms have simple leaves, and none are modified as spines, tendrils, or storage organs.

The absence of substantial diversity in the vegetative features of gymnosperms appears to have limited their ability to adapt to diverse or extreme habitats. The absence of vessels in most gymnosperms, and hence the less efficient water transport system than that found in the angiosperms, is one example. In fact, the only gymnosperms with vessels, the Gnetales, is the only group that contains vines and the only group that deviates from the usually woody trunk growth form. The absence of vessels in angiosperms, however, is rare; the few groups without vessels are small trees or shrubs with limited distribution, as in the Winteraceae. Another factor contributing to the limited distribution of gymnosperms is that they do not produce reproductive structures until several years after the seed germinates; therefore, a woody habit is required to achieve sexual maturity. Finally, the gymnosperms also require a relatively stable environment for growth. Thus, restraints imposed by anatomy and life cycle have probably limited morphological diversity among the gymnosperms.

Widespread distribution

The wide variation in the angiosperm form is reflected in the range of habitats in which they grow and their almost complete worldwide distribution. The only area without angiosperms is the southern region of the Antarctic continent, although two angiosperm groups are found in the islands off that continent. Angiosperms dominate terrestrial vegetation, particularly in the tropics, although submerged and floating aquatic angiosperms do exist throughout the world. Angiosperms are the principal component of salt marshes, tidal marshes, and mangrove marshes. The only vascular marine plants are a few submerged marine angiosperms that occur in shallow waters of coastal areas throughout the world; for example the sea grasses (*Zostera* and *Cymodocea;* Najadales). The various terrestrial biomes (defined primarily based upon the type of vegetation and climate) are composed mainly of herbaceous and woody angiosperms, except for taiga (boreal forest), temperate rain forest, and juniper savanna, where conifers (a gymnospermous division) dominate the woody component and angiosperms dominate the herbaceous and shrub components.

Morphological and habitat diversity, together with cosmopolitan distribution, contributes to the wide ecological tolerance of the angiosperms—adapting to Alpine tundra regions and salt marshes, from the Arctic Circle to the lowland tropical rain forests. The importance of angiosperms in the terrestrial portion of the biosphere is rarely rivaled by any other group of organisms.

All but a few angiosperms are autotrophs: they are green plants (primary producers) that use solar radiation, carbon dioxide, water, and minerals to synthesize organic compounds; oxygen is a by-product of these metabolic reactions. The few exceptions are either saprophytes (*e.g.,* the Indian pipe *Monotropa uniflora;* Ericales) that use connections with mycorrhizal fungi (fungi that form an association with the roots of certain plants) to obtain carbohydrates from dead organic material or parasites that develop specialized roots (haustoria), which penetrate the host plant and absorb food and other materials (*e.g.,* the dodder [*Cuscuta salina;* Solanales]).

The food chain

Because angiosperms are the most numerous component of the terrestrial environment in terms of biomass and number of individuals, they provide an important source of food for animals and other living organisms. Organic compounds (carbon-containing compounds, principally carbohydrates) not only are used by the plant itself for synthesizing cellular structures and for fueling their basic metabolisms but also serve as the only source of energy for most heterotrophic organisms. (Heterotrophs require an organic source of carbon that has originated as part of another living organism, in contrast to autotrophs, which require only an inorganic source of carbon—CO_2.) Solar energy is trapped by the photosynthetic pigments in the plant cells and converted into chemical energy, which is stored in the tissues of the plant. The trapped energy is transferred from one organism to the next as herbivores consume the plant, carnivores consume herbivores, and so on up the food chain. In a temperate forest, one angiosperm tree supports many thousands of animals (the majority being insects, birds, and mammals), a relationship that underscores the basic importance of the angiosperms to the food chain.

The angiosperm body contributes to the food chain in many ways. The vegetative parts (the nonreproductive organs, such as stems and leaves) are consumed by, and support, plant-eating animals. Vast numbers of insects and other invertebrates depend on shoots for food during all or part of their life histories. The reproductive organs (flowers, fruits, and seeds) also provide an energy source for many animals. The pollen supports many pollinating insects, particularly bees.

The flowers provide food from floral nectaries that secrete sugars and amino acids. These flowers often produce fragrances that attract pollinators which feed on the nectar. Nectar-feeding animals include many insect groups (bees, butterflies, moths, flies, and even mosquitoes), many mammal groups (bats, small rodents, and small marsupials), and birds (honeyeaters, hummingbirds, and sunbirds). Nectaries also occur on the nonfloral, or vegetative, parts of some angiosperms, such as the leaves and the petioles of bull's-horn thorn (*Acacia collinsii;* Fabales). Ants live inside the hollow modified spinous structures of bull's-horn thorn and feed on the nectar. In return for this food source, they attack and destroy animals of all sizes as well as other plants that contact the acacia plant. In doing so, the ants protect the bull's-horn thorn from herbivores and other plants competing for the available space, light, and minerals.

Fruits produced by angiosperms are the principal food for many bats, birds, mammals, and even some fish. Seeds are also an important food source for many animals, particularly small rodents and birds. These animals often carry the fruits and seeds of the angiosperms they consume to new areas, where the angiosperms propagate.

Another aspect of angiosperm diversity is found in the production of secondary compounds, such as alkaloids, quinones, essential oils, and glycosides. Angiosperms have evolved a comprehensive array of unpalatable or toxic secondary plant compounds that protect the plants from foraging herbivores. Some insects, however, successfully store these secondary compounds in their tissues and use them as protection from predation.

Secondary compounds

As the principal component of the terrestrial biosphere, the angiosperm flora determines many features of the habitat, some of which are available food, aspects of the forest canopy, and grazing land. They supply nesting sites and materials for a wide range of birds and mammals, and they are the principal living spaces for many primates, reptiles, and amphibians. The tank bromeliad, which traps water in its crowns, provides a habitat for salamanders, frogs, and many aquatic insects and larvae. The animal inhabitants of the water-filled, insectivorous pitcher-plant leaves (Nepenthales) have adapted to the hostile environment of the leaves' digestive fluids.

Angiosperms are as important to humans as they are to other animals. Angiosperms serve as the major source of food—either directly or indirectly through consumption by herbivores—and, as mentioned above, they are a primary source of consumer goods, such as building materials, textile fibres, spices, herbs, and pharmaceuticals.

Among the most important food plants on a global scale are cereals from the grass family (Poaceae); potatoes, tomatoes, eggplant, and red or chili peppers from the potato family (Solanaceae); legumes or beans (Fabaceae); pumpkins, melons, and gourds from the squash family (Cucurbitaceae); broccoli, cabbage, cauliflower, radish, and other vegetables from the mustard family (Brassicaceae, or Cruciferae); and almonds, apples, apricots, cherries, loquats, peaches, pears, raspberries, and strawberries from the rose family (Rosaceae). Members of many angiosperm families are used for food on a local level, such as ullucu (*Ullucus tuberosus*) in the Andes and cassava (*Manihot esculenta*) throughout the tropics. Tropical angiosperm trees are an important source of timber in the tropics and throughout the world. (D.W.St.)

The flowering plants have a number of uses as food, specifically as grains, sugars, vegetables, fruits, oils, nuts, and spices. In addition, plants and their products serve a number of other needs, such as dyes, fibres, timber, fuel, medicines, and ornamentals. Many plants serve more than one function—for example, the seeds of the kapok fruit (*Ceiba pentandra;* Bombaceae), yield a water-repellent fibre used in sound and thermal insulation and an edible oil used in cooking, lubricants, and soap; the oil cake is rich in protein and is fed to livestock; and the soft, light wood is used to make furniture and boats.

The angiospermous plant converts the energy of the sun into starch, the energy-rich storage form of sugar, and reserves it in the endosperm of the seed for the time when the seedling germinates and grows. Among the most economically important grains throughout the world are corn, wheat (*Triticum*), rice (*Oryza*), barley (*Hordeum*), oats (*Avena*), sorghum (*Sorghum*), and rye (*Secale*), all members of the grass family, Poaceae.

Corn provides food for humans and domesticated animals, and its derivatives (*e.g.,* cornstarch and corn oil) are used in making cosmetics, adhesives, varnishes, paints, soaps, and linoleum. Among the many cultivars of *Zea mays,* dent corn, variety *indentat,* is a widely used feed type in the United States. Wheat, barley, and rye are all members of the same tribe (Triticeae) within the family Poaceae (Cyperales). Wheat is among the oldest of the cultivated food crops. Barley is used for human consumption, livestock feed, and malting. Rye is usually used as a livestock feed, but can be used in baking and distilling liquor. Rice is a semiaquatic annual grass and is one of the major cereal crops of the world.

Vegetables constitute perhaps the greatest diversity of form and nutritional content and are grown for one or more of their parts—the flowers, shoots, or leaves; or the underground parts, such as tuberous roots, bulbs, rhizomes, corms, and tubers.

The globe, or French, artichoke (*Cynara scolymus;* Asteraceae, also known as Compositae) is an immature flower bud and receptacle overlaid by bracts. Asparagus (*Asparagus officinalis;* Liliaceae) is a perennial plant cultivated for its succulent green shoots (spears) that arise from underground stems called crowns.

The mustard family (Brassicaceae, also known as Cruciferae) contains a number of important vegetables—broccoli, brussel sprouts, cabbage, cauliflower, collards, kale, and kohlrabi—all members of *Brassica oleraceae* and comprising a group of vegetables called the cole crops, a term that probably reflects the fact that they are principally stem plants. The flower heads and stalks of broccoli and cauliflower are eaten, the two plants differing in that the white head of the cauliflower consists of malformed (hypertrophied) flowers that form in dense clusters. Brussel sprouts continually form many small heads in the axils of the leaves throughout the growing season. The cabbage head is a large terminal bud.

The edible portion of celery (*Apium graveolens;* Umbelliferae) is the petiole (leaf stalk) that arises from a compact stem. Rhubarb (*Rheum rhabarbarum;* Polygonaceae) is a leafy plant also grown for its leaf petioles.

Parsley (*Petroselinum crispum;* Umbelliferae), spinach (*Spinacia oleracea;* Chenopodiaceae), and swiss chard (*Beta vulgaris;* Chenopodiaceae) are cultivated for their leaves, and the leek (*Allium ampeloprasum;* Liliaceae), a close relative of the onion, is cultivated for its leaf bases.

Root crops are grown for their fleshy subterranean storage bodies: tuberous roots, bulbs, rhizomes, corms, and tubers. The potato is a tuber found in Solanaceae, the potato family. Other important root crops include the beet (*Beta vulgaris;* Chenopodiaceae), the sweet potato (*Ipomoea batatas;* Convolvulaceae), and the radish (*Raphanus sativus*), turnip (*Brassica rapa*), and rutabaga (*B. napus*), the latter all of the family Brassicaceae.

Bulb crops are underground leafy scales attached to short compressed stems; food is stored in the leaves rather than the roots, causing them to enlarge into bulbs. Onions (*Allium cepa;* Liliaceae) and garlic (*A. sativum*) are the most obvious examples of the bulb vegetable.

Many plants classified popularly as vegetables are in actuality fruits because they develop from the reproductive structures of the plant. The genus *Cucurbita* (Cucurbitaceae) includes the pumpkins, squashes, and gourds, of which *C. moschata* (winter squash, or crookneck pumpkin), *C. pepo* (summer squash, or marrow), and *C. mixta* (the pumpkin, or mixta squash) are some of the common types. Breadfruit (*Artocarpus altilis;* Moraceae), a plant native to the Pacific Islands, is a staple, providing a rich source of calcium and starch.

The common bean (*Phaseolus vulgaris*), including the French, or kidney, bean, the string bean, and the navy bean, is the edible fleshy pod containing the bean seeds. It provides a good source of protein. Lima beans (*P. lunatus*) probably originated in Central America and are now found in the United States, the lowland tropics, and Africa.

The cucumber (*Cucumis sativus;* Cucurbitaceae) produces a fruit that develops from a branching vine. Okra (*Abelmoschus esculentus;* Malvaceae) is a warm-weather crop that produces small fruit pods.

The garden, or English, pea (*Pisum sativum;* Fabaceae, also known as Leguminosae) is an annual, cool-weather plant cultivated for its edible green seed or pod. The pea is found throughout most temperate and tropical regions.

The family Solanaceae contains the important fruit vegetables—eggplants (aubergines), peppers, and tomatoes—all herbaceous plants, which are perennial in the tropics and annual in temperate zones. (The family also contains the potato, which is a root crop.) The eggplant (*Solanum melongena*) remains an important food crop in Asia.

The pepper (*Capsicum;* Solanaceae) includes the sweet, or bell, pepper (which is green when immature, but red or yellow when ripe), and the red, or chili, pepper. A native of Central and South America, this herbaceous plant is a perennial in the tropics and an annual in temperate zones. Pepper plants are cultivated for their fruits, some of which are extremely pungent owing to the presence of capsaicin found in the septa, in the placenta, and, to a lesser extent, in the seeds, but not in the wall, of the fruit.

The tomato (*Lycopersicon esculentum;* Solanaceae), a native to South America, was at one time wrongly reported to bear poisonous fruits. The fruit is a fleshy berry invested with many small seeds.

Plants cultivated for their fruits are found in temperate, tropical, or subtropical regions. Temperate plants are generally deciduous and either tolerate or require a cool period for growth. Apples (*Malus*) and pears (*Pyrus*) are important pome fruits of the family Rosaceae. Some well-known stone fruits of the family include the peaches and nectarines (*Prunus persica*), plums (*P. domestica*), and cherries (*P. avium*). Other temperate fruits grown on bushes, vines, or low plants include the grapes (*Vitis;* Vitaceae), strawberry (*Fragaria;* Rosaceae), blueberries (*Vaccinium*), and cranberries (*V. macrocarpon*), both from Ericaceae.

Tropical fruits tend to be grown on evergreen plants and can survive temperatures only above freezing. Subtropical plants are either deciduous or tropical and are not as susceptible to temperatures slightly below freezing. *Citrus* (Rutaceae), avocados (*Persea americana;* Lauraceae), olives (*Olea;* Oleaceae), dates (*Phoenix dactylifera;* Palmae, also called Arecaceae), fig (*Ficus;* Moraceae), pineapple (*Ananas comosus;* Bromeliaceae), banana (*Musa;* Muscaceae), and papaya (*Carica;* Caricaceae) are tropical and subtropical plants.

Commercially important plants cultivated for the nuts they produce are almonds (*Prunus dulcis;* Rosaceae), walnuts (*Juglans regia;* Juglandaceae), pecans (*Carya illinoinensis;* Juglandaceae), macadamias (*Macadamia;* Proteaceae), and filberts (*Corylus;* Betulaceae).

Sugarcane (*Saccharum officinurum;* Poaceae) and sugar beet (Chenopodiaceae) are rich sources of natural sugar.

Peanuts (*Arachis*) and soybeans (*Glycine*), both members of Fabaceae, the legume family, of the order Fabales, produce edible seeds that are important for their rich supply of protein or oil. Other plants rich in oil and important economically are the castor bean (*Ricinus;* Euphobiaceae), coconut (*Cocos nucifera;* Palmae), corn, cotton (*Gossypium;* Malvaceae), flax (*Linum usitatissimum;* Linaceae), olives, oil palm (*Elaeis guineensis;* Palmae), sesame (*Sesamum;* Pedaliaceae), and sunflowers (*Helianthus;* Asteraceae).

(Ed.)

Herbs and spices

As noted earlier, some plants produce toxic secondary compounds for protection. Some of the secondary compounds produced by angiosperms are not toxic, however; in fact, many are found in herbs and spices, as, for example, cloves, the dried flower buds of *Syzygium aromaticum* (Myrtales). The use of herbs and spices in cooking predates recorded history. Herbs are usually leaves or young shoots of nonwoody plants, although bay leaves and a few other leaves from woody plants are also considered herbs. Spices are the highly flavoured, aromatic parts of plants that are usually high in essential oil content. Spices are derived from roots, rhizomes, leaves, bark, seeds, fruits, and flower parts. The search for spices and alternative shipping routes for spices played a major role in world exploration in the 13th to 15th centuries. Many beverages are also derived from angiosperms; these include coffee (*Coffea arabica;* Rubiales), tea (*Camellia sinensis;* Theales), most soft drinks (*e.g.,* root beer from the roots of *Sassafras albidum;* Laurales), and most alcoholic beverages (*e.g.,* beer and whiskey from cereal grains and wine from grapes).

The angiosperms provide valuable pharmaceuticals. With the exception of antibiotics, almost all medicinals either are derived directly from compounds produced by angiosperms or, if synthesized, were originally discovered in angiosperms. This includes some vitamins (*e.g.,* vitamin C, originally extracted from fruits); aspirin, originally from the bark of willows (*Salix;* Salicales); narcotics (*e.g.,* opium and its derivatives from the opium poppy, *Papaver somniferum;* Papaverales); and quinine from *Cinchona* bark. Some angiosperm compounds that are highly toxic to humans have proved to be effective in the treatment of certain forms of cancer, such as acute leukemia (vincristine from the Madagascar periwinkle, *Catharanthus roseus;* Gentianales); and of heart problems (digitalis from foxglove, *Digitalis purpurea;* Scrophulariales). Muscle relaxants derived from curare (*Strychnos toxifera;* Gentianales) are used during open-heart surgery.

The contribution of the angiosperms to biodiversity and habitat is so extremely important that human life is totally dependent on it. A significant loss of angiosperms would reduce the variety of food sources and oxygen supply in a habitat and drastically alter the amount and distribution of the world's precipitation. Many sources of food and medicine doubtless remain to be discovered in this group of vascular plants.

Structure and function

The wide diversity in the morphological features of the plant body has been discussed above. This section will outline the underlying structural (anatomic) diversity among angiosperms.

VEGETATIVE STRUCTURES

There are three levels of integrated organization in the vegetative plant body: organ, tissue system, and tissue. The organs of the plant—the roots, stems, and leaves—are composed of tissue systems (dermal tissue, ground tissue, and vascular tissue; see below *Tissue systems*). The tissues of each of these systems are composed of cells of one or more types (parenchyma, collenchyma, and sclerenchyma; see below *Tissue systems: Ground tissue*). Tissues composed of only one cell type and performing only one function are simple tissues, while those composed of more

From (top) E.M. Gifford and A.S. Foster, *Morphology and Evolution of Vascular Plants*, 3rd ed. (1988), W.H. Freeman and Co., New York City, redrawn from Zimmermann, *Jahrbuch fur wissenschaftliche Botanik*, vol. 68, p. 289 (1928); (bottom) N.A. Campbell, *Biology* (1987), The Benjamin/Cummings Pub. Co., Inc.

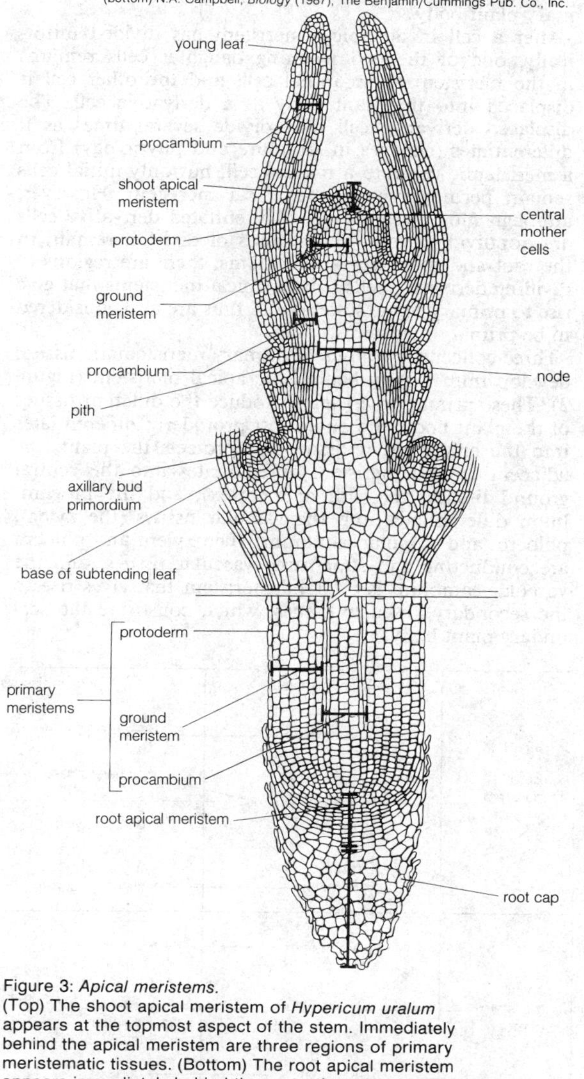

Figure 3: *Apical meristems.*
(Top) The shoot apical meristem of *Hypericum uralum* appears at the topmost aspect of the stem. Immediately behind the apical meristem are three regions of primary meristematic tissues. (Bottom) The root apical meristem appears immediately behind the protective root cap. Three primary meristems are clearly visible just behind the apical meristem.

than one cell type and performing more than one function, such as support and conduction, are complex tissues. Xylem and phloem are examples of complex tissues.

The plant develops from a fertilized egg, called a zygote, which undergoes mitotic cell division to form an embryo—a simple multicellular structure of undifferentiated cells (*i.e.,* those that have not developed into cells of a specific type)—and eventually a mature plant. The embryo consists of a bipolar axis that bears one or two cotyledons, or seed leaves; in most dicots the cotyledons contain stored food in the form of proteins, lipids, and starch, or they are photosynthetic and produce these products, whereas in most monocots and some dicots the endosperm stores the food and the cotyledons absorb the digested food. The embryos of dicotyledons have two seed leaves, while those of monocotyledons have only one.

Apical meristems

As the embryo continues to develop and new cells arise, the angiospermous plant develops specialized regions in which only cell division takes place and other areas in which nonreproductive (vegetative) activities, such as metabolism, respiration, and storage, occur. The areas of dividing cells, essentially permanently embryonic tissue, are called meristems, and their cells are termed initials. In the embryo they are found at either end of the bipolar axis and are called apical meristems. As the plant matures, apical meristems in the shoots produce new buds and leaves, and apical meristems in the roots are the points of active growth for roots (Figure 3). All growth produced by the apical meristems is primary growth and results in more primary tissues, which essentially extends the primary plant body.

After a cell in an apical meristem has divided mitotically, one of the two resulting daughter cells remains in the meristem as an initial cell, and the other cell is displaced into the plant body as a derivative cell. The displaced derivative cell may divide several times as it differentiates (changes in structure and physiology) from a meristemic cell into a mature cell, but only initial cells remain permanently in the apical meristem. However, although most permanently differentiated derivative cells are nondividing cells, and regions of division remain in the root and shoot apical meristems, there are regions of dividing derivative cells behind apical meristems that give rise to primary tissue systems and thus are also considered to be primary meristems.

Three concentric regions of primary meristematic tissues develop immediately behind the apical meristem (Figure 3). These primary meristems produce the different tissues of the plant body: the outermost protoderm differentiates into the epidermis, a tissue that protects the plant; the adjacent ground meristem differentiates into the central ground tissues (the pith and cortex); and the procambium differentiates into the vascular tissues (the xylem, phloem, and vascular cambium). The xylem and phloem are conducting and supporting vascular tissues, and the vascular cambium is a lateral meristem that gives rise to the secondary vascular tissues, which constitute the secondary plant body.

Lateral meristems

Lateral meristems, called cambia, run the length of the stems and roots of vascular plants and produce secondary tissues, which develop after a plant organ—or part of a plant organ—has ceased to elongate. Secondary growth is essentially an increase in girth. The vascular cambium produces secondary xylem and secondary phloem, and the cork cambium (phellogen) produces cork cells, from which bark develops. Figure 4 summarizes the patterns of primary and secondary growth from root and shoot apical meristems. (For a complete discussion of primary and secondary plant growth, see below *Tissue systems: Vascular tissue.*)

TISSUE SYSTEMS

As mentioned above, three areas of meristematic tissue are derived directly from the apical meristem: the ground meristem, procambium, and protoderm. These meristematic tissues differentiate into the three primary tissues that constitute the primary plant body: ground tissue (pith and cortex), vascular tissue (xylem, phloem, and eventually the lateral, or secondary, meristem called the vascular cambium), and dermal tissue (epidermis), respectively.

Ground tissue. The ground tissue system arises from a ground tissue meristem and consists of three simple tissues: parenchyma, collenchyma, and sclerenchyma (Figure 5). The cells of each simple tissue bear the same name as their respective tissue.

Parenchyma, often the most common ground tissue, takes its name from the Greek *para,* meaning beside, and *egchnma,* meaning the contents of a pitcher (literally, something poured beside), indicating its ubiquitous nature throughout the plant body. It forms, for example, the cortex and pith of stems, the photosynthetic tissue layer within the epidermis of the leaves (mesophyll), the cortex of roots, the pulp of fruits, and the endosperm of seeds. Parenchyma is composed of relatively simple, undifferentiated parenchyma cells. In most plants, metabolic activity (such as respiration, digestion, and photosynthesis) occurs in these cells because they, unlike many of the other types of cells in the plant body, retain their protoplasts (the cytoplasm, nucleus, and cell organelles) that carry out these functions.

Parenchyma cells are capable of cell division, even after they have differentiated into the mature form. They can therefore give rise to adventitious buds and roots at some distance from the apical meristem at the tips of shoots and roots. Parenchyma cells are also capable of further differentiation into new cell types under appropriate conditions, such as after trauma. (For information concerning the development of bark during the secondary growth of tissues, see below *Vascular tissue.*) Parenchyma cells are active in secretion, photosynthesis, and water and food storage (especially in fleshy fruits). They have large fluid-filled vacuoles that maintain cell turgidity; when a plant wilts, for example, it is because the vacuoles in the parenchyma cells have lost water and have become flaccid. Thus, parenchyma also functions in plant support. However, parenchyma cells do not have a secondary cell

From N.A. Campbell, *Biology* (1987); The Benjamin/Cummings Pub. Co., Inc.

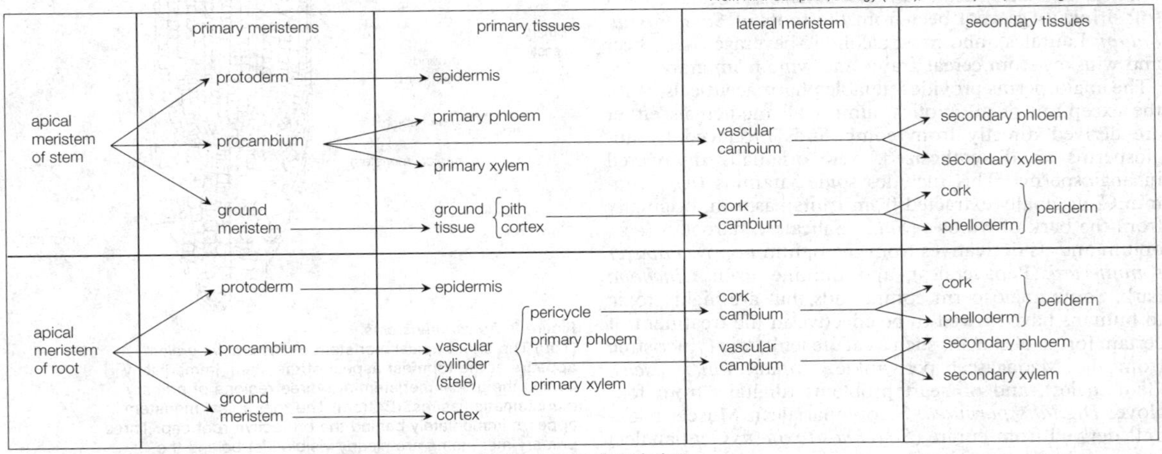

Figure 4: A summary of the primary and secondary growth of a woody dicotyledon.

wall at maturity and thus remain flexible and capable of elongation.

Prosenchyma cells are starch-containing parenchymal cells whose cell walls have become lined with lignin, as occurs in the stems of *Bougainvillea* (Caryophyllales). A specialized type of parenchyma cell, called a transfer cell, is involved in the short-distance movement of solutes by cell-to-cell transfer. Transfer cells occur in association with veins in leaves and stems and also in many reproductive parts.

Collenchyma tissue (Figure 5) consists of collenchyma cells that also have retained their protoplasts. They are closely related to parenchyma, although they have thick deposits of cellulose in the corners of their primary cell walls, and the two types often intergrade in areas of continuity. (D.W.St.)

Collenchyma is found chiefly in the cortex of stems and in leaves. For many herbaceous plants it is the chief supporting tissue, especially during early stages of development. In plants in which secondary growth occurs, the collenchyma tissue is only temporarily functional and becomes crushed as woody tissue develops. Collenchyma is located along the periphery of stems beneath the epidermal tissue. It may form a complete cylinder or occur as discrete strands that constitute the ridges and angles of stems and other supporting structures of the plant.

Collenchyma cells, polygonal in cross section, are much longer than parenchyma cells. The strength of the tissue results from the unevenly thickened cell walls and the longitudinal overlapping and interlocking of the cells. The wall is not uniformly thick in all cells, and thickening may occur predominately in longitudinal strips at the corners of the cell, on the tangential (*i.e.,* outer, toward the stem exterior) surface of the cell, or around the spaces between adjacent cells. Pits are present in the cell wall and provide a mechanism for intercellular communication. An important feature of collenchyma is that it is extremely plastic—the cells can extend and thus adjust to increase in growth of the organ. Because collenchyma cells are alive at maturity, these thickenings may be reduced when meristematic activity is resumed as in formation of a cork cambium or in response to wounding.

Scleren-chyma

Sclerenchyma tissue (Figure 5) is composed of sclerenchyma cells, which are usually dead at maturity (*i.e.,* have lost their protoplasts). They characteristically contain very thick, hard secondary walls lined with lignin; consequently, sclerenchyma provides additional support and strength to the plant body.

The two principal types of sclerenchyma cells are sclereids and fibres. Sclereids vary in shape and size and may be branched. They are common in seed coats and nutshells. Apart from providing some internal support for various plant organs, sclereids deter desiccation of hard seeds, such as beans, and discourage herbivory of certain leaves.

Fibres are slender cells, many times longer than they are wide. They are highly lignified cells with tapering (oblique) end walls. The side walls of fibres are often so thick that the centre of the cell (the lumen) is often occluded. Fibres have great tensile strength and yet are also elastic. These qualities are significant in the flexible support of the stems of large herbs and leaves of many monocotyledons, such as palms. Leaf fibres are the source of Manila hemp (*Musa textilis;* Zingiberales), sisal (*Agave sisalana;* Liliales), and many other fibre products. Fibres are found in various parts of the plant and are particularly common in the vascular tissues (see below *Vascular tissue*).

(M.H.Z./D.W.St.)

Vascular tissue. *Evolution of the transport process.* Water and nutrients flow through conductive tissues (xylem and phloem) in plants just as the bloodstream distributes nutrients throughout the bodies of animals. This internal circulation, usually called transport, is present in all vascular plants, even the most primitive ones.

The importance of transport processes in plants increased as multicellular plants evolved and became larger and their tissues acquired specialized functions. As land plants developed, long-distance transport assumed an important role; not only are carbohydrates transported from the organs in which they are formed (the leaves) to other parts—

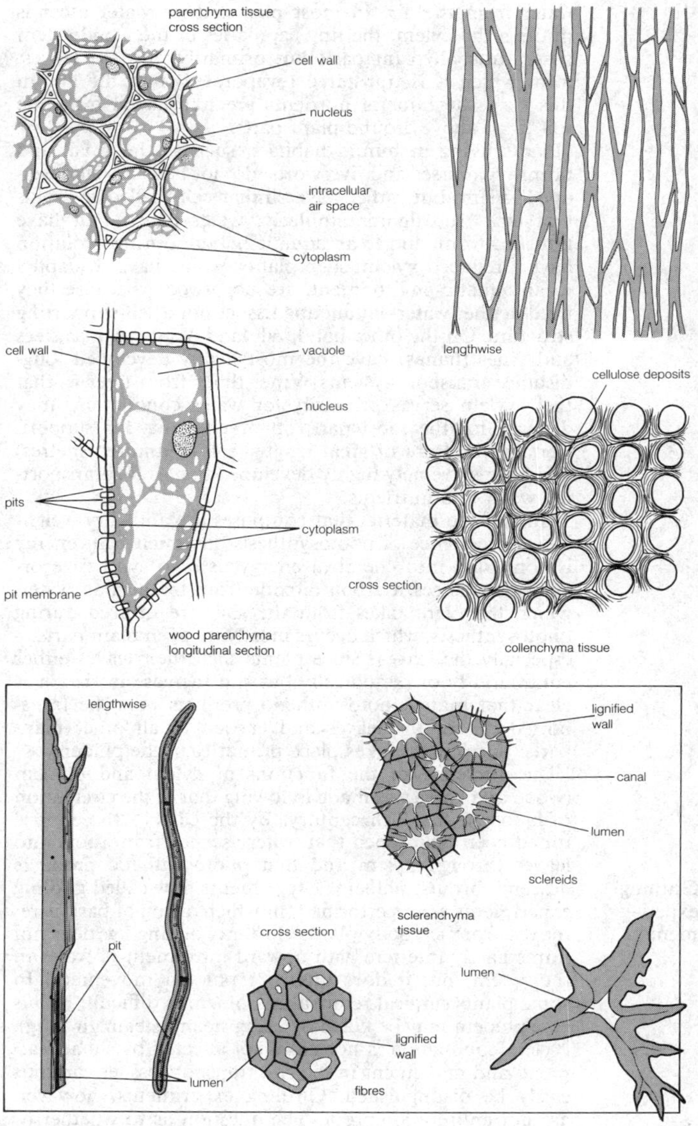

Figure 5: Cell types and tissues.
From T. Weier, C. Stocking, and M. Barbour, *Botany* (1970); John Wiley & Sons, Inc., New York City

such as reproductive organs (flowers and fruits), stems, and roots—but water and minerals must be transported to leaves, which are not submerged in water (as are those of most primitive nonvascular plants) but are in a relatively dry air environment. Highly developed land plants have two types of tissues specialized for long-distance transport: the xylem and the phloem. Water and dissolved mineral nutrients ascend in the xylem (the wood of a tree, such as an oak or a pine), and products of photosynthesis, mostly sugars, move from leaves to other plant parts in the phloem (the inner bark of a tree).

Xylem and phloem

Evolving land plants faced not only the problem of transport but also the problem of supporting their weight. Aquatic plants are supported by their buoyancy in water and do not need a rigid stem; flotation devices such as gas-filled stomata and intercellular spaces hold them upright and enable them to grow toward the water surface and obtain sufficient sunlight for photosynthesis. On land, a rigid, self-supporting structure is necessary for plants; this structure, the xylem, consists of tiny rigid tubes through which water and dissolved mineral nutrients can move. The rigidity of the tubes within a stem is sufficient to make it self-supporting.

Land plants take up water from the soil through the roots; some exceptions, such as some plants of the Peruvian desert that grow in dry soil and epiphytes that grow in tree canopies, rely on adaptations that enable them to obtain water from the air. In most plants, then, water ascends through the xylem, the tiny capillaries of the woody stem tissue, into all plant parts but primarily into the leaves, from which it is transpired (evaporated) into the air. In this way, the mineral nutrients are transferred from the soil to all above-ground plant parts.

Plants living in humid habitats, such as the small and primitive mosses and liverworts, do not have a well-developed xylem, but rather have similar cells called hydroids that lack true lignin. Similarly, water plants that have returned from land to an aquatic habitat during evolution have a reduced xylem; such plants, which have readapted to an aquatic environment, are not woody, because they need neither water-conducting tissues nor a self-supporting structure. On the other hand, tall land plants such as trees and vines (lianas) have the most highly developed long-distance transport systems. Vines differ from trees in that their xylem serves primarily for water conduction; they depend, for the most part, on other plants for support. Certain vines are of great length (a few hundred metres) and have extremely highly developed tissues for transporting water and nutrients.

Most of the material that composes a plant's dry weight is a consequence of photosynthesis, in which light energy is converted into chemical energy used to synthesize organic substances. Carbon dioxide from the air and water, which the plant takes from the soil, are utilized during photosynthesis, which occurs mostly in green plant parts—especially the leaves. Since plants shed their leaves either continuously or periodically but still increase in size, it is clear that many photosynthetic products must be transported out of the leaves and carried to all other plant parts; this process takes place primarily in the phloem.

The discovery of the functions of xylem and phloem (wood and bark) was made following that of the circulation of blood in the 17th century. By the early 19th century, it had been established that water ascends from roots into leaves through xylem and that photosynthetic products descend through phloem. Experiments now called girdling experiments were performed, in which a ring of bark is removed from a woody plant. Girdling, or ringing, does not immediately interfere with upward movement of water in the xylem, but it does interrupt phloem movement. In some plants surgical removal of phloem is difficult; in this case phloem may be killed by using steam (steam girdling). Xylem conduction is normally not affected by such treatment, and movement in the two transport tissues can thus easily be distinguished. Girdling experiments, however, are not entirely foolproof. The question as to whether or not mineral nutrients can ascend in the phloem illustrates the kinds of difficulties that may be encountered. Much smaller amounts of mineral nutrients reach the leaves in girdled plants than in ungirdled ones. From this observation it might be concluded that some nutrients ascend in the phloem of ungirdled trees; girdling, however, interrupts the flow of sugars into roots. Roots are thereby starved and take up fewer mineral nutrients; the reduced flow of mineral nutrients to the leaves of girdled plants can thus be explained as a secondary effect.

Girdling experiments

It was once widely believed that flogging a fruit tree increases the crop. The rational explanation of this is simple: flogging a tree damages the phloem—*i.e.,* it girdles the tree, perhaps partially. Girdling increases the sugar concentration of the leaves by restricting downward transport to the roots and may thus directly or indirectly stimulate flowering or, if done after fruit-set, may increase fruit size by reallocating sugars destined for the roots to the developing fruits.

Structural basis of transport. Two features of plant cells differ conspicuously from those of animal cells. In plant cells the protoplast, or living material of the cell, contains one or more vacuoles, which are vesicles containing aqueous cell sap. Plant cells are also surrounded by a relatively tough but elastic wall. Water entering the vacuole by osmosis (*i.e.,* movement of water across a membrane from regions of higher water concentration into regions of lower water concentration that normally contain dissolved substances, such as cell interiors) expands the protoplast and consequently the cell wall until the internal pressure is balanced by the elastic counterpressure of the wall. Spaces between and within cell walls are sufficiently large to permit water to flow around all cells. The space available for free water flow is called apoplast. Water in apoplast originates from the roots and contains nutrients taken up by them. Nutrients enter a cell by crossing the outer cytoplasmic membrane (the plasmalemma or plasma membrane).

Most of the metabolic activities of the cell—the chemical reactions of living systems—occur within protoplasts. Substances can enter a protoplast by their cytoplasmic connections between neighbouring cells (plasmodesmata) or by active transport mechanisms requiring energy and a group of enzymelike compounds called permeases. Plasmodesmata may penetrate neighbouring cell walls at areas called primary pit fields. Also, some substances pass out of cells into the apoplast and are transported by energy-requiring processes into the protoplast of another cell.

Cell-to-cell transport

Cell-to-cell transport takes place in all plants, but it is a slow process; the higher plants evolved the specialized tissues, xylem and phloem, for rapid long-distance transport. The woody tissue, xylem, contains highly specialized cells for water conduction. The cells are long and reinforced by strong, woody (lignified) walls; their protoplast breaks down and dissolves after wall growth is completed, so that the entire inside of the cell becomes available for rapid water conduction. In other words, the water-conducting cells of xylem are dead when functional. In the more primitive conifers the xylem consists largely of spindle-shaped cells called tracheids, which have a diameter around 0.04 millimetre (0.0016 inch) and a length of about 3 millimetres (0.12 inch). Flowering plants have a more highly specialized xylem, in which the mechanical function and the water-conduction function have been separated during evolution. Tracheids, the primitive conducting cells, have evolved into fibres for mechanical strength and vessels for water conduction, particularly in angiosperms. Vessel elements are barrellike cells with widths of up to 0.5 millimetre (0.02 inch) in some plants. Vessel elements are arranged end to end; their end walls are partly or wholly dissolved, and rows of such cells thus form long capillaries (tubes) up to several metres in length. These tubes are the vessels.

Numerous vessels of limited length thus provide a certain protection against injury—that is, since water pressures in the xylem are often well below zero (*i.e.,* the water is under tension), air will be sucked into any injured xylem vessel and spread immediately throughout it but cannot pass through the wet pit membranes into the uninjured units. Damage is thus confined to the units that are injured and cannot easily spread. In addition, the smaller the conducting unit, the more confined is the damage. Plants with large, highly efficient vessels are much more vulnerable to injury, as is evident, for example, from the vulnerability of the elm, which has large vessels, to Dutch elm disease, in which the water-conduction vessels are injured by beetle activity and fungal growth. In general, both the less efficient but safer coniferous wood and the more highly efficient but more vulnerable wood of flowering plants have been successful during evolution. Very tall trees occur in both groups—*e.g., Sequoia* among the conifers and *Eucalyptus* among the flowering plants.

The conducting elements of the phloem underwent evolutionary changes somewhat similar to those of the xylem. The conducting elements of conifers, called sieve cells, are similar in shape and dimensions to tracheids. They do not have a woody wall, however, and they are alive at functional maturity even though their cytoplasm may be highly specialized and the cells have usually lost their nucleus during development. In flowering plants the conducting elements in the phloem are called sieve elements and consist of sieve cells and sieve-tube members, the latter differing in having some sieve areas specialized into sieve plates (generally on the end walls). Sieve-tube members are arranged end to end to form sieve tubes, a name derived from the sievelike end walls through which passage of food from one cell to the next occurs. Sieve elements are almost invariably accompanied by special companion cells believed to control, to a certain extent, the metabolism of the nucleus-free conducting cells. (M.H.Z.)

Organization of the vascular tissue. Vascular tissue is organized into discrete strands called vascular bundles, each containing xylem and phloem. In stems, the vascular tissue is organized into many discrete vascular bundles. In the roots, the vascular tissue is organized within a single central vascular cylinder. The anatomy of roots and stems is discussed in their respective sections below.

Xylem

The xylem conducts water and minerals within the primary plant body, and the phloem conducts food. The xylem cells are arranged end to end to form a longitudinal continuum throughout the plant. The phloem cells form a similar continuum. Thus, water enters the xylem cells in the roots and travels to the leaves via the stems, and photosynthates (products of photosynthesis) enter the phloem cells in the leaves and are translocated to the roots via the stems. Storage parenchyma and fibres are generally present, and sclereids rarely are.

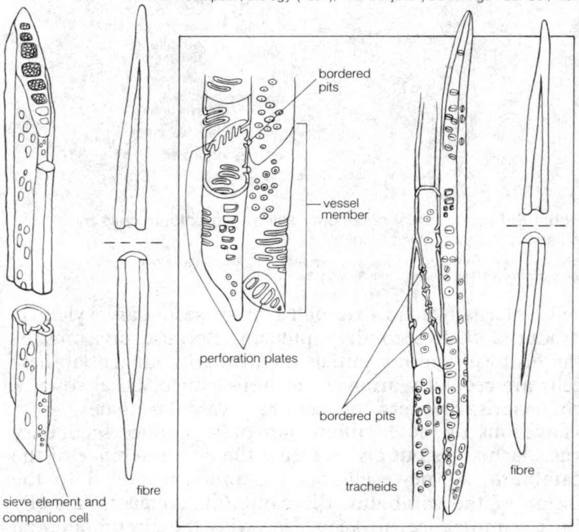

Figure 6: Cells of the (left) phloem and (right) xylem.

Primary xylem (Figure 6) consists of lignified tracheary elements (tracheids and vessel elements), which are dead at maturity (they have lost their protoplasts). Parenchyma cells also are interspersed throughout the tissue. Both tracheids and vessel elements are long hollow cells with tapered end walls. The end walls of adjacent tracheids contain paired small, rimmed, nonperforated pores, called bordered pits; water diffuses through a shared central membrane. The side walls have five patterns of thickening, which represent a developmental sequence from the initial xylem (protoxylem) to the final mature xylem (metaxylem): annular (a series of rings), helical (a long continuous spiral), reticular (a network), scalariform (a series of elongated bordered slits), and circular bordered pitting. Individual species may omit some of these patterns.

Vessel elements differ from tracheids in that the end walls are modified into perforation plates, an area or areas in which there is no shared wall material or membrane. Vessel elements join to form continuous vessels. The perforations are much larger than those of the bordered pits of tracheids and are of four types: scalariform (slitlike), foraminate (circular), reticulate (a network), or simple (single). The bordered pitting of the side walls of vessel members is either scalariform or circular (generally scalariform bordered pitting is associated with scalariform, foraminate, or reticulate perforation plates). Vessel elements are found in the late metaxylem (the final, or most developed, form of the primary xylem).

The most common type of perforation plates in the angiosperms are scalariform and simple; the other types are rare. The putatively primitive angiosperms are without vessels and evolved from a condition in which only tracheids were present to one in which a series of long vessel elements had scalariform lateral walls and highly inclined end walls with many scalariform perforations, to short vessel elements with circular bordered pits in lateral walls and simple perforation plates in horizontal end walls.

This series of specializations has increased the efficiency with which water moves through the vessels: from the more generalized method of water diffusion through pit membranes of narrow tracheids to mass movement of water through the perforated end walls of relatively narrow scalariform vessels and then to relatively wide simple vessels with large single perforated end walls. This simple form is a rather streamlined system that facilitates the maximum movement of water in terms of amount and speed with the minimum amount of resistance, allowing for greater efficiency and effective water transport.

Phloem

The primary phloem (Figure 6) is composed of sieve elements and fibres. Parenchyma cells are interspersed throughout. Sieve elements are longitudinal cells that transport food. They are composed of sieve cells and sieve-tube members. Sieve-tube members have clusters of pores in the cell walls known as sieve areas, which have either small pores or large pores; the latter are known as sieve plates. Sieve plates are mostly located on the overlapping adjacent end walls. As sieve-tube members differentiate, they lose their nucleus, ribosomes, vacuoles, and dictyosomes (the equivalent of the Golgi apparatus in animals); they are not dead, however, and remain metabolically active. Each sieve-tube member has an associated specialized parenchyma cell called a companion cell. They are derived by mitosis from the same parent cell and remain connected with each other. Photosynthates are actively secreted into, and actively removed from, sieve-tube members by their companion cells. Other unspecialized parenchyma cells also are present in primary phloem and provide storage.

Finally, the primary vascular tissue system usually has fibres, particularly in herbaceous plants. The fibres occur in groups either around vascular bundles or as a cap over the phloem (phloem fibres).

The primary vascular system (Figure 7) serves three functions. First, the sieve tubes conduct photosynthates via companion cells from green stems and leaves to nongreen areas (usually roots, lateral meristems, and shoot apical meristems) to promote growth and development. Second,

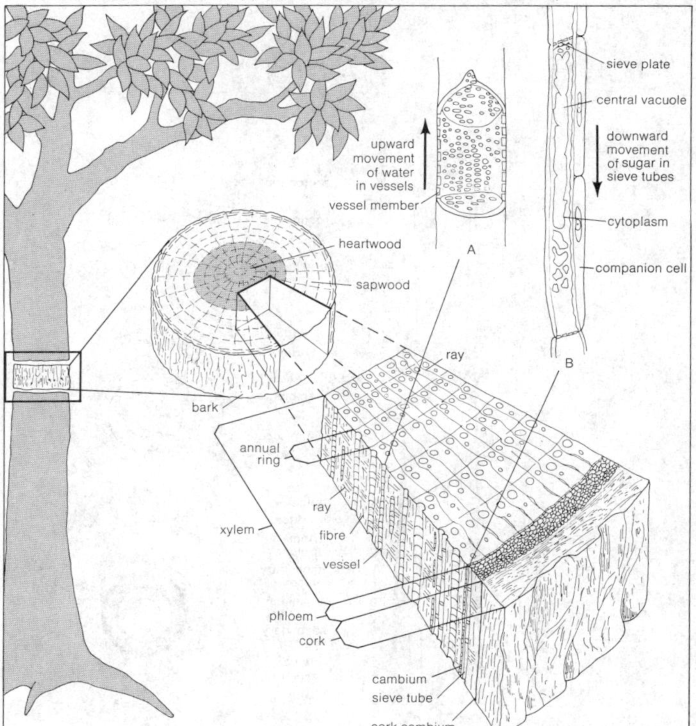

Figure 7: *Internal transport system in a tree.*
(A) Enlarged xylem vessel. (B) Enlarged mature sieve element.

tracheary elements provide a water-conducting system and a support system as a result of their rigid lignified cell walls. Third, fibres provide additional support.

Vascular cambium

In woody plants, a vascular system of secondary vascular tissue develops from a lateral meristem called the vascular cambium (Figure 8). The vascular cambium, which produces xylem and phloem cells, originates from procambium that has not completely differentiated during the formation of primary xylem and primary phloem. The cambium is thought to be a single row of cells arranged as a cylinder that produces new cells: externally the secondary phloem and internally the secondary xylem. Because it is not possible to distinguish the cambium from its immediate cellular derivatives, which also divide and contribute to the formation of secondary tissues, the cambium and its immediate derivatives are usually referred to as the cambial zone.

Unlike the apical meristems, which consist of a population of similar cells, the cambium consists of two different cell types; the fusiform initials and the ray initials (Figure 9). The fusiform initials are elongated tapering cells that give rise to all cells of the vertical system of the secondary phloem and xylem (secondary tracheary elements, fibres, and sieve cells and the associated companion cells). The ray initials are isodiametric cells—about equal in all dimensions—and they produce the vascular rays, which constitute the horizontal system of secondary tissues; this horizontal system acts in the translocation and storage of food and water.

The fusiform and ray initials of the cambium divide in a plane tangential to the surface of the stem, with the long axes of the fusiform and ray initials parallel to the long axis of the plant organ. The cambium generates xylem mother cells toward the inside and phloem mother cells toward the outside. These cells in turn continue to divide tangentially, producing new cells that add to the xylem and to the phloem. Divisions of the cambium cells and xylem and phloem mother cells do not result in the production of equal amounts of secondary xylem and secondary phloem; because the cambium produces more cells internally than externally, more secondary xylem is produced than secondary phloem. Because divisions in the fusiform and ray initials are primarily tangential, new cells are regularly arranged in well-defined radial rows, a characteristic pattern for secondary vascular tissues.

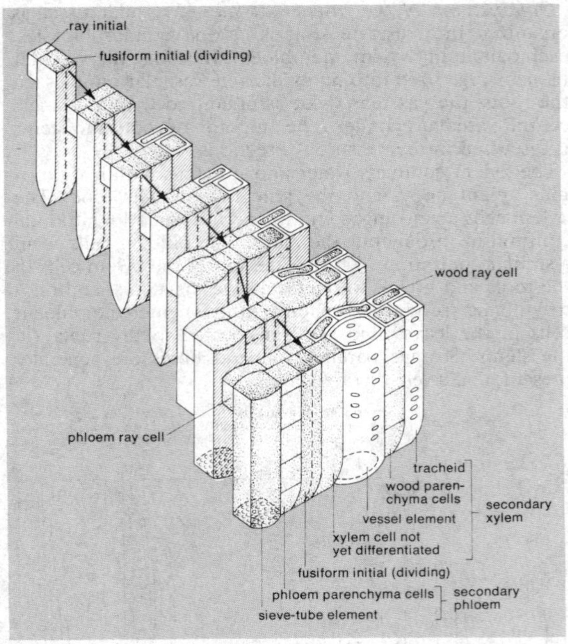

Figure 9: Production of secondary xylem and phloem cells by initials of the vascular cambium.

From P.M. Ray, *The Living Plant*, copyright © 1963 Holt, Rinehart and Winston, Inc., reprinted by permission of Holt, Rinehart and Winston, Inc.

From W.H. Mueller, *Botany*, copyright © 1968 W.H. Mueller, reprinted with permission of the Macmillan Pub. Co., Inc.

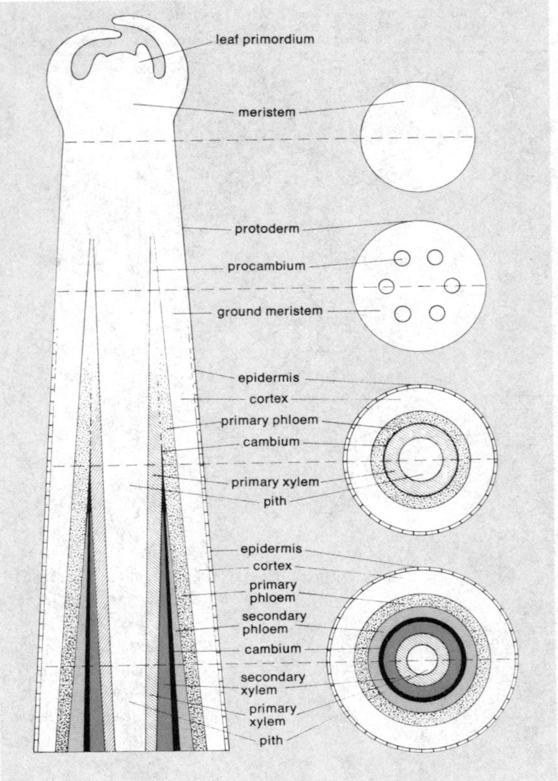

Figure 8: *Tissue organization in a stem tip.*
(A) Longitudinal section. (B) Cross section at different levels.

Divisions in the cambium not only produce secondary vascular tissues but also increase the circumference of the cambium. As new cells are continuously added to the inside of the cambium, the cambium increases laterally (in circumference) to keep pace with the circumferential growth of the stem. In some plants, this is accomplished simply by radial division of the fusiform and ray initials. In other plants, the mechanism for increasing cambial diameter or increasing the number of cambial cells is more complex. If cambial activity is extensive, the primary tissues lying outside the cambium, such as primary phloem, cortex, and epidermis, are crushed by the pressure of new secondary tissue growth or become torn and obliterated because they cannot accommodate the rapidly increasing diameter of the plant.

As growth proceeds, the cork cambium forms in living cells of the epidermis, cortex, or, in some plants, phloem and produces a secondary protective tissue, the periderm. The cork cambium is, like the vascular cambium, a lateral meristem that produces cells internally and externally by tangential divisions. Unlike the cambium, the cork cambium consists of one cell type.

Intercalary meristems

Another type of meristem active in certain plants, especially grasses, is the intercalary meristem. These cells possess the ability to divide and produce new cells, as do apical and lateral meristems. They differ, however, in being situated between regions of mature tissue, such as at the base of grass leaves, which are themselves located on mature stem tissue. In many instances intercalary meristems function for only a short time and eventually completely differentiate into mature tissues. Intercalary meristems are usually located at positions on the stem where leaves have emerged (nodes) and are largely responsible for elongation in grass shoots and leaves. Intercalary meristems are the internode regions where cell division of the ground meristem persists for a longer time than in other areas of the internode. In rosette plants, intercalary meristems are lacking.

Secondary xylem is composed of tracheary elements, rays, fibres, and interspersed axial parenchyma cells. The tracheary elements consist of only tracheids, as in the few vessel-less angiosperms (*e.g.*, Winteraceae), or of both tracheids and vessel elements, as in the vast majority of angiosperms. Axial parenchyma may surround the vessel elements (paratracheal) or be randomly dispersed among the vessel elements (apotracheal).

Tyloses are balloonlike outgrowths of parenchyma cells that bulge through the circular bordered pits of vessel members and block water movement. The presence of tyloses in white oaks makes their wood watertight, which is why it is preferred in casks and shipbuilding to red oak, which lacks tyloses and does not hold water. In trunks and branches that lean, there is eccentric growth of tension wood on the upper surface; tension wood is a type of reaction wood found in angiosperms that contains gelatinous fibres which shrink and pull.

Growth rings

Growth rings in the secondary xylem of temperate woody angiosperms are usually annual, but under environmental fluctuations, such as drought, more than one can form, or none at all. Growth rings result from the difference in density between the early wood (spring wood) and the late wood (summer wood); early wood is less dense because the cells are larger and their walls are thinner. Although the transition of early wood to late wood within a growth ring may be obscure, that demarcation between the adjacent late wood of one ring and the early wood of the next ring is clear. Diffuse-porous wood occurs when the size of the vessels (pores) in a growth ring are fairly uniform and evenly distributed (*e.g.,* red maple, *Acer rubrum;* Sapindales). Ring-porous wood occurs when the pores of the early wood are distinctly larger than those of the late wood (*e.g.,* black walnut, *Juglans nigra;* Juglandales). (D.W.St.)

Both xylem and phloem have limited longevity. The oldest phloem layers are the outermost—the dead bark of the stem surface. The yearly amounts of xylem visible as distinct rings in cross sections of stems are known as annual rings. The oldest xylem layers (*i.e.,* the oldest annual rings) are in the dead central core, or heartwood, of the woody stem, which can often be recognized by its darker coloration. The lighter-coloured sapwood is living and functions as storage tissue and, especially in the outermost sapwood, as conducting tissue; the younger annual rings make up the sapwood. In some highly specialized tree species with large vessels (such as some oaks, ashes, and others), only the very outermost growth ring functions in water conduction.

Conducting tissues seldom run straight along a tree stem; usually they are arranged in a helical or spiral pattern, sometimes called the spiral grain of a tree. The angle of the spiral arrangement usually changes from year to year; the path of water up a tree stem may therefore be very complicated if more than one growth layer acts as a conducting tissue. Functionally, the effect of the variable spiral grain is to distribute water to all parts of the tree from any root. (M.H.Z.)

The secondary phloem of angiosperms consists of sieve-tube members, companion cells, scattered parenchyma, ray parenchyma, and fibres. The fibres usually occur in clusters or as bands alternating with bands of sieve tubes and parenchyma cells. As the vascular cambium continues to produce more secondary xylem to the inside, the older (most exterior) portions of the secondary phloem are crushed, die, and are sloughed off as part of the bark. Successive cork cambiums (see below *Dermal tissue*), essentially lateral meristems from which the bark arises, originate in the parenchyma of the phloem and produce additional cork. (D.W.St.)

Uptake of water and mineral nutrients from the soil. Water uptake from the soil by root cells is passive, in that water may be pulled into the root by low xylem pressure and also follows osmotic gradients caused by the mineral nutrients, which are taken up actively (*i.e.,* with the expenditure of metabolic energy) across root cell membranes. As the mineral nutrients—the ions (charged components) of inorganic salts—are taken up, they are largely incorporated into organic molecules. Thus, the solutes in xylem sap are mostly complex organic substances, sometimes of a specific nature; for example, nicotine synthesis takes place in the roots of tobacco plants, where nitrogen is incorporated into compounds that have moved to the roots through the phloem as sugars. If a tomato shoot is grafted onto a tobacco rootstock, nicotine-containing tomato leaves are formed. On the other hand, a tobacco shoot grafted onto a tomato rootstock results in a plant with nicotine-free tobacco leaves. Many other specific nitrogen-containing substances originate in the roots; in most plants, however, nitrogen is transported to the leaves from the roots in the form of compounds known as amino acids and amides.

The major chemical elements needed by a plant are carbon, hydrogen, oxygen, phosphorus, potassium, nitrogen, calcium, iron, and magnesium; in addition, many other elements are required in very small amounts. A lack of any element may result in deficiency diseases. A few elements taken up by plants are of no nutritive value and usually are eliminated or crystallized (*e.g.,* silica), sometimes by deposition in special cells.

The plant is able to control to some extent the substances that enter. If equal amounts of sodium and potassium are available to roots of plants, and the amount of the two elements inside the plant is analyzed, less sodium is likely to be found than potassium. The structural basis for the control of uptake of substances into roots is the so-called Casparian strip, a conspicuously thickened wall area one cell layer deep surrounding primary roots; it prevents excess soil solution from being pulled directly into the central part of the root where the xylem is located. As a result, the soil solution has to pass through a cell barrier in which uptake can be metabolically controlled. After nutrients are inside living root cells and have been converted to appropriate compounds, the latter are released into the xylem and move to above-ground parts.

Casparian strips

Process of xylem transport. The total amount of conducting tissue remains about the same from roots to leaves. In terms of water movement, the velocity of movement might be expected to be uniform throughout the entire axial system of stem, branches, and twigs. Because some trees (*e.g.,* oaks) have thick twigs, however, the velocity of water movement is greater in the stem than in the twigs at any time. Similarly, in tree species with slender branches (such as birches), the reverse is true. Normally the proportion of xylem to leaves supplied by that xylem is greater in plants growing in dry habitats than in plants found in wet ones and may be as much as 700 times greater in certain desert plants than in aquatic plants and herbs of relatively humid forest floors. The leaves of dry-habitat plants thus are more richly supplied with water-conducting xylem tissue than are those of moist habitats.

The velocity of sap movement in trees varies throughout a 24-hour period. During the night, especially a rainy night, sap flow may stop; velocity increases with daylight, peak rates being found in the early afternoon. Peak velocities correlate with vessel size; the rate of sap flow in trees with small vessels is about 2 metres (7 feet) per hour; that in trees with large vessels, about 50 metres (160 feet) per hour. The energy required to lift water in both cases is comparable; in trees with large pores, water simply moves faster through fewer and larger vessels.

Mechanism of sap ascent

It was demonstrated about 1900 that living cells of the stem are not responsible for water movement. It is now generally recognized that water in the xylem moves passively along a gradient of decreasing pressures. Under certain special conditions, water is pushed up the stem by root pressure. This may be the case with herbaceous (nonwoody) plants in the greenhouse under conditions of ample water supply and little transpiration. In nature, these conditions may be met in early spring before the leaves emerge, when the soil is wet and transpiration is low. Under such conditions, water movement is caused by active uptake of ions (charged particles) and by the entry of water from the soil into the roots. Most of the time, however, water is pulled into the leaves by transpiration. A gradient of decreasing pressures from the base to the top of a tree can be measured, even though pressures are low.

A vacuum pump cannot pull water to a height of more than 10 metres (about 33 feet). Since many trees are far taller than 10 metres, the mechanism by which they move water to their crowns has been investigated. Is it possible for trees to pull water into their crowns along a decreasing pressure gradient or do they employ some other mechanism? If trees pull water, that in the xylem would have to be held on the tracheid and vessel walls by adhesion, and water molecules would have to hold together by cohesion. The hypothesis that water is pulled upward along a pressure gradient during transpiration has been called the cohesion theory. Two critical requirements of the cohesion mechanism of water ascent are (1) sufficient cohesive strength of water and (2) existence of tensions (*i.e.,* pressures below zero) and tension gradients in stems of transpiring trees.

Although the tensile strength of water is very high, an excessive pull exerted on a water column will break it. The tallest trees are about 100 metres (330 feet) high. A nonmoving water column at an atmospheric pressure of 1 atmosphere at the base of the tree is exposed to a pressure of −9 atmospheres (*i.e.,* a tension of 9 atmospheres) at the top. Under conditions of peak flow at midday, this gradient increases by about 50 percent; in other words, a transpiring sequoia would have a pressure in the xylem of at least −14 atmospheres at the top if the basal pressure is 1 atmosphere. If the pressure at the base is −10 atmospheres because of dry soil, however, the pressure at the top drops to −25 atmospheres. It has been demonstrated that water columns in the xylem can withstand this tension, or pull, without breaking.

Negative pressures and gradients of negative pressures have been shown to exist in trees with an ingeniously simple device called the pressure bomb. A small twig is inserted in a container (the pressure bomb), its cut stump emerging from a tightly sealed hole. As pressure is applied to the container and gradually increased, water from the xylem emerges from the cut end as soon as the pressure being applied is equal to the xylem tension that existed when the twig was cut. This method has been used to measure gradients of negative pressures in trees. Movement in the xylem is by mass flow of the whole solution, and the force is either the tension pull of transpiration or root pressure, or both. In general, however, water movement in the xylem is by transpiration pull. The mechanism of phloem transport remains unclear (see below).

Process of phloem transport. Products of photosynthesis (primarily sugars) move through phloem from leaves to growing tissues and storage organs. The areas of growth may be newly formed leaves above the photosynthesizing leaves, growing fruits, or pollinated flowers. Storage organs are found in roots, bulbs, tubers, and stems. Thus the movement in the phloem is variable and under metabolic control (whereas movement in xylem is always upward from the roots).

The rate at which these substances are transported in the phloem can be measured in various ways—*e.g.,* as velocities in distance traveled per unit time or as mass transfer in (dry) weight transported per unit time. Velocities appear to be graded—*i.e.,* some molecules move faster than others within the same channel. Peak velocities of molecules usually are of the order of 100 to 300 centimetres (40 to 120 inches) per hour. Average velocities, more difficult to measure but significant in mass-transfer considerations, are lower.

Velocity of phloem transport

Mass transfer can be measured by weighing a storage organ, such as a potato tuber or a fruit, at given time intervals during its growth. Mass transfer per cross-sectional area of conducting tissue is referred to as specific mass transfer and is expressed as grams per hour per square centimetre of phloem or sieve tubes. With a given specific mass transfer, the velocity with which a liquid of a certain concentration flows can be calculated; in dicotyledonous stems, for example, specific mass transfer is between 10 and 25 grams per hour per square centimetre of sieve tube tissue at times of peak performance. In certain tree species the sieve tubes can be tapped to obtain an exudate. The concentration of this exudate, multiplied by the measured average velocity, is of the same order of magnitude as specific mass transfer, indicating that liquid movement through sieve tubes could account for transport.

Much of the experimental work on phloem transport now is done with the aid of radioactive substances; for example, when radioactive carbon dioxide administered to an illuminated leaf is incorporated into sugar during photosynthesis and carried from the leaf, the velocity of this movement can be measured by determining the arrival of radioactivity at given points along the stem. Whole plants, as long as they are reasonably small, can be pressed against photographic film after the conclusion of a similar experiment, and the photographic image will indicate the areas to which radioactive sugar has moved.

Mechanism of phloem transport

The mechanism of phloem transport has been studied for many years. A number of hypotheses have been put forth over the past years, but none is entirely satisfactory. One fundamental question is whether sugars and other solutes move en masse as a flowing solution or whether the solvents diffuse independently of the solvent water. The phenomenon of exudation from injured sieve tubes supports the first possibility, which has been further supported by a discovery involving aphids (phloem-feeding insects): when aphids are removed from plants while feeding, their mouthparts remain embedded in the phloem. Exudate continues to flow through the mouthparts; the magnitude of the rate of this exudation indicates that transport within the sieve tube to the mouthparts occurs as a flow of solution.

Evidence against solution flow is the movement of substances in opposite directions through a section of phloem at any one given time. This, however, has never been convincingly demonstrated in just one sieve tube. On the other hand, attempts to find simultaneous movement of sugars and water along a phloem path, in order to demonstrate solution flow, have been only partially successful.

Mass-flow hypotheses include the pressure-flow hypothesis, which states that flow into sieve tubes at source regions (places of photosynthesis or mobilization and exportation of storage products) raises the osmotic pressure in the sieve tube; removal of sugars from sieve tubes in sink regions—*i.e.,* those in which sugars are removed or imported for growth and storage—lowers it. Thus a pressure gradient from the area of photosynthesis (source) to the region of growth or storage (sink) is established in sieve tubes that would allow solution flow. The electroosmotic hypothesis postulates that solution is moved across all sieve plates (areas at which individual sieve elements end) by an electric potential that is maintained by a circulation of cations (positively charged chemical ions), such as potassium. Transport hypotheses postulating solute movement independent of solvent water include the spreading of solute molecules between two liquid phases and the active transport of molecules by a type of cytoplasmic movement that is often referred to as cytoplasmic streaming.

During the life of a leaf, its role as a sink or a source changes. A young developing leaf before it is photosynthetic is a sink for sugars produced by older leaves. After the leaf begins to expand and turn green, it is both a sink (importer of sugar) and a source (exporter of sugar) as a result of its own photosynthetic capacity. When mature and fully expanded, the leaf then becomes a source of sugar production.

Storage and circulation

Transport and plant growth. It is important to realize that the plant, with its two transport systems, xylem and phloem, is able to move any substance to virtually any part of its body; the direction of transport is usually opposite in the two systems, and transfer from one system to the other takes place easily. An exception is transport into flowers and certain fruits, in which flow in each system is unidirectional.

Numerous substances move from roots to mature leaves through xylem and are transferred from the leaves, together with sugars, through the phloem to other plant parts. In the autumn months in temperate regions, plants store most of the products resulting from photosynthesis during the summer months in structures such as stems, bulbs, and tubers and mobilize it in the spring when new growth begins. A few plants, such as some tropical monocotyledons (certain palms, for example), store food for many years for use at the time of flowering and fruit-set at the end of their lives.

Plant hormones, or growth regulators, are effective in very small amounts; they induce or enhance specific growth phenomena. Because the site of hormone synthesis is different from its place of action, hormones must be transported before they can exert their effects. There are several groups of plant hormones; each has different effects on plant growth. The best-known plant hormones are the auxins, the most common of which is called indoleacetic acid. Auxins are formed in young, growing organs, such as opening buds, and are transported away from tips of shoots toward the base of the plant, where they stimulate the cells to elongate and sometimes to divide. Responses to gravity and light are also under auxin control. Auxins move to the lower side of a leaning stem; cells on the lower side then elongate and cause the stem to bend back to a vertical position. Response to gravity in many roots is the opposite of that in shoots; the same mechanism of auxin distribution is responsible, but roots react to different quantities of the hormone than do shoots. Similar auxin distributions are responsible for phototropic responses—*i.e.,* the growth of plant parts such as shoot tips and leaves toward light. In certain cases auxin may be destroyed on the illuminated side, and the unilluminated side with more auxin elongates, causing the shoot to bend toward the light.

Auxin transport

Auxins are not normally transported through vascular tissue; moreover, transport is polar—*i.e.,* it takes place along the stem from tip to base, regardless of the stem's position. Velocities of transport are of the order of 5 to 10 millimetres (0.2 to 0.4 inch) per hour, and transport requires the expenditure of metabolic energy. There is evidence that most growth hormones can be transported through xylem or phloem, but, at least in the case of auxin, the transport mechanism is specific directionally from morphological top to bottom.

Hormone transport is also involved in the stimulation of flowering. In some plants, flowering is triggered by short or long days. The receptor of this stimulus is in the leaves. A chemical substance, probably a flowering hormone of an as-yet-unknown nature, then moves to the shoot apex and causes a transformation of the vegetative growing point into a flowering shoot.

Many growth-correlating phenomena are effected by transported hormonal stimuli. A vigorously growing terminal (topmost) shoot may inhibit lateral buds lower down from growing out and may force later branches to bend down. If the terminal shoot is removed, laterals grow out and topmost lateral branches bend upward. In leaning trees with secondary tissue (wood), the cambium produces compression wood on the lower side (in conifers) or tension wood on the upper side (in dicotyledons) in response to a hormone; the stem responds by pushing (in conifers) or pulling (in dicotyledons) itself upright. Transport of growth-regulating substances is thus largely responsible for the characteristic shape of each plant species. (M.H.Z.)

Dermal tissue. The dermal tissue system—the epidermis—is the outer protective layer of the primary plant body (the roots, stems, leaves, flowers, fruits, and seeds). The epidermis is usually one cell layer thick, and its cells lack chloroplasts.

As an adaptation to a terrestrial habitat, the epidermis has evolved certain features that regulate the loss of water, carbon dioxide, and oxygen. Cutin and waxes are fatty substances deposited in the walls of epidermal cells, forming a waterproof outer layer called the cuticle. Often, epicuticular waxes, in the form of sheets, rods, or filaments, are exuded over the cuticle, giving some leaves their whitish, greenish, or bluish "bloom." The cuticle and epicuticular waxes minimize transpiration from the plant. The waxy deposits can be thin or thick, depending on the requirements of the plant; for example, desert plants usually have heavy wax coatings.

The plant, however, must have some means of exchanging water vapour, carbon dioxide, and oxygen through this cuticle barrier. Dispersed throughout the epidermis are paired, chloroplast-containing guard cells, and between each pair is formed a small opening, or pore, called a stoma (plural: stomata). When the two guard cells are turgid (swollen with water), the stoma is open, and, when the two guard cells are flaccid, it is closed. This controls the movement of gases, including water vapour in transpiration, into the atmosphere. Guard cells and stomata are found on aerial plant parts, most frequently on leaves, but are not known to occur on aerial roots.

Guard cells and stoma

The trichomes (pubescences) that often cover the plant body are the result of divisions of epidermal cells. Trichomes may be either unicellular or multicellular and are either glandular, consisting of a stalk terminating in a glandular head, or nonglandular, consisting of elongated tapering structures. Leaf and stem trichomes increase the reflection of solar radiation, thereby reducing internal temperatures, and thus reduce water loss in plants growing under arid conditions.

Epiphytic bromeliads (air plants such as Spanish moss, *Tillandsia usneoides;* Bromeliales) absorb water and minerals via foliar trichomes. The glandular trichomes produce and secrete substances such as oils, mucilages, resins, and, in the case of carnivorous plants, digestive juices. Plants growing in soils with high salt content produce salt-secreting trichomes (*e.g.,* saltbush, *Atriplex vesicaria;* Caryophyllales) that prevent a toxic internal accumulation of salt. In other cases, trichomes help prevent predation by insects, and many plants produce secretory (glandular) or stinging hairs (*e.g.,* stinging nettle, *Urtica dioica;* Urticales) for chemical defense against herbivores. In insectivorous plants, trichomes have a part in trapping and digesting insects. Prickles, such as those found in roses, are an outgrowth of the epidermis and are an effective deterrent against herbivores.

As defined above, the epidermis is the outermost protective layer of the primary plant body. At a certain stage in their life cycle, woody plants cease to grow in length and begin to add to their girth, or width. This is accomplished not by the addition of more primary tissue but by the growth of secondary vascular tissue around the entire circumference of the primary plant body. The secondary vascular tissue arises from the vascular cambium, a layer of meristematic tissue insinuated between the primary xylem and primary phloem (see above *Vascular tissue*). Secondary xylem develops on the inner side of the vascular cambium, and secondary phloem develops on the outermost side. A second lateral cambium, called the phellogen or cork cambium, is the source of the periderm, a protective tissue that replaces the epidermis when the secondary growth displaces, and ultimately destroys, the epidermis of the primary plant body.

Cork cambium

In woody plants, the phellogen, or cork cambium, arises in any of the three tissue systems near the surface of the plant body. The cork cambium produces cork cells toward the outside and parenchyma cells toward the inside. As a unit, the cork cambium, cork cells, and parenchyma (phelloderm) form the periderm. Like the epidermis, the periderm is a protective tissue on the periphery of the plant body; however, because the periderm is produced by a lateral meristem, it is considered to be of secondary origin (in contrast to the primary origin of the epidermis from the protoderm). At maturity the cork cells are nonliving, and their inner walls are lined with suberin, a fatty substance that is highly impermeable to gases and water (which is why cork is used to stop wine bottles). The walls of cork cells may also contain lignin.

In stems, the first cork cambium usually arises immediately inside the epidermis or in the epidermis itself. In roots, the first cork cambium appears in the outermost layer of the vascular tissue system, called the pericycle (see below *Plant organs: Roots*).

The meristematic tissue of the cork cambium produces more and more derivatives of cork cells and parenchyma and displaces them into the outer margins of the plant body. Because the epidermal cells do not divide, they cannot accommodate an increase in stem diameter. Thus, the epidermal cells soon become crushed by the growing number of cork cells derived from the cork cambium, eventually die, and are sloughed off.

The epidermis is then replaced by cork cells until eventually the original cork cambium ceases to produce derivative cork and is itself destroyed. A new cork cambium eventually arises in the secondary phloem situated just behind the old cork cambium. That portion of the secondary phloem that forms between the new cork cambium and the old one becomes crushed and displaced externally as well. This process is repeated often each growing season.

Cork

The term cork is used to denote the outer derivatives of

the cork cambium specifically. Bark, on the other hand, is an inclusive term for all tissues outside of the vascular cambium. The two regions of the bark are the outer bark, composed of dead tissues, and the inner bark, composed of living tissues of the secondary phloem. Outer bark is shed continually from a tree, often in a distinctive pattern, as the circumference increases because its dead cells cannot accommodate the increased diameter. Bark contributes to the support of the tree and protects the living tissue of the active secondary phloem and vascular cambium from desiccation and from such environmental disturbances as fire.

PLANT ORGANS

Roots. The root apical meristem, or root apex, is a small region at the tip of a root in which all cells are capable of repeated division and from which all primary root tissues are derived. The root apex is protected as it passes through the soil by an outer region of living parenchyma cells called the root cap. As the cells of the root cap are destroyed and sloughed off, new parenchyma cells are added by a special internal layer of meristematic cells called the calyptrogen. Root hairs also begin to develop as simple extensions of protodermal cells near the root apex. They greatly increase the surface area of the root and facilitate the absorption of water and minerals from the soil.

Along the longitudinal axis of a root, beginning with the root cap and leading away from the root tip, there are five distinct zones in which certain specific growth patterns dominate: cell division, cell elongation, primary tissue maturation, mature primary tissues, and secondary tissue growth (the latter is found in woody roots—*i.e.,* those of perennial dicotyledons). There is a gradual transition between these regions.

The region of cell division includes the apical meristem and the primary meristems—the protoderm, ground meristem, and procambium—derived from the apical meristem. As is generally true of nonmeristematic regions elsewhere in the plant body, root length in the second region is increased as a result of cell elongation rather than by cell division. The region of maturation that follows is where the cells differentiate (*i.e.,* change in structure and physiology into cells of a specific type) and where the first primary phloem and xylem, as well as mature root hairs, are clearly seen. The region of mature primary tissues is where the anatomy of the primary body of the root is most obvious and where all the elements of the vascular cylinder, cortex, and epidermis are evident. Finally, in the region of secondary growth, the secondary xylem and phloem as well as the periderm add girth to the plant.

The vascular cylinder

There are many individual vascular strands (or vascular bundles) in the primary body of the stem (see below *Stems*), and they all converge into a single central vascular cylinder in the root, forming a continuous system of vascular tissue from the root tips to the leaves. At the centre of the vascular cylinder of most roots is a solid, fluted (or ridged) core of primary xylem (Figure 10). The primary phloem lies between these flutes or ridges. Parenchyma cells are dispersed throughout the vascular cylinder.

The vascular cylinder of the root is surrounded by a layer of parenchymatous pericycle cells. As the root ages, many of these cells become fibres, particularly in monocotyledons and many herbaceous dicotyledons. As defined above (see *Tissue systems: Ground tissue*), a characteristic feature of parenchyma cells is their ability to differentiate into cells of a different type under appropriate conditions. The parenchyma cells of the pericycle, then, can be considered meristematic in that they give rise to new lateral meristems and lateral roots. In woody roots, the vascular cambium (the lateral meristem that gives rise to secondary phloem and secondary xylem) originates in the pericycle as well as in the procambium; the procambium is the primary meristematic tissue between the primary phloem and xylem. The first cork cambium is a lateral meristem that arises in the pericycle; the successive cork cambia arise in the secondary phloem. Because lateral roots are initiated in the pericycle and grow out through the cortex and epidermis, they are said to have an internal, or endogenous, origin, in contrast to the external, or exogenous, origin of leaves and the apical meristem of stems (see below *Stems*).

From P. Alexander *et al., Biology: The Living World* (1986); Prentice-Hall, Inc., Englewood Cliffs, New Jersey

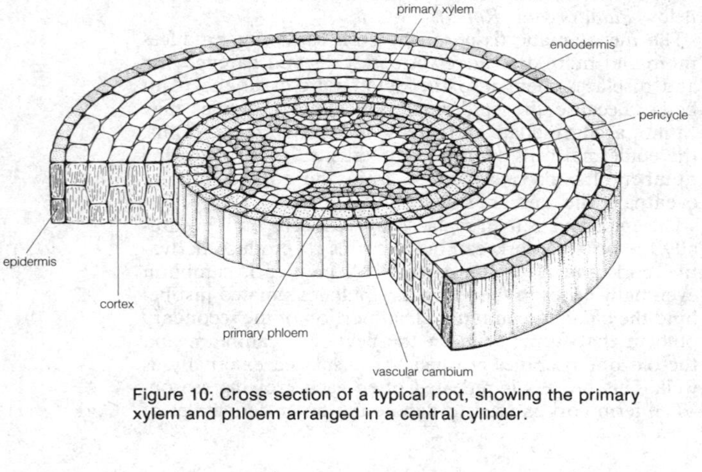

Figure 10: Cross section of a typical root, showing the primary xylem and phloem arranged in a central cylinder.

The cortex

Ground tissue called the cortex surrounds the vascular cylinder and pericycle. The cortex of roots generally consists of parenchyma cells with large intercellular air spaces. The endodermis (the innermost layer of the cortex adjacent to the pericycle) is composed of closely packed cells that have within their walls Casparian strips, water-impermeable deposits of suberin that regulate water and mineral uptake by the roots. The cortex is surrounded by the dermal system consisting of a single layer of epidermal cells.

The few variations that occur in root anatomy are mainly found among the monocotyledons. The roots of monocotyledons lack secondary growth. Monocotyledons also generally have a parenchymatous pith in the centre of the vascular cylinder and fibres or sclereids, or both, in the cortex; and extensive well-developed pericyclic fibres. Orchids have a multiple-layered epidermis called a velamen, which consists of nonliving compact cells with lignified strips of secondary walls. These cells provide support, prevent water loss, and assist the plant in absorbing water. When dry, the orchid root appears white, and, when wet, the root appears green, because the cells of the velamen absorb water, become translucent, and reveal the green cortical cells.

Stems. The shoot apical meristem and the primary meristems lie at the apex of the shoot and give rise to the primary tissues of the stem. The shoot apical meristem produces leaves and axillary buds exogenously; as a result, the epidermis of stems and leaves is continuous. (In contrast, as mentioned above, the lateral roots are produced endogenously and the dermal system of the lateral roots is discontinuous with that of the parent root.)

The stem has growth periods similar to those of the root, but longitudinal regions are not as obvious as in the root until the nodes become differentiated and internode lengths increase. Elongation of internodes involves many cell divisions and is followed by cell elongation. At this point, growth in thickness involves some radial cell division and cell enlargement.

The primary tissue systems appear after internode elongation. The procambium differentiates as a basically continuous hollow cylinder or discrete procambial strands, which differentiate into primary xylem and phloem. The ground tissue that lies outside the procambial cylinder is the cortex, and that within is the pith. Ground tissue called the interfascicular parenchyma lies between the procambial strands and remains continuous with the cortex and pith. As the vascular tissue grows, xylem and phloem develop, the vascular bundles mature, the single-layered epidermis differentiates as epidermal cells, trichomes, and a few stomata, and the parenchymatous pith may develop as collenchyma or contain sclereids or fibres or both; unequal pith proliferation and expansion produces the flattened stems (pads) of prickly-pear cacti (*Opuntia;* Cactaceae). The parenchymatous cortex also may develop some collenchyma, sclereids, or fibres; unequal growth and expansion of the cortex produces the cladodes of epiphytic cacti (*e.g.,* night-blooming cereus, *Selenicereus;* Cactaceae). In most aquatic angiosperms, the parenchymatous cortex contains large intercellular spaces. As a rule, angiosperm stems have no endodermis or definable pericycle.

Collateral bundle

The most common arrangement of the primary xylem and phloem is called a collateral bundle; the outer portion of the procambium (adjacent to the cortex) becomes phloem, and the inner portion (adjacent to the pith) becomes xylem. In a bicollateral bundle, the phloem is both outside and inside the xylem, as in Solanaceae (the potato family) and Cucurbitaceae (the cucumber family). In the monocots, the phloem may surround the xylem, or the xylem may surround the phloem.

The vascular bundles of the stem are continuous not only with the primary vascular system of the root but also with the vascular bundles of the leaves. At each node, one or more longitudinal stem bundles enter the base of the leaf as leaf traces, connecting the vascular system of the stem with that of the leaf. The point at which the stem bundle diverges from the vascular cylinder toward the leaf is a leaf gap, called a lacuna. The number of lacunae varies among angiosperm groups and remains a characteristic for classifying the various species.

Several leaves in a line along the stem have common stem bundles. In some species all stem bundles and their associated leaf traces are interconnected, while in others each stem bundle and the associated leaf trace remains laterally independent of the others. An arrangement of two trace leaves and a single lacuna is found among several primitive angiosperm families and throughout the gymnosperms and is the organization from which other nodal patterns are derived.

In woody dicots, the vascular cambium is formed in parts that grow toward each other and unite. Each vascular bundle develops a meristematic area of growth from an undifferentiated (parenchymatous) layer of cells between the primary xylem and primary phloem, called a fascicular cambium. This meristematic area spreads laterally from each bundle and eventually becomes continuous, forming a complete vascular cambium.

The arborescent (treelike) stems of monocotyledons have a different growth pattern and anatomy from dicotyledons. Scattered throughout the ground tissue are vascular bundles with no fascicular cambia and no definable pith or cortex. Secondary growth, when it occurs, is different because a secondary thickening meristem forms under the epidermis. This secondary thickening meristem produces secondary parenchyma (conjunctive tissue) to the inside, and then secondary vascular bundles develop within this conjunctive tissue. Thus, there are no rings of secondary xylem or secondary phloem as in woody dicotyledons.

Many arborescent monocots have only massive primary growth without secondary growth. This primary growth is derived from a primary-thickening meristem under the leaf bases that is a lateral continuation of the apical meristem. This primary-thickening meristem produces vast amounts of parenchyma to the inside, through which the leaf traces differentiate.

Leaves. Leaves initially arise from cell divisions in the shoot apical meristem. A slight bulge (a leaf buttress) is produced, which in dicots continues to grow and elongate to form a leaf primordium. (Stipules, if present, appear as two small protuberances.) Marginal and submarginal meristems on opposite flanks of the primordium initiate leaf-blade formation. Differences in the local activity of marginal meristems cause the lobed shapes of simple leaves and the leaflets in compound leaves. An increase in width and in the number of cell layers is brought about by marginal meristems. Subsequent expansion and increase in length is achieved by cell division and the general enlargement of cells throughout the blade.

Leaf-blade formation

Leaf growth is determinate; the tip matures first, and maturation then progresses toward the base, after which the leaf cells cease to grow and divide. (Stem growth is generally indeterminate since the meristems are active indefinitely.) The petiole, when present, and the leaf base become thickened, and often the latter expands laterally and fully or partially encloses the stem. Soon after the cells of the marginal meristems begin to divide, procambial strands differentiate into the leaf from the stem bundles to form the midvein, or midrib. The smaller lateral veins of the leaf are initiated near the leaf tip; subsequent major lateral veins are initiated sequentially toward the base, following the overall pattern of leaf development. A major lateral vein may have one or more orders of smaller veins, which also are initiated in size from larger to smaller. This results in the netlike venation patterns characteristic of dicotyledonous leaves.

Adaptations to water availability

The anatomy of a mature dicot leaf generally reflects the habitat, especially the availability of water. Mesomorphic leaves are adapted to conditions of abundant water and relatively humid conditions; xeromorphic leaves are adapted to dry conditions with relatively low humidity; and hydromorphic leaves are adapted to aquatic situations, either submerged or in standing water. Mesomorphic leaves (the most common type) are characteristic of crop plants, such as tomatoes and soybeans. Their veins (vascular bundles) permeate the ground tissue of the dermal system—a single layer of epidermal cells with interspersed guard cells. The ground tissue system, the mesophyll, is divided into two regions: the palisade parenchyma, located beneath the upper epidermis and composed of columnar cells oriented perpendicular to the leaf surface, and spongy parenchyma, located in the lower part of the leaf and composed of irregularly shaped cells. The veins contain primary xylem and phloem and are enclosed by a layer of parenchyma called the bundle sheath. Only the midvein and some large lateral veins have any secondary growth.

The anatomy of mesomorphic leaves is designed to function optimally for water uptake and gas exchange in photosynthesis under mesic (moist) conditions. The spongy mesophyll with irregularly shaped cells provides increased surface area internally, while the elongate palisade cells provide optimal exposure of chloroplasts to light.

The anatomy of hydromorphic leaves is simplified: the cuticle is thin or lost; the guard cells are raised and are found only on the upper surface in floating leaves (they are lost in most submerged leaves); the mesophyll contains aerenchyma (an adaptation to promote water loss) and little or no collenchyma or sclerenchyma; and the vascular system (particularly the water-conducting element of the vascular system, the xylem) is only weakly developed since the water provides much of the mechanical support to the plant normally provided by the xylem. The abundance of water means that there is no need for mechanisms that prevent water loss and little need for additional supports. The leaves generally become large and thin, and the reduction or loss of cuticle, vascular tissue, and ground tissue (mesophyll) permits the rapid loss of water vapour (transpiration). The guard cells on the upper surface of floating leaves also monitor the rate of water loss through the central stomata. Such plants may wilt if the turgor (water) pressure is reduced. Water lilies (Nymphaeales) and rice crops contain hydromorphic leaves.

Xeromorphic adaptations to arid conditions are quite varied and tend to prevent water loss during periods when water is limited and must be conserved by the plant. There are many modifications limiting transpiration: two examples are a multilayered epidermis covered by thick layers of epicuticular wax or mucilages secreted into stomates; another is dense mats of trichomes on both surfaces of the leaf and guard cells and stomata sunken into the lower surface and often lined with numerous trichomes, which trap moisture, thereby inhibiting total water loss. Mesophyll modifications provide a means of storing water. Most xeromorphic leaves have a high volume-to-surface ratio—*i.e.,* they are small and compact. In addition, many are fleshy and often oval to round in shape.

The development of monocotyledonous leaves after initiation of cell division on the shoot apical meristem is different from that of dicotyledons and results in leaves with different morphologies from those of dicotyledons. Leaves in monocotyledons have either a radial leaf tip or are expanded in the same plane as the stems instead of at a right angle to the stem, as in dicotyledons. The leaf buttress begins as a ring that encloses the stem. The upper portion of the buttress develops a meristem on the side facing the stem (adaxial meristem). Growth at this adaxial meristem forms the flattened leaf with the radial

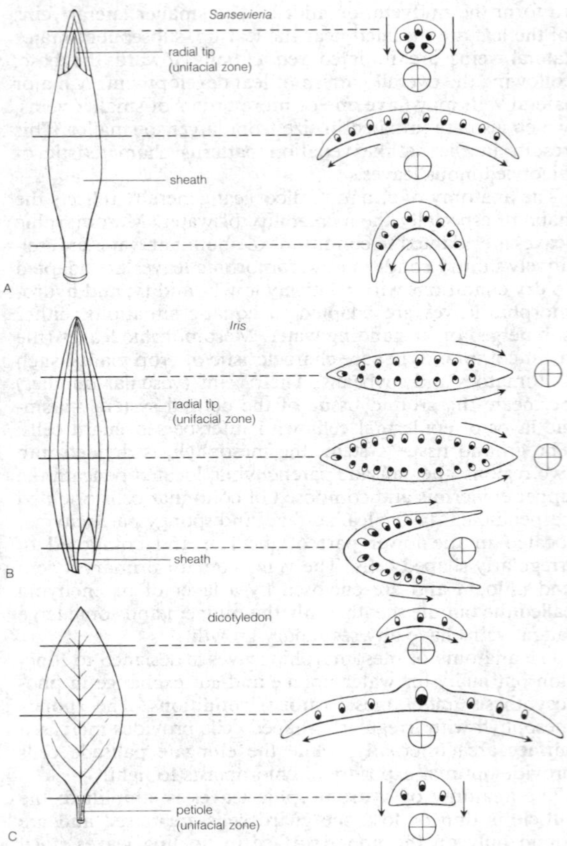

Figure 11: *Transections of various leaf types showing principal direction of development.*
(A) In *Sansevieria,* apical and marginal growth cease early in leaf development in favour of radial development from a meristem on the face of the leaf nearest to the stem (adaxial meristem). Cell division from marginal meristems pushes the direction of lamina development outward (middle transection) and then from adaxial meristems into a collarlike structure (topmost transection). (B) At the base of the *Iris* leaf, cell division takes place in both directions, during which the leaf begins to encircle the stem. Marginal growth in the upper part of the developing leaf is suppressed in favour of development from adaxial meristems. Radial development does not take place. (C) In many dicotyledenous plants, a peglike protuberance develops near the origin of the leaf, which is often flattened on the adaxial side. Apical growth ceases early in favour of elongation of the central leaf axis at the two margins (middle transection), during which the lamina expands laterally. Throughout, vascular bundles are the shaded circles, xylem is shown in black, phloem in white, and stem placement in relation to the leaf is shown by a circle divided by a cross. Direction of growth is indicated by arrows.

(cylindrical) leaf tip typical of the monocotyledons. If the adaxial meristem is long-lived (Figure 11), long flat leaves in the same plane as the stem are formed (*Iris;* Liliales); if short-lived (Figure 11), flat leaves with short cylindrical tips develop (snake plant, *Sansevieria trifasciata;* Liliales). When the radial (topmost aspect of the leaf) is short, the base becomes flattened because the marginal meristems (those on either side of the midvein) continue to expand outward. A monocot leaf grows either radially or along the margins, but not both in the same region. The monocot leaf grows in length from a meristem at its base, which is why it is possible to mow grass and have the leaf blades continue to grow.

The developmental pattern from a basal intercalary meristem has placed constraints on the anatomy of monocot leaves, particularly with respect to venation and the position of stomates. This has produced a leaf anatomy characteristic of the monocots. There is no midvein, and veins are longitudinally parallel. The stomates are in rows between the veins, and the mesophyll is often poorly developed and mostly parenchymatous with scattered bundles of fibres. Thus, most monocot leaves are uniform in appearance and texture. Most of the hydromorphic and xeromorphic modifications found among dicot leaves, however, also occur in monocot leaves in similar environments.

REPRODUCTIVE STRUCTURES

General features. The broad range of variation in the morphology and structure of nonreproductive (vegetative) organs within the angiosperms has been outlined above. There is a similarly broad range in the morphology and structure of the reproductive organs of the plant.

Many vegetative buds sooner or later become flower buds. Flower buds are modified leaves borne on a short axis with very short internodes and no axillary buds. The floral axis has determinate growth, in that at some point it ceases to grow.

Flowers, the reproductive tissues of the plant, contain the male and/or female organs. They may terminate short lateral branches or the main axis or both. Flowers may be borne singly (as in the daffodil and *Magnolia*) or in clusters called inflorescences (*e.g.,* bromeliads, snapdragons, and sunflowers). Fruits are derived from the floral parts of the angiospermous plant. Flower diversity

A complete flower is composed of four organs attached to the floral stalk by a receptacle (Figure 12). From the base of the receptacle upward these four organs are the sepals, petals, stamens, and carpels. In dicots the organs are generally grouped in multiples of four or five (rarely in threes), and in monocots they are grouped in multiples of three.

The sepals, the outermost layer, are usually green, enclose the flower bud, and collectively are called the calyx. Petals are the next layer of floral appendages internal to the calyx; they are generally brightly coloured and collectively are called the corolla. The calyx and corolla together compose the perianth. The sepals and petals are accessory parts or sterile appendages because, though they protect the flower buds and attract pollinators, they are not directly concerned with sexual reproduction. When the colour and appearance of sepals and petals are similar, as in the tulip tree (*Liriodendron tulipifera*) and Easter lily (*Lilium longiflorum*), the perianth is said to be composed of tepals.

Internal to the corolla are the stamens, spore-producing structures (microsporophylls) that are collectively called the androecium. In most angiosperms, the stamens consist of a slender stalk (the filament) that bears the anther (and pollen sacs), within which the pollen is formed. Small secretory structures called nectaries are often found at the base of the stamens and provide food rewards for pollinators. In some cases the nectaries coalesce into a nectary or staminal disc. In many cases the staminal disc forms when a whorl of stamens is reduced into a nectiferous disc, and

From (top row at left; bottom row) E.M. Gifford and A.S. Foster, *Morphology and Evolution of Vascular Plants,* 3rd ed. (1989), W.H. Freeman and Co., New York City

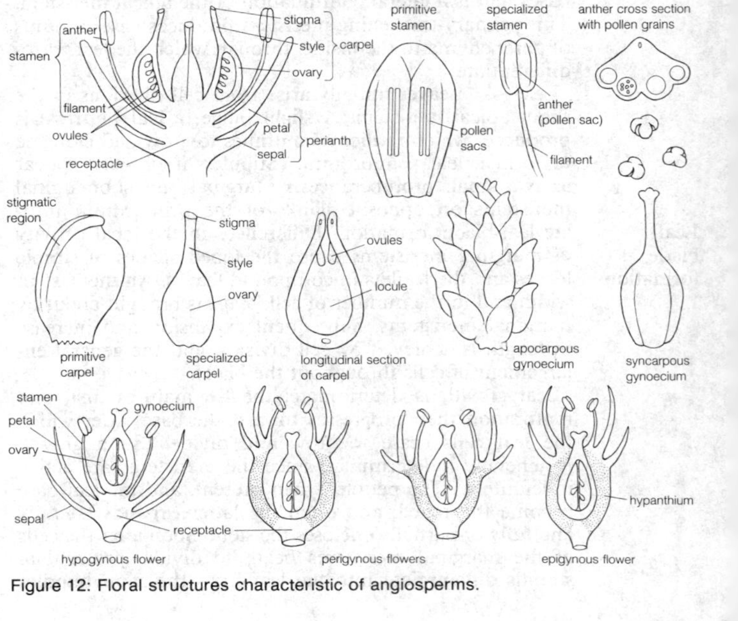

Figure 12: Floral structures characteristic of angiosperms.

in other cases the staminal disc is actually derived from nectary-producing tissue of the receptacle.

At the centre of the flower are the carpels, collectively called the gynoecium. Carpels are megasporophylls that enclose one or more ovules, each with an egg. After fertilization, the ovule matures into a seed, and the carpel matures into a fruit. Carpels (and thus fruit) are unique to angiosperms. The androecium and gynoecium are essential, or fertile, parts of the flower.

A complete flower contains all four organs, while an incomplete flower is missing at least one. A perfect flower has both stamens and carpels, and an imperfect flower lacks either stamens (called carpellate) or carpels (called staminate). Species with perfect flowers (*e.g., Magnolia*) or with both staminate flowers and carpellate flowers on the same plant (*e.g.,* corn) are monoecious. Species in which the staminate flowers are on one plant and the carpellate flowers are on another are dioecious.

Floral organs are often united or fused: connation is the fusion of similar organs—*e.g.,* the fused petals in the morning glory; adnation is the fusion of different organs—for example, the stamens fused to petals in the mint family (Lamiaceae). The basic floral pattern consists of alternating whorls of organs positioned concentrically: from outside inward, sepals, petals, stamens, and carpels (Figure 13). It is possible in most cases to interpret the flower with respect to missing parts and/or the modification of parts to function as missing parts simply by positional relationships. In a complete five-part flower (starting from the outside) there would be a whorl of five sepals, followed by an alternating whorl of five petals, followed by an alternating set of five stamens. In the floral diagram (Figure 13), the midline of each petal is midway between the midlines of two adjacent sepals. Because the whorls alternate, the midline of each stamen of the stamen whorl is between the midlines of two adjacent petals and on the midline of each sepal. When the petals are missing and bracts appear coloured and petaloid as in the *Bougainvillea,* one of the three whorls is missing: there are only two whorls of five organs instead of the three whorls of five organs described above. Because one whorl of the flower is obviously composed of stamens that bear functional pollen and the other whorl is composed of a brightly coloured set of organs that resemble petals one might conclude that the sepals are missing. But examination of positional relationships between the whorls reveals that the midline of each stamen is on the same line as the midline of the organs of the brightly coloured set. Thus, position tells us that the brightly coloured whorl represents a sepal whorl and that the sepals have assumed the function of the missing petals.

Most of the floral arrangements are derived independently in unrelated families and represent general evolutionary trends within the flowering plants.

The receptacle. The receptacle is the axis (stem) to which the floral organs are attached. Floral organs are attached either in a low continuous spiral, as is common among primitive angiosperms, or in alternating successive whorls, as is found among most angiosperms.

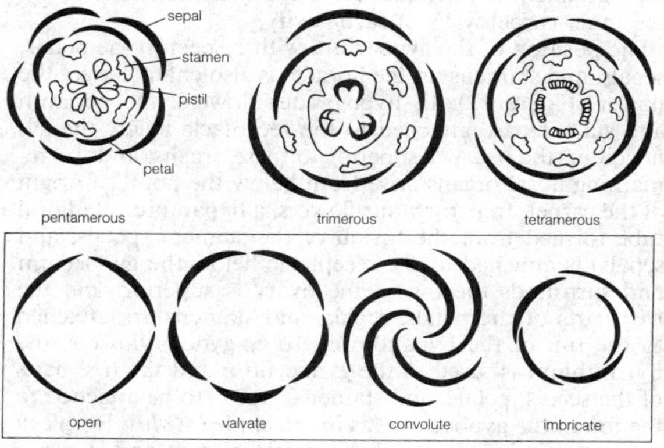

Figure 13: *Arrangement of floral parts.*
(Top) Floral diagrams showing different arrangements of flower structures. (Bottom) Types of arrangement (aestivation) of sepals and petals in flower buds.

The peduncle

The peduncle is the stalk of a flower or an inflorescence. When a flower is borne singly, the internode between the receptacle and the bract (the last leaf, often modified and usually smaller than the other leaves) is the peduncle. When the flowers are borne in an inflorescence, the peduncle is the internode between the bract and the inflorescence; the internode between the receptacle of each flower and its underlying bracteole is called a pedicel. Thus, in inflorescences, bracteole is the equivalent of bract, and pedicel is the equivalent of peduncle.

Often the bract subtending an inflorescence is brightly coloured, as in the poinsettia (*Euphorbia pulcherrima*; Euphorbiales), or provides protection, as in the woody, boat-shaped bracts in many palms. Bracteoles in the inflorescence of *Bougainvillea* also are brightly coloured to attract pollinators. In some angiosperms, the receptacle becomes fleshy; in the strawberry, for example, the receptacle is the fleshy edible part of the strawberry and, when eaten by small mammals and birds, aids in seed dispersal. In others, the peduncle or pedicel becomes fleshy; in the cashew (*Anacardium occidentale*), for example, the pedicel is made into a drink in the Neotropics, and it also aids in fruit dispersal of the much smaller cashew nut. In cacti (*e.g.,* prickly pear), the fleshy part of the edible fruit forms from the receptacle and peduncle, and several internodes below that grow up and surround the carpels; this is why there are axillary buds in cacti (areoles) with spines on the fruit surface.

The calyx. The sepals (collectively called the calyx) most resemble leaves because of their generally green colour. From their base and along most of their length, sepals remain either separate (aposepalous, or polysepalous) or marginally fused (synsepalous), forming a tube with terminal lobes or teeth. The number of calyx lobes equals the number of fused (connate) sepals.

The sepals enclose and protect the unopened flower bud. The calyx is commonly persistent and evident when the fruit matures (*e.g.,* persimmon, *Diospyros virginiana;* Ebenales), in contrast to the more short-lived petals and stamens. Sepals may be brightly coloured and function as petals when true petals are missing—for example, the virgin's bower (*Clematis*) and the *Bougainvillea.* Petaloid sepals in this case differ from tepals because the first group of stamens are on the same radii as the sepals, indicating the absence of the petals, which would normally be positioned on alternating radii in the next floral whorl.

Petals

The corolla. The petals composing the corolla are typically brightly coloured or white and attract insects and birds for pollination (see below *Reproduction: Pollination*). The number of petals is usually the same as the number of sepals. Floral symmetry is defined by the petals (Figure 14). When the petals of the corolla are of the same size and shape and when they are equidistant from each other, the flower has radial symmetry, and the flower is called regular or actinomorphic (*e.g.,* buttercup, *Ranunculus;* Ranunculales). In regular flowers, any line drawn through the centre will divide the flower into two identical halves. When at least one petal of the corolla is different, the flower has bilateral symmetry and is called irregular or zygomorphic (*e.g.,* violets, *Viola;* Violales).

The petals of the corolla may be separate, or apopetalous, or marginally fused (fusion of like floral parts is called connation), or sympetalous, for all or part of their length. When joined, they form a tubular corolla with terminal lobes. A tubular corolla may be present in regular flowers (*e.g.,* blueberries, *Vaccinium;* Ericales) or irregular flowers (*e.g.,* sage, *Salvia officinalis;* Lamiales). Stamens are commonly united to a tubular corolla (fusion of two unlike floral parts is called adnation). A marginally fused (synsepalous) calyx, a marginally fused (sympetalous) corolla, and stamens may fuse to form a cuplike floral tube called a hypanthium that surrounds the carpels, as in cherries (*Prunus;* Rosales), for example. Fusion and reduction of flower parts is considered to be more advanced in an evolutionary sense. Many wind-pollinated angiosperms do not have petals, nor do they have floral parts modified as petals; examples of wind-pollinated species include the amaranth family (Amaranthaceae) and the birch family (Betulaceae).

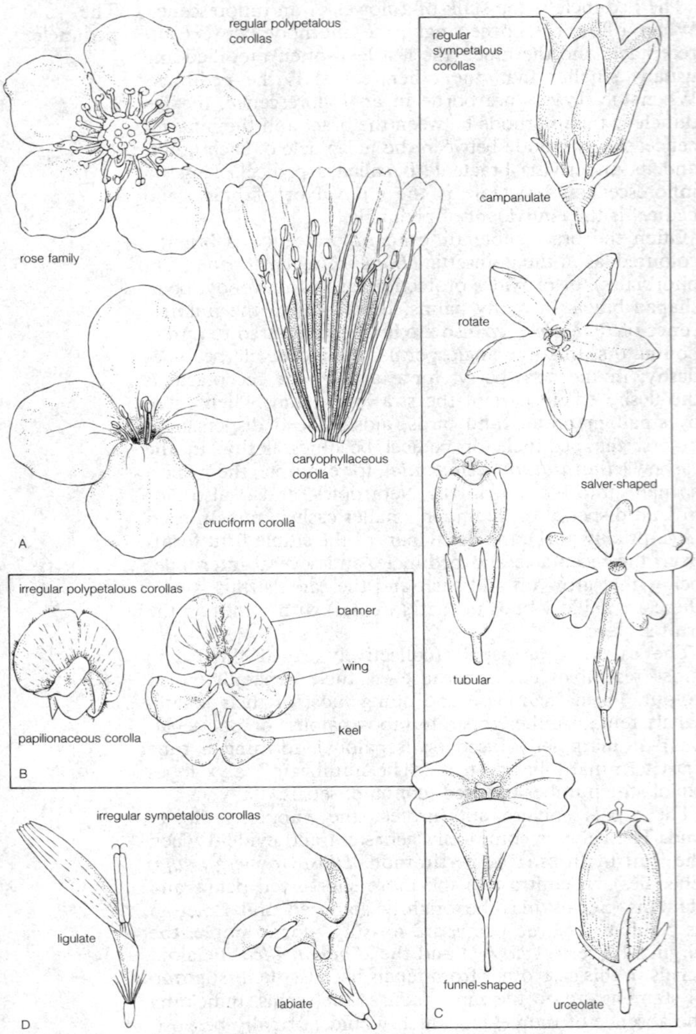

Figure 14: *Representative forms of the corolla.*
(A) The regular polypetalous corollas include those of the rose family (Rosaceae), with five petals (except in horticultural varieties); the caryophyllaceous corolla, as in the pinks (*Dianthus*), in which there are five clawed petals; and the cruciform corolla, having four petals in the form of a cross, as in the wallflower (*Cheiranthus*). (B) A marked example of the irregular polypetalous corolla is the papilionaceous form, as in some members of the legume family (Fabaceae), where one petal is upstanding (the banner), two are lateral (wings), and two are ventral and united (the keel). (C) Regular sympetalous corollas may exhibit various degrees of fusion: campanulate, or bell-shaped (*e.g.,* bellflower, *Campanula*); salver-shaped, the corolla tube being long and the shorter limb at right angles to it (*e.g.,* primrose, *Primula*); rotate, essentially salver-shaped, but with a short corolla tube (*e.g.,* potato, *Solanum tuberosum*); tubular (*e.g.,* comfrey, *Symphytum*); funnel-shaped (*e.g.,* four-o'clock, *Mirabilis;* morning glory, *Ipomoea*); and urceolate, or urn-shaped (*e.g.,* heaths, *Erica*). These forms may become irregular as a result of some parts developing more than others. There are, in addition, at least two forms of irregular sympetalous corollas, (D) ligulate and labiate; the former is a tubular corolla with a flattened strap-shaped extension (*e.g.,* ray flowers of the dandelion, *Taraxacum*), and the latter has two limbs, the upper usually of two united petals, and the lower of three, separated by a gap (as in the mint family, Lamiaceae).

Petals often bear nectaries that secrete sugar-containing compounds and petals also produce fragrances to attract pollinators; the fragrance of a rose (*Rosa;* Rosales) is derived from the petals. Petals often develop a nectar-containing extension of the tubular corolla, called a spur. This may involve one petal, as in the larkspur (*Delphinium*), or all the petals, as in columbine (*Aquilegia*), both members of the order Ranunculales.

The androecium. Stamens (microsporophylls) are structures that produce pollen in terminal saclike structures (microsporangia) called anthers. The number of stamens comprised by the androecium is usually the same as the number of petals. There are two pairs of spore-containing sacs (microsporangia) in a young stamen; during maturation the partition between the adjacent microsporangia of a pair breaks down so that there are only two pollen-containing sacs (one in each lobe of the anther) at the time the stamen releases the pollen. Stamens

The least-modified stamens are similar to leaves, with the paired microsporangia located at or near the margins; an example is found in the magnolia family (Magnoliaceae). In apomorphic (derived) stamens, the blade has become modified into a slender stalk, the filament, with the microsporangia at or near the filament apex. The filaments are very often united with the corolla, but with the anthers either separate, as in primroses (*Primula;* Primulales), or united with each other to form a staminal tube that encloses the gynoecium, as in the mallow family (Malvaceae). In thistle (*Cirsium;* Asterales) and in other members of the sunflower family, the staminal tube is fused to the lower half of the corolla tube.

There are several trends in stamen modification. In many angiosperms, one or more of the stamens is modified and lacks functional anthers. In the most common modification, the filament is expanded to form a petallike blade called a staminode (in the same manner that a sepal forms a petallike blade in some flowers without true petals). The apparent petals in some angiosperm families, such as are found in many members of the pink family (Caryophyllaceae), are staminodial in origin. Wild roses have only five petals and many stamens; however, cultivated roses have been selected for the many apparent petals (but actually staminodes) and few functional stamens. In other cases, stamens have been modified into sterile nectaries involved in pollination. If flowers have a large number of stamens, then the stamens often occur in groups or clusters (fascicles), as in the myrtle family.

The gynoecium. The gynoecium is composed of carpels. In more primitive families (*e.g.,* Magnoliaceae) the carpels are spirally arranged, and in more advanced families they tend to be arranged in a single whorl. Carpel number varies from one (*e.g.,* bean or legume family [Fabaceae]) to many (*e.g.,* buttercups or raspberries [*Rubus*]). Carpels

At the base of a carpel is the ovary, within which develop one or more multicellular structures called ovules that each contain an egg. The upper part of the carpel, the stigma, receives the pollen. A slender stalk called the style often connects the ovary and stigma. The carpels may be separate (apocarpous) or fused together (syncarpous) with the individual carpel walls and cavities (locules) still present. Syncarpy may involve only the ovaries, leaving the styles and stigmas free, as is found in the wood sorrel (*Oxalis*), or it may involve both the ovaries and styles, leaving only the stigmas free, as in the waterleaf (*Hydrophyllum*). The number of carpels in a syncarpous (or compound) ovary equals the number of locules; in an orange or a grapefruit, for example, the juice sacs are actually trichomes that line the inner carpel walls of each cavity.

The position of the gynoecium with respect to the petals, sepals, and stamens on the floral axis also characterizes the flower (Figure 12). In hypogynous flowers, the perianth and stamens are attached to the receptacle below the gynoecium; the ovary is superior to these organs, and the remaining floral organs arise from below the point of origin of the carpel. In perigynous flowers, a hypanthium (a floral tube formed from the fusion of the stamens, petals, and sepals) is attached to the receptacle below the gynoecium and surrounds the ovary; the ovary is superior, and the free parts of the petals, sepals, and stamens are attached to the rim of the hypanthium. In epigynous flowers, the hypanthium is fused to the gynoecium, and the free parts of the sepals, petals, and stamens appear to be attached to the top of the gynoecium, as in the apple (*Malus;* Rosales); the ovary is inferior, and the petals, sepals, and stamens appear to arise from the top of the ovary.

Fruits. Fertilization of an egg within a carpel by a pollen grain from another flower results in seed development within the carpel. (Formation of fruit without the fertilization of an egg and seed development is called parthenocarpy.) A fruit is a ripened ovary (or compound ovary) and any other structure, usually the hypanthium, that ripens and forms a unit with it. This clearly separates a fruit from a vegetable, because a vegetable is derived only from vegetative (nonreproductive) organs. Tomatoes, eggplants, and squashes are fruits, because they are derived from floral parts, whereas carrots, turnips (*Brassica rapa*), and beets are vegetables, because they are roots modified as storage organs in the same manner that potatoes, ginger (*Zingiber officinale*), and onions are modified stems.

Simple fruits develop from a single carpel or from a compound ovary. Aggregate fruits consist of several separate carpels of one apocarpous gynoecium (*e.g.,* raspberries where each unit is a single carpel). Multiple fruits consist of the gynoecia of more than one flower and represent a whole inflorescence, such as the fig and pineapple. Accessory fruits incorporate other flower parts in the development of the mature fruit; for example, the hypanthium is used in forming the pear (*Pyrus*), and the receptacle becomes part of the prickly pear.

The form, texture, and structure of fruits are varied (notably in simple fruits), but most fall within a few categories. The fruit wall, or pericarp, is divided into three regions: the inner layer, or endocarp; the middle layer, or mesocarp; and the outer layer, or exocarp. These regions may be fleshy or dry (sclerified) or any combination of the two, but they are classified as either one or the other.

Fleshy and dry fruit

The three main types of fleshy fruits are berries, drupes, and pomes. Berries are many-seeded simple fruits composed of one carpel or a syncarpous ovary. They are fleshy throughout, but the exocarp ranges in texture: a soft, thin exocarp as in tomatoes (a berry); a leathery exocarp, as in oranges (an hesperidium); and a somewhat hard exocarp, as in pumpkins (a pepo). In drupes, or stone fruits, there is usually only one seed per carpel or locule. Drupes are aggregate fleshy fruits and consist of an inner stony or woody endocarp, which adheres to the seed (peaches, plums, and cherries). The term druplet is used for each unit of aggregate fruit of this type (*e.g.,* raspberries and blackberries). Pomes are multiple fleshy fruits of the rose family (Rosaceae) in which an adnate hypanthium becomes fleshy (apples and pears).

Simple dry fruits are either dehiscent or indehiscent. They are dehiscent if the pericarp splits open at maturity and releases the seeds or indehiscent if the pericarp remains intact when the fruit is shed from the plant. The three principal types of dehiscent fruits are follicles, legumes, and capsules. Follicles and legumes are each derived from a single ovary (carpel), and a capsule is derived from several united carpels. As the fruit matures, the pericarp dries and the fruit splits. Whereas follicles split along a single side of the fruit, such as in the milkweeds, columbines, and magnolias, legumes split along both sides, as in the bean family. Capsules have two or more carpels and split open to release their seeds in various ways. They may open longitudinally to expose the seeds within each locule (cavity) or longitudinally along each septum between the locules, as in the agave (*Agave;* Liliales). Still others form an operculum (a lid) at the top of the ovary, as in the Brazil nut (*Bertholletia excelsa;* Lecythidales).

Indehiscent fruits are derived from either single carpels or compound ovaries. Single carpel forms include the achene, the samara, and the caryopsis. Forms derived from a compound ovary include nuts and schizocarps. An achene is a fruit in which the single seed lies free in the cavity, attached only by a single point. The strawberry, for example, is really an aggregate fruit, and each "seed" is an achene. The samara is a winged achene and is found in the tree of heaven (*Ailanthus altissima;* Sapindales) and ash (*Fraxinus;* Scrophulariales). In the caryopsis, or grain, the seed adheres to the fruit wall (pericarp). The caryopsis is found among the cereal grasses, such as corn. Nuts have a stony pericarp, and usually only a single seed in each carpel matures, as in acorns of oaks (*Quercus;* Fagales) and hazelnuts (*Corylus avellana;* Fagales). Schizocarps are fruits in which each carpel of a compound ovary splits apart to form two or more parts, each with a single seed. Schizocarps are found in the carrot family (Apiaceae). Winged schizocarps are found in maples.

Seeds. Seeds are the mature ovules. They contain the developing embryo and the nutritive tissue for the seedling. Seeds are surrounded by one or two integuments, which develop into a seed coat that is usually hard. They are enclosed in the ovary of a carpel and thus are protected from the elements and predators.

The ovule is attached to the ovary wall until maturity by a short stalk called the funiculus. The area of attachment to the ovary wall is referred to as the placenta. The arrangement of placentae (placentation) in the compound ovary of angiosperms is characterized by the presence or absence of a central column in the ovary and by the site of attachment (Figure 15). In axile placentation the placentae are located on a central column; partitions from the central column to the ovary wall create chambers (locules) that separate the placentae and attached ovaries from each other. Free-central placentation resembles axile placentation; however, the column is not connected by partitions to the ovary wall, and thus no locules are formed. In basal placentation ovules are attached to the base of the ovary, and in parietal placentation the placentae are located directly on the ovary wall or on its extensions.

Adapted from A. Cronquist, *The Evolution and Classification of Flowering Plants,* copyright © 1978, The New York Botanical Garden

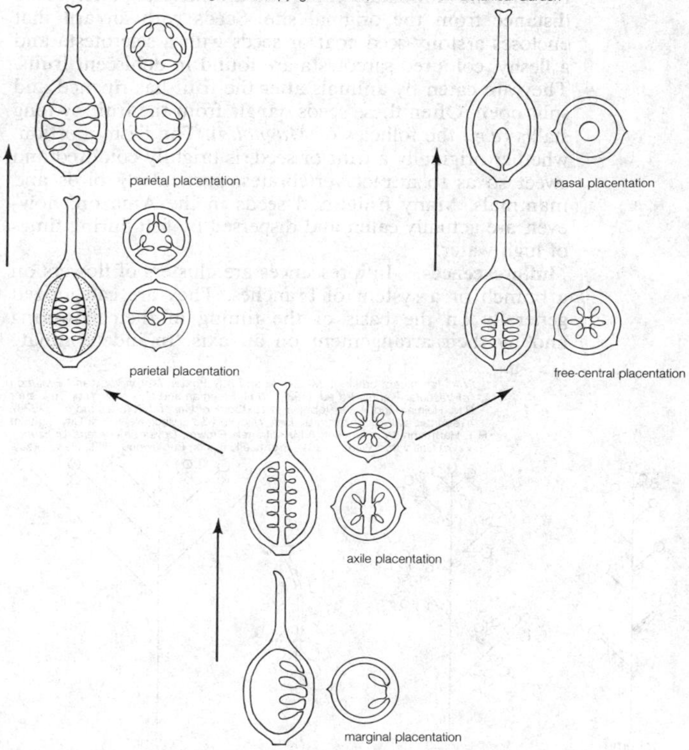

Figure 15: Evolutionary relationships among some types of placentation.

Mature seeds are enclosed in integuments that may become hard and stony or that may have an outer fleshy, usually brightly coloured sarcotesta with an inner stony sclerotesta. Seed coats also may be winged or variously ornamented with prickles or sclerified hairs. In some seeds, there may be an extra covering, the aril, which is an outgrowth of the funiculus (*e.g.,* the spice mace is derived from the red aril of *Myristica fragrans;* Magnoliales). The aril of tomato seeds makes them slippery, unlike the drupelets of raspberries.

Mechanisms of dispersal. Fruits and seeds are the primary means by which angiosperms are dispersed. The chief agents of dispersal are wind, water, and animals. Some fruits and seeds have modifications that aid in wind dispersal. Fruit modifications include samaras, samaroid schizocarps, and the feathery calyx lobes (*e.g.,* dandelion). Seeds may be modified in various ways to promote dispersal: they may be extremely small and light (*e.g.,* orchids,

Agents of dispersal

Orchidaceae), winged (*e.g.,* common catalpa, *Catalpa bignonioides;* Scrophulariales), plumed (*e.g.,* milkweed), covered with woolly hairs (*e.g.,* willows), or surrounded by explosive capsules that forcefully eject them into the air, as, for example, the touch-me-not (*Impatiens;* Geraniales) and the witch hazel (*Hamamelis;* Hamamelidales). The fruits or seeds of many aquatic and shore plants are adapted to float on water as a means of dispersal; for this reason, coconuts (*Cocos nucifera;* Arecales) are readily transported across oceans to neighbouring islands. Adaptations for water dispersal include aerenchyma in fruits or seeds and light weight (*e.g.,* water chestnut, *Trapa natans;* Myrtales).

Animals disperse fruits and seeds either by ingesting and subsequently excreting them or by passively transporting them once they have adhered to an external part of the body, such as the fur or a claw. The evolution of fleshy fruits and seeds exemplifies the coevolution of plants and their animal agents of dispersal. An animal diet often consists solely of fruits and seeds that are designed to be eaten and dispersed, and in many cases these seeds require full or partial digestion to stimulate germination. Most fruits with a fleshy pericarp are eaten whole by vertebrates, including the stony endocarp or the stony seed coat. The seeds are then either regurgitated by the animal or pass through the alimentary canal and are excreted, often some distance from the original site. Seeds with an aril that encloses a stony seed coat or seeds with a sclerotesta and a fleshy, coloured sarcotesta are found in dehiscent fruits. They are eaten by animals after the fruit has ripened and split open. Often these seeds dangle from the fruit by long stalks (*e.g.,* the follicles of *Magnolia*). The fleshy portion, whether originally a fruit or seed, is brightly coloured and sweet so as to attract vertebrates, particularly birds and mammals. Many fruits and seeds in the Amazon, however, are actually eaten and dispersed by fish during times of high water.

Inflorescences. Inflorescences are clusters of flowers on a branch or a system of branches. They are categorized generally on the basis of the timing of their flowering and by their arrangement on an axis. In indeterminate inflorescences, the youngest flowers, and therefore the last to open, are either at the top of the inflorescence (in elongated axes) or in the centre (in truncated axes). Branching and the associated flowers develop at some distance from the main stem (monopodial growth). Indeterminate inflorescences are of varied types: racemes, panicles, spikes, catkins (or aments), corymbs, and heads (Figure 16).

Indeterminate inflorescences

A raceme is an inflorescence in which a flower develops at the axil of each leaf along an elongated, unbranched axis. Each flower terminates a short stalk called a pedicel. The main axis has indeterminate growth; therefore, its growth does not cease at the onset of flowering. A spike is a raceme except that the flowers are attached directly to the axis at the axil of each leaf rather than to a pedicel. An example of a spike is the cattail (*Typha;* Typhales). The fleshy spike characteristic of the Araceae (*Philodendron;* Arales) is called a spadix, and the underlying bract is known as a spathe. A catkin (or ament) is a spike in which all the flowers are of only one sex, either staminate or carpellate. The catkin is usually pendulous, and the petals and sepals are reduced to aid in wind pollination when the inflorescence as a whole is shed. An example of a catkin is found in oaks. A corymb is a raceme in which the pedicels of the lower flowers are longer than those of the upper ones so that the appearance of the inflorescence overall is that of a flat flower. The lower flowers open first, and the axis of a corymb continues to produce flowers (indeterminate growth). Corymbs are found in the hawthorn (*Crataegus;* Rosales).

If the axis is short or stunted, the flowers arise from a common point and appear to be at approximately the same level. This pattern, called an umbel, is actually a flattened raceme because the internodes of the axis, or peduncle (the point of origin of the leaves and flower axes), are shortened so that the pedicels are of the same length (*e.g.,* the carrot family). A head is a raceme in which the peduncle is flattened and the flowers are attached directly to it (*e.g.,* aster family; Asteraceae). This results in a grouping of small flowers in such a way as to appear as a single flower. In many members of the family Asteraceae (*e.g.,* sunflowers, *Helianthus annuus*), for instance, the outer (or ray) flowers have a well-developed zygomorphic corolla, and the inner (disk) flowers have a small actinomorphic corolla. The inner disk flowers generally are complete flowers, and the ray flowers generally are sterile.

In the compound indeterminate inflorescences, the main axis is branched so that the many inflorescences form off the main axis. A panicle is a branched raceme in which the branches are themselves racemes (*e.g.,* yuccas; *Yucca*). In a compound umbel, all the umbel inflorescences arise from a common point and appear to be at about the same level (*e.g.,* wild carrot). This organization is the same for compound spikes, catkins, corymbs, and heads. The change from elongated axes (racemes and panicles) to flattened axes (corymbs and umbels) results in inflorescences in which the flowers are arranged close together. This close association encourages efficient pollination, and the extreme condensation of the inflorescences as in the head gives rise to an inflorescence that appears to be a single flower (*e.g.,* sunflowers).

In the determinate (cymose) inflorescences, the youngest flowers (those that are the last to open) are at the bottom of an elongated axis or on the outside of a truncated axis (*e.g.,* in the cymose umbel of onions, *Allium;* Liliales). These inflorescences are determinate because, at the time of flowering, the whole apical meristem produces a flower; thus, the entire axis ceases to grow. Each unit of a cyme consists of a dichasium, which has a central flower and two lateral flowers. The branching is primarily sympodial, and the inflorescence may be compound (*e.g.,* catchfly, or campion, *Silene;* Caryophyllales). Many monocotyledons have a one-sided cyme called a helicoid cyme. A cymose inflorescence arranged in pairs at the nodes, in the manner of a false whorl, is called a verticillaster. Finally, there are mixed inflorescences, as, for instance, the cymose clusters arranged in a racemose manner (*e.g.,* lilac, *Syringa vulgaris;* Scrophulariales) or other types of combinations.

Evolutionary trends. The evolutionary relationship (homology) of floral organs with leaves, first postulated by

From (all except catkin) E.M. Gifford and A.S. Foster, *Morphology and Evolution of Vascular Plants*, 3rd ed. (1989), W.H. Freeman and Co., New York City, after R.M. Holman and W.W. Robbins, *A Textbook of General Botany*, 2nd ed. (1928), reprinted with permission of John Wileyand Sons, Inc., New York City; (catkin) H.T. Hartmann, W.J. Flocker, A.M. Kofranek, *Growth, Development, and Utilization of Cultivated Plants* (1981), Prentice-Hall Inc., Englewood Cliffs, New Jersey.

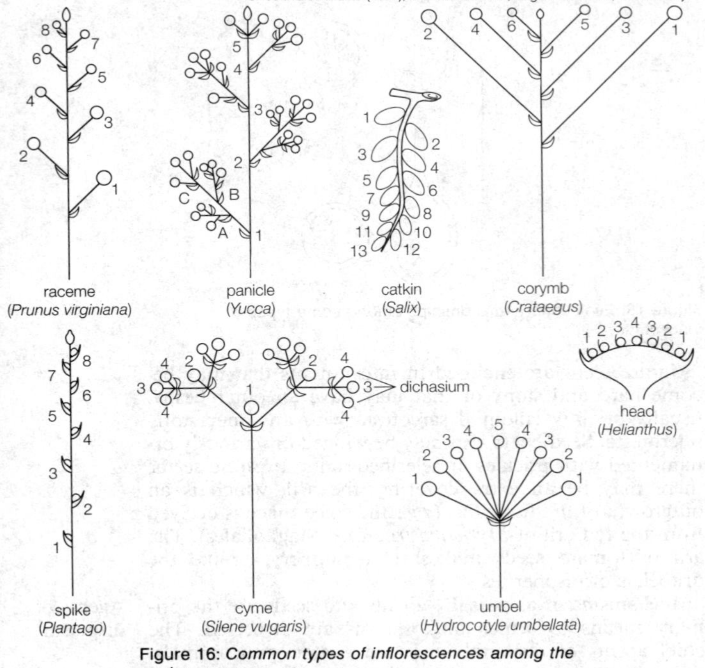

Figure 16: *Common types of inflorescences among the angiosperms.*
Flowers are represented by circles, and their order of development is indicated in numerical sequence: in each inflorescence, flower 1 is the oldest in the group. The letters *A, B,* and *C* in the diagram of the panicle depict the sequence of flower development in one of the lowest branches.

Johann Wolfgang von Goethe in 1790, is supported by the patterns of development of the floral parts (ontogeny) as well as by characteristics of their mature anatomy. Certainly, sepals and petals look like leaves and have a vascular pattern and anatomy resembling leaves. The similarity between leaves and floral organs becomes even more evident among many members of one of the most primitive angiosperm orders, Magnoliales (Magnoliidae). These plants have relatively simple and unspecialized stamens and carpels that bear little resemblance to the specialized reproductive organs of more advanced angiosperms. The carpels of *Tasmannia* (Winteraceae), for example, have thin, unsealed margins that are simply folded along the midrib, with ovules borne on the inner surface. The carpels of other members of the Winteraceae (*e.g., Degeneria*) are very similar; in addition, matted hairs along the entire margin of the unsealed carpel receive pollen grains in the manner of a stigma in the more specialized carpels of the higher flowering plants. Stamens of these flowers have an expanded blade (lamina) that bears anthers and a vascular pattern similar to that of leaves.

Floral development over time

The flower of the Magnoliales typifies one of the early lines of floral evolution. The early flowers consisted of an axis with many floral parts arranged spirally. The perianth consisted of individual tepals, leafy stamens, and apocarpous gynoecium of incompletely closed, leaflike carpels. The evolution of the flower and the specialization of its parts has proceeded independently in many lineages, accounting for the seemingly infinite diversity of flower design among the angiosperms.

Despite the multitude of floral forms, major evolutionary trends are apparent. The more primitive flowers tended to have many parts on an axis. Over time this condition evolved into one in which a few parts were arranged in a circle in the same plane. As illustrated above, early stamens were leafy (laminar); these gradually gave way to a filamentous form. These early stamens were functional but eventually became sterile (staminode)—*e.g.,* produced no pollen. In these cases, pollen production took place either on filamentous stamens or in the male flowers. The carpels originally were simply folded structures with open margins. They evolved into a closed form in which the ovary and the enclosed ovule were isolated from easy contact with pollen grains.

The symmetry of the flower also evolved. Whereas the early lineages tended to have radial symmetry, in that they could be divided into equal halves along more than one axis through the circumference of the flower, more advanced flowers tended to have bilateral symmetry and could be divided along only a single axis. This was reflected in the degree of fusion of parts of the flower: the floral parts of early flowers generally remained unfused; as the flowers evolved, the floral parts, whether similar or different, tended to become fused to an increasing extent.

The ovary of early flowers tended to be superior (hypogynous flowers). Gradually the ovaries of more advanced plants evolved to an inferior (epigynous flowers) or a lateral position with the petals and sepals. The ovary gradually became a less apparent part of the mature fruit, evolving from a dry, dehiscent fruit to a fruit in which the major portion is tissue other than that of the ovary. Finally, single flowers gave way to inflorescences; pollination was further encouraged by the evolution of more compact inflorescences from a more open organization.

Reproduction

GENERAL FEATURES

Life cycle

The vast array of angiosperm floral structures is for sexual reproduction. The angiosperm life cycle consists of a sporophyte phase and a gametophyte phase. The cells of a sporophyte body have a full complement of chromosomes (*i.e.,* the cells are diploid, or $2n$); the sporophyte is the typical plant body that we see when we look at an angiosperm. The gametophyte arises when cells of the sporophyte, in preparation for reproduction, undergo meiotic division and produce reproductive cells that have only half the number of chromosomes (*i.e.,* haploid, or n). A two-celled microgametophyte called a pollen grain germinates into a pollen tube and through division produces the haploid sperm. (The prefix micro- denotes gametophytes emanating from a male reproductive organ.) An eight-celled megagametophyte called the embryo sac produces the egg. (The prefix mega- denotes gametophytes emanating from female reproductive organs.)

Angiosperms are vascular plants, and all vascular plants have a life cycle in which the sporophyte phase (vegetative body) is the dominant phase and the gametophyte phase remains diminutive. In the nonvascular plants, such as the bryophytes, the gametophyte phase is dominant over the sporophyte phase. In bryophytes, the gametophyte produces its food by photosynthesis (is autotrophic) while the nongreen sporophyte is dependent on the food produced by the gametophyte. In nonseed vascular plants, such as ferns and horsetails, both the gametophyte and sporophyte are green and photosynthetic, and the gametophyte is small and without vascular tissue. In the seed plants (gymnosperms and angiosperms), the sporophyte is green and photosynthetic and the gametophyte depends on the sporophyte for nourishment. Within the seed plants, the gametophyte has become further reduced, with fewer cells comprising the gametophyte. The microgametophyte (pollen grain), therefore, is reduced from between 4 and 8 cells in the gymnosperms to a 3-celled microgametophyte in the angiosperms. A parallel reduction in the number of cells comprising a megagametophyte (ovule) has also taken place: between 256 and several thousand cells in the gymnosperms to an 8-celled megagametophyte in the angiosperms. The significance of the reduction in megagametophyte cells appears to be related to pollination and fertilization. In many gymnosperms, pollination leads to the formation of a large gametophyte with copious amounts of stored starch for the nourishment of the potential embryo regardless of whether fertilization of the ovule can actually take place (*i.e.,* whether the pollen is from the same species as the ovule). If the pollen is from a different species, fertilization or embryo development fails, so that the stored food is wasted. In angiosperms, however, the megagametophyte and egg are mature before the food is stored, and this is not ever accomplished until after the egg has been adequately fertilized and an embryo is present. This reduces the chances that the stored food will be wasted.

The process of sexual reproduction (Figure 17) depends on pollination to bring these gametophytes in close association so that fertilization can take place. Pollination is the process by which pollen that has been produced in the anthers is received by the stigma of the ovary. Fertilization occurs with the fusion of a sperm with an egg to produce a zygote, which eventually develops into an embryo. After fertilization, the ovule develops into a seed, and the ovary develops into a fruit.

Anthers. A transverse section of the anther reveals four areas of tissue capable of producing spores. These tissues are composed of microsporocytes, which are diploid cells capable of undergoing meiosis to form a tetrad (four joined cells) of haploid microspores. The microspores eventually separate and become pollen grains.

During pollen development, the layer of cells beneath the dermis of the anther wall (the endothecium) develops thickenings in the cell walls. The cell layer immediately inside the endothecium (the tapetum) develops into a layer of nutritive cells that either secrete their contents into the area around the microsporocytes or lose their inner cell walls, dissociate from each other, and become amoeboid among the microsporocytes. The pollen grains develop a thick wall of at least two layers, the intine and the exine. The intine, or inner layer, consists primarily of cellulose and pectins. The exine, or outer layer, is composed of a highly decay-resistant chemical called sporopollenin. The exine has one or more thin areas, or pores, through which the pollen tubes germinate, and the thick area of the exine is usually highly sculptured. The number of pores and pattern of exine sculpturing are characteristic within an angiosperm family, genus, and often within a species.

The terminology to describe the various sculpturing patterns and position and number of pores is highly complex and only a basic description as related to functional as-

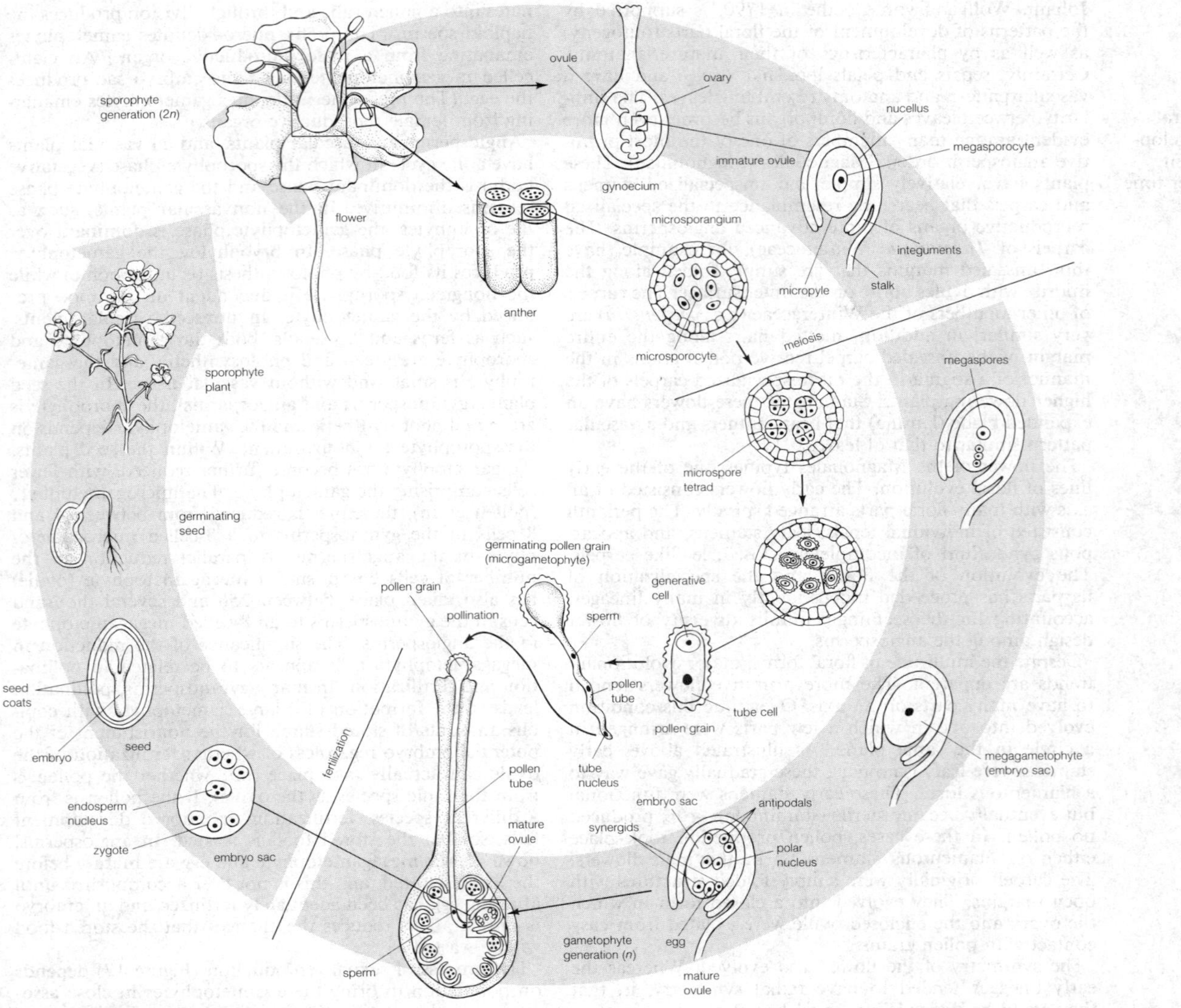

Figure 17: Typical angiosperm life cycle (see text).
Adapted from M.J. Nadakavukaren, *Botany, An Introduction to Plant Biology* (1985); West Publishing Co.

pects of sculpturing is given here. For example smooth or essentially smooth pollen is loosely correlated with wind pollination, as in oaks (*Quercus*) and grasses (corn, *Zea mays*). Many plants pollinated by birds, insects, and small mammals have highly sculptured patterns of spines, hooks, or sticky threadlike projections by which pollen adheres to the body of the foraging pollinator as it travels to other flowers.

Each microspore (pollen grain) divides mitotically to form a two-celled microgametophyte; one cell is a tube cell (the cell that develops into a pollen tube), and the other is a generative cell, which will give rise to two sperm as a result of a further mitotic division. Thus, a mature microgametophyte consists of only three haploid cells—the tube cell and two sperm. Most angiosperms shed pollen at the two-celled stage, but in some advanced cases it is shed at the mature three-celled stage. When the pollen grains are mature, the anther wall either splits open (dehisces) longitudinally or opens by an apical pore.

Because the sporopollenin is resistant to decay, free pollen is well represented in the fossil record. The distinctive patterns of the exine are useful for identifying which species were present as well as suggesting the conditions of early climates. The proteins in the pollen walls are also a major factor in hay fever and other allergic reactions, and the spinose sculpturing patterns may cause physical irritation.

Ovules. An ovule is a saclike structure that produces the megaspores and is enclosed by layers of cells. This megasporangium is called the nucellus in angiosperms. After initiation of the carpel wall, one or two integuments arise near the base of the ovule primordium, grow in a rimlike fashion, and enclose the nucellus, leaving only a small opening called the micropyle at the top. In angiosperms, the presence of two integuments is plesiomorphic (unspecialized) and one integument is apomorphic (derived). A single large megasporocyte arises within the nucellus near the micropyle and undergoes meiotic division, resulting in a single linear tetrad of megaspores. Three of the four megaspores degenerate, and the surviving one enlarges. The resulting megagametophyte produces the female gametes (eggs). This development (called megagametogenesis) involves free-nuclear mitotic divisions. The cell wall remains intact while the nucleus divides until the megagametophyte, or embryo sac, with eight nuclei is formed. Free-nuclear mitotic division is also found in gametophyte formation in gymnosperms.

Mega-gametogenesis

Four nuclei migrate to either end of the embryo sac. One nucleus from each group then migrates to the centre of the embryo; these become the polar nuclei. The two polar nuclei merge to form a fusion nucleus in the centre of the embryo sac. A cell wall develops around the fusion nucleus, leaving a central cell in the sac. Cell walls form around each of the chalazal nuclei to form three antipodal cells. During development, enlargement of the embryo sac leads to the destruction of most of the nucellus. This sequence of megasporogenesis and megagametogenesis, called Polygonum type, occurs in 70 percent of the angiosperms in which the life cycle has been charted. Variations found in the remaining 30 percent represent derivations from the Polygonum type of seed development.

POLLINATION

Effective pollination involves the transfer of pollen from the anthers to a stigma of the same species and subsequent germination and growth of the pollen tube to the micropyle of the ovule.

Pollen transfer is effected by wind, water, and animals, primarily insects and birds. Wind-pollinated flowers usually have an inconspicuous reduced perianth, long slender filaments and styles, covered with sticky trichomes and often branched stigmas, pendulous catkin inflorescences, and small, smooth pollen grains.

Wind pollination is derived in angiosperms and has developed independently in several different groups. For example, within the aster family wind pollination accompanied by floral reduction has developed independently in the tribes Heliantheae and Anthemideae. Water pollination occurs in only a few aquatic plants and is highly complicated and derived.

There is a wide range of animal pollinators of angiosperms as well as a wide range of adaptations by the flowers to attract those insect pollinators. Most of the living unspecialized families of Magnoliidae (*e.g.,* Magnoliaceae) are pollinated by beetles. The beetles forage and feed on pieces of the perianth and stamens. There are no nectaries but rather food bodies on these organs. The ovule-containing carpels are protected from the foraging beetle by the development of an ovary that is at or below the level of insertion of the sepals, petals, and stamens (perigynous and epigynous gynoecia).

Bees are responsible for the pollination of more flowers than any other animal group. Bees usually feed on nectar and in some cases on pollen. They may be general pollinators by visiting flowers of many species, or they may have adapted (*i.e.,* elongated) their mouthparts to different flower depths and have become specialized to pollinate only a single species. Flowers pollinated by bees commonly have a zygomorphic, or bilaterally symmetrical, corolla with a lower lip providing a landing platform for the bee. Nectar is commonly produced either at the base of the corolla tube or in extensions of the corolla base. The bees partially enter the corolla mouth to feed with their long tongues on the nectar, at which point they deposit pollen picked up from other flowers and collect pollen from the new flower. Flowers pollinated by bees are often blue or yellow or exhibit patterns of both. Particular pattern markings and ultraviolet reflection patterns serve as recognition guides.

Coevolution

A high degree of coevolution is common in orchids (*e.g., Ophrys speculum*), where the flower not only appears to resemble the female wasp of a particular species but also produces the pheromone released by the insect to attract males of the species. The male wasp effects pollination by pseudocopulation with the orchid flower. Other insect pollinators include flies, butterflies, moths, and mosquitoes. Many flowers pollinated by flies are called carrion flowers because they look and smell like rotting meat. The skunk cabbage (*Symplocarpus foetidus*) and the carrion flowers (*Stapelia schinzii*) have evolved these characteristics independently.

Vertebrate pollinators include birds, bats, small marsupials, and small rodents. Many bird-pollinated flowers are bright red, especially those pollinated by hummingbirds. Hummingbirds rely solely on nectar as their food source. Flowers (*e.g., Fuschia*) pollinated by birds produce copious quantities of nectar but little or no odour because birds have a very poor sense of smell. Flowers pollinated by bats produce large quantities of nectar and strong fragrances. They generally open only at night, when bats are the most active, and often hang down on long inflorescence stalks, which provide easy access to the nectaries and pollen. Some eucalypts (*Eucalyptus*) are pollinated by small marsupials (*e.g.,* honey possums).

Whatever the agent of dispersal, the first phase of pollination is successful when a pollen grain lands on a receptive stigma. The surface of the stigma is usually wet and often composed of specialized glandular tissue, and the style is lined with secretory transmitting tissue. Their secretions provide an environment that nourishes the pollen tube as it elongates and grows down the style. If mitosis in the generative cell has not yet occurred in the pollen grain, it does so now.

To prevent self-fertilization, many angiosperms have developed a chemical system of self-incompatibility. The most common type is sporophytic self-incompatibility, in which the secretions of the stigmatic tissue or the transmitting tissue prevent the germination or growth of incompatible pollen. A second type, gametophytic self-incompatibility, involves the inability of the gametes from the same parent plant to fuse and form a zygote or, if the zygote forms, then it fails to develop. These systems force outcrossing and maintain a wide genetic diversity.

The pollen tube ultimately enters an ovule through the micropyle and penetrates one of the sterile cells on either side of the egg (synergids). These synergids begin to degenerate immediately after pollination. Pollen tubes can reach great lengths, as in corn, where the corn silk consists of the styles for the corn ear and each silk thread contains many pollen tubes.

FERTILIZATION AND EMBRYOGENESIS

After penetrating the degenerated synergid, the pollen tube releases the two sperm into the embryo sac, where one fuses with the egg and forms a zygote and the other fuses with the two polar nuclei of the central cell and forms a triple fusion, or endosperm, nucleus. This is called double fertilization because the true fertilization (fusion of a sperm with an egg) is accompanied by another fusion process (that of a sperm with the polar nuclei) that resembles fertilization. Double fertilization of this type is unique to angiosperms. The zygote now has a full complement of chromosomes (*i.e.,* it is diploid), and the endosperm nucleus has three chromosomes (triploid). The endosperm nucleus divides mitotically to form the endosperm of the seed, which is a food-storage tissue utilized by the developing embryo and the subsequent germinating seed.

Double fertilization

The three principal types of endosperm formation found in angiosperms—nuclear, cellular, and helobial—are classified on the basis of when the cell wall forms. In nuclear endosperm formation, repeated free-nuclear divisions take place; if a cell wall is formed, it will form after free-nuclear division. In cellular endosperm formation, cell-wall formation is coincident with nuclear divisions. In helobial endosperm formation, a cell wall is laid down between the first two nuclei, after which one half develops endosperm along the cellular pattern and the other half along the nuclear pattern. Helobial endosperm is most commonly found in the Alismatidae of the Liliopsida (monocotyledons). In many plants, however, the endosperm degenerates, and food is stored by the embryo (*e.g.,* peanut [groundnut], *Arachis hypogaea*), the remaining nucellus (known as perisperm; *e.g.,* beet), or even the seed coat (mature integuments). Cellular endosperm is the least specialized type of endosperm with nuclear and helobial types derived from it.

Embryogenesis

The zygote undergoes a series of mitotic divisions to form a multicellular, undifferentiated embryo. At the micropylar end there develops a basal stalk or suspensor, which disappears after a very short time and has no obvious function in angiosperms. At the chalazal end (the region opposite the micropyle) is the embryo proper. Differentiation of the embryo—*e.g.,* the development of cells and organs with specific functions—involves the development of a primary root apical meristem (or radicle) adjacent to the suspensor from which the root will develop and the development of one cotyledon (in monocotyledons) or two cotyledons (in dicotyledons) at the opposite end from the suspensor. A shoot apical meristem then differentiates between the two cotyledons or next to the single cotyledon and is the site of stem differentiation.

The mature embryo is a miniature plant consisting of a short axis with one or two attached cotyledons. An epicotyl, which extends above the cotyledon(s), is composed of the shoot apex and leaf primordia; a hypocotyl, which is the transition zone between the shoot and root; and the radicle. Angiosperm seed development spans three distinct generations, plus a new entity: the parent sporophyte, the gametophyte, the new sporophyte, and the new innovation—namely, the endosperm.

SEEDLINGS

Mature seeds of most angiosperms pass through a dormant period before eventually developing into a plant. The life span of angiosperm seeds varies from just a few days (*e.g.,* sugar maple, *Acer saccharum*) to over a thousand years (*e.g.,* sacred lotus, *Nelumbo nucifera*). Successful germination requires the right conditions of light, water, and temperature and usually begins with imbibition of water and the subsequent release from dormancy. During its early growth stages and before it has become totally independent of the food stored in the seed or cotyledons, the new plant is called a seedling.

Seed germination

Two patterns of seed germination occur in angiosperms, depending on whether the cotyledons emerge from the seed: hypogeal and epigeal. In hypogeous germination, the hypocotyl remains short and the cotyledons do not emerge from the seed but rather elongate and force the radicle and epicotyl axis out of the seed coat. The seed, with the enclosed cotyledons, remains underground, and the epicotyl grows up through the soil. When the cotyledons contain seed-storage products, these products are transferred directly to the developing radicle and epicotyl (*e.g.,* garden pea). When the endosperm or perisperm contains the storage products, the cotyledons penetrate the storage tissues and transfer the storage products to the developing radicle and epicotyl (*e.g.,* garlic, *Allium sativum*).

In epigeous germination, the radicle emerges from the seed and the hypocotyl elongates, raising the cotyledons, epicotyl, and remains of the seed coat above ground. The cotyledons may then expand and function photosynthetically as normal leaves (*e.g.,* castor bean, *Ricinus communis*). When the cotyledons contain seed-storage products, they transfer them to the rest of the seedling and degenerate without becoming significantly photosynthetic (*e.g.,* garden beans, *Phaseolus*). Eventually, the seedling becomes independent of the seed-storage products and grows into a mature plant capable of reproduction. Although the dispersal of seeds is essential in the reproduction and spread of angiosperm species, it is equally important for successful germination and seedling establishment to take place in an appropriate habitat. (D.W.St.)

Paleobotany and evolution

The origins and diversity of flowering plants can best be understood by studying their fossil history. The fossil record provides important data to help show when and where early angiosperms lived, why flowering plants came to exist, and from what group or groups of plants they evolved.

Earliest known angiosperms

The earliest plants generally accepted to be angiospermous are known from the Early Cretaceous Period (144 to 97.5 million years ago). Fossil pollen of angiosperms is first found in the Hauterivian and Barremian ages, which spanned from about 131 to 119 million years ago. A very few angiosperm leaves and flowers are found in layers dating to the early Aptian Age (about 119 to 113 million years ago). Many of the earliest fossils of angiosperms are most similar to small bushes or small herbaceous plants, such as those in the Chloranthaceae (Piperales), Ceratophyllaceae (Nymphaeales), and Ranunculaceae (Ranunculales) families. More diverse flora showing a larger variety of pollen, leaves, and reproductive organs with angiospermous affinities developed during the Albian Age (113 to 97.5 million years ago).

From the end of the Albian (the close of the Early Cretaceous) and the beginning of the Late Cretaceous (97.5 to 66.4 million years ago), angiosperms further diversified and dispersed. Many woody angiosperms evolved at that time, as did several modern groups, such as the magnolia, laurel, sycamore, and rose families. Herbaceous plants, such as the water lilies (Nymphaeales), the family Ceratophyllaceae, and some of the early monocotyledons also persisted from the Albian until today.

Angiosperms are thought to have radiated from the Equator and spread to either pole because some of the oldest and most diverse angiosperm floras are found in Africa near the Equator, followed by low-latitude, angiosperm-dominated floras in North America. The angiosperms developed a close association with insect pollinators early in their evolution. This promoted outcrossing resulting in genetically vigorous offspring. Also, the relatively short generation time in which the angiosperms reproduce—permitting rapid population growth and easier colonization of disturbed habitats—gave the flowering plants an adaptive advantage over the gymnosperms, which were dominant during the Early Cretaceous. The seeds of angiosperms were small and were probably eaten and carried to new areas by animals. Thus, the angiosperms were able to migrate into and occupy new areas of the world. At the beginning of the Cenomanian Age (about 97.5 to 91 million years ago), angiosperms probably formed dominant pockets of vegetation along many low coastal tropical and warm temperate areas of the world. During the Cenomanian, the angiosperms also spread to inland continental areas as well as northward and southward along the coasts. By the Middle to Late Cenomanian (about 95 to 91 million years ago), angiosperms became the dominant form of vegetation in many areas of the world.

One of the most conspicuous features of angiosperms is the flower. Most frequently flowers are brightly coloured, often scented structures containing nectar and the male and female reproductive organs. Because it is essential for the genetic integrity of a plant that it avoid pollinating itself or a nearby, possibly closely related, neighbour, pollen from one plant must be moved some distance to an unrelated flowering plant. Wind is often an effective but an imprecise pollination mechanism. Frequently, flowering plants are more accurately pollinated by animals, which carry the pollen some distance to another flower. Thus, development of showy flowers has involved the coevolution of insects or other animals and the early ancestors of the angiosperms.

Possible ancestors

Various groups of extinct seed plants have been proposed as the ancestral stock at different times in the evolution of the angiosperms. The Pteridospermales (seed ferns) are a group of extinct early seed plants that resemble small trees and shrubs with fernlike foliage. They bore seeds on their leaves or in specialized structures derived from leaves and had specialized pollen-bearing organs or simple anthers. The ovules and pollen organs were separate reproductive units, and wind may have been the most common agent of pollen transfer. Some seed ferns of the Paleozoic Era (about 570 to 245 million years ago) contained pollen grains that were much too large to be effectively dispersed by the wind. These plants probably depended on insects to carry the pollen grains from one plant to another.

The Cycadeoidophyta are a group of extinct seed plants that contain members that have widely different reproductive structures. In some, the female and male reproductive organs were separate, while in others, the reproductive structures were organized into a common reproductive unit in which the male organs surrounded the female organ. These reproductive organs sat on a receptacle similar to that in flowering plants and often were surrounded by sterile bracts or leaflike tissue, which may have opened to form a flowerlike structure in the genus *Williamsoniella* (Cycadeoidales). Some extinct Cycadeoidales may have been pollinated by insects. The female and male reproductive organs tend to be clustered when insect pollination is involved, which is probably why most flowers are bisexual.

It is not clear whether the flowering plants are derived from the Pteridospermales or the Cycadeoidales; however, in both groups, the potential existed for the modification of the plant body and the reproductive tissue to be responsive to both the physical and biological environments of the Mesozoic Era (245 to 66.4 million years ago). The pollen evidence suggests that the Gnetales, a modern group of gymnosperms closely related to the angiosperms, were present during the Triassic Period (245 to 208 million years ago). Thus, the evolution that produced the plants which were eventually recognized as the angiosperms must have been taking place during the Triassic, Jurassic, and earliest Cretaceous periods (which span from 245 to 97.5 million years ago).

The ancestral stock probably was a small to medium-size plant in which large leafy shoots contained individual fertile female, fertile male, and sterile leaves. The form

A blue iris (*Iris*) with contrasting yellow nectar guides indicating the location of the nectar to the honeybee (*Apis mellifera*). Flecks of pollen grains dislodged from the stamens by the foraging bee can be seen on the bee's body.

Orange-tailed butterfly (*Eurema proterpia*) on an ash-colored aster (*Machaeranthera tephrodes*). The upstanding yellow stamens are tipped with pollen, which brushes the body of the butterfly as it approaches the centre of the flat-topped aster to feed on the nectar.

An evening primrose (*Oenothera biennis*) seen (top) in visible light and (bottom) in ultraviolet light; the latter reveals nectar-guide patterns that are discernible to the moth pollinating this flower but not to the human eye.

An epauletted fruit bat (*Epomophorus wahlbergi*) approaching the pendulous flower of the baobab tree (*Adansonia digitata*) to feed on its nectar, which is stored where the stamens and stigma are positioned, forward of the reflexed petals. In attaching itself to the flower in order to feed, the bat becomes covered with pollen, which it will spread as it visits other flowers in search of nectar.

The labellum of the mirror ophrys (*Ophrys speculum*). The colouring so closely resembles that of the female wasp *Colpa aurea* that males of the species are attracted to the flower and pick up pollen during their attempts at copulation.

Costa's hummingbird (*Calypte costae*) foraging for nectar in the bright red tubular flowers of ocotillo (*Fouquieria splendens*). Pollen is displaced onto the beak and head of the bird as it inserts its long tongue into the corolla tube, where the nectar is located.

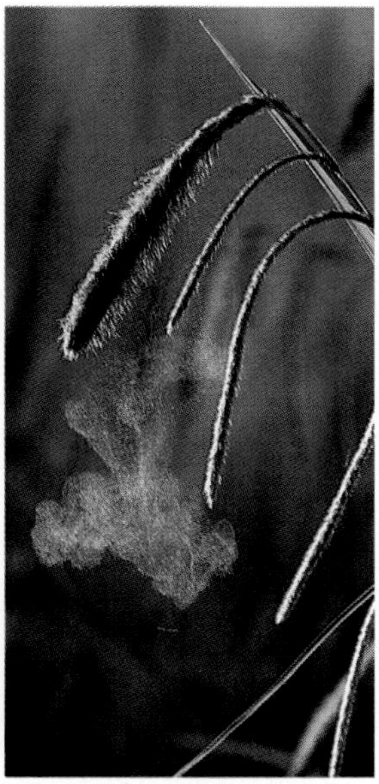

Spikes of sedge (*Carex pendula*) showing reduced floral parts adapted to wind pollination. The pollen bursts forth from the pendulous inflorescences as they sway in the wind.

Pollination

Degeneria roseiflora. The male phase of the flower, with whorls of showy rose-coloured petals, rose-coloured leaflike stamens, and purple staminodes. The single carpel in the centre is obscured by the tightly clasped staminodes. Pollen lines the microscopic furrows in the centre of each stamen.

Degeneria vitiensis. The female phase of the flower, showing conspicuous petals, fleshy staminodes coated with brilliant yellow exudate, and a single central carpel. Ovules are arranged within the fleshy carpel.

Hypericum calycinum (rose of Sharon). The brilliant regular flower of *Hypericum* develops a superior ovary with five spreading styles at its apex and numerous stamens arranged in five clusters (fascicles) emanating from below the base of the ovary.

Abutilon megapotamicum. A conspicuous red calyx tube envelops the closed yellow petals of this bell-shaped drooping flower. The anthers are attached to the apex of the exserted staminal column.

Variations in floral morphology

Salix discolor (pussy willow). Each flower of this dense inflorescence of male flowers consists of only two stamens in the axil of a small hairy bract. The appearance of the conspicuous yellow pollen-tipped stamens in early spring attracts pollinating insects.

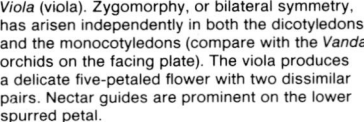

Viola (viola). Zygomorphy, or bilateral symmetry, has arisen independently in both the dicotyledons and the monocotyledons (compare with the *Vanda* orchids on the facing plate). The viola produces a delicate five-petaled flower with two dissimilar pairs. Nectar guides are prominent on the lower spurred petal.

Plate 2: (Top left, top right) John M. Miller in *National Geographic Research* 5(2): 218–231, 1989, (centre left, bottom right) E.S. Ross, (centre right) Jo-Ann Ordano—PHOTO/NATS, (bottom left) Bill Larkin—PHOTO/NATS

Plate 3: (Top left, lower middle left, bottom left) E.S. Ross, (top right) Horticultural Photography, Corvallis, Oregon, (upper middle left, centre right) © Robert and Linda Mitchell, (bottom right) © Harry Haralambou/Peter Arnold, Inc.

Rosa eglanteria (sweetbrier, or eglantine). These regular, bisexual flowers generally develop as single flowers with floral parts in multiples of five. Five broad petals and multiple stamens line the edge of the hypanthium (floral tube) from which many pistils arise. Sweetbrier is the parent for a number of cultivated hybrid roses.

Fuchsia. The floral parts of this showy flower are arranged in multiples of four. An inferior ovary at the base of the flower precedes the floral tube formed by the four sepals and four petals. Eight stamens of unequal length and a prominent four-lobed stigma emanate from the centre of the flower.

Hymenocallis liriosme (spider lily). A delicate staminal cup formed by the filaments near their base is the prominent feature of this showy flower. A spidery perianth frames the centre.

Campsis radicans (trumpet creeper, or trumpet vine). The petals of this delicate flower form a corolla tube with five spreading lobes. A shortened calyx tube covers the base of the flower.

Vanda. Orchids exhibit bilateral symmetry similar to that seen in *Viola,* on the facing plate. The two dissimilar pairs of petals and the single petal parallel the form seen in the genus *Viola.*

Tulipa (tulip). A perfect flower with floral structures in multiples of three, *Tulipa* has a three-lobed stigma, six stamens, and six distinct perianth parts.

Commelina communis (Asiatic dayflower). An irregular flower having three petals of unequal size (two large and one small), the dayflower also has six dimorphic stamens, of which three are long and fertile (one curves inward) and three are infertile and bear cross-shaped anthers.

A raceme of lily of the valley (*Convallaria majalis*).

Panicles of astilbe (*Astilbe*).

Spikes of false dragonhead, sometimes known as obedience plant (*Physostegia angustifolia*).

A drooping male catkin (left) and the small red female inflorescence (right) of hazel (*Corylus avellana*).

Verticillasters (a false whorl of inflorescences found at the nodes) of the hedge nettle (*Stachys bullata*).

Inflorescences

Corymbs of yarrow (*Achillea taygetea*).

Simple umbels of the Texas, or white, milkweed (*Asclepias texana*).

Compound umbels of cow parsnip (*Heracleum sphondylium*).

A dichasium (the basic unit of a cyme) of the wood stichwort (*Stellaria nemorum*).

A compound cyme of the elderberry, or European common elder (*Sambucus nigra*).

A helicoid cyme of the fiddle-neck (*Amsinckia intermedia*), a type of determinate inflorescence in which the flowers develop on one side of the axis, causing the inflorescence to curve.

The ligulate head of the dandelion (*Taraxacum officinale*), which is composed of only ligulate flowers.

The radiate head of the treasure flower (*Gazania rigens*), a daisylike inflorescence composed of disk flowers in the centre surrounded by marginal ray flowers.

The discoid head of the globe thistle (*Echinops*), which is composed of only disk flowers.

The mature spikes of barley (*Hordeum vulgare*).

Clusters of heads of the common tansy (*Tanacetum vulgare*) showing a mixed sequence of flowering. Within each head, flowering begins with the outer flowers, spiraling progressively toward the centre (racemose). Flowering among the heads, however, begins with the terminal head, advancing outward to the lateral heads (cymose).

Plate 4: (Top left) © Nell Bolen—The National Audubon Society Collection/Photo Researchers, (top centre) © E.R. Degginger, (top right, bottom centre) © Robert and Linda Mitchell, (centre left) © Richard Packwood—Oxford Scientific Films, (centre right) E.S. Ross, (bottom left) S. Rannels—Grant Heilman Photography, Inc., (bottom right) © Kent and Donna Dannen—The National Audubon Society Collection/Photo Researchers

Plate 5: (Top left) © David Woodfall/Natural History Photographic Agency, (top centre) © Stephen Dalton/Natural History Photographic Agency, (top right) © Robert Lee—The National Audubon Society Collection/Photo Researchers, (centre left) A–Z Collection/Alan Punton, (centre) E.S. Ross, (centre right) A–Z Collection/Maurice Nimmo, (bottom left) Grant Heilman—Grant Heilman Photography, Inc., (bottom right) J. and M. Bain/Natural History Photographic Agency

A hyacinth (*Hyacinthus*) bulb, an underground stem that produces aerial foliage. The foliage dies back to the bulb, which houses a maturing flower bud. The bulb is common in herbaceous perennials that become dormant in response to a seasonal change in climate or water availability.

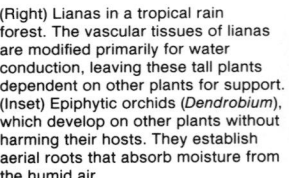

(Right) Lianas in a tropical rain forest. The vascular tissues of lianas are modified primarily for water conduction, leaving these tall plants dependent on other plants for support. (Inset) Epiphytic orchids (*Dendrobium*), which develop on other plants without harming their hosts. They establish aerial roots that absorb moisture from the humid air.

(Far left) Black mangroves (*Avicennia germinans*), typical of halophytes found in the tree-dominated tropical mangrove swamps. (Inset) Pneumatophores encrusted with salt and a young green seedling projecting above the surface of the water. Complex mechanisms that regulate the osmotic tensions in the plant permit mangroves to exclude most of the salt despite the high salinity of the water that bathes the roots.

Adaptations to the environment

(Far right) Water lilies (*Nymphaea*) growing in a garden pond. (Inset) The floating leaf of a water lily (*Nymphaea odorata*) facing downward to show the attachment of the leaf stalk near the centre of the leaf. Hydromorphic leaves are thin and the vascular tissues are scant because the surrounding water provides mechanical support for the plant.

(Far right) *Agave shawii* growing in a desert in North America. (Inset) *Echeveria,* a succulent with thick, fleshy leaves and epicuticular waxes ("bloom"). Plants adapted to arid habitats are called xerophytes. They develop highly cutinized fleshy leaves and stems for water storage with which they modulate the effects of strong sunlight, low humidity, and scant water.

The stinging nettle (*Urtica ferox*), showing secretory (glandular), or stinging, hairs (trichomes). Most herbivores are discouraged from grazing on this plant because of irritating toxins secreted by the trichomes.

Pinesaps (*Monotropa hypopitys*) are saprophytes with little photosynthetic tissue. Unlike green plants, saprophytes are unable to manufacture carbohydrates. They rely on their associations with mycorrhizal fungi, which synthesize carbohydrates from the rich organic leaf litter.

The dodder (*Cuscuta gronovii*), a parasitic plant that penetrates the tissues of the host plant using specialized roots called haustoria. This parasite is so effective in removing nutrients from its host that over time the roots that secure it to the ground degenerate, leaving the dodder completely dependent on its host.

Plate 6: (Top left) Park Seed Co., Greenwood, South Carolina, (top centre) © E.R. Degginger, (top right) © Gary Braasch, (centre left, centre right) Thomas Eisner, (bottom left) © Thomas C. Boyden, (bottom right) Horticultural Photography, Corvallis, Oregon

Plate 7: (Top left, centre, centre right) © E.R. Degginger, (top right) © Robert and Linda Mitchell, (centre left) G.R. Roberts, Nelson, New Zealand, (bottom left) © Jan van de Kam/ Bruce Coleman Ltd., (bottom right) Hans Reinhard/Bruce Coleman Ltd.

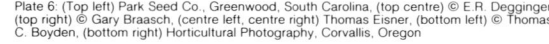

(Far left) Sea lavender (*Limonium vulgare*) growing with glasswort (*Salicornia europaea*), two herbaceous halophytes that are typical of temperate salt marshes. (Inset) A close-up of the glasswort showing the jointed, bright green stems specked with salt crystals.

Tendrils of catbrier (*Smilax rotundifolia*). The stipules elongate and coil around other plants for support.

Stipules of the tulip tree (*Liriodendron tulipifera*). Stipules develop at the base of a leaf and protect the developing blade.

A cladode of the orchid, or leaf, cactus (*Epiphyllum*). The stem does not bear leaves but rather becomes flattened and leaflike, assuming the plant's photosynthetic functions.

Passive traps of the slender pitcher plant (*Nepenthes gracilis*), a carnivorous plant. The leaf blade narrows into a tendril that transforms into an upright pitcher.

Bracts of the bougainvillea (*Bougainvillea*). Each cluster of three small tubular flowers is surrounded by colourful petallike bracts.

Bracts of the flowering dogwood (*Cornus florida*). The small green flowers are surrounded by four petallike white bracts.

Modifications of the shoot system

Active traps of the Venus' flytrap (*Dionaea muscipula*), a carnivorous plant. If depressed at least twice, thin pressure-sensitive hairs in the trap stimulate the lobes to clamp tightly over an insect.

An active trap of the sundew (*Drosera capensis*), a carnivorous plant. Sensitive tentacles topped with red mucilage-secreting glands fold over to secure and digest the struggling insect.

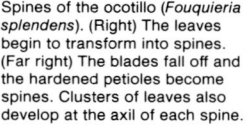

A large, white leafy spathe underlies a spadix in *Spathiphyllum*. The fleshy spike develops male flowers above and female flowers below.

Spines of the ocotillo (*Fouquieria splendens*). (Right) The leaves begin to transform into spines. (Far right) The blades fall off and the hardened petioles become spines. Clusters of leaves also develop at the axil of each spine.

Plate 8: (Top left) Runk/Schoenberger—Grant Heilman Photography, Inc., (top centre) G.R. Roberts, Nelson, New Zealand, (top right, lower middle right) © Thomas C. Boyden, (upper middle left, lower middle left, bottom centre, bottom right) © Robert and Linda Mitchell, (centre) © Stephen Dalton/Natural History Photographic Agency, (upper middle right) © John Shaw/Natural History Photographic Agency, (bottom left) © Sydney Karp—PHOTO/NATS of the plant was modified: the leaf size was reduced, and some shoots were modified so that the ovules remained enclosed inside the leaf tissue, which was shortened so that the ovule and pollen organs were borne close together. The sterile leaves may have been lost in some evolutionary lines or may have evolved into sepals and petals in others. The pollen-bearing organs (stamens) or ovule-bearing organs (carpels) may have been lost in some lines of evolution, resulting in unisexual flowers, or both may have been retained together in others to produce bisexual flowers.

Those early lines of angiosperm evolution in which wind may have functioned in pollination retained small, inconspicuous, often unisexual flowers, while in those evolutionary lines that developed close associations with specific insect pollinators, the organs become dramatically modified. Small, inconspicuous bisexual or unisexual flowers are known from the Aptian Age. Large petals developed by the late Albian (about 105 million years ago). In insect-pollinated flowers and bisexual flowers that contain their characteristic nectaries, very large petals and anthers with abundant small pollen are known from the earliest Cenomanian Age. The presence of small inconspicuous unisexual flowers, probably pollinated by wind or water, from the Aptian and late Albian suggests that the form and mode of reproduction of angiosperms were beginning to diverge from those of their ancestors even before this is attested to in macrofossils.

The special features of flowering plants that enhanced the coevolutionary links with animals evolved at various times in different groups of angiosperms. There were, however, three major nodes of coevolution in the development of flowering plants: the evolution of showy flowers attractive to animal (mainly insect) pollinators, the evolution of bilaterally symmetrical flowers with variously fused parts to direct the behaviour of particular animal pollinators (especially social insects and birds), and the evolution of larger energy-rich animals (especially mammals and birds) to disperse fruits and seeds. Each of these events had a dynamic effect on the evolution of angiosperms, increasing their diversity at different times in different groups and affecting their floral and fruit morphology in various ways.

Coevolutionary adaptations

The early angiosperms appear to have had few and radially arranged flower parts. The flowers were unisexual or bisexual, endowed with superior ovaries, loosely closed to fully closed carpels, free flower parts, and small fruits and seeds. The fossil record of the early evolution of the flower demonstrates a tendency toward an increased number of flower parts, a loose to complete fusion of carpels, the development of a style, the elevation of the stigmatic surface upon the style, a slight increase in seed size, and a diversity of ways in which flowers were borne upon the plant.

The evolution of both female and male reproductive organs in the same flower was both beneficial and problematic in the early angiosperms. Insects visiting a unisexual flower either picked up pollen or deposited pollen, depending on the sex of the flower visited. Insect visits therefore only randomly fertilized flowers as the insect alternated between male and female flowers. It became beneficial to the flower to evolve a place for both sexes in a single flower so that each insect visit would deposit and remove pollen. When both sexes are present in a single flower, however, there develops a strong possibility that the flower may pollinate itself, a situation that would cause inbreeding depression, thereby reducing the vigour of the offspring over successive generations. It was probably very early in the evolutionary history of flowering plants that self-incompatibility was evolved, a mechanism that prevents flowers or plants from self-pollinating. The pollen of many modern insect-pollinated bisexual flowers is incompatible with the flower in which it is produced.

Another feature of flowers that developed as a result of insect pollination is pollen-tube competition. When a pollen load of 50–200 pollen grains is deposited on a stigma at one time, each pollen grain grows a pollen tube into the stigmatic tissue. The pollen tubes that grow the fastest reach the ovules first and effect fertilization. It has been demonstrated that the pollen grain with the fastest-growing pollen tube carries genes that produce more vigorous offspring. By the Early Cenomanian the stigmas of some insect-pollinated flowers were elevated on styles, effectively establishing some distance for the pollen tubes to travel. This would establish pollen-tube competition as a selective mechanism within some early flowers.

Pollen-tube competition

During the first 70 million years of angiospermous evolution all the known flowers were radially symmetrical. It is only in the Tertiary (66.4 to 1.6 million years ago) during the late Paleocene and early Eocene (63.6 to 52 million years ago) that the first evidence of bilaterally symmetrical flowers is found. The evolution of bilateral flowers, as, for example, those of the legumes and orchids, is an adaptation for specialized pollinators such as social insects (bees) and some birds. The sterile organs (sepals, petals) are modified to present a certain flower orientation to the pollinator, enabling the pollinator to enter the flower where the pollen organs and pollen-receptive tissue are positioned to maximize effective pollination. During the early Tertiary, the bilateral organization of floral organs coevolved with animal behaviour independently at different times and in various groups of angiosperms.

The evolution of mammals and birds also influenced the evolution of flowering plants in the early Tertiary. During the first 70–80 million years of their existence, the fruits and seeds of the angiosperms were small. The initial radiation of larger energy-rich fruits and seeds, such as the acorns, chestnuts, walnuts, legume pods, and the earliest grasses, took place during the Eocene. These fruits appeared over a short period of time contemporaneously with the diversification of seed- and fruit-eating mammals and birds. Seeds of fleshy fruits, such as grapes, also became common in the Eocene (about 45 million years ago). This fact demonstrates that a second important node of plant and animal coevolution developed about 50–60 million years ago, when angiosperms began to produce fruits and seeds that were attractive to animals. The animals served as agents to carry fruits and seeds some distance from the parent plant, further enhancing the potential for outcrossing and aiding in the dispersal of angiospermous plants to new areas of the world.

In summary, the evolutionary history of angiosperms is intimately, but not exclusively, tied to their coevolution with animal pollinators and agents of fruit and seed dispersal. Wind and water pollination and fruit and seed dispersal also continued throughout the entire evolutionary history of flowering plants. This network of evolutionary pressures resulted in the variety of flowers and fruits representative of present-day angiosperms. Accordingly, some of the most useful characters in determining the particular taxon to which living angiosperms belong are flowers, fruits, and seeds. The evolution of such vegetative characteristics as wood and leaves is more complex and less well understood. (D.L.Di.)

Classification

DIAGNOSTIC CLASSIFICATION

The angiosperms are a well characterized, sharply defined group. There is not a single living plant species whose status as an angiosperm or non-angiosperm is in doubt. Even the fossil record provides no forms that connect with any other group, although there are of course some fossils of individual plant parts that cannot be effectively classified.

Most typically, angiosperms are seed plants. This separates them from all other plants except the gymnosperms, of which the most familiar representatives are the conifers and cycads.

The ovules (forerunners of the seeds) of angiosperms are characteristically enclosed in an ovary, in contrast to those of gymnosperms, which are exposed to the air at the time of pollination and never enclosed in an ovary. Pollen of angiosperms is received by the stigma, a specialized structure that is usually elevated above the ovary on a more slender structure known as the style. Pollen grains germinate on the stigma, and the pollen tube must grow through the tissues of the style (if present) and the ovary to reach the ovule. The pollen grains of gymnosperms, in contrast, are received at an opening (the micropyle) atop the ovule.

The female gametophyte of angiosperms (called the embryo sac) is tiny and contains only a few (typically eight) nuclei; the cytoplasm associated more or less directly with these nuclei is not partitioned by cell walls. One of the several nuclei of the embryo sac serves as the egg in sexual reproduction, uniting with one of the two sperm nuclei delivered by the pollen tube. Two other nuclei of the embryo sac fuse with the second sperm nucleus from the pollen tube. This triple-fusion nucleus is characteristically the forerunner of a multicellular food-storage tissue in the seed, called the endosperm.

The process in which both nuclei from the pollen tube fuse is referred to as double fertilization. This is perhaps the most characteristic single feature of angiosperms and is not shared with any other group. Gymnosperms, in sharp contrast, have a multicellular female gametophyte that consists of many hundreds or even thousands of cells. Double fertilization does not take place in this case, and the female gametophyte develops into the food-storage tissue of the seed.

Furthermore, angiosperms have a more complex set of conducting tissues than do gymnosperms. The water-conducting tissue (xylem) ordinarily includes some long tubes called vessels. Only one small group of gymnosperms, the Gnetophyta, has vessels. The food-conducting tissue (phloem) of angiosperms characteristically has companion cells that bear a direct ontogenetic relationship to the sieve tubes through which the actual conduction takes place. The phloem of gymnosperms has less specialized sieve cells and lacks companion cells.

Recognition that the angiosperms fall into two major groups, the dicotyledons and monocotyledons, has a long history and is embodied in all major systems of classification proposed since the late 18th century. The principal differences between the two groups, here treated as the classes Magnoliopsida and Liliopsida, respectively, are shown in the table below. All of the differences are individually subject to failure, but collectively they provide a reasonably clear distinction.

Only the position of the order Nymphaeales remains controversial. The traditional and still dominant view among authorities is that the Nymphaeales are dicotyledons, but there is a persistent minority opinion that in spite of their two cotyledons they belong with the monocotyledons instead.

ANNOTATED CLASSIFICATION

The classification here presented is based on that of Arthur Cronquist (1981, 1988). A complete listing of all angiosperm orders and families is given below. Additional articles about the most important groups contain more detailed information on their natural history, economic importance, structure, and evolution.

DIVISION MAGNOLIOPHYTA (angiosperms)
The entire range of flowering plants, with more than 200,000 species of worldwide distribution on land and along shore.

Class Magnoliopsida (dicotyledons)
Seeds typically with 2 cotyledons (seed leaves). Other characteristics as in Table 1. The class is named for the genus *Magnolia*. There are 6 subclasses.

Subclass Magnoliidae
Dicotyledons that have retained 1 or more features of a syndrome of putatively primitive characteristics and that are not obviously related to some more advanced group. Eight orders. (See the section below entitled *Subclass Magnoliidae.*)

Order Magnoliales (*Annonales*). The most archaic order of angiosperms, comprising those families of Magnoliidae that have ethereal oil cells in the parenchymatous tissues, pollen with a single aperture (or 2 or no apertures, never 3), and usually hypogynous flowers with a well-developed perianth of usually separate sepals. Ten families: Winteraceae, Degeneriaceae, Himantandraceae, Eupomatiaceae, Austrobaileyaceae, Magnoliaceae (magnolia), Lactoridaceae, Annonaceae (custard apple), Myristicaceae (nutmeg), and Canellaceae. (See the section below entitled *Magnoliales.*)

Order Laurales. Closely related to Magnoliales, but the flowers mostly perigynous or epigynous and the pollen never uniaperturate. Eight families: Amborellaceae, Trimeniaceae, Monimiaceae, Gomortegaceae, Calycanthaceae (strawberry shrub), Idiospermaceae, Lauraceae (laurel), and Hernandiaceae. (See the section below entitled *Laurales.*)

Order Piperales. More than half of the species are herbs or half-shrubs, in contrast to the mostly woody Magnoliales and Laurales. Small flowers often crowded into a spadixlike inflorescence. Three families: the Piperaceae (pepper) and Saururaceae (lizard's tail) form a closely related pair, but the Chloranthaceae are more distant and have often been treated as a separate order, Chloranthales.

Order Aristolochiales. Woody vines, less often herbs or shrubs. Flowers mostly with an inferior ovary, an often irregular and corolla-like calyx, and reduced or no petals. A single family, Aristolochiaceae (birthwort).

Order Illiciales. Woody Magnoliidae with 3 or 6 apertures in the pollen grains. Two families, the Illiciaceae and Schisandraceae.

Order Nymphaeales. Herbaceous and aquatic, mostly without vessels. Five families: Nelumbonaceae (lotus lily, sometimes taken as a separate order, Nelumbonales), Nymphaeaceae (water lily), Barclayaceae, Cabombaceae (water shield), and Ceratophyllaceae (hornwort).

Order Ranunculales. Herbaceous or secondarily woody with triaperturate (or triaperturate-derived) pollen; flowers usually with separate carpels and more than 2 sepals. Eight families: Ranunculaceae (buttercup), Circaeasteraceae, Berberidaceae (barberry), Sargentodoxaceae, Lardizabalaceae, Menispermaceae (moonseed), Coriariaceae, and Sabiaceae, the latter 2 families only doubtfully placed here. (See the section below entitled *Ranunculales.*)

Comparison of Dicotyledons and Monocotyledons

	Magnoliopsida (dicotyledons)	Liliopsida (monocotyledons)
Embryo	usually two cotyledons	one cotyledon
Leaves	usually reticulate (netted) venation (pinnate or palmate)	usually parallel venation
	seldom sheathed at the base	often sheathed at the base
	petiole usually well developed	petiole seldom developed
Bracteoles	when present, usually two; lateral	when present, usually one; adaxial
Vascular bundles	usually borne to a ring with a persisting cambium	generally scattered or seldom in two or more rings; usually without a cambium
	cortex and pith are usually well differentiated	usually no definable cortex or pith
Primary root	generally persistent and becoming a taproot	short duration, soon replaced by adventitious roots
	rootcap and piliferous layer have a common origin, with the exception of Nymphaeales	rootcap and piliferous layer have different origins
Habit	woody and herbaceous (primarily woody)	herbaceous and arborescent (primarily herbaceous)
Floral parts	usually borne in sets of five or four, seldom three or fewer	typically borne in sets of three, seldom four and never five
Nectaries	of various types, frequently transformed stamens and rarely of the septal type	chiefly of the septal type and occur in the septa between carpels
Pollen grains	usually tricolpate or tricolpate-derived (monocolpate only in a few primitive families)	monocolpate or monocolpate-derived (never tricolpate)

Order Papaverales. Differing from Ranunculales in typically having 2 sepals and 2 united carpels and in producing the isoquinoline alkaloid protopine. Two families, Papaveraceae (poppy) and Fumariaceae (fumitory).

Subclass Hamamelidae

Dicotyledons with reduced, often unisexual flowers that are often borne in catkins and never have numerous seeds on parietal placentas; pollen grains often with round germ pores, and the wall often with granular infrastructure. Eleven orders. (See the section below entitled *Subclass Hamamelidae.*)

Order Trochodendrales. Vesselless wood. Two families with a single species each, Trochodendraceae and Tetracentraceae.

Order Hamamelidales. Several fruits or a single dehiscent fruit per flower. Five families: Cercidiphyllaceae, Eupteleaceae, Platanaceae (plane tree), Hamamelidaceae (witch hazel), and Myrothamnaceae.

Order Daphniphyllales. Drupes, abundant endosperm, and a minute embryo. A single family, Daphniphyllaceae, in the past often associated with Euphorbiaceae.

Order Didymelales. Open-paniculate, bistaminate male flowers; very short, united filaments; drupes composed of a single carpel; seeds without endosperm. A single family, Didymelaceae.

Order Eucommiales. Naked, unisexual flowers racemosely arranged on the proximal, bracteate part of a distally leafy shoot. A single family, Eucommiaceae, with a single species; the insufficiently studied small family Physenaceae, from Madagascar, has a similar inflorescence and may belong here.

Order Urticales. Plants woody or often herbaceous, all other Hamamelidae being woody. Separate stamens; 1 ovule per locule; usually a single indehiscent fruit per flower; and a well-developed embryo. Six families: Barbeyaceae, Ulmaceae (elm), Cannabaceae, Moraceae (mulberry), Cecropiaceae, and Urticaceae (nettle). (See the section below entitled *Urticales.*)

Order Leitneriales. Secretory canals in the pith, petioles, and leaf veins. Flowers in catkins, the pistillate ones with a single carpel. A single family, Leitneriaceae, with only *Leitneria floridana.*

Order Juglandales. Pinnately compound leaves; at least the staminate flowers in catkins; ovary with a single ovule at the top of a partial partition. Two families, the Rhoipteleaceae and Juglandaceae (walnut).

Order Myricales. Much like the Juglandales, but the leaves simple and the ovary unilocular, with a basal ovule. One family, the Myricaceae (bayberry).

Order Fagales. Simple, mostly alternate leaves; flowers in catkins; 2 or more ovules in an ovary with 2 or more chambers. As many as five families: Balanopaceae (sometimes taken as a distinct order), Ticodendraceae, Fagaceae (beech), Nothofagaceae, and Betulaceae (birch). (See the section below entitled *Fagales.*)

Order Casuarinales. Whorled leaves that are reduced to scales. Ovule typically with multiple embryo sacs (unique in this feature). A single family, Casuarinaceae (she oak).

Subclass Caryophyllidae

An affinity group of 3 orders. (See the section below entitled *Subclass Caryophyllidae.*)

Order Caryophyllales. The core group of Caryophyllidae, with a syndrome of specialized embryological features, unique in that the sieve-tube plastids contain a subperipheral ring of proteinaceous fibrils; often producing betalains, not known in other vascular plants except Solanales. A well-defined order, with 12 families: Phytolaccaceae (pokeweed), Nyctaginaceae (four-o'clock), Achatocarpaceae, Didiereaceae, Aizoaceae (fig marigold), Cactaceae (cactus), Chenopodiaceae (goosefoot), Amaranthaceae (amaranth), Portulacaceae (purslane), Basellaceae, Molluginaceae, and Caryophyllaceae (pink). (See the section below entitled *Caryophyllales.*)

Order Polygonales. Perianth not clearly differentiated into calyx and corolla; ovary mostly tricarpellate, unilocular, with a single basal ovule. A single family, Polygonaceae (buckwheat). (See the section below entitled *Polygonales and Plumbaginales.*)

Order Plumbaginales. Corolla sympetalous, with 5 stamens opposite the lobes; ovary with 5 carpels and a solitary basal ovule. A single family, Plumbaginaceae (leadwort). (See the section below entitled *Polygonales and Plumbaginales.*)

Subclass Dilleniidae

A loosely knit affinity group, more advanced than the Magnoliidae but less so than the Asteridae. Thirteen orders. (See the section below entitled *Subclass Dilleniidae.*)

Order Dilleniales. Carpels mostly distinct, unlike nearly all other Dilleniidae. Two families, Dilleniaceae and Paeoniaceae (peony).

Order Theales. Mostly hypogynous or somewhat perigynous flowers with imbricate (spiraled, with overlapping margins) sepals; usually axile placentation. Eighteen families: Ochnaceae, Sphaerosepalaceae, Sarcolaenaceae, Dipterocarpaceae, Caryocaraceae, Theaceae (tea), Actinidiaceae, Scytopetalaceae, Pentaphylacaceae, Tetrameristaceae, Pellicieraceae, Oncothecaceae, Marcgraviaceae, Quiinaceae, Elatinaceae (waterwort), Paracryphiaceae, Medusagynaceae, and Clusiaceae (mangosteen). (See the section below entitled *Theales.*)

Order Malvales. Valvate sepals (the edges adjoining rather than overlapping); stamens often all joined by their filaments. Seeds commonly contain cyclopropenyl fatty acids, apparently unique to this group. Five families: Elaeocarpaceae, Tiliaceae (linden), Sterculiaceae (cacao), Bombacaceae (kapok tree), and Malvaceae (mallow). (See the section below entitled *Malvales.*)

Order Lecythidales. Epigynous flowers, imbricate (overlapping) sepals, separate petals, and numerous stamens united by their filaments. A single family, Lecythidaceae (Brazil nut).

Order Nepenthales. Insectivorous herbs or shrubs. Three families: Sarraceniaceae (pitcher plant), Nepenthaceae (East Indian pitcher plant), and Droseraceae (sundew).

Order Violales. Parietal placentation; most often 3 carpels; without the mustard oils and replum of Salicales. Twenty-four families: Flacourtiaceae, Peridiscaceae, Bixaceae, Cistaceae, Huaceae, Lacistemaceae, Scyphostegiaceae, Stachyuraceae, Violaceae (violet), Tamaricaceae (tamarix), Frankeniaceae, Dioncophyllaceae, Ancistrocladaceae, Turneraceae, Malesherbiaceae, Passifloraceae (passion flower), Achariaceae, Caricaceae (papaya), Fouquieriaceae (ocotillo), Hoplestigmataceae, Cucurbitaceae (cucumber), Datiscaceae, Begoniaceae (begonia), and Loasaceae. (See the section below entitled *Violales.*)

Order Salicales. Woody with flowers in catkins. Ovary with parietal placentation and usually more or less numerous ovules. One family, Salicaceae (willow).

Order Capparales. Plants producing mustard oils. Fruit most often a specialized type of capsule with a replum (a framelike margin that persists on the pedicel after the sides of the fruit have fallen off). Five families: Tovariaceae, Capparaceae (caper), Brassicaceae (mustard), Moringaceae, and Resedaceae (mignonette). (See the section below entitled *Capparales.*)

Order Batales. Plants producing mustard oils. Flowers tiny, unisexual; pollen with a solid exine (outer wall). Two families, Gyrostemonaceae and Bataceae.

Order Ericales. Strongly mycotrophic plants (modified in association with mycorrhizal fungi) with a syndrome of otherwise uncommon embryological features. Eight families: Cyrillaceae, Clethraceae, Grubbiaceae, Empetraceae (crowberry), Epacridaceae, Ericaceae (heath), Pyrolaceae (shinleaf), and Monotropaceae (Indian pipe). (See the section below entitled *Ericales.*)

Order Diapensiales. Herbaceous or partially woody with 5 stamens attached to the corolla tube alternate with the lobes and usually 5 staminodes opposite the lobes; some embryological features shared with Ericales. One family, Diapensiaceae.

Order Ebenales. Woody with the flowers generally bearing at least 1 cycle of stamens opposite the corolla lobes; placentation axile. Five families: Sapotaceae (sapodilla), Ebenaceae (ebony), Styracaceae (storax), Lissocarpaceae, and Symplocaceae (sweetleaf).

Order Primulales. Functional stamens opposite the corolla lobes; placentation free-central or basal. Three families: Theophrastaceae, Myrsinaceae, and Primulaceae (primrose).

Subclass Rosidae

A loosely knit affinity group parallel to the Dilleniidae, more advanced than the Magnoliidae, less so than the Asteridae. Eighteen orders. (See the section below entitled *Subclass Rosidae.*)

Order Rosales. An exceedingly diverse order, standing at the evolutionary base of its subclass. Twenty-four families: Brunelliaceae, Connaraceae, Eucryphiaceae, Cunoniaceae, Davidsoniaceae, Dialypetalanthaceae, Pittosporaceae, Byblidaceae, Hydrangeaceae (hydrangea), Columelliaceae, Grossulariaceae (currant), Greyiaceae, Bruniaceae, Anisophylleaceae, Alseuosmiaceae, Crassulaceae (stonecrop), Cephalotaceae, Saxifragaceae (saxifrage), Rosaceae (rose), Neuradaceae, Crossosomataceae, Chrysobalanaceae, Surianaceae, and Rhabdodendraceae. (See the section below entitled *Rosales.*)

Order Fabales. Legumes; mostly compound, stipulate leaves, flowers with a single carpel, the fruit most commonly dry and opening along 2 sutures; many members have nitrogen-fixing bacteria in root nodules. The Cronquist system recognizes 3 families: Mimosaceae (mimosa), Caesalpiniaceae, and Fabaceae (bean); an alternate classification used in this article recognizes three subfamilies (Caesalpinioideae, Mimosoideae, and Papilionoideae) in a single family, Leguminoseae (Fabaceae). (See the section below entitled *Fabales.*)

Order Proteales. Mostly 4 valvate sepals and reduced or no petals; ovary of a single carpel. Two rather different families, which may not properly belong together: the Elaeagnaceae and Proteaceae.

Order Podostemales. Highly modified aquatic herbs, often not clearly differentiated into roots, stems, and leaves. Flowers very small, perfect, hypogynous, and usually with numerous ovules. A single family, Podostemaceae.

Order Haloragales. Flowers minute, epigynous, with a single ovule per locule of the ovary. Often aquatic. Two families, Haloragaceae (water milfoil) and Gunneraceae.

Order Myrtales. Mostly strongly perigynous to epigynous flowers; stem with internal phloem (next to the pith) as well as phloem outside the xylem; vessels with vestured pits. Fourteen families: Sonneratiaceae, Lythraceae (loosestrife), Rhynchocalycaceae, Alzateaceae, Penaeaceae, Crypteroniaceae, Trapaceae (water chestnut), Myrtaceae (myrtle), Punicaceae (pomegranate), Onagraceae (evening primrose), Oliniaceae, Melastomataceae, Combretaceae (Indian almond), and, depending on the classification used, either Memecylaceae or Thymelaeaceae. (See the section below entitled *Myrtales.*)

Order Rhizophorales. Woody with simple, opposite leaves and interpetiolar stipules. Includes some important mangrove species. A single family, Rhizophoraceae.

Order Cornales. Mostly woody with simple leaves, generally without stipules; flowers epigynous, the ovary with as many ovules as carpels. Three families: Alangiaceae, Cornaceae (dogwood), and Garryaceae; a number of small satellite families are sometimes segregated from the Cornaceae.

Order Santalales. A group showing progressive adaptation to parasitism, with concomitant vegetative and floral reduction; ovary with only a few ovules; embryology often complex and unusual. Ten families: Medusandraceae, Dipentodontaceae, Olacaceae, Opiliaceae, Santalaceae (sandalwood), Misodendraceae, Loranthaceae, Viscaceae (Christmas mistletoe), Eremolepidaceae, and Balanophoraceae.

Order Rafflesiales. Nongreen parasites, often with only the flowers emergent from the host; ovules very numerous; pollen extraordinarily diverse. Three families: Hydnoraceae, Mitrastemonaceae, and Rafflesiaceae; *Rafflesia* has very large flowers, sometimes 1 metre wide.

Order Celastrales. Woody with simple leaves and mostly hypogynous or somewhat perigynous, regular flowers, the stamens alternate with the petals; ovary mostly with 1 or 2 ovules per locule. Twelve families: Geissolomataceae, Celastraceae, Hippocrateaceae, Stackhousiaceae, Salvadoraceae, Tepuianthaceae, Aquifoliaceae (holly), Icacinaceae, Aextoxicaceae, Cardiopteridaceae, Corynocarpaceae, and Dichapetalaceae.

Order Euphorbiales. A vegetatively diverse order of Rosidae (sometimes associated with the Dilleniidae instead) with reduced, unisexual, hypogynous or naked flowers that are grouped into pseudanthia (false flowers consisting of many tiny flowers arranged to simulate a single flower). The very large family Euphorbiaceae (spurge), the closely related small family Pandaceae, and 2 additional small families of more doubtful relationships, Buxaceae (boxwood) and Simmondsiaceae (jojoba). (See the section below entitled *Euphorbiales.*)

Order Rhamnales. Single set of stamens opposite the petals; with 1 or 2 ovules in each locule of the ovary. Three families: Rhamnaceae (buckthorn), Leeaceae, and Vitaceae (grape).

Order Linales. Simple leaves and hypogynous, usually regular flowers; stamens usually with connate filaments; ovules 1 or 2 per locule. Five families: Erythroxylaceae (coca), Humiriaceae, Ixonanthaceae, Hugoniaceae, and Linaceae (flax).

Order Polygalales. Simple leaves and hypogynous or perigynous, often strongly irregular flowers; ovules mostly 1 or 2 per locule. Seven families: Malpighiaceae, Vochysiaceae, Trigoniaceae, Tremandraceae, Polygalaceae (milkwort), Xanthophyllaceae, and Krameriaceae.

Order Sapindales. Mostly woody with usually compound or cleft leaves and hypogynous flowers with few (commonly only 1 or 2) ovules per locule. Fifteen families: Staphyleaceae (bladdernut), Melianthaceae, Bretschneideraceae, Akaniaceae, Sapindaceae (soapberry), Hippocastanaceae (horse chestnut), Aceraceae (maple), Burseraceae (frankincense), Anacardiaceae (sumac), Julianiaceae, Simaroubaceae, Cneoraceae, Meliaceae (mahogany), Rutaceae (rue), and Zygophyllaceae (creosote bush). (See the section below entitled *Sapindales.*)

Order Geraniales. Mostly herbaceous with the leaves in most families compound or conspicuously cleft; flowers mostly hypogynous, with a compound ovary. Five families: Oxalidaceae (wood sorrel), Geraniaceae (geranium), Limnanthaceae, Tropaeolaceae (nasturtium), and Balsaminaceae (touch-me-not).

Order Apiales. Mostly compound or cleft leaves and an epigynous ovary with a single ovule in each locule; flowers often in umbels. Two families: Araliaceae (ginseng), and Apiaceae (also known by the irregular name Umbelliferae; carrot).

Subclass Asteridae

Dicotyledons with sympetalous flowers and with the stamens alternate with (or fewer than) the corolla lobes. Eleven orders. (See the section below entitled *Subclass Asteridae.*)

Order Gentianales. Opposite or whorled leaves and internal phloem; flowers mostly regular and with as many stamens as corolla lobes. Five families: Loganiaceae, Gentianaceae (gentian), Saccifoliaceae, Apocynaceae (dogbane), and Asclepiadaceae (milkweed).

Order Solanales. Alternate leaves, mostly regular flowers with as many stamens as corolla lobes, and a hypogynous ovary that does not have the special features of the Lamiales. Nine families: Duckeodendraceae, Nolanaceae, Solanaceae (potato), Convolvulaceae (morning glory), Cuscutaceae (dodder), Retziaceae, Menyanthaceae (buckbean), Polemoniaceae (phlox), and Hydrophyllaceae (waterleaf). (See the section below entitled *Solanales.*)

Order Lamiales. Hypogynous ovary, each locule divided into 2 locelli with a single ovule each. Four families: Lennoaceae, Boraginaceae, Verbenaceae (verbena), and Lamiaceae (also called Labiatae; mint); a number of small satellite families are sometimes segregated from the Verbenaceae.

Order Callitrichales. Aquatic or semiaquatic herbs with much reduced flowers. Three families: Hippuridaceae (mare's tail), Callitrichaceae (water starwort), and Hydrostachyaceae.

Order Plantaginales. Mostly wind-pollinated flowers with a small, papery, persistent, 4-lobed corolla; leaves parallel-veined, often all basal. A single family, Plantaginaceae (plantain).

Order Scrophulariales. Hypogynous ovary and a usually irregular corolla with fewer stamens than corolla lobes. Twelve families: Buddlejaceae, Oleaceae (olive), Scrophulariaceae, Globulariaceae, Myoporaceae, Orobanchaceae (broomrape), Gesneriaceae, Acanthaceae, Pedaliaceae, Bignoniaceae, Mendonciaceae, and Lentibulariaceae (bladderwort). (See the section below entitled *Scrophulariales.*)

Order Campanulales. Epigynous ovary, mostly alternate leaves without stipules, and a pollen-presentation mechanism similar to that of the Asterales. Seven families: Pentaphragmataceae, Sphenocleaceae, Campanulaceae (bellflower), Stylidiaceae, Donatiaceae, Brunoniaceae, and Goodeniaceae.

Order Rubiales. Epigynous ovary, opposite leaves, and interpetiolar stipules (or whorled leaves and no stipules). Two families, Rubiaceae (madder) and Theligonaceae.

Order Dipsacales. Epigynous ovary; opposite or whorled, mostly exstipulate leaves; and without the specialized pollen-presentation mechanism of Calycerales or Asterales. Four families: Caprifoliaceae (honeysuckle), Adoxaceae (moschatel), Valerianaceae (valerian), and Dipsacaceae (teasel).

Order Calycerales. Much like Asterales but the single ovule pendulous from the top of the single locule. Plants producing iridoid compounds. A single family, Calyceraceae.

Order Asterales. Flowers borne in involucrate heads and with a characteristic complex pollen-presentation mechanism; ovary epigynous, with a single basal ovule. Plants with special secondary metabolites but not iridoid compounds. A single very large family, Asteraceae, often called Compositae (aster). (See the section below entitled *Asterales.*)

Class Liliopsida (monocotyledons)

Seeds typically with a single cotyledon; other characteristics as given in the accompanying table. The class is named for the genus *Lilium.*

Subclass Alismatidae

Either aquatic or semiaquatic. Separate carpels; vascular system often poorly developed; endosperm wanting except in Triuridales. Four orders. (See the section below entitled *Subclass Alismatidae.*)

Order Alismatales. Hypogynous flowers; perianth differentiated into sepals and petals. Three families: Butomaceae (flowering rush), Limnocharitaceae (water poppy), and Alismataceae (water plantain).

Order Hydrocharitales. Epigynous flowers. Includes some coastal marine as well as freshwater genera. One family, Hydrocharitaceae.

Order Najadales. Hypogynous flowers; perianth, when present, not differentiated into sepals and petals. Ten families: Aponogetonaceae, Scheuchzeriaceae, Juncaginaceae (arrow grass), Potamogetonaceae (pondweed), Ruppiaceae (ditch grass), Najadaceae (water nymph), Zannichelliaceae (horned pondweed), Posidoniaceae, Cymodoceaceae (manatee grass), and Zosteraceae (eel grass), the latter 3 families coastal-marine.

Order Triuridales. Terrestrial mycotrophic Alismatidae, without chlorophyll (unique in the subclass). Two families: Petrosaviaceae and Triuridaceae.

Subclass Arecidae

A loose affinity group characterized by small flowers that are often aggregated into a spadix; vessels commonly present in the first 3 orders. Four orders. (See the section below entitled *Subclass Arecidae.*)

Order Arecales. Very often unbranched trees with a terminal crown of large leaves, these with a plicate blade reflecting an ontogeny unique to this and the Cyclanthales. Inflorescence usually large and branched. One family, Arecaceae (often called Palmae; palms). (See the section below entitled *Palmae.*)

Order Cyclanthales. Related to the palms, but the inflorescence a spadix, the plants usually herbaceous and leaves often 2-parted. One family, Cyclanthaceae (Panama hat plant).

Order Pandanales. Leaves firm, narrow, appearing to be in 3 or 4 spirals because of the unique, spiral growth of the stem. One family, Pandanaceae (screw pine).

Order Arales. Mostly herbs, often with net-veined leaves. Two families, Araceae (arum) and Lemnaceae (duckweed), the latter consisting of small, free-floating plants of simple structure.

Subclass Commelinidae

Flowers mostly without nectar; perianth often small and inconspicuous; ovary hypogynous; endosperm with compound starch grains; vessels generally present in all vegetative organs. Seven orders. (See the section below entitled *Subclass Commelinidae.*)

Order Commelinales. Showy, mostly perfect flowers adapted to pollination by insects (unique in the subclass). Four families: Rapateaceae, Xyridaceae (yellow-eyed grass), Mayacaceae, and Commelinaceae (spiderwort).

Order Eriocaulales. Strictly basal leaves that lack a sheath (unique in the subclass). Tiny flowers borne in dense heads. One family, Eriocaulaceae (pipewort).

Order Restionales. Small flowers and a solitary ovule pendulous into each locule of the ovary; anthers often with a single pollen sac (unique in the subclass). Four families: Flagellariaceae, Joinvilleaceae, Restionaceae, and Centrolepidaceae.

Order Juncales. Small flowers with an evident, biseriate, chaffy perianth; pollen grains in tetrads. Capsular fruits have more seeds than locules. Two families, Juncaceae (rush) and Thurniaceae.

Order Cyperales. Pluricarpellate but unilocular ovary, containing a single ovule, ripening into an indehiscent fruit. Two families: Cyperaceae (sedge) and Poaceae (also called Gramineae; grass). (See the sections below entitled *Cyperaceae* and *Poaceae.*)

Order Hydatellales. Small flowers and a solitary ovule pendulous from the top of the ovary; seeds with perisperm (unique in the subclass); vascular system poorly developed. A single family, Hydatellaceae.

Order Typhales. Small flowers and a solitary ovule pendulous near the top of the ovary; seeds with endosperm. Two families, Sparganiaceae (bur reed) and Typhaceae (cattail).

Subclass Zingiberidae

Flowers mostly adapted to pollination by insects or other animals; sepals usually well differentiated from the petals; septal nectaries often present; endosperm typically with compound starch grains. Two orders. (See the section below entitled *Subclass Zingiberidae.*)

Order Bromeliales. Xerophytes and epiphytes with narrow, often firm and spiny-margined leaves; regular or somewhat irregular flowers with 6 functional stamens. One family, Bromeliaceae (bromeliad). (See the section below entitled *Bromeliales.*)

Order Zingiberales. Mesophytes and emergent aquatics. Irregular flowers with 1 or 5 functional stamens. Leaf blades with a prominent midrib and numerous primary lateral veins in a pinnate-parallel arrangement. Eight families: Strelitziaceae, Heliconiaceae, Musaceae (banana), Lowiaceae, Zingiberaceae (ginger), Costaceae, Cannaceae (canna), and Marantaceae (prayer plant). (See the section below entitled *Zingiberales.*)

Subclass Liliidae

Flowers mostly adapted to pollination by insects or other animals; sepals usually like the petals; nectar (often from septal nectaries) generally present; endosperm, when present, usually very hard, in any case without compound starch grains. Two orders. (See the section below entitled *Subclass Liliidae.*)

Order Liliales. Seeds usually with a well-developed embryo and endosperm. Fifteen families: Philydraceae, Pontederiaceae (water hyacinth), Haemodoraceae (bloodwort), Cyanastraceae, Liliaceae (lily), Iridaceae (iris), Velloziaceae, Aloeaceae (aloe), Agavaceae (century plant), Xanthorrhoeaceae, Hanguanaceae, Taccaceae, Stemonaceae, Smilacaceae (catbrier), and Dioscoreaceae (yam). (See the section below entitled *Liliales.*)

Order Orchidales. Strongly mycotrophic; seeds very numerous and tiny, with minute embryo and little or no endosperm. Four families: Geosiridaceae, Burmanniaceae, Corsiaceae, and Orchidaceae (orchid). (See the section below entitled *Orchidales.*)

CRITICAL APPRAISAL

Based on both comparative morphology and the fossil record, it appears that the evolutionary diversification of the angiosperms began more than 120 million years ago during the Early Cretaceous Period (144 to 97.5 million years ago). The ancestors of the angiosperms must by definition have been gymnosperms, since all the features that distinguish the two groups from each other appear to reflect evolutionary advances in the angiosperms. A precise connection to a particular group of gymnosperms remains to be established.

Inasmuch as all gymnosperms are woody and have secondary thickening in the stem, it is reasonable to suppose that the first angiosperms were also woody. The fossil record suggests that the divergence of the monocots as an essentially herbaceous, possibly aquatic group was the first major dichotomy in the evolutionary history of flowering plants. The herbaceous habit, scattered vascular bundles, and the absence of a vascular cambium in monocots may all reflect the putatively aquatic ancestry.

Herbaceous dicots appear to have originated subsequently many times from woody ones in open terrestrial habitats. Most of these have the vascular bundles in a ring (as seen in cross-section of the stem), and in many the vascular cambium actively dividing to some degree. Anatomical evidence shows that some of these herbaceous dicots have reverted to a woody habit.

The higher taxa of angiosperms (especially the orders and subclasses) do not show the same degree of correlation of structure, way of life, and evolutionary history that zoologists are accustomed to finding among animals. Some sort of organization is required to put together the things that are most alike and to separate them from things they are progressively less alike. The resulting major groups of plants, however, are often poorly characterized and subject to reasonable difference of opinion. Even at the level of genera and species, the competitive exclusion among related taxa that permeates the classification of higher animals is much more muted in plants.

Many of the characters that botanists have come to consider important in marking natural, evolutionarily significant groups are difficult to interpret in terms of survival value. Furthermore, evolutionary parallelism is so pervasive among angiosperms that it is often difficult to know whether a particular similarity between two groups reflects common ancestry or parallelism.

The subclasses within the dicotyledons and monocotyledons are conceptually necessary to provide a mental arrangement of the numerous orders, but they have little ecological significance. There are tendencies and averages, but it is difficult to find anything to say about a particular subclass as a whole that is not also true of some members of other subclasses. Some of the orders are relatively well marked, but others are mere affinity groups like the subclasses. There are still major differences of opinion among botanists as to which families belong in which order and, in particular, as to which order belongs in which subclass.

The families of angiosperms are for the most part more stable, and the same genera tend to show up in the same family in all modern systems of classification. Differences among systems in this regard primarily reflect the degree of lumping (recognition of large, inclusive, diversified groups) or splitting (recognition of smaller, more sharply limited groups) that appeals to different minds.

The general system of classifying angiosperms most widely used during the last decade of the 19th century and the first two-thirds of the 20th century was that of Adolf Engler and his associates. The first edition of Engler's *Syllabus . . .*, presenting an outline of the classification down to the level of families, was published in 1892. A more detailed scheme, down to the level of genera, was published seriatim in *Die natürlichen Pflanzenfamilien . . .* between 1887 and 1909. Engler initially considered flowers of simple structure—unisexual, without perianth—to be primitive, and his system was based on that assumption. Later he came to recognize (at least to some extent) the significance of floral reduction, but he did not modify his system accordingly.

A contrary opinion, holding that primitive flowers had indefinite numbers of free and distinct sepals, petals, stamens, and carpels, takes its origin in the pre-Darwinian concepts of Augustin Pyramus de Candolle (1813). An explicitly evolutionary version of Candolle's views has come to be called the strobilar hypothesis of floral evolution, from a comparison of the flower to a strobilus (cone) of gymnosperms.

The first general system of angiosperm classification embodying the strobilar hypothesis was presented by Charles E. Bessey in 1897 and further elaborated in the early 1900s. Although his system was never widely adopted, most of his principles are now generally accepted. Even the most recent edition of the Engler *Syllabus* (1954–64), prepared by Engler's successors in Berlin, was substantially modified in Besseyan direction.

John Hutchinson independently (1926–34, 1959, 1973) developed a system and set of precepts conceptually similar to Bessey's. Although Hutchinson's system attracted some support, it was not generally adopted, partly because other botanists did not accept his idea of an early and fundamental evolutionary dichotomy between woody and herbaceous dicotyledons.

During the past several decades a number of new partial or complete systems following essentially Besseyan principles have been presented by different authors, and the climate of professional opinion favours one or another such variant. Perhaps the most influential of these newer systems have been those of Armen Takhtajan (as exemplified by his books of 1966 and 1987) and Arthur Cronquist (1968, 1981, 1988), whose systems have much in common. (A.Cr./Ed.)

CLASS MAGNOLIOPSIDA: THE DICOTYLEDONS

The division Magnoliophyta, or angiosperms, is composed of the classes Magnoliopsida (dicotyledons, or dicots) and Liliopsida (monocotyledons, or monocots). Magnoliopsida is the larger of the two, containing approximately 175,000 species, although this number will surely increase as exploration of the biodiversity within the tropics continues into the 21st century.

Similarities with monocots

The similarities between the dicots and the monocots are far greater than their differences. In fact, there is no single character that separates all monocots from all dicots. The most consistent character is the number of cotyledons; however, one cotyledon does not a monocot make. Some dicots, such as the lotus (*Nelumbo* of the family Nelumbonaceae) have only a single cotyledon as the result of the fusion of the cotyledons. Other dicots, such as those of the mustard family Brassicaceae, may have only a single cotyledon after one of the two original cotyledons aborts. Since all other characteristics of the families mentioned above are dicotyledonous, they are so classified.

The dicots have net-veined leaves, while monocots generally have leaves with parallel veins. Some monocots have net-veined leaves, but this pattern is derived from cross-connections between parallel veins just as the parallel veins of some dicots are derived from net-veined patterns that have been reduced as the plant matures.

Other characteristics of dicots are a taproot and/or adventitious root systems and tricolpate or tricolpate-derived pollen. Also characteristic of the dicots is the arrangement of the vascular tissue within the primary and secondary plant body. In dicots the vascular tissue is segregated into discrete bundles of xylem and phloem, which are usually arranged in a ring around a central pith, whereas in monocots the vascular bundles (also containing bundles of xylem and phloem) are scattered throughout the parenchyma and a pith does not characteristically develop. The most obvious feature of dicots, however, is the growth pattern of secondary tissue, often called wood, which distinguishes the generally woody dicots from the generally herbaceous monocots. The dicots usually develop a vascular cambium between the primary xylem and phloem, from which secondary vascular tissues (wood) develops. In monocots, however, secondary growth, when it occurs, usually results from thickenings of the meristematic tissues rather than from the primary vascular tissues.

Exceptions to these basic characteristics are usually just that—exceptions to one character in a particular species, genus, or family. Most exceptions that do occur are monocot characteristics showing up in members of the dicots. The reason for this is that the monocots are related to a common ancestor within the dicots, probably within the order Nymphaeales. (D.W.St.)

Subclass Magnoliidae

Members of the subclass Magnoliidae are dicotyledonous plants that retain some primitive anatomic and morphological characteristics and are not closely related to more advanced groups of flowering plants. Although the subclass contains the most primitive families of flowering plants, no plant in this group is considered to be the most primitive angiosperm because none is most primitive in all its features. The fossil record suggests that the primitive woody Magnoliidae shared characteristics from which all other flowering plants evolved. Magnoliidae also contain the most primitive herbaceous angiosperms—the water lilies (Nymphaeales) and buttercups and their relatives (Ranunculales).

Orders of the Magnoliidae

There are 8 orders, 39 families, and approximately 12,000 species within the subclass Magnoliidae. The orders, arranged more or less from the most primitive to the most advanced, are Magnoliales, Laurales, Piperales, Aristolochiales, Illiciales, Nymphaeales, Ranunculales, and Papaverales. Such a linear sequence of orders does not imply, however, that one order has necessarily evolved from certain members of the preceding one. For example, although it is commonly considered that the Papaverales have been derived from the Ranunculales, it is also thought that the Laurales, Piperales, and Nymphaeales evolved independently from different members of the Magnoliales. The largest orders, the Magnoliales, Laurales, and Ranunculales, together contain more than two-thirds of the species in the subclass.

GENERAL FEATURES

Diversity of structure. The Magnoliidae illustrate much of the diversity that characterizes the dicotyledonous plants as a whole. Evergreen and deciduous trees and shrubs are found in the Magnoliidae, as are perennial herbs and a few annual herbs. Trees, shrubs, and vines are characteristic of Magnoliales, Laurales, Illiciales, and Ranunculales; the latter also contains herbs. Aristolochiales contains only woody vines; Nymphaeales, only aquatic herbs; and Papaverales, only herbs and soft-wooded shrubs. Piperales contains trees, shrubs, and herbs.

Primitive features

Most Magnoliidae have features of a relatively archaic nature: in the flowers, the usually unfused carpels are surrounded by either many petals or none at all; the numerous, sometimes leaf-shaped, stamens release two-celled pollen that often contain only a single aperture; the ovules are surrounded by two integuments; and the mature seeds usually contain a small embryo and usually copious endosperm. Biochemically, Magnoliidae are characterized by the presence of benzylisoquinoline or aporphine alkaloids, which are secondary metabolites with a defensive function and are rare in other groups. Only rarely do the Magnoliidae produce tanniferous substances, and betalains, iridoid compounds, or mustard oils are not evident. These different classes of defensive agents do, however, occur in some other groups.

Distribution. The subclass Magnoliidae has members throughout the world, especially in tropical, subtropical, and temperate areas. This is true of Annonaceae, Myristicaeae, and Magnoliaceae, three of the largest families in the order Magnoliales. A few species are found in Australia, New Guinea, and Fiji. Winteraceae (Magnoliales) is principally found in the southwestern Pacific, including New Guinea, New Caledonia, and Australia. A few species occur in Central and South America. Piperales and Aristolochiales occur almost exclusively in the tropical and temperate areas of the world, as does Laurales, which can be found in Australia and the subtropics as well. Some families of Nymphaeales are cosmopolitan, but many are generally found only in Asia. Ranunculales inhabits north temperate, tropical, and temperate areas, including South America and Southeast Asia. Papaverales thrives in temperate regions of the Northern Hemisphere, South Africa, and Australia. Illiciales is predominant in Southeast Asia, the southeastern United States, and the Caribbean.

NATURAL HISTORY

Reproduction and life cycles. The reproduction and life cycles of the more primitive extant members of the Magnoliidae reflect stages in the life histories of the early angiosperms that cannot be found in the fossil record. The more primitive families of the subclass also exhibit some of the basic, primitive features of the angiosperms as a whole.

Pollen development

There are usually two pairs of microspore- (pollen-) producing sacs in an immature, developing stamen, each divided by a partition to make four compartments. The stamens of the most primitive Magnoliidae have four pollen sacs, although some genera of a few families have only two pollen sacs as a derived condition. The tapetum, the nutritive layer of cells that lines the inner wall of the pollen sac, is of the secretory, or glandular, type in the Magnoliales and other primitive members of the Magnoliidae (see above *Reproductive structures*). The tapetal cells remain intact but become absorbed as they supply nutrients to the developing pollen grains. An amoeboid tapetum, on the other hand, breaks down early, and the contents of the cell (protoplasm) extrude between the young pollen grains, providing a more efficient way of nourishing them. This type of tapetum has been found in the Lauraceae (Laurales), where both types of tapetum occur, and in Ceratophyllaceae (Nymphaeales).

In the more primitive angiosperms, and in all Magnoliidae, pollen grains are released in the two-celled condition (one tube cell, which expands to form the pollen tube at germination, and one generative cell, which divides to form two sperm cells); in advanced subclasses of flowering plants, they are released in a three-celled condition (one tube cell and two sperm cells), because sperm cells are formed before the pollen is released. An exception of sorts occurs in *Laurelia* (Monimiaceae) and *Beilschmiedia* (Lauraceae) of the Magnoliidae order Laurales; in some of these, pollen grains are two-celled; in others, they are three-celled; and in still others, the sperm cells are in the process of forming as the pollen is liberated.

In the most primitive Magnoliidae, three of the four megaspores formed from the megakaryocyte (megaspore mother cell) degenerate. A female gametophyte of eight nuclei, including the ovum (egg), develops from the surviving megaspore (see above *Reproduction*). About 70 percent of angiosperms have this type of female gametophyte development. With few exceptions in the subclass, two integuments form the seed coat of the ovule. In some plants of more advanced subclasses, a single integument is found (*e.g.,* Asteridae). The few exceptions in the subclass occur in some more advanced herbaceous genera of Nymphaeales, Ranunculales, and parasitic genera of Aristolochiales. The single-integument condition has evolved separately several times in flowering plants, and therefore families in which it occurs are not necessarily closely related.

Inverted ovules

In Magnoliidae, the ovules are inverted, so that the opening in the ovule through which the pollen tube enters (the micropyle) remains alongside the stalk (funiculus, or funicle) that attaches the ovule to the ovary. This contrasts with the gymnosperms and some advanced groups of angiosperms, where the ovule does not bend back upon itself, but rather remains erect, with the micropyle at one end and the funiculus at the other.

The endosperm is a copious embryonic nutritive tissue that occupies much of the mature seed in more primitive angiospermous plants. It provides nourishment for the developing embryo and forms with the embryo during double fertilization, a reproductive process unique to angiosperms.

The more primitive Magnoliidae have a cellular type of endosperm. In the nuclear type of endosperm, repeated nuclear divisions take place before cell wall formation. Nuclear endosperm occurs in the Myristicaceae (Magnoliales); Ranunculaceae, Berberidaceae, Menispermaceae, and Coriariaceae (Ranunculales); and Papaveraceae and Fumariaceae (Papaverales). Both cellular and nuclear endosperm have been found among the Lauraceae (Laurales), Piperaceae (Piperales), and Nymphaeaceae (Nymphaeales), lending support to the theory that one type has evolved from the other, and vice versa, many times.

The seed of a primitive angiosperm, such as Winteraceae and Degeneriaceae (Magnoliales), contains a minute, relatively undifferentiated embryo, which occupies only a small part of the seed at maturity. Such plants are at a disadvantage. Because the embryos are so extremely small at the time that the seeds are shed, considerable time is lost while the embryo develops further—*i.e.,* before the actual rupture of the seed coat occurs and a seedling can arise. Also in these primitive plants, the pattern of embryo development is rather irregular and inconsistent—*e.g.,* in *Degeneria vitiensis, Drimys winteri.* In some of the more advanced Magnoliidae, as, for example, *Cinnamomum* of the Lauraceae (Laurales), the seeds contain large embryos and little or no endosperm. These angiosperms also have an established pattern of development from an early stage. This means that one can predict not only which cell or cells of a young embryo will be the next to divide, but also what their plane of division will be. In all but a few of the primitive Magnoliidae groups, embryo development has a set pattern and follows one or the other of the types described for flowering plants in general.

Cotyledon number

It has been argued that the hypothetical primitive dicotyledonous plant had three or four, rather than two, cotyledons. One of the most primitive angiosperm orders, Magnoliales, has members in which the embryos contain three or four (very rarely two) cotyledons, such as *Degeneria* (Degeneriaceae). *Idiospermum* (Idiospermaceae) of the Laurales has three or four cotyledons as well. On the other hand, embryos in some of the more advanced angiosperms also contain more than two cotyledons—*e.g.,* Pittosporaceae (Rosales; Rosidae), in which it seems certain that the polycotyledonous condition evolved from the dicotyledonous one, because the more primitive relatives of these plants have two cotyledons. Whether angiosperms first had three or four, rather than two, cotyledons remains uncertain.

Germination

In the few primitive families of Magnoliales that have been investigated to this point (*e.g.,* Winteraceae and Eupomatiaceae), the cotyledons emerge from the seed and are elevated above the surface (epigeal development), where they become green and capable of photosynthetic activity. In an alternate form of seed development, hypogeal germination, the cotyledons remain inside the seed coat. This also occurs within the Magnoliidae, as in some Annonaceae (Magnoliales). There is an intermediate form of seed germination, as seen in some species of *Peperomia* (Piperaceae; Piperales), in which one cotyledon remains inside the seed and functions as an absorbing organ and the other becomes the first leaf of the seedling.

In some angiosperms, the fruits are dispersed whole with their included seeds; in others, the fruit opens to release the seeds. The most primitive angiosperm fruit is often said to be a follicle. This consists of a single carpel that opens along a ventral suture to release individual seeds. Although follicles are found in some primitive members of Magnoliidae, such as Magnoliaceae (Magnoliales), and occur in the early fossil history of flowering plants, many other types of fruit are seen in the subclass as well. Most Magnoliidae, however, have indehiscent fleshy fruits, predominantly berries, which are dispersed by birds.

Ecology and habitats. The Magnoliidae occupy a wide range of habitats and are found in most countries. They occur in most habitats where other flowering plants exist, except in salt water, where only a few specialized angiosperms can survive. The Magnoliidae include short, medium, and tall trees; shrubs, some in Alpine regions; scramblers, vines, and climbers—a few of which are root parasites; annual and perennial herbs; and rooted and free-floating freshwater plants. They occur in tropical, subtropical, and temperate forests from low to high altitudes; in shrub lands from sea level to Alpine regions; and on stream banks, grasslands, lakes, bogs, marshes, and mountain slopes. Some of the Papaveraceae thrive in deserts.

Endangered species

Some of the more primitive angiosperms are considered to be rare and endangered species. One of the most vulnerable is *Lactoris fernandeziana* (Lactoridaceae), a family distantly related to other families of the order Magnoliales. The plant grows on a single island, Nearer Land Island of the Juan Fernández Islands, 650 kilometres west of Chile. A tiny shrub, *Lactoris* is sparsely distributed in fog-swept forests and grows under the shade of shrubs and ferns. The principal mechanisms of extinction may be grazing animals and competition from hardier plants.

A relict genus may rely on a particular pollinator for its continued existence, the absence of which may mean the extinction of the dependent plant species. The Eupomatiaceae, another family quite isolated taxonomically from others, contains two species of *Eupomatia,* both of which occur in eastern Australia and one of which is also in New Guinea. *Eupomatia* species are pollinated by a single genus of beetles (*Elleschodes*); if the beetles become extinct, so probably will *Eupomatia.*

Winteraceae is generally considered to be the most primitive group of the flowering plants and is found farther back in the fossil record than any other known family. *Takhtajania* is unusual in the family in apparently having a flower with an ovary consisting of two fused carpels with peripheral ovules. There have been conflicting views on its nature. Full details may never be known, for *Takhtajania,* which is confined to Madagascar, is known only from a pressed and dried specimen.

The greatest number of species of Magnoliidae are native to tropical regions, and there probably remain many undescribed members of the subclass in that area. With the rapid clearing of tropical forest for agriculture, and with the populations of most tropical countries increasing steadily, many members of this group face extinction in the future.

FORM AND FUNCTION

Vegetative structures. The tracheid is the basic conducting element in the xylem of vascular plants. It is an elongated, water-conducting cell, dead at maturity and surrounded by a lignified secondary wall. The vesselless tracheids of gymnosperms permit relatively slow water movement, making these plants vulnerable to wilting when water transpires from leaves faster than it can be replaced from the roots. Thus, the greatest limitation on gymnosperms has been not in geographic range but on the habitats they can occupy and on the life forms they can exhibit. (Gymnosperms, for example, are not annuals, and they have adapted small leaves and thick cuticles as protection from desiccation.) Angiosperms, on the other hand, have evolved a vessel system from the tracheids, which has enabled them to occupy the widest possible range of habitats (see above *Structure and function*). The two characteristic conducting structures of the angiosperm tracheary elements are vessel members and the tracheids. Vessel members resemble the tracheids but have perforations usually confined to the end walls of the cell (tracheids have pits, which are thinner parts of the wall but not perforations, along the length of the cell). Several vessel members are joined end-to-end to form vessels, providing more efficient water conduction. Vessels do occur in one small group of gymnosperms, the Gnetophyta. This does not, however, imply a relationship with angiosperms, for the vessels of these gymnosperms evolved from a different type of tracheid.

Vessel system

Vessels have evolved only to the level of conductiveness required by a particular plant. Stages in their evolution are therefore preserved in extant plants, especially the primitive Magnoliidae. The most primitive vessel members, *e.g.,* in *Eupomatia* (Eupomatiaceae), resemble the tracheids from which they evolved, being long and narrow with long, sloping end walls. The only difference is that, in vessel members, perforations replace the membranes inside the many bordered pits, forming scalariform vessels with which to expedite the movement of water through the vessel member.

Fewer than 200 species of angiosperms have the primitive feature of vesselless wood. With two exceptions, all vesselless angiosperms occur in the Magnoliidae. The exceptions, *Trochodendron* (Trochodendraceae) and *Tetracentron* (Tetracentraceae), show definite links with the Magnoliidae, but are classified in the most primitive order of the subclass Hamamelidae. Of the Magnoliidae, all Winteraceae (Magnoliales), Amborellaceae (Laurales), and Nymphaeales lack vessels, although vessels are in the roots of *Nelumbo.* Magnoliidae with primitive vessels usually grow on deep shady sites close to water, where there is a minimum of water stress; an example of such is *Illicium* (Illiciales). (Water stress occurs when there is a considerable difference between the amount of water available to the plant via the roots and the amount of water lost from the plant at its leaves by evapotranspiration.)

As they evolved, vessel members became shorter, wider, and rounder. The many transverse slitlike perforations arranged one above the other like rungs in a ladder (scalariform perforation plates) in the long sloping end walls were gradually replaced by fewer, larger, rounder perforations in more transverse end walls, leading to transverse walls with a single large perforation (simple perforation plates). Such vessels are weaker. Large woody plants that possess them compensate by having many fibres or fibre-tracheids in their wood.

Only in angiosperms are sieve tubes and companion cells found in the phloem (see above *Tissue systems: Vascular tissue*). In other vascular plants, parenchyma cells function in the same way as companion cells (that is, as the sieve cell's living protoplasm), but they are not derived from the same mother cell as the sieve element. The sieve cells of gymnosperms and pteridophytes are less efficient conductors of food materials than the sieve-tube members of angiosperms, because they do not have enlarged sieve pores in their more sloping end walls. The only angiosperm to have parenchyma cells with the same function as companion cells is *Austrobaileya* (Austrobaileyaceae) in the order Magnoliales. *Austrobaileya* seems to retain a stage in the evolution of phloem in angiosperms, for a few companion cells have recently been found in its phloem as well.

A wide range of leaf types are found in the Magnoliidae, some resembling those of early fossils. The types of stomata also range widely, sometimes even within a single family (*e.g.,* Winteraceae). There is, however, no clear way to discern the primitive from the advanced types of stomata. Most Magnoliidae contain ethereal oil cells, commonly with isoquinoline alkaloids, in their leaves and often in other aerial parts as well. Such ethereal oil cells are not found in other subclasses. It has been suggested that they form a chemical defense mechanism against predators and pathogens.

Ethereal oil cells

Reproductive structures. The archetypal angiosperm flower may well have lacked sepals and petals, for some primitive Magnoliidae seem to lack sepals and petals (a perianth) or tepals. In *Eupomatia* (Magnoliales), for example, the young flower bud is covered by a floral leaf (bract) that drops off at the time of flowering, exposing a naked flower (with stamens and carpels). Although the flower appears to have petals, it is actually a false, or pseudo- , perianth because it lies between the stamens and carpels rather than surrounding these reproductive structures; the pseudoperianth is thought to have evolved from sterile stamens (staminodes). It releases odours that attract beetle pollinators and is partially eaten by them. *Trimenia* has what appears to be a stage in the derivation of a perianth from bracts. Bracts cover the whole flower stalk (pedicel) and invest the flower bud. Those bracts closest to the flower appear to more closely resemble the petals and sepals in shape and arrangement, and all are shed at the time of flowering. Some primitive Magnoliidae have a dull perianth, while others, such as *Magnolia*, have a showy petallike one; in woody Magnoliidae, however, there is never a clear differentiation into typical sepals and petals.

Early fossil flowers and the vast majority of Magnoliidae are bisexual, although the fossil record indicates that early flowers could revert to unisexuality. This has occurred in some primitive families. For example, unlike other Winteraceae, most species of *Tasmannia* have unisexual flowers. The flowers indicate their bisexual origins by the presence of sterile carpels in the centre of the male flowers. In the Magnoliidae, as in early fossil flowers, the number and arrangement of floral parts varies; in other subclasses these characteristics are more fixed. For example, members in each of the more than 350 genera and some of the more than 3,000 species in the family Brassicaceae (Dilleniidae) have the same number and arrangement of petals. Although it seems that the perianth has evolved from bracts in most Magnoliidae, some investigators believe that the petals of Nymphaeaceae (Nymphaeales), the water lilies, have evolved from sterile stamens. Possible evidence for this lies in the presence of petallike structures with tiny pollen sacs intermediate between stamens and petals in extant *Nymphaea* flowers and in the evolution of these petallike organs from staminodes (as in *Eupomatia*; Magnoliales), albeit inside the stamens. It also seems possible that outer staminodes differentiated into typical petals in the Ranunculaceae and in most advanced dicotyledons.

Possible primitive angiosperm ancestor

The discovery of *Degeneria* (Degeneriaceae) in Fiji in 1942 by the American botanists Irving W. Bailey, Albert C. Smith, and others renewed researchers' interest in the Ranunculales as the most primitive dicotyledonous plant group. *Degeneria* is an example of a vanulean angiosperm with primitive stamens and carpels. It has leaflike, three-veined stamens and carpels rather than the obvious filaments and anthers of more modern groups. A pair of pollen sacs embedded between the midvein and each lateral vein run most of its length. In the leaflike carpels, a row of ovules is embedded on either side of the midvein, and the carpel is folded in along the central axis, with the seams facing the centre of the flower (a conduplicate carpel). This primitive carpel has been found in a Cretaceous fossil and in some of the Winteraceae (Magnoliales). Conventional carpels—with stigma, style, and ovary—evolved in a number of families of Magnoliales, including the Magnoliaceae. Similarly there are members in the Magnoliales and Nymphaeales that exhibit leaflike stamens and stages in evolution of stamens from the leaflike, three-veined condition to the conventional single-veined stamens with anther and filament, even within a single family (*e.g.,* Nymphaeaceae; Nymphaeales). The number of carpels per flower varies considerably in the subclass. The carpels are not fused in almost all of the Magnoliales, Laurales, and Illiciales, but in some Piperales, Aristolochiales, Nymphaeales, and Ranunculales and in all Papaverales they are fused.

Pollen

Pollen structure is diverse within the Magnoliidae. Pollen with three elongated apertures equidistant from one another (tricolpate pollen) and related forms are dominant in the more advanced angiosperm subclasses but are almost absent in monocotyledons as well as in all but a few of the Magnoliidae. The most frequent pollen types found in Magnoliidae and in the earliest angiosperm fossil pollen are monosulcate (in which grains have a single elongated aperture), inaperturate (without apertures), polyforate (with many round apertures), and biaperturate pollen. These types are not fundamentally different, for *Trimenia* (Laurales) has pollen that is inaperturate, polyforate, or disulculate (a biaperturate type). Such forms would have evolved from one to another many times over.

There is increasing evidence that early flowers were pollinated by insects and that this was one of the early events that triggered the evolution of the flowering plants. Some insect groups were well-established before angiosperms evolved, especially beetles (Coleoptera) and flies (Diptera). The Hymenoptera (wasps and bees) appeared in the Triassic (245 to 208 million years ago), although it seems that they and Lepidoptera (butterflies and moths) only came into prominence near the end of the Cretaceous Period (144 to 66.4 million years ago). Pollination by beetles is found in many primitive Magnoliidae, including *Magnolia, Eupomatia, Calycanthus,* and possibly *Degeneria.* Pollination in various members of the Winteraceae is carried out by beetles, primitive moths, flies, thrips, and even caterpillars. Plants highly adapted for wind pollination, such as grasses (Poaceae), did not appear until later in the evolution of the angiosperms.

EVOLUTION

Oldest known fossils

The oldest definitive angiosperm fossils are from the Early Cretaceous (144 to 97.5 million years ago). The most abundant fossils are pollen grains (this is because the outer coat, or exine, contains sporopollenin, a chemical that is extremely resistant to decay). Leaves, wood, and well-preserved flowers also have been recovered from Early Cretaceous sediments. At one time, angiosperms were thought to have appeared suddenly ("explosively") and were so diverse in structure that it was theorized that they must have originated well before their earliest remains appeared in the fossil record. When the first definitive angiospermous pollen grains and leaves were discovered, however, they were in fact similar to each other and accounted for a small proportion of the fossil plant material. This would suggest that they had evolved from their ancestors not long before they first appeared as fossils. During the course of the Cretaceous (*i.e.,* over a span of 80 million years) many families emerged, and significant structural variations became evident.

The earliest definitive angiospermous pollen grain is known as *Clavatipollenites,* which recent studies suggest is probably most closely related to the order Laurales, although it shows some links to the Magnoliales. It first appeared in the rocks of the Barremian, or in those of the slightly earlier Hauterivian, of the Early Cretaceous, about 130 million years ago, and in such diverse regions as England, Australia, and the United States. *Clavatipollenites* was the oldest known pollen to show a typical angiosperm construction of the outer exine into a perforated tectum

From E.M. Gifford and A.S. Foster, *Morphology and Evolution of Vascular Plants*, 3rd ed. copyright © 1989 by W.H. Freeman and Company, reprinted with permission; after D.L. Dilcher and P.R. Crane, "*Archaeanthus*: An Early Angiosperm from the Cenomanian of the Western Interior of North America," *Annals of the Missouri Botanical Garden*, vol. 71 (1984), after Megan Rohn

Reconstruction of *Archaeanthus linnenbergeri*, a primitive plant with a magnolia-type flower from the mid-Cretaceous. (Left) A leafy shoot and terminal flower. (Right) A leafy twig bearing numerous conduplicate carpels.

(roof)—giving the surface of the grains a network (reticulate) appearance—columellae (pillars), and foot (floor). It had a single elongated aperture (monosulcate) and closely resembled the pollen of *Ascarina* (Chloranthaceae).

Other types of pollen appeared a little later in the Cretaceous, between 108.5 and 100.5 million years ago. Also appearing around this time were the oldest fossils of the Magnoliales so far discovered—pollen grains of the Winteraceae. Another monosulcate pollen type that arose early in the fossil record in some primitive Magnoliidae, including Degeneriaceae, Eupomatiaceae, and some Annonaceae, resembles that found in some gymnosperms, having a smooth unperforated surface and a more or less homogenous (structureless) exine. It is debatable which pollen type is more primitive (the tectate-columellate or homogenous type), but they are not fundamentally different from one another because both have been found within *Polyalthia* (Annonaceae).

There are evolutionary advantages in the tectate-columellate type of pollen. These grains more easily expand and contract with changes in humidity, contributing to the longevity of the pollen. Incompatibility proteins operate via two basic methods to promote cross-pollination. In the most common method the proteins, which are stored beneath the tectum in the pollen of many plants, are "recognized" by matching proteins produced in the stigma or styles; this mechanism prevents self-pollination and contributes to greater genetic diversity. Triaperturate pollen, found among the other dicotyledon classes, began to appear later.

Leaves as well as rather inconspicuous flowers also appeared during the Cretaceous. The first angiosperm leaves evolved contemporaneously with the tectate-columellate pollen described above. They had irregular, basically pinnate venation with a midrib and a secondary vein. Secondary and smaller tertiary veins were poorly defined. The leaves were small and of a simple elliptical or ovate shape. Leaves with features characteristic of Magnoliales also appeared during this time in rock strata of the eastern United States.

In 1990 Aptian deposits in Australia revealed a small fossil with very thin herbaceous stems, leaves, and female inflorescences. *Clavatipollenites* pollen was the only angiospermous type found in the same strata. This new fossil has been linked with several extant angiospermous families; its leaves resemble those of Sauruaceae, Piperaceae (Piperales), and Aristolochiaceae (Aristolochiales), and its reproductive organs resemble Chloranthaceae (Piperales). If the new fossil had also contained the *Clavatipollenites* pollen, further links with Chloranthaceae and Aristolochiaceae would have been suggested. An ancestor of such a plant, with a small, rhizomatous perennial form and diminutive reproductive organs, might represent the ancestral angiosperm from which the first monocotyledons and rhizomatous-herbaceous dicotyledons diverged. Furthermore, as the lack of pre-Albian fossil angiosperm wood might indicate, weedy dicotyledon shrubs, which had been considered ancestral to other angiosperms, may have evolved from a plant similar to this Australian fossil.

REPRESENTATIVE GROUPS

Magnoliales. *Distribution and abundance.* The order Magnoliales, which is generally regarded as including the most primitive angiosperms, contains 10 families, 181 genera, and about 3,050 species. All are woody shrubs, climbers, or trees. The families are Winteraceae, Degeneriaceae, Himantandraceae, Eupomatiaceae, Austrobaileyaceae, Magnoliaceae, Lactoridaceae, Annonaceae, Myristicaceae, and Canellaceae.

Largest family

The Annonaceae, or custard apple family, contains approximately 70 percent of the total genera (130) in the order and 75 percent of the species (2,300). The family Annonaceae includes the cherimoya, soursap, ylang-ylang, and lancewood. Members of the Annonaceae grow throughout the tropics. They are particularly characteristic of lowland evergreen forests in Asia and Africa. Five of the 130 genera contain more than one-third of the species; they are *Guatteria* (250 species), *Uvaria* (175 species), *Xylopia* (100–150 species), *Polyalthia* (150 species), and *Annona* (120 species). *Asimina* (the dog apple) reaches temperate regions, extending as far north as New York.

The next two largest families, Myristicaceae (the nutmeg family) and Magnoliaceae (the magnolia family), together account for less than 20 percent of the species in Magnoliales. Myristicaceae is a tropical family with members in Central America, the northern half of South America, Central Africa, Asia (including most of India, Japan, Indonesia, and the Philippines), New Guinea, and northern Queensland, Australia. The largest genus, *Myristica* (including *M. fragrans,* the source of nutmeg and mace), has about 100 species. Approximately 80 percent of the Magnoliaceae, or magnolia family, consists of nine genera distributed in temperate and tropical southeast Asia from the Himalayas to Japan, Malaysia, Indonesia, and New Guinea. Other species are found in the temperate southeastern United States, Central America, northern South America, and Brazil. The largest genera are *Magnolia* (80 species), *Talauma* (50 species), and *Michelia* (40 species). *Liriodendron* (2 species), the tulip tree, has one species in China and the other in the eastern United States. Such a bicentric dispersal reflects a more continuous distribution in the past. *Magnolia* is widely cultivated, though some species are found in the native state. The bull bay, *Magnolia grandiflora,* also known as the evergreen magnolia or laural bay, for example, grows in forests from southern Virginia to eastern Texas and extends into the West Indies. Another American species, *Magnolia ashei,* however, is found only in a few counties in Florida. One Japanese species, *Magnolia pseudokobus,* has disappeared from its native habitats, and by 1986 a single cultivated plant was the only one known.

The Winteraceae, the most ancient extant family of angiosperms so far discovered, has a rather scattered distribution. *Takhtajania,* a genus with a single species, occurs in Madagascar and may be extinct (see above *Ecology and*

From (stamens and carpels, carpel) A. Cronquist, *An Integrated System of Classification of Flowering Plants*, copyright © 1981 The New York Botanical Garden, Columbia University Press; (*Magnolia grandiflora*) L.H. Bailey, *Manual of Cultivated Plants* (1969), reprinted with permission of The Macmillan Pub. Co.; (others) drawn by M. Pahl

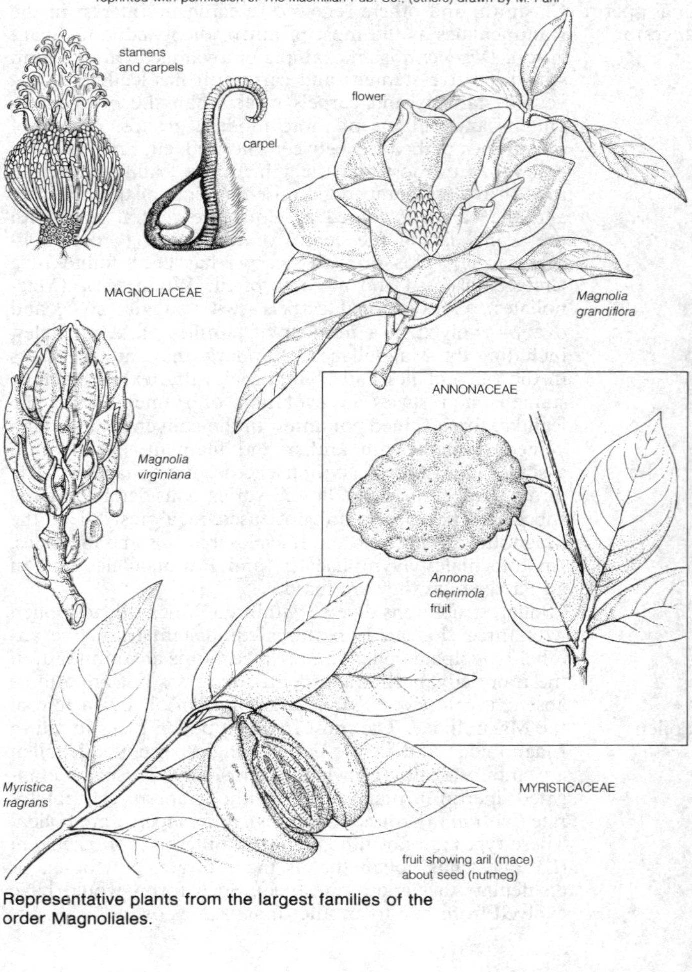

Representative plants from the largest families of the order Magnoliales.

habitats). *Drimys* occurs in Central and South America, from Mexico to Tierra del Fuego; one species is restricted to the Juan Fernández Islands off the coast of Chile and is one of the most common forest trees. *Tasmannia* extends from the Philippines to Australia (including Tasmania) and reaches its greatest diversity in New Guinea. *Zygogynum* and *Exospermum* are restricted to New Caledonia. *Bubbia* occurs from the Moluccas to New Caledonia and Australia, with one species confined to Lord Howe Island, where it is abundant. *Belliolum* occurs in New Caledonia and the Solomon Islands, and *Pseudowintera* is restricted to New Zealand.

The Canellaceae has one genus each in tropical Africa (*Warburgia*) and Madagascar (*Cinnamosma*), two genera in tropical South America (*Capsicodendron* and *Cinnamodendron*), and two in the Caribbean (*Canella* and *Pleodendron*). The Degeneriaceae (one genus) occurs in Fiji. *Degeneria vitiensis,* as the species name indicates, was found on Viti Levu, the largest island of the Fijian archipelago. It is a relatively common tree that occurs mostly in upland forests on steep slopes, and it has been used for timber. A second species, *Degeneria roseiflora,* was described in 1988 on different Fijian islands—namely, Vanua Levu and Taveuni. It is also a fairly common timber tree that differs from the first species in having magenta or pink flowers (as its name suggests), smaller fruits, and a different-coloured bark. The Himantandraceae contains one genus, *Galbulimima* (*Himantandra*), found in the Molucca Islands of Indonesia, Malaysia, New Guinea, and northeastern Australia.

Degeneria

The Eupomatiaceae consists of one genus, *Eupomatia,* with two species. *Eupomatia laurina* is a common rainforest shrub in New Guinea and Australia, from southern Australia along the eastern coast as far north as tropical Queensland. The other, *Eupomatia bennettii,* is much less common and is restricted to Australia, where it occurs near the coastal regions of northern New South Wales and Queensland. The Austrobaileyaceae consists of a single species, *Austrobaileya scandens. Austrobaileya* is a climbing vine found in some rain forests in Queensland, Australia. The Lactoridaceae (see above *Natural history*) consists of single species, *Lactoris fernandeziana,* which is found on a single island of the Juan Fernández group and may well become extinct in the near future. *Lactoris* pollen has been recovered in southern Africa from sediments dating back to the Late Cretaceous.

Economic and ecological importance. Most members of Winteraceae have little economic importance. *Drimys winteri* (variety, *chilensis*) is cultivated in many parts of the world in gardens and arboretums. A small, bushy tree in cultivation, it flowers for most of the year and has attractive white-petalled flowers about three centimetres in diameter. The bark was once used by sailors as a tonic and scurvy preventative; hence its common name of Winter's bark. It still has some use as an astringent and stimulant. The species name refers to Captain John Winter, who obtained specimens from the Straits of Magellan on Sir Francis Drake's voyage in 1578.

The leaves of many Winteraceae have a peppery taste, which discourages browsing animals. In parts of New Zealand, where introduced deer have had serious effects on the shrubs and young trees in native forests, the presence of *Pseudowintera* has increased because it is unpalatable to the deer.

No economic uses are known for Austrobaileyaceae. Both species of *Degeneria* (Degeneriaceae) have been milled for timber, which has been used in building construction and for furniture and veneer. They are too scattered, however, to be deliberately sought for timber. *Galbulimima* (Himantandraceae) wood has been used in Australia for cabinetmaking. The leaves and bark contain piperidine derivatives, which have narcotic and hallucinogenic effects. In Papua New Guinea, *Galbulimima* used in combination with the leaves of *Homalomena* (Araceae, Arecidae) causes violent intoxication, followed by sleep with visions and dreams. The wood of *Eupomatia laurina* (Eupomatiaceae) is used for furniture making in regions where it grows.

The American tulip tree, or tulip poplar, *Liriodendron tulipifera* (Magnoliaceae), the wood of which is sometimes called yellow poplar, reaches a height of 46 metres (150 feet) to a maximum height of 60 metres (198 feet) and a diameter at its base of 3 metres (10 feet). It is widely cultivated in many temperate regions. The durable timber, widely used in the United States, is light yellow to tan, with a creamy white margin of sapwood. Tulip tree wood is often used as weatherboard siding for houses, and large logs are suited for the manufacture of rotary-cut veneers for cabinetwork and millwork. The wood also has been used to a lesser extent in making paper.

Other genera of Magnoliaceae have been used for timber in regions where it grows naturally, including *Magnolia grandiflora* and *Michelia champaca,* the champac, or sapu. The wood of *M. grandiflora* was once used in the manufacture of venetian blinds because of its uniform texture, hardness, and ability to resist warping. It is in horticulture, however, that the Magnoliaceae are best known. *Magnolia* (magnolia) is a well-known genus of cultivated trees and shrubs, and *M. grandiflora* is one of the most popular garden varieties. The flowers, leaves, and fruit of *M. grandiflora,* also called the bull bay, evergreen magnolia, loblolly, laurel magnolia, or southern magnolia, create one of the most splendid ornamental trees in American forests. Large creamy-white flowers, 15–23 centimetres in diameter when fully open, are borne singly at the ends of branches and surrounded by persistent dark green, leathery leaves. Reddish fruits open to expose dangling scarlet seeds attached by thin threads. *M. grandiflora* can reach a height of 24–30 metres in its natural habitat, which consists of a strip about 161 kilometres (100 miles) wide from North Carolina through northern Florida, along the Gulf Coast to eastern Texas. It is cultivated in almost all temperate regions of the world and flowers five to seven years from planting. Another cultivated magnolia native to the United States is the cucumber tree, *M. acuminata,* which grows in open woods in the Appalachian region, Ozark Mountains, and Ohio and Mississippi river valleys. *M. acuminata* derives its popular name from its 5–7.5-centimetre-long fruit.

Magnolia

Many of the cultivated magnolias are hybrids. Probably the most widely cultivated of these is *Magnolia* × *soulangeana,* or saucer magnolia, a spreading deciduous shrub with leaves that measure up to 15–20 centimetres long. Its flowers appear in early spring before the leaves, and this flowering continues after the leaves have developed. The flowers are typically white at their tips, with dark pink staining the bases of the perianth. This hybrid was formed in 1820 by crossing *M. denudata* with *M. liliflora.* The cross took place by chance in the garden of a château belonging to Étienne Soulange-Bodin, founder of the National Horticultural Society of France. The stock soon flowered and was purchased by a British nursery that paid 500 guineas for it, a considerable sum in those days. The hybrid is tolerant of most soils and atmospheric pollution. There are now many forms of this hybrid, with flowers ranging from completely white to claret-purple. Another well-known hybrid is *Magnolia* × *veitchii,* which was formed by crossing *Magnolia campbellii* with *M. denudata.*

Another genus of the Magnoliaceae family that is widely cultivated in tropical regions is *Michelia.* Although the flowers are not as grandiose as those of the genus *Magnolia,* they more than make up for this deficiency by their abundance and extreme fragrance. They also differ from the flowers of *Magnolia* in that they develop in dense clusters in the axils of leaves, rather than singly at the ends of branches. The champac is supposedly native to India and Myanmar, but it has been in cultivation for so many centuries that its original natural range is difficult to determine. This tree is a handsome ornamental with evergreen leaves and profuse, highly scented yellow flowers that are the source of champak, an exotic East Indian perfume. In addition, the timber from this species has some local uses in making light furniture and plywood. The banana shrub (*Michelia figo,* sometimes known by the synonym *M. fuscata*) from southern China also is cultivated to some extent as a tropical ornamental with fragrant flowers.

Because the family Annonaceae is by far the largest in the Magnoliales order, it is not surprising that this group includes the most species that yield some type of economic product. The wood of many members of the Annonaceae is very pliable, and many of the edible fruits have commercial value. Lancewood (*Oxandra lanceolata*), from northern South America and the West Indies, is undoubtedly the most important commercial timber source in this family. The wood is yellow to olive-yellow, hard, heavy, and of fine texture, and has a very straight grain. These characteristics make the wood suitable for use in scientific instruments, turnery (objects shaped by lathe), tool handles, and such sporting goods as archery bows and fishing rods. Solera, or Colombian lancewood (*Guatteria boyacana*), has most of the same properties and uses but is not as well known in the timber trade. African whitewood (*Enantia chlorantha*), a yellowwood from Liberia, Côte d'Ivoire, and Cameroon, all in western Africa, produces a sulfurous yellow dye; the wood also is used locally to make unpainted furniture and veneers. Otu (*Cleistopholis patens*) yields a soft, light wood from western Africa that finds some of the same uses as balsa wood—*e.g.*, in buoys, life rafts, and floats. The fibrous inner bark is of some value for cordage and coarse netting.

Lancewood

Polyalthia longifolia is a tall, handsome tree with pendent linear leaves, which is cultivated in most parts of Sri Lanka and India as an avenue tree and around temples, where it has a religious significance. Although the wood is not very durable, it is utilized to some extent in making matches, boxes, and packing crates. Other woods of the Annonaceae family in India and Myanmar that have some commercial value are derived from the genera *Miliusa, Sageraea, Mitrephora, Saccopetalum,* and *Cyathocalyx.* Because of their tough and elastic qualities, these woods are utilized in the manufacture of tool handles, wheel spokes, and sporting goods.

The wood of *Xylopia aethiopica* is quite flexible and has some local use in west-central Africa for masts, boat paddles, and rudders. It has been described as termite-proof and, accordingly, is used for house posts and beams. The dried black fruits of this species are called guinea peppers and were once of commercial importance in Europe as a tangy condiment and drug.

The most widely known economic products of the Annonaceae family in the tropics are its edible fruits, especially the fruits of the genus *Annona* (the custard apple). One of the most important of these is the West Indian bullock's-heart (*Annona reticulata*), which is well adapted to hot climates, producing fruit only three years after planting. The common name is suggestive of the round to heart-shaped appearance and size (up to 12 centimetres in diameter and length) when ripe. When the fruit is ripe and the yellow-brown skin has begun to blacken, its white to cream-coloured pulp becomes sweet and aromatic and resembles ice cream when chilled. The sweetsop, or sugar apple (*Annona squamosa*), although native to northern South America, Central America, and the Caribbean region, is even more widely cultivated and highly esteemed in India and Pakistan. The conical fruits break into segments when ripe and expose a cream-coloured sweet pulp in which dark brown glossy seeds are embedded. Among the natives of the tropics the sugar apple tree is reputed to be of medical value. Tea made from the roots is highly purgative, while that made from the leaves is a mild laxative and is also considered to have a general tonic effect on the digestive tract. Poultices of the leaves are used in dressing infected wounds.

Tropical edible fruits

The cherimoya is the fruit of a rather small tree, *Annona cherimola,* which is native to the cool (but frost-free) mountain valleys of Peru. Although it is grown in southern Florida, it does not produce fruit well there because of the high humidity; it is currently commercially grown on a small scale in southern California. The fruits, however, are quite perishable and ferment readily. Like the sugar apple, it is now well-established in the Old World tropics. Although the fruit does not break into segments when ripe the way that of the sugar apple does, the flesh is of a more creamy consistency (it is thought to contain up to 18 percent sugar) and has fewer seeds. Under ideal conditions, the fruit may attain a large size, weighing up to 7 kilograms (16 pounds).

The soursop, or guanabana (*Annona muricata*), also is native to the American tropics; it probably originated in Brazil or the Antilles. In a commercial setting, it must be pollinated by hand. The fruit, the largest of the genus, weighs between 1.3 and 3.6 kilograms (3 to 8 pounds) and reaches 15 to 20 centimetres (6 to 8 inches) in length. It is tapering and heart-shaped, and the green skin is covered with spiny protuberances. The aromatic flesh, white and somewhat fibrous, is strained to make custards and ice cream; the acidulous juice is usually extracted to make a refreshing drink, which has been described as a combination of the flavours of strawberries, pineapples, and cinnamon. The fruit is approximately 12 percent sugar, mostly glucose, and is a good source of niacin, riboflavin, and vitamin C. The black seeds contain toxins that have a purported use locally as a repellent against parasites. The hybrid atemoya (*Annona squamosa* × *A. cherimola*), is a native of Central America and the Antilles (West Indies); reputedly the fruit contains the best features of both parents. Extracts of the root and leaves have a laxative effect, and poultices of the leaves are used to dress infected wounds. The alligator, or pond, apple (*A. glabra*) grows plentifully in the Florida Everglades and on the Florida Keys, where its fruits have been described as "edible but not very palatable." The tree's prime use in Florida is as a rootstock for *A. reticulata* and *A. squamosa* when the soil is deep and sandy.

Soursop

Other species of *Annona* that produce comparatively inferior fruit but are eaten locally include: *A. montana,* the mountain soursop (West Indies and South America); *A. longiflora* (Mexico); *A. paludosa* (Brazil); *A. testudinea* (Honduras); *A. nutans* (Paraguay); *A. senegalensis* (East and West Africa); and *A. diversifolia,* the ilama, which was first cultivated long ago by the Aztecs of Mexico.

Two species of *Rollinia* (*R. mucosa* and *R. pulchrinervis*) have edible fruits that reach 10 centimetres in length and bear some resemblance to those of the soursop, except that the spines are softer and more blunt. *R. mucosa* is a large tree native to the West Indies and northern South America, whereas *R. pulchrinervis* is restricted in the wild state to the Amazon River basin. Both species are referred to by the common name biriba, and both are widely cultivated, particularly throughout Brazil, for their delicious fruits.

Asimina triloba (the papaw, or pawpaw) of eastern North America produces edible fruits of various sizes, colours, and palatabilities. (*A. triloba* is not the common pawpaw, *Carica papaya,* or papaya, of the family Caricaceae, order Violales.) Two general types of papaw have been observed: large, yellow-fruited, highly flavoured, and early-ripening; and relatively small, white-fleshed, mild-flavoured, and late-ripening. A number of selected clones (groups of plants of identical genetic makeup that are vegetative divisions of one plant), propagated by grafting, are cultivated, principally in southern Pennsylvania, Ohio, Illinois, and Indiana (where the yellowish fruits are referred to as Indiana bananas). An alcoholic beverage may be made from the papaw.

Certain Asiatic species of *Polyalthia* (*P. cerasoides* and *P. korinti*), *Uvaria* (*U. burahol, U. dulcis,* and *U. heterophylla*), and *Artabotrys* produce edible fruit, as do African species of *Uvaria* (*U. chamae* and *U. globosa*).

The ylang-ylang tree (*Cananga odorata*) ranges from the tropical parts of eastern India through Malaysia to the Philippines. The name means "flower of flowers" because the yellowish green, bell-shaped flowers yield an exceedingly delicate and evanescent fragrance that is highly valued in the manufacture of perfumes. Ylang-ylang, or cananga, oil is derived by simple distillation from the petals of fully opened flowers. Although the tree blossoms throughout the year, the flowers picked in May or June yield the highest amounts of the cananga oil. Long known to the peoples of East Asia, this oil first reached Europe about 1864.

Ylang-ylang tree

In the upper Amazon region, Indian tribes use an extract from the tree *Unonopsis veneficiorum* to tip their poison blowgun darts and arrows; this substance is said to have the same paralyzing effect on humans and other animals as that caused by curare, which is obtained from the genus *Strychnos* of the Loganiaceae family (Gentianales).

Although many trees in the family Myristicaceae (nutmeg family) reach timber size, the wood is not of much value in world trade. Nevertheless, *Dialyanthera otoba* (otobo), *Iryanthera sagotiana* (marakaipo), and *Virola koschnyi* (banak) from tropical regions of South and Central America, *Pycnanthus kombo* and *Staudtia gabonensis* from West African countries, and Chuglum (*Myristica irya*) from the Andaman Islands in the Bay of Bengal find local use in the manufacture of furniture, millwork, flooring, and general carpentry.

By far the most important plant in this family is *Myristica fragrans,* a native of the Moluccas, or Spice Islands, in the Indonesian Archipelago but which is now grown in the tropics of both hemispheres. The seeds of *M. fragrans* are the source of nutmeg and mace. While these spices are still exported from Indonesia, the greatest production today is in the West Indies, principally the island of Grenada.

Nutmeg tree

The nutmeg tree (*Myristica fragrans*) is a handsome evergreen with dark leaves and reaches a height of 9 to 18 metres. The small, yellow, fleshy flowers are unisexual, and the plants producing them are dioecious—*i.e.,* the male and female flowers are produced on separate trees. The ripe fruits are golden yellow and resemble apricots or pears. As the fruits dry out, they split open, revealing the single shiny brown seed covered with a bright red fleshy structure called an aril. Inside the seeds are the kernels, which are the nutmegs of commerce; the aril is the source of mace. The pulverized seed finds much use for seasoning such food items as spiced fruits, sausages, pastries, puddings, and eggnog. Mace is one of the most delicately flavoured spices and is used in making baked goods, pickles, ketchups, and sauces. Nutmeg and mace contain myristicin, a substance poisonous in large amounts. Myristicin is described by some as a hallucinogen. Nutmeg butter is derived from the seeds and is used in ointments and in candles.

The family Canellaceae is of relatively little economic importance. The leaves and bark of the wild cinnamon (*Canella alba,* known sometimes by the synonym *C. winterana*) from the West Indies still have some use as a condiment and for medicinal purposes. The small trees of this species are cultivated to a limited extent in southern Florida, as ornamentals prized for their reddish purple flowers and blue-black berries.

The sole economic product from the Winteraceae family is Winter's bark from *Drimys winteri* of South America; it still finds some use as an astringent and a stimulant.

(J.E.Ca./F.B.S.)

Characteristic morphological features. Magnoliales are woody plants with simple (seldom lobed) leaves and ethereal oil cells in the parenchymatous tissues of the plant body. The ovary is usually placed above the base of the stamens in the flower (hypogynous) and the perianth is well developed. The pollen is typically uniaperturate (sometimes biaperturate or inaperturate), and the seeds have a small embryo and abundant endosperm.

Primitive features

All apparently primitive features of the angiosperms can be found in the Magnoliales. The Winteraceae are evergreen trees and shrubs with alternately arranged leaves and primitively vesselless wood (see above *Form and function*). To restrict transpiration, most species of Winteraceae grow in damp, shady habitats, and their stomata (restricted to the underside of the leaves) are partly obstructed by a somewhat porous, waxy material (cutin) that resembles a sponge under high magnification. Except in *Tasmannia,* the flowers are bisexual with a small cup of sepals fused to varying degrees, and spirally arranged, mostly white petals. One member, *Belliolum,* has leaflike stamens somewhat similar to *Degeneria* (see above *Form and function*). Except in *Belliolum,* the stamens have terminal pollen sacs and, except in a few species of *Zygogynum,* the distinctive pollen is in tetrads with reticulate sculpturing on the exposed surface. The carpels may be conduplicate (*Tasmannia*) or fused (*Zygogynum*), and most fruit of the family is indehiscent and berrylike.

The two plants in Degeneriaceae are large trees and share some features with Winteraceae (*e.g.,* conduplicate carpels). The many differences include the presence of primitive vessels (*Degeneria*), single pollen grains with an elongated aperture and a homogenous (structureless) exine, and sterile stamens (staminodes) between the fertile stamens and the central single carpel. The unusual kidney-shaped fruits of *Degeneria* measure up to 12 centimetres long; they split open along one side to reveal orange or red seeds embedded in a pulp. The seeds hang down from the open fruit and are dispersed by birds. The embryos have three or four cotyledons, a most unusual feature.

Himantandraceae consists of a single genus of large trees, *Galbulimima* (*Himantandra*). The vessels of the mature wood have simple perforations (a more advanced feature than in *Degeneria*). The alternate leaves have their lower surfaces covered with characteristic shield-shaped hairs. Flowers are usually solitary, as in *Degeneria,* and have two unusual leathery sepals that fall off when the flower opens. There are about 7 to 9 petals; the stamens resemble the petals in shape and texture and the 4 pollen sacs are restricted to the lowermost part of the stamen, an unusual feature. The 6–10 spirally arranged carpels, with 1 (or, rarely, 2) ovule, fuse to form a globe-shaped, fleshy fruit.

Members of Eupomatiaceae are shrubs to small trees. *Eupomatia laurina* reaches heights of up to 5 metres, but *E. bennettii* rarely exceeds 50 centimetres. It often has only one leafy shoot, which produces a single flower each year. The flowers lack a perianth but have petallike staminodes between the stamens and carpels. The stamens are short, with broad flat bases; the carpels are fused along the sides and are enclosed by a cup-shaped receptacle, so that only their receptive stigmatic apexes are exposed to the beetles that pollinate them. The carpels are a modified conduplicate type without a style. The pollen of both species is subspheroidal with a bandlike, encircling aperture around the middle of the grain. Each fruit is a globose berry consisting of the fused spirally arranged carpels.

Austrobaileya scandens (Austrobaileyaceae) is an evergreen, woody, rain-forest vine with opposite leaves and small deciduous stipules. The flowers have a greenish perianth, leaflike stamens, and from 6 to 14 unfused carpels, each containing 8 to 14 ovules arranged in two rows. A few carpels develop into large orange berries, up to eight centimetres long.

Unlike the other families of Magnoliales except Austrobaileyaceae, the Magnoliaceae have stipules. These are comparatively large and fall off when the leaf expands, leaving a characteristic scar. Some Magnoliaceae are evergreens; most are deciduous trees or shrubs. The tulip tree (*Liriodendron*) has lobed leaves, an unusual feature for Magnoliales. Flowers are mostly bisexual and showy, usually solitary, with a petallike perianth. Stamens are leaflike, numerous, and spirally arranged. Many spirally arranged free or partly fused carpels are attached to a conelike receptacle. Pollen grains have a single elongated aperture with an exine ranging from structureless to tectate-columellate. The fruit is composed of separate or united carpels, which in most genera split longitudinally to expose the seeds attached by silky threads.

Tulip tree

Lactoris (Lactoridaceae) has small stipulate, alternate leaves and bisexual or unisexual flowers. Flower parts differ from those of the families above in that they are arranged in threes: three sepals, no petals, four stamens, and three free carpels, each with four to eight ovules. Pollen grains, as in Winteraceae, are in permanent tetrads but have an elongated, poorly defined aperture. The fruit is a follicle.

In Annonaceae, the alternate leaves are without stipules and frequently have a characteristic metallic sheen. The fragrant, often pendulous flowers frequently open before all the parts are mature. Flower parts are mostly in threes, as in Annonaceae. Stamens usually have a short, stout filament and a connective that is expanded above the pollen sacs. Pollen is more varied than in any other family of Magnoliales. The fruits are berries, which may, as in custard apples (*Annona*), be fused to form aggregate fruits.

Myristicaceae have unisexual flowers that are usually situated on separate plants. Many trees have a distinctive growth pattern with whorled, almost horizontal, branches. The fruits of nutmeg, the best-known member of the family, are described above.

Members of the family Canellaceae have leathery alternate leaves, commonly with translucent spots. The flowers contain 3 sepals, 4 to 12 petals (either arranged in a spiral or a whorl), and 6 to 40 stamens, which are united into a tube, a characteristic feature for the family. The pollen has only a single aperture. Between 2 and 6 carpels are fused to form a single locule in which the ovules are attached to the inner surface of the locule wall (parietal placentation).

Evolution. Some features, found within the more primitive extant members, differ little from those detected in early fossils. Apparent evolutionary trends from primitive features to considerably more advanced ones occur within the Magnoliales. For example, the Winteraceae are entirely without vessels in their wood, the Eupomatiaceae illustrate a primitive type of vessel with scalariform perforation plates, the Annonaceae have vessels with simple perforations, and the Magnoliaceae have vessels with both scalariform and simple perforation plates. Large evolutionary trends are apparent even within a family. In the Winteraceae, for example, stamens range from the putatively primitive leaflike form (*Belliolum*) to more advanced forms having an elongated filament and terminal anther (*Tasmannia*). The Magnoliaceae exhibit trends in the evolution of a style and terminal stigma from the conduplicate carpel type. Pollen varies from those with a structureless exine to a more advanced tectate-columellate structure in the Magnoliaceae and Annonaceae; however, tricolpate pollen, characteristic of so many advanced groups of dicotyledons, is absent in the Magnoliales. Similarly, although there is a range of flower types and a range of pollinators, bird-pollinated flowers with inferior ovaries (those inserted below the base of the stamens), are absent in the Magnoliales. Magnoliales contains only trees, shrubs (both evergreen and deciduous), and a few woody vines. The only plant that resembles an herb is *Eupomatia bennettii,* although it is actually more a woody shrub that grows only as tall as 30 centimetres.

Evolutionary trends

The fossil record suggests that there are some extant plants which have changed little since their ancestors evolved in the Early Cretaceous, some 144 to 97.5 million years ago. Because of the comparative paucity of fossils, it is difficult, if not impossible, to gauge the rate of evolution of any feature in an angiosperm. In 1990, remarkably well-preserved fossil leaves of *Magnolia* were obtained in northern Idaho from Miocene fossil lake beds (those 5.3 to 23.7 million years old). Their exceptional preservation was attributed to the cold temperatures and low oxygen content of the water in which they were deposited. The leaf tissues were often bright green in colour, despite being about 20 million years old. The leaves and a few female parts of the flower of this fossil species, *Magnolia latahensis,* closely resembled those of several extant magnolias from the eastern United States, including *M. grandiflora* and *M. virginiana.* Deoxyribonucleic acid (DNA) testing of a chloroplast gene from the fossil leaves confirmed the similarity of the fossil to the extant magnolias.

Winteraceae, Degeneriaceae, Himantandraceae, Magnoliaceae, and Annonaceae are generally acknowledged to be reasonably closely related, though unmistakably distinct from one another. Canellaceae and Myristicaceae may be more closely related to the Annonaceae. The remaining families, Eupomatiaceae, Austrobaileaceae, and Lactoridaceae, are rather isolated.

Laurales. *Distribution and abundance.* The order Laurales contains 8 families, between 72 and 97 genera, and about 2,600 species. Like the Magnoliales, the Laurales are trees, shrubs, or woody vines. Most members are found in tropical or warm temperate climates and are especially abundant in regions with moist equable climates. The families in the Laurales are Amborellaceae, Trimeniaceae, Monimiaceae, Gomortegaceae, Calycanthaceae, Idiospermaceae, Lauraceae, and Hernandiaceae. Lauraceae and Monimiaceae together constitute most of the genera in this order.

The largest family, the laurel family, Lauraceae, contains 50 percent of the genera (approximately 45) and about 85 percent of the species (2,200) in the order, which are distributed throughout tropical and subtropical regions; principally Southeast Asia and tropical America, particularly Brazil. Some 66 percent of the species occur in only 6 genera: *Ocotea* has more than 400 species in trop-

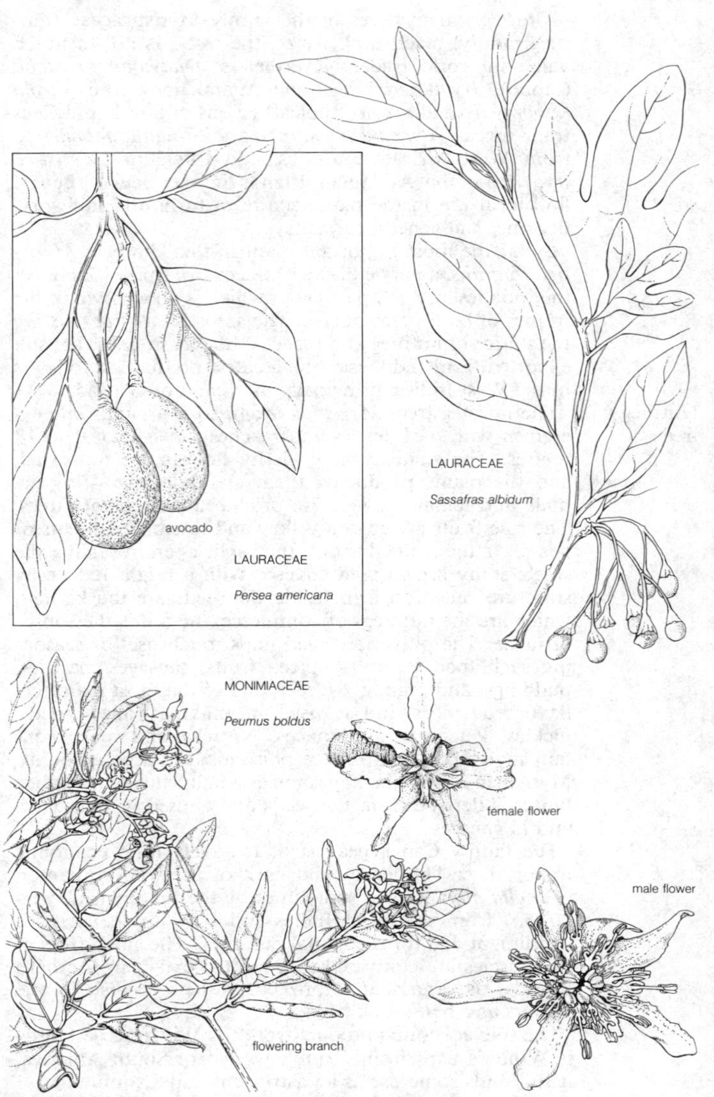

Representative plants from the two largest families of the order Laurales.

From (Monimiaceae), A. Cronquist, *An Integrated System of Classification of Flowering Plants* copyright © 1981, The New York Botanical Garden, Columbia University Press

ical America as well as South Africa and the Mascarene Islands; *Litsea* has more than 250 species distributed in Asia, Australasia, and America; *Persea* (avocado plant), *Cryptocarya,* and *Cinnamomum* (the source of camphor and the spice cinnamon) each contain about 200 species; *Persea* and *Cryptocarya* are found in many tropical regions, and *Cinnamomum* is distributed in Europe and Asia eastward to Australia; and *Beilschmiedia* contains 150 species throughout many tropical regions as well as Australia and New Zealand. *Cassytha,* a rootless vinelike stem parasite without proper leaves, is the most unusual member of the family. *Laurus* (laurel) consists of 2 species, one of which is the bay laurel (or bay tree, or sweet bay; *L. nobilis*), a native of the Mediterranean. The leaves of the bay laurel were once formed into laurel crowns by the ancient Greeks. *Sassafras* (sassafras), one of the few economically important genera of the family, has 2 species in eastern Asia and 1 in eastern North America.

Bay laurel

The second largest family, Monimiaceae, contains 36 percent of the genera (30–35) and 12 percent of the species (450) of Laurales. This family also is found in tropical and subtropical regions but is less extensively distributed and occurs mainly in the warmer areas of the Southern Hemisphere. The type genus, *Monimia,* is restricted to the Mascarene Islands. *Siparuna,* the largest genus in the family, with at least 150 species, is found from Mexico to Brazil, Bolivia, and Peru.

The remaining 6 families have fewer than 100 species in

total, with 3 families each containing a single species. The Hernandiaceae is a pantropical family of trees, shrubs, and some lianas. *Hernandia* consists of 24 species, distributed in Central America, the West Indies, Guiana, West Africa, Indo-Malaysia (a region comprising India, South China, and Southeast Asia), and the Pacific Islands. The Calycanthaceae (the strawberry shrub family) have a discontinuous distribution: *Calycanthus* (strawberry shrub, sweet shrub, or Carolina allspice) is found in California and in the southeastern United States, and *Chimonanthus* and *Sinocalycanthus* occur in China. Idiospermaceae is closely related to Calycanthaceae, and some authorities include *Idiospermum,* the sole genus, in that family. It occurs in Queensland, Australia, where it has a restricted distribution in several localities and has been classified as a vulnerable species, not presently endangered but at risk over a longer period. The Trimeniaceae is a small western Pacific family ranging from Indonesia in the west to New Guinea, the Solomon Islands, eastern Australia, New Caledonia and Fiji, Samoa, and the Marquesas Islands in the east. The Amborellaceae contains a single member, *Amborella trichopoda,* which is native to New Caledonia and has a scattered distribution through much of the central elevated part of the island. The Gomortegaceae (the queule family) also consists of a single species, *Gomortega keule* (*G. nitida*), which is a native of central Chile.

Applications

Economic and ecological importance. Various members of the family Monimiaceae are important locally for their timber and fruits and in making perfumes, medicine, and dyes. *Peumus boldus* (*Boldea fragrans*), a native of Chile, is the source of boldo wood, a hardwood used in cabinetmaking. A dye is obtained from its bark, and the leaves contain an essential oil and the alkaloid boldine, which are employed medicinally as a digestive aid and stimulant. A decoction of the bark of *Siparuna cujabana* from Brazil is used by local residents to induce sweating and as an abortifacient. The South American species *Laurelia sempervirens* (sometimes called *L. aromatica*) is known as Chile laurel or Peruvian nutmeg, and its seeds are ground up and used as a spice. *Laurelia novae-zelandiae* is used in New Zealand for boat building and furniture making. The wood is a light, hard wood that is difficult to split and dents, rather than breaks, upon impact. The bark contains an alkaloid, pukateine (after pukatea, the Maori name for the plant), which has strong pain-killing properties, similar to morphine. At one time the bark was boiled in water and used to treat ulcers, skin ailments (including boils and ulcers), toothache, and neuralgia. The leaves of *Doryphora sassafras* and *D. aromatica,* both known in eastern Australia as sassafras, produce a sarsaparilla-like odour when crushed. An essential oil containing safrole is distilled from the leaves and bark of *D. sassafras* and used in perfumery, and the fragrant wood is used in furniture making and woodturning.

Calycanthus floridus (Carolina allspice) and *Calycanthus occidentalis* (California allspice), both members of Calycanthaceae, are grown as ornamental shrubs valued for their sweetly fragrant summer flowers. The flowers of this family are remarkably adapted for pollination by beetles. The dark reddish brown flowers of *C. floridus* and the slightly paler flowers of *C. occidentalis* resemble a lobster pot in which the petals are aligned so that they permit easy entry but block the insect's escape. A beetle (*Colopterus truncatus* is the beetle that pollinates *C. occidentalis*) enters the flower and transfers pollen gathered from a flower it visited earlier to the stigma. After pollen is shed by the flower and lands on the beetle, the inner parts of the flower fold back and the beetle escapes. By this time the stigmas have withered, preventing further pollen germination and ensuring cross-pollination. The innermost parts of the perianth—the stamens and staminodes—have white granular food bodies at their tips on which the beetles feed. The aromatic bark of *C. floridus* is used as a spice (Carolina allspice). *Chimonanthus praecox* (*C. fragrans*), the wintersweet, is a cultivated deciduous shrub that flowers in winter before the leaves are produced. The light yellow flowers are popular for their spicy fragrance.

The Lauraceae is by far the most economically important family in the Laurales. *Persea americana,* known variously as the avocado, avocado pear, alligator pear, ahuacatl, or aguacate, is a highly nutritional fruit rich in proteins and fats and low in sugar. The total food value is high; it provides nearly twice the energy of an equivalent weight of meat as well as an abundance of several vitamins, such as A, B, C, D, and E. There are several wild species of *Persea* in Central America. Cultivated varieties were developed in Mexico and Guatemala by American Indians many thousands of years ago. (Seeds found in the caves of the Tehuacán Valley, south of Mexico City, have been determined to be nearly 10,000 years old and are cited as proof of the early use of the avocado fruit by humans.)

The avocado

Avocado trees are of medium size, generally not exceeding about 20 metres in height, with simple evergreen elliptical leaves 16 to 20 centimetres long. Mature fruits can be spherical and about 8 centimetres long or pear-shaped and up to 22 centimetres long. The fruit has a large central woody seed, typically the size of a hen's egg. There are a number of cultivars of avocados, each of which can be placed into one of three groups. "Mexican" species are hardy trees capable of withstanding cold weather to −6° C and poor growing conditions. "Guatemalan" species are a little less resistant, withstanding temperatures only to about −4.5° C, and produce large fruits with thick, rough skins. The "West Indian" species are the most susceptible of all to cold weather, succumbing to temperatures below −2° C; they produce large fruits with smooth, tough skins. Some species are picked when the fruits are beginning to soften; others, like the "Hass" and "Fuerte" cultivars, may ripen, but remain hard until picked.

The largest avocado plantations are in California and Florida, where a number of varieties have been developed. The United States produces about 10 percent of the world's supply of avocados. World consumption of the avocado increased substantially from 1960 to 1980, and by 1990 production reached approximately 1.46 million metric tons. A serious disease of avocado trees, caused by the fungus *Phytophthora cinnamomi,* affects trees grown in soils with a high degree of moisture. The fungus invades the vascular system of the roots, and, in most cases, the entire tree eventually dies.

Cinnamon and camphor

The leaves of the bay laurel of the Mediterranean are dried and used as a flavouring for cooking, particularly for meat and fish dishes. A fat extracted from the seeds is used to make soap. Cinnamon spice is derived from the inner bark of *Cinnamomum zeylanicum,* the cinnamon tree, a native of Sri Lanka and southern India. The bark is removed from two-year-old shoots during the monsoon season, as at that time the vascular cambium is actively growing and the bark can be removed more easily. Extraneous outer tissue is removed and the bark is dried to form quills or ground to make powder. Several thousand tons are produced annually, mostly from Sri Lanka, Madagascar, and the Seychelles. Cinnamon oil is distilled from bark chips and used to alleviate stomach upsets. Cinnamon was used by the ancient Egyptians during the embalming process. Eugenol, an oil distilled from the green leaves, is used as a substitute for clove oil, as an ingredient in some perfumes, and as a flavouring for sweets, foods, and toothpaste. Camphor is derived from *Cinnamomum camphora,* the camphor tree, of China, Taiwan, and Japan. It is obtained by steam distillation of wood chips. The wood of the camphor tree may contain up to 5 percent of the crude oil, and a single tree can yield up to three tons of the oil, which settles from the distillate and crystallizes. The oil can be redistilled to yield other compounds, notably safrole, which is used in perfumes and for flavourings (see below). Camphor was one of the raw materials used in making celluloid, which has now been replaced by other plastics. Camphor is employed in pharmaceuticals, especially in liniments and insecticides.

Many other species of *Cinnamomum* have uses as spices and medicines. *Cinnamomum cambodianum* bark is used to make joss sticks, which are burned as incense. Oil of sassafras is distilled from the bark enclosing the roots of *Sassafras albidum* (*S. officinale*), a plant native to Canada and the United States. The oil serves as a flavouring for sweets, medicines, toothpastes, root beer, and sarsaparilla, a drink derived from a genus of monocotyledonous plants,

Smilax (Liliidae). The plant is cultivated as a commercial source of safrole, which comprises 80 percent of the oil.

To say that the wood of all trees of Lauraceae is suitable for industrial purposes seems to be only a slight exaggeration. Most of the best-known timbers of Lauraceae are now depleted because they have been overexploited and are not likely to remain economically important in the future. Many species of the widespread genus *Ocotea* have been utilized for timber. Greenheart, *Ocotea rodiaei,* an olive-green to black wood from northern South America, is a very durable, strong, dense wood ideally suited to underwater applications, such as boats and wharf pilings. Bebeerine, a highly poisonous alkaloid produced as a secondary compound, has been extracted from several species of *Ocotea,* including greenheart. *Ocotea venenosa* is the source of a poison used for the tips of arrows by Brazilian natives. Because alkaloids are present in many woods of Lauraceae, timber workers who process them are susceptible to dermatitis and serious irritations of the respiratory tract.

Characteristic morphological features. Despite the great diversity of structure among families of the order, some structural features common to all distinguish the Laurales from other orders. Except for the twining, rootless stem parasite *Cassytha* (Lauraceae), all members of the Laurales order are woody and have ethereal (aromatic) oil cells with pollen grains having either two apertures or no apertures and a primitive nodal anatomy (arrangement of vascular bundles at the juncture of leaf and stem) of the type called unilacunar. Members of the Laurales characteristically have perigynous or epigynous flowers. (In perigynous flowers the "semi-inferior" ovary region is surrounded by the hypanthium (a cup-shaped extension of the receptacle), on the rim of which the perianth and stamens are inserted. In epigynous flowers the ovary is enclosed by the hypanthium and fused to it, and the perianth and stamens arise from the top of the hypanthium above the "inferior" ovary.) The stamens of many members have nectar-bearing appendages, and, in most species, the anthers split open when ripe by means of valves. The female structures usually have only a single carpel. Unlike the Magnoliales order, which has generally primitive leaflike carpels and stamens, most Laurales species have more specialized floral organs. The Laurales are closely related to the Magnoliales; in fact, several families, such as Austrobaileyaceae and Lactoridaceae, have been classified within this order by some authorities, rather than in the Magnoliales as in this article.

Perigynous and epigynous flowers

The sole member of the family Amborellaceae, considered the most primitive family in the order, is *Amborella trichopoda,* a plant endemic to New Caledonia. *Amborella trichopoda* is the only member of the order that lacks vessels. The separate male and female flowers are 5 millimetres (0.2 inch) or less in diameter and occur in small clusters in the axils of the leaves. They have 5 or 6 tepals enclosing 11 to 14 stamens or between 5 and 8 carpels. Both stamens and carpels are relatively primitive. The stamens are triangular and flattened and lack a filament. The stigma is attached directly to the top of the ovary (there is no intermediate, elongated style), and the single-seeded fruits that develop from each carpel are red at maturity and only 1 centimetre long and 3 millimetres wide. Unlike in most other members of Laurales and Magnoliales, ethereal oil cells are apparently absent.

Members of the family Trimeniaceae are trees (*Trimenia*) or vines (*Piptocalyx*) of tropical or subtropical rain forests. The leaves are simple and entire or toothed, and they are arranged in an opposite or subopposite manner. The flowers are bisexual or unisexual and exhibit what seems to be a stage in the evolution of a perianth from bracts (see above *Natural history; Reproductive structures*). There are many spirally arranged, broad stamens, and long filaments are not present. The bisexual and female flowers normally have a single styleless carpel (rarely two) consisting of an ovary and a terminal tuftlike dry stigma. Flowers are probably predominantly wind-pollinated, an unusual feature for the Laurales. The fruits are single-seeded berries.

The Monimiaceae is considered to be the family most critical to an understanding of the Laurales. Although it is not as large as the Lauraceae, members of each of the other families of Laurales reflect features found among the Monimiaceae. The Monimiaceae is rather heterogeneous.

The Monimiaceae

Members of the Monimiaceae are evergreen trees or shrubs, rarely rooted vines (lianas). The leaves are simple and oppositely arranged, with each pair at right angles to the previous pair (decussate). Ethereal oil cells are present. The flowers are unisexual or bisexual and are usually perigynous with a well-developed receptacle. The tepals are inconspicuous and rarely differentiated into sepals and petals. The stamens have two or four pollen sacs that open either by longitudinal slits or by the outward bending and lifting upward of oval flaps of tissue, hinged at the tip of each sac (valvular dehiscence). Paired ear-shaped appendages, often attached near the base of the short filaments, act as nectaries. The female flowers may have sterile stamens (staminodes) with attached nectaries to attract pollinators, although occasionally they have one or two functional stamens (*e.g., Laurelia*). Each carpel has a single ovule, and the outer carpels of female flowers are sometimes sterile. After fertilization, an enlarged perigynous receptacle may enclose the fruits; this false fruit splits open in some members and small feathery fruits are released and dispersed by the wind. Mature seeds of the Monimiaceae have copious endosperm and a smallish embryo, which sometimes has cotyledons with serrated margins.

Gomortega keule, the only member of the family Gomortegaceae, differs from other members of the Monimiaceae in having an inferior ovary and perfect (bisexual) flowers with only two or three carpels that are fused to form a compound ovary. As in many Monimiaceae, the pollen sacs of the stamens have valvular dehiscence.

The Calycanthaceae and Idiospermaceae differ from the families above in having seeds with a large embryo and little, if any, endosperm at maturity. These families have biaperturate pollen and pollen sacs opening by longitudinal slits. Each family has characteristic flower and fruit structure: the Calycanthaceae have 5 to 35 carpels per flower and an embryo with two cotyledons; the Idiospermaceae have 1 or 2 (rarely 3) carpels per flower and an embryo with 3 or 4 cotyledons.

The vast majority of species of Lauraceae differ from the other families of Laurales in possessing leaves that are alternately arranged, although a few have opposite or whorled leaves. They resemble the Calycanthaceae and Idiospermaceae in having a seed with a large embryo and no endosperm at maturity. Pollen of Lauraceae is inaperturate and surrounded by a reduced exine; it is, therefore, seldom found in the fossil record because it decays so readily. Leaves of Lauraceae are usually leathery and evergreen with numerous ethereal oil cavities, which accounts for the aromatic nature of many species. The generally small green, yellow, or white flowers are usually arranged in clusters, and the floral parts develop in multiples of three. The perianth is not differentiated into sepals and petals. There are between 3 and 12 stamens per flower, and the filament of each stamen often has paired nectariferous appendages attached near the base, as in many Monimiaceae. Stamens may have two (*Beilschmiedia*) or four (*Litsea*) pollen sacs, each with valvular flap dehiscence, again in common with various members of the Monimiaceae. Unlike the latter family, however, the flowers of Lauraceae have a single carpel. The single-seeded fruits are mostly fleshy berries or drupes.

Hernandiaceae shares a number of features with Lauraceae, including alternate leaves (which are sometimes lobed or palmately compound) and a single carpel per flower. Members of the family also have inaperturate pollen and develop stamens with valvular dehiscence and nectariferous appendages. Hernandiaceae differ in having an inferior ovary and indehiscent dry fruits (which are found in a very few Lauraceae).

Evolution. Although closely related to the Magnoliales, most of the Laurales are more advanced than the majority of Magnoliales in several respects. Floral evolution has advanced to perigyny in most members and even epigyny (inferior ovaries) and fused carpels in some. Instead of being predominantly uniaperturate, pollen is inaperturate or biaperturate. The number of ovules per carpel has been reduced; in fact, there is only a single functional ovule in many Laurales. The stamens are no longer leaflike, except in Amborellaceae, and many have the unusual feature of valvular dehiscence. In addition, many stamens have paired appendages near the base of the stamen filament, which function as nectaries in most plants. The morphological nature of these appendages has been debated: Did they arise de novo or is each the remains of a sterile stamen?

Pollination mechanisms

Pollination ecology in Laurales is similar to that in the Magnoliales. Insect pollination predominates, although there is evidence that wind pollination occurs in the Trimeniaceae and in some of the Monimiaceae. Bird pollination does not seem to take place. As in the Magnoliales, the form has not evolved beyond trees, shrubs, and vines. The anatomy of the wood ranges from being without vessels (*Amborella*) to having advanced vessels with simple perforation plates. The leaves of Laurales are almost all simple, sometimes toothed, but seldom lobed; compound leaves are rare. A feature common to all Laurales is unilacunar nodal anatomy; trilacunar or multilacunar nodal anatomy occurs in the Magnoliales. The two orders are so closely related that several families have been shifted from one order to the other by various authorities. The classification revised by Cronquist and reflected in this article appears to be gaining widespread acceptance.

Amborella, the sole member of the Amborellaceae, was once classified within the Monimiaceae. It is the most primitive member of Laurales, having vesselless wood, alternate leaves, hypogynous flowers, leaflike stamens dehiscing by longitudinal slits, and several carpels. Advanced members of the Laurales evolved from an archetype that shared these features with *Amborella.*

Ranunculales. *Distribution and abundance.* The order Ranunculales contains 8 families, 167 genera, and about 3,200 species. They range from annual and perennial herbs, to herbaceous or woody vines, to shrubs, and, in a very few cases, small trees. The families are Ranunculaceae, Circaeasteraceae, Berberidaceae, Sargentodoxaceae, Lardizabalaceae, Menispermaceae, Coriariaceae, and Sabiaceae. The Ranunculales are of considerable interest because they are abundant in most temperate areas, often forming a characteristic element of the floras. They also include many ornamentals, which are grown in gardens in many parts of the world. Several species are common and noxious weeds, particularly in Europe and North America; indeed, many species contain compounds (mainly alkaloids) that are poisonous to humans or to livestock. Some of these compounds are also important in folk medicine.

The buttercup family

The buttercup family, Ranunculaceae, contains more than half the species (2,000) and approximately a third of the genera (58) in the order. Members of the family are distributed throughout the world but are centred in temperate and cold regions of the Northern and Southern hemispheres. The largest genera are *Ranunculus* (ranunculus, buttercup, or crowfoot) and *Delphinium* (delphinium, or larkspur), each with about 250 genera. Ranunculus is cosmopolitan in distribution and found principally in cold temperate regions and tropical mountains; delphinium is found in northern temperate regions. Other large genera include *Clematis* (clematis, or traveler's joy), with about 230 species in temperate regions especially in the Northern Hemisphere and in tropical mountains of Africa; *Anemone* (anemone), with about 120 species cosmopolitan in distribution; and *Aconitum* (monkshood, or wolfsbane) with about 100 species distributed in northern temperate regions. *Thalictrum,* with 85 species in northern temperate regions, tropical America, tropical Africa, and South Africa, and *Aquilegia* (columbine) with about 70 species distributed in northern temperate regions, are also large.

The 15 genera and 570 species of the barberry family, Berberidaceae, are widespread, particularly the herbaceous species in northern temperate regions. Shrubby species extend south through the Andes in South America to Tierra del Fuego. *Berberis,* the barberry, with about 450 species, is the largest genus by far, and its distribution covers nearly the entire range of the family. *Mahonia,* another shrub, but thornless, was at one time included within *Berberis.* It consists of about 70 species found from the Himalayas to Japan and Sumatra and North and Central America. *Epimedium,* a genus of 21 species, many of which are cultivated, occurs in Europe, the Mediterranean, and Asia. The 3 species of *Vancouveria* and the 2 species of *Jeffersonia* are well-known ornamentals native to North America. *Jeffersonia* occurs in Asia as well. The single species of *Nandina,* the so-called heavenly bamboo, or sacred bamboo, is widely cultivated and is native to regions from India to Japan.

The family Circaeasteraceae consists of two genera, *Circaeaster* and *Kingdonia,* each with a single species. *Circaeaster* is distributed from the northwestern Himalayas to northwestern China and *Kingdonia* in northern and western China. The Sargentodoxaceae consists of a single plant, *Sargentodoxa cuneata,* which is a twining woody vine native to China, Laos, and Vietnam. Members of the Lardizabalaceae are woody vines or shrubs found from the Himalayas to Vietnam, southeastern China, Taiwan, Korea, and Japan. Two genera, *Boquila* and *Lardizabala,* occur in central Chile and appear to be more advanced morphologically than most other members of the family. They are climbing plants with male and female flowers on separate plants (dioecious). *Stauntonia,* with six species, is the largest member of the family. It, too, is a liana with separate male and female flowers, but these are borne on the same plant (monoecious). It grows in eastern Asia. One of the two species of *Akebia,* also a native of eastern Asia, *A. quinata,* is grown as a porch vine in the eastern United States. *Decaisnea,* considered the most primitive member of the family, is a shrub rather than a vine. The two species are native to Asia.

The moonseed family

The moonseed family, Menispermaceae, contains more genera (78) than any other family of Ranunculales. The family is widespread in tropical and subtropical countries, with only a few species in temperate regions. Most species are twining vines, but a few are shrubs, small trees, or herbs. The largest genera, with between 20 and 40 species each, are principally tropical, and include *Stephania, Tinospora, Abuta, Cyclea, Tiliacora,* and *Cissampelos.*

Coriariaceae comprises the single genus *Coriaria,* with about 15 species. *Coriaria* has a discontinuous distribution pattern, for it grows in the western Mediterranean, Asia, New Guinea, New Zealand, and some South Pacific islands, as well as in Central and South America.

The four genera of the family Sabiaceae occur in Southeast Asia, including Korea and Japan (*Sabia* and *Meliosma*), the Solomon Islands, and tropical regions of

From (*Ranunculus sceleratus, Aconitum napellus*) Baillon, Eichler, Firbas, Rassner, Troll, Warming and (*Podophyllum peltatum*) Eichler, A. Gray, Hegi, Maout et Decaisne, Schumann, Warburg, Warming, Wettstein in A. Engler, *Syllabus der Pflanzenfamilien II* (1964), Gebruder Borntraeger, Berlin; (others) G.H.M. Lawrence, *Taxonomy of Vascular Plants* (1969), The Macmillan Company

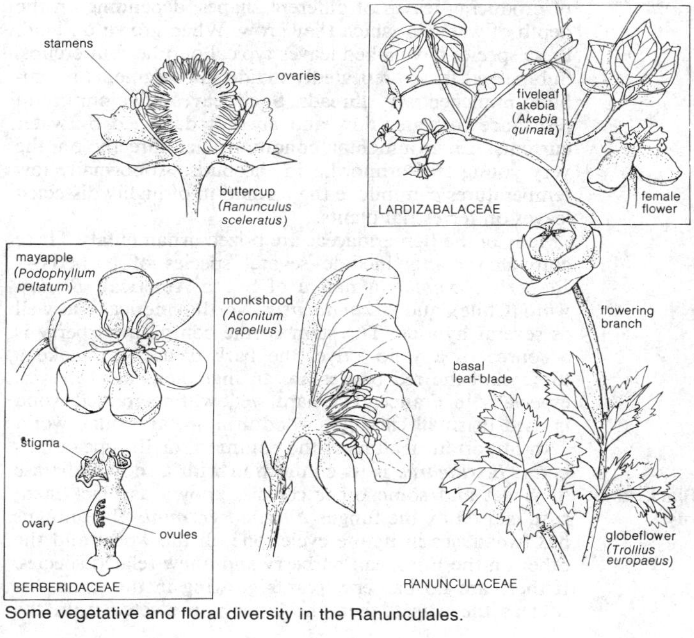

Some vegetative and floral diversity in the Ranunculales.

South America and Mexico (*Ophiocaryon*). The largest genus in the family is *Sabia,* with 19 species; the smallest is *Ophiocaryon.*

Economic and ecological importance. Among the many popular garden ornamentals in the family Ranunculaceae are the ranunculus; anemones; Christmas rose (or black hellebore, or winter rose; *Helleborus niger*); delphinium; love-in-a-mist (or devil-in-a-bush; *Nigella damascena*); clematis; monkshood; columbine; adonis (or pheasant's-eye; *Adonis*); globeflower (*Trollius*); and marsh marigold (or cowslip; *Caltha palustris*). Many members also have medicinal uses. A species of monkshood, *Aconitum napellus,* for instance, is the source of aconite, a drug used in treating heart conditions; an infusion of a distillate of the plant was once used to execute criminals. A number of deaths have occurred because monkshood tubers have been mistaken for Jerusalem artichokes (*Helianthus tuberosus,* or sunflower genus, a member of the family *Asteraceae*). Wolfsbane, *A. vulparia,* contains a number of alkaloids and is used as a narcotic in China. Black hellebore is helleborein, derived from the roots and underground stems (rhizomes) of the Christmas rose, are used as a drastic laxative and heart stimulant. The seeds and vegetative parts of several species of delphinium contain the alkaloid delphinine (delphine), which is employed as an insecticide. A tincture of baneberry, *Actaea spicata,* a native of temperate regions of Europe and Asia, has effects against pulmonary tuberculosis, muscular rheumatism, whooping cough, and angina pectoris. Black caraway, a seasoning used in foods, is obtained from the seeds of *Nigella sativa.* The marsh marigold, which occurs in North America, Europe, and temperate Asia, is edible: the flower buds, pickled in vinegar, are used as a substitute for capers, and the roots are eaten locally in Japan. The bleached stems and leaves of *Ranunculus ficaria,* commonly called the lesser celandine or pilewort, are occasionally used as a vegetable in Europe and the roots of *R. pallasii* are eaten by the Eskimo. One species, *R. sclereratus,* the blister buttercup (sometimes called the cursed crowfoot), is a native of temperate regions of Europe and received its common name because the juice of the plant causes blisters when rubbed on the skin. Some rare and endangered members of Ranunculaceae include 10 species of *Ranunculus* in Australia. One of the rarest members of the family, *Clematis marmoraria,* a small herb that occupies rock crevices, grows only near the rather inaccessible summits of two marble-topped mountains in an uninhabited part of New Zealand.

Aquatic species

The few aquatic species of *Ranunculus, R. aquatilis* in Europe and *R. flabellaris* in the United States, are among the most remarkable angiosperms from an ecological point of view. These aquatic species are capable of producing leaves of different shapes, depending on the depth of water in which they grow. When grown on land, these species have lobed leaves typical of other buttercups. Submerged leaves repeatedly divide into segments resembling branched wiry threads. Such leaves offer minimum resistance to water flow and are not damaged by water currents. Environmental conditions act directly on the very young leaf primordia in the buds. Abnormally low temperatures can induce the formation of highly dissected leaves on terrestrial plants.

Many of the Berberidaceae are prized ornamentals. These cultivated plants include several species of barberry—*Berberis buxifolia* (a native of South America), *B. darwinii* (Chile), and *B. canadensis* (North America)—as well as several hybrids. The stem of the common barberry is a source of a yellow dye, the bark is used to make a tonic, and the red berries are an ingredient in preserves, especially in France. The hard, yellow, fine-grained wood is used in small carvings, woodturnings, and inlay work.

An important feature of the common, or European barberry, *B. vulgaris,* is its connection with a serious disease of wheat and some other cereals, known as black stem rust, caused by the fungus *Puccinia graminis.* The fungus has two stages in its life cycle, one on the wheat and the other on the European barberry and a few related species. If there are no barberry plants growing in the same district as the wheat, then the latter is protected from the devastating effects of the fungus. In a single year the loss to wheat growers in Canada and the United States was eight million metric tons of grain. The disease was known as early as AD 100, when Pliny described it as the greatest pest of the crops. The association between barberry and the rust has been known for a long time, and in the mid-1700s the colony of Massachusetts passed a law stating that any barberry bushes in the colony must be destroyed. Plant pathologists have attempted to control the fungus by breeding wheat varieties that are resistant to the fungus, but mutation and genetic recombination readily produce new fungal strains that attack the new varieties of wheat. It is therefore important to eliminate barberry from wheat-growing areas. Under certain conditions, however, the life cycle of the fungus can be short-circuited without it being necessary for the barberry to be an intermediary. This occurs when wheat is growing in different places throughout the year—for example, when rust spores from winter wheat in the southwestern United States and Mexico drift north in the spring to reach crops in southern Manitoba, Can., and then drift to Alberta and finally south again at the end of summer to the winter wheat crops.

Black stem rust

Other popular cultivated plants of the Berberidaceae include several species of *Mahonia* and the heavenly bamboo, which is not, botanically, a bamboo, but a much-branched shrub from Japan. Deerfoot, or vanilla leaf, *Achlys triphylla,* a North American plant, is a popular ornamental as well.

A number of genera of the Berberidaceae have medicinal uses. The rhizomes of the *Podophyllum hexandrum* (*P. emodi*), a Himalayan species, and the mayapple, *P. peltatum,* a North American species, contain podophyllin, which is incorporated into some commercial laxatives for its drastic purgative and emetic properties. The Himalayan mayapple has been used as a medicine by the Hindus since ancient times. The American mayapple was used by the North American Indians to treat warts and is now employed in the treatment of testicular cancer. The dried rhizome of the squawroot, or papooseroot, *Caulophyllum thalictroides,* has been used as a diuretic. Extracts from the roots of *Leontice leontopetalum,* a native of Asia and the Middle East, have a variety of uses, as for example, in the treatment of leprosy, as an antidote to the effects of opium, and as a stain remover.

A decoction from the stems and roots of *Sargentodoxa cuneata* (Sargentodoxaceae) has been used as a treatment for rheumatism. Some of the edible fruits of Lardizabalaceae include *Akebia lobata,* the leaves of which are made into a tea by the Japanese; the young shoots, after bleaching, are woven into baskets. The fruits of *Lardizabala biternata* from South America and those of the East Asian staunton vine, *Stauntonia hexaphylla,* are sweet and juicy. All species of *Akebia* are deciduous, with separate male and female flowers on the same plant. The female flowers have a fragrant perfume, and the sausage-shaped fruits have a grayish violet skin and a white pulp. One of the most popular ornamentals in the genus is *Akebia quinata.* Some species of *Holboellia* have edible fruits, and several species of this woody Asian liana are cultivated.

The most important product from the family Menispermaceae is curare (tubocurarine chloride), which is obtained mostly from *Chondrodendron tomentosum,* a plant native to Brazil and Peru. The drug is used to treat certain neurological conditions and as a muscle relaxant during surgery; it has not yet been artificially produced. Some tribes of South American Indians taint their arrowtips with the curare poison. Picrotoxin, a poison present in the berries of the Southeast Asian fish berry, or cocculus, *Anamirta cocculus* (*A. paniculata*), can be used to stun fish, and the dried berries have some effect on internal parasites.

Curare

Several species of the tropical vine *Cissampelos* have medicinal applications. For example, in South America, a poultice made from *C. pareira* (*C. acuminata*) is an antidote for snakebite, and a decoction of the roots helps to reduce uterine bleeding and excessive menstrual flow. The plant contains the alkaloid bebeerine (pelosine). *C. capensis* is used by certain South African peoples to treat snakebite. Local farmers have utilized the leaves to make an emetic and laxative.

Most, perhaps all, species of *Coriaria,* the only member of the family Coriariaceae, are extremely poisonous, eliciting convulsions similar to those produced by strychnine. Tutin, a poison producing violent reactions, was isolated from a New Zealand species of *Coriaria* in 1901. Fruits of *Coriaria myrtifolia,* a plant native to the Mediterranean, contain corimyrtin, a convulsant in humans; the fruits are crushed in water to make a poison that kills flies. The leaves are rich in tannins and used for making ink and for curing leather. *Coriaria japonica,* a small shrub with attractive autumn leaf colours and red to black fruits, is grown as an ornamental.

Some members of Sabiaceae are cultivated, including several species of *Sabia* with attractive blue fruits and several species of *Meliosma.* The seeds of snakenut or snakeseed, *Ophiocaryon paradoxum,* have been imported from South America to Europe as a novelty under the name snakeseed, a reference to the coiled appearance of the embryo.

Characteristic morphological features. In contrast to the Magnoliales and Laurales, the Ranunculales lack ethereal oil cells, and the pollen either has three apertures or is derived from this type. Petals seem to have evolved from staminodes (sterile stamens), rather than bracts (floral leaves). The leaves are usually alternately arranged and lack stipules. The carpels are not fused in most Ranunculales. Seed are dispersed in various ways in the order, depending on the nature of the fruit. Fleshy fruits are eaten by animals (Berberidaceae), some fruits have spiny surfaces and are dispersed by adhering to the fur of animals (Ranunculaceae), and others show adaptations to wind dispersal (clematis). Most Ranunculales are herbaceous, and woody members of the order probably evolved from herbaceous ones. Alkaloids are generally present.

Seed dispersal

Most members of the buttercup family, Ranunculaceae, are herbs, some aquatic, but a few are low shrubs or vines (clematis). This large family, though considered a natural group, has been divided into subfamilies, the number of which varies from two to six in recent classifications.

The leaves in species of Ranunculaceae are generally arranged alternately (opposite in clematis), and most show net venation. There is considerable variation in leaf form, from simple leaves to lobed leaves, to much dissected leaves (especially in aquatic species). Many clematis species have leaves with twining petioles, forming tendrils used for climbing. In some clematis species, the entire leaf is modified into a tendril, and all photosynthesis is carried out by the green stems. The flowers are principally bisexual (rarely unisexual), with nonfleshy petals that often secrete nectar. The stamens are numerous and spirally arranged, and the pollen sacs open along longitudinal slits. There are normally at least two carpels—rarely, one—which are usually unfused. However, in some genera (*e.g., Nigella*) fusion of carpels occurs to varying degrees. Perennial herbaceous species usually persist over the winter by means of a rhizome or condensed rootstock, so that, with the death of the aerial shoots after flowering, a bud emerges from the rhizome or rootstock to give rise to the following year's shoots. Most members of the family are pollinated by insects, which visit them for their nectar or pollen. There are some wind-pollinated species. Although some species are self-pollinated, in many flowers the pollen is shed before the stigmas of the carpels are receptive to pollen (protandrous; *e.g., Delphinium ambiguum*), a mechanism favouring cross-pollination and outbreeding. Pollen grains have at least three apertures. The seeds contain well-developed endosperm. The mechanism of fruit and seed dispersal varies considerably; in clematis, the long, narrow, feathery fruits are highly adapted for wind dispersal.

Evolutionary features

The importance of the Ranunculales is related not only to its botanical and economic interest but to its evolutionary features as well: the group exhibits a series of structural features that might be construed as showing the origin of flower petals from sterile stamens. Almost the whole series is shown by the Ranunculaceae. The simplest stage in this series is embodied by genera such as anemone and *Pulsatilla,* in which the perianth consists of tepals; these are usually coloured and serve to attract insects. The stamens are numerous, and all are fertile. Many species of clematis are similar, but others have the outer stamens sterile and somewhat broader than the fertile inner ones. In the globeflower, the outer stamens are somewhat flattened and are sterile, the anther-bearing portion being represented by a nectar-secreting pit on the inner surface, near the base. These organs are coloured and very petallike, though the main insect-attracting organs are still the larger and brightly coloured sepals. In the genus *Ranunculus* the process is carried further, the sepals being small and usually greenish, whereas the nectar-secreting organs are larger and coloured and take on the main insect-attracting function. Like those of the globeflower, these organs each bear a nectar-secreting pit on the inner surface, near the base, often covered by a fold or flap of tissue. These organs, which are clearly homologous with sterilized stamens, occur in a close spiral between the sepals and the fertile stamens. They are generally few in number (usually five) and alternate in position with the sepals.

In columbines the petals are more or less tubular structures, with an expanded and flattened forward portion and backwardly projecting spurs, at the base of which nectar is secreted. The petals are only slightly larger than the sepals, and both series are coloured and serve to attract insects. In *Helleborus, Nigella,* and related genera, the petals are again tubular but much smaller than the usually coloured sepals. They are often of very elaborate construction and serve only to secrete nectar. In those genera with highly zygomorphic (irregular or bilaterally symmetrical) flowers, for example, *Aconitum, Consolida,* and *Delphinium,* the petals are much-modified nectar-secreting structures, often enclosed in and hidden by the large coloured sepals.

Thus, there is a series of elaboration of nectar-producing structures and petallike structures. It must be emphasized, however, that this series cannot be directly interpreted as showing an evolutionary lineage. What it does show, however, is various stages of a process of stamen sterilization and nectary and petal formation that may have taken place in the earliest angiosperms or in plants ancestral to the angiosperms.

Two members of Circaeasteraceae (*Circaeaster* and *Kingdonia*) differ from the Ranunculaceae in having leaves with dichotomous veins (in which a vein divides into two equal branches, which themselves divide into two equal branches, and so on). They differ also in having ovules that are straight (orthotropous) rather than curved and have one rather than two integuments. Both of these differences are advanced features. The flowers are reduced, without petals or petaloid nectaries.

The Berberidaceae also have many features in common with the Ranunculaceae. They differ in having flowers with a single carpel and fewer stamens (4–18, mostly 6) with pollen sacs that generally open by valves, which lift upward from the base. Leaves are simple or compound, but transformed into spines on the long shoots of *Berberis,* the barberry. There are several whorls of perianth parts, and the innermost whorl is usually more petallike and has nectaries. Pollen grains have a varied morphology.

Pollination in *Berberis* and *Mahonia*

In the Berberidaceae family (at least in the two shrubby genera *Berberis* and *Mahonia*) a mechanism involving sensitive stamens is employed to bring about pollination. Nectar is secreted in pits on the inner petals, and insects are attracted by the brightly coloured sepals and petals. Each of the six inner petals has two nectary pits near the base. The stamens are opposite these petals, the base of the filament lying above the line of junction of the two nectary pits. An insect visiting the flower to obtain nectar will necessarily touch the base of the filament. This area is sensitive to touch, and the stimulus causes the filament to spring rapidly into an erect position, thus depositing pollen on the body of the insect. The pollen may then be transferred to another flower by the insect, thus effecting cross-pollination.

Sargentodoxa cuneata, the only member of the Sargentodoxaceae, differs from the members of the three families of Ranunculales discussed above in having unisexual flowers and in being a twining woody vine bearing leaves made up of three leaflets. The small male and female flowers are on separate plants and are in drooping clusters. The male flowers have central sterile carpels and the female flowers have six staminodes, indicating their derivation from bisexual flowers. The fruits are single-seeded berries borne on a receptacle that is also fleshy and fruitlike. The Lardizabalaceae, which are allied to the Sargentodoxaceae, have fewer carpels—normally 3 in a single whorl but sometimes 6 to 15 in several whorls—and more than 1 ovule per carpel. Lardizabalaceae are woody vines with separate male and female flowers, except for *Decaisnea,* which is a shrub that contains bisexual flowers as well as unisexual flowers. The alternate leaves are compound (made up of leaflets), and the small flowers are in drooping bunches. There are six stamens on each male flower and their filaments are usually fused to form a hollow cylinder. They have short, pointed, sterile appendages above the pollen sacs. The carpels lack a style, and the stigma is inserted on the top of the ovary. *Akebia* has putatively primitive conduplicate carpels. Its fleshy fruits are either dehiscent (follicle type) or indehiscent berries. Pollen grains have three elongated apertures and the seeds have small embryos and abundant endosperm, both features shared with the Sargentodoxaceae.

The Menispermaceae are also twining woody vines or shrubs, although some are small trees, herbaceous vines, or perennial herbs. This family differs from the Sargentodoxaceae and Lardizabalaceae in having mostly simple leaves and drupes (fleshy fruits with a stony inner layer enclosing the seed) or nuts. The flowers are small and mostly unisexual, with parts arranged in whorls of three. There are two ovules per carpel, but one does not develop to maturity, so that single-seeded fruits are formed. The seeds contain large curved or coiled embryos.

The Coriariaceae differ from the six families already discussed in having opposite or whorled leaves and petals that enlarge and become fleshy at the fruit stage, forming a false fruit, enclosing up to five hard-walled indehiscent fruits. Moreover, the flower parts are in groups of 5, consisting of 5 sepals, 5 petals, 10 stamens in 2 whorls, and usually 5 carpels. The sole genus, *Coriaria,* is a shrub or perennial herb with elliptical to ovate leaves. Most have nitrogen-fixing bacteria in root nodules and can therefore grow well in nitrogen-deficient soils, as in some Alpine regions of New Zealand. *Coriaria arborea,* a native of New Zealand, is an extremely poisonous plant to humans and animals. In some parts of New Zealand, beekeeping has been prohibited by law where *Coriaria* is abundant because of outbreaks of honey poisoning. The bees do not visit flowers but collect "nectar" from branches, where it has been excreted by aphids that have fed on phloem sap.

The Sabiaceae are the only Ranunculales with a compound ovary of two, sometimes three, fused carpels and a nectary disc surrounding its base.

Evolution. In Ranunculales, one of the most advanced orders of the subclass Magnoliidae, the general evolutionary trend from woody to herbaceous plants appears to have been reversed. Although it is generally considered that herbaceous Ranunculales have evolved from woody ancestors, there is evidence that some of these herbs have undergone further evolutionary reversion to woody Ranunculales. Most of these woody plants possess broad medullary rays in their wood, which may indicate their herbaceous ancestry. The Ranunculales and Papaverales, another advanced order of Magnoliidae, have a preponderance of triaperturate pollen, an advanced type of pollen. Ethereal oil cells, which are so characteristic of the more primitive order, are absent in the Ranunculales and Papaverales.

Secondary reversion from herbaceous to woody plants

It has been suggested that the Ranunculales must have evolved from the Magnoliales through a group of woody plants that had triaperturate pollen, a condition fulfilled among the surviving groups only by the order Illiciales. The fossil record has not yet provided helpful information. The oldest (and only) fossil pollen referable to the Ranunculales is the *Ranunculus* type of pollen from the Early Miocene (23.7 to 16.6 million years ago).

Ranunculaceae is a large, diverse family considered to be the basal one in the order. The Circaeasteraceae could, arguably, be incorporated within it. There is general agreement that the Berberidaceae are closely related to the Ranunculaceae but are more advanced. The Sargentodoxaceae and Lardizabalaceae are thought to be closely related; the Sargentodoxaceae is more primitive in having numerous spirally arranged carpels but more advanced in having carpels with a single ovule. The Menispermaceae is probably also quite closely related to the families considered above; however, Coriariaceae and Sabiaceae diverge from these families. (F.B.S.)

Subclass Hamamelidae

The Hamamelidae is the smallest of the six subclasses in the class Magnoliopsida. Among its members are the witch hazel family (Hamamelidaceae), the hemp family (Cannabaceae), the nettle family (Urticaceae), the walnut family (Juglandaceae), the bayberry family (Myricaceae), the beech family (Fagaceae), and the birch family (Betulaceae).

Because of the presence of catkins, or aments, many members of the Hamamelidae, plus a number of unrelated families, were previously classified in an artificial group called the Amentiferae, or Amentaceae. The chief features of the members of the Amentiferae were staminate flowers, and frequently also pistillate flowers, in catkins, the sepals and petals reduced or absent, and a general trend toward wind pollination (anemophily). The taxa included in the Amentiferae varied with individual usage but often included the Piperaceae (Magnoliidae); the Saururaceae, Myricaceae, Juglandaceae, and Leitneriaceae (Hamamelidae); the Salicaceae (Dilleniidae); the Garryaceae, and Julianiaceae (Rosidae); and other groups. The amentiferous syndrome exhibited by these disparate families is now considered to have arisen through convergent evolution and thus does not indicate close relationships between the families.

The members of Hamamelidae are woody or herbaceous, usually with simple leaves, less often with the leaves pinnately or palmately compound. The stamens usually consist of well-defined filaments and anthers and are not thin and flat (laminar) as in some members of the Magnoliidae, the subclass containing the greatest number of species with features considered to be primitive within the angiosperms. The Hamamelidae produce tannins (proanthocyanins, ellagic acids, and gallic acids), presumably as a defense mechanism against the attack of insects and other pests, and rarely alkaloids. The flowers in the Hamamelidae are frequently very small, often unisexual and with the perianth reduced or absent, and are often borne in catkins. Wind pollination is common in the group. The seeds are never numerous and are not borne on parietal placentas.

Lack of consensus on classification of Hamamelidae

There is currently no consensus on the composition and classification of the subclass Hamamelidae. Based on various kinds of studies, especially on leaf architecture for example, some researchers are even of the opinion that the group has more than one origin (polyphyletic). Arthur Cronquist and Robert Thorne, two American botanists who have devoted much of their careers to interpreting the evolutionary history of the angiosperms, have developed systems of classification that take into account all available biological evidence. They disagree, however, in major ways on the contents and classification of the Hamamelidae. In Cronquist's scheme (which is followed in this article), which is basically the same as the system proposed by the Armenian botanist Armen Takhtajan, the Hamamelidae contain 11 orders (Casuarinales, Daphniphyllales, Didymelales, Eucommiales, Fagales, Hamamelidales, Juglandales, Leitneriales, Myricales, Trochodendrales, and Urticales). Within the Hamamelidae, Cronquist's Hamamelidales is basal to all other orders except the Trochodendrales, which appears to be a dead-end side branch that arose directly from the line leading from the ancestors of the subclass Hamamelidae to the present-day order Hamamelidales.

The approximately 3,400 species in about 26 families in the Hamamelidae are distributed unequally among 11 orders. The Urticales with roughly 2,200 to 2,300 species and the Fagales with about 1,100 species are by far the 2 largest orders. Within the remaining 9 orders are many small, isolated families that have only 1 or 2 species. Among these are the Tetracentraceae, Eucommiaceae,

Cercidiphyllaceae, and Leitneriaceae, all thought to be primitive and suggesting links to the most primitive group of flowering plants, the Magnoliidae. The Hamamelidae are thought by some to have arisen along with the Rosidae from among magnoliid ancestors during the later part of the Early Cretaceous (about 100 million years ago) and to have branched off and become fully distinct during the earliest part of the Late Cretaceous (97.5 to 66.4 million years ago).

Thorne's classification of the Hamamelidae differs considerably from the system proposed by Cronquist, not so much in that it treats the entire Angiospermae as a single class with two subclasses, the Dicotyledoneae and Monocotyledoneae, but in the placement and contents of the orders included in the Hamamelidae. At the level of classification equivalent to Cronquist's subclass, Thorne uses the category superorder, and it is within the superorder Rosanae that he places the orders Casuarinales, Fagales, Hamamelidales (including the Eucommiales and Trochodendrales), Pittosporales (including the Daphniphyllales and Didymelales), and Rosales. The Juglandales are placed in the superorder Juglandanae and the Urticales in the superorder Malvanae. A third system, proposed by the Swedish botanist Rolf Dahlgren, is similar to Thorne's in postulating close relationships between the Urticales, Malvales, and Euphorbiales.

Proponents of the systems of Cronquist and Thorne are about evenly divided. Making it even more difficult to arrive at a clear circumscription of the Hamamelidae is the fact that reasonable evidence, seemingly proving or disproving one point of view or the other, can be presented by either side. Until conclusive evidence becomes available to support the recognition of a single system of classification, it seems best to allow that each has merits.

GENERAL FEATURES

Diversity of structure. Members of the subclass Hamamelidae include small annual or perennial herbs, herbaceous or woody twining vines, weak-stemmed shrubs, and massive trees. Apart from the Urticales, however, all Hamamelidae orders are made up of trees or shrubs. Although a few families, such as the Fagaceae (beech family), Betulaceae (birch family), Moraceae (mulberry family), and Urticaceae (nettle family), contain hundreds of species, most families are small, frequently comprising only one or two species. The woody plants of most Hamamelidae retain many primitive features, and the subclass is believed to exhibit characteristics intermediate between the most primitive and most advanced groups of angiosperms, although they are not considered to represent a transitional stage between them.

Representative members

The Hamamelidae contain such familiar plants as the witch hazel (*Hamamelis virginiana*), fig (*Ficus*), breadfruit (*Artocarpus altilis*), mulberry (*Morus*), marijuana or hemp (*Cannabis sativa*), birch (*Betula*), elm (*Ulmus*), oak (*Quercus*), beech (*Fagus*), chestnut (*e.g., Castanea sativa*), plane tree (*Platanus*), alder (*Alnus*), hazelnut (*Corylus*), walnut (*Juglans*), hickory (*Carya*), nettle (*Urtica*), and a few ornamental house plants grown for their foliage, such as species of *Pilea* and *Elatostema.* The subclass is largely tropical and subtropical in distribution, but, with the exception of *Ficus,* the temperate species are the best known members.

Plants of the subclass Hamamelidae range from tiny annual herbs only a few centimetres (one or two inches) tall and occupying weedy or transitional habitats to massive trees with great buttressed trunks forming a conspicuous element in tropical rain forests. Within the Hamamelidae, only the Urticales contain herbaceous plants, and nearly all of these are restricted to the family Urticaceae.

The order Trochodendrales contains only two families, Tetracentraceae and Trochodendraceae, each with a single species, both of which are trees. These two families are considered to be the most primitive in the Hamamelidae. They show many characteristics of the subclass Magnoliidae, the most primitive subclass of angiosperms, especially in wood structure. The venation of the leaves of *Trochodendron,* considered to be the most primitive type in the Hamamelidae, also is similar to that in members of the Magnoliidae. However, features of the flowers, pollen, and particularly the seed coat have been used to place the two families in the Hamamelidae and may provide clues to the ancestry of the Hamamelidaceae. *Tetracentron sinense* (Tetracentraceae) is a large deciduous tree ranging from central and south-central China through the Himalayas to Nepal. *Trochodendron aralioides* (Trochodendraceae) is a small evergreen tree restricted to Japan, Korea, and Taiwan.

The five families of the order Hamamelidales contain woody shrubs or trees that range in size from small to large. The members of Hamamelidales apparently occupy an intermediate position between members of other subclasses with extreme types of floral organizations—for example, the primitive woody plants with large, petaled flowers (the magnolias, buttercups, saxifrages, and roses) and the plants without petaled flowers, such as the catkins found in the beeches, birches, alders, and oaks.

The katsura tree family Cercidiphyllaceae, now restricted to China and Japan, is abundantly represented in the fossil record from the extreme north in Canada, dating back to at least the Paleocene Epoch (66.4 to 57.8 million years ago).

Sycamores

Plane trees, or sycamores (*Platanus,* family Platanaceae), are often massive trees with a characteristic smooth bark that flakes off in large sheets or plates. With the death of many American chestnut trees from chestnut blight (a disease caused by the fungus *Endothia parasitica* and introduced into North America in the early 1900s), the sycamore is now the most massive, though not the tallest, tree in eastern North America. The carpels of *Platanus* are incompletely closed and are considered to be at a more primitive stage of development than those found in other members of the Hamamelidaceae. The wood, however, shows more advanced features. Although the leaves of *Platanus* resemble those of some of the maples and are rather uniform in having three to five lobes, *Platanus kerrii* of Vietnam and Laos differs dramatically in that their leaves are lance-shaped.

The Hamamelidaceae contain 26 genera, half of them with only a single species, and 6 other genera with only 2 species. Some of the genera contain species that are very large trees, but most contain only shrubs. The sweet gums, *Liquidambar,* often reach up to 45 metres in height. *Liquidambar styraciflua* is a dominant tree in wet woods in the eastern and southeastern United States and in Central America. The other four species in the genus reach similar or larger sizes in scattered localities in Asia from Taiwan to the Caucasus region but rarely occur in such large stands.

Liquidambar is one of about 120 genera of flowering plants in which very closely related species occur on opposite sides of the world, in this case in eastern Asia and eastern North America. Three species of *Liquidambar* are found in Asia, *L. formosana* and *L. acalycina* in China and *L. orientalis* in Turkey and Greece, but the latter two are morphologically more similar, and presumably also more closely related, to *L. styraciflua* of eastern North America and *L. macrophylla* of Mexico and Central America than they are to *L. formosana.* The members of the genus *Hamamelis* (witch hazel) also show this pattern of distribution; of the six species in the genus, two are in eastern and south central North America and Mexico and the others are in eastern Asia.

Factors in plant distribution

Distribution. The American botanist Asa Gray put forward a theory in the mid-1800s which suggested that the ancestors of such plants in the Hamamelidae migrated across the Bering Strait at a time when sea levels were lower. After fossils of many of these genera were also found in northern Canada and Greenland, it was postulated by the German botanist Adolf Engler that the members of this distribution pattern had once lived under fairly equitable climatic conditions in forests that circled the globe at high latitudes early in the Tertiary Period (66.4 to 1.6 million years ago). Plants now restricted to Asia and the southeastern United States are common in the high-latitude fossil record from the early Tertiary. Rising mountains in western North America eventually created extensive rain-shadows that eliminated many plants unable to adapt to increasingly dry conditions from the western part of the continent. Cooling of the global climate resulted in further migrations of the members of these forests southward and in the extinction of plants unable to migrate or adapt. This led to further restricted distribution ranges.

Recurring continental glaciations during the Pleistocene in Europe and North America were the final major climatic event that dramatically affected plant distributions. In North America, where mountain ranges run in a north-south direction, the Gulf of Mexico is the only barrier to southern migration. Many plants were able to survive in suitable habitats along the Gulf Coast well south of the glaciers, which reached their southernmost limits across the northern part of the United States. In Europe, plant migration in front of the advancing ice sheets was blocked by the tall mountain ranges that run in an east-west direction and by the Mediterranean Sea, both at fairly high latitudes. Many plant species were unable either to survive the deteriorating climate or to migrate southward. Pleistocene glaciation in Asia was much less severe. In China where the ice sheets did not span the continent, most glaciers were restricted to high mountains. In addition, the great extent of continuous, relatively unobstructed land surface at lower latitudes in Asia allowed plants to migrate much more easily in response to changing climates than was possible in either North America or Europe. Migration has continued to occur in response to climate-induced shifts in suitable habitats since the retreat of the ice sheets. The result is the widely separated occurrence of many closely related plants, including many in the Hamamelidae, in favourable habitats on opposite sides of the Earth.

The Myrothamnaceae contain two species, one on the African continent and the other on Madagascar. The species of Myrothamnaceae are remarkable in being among the most drought-resistant of all seed plants and ferns. The leaves fold like an oriental fan and become black and brittle during the dry season. The twigs and leaves can dry out and remain in that condition for several years without dying. Once rain falls, they revive and the leaves become green again. Although the family differs from the Hamamelidaceae in having opposite leaves, in its extreme xerophytic habit, and in other minor ways, it could perhaps still be placed in the Hamamelidaceae.

Daphniphyllales, Didymelales, and Eucommiales each contain only a single family and have features that suggest some association with one or more members of the subclass Rosidae. (P.K.E./D.E.Bo.)

The nettle order

Plants of the nettle order, Urticales, range from small herbaceous (nonwoody) species to large trees. The family Ulmaceae consists of shrubs and trees, including the elms (*Ulmus*) and hackberries (*Celtis*), some of which grow to 45 metres in height. A great diversity of mainly woody plants is found in the mulberry family (Moraceae), which contains about 800 species of figs. Figs are great trees of the tropical forests; some are buttressed by wide-ranging, and often finlike, spreading roots, as exemplified by *Ficus elastica,* the well-known India rubber tree. Many figs grow at first as epiphytes, or air plants, upon the branches of other trees, from seeds dropped by birds or bats. As these young plants develop, they send aerial roots along the trunk of the supporting host tree. Over time the ever-enlarging roots gradually crush the host to death. These are the so-called strangler figs, vinelike in youth but self-supporting large trees at maturity. The banyan (*F. benghalensis*) is another wide-spreading tree, an old specimen of which comes to resemble a dense grove of trees as thick prop roots are dropped from its spreading branches. Some of the tree species bear long, sharp thorns, and are employed as hedgerow or fencerow trees to enclose livestock or discourage trespassers (for example, *Maclura pomifera,* osage orange).

The nettle family (Urticaceae) is well known for its stinging hairs, which can cause severe pain on contact. Although the nettle family is most abundant in the tropics, where its species are shrubs and trees, the temperate regions of the Northern Hemisphere support large numbers of the herbaceous nettles, seldom more than a few metres tall and often resembling weeds. The hemp family (Cannabaceae) is also herbaceous: one genus, *Humulus lupulus* (hops), is a vine, and the other, *Cannabis sativa* (hemp), is a tall herb. (F.K.A.)

The family Barbeyaceae contains only a single species and is restricted to northeastern Africa and southeastern Arabia. Cronquist places it in the Urticales, while Thorne treats its taxonomic position as uncertain. The leaves of *Barbeya* bear a striking resemblance to the leaves of the olive tree, *Olea europaea,* in the certainly unrelated family Oleaceae (Scrophulariales; Asteridae).

The Leitneriales, another order with only a single family and a single species, corkwood (*Leitneria floridana*), are colonial shrubs restricted to the southern United States. Some authorities (and the classification used in this article) place the family in the Sapindales (Rosidae), others place it in the Rutales. The wood of *Leitneria,* at 208 kilograms per cubic metre (13 pounds per cubic foot), is the lightest of any plant native to the United States and is even lighter than cork. Although native to the southern United States, it thrives in cultivation as far north as the Canadian border.

The Juglandales, Myricales, and Fagales are about as often associated with the Hamamelidae as they are with the Anacardiaceae and related families in the subclass Rosidae. The Myricaceae usually have root nodules that fix nitrogen and are therefore able to grow in nutrient-poor soils. In *Myrica* (bayberry and wax myrtle), the fleshy or waxy protuberances on the fruit wall may have originated as modified appendages of the inflorescence axis and may be homologous to the scales of the cupules in *Quercus* (oaks). The fleshy fruits of a few species of *Myrica* are edible. The Juglandaceae contain about 60 species in 7 or 8 genera. Fruits in the family are either small and winged and dispersed by wind or large and heavy and dispersed by animals. Familiar examples of the latter are walnuts (*Juglans*) and pecans (*Carya illinoinensis*) and hickory nuts (*Carya*). Plants in the Juglandales and Myricales have resinous glands and are aromatic. In the northeastern United States, the wax obtained from bayberry, *Myrica pennsylvanica,* is gathered and made into fragrant candles.

The Fagales

The Fagales contains 3 families of trees or shrubs: Fagaceae, with 6–9 genera and about 1,000 species; Betulaceae, with 6 genera and about 130 species; and Balanopaceae, with 1 genus and about 9 species. *Balanops,* the single genus of Balanopaceae, is restricted to the southwestern Pacific, particularly New Caledonia. The primitive wood of *Balanops* is similar to that in the Hamamelidaceae, but the classification of the family with the Fagaceae and Betulaceae is open to question. The drupelike fruit in the Balanopaceae separates it from Fagaceae and Betulaceae. In addition, while the cupule which subtends the fruits of *Balanops* bears some resemblance to the cupule of Quercus (Fagaceae), it is considered to be of a different morphological origin.

The Fagaceae arose from among the more advanced Hamamelidae but bear considerable resemblance to the more primitive members of the subclass Rosidae. The American botanist Kevin Nixon has proposed that Rosidae and Hamamelidae cannot be maintained as separate subclasses. The Fagaceae are easily recognized by the distinctive cupules (or hulls) covering the hard or leathery nuts. In some of the oaks (*Quercus*) and tanbark oaks (*Lithocarpus densiflora*), the cupule barely covers the base of the nut (acorn). In other species of these genera and in other genera of the family, the nut is completely enclosed and protected by a scaly or spiny husk that is believed to be derived from a coalesced branch system and its associated leaves. In genera of the Betulaceae in which the fruits are covered by a husk (*e.g.*, in *Corylus;* hazelnuts, or filberts), the husk is believed to be derived from two or three bracts. Members of the Betulaceae frequently have both the male (staminate) and female (pistillate) flowers in catkins; in the Fagaceae, only the male flowers are in catkins.

Casuarinales is an order that consists of a single family of 4 genera (*Gymnostoma, Ceuthostoma, Casuarina,* and *Allocasuarina*) with 96 species ranging from Australia and a few Pacific islands to as far north as Myanmar on the Asian mainland. Casuarinales has no clear relationships with any other order in the Hamamelidae but has more in common with members of this subclass than with any other. The Casuarinaceae were once considered to be among the most primitive flowering plants because of the extreme reduction in their floral and vegetative features. The resemblance of the conelike fruiting clusters to the cones of some gymnosperms and the outward similarities of the jointed branch system to the stems of *Equisetum* (horsetails) were considered to be especially indicative of an ancient origin.

NATURAL HISTORY

Predominance of wind-pollinated plants

Reproduction and life cycle. The Hamamelidae contains many families and genera of woody, wind-pollinated flowering plants. Generally the individual flowers are greatly reduced in size, and one or many of the whorls of floral parts (petals and sepals) are reduced or absent. Frequently, the flowers are odourless, produce no nectar to attract insects, and are green throughout. The flowers tend to be unisexual with the staminate (male) and pistillate (female) flowers often borne in different types of inflorescences, and the plants are either monoecious or dioecious. The staminate flowers are usually in elongate pendulous catkins and the pistillate flowers are solitary or in tight clusters of only a few flowers, or sometimes also in elongate, pendulous inflorescences. Stigmas of wind-pollinated plants are usually large, prominently displayed, and feathery or brushlike, all characteristics that facilitate the interception of windblown pollen grains. The pollen of these wind-pollinated plants is small and frequently porate with a smooth surface. Species with this combination of characters are often woody plants, frequently (especially in temperate regions) deciduous, and are often abundant as either the dominant tree or one of the dominant trees in a particular habitat. Individuals sometimes occur in pure stands. Familiar examples in temperate areas are the oaks, chestnuts and their relatives, hickories and walnuts, and birches.

Earlier botanists had regarded this suite of characteristics, shared by many wind-pollinated plants, as an indication of a common origin and close relationship. These workers had even equated the similarities in the reproductive structures in strobili (in gymnosperms) to the mode of pollination, absence of perianth parts, and arrangement of flowers into catkins (in the angiosperms) in order to relate the gymnosperms to the angiosperms. The structurally simple, apetalous flowers devoid of bright colours and nectar were thought to have reflected the primitive angiospermous condition from which other, more complex flowers had evolved. Current evidence makes it clear that certain catkin-bearing families placed in an artificial category, Amentiferae, by early botanists do have diverse origins, although some families clearly belong in the Hamamelidae. It is now fairly certain that the primitive angiosperms bore insect-pollinated flowers and that wind pollination was a later development.

Evolution from insect-pollinated ancestors

Although the earliest angiosperm flowers are thought to have been pollinated by insects, Cronquist has speculated that the earliest Hamamelidae flowers may have been wind-pollinated and that animal pollination evolved within the group at a later time. Others, notably the Swedish botanist Peter K. Endress, who has made a specialized study of the Hamamelidae, believe that wind pollination was derived from insect-pollinated ancestors. Various studies have suggested that the primitive Hamamelidae (and Rosidae) were insect-pollinated and had small, nectar-producing flowers with differentiated sepals and petals, an undifferentiated number of floral parts, and unfused carpels. The primitive inflorescence type in the group is believed to have been a spike, from which other inflorescence types evolved.

In the order Hamamelidales, adaptations of the primitive flower and inflorescence have evolved for animal pollination (*e.g.,* birds, bees, and flies) and for wind pollination. *Corylopsis* (Hamamelidaceae), a genus of Asian plants with some species that are used as ornamental shrubs in temperate areas, has nectar-producing flowers with sepals and yellow petals. The flowers face downward in pendulous spikes, resembling catkins, and are visited by bees. In the genus *Rhodoleia* (Hamamelidaceae), the individual flowers are arranged in heads (capitula), resembling inflorescences found in the unrelated family Asteraceae (Asterales; Asteridae). Because only the outer flowers produce petals, the whole inflorescence has the appearance of a single large flower. Each individual rose-pink flower produces abundant nectar, and the inflorescences, subtended by brown scales and resembling a brush, are especially attractive to birds, the reported pollinating agents. *Disanthus,* another small Asian genus, has small dark red or purple petals, and witch hazel, in Asia and North America, has yellow or greenish, strap-shaped petals. The flowers of both genera have shiny areas on their surfaces—on the base of the petals in *Disanthus* and at the base of the sepals and staminodia in *Hamamelis.* The flowers in both genera produce nectar and are reported to give off an unpleasant odour that attracts flies.

Some genera pollinated by bees present pollen rather than nectar as the attractant. In *Fothergilla* (Hamamelidaceae), the petals are completely lacking and the stamens are increased in number. No nectar is issued from these flowers, but pollen is produced in great quantities. In collecting the pollen for food, the bees invariably carry some grains from the anthers of one flower to the stigmas of others. In *Parrotiopsis* (Hamamelidaceae), there are fewer stamens, but the headlike inflorescence is surrounded by showy bracts providing a visual stimulus for insects.

Wind pollination occurs in the tribe Liquidambaroideae of the Hamamelidaceae (where the perianth is almost totally lacking and the unisexual flowers are in globose or pyramidal clusters), in the genera *Parrotia, Sinowilsonia,* and *Sycopsis,* and in the families Cercidiphyllaceae, Eucommiaceae, Eupteleaceae, and Platanaceae. Members of the Cercidiphyllaceae and Eucommiaceae have male and female flowers on different plants (dioecious); the Platanaceae have male and female flowers on the same plant (monoecious).

Periods of flowering

Many of the plants in the Hamamelidae are notable in producing flowers either very early or very late in the year. Flowers produced in the spring on many deciduous species appear before or just as the leaves begin to develop, an ideal adaptation for plants dependent on wind for pollen transport. Even many of the insect-pollinated species (*e.g.,* some species of *Hamamelis, Corylopsis, Loropetalum,* and *Fothergilla*) flower very early in the year, or even during the winter, when insects are less likely to be active, and a few (*e.g., Disanthus* and *Hamamelis virginiana*) flower late in the autumn after nearly all other plants have finished flowering.

Most wind-pollinated flowering plants are distributed in the Northern Hemisphere, where wind pollination must have originated. The tropics appear to have been an effective barrier to the southward migration of wind-pollinated plants. Of the few wind-pollinated groups in the Southern Hemisphere, three members of the Hamamelidae (the Balanopaceae, the Casuarinaceae, and the Nothofagaceae) have been among the most successful. They or their predecessors evidently migrated across the Equator, since fossil evidence, in concert with modern distribution patterns, seems to indicate a Laurasian origin for the Hamamelidae.

In the genera of Hamamelidaceae with one seed per carpel, seed dispersal takes place by an ejecting mechanism. As the fruit opens, the bony endocarp (inner layer) bends in a characteristic manner and presses against the hard, smooth surface of the seeds. The seeds are then forcibly discharged over distances of several metres. In contrast, the small, winged seeds of the many-seeded fruits of *Liquidambar* are distributed by wind. In *Platanus* the tufted nutlets are wind-dispersed. In many species of the family Hamamelidaceae, seed germination is usually delayed because of the hard and impervious seed coat; the seeds sometimes take one or two years to germinate.

(F.K.A./D.E.Bo.)

Ecology. The family Platanaceae and most members of the family Hamamelidaceae grow in moist woodlands, especially on stream banks and steep woody slopes. Other species grow best on drier rocky soils. The exact ecological range is unknown for most species. Many members of the family Hamamelidaceae grow in tropical and subtropical mountain regions, particularly in undisturbed forest areas. In general, representatives of the families Hamamelidaceae and Platanaceae are not specialized for extreme habitats,

Adaptation to arid habitats

but, as mentioned above, the species of Myrothamnaceae are quite remarkable in being among the most extremely drought-resistant of all seed plants and ferns—twigs and leaves can remain in a dry condition for several years without dying. They are found in the arid regions of tropical and southern Africa and Madagascar.

Members of the Hamamelidae are ecologically diverse, although they rarely occupy extreme environments. Members of the Platanaceae (*Platanus*), Cercidiphyllaceae, Eupteleaceae (*Euptelea*), some Hamamelidaceae, some Fagales, and many Urticales are frequently found in mineral-rich soil along large or small streams or in other moist habitats. In the Fagales, especially in the oaks, adaptations to a wide variety of habitats have evolved. Some of the oaks grow in very arid habitats under near-desert conditions, others grow in tropical or subtropical, more drought-resistant environments in steppe-savanna situations, while still others may be the dominant tree in swamps in very humid climates. The greatest number of species in the subclass are tropical and subtropical in distribution. The Fagaceae (*Castanea, Castanopsis, Fagus, Lithocarpus,* and *Quercus,* for example), particularly in association with the Lauraceae (subclass Magnoliidae), frequently form the dominant vegetation type in mountainous tropical regions.

FORM AND FUNCTION

Vegetative characteristics. All species of the subclass Hamamelidae, apart from the order Urticales, are woody plants ranging from small shrubs to massive trees; the Urticales contain both woody and herbaceous species. The vessel elements (water-conducting cells) have scalariform or simple perforations, but they are absent in the order Trochodendrales. The sieve tubes in the phloem (the food-conducting tissue) have S-type plastids—that is, plastids that lack protein accumulations. Plastids that store protein accumulations are called P-type plastids. The leaves are simple except in the Juglandales, where they are pinnately compound, and in *Cannabis* (family Cannabaceae, order Urticales), where they are palmately compound. Stipules, which are small appendages at the base of the petiole, are present in some members of the subclass.

Flower and fruit characteristics. In the family Hamamelidaceae, the flowers range in size from medium to small and are usually borne in dense flower clusters or in spikes. Many species in the family have flowers with sepals, petals, stamens, and pistils, but there is a clear series within the family with the loss of one or more floral whorls from the flowers of some genera. Both sepals and petals are absent in some genera. In the remaining families of the subclass, the flowers are usually extremely reduced in size and often in numbers of parts. In some plants that are functionally unisexual, rudiments of the other sex are present. For example, in the pistillate flowers of *Liquidambar styraciflua* the calyx lacks lobes, petals are absent, and the stamens are reduced in size and produce no pollen. Frequently the petals, and sometimes also the sepals, are absent. When present, the petals are usually small and insignificant. There is rarely a single stamen per flower, more often there are two to many; all have distinct filaments and anthers. The tissue that separates the anthers is frequently extended beyond the apex of the anther sacs. In the Urticaceae, and in some Moraceae, the stamens are often inflexed within the bud and spring open as the flowers reach maturity, forcibly ejecting the pollen, which is often clearly visible as a smokelike puff. In pistillate flowers of some genera of the tribe Elatostemeae of the Urticaceae, the sterile stamens (staminodes) behave in a similar manner in ejecting the mature achenes.

Unisexual varieties

The pollen grains have two or three nuclei and three to many furrows or pores, through which the pollen tube germinates. The carpels (the ovule-bearing structures) are separate from each other in the flowers of some species, but most often the carpels are fused, at least at the base, to form a compound ovary. In the flowers of many species of Hamamelidae, the carpels appear to be solitary but are actually falsely solitary because the development of adjacent ovaries is suppressed. The ovules are attached to axillary, basal, or apical placentas in the ovary, or occasionally to marginal placentas or to placentas located on the inner wall of the ovary. The ovule is bent so that the opening for the pollen tube (the micropyle) and the stalk that supports the ovule (the funiculus) are adjacent to each other or the ovule is straight so that the micropyle and funiculus are at opposite ends. The wall that encloses the ovule (the nucellus) is several cell layers thick and the ovule has two integuments or, infrequently, only one. The seeds may or may not have endosperm. The embryo is usually well developed and contains two very large cotyledons (oaks, chestnuts, beeches, walnuts, pecans); less frequently the embryo is small and contains highly reduced cotyledons.

Drawing by M. Pahl based on (*M. moschata*) *Beitrage zur Biologie der Pflanzen* (1966), Duncker and Humbolt; and (*P. occidentalis* flowers) G.H.M. Lawrence, *Taxonomy of Vascular Plants* (1951), The Macmillan Company

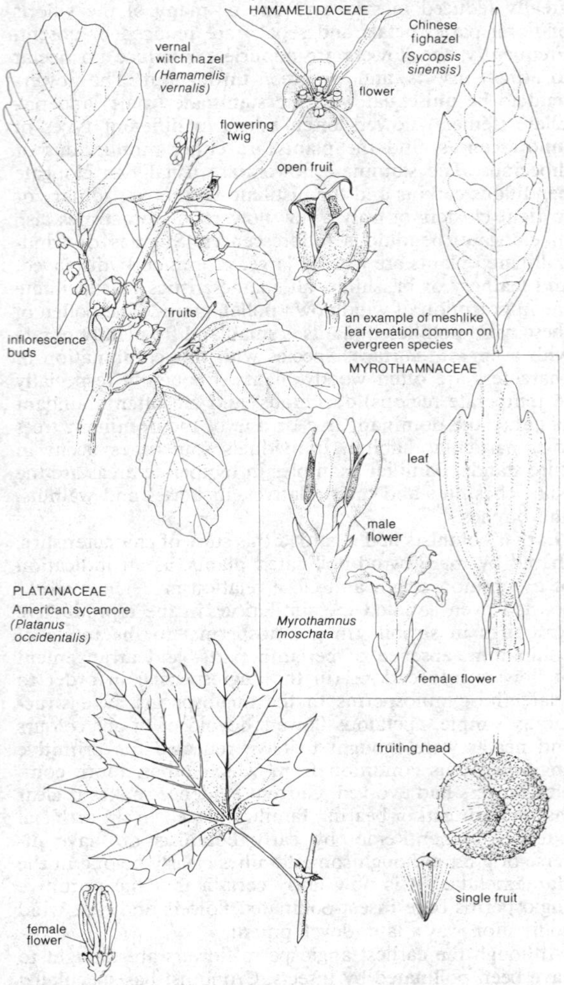

Vegetative, floral, and fruiting structures of three families of the order Hamamelidales.

All families of the Hamamelidae share these general features but differ in a number of important and unique ways. All members of the subclass have vessels, except for Trochodendrales, which has primitively vesselless wood. In the Platanaceae and Eucommiaceae the carpels are not completely sealed, a feature considered primitive and linking the Hamamelidae with Magnoliidae. The carpels show various degrees of fusion throughout the subclass, ranging from completely distinct (Cercidiphyllaceae) to partially fused (Tetracentraceae and Trochodendraceae, which are joined laterally but are distinct at their apex) to completely fused (Ulmaceae and Fagaceae).

Diversity of fruit forms

The fruits are extremely diverse in the Hamamelidae and include dry fruits such as single-seeded achenes (Urticaceae), nuts (walnuts and pecans), acorns, samaras, capsules, and follicles and fleshy fruits such as drupes, syconiums (figs), and fleshy berrylike fruits.

Members of the Hamamelidales reflect this variety. The fruits of *Platanus* (Platanaceae) are tiny, densely hairy nutlets borne in globose heads. The hairs apparently aid in the wind dispersal of the fruits, although the globose clusters often fall from the trees intact. In the genera with one seed per carpel and in the Hamamelidaceae the capsules frequently eject the seeds forcibly. In the Hamamelidaceae, and in other families where the seed coats are very hard and impervious, germination is often delayed; the seeds of Hamamelidaceae frequently take up to two years to germinate. The separate follicles of the Cercidiphyllaceae bear numerous, flattened, winged seeds containing oily endosperm. In the Eupteleaceae the endosperm is proteinaceous and also oily and the tiny embryo bears two poorly developed cotyledons. The fruits are scimitar-shaped because of the uneven growth and development of the marginal wing after fertilization. The Eucommiaceae (Eucommiales) and most members of the subfamily Ulmoideae of the Ulmaceae (Urticales) have dry, winged fruits called samaras.

Single-seeded fleshy fruits (drupes) are found in the Daphniphyllaceae (Daphniphyllales), Leitneriaceae (Leitneriales), and Didymelaceae (Didymelales). In the Daphniphyllaceae, the endosperm is oily and proteinaceous. The Didymelaceae lack endosperm, but the embryos have thick cotyledons; in the Leitneriaceae, where the drupes are dry and leathery, the endosperm is dry and starchy. The subfamily Celtidoideae of the Ulmaceae have drupes for fruits. Seeds in the elm family (Ulmaceae) have little or no endosperm.

In the Juglandales, the fruit is a nut or is sometimes drupelike. In several members of this order the nutlets are small, bear wings, and are dispersed by the wind, while in walnuts, hickories, and pecans the large, unwinged fruits are dispersed by animals. Both wind and animal adaptations for dispersal have been found in fruits of late Paleocene to early Eocene age (57.8 million years ago). For example, the Paleocene ancestors of *Carya* and *Juglans* had rather thin, smooth-walled shells. Over time and with the increasing development of the rodents and the appearance of the first squirrels, the shells became thicker, more complex, and more convoluted internally, presumably as a deterrent to these foraging animals. Recent selective breeding by humans has reversed the thickened seed coats of cultivated walnuts and pecans.

The most complex fruits in the Hamamelidae are found among the Urticales. Multiple fruits are formed as the gynoecia of several flowers fuse. Examples in this order include the mulberry (*Morus*), breadfruit (*Artocarpus altilis*), breadnut (*Brosimum*), fig (*Ficus*), and osage orange (*Maclura pomifera*). The jackfruit, or jakfruit (*Artocarpus heterophyllus*), is a multiple fruit that is unusual in still another way: it is produced along the main trunk of the tree, since such large fruits cannot be supported on the branches. In the fig, each "seed" is actually an individual fruit; the fig itself is the receptacle developed into a fruitlike structure. In the family Ulmaceae, the elms have dry, membranous, windblown fruit called samaras, and *Celtis* and others have a fleshy drupe, or stone-pitted fruit, spread by birds and other animals. Some members of the Urticaceae (*Soleirolia, Hesperocnide, Myriocarpa,* and *Phenax,* for example) have hooked hairs on the fruiting perianth that attach to the fur of passing animals. Others have various kinds of fleshy drupes, fleshy infructescences, or a fleshy perianth and are eaten by birds and animals. In a few genera—*i.e., Ficus, Coussapoa,* and *Poikilospermum* (the latter two genera belonging to the Cecropiaceae)—a mucilaginous layer surrounds the seed. This is a common feature in many plants that are epiphytic or parasitic. The mucilage-covered seeds stick to the beaks of birds that eat the fruits of these species. In cleaning their beaks the birds transfer the mucilage-covered seeds to tree branches, where they germinate.

Some plants in various genera of the Urticaceae and Moraceae may be dispersed by water; for example, in *Boehmeria cylindrica,* which grows in or near water, the perianth completely surrounds the seeds and becomes corky at maturity and is capable of drifting on water for long distances.

Cupule An important distinguishing feature of the order Fagales is the occurrence of a so-called cupule, a structure so characteristic that it provided the origin of the old family name Cupuliferae for the family Fagaceae. The cupule surrounds the fruit (*e.g.,* the acorn or nut) as a cup and on the outer side bears scales, spines, thin plates, or fused concentric rings of overlapping scales. In the genus *Lithocarpus,* each fruit is included in a cupule; the different cupules of an inflorescence may, however, be more or less grown together forming a hard stonelike mass (hence the name of the genus). Similar cupules are found in the oaks (*Quercus*), but they remain separate at maturity. In *Castanopsis* and *Castanea,* the whole female inflorescence is surrounded by a common cupule, which bursts open when the fruit matures. In *Chrysolepis,* the cupule is a compound structure with separating walls between the fruits.

The fruits in the Betulaceae range from the small, windblown two-winged samaras of alders and birches to clusters of nuts retained in tight husks in *Corylus* (filbert, hazelnut). The nutlets of *Carpinus* (hornbeam, or ironwood) and *Ostrya* (hop hornbeam) are attached to papery bracts on pendulous spikes. At maturity the bracts, attached to the small nutlets, separate from the inflorescence axis and are dispersed by the wind. The conelike structures of the Casuarinaceae consist of firm, woody bracteoles closed tightly around the fruit until maturity. At maturity the bracteoles spread apart and give the appearance of a cluster of dehiscing capsules, releasing the single-seeded, winged fruit.

EVOLUTION

The angiosperm subclass Hamamelidae extends back more than 100 million years to the Albian Age of the Cretaceous Period through ancestors similar to the extant Platanaceae (Hamamelidales). The Hamamelidae appear to have originated within the fossil *Normapolles* group. The group is noted for its distinctive small, smooth pollen with porate apertures, features considered to be adaptations to wind pollination. *Normapolles* pollen has been found in the middle latitudes of Europe and western Asia and the eastern part of North America and, if the Hamamelidae did arise from a member of this assemblage, it would indicate that the Hamamelidae originated in the Northern Hemisphere. The oldest pollen of this type has been found in sedimentary rocks of Cenomanian Age (about 97.5 to 91 million years old) from the earliest part of the Early Cretaceous and became particularly widespread during later stages of the Late Cretaceous. Origin

The *Normapolles* group rapidly differentiated during the end of the Cretaceous and then declined, being replaced by grains of more modern aspect, which in turn become more widespread in the fossil record. Presumably the evolution of pollen proceeded in concert with the evolution of the plants producing it, resulting in such modern genera as *Betula* and *Alnus* of the Betulaceae and *Myrica* of the Myricaceae.

The earliest Hamamelidae are thought by some to have differentiated from Magnoliidae stock at the same time as the ancestors of the Rosidae, a group having many members with pinnatifid or pinnately compound leaves. The two subclasses have been linked in their early stages of differentiation through fossils of palmately lobed leaves referred to *Platanus* (Hamamelidae) and pinnately compound leaves of *Sapindopsis* (Rosidae). These two subclasses are not clearly distinguishable from each other until the Cenomanian Age of the Late Cretaceous.

It has been suggested that the Hamamelidae, or at least the primitive Hamamelidae, are a transitional group between the Magnoliidae and both the Rosidae and Dilleniidae. The extant orders and families of the Hamamelidae are often quite different and frequently do not show clear relationships within the subclass. One of the explanations proposed for this is that most of the families and orders have had very long, independent evolutionary histories, sometimes dating back to the Cretaceous, since diverging very early from an ancestor from the Magnoliidae. Few shared derived characteristics hold the group together; instead, they share a series of rather unspecialized, more or less primitive characteristics that link them to an earlier stock transitional to the Magnoliidae. It has been further speculated that the Rosidae and Dilleniidae also branched off from this same transitional stock from which the extant Hamamelidae are derived.

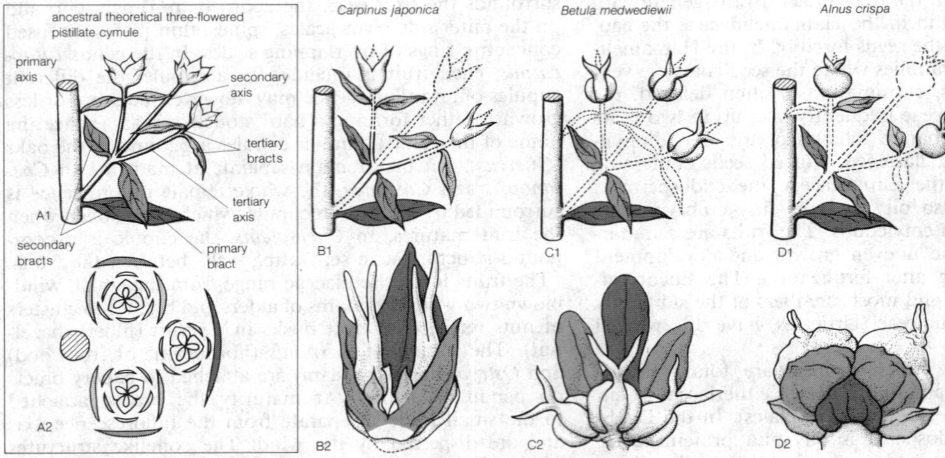

The evolutionary reduction series from the hypothetical ancestral condition to extant members of Betulaceae.
A1 is a schematic of the hypothetical inflorescence. The ancestral inflorescence is a cyme. A2 represents an overhead view in cross section and shows the three locules in the ovaries of the cymules. B1, C1, and D1 are schematic diagrams of the pistillate cymules believed to be ancestral to the extant cymules of B2, C2, and D2, respectively. Broken lines indicate the parts that were lost or reduced over time. Each cymule bears a basal primary bract on the primary axis, a secondary axis that bears secondary bracts and a flower, and flowers subtended by tertiary axes and bracts. B2, C2, and D2, all extant members, differ from the ancestral cymule in having lost, by suppression or condensation, one or more of the axes or bracts. The cymule is two-flowered in *Carpinus* and *Alnus,* and three-flowered in *Betula.* The result in extant members is an inflorescence that does not resemble a true cyme because the parts appear to be superposed on one another.

From G.H.M. Lawrence, *Taxonomy of Vascular Plants* (1951), The Macmillan Pub. Co.; after E.C. Abbe, "Studies in the Phylogeny of the Betulaceae," *Botanical Gazette,* vol. 97 (1935)

Several orders (Fagales and Urticales especially) have met with considerable evolutionary success and are highly diversified and widely distributed around the world. Others, however, are on the verge of extinction—*e.g.,* Trochodendrales (two species), Leitneriales (one species), Didymelales (two species), and Eucommiales (one species). The order Trochondendrales is phylogenetically significant for the absence of vessels in the wood, a primitive feature among vascular plants. It has been argued that the vesselless condition is actually an advanced condition in the angiosperms and that all primitive angiosperms possessed vessel elements. This is not the general consensus, however. The only other families regarded as primitively vesselless in the angiosperms—the Amborellaceae and Winteraceae—are placed in the subclass Magnoliidae.

REPRESENTATIVE GROUPS

Urticales. *Distribution and abundance.* The Urticales, with 6 families (Barbeyaceae, Cannabaceae, Cecropiaceae, Moraceae, Ulmaceae, and Urticaceae) and approximately 2,200 to 2,300 species, is the largest order in the subclass Hamamelidae. Alternative classifications link the Urticales with the Malvales (subclass Dilleniidae) and Euphorbiales (subclass Rosidae), and even Violales (subclass Dilleniidae), a relationship first proposed in the mid-1800s. It is largely because of the traditional association of the order with other members of the Amentiferae that it continues to be retained in the Hamamelidae. The Barbeyaceae are rather unusual in the order, but have been placed in the Urticales by some botanists for lack of a better alternative classification. The relationship of the other five families to each other has not been seriously questioned, although the Ulmaceae are usually considered to be somewhat distantly related to the other four.

Alternative relationships

Besides containing most of the herbaceous members of the Hamamelidae, the Urticales are unusual within the subclass Hamamelidae in flowering mostly from late spring to early fall. Whether or not this is a significant means of classifying the Urticales with the Hamamelidae, it may be more than coincidental that members of the orders Malvales (Dilleniidae) and Euphorbiales (Rosidae), considered by some taxonomists to be the closest relatives of the Urticales, also display peak flowering during the warmer parts of the year and after the leaves have fully developed.

The Ulmaceae contain about 150 species, all woody, in about 15–18 genera. The majority of the species are in only 3 genera, *Celtis, Trema,* and *Ulmus.* The family is widely distributed in temperate and tropical areas but occurs especially in the Northern Hemisphere. The genus *Celtis* (the hackberries) is the largest in the family, with about 70 species distributed in the Northern Hemisphere and in southern Africa. The elms consist of about 45 species in north temperate areas but extend as far south as the Himalayas and Indochina in Asia and Mexico in North America. Other genera in the tropics and subtropics include *Trema,* 15 species; *Gironniera,* 6; *Ampelocera,* about 5; *Parasponia,* 5–6; and *Chaetachme,* 4. The genus *Zelkova,* with about 3 species, has a discontinuous distribution and is found from the eastern Mediterranean region to the Caucasus, and in eastern Asia. The genus once had a much wider distribution, dating back to the Early Tertiary (about 60 million years ago), and is known in the fossil record from several sites in North America and Eurasia. *Pteroceltis,* with one species, is restricted to eastern Asia, and *Planera,* also with a single species, the planer tree, or water elm (*P. aquatica*), is native to the southeastern United States. Species of *Ulmus, Zelkova,* and *Celtis* are frequently cultivated as ornamentals.

The Moraceae, with about 40 genera and 1,000 species, are found principally in the tropics and subtropics, but a few genera, such as *Morus,* the mulberry (the food plant of the silk moth, *Bombyx mori,* in Asia), and *Broussonetia* (a source of fibres for paper in Asia), are primarily distributed in temperate regions. *Ficus,* the largest genus, contains between 700 and 800 species. It is a taxonomically complex group that includes trees, shrubs, lianas, and strangler figs and contains food plants (the common fig, *Ficus carica*), ornamentals (India rubber tree, *Ficus elastica;* the weeping fig, *F. benjamina,* and the sycamore fig, *F. sycomorus*), and the bo tree, or sacred fig (*F. religiosa*), of religious significance to Buddhists and Hindus, and under which the Buddha is believed to have received enlightenment. The banyan (*F. benghalensis*) spreads by dropping aerial roots from the branches to the ground to become accessory trunks. The branches continue to grow horizontally so that a single individual eventually resembles a grove of trees. The famous banyan in the Indian Botanic Garden in Calcutta is more than 300 metres in circumference. Osage orange of the south-central United States is occasionally cultivated. Breadfruit is an important dietary staple in the Old World tropics, and mulberries

Ficus

are a source of juicy fruits to birds, animals, and humans in temperate regions.

The Urticaceae can be divided into 5 tribes containing about 45 genera and between 800 and 1,000 species, which are mostly herbs but are occasionally shrubs or even trees. The genera *Pilea* and *Elatostema* each contain less than 300 species and are almost entirely tropical and subtropical. Some of the tropical and subtropical species of Urticaceae are shrubs or trees; many of the herbaceous species form dense ground covers in moist climates or grow as epiphytes on moss-covered tree trunks and tree branches in humid regions. Although there are not many species in temperate areas, the often weedy family may occupy extensive areas and may become so dense as to prevent the growth of other species of plants. The stinging nettles (*Urtica*) can be especially common, widespread, and often abundant. Single plants of *Urtica dioica* are able to form extensive colonies within a short time by growing underground stems called rhizomes.

Genera of the family Cecropiaceae often have been placed within either the Moraceae or Urticaceae, although they do form a tightly circumscribed and concordant natural group. The Cecropiaceae (6 genera and about 300 species) consist of trees, shrubs, or woody vines. The sexes are found on separate plants (dioecious), in contrast to members of the Moraceae and Urticaceae, where most members retain both sexes on the same plant, but in different flowers. The largest genus, *Cecropia,* with about 100 species of large, palmately lobed leaves, comprises fast-growing pioneer trees that are prominent in disturbed areas in the New World tropics. The Cecropiaceae produce mucilaginous sap (latex).

Cecropia

The Cannabaceae, although consisting of only two genera and three species, are well known and economically important for hops (*Humulus lupulus*) and marijuana or hemp (*Cannabis*). *Cannabis* contains a single species with two subspecies, *C. sativa* and *C. indica,* the former selected for its fibres (the source of hemp) and the latter selected for its high concentration of the compound Δ^9-tetrahydrocannabinol (THC), a drug that exerts effects on the central nervous system and cardiovascular system. Both subspecies are coarse, erect, annual, dioecious herbs with opposite and alternate leaves. Species of *Humulus* are twining or scrambling herbs. The leaves are palmately compound in *Cannabis;* in *Humulus,* they are palmately lobed.

The taxonomic position of the family Barbeyaceae, with one species in northeastern Africa and adjacent Arabia, is uncertain. The separate or partially fused carpels and primitive phloem are unusual in the Urticales, and some taxonomists have preferred to defer on the placement of the family until additional evidence becomes available.

Economic and ecological importance. Members of the Moraceae are distributed in the tropics and subtropics of both hemispheres, with some genera extending into temperate regions. In the Ulmaceae, a family often divided into two subfamilies, the genus *Ulmus* (elm) is widely distributed in north temperate areas, as are its closest relatives; members of the other subfamily, which includes the large genus *Celtis,* are for the most part confined to the tropics and subtropics. The Urticaceae are widespread in most tropical regions of the world, where some are troublesome weeds.

Wood products

Several genera in the mulberry family are valuable sources of timber. In Africa, the wood of *Antiaris,* while not highly durable, is suitable for veneer and plywood, furniture components, and light construction. The light wood of the umbrella tree, *Musanga cecropioides,* is used as a substitute for cork in floats and rafts, insulation, and model-making; it is a short-lived tree, suitable for plantation culture. Two species of iroko, *Chlorophora excelsa* and *C. regia,* cover the breadth of tropical Africa and produce durable heartwood used in joinery, boat-building and marine work, flooring, furniture, and veneer; it is often used as a substitute for oak and teak. Another species in tropical America, *C. tinctoria* (fustic), is used in heavy construction, planking, and flooring. In Southeast Asia and Oceania, species of *Artocarpus,* the same genus cultivated for the breadfruits and jackfruits, produce woods of variable durability used in joinery, furniture and cabinetwork, and musical instruments. In the American tropics, *Bagassa, Brosimum, Clarisia, Helicostylis,* and *Poulsenia* are all sources of wood for general construction. *Brosimum guianense* (letterwood, also called leopardwood or snakewood), is employed in inlays, turnery, fancy handles for cutlery, and violin bows, while *B. paraense,* the Brazilian redwood, is used for furniture. Species of *Trophis* are used locally in Venezuela. In the *Cecropia* family (Cecropiaceae), *C. peltata,* or trumpetwood, resembles the North American black cottonwood (*Populus trichocarpa;* Salicaceae) in density and mechanical properties and is used in making boxes, plywood, and particle-board stock. In the Ulmaceae, most species of *Ulmus* produce a superior timber with a distinctive grain and a strong resistance to decay; several species in North America provide wood for boxes, baskets, veneer for fruit and vegetable containers, and the bent parts in furniture. The American elm, *U. americana,* once an important street tree prized for its graceful form and stature, has been nearly eliminated by Dutch elm disease. Hackberry (*Celtis*) wood, similar to that of elm in structure, is usually cut into lumber for furniture and containers; *C. mildbraedii* of western, central, and eastern Africa, while not durable, has good strength properties and can be used for flooring, commercial plywood, and veneer. In tropical America, the San Domingo boxwood, *Phyllostylon brasiliensis,* has been suggested as a substitute for true boxwood (*Buxus;* Rosidae). It produces a fine-textured, lemon-yellow, straight-grained wood valued for the high polish it will accept; stained black, it has been used as a substitute for true ebony. The wood of *Planera aquatica* is fragrant and used in cabinetmaking. The lightweight wood of *Chaetachme microcarpa,* a shrub of central and southern Africa, is used for the manufacture of guitars and other instruments. The wood of *Ficus* is soft and of comparatively little value, but it does find use as lumber. *Ficus benghalensis* has wood that is durable in water. The wide, flat, finlike buttress roots of large individuals of *F. elastica*—the rubber tree grown as a houseplant—are used in tropical regions to make planks. *Ficus sycomorus,* a wood of great durability, was used by the Egyptians to make mummy cases.

Fibre crops

Hemp, or cannabis (*Cannabis*), has been cultivated since ancient times for the strong fibre, similar to flax, produced in its stems. Peak production was reached in the mid-20th century; costly spinning methods and competition from other fibres, both natural and synthetic, have contributed to the decline in its use. The plant is now increasingly known for the nonfibre-bearing subspecies that is grown for the narcotic drug marijuana, derived from the upper leaves and flowers. The fibre of the ramie plant, *Boehmeria nivea,* is currently cultivated mainly in China, the Philippines, and Brazil. Because the fibres must be separated from gums and pectins within the plant before they can be spun, the extraction process is more complicated than that for flax or jute; however, the tensile strength of ramie seems to compare well with that of cotton, flax, and hemp, and it is especially suitable for blending with synthetic fibres. The fibres also are used to produce papers, cordage, and industrial bagging. Other plants with fibres like those of ramie are sometimes used as substitutes; they include *Sarcochlamys pulcherrima* (duggal fibre) and *Pouzolzia occidentalis* (yaquilla). Olona (*Touchardia latifolia*) was formerly an important fibre plant of Hawaii, used for cloth, cordage, and especially fishnets because of its durability in water. Several other members of the Urticaceae also yield fibres.

Medicinal properties

The latex of the figs *Ficus glabrata* and *F. laurifolia* contains the proteolytic enzyme ficin, which digests *Ascaris* (roundworm) without harming the human host. It is used extensively in South America and Panama. In Mexico, the caustic latex of trumpetwood is used to remove warts. The latex of several members of the mulberry family—*e.g., Artocarpus cummingiana* in the Philippines and *Ficus platyphylla* in Africa—is variously treated and used as chewing gum. The fustic in tropical America, and *Ficus* species in Fiji and China, are used to treat toothache. The latex of *Antiaris toxicaria,* the upas tree, contains an extremely toxic cardiac glycoside, which has the effect of

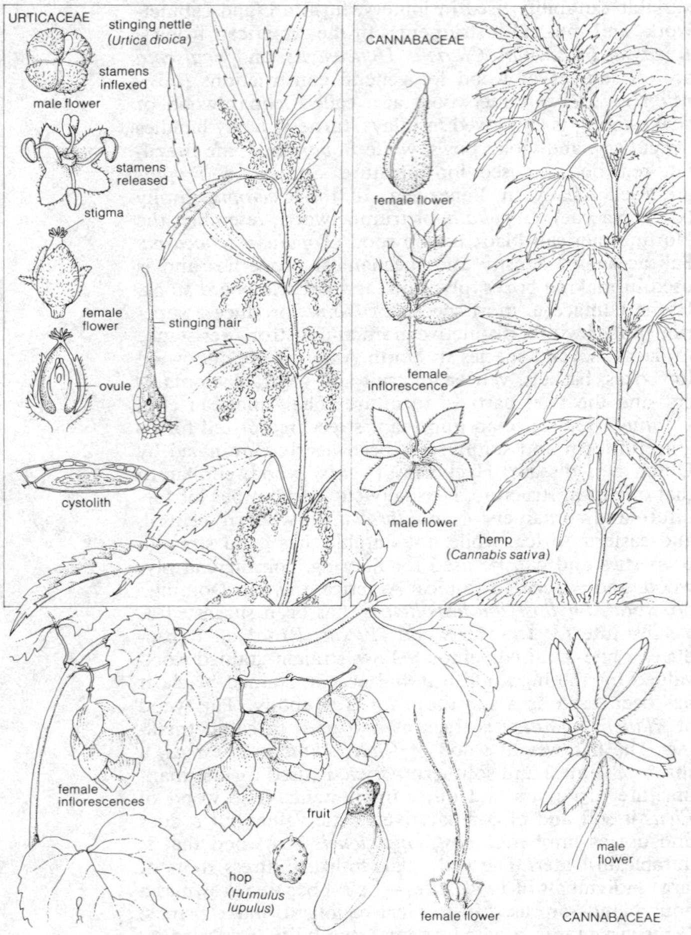

Representative plants of the families Urticaceae and Cannabaceae.

From (female flower, stinging hair) A. Engler, *Syllabus der Pflanzenfamilien* (1964), Gebruder Borntraeger Verlag Berlin-Stuttgart; and (cystolith) A.B. Rendle, *The Classification of Flowering Plants* (1967), Cambridge University Press

increasing the force of contraction of the muscles of the heart; in tropical Asia, it is a valuable source of poison for arrows and darts. Osage orange of central North America is suspected of being toxic to livestock; its milky latex can also irritate skin. The wind-borne pollen of many members of the Urticales, especially the elm and mulberry families, is responsible for attacks of allergic rhinitis and bronchial asthma. The irritants in the stinging hairs or spines of many genera in the Urticaceae, including *Laportea* (nettle tree), *Hesperocnide, Urera,* and *Urtica* (nettle) cause painful inflammatory skin reactions that can last from a few seconds to several days. *Ficus carica,* the common fig, can provoke phytophotodermatitis, and hops (*Humulus lupulus*) can cause contact dermatitis.

Food products

The Moraceae contain several highly valued tropical species long cultivated for their fruits. The fig (*Ficus*) is considered to be one of the first foods to be preserved by drying. Production of *Ficus carica,* the only fig grown commercially as food, is highest in the Mediterranean region (Turkey, Greece, and Italy) and the United States. The breadfruit, *Artocarpus altilis,* is an extremely important food source throughout Southeast Asia and the Pacific; more recently it has been widely cultivated in the New World tropics and in Africa. The fruit, usually about the size of a grapefruit and seedless, consists of a starchy, pulpy white mass that is customarily cooked before eating. In the seeded form, the seeds are boiled or roasted and have a flavour similar to that of the chestnut. The jackfruit, or jakfruit, tree, *Artocarpus heterophyllus,* bears one of the largest known edible fruits and has been cultivated for centuries throughout much of southern Asia. While it has not gained the popularity of the breadfruit, its pulp and seeds are used in cooking. A number of lesser fruits of the order also are eaten; examples of such include the breadnut (*Brosimum alicastrum*), mulberries (*Morus alba,* the white mulberry; *M. rubra,* the red mulberry; and *M. nigra,* the black mulberry), and hackberries (*Celtis occidentalis, C. selloviana* and *C. iguanaea*). In addition, the fruits of the following plants are edible: *Debregeasia edulis,* a Chinese and Japanese shrub that produces red or yellow fruits resembling raspberries; *Pourouma cecropiifolia,* a Brazilian tree with round, fleshy berries; *Cudrania javanensis; Myrianthus arboreus;* and *Sahagunia strepitans.*

Other uses

Moraceae contains a number of latex-producing plants. Although *Ficus elastica* was used as an early source of rubber, especially during World War II, the bulk of the world's rubber now comes from the para rubber tree, *Hevea brasiliensis,* a member of the family Euphorbiaceae (Rosidae). Several species of *Castilla,* notably *C. elastica,* are still used locally for rubber production. Latex from *Ficus* species and *Artocarpus altilis* is also employed in chewing gums, in glues and caulking compounds, and in birdlime, a sticky substance used to ensnare birds. *Brosimum galactodendron,* the cow tree or milk tree of South America, produces an abundance of latex similar in taste to ordinary milk.

Another plant of great economic importance is the hop, *Humulus lupulus,* the female flowers of which are used to flavour beer and to clarify it by precipitating the protein materials that cause turbidity. The active principles of the hop also help prevent spoilage by retarding the growth of bacteria in the beer. The leaves of the mulberry (*Morus*) are the principal food of silkworms, and the inner bark of the paper mulberry, *Broussonetia papyrifera,* is used to make paper. Several members of the Urticales serve as ornamentals. The breadfruit is also a handsome ornamental with a luxuriant crown of large leathery leaves. Elms are often planted for their stately appearance. Several species of *Ficus* are important in the horticulture trade; these include *F. elastica* (the India rubber plant), *F. lyrata* (fiddleleaf fig), *F. pumila* (creeping or climbing fig), and *F. benghalensis* (banyan).

Characteristic morphological features. Plants of the Urticales are evergreen or deciduous trees, shrubs, vines (both woody and herbaceous), or herbs (mostly in the family Urticaceae). They commonly have mucilage cells and canals and often have cystoliths (which probably serve as protection from insects), as in the Urticaceae, or laticifers (latex cells), as in Moraceae. The leaves are usually alternate, rarely opposite, in the Moraceae and Ulmaceae, but commonly opposite in the Urticaceae and Cannabaceae. Most leaves are simple and often oblique at the base. A few species have pinnatifid or palmately incised leaves (palmately lobed in *Humulus,* palmately compound in *Cannabis*).

The flowers are wind-pollinated or insect-pollinated, with a complex and highly evolved method of pollination in *Ficus.* The small, inconspicuous, and usually unisexual flowers are typically arranged in cymose inflorescences (the flowers are rarely solitary or perfect). There are usually 4 or 5 tepals (sepals?), or sometimes as few as 2 or as many as 12, arranged in 1 or 2 whorls and sometimes fused with each other (connate) at the base. Tepals are rarely absent, although the flowers in the Urticales lack petals. The stamens are attached opposite the tepals and are equal to them in number; rarely are the stamens greater or less in number than the tepals. The pollen grains have at least two apertures. The ovary may be inferior or superior, usually with one or two styles. There is a single locule in each ovary and one ovule in each locule.

Endosperm development is of the nuclear type; *i.e.,* nuclei are formed by nuclear division, after which cell walls may form. The seeds may or may not contain endosperm. The fruits range from fleshy syconiums (figs), to dry achenes, to drupes (or drupelets), or frequently multiple fruits (fruits in which the ripened ovaries of many adjacent flowers are borne in clusters; these resemble the fruits of blackberries or raspberries, but in these the clusters are made up of the ripened ovaries of only a single flower).

The family Ulmaceae is often divided into two subfamilies, the Celtidoideae and Ulmoideae (as in this article's classification), or sometimes even into two separate families, the Celtidaceae and Ulmaceae, on the basis of leaf venation, pollen characteristics, chemical composition, chromosome number, and fruit types. In the subfamily Celtidoideae the fruits are drupelike (fleshy, with one seed), and there are three strong main veins arising from the base of the leaf in addition to the pinnately arranged veins branching from the midvein. In the Ulmoideae, the fruits are dry, often winged, and the leaves are strictly pinnately veined.

Stinging hairs

Members of the tribe Urereae (also known as Urticeae) are among the most conspicuous members of the family Urticaceae (the nettle family) because of their stinging hairs. The stings are frequently a short-term irritant, but contact with some species can cause pain or numbness that lasts for several days. Fatalities have been reported in humans and domesticated animals from contact with the stinging hairs of *Urtica ferox* and some species of *Dendrocnide* and *Laportea.* The stinging hairs commonly have a bulbous or enlarged base and a slender tubular portion containing silica bodies. The tips of the stinging hairs break off on slight contact, leaving a sharp point that readily penetrates the skin, much like a hypodermic needle, allowing the fluid of the stinging-hair cell to enter the flesh. The compounds producing the stinging sensation in the Urticaceae have been reported to be histamine, acetylcholine, serotonin, and an unknown substance that also causes pain. Although the stinging members of the Urticaceae are among the most noticeable because of their irritating nature, they amount to only about 108 species (10 percent of the family).

Cystoliths

In addition to the stinging members of the nettle family, a few other plants in the order Urticales can cause skin irritations on contact. The fruits or leaves of the osage orange, for example, cause dermatitis in susceptible persons. Another feature characteristic of the nettle family and many members of the mulberry family (Moraceae) is the presence of cystoliths, deposits of calcium carbonate inside enlarged epidermal (surface) cells. They are visible as dots or variously shaped marks, especially in pressed, dried leaves. Their function in the plant is unknown. Calcium carbonate deposits occur in another form in *Chlorophora excelsa* (Moraceae), the source of iroko wood, which is very durable and practically immune to termites and wood-rotting fungi. The wood in about 3 percent of the trees carries streaks or lumps of calcium carbonate called iroko stones, which are hard enough to dull woodworking tools.

Explosive stamens

Most members of the order Urticales are wind-pollinated, and some species have adaptations that enhance this process. *Pilea microphylla* (Urticaceae), the artillery plant, for example, ejects its pollen in tiny explosive puffs. Many genera, particularly in the family Urticaceae, exhibit the same phenomenon. In the flower buds of the nettles (especially species of *Urtica*), the stamens (male, pollen-producing structures) are bent inward and held under tension (inflexed) in the bud. When the flower opens, the stamens are suddenly released and spring out with such violence that the anthers, or pollen sacs, are turned inside out, ejecting their pollen in a cloud. The pollen is then carried by the wind to the large, brushlike stigmas of other flowers. Like most wind-pollinated flowers, these flowers tend to be inconspicuous, green, and petalless.

The flowers of the genus *Parietaria,* unlike those of most other members of the family Urticaceae, are bisexual in that they have the functional organs of both sexes. Self-fertilization is averted by the early maturation of the pistil, a condition known as protogyny. In this process of fertilization, the elongated upper part of the pistil (the style and stigma) projects from the tip of the unopened flower bud ready to receive pollen from mature flowers. When the flower opens, the stamens have fully developed and release their pollen explosively, but the ovules of these flowers have already been fertilized and the style has dropped off.

Most of the species in the Moraceae (the mulberry family) are trees, shrubs, lianas, or, rarely, herbs. All except the herbaceous genus *Fatoua* produce a milky latex in special cells (laticifers) found in most parts of the plant. Plants in the Moraceae sometimes produce alkaloids and usually tannins (at least proanthocyanins).

Some species of the Moraceae are pollinated by insects, particularly the figs (*Ficus*), where complex interdependencies between the plants and their insect pollinators have evolved. Pollination is accomplished by small wasps called fig wasps or gall wasps (*Blastophaga psenes*). In the figs, separate male and female flowers are borne in a specialized inflorescence that consists of a hollow, pear-shaped stem tip with the flowers on the inside. This structure, called a syconium, ultimately matures into a fig. The male flowers are usually arranged near the small opening at the upper end of the syconium, and the female flowers, much more numerous, line the interior. The female flowers are of two types, long-styled fertile flowers and short-styled sterile ones. The long-styled flowers eventually produce a single, small, one-seeded, hard-shelled fruit termed the achene. The fig itself is actually a collection of many of these achenes surrounded by the fleshy tissue of the syconium. The short-styled flowers are called gall flowers; they do not develop fruits but are used as egg-laying sites by the gall wasps, which pollinate the other flowers while laying their eggs. The gall flowers then become a mass of pulpy, abnormal plant tissue, the gall, on which the wasp larvae feed and in which they develop.

Pollination of the fig by wasps

The three flower cluster types—male, long-styled female, and short-styled female (or gall flowers)—are produced in three distinctive syconia. The first type of syconium, produced in the spring, contains male flowers and gall flowers; each of the latter may contain one of the fig wasp eggs, deposited there in the spring by wasps that had just emerged from overwintering in another type of fig. These eggs produce wingless male and winged female wasps later in the summer. The male wasp bites through the wall of a gall containing a female wasp and mates with her. On leaving the fig to search for a suitable place to lay eggs, the female wasp becomes covered with pollen from the male flowers near the small exit hole at the tip of the fig. The second type of syconium, the true fig, bears only long-styled fertile female flowers. The female wasp, searching for egg-laying sites in summer, enters these figs and pollinates the flowers inside but does not lay eggs, because the styles are too long to suit the egg-depositing anatomy of the insect. The third type of syconium, produced in the autumn, contains only short-styled gall flowers. The eggs that are laid develop in the gall flowers and produce the following year's fig wasps.

Another symbiotic relationship exists between species of *Cecropia* (Cecropiaceae) and ants of the genus *Azteca.* The ants establish colonies within the hollow trunks and stems of the *Cecropia* plants and consume the glycogens and proteinaceous substances produced by these trees. This food is continually replaced as it is eaten. There are thin areas in the stem walls through which the fertile female ants burrow to lay their eggs inside the stem. The ants provide a form of protection for the tree by viciously attacking and biting insects that would otherwise eat the plant and animals that would brush against it. The ants also chew through vines that twine around their host and clear away other vegetation that comes in contact with, and threatens to shade, the *Cecropia* plants. Other *Cecropia* plants that do not harbour *Azteca* ants are protected against leaf-cutting ants by a thick coating of wax on the stem, which prevents the latter from climbing up.

Evolution. The herbaceous habit and preference for moist environments, particularly in tropical and subtropical lowlands, are unusual in the Hamamelidae and are believed to have been important factors in the diversification of the Urticales. The order, which comprises approximately two-thirds of the Hamamelidae, is allied to other members of the subclass in floral features and resembles particular families (Betulaceae and Fagaceae) in its leaf venation. Pollen of the Urticales resembles fossil pollen of the *Normapolles* group.

Thorne and Dahlgren have allied the anatomical features of the Urticales with the orders Malvales (Dilleniidae) and Euphorbiales (Rosidae). The curved embryos in the Urticales, Malvales, and Solanales are considered to be important in indicating close relationship among these groups. Thorne suggests that the Urticales show no close relationship to the Hamamelidae. The features he considers important in linking the order to the Malvales are the palmately veined, alternate, oblique, broad, stipulate leaves; the mucilage receptacles and cells and clustered crystals in the leaves and stems; extruded nucleoli in the sieve-tube elements; the alternating fibrous and nonfibrous layers in the phloem; and the often large and straight, bent, or folded embryos and other embryological features. The fossil record has not been particularly helpful in clarifying the relationships of the Urticales.

Fossils considered to belong to the family Ulmaceae date back to the Turonian Age of the Late Cretaceous (roughly 90 million years ago), and extant genera such as *Ulmus* (elms), *Zelkova* (keaki), *Celtis* (hackberries), *Aphananthe,* and *Gironniera* are known from the early Tertiary. In contrast, the early history of the Moraceae, Cannabaceae, and Urticaceae is not well known. The earliest record of the Moraceae is in pollen assigned to the family reported from the middle Eocene (about 45 million years ago), but both Moraceae and Cecropiaceae pollen have been reported from 2 million to 6.5 million years ago.

Fossil record of the Urticales

Overall, the fossil record of the Urticales is poor: only a single fossil flower, preserved in amber, from the Late Eocene (*i.e.,* 40 to 37 million years ago) seems to be unquestionably of the Urticaceae. Fossils attributable with fair certainty to extant Urticales are found in deposits from the early to middle Tertiary. The oldest fossil woods of the Urticales, those of the genus *Ficoxylon* in the Moraceae, are from the Paleocene to Miocene of Africa and Madagascar. More recent woods of this genus are also known from North America, Europe, and Cambodia.

Fruits are among the best fossils for certain identifications, but for the Urticales these, too, are scarce before the Eocene. From the late Eocene onward, however, the fossil record for the order improves considerably, and many fossil fruits representative of extant genera have been identified with certainty.

Fagales. *Distribution and abundance.* The order Fagales contains three families, the Balanopaceae, Betulaceae (the birch family), and Fagaceae (the beech family), which together include about 1,100–1,200 species. *Nothofagus,* the southern, evergreen, or New Zealand, beech, from the Southern Hemisphere, is sometimes recognized as a family distinct from the Fagaceae. The smallest family, the Balanopaceae, comprises only the genus *Balanops* with about 9 species restricted to the southwestern Pacific region, primarily New Caledonia.

The family Betulaceae contains 6 genera and about 120–150 species. It can be divided into 2 tribes, the Betuleae (with the genera *Alnus* and *Betula*) and the Coryleae (with *Carpinus, Corylus, Ostrya,* and *Ostryopsis*)—the Cronquist classification recognizes a third tribe, Carpineae—which at times have been recognized as separate families. The Betulaceae have occasionally been placed in a separate order, the Betulales. Members of the family are conspicuous elements in the colder parts of the Northern Hemisphere, where they are among the dominant woody plants in Arctic and Alpine regions, but the family is not restricted to those areas.

The birches

The genus *Betula* (the birches), with about 60 species, is the largest in the family. One species, *B. nana* (dwarf birch), a creeping shrub with tiny rounded leaves, reaches the northern limit of woody plants and appears to be nearly circumpolar in distribution. The genus *Alnus* (alders) is north temperate in distribution but ranges south through the Andes to about latitude 20° S. It is only in the Americas that members of the family extend along the mountains into the Southern Hemisphere.

Most genera in the family, with the exception of *Ostryopsis,* are widespread in their distribution. In *Betula,* for example, the silver birches (*B. pendula*) and the dwarf birches are circumboreal (*i.e.,* extending to the northern limit of the tree line); the two species very nearly coincide in their ranges, with the dwarf birches extending farther into the Arctic. They now occupy most areas that were glaciated until about 10,000 years ago. The greatest diversity in the family Betulaceae, however, is in the moist temperate forests of eastern Asia, particularly in China, where all six genera (including *Carpinus, Ostryopsis, Ostrya,* and *Betula*) are well represented. It has been speculated that *Alnus* may have originated in southeastern, eastern, or central Asia since the greatest morphological diversity in the genus, as well as the species considered to be the most primitive, occurs in that region.

Corylus contains about 15 species, including *C. avellana,* the hazelnut, filbert, or cobnut, distributed throughout the Northern Hemisphere. Species of *Corylus* are mostly shrubs or small trees that spread by means of sucker shoots and are able to form large colonies; however, the Turkish hazel (*C. colurna*) is a tree that may reach a height of about 24 metres, and a close relative in China (*C. chinensis*) grows up to about 20 metres tall.

The family Fagaceae, the beeches, contains about 1,000 species unevenly distributed among 9 genera (10 genera if *Nothofagus* is retained as a genus in the Fagaceae). The Fagaceae can be divided into 2 subfamilies. The first, Fagoideae, contains the genera *Fagus,* or beeches; *Quercus,* or oaks; *Colombobalanus; Formanodendron;* and *Trigonobalanus.* The second, Castaneoideae, contains *Castanea, Castanopsis, Chrysolepis* (which some experts include in the genus *Castanopsis*), and *Lithocarpus. Trigonobalanus verticillata,* restricted to Borneo, Sumatra, Celebes, and the Malay Peninsula, is unusual in the family in having the leaves arranged in whorls.

Fagus (the beeches) is a genus of about 10 species in the Northern Hemisphere, with the greatest diversity in China and Japan, where about 7 species are found. A single variable species, *F. grandifolia* (the American beech), occurs in eastern North America and Mexico, and another, *F. sylvatica,* is found in Europe.

The oaks

The largest genus in the Fagoideae, and in the entire Fagaceae, is the genus *Quercus* (the oaks), with about 450 species, mostly limited to the warmer parts of the Northern Hemisphere. The greatest concentrations of species of oaks are in the southeastern to southwestern United States and Mexico; in eastern Asia (China and Japan); and in the area from the Mediterranean to Caucasia.

In the Castaneoideae, the 12 or so species of the genus *Castanea* also show a worldwide distribution in temperate areas of the Northern Hemisphere, again with the greatest diversity in eastern Asia. The 2 species of *Chrysolepis* are confined to the western United States. The 2 remaining genera in the subfamily, *Lithocarpus,* with perhaps as many as 300 species, and *Castanopsis,* with about 120 species, are almost exclusively restricted, to eastern and southeastern Asia and the Indomalesian region (a region composed of India, Malaysia, New Guinea, Indonesia, the Philippines, and Borneo), mostly west of Wallace's Line (*i.e.,* Borneo, Java, and Bali, but not extending to Celebes).

Extant species of *Nothofagus* are scattered throughout southern South America, Australia, New Zealand, New Caledonia, and the mountains of New Guinea. The history of the genus has frequently been cited as evidence of continental drift after the breakup of the single large continent called Gondwanaland (or Gondwana) during the Middle Jurassic (187 to 163 million years ago). Because the fruits of *Nothofagus* are highly susceptible to damage by seawater, the plants could occur where they do only by the rafting of the continents or by the unlikely event that their seeds were transported by birds across vast distances of open ocean.

Economic and ecological importance. Members of the Fagaceae form a significant part of the broad-leaved forests characteristic of mid-latitudinal areas of the Northern Hemisphere and parts of the Southern Hemisphere. Much of the mixed deciduous forest region of North America is dominated by species of *Quercus. Fagus, Quercus,* and *Castanea* are prominent forest species in Europe, as is *Nothofagus* in the Southern Hemisphere. In the tropical forests of Southeast Asia, evergreen members of the family thrive in the mixed mountain forests. The Betulaceae generally occupy much of the same latitudes as the oak family in the Northern Hemisphere, but they extend into more northern latitudes where they are often part of forests at the northernmost limit of tree growth. The family extends into South America.

The oaks and birches are sources of some of the world's most valuable timbers. In both temperate and tropical America, many species of oak provide highly durable timber for use in construction, flooring, veneer, and millwork, as well as in the building of ships and boats. Members of the white oak group, including *Quercus alba, Q. macrocarpa,* and *Q. prinus,* among others, are especially valued in temperate America. In tropical America as well as in Southeast Asia and the Pacific Islands, the southern beech, *Nothofagus,* is used for flooring, cabinetwork, and millwork; it is an all-purpose timber in Chile. The wood of the genus *Castanopsis,* while susceptible to decay, is used in India, Malaysia, and the Philippines for general indoor construction. Several species of *Lithocarpus* provide timber in the same region. The American beech, *Fagus grandifolia,* and yellow birch, *Betula alleghaniensis* (*B. lutea*), are two of the three important northern hardwoods of the United States and are widely employed in flooring, veneer, woodenware, and millwork; in the Pacific Northwest, the principal wood is red alder (*Alnus rubra*). In East Asia, *Fagus crenata* is an important source of timber. While the American chestnut, *Castanea dentata,* was a highly valued timber in the past, its importance has diminished considerably since the advent of the chestnut blight. The Asian *Castanea crenata* and *C. henryi,* however, are important sources of timber.

Cork and tannins

Since the time of Confucius, cork has been used for a variety of purposes, from insulation to decoration. Commercial cork is obtained almost exclusively from the bark of the cork oak, *Quercus suber,* native to and cultivated in the Mediterranean region; however, other species also produce cork. The bark is first stripped from the trees when they are about 20 years old, although the first quality cork is not produced for another 8 to 10 years. Trees may produce cork for an average of 150 years. Oaks are also valuable sources of tannins (chemical compounds valued for, among other things, their ability to condition animal skins into leather. In America, the bark of *Lithocarpus densiflorus* (tanbark oak) as well as several species of *Quercus* are sources of tannin. The nutgalls produced on many *Quercus* species are excellent sources of tannin. Other chemical products were obtained at one time; for example, methyl alcohol, acetic acid, creosote, guaiacol, and tar were extracted from *Fagus;* and acetic acid was obtained from *Quercus robur.* Several species in the order have been used in dyeing—*e.g., Quercus velutina* in North America and *Castanea crenata* (Japanese chestnut) in East Asia.

Food products

Many members of the Fagales produce edible fruits, some of which have been cultivated since ancient times. The European (*Castanea sativa*) and Chinese (*C. mollissima*) chestnuts are economically important crops, although susceptibility to the chestnut blight fungus has somewhat diminished production of *C. sativa.* In North America, both the American chestnut (*C. dentata*) and the chinquapin (*C. pumila*) were used extensively by the native Indians for a variety of foods, from roasted nuts to breads; however, the advent of the blight and the subsequent destruction of vast stands of *C. dentata* virtually eliminated it as a source of food. Today, most of the commercial orchards in the United States grow cultivars of the Chinese species, and many of the roasted nuts sold in the United States are imported from Italy. *Corylus* (Betulaceae) is the source of the filbert, or hazelnut, grown for many centuries in parts of Europe. *C. avellana* is the source of most commercial nuts. By the 1990s, about 70 percent of the world's crop came from a small area in Turkey along the Black Sea.

Although not a commercial crop, the acorns produced by most species of oak (*Quercus*) are edible, but many require some preparation to remove the tannins. In North America, acorns were used extensively by the native Indians; the nuts of the "sweet" members of the white oak group were often consumed directly, while the bitter nuts of other species were ground and soaked before being made into mush or bread. Early American farmers valued acorns as a highly nutritional animal feed. During the American Civil War, acorns of the white oak were roasted and used to make a coffee substitute; roasted acorns continue to be used as a coffee substitute. Throughout the world, several species are used as feed for livestock and are important to local wildlife populations. The nuts of several *Lithocarpus* and *Castanopsis* species are a food source in their home countries of China and southeast Asia.

Other uses

Some oak species of East Asia are of indirect importance for humans. The logs of some species are used for the cultivation of edible fungi, especially shiitake mushrooms (*Lentinus edodes*) in Japan. In Tierra del Fuego, another edible fungus, *Cyttaria darwinii,* thrives on *Nothofagus* species. Some species of Fagales are used for silkworm culture in Asia, for example, *Quercus aliena* and *Q. fabri* in China; *Quercus* (*Cyclobalanopsis*) *glauca, Quercus acutissima,* and *Castanea crenata* (Japanese chestnut) in Japan; and *Q. semecarpifolia* in India. Others are cultivated as ornamentals for their distinctive form and foliage colour, such as many species of *Fagus, Quercus, Betula, Ostrya,* and *Corylus.*

Medicinal properties

The bark of *Alnus* was used by North American Indians to relieve indigestion, and that of *Quercus alba* has been used to make an extract for treating sore lips and mouth. In England, the inner bark of *Alnus glutinosa* (black alder) is employed as a mouthwash and as a treatment for inflamed gums or toothache. Both the American and the European beeches (*Fagus grandifolia* and *F. sylvatica,* respectively) are sources of the antiseptic creosote. Chewing sticks for cleaning teeth are made from the twigs of *Betula lenta* (American black birch, or cherry birch) and *B. alleghaniensis* (yellow birch) of eastern North America. For many centuries, the practice of using *ohaguro* ("tooth-black") in Japan was not only popular but was believed to preserve teeth and prevent decay; the acorns of *Quercus cyclophora* and the nutgalls of Chinese oaks were often the source of the tannin in this solution. North American Indians used the bark or nutgalls of several *Quercus* species to combat dysentery; the astringent properties of the tannins served as a powerful medicine.

Members of the Fagales are also known to be harmful. The pollen of almost all of the temperate genera—*Alnus, Betula, Carpinus, Corylus,* and *Ostrya* in the birch family, and *Fagus* and especially *Quercus* in the beech family—have been reported to cause allergic reactions.

Characteristic morphological features. The Fagales are all trees or shrubs with simple leaves usually arranged alternately (rarely opposite or whorled). Each plant generally contains tiny flowers of each sex (monoecious); unisexual flowers are primarily pollinated by the wind. The staminate often, and the pistillate sometimes, are arranged in catkins (aments). The perianth is absent or represented by a single rudimentary whorl of tepals. The pistillate flowers are often subtended by a cupule (hull), which sometimes partially or completely encloses the fruit. There are generally 2 to many distinct stamens in each flower, although in some cases there is only 1. The pistillate flowers (*i.e.,* those

Drawing by M. Pahl based on H. Hjelmqvist, "Studies on the floral morphology and phylogeny of the Amentiferae," *Botanical Notiser* supp. 2:1 (1948)

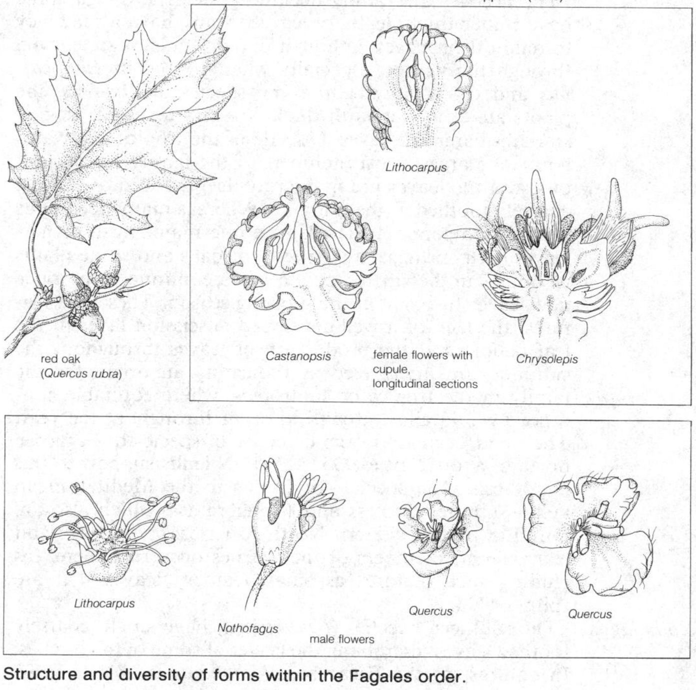

Structure and diversity of forms within the Fagales order.

without a functional stamen) contain 2, 3, or 6 (to 12) carpels, with the carpels united to form an inferior ovary with as many locules (cavities) as carpels, at least in the lower part of the ovary, but with the partitions often not reaching the summit of the ovary. The styles are distinct or united at the base, and there are 1 or 2 ovules in each locule. The fruit is a nut, samara, or drupe, often one or several together surrounded by a hull or cupule. The seeds contain a large embryo and little or no endosperm.

Fagales families

Three families—Fagaceae, Betulaceae, and Balanopaceae (Balanopsidaceae)—make up the order. (The latter family is placed in a separate order, the Balanopales, by Armen Takhtajan.) The most distinguishing feature of the Fagales is the cupule (hull) subtending or surrounding the fruit. The structure is believed to be of a different origin in each of the three families: in the Balonopaceae it consists of a tight, spirally arranged series of bracts; in the Fagaceae it is derived from a highly modified and reduced branch system with its associated modified leaves or bracts, at least in the genus *Quercus;* and in the Betulaceae the husks are thought to be made up of several modified bracts. It also has been suggested that the four-valved cupule of *Nothofagus* is derived from the four stipules at the base of the two bracts borne beneath the inflorescence. The interpretation is that bracts themselves are highly reduced or absent, while the stipules are greatly enlarged and modified. The Balanopaceae differ from other families in the order in having basally attached ovules and fleshy fruits containing more than one seed. The Fagaceae and Betulaceae have pendulous ovules and dry fruits that are either nuts or samaras and bear a single seed.

Of the extant genera of Fagaceae, *Chrysolepis* is considered to exhibit the most primitive features in the pistillate (female) flowers. The basic structure of the pistillate inflorescence is believed to be a three-flowered dichasium (an older central flower and a pair of opposite lateral branches bearing flowers). At one stage in the history of the family the primitive flower (and subsequent fruit) is thought to have been surrounded by three valves. From this basic condition it is surmised that two of the flowers of each dichasium have become lost in the course of evolution. No living member of the Fagaceae exhibits this primitive condition, but in *Chrysolepis* the three flowers are surrounded by five outer and two inner valves, presumably exhibiting the condition where one outer and one inner valve have already been lost. From this condition it is easy to postulate the reduction and loss of parts in concert with the fusion of the remaining ones to arrive at the types of fruiting structures seen in the Fagaceae today.

The beeches are tardily deciduous trees, although some have rather thick, leathery leaves. Many have a tendency to retain their leaves, although in a dry, lifeless state, even through the winter, especially when young. In *Lithocarpus* and *Chrysolepis,* and some species of *Quercus,* the plants are evergreen with thick, leathery-textured, usually smooth-margined leaves. Outside of the tropics and warm temperate areas, most members of the family are deciduous, and the leaves are frequently deeply lobed or at least coarsely toothed at the margins. Whereas many deciduous trees in temperate areas produce one major flush of new leaves each spring, many species of oaks and some plants in other families in temperate areas continue to produce new leaves throughout the growing season. These two features, the lack of a well-developed abscission layer in the leaf petiole and the production of leaves throughout the summer, are interpreted as indicating an origin for the family in the tropics or subtropics, where equitable conditions would allow growth to occur throughout the year. The rapid decrease in the diversity of species of Fagaceae north of about latitude 35° to 40° N lends support to this hypothesis. The special conditions in the Mediterranean area—summer dryness and winter rains—which also are found in part of western North America, give a dry habit character to members of the Fagales occurring there, including such features as small leathery leaves that are spiny or hairy.

Nothofagus

The southern beeches (*Nothofagus*) have small, coarsely toothed leaves resembling the leaves of some of the birches. In contrast to the Fagaceae, *Nothofagus* is able to grow in cold, inhospitable climates, even adjacent to the snow line in the mountains of South America. In this respect, the genus is more similar in ecological preference to the family Betulaceae than to the Fagaceae and perhaps can be thought of as the Southern Hemisphere counterpart of the birches. This fits in with other evidence that indicates a closer kinship for *Nothofagus* with the Betulaceae than with the Fagaceae.

The inflorescences of the Betulaceae comprise a central axis on which are borne a series of greatly reduced and compressed, spirally arranged cymules. The hypothetical ancestral inflorescence consisted of three flowers, each on a separate stalk, with each of these joined to a main stalk, and seven leaflike bracts. The extant inflorescence in the Betulaceae is believed to have been derived through the evolutionary loss of the flower stalks, peduncle, and one or more of the bracts, reduction in size of the flowers, and compression of the main axis of the inflorescence. In all genera except *Betula* the cymes have been reduced to two flowers. *Betula,* with three-flowered cymes, retains the ancestral arrangement. All the original bracts are still present in the female flowers of *Carpinus, Ostrya,* and *Ostryopsis;* the uppermost bracts have been lost in *Betula;* and one bract is lost in *Corylus.* The tepals are still present in the flowers of *Carpinus, Corylus, Ostrya,* and *Ostryopsis* but have been completely lost in the course of evolution in *Alnus* and *Betula.*

From (*Betula occidentalis*) *Taxonomy of Flowering Plants,* 2nd ed., by C.L. Porter, W.H. Freeman and Company, Copyright © 1967, and (others) C. Sargent, *Manual of the Trees of North America* (1922), Dover Publications, Inc.

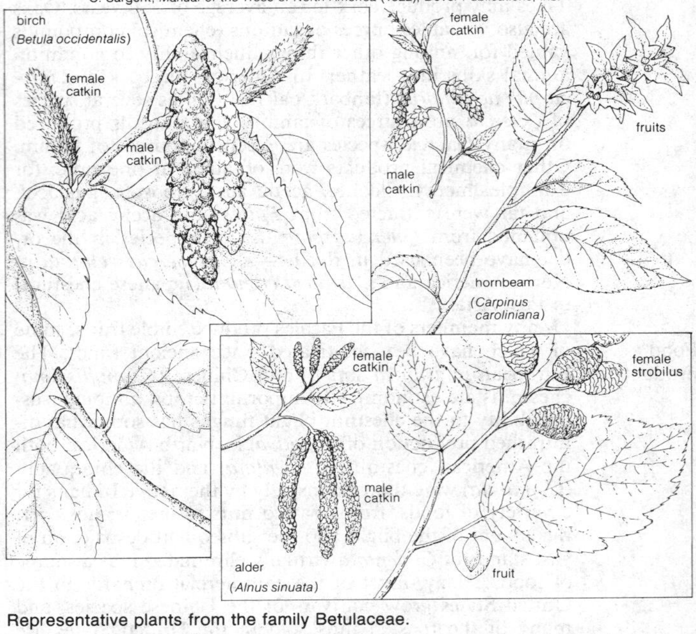

Representative plants from the family Betulaceae.

In *Betula* and *Alnus,* which have the smallest fruits in the Fagales, both the female and male flowers are borne in catkins. The catkins of the female flowers of *Alnus* are woody and reminiscent of the cones of some gymnosperms. The scales spread apart at maturity to release the ripe fruit. In *Betula,* the bracts of the catkins are deciduous, and the mature catkin shatters to release the winged fruit. In the remaining genera of Betulaceae, the fruits are nuts or nutlets borne in saclike husks or attached to leaflike bracts.

The husk that surrounds the nuts of *Corylus ferox* produces long spines and bears a striking resemblance to the husk of the fruits of *Castanea* and some species of *Castanopsis* in the Fagaceae, but in other species of *Corylus* the husks are more leaflike in appearance or tubular and flask-shaped. Although they are not spiny, the husks frequently bear numerous multicellular, glandular hairs, which exude a sticky substance that may deter predation of the nuts.

Evolution. Since the pollen of Fagaceae and Betulaceae show a marked similarity to the pollen of *Normapolles* from the Cretaceous Period (144 to 66.4 million years

Earliest known fossils

ago), it is thought by some that they may have originated from within that assemblage. The earliest known fossils of the Fagales are pollen specimens from the Campanian Age (84 to 74.5 million years ago) of the Late Cretaceous, while the *Normapolles* group was still in existence, but no forms transitional to modern forms are known. Various other fossils date to the end of the Cretaceous.

The earliest unquestionable remains of the subfamily Castaneoideae (Fagaceae) date about 57.8 million years ago to the Paleocene-Eocene border. These fossils from western Tennessee resemble most closely the extant genus *Castanopsis* (now restricted to eastern Asia). Pollen typical of this subfamily also has been found in association with the macrofossil remains, which some suggest supports the theory that extant members of subfamily Castaneoideae resemble the ancestral condition.

Associated with the fossils of the Castaneoideae are other fossils of Fagales, including some that closely resemble *Trigonobalanus, Colombobalanus,* and *Formanondendron.* The Castaneoideae and members of *Trigonobalanus* made up most of the Fagales until the Oligocene-Miocene, when the flora of Fagales took on a more modern aspect and began making an appearance in the fossil record by groups resembling the beeches (*Fagus*) and white oaks (*Quercus*). With the expansion of these groups, both the Castaneoideae and the members of *Trigonobalanus* declined in numbers, with the members of *Trigonobalanus* nearly becoming extinct and now being restricted to three very widely separated and localized areas.

Pollen characteristic of *Alnus* (alders) in the tribe Betuleae from the Santonian and Campanian ages (roughly 87.5 to 74.5 million years ago) of the Late Cretaceous in Japan and North America represents the earliest record of the family Betulaceae. Fossil leaves similar to those of the Betuleae have been found in deposits from about 70 million years ago and from the Paleocene in the early Tertiary (about 60 million years ago) but are not associated with the reproductive structures that would make identification certain. Reproductive structures of *Alnus* have been found in Paleocene deposits in Alaska and in the former U.S.S.R. The oldest fossil inflorescences and leaves to be identified with certainty as *Betula* are found in Eocene deposits in British Columbia and eastern Oregon.

Fossils of pollen and wood from the Campanian-Maastrichtian (*i.e.,* Late Cretaceous) of western North America have been attributed tentatively to the tribe Coryleae, but it is not until the early Tertiary that the fossil record of the Coryleae is more certain. Fruits resembling those of *Corylus* and *Carpinus* from several localities in North America, Greenland, and western Europe have been found. Definite *Carpinus* fruits with attached bracts are known from the late Eocene of Japan, and *Ostrya* is first definitely recognized in Oligocene deposits in western North America.

Apparent evolutionary pathway to wind pollination

Despite the absence of fossils showing a clear transition, the Swiss botanist Peter Endress and others consider the catkins and the reduced and simplified flowers and inflorescences in the Fagaceae and Betulaceae to represent the culmination of an evolutionary pathway leading to wind pollination from insect-pollinated ancestors. In members of the Betulaceae and Fagaceae numerous staminate (pollen-producing) flowers are borne in pendulous catkins, and the pistillate flowers generally show modifications, such as elongate styles and enlarged or feathery stigmas, to receive wind-transported pollen grains. All the earliest fossils attributed to the Fagales already manifest these changes, and so it is impossible to know exactly how the changes took place. Based on the available evidence, Endress speculates that the Fagales arose either from temperate, deciduous, insect-pollinated ancestors in the Hamamelidaceae or from an earlier group that gave rise to the Hamamelidaceae. The adaptations to wind pollination allowed the Fagales to rapidly diversify so that by the early Tertiary they were already one of the dominant groups over a large portion of the Earth. (D.E.Bo.)

Subclass Caryophyllidae

The subclass Caryophyllidae consists of three orders, Caryophyllales, Polygonales, and Plumbaginales, although the vast majority of its members are found in the order Caryophyllales.

POLYGONALES AND PLUMBAGINALES

Morphological features

The order Polygonales comprises a single family, Polygonaceae, the buckwheat, or dock, family, with about 30 to 40 genera and about 1,000 species. Consisting mostly of herbs and some trees, shrubs, and vines, Polygonaceae is prevalent in north temperate areas. The leaves of this family alternate along the stem, and the stipules are usually united into a sheath that surrounds the stem at the base of the leaf petiole. The inflorescences are generally cymes or racemes, and the individual flowers are bisexual with a superior ovary consisting of three united carpels at the base of which is a single ovule.

Although small, the order consists of some popular vegetables and cultivated ornamentals. One of the best known vegetables in the order is rhubarb (*Rheum × cultorum*), a hybrid cultivated for its edible leafstalks; sorrel (*Rumex acetosa*), is used as a green vegetable in salads, and buckwheat (*Fogopyrum esculentum*) is grown for the flour produced from it. Seaside grape (*Coccoloba uvifera*) develops an edible fruit used in making jellies. Redshank, or willowweed (*Polygonum persicaria*), is a common weed in the United States but is grown as an ornamental in many parts of Europe.

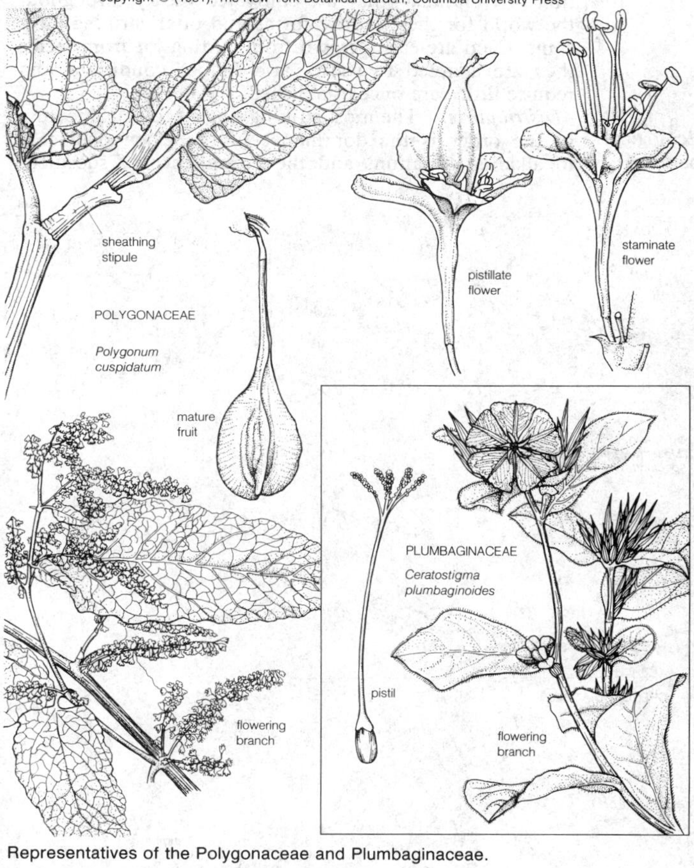

Representatives of the Polygonaceae and Plumbaginaceae.

Plumbaginales contains a single family, Plumbaginaceae, or the leadwort family. Although common throughout the world, members of the order thrive along seashores and in other saline environments. The family consists of perennial herbs, shrubs, and leaves. The leaves are simple and entire and without stipules; they form rosettes at the base of the stem or grow in an alternate pattern on branched stems. The flowers are regular with a superior ovary and form racemes, cymes, or panicles. The largest genera, *Plumbago* (leadwort) and *Limonium,* are popular garden plants.

Caryophyllales is by far the largest and most diverse order and will be discussed separately below. (Ed.)

CARYOPHYLLALES

General features. *Diversity of structure.* The order Caryophyllales (the pink order) is a group of dicotyledonous plants, ranging from garden subjects and vegetables to bizarre succulent plants that resemble stones. The garden plants include carnations, pinks, four-o'clocks, amaranths, portulacas, and Madeira vines. Vegetables in the order include beet, spinach, and Swiss chard. The fig marigold family (Aizoaceae) includes ice plants, sea figs (also called beach apples), and living stones. The cacti (family Cactaceae) are included in this order as well, although some authorities place them in a separate order, Cactales.

The Caryophyllales include mostly herbs, but various families have shrubs, vines, and trees. On the whole, the order is not noted for the size attained by its members. Commonly, the species are most prevalent in moist temperate or tropical environments, but many members of the goosefoot family (Chenopodiaceae) are restricted to salty, alkaline soil. In some salt-tolerant species, the leaves are succulent (fleshy). Leaf succulence is also common in the family Aizoaceae and remarkably so in its numerous southern African members.

The cacti are curious, often thorny (spiny), fleshy-stemmed plants constituting the family Cactaceae, characteristic of and well adapted to dry regions. Although the cacti are native to the Americas—with the possible exception of *Rhipsalis*—they are cultivated widely throughout the world for their bizarre forms and often striking blossoms. Cacti are easily grown from cuttings or from seeds; they are adapted to warm, arid indoor conditions and require little care once established.

Ecological patterns

Distribution. The most striking single ecological feature in the order is the dominance of the Chenopodiaceae in alkaline situations and the prominence of succulent Aizoaceae in the deserts of southern Africa. The other members of the order occur in any of several types of habitat, but in general none is conspicuous. Even the Aizoaceae in the southern African deserts are not conspicuous except when they are in flower.

Drawing by M. Pahl

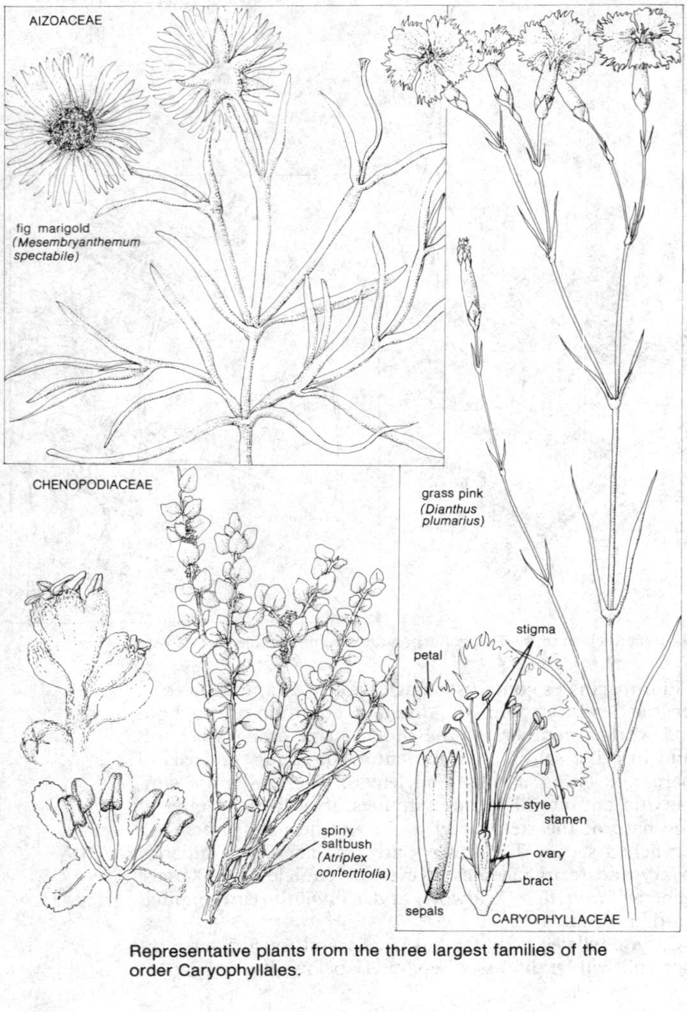

Representative plants from the three largest families of the order Caryophyllales.

Characteristic geographic distribution patterns occur in individual families, but none is typical of the order as a whole. The pokeweed family (Phytolaccaceae) and the Madeira vine, or basellar, family (Basellaceae) include plants primarily of the American tropics. The amaranth family (Amaranthaceae) is most highly developed in tropical America and tropical Africa. The four-o'clock family (Nyctaginaceae) is common throughout the tropics but occurs also in the warmer temperate regions. The fig marigold family (Aizoaceae) occurs over most of the Earth, but its chief centre of distribution is in desert and temperate latitudes of southern Africa. The Caryophyllaceae (pink family) and the Portulacaceae (purslane family) are characteristic of temperate regions. The carpetweed family (Molluginaceae) is found in tropical and temperate areas, especially in Africa. The Didiereaceae is centred in Madagascar, and Achaocarpaceae is found in the temperate regions of America. The goosefoot family (Chenopodiaceae) occurs throughout the world, but its greatest development is in salty or alkaline areas, particularly those of coastal salt marshes and deserts.

The Cactaceae are native through most of the length of North and South America, from British Columbia and Alberta southward. The northernmost limit is along the Peace River in Canada; the southernmost limit extends far into Chile and Argentina. The only representatives of the family possibly native to the Old World are members of the genus *Rhipsalis,* occurring in East Africa, Madagascar, and Sri Lanka. Whether these plants are native or were introduced in these tropical areas is a matter of disagreement, as is the possibility of dispersal of this highly specialized group from the Western Hemisphere to the Eastern Hemisphere.

Various species of *Opuntia* (prickly pear cactus and chollas) and some other genera have been introduced into the Mediterranean region, and some have grown wild there since shortly after the discovery of America. Species of *Opuntia* are widely naturalized in India, the Malayan region, Hawaii, and Australia. In Australia and eastern Cape Province in South Africa, they have become pests and are controlled largely by larvae of moth species from *Opuntia*'s original native habitat.

Economic and ecological importance. The order Caryophyllales includes a number of important plants known for their unusual beauty, nutritional value, or peculiar adaptations to difficult habitats. Many members are used to produce medicines, while others cause disease or even death.

Perhaps the best known ornamental of the order is *Dianthus* (Caryophyllaceae), the pinks, a strongly scented group of plants when found in nature. Native to Europe and Asia, *D. chinensis* (the Chinese pink), *D. plumarius* (the clove pink), *D. deltoides* (the maiden pink), and *D. barbatus* (sweet William) all develop in clumpy growths with numerous colourful flowers. Although perhaps less fragrant than the wild pinks, *D. caryophyllus,* the carnation, is commercially grown in large numbers and is a popular cut flower. Another important cut flower in the family is baby's breath (*Gypsophila paniculata*), native to Europe, Asia, Australia, and New Zealand. *Minuartia* and *Stellaria* (both known as chickweed), and *Sagina* (pearlwort) are herbaceous plants in this family and are well adapted to rock gardens, although species do develop as weeds. *Gypsophila rokejeka,* in combination with sesame seeds and honey, is used in making the confection halvah. *G. struthium* is found in Europe and the United States and may have some curative effects on certain skin diseases. *Arenaria rubra* (sandwort) is a common member of sandy heaths near the sea in Europe, Asia, North America, and Australia and has been used as a folk medicine to cure acute and chronic cystitis. *Saponaria officinalis* (soapwort) is common in central and southern Europe, and its dried roots and flowers are purported to cure skin problems.

Popular cut flowers

The bougainvillea (*Bougainvillea;* Nyctaginaceae) is a

climbing plant found in tropical America and is unusual in that its insignificant flowers arise from brightly coloured, long-lasting bracts (specialized leaves subtending flowers) arranged in groups of three to resemble a flower. The leaves of *Neea theifera* are used as a tea in Brazil. *Mirabilis,* the four-o'clock flower, is a night-flowering herbaceous perennial from tropical America. The white, pink, red, or yellow funnel-shaped flowers of the four-o'clock flower open late in the afternoon and close the following morning. The plant develops tuberous roots from which it can be propagated. The root tea of *M. nyctaginea* was used by the American Indians to treat burns and fever and as an anthelmintic. *M. nyctaginea* is considered to be extremely poisonous. Various species of *Mirabilis* and *Neea* are edible.

The family Chenopodiaceae contains a number of important plants. Species of the saltbush (*Atriplex*) are extremely tolerant of environments with a high salt concentration and do exceedingly well near coastal areas. *A. halimus,* the sea orach, is cultivated for its beautiful foliage and silvery-gray stems; its flowers remain green and rather insignificant. *A. hortensis,* the garden orach, was at one time used as a cure for gout. Another genus containing interesting ornamentals, *Bassia,* includes the summer cypress and the burning bush; the leaves of the latter turn a beautiful red in autumn.

Importance as vegetable crops

Beta, also a member of Chenopodiaceae, contains two important vegetable crops. *B. vulgaris,* subspecies *vulgaris,* is the sugar beet or beetroot, a plant derived from the wild sea beet (*B. vulgaris* subspecies *maritima*). Beetroot is a native of southern Europe and is cultivated for the high concentration of sugar in the root (the sugar content in the root may constitute up to 20 percent of the weight of the plant). The boiled leaves are similar in taste to spinach. The beet can be stewed, boiled, pickled, or baked; in eastern Europe, it is used in a soup called borscht. Cultivars of the beetroot include Forono, Cylindia, Boltardy, Detroit Globe, and Monopoly. *Beta vulgaris,* subspecies *cicla,* or Swiss chard, is grown only for its leaves; cultivars include Rhubarb Chard and Ruby Chard. Spinach (*Spinacia oleracea*) is a cultivated leafy vegetable with a high content of iron. *Chenopodium* (goosefoot) contains succulent herbs that commonly develop as weeds along seacoasts and salt marshes. *C. quinoa* is a native of the Andes in South America and is cultivated as an important nutritious grain crop by people in that region. The American Indians used the whole herb of the goosefoot in a decoction for painful menstruation; the essential oil was once used for its anthelmintic properties but has since been replaced by synthetic medicines.

The leaves of *Amaranthus hybridus* (smooth pigweed; Amaranthaceae) are used as a leafy vegetable similar to spinach and can be made into a tea that is purported to have astringent properties and to cure dysentery, diarrhea, and ulcers. The word amaranthus is from the Greek for "unwithering," and the plant was used as a symbol of immortality. The ancient Greeks held *A. hypochondriacus* (love-lies-bleeding, or the prince's feather) as sacred for its healing properties and used it to decorate tombs and images of gods. *Alternanthera philoxeroides* (the alligator weed) was introduced into North America as a cultivated ornamental, but its rapid growth habit in watery environments has often caused it to be considered a weed. *Gomphrena globosa* (the globe amaranth; Amaranthaceae) is from tropical Asia, Australia, and America. It is unusual in that the flower heads of tiny pink, white, or purple flowers are subtended by two coloured leafy bracts.

Phytolacca (pokeweed, poke, or the red inkberry; Phytolaccaceae) is a hardy perennial native to the United States. It is a poisonous, invasive plant with an unpleasant smell, although its oval, green, red-tinged leaves and erect red stems with spikes of white flowers are very attractive. The American Indians brewed the berries of *P. americana* into a tea that was used to treat rheumatism, arthritis, and dysentery. All parts of the plant, however, are considered to be extremely poisonous if not prepared carefully.

Lewisia (the tobacco root; Portulacaceae) is a native of North America. It was named in honour of Captain Meriwether Lewis, a leader of the Lewis and Clark Expedition of the Missouri River and northwestern United States from 1804 to 1806. The root is highly nutritious and was eaten by the American Indians. *L. rediviva* (bitterroot) develops a thick, starchy edible root and is often grown as an ornamental in rock gardens. *Claytonia lanceolata* develops corms that were once eaten by North American Indians, and *C. virginica* (spring beauty) is a cultivated ornamental.

Anredera cordifolia (the Madeira vine; Basellaceae) is a native of South America and is cultivated for its beautiful viny habit. *Basella alba* (Basellaceae) is the nightshade (a common name also given to members of the genus *Solanum* of the order Solanales).

Economic value of cacti

As mentioned above, the cacti are an unusual group of plants well adapted to their generally harsh, arid environments. Cacti are economic plants in Mexico, parts of Central and South America, and the Caribbean region. Various species are cultivated for food, including vast complexes of prickly pears, especially of *Opuntia ficus-indica,* and the torch cactus (*Cereus*). Drinks prepared from some cactus fruits have been a popular native medicine for fevers. In Mexico, leaves of chollas, resembling string beans, are eaten. In Latin America, species of *Opuntia, Cereus,* and other genera are planted around houses, often forming an impenetrable barrier. Barrel cacti (*Echinocactus* and *Ferocactus*) are a source of water in emergencies.

Cacti are cultivated chiefly for their ornamental features and general hardiness. They can be grafted easily, and many rare species are propagated by grafting upon more vigorous stocks. Many small cacti are suitable for home cultivation. Without water, most cacti persist but do not grow. Some species, however, do require periodic drought. Many species grow well in warm weather in full sun, pro-

(*Ferocactus wislizenii, Cereus, Cereus giganteus*) drawn by M. Pahl

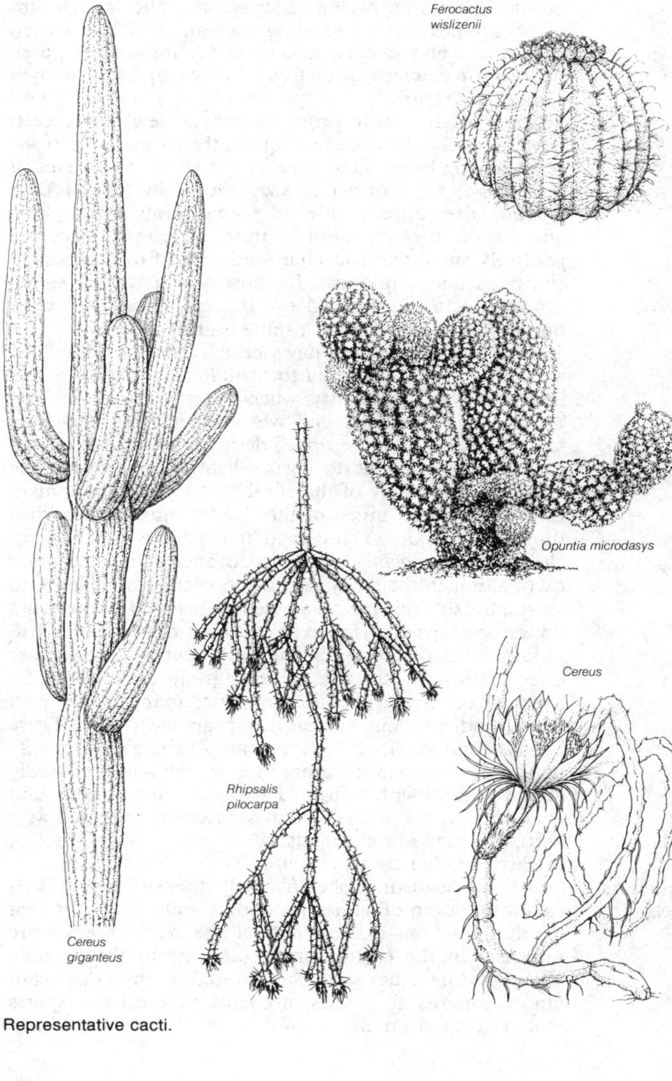

Representative cacti.

vided there is adequate soil moisture, but others require some shade.

Form and function. *Vegetative structures.* The external vegetative characteristics of the plants in the Caryophyllales vary greatly; no specific feature can be singled out as indicative of the group. Certain tendencies are noteworthy but not distinguishing. Only rarely do the leaf bases bear stipules (leaflike tabs). Succulents occur in the Cactaceae, Aizoaceae, and Didiereaceae (a small Madagascan family), as well as in some of the Portulacaceae, Chenopodiaceae, Basellaceae, and Phytolaccaceae. The leaves are usually alternate or opposite and simple and entire.

The cacti are succulent perennials with herbaceous or woody chlorophyll-containing stems. Because almost all cacti (except *Pereskia* and a few other primitive cactus genera) do not develop functional leaves, the stem has taken over the photosynthetic function of the plant.

Morphological features of cacti

Cacti vary greatly in size and general appearance. *Opuntia* and other genera are jointed with short stem segments or pads that break apart easily. The creeping cacti spread quickly above ground; where they contact the ground they send out new roots. Epiphyte cacti grow on other plants or on hard substrates such as rocks. They generally have thin, flat stems for easy absorption of water, and the protective spines prevalent among ground cacti are replaced by hairs or bristles. Climbing cacti, such as the orchid, or leaf, cactus (*Epiphyllum*) and some *Rhipsalis* species are found in forests and develop few internal structural supports but support themselves with spines and aerial roots. In addition, cacti show an overall gradient in design from flattened, nonbranching discs to globes through various degrees of columnar forms, including branching at or below ground level in the more elongate forms, to bushy and arborescent forms. Examples include the peyote, or mescal, button (*Lophophora*) and low clumps of prickly pear cactus to upright columns of barrel cacti (*Ferocactus* and *Echinocactus*) and the imposing saguaro (*Carnegiea gigantea,* sometimes known by the synonym *Cereus giganteus*).

Except for the more primitive genera, few of the cacti have functional leaves, the photosynthetic functions of the plant having been taken over by the stem. The leaves, if discernible, are reduced in size (except in *Pereskia*). In *Opuntia* they appear only on young joints of the stem and fall off after a month or more of growth. They are relatively small and succulent and range from conical to elongated and cylindrical. In most genera the leaves are not visible to the unaided eye but are represented by a hump of tissue just below a spine-bearing areole.

Some succulent stems have been further modified by an overall ribbed design, a form uniquely adapted to extremes in water variability; when water is scarce the folds between the ribs sink, and when water is available the folds swell. Further, the ribbed design increases the overall surface area available to absorb light. The stems of the epiphytes and many of the climbing cacti usually remain thin, however, as much of their water must be absorbed through the walls. Those cacti that have evolved tubercles (*e.g., Ferocactus*) are more advanced than the other cacti; although they may bear a superficial resemblance to leaves, the tubercle has an areole (see below) from which a flower develops and is therefore a shoot rather than a leaf.

Many other plants, succulent and essentially leafless, are often confused with cacti. A large group of spurges (*Euphorbia*) occurring in Africa includes many plants with long cylindrical stems similar in appearance to cacti. These plants, common in cultivation, are distinguished readily by their milky juice, a feature rare in cacti and supposedly absent in cacti with elongated stems. Yuccas (Yucca) and the agave (*Agave;* both of Liliales) often are confused with cacti, but they are distinguished readily by succulence of the leaves rather than the stem.

Spines in cacti

Cacti can be distinguished from all other succulent plants by the presence of spines in areoles, small cushions that develop from an axillary bud of the stem. Areoles are universal in the cactus family (at least in the juvenile phase) and have not so far been found in any other plant family. Almost all species of cactus have tufts of spines that develop from the areoles. These spines are of two basic types, stiff central spines located in the middle of the areole, and radial spines, which grow out laterally from the edges of the areole; the former are probably protective or when brightly coloured attract pollinators, while the latter are often white and reflect sunlight, providing shade and protecting the plant body from solar radiation. In addition, these spines may be variously modified, depending on the species; for example, they may be curved, hooked, feathery, bristly, flattened, sheathed, or needlelike. The only generally spineless cacti are the epiphytes, in which the protection afforded by the spines is not required in the relatively protected environment of the host plant, and various cacti that have developed aggressive chemical defenses.

The large, flat pads of the prickly pear cactus collect water from condensation and channel it to the joints between the pads; the water then drips or streams to the soil just under the plant. Some species of cacti have spines that point downward; water collected on the spines, even from light mists, is directed in droplets to the ground. The saguaro's downward-pointed spines during its earlier years of growth collect water and repel rodents that might eat the succulent stems to secure water. In older saguaros the stem above the approximately 1.2- to 1.5-metre level produces another, not downward-directed, type of spine. For plants growing near the lower edge of a rock or a crack between rocks, the amount of water available from a relatively light rain may be greatly increased, as it would be for a plant living under the edge of a roof.

The root systems of cacti are generally thin, fibrous, and shallow, ranging widely and absorbing superficial moisture. Some cacti develop extremely long taproots that exploit deep underground water supplies. In addition, some cacti, such as *Lophophora,* develop water storage organs in their roots. Substances from the roots of some desert plants, and perhaps some of the cacti, prevent the invasion of any other plants nearby, thus increasing the chance of continued survival. The absence of leaves reduces the ratio of plant surface to internal plant volume, as does the thickening of the stems, thus discouraging transpiration and aiding water retention.

Within their natural range, cacti occur in a wide variety of soil types. Frequently, a species is restricted to a particular type of rock formation, such as limestone or igneous rock. A few species are confined to localized rock outcroppings, a limitation particularly striking in the genus *Pediocactus* (snowball cactus), in which most of its species are found on special rock ledges on the Colorado Plateau or on gypsum-rich soil.

Some species of Cactaceae are associated with subtropical rain forests, as in the Everglades in Florida, where species of *Opuntia* and torch cactus occur at points at which the water table may be only several centimetres below the surface. Most species are sensitive to cold, but many grow in regions with cold winters, as in the United States on the Great Plains and in the Great Basin and the Rocky Mountains.

Betalains in Caryophyllales

In most flowering plants, colours ranging from nearly red to nearly blue (*i.e.,* from violet to purple) are dependent on the presence of chemical compounds called anthocyanins; colours ranging from yellow to reddish orange are dependent on compounds called anthoxanthins. A distinct but parallel series of pigments occurs only in a large number of Caryophyllales, including the cacti, and a limited number of other families of the flowering plants. These substances, known as betalains, include betacyanins, which produce colours from near red to near blue, and betaxanthins, which produce colours in the yellow to reddish orange series. The presence of betacyanins especially, rather than anthocyanins, is presumed to be of taxonomic significance. Betacyanins have been found in many of the Caryophyllales but not in any members of the family Caryophyllaceae or the Molluginaceae. Their presence also in the cacti is an indication of the relationship of these plants to the Caryophyllales.

Reproductive structures. Throughout most of the order, the flowers have true sepals but no true petals. Some families that display what appear to be petals, such as Portulacaceae and Nyctaginaceae, are thought to have greatly modified sepals, in which case the sepallike appendages are then interpreted as bracts. The Caryophyllaceae, however, apparently have true petals developed by the usual means—that is to say, through modification of individual stamens or portions of them.

Frequently the flowers of Cactaceae are large, attractive, and white or brightly coloured. Except in the most primitive genera, the flowers grow directly on the stem at the areoles. All the genera have a floral (perianth) tube that invests the ovary, and, except in *Pereskia,* adheres to its surface (the ovary is inferior, and the flower is said to be epigynous). The portion of the tube covering the ovary usually develops small, inconspicuous scales, which increase gradually in size upward on the free portion of the floral tube above the ovary. They grade into flower parts that resemble sepals and, farther up, into parts that resemble petals. There are many conspicuous stamens and 3 to 20 or more stigmas. In some groups, especially *Opuntia,* there is only a short floral tube above the ovary, but in others, as with some species of torch cactus, the tube may be very long.

In most members of the order, the stamens are in one or two series (concentric circles around the central axis of the flower) or sometimes in three series of three; in some cases, however, as in many of the Aizoaceae, there are numerous stamens.

The carpels are united and commonly enclose a single locule, but there may be 3 to 12, 1 for each carpel. Usually, there are as many styles as carpels, and they are not united. The structure and positioning of the ovule in most members of the Caryophyllales differ from the common type in the flowering plants in being curved or coiled in a special way. The ovule is surrounded by two coverings (integuments), the inner being longer than the outer. The embryo lies toward the outside of the ovule, surrounding the food-storage tissue, which usually is not formed from a nutritive tissue (endosperm) during fertilization, as in most flowering plants. Commonly, most of the food is stored in the perisperm. The features of the ovules, embryos, and seeds are similar to those of the cacti, which further strengthens the case for a relationship.

The ovary and the investing floral tube of the Cactaceae may develop into a fleshy and often edible fruit. The ovary is one-chambered, and the numerous ovules borne on the walls give rise to numerous seeds. The ovules usually are campylotropous—that is, curved between the hilum (point of attachment to the funiculus) and the opening through which the pollen tube enters (micropyle).

The characteristic feature of cactus seedlings is the pair of large seed leaves (cotyledons), which tend to be succulent, sometimes markedly so. From seed some species reach the flowering stage in two or three years, and both flowers and fruits may be developed even on stems that still retain juvenile characters. (This curious feature led to the misleading naming of many supposed species on the basis of plants that seemed to be mature because of reproduction but that did not have the expected type of thorns.)

Usually within a few years the succulent stem assumes the characteristic form and appendages of the species. In the prickly pears, in which the adult stem is composed of flattened pads arranged end to end, the portion developed in the first year of growth is cylinder-like for several months, the upper portion gradually becoming flattened, and the joints developed later being flat.

Most cacti reach a considerable relative size within 5 or 10 years, but some grow much slower. Information concerning the age of older plants usually is lacking because the woody parts are very thin; counting of growth rings requires sectioning and careful study with a compound microscope. The saguaro, or giant cactus, is alleged to attain ages in the hundreds of years.

Pollination of the Cactaceae is mostly by insects or birds, though sometimes by other animals such as bats. Because there is no precise mechanism governing the pathway of pollinators, the process of pollination tends to be haphazard, at least in most of the larger flowers of the open (as opposed to the tubular) types. Most flowers open in the daytime and are visited by day-flying insects or birds, but many, especially such species as the saguaro and the various species of *Cereus,* open at night. As with other night-pollinated plants, the night-blooming cacti tend to be white-flowered.

Evolution. As is true of most other chiefly herbaceous orders of flowering plants, the Caryophyllales have left virtually no fossil record. Any evidence of phylogeny, therefore, must come primarily from a consideration of the living members of the order. The origin of the Caryophyllales, in consequence, is largely a matter of speculation. The order was presumably derived from the ancestral complex of the buttercup family (Ranunculales; sometimes classified as an order, Ranales), but the present relationship of these orders is not close, and the lines of origin of the Caryophyllales are obscure.

Origin of the Caryophyllales

The evolutionary course of the cacti is also difficult to trace. One *Opuntia*-like fossil has been uncovered, but evidence suggests that it may not represent a cactus at all. Primitive living cacti may suggest lineage. The greatest number of primitive features is preserved in *Pereskia.* The flowers of some species are perigynous (floral tube surrounds the ovary) instead of epigynous; the stems are only moderately succulent; the leaves, though succulent, are similar to those of many other plants. The wood and reproductive parts reveal other primitive features. Of particular significance is the similarity of the carpels of *Pereskia pititache* to those of the primitive tropical woody plants of the Ranunculales. The carpels are unsealed, which may indicate origin of the cacti from a very primitive stock and an early separation in evolutionary development from the Ranunculales or from developmental lines ancestral to the Ranunculales and to related groups. (L.Be./Ed.)

Subclass Dilleniidae

The subclass Dilleniidae in the system used in this article contains 13 orders, 78 families, and about 25,000 species. Among its members are such plants as the peony, cacao, kapok (also known as the silk-cotton tree), mallow, brazil nut, nearly all the genera of pitcher plants except for *Cephalotus* (Rosidae), the sundew, violet, papaya, cucumber, begonia, willow, caper, mustard, heath, ebony, and primrose. The largest orders are the Violales, Capparales, Ericales, Theales, and Malvales, each of which has more than 3,000 species.

Familiar members

Apart from certain relatively small families that may ultimately be found to belong to another subclass of Magnoliopsida, the members of the Dilleniidae form a coherent taxon. It is more advanced in some respects than the subclass Magnoliidae, but less advanced than the subclass Asteridae. Unlike most members of the subclass Magnoliidae, the carpels (ovary components) in most Dilleniidae are fused (syncarpous), the exception being the Dilleniales. The pollen of the Dilleniidae has three pores and/or slits (triaperturate) or a derivation of this type, which is an advancement over the single pore that is seen frequently in the pollen of the Magnoliidae. Unlike Magnoliidae, the Dilleniidae have few alkaloids and are completely devoid of the benzylisoquinoline alkaloids characteristic of the Magnoliidae. They contain ellagic acid and raphides, all of which are concerned with defense against predators and are lacking in most of the Magnoliidae. The Dilleniidae, unlike the Caryophyllidae, do not contain betalains (red to blue flower colour being produced by anthocyanins), nor do they exhibit free-central placentation, except in the relatively advanced order Primulales (*e.g.,* the primroses). The boundary between the members of Dilleniidae and those of Rosidae is more difficult to fix, however. Most Dilleniidae have simple leaves; those members with compound leaves, especially those with distinct leaflets, are derived from various ancestors that had simple leaves. Compound leaves, on the other hand, are a common and probably basic feature in the Rosidae. In the Dilleniidae, the flower petals are partly or completely fused (sympetalous) in about a third of the group, although petalless flowers (apetalous) are also found, as in *Glaux* (Primulaceae) and the family Salicaceae (poplars and willows). In nearly all Rosidae, on the other hand, the petals are separate and unfused (polypetalous), although they may be absent or inconspicous. Parietal placentation (in which the ovules are directly attached to the inner wall of the ovary) and latex secretion are common in the Dilleniidae and relatively rare in the Rosidae. The nectary disc (the nectar-secreting structure) that is so frequent in the Rosidae is absent in the Dilleniidae, but other nectar-secreting structures do occur. The marginal teeth (serration) of leaves belonging to Dilleniidae are basically narrow, whereas in the Rosidae the leaf teeth are initially narrow and then become broad. The major distinguishing characteristic between the Dilleniidae and Rosidae, however, is the direction of stamen development in flowers with a large number of stamens: in Dilleniidae it is usually from the inside outward, whereas in Rosidae it is usually from the outside inward.

GENERAL FEATURES

Diversity of structure. The Dilleniidae are woody or herbaceous dicotyledons with simple leaves that are often unlobed. The leaf margins are smooth or serrated and the venation is pinnate to palmate or sometimes flabellate (fan-shaped) or parallel. The flowers are solitary or in simple or compound cymose or racemose inflorescences. The petals are usually separate and unfused but may rarely be completely or partially fused. The flowers may occasionally be petalless but sepals are rarely absent. The floral organs are arranged in groups of five in more primitive flowers, but can number fewer and sometimes more. The stamens are often numerous and frequently occur in groups or clustered in bundles originating from a common point (fascicles), although flowers with one or two whorls of single stamens are not rare. Those stamens that are fertile never appear as thin flattened leaflike structures as they can in some members of the primitive subclass Magnoliidae. The carpels are usually united (though sometimes free) and are in most cases equal in number to the parts in the outer whorls. The ovary may be located above or below the flower petals (hypogynous or epigynous, respectively), and the carpels may be fused.

General trends

Orders and families. The Dilleniidae show a general progression through the 13 orders of the aforementioned classification system from Dilleniales to Primulales (*i.e.,* from the relatively primitive members of the group to the more advanced): free (unfused) carpels to united carpels with the ovules attached at the inner angle of the compartment (axile placentation), or with the ovules attached either to the wall or base of the ovary or around a central, free-standing column (parietal, basal, or free-central placentation, respectively); multiple stamens in close clusters (fascicles) or apparently free and inserted on the receptacle (the portion of the flower stalk on which the flower is borne) to five stamens inserted on the petals or corolla; and free sepals and petals to united sepals and petals.

The order Dilleniales comprises two very disparate families, Dilleniaceae (the chief genera being *Dillenia, Doliocarpus, Hibbertia,* and *Tetracera*) and Paeoniaceae (the peony family). The Dilleniales are basic to the subclass in that the carpels are wholly or at least mostly free and the leaves are without true stipules. The 350 species of Dilleniaceae are tropical and subtropical woody plants, except for the herbaceous *Acrotrema,* and their leaves are entire, toothed (serrated), or, rarely, pinnately lobed. The perianth and the fascicles (clusters) of stamens normally occur in multiples of five, although the fascicles usually merge to form a uniform ring of stamens. There may be as many as 20 carpels, and they remain free or only partially united. The fruits usually split open to release their contents (dehisce), and the seeds bear a crested or fringed exterior appendage or covering (aril). The single genus of the north temperate Paeoniaceae, *Paeonia* (the peony), in contrast, is soft-wooded or herbaceous. The leaves are compound with the leaflets arranged in threes (ternately compound). The perianth and stamens are usually organized in multiples of five but may vary, especially in the number of petals. A fleshy lobed, nonsecreting (*i.e.,* nonnectary) disc partially envelops the carpels; each carpel matures into a fruit (a follicle) that splits open to release the large seeds. It is quite possible that the Paeoniaceae may not belong in the Dilleniidae.

Theales is a large and diverse order that is more advanced than Dilleniales in having united carpels, although the walls separating the individual carpels have not been lost so that the ovules attached to a central column remain segregated into separate chambers (axile placentation). Theales is regarded by Cronquist as basic to the remaining orders in this subclass. There are 18 families in the order Theales, of which Clusiaceae (the mangosteen family, sometimes given the name Guttiferae), with some 1,500 species, and the Theaceae (the tea family) and Dipterocarpaceae (the meranti family), each with 600 species, are the largest. A very diverse order, Theales can be divided into three groups of families principally on the basis of the general presence or absence of stipules. Doubtful members of the order include Dipterocarpaceae, Scytopetalaceae, Sphaerosepalaceae, Sarcolaenaceae, and Elatinaceae.

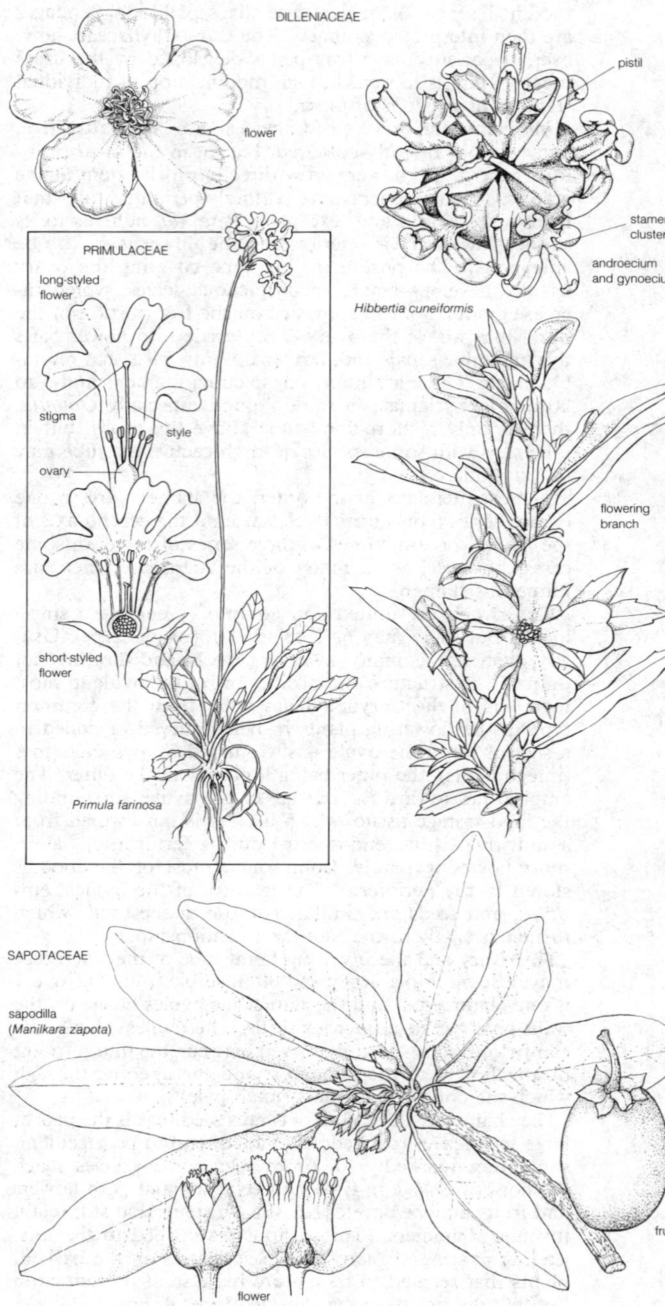

Representative plants from the three principal orders of the subclass Dilleniidae (Dilleniales, Ebenales, and Primulales, respectively). *Hibbertia cuneiformis,* of the family Dilleniaceae, is a genus having a theoretical position near the base of the subclass. Sapotaceae has many more-advanced, characteristics, and Primulaceae is the most advanced family of the subclass.

From (Dilleniaceae) A. Cronquist, *An Integrated System of Classification of Flowering Plants,* copyright © 1981 The New York Botanical Garden, Columbia University Press; (others) drawn by M. Pahl

Families Five families and between 3,000 and 3,500 species constitute the core group of the order Malvales, including the Sterculiaceae (the cacao family), Bombaceae (the kapok tree family), Malvaceae (the mallow family), Elaeocarpaceae, and Tiliaceae. Except in the primitive groups, the leaves have stipules and palmate venation and are often palmately compound. The antesepalous whorl of stamen fascicles is absent in the core families, and the members of the antepetalous whorl are often united, forming a tube (see below *Form and function: Floral structures*). The families Elaeocarpaceae and possibly Dipterocarpaceae and Scytopetalaceae (which is a member of the Theales according to Cronquist but is placed in Malvales by some authorities) form a transitional group to the true members of the Malvales, having only some of the characteristics of the order.

The Lecythidales usually differ from the orders mentioned above in having an inferior ovary with respect to the sepals, petals, and stamens. The order Lecythidales contains a single family, Lecythidaceae (the brazil nut family), with about 400 species found in tropical regions, especially South American rain forests. Members of the order do not have internal phloem (*i.e.,* phloem occurring inside the cambium), unlike the Myrtales (Rosidae), in which the Lecythidaceae used to be classified.

The three families of the order Nepenthales—Sarraceniaceae (the pitcher plant family), Nepenthaceae (the East Indian pitcher plant family), and Droseraceae (the sundew family)—constitute about 200 species and appear to have little in common except that they all trap and digest insects as a method of nutrition.

Violales Members of the large and varied Violales include the families Violaceae (violet), Passifloraceae (passion flower), and Cucurbitaceae (cucumber). They usually have stipules as well as ovules on a placenta that is attached directly to the ovary wall (parietal placentation). A large order of 12 to 24 families, depending on the classification used, the Violales mostly have stamen filaments that remain separate. As in the Malvales, the leaf venation is typically palmate. Some families (Bixaceae, the lipstick tree family; Cistaceae, the rock rose family; and Huaceae, the garlic tree family) do not have all the characteristics of the order and have sometimes been classified in the Malvales. Families doubtfully placed in the Violales include Fouquieriaceae (the ocotillo family), Ancistrocladaceae, Dioncophyllaceae, Hoplestigmataceae, and Loasaceae. The Violales are ancestral to three other orders: Salicales, Capparales, and Batales.

The order Salicales contains the single family Salicaceae, the willow family, and 2 genera, *Salix* (willows) and *Populus* (poplars), together comprising about 350 species distributed in north temperate regions. The family apparently is derived from the family Flacourtiaceae of the order Violales. The group consists of shrubs and trees propagated by wind pollination. Each flower of the usually unisexual catkins are apetalous (petalless) and subtended by a scale-like bract. (Although they are apetalous, it is not strictly true to call the Salicaceae asepalous, as the nectariferous scales in *Salix* are vestigial sepals that correspond to the vestigial annular or cupular calyx in *Populus.*) The fruit is in the form of a capsule with silky threads attached to the seeds.

The order Capparales, consisting of 5 families and 4,000 species, includes the families Capparaceae (caper), Brassicaceae (mustard), Moringaceae (horseradish tree), Resedaceae (mignonette), and Tovariaceae. The order differs essentially in having floral whorls in multiples of two, four, six, or eight rather than of five (as above) and in containing mustard oils produced by hydrolysis through mediation of the enzyme myrosin, typically located in specialized myrosin cells. The basically woody family Capparaceae also has numerous stamens, a single style, and an ovary with between 2 and 12 parietal placentae. Other families are herbaceous to some degree and the ovary is sessile (*i.e.,* stalkless), except in Tovariaceae.

The order Batales consists of only two families, Gyrostemonaceae and Bataceae (the saltwort family), with only 6 genera and 20 species. The flowers are petalless and the plants contain mustard oils, although not in myrosin cells.

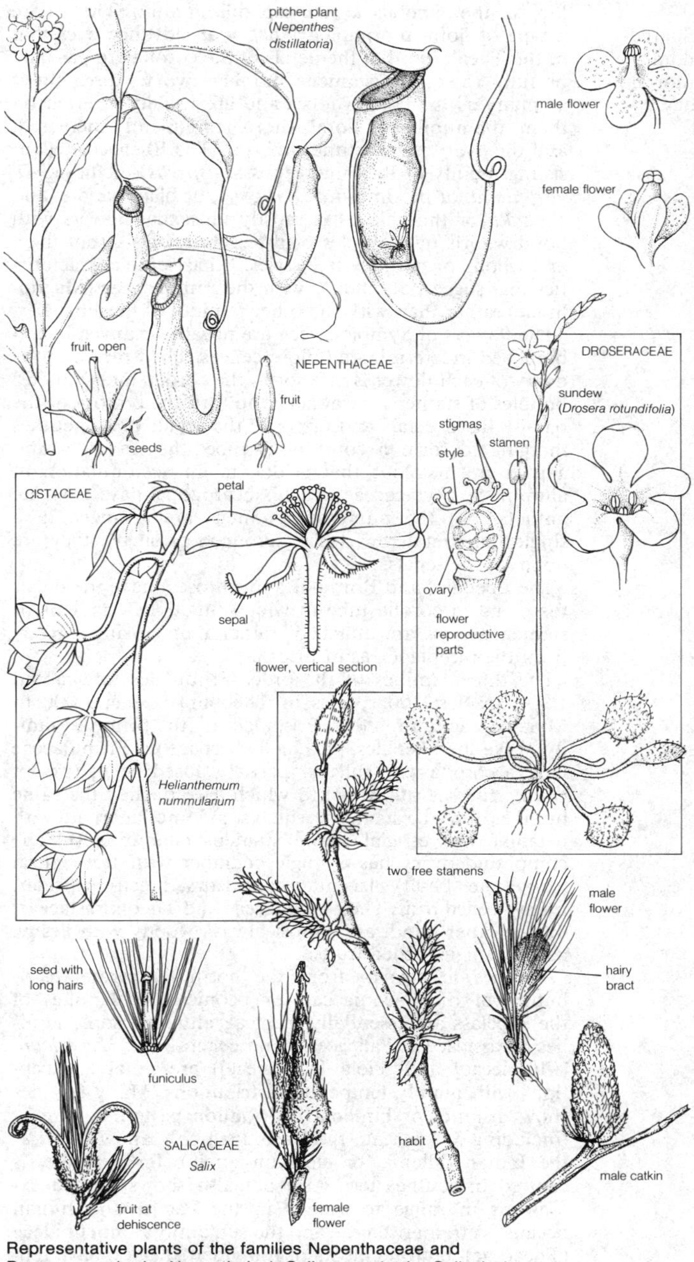

Representative plants of the families Nepenthaceae and Droseraceae (order Nepenthales), Salicaceae (order Salicales), and Cistaceae (order Violales).

From (Cistaceae) G.H.M. Lawrence, *Taxonomy of Vascular Plants* (1951), reprinted with permission of The Macmillan Pub. Co., drawn by M. Pahl; (Salicaceae) M. Hickey and C. King, *100 Families of Flowering Plants* (1988), Cambridge University Press; (others) drawn by M. Pahl

The remaining orders (Ericales, Diapensiales, Ebenales, and Primulales) are directly related to the Theales in the classification system used in this article.

The order Ericales consists of 8 families; of the 4,500 or so species in the order, 3,500 belong to the Ericaceae (the heath family) and 400 belong to the Epacridaceae (the epacris family). Principally woody shrubs or small trees, most members have perianth whorls in multiples of four or five, a corolla of fused petals, and stamens in multiples of four or five and inserted on the receptacle. Some members of the Ericales are herbaceous, and the order as a whole shows a trend toward increasing dependence on a fungal association for nutrition. The small order Diapensiales (which contains only one family, Diapensiaceae) is closely related to the Ericales and is perhaps derived from the Clethraceae.

The five families of the order Ebenales—Sapotaceae, Ebenaceae (the ebony family), Styracaceae (the storax family), Lissocarpaceae, and Symplocaceae (the sweetleaf family)—comprise about 1,700 species, of which 800 be-

Shared floral morphology

long to the Sapotaceae (the sapodilla family). They share a type of floral morphology that is an advance over that of the Theales in that the petals of the corolla are partially or fully fused, the stamens number two to three times as many as the corolla lobes and are usually inserted on them, the number of floral whorls is frequently increased, and the ovary is sometimes inferior. The Ebenaceae, consisting mainly of the large genus *Diospyros* (including *D. virginiana,* or persimmon; *D. digyna,* or black sapote; and *D. kaki,* or the kaki), has mostly unisexual flowers with floral whorls in multiples of three, four, or six (not five), and wholly or partially free styles. It has some characteristics that suggest an affinity with the Annonaceae (Magnoliidae) rather than with the other families of the Ebenales.

The flowers of Symplocaceae are usually arranged in unbranched indeterminate inflorescences called racemes; the ovary of each flower is inferior to the corolla and stamens, bundles of stamens are attached toward the bottom of the basally fused petals and opposite the sepals or sometimes merging to form a continuous tube; the leaves exhibit a pale green colour that is due to an accumulation of aluminum. Styracaceae and Lissocarpaceae have elongate anthers, but the numerous stamens are arranged in a single horizontal row, where, grouped or single, they are opposite the sepals.

The Ebenales and Primulales (primroses) have the petals fused into a corolla tube to which functional stamens or stamen groups are attached, rather than arising directly from the receptacle, as in Ericales.

The three families of the order Primulales total about 1,900 species: 100 species in Theophrastaceae; 1,000 in Myrsinaceae; and 800 in Primulaceae (the primrose family). Like the Ebenales, the chiefly herbaceous Primulaceae have a corolla with fully or partially fused petals (except *Glaux,* the sea milkwort) to which are attached the same number of fertile stamens, which sometimes alternate with petallike or vestigial sterile stamens (staminodes). The compound ovary has a single chamber with free-central (sometimes basal) placentation and dry, mostly capsular, many-seeded fruit. The Myrsinaceae and Theophrastaceae, on the other hand, are almost always woody with fleshy, usually single-seeded fruits.

Distribution. Apart from the north temperate distribution of the Paeoniaceae, or peonies, the families of the subclass are essentially tropical, although some families (Brassicaceae, Salicaceae) and genera (*e.g., Hypericum* [Clusiaceae] and Viola [Violaceae]) are notable exceptions with mainly temperate distributions. Many families show disjunct or bimodal distribution patterns. *Dillenia* (including *D. obovata,* the Burma simpoh, and *D. indica,* the Indian dillenia, or elephant apple), for example, is centred in southeastern Asia but also shows limited extensions in range to islands in the Pacific and Indian oceans. Tetrameristaceae and the subfamily Bonnetioideae (Theaceae), both members of the order Theales, have representatives in tropical America and in tropical East Asia. Lecythidaceae (Lecythidales) is one of many families that have members in America and the Old World. None of the more primitive families in the subclass contain members that are native to the north temperate regions, except for Paeoniaceae.

Habitats

Members of the subclass occupy almost all habitats where angiospermous plants can be found, except deep water. Mangroves of the order Theales (Pellicieraceae) and Primulales (Myrsinaceae) grow in shallow salt water. Microphyllous (small-leaved) salt-secreting inhabitants of maritime and saline regions occur in the Violales (Tamaricaceae and Frankeniaceae); and in the Namib desert of southwestern Africa is found a shrubby, spiny member of the Violales, the nara, or narras (*Acanthosicyos horridus,* or *horrida;* Cucurbitaceae).

NATURAL HISTORY

Although the members of the subclass Dilleniidae have no general features of their life cycles that distinguish them from other subclasses of the dicotyledons, there are groups in which the normal processes of nutrition are supplemented or replaced by other methods.

In the Ericales, the Ericaceae and related families have become increasingly dependent on a relationship with fungi for their nutrition, a relationship that is associated with the acid, mineral-poor soils in which most members of these families grow. The fungi (mycorrhizae) facilitate the absorption of nitrogen and phosphorous in such soils, at the same time reducing or preventing the absorption of potentially toxic metallic ions (aluminum, copper, zinc). In the Monotropaceae (*e.g., Monotropa*), where chlorophyll is completely absent, the plant is wholly dependent on the mycorrhizae for nutrition. These mycorrhizae often form an association with tree roots in addition to its association with the monotropoid plant, thus allowing the plant to parasitize the tree. In these instances there is evidence of transfer of carbon to the ericalean species from its host. This fungal dependency is evident at the seed stage of the life cycle. All families of Ericales have small seeds with either a thin outer seed coat (testa) consisting of one or two layers of cells or, in Cyrillaceae, no testa at all, permitting early association of the fungi and embryo. In the herbaceous Pyrolaceae, a group related to Ericaceae, the growing embryo's dependency on the fungi has gone a stage further in that the tiny embryo does not develop cotyledons (the main food-storage organs) until after the seed is dispersed. In the Monotropaceae, the dependency becomes total with the complete absence of chlorophyll and an embryo that never develops cotyledons.

The order Nepenthales includes three families in which growth in an environment poor in available nitrogen and thus inhospitable to normal methods of nutrition is associated with adaptations for trapping and digesting insects. Apart from this means of accessory nutrition, they have little in common, however. Indeed, while many Droseraceae (sundews) adopt the flypaper principle of trapping their prey on sticky hairs, other members have active trap mechanisms that close over the hapless victim (*Dionaea, Aldrovanda*), and members of the remaining two families (the pitcher plant family and East Indian pitcher plant family) passively ensnare their prey and drown their victims in liquid-filled pitcher-shaped modifications of their leaf bases (Sarraceniaceae) or leaf apices (Nepenthaceae).

Pitcher plant family

Although they are members of the same family, Sarraceniaceae, the three genera of the pitcher plant family (*Sarracenia, Heliamphora,* and *Darlingtonia*) have distinct, interesting modifications. The leaves of the Sarraceniaceae are borne in a rosette at the base of the plant (*Sarracenia*), or on a short, thick, ground-level or more or less elongate perennial stem (*i.e.,* they have no stalk) in some *Heliamphora* species, with the lower part forming a tube and the upper part a lid; in *Darlingtonia,* the upper part simulates a hood and has a forked tip. Resemblances to the Ranunculales (subclass Magnoliidae), as indicated in the classification scheme devised by the Armenian botanist Armen Takhtajan, are readily apparent. Some Andean species of the buttercup family, Ranunculaceae (Magnoliidae), such as *Krapfia cochlearifolia* (*Ranunculus macropetalus*), for example, have leaves that resemble an unfolded *Sarracenia* leaf. The Sarraceniaceae develop a single large flower on a leafless stalk that emerges at ground level, or occasionally a few-flowered raceme in some *Heliamphora* species.

The East Indian pitcher plant family, Nepenthaceae, contains only a single genus, *Nepenthes.* The family comprises shrubs, climbers, and epiphytes (nonparasitic plants that grow on top of other plants) distributed throughout rainforest areas of Southeast Asia and Madagascar. The leaves are highly modified in a way different from other pitcher plants. The petiole (leaf stalk) is attached directly to the clambering stem. The leaf blade is flat and narrowed at the apex into a stout tendril that usually connects to a large, open, brightly coloured pitcher with an expanded, flattened operculum (lid). The bright red and green pitchers are the most conspicuous parts of the plant. The small, unisexual flowers are arranged in inflorescences (racemes or panicles) with the male and female flowers on separate plants. The individual flowers have no petals but do have sepals with fragrant nectary glands, which also occur on the lower surface of the lid in some species. All the floral characteristics of *Nepenthes* can be matched in different families of the Ranunculales (subclass Magnoliidae).

The flypaper trapping and digesting mechanism of some members of the sundew family, Droseraceae, is quite different from that of the pitcher plants. The sundews are usually perennial herbs. The leaves usually have stipules and are variously covered with hairs tipped by sticky fluids, as in *Drosophyllum* (Portuguese sundew) and *Drosera* (sundew), or forming an active trap, as in *Dionaea* (Venus' flytrap) and the rootless aquatic insectivore *Aldrovanda.* The stipules, parietal placentation, flowers, and branching styles all suggest that they belong in the Violales, while the leaf venation suggests an affinity with the Theales. For example, *Triphyophyllum,* one of the three monotypic genera of the West African family Dioncophyllaceae (Violales), has multicellular, stalked, or sessile glands that cover the narrow leaves and stem, secreting a sticky acid mucilage that traps and may digest insect prey. These glands are similar to the insect-trapping glands of Droseraceae, and the leaves are not essentially different from those of the northwest Mediterranean semishrub *Drosophyllum.* It thus appears that the pitcher-bearing families of the Nepenthales (Sarraceniaceae and Nepenthaceae) might have a place in the subclass Magnoliidae, affiliated to some degree with the order Ranunculales, and the sundew family (Droseraceae) should perhaps be placed in the Dilleniidae orders Violales or Theales.

Pollination

The primitive members of Dilleniidae have open pollinated pollen flowers (flowers with pollen freely available to all flower visitors—*i.e.,* without any particular adaptation, such as a corolla tube, that restricts pollen availability to pollinators of certain species), and, even when in more advanced families the pollination mechanism has become more specific and includes nectar secretion, the nectar-secreting region is never a stamen disc, as it is in many members of the subclass Rosidae. The nectar-secreting region is usually on the receptacle, but it can be elsewhere, such as in the spur of the violets (*Viola;* Violales). Wind-pollination is rare, being confined to trees with pendulous catkins, such as the poplars and cottonwoods (*Populus*), which belong to the family Salicaceae. Self-pollination occurs in many annuals, as, for example, in the mustard family (Brassicaceae).

Plants that have both male and female flowers on separate plants (*i.e.,* that are dioecious) are less common in the subclass than in Hamamelidae or Rosidae. Dioecism is characteristic of Salicales and common in Violales. Heterostyly—*i.e.,* the occurence in the same species of flowers with different lengths of stamens and styles (which prevents or at least discourages self-pollination)—occurs in some members of Clusiaceae and in Primulaceae. In Clusiaceae, dioecism and heterostyly are alternative methods of pollination specialization in different subfamilies. In Marcgraviaceae (Theales), the shingle plant family, modified leaves called bracts subtend the inflorescences and usually are associated with sterile flowers; they are converted into sac-shaped or pitcherlike nectar-containing structures that are or originally were attractive to hummingbirds, which are instrumental in pollination.

FORM AND FUNCTION

Vegetative structures. The Dilleniidae vary from tall forest trees (*e.g.,* in Dipterocarpaceae) to shrubs and perennial or annual herbs (*e.g.,* in Brassicaceae). Even the Dilleniaceae exhibit a range from evergreen trees (*Dillenia*) to herbs (*Acrotrema*). Theales is almost wholly woody except for *Sauvagesia* (Ochnaceae) and *Hypericum* and *Triadenum* (both of Clusiaceae). *Hypericum* ranges from trees up to 10 metres in height in the East African mountains (*H. bequaertii*) to annual herbs such as the North American *H. mutilum.* Ebenales, Batales, Lecythidales, and Salicales are wholly woody, but the remaining orders range from woody to herbaceous. Some members of the Violales develop underground storage organs or swollen stems, especially in the Passifloraceae (passion flowers, *e.g., Adenia*) and Cucurbitaceae (gourds, melons, and squashes). Succulence occurs more rarely than in the subclasses Caryophyllidae or Rosidae and is found only among members of the Violales. Apart from Fouquieriaceae, whose membership in the subclass is in doubt, there are no cactuslike genera; the tree habit is confined in Cucurbitaceae to a single genus (*Dendrosicyos*); and stem succulence occurs in watery-stemmed genera in Cucurbitaceae, Passifloraceae, and *Begonia.* One particularly unusual habit occurs in *Caloncoba* (*Paraphyadanthe*), a West African tree in Flacourtiaceae (Violales), in which the inflorescences are borne at the end of shoots that radiate underground from the base of the trunk before emerging above the soil.

Leaf arrangement

The arrangement of leaves along the axis of a shoot is primarily spiral in the more primitive orders but becomes opposite and alternating at right angles or whorled in some Theales, Malvales, Violales, and Batales, and in many Primulales. Most Dilleniidae have simple leaves. The formation of compound leaves appears to have evolved suddenly in several groups, with no intermediate stages evident in related taxa. In the Violales, Capparales (except Capparaceae), and Malvaceae (Malvales), however, compound leaves apparently evolved by gradual subdivision with intermediate stages. In the peony, the compound leaves, with main divisions in threes and often much further divided, are unmatched in the Dilleniidae but common in the Ranunculales.

Although some paleobotanists have held that in the class Magnoliopsida (the dicotyledons) stipulate leaves are a primitive feature that has been lost in various evolutionary lines, the evidence in the subclass Dilleniidae is to the contrary. It seems likely that stipules have originated independently in the ancestors of many lines of descent within the subclass.

No members of the subclass Dilleniidae have vesselless wood, so that to this extent the subclass is more advanced than the subclass Magnoliidae, usually considered to be the most primitive subclass of the flowering plants. The limited degree of this anatomical advancement in various genera, however, indicates that if the Dilleniidae are indeed derived from the Magnoliidae, this evolution could only have taken place from the least-specialized members of the subclass Magnoliidae; the Dilleniaceae, Theaceae, and *Saurauia* (Actinidiaceae) have exceedingly primitive vessel members, and those of the Ericales are only slightly more advanced. The majority of latex-secreting plants are found among the subclass Dilleniidae, most of the others being in the Asteridae (Campanulales and Asterales).

Floral structures. The primitive Dilleniidae families include several species with large single flowers, but it is unlikely that this is the primitive state in these families or in the Dilleniidae as a whole. The type and appearance of inflorescences tend to vary considerably but racemes or panicles, both of which are indeterminate, appear to be universal in Ericales.

In Dilleniidae, the perianth of a single flower consists basically of five sepals and five petals, all free (unfused), the members of each whorl typically overlapping in bud. Modification has occurred as a result of a reduction in the number of sepals and/or petals; an increase in the number in one or both whorls, usually from four to six or more; an alteration of the arrangement of sepals or petals in the bud from overlapping to valvate or, in petals, the alteration to overlapping in the same direction; or the union (fusion) of sepals or petals. In some genera, the perianth is made up of tepals (*i.e.,* the sepals and petals are not distinguishable); in others, the petals are absent or both whorls are virtually absent. A bilaterally symmetrical (zygomorphic) perianth or corolla is found in Violales, Ericales, and Primulales.

Dilleniidae flowers

In flowers of the Dilleniidae with numerous stamens, the direction of development is nearly always from the inside outward. This type of development, which also occurs among members of other subclasses, such as Caryophyllidae, Rosidae, Magnoliidae, and Alismatidae, is associated with the presence of trunk vascular bundles in the receptacle of the flower, which in turn is associated with bundles (fascicles) of stamens.

The basic androecium of the Dilleniidae consists of two whorls of five stamen fascicles—one whorl opposite the sepals and the other opposite the petals—that are variously fertile or sterile, separate or united, or absent. In the Malvales, for example, the antesepalous whorl is absent and the antepetalous whorl is united to form a tube (the mallow family, Malvaceae), is free (the linden family, Tiliaceae), or is merged into a mass of stamens (also in Tiliaceae) or reduced to single stamens (the cacao family, Sterculiaceae). The number of stamens in a fascicle remains relatively unlimited, so that increases as well as decreases are not uncommon. Thus, in Bombacaceae (which includes the kapok tree and baobab of the order Malvales), the number of stamen fascicles has increased considerably in association with bat pollination; whereas in Lecythidaceae (Lecythidales) the androecium has become more and more zygomorphic in relation to pollination by particular insects, especially euglossine bees.

The pollen in Dilleniidae is most often binucleate, but in some orders it may be trinucleate. It is normally shed as single grains except in most Ericales, where four grains cohere in tetrads. The sculpturing of the outer surface of the pollen grain is related to the method of dispersal—*e.g.,* smooth in wind pollination and covered with spines in insect pollination.

The carpels in the subclass are united and usually number five or fewer, although in the order Dilleniales, the carpels are basically free; in *Hibbertia* and *Dillenia* (Dilleniaceae), they have increased in some species to as many as 20 and have become partly united in *Dillenia.* The carpels are arranged in a single whorl, except apparently in some members of the family Malvaceae (*e.g., Malope*). Placentation is axile or parietal and the ovules vary from many to one per locule. The styles range from being free to wholly united.

The unfused nature of the carpels in Dilleniales results in fruits that are clusters of follicles or achenes. In all other families of the subclass, the fruit is characteristic of a flower with fused carpels (*i.e.,* capsules, berries, or drupes). In addition, other parts of the flower may be involved in forming the actual fruit: for example, enlarged winged sepals in Dipterocarpaceae (the meranti family), the fleshy apex of each flower stalk (pedicel) of *Endodesmia* (Clusiaceae), and the calyx and fleshy receptacle of each flower of *Ochna* and *Ouratea* of the family Ochnaceae.

Seeds may be numerous and small, especially in thin-walled capsules or berries, or they may be few and large in thick-walled capsules or drupes. The seeds may be patterned because the seed coat is deeply sculptured, or the seed coat may be elongated to form a wing. Fleshy arils are found among the Dilleniales and Theales. In some berry-producing Clusiaceae, the whole seed coat becomes fleshy, as in the mangosteen (*Garcinia mangostana*). Hairy seed appendages are confined to the Malvales, Violales, and Salicales, except for some species of *Marila* (Clusiaceae).

EVOLUTION

Although tricolpate pollen is known from the Barremian and Aptian ages (124 to 113 million years ago) of the Early Cretaceous Period (144 to 97.5 million years ago), the record of those fossils recognized as Dilleniidae goes back no farther than the Cenomanian Age (97.5 to 91 million years ago) of the Late Cretaceous Period (97.5 to 66.4 million years ago). By this time, families in all parts of the subclass were apparently in existence—Tiliaceae, Bombacaceae, Sterculiaceae, Passifloraceae, Salicaceae, Capparaceae, Ericaceae, Ebenaceae, Sapotaceae, and Myrsinaceae, as well as some families that have been included in the subclass by certain experts (*e.g.,* Aquifoliaceae, which is placed in the subclass Rosidae in this article's classification system). The evolutionary history of the subclass therefore is based largely, if not entirely, on evidence from recent (*i.e.,* nonfossil) groups.

Fossil record

Members of the Dilleniidae are an essentially monophyletic group—*i.e.,* they have a single common ancestor. This ancestor must have originated no later than the Early Cretaceous Period (144 to 97.5 million years ago). The current distribution of families and genera throughout the world, however, would seem to indicate an earlier origin, before the breakup of Gondwana in the Jurassic Period (208 to 144 million years ago) or the Early Cretaceous. There is no clear fossil evidence for the existence of angiosperms at such an early date, however.

There is no obvious morphological link between the uniaperturate pollen of the early Magnoliidae and that of the Dilleniales, and so triaperturate pollen may have originated independently in these subclasses. If the Dilleniidae are related to the early Hamamelidae, however, as has been suggested on grounds of leaf architecture, then such a double origin hypothesis is not necessary. It is clear from studies on the Hamamelidae in particular that palmate leaf venation is relatively less common in recent members than in Cretaceous members; because of this some experts have theorized that angiosperm leaves were originally fan-veined. Certainly, some dilleniid leaf types are difficult to interpret by the current hypothesis that pinnate venation is primitive in the Magnoliidae, as is supported by the venation in some otherwise primitive species of *Bonnetia* and *Hypericum* (both of Theales), and *Richea* (Ericales).

It has been suggested that the Dilleniidae may have evolved from hamamelid-like ancestors with two whorls of five single stamens. Based on this theory, the 10 stamen fascicles that are a basic feature of the subclass have arisen from single stamens (via secondary polyandry or "dédoublement") in response to the demands of the pollinators, especially beetles. The perhaps superficial similarities in leaf architecture between species of *Hibbertia* (Dilleniales) and *Euptelea* (Hamamelidales) have led some botanists to regard *Euptelea* and that genus's fossil relatives as the sister-group to both the Dilleniidae and Rosidae. The flowers of *Hibbertia,* however, are quite unlike those in the Hamamclidae. The androecium of the flowers of the Dilleniidae are also quite different from those of the Magnoliidae (excepting members of the family Paeoniaceae). For these reasons it seems unlikely that the dilleniid stamen fascicles arose from single stamens—either from a polyandrous magnoliid androecium by grouping or from the hamamelid androecium by dédoublement. The relations of the Dilleniidae with the other subclasses must therefore remain sub judice for the present.

The Dilleniidae can be divided into four groups based on leaf architecture and the presence or absence of stipules: theoid, ericoid, ochnoid, and malvoid. The theoid group is basically exstipulate with fan-shaped or pinnate venation, perhaps not all derived from the (pinnate) Dilleniaceae; it consists of the entire-margined clusioid line (including the family Clusiaceae and the subfamily Bonnetioideae of the family Theaceae—both of Theales—and the order Lecythidales) and the dentate-margined theoid line (including Primulales and some or all of Ebenales). The ericoid group is basically exstipulate with pinnate venation (the venation is perhaps secondarily parallel in some members of the Epacridaceae). The ericoid group apparently is derived indirectly from Dilleniaceae through Actinidiaceae and, unlike the theoid group, also produces iridoid substances. It consists of the families Actinidiaceae and Oncothecaceae (both of Theales), the orders Ericales and Diapensiales, and probably the family Aquifoliaceae (which is placed in Rosidae in Cronquist's classification). The ochnoid group is basically stipulate with pinnate venation, derived either directly from Dilleniaceae or from an early member of the theoid group. The group consists of the family Ochnaceae (possibly including *Diegodendron* but not *Strasburgeria*), Quiinaceae, and possibly Dioncophyllaceae and Droseraceae. The malvoid group is basically stipulate, and all but the early families have palmate venation, apparently relating to the Dilleniaceae or the ochnoid group. It consists of Malvales (including Dipterocarpaceae, Scytopetalaceae, and possibly Sphaerosepalaceae and Huaceae); Violales; Salicales; Capparales; Batales; and probably Euphorbiales, which is possibly related to both Malvales and Violales; and Urticales, which is possibly related to early Malvales.

There are morphological trends from a woody to herbaceous habit, alternate to opposite and rarely whorled leaves (except in the ericoid group), floral parts in fives to fewer or sometimes more numerous and free to united, and a reduction of stamens in each fascicle to one, combined with sterilization and/or elimination of one androecial whorl.

If certain families are excluded (Paeoniaceae, Nepenthaceae, Sarraceniaceae, and possibly Strasburgeriaceae [placed by Cronquist in Ochnaceae], Ebenaceae, Symplocaceae, and Fouquieriaceae) and certain other families are included, the Dilleniidae form a homogenous, probably monophyletic, basically simple-leaved group as opposed to the basically pinnate-leaved subclass Rosidae. Evidence is accumulating that the Euphorbiales and Urticales probably should be included in the subclass, as perhaps should the Myrtales and Celastrales. (N.K.B.R.)

REPRESENTATIVE GROUPS

Violales. *Distribution and abundance.* The order Violales has recently been considered to be an offshoot of the order Theales; the families of Violales have been thought to be ancestors of, or transitional to, a dozen other orders in the Dilleniidae and other subclasses. The Violales nearly merge with the Theales, Malvales, Salicales, Capparales, and possibly others through various transitional genera and families.

Hardly any list of characteristics will define the limits of the order. The more ancient or primitive members are trees that have alternate leaves and stipules. The flowers have compound pistils with superior ovaries, parietal placentation, numerous petals, and multiple stamens that often develop from the inside outward (centrifugal). The seeds typically contain well-developed endosperm. These features, however, are not common to all the families in Violales, and not even to all the genera of Flacourtiaceae, which is considered to be the oldest family of the order.

The Violales have accommodated as many as 24 or as few as 9 families in authoritative classifications. A few small families that recently split from the Flacourtiaceae are not included in this discussion. A conservative listing of the core families constituting Violales includes Achariaceae, Caricaceae, Cucurbitaceae, Dipentodontaceae (this family is placed in Santalales [Rosidae] in Cronquist's classification), Flacourtiaceae, Lacistemataceae, Malesherbiaceae, Passifloraceae, Peridiscaceae, Scyphostegiaceae, Turneraceae, and Violaceae (the violet family). The families Huaceae (the garlic tree family), Cistaceae (the rockrose family), and Bixaceae (the lipstick tree family) do not show all the features of the order and are sometimes placed in Malvales.

Core families of the Violales

The Achariaceae include only three genera of subshrubby, stemless, or climbing herbs: *Acharia, Ceratiosicyos,* and *Guthriea,* each with a single species and all found only in South Africa. Caricaceae comprise four genera and about 30 species: one genus, *Cylicomorpha,* has two species, both with hollow spiny trunks that may house bee's nests, and both species are confined to tropical Africa; the remaining three genera (*Carica* [papaya], *Jacaratia,* and *Jarilla*) are limited to tropical America.

The Cucurbitaceae have about 90 genera and 700 species of gourds, melons, squashes, and pumpkins and is occasionally placed in its own order. The species are widespread in tropical and subtropical regions, with only a few reaching into temperate or cool climates. Aerial parts of all species are sensitive to frost. None of the genera have more than 100 species, and many are known primarily from domesticated species. *Bryonia* with 12 species is found in Eurasia, North Africa, and the Canary Islands; *B. alba* extends to Scandinavia, the northern limit of the family. *Citrullus* (watermelon) has three species in tropical and southern Africa. *Cucumis* (cucumbers and muskmelons) has 30 species and is native to the Old World tropics. *Cucurbita* (pumpkins and squash), probably the most important genus in an economically important family, has 27 species native to tropical and subtropical America. *Cyclanthera* has 15 species restricted to tropical America. *Lagenaria* (gourd) is noteworthy for having 6 species that range from tropical Africa to Madagascar. *Luffa* (loofah, or vegetable sponge) has six species that are also widespread throughout the tropics. *Dipentodon sinicus,* the sole member of the Dipentodontaceae, ranges from the eastern Himalayas to Myanmar and southwestern China.

Flacourtiaceae has 89 genera and about 800 to 875 species, and is widely distributed in the tropics and subtropics. A few species extend to temperate regions. Large or representative genera include *Casearia,* with 160 species widespread in the tropics; *Homalium,* with 200 species in the tropics and subtropics; and *Xylosma* with 85 species in warm regions. Smaller but significant genera include *Hydnocarpus,* with 40 species in Indo-Malaysia; *Scolopia,* with at least 37 species in tropical and southern Africa, Asia, and Australia; and *Flacourtia,* with 15 species

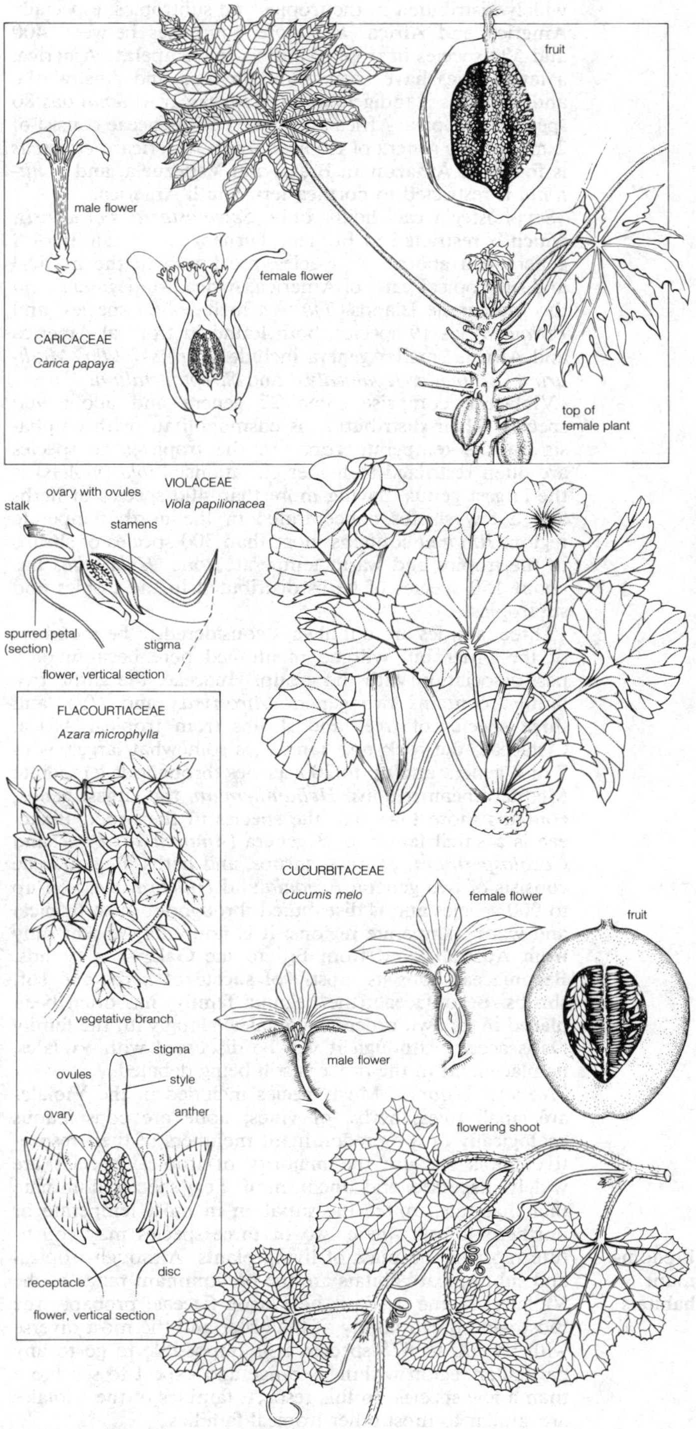

Vegetative, floral, and fruiting features of the order Violales.

From (*Caricaceae,* Cucurbitaceae) J.W. Purseglove, *Tropical Crops: Dicotyledons I* (1968), reprinted with permission of John Wiley & Sons, Inc., New York City; (others) G.H.M. Lawrence, *Taxonomy of Vascular Plants* (1951), reprinted with permission of The Macmillan Pub. Co., drawn by M. Pahl

in tropical and southern Africa, the Mascarene Islands, Southeast Asia, Malaysia, and Fiji. Lacistemataceae is a small family of 2 genera and about 14 species native to tropical America and the West Indies; *Lacistema* includes more than 10 species, and *Lozania* about 3 species. The genera are included by some authorities within the Flacourtiaceae. Malesherbiaceae contains about 27 species in 1 or 2 genera. The family is native to western subtropical South America; *Malesherbia* is often considered to hold all the species, but some authorities recognize the genus *Gynopleura.*

Passifloraceae (passion flowers) is a large family, with about 20 genera and approximately 600 species, and is

Passion flowers

widely distributed in the tropics and subtropics, especially America and Africa. *Passiflora* comprises between 400 and 500 species in tropical and warm temperate America; a few species have been found in Asia and Australasia, and 1 species is indigenous to Madagascar. *Adenia* has 80 species in tropical Africa and Asia. Peridiscaceae consist of 2 monotypic genera of tropical South America: *Peridiscus* is found in Amazonian Brazil and Venezuela, and *Whittonia* is restricted to northeastern South America.

Scyphostegiaceae holds only *Scyphostegia borneensis,* which is restricted to Borneo. Turneraceae, a family of 8 genera and about 100 species, are found in the tropical and subtropical parts of America, Africa, Madagascar, and the Mascarene Islands. *Turnera* includes 60 species, and *Piriqueta* has 19 species, both found in tropical America and Africa. Smaller genera include *Wormskioldia, Mathurina, Erblichia, Hyalocalyx,* and *Streptopetalum.*

Violaceae comprise some 22 genera and about 900 species. Their distribution is cosmopolitan, with emphasis on the temperate zone. In the tropics, the species are often restricted to higher elevations. *Viola* (violets) is the largest genus, having more than 400 species of herbs and a few shrubs concentrated in the north temperate region. *Rinorea* contains more than 300 species of shrubs in the tropics and warm temperate zone. *Hybanthus* has about 150 species of herbs distributed in the tropics and subtropics.

Three families are not always considered to be members of the order but will be mentioned here because of a past association with the group. Huaceae, the garlic tree family, contains two genera, *Afrostyrax* and *Hua,* and three species of trees and shrubs from tropical Africa. Cistaceae, the rock rose family, is somewhat larger, with 7 or 8 genera and up to 200 species throughout temperate Mediterranean regions. *Helianthemum,* the largest genus, contains more than half the species in the order. Bixaceae is a small family of 3 genera (*Amoreuxia, Bixa,* and *Cochlospermum*) of trees, shrubs, and herbs. Begoniaceae consists of two genera, *Begonia* and *Hillebrandia,* and up to 900 species and is distributed throughout most tropical and warm temperate regions; it is noticeably absent only from Australia and from Fiji to the Galápagos Islands. Begoniaceae consists mostly of succulent herbs and soft shrubs. Begoniaceae (the begonia family) has often been placed in its own order (Begoniales) along with the family Datiscaceae. Although it will be discussed with Violales, its placement in the order is still being debated.

Natural history. Most species included in the Violales are small trees, herbs, or vines; none are conspicuous ecologically or are predominant members of their respective floras because the majority of tropical species are widely dispersed and uncommon. Few species dominate their habitats, unlike the situation in most temperate or northern forests where two or three species may constitute most of the mass of living plants. Although tropical and subtropical habitats are the predominant range of the Violales, in the case of the Flacourtiaceae, probably the most widespread family of the order and the most diverse with its 800 to 875 species, it is impossible to go to any particular region within its range and expect to see more than a few species. In this respect, families of the Violales are similar to most other tropical families.

Predominant habitats

Economic and ecological importance. Four families of Violales yield a variety of products of modest importance to world markets. Only Cucurbitaceae produces domesticated crop plants that contribute significantly to human food supplies worldwide.

The seeds of *Hydnocarpus* (Flacourtiaceae), found in the Philippines, China, and India, are a source of chaulmoogra oil, at one time important in the treatment of leprosy. The presumed active agent in the oil was hydnocarpic acid, which is believed to have antibiotic properties. The seed oil of *Casearia sylvestris* of Brazil was used for the same purpose and for treating wounds. The seeds of *Oncoba echinata,* cultivated throughout the tropics, and of *Caloncoba echinata,* of west central Africa, are the sources of gorli oil, which was also used in the treatment of leprosy. These old treatments for leprosy have been replaced by sulfone drugs and other modern antibiotics.

Chew sticks are twigs of *Casearia* and *Rinorea* and other genera that are widely sold in small bundles in West African markets and used instead of toothbrushes. Many of the species used prevent tooth decay. One member of the Flacourtiaceae, *Ryania angustifolia* of the American tropics, is noted for having an extremely toxic and violent gastric poison in all parts of the plant, a poison that is used to kill alligators; the poisonous agent, ryanodine, is an effective insecticide.

The West Indian boxwood (*Casearia praecox*), a firm, close-grained wood popular among woodworkers, is native to Venezuela and the West Indies. It is often substituted for true boxwood, *Buxus sempervirens,* a member of the order Euphorbiales (subclass Rosidae), in the making of veneers, carvings, and keyboards. *Passiflora* (Passifloraceae) has more than 350 species from the tropics but is recognized by gardeners for the large, beautiful, and bizarre passion flowers. They were given their common name by early Roman Catholic missionaries who traveled to South America from Spain. Their name is based upon the passion of Christ; the three stigmas are held to represent the nails of the Crucifixion of Christ; the five anthers, the five wounds; the corona, the crown of thorns; and the five sepals and five petals together, the 10 apostles held by religious tradition to have been present at the Crucifixion. Various species of *Passiflora* from the American tropics produce passion fruit, especially the banana passion fruit (*P. mollissima*). *Passiflora edulis,* the purple granadilla, is probably the most important cultivated species of *Passiflora* grown in the subtropics. The long, yellow fruit of *Passiflora quadrangularis* is eaten as a vegetable when immature, although the mature fruit has been known to be poisonous. *Passiflora incarnata* has an ingredient used in sedatives. Distillations of the root of *Paropsia* (South Africa) and distillations of the twig bark of *Smeathmannia* (Liberia) are used to relieve toothaches. *Adenia volkensii* of tropical Africa is poisonous to humans, although other species of that genus are used medicinally.

The family Caricaceae is noted for the papaya (or papaw) *Carica papaya,* a native of Central and South America. The green fruits yield a milk sap, which is dried and from which papain (a proteinase—*i.e.,* an enzyme that breaks down proteins) is derived for use as a meat tenderizer.

Viola, a large genus of the family Violaceae, is commonly grown as an ornamental (violets and pansies) in north temperate regions. *Viola odorata* has rhizomes and seeds that are poisonous and cause gastroenteritis.

Viola

The family Cucurbitaceae contains a vast array of domesticated plants, demonstrating that humans have cultivated them for millenia. *Benincasa hispida* (the wax, or white, gourd) is an annual plant native to tropical Asia. The fruits, young leaves, and flower buds are boiled and eaten as vegetables, and the seeds are fried. *Citrullus lanatus* (*C. vulgaris*), the watermelon, is native to tropical and subtropical Africa. It has long been cultivated in the Mediterranean basin (it was grown in Egypt in prehistoric times) and throughout the tropics since Columbus' contact with the New World. It is grown seasonally in temperate zones. *Citrullus colocynthis* (the bitter apple) and other species produce a pulp that, when dried, is a purgative that has long been used in India and the Mediterranean. The large genus *Cucumis* produces gherkins, melons, and cucumbers. West Indian gherkins (*C. anguria*) are not the immature cucumbers (*Cucumis sativus*) that are often called gherkins; they are commonly used as pickles but are also eaten as cooked vegetables and used in curries. *C. anguria* originated in West Africa and may have been introduced in the New World during the slave trade. *C. melo* produces several varieties of melon, including cantaloupes, muskmelons, winter melons, and honeydew melons. They appear to have originated in Africa and were later introduced into Europe and the Middle East. Varieties of *C. melo* are now cultivated throughout the world. As the fruit matures, it accumulates sugars, and, upon ripening, the fruit softens. *Cucumis sativus,* the cucumber, yields fruits that are eaten as vegetables or (in their immature form) made into pickles. This plant may have been domesticated in northern India and was spread as far as Egypt and China. It is now cultivated throughout the world. *C. sativus* is a monecious, annual, trailing vine that reaches a length of 1 to 3 metres (3 to 10 feet). It is usually pollinated by bees.

The genus *Cucurbita,* a native of the New World, produces a variety of important gourds, melons, squashes (vegetable marrows), and pumpkins and is now grown around the world. (The terms squash and pumpkin are used for more than one species and variety of *Cucurbita.*) The ancestral wild forms are not known with certainty for any species or varieties of *Cucurbita. C. maxima,* probably domesticated in South America, contains a number of varieties. *C. moschata,* probably domesticated in southern North America and spread throughout the Americas, contains other varieties of squashes. *Cucurbita mixta* was domesticated in Mexico within the past 2,000 years. *Curcurbita pepo,* which provides summer squash, winter squash, zucchini (courgette), common pumpkin, and ornamental gourds, was cultivated as early as 5,000 years ago in Mexico.

The bottle gourd

The hard dry shell of the mature fruit of *Lagenaria siceraria* (the bottle gourd), has been a source of bowls, ladles, spoons, and many other utensils by peoples living throughout the tropics; it has been a cultivated plant of both the Old and New worlds for thousands of years. Some varieties are used as food, but the pulp of most varieties is too bitter. It may be used locally as a purgative in Africa.

Less important cucurbits include the smooth loofah (*Luffa cylindrica*), or vegetable sponge, which has a network of vascular bundles that mimic the appearance of the marine sponge. Some species of *Luffa* grown in Asia produce tender fruits that are used as a vegetable. *Momordica charantia,* the bitter gourd or balsam pear, is cultivated in India and East Asia, where it is often an ingredient in curries or pickled fruit. *Sechium edule,* or chayote, is native to Mexico and Central America. It produces a large pear-shaped fruit with a single seed (an unusual feature among the cucurbits) as well as a large tuberous root, both used in the tropics as vegetables. *Trichosanthes cucumerina* (also known as *T. anguina*), the snake gourd, the fruit of which may grow to nearly two metres in length, has long been cultivated from India to East Asia. The immature fruit is eaten as a boiled vegetable. (R.C.Ke.)

A member of the Bixaceae family (*Bixa orellana*) is used to produce a red annatto dye, which is extracted from the pulp around the seeds. It is native to tropical America, but it has been widely planted elsewhere in the tropics. The family Cistaceae provides many species of small ornamentals for rock gardens, especially from the genus *Cistus* (rockrose). At least 17 species native to the Mediterranean region have been introduced into North American gardens. Another genus of this family, *Helianthemum* (sunrose), also is occasionally planted. (N.H.R.)

The Begoniaceae family

The family Begoniaceae is of considerable horticultural interest, many species and hybrids being prized as house or garden plants. The leaves of some African and Asian *Begonia* species are eaten; in South America, some species are eaten to prevent scurvy. Rhizomes of certain species in South America are used for their medicinal qualities as astringents, as treatment for fever, as antisyphilitics, and as laxatives.

The ornamental value of the plants is also based on diversity in growth habit; leaves, including colour patterns; inflorescence (flower-cluster) type; flower size and colour; and length of blooming period. Classifications of begonias for horticultural purposes are quite different from those for botanical studies. In fact, the species are valued for their potential in producing hybrids. Three groups of species are of interest to horticulturists. One is cultivated for its leaves (including especially *Begonia rex*). Another, valued for its flowers, is subdivided into a group of small-flowered plants centred on *B. cucullata* (more commonly called *B. semperflorens*) and a group of large-flowered plants, including the tuberous begonias such as *B. rosaeflora, B. veitchii,* and *B. boliviensis.* A third group has both ornamental flowers and decorative leaves and includes *B. scharffiana* and *B. metallica,* from which was produced the hybrid *B. × credneri,* now more widespread than either of its parents.

Modern growers use four group classifications for begonias: (1) fibrous-rooted, including the wax (*B. semperflorens*), the cane-stemmed, and the hirsute, or hairy; (2) the rhizomatous; (3) the rex-cultorum, or rex; and (4) the tuberous rooted. Such horticultural classifications are not used by botanists because they often separate related taxa (genera, species, groups of species, and so forth). (B.G.S./L.B.Sm.)

Characteristic morphological features. The majority of plants of the order Violales are shrubs or small trees, which are variously evergreen or deciduous. Annual or perennial herbs are prominent in the Violaceae and are present in the Malesherbiaceae and Turneraceae. Species of Achariaceae are climbing or stemless herbs with some species tending toward shrubbiness. Woody or herbaceous vines occur in the Passifloraceae, which are also noted for having axillary tendrils that are considered to be modified inflorescences or parts of inflorescences. The Cucurbitaceae are mostly herbaceous or woody plants with a viney or trailing habit. Each node often has one spirally coiled tendril.

Plants are often glabrous, though hairs or glands may be present. The Turneraceae, for example, are noted for having a variety of hair types. The Lacistemataceae have multicellular unbranched hairs with basal cells having elongated pits.

Leaf structure

Leaves are most commonly alternately arranged; pinnately or palmately veined; elliptical and entire or toothed; and leathery or thin. These characteristics may vary even within a single family; the diversity within the Flacourtiaceae, for instance, is substantial—enough that leaves may be very large or small and occasionally whorled or oppositely arranged. The leaves of Cucurbitaceae, Passifloraceae, and Caricaceae may be palmately veined and lobed and occasionally compound. Leaves of the Malesherbiaceae range from simple to deeply pinnatifid. The leaves of Violaceae vary from entire to lobed to highly dissected and the inner epidermal cells of the family characteristically are mucilaginous (they secrete or contain gums or gelatinous substances that absorb water and become bulky). The epidermis is also mucilaginous in the Turneraceae. Nectaries or glands outside the flowers are associated with the leaves of Cucurbitaceae and Turneraceae (as a pair at the base of the leaf), and with Passifloraceae (on the petiole).

Inflorescences show very little systematic organization in this order. In the Flacourtiaceae, flowers are small (occasionally large) and solitary or in cymose or racemous inflorescences located predominately at the axils or at the apex. A few African genera have solitary flowers attached to the midribs of large leaves. Other noteworthy patterns include tiny unisexual flowers arranged in compound racemes in Scyphostegiaceae. Throughout the order, inflorescences may be axillary or terminal, panicles, cymes, racemes, or spikes. Unisexual flowers are found in the Cucurbitaceae where the plants are either monoecious or dioecious.

Flowers are regular (*i.e.,* exhibit radial symmetry) in most members of the order, although bilateral symmetry is found in the genus *Viola,* which has a spur petal. Perfect flowers are found in most families of the order, and unisexual flowers occur in families that also have bisexual flowers. Perianth parts are generally distinct and unfused in all families. The number of sepals and petals in the Flacourtiaceae—3 to 8 or occasionally up to 15—exceeds the range of variation (3, 4, or 5 of each) found in any other members of the order. In Peridiscaceae and Lacistemataceae, petals may be entirely absent. Modifications are also found in the group: some petals are spurred in species of *Viola;* the Passifloraceae have a distinct ornamental corona placed between petals and stamens; and a toothed corona also occurs in the Malesherbiaceae.

Stamens are often numerous in the Flacourtiaceae, Peridiscaceae, and in some Passifloraceae. This condition is often considered a primitive condition in flowering plants. In Flacourtiaceae, stamens develop from the inside outward, a phenomenon held by some botanists to be a later development that increases the number of stamens from a less numerous primitive state. Five stamens is otherwise average, and the number usually equals the number of petals or sepals. Only a single stamen is found in the Lacistemataceae.

Gynoecium features

The gynoecium in the order shows similar features in nearly all the families. The gynoecium is a compound organ comprising a circular fusion of the carpels. Carpels are primitive leaflike organs that bear ovules. From 2 to 13 carpels make up the ovary wall, and the attachment of the ovules along the carpels internal margins results in the condition called parietal placentation (a single locule, or chamber, is filled with ovules suspended inward from the outer wall); the old name for Violales was Parietales, based on such a shared ovary structure. Carpels numbering 3, 4, or 5 are common for the order, with up to 10 in the Flacourtiaceae and 13 in the Scyphostegiaceae.

In many species of the large genus *Viola,* the normal open pollinated flowers (flowers pollinated when open) are formed early in the spring and are followed by the formation of unusual flower buds that never open. These flowers, called cleistogamous, fertilize within the bud; as a result, the seeds are genetically identical to the successful parent that produced them. This unusual versatility is one of the reasons for the distinctive success that violets bring to their shady moist habitats.

Fruits of the Violales are most commonly berries or dry capsules with a variety of other types less commonly found. In addition to the above types, the Flacourtiaceae also have drupes. The Violaceae occasionally have nutlike fruits in addition to berries and capsules. The berry commonly found in the Cucurbitaceae usually has a leathery rind and is considered a unique type called the pepo. The seeds are large or small and range from one to many per fruit. Arils are associated with seeds in many Flacourtiaceae, Violaceae, Turneraceae (a membranous aril), and Scyphostegiaceae. In most seeds of the order, abundant fleshy and oily endosperm is present with the embryo. In the Flacourtiaceae and Caricaceae, the endosperm also contains protein. (R.C.Ke.)

Apart from the core families of the Violales, Huaceae and Begoniaceae also have distinctive features. Huaceae has a distinctive ovary composed of five carpels enclosing a single cell. There is one basal ovule in the genus *Hua* and up to six in *Afrostyrax.* The fruit opens by five valves or is indehiscent; the seeds smell strongly of garlic.

Begonias vary in size from several centimetres in height (such as *Begonia steyermarkii* of Venezuela, an herb) to the five- to six-metre height of somewhat woody shrubs or what are virtually small trees (such as *B. pentaphylla* and *B. digitata* of Brazil). The growth habits of the plants of the order vary as widely as their size. Included in the family Begoniaceae are plants with stems that are upright, creeping, or developed into underground rhizomes (horizontal rootlike stems); stemless plants with basal tubers; and plants that climb by means of true roots or prop roots or by hooks developed from bent and elongated axillary buds—buds located in the upper angle between stems and leafstalks.

The leaves of begonias vary from simple to compound (*i.e.,* single-bladed or with several leaflets, respectively) and essentially are smooth-margined to much-lobed. They generally have one lobe noticeably larger than the other. Characteristically, all leaves on one side of a branch have the larger lobe on the same side of the leaf, and those on the other side of the branch have the larger lobe on the opposite side; the leaves, in effect, form mirror images of each other.

Unisexual flowers of the Begoniaceae

Flowers of all the Begoniaceae are unisexual. There are almost no records of abnormalities in nature involving abortive members of one sex appearing in flowers of the other. The plants are usually monoecious—with flowers of both sexes developing on the same plant—but normally the two sexes come to maturity at different times. In some cases the plants are dioecious. In monoecious plants, flowers of both sexes may, depending on the species, develop on the same inflorescence, or the inflorescences may bear flowers of only one sex.

Even though flowers of both sexes are often borne on the same plant, self-pollination does not usually occur because of the difference in the flowering time of the sexes. Some inflorescences are protandrous (*i.e.,* the male flower parts mature before the female of the same inflorescence), and the pollen is completely shed by the time the female flowers are receptive. Other inflorescences, however, which have the staminate (male) flowers on upper branches and carpellate (female) ones on lateral branches, are protogynous—the female parts mature first—and the fruits are completely mature before the pollen is shed.

Few records have been made of pollinating agents, though three different genera of bee visitors (*Apis, Bombus,* and *Anthophora*) have been reported. In cultivation, it is thought that self-pollination may occur occasionally by a trickling down of pollen to the stigmas (the sticky pollen-receiving surfaces of the female flower parts).

Mature seeds, mostly less than one millimetre long, are borne in large numbers, usually in capsules, which become dry and split open. The small, characteristically patterned, lightweight seeds seem not to be transported over very great distances, though there are some records of bird dispersal.

Many members of the Begoniaceae contain free organic acids (including oxalic and malic) in the cell sap. It has been suggested that the presence of these acids may be an active deterrent to insect attack. Other cell contents of interest include crystals of calcium oxalate. (B.G.S./L.B.Sm.)

Evolution. The Violales have vague boundaries separating them from other orders and the criteria currently used often seem arbitrary or inadequate. The principal criterion used to separate the Violales from the Theales involves the position of attachment (placentation) of the ovules. Individual carpels, the ovule-bearing leaflike structures, bear two rows of ovules close to their margins. When normally closed, the two rows of ovules appear close together along the adjacent fused margins, as in the case of a pea pod. The Theales and the Violales both have compound ovaries made of several carpels. If the carpels were separately sealed before they became part of a compound organ, the placentation is near the centre and the ovules are suspended facing outward in separate locules. This type of placentation is called axile and is characteristic of many families of the order Theales. If the carpel walls were not individually sealed before becoming part of a compound pistil, there is a single locule and the ovules are suspended facing toward the centre. This position is called parietal and is characteristic of the Violales. There are exceptions in both orders. In some classifications, the parietal type is considered to be derived from the axile type, but this is an assumption and there is no hard evidence that the Theales are antecedent to the Violales. The two orders house clusters of families that are related to each other and both probably have an equal evolutionary distance from the basal family of the subclass Dilleniidae, the Dilleniaceae.

Paleobotany

Flacourtiaceae is ancestral or near ancestral to all other families of the Violales and, in its great diversity, is well connected to most of the other families listed here. The Passifloraceae seem related to the Flacourtiaceae through the tribe Paropsieae, which form a good link between the families. The presence of the corona in the flower and certain pollen characteristics define the boundaries of the Passifloraceae. The Turneraceae and Malesherbiaceae, with the Passifloraceae, form a cluster of three related families. The Caricaceae also may be related to the Passifloraceae, with the genus *Adenia* of the latter family representing the closest link. The Peridiscaceae is close to the Flacourtiaceae but is more specialized in its possession of apical placentation and anthers with two locules instead of the usual four. The Lacistemataceae may be related to the Flacourtiaceae through the genus *Prockia.*

The single species of Scyphostegiaceae has a very distinctive ovary with a flat, discoid stigma with radiating ridges and numerous basal erect ovules. It is somewhat isolated. The Achariaceae are probably related to the Passifloraceae and show some similarity to the Cucurbitaceae. The proper classification of the Cucurbitaceae is probably the most controversial of any family in the order. The family is sharply defined, having no clear connecting link to presumed neighbours. Current concensus places it closest to the Passifloraceae, and embryological characters support its placement in the Violales. Relationships to the Begoniaceae, Loasaceae, Grossulariaceae (Rosales; Rosidae), or Sapindaceae (Sapindales; Rosidae), however, have not been ruled out. Families variously placed in the Violales include Stachyuraceae, Tamaricaceae, Frankeniaceae, Dioncophyllaceae, Ancistrocladaceae, Fouquieriaceae, Hoplestigmataceae, Datiscaceae, and Loasaceae. (R.C.Ke.)

Capparales (caper order). *Distribution and abundance.* Capparales, the caper order of flowering plants, consists of 5 families, 427 genera, and 4,000 species. Although the largest family is Brassicaceae, with 3,000 species, perhaps the best known is Capparaceae, a family with 800 species that derives its name and importance from *kapparis,* the name used by the Greek physician Dioscorides in his *Materia Medica* (*c.* AD 60) for *Capparis spinosa,* the source of commercial caper. The genus *Capparis* is often confined to arid regions of the tropics and subtropics and includes diverse growth forms such as trees, shrubs, and scramblers. The cabbage, cauliflower, kohlrabi (which are all varieties of *Brassica oleracea*), turnip (a cultivar of *B. rapa*), and radish (*Raphanus sativus*), all of which are members of the family Brassicaceae (sometimes called the Cruciferae), are important vegetables, rich in sulfur compounds and vitamin C. The edible mustard oil is from the seeds of *Brassica juncea* and *B. rapa* subspecies *campestris.* The horseradish tree (*Moringa oleifera;* Moringaceae) is cultivated for its edible roots and fruits and for ben oil, used as a lubricant for watches. The mignonette (*Reseda odorata;* Resedaceae) is a garden plant widely cultivated for its flowers. Tovariaceae is represented by a single genus, *Tovaria,* a plant with mustard oil glands and a fetid odour, this plant is found in tropical America.

Key families

Diversity of structure and habit. Members of the order Capparales grow in varied ecological conditions. Trees, shrubs, and climbers occur in tropical rain forests, tropical deserts, rock clefts, and sandy hillocks, along the seashore

Drawing by M. Pahl

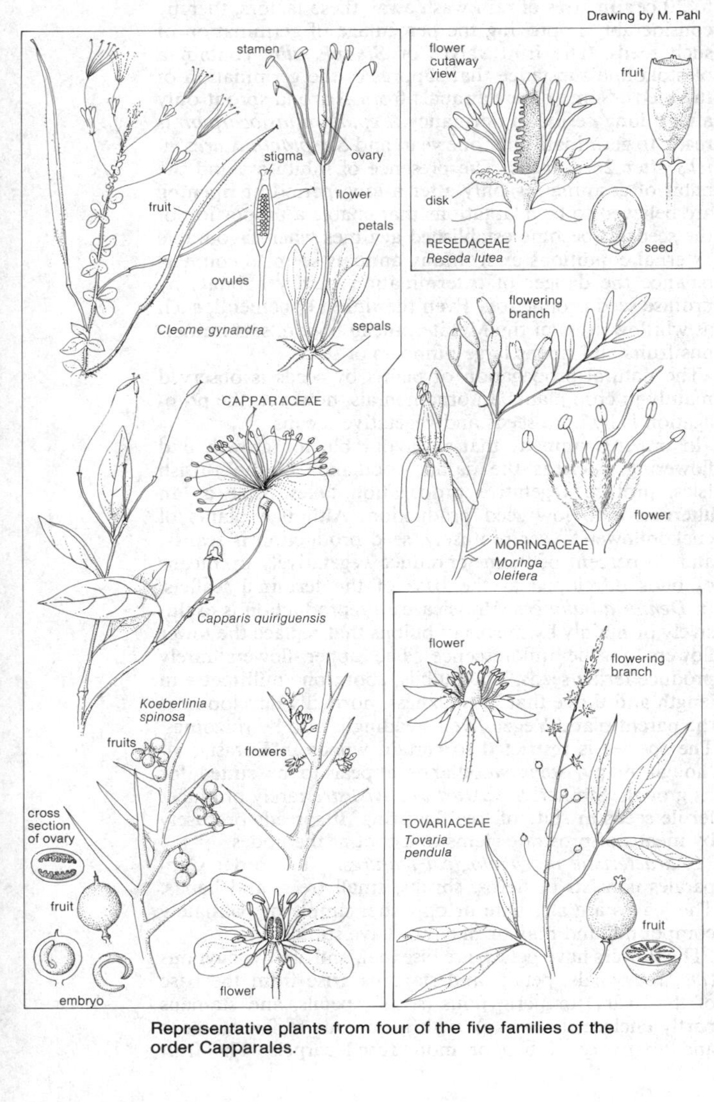

Representative plants from four of the five families of the order Capparales.

(enduring low concentrations of salts and the consequent physiological dryness), and in Arctic regions (withstanding continuous light during summer and low temperatures and dry winds in winter).

The members of the order exhibit diverse growth features. Some, such as *Moringa oleifera,* are small, deciduous trees, cultivated in the tropics and subtropics. Many others are thorny shrubs. The thorns are the paired, recurved modifications of the stipules, as in Capparaceae: *Capparis spinosa, C. micrantha,* and *Apophyllum anomalum,* which are distributed in the Mediterranean region, Africa, and Australia, respectively. The thorns may also consist of the branch tips in *Zilla myagroides* (Brassicaceae) of the Nubian Desert of Africa and *Koeberlinia spinosa* (Capparaceae) of the southwestern deserts of North America. The leaves are short-lived in many of these species.

Capparales is also rich in stragglers (sprawling, vinelike forms), such as *Capparis sepiaria* of India, *C. cucurbitina* and *C. scortechinii* of Malaysia, and woody lianas, such as *Maerua arenaria* of India, and *Ritchiea fragrans* of tropical Africa. *Cleome* (spiderflower) and allied genera are mostly glandular, annual (short-lived) herbs; *Cleome arborea* (sometimes known by the synonym *Isomeris arborea*), a close ally, is a shrub in the Mexican desert. (All four genera are in the family Capparaceae.) Within the Brassicaceae, the herbaceous annuals also are represented widely by *Capsella bursa-pastoris* (shepherd's purse), the herbaceous perennials by *Cheiranthus cheiri* (wallflower) and *Cochlearia officinalis* (scurvy grass), and the woody perennials by *Alyssum spinosum* and *Vella spinosa.* All of the above Brassicaceae, with the exception of *Alyssum spinosum,* belong to the north temperate zone.

The common aquatic forms are found in Brassicaceae: *Rorippa palustris* (sometimes known as *R. islandica;* marsh cress), *Cardamine pratensis* (cuckooflower), *C. rotundifolia* (mountain watercress), *Nasturtium officinale* (watercress), and *Subularia aquatica* (awlwort), which are all found in temperate regions and on tropical mountains. Watercress has spreading stems that root at the nodes ("joints" of a stem) and pinnate leaves. The awlwort has long, narrow, centric (shieldlike) leaves; its flowers either project above water or remain submerged and then rely on self-fertilization, because they remain closed. There are tufted xerophytes (plants adapted to dry habitats) such as *Erophila verna* (whitlow grass) and *Anastatica hierochuntica* (rose of Jericho, sometimes called the resurrection plant) of Europe and the Mediterranean region, which have hairy or fleshy leaves and grow on sand dunes. Saline (salty habitat) succulents, such as *Cakile maritima* (sea rocket) and *Crambe maritima* (sea kale), are found along the Atlantic and Baltic shores and in the Mediterranean region.

Common aquatic forms

Economic importance. The pickled flower buds of *Capparis spinosa* are the commercial capers. The root bark is bitter and has been used to treat rheumatism, paralysis, toothache, and disorders of the liver and spleen. The fruits and flower buds of *C. decidua* are edible and are often preserved in salt vinegar. The flower buds are used as potherbs. The fruit is an astringent and has been used to treat heart disorders, and the hard, heavy wood makes excellent tool handles and boat knees (a bent piece of wood used as a brace in boat construction) because it is resistant to termite attack. *C. sepiaria,* the Indian caper, is cultivated as a hedge, and it has been used to decrease fevers and to treat skin diseases. The fruits of *C. zeylanica* are edible and are an ingredient in curries. The root bark has been used as a sedative and is effective against cholera. The fruits of *C. mitchellii* are consumed in Australia and Tasmania and the flower buds of *C. corymbifera* are preserved in salt vinegar and eaten.

Edible and useful products

The leaves and twigs of *Cadaba farinosa* (Capparaceae) are pounded into a coarse mixture and made into cakes, puddings, and cereals; as food, the plant is called forsa or balambe in the Arabian Peninsula and tropical Africa. The leaves and seeds of *Cleome icosandra* are useful as external applications for wounds and skin ulcerations. The seeds are also an ingredient in curries. *C. spinosa* is grown as an ornamental. The ashes from the stems and leaves of *Courbonia virgate* serve as a source of salt in parts of The Sudan and Arabia.

Of the Brassicaceae, garlic mustard, *Alliaria officinalis,* is used to treat gangrenous infections. *Armoracia rusticana* is the well-known horseradish, whose roots are used for flavouring food. *Barbarea verna* (winter cress, or Belle Isle cress) is used as a vegetable. *Brassica campestris* variety *sarson* (yellow sarson, or Indian colza) provides seed oil for cooking and oil cake for cattle feed; the tender leaves and shoots are eaten as a vegetable. *B. campestris* variety *toria* (Indian rape) has similar uses. The tender leaves and shoots of *B. hirta* (white mustard) are used as a vegetable; the seeds yield a fatty oil. *B. juncea* (Indian mustard) seed oil is employed for cooking. *B. napus* (rape) leaves can be eaten as vegetables. The seeds of *B. nigra* (black mustard) are used as a spice and condiment. *B. oleracea* variety *acephala* contains the vegetables borecole, or kale, and collard greens. *B. oleracea* variety *botrytis* contains cauliflower and cauliflower-heading broccoli. These are grown for their edible inflorescences (flower clusters); the latter vegetable is grown widely only in Europe. *Brassica oleracea* variety *Italica* is the green-sprouting, or Italian, broccoli that is commonly eaten by North Americans. *B. oleracea* variety *capitata* is cabbage; *B. oleracea* variety *gemmifera* is Brussels sprouts, a bud-bearing cabbage the young shoots, buds, and leaves of which are edible; *B. oleracea* variety *gongylodes* is kohlrabi, or knol kohl, the short, swollen stem of which is edible; *B. pekinensis* is Chinese cabbage; *B. rapa* is turnip; and *Raphanus sativus* is the common radish.

Plants related to cabbage

Adaptations for pollination. The flowers, fruits, and seeds are efficiently adapted for pollination and dispersal. In the family Capparaceae, insects attracted by dense aggregates of flowers, brightly coloured petals, and nectar pollinate the flowers while feeding. The male and female organs of a flower mature at different times in many members, favouring cross-pollination; in *Cleome spinosa* the production of male flowers alternates with female and bisexual flowers in succession. In the family Brassicaceae, both cross- and self-pollination of the flowers occur. The twisting of stamens to one side may favour cross-pollination. In such instances, however, the slightest irregularity in the movement of the visiting insect may cause self-pollination because of the close proximity of the anthers to the stigma. *Pringlea antiscorbutica* (Kerguelen cabbage; Brassicaceae) is wind-pollinated in the absence of insects suitable for its pollination. The flowers are without petals but have exerted (long, extended past the end of the flower) anthers and long, filiform (threadlike), stigmatic pollen-catching structures. In the cuckooflower self-sterility favours cross-pollination. In mignonette different parts of the flower play different functions in the process of pollination. Nectar is secreted by the large, posteriorly projected petallike disc. The white, fringed edges of the petals, the colourful anthers, and the strong odour attract the insect visitors. The pistil, with terminal, papillose (nipplelike) stigmas, projects from the centre, and the stigmas receive the pollen carried by insect visitors. If the insects fail to visit the flowers, the stigmas, which lie directly below the anthers, eventually receive pollen from them and achieve self-pollination.

Adaptations for dispersal

The family Brassicaceae provides examples of the tremendous diversity in the mechanisms of fruit and seed dispersal in the Capparales order. The wind is the chief agent of dissemination in the desert. In North African deserts, fruits and seeds are either winged or are light or hairy; a pair of wings usually surrounds the fruit in *Zilla macroptera.* In *Morettia phileana* of the Nubian Desert in northeastern Sudan and *Sisymbrium altissium* (tumble mustard) of Europe and North America, the withered plants and their inflorescences are blown about, scattering the fruits and seeds. In the rose of Jericho of the deserts of the Middle East and North Africa, the plants curve into balls, or "roses," in drought and are blown along by the wind until they reach a wet spot; there the balls unfold along with the valves of the fruit, dispersing the seeds. In *Biscutella californica* the fruits are edged with hairs. In *Cochlearia,* the four- to six-seeded locules are dispersed by the valves acting as wings. The seeds of *Matthiola incana* (stock) and watercress in Malaysia, Myanmar, and Indochina are dispersed by river waters. The seeds of *Cakile maritima* and *Crambe maritima* and the fruits of *Raphanus maritimus* are disseminated by ocean tides. In *Nasturtium lacustre* and the cuckooflower the leaves with bulbils or adventitious buds float and develop into new plants elsewhere. Animals act as agents for the dispersal of seeds in the order Capparales through their excreta. Seeds of *Sisymbrium sophia* and shepherd's purse, for example, are distributed through the excreta of cattle; fruits of *Draba alpina* and seeds of *Cardamine bellidifolia* and *Cochlearia arctica* are dispersed in the excreta of birds. The seeds of Capparales may also be dispersed by simple adhesion to the feet of humans or cattle and to the wheels of carts. The mucilaginous seeds of shepherd's purse stick to the feet of gulls, and those of *Cardamine* (bitter cress) and *Lepidium perfoliatum* (peppergrass) to seashore birds.

The propagation of plants by seeds is strongly handicapped in saline and arid conditions because of incomplete seed ripening in mother plants at times; low soil moisture; hard, nonabsorbing soil crusts; high concentrations of soluble salts; or destruction of seedlings due to various factors such as irregular rainfall, animals, wind erosion, and deposition of mud. Large seeds with large food supplies (endosperm) may be at an advantage in establishing seedlings in spite of such negative factors as competition for light and moisture, predation by animals, and wind erosion. The large seed of sea kale (*Crambe maritima;* Brassicaceae), for example, sends down an extensive root enabling the species to colonize adverse habitats.

Germination inhibitors

Many of the desert seeds possess germination-inhibiting substances, and the family Brassicaceae shows good examples of this ability. The seeds of *Eruca boveana* and *Carrichtera annua* of the dry Mediterranean, Arabian, and Persian regions contain inhibiting factors; as much as 10 to 20 centimetres of rain wash away these factors, thereby considerably improving the percentage of germination of such seeds. The fruit valves of *Sinapis alba* contain a blastokoline substance that suppresses the germination of the seeds. Some desert annuals from Arizona sprout only after a long period of dormancy. *Lepidium lasiocarpum* is ready to germinate after one year, and *Streptanthus arizonicus* after 26 months. The presence of inhibitors and the habit of germinating only after a long period of ripening are believed to be adaptations that enable a proportion of the seeds to become established at times when favourable external conditions exist. Many annuals seem to counterbalance the danger of extermination in dry habitats by profuse seed production. Even the tiniest ephemeral, such as whitlow grass of the Mediterranean region, sets numerous fruits and ripens large numbers of seeds.

The natural propagation of plants by seeds is observed mainly in crop plants. In ornamentals, however, the propagation is by both seeds and vegetative means.

In an environment that is favourable for growth and flowering, such as the damp woodlands of the British Isles, profuse vegetative propagation takes place as an alternative to low seed production. Although plants of cuckooflower flower profusely, seed production is scanty, and 70 percent of them reproduce vegetatively by means of buds developed at the base of the terminal leaflets. In *Dentaria bulbifera* (Brassicaceae) reproduction is exclusively or mainly by means of bulbils that replace the lower flowers on the inflorescence. The upper flowers rarely produce fertile seeds. The bulbils, about one millimetre in length and thrice that in thickness, normally develop near the parent plant. Vegetative spreading is also by rhizomes. The species is restricted to certain woods in Eurasia, although many other woodlands appear to be suited for its growth. Similarly, *Nasturtium sylvestre* rarely produces fertile seeds in spite of free flowering. It spreads profusely by means of prostrate stems that root at the nodes.

Characteristic morphological features. The order Capparales consists of herbs, shrubs, small trees, and lianas. The leaves are alternate or opposite, simple or palmately compound, and may or may not have stipules.

The flowers have petals, are bisexual, and are hypogynous (*i.e.,* the sepals, petals, and stamens arise from the base of the ovary) or perigynous (sepals, petals, and stamens partly enclose the ovary), with numerous to few stamens and an ovary of two or more fused carpels. The fruit may be a fleshy berry or drupe or a dry silique (a dry, dehiscent, two-celled fruit), silicle (a dry, dehiscent fruit that has greater width than length), or capsule—fruits that open along one or more sutures. The seeds are curved or straight, winged or nonwinged.

Dry habitat adaptations

In desert species such as *Capparis decidua,* spiny, leafless, green stems form thickets, and there are strongly developed taproots. *Apophyllum anomalum* of Australia is also leafless but is covered with a thick coat of plant hairs. In *Zilla spinosa* and *Ochradenus baccatus* the leaves of the rainy season are replaced by smaller summer leaves. The seaside *Cakile maritima* and the dune-inhabiting *Cochlearia officinalis* are succulents; by storing water in their stems and leaves, the former resists high salt concentrations and the latter drought.

The Arctic and Alpine members of *Draba alpina, Cochlearia nudicaulis, C. fenestrata,* and *Cardamine bellidifolia* have thick, small, cushionlike stems and short, leathery leaves with concealed stomata (pores).

Evolution. The families Capparaceae and Brassicaceae form the core of the order Capparales. They have many common vegetative and floral features and cells, and other shared features suggest that Capparaceae is ancestral to Brassicaceae.

There are many taxonomic problems in this order. The orders Capparales and Violales are regarded by some authorities as parallel offshoots of the order Theales. Others, however, consider the Capparales to have originated from the most primitive members of the order Violales, similar to the family Flacourtiaceae of that order.

The Cleomoideae, a subfamily of the Capparaceae, closely resemble the family Brassicaceae in their herbaceous habit and capsular fruit with central partitions. Some authorities raise the Cleomoideae to the rank of family, called Cleomaceae, which is considered to be closely related and basic to the family Brassicaceae. This treatment needs support from other enquiries into floral anatomy, embryology, and pollen morphology, however.

The resemblance and position of the family Tovariaceae with respect to the family Capparaceae could be better understood if the vascular anatomy of the axile placentation and eight-parted flower were better known. (H.S.N./Ed.)

Theales. *Distribution and abundance.* The order Theales comprises 18 families, arranged into about 175 genera and 3,400 species, of which just 3 families—Theaceae, with 40 genera and 600 species; Clusiaceae, with 50 genera and 1,200 species; and Dipterocarpaceae, with 16 genera and 600 species—include two-thirds of the species, and 2 other families—Ochnaceae, with 30 genera and 430 species; and Actinidiaceae, with 3 genera and 300 species—contain most of the remainder of the order. Each of these major families is distributed throughout the tropics; some occur in the subtropics as well. Most of the small families (containing 5 or fewer genera) are geographically restricted in distribution. Marcgraviaceae, Quiinaceae, and Caryocaraceae are restricted to the Neotropics; Scytopetalaceae is found in tropical West Africa; Sphaerosepalaceae is endemic to Madagascar; Pentaphylaceae is found in China, Sumatra, and the Malay Peninsula; Pellicieraceae occurs along the Pacific coast of Central America; Medusagynaceae is found in Seychelles; Oncothecaceae and Paracryphiaceae are endemic to New Caledonia; Elatinaceae grows throughout the tropics; and the Tetrameristaceae are native to Malaysia and Venezuela.

Economic and ecological importance. Several of the world's most economically important plants are found in the order Theales. For example, the family Dipterocarpaceae contains various genera, principally *Dipterocarpus, Hopea, Shorea,* and *Vatica,* that occur together in dense stands, where they are often dominant trees in tropical Asia.

Source of hardwoods

These mixed forests of Dipterocarpaceae are the most important source of tropical hardwoods in the world and are highly endangered as the demand for these timbers increases. No other family in the Theales is so important internationally for timber as the Dipterocarpaceae; however, several families have species that are prized locally for their wood. The wood of *Scytopetalum tieghemii* (Scytopetalaceae), for instance, is used in Sierra Leone and Ghana for house poles because of its decay-resistant qualities. A locally important wood in Madagascar is provided by *Leptolaena pauciflora* (Sarcolaenaceae); this species, which formerly dominated the slope forests of high plateaus in Madagascar, is now endangered as the habitat is burned to form pasture. The timber of the two species of *Lophira* (Ochnaceae), known as the ekki, or African oak, is a significant commercial product, especially in the construction of bridges, pilings, and other structures in constant contact with water.

The most economically important plant in the Theales is certainly *Camellia sinensis* (Theaceae), the leaves of which are the source of tea. *C. sinensis* is a native of Assam (a state in northeastern India) but was first cultivated by the Chinese, from whom India and Ceylon (Sri Lanka) imported seeds. Tea is also grown in several other countries (*e.g.,* Turkey and the Caucausus republics and the republics of Central Asia). Various species in the Theales are highly prized ornamentals, such as *Gordonia* (loblolly bay), *Stuartia,* and *Camellia japonica* (the common camellia; Theaceae), Chinese gooseberry (*Actinidia chinensis;* Actinidiaceae), *Hypericum* (Clusiaceae), and *Ochna* (Ochnaceae). The latex from some members of Clusiaceae is used medicinally, and resin from several species of Dipterocarpaceae, known commercially as dammar, is used in the varnish, paint, and linoleum industries.

The Theales do not contain any internationally important food plant species, but several are quite important within local and national economies. In South America the Caryocaraceae is the source of souari nuts, which are collected in the wild and cultivated (*Caryocar nuciferum* and *C. amygdaliferum*). In the Clusiaceae the principal edible fruits are mammee apples (*Mammea americana*) and

Drawing by M. Pahl; *G. punctata* and *G. delpyana* based on A. Engler, *Syllabus der Pflanzenfamilien;* floral details of *G. mangostana* based on L.H. Bailey, *Manual of Cultivated Plants* (1949); The Macmillan Company

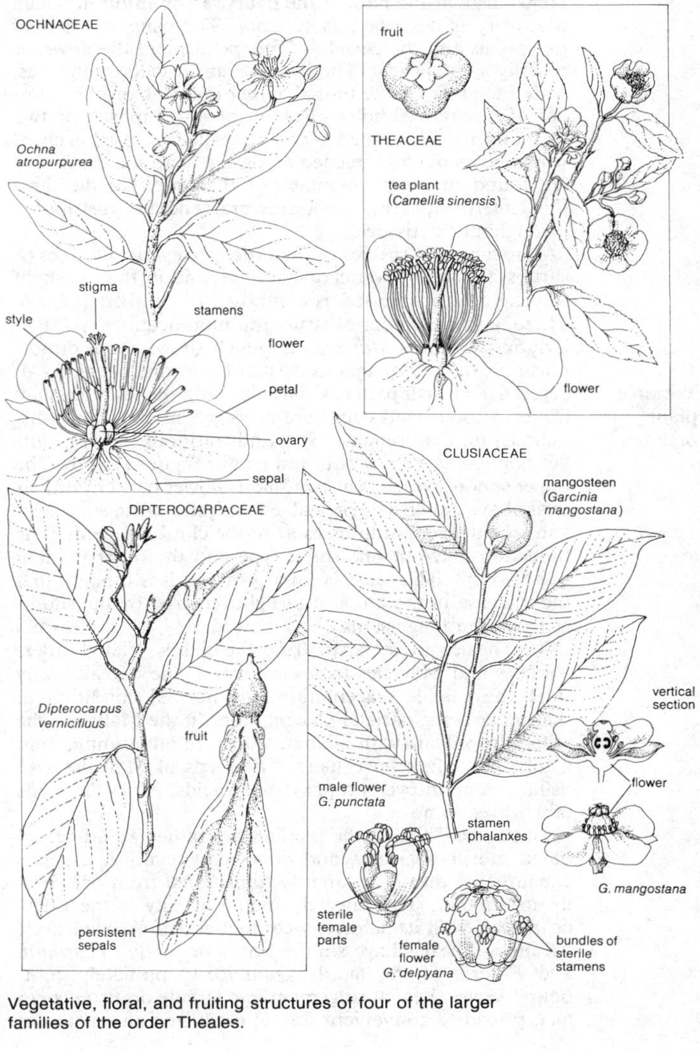

Vegetative, floral, and fruiting structures of four of the larger families of the order Theales.

mangosteens (*Garcinia mangostana*), although the fruits of other species of *Garcinia* also are edible. A substitute for cocoa butter is extracted from the fruits (known as illipe nuts) of certain species of *Shorea* (Dipterocarpaceae). Species of Elatinaceae are often important economically as weeds in rice fields and irrigation ditches, where they also play an important ecological role in the prevention of soil erosion. Most families of Theales, however, do not have such a distinct ecological role as the Elatinaceae. Other important generalizations that can be made include the mixed forests of Dipterocarpaceae in Malaysia mentioned above, the neotropical Pellicieraceae, which are restricted to mangroves, and Marcgraviaceae, which are largely lianas in rain forests. Most other families comprise principally rain-forest species of mostly trees and shrubs but occasionally herbs as well.

Prevention of soil erosion

The order Theales comprises such a diverse group of plants that few generalizations can be made about reproductive ecology. Both fleshy fruits (*e.g.,* in Quiinaceae) and dry, capsular fruits (*e.g.,* in Elatinaceae) are found, so that both wind and animals are responsible for fruit and seed dispersal in the order. Some dry fruits (notably those of Dipterocarpaceae) have spectacularly elongated winglike sepals that are obviously adapted for wind dispersal.

Characteristic morphological features. The flowers in the order Theales almost always have multiple petals, sepals that usually overlap, filaments that are distinct or fused into groups and without hairs, carpels generally fused to form a compound hypogynous or perigynous ovary, and mostly axile placentation. (B.M.Bo.)

The plants are usually woody, often with evergreen foliage. The leaves are usually simple, and resins are often present in the tissues. The bisexual flowers are mostly hypogynous—*i.e.,* the sepals, petals, and male parts (stamens) arise at the base of the ovary, a condition in which the ovary is described as superior. The calyx consists of free sepals and the corolla of free petals, and the flower is radially symmetrical. The stamens are usually numerous, with a tendency to be united, either in a ring or in a number of separate bundles. The ovary is composed of two to many usually united segments called carpels, each of which bears ovules attached along the central axis. Resins are found in many members of the order; in the family Dipterocarpaceae, the resins are generally distributed throughout the tissues.

Although most species of the order are evergreen trees or shrubs, the family Marcgraviaceae, found in the forests of tropical South America, is composed of climbers (lianas). These have a number of structural modifications, particularly in the genus *Marcgravia,* which shows shoot dimorphism, a condition that consists of two distinct types of vegetative growth patterns. The climbing shoots bear small leaves without stalks that are arranged in two rows (distichous) on the branches. Short adventitious (aerial) roots develop along these shoots and enable them to climb. The upper shoots, which bear pendulous flower clusters at their ends, have much larger, stalked, spirally arranged leaves and lack the adventitious roots of the climbing stems. The transition between one shoot type and the other is often quite abrupt. The cause is unknown, but it is thought that the increase in the amount of light received by the shoots as they climb higher may be involved. (J.Cul.)

Variable plant organs

The Theales are set apart from the closely related orders Violales and Malvales in several ways. The Violales only rarely have axile placentation, the normal condition in that order being parietal placentation. In the Malvales, the sepals are valvate with filaments that are often united into a tube and often have hairs. The seeds of Malvales also usually contain cyclopropenyl fatty acids, while the seeds of Theales do not.

Within the Theales, the families are rather well-differentiated morphologically, and only occasionally is a genus encountered that is apparently transitional from one family to another. The most distinctive family is the Caryocaraceae, with its palmately compound trifoliolate leaves. All other Theales have simple leaves or rarely (*Touroulia* and *Froesia* of the family Quiinaceae) pinnately compound leaves. Leaf arrangement and stipule occurrence, in fact, provide a convenient way to organize a discussion of the morphology of the remaining 17 families in the order.

Only four of the families in Theales have leaves that are mostly alternate and with stipules. One of these, the Dipterocarpaceae, is distinguished in having the connective of the anthers exserted, sepals that are often enlarged and persistent in the fruit, becoming winglike, and seeds that usually lack endosperm. Of the remaining three families, the Sarcolaenaceae usually has flowers with an extrastaminal disc (*i.e.,* the disc is located outside, or distal to, the stamens), while the Ochnaceae and Sphaerosepalaceae have flowers with an intrastaminal disc (*i.e.,* the disc is located inside, or proximal to, the stamens) or with no disc at all. The latter two families are easily distinguished from one another. The Ochnaceae has anthers with a normal connective that frequently open by terminal pores and flowers that often have a style which originates between the lobes of a deeply lobed ovary (gynobasic style). The Sphaerosepalaceae, on the other hand, has anthers with a broad, glandular connective tissue that separates the pollen sacs and flowers that rarely have a gynobasic style.

Leaf structure

Those families of Theales with alternate simple leaves and no stipules are twice as numerous as the stipulate families mentioned above. The most anomalous of these, the Marcgraviaceae, has a lianoid or epiphytic growth habit with floral bracts that are highly modified into pitcherlike, spurred, or hooded structures. The remaining seven families of this grouping are usually trees or shrubs and do not have the floral bracts so modified. Three of these families (Theaceae, Actinidiaceae, and Scytopetalaceae) have numerous stamens (10 or more) and usually 2 (sometimes 1) to many ovules in each locule of the ovary. The Scytopetalaceae are distinguished from the others in having valvate petals, and the Actinidiaceae are distinguished from the Theaceae in having inverted, deeply sagittate anthers that open by terminal pores, ridged seeds, and an oft-climbing growth habit. The four remaining families in this grouping have only four or five stamens per flower and only one to four ovules per locule. The family Oncothecaceae stands out immediately because of its sympetalous corolla (in which the petals are partially or completely fused), an extremely rare condition in the Theales. Of the other three families, the Pentaphylacaceae family is distinctive in having pollen sacs that open by a terminal pore and in lacking the ridged seeds and specialized flask-shaped sepal glands found in the other two families, the Tetrameristaceae and the Pellicieraceae. The latter two families, which would never be confused on ecological or geographic grounds, are equally well separated on morphological criteria: the Tetrameristaceae have fleshy fruits with one seed in each of the four or five locules, the seeds having copious endosperm; the Pellicieraceae have dry, seeded fruits with a single seed having no endosperm.

The remaining five families of the Theales all have opposite or whorled leaves. Two of these, the Quiinaceae and Elatinaceae, have stipules and are quite easily distinguished. The growth habit of the former includes trees, shrubs, and lianas, 15 or more stamens per flower, two ovules in each locule, and fleshy fruits; the growth habit of the latter includes herbs and subshrubs, fewer than 15 stamens per flower, numerous ovules in each locule, and dry, capsular fruits.

Three families of Theales have opposite or whorled leaves but do not have stipules (except for the genus *Mahurea* in Clusiaceae). Of these, only one family is commonly encountered, the Clusiaceae, and it is distinguished by generally having an ovary with three to five locules and well-developed secretory canals or cavities in almost all organs. The other two families, the Paracryphiaceae and Medusagynaceae, have fruits with 8 to 25 locules and no secretory canals or cavities. The former is distinguished from the latter by having 4 ovules (versus 2) per locule, an ovary with 8 to 15 locules (versus 17 to 25), and generally 8 stamens in a single cycle (versus many). (B.M.Bo.)

Pollination

A number of notable structural developments seem to be related to pollination. The most simple is the uniting of the stamens (male parts) either in a ring, as in the cultivated camellias, or in bundles, as in the common Saint-John's-wort (*Hypericum*) and in many tropical members of the order. In some members of the family Clusiaceae the stamens are united into very condensed groups known as phalanxes. A further adaptation, presumably effective in pollination, is the extreme elongation of the stamens of the family Caryocaraceae; these project considerably beyond the petals and are also united at the base.

The most remarkable pollination adaptations are found in members of the Marcgraviaceae, in which the floral bracts, small leaflike structures located just below the flowers, are transformed into nectar-secreting organs that are of various shapes but are always hollow and somewhat pitcherlike. In the simplest case (found in three genera), a bract subtends each flower. In the genus *Marcgravia,* however, the flower cluster is pendulous and umbellate—the flowers are on stalks that radiate from a common point, umbrella fashion. The central flowers of the umbel are sterile, and their bracts are enlarged to form erect, pitcherlike structures, superficially very like the insectivorous pitchers of *Nepenthes,* which hang below the outer ring of fertile flowers. The nectar-filled pitchers of *Marcgravia* attract hummingbirds, which were once thought to pollinate the fertile flowers as they hovered, drinking the nectar. However, in at least two Guyanese species, the hummingbirds approach the pitchers from above the fertile flowers and do not come into contact with the stamens or the stigmata. In these two species, the stamens open in the late bud stage, and the flowers are actually self-fertilized.

Seed dispersal

Various dispersal mechanisms occur in the order, but only two are noteworthy. In most families, the aging sepals persist around the ripening fruit, and in various groups, notably the families Dipterocarpaceae and Ochnaceae, two or more of them enlarge above the fruit, producing a two-winged structure that is distributed by the wind.

Evolution. The oldest pollen thought to represent a family of the Theales dates from the Eocene Epoch (57.8 to 36.6 million years ago). However, the pantropical distribution of the families Clusiaceae, Theaceae, Ochnaceae, Elatinaceae, and Actinidiaceae, together with the recent discoveries of disjunct taxa in the Neotropics of what had generally been thought to be strictly Paleotropical families (Tetrameristaceae and Dipterocarpaceae), suggest an origin in the mid-Cretaceous (about 97.5 million years ago).

Broad trends in the evolution of the order can be seen in several structures, such as the leaves (alternate to opposite), stipules (present to absent), stamens (numerous to few), corolla (unfused petals to fused), and latex (absent to present). There are, however, so many character state reversals possible in the heterogenous assemblage represented in the Theales that evolution of the order is best considered on a family-by-family basis. The sequence in which the families are mentioned below is not strictly primitive to advanced because not only is it impossible to present adequately the evolution of the order in this linear fashion, but more importantly the relationships among the numerous, small, isolated tropical families are especially poorly known.

The Ochnaceae, which in this article includes a number of small families occasionally recognized in their own right (Diegodendraceae, Lophiraceae, Luxemburgiaceae, Strasburgeriaceae, Sauvagesiaceae, and Wallaceaceae), lies at the base of the Theales and is clearly primitive in its often nearly separate and unfused carpels (apocarpous gynoecium). Within the family Ochnaceae there appear to be two lines of evolution: (1) those taxa with a terminal style and usually capsular fruit, and (2) those with a gynobasic style and fruit with separate, indehiscent cocci. Evidence from pollen morphology suggests affinity of the family to the Actinidiaceae, Marcgraviaceae, and Theaceae.

(J.Cul./B.M.Bo.)

Ericales. *Distribution and abundance.* The Ericales is an order of about 4,500 species of plants arranged in 8 families with about 160 genera. The vast majority of the species belong to the family Ericaceae and most of the remainder to the family Epacridaceae. The remaining 6 families have less than 200 species in total.

Predominance of shrubs or small trees

The order consists primarily of shrubs (sometimes climbing and vinelike) or small trees, but it also includes perennial herbs, undershrubs (sometimes trailing or creeping from underground stems), epiphytes (plants that grow on other plants), and mycotrophic herbs (nonphotosynthetic plants that obtain nourishment through their intimate association with fungi). A few tree species may reach heights of 20 to 35 metres. The order contains many of the most beautiful horticultural plants throughout the world, including azaleas and rhododendrons (*Rhododendron*), and some economically important species such as blueberries and cranberries. As a general rule, plants in this order prefer partially exposed, moist habitats, acidic soils, and an association with endotrophic mycorrhiza (where fungal cells penetrate the cells of the host root tissues). Widely distributed throughout the tropics and temperate regions of the Northern and Southern hemispheres, a few genera extend into the Arctic and Antarctic regions.

The Cyrillaceae (the cyrilla family) consists of 3 genera and 14 species and occurs in northern South America, Central America, the West Indies, and on the coastal plain of the southeastern United States. The single genus of Clethraceae (the clethra family), *Clethra,* has about 65 species; these are found from tropical South America north to Mexico and the southeastern United States, as well as in tropical and subtropical southeastern Asia and the East Indies.

Grubbiaceae (the grubbia family) also is composed of a single genus. Known as *Grubbia,* it has three species, all of which are indigenous to the Cape region of South Africa.

Empetraceae (the crowberry family) includes three genera and about five species and is widespread in the colder parts of the Northern Hemisphere, southern South America, and the coastal plain of the southeastern United States.

The 30 genera and 400 species of Epacridaceae (the epacris family) make this family second only to Ericaceae. The family is found primarily in Australia and New Zealand but also reaches north to the Philippine Islands and mainland Southeast Asia and extends east to the Hawaiian Islands and Patagonia.

The Ericaceae (the heath family) consists of about 110 genera and 4,000 species. Abundant and widespread throughout the temperate regions of the Northern and Southern hemispheres, it is a conspicuous element in the subartic circumpolar vegetation and in subtropical and tropical mountains. The blueberry (*Vaccinium*) group is most abundant in the tropics of the New World, Malaysia, and southeastern Asia. There they usually develop as epiphytic shrubs in the cool, moist montane regions known as cloud forests, although a few species range into typically tropical environments. The largest blueberry genus is *Vaccinium,* with some 450 species scattered throughout the world but especially in tropical Asia (*i.e.,* in Southeast Asia) to Malesia (the Malay Peninsula and the Malay Archipelago). The heath group is confined to Africa and Europe, with a proliferation of more than 650 species of *Erica* in the Cape region of southern Africa. The rhododendron group consists of primarily the ornamental genus *Rhododendron* (including the azaleas), which contains more than 800 species in the Himalayas and western China, as well as on the island of New Guinea.

Rhododendrons

The Pyrolaceae (the shinleaf family) is composed of 4 genera and about 45 species and is endemic to the Northern Hemisphere and most diverse in the north temperate and boreal regions.

The Monotropaceae (the Indian pipe family) consists of 10 genera and 12 species, most of which occur in the temperate and boreal regions of the Northern Hemisphere; 1 New World species ranges south, nearly approaching the Equator in Colombia, while 1 Old World species nears the same latitude in the Malay Peninsula. The family lacks chlorophyll (green, food-producing plant pigment) and is best known for the Indian pipe genus (*Monotropa*).

(J.L.L.)

Economic and ecological importance. Members of Ericale have served as tea substitutes; early explorers of Canada and the eastern and northern regions of the United States, for example, brewed tea from the leaves of Labrador tea, or bog tea (*Ledum palustre* or *L. groenlandicum*); Lapland rosebay (*Rhododendron lapponicum*); and checkerberry, or wintergreen (*Gaultheria procumbens*). The Ojibwa Indians used bog rosemary (*Andromeda glaucophylla*) and leatherleaf (*Chamaedaphne calyculata*) as

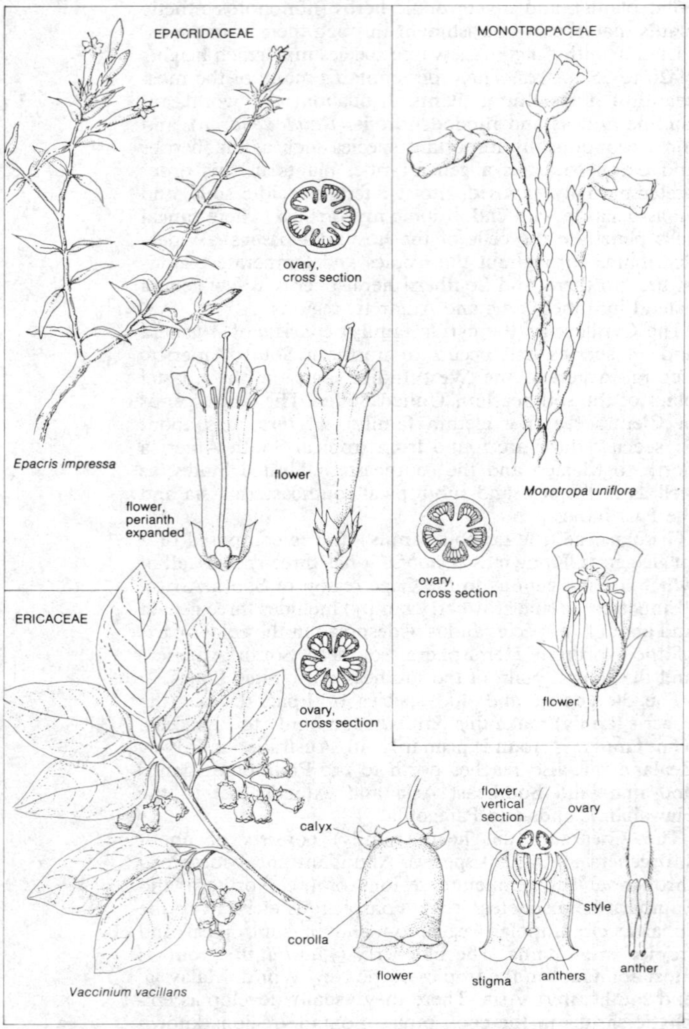

Representative plants from three of the principal families of the order Ericales.

Drawing by M. Pahl based on (Epacridaceae, Ericaceae all but ovary) G.H.M. Lawrence, *Taxonomy of Vascular Plants* (1951); The Macmillan Company, (Ericaceae ovary) J. Hutchinson, *The Families of Flowering Plants;* The Clarendon Press, Oxford

tea; however, care must be taken not to boil the leaves as this extracts andromedotoxin, a naturally occurring plant poison that is extremely toxic to humans. For centuries the best material for making briar pipes has been wood from burls of *Erica arborea* or related Mediterranean species.

Edible berries

Plants belonging to the Ericales have been and still are most important to humans as foodstuffs and as cultivated ornamentals. Checkerberry, certain of the bearberries *(Arctostaphylos* species), and creeping snowberry or moxie plum (*Gaultheria hispidula*) produce edible fruits. The huckleberries, the blueberries, and the cranberries are most prized as fresh fruits or as jellies or preserves.

Cranberries (*Vaccinium macrocarpon*) are cultivated in North America in Massachusetts, especially on Cape Cod; in New Jersey; in Wisconsin; and in the Pacific Northwest. They are also harvested from wild stands in these areas. In harvesting the cranberries, the bogs are flooded and the mature red berries then float in the water, thus lending themselves to harvesting by machine. Most cranberries are now processed for fruit drinks. The tart fresh berries are also processed with sugar and sold as cranberry sauce or jelly. Cranberries, first cultivated in New England in the early 18th century, are still one of the leading exports of Massachusetts. Cranberry sauce and jelly have come to be thought of as uniquely American, but the Scandinavians hold in high esteem their native lingonberry (*V. vitis-idaea*), the berry of which is similar to, but spicier than, the American cranberry.

Huckleberries (*Gaylussacia baccata*) are harvested only from wild stands in the eastern United States and Canada. Although the flesh of the fruit is generally considered to be sweet and delicious, the "berry" is actually a drupe, or stony-seeded fruit, with 10 large, hard nutlets, making it less desirable and marketable than blueberries.

Blueberries of many types are harvested from wild stands in New England and the eastern states and from northern California into western Canada. Several species of *Vaccinium* are involved. They range from lowbush (*V. angustifolium*) to highbush (*V. corymbosum*) species and from diploid to hexaploid forms (*i.e.,* genetic variants with two to six sets of chromosomes, respectively). Blueberries, with their small and insignificant seeds, are widely considered a delicacy, and their production is economically significant, especially in New England.

Ornamental uses

The other major use of the Ericales is as ornamentals. Several species of sweet pepperbush (*Clethra*) are used horticulturally to take advantage of the highly fragrant summer flowers. The leatherwood (*Cyrilla racemiflora*) and buckwheat tree (*Cliftonia monophylla*) are used similarly and also are desirable for their showy autumn coloration of foliage. The sourwood (*Oxydendrum arboreum*), one of the few trees in the order, is also cultivated because of the brilliant colour of its foliage in autumn. Mountain laurel (*Kalmia latifolia*), the most popular and best-known garden laurel, is considered by many to be the most beautiful flowering shrub in North America. Trailing arbutus, also called mayflower or ground laurel (*Epigaea repens*) is used as ground cover in many gardens. In Europe and New England, the heather (*Calluna vulgaris*) and some of the low bushy heaths (*Erica* species) are used as garden border plants. Many members of the Ericales are planted in gardens as novelties or to provide variation in foliage colour and texture.

The most important ornamentals in the entire order, however, are found in the genus *Rhododendron,* the azaleas and the rhododendrons, about 850 species of which are or have the potential to be ornamentals. Some of the most spectacular flower clusters known are produced by these shrubs, and they are widely used not only for the beauty of their blooms but also for the value of the many evergreen species as effective background shrubs. Natural species are cultivated, and many hybrids have originated in cultivation; it is thus difficult to develop a classification that includes all species, varieties, and forms. It is safe to say, however, that there are at least 6,000 varieties of rhododendrons and azaleas in cultivation.

Ecologically, the Ericales are often prominent features in the vegetation throughout the world. In many cases, they dominate a major vegetation type of tropical montane region known as the "ericaceous belt," and, because of their sun-loving ecology, they are frequently found as pioneers near the craters of volcanoes or in recent landslide areas. Heather (*Calluna vulgaris*) often dominates large areas of well-drained acidic soil, forming heaths or moors in Britain and over continental Europe. The true heaths (*Erica* species) form a distinctive part of the vegetation around the shores of the Mediterranean Sea and dominate the landscape in parts of the Cape region of South Africa. The circumpolar boreal forests and subarctic vegetation include only a few widespread species, especially blueberries (*Vaccinium* species) and bearberry (*Arctostaphylos*), but these frequently dominate in a number of plant communities. In some forests in the Himalayas, *Rhododendron* trees 12 metres tall may dominate the upper story; at higher altitudes they may be shorter, forming impenetrable shrubberies 5 to 6 metres tall; these may pass into shorter shrubberies in the Alpine zone.

Noxious plants

The order contains a few species harmful to humans or animals. Some contain a toxic substance identified as andromedotoxin. This compound is known to occur in certain species of *Rhododendron, Leucothoe, Menziesia, Ledum* (marsh rosemary), and *Kalmia* (mountain laurel), and it is probably more widespread in the order than is now known. The leaves, twigs, flowers, and pollen all contain andromedotoxin. Poisoned honey has been reported in areas in which bees visit large rhododendron or mountain laurel stands, but the honey is so bitter that very little of it can be eaten. The poison causes watering of the mouth, eyes, and nose; vomiting; slow pulse; and depressed blood pressure. Massive ingestion of andromedotoxin results in convulsions and slow and progressive paralysis until death; fatalities, however, are rare.

Several species of laurel long have been known to be poisonous to domestic animals. *Kalmia angustifolia* is known colloquially as sheepkill, lambkill, or calfkill, and one common name of *K. latifolia* is poison laurel. Sheep and cattle may become ill and die from eating foliage of these plants, but deer do not seem to be affected. The course of the disease parallels that in humans who have ingested a massive amount of andromedotoxin—convulsions, progressive paralysis, and death. Laurel poisoning is not a serious problem in sheep or cattle, however, probably because the tough, leathery leaves are not desirable except in the absence of more palatable foliage. Cases of poisoning are more frequent in sheep than in cattle.

Characteristic morphological features. Although there are exceptions to most features, and most or all of them occur in other orders, it is the combination of features, rather than any individual one, that distinguishes the bulk of the Ericales from other orders. The Ericales generally are shrubs or rather small trees that have a strong tendency to form mycotrophic associations (*i.e.,* the roots are associated with certain fungi that assist in providing nutrients to the plant) and commonly produce tannins (a natural plant compound used in tanning). The leaves are alternate, simple, and leathery, and the flowers are regular (radially symmetrical) with a four- or five-parted corolla (collection of petals) of partly fused petals. The flowers have functional (fertile) structures of both sexes. The stamens number twice the number of corolla lobes and usually are attached directly to the receptacle at the edge of a nectar-producing disc. Anthers commonly become inverted during early development and open lengthwise or by terminal pores to discharge the pollen grains, which are borne in tetrads. The single pistil consists of a compound ovary at its base with one hollow style and a simple stigma to which the pollen will adhere. The ovules are numerous and are attached along the central axis of the ovary. Fruits are of various types, including capsules (dry dehiscent fruit), berries, and drupes, and the enclosed seeds are small. Most members of the Ericales have a long series of embryological features in common, although the only characteristics shared by all species of the Ericales are that the ovule has only one integument (or covering cell layer) and the nucellus (central part of the ovule) is a single cell layer thick.

The flowers of most members of the Ericales are showy or colourful and produce abundant nectar, pollen, or both; a few also produce pleasant odours. These features are special adaptations to attract insects or birds that pollinate the plant while seeking food. In some rhododendrons, where the flowers are horizontally oriented and the stamens are exposed, the pollen tetrads are linked together by sticky threads. Thus, when a butterfly or bee visits the flower seeking food, it snags the entire pollen mass, which is then pulled from the anther like pearls on a string and transferred to the stigma of a neighbouring flower.

Compared with some of the very highly specialized plant groups, such as the orchids, few unusual or unique features exist in the life cycle of the Ericales. There has been only the slightest tendency toward development of irregular flowers, and highly involved and complicated methods of pollination are rare.

Probably most members of Ericales may be pollinated in more than one way, but studies on pollination in the Ericales have been sketchy. In the heather, or ling (*Calluna vulgaris*), the nectary in the flower is a continuous, fleshy ring around the base of the ovary, and the lower parts of the petals and stamen filaments (basal parts of the male structures) are also succulent. An insect forcing its proboscis into the flower shoves the anthers apart. Anther chambers open laterally, and hornlike appendages attached to the anthers help deposit pollen on the insect's proboscis by acting as levers. Pollen is carried to another flower by the insect and deposited on the stigma as the insect probes for nectar in the flower.

Insect pollination

Nectar production decreases near the end of the pollination period. The filaments then elongate and extend the open anthers beyond the confines of the flower; thereafter wind pollination occurs.

Another kind of pollination also takes place in the same heather flower. Certain small insects (*Taeniothrips ericae* [Thysanoptera]) appear to be present at all times in *Calluna* flowers. These tiny insects are very lively, move about actively, and reach parts of the flower inaccessible to larger insects. Pollen discharged during their activity adheres to their bodies, which become sticky with nectar.

The males of *T. ericae* are much rarer than the females and cannot fly. Females fly from flower to flower searching for males. They depart from projecting stigmas, their bodies heavily laden with pollen, and presumably land on stigmas, thereby probably being able to effect both self- and cross-pollination. After fertilization the females lay their eggs in the fleshy basal region of the petals. The eggs pass the winter in the persistent corolla, and the larvae emerge the following year. Thrips are thus able to spend their entire life cycle within the heather flower.

The mountain laurels have two pouches in each of the five partly fused petals. Anthers are retained under tension in these pockets until the flower opens; then the filaments snap the anthers up, and pollen is forcibly ejected. Laurel flowers are visited by bees that almost certainly effect pollination. Presumably elevation of the anthers above the saucer-shaped flowers of the laurel also permits wind pollination.

The flowers of many tropical American blueberries display a number of morphological features associated with pollination by hummingbirds. The flowers are odourless (hummingbirds have no sense of smell) and relatively showy; flowers and their associated bracts often have contrasting colours in some shade of red, violet, or orange, which attract hummingbirds and are not particularly alluring to insects; the corollas are regular and tubular with a constricted throat and spreading lobes to exclude large insects; the flowers are pendant or arching in habit and are arranged in open, elongate or few-flowered clusters, a condition suited to hummingbirds, which feed in flight; a nectar-secreting disc is located on top of the ovary at the base of the corolla so that the visiting bird requires a proboscis for access; corolla tubes are thick and fleshy to protect them from damage by a probing bill; corollas correspond well to the size and proportions of the bills of visiting hummingbirds; and sugar concentrations in the nectar fall into the range preferred by hummingbirds. In connection with hummingbird pollination, nectar-thieving mites (*Rhinoseius*) spend virtually the entire life cycle within the flowers of certain plants of this order frequented by hummingbirds. The mites depend not only on the flowers as a source of nectar but also on the birds themselves, as their primary means of dispersal is on the bills or in the nasal cavities of hummingbirds.

Mycorrhizal relationships

Mycorrhizae are structures formed by plant roots and the fungi that live in close association with them. It has been suggested that probably all Ericales members are in some mycorrhizal relationship; the relationship is obligate in the few members of the family Pyrolaceae that occasionally lack chlorophyll and in the family Monotropaceae, all of whose members lack chlorophyll. In addition to these families, mycorrhizae have been reported in the Ericaceae (in which it is widespread), Epacridaceae, and Empetraceae. The structure of the mycorrhiza of the Ericales has been described as being intermediate between the conditions called ectotrophic and endotrophic, and the term ectendotrophic has been used to describe the mycorrhiza of *Monotropa.* Host roots are enveloped by masses of fungal hyphae (filaments of fungus cells) as in ectotrophs, but hyphae penetrate the cells of the host root tissues, as in endotrophs. The fungi involved in the relationship are members of the fungal classes Deuteromycetes and Basidiomycetes. A number are of the genus *Rhizoctonia.* Little is known as yet of the physiological relationships between the fungus and the plant. The view that species of *Phoma,* a deuteromycetes associated with some members of Ericales, serve to fix free atmospheric nitrogen appears to be unfounded. In some species the fungi may serve to synthesize various carbon-containing materials from the soil, which are then passed along to the host plant. This explanation is especially attractive in explaining saprophytic situations of nongreen members of Ericales. It must be assumed that the fungus utilizes organic compounds from the soil and transfers its products in forms useful to the plant. (H.T.C./J.L.L.)

Evolution. The fossil record of Ericales is not enormous, especially considering the number of extant species in the order; in fact many species placed in Ericales require careful reconsideration as their affinities with the order are doubtful. The Cyrillaceae are well documented in the fossil record with pollen grains occurring as far back as the Maastrichtian of the Late Cretaceous (74.5 to 66.4 million years ago) and wood dating from the Late Oligocene (30 to 23.7 million years ago). Fossil seeds of *Rhododendron* and *Vaccinium* have been found in Paleocene strata (*i.e.,* 57.8 to 66.4 million years old), and pollen representing the Ericaceae, Epacridaceae, or Clethraceae dates from the Maastrichtian and the Eocene (57.8 to 36.6 million years ago). There are no positive fossil records for Clethraceae, Grubbiaceae, Empetraceae, or Epacridaceae. Therefore, the fossil record is of little help in tracing phylogenetic relationships within the order or between the Ericales and other orders. Any such relationships must continue to be determined largely from comparative morphological, biochemical, and genetic studies of living forms.

Major variables of taxonomic significance in the Ericales are the presence or absence of chlorophyll, the number of floral parts, the degree of fusion of floral parts, the structure and position of the ovary, the degree of fusion of floral parts with the ovary, the type of anther dehiscence, the structure of pollen; the type of fruit, and the structure of the embryo.

The three core families comprise some 4,465 species, or more than 99 percent of the approximately 4,500 species of the order. Since the 1960s there has been almost universal acceptance for including the family Empetraceae in the group of core families, based on habit, embryology, and pollen morphology. The placement of the family Cyrillaceae in the Ericales, after previous assignment to the Celastrales, also has been based on studies of the embryology and pollen.

Reclassification of the family Grubbiaceae

The family Grubbiaceae has been included in Ericales only fairly recently, and there is still some question as to its exact relationships. The family has often been placed in the order Santalales because of the structure of its pistil: the inferior ovary begins its development with two chambers but as it matures only a single chamber with free-central placentation and two pendulous ovules develops. This ovular structure is typical of Santalales and completely atypical of Ericales. There are, however, other features that cause the Grubbiaceae to be misplaced in the Santalales, including anatomical differences, its autotrophic (producing its own food) rather than parasitic habit, and its lack of close relationships to any other family in the Santalales. On the other hand, Grubbiaceae are similar to the Ericales in habit, embryology, and pollen and in the inverted position of the anthers during development.

In addition, then, to the eight families of Ericales, Actinidiaceae and Diapensiaceae are sometimes included within the Ericales, in which case Actinidiaceae (including the Saurauiaceae) would be the most archaic family. The Diapensiaceae, although related to the Ericales, are removed from them because of such differences as those of embryology, stamens, and pollen. They too are probably better associated with the Theales.

The American botanist Arthur Cronquist has suggested that:

> The Ericaceae, Pyrolaceae, and Monotropaceae represent progressive stages in dependence on a mycorrhizal fungus. The Ericaceae require the fungus for successful growth, but they have green leaves, and the morphology of their aerial parts in general does not obviously reflect their mycotropic habit. The Pyrolaceae and Monotropaceae have the reduced embryo that so often accompanies parasitism or extreme mycotrophy in other groups. The Pyrolaceae usually have green leaves, although some species of *Pyrola* have leafless as well as leafy forms. The Monotropaceae have reduced, scalelike leaves and are wholly without chlorophyll.

(J.L.L.)

Malvales. *Distribution and abundance.* The Malvales are a moderately large order of flowering plants, including some 4,700 species of mainly shrubs and trees. The order is most strongly represented and exhibits its greatest morphological and ecological diversity in the tropical and warm temperate regions of the world, but it also extends into the cool temperate zones of the Northern and Southern hemispheres. Species occupy a wide variety of habitats, ranging from deserts to tropical rain forests, and are found from near sea level to Alpine elevations in Andean South America. The Malvales take their name from the Latin word *malva,* which is of Greek origin and means mallow, a name that refers to the mucilaginous nature of most species. A number of plants in this order are economically or aesthetically important—for example, the cotton genus

From (*Malva neglecta, Tilia platyphylla*) S. Ross-Craig, *Drawings of British Plants,* part VI (1952), G. Bell and Sons LTD; (*Adansonia digitata, Theobroma cacao*) drawing by M. Pahl based on H. Baillon, *The Natural History of Plants,* vol. 14 (1875), L. Reeve & Co., Ltd.; (*Dombeya rotundifolia*) H. Wild, "Sterculiaceae," in A.W. Exell and H. Wild (eds.) *Flora Zambesiaca,* vol. 1, part 2 (1960–1961), Crown Agents for Overseas Governments and Administrations, London; (*Gossypium barbadense*) A. Robyns, "Family 115. Malvaceae," of R.E. Woodson, Jr., and R.W. Schery, "Flora of Panama," in *Annals of the Missouri Botanical Garden,* vol. 52, no. 4 (1966)

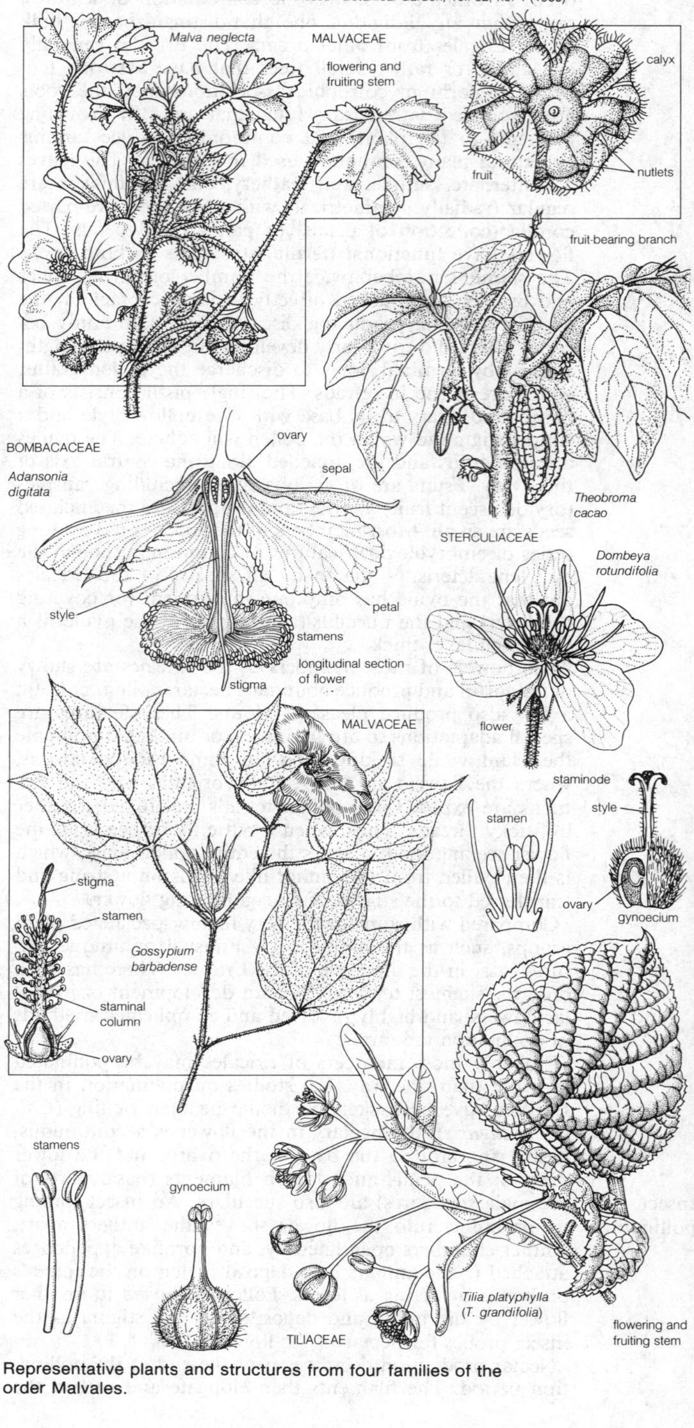

Representative plants and structures from four families of the order Malvales.

(*Gossypium*), the source of chocolate (*Theobroma cacao*), and plants cultivated for their beautiful flowers (including *Hibiscus* and *Alcea*).

Opinions differ concerning the number of families that should be included in the Malvales; however, most recent authors agree that 5 families, the Elaeocarpaceae, Tiliaceae, Sterculiaceae, Bombacaceae, and Malvaceae, containing about 3,000–3,500 species in total, constitute the core of the order. Sometimes the Elaeocarpaceae are included in the Tiliaceae, and on occasion a separate family, the Byttneriaceae, is separated from the Sterculiaceae. Of the five families, the Elaeocarpaceae are morphologically the least specialized, the Malvaceae the most. The Tiliaceae, Sterculiaceae, and Bombacaceae are intermediate and are progressively more specialized, with the Bombacaceae grading into the Malvaceae.

The Elaeocarpaceae include about 400 species in 10 genera but are dominated by *Elaeocarpus*, with about 250 species, and *Sloanea*, with about 100. The Tiliaceae (the linden family) are only slightly more numerous but are more variable in their composition, with some 450 species distributed in 50 genera. The major genera are the tropical *Triumfetta* and *Grewia*, with about 70 and 150 species, respectively, and the principally temperate-zone *Tilia*, the lindens, basswoods, or limes (not to be confused with the unrelated tropical limes, *Citrus aurantiifolia* [family Rutaceae, order Sapindales]), with about 50 species. The Sterculiaceae (the cacao family) include about 66 genera and 1,100 species. The largest genera are *Sterculia* and *Dombeya*, each with 200 species. The Bombacaceae (the bombax or kapok tree family) are a small family of about 25 genera and some 200 species. *Quararibea* (including the plants which some experts place in the genus *Matisia*) of tropical America, with 75 species, is the largest genus, but smaller genera, such as *Adansonia* (the baobab), *Bombax, Ceiba* (the kapok tree), and *Durio*, are better known. The Malvaceae (the mallow family) are the largest of the core families, with more than 100 genera and up to 2,000 species. The principal genera are *Hibiscus, Sida*, and *Pavonia*, each with some 150 or more species, and Abutilon, with more than 100 species. Economically, *Gossypium*, the cottons, with about 40 species, is the most important genus of the family and the order.

Each of the core families of the Malvales is found in both the Old and New World tropics and subtropics. The Elaeocarpaceae, however, are absent from Africa. The Bombacaceae are most diverse in the New World and, unlike the other families, do not extend into temperate regions. The Malvaceae, in contrast, are common not only in the tropics but also in temperate regions, and there they are represented by such genera as *Malva, Lavatera, Althaea*, and *Sidalcea* in the Northern Hemisphere, *Plagianthus* and *Hoheria* in New Zealand, and others elsewhere in the Southern Hemisphere. In the Andean regions there are two genera of Alpine, cushion- or mound-forming plants, *Nototriche* and *Acaulimalva*.

Up to 5 additional families, the Sphaerosepalaceae (including the Rhopalocarpaceae), Sarcolaenaceae (including the Chlaenaceae), Dipterocarpaceae, Scytopetalaceae, and Huaceae, with a total of about 575 species, are included in the Malvales by some authors. Of these families, the Dipterocarpaceae, with more than 500 species (507 by some estimates), is the largest. This family, together with the Sphaerosepalaceae, Sarcolaenaceae, and Scytopetalaceae, can be allied variously to the Tiliaceae. When not classified as Malvales, they are generally placed in the order Theales. The Huaceae stand apart from all other families of Malvales and often are allied with the order Violales.

Economic and ecological importance. Members of the Malvales are common components of many ecosystems but tend not to be the dominant elements, except in local or specialized habitats. For example, the *Hibiscus tiliaceus* (majagua, or mahagua), native to low-elevation, coastal sites in the Pacific islands but now widely naturalized in tropical regions, may form essentially pure stands, as may *Thespesia populnea* (Malvaceae), the portia tree, in coastal tidal zones of the Pacific islands.

Important sources of nectar and pollen

Species of Malvales are important sources of nectar and pollen for birds, bats, and insects, especially bees and beetles, all of which may act as pollinators. Pollination by hummingbirds, sunbirds, and others is common in tropical species. The red flowers of *Malvaviscus* (watmallow, in Malvaceae), which have a relatively narrow tube formed by the overlapping petals and protruding stamens and styles, are an excellent example of adaptation to pollination by hummingbirds. Among the Malvaceae endemic to Hawaii, *Hibiscus kokio, Abutilon menziesii, Kokia*, and *Hibiscadelphus* apparently owe their floral evolution to the native honeycreepers (family Fringillidae) and honey eaters (family Meliphagidae).

Bat pollination is widespread in the Bombacaceae, and adaptations to this have taken place. In the genus *Adansonia*, for example, a large anther mass hangs down from the white flowers below the foliage where bats can easily reach them. The dark purple flowers of *Sterculia* (Sterculiaceae) and other genera emit a fetid odour that attracts flies.

Seed dispersal in the Malvales is accomplished by dispersing whole fruits or individual seeds. The fruits are generally dry capsules or sometimes schizocarps (*i.e.*, fruits that separate into individual carpels called mericarps when mature). The mericarps may be winged, which can aid in wind dispersal, or bear hairs or hooks, which can be a factor in animal dispersal. Elongate seed hairs may have a similar function. In some instances, the fruits are indehiscent, and in the case of *Thespesia populnea* they are especially adapted to ocean dispersal. Occasionally, the fruits are fleshy and drupaceous or even berrylike, or the seeds, as in *Hampea* (Malvaceae), are arillate (they bear a fleshy covering), which suggests animal dispersal.

The Malvales are directly useful to humans as a source of a wide range of extracted compounds and other products, such as wood; bast (phloem) fibres; seed surface fibres; extractives, such as oils, resins, gums, alkaloids, and other chemical compounds; foods and beverages; medicines; and ornamental plants.

Valuable woods are harvested from a number of species. The New World tropical balsa tree (*Ochroma pyramidale;* Bombacaceae) is a source of balsa wood, the lightest of all timbers. In temperate regions of the Northern Hemisphere, the genus *Tilia* (Tiliaceae), the linden tree, particularly *T. americana* (the American lime or basswood), is a timber source and sometimes a source of bast fibres. The nectar of the sweetly scented flowers, gathered by bees, produces honey.

Cotton

Cotton, still the basic natural fibre in the world's textile industry, is composed of the elongate, twisted, cellulosic seed hairs (lint) of some species of *Gossypium* (Malvaceae). The lint of the domesticated cottons, which is especially suited for spinning by machine, played a crucial role in the industrialization of Europe and the United States during the 18th and 19th centuries. Two New World species, *G. hirsutum* (the upland cotton) and *G. barbadense* (the Sea Island cotton), are the principal domesticated species, although two Old World species, *G. herbaceum* (levant cotton) of Africa and *G. arboreum* (tree cotton) of the Indian subcontinent, produce a short, coarse lint and were important at one time. *Gossypium hirsutum* and *G. barbadense* apparently were derived in prehistorical periods from natural hybridization between the Old World *G. herbaceum* and a New World species. Approximately two-thirds of the cotton grown in the world and most grown in the United States is *G. hirsutum*, a species that originated in Central America as a perennial shrub but through breeding was altered to an annual plant.

Kapok are moisture-resistant fibres derived from the seeds of *Ceiba pentandra* (Bombacaceae), the silk cotton, or kapok tree. Kapok fibres can be spun into yarn and textiles; however, their resiliency, buoyancy, and resistance to water make them an ideal natural fibre for insulating and as filler, as in mattresses and life preservers. The kapok is a tall, widely buttressed tree native to tropical America, although it is now widely distributed throughout the tropics. Various species of *Bombax* (Bombacaceae) produce an inferior kapok such as *Bombax ceiba* (*B. malabaricum*), the silk cotton tree, of tropical Asia.

Bast fibres are soft, flexible phloem strands extracted from just beneath the outer bark of many orders of flowering plants, especially flax (Linales), ramie (Urticales), hemp (Urticales), and jute (Malvales). They are used to make twine, ropes, textiles, and other fibre products and are important in commerce and in subsistence cultures. Many species of Malvales are used to make jute or jute-like fibres. Jute is second only to cotton as the most important commercial natural fibre crop and is used in the manufacture of twine, rope, burlap, backing for carpeting, and webbing for upholstered furniture. The bast fibres of *Corchorus capsularis* and *C. olitorius,* tossa jute, or Jew's mallow (Tiliaceae) are the chief source of jute and are widely cultivated in India, Bangladesh, and elsewhere. The plants are sparsely branched annuals that grow to heights of three metres or more. When mature, the stems are cut and retted in water (a rotting process that loosens the fibres from the surrounding tissues). Other important sources of bast fibres include species of *Tilia* and *Grewia* in Tiliaceae; *Abroma* (*Ambroma*) in Sterculiaceae; and *Abutilon* (including Chinese jute), *Hibiscus, Malachra, Sida* (including Queensland hemp), and *Urena* (including the Congo jute) in Malvaceae.

Among the extracted products of the Malvales are seed oils, including cottonseed oil (*Gossypium*), the residue of which, cottonseed-oil presscake, is used to feed cattle. Resins (terpenoid compounds distilled from the crude exudate of a wounded tree) are derived from members of Dipterocarpaceae, especially by tapping into the trunk. Karaya gum, a complex polysaccharide, is obtained from species of *Sterculia,* especially *S. urens,* in India and Africa. It is used primarily in pharmaceuticals.

Cacao

The seeds of the cacao, *Theobroma cacao* (Sterculiaceae), commonly called beans, are native to the New World tropics and are the source of chocolate and cocoa. The large, tough, berrylike fruits containing the seeds are borne directly on the tree trunks or major branches. An oil, known as cocoa butter, is pressed from the seeds. Alone, it is the base of fine chocolate confections; incompletely extracted, cocoa butter is ground with seed kernels and then combined with other ingredients to make milk chocolate and cocoa.

The genus *Cola* (Sterculiaceae), especially *C. nitida* and *C. acuminata,* native to West Africa, is the source of seeds known as kola, or cola, nuts. They are widely used in tropical Africa as a flavourful masticatory (something chewed, like gum) but also are a commercial source of the alkaloid caffeine and of a flavouring for certain carbonated beverages.

One edible plant is the okra, an immature, mucilaginous, fruiting capsule of *Abelmoschus esculentus* (Malvaceae). The leaves and young shoots of various members are used as potherbs; *Corchorus olitorius* (Tiliaceae), for example, has long been cultivated for this purpose. Interestingly, the seeds of *C. olitorius* are poisonous, containing a cardiac glycoside (heart stimulant) of the type found in *Digitalis* (Scrophulariales; Asteridae). The fleshy red calyx of *Hibiscus sabdariffa* (Malvaceae), the roselle, is used as the base of a refreshing beverage or relish. *Durio zibethinus* (Bombacaceae), the durian, a large buttressed tree native perhaps in Sumatra and Kalimantan, is sought for the fleshy, odoriferous, sweet or tangy arils surrounding the seeds.

Medicinal uses of the Malvales relate primarily to the soothing qualities of the mucilage. Crushed plants or extractions are used as emulsifiers to treat irritated mucous membranes and skin lesions and as laxatives. Gossypol, derived from *Gossypium,* is used as a male contraceptive in China. Caffeine and the related alkaloids, such as theobromine, are used as stimulants and as diuretics (substances that increase urine flow).

Plants cultivated for their pleasing foliage and flowers include a number of flowering trees, examples of which include *Elaeocarpus* and *Crinodendron* (Elaeocarpaceae), especially *C. hookeranum,* the lantern tree, a native of Chile; *Tilia* (Tiliaceae); *Brachychiton* (Sterculiaceae), including *B. acerifolius,* the Australian flame tree; and *Chorisa speciosa* (Bombacaceae), the floss-silk tree of Brazil and Argentina. Shrubs with especially striking flowers include species of *Hibiscus* (Malvaceae); for example, *H. syriacus,* the rose-of-Sharon, in temperate regions, and *H. rosa-sinensis,* the China rose, in tropical and subtropical regions. The family Malvaceae contains several garden favourites, including *Alcea rosea* (hollyhocks), a native of the eastern Mediterranean region.

Characteristic morphological features. The Malvales are mostly shrubs and trees, and a few are lianas. As shrubs, they may be soft woody or woody only at the base. Some members of Malvales are herbaceous perennials, but rarely annuals.

The primary leaf venation is often palmate (radiating fanlike from a common point), at least in the advanced core families. The surface of the plant body (indumentum) in most families includes stellate hairs or peltate scales, as well as simple hairs. Most families have mucilage-containing cells, cavities, or canals. The phloem is commonly tangentially stratified (alternating bands of phloem cells and fibres) with wedge-shaped rays. Stratified phloem apparently functions no differently than unstratified phloem. Practically, the clumping of the fibres permits them to be relatively easily extracted from the bark.

Floral structure

The flowers are sometimes subtended by a series of bracts (an epicalyx). There are generally five sepals, which touch edge to edge in bud (valvate). The nectaries are commonly borne at the base of the sepals. There are also normally five petals rolled together lengthwise, overlapping, or valvate (margins touching but not overlapping) in bud. The stamens may be as few as five but more commonly are many in number, in which case they develop from the inside outward. The stamen filaments are free, or somewhat fused at the base (often in groups of five), or united to form a tube around the central style. The superior ovary is generally composed of five or more united or (rarely) distinct carpels, each of which contains one or more ovules arranged in axile placentation. The style is generally simple but also may be deeply lobed or branched. The dry, dehiscent fruit is generally a capsule or schizocarp, but the fruit may be indehiscent and occasionally fleshy.

The Tiliaceae largely embrace those characteristics considered generalized for the order, and thus the family serves as a point of reference against which the other families may be compared. The Tiliaceae usually have mucilage cells, and the plant surface (indumentum) may consist of simple and stellate hairs and peltate scales. The phloem is stratified, and the rays are wedge-shaped. The flowers usually lack a subtending whorl of bracts that resemble the calyx (epicalyx), and the sepals are valvate in bud. The stamens are usually numerous, and the filaments are free or united only at the base. The anthers contain two pollen sacs. The ovary is compound and the style is single. The fruit is dry or fleshy and indehiscent or capsular.

The Elaeocarpaceae are distinguished from the Tiliaceae primarily in having unstratified phloem that lacks wedge-shaped rays, an absence of mucilage cells except in epidermal leaf tissue, an indumentum of simple hairs, and normally valvate petals, which often are fringed or divided at the tip. The stamen filaments of the Sterculiaceae are often fused to form a tube but also may be numerous and arranged into two whorls, with those of the outer whorl often sterile (staminodes). The leaves may be palmately compound. Some authors restrict the Sterculiaceae to only those genera with unisexual, apetalous flowers, smooth pollen, and fruits in which the carpels are free from one another. The genera remaining, constituting the Byttneriaceae, have bisexual, usually petaloid flowers, with smooth to spiny pollen, and fruits formed from united carpels.

The Bombacaceae and Malvaceae are distinguished from all families of the order in that they have anthers with a single pollen sac. The Bombacaceae are typically trees. The flowers are often subtended by an epicalyx. The stamens are generally fused into a single tube or column, the pollen is smooth or nearly so, the carpels number five to eight, the style is simple or lobed, and the fruit is a capsule. The Malvaceae are principally shrubs, the pollen is typically spiny, the carpels number two to many, the style is simple or branched to near the base, and the fruit is generally a capsule or schizocarp.

The pollen grains of the Malvales, as far as is known, are binucleate. They vary in shape from more or less flattened spheres to spherical but in the Bombacaceae are sometimes elongate or angular. The surface is smooth or reticulate ridged, but in most Malvaceae and some members of the Sterculiaceae the grains are spiny. In the Malvaceae and some Sterculiaceae and Bombacaceae, the pores are numerous and distributed over the surface of the pollen grain.

The chemistry of the Malvales is highlighted by the general occurrence of fatty acids containing a cyclopropenyl ring (a structure unique to the order) in the families Tiliaceae, Sterculiaceae, Bombacaceae, and Malvaceae. Alkaloids (physiologically active compounds) have been reported in several genera, most notably *Theobroma* and *Cola,* but also in others of Sterculiaceae and some of the Elaeocarpaceae, Tiliaceae, and Malvaceae. The presence of gossypol is a defining character of *Gossypium* (Malvaceae). Some Malvales have tannins, generally with ellagic and gallic acids. Calcium oxalate crystals are sometimes present in the order.

Evolution. While the existence of Malvales by the Late Cretaceous (97.5 to 66.4 million years ago) is generally assumed, the fossil record from that period is problematic, although petrified wood classified as *Hibiscoxylon niloticum* has been attributed to the order, as have leaf impressions resembling the extant genus *Sterculia.* Fossil pollen attributed to the Bombacaceae has been recorded from the close of the Cretaceous, about 66.4 million years ago, and that of the Tiliaceae and Sterculiaceae enters the record during the Tertiary Period.

Fossil record

From the Eocene onward, beginning about 57.8 million years ago, leaf impressions and plant parts of the Malvales, including some fruits, became increasingly common. From later Tertiary beds (those of the Miocene onward, beginning about 23.7 million years ago), numerous fossils of the Malvales have been reported from many different parts of the world, including Europe, North and South America, Central and East Asia, and Australia, with remains increasingly attributable to modern genera.

In spite of a reasonable knowledge about the families of the Malvales, understanding of the origin and subsequent evolution of the order remains uncertain, and conclusions are speculative. The intercontinental distributions of the relatively specialized core families and the restriction of the presumably less specialized and relict families Sarcolaenaceae, Sphaerosepalaceae, and Scytopetalaceae to the Southern Hemisphere supports the hypothesis that the Malvales evolved and diversified in Gondwana prior to the breakup of that great southern landmass.

Unresolved questions concerning the boundaries and the ordinal affiliation of the Malvales are: Should the order be restricted to the core families or expanded to encompass families included in other orders? And which order of the Dilleniidae was the ancestor of Malvales—Theales or Violales? Two of several defensible hypotheses are considered here.

One hypothesis derives the Malvales from the Theales and restricts the order to the five core families (Elaeocarpaceae, Tiliaceae, Sterculiaceae, Bombacaceae, and Malvaceae). In this scheme the Malvales, defined largely by the presence of valvate sepals and fatty acids of a unique kind, are distinct from the morphologically more heterogeneous Theales, in which the sepals are largely imbricate and cyclopropenyl fatty acids are absent. Such an approach does not fully resolve the placement of the Elaeocarpaceae, since they also lack cyclopropenyl fatty acids, nor does it suggest which family of the Theales might be ancestral to the Malvales.

A second hypothesis argues for greater heterogeneity in the Malvales by including in it the core families in addition to the Huaceae and those excluded above, with the corollary that no single character is sufficient to define the order. In this case, the Malvales are derived from the Violales through an often perceived relationship between the Elaeocarpaceae and the Flacourtiaceae, the latter being among the least specialized families of the Violales. Such a derivation would require a change from the parietal arrangement of the ovules of the Violales to the axile arrangement of the Malvales.

Evolutionary problems similar to those encountered at the ordinal level exist within the Malvales. These problems are concerned with the boundaries and relationships of families and the relationships of genera within families. It is likely that future analyses of the genera comprising the Malvales, in the broad sense, will result in a modest redefinition of the families and a more definitive understanding of their phylogeny. (D.M.Ba.)

Subclass Rosidae

GENERAL FEATURES

Rosidae is 1 of the 6 subclasses in the class Magnoliopsida. It consists of 18 orders, 116 families, and more than 60,000 species. Rosidae includes the largest number of families of all the subclasses, although the vast majority of species belong to only 5 large orders: Fabales (18,000), Myrtales (9,000), Euphorbiales (8,000), Rosales (6,600), and Sapindales (5,400). The 18 orders that make up the Rosidae have natural affinities, except perhaps for the Euphorbiales and Rafflesiales, the former because of some similarities to the Malvales (Dilleniidae), the latter because, as parasites, they have lost certain characteristics that might otherwise clarify their affinities. Members of the Rosidae tend to be more advanced than the Magnoliidae, and the Rosidae and the Dilleniidae constitute two natural groups derived separately from that ancestral stock. The Rosidae are found in most habitats.

Makeup of the subclass

Evolution. There are two theories on the evolutionary origin of the Rosidae; in both scenarios the Rosidae arise eventually from the Magnoliidae, but in one theory they arise from that subclass directly, while, in the other, a stage interposed between the two subclasses resembles the Hamamelidae in having reduced flowers and a loss of petals. The petals of Rosidae, Dilleniidae, and petaled members of Hamamelidae appear to be derived from modified stamens, in contrast to those of the Magnoliidae, which in general are derived from sepals, supporting to some extent the latter scenario. The fact that fossil flowers remain relatively scarce continues to undermine a solid interpretation of the evolution of the Rosidae.

The Rosidae appear to have diverged from the ancestral Magnoliidae some 113 to 97.5 million years ago. The earliest ancestor is thought to be *Sapindopsis* based on the pinnate leaf form, a growth pattern thought to be a basic characteristic of the group, derived from the simple leaves of the ancestral Magnoliidae and ancestral to the simple leaves of modern families.

Diversity of structure and distribution. *The order Proteales.* The Proteales consists of two families, Elaeagnaceae and Proteaceae, although this might not be a natural affiliation. The Proteaceae is composed of about 75 genera and more than 1,000 species distributed throughout tropical and subtropical regions of the world, especially in South Africa and Australia. They are evergreen woody plants that thrive in nutrient-poor soils in regions with alternating wet and dry seasons. In some members (*e.g., Protea*), the flowers are arranged into large heads. The ovary consists of only one carpel, which may not be fully sealed. Fossil pollen of Proteales is thought to be found from the Late Cretaceous Period, more than 80 million years ago. Economically important members of the order include the Australian genus *Macadamia,* from which macadamia nuts are obtained. Several genera also have local importance as ornamental trees in warm regions of the world.

The Elaeagnaceae is a small family of trees and shrubs with only about 50 species. It is found in temperate and subtropical regions of the Northern Hemisphere, although it extends into tropical Asia and even to northern Australia. The plants are invested with scales or hairs, and the fruit is typically a pseudodrupe—that is, a dry achene surrounded by the fleshy or mealy base of the hypanthium.

The ovary of the Elaeagnaceae appears to have only one carpel. The Elaeagnaceae probably appeared more recently than the Proteaceae; pollen enters the fossil record in the Oligocene, 36.6 to 23.7 million years ago. Several members of the family are cultivated ornamentals, notably the Russian olive (*Elaeagnus angustifolia*).

The order Podostemales. The Podostemales consists of only 1 family, Podostemaceae (the river weed family), and fewer than 200 species. Although widespread throughout tropical and subtropical areas of the world, some members are found in more temperate climates. The family consists

Aquatic herbs

of aquatic herbs, which thrive in fast rivers with a stony bed; they are mostly submerged or with some parts floating, and they produce small aerial flowers and fruits when the water level is low. Although their form and organization is diverse and relatively simple, it is sometimes only with some difficulty that the parts can be recognized as modified roots, stems, and leaves. Most authors agree that they are related to the Saxifragaceae and Crassulaceae, families assigned to the order Rosales.

The order Haloragales. Within this order are placed 2 families, the Haloragaceae and Gunneraceae, with a total of fewer than 200 species. The minute flowers have an inferior ovary with one to four locules and two to four distinct styles, each locule with a single pendulous ovule. Most members are aquatic herbs, often with dissected leaves. *Myriophyllum aquaticulm,* parrot's-feather, is a popular aquarium plant.

The family Gunneraceae, on the other hand, contains terrestrial herbs. Some species of *Gunnera* in moist, mild climates develop leaves as large as three metres across. Fossil pollen of *Gunnera* dates from the Turonian Age of the Late Cretaceous, some 90 million years ago.

The order Rhizophorales. This order consists of only 1 family, Rhizophoraceae, with about 100 species distributed throughout tropical regions. The members are woody plants with simple, entire, opposite leaves, interpetiolar stipules, separate petals, and at least twice as many stamens as petals. The ovary consists of multiple locules, each with two ovules.

There are 4 mangrove genera containing a total of 17 species in Rhizophoraceae. Although the mangroves constitute the most familiar members of the family, the majority of the genera and species of Rhizophoraceae are inland plants that are not mangroves. *Rhizophora mangle,* of tropical America, is one of the most common mangroves, but this habit is found in other families as well. The family probably originates in the Rosales and is thought to date from the Late Eocene, 40 to 36.6 million years ago.

The order Cornales. It has at least 3 families and fewer than 150 species. The largest family, Cornaceae, is only

Drawing by M. Pahl

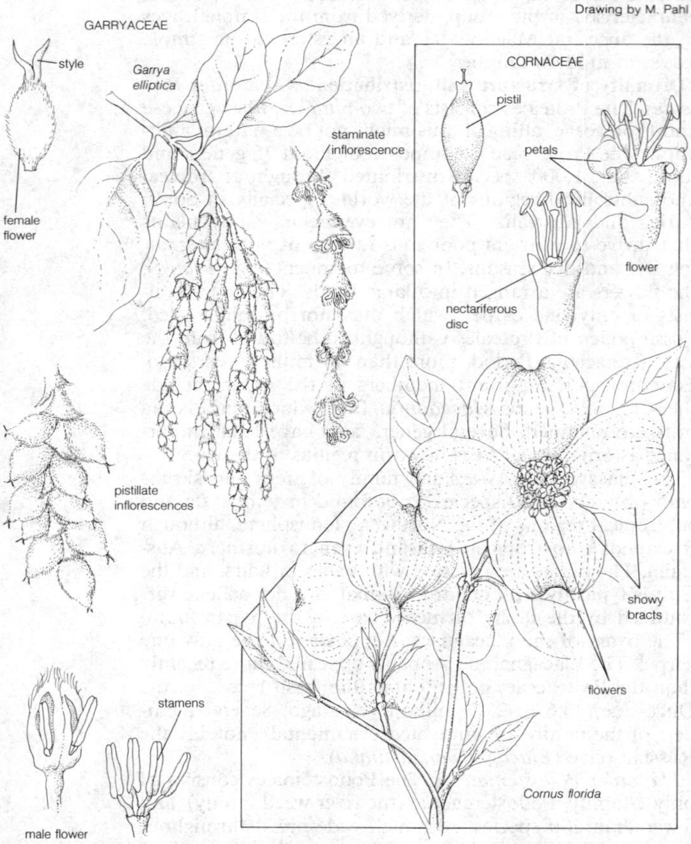

Representative plants from the families Cornaceae and Garryaceae of the order Cornales.

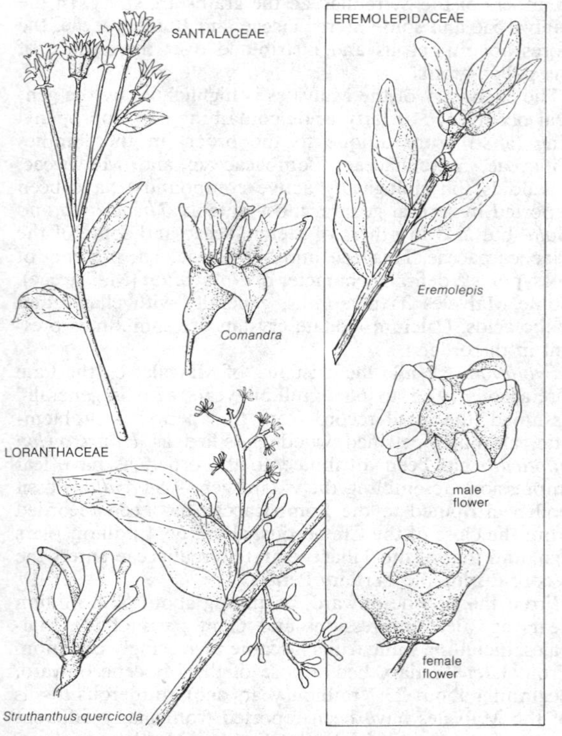

Floral characteristics in representative families of the order Santalales.

Drawing by R. Findahl

loosely allied, and 11 of its 14 genera have been placed in single families by some authorities. The order consists of woody plants with simple leaves, usually without stipules, and flowers with parts in multiples of four. The petals, when present, are usually distinct, and the ovary is inferior and contains several carpels with as many locules and ovules as carpels. The order is considered to be derived from the Rosales, with the diversification of the order into families and genera having been well under way by the Late Cretaceous, 97.5 to 66.4 million years ago. Species of *Cornus* (dogwood) and *Aucuba* (gold-dust tree) are often cultivated as ornamentals. The flowering dogwood (*Cornus florida*) has four large, petallike white or pink bracts subtending each close cluster of small flowers.

The order Santalales. The Santalales includes 10 families and about 2,000 species, although the inclusion of Medusandraceae, Dipentodontaceae, and the small nongreen family Balanophoraceae has been debated. The remaining 7 families show a natural alliance, as well as a progressive adaptation to a parasitic mode of nutrition. The Olacaceae, Opiliaceae, and Santalaceae are terrestrial parasites that attach themselves to the roots of other plants and have green leaves. The mistletoes (Misodendraceae, Loranthaceae, Viscaceae, and Eremolepidaceae) are green-leaved or green-stemmed aerial parasites that attach themselves to the branches of their hosts. The ovary contains only a few ovules borne on or in a free-central or basal placenta or pendulous from near the top of a columnar placenta that extends upward beyond the basal partitions. The order is thought to be derived from the Rosales or an allied order and dates from the Maastrichtian Age of the Late Cretaceous, 74.5 to 66.4 million years ago, although most familes are of more recent origin. Sandalwood (*Santalum album;* Santalaceae), a small tree found in tropical southeastern Asia, contains a yellow aromatic oil and wood, both of which are prized for a variety of uses. Mistletoes are considered to be significant pests to forest communities. The common Christmas mistletoe of the United States (*Phoradendron serotinum*) is a popular symbol of the holiday season.

Parasitic plants

The order Rafflesiales. This order is comprised of 3 families and perhaps 60 species, most of which belong to the Rafflesiaceae. The members are nongreen parasitic plants so modified that only the flowers or the inflorescence emerges from the host. The vegetative (nonreproductive) body of 2 families (Rafflesiaceae and Mitrastemonaceae) is largely filamentous, resembling a fungal mycelium that permeates the tissues of the host. In the Hydnoraceae, on the other hand, the body is external to the host, and the slender roots that emerge parasitize the roots of other plants. *Rafflesia* has notably large flowers, and *Rafflesia arnoldii* is a plant from Sumatra that is famous for having some of the largest individual flowers in the world, sometimes measuring nearly one metre across.

The order Celastrales. The Celastrales consists of up to 12 families and a little more than 2,000 species, of which Celastraceae, Hippocrateaceae, Aquifoliaceae, and Icacinaceae comprise the bulk of the order. The members are generally woody plants with simple leaves and regular flowers with fused petals. There is usually a single set of stamens that normally alternate with the petals. The order first appears early in the Late Cretaceous, some 90 million years ago, in the form of the genus *Ilex* (holly) of the family Aquifoliaceae. Several evergreen species of *Ilex* are popular ornamentals, such as the English holly, *I. aquifolium.* Maté, a tealike beverage, is brewed from the leaves of *I. paraguariensis,* which is native to warm temperate regions of South America.

The order Rhamnales. This order has 3 families and about 1,700 species, of which the majority are found in Rhamnaceae, with 900 species, and Vitaceae, with 700 species. Leeaceae contains only 70 species. Most members have as many stamens as petals with a stamen situated in front of each petal. The order is thought to be derived from the Rosales in common with ancestors of the Celastrales and Sapindales. The history of the order dates only from the Eocene Epoch of the Tertiary Period, about 50 million years ago. The Rhamnaceae and Vitaceae are of considerable economic importance. *Rhamnus* (buckthorn) is a popular cultivated plant, and the berrylike fruits of the European species (*R. cathartica*) and the bark of the western North American species (*R. purshiana*) contain a potent laxative. *Ceanothus* species are found in the chaparral vegetation of southern California. *Vitis* species (grapes) are eaten for their sweet fruits and are used in making wines. The Virginia creeper, *Parthenocissus quinquefolia,* is a well-known ornamental vine.

Families of economic importance

The order Linales. The Linales consists of 5 closely related families and about 550 species. The 2 largest families, Linaceae and Erythroxylaceae, contain about 200 species each, and some of the smaller families (Humiriaceae, Ixonanthaceae, and Hugoniaceae) have been included in the Linaceae by different authorities. The members are plants with simple leaves and regular flowers that house a compound ovary. The stamens are usually fused by their filaments, at least toward the base. The order dates to the Maastrichtian Age of the Late Cretaceous Period. *Erythroxylum coca* and its relative *E. novogranatense* are the source of cocaine. Flax, *Linum usitatissimum,* is a plant cultivated for its fibre and oil.

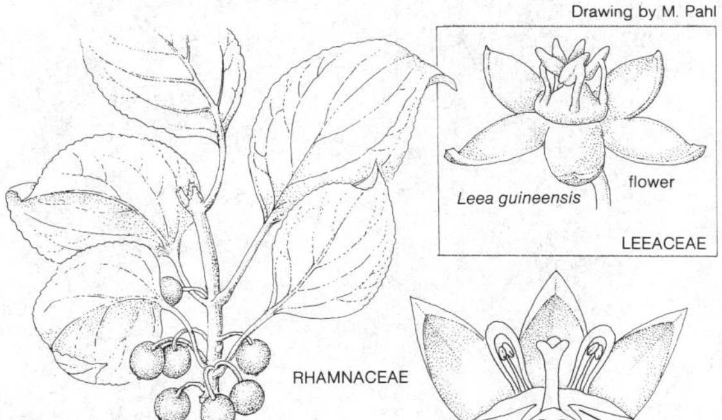

Representative plant structures of the order Rhamnales.

The order Polygalales. It has 7 families and about 2,300 species, most found in the families Malpighiaceae (with 1,200 species), Polygalaceae (with 750 species), and Vochysiaceae (with 200 species). The remaining families are Trigoniaceae, Tremandraceae, Xanthophyllaceae, and Krameriaceae, together containing fewer than 100 species. The members have simple leaves and irregular flowers. The petals are distinct and often have a claw at their base. The compound ovary is situated at or below the point of petal insertion. The family is extremely diverse, containing small trees, shrubs, herbs, climbers, and even some nongreen mycoparasites. The family Polygalaceae appears to have originated in the Paleocene Epoch of the Tertiary Period, about 60 million years ago. The order is relatively unimportant economically. The fruit of *Malpighia glabra* (Barbados cherry, or acerola) is edible and has a high content of vitamin C.

The order Geraniales. This order has 5 families and 3,600 species, which are found principally in Oxalidaceae, Balsaminaceae, and Geraniaceae, the former families with 900 species each and the latter with 700. Tropaeolaceae and Limnanthaceae together have only about 100 species. Most of the members are herbaceous with a superior compound ovary and one to two ovules per locule. The Geraniaceae is a relatively recent family, developing only 10 million years ago during the Late Miocene of the Cenozoic Era. A number of species are cultivated ornamentals, including *Geranium, Pelargonium, Oxalis, Impatiens,* and *Tropaeolum majus* (garden nasturtium). *Oxalis tuberosa* (oca) and *Tropaeolum tuberosum* (añu) are grown in the Andes for their edible tubers.

The order Apiales (*Umbellales*). Within the Apiales are 2 families, Apiaceae (Umbelliferae), with about 3,000 species, and Araliaceae, with about 700 species. The plants have compound or cleft leaves and an inferior ovary. The common arrangement of the flowers is into umbels and compound umbels, although other inflorescences are known. Members of the Apiaceae have odours that are uncharacteristic of other families. Among the species cultivated for food or spice are *Anethum graveolens* (dill), *Apium graveolens* (celery), *Carum carvi* (caraway), *Coriandrum sativum* (coriander, or cilantro), *Daucus carota* (carrot), *Petroselinum crispum* (parsley), and *Pastinaca sativa* (parsnip). Other members are poisonous, including *Cicuta* and *Conium* (hemlock). Within the Araliaceae are *Schefflera, Polyscias, Hedera helix* (English ivy), *Oplopanax horridus* (devil's club), and *Panax ginseng* (ginseng). The order dates to between 60 and 70 million years ago.

Source of food and spice

REPRESENTATIVE GROUPS

Fabales. The Fabales (legumes) may be considered a single family (Leguminosae or Fabaceae) as defined in 1981 by the British botanist R.M. Polhill and the American P.H. Raven and in this article, or they may be divided into three families as in the taxonomic system proposed by Arthur Cronquist. Including about 18,000 species in approximately 650 genera, the Leguminosae is the third largest family of angiosperms, exceeded only by the Asteraceae (aster or sunflower family) and Orchidaceae (orchid family). Although approximately coeval (contemporary) with the grass family (Poaceae), the legume family is the most important of any in the production of food for humans and livestock, as well as in the production of industrial products. Because they develop bacteria-harbouring root nodules that maintain the nitrogen balance in the soil which is necessary for plant growth, the legumes are also an essential element in nature and in agriculture. Legumes are perhaps best known by their more common cultivated names, such as peas, beans, soybeans, peanuts (groundnuts), alfalfa (lucerne), and clover.

In any large group of organisms, evolutionary byways give exceptions to any useful generalities. This will be true of the following discussion. The common name "legume"

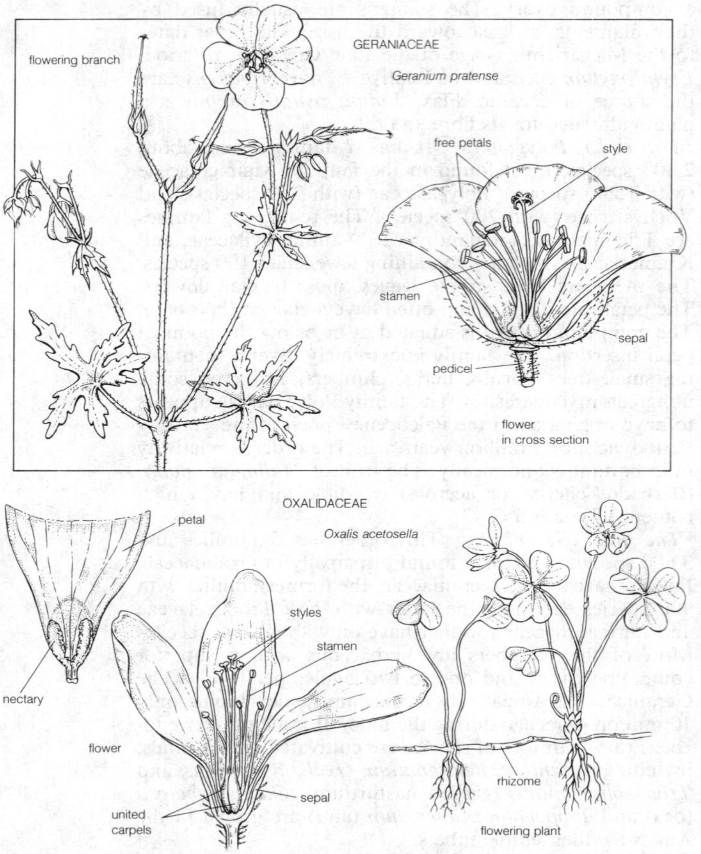

Two families, Geraniaceae and Oxalidaceae, in the order Geraniales.

From M. Hickey and C. King, *100 Families of Flowering Plants,* 2nd ed. (1988); Cambridge University Press

used here much of the time is synonymous with the order Fabales as a whole.

Distribution and abundance. Legumes occur in all terrestrial habitats occupied by plants, although the greatest number of species is in the tropics, where the group probably originated. But there are many legumes in the temperate plains, woodlands, and deserts. A few not only survive but succeed as weeds, in the human-made farming, industrial, and urban environment. They are less common in the northern boreal (taiga) evergreen forests and almost absent from aquatic habitats. Beyond their natural occurrence, many legumes—*e.g.,* soybeans (*Glycine max*), and beans (*Phaseolus,* several species)—are cultivated every year on a single, perhaps vast, area of land (monoculture). Many species are seeded as pasture components; others are planted for soil improvement or to prevent erosion; woody species are grown for firewood and timber in developing countries; and dozens of species are popular ornamentals. Thus legumes are cosmopolitan, not only in the wild but also in the human environment that has replaced the wilderness throughout much of the world.

Types of plants in the order

Characteristic morphological features. The Fabales include trees, herbaceous or woody vines, and perennial or annual herbs. The leaves are usually compound—that is, they are divided into leaflets, and in some the leaflets are secondarily compound. The simple leaves of some are presumably reduced from the compound forms. The most striking of these modified leaf forms are the several hundred species of Australian acacias (*Acacia*) in which the apparently simple leaf represents the flattened and modified axis of a compound leaf. Stipules, a pair of appendages subtending the leaf petiole, are usually present. The flowers may be solitary or bunched in leaf axils. The inflorescences, when present, are of various kinds, simple or branched in diverse ways. The flowers are usually perfect (bisexual) but unisexual flowers occur sporadically throughout the family. Some legumes produce two kinds of flowers, commonly on the same plant. The typical kind have conspicuous petals that open so that cross-pollination (in some, an obligatory mechanism of propagation) is possible (chasmogamous); in others all parts are reduced and the petals do not open, thus enforcing self-pollination (cleistogamous). In the chasmogamous flowers, the sepals are most commonly partly fused, and the 5 petals alternate in position with the sepals. There are commonly 10 stamens, but there may be fewer or more. The stamens may remain free or they may be fused into a single tubular structure (monadelphous) or into a group of 9 united stamens with a free stamen above this (diadelphous).

Most of these floral features, however, also can be found in other plant families. It is the pistil, or gynoecium, of the Fabales that is unique. The single carpel develops into a fruit (the pod, or legume) that splits open (dehisces) along one or both edges (sutures) at maturity, releasing the seeds that have developed from the ovules. This basic legume type is idealized in a pea or bean pod, which bears two rows of marginally placed ovules along the upper suture. But evolution within the family has variously modified many legume fruits, and they bear but scant resemblance to that of a bean or pea. Some retain the form of the basic type but do not split open when ripe (indehiscent), as with locusts (*Robinia*) and redbud (*Cercis*). In many Fabales, as, for instance, the sweet clover (*Melilotus*), the fruit has been reduced to a single-seeded indehiscent structure that resembles a tiny nutlet. In others, it is several-seeded and indehiscent but is divided transversely into single-seeded segments that break apart at maturity (*e.g.,* tick trefoil, *Desmodium*). In another variant, the fruit coat becomes fleshy and plumlike as in the tropical *Andira* (angelin tree). There are species in which the fruit is flattened and winged, facilitating wind transport; it is analogous to the winged fruits, or samaras, of maples (*Acer;* Sapindales) or ashes (*Fraxinus;* Asteridae). A few legumes have fruits that are produced or that mature underground; the peanut is the best-known example. The peanut flower is actually produced above ground but assumes a position close to the soil surface as it ages. The ovary elongates and develops as a subterranean pod. All of these and other modifications are derivative and can be traced back to the basic, dehis-

Drawing by M. Pahl

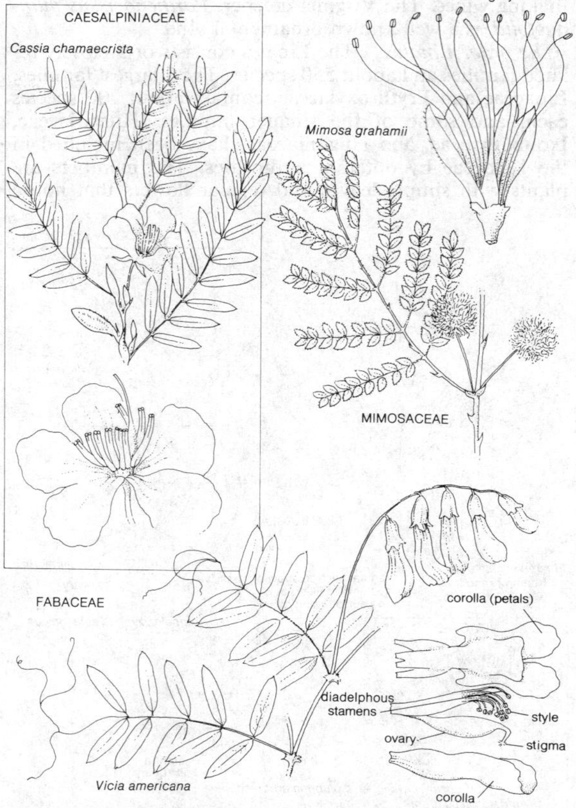

Floral and vegetative structures representing plants from the three families of the order Fabales.

cent pod of the pea or bean. This type of fruit remains the fundamental feature of the Fabales, which, together with correlative features, clearly distinguishes them from any other plant order.

Legume seeds

Seeds within the legumes are also variable, ranging from the size of a pinhead to that of a baseball. Legume seeds are sometimes quite colourful; the *Abrus precatorius* and *Ormosia* species, for example, produce striking black and red seeds. These seeds have been used as currency by primitive peoples and in the production of beads and handbags, especially in the more tropical regions. They may be quite poisonous if eaten, however.

As stated initially, the Fabales fall into three relatively discrete groups, each of which may be considered a plant family or, alternatively, may be treated as a subfamily. The difference in view is perhaps philosophical or possibly semantic. The interpretation of the order Fabales followed here classifies the Caesalpinioideae, Mimosoideae, and Papilionoideae as separate subfamilies of a single family, the Leguminosae (Fabaceae).

Classification. The rationale for plant family classification derives not only from conspicuous morphological features but from numerous cryptic characters as well. Chromosome numbers are often useful in evaluating the relationship of plant taxa. The legumes are no exception. The legumes produce many kinds of chemical substances—*e.g.,* alkaloids, flavonoids, tannins, and the free amino acid canavanine (the latter found only in legumes). The function of those that are physiologically active (*i.e.,* often poisonous) in animals seems usually to be that of predator defense. The medical potential (especially of the alkaloids) of some of these substances, or of their synthetic derivatives, has been extensively studied. The absence or presence and distribution of these substances in the various groups also is used in legume classification. Information about other cryptic features, such as pollen and plant anatomy, contributes to scientific knowledge of legume evolution as well. The floral types in this order are quite variable, with flowers ranging from regular (*i.e.,* actinomorphic, radially symmetrical) in the Mimosoideae to highly irregular (*i.e.,* zygomorphic, bilaterally symmetrical) in the family Papilionoideae. Flowers of the Caesalpinioideae are somewhat intermediate between these extremes as regards symmetry.

The subfamily Caesalpinioideae (classified as a family, Caesalpiniaceae, by some authorities) is a heterogeneous group of plants with about 150 genera and some 2,000 species. They are found throughout the world but primarily as woody plants in the tropics. Their moderate secondary invasion of temperate regions is mostly by herbaceous (nonwoody) evolutionary derivatives. The presence of the ancient and presumed relict honey locusts (*Gleditsia*) and of the related Kentucky coffee tree (*Gymnocladus dioica*) in temperate regions is a striking exception to this generalization, however.

The caesalpinioids

The caesalpinioids, probably progenitors of other Fabales, are more variable than the other two subfamilies. The leaves are usually divided into leaflets (compound) or else the leaflets are again divided into leaflets (bicompound), but redbud and the orchid trees (*Bauhinia*) and its relatives have simple leaves. The flowers also vary in symmetric form, from nearly radial to bilateral to irregular (symmetric in no plane). The sepals are usually separate and imbricate (overlapping in the bud). There are generally 5 separate imbricate petals, the upper one inside of the lateral petals in the bud. The 10 or fewer stamens are exposed, although not as conspicuously as in many of the members of the subfamily Mimosoideae described below. The fruit conformation is diverse. Bacterial nodulation is much less prevalent than in either of the other two subfamilies. Canavanine is not present. Many caesalpinioids are prized ornamentals in the tropics, such as the royal poinciana (*Delonix regia*), the pink shower group (*Cassia*), and the orchid trees. Redbud and honey locust are well known in temperate regions.

The subfamily Mimosoideae (classified as a family, Mimosaceae, by some authorities) includes about 60 genera and 3,000 species. Like the caesalpinioids, the mimosoid legumes are primarily woody plants of the tropics, and the few species native to temperate parts of the world are mostly herbaceous. The majority of the mimosoids have large leaves that are divided into secondary (compound) leaflets, and in many these leaflets are again divided (bicompound) and have a feathery, sometimes fernlike appearance. A striking exception is that of most of the Australian acacias (but not of the American kinds) mentioned above, in which the compound leaves have become modified, losing all their leaflets and appearing to be undivided, or simple. The flowers of the family are radially symmetrical and are usually most easily recognized by the long stamens that extend beyond the rest of the flower. The calyx and corolla are both valvate in bud, contrasting with the usual condition in both of the other subfamilies. The petals are small and often not noticed except by close examination. Many of these plants have nodules containing the nitrogen-fixing bacterium *Rhizobium* on their roots. The sensitive plant (*Mimosa pudica*) is sometimes grown as a novelty because its leaves quickly fold up when touched. The mimosa, or silk, tree (*Albizia julibrissin*), a widely planted ornamental in the southern United States, folds its leaves together at dusk, decreasing by at least half the amount of leaf surface exposed to the atmosphere. The movement is caused by changes in water pressure in specialized structures at the base of the petioles and leaflets.

The subfamilies Caesalpinioideae and Mimosoideae do not contain many food crops and are perhaps best known for their shade and ornamental species, such as the Judas tree or redbud, orchid tree, and huisache (*Acacia farnesiana*), although some of the more rapid-growing weedy species—for example, the white popinac (*Leucaena leucocephala*) and *Albizia* species—are widely employed as green manure and fodder crops. *Acacia* species are used extensively in the production of gum exudates and wood, especially in South Africa and Australia, where the species are known as wattle trees.

Largest group of legumes

The subfamily Papilionoideae, also called Faboideae (classified as a family, Papilionaceae or Fabaceae, by some authorities), is the largest group of legumes, consisting of about 420 genera and 12,000 species grouped in 32 tribes. The name of the group probably originated because of the flower's resemblance to a butterfly (Latin: *papilio*). It is the unique bilaterally symmetrical (zygomorphic) flowers that especially characterize the group, so that thousands of species can be recognized as a papilionoid at a glance. The sweet pea (*Lathyrus*) flower provides an example. It has a large petal at the top, called the banner, or standard, that develops outside of the others before the flower has opened, two lateral petals called wings, and two lower petals that are usually fused and form a keel that encloses the stamens and pistil. The whole design is adapted for pollination by insects or, in a few members, by hummingbirds. Sweet nectar, to which the insects are cued by coloured petals, is the usual pollinator attractant. Various locking and releasing devices of the keel and wing petals control pollination in diverse ways favouring (or enforcing) either outcrossing or self-pollination—*e.g., Trifolium* (clovers), *Medicago* (alfalfa), and *Lotus corniculatus* (bird's-foot trefoil). The most effective kind of obligate self-pollination, however, is that of cleistogamous flowers which do not open and thus prevent the entry of insects. Lespedeza (*Lespedeza*) and many other genera of papilionoid legumes bear both kinds of flowers, generally on the same plant. Enforced inbreeding serves to fix and maintain successful strains; outbreeding provides evolutionary diversity that may facilitate habitat or range expansion or may serve to provide flexibility for environmental changes.

The calyx is composed of fused sepals. The stamens are 10 or fewer and are free in a few tribes but are most commonly fused at their filaments (monadelphous) or fused at all filaments but one, which remains free (diadelphous). The ovary has a single carpel and develops into various fruit types.

Like the other subfamilies, the papilionoids have their origins in the tropics, but their occupation of the arid and temperate parts of the world, mostly as herbaceous plants, is far more extensive. In the forests, prairies, and deserts, they are among the most common plants. These temperate legumes have mostly pinnate leaves among which those with 3 leaflets (trifoliolate) are common—*e.g.*, beans and soybeans. Trifoliolate leaves rarely occur in the other subfamilies. The large genus of lupines (*Lupinus*) generally has 5 to 11 (occasionally up to 15) palmate leaves. The leaves of clovers are most commonly palmately trifoliolate, as are those of *Baptisia*. In one tribe the leaf axis terminates in a tendril, which facilitates climbing; members include the sweet pea and vetches (*Vicia*). The symbiotic relationship between *Rhizobium* and the plant, which takes place in root nodules and "fixes" atmospheric nitrogen into compounds useful to the plant, is most strongly developed in the papilionoid legumes.

Speculations about origin

Evolution. The origin of the Fabales and its relationship to other plant families and orders are speculative. Traditionally the Fabales have been thought to have derived from the order Rosales, and even specific groups of the Rosaceae family have been postulated. A careful evaluation by the American botanist William C. Dickison has compared the Fabales with three families of the Rosales (Connaraceae, Chrysobalanaceae, and Crossosomataceae), but none fit sufficiently well to be placed with confidence. Dickison also has found numerous shared characteristics with the family Sapindaceae (Sapindales). Although the relationship between the two groups is tentatively favoured by several specialists, a possibly fatal flaw in this view is that the Sapindaceae have compound ovaries with 2 or 3, or sometimes 6 carpels, whereas the Fabales have but a simple ovary derived from a single carpel. Nothing among legumes has been found to suggest that the single carpel condition can be traced through the multicarpellate one of the Sapindales, or vice versa. The view that the legume is primitively simple is unanimous.

Considerations of the evolutionary relationships within the legumes necessarily must postulate which of the subfamilies is primitive and which members of that group seem to best approximate the hypothetical original legume(s). The theory that the Caesalpinioideae is the basic group is usually accepted on a number of bases, including its extraordinary diversity in the tropics, an extended fossil record, and the wide variation of floral and vegetative structures beyond the specializations in the other two subfamilies. The unique *Rhizobium* nitrogen fixation symbiosis is much less developed in the caesalpinioids than in the other groups; indeed, it seems to have originated in this subfamily.

Postulates about the basic genera or tribes within the caesalpinioids are equivocal, however. In angiosperm evolution, reduced flowers usually appear later in geologic time than those with a well-developed corolla. The abundance of petaliferous (petal-bearing) caesalpinioids in the tropics favours this view and suggests that temperate plants, such as honey locust and Kentucky coffee tree, which have tiny unisexual flowers, had petal-bearing ancestors and are therefore more recent. But fossil representation of the honey locust in the Cretaceous Period (some 144 to 66.4 million years ago) suggests that it is an ancient genus, and some authorities favour the view that these genera may resemble the original legumes. The question remains unresolved.

The unity of the mimosoids is convincing. It is presumed that the mimosoids were derived from caesalpinioid types through now-extinct taxa.

Most Papilionoideae can be easily recognized by the specialized corolla described above and might seem to be independent of the other two subfamilies; this is not true, however. They plainly owe their origin to the Caesalpinioideae. The Papilionoideae, as defined above, is the dominant subfamily of legumes, the one that has most thoroughly invaded temperate regions and the one in which *Rhizobium* nodulation is most firmly established.

Ecological and economic importance. The unique ecological role of the Fabales is in nitrogen fixation. Nitrogen is an element of all proteins and is an essential component in both plant and animal metabolism. Although elemental nitrogen makes up about 80 percent of the atmosphere, it is not directly available to living organisms; nitrogen that can be metabolized by living organisms must be in the form of nitrates or ammonia compounds. Through a mutual benefit arrangement (symbiosis) between legumes and *Rhizobium* bacteria, nitrogen gas (N_2) is fixed into a compound and then becomes available to the biotic world. The legume plant furnishes a home and subsistence for the bacteria in root nodules. In a complex biosynthetic interaction between the host plant and the bacterium, nitrogen compounds are formed that are used by the host plant. These compounds are also available to other plants after decayed roots (and other plant parts) of the host plant have allowed these nitrogen products to be released into the soil. Animals obtain compound nitrogen by eating plants.

Nitrogen fixation

Consequently, the vegetation of the forests, prairies, and deserts of most of the world is primarily dependent on the legume component of their vegetation and could not exist without it. Only in a few ecosystems—those that include but few legume species—have substitute biological nitrogen-fixing arrangements evolved. These include symbiotic relationships between miscellaneous woody species other than legumes, and certain actinomycetes bacteria and are limited mostly to boreal evergreen forests, certain coastal areas, and acid bogs. Nitrogen fixation by free-living cyanobacteria seems to be important in aquatic ecosystems. On a worldwide scale, however, these alternate arrangements of nitrogen fixation are relatively minor compared to those supported by legumes.

Legume nitrogen fixation is also of prime importance in agriculture. Before the use of synthetic fertilizers in the industrial countries, the cultivation of crop plants, with the exception of rice, was dependent on legumes and plant

Drawing by M. Pahl (all except *Entada spicata, Millettia dielsiana, Erythrina rubrinervia*) based on J. Hutchinson, *Evolution and Phylogeny of Flowering Plants* (1969); Academic Press Inc.

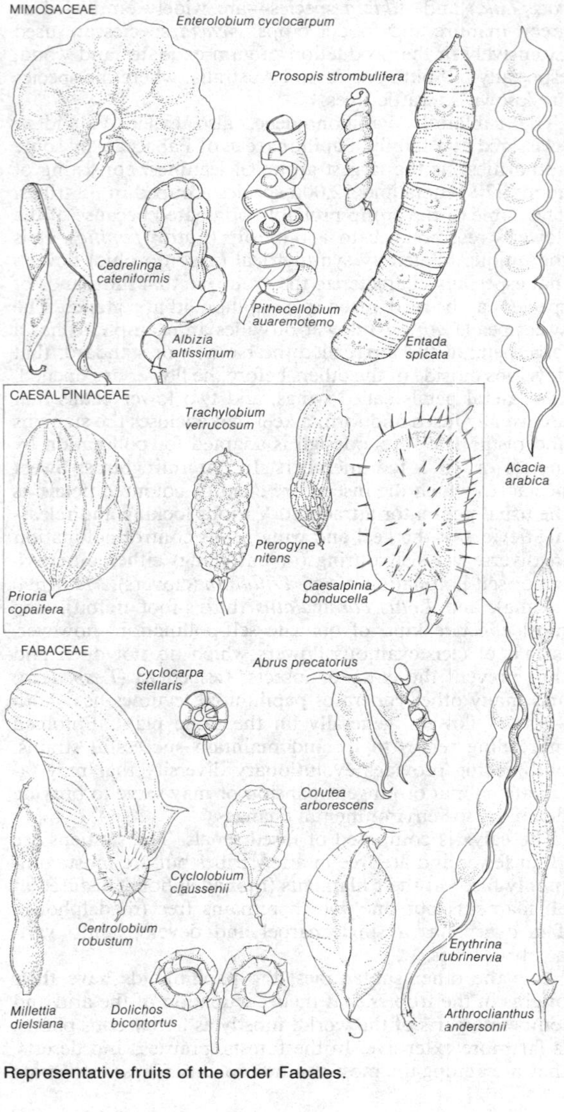

Representative fruits of the order Fabales.

and animal wastes (as manure) for nitrogen fertilization. A common procedure was the use of crop rotation, usually the alternation of a cash grain crop such as corn (maize) with a legume, often alfalfa (*Medicago sativa*), in the temperate world. Apart from the nitrogen contribution, the legume in this case furnishes animal forage (hay or silage). Pastures or other grazing areas must have legume components, such as a clover (*Trifolium*), as well as a grass component.

The 20th-century substitution of petroleum-derived synthetic nitrogen fertilizers is partly a consequence of economics in that a cash grain, such as corn or wheat, planted every year provides a higher fiscal return than alternating it with a legume crop. In addition, legume-rhizobium fixation is inhibited when the level of nitrogen in the soil is high and is not sufficient for maximum yields of a grass crop. Therefore, in developed countries chemical fertilizers have largely replaced biological fixation in row-crop culture. On a worldwide basis, however, dependence on legumes is still preeminent. Even in the United States, it has been estimated that, including range land and pasture agriculture, nitrogen production by biological fertilizers still exceeds chemical application. The role of synthetic fertilizers in agriculture is being investigated because of their vastly increasing costs and environmental effects.

Other benefits accrue from the use of legumes to maintain soil nitrogen. Weed control is facilitated by a crop sequence that alternately changes the growing environment. Such legumes as alfalfa may be harvested for forage (hay or silage) or grazed by livestock. As cover crops, legumes prevent or reduce soil erosion and may be plowed under as "green manure." Even though starch-producing grasses such as corn are more efficient, under favourable conditions, in producing energy foods, grain legumes are commonly grown in the tropics because they are more successful in depleted, nitrogen-deficient soils.

Human and animal foods

Legume seeds constitute a part of the diet of nearly all humans. Their most vital role is that of supplying most of the protein in regions of high population density and in balancing the deficiencies of cereal protein (Poaceae). Except for the soybean and peanut, the order is not noted for the oil content of the seeds since most seeds have only about 10 percent oil content by weight. The legume seeds generally are highest in carbohydrate compounds, followed by protein and fat. Legumes are thus considered to be energy foods. Most legumes that are used for foods are multipurpose plants, serving for animal forage and soil improvement as well. Some, notably the soybean, are also important industrial crops. The family Fabaceae contains the more important crop plants, such as soybeans; beans; cowpeas (*Vigna*); pigeon pea (*Cajanus cajan*); chick-pea, or garbanzo (*Cicer arietinum*); lentils (*Lens culinaris*); peas (*Pisum sativum*); and peanuts.

Forage legumes (which concentrate their vitamins and proteins in their young growing parts) also are grown as animal feed. Their role as such is especially common in countries that can afford the luxury of red meat—derived from the process of first passing the nutrient through an animal rather than eating it directly is a relatively inefficient mechanism of nutrition. Some major forage legumes of the temperate world include clovers, alfalfa, bird's-foot trefoil (*Lotus corniculatus*), and vetches. In the tropics or arid regions, some of the important elements of the habitat are species of *Glycine* (soybean), *Stylosanthes*, and *Desmodium* (tick trefoil).

Apart from the legume plants of worldwide importance, the following are examples of locally significant legume species that are cultivated or gathered from the wild. Some would plainly have substantial potential were they subject to genetic evaluation and development through modern breeding techniques. They are still in the same stage as teosinte (the ancestor of corn) or einkorn and emmer (the ancestors of the modern varieties of cultivated wheats) in yield and utilization potential.

Notable among the locally useful plants of the legume family is the Bambara groundnut, *Vigna* (*Voandzeia*) *subterranea*, a leguminous plant that develops underground fruits in the arid lands of Africa. Important, too, are the seeds of *Bauhinia esculenta;* they are gathered for the high-protein tubers and seeds. The moth bean and rice bean (*Vigna aconitifolia* and *V. umbellata*) are much used in the tropics for forage and soil improvement, and their seeds are palatable and rich in protein. The winged bean (*Psophocarpus tetragonolobus*) is collected in Southeast Asia for the edible fruits and protein-rich tubers. The yam bean (*Pachyrhizus*) is a high-yield root crop of Central America.

Various forms of leucaena (*Leucaena leucocephala*) have been developed for animal forage, firewood, and construction, as well as for the high production of nitrogen that enriches impoverished soils, especially in the Asiatic tropics. Other important plants are acacia, used for animal food (both pods and leaf forage), for soil improvement and revegetation, and as a source of tannin and pulpwood; yeheb (*Cordeauxia edulis*), an uncultivated desert shrub of North Africa that has been so extensively exploited for food (seeds) that it is in danger of extinction; carob (*Ceratonia siliqua*), a Mediterranean plant whose fruits are used as animal and human food and in the manufacture of industrial gums; and the tamarind (*Tamarindus indica*) of Africa, now primarily grown in India, which has agricultural uses and is also used as an industrial gum.

Endangered species

The soybean is a bushy annual whose seeds are an important source of oil and protein. An edible oil pressed from the seeds is used to make margarine and as a stabilizing agent in the processing of food and the manufacture of cosmetics and pharmaceuticals. The oil is employed in such industrial products as paint, varnish, printing ink, soaps, insecticides, and disinfectants. Oil cakes pressed from the seeds are used as protein concentrate in the mixed-feeds industry. The soybean is a good source of vitamin B and is dried to produce soya milk, which is used in infant formulas. Fermented pods are used in making soy sauce, a flavouring commonly employed in Asian cooking.

The peanut, a native of South America, is high in vitamin B complex, proteins, and minerals. The peanut is eaten raw or roasted or is processed into peanut butter. An edible oil is pressed from the seed and is used as a cooking oil and in processing margarine, soap, and lubricants. The oil also is employed by the pharmaceutical industry in making medications. Pressed oil cake is fed to livestock. Peanuts are commercially grown in the United States, Asia, Africa, and Central and South America.

Legumes in general are used to revitalize nutrient-depleted soils, especially abandoned or abused agricultural and grazing lands. A more stringent revegetational challenge is that following strip mining. Generally speaking, native legumes are common in these habitats because they are better able to thrive in nitrogen-poor soils than other plants. (D.Is.)

As mentioned above, the legumes produce secondary compounds of an irritating or poisonous nature that provide protection against predators. These secondary compounds are being studied for their pharmacological potentials. They are found in the leaves and fruiting parts and include flavonoids, alkaloids, terpenoids, nonprotein amino acids, and others. Some of these, as, for example, the amino acid canavanine, may comprise up to 5 percent of the dry weight of seeds. The chemical compound rotenone, which is toxic to a number of organisms, is sufficiently abundant in the roots and stems of certain species belonging to the Papilionoideae that primitive peoples often used these plants to poison fish. More recently it has been shown that serious bone and neural diseases afflicting humans (*e.g.*, lathyrism) and livestock may be caused by the ingestion of unusually large amounts of certain free amino acids. In sheep, ingestion of large quantities of the amino acid mimosine, found in *Leucaena glauca* and some other species of the Mimosoideae, apparently halts the growth of hair or wool, and in certain cases the fleece itself has been observed to shed. A wide variety of alkaloids are found in the order, most of them restricted to the family Fabaceae, however. Some alkaloids occur in sufficient concentration in range plants to be poisonous to livestock, especially in species belonging to the large genus *Astragalus*. Species of *Astragalus* are commonly referred to as locoweed in North America because, following excessive consumption of these plants, cattle seem to be-

Poisonous plants

come unmanageable and "go crazy" or "loco." *Astragalus* is poisonous in any of three ways: by promoting selenium accumulation, through locoine, and through several nitrogen-containing toxins. In the early 20th century, several African species of *Crotalaria* were brought to the United States for use as soil improvement plants. Their poisonous qualities were discovered owing to animal stock loss, and their development was then halted, but several persist as common noxious weeds.

An interesting biochemical component of the legume seed is phytohemagglutinin, a large protein molecule that is specific in its capacity to agglutinate certain human blood types. Approximately 60 percent of the several thousand seeds belonging to this order tested to date contain the compound. Phytohemagglutinin is particularly abundant in the common bean and has been extracted in a relatively pure state on a commercial scale from species belonging to this genus. In addition to its agglutination properties, the compound has been of interest because of its other biological effects. It is toxic to rats, inactivates some human tumour cells, and has beneficial effects in the treatment of aplastic anemia, the shortage of blood cells in humans due to the destruction of blood-forming tissues.

(B.L.T./D.Is.)

Myrtales (myrtle order). *Distribution and abundance.* The myrtle order (Myrtales) comprises some 14 families and 10,400 species, the vast majority of which are assigned to just 2 families, Melastomataceae and Myrtaceae. Its representatives are chiefly shrubs and trees of the tropics and subtropics. Some of the most important sources of pulp and timber in these areas, such as eucalypts, belong to the order. The Myrtales have few representatives in temperate regions and almost none in cold zones; however, some species occur in Tasmania and others reach the timberline in southern Australia.

Drawing by R. Findahl

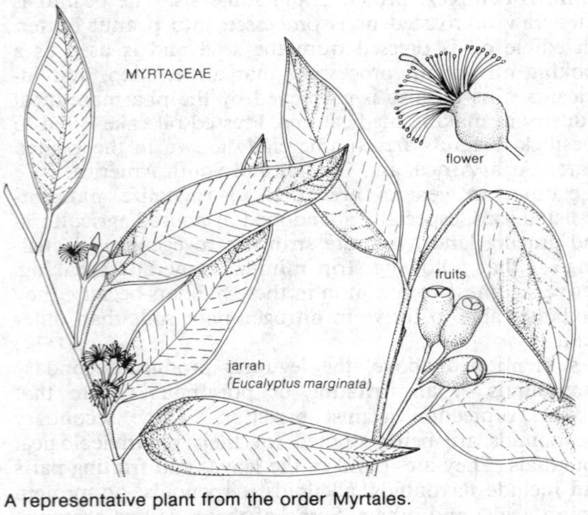

A representative plant from the order Myrtales.

The Myrtaceae

The Myrtaceae (including the genera belonging to groups that some experts place in the separate families Psiloxylaceae and Heteropyxidaceae), with 147 to 155 genera and 3,000 to 3,600 species, are particularly abundant in Australia and tropical America. In Australia some 75 genera and 1,500 species are found. In tropical America approximately 2,400 species occur. Dry-fruited species predominate in Australia, whereas berry-fruited members are found in tropical America. The genus *Eucalyptus,* very much an Australian specialty, contains more than 600 species and forms large forests from the semiarid to the wet coastal zones and up to the tree line. Another large genus, *Eugenia,* has more than 500 species. *Myrtus* grows in the warmer regions of both hemispheres, and the myrtle (*M. communis*) is an important element in Mediterranean vegetation.

The Melastomataceae family contains some 4,700 species in about 190 genera. Its members are found along the entire humid tropical belt but are most diverse in the New World, where two-thirds of the species are found. The largest genus—and one of the largest in the flowering plants in general—is *Miconia* with 1,000 species. Most members of the family are shrubs or small trees, but there are some large trees as well as herbaceous perennials and annuals (plants that complete an entire life cycle in one growing season), root climbers, and true epiphytes (nonparasitic plants that live on other plants).

The Memecylaceae family, which was formerly included in the Melastomataceae, has perhaps 430 species in 6 genera. Its main centre of development is in tropical Asia, with a second centre in the Amazon basin. Most of its members are trees of lowland rain forests.

The Crypteroniaceae family, with about 10 species of trees in 3 genera, is found entirely in Southeast Asia. The Alzateaceae family consists of a single species, a scrambling shrub or treelet that occurs from Bolivia, throughout the Andes, to Costa Rica. Both families belong in the general alliance of the Lythraceae. Another small systematic entity, occurring in the eastern parts of South Africa, is the Rhynchocalycaceae family, which is very closely related to the Lythraceae and consists of 1 tree species. The Combretaceae (white mangrove, or Indian almond) family, with about 450 species in 18 to 20 genera of mostly trees and shrubs, is especially important along tropical seacoasts, in African savannas, and in Asiatic monsoon forests. It comprises mangrove species of muddy shores or estuaries; examples include *Laguncularia,* the white mangrove, and *Lumnitzera,* the eastern mangrove, as well as genera of large trees such as *Terminalia,* with about 150 species, and *Combretum,* with some 250.

The Lythraceae, or loosestrife family, occurs primarily in warmer regions of both the Old World and New World and is especially diverse in South America and Africa. The very closely related Punicaceae family, consisting of 2 species of *Punica* (pomegranate), and the Sonneratiaceae family, comprising 7 species of two mangrove and tropical rain forest genera, *Sonneratia* and *Duabanga,* are confined to the Old World. Lythraceae comprises about 600 species in 27 genera of trees, small shrubs, and perennial herbs; many of the latter are aquatic or semiaquatic. The largest genus, *Cuphea,* has approximately 260 species in the American tropics. *Lythrum salicaria* (purple loosestrife) is originally from the Old World but its range has extended from Europe and Asia into North America and southeastern Australia.

Evening primrose

The mostly herbaceous Onagraceae, or evening primrose, family has 675 species in 17 genera widely distributed in nature, although it is chiefly found in the temperate zones of the Americas, particularly in the western regions. The largest genus of the family, *Epilobium* (willowherbs), has approximately 185 species and is distributed in temperate zones throughout the world. *Fuchsia,* with mostly woody members, has 100 species and is mainly distributed throughout the region of the Andes Mountains in South America with some species in New Zealand and southeastern Brazil. The evening primrose family also comprises several marsh plants and aquatics—*e.g.,* in the genus *Ludwigia.* The genus *Trapa* (water chestnut), with 3 species of aquatic herbs found from central and southern Europe to eastern Asia and from tropical to subtropical Africa, is the sole member of the family Trapaceae, which is considered to be close to the Onagraceae. It has become naturalized in North America and Australia.

Africa is home to the last 2 families in the order: Oliniaceae, found in eastern and southern Africa and on the island of St. Helena with 5 species of the single genus *Olinia;* and Penaeaceae, consisting of *Penaea* and 5 or 6 other small genera with a total of about 20 species of low shrubby habit adapted to life in the dry parts of southwestern and southern Africa.

Economic and ecological importance. The most economically important single genus in the order is *Eucalyptus,* a hardwood plant. The growing demand for wood, pulp, and paper as well as other reconstituted uses, such as hardboard, has made the genus one of the most widely cultivated plants in warm temperate and tropical parts of the world. One reason for this is its fast growth rate. Several species of trees are 30–50 metres tall; the Australian mountain ash of Victoria and Tasmania, *E. regnans,* for example, may attain a height of more than 90 metres.

Ethereal oils with fever-controlling and germicidal properties, gums, and resins are extracted from *Eucalyptus* leaves and wood. Some species are an important source of nectar and pollen for honeybees. Other members of the order used for timber are *Metrosideros, Angophora,* and *Syzygium* (Myrtaceae); the tulipwood tree of Brazil (*Physocalymma scaberrima*), and *Lagerstroemia flos-reginae* (pride-of-India) of eastern India (Lythraceae); as well as several species of *Terminalia* (Combretaceae), *T. alata* (the Indian laurel), *T. procera* (white bombway), and *T. superba* (afara, or limba); *T. brassii* (the swamp oak), for example, originally from the Bismarck Archipelago (northeast of New Guinea), is used in reforestation programs in swampy tropical lowlands.

Edible fruits

Although the order is not an important source of food, edible fruits are produced by some of its members. The most widely known is probably the pomegranate (*Punica granatum*), which is now cultivated in the warmer regions of the world for its fruit and also as an ornamental shrub. In the Myrtaceae family, the guava (*Psidium guajava*); strawberry guava (*P. cattleianum*); feijoa, or pineapple guava (*Feijoa sellowiana*); and many species of *Eugenia* and *Syzygium* are of local value, such as the Brazilian cherry (*Eugenia dombeyi*); the Surinam-cherry (*E. uniflora*); the rose apple (*Syzygium jambos*); and the Malay apple (*S. malaccense*). The fruits are eaten raw or cooked and are used for making jellies, preserves, or beverages. Small industries have grown around *Psidium guajava* in many warmer parts of the world, such as Florida (U.S.), Colombia, and Brazil; the guava contains more vitamin C than most citrus fruits. The boiled fruits of the water chestnut (*Trapa*) are popular from southern China to Thailand; in northwestern India and Kashmir, flour is prepared from them. Although the fruits of all of the berry-fruited melastomes are edible, only one species, *Bellucia pentamera* (*B. axinanthera*), has been considered a potential fruit crop and was introduced for this reason into the Old World by the Dutch. The family Combretaceae supplies the Indian, or country, almond (*Terminalia catappa*), and in tropical Africa, a butterlike substance called chiquito is obtained from the fruits of *Combretum butyrosum.*

Because of the essential oils present in secretory cavities in members of the Myrtaceae, this family provides valuable spices such as the dried flower buds of *Syzygium aromaticum,* the cloves of the spice commerce. Clove oil, however, which used to be commercially extracted from young parts of *S. aromaticum,* is now synthetically produced. Medicinally important oils containing cineole, limonene, or citral are extracted from several species of *Eucalyptus,* including *E. dives* (broad-leaved peppermint) and *E. radiata* (narrow-leaved peppermint). *Pimenta* is a genus of aromatic trees. *Pimenta racemosa,* for example, yields bay oil, which is used by the perfume industry, as are the oils of some eucalypts, and the powdered unripe fruit of *P. dioica* is allspice (pimento).

Lawsonia inermis, of the family Lythraceae and native to northeastern Africa, is the henna of commerce, yielding an orange-red dye that has been used for centuries in the Middle East and East Asia for colouring the hair, fingernails, and soles of the feet. The leaves contain a substance that reacts directly with the keratin of human hair and skin to form the bright pigment. Chemically altered henna is now used as the base for a wide array of hair colorants. Tannins for tanning hides are extracted from the bark and foliage of the Australian *Eucalyptus astringens* and from the fruits (myrobalans) of *Terminalia chebula.*

Crape myrtle

The crape myrtle, *Lagerstroemia indica* (Lythraceae), originating in tropical Asia and Australia, is a popular garden shrub or tree widely cultivated for its beautiful pink, purple, or white flowers arranged into panicles and for its smooth gray bark. Species of *Quisqualis* and *Terminalia catappa* (Combretaceae), the former a liana and the latter a tree, are also cultivated in the tropics. Other horticulturally important plants in the Myrtales order are species of *Eucalyptus,* myrtle, Geraldton waxflower (*Chamaelaucium*), bottlebrush (*Callistemon*), feijoa (*Feijoa*), and many other Myrtaceae, including several horticultural hybrids of *Leptospermum.* Eucalyptus has six subgroups that are derived from six different bark types: peppermints, with fibrous bark; stringbarks, with stringlike fibrous bark; boxes, with rough bark; bloodwoods, with rough, scaly bark; gums, with smooth bark; and ironbarks, with hard bark. The family Melastomataceae contains the glory bush (*Tibouchina*), with its striking purple to violet flowers and purple anthers, often cultivated outdoors in the southeastern United States and elsewhere in the warm tropics. Some of the more beautiful greenhouse plants of the family Melastomataceae are *Medinilla magnifica,* whose purple flowers are arranged in pendulous panicles up to one foot long and subtended by pink bracts between one and four inches long, and various species of *Bertolonia, Monolena,* and *Sonerila,* cultivated for their interesting foliage. Herbaceous annuals or perennials of the Onagraceae family, such as those found in the genus *Oenothera* (evening primroses), are popular cultivated ornamentals in which the scented flowers open in the evening. Another ornamental in the family is *Clarkia* (*Godetia*). The shrubby *Fuchsia* is a cultivated plant familiar throughout the world for its showy flowers in delicate, usually pendulous inflorescences. The flowers generally are in shades of red and purple, with some parts white. The calyx tube (hypanthium) is bell-shaped to tubular and prolonged beyond the ovary. The four calyx lobes remain free and spreading; in some species, the petals are lost. The stamens, style, and stigma are prominent.

Natural history. In general, the flowers of Myrtales are adapted for pollination by animals because they frequently provide abundant nectar or pollen and are shaped so as to facilitate pollen deposition on the stigma while the animals forage on these foods. A highly specialized mechanism for promoting outcrossing is widespread in the Lythraceae, where members of *Lythrum, Decodon* (swamp loosestrife), and *Nesaea* have three flower forms on different plants (trimorphism); plants with two flower forms (dimorphic) are known in *Rotala* (toothcup) and in *Lythrum.* As such, the style and stamens of a flower differ in length, and the pollen of the different stamen whorls differ in size and chemical characteristics, as do the stigmatic papillae. Only pollinations between anthers and stigmas of the same height (necessarily from different plants) result in the production of seed. The pollen from the different anther levels is carried on different places on the bees and butterflies that visit the flowers for the nectar and thus effect the obligate cross-pollination. Although Lythraceae flowers normally open when mature, the opposite condition, of mature flowers remaining closed (cleistogamy), occurs in *Ammannia* and is thought to occur in the apetalous species of *Rotala, Lythrum,* and *Nesaea.*

Mechanisms of pollination

Most species of the Combretaceae family are pollinated by insects, although some are pollinated by birds. This is also true of the Onagraceae family—*e.g., Fuchsia* and some evening primroses and *Epilobium* (willow herbs) species are bird-pollinated. In addition, some species of *Epilobium* have many small-flowered, largely self-pollinated species. The transfer of pollen in the Myrtaceae is usually accomplished by insects, chiefly bees, and to a lesser extent by moths and butterflies. Some species of *Eucalyptus* and *Metrosideros* are visited for nectar and pollinated by birds, especially honey eaters. Memecylaceae and most Melastomataceae have nectarless flowers adapted to pollination by pollen-collecting bees. In many members of Melastomataceae, the stamens bear conspicuous, often yellow appendages and may be of two lengths or different colours; it is not clear whether these elaborations have a function in the pollination mechanism beyond that of enhancing the visual attractiveness of the flowers and making the stamens easier for the bees to grasp. Some 80 species in perhaps 11 genera of the family Melastomataceae offer nectar as a reward to pollinators; they are pollinated by hummingbirds, bats, and rodents, as well as bees and wasps. Flowers of *Trapa* (Trapaceae) are predominantly self-pollinated, and those of the other small families of the order are pollinated by birds (some Penaeaceae) or insects (Alzateaceae, Crypteroniaceae, and Rhynchocalycaceae). *Sonneratia* is pollinated by bats and hawk moths. The pollinating mechanisms of Oliniaceae are not completely known.

Seed dispersal in the order is by wind, water, or animals,

depending on whether the fruits are dry and capsular or fleshy—both types often occur within the same family. Melastomataceae and Myrtaceae berries, particularly those from underlying low-growth vegetation in forests, are important food for birds; their seeds are viable after passing through the gut. Seeds of many members of the Lythraceae and Combretaceae families are well suited to water dispersal by means of winglike expansions of the seed coat or by buoyant airy tissues on the outer seed coat. Some seeds of *Terminalia* (Combretaceae) are able to float for several months in seawater without adverse affects on germination.

In some members of the Melastomataceae family, such as *Maieta, Tococa,* and certain *Clidemia,* the leaf bases develop saclike outgrowths that serve as shelters for ants, which enter them through two small holes on the lower surface. The ants protect the leaves from herbivores such as caterpillars, which they kill or drive away.

Characteristic morphological features. The wood of all Myrtales is characterized by the presence of phloem tissue on each side of the xylem vessels (included, intraxylary phloem), in contrast with the presence of only one phloem layer in most angiosperms. In addition, in the Myrtales, the pits of vessels have a sievelike appearance owing to minute outgrowths from their borders, which arch over the pit cavity. Bordered pits with such processes are called vestured pits. This combination of wood anatomical characteristics is otherwise very rare in angiosperms and is used to help define the order.

Vegetative features

An unusual feature seen in most species of *Eucalyptus* and some other Myrtaceae is the presence of lignotubers. These organs are large, woody, rounded outgrowths, up to several centimetres in diameter, surrounding the base of the young tree trunk. The lignotuber consists of a mass of vegetative buds and associated vascular tissue and contains substantial food reserves. If the top of a seedling, which has developed a lignotuber, is destroyed by fire, drought, or grazing, growth is vigorously renewed by the development of new shoots from the lignotuber. It is evident that this organ is of considerable value in an environment where fire and drought are frequent.

The root systems of mangroves that grow in tidal mud flats, such as *Sonneratia* (Sonneratiaceae) and *Laguncularia* (Combretaceae), are characterized by the presence of "breathing roots" (pneumatophores), portions of the root that grow upward until they project some inches above the low-tide level. They have small openings (lenticels) in their bark so that air can reach the rest of the plant's root system. Another feature of most mangroves is aerial prop roots, which form a tangled jungle, even after the main roots and stem bases of the trees have decayed. In the Onagraceae family, a similar adaptation to an oxygen-deficient environment is seen in *Ludwigia,* a genus of plants found in wet areas. When plants grow in water, air spaces develop in the tissues of the roots and submerged stems, and in *L. repens* special spongy-tissued respiratory roots grow to the surface of the water. Under ordinary dry-land conditions, however, the same plants do not exhibit these features. Loose internal cell tissue that contains air spaces also occurs in the submerged portions of the stems and roots of marsh-inhabiting species of the family Melastomataceae.

Leaf arrangement

Most members of the order bear opposite, simple, and entire leaves, but there is considerable variation in leaf arrangement between families and within species or even individuals. For example, within a single genus, *Quisqualis* (Combretaceae), alternate leaves are borne on the stem and opposite leaves are borne on the flowering shoots. In *Eucalyptus,* young branches have opposite leaves, whereas the leaf arrangement on older branches is alternate.

Whorled leaves occur in a few genera, and quite often the leaves are disjunct-opposite, or "scattered," as in many Myrtaceae, Onagraceae, Combretaceae, and some Lythraceae. In most of the families in the order, stipules are diminutive, only rarely reaching a length of more than a few millimetres; they are absent in the Combretaceae, Onagraceae, Melastomataceae, and Memecylaceae. The upper leaves of *Trapa* and some *Ludwigia* species have inflated petioles that act as a float, while the submerged leaves are finely divided and resemble roots. In most Melastomataceae and in some Myrtaceae, there are several main secondary veins that branch out from the base of the blade and many tertiary veins that run in a transverse pattern across the leaf blade. This venation pattern gives the leaves of nearly all melastomes a highly characteristic appearance. Leaves of Myrtaceae are further characterized by large, scattered oil-containing cells, that are visible as translucent spots when the leaves are held up to the light.

Reproductive features

The inflorescences found in the Myrtales order are extremely variable, but the panicle seems especially frequent. In some members of the Myrtaceae and Melastomataceae, flowers and fruits are borne directly on the old wood of the trunk; this is known as a cauliflory. The flowers of most species of Myrtales are bisexual (*i.e.,* they have both male and female parts in the same flower), but those of some species of Myrtales—*e.g., Eucalyptus calophylla, Pimenta dioica,* some *Sonneratia* species, and very few Melastomataceae and Crypteroniaceae—have flowers of only one sex; structures of the opposite sex, though originally present, fail to mature in these cases.

In the Myrtales, the floral tube (hypanthium) surrounds the ovary either tightly or loosely or is fused to the ovary walls for varying lengths. The rim of the hypanthium bears calyx lobes (free sepals), petals, and either one or two whorls of stamens or numerous stamens. Flowers in which the flower parts appear to arise at the top of the ovary rather than at its base (epigynous) are considered the most advanced, and perigyny (the flower parts appear to arise at the same level as the ovary) is undoubtedly the ancestral condition in the Myrtales. The flowers commonly contain four or five parts (4- or 5-merous) and very often have two whorls of stamens or stamens grouped in fascicles (bundles). The calyx lobes are sometimes shed as a cap when the flower blooms; the cap may be woody (*Eucalyptus*) or herbaceous (several genera of Melastomataceae).

Pollen characteristics of the Onagraceae

Myrtales pollen is usually in the two-celled state when mature and liberated from the anthers; *i.e.,* it consists of a large vegetative or pollen tube cell and a smaller generative cell. Only in the Combretaceae family do some species have three-celled pollen grains (with the generative cell having divided to form the two sperm cells). Members of the Onagraceae are very distinct in the order in their pollen characteristics. In most flowering plants, the four haploid cells resulting from the nuclear reduction divisions (meiosis) in the anthers, and from which the pollen grains (the male gametophytes) develop, remain joined together for only a very brief period before separating as four individual pollen grains. In the Onagraceae, however, they form permanent tetrads and, in most members of the family, the pollen is furthermore connected by viscid threads that stick to a visiting insect; thus, hundreds of pollen grains are drawn out of the anther at the same time.

Following fertilization, nuclear endosperm, a tissue with nutritive function for the developing embryo, is formed in the embryo sac. This tissue is depleted during seed development, and the mature seeds are generally without any or with a very thin layer of endosperm. In the water chestnut, however, endosperm formation hardly takes place. Instead, the embryo sac becomes prolonged and invades the surrounding tissues from which the embryo is then supplied with nutrients. Although normally the embryo in Myrtales species has two cotyledons and stores fatty oils and aleurone, the water chestnut has only a single rudimentary cotyledon and the embryo stores starch. Starchy embryos also occur in some Myrtaceae and Memecylaceae (which is considered to be a part of the family Melastomataceae in this article's classification system).

In *Eucalyptus,* only relatively few of the ovules present in each ovary develop into seeds; the majority are sterile. The sterile ovules, called ovulodes, remain small and form chaff. The amount of mature seed to chaff by weight is often as little as 5 percent. Polyembryony, the presence of several embryos in each seed, on the other hand, also occurs in several families of the order and is very common in myrtle and the genus *Eugenia* (including the Brazilian and Surinam cherries). In *E. paniculata,* up to 21 embryos have been found in a seed, and it is unusual for there to be only one.

Viviparity, a feature of mangroves such as *Sonneratia* and *Laguncularia,* is seed germination inside the fruit while it is still retained on the tree; following the growth of the seed leaves, the root end of the embryo elongates and passes through the opening in the seed (micropyle) and then through the ovary wall. It may grow a considerable length before the seedling drops into the mud, where it establishes itself at once.

Fossil record

Evolution. Among fossil flowers and fruits from the Maastrichtian Age (74.5 to 66.4 million years ago) of the Late Cretaceous, the Myrtales are especially well represented, and pollen of the Myrtaceae family has been reported from the Santonian Age (87.5 to 84 million years ago). Even aquatic plants, like *Decodon* (Lythraceae) are represented among fossils from the late Paleocene Epoch (63.6 to 57.8 million years ago) of the Tertiary Period. Thus, the families of Myrtales, as they are now defined, were probably all in existence by Tertiary times, and their common ancestors existed in Gondwana before the separation of South America from Africa during the Jurassic Period (208 to 144 million years ago).

The origin and systematic position of the order, however, are still a matter of divergent opinions. Generally, the Myrtales are placed in the flowering plant subclass Rosidae, and it is agreed that they are more or less closely related to the Rosales, as well as to the Haloragales, Rhizophorales, and Lecythidales. Conspicuous similarities with the Rosales are the prominently developed floral tube and the degree of its fusion with the ovary wall, as well as other features of floral morphology. Problems encountered in attempting to define and place the order result mainly from conflicting data from wood anatomy, embryology, and phytochemistry. (S.S.R.)

Euphorbiales. *Distribution and abundance.* The order Euphorbiales, in the strict sense, includes only one family, the Euphorbiaceae (spurge). However, traditionally a number of other families, especially Buxaceae (boxwood), have been included by various authors; these will be discussed below.

Euphorbiaceae, one of the larger families of dicotyledons, contains about 7,500 species in 275 genera mostly distributed throughout tropical regions, although species of a few genera, especially euphorbia (*Euphorbia*), are found at high latitudes and elevations. Although the family is diverse in vegetative structures, certain floral characteristics distinguish it. The flowers are invariably unisexual (hermaphroditic flowers occur only sporadically) and hypogynous (or slightly perigynous); the ovary is usually 3-chambered with axile placentation (although the carpel number varies from 1 to 20), and each contains 1 or 2 ovules inverted and positioned along the stalk, or funiculus, that attaches it to the placenta; and, in most genera, the fruit is a dehiscent capsule. Other reproductive characteristics vary widely: sepals, petals, and floral nectaries may be present (free, or separate) or absent, the number of stamens per flower can range from 1 to 500 or more, and the seeds can be with or without endosperm and a fatty terminal appendage (caruncle), which in some genera serve to attract ants for seed dispersal. Observations using scanning electron microscopy have shown great diversity in the form of pollen grains, perhaps more than in any other angiosperm family; these characteristics are important in the classification of subdivisions of the family.

Inflorescence characteristics

Characteristic morphological features. An inflorescence of Euphorbiaceae is characteristically cymose, with flowers terminating the axes of forked branches (dichotomous); this is especially prominent in genera such as jatropha (*Jatropha*), but in many taxa the cymes are reduced to clusters of flowers (glomerules) that develop in the axil, or angle, between the leaf and the stem. Euphorbiaceae do not display self-compatibility, but cross-pollination is furthered by the opening of female flowers before the male flowers (protogyny) and sometimes by the occurrence of male and female flowers on separate plants. Although the familiar castor-oil plant (*Ricinus*) is wind-pollinated, the vast majority of Euphorbiaceae are insect-pollinated; pollination by hummingbirds is reported in *Pedilanthus* (slipper plant, or bird cactus), a succulent shrub, and by bats in *Hura* (sandbox tree).

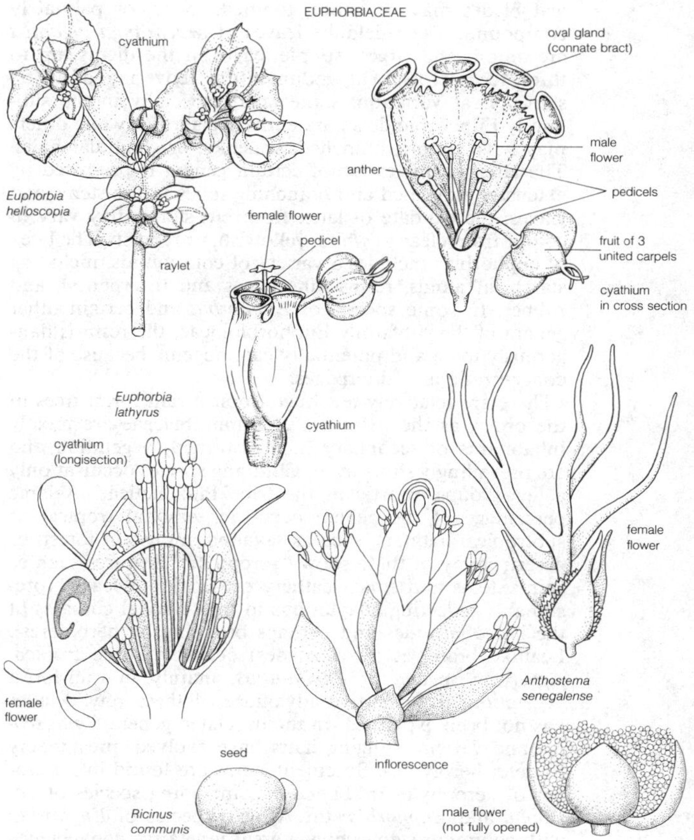

Vegetative and floral structures of the family Euphorbiaceae.

From (*Euphorbia helioscopia*) M. Hickey and C. King, *100 Families of Flowering Plants*, 2nd ed. (1988), Cambridge University Press; (*Euphorbia lathyrus, Anthostema senegalense, Tapura guanensis*) H. Baillon, *The Natural History of Plants* (1871), L. Reeve & Co., Ltd.

In a number of genera of Euphorbiaceae, the inflorescence is highly modified into a flower cluster that mimics a single flower (pseudanthium). Perhaps the most familiar example is the cyathium of euphorbia and related genera of tribe Euphorbieae, including the commonly cultivated poinsettia (*Euphorbia pulcherrima*). The "calyx" of the cyathium is formed by 5 connate (united) bracts, and the "corolla" is formed by oval or crescent-shaped glands, frequently with coloured appendages. The central "pistil" is in reality a female flower containing 3 carpels and only a rudimentary or suppressed perianth, and the lateral "stamens" are really male flowers reduced to a single stamen and borne on 5 specialized cymes. The cyathium of euphorbia may therefore be interpreted as an inflorescence that has a single terminal female flower lacking a perianth, with 4 or 5 lower cymes of male flowers, each in the axil of one of the bracts that are fused into a calyxlike cup. The cyathium of euphorbia is radially symmetrical, but bilaterally symmetrical pseudanthia are found in the related genus *Pedilanthus* and in the unrelated genus *Dalechampia*. In the *Dalechampia,* the 2 involucrate bracts are not united as in euphorbia, and they subtend a lower cyme of 3 female flowers as well as an upper cyme of 5 to 15 male flowers. The male cyme of *Dalechampia* is remarkable in that the minor bracts produce resin that is gathered by female bees (primarily the families Apidae [honeybees or bumblebees] and Megachilidae [leaf-cutting bees]) for nest-building; other than the genus *Clusia* (Clusiaceae), this is the only known example of the use of resin as a floral reward for insects.

Great diversity of vegetative structure

Vegetatively, the Euphorbiaceae are extremely diversified, including trees, shrubs, lianas, and annual and perennial herbs; this variety of life-forms reflects adaptations to a wide variety of habitats. A few characters, such as stipules (sometimes modified into glands or spines) at the base of the leaves, are widespread throughout the family, but other features, such as the presence of milky latex in the stems, are restricted to certain subfamilies (mainly Crotonoideae and Euphorbioideae). Leaf size and shape vary greatly;

leaf blades may be entire, toothed, lobed, or palmately compound. The shieldlike leaves of *Macaranga gigantea* are among the largest simple leaves in the dicots, up to three feet across. The indumentum (covering of hairs) shows great variation; some taxa (especially in the subfamily Euphorbioideae) are entirely glabrous, while others may have simple, branched, scalelike, or glandular hairs. The latex characteristic of certain genera is produced by extensive elongated and branching tubes in the stems and leaves; the exudate of latex from cut stems may vary in colour from clear to white, yellowish, or reddish. The latex of euphorbias includes a variety of compounds, including starch, alkaloids, resins (diterpenes and triterpenes), and rubber. In some species of *Euphorbia* and certain other genera of the subfamily Euphorbioideae, the resin is dangerously toxic and potentially carcinogenic because of the concentrations of diterpenes.

There are relatively few huge tropical rain forest trees in the order, as the members of Euphorbiaceae are mostly inhabitants of secondary (*i.e.,* disturbed) vegetation and are prevailingly short-lived. Climbing species occur in only a few groups, mostly in the tribe Plukenetieae. A large percentage of the genera occur in seasonal tropical or subtropical habitats, such as savanna, monsoon forest, or desert; many of these show "xerophytic" features such as spiny stems and small leathery or deciduous leaves (presumably reflecting adaptations to the seasonal climates of the horse latitudes and perhaps browsing by herbivores). Leaflike branches (phylloclades) occur in some tropical American species of *Phyllanthus,* mainly in rain-forest vegetation; the adaptive advantage of these phylloclades has not been explained. In the unrelated genera *Cnidoscolus* and *Tragia,* stinging hairs have evolved, presumably to deter herbivores. Succulent stems are found in a number of xerophytes in *Euphorbia,* including species of *Jatropha* and *Euphorbia;* the African species of *Euphorbia* with columnar stems show a great vegetative convergence on the columnar cacti of the Americas in having fleshy stems of different shapes armed with spines. The cactus-like euphorbias differ from cacti in that their spines are branches or pedicels (not modified leaves as in cacti); a small number of spineless succulent euphorbias are similar to stapelias (*Stapelia,* in the Asclepiadaceae) but differ in their very dissimilar inflorescences and flowers. There are also a considerable number of Euphorbiaceae that flourish in riparian or aquatic habitats; the most outstanding genus is *Phyllanthus,* which includes one Amazonian floating species (*Phyllanthus fluitans*) that mimics a water fern (*Salvinia*).

Economic and ecological importance. The Euphorbiaceae include a number of economically important plants. Rubber from the latex of the Para rubber tree (*Hevea brasiliensis*) is still important for some uses (such as in the manufacture of truck tires) despite the prevalence of synthetic rubber. Cassava (manioc; *Manihot esculenta*), a starchy root crop of South American origin, is now an important carbohydrate source in West Africa and other tropical regions. Minor tropical fruits are produced by species of *Antidesma, Baccaurea,* and *Phyllanthus.* The seeds of *Ricinus communis,* although producing an extremely powerful toxin (ricin) in the seed coat, have a valuable oil (castor oil) in the endosperm. Other commercially important seed oils are produced by species of the tung tree (*Aleurites*); and commercial waxes are obtained from the seeds of the tallow tree (*Sapium sebiferum*) and the stems of the Mexican *Euphorbia antisiphilitica.*

Source of medicines and poisons

Euphorbiaceae are important medically as a source of toxins and of medicines. Purgatives are produced by the seeds of croton (*Croton*), euphorbia, jatropha (especially the physic nut, or Barbados nut, *Jatropha curcas*), and castor-oil plant. Poisoning of humans and livestock has been reported for these genera and others, including *Excoecaria, Hyaenanche, Manihot,* and *Sapium.* Diterpene resins from croton have been used experimentally in studies of tumour initiation and may conceivably prove to be useful in cancer therapy. Because of the biochemical diversity of the family, it seems probable that additional medicines may be discovered, as is suggested by reports of uses by peoples of tropical America, Africa, and Asia. For example, it appears that an obscure weed (*Phyllanthus amarus*), hitherto regarded as worthless, may have a compound useful in the treatment of hepatitis.

The 275 genera of Euphorbiaceae are classified in 45 tribes assigned to five subfamilies. These subfamilies, and the characteristic genera, are listed below.

There are 55 genera with approximately 2,000 species in the subfamily Phyllanthoideae. Their petals may be present or absent, the pollen grains are not spiny, there are two ovules per chamber (locule), and the seeds do not develop a caruncle. None of the members exude latex. Among the most important species are *Antidesma, Baccaurea, Bridelia, Glochidion,* and *Phyllanthus.*

The subfamily Oldfieldioideae contains 25 genera totaling 100 species. The members of this subfamily do not have petals, the pollen grains are spiny, the carpels contain two ovules per locule, and the seeds often develop a caruncle. These plants do not exude latex. *Hyaenanche* and *Oldfieldia* are representative genera.

Acalyphoideae, one of the largest subfamilies with 100 genera and approximately 1,500 species, has members in which the petals may be present or absent, the pollen grains are not spiny, the carpel contains only a single ovule per locule, and the seeds often develop a caruncle. Latex is usually absent in this group. *Acalypha, Alchornea, Dalechampia, Macaranga, Panda, Ricinus,* and *Tragia* are important genera.

There are 50 genera and approximately 1,500 species in the subfamily Crotonoideae. The members usually have petals, the pollen grains mostly have knoblike projections, the carpel contains a single ovule per locule, and the seeds generally develop a caruncle. Latex is usually exuded in the members of this group. *Aleurites, Cnidoscolus, Croton, Hevea, Jatropha,* and *Manihot* are representative genera.

The subfamily Euphorbioideae contains 35 genera and more than 2,000 species. Its members do not have petals, the pollen grains are not spiny, the carpels contain a single ovule per locule, and the seeds generally develop a caruncle. Latex is exuded in this group. *Chamaesyce, Euphorbia, Excoecaria, Hura, Mabea, Pedilanthus,* and *Sapium* are representative genera.

Phylogenetic relationships

Phylogeny and biogeography. The phylogenetic relationships and biogeographic history of the Euphorbiaceae have been debated since the classic essay published by the British botanist George Bentham in the *Botanical Journal of the Linnean Society* (London) in 1878. The family Buxaceae (boxwood) has been assigned to the Euphorbiales by many authors, perhaps influenced by Bentham's treatment. However, although the unisexual flowers of Buxaceae are superficially similar to those of the Euphorbiaceae, the boxwoods are fundamentally different in their floral morphology (perianth homology, pollen morphology, gynoecial structure, and ovule orientation), embryology, and biochemistry. The closest relationships of the Buxaceae are with members in the subclass Hamamelidae, not the Euphorbiaceae. The family Simmondsiaceae, a segregate of the Buxaceae, shows many of the same differences from Euphorbiaceae and is of dubious affinity. The small Old World family Pandaceae has been recognized as distinct from the Euphorbiaceae, but *Panda* and its relatives are probably best regarded as aberrant Euphorbiaceae.

The geographic distribution of living Euphorbiaceae displays some recurrent patterns that suggest possible models for the origin and dispersion of the family. There are a number of instances of paired (vicarious) taxa shared between South America and Africa: *Amanoa, Maprounea, Tetrorchidium* (South America and West Africa), *Savia* (West Indies and Madagascar), and species of croton (South America and Madagascar). The classic model of Bentham postulating an African origin and early dispersal to South America is still valid, although it requires modification that for subfamilies Crotonoideae and Euphorbioideae the direction of migration was reversed.

The phylogenetic relationships of the Euphorbiales with other major taxa of the dicotyledons remain controversial. A number of phylogenists have regarded the Malvales as closely related, but many of the cited resemblances in leaf form and floral morphology seem due to convergence. There is considerable resemblance in basal floral plan to families in the Geraniales or Linales (especially the Ixonanthaceae). On the other hand, the family Thymelaeaceae shows some remarkable similarities in biochemistry (terpenes) and pollen morphology, and so the order Thymelaeales can perhaps make an equally strong claim for affinity with Euphorbiales. (G.L.W.)

Rosales. The classification of the order Rosales followed in this article comprises 24 families totaling approximately 321 genera and 6,700 species. The accompanying table summarizes the geographic distributions and gives the estimated number of genera and species in each family of the order. The sizes of the families vary greatly. Three of them are monotypic—that is, they have only one species—and nearly half of the families have 10 or fewer species. At the other extreme, the rose family (Rosaceae) includes about 45 percent of the species in the order, the 3 largest families contain two-thirds of the species, and the largest 7 families comprise more than 90 percent of the members of the order.

Distribution and abundance. Members of the Rosales are distributed throughout the world, and they grow on all continents and many islands. Their distribution ranges from Arctic regions to the tropics, from sea level to high mountains, and from forests to grasslands and deserts. Representatives of this order are frequent, and sometimes dominant, members of a variety of ecological communities. While the order as a whole can be found almost anywhere in the world, the geographic distribution of specific families and genera are more restricted. Several types of distribution patterns are found, some based on geography, others on climate.

North Temperate Zone

The vast majority of species in the order are found in the North Temperate Zone, especially because the Rosaceae, Saxifragaceae, and to a lesser degree, the Hydrangeaceae, Grossulariaceae, and Crassulaceae are most diverse in this region. A few groups are widespread across most of the zone, being found in a variety of habitats. For example, *Prunus,* which includes cherries, plums, and peaches, is one of the most widely distributed genera of the order. It is most abundant in North America, Asia, and southern Europe but is also well represented in the subtropics, extending southward to Malaysia and northern Australia and through Central America to Brazil and Chile. Another widespread genus is *Crataegus* (hawthorns), which is particularly abundant, both in terms of individuals and diverse forms, in eastern North America. Various kinds of hawthorns also exist westward across the continent, southward to Mexico and the Andes Mountains, throughout much of Europe, the Middle East, and Asia.

The family Saxifragaceae is widespread but is most common in temperate and cold climates, especially in mountainous and Arctic regions. The genus *Saxifraga* contains about half of the species in the family, and many are known for their tenacious ability to grow and thrive on exposed rocky crags and in the fissures of rocks (the name *Saxifraga* literally means "rock breaker"). Several species of *Saxifraga* have a circumpolar distribution—that is, they range all around the globe in the Arctic regions of North America, Europe, Asia, and intervening islands.

Some genera and species of Rosales frequently grow on more than one continent, but there are discontinuities, or gaps, in their ranges. For instance, the genera *Waldsteinia* (barren strawberry) and *Philadelphus* (mock orange) occur in areas that are widely separated geographically: eastern North America, western North America, southeastern Europe, and eastern Asia. *Physocarpus* (ninebark) and *Boykinia* (brook saxifrage) follow the same pattern, except that they are absent from Europe. Native only in eastern North America and in eastern Asia are the genera *Penthorum* (ditch stonecrop), *Astilbe* (astilbe, or false goatsbeard), and *Itea* (sweet spire or Virginia willow). This overall distribution pattern developed near the beginning of the Tertiary Period, about 60 million years ago, at which time the Bering Strait served as a bridge between western North America and Asia, and Europe and North America as well were closer geographically than at present; there was a widespread forest across Europe, Asia, and North America, and plants could readily migrate over time between the regions. With subsequent changes in climate and the advance of glaciers over much of the Northern Hemisphere, many plants that were broadly distributed became eliminated from some areas, while persisting as relicts in others.

A number of Rosales have restricted geographic ranges, from continents to extremely local areas. For example, *Heuchera* (alumroot) is strictly North American, yet the genus is found over nearly the whole continent from the Atlantic to the Pacific and from Alaska and Canada to the southern United States and Mexico. The genus *Gillenia* is confined to eastern North America; one species, *G. trifoliata,* is found mostly in the mountains and upper Piedmont region of the Appalachian Mountains and the remaining species, *G. stipulata,* grows mostly west of the Appalachians. As implied by its common name, elf orpine, *Diamorpha smallii* is a tiny annual less than 10 centimetres tall. It is restricted to North and South Carolina, Georgia,

From (Saxifragaceae) A. Cronquist, *An Integrated System of Classification of Flowering Plants* copyright © 1981 The New York Botanical Garden, Columbia University Press; (Chrysobalanaceae, fruit and flower cross-section of *Rosa canina*) A. Engler, *Syllabus der Pflanzenfamilien,* drawn by M. Moran; (Grossulariaceae, flowering branch of *Rosa canina* and, *Fragaria chiloensis*) G.H.M. Lawrence, *Taxonomy of Vascular Plants* (1951), reprinted with permission of The Macmillan Pub. Co., drawn by M. Moran

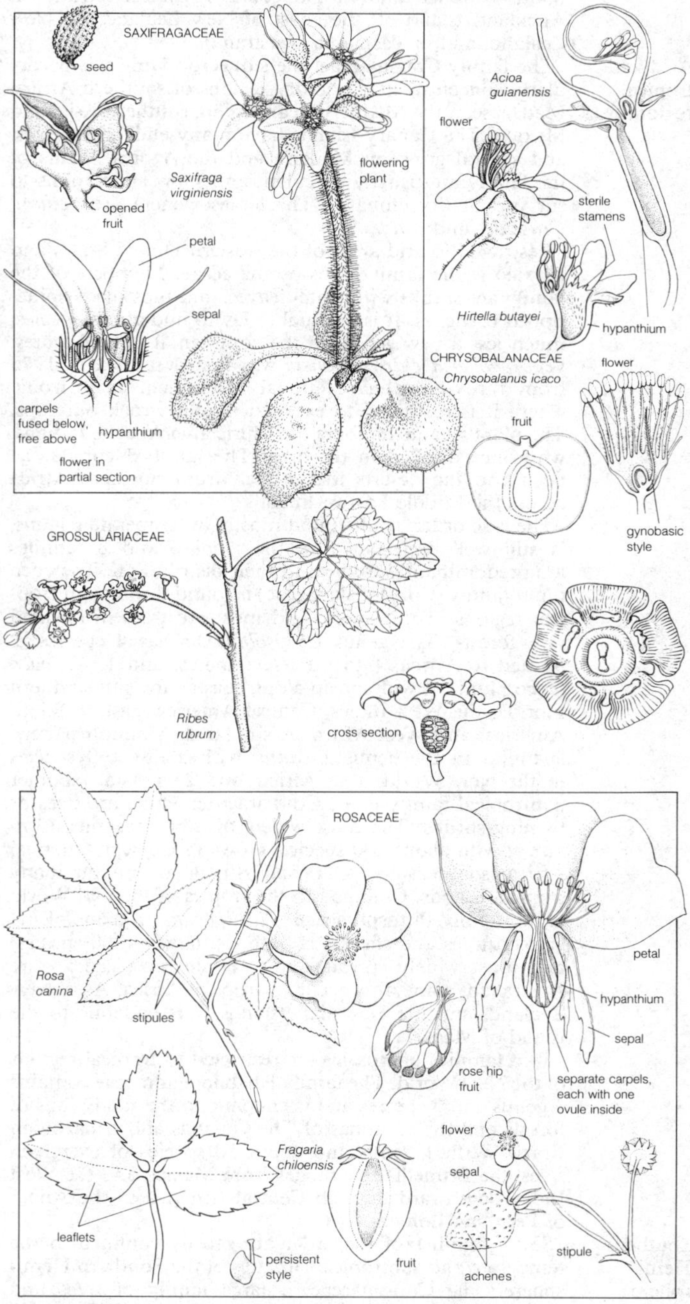

Vegative and floral features of four families in the order Rosales.

Alabama, and Tennessee, where it grows in depression pits of granite and sandstone outcrops. Some Rosales are endemic to islands, such as box-of-the-rocks (*Chamaemeles*) on Madeira and Catalina ironwood (*Lyonothamnus*) on the offshore islands of southern California. Many other genera of Rosales also have restricted ranges, particularly in western North America and eastern Asia.

Some members of the Rosales are distributed in temperate climates of both the Northern and Southern hemispheres but not in between. The genus *Chrysosplenium* (golden saxifrage) contains creeping perennial herbs and is widespread in the Arctic and temperate regions of the Northern Hemisphere, with two species occurring disjunctly in Chile and Patagonia (in southern Argentina). A species of wild strawberry (*Fragaria chiloensis*) is found in three discrete areas: Chile and Argentina, California northward to the Aleutian Islands, and the Hawaiian Islands. The genus *Geum* (avens) has a distribution ranging across North America, Europe, and eastern Asia, but, in addition, some species grow in the Andes Mountains of South America and in Patagonia, in South Africa, on Auckland Island off the coast of New Zealand, on New Zealand, and in Tasmania (Australia).

Arid and tropical regions

The family Crassulaceae, the stonecrop family, is particularly concentrated in the dry regions of southern Africa, Madagascar, the Mediterranean region, southern Asia, and Mexico. The Canary Islands have many endemic species, and several grow on Madeira and the Azores. Plants of the family are usually succulent and show adaptations to survival in dry climates. The largest genera are *Sedum, Crassula,* and *Kalanchoe.*

Restricted to arid areas of the western United States and Mexico is the family Crossosomataceae. Members of the family are shrubs with small leaves, and most have spine-tipped branches. It is unusual today to find a new species, much less a new genus, in the continental United States, yet *Apacheria chiricahuensis* was first described in 1975 from the Chiricahua National Monument in Arizona, where it is restricted to exposed rhyolitic rock outcrops. The plant's name honours the Chiricahua Apache Indians, who once dwelled in the area. The family Neuradaceae occurs in the deserts that stretch from northern Africa across the Middle East to India.

The rose order, while found mostly in temperate regions, is still well represented in the tropics, and 8 families are predominantly tropical in their distribution. The coco plum family (Chrysobalanaceae) is found throughout tropical regions of the world, and most are trees in lowland rain forests. The genus *Chrysobalanus* has 4 species, 2 limited to Africa, 1 to the West Indies, and 1, *C. icaco* (coco plum), is widespread along coastal areas in southern Florida, the West Indies, Central America, eastern South America, and West Africa. A similar distribution pattern is found in the genus *Licania,* with about 160 species in the New World, 1 in Africa, and 2 in Asia. Another pantropical family is the Connaraceae, which are trees or twining shrubs. The most widely distributed genus, *Connarus,* with about 100 species, grows in tropical America, Africa, southeastern Asia, and Australia, and on many tropical islands. Confined to the tropics of the Old World is the family Pittosporaceae. *Pittosporum,* a genus of evergreen trees and shrubs, is both the largest (200 species) and most widely spread genus. While most species are Australian, some also occur in tropical Africa, Asia, New Zealand, and the Hawaiian Islands; 1 is endemic to the island of Madeira.

Two families of Rosales are restricted to tropical regions of the New World. The family Rhabdodendraceae contains 1 genus and 3 species and is endemic to the sandy soils of forests and the savannas of The Guianas and Amazonian Brazil. With 1 genus and about 50 species of evergreen trees, the Brunelliaceae ranges from Mexico and the West Indies southward through Central America to the Andes of Peru and Bolivia.

Southern Hemisphere

Seven families of the order are mostly confined to the temperate and subtropical climates of the Southern Hemisphere. The Cunoniaceae, a large family of trees and shrubs, is especially diverse in Australia, New Guinea, and New Caledonia, but it also extends from southern South America northward to Mexico and the West Indies. Two families of the order, Greyiaceae and Bruniaceae, are endemic to southern Africa. Australia also has two endemic families of Rosales, Cephalotaceae and Davidsoniaceae. Byblidaceae occurs in both South Africa and Australia. Restricted to New Zealand and New Caledonia is the family Alseuosmiaceae.

The genus *Escallonia* of Grossulariaceae (the currant family) has nearly 50 species and is confined to South America, except for 1 species that reaches Costa Rica. The genus is found chiefly in mountainous regions, but in the southernmost part of its range it grows in a temperate climate near the sea. In the cordilleras of the Andes Mountains, plants of *Escallonia* grow as low shrubs at an elevation in excess of 4,000 metres, extending above the tree line and into the high treeless plains. They also grow in the upper cloud-forest border in subalpine meadows with many members of the Ericaceae (heaths).

Economic and ecological importance. The order Rosales is perhaps the third most economically important group, after Poaceae (the grass family) and Fabales (the legume order). While no member of the Rosales is a staple food, the diets of many peoples of the world are enriched by its fruits. Most of the major fruit crops in temperate regions belong to the rose family, Rosaceae. Cherries, peaches, apricots, nectarines, plums, and almonds are fruits from species of *Prunus* and blackberries, raspberries, loganberries, and dewberries, from *Rubus.*

Food plants

Apples, pears, quinces, and strawberries also belong to the rose family. Apples (*Malus domestica*) make up about half of the fruit-tree production in temperate climates. Contrary to the popular saying "as American as apple pie," the commercially grown apple is a native of the Old World, probably originating in western Asia. While more than 6,500 varieties of apples have been named, very few are widely available for sale in supermarkets. Pears (*Pyrus communis*) have long been a favourite fruit in England and Europe, and they are becoming more popular in North America as a wider selection of juicy and flavourful varieties are now grown commercially. Quinces (*Cydonia oblonga*) are better appreciated in the warmer parts of Europe than in North America. The flesh of quince is extremely fragrant but hard, gritty, and generally too tart to eat fresh; hence, most quince is made into jelly, jam, and marmalade. In Turkey, finely ground quince pulp is mixed with sugar, cooked, and spread out to dry, forming the gummy or jellylike confection known as Turkish delight.

The cultivated strawberry is a favourite fruit, but the strawberry as it is known today is far different from the wild types. About a dozen species of strawberries are distributed in the North Temperate region, extending southward in the mountain ranges of Central and South America. Among the plants that explorers sent back to Europe in the mid-18th century were wild strawberries from Chile (*Fragaria chiloensis*). These proved to be barren in European gardens because the plants that were sent had only female flowers. Meanwhile, wild strawberry plants from the eastern United States (*F. virginiana*) were sent to France. In a botanical garden in Paris, it was found that pollen of the latter would cause the Chilean strawberry to set fruit. Plants grown from the seeds of these fruits produced much larger fruit, and it was realized that a new hybrid type of strawberry had developed (*F.* × *ananassa*). Modern cultivated strawberries are developed from this hybrid and similar crosses between these two wild species.

Currants and gooseberries are produced by the shrubs belonging to the genus *Ribes* (Grossulariaceae) and are of considerable commercial importance, particularly in Europe. The European gooseberry (*R. uva-crispa,* formerly *R. grossularia*) has a tart, translucent, yellow-green or reddish fruit that is used in baking and preserves. Some modern varieties develop fruits nearly the size of marbles. Both red (*R. sativum*) and black (*R. nigrum*) currants are small and are eaten fresh or used to make jams. A sweet liqueur, crème de cassis, is produced from the strong, slightly smoke-flavoured black currant. Dried currants are used much like raisins in cookies, scones, and cakes.

Originally from central China, the loquat (*Eriobotrya japonica*) is widely cultivated in southern Florida, California, and in warm regions throughout the world. The succulent yellow-orange fruits are about 5 centimetres long, have a pleasant, mildly acid taste, and are eaten fresh, stewed, or used to make jelly and jam. A liqueur is made from the fruits in Bermuda. A delicately flavoured jelly can be made from the partly ripe fruits. Coco plum is found along beaches in tropical America. The fruits are used to make jam and jelly, although some can be eaten fresh when fully ripe.

Besides providing food for humans, the fruits of many members of the rose order are important elements in the diets of wildlife. The fleshy fruits of mountain ashes (*Sorbus*), cherries and plums (*Prunus*), crab apples (*Malus*), hawthorns (*Crataegus*), and shadbush (*Amelanchier*) are relished by birds, and strawberries are a favourite food of turtles and other ground-dwelling animals. The thick, dense, thorny plants of hawthorns and brambles provide excellent cover for wild animals. In the dry areas of western North America, mountain mahogany (*Cercocarpus*), cliff rose (*Cowania*), and bitterbrush (*Purshia*) are important browse plants for deer and other mammals.

Flowers of certain roses are wonderfully fragrant. Rose petals from the damask rose (*Rosa damascena*) or the cabbage rose (*R. centifolia*) are placed in a still and subjected to distillation, which extracts the volatile oils and produces attar of rose, a major ingredient in many perfumes. It is costly to produce: 4,000 kilograms of rose flowers yield only a single kilogram of attar of rose. The water that remains after distillation has some rose fragrance and is sold as rose water. Dried rose petals kept in potpourri jars or among clothing items slowly release their fragrance.

A large number of ornamental plants widely cultivated in temperate regions belong to the Rosales. Small to medium-size trees and shrubs grown for their flowers or fruit include spirea, meadowsweet, and hardhack (*Spiraea*); pearl bush (*Exochorda*); jetbead (*Rhodotypos*); crab apples; flowering cherries (*Prunus*); shadbush; Japanese quince (*Chaenomeles*); cotoneasters (*Cotoneaster*); fire thorns (*Pyracantha*); mountain ash, rowan trees, and whitebeams (*Sorbus*); photinias (*Photinia*); Christmas berry (*Heteromeles*); escallonias (*Escallonia*); mock orange; Virginia willow; tree anemone (*Carpenteria*); and fendleras (*Fendlera*).

Roses

None, however, are more widespread or appreciated than the cultivated roses, which have long been one of the favourite flowers of peoples of many lands and cultures. Roses often figure in song, poetry, literature, painting, and even historical events; the cottage rose (*Rosa* × *alba*) was adopted as a symbol by the Yorkists in the English War of the Roses. There are perhaps 120 species of wild roses, and over the centuries, humans have deliberately selected and bred these wild roses to produce a wide variety of cultivated roses.

The roses commonly grown today fall into several different categories. Many wild species, or direct descendants of them, are grown as species roses. Examples include Austrian Copper rose (*Rosa foetida,* variety *bicolor*); Father Hugo rose, (*R. hugonis*); saltspray, or rugosa, rose (*R. rugosa*); red-leaved rose (*R. rubifolia*); Scotch rose (*R. spinosissima*); and Harison's yellow rose, or yellow-rose-of-Texas (*Rosa* × *harisonii*). Old roses, as a group, are various sports, mutations, or hybrids of species roses. A few types of old roses are the alba, or cottage, roses, derived from *Rosa* × *alba;* the damasks, originating from *R. damascena;* the French, or gallica, roses from *R. gallica;* the hybrid musks, from *R. moschata;* and the cabbage, or Provence, roses, from *R. centifolia.* The moss rose, with its sepals and flower stalks covered with dense, mosslike hairs, is a mutation of the cabbage rose.

Perhaps the most familiar cultivated roses are the hybrid teas. These are of complex hybrid origins, involving up to seven wild species. In this breeding process, roses from eastern Asia were crossed with those from Europe. The flowers of Asiatic roses have urn-shaped buds, high-centred open flowers, and a peppery scent or the fragrance of crushed tea leaves. The Asiatic roses blossom heavily throughout the growing season, but they cannot withstand extremely cold winter temperatures; some have a rather vinelike climbing habit. European roses, on the other hand, are much more winter-hardy, usually produce only one flush of blooms in the spring, and have flat flowers with little fragrance. The Bourbon, Portland, hybrid China, tea, and hybrid perpetual roses are the products of the many crosses made between the Asiatic and European roses. Hybrid tea roses emerged primarily from crosses between tea and hybrid perpetual roses.

Floribunda roses, with clusters of numerous rather small flowers, have their basic origin in hybrids between hybrid teas and ultimately *R. multiflora,* while grandiflora roses are hybrids between floribundas and hybrid teas. Consequently, grandifloras have flowers that are larger and less numerous than floribundas but that are smaller and more plentiful than hybrid teas.

Today, garden roses have a wide range of colours, but this was not always the case. In the 19th century, roses exhibited a continuous range from white to pink through dark mauve-red, with some soft yellows. The first bright yellow garden rose was introduced in the early 1900s, as a result of hybridizing the cultivated variety Antoine Ducher with the Persian yellow rose (*R. foetida* variety *persiana*). While people often speak of "red" roses, true bright red roses are a relatively recent phenomenon. There are no wild species of roses with red flowers; in fact, red flowers are absent from the whole rose family. This is because the family lacks the gene for the pure red pelargonidin pigment. However, a natural genetic mutation occurred about 1930 that produced pelargonidin. Through rose-breeding programs, this gene was rapidly incorporated into modern cultivated roses, resulting in the vibrant red colours seen today.

One flower colour still missing in roses (both wild and cultivated) is blue, again because the gene for producing the proper pigment, delphinidin in the case of blue, is lacking in the rose family. Scientists are currently attempting to use genetic engineering methods to transfer the delphinidin gene from petunias (*Petunia,* Solanaceae) or delphiniums (*Delphinium,* Ranunculaceae) to roses.

Hydrangeas

Hydrangeas (*Hydrangea*) are known to most gardeners as shrubs, although some are woody vines or small trees. In the early spring the common hydrangea, or hortensia, that is popular with horticulturalists (*H. macrophylla*) is sold as a potted plant in northern cities. Hydrangea flowers are produced in large, showy white, blue, or pink clusters. In some species, flower colour seems to be related to soil acidity. The pink-flowered hortensias, for example, show a tendency to turn blue when iron filings or alum are added to the soil to increase acidity. Two other members of the hydrangea family often grown in gardens are mock orange, or sweet syringa, and *Deutzia.* These shrubs and their many cultivated varieties are widely planted in shrub borders for the white flowers that appear in late spring.

Several species of *Pittosporum* are commonly grown outdoors in California, Florida, and other warm regions. Japanese pittosporum, or tobira (*P. tobira*), makes an excellent hedge; it is also used to decorate the lobbies of hotels and office buildings. Karo (*P. crassifolium*), of New Zealand, is suitable as a windbreak or shelter near the sea because it is resistant to strong winds and salt spray.

Perennial borders contain many herbaceous representatives of the rose order. A few garden favourites are goatsbeard; agrimony (*Agrimonia*); lady's mantle (*Alchemilla*); Indian strawberry (*Dalibarda*); avens; queen of the prairie, meadowsweet, and dropwort (*Filipendula*); cinquefoils (*Potentilla*); burnet (*Sanguisorba*); saxifrages, rockfoils, and strawberry begonia (*Saxifraga*); bergenias and winter begonia (*Bergenia*); astilbes (*Astilbe*); and pickaback plant (*Tolmiea*).

Many members of the family Crassulaceae are grown as potted plants and in rock and succulent gardens. Having their origins in mostly arid and rocky regions, the leaves are typically fleshy, and the plants have a succulent appearance. Some examples include aeoniums (*Aeonium*); crassulas, jade tree, propeller plant (*Crassula*); escheverias and hen and chickens (*Echeveria*); kalanchoes (*Kalanchoe*); stonecrops and orpines (*Sedum*); and houseleeks and live-forevers (*Sempervivum*). In some species of *Kalanchoe* and *Bryophyllum,* young plants appear in notches around the margins of leaves still attached to the parent plant. The plantlets either drop off naturally and become established below the main plant, or they can be removed from the parent leaf and planted.

Several kinds of useful and beautiful wood come from members of the rose order. The wood of black cherry (*Prunus serotina*), native to North America, has a reddish brown colour and a warm lustre when finished. It also resists shrinkage and warping and has excellent working properties. Black cherry is a favourite wood for furniture, paneling, woodenware, tool handles, and musical instruments. Wood of the European wild cherry (*Prunus avium*) is brownish with a golden sheen and is used for high-quality furniture, either as solid cherrywood or cherry veneer. Pearwood has a rich pinkish red colour and a very smooth grain. Because pearwood has a smooth, hard, and stable surface, it was formerly widely used for rulers, T-squares, and drawing boards. Although plastics have generally replaced it for these uses, pearwood is still used for bowls, other kinds of wooden tableware, and in making veneers. Because of its colour, pearwood is often used in marquetry work. The apple tree produces wood that is reddish brown, hard, and rather heavy. It is prone to warping and splitting if not dried carefully, but properly cured applewood is used in the heads of the best golf clubs.

Black cherry

Trees of several species of *Weinmannia* occur in the tropics of both the Old World and the New World, and the timber is suitable for furniture and for interior construction. The wood of many other members of the Rosales is used locally, and limited amounts enter the commercial lumber market.

Many plants from the rose order are used locally as medicines in different parts of the world. Although several remedies have been ascribed to these plants, it remains to be proved scientifically that more than a few have therapeutic value. A tea or infusion made from strawberries, ocean spray (*Holodiscus discolor*) flowers, and the bark of crabapple (*Malus fusca*) was used by Indians in Washington to treat diarrhea. Other North American Indians used decoctions from blackberries and raspberries and alumroot (*Heuchera americana*) for the same purpose. Common agrimony (*Agrimonia eupatoria*) from Europe was looked upon in past ages as a general cure for any sort of wound or snakebite and for wart removal, liver ailments, and diarrhea. Twigs of *Parinaria curatellifolia* are chewed in West Africa as an antimalarial tonic, blood tonic, and cardiac stimulant and to treat respiratory ailments.

Kalanchoe laciniata is employed as an external medicine in India. The Malays use this plant to attract good spirits by placing twigs in houses to encourage the return of such spirits after a death. The same process is followed to drive away evil spirits and ward them off during serious illnesses such as cholera and smallpox. Children are bathed in water containing leaves of the plant, and a poultice of the leaves is applied to the chests of persons with coughs or colds. Pulped leaves are used in the Philippines to treat chronic ulcers, sores, and headaches.

Poisonous and disease-causing plants

Many members of the family Rosaceae produce chemicals called cyanogenetic glycosides (glycosides capable of releasing hydrogen cyanide gas, HCN, upon hydrolysis). The best known is amygdalin, which upon hydrolysis yields sugar, benzaldehyde, and cyanide. Benzaldehyde is a nonpoisonous compound providing almond, or amaretto, flavour and aroma. Cyanide, however, is a dangerous poison that blocks the activity of an enzyme which is directly involved in oxygen uptake during respiration, resulting in cyanosis and asphyxiation. Amygdalin develops in the seeds and pits of many plants, including cherries, plums, apricots, and apples. Hence, these seeds are potentially dangerous when consumed in quantity.

Almonds, which come from the pits of *Prunus amygdalus,* are of two kinds, bitter and sweet. Almond oil, used for flavouring, is extracted from the bitter almond. The crude oil contains considerable amygdalin and is poisonous, but this is removed during refining. The almonds eaten as nuts come from sweet almond varieties, which do not contain amygdalin and are safe to eat. Cyanogenic compounds also appear in the leaves of many of the rose family. Wilted or damaged leaves contain the highest concentrations. Occasionally cattle become ill or even die from eating the foliage of these plants.

White pines, whose needlelike leaves are produced in clusters of five, are important forest and timber trees in North America. They are, however, susceptible to the white pine blister rust, which can cause much damage. This disease is caused by a parasitic fungus, *Cronartium ribicola,* and requires that the members of the genus *Ribes* (currants and gooseberries) and the pine trees be in close proximity. Certain stages in the growth of the fungus take place on plants of *Ribes;* others are restricted to white pines. The fungal spores that carry the disease from *Ribes* to pine are relatively large and can be carried only about 90 to 275 metres by the wind, while those that spread the disease from pine to currant are much smaller and can be wind-blown hundreds of kilometres. Thus, once the pines are infected, disease can be spread much further afield. This disease is generally not a problem with ornamental pines in cities as the air contains pollutants that are not favourable to the fungus. Certain varieties of currants are evidently immune to the disease, and some white pines are showing resistance.

Characteristic morphological features. Practically all growth forms are found in the Rosales, including small to large trees, shrubs, stout woody vines, succulents, and annual and perennial herbs. Only the parasitic habit is absent. The complete range of habits is usually not found within a single family. Members of the Rosaceae are generally woody plants, mostly shrubs or small to medium-size trees, some of which are armed with thorns, spines, or prickles to discourage herbivores. The genus *Rubus* (blackberries, raspberries, and brambles) contains chiefly arching shrubs or scramblers of irregular, often tangled appearance. The woody habit predominates in most of the other families of the order. Members of the Brunelliaceae, Eucryphiaceae, Pittosporaceae, and Chrysobalanaceae are evergreen trees and shrubs. The Bruniaceae are heathlike shrubby plants of the Table Mountain region of South Africa with small, rigid, needlelike leaves. Xerophytic shrubs predominate in the Crossosomataceae, native to the chaparrals and deserts of the western United States and Mexico.

Woody climbers are rare in the rose order, being found in the Cunoniaceae and Hydrangeaceae. *Decumaria, Pileostegia, Schizophragma,* and a few species of hydrangea are woody shrubs that climb by aerial rootlets put out along the stems. They attach themselves to tree trunks, walls, and fences, and some kinds can climb to a height of 25 metres. A few cultivated roses also are climbers.

Aerial rootlets for climbing

Herbaceous perennials are found in several rosaceous genera, most notably *Fragaria, Potentilla, Geum,* and *Aruncus.* The genus *Aphanes* (parsley piert) has only annual species; a few kinds of cinquefoils also are annuals. Herbaceous plants also occur in the Neuradaceae (annuals) and the Saxifragaceae (mostly perennials).

The Crassulaceae has a wide variety of growth forms, including annuals, biennials, perennials, and even a few small shrubs or treelike members. Many plants of this family are succulent with thick, fleshy, evergreen leaves adapted to dry climates. Adaptations that allow plants to live through long dry periods include leaf surfaces often covered with hairs, papillae, bristles, or wax. The leaves, and often the stems, have an abundance of water-storage tissue. Stomata open primarily at night to reduce water loss.

Few truly aquatic plants are found in the order. One species, the Australian swamp stonecrop (*Crassula helmsii,* sometimes listed as *Tillaea recurva*) has been widely sold in Britain and Europe, where it is placed in ponds as an oxygenating plant. Unfortunately, its extremely fast growth rate and lack of diseases or insect pests enable the species to choke ponds, eliminate existing natural vegetation, and fill the ponds with a single large, weedy mass.

A few members of the rose order have special adaptations to trap and externally digest insects. Insectivorous plants usually grow in soils deficient in nitrogen. By capturing insects and absorbing the proteins from their bodies, these plants obtain a supplemental source of nitrogen. The Australian pitcher plant, *Cephalotus follicularis* (Cephalotaceae), is restricted to acid, boggy areas along coastal areas of western Australia. Two kinds of leaves are produced, foliage and pitcher. The pitchers are fully formed in summer, when the insects they capture, mostly ants, are plentiful. A lid overhangs the opening of the pitchers and has windowlike areas framed in green. Insects are probably attracted to the windows and then fall into the pitcher, where they cannot escape because of teeth around the rim. Trapped insects land in a liquid held within the pitcher and drown. This liquid contains digestive enzymes that slowly dissolve the soft parts of the insects, releasing nitrogen compounds which are then absorbed by the plant.

Rainbow plants belong to the genus *Byblis* (Byblidaceae) of Australia. Many sticky glands cover the long, linear yellow-green leaves, giving the leaf a glistening appearance that shimmers as the glands split the sunlight into all the colours of the spectrum. Each plant has two types of glands, stalked and unstalked. When an insect comes into contact with the stalked glands, it is trapped by a sticky covering. The unstalked glands then secrete a less viscous liquid containing digestive enzymes that break down proteins in the bodies of the trapped insects, thus making nitrogen available to the plant. A group of small, wingless capsid insects (members of the Heteroptera) often infest plants of *Byblis*. Although other small insects are ensnared in the mucilage, capsids appear to be able to move unhindered over the surface of the leaves.

Stalked and unstalked glands

A remarkable example of convergent evolution is found in goatsbeard (*Aruncus dioicus*) and false goatsbeard (*Astilbe biternata*) in the southeastern United States. Both species grow in or along the edges of rich, moist woods. They have a similar aspect, being tall perennial herbs with large, irregularly compound leaves and many small flowers arranged into showy flower clusters at the ends of the stems. A close examination shows that this resemblance is superficial. False goatsbeard has glandular hairs on the leaves, 10 stamens, and 2 or 3 partly united carpels, while goatsbeard has simple hairs, 20 stamens, and 3 to 5 free carpels. Goatsbeard is a member of the Rosaceae, whereas false goatsbeard belongs to the Saxifragaceae. Both false goatsbeard and goatsbeard also are variable in China, Japan, and the Himalayas, but the degree of convergence of these Asiatic species has not yet been studied.

A wide variety of leaf types can be found in the rose order. Simple leaves with entire margins are found in many species. A few families typically have such leaves—for example, Dialypetalanthaceae, Pittosporaceae, Anisophylleaceae, Crassulaceae, Crossosomataceae, Chrysobalanaceae, Surianaceae, and Rhabdodendraceae. Simple leaves with toothed margins are common in the order, as are shallowly to deeply lobed leaves. Several families have compound leaves, including the Brunelliaceae, Connaraceae, Cunoniaceae, and Davidsoniaceae. The leaves of the Davidsoniaceae are extremely large, reaching up to one metre in length. The family Rosaceae shows the greatest diversity of leaf types in the order; simple, lobed, and ternately, pinnately, and palmately compound leaves are found within the family.

Leaves in the Rosales may be alternate, opposite, or, rarely, whorled in arrangement. Within a given plant family, one type of arrangement usually dominates. As examples, most members of the Rosaceae have alternate leaves, with opposite leaves being found in a very few species, while the reverse situation prevails in the Hydrangeaceae. Small, leaflike structures called stipules can be present at the base of the leaf stalks. Some families, like the Rosaceae and Chrysobalanaceae, routinely have stipules, while others, including the Saxifragaceae and Hydrangeaceae, lack them.

The flowers in the rose order vary from small to large and range from white to various shades of yellow, pink, orange, lavender, or red. Blue flowers are rare in the order. Typically, the flowers are rather flat or shallowly cup-shaped, produce nectar, and are pollinated by a variety of kinds of insects. The basic structure of flowers in the order is relatively primitive. They are almost always bisexual with both male (stamens) and female parts (carpels) present in the same flower. When separate male and female flowers exist, they may be on the same or on different plants. The flowers are usually radially symmetrical, but bilaterally symmetrical flowers are seen in some saxifrages, alumroot and coralbells (*Heuchera*), Indian physic, and most Chrysobalanaceae. Elongate or tubular flowers are found in gooseberries and currants, escallonias, pittosporums, and some kalanchoes. The sepals and petals usually number four or five. The sepals are free from each other or united. The petals are usually free; only rarely are they united at the base or into a tube. In a few cases, the petals are absent. Many flowers of the order have some type of hypanthium or floral cup, from whose rim the sepals, petals, and stamens arise. The hypanthium is often lined with nectar-producing tissue. Specialized nectar glands are also frequent in the order.

Flower structure

The stamens are often numerous, a feature rare elsewhere in the subclass Rosidae, and they occur in whorls of four or five. The filaments are usually free; when a hypanthium is present, the stamens attach to its rim. In several genera of the Chrysobalanaceae, the filaments are joined at the base to varying degrees, and in one genus, *Acioa*, they are joined completely in a ribbonlike structure on one side of the flower. In the few cases where the petals are fused into a tube, the bases of the filaments attach to the tube, such as the genus *Kalanchoe*.

Each flower typically has two to many carpels. Only a few groups have one carpel, notably the genus *Prunus* (plums, cherries, peaches, and apricots). The carpels are free from each other in most cases, as exemplified by the spirea and rose subfamilies of the rose family. In the family Saxifragaceae, the carpels usually are united at the base but free above. In several families, such as the Pittosporaceae, the carpels are completely united into a compound gynoecium. The ovary is most often superior, and the sepals, petals, and stamens are inserted below the base of the ovary. When a hypanthium is present, the flowers parts (the sepals, petals, and stamens) are attached to the rim (perigynous), although they may appear to be attached to the ovary. The apple subfamily of the rose family normally has a distinctly inferior ovary with the sepals, petals, and stamens arising above the gynoecium. The Chrysobalanaceae is unusual since there are three carpels, of which only one usually develops fully, and the single style is inserted at the base of the developed carpel; the carpel may be attached at the base, middle, or mouth of the hypanthium.

Fruit types

The rose order shows a wide diversity of fruit types. Many have dry fruits, follicles, and capsules that split open at maturity to release the seeds for dispersal; follicles come from one simple carpel while capsules are produced by a compound gynoecium of fused carpels. Some members of the Saxifragaceae, Crassulaceae, and Hydrangeaceae have unusual fruits in that they are capsular below and follicular above. Some dry fruits in the order do not open at maturity, examples being the achenes of some Rosaceae and Surianaceae and the several-seeded fruits of the Neuradaceae. Fleshy fruits are frequent in the order. Drupes, characteristic of *Prunus* and the Chrysobalanaceae, and druplets, like raspberries and blackberries of the genus *Rubus*, develop from simple carpels, while berries, such as gooseberries and currants (*Ribes*), are produced by a compound gynoecium.

The rose family is divided into four very distinct subfamilies based primarily on fruits: Spiraeoideae (spirea subfamily), with follicles; Rosoideae (rose subfamily), with achenes or, in *Rubus*, druplets; Amygdaloideae, also called Prunoideae (plum subfamily), with drupes; and Maloideae (apple subfamily), with pomes. As a member of the Rosoideae, strawberries have achenes, although this is not obvious to the casual observer as they are tiny and occur on the surface of the enlarged flower axis, or receptacle. The pome is unique to the Maloideae and is a fleshy fruit in which the carpels are surrounded by an enlarged hypanthium. In most, but not all, Maloideae, the carpels are partly to completely fused to each other and to the sides of the hypanthium and are thus inferior to varying degrees. Some pomes are fleshy throughout, others have a membranous, or papery, core, and others contain hard nutlets. Examples of pome fruits are apples, pears, quinces, loquats, serviceberries (also known as juneberries), mountain ashes, hawthorns, and fire thorns.

The evolutionary success of the rose order rests on a variety of adaptive features. Among these is the variety of mechanisms for the dispersal of seeds away from the parent plant. In some instances, the seeds themselves are dispersed directly, while in others the fruit or some other structure is the unit of dispersal, with the seeds held within. Tiny, light seeds (*Spiraea,* many Saxifragaceae, Crassulaceae, and Hydrangeaceae) or large, winged seeds (*Quillaja, Eucryphia*) are produced by many members of the order, and they are spread by the wind. Fruits may also have wings (*Margyricarpus,* the pearl fruit), plumelike appendages (*Geum* and *Dryas*), or many hairs (*Holodiscus*) that aid in wind dispersal. Tiny hooks or barbs on seeds and fruits allow them to attach to the fur of animals as they pass by, transporting the seeds and fruits to other places. Some examples include the bristly seeds of the pickaback plant (*Tolmiea*), hooked styles in some species of avens, and barbs on the hypanthium in agrimony. Certain species of cinquefoil have fleshy oil-containing structures called elaiosomes on the achenes, and ants pick up these achenes and carry them back to their nest to feed on them. The large achenes of *Purshia* are collected by pack rats and placed in caches; those not eaten may eventually germinate and grow into new plants.

Dispersal mechanisms

In many Saxifragaceae, capsules held erect at the tips of flexible stems wave in the wind, tossing out the seeds as they move. *Chrysosplenium* and *Mitella* (Saxifragaceae) have small, cup-shaped fruits that point upward; raindrops that fall into the cups splash out the seeds. The elongated lower valve on the capsules of false miterwort (*Tiarella*) functions as a springboard for the seeds, powered by falling raindrops. The large, red hips of *Rosa rugosa* are buoyant and can float for extended periods, and the thick-walled achenes protect the seeds from fresh and salt water. A native of eastern Asia, this plant has become naturalized along beaches in eastern North America.

Fleshy fruits are ingested by animals, and some seeds pass unharmed through the digestive tract; in fact, many seeds require such treatment before they will germinate. The druplets of *Rubus* and the drupes of *Prunus* and the Chrysobalanaceae have thick pits or stones to protect the seeds. Other examples of fleshy fruits in the order include currants, strawberries, and the pomes of the Rosaceae subfamily Maloideae.

Fossil record

Evolution. Angiosperms first appear in the fossil record during the early Cretaceous Period, some 144 to 97.5 million years ago. While the Rosales are relatively primitive, fossil remains that can be assigned to the order are not known to exist before the Paleocene and Eocene epochs (66.4 to 36.6 million years ago) of the Tertiary. Fossils of the order are particularly frequent in both European and North American formations of Eocene to Pleistocene epochs (57.8 to 1.6 million years ago).

Members of all four subfamilies of the Rosaceae are represented in the fossil record. The genus *Spiraea* of the subfamily Spiraeoideae is known from fossil fruits and leaves, and the related genus *Physocarpus* is represented in fossils of the mid-Tertiary. In the subfamily Maloideae, fruit and seed remains have been recognized from the genera *Crataegus* and *Pyrus.* Leaf fossils are described for *Cydonia, Amelanchier,* and *Crataegus.* In the subfamily Rosoideae, fruits of *Potentilla* and *Rubus* are known from the Pliocene (5.3 to 1.6 million years ago) and Oligocene (36.6 to 23.7 million years ago) epochs of western Europe, respectively. Leaves, thorns, branchlets, calyx fragments, and fruits of *Rosa* are frequently found in North America, Europe, and Asia dating from the Eocene Epoch to the end of the Tertiary (57.8 to 1.6 million years ago). The subfamily Amygdaloideae is represented by fossil fruit pits of *Prunus* from the Eocene to the Pleistocene and of *Prinsepia* from the Oligocene to Pliocene. The Chrysobalanaceae, today confined to the tropics and subtropics, is represented by leaf fossils in the late Eocene flora of Oregon in the northwestern United States.

Various fossilized fruits and leaves of *Saxifraga* and *Chrysosplenium* of the Saxifragaceae have been found in many European deposits of Tertiary age. The family Hydrangeaceae is represented in the fossil record by *Philadelphus, Deutzia, Schizophragma, Decumaria,* and *Hydrangea* from many European, Russian, Japanese, Alaskan, and North American localities. Fossils thought to be referable to *Ribes* and *Itea* of the Grossulariaceae date from the Tertiary, and those of the same family *Escallonia* and *Quintinia* are known from the Pliocene of Bolivia and New Zealand, respectively. Leaf and stem fossils of the family Crassulaceae are known from France and The Netherlands in Tertiary deposits. A flower of *Billardiera* of the family Pittosporaceae has been found in amber of Miocene age (*i.e.,* 5.3 to 23.7 million years old) from the Småland peninsula of the Baltic coast of Sweden.

Phylogeny

The Rosales are considered to be the most ancient order of the subclass Rosidae, evidently derived from the Magnoliidae. The order is very diverse, and the families that make up the order are held together by a pattern of overlapping similarities, rather than by characteristics held in common by all families. In general, the families that comprise the order are relatively primitive and are what are left after the more advanced and specialized families of subclass Rosidae have been delimited. Most of the morphological features found in the more advanced orders of the subclass Rosidae, and even the subclass Asteridae, can be found individually in the rose order, such as sympetalous corollas (in which two petals are united, at least at the base), united carpels, inferior ovaries, and bilaterally symmetrical flowers. In the Rosales, however, these advanced features are not in the combinations characteristic of more advanced groups.

There is considerable controversy as to how the Rosales should be defined. The scheme used here, in which 24 families are recognized, follows the 1981 classification devised by the American botanist Arthur Cronquist. Other authors have divided these 24 families into as many as 42 families distributed among 17 orders. For example, Hydrangeaceae, Columelliaceae, Byblidaceae, and Pittosporaceae have been allied with Cornales; *Brexia* of Grossulariaceae with Celastrales; Connaraceae, Surianaceae, and Rhabdodendraceae with Rutales; Anisophylleaceae with Rhizophorales; and Chrysobalanaceae with Theales. Clearly, much research remains to be done to clarify the relationships and evolutionary history of plants currently included in the Rosales. (K.R.R.)

Sapindales. The order Sapindales consists of 15 families, approximately 500 genera, and some 6,200 species. More than half of the species belong to 2 families, the Sapindaceae (with 2,000 species) and the Rutaceae (with 1,700 species). Most of the remaining species belong to 6 other well-known families, the Anacardiaceae (with 650 species), Burseraceae (with 600 species), Meliaceae (with 575 species), Zygophyllaceae (with 270 species), Aceraceae (with 200 species), and Simaroubaceae (with 150 species). The remaining 7 families together total fewer than 100 species.

Distribution and abundance. The Sapindaceae (soapberry family), with about 150 genera and 2,000 species, occurs mainly in the tropical areas of the world and is especially abundant in the American tropics. Species range from trees and shrubs to lianas or herbaceous vines. The family is found throughout the wetter tropics and subtropics, extending north to Japan and south to New Zealand. The largest genera are *Serjania* (about 230 species), which occurs from the southern United States to tropical South America and has a main centre of diversity in southeastern Brazil, and *Paullinia* (about 190 species) in the American tropics and subtropics. Both are lianas or vines. *Allophylus,* another tropical and subtropical vine genus, may have as many as 190 species or as few as 1, depending on the authority.

The citrus family

The Rutaceae (the citrus, or rue, family) consists of shrubs, trees, and a few herbs. It has about 160 genera and 1,700 species, which are widespread in distribution but occur primarily in tropical and warm-temperate areas. The largest numbers of genera and species are found in southern Africa and Australia. Many of these grow in semiarid woodlands. The largest genus, *Zanthoxylum* (*Fagara*), has about 280 species and occurs in temperate North America and East Asia and throughout the tropics. *Agathosma* (135 species) is endemic to South Africa. Other genera with about 70 species each are *Pelea,* which occurs in

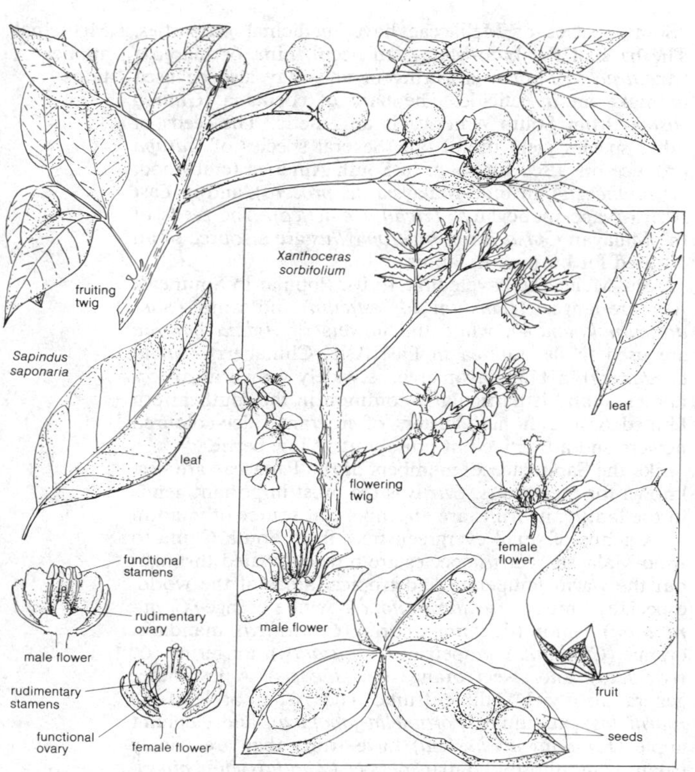

Representative plants from the family Sapindaceae, the largest family of the order Sapindales.

Drawing by R. Findahl; from (*Sapindus saponaria*) A. Engler, *Syllabus der Pflanzenfamilien*

the Pacific Islands (mainly the Hawaiian Islands); *Haplophyllum,* which occurs from the Mediterranean region to eastern Siberia; *Melicope,* occurring from Indo-Malaysia through Australia and New Zealand to the Pacific Islands; and *Boronia,* one of the largest endemic Australian genera.

The Anacardiaceae (the sumac family) consists of perhaps 70 genera and 650 species of trees, shrubs, or woody vines. They occur mostly in the tropics and subtropics, but a few genera extend into both the North and South Temperate zones. The largest genus by far is *Rhus,* with about 250 species in the subtropics and warm-temperate areas of the world. There are no other genera of comparable size, but *Semecarpus* (occurring from Indo-Malaysia to Micronesia) has about 60 species, *Mangifera* (occurring in Southeast Asia and Indo-Malaysia to the Solomon Islands) has 40, and *Schinus* (occurring from Mexico to Argentina) has 30.

The Burseraceae (the frankincense family) has 16 genera and 600 species of trees and shrubs. The family occurs throughout the tropics and is especially common in tropical America and northeastern Africa, Madagascar, and the Arabian Peninsula. Many species dominate the forests or woodlands in which they grow. The largest genus, *Commiphora* (150–200 species), is found mostly in the drier areas of northeastern Africa, Madagascar, and from Arabia to India. Three genera with about 100 species each are: *Bursera,* occurring in tropical America with its centre of diversity in Mexico; *Protium,* occurring mostly in wet lowland tropical America but with a few species in Madagascar and Malaysia; and *Canarium,* occurring in the forests of the Old World tropics.

The mahogany family

The Meliaceae (the mahogany family) has 51 genera and about 575 species of trees and shrubs and a very few perennial herbs. Many are large, widespread, and common or dominant trees in tropical and subtropical, primary and secondary forests, with only a few species in temperate areas. About three-quarters of the species occur in the 6 largest genera: *Aglaia* (100 species) in Indo-Malaysia (a region comprising India, South China, and Southeast Asia) and tropical Australia; *Trichilia* (about 90 species), which occur commonly as understory trees in lowland forests from Mexico to the West Indies, tropical South America, and tropical Africa; *Dysoxylum* (about 75 species) from Indo-Malaysia to the islands of the Pacific; *Turraea* (60 species) in tropical and southern Africa to Australia; *Chisocheton* (51 species) in Indo-Malaysia; and *Guarea* (40 species) in tropical America and tropical Africa.

The Zygophyllaceae (the bean caper, or creosote bush, family) contains 27 genera and 270 species of mostly shrubs, but a few are trees or annual or perennial herbs. They are widespread in the warmer, drier areas of the world, where some species are extremely abundant. Creosote bush (*Larrea tridentata*) is the most common species in the warm deserts of North America. The largest genus, *Zygophyllum,* contains about 100 species and is found from northern and southern Africa to Central Asia, India, and Australia. *Fagonia* (which has 40 species) is widespread, occurring in the warm deserts of North and South America, the Canary Islands, the Mediterranean region, southwestern Africa, and southwestern Asia to northwestern India. *Balanites* (containing 25 species) is found from tropical Africa to Myanmar, and is separated into its own family, Balanitaceae, by some authorities.

The maple family

The Aceraceae (the maple family), with 2 genera and about 200 species, is not a large family, but its trees dominate many areas of North Temperate forest. *Acer* (maple), with about 200 species, is found across the North Temperate region from western North America to Japan, and trees of the genus form an important component of the deciduous forests of North America, Europe, and Asia. The genus dips southward to Guatemala and through Southeast Asia to Malaysia and the Philippines, where species may be abundant in tropical mountain forests. The major centre of distribution for the genus is China, where half of the species occurs; about 90 percent of the species are Asian. There are eight species of *Acer* with compound leaves that are sometimes placed in a separate genus, *Negundo*. *Dipteronia* is a genus of central and southern China with only one or two species.

The Simaroubaceae (the quassia family) is a family of trees and shrubs with about 20 genera and 150 species that are mostly tropical in distribution. *Picramnia,* shrubs and small trees found from Mexico and the West Indies to tropical South America, has about 55 species. The only other genus of any size is *Quassia,* with 40 species in the rain forests of tropical America and Africa.

The Staphyleaceae (the bladdernut family) contains 5 genera and about 60 species of mainly North Temperate and tropical trees and shrubs that occur irregularly from western North and South America to Europe, eastern Asia, and Japan. The largest genus, *Turpinia,* contains about 40 species in Central and South America and in Asia from Sri Lanka to Japan. *Staphylea* has 9 or 10 species in the North Temperate region.

The Hippocastanaceae (the horse chestnut family) has only 2 genera of trees and shrubs. *Aesculus,* with about 13 deciduous species, has an interrupted distribution in temperate forests from western and eastern North America (7 species) to the Balkan Peninsula in Europe (1 species) and in Asia from India to China and Japan (5 species). The 2 evergreen species of *Billia* occur as isolated trees in tropical forests from southern Mexico to northern South America.

The Melianthaceae (the honeybush family) has 2 genera of shrubs or small trees. *Melianthus* has 7 species in southern Africa. *Bersama* has a great deal of morphological variability. Some botanists recognize 2 species; others recognize 30. These are widespread in southern and west-tropical Africa.

The Julianiaceae (the huachalata family) contains 2 genera and 5 species of tropical shrubs or small trees. *Amphipterygium* (with 4 species) occurs in southern Mexico and Guatemala, while *Orthopterygium* (with 1 species) grows in Peru. They are characteristic trees of tropical deciduous forests.

The Cneoraceae (the spurge olive family) has only 2 genera and 3 species of shrubs: *Cneorum,* with 2 species, one in the western and central Mediterranean and one in Cuba, and *Neochamaelea,* with one species in the Canary Islands.

The Bretschneideraceae (the bretschneidera family) is one of the two families of the Sapindales with only one genus and one species, *Bretschneidera sinensis,* a deciduous tree found in low mountain forests of southwestern China. The Akaniaceae (the akania family) is the other family in the order with only a single genus and species. *Akania lucens* is a small tree common in subtropical coastal rain forests in eastern Australia.

Economic and ecological importance. Many members of the order are important economically, particularly for their timber or fruits. A few tropical species of the family Sapindaceae produce useful wood for construction, furniture, or fuel, but many are better-known for their fruits. Akee (*Blighia sapida*) from West Africa, wild prune (*Pappea capensis*) from tropical and southern Africa, and *Pometia pinnata* from New Guinea are the larger trees of the family that provide timber. The akee and *Pometia* also have edible fruits. The akee, which looks and tastes like scrambled eggs when cooked, is the national fruit of Jamaica, where it is widely grown and eaten; it is, however, poisonous if not cooked at the correct stage of ripeness—*i.e.*, after the fruit has opened naturally and is still fresh. Only the fleshy aril around the seed is eaten.

Sources of timber and fruits

Other popular tropical fruits from the Sapindaceae come from litchi (*Litchi chinensis*), longan (*Dimocarpus longan*), rambutan (*Nephelium lappaceum*), and Senegal cherry (*Aphania senegalensis*) from the Old World, and mamoncillo (*Melicoccus bijugatus*) from the New World. Many of these are widely cultivated. Useful oils are expressed from the seeds of wild prune and Ceylon oak (*Schleichera oleosa*); the latter is the source of macassar oil, and this species harbours the lac insect (*Laccifer lacca*), which produces lac, a resinous excretion that is a source of shellac. The seeds of the Brazilian and Paraguayan vine guarana (*Paullinia cupana*) are ground to make a beverage, guarana, a popular drink in the region that contains three times more caffeine than does coffee. The bark of yoco (*P. yoco*) is used for the same purpose.

The fruits of soapberry (*Sapindus saponaria*), a tropical American species, contain saponins (chemical substances that produce soapy lather in water) and are used as soap. The genus name *Sapindus* means "soap of the Indians." A number of members of the family Sapindaceae have saponins in their tissues. In the American tropics, the native peoples sometimes crush the leaves and branches of *Paullinia, Serjania,* and related genera and throw them into pools or small streams to stun fish.

A few species of Sapindaceae also are grown as ornamentals. Golden rain tree (*Koelreuteria paniculata*), a small tree from China, Korea, and Japan, is commonly cultivated in temperate regions for its large pyramidal clusters of yellow flowers and conspicuous bladderlike fruits. Balloon vine (*Cardiospermum halicacabum*), an annual from the tropics and subtropics, is grown for its small balloonlike fruits in many areas, where it sometimes escapes and becomes naturalized. Hopbush (*Dodonaea viscosa*), a widespread tropical shrub, is cultivated in warmer areas for its colourful foliage. The akee is grown not only for its fruits but also as a shade tree.

Many tropical species of the family Meliaceae are important timber trees. The best known, West Indian mahogany (*Swietenia mahagoni*), a native of the West Indies, is one of the world's most valuable woods. Honduras mahogany (*Swietenia macrophylla*), from Mexico to Bolivia, is also well known. Other valuable timbers of the Meliaceae from the American tropics are derived from species of *Cedrela;* West Indian cedar (*C. odorata*), for example, is the source of wood used for making cigar boxes.

The eight species of *Khaya* in tropical Africa and Madagascar, including African mahogany (*K. senegalensis*), produce a wood like that of mahogany, as do the nine species of omu, sapele, and utile mahoganies (*Entandrophragma*). Important Asian timber trees are toon (*Toona ciliata*) in India, chittagong wood (*Chukrasia tabularis*) in China to Indo-Malaysia, and Indian redwood (*Soymida febrifuga*) in Indo-Malaysia. Australian mahogany (*Dysoxylum fraserianum*) is a timber tree of the forests of northern and eastern Australia. The wood of these genera, all of Meliaceae, is typically reddish in colour, lustrous, easy to work, and free of warping under changes in relative humidity. Such characteristics make the wood highly suited for cabinetmaking.

Some species of Meliaceae have medicinal properties. The bark of the Indo-Malaysian neem, nim, or margosa (*Azadirachta indica*) is astringent and may also be used to make an insecticide. The bark of cocillana (*Guarea rusbyi*) from South America is an emetic. The seeds of other species yield useful oils. Several species of *Carapa* produce oils used for soap: in South America (crabwood, *C. guianensis*), in Indo-Malaysia (*C. procera*), and in East Africa (cape mahogany, *Trichilia emetica*). The seeds of the Malayan *Chisocheton macrophyllus* are a source of an oil used for burning in lamps.

Medicinal applications

A few Meliaceae have edible fruits. Popular in Southeast Asia are langsat (*Lansium domesticum*) and santol (*Sandoricum koetjape*), while the flowers of *Aglaia odorata* are used to flavour tea in East Asia. Chinaberry (*Melia azedarach*), a Himalayan tree, is widely grown as an ornamental and is particularly common in the southeastern United States. It has clusters of fragrant, lilac-coloured flowers and attractive but poisonous yellow berries.

Like the Sapindaceae, members of the Rutaceae are best known for their fruits. *Citrus* is the most important genus in the family; its fruits are an important source of vitamin C. A genus of small evergreen trees from South China to Indo-Malaysia, *Citrus* species are now cultivated throughout the warm temperate and tropical areas of the world, especially lime (*Citrus aurantifolia*), Seville orange (*C. aurantium*), lemon (*C. limon*), citron (*C. medica*), mandarin orange (*C. nobilis*), grapefruit (*C. paradisi*), tangerine (*C. reticulata*), and sweet orange (*C. sinensis*). A few other genera also yield edible fruits. The Asian bael (*Aegle marmelos*), kumquat (*Fortunella japonica*), and elephant apple (*Limonia acidissima*) have fruits that are widely eaten, while those of Japan pepper (*Zanthoxylum piperitum*) are used as a condiment.

The fruits of *Aegle* are used medicinally, as are those of the Chinese hardy orange (*Poncirus trifoliata*). Many species of Rutaceae have bitter bark that is medicinal, including the tropical American angostura (*Angostura febrifuga*) and casparia (*Galipea officinalis*). The bark of several North American species of *Zanthoxylum* is chewed for toothache.

Essential oils found in the tissues of Rutaceae are the source of the characteristic flavours of fruits, bark, gums, and leaves. The leaves of rue (*Ruta graveolens*) are a flavouring herb in Europe, and oil of rue is distilled from them. Leaves of orange jasmine (*Murraya koenigii*) are used in curries. Citrus oils are commonly expressed from the rinds of different citrus fruits or from their flowers. Perhaps the best known is oil of neroli from the Seville orange, widely used in perfumery in France.

A few species of Rutaceae are grown as ornamentals in temperate regions. *Poncirus* is a spiny hedge shrub, while Japanese skimmia (*Skimmia japonica*) and Chinese skimmia (*S. reevesiana*) have white flowers and red berries, the North American hoptree (*Ptelea trifoliata*) has attractive winged fruits, and the northeast Asian Amur cork tree (*Phellodendron amurense*) is a valuable shade tree. Burning bush (*Dictamnus albus*) is one of the few members of the family that is not woody. This poisonous perennial herb, native from southern Europe to northern China, is grown not only for its attractive whitish flowers but also for its ethereal oil; the glands of this plant can be squeezed and the oil expressed into the air and ignited by a match—hence the common name.

Only a few species of Rutaceae are important timber trees. The Indo-Malaysian satinwood (*Chloroxylon swietenia*), eastern Australian yellow wood (*Flindersia oxleyana*), and Caribbean West Indian silkwood (*Zanthoxylum flavum*) are used for veneering and cabinetmaking.

The Anacardiaceae, like the Rutaceae and Sapindaceae, are known for their fruits. Cashew (*Anacardium occidentale*), a tropical South American tree, was one of the first fruit trees to be distributed throughout the tropics by early Spanish and Portuguese adventurers. The seed produces the cashew nut, while the reddish, swollen axis under the fruit proper is the cashew apple. The former is roasted and eaten, while the latter is crushed, strained, and added to water and sugar to make a refreshing drink consumed throughout tropical America. Mango (*Mangifera indica*),

Cashew

native to Indo-Malaysia, now also is cultivated throughout the tropics. The fruit of this large tree has a thick, aromatic, tasty flesh; it has been called the queen of the tropical fruits. Several species of the tropical genus *Spondias* (hog plum, Jamaica plum, mombin, otaheite apple, and Spanish plum) are cultivated for their fleshy fruits, eaten fresh or cooked. The pistachio nut (*Pistacia vera*) is a temperate tree, native from the Mediterranean to Afghanistan, but now also cultivated in North America for its edible seeds.

The Peruvian pepper tree (*Schinus molle*) has fruits that are not eaten directly, but they are the source of a fermented alcoholic drink. This is a commonly grown ornamental in subtropical America, where it has frequently become part of the natural habitat. It is grown for its feathery, evergreen, compound leaves and red berries (of the female tree). The ground seeds are used as a condiment or as an adulterant in pepper. It grows well on poor soils. The dhobi nut (*Semecarpus anacardium*) has young fruits with a black resin insoluble in water that is used as a marking ink in Southeast Asia.

Other species of Anacardiaceae are also grown as ornamentals. The smoke tree (*Cotinus coggygria*), from southern Europe to central China, is a shrub with purplish foliage and large, diffuse inflorescences that give the "smoky" appearance. It is commonly planted in temperate regions. Several species of sumac (*Rhus*), particularly those from North America, are cultivated as shrubs, especially for their colourful reddish autumn foliage.

Few Anacardiaceae species are exploited for their wood for building or for cabinetmaking; however, many of them have valuable tannins that are extracted for tanning leather. Quebracho (*Schinopsis quebracho-colorado*) is a major source of tannins in South America, as is sumac (*Rhus coriaria*) in southern Europe. Species of *Cotinus, Pistacia, Rhus,* and *Schinopsis* are important sources of tannins for the leather industry.

Exudates from the stems of various species of Anacardiaceae yield lacquers, resins, or gums. The art of lacquering began in China centuries ago, reaching its climax of development during the Ming dynasty, AD 1368–1644. The lacquers used were obtained from the varnish tree (*R. vernicifera*). The milky exudate from this tree darkens and thickens rapidly on exposure to air. Lacquer, when applied as a varnish, provides remarkable protection, as it is unchanged by acids, alkalies, alcohol, or heat up to 70° C (158° F). The Burmese lacquer tree (*Gluta usitata*) produces a more slowly drying lacquer. The mastic tree (*Pistacia lentiscus*), from the Mediterranean region, produces mastic, a varnish used for coating metals and oil and watercolour pictures. It is one of the most expensive resins to produce. The tropical American *Anacardium humile, A. occidentale,* and *A. nanum* produce cashew gum, a substitute for gum arabic. Not only are they good adhesives, but they also contain a small amount of cashew oil, which can be used as an insect repellent or as a lubricant in the electrical insulation of airplanes.

Mastic tree

Many people know the Anacardiaceae because of the dermatitis caused by the resins of some species. The most notorious probably are poison oak (*Toxicodendron diversiloba*) of western North America and poison ivy (*T. radicans*) and poison sumac (*T. vernix*) of eastern North America. (*Toxicodendron* means "poison tree.") The resin will disperse in the smoke of the burning wood of these plants and may even volatilize from their tissues on hot, dry days. Mangoes and cashew apples will cause dermatitis in those sensitive to their resins, as will their wood or leaves. Many people are also sensitive to liquid lacquer or mastic.

Like some of the Anacardiaceae, most of the Burseraceae are known for their aromatic resins or gums. The most famous of these are *Boswellia carteri* and related species, the sources of frankincense, while *Commiphora abyssinica* and related species yield myrrh. *C. opobalsamum* furnishes balm of Gilead. All grow naturally or are cultivated in arid areas from Ethiopia to India with other species that produce resins, also used in incense and perfumes. Resin collecting is an important part of the economy in Ethiopia and Somalia. In tropical America, copal (*Protium copal*) and other protiums are tapped for their resins, which have been used in Central America as incense for religious purposes since pre-Columbian times. Likewise, indio desnudo (*Bursera simaruba*) and other burseras are exploited for turpentine or elemi (an oily resin) in tropical America. Some contain such large amounts of resin and burn so fiercely that they are known as torchwoods. The Indian black dammar tree (*Canarium strictum*) and Java almond (*C. commune*) of Indo-Malaysia, a source of Manila elemi, also produce commercially valuable resins. The seed of the latter, which is cultivated in Australia, is edible, as are those of several other East Asian species, which also may be processed to produce cooking oil. The fruits of *C. album* are eaten like olives.

A few Burseraceae are important timber trees. Probably the most important of these is gaboon mahogany (*Aucoumea klaineana*), from West Africa, used for veneers and plywood.

Timber trees of the Western Hemisphere

Within the family Zygophyllaceae are several valuable New World timber trees. The most famous of these is lignum vitae (*Guaiacum officinale*), a Caribbean tree with very hard, dense, and durable wood. It is used in making the bushings for ships' screws and for mallets. The wood contains gum guaiac, a resin that has been used medicinally since the 15th century as a specific, but ineffective, cure for syphilis. The guaiac test is still used, however, to detect blood in feces. The wood of holywood lignum vitae (*Guaiacum sanctum*), from the northern Caribbean and Central America, is used for making small objects that require weight, hardness, and strength. Maracaibo lignum vitae (*Bulnesia arborea*) is utilized for the same purpose in Colombia and Venezuela. The wood of Paraguay lignum vitae (*B. sarmientoi*) is the source of guaiac wood oil, which has a roselike scent and is used in soaps and perfumes.

A few species of Zygophyllaceae are edible. The fruits of several African species of *Balanites* and Asian species of *Nitraria* are sometimes eaten, and their seeds produce oils used in cooking or soap manufacture. The pickled buds of the North African bean caper (*Zygophyllum fabago*) are used as a substitute for capers. The seeds of harmal (*Peganum harmala*), a small shrub that grows naturally from North Africa to the Middle East and is a weed (not indigenous) elsewhere, are reputedly narcotic. They also produce the dye Turkey red. Some species of other genera also are weedy, but the most pernicious of these is puncture vine (*Tribulus terrestris*). This native of the Mediterranean region has been disseminated to all the drier warm areas of the world. It has hard fruits with sharp spines that easily attach to automobile and airplane tires and to the feet of grazing animals. The spines can injure an animal externally if touched or internally if eaten. Livestock that eat the plant may become very sensitive to light; ingestion of the fruits may cause death in these animals.

Sugar maple

The best-known member of the Aceraceae is sugar maple (*Acer saccharum*). It has sugar-rich sap that is tapped in the early spring in eastern North America in order to make maple syrup and maple sugar. Sugar maple has been described as the most valuable hardwood in North America. Its figured wood (curly maple and bird's-eye maple) is valued for cabinetry and furniture; the plain wood is used for construction, flooring, and interior finish. The hard, strong, heavy, close-grained wood is often beautifully patterned. The sugar maple is a valuable ornamental and shade tree because of its thick, shapely crown and the bright yellow, orange, and red autumnal coloration. In addition, it yields valuable firewood.

Other North American maple species are less important as timber, paper pulp, sugar-producing, and ornamental trees. A few European species, and more Asian species, are sources of timber or grown as ornamentals for their foliage and leaf colours.

The Simaroubaceae is a family known for its medicinal plants, although the southern African white syringa (*Kirkia acuminata*) has wood that is worked into veneer, furniture, flooring, or household articles. Decoctions of the bark and wood of quassia wood (*Quassia amara*) are used to make an antimalarial tonic in tropical America. This species is widely cultivated for its red flowers and bitter bark. Likewise, bitters are prepared from the bark of cedron (*Simaba cedron*) in Central America and Jamaica quassia (*Picrasma excelsa*) in the West Indies. At one time, the bitter leaves and licorice-flavoured bark of the West Indian and Central American cascara amarga (*Picramnia antidesma*) were exported to Europe as a treatment for venereal disease. The astringent seeds of *Brucea amarissima* and *B. sumatrana* are used to treat dysentery in southeastern Asia.

The Staphyleaceae has a few members of minor economic importance. Several species of bladdernut (*Staphylea*) are grown as ornamental shrubs in temperate areas. *Turpinia* species are used locally in Asia and the West Indies for their timber. In China and Japan, the fruits of gonzin zoku (*Euscaphis japonica*) are used medicinally.

Next to the Aceraceae, the Hippocastanaceae probably have the most economic significance in temperate areas, in spite of the small size of the family. The horse chestnut (*Aesculus hippocastanum*) of the Balkan mountain region and the North American Ohio buckeye (*A. glabra*) and

From (Zygophyllaceae) H. Baillon, *Histoire des Plantes* (1867–1895), Librairie Hachette, drawn by M. Moran; (Burseraceae, Simaroubaceae) drawn by M. Pahl

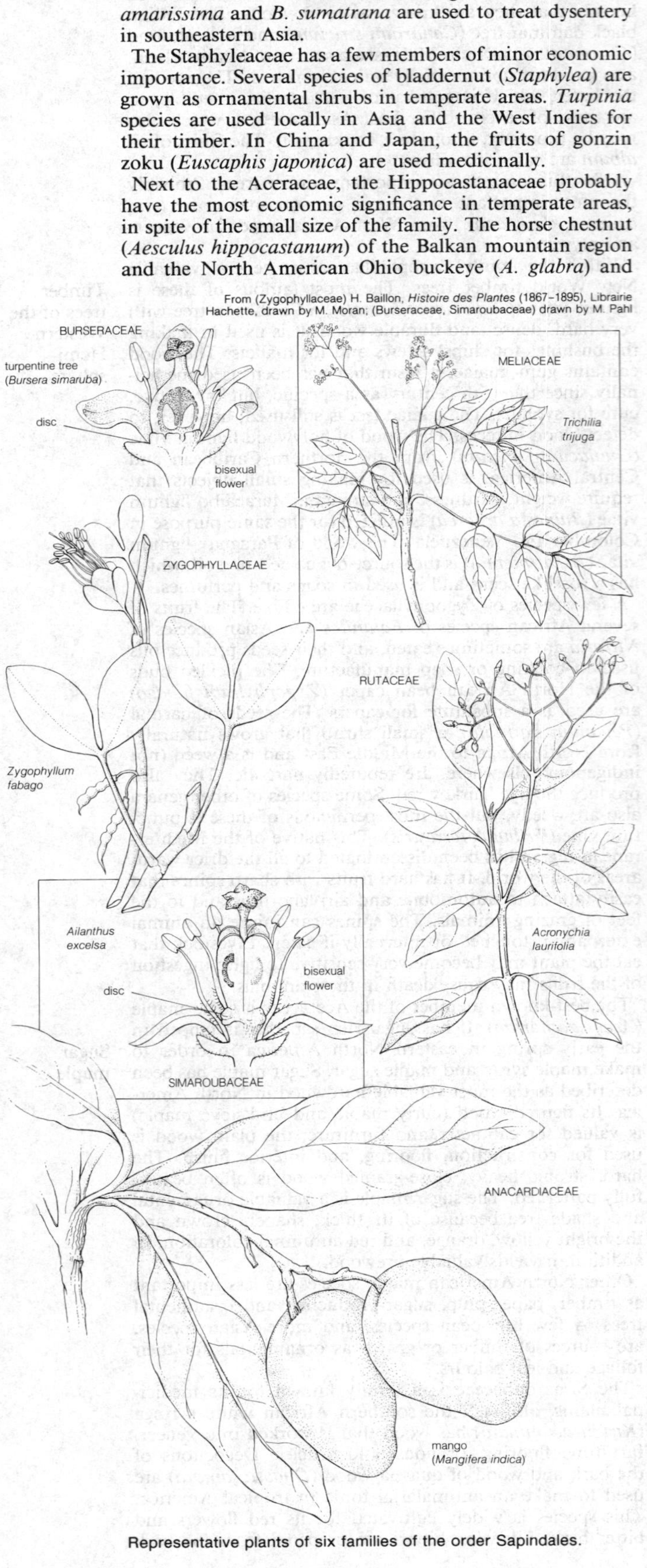

Representative plants of six families of the order Sapindales.

yellow buckeye (*A. flava*) have light, soft, tough, fine-grained wood. Once used for artificial limbs, splints, and various kinds of woodware, the wood is now most important as a source of paper pulp. The leaves and seeds are poisonous, and extracts from them are employed by certain native peoples to stun fish. Selected varieties and hybrids of *Aesculus* are frequently cultivated as ornamentals for their flowers or foliage or as shade trees.

Honey bush and touch-me-not

The African family Melianthaceae has a few species of shrubs that are sometimes cultivated in warm-temperate areas. Honey bush (*Melianthus major*) and touch-me-not (*M. comosus*) have long racemes of reddish flowers that are attractive to honeybees. A decoction of the leaves of the honey bush is used for healing wounds, while the root, bark, and leaves of the touch-me-not are used in southern Africa for treating snake bites. Bitter bark (*Bersama abyssinica*), a tree, produces a hard, heavy wood suitable for house construction in West Africa.

In the family Julianiaceae, the Mexican huachalata (*Amphipterygium adstringens*) has a bark that can be applied medicinally as an astringent, for treating malaria, and for toughening the gums. It also contains tannins and a red dye. *Cneorum tricoccon*, a western and central Mediterranean species of the family Cneoraceae, has leaves and fruits that are used locally as a purgative. Neither of the single species of the families Akaniaceae or Bretschneideraceae appears to have any economic uses.

Characteristic morphological features. The order Sapindales is overwhelmingly composed of woody plants, mostly trees, large shrubs, or woody climbers. The latter are particularly common in the Sapindaceae (*Paullinia, Serjania,* and *Urvillea*) and Anacardiaceae (*Toxicodendron*). Small subshrubs and herbs are rare, although they are common in the family Zygophyllaceae. Many beautiful forest trees belong to this order. The largest trees are in the family Sapindaceae; they include the Ceylon oak (to 60 metres) in Myanmar, *Pometia pinnata* (to 50 metres) in Malaysia, and *Tristiropsis canarioides* (to 45 metres) in New Guinea. Several species of the Anacardiaceae, such as the Old World tropical *Campnosperma auriculata, Mangifera lagenifera,* and *Buchanania lucida,* may reach heights of 33 metres. In North America, the sugar maple may grow to 35 metres high. At the other extreme are a few genera of the Zygophyllaceae (*Kallstroemia, Tribulopis,* and *Tribulus*) with species that are prostrate annual herbs.

Most species of Sapindales have pinnately compound leaves (with the leaflets of each compound leaf arranged along both sides of a central axis). They are rarely palmately compound (the leaflets radiating from the petiole apex) or simple. Leaves are generally alternately arranged along a stem and are only rarely opposite or whorled. An interesting form of leaf is found in *Citrus,* where the simple blade is separated from the petiole by a joint. Because this type of leaf occurs in other genera of the Rutaceae with compound leaves, it is believed that this is reduced from a compound form. Reduction goes still further in *Citrus,* in which the first one or two leaves of an axillary bud (a bud located in an axil, or upper angle, between a stem and a branch or leaf) are reduced to spines. Leaves of the Asian genus *Chisocheton* (Meliaceae) show indeterminate or continuous growth. Stipules are usually absent from the leaves of members of the Sapindales, but the Melianthaceae, Staphyleaceae, and Zygophyllaceae rarely lack them.

Predominance of insect pollination among the Sapindales

The flowers may be single in the axils of the leaves, or they may be arranged in racemes (spikelike clusters that bloom from the base upward), cymose spikes (clusters blooming from the top downward), or panicles (many-branched clusters). Flowers of most Sapindales appear to be pollinated by insects. The coloured petals and sometimes stamens of many of these flowers make them conspicuous; fragrance makes others attractive to insects. The disc at the base of the pistil often secretes an abundance of nectar attractive to insects as well. In some species, cross-pollination is favoured by protandry (maturation of the stamens before the stigma of the same flower is receptive to pollen) or protogyny (the stigma matures first). In *Kallstroemia* (Zygophyllaceae) the petals and stamens spread horizontally from the pistil when the flower opens in the morning. The stigma is receptive to pollen carried in by insects (bees, wasps, butterflies, and flies) visiting the open flower for its nectar. By early afternoon the flowers begin to close, and the petals and stamens bend back upward, causing appression of the stamens, and what pollen they may still contain is placed onto the stigma, effecting self-pollination. This is a remarkable instance in which seed formation is ensured by self-pollination if necessary, but cross-pollination is first attempted. This is an important adaptation in a genus of plants growing in arid areas where their pollinators might not be present or abundant.

In a number of families and genera throughout the order, there is a strong tendency toward obligate cross-pollination through the progressive development away from the typical floral bisexuality, in which both sexes are present and functional in the same flower. This culminates in dioecism, a condition where male and female flowers in the species are borne on separate plants. Dioecism has evolved independently in most families. Many members of the order have bisexual and unisexual flowers on the same plant (polygamous). In some inflorescences, for example, the terminal flower is bisexual, while the others are all male or female. This combines the advantages of maximum fertility through inbreeding with increased variability through outcrossing. Many structurally bisexual flowers, as in many maples for example, are functionally unisexual, as either the stamens do not produce fertile pollen, the stigmas are not receptive, or the pistils do not contain ovules. Some species (*e.g., Acer platanoides,* Norway maple; *A. saccharinum,* silver maple; and *A. spicatum,* mountain maple) are self-sterile and must be outcrossed. Most unisexual flowers in the order have become that way after either the pistil or the stamens fail to mature, as the flowers often retain the rudimentary remains of the nonfunctional organ. Thus, although many species of the Sapindales have insured cross-pollination and outbreeding, most have not achieved complete anatomical dioecism.

Floral structure

Flowers in the Sapindales are either radially or bilaterally symmetrical and are typically small, although there are a number of exceptions to the latter. Generally, both sepals and petals are present. They are usually free, but in some genera sepals may be fused into a calyx or petals into a corolla (*e.g.,* the tropical American genera of Burseraceae, *Tetragastris* and *Trattinnickia*). Petals may be lacking in some (*e.g., Acer negundo,* box elder).

Stamens are usually double in number of petals, with an outer whorl opposite the sepals and an inner whorl opposite the petals. In some they are equal to the number of petals and alternate with them, while in others there may be three whorls of stamens or there may be a larger number with whorls that are difficult to distinguish. Filaments are usually free, but they may be fused into a tube in most Meliaceae and some Rutaceae. In many Zygophyllaceae, filaments have a basal appendage. Anthers have two locules and open lengthwise. In species with unisexual flowers, staminodes (sterile stamens) are usually present in female flowers. There is almost always a nectar-producing disc between the stamens and the pistil.

The pistil is usually compound, but in a few genera (*e.g., Zanthoxylum,* Rutaceae) there are separate simple pistils in the flower. The ovary is almost always superior and is composed of 1 to 20 carpels. The ovary is usually multilocular, but it may be multilocular at the base and unilocular above in several members of the Meliaceae. It is unilocular in simple pistils. Ovules are typically two per locule, although they may be one or several. Styles are usually united and the same number as the carpels. Functionally male flowers often contain a pistillode (sterile pistil).

The fruit in Sapindales is basically a capsule that splits open between the internal partitions, although it has been modified into a number of other types in most families. For example, in the Rutaceae one finds capsules (*e.g., Ruta,* rue), follicles (*Zanthoxylum,* prickly ash), drupes (*Amyris,* torchwood), berries (*Triphasia,* limeberry), samaras (hop tree), and schizocarps (*Helietta,* barreta). The fruit of *Citrus* is a modified berry with a thick rind called a hesperidium (after the golden apples of the Hesperides). In the myth of the Greek hero Heracles, one of Heracles' 12 Labours was the fetching of the golden apples kept by the Hesperides. These mythical apples may well have been based upon oranges, which were not grown in the West in ancient times, but which the Greeks may have been aware of owing to their trade with the East.

When mature, the seeds of Sapindales may be with or without endosperm, the starchy nutrient tissue that supplies energy for the developing embryo. There are commonly one or two seeds per locule. Some genera of Rutaceae (*e.g., Citrus* and *Zanthoxylum*) and Anacardiaceae (*Mangifera*) contain many embryos in a single seed; these embryos may come from different parts of the ovule besides the fertilized egg. (The formation of an embryo from tissue other than the fertilized egg is called apomixis.) The seeds of Meliaceae are often winged and dispersed by wind. In many Sapindaceae and Burseraceae, the seed is surrounded by a colourful fleshy aril that is attractive to birds, which disperse these seeds. Most families have fleshy fruits attractive to mammals and birds and hard seeds that will pass through their alimentary canals without harm.

Evolution. The evolutionary relationships among the families placed in the Sapindales, and between them and other orders, are still somewhat obscure. No two authors of contemporary systems of classification seem to be able to agree on the circumscription of the order and its close relatives. Many of the tropical genera, in particular, are still poorly known. In spite of this, the families have many morphological and anatomical features in common. New data from such research areas as comparative biochemistry, palynology, paleobotany, embryology, and the natural history of sexuality, pollination, and seed dispersal are helping to establish their relationships.

Disagreement in classification

The Sapindales consists of basically two groups of related families that have been placed together historically because of their morphological resemblances. One group is clustered around the Sapindaceae (Staphyleaceae, Melianthaceae, Bretschneideraceae, Akaniaceae, Hippocastanaceae, and Aceraceae), the other around the Rutaceae (Burseraceae, Anacardiaceae, Julianiaceae, Simaroubaceae, Cneoraceae, Meliaceae, and Zygophyllaceae).

The Staphyleaceae is the most primitive family in the Sapindales, with its unspecialized wood structure, mostly stipulate leaves, sometimes unfused carpels, usually several ovules per ovary locule, and well-developed endosperm. These are very primitive features for the Sapindales. Evidence from leaf and stem anatomy and flower morphology and anatomy indicate that the Staphyleaceae also shows close relationships with the Cunoniaceae (the cunonia family) and Saxifragaceae (the saxifrage family) of the order Rosales. Thus, the ancestory of the Sapindales may lie close to these families. In the Sapindales, the Staphyleaceae is most closely related to the Sapindaceae complex of families.

Morphologically, anatomically, and chemically, the Melianthaceae, Bretschneideraceae, Akaniaceae, Sapindaceae, Hippocastanaceae, and Aceraceae form a close-knit group of families. Indeed, there is evidence that the Aceraceae and Hippocastanaceae are so similar to the Sapindaceae that they should not be recognized as separate families but be placed in it. *Akania* and *Bretschneidera* also are placed by some in the Sapindaceae.

Morphologically and anatomically, the remaining families form another more or less cohesive complex. Chemically, however, they appear to form two groups, with the Burseraceae, Anacardiaceae, Julianiaceae (often put in the Anacardiaceae), and perhaps Zygophyllaceae in one group, and the Simaroubaceae, Cneoraceae, Meliaceae, and Rutaceae in another. In spite of this, the overall evidence indicates that the Zygophyllaceae is most closely related to the Rutaceae. The Zygophyllaceae has a number of herbaceous species and because of this and other derived characteristics, it is clearly the most advanced family of the Sapindales. (D.M.Po.)

Subclass Asteridae

GENERAL FEATURES

The subclass Asteridae, one of the six subclasses in the class Magnoliopsida (dicotyledons), consists of 11 orders,

49 families, and nearly 60,000 species. About one-third of the species of Asteridae belong to the family Asteraceae (of the order Asterales), which is the largest family of dicotyledons and one of the two largest families of flowering plants.

Diversity of structure. The Asteridae are the best characterized and defined subclass of Magnoliopsida. In the vast majority of its members, the flower petals are joined together toward the base and the tips remain separate (sympetalous). Almost invariably, the stamens (male, or pollen-producing, organs) number as many as the corolla lobes, with the stamens alternating with the lobes, or the stamens may number fewer than the corolla lobes. More than 99 percent of the species of Asteridae meet these criteria, and probably not more than 1 percent of the species that have this combination of characters do not belong to the Asteridae. In most of the Asteridae, the ovule tissue (the nucellus) is only one cell thick and is surrounded by one large integument (the forerunner of the seed coat), an otherwise uncommon combination of characteristics; there are, however, more exceptions in these characteristics.

Aside from their consistent floral features, the Asteridae are a highly diversified group of plants. They include trees, shrubs, herbs, and vines, and they grow in a wide range of habitats.

Chemical features

The Asteridae frequently have iridoid compounds but usually are without ellagic acid and proanthocyanins. Betalains, mustard oils, and benzylisoquinoline alkaloids are apparently absent. The absence of betalains and benzylisoquinoline alkaloids tends to distinguish the Asteridae from Caryophyllidae and Magnoliidae, respectively, and the absence of ellagic acid and proanthocyanins tends to distinguish Asteridae from the subclasses Rosidae, Dilleniidae, and Hamamelidae. Iridoid compounds are not found in Asteraceae and are probably present in only about half of the species of the subclass. Iridoids also develop in some members of Rosidae, Dilleniidae, and Hamamelidae.

It may be theorized that the Asteridae abandoned the traditional chemical deterrents of tannins (including ellagic acid and proanthocyanins), saponins, and cyanide, to which herbivores developed a tolerance, in favour of the iridoid compounds and the chemically related alkaloids, chemical compounds not previously widespread. One may further hypothesize that many herbivores had developed a tolerance to iridoids and alkaloids about the time of the origination of Asteraceae (toward the end of the Oligocene Epoch, 23.7 million years ago), prompting another shift in defensive chemical weaponry.

Evolution. The order Rosales (taken in the broadest sense) in the subclass Rosidae is probably the ancestor of the Asteridae. That is to say, if investigators had the common ancestor of the Asteridae (or its immediate predecessor) at hand, they would probably refer it to the Rosales. Iridoid compounds, a sympetalous corolla, stamens of the same number as petals and alternating with them, a compound ovary with numerous ovules on axile placentas, ovules with a single integument, and ovules with a very thin nucellus are all found among members of the Rosales. These are common features of the Asteridae, or at least of their more archaic members. The nectary disc around the ovary and the simple, stipulate, opposite leaves among the oldest Asteridae are also found in some members of Rosidae. It is the combination of these features in a single species, however, that signals the evolutionary transition from the ancestral Rosales to the early Asteridae. Each of the remaining orders of the subclass Rosidae is already too advanced in one or another respect to serve as a plausible ancestor of the Asteridae.

The Asteridae probably did not develop before the outset of the Tertiary Period (which began about 66 million years ago). The Asteridae came into prominence during the Oligocene Epoch (which began a little more than 36 million years ago).

Results of comparative studies

Ongoing comparative studies on the structure of chloroplast deoxyribonucleic acid (DNA) are beginning to shed some light on relationships among the orders of Asteridae, but by the early 1990s had not yet warranted a comprehensive reconsideration of the phylogeny.

Classification and representative groups. *Gentianales.* The order Gentianales (commonly consisting of the families Loganiaceae, Gentianaceae, Saccifoliaceae, Apocynaceae, and Asclepiadaceae; Retziaceae has been occasionally included in this order) is ancestral to the other orders in the subclass Asteridae. The superior ovary (*i.e.,* attached above the other floral parts), regular corolla, isomerous stamens (*i.e.,* stamens having the same number as the corolla lobes), fairly numerous ovules, and iridoid compounds are all features found among characteristic members of the order and appear to be primitive for the subclass as a whole, as does the absence of a nutritive tissue in the developing ovule that is derived from the integument (integumentary tapetum) in all members except Apocynaceae (the dogbane family). None of the remaining orders of the subclass provides this collection of putatively primitive characteristics. On the other hand, the opposite leaves, internal phloem, and nuclear pattern of endosperm development are not necessarily primitive in the subclass.

Gentianales is found in a wide range of habitats that are also occupied by various other orders. The Gentianales heavily exploit iridoid compounds, cardenolides (cardiotonic glycosides), and certain groups of alkaloids to deter herbivores.

Within the order Gentianales, the Apocynaceae and Asclepiadaceae (milkweed family) form a sequential pair of families marked by a well-developed latex system and the usual production of cardenolides as well as alkaloids. Further, there exists a series of progressive evolutionary changes in the structure of the pistil: the older members of the Apocynaceae have a fairly ordinary kind of ovary with a simple style and stigma; within the family there is a progressive separation of the carpels, beginning at the bottom and leading to a condition in the more advanced members in which the carpels are separate except for the thickened apex of the style.

Floral specialization

The Asclepiadaceae show a further progressive series of floral specialization related to pollination by animals. There is usually an extra set of petallike structures (corona) between the corolla and the stamens. The anthers cohere (or unite) into a sheath that adheres to the thickened style. The pollen grains within cohere, forming a cluster called a pollinium. An acellular, yoke-shaped structure called a translator attaches to the adjacent pollinia of two different, adjacent anthers. The translators become entangled on the legs of visiting insects so that the departing insect carries a pair of pollinia joined by the translator. When the insect visits the next flower, the pollinia may be transferred to the stigmas, which are borne on the stylehead and alternate with the anthers. This complex method of pollination is uncertain in operation and often fails, but great numbers of pollen grains are transferred when it works, resulting in the production of large numbers of seeds.

The association of the monarch butterfly (*Danaus plexippus*) with plants of the genus *Asclepias* (milkweed) illustrates the continuing evolution of adaptations in the battle between plants and predators. Although cardenolides in the latex of the milkweeds are highly poisonous, the monarch caterpillar is able to eat the plant and concentrate the poison in the wings and abdomen of the adult, where it does not interfere with metabolism; in fact, the cardenolides give the caterpillar and butterfly a nauseous taste, causing them to be avoided by birds, which might otherwise eat them. The learning process experienced by individual birds necessarily causes some attrition in the population of caterpillars and butterflies, but the death of a few protects the others. The poisons produced by the milkweed have, in effect, reserved the herbage for a particular kind of predator-parasite, the caterpillar of the monarch butterfly.

As is so often true, this beautiful evolutionary adaptation is less than perfect. Different species of milkweed produce different kinds and amounts of the poisonous cardenolides, conferring greater or lesser protection on the caterpillars and butterflies. Some birds have learned to pluck out the internal organs of the butterflies, avoiding the highly poisonous wings.

The remaining families of the Gentianales, aside from the Apocynaceae and Asclepiadaceae, do not have latex or cardenolides, and the pistil is of more ordinary structure, with the carpels generally fully united except in some cases for the stigmas.

In the Loganiaceae, the stipules are characteristically attached directly to the stem between the leaves or petioles (interpetiolar stipules), rather than being obvious parts of the leaves. The ovary has two or more seed cavities, and the ovules are attached to the central axis of the ovary (axile placentation). They commonly produce iridoid compounds and various sorts of alkaloids, especially tryptophan alkaloids. The family is largely tropical and subtropical. *Gelsemium sempervirens,* the Carolina yellow jessamine, is a familiar cultivated climbing vine in the southern United States. *Strychnos,* a large genus of tropical trees, shrubs, and vines, is especially notable for its poisonous alkaloids. Strychnine is obtained from the seeds of *Strychnos nux-vomica,* a native of South Asia, and some components of curare are obtained from *S. toxifera* and closely allied species.

Source of poisonous alkaloids

The Gentianaceae lack both stipules and alkaloids, but do have iridoid compounds. The placentation is parietal, so that the ovules are attached to the wall of the single-seeded cavity or to the inner walls of partial partitions that extend inward from the outer wall without meeting in the centre. The family is cosmopolitan but is most common in temperate and subtropical regions and in tropical mountains. Various species of the large genus *Gentiana* (gentian) are cultivated as garden ornamentals.

The bizarre family Saccifoliaceae, with only a single genus and species, *Saccifolium bandeirae,* is confined to the summit of an isolated Guyana mountain in southern Venezuela. The plants are low shrubs, with flowers much like the Gentianaceae except that the ovary has two seed cavities and axile placentation. Unlike nearly all the other members of the Gentianales, *Saccifolium* has alternate leaves. The leaves are small and are crowded toward the ends of the twigs. The margins of the leaf closest to the stem are curved downward; farther away from the stem these margins join, so that the end of the leaf is hollow with an opening toward the base on the lower side. The functional significance of this structure is not known.

Lamiales. The order Lamiales consists of three fairly large families, the Boraginaceae, Verbenaceae, and Lamiaceae, in addition to one very small family, the Lennoaceae. The Lennoaceae are fleshy parasites that invade roots. They have small, scalelike leaves and are without chlorophyll. Members have a relatively large number of carpels (from 6 to 14); like the other members of the order, however, they have only 2 ovules in each carpel, with a partition between the 2 ovules so that the ovary has twice as many seed cavities as carpels. The family is confined to the New World, from the southwestern United States to Colombia and Venezuela.

Aside from the Lennoaceae, members of the Lamiales are green plants with a superior ovary composed of a small number of carpels (typically two), with each carpel forming two small compartments that contain a single ovule each. The fruit very often consists of single-seeded, half-carpellary nutlets.

Within the order Lamiales, the families Verbenaceae and Lamiaceae (also called Labiatae) are closely related, both with opposite leaves. The flowers generally have an irregular corolla (*i.e.,* it is not radially symmetrical) and only two or four stamens. The Lamiaceae (mint family) is generally thought to have begun with the Verbenaceae.

In the Verbenaceae, the style is terminal on the ovary, or nearly so, and the ovary is unlobed or only shallowly lobed at the top. The plants are seldom aromatic, and the fruit is not as consistently specialized as that found in the Lamiaceae. There is considerable variation in the structure of the ovary and fruit of the Verbenaceae (within the general confines of the order Lamiales), and some authorities have split off a number of smaller separate families. Inclusion of these groups in the Verbenaceae (as here) or their exclusion as satellite families is purely arbitrary. Only a few members of the Verbenaceae are economically significant. Teak (*Tectona grandis*), originally from India and Myanmar (Burma), is well known for its hard, heavy, durable wood. A number of species of *Verbena* (vervain) are cultivated ornamentals.

Teak

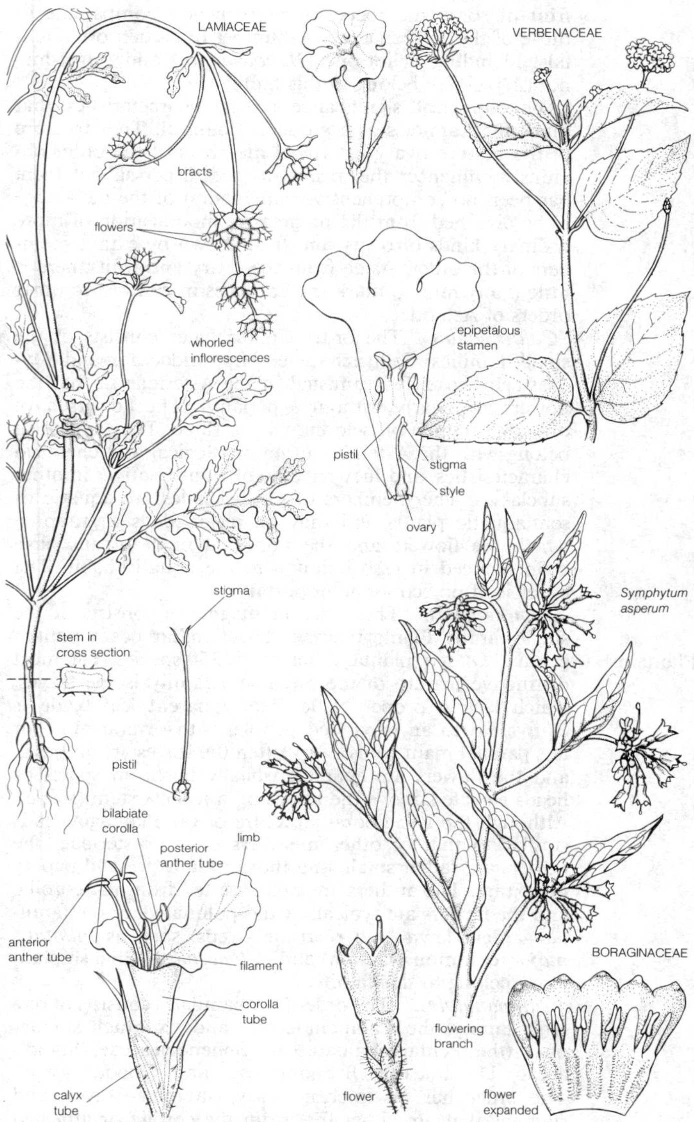

Representative members of the order Lamiales.

From (Lamiaceae, Verbenaceae) A. Engler and K. Prantl, *Die Naturlichen Pflanzenfamilien,* 2nd ed., vol. 19c (1931), Duncker & Humblot; (Boraginaceae) L.H. Bailey, *Manual of Cultivated Plants,* rev. ed. (1969), reprinted with permission of The Macmillan Pub. Co.

Members of the Lamiaceae commonly have a style that originates between the deep lobes of the ovary (gynobasic style), uniting the four otherwise essentially distinct lobes of the ovary. The fruit typically consists of four half-carpellary nutlets. In some genera that mark a transition from Lamiaceae toward the Verbenaceae, only the top of the ovary is indented (one-third of its length or more) to form four lobes, and the style is seated between the lobes. The four parts of the ovary separate at maturity to form nutlets just as in the other members of the family. Members of the mint family are characteristically aromatic, and many of them are cultivated for their ethereal oils. Among these are peppermint, spearmint, and pennyroyal (all species of *Mentha*); lavender (*Lavandula*); horehound (*Marrubium vulgare*); thyme (*Thymus vulgaris*); sage (*Salvia officinalis*); and catnip (*Nepeta cataria*). Some members of the mint family, including species of *Salvia* and *Coleus,* are cultivated ornamentals.

The Boraginaceae stand somewhat apart from the Verbenaceae-Lamiaceae pair. They have alternate leaves and usually regular flowers that have five equal corolla lobes and five stamens. The Boraginaceae also have their own set of secondary metabolites (chemical compounds used as defense), commonly including pyrrolizidine alkaloids, and (in the roots) a red naphthaquinone called alkannin. Most of them have a gynobasic style and a fruit of four separating nutlets, as in the Lamiaceae, but the ovary and fruit of some members are more nearly comparable to those of the Verbenaceae. A number of garden ornamentals, including heliotrope (*Heliotropium*) and forget-me-not (*Myosotis*), belong to this family.

The biological significance of the characteristics that mark the Lamiales as a group is doubtful. The structure of the mature ovary in typical members of the order obviously influences the means of seed dispersal, but there has been no comprehensive explanation of the advantage to be obtained from the progressive modification of more ordinary kinds of ovary and fruit shown by extant members of the order. Aside from the ovary and fruit, there is little if anything to mark the Lamiales in contrast to other orders of Asteridae.

Callitrichales. The order Callitrichales consists of the small families Callitrichaceae, Hippuridaceae, and Hydrostachyaceae. It is unusual in the Asteridae in that the flowers are nearly without a perianth. The flowers have only one stamen or, seldom, two or three. They appear to belong with the Asteridae in embryological and chemical characteristics, and they have no obvious relatives in other subclasses. The members of Callitrichales are aquatic or semiaquatic plants and may be regarded as a group in which the flowers and the nonfloral plant organs have been reduced in association with the aquatic habit. The order is of no economic importance.

Plantaginales. The order Plantaginales consists of the single family Plantaginaceae. The familiar cosmopolitan genus *Plantago* (plantain) has about 250 species. The most distinctive feature of the order and family is the leaves, which lack a proper blade. The apparent leaf blade is equivalent to an expanded petiole, with several more or less parallel main veins. Very often the leaves are all basal, and the flowers are characteristically borne in spikes or heads elevated above the leaves on a leafless stem (scape). Although the basic floral structure of the Plantaginales is similar to that of other members of the Asteridae, the flowers are rather small, and the corolla is dry and papery in texture. The anthers are well exserted from the corolla, and the flowers are typically wind-pollinated. Some familiar garden, lawn, and roadside weeds, such as *Plantago major* (common plantain) and *P. lanceolata* (English plantain), belong to this family.

Plantains

Campanulales. The order Campanulales consists of one large family, the Campanulaceae, and six much smaller ones (the Pentaphragmataceae, Sphenocleaceae, Stylidiaceae, Donatiaceae, Brunoniaceae, and Goodeniaceae). The order has an inferior ovary, alternate leaves, and stamens that are either free from the corolla or attached at the base of the corolla tube. Inulin is the stored form of carbohydrates. Most of them (including not only the Campanulaceae but also the next largest family, the Goodeniaceae) have a characteristic type of pollen-presentation mechanism comparable to that of the Asterales. There are differences in detail, but in general the pollen is discharged into the anther tube and is pushed out as the style grows. The Campanulales have often figured in speculation regarding the ancestry of the Asterales. A number of species of *Campanula* (bellflower) and *Lobelia* (lobelia) are familiar garden ornamentals, but otherwise the order is not of much economic importance.

Rubiales. The order Rubiales consists of the large family Rubiaceae and the small, highly modified family Theligonaceae. The Rubiaceae are Asteridae with opposite leaves and interpetiolar stipules (stipules borne at the nodes on the stem between the leaves), or with whorled leaves and no stipules. Whorled leaves, as in the genus *Galium,* reflect the transformation of the interpetiolar stipules into ordinary leaves. Once the pattern of four leaves in a whorl is established, the number may be increased by changes in the growth pattern of the apical meristem of the shoot. Stipules of the Rubiaceae commonly have colleters (stout, short, glandular hairs) on the inner surface that help to protect the developing shoot tip from insects. The flowers of the Rubiaceae have an ovary borne below the other flower parts and the stamens are attached to the corolla tube and alternate with the lobes. The flower is typically regular (radially symmetrical), as in the Gentianales.

The most economically important genera in the Rubiaceae are *Cinchona* and *Coffea.* Bark of several species of *Cinchona* provides the closely related alkaloids quinine and quinidine, used to treat malaria and to regulate heart rhythm, respectively. Coffee is derived from the dried fruits of several species of *Coffea,* notably *C. arabica. Rubia tinctorum* (madder) is the traditional source of a red dye, alizarin, now prepared synthetically.

Coffee plant

The family appears to have dispersed widely after the close of the Eocene (*i.e.,* within the past 35 million years), although evidence of the family is thought to exist from the Eocene Epoch (about 57.8 to 36.6 million years ago).

The family Rubiaceae forms a connecting link between the orders Gentianales and Dipsacales and would be an aberrant element in either order. The family Loganiaceae (Gentianales) appears to be near the ancestry of the Rubiaceae, and indeed there are two genera, *Gaertnera* and *Pagamea,* that seem to connect the two families. These genera have an ovary borne above the other floral parts, as in the Loganiaceae, but their probable closest relatives have an inferior ovary and belong to the Rubiaceae.

Drawing by M. Moran

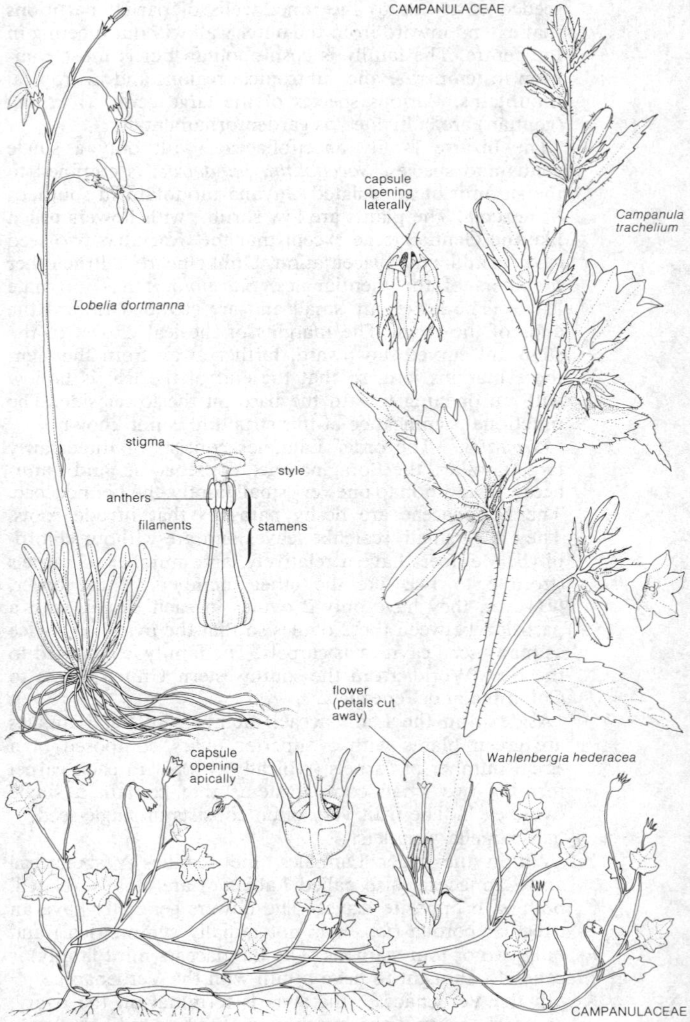

Representative plants and floral structures of the largest family in the order Campanulales.

Dipsacales. The order Dipsacales consists of four families (the Caprifoliaceae, Valerianaceae, Dipsacaceae, and Adoxaceae) and are Asteridae in having an inferior (or partly inferior) ovary and opposite or whorled leaves mostly without stipules and, in any case, without colleters. The Dipsacales show strong tendencies toward the development of an irregular corolla and toward having fewer stamens than corolla lobes. Both of these features are phyletically advanced as compared with the related order Rubiales.

Some familiar genera of the Dipsacales are *Lonicera*

(honeysuckle), *Sambucus* (elder), *Symphoricarpos* (snowberry and coralberry), *Viburnum* (viburnum), and *Weigela* in the Caprifoliaceae; and *Dipsacus* (teasel) in the Dipsacaceae. Extracts or infusions of *Valeriana*, or valerian (especially the European species, *V. officinalis*) have long been used as a tonic in folk medicine and to some extent in more formal medicine but have not been much favoured in recent years in the United States.

On the basis of pollen and seeds, it appears that the Caprifoliaceae can be traced back to the Middle Eocene, about 45 million years ago. Dipsacaceous pollen also dates from this time.

The family Calyceraceae

Calycerales. The order Calycerales, with only the small family Calyceraceae (about 60 species), is of interest because of its role in speculation concerning the ancestry and relationships of the family Asteraceae. The family Calyceraceae has sometimes been included in the Campanulales or in the Dipsacales, but it does not fit well in either.

The solitary, apical, pendulous ovule in the ovary of the Calyceraceae is in full harmony with the Dipsacales but would be unique in the Campanulales. The Calyceraceae are also more nearly in harmony with the Dipsacales than the Campanulales in having the filaments attached near the summit of the corolla tube and in a series of embryological details. On the other hand, the Calyceraceae resemble the Campanulales, and differ from the Dipsacales, in their alternate leaves, in producing the storage carbohydrate inulin (found also in the Asteraceae), and in their pollen-presentation mechanism (found also in the Asteraceae and some Rubiaceae).

The flowering heads are centripetal (*i.e.,* they bloom from the outside inward or from the base upward) and are subtended by whorls of bracts (involucrate) in the Calyceraceae, and this strongly suggests the Asteraceae, as does the pollen-presentation mechanism described for that family. Furthermore, the pollen is like that of many Asteraceae in the structure and ornamentation of the wall. Characters that oppose a close relation of the Calyceraceae to the Asteraceae are the terminal, pendulous (rather than basal and erect) ovule of the former group, the production of iridoid compounds in the Calyceraceae, and the absence of polyacetylenes and sesquiterpene lactones (characteristic of the Asteraceae). The weight of the evidence is considered to suggest that the similarities between the Calyceraceae and Asteraceae more nearly reflect evolutionary parallelism than joint inheritance from a common ancestry.

REPRESENTATIVE GROUPS

Asterales. The order Asterales consists of a single large family of flowering plants called the Asteraceae, also known as Compositae. The number of species is not accurately known but is estimated to be about 20,000. The only other family with a comparable number of species is the orchid family, Orchidaceae (Liliidae). Asterales is the principal order for the subclass Asteridae. The order includes many familiar garden ornamentals, such as asters, chrysanthemums, dahlias, daisies, marigolds, sunflowers, and zinnias. Some other members of the group, such as dandelions, ragweeds, and thistles, are familiar weeds. Lettuce and safflower are examples of economically important crop plants of the order.

Unique flowers a distinguishing characteristic

General features. The most obvious and outstanding general feature of the Asterales is that the flowers are characteristically grouped into compact inflorescences (heads) that superficially resemble individual flowers. The name Compositae refers to this feature; what appears to be a distinct flower is actually a composite flower cluster. Each such head is ordinarily subtended by an involucre of small modified leaves (bracts), usually green, which bear the same relation to the flower head that the green sepals do to a flower in other families. Furthermore, in more than half the members of the order, the flowers in the outermost row or rows of the head have a modified, mainly flat and elongate corolla that more or less resembles an individual petal of most other flowers. The "petals" of a daisy or sunflower are actually these outermost flowers of the head. Various members of the order may produce anywhere from one to more than several hundred of these composite-flowered heads, each with several to many flowers; rarely does a head have only a single flower.

Several families or individual genera of angiosperms have the flowers grouped in heads more or less resembling those of the Asterales, but they lack the other features that characterize the order, as described below, and most of them especially lack the complex pollen-presentation mechanism of the Asterales.

Members of the Asterales are diverse in habit and habitat. They are most characteristically herbs of sunny places in temperate to subtropical regions, but they are not all so restricted. Not many are large trees, and only a few are adapted to life in undisturbed moist tropical forests, but otherwise they are ubiquitous. They are trees, shrubs, herbs, or woody or herbaceous vines. The leaves are simple or occasionally compound, and their arrangement along the stem may be opposite, alternate, or, less commonly, whorled; not infrequently they are opposite toward the base of the stem and alternate above.

Distribution. Members of the Asterales occur from the Arctic to the Antarctic and from above the mountain timberline to the ocean shores. In addition to the more ordinary habitats, some of them are adapted to growth in sand dunes; others to cliff crevices; others to talus slopes; others to seleniferous, gypsiferous, or alkaline soils; and others to fields or disturbed sites around human habitations. Only a few species are aquatic.

Centres of diversity

In most temperate regions more than 10 percent of the species of angiosperms belong to the Asterales. In tropical regions the percentage is smaller but still significant. The greatest centres of diversity in the order are the dry highlands of Mexico, where the primitive Heliantheae is especially well represented, and the Mediterranean–Middle East region.

Economic and ecological importance. The greatest economic importance of the Asterales order lies in the use of many of its members as garden ornamentals. Species and garden hybrids of *Aster* (Michaelmas daisy), *Bellis* (English daisy), *Callistephus* (China aster), *Chrysanthemum* (chrysanthemum), *Cosmos* (cosmos), *Dahlia* (dahlia), *Helianthus* (sunflower), *Rudbeckia* (coneflower, black-eyed Susan), *Tagetes* (marigold), and *Zinnia* (zinnia) are well-known garden favourites. *Achillea* (yarrow), *Ageratum* (ageratum), *Anaphalis* (pearly everlasting), *Anthemis* (golden marguerite), *Artemisia* (wormwood), *Calendula, Centaurea, Echinops* (globe thistle), *Erigeron, Eupatorium, Gaillardia* (blanketflower), *Helichrysum* (strawflower, everlasting), *Liatris* (button snakeroot), *Ratibida* (one of several genera with the common name of coneflower), *Santolina* (lavender cotton), and *Stokesia* (Stokes' aster) are also familiar in gardens. The florists' cineraria, a popular wintertime potted flower, is *Senecio cruentus,* originally from the Canary Islands.

The most important food plant in the Asterales is lettuce, *Lactuca sativa,* a European cultigen. Second in importance is the common sunflower, *Helianthus annuus,* a native of the United States. Sunflower seeds are excellent poultry food, and a light-golden oil made from them is used as a salad oil and in cooking as well as in the manufacture of margarine, soap, paint, and varnish. Oil cake is fed to livestock, and the whole plant is used as ensilage. Flowers of the safflower, *Carthamus tinctorius,* are the source of red and yellow dyes, and the seeds produce an edible oil that is also used in soap, paint, and varnish. Several other members of the order, including the artichoke (*Cynara scolymus*) and the Jerusalem artichoke (*Helianthus tuberosus*), are of minor importance as food plants.

Chemical compounds derived from Asterales

Pyrethrum, an insecticide that does not produce the environmental problems associated with many synthetic products, is obtained from the flowers of several species of chrysanthemum, particularly *Chrysanthemum cinerariaefolium.* Extracts from several species of wormwood, notably *Artemisia cina* from the Middle East, have been much used to expel intestinal worms, the source of its common name. *Artemisia absinthium* is the source of a poisonous oil used to give the liqueur absinthe its distinctive character. A sesquiterpene extracted from *A. annua* (a Eurasian weed) is increasingly used in the treatment of quinine-resistant malaria.

The ragweeds (*Ambrosia*), dandelions (*Taraxacum*), and thistles (*Carduus, Cirsium,* and *Onopordum*) are the most troublesome weeds in the Asterales order. *Ambrosia artemisiifolia* (common ragweed) and *Ambrosia trifida* (giant ragweed) are two of the most significant plant species, causing the allergic reaction known as hay fever.

Characteristic morphological features. The flower petals of the Asterales are joined together by their margins, forming a tubular or mainly strap-shaped corolla (a sympetalous corolla) that often has apical teeth representing the petal tips. The other floral parts are attached to the top of the ovary (epigynous) rather than beneath it. These two features occur individually in various other groups of flowering plants, but their occurrence in combination is much more limited.

Drawing by M. Pahl

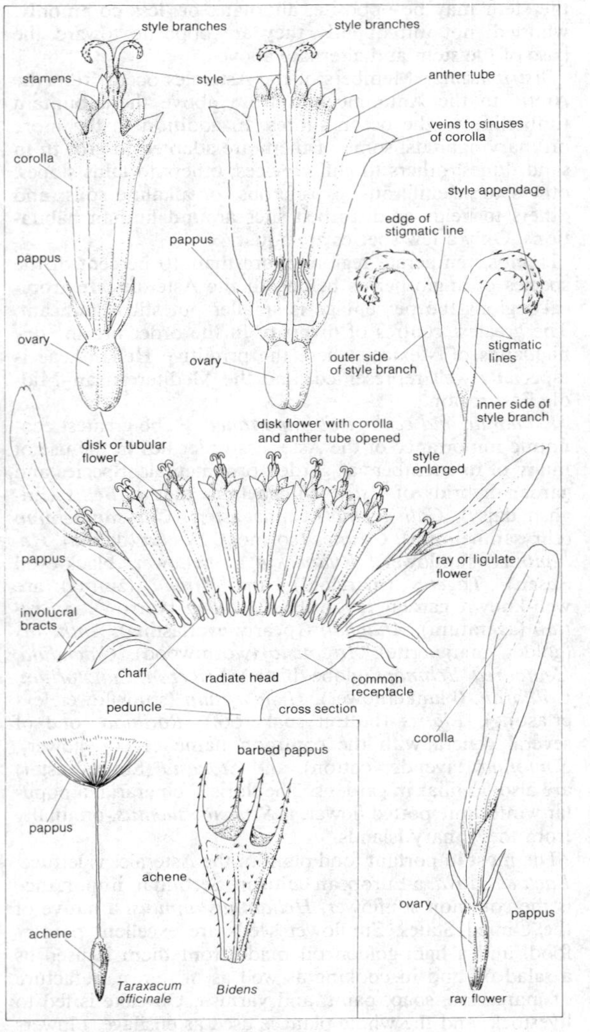

Floral structures of the Asterales.

The calyx (sepals) of the Asterales is so highly modified, in contrast to that of other orders, that it is given a different name, the pappus. The pappus consists of one to usually several or many dry scales, awns (small pointed processes), or capillary (hairlike) bristles; in some, the scales may be joined by their margins to form a crownlike ring at the summit of the ovary. In only a few genera (*e.g., Marshallia*) of the archaic tribe Heliantheae does the calyx consist of five regularly placed scales that are obviously homologous with sepals. The pappus is often completely wanting. When the pappus consists of numerous capillary bristles, as in the common dandelion (*Taraxacum officinale*), it facilitates distribution of the achenes (seedlike fruits) by the wind. In some other genera, such as *Bidens* (beggarticks), the pappus awns are barbed, permitting them to stick in fur or clothing, and some achenes are thus transported by animals. In many other genera, especially those with the pappus of scales or a crown, the function of the pappus is obscure.

The pistil (female structure) is composed of two carpels, united to form a compound ovary with a terminal style. There is usually a nectar-producing region (nectary) in the form of a minute ring surrounding the style atop the ovary. The ovary has only one locule (seed cavity), with a single ovule arising from the base. The fact that the ovule is basal is the best single feature distinguishing the Asterales from the related order Calycerales, which also has involucrate heads with a similar pollen-presentation mechanism but has the ovule pendulous from the top of the ovary.

As in most flowering plants, the ovule is curved back on itself so that the apical opening (micropyle) is alongside the stalk (funiculus), a condition known as anatropy. As in other members of the subclass Asteridae, the ovule has a single, rather thick outer covering layer (integument), the forerunner of the seed coat, rather than the double integument found in so many other orders. The seed has virtually no endosperm; its reserve food is stored largely in the two cotyledons (seed leaves) of the embryo.

The pollen-presentation mechanism of the Asterales is especially characteristic, being shared only by the orders Campanulales and Calycerales and some genera of the family Rubiaceae (Rubiales). The stamens are generally joined by their anthers to form a tube; the anthers open toward the centre by lengthwise slits, releasing the pollen into the tube. The style grows up through the tube, pushing the pollen out ahead of it. The style usually has two branches that separate after it has grown up through the anther tube. Pollination

The pollen-receiving surfaces (stigmas) are usually arranged in lines along the inner margins of these branches, well back from the sterile tips (style appendages), which are the structures that push out the pollen. The stigmatic lines later become exposed to the air, when the style branches spread apart.

Pollination is effected by diverse agents, most commonly various sorts of insects. The individual flowers of most species are relatively small, and the nectar within the corolla tube is thus readily available to most insect visitors; no long tongue is needed to reach it. The pollen itself is freely exposed on the surface of the head, and a single head is likely to be visited by several kinds of insects. A considerable minority of the members of the order are wind-pollinated; these generally have small and inconspicuous flower heads.

Some species are pollinated by both wind and insects. *Solidago speciosa,* one of the common goldenrods of the eastern United States, for example, produces a considerable amount of airborne pollen in addition to attracting insect visitors. The goldenrods, like the ragweeds, generally flower in late summer and fall. Because they are common and conspicuous when the ragweeds release pollen into the wind, they have often been blamed for the allergies that are actually caused primarily by the ragweed.

A relatively few species are regularly self-pollinated; the genus *Psilocarphus* is an example of this method. Bird pollination is also uncommon, but the tropical American genus *Mutisia* is bird-pollinated.

Various genera and individual species of the order are known to be reproduced by apomixis (the setting of seed without fertilization), either completely or in addition to normal sexual means. The genus *Antennaria* (pussytoes), well known in the Northern Hemisphere, is dioecious, and some of the species are represented in large parts of their range only by pistillate (female) plants. In this genus, normal sexual reproduction yields equal numbers of staminate and pistillate plants, but apomictic reproduction yields only pistillate plants. Among the members of the Asterales order, as in other orders, apomixis is often associated with polyploidy (the presence of three or more complete sets of chromosomes in every cell) and a past history of hybridization.

The fruit of the Asterales is an achene; *i.e.,* it is dry, contains only one seed, and does not open at maturity. The apparent seeds of the sunflower, for example, are actually achenes. The hull is the achenial wall, and the proper seed

Seed dispersal

coat surrounding the embryo is thin and insignificant. In speaking of seed dispersal of the Asterales, it should be realized that it is actually the achenes, each containing a seed, that are dispersed.

The seeds of many Asterales species are distributed by wind, having fluffy or parachute-like structures (mainly the pappus) that provide buoyancy. In others, such as *Coreopsis* (tickseed), the achene is thin and flat, and the surface area is increased by the presence of an even thinner expanded margin (wing). Some have barbed structures or are provided with hooks or spines, as in cocklebur (*Xanthium strumarium*) or burdock (*Arctium*), engaging humans or animals as means of transport. In cocklebur and burdock, the protective bracts surrounding the developing head (involucre) are provided with hooks, and the whole head is distributed intact. The hooked heads of burdock are said to have inspired the invention of Velcro, a modern fabric fastener utilizing tiny hooks attaching to a fuzzy base.

Other means of seed dispersal are less common. The achenes of species that grow in wet places may be carried in mud on the feet of migrating waterfowl; those of some streamside species are buoyant, achieving dispersal by floating until they become waterlogged. In *Centaurea* and some related genera, the achenes are attractive to ants, which carry them about and feed upon special parts of the wall. The achenes of some field weeds have been widely distributed by becoming mixed with the seeds of cultivated crops. Many other members of the order have no obvious means of seed dispersal.

The secondary inflorescence of the Asterales is typically cymose (determinate). The terminal head on the main axis blooms first, followed by the terminal heads of the main branches. After that, the sequence is less clear, not infrequently being mixed, with both cymose and racemose (indeterminate) components. Only rarely, and then clearly as a derived condition, is the secondary inflorescence racemose throughout, with the lowest heads blooming first and the terminal ones last.

The sequence of flowering within the individual heads, on the other hand, is always racemose (indeterminate, centripetal). The outer flowers bloom first, and there is a progressive spiral of flowering thence to the centre of the head. The head is in essence a compact shoot, with spiral (alternate-leaved) phyllotaxy. The involucral bracts are more or less modified leaves, and very often they are green and leafy in texture. Sometimes the flowers in the outermost row of the head are borne in the axils (angles) of involucral bracts, sometimes not.

In many members of the order, especially the archaic tribe Heliantheae, the common receptacle (the short stem tip, on which all the flowers of the head are borne) is also provided with bracts, to which the individual flowers of the head are axillary. The receptacle is said to be chaffy when these bracts are present and naked (or sometimes bristly) when they are not. Sometimes the receptacle is chaffy only toward the margin or only toward the centre. In some genera (notably of the tribe Cynareae) the receptacle is bristly—*i.e.,* it is set with bristles that are difficult to interpret in terms of bracts, although that may be their evolutionary origin.

Individual heads of most members of the Asterales order are said to be ligulate, radiate, discoid, or disciform, according to the kinds of flowers they contain. The simplest type is the discoid head, with all the flowers having a regular, tubular corolla, the generally four or five apical teeth representing the tips of the petals. This kind of flower is called a disk flower. Ordinarily the flowers in a discoid head are all perfect (bisexual) and fertile. Thistles and ageratums are examples of Asterales species with discoid heads.

The radiate head has disk flowers in the centre, surrounded by one or more marginal rows of another kind of flower, the ray flower. The corolla of ray flowers is very irregular. It is tubular at the base but prolonged on the outer side into a generally flat projection, the ray, or ligule. These rays are the petallike parts, in a comparison of the flower head to an ordinary flower. The ray in radiate heads represents only three lobes of the corolla;

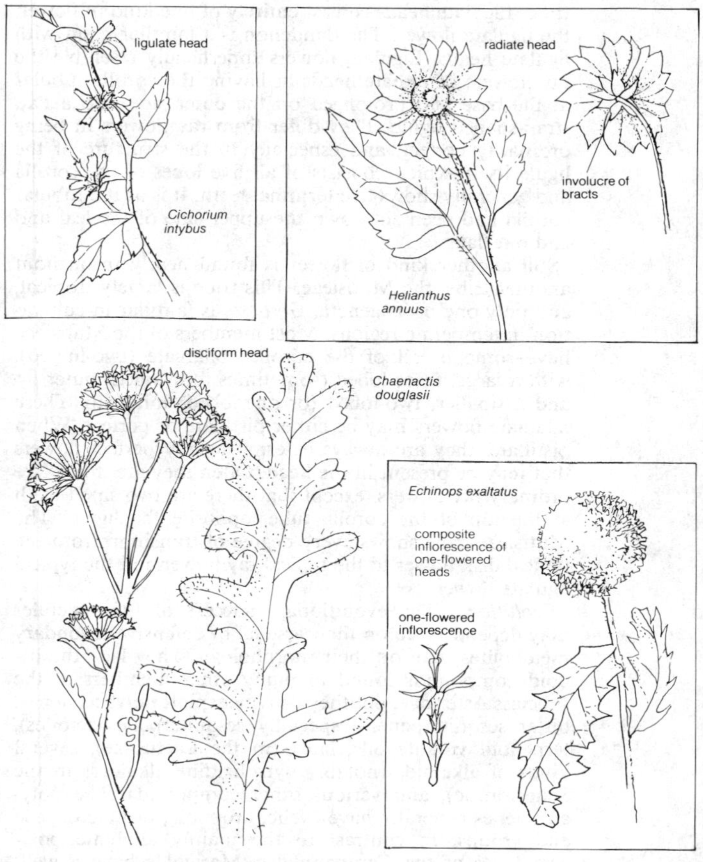

Inflorescence types in the order Asterales.

Drawing by R. Findahl based on (*Cichorium, Helianthus* radiate head, *Echinops*) G.H.M. Lawrence, *Taxonomy of Vascular Plants* (1951), reprinted with permission of The Macmillan Pub. Co.; (*Helianthus* involucre of brachts) J. Craighead, F. Craighead, Jr., and R. Davis, *A Field Guide to Rocky Mountain Wildflowers* (1963), reprinted by permission of Houghton Mifflin Co.

often there are two or three minute apical teeth. The other two corolla teeth (those toward the centre of the head) are much reduced or, often, wanting. Ray flowers in radiate heads are never perfect. Instead, they are pistillate (female) or neutral (with a vestigial, nonfunctional ovary and no style). Disk flowers in a radiate head are usually perfect, but sometimes they are functionally staminate, with a normal pollen-presentation mechanism but without a functional ovary.

"Double-flowered" plants

Occasional mutant forms of species that normally have radiate heads have most or all of the disk flowers more or less transformed into ray flowers, with only a few (or no) normal disk flowers in the centre. These "double-flowered" forms do not long survive competition in nature, but they are valued and perpetuated horticulturally because of their more showy flower heads. The "daisy-flowered" chrysanthemums, with only a single marginal row of ray flowers, have the normal type of radiate head, but the more commonly cultivated kinds of mums are double-flowered. The garden dahlia is another member of the Asterales order that is cultivated in both normal and double-flowered types, with the double-flowered ones being more frequent. China asters, marigolds, and zinnias are also commonly cultivated in double-flowered forms.

The disciform head, a special derivative of the radiate type, resembles the discoid head in lacking the marginal rays, but the outer flowers are pistillate, with a tubular, rayless corolla. Plants of the genus *Gnaphalium* (cudweed) have disciform heads. Some varieties of a species, such as *Erigeron compositus,* show a complete series of transitions from the radiate to the disciform type of head, with varying degrees of suppression of the ligule on the pistillate flowers.

Radiate, discoid, and disciform heads occur in various tribes of the Asteraceae family. The ligulate head, on the contrary, is almost entirely restricted to one tribe, the Lactuceae (Cichorieae), and is found in all members of that tribe. Ligulate heads consist entirely of one kind of flower, the ligulate flower. The dandelion is a familiar plant with ligulate heads. Ligulate flowers superficially resemble the ray flowers of radiate heads in having the corolla tubular at the base and prolonged on the outer side into a flat, strap-shaped ligule. They differ from ray flowers in being ordinarily perfect, and especially in the structure of the ligule itself, which consists of all five lobes of the corolla and generally shows five terminal teeth. It is as if a tubular corolla had been slit down the upper side of the leaf and laid out flat.

Still another kind of flower is found nearly throughout another tribe, the Mutisieae. This tribe is largely tropical, and only one of its genera, *Gerbera,* is familiar in cultivation in temperate regions. Most members of the Mutisieae have some or all of the corollas bilabiate (two-lipped), with a large, three-lobed (sometimes four-lobed) outer lip and a smaller, two-lobed (or one-lobed) inner lip. These bilabiate flowers may be either pistillate or perfect. When pistillate, they are always external to any perfect flowers that may be present in the head. Often they are much like ordinary ray flowers, except that there are two small teeth at the top of the corolla tube, opposite the ligule. The Mutisieae tribe shows every degree of transition from the typical disk flower to the typical ray flower and the typical ligulate flower.

Evolution. The evolutionary success of the Asterales may depend more on their arsenal of defensive secondary metabolites than on their morphology. They lack the iridoid compounds found in many other members of the subclass Asteridae, but they heavily exploit polyacetylenes, bitter sesquiterpenes (especially sesquiterpene lactones), terpenoid volatile oils, latex (in the Lactuceae), several kinds of alkaloids (notably pyrrolizidine alkaloids in the Senecioneae), and various other compounds. The polyacetylenes generally have cyclic, aromatic, or heterocyclic end groups, in contrast to the mainly aliphatic polyacetylenes of the Campanulales. Marigolds have a well-justified reputation for killing nematodes in the soil by releasing terpenoid compounds from the roots.

Fossil record

The fossil record of the Asterales is not especially useful at present in helping to understand the origin or evolutionary history of the group. The floral structures that would permit identification of the order on critical technical features are rarely part of the fossil record. Pollen considered to represent the Asterales enters the fossil record at many locations throughout the world about the end of the Oligocene Epoch, some 30 to 25 million years ago. The distinctive pollen of the tribe Lactuceae is more recent, entering the fossil record in the later part of the Early Miocene Epoch, some 18 million years ago. All the macrofossils that predate the Miocene and are thought to represent the Asterales are debatable at best.

The ancestry and relationships of the Asterales have been vigorously, but inconclusively, debated, although it is agreed that they form an advanced order of the subclass Asteridae. The small order Calycerales is often regarded as a close ally derived through parallel evolution with Asterales but not as ancestral to Asterales. The two orders most often considered as possibly ancestral are the Rubiales and Campanulales. These alternative choices imply different views as to the trends of evolution within the order, inasmuch as the Rubiales are a primarily woody group with opposite leaves, whereas the Campanulales are an essentially herbaceous group with alternate leaves. The view that the tribe Heliantheae is the earliest group within the family has a long history, going back to the British botanist George Bentham in 1871, and is being investigated using studies that map the DNA sequences in the chloroplast.

Despite the overall diversity within the order Asterales, it is sharply defined. There is not a single species about which there is any doubt as to whether or not it should be placed in the order. Although the casual observer may be struck by its diversity and infer that it must be an artificial rather than a natural group, serious students are agreed that its members have highly natural associations.

The species are not easily organized into genera and tribes, however, and it is customary to sort the often ill-defined genera into about 13 tribes: Anthemideae, Arctotideae, Astereae, Calenduleae, Cynareae, Eupatorieae, Heliantheae, Inuleae, Lactuceae, Liabeae, Mutisieae, Senecioneae, and Vernonieae. (A.Cr./Ed.)

Scrophulariales. *Distribution and abundance.* The Scrophulariales order of flowering plants is most prominent for certain agriculturally important parasitic weeds (broomrapes [*Orobanche*], witchweeds [*Striga*]); for the many ornamentals it contains; for the food plants sesame (*Sesamum orientale*) and olive (*Olea europaea*); for species of *Digitalis* (foxglove), the source of the drugs digoxin and digitoxin; and for a few timber trees. In the circumscription accepted here (that of Cronquist 1988) the order contains about 10,000 species and 750 genera distributed among 12 families. About three-fourths of the species belong to three large families: the figwort family, Scrophulariaceae (4,000); the acanthus family, Acanthaceae (2,500); and the gesneria family, Gesneriaceae (2,500). In variety of form and colour, some flowers of the order rival the orchids.

Members of the order Scrophulariales occur on all the landmasses of the Earth except Antarctica. About two-thirds of the species are found in the tropics, the remainder in temperate regions. About 50 species occur in the Arctic; of these, only a few species of lousewort (*Pedicularis*) reach the most northern lands.

Life span categories

In life span, members of the order range from short-lived desert herbs to long-lived tropical trees. Many are annuals, completing their life cycle from seed to seed in a single growing season. A few are biennials, producing flowers and fruit the second year, after which they die. Most, however, are perennials, surviving for several years and withstanding adverse seasons by means of underground parts (*e.g.,* the herbaceous perennials) or by means of long-lived aboveground parts (*e.g.,* woody perennials). Of the perennials, most come into flower year after year. A few live for several years—15 to 20 in certain cases (*e.g., Boea*)—before flowering and then die after flowering once. Various species of bladderworts can reproduce for years without flowering. Instead, they may form turions, spherical or egg-shaped structures 2 to 30 millimetres long, consisting of many small and tightly packed leaves. The turions overwinter and grow into new plants the following spring.

Size range and diversity of structure. The plants range in size from the diminutive aquatic bladderwort, *Utricularia olivacea,* one of the smallest in bulk of all flowering plants, with threadlike stems to about 10 centimetres in length with a very few minute leaves, to large trees, of which the largest may be the tabebuia, or guayacan (*Tabebuia*), which reaches about 50 metres in height and 2 metres in trunk diameter.

Flower size is also diverse. The smallest flowers are perhaps those of the aquatic *Micranthemum umbrosum,* which reaches about 1.5 millimetres in length. Among the largest are those of the mangrove trumpet tree (*Dolichandrone spathacea*), which reach 18 centimetres in length; and the escobedias (*Escobedia*), to 15 centimetres.

Fruits of the order range from the minute globose capsules of *Micranthemum,* less than about 1 millimetre in length, to the elongated pods of the midnight horror (*Oroxylum indicum*), 60 to 120 centimetres long but only about 8 centimetres wide, and the sausage-shaped fruits of the sausage tree (*Kigelia pinnata*), which attain 90 centimetres in length and sometimes exceed 7 kilograms in weight.

About two-thirds of the species in the order are herbaceous. Most of the woody species are shrubs; there are few woody vines except in the bignonia family (Bignoniaceae). Trees are few, and most, except for some in the bignonia family, are small, 12 metres or less in height.

Especially well known among the aquatic plants of the order are the bladderworts, which are among the few "carnivorous" plants and the only ones that capture their prey underwater. The leaves of most bladderworts have small, pear-shaped bladders provided with a trap door. These bladders trap tiny organisms, such as protozoans, crustaceans, worms, and even newly hatched fish, where they are digested. Whether this occurs by bacterial action or through the action of enzymes secreted by the plant is not certain. Nitrogenous end-products of the digestion are presumably absorbed by cells in the walls of the bladder and provide a nutritional supplement to the plant.

Parasitic species

Parasitic species are known in 14 families of flowering plants. Two of these families, the broomrape family (Orobanchaceae) and the figwort family (Scrophulariaceae), are in the order Scrophulariales. Plants of the broomrape family lack chlorophyll and are unable to carry on photosynthesis, depending entirely on their host for organic food materials, a condition known as holoparasitism (see below *Economic and ecological importance*). Important members of the family include the broomrapes and beechdrops (*Epifagus virginiana*).

In the figwort family, parasitism is known in 26 genera. Among these, all degrees of parasitism exist, ranging from holoparasitism (*Harveya, Hyobanche*) to semiparasitism—in which the parasite has some chlorophyll and can carry on photosynthesis but relies to a greater or lesser extent on the host plant for at least water and minerals. Semiparasitic members of the figwort family include the witchweeds (*Striga*), Indian paintbrushes (*Castilleja*), gerardias (*Agalinis*), eyebrights (*Euphrasia*), bartsia (*Bartsia*), and yellow rattles (*Rhinanthus*).

All members of the broomrape family, so far as is known, and the witchweeds of the figwort family produce seeds that germinate only when close to a host root. They are stimulated to do so by substances secreted by the root. The emerging root of the parasite grows toward the host root and eventually may penetrate it, establishing a haustorial union.

Epiphytes, plants that grow upon other plants for support, are infrequent in the order except in the family Gesneriaceae. A few bladderworts are also epiphytes, growing among mosses and ferns on tree trunks in rain forests.

Economic and ecological importance. The broomrape and figwort families contain all of the world's agriculturally important root parasites—*i.e.,* parasites whose roots are attached to the roots of their host by means of haustoria. The broomrapes are serious pests on various crop plants—tobacco, tomato, eggplant, hemp, and sunflower—and on various fodder plants. *Aeginetia* attacks sugarcane in Asia; in the Philippines, sugarcane is parasitized also by *Christisonia.* The most important parasites in the figwort family are the semiparasitic witchweeds, natives of the Old World that attack many grasses, including corn (maize), sugarcane, rice, and sorghum, and certain broad-leaved plants, such as peanut (groundnut), soybean, and tobacco. The mealie witchweed (*Striga asiatica*) has been introduced into the United States, where, starting in 1956, it was reported on corn in the Carolinas. Another witchweed, *S. gesnerioides,* was reported from Florida in 1970.

Ornamental herbaceous plants (annuals, biennials, and perennials), shrubs, trees, and vines are well represented in the order Scrophulariales. Among the best-known herbaceous garden and greenhouse plants are acanthus (*Acanthus*), African violet (*Saintpaulia*), calceolaria (*Calceolaria*), foxglove, gloxinia (*Sinningia*), monkey flower (*Mimulus*), mullein (*Verbascum*), nemesia (*Nemesia*), penstemon (*Penstemon*), snapdragon (*Antirrhinum*), torenia (*Torenia*), and veronica (*Veronica*).

Ornamental shrubs of the order include the butterfly bush (*Buddleja*), cape fuchsia (*Phygelius capensis*), caricature plant (*Graptophyllum pictum*), coral plant (*Russelia equisetiformis*), forsythia or golden bells (*Forsythia*), hebe (*Hebe*), jasmine (*Jasminum*), leucophyllum (*Leucophyllum*), lilac (*Syringa*), and privet (*Ligustrum*).

Ornamental tree species

Members of the Scrophulariales are among the showiest of tropical ornamental trees. Among them are the jacaranda (*Jacaranda mimosifolia*), widely used as a street tree for its blue flowers and lovely foliage; the white-flowered Indian cork tree (*Millingtonia hortensia*), once described as the handsomest of India's flowering trees; the African tulip tree (*Spathodea campanulata*), with scarlet flowers; and the New World tabebuia, with white, pink, lavender, purple, red, or yellow flowers. In temperate regions the catalpas (*Catalpa*), with their white flowers and large leaves, and the princess tree (*Paulownia tomentosa*), with blue flowers, are well known.

Both herbaceous and woody vines are frequent in the order. Some rank with the world's most beautiful flowering vines, including clock vine (*Thunbergia grandiflora*), with an abundance of sky-blue flowers; cat's-claw (*Doxantha unguis-cati*), with golden yellow flowers; and flame vine (*Pyrostegia venusta*), with orange flowers. Woody vines are especially common in the bignonia family. Most of the vines in the order Scrophulariales are tropical, but in the United States the native cross vine (*Bignonia capreolata*) and trumpet creeper (*Campsis radicans*) are well known. Vines in the order support themselves by tendrils (*Bignonia*), by twining leafstalks (*Maurandya*), by aerial clinging roots (*Campsis*), or simply by leaning on other plants.

Food plants

The only widely known food plants of the order are sesame and olive, both native to the Old World and cultivated since antiquity. The sesame plant is grown in many warm regions for its edible, oil-rich seeds. The oil is used largely in cooking; the seeds are used in confections and as a garnish on baked goods. Fruits of the olive tree are the source of one of the best-known and most widely used vegetable oils and are a pleasant food, both green and ripe, after treatment to preserve them has taken place.

The order contains only two plants that yield drugs of worldwide significance, the foxgloves: *Digitalis lanata,* the source of digoxin, and *D. purpurea,* the source of digitoxin. These drugs are important medicines in the treatment of irregular heart rhythms. Foxgloves are also among the few poisonous plants in the order. A few trees in the order are useful for timber, including the catalpas of North America, East Asia, and the West Indies; the ashes (*Fraxinus*) of the

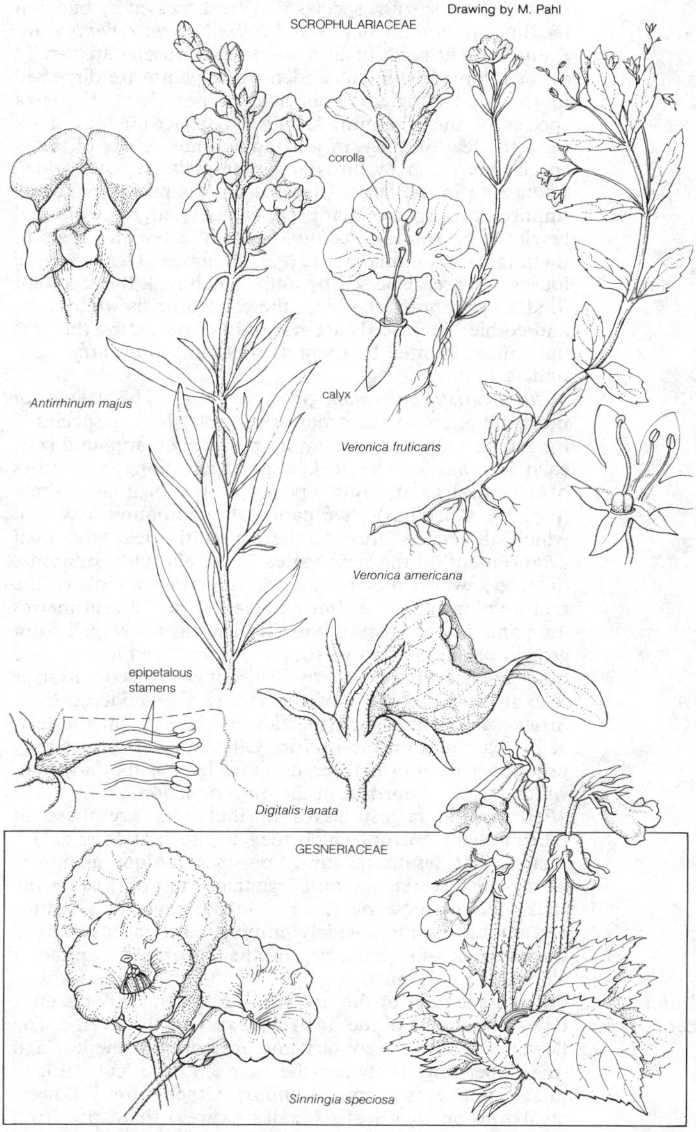

Some representative members of the order Scrophulariales.

North Temperate Zone; the bastard sandalwood (*Myoporum sandwicense*) of Hawaii; and the tabebuias (*Tabebuia*) and the jiggerwood (*Bravaisia*) of tropical America.

Natural history. Pollination mechanisms in the order are varied. In addition to flowers that normally open for pollination (chasmogamous), a few species regularly produce cleistogamous flowers—*i.e.,* flowers that never open but nonetheless develop viable seeds because they are self-pollinated in the bud (*e.g., Amphianthus* and *Limosella*). Such flowers characteristically are smaller and somewhat different in structure from chasmogamous flowers of the same species. In most members of the order Scrophulariales, the flowers open normally and then depend on various agents for pollination. None is known to rely on water. A few species are wind-pollinated. Most members of the order rely on animals for pollination, especially insects, including bees, flies, moths, and butterflies. Some are pollinated by hummingbirds. A few are pollinated by bats; outstanding among these are the sausage tree and the midnight horror.

Seed dispersal

The range of seed-dispersal mechanisms is great. In the family Acanthaceae seeds are thrown for short distances by the sudden—"explosive"—opening of the seed capsule. Most other plants of the order, however, rely on external agents, such as wind, water, or animals, for dispersal. Those that are wind-dispersed may have dustlike seeds or seeds with wings or netlike coats that increase their buoyancy. Those that are spread by water include the mangrove trumpet tree, whose seeds owe their dispersal at least in part to ocean currents; some species may be dispersed by buoyant seedlings (*Mimulus luteus* and *Scrophularia aquatica,* for example). The seeds of animal-dispersed species are carried on or in animals. Small-seeded water plants are dispersed in the mud clinging to the feet of waterfowl. Fruits of species of the sesamum family (Pedaliaceae) may hook onto the feet and legs of grazing animals. Seeds of many species are eaten by birds and mammals and are voided undigested in the feces. Dispersal in this way is especially important for species that produce juicy, brightly coloured berries (*e.g., Halleria lucida*). Seeds of a few members of the family Scrophulariaceae (*e.g.,* veronica, *Melampyrum,* lousewort) are dispersed by ants, which seek the seeds for food. A portion of the seed, the elaiosome, is white, oily, and edible. Such seeds are not only dispersed by the ants but can be planted by them as well—the ants carry them underground.

Characteristic morphological features. The leaves of most members of the order are simple. In few species—*e.g.,* some louseworts—they are pinnately compound (*i.e.,* each leaf has smaller leaflets arranged along both sides of a central axis). Some species of the bignonia family (*e.g.,* the tabebuias) have palmately compound leaves in which all leaflets arise at the tip of the leafstalk. Leaf arrangement on the stem varies, being alternate, opposite, or, rarely, whorled or in rosettes. In certain members, the mature plant possesses but one leaf, up to 76 centimetres long and 56 centimetres wide, which has developed from growth of one of the two cotyledons, or "seed leaves"; the other cotyledon aborts early. This single-leaf condition is seen in several genera of the family Gesneriaceae (*e.g., Streptocarpus*) in which the flowers develop on the leaf, at the base and on the midrib. Other related species may produce a rosette of three or more leaves, the largest of which has developed from the one cotyledon.

Perhaps the largest leaves in the order are those of the midnight horror, which may measure as long as 1.5 metres. The sesamum family possesses unique glandular hairs, which secrete the mucilage that is responsible for the sticky feel of these plants. The lobed leaves of acanthus are among the most widely employed art motifs derived from plants—for example, in the decorative capital of Corinthian columns.

Inflorescence types

In arrangement of the flowers—*i.e.,* in the inflorescence type—the plants of the order are exceedingly diverse. The flowers of some are solitary and are borne in the leaf axil (the upper angle between the stem and the leafstalk), as in the monkey flowers (*Mimulus*). Other solitary flowers are borne on long leafless stalks (scapes) that arise from a rosette of leaves, as in African violets and butterworts (*Pinguicula*). In the majority, however, the flowers are grouped into clusters of various kinds.

The flowers are almost always complete and perfect (bisexual); only in certain members of the olive family (Oleaceae), such as some ashes, are the flowers incomplete (the petals being absent) and dioecious (unisexual and on separate plants). Flowers of the order are generally irregular (bilaterally symmetrical) in shape, sometimes strikingly so, or, less often, regular (radially symmetrical). The flowers of most members of the order have superior ovaries (hypogynous). In contrast, the flowers of *Trapella* and of some members of the gesneria family have inferior ovaries (epigynous).

The calyx (sepals) is regular to highly irregular. Typically it is composed of five (or, less frequently, four) free to variously united sepals. In some species, the four-sepalled condition arises as a result of the loss of one or more sepals, as in many veronicas, in which the upper sepal is absent. In bladderworts, the calyx is strongly two-lipped, the upper lip being formed from the union of three sepals and the lower lip from the union of two sepals; the whole suggests a calyx of only two parts. Rarely, as in some ashes, the calyx is absent.

The corolla (petals) is regular or essentially so in the olive family, the butterfly bush family (Buddlejaceae), the mendoncia family (Mendonciaceae), and some species of the gesneria family; in the rest of the order it is typically irregular. It is composed of five or, less frequently, four petals, these mostly united (essentially distinct in some ashes). The union ranges from partial (only at the base, the five-petalled condition being evident) to complete (the five-petalled condition being obscure). The corolla, when composed of completely fused petals (the five-petalled condition being thus obscure), is more or less trumpet- or funnel-shaped, as in the ruellias (*Ruellia*). The five-petalled condition is also obscure in some of the highly irregular flowers of the order. The base of the corolla may bear a backwardly projecting spur, as in Kenilworth-ivy (*Cymbalaria muralis*), linarias (*Linaria*), bladderworts, and butterworts; the spur is the site of nectar production. In many species, the corolla has more or less two lips; the upper lip is composed of two petals, the lower of three. The number of petals in each lip may or may not be obvious. The lips may be the same size, or one or the other may be larger, sometimes markedly so. An upward bulge, the palate, in the central portion of the lower lip may be pronounced in some species, such as the snapdragon, in which it closes the corolla throat. In some genera (*e.g.,* veronica) the corolla appears to be composed of four petals; in these, however, the upper "petal" is really two completely united petals.

Variation in the number of stamens

In some families of the order, the androecium (stamens) is constructed on a two-part (dimerous) or a four-part (tetramerous) plan, both associated with corollas that are regular or essentially so. Thus, species of the olive family—*e.g.,* the ashes, forsythias, and lilacs—have typically two stamens; species of the butterfly bush family, typically have four. In other families of the order, the androecium is constructed on a five-part (pentamerous) plan, associated mostly with corollas that are irrregular. In these species, departures from a full set of five stamens derive clearly from the suppression of one or more of the five. Thus, a few members of the families have five stamens (as in the mulleins), but most have only two or four. Species having four stamens (an upper pair and a lower pair) lack only the uppermost stamen. Other species lack the uppermost stamen and either the upper or the lower pair, leaving only two stamens. Any of the lost stamens may be represented by a staminode, or sterile stamen, borne in place of a normal stamen but not producing pollen. Depending on the species, a staminode may range from a minute projection on the inner surface of the corolla to an elongated filament-like structure equal in size and conspicuousness to the normal stamens (*e.g.,* penstemon). In most species of the order, the stamen filaments are united with the petals (epipetaly), the degree of union ranging from slight to considerably over one-half the length of the stamen. The stamens are alternate with the lobes of the corolla—*i.e.,* they are attached between the petals. In some highly irregular flowers, the alternate arrangement is difficult to see. The anthers of all members of the order have four pollen sacs. Pollen form and structure is exceedingly diverse. One family of the order, the acanthus family, is alleged to show a wider range of pollen morphological features than does any other flowering plant family.

In most members of the order, the pistil is composed of two united carpels, or sections. Most species have an ovary with two locules, or chambers, each locule representing a single carpel. In the globularia family (Globulariaceae) and some members of the mendoncia family, one locule of the ovary may be reduced or even suppressed, giving the ovary the appearance of being one-loculed. Most species of the order have axile placentation; in some, however, notably the broomrape family and the gesneria family, placentation is parietal. The bladderwort family is characterized by free-central placentation, in which the ovules are borne on a central stalk that arises from the base of the single locule.

Depending on the species, the number of ovules in each ovary may range from 1 to about 70,000 (in *Aeginetia*). In most members of the globularia family, a solitary ovule is pendulous from the apex of each locule; in the olive, mendoncia, and myoporum families, there are commonly 2 ovules in each locule.

Most Scrophulariales species are characterized by a capsular fruit. The capsule may open by splits or pores in its wall. Other fruit types of the order are berries (*Halleria lucida*), samaras (ashes), and drupes (the mendoncia family). Fruits of *Globularia* and *Lagotis,* when one-seeded, resemble achenes.

Although most Scrophulariales species produce several to many seeds per fruit, a few produce only one (ashes, some species of *Globularia*). Perhaps the record for seed production in the order goes to *Boschniakia rossica* (broomrape family), an average plant of which is said to mature more than 333,000 seeds. In size, the seeds of the order range from those of some members of the bignonia family, which may be several centimetres long, though thin and light, to the dustlike seeds of broomrapes, which are about 0.3 millimetre long.

Evolution. Families of the order Scrophulariales are poorly represented as fossils and do not appear until the mid-Tertiary Period (starting from about 52 million years ago).

The order Scrophulariales is closely related to the order Solanales. Within the order, the acanthus, bignonia, broomrape, figwort, and globularia families are clearly related to each other, being interconnected by transitional genera or groups of genera; the boundaries between these families are thus not well-defined. The other families of the order—bladderwort (Lentibulariaceae), butterfly bush, gesneria, mendoncia, myoporum, olive, and sesamum—are rather well circumscribed.

Controversial position of some families

The relationships of several families in the order are controversial; for example, the butterfly bush family is sometimes placed in the order Gentianales. The plantain family (Plantaginaceae), excluded from the Scrophulariales by Cronquist, is included there by Thorne and Takhtajan. These differences of opinion have not yet been settled.

The order Scrophulariales, as recognized by Cronquist, is defined on the basis of a combination of features, none of which is unique to the order. Its families generally have flowers with both sepals and petals; irregular corollas; fewer than five stamens; leaves which are opposite, alternate, or sometimes whorled; and superior, two-loculed ovaries. The flowers are pollinated mainly by insects or birds. Orobanchin and iridoid compounds are frequently present, but alkaloids seldom are. Internal phloem and opposite leaves do not appear together.

One of the orders in the Engler system of classification (dating from the close of the 19th century) is the Tubiflorae, which includes among its 26 families those 12 families identified here with the Scrophulariales. The order, as defined by Engler, embraces those dicotyledons with united petals, perfect flowers, regular or irregular corollas, united stamens, petals often fewer in number than the stamens, superior or inferior ovary, and ovules with one integument. In more recent systems, the Tubiflorae, considered too unwieldy and unnatural as a single order, has been divided into three or more smaller orders, of which the Scrophulariales, as presented here, is one. The size and composition of these orders depend on the features emphasized; the evidence is not overwhelmingly in favour of any one of these views. Because botanists subdivide the old group Tubiflorae differently, the exact equivalent of the Scrophulariales, as defined by Cronquist, is not to be found among the orders recognized by other authorities. It is most closely equivalent to the suborder Solanineae of the order Tubiforae, but it differs from it mainly by the exclusion of the potato family (Solanaceae) and the nolana family (Nolanaceae). (J.W.Th.)

Solanales. The order Solanales includes the Solanaceae and usually some other families from the large 19th-century order Tubiflorae (see below *Evolution*). Evolutionary botanists have differed greatly as to which families should be included in the Solanales, but however the order is construed it includes some of the most important plants to human well-being. Representative species are found and used in almost every country. The most im-

From (*Solanum dulcamara*) M. Hickey and C. King, *100 Families of Flowering Plants* (1988), Cambridge University Press; (*Capsicum frutescens*) drawn by M. Pahl; (*Lycopersicon esculentum, Ipomoea leari*) L.H. Bailey, *Manual of Cultivated Plants,* rev. ed. (1969), reprinted with permission of The Macmillan Pub. Co.

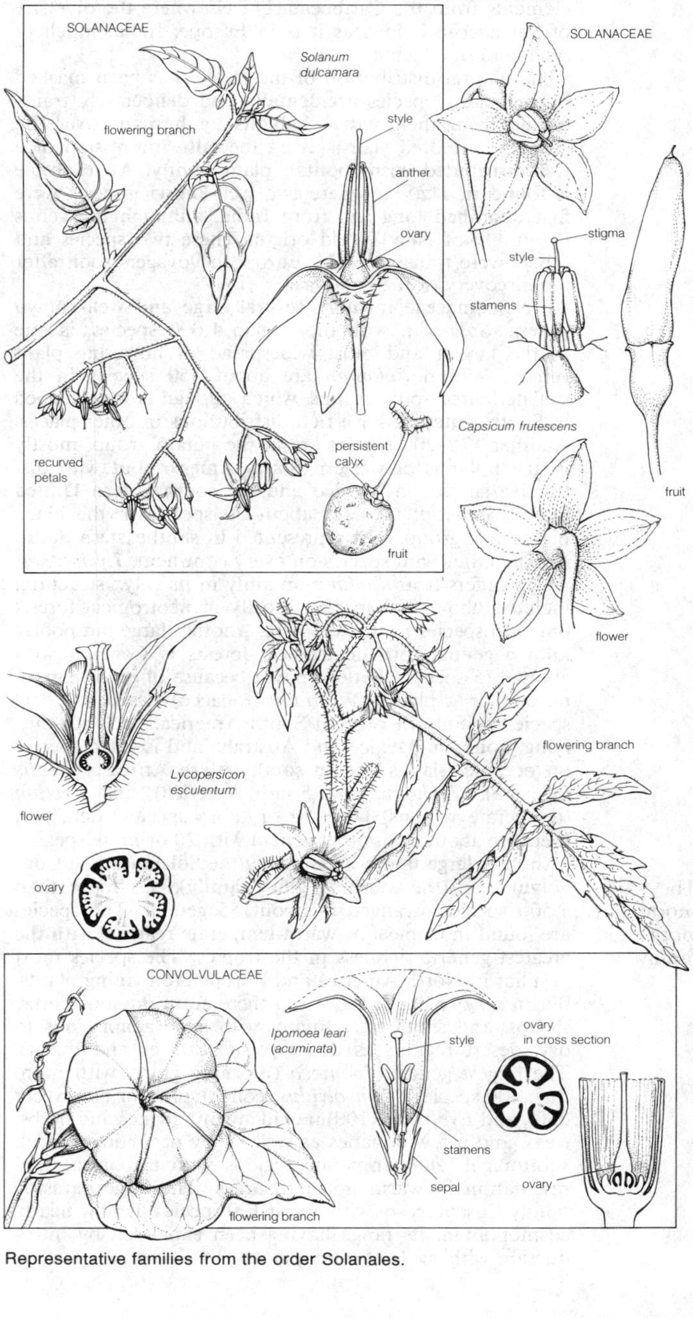

Representative families from the order Solanales.

portant and best-known families usually included in the Solanales are the Solanaceae (nightshades) and Convolvulaceae (morning glories).

The potato family

Distribution and abundance. The largest family in the Solanales is the Solanaceae (the potato family), which includes about 95 genera and 2,400 species. The majority of these are tropical, but the family is also well represented in temperate regions. The greatest diversity is found in western South America, and many groups are restricted to temperate parts of the continent. Many genera and species extend from South America into Central America and southern Mexico, where the diversity of Solanaceae is also rich. Other important regions of generic diversity are temperate Mexico and southwestern Australia. A small but distinctive group of temperate Solanaceae extends across Europe and Asia. In Africa, Australia, Mexico, and eastern South America, there is a rich development of spiny, stellate-haired species of *Solanum* (nightshades) that tolerate dry conditons. In New Guinea and in Madagascar, there are many spineless species of nightshade in wet forests. Many of the more rare and unusual members of the family are restricted to limestone substrates.

In the United States, the Southwest has elements from the groups in temperate Mexico and the Southeast has elements from the Caribbean, but elsewhere the diversity of Solanaceae is low, as it is in Europe, India, much of Asia, and the Pacific.

The natural distribution of the family has been masked by the many species accidentally and deliberately transported from their native habitats by humans over the past few hundred years, giving the false impression of a well-distributed cosmopolitan plant family. An example is found in *Datura,* where two well-known species were first described long ago from India, although the genus is entirely of New World origin. These two species and others were transported by European voyagers soon after the discovery of the Americas.

The Solanaceae includes several large and well-known genera. *Solanum,* with more than 1,000 species, is one of the largest and most widespread of flowering plant genera. Within *Solanum* are about 450 species in the stellate-haired spiny groups, which, though best developed in South America, have rich distributions in other places. Another 175–200 species are in the potato group, mostly in the uplands of western South America but with distinctive species in Mexico and the southwestern United States. *Solanum* includes about 30 species in the black nightshade group, best represented in southeastern South America, but with species on every continent. *Lycianthes,* which differs from *Solanum* mainly in its calyx structure, includes about 200 species, mostly of neotropical forests but with species in tropical Asia. Another large but poorly known genus from neotropical forests is *Cestrum* with about 175 species. Better known because of its ornamental and drug plants, *Nicotiana* (tobacco) has nearly 100 species, mainly in western South America, but with outlying groups in Mexico and Australia and isolated species on oceanic islands and in southwestern Africa. *Physalis* (Mexico), *Cyphomandra* (South America), and *Lycium* (temperate regions) have 50 or more species each, and there are about eight other genera with 20 or more species.

The morning glory family

Another large family comprising the Solanales, the Convolvulaceae (the morning glory family), has more than 1,500 species arranged in about 55 genera. The species are found in tropical or warm-temperate regions, with the greatest generic richness in the tropics. The species most familiar in North America and Europe are twining plants, but in other parts of the world there are numerous herbs, shrubs, and small trees, many with such adaptations to dry, desert regions as dense plant surfaces and thorns. The largest genera, *Ipomoea* (morning glory, with more than 400 species), *Convolvulus* (convolvulus, or bindweed; 250), and *Evolvulus* (100) include twining vines and herbs, trees, and a few aquatics as well. They occur in tropical, subtropical, and temperate regions with important representation in warm northern areas. The large parasitic family Cuscutaceae (with about 100 species) is now nearly cosmopolitan, its range having been expanded by introduction with seeds of other plants.

Two small families that appear to have a relationship in the Solanales, the Goetzeaceae and Duckeodendraceae, are poorly known. The Goetzeaceae consists of about five or seven species of small trees or shrubs from the Greater Antilles; most of these are now extinct or seriously endangered. *Duckeodendron,* the only genus of Duckeodendraceae, a family of tall trees, includes one species, which occurs in Amazonian rain forests.

Several other families have been proposed as belonging to the Solanales. Polemoniaceae (the phlox family) includes about 300 species of herbs and some shrubs, lianas, and small trees arranged in between 15 and 20 genera. Most of the species are from western North America, with extensions of the family into Siberia and tropical America. At least one species reaches Chile. Hydrophyllaceae (the waterleaf family) includes about 250 species of herbs arranged in about 20 genera. Most of the species are from western North America, but a few are found in the Andes, in Africa, and in Asia. Most are adapted to dry environmental conditions (xerophytic), but *Hydrolea,* with 20 species in the tropics, is an aquatic. The Menyanthaceae (the buckbean family), which is sometimes included in the Gentianaceae (Gentianales), includes about 40 species arranged in about 5 closely related genera. The family is cosmopolitan. The floating aquatics, *Fauria* (*Nephrophyllidium*) and *Nymphoides,* occur in the southeastern and northwestern United States, respectively. The Retziaceae, with one species of shrubs in southern Africa, is now sometimes excluded from the Solanales.

Economic and ecological importance. Plants of the Solanales are important for food, drug, ornamental, and laboratory uses. The order includes major crop plants: potatoes, tomatoes, bell peppers, eggplants, tobacco, the garden petunia (Solanaceae), and sweet potatoes (Convolvulaceae), as well as many other well-known plants of lesser importance.

Potatoes (*Solanum tuberosum*) were first domesticated in western South America and were introduced to Europe before the 16th century but did not become important there for more than a century. (The term potato comes from *batatas,* an American Indian word for the sweet potato.) Most potatoes grown today are a single species, but several other tuber-bearing species are still cultivated by indigenous peoples in the upland regions of Peru. The edible tubers are the underground stem of a sprawling, strong-smelling herb. Plants are grown from the "eyes," which are actually buds. A plant is sometimes susceptible to late blight, a rotting disease caused by the fungus *Phytophthora infestans.* This disease brought about the Irish potato famine and decimated European potato crops between 1845 and 1860. More than a million lives were lost through starvation. Apart from its use as food, starch milled from the potato is used in the manufacture of paper, textiles, confections, and adhesives. Potatoes are also an important cattle feed. Potatoes have a world crop importance comparable to rice, wheat, or sweet potatoes.

Tomato plants

Tomatoes (*Lycopersicon esculentum*) belong to a genus native to western South America. Domestication, however, took place in Mexico from the cherry tomato (*Lycopersicon esculentum* variety *cerasiforme*), the only element of the genus occurring naturally north of South America. Because they were once thought to be poisonous, tomatoes did not become a popular food item in Europe and North America until the 19th century. The tomato is actually a fruit, although it is used as a vegetable. It is produced in abundance on a sprawling vine. The genus *Lycopersicon* is closely related to *Solanum,* and some scientists actually have named the tomato *Solanum esculentum.* The term tomato is from the Native Mexican *tomatl,* which referred to several similar, mostly juicy, edible fruits.

Peppers belong to the South American genus *Capsicum.* As with the tomato, the garden pepper was domesticated in Mexico rather than in South America where the major range of the genus occurs. Botanists disagree on whether peppers constitute one species or three, *Capsicum annuum* (sweet peppers), *C. frutescens* (hot peppers), and *C. sinense.* The bird pepper (*C. annuum* variety *aviculare*), the parent stock of the garden pepper, occurs from Florida and Texas to as far south as Argentina. Its fruits are hot.

The pungent principle in hot peppers, capsaicin, can be corrosive to the skin and is found in the tissue under the seeds (placenta). It is sometimes used in medicine as a stimulant, and it is the active principle in cayenne pepper. Chili peppers also yield the spice paprika. (Black pepper is from the vine *Piper nigrum,* a plant unrelated to the Solanales.) The term chili is from the native Mexican-language word for this plant.

Tobacco is perhaps the world's most economically important drug plant, generating huge incomes in the agricultural, manufacturing, and merchandising sectors in most world economies, and also huge outlays in health sectors in treating the effects its use has on human populations.

Tobacco species

The tobacco smoked, sniffed, and chewed is from *Nicotiana tabacum,* a species of tobacco not known in the wild. Its closest relatives are found in western South America. Another species, *Nicotiana rustica,* was the tobacco first brought to Europe by the Spanish in 1558; this tobacco continued to be used long after the milder Virginia tobacco (*Nicotiana tabacum*) was generally accepted. Tobacco is a robust, erect annual herb. Its leaves are prepared for use by any of several fermentation processes, which may take as long as four years to complete.

The alkaloid with the best-known effects is nicotine, but tobacco contains many other alkaloids, some of them even more toxic; in some tobacco, for example, powdered leaves or extracted nicotine is used as an insecticide. The name tobacco is from a West Indian name for a device for snuffing dried leaves.

Eggplant, also called aubergine (*Solanum melongena*), was domesticated from a group of spiny *Solanum* species of tropical Asia where the fruits come in many shapes, colours, and textures (smooth or hairy). All the fruits are yellow when fully ripe. (This stage occurs after the normal eating stages.) Some fruits, especially from plants subjected to drought, may have high levels of alkaloids that cause nightmares. The name eggplant was given to forms with white fruits resembling a hen's egg that are still grown in Thailand and other parts of Asia.

Sweet potato (*Ipomoea batatas*) is of South American origin, appearing in the Old World soon after European contact. The sweet potato is the swollen root of a vine that trails along the ground. A popular vegetable, especially in the southern United States, it is a staple in Japan, China, and the islands of the South Pacific. In many places it rivals or exceeds rice as the main dietary item. In the United States, races with orange to red, moist, and sweet flesh are erroneously known as yams, a term that correctly refers to the tubers or rhizomes of the monocotyledonous genus *Dioscorea*. Other races have floury yellow flesh, and still others are important for fodder, all parts of the plant being utilized. The American Indian word for the sweet potato was *batatas.*

Medicinal plants

The Solanales contain an exceptionally rich array of medicinal plants. Important alkaloids derived from the Solanales include some tropanes such as atropine, which is used as a muscle relaxant and as an antidote for several types of poisons (*e.g.,* nerve gas poisoning). Many species are toxic; deaths have been attributed to green-fleshed potatoes, deadly nightshade (belladonna), and other species. Tobacco has been linked to cancer and other illnesses. Various Solanaceae were implicated in witchcraft practices in medieval Europe, in South America, and elsewhere. The term jimsonweed (*Datura stramonium*) dates from 17th-century British troops who displayed hallucinating behaviour after eating the plant following the fall of Jamestown. Members of Convolvulaceae and Solanaceae have occasionally been used as hallucinogens. *Ipomoea purga* supplies jalap, an emetic drug.

Common members of the Solanales are notable experimental plants in theoretical biology. They have been crucial in many advances in plant science. They also are important tools in maintaining other systems under study, such as plant viruses and bacteria, by forming the basis of agars and cultures. Because there is such a large base of knowledge about each of these plants, their continued use as experimental species seems assured.

Most families constituting the Solanales include commonly known ornamentals. The Solanaceae includes *Brugmansia, Cestrum, Nicandra, Nicotiana, Nierembergia, Petunia, Salpiglossis, Schizanthus, Solandra,* and *Solanum* (*S. pseudocapsicum,* the Jerusalem cherry). The species of *Nicotiana* grown as ornamentals are different from those that produce tobacco. The Convolvulaceae includes many ornamental vines of morning glory (*Ipomoea*), convolvulus (*Convolvulus*), and moonflower (*Calonyction* and *Ipoema alba*). The Polemoniaceae (*Phlox, Polemonium, Loeselia, Gilia, Collomia, Cantua,* and *Cobaea*), and Hydrophyllaceae (*Phacelia, Hydrophyllum*), sometimes included in the Solanales, have well-known ornamental species grown mainly as bedding plants.

Many members of the order have minor uses. Tomatillos (*Physalis philadelphica*) and tamarillos, or tree tomatoes (*Cyphomandra betacea*), are sold in North America and elsewhere. Some Mexican species of *Ipomoea* (Convolvulaceae) yield resins, and some *Convolvulus* species yield rosewood oil.

Nightshades, jimsonweeds, henbanes (*Hyoscyamus niger*), and other weed species interfere with crops and pastures, and bindweeds (*Convolvulus*) and sweet potato vine (*Ipomoea pandurata*) are notorious for tying other plants into unmanageable masses. Dodder (*Cuscuta;* Cuscutaceae) is a widespread parasite that causes economic losses in crops and orchards.

Except for the weedy propensity of many species to colonize newly disturbed sites, plants of the Solanales are of scant ecological importance.

Characteristic morphological features. The Solanales share a number of features also found in other orders: included phloem (*i.e.,* phloem in strands included within the secondary xylem); alternate leaves that generally lack stipules; typically pentamerous flowers with parts of the calyx, corolla, and the stamens alike in number; the calyx often fused; the corolla and stamens usually fused, at least basally; the stamens alternating with the corolla lobes and inserted on the corolla tube; the anther tapetum secretory; the ovary mostly superior; mostly 2–3 locules in the carpels; a single style; ovules with vascular tissue in the integuments; the embryogeny of various types; and seeds with endosperm. Plants of the order also tend to contain alkaloids but not iridoid alkaloids.

Many of the other families that have been included in the Solanales in past decades also have most of these characteristics, although many lack included phloem and their alkaloids are either different or absent—*e.g.,* the Polemoniaceae.

Principal agents of pollination

Flowers of the Solanales are pollinated mainly by insects, but birds and bats pollinate a few tropical species. Both wide-open flowers that attract generalist pollinators and irregular corollas with narrow openings that attract specialized bees are present in the order. Several groups have tubular or night-scented corollas that attract moths. Nectar is commonly produced from the disc that subtends the ovary. A large number of species have anthers with terminal pores that are "buzz pollinated" by many unrelated groups of bees (not honeybees). In this action, the bee grasps the anthers and by shivering her indirect flight muscles causes a cloud of pollen to be resonated out of the pore. The species with terminal anther openings usually do not produce nectar.

The Solanaceae are mostly herbs, shrubs, or woody epiphytes, but some are trees. Although a few species are vines or hemiepiphytes, these are seldom twining. Latex is absent. Leaves are alternate but are often in unequal pairs, the smaller leaves sometimes resembling stipules. The leaves may be entire or variously divided, and bracts are sometimes present, but bracteoles seldom occur. Flowers are mostly perfect, and the floral parts occur in multiples of four or five. They may be regular. The calyx lobes are united to various degrees. The anthers often dehisce by terminal pores, and a nectary disc is present when anthers are longitudinally dehiscent. The ovary generally consists of two fused carpels with several to many ovules in each locule. The ovules are erect, anatropous, or semianatropous, and surrounded by only one integument. The fruit is a berry or capsule and generally contains many seeds.

The Solanaceae have some unusual and enigmatic characteristics. A calcium-accumulating resorption tissue is present in the anthers of almost all species of Solanaceae. Its function is not known. This unusual feature is also known in the family Ericaceae (Ericales). Many Solanaceae have single degenerate guard cells in the leaf epidermis, a feature that is shared with the Verbenaceae (Laminales). These have no evident function (two guard cells are required for a functional stoma).

The Convolvulaceae tend to have conduplicate aestivation (folding of the corolla in bud), but this also occurs in several Solanaceae.

The included phloem in Solanaceae and Convolvulaceae appears to be similar, but it has different origins and may not be homologous. Included phloem is sometimes mislabeled as internal phloem, which occurs in a different series of families unrelated to the Solanales. The Convolvulaceae have a complicated seed coat structure quite unlike that of the Solanaceae or other members sometimes placed in the Solanales.

About half of the species in the largest genus, *Solanum,* have spines and/or pubescence of stellate hairs, and many species in this group have heterostyly (some flowers with pollen but no functional ovary). Many species in the same genus have underground tubers.

The Solanaceae is broken down into the subfamilies Solanoideae, Cestroideae, and Nolanoideae.

The Solanoideae (with 61 genera containing more than 1,700 species) usually have regular flowers, berry fruits, compressed seeds, and curved embryos. The subfamily includes four genera with anthers that dehisce by terminal pores, one of which is the genus *Solanum,* which comprises about half the species in the family. The subfamily is near cosmopolitan. Other well-known members of this subfamily are *Capsicum* (red pepper), *Physalis* (groundcherry and tomatillo), *Datura* (jimsonweed), *Hyoscyamus niger* (henbane), *Atropa belladonna* (deadly nightshade), and *Cyphomandra betacea* (tamarillo, or tree tomato). The tribe Hyscyamae have mostly capsular fruits.

The Cestroideae (with 33 genera containing about 500 species) usually have irregular flowers, capsular or berrylike fruits, often minute seeds, straight embryos, and many different chromosome numbers. This group occurs mainly in the Americas but also has representatives in the Australian region. The largest genus, *Cestrum,* is made up of shrubs with few-seeded berries, but most other genera, including *Nicotiana,* have capsules with numerous, minute seeds. The subgenus also includes *Petunia, Browallia, Salpiglossis,* and other ornamental plants, mostly from South America. The Australian genera related to *Anthocercis* are a unified group distinctive from the rest of the subfamily.

The Nolanoideae (with 2 genera, 22 species), which otherwise resembles the Solanoideae, has a compound ovary and distinctive fruit. It is restricted to the desert areas of Peru and Chile.

The Convolvulaceae

The Convolvulaceae are twining vines, herbs, or small trees, a few spiny and a few aquatic. Some have tuberlike roots or rhizomes. Many have latex. The leaves are alternate, mostly without stipules and with axillary buds, often with extrafloral nectaries. The inflorescences usually have bracts and bracteoles. The flowers are mostly perfect, with floral parts in multiples of five. The calyx lobes are free, imbricate, the corolla often almost entire, often induplicate-valvate in bud, a nectariferous disc usually is present. The ovary consists mostly of two to five fused carpels with one or two ovules in each locule. The ovules are erect, anatropous or semianatropous, and one is surrounded by a single integument. The fruit is a berry, nut, or capsule.

The Convolvulaceae are divided into the four subfamilies Humbertioideae, Dichondroideae, Cuscutoideae, and Convolvuloideae, each of which has been recognized as a distinct family by authorities during the 20th century. Sometimes the Convolvulaceae are divided further into nine or so tribes.

Humbertoideae comprises a single species (*Humbertia*) restricted to Madagascar. This is a tree with carpels having many ovules, and woody fruit. Dichondroideae consist mainly of *Dichondra,* a creeper common in lawns in warm temperate areas of America, including Florida. It is distinguished by its deeply divided carpels and subgynobasic styles. Cuscutoideae comprises the large cosmopolitan genus *Cuscuta* (more than 150 species), or dodder, leafless parasites that send yellow or orange stems twining around other plants and draw nourishment from them through specialized rootlike structures called haustoria. Convolvuloideae, the most familiar subfamily, includes herbs, vines, and a few shrubs. Here are the genera *Ipomoea, Convolvulus,* and others with garden subjects, food plants, and noxious weeds.

Two other poorly known groups are sometimes included in the order. The Goetzeaceae are small shrubs with many-veined, entire leaves, sometimes showy flowers, and one- or two-seeded berries. *Duckeodendron cestroides* consists of large trees with alternate, entire leaves, tubular flowers, and a bony one-seeded fruit.

Evolution. The Solanales represents one of the several subaggregations of families from a 19th-century order "Tubiflorae," which have been proposed as separate orders in the late 20th century. There is a growing consensus that the order should include the two large families, Solanaceae (Nolanaceae as subfamily Nolanoideae) and Convolvulaceae (Cuscutaceae as subfamily Cuscutoideae), and perhaps the Duckeodendraceae and Goetzeaceae. Most schemes have included other families, while some have placed its families in other orders—*e.g.,* Polemoniales and Scrophulariales. Thus, it is important to ascertain just which families are meant in the term Solanales.

Research carried out in the 1990s that made use of macromolecular methodology laid the groundwork for a new assessment of orders in the Asterideae. Early findings support the above configuration and tend to remove other families (*e.g.,* Polemoniaceae, Hydrophyllaceae, and Menyanthaceae) from the closest relationship with the Solanaceae and hence from the order Solanales. The closest relatives to the Solanales and the families from which they might have arisen is yet to be agreed upon.

The Solanaceae and Convolvulaceae have a number of characteristics usually considered to be advanced: fused calyx and corolla; stamens adnate to the corolla, and sometimes fused; mostly two to three fused carpels; fused styles and stigmas; and usual reduction to five of calyx, corolla and androecium parts. They also have primitive characteristics: occasionally or often numerous ovules and seeds, and usually superior ovaries. Thus, the Solanales are at a relatively high, but not the highest, level of morphological advancement in the angiosperms. Because many genera of the Solanaceae have bilaterally symmetrical (zygomorphic) flowers while the Convolvulaceae have few, and the Convolvulaceae usually have only one or two seeds and the Solanaceae many, the two families could be considered to be about equally advanced.

Fossil record

Few fossils are known for the Solanales (Convolvulaceae from the Tertiary, about 66.4 to 1.6 million years ago); thus views on the time and place of origin of the order are speculative. Fossils dated to the Late Cretaceous (97.5 to 66.4 million years ago) have many of the advanced features found in the Solanales; insects with musculature that might have permitted buzz-pollination of anthers with terminal pores have been recorded much earlier than this. Therefore, the nearly complete lack of a fossil record for the order cannot be used to argue a recent origin.

The geography of the two main families in the order suggests a history related to the ancient supercontinent Gondwana, which separated into the present-day continents of the Southern Hemisphere. Because the Solanaceae has a rich diversity in South America and Australia and the Convolvulaceae also has significant diversity in Africa and Madagascar (all Gondwanan areas), ancestors of these plants were probably present on the southern supercontinent before its breakup. Both families are well represented in Africa by xeric-adapted groups. (W.G.D'A.)

CLASS LILIOPSIDA: THE MONOCOTYLEDONS

The class Liliopsida is one of the two classes that collectively make up the division Magnoliophyta, or angiosperms. The Liliopsida have also been known under the more descriptive taxon name Monocotyledoneae, or monocotyledons (monocots). The term refers to the most characteristic single feature of the group, the single cotyledon in the embryo of the seed. The Magnoliopsida, or dicotyledons, in contrast, ordinarily have two cotyledons.

The monocotyledons were first collectively treated as a taxonomic group by the French botanist Antoine-Laurent de Jussieu in 1774. Jussieu's arrangement has an antecedent in the *Methodus Plantarum Nova,* published by the English botanist John Ray in 1682. Ray differentiated herbaceous flowering plants into dicotyledons and monocotyledons, but he grouped woody plants on other bases, while noting that the palms differ from other woody plants in being monocotyledonous.

There are about 50,000 species of monocots, less than one-third the number of dicot species. These 50,000 species are considered in this article to form 5 subclasses, 19 orders, and 66 families. Any estimate of the number of species is highly subjective because the classification, especially of the larger families, is still in a state of flux.

Despite the general agreement among botanists about what should be included in the monocots, the group cannot be characterized in any absolute way. The usual differences between monocots and dicots are shown in the table entitled *Comparison of dicotyledons and monocotyledons* (see above *Classification*) on an earlier page, but all characteristics are subject to exception.

It is now widely believed that the monocots were derived from primitive dicots. The single cotyledon, parallel-veined leaves, scattered vascular bundles in the stem, the absence of a typical cambium, and the adventitious root system of monocots are all regarded as derived characteristics within the angiosperms, and any plant more primitive than the monocots in these several respects would certainly be a dicot.

Root structure

Form and function. The roots of a monocot lack a vascular cambium (the area of secondary xylem and phloem, or secondary vascular tissues, development) and therefore have no means of secondary thickening. In other structural respects, monocot roots are essentially similar to those of dicots. Many dicots have a taproot or several strong roots, with several orders of branch roots, all originating eventually from the embryonic root (radicle). The taproot or primary roots in such a system have a vascular cambium and are thickened by secondary growth. This kind of root system is not available to monocots. Instead, the primary root that originates from the radicle of the embryo soon aborts or is undeveloped, so that no primary root is produced. The root system of monocots is thus wholly adventitious—*i.e.,* the roots originate laterally from the stem or from the hypocotyl (the region of transition between the root and the stem in the embryo). The roots are all slender, and the plant is said to be fibrous-rooted. Many herbaceous dicots likewise have a fibrous root system composed of adventitious roots, but the dicots have other types of root systems as well.

Monocot stems typically have numerous small vascular bundles that may be arranged in two or more concentric rings but are more often scattered throughout the fundamental tissue. In the latter case, there is neither a well-defined cortex nor a well-defined pith. The vascular bundles of monocots are not open to further growth (*i.e.,* secondary growth). This is in contrast to the vascular bundles of many dicots, which increase in thickness by cell division in the vascular cambium.

In herbaceous monocot stems the fundamental tissue is usually parenchymatous—*i.e.,* it is composed of soft, thin-walled cells—but often there is a layer of hard, thick-walled cells not far from the outside of the stem. In woody monocot stems, the cells of the fundamental tissue commonly become hard and thick-walled. Usually only a small part of the tissue of the monocot stem is formed directly from the apical meristem (a region of cell division and growth). A primary thickening meristem, shaped like an inverted thimble, is more or less continuous at the top with the small apical meristem. The leaf primordia and axillary buds originate from the apical meristem, but the apical region of the stem is thickened chiefly from cell division in the cap of the primary thickening meristem. Activity of this meristem decreases progressively in the region of elongation (corresponding to the sides of the thimble) and usually ceases in the region of maturation.

In a few herbaceous monocots, such as aloe (*Aloe*) and snake plant (*Sansevieria*), the thickening meristem continues to function more or less indefinitely. In the mature region of the stem, this meristem is continuous with the primary thickening meristem. It does not, however, pass through each vascular bundle. This meristem of monocots produces parenchyma and vascular bundles toward the inside, and usually only a small amount of parenchyma toward the outside.

Woody monocot stems have scattered vascular bundles, just as do herbaceous ones. The tissue in which the bundles are embedded characteristically becomes hardened with thick-walled cells, instead of remaining largely parenchymatous. Some woody monocots, such as most palms, show little or no secondary growth, but others have a slow secondary growth of the type described for some herbaceous monocots. Sometimes, as in species of yucca (*Yucca*) and dracaena (*Dracaena*), the secondary tissues eventually constitute the bulk of the stem.

Leaf structure

Monocot leaves typically have a narrow blade with numerous parallel longitudinal veins and a sheathing base that wraps around the stem, without a clearly marked leaf stalk (petiole). The longitudinal veins are connected by numerous small cross veins, but these are usually inconspicuous and easily escape attention. Thus, the standard parallel-veined versus net-veined contrast between the leaves of monocots and dicots is misleading if taken too literally. Ordinary parallel-veined monocot leaves also have a network of veins. As noted below, there are several ways by which some monocots escape, to some degree, the constraint of narrow blade and parallel venation. In some members of the family Araceae, the leaves are essentially like those of typical dicots, with a definite petiole and a broad, pinnately net-veined blade.

Flowers of monocots differ from those of dicots mainly in the number of parts of each kind. Monocot flowers most often have the parts in sets of three, occasionally four, but almost never five. The numbers are especially characteristic of the sepals and petals. The stamens and pistils may be numerous even when the perianth is trimerous (in sets of three), or the single ovary may have only two carpels instead of three. Often there are six stamens, representing two whorls of three. Dimerous flowers (parts in sets of two) are also known, as in *Maianthemum,* of the Liliaceae (lily family).

The unique septal nectary of many monocots not only helps to unify the class but also to strengthen the theory held by some that the subclass Alismatidae is near-basal (*i.e.,* among the earliest members of the class). Septal nectaries develop in the partitions between the locules of a compound ovary, in places where the adjacent walls of the carpels have not fused. They discharge nectar to the outside through small openings.

Septal nectaries are characteristic of those Arecales (palms) that produce nectar and of the Liliales, Bromeliales, and Zingiberales. Not every genus in every family of these orders has septal nectaries, but they are common enough so that their absence is exceptional rather than typical. The complex, external nectaries at the top of the ovary in some Zingiberales are evidently derived from septal nectaries. Some of the Orchidales also have septal nectaries.

Septal nectaries probably have their origin in the subclass Alismatidae. Arrowhead (*Sagittaria*) and some other Alismatidae have nectaries between the petals and staminodes and between and around the staminodes and lower carpels.

Water plantain (*Alisma*), with a single whorl of carpels, has a nectary at the base of the slit between any two adjacent carpels. The palms, in which the carpels range from being separate to united, have corresponding nectaries, either resembling those of the Alismatidae or those that are septal. Presumably a similar change occurred in the lines leading to the Zingiberidae and Liliidae.

Evolutionary diversification

Evolutionary diversification among the monocotyledons appears to have been constrained by a number of fundamental features of the group, most notably the absence of a typical vascular cambium and the parallel-veined rather than net-veined leaves. Within these constraints, the monocots show a wide range of diversity of structure and habitat. They are cosmopolitan in their distribution on land. They also grow in lakes and ponds and rivers, sometimes free-floating, but more often rooted to the bottom. Some of them grow in the intertidal zone along the seashore, and a few are submerged marine plants rooted to the bottom in fairly shallow water along the shore.

Lacking a typical cambium, and thus lacking normal secondary thickening, the monocots cannot exploit the taproot growth habit, and their exploitation of the woody growth habit is severely limited. Only the palms form a fairly large group of woody monocots, but even these cannot have stems that thicken year by year through the production of growth rings. The numerous vascular bundles in the trunks of palm trees are not open to secondary growth and are scattered in a primary ground tissue that often includes many very hard, silicified fibres. The slender trunk of even the tall palms reflects the absence of a cambium. Because they do not have a mechanism for secondary growth, the roots cannot persist, enlarge, and ramify (branch). Thus, the principal growth habit for monocot roots is a diffuse fibrous system.

Monocots are generally thought to have had as their common ancestor an aquatic dicot of the family Nymphaeaceae. As such, they have what appear to be vestigial, primitive vessels in the roots. Upon returning to a terrestrial habit, some monocots developed a vessel system in the shoot to provide support and transport nutrients and water throughout the plant structure. Further, expanded net-veined leaves, an arborescent growth habit, or some degree of secondary thickening additionally adapted these groups to a land-based habit.

On the assumption that parallel venation in a leaf blade is the ancestral condition in monocots, terrestrial monocots with net-veined blades are derived from this ancestral form. There are three ways in which monocots are presumed to have evolved a more net-veined pattern and broader leaf blades which allowed them to escape the constraints to an aquatic habitat that strictly parallel venation would have imparted. Traces of the ancestral parallel-veined pattern, however, can usually be found.

In one avenue of development that results in a leaf that is broader and somewhat net-veined, the main veins of the leaf blade spread farther apart, while the small cross-connections between them are amplified. Subsequently, the main veins fade out before reaching the leaf tip, establishing a more or less palmate venation. Water plantain (*Alisma*), arrowhead (both of Alismatidae), yam (*Dioscorea*), catbrier (*Smilax*), and trillium (*Trillium;* Liliidae) reflect this evolutionary development. Some of the Araceae are further modified to produce pinnately net-veined leaves like those of many dicots. Throughout the monocots, many transition stages are evident.

In a second avenue of development, closely set parallel veins diverge in turn toward the margin, beginning with the outermost veins and ending with those closest to the midvein. The superficial structure resembles a pinnately veined leaf with closely parallel lateral veins, as is found among the Zingiberales, especially the banana (*Musa*). Such pinnately veined leaves tend to be fragile and subject to fraying because the connections between adjacent primary lateral veins remain slender and weak.

A third avenue of development is found only in the fanlike leaves of the palms and the related order Cyclanthales. It differs from the second type of development in the way in which new tissue develops between the lateral veins early in the growth of the leaf.

Fossils and phylogeny

Evolution and paleobotany. The early macrofossil record of monocots is fragmentary and subject to diverse interpretations. Only the fossil pollen, often preserved in exquisite detail, seems to provide substantial, reliable evidence. The pollen of early angiosperms was provided with a single long furrow, and no other aperture (monosulcate, also called monocolpate) with a sculptured outer wall (exine). This pattern appears to be basic to monocots and is still represented in some archaic present-day dicots. In the context of the rest of our information, the details of sculpturing of the exine in fossil and modern groups suggest that the origin of monocots from primitive dicots in Aptian-Albian time, more than 100 million years ago, was the first important dichotomy in the evolutionary diversification of the angiosperms.

One of the most obvious pieces of evidence indicating the ongoing diversification of the Liliopsida during the Early Cretaceous and throughout the Late Cretaceous (roughly 98 to 66 million years ago) is the enormous variety of monocotyledonous leaves. Most of these leaves, however, cannot be placed with any certainty into a modern group. Although Arecaceae (palms) is the first modern family of monocotyledonous plants represented in the fossil record—this occurring in strata dating to the Santonian (or perhaps the Coniacian) Age of the Late Cretaceous, nearly 90 million years ago—the palms do not represent the most primitive monocotyledons. They are clearly represented in the fossil record only because their large, distinctive leaves are easy to recognize in all phases of their development.

A scenario that attempts to explain the evolutionary history of monocots has them originating during the Aptian-Albian interval of the Lower Cretaceous from aquatic dicots similar in many respects to the modern dicot family Nymphaeceae (water lilies). The existence of Albian angiosperms, presumably dicotyledons, with leaves much like those of the modern Nymphaeales is well documented in the fossil record. Modern Nymphaeales lack secondary growth and are wholly herbaceous. Furthermore, they have scattered vascular bundles in the stem and are almost wholly without vessels. If the Albian "nymphaeaphylls" were similar to the modern Nymphaeales in these respects, they would provide a good basis for the origin of monocots. Although there is still some controversy, it is generally believed that both monocots and dicots were primitively vesselless and that vessels evolved independently from tracheids in both groups.

Two important changes would have been necessary to set the monocotyledons apart from their possible ancestors among the aquatic dicotyledons: reduction of the two cotyledons to a single cotyledon and the substitution of a narrow, parallel-veined leaf for the broad, net-veined leaf of the nymphaeaphylls.

Morphological changes

Reduction in the number of cotyledons from two to one has occurred in several small groups of Magnoliopsida (dicotyledons), and evidently in more than one way. One of the cotyledons may be gradually reduced by a series of short evolutionary steps, or one cotyledon may abort, being represented only by a vestige, or there may be a simple change in symmetry, so that the apical meristem of the embryo produces only one cotyledon instead of two. Thus the reduction of two cotyledons to one during the origin of the monocots does not seem to present a difficult evolutionary problem.

In the Nymphaealean scenario, still another means of reduction to one cotyledon may be envisaged. In the modern Nymphaeales, the two cotyledons arise from a ring-shaped common primordium, and often they are more or less connate below to form a bilobed tube. Reduction of one of the lobes would result in a single cotyledon with a sheathing, tubular base. The sheathing leaf base of so many monocots might conceivably reflect a continuation of the embryonic pattern into maturity.

In the scenario presented in this article, the leaf blade of monocots is equivalent to the leaf petiole of dicots. The pattern of development of typical monocot leaves from inception to maturity lends some support to this theory. The blade typically develops from a portion of the leaf primordium somewhat behind the tip of the primordium and matures toward the base. The primordial tip is inactive or produces only a terminal point or small appendage on the blade.

A possible recapitulation of evolutionary history here is provided by some species of the modern aquatic genus *Sagittaria* (arrowhead) in the family Alismataceae of the order Alismatales. Several species of *Sagittaria* show all transitions, within a single local population, between a normal leaf with blade and petiole and a typical narrow monocotyledonous leaf with parallel veins. Depending mainly on the depth of the water, the blade is either well developed or progressively reduced and lost, with a concomitant change in the structure of the petiole. Here the parallel-veined, submerged leaf is clearly nothing but a modified, bladeless petiole. Unfortunately for this comparison, the leaf blade of *Sagittaria* itself is probably only a secondarily expanded petiole tip not strictly homologous with the blade of dicots. *Sagittaria* may provide an example of how the parallel-veined leaf of monocots may have originated, but it is only an example, not a direct link. Parallel-veined leaves in some modern dicots, such as plantain (*Plantago*), also are considered to be expanded, bladeless petioles.

The fossil record suggests that, aside from aquatic groups like the Nymphaeales, there were not many herbaceous dicots before about the end of the Oligocene Epoch, some 30 to 24 million years ago. In the scenario here presented, the monocots thus had an evolutionary opportunity, lasting many millions of years, to return as herbs to a land habitat, occupying an ecological zone in which their principal competitors were ferns and other vascular spore-producing plants (cryptogams).

Economic importance. Grasses (family Poaceae) are economically the most important group of monocots and, indeed, of all plants. The cereal grains, sugarcane, and lawn, pasture, and forage grasses, are discussed under that family. In some tropical regions the palms (family Arecaceae) provide much of the sustenance of life. The coconut palm (*Cocos nucifera*) and the date palm (*Phoenix dactylifera*) are of special importance, as noted under that family. The lily family (Liliaceae) and orchid family (Orchidaceae) provide many spectacular ornamentals. Other economically important plants occur in diverse families. (A.Cr./Ed.)

Subclass Alismatidae

GENERAL FEATURES

Members of the subclass Alismatidae are generally considered to comprise one taxon, whether this taxon is ranked at the order, superorder, or subclass level. The individuals are most commonly found in aquatic or wetland habitats, except for members of the order Triuridales, which are tropical and subtropical terrestrial mycotrophs (*i.e.,* plants that obtain food from nonliving organic matter through their association with fungi).

One characteristic alone holds most of the subclass together, that being the method of endosperm development. Endosperm, the food source of the developing embryo, originates from a process essentially unique to flowering plants called double fertilization. In this process, two events take place. In one phase, a sperm nucleus from the pollen grain unites with the egg (ovule) to produce a zygote. In another phase, a second sperm nucleus from the pollen grain unites with two other nuclei (polar nuclei) of the embryo sac to produce a triploid cell that gives rise to the endosperm by division. (A triploid cell has a nucleus with three sets of chromosomes.)

The two main paths of endosperm development are cellular and nuclear. In cellular development, the triploid cell divides to produce two new cells, each with a nucleus surrounded by a cell wall. This process continues until the embryo sac is filled with cellular endosperm. Nuclear endosperm development results when the triploid cell divides quite rapidly by nuclear division but is not followed immediately by cytokinesis (cytoplasmic division). Nuclear division continues until the entire embryo sac is filled with nuclei that are not surrounded by cell walls. Cytokinesis begins once nuclear division nears completion

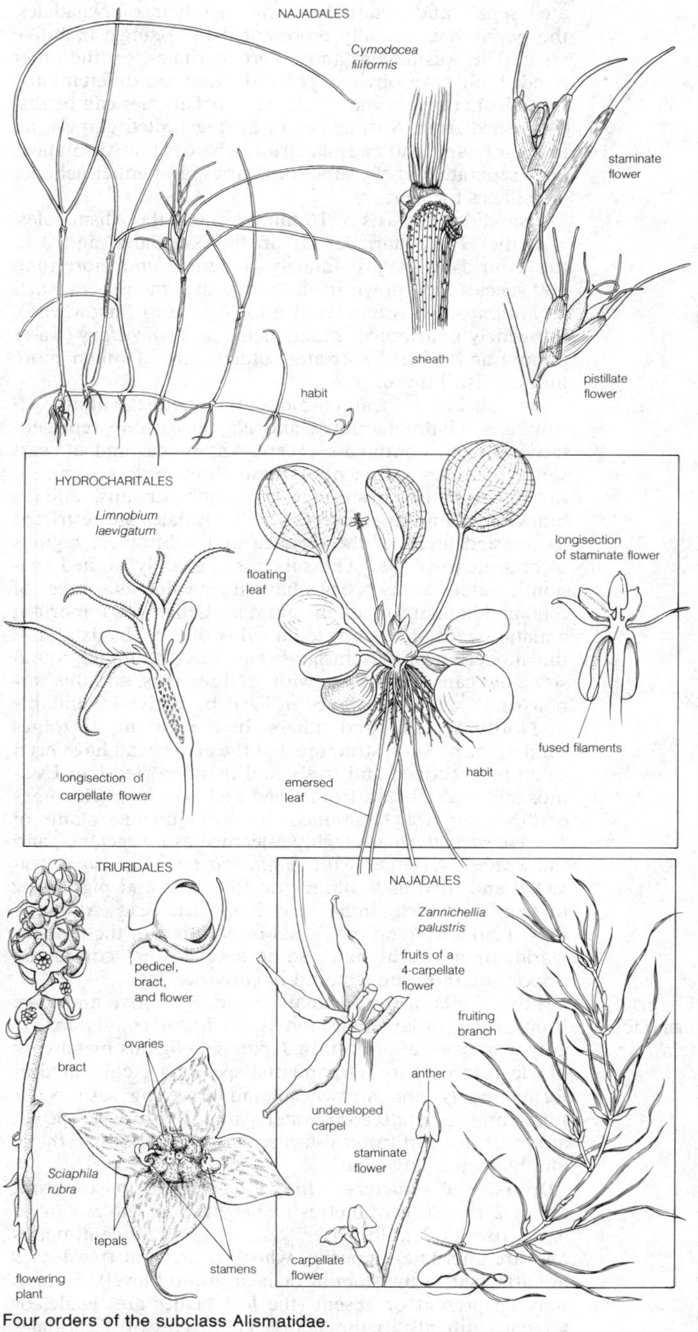

Four orders of the subclass Alismatidae.

From (*Cymodocea filiformis*) R.K. Godfrey and J.W. Wooten, *Aquatic and Wetland Plants of Southeastern United States: Monocotyledons* (1979), The University of Georgia Press; (Hydrocharitales) R.R. Haynes and L.B. Holm-Nielsen, "Hydrocharitaceae," in G. Harling and L. Andersson (eds.), *Flora of Ecuador,* no. 26 (1986); (Triuridales) P.J.M. Mass and T. Rubsamen, *Flora Neotropica: Triuridaceae,* vol. 40 (April 1986) copyright © The New Botanical Garden; (*Zanichellia palustris*) R.R. Haynes and L.B. Holm-Nielsen, "The Zannichelliaceae in the Southeastern United States," in *Journal of the Arnold Arboretum,* vol. 68 (April 1987) copyright © 1987 President and Fellows of Harvard College

and continues until all nuclei are surrounded by cell walls.

Alismatidae endosperm development is usually helobial, a combination of the two major types. Triuridales differs from the other orders of Alismatidae in having only nuclear endosperm development.

Orders

The subclass is divided into four orders: Alismatales, Hydrocharitales, Najadales, and Triuridales. The Triuridales is the most distinct order in having seeds with well-developed endosperm and in being saprophytes without chlorophyll. The order is so distinct, in fact, that several authorities consider the order to comprise a separate subclass or superorder. The American botanist Arthur Cronquist suggested in the early 1980s that Triuridales may eventually become established as a separate subclass.

The characteristic that distinguishes Najadales from the Alismatales and Hydrocharitales is the lack of differentiated sepals and petals. In some members of Najadales, the perianth is actually represented by a single bractlike tepal. The Alismatales and Hydrocharitales, on the other hand, both have obvious perianths that are differentiated into distinct sepals and petals. Hydrocharitales can be distinguished from Alismatales in having united carpels, an inferior ovary, and capsular fruit, whereas the Alismatales have separate carpels, superior ovaries, and either achenes or follicles for fruit.

Alismatidae consists of 16 families: 3 in the Alismatales, 1 in the Hydrocharitales, 10 in the Najadales, and 2 in the Triuridales. Approximately 60 genera and more than 400 species are known in the subclass; some genera, such as *Potamogeton* (pondweed) and *Sagittaria* (arrowhead), are widely distributed; others, such as *Hydrocleys* (water poppy) and *Stratiotes* (water soldier), are of much more limited distribution.

The subclass is near cosmopolitan in distribution. Alismatales, Hydrocharitales, and Najadales have representatives on all continents except Antarctica, and at least some members of each of these three orders occur in marshy habitats, freshwater lakes and streams, and in brackish and marine waters. The Triuridales are restricted to forested areas of the tropical and subtropical regions of both hemispheres. The subclass is of only limited economic value. Many species have their value as sources of food and habitat for aquatic animals. Others are important aquatic weeds. The nutritional value of the Alismatales in the modern world is insignificant, but the underground storage organs are swollen with food reserves, and this carbohydrate source was once utilized by native inhabitants of North America and others. In the Orient, rhizomes (underground stem structures) of the arrowhead have been eaten both cooked and fresh, and it is reported that Eskimos still make bread from dried and powdered rhizomes of flowering rush (*Butomus*). In Java, juvenile plants of *Limnocharis flava* are highly esteemed as a vegetable, and this species, together with *Sagittaria trifolia,* also is collected and used as fertilizer and for cattle and pig fodder in tropical Africa, India, and Southeast Asia. Although these plants have no medicinal importance in the modern world, in medieval times some species were considered important and were featured in early herbals.

Use as ornamentals

Many plants of the Alismatales are decorative and have been used as ornamental models; *Sagittaria trifolia,* for example, appears as a motif in Japanese religious metalwork of the 16th century. Ornamental species are cultivated in formal pools, and arrowhead and flowering rush occur frequently in landscaped water gardens. Tropical species are much used in tropical-fish aquariums to both aesthetic and biological advantage.

Diversity of structure. Individuals range in size from about 2 to 180 centimetres in height. The leaves can be as narrow as 2 millimetres to as wide as 50 centimetres and are alternate, opposite, whorled, or basal (the leaves are attached to the stem at or near ground level). Petioles may be present or absent (the leaf blades are sessile, or attached directly to the stem). The leaves of Triuridales are small and scalelike. The leaves are either submerged, floating, or emersed in the remaining three orders, and more than one form may be present on an individual plant. At least some members have linear sessile leaves or leaves with leaflike petioles. Stomata are generally absent on submerged leaves and on the lower surface of floating leaves, but stomata are present on the upper surface of floating leaves and on both surfaces of emersed leaves.

Large air spaces surrounded by tissue (aerenchyma) are abundant in all orders except Triuridales, comprising almost 80 percent of the total plant volume. Vascular tissue is universally present, although xylem, the water-conducting tissue, is primitive and may be nearly or completely absent in submerged species. Distribution of vascular bundles varies among the orders: they are randomly scattered in most Najadales, although some members of the order have the number of bundles reduced to one, as they are in the Hydrocharitales; most Alismatales and Triuridales have the vascular bundles arranged in arcs or circles.

Mechanical tissue (mostly schlerenchymatous tissue for providing support) is reduced in all members of the sub-

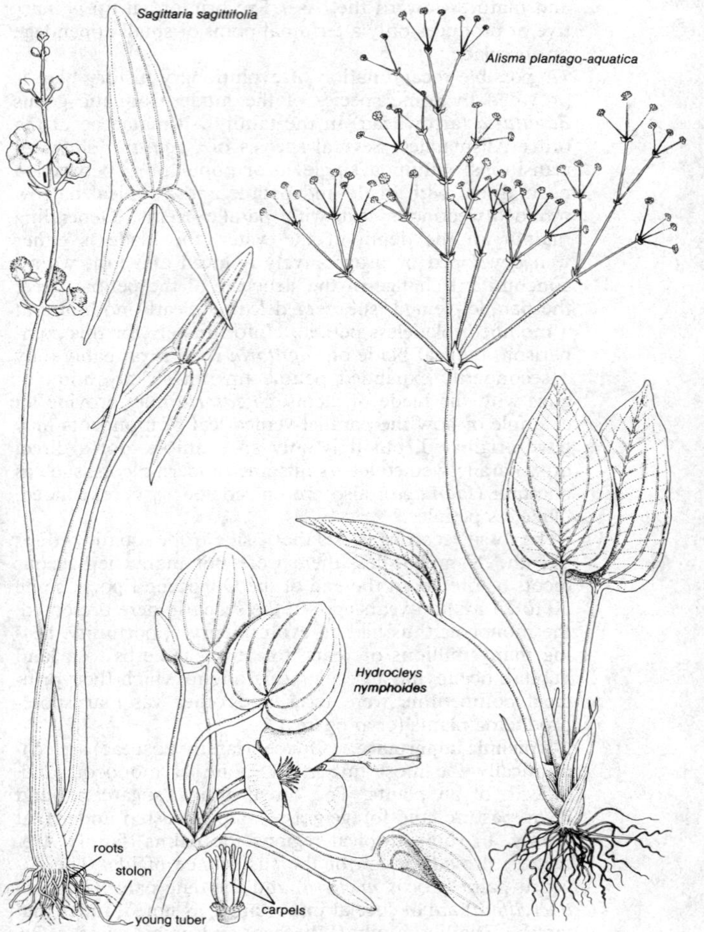

Typical plants and structures of the order Alismatales.
Drawing by M. Moran

class, and there is an absence of cell-wall thickening in conducting tissue. Secretory canals that exude a type of latex are frequent in parts of the Alismataceae and Limnocharitaceae of the Alismatales.

Distribution. The subclass is broadly distributed throughout temperate and tropical regions and includes many familiar water plants. The Alismatales consist of three families, Alismataceae, Limnocharitaceae, and Butomaceae. The Alismataceae occur throughout the Americas, Asia, Australia, Africa, and Europe. Common genera include *Sagittaria* (arrowhead), *Alisma* (water plantain), and *Echinodorus* (burhead). Water plantain and arrowhead are most common in temperate regions, whereas burhead has its centre of distribution in the Neotropics (New World tropics). Limnocharitaceae consist of three genera, *Butomopsis* (*Tenagocharis*) of the Paleotropics (Old World tropics) and *Limnocharis* and *Hydrocleys* (water poppy) of the Neotropics. *Limnocharis* has been introduced into the Asian tropics, however. Butomaceae, native to Europe, consists of one species, *Butomus umbellatus* (flowering rush). The species has become naturalized in temperate North America.

Water plants

The Hydrocharitales comprises a single family, Hydrocharitaceae. Common genera include *Vallisneria* (tape grass), *Elodea* (waterweed), *Ottelia,* and *Thalassia* (turtle grass). Tape grass and waterweed are mostly found in temperate regions, although representatives of each occur in the tropics, with tape grass being native to both the Eastern and Western hemispheres and waterweed being native to the Western Hemisphere. Waterweed and *Ottelia* originate in the tropics, with the former being native to South America and *Ottelia* having its centre of distribution in the Paleotropics. Turtle grass, *Halophila,* and *Enhalus* are marine seed plants; they occur to depths of 30 metres (when the water is adequately clear) in warm temperate and tropical waters throughout the world. Members of the family, such as *Egeria, Ottelia,* waterweed, and tape grass, are important aquarium plants.

Ten families make up the Najadales. The family Aponogetonaceae consists of *Aponogeton* (lattice plant) with about 40 species that are native to the fresh waters of the Paleotropics and South Africa. Several species are aquarium plants. *Scheuchzeria palustris,* a circumpolar species that is frequently found in quaking bogs in the Northern Hemisphere, is the only taxon in the family Scheuchzeriaceae. A closely related family, the Juncaginaceae, is widespread in the Northern and Southern hemispheres, especially in colder climates. The family consists of 5 genera, the most widespread of which are *Triglochin* (arrow grass) and *Lilaea.* Other than producing hydrogen cyanide, which occasionally poisons livestock, members of this family are of little economic importance. The largest family of the order, Potamogetonaceae, has 2 genera, *Groenlandia,* with the single species, *G. densa,* a native of western Europe, and *Potamogeton* (pondweed), a cosmopolitan genus with about 100 species and the most important native plant in freshwater ecosystems, particularly in relation to food for aquatic animals. A few species are also important aquarium plants. The closely related Ruppiaceae have often been combined with this family. Ruppiaceae consist of a single genus, *Ruppia* (ditch grass), which is essentially worldwide in aquatic systems that have a high mineral content, especially of sodium, calcium, or sulfur. *Najas* (water nymph), the only genus of the Najadaceae, is a nearly cosmopolitan genus of fresh or brackish waters and comprises approximately 35 species. The genus is of little economic importance. The horned pondweed family, Zannichelliaceae, consists of 4 genera, 1 of which, *Zannichellia* (horned pondweed), is nearly cosmopolitan. The other genera are native to the Mediterranean region, Australia, and South Africa.

Pondweed species

The three remaining families of the order, Posidoniaceae, Cymodoceaceae, and Zosteraceae, are small families of marine habitats. *Posidonia,* the only genus of the Posidoniaceae, is native to the Mediterranean and to coastal Australia. The family Cymodoceaceae contains five genera and is native to tropical and subtropical seacoasts around the world. *Halodule* and *Syringodium* are widespread in shallow waters of the Gulf of Mexico and the western Atlantic Ocean. The family Zosteraceae is widely distributed in marine waters around the world. The family is most common in cold temperate waters of the Northern Hemisphere. The genera that make up the family are *Zostera* (eelgrass), which is nearly worldwide, *Phyllospadix,* which is widely distributed throughout the northern Pacific Ocean, and *Heterozostera,* which is distributed in the temperate waters off of Australia and Chile.

The remaining order of the subclass, Triuridales, comprises two families: Petrosaviaceae, containing the single genus *Petrosavia,* with two species native to subtropical and tropical Asia, and Triuridaceae, which consists of seven pantropical genera.

NATURAL HISTORY

Sexual reproduction. Vascular water plants betray their land-based ancestry in the reproductive phase. The form and structure of their vegetative organs are modified in relation to their aquatic habitat, but the reproductive organs are remarkably similar to those of related land plants in both general organization and microscopic structure. The flowers are adapted to aerial life and are pollinated by insects or wind. Some flowers, however, are entirely submerged, and the surrounding water is the medium of pollen transport.

The Alismatales generally produce perfect flowers with obvious perianth structures; when imperfect, both staminate and carpellate flowers are produced on the same plant (monoecious). The flowers are aerial and produced in whorls or umbels on erect or floating axes. The flowers have attractive, though occasionally small, petals and are usually pollinated by flies, beetles, and butterflies.

The order Hydrocharitales is unique in the subclass in having flowers with an inferior ovary; the ovary itself is composed of several united carpels. The flowers are either perfect or imperfect; species with imperfect flowers may be either monoecious or dioecious (unisexual flowers on different plants). Flowers usually develop on stalks that originate in the leaf axes. These flowers are often solitary on the axis, with only a few axes producing flowers on a plant. Such flowers may be either aerial or floating. Occasionally, however, flowers are enclosed within one fleshy modified leaf or two connate leaves, called a spathe, which is produced on a stalk (peduncle) from a leaf axis. These peduncles often arise from basal leaves that are attached to the system at the substrate in several metres of water; such a peduncle elongates until it is at the surface of the water. Other peduncles are very short so that the flowers develop entirely under water.

Pollinating mechanisms in the Hydrocharitales range from simple insect-pollen transfer to quite elaborate transfer mechanisms in which water is the transfer vector. Species with aerial flowers are principally pollinated by insects or occasionally by wind. Insects are also thought to have a role in pollination even for the showy floating flowers of *Ottelia.* Some individuals of this genus, and probably of others, are known to accomplish self-pollination in the bud. The flowers subsequently open fully. Pollinating mechanisms are often much more elaborate, however, for the majority of species that have floating or submersed flowers, with water generally being important to some degree in pollen transfer. These species usually have fairly small, inconspicuous flowers, many, if not most, of which are imperfect. Generally, though not universally, in species with imperfect floating flowers the staminate flowers are produced below the surface of the water on one or more short peduncles. The carpellate flowers float on the water's surface attached usually by elongated peduncles. The weight of the carpellate flower and the downward pressure on the flower caused by the pull of the peduncles result in a very slight depression (or meniscus) in the surface of the water on which the flower floats. When the pollen matures, the staminate peduncle breaks, and the staminate flower or spathe with the enclosed staminate flowers rises to the surface of the water. As the flower or spathe reaches the water's surface, the change in water pressure causes the flower or spathe (or both) to open, with the perianth becoming almost reflexed. This opening of the staminate flower results in the flower essentially floating on a "boat" formed by the reflexed perianth. The staminate flower is blown along the surface of the water by the wind, possibly eventually approaching a meniscus, formed by a carpellate flower; the meniscus is important in pollen transfer. As the flower enters a meniscus, the staminate flower tips because of the lower water level in the meniscus, and pollen transfer is accomplished, either by contact between the anther and stigma or by pollen falling from the staminate flower onto the carpellate flower.

Role of water in pollen transfer

In marine species of Hydrocharitales, the flowers are permanently submerged, and the plants are dioecious; pollen released from the staminate flowers adheres in chains, forming what is functionally one long pollen grain. These chains are suspended in the water and move along with the water current. (Elongate structures are much more likely to contact a stigma that is an individual grain.) Pollination is accomplished when one such chain contacts a stigma.

Flowers of the Najadales are generally small and inconspicuous, and are either perfect or imperfect, and either aerial or submerged. Aerial flowers are usually arranged in compact spikes and are projected by a peduncle several centimetres or more above the water surface. Aerial flowers are usually considered to be wind-pollinated, although the mechanisms are not fully understood. Submerged flowers of pondweed are pollinated in the bud, whereas pollen grains of those of other genera are transferred by water (these genera usually have imperfect flowers). Staminate flowers of water nymph are generally found in the upper axes, and carpellate flowers in lower axes. Pollen of water nymph has a greater specific gravity than water because of its rich starch content, so that as it is released from the anthers it sinks slowly in the water column. If a grain contacts a stigma as it sinks, pollination is accomplished. Water nymph grows in very dense colonies, increasing the chances of pollination. In horned pondweed, both staminate and carpellate flowers are produced in the same leaf axil. The filament of the staminate flower is much longer than the carpels of the carpellate flower. The filament bends slightly, projecting the anther directly over the funnel-shaped stigmas of carpellate flowers. Pollen is released in a gelatinous mass, one mass from each locule, and falls onto a stigma, effecting pollination. The marine species are dioecious; staminate plants release pollen into the water current, as do marine Hydrocharitales. Individual pollen grains of marine Najadales are elongate rather than adhering in chains, thereby accomplishing the same result.

Nothing is known about the pollination of Triuridales, although it is probably accomplished by some insect vector since the flowers have attractive structures and emit a fragrance.

Fruit characteristics

Fruits develop aerially for emergent species and at or below the water surface for floating and submerged species. In the Alismataceae, Potamogetonaceae, Najadaceae, Zosteraceae, Cymodoceaceae, and Zannichelliaceae, separate carpels develop into a cluster of one to many one-seeded fruits. The fruits of both Potamogetonaceae and Zannichelliaceae are druplets, which are fleshy. The separate carpels of the Limnocharitaceae, Scheuchzeriaceae, Juncaginaceae, Butomaceae, and Triuridales develop into a cluster of pods, each of which contains many seeds. Except for the indehiscent pods of Juncaginaceae, the clusters open at maturity, releasing these seeds. The united carpels of the Hydrocharitales develop into one capsule, a multiseeded fruit that dehisces at maturity.

During fruit maturation, the peduncle of true aquatic vascular plants usually coils or reflexes, pulling or pushing the developing fruit into the water. In many species of true aquatic plants, the viability of a seed is greatly reduced by drying. Such a reflexing or coiling of the peduncle is an adaptation that prevents drying and maintains the viability of the seeds.

Seeds of many species have a prolonged dormancy. Single-seeded indehiscent achenes (dry, one-seeded fruits that do not open at maturity) have a hard fruit wall that is thick and tight-fitting. Some fruits retain their viability even after being frozen in ice or mud for some weeks.

Asexual reproduction. Asexual, or vegetative, reproduction is reproduction in which no union of sperm and egg occurs. Such reproduction may occur as a result of vegetative features (*e.g.,* stems or leaves) developing adventitious roots and growing into a new plant or by a cell in the gynoecium beginning cell division and growing into an embryo. This embryo may be surrounded by a seed coat. The latter is an example of vivipary if the gynoecium develops into a fruit. If a cell in the flower but outside of the gynoecium begins cellular division, no fruit will be formed, and a new small plant or plantlet will be produced in place of the flower. Such asexual reproduction is termed pseudovivipary.

Aquatic plants resort to vegetative reproduction more frequently than do land plants, although methods of propagation are fairly universal. The uniform environment and abundance of carbon dioxide and water encourage leaf development and sustain vegetative growth. Vegetative reproduction is facilitated by fragmentation of the plant body followed by regeneration from any small part bearing a bud.

Multiplication by means of modified stems such as rhizomes, stolons, and runners is widespread in temperate species. These specialized organs also serve the purpose of sustaining plants during adverse conditions. In hot climates vegetative growth may be more continuous. Vegetative parts that can grow into new plants may be transported by water or animals, further contributing to the distribution of a species.

Pseudovivipary

There are many instances of pseudovivipary, wherein asexual reproductive units replace some or all of the normal sexual flowers in the inflorescence. This method is common in the family Alismataceae, in which the inflorescence may set seed above water but bear young plantlets when submerged.

In many genera there is an abbreviated axis from which arises the crown of leaves. This rootstock becomes swollen with starch grains and serves as a storage organ during the resting period when foliage dies down. Many plants with underground stems reproduce vegetatively and spread horizontally by means of runners at the soil-surface level or by similar underground stems. These become erect at intervals to form new plants with adventitious roots. Later, intermediate parts may disintegrate and the secondary plants become independent.

Species of *Sagittaria* remain alive during adverse seasons by the production of special terminal tubers behind the apical bud. These structures are two to five centimetres long and may be brightly coloured blue and yellow. They remain dormant during the winter but sprout into a new plant the following spring.

Many species of Potamogetonaceae produce turions, or winter buds, at the apex of erect stems and branches. These hardened terminal buds break off of the stem and fall to the substrate, where they lie dormant over the unfavourable conditions and germinate into a new plant during the next growing season.

Vegetative reproduction is of the utmost importance in the maintenance and spread of some species. In all three families of the order Alismatales it is correlated with aquatic existence, and this perhaps accounts for its success and frequency in comparison with sexual reproduction, which is not adapted to aquatic conditions.

Apparently little or no vegetative reproduction takes place in the Triuridales. The majority of the life history of Triuridales is spent underground; the plant emerges only when conditions are favourable for flowering and fruiting.

Ecology. Plants in which the shoots are generally emersed, such as arrowhead and *Limnocharis,* are found mostly in silted substrata with fairly shallow water. Floating-leaved and submerged species, such as pondweed and water nymph, occur in deeper waters, including rivers with moderate currents. Members of this subclass often dominate submerged communities.

Temperature is uniform in aquatic environments and may partly explain the vast geographic range and latitudinal extension of some species. The requirement for water itself is perhaps the most restrictive factor in the occurrence of these plants.

A factor almost as important as the presence of water is the availability of carbon dioxide, a compound essential in the process of photosynthesis. Although the total concentration of carbon dioxide in the surface water is about equal to that in the air immediately above the water, the diffusion rate of carbon dioxide in water is much less than that in air. Thus, as photosynthesis takes place in submerged plants, the carbon dioxide in the water surrounding the leaves is depleted; diffusion or the movement of carbon dioxide from distant areas with higher concentration takes place at a much slower rate than it does in the atmosphere. In addition, a relatively static layer of gas or water surrounding a leaf is about 10 times thicker in water than in the atmosphere. Water rich in carbon dioxide, therefore, is only slowly regenerated around a leaf.

Adapting to reduced availability of carbon dioxide

Aquatic vascular plants have adapted to the reduced availability of carbon dioxide by increasing the ratio of surface area to volume. Such morphological adaptations include long, narrow, thin leaves or compound leaves divided into filiform segments.

Another feature of the aquatic environment that limits available carbon dioxide is pH. A pH value of 10 or greater (basic) will remove all free carbon dioxide from the water. Aquatic vascular plants have evolved several physiological adaptations to such limited carbon dioxide availability. In one such adaptation, bicarbonate ions are used as a carbon source. Only certain species of aquatic vascular plants, however, can use such ions in this way; these species occur in waters that commonly have a pH of 9 or better.

Triuridales have developed a saprophytic relationship with mycorrhizal fungi and live on the forest floor of tropical rain forests. The fungal mycelium (body) penetrates the root hairs and other epidermal cells of the Triuridales plant. The fungi absorb organic matter and nutrients from the substrate and enzymatically convert them into substances that the vascular plant can use. The vascular plant then digests the fungus to obtain the nutrients. The

Triuridales are in fact, therefore, parasitic on the fungus. The fungus, however, does derive some benefit from its association with the roots of the vascular plant, in that competition from the soil environment is greatly reduced, permitting the fungus to obtain nutrients more easily.

FORM AND FUNCTION

Vegetative structures. The plants of this subclass are nonwoody annuals or perennials. Alismatales generally have basal leaves from an underground rhizome or abbreviated axis. They are characterized by a structural uniformity that adapts them to an aquatic existence. Variations in leaf form and shape are associated with the degree of immersion in water, and some species have leaves of two or more forms. Submerged leaves, if present, are usually produced first, followed by floating or emergent leaves. When a plant that normally develops emergent leaves is grown in relatively deep water, only submerged leaves are produced and flowering does not generally occur. For example, *Butomus umbellatus* (flowering rush), a species that normally develops erect emergent leaves, grows in water up to about one metre deep in Lake Erie. These submerged plants are not known to flower and have been given the name *Butomus umbellatus* forma *vallisneriifolius.* (Forma is a taxonomic category below variety.) However, when these plants are transplanted into clay pots and kept in water just deep enough to cover the soil, emergent leaves and flowering stems develop.

Butomaceae has a broad, horizontally creeping, underground stem with thick, fibrous roots from which arise tall leaves in two vertical series. Leaves are linear, erect, and triangular in section but are not differentiated into a separate leaf and blade. The leaf base is broadly sheathed (*i.e.,* it wraps around the stem), and the tip may be slightly flattened. Because the leaf and blade are not differentiated, the whole leaf is morphologically equivalent to the petiole (leafstalk) of other genera and is thus called a phyllode (a flattened leafstalk that functions as a leaf blade).

Limnocharitaceae consist of a short root stock with fine basal roots. The leaves arise from the apex of the root stock, have a long petiole, and are either emergent (as in *Limnocharis* and *Butomopsis*) or floating (as in water poppy). The emergent leaves are often massive, with the entire blade and upper petiole growing out of the water; the petiole is sturdy, and the blade varies in shape from broadly oval to elongated lance-shaped. Floating leaf blades have long, flexible, sinuous rounded or triangular petioles and flattened blades that rest horizontally on or near the surface of the water, with their upper surfaces exposed to the atmosphere.

Leaf forms

Leaves of the Alismataceae are quite variable, ranging from submerged leaflike petioles (phyllodia) to emersed phyllodia to floating or emergent leaves with expanded blades. These leaf forms are widespread within the family, often all forms occurring within one genus (*i.e.,* arrowhead); two forms commonly occur on a single plant. Emergent leaves, especially in the tropics, may become quite large, growing to a height of 1.5 to 1.8 metres and developing a blade width of 30 centimetres. Emergent leaves of burhead (*Echinodorus*) commonly are covered with large stellate (branched) hairs.

Leaves of the Hydrocharitales are mostly submerged (as in *Hydrilla,* waterweed, and *Ottelia*) or emergent (as in *Limnobium*). Juvenile leaves of *Limnobium* (frogbit) often float on the surface of the water and have large air spaces interspersed among the cells (aerenchyma) on the lower surface of the blade. Emergent leaves are usually supported by a round sheathing petiole with an expanded blade. Submerged leaves either originate at the base of the stem or are scattered along an upright or trailing stem (cauline). Basal leaves may be flattened phyllodia (as in tape grass and turtle grass) or have an angular petiole with an expanded blade (*Ottelia*). Cauline leaves are almost always linear, sessile (without a petiole), and whorled (three or more arising at a point along the stem).

Najadales leaves vary from emergent phyllodia (as in Juncaginaceae and Scheuchzeriaceae) to submerged (Najadaceae) to petiolate with floating blades (as in pondweed [Potamogetonaceae]). The leaves are either sessile or petiolate with a basal sheath that may or may not be fused to the blade or petiole. Emergent phyllodia are usually sessile, basal, and round, although the larger leaves are occasionally slightly flattened. Submerged leaves are mostly cauline and essentially alternate, although some appear to be opposite (as in water nymph and horned pondweed). The leaves of most submerged genera are linear and not attached to the stem by means of a petiole (water nymph). Others are thin and almost threadlike (filiform), as in horned pondweed and ditch grass. Pondweed has petiole or sessile submerged leaves, some of which have the sheath united to the blade or petiole. The submerged leaves of pondweed range from filiform to linear to nearly elliptic. In addition to submerged leaves, some species of pondweed develop leaves with floating blades. These blades contain considerably more cuticle (a thin layer of waxy substance that functions to prevent loss of water by evaporation) than do submerged leaves and are generally elliptical.

Triuridales have very small, sessile leaves with a triangle to ovate shape. There are usually few leaves on the stem, and these probably are unimportant to the plant.

Reproductive structures. The flowers of the Alismatidae vary widely in morphology. The apparently more primitive type (*i.e.,* Limnocharitaceae) have numerous separate stamens and carpels and two whorls of perianth parts (sepals and petals). Evolutionary gradation to more advanced types apparently results in an absence of perianth parts and a single carpel and stamen, such as occurs in the Najadaceae.

The flowers of the Alismatales are generally more primitive than those in the other orders. All parts are separate, and the perianth is obvious. Burhead and *Limnocharis* have numerous stamens and carpels; these numbers decrease within the order to three carpels and six stamens in some water poppies. Some species of arrowhead have imperfect flowers; the staminate flowers are arranged above the carpellate flowers of an inflorescence. Stamens, petals, and sepals all arise below the ovary without any fusion to the ovary.

Perianth structure

Some flowers of Hydrocharitales also have obvious perianth parts divided into sepals and petals (*Ottelia*). However, other members of the order (*i.e.,* turtle grass) have flowers without perianth parts. Although some species within the order develop perfect flowers, there is a trend toward imperfect flowers, culminating in carpellate and staminate flowers on separate plants (dioecious). The number of stamens and carpels is usually low (3 to 6), although some members may develop numerous stamens and up to 20 carpels. The carpels are fused into a single compound ovary, and the stamens and perianth parts are fused to the ovary.

Flowers of Najadales are fairly reduced; the perianth may be represented as two whorls of scalelike parts, reduced to one scale that is adnate (fused) to the stamen, or, as in most genera, absent. The number of stamens and carpels ranges from one to six; all are separate and free, except for pondweed, in which the perianth is fused to the stamens. The trend in the order is from perfect flowers with all the perianth parts present and three to six stamens and carpels to imperfect flowers with no perianth and one stamen or carpel, ultimately culminating in the dioecious condition. An unusual and interesting situation is found in horned pondweed, a plant with several imperfect flowers in the axis of a leaf; three to four carpellate flowers are usually surrounded by a spathe. Outside the spathe is a single staminate flower that grows over the carpellate flowers.

The saprophytic Triuridales generally have imperfect flowers with 3 to 10 somewhat basally fused perianth parts in one or two series. There are 3 to 6 stamens fused to the perianth. Three to many separate or basally united carpels develop over a flat to globose receptacle.

EVOLUTION

It has been suggested that the dicotyledon group that gave rise to monocotyledons must have had many features in common with the plants of Alismatidae. The Nymphaeales order is such a group and itself was probably derived from some ancient, vesselless stock of the Magnoliales order. Nymphaeales plants are aquatics without vessels and show tendencies toward cotyledon (seed-leaf) fusion. It is certainly feasible that an ancient stock of plants resembling the modern Nymphaeales order gave rise to the Alismatidae.

Monocots are considered to be of aquatic ancestry, later evolving land forms that in turn gave rise to groups that have returned to the water. The Alismatidae shows a progressive adaptation to an aquatic habitat.

One of the fundamental differences between the two great groups of flowering plants, the monocots and dicots, is the difference in leaf-vein arrangement between them. The Alismatidae is important in being positioned, in an evolutionary sense, near the bottom of the monocot sequence; some of its members exhibit a leaf structure that can be viewed as showing the evolution of the parallel-veined monocot leaf from the dicot leafstalk.

Phylogeny

Phylogenetic trends within the subclass Alismatidae are difficult to discern because they are masked by characters that are more easily altered by ecological factors. Among the aquatic or wetland members of the subclass, the Alismatales and Hydrocharitales are most closely related by the obvious perianth that is differentiated into sepals and petals and the flowers that are generally subtended by bracts. Among the Alismatales, the Butomaceae and Limnocharitaceae have characteristics that appear to make them more primitive than the Alismataceae: laminar placentation (ovules scattered along the inner wall of the carpel, rather than being in one row) and follicular fruits. The Butomaceae probably branched from the main line of the order early by loss of glands that produce milky sap (lactifers) and by the adoption of shorter and wider vessel elements. The order Hydrocharitales is more advanced, with an inferior ovary, united carpels, a trend toward the dioecious condition, and some species of marine habit.

The order Najadales is the most advanced order of the subclass, having a perianth of one to four tepals in a single series or six distinct tepals in two sets of two or three, a reduced number of carpels, and a trend toward single-seeded fruits and a submerged habit that culminates in an adaptation to the marine habitat. The family with the most primitive characteristics is the Aponogetonaceae: obvious, often coloured, perianth parts; usually perfect flowers; spherical pollen grains; and follicular fruits. Zosteraceae, probably the most advanced family, on the other hand, has a set of widely contrasting characteristics: a dioecious habit in *Phyllospadix,* an absence of perianth parts, linear pollen grains, single-seeded fruit, and a marine habit.

The Triuridales—with nuclear endosperm development, endosperm present in mature seed, saprophytic and terrestrial habit, and lack of chlorophyll—appear to be an early branch, not apparently in the main line of evolution of the subclass.

As is true of other water plants with soft vegetative organs, many members of the Alismatales order have rarely been preserved in fossil deposits. In the absence of woody parts, it usually happens that only resistant hard fruits, seeds, or pollen grains remain, the identification of which is uncertain. (M.Y.S./R.R.H.)

Subclass Arecidae

GENERAL FEATURES

Smallest angiosperm subclass

The Arecidae, the smallest and least homogeneous subclass in the angiosperms, includes four orders, of which three have only a single family and the fourth has three families. Together the six families encompass about 4,800 species. Arranged from largest to smallest, the orders are Arecales, including the Arecaceae, or Palmae, with 202 genera and about 2,800 species; the Arales, including three families, the Araceae with 110 genera and 1,100 species, the Lemnaceae with 6 genera and 29 species, and the Acoraceae with 1 genus and 2 species; the Pandanales, including one family, the Pandanaceae with 3 genera and about 700 species; and the Cyclanthales, including the family Cyclanthaceae with 11 genera and about 200 species.

The families were originally placed together on the basis of a woody habit with leaves in terminal clusters and presumably similar inflorescence structure. Subsequent study, however, has revealed that the architecture, leaf, inflorescence, flowers, and seeds are structurally different in these families. The classification into separate orders reflects their distinctiveness.

Diversity of structure. The orders include trees, shrubs, perennial herbs, and vines, and the genera of Lemnaceae have thalloid plant bodies. The woody forms may have some diffuse secondary growth but do not develop new vascular tissue.

Members of the subclass are outstanding for several reasons. They include one of the largest angiosperm leaves (the jupati; *Raphia*), inflorescence (*Corypha*), and seed (the double coconut; *Lodoicea*), all found in the Palmae, as well as the smallest known flowering plant (the watermeal; *Wolffia;* Lemnaceae). The family Palmae, or Arecaceae, exhibits more diversity than most monocotyledonous subclasses and generally is regarded as second among the monocots only to the grasses in economic importance. The palms also are of special interest because of their long fossil record and structural diversity.

The members of the Arecales are distinctive in geography and habit; all but a very few species are restricted to the tropics and subtropics, where they make up a prominent part of the vegetation. Characteristically woody, they stand out within the largely herbaceous monocotyledons. The family is fifth among monocotyledonous families in size, after the Orchidaceae, Gramineae, Cyperaceae, and Liliaceae. Palms have been difficult to study for several reasons. Their large size and extreme hardness deterred early collectors and led Liberty Hyde Bailey, an eminent American horticulturist during the early 20th century, to call them the big game of the plant world. Many genera are island endemics. Notwithstanding their importance, they remained poorly known until air travel to remote tropical areas became feasible. Increased botanical exploration of the tropics in the 1980s established the importance of palms and has resulted in measures for studying and conserving them.

The remaining three orders include unusual forms but their structures lack the range (from primitive to advanced) occurring in the Palmae. Each order is specialized in its own distinctive fashion, however. The single genus, *Acorus,* of the Acoraceae (Arales) has usually been placed in the Araceae, but it is now realized that *Acorus* differs in several respects—notably, in having unifacial rather than bifacial leaves, introrse (with the anther opening turned toward the inside of the flower) rather than extrorse (with the anther opening turned toward the outside of the flower) anthers, dry rather than fleshy fruits, ethereal oils and not raphides, and apical rather than basal placentation. Given these differences, a separate family is considered justified by most authors. Members of the Araceae are worldwide, though mostly tropical and subtropical, in distribution, largely herbaceous, and of considerable importance as food plants and ornamentals. The third family of the Arales, the Lemnaceae, brings a new dimension to the subclass in its thalloid form, which lacks stems and sometimes also roots. The third order, Cyclanthales, is restricted to the New World tropics and includes herbaceous or slightly arborescent plants, and a few lianas or subshrubs. Because their leaves are plicate (fanlike), the Cyclanthaceae are often considered to be related to palms, but there are developmental differences in the leaves of the two families and the similarities may be due to convergent or parallel evolution. In contrast to the Cyclanthales, the three genera of the Pandanales—*Pandanus* (screw pine), *Freycinetia* (freycinetia), and *Sararanga*—inhabit Old World coastal and marshy areas and exhibit unusual growth forms and architecture. Their largely dioecious breeding systems and questionable position in monocotyledonous evolution make them of special interest. Because of the distinctiveness of these orders, each is discussed separately in the following sections; the Arales, Cyclanthales, and Pandanales are treated in the section below, and the Palmaceae is considered in more detail as the representative group of the subclass Arecidae.

Distinctive features of the Pandanales

Distribution and economic importance. *Acorus calamus* (sweet flag), the only genus of the family Acoraceae, occurs in the wetlands of North America and from India to Indonesia in the Old World. Extracts of whole plants of sweet flag have been employed for medical purposes since the time of ancient Greece, and its leaves have provided floor covering as well.

Members of the family Araceae are widely distributed; some are temperate but most occur in subtropical and tropical regions of the Old and New worlds with a definite centre in the Old World tropics. Many genera occur in moist, humid areas in rain forests, where they may be dominant. Four genera, *Anthurium* (anthurium), *Arisaema* (jack-in-the-pulpit), *Amorphophallus* (devil's-tongue), and *Philodendron* (philodendron), account for over half the species in the family. The largest genus, *Anthurium,* consists of terrestrial or epiphytic rain-forest plants and has about 500 species that range from northern Argentina to Mexico. The family exhibits great variety in vegetative habit: most genera are herbaceous perennials, a few are woody, a number are climbers, some are epiphytes, and one (*Pistia,* water lettuce) is a floating water plant. Stems of the Araceae are aerial or underground and may develop rhizomes or tubers. Roots fall into two types: one form grows downward toward the soil and the other grows upward and is often green and climbing.

The family includes a number of economically important members. Throughout the tropics, the starchy tuberous corms of several genera (*Colocasia* [taro], *Xanthosoma* [tania, or yautia], *Alocasia* [giant taro], *Amorphophallus* [elephant yam], and *Cyrtosperma*) are grown as food. In some countries taro and tania are produced commercially. Taro (*C. esculenta*) of Asian origin has many varieties, some adapted to upland areas and others to flooded lowlands. The starch grains of this species are small and thus a more desirable food source for infants or invalids. Calcium oxalate crystals must be removed from the corms by boiling or baking. The South American equivalent, tania (*X. sagittifolium, X. atrovirens,* and *X. violaceum*), produces larger tubers and starch grains. The inflorescence ("fruit") of *Monstera* (ceriman) has a delicate flavour. Other genera, *Dracunculus* (dragon arum), philodendron, and *Zantedeschia aethiopica,* the arum, or calla, lily of florists, are important members as well. Philodendron and *Dieffenbachia* (dieffenbachia, or dumb cane) are popular houseplants because of their attractive foliage and low light requirements. Dieffenbachia, however, contains a proteinaceous poison and highly irritating raphides that can cause swelling of the tongue and mouth, even to the point of strangulation. Philodendron is also poisonous; children and pets may die from eating the leaves of either genus.

Poisonous species

The third family of the Arales, Lemnaceae, has six genera, which are cosmopolitan, occurring in fresh water throughout the world. The floating or submerged plants have little economic importance but serve to some extent as food for waterfowl and fish. Some (especially duckweed; *Lemna minor*) are used extensively in physiologic and genetic research, where the small size is a great advantage.

Most members of the Pandanales are distributed along coastal or in marshy areas in the tropics and subtropics of the Old World. They are abundant in the Malay Archipelago, Melanesia, and Madagascar and have a few species in New Zealand, southern China, and Japan. Fibre from the leaves and roots of the screw pine is used for mats, baskets, cording, and fishing nets. A few species (*Pandanus leram, P. andamanensium,* and *P. utilis*) have edible starchy fruits. Leaves of the most common, *P. odoratissimus,* are used to make an Indian perfume (kewda attar). Several are ornamentals, including *P. veitchii,* appreciated for its dark green glossy leaves with silvery white borders, and *Freycinetia banksii,* which is trained to grow around peat-covered pillars in New Zealand. Cyclanthales is restricted to the Neotropics, extending from southern Mexico south through Central America, the West Indies, and northern South America to central Bolivia and southeastern Brazil. Its single family, Cyclanthaceae, is centred in Colombia, where two endemic genera are found. The young leaves of *Carludovica palmata* (Panama hat plant) have long been used for making Panama hats. Ecuador, where the species is widely cultivated for the fibres known as "toquilla straw," exports more than one million hats each year. Older leaf fibres are used to make mats and baskets. Other uses include the making of brooms in Guiana from leaves of *C. sarmentosa* and thatching using the leaves of *C. angustifolia* in Peru.

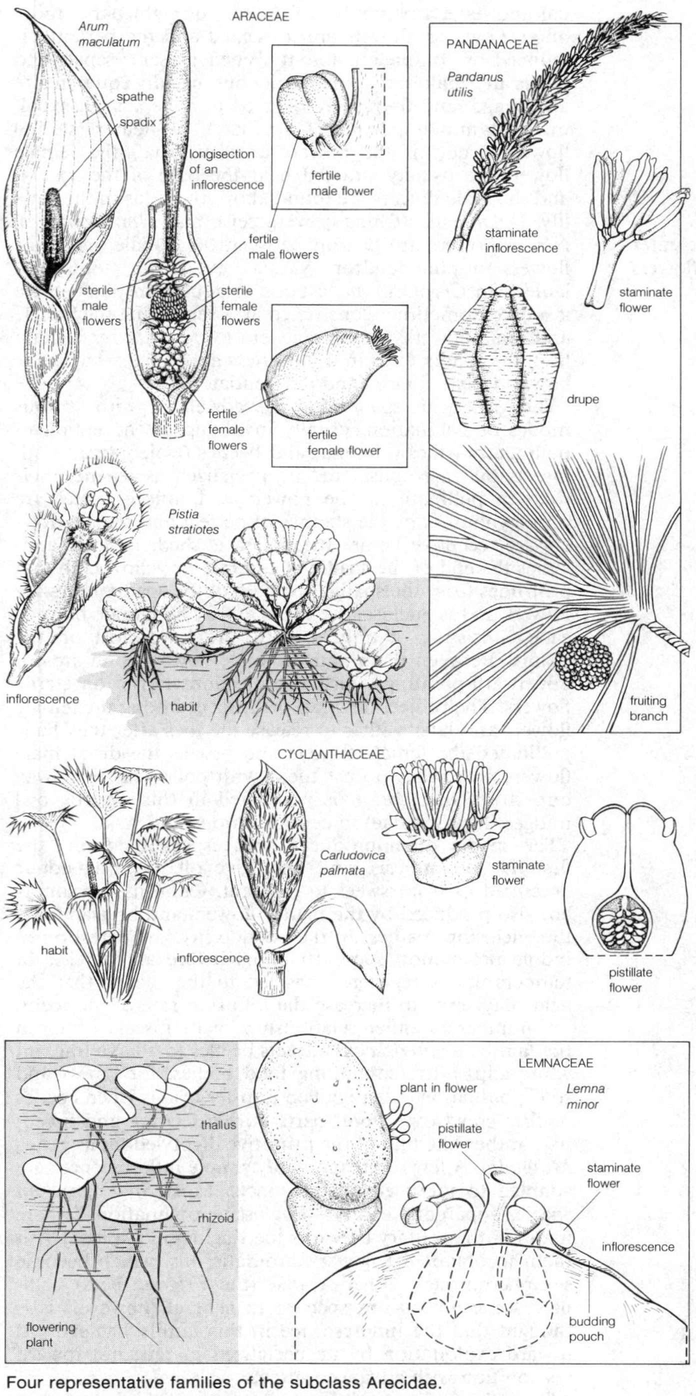

Four representative families of the subclass Arecidae.

From (*Arum maculatum*) M. Hickey and C. King, *100 Families of Flowering Plants,* 2nd ed. (1988), Cambridge University Press; (Pandanaceae, Cyclanthaceae, and *Pistia stratiotes*) L.H. Bailey, *Manual of Cultivated Plants,* rev. ed. (1969), reprinted with permission of The Macmillan Pub. Co.; (Lemnaceae) G.H.M. Lawrence, *Taxonomy of Vascular Plants* (1951), reprinted with permission of The Macmillan Pub. Co.

NATURAL HISTORY

Reproduction. The inflorescence characterizing all members of the Araceae is an unbranched fleshy axis bearing sessile flowers, usually known as a spadix. The spadix is wholly or partly enclosed by a more or less tubular bract called the spathe. The simplest, and supposed ancestral, state in the Araceae is a spadix closely covered to its tip with perfect (bisexual) flowers, as in *Pothos,* anthurium, and *Spathiphyllum;* a similar unspecialized inflorescence form is found in *Acorus.* Great variation in the spathe and spadix has developed from this basic form, especially in flower structure and position. The flowers may be bisexual and have a perianth of four, six, or eight parts; more often, however, flowers are unisexual and the perianth is reduced or completely absent. When present, sepals and petals are small, rather inconspicuous, usually equal in size and shape, and frequently referred to as tepals. Bisexual, male (staminate), female (carpellate), or neuter (sterile) flowers occur. If the flowers are unisexual, the female flowers are usually situated near the base of the spadix, and the male flowers are found above them (as in the calla lily, *Aglaonema* [Chinese evergreen], and *Homalomena*).

Neuter flowers

Neuter flowers are present between the female and male flowers in philodendron, yautia, and *Arum* (lords-and-ladies). In *Cryptocoryne,* a popular aquarium plant, there is a bare, sometimes constricted area separating the female and male flowers. In some genera (*Sauromatum;* voodoo lily), the spadix ends in a flowerless appendix, which may be variously coloured and differentiated.

The variety in spadix form is correlated with various modes of pollination, usually involving the deception of pollinators—flies (Diptera) and beetles (Coleoptera), both insects that are considered unspecialized as regards their roles in pollination. The flowers and inflorescences are protogynous—*i.e.,* the stigmas of perfect and female flowers are receptive before the pollen is shed. In lords-and-ladies the end of the spadix is a purple or yellow club that protrudes from the spathe; the base of the spadix bears the flowers and is enclosed by the spathe. The female flowers, each consisting of only a pistil, are lowermost on the spadix. Between them and the male flowers is an area of downward-pointing, hairlike projections borne on sterile flowers. The projections trap the insects among the female flowers and later wither to release the flies after they have pollinated the female flowers and just as the distal male flowers are ready to dust them with pollen on their way out. *Arum maculatum* is pollinated in this way by owl midges (Psychodidae) in central Europe and Asia.

The spadix often produces heat, especially during the first day of anthesis, and may give off a strong odour described as from sweet to pungent. Odorous substances are also produced by the neuter flowers and by glands on the enclosing spathes. In the voodoo lily, the detection of indole production some 10 hours before an increase in temperature is registered has led to the theory that the heat may serve to increase the diffusion rate of the scent.

A number of other relationships with insects occur in the family. *Zantedeschia* attracts beetles to a large fragrant white cup, often containing food bodies, for "mess and soil" pollination (where pollen transfer results when beetles or flies crawl over floral parts during feeding and breeding), rather like that of the primitive dicotyledonous genus *Magnolia.* A few of the reputedly simple inflorescences are adapted to more advanced insects. Most *Spathiphyllum* species apparently exhibit "Euglossine pollination," where males of the solitary bees of tribe Euglossini (Apidae) visit them to obtain the flower's aromatic oils, which become sex pheromones. Other Apidae (the *Trigona* bees) pollinate some anthurium species. In general, however, it is thought that the inflorescence in this family has evolved toward exploitation by unspecialized insects, not toward coevolution with advanced insects.

The inflorescence and flower structure of the Lemnaceae are the most reduced of any in the subclass. In one subfamily, the Lemnoideae, the inflorescence is borne in a pouchlike cavity and consists only of two male flowers and a lateral female flower surrounded by a membranous spathe. The flower structure is extremely simple. The male flower consists of a single stamen with a bilocular anther; the female flower is a pistil with a short style and single locule. The inflorescence in the other subfamily, the Wolffioideae, is borne in a dorsal cavity, not in a pouch, lacks a spathe, and bears only two flowers: the male consisting of a single stamen and the female of one pistil. Reproduction in Lemnaceae is frequently by vegetative budding. The plants rarely flower in the wild. When flowering occurs, the stamens and the pistil are not receptive at the same time. Pollination has been reported to be by water insects or to result from the forcing together of male and female flowers by wind or water movements.

The inflorescence of the Cyclanthales, also described as a spadix, has a very different structure from that of the Arales. The spadix varies in shape from more or less spherical to long-cylindrical and bears two to eight spathes that differ in size and may be red, white, yellow, or green in colour. The plants are monoecious, each bearing both male and female flowers. In all but one genus (*Cyclanthus;* cyclanthus), the flowers are borne in sessile groups of a female flower surrounded by four males. The groups are closely appressed in a spiral from the base to the apex of the spadix.

Structural variations among inflorescences

The spadix of cyclanthus is unusual both in the family and in monocotyledons as a whole. Its form is difficult to interpret. Male flowers, consisting of single stamens, are in four rows in a cycle around the spadix. The female flowers consist of ovaries, which are fused into female cycles, alternating with the male cycles and separated from them by thin wings, which are thought to represent perianth members.

Ecology. Many of the species of Cyclanthaceae grow on river banks and a few in mangrove communities along coasts. A strong scent produced by the flowers attracts weevils (Coleoptera), which appear to be the pollinators. Heat is also produced by the inflorescences, and the coloured spathes probably serve as attractants. Dispersal of seeds is largely by ants, which visit the fruiting inflorescences. Seeds of the riverside species are probably dispersed by water, although birds, mammals, and other animals may also be involved.

In the Pandanales, *Pandanus* and *Sararanga* are dioecious. The third genus, *Freycinetia,* was long thought to be dioecious, but bisexual inflorescences have recently been discovered in *F. reineckei* in Samoa. *Pandanus,* a genus of between 500 and 600 species, occupies many habitats. Its species, known as the screw pines, occur along seashores and lagoons, in mangrove fringes and lowland swamps, along rivers, in mountain forest, and in shady forest, where they may be understory shrubs. They represent a diversity of growth forms. Many are trees, reaching up to 20 metres with leaves 5 metres or more long. Most species have large stilt roots that support the trunk. The stem terminates in several equal branches, each of which ends in a dense crown of leaves. Coastal species often have spreading branches supported by lateral roots. Such branches may separate and form new individuals in a kind of vegetative reproduction.

An unusual growth form is found in deep swamps and gallery forests in Madagascar where 13 endemic, closely related species occur. In these species, a columnar trunk up to 15 metres high ends in a large rosette of leaves and bears lateral, horizontal, forked branches that have leaves which are smaller than those of the terminal trunk. Inflorescences are borne only on the lateral branches, a somewhat conifer-like habit that is unique in the family and in monocotyledons as a whole.

The genus is thought to be pollinated by the wind; however, white to pink spathes enclose the inflorescences, and an odour is known to be emitted from some inflorescences (such as *P. odoratissimus*), and so insects or animals probably pollinate the flowers to some degree. Animals and sea currents disperse the yellow, pink, or red drupes. The genus *Sararanga* has only two species: *S. sinuosa* from New Guinea, the Solomon Islands, and the Admiralty Islands, and *S. philippinensis* from the Philippines. The plants grow inland in mountain forest and on woody slopes near the sea. Both species are trees with long, narrow leaves. The inflorescences are pendant and borne in panicles and the flowers have a cupule apparently representing a perianth. The greenish white inflorescences are assumed to be wind-pollinated.

The genus *Freycinetia*

The third genus, *Freycinetia,* is found from Sri Lanka through Southeast Asia to northern Australia, Polynesia, and New Zealand. The woody plants climb by means of flattened, often long and wiry roots. Their leaves, which are less than two metres long, are linear, obovate (the widest axis above the middle), or ovate (the widest axis below the middle) in shape. They have membranous ear-like appendages near the base and spiny margins, at least near the tip. The inflorescence in freycinetia is a terminal spadix, usually borne in groups of three, but rarely solitary. The spadix bears several bracts; the lower ones are leaflike, the next higher variously coloured (orange, pink, salmon, red, yellow, lavender). The uppermost are often fleshy and edible, containing hexose (sugar). Female spadices bear single or united carpels and the males bear densely crowded stamens, each with a minute filament, globose, linear, or oblong anther, and a blunt tip. No perianth is evident at maturity in either male or female flowers. The stamens and pistils are so closely crowded that definition of single flowers is very difficult. However, study of young stages of the flowers using the scanning electron microscope (SEM) has helped resolve their structure and limits; a six-part perianth was observed in early stages. Very small staminodes are present in *F. caudata, F. urvilleana,* and *F. banksii,* and pistillodes were found on the staminate spikes of *F. sumatrana* and *F. funicularis.* These structures are obscured as the flowers subsequently enlarge and are absent in mature flowers. Their presence at immature stages suggests that the flowers represent modifications of bisexual flowers with parts in multiples of three, the basic form in the monocotyledons.

The inflorescences of freycinetia are usually crowded together and surrounded by a number of bracts; this telescoping results in a clustering of food bodies and presumably accommodates vetebrate pollination. Pollination of freycinetia by birds and bats has been reported in Indonesia, Samoa, Hawaii, and New Zealand. Bats and birds are both attracted by the edible bracts and by the pollen that is borne in a waxy matrix of edible oils. Flying foxes, also known as fruit bats (*Pteropus samoensis*), some of the largest known bats, pollinate *F. reineckei* in Samoa. The bats eat the terminal sugar-rich bracts and the staminate and bisexual inflorescences. They devour the bracts but not the flower-bearing parts of pistillate inflorescences. This sexual discrimination by the pollinators is hypothesized as leading to the establishment of separate sexes on different plants (dioecy). The fruits of freycinetia are berries, which are red, yellow, or white in colour and borne in dense heads.

FORM AND FUNCTION

Stem and root. The families of the Arales differ in stem patterns and root development. In Acoraceae the stem is underground and sympodial (*i.e.,* the extension of the stem is by development of a lateral bud rather than by increased growth of its apex). Both underground and aerial stems develop in the Araceae. The underground stems are corms or tubers of varying sizes. Aerial stems may be trailing (*Anthurium radicans*), erect (dieffenbachia), or climbing (ceriman, *Raphidophora,* and *Scindapsus*). Young plants seem first to exhibit monopodial growth and to produce a terminal inflorescence, after which the growth of the stem is sympodial. Some members of the subfamily Pothoideae have monopodial growth throughout. Vegetative adventitious buds are formed occasionally. They have been found on stems (*Xanthosoma viviparum*), leaves (*Amorphophallus bulbifer*), and on special branches of tubers (*Remusatia vivipara*).

Sympodial stems

Many different features of vegetative anatomy are found in the Araceae. Simple or uniseriate lactifers (latex-secreting glands) occur in certain taxonomic groups. Distinctive T- or H-shaped fibrelike cells characterize other genera, and still other genera have resin ducts and rows of mucilage cells. Silica bodies in specialized cells have not been reported. In some genera, there are compound vascular bundles in which two or three vascular strands are enclosed in a single common fibrous bundle sheath, with only one of the bundles having normally oriented phloem. The adaptive significance of these unusual bundles is not known, but they are useful as diagnostic characters.

Vessels, the special water-conducting cells characteristic of most seed plants, are found only in roots and have scalariform plates, the least specialized form of end wall. Needle-shaped crystals of calcium oxalate (raphides) are almost universally present; they may deter herbivores and other predators. Some crystals are diagnostic for families. The flavonoid tricin, common in palms, has not been found in Araceae, and chelidonic acid also is lacking. Steroidal saponins, however, have been reported, and cyanogenic compounds are common. Some other distinctive flavonoids occur as well.

Stems and leaves as such do not occur in the Lemnaceae. The plant body consists of a green, flat platelike structure, or thallus. These structures, often called fronds, float on the surface of the water or are slightly submerged and can form large floating mats that may become a nuisance in still water. Budding pouches, or grooves in the fronds, develop the inflorescences and the vegetative buds, from which new plant bodies form.

Stems are lacking in some Cyclanthales; in others the stems are short, and in a few they are long slender lianas, reaching 30 metres in *Thoracocarpus.* The stems lack vessels—except for *Thoracocarpus,* which has vessels with scalariform plates—and often develop cork. Their vascular bundles are compound (*i.e.,* two or more bundles are closely associated) and fused at the base. The rhizomes of the apparently stemless genera and those with short aerial stems bear adventitious roots; the lianas have many short climbing roots as well as some long rope roots. Cortical air cavities and usually scalariform vessels are present in the roots. Raphides are found throughout the family. Other forms of crystals also occur: styloids (elongated crystals) are numerous in *Evodianthus,* and druses (clusters of crystals) in leaves of *Cyclanthus.* Silica bodies are lacking. The chemistry of the family is not well known, however; cyanogenic compounds and small quantities of *p*-coumarin acid have been reported in the Panama hat plant.

Presence of crystals

Most members of the order Pandanales have branched stems, which are woody except in a few reedlike species of freycinetia. Their branching is usually sympodial with an inflorescence formed from each stem apex; vegetative branches arise laterally from the leaf axils. Some unusual patterns of development occur. Lateral buds may develop into short-lived shoots (*Pandanus gemmiferus*). In a group of species from Madagascar, only the lateral shoots produce inflorescences. The stems do not have secondary growth; the diameter of the trunk increases as a result of primary thickening growth before the trunk elongates, as in most palms. The three genera are alike anatomically. They all have compound vascular bundles, which are not fused basally as are compound bundles in Cyclanthaceae, and they have a more regular pattern than those in Araceae in which compound bundles are less frequent. It may be noted that in the vascular bundles of the stems in palms the phloem is arranged only on one side of the xylem (collateral), as in dicots, but compound bundles are found in at least some members of the other three orders.

The leaf. Leaf structure is different and distinctive in each of the six families of the subclass. In Acoraceae both the leaves and the scapes are ensiform (sword-shaped). Leaves in Araceae usually have a basal sheath, a petiole, and a flat blade. The blade is lanceolate to broadly ovate or rarely linear or strap-shaped. The base of the blade may be heart-shaped (cordate), arrowhead-shaped (sagittate), or enlarged basally with two acute lobes that resemble the barbed head of an arrow (hastate). The broadly wedge-shaped, sessile leaves of the water lettuce (*Pistia*) are unusual. Water lettuce also has stipules. *Piptospatha* has a true ligule, but otherwise ligulelike structures occur rarely (jack-in-the-pulpit, dieffenbachia). Intravaginal scales are found in philodendron, *Cryptocoryne,* and *Lagenandra.* Many genera show leaves of different sizes and shapes on the same plant, having entire young leaves and cordate or lobed mature leaves. Reticulate venation, unusual in monocotyledons, is common in Pothoideae, Monsteroideae, Calloideae, Lasioideae, and Aroideae.

In the Cyclanthales, the arrangement of leaves is spiral or rarely distichous. Petioles are universally present and may be long (Panama hat plant) or short. The blade is always plicate and varies from entire and small (*Ludovia* and *Pseudoludovia*) to bifid or palmately split (Panama hat plant). There are usually one to three major ribs (costae), but the genus *Cyclanthus* has strongly bifid leaves in which the central costa divides near the base, each branch running to the tip of its segment. In Pandanales, the spiral ranks of leaf bases that are pressed closely together are distinctive. The leaves are alternate and arranged in three rows, except in *Sararanga,* where they are arranged in four. The leaf sheath is not well differentiated except in freycinetia, and petioles are absent. The simple leaf blades are very long and narrow and usually leathery and rigid, with fibrous spines along the margins and midrib. Silica has not been observed in the family, but calcium oxalate is abundant as raphides and other crystalloid forms. Cyanogenic compounds are reported in some species of screw pine; otherwise, the chemistry is unknown.

The inflorescence. The Palmae inflorescences, as described below, may be huge and branched to six levels. A panicle also occurs in freycinetia (Pandanaceae); elsewhere in the subclass, inflorescences are more or less fleshy spikes, usually with associated spathes, and can be described as spadices. Thirty-five genera of palms bear spadixlike inflorescences and associated spathelike bracts. Spathes in the Palmae, however, are bracts of different kinds and are therefore not always homologous either to each other or to spathes of the other orders. The spathes of all the orders may be large and colourful or rather leaflike, and they function to protect the flowers as well as to encourage animal pollination. Differences in the arrangement of the flowers on the spadix and in flower structure distinguish the four orders of the subclass.

Palmae spathes

The fruit and seed. The fruit in Acoraceae is dry. The fruit in Araceae is generally a fleshy berry, although in water lettuce the fruits are rather dry and juiceless drupes, and a few others have nutlike fruit walls. The outer seed coat may be fleshy and sticky or dry and then usually develops longitudinal ridges. Endosperm is not always present in the ripe seeds of various Araceae. It does occur in the ripe seeds of the Lemnaceae, which has rather dry fruits.

The fruits of Cyclanthales, also berries, cohere to varying degrees within the spadix but become free in a few genera. In the Panama hat plant the orange fruits stick together and peel off the pink spadix in thick sheets, a colourful and structurally bizarre mode of dispersal. The female cycle of flowers in *Cyclanthus* gives rise to a hollow ring of united fruits (a syncarp), which becomes filled with seeds that are shed when the ripe syncarp splits into halves. Seeds in the family vary in shape. In species of *Sphaeradenia* they are crescentic, rectangular, elliptic, or ovoid. Seeds of *Stelestylis* have long terminal appendages. The seed coat varies in thickness, and the abundant endosperm contains both fatty oils and proteins. The small to medium-size embryo is straight and cylindric or, rarely, curved. Endosperm and embryo both contain starch in *Dicranopygium.*

In the Pandanales the fruits of freycinetia are berries with from 10 to 1,000 aggregated in a head. Drupes are formed in *Sararanga* and screw pine. *Sararanga* may have 12–80 pits (stony endocarps) in a single fruit. In the screw pine, the drupes either are formed from one carpel and have a single seed or are formed from phalanges of carpels and then have many seeds with separate or united bony endocarps. Abundant oily endosperm is present in seeds of the screw pine and *Sararanga* and starchy endosperm in freycinetia.

EVOLUTION

Fossil record

The Palmae have the longest and most extensive fossil record of any family of the subclass Arecidae, extending some 80 million years ago to the middle Late Cretaceous. The Palmae are structurally the most diverse and also the most distinctive group in the subclass. They differ from members of the other orders in always lacking sympodial branching below a terminal inflorescence; in having leaves with a nonplicate (non-fan-shaped) marginal strip that is shed during development; and in having a completely tubular leaf sheath. Palms also have collateral rather than compound vascular bundles in their stems, and silica bodies that are borne in specialized cells (stegmata) throughout. Vessels, often with simple perforation plates, are found in roots, stems, and leaves. No root climbers are known in the family.

The other three orders are younger and less variable. They do not show the large number of evolutionary sequences that are present in palms; rather, each order is specialized along certain lines. Macrofossils of the Cyclanthales are known from the Eocene Epoch (57.8 to 36.6 million years ago); fossil pollen has not been reported. The fibrous plicate leaves and possession of a spathe and spadix led to the inclusion of this order in the Arecidae. Sympodial branching below a terminal inflorescence and a few monopodial stems are found. Studies of the embryonic development of the leaves have shown that the origin of plications (longitudinal folding) in leaves is similar in Cyclanthales and Palmae and that an adaxial hastula (a ridgelike flap of tissue borne at the end of the petiole) may be present in both; however, the leaf sheath remains open in Cyclanthales and a nonplicate marginal strip is absent. Similarities in leaf structure between Palmales and Cyclanthales appear to represent parallel evolution. The Cyclanthales lack both silica bodies and cuboidal crystals but usually have mucilage cavities and sometimes other features, such as styloids and lactifers. Stem bundles are compound and basally fused in a distinctive way. Cyclanthales is generally thought to be an isolated order. Similarities to the genus *Freycinetia* (Pandanales) have been noted in flowers, seed characters, vegetative anatomy, embryology, and pollen morphology. Further studies are needed to determine whether these represent parallel developments.

Several genera of Araceae, represented by leaves referred to philodendron and *Peltandra* and some aroid spadices, have been found in the United States in strata dating to the Eocene. Fragments of probable leaves from this order have been observed in Paleocene deposits (*i.e.,* those dated at about 57.8 to 66.4 million years old) in Kazakhstan, and pollen referred to *Spathiphyllum* are known from Paleocene strata in Colombia. Araceous seeds (*Keratosperma*) have been described from the mid-Eocene of British Columbia in Canada; elsewhere, aroid pollen occurs in deposits of Miocene age (about 5.3 to 23.7 million years old) or younger. A fleshy spadix with a single spathe is a synapomorphy (shared derived characteristic) that occurs in all Araceae. The family is largely herbaceous while other members of the subclass are arborescent. Vegetative anatomy is diverse and not yet well investigated. Floral evolution has involved the loss of the perianth and the reduction and fusion of carpels and stamens. It is generally agreed that the Lemnaceae and Araceae may share a common ancestor. The genus *Pistia,* though not in itself ancestral to Lemnaceae, suggests such a possibility. In general the Araceae have few affinities with members of the other orders and may be more closely related to primitive Liliidae or perhaps to the Alismatidae.

The Pandanales have the second longest fossil record in the subclass, with pollen found in the Maastrichtian (74.5 to 66.4 million years ago); fossil fruit of this order have been identified in strata of early Eocene age. Their habit is often described as palmlike, but branching is always sympodial and there are no similarities in reproductive structures, except for the spathe, which is rarely present in the palms. The Pandanales exhibit dioecy, loss of a perianth, and a possible increase in the number of stamens and carpels. The family is characterized by an open leaf base, compound stem bundles without basal fusion, cuboidal crystal bodies, and an apparent lack of vessels in stems and leaves.

Obscure evolutionary relationships

The evolutionary relationships of these orders remain obscure. There is no one characteristic that unites them in a monophyletic group. Similarities include the occurrence of arborescent forms and lianas, tetracyclic stomata, usually indehiscent or fleshy fruits, similar embryos, and hypogeal germination (in which the cotyledons remain underground). In leaf anatomy, all have well-developed bundle sheaths and frequent nonvascular fibres, but these characteristics may relate to the mechanics of large, long-lived leaves.

The fossil records of the orders support the theory, based on structure, that the Palmales is older and stands apart from the other orders. As yet, there is no clear evidence relating the orders to each other or indicating their relationships to other monocotyledons. They all show evidence of the basic monocotyledonous trimerous floral plan and of a vascular system that has been determined to be distinctive to monocotyledons and quite unlike the vasculature of the dicotyledons. Perhaps these orders radiated separately from a widespread group of early monocotyledons. Modern studies are promising. Similar patterns in epicuticular wax, in certain organic acids found in cell walls, in flavonoid compounds, and in some parasites have led to the suggestion that palms may have had a common ancestry with some Commelinidae. Further developmental studies, cladistic analyses, and studies of DNA that are being undertaken are expected to lead to more insights on the evolution and relationships of these unusual plants.

(N.W.U.)

REPRESENTATIVE GROUP

Palmae. *Distribution.* The great centres of palm distribution are in America and in Asia from India to Japan and south to Australia and the islands of the Pacific and Indian oceans, with Africa and Madagascar as a third but much less important palm region. These centres are bounded roughly by latitudes 44° N and 44° S, though the greatest abundance lies primarily between latitudes 30° N and 30° S. These distributions correspond more or less with zones having mean annual temperatures of 15° and 21° C (60° and 70° F) and, with rare exceptions, to areas having 50 centimetres or more of rainfall per year.

The northernmost palm is the European fan palm (*Chamaerops humilis*), which grows about the Mediterranean in Europe and North Africa; the southernmost is the nikau palm (*Rhopalostylis sapida*), of New Zealand and the Chatham Islands. Although there are species with extensive ranges, especially in America, most are restricted in range, and those of islands, in particular, are frequently found nowhere else. One species, *Maxburretia gracilis,* is limited to a few limestone outcroppings in the Langkawi Islands off the Malay Peninsula. The island of New Caledonia has 17 genera and 32 species of palms, all of them endemic. The palms of Madagascar are not yet well known, but 130 species belonging to 21 genera are recorded and at least 14 of the genera are found only on the island. No species, except the European fan palm and the pantropical cultivated coconut (*Cocos nucifera*), occurs on more than one continent; the genera transcending continental bounds are *Chamaerops* in Europe and Africa, *Elaeis* (oil palm) and *Raphia* (raffia palm, or jupati) in Africa and America, and *Borassus* (palmyra palm), *Calamus* (rattan palm), *Hyphaene* (doum palm), and *Phoenix* (date palm) in Africa and Asia. Numbers of individuals of a species may be few or many.

Centres of concentration

Centres of abundance in numbers of species occur in mixed tropical and subtropical forests in both the American and the Asian tropics. The lowland rain forests of New Guinea and the Sunda Islands and the rain forests of Central and South America are richest in palm species. The Chocó region of western Colombia and parts of the island of Borneo have extraordinary numbers of palms. In the Gunung Mulu National Park, Malaysia, an area of rain forest spanning about 52,864 hectares, has 111 species representing 20 genera. In the western part of the Antioquia region of northwestern Colombia, 89 species representing 34 genera of palms occur in an area of 19,000 square kilometres. It is noteworthy that palms are not the dominant elements in these forests. Large stands of single species do dominate certain types of vegetation in the tropics and subtropics. The carnauba wax palm (*Copernicia alba*) occurs in solid stands hundreds of square kilometres in extent in the northeastern section of the Paraguayan Chaco Boreal and adjacent Bolivia and Brazil, the largest stands in this region alone containing possibly 500 million plants.

In the eastern tropics, *Nypa fruticans* may form dense colonies on estuarine muds; these pure stands of nipa palm (*Nypa*) extend for hundreds of hectares in eastern Sumatra and parts of Borneo. In other situations, dicotyledonous mangrove species occur with the nipa palm. The genus *Manicaria* (bussu palm) occupies similar habitats in some New World areas. Palms are dominant in another type of vegetation on the landward fringe of mangrove swamps in the western Malay Archipelago, where *Oncosperma tigillarium* and *Calamus erinaceus* (and, in Borneo, *Daemonorops longispathus*) are found. In the Amazon estuary *Raphia taedigera* covers extensive areas; other species of the raffia palm dominate similar habitats in West Africa. The raffia palm occurs in nearly pure stands between marsh and dicotyledonous swamp forests along the Caribbean and Pacific coasts of Costa Rica, and *Mauritia flexuosa* is found in vast stands in inland parts of the Amazon basin. On riverine flats and coastal plains of Africa, *Hyphaene compressa* and *Borassus aethiopum* occur, often in great abundance. Freshwater swamplands in parts of New Guinea are dominated by *Metroxylon sagu.* Both the doum palm and the sago palm (*Metroxylon*) are useful, and their distribution may be due in part to human activities. *Eugeissona utilis* grows in dense local stands to the exclusion of other trees in the uplands of Borneo. The vegetation dominated by *Prestoea montana* is distinctive in the montane forests of the Caribbean. Many of these palms are economically useful, and their natural or seminatural stands may be immensely important in local economies.

The abundance of palms may also be considered in relation to numbers of species per genus, in that a few palm genera have large numbers of species. *Calamus* with about 379 is the largest and *Bactris* (the peach palm) with approximately 239 is second. Several other genera, *Licuala, Pinanga, Chamaedorea,* and *Daemonorops* have more than 100 species each. Nearly a third of the genera (64), however, have only a single species, and more than half have fewer than 5 species each. The small number of species per genus reflects the large amount of endemism in the family.

Economic importance. The palms with the greatest importance in world commerce are the coconut and the African oil palm (*Elaeis guineensis*); both are prime sources of vegetable oil and fat. Few plants are as versatile as the coconut. The husk of the fruit is the source of coir, used for ropes and mats; the hard inner fruit layer (endocarp) is used as fuel and to make charcoal, cups, bottles, and trinkets; the coconut milk (liquid endosperm) is used as a beverage and in cooking; the coconut flesh (solid endosperm) is used as raw food or dried to form copra, a source of oil and oil cake, the latter used as cattle feed. The sap obtained from tapping the inflorescence, or flower stalk, is drunk unfermented or fermented (toddy) and is a source of sugar, alcohol, and vinegar. Trunks are used in construction and furniture making, and leaves are used in a variety of ways in domestic economies. The African oil palm is important chiefly for the palm oil obtained from the fruit coat and for kernel oil from the seed.

Coconut and African oil palms

Other palms are used extensively in both the Old and New worlds. Sugar and alcohol are obtained by tapping inflorescences of the sugar palm (*Arenga pinnata*), the palmyra palm (*Borassus flabellifer*), the wild date (*Phoenix sylvestris*), the toddy palm (*Caryota urens*), the nipa palm, and the gebang and talipot palms (*Corypha elata* and *C. umbraculifera*). Wine is made from species of the raffia palm in Africa and from the gru gru palm (*Acrocomia*) and the coquito palm (*Jubaea*) in America. The sago palm and, to a lesser extent, the sugar palm and the gebang palm are sources of starch obtained from the pith. The fruit of the date palm (*Phoenix dactylifera*) is a staple in parts of Asia Minor, the Arabian Peninsula, and North Africa and is also an article of commerce. Fruits are also widely used fresh, as sources of oil, and in the preparation of refreshing drinks and ice cream. Throughout much of the Asian tropics and even in parts of East Africa, the seed of the betel palm (*Areca catechu*) is used, with lime and the leaf of the betel pepper (*Piper betle*), as a chewing substance. Trunks and leaves serve in local construction, in the making of weapons, and as sources of wax (the wax palm, *Ceroxylon;* the carnauba wax palm). Leaves of the gebang palm are made into umbrellas and books; others provide material for rain capes, baskets, raffia (*Raphia farinifera*), hats, hammocks, and the fibre known as piassava.

Palms seem destined to continue to be extremely valuable economically, but in increasingly different ways. For centuries they have provided most of the necessities of life for humans in the tropics. Within rain forests and along their borders, whole communities have depended on palms for their livelihood. Except for the pantropical coconut, different genera have served in different tropical areas. The number of uses is legion. The sugar palm is used in more than 40 ways in Asia; the babassu palm (*Orbignya*) in Brazil yields 28 products of edible and chemical value. Native palm products are now contributing substantially to local economies. In 1979 the value of the harvest from six native palm genera (the black palm, *Astrocaryum;* the piassava palm, *Attalea;* the carnauba wax palm, *Copernicia; Euterpe; Mauritia;* and the babassu palm) was more than $100 million. Entrepreneurs recognized during the 1980s that several genera that have been utilized only from natural stands might be enhanced by the selection, cultivation, and mechanical harvesting that could be afforded them as major plantation crops. Certain neotropical palms, which are reported to have several times the potential yield of the traditional oil seeds such as peanuts and soybeans, are a good example. Perhaps 200 species of palms are potential oil producers, but only about 20 have been exploited, and, except for the oil palm (*Elaeis*), which is a plantation crop, oil has been extracted from wild specimens. The oil from the seeds of one species, *Jessenia bataua,* is physically and chemically much like olive oil, and the mesocarp pulp from the fruits of *Jessenia* and the closely related *Oenocarpus* is reported to have a protein content similar to that of meat. Large-scale production of such genera has been advocated.

Significance for local economies

Several genera show excellent potential for silviculture and agroforestry in land use systems where they are mixed with other species, sometimes also with animal components. A further advantage is that some useful palms grow on land not suitable for other crops, such as *Mauritia flexuosa* in waterlogged soils, the black palm in seasonally inundated areas, and *Euterpe chaunostachys* in swamps. Many palms, such as the sugar palm, the palmyra palm, and the sago palm, are multipurpose trees. In tropical America, the peach palm (*Bactris gasipaes*) is widely grown for hearts of palm and fruits, both in plantations and on small farms. The wood is valuable, and the peach palm also is grown as shade for several crops, such as coffee (*Coffea arabica*), citrus (*Citrus*), and breadfruit (*Artocarpus altilis*); it is especially successful with cacao (*Theobroma cacao*). In Ecuador, palms that are grown by the agroforestry industry include the peach palm; the tagua, or ivory, palm (*Phytelephas aequatorialis*) grown for vegetable ivory; and a fibre palm (*Aphandra natalia*). In Southeast Asia the production of rattan from species of *Calamus* (*C. caesius, C. manan,* and *C. trachycoleus*) is a promising industry. Commercial production of sago from trunks of *Metroxylon* has been investigated. Palms are sources of many products; indeed, no other plant family provides such a diversity. Their use in agroforestry may help conserve rain forests while providing an income for small farmers. The potential for their development is enormous.

Apart from commercial or local uses, palms are extensively planted for ornament in warm regions or indoors when a tropical effect is desired. Several hundred species are used as ornamentals in outdoor gardens as well.

Ecology. Palms have adapted to many habitats within their geographic limits. To the dweller in temperate regions, they tend to be associated with jungle or with tropical shores, where the coconut is often a prominent feature of the landscape. Most palms are inhabitants of tropical forests. There they thrive on well-drained acid soils in regions of high though often seasonal rainfall. They range from the lowlands to mountain and cloud forests up to altitudes of 1,800 metres. Rarely, as in the wax palm and some species of *Geonoma,* they grow at elevations as high as 3,000 metres in the Andes. There are exceptions, however, for palms are also found in swamps or poorly drained areas (bussu palm, *Mauritia,* date palm, sago palm, raffia palm) or brackish estuaries and lagoons (nipa palm) or areas subject to alternate flooding and drying (carnauba wax palm). They also occur in deserts or on seashores when underground water is present (doum palm, *Washingtonia,* coconut palm), or in open savanna, grassland, or gallery forest, or restricted to such special habitats as limestone outcrops (*Maxburretia rupicola*), serpentine soils (*Gulubia hombronii*), or river margins (*Astrocaryum jauari, Leopoldinia pulchra*) where competition is limited.

Habitats occupied by palms

Palms were long assumed to be wind-pollinated, but recent studies are showing that, while some (the thatch palm, *Thrinax*) are indeed anemophilous, wind is only one of a diversity of mechanisms of pollination. Some genera, such as the coconut and babassu palms, are pollinated by both insects and wind. Beetles are implicated in *Astrocaryum mexicanum, Bactris, Cryosophila albida, Rhapidophyllum hystrix,* and *Socratea exorrhiza.* Syrphus flies apparently pollinate *Asterogyne martiana* in Costa Rica, and drosophila flies are thought to pollinate the nipa palm in New Guinea. Bees pollinate several species (*Sabal palmetto* and *Iriartea deltoidea*). Studies of pollination are difficult because of the large number of insects that are associated in some way with most palms. Few modern studies have been done, but obvious adaptations for insect pollination can be found in many palms. Bats have been found to pollinate *Calyptrogyne* in Costa Rica.

In most palm fruits only one ovule matures into a seed, although a few genera are known to have 2- or 3-seeded fruits and up to 10 seeds may develop in *Phytelephas.* The black or brightly coloured fruits are dispersed by many different animals. The African elephant feeds on fruits and is important in dispersing *Phoenix reclinata, Borassus aethiopum,* and species of *Hyphaene.* Shrikes feed on fruits of the date palm, and in northeastern Queensland, Australia, the cassowary ingests fruits and disperses seeds of several rain-forest palms (*Calamus* and *Linospadix*). The black bear (*Ursus americanus*) disperses *Sabal, Rhapidophyllum hystrix,* and *Serenoa repens* in Florida, U.S. Fruits of *Euterpe* in northern South America are sought by fish and by the electric eel (*Electrophorus electricus*). Wild dogs (family Canidae) and palm civets (*Paradoxurus*) devour fruits of *Arenga* and *Caryota* in Asia. Studies of fruit dispersal are in their infancy, but a large number of interesting associations have been noted.

In tropical forest ecosystems palms are important in many ways. Breathing roots help aerate waterlogged soils. *Orbignya cohune* is known to be important in the development of the soil profile—stems are initially geotropic and buried to depths of one metre during establishment growth. The large cavities that are formed when palms in a population die result in considerable soil turnover. Many palms accumulate leaf litter in their crowns (*Asterogyne martiana, Eugeissona minor, Pinanga ridleyana,* and *Daemonorops verticillaris*), presumably trapping important nutrients. Some palms (*Orbignya phalerata*) contribute large amounts of dry matter, which, when recycled, adds to soil fertility.

Importance of palms in research

During the 1980s the value of palms in demographic studies was realized. Palms are easily identified within the forest. Their age can be estimated by determining the length of time needed to produce a leaf and counting the leaf scars. This method, however, must be used with considerable caution since studies are beginning to show that the rate of leaf production can vary with environmental factors. Some palms have very long lives; life spans of 50 to 100 years are common. In the Seychelles, specimens of the double coconut, *Lodoicea maldivica,* have lived for up to 350 years, and *Livistona eastonii* in Australia has lived to be as old as 720 years.

Palms are important in determining the composition of the forest community. Forest understories are sometimes dominated by a single species, as is the case with *Astrocaryum mexicanum* in Veracruz, Mex. Competition between young palms and ultimate canopy components may be an important factor in forest regeneration. Some palms that grow near the forest floor (*Asterogyne martiana* and *Geonoma cuneata,* for example) are being used to study light relationships, especially as regards simple versus dissected leaves. These studies are promising but in their preliminary stages.

Characteristic morphological features. The life cycle of a palm is like that of most flowering plants except that the early vegetative phase is often prolonged because the palm stem generally attains its maximum girth below ground before it begins to grow upward. This establishment growth is necessary because palms, unlike woody broad-leaved plants, do not have the means for growing a thicker trunk; moreover, they have only a single growing point. There is usually an accompanying change from the small and sometimes strap-shaped leaf of the seedling to the leaf of the adult.

Stem and root

Most palm stems are erect and solitary or clustered, but some grow horizontally, becoming procumbent, or trailing, at or below the surface of the soil and producing the crown at ground level, while others are high-climbing vines. Rare instances of regular branching (in *Allagoptera, Chamaedorea, Hyphaene, Nannorrhops, Nypa, Vonitra*) appear to involve equal or subequal division at the apex that results in a forking habit. The two newly formed branches may continue equally, or one may be overtopped by the other (*Nannorrhops*). When thickening occurs, as in the royal palms (*Roystonea*) or in the few that produce conspicuous swellings or "bellies" such as *Colpothrinax,* it is due to an increase in number or size of internal cells and not to new cell production at a cambium, or growing, layer. The cortex, or "bark," may be smooth or rough, and it is sometimes fiercely armed with spines or covered with old leaf bases. Nodes are marked by often prominent and ringlike leaf scars.

A typical palm stem, unlike the woody cylinder of a hardwood tree, is composed of hundreds to thousands of conducting strands scattered in softer ground tissue. There are usually two unequal regions, however. The central region is larger and softer than the outer region, which often is composed of densely packed fibres so hard that they quickly dull any cutting instrument. Thus, palms are often left in place when forests are cleared for cultivation. Such a construction accounts for the ability of palms to withstand winds that break ordinary trees.

The unusual nature of roots in the palms

The first root of palms, unable to increase in diameter as do roots of broad-leaved plants, is eventually replaced by adventitious roots from the basal nodes of the stem. Most roots penetrate the ground, but, in some palms, adventitious roots may form a mound above ground or appear at intervals along the stem. In *Cryosophila* and *Mauritia,* roots along the stem are transformed into spines. Stout prop roots forming a dense or open cone are found at successive nodes along the stem of certain varieties of palms.

Leaves in the Palmae have a characteristic aspect but are diverse in size, shape, and division. Most have a sheath, petiole or leafstalk, and blade. Sheaths sometimes are elongate or tubular, and when they appear to form a continuation of the stem, they are referred to as a crownshaft. The petiole is discernible above the sheath as a supporting axis devoid of leaflets.

The terminal portion or blade of the palm leaf is always plicate and may be either pinnate (featherlike) or palmate (fanlike). The first category embraces those that have distinct pinnae or leaflets or are bipinnate (*Caryota*) or merely pinnately veined. The second includes blades with relatively elongate central veins or ribs (costapalmate) or those in which segments radiate from a central region at the tip of the petiole. Many palmate and costapalmate leaves have a prominent, often spear-shaped, ridge of tissue at the apex of the petiole known as the hastula.

Leaves are sometimes armed with spines or marginal teeth on sheath, petiole, or blade, or on all parts. Pinnae may be modified into recurved hooks (*Desmoncus*), or the tip of the central axis may be produced into a long slender whiplike strand armed with recurved spines in climbing palms such as the rattan palm.

The inflorescence, the structure that bears the flowers, may be a large and complex panicle with numerous small leaflike bracts and branches to the sixth order, or it may be reduced to a head or to a spikelike axis with a single bract, or, as in the rattan palm, it may become a slender, clawed climbing organ or cirrus (tendril). The usual inflorescence has a supporting peduncle, or main axis, on which is borne a two-keeled first bract that is known as a prophyll and usually one or more other sterile bracts below the flowering portion. The flowering portion is composed of a central axis with branches of one or more orders and bracts associated with each branch.

A small bract usually subtends the flower or flower cluster. More rarely, the flowers are sunken in pits formed by the union of prominent bracts or by differential growth of the branch.

Palm flowers

Flowers of the Palmae are attached directly to the flowering branch or more rarely may have short supporting stalks. In either case they are very diverse in structure, size, and colour and are usually based on a three-part plan. Most are less than 2.5 centimetres in length, but the female flowers of *Phytelephas* may be 25 centimetres long. The least specialized flowers are those with a calyx of three sepals, a corolla of three petals, a male complement of six stamens, and a female structure of three distinct carpels, each with one ovule. Unisexual flowers are often markedly dimorphic (*i.e.,* the male and female forms are very different).

The sepals in all flowers are either overlapping or joined in a lobed cupule and are 3, rarely 2 or up to 10, in number. Petals, similarly, are usually 3, but may be 2 or up to 10; these are usually thicker than sepals, fibrous, and whitish or coloured. They may be distinct and overlapped or they may meet without overlapping, especially in male flowers. Petals also are sometimes partially to completely united. In a few palms the sepals and petals are reduced and united into a lobed cupule.

Stamens, though most often 6 in number, may rarely be 3 (*Areca triandra, Geonoma triandra, Nypa fruticans*) or more numerous, ranging from 6 to 36 in *Heterospathe,* to more than 200 in such groups as *Caryota, Phytelephas,* and *Veitchia.* Sterile stamens may differ only slightly from fertile stamens, or they may consist of a filament alone without an anther, or be united in a cup about the base of the female structure or in a tube joined to the petals,

From N.W. Uhl and J. Dransfield, *Genera Palmarum: A Classification of Palms Based on the Work of Harold E. Moore, Jr.* (1987); Allen Press, Lawrence, Kansas

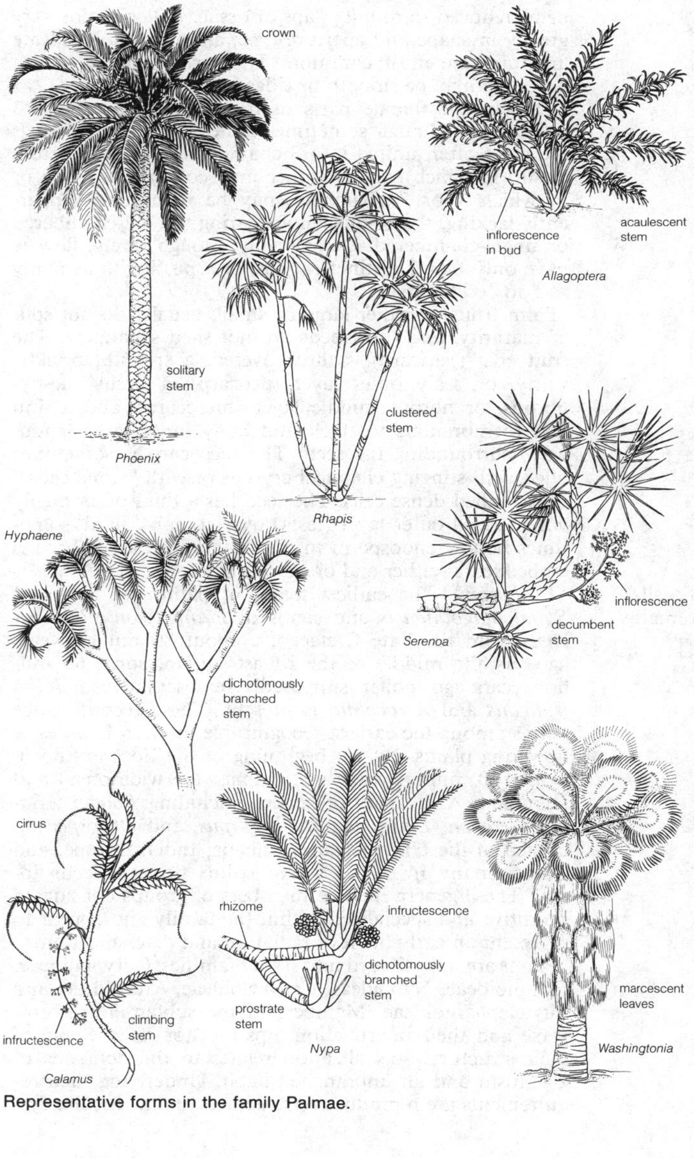

Representative forms in the family Palmae.

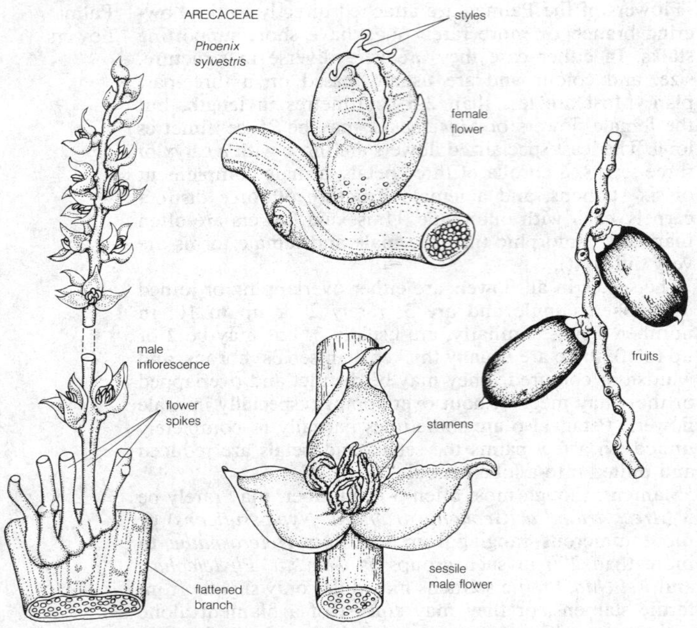

Representative floral structures for the family Palmae.

From M. Hickey and C. King, *100 Families of Flowering Plants*, 2nd ed. (1988); Cambridge University Press

or be reduced to minute flaps of tissue. Pollen grains vary greatly in shape and aperture type, although monosulcate apertures are most common. The surface of the grains, however, may be smooth or ridged to warty or spiny.

Carpels, the female parts of the flower, are usually 3 in number. Though sometimes quite distinct, the carpels are most often united in a 3-chambered female structure (pistil) in which each chamber may contain an ovule or in which 1 or 2 chambers may be reduced or apparently lacking, the pistil then appearing to be 2-chambered or single-chambered. Occasionally, though rarely, flowers have only 1 or 2 distinct carpels, or a pistil with as many as 5 to 10 chambers.

Palm fruits, whether large or small, usually do not split at maturity, and thus seeds are not shed separately. The fruit coat (pericarp) is three-layered: a smooth, prickly, warty, or scaly outer layer (exocarp); a fleshy, fleshy-fibrous, or fibrous middle layer (mesocarp); and a thin and membranous to thick and bony inner layer (endocarp) surrounding the seed. The mesocarp is sometimes filled with stinging chemical crystals or with "stone cells," thick-walled dense cells. The seed has a thin, often highly vascularized outer layer (testa) over copious, hard, sometimes hollow endosperm in which the pluglike embryo is embedded at either end or on one side.

Fossil remains

Evolution. The earliest fossils of palms are leaves of *Sabal magothiensis* and stems of *Palmoxylon cliffwoodensis* from the Late Cretaceous, about 80 million years ago. By the middle of the Maastrichtian, some 69 million years ago, pollen supposedly representative of *Nypa fruticans* and *Acrocomia* is present. These records place palms among the earliest recognizable modern families of flowering plants. By the beginning of the Eocene Epoch, nearly 60 million years ago, palms were widespread and abundant. A diversity of genera, including *Phoenix, Sabal, Serenoa, Livistona, Trachycarpus,* and *Oncosperma,* existed in the United States, Canada, India, Europe, and China, many in places where palms do not occur today. These genera include members of groups considered primitive and specialized within the family and appear to represent an early burst of radiation and diversification.

Palms are now divided into six subfamilies: Coryphoideae, Calamoideae, Nypoideae, Ceroxyloideae, Arecoideae, and Phytelephantoideae. Members of the subfamilies are diverse and their interrelationships are not clear. Some of their structural specialization relates to the demands of gigantism and an unbranched habit. Underlying such requirements are reproductive structures and a vascular system that are characteristic of all monocotyledons. Thus, the study of palms may be valuable in interpreting monocotyledonous evolution. It has been suggested that the palms, like the other families in the Arecidae, may represent a fragment of an early monocotyledonous radiation. The Palmae was separated earlier then the other families and has developed more specialized features, although within its own special constraints. (H.E.M./N.W.U.)

Subclass Commelinidae

GENERAL FEATURES

Orders

The subclass Commelinidae as defined in the taxonomic system of Arthur Cronquist consists of seven orders, of which the Cyperales (families Poaceae and Cyperaceae) accounts for the majority of the members. Commelinales, the basal and oldest order in the group, has flowers pollinated by pollen-collecting insects. The other orders in the subclass, Juncales, Restionales, Eriocaulales, Typhales, and Hydatellales, are significant for their gradual reduction in floral organs as they exhibit adaptations to pollination by wind dispersal.

Because of their significant place within the subclass, the Poaceae and Cyperaceae will be discussed separately below.

REPRESENTATIVE GROUPS

Cyperaceae (the sedge family). *Distribution and abundance.* The Cyperaceae, among the 10 largest families of flowering plants, contain about 5,000 species and, depending on the classification used, between 70 and 115 genera. The members are distributed throughout all the continents except Antarctica. Although there is a large number of species in Arctic, temperate, and tropical regions, the diversity of genera is far greater in tropical regions. Many species of sedges that occur in northern latitudes have circumpolar distributions. Species occurring in tropical or warm temperate regions, except for those that are widespread agricultural weeds, are generally confined to a single continent.

The six largest genera within the Cyperaceae account for about 3,500 species, nearly three-quarters of the total species: *Carex* (sedges), with about 2,000 species; *Cyperus,* with nearly 650 species; *Rhynchospora* (beak rushes), with roughly 250 species; and *Fimbristylis, Eleocharis* (spike rushes), and *Scleria* (nut rushes), each with about 200 species. Other large genera are *Bulbostylis,* with approximately 100 species; *Schoenus,* also with about 100 species; and *Mapania,* with up to 80 species.

Each of the six large genera except for *Carex* are primarily found in warm temperate or tropical regions, with only a few cold temperate species. *Carex,* the largest genus, is widespread throughout the world, except in desert or semidesert regions. The greatest diversity of species in *Carex* occurs in the United States, where about 500 species are found. About the same number occur in eastern Asia, from Siberia through China to Japan. In the tropics, *Carex* is uncommon in lowlands, although often diverse in montane regions. *Eleocharis* also has a number of species in cold temperate or even Arctic regions, although the great bulk of its 200 species are confined to warmer areas. Other large genera are basically distributed throughout the tropical regions of the Earth, with only a few outlying species in cold temperate regions. *Schoenus* is basically found in the Old World, with only a few of its species located in the New World.

Most of the remaining genera of Cyperaceae are quite small, almost all with less than 30 species, and many with only a single species. The limits of these genera are also somewhat unsettled, with the circumscription and limits of such well-known genera as *Cyperus* and *Scirpus* (bulrushes or clubrushes) being somewhat controversial. In some classifications, for example, up to 300 species have been included in broad definitions of *Scirpus;* however, as so defined, *Scirpus* is extremely diverse and includes several different embryo types (defined by shape and relative orientation of the parts) and a number of fundamentally different morphological forms. In this article, *Scirpus* is recognized in a narrow sense to include only the leafy bulrushes (about 40 species) in order to more accurately reflect the evolutionary relationships within the family. Genera recognized here that are sometimes included in *Scirpus* are *Bolboschoenus, Isolepis, Schoenoplectus,* and *Trichophorum* (club rushes). *Cyperus* is recognized here in a broad sense, although the genus *Kyllinga* is not included with it. All *Cyperus* have a uniform embryo type and a relatively consistent morphology.

Ecological diversity

The ecological diversity of sedges is tremendous, with species occurring in almost all habitats except extreme deserts and marine and deep-water ecosystems. A majority of sedges, however, are plants of sunny, moist to wet habitats such as fresh and salt marshes, pond and lakeshores, meadows, bogs, fens, wet prairies and savannas, and moist to wet tundra. Species preferring moist, sunny sites may also occur in man-made habitats such as ditches and canal banks. Many species of sedges also occur in understories of diverse types of forest, both temperate and tropical. Some are adapted to specialized habitats, including sand dunes, freshwater lakes and streams, and cliffs. Epiphytes are very rare among the sedges, occurring primarily in the South American genus *Everardia*.

Economic and ecological importance. Few sedges are crop plants. Of these, by far the most important are the Chinese water chestnut (*Eleocharis dulcis*) and chufas or tiger nuts, cultivars of the yellow nut sedge (*Cyperus esculentus*) grown primarily in Africa. In both species, the edible parts are underground tubers. In boreal regions and mountainous areas, species of *Carex* are often important pasture and rangeland plants and may even be managed, as, for example, meadows of *Carex lyngbyei* in Iceland.

Throughout the world many species of Cyperaceae have regional importance in weaving mats, baskets, screens, and even sandals because of their strong, fibrous stems and leaves. Genera used for these purposes include *Carex, Cyperus, Eleocharis, Schoenoplectus,* and, in Malaysia, the species *Rhynchospora corymbosa. Cyperus tegetum* is cultivated in India for this purpose, but the other genera are gathered from wild stands. Indigenous peoples on Lake Titicaca, in the Andes, use tatora (*Schoenoplectus tatora*) to construct small boats called balsas for traversing the lake.

Papyrus (*Cyperus papyrus*) was used in ancient Egypt for making paper and for constructing boats; it apparently was the bulrushes referred to in the biblical story of the infant Moses. Papyrus is still of local importance in Africa as a fuel source and is cultivated throughout the tropics and in conservatories in temperate regions as an ornamental for ponds. Several other species of *Cyperus* also are cultivated as ornamentals, including *Cyperus involucratus* (umbrella plant), a native of Africa, and, less commonly, *Cyperus albostriatus* and *C. isocladus.*

Use as ornamentals

A number of species of *Carex,* often those forms with variegated leaves, are cultivated as ornamentals in temperate gardens, especially along the shores of streams and ponds, as edgings, in rock gardens or woodland gardens, or as ground covers. The most significant of these are variegated forms of several Japanese species, *Carex conica, C. morrowii,* and *C. phyllocephala,* which are grown as edging or accent plants. The variegated form of the European *C. ornithopoda* serves the same function. The European Alpine species *C. baldensis,* with decorative white heads, and the variegated form of *C. firma,* with shiny, short, stiff leaves, are sometimes grown as ornamentals in rock gardens. Yellow-leaved forms of the large European species *C. riparia* and *C. elata* are popular waterside plants. Several New Zealand *Carex,* especially *C. buchananii, C. comans, C. flagellifera,* and *C. secta,* have wiry, brown or copper-coloured leaves and are grown in mild temperate climates as accent plants under the collective name New Zealand bronze sedges. Species of woodland *Carex,* notably the eastern North American *C. grayi* and *C. plantaginea,* the eastern Asian *C. siderosticta,* and the European *C. pendula,* are also grown as edgings or accent plants in shaded areas. *Carex baccans,* a Southeast Asian tropical species with fleshy, red to purplish fruiting structures in large clusters, is sometimes grown in greenhouses.

Species of other genera of Cyperaceae also are cultivated. A variegated form of the great bulrush, *Schoenoplectus lacustris,* is occasionally grown in ponds. The dwarf, tufted *Isolepis cernua* is commonly grown as a greenhouse edging or potted plant. The monotypic eastern North American *Cymophyllus fraseri,* with white inflorescences, is sometimes grown in shady wildflower gardens, and *Eriophorum* (cotton grasses) and the whitetop sedges, *Rhynchospora* section *Dichromena* (genera with a large number of species may be divided into sections), are popular plants of bog gardens.

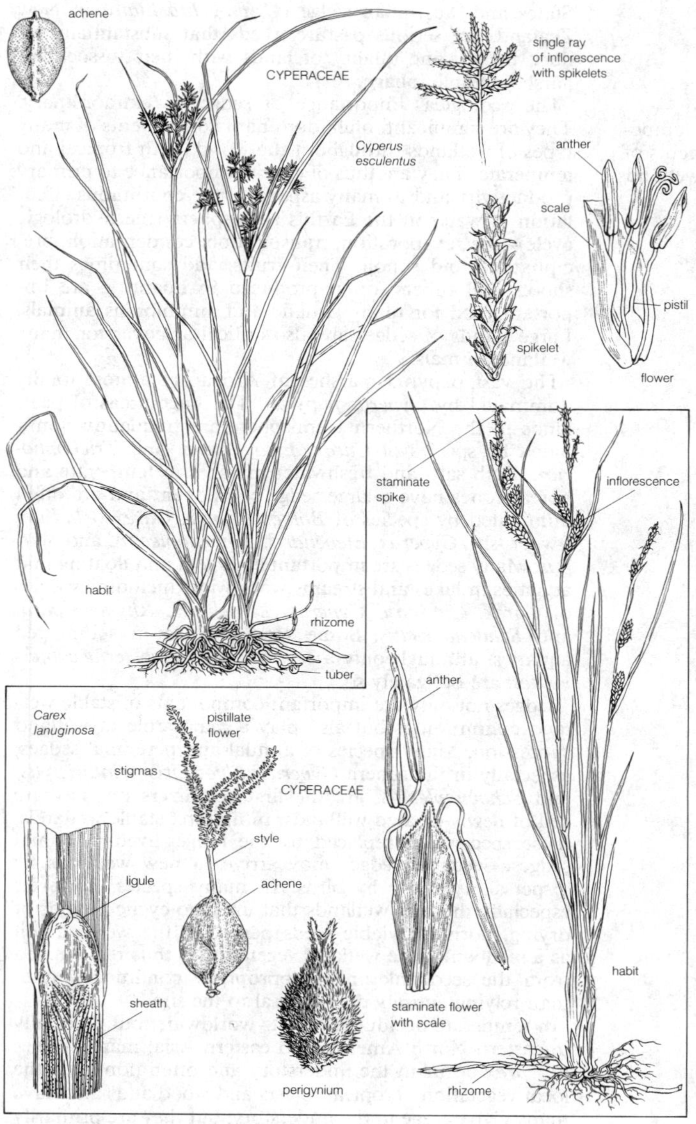

Representative genera of Cyperaceae.

From H.L. Mason, *A Flora of the Marshes of California* (1957); University of California Press, Berkeley

Some large, fast-growing wetland sedges, especially *Schoenoplectus lacustris* and some *Carex* species are grown in pond and tank treatments of domestic wastewater because of their capacity to absorb excess nutrients (notably phosphorus and nitrogen).

A substantial number of sedges are economically important because they are weeds. Purple nut sedge (*Cyperus rotundus*), arguably the world's worst weed, infests crops throughout tropical and warm-temperate regions of the world. The yellow nut sedge (*Cyperus esculentus*), also a weed, is a serious threat in cooler climates, causing considerable crop loss. Many other species of *Cyperus* grow in bare soils in areas that have had their vegetative cover removed or disrupted and also occasionally invade cultivated sites. A few *Cyperus* species, as well as species of *Fimbristylis* and *Schoenoplectus,* are significant weeds of rice paddies. Several coarse species of *Carex,* including wolf tail (*C. cherokeensis*) in the southeastern United

States and Australian sedge (*C. longebrachiata*) in New Zealand, are serious pasture weeds that substantially reduce the grazing quality of lands with their tussocks of harsh, inedible foliage.

Components of wetlands

The ecological importance of sedges is extraordinary. They are significant, often dominant components of many types of wetlands throughout the world, both tropical and temperate. They are thus of crucial importance to primary productivity and to many aspects of the continuous circulation of water in the Earth's atmosphere (the hydrologic cycle)—*i.e.*, evaporation, transpiration, condensation, precipitation, and runoff. Their fruits, and sometimes their shoots and tubers, often produced in quantity, are important food for many aquatic and amphibious animals. Large stands of sedges are also critical as cover for many wetland animals.

The vast papyrus marshes of Africa are almost totally dominated by *Cyperus papyrus*. The huge areas of peatlands in the Northern Hemisphere are frequently dominated by species of *Carex, Eriophorum,* and *Trichophorum.* Both salt- and freshwater marshes in temperate and boreal zones have a large sedge component and are often dominated by species of *Bolboschoenus, Carex, Cladium* (twig rush), *Cyperus, Eleocharis, Schoenoplectus,* and *Scirpus.* Many sedges are important emergent and floating mat aquatics in lakes and streams worldwide, including species of *Carex, Cladium, Cyperus, Eleocharis, Rhynchospora,* and *Schoenoplectus.* Some species are even submerged aquatics, although only a few, notably *Websteria confervoides,* are obligately so.

Sedges not only are important components of stable wetland communities but also play a major role in wetland succession. Many species of annual and perennial sedges, especially in the genera *Cyperus, Eleocharis, Fimbristylis,* and *Schoenoplectus,* are the first colonizers on the bare soil of newly created wetlands. In mature, stable wetlands, these species are replaced by the longer-lived perennial sedges. Seeds of sedges may arrive in new wetlands by dispersal, typically by birds. In many species, however, especially those of wetlands that undergo cyclic periods of drying, dormant viable seeds persist in the wetland soil as a seedbank. The wetland vegetation is thus rejuvenated from the seedbank under appropriate conditions rather than relying entirely on dispersal to the site.

In temperate deciduous forests worldwide, but especially in eastern North America and eastern Asia, many species of *Carex* occur in the understory and often dominate the local vegetation. Tropical forests and woodlands also have many Cyperaceae in the understory, but they are primarily species of *Cyperus, Hypolytrum, Mapania, Rhynchospora,* and *Scleria.*

Other habitats in which sedges are important are temperate and tropical grasslands and savannas, especially in moist sites. In dry or seasonally dry grasslands or savannas, especially in sandy soils or thin soils over rock, genera such as *Abilgaardia, Bulbostylis,* and some species of *Cyperus, Lagenocarpus, Scleria,* and, in Australia, *Gahnia* and *Lepidosperma* are important. Moist-to-wet zones along lakeshores and streambanks essentially worldwide also may have an important sedge component, as do various moist Alpine habitats, including paramo—the distinctive Central and South American alpine grasslands dominated by bunch grasses.

Characteristic morphological features. Although the Cyperaceae are similar in appearance to grasses (family Poaceae) and placed in the same order, there is a growing body of evidence that suggests that the closest relatives of Cyperaceae are the rushes (family Juncaceae). Rushes share with sedges a number of specialized anatomic and developmental features. Both families have chromosomes with a very peculiar structure. The centromeres, the point of attachment of the spindle fibres during meiosis, are not localized at one point near the middle but rather are distributed diffusely over the length of the chromosomes. Both the Cyperaceae and the Juncaceae have pollen that is dispersed as tetrads, although in the Cyperaceae three of the four nuclei produced by meiosis degenerate to leave only one functional nucleus in the tetrad. Both families also have tristichous phyllotaxy (leaves in three ranks).

Grasses

Grasses differ from sedges in many features, most obviously in their sheaths and the arrangement of the leaves on the stem. In the grasses leaf initiation begins on one side of the stem and the leaf margins grow around the stem from both sides of the centre of initiation until they encircle the stem, the margins overlapping when they meet. For the sedges, growth is as in grasses except that the leaf margins fuse when they meet around the stem on the opposite side of the centre of initiation. In grasses, the leaves are arranged alternately and in two ranks (distichous); that is, successive leaves arise on opposite sides of the stem, creating two vertical rows of leaves. In the sedges, three vertical rows are created (tristichous), with successive leaves developing at 120 degrees around the circumference of the stem.

The stems of Cyperaceae are often triangular and mostly solid, whereas those of grasses are never triangular and are usually hollow except at the nodes. In spikelets of Cyperaceae the individual flowers are subtended by a single scale, whereas the individual flowers of the grasses usually are subtended by two scales. Grasses have localized centromeres and single-celled pollen grains.

A majority of sedges have the morphological appearance of grasslike herbaceous perennials with fibrous roots, triangular stems, and three-ranked, linear leaves. A significant number are annuals, especially those of weedy or seasonal habitats. Many species have rhizomes of varying lengths; in a number of species, these rhizomes are important food storage organs and may even be tuberous. In many species, these rhizomes form extensive underground systems that are very important in local vegetative dispersal. In those species adapted to dunes or other sandy sites, the rhizome systems play an important role in dune formation and soil stabilization. Some species, especially in the genera *Eleocharis* and *Schoenoplectus,* have round stems, and a few species such as *Eleocharis quadrangulata* have four-angled or polygonal stems. Most sedges have solid stems or stems with only a small, irregular cavity, but a few, such as the three-way sedge (*Dulichium arundinaceum*), have hollow stems.

Sedges range in size from tiny plants less than 1 centimetre (0.4 inch) high found in a number of genera, such as *Eleocharis, Lipocarpha,* and *Abildgaardia,* to the giant papyrus, which can attain a height of 5 metres (16 feet). Some species of *Scleria,* for example, the African *S. boivinii,* are scrambling vines up to 10 metres long. Unlike grasses, which have extensively exploited the woody habit in the bamboos, very few sedges are woody. A few species of *Gahnia* have woody stems, and the remarkable West African *Microdracoides squamosus* is a woody shrub up to 1.5 metres tall with a form resembling a miniature Joshua tree.

All sedges have sheathing leaves, usually with blades; but members of a substantial number of genera, including *Caustis, Eleocharis, Lepironia, Schoenoplectus,* and *Trichophorum,* may be bladeless or nearly so. The sheaths are uniformly closed except in the small African genus *Coleochloa.* As in grasses, many genera have a small flap of tissue or fringe of hairs called a ligule that extends from the top of the sheath; the blade elongates above the ligule.

Varied forms of sedge leaf blades

Leaf blades of sedges are highly variable in form. Most are linear, less than 1.5 centimetres wide, and flat or folded at the main veins. In a number of genera, especially those of dry or seasonally dry habitats, the leaf blades are stiff and circular in cross section or are strongly rolled inward. Sedges adapted to shady habitats, especially species of tropical forests and the deciduous forests of eastern North America and eastern Asia, may have expanded (broad) blades; this includes a number of species of *Carex* in temperate forests and species of *Hypolytrum, Mapania,* and *Scleria* in tropical woodlands. In some instances, including species of *Carex* such as the Southeast Asian *C. scaposa* and species of *Mapania,* the leaves may be contracted into a false petiole. The leaf of the remarkable genus *Cymophyllus* from the eastern United States appears to be a broad, flat blade without a sheath, midrib, or ligule; however, the apparent blade is evidently an expanded and opened bladeless sheath.

The flowers in Cyperaceae are highly reduced in size and

complexity and are either unisexual or bisexual. The perianth (the calyx and corolla or the tepals) is either absent altogether or represented by up to six (though sometimes one) hairlike to stiff, sometimes barbed bristles. In *Eriophorum,* the bristles are extremely long, white to russet, and up to 50 in number. A few sedges, including most species of *Fuirena* (umbrella grass) and *Oreobolus,* have small scales instead of bristles. The flower usually has 3 stamens, although sometimes as few as 1 or 2 or very rarely (in the Australian genus *Evandra*) as many as 20. The single unilocular ovary has a terminal style with two or three stigmatic branches or very rarely one or up to as many as eight styles (in *Evandra*). Underlying each flower is a chaffy floral bract.

The flowers are arranged along a shortened axis, called a rachilla, that arises from the central stem of the plant. From a few to many flowers are arranged along the rachilla (rarely only a single flower), forming the spikelet, the basic unit of a sedge inflorescence. Spikelets are arranged into inflorescences of variable size and form: from small, tight heads in many genera to panicles, the usual form of the inflorescence; panicles as long as one metre or more can be found in some species of *Cladium* or *Gahnia.* Leaflike bracts often also underlie the major branches of the inflorescences. The reduction of an inflorescence to a single spikelet has occurred repeatedly in different evolutionary lines, usually in conjuction with a reduction in the size of the plant or as an adaptation to extreme habitats, or both. In some sedges, the spikelets are reduced to the point where they simulate a single flower (a pseudanthium), and these highly reduced flowerlike spikelets may then also be arranged, as if they were true flowers, into structures that simulate spikelets formed from true flowers. These structures are called pseudospikelets and become the basic units of compound inflorescences. The subfamily Mapanioidieae, an important tropical group, contains a number of examples of sedges with pseudospikelets.

The vast majority of sedges are wind-pollinated and have adaptations reflecting this fact, including abundant pollen production, nonsticky pollen, exserted anthers, and open inflorescences. In the few genera of Cyperaceae that are insect-pollinated, the inflorescences are contracted into dense heads, and the scales are usually white or sometimes yellow. If leaflike bracts are present in the inflorescence, these also may be white or yellow and are usually clustered together beneath the heads and arrayed radially at right angles to the stem. The coloration attracts the pollinator, and the arrangement of the flowers permits access to the most pollen per visit. Whitetop sedges (*Rhynchospora* section *Dichromena*), which occur from the southeastern United States to South America, are the best-known examples of insect-pollinated sedges. Species of *Ascolepis* and *Ficinia* in Africa, a number of tropical and subtropical species of *Cyperus* and *Kyllinga,* and even *Cymophyllus fraseri* in the eastern United States and *Carex baldensis* in the Alps have white heads (sometimes yellow or orange in *Ascolepis* and *Ficinia*) and are in all likelihood primarily insect-pollinated.

The inflorescences of insect-pollinated Cyperaceae

Fruits of sedges are most commonly achenes (nutlets), but in a few genera, notably *Mapania* and *Scirpodendron,* are single-seeded fleshy fruits called drupes. In many instances, the achenes have no obvious dispersal mechanism and are probably eaten and dispersed by birds and small mammals. In *Carex,* the achenes are enclosed in a sac called a perigynium, a modified tubular bract. The perigynium may tightly envelop the achene or it may be inflated like a bladder, flattened and scalelike, or even fleshy and edible. Many woodland species of *Carex* have food bodies (elaiosomes) at the base of the perigynium for ants, which disperse the perigynia. Species of *Lepidosperma* also have elaiosomes. In some species of *Cyperus,* the achenes are partly enclosed by the corky rachilla; at maturity the rachilla breaks apart to produce many rachilla segments and their attached achenes, which are then dispersed by water. When present, bristles may be barbed and cling to animal fur to disperse the nutlets, as in *Rhynchospora,* or they may be long and silky and act as parachutes for wind dispersal, as in *Eriophorum* and some species of *Scirpus* and *Trichophorum.*

Evolution and classification. Although fossil sedges are known from as early as the Eocene, they are as yet of little use in interpreting evolution in Cyperaceae because they are both fragmentary and apparently closely resemble modern groups. The rather uniform morphology of the nonreproductive parts of the plant body as well as the highly reduced flowers make deduction of evolutionary patterns from living sedges difficult. Thus, most theories on the evolution of the Cyperaceae at this point are derived from studies of the morphology and development of the spikelets.

Current systems of classification of the Cyperaceae divide it into two to five subfamilies. A division of the family into two subfamilies would result in the subfamily Cyperoideae with usually bisexual flowers and the subfamily Caricoideae with unisexual flowers, but many botanists consider this to be a rather arbitrary division. Four subfamilies are recognized in this article. The Cyperoideae, the largest subfamily including about 70 genera and 2,400 species, has usually perfect flowers in simple spikes with often numerous spirally arranged or two-ranked scales. The Caricoideae, the next largest subfamily, has 2,100 species dispersed among only 5 genera and is characterized by unisexual flowers with the female in single-flowered spikelets enclosed by a bract. The subfamily Sclerioideae has about 14 genera and 300 species; its flowers also are unisexual, but its fruit is not enveloped by a similar bract. The smallest subfamily, the Mapanioideae, has about 170 species in 14 genera. The highly reduced, unisexual flowers are grouped together tightly in such a way as to simulate a single flower (pseudanthium).

Cyperoideae

The most primitive type of spikelet is found in the genus *Scirpus* (bulrushes) and its relatives in the subfamily Cyperoideae. *Scirpus* has many-flowered spikelets with all but the topmost bracts bearing flowers. From this basic type, the remaining, more advanced members of the family can be derived by a reduction in the number of flowers, by the sterilization of flowers, and by the evolution of unisexuality in the loss of stamens or pistils within a flower.

The *Scirpus* spikelet is not the only type found in the subfamily Cyperoideae. The spikelet found in *Cyperus* and several related, smaller genera is similar, but the lowermost bract does not bear a flower. Spikelets characteristic of *Rhynchospora* and its allies and *Cladium* and its allies are derived by a reduction in the number of flowers per spikelet and a sterilization of lowermost or uppermost flowers, as well as by the conversion of some bisexual flowers to staminate only; in *Rhynchospora,* for example, male flowers are above the perfect flowers, and in *Cladium* male flowers are below.

The caricoid spikelet, characteristic of *Carex* and its satellite genera in the subfamily Caricoideae, is a highly specialized, reduced spikelet with uniformly unisexual flowers. The female flowers are always solitary and borne within a perigynium derived from the partly or wholly closed first leaf (prophyll) of the spikelet axis. Male flowers occur in the axils of bracts either on the rachilla extending beyond the female flower or on axes bearing perigynia. The evolutionary relationships of the Caricoideae are unclear. The spikelet of the Caricoideae can, in theory, be derived from the *Scirpus*-type by a reduction in flower number and conversion to unisexual flowers, and its relationships are probably with the Cyperoideae subfamily. The uniformly unisexual flowers, however, have also prompted botanists to align it with the subfamily Sclerioideae, which has unisexual flowers as well.

Mapanioideae

The subfamily Mapanioideae has a pseudanthium, or false flower, composed of a single terminal female flower surrounded by a number of naked stamens, each of which is subtended by a bract with the lowest two stamens situated opposite each other. In the genus *Hypolytrum,* only the two opposite stamens and their subtending bracts are present beneath the female flower. The pseudanthium is thought to be derived from a hypothetical prototype inflorescence in which a single female flower terminates an axis along which numerous male flowers are situated in the axils of bracts. The inflorescence then underwent reduction so that the male flowers were represented by only a single stamen each and the axis between them became greatly shortened. The reduction in the inflorescence was so extreme that it strongly resembles a flower—hence the term pseudanthium. This subfamily is highly specialized and entirely tropical.

The subfamily Sclerioideae also has inflorescences with terminal female flowers but the branches housing the male flowers below the female flowers are slightly more extended, though still short. This subfamily may have originated from plants with branched inflorescences similar to the hypothetical prototype ancestral to the subfamily Mapanioideae; however, the male flowers immediately below the terminal female flower were reduced to bracts, while branches below this point on the inflorescence have lost their terminal female flower and bear a few male flowers and one or a few distal bracts. In the tribe Bisboekelereae, the bracts below the terminal female flower are united to form a perigynium somewhat similar to that of the subfamily Caricoideae, though evolved independently. The subfamily Sclerioideae is almost entirely tropical, with only a few species of *Scleria* occurring in the temperate zone.

Some authorities have proposed a hypothesis of evolution in the Cyperaceae that is essentially the reverse direction of evolution to that presented above—that is, that unisexual flowers were the primitive condition. They suggest that inflorescences of the subfamily Mapanioideae, with their pseudanthia composed of tiny, unisexual flowers, represent the primitive condition in the Cyperaceae. The apparent flowers of other genera of Cyperaceae are thus also pseudanthia, and the seemingly simple, bisexual flowers of, for example, *Scirpus,* with three stamens and a single ovary, is actually a pseudanthium composed of three male flowers each with one anther and one female flower of a single pistil.

This hypothesis is based on the observation that unisexual flowers in the Cyperaceae apparently have no vestiges of the other sex. Also, it assumes that the broad-leaved tropical lowland species of the subfamily Mapanioideae are the most primitive representatives of the family. This hypothesis is thought by many, including Arthur Cronquist, to introduce unnecessary complexity in floral morphology for which there is little support. (A.A.R.)

Poaceae (the grass family). The Poaceae (also called the Gramineae), or grasses, rank among the top five families of flowering plants in terms of the number of species, but they are clearly the most abundant and important family of the Earth's flora. They grow on all continents, in desert to freshwater and marine habitats, and at all but the highest elevations. Plant communities dominated by grasses account for about 24 percent of the Earth's vegetation.

Ubiquity of the grasses

Distribution and abundance. There are about 8,000 to 10,000 species of grasses, most of them confined to a single continent. An exception, the cosmopolitan species *Phragmites australis,* the giant reed grass, has the widest geographic range of any flowering plant. This remarkably versatile species extends north to south in a wide band around the Earth between latitudes 70° N and 40° S and is most abundant in the Old World temperate regions; it is not native to the extreme south of South America, the Amazon basin, New Zealand, Polynesia, and parts of Australia, however. Humans have played an important role in expanding the range of many grasses, including weeds such as *Digitaria sanguinalis* (crabgrass), *Echinochloa crus-galli* (barnyard grass, or cockspur), and *Poa annua* (bluegrass). Endemism, or restricted geographic distribution, is fairly common among grasses, especially at the southern tips of continents and on mountain ranges.

The 500 to 650 genera of grasses fall into three distributional patterns. Nearly three-quarters are confined to one of seven basic centres of distribution: Africa, Australia, Eurasia north of the Himalayas, South and Southeast Asia, North America, temperate South America, and tropical America. About one-fifth of the genera encompass even broader distribution patterns throughout temperate or tropical regions of the world. Somewhat less than one-tenth of the genera have established discontinuous distributions on adjacent continents; 12 genera, for example, have such disjunct distributions between North and South America, 11 genera show these patterns between North America and Europe, and 7 genera are discontinuous between North America and northern Asia. *Brachyeletrum erectum* exemplifies the latter distributional pattern. This attractive herb inhabits woodlands of eastern North America and eastern Asia, a common pattern in many plant groups that is thought to represent the remnants of a once more continuous distribution around the Northern Temperate Zone.

There is general agreement that grasses cluster into five major groups. These subfamilies are more or less distinctive in structural features (especially in the anatomy of the leaves) and geographic distribution. The subfamily Bambusoideae differs from other grasses in its specialized leaf anatomy and structure, well-developed rhizomes (underground stems), often woody stems, and unusual flowers. Although the geographic range of the subfamily is between latitudes 48° N and 47° S, up to elevations of 4,000 metres, including regions with snowy winters, it is most prevalent in tropical forests. The core of the grasses of this subfamily consists of two more or less distinct major groups: the bamboos, or tree grasses, which are members of the canopy of tropical forests and of other vegetation types, and the herbaceous grasses of the Bambusoideae, which are restricted to the tropical forest understory. Of the 1,000 species of bamboos, somewhat less than half are native to the New World. Almost 80 percent of the total diversity of the herbaceous Bambusoideae subfamily, however, is found in the neotropics. The coastal, moist forests of Bahia, a state in Brazil, are home to the greatest bamboo diversity and endemism in the New World.

A peripheral subgroup of the Bambusoideae is sometimes segregated as the subfamily Oryzoideae owing to the distinctive spikelets and aquatic or wetland herbaceous habit of these tropical and warm-temperate plants. The best-known members of this subgroup of only about 70 species are rice, *Oryza sativa,* a native of Asia, and wild rice, *Zizania aquatica,* of North America.

Four of the major cereals—wheat (*Triticum aestivum*), barley (*Hordeum vulgare*), rye (*Secale cereale*), and oats (*Avena sativa*)—and many lawn and forage grasses come from the Pooideae. This subfamily contains almost 3,300 species and is clearly defined by various features, including the absence of the distinctive two-celled hairs found on the leaf epidermis in the rest of the family. The Pooideae reigns in temperate climates and is the only subfamily to have seriously invaded very cold areas.

Most members of the two subfamilies Chloridoideae and Panicoideae tolerate relatively warm and dry habitats through special adaptations for photosynthesis. Both subfamilies are concentrated in the tropics, and those that do extend into higher latitudes flower and grow mostly during the warmest part of the growing season. The 1,300 species of the Chloridoideae share unusual features of leaf anatomy, and many of the species are especially tolerant of drought and high soil salinity.

The Panicoideae include almost 3,300 species and are remarkably consistent in the nature of their spikelets. This enormously successful group divides naturally into two tribes, the Paniceae and Andropogoneae. Most of the former tribe has become specialized for savannas in tropical, humid zones, especially South America, and the latter is most abundant in areas of the tropics with pronounced seasonal rainfall, most notably India and Southeast Asia.

The last subfamily, Arundinoideae, is not nearly as sharply defined as the other subfamilies. The 600 species of this heterogeneous group of primitive grasses grow mostly in the tropics and Southern Hemisphere. *Phragmites australis* belongs in this subfamily.

The success of the grasses results from their tolerance of grazing herbivores and fire, their varied means of reproduction, and their versatility in photosynthesis. In most flowering plants, new growth in the aerial plant body occurs at the shoot tips only. If the tip is removed, buds in the axils of lower leaves may start growing, but the original shoot stops growing. However, the growing points, or meristems, of grasses lie at the base of each stem between the leaves so that regrowth is possible following removal of the tip by grazers, fire, or lawnmowers. The meristems of the grass leaf are also basally positioned and therefore similarly protected.

Seed production

Grasses produce seed through cross-pollination between plants (the most common reproductive condition in plants) and by two other methods: self-fertilization and asexual reproduction. Many grasses, including some weeds and cereals, have developed the capacity for self-fertilization, not only making it possible for a single plant to reproduce after long-distance dispersal but also enhancing the chances of preserving successful gene combinations, or genotypes, that crossing would disrupt. This fixation of successful genotypes benefits weeds because genes permitting effective colonization of an available site persist through generations.

Grasses in about 35 genera produce seed without fertilization; the egg contains a full complement of genes and does not need to fuse with a sperm to produce a zygote. This unusual reproductive mode, called apomixis, leads to clonal reproduction in that all offspring are by and large genetically identical to the parent. Apomicts such as several species of *Poa* (bluegrass) and *Sorghum* (sorghum) enjoy the same advantages as self-pollinators in being able to establish themselves after long-distance dispersal and in the perpetuation of successful genotypes. In addition, many apomicts are also capable of sexual reproduction for a flexible reproductive pattern.

Clonal reproduction

Many grasses reproduce clonally through vegetative parts. The most common means of such spreading involve rhizomes (horizontal underground stems that send shoots aboveground) and stolons (horizontal aboveground shoots that may produce vertical shoots). *Phragmites australis* is not only one of the most widely distributed plants—its fruits are borne in parachute-like containers that are carried by the wind—but also one of the most successful at dominating appropriate habitats. Its rhizomes rapidly infest moist-to-saturated soils of swamps, ponds, streams, and banks to the eventual exclusion of almost all other plants.

Grasses display a wide variety of adaptations for dispersal and establishment of seeds. Awns (bristlelike projections), hairs, spines, and barbs on the spikelets or their parts catch onto the fur of passing animals. Members of the genus *Cenchrus* are commonly known as bur grass or sandburs because they grow in sandy areas, such as beaches, and their spikelets are beset with barbed spines that readily cling to animal fur or painfully attach themselves to the feet of people walking on the beach. Hairs may also perform like parachutes in retarding the fall and thereby increasing the dispersal of seeds. Large grazing animals, birds, small mammals, and other animals eat grasses and disperse the seeds that pass through their digestive tract.

Economic and ecological importance. Grasses dominate large expanses of the middle of continents, such as the North American prairies, South American pampas, African veld, and Eurasian steppes. No single climate generates grasslands; they develop in areas with wide ranges of rainfall (from semiarid to subhumid) and temperature.

Native grasslands develop where there are frequent fires and droughts, level to gently rolling topography, and in some instances grazing animals and special soil conditions. Fire is pervasive in natural grasslands—early settlers of the North American grasslands, for example, recorded spectacular annual fires—and beneficial in that a fire recycles nutrients bound in dead plants into the soil for use by living plants. Persistence of grasslands depends on the exclusion of competing woody species that would supplant the grasses. Because fires tend to occur most readily during dry seasons when grass roots, rhizomes, and seeds are protected in the soil and woody plant stems are fully exposed, they tend to do more damage to woody plants than to grasses. Fire alone, however, will not maintain grasslands, because some trees are tolerant of fire. Periodic drought damages the exposed stems of woody vegetation more than the buried underground parts or seeds of grasses. Further, the composition of grasslands has been partially regulated by large herbivores, such as the buffalo on the North American prairie whose grazing suppresses the invasion of woody plants into the grassland and, like fire and drought, may actually stimulate the growth of grasses.

Often, a small number of species dominates a grassland. For example, on the true North American prairie, which stretches from southern Manitoba to Texas and forms the eastern edge of grasslands in North America, *Andropogon gerardi* (big bluestem), *Schizachyrium scoparium* (little bluestem), *Sporobolus heterolepis* (prairie dropseed), and *Stipa spartea* (porcupine grass) are the primary grasses. These species occur in varying proportions and are joined by other grasses, depending on climatic and other factors.

Adaptation to environmental extremes

Grasses have adapted to the full range of environmental extremes occupied by plants, from the coldest regions and highest elevations where plants grow to equatorial heat, and from fully aquatic habitats to deserts. These remarkably adaptable plants play significant, sometimes dominant, roles in many plant communities, such as freshwater and saltwater marshes, tundras, meadows, and disturbed habitats. In addition, civilization creates temporary habitats for many grasses including not only lawn, pasture, and crop species but also weeds. The competitive ability and adaptability that has made grasses dominant over much of the Earth have produced some of the world's most pernicious weeds. Weedy grasses invade and colonize disturbed habitats. While this is not a concern on roadsides, abandoned farmlands, vacant lots, and other low-value land, weedy grasses do seriously devalue cultivated areas such as lawns, pastures, and croplands. *Phragmites australis,* for example, is spread vigorously by rhizomes, threatening agriculture wherever there are lowlands or bodies of water near arable fields or pastures.

Natural forces, such as windstorms or fire, may disturb forests and other vegetation not dominated by grasses and thereby open a habitat for weedy grasses. The ancestors of modern weedy grasses may have evolved as a result of such natural disturbances.

Except for the woody bamboos, grasses lack the stature needed to compete with trees for light and to elevate their flowers into the forest canopy for wind-dispersal of pollen. All major habitats of grasses are open and largely devoid of trees. Nevertheless, many grasses normally grow in the understory of temperate and tropical forests. Herbaceous grasses of the subfamily Bambusoideae are generally limited to lowland tropical forests, and some of them (*e.g., Pariana*) have overcome the relative absence of wind currents by evolving adaptations to insect pollination.

The economic importance of grasses lies in their role as an important food source. Up to 70 percent of the world's agricultural land is given to crop grasses, and more than 50 percent of the world's calories come from grasses, particularly the cereals. Most grasses produce an edible grain, the bulk of which, the endosperm, provides a rich source of carbohydrates for the germinating embryo. Also called the germ, the embryo contains protein, oil, and some vitamins.

At least 300 grass species are known to be harvested in the wild as cereals, and about 35 are or have been domesticated. Ironically, most crop grasses were originally successful weeds. Some of the traits that have made weeds successful, such as their ability to colonize rapidly and to produce an abundance of seeds, are also desirable in crops. Domestication, the propagation of selected individuals, leads to uniform population maturity, loss of natural seed dispersal, and an increase in the yield of harvestable seed. These changes enhance the quality of cereal crops. Grasses that produce desirable grain but that are not adaptable to agricultural habitats, however, have not become domesticated. *Zizania aquatica,* the wild rice of North America, has been harvested extensively from wild stands, but its requirement of deep-water habitats precluded its domestication until recently.

Cereal cultivation

Cultivation of the cereals began about 10,000 years ago as a major part of the shift from hunting and gathering to plant and animal husbandry, a transition that stimulated rapid social and cultural evolution. From the beginning of their domestication, bread wheat (*Triticum aestivum*), barley (*Hordeum vulgare*), oats (*Avena sativa*), and rye (*Secale cereale*) in the Middle East; sorghum (*Sorghum bicolor*) in Africa; rice (*Oryza sativa*) in Southeast Asia; and corn (maize [*Zea mays*]) in Central America have supported the rise of many civilizations.

The earliest evidence of cereal domestication appears in Southwest Asia about 7000 BC, when domesticated barley that was totally dependent on humans for seed dispersal first appeared in several Middle Eastern sites. (Some investigators believe the domestication of barley may have originated in Ethiopia.) Over the next 4,000 years the practice of growing wheat and barley spread north and west to Europe, and by 3000 BC these cereals had reached China. Bread wheat, known widely in the Middle East by 6000 BC, is strictly a domesticated species; it arose serendipitously when different species of wheat were grown together.

The processes of hybridization and polyploidization have produced many valuable crops. Normally during sexual reproduction, two haploid gametes (n) fuse to form a diploid zygote ($2n$). In polyploidy, one or both gametes remain diploid because the chromosomes fail to separate during an early stage of meiosis. Consequently, fusion of three or more complete sets of chromosomes produce offspring that may be incapable of reproducing with the parent strain and thus constitute a new species. The importance of this condition rests in the larger store of genes, which imparts a greater evolutionary potential on the hybrid. Hybridization is important because, in crossing breeds, a more uniform product replaces the often heterogenous parent generations.

An example of the improvement that results from these two evolutionary processes can be found in the gradual domestication of wheat. Among wheats there are three levels of ploidy, or sets of chromosome complements: diploid ($2n$), the normal condition; tetraploid ($2n = 14$, resulting from the fusion of diploid gametes); and hexaploid ($2n = 21$). An example of a domesticated diploid wheat is einkorn wheat (*Triticum monococcum*), one of the earliest domesticated wheat species. Hybridization of a diploid wheat with *Aegilops speltoides* (a closely allied species of grass), followed by doubling of the chromosome complement, produced tetraploid wheats. In one of these, emmer wheat (*T. dicoccon*), the grain is tightly clasped by the hull (lemma and palea), a characteristic of wild species that depend on the hull for dispersal. Threshing and winnowing—the separation of chaff from grain—is far easier when the hull separates freely from the grain, as in the cultivated tetraploid macaroni wheat (*T. durum*), a major commercial wheat species. The development of bread wheat (*T. aestivum*), a hexaploid wheat, involved the hybridization of a tetraploid wheat with *A. tauschii*, a closely allied diploid species of grass, followed by chromosome doubling to 42.

Plant breeders have developed many cultivars of wheat closely adapted to different growing conditions; there are more than 200 cultivars grown in North America alone. Many others were mainstays of the Green Revolution of the late 1960s and early 1970s, which bred wheat and other crops specially adapted to the ecological conditions in the agriculturally less developed parts of the world. What makes bread wheat the most widely cultivated plant in the world today is its adaptability to a wide range of growing conditions, ease of harvesting and handling, and high nutritional value. Gluten, its seed protein, forms the elastic matrix of leavened bread.

Domestication of rice

The domestication of rice dates to about 4000 BC in mainland Southeast Asia (Thailand, Myanmar [Burma], and South China). Cultivation of this species usually involves flooded conditions in paddies, although it is also grown in upland conditions. Almost half of the world's rice cultivation takes place in China and India and less than 1 percent in the United States. The immediate product of harvesting, brown rice, may be converted to white rice for a visually appealing but nutritionally inferior grain, with reduced protein and B vitamins. The thousands of rice cultivars supply the basic food for more than half of the world.

Corn (maize) was first grown in the highlands of west-central Mexico about 6000 to 5000 BC. (The term corn is confusing outside of the United States, where it refers to cereals in general.) Corn differs strikingly from Middle Eastern cereals as it is much larger, and as a member of the Panicoideae it is adapted to warm seasons. Its flowers are unisexual—staminate (male) flowers are clustered in a tassel, and pistillate (female) flowers are found in an ear. Considerable controversy surrounds the origin of the totally unique ear of corn. A leading hypothesis derives the ear from the tassel of a teosinte (*Zea maya* subspecies *parviglumis*), a wild relative of corn. Its large grain is naked (not enclosed in a husk) and it remains attached to the axis or cob at maturity.

With its high nutritional value and adaptability, corn became the staple crop of all agricultural peoples in the Western Hemisphere by the 1st century BC. One of the first uses of the corn kernels was for popping. Corn can be ground into tortillas, an unleavened "bread," parched, or prepared with wood ashes or shells to make a hominy. The use of lime from wood ashes or another source played a significant role in the diets of people who depended on corn as a staple because, without the lime treatment, it lacks a sufficient amount of the vitamin niacin. Corn breeders have exploited the vigour inherent in hybrid lines to generate tremendous yields of the grain.

Sorghum cultivation extends back to about 3000 BC in northern and eastern Africa. It is now the fourth largest cereal crop. Its wild ancestors include several subspecies that persist in the wild on African savannas. Sorghum grains are a rich source of protein (approximately 15 percent of its weight), and its sap is concentrated into molasses. Broomcorn is a cultivar of sorghum grown for the stalks that are used to make brooms.

Millets

The centres of early domestication of the major cereals were the sites of other cultivated grasses as well, the most notable being the millets: proso millet (*Panicum miliaceum*) and foxtail millet (*Setaria italica*) in Asia; pearl millet (*Pennisetum americanum*) and finger millet (*Eleusine coracana*) in Africa and India; and Job's tears (*Coix lacryma-jobi*) in Asia. Like sorghum, all these so-called minor cereals belong to the Chloridoideae or Panicoideae. In each of these agricultural centres, members of the pea or bean family (Fabaceae, also called Leguminosae), such as lentils, soybeans, chickpeas, peas, and various beans, were almost as important as the grains.

In terms of world production, four of the best known crops are members of the grass family: sugarcane (*Saccharum officinarum*), wheat, rice, and corn (maize). Barley and sorghum are among the top 20 grains in terms of production. Domestication of sugarcane is thought to have occurred in Southeast Asia after it was discovered that the stem is a rich source of sugar. This crop produces more calories per acre than any other crop, calories that are used in the form of table sugar, to generate alcohol to power automobiles, and for the manufacture of rum. Alcoholic beverages are distilled from other crop grasses: barley provides beer malt, rice is used in the production of sake, and corn for bourbon. Wheat, rye, corn, and barley contribute to the making of whiskeys and vodka.

While the cereals and sugarcane are a primary food source, bamboos provide a remarkable range of useful products. It has been suggested that the tree grasses (or bamboos) provide more and more varied uses than any other plant on Earth. Young shoots of several species of *Bambusa, Dendrocalamus,* and *Phyllostachys* are important vegetables in the daily diet of the peoples of China, Japan, and Taiwan and a gourmet item in other parts of the world. In China, Southeast Asia, and Brazil, bamboos have been used in papermaking, and in India the majority of the pulp for paper production comes from bamboos, especially *Dendrocalamus strictus*. The extraordinary strength and lightness of bamboo stems make them an excellent building material in the construction of houses and temples, woven mats, and bowls, trays, and other vessels.

Grasses also are used for livestock feed, erosion control, and turf.

Characteristic morphological features. Although grasses superficially resemble other plants, most notably the rushes (family Juncaceae) and sedges (family Cyperaceae), these similarities are far outweighed by the numerous less-conspicuous differences in the structure and arrangement of reproductive parts, pollen development and structure, chromosome structure, and embryology.

Root system

Grasses are perennial or annual and usually terrestrial and free-standing; they are rarely vines or aquatics. The root system consists not of a taproot, as in many dicotyledons, but of fine, fibrous roots. Corms and bulbs are sometimes present and prop roots may develop from the lower nodes or joints of the stem, as in corn. Grass stems, sometimes called culms, are herbaceous or woody, and they range from about 2 centimetres (0.79 inch) in some grasses of severe climates (*Aciachne pulvinata*) to 40 metres (131 feet) in height and 30 centimetres in diameter in bamboos (species of *Dendrocalamus*).

As is true of other monocotyledons, woodiness or lignification does not develop from the annual production of lignified layers of tissue as in broad-leaved trees of such dicotyledons as oaks and maples. Instead, blocks of tough, fibrous cells associated with the xylem (water-conducting tissue), some lignification of the most common type of cells (parenchyma) in the stem, and silicification of the epidermis (outermost layer of cells) provide the structural rigidity of bamboo stems.

The stems of grasses range from fully erect to prostrate. They are solitary to densely clumped, as in the so-called bunch grasses. Many grasses produce horizontal stems, either below ground (rhizomes) or above ground (stolons).

The internodes, or stem regions between the nodes, are usually round in cross section and either hollow or filled with a spongy pith. What makes the grasses unusual, however, is their method of growth: they elongate by means of cell division and enlargement at the basal point of growth.

Some of the structural strength required for grass plants to stand erect comes from the leaves, particularly the leaf sheaths. Arising at nodes and encircling the internode above, sheaths counter the tendency for the internode to bend at the basal growing point, where it is weakest.

Grass blade

The other major part of the grass leaf is the blade. Grass leaves are borne singly at the nodes and, with minor exception, are arranged in two vertical ranks. Thus, a leaf, and most conspicuously its blade, is positioned directly under the blade two nodes above it. Structurally, this means that the point of leaf initiation alternates with each node; the leaf sheath grows to encircle the stem and overlap when the two points meet. Grass leaf blades are usually long and narrow, with parallel margins, but occasionally are in the shape of a lance, egg, arrow, or heart. The blades may be shorter than one centimetre or less than five metres in the larger bamboos. In grasses of such arid areas as the desert, the leaves may roll up to form long, thin tubes, thereby reducing surface area and water loss.

The leaf veins (vascular bundles that transport water and nutrients) run parallel to one another. Special cells in the outermost cell layer of grass leaves contain silica bodies, which range from saddle-shaped to crescent- or dumbbell-shaped. These shapes are often used to distinguish large groups of grasses from one another. While silica bodies occur in the epidermis of other monocots, such as sedges, they do not show the great variability of form found among the grasses.

At the junction of leaf sheath and blade, designated as the collar of the leaf, and on the side facing the stem, grass leaves bear a ligule, a small flange or ring of hairs, depending on the species, that may have evolved to prevent the entry of water into the leaf sheath. At the base of the blade, in some grasses, especially members of the subfamily Bambusoideae, the leaf is constricted and resembles a stalk or petiole. This pseudopetiole moves the leaf downward or upward at night, depending on the species.

Internal structural differences associated with photosynthetic pathways

The most significant variation in the internal structure of grass leaves involves anatomical differences associated with two photosynthetic pathways: the pathway that synthesizes a four-carbon (C-4) compound and that which synthesizes a three-carbon (C-3) compound. The chief distinction between these two pathways is the presence of specialized, thick-walled photosynthetic cells located in sheaths surrounding vascular bundles in C-4 plants. These cells participate in the mechanism for assimilation of carbon dioxide from the atmosphere into a four-carbon compound. Hence, plants with these features are called C-4 plants, as opposed to C-3 plants, which take up carbon dioxide into a three-carbon compound.

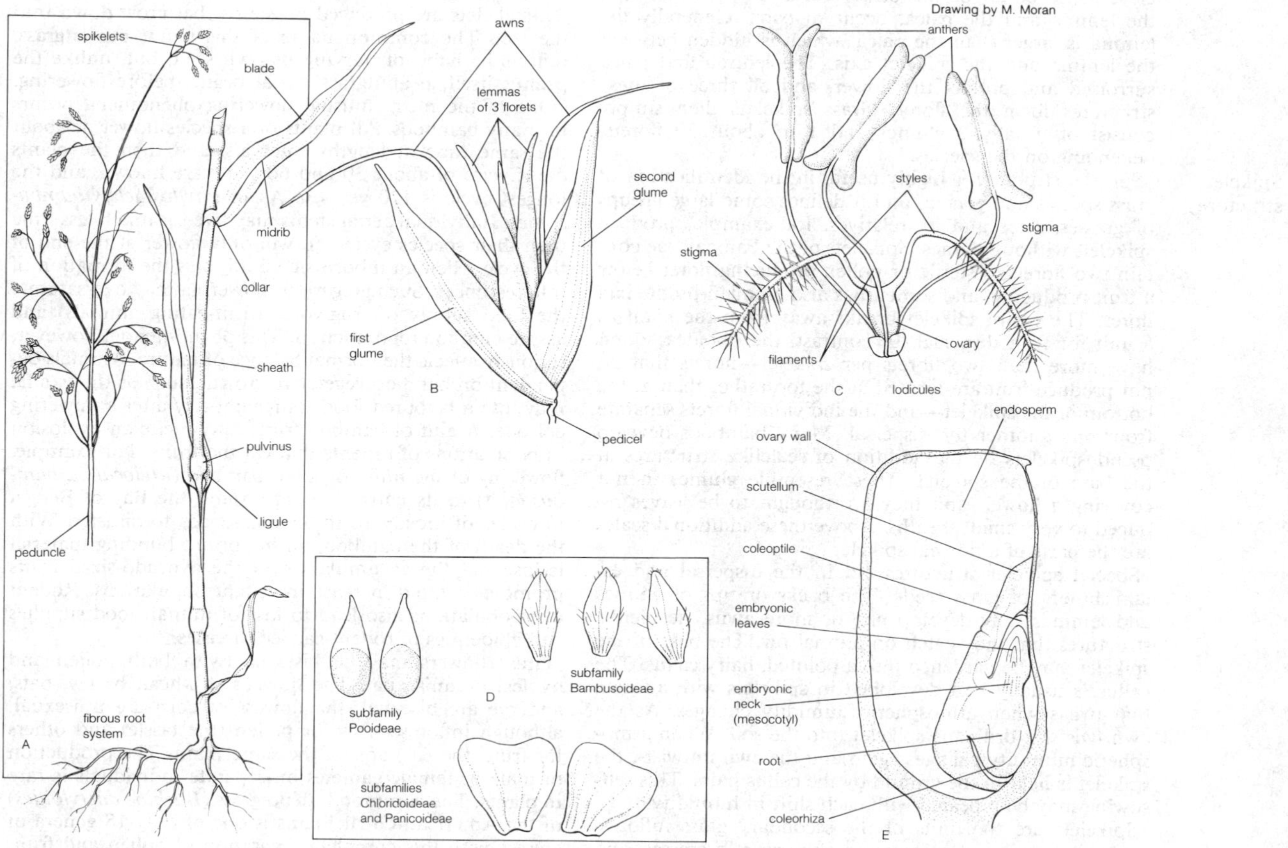

Grass structures.
(A, left) Grass inflorescence (panicle); (right) culm bearing leaves. (B) A common type of grass spikelet. (C) A grass flower. (D) Grass lodicules (modified petals) from the four largest grass subfamilies. (E) A mature caryopsis, or grain (longitudinal section).

It is important to understand that both C-3 and C-4 plants use the C-3 route of CO_2 fixation, the ultimate aim of which is the synthesis of sugars. In the C-4 cycle, however, there are additional steps before the CO_2 is fixed into a three-carbon compound. In C-4 plants, carbon dioxide is fixed into a four-carbon compound (oxaloacetate) in the mesophyll and reduced to malate or aspartate, which is then transferred to the sheaths surrounding the vascular bundle. Here CO_2 is removed from the malate or aspartate (decarboxylation) and refixed in the C-3 cycle, which produces 3-phosphoglycerate, a three-carbon compound.

Although the C-4 cycle uses more energy in the form of adenosine triphosphate (ATP), it is advantageous in hot tropical conditions. Under such conditions, plants tend to close their stomata when it is hot or dry, decreasing the flow of carbon dioxide into the bundle sheaths. The mesophyll readily fixes the carbon dioxide, which is concentrated as malate or aspartate in the mesophyll and is removed to the bundle sheaths, where the C-3 cycle proceeds. The higher concentration of carbon dioxide in the bundle sheaths facilitates the C-3 cycle, enabling the tropical plants to grow faster than their C-3 relatives.

C-4 plants are more efficient at taking up carbon dioxide than are C-3 plants and tend to fare better in hot or dry climates. This climatic association of the C-4 syndrome is consistent with the fact that all members of subfamily Chloridoideae and most of the Panicoideae, the two large tropical subfamilies, are C-4 plants. A very small number of Arundinoideae are C-4 plants, while all the Bambusoideae and Pooideae are C-3 plants. The C-4 pathway represents an evolutionary specialization that has evolved in about 10 families of flowering plants and is particularly common in the grasses.

The primary inflorescence of grasses is the spikelet, a small structure consisting of a short axis, the rachilla, to which are attached chaffy, two-ranked, closely overlapping scales. There are three kinds of scales. The lowermost, called glumes, are usually two in number, and they enclose some or all of the other scales. The other scales, the lemma and the palea, occur in pairs. Generally the lemma is larger than the palea, which is hidden between the lemma and the spikelet axis. The lemma and palea surround and protect the flower, and all three of these structures form the floret. Grass spikelets then simply consist of usually 2 glumes and 1 to about 50 florets, depending on the species.

Spikelet structure

Spikelet structure is highly useful in the identification of grass species and genera, and it defines some large groups of grasses. Rice and its relatives, for example, produce spikelets without glumes. Spikelets of the Panicoideae contain two florets, a sterile or pollen-producing floret below a fruit-producing, and sometimes also a pollen-producing, floret. The entire spikelet breaks away from the plant as a unit for fruit dispersal. In contrast, the Pooideae often have more than two florets per spikelet—florets that do not produce fruit are located at the top rather than at the bottom of the spikelet—and the individual florets separate from one another for dispersal. Many bamboos develop pseudospikelets by the addition of scalelike structures at the base of the spikelet. These resemble glumes in not covering a flower, and they are thought to be leaves reduced to very small sheaths. Above these additional scales are the parts of a normal spikelet.

Special spikelet structures aid in the dispersal and establishment of grass seeds. The backs or tips of glumes and lemmas may develop one or more awns, needlelike structures that may catch on animal fur. The base of the spikelet may be hardened into a pointed, hairy callus. The callus is usually best developed in spikelets with an awn that twists when atmospheric humidity changes. As the awn twists, it drills the spikelet into the soil. When atmospheric humidity changes again and the awn untwists, the spikelet is held in the ground by the callus hairs. This self-sowing may be repeated with each shift in humidity.

Spikelets are the units of the secondary grass inflorescence. All major inflorescence types occur in grasses, and a certain type or variant of that type is often characteristic of a species or group of species. In the wheats, for example, the spikelets are attached to a central axis without a stalk or pedicel. This kind of inflorescence also characterizes relatives of wheat, such as barley and rye. The bluegrasses of the genus *Poa,* in contrast, have a panicle inflorescence, with the spikelets borne on distinct pedicels.

Grass flowers are minute and highly simplified compared with the flowers of most other plants. Hidden within the lemma and palea, they are evident only by the brief appearance of some of their parts during flowering. In place of the petals there are translucent structures called lodicules. They are two or three (rarely none or up to six) in number and too small to be seen well without magnification. They vary in shape, but all function similarly in that they swell rapidly when the flower is mature and force apart the lemma and palea. Opening of the floret makes possible exsertion of the anthers (pollen sacs) on their filaments and stigmas (the receptive surface for pollen) for exchange of pollen between individuals (cross-pollination).

Grass flowers

Grass flowers are adapted for wind-pollination. There are no brightly coloured or strongly scented parts to attract animal pollinators, nor is there any nectar to reward animals for transporting pollen between flowers. Instead, there is an abundance of pollen contained in usually 3, less commonly as few as 1 or as many as 6, and exceptionally up to 120 (in *Ochlandra*), anthers. The smooth, lightweight pollen travels well on air currents, and two (less often three) feathery stigmas catch the airborne pollen. The stigmas of corn, collectively referred to as the silk, are unusual in two ways: there is only one stigma per flower, and they are very long. Pollen tubes must grow as long as 25 centimetres to reach the ovary. After pollen shedding and reception, the lodicules shrink and the floret closes to protect the developing fruit.

In more than 300 grass species, some of the florets do not open at flowering because they are confined (cleistogamous). Most commonly, retention of spikelets within leaf sheaths prevents their opening and enforces self-pollination, but in a few species, such as *Amphicarpum purshii* of the Atlantic coastal plain of North America, some of the spikelets are produced on stems that grow down into the soil. The common name of this plant, peanutgrass, reflects its habit of burying its own seed, but, unlike the peanut itself, peanutgrass burial begins before flowering.

One of the most unusual flowering phenomena occurs in many bamboos. All plants of a species flower at about the same time at lengthy intervals, and then the plants die. Cycles of about 30 and 60 years are known, and the longest cycle is 120 years in Asian *Phyllostachys bambusoides.* Individual aerial stems may live for much less time than their species cycle and will only flower at the end of the cycle when an inborn signal initiates the formation of inflorescences. Such gregarious flowering may oversaturate the food supply of frugivores (fruit-eating animals) and assure bamboo reproduction. This phenomenon, however, seriously affects the normal balance of nature. Animals dependent on bamboo vegetative growth, such as the panda, may lose a favoured food source entirely after a flowering episode. A glut of bamboo fruits may incite an explosion in populations of rodents that eat the fruits. For example, flowering of the muli, or terai, bamboo (*Melocanna bambusoides*) in its native habitat around the Bay of Bengal in cycles of mostly 30 to 35 years leads to disaster. With the death of the bamboo, an important building material is lost and the accumulation of the avocado-sized fruits promotes a rapid increase in rodent populations. Rodent overpopulations also lead to loss of human food supplies and epidemics of rodent-carried diseases.

Grass flowers may be bisexual (with both pollen and ovules) or unisexual. The flowers of wheat, barley, oats, and rye are bisexual; the flowers of corn are unisexual, although inflorescences for pollen (the tassle) and others for fruit (the ear) are on the same plant. The production of male or female gametes on separate individuals is rare in plants. The common buffalo grass (*Buchloe dactyloides*) of the American Great Plains is one of only 18 genera of grasses with this complete separation of pollen and fruit.

Grass fruits

Grass fruits, also called grains or caryopses, are unusual among plants in that the fruit wall completely adheres to the single seed. Caryopses are generally dry. In some grasses, the fruit does not fuse with the seed coat, and in some bamboos the fruit is a berry since the fruit wall becomes juicy.

The seed itself consists of two major parts, endosperm and embryo. Endosperm is a starchy, storage tissue (popcorn is exploded endosperm). The embryo lies between the endosperm and fruit wall with the large scutellum facing the endosperm. The scutellum is thought to be a modified cotyledon, or seed leaf. In grasses this seed leaf never develops into a green structure but serves only to digest endosperm and transfer nutrients to the rest of the embryo. The remainder of the embryo is an axis with primordial shoot and root systems. The shoot system consists of the shoot apex and its embryonic leaves, which are covered by the coleoptile. The mesocotyl connects the shoot system to the point of attachment of the scutellum. The primary root, which is replaced by secondary, fibrous roots after germination, is covered by the coleorhiza (root sheath).

Evolution. There is no clear evidence for the geographic place of origin of the grasses. Some authorities have suggested that grasses evolved within or on the margins of tropical forests. As Bambusoideae generally grow in forests and retain primitive features in their flowers, they were possibly the first grasses. However, they may be the most primitive extant grasses, numerous specializations reveal considerable evolutionary advancement. From these forest dwellers an early offshoot, perhaps similar to modern Arundinoideae, extended into savannas and gave rise to, and was partially supplanted by, Chloridoideae and Panicoideae in the tropics and pooids at higher latitudes. Alternately pooidlike grasses may have come first, evolving on tropical mountains and spreading to plains and temperate regions.

The meagre fossil remains of grasses do little to resolve questions of the origin of the family, its geologic age, relationships with other monocots, and evolution within the family. The oldest records of grass pollen are from about 60 million years ago during the Late Paleocene, but they did not become abundant until about 30 million years ago near the beginning of the Late Oligocene. The apparent upsurge of grasses likely stemmed from their coevolution with the then newly evolved groups of grazing animals and the aridification of the Earth's surface due to the rain shadow created by new mountains and growth of polar icecaps.

Relationships between grasses and sedges

Grasses have long been assumed to be closely related to sedges (family Cyperaceae) because they both are primarily herbaceous with long narrow leaves and minute wind-pollinated flowers borne in spikelets. Similarities between these two great families, however, most likely evolved as independent responses to the same environmental conditions. The closest extant relatives of grasses probably belong to a group of small families centred around the southern Pacific Ocean. One family in particular, the Joinvilleaceae, resembles grasses in some anatomical features of the leaves and embryos. Its flowers, however, have a well-developed perianth, and it lacks the other distinctive, easily recognizable features that mark grasses.

Current geographic distribution of grass subfamilies, tribes (groups of genera within subfamilies), and even some modern genera on all or most continents suggests that these groups evolved well before the first half of the Tertiary Period, roughly 66 to 36 million years ago, when continents had become sufficiently separated to prevent dispersal between them.

There are a number of reasons why so many genera and species of grasses exist today. In addition to the adaptations that make grasses ecologically successful, the grass spikelet has apparently been a competent means of protecting the flower, developing the fruit, and dispersing the seed. It has evolved into a myriad of forms by addition, loss, and modification of parts. Hybridization and polyploidy have undoubtedly spawned many grass species, as, for example, the wheats. Polyploidy and hybridization are usually linked because interspecific hybrids are often sterile, and fertility may be restored by chromosome doubling. An estimate of the incidence of polyploidy in the family, which is up to about 80 percent, indicates how frequently hybridization has taken place in grasses. (C.S.C.)

Subclass Zingiberidae

Although placed in the same subclass in this classification scheme, Zingiberales and Bromeliales are sufficiently different to warrant separate treatment. These two orders are discussed below.

ZINGIBERALES

General features. The order Zingiberales includes 8 families, 66 genera, and about 1,800 species. Plants of the order are abundant and conspicuous throughout the wet tropics, and some are also found in the seasonally dry tropics. In many cases, the plants and their leaves are very large. They are herbaceous perennials in the sense that most of them have little or no woody tissue; in the wet tropics they are evergreen. Because their stems do not develop secondary vascular tissues, their possible growth habits are restricted, but within these limits they are remarkably varied. Within the order are the cultivated bananas, Manila hemp (*Musa*), and cultivated ornamentals.

The family Strelitziaceae contains one of the most spectacular ornamental plants, the bird-of-paradise (*Strelitzia*). In addition, *Ravenala,* the traveler's-tree, is a large and dominant member of the tropical forests of Madagascar. Musaceae, or the banana family, contains important fruit and fibre plants in tropical and subtropical areas of the Old World. Zingiberaceae, or the ginger family, the largest family in the order, is known for ginger (*Zingiber officinale*), the spice and yellow dye called tumeric (*Curcuma domestica*), East Indian arrowroot starch (*Curcuma angustifolia*), and cardamom (*Amomum* and *Elettaria*). Marantaceae, or the prayer plant family, is known for a number of important products, among them are West Indian arrowroot starch (*Maranta arundinacea*), wax and edible tubers and flowers (*Calathea*), and decorative houseplants (*Maranta leuconeura*). Cannaceae, a family with a single genus, *Canna,* is known for the starchy edible tuberous rhizomes of *C. edulis.* Heliconiaceae, Lowiaceae, and Costaceae have members of lesser worldwide importance.

The ginger family

Size range and structural diversity. The largest plants of the order are the traveler's-tree (*Ravenala madagascariensis*), which has a woody trunk about 9 metres (30 feet) or more tall and a fan-shaped array of 20 or more leaves 4 to 5 metres in length, and the gigantic *Musa ingens* of New Guinea with its false trunk about 9 metres tall—*Musa* species are actually herbaceous, nonwoody plants whose rolled leaf bases and sheaths form what appears to be an aerial stem. The smallest Zingiberales are the lowly herbs of *Kaempferia* (Zingiberaceae) and some members of the family Marantaceae that raise their upward-facing leaves only a few centimetres above the ground. The leaves of *Musa* and *Canna* spread in all directions from the stem, but most other genera have them arranged in two ranks (one leaf is positioned directly below another leaf two nodes above it); variety in appearance is caused by close or wide spacing of the leaves, size of leaf blades, short or long leafstalks, vein patterns, and (especially in Marantaceae) colour variegation of leaves.

The inflorescence (flower cluster) always terminates on an erect stem, but sometimes these stems are very short and are separate from the leafy ones. Flower clusters are located in the axils (the angle between two organs) of the main inflorescence bracts and vary from compact to spreading with well-spaced flowers. In many species the cluster is reduced to a single flower. Similarly, the size of flowers and the relative size of their parts show great differences as between the various families, although all have the same basic pattern. The basic flower pattern is further complicated by a reduction of the basic number of six stamens and the replacement of some of them by petallike staminodes (sterile stamens). At the extremes are the large and spectacular blossoms of the bird-of-paradise flower with two erect much-modified petals and only one stamen missing, and the very small flowers of some Marantaceae species, which have staminodes of four different shapes and only half a functional stamen. *Maranta* flowers are thus asymmetric, and, as if to compensate for this lack of symmetry, they are produced in pairs, each flower a mirror image of the other.

Variation among flowers

Distribution. Although the order is represented by conspicuous plants throughout the tropics, the distribution of the constituent families is diverse. Probably the woody members of the order, found in the family Strelitziaceae, are the oldest in an evolutionary sense, and they have a curiously discontinuous distribution. The family is thought to have at one time contained more species than at present and was probably more widely distributed. Two of the genera (*Ravenala* in Madagascar and *Phenakospermum* in South America) have each only one species; the third genus, *Strelitzia,* has five species in southern Africa. Musaceae species are confined, as wild plants, to the Old World tropics, with a centre of distribution in the region of Myanmar, Thailand, and Malaysia, but cultivated bananas have been carried by humans to all parts of the tropics and some subtropical regions. The only genus of Musaceae in Africa (*Ensete*) has no part in the production of edible bananas, but its leaf sheaths are a source of food in Ethiopia. The family Heliconiaceae mainly occurs in tropical America, but there is one variable species in the western Pacific (New Guinea to the Samoa Islands), some forms of which have been widely cultivated for decorative purposes. Zingiberaceae is found throughout the tropics but is predominantly Asian; the related family Costaceae, also worldwide tropical, is most numerous in America. Marantaceae, the second family in order of size, is most diversified in the New World but also occurs in the Old World. (The American species have been better studied and are the only ones in cultivation.) The family Cannaceae is confined to the Americas. The family Lowiaceae consists of six little-known species in the forests of Malaysia; its short-lived, foul-smelling flowers are orchidlike but have five stamens. The only plants of the order that are hardy in north temperate regions are species of *Roscoea* (Zingiberaceae) from the Himalayas.

Natural history. *Life cycle.* With the exception of the genus *Ensete,* all plants of the order have the same basic growth habit, but this is disguised by differences in foliage and rhizome development. The growth of each leafy stem is limited because it does not increase in thickness; the main root is similarly limited, but additional roots are produced from nodes at the base of the stem. New growth is initiated in a bud at the axil of a basal leaf; this new growth must develop horizontally to become clear of the parent stem. If its end turns up close to the parent stem, the new shoot is called a sucker; if horizontal growth is extended, it is called a rhizome or stolon. In either case, the horizontal part and the base of the new erect stem bear new roots at the nodes; thus every new leafy stem has its own new complement of roots.

Limited manner of growth

The first erect shoot of a seedling is usually small, successive ones becoming larger until the mature size is reached, after which the pattern is repeated indefinitely, the rhizomatous species at least being potentially immortal; how long individual plants live in nature, however, is not known. This kind of growth is called sympodial; a horizontal rhizome may ultimately appear continuous, but it is built up from a series of elements, each of which grows upward at its tip. *Musa* and *Ravenala* plants produce suckers that grow up close to the parent stem; some species of the family Zingiberaceae have quite long rhizome elements, and the leafy shoots are far apart. This sympodial growth is common to most monocotyledons, though often it is more modified than in the order Zingiberales.

Ecology. The majority of species are shade plants of the rain forest of evergreen tropical regions, although some grow mainly on forest margins, in clearings, or on riverbanks. Within a single genus (*e.g., Musa, Costus*) some species may grow only in shade while others grow in more open places. In Malaysia, many members of the family Zingiberaceae that have tall leafy stems produce their flowers on separate, short, sheath-covered stems that

Drawing by M. Pahl based on (Musaceae) *Curtis's Botanical Magazine* (1898), (*Zingiber ortensii*) R.E. Holttum, *Plant Life in Malaya* (1953); Longman Group Ltd., (*Ravenala madagascariensis, Musa paradisiaca*) A.B. Rendle, *The Classification of Flowering Plants* (1967); Cambridge University Press, (A–E) *Evolution* (1962)

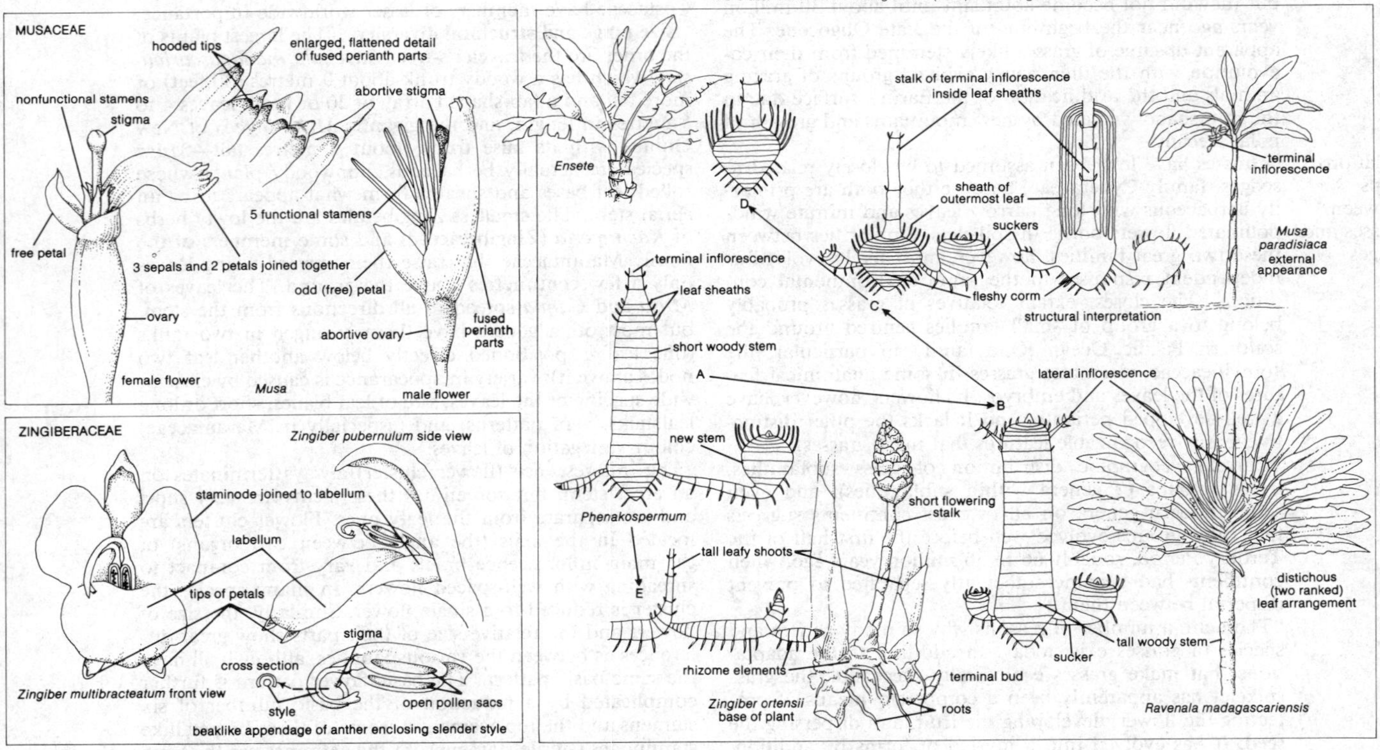

(Left) *Floral structures of two families and* (right) *growth habits in the order Zingiberales.*
In the right-hand figure a diagrammatic interpretation of the evolution of the various growth habits is shown by the stem structures (not to scale). The arrows indicate the direction of evolution according to the concept that woody plants were primitive in the order.
(A) *Phenakospermum,* with a short woody stem and terminal inflorescence. New stems occur at the ends of rhizome elements. (B) *Ravenala,* with tall, woody stem and lateral inflorescence. New stems appear as suckers near the parent stem. (C) *Musa,* with stem consisting of a large, fleshy corm bearing a terminal inflorescence and suckers. (D) *Ensete,* with growth habit as in *Musa* but lacking suckers. (E) The nonwoody rhizomatous habit of *Zingiber,* of the family Zingiberaceae, and most other members of the order.

arise from buds on the rhizome; the flowers are protected by overlapping bracts, the whole inflorescence often being shaped like a pinecone. In species having long rhizome elements the inflorescence may appear some distance from the nearest leafy stem. In the genus *Etlingera,* the inflorescence shoots are so short that they do not emerge from the ground and all that can be seen is a circlet of flowers with prominent, bright red petallike structures (labella) radiating outward, the flower tubes and ovaries being below ground level. Fruits ripen below ground and the seeds are thought to be dispersed by wild pigs or other animals. The leafy shoots may be three to five metres tall, so that the leaves are high in the air, even though the flowers are partially buried in the ground. In the genus *Hornstedtia* the inflorescences are wholly just above ground level, with firm empty outer bracts forming a spindle-shaped structure out of the top of which the flowers emerge, one or two at a time. In one Malaysian species of *Hornstedtia,* however, the whole rhizome is raised 50 centimetres or more above the ground by thick red stilt-roots so that the flowers are also raised. In nearly all such inflorescences, the overlapping bracts hold water in which flower buds and, later, fruits develop. Alternatively, moisture may be provided by the rotting of main bracts (*e.g.,* in some species of *Amomum*) so that fruits develop in a mass of black putrescence maintained in a wet state by frequent rains. In species that flower at the top of leafy stems, the main inflorescence bracts are often small or lacking and the flowers are fully exposed. The inflorescence develops inside the tube of overlapping leaf sheaths and appears at the top of the plant with flowers fully formed; the leaf sheaths thus take over the protective function of the main bracts. All members of the family Zingiberaceae have brightly coloured flowers and slender flower tubes full of nectar. They are probably mostly pollinated by butterflies. Flowers are, in all cases, short-lived, often lasting only a few hours.

Water-storing structures

The small flowers of Marantaceae, usually white, have a curious mechanism that is little understood but is doubtlessly connected with pollination by small insects. The style develops an internal tension but is held straight by the hooded staminode; when the latter is touched, the style escapes and instantly bends so that the stigma (the sticky pollen-receiving surface) faces downward. Pollen is deposited from the ripe stamen on the style below the stigma before the flower opens and may be removed by a visiting insect, but self-pollination is impossible.

Musa flowers are individually not conspicuous but the large main bracts are so; the bracts curl back in turn to expose the flowers they have protected while in bud. *Musa* species (including cultivated bananas) with pendulous inflorescences and dull purplish bracts have flowers with a rank odour and copious nectar; they open at night and are pollinated by bats. An important character of the cultivated bananas is that fruits develop without pollination; if pollinated by bats (as they often are), they do not form seeds. Other species of *Musa* have erect inflorescences and brightly coloured bracts; such appear to be bird-pollinated, though the flowers are also visited by bees for pollen. The large flowers of *Strelitzia* are thought to be bird-pollinated.

The curious genus *Orchidantha* consists of rather small plants found in Malaysian forests. One species has quite large flowers with dull purplish sepals and creamy white labellum, both as long as 12 centimetres. The flowers have a strong unpleasant odour and probably attract flies, but no observations on pollination have been made and few fruits have been found. The ovary has a long solid neck to which the other parts of the flower are attached.

Drought resistance

The species of the order that occur in seasonal parts of the tropics are adapted to withstand drought. Some of them (*e.g., Kaempferia, Curcuma,* and *Zingiber* species) lose their leafy parts and survive the dry season as underground rhizomes. Some *Curcuma* and *Kaempferia* species also produce tuberous roots, which act as an additional store of food and water. Many such plants produce their inflorescences in the latter part of the dry season before the new leafy shoots appear. An African species of *Costus* produces downward-growing rhizome branches that function as tubers and do not end in leaf shoots. *Ravenala* plants grow in open places in Madagascar but are evergreen; they may be adapted to withstand dry seasons by virtue of the water they produce and store in their closed sheathing leaf bases, about a litre in each. *Phenakospermum* is a swamp plant.

Epiphytes (plants that are not rooted in soil but grow on the branches of other plants or in other aerial locations) in the wet tropics, like plants of seasonally dry climates, need to have some method of withstanding drought, because their roots are exposed. The few species of Zingiberaceae that grow epiphytically (at least two species of *Hedychium* in Malaysia) have thick fleshy roots not unlike the tubers of some *Kaempferia* species, but they probably serve to store water rather than food. The plants are evergreen and do not grow in places exposed to strong sun and wind.

Form and function. *Vegetative structures.* Leaves normally consist of a broad blade with a conspicuous midrib and a stalk that grades into a long sheathing base, but leaves at the base of a new shoot consist only of sheaths. One of the common characteristics of this order is the arrangement of tissues in the leafstalk, an arrangement that typically includes prominent arcs of vascular bundles and air canals. Each new leaf grows up inside the sheath of the preceding one. In this position its blade has to be tightly rolled, one half being rolled inward, the other being rolled entirely outside the inner one; this is another peculiar characteristic common to all members of the order. As a consequence, the halves of a fully expanded leaf are often slightly unequal, or the base of the blade is asymmetric. There are other anatomical characteristics common to all members of the order, as well as some peculiar to each family. Each leaf in the family Marantaceae, for example, has a peculiar firm, specialized tissue called a pulvinus at the junction of the blade with the midrib or stalk; this consists of elongate cells arranged obliquely to the surface, and it serves to fix the angle between the blade and stalk. In the family Cannaceae, which on other grounds also shows relationship to Marantaceae, there are similar cells on the lower surface only.

Leaf arrangement

In almost all members of the order, the long leaf sheaths overlap, so that the true stem bearing them is not exposed. The stem is slender and lacks firm tissues, the leaf sheaths (the inner ones of which are very long) providing the necessary rigidity. As a consequence, the only fully exposed stems occur where the flowering stalk projects above the false stem of leaf sheaths. Exceptions to this rule are found in the genera *Costus* and *Canna* and in some species of the family Marantaceae. Plants of *Donax* (Marantaceae) in Malaysia have one stem section at least two to three metres from the ground to the first bladed leaf; these slender, firm structures are much used locally in constructing mats and baskets and are known by the Malay word *bembans.*

Reproductive structures. The inflorescence terminates the growth of a stem in most members of the order. The exceptions are the axillary inflorescences of *Ravenala* and some *Strelitzia* species and those of the family Zingiberaceae in which the leafy shoots bear no inflorescence. The basic inflorescence type consists of an erect axis bearing main bracts in the axil of each of which is a monochasial cyme: a flower cluster in which the first flower is located at the end of the axillary shoot attached to the main axis of the plant, the second flower arises in the axil of a bract located on this shoot below the first flower, the third flower similarly arises below the second, and so on for many additional flowers. In some cases there may be branch inflorescences, each like the top of the main one, in the axils of lower main bracts. This arrangement can produce a great variety of different floral displays. The main bracts may be large or small, absent (some Zingiberaceae), reduced to one (*Strelitzia reginae*), closely overlapping or widely spaced, green or brightly coloured. Some species are cultivated because of their decorative bracts (*Heliconia* and species of *Etlingera*). The cyme within each main bract may be very condensed so that its branching is hardly detectable, or it may be reduced to a single flower; in other cases (*Alpinia* and *Globba* in the family Zingiberaceae), the cyme is extended and the branching conspicuous. In *Musa,* the flowers are functionally unisex-

Basic inflorescence type

ual (the stamens, although present in the female flowers, lack pollen), and the cyme within each main bract lacks all minor bracts, but a careful study of the sequence of development of flower buds shows that the arrangement is cymose. The terminal part of the inflorescence, usually pendulous, bears only male flowers; the tip of this male inflorescence can be cut off and cooked for food.

Zingiberales flowers have three sepals, three petals, up to six stamens in two whorls of three each, some being represented by sterile structures of varying form, and three carpels; the members of successive whorls are alternating. The female structure, or ovary, is enclosed by the united basal portions of the other flower parts, which thus appear to arise at the upper end of the ovary (an inferior ovary). The calyx is always different in shape and size from the corolla, and the sepals are free from each other in all families except Zingiberaceae, which has a tubular calyx with small free lobes. The flowers are mostly bilaterally symmetric (zygomorphic), but in some cases they are asymmetric. There are six stamens only in the genus *Ravenala;* the rest of the order exhibit either five stamens (four families) or one functional stamen, the other stamens represented by a varying array of petallike sterile stamens called staminodes, which form the conspicuous part of the flower (four families).

Variations on the basic flower structure pattern exist in the families with five and with one stamen. In the former, sepals and petals are the conspicuous parts of the flower; they are often large, and the paired petals are larger than the median one except in *Musa* and the family Lowiaceae. The families with one stamen and a varied number of petallike staminodes show a great range of floral form. The most conspicuous part of the flower in the family Zingiberaceae is usually called the labellum; this structure, however, does not consist of the same floral parts as the labellum in the family Lowiaceae and in orchids, in which it is a petal. The labellum represents two or three united stamens, and in many genera there is a pair of smaller but conspicuous petallike staminodes, each representing one stamen (in the genus *Zingiber* they are joined to the labellum); the result is a flower of orchidlike aspect, but the parts concerned in orchid and ginger flowers are different, and undoubtedly the two have developed along quite different evolutionary lines. In the families Marantaceae and Cannaceae, the single stamen is only half functional, the other half being more or less petallike. In both families the staminodes are of varying size and shape, so that their status is not easily decided, and there have been differences of opinion about them. In the family Costaceae the large labellum represents a union of all five nonfunctional stamens, and in some cases it can be seen to be five-lobed.

The Zingiberaceae labellum

The fruit is usually dehiscent (splitting open along definite lines), except in *Musa* and *Heliconia,* with several seeds that have attached growths, called arils, of various forms (in the family Marantaceae the arils assist the dehiscence of the fruit). Reduction in the number of seeds, in a few cases to one, occurs independently in the family Heliconiaceae, in various subdivisions of Zingiberaceae and in Marantaceae. The seeds have abundant endosperm (food storage tissue). The hard seed coat has a little plug opposite the radicle of the embryo (the portion of the embryo that will become the root), and in germination the base of the cotyledon (the so-called seed leaf) elongates far enough to bring the aerial bud clear of the seed, the cotyledon tip remaining in the seed as an absorbing organ.

Evolution. The order Zingiberales has spread to seasonal parts of the tropics, where they have evolved adaptations involving a period of rest during seasons when growth is impossible because of drought. Other groups of monocotyledons have evolved further by the development of resting organs (rhizomes, corms, and bulbs) that can withstand cold, the result being that monocotyledons of temperate regions (except grasses) are often thought to be characterized by such storage organs and by an adaptation to seasonal growth alternating with dormancy. It seems probable that monocotyledons began their existence in the wet tropics and that continuous growth on a sympodial pattern is their basic life form. Zingiberales show how this life form can be the basis for evolution of resting organs; there can be no doubt that this order began its diversification in the wet tropics, where it has left no certain fossil record.

It has been stated that the order Zingiberales shows resemblances to the subfamily Asphodeloideae of the Liliaceae (order Liliales). The members of that subfamily, however, are temperate or subtropical plants, mostly geophytes (plants that overwinter below the ground surface) of seasonal growth; furthermore, they do not share any of the peculiar characters common to all Zingiberales species. Evidence has been produced that the woody species of the family Strelitziaceae represent the most primitive element in Zingiberales; if that is so, a common ancestor with the family Liliaceae must go back farther than the beginning of the present great diversity of Liliaceae. Some authorities have also suggested that the possibility exists that the monocotyledons as a whole have descended from treelike ancestors. It is, however, equally possible that the woody Strelitziaceae, the palms, and the pandans are independent evolutionary developments exhibiting woody structure and that the original monocotyledons were ancient herbaceous (nonwoody) dicotyledons similar to the family Nymphaeaceae (order Nymphaeales) but more primitive and less reduced.

Examples of fossil Zingiberales are not known with certainty, although there are fossil leaves that may belong to this order. The most likely records are fossil fruits and seeds from deposits of the Early Oligocene to the Middle Eocene (50 million to 30 million years ago) in southern England and elsewhere in Europe; these have been given the name *Spirematospermum.* The fruits are somewhat like small bananas, but the inflorescence is more like that of some members of the family Zingiberaceae allied to *Alpinia;* the seeds also resemble those of *Alpinia.* Leaves similar to those of *Musa* have been found in the same formations as these fruits. (R.E.H./Ed.)

BROMELIALES

General features. The order Bromeliales contains a single family, the Bromeliaceae, with about 50 genera and almost 2,600 species. Members of the family are commonly referred to as bromeliads; the family as a whole is often called the pineapple family. Apart from the pineapple (*Ananas comosus*), a number of the genera (*e.g., Aechmea, Cryptanthus,* and *Tillandsia*) are of horticultural interest, mostly owing to their curious growth forms and brightly coloured floral displays. The Bromeliaceae is one of the few angiosperm families where epiphytes (nonparasitic plants that grow on other plants) are common. It is estimated that at least half of the species are epiphytes.

The pineapple family

The order Bromeliales was established to accommodate Bromeliaceae, a family that has no obvious close relationship to any other family. This taxonomically isolated position for the Bromeliaceae is reflected in the placement it receives in upper-level classification systems. For example, the Swedish botanist Rolf Dahlgren has placed the Bromeliales into the superorder Bromeliiflorae, along with five other, mostly single-family orders (Velloziales, Haemodorales, Philydrales, Pontederiales, and Typhales). The American botanist Arthur Cronquist has placed the Bromeliales, along with the order Zingiberales (including the families Cannaceae, Costaceae, Heliconiaceae, Lowiaceae, Marantaceae, Musaceae, Strelitziaceae, and Zingiberaceae) into the subclass Zingiberidae. Thus, these two experts have proposed two completely different sets of families as being the most closely related to the Bromeliaceae; however, three subfamilies, are currently recognized within the Bromeliaceae: Bromelioideae, Pitcairnioideae, and Tillandsioideae. A fourth subfamily, Navioideae, has been proposed to accommodate the genus *Navia* (which is now placed in Pitcairnioideae).

The subfamily Bromelioideae contains 30 genera and about 720 species. Members of the Bromelioideae are mostly epiphytic and have leaves with toothed margins. The ovary is inferior, the fruit is a berry or, seldom, a multiple fruit (*e.g.,* pineapple), and the seeds have neither wings nor appendages. Important genera include *Aechmea* (200 species), *Ananas* (7 species), *Neoregelia* (94 species), and *Billbergia* (61 species).

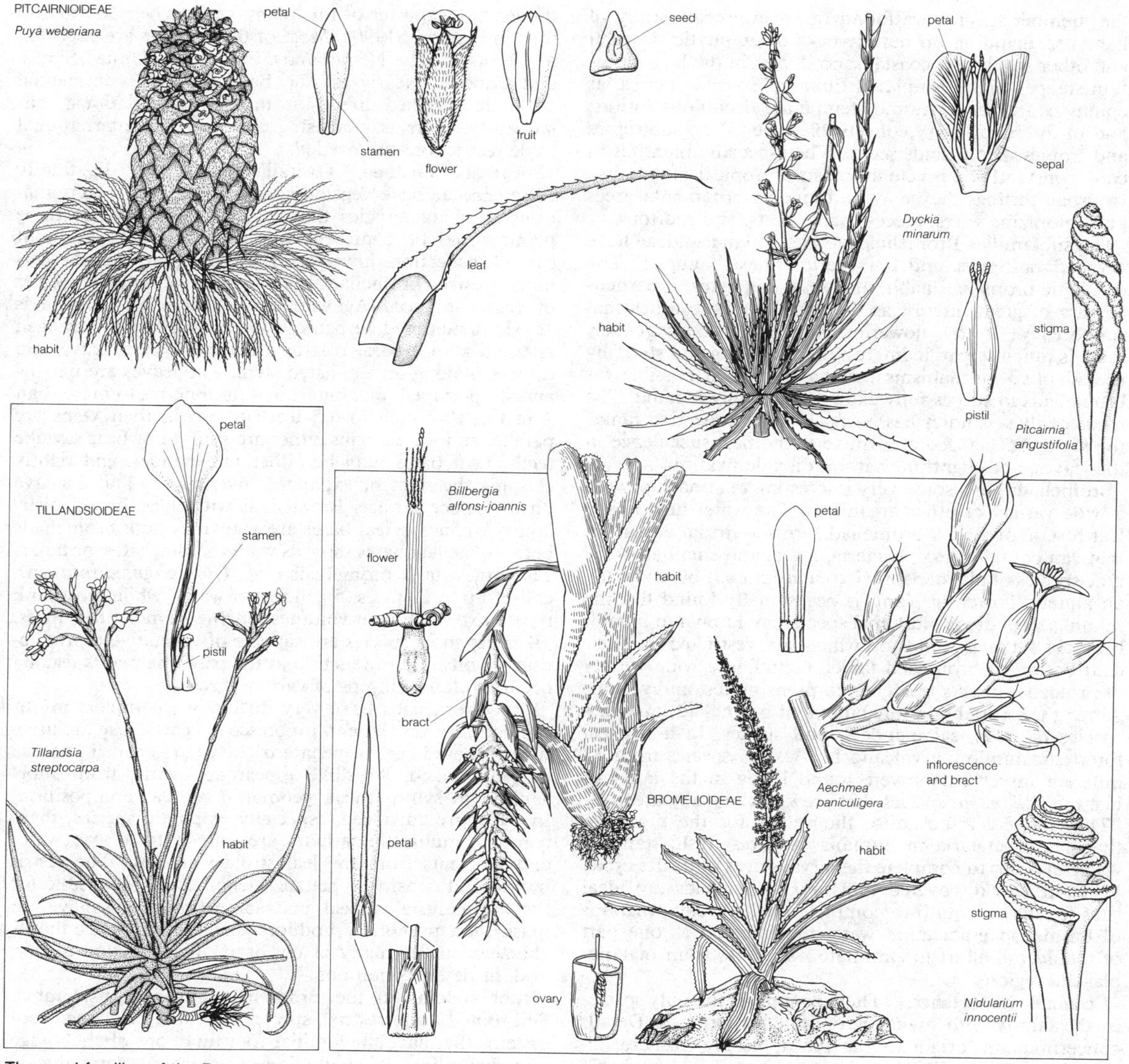

Three subfamilies of the Bromeliales.

From (*Puya weberiana, Dyckia minarum*) L.B. Smith and R.J. Downs, *Flora Neotropica: Pitcairnioideae (Bromeliaceae)*, no. 14, part 1, copyright © 1974 The New York Botanical Garden; (*Pitcairnia augustifolia, Nidularium innocentii*) G.K. Brown and A.J. Gilmartin, "Stigma Structure and Variation in Bromeliaceae—Neglected Taxonomic Characters," *Brittonia*, vol. 36, copyright © 1984 The New York Botanical Garden; (*Tillandsioideae*) L.B. Smith and R.J. Downs, *Flora Neotropica: Tillandsioideae (Bromeliaceae)*, no. 14, part 2, copyright © 1977 The New York Botanical Garden; (*Aechmea paniculigera, Billbergia alfonsi-joannis*) L.B. Smith and R.J. Downs, *Flora Neotropica: Bromelioideae (Bromeliaceae)*, no. 14, part 3, copyright © 1979 The New York Botanical Garden

The subfamily Pitcairnioideae contains 15 genera and 860 species. The species in this subfamily are almost all terrestrial and have leaves with toothed margins. The ovary is superior, the fruit is a capsule, and the seeds are either winged or tailed. The exception is the genus *Navia,* which has naked seeds. Important genera in the Pitcairnioideae include *Pitcairnia* (314 species), *Puya* (190 species), *Dyckia* (116 species), and *Navia* (101 species).

Tillandsioideae contains 6 genera and 1,020 species. The species in this subfamily are mostly epiphytic, and the leaves have smooth margins. The ovary is superior, the fruit a capsule, and the seeds have a feathery crown of hairs at one end. Important genera in the Tillandsioideae include *Tillandsia* (540 species), *Vriesea* (295 species), and *Guzmania* (158 species).

Size range and diversity of structure. Bromeliads display an impressive degree of morphological variation. In terms of size, this ranges from tiny plants with a mosslike habit (*Tillandsia bryoides*) that rarely exceed five centimetres (two inches) in length and produce a single small flower, to huge plants, like *Puya raimondii,* with a stem up to four metres in length, a rosette of leaves that exceeds two metres in diameter, and a massive inflorescence that will grow to over four metres tall.

Adaptation to diverse habitats

Bromeliads span a broad spectrum of habitat adaptation, from soil-rooted terrestrial species, especially in the subfamily Pitcairnioideae, to species that can be either terrestrial or epiphytic (facultative epiphytes), to species that are obligate epiphytes, as in the Tillandsioideae and Bromelioideae. Furthermore, epiphytic species can be described in two general categories: tank, or water-collecting epiphytes, and atmospheric epiphytes. Atmospheric epiphytes, or air plants, include those gray- or silver-leaved species of *Tillandsia* and *Vriesea* that do not collect water; their colour results from a dense covering of the absorptive peltate trichomes, which in their dry state reflect light. These atmospheric epiphytes are typically found in arid habitats, and they procure their water and mineral nutrition via the absorptive trichomes.

Distribution. The Bromeliaceae are native to the New World, except for a single species, *Pitcairnia feliciana,* that grows in tropical West Africa. Most of the species occur in tropical and subtropical latitudes; however, the range limits extend from the extreme southeast coastal region of Virginia (approximately latitude 37° N) in North America to the south-central coastal region of Argentina (latitude 44° S) in South America. The native elevational range for bromeliads spans from sea level to about 4,500 metres in tropical South America. The regions with the greatest diversity of bromeliad species are southern Mexico through Central America, the Andes Mountains from Colombia to Peru, the Guiana Highlands of Venezuela, and extreme eastern Brazil.

While the family is not continuous in this distribution,

the member species are found in an impressive array of habitats, including on desert rocks or epiphytic on cacti and other shrubs; on coastal sand dunes; in the high elevation steppe, or the Altiplano, Puna, of South America; as epiphytes in warm, humid, temperate deciduous forests; and in forests of every conceivable type in the subtropics and tropics. Bromeliads seem to be especially plentiful in cool, constantly damp cloud forests of tropical mountains. In urban settings they may be found in ornamental trees and colonizing wires, fences, walls, posts, and rooftops.

The subfamilies Bromelioideae and Tillandsioideae have invaded both wet and dry (xeric) forest canopies. The epiphytic bromeliad habit, and xeric epiphytes in particular, are of great interest as they occur on substrates that support few, if any, flowering plants. As a consequence, there is much scientific interest in identifying and studying the adaptive mechanisms that have made it possible for bromeliads to successfully exploit the epiphytic habit. The focus of these studies has been on water-collecting tanks, the highly specialized absorptive trichomes, succulence in the leaves, and nighttime carbon dioxide fixation.

Habitation of bromeliad tanks

Bromeliads have some very interesting relationships with a wide variety of other organisms. The water held in the leaf rosette of a tank bromeliad forms a virtual aquarium that can contain fungi, bacteria, algae, and small animals. One species of bladderwort (*Utricularia;* Lentibulariaceae), an aquatic flowering plant, is occasionally found floating in tanks. Hundreds of animal species are known to inhabit bromeliad tanks, some of which are restricted in their distribution to bromeliad tanks, including a wide variety of protozoa, insects, spiders, scorpions, mites, and worms. Among the vertebrate inhabitants of bromeliad tanks are species of frogs, salamanders, and snakes. In a tropical forest surrounding a volcano in Mexico, species from 12 different insect orders were found living in the tanks of just the *Tillandsia* species that grow in the study area.

The *Anopheles* mosquito, the vector for the organism that causes malaria in humans, requires fresh, standing water in order to complete the larval stages of its life cycle. When it was discovered that tank bromeliads are ideal sites for the mosquito to complete its life cycle, programs of bromeliad eradication were implemented as one part of the overall effort to eliminate *Anopheles* from malaria-plagued regions.

Economic importance. The pineapple is the only species in the family with major agronomic importance. Details concerning the origin of the pineapple are obscure, although it appears likely to have originated in Brazil. No native or wild populations of pineapple are known, and it is probably a cultivated species that developed under conditions of artificial selection. The generic name *Ananas* comes from Tupian word of the South American Guariní Indians for "excellent fruit." Today pineapples are cultivated throughout the tropics.

A number of bromeliads have been exploited for their leaf fibres. Some of these (*e.g., Aechmea magdalenae, Bromelia pinguin,* and *Neoglaziovia variegata*) continue to be useful for cordage fibres or for fishnet construction in local South American markets. In the Philippines, fibres from the leaves of the pineapple plant are woven into an exquisite fabric called piña cloth, which is used to make shirts, shawls, and scarfs. Spanish moss (*Tillandsia usneoides*) constituted a minor fibre industry in the Gulf Coast region of North America, peaking in 1936, the year of the largest Spanish moss harvest in the United States, with an estimated 10,000 tons worth $2.5 million processed for use in upholstery stuffing and fishnet repair. An estimated 50 tons are still processed annually in Louisiana for use in fish hatcheries to collect and preserve eggs from spawning females. Some Spanish moss is also collected for sale to flower shops and plant nurseries, which use it as decorative material in potted plants or floral arrangements.

Worldwide the commercial horticultural trade of bromeliads is extensive, with the greatest interest being in Europe and North America. The species found in the horticultural trade are mainly from the subfamilies Bromelioideae and Tillandsioideae, with species from the genus *Tillandsia* being the most widely sought. It is estimated that the annual amount of *Tillandsia* exported from Guatemala, the leading exporter of this plant, approached 160 to 180 tons in the early 1990s. Most of these plants are exported to Germany, The Netherlands, France, the United States, and Canada. Nearly all the bromeliads in commercial trade are collected directly from native populations; consequently, there is increasing concern that international trade restrictions are needed.

Form and function. Overall, members of the family Bromeliaceae have vegetative and reproductive combinations of characteristics that make it unlikely that these plants could be confused with nonbromeliads. Without careful inspection, however, it is possible to mistake certain terrestrial bromeliads in the vegetative state for species of *Agave* or *Yucca* (Agavaceae; Liliales). Most bromeliads are short-stemmed herbaceous plants with leaves arranged alternately in a basal rosette. In some species, leaves are dispersed along an elongated stem. The leaves are narrow and strap-shaped, ranging from 4 millimetres to more than 2 metres (0.2 inch to 6.5 feet) in length; their veins are parallel and the margins either are smooth or bear sawlike teeth. Leaf bases may be either unexpanded and tightly clasping the stem or expanded, overlapping and concave on the upper surface. Bromeliads with these broad, overlapping, concave leaf bases are known as tank bromeliads because the leaf bases serve as water-holding sites, or tanks. The largest tank bromeliads (*e.g., Glomeropitcairnia*) can collect up to 20 litres (5 gallons) of water, while most tank types have catchment volumes ranging from 0.1 to 5 litres.

Distinguishing vegetative and reproductive characteristics

Because most species are capable of vegetative reproduction via offshoot production at the base, the plants usually occur in clonal clumps of various sizes.

Most bromeliads have very distinctive, complex, multicellular hairs on leaf and inflorescence parts. The architecture of these hairs, or peltate trichomes (so called because of their stalked, shieldlike appearance) varies from unorganized to symmetrical, geometric cellular composition. In the more advanced, especially epiphytic species, these complex multicellular hairs are known to absorb water and nutrients from the leaf surface or tank. The distribution and density of peltate trichomes is responsible for the horticultural appeal that some bromeliads have. In mass, these trichomes produce a silvery appearance that is characteristic of many of the bromeliads adapted to dry, arid, or desert conditions.

Root systems in the Bromeliaceae vary considerably. Soil-rooted, or terrestrial, species have well-developed root systems that have the familiar root functions of anchorage and absorption. In epiphytic and saxicolous (growing on bare rock) bromeliads, the roots generally serve to anchor the plant to the supporting branch, rock, or other substrate, and have limited or no absorptive function. Some epiphytic species (*e.g., Tillandsia usneoides*) do not form roots or do so only briefly as seedlings.

Natural history. *Reproductive characteristics.* Flowers of the Bromeliaceae are typically bisexual and regular, although unisexual flowers are known from three genera (*Hechtia, Catopsis,* and *Dyckia*), and somewhat irregular flowers are found in *Pitcairnia.* The bromeliad perianth is clearly differentiated into three sepals and three usually brightly coloured petals. Small paired or single outgrowths from the base of each petal, known as petal scales or petal appendages, are common. Stamens develop in two whorls of three each with each stamen clearly composed of both filament and anther. Each flower contains one ovary consisting of three fused carpels. The ovary, which may be superior or inferior, houses three locules; each chamber contains many ovules with axile placentation. The ovary supports a single style with three stigmatic lobes (surfaces receptive to pollen) in one of five possible organizational types. Conduplicate-spiral stigma organization, which is unique to the Bromeliaceae, is the most common stigma form found in the family. In this organization, three flattened style branches are each folded along the long axis, and the three folded branches are spiraled together. The fruit is a capsule or a berry. In the pineapple, the individual berry-fruits are fused to form the large fleshy multiple fruit known as the pineapple. The seeds of bromeliads range from naked to variously appendaged with wings, tails, or a feathery crown of hairs.

Conduplicate-spiral stigma organization

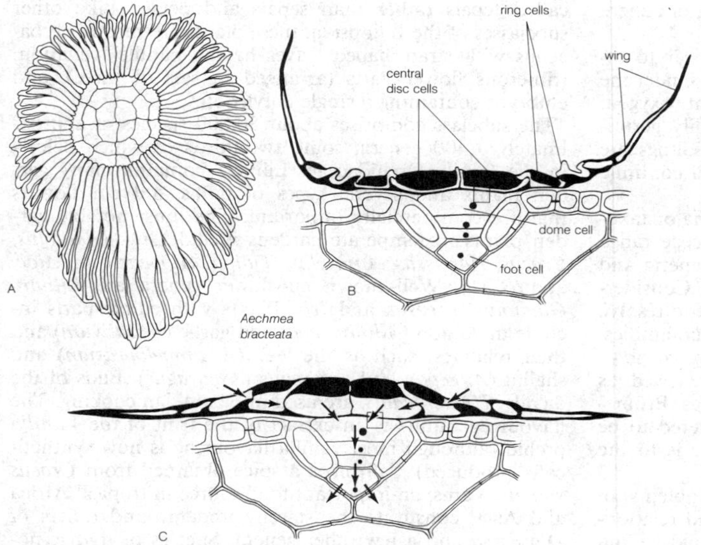

Water movements through an absorbing trichome and a sectional view of the foliar hair of Aechmea bracteata.
(A) Upper surface of a flattened shield (hydrated state).
(B) Median section through a trichome (dry leaf surface).
(C) Same trichome when the surface is moist and water movement through the hair into the leaf is as depicted by arrows. As water falls onto a shoot, it enters the shield cells, which swell from the flow of water. The disc cells and ring cells, previously collapsed, rise and afford a pathway for water movement.

D.H. Benzing, *The Biology of the Bromeliads*, © 1980 D.H. Benzing, Mad River Press, Eureka, Calif.

Each flower is subtended by a usually conspicuous bract, which is often as showy, or more so, than the flower. The terminal inflorescence is produced from the centre of the leaf rosette and ranges from a solitary flower to a spike, raceme, or panicle. The inflorescence stalk, branches, and accompanying bracts are often brightly coloured.

Life cycle. Bromeliads are generally slow-growing plants; the average life span for a healthy individual plant is usually several years. Individuals from some species do, however, exhibit greater longevity. The giant *Puya raimondii,* for example, takes 50 to 70 years to reach maturity, and many species of tank bromeliads, where the rosette of leaves approaches or exceeds one metre in diameter, require at least 10 to 20 years to reach maturity.

When a plant reaches reproductive maturity, the flower cluster, or inflorescence, forms in the centre of the leaf rosette. As a rule, inflorescence formation terminates the growth of the rosette producing it. The length of time during which an individual inflorescence will produce flowers, and thus be potentially sexually reproductive, varies considerably. In most species, where the inflorescence is multiflowered, the sexually reproductive period will last from about a week to up to three months. Some species, however, will produce flowers for several months to more than one year. Termination of flowering in the inflorescence signals the start of an eventual physiological decline in the rosette producing the inflorescence, and the eventual death of the rosette. This dying process is usually a gradual one that spans several months to well over a year.

Nearly all bromeliads reproduce by vegetative means (asexually) at some point in their life cycle. Depending on the species, each leaf rosette, or mother plant, usually produces a few offshoots; some species can produce 100 or more offspring per mother plant. Offshoot production is associated with the flowering or postflowering period; the offshoots usually appear at the base of the mother plant. A few species produce offshoots in the bracts associated with the inflorescence. For some species, vegetative reproduction via offshoot production is ongoing and is not associated with episodes of flower production. The dead axis of a mother plant often remains attached to the new generation of offshoots to form a tight clump of plants. In more exceptional cases, multiple generations of offshoots are attached, forming large, dense clusters.

Considering the large size, common occurrence, and conspicuous nature of the Bromeliaceae, relatively little is known about their pollination biology. Hummingbirds are frequently reported to visit bromeliad flowers, and some experts consider the family to be predominately bird-pollinated. There are, however, reports of bat- and insect-pollination based on observed visitations by bats, bees, bumblebees, moths, and butterflies. At present, there are no verified reports of wind-pollination in bromeliads. In most cases, pollination has not been documented but only assumed; thus, for the great majority of bromeliad species, the potential pollinator type is simply inferred from the floral and inflorescence syndrome, which is known in other flowering plant species in which the pollinator has been documented.

Agents of pollination

Seed dispersal mechanisms differ for the three bromeliad subfamilies because of the differences in fruit type and seed morphology. In the Pitcairnioideae, the mature capsule splits open to release the seeds, which are dislodged by gravity or wind agitation or by both. Dispersal of the seed, because of the wing or taillike appendage, is aided by wind. The capsule fruit in the Tillandsioideae also splits open to release seeds; however, because these seeds have a feathery crown of hairs at one end that acts like a parachute, wind dispersal is more effective. The hairs on these Tillandsioideae seeds, which have been referred to as "flight hairs," have also been shown to be important in the adherence of the seed to a potential germination substrate. A high percentage of Tillandsioideae species are epiphytic or saxicolous, and these hairs are easily caught in the rough textures of tree bark, clusters of cactus spines, rock or cliff surfaces, and even wooden telephone poles, fences, and wires. In the subfamily Bromelioideae, the fruits are attractive fleshy berries, and the seeds, while lacking appendages, are coated with a sticky material. In these plants, seed dispersal appears to be mostly a matter of fruit dispersal in that birds (the principal agent of seed dispersal) and bats are known to utilize the berries as a food source. It has not yet been demonstrated that Bromelioideae seeds remain viable after passing through the digestive systems of these animals, but circumstantial evidence strongly indicates that they do. It is also possible that during the berry-eating process the seeds, with their sticky coat, can be separated accidently from the fruit and stick to potential germination substrates in trees, or adhere to the animal and fall off later.

Fully mature Bromeliaceae seeds do not appear to require any dormancy period before germination. Under the proper combination of temperature, water, light, oxygen, and substrate, most bromeliad seeds will readily germinate. If suitable growth conditions for the seedlings are maintained, the long period of slow growth will continue until the plant reaches reproductive maturity.

Evolution and classification. The scope of major taxonomic problems associated with the Bromeliaceae range from ordinal and subfamily relationships to generic and subgeneric circumscriptions and relationships. Considerable research has been conducted in an attempt to resolve the evolutionary relationships among the three subfamilies. Thus far, however, these efforts have proven equivocal.

Traditionally, the Pitcairnioideae has been viewed as the most primitive subfamily, and subfamilies Bromelioideae and Tillandsioideae have been considered to be more closely related to each other than either is to the Pitcairnioideae.

Major taxonomic problems

Currently, the most pressing taxonomic problems in the pineapple family concern generic limits and relationships, especially within the subfamilies Bromelioideae and Tillandsioideae; for example, most members of the Pitcairnioideae can be identified to the genus level even while in fruit, whereas most Tillandsioideae require mature flowers in good condition for such a level of identification. Generic determination in the Bromelioideae is the most difficult, because the genera are so poorly defined. Even with a complete specimen (vegetative material, flowers, and fruit), it is difficult to assign some Bromelioideae specimens to a genus.

Many of the problems surrounding the limits of the genus and the relationships of the genera within the Bromelioideae and Tillandsioideae appear to be directly related to an overemphasis on the use of one floral characteristic to separate certain genera, in this instance the petal scales or petal appendages. *Tillandsia* and *Vriesea*, for example, are two genera from the Tillandsioideae that differ only by the absence (*Tillandsia*) or presence (*Vriesea*) of petal appendages. This use of petal appendage presence or absence to define genera is similarly repeated in the Bromelioideae. Petal appendage occurrence as the sole or primary criterion for establishing generic limits has been criticized as arbitrary. Recent, detailed studies of bromeliad petal appendages support these criticisms, and it is likely that major generic realignments will be forthcoming as bromeliad taxonomists continue to seek new or underutilized characteristics and to evaluate multiple character correlations.

The fossil record for the Bromeliaceae is nearly nonexistent. A few putative bromeliad macrofossils (leaves) have been described, but placement of these fossil materials within the Bromeliales is highly questionable. Microfossil (pollen) evidence has been reported from Late Eocene sediments in Panama dated at about 40 million years. The Bromeliaceae remain an isolated family with no clear evolutionary relationships with other monocot families. Different interpretations of morphological, anatomical, chromosomal, and biogeographic data have resulted in suggestions that any one of a few families (*e.g.*, Commelinaceae, Rapateaceae, Velloziaceae, or Zingiberaceae) could have the closest evolutionary relationship to the Bromeliaceae. New molecular data, and the analyses of these data, now point to the Rapateaceae as the family most closely related to the Bromeliaceae. (G.K.B.)

Subclass Liliidae

GENERAL FEATURES

Subclass Liliidae constitutes a group of plants loosely referred to as the petaloid monocots. The flowers are generally conspicuous and colourful; even when not large and brightly coloured, the inner and outer whorls of the perianth are typically petallike, lacking the classic distinction between a green calyx and a variously coloured corolla. Because the only distinction between these two whorls is in their position, the segments of the perianth are usually called tepals rather than sepals and petals. Like other subclasses of the Liliopsida, these plants are mostly herbaceous with strap-shaped leaves having parallel venation, trimerous flower parts (arranged in sets of three), and embryos containing a single cotyledon.

The subclass comprises about 30,000 species in approximately 1,400 genera, some two-thirds of which belong in the family Orchidaceae. Liliidae contains many garden plants and several types of bulbs and cut flowers that are commercially important. The most notable garden plants in temperate gardens include *Iris, Gladiolus, Crocus, Narcissus, Amaryllis, Tulipa, Hippeastrum, Aloe,* and *Hosta.* Well-known cut-flower genera are *Lilium, Gladiolus, Freesia,* and *Iris*. Plants with edible parts include the onion (*Allium cepa*) and garlic (*A. sativum*) and their relatives, such as the leek (*A. ampeloprasum*) and shallot (*A. cepa*), and asparagus (*Asparagus*). Buds of the daylily, *Hemerocallis,* are used in East Asian cooking. The flavouring vanilla is an extract of the fruit of the *Vanilla* orchid (although most vanilla flavouring is now synthetically produced). Saffron is a spice obtained from *Crocus sativus*. Yams, an important food source in tropical Africa and Asia, constitute the starchy underground tubers of *Dioscorea* and a few other genera. Species of *Agave,* notably *A. sisalana,* yield a fibre used in matting and cordage and are extensively grown in the tropics. In Mexico the sap of other species of *Agave* is used to produce pulque (a beverage made from fermented sap), mescal, and tequila.

Liliidae are also a source of a number of pharmaceutical products. Colchicine, an alkaloid used in medicine, is obtained from *Colchicum* (meadow saffron). Several steroid compounds were originally obtained from *Dioscorea* to manufacture contraceptives and medicines. Many more are folk medicines in some parts of the world.

Diversity of structure. Liliidae are diverse in growth form and include vines, shrubs, a few trees, as well as herbs. Specializations of the underground parts include rhizomes, tubers, corms (all modified stems), and bulbs (modified shoots with leafy tissue).

The classifications of Cronquist and Dahlgren

Perhaps no other group of the flowering plants evokes so much diversity of opinion about overall circumscription and internal classification as the Liliidae. Of contemporary classifications, that of the American botanist Arthur Cronquist is the broadest, recognizing just 2 orders, Liliales, with 15 families, and Orchidales, with 4. The major families of the order Liliales recognized in this system are Liliaceae, Iridaceae, and Dioscoreaceae. Three additional groups are sometimes recognized as separate families because of their treelike or predominantly treelike habit: the mostly African Aloeaceae, the American Agavaceae, and Australasian Xanthorrhoeaceae. Of the remaining families in the order, Velloziaceae (indigenous to Africa, Madagascar, and South America), Haemodoraceae, Philydraceae, and the aquatic Pontederiaceae are now generally thought to belong to other subclasses.

At the opposite extreme is the classification of the Swedish botanist Rolf Dahlgren and his colleagues, the Australian Harold Trevor Clifford and the Briton Peter F. Yeo, who regard the Liliidae as comprising five orders: Dioscoreales (5 families), Asparagales (31 families), Melanthiales (2 families), Liliales (11 families including Orchidaceae), and Burmanniales (3 families). Dahlgren, Clifford, and Yeo place Haemodoraceae, Philydraceae, and Velloziaceae in orders close to Bromeliales in a superorder Bromeliiflorae (equivalent to Cronquist's taxon subclass).

The Dahlgren system has considerable merit in recognizing many natural genetic assemblages within Liliidae at equivalent taxonomic rank. In contrast, the Liliaceae of Cronquist includes the majority of species of Liliales but excludes from the family groups that are closely related to different groups of species within Liliaceae on the basis of their arborescent habit. Notably, Cronquist does not recognize Amaryllidaceae, a family important for the many horticultural subjects, but does recognize Iridaceae, an alliance of about the same size and importance and equally easy to distinguish. The development of a useful but scientifically acceptable classification of Liliidae is an important problem for current science.

Orchidales consists of four families, as mentioned above:

Geosiridaceae, Burmanniaceae, Corsiaceae, and Orchidaceae. The former families together account for fewer than 30 genera, while Orchidaceae is by far the largest family, with as many as 1,000 genera.

Because the systems of Cronquist and Dahlgren each have considerable merit, both will be mentioned below when appropriate in discussing a particular genus. Cronquist will be followed in discussion and Dahlgren given in parentheses after the first mention of the genus.

Ecology. Members of Liliales are typically perennial herbs with fleshy to fibrous stems arising from any of various types of underground storage or perennating organs. Herbaceous climbers are rare, but nearly all species of Dioscoreaceae and Smilacaceae are vines, among which *Smilax* is often a significant component of the vegetation. A few Liliaceae are also climbers, including the African genera *Gloriosa* and species of *Littonia* (Colchicaceae) and *Walleria* (Tecophilaeaceae). *Bomarea* (Alstroemeriaceae), found from Mexico to tropical America, is a climber. Some species of *Dracaena* and *Protasparagus* also may be regarded as vines, as they scramble through the forest or bush canopy, but neither has tendrillike adaptations for climbing.

Aquatic forms

Aquatics are uncommon and are largely confined to Pontederiaceae, a tropical family that includes rooted and free-floating species. The water hyacinth, *Eichhornia crassipes,* a native of Brazil, has become a nearly pantropical weed of still waters. Elsewhere in Liliidae, aquatics are common in *Crinum,* many species of which grow in permanent or seasonal stands of water. Their bulbs permit them to survive the dry season when ponds, streams, and marshes dry out.

Annual plants are particularly rare. A few species of *Sisyrinchium* of Iridaceae are true annuals with fibrous roots and some have become weedy in many parts of the world. Some Burmanniceae and the Brazilian *Hydrothrix* of Pontederiaceae are also annuals.

The seeds of the Orchidales do not contain sufficient endosperm (food reserves) to support the growth of the developing embryo. Many Orchidales have developed symbiotic relationships with certain fungi (mycotrophy), which supply the host plant with essential nutrients during germination by means of a method of nutrition called saprophytism, the absorption of dissolved organic materials from dead and decaying organisms. Burmanniaceae, Corsiaceae, some Orchidaceae, and a few Liliaceae have no chlorophyll (achlorophyllous) and remain saprophytic throughout their lives.

Arborescent or shrubby Liliidae are unusual but are known, for example, in some species of the predominantly African genera *Dracaena* of Agavaceae and *Aloe* of Aloeaceae, the latter having succulent leaves. The stems form fairly thick trunks composed of fibrous rather than woody tissue, a distinction that clearly differentiates them from true (dicotyledenous) trees. In the Americas, some species of *Yucca, Agave, Furcraea,* and *Nolina* of Agavaceae have a similar arborescent habit, as does *Xanthorrhoea* and *Kingia* of Xanthorrhoeaceae in Australia. In the arborescent Liliidae, a certain amount of stem girth may be due to secondary thickening from a lateral cambium layer (region of secondary growth). While the majority of monocotyledons do not form lateral meristems (and thus secondary vascular tissues), they do undergo diffuse secondary growth by the continued division and enlargement of the ground parenchyma cells. The members of a number of the Liliidae, however, undergo true secondary growth that involves a secondary meristem, the lateral cambium layer that forms below the secondary thickening meristem and extends to the base of the plant (*i.e.,* it develops in the primary plant body that has already completed its elongation). Unlike the vascular cambiums in the dicotyledons, in which the secondary xylem develops internally and secondary phloem develops externally, the cambium of monocots divides and forms largely fibrous parenchymatous tissue toward the outside of the central pericycle, or cortex, and parenchyma and vascular bundles more or less typical of monocotyledonous bundles toward the inside. Usually the secondary bundles form radial rows in the secondary tissue.

A few Iridaceae in southern Africa, notably *Nivenia,* also have a shrubby habit. These genera have brittle woody stems. In spite of the similar pattern of secondary growth in these few monocots, it is likely that the condition arose independently in each group.

Epiphytes abound in Orchidaceae but are rare in other families of Liliidae. Largely found in the subfamily Orchidoideae, epiphytes are extraordinarily richly developed in the moist and wet tropics and have diversified into numerous genera and species, often with remarkable floral elaborations.

FORM AND FUNCTION

Rhizome

Underground adaptations. Specialized underground storage organs are particularly common in the Liliaceae and Iridaceae, the basal form probably being a rhizome—that is, a more or less prostrate stem that produces roots from the lower surface and a cluster of leaves from the apex. Bulbs have evolved repeatedly in several lines and occur among most members of Liliaceae. In Iridaceae, bulbs occur in some species of *Iris* and in the New World

Drawing by M. Moran; (far right) from J. Hutchinson, *Families of Flowering Plants,* © 1959 by The Clarendon Press, Oxford, reprinted by permission

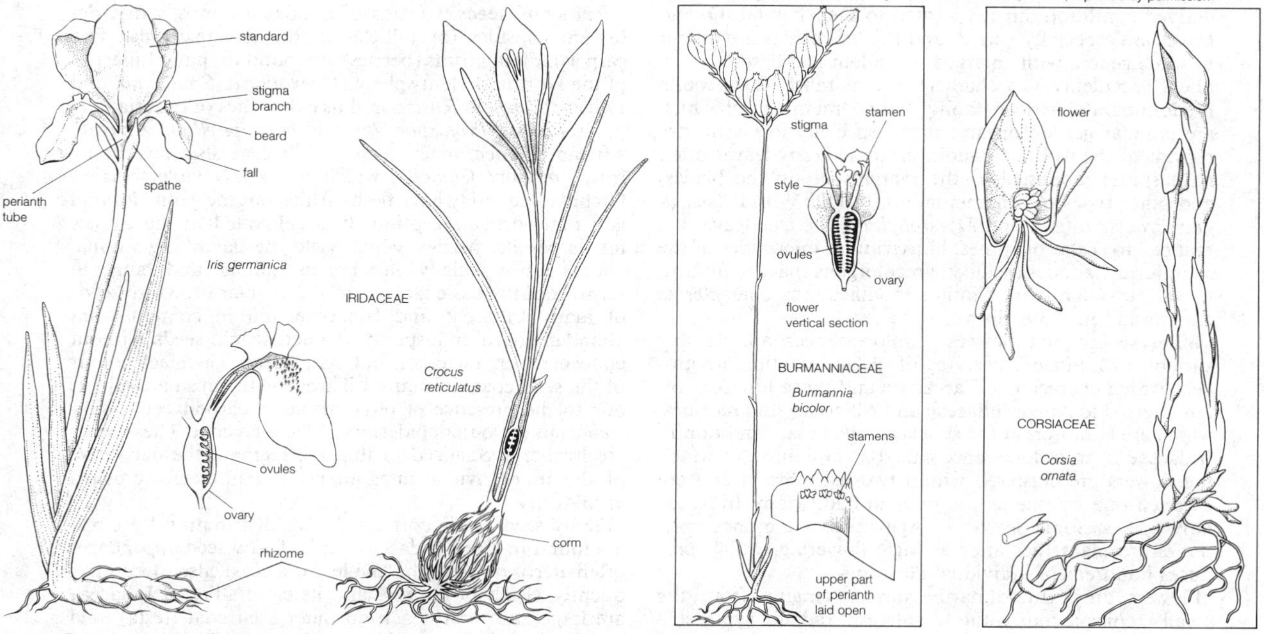

Representative plants and structures from three families of the subclass Liliidae.

tribe Tigridieae. Although the swollen and fleshy leaf bases or the protective bud scales (cataphylls) make up most of the bulb, a basal plate of stem tissue to which the leaves are attached is always present. Corms, which are largely composed of stem tissue, characterize many Iridaceae and those Liliaceae sometimes separated into the families Colchicaceae and Tecophilaeaceae. Corms are usually dry and starchy and are surrounded by coverings (tunics) that are derived from the remains of decayed leaf bases or are produced by specialized leaves. The tunics may be fibrous, membranous, or even woody. While corms are generally compact, round, and are replaced annually, tubers, which may also be composed of stem tissue, are often irregular in shape, are without special coverings, and persist for several years. The distinction between corms and tubers is not always obvious.

Aerial stem. In the majority of Liliidae, the flowers are borne in terminal inflorescences on aerial stems that may carry normal or reduced leaves; if leafless, the flowering stem is often called a scape. Scapose inflorescences characterize many of the species that have bulbs and are typical of those Liliaceae sometimes placed in Amaryllidaceae, Alliaceae, and Hyacinthaceae. The aerial stem is drastically shortened (reduced) in some Liliaceae, Iridaceae, and Orchidaceae. As a result, the flowers are borne at ground level, often with the ovary below ground and at the base of a long-tubed flower. Among the well-known stemless genera are *Crocus* of Iridaceae and *Colchicum* of Liliaceae. Many more examples can be found in parts of the world with arid climates, such as southern Africa and the Middle East. Although the ovary may be underground at flowering, the flower stalk (peduncle) usually elongates so that the ovary is a short distance above the ground as the seeds develop and ripen.

Leaves. In being characteristically strap-shaped and having parallel venation, the leaves of Liliidae are typical of the monocotyledons. Leaves are reduced to scales in most saprophytic Liliidae and have no photosynthetic function. Iridaceae and Philydraceae stand out in having their leaf blade compressed in the same plane as the stem (equitant), the basic condition for these families. Similar leaves characterize Haemodoraceae and also occur in a few Liliaceae and Orchidaceae. The leaves of *Alstroemeria* and *Bomarea* are twisted so that the leaf undersurface is twisted to face upward (resupinate). Leaves of some species of Taccaceae and *Alstroemeria* are elaborately lobed and even pseudocompound. Dioscoreaceae often have truly compound leaves. The leaves of Smilacaceae, Dioscoreaceae, Stemonaceae, and several genera of Liliaceae, notably those of forest habitats, are broad and have more or less pinnate-reticulate venation, probably a derived condition directly related to their habitat. Orchid leaves are especially varied, and the leaf blades are absent in some genera with enlarged, succulent leaf bases.

Leaf succulence is a characteristic of most Aloeaceae, a predominantly African family, many members of which are popular garden ornamentals, especially in warm, dry regions of the world. In addition, these fleshy leaves often have spines (confined to the margins or on the blades) and other types of ornamentation. In Old World *Asparagus, Protasparagus,* and *Myrsiphyllum,* the true leaves are reduced to scales or spines, but terminal internodes of the stem form cladodes (leaflike, green organs that are filiform to variously laminar). Similar modifications characterize *Ruscus* and its close allies.

Inflorescence and flowers. Inflorescences are notably variable in Liliidae. Deserving of special mention are umbels, which characterize Taccaceae and those Liliaceae often referred to Amaryllidaceae and Alliaceae, and racemes, which are common in the subclass. The basal condition in Iridaceae is an inflorescence called a rhipidium, in which the flowers are clustered within two leafy bracts and are exserted one by one as the buds unfold. Many Iridaceae have spikes. Some species of Agavaceae are monocarpic; the entire plant dies after a single flowering, which produces hundreds of individual blossoms.

Umbels and racemes

Flowers are extraordinarily varied, ranging from the small inconspicuous white to greenish, radially symmetrical (actinomorphic) flowers of most Dioscoreaceae to the large brightly coloured flowers of Orchidaceae and Iridaceae and some Liliaceae. A corona, which is a petaloid extension of some or all the tepals and perhaps most obvious as the trumpet portion of the flowers of *Narcissus,* occurs in some Liliaceae and Velloziaceae.

Although radial symmetry is the rule, most members of the Iridaceae subfamily Ixioideae and most Orchidaceae have bilaterally symmetrical (zygomorphic) flowers. Another frequent condition in Orchidaceae is floral resupination, in which the ovary is twisted 180 degrees so that the undersurface of the ovary faces upward.

Floral variation is closely correlated with pollination strategy. Further, floral zygomorphy and floral-tube length are associated with restriction to specific pollinators. Nectaries located on the tepals (perigonal nectaries) occur in some Liliaceae and Iridaceae and in many Orchidaceae. They are either superficial or confined to folds, pouches, or spurs, the latter being especially characteristic of Orchidaceae. Septal nectaries, embedded in the ovary, occur in many Iridaceae and Liliaceae.

The basal condition in the male organs (androecium) is the presence of two whorls of three stamens each, these alternating with the perianth whorls. Anther dehiscence is typically longitudinal, but may be introrse (the anther opening facing the inside of the flower) or extrorse (the opening facing outward). Pollen grains are typically shed as monads.

The gynoecium comprises three carpels, which are frequently united but are free in a few generally unspecialized, primitive Liliaceae, notably some species of the Northern Hemisphere genus *Tofieldia* of Liliaceae (Melanthiaceae). Styles may be free or, more often, united, and they may be either with discrete stigmatic lobes or simple, which is the most common condition in those Liliaceae treated by Dahlgren as Asparagales. In many members of the Iridaceae subfamily Iridoideae, the style is divided into three broad, flattened petaloid lobes, which are extended above into paired appendages (crests); the stigma is a small lobe on the undersurface of each style branch. Septal nectaries located within the walls of the ovary are widespread in the subclass; they are, however, rare in Orchidaceae where nectaries located on the tepals are frequent. Perigonal nectaries also characterize most groups of Liliaceae that lack phytomelanic seeds (see below) and one subfamily of Iridaceae.

The ovary usually has three locules with axile placentation. Parietal placentation characterizes subfamilies Cypripedioideae and Orchidoideae of Orchidaceae but is rare elsewhere in Liliidae. An inferior ovary characterizes Orchidaceae, Velloziaceae, Dioscoreaceae, Taccaceae, most Iridaceae, and some Liliaceae.

Characteristics of the ovary

Fruits and seeds. Fruits of Liliidae are mostly dry, dehiscent capsules (or follicles in the few taxa with free carpels). Fleshy fruits (berries) are found in many Liliaceae of the Northern Hemisphere (*Convallaria, Smilacina,* and *Polygonatum*), in *Ruscus* and its close allies of Eurasia, and in *Asparagus, Protasparagus,* and *Myrsiphyllum,* a largely African alliance. A few tropical Liliaceae also have fleshy fruits, notably *Dianella,* which has glossy violet berries. Orchidaceae rarely have fleshy fruits, but the genus *Vanilla* is a noteworthy exception. It is cultivated in the tropics for its podlike berries, which yield the flavouring vanilla.

Seeds are especially variable in Liliidae and range in form from the basic globose to the angular brownish seeds of many Liliaceae and Iridaceae and in content from abundant hard endosperm to microscopic seeds without endosperm characteristic of Orchidaceae. The black colour of the seed coats in many Liliaceae with capsular fruits is due to the presence of phytomelan, a carbonaceous substance, in the outer epidermis of the seed coat. These seeds are further specialized in that the tegmen (the derivative of the inner ovular integument) is completely crushed at maturity.

Fleshy seed coats, correlated with distribution by birds, are found in a few Iridaceae. Arils (fleshy seed appendages often derived from the ovule funiculus) also occur frequently. Seeds of *Crinum* and its close allies in Liliaceae are large and fleshy, lack an outer seed coat (testa), and have lost their ability to become dormant. They germinate rapidly after being shed, sometimes even within the capsules, and the young seedlings develop rapidly from small bulbs, ensuring survival in the dry season, the onset of which may be quite soon after fruiting.

Seeds of the saprophytic Liliidae, Burmanniaceae, Corsiaceae, and Geosiridaceae are numerous and minute and usually lack endosperm. This is also the case with Orchidaceae in which only the outer layer of the outer integument generally persists as a membranous seed coat. Seeds of Orchidaceae have little or no endosperm; thus, under natural conditions they only germinate after a symbiotic relationship has been established with a specialized fungus, which supplies nutrients to the developing seedling.

Embryology. Ovules are basically crassinucellar (with ample nucellar tissue) but the tenuinucellar condition (without a parietal cell) has evolved repeatedly within several families. Both successive and simultaneous microsporogenesis (pollen production) occur in Liliidae, and the resulting pollen grains are typically two-celled. Frequently endosperm is formed by free-nuclear divisions, followed later by cell wall formation (nuclear endosperm formation), but helobial endosperm formation (mitosis) occurs in several lineages. Endosperm generally consists of hemicelluloses in thick cell walls; oil and protein and the seeds typically contain considerable endosperm and small embryos. The seeds of Orchidaceae, already mentioned, are tiny and contain little or, more often, no endosperm or any other storage material. Starchy endosperm is characteristic of the seeds of Philydraceae, Pontederiaceae, Haemodoraceae, and Velloziaceae. Embryos generally have a single terminal cotyledon and a tiny lateral, sometimes sunken primary bud (plumule).

Endosperm formation

Phytochemistry. As might be expected from so large a group, Liliidae are very diverse in their flavonoids. These compounds have systematic importance only at the generic level. The unusual steroid saponins, however, characterize Liliidae to a remarkable degree, although they are absent from several groupings—notably *Lilium* and its close allies as well as several genera with alkaloids sometimes segregated as Colchicaceae and Amaryllidaceae. Steroid saponins are particularly notable in Dioscoreaceae and are of commercial importance. They are a source of steroid compounds used as drugs and medication. Chelidonic acid is very characteristic of Liliaceae, Aloeaceae, and Agavaceae as well as Haemodoraceae but is absent in Orchidaceae and Burmanniaceae. Chelidonic acid is rare or absent elsewhere in the Liliidae and other monocotyledons. Characteristic alkaloids are found in several genera of Liliidae. Colchicine, an important medicinal compound, and related alkaloids characterize a group of Old World genera, including *Colchicum* and *Gloriosa.* A group of genera that is frequently treated as a separate family, the Amaryllidaceae, has a different series of alkaloids. Other alkaloid-containing Liliaceae are the bulbous genera (sometimes treated as Hyacinthaceae), including highly toxic members such as *Drimia* (also called *Urginea*), *Scilla,* and *Ornithogalum.* Their toxicity stems from the cardiac glycosides (heart stimulants) they produce, which also occur in a few genera of African Iridaceae. A number of genera of the Northern Hemisphere including *Veratrum* and *Zigadenus* have the alkaloid veratrine and similar compounds. Allylic sulfides, responsible for onion- or garlic-type odours, characterize *Allium* and other genera sometimes included in a separate family Alliaceae.

NATURAL HISTORY

The many types of underground organs of Liliidae permit these plants to survive beneath the ground during unfavourable seasons and enable rapid regeneration of the aerial plant body when conditions are suitable for growth. Liliidae seem particularly adapted to Mediterranean climatic zones, and they have radiated explosively in the Mediterranean basin and the Cape region of southern Africa. Underground organs also often act as reproductive structures in the sense that they fragment into new individual plants. Bulbs and corms are preferred foods of porcupines (*Hystrix*) and mole rats (*Cryptomys, Bathyergus, Georychus,* all of Bathyergidae) of Africa, which disperse bulbils and corm fragments in the process.

The variety of insect pollinators (the principal animal pollinator of Liliidae) is extensive, but the most frequent is the bee. Among the adaptations that the flowers have developed for this mode of pollination are bright colours (except reds, which bees cannot distinguish from black), contrasting markings (nectar guides), and often a sweet odour. In some Orchidaceae—for example, *Ophrys*—the colouring and shape of the labellum (lowest of three petals) resembles a female bee of a particular species; the flower is pollinated during pseudocopulation by the male bee. In many American genera of Orchidaceae and Iridaceae, sweet (sugar-containing) nectar may be supplemented by oils secreted by stalked glands in the nectaries. Some of the Neotropical Orchidaceae that produce aromatic compounds are pollinated by male bees which utilize them for marking territory and probably in mating behaviour; the nectar or pollen or both may be the reward offered. Carrion fly pollination is relatively uncommon, but in Africa pollination by flies of several families with long proboscises is common. Flowers with a long, thin perianth tube are typical of this pollination syndrome, especially in Iridaceae.

Insect pollination

Birds are also an important but less frequent pollinator. Pollination by passerine sunbirds is relatively common in African Aloeaceae, such as *Aloe* and *Kniphofia,* for example, and Iridaceae, notably in *Gladiolus* and *Watsonia,* and in some Australian Haemodoraceae, such as *Anigozanthos,* and Liliaceae, such as *Blandfordia.* In the New World, hummingbird pollination occurs in several Liliaceae, including *Bomarea, Stenomesson, Phaedranassa,* some Agavaceae, including *Beschorneria* and *Polianthes,* and a few Iridaceae, as in *Rigidella.* Bird-pollinated species generally have a red perianth; a long, wide tube; and exserted stamens and stigmas. Despite the great floral diversity in Orchidaceae, bird pollination is rare.

Pollination by hawkmoths (sphingophily) occurs in many orchids that have long nectar-bearing spurs and in some Liliaceae and Iridaceae with long perianth tubes. In addition, the flowers have a white or yellow perianth and a strong, sweet scent. The *Yucca* (Agavaceae) has an unusual pollination syndrome. Females of the moth *Tegeticula* lay eggs in the ovary and then carefully transfer pollen to the stigmas. Bat pollination is rare in Liliidae but recorded in some species of Agavaceae.

Seed dispersal is not markedly developed in Liliidae, but the fleshy fruits of many Liliaceae and the fleshy or brightly coloured seeds of some Iridaceae are dispersed by birds. Very small seeds, or those with wings, as in several genera of Liliaceae and *Gladiolus,* are adapted for wind dispersal. Elaiosomes (fleshy white arils) are found in a few genera, notably many species of *Iris* and *Lachenalia.* These adaptations are thought to relate to dispersal by ants, which store the seeds in their nests and eat only the fleshy part. Adaptation for water dispersal is developed in a number of genera that have corky or spongy seed coats (*e.g., Crinum*) and some species of *Iris.* For the majority of the subclass, however, dispersal is poorly understood, and the predominant mechanisms may be passive.

CLASSIFICATION AND EVOLUTION

Taxonomic status. Few groups of angiosperms are in such taxonomic ferment as the Liliidae, the delimitation and division of which is unsettled. The 1981 system favoured by Cronquist and represented in this article takes a broad view of the variability in the subclass and recognizes 2 orders: Liliales, with 15 families, and Orchidales, with 4.

Diverse systems of classification

The most critical and extensive modern treatment of the families of the monocotyledons, that of Dahlgren, Clifford, and Yeo, differs in two important ways. First, Philydraceae, Pontederiaceae, Haemodoraceae, and Velloziaceae are not included in Liliidae. Second, the arrangement of the remaining families into orders is substantially different: three major orders are Dioscoreales, Asparagales, and Liliales, and two smaller orders are Burmanniales and Melanthiales. A compromise between these systems will be achieved only slowly.

The assignment of families into orders, however, seems less important in Liliidae. The lack of clearly defined family clusters may mean that too few discontinuities exist among the families to merit more than a single order.

A resolution of the question of subclass assignment for Philydraceae, Pontederiaceae, Haemodoraceae, and Velloziaceae, however, is important; Dahlgren stresses the differences between these families and the other orders in Liliidae in terms of the presence of starch in the seeds, epicuticular waxes, of the type found in *Strelitzia* of Zingiberidae, and the presence of ultraviolet fluorescent compounds in the cell walls. These characteristics are common in the subclass Zingiberidae and differ from other Liliidae. In addition, these four families exhibit helobial endosperm formation, paracytic stomata (*i.e.,* stomata with two guard cells), both common in Zingiberidae, whereas nuclear endosperm formation and anomocytic stomata are typical in Liliidae. To this series of characters may be added the presence of an amoeboid tapetum in Pontederiaceae and Haemodoraceae, a rare characteristic elsewhere in the monocotyledons.

Evolution. Lacking woody tissues for the most part, Liliidae make poor fossils and their geologic record is consequently incomplete. The first pollen type that can be ascribed to the monocotyledons, that of the fossil genus *Liliacidites,* possesses characteristics typical of the grains of Liliidae (monosulcate and coarsely reticulate) and appeared as early as the Albian Age of the Early Cretaceous Period (approximately 113 million years ago). Pollen grains that probably represent Liliaceae or Agavaceae are known from the Maastrichtian Age of the Late Cretaceous (74.5 to 66.4 million years ago). Pollen grains thought to belong to Liliaceae have also been recorded in deposits of Late Eocene age (36.6 to 43.6 million years old) and of more recent times, but the family and subclass are no doubt considerably older. Fossils assigned to Dioscoreaceae are known from the Eocene and later. Fossil leaves from eastern European deposits dating to the Miocene (23.7 to 5.3 million years ago) have been assigned to Dioscoreaceae and Smilaceae.

Within the monocotyledons, Liliidae are regarded as a very specialized group by Cronquist, who considers that the most primitive members of Liliopsida are the largely aquatic and entirely herbaceous Alismatidae. Among Liliidae, the most primitive members fall within the Liliales where a herbaceous habit, narrow parallel-veined leaves, flowers with a petaloid perianth, six stamens, and three free carpels with individual styles probably constitute the basal condition.

Primitive members

The primitive type of endosperm for Liliidae is, according to Cronquist, probably fleshy or cartilaginous with reserves of oil and protein; both hard seeds with reserves of hemicellulose in thick walls and strongly starchy seeds are specialized. Dioscoreaceae, Taccaceae, and Stemonaceae seem specialized in their habit, petiolate leaves with broad blades and, except in some Stemonaceae, inferior ovaries, yet the embryos with terminal plumules and no hemicellulose are unspecialized.

The four families with starchy endosperm—Philydraceae, Pontederiaceae, Haemodoraceae, and Velloziaceae—seem rather isolated from other Liliales in other features as well. For these reasons, Dahlgren has preferred to exclude them from Liliidae altogether.

The opinion of Dahlgren, Clifford, and various other authorities in the early 1980s differs with the generally traditional view favoured by Cronquist. They regard members of their order Dioscoreales (including Dioscoreaceae, Stemonaceae, Taccaceae, and Smilacaceae) as being among the most primitive of the Liliidae and perhaps close to the basic type of the whole class. Their hypothesis holds that petiolate leaves with broad blades are more primitive than narrow leaves without petioles. This is consistent with the apparently primitive embryos and seed reserves of the order. The vining habit and inferior ovary are clearly specialized here, as is a complex chemistry, but they find nevertheless more similarities with primitive dicotyledons within this alliance than any other alliance in the Liliopsida.

The arborescent habit has evolved several times in Liliidae, evidently from different ancestors within Liliaceae. The major assemblages with arborescent members are accorded family status by Cronquist. In Iridaceae, however, where a comparable development has occurred, shrubby members are not removed from the family. When the immediate ancestry of the arborescent or shrubby allies of Liliaceae was evident, Dahlgren preferred to unite them with their closest herbaceous relatives, thus including Aloeaceae within Asphodelaceae. In other cases, lacking clear evidence of ancestry, they created additional families defined by the arborescent condition, resulting in a proliferation of rather similar and broadly related families.

It is clear from the divergence of opinion that the broad pattern of evolution among the monocots (Liliopsida) is far from clear. No doubt the class is very ancient, perhaps having diverged not long after the origin of the flowering plants. With its scant fossil record and convergence in many lineages for diverse character combinations, it is not surprising that the phylogeny of Liliidae remains poorly known. Details of the evolutionary relationships among the families of the subclass are equally meagre, making it impossible to allow an informed choice about which systems of classification best reflect phylogeny. (Pe.G.)

REPRESENTATIVE GROUPS

Liliales (the lily order). The order Liliales is a vast assemblage of plants whose flowers usually have three petals and three sepals—the sepals usually resembling the petals in shape and colour—and whose leaves are generally linear or strap-shaped with parallel veins. Within this large order, exemplified by the lily, are more than 400 genera and 8,000 species, including erect perennial herbs, climbers, shrubs, and a few trees. The group contains many common garden plants and vegetables, such as the lily, hyacinth, narcissus, amaryllis, asparagus, onion, and yam. Other economically important members include the agaves, fibre crop plants; *Colchicum,* from which the drug colchicine is extracted; and *Smilax,* from which the flavouring sarsaparilla is derived.

Distribution and abundance. Liliaceae, the largest family in the order, consists of some 280 genera and 4,000 species of herbs, shrubs, or trees distributed throughout the world, predominantly in temperate and subtropical areas. Liliaceae develop rhizomes, bulbs or corms, linear to lanceolate leaves, and occasionally petiolate flowers that are often arranged in panicles, racemes, or umbels. Its flowers are occasionally zygomorphic (bilaterally symmetrical). Important genera include *Lilium, Narcissus, Allium, Hemerocallis,* and *Tulipa.* Liliaceae is a very diverse family with an unsettled taxonomic composition. Dahlgren and his coworkers regard Liliaceae as comprising three orders and many families.

Liliaceae

Iridaceae, the second largest family, contains 80 genera and an estimated 1,700 species. Nearly worldwide in distribution, the Iridaceae are best developed in Africa. Among the important genera in the family are *Iris, Tigridia, Sisyrinchium, Gladiolus, Watsonia,* and *Freesia.* Iridaceae includes geophytic herbs (perennial buds situated on corms or bulbs) or rhizomes and flowers arranged in rhipidia (fanshaped cymes) or spikes. The often highly coloured flowers are extremely diverse and frequently zygomorphic and tubular.

Agavaceae contains 18 genera and 600 species distributed throughout the world, although principally in semiarid tropical regions. Important members include *Dracaena* and *Agave* (the source of a fibre called sisal and of alcoholic beverages such as mescal, pulque, and tequila).

Haemodoraceae, included in Bromeliales by Dahlgren, is a family of approximately 14 genera and 100 herbaceous species found principally in Australia, South Africa, and North America. The flowers and inflorescences are frequently hairy, and the perianth is often tubular but sometimes zygomorphic.

The remaining families, Pontederiaceae, Xanthorrhoeaceae, Velloziaceae, Aloeaceae, Phylidraceae, Stemonaceae, Hanguanaceae, Taccaceae, Cyanastraceae, Smilacaceae, and Dioscoreaceae have 10 or fewer genera each. Aloeaceae, however, has approximately 700 species and is centred in Africa. The leaves are usually succulent and crowded in rosettes, and the often tubular flowers are simple or branched spikes or racemes. Among the important

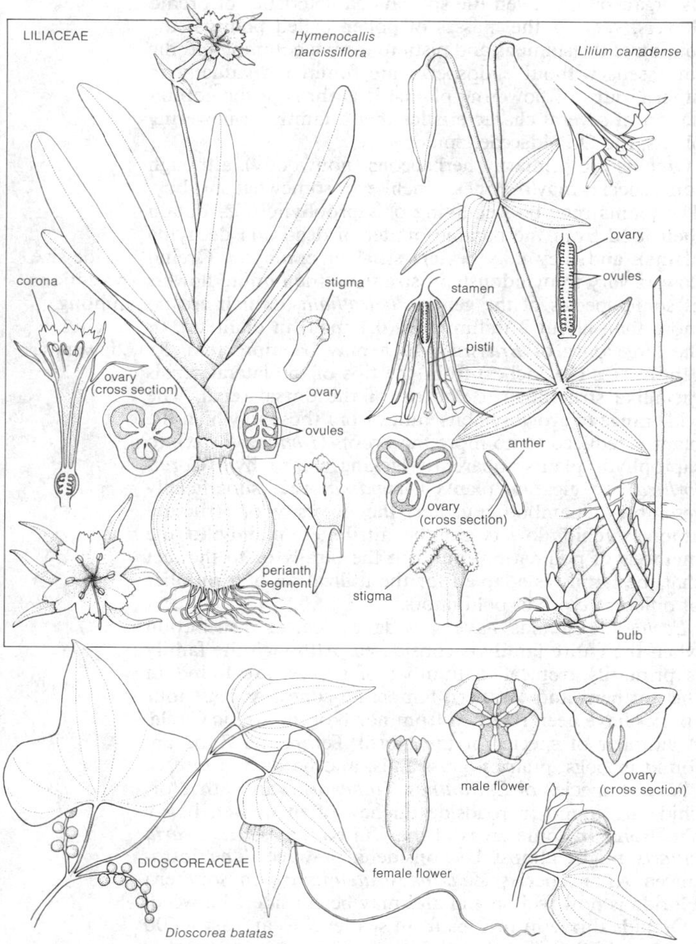

Representative plants from two major families of the order Liliales.
Drawing by M. Moran

genera are *Aloe* and *Haworthia.* Pontederiaceae is a family of aquatic herbs, with emergent, floating, or submerged leaves; it has been allied with the Bromeliales by Dahlgren.

Species of the Liliales are usually perennial herbs, with fleshy stems arising from various kinds of underground stems. The order also contains succulents such as the *Aloe* and *Agave* species. Agaves include some of the largest members of the Liliales: the flower stalk of the so-called century plant (*Agave americana*) may attain 6 metres (20 feet) in height. *Yucca* and *Dracaena* species are often woody and treelike, such as the Joshua tree (*Yucca brevifolia*) and the dragon tree (*Dracaena draco*).

The lily order is cosmopolitan in distribution, although most of its members are found in temperate and subtropical regions. The extreme range is as far north as northern Greenland (*Tofieldia coccinea*) and as far south as the southern tip of South America and New Zealand (*Luzuriaga marginata*). In numbers of species and individuals the order is best represented in southern Africa, North America, western Asia, and Australia.

Economic importance. The lily order is notable for species producing food and other useful products, on the one hand, and its many showy cultivated ornamental plants, on the other. The outstanding food crops include the onion (*Allium cepa*), garlic (*A. sativum*), leek (*A. ampeloprasum* variety *porrum*), chive (*A. schoenoprasum*), *rakkyo,* or *ch'iao* (*A. chinense*), Chinese chive (*A. tuberosum*), and asparagus (*Asparagus officinalis*).

Agave species

The more than 100 species of *Agave,* ranging from the United States to tropical South America, and the related 20 species of *Furcraea* provide important commercial fibres, obtained by processing the leaves. Sisal hemp is obtained from *Agave sisalana,* native to Yucatán; henequen from *A. fourcroydes,* Mexico; Mauritius hemp from *Furcraea foetida* (sometimes called *F. gigantea*), the tropics; and Ceylon bowstring hemp, from *Sansevieria zeylanica,* Sri Lanka.

Many other *Agave* species are cultivated or harvested from native stands mostly for local fibre needs or for fermented beverages. Several species are used in making pulque, the national drink of Mexico; the alcoholic liquor mescal is distilled from pulque.

The water hyacinth (*Eichornia crassipes*), with its bladderlike leaf bases, has been recommended as a source of cellulose for papermaking and other uses.

Dracaena cinnabari, a tree native to the island of Socotra, in the Indian Ocean, is the source of a red resin called dragon's blood, or Socotra resin, which is used in varnishes and also as an astringent and to stop hemorrhage. *Dracaena draco,* a tree native to the Canary Islands, is the source of a red resin, also known as dragon's blood, which is used in the varnish industry, for pigment in papermaking, and in medicine.

Drug products include many crude drugs used locally. Aloe juice, obtained from various *Aloe* species, is used as a purgative. The flowers of lily of the valley (*Convallaria majalis*) serve as a cardiac tonic in place of digitalis; squill, from the bulbs of *Urginea scilla,* is, among other things, a cardiac stimulant. White hellebore (*Veratrum album*), *min-mun-tung,* from the tubers of *Ophiopogon japonicus,* and chinaroot, from the dried rhizomes of *Smilax china,* have been used medicinally in China since ancient times. The seeds and corms of the meadow saffron (*Colchicum autumnale*) are used to treat gout. The active chemical is the alkaloid colchicine, which is one of the most efficient chemicals yet discovered for causing the doubling of chromosomes in cells.

Finally, the lily order is outstanding for its many ornamental plants, cultivated from most of the 15 families; the more important ones, however, are found in the Liliaceae and Iridaceae (*e.g.,* tulip [*Tulipa*], hyacinth [*Hyacinthus*], crocus [*Crocus*], lily [*Lilium*], and daylily [*Hemerocallis*]); in Aloeaceae (*e.g.,* aloe [*Aloe*]); and in Agavaceae (*e.g.,* agave [*Agave*], yucca [*Yucca*], hosta, or plantain lily [*Hostu*], dracaena [both *Dracaera* and *Cordyline*], and snake plant, or mother-in-law's tongue [*Sansevieria*]).

In The Netherlands there is a significant export business based on certain bulbous and cormous plants of the Liliales. In the United States, lily breeding for the domestic and export trade has developed into a considerable industry. Locally, the growing of plants of the lily order is active in season, particularly the forcing and marketing of lilies, tulips, hyacinths, narcissus, and amaryllis.

Natural history. The life cycle of members of the Liliales is similar to that of other monocotyledonous plants. Pollination is usually by insects or by other small animals, but cleistogamy, a condition in which self-fertilization takes place within unopened flowers, occurs in the genera *Heteranthera* and *Hydrothrix,* of the Pontederiaceae.

One of the outstanding features of a large number of the Liliales is the manner in which they have adapted to the seasonal peculiarities in different parts of the world. The most primitive Liliales are usually herbaceous perennials having short rhizomes with fibrous roots; they are adapted to humid climates. Organs for moisture and food storage have been evolved to permit the plant to survive unfavourable periods when growth is inhibited by dry or cold weather. These include creeping rhizomes, as in daylilies and lily of the valley; bulbs, as in *Lilium* and *Allium;* corms, as in *Brodiaea, Milla,* and *Tecophilaea;* tubers, as in *Gloriosa;* and tuberous roots with buds at the stem end, as in *Alstroemeria* and *Dioscorea.*

Food and water storage

In the agaves and aloes, the problem of surviving in a dry desert climate has been successfully solved by the evolution of tough, thick succulent leaves and a tough, thick stem for food and moisture storage. The American *Agave* species have assumed the outward shape, within limits, of the thick succulent-leaved African *Aloe* and allied genera of the family Liliaceae.

Extreme drought resistance is shown by *Leucocoryne,* native to the extremely dry Atacama Desert of Chile, where scant rainfalls occur years apart. When limited rains do occur after prolonged droughts, the bulbs, dormant for years, quickly sprout, come into flower, and produce seed. Another interesting adaptation to an arid climate is found in certain species of *Vellozia,* in which the upper parts of the stems are covered with fibrous sheaths of the leaves, and the lower parts with a covering of aerial roots a number of centimetres deep. When water falls on the aerial roots, it disappears as if into a sponge. The plant is thus able to supply itself with moisture in the form of dew and occasional light rainfall as well as from moisture condensed on the aerial roots.

Miscellaneous adaptations

Vivipary, in the sense of bulblets sprouting from buds in a flower cluster (inflorescence) almost to the total exclusion of the regular florets in the inflorescence, is found in some *Allium* species. It is by such means that European wild garlic (*Allium vineale*) has been naturalized as a noxious weed over wide areas in North America and elsewhere. The Pontederiaceae are adapted for life in an aquatic habitat. In the water hyacinth, for instance, the swollen petioles enable the plant to float, and floating has led to very wide distribution of this species.

Characteristic morphological features. The rootstock varies from creeping rhizomes, bulbs, corms, and tubers, all of which are modifications of the stem, to thickened storage roots with buds at the stem end. The plants are usually perennials, very rarely annuals, ranging from herbs to shrubs and climbers or rarely to types with a woody stem that is branched and treelike. The leaves are usually linear or strap-shaped, with longitudinal veins; in a few cases, the leaves are broader and have a stalk (petiole), with longitudinal veins separated by netted venation.

Floral variations

The flower varies from small and in loose clusters to large and solitary. When showy, the perianth (petals and sepals collectively) is usually arranged in six parts (rarely three parts or fewer); when the perianth segments are similar, they are sometimes united below into a tube. Occasionally there is a floral structure called the paraperigone, consisting of inward extensions of the lower part of the perianth tube; or scales or bristles may be present at the base of the filaments.

The stamens usually number six, rarely three or fewer; each stamen consists of an anther and a filament. The filaments may be variously modified, united into a tube below or into a conspicuous staminal cup. The pistil (usually one to a flower) consists of a three-part ovary formed of three greatly modified leaves (carpels) and a stalk (style) capped by a pollen-receptive tip (stigma). Pollination is accomplished by small animals, including birds, insects, and arachnids. Fertilization follows pollination. Most of the Liliales depend on cross-pollination, and thus fertilization follows flower opening; rarely are the flowers cleistogamous. The fruit is usually a dry, three-part (rarely a one-celled) capsule, sometimes a fleshy berry, very seldom a nut; the seeds are sometimes winged. (H.P.Tr./Ed.)

Orchidales (orchid order). *Distribution and abundance.* The order Orchidales consists of four families. The largest, Orchidaceae, consists of approximately 1,000 genera and 20,000 species distributed throughout the world, especially in wet tropics. The orchids are generally terrestrial or epiphytic herbs (*i.e.,* those not rooted in soil), rarely vines, and occasionally saprophytes. Often, the orchids develop corms or tubers. The leaves are occasionally reduced to scales, and the flowers are arranged in racemes, spikes, or panicles and are usually strongly zygomorphic (bilaterally symmetrical). Burmanniaceae is a pantropical family consisting of 21 genera and 165 species. Its members are autotrophic or often saprophytic herbs with rhizomes or tubers and, occasionally, zygomorphic tubular flowers. Corsiaceae, a family having a likely affinity with Burmanniaceae, contains two genera and 26 species in New Guinea, eastern Australia, and Chile. They are generally saprophytes with rhizomes, and the plant body develops scalelike leaves and zygomorphic, sometimes unisexual flowers. Geosiridaceae, a family of one genus and species, is a saprophyte in the wet forests of Madagascar. It is thought to be allied to the Iridaceae and Burmanniaceae by some authorities.

Structural diversity. As a group, the orchids are different from other plants but only in the morphological (structural) characteristics associated with the flower and its organization. Even the special characteristics of orchid flowers, such as the masses of pollen called pollinia, the joining of the stamens and pistil to form a column, and the tiny seeds without endosperm are found individually in other groups of flowering plants. It is through the combination of several characteristics that a family of flowering plants, the Orchidaceae, emerges.

Orchids are primarily herbaceous (nonwoody), although some species may be vines, vinelike, or somewhat shrubby. The plants may be free-living or saprophytic (*i.e.,* obtain their food from the organic matter of dead and decaying plants), and they may be terrestrial or epiphytic. Orchid flowers vary tremendously in size from the minute flowers of some species of the genus *Pleurothallis,* which are no more than about 2 millimetres (0.1 inch) in diameter, to the large ones of *Brassia,* which may be more than 38 centimetres (15 inches) from the tips of the lateral sepals (petallike structures) to the tip of the dorsal sepal. The wide range of growth habits varies from those in which the plant is reduced to no more than roots (*Dendrophylax*), to saprophytic plants apparently lacking chlorophyll (*Corallorhiza*), to gigantic plants (*Arundina*) that superficially resemble a bamboo. Further, the diversity of structure among orchid flowers can be attributed mainly to the methods of pollination found in the family or to the fact that the family is adapted for the utilization of a number of different types of pollinators.

Wide size variations among orchid flowers

Ecology. Orchids have a wide ecological distribution when the entire family is considered. Although the family is primarily tropical, a number of species are found in the northern and southern temperate zones. At least four species have been reported from north of the Arctic Circle. A number of species of the North Temperate Zone are found in bogs, prairies, grasslands, and hardwood forests.

Several species of *Spiranthes, Habenaria,* and other orchids are found in roadside ditches, often in wet, boggy situations. In some areas of the United States, *Habenaria ciliaris* might almost be considered a weed. The introduced Asian species *Zeuxine strateumatica* in southern Florida is now widespread and may be considered a weed.

Orchids thrive in regions from sea level to at least 4,600 metres (15,000 feet) in elevation. The greatest number of orchid species is found in cloud-forest associations in tropical regions, usually on mountainsides where the clouds brush the mountain day and night. Such forests are literally covered with mosses and lichens, and the inclination of the ground permits sunlight to penetrate through the vegetation to the ground. This is a perfect habitat for epiphytic orchids as well as members of the family Gesneriaceae and Araceae, ferns, and numerous other epiphytic plants.

Contrary to popular belief, rain forests on generally flat terrain are poor localities for orchids. At Iquitos, on the Amazon River in Peru, only about 125 species of orchids have been reported, and many of these are quite rare. Orchids that do occur in rain forests tend to be in the tops of large trees; often great quantities of a single species inhabit a tree, while another nearby tree may have only one or two additional species. The tropical-deciduous seasonal hardwood forests of the tropics, where marked wet and dry periods occur, often have numerous orchid species; however, this also tends to be the best farmland, and therefore forests do not last long after cultivation.

A wide range of ecological tolerance is shown by orchids. In addition to those species found above the Arctic Circle, a few species of orchids thrive in desert conditions; for example, in the dry areas of northern Peru, several species of orchids are found that are epiphytic on cacti. On the Santa Elena Peninsula in western Ecuador, two species of *Oncidium* as well as one species of *Brassia* are found on cacti. In parts of Central America one species of *Brassavola* is found growing on mangrove roots, often at, or only slightly above, the level of high tide. In Jamaica several species are found growing on bare rocks. In the Everglades of Florida in the United States, on the other hand, one species of *Habenaria* is almost aquatic. In western Mexico, one species of *Pleurothallis* is epiphytic on lichens.

Orchids vary from those species that are very widespread,

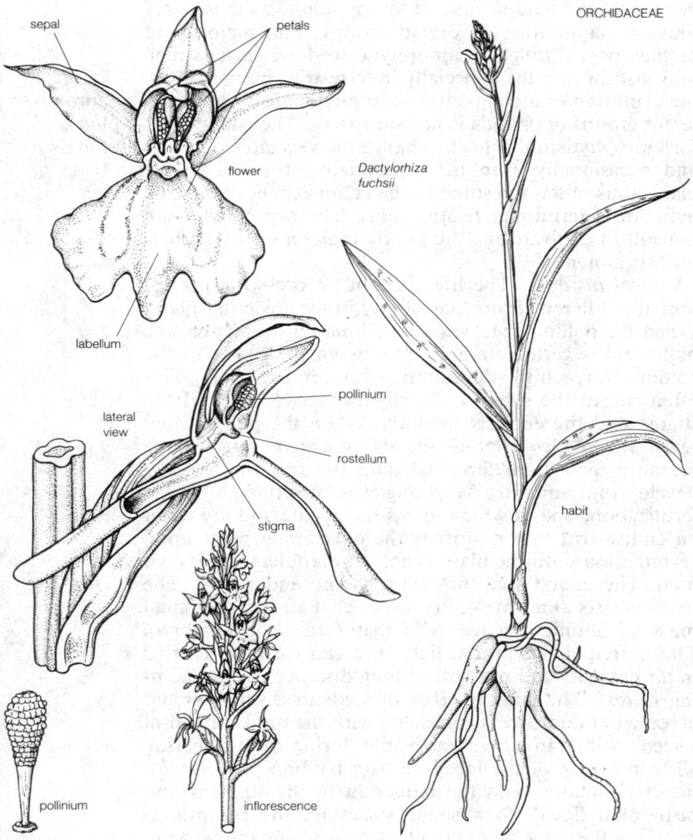

A representative orchid.

From M. Hickey and C. King, *100 Families of Flowering Plants*, 2nd ed. (1988); Cambridge University Press

such as the species found throughout most of the tropical regions of the Western Hemisphere (*e.g., Ionopsis utricularioides*), to some species that seem to be restricted to a single mountain. In the West Indies, each of the major islands have a fair number of such restricted species.

Economic importance. The orchid family is probably one of the most important of plant families from a horticultural point of view. Other than the horticultural uses to which orchids are put, the family is notably lacking in species from which products are derived. The only commercially important product derived from orchids is vanilla. Most vanilla is produced from one species, *Vanilla planifolia,* although two additional species are also cultivated commercially (*V. pompona* and *V. tahitensis*). The principal vanilla-growing areas are Madagascar, Mexico, French Polynesia, Réunion, Dominica, Indonesia, the West Indies, Seychelles, and Puerto Rico. Vanilla is grown from sea level to about 600 metres in elevation. The plant is a climbing vine that is indigenous to the tropical regions of the Western Hemisphere.

Source of vanilla

Various other orchids are used for a variety of folk medicines and cures. In the West Indies, the bulbs of *Bletia purpurea* are boiled, and the liquid is thought to cure poisoning from fish. In Malaysia, women take a drink made from the boiled leaves of *Nervilia aragoana* to prevent sickness after childbirth. In Melaka (formerly Malacca), a state in western Malaysia, boils are treated with a poultice made from the entire plant of *Oberonia anceps.* In Chile, *Spiranthes diuretica* is known to be a strong diuretic. In certain parts of Ecuador, the mucilage from *Catasetum* is thought to be good for broken bones. In various parts of the world, certain orchids are also used for food or food supplements. In Malaysia, the leaves of one species of *Anoectochilus* are sold as a vegetable, and the leaves of *Dendrobium salaccense* are cooked as a seasoning with rice. In certain parts of the Asian tropics, the tubers of some species of *Gastrodia* are eaten like potatoes. Throughout the world several species of orchids are used as a glue substitute. In most cases, the glue is derived from the pseudobulbs. Salep is derived from the tubers of several species of *Orchis.* The tubers are boiled, then dried and powdered. The resulting preparation is often used as a flour substitute.

Characteristic morphological features. The primary characteristics that distinguish the orchids as a group are found in the flower. At the bottom of an unspecialized non-orchid flower is the stem that supports it, called the pedicel. Directly above, and at the base of the flower itself, is a whorl of green, leaflike organs called sepals. Above and inside the sepals is a second whorl of coloured petals. Together the sepals and petals are called the perianth, which constitute the nonreproductive parts of the flower. The perianth protects the flower or attracts pollinators or both. Inside (also arranged in whorls) are the sexual portions of the flower. First are the pollen-producing stamens in up to several whorls; each stamen consists of an anther on a long slender filament. In the centre of the flower is the female pistil, which consists of an enlarged inferior ovary topped by a stalklike style with a stigma at its apex. The sepals and petals are usually similar, often highly coloured, and in sets of three. One petal is developed as a landing platform for the pollinator and is called the lip (or labellum).

Distinctive flower

The sexual portions of the orchid flower are quite different from other generalized flowers, and they tend to characterize the family. The filaments, anthers, style, and stigma are reduced in number and are usually fused into a single structure called the column. The majority of the orchids retain only a single anther at the apex of the column.

In the orchid the ovary is composed of three carpels fused so that the only outward evidence of their existence is the three ridges on the outside of the seed pods. The mature seed pod opens down the middle between the lines of juncture. The ovules are arranged along the ridges inside the ovary and do not develop until some time after the flower has been pollinated, thereby contributing to the long delay between pollination and the opening of a ripened pod.

The sepals and petals are usually quite distinct and therefore retain their separate identification. The petal opposite the fertile stamen is called the lip, or labellum. Often two, or even all three, of the sepals are joined, and the lip, petals, or the sepals may be joined to the column for some distance. One of the characteristic differences between the orchid family and other advanced monocots is that the fertile stamen or stamens are on one side of the flower opposite the lip. This makes the flower bilaterally symmetrical.

The lip is oriented upward in the bud, but, as it later develops, the pedicel or ovary twists so that the lip is usually oriented downward by the time the flower opens, a process called resupination.

There are several types of nectaries in the orchids, including extrafloral types that secrete nectar on the outside of the buds or inflorescence (flower cluster) while the flower is developing. Shallow cuplike nectaries at the base of the lip are common. Some nectaries are in long spurs that develop either from the joined sepals or from the base of the lip. Members of the *Epidendrum* complex have long tubular nectaries embedded in the base of the flower alongside the ovary. Nectaries on the side lobes of the lips are known, and general nectar secretion along the central groove of the lip is common. The nectaries of the Orchidales are present on the sepals or petals, if they are present at all.

Nectaries

In most orchids the anther is a caplike structure at the apex of the column. The anther of some of the more primitive orchids is superficially similar to that of a lily or amaryllis. In *Habenaria* and its allies the anther projects beyond the apex of the column but is thoroughly attached.

The pollen grains are usually bound together by threads of a clear, sticky substance (viscin) in masses called pollinia. Two basic kinds of pollinia exist: one has soft, mealy packets bound together to a viscin core by viscin threads and is called sectile; the other kind ranges from soft, mealy pollinia, through more compact masses, to hard, waxlike pollinia; the latter usually have some mealy pollen with viscin strands that attach the pollinia to each other or to a viscidium. This portion of the pollinium is called the caudicle.

The stigma, usually a shallow depression on the inner sides of the column, is composed of three stigmatic lobes (as in the typical monocot flower); however, the three lobes are fused together in the orchids. Faint lines often can be seen on the surface of the stigma, indicating its three-part structure.

In the majority of the orchids, a portion of one of the three stigma lobes forms the rostellum, a flap of tissue that projects down in front of the anther separating the stigma and the anther. As the visiting insect backs out of the flower, it brushes the rostellum, which is covered with sticky stigmatic liquid. The pollinia are then picked up from the anther and adhere to the body of the insect. Some primitive species have no rostellum, and the pollinia simply stick to stigmatic liquid that is first smeared on the back of the insect. A further specialization occurs in more advanced orchids in which the caudicles of the pollinia are already attached to the rostellum and a portion of it comes off as a sticky pad called a viscidium. In the most advanced genera a strap of nonsticky tissue from the column connects the pollinia to the viscidium. This band of tissue is called the stipe and should not be confused with the caudicles, which are derived from the anther. Orchids that have a stipe also have caudicles that connect the pollinia to the apex of the stipe. The pollinia, stipe, and viscidium are called the pollinarium.

Mycorrhiza and seed germination

Orchid seeds are extremely small and contain an undifferentiated embryo that lacks endosperm. A single seed pod produces a large number of small seeds, which are ideally suited for dispersal by wind. Orchid seeds need the presence of a fungal mat (mycorrhiza) in order to germinate and grow in nature. The fungus apparently penetrates the seed and contributes to the growth of the seedling by producing or supplying some of the necessary nutrients for growth. It has not yet been firmly established whether or not the fungus is necessary for the continued growth of the mature plant, but it appears likely that the presence of the fungus aids in the uptake of nutrients and prevents the leaching of nutrients from the root material of epiphytic species. In some cases the presence of a specific species of fungus is necessary, while in other cases several fungi may have the ability to become involved in the process. It is possible to grow and germinate some orchids without the fungus in artificial cultures that supply the required nutrients.

The majority of the tropical orchid species are epiphytes; nearly all the orchids in the temperate zones, however, are terrestrial.

The predominant and perhaps primitive growth form in a wide range of monocots is sympodial growth, a creeping habit consisting of an axis that appears to be continuous but is actually made up of a succession of elements. Each of these elements originates not from a terminal bud but as a fork of a dichotomy, the other fork being weaker in growth or suppressed entirely. The usual form of a sympodium is a horizontal rootlike stem structure called a rhizome that terminates each "branch." Most primitive orchids have a rather ordinary monocot appearance with a short rhizome stem and erect, nonthickened annual stems having scattered, spirally arranged leaves and a terminal inflorescence (flower cluster).

Another growth form found in the orchid order is the monopodial habit, in which the stem has unlimited apical growth and the roots are not restricted to its basal portion.

A great many orchids, especially the epiphytes, show variously thickened stems, or "pseudobulbs." While these structures are quite diverse in form, they fall into a limited number of morphological types and seem to show some evolutionary trends. One of these seeming trends is from pseudobulbs (or corms, bulblike stem structures) of several or many internodes (nodes are stem regions at which leaves attach, internodes are the stem areas between such nodes) to pseudobulbs of a single internode. Thickened stem bases may be found in either terrestrial or epiphytic groups, but pseudobulbs of a single internode are restricted to primarily epiphytic groups.

Saprophytic orchids

Saprophytic orchids, those that obtain their food from dead organic matter instead of by photosynthesis, are found in a number of orchid groups. The majority of orchids pass through a saprophytic seedling stage, which may last for months, especially in terrestrial species. Thus, the evolution of a completely saprophytic life cycle in different groups of orchids is not surprising. The adaptations for saprophytism drastically change the vegetative features and occasionally even the reproductive features of the plant, thus obscuring some of the characteristics normally used for determining relationships. The saprophytes are difficult to cultivate and are poorly represented by herbarium specimens.

Natural history. The life cycle of an orchid is not essentially different from that of any other flowering plant. When the pollinator leaves the pollinia on the stigma, the pollen tubes germinate and grow down the centre of the column to reach the developing ovules in the ovary. This often causes the sides of the stigma to swell around the stigma and the enclosed pollinia. When the pollen tubes reach the ovules after about six weeks or longer, one or more ovules are fertilized, and the resulting zygotes develop into embryos. Most angiosperms undergo double fertilization, one of which forms the zygote and the other an endosperm that nourishes the developing plant upon germination until the plant is able to manufacture its own food. The orchid seed, however, has no endosperm. The seed consists of a simple, dry, outer coat enclosing a small mass of undifferentiated cells that form a pro-embryo. This extremely small and light unit can easily be carried in air currents and may travel long distances before coming to rest. The large number of seeds in a single orchid capsule undoubtedly is correlated with the unlikelihood of a seed's falling in a favourable spot during wind dispersal.

The presence of the labellum as a landing platform for insect pollinators and the reduction of the stamens and pistil of a flower to a single structure, the column, is certainly the apex of floral adaptation to insects as pollinating agents. Once achieved, this combination provides a foundation for all kinds of specializations for attracting of specific pollinators.

The function of pollen deposition is centralized precisely in the median plane opposite the labellum. Being directed back toward the centre of the flower, the anther deposits pollen on the most advantageous side of the visitor, considering efficiency in reception and deposition. This precision is also expressed by a tendency of orchids to deposit the pollen as one mass, the pollinarium.

Orchids as a group use nectar as the major attractant, whereas pollen, sought by pollinators among more primitive plant families as a protein-rich food, has been withdrawn. This is tied to the exactness of the mechanics of pollination, but it also means that orchids can no longer provide the only source of sustenance for the pollinator, and other flowers must be present in the biosphere to maintain visitors.

Nectar is provided in tubular nectaries (*Brassavola, Angraecum, Comparettia,* and other genera), in grooves on the labellum (*e.g., Listera* and *Epipactis*), and at the base of the column and lip (*e.g., Dendrobium* and *Scaphyglottis*). A large number of orchids are nectarless and have developed other means of attracting pollinators, largely consisting of deceptive attractants in one form or another.

The function of pseudopollen

Many orchids attract pollinators with pseudopollen, a powdery mass resembling pollen that is found on the labellum of a number of species of *Maxillaria* and *Polystachya.* Sometimes the grains are detached outgrowths called papillae, and sometimes they are disintegrated multicellular hairs that are filled with starch.

Flowers pollinated by bees open during the day and tend to have similar characteristics: agreeable odours, bright colours (except red, which bees see as black or gray), a landing platform, nectar guides in the form of coloured lines running into the depths of the flower, and concealed nectaries. The basal portions of the orchid lip are usually formed into a tunnel with the column constituting its upper side. The bee enters the tunnel to get at the nectary, and as the bee backs out some of the stigmatic fluid may be rubbed on its back. As the bee backs farther, the pollinia become attached to the sticky material and are carried with the bee to the next flower. In more advanced orchids the pollinia may be attached to a sticky pad, the viscidium, which becomes detached from part of the stigma and sticks to the pollinator.

Some species of orchids are pollinated by bees that are attracted by means of deception. The flowers of the large genus *Oncidium,* for example, are pollinated by male *Centris* bees in what appears to be a case of pseudoantagonism. The flower seems to simulate an enemy insect, which the male bee tries to drive away from his territory. As the bee strikes at the flower, the pollinia are attached to the head of the bee.

The most exciting and unusual examples of deceit, traps, and manipulation of pollinators are to be found in those orchids that are pollinated by male euglossine bees (species of the bee tribe Euglossini). The syndrome of flowers that are pollinated by male euglossini is based on the attraction of the male bees to the odour of the flower. In no case does the male euglossine bee receive food from the orchid that it visits. The euglossine male bees visit other nectar-producing flowers for their food, but, when the male bees visit the non-nectar-producing orchid flowers, they rub the surface of the lip with their front feet and collect in special tarsal brushes the odour that is produced there. The bees then launch themselves into the air and transfer the odour to their hind tibiae (leg segments), which have become noticeably swollen. It is in the process of transferring the odour to the hind tibiae that the bee is manipulated by the orchid.

Another variation of pollinator manipulation by orchids is found in the genus *Coryanthes.* The flowers are very large and might even be considered grotesque. The sepals and petals fold back out of the way when the flower opens—like sails on a boat—revealing a strangely formed lip divided into three parts: a globular- or hood-shaped portion called the hypochile above; an elongate, sometimes fluted part, the mesochile; and a bucket-shaped epichile. The epichile is partially filled with water during the last few hours before the flower opens and for a short time afterward by two faucetlike organs located at the base of the column, which drip water. Male euglossine bees are attracted by the strong odour produced by the hypochile, where they scratch. In trying to launch into the air to transfer the odour to their hind legs, the bees occasionally fall into the water-filled bucket. The sides of the bucket are vertical and are very waxy, so that the bee is not able to climb out of the bucket. The only way for the bee to get out is through a small tunnel formed by the apex of the column and the apex of the epichile of the lip. As the bee forces its way out of the tunnel, the pollinarium is deposited on its thorax. The pollinia may then be deposited in the stigma of another flower on a next visit, provided the original pollinia of that flower have already been removed and the stigmatic cleft has opened sufficiently to become receptive.

Moth and butterfly pollination

Because moths normally fly at night, they are attracted to flowers that produce strong odours and are white or light-coloured. Moths hover in front of the flower while extracting the nectar. The typical moth-pollinated flower has a long, slender nectar tube containing abundant nectar. The fragrance produced is typically sweet or musky, and the flowers usually are horizontal or hanging. Butterflies, on the other hand, are day fliers and are attracted to highly coloured flowers that may or may not be fragrant. Butterflies tend to be somewhat erratic fliers and, lacking the ability to hover, usually land on the flower. The flowers are, therefore, usually erect and provide platforms for landing. Often the platform simply consists of a head of erect, densely packed flowers. Butterflies detect colours well, and butterfly-pollinated flowers are usually brightly coloured with red, orange, or yellow predominating. Nectar is commonly abundant and is hidden in deep nectar tubes. In most of the moth- and butterfly-pollinated orchids, the nectar tube is arranged to guide the tongue or beak in such a manner that the pollinia are correctly attached to the pollinating organism.

In an oft-cited case, Charles Darwin, the English naturalist, predicted that a moth with a 25-centimetre-long proboscis would eventually be found on the island of Madagascar as the pollinator of the orchid *Angraecum sesquipedale,* since a moth would need a long tongue to reach the nectar hidden in the very long nectary at the base of the lip. Such a moth has been found but has not yet been observed to pollinate the flowers of this amazing orchid.

Flowers adapted to pollination by birds are usually brightly coloured, with reds, blues, and yellows predominating. They are usually tubular in form, often with a long nectary, and nectar is almost always present. Birds have little or no sense of smell, and bird-pollinated flowers tend to lack odour; however, the bright colours serve to attract the birds. Bird-pollinated orchids tend to follow the pattern of other bird flowers, but in some cases they diverge considerably. Many orchids of the Western Hemisphere appear to have adapted to bird pollination as an extension of butterfly pollination, and, as in the case of *Epidendrum secundum,* birds and butterflies act as copollinators. In such cases, orchid flowers already adapted to butterflies are not greatly changed morphologically. On the other hand, orchids that have adapted directly to hummingbirds from bee-pollinated ancestors have changed fundamentally. The genera *Cochlioda, Sophronitis, Elleanthus, Isochilus, Comparettia, Hexisea,* and *Meiracyllium* are all bird-pollinated and are remarkably similar in certain aspects. All have bright colours, tubular form, and a callus or hump in the interior of the tube, on the lip, which acts to force the beak of the bird against the column.

Some flies are important pollinators of flowers, and certain families of flies (*e.g.,* the Syrphidae and Bombyliidae) are restricted to flowers for their food. Unspecialized flowers may attract flies to nectar, which is present in open, shallow nectaries and may emit sweet odours. The flies eat the nectar and do not store it as do bees. More specialized fly flowers may attract flies through deception, imitating decaying substances, dung, or carrion. Many kinds of flies are then attracted and act as effective pollinators.

Adaptations to fly pollination

Fly-pollinated flowers have often developed traps for catching and holding unadapted visitors. They commonly have large landing surfaces and "tails" produced from the flower parts, which function as guides. Their colours are usually checkered or blotched and tend toward dull green, brown, purple, or red. The odours produced are commonly putrescent. Orchids pollinated by flies are common throughout the world. In most fly-pollinated orchids, special adaptations have developed—superimposed on the basic pattern of the bee-pollinated orchid flower—to guide the somewhat poorly oriented flies. Certain of the five petals may be long and taillike (as in *Bulbophyllum* and *Masdevallia*) or joined to form a flat radial flower (as in *Stelis*). The flowers themselves may be arranged to form a larger radial, compound "flower" (as in *Cirrhopetalum*). The petals or lip may be fringed with motile clublike hairs that vibrate in the wind and attract the flies (*Bulbophyllum*). Often the sepals are joined or the lip is saccate to form a trap (*Pterostylis*) into which the flies fall and from which they must crawl by way of a tunnel that passes the stigma and anther. A common contrivance by which orchids exploit flies is a hinged, balanced lip that tips with the weight of the fly and launches the pollinator into the flower.

In orchids it is often difficult to decide when simple fly pollination ends and deception that is based on carrion mimicry begins. Many genera have some species whose pollination is based simply on attracting various kinds of flies by means of sweet odours and nectar production, while others attract flies on the basis of rotten odours but provide no food.

Three major groups of orchids have become predominantly fly-pollinated: the subtribe Pleurothallidinae in tropical America, containing about 1,000 species pollinated by flies; the *Bulbophyllum* group of about 1,000 species found mainly in the Old World; and the large genus *Pterostylis* and its relatives in Australia.

Self-pollination occurs in a significant number of orchids. Several degrees of this phenomenon may be found in a single genus, from species in which accidental self-pollination results in fertilization to those in which the flowers never open, yet are capable of producing fertile seed. In many orchids, self-fertilization is not possible because of genetically controlled self-incompatibility, in which pollen from a plant having a particular combination of genetic factors will not fertilize its own ovules or those of any other plant having the same combination.

In most species the pollen is kept separate from the stigma by the rostellum. This physical barrier is normally quite effective; but, in some species, forms occur in which the rostellum degenerates or becomes stigmatic, and self-pollination results when the pollen germinates on the stigmatic fluid. In most of these forms, normal plants are also found in the same population. Self-pollination may also occur as a result of simple falling of old pollinia, a means of averting sterility at the end of a long normal period when the flower is open but no pollinator arrives.

A kind of mechanical self-pollination occurs in some orchids in which the tissues connecting the viscidium and the pollinia bend down and carry the pollinia into place on the stigma. Generally speaking, self-fertilization in orchids seems to be a means of averting extinction in plants growing under conditions adverse for normal pollination relationships. Examples include some species of *Orchis* in Europe and several orchids in Florida, such as *Epidendrum nocturnum* and *Bletia purpurea,* all of which have cross-pollinated forms in other areas. Seeds blow into Florida from the Caribbean area where normal pollinators exist, but the plants that survive tend to be self-pollinated because they lack their customary pollinators, which are not found in Florida.

Mimicry and deception

Flowers of the genus *Ophrys* deceive and manipulate pollinators mainly through odours, imitating those produced by the abdominal glands of female bees or wasps. Flower shapes, colours (including ultraviolet reflection), and tactile stimuli by the hairs on the lip operate on the sensory organs of the visiting males, leading ultimately to the same behaviour as that observed during the initial phases of copulation with female bees. No ejection of sperm occurs, however, but the supernormal olfactory stimulation ensures that the male will remain for a long stay on the flower.

This act of pseudocopulation takes place in such a way that the pollinia are carried off and redeposited on a different plant. Four genera of solitary bees and wasps appear to be the principal pollinators. The orchid species of *Ophrys* that are pollinated by the wasps *Trielis* and *Gorytes,* and the bee *Eucera* induce the insects to attempt copulation with the apex of the lip. Those orchids pollinated by *Andrena* appear, for the most part, to stimulate the bee to reverse its position and copulate with the base of the lip. In the former group the pollinarium is affixed to the head of the pollinator, while in the latter it is attached to the abdomen. Only the introductory behaviour is necessary for pollination of the flower, and the bees do not encounter structures that lead to ejection of sperm. The behaviour is elicited by tactile stimulation from the hairs on the labellum, but the male "suitor" requires simultaneous and continued olfactory stimulation. The glistening pseudonectaries apparently imitate the eyes of the female bee. Metallic-blue mirror spots similar to those found in the females enhance the effect. Dimensions of the flowers in the various species of *Ophrys* help in determining specificity and success.

Australian orchids of the genus *Cryptostylis* are pollinated by ichneumon wasps of the genus *Lissopimpla.* The wasp, after backing into the stigma, attempts to copulate with the flower by bending its body into an arch, with the base of the lip of the flower held by the claspers of the wasp. The upper side of the apex of the abdomen comes in contact with the viscidium, and the pollinarium becomes cemented in place. The wasp, after a short pause, then flies to another flower, and the same behaviour delivers the pollinia to the stigma.

Orchid flowers resembling female flies

The South American orchid *Trichoceros antennifer* has flowers that simulate the female flies of the genus *Paragymnomma* to a remarkable degree. The column and base of the lip are narrow, barred with yellow and red-brown, and they extend laterally to simulate the extended wings of a sitting fly. The base of the lip has no particular similarity to the head and thorax of a fly, but this is probably not necessary to complete the illusion. The stigma of the flower is located more or less at the apex of the "false abdomen" of the flower and reflects sunlight, as does the genital orifice of the female fly. The viscidium, extended over the stigma on the slender rostellum, projects up through the bristles and becomes attached to the basal portion of the abdomen of the fly. The viscidium is flat and padlike in this genus. The male flies, deceived by the simulated female fly and stimulated by the signal from the genital-orifice-like stigma, strike the flower for only a moment and then pass on to other flowers in the same area. The action is sufficient, however, to pick up the pollinarium. The long, slender stipe of the pollinarium bends down slightly and is forced into the stigma when the fly visits a succeeding flower.

A number of species of orchids have developed nectaries located in other places on the plant body than the flower. These seem to attract ants, which in turn scare away bees that would otherwise rob the flower of its nectar by cutting into the tissues of the flower. Such extrafloral nectaries also attract wasps, which also scare away insects that might steal the nectar from the flower. These ants and wasps are also thought to keep away grasshoppers, crickets, caterpillars, and other insects that eat the flowers. The symbiotic relationship (*i.e.,* two organisms living together with mutual benefit) between ants and the orchids that grow only in ant nests (*e.g., Coryanthes* and some species of *Gongora, Epidendrum,* and *Schomburgkia*) may depend on this defensive mechanism. The plants and flowers of these orchids are extremely susceptible to damage by chewing insects if the ants are destroyed. The ants involved in this relationship do not pollinate the orchids; indeed, no ants are known to pollinate orchids. (C.H.D./Ed.)

BIBLIOGRAPHY

General works. Overviews of various aspects of plant life with discussions of angiosperms include PETER H. RAVEN, RAY F. EVERT, and SUSAN E. EICHHORN, *Biology of Plants,* 5th ed. (1992), an excellent general treatment; ARMEN TAKHTAJAN (A.L. TAKHTADZHIAN), *Floristic Regions of the World* (1986; originally published in Russian, 1978), a comparative study of the world's endemic floras, including the flowering plants; KNUT NORSTOG and ROBERT W. LONG, *Plant Biology* (1976); and D.J. MABBERLEY, *The Plant-Book* (1987), an excellent source for specific information on genera and families, arranged alphabetically with common-name entries. Descriptive, illustrated listings of plants may be found in KENNETH A. BECKETT *et al., The RHS Encyclopedia of House Plants* (1987); JACQUELINE HÉRITEAU *et al., The National Arboretum Book of Outstanding Garden Plants* (1990); and PIERRE ANGLADE (ed.), *Larousse Gardening and Gardens* (1990).

Economically important plants of all families are addressed in JOHN C. ROECKLEIN and PINGSUN LEUNG, *A Profile of Economic Plants* (1987); GEORGE USHER, *A Dictionary of Plants Used by Man* (1974); F.N. HOWES, *A Dictionary of Useful and Everyday Plants and Their Common Names* (1974); RICHARD M. KLEIN, *The Green World: An Introduction to Plants and People,* 2nd ed. (1987); CHARLES B. HEISER, JR., *Of Plants and People* (1985), and *Seed to Civilization: The Story of Food,* new ed. (1990); BERYL BRINTNALL SIMPSON and MOLLY CONNER-OGORZALY, *Economic Botany: Plants in Our World* (1986); N.T. GILL and K.C. VEAR, *Agricultural Botany,* vol. 1, *Dicotyledonous Crops,* and vol. 2, *Monocotyledonous Crops,* 3rd ed. rev. (1980); MAS YAMAGUCHI, *World Vegetables* (1983); MARTIN CHUDNOFF, *Tropical Timbers of the World* (1984); DOUGLAS PATTERSON, *Commercial Timbers of the World,* 5th ed. (1988); JAMES M. DEMPSEY, *Fiber Crops* (1975); LESLIE S. COBLEY, *An Introduction to the Botany of Tropical Crops,* 2nd ed. rev. by W.M. STEELE (1976); STEVEN NAGY and PHILIP E. SHAW, *Tropical and Subtropical Fruits: Composition, Properties, and Uses* (1980); J.A. SAMSON, *Tropical Fruits,* 2nd ed. (1986); LAWRENCE K. OPEKE, *Tropical Tree Crops* (1982); FREDERIC ROSENGARTEN, JR., *The Book of Edible Nuts* (1984), and *The Book of Spices,* rev. ed. (1973, reissued 1981); J.W. PURSEGLOVE *et al., Spices,* 2 vol. (1981); and GERHARD RÖBBELEN, R. KEITH DOWNEY, and AMRAM ASHRI (eds.), *Oil Crops of the World* (1989).

Poisonous and medicinally useful plants are described in WALTER H. LEWIS and MEMORY P.F. ELVIN-LEWIS, *Medical Botany: Plants Affecting Man's Health* (1977); JAMES W. HARDIN and JAY M. ARENA, *Human Poisoning from Native and Cultivated Plants,* 2nd ed. (1974); KENNETH P. LAMPE and MARY ANN MCCANN, *AMA Handbook of Poisonous and Injurious Plants* (1985); and WILL H. BLACKWELL, *Poisonous and Medicinal Plants* (1990).

Insectivorous varieties are treated in ADRIAN SLACK, *Carnivo-*

rous Plants, rev. ed. (1988); JAMES PIETROPAOLO and PATRICIA PIETROPAOLO, *Carnivorous Plants of the World* (1986); and B.E. JUNIPER, R.J. ROBINS, and D.M. JOEL, *The Carnivorous Plants* (1989).

Overview. *General features:* V.H. HEYWOOD (ed.), *Flowering Plants of the World* (1978, reissued 1985), is an illustrated guide to flowering plant families with distribution maps and uses. Flowering plants from several families are discussed together in PETER BERNHARDT, *Wily Violets & Underground Orchids* (1989), a popular treatment of forest cyclicality, North American grassland pollination, Australian mistletoe, Amazonian giant water lilies, violets, and orchids. C.D. SCULTHORPE, *The Biology of Aquatic Vascular Plants* (1967, reprinted 1985), is a comprehensive monograph on water plants.

Structure and function: Discussions of angiosperm anatomy are included in ARTHUR J. EAMES, *Morphology of the Angiosperms* (1961, reprinted 1977), emphasizing floral structure and diversity; KATHERINE ESAU, *Anatomy of Seed Plants*, 2nd ed. (1977), emphasizing developmental vegetative anatomy and growth; ERNEST M. GIFFORD and ADRIANCE S. FOSTER, *Morphology and Evolution of Vascular Plants*, 3rd ed. (1989), a succinct comparative treatment of reproductive and vegetative anatomy, morphology, and evolution; A. FAHN, *Plant Anatomy*, 4th ed. (1990), covering all aspects of reproductive and vegetative plant anatomy; F. WEBERLING, *Morphology of Flowers and Inflorescences* (1989; originally published in German, 1981), a thorough treatment of flower and inflorescence structure, development, and diversity; P.H. RAVEN, "The Bases of Angiosperm Phylogeny: Cytology," *Annals of the Missouri Botanical Garden*, 62(3):724–764 (1975), a comprehensive discussion of basic chromosome numbers in the angiosperms, although it does not go into great detail; GHILLEAN TOLMIE PRANCE and KJELL B. SANDVED, *Leaves* (1985); and FRANCIS E. PUTZ and HAROLD A. MOONEY (eds.), *The Biology of Vines* (1992).

Reproduction: K. FAEGRI and L. VAN DER PIJL, *The Principles of Pollination Ecology*, 3rd rev. ed. (1979), provides a thorough treatment of pollination biology and plant-animal interactions. B.M. JOHRI (ed.), *Embryology of Angiosperms* (1984), summarizes recent advances in the knowledge of flowering plant reproduction. Also useful are GWENDA L. DAVIS, *Systematic Embryology of the Angiosperms* (1966); and BASTIAAN MEEUSE and SEAN MORRIS, *The Sex Life of Flowers* (1984).

Paleobotany and evolution: The fossil record is analyzed in a number of books, including ARMEN TAKHTAJAN (A.L. TAKHTADZHIAN), *Flowering Plants: Origin and Dispersal* (1969; originally published in Russian, 2nd ed., 1961), and *Evolutionary Trends in Flowering Plants* (1991); CHARLES B. BECK (ed.), *Origin and Early Evolution of Angiosperms* (1976); NORMAN F. HUGHES, *Palaeobiology of Angiosperm Origins: Problems of Mesozoic Seed-Plant Evolution* (1976); WILSON N. STEWART, *Paleobotany and the Evolution of Plants* (1983); and ELSE MARIE FRIIS, WILLIAM G. CHALONER, and PETER R. CRANE (eds.), *The Origins of Angiosperms and Their Biological Consequences* (1987); and in such articles as PETER H. RAVEN and D.I. AXELROD, "Angiosperm Biogeography and Past Continental Movements," *Annals of the Missouri Botanical Garden*, 61:539–673 (1974); D.L. DILCHER, "Early Angiosperm Reproduction: An Introductory Report," *Review of Palaeobotany and Palynology*, 27(3–4):291–328 (1979); J. MULLER, "Fossil Pollen Records of Extant Angiosperms," *The Botanical Review*, 47(1):1–142 (1981); *Annals of the Missouri Botanical Garden*, vol. 71, no. 2 (1984), the entire issue devoted to papers on angiosperm paleobotany; P.R. CRANE, "Phylogenetic Analysis of Seed Plants and the Origin of Angiosperms," *Annals of the Missouri Botanical Garden*, 72:716–793 (1985); PETER K. ENDRESS, "The Early Evolution of the Angiosperm Flower," *Trends in Ecology & Evolution*, 2(10):300–304 (1987), written for the general reader; and D.W. TAYLOR and L.J. HICKEY, "An Aptian Plant with Attached Leaves and Flowers: Implications for Angiosperm Origin," *Science*, 247(4943):702–704 (1990).

Classification: Taxonomy is addressed by ARTHUR CRONQUIST, *The Evolution and Classification of Flowering Plants*, 2nd ed. (1988), and *An Integrated System of Classification of Flowering Plants* (1981), the full-dress exposition of his system; ADOLF ENGLER, *Syllabus der Pflanzenfamilien*, vol. 2, *Angiospermen*, 12th ed. rev. by HANS MELCHIOR (1964), the most recent edition of this work; J. HUTCHINSON, *The Families of Flowering Plants*, 3rd ed., 2 vol. (1973), the final version of his system; TOD STUESSY, *Plant Taxonomy: The Systematic Evaluation of Comparative Data* (1990); ARMEN TAKHTAJAN (A.L. TAKHTADZHIAN), *Система и филогения цветковых растений* (1966), the first full-length version of his system, and *Система магнолиофитов* (1987), the most recent full-dress version. Short versions of Takhtajan's system have appeared at various times in English, *e.g.*, ARMEN TAKHTAJAN, "Outline of the Classification of Flowering Plants (Magnoliophyta)," *The Botanical Review*, 46(3):225–359 (1980). Other journal articles on angiosperm taxonomy include ARTHUR CRONQUIST, ARMEN TAKHTAJAN, and W. ZIMMERMANN, "On the Higher Taxa of Embryobionta," *Taxon*, 15:129–134 (1966); ROBERT F. THORNE, "A Phylogenetic Classification of the Angiospermae," *Evolutionary Biology*, 9:35–106 (1976), "An Updated Phylogenetic Classification of the Flowering Plants," *Aliso*, 13(2):365–390 (1992), and "Classification and Geography of the Flowering Plants," *The Botanical Review*, 58(3):225–348 (1992); F. EHRENDORFER and R.M.T. DAHLGREN (eds.), "Symposium on New Evidence of Relationships and Modern Systems of Classifications of the Angiosperms," *Nordic Journal of Botany*, 3(1):1–155 (1983), a series of papers that gives useful discussions on and bibliographies of modern angiosperm classifications; and three articles from *The Botanical Journal of the Linnean Society:* E.J.H. CORNER, "Angiosperm Classification and Phylogeny: A Criticism," 82(1):81–88 (1981); and R.M.T. DAHLGREN, "A Revised System of Classification of the Angiosperms," 80(2):91–124 (1980), and "Angiosperm Classification and Phylogeny: A Rectifying Comment," 82(1):89–92 (1981).

Class Magnoliopsida: the dicotyledons. Discussions of aspects of the dicotyledons are contained in C.R. METCALFE and L. CHALK, *Anatomy of the Dicotyledons*, 2nd ed., 3 vol. (1979–87); AARON GOLDBERG, *Classification, Evolution, and Phylogeny of the Families of Dicotyledons* (1986); GERTRUDE DAHLGREN, "The Last Dahlgrenogram: System of Classification of the Dicotyledons," in KIT TAN (ed.), *The Davis & Hedge Festschrift . . . : Plant Taxonomy, Phytogeography, and Related Subjects* (1989), pp. 249–260; and J.W. PURSEGLOVE, *Tropical Crops: Dicotyledons*, 2 vol. (1968, reissued in 1 vol., 1974).

Magnoliidae: Coverage is provided by PETER K. ENDRESS, "Evolution of Reproductive Structures and Functions in Primitive Angiosperms (Magnoliidae)," *Memoirs of the New York Botanical Garden*, 55:5–34 (February 1990), an extremely useful up-to-date summary; F.B. SAMPSON, J.B. WILLIAMS, and POH S. WOODLAND, "The Morphology and Taxonomic Position of *Tasmannia glaucifolia* (Winteraceae), a New Australian Species," *Australian Journal of Botany*, 36(4):395–414 (1988), a rather specialized discussion of the reasons for keeping *Drimys* and *Tasmannia* as separate genera in the Winteraceae and a description of a new and unusual species of this most primitive of extant families; J.M. MILLER, "The Archaic Flowering Plant Family Degeneriaceae: Its Bearing on an Old Enigma," *National Geographic Research*, 5(2):218–231 (1989), a fascinating and readable account of *Degeneria*, including the discovery of a new species by the author, with excellent colour illustrations; and JAMES M. GARDINER, *Magnolias* (1989).

Hamamelidae: A good, all-inclusive work with many important references is PETER R. CRANE and STEPHEN BLACKMORE (eds.), *Evolution, Systematics, and Fossil History of the Hamamelidae*, 2 vol. (1989), containing a collection of papers by specialists, including one by ROBERT F. THORNE, "'Hamamelidae': A Commentary," vol. 1, pp. 9–16, an alternative to Cronquist's system of classification, less detailed, slightly more technical, and less descriptive. Useful journal articles are B.S. FEY and PETER K. ENDRESS, "Development and Morphological Interpretation of the Cupule in Fagaceae," *Flora (Jena)*, 173(5–6):451–468 (1983); B.H. TIFFNEY, "Fruit and Seed Dispersal and the Evolution of the Hamamelidae," *Annals of the Missouri Botanical Garden*, 73:394–416 (1986); ROBERT F. THORNE, "The 'Amentiferae' or Hamamelidae as an Artificial Group: A Summary Statement," *Brittonia*, 25(4):395–403 (1973); and two articles from *Plant Systematics and Evolution, Supplementum*, vol. 1 (1977): PETER K. ENDRESS, "Evolutionary Trends in the *Hamamelidales-Fagales* Group," pp. 321–347, a very good account of similarities, with many clarifying illustrations; and C.C. BERG, "*Urticales*, Their Differentiation and Systematic Position," pp. 349–374.

Caryophyllidae: Cactaceae: The cacti are described in WILLY CULLMANN, ERICH GÖTZ, and GERHARD GRÖNER, *The Encyclopedia of Cacti* (1986; originally published in German, 5th rev. ed., 1984); ARTHUR C. GIBSON and PARK S. NOBEL, *The Cactus Primer* (1986); J. ŘÍHA and R. ŠUBÍK, *The Illustrated Encyclopedia of Cacti & Other Succulents* (1981); GÜNTER ANDERSOHN, *Cacti and Succulents* (1983); and LYMAN BENSON, *The Cacti of the United States and Canada* (1982).

Dilleniidae: The subclass is addressed in FRIEDRICH EHRENDORFER, "New Ideas About the Early Differentiation of the Angiosperms," *Plant Systematics and Evolution, Supplementum*, 1:227–234 (1977), which suggests that the Dilleniales have originated from the Hamamelididae by secondary polyandry (multiplication) of 10 single stamens in response to visits from pollen-collecting insects. Alternative views based on various vegetative characters include, on leaf venation and marginal toothing, R. MELVILLE, "Leaf Venation Patterns and the Origin of the Angiosperms," *Nature*, 224(5215):121–125 (1969); L.J. HICKEY and J.A. WOLFE, "The Bases of Angiosperm Phylogeny:

Vegetative Morphology," *Annals of the Missouri Botanical Garden,* 62(3):538–589 (1975); and J.A. WOLFE, "Leaf-architecture Analysis of the Hamamelididae," in the work ed. by Crane and Blackmore cited above, pp. 75–104; and, on fasciculate (bundled) stamens, C.L. WILSON, "The Floral Anatomy of the Dilleniaceae: I. *Hibbertia* Andr.," *Phytomorphology,* 15:248–274, and "The Floral Anatomy . . . : II. Genera Other Than *Hibbertia,*" *Phytomorphology,* 23:25–42 (1973); and N.K.B. ROBSON, "Evolutionary Recall in *Hypericum* (Guttiferae)," *Transactions of the Botanical Society of Edinburgh,* 41(3):365–383 (1972), and "Studies in the Genus *Hypericum* L. (Guttiferae): 2. Characters of the Genus," *Bulletin of the British Museum (Natural History), Botany Series,* 8(2):55–226 (March 1981).

Representative orders are treated in the following works: on the Violales, W.H.A. HEKKING, *Violaceae,* pt. 1, *Rinorea and Rinoreocarpus* (1988); JOHN VANDERPLANK, *Passion Flowers and Passion Fruit* (1991); CHARLES B. HEISER, JR., *The Gourd Book* (1979); DAVID M. BATES, RICHARD W. ROBINSON, and CHARLES JEFFREY (eds.), *Biology and Utilization of the Cucurbitaceae* (1990); MILDRED L. THOMPSON and EDWARD J. THOMPSON, *Begonias: The Complete Reference Guide* (1981), a general, well-documented and well-illustrated reference; and LYMAN B. SMITH *et al., Begoniaceae* (1986), the most inclusive set of keys to all recognized species and varieties of *Begonia,* with illustrations; on the Capparales, J.G. VAUGHAN, A.J. MACLEOD, and B.M.G. JONES (ed.), *The Biology and Chemistry of the Cruciferae* (1976); and P. FEENY, "Defensive Ecology of the Cruciferae," *Annals of the Missouri Botanical Garden,* 64:221–234 (1977); on the Theales, T. EDEN, *Tea* (1976), an excellent overview of tea, both as plant and product; DAVID L. FEATHERS and MILTON H. BROWN, *The Camellia* (1978), a standard text covering history, culture, genetics, and prospects for the future; and BASSETT MAGUIRE *et al.,* "The Botany of the Guyana Highland: Part IX, Tetrameristaceae," *Memoirs of the New York Botanical Garden,* 23:165–192 (1972), a technical account of the discovery and description of a new genus in this small family, capturing the excitement of the dramatic botanical discoveries that result from exploration in the tropics; on the Ericales, FRED C. GALLE, *Azaleas,* rev. and enlarged ed. (1987), a well-illustrated book for a general audience on native and cultivated azaleas; PETER A. COX, *The Larger Rhododendron Species,* rev. ed. (1990); H.H. DAVIDIAN, *The Rhododendron Species,* 3 vol. (1982–92); RICHARD A. JAYNES, *Kalmia* (1988), also well illustrated and for a general audience, on the mountain laurels and their cultivated forms; A.H. BAKER and E.G.H. OLIVER, *Ericas in Southern Africa* (1967), a technical book with detailed scientific descriptions; J.L. LUTEYN, "Speciation and Diversity of Ericaceae in Neotropical Montane Vegetation," in L.B. HOLM-NIELSEN, I.C. NIELSEN, and H. BALSLEV (eds.), *Tropical Forests: Botanical Dynamics, Speciation, and Diversity* (1989), pp. 297–310, a technical account of the South American members of this family and how they have adapted to montane habits; and P.F. STEVENS, "Phytogeography and Evolution of the Ericaceae of New Guinea," in J.L. GRESSITT (ed.), *Biogeography and Ecology of New Guinea,* vol. 1 (1982), pp. 331–354, a technical account; and on the Malvales, BERTHA S. DODGE, *Cotton, the Plant That Would Be King* (1984), a nontechnical account of the social and economic history of cotton; PAUL A. FRYXELL, *The Natural History of the Cotton Tribe (Malvaceae, Tribe Gossypieae)* (1979), a detailed but highly readable account, including discussion of characters, adaptations, and evolution, and *Malvaceae of Mexico* (1988), a comprehensive, technical treatment, but with general value that goes well beyond its geographical limitation; and JOHN M. MUNRO, *Cotton,* 2nd ed. (1987).

Rosidae: A number of mangrove species occur in the Rosidae subclass and are addressed in P.B. TOMLINSON, *The Botany of Mangroves* (1986); and PATRICIA HUTCHINGS and PETER SAENGER, *Ecology of Mangroves* (1987).

Representative orders are analyzed in the following works: on the Fabales, O.N. ALLEN and ETHEL K. ALLEN, *The Leguminosae: A Source Book of Characteristics, Uses, and Nodulation* (1981), a descriptive summary, with an alphabetical listing of legume genera; J.B. HARBORNE, D. BOULTER, and B.L. TURNER (eds.), *Chemotaxonomy of the Leguminosae* (1971); R.M. POLHILL and P.H. RAVEN (eds.), *Advances in Legume Systematics* (1981–), an updated evolutionary classification of the Fabales; R.J. SUMMERFIELD and A.L. BUNTING (eds.), *Advances in Legume Science* (1980); C.H. STIRTON and J.L. ZARUCCHI (eds.), *Advances in Legume Biology* (1989); JAMES A. DUKE, *Handbook of Legumes of World Economic Importance* (1981), also with an alphabetical listing of genera; D. ISELY, "Leguminosae and *Homo sapiens,*" *Economic Botany,* 36(1):46–70 (1982), a succinct summary of the contributions of legumes to human welfare; NATIONAL RESEARCH COUNCIL (U.S.), ADVISORY COMMITTEE ON TECHNOLOGY INNOVATION, *Tropical Legumes: Resources for the Future* (1979), a descriptive listing of utilized but undeveloped tropical legumes; J. SMARTT, *Tropical Pulses* (1976); HAROLD J. EVANS (ed.), *Enhancing Biological Nitrogen Fixation* (1975); J.R. POSTGATE, *The Fundamentals of Nitrogen Fixation* (1982); R.O.D. DIXON and C.T. WHEELER, *Nitrogen Fixation in Plants* (1986); J.M. VINCENT (ed.), *Nitrogen Fixation in Legumes* (1982); W.J. BROUGHTON (ed.), *Nitrogen Fixation,* vol. 3, *Legumes* (1982); J. SMARTT, *Grain Legumes: Evolution and Genetic Resources* (1990); A. GEOFFREY NORMAN (ed.), *Soybean Physiology, Agronomy, and Utilization* (1978); and C. WEBB and G. HAWTIN (eds.), *Lentils* (1981); on the Myrtales, articles in *Annals of the Missouri Botanical Garden,* vol. 71, no. 3 (1984), authoritative reviews of the botanical characters used in the classification of all myrtalean families; LINDSAY D. PRYOR, *The Biology of Eucalypts* (1976), descriptions of distribution, uses, and characteristics of the genus *Eucalyptus;* and STAN KELLEY, G.M. CHIPPENDALE, and R.D. JOHNSTON, *Eucalypts,* new rev. ed., 2 vol. (1983); on the Euphorbiales, G.L. WEBSTER, "The Genera of Euphorbiaceae in the Southeastern United States," *Journal of the Arnold Arboretum,* 48(4):303–430 (1967), and "The Saga of the Spurges: A Review of Classification and Relationships in the Euphorbiales," *The Botanical Journal of the Linnean Society,* 94:3–46 (1987); and S.L. JURY *et al.* (eds.), *The Euphorbiales: Chemistry, Taxonomy, and Economic Botany* (1987), both general treatments; ALAIN WHITE, R. ALLEN DYER, and BOYD L. SLOANE, *The Succulent Euphorbisae (Southern Africa),* 2 vol. (1941); and articles in *The Euphorbia Journal* (annual); on the Rosales, K.R. ROBERTSON, "The Genera of Rosaceae in the Southeastern United States," *Journal of the Arnold Arboretum,* 55(2):303–332, 55(3):344–401, and 55(4):611–662 (1974); and on the Sapindales, TERENCE D. PENNINGTON, *Meliaceae* (1981), a monographic treatment of the New World members of the ecologically and economically important mahogany family; PETER G. WATERMAN and MICHAEL F. GRUNDON (eds.), *Chemistry and Chemical Taxonomy of the Rutales* (1983), an excellent example of how chemistry can be used to aid in classification; D.M. PORTER, "Disjunct Distributions in the New-World Zygophyllaceae," *Taxon,* 23(2/3):339–346 (1974); M.F. DAS GRACAS FERNANDES DA SILVA, O.R. GOTTLIEB, and F. EHRENDORFER, "Chemosystematics of the *Rutaceae:* Suggestions for a More Natural Taxonomy and Evolutionary Interpretation of the Family," *Plant Systematics and Evolution,* 161(3–4):97–134 (1988); STEVEN NAGY, PHILIP E. SHAW, and MATTHEW K. VELDHUIS (eds.), *Citrus Science and Technology,* 2 vol. (1977); and papers in the *Journal of the Arnold Arboretum* on sapindalian genera: G.K. BRIZICKY, "The Genera of Sapindales in the Southeastern United States," 44:462–501 (1963), a thorough discussion of the Aceraceae, Hippocastanaceae, and Sapindaceae of the area, "The Genera of Rutaceae in the Southeastern United States," 43:1–22 (1962), "The Genera of Simaroubaceae and Burseraceae in the Southeastern United States," 43:173–186 (1962), and "The Genera of Anacardiaceae in the Southeastern United States," 43:359–375 (1962); S. SPONGBERG, "The Staphyleaceae in the Southeastern United States," 52:196–203 (1971); and D.M. PORTER, "The Genera of Zygophyllaceae in the Southeastern United States," 53:531–552 (1972).

Asteridae: Classification of the subclass is the subject of GERHARD WAGENITZ, "New Aspects of the Systematics of the Asteridae," *Plant Systematics and Evolution, Supplementum,* 1:375–395 (1977). M.N. CLIFFORD and K.C. WILLSON (eds.), *Coffee* (1985), explores an important crop.

Representative orders are examined in these works: on the Asterales, ARTHUR CRONQUIST, "Phylogeny and Taxonomy of the Compositae," *The American Midland Naturalist,* 53:478–511 (1955), and his updating of this synthesis, "The Compositae Revisited," *Brittonia,* 29(2):137–153 (1977); and V.H. HEYWOOD, J.B. HARBORNE, and B.L. TURNER (eds.), *The Biology and Chemistry of the Compositae,* 2 vol. (1977), a multiauthor symposium; on the Scrophulariales, JOHANN VISSER, *South African Parasitic Flowering Plants* (1981), an illustrated account of their biology, including members of the order Scrophulariales; JOHN L. FIALA, *Lilacs: The Genus Syringa* (1988); and three review articles on genera in the southeastern United States, with many references, in the *Journal of the Arnold Arboretum:* K.A. WILSON and C.E. WOOD, "The Genera of Oleaceae in the Southeastern United States," 40:369–384 (1959); and JOHN W. THIERET, "The Genera of Orobanchaceae in the Southeastern United States," 52(3):404–434 (1971), and "The Martyniaceae in the Southeastern United States," 58(1):25–39 (1977); and on the Solanales, WILLIAM G. D'ARCY (ed.), *Solanaceae: Biology and Systematics* (1986); J.G. HAWKES, R.N. LESTER, and A.D. SKELDING (eds.), *The Biology and Taxonomy of the Solanaceae* (1979); J.G. HAWKES *et. al., Solanaceae III: Taxonomy, Chemistry, Evolution* (1991); CHARLES B. HEISER, JR., *Nightshades, the Paradoxical Plants* (1969); PAUL H. LI (ed.), *Potato Physiology* (1985); W.G. BURTON, *The Potato,* 3rd ed. (1989); J.G. HAWKES, *The Potato: Evolution, Biodiversity, and Genetic Resources* (1990); B.C. AKEHURST, *Tobacco,* 2nd ed. (1981); and JEAN ANDREWS, *Peppers: The Domesticated Capsicums* (1984).

Class Liliopsida: the monocotyledons. General overviews of the monocotyledons include R.M.T. DAHLGREN, H.T. CLIFFORD, and P.F. YEO, *The Families of Monocotyledons: Structure, Evolution, and Taxonomy* (1985); R.M.T. DAHLGREN and H. TREVOR CLIFFORD, *The Monocotyledons: A Comparative Study* (1982); C.R. METCALFE, *Anatomy of the Monocotyledons* (1960–); J.W. PURSEGLOVE, *Tropical Crops: Monocotyledons*, 2 vol. (1972, reprinted 1988); C.P. DAGHLIAN, "A Review of the Fossil Record of Monocotyledons," *The Botanical Review*, 47:517–666 (1981); R.M.T. DAHLGREN and FINN M. RASMUSSEN, "Monocotyledon Evolution: Characters and Phylogenetic Estimation," *Evolutionary Biology*, 16:255–395 (1983); and M.S. ZAVADA, "Comparative Morphology of Monocot Pollen and Evolutionary Trends of Apertures and Wall Structures," *The Botanical Review*, 49:331–371 (1983).

Alismatidae: Accounts of this subclass are found in R.R. HAYNES and L.B. HOLM-NIELSEN, "A Generic Treatment of the Alismatidae in the Neotropics with Special Reference to Brazil," *Acta Amazonica*, 15(Supp. 1–2):153–194 (1985), and "Speciation of Alismatidae in the Neotropics," in L.B. HOLM-NIELSEN, I.C. NIELSEN, and H. BALSLEV (eds.), *Tropical Forests: Botanical Dynamics, Speciation, and Diversity* (1989), pp. 211–219; and P.J.M. MAAS and T. RÜBSAMEN, "Triuridaceae," in P.J.M. MAAS *et al.*, *Saprophytes pro parte*, pp. 1–55 (1986).

Arecidae: The representative order Arecales is examined in MICHAEL J. BALICK (ed.), *The Palm—Tree of Life: Biology, Utilization, and Conservation* (1988), detailed discussions of a number of important palms, with a section on worldwide endangerment of useful palms; MICHAEL J. BALICK, *Systematics and Economic Botany of the Oenocarpus-Jessenia (Palmae) Complex* (1986), a treatment of two important American oil palms; MICHAEL J. BALICK *et al.*, *Useful Palms of the World: A Synoptic Bibliography* (1990), an extensive annotated list of uses of palms, incomplete but very informative; A. HENDERSON, "A Review of Pollination Studies in the Palmae," *The Botanical Review*, 53(3):221–259 (1986), a recent summary that shows which genera have been studied and the diversity of mechanisms; DAVID JONES, *Palms in Australia* (1984), a horticultural treatment that provides a good, well-illustrated, nontechnical introduction, giving for each palm a short description, notes, distribution, distinguishing features, confusing species, cultivation, and propagation; H. BORGTOFT PEDERSEN and H. BALSLEV, *Ecuadorean Palms for Agroforestry* (1990), an enlightening discussion of the potential of palms in agroforestry; P.B. TOMLINSON, *The Structural Biology of Palms* (1990), a masterful, detailed synthesis of palm structure, its biological implications, and the author's prognosis for the future; H.E. MOORE and NATALIE W. UHL, "Major Trends of Evolution in Palms," *The Botanical Review*, 48:1–69 (1982); and NATALIE W. UHL and JOHN DRANSFIELD, *Genera Palmarum* (1987), a classification reference book, including treatment of morphology, anatomy, fossil record, distribution, ecology, and evolution.

Commelinidae: Representative families in the Cyperales order are treated in the following: on the Cyperaceae, L.T. EITEN, "Inflorescence Units in the Cyperaceae," *Annals of the Missouri Botanical Garden*, 63(1):81–112 (1976); I. KUKKONEN, "On the Inflorescence Structure in the Family Cyperaceae," *Annales Botanici Fennici*, 21(3):257–264 (1984); and G.C. TUCKER, "The Genera of Cyperaceae in the Southeastern United States," *Journal of the Arnold Arboretum*, 68(4):361–446 (1987); and on the Poaceae, RICHARD W. POHL, *How to Know the Grasses*, 3rd ed. (1978), a nontechnical guide to grass identification; W.D. CLAYTON and S.A. RENVOIZE, *Genera Graminum: Grasses of the World* (1986), exhaustive, up-to-date, and admirably prepared; G.L. STEBBINS, "Co-evolution of Grasses and Herbivores," *Annals of the Missouri Botanical Garden*, 68(1):75–86 (1981), a relatively nontechnical but thorough discussion of the evolutionary interaction of grasses and grazers; J.M.J. DEWET, "Grasses and the Culture History of Man," *Annals of the Missouri Botanical Garden*, 68(1):87–104 (1979), a relatively nontechnical but thorough discussion of the domestication of cereals; FRANK W. GOULD and ROBERT B. SHAW, *Grass Systematics*, 2nd ed. (1983), covering all aspects of the study of grasses, with keys to the grass genera of the United States; JAMES R. ESTES, RONALD J. TYRL, and JERE N. BRUNKEN (eds.), *Grasses and Grasslands: Systematics and Ecology* (1982), a technical treatment of some aspects of grass evolution, classification, and ecology, covering structural and biochemical diversity, reproductive biology, evolution, systematics of major groups, taxonomic data and analysis, and the past, present, and future of the study of grasses; T.R. SODERSTROM and C.E. CALDERON, "A Commentary on the Bamboos (Poaceae: Bambusoideae)," *Biotropica*, 11(3):161–172 (1979), a general account of bamboo biology; F.A. MCCLURE, *The Bamboos: A Fresh Perspective* (1966), a detailed discussion of their growth, reproduction, and classification; CHRISTOPHER S. CAMPBELL, "The Subfamilies and Tribes of Gramineae (Poaceae) in the Southeastern United States," *Journal of the Arnold Arboretum*, 66(2):123–200 (1985), a technical treatment discussing biology, distribution, anatomy, morphology, evolution, and classification; THOMAS R. SODERSTROM *et al.* (eds.), *Grass Systematics and Evolution* (1987), the most thorough treatment of the systematics and evolution of the family; PAUL C. MANGELSDORF, *Corn: Its Origin, Evolution, and Improvement* (1974); ROBERT W. JUGENHEIMER, *Corn: Improvement, Seed Production, and Uses* (1976, reprinted 1985); FRANK BLACKBURN, *Sugar-Cane* (1984); D.H. GRIST, *Rice*, 6th ed. (1986); and D.E. BRIGGS, *Barley* (1978).

Zingiberidae: The two orders in this subclass are detailed in the following books: on the Bromeliales, DAVID H. BENZING, *The Biology of the Bromeliads* (1980), a good, general introduction to the Bromeliaceae addressing nearly every aspect of bromeliad biology; WERNER RAUH, *Bromeliads for Home, Garden, and Greenhouse* (1979; originally published in German, 2 vol., 1970–73), with a good introduction to the general morphology of bromeliads, keys for identification, and short descriptions of genera and many species, with numerous illustrations; J.L. COLLINS, *The Pineapple: Botany, Cultivation, and Utilization* (1960), a comprehensive and interesting treatment; LYMAN B. SMITH and ROBERT JACK DOWNS, *Pitcairnioideae (Bromeliaceae)* (1974), *Tillandsioideae (Bromeliaceae)* (1977), and *Bromelioideae (Bromeliaceae)* (1979), the only complete, modern taxonomic treatment for the Bromeliaceae, with keys to genera and species, complete technical descriptions, distribution maps, and drawings; PAUL T. ISLEY III, *Tillandsia: The World's Most Unusual Air Plants* (1987), dealing specifically with the genus *Tillandsia*, geared toward the hobbyist, but with photographs providing examples of the variations found in the family; and VICTORIA PADILLA, *Bromeliads* (1973, reissued 1986); and on the Zingiberales, N.W. SIMMONDS, *The Evolution of the Bananas* (1962), an account of the natural subdivisions of the genus *Musa*, based on cytotaxonomic and genetic studies and on the origin of cultivated bananas; and R.H. STOVER and N.W. SIMMONDS, *Bananas*, 3rd ed. (1987).

Liliidae: The two orders in this subclass are explored in the following works: on the Liliales, P. GOLDBLATT *et al.*, "Affinities of the Madagascan Endemic *Geosiris*. Iridaceae or Geosiridaceae," *Bulletin du Muséum National d'Histoire Naturelle*, sect. B, *Adansonia, Botanique, Phytochimie*, 9(3):239–248 (1987); PARK S. NOBEL, *Environmental Biology of Agaves and Cacti* (1988); FRITZ KÖHLEIN, *Iris* (1987); and DIANA GRENFELL, *Hosta* (1990); and on the Orchidales, HELMUT BECHTEL, PHILLIP CRIBB, and EDMUND LAUNERT, *The Manual of Cultivated Orchid Species*, 3rd ed. (1992; originally published in German, 1980), a well-illustrated encyclopaedic treatment of cultivated orchids; ROBERT L. DRESSLER, *The Orchids: Natural History and Classification* (1981, reissued 1990); FLOYD S. SHUTTLEWORTH, HERBERT S. ZIM, and GORDON W. DILLON, *Orchids*, rev. ed. (1989), containing illustrated general information and a survey of the principal orchid genera and species; L. VAN DER PIJL and CALAWAY H. DODSON, *Orchid Flowers: Their Pollination and Evolution* (1966), a detailed treatment; and the series *Orchid Biology: Reviews and Perspectives*, ed. by JOSEPH ARDITTI (1977–).

(D.W.St./D.L.Di./A.Cr./F.B.S./D.E.Bo./N.K.B.R./
R.C.Ke./B.M.Bo./J.L.L./D.M.Ba./D.Is./S.S.R./
G.L.W./K.R.R./D.M.Po./J.W.Th./W.G.D'A./
R.R.H./N.W.U./A.A.R./C.S.C./G.K.B./Pe.G./Ed.)

Animals

Animals make up one of the three kingdoms of multicellular eukaryotic organisms (*i.e.,* as distinct from bacteria, their deoxyribonucleic acid, or DNA, is contained in a membrane-bound nucleus). Unlike fungi (Mycota) and plants, the other two kingdoms of multicellular eukaryotes, animals have developed muscles and hence mobility, a characteristic that has stimulated the further development of tissues and organ systems.

Animals dominate human conceptions of life on Earth not simply by their size, abundance, and sheer diversity but also by their mobility, a trait that humans share. So integral is movement to the conception of animals that sponges, which lack muscle tissues, were long considered to be plants. Only after their small movements were noticed in 1765 did the animal nature of sponges slowly come to be recognized.

In size animals are outdone on land by plants, among whose foliage they may often hide. In contrast, the photosynthetic algae, which feed the open oceans, are usually too small to be seen, but marine animals range to the size of whales. Diversity of form, in contrast to size, only impinges peripherally on human awareness of life and thus is less noticed. Nevertheless, animals represent three-quarters or more of the species on Earth, a diversity that reflects the flexibility in feeding, defense, and reproduction which mobility gives them. Animals follow virtually every known mode of living that has been described for the creatures of Earth.

Animals move in pursuit of food, mates, or refuge from predators, and this movement attracts attention and interest, particularly as it becomes apparent that the behaviour of some creatures is not so very different from human behaviour. Other than out of simple curiosity, humans study animals to learn about themselves, who are a very recent product of the evolution of animals.

For coverage of related topics in the *Macropædia* and *Micropædia,* see the *Propædia,* section 313, and the *Index.*

This article is divided into the following sections:

The animal kingdom 766
- A definition of animals
- History of classification

Animal diversity 767
- Parazoa: a cellular level of organization
- Radiata: a tissue level of organization
- Bilateria: an organ level of organization
- Social levels of organization

Form and function 768
- Support and movement
- The nervous system
- The senses
- Hormones
- Digestion
- Water/vascular systems
- Reproduction and life cycles

Ecology and habitats 773
- Competition and animal diversity
- Evolution of ecological roles
- Humans and the environment

Evolution and paleontology 774

Classification 776
- Diagnostic features
- Annotated classification
- Critical appraisal

Bibliography 777

THE ANIMAL KINGDOM

Animals evolved from unicellular eukaryotes. The presence of a nuclear membrane in eukaryotes permits separation of the two phases of protein synthesis: transcription (copying) of deoxyribonucleic acid (DNA) in the nucleus and translation (decoding) of the message into protein in the cytoplasm. Compared to the structure of the bacterial cell, this gives greater control over which proteins are produced. Such control permits specialization of cells, each with identical DNA but with the ability to control finely which genes successfully send copies into the cytoplasm. Tissues and organs can thus evolve. The semirigid cell walls found in plants and fungi, which constrain the shape and hence the diversity of possible cell types, are absent in animals. If they were present, nerve and muscle cells, the focal point of animal mobility, would not be possible.

A definition of animals. A characteristic of members of the animal kingdom is the presence of muscles and the mobility they afford. Mobility is an important influence on how an organism obtains nutrients for growth and reproduction. Animals typically move, in one way or another, to feed on other living organisms, but some consume dead organic matter or even photosynthesize by housing symbiotic algae. The type of nutrition is not as decisive as the type of mobility in distinguishing animals from the other two multicellular kingdoms. Some plants and fungi prey on animals by using movements based on changing turgor pressure in key cells, as compared with the myofilament-based mobility seen in animals. Mobility requires the development of vastly more elaborate senses and internal communication than are found in plants or fungi. It also requires a different mode of growth: animals increase in size mostly by expanding all parts of the body, whereas plants and fungi mostly extend their terminal edges.

Importance of mobility

All phyla of the animal kingdom, including sponges, possess collagen, a triple helix of protein that binds cells into tissues. The walled cells of plants and fungi are held together by other molecules, such as pectin. Because collagen is not found among unicellular eukaryotes, even those forming colonies, it is one of the indications that animals arose once from a common unicellular ancestor.

The muscles that distinguish animals from plants or fungi are specializations of the actin and myosin microfilaments common to all eukaryotic cells. Ancestral sponges, in fact, are in some ways not much more complex than aggregations of protozoans that feed in much the same way. Although the sensory and nervous system of animals is also made of modified cells of a type lacking in plants and fungi, the basic mechanism of communication is but a specialization of a chemical system that is found in protists, plants, and fungi. The lines that divide an evolutionary continuum are rarely sharp.

Mobility constrains an animal to maintain more or less the same shape throughout its active life. With growth, each organ system tends to increase roughly proportionately. In contrast, plants and fungi grow by extension of their outer surfaces, and thus their shape is ever changing. This basic difference in growth patterns has some interesting consequences. For example, animals can rarely sacrifice parts of their bodies to satisfy the appetites of predators (tails and limbs are occasionally exceptions), whereas plants and fungi do so almost universally.

History of classification. Except perhaps for the possession of collagen, the criteria used above to distinguish animals from other forms of life are not absolute. The first catalogs of animal diversity were based on overall form and similarity. Aristotle and other early biologists regarded all organisms as part of a great chain, divisions of which were more or less arbitrary. The 18th-century Swedish botanist Carolus Linnaeus divided all animals into six classes: Mammalia, Aves, Amphibia (including reptiles), Pisces, Insecta (Arthropoda), and Vermes (other invertebrates). In the early 1800s the French zoologist Georges Cuvier recognized that vertebrates were substantially different from invertebrates, and he divided most animals on the basis of form and function into four branches: vertebrates, arthropods (articulates), mollusks, and radiates (animals with radial symmetry). Cuvier's divisions formed the basis for all subsequent classifications.

Just after Cuvier's classification, the French naturalist Étienne Geoffroy Saint-Hilaire outlined the importance of homologous structures. Homology is correspondence between features caused by continuity of information. Thus, a bird's wing is homologous to a bat's wing insofar as both are forelimbs, but they are not homologous as wings. Homologous structures need not resemble each other; for example, the three bones in the middle ear of humans are homologous to three bones in the jaw apparatus in fishes because the genetic and developmental information controlling them has been continuous through evolutionary change.

Homology

Before evolution was generally accepted, homologies among different animals, when they were recognized at all, were regarded as aspects of God's pattern. Evolution provided a testable explanation for homologies. By carefully tracing selected homologies, it has been possible to show that previously proposed classifications established inappropriate relationships based solely on form or function, or both; for example, the radial symmetry of starfishes is not homologous to that of coelenterates (such as jellyfish).

Protozoans were once considered to be animals because they move and do not photosynthesize. Closer study has shown, though, that their movement is by means of nonmuscular structures (cilia, flagella, or pseudopods) and that photosynthesis in them has often been lost and gained. Protozoans do not, therefore, form a natural group but with algae form a eukaryotic kingdom separate from plants and animals, called Protista.

Like plants and animals, fungi arose from protists and are now accorded a kingdom of their own.

ANIMAL DIVERSITY

The diverse appearance of animals is mostly superficial; the bewildering variety of known forms, some truly bizarre, can be assorted among a mere half-dozen basic body plans. These plans are established during the embryonic stages of development and limit the size and complexity of the animals. Symmetry, number and relative development of tissue layers, presence and nature of body cavities, and several aspects of early development define these fundamental modes of organization.

Parazoa: a cellular level of organization. Although the two phyla in this subkingdom, Porifera (sponges) and Placozoa, lack clearly defined tissues and organs, their cells specialize and integrate their activities. Their simplicity has been adaptive, and sponges have remained important in benthic marine habitats since their origin. The sessile, filter-feeding way of life shown by sponges has favoured a body plan of radial symmetry, although some members have become asymmetrical. The shape of the creeping, flattened placozoans is irregular and changeable.

Radiata: a tissue level of organization. The two coelenterate phyla (Cnidaria and Ctenophora) advanced in complexity beyond the parazoans by developing incipient tissues—groups of cells that are integrally coordinated in the performance of a certain function. For example, coelenterates have well-defined nerve nets, and their contractile fibres, although only specialized parts of more generalized cells, are organized into discrete muscle units. Because discrete cells of different types do not carry out the internal functions of the animals, coelenterates are considered to be organized at only a tissue level.

The integration of cells into tissues, particularly those of nerve and muscle, permits a significantly larger individual body size than is possible with other modes of body movement. Flagella and cilia become ineffective at rather small size, and amoeboid movement is limited to the size a single cell can attain. Muscles contract by a cellular mechanism basically like that used in amoeboid locomotion—interaction of actin and myosin filaments. Through coordinated contraction of many cells, movement of large individuals becomes possible.

Coelenterates, like parazoans, have only two body layers, an inner endoderm primarily for feeding and an outer ectoderm for protection. Between the endoderm and the ectoderm of coelenterates is the mesoglea, a gelatinous mass that contains connective fibres of collagen and usually some cells. Both layers contain muscle fibres and a two-dimensional web of nerve cells at the base; the endoderm surrounds a central cavity, which ranges from simple to complex in shape and serves as a gut, circulatory system, and sometimes even a skeleton. The cavity is also used for gamete dispersal and waste elimination.

Endoderm, ectoderm, and mesoglea

Cleavage of a fertilized egg produces a hollow sphere of flagellated cells (the blastula). Invagination of cells at one or both poles creates a mouthless, solid gastrula; the gastrula is called the planula larva in species in which this stage of development is free-living. The inner, endoderm cells subsequently differentiate to form the lining of the central cavity. The mouth forms once the planula larva has settled. Although the details of early development are different for parazoans and coelenterates, most share a stage in which external flagellated cells invaginate to form the inner layer, which lines the cavity, of these diploblastic (two-layered) animals. This is characteristic of invagination during the development of all animals.

All coelenterates are more or less radially symmetrical. A radial form is equally advantageous for filtering, predatory, or photosynthetic modes of feeding. Tentacles around the circumference can intercept food in all directions.

Bilateria: an organ level of organization. All animals except those in the four phyla mentioned above have bilaterally symmetrical ancestors and contain three body layers (triploblastic) with coalition of tissues into organs. The body plans that are generally recognized are acoelomate, pseudocoelomate, and coelomate.

Acoelomates have no internal fluid-filled body cavity (coelom). Pseudocoelomates have a cavity between the inner (endoderm) and the middle (mesoderm) body layers. Coelomates have a cavity within the mesoderm, which can show one of two types of development: schizocoelous or enterocoelic. Most protostomes show schizocoelous development, in which the mesoderm proliferates from a single cell and divides to form a mass on each side of the body; the coelom arises from a split within each mass. Deuterostomes show enterocoelic pouching, in which the endoderm evaginates and pinches off discrete pouches, the cavities of which become the coelom and the wall the mesoderm. The animals in these major divisions of the Bilateria differ in other fundamental ways, which are detailed below.

Unlike sessile sponges or floating jellyfish, the Bilateria typically move actively in pursuit of food, although many members have further evolved into sessile or radial forms. Directed movement is most efficient if sensory organs are located at the head or forward-moving end of the animal. Organs of locomotion are most efficiently arranged along both sides, a fact that defines the bilateral symmetry; many internal organs are not in fact paired, whereas muscle layers, limbs, and sensory organs almost invariably are. The diffuse nerve net of coelenterates coalesces into definite tracts or bundles, which run posteriorly from the anterior brain to innervate the structures of locomotion.

Acoelomates. Flatworms (phyla Platyhelminthes, Nemertea, and Mesozoa) lack a coelom, although nemerteans have a fluid-filled cavity at their anterior, or head, end, which is used to eject the proboscis rapidly. The lack of a fluid-filled cavity adjacent to the muscles reduces the extent to which the muscles can contract and the force they exert (see below *Support and movement*). Because most also lack a circulatory system, supplying muscle tissues with fuel and oxygen can be no faster than the rate at which these substances diffuse through solid tissue. Flatworms are thus constrained to be relatively flat and comparatively small; parasitic worms, which do not locomote, can achieve immense lengths (*e.g.,* tapeworms), but they remain very thin. The larger of the free-living flatworms

Flatworms

have extensively divided guts, which reach to within a few cells of the muscles, thus compensating for the lack of a circulatory system. Most flatworms have but one opening to the gut. Nemerteans, in addition to a coelom-like housing for their proboscis, have attained a one-way gut and a closed circulatory system. Both increase their ability to move food and oxygen to all parts of the body. Flatworms are considered to be the ancestors of all other Bilateria.

Pseudocoelomates, or aschelminths. The pseudocoelomates include the nematodes, rotifers, gastrotrichs, and introverts. Some members of some other phyla are also, strictly speaking, pseudocoelomate. These four phyla of tiny body size (many species no larger than the bigger protozoans) are placed together in part because they lack mesoderm on the inner side of the body cavity. Consequently, no tissue, muscular or connective, supports the gut within the coelomic fluid. For tiny organisms, this is advantageous for conservation of tissue: there is no reason to evolve or to maintain a tissue that is not functionally important. The inconspicuousness of most of these phyla has led to a slow advancement in understanding their phylogenetic position in the animal kingdom.

Coelomates. The advantage of a true coelom is the ability of the inner mesenteric (mostly connective tissue) layer to suspend the central gut in the middle of the animal. Otherwise, in those animals with a body cavity used in locomotion, gravity would pull the gut down and severely curtail body size. Coelomates have attained vastly larger body sizes than has any other group of animals. Within the coelomates, the coelom has been of variable significance to the form and diversity of the various phyla. For example, it is essential for the burrowing abilities of annelids and related phyla. It has largely lost this significance in the arthropods, however, which have transferred locomotion to limbs supported by an exoskeleton rather than a coelomic hydroskeleton. Suspension is the main function of the coelom in vertebrates, which achieve the largest body sizes among animals by virtue of an endoskeleton that does not need to be shed during growth.

Protostome and deuterostome coelomates

The protostome coelomates (acoelomates and pseudocoelomates are also protostomes) include the mollusks, annelids, arthropods, pogonophorans, apometamerans, tardigrades, onychophorans, phoronids, brachiopods, and bryozoans. Deuterostomes include the chaetognaths, echinoderms, hemichordates, and chordates.

In early development protostome coelomates mostly differ from deuterostome coelomates in the following ways: (1) The mouth of protostomes is the blastopore, the original opening into the developing gut which is formed during the invagination of cells during gastrulation; that of deuterostomes is a secondary opening, with the blastopore becoming the anus. (2, 3) Early cleavage is typically spiral and determinate in protostomes, which means that the dividing cells are oriented at an angle to one another and that the ultimate fate of the cells is mostly determined from the beginning. Deuterostomes, in contrast, show indeterminate, radial cleavage, with the dividing cells becoming layered and the fate of early cells a product of where they are positioned later in development. (4) Coelom formation is schizocoelous in most protostomes, whereas enterocoelous development is typical of deuterostomes. (5) For those with a larval stage, the characteristic larval forms also differ.

The two phyla that have clearly dominated both land and sea since nearly the beginning of animal evolution are the arthropods and chordates, protostomous and deuterostomous coelomates, respectively. A key to arthropod success has been the differentiation of many serially repeated parts, in particular jointed appendages with a rigid exoskeleton, to perform the varied functions necessary to maintain life. The exoskeleton, however, sets a moderate upper limit to body size. In contrast, vertebrates share all habitats with arthropods by virtue of the larger maximum size permitted by the development of an internal rigid skeleton. More than does a coelom, the evolution of rigid, jointed skeletons has allowed these two phyla to dominate most animal communities.

Social levels of organization. Large size is often competitively advantageous but unobtainable by many animals because of constraints of basic body plan. Intrinsically small animals sometimes become large in the same way that protozoans evolved into metazoans: they multiply the number of individuals by asexual reproduction (thus maintaining the same genotype) and remain attached, with the option that individuals can be modified during their development for a specialized function. This type of asexual sociality forms the colonoids of sponges, coelenterates, bryozoans, hemichordates, and tunicate chordates, all of which were primitively small, sessile filter feeders. Staying together after asexual budding of new individuals gave a competitive edge to monopolizing available space. With slight modifications so that all individuals in the colony could share equally in the gains, these larger entities had the energy reserves necessary to outcompete smaller organisms for space. This type of sociality has evolved in ways that complicate the definition of individuality. For instance, Portuguese men-of-war and their kin (some hydrozoan coelenterates) look and act like single individuals, yet their components develop as genetically identical units, each homologous to a whole jellyfish or polyp. It is a question whether such an animal should be considered one individual or many.

Sociality among large individuals

A different type of sociality emerged among mobile complex animals that can individually attain large size. In fact, the largest known living animals, the whales and elephants, comprise two of a very few mammalian orders that contain only social species. The pattern of evolution on Earth has favoured sociality in the smallest and the largest (mostly vertebrates) of animals, albeit for different reasons. The smallest seek the advantages of being large, as protozoans did to form the first animals. The large animals can communicate; they spread out to find food, which all can share, and they protect one another. Among the social groups of large animals, only humans have differentiated their functions to such an extent that their societies begin to behave as individuals.

Insect societies show behaviours halfway between societies based on genetically identical members and those created by genetically different individuals; such properties largely reflect their intermediate degree of genetic relatedness. Insects are more cooperative and show a greater degree of altruism than is true of vertebrate societies.

FORM AND FUNCTION

To stay alive, grow, and reproduce, an animal must find food, water, and oxygen, and it must eliminate the waste products of metabolism. The organ systems typical of all but the simplest of animals range from those highly specialized for one function to those participating in many. The more basic functional systems are treated below from a broadly comparative basis.

Support and movement. A skeleton can support an animal, act as an antagonist to muscle contraction, or, most commonly, do both. Because muscles can only contract, they require some other structure to stretch them to their noncontracted (relaxed) state. Another set of muscles or the skeleton itself can act as an antagonist to muscle contraction. Only elastic skeletons can act without an antagonist; all antagonistic muscles act through a skeleton, which can be either rigid, flexible, or hydrostatic.

Types of skeletons and their distribution. Hydrostatic skeletons are the most prevalent skeletal system used by animals for movement and support. A minimal hydroskeleton resembles a closed container. The walls are two layers of muscles (antagonists) oriented at right angles to one another; the inside contains an incompressible fluid or gel. The contraction of one set of muscles exerts a pressure on the fluid, which is forced to move at right angles to the squeezing antagonist. The movement of the fluid stretches the other set of muscles, which can then contract to stretch its antagonist back to its relaxed position. The net result is an alternating change in the shape of the container. Locomotion as varied as crawling, burrowing, somersaulting, looping, or even walking is possible when the container has some means of traction against a substrate: the system extends forward from the point of attachment, attaches at a more forward point, releases posteriorly, and contracts forward. Hydroskeletons are also important

Importance of hydroskeletons

in nonlocomotory muscular systems, such as hearts or intestines, which move blood or food, respectively. Contraction-relaxation cycles push in one direction only when the system has structures that prevent backflow.

Hydroskeletons become less efficient when fluid is lost. The optimal volume of fluid for a particular system must remain constant for effective contraction and expansion of the antagonistic muscles. If too much fluid is lost, the animal becomes limp and neither muscle can stretch; when too much fluid is gained, the animal becomes bloated and neither muscle can contract. Those coelenterates that use a hydroskeleton regularly face a loss of pressure because their skeleton is also their gut. Freshwater animals tend to become bloated as water diffuses into their salty cells, but terrestrial animals with hydroskeletons tend to become limp as they dry. Solutions to water loss tend to be partial because impermeable barriers, such as a shell, tend not to be very flexible, thus negating the use of a hydroskeleton for movement. Terrestrial animals with locomotory hydroskeletons (*e.g.,* snails and earthworms) are restricted in their activity to moist conditions.

Partitioning a hydroskeleton into many small, separate, but coordinated units facilitates locomotion. In an earthworm, for example, a front group of segments narrows together, thereby elongating that part of the worm. If there were no partitions between the segments, the fluid would flow farther back, providing little elongation. Widened segments behind these initial segments anchor the worm, and its head moves forward. The process then reverses in a wave, and the posterior end moves forward. Metamerism, or the partitioning of the coelom, is thought to have evolved in ancestral annelids to improve their ability as burrowers in the bottom mud of the ocean. It undoubtedly explains the unrivaled success of this phylum among worms and helps to explain the extraordinary success of one of its relatives, the arthropods, which remained segmented even after the skeletal function of the coelom was lost.

Elastic skeletons do not change shape but simply bend when a muscle contracts. Muscle relaxation results either from a muscle contracting in the opposite direction to its antagonist or from the skeleton resuming its original position. The tentacles of many hydrozoan coelenterates, the mesoglea of jellyfish, the hinge of clamshells, and the notochord of chordates are examples. The high-pressured coelom contained in the rigid but flexible cuticle of nematodes also functions like an elastic skeleton.

Rigid, jointed skeletons

Rigid, jointed skeletons achieve movement through a lever system. The elements of the skeleton are rigid segments attached together by flexible joints. Muscles span the joints and attach at each end to different elements. The more stable attachment site of a muscle is called the origin, the other the insertion. One muscle contracts and moves the skeletal element on which it is inserted, and an antagonistic muscle contracts and moves the skeletal element in the opposite direction. The biceps and triceps of the upper arm in humans are such a set of antagonistic muscles that bend and straighten, respectively, the lower arm. The control of movement can be quite precise with jointed skeletons. Muscles can bend or rotate skeletal elements whose length, shape, and number contribute to the resulting action. The dexterity of the hands is an example of the complexity of controlled movements made possible by a jointed skeleton.

Important to the speed and force of a movement are the length of the skeletal element and the size of the contracting muscle. Short limbs with thick muscles have more power than long limbs with slender muscles, but the latter have more speed. Limbs thus reveal a great deal about how an animal moves. Likewise, the relative massiveness of jaws reflects the toughness of the food eaten.

Two animal phyla, Chordata (vertebrates only) and Arthropoda, exploit jointed skeletons. Although the skeleton is internal in vertebrates and external in arthropods, the principles of movement are the same. A jointed skeleton is ideal for moving on land because adaptations for protection against dehydration (such as the cuticle) do not interfere with the action of the skeletal system. Indeed, the arthropod cuticle serves jointly a protective and a skeletal role. Moreover, the diverse range of precise movements made possible by this skeleton facilitates all sorts of locomotory patterns: swimming, digging, running, climbing, and flying. Jointed skeletons are also used directly for feeding (jaws). Arthropod jaws are derived from legs, while vertebrate jaws are derived from gill arches.

Translating movement into locomotion and feeding. Although all animals can move, not all locomote or displace the body over a distance. Locomotion serves the animal in finding food and mates and in escaping predators or unsuitable habitats. These functions of locomotion are typically correlated among different animals, so that those using the same mechanism of locomotion usually also feed, seek mates, and avoid danger in similar ways.

Some of the correlations between mode of locomotion and mode of feeding are described here, but space precludes discussion of the rich diversity found among animals past and present. The locomotory/feeding system of animals is the heart of their adaptation to their physical and biotic environments. Locomotory strategies for finding or gathering food include the following techniques.

Methods for finding food

Sitting still and waiting for food to arrive is particularly prevalent in aquatic habitats but is not rare on land. Sessile animals tend to develop strong defenses that are sometimes incompatible with effective locomotion. They rely on water or air currents or on the locomotion of their potential prey to bring food within reach. Because food may come from any direction, many sessile animals evolve radial symmetry. Settlement may be permanent or temporary, but in all cases one stage of the life cycle is capable of moving actively or passively from its place of origin. The choice of attachment site can also be active or passive; passive choice is often associated with an ability to grow in such a way as to maximize feeding efficiency. As with plants, passive settlers do well only with luck. The retention of locomotory capabilities requires energy and nutrients that can otherwise be diverted into growth or the production of offspring. Sessile feeders need to move if feeding and resting sites differ. Sessile animals include filter feeders, predators, and even photosynthesizers; the latter include corals that house symbiotic algae. Internal parasites are usually sessile because they live within their lifetime food supply. Mobile animals that pursue sedentary strategies for seeking prey include web-spinning spiders (a terrestrial mode of filter feeding) or deep-sea fishes with morphological adaptations that lure prey.

Burrowing animals typically eat the rich organic substrates they move through. Others burrow for protection and either temporarily emerge and gather organic sediments at the top of their burrows or pump water with potential food through the burrow. Instead of digging or finding burrows, some animals move into the centre of sponges, where they find protection and a renewing source of food.

Active movement in search of food requires energy, but this expenditure is more than made up for by an ability to seek out areas of concentrated food. This method of feeding applies to burrowing animals that eat the substrate through which they move, as well as to animals that move over solid surfaces, swim, or fly. Actively moving animals can feed on organisms that do not move, a rich variety coating virtually the entire solid surface of the Earth from the depths of the oceans to the peaks of many mountains. The main problem with this most productive avenue of food gathering is protection. Shells and poisons are the major types of defenses, although innovative detoxification metabolism and jaws of various kinds breach the defenses in part. This is an escalating battle, with the defenses, as well as the weapons to penetrate them, continually improving. Nudibranchs, shell-less marine snails, incoporate the defensive stinging cells of prey cnidarians into their own skin. Poisonous plants are eaten by specialized insects that avoid or detoxify the poison. In fresh water, for reasons not known, the arms race has not proceeded as far as in the sea.

Cooperation among animals

Cooperation of individuals enables social animals to obtain food in novel ways. Uncannily like humans, some ants farm and herd other organisms for food. For example, some cultivate a fungus on leaves they cannot directly digest, while others herd aphids from which they milk nectar (actually the phloem sap of plants). Some ants even raid the nests of other species and make slaves of them. Another form of cooperation is the mutualism between species that trade advantage for advantage. Some fishes feed on parasites on the surfaces of other fishes, which benefits all but the parasites. In many animals, including termites and ruminants, microorganisms thrive in the gut and digest cellulose for them.

The nervous system. Coherent movement results only when the muscles receive a sensible pattern of activating signals (for example, antagonists must not be activated to contract simultaneously). Animals use specialized cells called neurons to coordinate their muscular activity; nerves are bundles of neurons or parts thereof. Neurons communicate between cells by chemical messengers, but within a single cell (often extremely long) they can send high-speed signals through a wave of ionic polarization (analogous to an electric current) along their membranes, a property inherent in all cells but developed for speed in nerve cells by special modifications.

A system of communication requires three parts: a collector of outside information, an integrator to evaluate that information and decide upon its relevance, and a transmitter to convey the decision to the motor unit. In animals, sensory nerves and organs such as eyes collect the information; associative nerves usually concentrated into a brain integrate, evaluate, and decide its relevance; and effector or motor nerves convey decisions to the muscles or elsewhere. Although all three parts of the nervous system have kept pace with increases in the size and complexity of animals, the simplest systems found among animals (those of parazoans and coelenterates) are nevertheless capable of intricate feats of coordination. All ends of a coelenterate bipolar neuron can both receive and transmit an impulse, whereas the unipolar neurons of more derived animals receive only at one end (dendrite) and transmit at the other (axon). A neuron can have multiple dendrites and axons.

The earliest animals were probably radial in design, so that bipolar neurons arranged in a netlike pattern made sense. In such a design, a stimulus impinging at any point on the body can travel everywhere to alert a simple array of myofilaments to contract simultaneously. In the case of directed locomotion and relevant sensory input received at the head end of a bilateral animal, unidirectional transmission of nerve impulses to muscles becomes the only way to communicate effectively. The location of the brain in the head also reflects efficiency and the speed of receipt of information, because this position minimizes the distance between sensory and associative neurons as well as concentrates these two functions in a small, protected part of the body. In most animals nerve cells cannot be replaced if lost, although axons can be. Nerve cells tend to be concentrated centrally in ganglia or nerve cords, with long axons extending peripherally. Although certain animals may lose tails or limbs to predators or in accidents and then regenerate them, loss or damage to the central nervous system means death or paralysis.

Transmission of nerve impulses

The nervous system uses the transmission properties of neurons to communicate. Within a neuron, propagation of an impulse by an ion wave can be extremely rapid, but the wave can pass along the length of only one cell's membrane. To pass to the next cell at a synapse, where an axon meets a dendrite, a chemical transmitter is required. This molecule diffuses to the dendrites of a connecting neuron, where it initiates an ionic wave that propagates along the length of the cell's membrane. Although chemical transmission is considerably slower than the ionic wave, it is more flexible. For example, learning involves in part increasing the sensitivity of a particular nerve pathway to a stimulus. The sensitivity of a synapse can be altered by increasing the amount of transmitter released from the axon per impulse received, increasing the number of receptors in the dendrite, or changing the sensitivity of the receptors. Bridging the synapse directly by the formation of membrane-bound gap junctions, which connect adjacent cells, enables an impulse to pass unimpeded to a connecting cell. The increase in speed of transmission provided by a gap junction, however, is offset by a loss in flexibility; gap junctions essentially create a single neuron from several. The same result can be achieved more effectively by lengthening the axons or dendrites, making some nerve cells metres in length. Situations arise where gap junctions become desirable, however. Gap junctions are found in vertebrate cardiac and smooth muscles, both of which transmit impulses along their cells to others. This ability makes these muscles somewhat independent of nervous-system control. A body can thus be kept partly functioning for some time without the activity of a brain.

Nerve impulses travel faster along axons of greater diameter or along those with good insulation against ion leakage (except at spaced nodes required for recharging). Vertebrates use their unique myelinated axons to increase the transmission rate of nerve impulses, whereas invertebrates are limited to using axons of greater diameter. As a result, vertebrates can concentrate more small neurons into a body of a particular size, with the potential for greater complexity of behaviour.

Memory is still a poorly understood aspect of the nervous system. As in learning, both short- and long-term memories seem to involve alterations in the ease with which subsequent impulses travel a particular pathway after it has been used. Transfer of memory through direct ingestion of the brain has not been confirmed experimentally. Although the underlying mechanisms are only dimly understood, it is known that there is a correlation between learning and memory capacity. The capacities for both increase with the number of associative neurons and the number of branches or interconnections formed. Since learning is a process of associating incoming cues with appropriate motor or internal response, greater memory capacity of a brain gives a more rapid learning process. Memory of inappropriate responses to an incoming set of cues can be used without motor repeat.

The degree to which the neurons of a brain develop interconnections is correlated with the complexity of its environs while growing. Consequently, a brain with fewer neurons but with more interconnections can be more "intelligent" than one with more neurons. Basic, repeated behaviours are inherited or learned by the development of fixed pathways by which an environmental signal reaches the motor nerves rapidly with little or no variation (reflex arcs). Nonreflex behaviour requires a decision to be made in the brain, with the resulting pathway to the motor nerves becoming more fixed (habitual) as one particular decision seems always to be correct. Reflexes are faster than decisions, but their relative adaptiveness depends on context. Animals vary in the degree to which they use reflexes or make decisions, patterns that are strongly correlated to brain size. Habitual actions are perhaps the most prevalent response, a compromise between the speed of a response and its appropriateness to context.

The senses. Appropriate behaviour relies on receiving adequate information from the environment to alert an animal to the presence of food, mates, or danger. Although sensory nerves carry this information to the brain, they do not always directly perceive the external world. Other modified cells intervene to convert light waves into vision, pressure waves in air or water into sound, chemicals into smell or taste, and simple contact into touch. Some animals have other senses, as for electric or magnetic fields.

Vision

In vision, for example, a photosensitive molecule changes shape and thereby sets off a chain of reactions that ultimately depolarize the dendrite of a sensory nerve. The associative neurons in the brain interpret the pattern of incoming impulses into a composite picture. What is "seen" may not entirely map what is really there: a great deal of filtering occurs, with editing by the brain to eliminate less important details so that only the most important are perceived. The accuracy of what is seen increases with brain size and the complexity of the visual gathering system, or eyes. Animal eyes range from being able to discern only the presence or absence of light to being able to see objects in vivid colour and great detail. Some animals see in ranges beyond unaided human vision. Pollinating insects in particular discern the colour of flowers differently than do humans; the ultraviolet reflection patterns of flowers do not always coincide with their coloured ones. Bees and birds perceive polarized light and can orient themselves by it. Some animals perceive long wavelengths, which are associated with heat (infrared), and can locate the presence of warm-blooded prey by such a mechanism.

Chemoreceptors are usually little-modified sensory neurons, except for the taste receptors of vertebrates, which are frequently replaced cells in synaptic contact with permanent sensory neurons. Chemoreception is based on the recognition of molecules at receptor sites, lipid-protein complexes that are liberally scattered on the dendrites of a sensory neuron. When the receptor recognizes one particular molecule by shape and sometimes chemical composition, it fires an impulse. The pattern of firings set off in the receptors of a certain molecule provides the information that the brain interprets as an odour or a taste. The details of how animals smell and taste are not as well understood as are the other senses. In many animals, chemoreceptors are not concentrated into obvious organs as they are in vertebrates, making even their location difficult to discern. Most animals possess some sort of chemoreception, and in many the sense is a major part of the animal's perception of its environment, far more so than it is for humans.

Sounds are waves of molecular disturbance that move through air, water, or solids, and their perception by animals simply uses sensitive mechanoreceptors. (Loud sounds can also be felt by the general touch receptors of the body and thereby influence its sense of well-being.) Sound receptors are sensitive hair cells or membranes that depolarize a sensory neuron when bent by the passage of a sound wave. Direct deformation of the dendritic membrane or release of transmitters by the hair cells fire the sensory neurons. Aside from a few insects, only vertebrates have organs with which to hear. Fishes and aquatic amphibians use a lateral-line system, and other vertebrates use ears; both organs use hair cells as phonoreceptors. Sound waves directly stimulate the hair cells of lateral-line systems, while sound waves only indirectly stimulate the hair cells of ears through an amplifying system of membranes and bones, which reaches a peak of complexity in mammals. Some animals (*e.g.,* most bats and whales, and even whirligig beetles) use sound to "see" by echolocation. Sound is the preferred medium of communication between animals that hear. It can be used over longer distances than vision, and it can be used when vision is not possible. The signals decay more rapidly than do those of odours, and therefore the information can be more precise.

Mechanoreceptors

Mechanoreceptors also respond to touch, pressure, stretching, and gravity. They are located all over the body and enable an animal to monitor its state at any moment. Much of this monitoring is subconscious but necessary for normal functioning. Mechanoreceptors are often just sensory nerves, but other cells may be involved. Unlike other senses, that of touch is found in all animals, even sponges, where it reflects a general cellular trait of eukaryotes.

Hormones. Hormones are the chemical integrators of a multicellular existence, coordinating activities from daily maintenance to reproduction and development. The neurotransmitters released by axons are one class of chemical communicators that act on an adjacent cell, usually a muscle cell or another neuron. Hormones are a mostly distinct class of chemical communicators secreted by nerves, ordinary tissue, or special glands; they act on cells far removed from the site of their release. They can be proteins, single polypeptides, amines, or steroids or other lipids. Hormones travel to their place of action via the circulatory system and then match their particular configuration with a specific receptor molecule attached to a cell membrane or, more usually, located within the cell.

The nervous system coordinates the more rapid activities of animal life, such as movement, while the hormones integrate everything else. Only the larger, more complex animals, such as vertebrates and some arthropods, have special endocrine glands to produce hormones; other animals use nerve cells or tissues such as the gonads. Endocrine glands are another example of a partitioning of functions into separate organs, a system that increases efficiency but that requires a relatively large size to maintain. Greater specialization is also associated with greater difficulties in regenerating lost parts or preventing breakdowns in functions.

Although the list of hormones found in the mammalian body may seem large, the numbers are surprisingly low for the variety of functions they influence. Which of the multiple functions any one hormone regulates depends on the specificity of the receptors on or within cells. Because all hormones bathe all cells as a result of their transport by the circulatory system, it is more efficient to have a general messenger transported to a cell, where it elicits only one of many possible outcomes. As in the nervous system, the specificity of response lies in the organ that responds and not with the messenger that merely commands action.

Chemicals that allow communication among individuals are called pheromones. Sexual attractants are the most common, but there are many other kinds.

Digestion. In contrast to plants, the essential nutrients that animals require to sustain life and to reproduce come packaged with their source of energy—the flesh or organic remains of other organisms. More complex animals tend to shorten and even eliminate many synthetic pathways, because most of the essential building blocks of their own complex molecules are present in their food. Reducing synthetic flexibility, however, inhibits a radical alteration in diet. The digestive and synthetic chemistry of animals strongly reflects their diets; some of this design may be altered with diet, and some may not. No matter how many leafy vegetables humans consume, for example, the cellulose remains undigested because appropriate microorganisms are not present in the digestive tract and they cannot be obtained at will. Consequently, essential nutrients are species-specific and tend to include only molecules adequately available in the usual diet.

Purpose and structure of the gut

The structure of a digestive system reflects its typical diet. Its purpose is to process food only to the point at which it can be transported to other cells for use as either fuel or structural material. In the simplest animals, such as sponges or some coelenterates, digestion is entirely intracellular, and some of the products of digestion are transported to nondigestive cells. As animals began to catch larger types of food, more of the digestive process had to be handled extracellularly. At the simplest level, seen in coelenterates or flatworms, large food items are held in an internal cavity (the gut) or even externally where certain cells release digestive enzymes. The food is broken down only to the stage at which it can be ingested by cells, which finish the process intracellularly. In more complex animals extracellular digestion accounts for virtually all breakdown of food before the products are transported to nondigestive cells.

Chemical digestion, whether intracellular or extracellular, is a relatively slow way to decompose a large item. Thus, animals begin to break it apart mechanically before exposing it to digestive enzymes. Teeth, the molluscan radula, and muscular gizzards are organs that speed up the digestive process by macerating food into finer particles.

Very early in their evolution animals acquired a one-way gut (gastrointestinal system), with the mouth typically armed with the macerating equipment and the terminal stretch sometimes specialized to retrieve excess water or other nutrients. Often a single passage through the digestive system leaves a great deal of useful material unclaimed. Because food moves along at a characteristic rate, which is sometimes influenced by how much is coming in, not all can be fully digested. Some animals regularly eat their feces to retrieve nutrients that may have escaped during first passage. If not recycled by their owners, feces are consumed by a diverse set of organisms.

A common specialization of the gut is the stomach or crop—a highly extensible part of the digestive tract that is used to hold a large amount of food and partially digest it before it enters the intestines, where most of the chemical breakdown and absorption of nutrients occurs. Most animals eat intermittently; the less often they eat, the larger the relative stomach size. Internalizing as much food as possible when it is available prevents potential food from being taken by a stronger competitor or enables a feeder to retreat to safety while digesting its meal. Ceca and second stomachs provide symbiotic microorganisms with a safe area within the gut to digest cellulose. Excess microorganisms mixed in with the partly digestible wastes contribute a steady protein-rich fare to the host in exchange for an optimal place to consume cellulose.

Stomachs predominate as a gut specialization because they allow animals to keep food from competitors or other dangers, but a few animals have developed ingenious methods of digesting their food before ingesting it. Humans are latecomers to this practice and have not yet carried it very far. Starfish exploit secondary radial symmetry and tube feet to open bivalved mollusks only enough to inject their stomachs, digest their meal within the protected shell, absorb the products, and leave the wastes behind. Spiders immobilize prey by silk wrappings and venoms, inject digestive enzymes, and drink the brew. Some primitive animals, like placozoans and certain flatworms, simply hunch over their prey as they digest it externally, a practice that leaves them vulnerable to other predators.

Digestion before ingestion

Animals use surfaces in many ways but no more strikingly than in the gut. Nutrients enter the body proper through the surface membrane of the gut; the larger the animal, the larger this surface area must be. The gut is probably the system that best reflects an animal's ecology. The simplest guts, found in animals from sponges to flatworms, simply branch like trees as the animal increases in size; the gut itself reaches all parts of the body to within the distance of a few cells and thus can serve for nutrient transport. As muscle masses become more prominent, the gut is squeezed into a more compact form. The gut compensates for this lack of space by internalizing its foldings. For example, the lining of the mammalian small intestine, the major site of digestion and absorption, is not only folded but each cell also has numerous outpocketings (microvilli), which increase the surface area 25-fold. Mammals and birds that primarily eat plants have longer intestines than those that favour meat. Warm-blooded animals, which maintain constant internal temperatures, require a great deal more energy than cold-blooded ones and thus tend to concentrate more surface area into a gut. Although they are not efficient energy users, it is to their advantage to obtain more usable energy even if efficiency is lost in the process.

Water/vascular systems. Animals live in an aquatic environment even on land. Each cell is in contact with the ocean or its aqueous equivalent, which carries food and oxygen to the cells of the animal and carries its metabolic wastes away. The water/vascular systems found in animals vary from the nonexistent to the complex, with the complexity correlated with body size and level of activity. Smaller animals simply use the fluid-filled coelom for transport. Increasing size, however, places too many cells beyond diffusion distance from either the coelom or the outside. A muscular pump attached to muscular vessels has arisen in larger animals to move the interstitial fluid surrounding the cells. Most animals have open circulatory systems. Those few animals with closed circulatory systems have a continuous series of vessels to circulate fluid to the vicinity of all cells, whereas those with open systems have vessels only near the heart. (Actually, no system is entirely closed or open.) In open systems the interstitial fluid and the circulatory fluid are the same, but in closed systems the two fluids can differ considerably in composition.

Open and closed systems

Closed circulatory systems have several advantages that make them more appropriate than open systems for large, active animals: active animals, in fact, tend to possess closed systems even though their relatives may not. For example, cephalopods, alone among the mollusks, and nemerteans, the most active of acoelomates, have closed systems, as do all annelids and vertebrates. Decapod crustaceans, the largest living arthropods, have nearly closed systems. The most fully open systems have a heart with a few vessels leading from it, while fully closed systems both leak fluid (which is reclaimed by the open lymphatic system) and have open sections. For example, blood flow in the vertebrate liver is partly open.

In closed systems, blood flow can be both higher and directed more often to tissues that require a greater perfusion of blood. If blood is confined within discrete vessels, most of which are muscular, contractions can vary the flow rate according to need by altering the amount of constriction. Thus, the heart beats faster during exercise, when the muscles need more oxygen. Fear changes the distribution of blood flow to ready the muscles for possible imminent action. The more muscular arteries, which carry oxygenated blood to the tissues, can proliferate more finely in active tissues so that more cells are closer to the capillaries, where exchange takes place.

Another advantage of a closed system is the ability to carry a high density of oxygen-bearing cells. Such cells cannot flow smoothly through the sometimes tight interstitial spaces and thus are not much used by animals with open systems. A great deal more oxygen, however, can be carried if the oxygen carrier (such as hemoglobin) is packed into cells. The viscosity of the blood is a function of how many discrete particles are contained within it, and size is of little influence. If all the hemoglobin in the blood of humans were released by dissolving the cell membranes, it would be a thick gel unable to flow. Animals with open systems do aggregate their oxygen carriers into giant polypeptides, but single molecules have limits to their size. Myriapods and insects, highly active arthropods with open systems, circumvented this problem by evolving a tracheal system of respiration, as have some other groups: molecular oxygen is carried by branching tubes to within a few cell lengths of any cell.

A few types of cells protect organisms from a potentially hostile outside environment. Internal cells thus can eliminate any unnecessary ancestral life-support components as they specialize for various functions. This cooperation maintains an ideal internal environment for the members of the society of cells but only at the cost of active labour and expenditure of energy. In particular, the proper water/salt balance of the interstitial fluid is crucial to prevent the cell from shrinking or bloating.

Removal of ammonia

Problems of water/salt balance are usually handled by the same system that eliminates the poisonous ammonia derived from metabolizing nitrogen-containing compounds, such as nucleotides or amino acids. Ammonia dissolves readily in water and thus is removed from an animal that needs to rid itself of excess water anyway. (In small animals the ammonia diffuses into the surrounding water.) With large size or a need for water conservation, animals excrete urea, a less toxic compound but one that also contains carbon and oxygen and thus potential energy. Urea also is highly soluble in water, but its low toxicity means that it can be concentrated before being excreted. Terrestrial animals with problems of water conservation either convert urea into uric acid, a solid compound that can be stored indefinitely in the body or voided with the feces, or develop efficient excretory organs (*e.g.,* the mammalian kidney) that can concentrate the urea. Although water balance is usually handled by the kidney, salt balance is sometimes a specialized function of other organs. For example, because freshwater fish tend to lose a great deal of salt through their gills, they simply expend energy to concentrate salt against a gradient at this location.

Reproduction and life cycles. Primitive members of all major taxa of animals reproduced sexually, and virtually all animals still do at some time or another. In contrast to other activities, that of reproduction and life history may be most complex in the more simply structured animals. If little energy is put into complex maintenance systems, more is left for reproduction, the central focus of an animal's life. Thus, although locomotion constrains the reproductive strategy of an animal, the possibilities with any locomotory mode are diverse. For example, although sessile animals need not expend energy attracting a mate, they do face the problem of getting their gametes in contact with those of the opposite sex. Sometimes both sexes release gametes in immense swarms in which the probability of contact with the opposite sex is high. Often the female harbours large eggs, and the smaller, more mobile sperm are released to find them. In sponges, sperm simply enter with food. Hermaphroditism (the possession of both male and female capabilities) and parasitism by males are ways by which sessile, slow-moving, or sparsely distributed animals cope with finding mates. Barnacles, which are sessile crustaceans, elongate one limb to transfer sperm directly to another barnacle. (The hermaphroditism of barnacles lets any individual's neighbours be potential mates.) Some barnacles and other animals have small males that are parasitic on the females.

Mobile animals employ many kinds of devices for signaling their availability to the opposite sex. Pheromones, sound, and visual cues are used singly or in combination. Competition for mates may lead to elaborate courtship rituals, which enable a female to choose a suitable male; to size increases of males that fight for control of a harem; or even to size diminution and ultimately parasitism as males compete for a mate. In some species, sex changes with age, with males turning into females as they get larger. In a few animals, the sex depends on whether the individual settles on the substrate (becoming female) or on another individual (becoming a parasitic male).

Competition for mates

Finding a mate is but one aspect of a reproductive strategy. The size of eggs is intimately related to the stage of development at which the young emerge to independent life, which in turn correlates with the habitat or mode of locomotion. For example, marine animals at one extreme produce vast numbers of tiny eggs, which hatch at an early developmental stage (*e.g.,* the planula larva of coelenterates), or fewer, larger eggs, which hatch at a much later stage in the development toward adulthood. Smaller larvae spend more time feeding in the plankton before settling down to adult life, and during this time they are vulnerable to predation; however, they can disperse more widely, and their vast numbers give a positive chance that some will survive at each reproductive period. Terrestrial animals always produce relatively large, developmentally advanced young (spending the larval time in the egg), because the rigours of living on land demand immediately functional organ systems to sustain a free-living life.

Another problem faced by animals as well as plants is whether to breed only once during life, and thus to put all gathered energy into the effort, or to spend less energy during each reproductive period in order to grow and survive to reproduce for many years. A major factor affecting the evolution of a system of reproduction is whether the adult or the juvenile has the greater likelihood of survival. Some insects, such as mayflies, spend so little time as an adult (not much more than a day) that they have lost their feeding structures so as to allot more energy and space to reproduction. Breeding sooner means more descendants faster and more surely, so that mutations which are harmful late but helpful early are selected for. Therefore humans too senesce, unlike an amoeba.

Simple and complex life cycles

Simpler animals can pinch or bud off replicas of themselves, a mode of reproduction used by some animals that individually cannot get very large because of the simplicity of their organ systems. Such asexual reproduction is a form of growth but rarely of dispersal—the bud is usually sessile like the parent and thus remains adjacent to it. Mobility apparently requires such an integration of the nervous and muscular systems that it usually inhibits budding or fission.

Complex life cycles are an extreme variant on the usual life cycle of animals. The juvenile or larval stage is simply more prolonged and complex; it is also structurally quite different from the sexually reproductive adult. Transformation to the adult may occur by asexual budding (*e.g.,* coelenterates) or individual remodeling (*e.g.,* insects or frogs). A complex life cycle enables an animal to feed in two different environments. It is not usually equally advantageous for the animal in both environments, so that one stage typically lasts longer than the other. For example, insects can become parasites without the usual problems of dispersal to a new host; the winged adult is admirably suited to find the correct host. Frogs can take advantage of ephemeral ponds or ditches of water without competition from fish because in their terrestrial adult phase frogs can survive on land and thus locate new ponds when and where they become available. The cnidarian life cycle is also commonly one of alternation between a mobile and sessile form. Some animals alternate between reproduction from unfertilized eggs (all females) and sexual reproduction. The all-female generations can reproduce faster to take advantage of seasonally excessive resources (*e.g.,* aphids or many freshwater crustaceans).

ECOLOGY AND HABITATS

Animals evolved in the seas but moved into fresh water and onto land in the Ordovician Period, after plants became available as a food source. A simple history of animal ecology centres on the theme of eating some organisms for food while providing food for others. The realities of how animals have done so are richly varied and complex. The ecology of animals and other organisms is reflected in their phylogenetic radiations (*i.e.,* the diversification of lineages). Ecologies are as numerous as species, but, just as species can be grouped into higher taxa, so too can a classification be made of the ways by which animals find adequate food to reproduce and the ways they remain alive while doing so.

Competition and animal diversity. The majority of animal phyla are, and have always been, confined to the sea, a comparatively benign environment. Marine animals need not osmoregulate, thermoregulate, or provide against desiccation. The energy procured can thus be used mostly for growth, reproduction, and defense. Even reproduction can be simple: shunting millions of eggs and sperm into the water and letting them fend for themselves. Developing embryos do not need the protection of a womb because the ocean provides a suitable environment.

Despite the simplicity an animal's life can attain within the ocean, most oceanic animals have not remained simple. Competition and predation, two major components of any habitat, have complicated the lives of animals, leading to ever more novel ways of surviving. No matter how inimical to life, the physical components of environments are relatively predictable elements to which adaptation is often comparatively easy, if costly. Competition and predation, in contrast, relentlessly challenge all forms of life no matter how perfect they become for an instant in time. Adaptations often become obsolete as soon as they are successful, because successful life forms become a prime source of food for others.

Importance of competition

Given the simple thesis that competition drives much adaptation, the ecological diversity of animals can be sketched readily. Form, function, and phylogenetic history reflect the roles that animals assume in the evolutionary drama. Throughout a billion-year history, the animal actors have changed many times, but they perform variations on the same theme and the backdrops look much the same. For example, shortly after plants became well established, forests of giant lycopods (club mosses) and tree ferns provided food and shelter for numerous arthropods, including winged insects, on which four-legged amphibious vertebrates fed. Larger amphibians and reptiles later turned to smaller ones for food. Some of the arthropods and other terrestrial animals in turn were parasitic on the vertebrates. Later, different groups of plants, insects, and vertebrates enacted the same scene. First gymnosperms and then angiosperms became the dominant components of forests. Amphibians yielded dominance to mammallike reptiles (some of which became herbivorous), which gave in to dinosaurs; the latter were replaced by mammals and, most recently, by humans. In aquatic habitats the same drama has unfolded, with ever-changing actors. Reefs, for example, have entirely disappeared several times, with each subsequent avatar built mostly from different kinds of organisms. A historical perspective illustrates the underlying direction provided by competition and predation.

Evolution of ecological roles. Animals arose from protozoans and initially were simply larger, more complex, and successful competitors for the same sources of food. The early animals (parazoans, coelenterates, flatworms, and extinct groups) exhibited the same basic strategies of obtaining food as did the protozoans. Because of their larger size, however, they had an advantage over protozoans: they could prey on them and oust them from their attachment sites on the ocean floor. The early basic strategies of animal life reflected two different means of competing for food, that fixed by photosynthetic and chemosynthetic organisms and that provided by the wastes and decaying tissues of life forms. Almost all the free energy fixed is used by one organism or another, so that what one animal wins is lost to the rest. Animals do whatever they can to acquire all the energy they can use, and in this basic sense each is competing with all the others. Ultimately, predation is a mode of competition that simply involves eating the potential competitor rather than finding another way to share the same resource.

Ecological roles

Three early ecological roles of animals were as filter feeders, predators, and scavengers. The filtering of comparatively tiny organisms and organic detritus is a form of predation that was easily acquired when an animal became immense relative to potential food. Sponges were the earliest filter-feeding animals and still dominate certain marine habitats.

Predation on relatively large organisms relies on capture and subsequent subjugation of the prey until it can be ingested. Predation grades into filter feeding when the prey is very small in relation to the predator and into parasitism when very large. Among the early animals, coelenterates were the initial predators. Either attached to the bottom or floating near the surface, they paralyzed potential prey with their stinging and muscular tentacles and pushed it into their guts to digest it at leisure. Placozoans and flatworms preyed somewhat less effectively; they crept over a sessile or slow-moving potential prey, formed a pocket around it, and then ejected digestive enzymes to break it into smaller pieces that could be ingested.

Scavengers feed on the remains of dead organisms. A layer of energy-rich organic matter continuously settles on the ocean bottom, where it is recycled by diverse organisms. As animals evolved, they became essential as garbage eliminators because their remains (and those of plants and some fungi) are only slowly decomposed by microorganisms. Without animal scavengers, ocean bottoms and land surfaces would be cluttered with the refuse of dead organisms. Among the early animals, flatworms were the primary scavengers on the ocean bottoms.

Although the early radiation of animals admirably filled the major ecological roles, they had structural, physiological, and behavioral limitations that left some options open. For example, there were no potential predators of the surface-creeping flatworms or placozoans or of the cnidarians, with their stinging cells. There were no burrowers that could penetrate the layer of detritus which undoubtedly accumulated on the ocean floor. With the acquisition of a coelom or pseudocoel, animals could burrow into the detritus layer, consuming it as they went, as earthworms do on land.

Well-developed organ systems permitted an increase in body size, which gave rise to successive levels of predators. Quite early in the rapid diversification of animal life, protective hard shells appeared, a defense against predators but later also a means of enabling animals to expand outward from the seas. The intertidal areas, with partial exposure to the atmosphere, became a livable habitat. Jaws were an important innovation to predators. They are particularly central to the overwhelming success of arthropods and vertebrates, especially on land, where most plants and animals possess a tough drought- and injury-resistant covering. Most mollusks have a filelike radula that is well suited for breaking down tough plant or animal tissue into ingestible pieces and even adequate for drilling through the thick shells of their own group.

Large size, made possible by rigid skeletal support, particularly for reef-forming animals, provided shelter and thus more variations on the common themes. Corals and some other animals shelter algae, particularly in the nutrient-poor tropical seas, and obtain their food directly from their symbionts. This was probably more common in the Vendian (the last interval of the Precambrian, from 670 to 590 million years ago on certain geologic time scales), when thin animals could bask in the water without predators. Most of the deep sea is sparsely populated, its animals living on what settles down from above, but volcanic and other deep-sea vents emit gases that can be oxidized to provide energy. Some animals have symbiotic bacteria that do this, and they reach high densities there. Photosynthetic reef builders create forests in the seas that are analogous to those on land.

Parasitism

Large body size also favours the rise of parasitism, the consumption of living tissue that typically does not kill the host organism outright. Too heavy a load of parasites weakens an animal and makes it more susceptible to predation or other forms of death. Parasites have evolved in many phyla, the most important being platyhelminths, nematodes, and arthropods. Several taxa of high level are entirely parasitic. A disadvantage of parasitism, particularly on land, is dispersal to another host. Intermediate hosts are sometimes used if direct passage cannot be made. Enormous reproductive output is the rule (other organ systems can be minimal because the habitat is so congenial). The extraordinary number of species of winged insects attests to the success of the parasitic way of life. Insects can actually feed in the dispersal stage and thus survive longer while seeking the appropriate host.

Humans and the environment. Humans have had two major effects on their environment, neither of which is original but both of which are greater in consequence than those of any other single species. These two impacts are expected outcomes of natural selection, but their magnitude is of an unprecedented order.

All animals pollute their environs with their wastes, but only when animals are too crowded does a buildup of wastes impair their health. As mentioned above, the wastes of organisms normally become the food of others and thus usually are eliminated almost as rapidly as produced. Leaf litter in the humid tropics, for example, is almost nonexistent because of low seasonality, but elsewhere it can accumulate to some depth. Pollution becomes a problem only when waste cannot be eliminated. For example, the first great pollution episode in life's history, which formed oxygen, was a product of more efficient photosynthesis. Oxygen is a poison to cells, but it is also among the best acceptors of electrons in the breakdown of molecules for energy. Organisms thus developed defenses against oxygen so that they could use it advantageously in their metabolic pathways—a pollutant turned essential to most life.

Humans have only seriously started to pollute their environment in the past two centuries. By their sheer increase in numbers, humans crowd out many other species, particularly those that are large in size but also those that live in habitats humans preempt. Humans have eliminated countless tiny species without realizing their existence. The number of extinctions humans have been directly and indirectly responsible for ranks as one of the major extinction events in Earth's history.

EVOLUTION AND PALEONTOLOGY

Natural selection

All the adaptations in the living world have been produced by natural selection. This selection acts continuously, on many levels and time scales. Thus, an animal may become well adapted to an ecological niche that then disappears, forcing the animal either to evolve rapidly to fill another or, more likely, to become extinct. Another animal, adapted to a more permanent niche, survives. There is also long-term selection on the ability to adapt, as well as on current adaptation, for environments change, in both their physical and biotic components. Mass extinctions of the past testify to major changes, some perhaps catastrophic, the causes of which are still debated. These mass extinctions tended to eliminate more active and specialized groups, partly setting broad-scale evolution back and selecting for the inactive and resistant.

Evolution proceeds by the incremental acquisition of adaptations. It may be impossible for a lineage to evolve into a more effective way of life, because its present adaptations would have to be lost first. An adaptive zone is the niche of a (perhaps large) group of species; in general, the more different and basic the overall adaptive zone, the higher the rank of the taxonomic group. When an adaptive transition has occurred, a new group has arisen.

It is possible to turn this process around and to infer the course of evolution from its results. Species that share a derived character are likely to have had a common ancestor with that character, although there are many exceptions. Incorporating as much evidence as possible, morphological and molecular, makes the inference more likely. Fossils help too, letting scientists know what actually did live at each time. Only hard skeletons are ordinarily preserved intact or as fossils, though, so that groups without them have a sparse record or none. Simpler skeletons are sometimes ambiguous as to what animal they came from, and many groups have existed that have no close relatives today. There are nevertheless several dozen faunas through the geologic record that preserve soft-bodied animals and thereby help fill in the historical record of animals.

Animals first appeared in the Vendian, soft-bodied forms that left traces of their bodies in shallow-water sediments. The best-known are coelenterates of various sorts, including some that were more irregular than any today, and there are several groups with unclear affinities. At least some of the latter groups probably left no descendants. Most of the Vendian animals were thin, with each cell able to diffuse nutrients from the water, and many may have photosynthesized with symbiotic algae. No sponges are known to have existed in the Vendian, but they probably had already arisen from choanoflagellate protists.

First mass extinction

The first known mass extinction ended the Vendian. In the Cambrian Period (570 to 505 million years ago) began the great evolutionary radiation that produced most of the known phyla. Evolution occurred rapidly then, as it ordinarily does when adaptive zones are more or less empty and evolutionarily accessible. More soft-bodied faunas show that there were a number of sorts of animals that have no apparent relation to known phyla. It is unclear how many of these are aberrant members of known phyla and how many are more basically different. Although natural selection adapts the parts of animals to function and develop harmoniously with one another, at such an early time much of this internal coadaptation may not yet have occurred, making it easier to change in major ways. There were many groups of arthropods and echinoderms that also have unclear specific affinities with their longer-lasting relatives. Priapulid worms, a minute component of the modern free-living biota, were abundant and diverse. Coeloms evolved and many animals burrowed, and burrowing has increased throughout the Phanerozoic (from roughly 570 million years ago to the present). The Cambrian was also the time when hard skeletons originated in many groups and predators began to prowl the ocean floor.

The probability that a taxonomic family of animals would become extinct in a million years was highest in the Cambrian and declined exponentially until a mass extinction occurred in the late Permian Period (about 260 to 245 million years ago). It then declined again exponentially thereafter. This pattern is due entirely to the decline and extinction of whole groups that are more susceptible to extinction; within each group the probability of extinction stays about constant except during mass extinctions. The probability that a family will give rise to a new family usually has declined exponentially both within groups and overall, however, so that most groups tend to decline in large-scale diversity over time. There has been nevertheless an overall increase through the Phanerozoic in the number of taxa at levels from species to family as new groups like mammals and teleost fishes have originated and as others, like clams and insects, have gradually diversified. Extinction is the common fate of a lineage, while the survivors multiply disproportionately.

Sponges are first definitely known in the Cambrian, including a short-lived major group, the Archaeocyatha. They have not evolved much since then. Some of their larvae became sexually mature without growing up and gave rise to the coelenterates and perhaps the placozoans. Most groups of coelenterates also appeared early and evolved slowly. All corals of the Paleozoic Era (570 to 245 million years ago) belong to groups that are restricted to that era. After the Permian extinction, a group of sea anemones evolved a skeleton and diversified into modern corals. In the Cretaceous Period (144 to 66.4 million years ago), some clams became corallike, even with symbiotic algae, and for a while outcompeted the corals on reefs.

The fossil record is uninformative for flatworms and pseudocoelomates. The interrelations of these groups have also not yet been studied adequately by modern comparative methods. They probably form an adaptive radiation distinct from that of the coelomates, however. Some anatomic evidence suggests that the pseudocoelomates were all derived from gnathostomulid-like Platyhelminthes. The Introverta seem related to the rotifers, and the gastrotrichs to the nematodes. The Mesozoa may be an unnatural group, with its classes being simplified descendants of different phyla, while the Nemertea are probably derived from turbellarian Platyhelminthes.

Origin of coelomates

Coelomates appear to have had a single origin, probably from ancestral turbellarian Platyhelminthes. They were already diverse in the early Cambrian, and the hydroskeletal function of the coelom in small animals suggests that the ancestor was a burrowing worm. Segmentation arose very early in the group and is retained in its probably primitive form by most annelids. Leeches arose from freshwater oligochaetes, and oligochaetes probably from ancestral polychaetes. Annelid fossils merely show that they have been around since the Cambrian.

Arthropods have been the most diverse phylum since the Cambrian. Trilobites and crustaceans dominated then, with the former declining in abundance through the Paleozoic and the latter expanding into great adaptive diversity. Chelicerates also arose in the early Paleozoic and later radiated widely on land. Myriapods are a terrestrial group and gave rise to insects about 400 million years ago (during the Devonian). Insects were already diverse in the Carboniferous (360 to 286 million years ago), and modern orders have gradually originated and then replaced many of the earlier ones. The interrelations among the four major arthropod groups are unclear, as is the position of the Onychophora. The latter, a relative of annelids and known as early as the Cambrian, may be ancestral to myriapods, in which case the Arthropoda must be divided into two phyla. The position of the weakly segmented Tardigrada is even less clear, as they show special similarities to both the Onychophora and the Gastrotricha.

Segmentation has been reduced or lost in many groups. The Pogonophora retain segmentation mostly at their hind end. Another annelid relative known since the Vendian, this group has gutless members that get nutrients only from symbiotic bacteria and what is dissolved or suspended in the water. The Apometamera show traces of segmentation in the Echiura but none in the overall more-derived Sipuncula. Apometamera are also annelid relatives but may be even closer to mollusks. They lack useful fossils, unless the tube-forming Hyolitha, which may alternatively be annelids or a separate phylum and which lived throughout the Paleozoic, belong here.

Some living mollusks retain traces of segments, and the Machaeridia, an early Paleozoic group probably at the base of this phylum, were highly segmented. The Mollusca can be said to have originated when the radula did. The primitive Aplacophora lack a shell and are unknown as fossils, while their relatives the chitons come from the Cambrian. The Monoplacophora are mostly Paleozoic and gave rise to snails, cephalopods, and the Paleozoic class Rostroconchia of semibivalves. From the latter originated the clams (which have lost the radula) and the scaphopods, always a sparse group. Clams and snails have gradually expanded, the latter especially since the Cretaceous, when one group evolved a movable proboscis. Cephalopod evolution has been more rapid and complex, with nautiloids dominant in the early Paleozoic and ammonoids from then to their final extinction at the end of the Mesozoic Era (*i.e.*, 66.4 million years ago), after having nearly disappeared three times before. Octopuses and squids grow too rapidly to form an external shell, but one group with an internal shell is known to have thrived in the Mesozoic.

Three phyla of annelid relatives feed by a lophophore and are probably related to each other. They too have nearly lost segmentation. Phoronids lack a useful fossil record and probably have always been sparse. Brachiopods and the colonoid bryozoans, on the contrary, were the predominant filter feeders of the Paleozoic Era. Most brachiopods succumbed to the Permian extinction, and the phylum has never recovered. A group of bryozoans, though, has managed to diversify since the middle Cretaceous.

Chaetognaths, abundant but with few species, lack a useful fossil record (unless some Cambrian teeth came from them) but appear related in some way to the remaining phyla. Echinoderms had remarkable structural diversity in the early Paleozoic, with no less than 20 classes usually recognized then: some asymmetric, stalked, helical, mobile, or cemented down, with multiple origins of adaptively similar forms. Most were both rare and with few species, but blastoids were abundant in the later Paleozoic, and crinoids were a major group throughout that era. Blastoids became extinct in the Permian, and crinoids nearly so. Most later crinoids are free-swimming rather than stalked like their ancestors. An expansion of powerful general predators (crabs and fishes) in the Jurassic Period (208 to 144 million years ago) reduced the numbers of crinoids and some other groups.

Hemichordates are another group now inconspicuous but diverse in the Paleozoic. Most of the latter are called graptolites, colonoids abundant in the Ordovician Period (505 to 438 million years ago) and Silurian Period (438 to 408 million years ago). Hemichordates are very primitive deuterostomes related to both echinoderms and chordates. Of the latter, tunicates lack useful fossils, but a Cambrian cephalochordate shows the early existence of human ancestors. Small pelagic animals called Conodonta, with phosphatic teeth and segmented muscles but no hard skeleton, are most likely cephalochordates but may have been very primitive fishes. They also appeared in the Cambrian and were among the most abundant animals to the end of the Triassic Period (*i.e.,* 208 million years ago). They may have filtered through their spiny teeth rather than through their gills as their ancestors did.

Rise of vertebrates

Vertebrates are not known until the Ordovician, when the first of a series of mostly heavily armoured jawless fishes appeared, probably mud-grubbers and filter feeders. Predaceous jawed fishes appeared in the Silurian, perhaps even with a separate origin of bone, and divided into three large groups. One, the placoderms, was more or less dominant in the Devonian Period but rapidly became extinct at its end. Sharks and their relatives have had a series of adaptive radiations, each mostly replacing the previous. The same is true for bony fishes, but the teleosts have been successful to an unprecedented degree. Lungfishes are mollusk-crushers and have declined in numbers since the Devonian.

Amphibians crept from the water in the Devonian and fed on arthropods, which had done so first. They were derived from distant relatives of the modern coelacanth. Many archaic amphibians were large, a metre or two long. Frogs and salamanders first appeared in the early Mesozoic. Reptiles lay eggs that can withstand dry external conditions, and they evolved from amphibians early in the Carboniferous. They were subordinate until the drier Permian, when they began a series of adaptive radiations that put some groups back in the sea and others into the air. Dinosaurs arose in the Triassic and were cut down about the end of the Cretaceous, as were many other groups. Birds evolved from dinosaurs in the Jurassic but apparently expanded greatly only in the Cenozoic.

Mammals arose in the Triassic from reptiles that had separated from the rest in the Carboniferous. They too have undergone sequential adaptive radiations, some of which occurred in the Mesozoic when they were kept small by the dinosaurs. Placentals and marsupials began in the Cretaceous, the latter in North America, from which they invaded South America with some placentals at the beginning of the Cenozoic, replacing an archaic fauna there. They then went on alone across Antarctica to Australia, meanwhile becoming extinct in the north. Placentals themselves had an early radiation that was mostly replaced in the Eocene Epoch (57.8 to 36.6 million years ago) by the modern orders to which it had given rise.

CLASSIFICATION

Diagnostic features. Animals are multicellular eukaryotes whose cells are bound together by collagen. They have sperm and form polar bodies in oogenesis. Animals lack semirigid cell walls, and movement is effected through muscle and nerve cells. They usually gain energy from other organisms or their products. Animals are found almost anywhere on Earth where there is life.

Annotated classification.

Phylum Porifera (sponges)
Sessile; vary in form from amorphously matted to delicately sculptured; distinctive flagellated collar cells pump water and extract food; models of efficient flow design; 2 cell layers with gelatinous mesenchyme containing various types of cells, including those producing supporting spicules; colonoid; marine and some freshwater species; filter feeders; Cambrian to recent; 9,000 species.

Phylum Placozoa
Flattened, 2 flagellated cell layers; fluid mesenchyme with a few cells and connecting fibres; similar to the larvae of primitive animals, from which they may be derived; digestive method unknown; shape irregular and changing; marine; predators or scavengers; recent; 1 species.

Phylum Cnidaria
Possess tentacles with stinging cells (nematocysts) for paralyzing prey or repelling predators; sessile (polyp) and floating (medusa) forms; many have both stages alternating in complex life cycles; medusae with well-developed mesoglea used as elastic skeleton for jet propulsion; muscle cells epithelial; solitary to the most complex of animal colonoids; marine and freshwater species; predators or scavengers with some filter-feeding species; Vendian to recent; 9,000 species.

Phylum Ctenophora (comb jellies)
Long tentacles of most have sticky lasso cells (colloblasts) to secure prey; comb plates of fused cilia (ctenes) used for swimming; separate muscle cells; marine; predators; Devonian to recent; 100 species.

Phylum Platyhelminthes (flatworms)
Lack anus except perhaps in the class Gnathostomulida; no circulatory system; mouth ventral; mesoderm of loose cells (parenchyma); marine and freshwater species, with some terrestrial species known; predators or scavengers, with some parasitic species known; recent; 20,000 species.

Phylum Mesozoa
Among simplest animals; only organ the gonad; 2 classes probably arose separately; dicyemids with unique within-cell embryo formation; marine; parasitic; recent; 100 species.

Phylum Nemertea (Rhynchocoela; ribbon worms)
Proboscis in fluid-filled cavity not attached to gut; anus present; closed circulatory system; marine, with some freshwater and terrestrial species known; predators; Carboniferous to recent; 900 species.

Phylum Gastrotricha
Wormlike pseudocoelomates; ventral ciliation used to glide over surfaces; use muscular pharynx to pump in small prey or organic debris; marine and freshwater; predators or scavengers; recent; 450 species.

Phylum Nematoda (roundworms)
Found almost everywhere animals exist; thick, complex cuticle permits high pressure on internal fluid and acts as elastic skeleton; only longitudinal muscles; many internal structures reflect high internal pressure; unique type of excretory organ; some have jaws; marine, freshwater, and terrestrial species; predators or scavengers or parasites; Carboniferous to recent; 12,000 species.

Phylum Rotifera (wheel animals)
Distinctive corona of cilia used in pulling cellular food into gut; most have elaborate jaws; some with telescoping bodies; marine and freshwater; predators or filter feeders, with some parasitic species known; Eocene to recent; 1,800 species.

Phylum Introverta
Spiny retractable proboscis (or introvert) at head of wormlike body functions in burrowing through soft substrates or guts; marine and freshwater species; predators or parasites; parasitic forms lack a gut; Cambrian to recent; 900 species.

Phylum Annelida
Segmented worms; paired appendages or setae on segments used in locomotion; protonephridia or metanephridia; closed circulatory system; some with jaws; some sedentary or sessile; some secrete tubes around them; marine, freshwater, and terrestrial; predators, scavengers, or filter feeders, with some parasitic species known; Cambrian to recent; 15,000 species.

Phylum Pogonophora
Deep-sea, sedentary, tube-building worms with 3 body divisions; long, ciliated tentacles with microvillus-like extensions of single cells; no mouth or digestive system; symbiotic bacteria in characteristic organ; closed, well-developed circulatory system; Vendian to recent; 150 species.

Phylum Tardigrada (water bears)
Tiny; secrete cuticle; epidermal cell number constant; metameric nervous system; 4 pairs of legs; reduced coelom functionally replaced by hemocoel; extraordinary ability to withstand desiccation and other stresses; mostly terrestrial, with some marine and freshwater species known; predators or scavengers; Cretaceous to recent; 400 species.

Phylum Onychophora
Wormlike, with many pairs of stubby legs; jaws are modified legs; thin secreted cuticle; annelid-like body plan; tracheal respiratory system; terrestrial; predators; Cambrian to recent; 80 species.

Phylum Arthropoda
A rigid, jointed cuticle used as skeleton; lack epithelial cilia entirely; open circulatory system; segmented, with each segment bearing a pair of appendages primitively; much fusion of segments and use of appendages for functions other than locomotion; many with compound eyes; respiratory systems highly varied; complete range of habitats and feeding modes; Cambrian to recent; more than 1,000,000 species.

Phylum Mollusca
Ciliated epithelia; ventral surface forms muscular foot, primitively used for locomotion but variously modified; dorsal and lateral surfaces usually form shell-secreting mantle that protects external gills; unique chitinous scraping radula aids feeding and burrowing; coelom reduced; open circulatory system serves as hydroskeleton; many species moderate to large in size; marine, freshwater, and terrestrial species; predators, scavengers, filter feeders, and grazing species, with some parasitic species known; many derived forms are sessile; Cambrian to recent; 50,000 species.

Phylum Apometamera
Unsegmented worms; food-gathering proboscis with cilia below or in tentacles; sedentary tube dwellers; metanephridia; marine; filter feeders; Devonian to recent; 400 species.

Phylum Phoronida
Wormlike; sedentary in chitinous tube; lophophore; closed circulatory system; metanephridia; marine; filter feeders; Devonian? to recent; 15 species.

Phylum Bryozoa (moss animals)
All but a few commensal species are colonoid, forming large matlike or plantlike forms; sessile; lophophore; tiny individual zooids; reduced organ systems; marine and some freshwater species; filter feeders; 2 subphyla, Ectoprocta and Entoprocta; Ordovician to recent; 4,600 species.

Phylum Brachiopoda (lamp shells)
Calcareous, bivalved shell with mantle; lophophore; open circulatory system; metanephridia; marine; filter feeders; Cambrian to recent; 340 species.

Phylum Chaetognatha (arrowworms)
Swimming marine predators; head with grasping spines, jaws, and eyes; coelom lacks mesodermal lining; Cretaceous to recent; 100 species.

Phylum Echinodermata
Unique water/vascular system (tube feet) used mainly for locomotion and feeding; lack heads, brains, and segmentation; internal calcareous skeleton; circulatory system open; pentamerous, nearly radial symmetry in recent classes; marine; predators, scavengers, or filter feeders; Cambrian to recent; 7,000 species.

Phylum Hemichordata
Wormlike or colonoid; tripartite coelom; construct mucus-lined U-shaped burrows or proteinaceous tubes; open circulatory system; dorsal and ventral nerve cords, the dorsal one partly hollow; some with branched tentacles to gather food; pharyngeal gill slits used for exit of sediment-bearing water entering mouth and for gas exchange; marine; filter feeders; Cambrian to recent; 85 species.

Phylum Chordata
Elastic notochord used as skeleton when present; dorsal hollow nerve cord; postanal tail; pharyngeal slits used originally in feeding and later in gas exchange; all habitats and feeding modes, but rarely parasitic; 50,000 species.

<u>*Subphylum Tunicata*</u> (Urochordata)
Secrete a thick tunic or a filtering device of complex composition around body; most adults lack notochord and head; circulatory system open; coelom reduced; pharyngeal cavity well-developed; solitary or colonoid; sessile or pelagic; marine; filter feeders; Silurian? to recent; 3,000 species.

<u>*Subphylum Cephalochordata*</u> (Acrania)
Fishlike; persistent notochord; segmental muscles but no hard skeleton or heart; protonephridia; Cambrian to recent; 23 species.

<u>*Subphylum Vertebrata*</u> (Craniata)
Skeleton of bone or cartilage; heart; kidneys; myelinated axons; includes the agnathans, Chondrichthyes, Osteichthyes, amphibians, reptiles, mammals, and birds; Ordovician to recent; 47,000 species.

Critical appraisal. This classification includes only extant groups. Because the aschelminths have not been studied adequately by modern methods, there is no consensus on their classification, and the system used here differs in some respects from that in the article ASCHELMINTHS. The classification in this article is based on morphological work carried out in the late 1980s and remains to be tested by RNA sequence studies and other comparisons. This classification defines the phylum Introverta as containing the classes Kinorhyncha, Loricifera, Priapulida, and Acanthocephala and the phylum Nematoda as containing the classes Ademophorea, Secernenta, and Nematomorpha.

BIBLIOGRAPHY. Technical descriptions of almost all taxa to the family level are presented in SYBIL P. PARKER (ed.), *Synopsis and Classification of Living Organisms,* 2 vol. (1982). The most detailed survey of animals is found in PIERRE P. GRASSÉ (ed.), *Traité de zoologie: anatomie, systématique, biologie* (1948–), an ongoing multivolume work, published in parts. LIBBIE H. HYMAN, *The Invertebrates,* 6 vol. (1940–67), is a classic, unfortunately incomplete, but careful, fairly detailed, and still mostly accurate.

A survey of animal diversity is found in C. BARRY COX and PETER D. MOORE, *Biogeography, an Ecological and Evolutionary Approach,* 4th ed. (1985). Developments in the preservation of biological diversity are discussed in EDWARD O. WILSON and FRANCES M. PETER (eds.), *Biodiversity* (1988). Laws of physics that directly influence the size and shape of living organisms are addressed in STEVEN VOGEL, *Life's Devices: The Physical World of Animals and Plants* (1988); and R. MCNEILL ALEXANDER, *Animal Mechanics,* 2nd ed. (1983). KNUT SCHMIDT-NIELSEN, *Scaling: Why Is Animal Size So Important?* (1984), discusses the significance of animal body size.

For discussion of form and function, see ALFRED SHERWOOD ROMER and THOMAS S. PARSONS, *The Vertebrate Body,* 6th ed. (1986), a classic text; and E.J.W. BARRINGTON, *Invertebrate Structure and Function,* 2nd ed. (1979), a survey by system. ROBERT D. BARNES, *Invertebrate Zoology,* 5th ed. (1987) and RICHARD C. BRUSCA and GARY J. BRUSCA, *Invertebrates* (1990), are surveys by group. W.N. BEKLEMISHEV, *Principles of Comparative Anatomy of Invertebrates,* 2 vol. (1969; originally published in Russian, 1944; 3rd Russian ed. 1964), provides good coverage of invertebrate development. Research-level reviews of reproduction in many groups are available in ARTHUR C. GIESE and JOHN S. PEARSE (eds.), *Reproduction of Marine Invertebrates,* vol. 1–5 (1974–79), with a concluding synthesis provided in vol. 9 (1987) and intermediate volumes scheduled for publication in the 1990s. See also B.I. BALINSKY, *An Introduction to Embryology,* 5th ed. (1981), a standard text that focuses on vertebrates only. A review of research on energy metabolism in most major animal groups is offered in T.J. PANDIAN and F. JOHN VERNBERG (eds.), *Animal Energetics,* 2 vol. (1987). MARCEL FLORKIN and BRADLEY T. SCHEER (eds.), *Chemical Zoology,* 11 vol. (1967–79), surveys the chemicals important to animal structure, physiology, and behaviour, organized by taxonomic group. KNUT SCHMIDT-NIELSEN, *Animal Physiology: Adaptation and Environment,* 4th ed. (1990), is a comprehensive introduction.

For more detailed treatment of the fauna and ecology of major terrestrial and aquatic ecosystems, see the multivolume series *Ecosystems of the World,* published by Elsevier Scientific since 1977. F. HARVEY POUGH, JOHN B. HEISER, and WILLIAM N. MCFARLAND, *Vertebrate Life,* 3rd ed. (1989), presents a broad overview from paleontology to animal behaviour. ROBERT E. RICKLEFS, *Ecology,* 3rd ed. (1990), is an authoritative work. THOMAS C. CHENG, *General Parasitology,* 2nd ed. (1986), provides a detailed introduction to the subject.

For explorations of evolution and paleontology, see DOUGLAS J. FUTUYUMA, *Evolutionary Biology,* 2nd ed. (1986), a general introduction; MARTIN F. GLAESSNER, *The Dawn of Animal Life: A Biohistorical Study* (1984), a useful discussion of the first recorded radiation of animals; RUDOLF A. RAFF and THOMAS C. KAUFMAN, *Embryos, Genes, and Evolution: The Developmental-Genetic Basis of Evolutionary Change* (1983), a causal rather than descriptive approach to embryology in all animals; and ROBERT L. CARROLL, *Vertebrate Paleontology and Evolution* (1988), a standard survey. RAYMOND C. MOORE (ed.), *Treatise on Invertebrate Paleontology* (1953–), a basic source of information, with descriptions and illustrations to generic level, is an ongoing multivolume work published in parts; newly revised editions of some parts began to appear in 1970, ed. by CURT TEICHERT. Paleontological topics are thoroughly reviewed in RICHARD S. BOARDMAN (ed.), *Fossil Invertebrates* (1987); and STEVEN M. STANLEY, *Extinction* (1987). On the origin and diversification of hormones, see E.J.W. BARRINGTON (ed.), *Hormones and Evolution,* 2 vol. (1979). ERNST MAYR, *Populations, Species, and Evolution* (1970), is a revised abridgement of the author's classic book on speciation and other relevant topics.

(V.C.M./L.M.V.V.)

Annelids

The Annelida, or segmented worms, constitute a major invertebrate phylum of the animal kingdom. The group numbers more than 9,000 species and includes three classes: the marine worms (Polychaeta), which are divided into free-moving and sedentary, or tube-dwelling, forms; the earthworms (Oligochaeta); and the leeches (Hirudinea). Annelids, named for the transverse rings, or annulations, of the body, are segmented animals with a body cavity (coelom) and movable bristles (setae). The coelom is reduced in leeches, and setae are lacking in a few specialized forms, including leeches.

For coverage of related topics in the *Macropædia* and *Micropædia,* see the *Propædia,* section 313.

This article is divided into the following sections:

General features 778
- Distribution and abundance
- Size range and diversity of structure
- Importance

Natural history 779
- Life cycle
- Ecology
- Locomotion
- Food and feeding
- Behaviour and associations

Form and function 782
- External features
- Internal features

Evolution and paleontology 784

Classification 785
- Distinguishing taxonomic features
- Annotated classification
- Critical appraisal

Bibliography 787

GENERAL FEATURES

Distribution and abundance. Annelids are found worldwide in all types of habitats, especially oceanic waters, fresh waters, and damp soils. Most polychaetes live in the ocean, where they either float, burrow, wander on the bottom, or live in tubes they construct; their colours range from brilliant to dull, and some species can produce light. The feather duster (*Manayunkia speciosa*) inhabits the Great Lakes and some rivers of the United States. The polychaetes include more than 6,000 known species, which are about evenly divided between free-moving and tube-dwelling forms. The oligochaetes number about 3,250 known species. Oligochaetes, including earthworms, burrow into soil; certain small oligochaetes are found in fresh water, and a few are marine, usually inhabiting estuarial or other shallow waters. Leeches, which number about 300 species, inhabit freshwater or humid environments and are carnivorous or parasitic on other organisms—*e.g.,* all marine leeches are parasitic on fish.

Environments

Size range and diversity of structure. The length of annelids varies from a fraction of an inch to more than six metres (about 20 feet). The width may exceed 2.5 centimetres (about one inch) in the contracted state. Free-moving polychaetes and earthworms include the largest species. Leeches attain lengths of about 0.4 metre in the contracted state.

Polychaetes. The body of free-moving polychaetes (see Figure 3) consists of a head, or prostomium, which may bear two or more eyes; a preoral segment, with such appendages as antennae, tentacles, and palpi (fleshy sensory projections); a trunk divisible into distinct segments; and a tail, or pygidium, which may bear anal cirri (fleshy projections) or plaques and a terminal anus. Each body segment following the second segment (peristome) usually has paired parapodia; *i.e.,* fleshy, lateral outgrowths used in feeding, locomotion, or breathing. The parapodia, generally prominent in free-moving polychaetes, bear bundles of setae, which can be extended, and aciculae (needlelike structures), which are used for support.

The heads of sedentary polychaetes (see Figure 3) may be distinct or indistinct. Forms with a distinct head generally lack head appendages. Branchiae, or gills, which serve for respiration and as food-gathering organs, are well-developed in many of the tube-dwelling forms. Some have tentacles at the anterior (front) end, and gills arise from the dorsal (upper) surface of a few anterior segments. In these species food is gathered by the tentacles and respiration is confined to the gills. The rest of the body is divided into thoracic and abdominal regions. Parapodia, if present, are generally simple lobes; frequently the setae project directly from the body wall. Many sedentary polychaetes construct tubes made from a substance secreted from cells that constitute the epidermis, or skin. Tubes may consist of calcium carbonate, parchment, or mucus, to which sediment adheres. The anus is at the posterior tip. Tube dwellers generally have an external fecal groove along which fecal material passes forward. Eyes are occasionally present on gills, along the sides of the body, or on the pygidium in sedentary forms that do not live in tubes.

Tube construction

Oligochaetes. The body of oligochaetes (Figure 1) is uniformly segmented and has conspicuous segmental lines. The prostomium is usually a simple lobe overhanging the mouth and lacking appendages. The microscopically small eyes are scattered over the body. The clitellum, a saddle-shaped thickening of the body wall, is present at sexual maturity. The anus is at the posterior tip. Setae generally arise from the ventral (lower) surface of the body.

Leeches. Leeches (see Figure 4) have 34 segments, and elongation occurs by the subdivision of these segments. Leeches have a small sucker at the anterior end and a large sucker at the posterior end. A clitellum is present in the mid-region during the reproductive period. The poorly developed eyes are paired structures at the anterior end. Setae are absent.

Importance. Large earthworms, or night crawlers (*Lumbricus terrestris*), are cultivated and sold as bait for freshwater fishes and as humus builders in gardens. The sludge worm *Tubifex,* abundant near sewer outlets and thus an indicator of water pollution, is collected and sold as food for tropical fish. Polychaetes play an important role in turning over sediment on the ocean bottom.

The medicinal use of leeches, which dates from antiquity, reached its peak in the first half of the 19th century. The European species *Hirudo medicinalis* formerly was exported throughout the world, and native species also were used. Hirudin, an extract from leeches, is used as a blood anticoagulant.

Hirudin

The estuarine flats of Maine and Nova Scotia are the principal sources of the bloodworm (*Glycera dibranchiata*), which is used as bait for saltwater fishes. Reproduc-

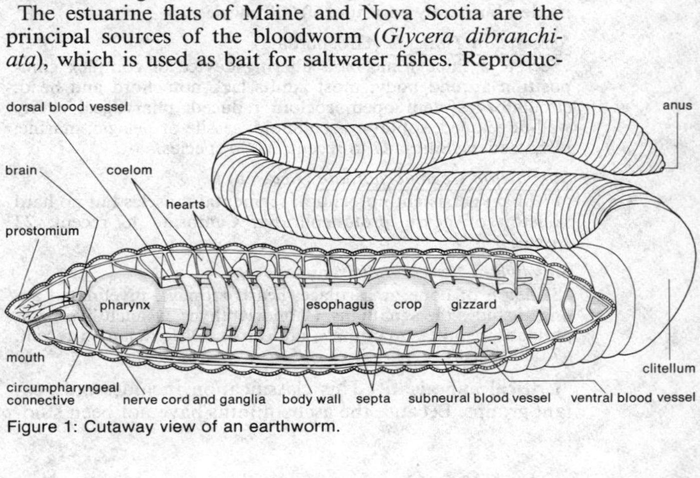

Figure 1: Cutaway view of an earthworm.

tive parts of the palolo (*Palola siciliensis*), which break off and are found in great numbers during the reproductive period, are used as food in Samoa in the south Pacific.

NATURAL HISTORY

Life cycle. *Reproduction.* In the polychaetes, sexes are usually separate but cannot be distinguished in the immature state until gametes (eggs and sperm) appear. Gametes are derived from the mesodermal linings around the digestive tract. The developing gametes are shed into the coelom, where they are nourished by nurse cells (eleocytes). The gametes, especially eggs, are nourished by the breakdown products of muscle tissue, which are passed on to the gametes via the eleocytes. Ripe eggs and motile sperm may leave the body through gonoducts, or tubes for the passage of reproductive cells; through excretory, or nephridial, pores; or through ruptures of the body wall.

Epitoky and stolonization in polychaetes

Most polychaetes shed their gametes into the water. Various major body changes may precede the emission of gametes, the two most profound being epitoky (maturation into a modified, fertile form) and stolonization (the development of stemlike growths). In species of *Nereis,* morphological changes include enlargement of the eyes, enlargement of a specific number of parapodia, replacement and alteration of setae, and development of an anal organ (rosette) for the emission of sperm. Morphological changes occur in species of *Syllis* as well, but they involve only the part that is shed in stolonization. At sexual maturity these polychaetes leave their burrows and swim in groups before releasing gametes.

The removal of the brain of a nereid that normally undergoes epitoky causes morphological changes without the subsequent formation of gametes. Nereids that normally do not undergo epitoky are unaffected by the removal of the brain. This suggests that apparently the hormone which stimulates epitoky is present only in species that normally undergo this phenomenon. In syllids, stolonization may produce one or more stolons, or stems, containing developing gametes; epitoky is controlled by a nerve ganglion in the proventriculus part of the digestive tract. Epitokous females produce a pheromone that stimulates the male to spawn. The presence of the sperm in the water initiates spawning in the female. Swarming in certain epitokous species coincides with a specific phase of the Moon, but the causes of such behaviour are unknown. Palolos of the Pacific, for example, swarm on a specific day at certain places each year, an event that can be predicted with precision.

Another type of epitoky occurs in some sedentary polychaetes; in these worms, the parapodial lobes develop long, thin setae. Either the entire animal or only the posterior portion (*e.g.,* the palolo) leaves the tube or burrow and swims before releasing gametes.

Hermaphroditism

Hermaphroditism—that is, the production of eggs and sperm in one individual—rarely occurs in polychaetes. The free-moving polychaete *Ophryotrocha,* however, shows marked sexual variability; individual males or females may exist in association with hermaphroditic forms. Experiments with *Ophryotrocha* suggest that the age at which transition from one sex to another occurs may differ among groups within certain species.

Asexual reproduction is known in a few sedentary polychaete species. In some genera—*Ctenodrilus, Pygospio,* and *Sabella*—fragmentation of the body occurs, sometimes forming single segments, from which new individuals can develop.

Reproduction in oligochaetes is primarily hermaphroditic; the number, arrangement, and location of the male and female gonads and their pores vary considerably among the various species. Lower oligochaetes (Microdrili) have one pair of testes and one pair of ovaries in successive segments. Higher oligochaetes (Megadrili) retain the two pairs of testes in segments 10 and 11 and the pair of ovaries in segment 13. Developing sperm are frequently stored in seminal vesicles before transfer to female receptacles. Sperm ducts lead from the seminal vesicles to male pores located one or more segments behind the testes. The ovaries are simple outpouchings (ovisacs), with oviducts leading to female pores in the next posterior segment.

Copulation in oligochaetes is reciprocal—that is, both sperm and eggs are exchanged—and takes place in a head to tail position, with the two ventral surfaces in contact (see Figure 2). In lower oligochaetes, the male pores of one worm and the female pores of another are opposite each other, and sperm pass directly from the male pores into the seminal receptacle of the female. Cells associated with the brain secrete a hormone that stimulates gamete development. The worms separate after the gametes have been exchanged.

Fertilization in earthworms

The clitellum of the earthworm secretes a case, or cocoon, into which is secreted a material that serves as nourishment for the young and a mucous substance that aids in copulation. The cocoon slips forward and receives eggs as it passes the female pores and sperm as it passes the male pores. Fertilization, therefore, takes place within the cocoon. The cocoon slides over the peristome, becoming completely sealed as it does so.

Asexual reproduction is common in aquatic oligochaetes; indeed, sexual reproduction is virtually unknown in certain naidid species. Some oligochaetes divide to form a chain of two or more individuals that later break off as young worms. In many genera, individuals lay self-fertilized eggs capable of development. Others exhibit parthenogenesis—the production of young without fertilization—a phenomenon associated with polyploidy (multiple sets of chromosomes) in earthworms and accompanied by degeneration of male gonads.

All leeches are hermaphroditic, and reproduction is always sexual. The testes, from four to 10 pairs, are arranged by segments, beginning with segment 12 or 13. The testes on each side of the body are connected with the vas deferens, a duct that leads indirectly to the male pore. The female reproductive system consists of one pair of ovisacs containing the ovaries, which, although located in front of the testes, may extend some length posteriorly, depending on the animal. The ovaries connect to form an oviduct that forms either a female pore or, in those species that copulate, a vagina.

In one leech family (Gnathobdellae), sperm are transferred by the penis of one animal into the vagina of another. In two other families (Rhynchobdellae and Erpobdellidae), sperm are transferred by sperm capsules, or spermatophores, onto the body of the leech, after which the sperm leave the spermatophore and enter the ovary through the female pore to unite with the eggs. Leech eggs, numbering from one to more than 100, are usually deposited in cocoons, which may be oval or elongated in shape and are generally attached to rocks or vegetation. Glossiphoniids produce a membranous cocoon and attach it to their ventral surface, where development takes place. A clitellum, which forms only during the reproductive period, secretes the cocoon and material (albumin) to nourish the developing young.

Determinate cleavage

Development. Annelid eggs, like those of flatworms and mollusks, exhibit spiral, or determinate, cleavage, so called because early differentiation of various regions occurs; in indeterminate cleavage (in echinoderm and chordate eggs), early differentiation does not occur.

In annelids, the first four cells (blastomeres) give rise, by alternating clockwise and counterclockwise divisions, to a cap of smaller cells, called micromeres, at one end of the egg and a cap of larger cells, called macromeres, at the other end.

All cells divide simultaneously during the early stages of annelid development; during later stages, however, macromeres divide more slowly than micromeres. As a result, a ball of cells (solid gastrula) forms as the mi-

From W. Kukenthal and T. Krumbach (eds.), *Handbuch der Zoologie;* by permission of Walter de Gruyter, Berlin-New York

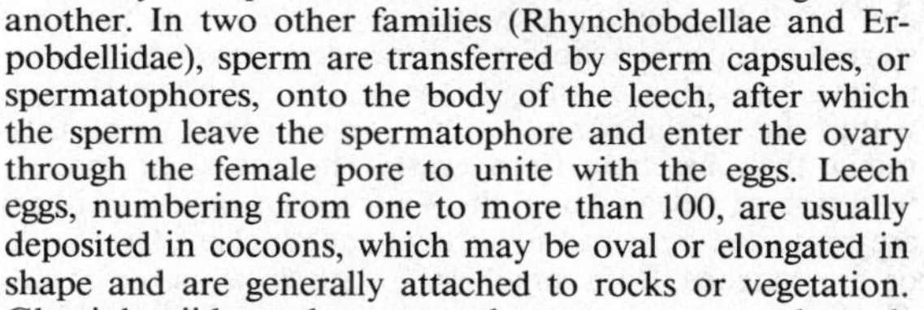

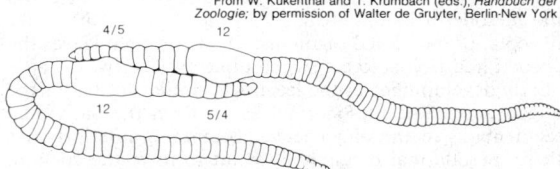

Figure 2: *Enchytraeus albidus* in copulation, the male pore, on segment 12, being directly opposed to the spermathecal pore of the other worm, between segments 4 and 5.

cromeres grow over the macromeres. The gastrula may form by invagination (infolding of cells), epiboly (overgrowth and lengthening), or by both processes. Some of the micromeres become arranged in a characteristic pattern known as the annelid cross.

Trochophore larva of polychaetes

A free-swimming immature form called the trochophore larva develops in the polychaete annelids and during the development of certain other invertebrate groups—mollusks, sipunculids, and lophophores. The trochophore larva of polychaetes is typically diamond-shaped with a circle of short, hairlike projections (cilia), called the prototroch, around the thickest part of the body. Cells bearing the prototroch develop from specific micromeres at the 16-cell stage. The four cells of the annelid cross frequently give rise to a so-called apical tuft of cilia at the anterior end. A tuft of cilia (the telotroch) may appear later at the posterior end.

The upper half of the trochophore—that portion above or in front of the prototroch—will become the prostomium (head) containing the brain, the eyes, and the prostomial appendages, if present in the adult polychaete. The lower half of the trochophore contains the digestive tract, excretory organs, and other internal organs; it is also the site of future segmentation. The mouth and anus form during the trochophore stage, but the digestive tract may or may not be functional at that point.

Typically, the first three segments form almost simultaneously in the lower half of the trochophore. Development of the parapodial lobe and the appearance of larval bristles (setae) follow shortly thereafter. The body grows in length by the addition of new segments from the preanal segment (pygidium or tail), which is the site of all additional segment formation. The setae generally fall off the first segment, which becomes the adult peristome, or first postoral segment. The parapodial lobes of this segment either develop peristomial appendages or atrophy, depending upon the polychaete species. Adult setae gradually replace larval setae on the second and third segments.

Although the features of the trochophore larva are relatively uniform among species within an order, the nature of the larva also depends upon other factors—*e.g.,* egg size and larval ecology. Species lacking a pelagic trochophore stage show special adaptive features—*e.g.,* protection by a parent, formation of an egg capsule, the discharge of eggs within one of the parent's tubes, or viviparity (live birth rather than hatching from eggs). The young of species with a short pelagic larval life—a few days or less—either are protected by a parent throughout much of larval life or are hatched from small eggs, with little or no yolk. The most common polychaete trochophore feeds and has a long pelagic life; food consists of microscopic organisms such as diatoms or dinoflagellates. Structural modifications, usually large numbers of setae or bands of cilia around each newly formed segment, facilitate the long pelagic life. After settling, the young polychaete quickly loses its trochophore characteristics and begins to resemble the adult.

Development of oligochaetes in cocoons

Development in oligochaetes takes place entirely within the cocoon; there is no free-living larval stage. The cocoon of the aquatic lower oligochaetes contains large eggs and relatively little albumin. The cocoon of the terrestrial higher oligochaetes contains small eggs but large amounts of albumin, which nourishes the developing embryos. The oligochaetes undergo a highly modified form of spiral cleavage. The ectoderm, endoderm, and mesoderm, however, arise in the same manner as in the polychaetes. The elongated gastrula has a ventral mouth at the front end and a posterior anus. At the gastrula stage, earthworms begin to feed on the albumin, the embryo elongates, and the mesoderm bands break into units to form the walls, or septa, of individual segments; the worm then leaves the cocoon and begins to construct a burrow nearby.

Early development in the leeches is similar to that of the oligochaetes. The mesodermal bands form the individual segments as in the oligochaetes, beginning anteriorly. As these mesodermal bands hollow out to form the coelom, mesenchymal cells from the lining of the coelom begin to form one large coelomic cavity extending the entire length of the worm; as the number of mesenchymal cells increases, however, the coelom becomes filled with them. This is the characteristic state of adults. Young leeches hatch from cocoons after feeding upon albumin.

Life-span. Since both the polychaetes and oligochaetes are able to regrow lost parts—*i.e.,* regenerate (see below)—it may appear that they are essentially ageless. Few longevity studies have been carried out with polychaetes, however. Most of the adults of species studied have a characteristic number of segments, which form rapidly during early life and prior to the appearance of gametes. Many polychaetes, especially among the nereids, reproduce only once and then die. In nature these worms, usually quite sluggish after spawning, are eaten by fish and other animals. Species of polychaetes are known to live from one month (*Dinophilus*) to three years (*Perinereis*). Species that form stolons (stems), such as the syllids, or whose posterior end breaks off, such as the palolo, are capable of repeating the process; but the number of times and the length of time they are able to do so have not been established. Most sedentary polychaetes survive following spawning, but, again, it is not yet known how often this process can be repeated.

Aging in oligochaetes

The life-span of oligochaetes is better established because they are frequently used in laboratory experiments. Asexual reproduction for 130 generations has been reported in one aquatic species. Some earthworms are believed to live as long as 10 years. Senescence, or aging, is known to occur in oligochaetes; *Eisenia,* for example, lives beyond a reproductive period with a progressive loss of weight. Aging oligochaetes darken in colour, largely as a result of an increase in pigment deposition. In addition, the metabolic rates decrease, and their physiological processes slow.

Little is known about the life-span of leeches. One species of *Erpobdella* requires a year to reach sexual maturity, after which it lays cocoons once and dies. Another species breeds once a year for two years and dies during the third.

Regeneration. It has been said that annelids are the most highly organized animals with the power of complete regeneration. The powers of regeneration are greater in the polychaetes and lower oligochaetes than in the higher oligochaetes; leeches lack the ability to regenerate. Most polychaetes and oligochaetes can regenerate a new tail. The ability to replace an amputated part is usually restricted to the anterior end, where lost segments are replaced either by the same number or fewer; if fewer segments form, internal reorganization of the organ system follows. Regeneration from a single segment occurs naturally in the polychaetes *Ctenodrilus* and *Dodecaceria.*

Steps involved in regeneration

The process of regeneration occurs in a series of steps. First the wound seals over; then a structure (blastema) forms on the surface of the wound. New tissue probably arises from preexisting parent tissue, although mesodermal regenerative cells known as neoblasts, which migrate to the site of the injury, are found in polychaetes and lower oligochaetes. As healing begins, RNA (ribonucleic acid) accumulates at the wound site, first in the epidermal cells and later in mesodermal cells. The amount of glycogen, a complex carbohydrate that serves as an energy source in animals, in the oligochaete *Eisenia* decreases markedly near the point of injury, returning to normal only after regeneration is complete.

There is evidence that specific hormones control regeneration in both polychaetes and oligochaetes. A hormone from the posterior part of the brain is essential for posterior regeneration; its presence is apparent only after the second or third day following injury. A mature *Nereis* is unable to regenerate unless brains from young worms with tails removed are implanted in its coelom.

Reversal of anterior–posterior polarity has been obtained in an earthworm (*Perionyx excavatus*). A piece removed from the anterior end regenerates a head at both cut ends if the cuts are made simultaneously. If the new anterior head then is removed, the posterior head becomes dominant and evokes tail regeneration at the surface from which the new anterior head was removed.

Ecology. There are no marine habitats containing specific polychaetes as there are for mollusks and echinoderms. Many species, such as *Neanthes arenaceodentata* and *Capitella capitata,* cosmopolitan in distribution, are found throughout the world. Aquatic oligochaete species are widespread in suitable environments; terrestrial forms are less widely distributed, except for the earthworm and others that have been transported to new habitats, generally inadvertently, by humans. The distribution of leeches is similar to that of oligochaetes, with the aquatic forms more widely distributed.

Mechanisms of adaptation

Some oligochaete species can secrete a tough mucous covering to protect themselves against either summer heat or winter cold. Some terrestrial burrowing forms burrow deeper into the ground during periods of adverse conditions. Some aquatic leeches burrow deep into the bottom of a pond or stream during the warm months. Polychaetes have no known mechanism for adapting to adverse conditions.

Locomotion. The basic features of locomotion in annelids are most easily observed in the earthworm because it lacks appendages and parapodia. Movement involves extending the body, anchoring it to a surface with setae, and contracting body muscles. When the worm begins a forward movement, circular muscles at the anterior end contract, extending the head forward. At the same time the anterior end lifts from the surface to facilitate forward movement. A wavelike contraction originating in the circulatory muscles then passes toward the posterior end. When the wave of contraction nears the mid-region of the body, longitudinal muscles contract, thereby shortening the region. A wave of contraction of longitudinal muscles follows, and the cycle is repeated. The setae of a segment are extended by certain body muscles to prevent backward movement of the segment during the contraction of the longitudinal muscles. The setae are retracted during the circular contraction period. Muscular movement is aided by the compartmentalization of the segment—coelomic fluid, confined by the segment walls, provides a substance against which the muscles can work. The earthworm is capable of reversing the direction of its movement; the waves of contraction pass forward.

Locomotion in free-moving polychaetes is accomplished by circular, longitudinal, and parapodial muscles and by coelomic fluid. When a worm such as *Nereis* moves slowly, the contractual force comes from the sweeping movement of the parapodia. The parapodia of each segment are not aligned, and the effective stroke is the backward one, in which the aciculae (needlelike processes) are projected beyond the parapodium and come in contact with the crawling surface. In the recovery, or forward, stroke, the aciculae retract, and the parapodium lifts free of the surface. When a parapodium ends its backward stroke, the next parapodium initiates one. Body undulations, which help the worm to move rapidly, are produced by the contraction of longitudinal muscles stimulated by the backward stroke of parapodium of a particular segment.

Locomotion in the burrowing polychaetes, especially those forms lacking anterior appendages, is similar to that of the earthworm. In tube-dwelling sedentary forms, such as the Sabellidae, locomotion is restricted to movement within the tube. In this group, the parapodia are reduced or absent; specialized setae, the uncini, function in much the same way as do parapodia in free-moving forms.

Use of suckers in leeches

Locomotion in the leech may be compared, in part, to that of the inchworm (immature members of the moth family Geometridae); the anterior and posterior suckers serve as points of contact. When the posterior sucker attaches to a surface, the circular muscles contract, beginning at the posterior end. The leech thus elongates and the anterior sucker fastens to the surface. When the posterior sucker is released, a wave of contraction of the longitudinal muscles moves in a forward direction; this completes one cycle. During swimming, the dorsoventral muscles maintain a contracted state, and undulations of the body are produced by waves of contraction of the longitudinal muscles.

Food and feeding. The nature of the food and feeding methods of the polychaetes is closely related to the structure of the species, particularly of the anterior end. Those species that feed on large particulate matter have a pharynx either with jaws (*Glycera*) or without (*Phyllodoce*); both types can be either herbivorous or carnivorous feeders. Those species that feed on fine particulate matter may be filter feeders, surface-deposit feeders, or burrowers. Filter feeders either capture floating material with ciliated tentacles (*Sabella*) or pump water through their burrows and capture the fine material on a mucous secretion, upon which they feed (*Chaetopterus*). Surface-deposit feeders may take in material through a pharynx provided with jaws (*Neanthes*), with an unarmed pharynx (*Cirriformia*), or with numerous long ciliated tentacles capable of extending one metre or more (*Terebella*). Burrowers have a structure similar to that of surface-deposit feeders and can be related species. *Pectinaria* lives with its anterior end in the sediments and feeds on fine material with its tentacles.

The diet and feeding mechanisms in oligochaetes are not as varied as those in polychaetes. Terrestrial oligochaetes, such as the earthworm, are scavengers and feed upon decaying organic material, especially of plant origin. Some aquatic oligochaetes, aside from being scavengers, feed on micro-algae or protozoans and other microscopic animals.

Leeches are primarily bloodsuckers. The medicinal leech *Hirudo* feeds principally on mammalian blood, but it also sucks blood from snakes, tortoises, frogs, and fish; when young, it may eat oligochaetes. Feeding is facilitated by the secretion of hirudin. The leech detaches after becoming engorged with blood, and it may not attempt to feed again for up to 18 months. Marine leeches attach to, and feed directly from, the gills of fish. Other leeches are carnivorous and feed on oligochaetes and snails.

Behaviour and associations. Various polychaetes (for example, *Syllis, Chaetopterus, Cirratulus, Terebella*) are bioluminescent—that is, capable of producing light. The phenomenon occurs within the cells of *Polynoe;* the lower surfaces of some scale worms (*Halosydna*) have special photocells that produce light when stimulated. *Odontosyllis* light production is related to sexual maturity and swarming, which is influenced by lunar cycles. The female produces a bright luminescence that attracts the luminescent male; light production decreases in the female following the release of gametes. In the order Chaetopterida, the process, which involves the discharge of a luminescent secretion from certain segments and from the antennae, is under nervous control; in *Chaetopterus,* light can be produced in the parapodia by stimulating the ventral nerve. The significance of light production in this genus is unknown, however, because it lives in a tube through which light rays cannot pass. When stimulated, some earthworms produce a luminescent slime from the mouth, anus, dorsal pores, or excretory pores; it is possible that the light is produced by bacteria living in the worm. Luminescence is unknown in leeches.

Bioluminescence

Polychaetes, especially the tube-dwelling Sabellida, generally respond to changes in light intensity by withdrawing into their tubes.

Aggressive behaviour has been reported in several species of nereids (a group of free-moving polychaetes); they respond to a stimulus by extending the proboscis (feeding organ) to expose the jaws. *Neanthes arenaceodentata* fights members of its own sex but not those of the opposite sex. The response may be related to spawning since this species does not swarm but lays gametes in the tube of another individual; fighting thus prevents the occupation of one tube by two individuals of the same sex.

Both polychaetes and oligochaetes can learn to choose between favourable and unfavourable environments. In an experiment earthworms try about 12 times to bring into their burrow a leaf made immobile by attachment to some object; when an unattached leaf is presented to the worm, it turns to it and ignores the immobilized leaf thereafter.

Commensalism and parasitism

Commensalism, a beneficial relationship between two types of organisms, is common among certain scale worms (Phyllodocida, an order of polychaetes). These worms may be found in the tubes of sedentary polychaetes, in the mantle cavity of mollusks, such as chitons and limpets; and on certain echinoderms, such as the starfishes and in the rectums of sea cucumbers. The scale worm *Arctonoe,* which normally lives on starfishes, is attracted to water flowing from the host starfish but not to that from other starfish species. It has been established that the attractant in the water is a chemical secreted by the host, but its nature is unknown. Tube-dwelling polychaetes, such as *Chaetopterus,* may be the host to scale worms, pea crabs, or fish, which eat material carried in by water currents produced by the host. Commensalism occurs in some aquatic oligochaete species. The posterior end of *Aspidodrilus,* for example, is modified as a large sucker for attachment to other worms.

Parasitism is rare in polychaetes. Myzostomida, an atypical polychaete group, are commensal or parasitic either on the surface of or within echinoderms, primarily the crinoids. Polychaete species that live on the surface feed on fine particles carried to the mouth of the crinoid. Parasites that live within crinoids may be found in the body wall, the coelom, or the digestive tract. Parasitic infestations by polychaetes are frequently severe enough to cause wartlike growths on the surface of the host; such growths have been noted on the surfaces of fossil crinoids of the Paleozoic Era (more than 225,000,000 years ago), indicating that these parasites established themselves early. Some forms, such as *Iphitime,* are parasitic in the branchial chamber of crabs. The young stages of the cosmopolitan polychaete species *Arabella iricolor* develop in the coelom of species of another polychaete (*Diopatra*). Some aquatic oligochaetes live in the ureters of toads or in the eyes of frogs. All members of the order Branchiobdellida are parasitic in the brood chambers of the crustacean isopods or on the gills of crayfish, where they suck blood. Many leeches, all of which feed on blood, attach to the host only during feeding. Marine leeches, however, attach permanently to their fish host.

FORM AND FUNCTION

External features. The body of an annelid is often described as a tube within a tube. The inner tube, or digestive tract, is separated from the outer tube, or body wall, by the coelom. The head region (prostomium) is followed by a series of segments similar to each other in appearance. The body in many species, especially in the sedentary polychaetes, is separated into two or three regions. The cells constituting the epidermis (outermost cell layer) are usually simple columnar epithelial cells covered by a cuticle; parts of the body may be ciliated, especially in smaller forms. The cuticle consists of thin layers of protein similar in composition to that of the collagen found in some vertebrate tissues.

Polychaete structure

The body form of polychaetes (see Figure 3) varies, depending on whether the polychaete is free-moving, sedentary, or pelagic (ocean-dwelling). The first segment, the prostomium, is in front of the mouth and may be a simple lobe or a highly developed projection. The next segment, the peristome, surrounds the mouth and is followed by a series of segments, the total number of which may be limited or unlimited. The parapodia, fleshy outgrowths on each segment following the peristome, contain bundles of setae (movable bristles), which differ in structure and function among species and thus provide a key to species identification. A seta consists of a basal portion within a follicle and a shaft projecting from the follicle; it is secreted from an epidermal cell, which encloses both the ciliary apparatus from which the seta arises and the lacuna in which the seta develops and through which it pushes to the outside. Composite, or pointed, setae are formed from two or more epidermal cells. New setae form in reserve follicles and move forward to replace old ones, which are discarded.

Branchiae, or gills, are not found in polychaete species that breathe through the body wall. When present, they are simple filaments or tufts near the anterior end of the worm. A mass of feeding structures in sabellid and serpulid polychaete worms, called a tentacular crown, functions both for food gathering and for respiration. Polychaete sensory receptors include eyes, lateral organs, dorsal ciliated ridges, statocysts (organs of balance), taste buds, papillae (blunt-shaped projections), and stiff hairs. The eyes, which range in complexity from simple pigment spots to eyes with lenses, may be found on the prostomium, on the peristome, on the pygidium, along the sides of the body, or on the tentacular crown.

Oligochaete structure

The oligochaete body (see Figure 1) is usually cylindrical, is sometimes flattened, and rarely has projecting structures. Segmental lines are usually conspicuous, and secondary segmentation may occur in larger forms. The

(A,D) Adapted from original drawings by Janice L. Findley; (B,C) from F.A. Brown, *Selected Invertebrate Types* (1950); John Wiley and Sons, Inc.

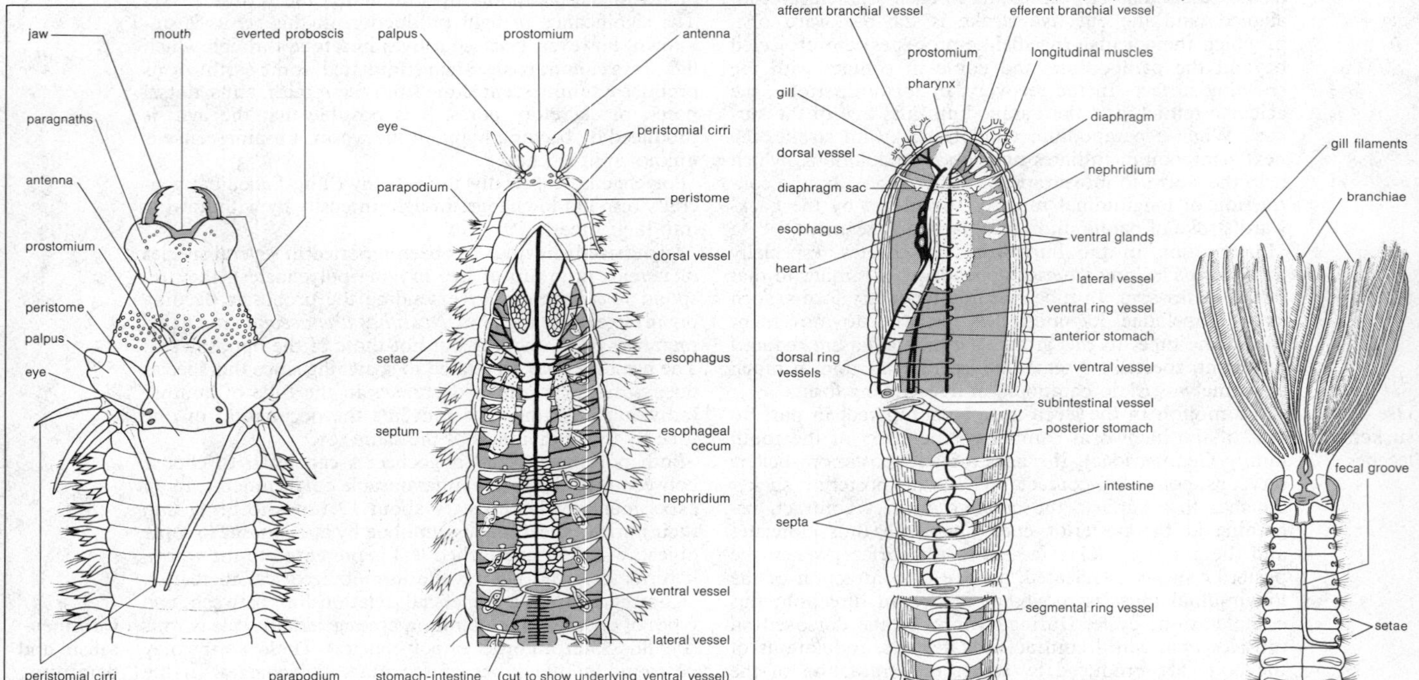

Figure 3: *The structure of polychaetes.*
(Left) Free-moving polychaetes. (A) *Neanthes,* (B) *Nereis.* (Right) Tube-dwelling (sedentary) polychaetes. (C) *Amphitrite,* (D) *Sabella.*

number of segments varies from seven in some aquatic species to 600 in the earthworms. Setae, embedded in the body wall, may be simple, S-shaped, forked, or hairlike. Except for the first, each segment may have either two pairs of S-shaped setae or a circle of setae. Many transitional forms of setal arrangement occur, and copulatory setae are found on some segments in certain species. All sexually mature oligochaetes have a clitellum (a glandular structure derived from the epithelium), which secretes the egg capsule; it may be saddle-shaped or ring-shaped. In lower oligochaetes it consists of a single layer of modified epithelial cells; in higher forms, such as earthworms, it may have many layers.

The ends of nerves, which probably respond to touch, heat, and pain, branch among the epidermal cells of oligochaetes. Epithelial sense organs resembling taste buds occur in the skin and mouth cavity; they probably function as chemoreceptors (*i.e.,* smell and taste receptors). Photoreceptors, or light-sensitive organs, are abundant at the anterior and posterior ends of earthworms. Earthworms respond negatively to strong light but are attracted to weak light. All oligochaetes are strongly stereotactic (attracted to surfaces). Some forms have pressure receptors, sensory hairs, and pits.

A leech (see Figure 4), which has 34 segments, may increase in length as a result of subdivision and elongation of the annuli, or rings, that divide each segment. The typical number of annuli per segment in the mid-region is three to five. The anteriorly located eyes usually vary in number from one to five pairs. The clitellum, which is present during reproduction, extends from segments 10 through 12. The most conspicuous of the external features of the leech are the small anterior and the large posterior suckers.

Internal features. *Tissues and fluids.* The body cavity of annelids is lined by epithelium. Successive body segments are separated by walls that correspond to the external rings. In grooves between the segments of some oligochaetes are dorsal pores through which coelomic fluid may be discharged. As the leech develops, its coelom becomes nearly filled with connective tissue. Internal features of the three annelid classes are shown in Figures 1 (oligochaetes), 3 (polychaetes), and 4 (leeches).

The coelomic fluid of annelids plays a role in many important functions—*e.g.,* locomotion and regulation of fluid transfer through the body wall (osmoregulation). Many metabolic processes occur in the coelom, which also serves as a site for temporary food storage, for excretion of nitrogen-containing wastes, and for maturation of gametes. The coelomic walls of earthworms contain cells, called chloragocytes, that store and metabolize oil and glycogen and produce ammonia and urea. The chloragocytes eventually disintegrate in the coelomic fluid, and their granules are taken up by amoebocytes, which increase in size, becoming large brown bodies that are never eliminated from the body.

Osmoregulation

The fluids of marine polychaetes have the same salt balance as (*i.e.,* are isosmotic with) the surrounding seawater and thus can tolerate no more than a moderate change in the salt (*i.e.,* ion) content of the salt water. Coelomic fluids contain little or no protein. Certain aquatic oligochaetes, however, which live exclusively in fresh water, are capable of regulating the internal medium because, although their coelomic fluid contains fewer salts than does that of polychaetes, it contains more proteins. Freshwater leeches have osmoregulatory mechanisms similar to those of oligochaetes.

The body wall of a typical marine polychaete, such as *Perinereis cultrifera,* which cannot adapt to salinity fluctuations of seawater, swells and bursts if salinity is reduced to 20 percent that of seawater because the worm has no physiological mechanism for the control of water intake. On the other hand, certain individual *Nereis diversicolor* worms are capable of tolerating intertidal changes of salinity because they have enlarged nephridia that enable them to excrete excess water.

Nervous system. The nervous system of free-moving polychaetes is similar to that of oligochaetes. It consists of a dorsal brain, or supraesophageal ganglion, which is a discrete mass of nervous tissue in the prostomium; a pair of nerves united ventrally to form the ventral subesophageal ganglion; and paired nerve cords with one ganglion per segment. In sedentary polychaetes, the brain may become highly modified.

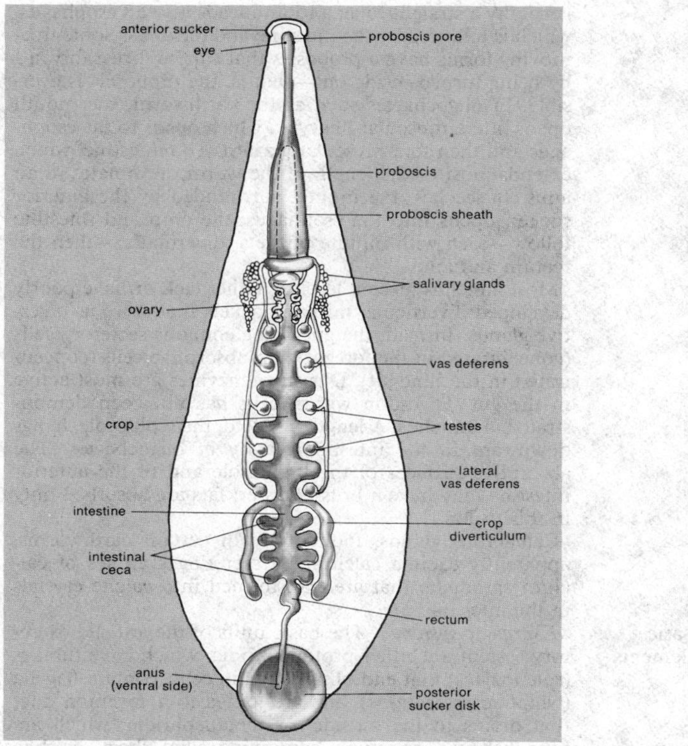

Figure 4: The internal structure of leeches.
From D.J. Reish, *Laboratory Manual for Invertebrate Zoology*

The muscles of annelids are coordinated both by the ventral nerve cord, which is composed of two strands and extends the length of the worm, and by a ganglion and nerves located within each segment. The nerves within each segment carry impulses away from the ganglion (motor nerves) or toward it from a sensory receptor (sensory nerves). The cell bodies of sensory nerves are located beneath the surface epithelium; those of motor nerves are either within the ganglion or in separate parapodial ganglia. Each segmental nerve innervates those components of the body wall, parapodia, and the digestive tract found in its segment.

The nerve cord of many annelids has giant nerve fibres (neurochords), which may have either a simple or a compound structure. Simple neurochords are very large single nerve cells; their axons arise from cells situated in either the brain or a segmental ganglion. Compound neurochords are multiple structures; each axon is connected to numerous cell bodies along its course. The function of the giant nerve cord is the rapid transmission of impulses from one end of the worm to the other; this enables the longitudinal muscles of each segment to contract at about the same time. The value of rapid contraction is evident in the escape reaction of tube-dwelling sedentary polychaetes.

Comparison with vertebrate fibres

Some giant nerve fibres convey impulses as fast as vertebrate nerve fibres (about 21 metres per second); annelid fibres, however, are larger in diameter (1.5 millimetres in *Myxicola*) and lack a thick insulating sheath (myelin). Not only is recovery from the passage of impulses slower in giant nerve fibres than in other annelid nerves but the former are also the last component to develop in the nerve cord of a growing worm. The nerve cord of *Myxicola* contains one giant nerve fibre, which is used to study the properties of the nerve impulse. In *Myxicola,* an impulse may be conducted in either direction along the nerve, unlike *Nereis* or the earthworm; may be initiated at any level; and is an all-or-none action.

Digestive system. The polychaete digestive system is

generally a straight tube; a mouth leads into an esophagus, which is followed by the intestine and the anus. Some free-moving forms have a proboscis that can be thrust forward by being turned inside out—that is, the proboscis is eversible. In oligochaetes such as the earthworm, the mouth opens into a muscular pharynx, which opens to the esophagus and then to a muscular gizzard. The intestine, which extends most of the length of the worm, terminates in an anus. In leeches, the mouth, surrounded by the anterior sucker, opens into the esophagus; the crop and intestine follow—each with minute pockets (diverticula)—then the rectum and anus.

Most annelids, except leeches, either lack or have poorly developed diverticula, minute pockets that serve as digestive glands. Instead, the gut lining contains secretory cells (concentrated in the foregut) and absorptive cells (concentrated in the hindgut). Digestive enzymes are most active in the gut. Digestion within cells has not been demonstrated in annelids. A lengthwise fold, the typhlosole, hangs downward in the intestinal cavity of oligochaetes. The absorptive surfaces of the typhlosole and of the anterior intestine may have a brush border; fats are absorbed only in this region.

Calciferous glands, found only in certain earthworms, apparently excrete calcium by secreting granules of calcium carbonate that are transformed into calcite crystals in the intestine.

Basic elements

Excretory system. The basic units of the annelid excretory system are either protonephridia, which have tubules (solenocytes) that end blindly within cells, contain flagella (whiplike projections), and are joined to a common duct that drains to the outside; or metanephridia, which are funnel-shaped structures containing cilia (short, hairlike processes) that open to the outside.

Ammonia is the chief nitrogen-containing end product of protein metabolism in aquatic annelids; earthworms, adapted to living in the soil, excrete more of another nitrogen-containing compound, urea, probably as part of a mechanism to control salt and water balance in the worm. The sea mouse *Aphrodita,* a polychaete, excretes 80 percent of its nitrogen as ammonia, which is also the primary nitrogenous excretory product in leeches (smaller amounts of urea also are excreted). Part of the ammonia excreted by leeches may come from bacteria in part of the leech's excretory system (nephridial capsules). The ability of leeches to withstand high concentrations of ammonia is believed to result from a protective effect provided by high levels of calcium in their cells.

Three aspects of nephridial function in annelids correspond to those of the vertebrate kidney—filtration, resorption, and secretion. Coelomic fluid filters through solenocytes. The ciliated funnels of metanephridia retain minute particles and those of moderate size. In oligochaetes, whose coelomic fluid contains proteins, particles are actively absorbed in the ciliated region of the tubule. The tubules of earthworms also resorb inorganic ions such as sodium and calcium and can selectively eliminate excretory products from both the coelomic fluid and the bloodstream.

Respiratory system. Gas exchange generally takes place through the skin, but it may occur through gill filaments in some polychaetes or through the rectum of aquatic oligochaetes. Although oxygen may be transported directly in the blood, it is usually carried by a respiratory pigment, either hemoglobin or chlorocruorin. Hemoglobin, the most common pigment, is present in most free-moving and some sedentary polychaetes and in most oligochaetes and leeches. Chlorocruorin is found in several polychaete groups (Flabelligerida, Terebellomorpha, and Serpulimorpha). A few free-moving polychaetes, some oligochaetes, and rhynchobdellid leeches have colourless blood. The blood of the polychaete *Serpula vermicularis* contains both pigments, the young having more hemoglobin and the old more chlorocruorin.

Respiratory pigments

Annelid hemoglobin molecules have several properties in common with the hemoglobin found in vertebrates but differ in molecular weight and in the relative amounts of certain constituents. Chlorocruorin differs from hemoglobin in having a lower affinity for oxygen and in being green in dilute solutions, red in concentrated ones.

The properties of annelid respiratory pigments are associated with the mode of life of the worm. The hemoglobin of the lugworm *Arenicola,* a polychaete, releases oxygen to the tissues only under conditions of extreme oxygen deficiency. The hemoglobin of some earthworms takes up oxygen from a normal atmosphere but releases it only when tissue oxygen is low and, thus, may protect the worm from oxygen poisoning.

Circulatory system. The circulatory system in the lower oligochaetes consists of a dorsal vessel that arises from a blood sinus or capillary network surrounding the intestine and conveys blood forward; a ventral vessel that conveys blood backward; and connective vessels between the two. The blood vessel walls consist of an outer membranous (peritoneal) layer containing muscle fibres, a middle region of collagenous material, and an inner lining of thin cells (endothelium). In higher oligochaetes, one or more pairs of hearts connect the dorsal and ventral vessels and propel the blood. In free-moving polychaetes the dorsal vessel is the chief propulsive force, and networks of small vessels connect the dorsal and ventral ones. In some leeches the blood is propelled by a dorsal vessel connected by loops at both ends to a ventral one.

Blood is moved by wavelike contractions of the blood vessels, by the beating of cilia, or by pumping provided by hearts. In *Arenicola* and the earthworm the heartbeat apparently is initiated in nerve cells rather than in muscle tissue, as occurs in vertebrates. The blood apparently carries nitrogen-containing products to the nephridia for excretion. The only blood cells are amoebocytes, which are free-moving cells that engulf particles.

Hormones. The brain contains several types of cells whose secretory activities relate to phases of the life cycle, especially those of reproduction, growth, and regeneration.

Neurosecretory cells

Neurosecretory cells, which are nerve cells that produce hormones, are found in the brain; their structure, similar to that of nonsecretory nerve cells, consists of fine projections (an axon and neurofibrils) and a cell body. The secretions of neurosecretory cells, which terminate in the walls of a blood vessel, in other fluid systems, or in the epidermis, are in the form of microscopic droplets or granules. Neurosecretory cells seem to be derived from epidermal secretory cells that have been incorporated into the central nervous system.

Inhibitor hormones are known in some Phyllodocida, and a stimulator substance has been identified in Drilomorpha, both of which are polychaete groups. (For a discussion of inhibitor hormones in nereids and syllids, see above *Reproduction.*) The maturation of gametes is apparently inhibited in nephtyid polychaetes by neurosecretions of the brain. The brain of the lugworm *Arenicola* stimulates maturation of gametes.

The brain has been shown to play a role in the regeneration of the posterior end of the body of polychaetes such as nereids and nephtyids, but the effect may be an indirect one involving the genital inhibiting hormone. Neurosecretory cells occur in the brain and subesophageal ganglia of several terrestrial and aquatic oligochaete species. Removal of the brain from sexually maturing earthworms causes degeneration of the clitellum and prevents gamete formation. The brain also plays a role in osmoregulation, as indicated by the increase in chloride concentration in the urine of oligochaetes lacking a brain. The neurosecretory cells in the brain of leeches control gamete formation.

EVOLUTION AND PALEONTOLOGY

Early development

The annelids are considered to have evolved in the sea, perhaps from an ancestral flatworm that evolved through the trochophore larva, the characteristic early stage of polychaetes. The oligochaetes are thought to have developed from polychaete stock; the leeches, which have the clitellum in common with the oligochaetes, probably evolved from the latter (see Figure 5).

The question of which polychaete order preceded the others remains unresolved. The Archiannelida were long considered to have been the earliest polychaete group because of their primitive condition; however, some members (*e.g., Polygordius*) that lack setae and external segmentation and have simple nervous, muscular, and circulatory

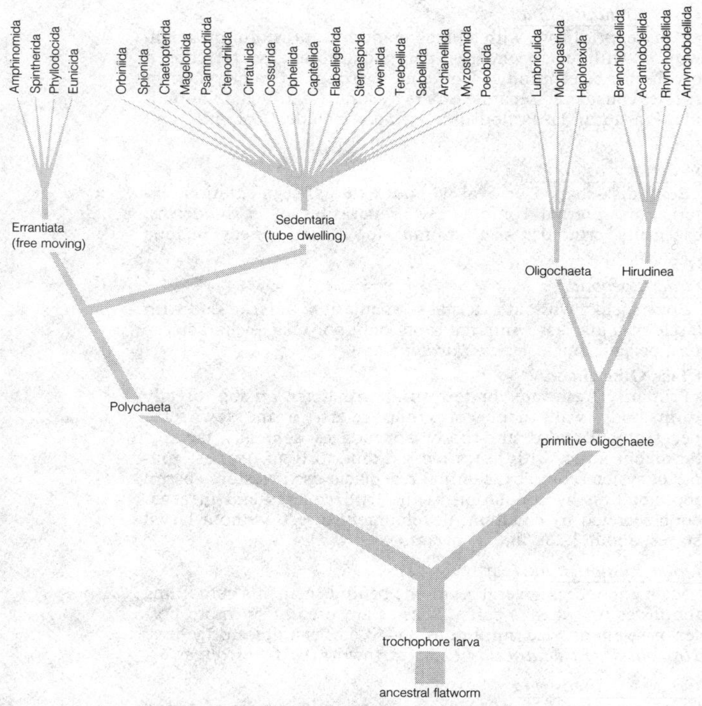

Figure 5: Possible origin of relationships among annelids.

systems are now considered to be a specialized group. *Polygordius* species typically are small in size; they have cilia on their surfaces for locomotion, respire through the skin, and have internal fertilization. Finally, the larvae undergo non-pelagic development. The polychaetes appear therefore to have undergone radiative evolution, in which every character has been modified independently of the others. There is thus little basis for regarding any one order as ancestral to the others.

Adaptation to fresh water

The evolution of oligochaetes from polychaetes may be related to the change from a marine to a freshwater habitat. One view is that oligochaetes evolved in marine swamps and were subjected to periodic drying; survival during dry periods would have been made possible by egg cocoons. A contrary hypothesis is that the primitive oligochaete was adapted to permanent freshwater conditions rather than to a terrestrial habitat. Some authorities consider the oligochaetes to have evolved from some members of the order Eunicida (*e.g.,* the family Lumbrineridae) or the order Capitellida (*e.g.,* the family Capitellidae), but this may result from a superficial resemblance in body form and thus may be of little evolutionary significance.

Reproductive structures provide not only the main criteria for understanding the course of evolution within the oligochaetes, but the basis for the classification of oligochaetes as well.

Each of the oligochaete orders, Lumbriculida, Moniligastrida, and Haplotaxida, is considered to have evolved separately from primitive oligochaetes. Many, however, believe that two paths of evolution occurred. In one pathway, the vas deferens (the tube carrying sperm from the testes) opened outward on the segment immediately behind the segment that contains the testes and evolved into two lines differentiated on the basis of whether the seminal receptacle (a storage cavity) opened in front of the testes, or at the same segment, or posterior to the testes. In the second principal pathway, the vas deferens opened a few segments behind the testes.

There is little doubt that the leeches evolved from the primitive oligochaetes, since both groups have a clitellum, at least during the reproductive period, and both are hermaphroditic. The Acanthobdellae are considered to be the link between the oligochaetes and leeches because they possess setae and walls between segments; the order contains only one known species, however. The three remaining orders of leeches evolved into two lines based on whether or not the animals have jaws.

Fossil record

The fossil record of annelids is limited because they have almost no hard body parts. Tubes constructed by polychaetes and polychaete jaws are the most commonly encountered fossil specimens. Most fossil records of oligochaetes are doubtful, and fossil leeches are unknown. Some burrows, or tubes, have been interpreted as belonging to wormlike creatures from Precambrian strata (more than 620,000,000 years old). Fossils resembling the scale worm *Halosydna* and the sea mouse *Aphrodita, Nereis*-like forms, and calcareous tubes similar to present-day *Serpula* and *Spirorbis* species have been described. The shells of Paleozoic mollusks (more than 230,000,000 years old) are occasionally marked by U-shaped tubes similar to those made by the polychaete *Polydora,* a modern-day pest of oysters. The tough jaws of polychaetes, containing minute spiny black teeth known as scolecodonts, occur from the Cambrian Period (about 570,000,000 to 500,000,000 years ago) onward.

CLASSIFICATION

Distinguishing taxonomic features. Classification of free-living and sedentary polychaetes relies almost exclusively on external characters, such as the shape of the head, and on the number and nature of structures, such as appendages (including anal ones), parapodia, and setae, and on tube construction. Oligochaete classification relies largely on internal structures, especially the arrangement and number of gonads, the position of the gonoducts, and particularly the location of the male pore. Setal characteristics are generally uniform among species. Leech classification is based on the presence or absence of setae and the nature of the mouth, proboscis (feeding organ), jaws, suckers, eyes, and reproductive system.

Annotated classification. The following classification incorporates the views of several authorities.

PHYLUM ANNELIDA (segmented worms)
Body wall covered with a cuticle secreted by the epidermis and containing an outer circular and inner longitudinal muscle layer; chitinous (tough, complex carbohydrate material) setae usually present, secreted by follicular cells and arranged segmentally; head or prostomium preoral, with or without appendages; closed circulatory system, with blood often containing a respiratory pigment; coelom, of schizocoelic origin, divided segmentally into compartments by walls, or septa; nervous system includes a dorsal, bilobed brain and a pair of connective nerves that encircle the digestive tract and unite to form a ventral nerve cord with 1 ganglion per segment.

Class Polychaeta (marine worms)
Paired lateral appendages, or parapodia, bearing chitinous setae; name of group refers to the many setae per segment; head with or without appendages; sexes generally separate with gametes discharged directly into the water, where fertilization and development occur; the free-swimming larva called a trochophore; more than 6,000 living species; free-moving and sedentary (tube-dwelling) forms.

Order Aphroditamorpha (scale worms)
Free-moving; dorsally rounded, with flattened pairs of scales more or less alternating with the dorsal cirri (slender projections); head with 1 or 3 tentacles, 2 palpi (fleshy sensory projections), and 4 tentacular cirri used for feeding and respiration; projecting (protrusible) proboscis cylindrical in shape, with border of soft papillae (nipplelike projections) and 4 chitinous jaws; size, 0.5 to 25 cm; examples of genera: *Aphrodita* (sea mouse), *Halosydna* (common scale worm), *Arctonoe.*

Order Amphinomida
Free-moving; prostomium with 1 to 5 antennae, 2 palpi, and a caruncle (posterior ridge) deeply set into anterior segments; parapodia with 2 lobes and branchiae (gills); size, 0.5 to 35 cm; examples of genera: *Eurythoe* (fireworm), *Euphrosyne.*

Order Spintherida
Body oval; median antenna on prostomium; pharynx retractable; dorsal surface with membranous ridges; ventral setae strongly curved; found on sponges; small; single genus, *Spinther.*

Order Phyllodocida
Free-moving; a large group characterized by a protrusible proboscis that may or may not be armed with chitinous jaws, teeth, or papillae; prostomium with 1 to 5 antennae, with palpi, and with 0 to 3 pairs of eyes; parapodia well developed into 1 or 2 lobes usually bearing compound setae; size, 0.2 to over 1 m; examples of genera: *Anaitides, Syllis, Hesione, Nereis, Glycera* (bloodworm), *Nephtys, Halosydna.*

Order Eunicida
Free-moving; head with or without appendages and eyes; proboscis with dorsal maxillae (upper jaws) of 1 to many paired pieces, a ventral pair of mandibles (lower jaws) more or less fused along the median line, and a pair of embedded maxillary carriers; parapodia single-lobed, often with many aciculae (needlelike structures); size, minute to 3 m; examples of genera: *Palola* (palolo), *Eunice, Stauronereis, Lumbineris, Onuphis.*

Order Orbiniida
Sedentary; head pointed or rounded without appendages; proboscis eversible and unarmed; body divided into distinct thorax and abdomen; gills arise dorsally from thoracic region; size, minute to 40 cm; examples of genera: *Scoloplos, Paraonis.*

Order Spionida
Sedentary; at least 2 long feeding tentacles adapted for grasping and arising from prostomium; size, 0.5 to 25 cm; examples of genera: *Spio, Polydora.*

Order Chaetopterida
Two to 3 distinct body regions; prostomium with palpi; modified setae on segment 4; tube dweller; examples of genera: *Chaetopterus* (parchment worm), *Spiochaetopterus.*

Order Magelonida
Long, slender bodies divided into 2 regions; prostomium flattened with 2 long palpi arising from the ventral surface at the junction of the prostomium and next segment; capillary and hooded hooks; single genus, *Magelona.*

Order Psammodrilida
Prostomium and peristome lack appendages; parapodia in mid-region long and supported by aciculae; minute; 2 genera, *Psammodrilus* and *Psammodriloides,* each with a single species.

Order Ctenodrilida
No prostomial appendages; no parapodial lobes; setae arise directly from body wall; all setae simple; minute; examples of genera: *Ctenodrilus, Zeppilina.*

Order Cirratulida
Sedentary; prostomium pointed and without appendages; 1 or more pairs of tentacular cirri arising from dorsal surface of anterior segments; gills, if present, long and slender, inserted above parapodia; size, minute to 20 cm; examples of genera: *Cirratulus, Cirriformia.*

Order Cossurida
No prostomial appendages; a single median tentacle arises from the dorsum between segments 2 and 6; parapodia biramous with weakly developed lobes; all setae simple; size, usually less than 2 cm; *Cossura.*

Order Opheliida
No prostomial appendages; body with limited number of segments; setae all simple; size, 1 to 10 cm; examples of genera: *Ophelia, Polyophthalmus, Scalibregma.*

Order Capitellida
No prostomial appendages; 1 or 2 anterior segments without setae; parapodia biramous; setae all simple; size, 1 to 20 or more cm; examples of genera: *Capitella, Notomastus, Arenicola, Maldane, Axiothella.*

Order Flabelligerida
Sedentary; setae of anterior segments directed forward to form a cephalic (head) cage; prostomium and peristome retractile, with 2 palpi and retractile branchiae; size, 1 to 10 cm; examples of genera: *Flabelligera, Stylariodes.*

Order Sternaspida
Sedentary; anterior setae short and thick; posterior end with ventral shield bearing radiating setae and anal branchiae; size, 3 cm; genera include *Sternaspis.*

Order Oweniida
Sedentary; anterior end with or without divided lobed membrane; anterior segments long; dwelling tube mucoid, coated with sand or shell fragments; size, 0.2 to 10 cm; genera include *Owenia.*

Order Terebellida
Sedentary; head concealed by filamentous tentacles; branchiae, simple or branched, arising from dorsal surface of anterior end; body divided into thorax and abdomen; tube of mucoid substance to which sediment adheres; size, 1 to 40 cm; examples of genera: *Amphicteis, Terebella, Pista, Thelepus.*

Order Sabellida (feather dusters)
Sedentary; head concealed with featherlike filamentous branchiae; body divided into thorax and abdomen; tube mucoid or calcareous; size, minute to 50 cm; examples of genera: *Sabella, Eudistylia, Serpula, Hydroides.*

Order Archiannelida
Minute, primitive, with ciliated epidermis; prostomium small, with or without appendages; parapodia absent; septa reduced or absent; size, minute. Contains 4 groups of poorly known species considered separate orders by some (Nerillida, Dinophilida, Polygordiida, Protodrilida); genera include *Dinophilus* and *Polygordius.*

Order Myzostomida
Body disk-shaped or oval without external segmentation; external or internal commensals or parasites of echinoderms, especially crinoids; size, minute to 1 cm; genera include *Myzostoma.*

Order Poeobiida
Body saclike without external segmentation; anterior end with circle of tentacles; 2 internal septa only polychaete characteristics; pelagic; single genus, *Poeobius.*

Class Oligochaeta
Primarily freshwater or terrestrial with setae arising directly from body wall; name of group refers to the few setae per segment; head and body appendages generally lacking; hermaphroditic, with testes located anteriorly to ovaries; gonoduct system complex; seminal receptacle used to store sperm; reproduction by copulation, with fertilized eggs laid in a cocoon secreted by clitellum; development direct, without larval stages; about 3,250 living species.

Order Lumbriculida (earthworms)
Male gonopores several segments behind segments containing the testes or, when 2 pairs of testes are present, in more posterior segment; size, minute to 30–40 cm; examples of genera: *Haplotaxis, Eisenia, Lumbricus* (earthworm), *Megascolides.*

Order Moniligastrida
Male gonopores, 1 or 2 pairs on segment posterior to testes; clitellum 1 cell thick; 4 pairs of setae per segment; size, minute to 3 m; examples of genera: *Moniligaster, Drawida.*

Order Haplotaxida
Chiefly aquatic worms; male gonopores in segment immediately behind testes; seminal receptacle at or near segment containing testes; size, minute to 1–3 cm; examples of genera: *Nais, Tubifex* (sludge worm).

Class Hirudinea (leeches)
Primarily freshwater, but also terrestrial and marine forms; small sucker at anterior end, large sucker at posterior end; fixed number of body segments at 34; body cavity filled with connective tissue; hermaphroditic, with fertilized eggs laid in a cocoon secreted by clitellum; development direct without larval stages; about 300 living species.

Order Branchiobdellida
Head modified as sucker with fingerlike projections; posterior segments also modified to form sucker; body with 14 to 15 segments; all species parasitic or commensal on freshwater crayfish; size, minute; *Stephanodrilus.*

Order Acanthobdellida
Primitive group; setae present on 5 anterior segments; no anterior sucker; parasitic on fish in Lake Baikal (U.S.S.R.); size, small; genera include *Acanthobdella.*

Order Rhynchobdellida
An eversible pharynx used to penetrate host tissue; jawless; distinct blood vessels contain colourless blood; freshwater or marine inhabitants; size, minute to 20 cm; examples of genera: *Glossisphonia, Piscicola, Pontobdella.*

Order Arhynchobdellida
Pharynx with 3 toothed jaws or none, noneversible; terrestrial or freshwater; bloodsuckers or carnivorous; size, minute to 20 cm; examples of genera: *Hirudo, Haemopis, Erpobdella.*

Critical appraisal. Most authors accept the annelids as having three major classes: Polychaeta, Oligochaeta, and Hirudinea. Older systems would place the polychaetes and oligochaetes under the class Chaetopoda because both groups possess setae. Other systems would join the oligochaetes and leeches in a single class, called the Clitellata, because both groups possess a clitellum. The Archiannelida and Myzostomida treated as polychaete orders in the classification system above have been considered as separate classes in the past. The Branchiobdellida are considered an order of Hirudinea, but they have been considered as a separate class in the past or as an order of Oligochaeta. Depending upon the author, annelids could consist of as many as six classes.

Orders were frequently ignored in the past, especially with the polychaetes, but authors have come to greater agreement as to the placement of families within orders. Placement of annelids within orders has been difficult because of the tremendous diversity in structure and specialization in habitat, especially in the polychaetes.

The class Polychaeta has also been divided into subclasses or orders, the Errantiata (free-moving forms) and Sedentaria (sedentary, or tube-dwelling, forms), based on the mode of living. This arrangement, while convenient, is not based on morphology and is not generally used. The classification system given above lists 23 orders (Archiannelida was considered as one order in the classification above, while other schemes divide the group into four orders). There are approximately 87 known families of polychaetes.

The oligochaetes are divided into three orders based especially on the placement of the male gonopores. There are approximately 43 families in the class. The families of leeches, organized into the four orders outlined above, are generally accepted.

BIBLIOGRAPHY. General overviews of annelids can be found in R. PHILLIPS DALES, *Annelids*, 2nd ed. (1967), a semipopular account; D.T. ANDERSON, *Embryology and Phylogeny in Annelids and Arthropods* (1973); P.J. MILL (ed.), *Physiology of Annelids* (1978), a review; ROBERT D. BARNES, *Invertebrate Zoology*, 4th ed. (1980), ch. 10, "The Annelids," pp. 263–341; R.O. BRINKHURST, "Evolution in the Annelida," *Canadian Journal of Zoology*, 60(5):1043–59 (1982), a summary of current scholarship; DONALD J. KLEMM (ed.), *A Guide to the Freshwater Annelida (Polychaeta, Naidid and Tubificid Oligochaeta, and Hirudinea) of North America* (1985), on ecology and taxonomy; and VICKI PEARSE *et al.*, *Living Invertebrates* (1987), ch. 16, "Annelid Body Plan," and ch. 17, "A Diversity of Annelids," pp. 387–437. For information on polychaetes, see KRISTIAN FAUCHALD, *The Polychaete Worms: Definitions and Keys to the Orders, Families, and Genera* (1977); KRISTIAN FAUCHALD and P.A. JUMARS, "The Diet of Worms: A Study of Polychaete Feeding Guilds," *Oceanography and Marine Biology*, 17:193–284 (1979); and ALBRECHT FISCHER and HANS-DIETER PFANNENSTIEL (eds.), *Polychaete Reproduction: Progress in Comparative Reproductive Biology* (1984), a collection of symposium papers. For oligochaetes, see R.O. BRINKHURST and B.G.M. JAMIESON, *Aquatic Oligochaeta of the World* (1971); C.A. EDWARDS and J.R. LOFTY, *Biology of Earthworms*, 2nd ed. (1977); and O. GIERE and O. PFANNKUCHE, "Biology and Ecology of Marine Oligochaeta: A Review," *Oceanography and Marine Biology*, 20:173–308 (1982). See also the proceedings of three international symposia on aquatic oligochaete biology: R.O. BRINKHURST and DAVID G. COOK (eds.), *Aquatic Oligochaete Biology* (1980); G. BONOMI and C. ERSÉUS (eds.), *Aquatic Oligochaeta* (1984); and R.O. BRINKHURST and R.J. DIAZ (eds.), *Aquatic Oligochaeta* (1987). For leeches, see KENNETH J. MULLER, JOHN G. NICHOLLS, and GUNTHER S. STENT (ed.), *Neurobiology of the Leech* (1981); and ROY T. SAWYER, *Leech Biology and Behaviour*, 3 vol. (1986), an extensive overview.

(D.J.R.)

Antarctica

Lying almost concentrically around the South Pole, Antarctica—the name of which means "opposite to the Arctic"—is the southernmost continent, a circumstance that has had momentous consequences for all aspects of its character. It is the fifth largest continent, covering about 5,500,000 square miles (14,200,000 square kilometres), and would be essentially circular except for the outflaring Antarctic Peninsula, which reaches toward the southern tip of South America (some 600 miles [970 kilometres] away), and for two principal embayments, the Ross Sea and the Weddell Sea. These deep embayments of the southernmost Pacific and Atlantic oceans make the continent somewhat pear shaped, dividing it into two unequal-sized parts. The larger is generally known as East Antarctica because most of it lies in east longitudes. The smaller, wholly in west longitudes, is generally called West Antarctica. East and West Antarctica are separated by the 1,900-mile-long Transantarctic Mountains. Whereas East Antarctica consists largely of a high, ice-covered plateau, West Antarctica consists of an archipelago of mountainous islands covered and bonded together by ice.

The continent is almost wholly overlain by a continental ice sheet, containing approximately 7,000,000 cubic miles (30,000,000 cubic kilometres) of ice and representing about 90 percent of the world's ice. The average thickness is about 6,500 feet (2,000 metres). Many parts of the deep embayments of the Ross and Weddell seas are covered by ice shelves, or ice sheets floating on the sea. These shelves—the Ross Ice Shelf and the Ronne and Filchner ice shelves—together with other shelves around the continental margins, constitute about 10 percent of the area of Antarctic ice. Around the Antarctic coast, shelves, glaciers, and ice sheets continually "calve," or discharge, icebergs into the seas.

Because of this vast ice, the continent supports only a primitive indigenous population of cold-adapted land plants and animals. The surrounding sea is as rich in life as the land is barren. With the decline of whaling and sealing, the only economic base in the past, Antarctica now principally exports the results of scientific investigations that lead to a better understanding of the total world environment. The present scale of scientific investigation of Antarctica began with the International Geophysical Year (IGY) in 1957–58. Although early explorations were nationalistic, leading to territorial claims, modern ones have come under the international aegis of the Antarctic Treaty. This treaty, which was an unprecedented landmark in diplomacy when it was signed in 1959 by 12 nations, preserves the continent for nonmilitary scientific pursuits.

Antarctica, the most remote and inaccessible continent, is no longer the most unknown area in the world. All of its mountain regions have been mapped and visited by teams of geologists, geophysicists, glaciologists, and biologists. Many hidden ranges and peaks are known from geophysical soundings of the Antarctic ice sheets. By using sophisticated radio-echo sounding instruments, systematic aerial surveys of the ice-buried terrains can be made, and some of these are almost as well mapped as the exposed ones.

The ice-choked and stormy seas around Antarctica long hindered exploration by wooden-hulled ships. No lands break the relentless force of the prevailing west winds as they race clockwise around the continent, dragging westerly ocean currents along beneath. The southernmost parts of the Atlantic, Pacific, and Indian oceans converge into a cold, oceanic water mass with singularly unique biologic and physical characteristics. Early penetration of this Antarctic (or Southern) Ocean, as it has been called, in the search for fur seals led in 1820 to the discovery of the continent. Icebreakers and aircraft now make access relatively easy, although still not without hazard in stormy conditions. Many tourists have visited Antarctica, and it seems likely that, at least in the short run, scenic resources have greater potential for economic development than do mineral and biologic resources.

The term Antarctic regions refers to all areas—oceanic, island, and continental—lying in the cold Antarctic climatic zone south of the Antarctic Convergence, an important boundary with little seasonal variability, where warm subtropical waters meet and mix with cold polar waters. For legal purposes of the Antarctic Treaty, the arbitrary boundary of 60° south latitude is used. The familiar map boundaries of the continent known as Antarctica, defined as the South Polar landmass and all its nonfloating grounded ice, are subject to change with future changes of climate. The continent was ice-free during most of its lengthy geologic history, and there is no reason to believe it will not become so again in the probably distant future. When it does, the inhabitants will know a continent (East Antarctica) and nearby island archipelago (West Antarctica) of about the size of Australia and Indonesia today.

This article is divided into the following sections:

Physical geography 788
- The land 788
  - Geologic record
  - Relief
  - Climate
  - Glaciers and seas
  - Plant life
  - Animal life
- Economic resources 797
  - Mineral resources
  - Biological resources
  - Other resources

History 799
- The "heroic era" of exploration 799
- From World War I to IGY 800
- IGY and the Antarctic Treaty 801
  - The development of IGY
  - The Antarctic Treaty
  - Post-IGY research

Bibliography 803

Physical geography

THE LAND

Geologic record. *Antarctica and continental drift.* The geological evolution of Antarctica has followed a course generally similar to that of the other southern continents. The earliest chapters in Antarctica's rather fragmentary record extend far back, perhaps as much as 3,000,000,000 years, into early Precambrian time. Similarity in patterns of crustal and biologic evolution in the southern continents extends up until some 150,000,000 years ago, and evolutionary courses began to diverge conspicuously by about 70,000,000 years ago, or the early Cenozoic Era. Plant and animal migration routes that had apparently freely interconnected all of the southern continents were largely cut off by the beginning of the Cenozoic. Antarctica became isolated at a time when land mammals diversified and flourished elsewhere, populating all the other continents of the world. Antarctica had long been thought to be a migratory path for marsupials moving between southern continents in early Cenozoic time. Documentation for the theory was not discovered, however, until 1982, when the

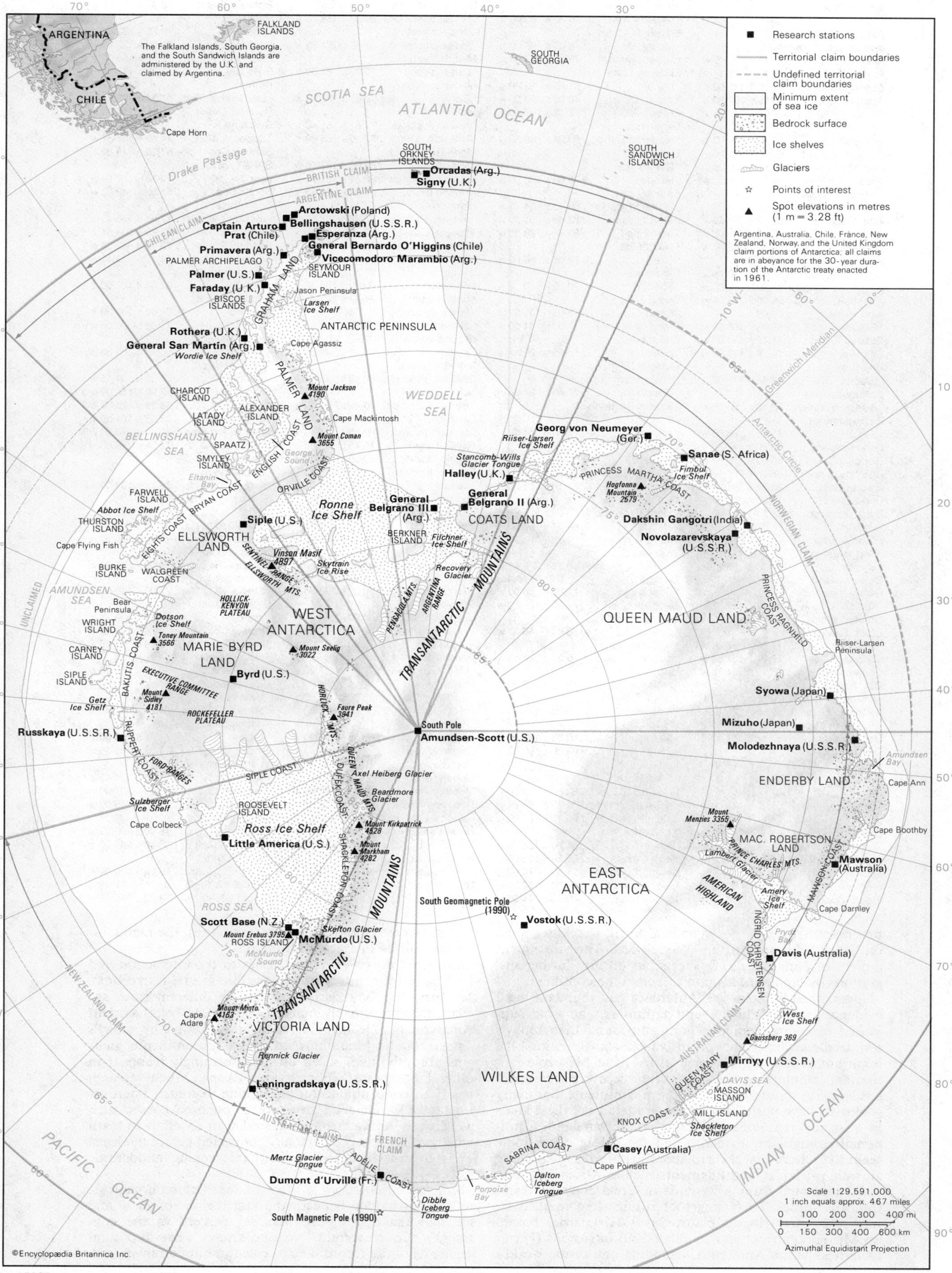

Research stations
Territorial claim boundaries
Undefined territorial claim boundaries
Minimum extent of sea ice
Bedrock surface
Ice shelves
Glaciers
Points of interest
Spot elevations in metres (1 m = 3.28 ft)
Argentina, Australia, Chile, France, New Zealand, Norway, and the United Kingdom claim portions of Antarctica; all claims are in abeyance for the 30-year duration of the Antarctic treaty enacted in 1961.
The Falkland Islands, South Georgia, and the South Sandwich Islands are administered by the U.K. and claimed by Argentina.
ARGENTINA
CHILE
FALKLAND ISLANDS
SOUTH GEORGIA
Cape Horn
SCOTIA SEA
ATLANTIC OCEAN
Drake Passage
SOUTH ORKNEY ISLANDS
SOUTH SANDWICH ISLANDS
BRITISH CLAIM
ARGENTINE CLAIM
CHILEAN CLAIM
NORWEGIAN CLAIM
AUSTRALIAN CLAIM
FRENCH CLAIM
NEW ZEALAND CLAIM
UNCLAIMED
Orcadas (Arg.)
Signy (U.K.)
Arctowski (Poland)
Captain Arturo Prat (Chile)
Bellingshausen (U.S.S.R.)
Esperanza (Arg.)
General Bernardo O'Higgins (Chile)
Vicecomodoro Marambio (Arg.)
Primavera (Arg.)
PALMER ARCHIPELAGO
SEYMOUR ISLAND
Palmer (U.S.)
Faraday (U.K.)
BISCOE ISLANDS
Jason Peninsula
Larsen Ice Shelf
GRAHAM LAND
ANTARCTIC PENINSULA
Rothera (U.K.)
General San Martín (Arg.)
Wordie Ice Shelf
Cape Agassiz
PALMER LAND
CHARCOT ISLAND
Mount Jackson 4190
LATADY ISLAND
ALEXANDER ISLAND
Cape Mackintosh
WEDDELL SEA
BELLINGSHAUSEN SEA
SPAATZ I.
Mount Coman 3655
ENGLISH COAST
George VI Sound
SMYLEY ISLAND
Eltanin Bay
ORVILLE COAST
BRYAN COAST
FARWELL ISLAND
Abbot Ice Shelf
THURSTON ISLAND
EIGHTS COAST
Ronne Ice Shelf
General Belgrano III (Arg.)
General Belgrano II (Arg.)
COATS LAND
Siple (U.S.)
ELLSWORTH LAND
BERKNER ISLAND
Filchner Ice Shelf
Cape Flying Fish
Vinson Masif 4897
SENTINEL RANGE
ELLSWORTH MTS.
Skytrain Ice Rise
BURKE ISLAND
WALGREEN COAST
Recovery Glacier
AMUNDSEN SEA
HOLLICK-KENYON PLATEAU
PENSACOLA MTS.
ARGENTINA RANGE
Bear Peninsula
Dotson Ice Shelf
WEST ANTARCTICA
WRIGHT ISLAND
Toney Mountain 3566
MARIE BYRD LAND
Mount Seelig 3022
CARNEY ISLAND
SIPLE ISLAND
Byrd (U.S.)
EXECUTIVE COMMITTEE RANGE
BAKUTIS COAST
Mount Sidley 4181
Getz Ice Shelf
ROCKEFELLER PLATEAU
HORLICK MTS.
Faure Peak 3941
Russkaya (U.S.S.R.)
RUPPERT COAST
FORD RANGES
SIPLE COAST
South Pole
Amundsen-Scott (U.S.)
QUEEN MAUD MTS.
DUFEK COAST
Axel Heiberg Glacier
Beardmore Glacier
Sulzberger Ice Shelf
ROOSEVELT ISLAND
Cape Colbeck
Ross Ice Shelf
Mount Kirkpatrick 4528
Little America (U.S.)
Mount Markham 4282
SHACKLETON COAST
ROSS SEA
Scott Base (N.Z.)
Mount Erebus 3795
ROSS ISLAND
McMurdo (U.S.)
McMurdo Sound
Skelton Glacier
TRANSANTARCTIC MOUNTAINS
Cape Adare
Mount Minto 4163
VICTORIA LAND
Rennick Glacier
Leningradskaya (U.S.S.R.)
Mertz Glacier Tongue
ADELIE COAST
Dumont d'Urville (Fr.)
South Magnetic Pole (1990)
PACIFIC OCEAN
Georg von Neumeyer (Ger.)
Riiser-Larsen Ice Shelf
Stancomb-Wills Glacier Tongue
Halley (U.K.)
Sanae (S. Africa)
Fimbul Ice Shelf
PRINCESS MARTHA COAST
Hogfonna Mountain 2579
Dakshin Gangotri (India)
Novolazarevskaya (U.S.S.R.)
QUEEN MAUD LAND
PRINCESS RAGNHILD COAST
Riiser-Larsen Peninsula
Greenwich Meridian
Antarctic Circle
Syowa (Japan)
Mizuho (Japan)
Molodezhnaya (U.S.S.R.)
Amundsen Bay
ENDERBY LAND
Cape Ann
Mount Menzies 3355
MAC. ROBERTSON LAND
Cape Boothby
PRINCE CHARLES MTS.
Lambert Glacier
Mawson (Australia)
MAWSON COAST
EAST ANTARCTICA
AMERICAN HIGHLAND
Amery Ice Shelf
Cape Darnley
South Geomagnetic Pole (1990)
Vostok (U.S.S.R.)
Prydz Bay
Davis (Australia)
INGRID CHRISTENSEN COAST
West Ice Shelf
Gaussberg 369
Mirnyy (U.S.S.R.)
QUEEN MARY COAST
DAVIS SEA
MASSON ISLAND
WILKES LAND
MILL ISLAND
Shackleton Ice Shelf
KNOX COAST
SABRINA COAST
Casey (Australia)
Cape Poinsett
Dalton Iceberg Tongue
Porpoise Bay
Dibble Iceberg Tongue
INDIAN OCEAN
Scale 1:29,591,000
1 inch equals approx. 467 miles
0 100 200 300 400 mi
0 150 300 400 600 km
Azimuthal Equidistant Projection
©Encyclopædia Britannica Inc.

MAP INDEX

Physical features and points of interest

Abbot Ice Shelf	72 45 s	96 00 w
Adare, Cape	71 17 s	170 14 E
Adélie Coast	67 00 s	139 00 E
Agassiz, Cape	68 29 s	62 56 w
Alexander Island	71 00 s	70 00 w
American Highland	72 30 s	78 00 E
Amery Ice Shelf	69 45 s	71 00 E
Amundsen Bay	66 55 s	50 00 E
Amundsen Sea	73 00 s	112 00 w
Amundsen-Scott, *research station*	90 00 s	0 00
Ann, Cape	66 10 s	51 22 E
Antarctic Peninsula	69 30 s	65 00 w
Arctowski, *research station*	62 09 s	58 28 w
Argentina Range	82 20 s	42 00 w
Atlantic Ocean	58 00 s	45 00 w
Axel Heiberg Glacier	85 25 s	163 00 w
Bakutis Coast	74 45 s	120 00 w
Bear Peninsula	74 36 s	110 50 w
Beardmore Glacier	83 45 s	171 00 E
Bellingshausen, *research station*	62 12 s	58 58 w
Bellingshausen Sea	71 00 s	85 00 w
Berkner Island	79 30 s	47 30 w
Biscoe Islands	66 00 s	66 30 w
Boothby, Cape	66 34 s	57 16 E
Bryan Coast	73 35 s	84 00 w
Burke Island	73 08 s	105 06 w
Byrd, *research station*	80 02 s	119 45 w
Captain Arturo Prat, *research station*	62 30 s	59 41 w
Carney Island	73 57 s	121 00 w
Casey, *research station*	66 17 s	110 32 E
Charcot Island	69 45 s	75 15 w
Coats Land, *region*	77 00 s	27 30 w
Colbeck, Cape	77 07 s	157 54 w
Coman, Mount	73 49 s	64 18 w
Dakshin Gangotri, *research station*	70 05 s	12 00 E
Dalton Iceberg Tongue	66 15 s	121 30 E
Darnley, Cape	67 43 s	69 30 E
Davis, *research station*	68 35 s	77 58 E
Davis Sea	66 00 s	92 00 E
Dibble Iceberg Tongue	65 30 s	135 00 E
Dotson Ice Shelf	74 24 s	112 22 w
Dufek Coast	84 30 s	179 00 w
Dumont d'Urville, *research station*	66 40 s	140 01 E
East Antarctica, *region*	80 00 s	80 00 E
Eights Coast	73 30 s	96 00 w
Ellsworth Land, *region*	75 30 s	85 00 w
Ellsworth Mountains	78 45 s	85 00 w
Eltanin Bay	73 40 s	82 00 w
Enderby Land, *region*	67 30 s	53 00 E
English Coast	73 30 s	73 00 w
Erebus, Mount	77 32 s	167 10 E
Esperanza, *research station*	63 24 s	56 59 w
Executive Committee Range	76 50 s	126 00 w
Faraday, *research station*	65 15 s	64 16 w
Farwell Island	72 49 s	91 10 w
Faure Peak	85 42 s	128 35 w
Filchner Ice Shelf	79 00 s	40 00 w
Fimbul Ice Shelf	70 30 s	0 10 w
Flying Fish, Cape	72 06 s	102 29 w
Ford Ranges	77 00 s	144 00 w
Gaussberg, *peak*	66 48 s	89 11 E
General Belgrano II, *research station*	77 46 s	34 34 w
General Belgrano III, *research station*	77 54 s	41 49 w
General Bernardo O'Higgins, *research station*	63 19 s	57 54 w
General San Martín, *research station*	68 07 s	67 08 w
Georg von Neumeyer, *research station*	70 37 s	8 22 w
George VI Sound	71 00 s	68 00 w
Getz Ice Shelf	74 15 s	125 00 w
Graham Land, *region*	66 00 s	63 30 w
Halley, *research station*	75 31 s	26 56 w
Høgfonna Mountain	72 45 s	3 33 w
Hollick-Kenyon Plateau	78 00 s	105 00 w
Horlick Mountains	85 23 s	121 00 w
Indian Ocean	63 00 s	90 00 E
Ingrid Christensen Coast	69 30 s	77 00 E
Jackson, Mount	71 23 s	63 22 w
Jason Peninsula	66 10 s	61 00 w
Kirkpatrick, Mount	84 20 s	166 25 E
Knox Coast	66 30 s	105 00 E
Lambert Glacier	71 00 s	70 00 E
Larsen Ice Shelf	67 30 s	62 30 w
Latady Island	70 45 s	74 35 w
Leningradskaya, *research station*	69 30 s	159 23 E
Little America, *research station*	78 42 s	164 05 w
Mac. Robertson Land, *region*	70 00 s	65 00 E
Mackintosh, Cape	72 53 s	60 03 w
McMurdo, *research station*	77 51 s	166 40 E
McMurdo Sound	77 30 s	165 00 E
Marie Byrd Land, *region*	80 00 s	120 00 w
Markham, Mount	82 51 s	161 21 E
Masson Island	66 08 s	96 35 E
Mawson, *research station*	67 36 s	62 52 E
Mawson Coast	67 40 s	63 30 E
Menzies, Mount	73 30 s	61 50 E
Mertz Glacier Tongue	67 10 s	145 30 E
Mill Island	65 30 s	100 40 E
Minto, Mount	71 47 s	168 45 E
Mirnyy, *research station*	66 33 s	93 01 E
Mizuho, *research station*	70 42 s	44 20 E
Molodezhnaya, *research station*	67 40 s	45 51 E
Novolazarevskaya, *research station*	70 46 s	11 50 E
Orcadas, *research station*	60 45 s	44 43 w
Orville Coast	75 45 s	65 30 w
Pacific Ocean	63 00 s	170 00 E
Palmer, *research station*	64 46 s	64 03 w
Palmer Archipelago	64 15 s	62 50 w
Palmer Land, *region*	71 30 s	65 00 w
Pensacola Mountains	83 45 s	55 00 w
Poinsett, Cape	65 46 s	113 13 E
Porpoise Bay	66 30 s	128 30 E
Primavera, *research station*	64 09 s	60 57 w
Prince Charles Mountains	72 00 s	67 00 E
Princess Martha Coast	72 00 s	7 30 w
Princess Ragnhild Coast	70 30 s	27 00 E
Prydz Bay	69 00 s	75 00 E
Queen Mary Coast	66 45 s	96 00 E
Queen Maud Land, *region*	72 30 s	12 00 E
Queen Maud Mountains	86 00 s	160 00 w
Recovery Glacier	81 10 s	28 00 w
Rennick Glacier	70 30 s	160 45 E
Riiser-Larsen Ice Shelf	72 40 s	16 00 w
Riiser-Larsen Peninsula	68 55 s	34 00 E
Rockefeller Plateau	80 00 s	135 00 w
Ronne Ice Shelf	78 30 s	61 00 w
Roosevelt Island	79 25 s	162 00 w
Ross Ice Shelf	81 30 s	175 00 w
Ross Island	77 30 s	168 00 E
Ross Sea	75 00 s	175 00 w
Rothera, *research station*	67 34 s	68 08 w
Ruppert Coast	75 45 s	141 00 w
Russkaya, *research station*	74 46 s	136 51 w
Sabrina Coast	67 20 s	119 00 E
SANAE, *research station*	70 18 s	2 24 w
Scotia Sea	57 30 s	40 00 w
Scott Base, *research station*	77 51 s	166 45 E
Seelig, Mount	82 28 s	103 54 w
Sentinel Range	78 10 s	85 30 w
Seymour Island	64 17 s	56 45 w
Shackleton Coast	82 00 s	162 00 E
Shackleton Ice Shelf	66 00 s	100 00 E
Sidley, Mount	77 02 s	126 06 w
Signy, *research station*	60 43 s	45 36 w
Siple, *research station*	75 56 s	84 15 w
Siple Coast	82 00 s	155 00 w
Siple Island	73 39 s	125 00 w
Skelton Glacier	78 35 s	161 30 E
Skytrain Ice Rise	79 40 s	78 30 w
Smyley Island	72 55 s	78 00 w
South Geomagnetic Pole	79 13 s	109 00 E
South Magnetic Pole	64 50 s	139 22 E
South Pole	90 00 s	0 00
Spaatz Island	73 12 s	75 00 w
Stancomb-Wills Glacier Tongue	75 00 s	22 00 w
Sulzberger Ice Shelf	77 00 s	148 00 w
Syowa, *research station*	69 00 s	39 35 E
Thurston Island	72 06 s	99 00 w
Toney Mountain	75 48 s	115 48 w
Transantarctic Mountains	85 00 s	175 00 w
Vicecomodoro Marambio, *research station*	64 14 s	56 43 w
Victoria Land, *region*	74 15 s	163 00 E
Vinson Massif	78 35 s	85 25 w
Vostok, *research station*	78 28 s	106 48 E
Walgreen Coast	75 30 s	107 00 w
Weddell Sea	72 00 s	45 00 w
West Antarctica, *region*	79 00 s	100 00 w
West Ice Shelf	66 40 s	85 00 E
Wilkes Land, *region*	69 00 s	120 00 E
Wordie Ice Shelf	69 15 s	67 45 w
Wright Island	74 03 s	116 45 w

first mammal remains, a marsupial fossil, were discovered on Seymour Island in the Weddell Sea. The subsequent growth of Antarctica's ice sheets cut off any further migrations by land animals into or across the continent.

Now bathed by polar ice, Antarctica has abundant fossil evidence that its climate and terrain at one time supported far more populous flora and fauna than today's few seedless plants and primitive insects. Remains of a luxuriant extinct flora, as well as fossils of Mesozoic reptiles and amphibians that have been discovered, compare so closely to those of other southern continents that many geologists have postulated former contiguity of these lands in a single, giant continent called Gondwanaland. Continental stratigraphic evidence and the dating of seafloors seem to indicate that the supercontinent broke apart along Jurassic rift faults, and fragments such as Africa and Australia separated from Antarctica in Cretaceous and early Cenozoic times. Early stages of rifting were marked by immense outpourings of plateau lavas (Kirkpatrick Basalt, on Mt. Kirkpatrick) and by related sill intrusions (Ferrar Dolerites) across Antarctica, including one of the world's largest layered gabbroic igneous complexes, the Dufek intrusion, in the Pensacola Mountains.

Modern theory ties mobile zones to the interaction and jostling of immense crustal plates (see PLATE TECTONICS). Modern plate boundaries may be far different from ancient ones presumably marked by old fold belts. Ancient Antarctic mobile belts, such as are followed by today's Transantarctic Mountains, terminate at continental margins abruptly, as if sliced off, and seemingly reappear in other lands across young ocean basins. Much research has been concentrated on attempting to match intercontinentally the detailed structure of opposed coasts, such as between Antarctica and Australia, in an effort to learn whether they had been actually connected before the latest cycle of crustal spreading from intervening midoceanic ridges.

Structural framework. Most of the Antarctic geologic record lies hidden beneath the vast regions of snow and ice that make up more than 95 percent of the continent's surface terrain. No one knows what important segments of the record lie concealed in buried ranges such

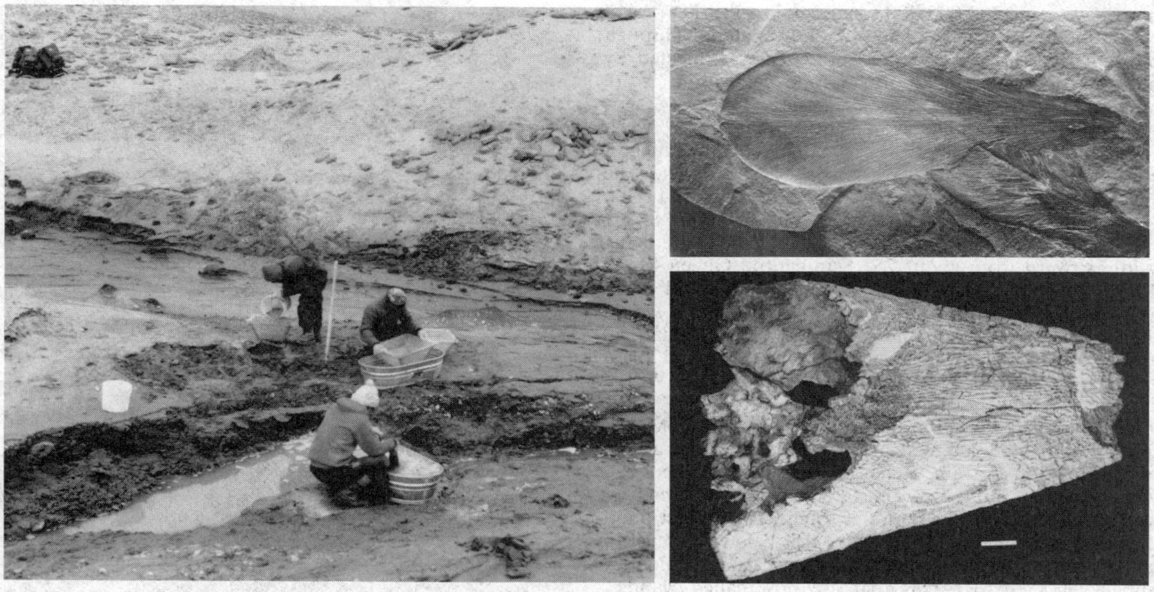

(Left) Researchers working on Seymour Island, where the fossil of a marsupial was discovered in 1982. Among the evidence of former plant and animal life on Antarctica are (top right) the fossil of a leaf, from southern Victoria Land, and (bottom right) the fossil of the skull, nearly 61 centimetres (24 inches) in length, of a capitosaurid amphibian, from the Transantarctic Mountains.

By courtesy of (left) William J. Zinsmeister, (top right) Edith L. Taylor, and (bottom right) William R. Hammer

as the Gamburtsev Mountains, the topography of which has been mapped only by seismic reflections through the great East Antarctic Ice Sheet. The extraordinarily thick cover, the extremely difficult working conditions, and the tremendous expense of mounting expeditions into remote areas have long held geologic knowledge of Antarctica far behind that of other continents. Great advances by geologists of many Antarctic Treaty nations, however, have yielded geologic maps of at least reconnaissance scale for virtually all exposed mountain areas.

From results mainly of British expeditions early in the 20th century, the concept arose that Antarctica is made up of two structural provinces—a long, stable Precambrian shield in East Antarctica and a much younger Mesozoic and Cenozoic mobile belt in West Antarctica—separated by the fault-block belt, or horst, of the Transantarctic Mountains. East and West Antarctica have come to be known respectively as the Gondwana and Andean provinces, indicating general affinities of each sector with other regions—that is, the east seems to have affinity with the Gondwana region of peninsular India, and the west seems to represent a southerly continuation of the South American Andes. As new expeditions study and restudy each range in ever-increasing detail, concepts of the geological structure are continually modified. Antarctica's structural record is now known to be more complex than that implied in the past by the simple two-fold continental subdivision.

Crustal thickness and mobility

The average thickness of the Earth's crust for both East and West Antarctica approximates that of other continents. Although it has been postulated that West Antarctica might be an oceanic island archipelago if the ice were to melt, its crustal thickness of about 20 miles indicates an absence of oceanic structure. This thickness is similar to that of coastal parts of other continents. The crust thickens sharply along the Transantarctic Mountains front, possibly a deep crustal fault system, and averages about 25 miles thick in East Antarctica. Significant earthquakes are not known along this or other faults in Antarctica, now the most seismically quiet of all continents. Seismic activity occurs chiefly along surrounding oceanic ridges, with rare minor activity associated with volcanoes of the continent or nearby islands.

The ancient crust of Antarctica must have been highly mobile and the configuration of the continent many hundreds of millions of years ago in the Precambrian far different from today's. Ancient marine and lake basins were filled with a variety of sedimentary and volcanic debris eroded from primeval lands. During mountain-building episodes these materials were complexly deformed and recrystallized deep within the crust to form, particularly in East Antarctica, great crystalline-rock complexes. At the surface, rocks were uplifted and mountains were carved by erosion as sediments filled new basins, and new folds of the Earth's crust were formed. Again and again this cycle was repeated during the evolution of Antarctica. Mobility ceased approximately 400,000,000 years ago in the Transantarctic Mountains. Between that time, in the Devonian Period, and about 160,000,000 years ago, in the Jurassic Period, a series of mainly quartzose sediments was laid down in ancient lakes and shallow seas in the sites of former mountain chains that had been carved away by erosion. Known as the Beacon Sandstone, this formation of platform sediments contains a rich record of extinct Antarctic life forms, including freshwater fish fossils in Devonian-age rocks; ancient, temperate forests of trees known as *Glossopteris* in coal deposits of Permian- and Triassic-age rocks (roughly 280,000,000 to 190,000,000 years ago); and large reptiles, such as *Lystrosaurus,* and amphibians in Triassic-age rocks. Tillites—rocks deposited by ancient glaciers—underlie Permian-age coal beds in numerous places in Antarctica just as they do in the other southern, including now tropical, continents. The widespread occurrence of glacial erratics, containing microfossils of Cretaceous and Cenozoic age, indicates the presence of rocks younger than the Beacon Sandstone under ice sheets near the Transantarctic Mountains. The youngest mountain chain in Antarctica is the southward extension of the Andes that makes up the Antarctic Peninsula, Ellsworth Land, and part of Marie Byrd Land.

Beacon Sandstone

Relief. There are two faces of the present-day continent of Antarctica. One, seen visually, consists of the exposed rock and ice-surface terrain. The other, seen only indirectly by seismic or other remote-sensing techniques, consists of the ice-buried bedrock surface. Both evolved through long and slow geological processes.

Effects of glacial erosion and deposition dominate everywhere in Antarctica, and erosional effects of running water are relatively minor. Yet, on warm summer days, rare and short-lived streams of glacial meltwater do locally exist. The evanescent Onyx River, for example, flows from Lower Wright Glacier terminus to empty into the nondrained basin of Lake Vanda near McMurdo Sound. Glacially sculptured landforms now predominate, as they must have some 300,000,000 years ago, in an earlier period of continental glaciation of all of Gondwanaland. Through most of its history, however, Antarctica was affected by more normal processes of erosion and deposition, as are other continents today.

Antarctica, with an average height estimated at between 7,000 and 8,000 feet above sea level, is the world's highest continent. (Asia, the next, averages about 3,000 feet.) The vast ice sheets of East Antarctica reach heights of 11,500 feet or more in two main centres: one at about 80° S in western Wilkes Land, the other in a belt stretching southeastward from about 75° S in central Queen Maud Land. Without its ice, however, Antarctica would probably average little more than about 1,500 feet. It would then consist of a far smaller continent (East Antarctica) and a nearby island archipelago. A vast lowland plain between 90° E and 150° E (today's Polar and Wilkes subglacial basins) would be fringed by the ranges of the Transantarctic Mountains and of the Gamburtsev Mountains, 6,500 to 13,000 feet high. The rest might be a hilly to mountainous terrain. Relief in general would be great, with elevations ranging from 16,864 feet (5,140 metres) at Vinson Massif in the Sentinel Range, the highest point in Antarctica, to more than 8,200 feet below sea level in an adjoining marine trough to the west (today's Bentley Subglacial Trench). Areas that are now called "lands," including most of Ellsworth Land and Marie Byrd Land, would be beneath the sea.

Volcanoes

Ice-scarred volcanoes, many still active, dot western Ellsworth Land, Marie Byrd Land, and sections of the coasts of the Antarctic Peninsula and Victoria Land, but principal activity is concentrated in the volcanic Scotia Arc. Only one volcano, Mt. Gaussberg (90° E), occurs along the entire coast of East Antarctica. Long dormant, Mt. Erebus, on Ross Island (see illustration), showed increased activity from the mid-1970s. Lava lakes have occasionally filled, but not overspilled, its crater, but the volcano's activity has been closely monitored because Antarctica's largest station (McMurdo Station, U.S.) lies on its lower flank. One of several violent eruptions of Deception Island, a volcanic caldera, in 1967–70, destroyed nearby British and Chilean stations. Whereas volcanoes of the Antarctic Peninsula and Scotia Arc are mineralogically similar to the volcanoes typical of the Pacific Ocean rim, the others in Antarctica are chemically like those of volcanoes along the East African Rift Valley. The differences are related to different styles of interaction between the Pacific and Antarctic crustal plates.

Climate. The unique weather and climate of Antarctica provide the basis for its familiar appellations—Home of the Blizzard and White Desert. By far the coldest continent, Antarctica has winter temperatures that range from −128.6° F (−89.2° C), the world's lowest recorded temperature, measured at Vostok Station on July 21, 1983, on the high inland ice sheet, to −76° F (−60° C) near sea level. Temperatures vary greatly from place to place, but direct measurements in most places are generally available only for summertime. Only at fixed stations operated since the IGY have year-round measurements been made. Winter temperatures rarely reach as high as 52° F (11° C) on the northern Antarctic Peninsula, which because of its maritime influences is the warmest part of the continent. Mean temperatures of the coldest months are −4° to −22° F (−20° to −30° C) on the coast, and −40° to −94° F (−40° to −70° C) in the interior, the coldest period on the polar plateau being usually in late August just before the return of the Sun. Whereas midsummer temperatures may reach as high as 59° F (15° C) on the Antarctic Peninsula, those elsewhere are usually much lower, ranging from a mean of about 32° F (0° C) on the coast to between −4° and −31° F (−20° and −35° C) in the interior. These temperatures are far lower than those of the Arctic, where monthly means range only from about 32° F in summer to −31° F in winter.

Wind chill—the cooling power of the atmosphere—is the major debilitating weather factor of Antarctic expeditions.

Winds

Fierce winds characterize most coastal regions, particularly of East Antarctica, where cold, dense air flows down the steep slopes off interior highlands. Known as katabatic winds, they are a surface flow that may be smooth if of low velocity but that may also become greatly turbulent, sweeping high any loose snow, if a critical velocity is surpassed. This turbulent air may appear suddenly and is responsible for the brief and localized Antarctic "blizzards" during which no snow actually falls and skies above are clear. During one winter at Mirny Station, gusts reached more than 110 miles per hour on seven occasions. At the Adélie Coast camp of Douglas Mawson's Australasian Antarctic Expedition (1911–14), velocities in the winter of 1912–13 averaged 40 miles per hour for 64 percent of the time. Gusts estimated at between 140 and 155 miles per hour on Dec. 9, 1960, destroyed a Beaver aircraft at Mawson Station on the MacRobertson Land coast. Winds on the polar plateau are usually light, with monthly mean velocities at the South Pole ranging from about nine miles per hour in December (summer) to 17 miles per hour in June and July (winter).

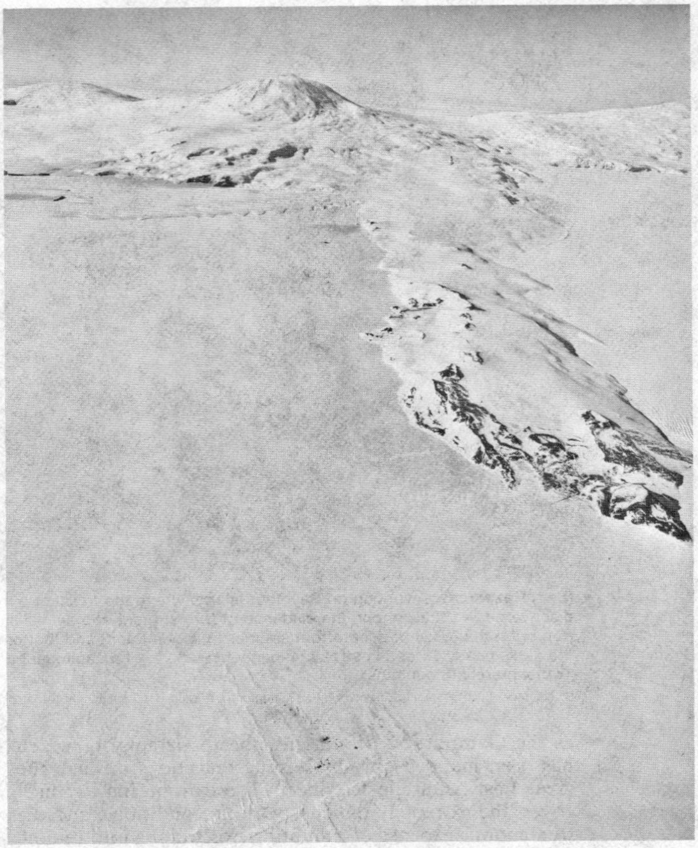

Ross Island seen across frozen McMurdo Sound. McMurdo Station is on the tip of the island at right with its aircraft runway in the foreground. The volcanic Mt. Erebus is in the upper centre.
By courtesy of the U.S. Navy

The Antarctic atmosphere, because of its low temperature, contains only about one-tenth of the water-vapour concentration found in temperate latitudes. This atmospheric water largely comes from ice-free regions of the southern oceans and is transported in the troposphere into Antarctica mostly in the 140° sector (80° E to 140° W) from Wilkes Land to Marie Byrd Land. Most of this water precipitates as snow along the continental margin. Rainfalls are almost unknown. Despite the tremendous volume of potential water stored as ice, Antarctica must be considered as one of the world's great deserts; the average precipitation (water equivalent) is only about two inches (50 millimetres) per year over the polar plateau, though considerably more, perhaps 10 times as much, falls in the coastal belt. Lacking a heavy and protective water-vapour-rich atmospheric layer, which in other areas absorbs and reradiates to Earth long-wave radiation, the Antarctic surface readily loses heat energy into space.

Many factors determine Antarctica's climate, but the pri-

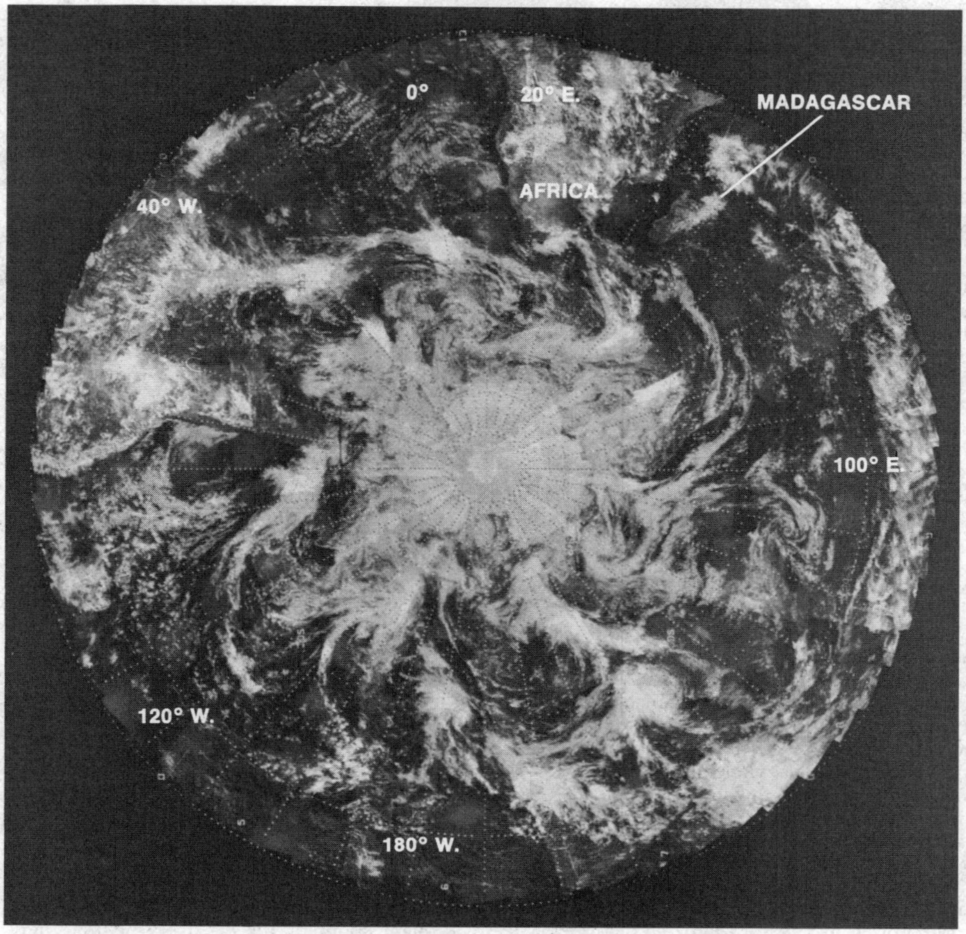

Cloud patterns around the South Pole as photographed by the U.S. satellite, ESSA 3, Jan. 28, 1967. At the top is the southern end of Africa and Madagascar.

By courtesy of the Commerce Department, National Oceanic and Atmospheric Administration, National Environmental Satellite Service, Washington, D.C.

mary one is the geometry of the Sun–Earth relationship. The 23.5° axial tilt of the Earth to its annual plane of orbit, or ecliptic, around the Sun results in long winter nights and long summer days alternating between both polar regions and causing seasonal variations in climate. On midwinter day, about June 21, the Sun's rays reach to only 23.5° (not exact, due to refraction) from the South Pole along the latitude of 66.5° S, a line familiarly known as the Antarctic Circle. Although "night" theoretically is six months long at the geographic pole, one month of this actually is a twilight period. Only a few coastal fringes lie north of the Antarctic Circle. The amount of incoming solar radiation, and thus heat, depends additionally on the incident angle of the rays and therefore decreases inversely with latitude to reach a minimum at the geographic poles. These and other factors are essentially the same for both polar regions. The reason for their great climatic difference primarily lies in their reverse distributions of land and sea: the Arctic is an ocean surrounded by land, while Antarctica is a continent surrounded by ocean. The Arctic Ocean, a climate-ameliorating heat source, has no counterpart at the South Pole, the great elevation and perpetually reflective snow cover of which instead intensify its polar climate. Moreover, during Antarctic winters, freezing of the surrounding sea effectively more than doubles the size of the continent and removes the oceanic heat source to nearly 1,800 miles from the central polar plateau.

Solar and terrestrial radiation

Outgoing terrestrial radiation greatly exceeds absorbed incoming solar radiation. This loss results in strong surface cooling, giving rise to the characteristic Antarctic temperature inversions in which temperature increases from the surface upward to about 1,000 feet above the surface. About 90 percent of the loss is replaced by atmospheric heat from lower latitudes, and the remainder by latent heat of water-vapour condensation.

Great cyclonic storms circle Antarctica in endless west-to-east procession, exchanging atmospheric heat to the continent from sources in the southern Atlantic, Pacific, and Indian oceans. Moist maritime air interacting with cold polar air makes the Antarctic Ocean in the vicinity of the Polar Front one of the world's stormiest. Few storms bring snowfalls to interior regions. With few reporting stations, weather prediction has been exceedingly difficult but is now greatly aided by satellite imagery.

A number of studies on the upper atmosphere of Antarctica have been leading toward solving problems that are worldwide in scope. Very low-frequency radio waves, called whistlers, which are generated by lightning at opposite, or conjugate, points in the Northern Hemisphere and received in Antarctica, are providing much information about the Earth's magnetosphere. Research in Antarctica has also made many contributions to knowledge of the ionosphere, geomagnetism, and solar cosmic radiation.

Glaciers and seas. *Glaciation.* Antarctica provides the best available picture of the probable appearance 20,000 years ago of northern North America under the great Laurentide Ice Sheet. Mountain glaciers, which formed on such highlands as the Sentinel Range perhaps as early as about 50,000,000 years ago, advanced down valleys to calve into the sea. Fringing ice shelves were built and later became grounded as glaciation intensified. Local ice caps developed, covering West Antarctic island groups as well as the mountain ranges of East Antarctica. The ice caps eventually coalesced into great ice sheets that tied together West and East Antarctica into the single continent that is known today. The continent has apparently been continuously glaciated since the first glaciers appeared.

Evolution of ice sheets

Causal factors leading to birth and development of these continental ice sheets and then to their decay and death are, nevertheless, still poorly understood (see ICE AND

ICE FORMATIONS). The factors are complexly interrelated. Moreover, once developed, ice sheets tend to form independent climatic patterns and thus to be self-perpetuating and eventually perhaps even self-destructing. Cold-air masses draining off Antarctic lands, for example, cool and freeze surrounding oceans in winter to form an ice pack, which reduces solar-energy input by increasing reflectivity and makes interior continental regions even more remote from sources of open oceanic heat and moisture. The East Antarctic Ice Sheet has grown to such great elevation and extent that little atmospheric moisture now nourishes its central part.

One hypothesis on the causes of continental glaciation ties periodic Northern Hemisphere ice ages, or glaciations, to periodic instability and surging of the Antarctic Ice Sheet. Instability is believed to occur when glacier buildup becomes so great as to cause pressure sufficient to melt the base of the ice sheet. Then, riding on water, the East Antarctic ice dome rapidly collapses, and, according to the hypothesis, the outflowing ice forms extensive ice shelves reaching perhaps to the Antarctic Convergence. The resulting increased reflectivity over such a large area would then cool the entire Earth. Once collapsed, the ice-dome base would no longer be at the pressure melting point, and the ice shelves, no longer fed, would soon disappear by calving and melting. Consequent decreased reflectivity over the Antarctic Ocean would then result in global warming and thus an interglacial period. The process could repeat itself many times.

The volume of South Polar ice must have fluctuated greatly at times since the birth of the ice sheets. Glacial erratics and glacially striated rocks on mountain summits now high above current ice-sheet levels testify to an overriding by ice at much higher levels. General lowering of levels caused some former glaciers flowing from the polar region through the Transantarctic Mountains to recede and nearly vanish, producing such spectacular "dry valleys" as the Wright, Taylor, and Victoria valleys near McMurdo Sound. Doubt has been shed on the common belief that Antarctic ice has continuously persisted since its origin by the discovery reported in 1983 of Cenozoic marine diatoms—believed to date from the Pliocene Epoch (about 7,000,000 to 2,500,000 years ago)—in glacial till of the Beardmore Glacier area. The diatoms are believed to have been scoured from young sedimentary deposits of basins in East Antarctica and incorporated into deposits of glaciers moving through the Transantarctic Mountains. If so, Antarctica may have been free or nearly free of ice as recently as about 3,000,000 years ago, when the diatom-bearing beds were deposited in a marine seaway; and the Antarctic Ice Sheet may have undergone deglaciations perhaps similar to those that occurred later during interglacial stages in the Northern Hemisphere. Evidence of former higher sea levels found in many areas of the Earth seems to support the hypothesis that such deglaciation occurred. If Antarctica's ice were to melt today, for example, global sea levels would probably rise about 150 to 200 feet.

Antarctic ice budget

The Antarctic Ice Sheet seems to be approximately in a state of equilibrium, neither increasing nor decreasing significantly according to the best estimates. Snow precipitation is offset mainly by continental ice moving seaward by three mechanisms—ice-shelf flow, ice-stream flow, and sheet flow. The greatest volume loss is by calving from shelves, particularly the Ross, Ronne, Filchner, and Amery ice shelves. Much loss may also occur by bottom melting from ice shelves, but its importance is controversial and some glaciologists believe ice shelves actually gain mass by bottom accretion.

The Antarctic ice sheets are, in effect, settling tanks for atmospheric constituents and extraterrestrial material. They contain a record of climates and ancient atmospheres, of global volcanic activity, and of cosmic-particle bombardment extending back for thousands of years. Upper layers of ice, for instance, record the effects of high-latitude pollution by industrial wastes and of fallout of radioactive strontium (strontium-90) from the testing of nuclear weapons. This record in ice has been studied in cores from deep holes drilled through the ice sheet.

The "heroic era" of exploration in Antarctica in the early 20th century has given way to an "extraterrestrial era" there, brought about by the discovery of thousands of meteorites on its ice sheets. Only five fragments had been found by 1969, but since then more than 7,000 have been recovered by Japanese and American scientists. In 1969 Japanese glaciologists began finding great numbers on blue-ice fields near their Syowa station, and an early recognition of the process by which the fragments are concentrated soon led to profitable searches in other areas, especially in the Transantarctic Mountains. Most specimens appear to have landed on Antarctic ice sheets between about 700,000 and 10,000 years ago. They accumulated and were carried by ice to areas near mountains where the ancient ice ablated and meteorites became concentrated on the surface. Probably only 1 to 10 percent of the finds, however, represent discrete meteorite falls. Most meteorites are believed to be from asteroids and a few from comets, but one found in 1982 is the first that is thought to be of lunar origin. Its composition and structure are like those of the soils on the Moon's surface collected by U.S. astronauts on the Apollo missions, and it seems likely that the meteorite came from material spalled off the Moon by some giant lunar impact and impelled into an Earth-crossing orbit. The discovery lends support to the hypothesis that meteorites from a rare class called shergottites had a similar origin from Mars; a few of the small handful known are from Antarctica. Antarctic ice is thus a rich storehouse of extraterrestrial samples. The cold, dry environment preserves them in a pristine state for great lengths of time, and they thus can provide much information about their parental bodies not available from meteorites collected elsewhere on Earth.

Meteorite discoveries

Wright Valley, a dry valley in the McMurdo Sound area.
By courtesy of the U.S. Navy

The surrounding seas. The seas around Antarctica have often been likened to the moat around a fortress. The turbulent "Roaring Forties" and "Furious Fifties" lie in a circumpolar storm track and a westerly oceanic current zone commonly called the West Wind Drift, or Circumpolar Current. The three major oceans, Atlantic, Pacific, and Indian, are bounded on the south by Antarctic shores. Warm, subtropical surface currents move southward in the

Ocean currents and convergences

western parts of these oceans and then turn eastward upon meeting the Circumpolar Current. The warm water meets and partly mixes with cold Antarctic water, called the Antarctic Surface Water, to form a mass with intermediate characteristics called Subantarctic Surface Water. Mixing occurs in a shallow but broad zone of approximately 10° latitude lying south of the Subtropical Convergence (at about 40° S) and north of the Antarctic Convergence (between about 50° and 60° S). The Subtropical Convergence generally defines the northern limits of a water mass having so many unique physical and biologic characteristics that it is often given a separate name, the Antarctic, or sometimes the Southern, Ocean; it contains about 10 percent of the global ocean volume.

The two convergences are well defined and important oceanic boundary zones that profoundly affect climates, marine life, bottom sedimentation, and ice-pack and iceberg drift. They are easily identified by rapid changes in temperature and salinity. Antarctic waters are less saline than tropical waters because of their lower temperatures and lesser evaporational concentration of dissolved salts. When surface waters move southward from the Subtropical Convergence zone into the subantarctic climatic belt, their temperatures drop by as much as about 9° to 16° F (5° to 9° C). In crossing the Antarctic Convergence, from the subantarctic into the Antarctic climatic zone, surface-water temperature drops further, lowering from about 46° to 39° F (8° to 4° C) in summer, and from about 37° to 34° F (3° to 1° C) in winter.

Whereas the pattern of surface currents, controlled largely by the Earth's rotation, winds, water-density differences, and the geometry of basins, is relatively well understood, that of deeper water masses is more complex and less well known. North-flowing Antarctic Surface Water sinks to about 3,000 feet beneath warmer Subantarctic Surface Water along the Antarctic Convergence to become the Subantarctic Intermediate Water. This water mass, as well as the cold Antarctic Bottom Water, spreads far north beyond the Equator to exchange with waters of the Northern Hemisphere. The movement of the Antarctic Bottom Water is identifiable in the Atlantic as far north as the Bermuda Rise. Currents near the continent result in a circumferential belt of surface-water divergence accompanied by upwelling of deeper water masses.

Two forms of floating ice masses build out around the continent: (1) glacier-fed semipermanent ice shelves, some of enormous size, such as the Ross Ice Shelf, and (2) an annually frozen and melted ice pack that in winter reaches to about 56° S in the Atlantic and 64° S in the Pacific. Antarctica has been called the pulsating continent because of the annual buildup and retreat of its secondary ice-fronted coastline. Pushed by winds and currents, the ice pack is in continual motion. This movement is westward in the coastal belt of the East Wind Drift at the continent edge and eastward (further north) at the belt of the West Wind Drift. Icebergs—calved fragments of glaciers and ice shelves—reach a northern limit at about the Subtropical Convergence. With an annual areal variation about six times as great as that for the Arctic ice pack, the Antarctic pack doubtless plays a far greater role in varying heat exchange between ocean and atmosphere and thus probably in altering global weather patterns. Long-term synoptic studies, now aided by satellite imagery, have been searching for long-period changes in the Antarctic ice-pack regimen and the possible relation of these changes to global climate changes.

By courtesy of the U.S. Navy

U.S. Navy icebreakers cutting a path through floating sea ice near Little America.

Deep-ocean drilling

As part of the Deep Sea Drilling Project conducted from 1968 to 1983 by the U.S. government, the drilling ship *Glomar Challenger* undertook several cruises of Antarctic and subantarctic waters to gather and study materials on and below the ocean floor. Expeditions included one between Australia and the Ross Sea (1972–73); one in the area south of New Zealand (1973); one from southern Chile to the Bellingshausen Sea (1974); and two in the Drake Passage and Falkland Islands area (1974 and 1979–80). Among the ship's most significant findings were hydrocarbons discovered in Tertiary sediments in the Ross Sea and rocks carried by icebergs from Antarctica found in late Oligocene sediments at numerous locations. Researchers inferred from these ice-borne debris that Antarctica was glaciated at least 25,000,000 years ago. A second long-term project that includes exploration of Antarctic waters, the Ocean Drilling Program, began operations in 1985.

Plant life. The cold-desert climate of Antarctica supports only an impoverished community of cold-tolerant land plants that are capable of surviving lengthy winter periods of total or near-total darkness during which photosynthesis cannot take place. Growth must occur in short summer bursts lasting only a few days, a few weeks, or a month or two, depending upon such diverse factors as latitude, seasonal snowpacks, elevation, topographic orientation, wind, and moisture, in both the substrate and the atmosphere. Moisture is the most important single variable and is provided mainly by atmospheric water vapour and by local melt supplies from fallen snow, drift snow, and permafrost. Stream runoff is exceedingly rare. Extreme cold, high winds, and aridity inhibit growth even in summer in most areas. There are, however, certain areas at high latitude and high elevation that have local microclimates formed by differential solar heating of dark surfaces, and these areas are able to support life. The importance of such microclimates was demonstrated by the second Byrd Antarctic Expedition (1933–35), which found that lichens in Marie Byrd Land grow preferentially on darker-coloured heat-absorbing rock.

Antarctic plants total about 800 species, of which 350 are lichens. Lichens, although slow growing, are particularly well adapted to Antarctic survival. They can endure lengthy high-stress periods in dormancy and almost instantly become photosynthetic when conditions improve. Bryophytes (mosses and liverworts), totaling about 100 species, predominate in maritime regions, but mosses can grow nearly everywhere that lichens grow. Liverworts are reported only from coastal and maritime regions. Numerous species of molds, yeasts, and other fungi, as well as freshwater algae and bacteria, complete the listing of Antarctic plants. These forms are extremely widespread and are reported as far as 87° S latitude. In addition, Antarctic seas are highly productive in plankton plant life, particularly in near-shore, nutrient-rich zones of upwelling. Diatoms, a type of algae, are especially abundant.

Although soils are essentially not of humic type, they commonly are not sterile either, in that they may contain such microorganisms as bacteria or a variety of blue-green algae. The blue-green algae *Nostoc* locally contribute minor organic compounds to soils.

Today's barren Antarctic landscape little resembles ancient Paleozoic and Mesozoic ones with their far greater floral displays. Antarctic glaciation, probably beginning 50,000,000 years ago, forced the northward migration of all vascular plants (ferns, conifers, and flowering plants). Only nonwoody forms have again populated subantarctic regions and have scarcely repenetrated the Antarctic zone.

Plant life in the subantarctic

In contrast to Antarctica, lying south of the Antarctic Convergence, the islands north of the Convergence in the subantarctic botanical zone—including the South Georgia, Crozet, Kerguelen, and Macquarie islands—are characterized by an abundance of vascular plants of many species, at least 50 being identified on South Georgia alone. Thus, whereas plants reproducing by spores are characteristic of Antarctica, seed plants chiefly characterize subantarctic regions.

Humans have greatly influenced the natural ecosystem in many Antarctic and subantarctic regions. A number of alien species of vascular plants near whaling stations have been introduced, and doubtless many alien microorganisms exist near all Antarctic stations. Alien herbivores, chiefly sheep and rabbits, have decimated plant communities on many subantarctic islands. Rabbits have exterminated the native cabbage *Pringlea antiscorbutica* over wide areas on Kerguelen, and sheep have decimated tussock communities on South Georgia.

Animal life. *Land fauna.* The native land fauna is wholly invertebrate. Apparently climatically less tolerant and less easily dispersed, the fauna follows plant colonization of newly deglaciated regions and therefore is not as widely distributed. The Antarctic microfauna includes heliozoans, rotifers, tardigrades, nematodes, and ciliate protozoans. The protozoans dominate soil and freshwater communities. The terrestrial macrofauna consists entirely of arthropods, many species being parasitic on birds and seals. The principal arthropod groups represented include Acarina (mites), Mallophaga (biting lice), Collembola (springtails), Anoplura (sucking lice), Diptera (midges), and Siphonaptera (fleas). Two species of beetles, probably alien, are known from islands near the Antarctic Peninsula. The dominant free-living forms, mites and springtails, live under stones and are associated with spore-reproducing plants.

Birds. About 45 species of birds live south of the Antarctic Convergence, but only three—the emperor penguin, Antarctic petrel, and South Polar (McCormick's) skua—breed exclusively on the continent or on nearby islands. An absence of mammalian land predators and the rich offshore food supply make Antarctic coasts a haven for immense seabird rookeries. Penguins, of the order Sphenisciformes, symbolize this polar region, though they live on seacoasts throughout the Southern Hemisphere. Of the 18 living species (of which two may only be subspecies), only the Adélie and emperor live along the Antarctic coastline. The habitats of five other polar species—king, chinstrap, gentoo, rockhopper, and macaroni—extend only as far south as the northern Antarctic Peninsula and subantarctic islands. The evolution of these flightless birds has been traced to the late Eocene Epoch, about 40,000,000 years ago, using fossils found on Seymour Island, off the northern tip of the Antarctic Peninsula, and at a few other places. The largest modern penguin, the emperor, standing between three and four feet in height, would be dwarfed by some of its extinct New Zealand and Seymour Island relatives, the fossil bones of which indicate that they reached heights up to five feet seven inches. Some authorities believe that penguins may have a shared ancestry with other birds of Antarctica, capable of flight, from the order Procellariiformes. Birds of that order, mainly species of petrels but also a few of albatrosses, make up more than half of the Antarctic and subantarctic breeding species. Other birds of the region include species of cormorants, pintails, gulls, terns, sheathbills, and pipits.

Penguins

By courtesy of A.B. Ford

Adélie penguins at Cape Royds rookery on Rose Island. In the background is Mt. Erebus.

Banding and recovery studies show that some Antarctic birds travel throughout the world. One giant petrel caught alive at Fremantle, Australia, had been banded as a nestling only two months previously in the South Orkney Islands. In that time span, it had learned to fly and had traveled some 10,000 miles, about halfway around the world. Rare sightings of skuas and petrels far in the continental interior, even near the South Pole, suggest that these powerful birds may occasionally cross the continent. Experiments show that Antarctic birds, including the flightless penguin, have strong homing instincts and excellent navigational capability; they apparently have a highly developed Sun-azimuth orientation system and biological clock mechanism that functions even with the Sun remaining continuously high. Adélie penguins released as far as 1,900 miles from their nests, for example, are known to have returned within a year. The mechanism fails to explain, however, how emperor penguins living south of the Antarctic Circle in winter can navigate during the long polar night.

Feeding habits of birds

Feeding habits vary widely from species to species. Most depend on the abundantly provisioned larder of the sea. The seabirds feed mainly on crustacea, fish, and squid, mostly at the surface or, in the case of cormorants and penguins, at depths of up to about 150 feet. Shore birds forage for mollusks, echinoderms, and littoral crustacea. Sheathbills, the southern black-backed gull, giant petrels, and skuas feed occasionally, as allowed, on other birds' unguarded eggs. The voracious skua and giant petrel are even known to attack the young or weak of other species, particularly penguins. Low aircraft overflights of rookeries are now prohibited because frightened adults leave chicks and nests undefended from predators.

Dependent upon seafood, most birds leave the continent each autumn and follow Antarctica's "secondary" coastline as the ice pack builds northward. The emperor penguins, however, are unique exceptions and remain behind as solitary guardians (other than humans) of the continent through the long winter night. The emperors, once thought rare, are now estimated to number more than 1,000,000 in about 25 known colonies. They congregate in close-packed hordes, females each autumn laying a single egg that their mates incubate by carrying on their broad feet beneath a warm fold of abdominal skin. Whereas other penguins build pebble nests for summer use, the emperors, without nests, have uniquely adapted to violent winter conditions in which nest maintenance would be impossible in the driving snows of Antarctic blizzards.

Sea life. The prolific zooplankton of Antarctic waters feed on the copious phytoplankton and, in turn, form the basic diet of whales, seals, fish, squid, and seabirds. The Antarctic waters, because of their upwelled nutrients, are more than seven times as productive as subantarctic waters. The most important organism in the higher food chain is the small, shrimplike krill, *Euphausia superba,* only an inch or two in length when mature. But for their habit of congregating in vast, dense schools, they would have little food value for the large whales and seals. Their densities are great, however, and a whale, with built-in nets of baleen and hairlike fibres, can strain out meals of a ton or more in a few minutes. During the three to four months spent in Antarctic waters, the original population of baleen whales alone could consume an estimated

Krill

150,000,000 tons of krill. Animals on the sea bottom of the near-shore zone include the sessile hydrozoans, corals, sponges, and bryozoans, as well as the foraging, crablike pycnogonids and isopods, the annelid worm polychaeta, echinoids, starfish, and a variety of crustaceans and mollusks. Winter and anchor ice, however, keep the sublittoral zone relatively barren to about 50 feet in depth.

Fishes

Of the nearly 20,000 kinds of modern fish, no more than about 100 are known from seas south of the Antarctic Convergence. Nearly three-fourths of the 90 or so sea-bottom species belong to the superfamily Notothenioidea, the Antarctic perches. At sea bottom there are also the Zoarcidae, or eel-pouts; the Liparidae, or sea snails; the Macrouridae, or rat-tailed fishes; and the Gadidae, or codlike fishes. Rare nonbony types in the Antarctic zone include hagfish and skates. Many species of deep-sea fish are known south of the Antarctic Convergence, but only three, a barracuda and two lantern fishes, seem to be confined to this zone. Antarctic fishes are well adapted to the cold waters; the bottom fish are highly endemic, 90 percent of the species being found nowhere else. This supports other biologic and geologic evidence that Antarctica has been isolated for a very long time.

Antarctic native mammals are all marine and include seals (pinnipeds), porpoises, dolphins, and whales (cetaceans).

Seals

Only one otariid, or fur seal, breeds south of the Antarctic Convergence; four species of phocids, or true seals—the gregarious Weddell seal, the ubiquitous crabeater seal, the solitary and aggressively carnivorous leopard seal, and the rarely seen Ross seal—breed almost exclusively in the Antarctic zone, and another, the southern elephant seal, breeds near the Convergence at South Georgia, Kerguelen, and Macquarie islands. The sea lion, an otariid, is plentiful in the Falkland Islands but probably never ventures into the cold Antarctic waters. The fur seal and the elephant seal are now regenerating after near extinction: the former have been estimated to number about 30,000 or more and the latter about 700,000. Weddell seals are thought to number about 500,000, the crab-eater about 5,000,000 to 6,000,000, and the Ross seals about 50,000. Weddell seals are unique in being able to survive under fast ice, even in winter, by maintaining open breathing holes with their teeth. The leopard seal, armed with powerful jaws and huge canines, is one of the few predators of adult penguins. A number of mummified seal carcasses, chiefly crab-eaters, have been found at distances of nearly 30 miles from the sea and elevations up to about 3,000 feet in the McMurdo dry valleys. Finding no food in such inland wanderings, the crab-eaters eventually died, and their leathery carcasses were preserved by the coldness and aridity of the climate.

E.E. Gless

Ross seal at Cape Hallett.

Whales

Whales and their cetacean relatives, porpoises and dolphins, range widely from Arctic to Antarctic waters and are found in all oceans and seas. A number of species range to, but generally not across, the Antarctic Convergence and so are considered only peripheral Antarctic types. Among the fish- and squid-eating toothed whales, or odontocetes, are a few peripheral Antarctic porpoises and dolphins and the pilot whale. More typical of Antarctic waters are the killer whale, sperm whale, and rare bottle-nosed, or beaked, whale. Seven species of baleen, or whalebone, whales also inhabit Antarctic waters, subsisting on the plentiful krill; these include the southern right whale, humpback whale, and four kinds of rorqual—the blue whale, the fin whale, the sei whale, and the lesser rorqual, or minke. The pygmy right whale is endemic to Antarctic and subantarctic waters. The killer whale, one of the most intelligent of marine animals, hunts in packs and feeds on larger animals, such as fish, penguins and other aquatic birds, seals, dolphins, and other whales. Despite its name, there have been no authenticated accounts of attacks on humans near Antarctica. Excessive slaughter in the past has drastically decimated stocks of the larger whales, particularly the giant blue whales. Near extinction, the blue whales have been protected by international agreement.

Alien mammals that now reside semipermanently in Antarctic and subantarctic regions include sheep, rabbits, dogs, cats, rats, mice, and human beings. Effects on local ecosystems are great, from pollution of station areas by human wastes to erosion from overgrazing by sheep and to decimation of bird populations by dogs and cats and of whale and fur-seal stocks by humans. Even so, Antarctica remains by far the least contaminated land on Earth. Under the Antarctic Treaty, it is designated as a special conservation area, and many former human activities have been prohibited in an attempt to preserve the natural ecological system of the unique environment.

Conservation

ECONOMIC RESOURCES

Antarctica, it has been suggested, may have become a continent for science because it was useful for nothing else. Certainly, the great success of the Antarctic Treaty and of the political experiment in international cooperation is in no small way attributable to the fact that exploitable resources have not been found. Articles of the treaty do not exclude economic activities, but neither do they set up jurisdictional procedures in the event that any are undertaken (see below *History*).

Increasing economic pressures have forced mineral and petroleum exploration into more and more remote regions as resources have gradually become depleted in other, more accessible lands. It is likely that market and technological conditions will make it economically feasible to carry the search to Antarctica and its continental shelves. The political volatility of the resource question, especially the problems of rights of ownership and development, has prompted proposals that range from sharing any found mineral wealth equally among nations to establishing the continent as a world park; it is understood that any significant mineral discovery will provide a severe test for the Antarctic Treaty.

Most early Antarctic expeditions through the 19th century were directly or indirectly of economic incentive. For some, it was the search for new trading routes; for others, it meant the opening of new fur-sealing grounds; still others saw a possibility of mineral riches. The exploitation of natural resources has centred in the subantarctic and Antarctic seas, and virtually none has yet occurred on the continent. In one analysis of resource potentials, "Antarctic natural resources" were defined as "any natural materials or characteristics (in the Antarctic region) of significance to man." By this broad definition, the term includes not only biologic and mineral resources but also the land itself, water, ice, climate, and space for living and working, recreation, and storage. "Economic" resources are those that can be used or exported at a cost that is less than their value. Any attempted appraisal must therefore

Economics of resource development

be continually reevaluated in terms of current market values, logistical costs, and technological developments. Few known Antarctic resources have any economic importance in terms of present-day estimates of these factors. The factors are complexly interrelated and difficult to assess for the present, let alone the future. For example, technological advances that could allow development in Antarctica might instead allow development of what are considered marginally economic resources in other regions. Moreover, by the time it might become feasible to develop an Antarctic resource, such as petroleum, other suppliers for the market might be found, such as, in this case, fusion reactors or solar or geothermal energy, which would greatly change cost factors.

Mineral resources. The geology of Antarctica is known sufficiently well to allow rather certain prediction of the existence of a variety of mineral deposits, some probably large. The fact that none of significant size, besides coal in the Transantarctic Mountains and iron near the Prince Charles Mountains of East Antarctica, is known to exist is largely the result of inadequate sampling. With the amount of ice-free terrain in Antarctica estimated at somewhere between 1 and 5 percent, the probability is practically nil that a potential ore body would be exposed. Moreover, whereas generations of prospectors have combed temperate and even Arctic mountains, Antarctic mountains have been visited mostly by reconnaissance parties since the IGY.

By courtesy of the U.S. Geological Survey

Exposed stratified rock of the Beacon Group in the Pensacola Mountains near the South Pole. Flat-lying Permian siltstone and coal measures are capped by Jurassic diabase sill.

Parallels between Antarctica and other continents

The high degree of certainty that mineral deposits do exist is based on the close geological similarities that have been observed between areas of Antarctica and of mineral-rich provinces of South America, South Africa, and Australia and on the consensus that has been reached on the configuration of the Gondwanaland landmass during Mesozoic times. The gold-producing Witwatersrand beds of South Africa may correspond to the terranes of western Queen Maud Land. The young mountain belt of the copper-rich South American Andes continues southward, looping through the Scotia Arc into the Antarctic Peninsula and probably beyond into Ellsworth Land. The mostly ice-covered areas of Wilkes Land may parallel the gold-producing greenstone belts and platinum-bearing intrusions of southwestern Australia. The Dufek intrusion, an immense layered gabbroic complex in the northern Pensacola Mountains, is geologically similar to, though much younger than, the Bushveld complex of South Africa, which is a leading producer of platinum-group metals, chromium, and other resources. Mineral occurrences have been found in some of these Antarctic areas, including antimony, chromium, copper, gold, lead, molybdenum, tin, uranium, and zinc. None approaches a grade or size warranting economic interest. Also noneconomic are the very large deposits of coal and sedimentary iron. Because of the high costs of polar operations, few conceivable resources—excepting those with high unit value such as platinum, gold, and perhaps diamonds—have any likelihood for exploitation.

Offshore petroleum resources

Offshore resources of petroleum, however, are a different matter. The finding of gaseous hydrocarbons in cores drilled in the Ross Sea by the *Glomar Challenger* in 1973 aroused considerable international interest. Cruises of the U.S. research vessel *Eltanin* had by then made a number of reconnaissance geophysical studies investigating the nature of the Antarctic continental margin. Since the late 1970s oceanographic research ships of many nations, including those of France, West Germany, Japan, and the United States, have undertaken detailed studies of the structure of the continental margin, using the sophisticated geophysical techniques of seismic reflection and gravity and magnetic surveys. Thicknesses of sedimentary rock needed for sizable petroleum accumulations may occur in continental-margin areas of the Ross, Amundsen, Bellingshausen, and Weddell seas and perhaps near the Amery Ice Shelf; and some may also exist in inland basins covered by continental ice, particularly in West Antarctica. It seems unlikely, however, that fields of a size needed for exploitation are present. If they should be found, any petroleum extraction would be difficult but not impossible in the offshore areas, as technologies have been developed for drilling for and recovering petroleum in Arctic regions. Drill ships and platforms would be more severely affected by iceberg drift and moving ice packs than in the Arctic. Icebergs are commonly far larger than those in the Arctic and have deeper keels; they scour the seafloor at deeper levels and would be more likely to damage seafloor installations such as wellheads, pipelines, and mooring systems. These problems, even though great, are far fewer than those that would be encountered in developing inland mineral resources of any kind. Thus, although petroleum is generally considered to be the most likely prospect for exploitation in Antarctica, there is little potential for its development before reserves are consumed from more accessible areas throughout the world.

Biological resources. Resources of the sea first attracted men to Antarctica and provided the only basis for commercial activity in this region for many years. Commercial fur sealing began about 1766 in the Falkland Islands and rapidly spread to all subantarctic islands in the zeal to supply the wealthy markets of Europe and China. Immense profits were made, but the toll was equally immense. Early accounts relate that millions of skins were taken from the Falklands during the mid-1780s. Within a century, however, the herds of fur seals had disappeared. Elephant seals were then hunted for their oil, and as their numbers dwindled the sealers turned to whaling. During the 20th century herds of some whale species (notably blue, fin, and sei) were largely driven from Antarctic waters, but commercial whaling was not effectively curtailed until catch quotas were imposed in the 1970s and 1980s. Although populations of many species of seals and whales have been regenerating, it appears unlikely that they will again become an exploitable resource.

Sealing and whaling

Commercial fishing, although little developed before 1970, has been rising in significance since then, especially with the increased use of factory ships, which can catch and process large quantities of fish. Catches of one species of Antarctic cod (*Notothenia rossii*) have been as high as 400,000 tons, prompting concerns about overfishing in Antarctic waters. Interest in fishing for Antarctic krill has also been growing. An almost unfathomable abundance of krill lives in the nutrient-rich coastal waters of Antarctica and the subantarctic islands. Predators (sea mammals, fish, and birds) take an enormous quantity of them annually, but their numbers are so great that there has been some activity, notably by the Soviet Union, toward establishing a krill-based fishing and processing industry.

Other resources. A rich imagination can see many possible uses of Antarctica and its materials. The continental ice sheet contains nearly 90 percent of the world's glacial ice—a huge potential supply of fresh water—but any economic value is precluded by delivery costs. Antarctica has been proposed as a long-term deep-freeze storage site for grain and other foods, but calculations show that such usage cannot be economic, because of excessive shipping, handling, and investment costs. The Antarctic Treaty prevents the continent from being used as a site for radioactive-waste disposal and storage. Antarctica and its nearby islands could play an important role in wartime, particularly in the Scotia Sea region and Drake Passage, for control of interocean shipping. In 1940–41, for example, German commerce raiders made considerable use of Kerguelen Island for this purpose. The Antarctic Treaty rules out military use, however, and the increasing capability of long-range aircraft, rocketry, and satellite surveillance and reentry decreases the possible military importance of Antarctica.

Tourism

Antarctica contains abundant scenic resources, and these have been increasingly exploited since the late 1950s. The tourist industry began in a modest way in January and February 1958, with tours to the Antarctic Peninsula area arranged by the Argentine Naval Transport Command. Since January 1966, yearly tourist ships have plied Antarctic coastal waters, stopping here and there for visits at scientific stations and at penguin rookeries. The number of visits by cruise ships has increased, and in the mid-1970s sightseeing flights by commercial airliners were inaugurated. Polar visionaries see an all-weather landing strip for wheeled jet aircraft at Marble Point near McMurdo Sound; one or more hotels nearby, perhaps in one of the McMurdo dry valleys and served by helicopter from the jet runway; and possibly even a centre for skiing and mountaineering. With such facilities, they believe, greatly increased numbers of tourists could be brought to the continent, and costs would be decreased accordingly. Many other problems, though, would be raised, including methods of sewage and waste disposal that would not affect highly sensitive local ecosystems; ways to ensure that Antarctic flora and fauna are not disturbed; provisions for search and rescue facilities; and a system for handling the civil and criminal cases that would inevitably arise.

History

A great many nations, large and small, played important roles in the discovery and exploration of Antarctica. Who first saw the continent is clouded in controversy. The Russian expedition leader Fabian Gottlieb von Bellingshausen, the Englishman Edward Bransfield, and the American Nathaniel Palmer all claim first sightings in 1820: Bellingshausen sighted a shelf edge of continental ice on January 20; two days later Bransfield caught sight of land that the British later considered to be a mainland part of the Antarctic Peninsula; and on November 18 Palmer unequivocally saw the mainland-peninsula side of Orleans Strait.

Terra Australis

In about AD 650, however, long before European geographers of the Middle Ages and the Renaissance were to conjecture about the mythical Terra Australis, Maori legend tells of a New Zealand Polynesian war canoe, under the command of one Ui-te-Rangiora, that sailed at least as far south as the frozen ocean. The legendary vast size of the continent shrank to nearly its present one when in 1772–75 the Englishman James Cook circumnavigated the globe in high southern latitude, proving that Terra Australis, if it existed at all, lay somewhere beyond the ice packs that he discovered between about 60° and 70° S.

The period from the 1760s to about 1900 was one dominated by exploitation of Antarctic and subantarctic seas, particularly along Scotia Ridge. Sealing vessels of many nations, principally U.S. and British but including Argentine, Australian, South African, New Zealand, German, and Norwegian, participated in hunting that eventually led to near extinction of the southern fur seal. Many also hunted whales, but the less profitable whaling industry climaxed following World War I after the decline of sealing. Among the few geographic and scientific expeditions that stand out during this period are those of Bellingshausen, commanding the Russian ships *Vostok* and *Mirny,* in the first close-in circumnavigation of Antarctica in 1819–21; Bransfield, on a British expedition charting part of the Antarctic Peninsula in 1819–20; Dumont d'Urville, on a French expedition in 1837–40, when Adélie Land was discovered and claimed for France; Charles Wilkes, on a U.S. naval expedition in 1838–42 that explored a large section of the East Antarctic coast; and James Clark Ross, on a British expedition in 1839–43 that discovered the Ross Sea and Ross Ice Barrier (now called Ross Ice Shelf) as well as the coast of Victoria Land.

THE "HEROIC ERA" OF EXPLORATION

The expeditions of Scott and Shackleton

During the first two decades of the 20th century, commonly called the "heroic era" of Antarctic exploration, great advances were made in not only geographic but also scientific knowledge of the continent. The Englishmen Robert F. Scott and Ernest Henry Shackleton led three expeditions between 1901 and 1913, pioneering routes into the interior and making important geological, glaciological, and meteorological discoveries that provided a firm foundation for present-day scientific programs. This era was preceded by two events that proved the feasibility of Antarctic overwintering: (1) the Belgian ship *Belgica,* under command of Capt. Adrien de Gerlache, became the first vessel to winter in Antarctic waters when, from March 1898 to March 1899, it was trapped and drifted in pack ice of the Bellingshausen Sea; and (2) a scientific party under Carsten E. Borchgrevink spent the next winter camped at Cape Adare, for the first planned overwintering on the continent.

Sledge probes deep into the interior were made by Scott on the British National Antarctic *Discovery* Expedition (1901–04) and by Shackleton on the British Antarctic *Nimrod* Expedition (1907–09) from base camps on Ross Island. New southing records were set by Scott, in company with Shackleton and E.A. Wilson, who reached 82°17′ S on Ross Ice Shelf on Dec. 30, 1902, and by Shackleton in a party of five, which reached 88°23′ S, a point within 97 miles of the pole, on Jan. 9, 1909. The aerial age in Antarctica was presaged by Scott in 1902, who went aloft in a captive balloon for aerial reconnaissance, and the mechanical age by Shackleton in 1908, who used an automobile at Cape Royds, Ross Island. The experimental use of hardy Manchurian ponies and the pioneering of a route up the great Beardmore Glacier to the polar plateau by Shackleton paved the way for the epic sledging trip of Scott in 1911–12 to the South Pole.

Discovery of the Antarctic poles

National and personal prestige in attaining the Earth's poles, as well as territorial acquisition and scientific inquiry, provided strong motivation for polar exploration in the early 1900s. The south magnetic pole, the point of vertical orientation of a magnetic dip needle, which was predicted by the German physicist Carl Friedrich Gauss to lie at 66° S, 146° E, inspired the unsuccessful quest, in about 1840, of the seafarers Wilkes, d'Urville, and Ross (Ross had earlier discovered the north magnetic pole). The point was later reached, on Jan. 16, 1909, at 72°25′ S, 155°16′ E, on the high ice plateau of Victoria Land by T.W.E. David and Douglas Mawson on a sledge journey from Cape Royds. The pole has migrated more than 550 miles since then to its present location near the Adélie Land coast. The South Pole of the Earth's rotation was the unattained goal of Shackleton in 1908–09 but was eventually reached on Dec. 14, 1911, by Roald Amundsen of the Norwegian Antarctic Expedition of 1910–12 and, a month later, on Jan. 17, 1912, by Scott of the British Antarctic *Terra Nova* Expedition of 1910–13. Whereas Amundsen's party of skiers and dog teams, using the Axel Heiberg Glacier route, arrived back at Framheim Station at Bay of Whales with little difficulty, Scott's man-hauling polar party—Scott, E.A. Wilson, H.R. Bowers, L.E.G. Oates, and Edgar Evans—using the Beardmore Glacier route, perished during a blizzard on the Ross Ice Shelf on the return march.

Shackleton's ship the *Endurance* caught in an ice pack in the Weddell Sea off Coats Land during his Imperial Trans-Antarctic Expedition, 1914.
By courtesy of the Royal Geographical Society; photograph, Underwood and Underwood, New York

Two other related discoveries were accomplished during the IGY. The south geomagnetic pole, the theoretical pole of the Earth's magnetic field, on the East Antarctic Ice Sheet at 78°28′ S, 106°48′ E, was reached by a Soviet IGY tractor traverse on Dec. 16, 1957. The pole of relative inaccessibility, the point most remote from all coasts, at 82°06′ S, 54°58′ E, was reached by a Soviet IGY tractor traverse on Dec. 14, 1958.

After Amundsen and Scott attained the South Pole, the idea that particularly haunted men's minds was that of an overland crossing of the continent. Conceived earlier by the Scotsman W.S. Bruce and the German Wilhelm Filchner to test the thought that a channel might exist connecting the Ross and Weddell seas, a trans-Antarctic expedition was finally organized in 1914 by Shackleton. His ship, the *Endurance,* was caught and crushed, however, in pack ice of the Weddell Sea, thus aborting one of the most ambitious polar expeditions hitherto planned. The idea lay dormant for several decades and came to fruition during IGY with the British Commonwealth Trans-Antarctic Expedition led by Vivian Fuchs. Using tracked vehicles and aided by aerial flights, the party left Shackleton Base on Filchner Ice Shelf on Nov. 24, 1957, and by way of the South Pole reached the New Zealand Scott Base on Ross Island on March 2, 1958. The continent was again crossed (1979–81) as part of the British Transglobe Expedition that undertook the first polar circumnavigation of the Earth.

Trans-Antarctic expeditions

FROM WORLD WAR I TO IGY

The period between World Wars I and II marks the beginning of the mechanical, particularly the aerial, age of Antarctic exploration. Wartime developments in aircraft, aerial cameras, radios, and motor transport were adapted for polar operation. On Nov. 16, 1928, the first heavier-than-air flight in Antarctica was made by the Alaskan bush pilot C.B. Eielson and George Hubert Wilkins in a wheel-equipped Lockheed Vega monoplane. This flight was quickly followed by the better-equipped, aircraft-supported expeditions of the American naval officer Richard E. Byrd (1928–30, 1933–35, 1939–41, and 1946–47), in which progressively greater use was made of ski-planes and aerial photography. Byrd, on Nov. 29, 1929, was first to fly over the South Pole (after having flown over the North Pole in 1926). His fourth expedition, called "Operation High Jump," in the summer of 1946–47, was the most massive sea and air exploratory assault hitherto attempted in Antarctica and involved 13 ships, including two seaplane tenders and an aircraft carrier, and a total of 25 airplanes. Ship-based aircraft returned with 49,000 photographs that, together with those taken by land-based aircraft, covered about 60 percent of the Antarctic coast, nearly one-fourth of which had been previously unseen. Innovations by Byrd included the use of an autogiro in 1933–34 and six helicopters in 1946–47. Meanwhile, the courageous flight of Lincoln Ellsworth, an American, and Herbert Hollick-Kenyon, a Canadian pilot, across uncharted lands and icefields on the first aerial crossing of the continent from Nov. 23 to Dec. 5, 1935, clearly demonstrated the feasibility of aircraft landings and takeoffs for inland exploration. These early aerial operations and the extensive use of ship-based seaplanes in Norwegian explorations of coastal Queen Maud Land during the 1930s were forerunners of present-day aerial programs.

The Byrd expeditions

The early discoveries led to a few controversies not only for territorial claims but also in geographical nomenclature. The struggle for national influence was especially acute in the slender peninsular landmass south of Scotia Sea that became known as O'Higgins Land (Tierra O'Higgins) to Chileans and San Martin Land (Tierra San Martín) to Argentines, named for national heroes who helped in gaining independence from Spain. To the English it was known as Graham Land, for a former first lord of the admiralty, and to Americans as Palmer Peninsula, for the sealer and explorer Nathaniel Palmer. By interna-

National rivalries

Territorial Claims in Antarctica

country	sector	date of claim
Norway (Queen Maud Land)	20°W–45°E	January 14, 1939, by Norwegian Order in Council (also claimed Bouvet Island on January 23, 1928, and Peter I Island on May 1, 1931)
Australia (Australian Antarctic Territory)	45°E–136°E, 142°E–160°E	February 7, 1933, by British Order in Council; and June 13, 1933, by Australian Antarctic Territory Acceptance Act
France (Adélie Land)	136°E–142°E	April 1, 1938, by official decree (placed under Governor of Madagascar in 1924)
New Zealand (Ross Dependency)	160°E–150°W	July 30, 1923, by British Order in Council
Chile (Antarctic Peninsula)	90°W–53°W	November 6, 1940, by official decree
Great Britain (British Antarctic Territory)	80°W–20°W	July 21, 1908
Argentina (Antarctic Peninsula)	74°W–25°W	1942

tional agreement, the region is now known simply as the Antarctic Peninsula, Graham Land its northern half and Palmer Land its southern half.

The first half of the 20th century is the colonial period in the history of Antarctica. Between 1908 and 1942, seven nations decreed sovereignty over pie-shaped sectors of the continent. Many nations—including the United States, the Soviet Union, Japan, Sweden, Belgium, and Germany—carried out Antarctic exploration without lodging formal territorial claims, even though claims may have been announced by some of their exploratory parties. The U.S. government, for example, has never taken up the claims made in 1929 by Richard Byrd's expedition in the Ford Ranges of Marie Byrd Land (an area presently unclaimed), nor those made by Lincoln Ellsworth on aerial landings on Nov. 23, 1935, in Ellsworth Land (an area now claimed by Chile) and on Jan. 11, 1939, in the American Highland near Amery Ice Shelf of East Antarctica (an area now claimed by Australia). The German Antarctic Expedition of 1939 aerially photographed an extensive segment of Princess Astrid and Princess Martha coasts of western Queen Maud Land and, dropping metal swastikas over the region, claimed it for the Hitler government (the area is now claimed by Norway). Other claims were transferred, such as that made in 1841 by James Ross, who, after discovering and naming the coastal Ross Sea region after Queen Victoria, claimed it for the British crown; the area was later transferred to, and is now claimed by, New Zealand.

After the French claim of Adélie Land caused Americans to demand retaliatory action, the United States' official position was announced in 1924 by the Secretary of State, Charles Evans Hughes:

> It is the opinion of this Department that the discovery of lands unknown to civilization, even when coupled with a formal taking of possession, does not support a valid claim of sovereignty, unless the discovery is followed by an actual settlement of the discovered country.

This policy has been reiterated many times since.

The conflicting claims of Britain, Argentina, and Chile

Few combative activities have marred the history of Antarctica. World War II brushed the continent lightly, only in that its nearby seas were used by Nazi commerce raiders. The threat of increased activity, however, prompted British warships to keep the northern Antarctic Peninsula under surveillance. On one visit to Deception Island in January 1943, it was discovered that Argentine visitors had been there the year before, leaving a brass cylinder with notice of claim to the peninsular region. The British obliterated the Argentine signs, hoisted the Union Jack, posted a notice of crown ownership, and returned the cylinder to the Argentine government. Reaction was swift. In London, growing concern that the territory might possibly be lost and that a pro-German Argentine government might control both sides of the vital Drake Passage linking Atlantic and Pacific sea routes resulted in a secret military plan, code-named "Operation Tabarin," to establish a base on Deception Island for closer watch. When the British returned to the island in February 1944, they found their earlier sign gone and an Argentine flag painted in its place. This they soon replaced with their own flag, and their base was established to back up the British claims to the region. Several other stations were built, and, with the conclusion of the war, the United Kingdom decided to maintain a continued presence in Antarctica.

Argentina and Chile both were stimulated to increase activities to back up their claims to the Antarctic Peninsula as a result of the British occupancy. (Chile had expressed a claim in 1940.) The Argentines had maintained a weather station in the South Orkney Islands continuously since 1903, and after 1947 they and the Chileans constructed bases at several sites. With the coming of the U.S. Ronne Antarctic Research Expedition (RARE) in 1947–48 to the old U.S. Antarctic Service East Base camp on Marguerite Bay, the peninsula protagonists—British, Argentine, and Chilean—became concerned that the United States might rejuvenate its claims. Any antagonism was soon overcome, and the Americans and British joined forces for an arduous sledging journey down the east side of the peninsula.

Military violence has flared on two occasions in the region and in both instances has involved Argentina and the United Kingdom. The first incident took place in 1952, when Argentine navy small-arms fire chased a British meteorological party that had landed at Hope Bay (at the northern end of the Antarctic Peninsula) back to its ship. The matter was resolved when the Argentine government agreed not to interfere with the party. The second, much more serious confrontation took place in 1982 in the Falkland Islands, a British colony that is also claimed by Argentina (called the Islas Malvinas by the Argentines). Argentine forces invaded the Falklands and South Georgia Island in early April. The British responded by sending a military task force, reoccupying the islands, and forcing the Argentines to surrender on June 14.

Claims by the 1950s

By the mid-1950s, many nations had active Antarctic interests, some commercial and some scientific but generally political. In 1947–48, Australia had established stations on Heard and Macquarie islands and in 1954 built Mawson Station on the mainland coast of MacRobertson Land as a basis for its vast territorial claim. South Africans raised their flag over Prince Edward and Marion islands. France established permanent bases by 1953 in the Kerguelen and Crozet islands and surveyed much of the Adélie Land coast. In 1955, with icebreaker aid, Argentina established General Belgrano Station on the Filchner Ice Shelf. A profusion of British, Chilean, and Argentine bases had been built in such proximity to one another on the peninsula and nearby islands that their purpose seemed more for intelligence activities than for science. The international Norwegian-British-Swedish Expedition of 1949–52 carried out extensive explorations from Maudheim Base on the Queen Maud Land coast in the territory claimed in 1939 by Norway. The United States had shown little interest in Antarctica since the Ronne expedition and the U.S. naval "Operation Windmill," both in 1947–48 (the latter expedition was to obtain ground checks on the aerial photography of the previous season's "Operation High Jump"), but it continued its policy of nonrecognition of any claims. The Soviet Union had shown little interest, other than whaling, in Antarctica since Bellingshausen's pioneer voyage. On June 7, 1950, however, the Soviet government sent a memorandum to other interested governments intimating that it could not recognize any decisions on the regime for Antarctica taken without its participation. Such was the political climate on the continent during the organizational years for the coming International Geophysical Year of 1957–58.

IGY AND THE ANTARCTIC TREATY

The importance of coordinating polar science efforts was recognized in 1879 by the International Polar Commission meeting in Hamburg, Ger., and thus the 11 participating nations organized the First International Polar Year of 1882–83. Most work was planned for the better known Arctic, and, of the four geomagnetic and meteorologic stations scheduled for Antarctic regions, only the German station on South Georgia materialized. The decision was made at that time to organize similar programs every 50 years. In 1932–33 the Second International Polar Year took place, with 34 nations participating, but no expeditions were mounted to Antarctica.

International Council of Scientific Unions

The development of IGY. The idea for more frequent programs was born in 1950, when it was proposed that scientists take advantage of increasing technological developments, interest in polar regions, and, not the least, the maximum sunspot activity expected in 1957–58. (The earlier, second polar year was a year of sunspot minimum.) The idea quickly germinated and grew: a formalized version was adopted by the International Council of Scientific Unions (ICSU), and in 1952 ICSU appointed a committee that was to become known as the Comité Spécial de l'Année Géophysique Internationale (CSAGI) to coordinate IGY planning. Plans widened to include the scientific study of the whole Earth, and eventually 67 nations showed interest in joining. Plans were laid for simultaneous observations, at all angles, of the Sun, weather, the aurora, the magnetic field, the ionosphere, and cosmic rays. Whereas in the first polar year observations were confined to ground level and in the second to

Snow-cat traverse party near the Dufek Massif in Ronne Ice Shelf during the International Geophysical Year (IGY), 1958.
By courtesy of the National Academy of Sciences

about 33,000 feet by balloon, during IGY satellites were to be launched by the United States and the Soviet Union for exploration of space. Several international data centres were established to collect all observations and make them freely available for analysis to scientists of any nation.

Two programs, outer space and Antarctica, were especially emphasized at an ICSU committee meeting in Rome in 1954. Antarctica was emphasized because very few geophysical studies had yet been made on the continent, because the south geomagnetic pole focuses auroral and cosmic-ray activity in the Southern Hemisphere, and because on the eve of IGY almost half the continent had not yet even been seen by humans. The First Antarctic Conference was held in Paris in July 1955 to coordinate plans for expeditions, the advance parties of which were soon to set sail for the continent. Early tensions, due in part to overlapping political claims on the continent, were relaxed by the conference president's statement that overall aims were to be entirely scientific. Plans were laid for extensive explorations: 12 nations were to establish more than 50 overwintering stations on the continent and subantarctic islands; the first regular aircraft flights to the continent were to be inaugurated (by the United States); massive tractor traverses were to be run in order to establish inland stations in West Antarctica (Byrd Station for the United States), at the south geomagnetic pole (Vostok Station for the Soviet Union), and the pole of relative inaccessibility (also for the Soviet Union); and an airlift by giant cargo aircraft was to be established in order to set up a station at the South Pole itself (Amundsen–Scott Station for the United States). Several major scientific programs were scheduled for Antarctica, dealing with the aurora and airglow, cosmic rays, geomagnetism, glaciology, gravity measurement, ionospheric physics, meteorology, oceanography, and seismology. Biology and geology were not primary studies of IGY.

First Antarctic Conference

Coastal bases were established in the summer of 1955–56 and inland stations the next summer for the official opening of IGY on July 1, 1957. For 18 months, until the end of IGY on Dec. 31, 1958, a frenzy of activity not only in Antarctica but all over the world and in space resulted in a multitude of discoveries that revolutionized concepts of the Earth and its oceans, landmasses, glaciers, atmosphere, and gravitational and geomagnetic fields. Perhaps the greatest contribution was the political moratorium by the governments and the cooperative interchange between scientists of participating nations.

The Antarctic Treaty. With the ending of IGY the threat arose that the moratorium too would end, letting the carefully worked out Antarctic structure collapse into its pre-IGY chaos. In the fall of 1957 the U.S. Department of State reviewed its Antarctic policy and sounded out agreements with the 11 other governments with Antarctic interests. On May 2, 1958, Pres. Dwight D. Eisenhower issued identical notes to these governments proposing that a treaty be concluded to ensure a lasting free and peaceful status for the continent. Preparatory talks by the 12 governments were held in Washington, D.C., beginning in June 1958 and continuing for more than a year. A final conference on Antarctica convened in Washington on Oct. 15, 1959. Agreement on the final draft was reached within six weeks of negotiations, and the Antarctic Treaty was signed on Dec. 1, 1959. With final ratification by each of the 12 governments (Argentina, Australia, Belgium, Chile, France, Japan, New Zealand, Norway, South Africa, Soviet Union, United Kingdom, and United States), the treaty was enacted on June 23, 1961.

The achievement of the Antarctic Treaty was an unprecedented landmark in political diplomacy: an entire continent was reserved for free and nonpolitical scientific investigation. Article I of the treaty provides for the peaceful use of Antarctica; Article II for international cooperation and freedom of scientific investigation; Article III for free exchange of plans, scientific results, and personnel; Article IV for the nonrenunciation of prior claim rights and for the prohibition of new claims and the citation of any activities during the treaty term as a basis for past or future claims; Article V for prohibition of nuclear explosions or waste disposal; Article VI for application of the treaty to all areas south of latitude 60° S, excluding the high seas, which come under international law; Article VII for open inspection of any nation's Antarctic operations by any other nation; Article XI for reference of disputes to the International Court of Justice if they cannot be settled by peaceful negotiation or arbitration by involved parties; and Article XII for a review of the treaty after it has been in force for 30 years, if such a review is requested by any contracting party.

Contents of the Antarctic Treaty

As stated in Article IV, the many territorial claims that existed before the signing of the treaty were not abrogated by signatory nations. Multiple claims in some regions have never been resolved by international courts, and a number of countries, including the United States, recognize the validity of no claims in the absence of permanent habitation and settlements on the continent. An important provision of the treaty requires periodic meetings of representatives of signatory nations to take up occasional problems. Such meetings have agreed upon important measures for conservation of Antarctic flora and fauna and for the preservation of historic sites. The granting of consultative status within the Antarctic Treaty, permitting full participation in its operation with that of the original 12 contracting states, began in 1977 with the addition of Poland, followed by West Germany (1981), and Brazil and India (1983). Several other nations have also acceded to the treaty and have been granted partial status.

Post-IGY research. In order to continue and coordinate the international Antarctic scientific effort in the post-IGY period, ICSU in September 1957 organized the Special Committee on Antarctic Research, or SCAR. (In 1961 the word *Scientific* was substituted for *Special.*) The foundations for the committee were laid at its first meeting in The Hague in 1958. SCAR, a nonpolitical body, coordinates not only research activities in Antarctica itself but also, through ICSU, those Antarctic programs that relate to worldwide projects, such as the International Years of the Quiet Sun, the World Magnetic Survey, the Upper Mantle Project, the International Biological Program, and the International Hydrological Decade. Member nations send representatives to periodic meetings of "working groups" for the various scientific disciplines. International scientific symposia are organized by SCAR for exchange of latest research results, on a timetable depending upon progress in the discipline. The great success of the political venture of the Antarctic Treaty depends in no small way on the achievements of SCAR and of the scientific and support teams in the field and laboratory.

Special Committee on Antarctic Research

Scientific knowledge of Antarctica has increased steadily. Many important problems relating to knowledge of the entire Earth can be resolved only in the polar region. As pointed out by R.F. Scott's son Peter on an Antarctic visit in 1966, about half the topics of modern polar research could not even have been guessed at in his father's era only a half century earlier. Who at that time but a Jules Verne could have foreseen the advent of jet aircraft, turbine-powered helicopters, ski-planes, and of data-recording machines powered by radioactive isotopes and polar-orbiting satellites that automatically collect meteorologic and upper atmosphere data across the continent and transmit it to a base collection station? The polar knowledge gained in the decades during and after IGY far outweigh that learned in the preceding millennia. The incredible advances in modern Antarctic science have only been possible by adapting to polar operation the great technological advances in aircraft, oceanographic technique, and remote data acquisition and telemetry systems (unmanned weather stations, satellite surveillance, and the like).

During the period of the Antarctic Treaty there has been a steady growth in the number and nature of cooperative international scientific projects (the International Antarctic Glaciological Project, Dry Valley Drilling Project, Biomass [Biological Investigations of Antarctic Systems and Stocks], International Weddell Sea Oceanographic Expedition); of the various SCAR working groups; and, notably, of projects at the interface of astronomy and atmospheric physics (the International Magnetospheric Study, Antarctic and Southern Hemisphere Aeronomy Year).

International programs

In addition to these internationally supported programs, there have been major increases in individual national programs, mostly among those countries with territorial interests in the continent but also among countries that had not for decades (or never) supported programs there. This latter group includes Italy, which mounted its first expedition during 1975–76; Uruguay, which made its first land expedition in 1975; Poland, which established marine and land programs during 1976–77; West Germany, which first undertook large-scale operations in 1980–81; India, which began work in the early 1980s; and China, which established its first station in 1984.

Virtually all of the physical sciences are represented in the studies carried out under these programs, often having direct impact on such disparate fields as meteoritics and planetary geology, continental drift, hydrology and world water balance, meteorology and climate history, or biology and population studies. The biological programs reflect both the inherent interest of the Antarctic subjects themselves and the interest elsewhere in the world in ecology and conservation. The history of Antarctic whaling had made apparent to scientists the necessity of conserving biological populations, and the area below 60° S had long contained nature reserves of greater or lesser extent, but the Convention on the Conservation of Antarctic Marine Living Resources (1982) gave especial impulse to the principle. One of the most unexpectedly fertile areas of research in the late 20th century was that of meteoritics, brought about by the Japanese meteorite discoveries in 1969. In less than a decade, the world's supply of meteorites available for study was doubled.

The gradual recognition by scientists of the extent of potentially exploitable mineral resources on Antarctica and on the seabed surrounding it, as well as the long, tortuous process that led to the final Law of the Sea Convention (1983), has induced consultative members of the treaty to initiate discussions that would eventually permit orderly exploitation of those resources within the conserving framework of existing agreements.

BIBLIOGRAPHY

General: The most complete guide to literature about the Antarctic is the U.S. LIBRARY OF CONGRESS, *Antarctic Bibliography* (irregular), which is continued monthly in *Current Antarctic Literature.* LOUIS O. QUAM (ed.), *Research in the Antarctic* (1971); and RICHARD S. LEWIS and PHILIP M. SMITH (eds.), *Frozen Future: A Prophetic Report from Antarctica* (1973), contain review articles by leading experts of most subjects of current research, the latter also with articles on resources, economics, politics, and the outlook for the future. A general review, RAYMOND PRIESTLEY, RAYMOND J. ADIE, and G. DE Q. ROBIN (eds.), *Antarctic Research* (1964), emphasizes British scientific achievements, particularly in the Antarctic Peninsula and Scotia Arc. *Атлас Антарктики,* 2 vol. (1966–69), is a comprehensive map collection in Russian, useful especially when complemented by the translation of legend matter and explanatory text from vol. 1, published as "Atlas of Antarctica," a special issue of *Soviet Geography: Review and Translation,* vol. 8, no. 5–6 (May–June 1967). Numerous folios of the AMERICAN GEOGRAPHICAL SOCIETY OF NEW YORK, *Antarctic Map Folio Series,* (1964–75); and volumes of the *Antarctic Research Series,* published by the AMERICAN GEOPHYSICAL UNION since 1964, provide modern maps and technical accounts of all phases of the research programs. Semitechnical to nontechnical reviews of current projects and exploration are in summary articles in the *Antarctic Journal of the United States* (five times per year); a general nontechnical review is provided by H.G.R. KING, *The Antarctic* (1969). F.M. AUBURN, *Antarctic Law and Politics* (1982), provides a comprehensive discussion of the legal aspects of the Antarctic Treaty, jurisdictional problems of crime, ecology, and tourism. J.F. LOVERING and J.R.V. PRESCOTT, *Last of Lands: Antarctica* (1979), examines resources, discovery and exploration, political geography, and future prospects. BARBARA MITCHELL, *Frozen Stakes: The Future of Antarctic Minerals* (1983), presents an account of polar politics and minerals and discusses possible regimes for regulating resource development. FRANCISCO ORREGO VICUÑA (ed.), *Antarctic Resources Policy: Scientific, Legal, and Political Issues* (1983), contains reports from the first symposium of its kind, a meeting of scientists, diplomats, and international lawyers at an Antarctic scientific station.

Geology and solid-earth geophysics: RAYMOND J. ADIE (ed.), *Antarctic Geology* (1964), and *Antarctic Geology and Geophysics* (1972); CAMPBELL CRADDOCK (ed.), *Antarctic Geoscience* (1982); and R.L. OLIVER, P.R. JAMES, and J.B. JAGO (eds.), *Antarctic Earth Science* (1983), are records of international symposia describing earth-science research by many nations. J.C. BEHRENDT and C.R. BENTLEY, *Magnetic and Gravity Maps of the Antarctic* (1968); and CAMPBELL CRADDOCK and V.C. BUSHNELL (eds.), *Geologic Maps of Antarctica* (1970), provide modern maps and texts, the latter work covering most mountain regions at 1:1,000,000 scale. SCRIPPS INSTITUTION OF OCEANOGRAPHY, *Initial Reports of the Deep Sea Drilling Project,* vol. 28 (1975), 35 (1976), and 36 (1977), contain results of drilling by the *Glomar Challenger* in Antarctic waters. A discussion of meteorite recovery through knowledge of glaciology is provided by WILLIAM A. CASSIDY and LOUIS A. RANCITELLI, "Antarctic Meteorites," *American Scientist,* vol. 70, no. 2, pp. 156–164 (March–April 1982).

Climate and meteorology: MORTON J. RUBIN (ed.), *Studies in Antarctic Meteorology* (1966); S. ORVIG (ed.), *Climates of the Polar Regions* (1970); and W.S. WEYANT, *The Antarctic Atmosphere: Climatology of the Surface Environment* (1967), include topical studies and a few general review articles.

Glaciology and oceanography: MALCOLM MELLOR (ed.), *Antarctic Snow and Ice Studies* (1964); and A.P. CRARY (ed.), *Antarctic Snow and Ice Studies II* (1971), are collections mainly of topical studies of greatly varied scope; JOHN H. MERCER, *Glaciers of the Antarctic* (1967), provides a general review of Antarctica's glaciers. A.L. GORDON and R.D. GOLDBERG, *Circumpolar Characteristics of Antarctic Waters* (1970); and JOSEPH L. REID (ed.), *Antarctic Oceanology* (1971), describe features of South Polar water masses, their currents, and their interactions with subtropical and subantarctic waters, as well as of the ocean floor and sediment carpet.

Biology: ERIC HOSKING and BRYAN SAGE, *Antarctic Wildlife* (1982), is an authoritative discussion of the fauna of Antarctica. MILTON O. LEE, GEORGE A. LLANO, and I. EUGENE WALLEN (eds.), *Biology of the Antarctic Seas* (1964–), is a continuing series of technical accounts of Antarctic sea life; a more popular summary is ROBERT C. MURPHY, "The Oceanic Life of the Antarctic," *Scient. Am.*, vol. 207, no. 3, pp. 186–194 (Sept. 1962). Technical accounts of terrestrial life are in J. LINSLEY GRESSITT (ed.), *Entomology of Antarctica* (1967); and S.W. GREENE *et al.*, *Terrestrial Life of Antarctica* (1967); a nontechnical review is provided by GEORGE A. LLANO, "The Terrestrial Life of the Antarctic," *Scient. Am.*, vol. 207, no. 3, pp. 212–218 (Sept. 1962). OLIVER L. AUSTIN, JR. (ed.), *Antarctic Bird Studies* (1968), is a technical publication, whereas JOHN SPARKS and TONY SOPER, *Penguins* (1967), comprehensively but nontechnically describes the characteristic flightless birds of subantarctic and Antarctic coasts. See also GEORGE GAYLORD SIMPSON, *Penguins Past and Present, Here and There* (1976), an authoritative, popularly written account of penguins and their fossil record.

History: A complete list of expeditions through the IGY is in BRIAN ROBERTS, *Chronological List of Antarctic Expeditions* (1958). A thorough general account is in C.H. GRATTAN, *The Southwest Pacific Since 1900* (1963); an account of early U.S. explorations is in KENNETH J. BERTRAND, *Americans in Antarctica, 1775–1948* (1971). An interesting and thorough history is WALTER SULLIVAN, *Quest for a Continent* (1957). (A.B.Fo.)

Antwerp

The second-largest city in the Kingdom of Belgium and the capital of the Belgian province of the same name, Antwerp (Flemish: Antwerpen; French: Anvers) is situated on the Schelde (Scheldt) River, about 55 miles (88 kilometres) from the North Sea. The Schelde, together with the Meuse and the Rhine, forms the biggest estuary in western Europe, and Antwerp is an essential part of an enormous harbour complex, one of the greatest in the world. The harbour installations of Antwerp grew especially after World War II. For many years this expansion took place on the right bank of the Schelde only, but during the 1970s and '80s there was much development on the left bank, indicating that Antwerp's harbour facilities will ultimately extend on both banks of the river to the Dutch frontier, almost 13 miles downstream. Because Antwerp lies in the Dutch- (Flemish-) speaking part of Belgium, the city plays the role of unofficial capital of Flanders. Antwerpians generally take this role very seriously, conscious as they are of the great importance of their city in the past and present. The pride and competitive attitude thus exhibited by the residents has led to their being designated by the nickname Sinjoren (from the Spanish *señores*).

This article is divided into the following sections:

Physical and human geography 805
The landscape 805
The city site
The city layout
The character of the city 805
The people 805
The economy 806
Industry and commerce
Transportation
Administration and social conditions 806
Government
Health and education
Cultural life 806
History 807
Early settlement and growth 807
From the 15th to the 19th century 807
The modern city 807
Bibliography 807

Physical and human geography

THE LANDSCAPE

The city site. Antwerp's site on the right bank of the generally south–north-flowing Schelde is a vast, flat alluvial plain. Since 1923, however, the city's territory also has included an area on the left bank of the river. Annexation of villages on the right bank north of Antwerp in 1929 and 1958 extended the city's territory to the Dutch frontier, and further annexation in 1983 of municipalities surrounding the original city added considerably to Antwerp's area and population. The total area of contemporary Antwerp measures 75 square miles (195 square kilometres), compared with 7 square miles before the beginning of the annexations. Only a part of this territory is completely built up. The extension of the agglomeration is continuing; many outlying villages have already lost their agricultural character and have grown in population as a result of emigration from the city.

Spread of the city

The city layout. Until 1859 Antwerp lay surrounded by its 16th-century fortified walls, which were transformed in the latter half of the 19th century into broad avenues as a larger half circle of fortifications was built. This later encircling belt was replaced after World War II by another system of ring roads, which connect with a network of national and international highways. Several tunnels connect the right bank of the city with the left bank, where considerable residential and industrial development has taken place since World War II. The city centre, however, remains on the right bank; it stretches westward from the Central (railway) Station along the lively artery constituted by the Keyserlei and the Meir into the old city and thence to the terraced right bank of the Schelde.

The old city, within the arc once formed by the 16th-century fortifications, has many narrow, winding streets and old buildings. This area contains the Cathedral of Our Lady, begun in the 14th century and restored in the 19th and 20th centuries; it is one of the nation's finest Gothic buildings. The 19th-century city, with broader and substantially right-angled streets, stretches beyond the old city and merges with some of the suburban extensions annexed in 1983. A third right-bank area spreads beyond the 19th-century fortifications and is characterized by numerous modern buildings.

The largest part of Antwerp, however, is the essentially nonresidential northern seaport complex. Most of the agricultural waterside villages incorporated by the city have been eliminated to make room for expanding, if somewhat bleak, areas of docks, industrial sites, and railway yards. Six locks connect this right-bank complex with the tidal Schelde River: the first, the Kattendijk, was opened in 1860; and the newest, the 1,640-foot (500-metre) Berendrecht, was when it opened in 1988 the largest lock in the world. Left-bank port and industrial facilities have access to the Schelde via the Kallo lock.

THE CHARACTER OF THE CITY

The unique flavour of Antwerp is derived from the combination of, and tensions between, the diverse aspects of its personality: a passionate commitment to commerce goes hand in hand with an abiding interest in the life of ideas and in the arts; respect and affection for the past are juxtaposed with a fervent desire to participate fully in the present and in the future; and awareness of being a truly European and cosmopolitan city, with a resulting openness and broad curiosity, coexists with a sense of tradition and of idiosyncratic particularity, which lend an almost provincial charm to life in the city. In its centre a lively social activity is conducted on the streets and in the countless cafés. The Schelde is the veritable heart and soul of Antwerp, the raison d'être not only of Antwerp's dynamic economic life but also of its sense of identity and of the deep attachment—touchingly expressed in many literary works—that Antwerpians tend to feel for their city.

THE PEOPLE

The residents of Antwerp generally speak the local Brabantian-Antwerp dialect of Dutch. Dutch as spoken in The Netherlands and by Dutch-speaking cultured Belgians, however, is taught in the schools and is gaining ground in economic life. Although French is still much used in commercial and industrial circles, it is losing steadily as a means of expression. This does not mean that Dutch-speaking Antwerpians do not know French or other languages, for the international character of the city implies a readiness of many of its residents to understand foreign languages.

Dialects and languages

Most of the foreigners living in Antwerp are Dutch, followed by Moroccans, Spaniards, French, and Germans; there are also small numbers of British, Americans, and Israelis. Unlike the other foreigners, the Moroccan and Spanish groups are largely unskilled workers who migrated to Belgium during periods of labour scarcity after World War II. There have been associated social tensions, notably concerning discrimination in housing.

The prevalent religion in Antwerp is Roman Catholicism. There are also small groups of various Protestant churches and a sizable Jewish group of different tendencies. (By the 19th century, Antwerp already had a great number of Jewish residents, but many Jews died in World War II German concentration camps.) A large and growing part of the population is nonreligious.

THE ECONOMY

Industry and commerce. Antwerp's economic life has long been closely connected with its existence as a seaport, and as such it is inseparable from the city's favourable geographic location and from the port's facilities and functions. In the 16th century the city developed an important sugar-refining industry, in which partially worked sugarcane was brought in by ship, refined, and reexported. The first petroleum refineries were established during the 1920s and '30s, and they were soon joined by automobile assembly plants. After World War II, industry expanded at a rapid pace. Larger petroleum refineries, closely followed by petrochemical industries, were established, together with chemical plants in the 1960s, and the automotive industry was restructured on a larger scale.

The diamond industry

Other important products include photographic and electronic equipment and cut diamonds, the latter for which Antwerp is world-famous. According to legend, the first diamond was cut in Antwerp in 1476. Since the 16th century, cutting and dealing establishments have thrived in the so-called diamond quarter adjacent to the Central Station, and Antwerp has become the international centre of the diamond industry.

Antwerp's complex of harbour and industrial activities is served by many commercial agencies, commission agents, import and export firms, banking establishments, insurance companies, road-transport enterprises, and railways.

Transportation. A dense network of railway lines and highways serves Antwerp's huge port and industrial complex, and the city is a rail and road centre for Belgian and international destinations. Antwerp is also well integrated into Europe's vast inland waterway network. The airport at Deurne is important for freight and passenger flights. On the local level, public transportation in the city consists of a network of bus lines and tramways; some of the tramways have been transformed into subway lines.

ADMINISTRATION AND SOCIAL CONDITIONS

Government. Like all Belgian municipalities, Antwerp is governed by an elected city council, which in turn elects a board of aldermen, headed by a burgomaster, nominated by the king on recommendation of the council. Generally the burgomaster is a member of the elected council, but this is not obligatory. Each alderman has a specified department to manage, but decisions and resolutions are always taken by the board as a whole. Under the board of aldermen is the town clerk, the chief official to whom the different administrative services report. The city is also the residence of the government of the province of Antwerp, headed by a governor appointed by the king; a provincial council, elected every four years; and its board of deputies, who have, in regard to the province, the same task as the city aldermen. The provincial recorder is the counterpart of the town clerk. A third kind of public service is the Commission for Public Relief. The members of the commission are appointed for six years by the city council.

Health and education. The Commission for Public Relief, responsible for public health and care of the aged and orphans, manages a series of institutions, among which are several large hospitals. Together with these official establishments, there are a number of independent, mostly Roman Catholic, institutions. This duality is also found in education. Besides the different schools of all grades (*i.e.*, kindergarten, primary and secondary schools, and technical institutions) managed by the city administration (and for a small part by the state), there exists an independent, essentially Roman Catholic, network. This is also the case at the university level: both an official (state) and an independent (Jesuit) institute were founded in 1965. Higher artistic training is given in the National Higher Institute and Royal Academy for Fine Arts (1663) and the Royal Flemish Conservatory of Music (1898).

CULTURAL LIFE

Museums

It is significant, in view of Antwerp's long-standing involvement with learning and with the arts, that two of the most important figures of its cultural past are still present in the modern city through the preservation of their homes and workshops as museums: the 16th-century humanist printer Christophe Plantin (Plantin-Moretus Museum) and the 17th-century painter Peter Paul Rubens (Rubens House). Rubens' works may be seen in the Royal Museum of Fine Arts, as well as in the Cathedral of Our Lady and many other Antwerp churches, such as the Church of St. James, where the painter is buried. Rubens united Italianate traits and an attachment to the Flemish artistic tradition to create a highly personal style. His students and coworkers included the three 17th-century Antwerpians Jacob Jordaens, Anthony Van Dyck, and Frans Snyders; their works also may be seen in the Royal Museum, which houses a vast collection from the 15th to the 20th century.

A number of other museums are located in historical buildings such as the Steen, the medieval riverside castle that is home to the National Maritime Museum; the 16th-century Butchers' Hall and Brewers' Hall, both of which house historic arts and artifacts; and the Maagdenhuis (Flemish: "Maidens' House"), a 16th-century charitable foundation for needy young women, where Renaissance art and furniture may be seen. Other small museums were established by 19th-century patrician families, such as the Mayer van den Bergh Museum, which contains sculpture, furniture, and paintings, notably Pieter Bruegel's famous "Dulle Griet" (or "Mad Meg"). Museums for folklore and for ethnography are located not far from the Schelde. For modern art, there is the Museum of Contemporary Art, installed in a 1920s Art Deco grain silo in the old dock area of the port, which is close to the Provincial Museum of Photography, housed in a former warehouse built in 1911. In the Middelheim Open-Air Museum of Sculpture, the permanent collection is displayed among the trees and lawns of a public park located south of the old city, and every other year a special exhibition features works by young contemporary sculptors. Antwerp's architecture ranges from Gothic to Postmodernism.

The performing arts in the city are represented by the Royal Flemish Opera House and by the Royal Dutch Theatre, and numerous theatrical and musical performances

Eric Carle—Shostal Assoc.

The Cathedral of Our Lady, Antwerp, with a statue of Peter Paul Rubens in the foreground.

of traditional as well as modern works take place in the framework of Antwerp's monuments, such as in the courtyard of the Rubens House. The city's zoological garden is one of Europe's oldest as well as most modern zoos.

History

EARLY SETTLEMENT AND GROWTH

The site of Antwerp was probably already inhabited, as excavations on the right bank of the Schelde have proved, in Gallo-Roman times, in the 2nd and 3rd centuries AD. After the great Eurasian migrations of the 4th and 5th centuries, the region was occupied and Germanized by Franks and possibly Frisians, who gave it its present name, from the Germanic prefix *anda* ("against") and a noun derived from the verb *werpen* ("to throw"), indicating a structure—possibly a predecessor of Antwerp's 9th-century fortified castle, the Steen—erected against something or someone.

Origin of the city's name

A more picturesque etymology for the name of the city involves the story of the evil giant Druon Antigoon, who severed the hands of the river's boatmen when they refused to pay his exorbitant tolls. The Roman soldier Silvius Brabo challenged him to a fight, cut off one of his hands, and flung it into the river, not far from the site of the present Steen, thus putting an end to the giant's extortion and giving the city its name: literally, "to throw a hand." Antwerp's coat of arms consists of a fortified castle with a hand on each side; and in the Great Market, in front of the 16th-century Town Hall, the Brabo Fountain (1887) depicts the legendary event.

The city probably developed from two nuclei: a southern one called Chanelaus–Caloes–Callo and a later northern nucleus grown around the Steen, which eventually became the more important of the two. Christianity was introduced in the 7th century. In the 9th century the region became a border county of the Holy Roman Empire. In 1124 the religious centre was transferred from Chanelaus to the northern nucleus. It was around the castle, built originally as a seat for the border county, that Antwerp developed, in the course of the centuries, in more or less concentric half circles.

Situated relatively far inland on the deep right bank of the Schelde, Antwerp was predestined to become a trade and shipping centre. This was already fully the case in the 13th century. At the end of that century and the beginning of the 14th, freedom of trade was given to the English, Venetians, and Genoese by the dukes of Brabant, who had made themselves masters of the county. The city of Antwerp became one of the duchy's capital cities, together with Louvain and Brussels, in Belgium, and the city of Hertogenbosch (Bois-le-Duc), in the Netherlands. In the first quarter of the 14th century, the Antwerp fairs began to flourish. These, together with the fairs of nearby Bergen op Zoom (now in The Netherlands) became one of the foundations of Antwerp's medieval economic growth.

FROM THE 15TH TO THE 19TH CENTURY

Antwerp succeeded in the 15th century in becoming the successor of Brugge (Bruges) in Flanders, which until then had been the mercantile metropolis of western Europe. At the end of the 15th century, when nearly all the Low Countries were united under the Burgundian and Habsburg dynasties, the economic preeminence of Antwerp over Brugge is indicated by the fact that the majority of foreign merchants transferred their residence from the old Flemish town to Antwerp. It quickly became the leading commercial centre of western Europe, profiting from the beginnings of colonial trade and stimulated by the great discoveries of the Portuguese and Spaniards. Toward the mid-16th century, the population totaled nearly 100,000, whereas there had been about 20,000 people in the city at the end of the 14th century. Extensive urbanization plans were developed to lodge the increasing population, who earned their livelihood in trade, transport, and industry.

Commercial ascendancy

The port underwent its first northward extension. New industries included breweries, malt factories, and bleaching works. Together with the already established finishing works of (English) cloth, tapestry, and silk factories, the sugar refineries, and the diamond industry, they made Antwerp one of the greatest industrial centres of western Europe. Antwerp also became a financial centre: its Stock Exchange (inaugurated 1531), a model for the younger London and Amsterdam exchanges, was the scene of dramatic and momentous events, in which financial agents and bankers of the Habsburg, Tudor, and Valois monarchs played their part, together with Antwerpian, English, French, Portuguese, Italian, Spanish, and German merchants. Antwerp also became a great cultural centre: its school of painting began to flourish at the end of the 15th century; the city's printing houses became known throughout Europe; and humanism began to thrive.

State bankruptcies in Spain, Portugal, and elsewhere, together with religious troubles and ensuing wars (Antwerp early in the 16th century became a centre of Protestant activity), brought about a decline. Antwerp became involved in the revolt of the Netherlands and was taken, in 1585, by Alessandro Farnese, duke of Parma, governor general for the Spanish king. The consequences of this strife with Spain were severe: from 1585 to 1589 the population diminished from 80,000 to 42,000. The Schelde, gateway to the sea, was closed by the Dutch, maintaining their positions against King Philip II of Spain. Capital and enterprise emigrated from Antwerp, mostly northward. The economic greatness of Amsterdam in the 17th century was due in part to Antwerp emigrants and their financial support, as was the case, to a lesser extent, for Hamburg, Frankfurt am Main, and other mercantile cities.

Yet Antwerp was not reduced to the status of a nonentity. The city remained the dynamic economic centre of the Spanish (later, in the 18th century, the Austrian) Netherlands. Antwerp became a more famous art centre than ever before: this was the time of Rubens, Van Dyck, Jordaens, and other major artists. The French Revolution and the Napoleonic period, followed by Belgium's temporary union with The Netherlands (1815–30), reversed the general decline in trade of the 18th century. With the Schelde once more freely navigable (restored by the French in 1792), the attraction of Antwerp as a seaport became evident again. Population grew, and the city began to expand and modernize.

Revitalization of the port

THE MODERN CITY

Since the second half of the 19th century, the growth of Antwerp's seaport has been interrupted only by the two world wars and associated German occupations; even the economic depression of the 1930s did not affect the expansion of port traffic and facilities. Immediately after liberation in 1944, Antwerp's nearly unharmed port was instrumental in the supply of the Allied armies aiming their final blow against Nazi Germany, although bombardment by German missiles devastated the city. Since World War II Antwerp, its suburbs, and its seaport have grown apace, spurred by a commercial, industrial, and maritime boom. Port facilities, highways, and inland waterways have all been extended and improved. Some of this expansion, however, has created ecological problems, which have been investigated and addressed to some degree.

BIBLIOGRAPHY. The economic history of the city is discussed by HERMAN VAN DER WEE, *The Growth of the Antwerp Market and the European Economy (Fourteenth–Sixteenth Centuries),* 3 vol. (1963). F. SUYKENS *et al., Antwerp, a Port for All Seasons,* trans. from Flemish (1986), gives the history of the harbour. Intellectual and cultural history is detailed in several books, among them THEODORE L. DE VINNE, *The Plantin-Moretus Museum: A Printer's Paradise* (1929); JOHN J. MURRAY, *Antwerp in the Age of Plantin and Brueghel* (1970); *Antwerp's Golden Age: The Metropolis of the West in the 16th and 17th Centuries* (1973?), an exhibition catalog with a large bibliography; and LÉON VOET, *Antwerp, the Golden Age: The Rise and Glory of the Metropolis in the Sixteenth Century* (1973; originally published in Dutch, 1973). JULIEN WEVERBERGH (ed.), *Museumgids voor Antwerpen* (1988), is a directory of Antwerp's museums.

Studies of Antwerp's history include WILFRID C. ROBINSON, *Antwerp: An Historical Sketch* (1904); JERVIS WEGG, *Antwerp, 1477–1559, from the Battle of Nancy to the Treaty of Cateau Cambrésis* (1916), with a good bibliography, and *The Decline of Antwerp Under Philip of Spain* (1924, reprinted 1979); and JAN VAN ACKER, *Antwerpen: van Romeins veer tot wereldhaven* (1975). (J.V.R./T.A.Sa.)

Arabia

Arabia is the name applied to the Arabian Peninsula (Arabic: Shibh Al-Jazīrah Al-ʿArabīyah), which is located in the extreme southwestern corner of Asia. The Arabian Peninsula is bounded by the Red Sea on the west and southwest, the Gulf of Aden on the south, the Arabian Sea on the south and southeast, and the Gulf of Oman and the Persian Gulf (also called the Arabian Gulf) on the northeast. Geographically the peninsula and the Syrian Desert merge in the north with no clear line of demarcation, but the northern boundaries of Saudi Arabia and of Kuwait are generally taken as marking the limit of Arabia there.

The peninsula's total area is about 1,000,000 square miles (2,590,000 square kilometres). The length, bordering the Red Sea, is approximately 1,200 miles (1,900 kilometres) and the maximum breadth, from Yemen to Oman, 1,300 miles. The largest political division is Saudi Arabia; it is followed, in order of size, by Yemen, Oman, the United Arab Emirates, Kuwait, Qatar, and Bahrain. The island of Socotra in the Indian Ocean, about 200 miles southeast of the mainland, has strong ethnographic links to Arabia; politically it is part of Yemen.

The geographic cohesiveness of the Arabian Peninsula is reflected in a shared interior of desert and a shared exterior of coast, ports, and relatively greater opportunities for agriculture. The fact that most of the peninsula is unfavourable for settled agriculture is of enormous significance. Competition for habitable land is keen, and efficient use of land and water is crucial to the welfare of each state. Social characteristics reinforce the geophysical factors that have created a somewhat similar environment throughout the peninsula: a homogeneity among the people is seen in a degree of similarity in language, religion, culture, and political experience.

The vast majority of Arabians are ethnic Arabs, and a large number are able to trace their ancestry back through many generations living in the same area. Nearly all speak Arabic, and differences in dialects, though substantial, do not bar mutual intelligibility. Since the Islāmic expansion of the mid-7th century, most Arabians have been Muslim. Differences in sects are important locally, as in Bahrain and Yemen, but the historic commitment of the peninsula to the faith of its son, the Prophet Muḥammad, has done more to unite than divide it.

Culture has found expression in forms that are the joint inheritance of all the peoples of the Arabian Peninsula, and that inheritance is shared with Arab and Muslim societies beyond the region. Poetry, religious laws and precepts, and values associated with heroism permeated the culture of the past, but the innovations associated with Western culture have reached the entire peninsula in the 20th century and have substantially influenced art, mores, and behaviour.

Most of the states of the peninsula share common political systems. Nearly all are or have been monarchies, based in large part on principles of religious legitimacy. In the 20th century, and especially since World War II, they have aimed at gradual change in political life while trying to achieve rapid economic and social advancement. Although the peninsula's available natural resources are not distributed equally among its states—those in the south and southwest derive far less wealth from oil, for example—similar economic transformations have taken place, or are taking place, in all the societies. Urbanization, greater access to health care and education, secularization, and the settling of many nomads have changed the fabric of daily life throughout the area.

The various sections of the Arabian Peninsula have only seldom been united under one government. In the 16th century, for instance, the Ottoman Empire was able to conquer most of the coasts, but it could take neither the interior of the peninsula nor the southeast. In the 19th century Great Britain or the Ottomans controlled much of the peninsula, but the central interior almost continually remained independent under the Saudis.

Arabia, from the advent of Islām in the 7th century, maintained close ties with other parts of the Middle East through commercial, religious, social, military, and political interactions. In modern times the Arabian Peninsula's growing importance to the rest of the world, resulting primarily from the petroleum discoveries of the 20th century, led to increased contacts with the West. The blending of Middle Eastern and external influences presents both opportunities and problems for the peoples and countries of the peninsula.

Despite the political disunity of the past and the considerable variety of national experiences in the present, the Arabian Peninsula continues to share an underlying unity of environment, society, culture, and faith. (W.L.O.)

This article is divided into the following sections:

The region 809
- Physical and human geography 809
  - The land
    - Geology
    - Relief, drainage, and soils
    - Climate
    - Plant life
    - Animal life
  - The people
  - The economy
- History and cultural development 815
  - Pre-Islāmic Arabia, to the 7th century AD
    - Prehistory and archaeology
    - Pre-Islāmic Yemeni kingdoms
    - Central and northern Arabia
  - Arabia since the 7th century
    - Arabian and Islāmic expansion
    - The Umayyad and ʿAbbāsid periods
    - Mamlūk and Ottoman influence
    - Omani expansion
    - The Wahhābīs
    - The Hejaz
    - Yemen
    - The gulf states
    - World War I
    - Wahhābī-sharifian dispute
    - Saudi Arabia
    - Yemen
    - Postwar Arabia, to 1962
    - Arabia since 1962

The countries of Arabia 823
- Bahrain 823
  - Physical and human geography
  - History
- Kuwait 825
  - Physical and human geography
  - History
- Oman 828
  - Physical and human geography
  - History
- Qatar 831
  - Physical and human geography
  - History
- Saudi Arabia 833
  - Physical and human geography
  - History
- United Arab Emirates 841
  - Physical and human geography
  - History
- Yemen 843
  - Physical and human geography
  - History

Bibliography 850

THE REGION

Physical and human geography

THE LAND

Arabia may be described as a vast plateau, edged with deeply dissected escarpments on three sides and sloping gently northeastward from the Red Sea to the eastern lowlands adjoining the Persian Gulf. The peninsula's highest peak, An-Nabī Shuʿayb, at 12,008 feet (3,660 metres), is located approximately 20 miles northwest of Ṣanʿāʾ in Yemen.

Geology. The bulk of Arabia consists of two main geomorphological areas: the Arabian shield in the west; and sedimentary areas dipping away from the shield to the northeast, east, and southeast into the great basin consisting of lower Iraq, the Persian Gulf, and the eastern part of the Rubʿ al-Khali (the Empty Quarter) desert. The eastern edge of the shield curves eastward from the head of the Gulf of Aqaba, a northern extension of the Red Sea, to a point midway across the peninsula and then trends southwestward and southward to the Yemeni highlands. Extinct volcanoes overlie the shield; their eruptions, which ceased seven centuries ago, produced the broad black lava beds (*ḥārrahs*) that are characteristic of the western Arabian landscape.

The sedimentary areas, younger in age than the shield, represent the deposits of ancient seas. The surface sedimentary strata have been extensively eroded. The harder members, more resistant to erosion, now stand as westward-facing escarpments following the curve of the shield. The sedimentary province consists primarily of limestone, together with much sandstone and shale. The first deposits are early Paleozoic (395 to 570 million years old), which in eastern Arabia dip to almost six miles below the surface. In the Jurassic and Cretaceous limestone (65 to 190 million years old) oil and gas occur at depths of two miles or less. Some of the limestone strata take in rainfall at outcrops in the western highlands and carry it underground to the Persian Gulf coastal areas.

The Yemeni and Omani highlands

The Yemeni highlands are physiographically very different from those of the shield; they are not mountains but the deeply dissected edge of the Arabian plateau. From the west the formations rise abruptly from the narrow coastal plain in Yemen; they reach heights of about 10,000 to 12,000 feet above sea level, and eastward they decrease gradually in elevation. The highlands along the southern coast are basically sedimentary in origin. The Omani highlands are geologically more closely related to the Zagros Mountains of western Iran than to other mountains in Arabia. (The sea is only about 50 miles wide at the Strait of Hormuz.)

Relief, drainage, and soils. *The Hejaz and Asir.* A virtually unbroken escarpment runs the length of the peninsula above the Red Sea. The stretch from the Gulf of Aqaba to a point about 200 miles south of Mecca is called the Hejaz (Al-Ḥijāz, meaning "The Barrier"), and the higher stretch from there to the Najrān region near the Yemeni border has acquired the name of Asir (ʿAsīr; from the name, meaning "Difficult," of a prominent highland tribal confederation). In places the escarpment has two parallel ranges, with the lower range closer to the coast. In Midian (Madyan), the northernmost part of the Hejaz, the peaks have a maximum elevation of nearly 9,500 feet. The elevation decreases to the south, with an occasional upward surge such as Mount Raḍwā west of Medina (Al-Madīnah). Wadi Al-Ḥamḍ, an intermittent river drawing water from the Medina Basin on the inner side of the escarpment, breaks through the mountains to reach the Red Sea. Another pass leads to Mecca and Aṭ-Ṭāʾif in the highlands. The mountains become higher again in Asir, where some peaks rise to more than 9,000 feet. The passes there are particularly difficult. A lava field descending from the mountains and reaching the sea near Ḥalī long formed the natural southern boundary of the Hejaz. The high plateau of Asir, within the area watered by the Indian Ocean monsoon, is more fertile than the rural Hejaz.

The Red Sea coastal plain

The Red Sea coastal plain is constricted throughout its length, attaining its greatest widths, 40 to 50 miles, south of Medina and south of Mecca. The name Tihāmah, used for the whole plain, is sometimes subdivided into Tihāmat Al-Ḥijāz and Tihāmat ʿAsīr. There are no natural harbours adequate for large vessels, but the many inlets are well suited for sailing craft. Islands are particularly numerous along the southern part of the coast, where the Farasān Archipelago lies, and coral reefs are common.

In the northwestern interior the sandstone plateau of Ḥismā has an elevation of about 4,000 feet. South of it are great lava fields such as the ʿUwayriḍ, while others ring Medina. Tongues of lava south of Medina, lapping over the mountains, descend almost to the coast. The sand plain of Rakbah unrolls south of the Kishb Lava Field, which is southeast of Medina. Among the lava fields east of Mecca is one surrounding the mountains of Ḥaḍan (Ḥiḍn), the traditional border area between the Hejaz and Najd.

Najd. The western part of Najd (Nejd, meaning "Highland"), known as Upper Najd, lies within the Arabian shield with an average elevation of 4,000 feet; the eastern part falls within the sedimentary province with the city of Riyadh (Ar-Riyāḍ), near the eastern edge, having an elevation of about 1,950 feet. The principal drainage of Najd consists of a number of eastward-flowing wadi systems that carry water only seasonally.

In the north, the parallel ridges of Ajāʾ and Salmāh tower above the plateau to form Jabal Shammar (named after the Shammār tribe), the northernmost district of Najd. Just south of the Mecca-Riyadh road are the An-Nīr Hills. East of the Hejaz highlands and Mecca lie the Subayʿ sand dunes (named after the tribe of Banū as-Subayʿ), which constitute the largest sand desert within the shield.

The Ṭuwayq Mountains

The broad mountain-studded plateau gives way in central and eastern Najd to a series of escarpments curving from north to south along the contour of the shield: Al-Khuff, Jilh Al-ʿIshār, the Ṭuwayq Mountains, and Al-ʿArmah. Of these the longest and highest are the Ṭuwayq Mountains, which with their length of 800 miles constitute the backbone of the most densely settled part of Najd. The steep western face of the Ṭuwayq, rising about 800 feet above the plains to the west, is pierced by half a dozen wadis, of which the most spectacular is Wadi Birk, a tributary of Wadi As-Sahbāʾ. West of the Ṭuwayq a series of sand deserts (*ʿirqs* and *nafūds*) forms an almost continuous link between the great desert known as An-Nafūd to the north and the Rubʿ al-Khali to the south; the sand deserts also conform to the curve of the shield.

An-Nafūd (Great Nafūd). The second largest sand desert in the Arabian Peninsula, An-Nafūd, marks the northern limit of Najd. Lying just beyond the shield, it occupies an area of about 25,000 square miles. Its sands almost reach the oasis towns of Taymāʾ (Taima) in the west, Al-Jawf and Sakākah in the north, and Ḥāʾil in the south. The sands are gradually moving toward the southeast, where they enter either the Mazhur sand dunes, the first of the deserts lying west of the Ṭuwayq Mountains, or Ad-Dahnāʾ.

Northern Arabia. The Wadi As-Sirḥān, a depression rather than a true wadi, is about 200 miles long and 1,000 feet below the adjacent plateau. Northeast of Wadi As-Sirḥān are wide lava fields and chert plains belonging to the southern part of Al-Ḥamād, the Syrian Desert. The basin containing An-Nafūd is rimmed on the north by escarpments, down the northern slope of which run the ʿAnizah Wadis (the wadis of the tribe of ʿAnizah), to empty into the Euphrates valley; among the largest of these are Wadi ʿArʿar and Wadi Al-Khurr.

Ad-Dahnāʾ. The Ad-Dahnāʾ belt, separating Najd from eastern Arabia, is a sand stream moving slowly over 800 miles from An-Nafūd to the Rubʿ al-Khali. Usually it is no more than 50 miles wide. The sands, frequently reddish in colour, vary greatly in form; particularly in the central stretches, long parallel ridges rise to heights of approximately 150 feet, while some dunes are three times that height. Ad-Dahnāʾ also provides pasture in winter

MAP INDEX

Asterisked entries (*) appear on inset map

Cities and towns

Abhā 18 13 N 42 30 E
Abqaiq (Buqayq) 25 56 N 49 40 E
Abu Dhabi 24 28 N 54 22 E
Aden (ʿAdan) 12 46 N 45 02 E
ʿAfīf 23 55 N 42 56 E
Aḥmadī, al- 29 05 N 48 04 E
Aḥwar 13 31 N 46 42 E
ʿAjmān 25 25 N 55 27 E
ʿAmrān 15 41 N 43 55 E
ʿArādah 22 59 N 53 26 E
ʿArʿar 30 59 N 41 02 E
Arṭāwī, al- 25 23 N 44 30 E
ʿAwālī 26 05 N 50 33 E
ʿAyn, al-* 24 13 N 55 46 E
Badanah 30 59 N 40 58 E
Badīʿ, al- 22 02 N 46 34 E
Bāḥah, al- 20 01 N 41 28 E
Bahlāʾ (Bahlah) 22 58 N 57 18 E
Balḥāf 13 58 N 48 11 E
Barkāʾ 23 43 N 57 53 E
Bayḍāʾ, al- 13 58 N 45 35 E
Bayt al-Faqīh 14 31 N 43 19 E
Biʾār, al- 22 39 N 39 40 E
Birkah 23 48 N 38 50 E
Buqayq,
see Abqaiq
Buraydah 26 20 N 43 59 E
Buraykah 22 21 N 39 20 E
Buraymī, al- 24 15 N 55 45 E
Ḍāliʿ, aḍ- 13 42 N 44 44 E
Dammām, ad- 26 26 N 50 07 E
Ḍank 23 33 N 56 16 E
Dawḥah, ad-,
see Doha
Dhahran
(aẓ-Ẓahrān) 26 18 N 50 08 E
Dhamār 14 33 N 44 24 E
Diqdāqah 25 40 N 55 58 E
Doha
(ad-Dawḥah) 25 17 N 51 32 E
Dubayy 25 16 N 55 18 E
Dukhān 25 25 N 50 47 E
Duqm 19 39 N 57 42 E
Fughmah 16 09 N 49 26 E
Fujayrah, al- 25 08 N 56 21 E
Ghayḍah, al- 16 13 N 52 11 E
Ghayl Bā Wazīr 14 47 N 49 22 E
Ghulayfiqah 14 26 N 43 01 E
Ḥabbān 14 21 N 47 05 E
Ḥadd, al-
(al-Ḥidd)* 26 15 N 50 39 E
Ḥafar al-Bāṭin 28 27 N 45 58 E
Ḥāʾil 27 33 N 41 42 E
Ḥāʾir, al- 24 23 N 46 50 E
Ḥajjah 15 42 N 43 36 E
Ḥalabān 23 29 N 44 23 E
Ḥarajah 17 56 N 43 21 E
Ḥawallī 29 19 N 48 02 E
Ḥawrāʾ 15 43 N 48 18 E
Hayjān 16 40 N 44 05 E
Haymāʾ 19 56 N 56 19 E
Ḥays 13 56 N 43 29 E
Ḥidd, al-,
see Ḥadd, al-
Ḥudaydah, al- 14 48 N 42 57 E
Hufūf, al- 25 22 N 49 34 E
Ibb 13 58 N 44 11 E
Ibrāʾ 22 43 N 58 32 E
ʿIbrī 23 14 N 56 30 E
Izkī 22 56 N 57 46 E
Jahrah, al- 29 20 N 47 40 E
Jawf, al- 29 48 N 39 50 E
Jiddah 21 29 N 39 12 E
Jīzān (Qīzān) 16 54 N 42 32 E
Juʿaydah, al- 19 40 N 41 34 E
Jubayl, al- 27 01 N 49 40 E
Kalbā 25 05 N 56 22 E
Khābūrah, al- 23 59 N 57 08 E
Khamīs Mushayṭ 18 18 N 42 44 E
Khaṣab 26 12 N 56 15 E
Khawkhah, al- 13 48 N 43 15 E
Khawr, al- 25 41 N 51 30 E
Khawr Fakkān 25 21 N 56 22 E
Khawr Rawrī
(Khor Rori) 17 02 N 54 27 E
Khawsh 18 59 N 41 53 E
Khīs, al- 23 00 N 54 12 E
Khubar, al- 26 17 N 50 12 E
Kuwait 29 20 N 47 59 E
Laḥij 13 04 N 44 53 E
Lawdar 13 53 N 45 52 E
Laylā 22 17 N 46 45 E
Luḥayyah, al- 15 43 N 42 42 E
Madāʾin Ṣāliḥ 26 48 N 37 57 E
Madīnah, al-,
see Medina
Madīnat
ash-Shaʿb 12 50 N 44 56 E
Madīnat Ḥamad* 26 08 N 50 30 E
Madīnat ʿĪsā* 26 10 N 50 33 E
Maḥwīt, al- 15 29 N 43 34 E
Majmaʿah, al- 25 54 N 45 20 E
Makkah,
see Mecca
Manama* 26 13 N 50 35 E
Manṣūrīyah, al- 14 42 N 43 17 E
Marāh 25 04 N 45 28 E
Maʾrib 15 25 N 45 21 E
Māriyah, al- 23 08 N 53 44 E
Maṣnaʿah, al- 23 47 N 57 38 E
Masqaṭ,
see Muscat
Maṭraḥ 23 37 N 58 34 E
Maydī 16 19 N 42 48 E
Mecca (Makkah) 21 27 N 39 49 E
Medina
(al-Madīnah;
Yathrib) 24 28 N 39 36 E
Midhnab, al- 25 52 N 44 14 E
Minʿar 16 43 N 51 18 E
Mirbāṭ 17 00 N 54 41 E
Mishʿāb, al- 28 12 N 48 36 E
Miskah 24 49 N 42 56 E
Mocha (al-Mukhā) 13 19 N 43 15 E
Mubarraz, al- 25 25 N 49 35 E
Mūdiyah 13 56 N 46 05 E
Muḥarraq, al-* 26 16 N 50 37 E
Mukallā, al- 14 32 N 49 08 E
Mukhā, al-,
see Mocha
Muṣābiḥ 18 42 N 42 01 E
Musayʿīd 25 00 N 51 33 E
Muscat (Masqaṭ) 23 37 N 58 35 E
Naʿjān 24 05 N 47 10 E
Najrān 17 26 N 44 15 E
Niṣāb 14 31 N 46 30 E
Nizwā (Nazwah) 22 56 N 57 32 E
Qaḍīmah, al- 22 21 N 39 09 E
Qalʿat-Bīshah 20 00 N 42 36 E
Qana 14 00 N 48 20 E
Qanā 27 47 N 41 25 E
Qaṭīf, al- 26 33 N 50 00 E
Qīzān,
see Jīzān
Qunfudhah, al- 19 08 N 41 05 E
Qurayyāt 23 15 N 58 54 E
Rābigh 22 48 N 39 02 E
Rafḥāʾ 29 38 N 43 30 E
Rakhyūt 16 44 N 53 20 E
Raʾs al-Khaymah 25 47 N 55 57 E
Ras Tanura 26 42 N 50 06 E
Raydah 15 50 N 44 03 E
Ridāʿ 14 25 N 44 50 E
Rifāʿ al-Gharbī, ar-* 26 07 N 50 33 E
Rifāʿ ash-Sharqī,
ar-* 26 07 N 50 34 E
Riyadh (ar-Riyāḍ) 24 38 N 46 43 E
Rumaythah, ar-* 25 55 N 50 33 E
Rustāq, ar- 23 24 N 57 26 E
Ruways, ar- 26 08 N 51 13 E
Ṣaʿdah 16 57 N 43 46 E
Ṣafrāʾ, aṣ- 24 02 N 38 56 E
Sahwah 19 19 N 42 06 E
Sakākah 29 59 N 40 12 E
Ṣalālah 17 00 N 54 06 E
Ṣalīf 15 18 N 42 41 E
Ṣanʿāʾ (Sana) 15 21 N 44 12 E
Ṣayḥūt 15 12 N 51 14 E
Saywūn (Sayʾūn) 15 56 N 48 47 E
Shabwah 15 22 N 47 01 E
Shahārah 16 11 N 43 42 E
Shaqrāʾ 13 21 N 45 42 E
Shāriqah, ash- 25 22 N 55 23 E
Shidād 21 19 N 40 03 E
Shiḥr, ash- 14 45 N 49 36 E
Shināṣ 24 46 N 56 28 E
Shuʿaybah, ash- 29 03 N 48 08 E
Ṣirwāḥ 15 27 N 45 01 E
Ṣuḥār 24 22 N 56 45 E
Sulayyil, as- 20 27 N 45 34 E
Ṣūr 22 34 N 59 32 E
Tabūk 28 23 N 36 35 E
Ṭāʾif, aṭ- 21 16 N 40 25 E
Taʿizz 13 34 N 44 02 E
Ṭāqah 17 02 N 54 24 E
Ṭarīf 24 03 N 53 46 E
Tarīm 16 03 N 49 00 E
Taymāʾ 27 38 N 38 29 E
Thamarīt 17 39 N 54 02 E
Ṭurayf 31 41 N 38 39 E
Turbah, at- 13 13 N 44 07 E
ʿUlā, al- 26 38 N 37 55 E
ʿUlyā, al- 14 36 N 47 09 E
Umm al-Qaywayn 25 35 N 55 34 E
ʿUnayzah 26 06 N 43 59 E
ʿUsfān 21 55 N 39 22 E
Wadhīl 23 03 N 54 08 E
Wakrah, al- 25 10 N 51 36 E
Yanbuʿ al-Baḥr 24 05 N 38 03 E
Yarīm 14 18 N 44 23 E
Yathrib,
see Medina
Zabīd 14 12 N 43 19 E
Ẓahrān 17 40 N 43 30 E
Ẓahrān, aẓ-,
see Dhahran
Ẓalim 22 43 N 42 10 E
Zilfī, az- 26 18 N 44 48 E
Zinjibār 13 08 N 45 23 E
Zuhrah, az- 15 44 N 43 00 E

Physical features and points of interest

Aden, Gulf of 12 00 N 48 00 E
Aḥsāʾ, al-,
see Hasa, al-
Ajāʾ Mountains 27 30 N 41 30 E
Akhḍar, Mount al- 23 15 N 57 20 E
Aqaba, Gulf of 29 00 N 34 30 E
Arabian
Peninsula 21 00 N 48 00 E
Arabian Sea 20 00 N 65 00 E
ʿAramah Plateau,
al- 25 30 N 46 30 E
ʿArʿar, Wadi 31 23 N 42 26 E
Asir, *region* 19 00 N 42 00 E
ʿĀtinah, Wadi 18 23 N 53 28 E
ʿAyn, Wadi al- 22 15 N 55 28 E
Bab el-Mandeb
Strait 12 35 N 43 25 E
Bādiyat ash-Shām,
see Syrian Desert
Bahrain, Gulf of
(Khalīj
al-Baḥrayn)* 25 45 N 50 40 E
Banā, Wadi 13 03 N 45 24 E
Bāṭin, Wadi al- 30 25 N 47 35 E
Bāṭinah, al-,
region 23 45 N 57 20 E
Bayḥān, Wadi 15 12 N 46 10 E
Bīshah, Wadi 21 24 N 43 26 E
Brothers, The
(al-Ikhwān),
islands 12 08 N 53 10 E
Būbiyān, *island* 29 45 N 48 15 E
Dabbāgh, Mount 27 52 N 35 45 E
Dahnāʾ Desert,
ad- 24 30 N 48 10 E
Ḍarbat ʿAlī, Cape 16 38 N 53 05 E
Dawāsir, Wadi
ad- 20 24 N 46 29 E
Dukhān Hill, ad-* 26 02 N 50 32 E
Empty Quarter,
see Rubʿ al-Khali
Desert
Farasān Islands 16 48 N 41 54 E
Ḥaḍan Lava Field 21 30 N 41 23 E
Ḥadd, Cape al- 22 32 N 59 48 E
Hadhramaut
(Ḥaḍramawt),
region 15 00 N 50 00 E
Ḥaḍramawt,
Wadi 16 00 N 48 53 E
Ḥaḍur Shuʿayb,
see Nabī Shuʿayb,
Mount an-
Ḥajar, al-,
mountains 23 10 N 57 30 E
Ḥajr, Wadi 14 04 N 48 40 E
Ḥamḍ, Wadi al- 25 58 N 36 42 E
Ḥanīsh Islands 13 45 N 42 45 E
Ḥarāsīs Plain, al- 19 45 N 56 30 E
Hasa, al-
(al-Aḥsāʾ),
region 26 35 N 48 10 E
Hasa Oasis, al- 25 20 N 49 38 E
Ḥawār Islands* 25 40 N 50 47 E
Hejaz (al-Ḥijāz),
region 24 30 N 38 30 E
Ḥismā Plateau 28 30 N 35 50 E
Hormuz, Strait of 26 34 N 56 15 E
Ikhwān, al-,
see Brothers, The
Jabal Shammar,
region 27 20 N 41 45 E
Jāfūrah Desert,
al- 25 00 N 50 15 E
Jawf, Wadi 15 50 N 45 30 E
Kamaran, *island* 15 21 N 42 35 E
Khalīj al-Baḥrayn,
see Bahrain,
Gulf of
Khalīj Maṣīrah,
see Masira,
Gulf of
Kharj Oasis, al- 24 10 N 47 30 E
Khaybar Lava
Field 25 30 N 39 45 E
Khurīyā Murīyā
Islands 17 30 N 56 00 E
Khurr, Wadi al- 32 03 N 43 52 E
King Fahd
Causeway* 26 10 N 50 20 E
Kishb Lava Field 22 47 N 41 30 E
Kuria Muria Bay 17 40 N 55 45 E
Lawz, Mount 28 41 N 35 18 E
Mahrāt Mountain 16 44 N 52 46 E
Masīlah, Wadi al- 15 10 N 51 08 E
Masira, Gulf of
(Khalīj Maṣīrah) 20 10 N 58 10 E
Maṣīrah, *island* 20 25 N 58 50 E
Maṭṭī Salt Flat 23 30 N 52 00 E
Mazhur Desert 27 25 N 43 55 E
Muḥarraq Island,
al- 26 16 N 50 37 E
Musandam
Peninsula 26 18 N 56 24 E
Nabī Shuʿayb,
Mount an- (Ḥaḍur
Shuʿayb) 15 17 N 43 59 E
Nafūd Desert, an- 28 30 N 41 00 E
Najd (Nejd),
region 25 00 N 44 30 E
Nawāṣīf Lava
Field 21 20 N 42 10 E
Oman, Gulf of 25 00 N 58 00 E
Persian Gulf 27 00 N 51 00 E
Qamar Bay, al- 16 00 N 52 30 E
Qarāʾ Mountains,
al- 17 15 N 54 15 E
Qitbīt, Wadi 19 15 N 54 23 E
Raḍwā, Mount 24 34 N 38 18 E
Rahaṭ Lava Field 23 00 N 40 05 E
Rakbah Plain 22 15 N 41 00 E
Rakhawt, Wadi 18 16 N 51 50 E
Ranyah, Wadi 21 18 N 43 20 E
Red Sea 25 00 N 35 00 E
Rimah, Wadi ar- 26 38 N 44 18 E
Rubʿ al-Khali
Desert (Empty
Quarter) 21 00 N 51 00 E
Sabʿatayn Desert,
Ramlat as- 15 30 N 46 10 E
Sahbāʾ, Wadi as- 23 44 N 49 53 E
Sanāʾil, Wadi 23 40 N 58 10 E
Sawdāʾ, Mount 18 18 N 42 22 E
Ṣawqirah Bay 18 35 N 57 00 E
Shaqāyā Peak,
ash- 29 08 N 46 40 E
Sirḥān, Wadi as-,
depression 30 30 N 38 15 E
Sitrah,* *island* 26 09 N 50 37 E
Socotra
(Suquṭrā), *island* 12 30 N 54 00 E
Subayʿ Desert 22 15 N 43 05 E
Ṣummān Plateau,
aṣ- 25 00 N 47 00 E
Suquṭrā,
see Socotra
Syrian Desert
(Bādiyat
ash-Shām) 32 00 N 40 00 E
Tathlīth, Wadi 20 35 N 44 20 E
Tihāmah Plain 22 00 N 40 00 E
Ṭuwayq
Mountains 23 30 N 46 20 E
Umm* an-Naʿsān,
island 26 09 N 50 24 E
Umm as-Samīm
Salt Flat 21 45 N 55 50 E
ʿUwayriḍ Lava
Field 27 00 N 37 30 E
Wahībah Dunes,
Āl, *desert* 21 56 N 58 55 E

Scale 1: 13,699,000
1 inch equals approx. 216 miles
0 50 100 150 200 mi
0 100 200 300 Km
Cities over 500,000
Cities 50,000 to 500,000
Cities under 50,000
National Capitals
International boundaries
International boundaries, undefined
Intermittent rivers
Bridges
Salt flats
Sand areas
Lava
Spot elevations in metres (1 m = 3.28 ft)
Lambert Conformal Conic Projection
BAHRAIN
Scale 1: 1,689,000
1 inch equals approx. 26 miles
Manama
Gulf of Bahrain
King Fahd Causeway
SAUDI ARABIA
QATAR
HAWĀR ISLANDS (Bahrain)
ar-Rumaythah
IRAQ
IRAN
KUWAIT
SAUDI ARABIA
ARABIAN PENINSULA
UNITED ARAB EMIRATES
OMAN
YEMEN
QATAR
JORDAN
ISRAEL
EGYPT
SUDAN
ETHIOPIA
DJIBOUTI
SOCOTRA (Yemen)
THE BROTHERS
RUB' AL-KHALI DESERT
AN-NAFŪD DESERT
AD-DAHNĀ' DESERT
AS-SUMMĀN PLATEAU
NAJD
HEJAZ
TIHĀMAH PLAIN
TUWAYQ MOUNTAINS
SYRIAN DESERT
Persian Gulf
Gulf of Oman
ARABIAN SEA
RED SEA
Gulf of Aden
Tropic of Cancer
Baghdad
Amman
Jerusalem
Kuwait
Riyadh
Doha
Abu Dhabi
Muscat
Şan'ā'
Mecca
Medina
Jiddah
Aden
Shīrāz
Eşfahān
Ahvāz
Dubayy
al-Mukallā
Iraq-Saudi Arabia Neutral Zone
Area administered by Sudan
© Encyclopaedia Britannica Inc.

The Rubʿ al-Khali sand desert, most of which lies within Saudi Arabia.
Lynn Abercrombie

and spring. In 1957 the Khurayṣ oil field was discovered beneath its sands.

The Rubʿ al-Khali. The largest uninterrupted sand desert in the world, the Rubʿ al-Khali covers an area estimated at about 250,000 square miles. The name Rubʿ al-Khali is not commonly used by the few nomadic Bedouins who live there; they call it simply Ar-Ramlah ("The Sand"). Shrub vegetation is widely spaced over the porous, sandy surfaces and is almost nonexistent on the occasional rock and salt surfaces. Only about 37 species have been identified, most of which are perennial. The desert has been intensively explored by oil companies since 1950.

"The Sand"

Some areas of the Rubʿ al-Khali may have droughts of more than 10 years' duration, while others sometimes have thunderstorms or high summer humidity. In the west the gravel plains of Raydāʾ and Abū Baḥr separate the Rubʿ al-Khali from the southern end of Ad-Dahnāʾ, while another gravel plain, Al-Jaladah, lies within the Rubʿ al-Khali. What appears to be a northern extension of the Rubʿ al-Khali, Al-Jāfūrah, is regarded by the Arabs as an independent desert. Southeast of Qatar the sands give way before the vast salt flat of the Maṭṭi salt marsh, which runs north about 60 miles to the Persian Gulf coast. East of the Maṭṭi the oasis hamlets of Al-Jiwāʾ (Liwāʾ in the United Arab Emirates) lie among the dunes on the desert's northeastern fringe. The largest dunes of the Rubʿ al-Khali are in the far east, where heights of more than 800 feet are reached and sand ridges extend for more than 30 miles, with salt flats as the usual floor in between. In the east, along the Oman edge of the desert, is the large salt flat of Umm As-Samīm. In the southwest, sand ridges reach a length of 150 miles.

Most of the Rubʿ al-Khali falls within Saudi Arabia, but boundaries with Oman in the south and Yemen in the southeast have been disputed. In 1974 Saudi Arabia and the United Arab Emirates reached an agreement over a disputed eastern boundary.

The Persian Gulf lowland. A low-lying region follows the Arabian shore of the Persian Gulf from Kuwait around to the Al-Ḥajar mountains of Oman at the mouth of the gulf. The gravel plain of Ad-Dibdibah lies inland southwest of Kuwait. Adjacent to Ad-Dahnāʾ is the low plateau of Aṣ-Ṣummān; between it and the coast scattered hills rise a few hundred feet. Broad patches of sand occur here and there, and salt flats are numerous along the coast. The Persian Gulf on this side provides no good deep-draft natural harbours, but many inlets offer shelter to sailing craft, and modern ports have been built in Kuwait, Saudi Arabia, Bahrain, and Qatar. This lowland region is relatively well supplied with underground water from springs and wells. Deep in the sedimentary strata enormous accumulations of oil and gas are found.

Yemen. Arabia's highest mountains occur in Yemen: An-Nabī Shuʿayb, northwest of Ṣanʿāʾ, reaches 12,008 feet. The Tihāmah in Yemen, broader and more habitable than the Tihāmah farther north in Saudi Arabia, supports some towns. Monsoon rains make the mountains and high plateaus of Yemen the most fruitful region in Arabia. The easy slope from the highlands to the southwestern corner of the Rubʿ al-Khali was the principal home of the pre-Islāmic civilization of southern Arabia, and the ruins of the Maʾrib dam, the greatest monument of that age, still stand there. The seaward descent from the mountains of Al-Kawr at the southern end of Yemen is precipitous.

The harbour of Aden is formed by two volcanic peninsulas of the lowland below the southern mountain face of Yemen. The coastal plain, about 30 miles wide behind Aden, is narrower nearly everywhere else. Along this coast the stream of Wadi Ḥajr, perhaps the only truly perennial river in Arabia, flows about 60 miles to the sea.

Aden harbour

Eastward the mountains of Al-Kawr merge with the highlands of Hadhramaut known as the *jawl* ("plateau"). Hadhramaut, strictly speaking, is a great interior valley cleaving through the *jawl,* with its lower course reaching the sea under the name Wadi Al-Masīlah. In the interior the sand desert of Ramlat As-Sabʿatayn lies on the slope descending from Al-Kawr to the Rubʿ al-Khali, which is gentle both here and going down from the *jawl.*

Dhofar (Ẓufār). The Qarāʾ Mountains in Dhofar, the southern province of the sultanate of Oman, are about 3,000 feet high, with one peak higher than 5,000 feet. The monsoon keeps the seaward (southern) side of the mountains, as well as the coastal plain, fertile. A gradual slope leads northward from the water divide to the Rubʿ al-Khali; valleys from the slope converge on Ramlat Al-Mughshin at the desert's edge.

Oman. The Al-Ḥajar mountain range is divided into Eastern Al-Ḥajar and Western Al-Ḥajar. The range, which exceeds a height of 9,000 feet in places, differs from other Arabian coastal highlands in being steep on both sides. Plains at the foot of the mountains fall away almost imperceptibly from the numerous towns of interior Oman to the Rubʿ al-Khali basin. No mountains bar Oman's outlet to the Arabian Sea in the south; the plateau along the coast has an average elevation of about 500 feet.

Climate. The Tropic of Cancer virtually bisects the Arabian Peninsula, passing just south of Medina. The summer heat is intense everywhere, reaching as high as 129° F (54° C) in places. Much of the interior is dry, but along the coasts and in some of the southern highlands and deserts the humidity is extreme in the summer. Fogs and dews occur in the humid areas, dew often serving as a substitute for rain. In the dry zones the sun blazes fiercely throughout the summer. Spring and autumn are pleasant

Extremes of humidity

seasons, and biting cold and snow are rare in winter, except at high elevations and in the far north.

Rainfall is scanty in all parts beyond the reach of the Indian Ocean monsoon, averaging only 3 to 4 inches (77 to 102 millimetres) a year. The desert rains are torrential on occasion, causing flash floods in the wadis; sometimes these rains turn into hailstorms. It is not unusual for a drought to last several years. The monsoon increases the precipitation fourfold or more in the southwest and south. Lying within the trade wind belt, northern Arabia receives westerlies from the Mediterranean that blow toward the Persian Gulf and then south and southwest through the Rubʿ al-Khali toward Yemen. The monsoon strikes Arabia from the opposite direction. In midwinter and again in early summer the Persian Gulf experiences seasonal winds laden with dust and sand similar to the Egyptian khamsin; in Arabia these are called *shamāl* ("north"), though the prevailing direction is actually from the north-northwest. In contrast to the *shamāl* is the less frequent *qaws* from the southeast. The wind regimes of Najd and the Rubʿ al-Khali are complex, particularly during spring. The winds may come from any point of the compass and vary in intensity from zephyr to gale.

Plant life. The date palm grows almost everywhere, except at very high elevations and in Dhofar, on the coast of which it is replaced by the coconut palm. The date is a source of food, and uses are found for the trunk, branches, and fibre of the date palm. Among places noted for high-quality date-palm production are Medina, Bīshah, and Al-Ḥasā. Alfalfa (lucerne), widely used as fodder, often fills the space between palms. The principal grains are wheat, sorghum, barley, and millet. Rice supplements wheat as a food, but little is raised locally. Cotton does well in a few places, such as Abyān near Aden. In general the people of Arabia have a greater fondness for fruits than for vegetables. Melons, pomegranates, and the jujube are particularly favoured, and Al-Buraymī is noted for its mangoes. Figs, grapes, bananas, prickly pears, and other fruits are also grown, and citron and Java almond flourish in the oases.

Although Arabia is no longer as renowned as formerly for its coffee, fair amounts are still cultivated on the terraced mountainsides of Yemen. In places coffee has given way to the more profitable *qāt* (khat; *Catha edulis*), the leaves of which produce a stimulant. Tobacco is a product of the Hadhramaut coast.

The world's chief source of incense in antiquity, Arabia still numbers various aromatics among its herbs, though the trade in frankincense and myrrh has long been languishing. Mimosas and acacias are widespread, but little advantage is taken commercially of their gums. Indigo and other native dyes are used in the south, both for cloth and for personal adornment. Cactus, cactiform *Euphorbia,* and the aloe grow profusely in some areas.

Lynn Abercrombie

Bedouin woman with Arabian camels near Madāʾin Ṣāliḥ, Saudi Arabia.

Arabia is not the most hospitable of lands for flowers, but the roses of Aṭ-Ṭāʾif are well-known, the oleander thrives in a desert environment, and other flowers sometimes brighten the general bleakness of the landscape.

The peninsula is almost devoid of trees. Clumps of junipers in the southwestern highlands make the closest approach to true forests. The tamarisk, which grows well without much water, is often planted in rows to retard the encroachment of drift sand. Trees are so rare that the standard Arabic word for tree, *shajar,* is ordinarily used by the Bedouin for bushes in the desert that furnish grazing for his animals and firewood for his tent. The leaves of varieties called *hamd* have enough salinity to satisfy the camel's need for salt. The tough perennials are as essential to life as the tender annuals nourished by the rains of winter and spring. The rains also assist in growing the truffle, which the Bedouins dig out of the ground.

Importance of the camel

Animal life. The camel has traditionally been the chief support of nomadic life in Arabia. Without the camel the Bedouin could never have moved far from water fit for human beings; with the camel he could survive for months on its milk and penetrate deep into the deserts. The camel also furnished food, clothing, fuel (dung), transportation, and power for drawing water or for plowing. For the Bedouin the camel represented the best form of capital and the most valuable article of commerce. The noblest breeds of camel came from Oman, but some of the more plebeian breeds showed greater stamina. Today, the camel, which has been for the most part supplanted as a means of transport by four-wheel-drive vehicles, is used primarily as livestock.

Sheep and goats, known collectively in Arabic as *ghanam,* are numerous, but they are kept in small numbers rather than in large herds. Mutton and lamb are the favourite meats, and goat's milk is used for making cheese. The Arabian horse, noted for its beauty and endurance, is a disappearing strain in Arabia, where only a few thousand remain, though the breed is now fostered in other countries. Many Bedouin own Salukis, a breed of speedy hunting dog; trained falcons are also used in the chase. Gazelles once ranged the plains in large numbers, but unrestricted hunting decimated them. Very few oryx are left in the Rubʿ al-Khali, their last stronghold, and the ibex has also become rare. Other large wild animals are the hyena, wolf, and jackal. The lion is frequently mentioned in early Arabic literature, but lions seem now to be extinct in the peninsula. Baboons were once abundant in the southern highlands. Among the smaller animals are the fox, ratel, rabbit, hedgehog, and jerboa.

Deadly desert snakes are the horned viper and a species of cobra differing considerably from the Indian. The striped sea snakes are also poisonous. Lizards include the large desert monitor and the smaller sand-swimming skink.

Ostriches have become extinct. Eagles, vultures, and owls are common, and the lesser bustard is often hunted with falcons. Flamingos, pelicans, egrets, and other sea birds frequent the coasts. Smaller birds found in the towns and oases include the pigeon, cuckoo, swallow, and hoopoe, while the sand grouse, lark, and courser inhabit the desert.

Swarms of locusts periodically descend as a plague, devouring every green plant in their path. Other common insects are the fly, which appears even in the depths of the desert, mosquito, tick, beetle, scorpion, and ant. In some places bees are kept for their honey.

The seas around Arabia contain mackerel, groupers, tuna, porgies, and other food fish, as well as shrimps. Sharks and sardines are plentiful off the southern coast, and whales occasionally enter the Persian Gulf.

(G.Re./B.K.N.)

THE PEOPLE

Origin of Arab tribes

In ethnographic terms, Arabs belong to the Mediterranean local race, a subgroup of the Caucasoid geographic race. According to tradition, Arabs are descended from a southern Arabian ancestor, Qaḥṭān, forebear of the "pure" or "genuine" Arabs (known as al-ʿArab al-ʿĀribah), and a northern Arabian ancestor, ʿAdnān, forebear of the "Arabicized" Arabs (al-ʿArab al-Mustaʿribah). A tradition, seemingly derived from the Bible, makes ʿAdnān, and perhaps Qaḥṭān also, descend from Ismāʿīl (Ishmael), son of Abraham. The rivalry between the two groups spread, with the Muslim conquests, beyond Arabia; it even recurred in northern Yemen in the 1950s when the Zaydī imams, descendants of the Prophet Muḥammad, a "northern" Arab, were called "ʿAdnānī."

A Veddoid, non-Mediterranean strain occurs in southern Arabia, where also are found the low-status groups called Akhdām and Ṣibyān. In the north are the Ṣulubah, known to the ancient Arabians as *qayn,* a low-status group regarded as being of non-Arab descent. In Oman the Zuṭṭ, a Gypsy folk, seem to be descendants of Indian emigrants to the gulf in the early 9th century, but the Balochi, whose ancestors immigrated more recently, have formed a sort of warrior tribe there. In the border regions of Oman and Yemen are the Mahra, Ḥarāsīs, Qarā, and others, speaking languages of the South Arabic group, and on the Musandam Peninsula are the Shiḥūḥ.

From ancient times African slaves were imported to Arabia; Saudi Arabia and the Yemens abolished slavery only in 1962. Some districts such as the oasis of Khaybar in the Hejaz and parts of the Tihāmah are largely populated by black cultivators. The ports always had a large element of Africans, Asians, and others. The oil era brought many Lebanese, Egyptians, Jordanians, and Iraqis with the education and skills the Arabians lacked, and great numbers of Yemenis moved into the oil-producing states as unskilled labourers. Palestinians make up between one-fifth and one-fourth of Kuwait's population, refugees from Yemen occupy entire streets in Abu Dhabi, and so many Pakistanis, Indians, Sri Lankans, Koreans, and Filipinos have flocked to the Persian Gulf states that often they considerably outnumber the native inhabitants. By contrast, almost no Jews, long settled in western Arabia, now remain.

Throughout Arabian history, even during phases of foreign rule, it was the free, arms-bearing tribesmen who dominated other classes of society, be the tribes nomadic or oasis dwellers, settled farmers in the highlands, or sailors, traders, and pirates gaining their livelihood at sea. The sultans, emirs, and sheikhs were drawn from the tribes, whom they had to cosset to obtain backing. There are, however, descendants of the Prophet Muḥammad, sayyids and sharifs, regarded as superior in the social scale to all others, who have at times exercised a theocratic type of rule as spiritual leaders.

Bedouin

An age-old antagonism exists between the settled peoples, *al-ḥaḍar,* and the nomadic or pastoral tribes, known as Bedouin (*al-bādiyah*), but many settled tribes also have nomadic branches. In Yemen, the fertile southwestern corner of Arabia containing more than one-third of its total population, the same antagonistic feelings exist between city dwellers and *qabīlīs*, arms-bearing tribes mostly settled in villages. Until after World War I the Bedouin of the northern deserts were able to keep the settled people in constant apprehension of their raiding; the tribes would even attack and plunder the pilgrim hajj caravans to the Holy Cities unless they were bought off or restrained by force. But modern weapons and airplanes, which can be used to search out tribesmen in their desert or mountain fastnesses, have altered the situation. Each tribe used to be at war or in a state of armed truce with others, and protection was required to enter another tribe's territory. Shortly before World War I Ibn Saʿūd, the founder of modern Saudi Arabia, began to establish the Bedouin in military and agricultural colonies called *hijrah,* encouraging them to abandon pastoral life, and programs aimed at the "sedentarization" of the Bedouin have been adopted by states like Jordan and Kuwait.

Contrary to commonly held belief, the tribes are not egalitarian, and some have the quality of *sharaf* or nobility in greater degree than others; some, such as the Hutaym and Sharārāt of the north, are despised by the noble tribes. A father will not accept a suitor who belongs to an inferior tribe for his daughter's hand, far less a *ḥāḍarī* suitor. This is the key to social standing in Arabia.

The nomadic tribes of Arabia are herders of camels, sheep, and goats. They move from pasture to pasture, but they visit tribal markets to purchase dates and grain and to sell their animals, wool, and clarified butter (ghee). The mountain peoples depend more on donkeys than camels, and they raise cattle, which they use to power agricultural and irrigation work, as well as sheep and goats.

Oil and ancient culture

Oil's vast revenues, poured into Arabia, have transformed and are fast destroying ancient patterns of living. The population of the Arabian Peninsula as a whole is now incomparably better off in terms of nutrition, welfare, amenities, and education, but the rapidity of the cultural change is unsettling, as are the shifts in the native population. Throughout the peninsula, the new urban centres are drawing in labour from the countryside, and the presence of large numbers of foreigners, many of whom enjoy much higher incomes than the natives, is resented. (R.B.Se.)

THE ECONOMY

The mineral resource of greatest value is oil. The Arabian Peninsula has the largest oil reserves in the world. With the exception of deposits in Yemen, the Arabian oil fields lie in the same great sedimentary basin as the fields of Iran and Iraq. Although oil was discovered in Iran in 1908, the first field on the Arabian side of the basin, in Bahrain, was not found until 1932. This inspired an intensive search in eastern Arabia that in time reached far into the interior. Oil was discovered in Saudi Arabia in 1938, in Kuwait and Qatar in 1940, on the mainland of the Saudi Arabia/Kuwait Neutral Zone in 1953, on the mainland of Abu Dhabi in 1960, in Oman in 1964, in South Yemen in 1983, and in North Yemen in 1984. In 1951 oil was

Oil refinery on the island of Ḥālū in the Persian Gulf, Qatar.

discovered in the Persian Gulf off Saudi Arabia, in 1958 in Abu Dhabi offshore, and in 1960 in the Saudi Arabia/Kuwait Neutral Zone offshore.

In association with the oil are enormous amounts of natural gas. Making use of this gas commercially requires extremely large investments. Some gas is liquefied for local consumption or for export, and some is reinjected into the oil-bearing strata for storage and to help maintain pressure for oil production.

The Arabian countries are attempting economic diversification, though the abundance of oil is a disincentive. Ancient mining sites bear witness to once-flourishing production of minerals: gold at the old mine of Mahd adh-Dhahab in the Hejaz; silver at a mine in the mountains west of Ma'rib; and very large copper production in Oman (until deforestation exhausted the supplies of wood for on-site smelting). Deposits of iron have been found in the northern Hejaz and Najd. Other resources, some of which are being exploited, are barite, gypsum, salt, lime for cement, clay for bricks and pottery, shale, quartz sand for glass, marble, and building stone.

Decline of the oyster trade

For many centuries the oyster beds of the Persian Gulf produced some of the world's finest pearls, and pearling was once a thriving and profitable occupation. Bahrain was the chief centre, and the Trucial States (now the United Arab Emirates), Qatar, and Saudi Arabia also participated. Since about 1931 the trade has declined continuously as a result of the world economic depression, the competition of Japanese cultured pearls, and the siphoning off of labour into other less onerous and more lucrative fields.

Even in the southwest, where rainfall is heaviest, the water supply is not constant enough for the generation of power. The scarcity of water and the poor quality of the soil have hampered the development of an export trade in agricultural produce. Progress has been made by individual states in improving irrigation systems and expanding cultivated areas. (G.Re./B.K.N.)

History and cultural development

Some time after the rise of Islām in the first quarter of the 7th century AD and the emergence of the Arabian Muslims as the founders of one of the great empires of history, the name "Arab" came to be used by these Muslims themselves and by the nations with whom they came in contact to indicate all people of Arabian origin. The very name Arabia, or its Arabic name Jazīrat Al-ʿArab, has come to be used for the whole peninsula. But the definition of the area, even in Islāmic sources, is not agreed upon unanimously. In its narrowest application it indicates much less than the whole peninsula, while in ancient Greek and Latin sources—and often in subsequent sources—the term Arabia includes the Syrian and Jordanian deserts and the Iraqi desert west of the lower Euphrates. Similarly, "Arabs" connoted, at least in pre-Islāmic times, mainly the tribal populations of central and northern Arabia.

Arabia has been inhabited by innumerable tribal units, forever splitting or confederating; its history is a kaleidoscope of shifting allegiances, although certain broad patterns may be distinguished. A native system has evolved of moving from tribal anarchy to centralized government and relapsing again into anarchy. The tribes have dominated the peninsula, even in intermittent periods when the personal prestige of a leader has led briefly to some measure of tribal cohesion.

Arabian culture and the trade route

Arabian culture is a branch of Semitic civilization; because of this and because of the influences of sister Semitic cultures to which it has been subjected at certain epochs, it is sometimes difficult to determine what is specifically Arabian. Because a great trade route passed along its flanks, Arabia had contact along its borders with Egyptian, Greco-Roman, and Indo-Persian civilizations. The Turkish overlords of the Arabic-speaking countries affected Arabia relatively little, however, and the dominant culture of western Europe arrived late in the colonial era.

Arabia was the cradle of Islām, and through this faith it influenced every Muslim people. Islām, essentially Arabian in nature, whatever superficial external influences

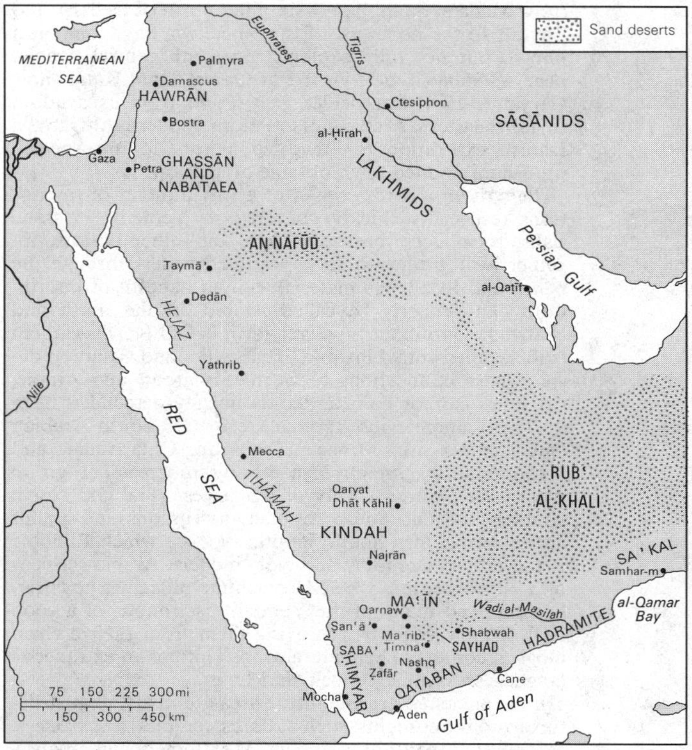

Principal sites in pre-Islāmic Arabia.

may have affected it, is Arabia's outstanding contribution to world civilization. (M.A.G./A.F.L.B.)

PRE-ISLĀMIC ARABIA, TO THE 7TH CENTURY AD

Prehistory and archaeology. At one time Arabia as a whole may have had greater rainfall and richer vegetation than it does today, as shown by the large dried-up watercourses intersecting the peninsula. But climatic conditions seem to have changed little in the past five millennia; human life—settled or nomad—has been a struggle to cope with the harsh realities of this vast subcontinent.

Stone Age settlements of fishermen and shellfish eaters going back to the 3rd millennium BC have been found on the northeast coast and in the islands of Faylakah and Bahrain. Surface scatters of flint implements are seen in many places in the peninsula, as are undatable but probably ancient rock drawings for which affinities have been thought to exist with rock drawings in the Sahara.

Southern Arabia (comprising Yemen and Oman) lies within the climatic zone of the Indian Ocean monsoons, which yield enough rainfall to make it potentially the most fertile part of Arabia. In Yemen, sophisticated irrigation techniques go very far back indeed; soundings in the silt deposits around the great dam of Ma'rib attest intensive agricultural exploitation there from at least 2000 BC.

The racial affinities of the Arabian populations are not traceable. A theory by which Arabia was considered the birthplace and homeland of the nations of Semitic culture is not now regarded as tenable. Arabian peoples have been held to be related to a variety of groups, with homelands in almost all directions outside Arabia: the view that sought to visualize all Arabians as a single race has never been valid. The oldest evidence indicates the presence of Africans in the Red Sea coastal plain, Iranians in the southeastern tip of the peninsula, and peoples of Aramaean stock in the north. The racial affinities of the ancient Yemeni peoples remain unsolved; the marked similarity of their culture to the Semitic cultures that arose in the Fertile Crescent to the north of the peninsula can be attributed to cultural spread rather than to immigration.

Apart from pursuing the few prehistoric evidences, archaeological research centres mainly on sites of the historic period, which is also attested by written records beginning in the first half of the 1st millennium BC. Some sites in the northern Hejaz, such as Dedān (now Al-ʿUlā), Al-Ḥijr (now Madā'in Ṣāliḥ, barely six miles north of Dedān), and Taymā' to the northeast of the other two, have long been known but not fully explored. In south central Arabia, near As-Sulayyil, a town site at Qaryat Dhāt Kāhil (now Qaryat Al-Fāw) has yielded rich results from excavation. In northeastern Arabia, inland from modern Al-Qaṭīf, a Danish expedition has revealed a hitherto unsuspected pre-Islāmic walled town of large dimension.

The written records consist of a vast number of inscriptions (especially thickly clustered in Yemen) on stone slabs, rock faces, bronze tablets, and other objects, together with graffiti on rock, scattered widely through the peninsula. In all this material, only a handful of inscriptions can properly be called Arabic. In the north and centre the dominant linguistic form is Old North Arabian (subclassified into Liḥyānic, Thamūdic, and Ṣafaitic); despite close connections between this group and Arabic, the latter cannot be regarded as lineally descended from it. The Yemenite inscriptions are in Old South Arabian (subclassified into Minaean, Sabaean, Qatabānian, and Hadhramautic), which is a wholly independent group within the Semitic family of languages. (The Old North Arabian and Old South Arabian inscriptions and graffiti are in scripts of a South Semitic type, of which Ethiopic is the only present-day survivor; modern Arabic script is of a North Semitic type.) Unscientific pillaging, however, has deprived many of the Yemeni inscriptions of a good deal of their value by removing them from their archaeological context. There are also inscriptions in extraneous languages: Aramaic, Greek, and Latin.

In the ancient Yemeni culture area are many great structures and monuments, such as dams, temples, and palaces, as well as a wealth of plastic art of extremely high quality. The motifs, such as the ubiquitous bull heads and ibex figures, are partly characteristic of Yemen, but from the 3rd century BC onward the style is markedly Hellenistic.

Ancient Yemeni art

Fresh data, both archaeological and epigraphic, appear every year and sometimes entail radical reappraisal of earlier hypotheses. Any attempt at a synthetic picture is therefore strictly provisional.

Pre-Islāmic Yemeni kingdoms. The Greek writer Eratosthenes (3rd century BC) described "Eudaimon Arabia" (*i.e.,* Yemen) as inhabited by four major peoples (*ethne*), and it is on the basis of his nomenclature for these groups that modern scholars are accustomed to speak of Minaeans, Sabaeans, Qatabānians, and Hadramites. The fourfold categorization does indeed correspond to the linguistic data (see above), but the political and historical facts are a good deal more complex. The capitals of the four peoples were not located in the centres of their respective territories but instead lay close together on the western, southern, and eastern fringes of a tract of sand desert known to medieval Arab geographers as the Ṣayhad (modern Ramlat As-Sab'atayn). This off-centre placing has been thought to originate from proximity to the trade route by which frankincense was conveyed from Hadhramaut first westward, then north to Najrān, then up the west coast of Arabia to Gaza, and across the peninsula to the east coast. The territories attached to the latter three of the capitals spread out fanwise into the mountainous regions.

Sabaeans. The people who called themselves Saba' (biblical Sheba) are both the earliest and the most abundantly attested in the surviving written records. Their centre was at Ma'rib, east of present-day Ṣan'ā' and on the edge of the sand desert. (In the indigenous inscriptions Ma'rib is rendered Mryb or Mrb; the modern spelling is based on an unjustified "correction" by medieval Arabic writers.) The town lay in a formerly highly cultivated area watered by the great Ma'rib Dam, which controlled the flow from the extensive Wadi Dhana basin.

Sabaean rulers—who are mentioned in Assyrian annals of the late 8th and early 7th centuries BC (although some scholars date Sabaean inscriptions to about the 6th century BC)—were responsible for impressive constructions both cultic and irrigational, including the greatest part of what is now visible of the dam; but there are traces of earlier dam works, and the silt deposits indicate agricultural exploitation far back in prehistory.

From the early historic period one ruler, named Karib'il Watar, has left a long epigraphic record of victories over peoples throughout the major part of Yemen, most importantly the Awsānian kingdom to the southeast, but the victories did not lead to permanent conquest. Nor did his campaigns ever extend into the Hadhramaut region or to the Red Sea coastal area. At no period of their history as an independent people did the Sabaeans have real control of those two areas; in the Red Sea coastal area the sole indication of their presence is a small temple near Zabīd, probably attached to a military outpost guarding a route down to the sea.

Two secondary centres were Ṣirwāḥ, on a tributary of the Wadi Dhana above the dam, and Nashq (now Al-Bayḍā'), at the western end of Wadi Al-Jawf.

From perhaps just before the Christian era, however, the highland regions, both north and west of Ṣan'ā', played a much more active part in Sabaean affairs, and some of the rulers belonged to highland clans. The early centuries of the Christian era also saw the emergence of Ṣan'ā' as a government centre and royal residence (in its palace, Ghumdān) almost rivaling the status of Ma'rib. Nevertheless, Ma'rib (with its palace, Salḥīn) retained its prestige into the 6th century AD.

Sabaean regnal style

Sabaean rulers of the early period employed a regnal style consisting of two names, each chosen from a very short list of alternatives; possible permutations were thus limited, and the same style recurs several times over. In drafting their own texts, the rulers adopted the title *mukarrib,* now generally thought to mean "unifier" (with allusion to the process of expansion of Sabaean influence over neighbouring communities). Persons other than the rulers never used this title in their texts but referred to the rulers by their regnal styles or occasionally as "king of Ma'rib." Later the title *mukarrib* disappeared, and the rulers referred to themselves, and were referred to by their subjects, as "king of Saba'."

As among the Minaeans, the early rulers were only one element in a legislature including both a council and representatives of the nation. The rulers' personal activity lay mainly in building and in leading wars. The first three centuries of the Christian era have yielded a more ample documentation than any other period, but during those centuries the Sabaeans were facing a strong threat from the Ḥimyarites to the south of them. The Ḥimyarites succeeded at times in gaining supremacy over the Sabaeans, and at the end of the 3rd century they definitively absorbed the Sabaeans into their realm. In the wars of the 1st century onward, the kings (whether Sabaean or Ḥimyarite) were supported both by a national army (*khamīs*) under their own command and by contingents raised from the associated communities led by *qayl*s, belonging to the aristocratic clans that headed each associated community. The oldest documents attest a number of other kingdoms. The most important was Awsān, which lay in the highlands to the south of the Wadi Bayḥān. An early Sabaean text speaks of a massive defeat of Awsān, in terms that attest its high significance. Yet the kingdom had a brief resurgence much later, around the turn of the Christian era, when it appears to have been wealthy and heavily influenced by Hellenistic culture. One of its kings of this period was the only Yemeni ruler to be (like the Ptolemies and Seleucids) accorded divine honours, and his portrait statuette is dressed in Greek garb, contrasting with those of his predecessors who are dressed in Arabian style, with kilt and shawl. Awsānian inscriptions are in the Qatabānian language (which might account for the fact that Eratosthenes gives no separate mention to Awsān in his list of the main *ethne*).

Minaeans. The Minaean kingdom (Ma'īn) lasted from the 4th to the 2nd century BC and was predominantly a trading organization that, for the period, monopolized the trade routes. References to Ma'īn occur earlier in Sabaean texts, where they seem to be loosely associated with the 'Āmir people to the north of the Minaean capital of Qarnaw (now Ma'īn), which is at the eastern end of the Wadi Al-Jawf and on the western border of the Ṣayhad sands. The Minaeans had a second town surrounded by impressive and still extant walls at Yathill, a short distance south of Qarnaw; and they had trading establishments at Dedān and in the Qatabānian and Hadramite capitals. The overwhelming majority of Minaean inscriptions come from Qarnaw, Yathill, and Dedān, and there is virtually no evidence of territorial possessions apart from the immediate vicinities of these three centres, which have more the aspect of typical "caravan cities." A thin scattering of Minaean inscriptions has been found in places just outside Arabia, such as Egypt and the island of Delos, all manifestly resulting from far-flung trading activities; and texts from Qarnaw refer to a number of important points on the caravan routes, such as Yathrib (Medina) and Gaza, and also to interruption of trade by one of the several phases of warfare between Egypt and the Seleucids of Syria. An explicit mention of caravans is perhaps found in the expression *mʿn mṣrn,* interpreted by the scholar Mahmud Ali Ghul as "the Minaean caravaneers."

Minaean trading activities

Minaean social structure differed from that of the other three, predominantly agricultural peoples. The latter were federations of communities (often termed by modern scholars "tribes," though they were not genealogically based) grouped under a leading community, with the nation as a whole designated by the name of the hegemonial community, followed by the phrase "and the [associated] communities." The Minaeans, however, were subdivided into groups of varying size and importance, some quite small, with none exercising a dominating role over the others. Among the other three peoples the office of "elder" (*kabīr*) was normally filled by the head of one of the associated communities in a national federation. Among the Minaeans, however, the *kabīr* was a biennially appointed magistrate controlling one of the trading settlements or, in some cases, invested with authority in all of them. Legislative functions were exercised by the king acting together with a council and representatives of all the Minaean social classes. Minaean inscriptions make no mention of wars undertaken by the king or the state; this suggests that Maʿīn may have enjoyed covenants of safe-conduct with their neighbours along the trade routes.

Qatabānians. The heartland of the Qatabān people was Wadi Bayḥān, with the capital, Timnaʿ, at its northern end, and Wadi Ḥarīb, immediately west of Bayḥān. As in the case of Maʿīn, the earliest references are in Sabaean inscriptions; native Qatabānian inscriptions do not seem to antedate the 4th century BC. Timnaʿ was destroyed by fire at a date not easy to fix; pottery evidence has been thought to suggest the 1st century AD, but epigraphy points to a survival of the kingdom at least until the end of the 2nd century. Its fortunes had fluctuated: in the earliest Sabaean phase it was "liberated" by the Sabaeans from Awsānian domination in the above-mentioned defeat of Awsān. At some periods the Qatabānians themselves dominated a federacy similar to the Sabaean one, and at a relatively late date a ruler whom his subjects called "King of Qatabān" styled himself *mukarrib* of Qatabān. Inasmuch as Eratosthenes says that this people extended to "both seas"—*i.e.,* the Red Sea and the Gulf of Aden—it might be inferred that there was some sort of Qatabānian presence in the southwest corner of the peninsula, an area later ruled by the Ḥimyarites.

Hadramites. Inscriptions from the Hadramite kingdom are scantier in number than from the Sabaean, Minaean, or Qatabānian. Yet the Hadramite was probably the wealthiest of them all. Hadhramaut and the Saʾkal area to the east (modern Dhofar province of the sultanate of Oman) are the only places in Arabia where climatic conditions make production of frankincense possible, and Pliny wrote that the whole of the produce was collected at the Hadramite capital, Shabwah, on the eastern fringe of the Ṣayhad sands, and taxed there before being handed over to the caravans that carried it to the Mediterranean and Mesopotamia. In addition, Hadhramaut was an entrepôt for Indian goods brought by sea and then forwarded by land. The caravan trade may have suffered to some degree from competition by Red Sea shipping, which, from the 1st century AD, began to sail through the Bab El-Mandeb Strait into the Indian Ocean. Nevertheless, as late as about AD 230 a king of Hadhramaut received missions from India and Palmyra (Tadmor), at the opposite ends of the long-standing trade route along which Hadhramaut occupied a central position. At Shabwah, French archaeological work begun in 1975 adjacent to the visible temple ruin has revealed a walled town of larger extent than any other ancient Yemeni site. The palace, on the opposite side of the town from the temple, was, according to the archaeological evidence, a truly magnificent building. The main port of Hadhramaut was at Cane on the bay of Biʾr ʿAlī; and the Hadramites had a settlement at Samhar-m (now Khawr Rawrī) on Qamar Bay in the Saʾkal region, founded about the turn of the Christian era.

Frankincense production

Ḥimyarites. Ḥimyar is the Arabic form of the name of a people who appear in the inscriptions as Ḥmyr and in Greek sources as Homeritai. They occupied the extreme southwest of the peninsula and had their capital at Ẓafār, a site some nine miles southeast of present-day Yarīm, on the motor road from Aden and Taʿizz to Ṣanʿāʾ. The first appearance of Ḥimyar in history is in Pliny's *Naturalis Historia* (latter half of the 1st century AD); a short time later the Greek document known to scholars as the *Periplus Maris Erythraei* mentions an individual who was "king of two nations, the Homerites and the Sabaeans." But this dual kingship was not definitive: throughout the 2nd and 3rd centuries there were phases of warfare between native Sabaean rulers and Ḥimyarite ones. Royal titulature in this period is confusing: alongside "kings of Sabaʾ" are found "kings of Sabaʾ and the Raydān," but the implications of the latter are still debated. A thesis advanced by the Arab scholar M.A. Bafaqih is that the former are native Sabaeans and the latter heads of a dual kingship over both peoples. Others have held that native Sabaean rulers sometimes claimed the longer title even when there was little reality behind it. Moreover, the Ḥimyarites, until the 6th century AD, used the Sabaean language for their epigraphic records, and there are no inscriptions or other monuments at Ẓafār or elsewhere in the true Ḥimyarite area that can be confidently dated before AD 300.

In the last decades of the 3rd century AD a Ḥimyarite ruler named Shammar Yuharʿish ended the independent existence of both Sabaʾ and Hadhramaut; and inasmuch as Qatabān had already disappeared from the political map, the whole of Yemen was united under his rule. Thereafter, the royal style was "king of Sabaʾ and the Raydān and Hadhramaut and Yamnat." Arabic writers call him and his successors the Tabābiʿah (singular Tubbaʿ), and, because in the centuries immediately preceding Islām Yemen was dominated by the Ḥimyarites, the Arabic writers (followed by many 19th-century Europeans) apply the term Ḥimyaritic to all pre-Islāmic monuments of Yemen, irrespective of date or location.

The Tubbaʿ kings. A major break with the past was made in the 4th century AD, when the polytheistic religion of the earlier cultures was replaced by a monotheistic cult of "The Merciful (Raḥmān), Lord of heaven and earth." There was also an increasing interest, both friendly and hostile, in central Arabia. Already in the 2nd and 3rd centuries AD Sabaean, Ḥimyaro-Sabaean, and Ḥimyarite rulers had employed central Arabian Bedouin mercenaries; and the first Tubbaʿ king, Shammar Yuharʿish, sent a diplomatic mission to the Sāsānian court at Ctesiphon.

Early Arabian monotheism

The kingdom of Aksum in Eritrea is mentioned in Sabaean texts of the 2nd century AD as having some not very definable link with Habashite ("Abyssinian") people settled in the Arabian coastal areas, who were throughout the 2nd and 3rd centuries a thorn in the flesh of both Sabaean and Ḥimyaro-Sabaean rulers, even at one point occupying Ẓafār. Tension between Aksum and Ḥimyar reached a climax in AD 517 or 522, with a Jewish Ḥimyarite king (traditionally said to have been a convert to Judaism) named Yūsuf Asʾar Yathʾar. It seems that the conflict escalated from what had been (in one account) a trade dispute. Yūsuf massacred the entire Ethiopian population of the port of Mocha and of Ẓafār and, about a year later, the Christians of Najrān. Aksum retaliated with invasion, leading to the defeat and death of Yūsuf (who is known in Arabic tradition mostly by the nickname Dhū Nuwās) and the establishment of a puppet kingdom in Yemen subject to Aksum. Somewhat later the Ḥimyarite king Abraha regained some measure of independence, and he was responsible for major repairs to the Ma'rib Dam in the 540s. His reign was followed by a fairly brief Persian occupation of Yemen. Early in the 7th century Yemen accepted Islām peacefully, and its antique native culture merged into the Islāmic culture.

Central and northern Arabia. The oasis of Taymā' in the northern Hejaz emerged briefly into the limelight when the Neo-Babylonian king Nabu-na'id (Nabonidus, reigned *c.* 556–539 BC) took up his residence there for 10 years and extended his power as far as Yathrib. A few important monuments of this time are known.

Dedān and Al-Ḥijr. It is possible that the Minaean settlement at Dedān (see above) coexisted with a native Dedānite town. But only one "king of Dedān" is recorded. This kingdom seems to have been replaced quite soon by a kingdom of Liḥyān (Greek: Lechienoi). The entire area, however, was not long in coming under the rule of the Nabataean kings of a dynasty (centred at Petra) covering the 1st century BC and the 1st AD; and the ancient town of Dedān was eclipsed by a new Nabataean foundation just to the north at Al-Ḥijr (Madā'in Ṣāliḥ). At the beginning of the 2nd century AD the Nabataean kingdom was annexed by Rome, the official decree of annexation being dated 111. The Nabataeans, like the Minaeans before them, had been involved in the caravan trade, and it would appear probable that for at least a time after the annexation they continued this role, under Roman aegis. Subsequent history of the area remains obscure.

Kindah. Kindah was a Bedouin tribal kingdom quite unlike the organized states of Yemen; its kings exercised an influence over a number of associated tribes more by personal prestige than by coercive settled authority. Its area of influence was south central Arabia, from the Yemeni border nearly up to Mecca. The discovery of the tomb of a king of Kindah (datable to perhaps the 3rd century AD) at Qaryat Dhāt Kāhil, on the trade route linking Najrān with the east coast, suggests that this site was in all likelihood the royal headquarters. Sabaean texts of the 2nd and 3rd centuries contain a number of references to Kindah, attesting relations sometimes hostile (as when an assault was made on Qaryat Dhāt Kāhil) and other times friendly (as evidenced by the supply of Kindite troops for the Yemenite rulers). This pattern of relationship seems to have continued down to the early 6th century, when the Kindite hegemony collapsed, partly as a consequence of tribal wars and partly perhaps as a result of the emergent power of the Meccan Quraysh at that time. The last Kindah king, the famous poet Imru' al-Qays, became a fugitive.

The collapse of Kindite hegemony

Al-Ḥīrah. Al-Ḥīrah was similarly a Bedouin tribal kingdom, the kings of which are commonly designated the Lakhmids. According to tradition, the founder of the dynasty was 'Amr, whose son Imru' al-Qays died in AD 328 and was entombed at An-Nimārah in the Syrian desert. His funerary inscription is written in an extremely difficult type of script. Recently there has been a revival of interest in the inscription, and a lively controversy has arisen over its precise implications. One thing that is certain is that Imru' al-Qays claimed the title "king of all the Bedouin" and claimed to have campaigned successfully over the entire north and centre of the peninsula, as far as the border of Najrān. In Muslim sources it is said that he was given by the Sāsānian king Shāpūr II a "governorship" over the Bedouin of northeast Arabia, being charged with the task of restraining their incursions into Sāsānian territory. Later kings of the dynasty settled themselves definitively in that area, at Al-Ḥīrah (near modern Kufah). They remained influential throughout the 6th century, and only in 602 was the last Lakhmid king, Nu'mān ibn al-Mundhir, put to death by the Sāsānian king Khosrow II (Parvīz) and the kingdom swept away. In the 6th century Al-Ḥīrah was a considerable centre of Nestorian Christianity.

Ghassān. The dynasty of the Ghassānids, though often called kings, were in fact Byzantine phylarchs (native rulers of subject frontier states). They had their headquarters well within the Byzantine Empire, a little east of the Sea of Galilee at Jābiyah in the Jawlān (Golan) area; but they controlled large areas of northwestern Arabia, as far south as Yathrib, serving as a counterpoise to the Sāsānian-oriented Lakhmids in the northeast. The Ghassānids were Monophysite Christians and played an important part in the religious conflicts of the Byzantine church. Their influence spanned the 6th century AD, and their most prominent member, al-Ḥārith ibn Jabalah (Greek: Aretas), flourished in mid-century. The last three phylarchs fell out with Orthodox Byzantium because of their Monophysite creed; in 614 the power of Ghassān was destroyed by a Persian invasion.

Quraysh. According to Muslim tradition, Mecca had at one time been in the hands of Jurhum, a people living on the central west coast recorded in Greco-Latin sources as Gorrhamites. But sometime about AD 500 ("five generations before the Prophet Muḥammad") Quṣayy ibn Kilāb, called al-Mujammi' ("The Unifier"), is credited with having brought together scattered groups of Bedouin and installed them in Mecca. They took over a role that had long before been played by Minaeans and Nabataeans, controlling the west coast trade routes; they sent annual caravans to Syria and Yemen. Authority in Quraysh was not royal but was vested in a mercantile aristocracy, not unlike the Venetian Republic. Their trading contracts ensured them considerable influence, and, when in the opening years of the 7th century the collapse of the Ḥimyarites, Lakhmids, and Ghassānids had left a power vacuum in the peninsula, Quraysh remained the only effective influence. There is, however, little doubt that the ancient traditions of Yemenite civilization contributed substantially to the consolidation of the Islāmic empire. (A.F.L.B.)

ARABIA SINCE THE 7TH CENTURY

Arabian and Islāmic expansion. In the 6th century Quraysh—the noble and holy house of the confederation of the Hejaz controlling the sacred enclave (*ḥaram*) of Mecca—contrived a chain of agreements with the northern and southern tribes that opened the highways of Arabia to commerce. Under Quraysh aegis, caravans moved freely from the southern Yemen coast to Mecca and thence northward to Byzantium or eastward to Iraq. Another agreement made trade with Axum (in what is now Ethiopia) and the African coast secure, as was also the Arabian coastal sea route. Furthermore, members of the Quraysh house of 'Abd Manāf concluded pacts with Byzantium, Persia, and rulers of Yemen and Ethiopia, promoting commerce outside Arabia. The 'Abd Manāf house could effect such agreements because of Quraysh's superior position with the tribes. Quraysh had some sanctity as lords of the Meccan temple (the Ka'bah) and were themselves known as the Protected Neighbours of Allāh; the tribes on pilgrimage to Mecca were called the Guests of Allāh.

Quraysh trade agreements

In its *ḥaram* Quraysh was secure from attack; it arbitrated in tribal disputes, attaining thereby at least a local preeminence and seemingly a kind of loose hegemony over many Arabian tribes. Temple privileges held by Quṣayy, who established the rule of Quraysh, passed to his posterity, the 'Abd Manāf house of which collected the tax to feed the pilgrims. The Ka'bah, through the additions of other cults, developed into a pantheon, the cult of other gods perhaps being linked with political agreements between Quraysh—worshipers of Allāh—and the tribes.

The life of Muḥammad. Muḥammad was born in 570 of the Hāshimite (Banū Hāshim) branch of the noble house of 'Abd Manāf; though orphaned at an early age and, in consequence, with little influence, he never lacked protection by his clan. Marriage to a wealthy widow improved his position as a merchant, but he began to make his mark in Mecca by preaching the oneness of Allāh. Rejected by the Quraysh lords, Muḥammad sought affiliation with other tribes; he was unsuccessful until he managed to negotiate a pact with the tribal chiefs of Medina, whereby he obtained their protection and became theocratic head and arbiter of the Medinan tribal confederation (*ummah*). Those Quraysh who joined him there were known as *muhājirūn* (refugees or emigrants), while his Medinan allies were called *anṣār* (supporters). The Muslim era dates from the *hijrah* (hegira)—Muḥammad's move to Medina in AD 622. (For more detail about the life of Muḥammad

Beginning of the Muslim era

and the rise of Islām, see ISLĀM, MUḤAMMAD AND THE RELIGION OF; and ISLĀMIC WORLD, THE.)

Muḥammad's men attacked a Quraysh caravan, thus breaking the vital security system established by the ʿAbd Manāf house, and hostilities broke out against his Meccan kinsmen. In Medina two problems confronted him—the necessity to enforce his role as arbiter and to raise supplies for his moves against Quraysh. He overcame internal opposition, removing in the process three Jewish tribes, whose properties he distributed among his followers. Externally, his ascendant power was demonstrated following Quraysh's failure to overrun Medina, when he declared it his own sacred enclave. Muḥammad foiled Quraysh offensives and marched back to Mecca. After taking Mecca he became lord of the two sacred enclaves (*al-ḥaramayn*); however, even though he broke the power of some Quraysh lords, his policy thenceforth was to conciliate his Quraysh kinsmen.

The rise of Islām. After Muḥammad's entry into Mecca the tribes linked with Quraysh came to negotiate with him and to accept Islām; this meant little more than giving up their local deities and worshiping Allāh alone. They had to pay the tax, but this was not novel because the tribal chiefs had already been taxed to protect the Meccan *ḥaram*. Many tribesmen probably waited to join the winner. Doubtless they cared little for Islām—many tried to break away (the so-called apostasy) on Muḥammad's death.

Islāmic expansionism

Islām, however, was destined for a world role. Under Muḥammad's successors the expansionist urge of the tribes, temporarily united around the nucleus of the two sacred enclaves, coincided with the weakness of Byzantium and Sāsānian Persia. Tribes summoned to the banners of Islām launched a career of conquest that promised to satisfy the mandate of their new faith as well as the desire for booty and lands. With families and flocks, they left the peninsula. Population movements of such magnitude affected all of Arabia; in Hadhramaut they possibly caused neglect of irrigation works, resulting in erosion of fertile lands. In Oman, too, when Arab tribes evicted the Persian ruling class, its complex irrigation system seems to have suffered severely. Many Omani Arabs about the mid-7th century left for Basra (in Iraq) and formed the influential Azd group there. Arabian Islām replaced Persian influence in the Bahrain district and Al-Ḥasā province in the northeast, and in Yemen.

As the conquests far beyond Arabia poured loot into the Holy Cities (Mecca and Medina), they became wealthy centres of a sophisticated Arabian culture; Medina became a centre for Qurʾānic study, the evolution of Islāmic law, and historical record. Under the caliphs—Muḥammad's successors—Islām began to assume its characteristic shape; paradoxically, outside the cities it made little difference to Arabian life for centuries. Sharīʿah (Islāmic law), promoted often by the Prophet's own descendants, developed in the urban centres; but outside them customary law persisted, sometimes diametrically opposed to Sharīʿah. In time the Hejaz and Yemen came to make notable contributions to Islāmic culture, but Islām's basically Arabian nature first shows in the early mosque, which resembles the pre-Islāmic temple, and in the pilgrimage rites, little altered from paganism.

Struggle for leadership. In Arabia offices were generally hereditary and elective; but on Muḥammad's death, Abū Bakr, the first caliph, aided by his own eventual successor, ʿUmar, gained the leadership that Quraysh might have lost to others. They were not of the house of Hāshim, which, from the outset, felt cheated of its rights. ʿAlī, Muḥammad's stepbrother and son-in-law, became the focus of legitimist claims to succeed the Prophet. ʿUthmān, however, the third caliph, was descended from both the Umayyah and Hāshim branches of ʿAbd Manāf. The latter half of ʿUthmān's reign coincided with a slackening in the tide of conquest. ʿUthmān was censured for diverting property, revenues, and booty in Iraq and Egypt to his Quraysh relatives. Squabbles with the tribes resulted in ʿUthmān's murder at Medina by opponents from Egypt. ʿAlī was proclaimed caliph by the *anṣār,* but he lost the political battle with ʿUthmān's powerful relative Muʿāwiyah, governor of Syria, who demanded retaliation against the murderers. ʿAlī was later murdered by a Khārijite, a member of a dissident group. ʿAlī had quitted Medina for Iraq, and the political power centre of Islām left the peninsula, never to return. ʿAlī's posterity, however, played a key role in subsequent Arabian history.

Departure of the caliphate

The Umayyad and ʿAbbāsid periods. *Regional centres.* Once Muʿāwiyah and the Umayyads had seized overlordship of the far-flung Islāmic empire, which they ruled from Damascus, the Holy Cities remained only the spiritual capitals of Islām. The Umayyad caliphs appointed governors over the three crucial areas of the Hejaz, Yemen, and Oman; but in Iraq occasional powerful governors managed to control the Persian Gulf provinces, the gulf being an important maritime trade route, especially under the ʿAbbāsids. Occasionally Bahrain, Al-Ḥasā, and Najd also became regional centres of power within Arabia.

The brief unity that Islām had imposed on the Arabian Peninsula was irrevocably broken as the main Islāmic sects took shape—the "orthodox" Sunnites and the "legitimist" Shīʿites (who were distinguished from the Sunnites principally by their tenet that the imam of the Muslim community must be descended from ʿAlī by Muḥammad's daughter Fāṭimah).

Umayyad forces defeated a Quraysh pretender, ʿAbd Allāh ibn az-Zubayr, who had been proclaimed caliph in the Hejaz. Medina was captured; Mecca was besieged, the *ḥaram* bombarded, and the Kaʿbah set on fire (the sacred Black Stone—an object of veneration probably appropriated from pre-Islāmic religion—was split in three places). The harsh Umayyad general al-Ḥajjāj captured the city, and the pretender perished. The violation of the sacred enclaves by troops, including Arab Christians, was an act of sacrilege, but it broke any power remaining with the tribal "supporters" in Medina. The Prophet's original simple mosque in Medina, already enlarged by the early caliphs, was rebuilt by the Umayyad al-Walīd (it has been much altered and restored since). The Umayyads spent lavishly on the Holy Cities and developed Hejaz irrigation.

Preservation of the Holy Cities

The Umayyads collapsed before the ʿAbbāsids in 750, a fall to which rivalry between the tribes, aligned as northern and southern Arabs, contributed materially. The ʿAbbāsids claimed adherence of the Legitimists, since their ancestor, the Prophet's uncle, was of the Hāshimite house. The ʿAbbāsids maintained a policy of strict adherence to religious observance, and they too devoted large sums to supporting and embellishing the Holy Cities, to which they sent annually a pilgrim caravan. Zubaydah, wife of the caliph Hārūn ar-Rashīd, celebrated for her public works, is said to have ordered the construction of the *qanāt,* a tunneled conduit that took water to Mecca. The threat of insurrection by Legitimist pretenders of the ʿAlīd branch of the Hāshimite house—who denied ʿAbbāsid claims to the caliphate as they had with the Umayyads—was a constant danger to the ʿAbbāsid caliphs. The ʿAlīd family developed both Sunnite and Shīʿite branches, but the latter split into a multiplicity of sects, of which the most important are the "Twelvers" (Ithnā ʿAsharīyah, or Imāmīs), who recognized 12 imams, and the Ismāʿīlite "Seveners" (Ismāʿīlīyah, or Ismāʿīlīs, for Imam Ismāʿīl ibn Jaʿfar), who acknowledged only seven.

Yemen. To quell a rising in Yemen, the ʿAbbāsid caliph al-Maʾmūn dispatched Ibn Ziyād, who refounded in 820 the southern city of Zabīd and became overlord of Yemen, Najrān, and Hadhramaut. About a century later, the Najāḥids—Ethiopian slaves or local Afro-Asians—supplanted the Ziyādids in Zabīd; however, though independent, neither dynasty renounced vague ʿAbbāsid suzerainty. The Banū Yaʿfur, lords north of Ṣanʿāʾ, expelled the Ziyādid governor and ruled independently from 861 to 997. Najāḥid rule ended when ʿAlī ibn Mahdī captured Zabīd in 1159.

The Qarmatians. A more serious loss to ʿAbbāsid power in Arabia was occasioned by the appearance of Ismāʿīlite propaganda in Yemen about 880, in eastern Arabia about 899, and even briefly in Oman. From Yemen, Ismāʿīlīs reached North Africa, where the Fāṭimid movement arose and conquered Egypt and for a time seriously threatened the ʿAbbāsids in Baghdad. The Qarmatians (Qarāmiṭah), an extremist offshoot of the Ismāʿīlīs, founded a state in Al-Ḥasā, in northeastern Arabia. They set out to subvert Sunnite Islām. They were alleged to oppose many of the teachings of the Prophet Muḥammad, and they encouraged social equality for nomads, townspeople, and peasants. In 930 the Persian Gulf Qarmatians plundered Mecca, carrying off the Black Stone to Al-Ḥasā; they later returned it under Fāṭimid pressure. The Qarmatians were overthrown in 1077–78 by local Sunnite tribes, but Qarmatian influence persisted in Bahrain. From the 13th century, Twelver, or Imāmī, Shīʿism spread in Al-Ḥasā and Bahrain, while political power was held by the Shīʿite Sevener Jarwānid dynasty (1305 to about 1450).

In 1037 ʿAlī ibn Muḥammad aṣ-Ṣulayḥī of Yemen proclaimed the Fāṭimid caliph al-Mustanṣir but set up a dynasty in Ṣanʿāʾ. The Ṣulayḥid dynasty ruled most of upper Yemen, warred with the pro-ʿAbbāsid Najāḥids, and gained control of Aden.

Oman. In the last decades of the 7th century the Ibāḍites (Ibāḍīyah), regarded as a moderate Khārijite sect, conquered southern Arabia, established a Kindite imam in Hadhramaut, occupied Ṣanʿāʾ, and took Mecca and Medina, before the Umayyads drove them back to Hadhramaut. Oman had early become Khārijite; the first Ibāḍite imam, al-Julandā ibn Masʿūd, was elected at about the beginning of the ʿAbbāsid caliphate. After the Ibāḍite invasion of southern Arabia in 893, Oman wavered between independence and subjection to the ʿAbbāsids and their Būyid or Seljuq supporters. By the 12th century the Seljuq hold had become rather precarious and local imams existed. During periods when the Indian trade used the Persian Gulf, Omani ports flourished; however, revenues diminished wherever trade was switched to the Red Sea. From the mid-12th century until 1406 the Nabhānid dynasty controlled the interior of Oman, but Turkic Oğuz (Ghuzz), Persians, and others variously possessed the coastal flank of the mountains.

The Zaydīs and ʿAlawīs. In Yemen lasting movements were being shaped by the close of the 9th century; the imam al-Hādī, a theocratic arbiter-ruler of traditional type, founded the ʿAlīd Zaydī dynasty in Ṣaʿdah of northern Yemen. About the mid-12th century a Zaydī imam extended his rule northward to Khaybar and Yanbuʿ (Yenbo) and southward to Zabīd.

In the mid-10th century a refugee from disturbances in Iraq, Aḥmad ibn ʿĪsā al-Muhājir, arrived in Hadhramaut, then under Ibāḍite domination, and founded the ʿAlawite (ʿAlawī) Sayyid house, which was instrumental in spreading the Shāfiʿite (Shāfiʿī) school of Islāmic law to India, Indonesia, and East Africa.

The Ayyūbids and Rasūlids. The Ayyūbids of Egypt, when they invaded Yemen in 1173, found it parceled out among several dynasties. Ayyūbid objectives were probably part political, to find themselves a haven and destroy the Ismāʿīlites, and part economic, to control the India trade route. They remained in power until about 1229, generally controlling Aden, Hadhramaut, the Tihāmah, and the districts south of Ṣanʿāʾ. They introduced an administrative centralization apparently adapted from Syro-Egyptian organization.

The Rasūlid period

With the Ayyūbids arrived the emir ʿAlī ibn Rasūl, probably of Oğuz origin, whose descendants, at first Ayyūbid governors, grasped independence (*c.* 1229). The Rasūlid period is the most brilliant era of Islāmic history in Yemen. These monarchs embellished their capital, Taʿizz, and other cities with fine buildings; several kings had a literary bent and, besides belles lettres, wrote treatises of some originality on various subjects. A fiscal survey still surviving provides an account of the trade through Ash-Shiḥr, Aden, and the Tihāmah ports, with budgets for maintaining castles, troops, and hostages kept as surety of good tribal conduct. Aden served as an important trade centre in a flourishing period of Arab and Jewish commercial enterprise. The Rasūlids kept the southern coast under loose control up to Dhofar, even holding Hadhramaut to some extent and maintaining a squadron against pirates.

The sharifs of the Holy Cities. At Mecca in the mid-10th century commenced the 1,000-year ascendancy of the ʿAlīd sharifian families. Mecca now became capital of the Hejaz, replacing Medina, the centre from which it had been ruled since the Prophet's days. The sharifs, though at times subject to such foreign overlords as the rulers of Egypt and of other parts of Arabia, exercised virtual independence. Throughout the ʿAbbāsid-Fāṭimid struggle, however, the sharifs took the opportunist line of supporting the side in ascendancy. When the Ayyūbid Saladin, after deposing the Fāṭimids in 1171, brought back orthodoxy, the sharifs again recognized the ʿAbbāsids and Ayyūbids, and from being Zaydīs turned Sunnite Shāfiʿī.

In 1181 the French crusader knight Reynaud de Châtillon raided Arabia. He intended to attack Medina but, switching his plan, raided in 1182 the Red Sea ports as far south as Bab El-Mandeb; Saladin destroyed Reynaud's vessels and so ended the threat to Mecca.

By the early 13th century the sharifs had conquered the Hejaz, extending their power southward to Ḥalī; but, when they sought support from Egypt, Syria, or Yemen, the Rasūlids managed temporarily to dispute the overlordship of Mecca with the Egyptians.

After Baghdad fell to the Mongols in 1258, the pilgrim caravan from Iraq lost all political significance for the Hejaz. As Iraq declined, Egyptian influence increased and the sharifs became steadily more dependent on the Mamlūks of Egypt.

Mamlūk and Ottoman influence. Although the Yemeni Rasūlids sometimes disputed with the Mamlūks the overlordship of the Holy Cities, the Mamlūks generally prevailed. Egyptians and Meccans attacked al-Mujāhid the Rasūlid on a pilgrimage in 1350, and he was held prisoner in Egypt though released later.

Mamlūk domination

The Mamlūks. During the 14th and 15th centuries the Mamlūks became the dominant power, maintaining a political agent in the Hejaz and a body of cavalry in Mecca. Eventually they made or unmade the sharifian rulers, though the local Egyptian commander's policy sometimes ran counter to that of Cairo. From the mid-15th century the Mamlūks took charge of the customs at Jiddah, Mecca's port, allotting a portion of the revenue to the pasha of that port. Sharif Muḥammad ibn Barakāt (ruled 1425–53), however, received one-quarter of the value of all wrecked ships, one-quarter of all gifts arriving from abroad for the Meccans, and one-tenth of all imported goods. About half his income was distributed among the leading sharifian families.

By the mid-15th century the foundering of the Rasūlid dynasty in Yemen made way for the Ṭāhirids; about the same time the Kathīrī tribe of southeastern Arabia controlled Hadhramaut on behalf of the new dynasty.

The beginning of the 16th century witnessed Portuguese penetration of the Indian Ocean and the Red Sea. Though they failed to capture Aden, the Portuguese blockaded the Indian trade routes to Europe via the Persian Gulf and Red Sea, eventually causing severe, lasting damage to the economy of Muslim Middle Eastern countries.

The Ottomans. In 1517 the Ottoman sultan Selim I conquered Egypt and proclaimed the Hejaz part of the Ottoman dominions. Sharif Barakāt II of Mecca sent his son to negotiate at the Ottoman court and was confirmed as lord of the Holy Cities and Jiddah, subject to recognizing the Ottoman sultan as overlord. Selim's successor, Süleyman I the Magnificent, at the zenith of Ottoman power, munificently subsidized the Holy Cities, devoting large sums to new building.

In Yemen the Mamlūks of Zabīd and Taʿizz acknowledged Ottoman authority, and Ottomans took over naval operations against the Portuguese in the Red Sea and Indian Ocean. They seized Aden and forced the Yemenis into the mountains, capturing Ṣanʿāʾ and Shahārah; ultimately, however, the Yemenis drove them back into the Tihāmah. The Ottomans adopted Mocha (Al-Mukhā) in southern Yemen as their base, and Aden declined in importance. After conquering Iraq in 1534–36, the Ottomans could operate in the Persian Gulf against the Portuguese, who had taken Hormuz and Muscat in 1507 and Bahrain in 1521 and freely harried the Arabian coasts.

The Ottomans reached as far as Al-Ḥasā by 1550 as they sought to curb Portuguese expansion. With Ottoman help, local merchants partially revived the spice trade, especially in pepper, but the Sunnite Banū Khālid expelled Ottoman forces in 1670. The Portuguese maintained themselves in Muscat until 1649, although they could hold Bahrain only until 1602, when they were expelled by Ṣafavid Iran, which ruled there until 1717. Many Bahraini Shīʿite scholars in the 17th century moved to Iran, where they led in the development of Shīʿite theology.

Coastal Arabia was coming into direct contact with other Christian European maritime nations, which had begun their commercial penetration of the Indian Ocean. The Dutch, English, and French followed the Portuguese. The Western nations traded with Yemen through Mocha, whose coffee trade began in the 17th century; later the Europeans opened trading stations, or "factories," there.

By 1635 the Zaydīs of Yemen, supported by the northern tribes, had expelled the Ottomans, and the Zaydīs had their first great, if short-lived, expansion when their tribes moved into much of southern Arabia. The broken terrain made it impossible for them to maintain their supremacy, and local tribes drove out Zaydī garrisons by about the second decade of the 18th century.

In the 17th century Mecca and Medina saw a sharing of power between the locally autonomous sharifs and Ottoman Sunnite governors. Mecca was important in the spread and development of Islāmic theology, even for Shīʿite thinkers, while the pilgrimage reinforced a common Muslim identity among the far-flung and diverse Muslim communities of the world. In the late 17th and 18th centuries, however, there was confusion and civil war in Mecca, with disputes among the sharifian tribes and struggles at Jiddah with Ottoman officials, who, notwithstanding the virtual independence of the sharifs, still dabbled in Hejaz politics. A new element was introduced in Najd (in central Arabia) in the mid-18th century with the rise of the puritan Wahhābīs, who, because the sharifs regarded them as dangerous heretics, for a time were refused permission to make the pilgrimage to Mecca.

Omani expansion. In Oman events took an independent course. The Yaʿrubid dynasty—founded about 1624 when a member of the Yaʿrub tribe was elected imam—expelled the Portuguese from Muscat and set to harrying Portuguese possessions on the Indian coast. Embarking on expansion overseas—to Mombasa in 1698, then to Pemba, Zanzibar, and Kilwa—the Omanis became the supreme power on the coastal regions of the Indian Ocean, and European merchants feared marauding Omani fleets.

The Persians captured Muscat in 1743. The Yaʿrubids dissolved into dynastic dispute, and a leader named Aḥmad ibn Saʿīd set to liberating Oman from the Persians. He became imam in 1749, founding the Āl Bū Saʿīd dynasty. This period in Oman is marked by the crystallization of the political alignment of the tribes of the Banū Ghāfir (Ghāfirī) against those of the Banū Hinā (Hināwī).

During the 18th century the growth of the East India Company and British paramountcy in India began to affect Arabian politics and commerce most directly in the southern coastal region, while the interior was little concerned at first. Coastal Arabia now came fully into the world economy through commerce in coffee, slaves, pearls, and dates and the continuing pilgrimage to Mecca. Oman, Iran, and Sunnite Arab tribes struggled to dominate the coasts of the Persian Gulf, while a series of agreements later paved the way for British control in that area.

The Wahhābīs. The Ottomans, clinging to the Hejaz for religious prestige and claiming to be custodians of the Holy Cities, had little power outside their garrisons in those cities and along the pilgrim route. The bribes they gave the nomads for allowing the caravans to pass, and the need to keep food subsidies for Mecca and Medina, however, prevented their expulsion.

Religious reform. The Wahhābī movement, which introduced a new factor into the pattern of Arabian politics, was founded by Muḥammad ibn ʿAbd al-Wahhāb, a reformer influenced by the writings of the 13th–14th-century pietist theologian Ibn Taymīyah, of the strict Ḥanbalī school of Islāmic law. It was ʿAbd al-Wahhāb's intention to purify Islām of polytheism and to return it to an idealized primitive state. Expelled from his hometown in Najd, he moved to Ad-Dirʿīyah, a village that had never been ruled by the Ottomans, and obtained the protection and the adherence of its chief, Muḥammad ibn Saʿūd.

Resistance to the Ottomans. Propagating the doctrines of ʿAbd al-Wahhāb, Ibn Saʿūd and his son mastered all Najd. Late in the 18th century the Wahhābīs began raiding Iraq and then besieged Mecca, which they definitively conquered in 1806. The Ottomans became so alarmed at the Saʿūdī-Wahhābī peril that they urged Muḥammad ʿAlī, viceroy of Egypt, to drive the Wahhābīs from the Holy Cities. Egyptian troops invaded Arabia, and after a bitter seven-year struggle the viceroy's forces recaptured Mecca and Medina. The Wahhābī leader was forced to surrender his capital and was then beheaded. Egyptian occupation of western Arabia continued some 20 years.

Second Saʿūdī-Wahhābī dominance

The second Saʿūdī-Wahhābī kingdom began when Turkī, of a collateral Saʿūdī branch, revolted and in 1824 captured Riyadh in Najd and made it his capital. He was succeeded by his son Fayṣal. By 1833 Wahhābī overlordship was generally recognized in the Persian Gulf, though the Egyptians remained in the Hejaz.

After Fayṣal's death the fratricidal ambitions of his two eldest sons allowed Ibn Rashīd, ruler of Ḥāʾil in Jabal Shammar to the north, to take Riyadh. Ibn Rashīd ruled northern Arabia until he died in 1897. Meanwhile, the Saʿūdīs in 1871 had lost the fertile Al-Ḥasā to the Ottoman Turks, and the family ultimately took refuge in nearby Kuwait.

Ibn Rashīd's son and successor became involved in a struggle with the sheikh of Kuwait, which enabled the greatest of the Saʿūdīs, Ibn Saʿūd (ʿAbd al-ʿAzīz II), to retake Riyadh in 1902 and establish the third Saʿūdī kingdom. By 1904, through raiding and skirmishing, Ibn Saʿūd had recovered much of the earlier Saʿūdī territory. In 1912, to bring the nomads under control, he set up agricultural settlements colonized by Wahhābī warrior groups called Ikhwān.

When World War I broke out, Kuwait renounced allegiance to the Ottoman Empire. Ibn Saʿūd fought the pro-Ottoman Rashīdīs but otherwise remained inactive.

The Hejaz. The Meccan sharifs were merely the nominees of Egypt until 1840, when the Egyptians evacuated Arabia. Thereafter the sharifs were usually semiautonomous beside the Ottoman governors of the Hejaz. Improved communications after the opening of the Suez Canal in 1869 allowed the Ottoman Empire to send troops by sea to Arabia. An attempt to establish direct administration in the Hejaz in the 1880s failed when the sharifs and the population objected to Ottoman reforms. Ḥusayn ibn ʿAlī, appointed grand sharif in 1908, also successfully resisted Ottoman measures aimed at centralization by means of the new Hejaz Railway from Damascus to Medina.

British control of Aden

Yemen. In 1839 the British took Aden, ruling it and the island of Socotra (at the entrance to the Gulf of Aden) from India; the port of Aden became valuable as a coaling station. In 1849 the Ottoman Turks occupied the Yemeni Tihāmah but could not hold Ṣanʿāʾ in the interior until 1872. They were never able to break the resistance of the Zaydī tribes completely and were forced to an accommodation with the imam, Yaḥyā ibn Muḥammad, a few years before World War I. Aden developed into a large town and port, especially after the Suez Canal opened. Protectorate treaties concluded with the independent tribes around Aden were gradually extended inland. Many Yemenis worked overseas, especially in India and Southeast Asia.

The gulf states. In 1835 the Qawāsim coastal tribes of the Persian Gulf, earlier conquered and inspired by the Wahhābīs, were induced to bind themselves by a maritime truce to end hostilities with the British by sea, and the truce was made permanent in 1853. In Oman, Sulṭān ibn Aḥmad, revolting against his uncle the imam in 1793, gained mastery of the coastal towns. The British made Omani Zanzibar, in East Africa, a protectorate in 1890. The extension of British influence over Bahrain culminated in 1900 with the opening of a British political agency. The British also persuaded the gulf states, Zanzibar, and the Ottomans to help suppress the slave trade.

World War I. The Ottoman Empire entered World

War I holding all of western Arabia and supported in central northern Arabia by the Rashīdīs of Ḥā'il. Earlier Ottoman attempts to extend the empire to eastern Arabia, however, had been countered by the British, who were then paramount in the gulf and in treaty relation with the Arab sheikhdoms there. Sharif Ḥusayn ibn ʿAlī of Mecca, with assurance of British support, revolted against the Ottomans in June 1916, taking Mecca but failing to capture Medina. The British also supported the Idrīsī in Asir against the Ottomans. In Yemen Ottoman forces entered the Aden Protectorate, but the war subsequently settled down to a stalemate.

Two sons of Sharif Ḥusayn of Mecca, Fayṣal and Abdullah, stirred up the Hejazi tribes against the Ottomans and, assisted by British supplies and liaison officers, including the famous T.E. Lawrence ("Lawrence of Arabia"), moved northward to Transjordan along the right flank of the British armies and into Damascus (1918). Fayṣal set up an Arab government there, only to be dislodged by the French in 1920. In 1921 he was made king of Iraq, Abdullah emir of Transjordan.

Wahhābī-sharifian dispute. During the war, relations between Sharif Ḥusayn and Ibn Saʿūd worsened. In 1919 the dispute broke into an open clash. The Wahhābīs won so decisive a victory that they might have advanced unopposed into the Hejaz but for pressures on Ibn Saʿūd by the British. Instead, Ibn Saʿūd concentrated his forces against Ibn Rashīd, mastering all Shammar territory and capturing Ḥā'il in 1921.

Meanwhile, the grand sharif refused the terms of a treaty with Britain, mainly because of the Balfour Declaration, which approved a national home in Palestine for the Jews. The Wahhābīs marched into the Hejaz in 1924, and by October Ḥusayn was ruler no longer.

Saudi Arabia. Ibn Saʿūd's zealous Wahhābī followers, arriving in the more cosmopolitan atmosphere of Hejaz society, were now exposed to the world of Islām at large. Ibn Saʿūd managed the resulting problems with firmness and tact. He had furthermore to enforce his rule over the tribes impatient with centralized government. His tough action with them won, and he set out to develop security, economic reform, and communications.

On Ibn Saʿūd's southern border the Idrīsī sayyids of Asir had risen to power in the first decade of the 20th century. When in 1926 and 1930 Ibn Saʿūd concluded agreements with the Idrīsī, rendering Asir a virtual dependency of Saudi Arabia, Imam Yaḥyā of Yemen took Al-Ḥudaydah and southern Asir. Saudi troops swept into the Yemeni Tihāmah, but they withdrew after the Treaty of Aṭ-Ṭā'if in 1934, which acknowledged Saudi rule over Asir.

In the postwar years Britain and Saudi Arabia concluded agreements defining the frontiers with the British mandates of Jordan and Iraq (though most Saudi borders remained uncertain), and by treaty in 1927 Ibn Saʿūd was recognized as a sovereign, independent ruler.

Yemen. Imam Yaḥyā had to virtually conquer Yemen, in the Zaydī interest, after the Ottoman departure; by stern measures he established security. He refused to recognize the British-backed border between the Aden protectorates and Yemen. The British in the later 1930s pacified and, to a limited degree, developed their protectorates.

Postwar Arabia, to 1962. The post-World War I settlement and centralization of power in the hands of Yaḥyā, Ibn Saʿūd, and the British gave Arabia a large measure of internal peace and external security, which endured until 1962. A new factor in the 1930s was the discovery of immense quantities of petroleum in the deserts. In Bahrain oil was struck in June 1932. The American-owned Arabian Standard Oil Company (later Aramco) discovered oil in the Dhahran area of Saudi Arabia, and the first shipments left in September 1938. The Kuwait Oil Company, a joint Anglo-American enterprise, began production in June 1946. Thereafter oil was discovered in many other places, mostly in the Persian Gulf. Vast petroleum revenues brought enormous changes to Saudi Arabia and transformed the gulf states. The market for labour brought migrants from Yemen and other Arab countries.

Discovery of oil

Egypt, and later Syria and Iraq, utilized resentment of Israel and the appeal of Pan-Arab nationalism in the 1950s and '60s to try to undermine "feudal" Arab kingdoms and to remove British and American influence from Arabia.

Arabia since 1962. Political changes in Yemen and Saudi Arabia during the early 1960s epitomized a vast transformation of the Arabian Peninsula that affected the lives of most of its inhabitants. In 1962 Egyptian-trained Yemeni officers led a coup d'état and invited Egypt to send troops to support the republic. The imam's forces, although backed by Saudi Arabia during five years of war against large Egyptian armies, ultimately lost, and the republic was triumphant. Following the death of King Ibn Saʿūd of Saudi Arabia in 1953, his ineffective heir, Saʿūd, was replaced in a royal family coup d'état in 1964 by another son, Fayṣal, who initiated a number of modernizing changes.

The power of governments increased in all the countries of the peninsula as oil production provided most ruling elites with unprecedented wealth. Religion and dynasty, the two pillars of most earlier regimes, were increasingly supplemented by the distribution to the people of oil revenues; individual national identities also began slowly to develop. Governments whose effective jurisdiction had often been limited to the coast now expanded their powers into the interior, while commercial, social, cultural, and diplomatic interactions with the rest of the world played a larger role in determining local matters.

President Gamal Abdel Nasser of Egypt applied political pressure to remove the British from Aden, and Britain left Aden and South Yemen in 1967. A violently leftist group, the National Liberation Front (NLF), proclaimed the People's Democratic Republic of Yemen (Yemen [Aden]), which became communist and formed links with the Soviet Union.

After a compromise between royalists and republicans, northern Yemen, with its capital at Ṣanʿā', was ruled by relatively liberal military governments, with army officers as presidents, including the long-lasting ʿAlī ʿAbd Allāh Ṣāliḥ, who first took office in 1978. North Yemen gained considerable income from the hundreds of thousands of Yemenis who worked in oil-rich Saudi Arabia; in the 1980s both Yemens discovered oil fields of their own.

Over several years a struggle for control of Yemen (Aden) waged within the ruling political party resulted in a brief civil war in 1986. The collapse of communism in Europe and the yearning of Yemenis for the union of the two parts of Yemen in the north and south, despite the great differences between them, resulted in the proclamation of their unification on May 22, 1990.

In Oman, after a palace revolution in 1970, the new sultan, Qābūs, opened a program of modernization, welfare, and reform. Much oil revenue initially had to be devoted to repelling rebel attacks, supported from Yemen (Aden), but the rebels were defeated in 1975. A mutual accord was signed in 1982.

At the entrance to the Persian Gulf, the Trucial States had acquired world importance from their vast oil riches. In the new alignments following Britain's withdrawal, the former Trucial States—Abu Dhabi, Dubayy, Ash-Shāriqah, ʿAjmān, Al-Fujayrah, and Umm Al-Qaywayn—proclaimed themselves the United Arab Emirates (UAE) in 1971. They were joined by Ra's Al-Khaymah in 1972.

British withdrawal

Kuwait saw the British withdraw in 1961, but Iraq claimed the country, and it was deterred only by British and later by Arab armed forces. In 1970–71 Bahrain and Qatar became independent and subsequently acquired control of Western oil concerns operating in their territories. Their way of life was transformed as oil revenues and the service sector of the economy grew.

The Iran-Iraq War. A fresh threat to the rich oil states of the gulf arose with the revolution in Iran in 1978–79 and with the outbreak of the Iran-Iraq War in 1980. Islāmic fundamentalism in the Ayatollah Ruhollah Khomeini's Iran struck an answering chord with Shīʿites and Iranian workers in the Arabian states, which gave financial support to Iraq. U.S. President Jimmy Carter and his successor in 1981, Ronald Reagan, pledged American support to keep open the Strait of Hormuz, through which some 60 percent of the industrial world's oil supply was being transported.

In response to the tensions of the Iran-Iraq War, Saudi Arabia and other gulf Arab states expanded their military power, but the small size of their populations limited their military effectiveness. In 1979 Saudi religious extremists seized the Al-Ḥaram mosque (Great Mosque) of Mecca and revolted against the Saʿūdi dynasty. They were forcibly repressed, and few changes were made in the Saudi government.

In March 1981 Kuwait, Bahrain, Qatar, Oman, Saudi Arabia, and the United Arab Emirates formed the Gulf Cooperation Council (GCC) to promote stability and cooperation in the gulf region; the GCC coordinated their economic and defensive efforts. Expected economic growth in the entire region was slowed by the fall in oil prices in the mid-1980s, and the countries of Arabia made plans to diversify their economies and to institute austerity measures in the face of falling prices. (R.B.Se./W.L.O.)

The 1991 Persian Gulf War. Following the end of the Iran-Iraq War in 1988, President Saddam Hussein of Iraq faced massive economic problems, including debts owed to Saudi Arabia and Kuwait. The Iraqi president also viewed himself as the leader of Pan-Arab nationalism and socialism, two ideologies firmly opposed by the conservative monarchies that controlled most of the Arabian Peninsula outside of Yemen.

Claiming that Kuwait had historically been part of Iraq and that Kuwaiti oil policy had robbed Iraq of much-needed revenue, Saddam Hussein ordered an invasion of Kuwait on Aug. 2, 1990. Kuwait itself fell quickly to the Iraqis, but the Kuwaiti royal family established a government-in-exile in Saudi Arabia, while hundreds of thousands of Kuwaitis fled to several gulf countries. Many Kuwaiti citizens remaining in the emirate engaged in guerrilla warfare against the invaders.

Initially Saudi Arabia and the other GCC countries reacted cautiously, but, when the United States suggested that Iraq might next invade Saudi Arabia, most Arabian Peninsula countries took a firm stand against the Iraqi annexation of Kuwait. Hundreds of thousands of soldiers and many warships and aircraft from a wide variety of countries acted under the authority of United Nations resolutions as they assembled in Saudi Arabia.

Since Yemen held a seat on the United Nations Security Council, its reluctance to authorize force to oust Iraq from Kuwait was particularly noteworthy; Saudi Arabia in retribution compelled hundreds of thousands of Yemeni workers to leave the kingdom. The GCC countries provided military facilities for the coalition armed forces. The military contingents coming from the various Islāmic countries acted together under the command of Saudi generals; troops from Western nations ultimately coordinated their activities under U.S. command.

Iraq attempted to link a solution of the Kuwait question to the resolution of the Palestinian Arab issue, but the coalition countries insisted on unconditional Iraqi withdrawal from Kuwait. After Iraq rejected this demand, the coalition launched an air war against Iraq and Iraqi-occupied Kuwait on Jan. 16–17, 1991. A ground campaign that began on February 24 lasted only four days and secured the eviction of Iraq from Kuwait. Iraqi military and civilian casualties were heavy, but the coalition armed forces suffered fewer than 1,500 killed or wounded in action.

The Arabian Peninsula countries had not seen such a far-reaching external military intervention in their affairs since the days of Muḥammad ʿAlī and the first Saʿūdī kingdom. As a result, the diplomatic, military, and political structures and patterns created after the withdrawal of the British imperial presence in the early 1960s were placed in question. (W.L.O.)

For coverage of related topics in the *Macropædia* and *Micropædia,* see the *Propædia,* sections 911, 922, 924, 962, 96/11, and 978.

THE COUNTRIES OF ARABIA

Bahrain

The State of Bahrain (Arabic: Dawlat Al-Baḥrayn), a small Arab state in the Persian (Arabian) Gulf, is an archipelago consisting of Bahrain Island—extending about 30 miles (48 kilometres) from north to south and 10 miles from east to west—and some 30 smaller islands. Its Arabic name, Al-Baḥrayn, means "Two Seas." It is situated in a bay on the southwestern coast of the Persian Gulf between the northeastern coast of Saudi Arabia to the west and the Qatar peninsula to the east. The King Fahd Causeway, 15 miles long, links Bahrain with Saudi Arabia. Bahrain's total land area is 267 square miles (692 square kilometres).

From earliest times Bahrain has been an important commercial and shipping centre in the gulf; its importance has increased since the discovery and development of the oil resources of the region. Although only a small producer of oil itself, Bahrain is placed to take advantage of the vast oil production in Saudi Arabia, and its own early development of oil production and refining has provided opportunities for the creation of related industries and services. The chief town, port, and seat of administration is Manama (Al-Manāmah), on the northeastern tip of Bahrain Island.

Bahrain became a fully independent Arab emirate in 1971. It is a member of the United Nations, the Arab League, and the Gulf Cooperation Council. The emir—the ruler of the state—is a member of the Khalīfah family (Āl Khalīfah), which has been paramount in Bahrain since 1783. The system of government might be described as a mixture of traditional Arab autocracy and a benevolent oligarchy much modified by Western influence.

PHYSICAL AND HUMAN GEOGRAPHY

The land. *Relief.* The state consists of two separate groups of islands. The 225-square-mile island of Bahrain is surrounded by smaller islands. Two of these—Al-Muḥarraq and Sitrah, both to the northeast—are joined to it by causeways that have encouraged their development for residence and industry; other islands in the group are Nabī Ṣāliḥ, Al-Muḥammadīyah (Umm Aṣ-Ṣabbān), Umm An-Naʿsān (linked by the King Fahd Causeway), and Jiddah. The second group consists of the Ḥawār Islands, which are situated near the coast of Qatar about 12 miles southeast of Bahrain Island; small and rocky, they are inhabited by only a few fishermen and quarry workers.

The archipelago

While all the small islands in both groups are rocky and low-lying, rising only a few feet above sea level, the main island is more varied in appearance. In geologic terms the island consists of a gentle anticline of arched layers of sedimentary rocks: limestones, sandstones, and marl (loose clay, sand, or silt) formed during the Cretaceous and Tertiary periods (from 144 to 1.6 million years ago). The central region rises to 440 feet (134 metres) above sea level at Ad-Dukhān Hill and is rocky and barren. The southern and western lowlands consist of a bleak sandy plain with some salt marshes. The northern and northwestern coasts afford a striking contrast; they form a narrow belt of date and vegetable gardens irrigated from prolific springs and wells that tap artesian water. The source of this water is rainfall on the western mountains of Saudi Arabia. This abundance of fresh water was the reason for the legendary fertility of Bahrain and its importance as a harbour and trading centre in the generally inhospitable environment of the Persian Gulf. Economic developments and population growth have outstripped the available artesian water in Bahrain, and some 60 percent of the water used now comes from seawater distillation plants powered by natural gas.

Climate. The summer climate is distinctly unpleasant on the many occasions when high temperatures coincide with high humidity. Midday temperatures from May to October generally exceed 90° F (32° C) and often reach 95° F (35° C) or higher. Summer nights are sultry and humid. Winters are cooler and more pleasant, with mean temperatures from December to March below 70° F

(21° C). Rainfall is confined to the winter months and averages only 3 inches (75 millimetres) per year, but this may vary from almost nothing to double this amount. On average, rain falls only about 10 days a year. Sunshine is abundant the year round. The predominant wind is the damp, northwesterly *shamāl* blowing on most summer days. The *qaws,* a hot, dry, and dusty south wind, is less frequent but brings sand dust and low humidity.

Plant and animal life. Some 200 different species of desert plants grow in the bare arid portions of the archipelago, while the irrigated and cultivated areas of the islands support fruit trees, fodder crops, and vegetables. The variety of animals is limited by the desert conditions. The gazelle and the hare are not yet extinct, and lizards and jerboas (desert rats) are common, while the mongoose—probably imported from India—is found in the irrigated areas. Birdlife is sparse except in spring and autumn, when many varieties of migratory birds rest temporarily in Bahrain while traveling to and from higher temperate latitudes.

Settlement patterns. The majority of the population now dwell in towns, but in the north and northwest of the main island, where irrigation has long been carried out using artesian water, there are numerous small villages and isolated dwellings where horticulture is the way of life. This area has an aspect of great fertility, which contrasts quite starkly with the bare desert appearance of much of the country. The villages consist, for the most part, of substantial houses built of stone or concrete with a flat roof. Some of the temporary settlements of fishermen and the very poor are still constructed of *barasti* (branches of the date palm). There is little permanent settlement either in the southern half of Bahrain Island or on the smaller islands.

About half the population lives in the two principal towns, Manama and Al-Muḥarraq. Manama, with its port of Mīnā' Salmān, is the principal town and contains the main government offices, the business and financial district, many large hotels, Western-style shops, and a traditional Arab souk. It has a distinctly modern appearance as compared with Al-Muḥarraq, which is densely settled and has many narrow, winding streets. Other major settlements are 'Awālī, near the centre of Bahrain Island, which was built largely for expatriate employees of the Bahrain Petroleum Company; Madīnat 'Īsā' (Isa Town), a new town built by the government since 1968; the sizeable settlements of Ar-Rifā' Ash-Shamālī (North Rifā'), Ar-Rifā' Ash-Sharqi (East Rifā'), and Ar-Rifā' Al-Gharbī (West Rifā'); and the new town at Ḥamad, completed in 1984.

The people. Some 70 percent of the population is Arab. Most of those are native-born Bahrainis, but some are Palestinians, Omanis, or Saudis. Foreign-born inhabitants are mostly Iranian, Indian, Pakistani, British, and American workers. In 1985 foreigners outnumbered Bahrainis among those holding regular full-time jobs.

The Muslim population is composed of both Sunnite and Shī'ite sects, with the latter in the majority. The ruling family and many of the wealthier and more influential Bahrainis are Sunnite, and this difference has been an underlying cause of local tension, particularly during the Iran-Iraq War in the 1980s. Arabic is the official language of Bahrain, but English is widely understood.

Tom Sheppard—Robert Harding Picture Library

Building a dhow in a boatyard on the coast of Bahrain.

The economy. The economy of Bahrain, like that of other Arab states in the Persian Gulf, has in recent times been based largely on the production of oil and natural gas and on refining petroleum products. It is therefore very sensitive to fluctuations in the demand for oil and in oil prices. With its long tradition of shipping and commerce, however, and because both its oil and gas reserves are relatively small, Bahrain has been more successful than some other states in the gulf in diversifying its economy to include manufactures and both commercial and financial services. It has long been the most important commercial and financial centre in the gulf.

Agriculture and fishing. The majority of Bahrain's food is imported, but agriculture contributes significantly to the local food supply. Dates, bananas, citrus fruits, mangoes, pomegranates, vegetables, and alfalfa (lucerne) are the main items. Cattle breeding and dairy and poultry farming are encouraged by the government, and camels and horses are bred for racing. The increasing pollution of the waters of the gulf has killed off important segments of the fishing industry, such as shrimp, which have virtually disappeared from the gulf. Pollution of the waters of the gulf by oil spillages from Kuwaiti oil installations during the Persian Gulf War has not proved as serious or as lasting as was first feared. Some Bahraini-owned trawlers now fish in the deep waters of the Indian Ocean.

Industry. The traditional industries of Bahrain were building dhows (Arab sailboats), fishing, pearling, and the manufacture of reed mats. Demand for the traditional products has decreased, however, as living standards have risen, and the traditional industries are now carried out on only a very small scale.

Oil was first discovered in Bahrain in 1932. The country's oil production has always been small by Middle Eastern standards, and the refining of crude oil imported from Saudi Arabia has been of much greater importance since the discovery of vast oil fields on the mainland. Bahrain's oil reserves are expected to last only until the year 2000, but the offshore natural gas supplies may have a longer life. An aluminum smelter operated by Aluminum Bahrain (ALBA), in which the government is a majority shareholder, began production in 1972 and is one of the largest non-oil industrial establishments in the gulf. As a further development of this industry, an aluminum rolling mill was opened in 1985 to manufacture aluminum products such as door and window frames. Ship repair is handled at Mīnā' Salmān, near Manama, and at a large yard operated on Al-'Azl Island. The yard can handle as many as 50 large tankers per year. Other industries include the production of building materials, furniture, soft drinks, plastics, and a wide range of consumer goods. The government has a significant financial stake in all these modern industries; the oil and natural gas resources and production are nationalized.

The aluminum industry

Finance and trade. The government has encouraged the growth of offshore banking, insurance, and other financial services, and consequently Bahrain has become an important financial centre. It has also been able to benefit from its long tradition as a commercial centre.

Bahrain's major import is the crude petroleum brought in by underwater pipeline from Saudi Arabia to be refined. Other major imports are machinery, food, alumina, chemicals, and a wide range of manufactured goods. The major export is refined petroleum products, and other exports include aluminum goods, machinery, and transport services. Banking, insurance, and financial services are becoming important in the country's balance of payments. A stock exchange was opened in 1989.

Transportation. Bahrain Island has an excellent system of paved roads, and its causeway connections to Al-Muḥarraq and Sitrah islands and to Saudi Arabia facilitate travel. The principal towns and villages are well served by bus and taxi services. A high percentage of residents own motor vehicles. Bahrain International Airport on Al-

Muḥarraq Island is one of the busiest airports in the Middle East and is used by most major international airlines. Manama is the headquarters of Gulf Air, owned by the governments of Bahrain, Oman, Qatar, and the United Arab Emirates. There is a military airfield in the south of the main island. Steamers run scheduled service from Bahrain to other gulf ports and to Karāchi, Pak., and to Bombay.

Administration and social conditions. The emir is assisted by a Cabinet, or council of ministers, which consists of the heads of various government departments, many of whom are members of the royal family. A constitution promulgated in 1973 created a National Assembly composed of members of the Cabinet and elected members, but after a period of industrial unrest and political agitation the assembly was dissolved by the emir in 1975. Public representation has reverted to the traditional Arab and Islāmic system of a *majlis,* through which citizens and other residents may present petitions to the emir. This system has survived subsequent sporadic outbursts of discontent fueled both by left-wing elements and by Shīʿite interests inspired by the 1979 Iranian revolution.

Education

Public education is free for both boys and girls at the primary, intermediate, and secondary level. Private schools are available as well. Institutions of higher education include the University College of Arts, Sciences, and Education; the Gulf Polytechnic; and the College of Health Sciences. Medical care is extensive and free, and there is provision for most forms of social security: pensions, sick pay, compensation for industrial injury, unemployment benefits, and maternity and family allowance payments.

Cultural life. In spite of its rapid economic development, Bahrain remains, in many respects, essentially Arab in its culture. The state television and radio stations broadcast most programs in Arabic, although there are channels in English. Football (soccer) is popular, and the traditional sports of falconry and of gazelle and hare coursing are still practiced by wealthier Bahrainis. Horse and camel racing are popular public entertainments.

Several weekly and daily papers are published in Arabic, and a small number appear in English. The museum in Manama contains local artifacts from ancient times such as ivory figurines, pottery, copper articles, and gold rings, many of which reflect various external cultural influences.

For statistical data on the land and people of Bahrain, see the *Britannica World Data* section in the BRITANNICA WORLD DATA ANNUAL.

HISTORY

Bahrain has been inhabited from prehistoric times, and several thousand burial mounds in the north of the main island probably date from the Sumerian period of the 3rd millennium BC. The archipelago was mentioned by Persian, Greek, and Roman geographers and historians. It has been Arab and Muslim since the Muslim conquest of the 7th century AD, though it was ruled by the Portuguese from 1521 to 1602 and by the Persians from 1602 to 1783. Since 1783 it has been ruled by sheikhs of the Khalīfah family, which originated in the Al-Ḥasā province of Arabia.

British intervention

Several times during the 19th century the British intervened in the government of the territory to suppress war and piracy and to prevent the establishment of Egyptian, Persian, German, or Russian influence. The first Bahraini-British treaty was signed in 1820; and Bahrain's British-protected status dates from 1861, with the completion of a treaty by which the sheikh bound himself to refrain from "the prosecution of war, piracy, or slavery." Britain thus assumed responsibility for the defense of Bahrain and for the conduct of its relations with other major powers; until 1947 this protection was, in effect, the responsibility of the government of British India, which had both commercial and strategic interests in the Persian Gulf. Until 1970 the government of Iran periodically advanced claims to sovereignty over Bahrain, but these were repudiated.

In August 1971 Bahrain proclaimed independence. A treaty of friendship was signed with the United Kingdom, terminating the British protectorate status, and Sheikh ʿĪsā was designated the emir. Bahrain then became a member of the United Nations and the Arab League. In 1981 Bahrain joined with five other Arab gulf states in forming the Gulf Cooperation Council (GCC), which has led to freer trading and closer economic and defense ties. Bahrain has a close political and defense relationship with Saudi Arabia. During the Persian Gulf War of 1991 Bahrain made its port and airfields available to the coalition forces that liberated Kuwait.

For later developments in the history of Bahrain, see the *Britannica Book of the Year* section in the BRITANNICA WORLD DATA ANNUAL. (C.G.S.)

Kuwait

The State of Kuwait (Arabic: Dawlat Al-Kuwayt), located at the upper northwestern corner of the Persian (Arabian) Gulf, has an area of 6,880 square miles (17,818 square kilometres) and is bounded on the west and north by Iraq, on the east by the Persian Gulf, and on the south by Saudi Arabia. A territory of 2,200 square miles along the gulf was shared by Kuwait and Saudi Arabia as a neutral zone until 1969, when a political boundary was agreed upon. Each of the two countries administers one-half of the territory (called the Divided Zone), but, as before, they share equally the revenues from oil production in the entire area. While the boundary with Saudi Arabia is defined, the border with Iraq remains disputed.

Kuwait is largely a desert, except for Al-Jahrah oasis, at the western end of Kuwait Bay, and a few fertile patches in the southeastern and coastal areas. The largest offshore islands are the uninhabited islands of Būbiyān and Al-Warbah. The island of Faylakah, near the entrance of Kuwait Bay, has been populated since prehistoric times.

The capital city of Kuwait, a true desert metropolis, is located on the southern shore of Kuwait Bay and derives its name from the diminutive of *kūt,* meaning "fort." With almost all of its population concentrated in or near the capital, Kuwait is one of the world's most highly urbanized states. The emir—the ruler of the state—is a member of the Ṣabāḥ family, which has governed Kuwait since the inception of a sheikhdom there in 1756.

Since the discovery of oil in Kuwait in the 1930s and the development of the petroleum industry in the years after World War II, oil has dominated the economy of the country, accounting for more than 90 percent of its export revenues until the 1980s. During the 1980s Kuwait began to earn more money from its now vast overseas investments than from the direct sale of oil. It was this investment income that sustained Kuwait during the Iraqi occupation of 1990–91 and the subsequent period when oil exports ceased. Historically Kuwait has been one of the largest oil producers in the world and has had one of the largest oil reserves of any producing country.

PHYSICAL AND HUMAN GEOGRAPHY

The land. *Relief.* The relief of Kuwait is generally flat or gently undulating, broken only by occasional low hills and shallow depressions. The elevations range from sea level in the east to 951 feet (290 metres) at Ash-Shaqāyā peak, in the western corner of the country. The Az-Zawr Escarpment, one of the main topographic features, borders the northwestern shore of Kuwait Bay and rises to a maximum height of 475 feet above sea level. Elsewhere in coastal areas large patches of salty marshland have developed. Throughout the northern, western, and central sections of Kuwait there are desert basins, which fill with water after winter rains; historically these basins formed important watering places for the camel herds of the Bedouin.

Vegetation. True soils scarcely exist naturally in Kuwait. Except in the new green belt of Kuwait city and in a few desert oases such as Al-Jahrah, where cultivation and irrigation are carried out, the vegetation consists of scrub and low bushes (and ephemeral grass in the spring). Halophytes (salt-loving plants) grow on the marshy stretches along the coast.

Climate. The climate is desert, tempered somewhat in the coastal regions by the warm waters of the gulf. If there is enough rainfall, the desert turns green from the middle of March to the end of April. But during the dry season, between April and September, the heat is severe—the temperature ordinarily reaching 111° F (44° C) during the day and on occasion going as high as 130° F (54° C). The winter is more agreeable (even frost can occasionally occur in the interior, though never on the seacoast). Annual rainfall averages only from 1 to 7 inches (25 to 180 millimetres), chiefly between October and April, though cloudbursts can bring more than two inches of rain in a day.

The frequent winds from the northwest are cool in winter and spring and hot in summer. Southeasterly winds, usually hot and damp, spring up between July and October; hot and dry south winds prevail in spring and early summer. The *shamāl,* a northwesterly wind, causes dramatic sandstorms.

Settlement patterns. The old town of Kuwait, although located in a harsh desert climate, opened onto an excellent sheltered harbour. Kuwait developed in the 18th and 19th centuries as a trading city, relying on the pearl banks of the gulf as well as on long-distance sea and caravan traffic. The old city—oriented toward the sea and bounded landward from 1918 to 1954 by a mud wall, with gates that led out only into the endless desert—was compact, only five square miles in area; its typical dwelling was a courtyard house. Following the discovery of oil in the 1930s and the rapid expansion of the oil industry after World War II, Kuwait city underwent a transformation. With the urban explosion of the years after 1951, the semicircular city wall was demolished (its gates were preserved as a reminder of the early years), and new suburbs were formally laid out. The government invested large portions of the oil revenues in infrastructure and urban development, creating in the process a modern, air-conditioned metropolis.

Urbanization and suburbanization

Kuwaitis are now scattered at a relatively low density throughout the urban area, with minor concentrations in the suburbs of Dasmah, Ash-Shāmīyah, and Al-ʿUḍaylīyah. Non-Kuwaitis, excluded from the restricted suburbs, live at higher densities in the old city and in the suburbs of Ḥawallī and As-Sālimīyah, mostly in apartments.

The people. Kuwait's national population is almost entirely Muslim; a law passed in 1981 limits citizenship to Muslims. The majority are Sunnite, but some 20 percent may be Shīʿite. Both the Iranian revolution of 1979 and the Kuwaiti government's heightened discrimination against Shīʿites in reaction to the revolution prompted a new sense of community in the Shīʿite population in the 1980s.

The native and official language is Arabic, and fluency in Arabic is a requirement for naturalization. English is the second basic language taught in public schools. Hindi, Urdū, and Fārsī (Persian) also are widely spoken among the foreign population.

Historically, Kuwait had several important class divisions. After the discovery of oil, most of these vanished as the state became the primary employer. The one class that remains politically important is the old merchant oligarchy.

Native Kuwaitis, who were only about one-quarter of Kuwait's residents before the Iraqi invasion, now make up slightly more than half of the country's total population. Until the Iraqi invasion of 1990, Palestinians, some of them third-generation residents of Kuwait, were the largest single expatriate group, numbering perhaps 400,000. After the invasion, the Kuwaiti government encouraged and coerced this group to leave. By mid-1991 their number had fallen to 50,000. They have largely been replaced by Egyptians and nationals of other states that supported Kuwait during the occupation. These non-nationals do not enjoy citizenship rights, which are reserved for "native" Kuwaitis—*i.e.,* those who can prove Kuwaiti ancestry from before 1920. Naturalization is strictly limited.

The economy. Virtually all of Kuwait's wealth is derived, directly or indirectly (through overseas investments), from oil. This income gives Kuwait one of the highest per capita incomes in the world. Although the downturn in the world oil market in 1986 substantially reduced the income from oil exports, Kuwait's economy did not suffer greatly. In part this was because the return on foreign investments had begun to exceed the income from oil. Kuwait's foreign investments are mostly in the United States and include a variety of holdings. It was this investment income that allowed the government to survive after the Iraqi invasion cut off oil imports. Even after liberation oil exports were slow to resume because of the damage done to the wells. The Kuwait Fund for Arab Economic Development, established in 1961, extends generous loan assistance to governments of Muslim and Third World countries, although no longer at the levels achieved in the 1970s, when aid disbursements reached as much as 15 percent of the gross national product.

The most dramatic aspect of Kuwait's economic development since the 1970s has been the expansion of its oil industry. By the mid-1980s, Kuwait was refining 80 percent of its oil at home and marketing 250,000 barrels a day in its own European retail outlets under the logo "Q8."

Domestically, Kuwait has invested its revenues in social services, including health and education (giving it one of the most literate populations in the region), in infrastructure, and only marginally in local industry.

Employment generated directly by oil production and export accounts for only a small percentage of the labour force. More than half of all employed Kuwaitis work for the state, most of these in the public administration, defense, and services sectors; about one-fifth of all jobs are in construction; and the trade, manufacturing, transportation and communication, finance, and agriculture sectors all employ more than the oil sector. In both the public and private sectors, Kuwait remains heavily dependent on foreign labour, although after the invasion the government reiterated more forcefully its formal goal of reducing this dependence.

Resources. Kuwait's proven, recoverable oil reserves are thought to be enough to sustain pre-invasion levels of production for more than 150 years. Kuwait also has considerable reserves of natural gas, almost all of it in the form of associated gas—*i.e.,* gas that is produced together with oil. There are no other important minerals. Naturally

© Burnett H. Moody/Bruce Coleman Inc.

The Kuwait Towers, containing two water reservoirs and a restaurant with a revolving viewing platform, Kuwait city, Kuwait.

occurring fresh water is scarce (and, until desalination plants were built after World War II, had to be imported).

Agriculture and fishing. The possibilities of agricultural development are severely limited. Only a very small percentage of the land is arable, and, because of the scarcity of water, deficiencies of soil, and lack of manpower trained in agricultural skills, an even smaller percentage of the land area is under actual cultivation. Agriculture's contribution to the output of the economy is insignificant.

Fish are plentiful in the Persian Gulf, and, before the discovery of oil, fishing in Kuwait was a leading industry. The Kuwait United Fisheries continues the tradition today. Shrimp was one of the few commodities besides oil that Kuwait continued to export after World War II. Shrimp production, however, was devastated by the environmental havoc wreaked in the gulf by the 1991 war.

Development of oil production

Industry. In 1934 the Kuwait Oil Company (KOC), the ownership of which was divided equally between the British Petroleum Company and the Gulf Oil Corporation (of the United States), obtained a concession covering the whole territory except the Neutral Zone. Oil was struck in 1938, but World War II deferred development until 1946. Thereafter, progress was spectacular. In 1953 the American Independent Oil Company and the Getty Oil Company, which jointly held concessions for the Neutral Zone, struck oil in commercial quantities; and in 1955 oil was discovered in northern Kuwait. By 1976 Kuwait had achieved 100 percent control of the KOC, with the former owners retaining the right to purchase at a discount. The government also achieved full ownership of the Kuwait National Petroleum Company (KNPC), which it had formed in 1960 with private Kuwaiti investors. The KNPC, designed to serve as an integrated oil company, controlled distribution and petroleum products supplies within the country and began marketing operations abroad. In 1980 the government founded the Kuwait Petroleum Corporation as an umbrella organization overseeing the KOC and the KPNC as well as the Kuwait Oil Tanker Company, the Petrochemicals Industries Company, and the Kuwait Foreign Petroleum Exploration Company.

The relatively low cost of oil production in Kuwait stems from certain unique advantages. First, there are a number of highly productive wells, the output of which can be varied at short notice, thus eliminating the need for large numbers of storage tanks. Most of the storage tanks themselves are placed on a ridge set back a few miles from the seacoast at a height of some 300 feet; this enables loading operations to be carried out by gravity and not through the use of pumps. There are also extensive refineries and bunkers for tankers. While retreating from Kuwait at the end of the Persian Gulf War, the Iraqis set fire to more than 700 of the country's 950 wells. By the fall of 1991, the fires, which had consumed 4 to 6 million barrels of oil per day, had been extinguished and limited production had returned, but recovery of the industry remained slow. In mid-1992 oil production stood at nearly 1 million barrels per day.

Natural gas and other industries

Massive volumes of natural gas are produced in association with crude oil. Although natural gas has great potential as a source of foreign exchange, its principal uses so far have been in reinjection in oil fields to maintain pressure, in the generation of electricity (as for water distillation), and in the production (as raw material) of petrochemicals and fertilizers.

For fresh water in earlier days people depended on a few artesian wells and on rainwater collected from the roofs of houses or from cisterns at ground level. Dhows manned by Kuwaiti seamen also brought fresh water from the Shaṭṭ Al-ʿArab near Basra, Iraq. With the rapid growth of population, however, the government of Kuwait built desalinization plants at Kuwait city, Ash-Shuʿaybah, and several other locations. Important sources of fresh water have been discovered at Ar-Rawḍatayn and Ash-Shaqāyā, but desalinization still provides the great majority of Kuwait's daily consumption of potable water.

The expansion of electric facilities also has been remarkable. Production is concentrated in several large, natural-gas-fired power stations, including one at Ash-Shuwaykh and another at Ash-Shuʿaybah.

Power

Trade and finance. Oil and oil-derived products account for all but a very minor portion of Kuwait's exports, with Asia and Europe being the most important markets. Kuwait's imports, largely manufactured goods, are principally from Japan, the United States, and several western European nations.

In addition to its Central Bank, Kuwait has specialized banks operating in the areas of savings and credit, industrial loans, and real estate. There are also commercial banks. No foreign banks may operate, with the exception of the Bank of Bahrain and Kuwait, based in Bahrain and owned equally by the two states. An Islāmic bank has also been established. Since before independence an officially sanctioned stock exchange has operated, growing to become one of the largest in the world. However, the fall of the unofficial but wildly popular stock market, the Suq Al-Manakh, in 1982 sent the local economy into a mild recession.

Transportation. Kuwait has a modern road system, linking it with its neighbours, and a large international airport. Kuwait Airways Corporation, a state-owned enterprise, serves a number of international routes. The country's port facilities and its fleet of oil tankers and general cargo ships have been expanded.

Administration and social conditions. Since gaining its independence from Britain in 1961, Kuwait has been a constitutional monarchy whose ruler, called the emir, has episodically shared some power with a National Assembly elected by adult male Kuwaitis. The reopening of this parliamentary body, suspended once in 1976 and again in 1986, became the goal of the prodemocracy Constitutionalist Movement in 1989–90. A compromise National Council, partially elected and partially appointed and with more limited power, was convened by the emir just prior to the Iraqi invasion in 1990 and reconvened following the liberation in 1991. This did not, however, placate the popular opposition, which prompted the emir to schedule elections for October 1992.

The legal system of Kuwait is based upon a number of diverse sources. Most matters of civil and personal status law are governed by the Sharīʿah, the Islāmic religious law based on the Qurʾān and the Ḥadīth (collected traditions of the Prophet Muḥammad). Commercial and criminal laws derive from Ottoman and several modern Arab sources and, through them, reflect elements of the French legal code and the English common law. There are several courts of first instance and courts of appeal at two levels. The emir acts as the final court of appeal.

Social welfare services

Kuwait has a comprehensive scheme of social welfare. For the needy there is financial assistance; for the handicapped there are loans to start a profitable business; for the disabled there are treatment and training; and for adult illiterates there is education. A huge program called the Limited Income Housing Scheme, which provides adequate houses fully equipped with modern facilities for native Kuwaiti families with limited incomes, has been one of the chief projects of the Ministry of Social Affairs and Labour. Kuwait has a comprehensive and highly developed free national health-care system. In 1990 the life expectancy in Kuwait was 73.4 years. Kuwait has established a Reserve Fund for Future Generations to provide for the welfare of its people. The fund receives 10 percent of the state's revenues annually, and both principal and interest were originally scheduled to remain untouched until the year 2001. The government found it necessary, however, to tap this fund during the Iraqi occupation.

General education in Kuwait is compulsory for native Kuwaitis between the ages of 6 and 14. It is entirely free and also includes school meals, books, uniforms, transportation, and medical attention. Non-Kuwaiti students attend government schools as space permits or attend private schools. Kuwait University was founded in 1962. About three-fourths of the university students are Kuwaitis, and more than half are women. Several thousand students attend colleges and universities overseas, principally in the United States, Britain, and Egypt, usually on state scholarships.

The Ministry of Information runs the government press and the radio and television broadcasting stations. It also has undertaken the task of reviving some of the outstanding literary works in Arabic.

For statistical data on the land and people of Kuwait, see the *Britannica World Data* section in the BRITANNICA WORLD DATA ANNUAL. (D.A.Sa./J.D.An./J.C.)

HISTORY

The origin of the city of Kuwait—and of the State of Kuwait—is usually placed at about the beginning of the 18th century, when the Banū ʿUtūb, a group of families of the ʿAnizah tribe in the interior of the Arabian Peninsula, migrated to the area that is now Kuwait. The foundation of the autonomous sheikhdom of Kuwait is dated from 1756, when the settlers decided to appoint a sheikh from the Ṣabāḥ family. During the 19th century Kuwait developed as a thriving, independent trading community. Toward the end of the century one ruler, ʿAbd Allāh II (reigned 1866–92), began moving Kuwait closer to the Ottoman Empire, although never placing his country under Ottoman rule. This trend was reversed with the accession of Mubārak the Great, who came to power by assassinating his brother ʿAbd Allāh—an act of uncustomary political violence in Kuwait. Mubārak cultivated a close relationship with Britain in order to keep both other European powers and the Ottomans at bay. An 1899 treaty granted Britain control of Kuwait's foreign affairs. Following the outbreak of World War I, Kuwait became a British protectorate.

At the 1922 Conference of Al-ʿUqayr, Britain negotiated the Kuwait-Saudi border, with substantial territorial loss to Kuwait. A 1923 memorandum set out the border with Iraq based on an unratified 1913 convention.

The first Iraqi claim to Kuwait surfaced in 1938—the year oil was discovered in the sheikhdom. Although neither Iraq nor the Ottoman Empire had ever actually ruled Kuwait, Iraq asserted a vague historical title. That year it also offered some rhetorical support to a merchant uprising against the emir. Following the failure of the uprising, called the Majlis Movement, Iraq continued to put forth a claim to at least part of Kuwait, notably the strategic islands of Būbiyān and Al-Warbah.

On June 19, 1961, Britain recognized Kuwait's independence. Six days later, however, Iraq renewed its claim, which was now rebuffed by first British, then Arab League forces. It was not until 1963 that a new Iraqi regime formally recognized both Kuwait's independence and, subsequently, its borders, while continuing to press for access to the islands.

The Iran-Iraq War of 1980 to 1988 represented a serious threat to Kuwait's security. Kuwait saw no alternative to providing Iraq substantial financial support and serving as a vital conduit for military supplies. Iran attacked a Kuwaiti refinery complex in 1981 and inspired terrorist acts of sabotage in 1983 and 1986. In 1985 a member of the underground pro-Iranian Iraqi radical group Ad-Daʿwa attempted to assassinate the ruler, Sheikh Jābir al-Aḥmad Āl Ṣabāḥ.

In September 1986 Iran began to concentrate its attacks on gulf shipping largely on Kuwaiti tankers. This led Kuwait to invite both the Soviet Union (with which it had established diplomatic relations in 1963) and the United States to provide protection for its tankers in early 1987. The effect of the war was to promote closer relations with Kuwait's conservative gulf Arab neighbours—Saudi Arabia, Bahrain, Qatar, the United Arab Emirates, and Oman. With them, in 1981, Kuwait had formed the Gulf Cooperation Council (GCC) to develop closer cooperation on economic and security issues.

Relations with Arab neighbours

With the end of the Iran-Iraq War in 1988, Iraqi-Kuwaiti relations began to deteriorate. On Aug. 2, 1990, Iraq unexpectedly invaded and conquered the country.

Although Iraq advanced several arguments for its actions, the basic causes of the invasion were the perennial ones that had led earlier Iraqi regimes to seek the same result: the desire to control Kuwait's oil and wealth; the military benefits to be gained from a greater frontage on the gulf; the urge to Pan-Arabism, which saw the acquisition of Kuwait as the first step toward the union of all the Arabs under Iraqi leadership; the prestige such an adventure, if successful, could confer on the political leadership in Baghdad; and the feeling held by most Iraqis (despite its historical inaccuracy) that Kuwait was genuinely part of Iraq. On August 8 Iraq announced the annexation of Kuwait, despite condemnations from the United Nations, the major world powers, the Arab League, and the European Community. The vehement anti-Iraqi feelings of virtually all Kuwaitis and diplomatic efforts by the Kuwaiti government-in-exile in Saudi Arabia did not stop Iraq from harshly imposing its rule on Kuwait.

On Jan. 16–17, 1991, a coalition of nations, acting under the authority of the United Nations and led by the United States and Saudi Arabia, began an air war against Iraqi forces. Just before the ground war began on February 24, Iraqi troops set afire hundreds of Kuwait's oil wells, creating an unprecedented ecological disaster. By February 27 Kuwait was liberated from Iraqi control. As hundreds of thousands of Kuwaitis returned from foreign refuges to their homes in May, the full extent of the damage created by the invasion, looting, and war became clear.

The invasion and occupation affected every aspect of Kuwaiti life. More than half the population fled during the war. Although most nationals returned during 1991, many non-nationals, notably the Palestinians, were not permitted to do so. A division emerged between those who had stayed behind in the resistance and those who had fled, and another between the apparent majority pressing for political liberalization (specifically, for parliamentary elections) and the ruling family, whose behaviour in exile had stirred considerable popular disfavour in Kuwait. The government's initial response—the institution of martial law and show trials—gave way as reconstruction proceeded to a cautious reopening of dialogue. The survival of the Iraqi regime in Baghdad spawned an ambient fear in Kuwait that the events of 1990–91 would someday be repeated.

In 1992 a United Nations commission formally delimited the Iraqi-Kuwaiti border in accordance with UN Security Council Ceasefire Resolution 687 (which had reaffirmed the inviolability of the Iraq-Kuwait border). The commission's findings were generally favourable to Kuwait, moving the Iraqi border 0.035 mile northward in the area of Safwān and slightly north in the area of the contested Ar-Rumaylah oil field, thereby giving Kuwait not only an additional six oil wells but also part of the Iraqi naval base of Umm Qaṣr. Kuwait accepted the UN's border designation; however, Iraq rejected it and continued to voice its claim to Kuwaiti territory.

For later developments in the history of Kuwait, see the *Britannica Book of the Year* section in the BRITANNICA WORLD DATA ANNUAL. (J.D.An./W.L.O./J.C.)

Oman

The Sultanate of Oman (Arabic: Salṭanat ʿUmān) is an independent sultanate that occupies the southeastern coast of the Arabian Peninsula. It is bounded on the southwest by Yemen, on the south and east by the Arabian Sea, on the north by the Gulf of Oman, on the northwest by the United Arab Emirates, and on the west by Saudi Arabia. In addition, in the Ruʾūs Al-Jibāl ("The Mountaintops") is a small enclave, occupying the northern tip of the Musandam Peninsula at the Strait of Hormuz; this territory gives Oman its only frontage on the Persian Gulf. Because the boundaries with Saudi Arabia are not fixed, the exact area of Oman cannot be determined; it is estimated to be about 120,000 square miles (300,000 square kilometres). Its offshore territories include Al-Maṣīrah Island to the east and the five Khurīyā Murīyā Islands, 25 miles off the south coast. Muscat (Masqaṭ), a port on the Gulf of Oman, is the capital.

PHYSICAL AND HUMAN GEOGRAPHY

The land. *Relief.* Northern Oman is dominated by three physiographic zones. The long, narrow coastal plain of Al-Bāṭinah stretches along the Gulf of Oman. The high, barren Al-Ḥajar Mountains extend southeastward, parallel to the gulf coast, from the Musandam Peninsula to a point near Cape Al-Ḥadd, at the easternmost tip of the Arabian

Peninsula; the great central divide of Wadi Sanā'il separates the Al-Ḥajar into a western and an eastern range. An inland plateau falls away to the west of the Al-Ḥajar Mountains into the great Rubʿ al-Khali (the Empty Quarter) desert, which the sultanate shares with Saudi Arabia. These zones are further subdivided into a number of unofficial provinces: Al-Bāṭinah; the mountains and associated valleys of the Eastern Al-Ḥajar and Western Al-Ḥajar; Oman province, or Al-Jawf (the central foothills and valleys on the inland side of the Al-Ḥajar Mountains and the historic heartland of Oman); Aẓ-Ẓāhirah (west of Oman province, next to the United Arab Emirates, and including Al-Buraymī oasis); Ash-Sharqīyah (lying east of Oman province behind the Al-Ḥajar Mountains); and Jaʿlān (fronting the Arabian Sea south of Cape Al-Ḥadd).

The Dhofar region

The fertile southern region of Dhofar (Ẓufār), incorporated into the sultanate only in the 19th century, is separated from the rest of Oman by several hundred miles of open desert. Three coterminous mountain ranges, rising to about 5,000 feet (1,524 metres), form a crescent in Dhofar around a long, narrow, coastal plain on which is located the provincial capital of Ṣalālah. Behind the mountains, gravel plains gradually merge northward into the southern reaches of the Rubʿ al-Khali.

Climate and plant and animal life. Generally, the climate is hot and dry in the interior and hot and humid along the coast. Summer temperatures in the capital of Muscat and other coastal locations often reach 97° F (36° C), with high humidity; winters are mild, with lows around 63° F (17° C). Temperatures are similar in the interior, although they are more moderate at higher altitudes. Dhofar is dominated by the summer monsoon that envelops the mountains in fog and mist for up to four months. Ṣalālah's climate is more moderate than that of northern Oman and is relatively constant throughout the year. Rainfall throughout the country is minimal, averaging about 4 inches (104 millimetres) a year. There are no permanent bodies of fresh water in the sultanate.

Because of the low rainfall, vegetation is sparse except where irrigated. Irrigation is provided by an ancient system of water channels known as *aflāj* (singular, *falaj*). The channels, which often run underground, originate in wells near the bases of the mountains.

Acacia trees form most of what little natural vegetation exists, and the soil is extremely rocky. The government protects rare species, such as the Arabian oryx, mountain goats, foxes, and the loggerhead turtle.

Settlement patterns. Oman is fundamentally a rural country. Settlements are typically located near the foothills of the Al-Ḥajar Mountains, where the *aflāj* provide irrigation. In addition to small villages, a number of sizable towns, including Nizwā, Bahlā', Izkī, and 'Ibrī, are found on the inland, or southwestern, side of the Western Al-Ḥajar. The Al-Bāṭinah coast provides opportunities for fishing, as well as irrigated cultivation. As a consequence it is rather more densely populated, with major towns at Shināṣ, Ṣuḥār, Al-Khābūrah, Al-Maṣnaʿah, and Barkā'. Traditional housing in the Al-Bāṭinah often consists of palm-frond huts, in contrast to the mud-brick structures of the interior. Ar-Rustāq, Al-ʿAwābī, and Nakhl are principal settlements on the Al-Bāṭinah side of the Western Al-Ḥajar.

At the eastern end of the Al-Bāṭinah lie the twin cities of Muscat and Maṭraḥ; both are ancient ports, but they have been transformed into a booming metropolis. To the east, the only major town is Ṣūr, a well-protected port that is still the hub of fishing and boatbuilding industries. A nomadic population occupies the land between the irrigated valleys and the desert, but the nomadic proportion of the total population is quite small. Some of Dhofar's residents are concentrated in towns along the coast, and some are seminomadic cattle herders in the mountains. A small nomadic population inhabits the inland plateaus along the Rubʿ al-Khali. Khaṣab is the only significant town in the sparsely populated Musandam Peninsula.

The people. Oman's population is principally Arab, although large numbers of ethnic Balochi live along the Al-Bāṭinah; both groups are exclusively Muslim. The Ibāḍite branch of Islām, a moderate variant of the Khārijite sect, claims the largest number of adherents, perhaps slightly less than half of the total population. In belief and ritual, Ibāḍism is close to Sunnite Islām (the major or orthodox body of Muslims), differing in its emphasis on an elected imam as the spiritual and temporal leader of the Ibāḍite community. Non-Ibāḍite Arabs and the Balochi, who have migrated to Oman from Iran and Pakistan over the last several centuries, are Sunnites.

Ibāḍism

The Muscat-Maṭraḥ conurbation has long been home to significant numbers of merchants of Indian origin, some of whom also live along the Al-Bāṭinah. Notable among these are the Khōja, originally from Sind but who have lived in Oman for about 400 years. The Indian communities are mainly Shīʿite, the most widespread Islāmic sect after the Sunnite, with a few Hindus. There are also several small Persian communities, and a number of Swahili-speaking Omanis born in Zanzibar and elsewhere in East Africa returned to Oman after 1970.

Several large Arab tribes predominate along Dhofar's coastal plain. The inhabitants of the Dhofari mountains are known as *jibālī*s, or "people of the mountains." They are ethnically distinct from the coastal Arabs and are related instead to the inhabitants of eastern Yemen. They speak South Arabic languages, which are largely unintelligible to speakers of modern standard (North) Arabic. Dhofaris are all Sunnite Muslims.

Since the influx of oil income and the palace coup of 1970, increasing numbers of expatriates reside in the country, particularly in the capital area. These include Western

A.C. Waltham—Robert Harding Picture Library

A *falaj* in a date grove on Mount Al-Akhḍar, Al-Ḥajar Mountains, Oman.

businessmen, government advisers, and army officers, as well as skilled and unskilled labourers from the Indian subcontinent, the Philippines, and elsewhere in Asia.

The economy. Oman is a rural, agricultural country, with fishing and overseas trading important for the coastal populations. Before 1970, thousands of Omanis left the country to find work in nearby oil-producing states. Oil in commercial quantities was discovered in Oman in 1964, however, and was first exported in 1967. Subsequently the production of oil rapidly came to dominate the country's economy. By the mid-1980s oil represented one-half of the gross domestic product and provided about 85 percent of the government's income.

Serious development planning began in 1976 with the first five-year plan (1976–80). The framework for the second five-year plan (1981–85) was laid in 1978. The plans included development of necessary social amenities, additional investment in the petroleum industry, and further economic diversification.

Natural resources. Several small copper mines and a smelter were opened in the early 1980s at an ancient mining site near Ṣuḥār, but copper reserves are not expected to last beyond the mid-1990s. Chromite is also mined in small quantities. Other mineral resources are insignificant.

Agriculture and fishing. Agriculture is mainly subsistence in nature and employs about one-half of the population. The *aflāj* irrigation system has long supported a three-tiered crop approach (three crops raised at different levels on the same plot), with date palms above; limes, bananas, or mangoes in the middle; and alfalfa, wheat, and sorghum on the ground. Dates (the country's leading crop) and limes grown in the interior oases have long been traded for fish from the coast as well as exported abroad. Grapes, walnuts, apples, and other fruits are grown in the high mountain plateaus. Dhofar also produces coconuts and papayas. Most rural families keep goats, as well as a few cows, and Oman is well known for camel breeding. Cattle are raised almost exclusively in Dhofar.

Labour migration has left fields to lie fallow and the irrigation systems to decay. Partly in an attempt to reduce food imports, the government has sought to stimulate agricultural production with the establishment of research stations and model farms along the Al-Bāṭinah coast and in Dhofar, as well as date-processing plants at Ar-Rustāq and Nizwā. The government has also sought to encourage commercial fishing by providing boats and motors, cold stores, and transportation; and fisheries production in the Gulf of Oman and Arabian Sea has increased.

Research stations and model farms

Industry. Crude oil production averaged about 300,000 barrels per day through the 1970s. The government's response to declining oil prices in the 1980s was to increase production; by the middle of the decade, production had climbed to nearly 600,000 barrels per day, a larger figure than some OPEC countries produced but still far behind the ranks of the world's largest oil exporters.

Industrial development began only with the change of government in 1970 and is oriented to such infrastructural projects as electricity generators, desalinization complexes, and the cement plants outside Muscat and Ṣalālah. The five-year plans have stressed private-sector development as well as joint ventures with the government. Traditional handicrafts, such as weaving, leatherworking, boatbuilding, and gold and silver work, are declining.

Finance and trade. After registering annual economic growth rates of 10 percent or more in the early 1980s, the country began to suffer balance-of-payment deficits in 1986 as a result of declining oil prices. The low level of foreign reserves forced the government to introduce regular budget cuts, devalue the Omani riyal by 10 percent in 1986, and issue treasury bills for the first time. Defense spending, which had averaged between 40 and 50 percent of the total budget since 1970, was trimmed somewhat, and expensive arms purchases were postponed.

Crude oil accounts for most exports, while imports consist of consumer goods, foodstuffs, and industrial equipment. Among the country's major trading partners are Japan, the United Arab Emirates, and the United Kingdom. Most businesses are family-owned.

Transportation. There are two modern ports, Port Qābūs in Maṭraḥ and Raysūt near Ṣalālah, both built in the early 1970s. Significant intercoastal trade is carried on by traditional wooden dhows. The two principal airports are located at As-Sīb, about 30 miles from Muscat, and at Ṣalālah. The government is a major stockholder in the international carrier Gulf Air and also operates Oman Aviation Services domestically. Since 1970 a modern road network of asphalt and gravel roads linking all the country's main settlements has been built up from virtually nothing, and a 480-mile highway between Muscat and Ṣalālah was completed in 1984.

Administration and social conditions. *Government.* Oman's government is a monarchy (sultanate). Cabinet ministers are typically chosen from among Muscat merchants, informal representatives of interior tribes, and Dhofaris. The country has no written constitution and there are no political parties or elections, but the State Consultative Council, formed by the sultan in 1981, includes members representing the government, the chamber of commerce, and the various regions of the country. Local government is carried out by a combination of traditional *wali*s (representatives of the sultan) and more recently established municipal councils.

The Sultan's Armed Forces, formed in 1958 from several smaller regiments, has grown since 1970 to about 21,500 personnel, spurred in part by the rebellion in Dhofar in 1964–76. The preponderance of Balochi soldiers, many of whom had been recruited from the sultanate's former enclave of Gwādar in Pakistan, was reversed in favour of Arabs, and a policy of Omanization steadily reduced the numbers of British officers.

Education. Education has expanded dramatically since 1970, when only 3 primary schools existed. By 1985 there were almost 200 primary schools, 300 preparatory schools, and 36 secondary schools serving some 200,000 students. Sultan Qābūs University was opened in September 1986.

Health and welfare. The post-1970 government also improved health care throughout the countryside. It has built hospitals, health centres, and dispensaries and equipped mobile medical teams to serve remote areas. The government also provides generous housing loans.

Cultural life. Oman is a tribal society and the individual Omani typically identifies foremost with his tribe. Women have been relatively freer in Oman than elsewhere in the Arab world. Attempts have been made to minimize the effect of development on the heavily traditional society through, for example, incorporating traditional elements of architecture in new buildings and passing a law (1986) forbidding Omani nationals to marry foreigners. The Ministry of National Heritage and Culture has been active in preserving historic buildings, excavating archaeological sites, and supporting traditional crafts.

Several Arabic-language newspapers are published on a daily and weekly basis, and there is an English-language daily. A colour television system was opened in 1974–75, and radio stations broadcast in Arabic and English.

For statistical data on the land and people of Oman, see the *Britannica World Data* section in the BRITANNICA WORLD DATA ANNUAL.

HISTORY

There are three principal themes in Omani history: the tribal nature of its society, the traditional Ibāḍite imamate form of government, and its maritime tradition. Archaeological evidence of civilization in Oman dates to the 3rd millennium BC, but Persian colonization in the 7th or 8th century BC seems to have been responsible for the creation of the *falaj* irrigation system, which has sustained Omani agriculture and civilization ever since.

Persian colonization

The history of Dhofar followed a separate track. Ancient south Arabian kingdoms controlled the production of frankincense from Dhofar's port of Sumharum from the 1st century AD, and the province remained oriented toward south Arabia until it was absorbed into the Āl Bū Saʿīd state in the 19th century.

The Omani tribal system. The origins of the Omani tribal system can be traced to the immigration of Arab tribes from south Arabia into the Jaʿlān region in the 2nd century AD. The tribes subsequently moved northward into the Persian-controlled area of Māzūn in Oman, where they were joined by tribes moving into Oman from the northwest. Arab dominance over the country began with the introduction of Islām in the 7th century.

The Ibāḍite imamate. A semblance of national political unity emerged only with the introduction of the Ibāḍite imamate in the mid-8th century. Oman's mountains and geographic isolation provided a refuge for then-extremist Ibāḍites, who proceeded to convert the leading tribal clans to their sect. The new Ibāḍite state was headed by an elected imam who served as both temporal and secular leader of the community. In actuality, selection of a new imam depended on agreement among the religious leaders and the heads of the major tribes, particularly the leaders of the two major tribal confederations, which came to be known as the Ghāfirīs and the Hināwīs.

A recurring pattern was established with the decline of the First Imamate, which reached its zenith during the 9th century. Elected imams tended to give way to hereditary dynasties, which then collapsed as a result of family disputes and the resurgence of Ibāḍite ideals.

The maritime tradition. Maritime trade, the third principal theme in Omani history, also contributed to dynastic decline. Virtually cut off from the rest of the Arabian Peninsula by vast deserts, Omani sailors plied the waters of the Indian Ocean, ranging as far as China in the medieval period. This maritime tendency was strongest when dynasties moved their capitals from the Ibāḍite heartland to the coast and focused their attention on acquiring territory elsewhere in the gulf, along the Arabian Sea, and on the East African littoral.

Arrival of the Portuguese. The Portuguese sacked Muscat in 1507 and soon controlled the entire coast. A century later, the Yaʿrubid dynasty drove the Portuguese from the Omani coast, recapturing Muscat in 1650, and then took over Portuguese settlements along the Persian and East African coasts. Their empire eventually crumbled in a civil war over succession in the early 18th century, enabling the Persian ruler Nādir Shāh to invade the country in 1737.

Aḥmad ibn Saʿīd, the governor of Ṣuḥār, drove out the Persian invaders and was subsequently elected imam about 1744, thus establishing the Āl Bū Saʿīd dynasty, which has ruled Oman ever since. His grandson, Saʿīd ibn Sulṭān (ruled 1807–56), reasserted Omani control over Zanzibar and eventually moved his residence there. Upon his death the Āl Bū Saʿīd empire was split between two sons, with one receiving Zanzibar, which remained under Āl Bū Saʿīd rule until 1964, and the other ruling Oman.

The fortunes of the Āl Bū Saʿīd state in Oman declined through the second half of the 19th century. The Āl Bū Saʿīd dynasty quite possibly would have collapsed if it had not been for the presence of the British, who propped up the Āl Bū Saʿīd sultans in Muscat against periodic revivals of the Ibāḍite imamate in the interior.

Tribal attacks in the name of the imam were made on Muscat and Maṭraḥ in 1895 and 1915. An agreement was negotiated by the British between the tribal leaders and Sultan Taymūr ibn Fayṣal (reigned 1913–32) in 1920. By its terms, the sultan recognized the autonomy, but not the sovereignty, of the Omani interior.

This situation lasted until 1954, when Imam Muḥammad al-Khalīlī, who had become imam in 1920, died. His weak successor, Ghālib, was influenced by his brother Ṭālib and a prominent tribal leader, Sulaymān ibn Ḥimyār, and the three enlisted Saudi Arabia's support against Sultan Saʿīd ibn Taymūr. The Saudis had occupied part of Al-Buraymī oasis, jointly administered by Oman and neighbouring Abu Dhabi (now part of the United Arab Emirates), in 1952, apparently in hopes of finding oil. In 1955 an international arbitration tribunal on Al-Buraymī broke down, and the British engineered the ouster of the Saudi garrison.

Saudi occupation

At the same time a regiment led by British officers moved into the Omani interior and reunited the sultanate. Remnants of the imamate's supporters, however, held strongholds in the Mount Al-Akhḍar Massif of the Western Al-Ḥajar mountains until they were forced to surrender in early 1959.

In the early 1960s another threat to the sultanate emerged in Dhofar. Sultan Saʿīd ibn Taymūr had moved to Ṣalālah permanently in 1958. The mountain *jibālīs* began to rebel openly against Sultan Saʿīd's petty restrictions in the mid-1960s. The Marxist Popular Front for the Liberation of the Occupied Arab Gulf (later the Popular Front for the Liberation of Oman; PFLO) gained control of the growing rebellion in 1968, with the help of neighbouring Marxist South Yemen (which gained independence from the British in late 1967) and first Chinese and then Soviet assistance. The seriousness of the Dhofar rebellion was a principal factor in the palace coup of July 23, 1970, which saw Sultan Saʿīd overthrown by his son, Qābūs ibn Saʿīd.

Qābūs, who had been trained in Britain at the Royal Military Academy, Sandhurst, quickly reversed his father's policy of isolation and set about to develop Oman. Additional British personnel and equipment were brought into the sultan's armed forces to help put down the rebellion in Dhofar, and these efforts were aided by Jordanian and especially Iranian troops. The plain around Ṣalālah was gradually freed from the threat of attack, the mountains were cleared of rebel activity, and the rebellion was crushed by late 1975.

In late 1970 Sultan Qābūs appointed the country's first true cabinet and took steps toward building a modern government structure. Qābūs first appointed his uncle Ṭāriq ibn Taymūr as prime minister, but he subsequently served as his own prime minister and as minister of defense and foreign affairs also. The Āl Bū Saʿīd are less heavily represented in government positions than other ruling families elsewhere in the gulf.

Oman joined the Arab League and the United Nations in 1971 but declined to join either the Organization of Petroleum Exporting Countries (OPEC) or the smaller Organization of Arab Petroleum Exporting Countries (OAPEC). It was one of six founding members of the Gulf Cooperation Council, established in 1981 to promote cooperation in economic, political, and security matters among its members. Oman has been closely linked to Britain since the early 19th century, and relations with the United States, established in 1833, have grown close since the early 1970s.

Oman's location gives it a particular interest in the safety of traffic through the Strait of Hormuz, and Oman attempted to maintain neutrality in the Iran-Iraq War.

For later developments in the history of Oman, see the *Britannica Book of the Year* section in the BRITANNICA WORLD DATA ANNUAL. (J.E.P.)

Qatar

The State of Qatar (Arabic: Dawlat Qaṭar) is an independent emirate on the west coast of the Persian Gulf. It occupies a desert peninsula that extends from the Arabian mainland north of eastern Saudi Arabia and the United Arab Emirates. Its area is about 4,400 square miles (11,400 square kilometres), including a number of small islands nearby in the Persian Gulf. The capital is Doha (Ad-Dawḥah) on the east coast, once a centre of pearling activity.

PHYSICAL AND HUMAN GEOGRAPHY

The land. The Qatar peninsula is about 100 miles (160 kilometres) from north to south and 50 miles from east to west. Most of its area is flat desert, but hills rise to about 130 feet (40 metres) along the western coast. Sand dunes and salt flats are the chief topographical features of the southern sector. Vegetation is found only in the north.

Doha, on the east coast, is Qatar's largest city and its commercial centre. It has a deepwater port and an international airport. The main oil port and industrial centre is Umm Saʿīd, to the south of Doha on the eastern coast. Dukhān, on the western coast, is the country's fourth major urban area. These three cities and many smaller settlements are linked by road.

The climate is hot and humid from June to September, with temperatures as high as 104° F (40° C). The spring and fall months—April, May, October, and November—are temperate. Rainfall is scarce.

The people. Qatar was originally settled by nomads

A minaret and houses in the capital city of Doha, Qatar.
© Peter Vine

from the central part of the Arabian Peninsula. Qatari citizens, most of whom are Sunnite Muslims, constitute only about one-fifth of the total population. The rest are foreign workers, whose stay in Qatar is temporary. About one-third of the population is of South Asian origin, largely Pakistani; almost one-fifth are Iranian (mostly Shī'ite Muslims); and about one-fourth are other Arabs. Few nomads remain, and only about 10 percent of the people live in rural areas. Of the total work force, some 90 percent is expatriate. Arabic is the official language, and the official religion is Islām.

The economy. Qatar's economic prosperity is derived from oil, which was discovered there in 1939 and was first produced in 1949. Before then, lacking any significant merchant class and any economic occupation apart from pearling, fishing, and some trade, Qatar's population was one of the poorest anywhere in the world. By the 1970s, however, the native Qataris enjoyed one of the highest per capita incomes in the world.

The original oil concession was granted to the Iraq Petroleum Company (IPC), comprising European and American companies. This and later concessions were nationalized in the 1970s. While the state-owned Qatar General Petroleum Corporation oversees oil operations, the private corporations continue to play an important role as service companies.

Nationalization of oil industry

Resources. Qatar's oil reserves, found both onshore along the western coast and offshore from the eastern coast, are modest, especially by the standards set elsewhere in the region, and are expected to last only until the second or third decade of the 21st century at present rates of production. Qatar's gas reserves are more significant, amounting by conservative estimate to 4 percent of the world's total.

Industry. To assure its future prosperity Qatar has sought to diversify its economy through industrialization. Most of the industrial sector comprises large firms of mixed state and foreign private ownership. For example, the Qatar Iron and Steel Company is co-owned by the Qatari government and two Japanese companies, which constructed the plant and took responsibility for production, marketing, and exporting. Flour milling and cement production have also been undertaken. Because the diversification is dependent for its success on the abundance of cheap energy to run the plants, it is tied to Qatar's hydrocarbon resources. Thus the future economic development and prosperity of the country are largely dependent on exploitation of the enormous offshore natural gas reserves of the North Field, beneath the Persian Gulf. The North Field is the single largest known natural gas field in the world.

Agriculture. The scarcity of fertile land and water imposes severe limitations on agriculture, and most food must be imported. Use of treated sewage effluent and desalinated water have helped expand production of fruits, such as dates and melons, and of vegetables, such as tomatoes, squash, and eggplants. The cultivation of vegetables has been so successful that Qatar even exports such produce to other gulf countries. Meat and milk production have increased, and some efforts at modernizing the fishing industry have been undertaken. Food production generates only about 1 percent of the gross domestic product, however.

Trade and finance. In the mid-1970s Japan supplanted Britain as Qatar's chief source of imports. The chief purchasers of Qatari exports are Japan, France, and Singapore. Other major markets for and suppliers of goods include Italy, The Netherlands, the United States, and Australia. Machinery and transport make up the largest category of imports, and crude petroleum accounts for more than 90 percent of exports.

The Qatar National Bank provides banking functions for the state; other banks are authorized to operate. Qatar has been generous in its foreign aid disbursements, particularly to other Arab and Islāmic countries.

Administration and social conditions. *Government.* Qatar is ruled by a hereditary emir who presides over a patriarchal political system. In large measure the country's political stability is made possible by the homogeneous nature of the native Qatari population. Moreover, several hundred male members of the ruling family, the Āl Thānī, dominate politics, and the Āl Thānī make up perhaps as much as 40 percent of the native Qatari population. Succession is within the family but not necessarily from father to son. The emir's power is constrained principally by the need to maintain the support of important members of the family, many of whom occupy ministerial and other high governmental posts.

The Āl Thānī

The constitution, originally adopted in 1970 and revised since, formally divides the government into branches, explicitly naming the executive and the judiciary. The constitution includes the legislative process among the functions of the emir. The emir appoints a Council of Ministers to manage the affairs of state and an Advisory Council to assist him in drafting and promulgating laws. Civil and criminal codes were introduced in 1971, and all civil and criminal cases fall within the purview of a system of secular courts. The Islāmic (Sharī'ah) courts are based on the interpretation of the Qur'ān and the sunna (customs derived from the sayings and actions of the Prophet Muḥammad), which narrowly and rigidly defines the scope and application of the religious law. The jurisdiction of the Sharīʿah courts in Qatar is now essentially confined to personal and family matters.

Qatar is a member of the Organization of Petroleum Exporting Countries (OPEC), the Organization of Arab Petroleum Exporting Countries (OAPEC), and the Arab League; membership in the Gulf Cooperation Council (GCC) links it closely to its fellow Arab gulf states—Kuwait, Saudi Arabia, Bahrain, the United Arab Emirates, and Oman. Although Qatar has a small defense force of about 6,000 men, for security against external threat it must depend on the protection of others. It follows very closely the lead of Saudi Arabia on most issues, in part because, like Qatar, Saudi Arabia adheres to the conservative Ḥanbalī school of Islāmic jurisprudence.

Education. Education is free and compulsory for all residents, citizens and noncitizens alike. Six years of primary school, three years of intermediate school, and three years of secondary school are required in both government-run and private schools. Classes are segregated by sex.

Qatar spends generously on education, having one of the highest per-pupil expenditures in the world. Its system has expanded rapidly. Two teacher-training colleges, one for men and one for women, were founded in 1973, and together they were given university status in 1977. The university has continued to expand, and a new campus was completed in 1985 in Doha.

The government also provides adult education classes in schools and centres throughout the country, with an emphasis on increasing adult literacy. The country's literacy rate is estimated to be about 75 percent.

Health and welfare. Health care and medical services are provided free to all residents through government programs. The government also funds recreational and cultural clubs and facilities for young people as part of its extensive "youth welfare" campaign.

Cultural life. Several agencies and departments oversee literary, artistic, and cultural activities as well as recreation and tourism. The Qatar National Museum, in Doha, includes displays of the country's history and archaeology, a lagoon in which Qatari sailing and pearling vessels are displayed, and a museum of the sea.

The government sponsors the fine arts, traditional arts and crafts, theatre, music, publishing, and libraries through various programs. Government-owned radio and television stations broadcast in Arabic, English, French, and Urdū. Several local daily newspapers and weekly publications are available.

For statistical data on the land and people of Qatar, see the *Britannica World Data* section in the BRITANNICA WORLD DATA ANNUAL.

HISTORY

Little is known of Qatar's history before the 18th century, when the region's population consisted largely of transient nomads and a few small fishing villages. Qatar's modern history begins conventionally in 1766 with the migration to the peninsula of families from Kuwait, notably the Āl Khalīfahs. Their settlement at the new town of Az-Zubārah grew into a small pearl-diving and trade centre. In 1783 the Āl Khalīfahs led the conquest of nearby Bahrain, where they remained the ruling family in the late 20th century. Following their departure from Qatar, the country was ruled by a series of transitory sheikhs, the most famous of whom was Raḥmah ibn Jābir al-Jalāhimah, whom the British regarded as a leading pirate of the so-called Pirate Coast.

Qatar came to the attention of the British in 1867 when a dispute between the Bahraini Āl Khalīfahs, who continued to hold some claim to Az-Zubārah, and the Qatari residents escalated into a major confrontation, in the course of which Doha was virtually destroyed. Until the attack, Britain had viewed Qatar as a Bahraini dependency. It now negotiated a separate treaty with Muḥammad ath-Thānī in 1868, setting the course both for Qatar's future independence and for the rule of the Āl Thānī family, who were until the treaty only one among several important families on the peninsula.

Ottoman forces, which had conquered the nearby Al-Ḥasā province of Saudi Arabia, occupied Qatar in 1871 at the invitation of the ruler's son, then left following the Saudi reconquest of Al-Ḥasā in 1913. In 1916 Britain signed a treaty with Qatar's leader that resembled earlier agreements with other gulf states giving Britain control over foreign policy in return for British protection.

Oil was discovered in Qatar in 1940; in 1935 a concession agreement had been signed with the Iraq Petroleum Company. Oil was not recovered on a commercial scale, however, until 1949. The revenues from the oil company, later named Petroleum Development (Qatar) Limited and then the Qatar Petroleum Company, rose dramatically. The distribution of these revenues stirred serious infighting in the Āl Thānī family, prompting the British to intervene in the succession of 1949 and eventually precipitating a palace coup in 1972 that brought Sheikh Khalīfah ibn Ḥamad ath-Thānī to power. In 1968 Britain announced plans to withdraw from the gulf. After negotiations with neighbouring sheikdoms—those comprising the present United Arab Emirates and Bahrain—Qatar instead declared independence on Sept. 1, 1971. The earlier agreements with Britain were replaced with a treaty of friendship. Later that same month Qatar became a member of the Arab League and of the United Nations. In 1981 it joined its five Arab gulf neighbours in establishing the Gulf Cooperation Council, an alliance formed to promote economic cooperation and to enhance both internal security and external defense against the threats generated by the Islāmic revolution in Iran and the Iran-Iraq War.

Qatari troops participated in the Persian Gulf War of 1991, notably in the battle for control of the Saudi border town of Raʾs Al-Khafji on January 30–31. Doha, which served as a base for offensive strikes against Iraq and Iraqi forces occupying Kuwait by French, Canadian, and U.S. aircraft, remained minimally affected by the conflict.

For later developments in the history of Qatar, see the *Britannica Book of the Year* section in the BRITANNICA WORLD DATA ANNUAL. (J.D.An./J.C.)

Saudi Arabia

The Kingdom of Saudi Arabia (Arabic: Al-Mamlakah Al-ʿArabīyah As-Saʿūdīyah) has an estimated area of 865,-000 square miles (2,240,000 square kilometres), occupying about four-fifths of the Arabian Peninsula. It is bordered by Jordan, Iraq, and Kuwait on the north; by the Persian (Arabian) Gulf, Qatar, the United Arab Emirates, and Oman on the east; by a portion of Oman on the southeast; by Yemen on the south and southwest; and by the Red Sea and the Gulf of Aqaba on the west. Portions of the borders with the United Arab Emirates, Oman, and Yemen are undefined. A territory of 2,200 square miles along the gulf coast was shared by Kuwait and Saudi Arabia as a neutral zone until 1969, when a political boundary was agreed upon. Each of the two countries administers one-half of the territory, but they equally share oil production in the entire area. The capital is Riyadh. Saudi Arabia is named for the house of Saʿūd, the founding and ruling dynasty that dates from the 18th century.

Saudi Arabia is a Muslim and an Arab state, and these two attributes have had a fundamental influence on the country's foreign relations. It is a founding member of the Arab League (1945) and of the Organization of the Islāmic Conference (1971). The kingdom exhibits a certain aloofness to outsiders: a foreigner can secure a visa to visit it only if invited by an individual or an organization within the country. Once inside, a visitor encounters a pervading sense of independence and pride. The extraordinary economic changes that occurred starting in the 1960s altered neither the government nor the centrality of religion.

Since the mid-20th century, however, the pace of life in Saudi Arabia has accelerated greatly. Mecca and Medina, the two holiest cities of Islām, have always provided the country with outside contacts, and such contacts have expanded with innovations in transportation technology and organization. More recently, petroleum has wrought irreversible domestic changes—educational and social as well as economic. Modern industrial skills, technology, and methods of organization have been superimposed on a traditional society by the introduction of millions of foreign skilled workers and by the employment of hundreds of thousands of Saudis in nontraditional jobs. In addition, tens of thousands of Saudi students have studied abroad, mostly in the United States. Television and radio have become common media of communication and education. Highways and airways have replaced traditional means of transportation, notably the camel caravan.

PHYSICAL AND HUMAN GEOGRAPHY

The land. *Relief.* The Arabian Peninsula is dominated by a plateau that rises abruptly from the Red Sea and dips gently toward the Persian Gulf. In the north the western highlands are upward of 5,000 feet (1,500 metres) above sea level, decreasing slightly to 4,000 feet in the vicinity of Medina and increasing southeastward to more than 10,000 feet. The watershed of the peninsula is only 25 miles (40 kilometres) from the Red Sea in the north, receding to 80 miles near the Yemen border. The coastal plain, known as the Tihāmah, is virtually nonexistent in the north, except for occasional wadi deltas, and it widens slightly toward the south. Wadis flowing to the Red Sea are short and steep, though one unusually long extension is made by Wadi Al-Ḥamḍ, which rises near Medina and flows inland to the northwest for 100 miles before turning westward. The imposing escarpment that runs parallel to the Red Sea is somewhat interrupted by a gap northwest of Mecca but becomes more clearly continuous to the south.

The Tihāmah

Toward the interior, the surface gradually descends into the broad plateau area of the Najd, covered with lava flows and volcanic debris as well as with occasional sand accumulations; it slopes down from an elevation of about 4,500 feet in the west to about 2,500 feet in the east. There the drainage is more clearly dendritic (*i.e.,* branching) and is much more extensive than that flowing toward the Red Sea. To the east, this region is bounded by a series of long, low ridges, with steep slopes on the west and gentle slopes on the east; the area is 750 miles long and curves eastward from north to south. The most prominent of the ridges are the Ṭuwayq Mountains (Jabal Ṭuwayq), which rise from the plateau at an elevation of some 2,800 feet above sea level and reach a height of more than 3,500 feet southwest of Riyadh, overlooking the plateau's surface to the west by 800 feet and more.

The interior of the Arabian Peninsula contains extensive sand surfaces. Among them is the world's largest sand area, the Rubʿ al-Khali (the Empty Quarter), which dominates the southern part of the country and covers more than 250,000 square miles. It slopes from above 2,600 feet near the border with Yemen northeastward down almost to sea level near the Persian Gulf; individual sand mountains reach heights of 800 feet, especially in the eastern part. A smaller sand area of about 22,000 square miles, called An-Nafūd (*nafūd* designating a sandy area or desert), is in the north central part of the country. A great arc of sand, Ad-Dahnā', almost 900 miles long but in places only 30 miles wide, joins An-Nafūd with the Rubʿ al-Khali. Eastward, as the plateau surface slopes very gradually down to the gulf, there are numerous salt flats (*sabkhah*s) and marshes. The gulf coastline is irregular, and the coastal waters are very shallow.

The Empty Quarter

Drainage. There are virtually no permanent surface streams in the country, but wadis are numerous. Those leading to the Red Sea are short and deep, but those draining eastward are longer and more developed except in An-Nafūd and the Rubʿ al-Khali. Soils are poorly developed. Large areas are covered with pebbles of varying sizes. Alluvial deposits are found in wadis, basins, and oases. Salt flats are especially common in the east.

Climate. Climatically, the kingdom is almost entirely a desert. In winter, cyclonic weather systems generally skirt north of the Arabian Peninsula, moving eastward from the Mediterranean, though sometimes they reach eastern and central Arabia and the gulf. Some weather systems move southward along the Red Sea trough and provide winter precipitation as far south as Mecca and sometimes as far as Yemen. In March and April some rain, normally torrential, falls. In summer the highlands of Asir (ʿAsīr), southeast of Mecca, receive enough rain from the monsoonal winds to support a steppelike strip of land.

Winters, from December to February, are cool, and frost and snow may occur in the southern highlands. Average temperatures for the coolest months, December through February, are 74° F (23° C) at Jiddah, 58° F (14° C) at Riyadh, and 63° F (17° C) at Ad-Dammām. Summers, from June to August, are hot, with daytime temperatures in the shade exceeding 100° F (38° C) in almost all of the country. Temperatures in the desert frequently rise as high as 129° F (54° C) in the summer. Humidity is low, except along the coasts, where it can be high and very oppressive. Precipitation is low throughout the country, amounting to about 2½ inches (64 millimetres) at Jiddah, a little more than three inches at Riyadh, and three inches at Ad-Dammām. These figures, however, represent mean annual precipitation, and large variations are normal. In the highlands of Asir more than 19 inches a year may be received, falling mostly between May and October when the summer monsoon winds prevail. In the Rubʿ al-Khali a decade may pass with no rain at all.

There are three climatic zones: (1) desert almost everywhere, (2) steppe along the western highlands, forming a strip less than 100 miles wide in the north but becoming almost 300 miles wide at the latitude of Mecca, and (3) a very small area of humid and mild temperature conditions, with long summers, in the highlands just north of Yemen.

Three climatic zones

Plant and animal life. Much of Saudi Arabia's vegetation belongs to the North African–Indian desert region. Plants are xerophytic and are mostly small herbs and shrubs that are useful as forage. There are a few small areas of grass and trees in southern Asir. The date palm (*Phoenix dactylifera*) is widespread, though about one-third of the date palms grown are in Ash-Sharqīyah province.

Animal life includes the wolf, hyena, fox, honey badger, mongoose, porcupine, baboon, hedgehog, hare, sand rat, and jerboa. Larger animals such as the gazelle, oryx, leopard, and mountain goat were relatively numerous until about 1950, when hunting from motor vehicles reduced these animals almost to extinction. Birds include falcons (which are caught and trained for hunting), eagles, hawks, vultures, owls, ravens, flamingos, egrets, pelicans, doves, and quail, as well as sand grouse and bulbuls. There are several species of snakes, many of which are poisonous, and numerous types of lizards. There is a wide variety of marine life in the gulf. Domesticated animals include camels (now little used for transportation), fat-tailed sheep, long-eared goats, salukis, donkeys, and chickens.

Settlement patterns. Four traditional regions stand out—the Hejaz, Asir, Najd, and Al-Ḥasā (transliterated more precisely as Al-Ḥijāz, ʿAsīr, Najd, and Al-Aḥsā'). The Hejaz, in the northwest, contains the two holiest cities of Islām, Mecca and Medina, as well as the kingdom's primary port and diplomatic centre, Jiddah. Asir is the highland region south of the Hejaz; its capital, Abhā, lies at an elevation of about 8,000 feet. Subregions in Asir are formed by the oasis cluster of Najrān—a highland area north of Yemen—and by the coastal plain, the Tihāmah. Najd occupies a large part of the interior and includes the capital, Riyadh. Al-Ḥasā is in the east along the Persian Gulf; the region includes the principal petroleum-producing areas.

Nomadism, the form of land use with which the kingdom is traditionally associated, has become virtually nonexistent, and the pattern of extensive land use traditionally practiced by the nomadic Bedouin has been supplanted by the highly intensive patterns of urban land use. More than 70 percent of Saudi Arabia's total population lives in cities, and almost all of the rest lives in government-supported agricultural enterprises.

Less than 1 or 2 percent of the total land area is used for crops. Of the cultivated land about 45 percent is worked by rain-fed dry farming (mostly in Asir), 40 percent is in tree crops, and the remainder is irrigated. Most of the irrigated areas, in the districts of Riyadh and Al-Qaṣīm, for example, and near Al-Hufūf in Ash-Sharqīyah province, utilize underground water.

Irrigation

The largest towns are cosmopolitan in character, and some are associated with dominant functions: Mecca and Medina are religious, Riyadh is political and administrative, and Jiddah is commercial and diplomatic. Dhahran

Mud dwellings with crenellated rooftops typical of Najrān, Asir region, Saudi Arabia.
Peter Ryan—Robert Harding Picture Library

(Aẓ-Ẓahrān), near the Persian Gulf coast in Ash-Sharqīyah province, is the administrative centre of the Arabian American Oil Company (Aramco), and nearby Al-Khubar and Ad-Dammām are important commercial coastal towns. Al-Jubayl on the Gulf and Yanbuʿ on the Red Sea are the terminus points of oil and gas pipelines, and large petrochemical industrial complexes are located there.

The people. *Language.* Arabic is a Semitic language. It originated in Arabia, where the language is presumed to be the "purest." Classical written Arabic is standard throughout the Arab world, while spoken Arabic varies considerably. Such colloquial variations are evident even within Saudi Arabia—in part because of the strength of traditional group allegiances and in part because of varying external influences in different parts of the kingdom. English is widely understood.

Ethnic homogeneity

Ethnic groups. Considerable ethnic homogeneity is evident. Saudi nomads are "pure" Arabs, or at least descendants therefrom. As in the case of language, variations have developed because of a long history of regionalism and tribal autonomy and because some localities have been subjected to important outside influences. Thus, the influence of black Africa is evident along the Red Sea littoral, and influences from Iran, Pakistan, and India are seen in the east.

An increasing number of outsiders enter and leave Saudi Arabia. By the late 1980s the estimated number of foreign workers was between one-fourth and one-fifth of the country's total population. At first most of these were Arab, such as Yemenis, Egyptians, Palestinians, Syrians, and Iraqis. Increasing numbers of non-Arab Muslims such as Pakistanis have been employed, as have large numbers of non-Muslim Koreans and Filipinos who are hired in group contracts for specified periods. Among specialized technical workers, most are Europeans and Americans. Also of note is the number of people making the annual pilgrimage (hajj) to Mecca. By the late 1980s the number approached 2.5 million a year, of whom about half traveled from Arab countries and half from African and Asian countries.

Religion. Saudi Arabia is the home of Islām, and its native population is almost entirely Sunnite Muslim (*i.e.,* adhering to the chief branch of Islām, Sunnism [Sunnah], called traditionalist or orthodox). The Wahhābī interpretation of Sunnite Islām is the one officially used. Wahhābism, as it is called in the West, is a puritanical interpretation and is named after Muḥammad ibn ʿAbd al-Wahhāb (1703–92). Islām is a political as well as a religious system, and it is the source of the government's legitimacy. The king upholds Islām, applies its precepts, and is subject to them.

Shīʿites, who are adherents of Shīʿism, the second major branch of Islām, make up about 4 percent of the population and are found mostly in the oases of Al-Ḥasā and Al-Qaṭīf. The only Christians are foreign industrial employees and businessmen. Public worship and display of non-Muslim faiths is prohibited.

Demography. Saudi Arabia's birth and death rates are, respectively, 42 per 1,000 and 12 per 1,000, giving an annual natural increase of about 3 percent. Infant mortality is about 110 per 1,000 live births, and life expectancy at birth is 61 years. About 45 percent of the population is under 15 years of age, and 4 percent is 60 years or older. The government's pronatal policy prohibits the use of birth control measures.

The major areas of population are in the central Hejaz, in Asir, in central Najd, and near the Persian Gulf. The largest cities include Riyadh, Jiddah, Mecca, Aṭ-Ṭāʾif, Medina, Ad-Dammām, Al-Hufūf, Tabūk, Buraydah, Al-Mubarraz, Khamīs Mushayṭ, Al-Khubar, Najrān, Ḥāʾil, Jīzān, and Abhā.

The economy. Long-range economic development is directed through the implementation of five-year plans. In contrast to most developing countries, in Saudi Arabia there is an abundance of capital. The first two five-year plans (1970–80) established most of the country's basic transport and communications facilities. Subsequent objectives were to diversify the economy (including the development of agriculture-based industry, such as flour milling); to reduce dependence on foreign labour (especially at the management level); to increase domestic food production; to improve education, vocational training, and health services; and to further connect the different regions of the country. Industrial development is centred on the towns of Al-Jubayl on the Persian Gulf and Yanbuʿ on the Red Sea coast, both of which are part of a plan to use natural gas to fuel industries.

Resources. The economy of Saudi Arabia is dominated by petroleum and its associated industries. In terms of oil reserves, Saudi Arabia ranks first, with almost one-fourth of the world's known reserves.

Oil deposits are located in the east, southward from Iraq and Kuwait into the Rubʿ al-Khali and under the waters of the Persian Gulf. Other mineral resources are known to exist, and the government has pursued a policy of exploration and production in order to diversify the economic base. Geologic reconnaissance mapping of the Precambrian shield in the west has revealed deposits of gold, silver, copper, zinc, lead, iron, titanium, pyrite, magnesite, platinum, and cadmium. There are also nonmetallic resources such as limestone, silica, gypsum, and phosphorite. Forest and rangeland resources are limited, the former covering a total of only about 600 square miles, mostly in Asir.

Non-petroleum mineral resources

Agriculture. The Kingdom of Saudi Arabia inherited the simple, tribal economy of Arabia. Many of the people were nomads, engaged in raising camels, sheep, and goats. Agricultural production was localized and subsistent. Domestic food production has been given special attention in the kingdom's development planning, and the government has made subsidies and generous incentives available to the agriculture sector. In the mid-1980s more than 50 percent of the native Saudi work force continued to be employed in agriculture, and agriculture contributed about 4 percent of the gross domestic product.

The kingdom has achieved self-sufficiency in wheat, eggs, and milk, among other items, though it still imports about 70 percent of its food needs. Wheat is the primary cultivated crop, followed by sorghum, barley, and millet. Watermelons, tomatoes, dates, grapes, onions, and pumpkins and squash are also important crops.

Two major constraints to cultivation are poor water supply and poor soil. Concrete and earth-filled dams have been built, primarily in the southwest, to provide irrigation. Agricultural expansion has been great in irrigated areas, while the amount of land given to rain-fed farming has decreased. Substantial resources of subterranean water have been discovered in the central and eastern parts of the country. Desalinization of seawater is almost entirely for urban and industrial uses. Riyadh's water supply, for example, is augmented by a pipeline from a desalinization plant in Al-Jubayl on the gulf.

Industry. The discovery of oil changed the entire economic situation of Saudi Arabia. As early as 1923 Ibn Saʿūd granted an oil-prospecting concession to a British company, but this concession was never exploited. Although oil was discovered in 1938, World War II curtailed activities until near its end. The Ras Tanura refinery was opened in 1945, and rapid expansion of the oil industry followed because of the increasing postwar demand.

Discovery of oil

In 1951 the Arabian American Oil Company (Aramco) discovered the first offshore field in the Middle East, at Ra's As-Saffānīyah, just south of the Saudi Arabia–Kuwait neutral zone, and oil was discovered in the zone itself in 1953. Al-Ghawār, just south of Dhahran and west of Al-Hufūf, is the world's largest oil field. The first portion of the Al-Ghawār oil field was discovered at ʿAin Dār in 1948. Intensive exploration of the Rubʿ al-Khali began in 1950, and oil fields were finally discovered in the area in the 1970s.

In 1950 Aramco put into operation the Trans-Arabian Pipe Line (Tapline), which ran from Al-Qayṣūmah in Saudi Arabia across Jordan and Syria to its Mediterranean terminal at Sidon, Lebanon. The line was in operation only sporadically during the 1970s, and in 1983 it ceased to function beyond supplying a refinery in Jordan. In 1981 Petroline, built to carry crude oil, was completed from Al-Jubayl on the Persian Gulf to Yanbuʿ on the Red Sea, greatly shortening the distance to Europe and obviating navigation through the gulf and the Strait of Hormuz. Petroline was built by the General Petroleum and Mineral Organization (Petromin), a government-owned corporation. Aramco constructed a massive gas-gathering system and, parallel to Petroline, a pipeline for transporting natural-gas liquids, which reached Yanbuʿ in 1981.

During the 1970s and early '80s Saudi Arabia gradually acquired complete ownership of Aramco, and in 1984 Aramco had its first Saudi president. In terms of production Saudi Arabia is among the world leaders.

The manufacturing sector has expanded widely. Manufactures include rolled steel, petrochemicals, fertilizers, pipes, copper wire and cable, truck assembly, refrigeration, plastics, aluminum products, metal products, and cement. Small-scale enterprises include baking, printing, and furniture manufacturing.

Finance. The Saudi Arabian Monetary Agency (SAMA) was established in 1952 as the kingdom's central money and banking authority. It regulates commercial and development banks and other financial institutions. Its functions include issuing and regulating money supply, stabilizing the value of currency, acting as banker for the government, and managing foreign reserves and investments. As an Islāmic institution its status is nonprofit. Under Islāmic law banks cannot charge interest, but they do charge fees for lending and they pay commission on deposits. Money supply and the tempo of business are dominated by government economic activity, though the government favours expansion of the private sector. Saudi Arabia is one of the world's largest lenders in terms of foreign aid and development assistance.

Trade. Exports consist almost entirely of petroleum and petroleum products. Major imports are machinery and appliances, foodstuffs and tobacco, transport equipment, textiles and clothing, metals and metal articles, and chemicals. The principal destinations of exports are Japan, the United States, Italy, France, and The Netherlands. The principal sources of imports are the United States, Japan, Germany, Italy, the United Kingdom, and Taiwan.

Transportation. About one-third of the country's roads are paved. The first coast-to-coast road connection, from Ad-Dammām on the gulf to Jiddah on the Red Sea, by way of Riyadh, was opened in 1967; it includes a spectacular descent of the western escarpment from Aṭ-Ṭā'if to Mecca. Other important connections are from Riyadh northwestward through Najd to Ḥā'il, from Riyadh southwestward to the Najrān region, between central Najd and Medina, from Medina northwestward through Tabūk to Jordan, from Medina westward and southward to Yanbuʿ and Jiddah, along the length of the Red Sea coast between the borders of Jordan and Yemen; from Aṭ-Ṭā'if southeastward along the edge of the plateau to the Najrān by way of Abhā, and from Ad-Dammān on the gulf northwestward along the Tapline to Jordan. A railroad passing through Al-Hufūf connects Riyadh and Ad-Dammām. A causeway, opened in 1986, connects the kingdom with the island nation of Bahrain.

Roads

Seaport capacity has been greatly expanded. Major cargo ports are Jiddah, Yanbuʿ, and Jīzān on the Red Sea and Ad-Dammān and Al-Jubayl on the gulf. The country has many small airports, of which fewer than half have paved runways. The national airline, Saudia, provides both domestic and international service. The chief international airports are at Dhahran, Riyadh, and Jiddah.

Administration and social conditions. *Government.* Saudi Arabia's government is based on the law of Islām, the Sharīʿah, derived from Muḥammad's pronouncements and practices and from the traditions of Islām's first adherents. Muslim law prescribes civil as well as religious rights, duties, obligations, and responsibilities for both ruler and ruled. Law is revealed and not created, and it is interpreted by the *ʿulamā'*, or learned religious men.

The person of the king combines legislative, executive, and judicial functions. As prime minister he presides over the Council of Ministers. This council is a legislative body, although it is also responsible for such executive and administrative matters as foreign and domestic policy, defense, finance, health, and education, which it administers through numerous separate agencies. Appointment to and dismissal from the council are prerogatives of the king. Major policy decisions are made by consensus, and opinion is sought primarily within the royal family (comprising the numerous descendants of the kingdom's founder, Ibn Saʿūd). Many members of the royal family hold sensitive government posts.

The monarchy

Succession to the throne is not hereditary; the crown prince, who also serves as deputy prime minister, is designated by the royal family with the support of the *ʿulamā'* and the Council of Ministers. The same consultative process also designates the second deputy prime minister, who is the second heir apparent after the deputy prime minister.

The kingdom is divided into administrative regions,

which in turn are divided into districts. Provincial governors are appointed and are responsible for such functions as finance, health, education, agriculture, and municipalities. The consultative principle operates at all levels of government, including the government of villages and tribes.

Justice. The Sharīʿah law is the basis of justice. Judgment usually is according to the Ḥanbalī tradition of Islām; the law tends to be conservative and punishment severe. In 1970 the Ministry of Justice was established; its work is assisted by a Supreme Judicial Council consisting of leading members of the *ʿulamāʾ*. There are more than 300 Sharīʿah courts across the country. Rapid changes since the mid-20th century have produced circumstances—such as traffic violations and industrial accidents—not encompassed by traditional law, and these have been handled by the issuance of royal decrees. These decrees have evolved into a body of administrative law. Avenues of appeal are available, and the monarch is both the final court of appeal and the dispenser of pardon.

The armed forces. Military service is voluntary. The army accounts for about three-fifths of the total military force. It experienced rapid modernization especially after the Arab-Israeli War of 1967. Army officers are trained at King ʿAbd al-ʿAzīz Military Academy just north of Riyadh. The air force was equipped largely by the British until the 1970s, when the kingdom began to buy aircraft from the United States. Major air bases are at Riyadh, Dhahran, Ḥafar Al-Bāṭin (part of the King Khālid Military City) near the border with Iraq and Kuwait, Tabūk in the northwest near Jordan, and Khamīs Mushayṭ in the southwest near Yemen. All three armed services are directed by the defense minister, who is also the second deputy prime minister. The National Guard is essentially an internal security force, though it can support the regular forces for national defense. One of its primary peacetime tasks is to guard the country's oil fields. It is administered separately, and its commander reports to the crown prince. The armed forces employ expatriate personnel in support and training positions.

Education. Education is free at all levels and is given high priority by the government. The school system consists of elementary (grades 1–6), intermediate (7–9), and secondary (10–12) schools.

Expansion in higher education

Higher education has expanded at a remarkable pace. Institutions of higher education include the King Saʿūd University (formerly the University of Riyadh, founded in 1957), the Islāmic University (1961) at Medina, and the King ʿAbd al-ʿAzīz University (1967) in Jiddah. Other institutes include the Higher Institute of Technology, the Higher Juridical Institute, the King ʿAbd al-ʿAzīz Military Academy, the College for the Arabic Language, the Technical Institute, and the College of Islāmic Jurisprudence, all at Riyadh; the King Fahd University of Petroleum and Minerals at Dhahran; the School of Ḥadīth (narrative traditions), the Sharīʿah College of Islāmic Jurisprudence, and the Saudi Arabian Institute for Higher Education, all at Mecca; the School of Applied Arts and the Teacher Training Centre, both at Medina; and schools of industrial education at Riyadh, Jiddah, Medina, and Ad-Dammām. Institutes for religious teaching are located in several towns. A college of medicine has been started in Jiddah. Many foreign teachers are employed, especially in technical and medical schools. Large numbers of students enroll in overseas universities.

Health and welfare. A great deal of attention has been given to health care since the 1970s. Between 1970 and 1980 the numbers of hospital beds, physicians, and nurses increased greatly. During the 1980s budgets made provision for the construction of many additional health institutes, hospitals, and health centres and the hiring of additional medical staff. A network of dispensaries serving communities of 10,000 or more persons is complemented by a system of mobile health services to reach small communities and the remaining nomadic populations. The government has also begun to train Saudis to replace foreign medical personnel. Of serious concern are a high rate of trachoma and occasional outbreaks of malaria, bilharzia, and cholera.

Saudi Arabia's population has traditionally been composed of nomads, villagers, and townspeople. Pervading this triad, however, is the patrilineal kinship principle, and superimposed on all is the administrative organization centred on the royal family. The kinship principle is pervasive in Saudi society, and the extended family is a strong social unit. Villages constitute local service centres and contain representatives from more than one tribal affiliation, though one group may tend to be dominant. Cities are not tribally organized, though the importance of kinship affiliation endures, and local affairs tend to be dominated and administered by a few families. Social stratification is more clearly developed in the cities than elsewhere. Before the effects of oil were felt on the economy, status was a matter of lineage and occupation rather than of wealth; with the development of the oil industry, however, wealth and material position have acquired an additional social value. The new technology and industry have produced a growing middle-income economic group of technocrats that is increasingly aware of the widening gap between the ruling families and the rest of the population.

Nomads, villagers, and townspeople

Cultural life. The cultural setting is Arab and Muslim. To preserve the country's purist religious position, many proscriptions of behaviour and dress are enforced. Alcoholic beverages are prohibited, for example, and the theatre and public cinema do not exist. Educated Saudis are well informed on issues of the Arab world, the Muslim world, and the world at large, but public expression of opinion about domestic matters is not encouraged. There are no public forums such as political parties or labour unions.

For a thousand years artistic expression usually perpetuated ancient forms. From the 18th century onward the strict Wahhābī religious outlook discouraged intellectual deviation from accepted purist positions. With the advent of the petroleum industry came exposure to outside influences, such as housing styles, furnishings, and clothes, and at the same time local craftsmen found themselves in competition with imported goods.

Music and dance have always been part of Saudi life. Visual arts are dominated by geometric, floral, and abstract designs and by calligraphy, the latter a sophisticated and learned enterprise. Not much diversity is seen in traditional architecture; typical features are decorative designs on doors and windows and wide use of crenellated walls. The wave of change starting in the 1960s influenced architectural styles, and stark linear motifs became common in office and residential buildings. The spectacular airport terminals at Jiddah and Riyadh, however, are testimony to the persistence and worth of traditional styles.

Several daily and weekly newspapers are published in Arabic and in English. Radio and television broadcasting is operated by the Ministry of Information, and there is a modern system of telecommunications.

For statistical data on the land and people of Saudi Arabia, see the *Britannica World Data* section in the BRITANNICA WORLD DATA ANNUAL. (B.K.N.)

HISTORY

The coastal parts of the territory that was to become Saudi Arabia participated in the broad trends of Arabian Peninsula history in the Islāmic period—the rise of Islām in western Arabia in the 7th century, the creation and expansion of the Islāmic empires to the 10th century, the establishment of separate and usually small Muslim states in the period leading to the 15th century, and the ordering of the Arab Middle East conducted by the Ottoman Empire starting in the 16th century. Central Arabia was linked commercially and intellectually with western Arabia and the Fertile Crescent but was often isolated from general political and military trends because of its remoteness and relative poverty. In the middle of the 18th century in central Arabia an alliance of Muslim Wahhābī religious reformers and the Saʿūdī dynasty formed a new state and society that resulted in the creation of three successive Saʿūdī kingdoms, including the modern country of Saudi Arabia, officially proclaimed in 1932.

The Wahhābī movement. *Origins and early expansion.* As the population of the oasis towns of central Arabia such as ʿUyaynah slowly grew from the 16th to the early 18th centuries, the *ʿulamāʾ* residing there increased in number and sophistication. Muḥammad ibn ʿAbd al-Wahhāb, the founder of the Wahhābī movement, was born in ʿUyaynah in 1703 to a family of religious judges and scholars and as a young man traveled widely in other regions of the Middle East. It was upon his return to ʿUyaynah that he first began to preach his revolutionary ideas of religious reformation on fundamentalist lines. His teaching was influenced by that of the Ḥanbalī scholar Ibn Taymīyah, who had died in 1328.

The ruler of ʿUyaynah, ʿUthmān ibn Muʿammar, gladly welcomed the returning prodigal and even adhered to his doctrines. But many opposed him, and ʿAbd al-Wahhāb's preaching was put to a number of severe tests. ʿUthmān received threats from the Banū Khālid chief of Al-Ḥasā, demanding the death of the innovator on pain of withholding annual gifts from the province and even of invasion. ʿUthmān, unable to face this danger but unwilling to kill his guest, decided to dismiss ʿAbd al-Wahhāb from his territory. ʿAbd al-Wahhāb went to Ad-Dirʿīyah, some 40 miles away, which had been the seat of the local prince Muḥammad ibn Saʿūd since 1726. In 1745 the people flocked to the teaching of the reformer. The alliance of theologian and prince, duly sealed by mutual oaths of loyalty, soon began to prosper in terms of military success and expansion.

Military success of the movement

One by one the enemies of the new dispensation were conquered. The earliest wars brought ʿUyaynah and portions of Al-Ḥasā under Wahhābī control, but Riyadh maintained a stubborn resistance for 27 years before succumbing to the steady pressure of the new movement. By 1765, when Muḥammad ibn Saʿūd died, only a few parts of central and eastern Arabia had fallen under more or less effective Wahhābī rule.

Muḥammad ibn Saʿūd's son and successor, ʿAbd al-ʿAzīz I (reigned 1765–1803), who had been largely responsible for this extension of his father's realm by his exploits as commander in chief of the Wahhābī forces, continued to work in complete harmony with Muḥammad ibn ʿAbd al-Wahhāb. It was indeed the latter who virtually controlled the civil administration of the country, while ʿAbd al-ʿAzīz himself, later in cooperation with his warlike son, Saʿūd I (reigned 1803–14), busied himself in the expansion of his empire far beyond the limits inherited by him. Meanwhile, in 1792, Muḥammad ibn ʿAbd al-Wahhāb died at the age of 89. Wahhābī attacks had begun to attract the attention of the Ottoman government, and in 1798 an Ottoman force invaded Al-Ḥasā, though it was compelled to withdraw. Qatar fell to the Saʿūdīs in 1797, and the latter also gained control through local allies over Bahrain and parts of Oman.

Struggle with the Ottomans. In 1801 the Wahhābīs captured and sacked the Shīʿite holy city of Karbalāʾ in Ottoman Iraq, and in the following year Saʿūd led his father's army to the capture of Mecca itself in the Ottoman Hejaz. It was soon after his return from this expedition that his father was assassinated by a Shīʿite in the mosque of Ad-Dirʿīyah in revenge for the desecration of Karbalāʾ.

Capture of Medina

The issue was now joined between the Ottomans and the Wahhābīs of Arabia. In 1804 Saʿūd captured Medina, and the Wahhābī empire embraced the whole of Arabia down to Yemen and Oman. Year after year Saʿūd visited Mecca to preside over the pilgrimage as the imam of the Muslim congregation. But the tide was soon to turn to his disadvantage. The sultan of the Ottoman Empire, preoccupied in other directions, consigned to Muḥammad (Meḥmet) ʿAlī Pasha, the virtually independent viceroy of Egypt, the task of crushing the "heretics." An Egyptian force landed on the Hejaz coast under the command of Ṭūsūn, the youthful son of Muḥammad ʿAlī Pasha. Saʿūd inflicted a severe defeat on the invaders, but reinforcements enabled Ṭūsūn to occupy Mecca and Medina in 1812. The following year Muḥammad ʿAlī assumed command of the expeditionary force in person. In the east, Britain severely curbed the naval allies of the Wahhābīs in 1809.

Saʿūd died at Ad-Dirʿīyah in 1814. His successor, his son ʿAbd Allāh ibn Saʿūd, was scarcely of his father's calibre, and the capture of Ar-Raʾs in Al-Qaṣīm by the Egyptians in 1815 forced him to sue for peace. This was duly arranged, but the truce was short-lived, and in 1816 the struggle was renewed, with Ibrahim Pasha, another of Muḥammad ʿAlī's sons, in command of the Egyptian forces. Gaining the support of the volatile tribes by skillful diplomacy and lavish gifts, he advanced into central Arabia. Joined by most of the principal tribes, he appeared before ad-Dirʿīyah in April 1818. Fighting ended in September with the surrender of ʿAbd Allāh, who was sent to Istanbul and beheaded. Local Wahhābī leaders were executed, Ad-Dirʿīyah was razed to the ground, and Egyptian garrisons were posted to the principal towns. The Saʿūdī family had suffered heavy losses during the fighting. A few had managed to escape before the surrender; the rest were sent to Egypt for detention along with descendants of Muḥammad ibn ʿAbd al-Wahhāb. The Wahhābī empire ceased to exist, but the faith lived on in the desert and in the towns of central Arabia in defiance of the new rulers of the land.

Second Saʿūdī state. The dynasty was restored and the second Saʿūdī state begun in 1824 when Turkī (1823–34), a grandson of Muḥammad ibn Saʿūd, succeeded in capturing Riyadh and expelling the Egyptian garrison. Thereafter, Riyadh remained the capital of the state. Turkī tried to maintain friendly ties with the Ottoman governors of Iraq and the British as he accepted nominal Ottoman sovereignty. Al-Ḥasā and Ḥāʾil fell again to the Saʿūdīs by 1830, as the town militias of central Arabia, which formed the bases of the Saʿūdī army, overcame the nomadic tribes. Literature, commerce, and agriculture flourished despite the crushing losses to society occasioned by the return of cholera.

In 1834 Turkī was murdered by an ambitious cousin, who then was deposed and executed by Turkī's son Fayṣal (1834–38; 1843–65). Fayṣal refused to pay the Egyptian tribute; in 1837 an Egyptian expeditionary force entered Riyadh, and Fayṣal was captured in 1838 and sent to Cairo. Khālid, son of Saʿūd and brother of ʿAbd Allāh, was installed as ruler of Najd by the Egyptians. Both Fayṣal and Khālid had been carried away into captivity in Egypt after the fall of Ad-Dirʿīyah, but the former had escaped in 1828 to rejoin his father and to play a prominent part in the reestablishment of the Wahhābī regime. Khālid had been released from prison to accompany the expeditionary force sent to restore Egyptian rule in Arabia as the ruler designate, on his undertaking to recognize the control by Egypt. So Fayṣal returned to Cairo for a second period of incarceration until his second escape and return to Najd in 1843.

Meanwhile the subservience of Khālid to his Egyptian and Ottoman masters was increasingly resented by his Wahhābī subjects; and in 1841 his cousin, ʿAbd Allāh ibn Thunayan, raised the standard of revolt. Riyadh was captured by a bold coup, its garrison was expelled, and Khālid, who was in Al-Ḥasā at the time, fled by ship to Jiddah. ʿAbd Allāh resisted when Fayṣal reappeared in 1843, only to be overpowered and slain. So Fayṣal resumed his reign after an interruption of five years, to rule basically unchallenged, despite occasional tribal uprisings and friction with the townspeople of Al-Qaṣīm, until his death in 1865. The Hejaz remained in Ottoman hands, while northern Arabia (the province of Jabal Shammar) was locally autonomous but acknowledged the supremacy of Riyadh. Fayṣal reestablished Saʿūdī authority for a short time in Bahrain and for a longer time in Al-Buraymī and the Oman hinterland. He extended his influence as far as Hadhramaut and the frontiers of Yemen. Only British intervention stopped the extension of direct Saʿūdī power over the western shore of the gulf.

Administration under Fayṣal was simple and involved few people, mostly members of the royal family and descendants of Muḥammad ibn ʿAbd al-Wahhāb. Justice in the provinces was enforced by officials appointed by Riyadh, even the tribes paid taxes, and the writing of poetry and history flourished.

Legacy of Fayṣal

In 1865, when his power was an acknowledged factor in Arabian politics, Fayṣal died. His sons disputed the succession. His eldest son, ʿAbd Allāh, succeeded first, maintaining himself against the rebellion of his brother Saʿūd II for six years until his defeat at the Battle of Jūdah in 1871. ʿAbd Allāh's flight left Saʿūd in possession, but the next five years saw the throne change hands no fewer than seven times in favour of different members of the Saʿūdī family. Drought in 1870–74 exacerbated the civil war's effects, as the unity of the Wahhābī community disintegrated. Meanwhile ʿAbd Allāh had appealed to the Ottomans in Baghdad, who came to his assistance but took advantage of the situation to occupy the province of Al-Ḥasā for themselves in 1871—an occupation that lasted for 42 years.

The Rashīdīs. Saʿūd II died in 1875, and after a brief interval of chaos ʿAbd Allāh II returned to the throne the following year, only to find himself powerless against the Rashīdī emirs of Jabal Shammar, with their capital at Ḥāʾil. The Rashīdīs had ruled there since 1836, first as agents for the Saʿūdīs, but subsequently they became independent, with strong links to the Ottomans and growing wealth from the caravan trade. Muḥammad ibn ʿAbd Allāh ar-Rashīd (reigned 1869–97) was undoubtedly the dominant figure in Arabian politics when ʿAbd Allāh II ibn Saʿūd returned to Riyadh for his third spell of authority. At first the Rashīdīs refrained from any forward action, but they soon intervened in the chaotic affairs of the Wahhābī state. And it was not long before ʿAbd Allāh was "invited" to be the "guest" of Ibn Rashīd at Ḥāʾil, while a representative of the Rashīdīs was appointed governor of Riyadh in 1887. ʿAbd Allāh was allowed to return to Riyadh and even was named governor of the city in 1889. ʿAbd Allāh did not live long in enjoyment of his restoration, however; he died in the same year, leaving to his youngest brother, ʿAbd ar-Raḥmān, the almost hopeless task of saving the realm of their ancestors.

ʿAbd ar-Raḥmān was soon embroiled in hostilities with the Rashīdīs. The Battle of Al-Mulaida (in Al-Qaṣīm) settled the issue between them decisively in 1891, and for the second time in the space of 70 years the Wahhābī state seemed to be completely destroyed. ʿAbd ar-Raḥmān fled with his family to take refuge in Kuwait as the guest of its rulers. Unlike the first Saʿūdī regime, which was ended by external conquest, the second Saʿūdī state fell chiefly because of internal disputes among members of the royal family.

Ibn Saʿūd and the third Saʿūdī state. ʿAbd al-ʿAzīz, the son of the exiled ʿAbd ar-Raḥmān, took advantage of his new location to learn useful knowledge of world affairs, while the new Rashīdī prince, ʿAbd al-ʿAzīz ibn ʿAbd Mitʿab, alienated the population of Najd. In 1901 the young ʿAbd al-ʿAzīz ibn ʿAbd ar-Raḥmān (he was about 22 to 26 years old) sallied out with a small force of 40 followers on what must have seemed a forlorn adventure. On Jan. 15, 1902, with a select body of only 15 warriors, he scaled the walls of Riyadh, surprised and defeated the Rashīdī governor and his escort before the gate of the Mismāk fort, and was hailed by the populace as their ruler.

ʿAbd al-ʿAzīz and the capture of Riyadh

Ibn Saʿūd. Thus began a reign destined to be one of the most famous in Arabian history. The following years witnessed the development of the struggle by the third Saʿūdī state to expand its control once again over most of the Arabian Peninsula and thereby reestablish the glories of the first Saʿūdī experiences in the 18th century. The first challenge was from the Rashīdīs, whose power was by no means spent and who received substantial help from the Ottomans in men and material. In 1904 the combined Rashīdī and Ottoman forces were defeated by Ibn Saʿūd (as ʿAbd al-ʿAzīz ibn ʿAbd ar-Raḥmān ibn Fayṣal ibn Turkī ibn ʿAbd Allāh ibn Muḥammad Āl Saʿūd became generally known outside Arabia); but in agreement with him the Ottomans placed garrisons in central Arabia for one year. Ibn Rashīd continued the struggle, but he was killed in battle in 1906, and thenceforth Ibn Saʿūd, who secured the withdrawal of Ottoman troops from Al-Qaṣīm in 1906, remained the undisputed master of central Arabia. Ibn Saʿūd bent himself to the task of regaining the whole realm of his ancestors. He was cautious enough to keep the fiction of acknowledging Ottoman overlordship, and by contacts with Britain he hoped to balance each power against the other.

Meanwhile he busied himself with the reorganization of the country's administration, including the inception of a plan designed to ensure the stability and permanence of his military force. In 1912 he established the first Ikhwān (Brethren) colony on the desert wells of Al-Arṭāwīyah, peopled entirely by Bedouin. The colony formed a militant cantonment dedicated to the service of God and prince. Within the next decade nearly 100 similar colonies organized around tribal group identity were founded throughout the country, providing Ibn Saʿūd with a formidable force. The Saʿūdī military also included, however, soldiers recruited from the towns and nomadic tribes.

Ibn Saʿūd's first spectacular conquest was the taking of Al-Ḥasā province from the Ottomans in 1913, although he was compelled to reaffirm Ottoman sovereignty over all of his territory in 1914. During World War I he was aided by British subsidies, but he managed by adroit diplomacy to be relatively quiescent, though surrounded by enemies. In 1919, however, he struck his first blow, against Sharif Ḥusayn ibn ʿAlī of the Hejaz, whose army was annihilated by the Ikhwān. In 1920 Ibn Saʿūd's son Fayṣal captured the province of Asir between the Hejaz and Yemen. In 1921 Ibn Saʿūd defeated the forces of Muḥammad ibn Talal, the last Rashīdī emir, and annexed the whole of northern Arabia, occupying Al-Jawf and Wadi As-Sirḥān in the following year. Kuwait experienced border raids and a Saʿūdī blockade over payment of customs duties. Meanwhile Fayṣal and Abdullah, the sons of Sharif Ḥusayn of Mecca, king of the Hejaz, had been placed on the thrones of Iraq and Transjordan, respectively, by the British government. These territories with the Hejaz served as a formidable British-protected cordon around the northern and western borders of the Wahhābī state, with the inevitable result of frequent border incidents.

In 1923 the British government invited all the rulers concerned in these sporadic hostilities to attend a conference at Kuwait and if possible to agree on a settlement of their differences. The British also made it clear that the subsidies theretofore paid to Ibn Saʿūd and Sharif Ḥusayn would be terminated.

The conference ended in complete disagreement, and in September 1924 the Wahhābīs attacked the Hejaz. They captured Aṭ-Ṭāʾif after a brief struggle but with an accompanying massacre of male civilians, and then they occupied Mecca without opposition. Ibn Saʿūd then laid seige to Jiddah and Medina, while Sharif Ḥusayn abdicated his throne in favour of his son ʿAlī. By the end of 1925 both Medina and Jiddah had surrendered to the Saʿūdīs. The ʿAqabah-Ma ʿān district adjacent to the northern Hejaz was occupied by Transjordan to prevent its falling into Wahhābī hands. On Jan. 8, 1926, Ibn Saʿūd, who had adopted the title of sultan of Najd in 1921, was proclaimed king of the Hejaz in the Great Mosque of Mecca. In 1927 he also changed his title of sultan to king of Najd and its dependencies, the two parts of his dual kingdom being administered for the time being as separate units. In the same year the Treaty of Jiddah, negotiated by him with Sir Gilbert Clayton, placed his relations with Great Britain on a permanent footing as the British fully acknowledged Saʿūdī independence. The results of Muslim conferences sponsored by the Saʿūdīs in the Hejaz were to legitimize their presence as rulers.

King of the Hejaz and Najd

Ibn Saʿūd found himself in difficulties with the more religious elements of Najd because of his association with Christian powers and his alleged complaisance in regard to the British-protected regimes in Iraq and Transjordan, which were still the objects of Ikhwān desire for conquest. Incidents on their frontiers created a state of virtual though undeclared war, in which British aircraft played a part in discouraging Wahhābī incursions. Ibn Saʿūd also on several occasions violently suppressed political and military opposition by the Ikhwan.

In 1928 and 1929 Fayṣal ad-Dawīsh, Sulṭān ibn Bijād, and other leaders of the Ikhwān, accusing Ibn Saʿūd of betraying the cause for which they had fought and opposing the taxes levied upon their followers, resumed their defiance of the king's authority. The rebels sought to stop the centralization of power in the hands of the king and keep the purity of Wahhābī practices against the innovations advocated by Ibn Saʿūd. The majority of the population rallied to the king's side, and this, with the support of the Najdi *ʿulamāʾ*, enabled him to defeat the rebels. The civil war, however, dragged on into 1930, when the rebels were rounded up by the British in Kuwaiti territory and their leaders were handed over to the king. With their defeat, power passed definitively into the hands of townspeople rather than the tribes.

Ibn Saʿūd was at last free to give his undivided attention to the development of his country and to the problems of foreign policy that beset him on all sides. Above all he was concerned to assert and maintain the complete independence of his country and in it the exclusive supremacy of Islām. Subject to their respect of these fundamental objectives, he was not only ready to cooperate with all nations but prepared to regard with sympathy some of the practices that had taken root in the Hejaz and other areas as the result of foreign contacts. The ban on music, for example, was progressively circumvented by the radio, which was also used as a tool to unite the kingdom and increase military efficiency. And so the latitudinarian spirit, slowly at first but with ever-increasing momentum, lessened a few of the inhibitions of the puritan regime.

On the other hand Ibn Saʿūd rigorously opposed any foreign intervention whatever in the internal politics of the regime. Aside from members of the royal family, and Najdi and Hejazi merchants, many of the king's chief advisers were foreign Muslims. Some of the foreign advisers were political refugees from their homelands and served Ibn Saʿūd for a very long time. (H.St.J.B.P./W.L.O.)

The Kingdom of Saudi Arabia. The history of the Kingdom of Saudi Arabia begins properly on Sept. 18, 1932, when by royal decree the dual kingdom of the Hejaz and Najd with its dependencies, administered since 1927 as two separate units, was unified under the name of the Kingdom of Saudi Arabia. The chief immediate effect was to increase the unity of the kingdom and to decrease the possibility of Hejazi separatism, while the name underscored the central role of the royal family in the kingdom's creation. No attempt was made to change the supreme authority of the king as the absolute monarch of the new regime; indeed, his power was emphasized in 1933 by his choice of his son Saʿūd as heir apparent.

Unification of the kingdom

Foreign relations, 1932–53. From the date of its establishment in September 1932, Saudi Arabia enjoyed full international recognition as an independent state, although it did not join the League of Nations.

In 1934 Ibn Saʿūd was involved in war with Yemen over a boundary dispute. An additional cause of the war was Yemen's support of a rising by an Asiri prince against Ibn Saʿūd. In a seven-week campaign the Saudis were generally victorious. Hostilities were terminated by the Treaty of Aṭ-Ṭāʾif, by which the Saudis gained the disputed district. Diplomatic relations with Egypt, severed in 1926 because of an incident on the Meccan pilgrimage, were not renewed until after the death of King Fuʾād of Egypt in 1936.

Fixing the boundaries of the country remained a problem throughout the 1930s. In tribal society, sovereignty was traditionally expressed in the form of suzerainty over certain tribes rather than in fixed territorial boundaries. Hence Ibn Saʿūd regarded the demarcation of land frontiers with suspicion. Nevertheless, the majority of the frontiers with Iraq, Kuwait, and Jordan had been demarcated by 1930. In the south no agreement was reached on the exact site of the frontiers with the Trucial States and with the interior of Yemen and Muscat and Oman.

After Saudi Arabia declared its neutrality during World War II, Britain and the United States subsidized Saudi Arabia, which later declared war on Germany in 1945, thus enabling the kingdom to enter the United Nations. Ibn Saʿūd also joined the Arab League, but he did not play a leading part in it since the religious and conservative element in Saudi Arabia opposed cooperation with other Arab states, even when Saudis shared common views, as in opposition to Zionism. In the Arab-Israeli War of 1948, Saudi Arabia contributed only one battalion.

Internal affairs, 1932–53. Although oil had been discovered in Al-Ḥasā near the shores of the Persian Gulf before World War II, it was not exploited energetically until after 1941. Revenues before the war were based primarily on the pilgrimage, customs duties, and taxes—much of which decreased as a result of the world economic depression of the 1930s. After 1944 a considerable number of employees of the oil company, known thereafter as Aramco (the Arabian American Oil Company), arrived in Saudi Arabia. The resulting sudden access of wealth from increased production was a mixed blessing. The country was itself unable to supply the oil company with sufficient skilled workers. When in 1949 Aramco paid more taxes to the U.S. government than the yield to Saudi Arabia in royalties the Saudi leadership obtained a new agreement in 1950 that required Aramco to pay an income tax of 50 percent of the net operating income to the Saudis.

Exploitation of oil reserves

Cultural life flourished, primarily in the Hejaz, which was the centre for newspapers and radio. The disturbance of traditional patterns caused by the cultural changes, new wealth from increased production of oil, inflation, and the movement of the population to the major cities was reflected in the government. Despite the new wealth, extravagant spending led to governmental deficits and foreign borrowing in the 1950s.

Ibn Saʿūd viewed this flood of wealth and the consequent changes in morality with distaste and bewilderment. He died on Nov. 9, 1953.

Reign of King Saʿūd ibn ʿAbd al-ʿAzīz. Ibn Saʿūd was succeeded by his eldest surviving son, Saʿūd, his second son, Fayṣal, being declared heir apparent. The two brothers were remarkably different. Saʿūd had been heir apparent since 1933; he had many ties among the desert tribes. Fayṣal, who had lived chiefly in the cities of the Hejaz, had often been abroad in his post as Saudi foreign minister. Saʿūd thus represented the ancien régime, while those advocating modernization supported Fayṣal.

As urbanization increased, the character of Riyadh and Jiddah was enormously changed. Roads, schools, hospitals, palaces, apartment buildings, and airports replaced the old alleyways and mud-built houses. Weaving and other crafts continued, but they were modified by the use of new patterns and materials.

At the royal court there was constant rivalry between Saʿūd and Fayṣal. In March 1958, as a result of pressure, Saʿūd issued a decree transferring all executive power to Fayṣal. In December 1960, however, Fayṣal was obliged to resign as prime minister, and the king himself assumed the office. In 1962–63 Fayṣal was once more given executive powers. Finally, on Nov. 2, 1964, King Saʿūd was deposed and Fayṣal was proclaimed king. The National Guard, the royal princes, and the *ʿulamāʾ* supported Fayṣal in the struggle for power against Saʿūd. Fayṣal was more competent than Saʿūd; it was he who developed the ministries of government and established for the first time an efficient bureaucracy.

Foreign affairs under Saʿūd and Fayṣal. Since the frontier between Saudi Arabia and Oman had never been demarcated and there was the possibility of discovering oil in the area, in 1952 Saudi Arabia occupied the oasis of Al-Buraymī. In January 1953, however, Britain and Oman reoccupied the oasis.

After World War II the United States became the most influential foreign power in Saudi Arabia. American interest was directed toward the oil industry, which was owned by U.S. companies. In 1960 Saudi Arabia helped found the Organization of Petroleum Exporting Countries (OPEC). The Saudis favoured the United States in the Cold War with the Soviet Union, but they opposed American support of Israel.

As a result of the rise to power of Egypt's Pan-Arab nationalist president, Gamal Abdel Nasser, Saudi relations with Egypt were often strained. Egyptian propaganda made frequent attacks on the Saudi system of royal government. When Egyptian troops were sent to North Yemen in 1962, tension between Saudi Arabia and Egypt became more acute. The Saudis helped the Yemeni royalists against the Egyptian-backed Yemen republic. King Fayṣal ultimately agreed to assist Egypt with financial aid provided Nasser withdrew his troops from Yemen.

Disputes with Egypt

Fayṣal, leader of the largest conservative Arab state, continued to warn against the danger of communist influence in Arab and Muslim countries. Saudi Arabia also acted against the United States, however, as a result of U.S. assistance to Israel during the Arab-Israeli War of 1973. The

Saudis and other Arab oil producers organized a short-lived oil boycott, and the price of oil quadrupled.

The Saudi government gained direct ownership of one-quarter of Aramco's crude oil operations in 1973. Ultimately, the Saudis achieved complete control of the company and, therefore, over their chief economic resource. By 1984 the president of Aramco was a Saudi citizen.

(H.St.J.B.P./J.B.Gl./W.L.O.)

Assassination of Fayṣal

Reigns of Khālid and Fahd. On March 25, 1975, King Fayṣal was assassinated; he was succeeded by his half-brother, Crown Prince Khālid, and Prince Fahd was made crown prince. During the new king's reign, economic and social development continued at an extremely rapid rate, revolutionizing the infrastructure and educational system of the country.

After the signing of the Egyptian-Israeli peace agreement on March 26, 1979, Saudi Arabia joined most of the other Arab nations in severing diplomatic relations with Egypt. The establishment of the Islāmic Republic of Iran in 1979 and the subsequent Iran-Iraq War of 1980–88 also caused the Saudi monarchy serious concern.

The only dramatic domestic challenge to the monarchy since World War II took place when the Al-Ḥaram mosque (Great Mosque) in Mecca, the holiest site in the world for Muslims, was seized by followers of a Saudi religious extremist. The rebels occupied the mosque for two weeks before they were defeated. Domestic unrest continued with rioting by Shīʿite Muslims in eastern Saudi Arabia in 1979 and 1980.

On June 13, 1982, King Khālid died and Crown Prince Fahd, who had long been influential in the administration of affairs, succeeded to the throne. Fahd maintained Saudi Arabia's foreign policy of close cooperation with the United States and increased purchases of sophisticated military equipment from the United States and Britain. In the 1970s and '80s the Saudi government played a major role in determining OPEC policy on oil production and pricing. Oil revenues were crucial to Saudi society as its economy was changed by the extraordinary wealth channeled through the government and derived from oil operations, notwithstanding a downturn in oil prices and production in the mid-1980s. Urbanization, mass public education, the presence of numerous foreign workers, and access to new media all affected Saudi values and mores. While society changed profoundly, however, political processes did not. The political elite came to include more bureaucrats and technocrats, but real power continued in the hands of the dynasty.

Saudi political leadership was challenged when Iraq, after rejecting attempted Saudi mediation, invaded neighbouring Kuwait on Aug. 2, 1990. The Kuwaiti government fled to Saudi Arabia, and King Fahd denounced the Iraqi invaders. Fearing that President Saddam Hussein of Iraq might invade Saudi Arabia next (despite Saudi assistance to Iraq during the Iran-Iraq War), the Saudis hurriedly invited the United States and other countries to send troops to protect the kingdom. By mid-November the United States had sent 230,000 troops, which were the most important part of the coalition armed forces that ultimately included soldiers from many other countries. The Saudis adroitly coordinated Arab and Muslim contingents and also established diplomatic ties with China, the Soviet Union and, later, Iran. King Fahd expanded his goal beyond the protection of Saudi Arabia to include the liberation of Kuwait and, if possible, the overthrow of Saddam Hussein.

The economic impact of the crisis was considerable, as Saudi Arabia housed and assisted not only foreign troops but also Kuwaiti civilians, while at the same time expelling Yemenis and Jordanians, whose countries supported Iraq diplomatically. Saudi Arabia purchased new weapons from abroad, increased the size of its own armed forces, and gave financial subsidies to a number of foreign governments. Total costs in 1990–91 ran to as much as $64 billion. Higher Saudi oil production and substantially higher prices in the world oil market provided some compensation for the Saudi economy. King Fahd made relatively few changes in the political structure of the country but promised future reforms.

With approval from Saudi Arabia secured in advance, the coalition, with some 800,000 troops (more than 540,000 from the United States), attacked Iraq by air on Jan. 16–17, 1991. Saudis flew more than 7,000 sorties and were prominent in the battles around the Saudi town of Ra's Al-Khafji. In the four-day ground war that began on February 24, Saudi troops, including the National Guard, helped defeat the Iraqis and drive them out of Kuwait. Despite the clear military victory, the full implications of the war for Saudi Arabia were unknown, and the diplomatic, military, economic, social, and political effects of such an unprecedented event would only gradually become apparent.

One of the first results of the altered situation in Saudi Arabia was King Fahd's March 1, 1992, issuance of decrees that were collectively entitled "A Basic System of Government," creating a quasi-constitution. The new laws changed the process used to select the heir to the throne, established a right to privacy, prohibited infringements of human rights without cause, and set a framework for a national consultative council to be appointed by the king. While the new council was to have the power to initiate and review laws and to approve or reject treaties and budgets, the monarch retained ultimate power, including the authority to dismiss the council at his will. These modest changes in government, combined with continuing economic growth, helped the regime maintain its base of popular support in spite of the challenges posed by the uncertain political environment in the Middle East resulting from the collapse of the Soviet Union and the continuing threat from Iraq.

For later developments in the history of Saudi Arabia, see the *Britannica Book of the Year* section in the BRITANNICA WORLD DATA ANNUAL. (W.L.O.)

United Arab Emirates

Seven tiny emirates along the eastern Persian (Arabian) Gulf coast of the Arabian Peninsula together form the United Arab Emirates (Arabic: Ittiḥād Al-Imārāt Al-ʿArabīyah). Formerly known as the Trucial States, Trucial Oman, or the Trucial Sheikhdoms, they are bordered by Qatar on the northwest, by Saudi Arabia on the west, south, and southeast, and by Oman on the southeast and northeast. Most of the union's area of 30,000 square miles (77,700 square kilometres) is occupied by Abu Dhabi, which stretches along the Persian Gulf coast. The six other emirates are clustered on the Musandam Peninsula, which separates the Persian Gulf from the Gulf of Oman; they are Dubayy, ʿAjmān, Ash-Shāriqah, Umm Al-Qaywayn, and Ra's Al-Khaymah on the Persian Gulf side, and Al-Fujayrah on the Gulf of Oman side. The population is concentrated in cities along both coasts, although the interior oasis settlement of Al-ʿAyn has grown into a major population centre as well. ʿAjmān, Ash-Shāriqah, and Dubayy have enclaves in Al-Fujayrah. Upon formation of the union, in 1971, the city of Abu Dhabi was chosen as the national capital for a period of five years (later extended).

PHYSICAL AND HUMAN GEOGRAPHY

The land. Nearly the entire union is desert, containing broad patches of sand and numerous salt flats. Along the eastern portion of the Musandam Peninsula, the northern extension of the Al-Ḥajar Mountains offers the only other major relief feature. Steep on all sides, the mountains rise to 5,000 feet in some places. The Persian Gulf coast is broken by shoals and dotted with islands that offer shelter to small vessels. There are, however, no natural deepwater harbours. The coast of the Gulf of Oman is more regular and has three natural harbours—Dībā Al-Ḥiṣn, Khawr Fakkān, and Kalbā.

Desert climate

The climate is hot and humid along the coast and is hotter still, but dry, in the interior. Rainfall averages only 3 to 4 inches (75 to 100 millimetres) annually. The average January temperature is 65° F (18° C), while in July the temperature averages 92° F (33° C). Summer temperatures can reach 115° F (46° C) on the coast and 120° F (49° C) or more in the desert. In midwinter and early summer, winds known as the *shamāl* blow from the north and northwest, bearing dust and sand.

Because of the desert climate, vegetation is scanty and largely limited to the low shrubs that offer forage to nomadic herds. In the oases date palms are raised together with alfalfa. Food grains include wheat, barley, and millet. Fruits are grown, and Al-ʿAyn oasis in Abu Dhabi is known for its mangoes. Animal life is largely restricted to domesticated goats, sheep, and camels, together with cattle and poultry, which were introduced in modern times. The gulf waters offer schools of mackerel, grouper, tuna, and porgies, as well as sharks and occasional whales.

The people. Only one-fifth of the union's residents are native and enjoy the rights of citizenship. The remainder are the mostly male foreign workers and their dependents, with South Asians, mainly Indians and Pakistanis, accounting for as much as half of the total population by some accounts. Arabs from countries other than the United Arab Emirates account for more than 10 percent, as do Iranians. Southeast Asians, including many Filipinos, have immigrated in increasing numbers to work in various capacities. The official language is Arabic.

Most of the population resides in the coastal cities. Al-ʿAyn, part of a grouping of oases on the Omani border (known in Oman as Al-Buraymī), is a rapidly growing city in the interior.

The economy. The union's economy is dominated by the oil produced in the Abu Dhabi and Dubayy emirates. The richest of the emirates, Abu Dhabi, contributes more than three-fifths of the national budget.

Oil reserves

Oil was first discovered in Abu Dhabi in 1958. The government of Abu Dhabi owns a controlling interest in all oil company operations in the emirate. The largest concessions are held by Abu Dhabi Marine Operating Company (Adma-Opco), which is partially owned by British, French, and Japanese interests. One of the main offshore fields is located in Umm ash-Shāʾif, 80 miles into the Persian Gulf and 20 miles from the island of Dās. Al-Bunduq offshore field is shared with neighbouring Qatar but is operated by Adma-Opco. A Japanese consortium operates an offshore rig at Al-Mubarraz, 70 miles west of Abu Dhabi city, and other offshore concessions are held by U.S. companies.

Onshore oil concessions are held by the Abu Dhabi Company for Onshore Oil Operations (ADCO), which is partially owned by U.S., French, and British interests. Other concessions are held by Japanese companies.

The production of oil in Dubayy began in 1969. There are offshore oil fields at Ḥaql Fatḥ, Fallah, and Rāshid, all located between 30 and 80 miles northwest of Dubayy. Dubayy owns a controlling interest in all oil companies in the emirate. Ash-Shāriqah began producing oil in 1974, and in 1980 another field, predominantly yielding natural gas, was discovered. In 1984 oil production began off the shore of Raʾs Al-Khaymah, in the Persian Gulf.

Agricultural production, largely centred in Raʾs Al-Khaymah emirate, Al-Fujayrah emirate, the enclaves of ʿAjmān, and Al-ʿAyn, has undergone a considerable expansion through the increasing use of wells and pumps to provide water for irrigation. Dates are a major crop, and the United Arab Emirates is close to self-sufficiency in much fruit and vegetable production. The country must import most of its grains, however. It has also greatly increased its production of eggs, poultry, and dairy products. The Arid Lands Research Centre, moved from As-Saʿdīyāt Island to Al-ʿAyn, experiments with raising crops in a desert environment. Most fishing is at Umm Al-Qaywayn.

The emirates have attempted to diversify their economy so as not to be completely dependent on oil. Abu Dhabi has begun to harness energy from natural gas for local use as well as for export. A petroleum industrial complex has opened in Ar-Ruways, 140 miles southwest of Abu Dhabi city, with a petroleum refinery, a gas fractionation plant, and an ammonia and urea plant. Dubayy's revenues have been invested in projects such as a dry dock and a trade centre; its airport has been expanded, and additional hotels have been built. The free trade zone of Mīnāʾ Jabal ʿAlī, 20 miles southwest of Dubayy city, was developed during the 1970s and early '80s. Ash-Shāriqah has built a cement plant, a plastic-pipe factory, and paint factories.

Finance. The United Arab Emirates Central Bank was established in 1980, with Dubayy and Abu Dhabi depositing one-half of their revenues in the institution. There are also commercial and foreign and domestic banks.

Trade patterns

Trade. Trade has long been important to Dubayy and Ash-Shāriqah. Even before the discovery of oil, Dubayy's prosperity was assured by its role as the gulf's leading entrepôt. It was known especially as a route for smuggling gold into India. Dubayy's Port Rāshid, adjacent to the city, is a large, modern port with a vast shipyard. Ash-Shāriqah city's more modest port is located a few miles north of the city on the Persian Gulf coast. Ash-Shāriqah's port of Khawr Fakkān, in an enclave on the Gulf of Oman coast, specializes in container shipping.

Exports are dominated by oil, primarily to Japan, the United States, and western Europe. Imports include machinery and transport equipment, basic manufactures, foodstuffs and live animals, mineral fuels, chemicals, and crude minerals. Major trading partners include Japan, western European countries, the United States, Bahrain, Australia, and Singapore.

Transportation. An excellent road system, developed in the late 1960s and '70s, carries vehicular traffic throughout the emirates and links the union to its neighbours. The addition of a tunnel to the bridge connecting Dubayy city and Dayrah facilitates the movement of traffic across the small saltwater inlet that separates them. The cities of Abu Dhabi, Dubayy, Ash-Shāriqah, and Raʾs Al-Khaymah have international airports.

Administration and social conditions. *Government.* The highest governmental authority is the Supreme Council, which is composed of the rulers of the seven emirates. The president and vice president of the union are elected by the Supreme Council from among its members. The president appoints a prime minister and a cabinet. The Federal National Council, an advisory body, is made up of members appointed by the emirates for two-year terms.

Justice. A provisional constitution was ratified in 1971 and has been extended periodically by the Federal National Council. The provisional constitution blends Western and Islāmic legal principles and calls for a legal code based on Sharīʿah (Islāmic law). At the federal level the judicial branch consists of a supreme court and several courts of first instance: the former deals with emirate-federal or interemirate disputes and crimes against the state, and the latter cover administrative, commercial, and civil disputes between individuals and the federal government. Other legal matters are left to local judicial bodies.

The armed forces. The Abu Dhabi and Dubayy defense forces have been merged with those of the other emirates as the Federal Defense Force; in practice, however, Dubayy's forces have remained independent of those of the other emirates. The Supreme Council has made the right to levy armed forces a power of the national government.

Education. Education in the emirates is free. Both boys and girls attend public school, and women constitute more than half of the student body at the United Arab Emirates University, opened in 1977. The literacy rate has reached about 70 percent.

Health. Medical services are concentrated in Dubayy, which has several hospitals and child-welfare clinics, and in Abu Dhabi, which has a large maternity hospital and other health facilities. Hospital services are free; there is little private medical practice, and most people are treated in hospital outpatient clinics.

Cultural life. The cultural life of the United Arab Emirates remains largely traditional. It is rooted in Islām and identifies with the wider Arab world, but it maintains ties especially with the neighbouring conservative, patriarchal states. Tribal identities remain fairly strong, despite urbanization, and the family is still the strongest and most cohesive social unit. The United Arab Emirates has experienced the impact of Islāmic resurgence, though Islām in the emirates is generally less austere than in Saudi Arabia. Camel racing remains a popular sport, with prize racers often selling for hundreds of thousands of dollars.

In a number of ways change is apparent in the nation's cultural life. Changes in attitudes toward marriage and employment of women are discernible. Some women are

Young boys preparing for a camel race in Dubayy, U.A.E.
Alain le Garsmeur—Tony Stone Worldwide

now given more opportunity for choice in a marriage partner, and education and some types of professional work have become available to women. New forms of entertainment, ranging from soccer matches to videotape recorders, have begun to alter patterns of taste and behaviour.

The news media are concentrated in Abu Dhabi, Dubayy, and Ash-Shāriqah. Several daily newspapers are published, in both Arabic and English. Daily radio and television programs are broadcast from Abu Dhabi, Dubayy, and Ra's Al-Khaymah, in Arabic and English.

For statistical data on the land and people of the United Arab Emirates, see the *Britannica World Data* section in the BRITANNICA WORLD DATA ANNUAL.

HISTORY

In the late 18th and early 19th centuries the dominant tribal faction was the Qawāsim, whose ships controlled the maritime commerce of the lower Persian Gulf and much of the Indian Ocean. Attacks on British and Indian shipping led to a British naval action in 1819 that defeated the Qawāsim forces.

The effect of this was not only to lessen the power of the Qawāsim but to favour the Banū Yās tribal confederation of Abu Dhabi. The Banū Yās were centred on the Al-Liwā' oases of Abu Dhabi, and their strength was land-based and largely Bedouin. Under the leadership of the Āl Nuhayyan, members of the Āl Bū Falāḥ tribe, they were the dominant element in the Trucial States from the mid-19th century. The sheikhs signed in 1820 a general treaty of peace, in 1853 the perpetual maritime truce, and in 1892 exclusive agreements restricting their foreign relations to Britain. In January 1968, after the British government announced that its forces would be withdrawn from the Persian Gulf by the end of 1971, Trucial Oman and the sheikhdoms of Qatar and Bahrain initiated plans to confederate. After three years of negotiations, however, Qatar and Bahrain decided on independent sovereign status. The former Trucial States, excluding Ra's Al-Khaymah, announced the formation of the United Arab Emirates in December 1971. Ra's Al-Khaymah joined the federation in February 1972.

A movement toward centralization was initiated by Abu Dhabi in December 1973, when after a change in Cabinet membership several of its former Cabinet members took positions with the federal government. In May 1976 the seven emirates agreed to merge their armed forces, and the constitution was amended in November limiting to the federal government the right to form an army and purchase weapons. Conflicts in 1978 prompted Dubayy and Ra's Al-Khaymah to refuse to submit their forces to federal command, and Dubayy began purchasing weapons independently. A proposal to form a federal budget, merge revenues, and eliminate internal boundaries was rejected by Dubayy and Ra's Al-Khaymah, despite strong domestic support. Dubayy's opposition was curtailed, however, when its ruler, Sheikh Rāshid, was offered the premiership of the federal government; he took office in July 1979.

The federation

The Khomeini regime in Iran and the Iran-Iraq War created significant danger for the United Arab Emirates. The resurgence of Islāmic fundamentalism posed a double threat to the union's stability by generating unrest among the many Iranian Shī'ites living in the emirates and by providing inspiration to the growing numbers of young activist Sunnites who found the existing political order to be insufficiently committed to Islāmic values. The Iran-Iraq War was brought within a few miles of the United Arab Emirates' coast when Iran and Iraq began to attack tankers in the Persian Gulf.

The intensity of such threats moved the United Arab Emirates to join with Oman, Qatar, Saudi Arabia, Bahrain, and Kuwait to form the Gulf Cooperation Council (GCC). The council, which held its first summit meeting in 1981, was designed to strengthen the security of its members and to promote economic cooperation.

For later developments in the history of the United Arab Emirates, see the *Britannica Book of the Year* section in the BRITANNICA WORLD DATA ANNUAL.

(W.H.I./V.E.I./J.D.An.)

Yemen

The Republic of Yemen (Arabic: al-Jumhūrīyah al-Yamanīyah) is situated at the southwestern corner of the Arabian Peninsula. The present Yemen came into being in May 1990, when the former Yemen Arab Republic, or North Yemen, merged with the former People's Democratic Republic of Yemen, also called South Yemen.

Present-day boundaries

Most of Yemen's northern frontier with Saudi Arabia traverses the great desert of the peninsula, the Rub' al-Khali (Empty Quarter) and remains undemarcated, as does the eastern frontier with Oman. In the west and the south, Yemen is bounded by the Red Sea and the Gulf of Aden, respectively. Its territory includes a number of islands as well, including the Kamaran group, located in the Red Sea near al-Ḥudaydah, and the most important and largest island, Socotra (Suqutrā), located in the Arabian Sea nearly 620 miles (1,000 kilometres) east of Aden.

Yemen's uncharted desert marches make its precise area impossible to determine. Most observers suggest a figure of about 156,000 square miles (405,000 square kilometres); the area of Socotra is 1,400 square miles.

By stipulation of the (re-) unification agreement of 1990, Ṣan'ā', formerly the capital of North Yemen, functions as the political capital of the new nation, while Aden, formerly the capital of South Yemen, functions as the economic centre.

The history, culture, economy, and population of Yemen have all been influenced by the country's strategic location at the southern entrance of the Red Sea—a crossroads of both ancient and modern trade and communications routes. In the ancient world, the states that occupied the area known today as Yemen controlled the supply of such important commodities as frankincense and myrrh and dominated the trade in many other valuable items, such as the spices and medicines of Asia. Because of its fertility as well as its commercial prosperity, Yemen was known in the ancient world as Arabia Felix (Latin: "Fortunate Arabia") to distinguish it from the vast forbidding reaches of Arabia Deserta ("Desert Arabia").

The two components of the Yemen Republic underwent strikingly different historical evolutions: North Yemen never experienced any period of colonial administration at the hands of a European power, while South Yemen was a part of the British Empire from 1839 to 1967. The contemporary borders are the consequence of British, Ottoman Empire, and Saudi Arabian foreign policy goals and actions, some of which date to the 18th and 19th centuries. These have had a substantial impact on many aspects of 20th-century Yemen.

PHYSICAL AND HUMAN GEOGRAPHY

The land. Yemen may be divided into five major regions: a coastal plain (known as the Tihāmah in northern Yemen), the western highlands, the central mountains (the Yemen Highlands), the eastern highlands, and finally, the eastern and northeastern desert regions.

The coastal plain ranges in width from 5 miles (8 kilometres) to as much as 40 miles (64 kilometres). Low mountains rising from 1,000 to 3,500 feet (300 to 1,070 metres) lie between the low hills of the plain and the great central massif, which has many peaks in excess of 10,000 feet; the highest is Mount An-Nabī Shuʿayb (more than 12,000 feet). Toward the east-northeast the mountains subside rather rapidly into the eastern highlands (2,500–3,500 feet), which drop off to the sandy hills of the Rubʿ al-Khali.

Major watercourses

The regular rainfall that occurs in some areas drains, in the northern section, westward toward the Red Sea through five major watercourses (wadis) and, in the southern sector, southward into the Gulf of Aden through three major watercourses. The largest of the latter is the Wadi Ḥaḍramawt (Hadhramaut Valley), which has been renowned since antiquity for its frankincense trees and which has been the locus of a number of sophisticated city-states. Together with their tributaries and lesser neighbours, these intermittently flowing channels slice the highlands and central massif into a large number of plateaus and ridges. In many places, there is evidence of volcanic activity from as recently as a few hundred years ago; the existence of hot springs and fumaroles attest to continued subterranean activity. Moreover, the country sits astride one of the most active fault lines in the Red Sea (Great Rift Basin) region and has experienced several severe earthquakes in modern times. The most recent one shook the Dhamar area in December 1982, killing roughly 3,000 people and largely destroying several villages and hundreds of smaller settlements.

The monsoon rainfall that causes the western slopes of the massif to be so well-dissected makes the area also the most densely populated. Fertile soils are another regional asset. In varying concentrations, Yemenis inhabit nearly all the country's geographic zones—from sea level to 10,000 feet and higher. In fact, the intricate variety of subregions and microclimates produces an agricultural base of astonishing diversity. In the coastal plain, citrus fruits, tobacco, corn (maize), sesame, cotton, and similar heat-tolerant crops predominate; the middle highlands support various grains (wheat, millet, sorghum) and a variety of fruits and vegetables, while the famous Yemeni coffee trees (*Coffea arabica*) and other specialty crops thrive in the cool upper highlands. In some areas, elaborate agricultural terraces cover the mountains from base to peak. The high productivity of this system is largely attributable to the soil that has been collected and composted over a period of centuries. In the modern period, neglect and civil conflict have taken their toll on the earthworks, which are also vulnerable to flooding.

Climate. Most of Yemen lies in the border zone between two main weather patterns: the regular northerly winds (from the Mediterranean basin) and the southwest monsoon winds. These create a fairly well-defined seasonal rhythm; the northerly winds predominate during the winter, while in the summer, the southwest monsoon brings the primary rains. Cut off from this pattern by the central mountains, the southern fringe areas on the Gulf of Aden experience a markedly tropical climate. In Al-Ḥudaydah and Aden, temperatures often exceed 100° F (38° C) with high humidity, whereas in Ṣanʿāʾ (at around 8,000 feet on the western face) the daytime temperature averages just under 70° F (21° C), and humidity is low. The higher northern elevations of the central massif experience frequent frosts and occasional snowfalls during the winter months.

In the northern Tihāmah, as well as in the coastal belt on the Gulf of Aden, the average annual rainfall is less than about 5 inches (133 millimetres); many years record no measurable precipitation. Rainfall increases with distance from the sea: the lower highlands receive about 15 to 20 inches (38 to 51 centimetres) per year; the southern uplands around Taʿizz average more than 30 inches annually. Different annual cycles characterize the northern and southern sections: whereas the north usually has two main rainy seasons (March–May and July–September), the south often receives no rainfall except sparse amounts in the summer months. Lengthy droughts are not unknown; there have been periods as long as five years when the precipitation was one-tenth the normal amount; the most recent serious drought occurred during the civil war of 1962–70 and had an important impact on the outcome of that conflict. Average rainfall

Plant and animal life. The distribution of vegetation roughly corresponds to the zones of elevation and precipitation. It is possible to distinguish three general regions:

Lynn Abercrombie

The mud-brick multistory houses of Shibam, Yemen.

(1) the coastal plain, in which dry-climate plants predominate (the date palm, citrus fruits, banana, and cotton, as well as euphorbia, acacia, tamarisk, and other drought-resistant species; the dry wadis of the eastern desert support similar flora), (2) the middle highlands, with a variety of food crops (melons, nuts, grapes, grains) as well as euphorbia, eucalyptus, sycamore, fig, and carob, and (3) the mountainous interior, with its temperate-zone crops, including coffee, *qāt* (see below *The economy: Agriculture*), and a variety of woody shrubs and trees. Yemen retained considerable forest cover into the early years of the 20th century, but less than approximately 6 percent of the country is forested today; the pressures generated by rapid population growth—notably the increased demand for stovewood and agricultural land—have largely depleted the forest legacy.

These same pressures have had a devastating effect on Yemen's wildlife. Evidence suggests the presence of such species as the panther, ostrich, various antelopes (including the Arabian oryx), the rhinoceros, and large cats (*e.g.*, lions) as recently as a century ago. The largest wild mammal still to be found in Yemen is the gelada baboon; among the smaller mammals are the hyena, fox, and rabbit. In two categories of wildlife—birds and insects—Yemen has a relatively abundant and varied population; many species remain uncatalogued. Probably the greatest diversity of fauna, however, inhabits the waters of the Red Sea and the Gulf of Aden. Among the many different species are tuna, shark, sardines, lobster, and squid.

Major groups

The people. The people of Yemen are overwhelmingly Arabic-speaking Muslims of Mediterranean stock. Yemenis of "northern" origin are thought to have descended from Mesopotamians who entered the region in the 1st millennium BC. The "southern" group represents the South Arabian stock, and the Arabic of the rural areas of former South Yemen is still heavily influenced by the ancient South Arabian languages. The two groups maintain disparate genealogies and historical traditions concerning their roles and origins: The northern Yemenis trace their ancestry to Ismāʿīl (Ishmael) through his descendant ʿAdnān, whereas their southern countrymen claim descent from Qaḥṭān (the biblical Joktan).

Ethnic minorities include the Mahra, a people of possibly Australian origin who occupy the eastern border areas of former South Yemen (as well as the island of Socotra) and who speak a variant of the ancient Himyaritic language. In the (northern) Tihāmah, in-migrations from Ethiopia and Somalia have occurred since World War II. There is a clear African admixture in a distinct social group known as the Akhdām, who perform menial tasks; some anthropologists consider this group the closest thing to a caste in Yemen. In the far north, there are still small remnants of Jewish communities, while in the area of Aden and the eastern regions of the former South Yemen there are distinct Indonesian as well as Indian elements in the population (attributable to economic and political ties extending back over two millennia).

Societally, the broadest distinctions among population groups are based not on ethnicity but on religious affiliation. The Sunnite (or Sunnī) sect of Islām, represented by the Shāfiʿī (Shāfiʿite) school, predominates. The Shīʿite minority comprises the Zaydī school, which has long been dominant in the mountainous highlands of the north, and the Ismāʿīlīs, now a relatively small group found in the Haraz region of North Yemen and in the mountainous area west of Ṣanʿāʾ (Jabal Manakhah).

Tribal affiliation is another deep-seated component of social identity. Some confederations of tribes have histories spanning more than two millennia. Such complexes served as the basis for political and social organization in former South Yemen until the postindependence government set out to eradicate what it considered to be reactionary cultural institutions. Although these efforts toward detribalization were at least in part effective, the events of the 1980s in both North and South Yemen indicated that such identifications were still socially and economically as well as politically relevant.

In many respects, the most important contemporary demographic trend has been the emigration of large numbers of males between the ages of 15 and 45 for employment in other countries. Although the number of such emigrants has varied since the late 1970s, when it reached its peak, there are still perhaps more than one million Yemeni nationals employed abroad—in countries of the Persian Gulf region, in Great Britain (in the industrial Midlands and Wales), and in the United States (in industrial areas of the Northeast and Midwest, and in the agricultural areas of California). The remittances of these emigrants have played an important role in the balance of payments, in radically increasing the purchasing power of most Yemenis, and in funding many local development projects. The drop in the price of oil in the early 1980s resulted in the return of many Yemenis to their homeland and a concomitant drop in remittance income for the country. Another reversal of the emigration pattern occurred during and after the Persian Gulf War of early 1991, when the Saudi Arabian government expelled hundreds of thousands of Yemenis in retribution for the votes that Yemen initially cast in the United Nations in support of Iraqi policy.

Population characteristics

In terms of the generally accepted statistical indicators, the population of Yemen continues to display characteristics typical of developing areas: high birth rate, high infant mortality rate, and generally poor standards of hygiene, sanitation, and public health service. Major programs funded by foreign governments and the United Nations attempt to address both structural and programmatic deficiencies, especially in the north, where the economy remained essentially preindustrial until after the 1962 revolution.

The economy. Despite the advances of the past two decades—most notably the commercial exploitation of oil and natural gas—Yemen is one of the world's least developed countries. The majority of Yemenis are subsistence agriculturalists. It is estimated that about 12 to 15 percent of the area of former North Yemen is arable, while the comparable figure for the former South Yemen is less than 1 percent. During the first half of the century, the northern imams established virtual self-sufficiency in food production for their region. A far different condition prevails in Yemen today. One important causative factor is the high cost of domestic labour, brought about by the exodus of much of the adult male labour force. The remittances of these emigrants fueled inflation, driving the prices of domestic food products above those of imported equivalents, such as U.S. grains and Australian meats.

Resources. Oil and natural gas, discovered near Shabwah in the former South Yemen in 1983 and near Maʾrib in the north the following year, now generate a major portion of the national income. Exploration and development by American, Korean, Japanese, and other foreign companies continues. A pipeline carries northern Yemen's oil to the Red Sea coast, and a similar line serving the southern region by way of Little Aden was under construction in the early 1990s.

Salt is extracted from underground mines near Ṣalīf in the Tihāmah and from surface deposits near Aden in the south; the market for salt, however, has been tenuous. There has never been a full scientific survey of Yemen to determine precisely what other mineral resources might be commercially exploitable. In the past, coal and iron deposits supported a small-scale steel industry (primarily for the manufacture of swords and daggers). There are deposits of copper, as well as some evidence of sulfur, lead, zinc, nickel, silver, gold, and perhaps other minerals.

Agriculture. Yemen's difficult terrain, limited soil, inconsistent water supply, and large number of microclimates have fostered some of the most highly sophisticated methods of water conservation and seed adaptation found anywhere in the world, making possible the cultivation of surprisingly diverse crops. The typical Yemeni farmer raises at least some livestock, typically the regional varieties of goats, sheep, or cattle; agricultural development programs sponsored by Western countries have introduced new varieties of dairy and beef cattle in the more temperate regions of the north.

The most common crops are cereals, such as millet, corn (maize), wheat, barley, and sorghum; myriad vegetables from a burgeoning truck farm industry have appeared on the market in recent years. There has also been extensive cultivation of fruits—both tropical (mangoes, plantains, bananas, melons, papayas, and citrus) and temperate (pears, peaches, apples, and grapes).

Principal cash crops

The two main cash crops are coffee and *qāt*. Coffee has for centuries been the most important and renowned export of Yemen. The finest varieties continue to take their name from Mocha, the city from which most of Yemen's coffee was exported between the 16th and 18th centuries (*i.e.,* before cultivation was introduced in South America, Africa, and Southeast Asia). The coffee tree grows best in the middle highlands (at elevations of 4,500 to 6,500 feet), where *qāt* also flourishes. The latter is an evergreen shrub whose young leaves (containing an alkaloid) are chewed as a mild stimulant. The production and consumption of *qāt* occupy a prominent position in Yemeni culture. The increased affluence of the past two decades has allowed an increasing percentage of the population to indulge in the habit, which the government has undertaken through various measures to discourage. Greater demand has fueled a substantial increase in *qāt* acreage. Older coffee plantations are often converted to *qāt* as their productivity declines. Much of the land being devoted to *qāt,* however, was formerly considered marginal for commercial agricultural purposes and now benefits from regular soil-enhancement programs. A portion of the *qāt* crop is exported to Ethiopia and Kenya.

In the past two decades, the cultivation of cotton—in both the Tihāmah in the north and the coastal plain east of Aden—was strongly supported by the respective national governments, and for a while it contributed significantly to national income. In the past few years there has been a significant decline in world prices, and the high costs of initiation and development have meant that the Yemeni cotton industry has not been competitive.

Another recent economic development has been the growth of the fishing industry. The waters of the Red Sea and the Gulf of Aden are extraordinarily rich in a wide variety of commercially desirable fish and crustaceans. In the past, very small quantities of some species were marketed locally; the foreign technical and financial assistance provided to the fishing industry (notably by the former Soviet Union) contributed markedly to its increased role in the national economy.

Industry. The traditional handicraft industry of Yemen achieved great renown in the past for the quality of its products in a large number of areas: fine textiles, jewelry (especially silver and gold filigree), leatherwork, carpets, glass, utensils, swords and daggers, and decorative materials for a variety of domestic and commercial uses. Modern industrial enterprises did not contribute significantly to the national income until the 1980s, with the exception of the oil refinery in Little Aden, built originally by British Petroleum in the 1950s (and nationalized in 1977), and the cotton industry established in former North Yemen in the last years of Imam Aḥmad ibn Yaḥyā's reign (1948–62).

The multiyear development programs of the preunification governments of Yemen concentrated on the establishment of more diversified industries; although most of these were designed as import-substitution enterprises (producing such items as aluminum ware, cement, plastics, paints, textiles, furniture, and tobacco products), some have, in the interim, become major contributors to the national income. The oil and natural gas industry entails—in addition to the foreign primary firms—an array of local subcontractors and allied services.

Integration of economic systems

Finance. One of the more important issues raised by the merger of the two Yemens was the integration of the south's communist (command) economy into the pronouncedly capitalist (market) economy of the north. During the last two decades of the People's Democratic Republic, the government had nationalized practically all land and housing, along with most industrial and business enterprises in the country; South Yemen had, in fact, one of the most centrally directed of all the command economies in the world. North Yemen occupied a position near the opposite pole: nearly all the remittances of the emigrant population were sent back to family members through "agents" who arranged such transfers. Consequently, the remittances escaped the domestic banking industry as well as efforts by the government to levy any taxes on them. In fact, for many years the government was so lacking in resources that it had to rely upon other countries (notably Saudi Arabia) to meet its budget. The major financial institutions are relatively new; for example, the Yemen Bank for Reconstruction and Development was founded in 1962, just after the revolution, and the Central Bank of Yemen, which is responsible for issuing currency and managing the government's foreign exchange and other financial operations, was not established until 1971.

Trade. Trade was for centuries the major source of wealth for the states that occupied the southwestern corner of the Arabian Peninsula. In the ancient world, the merchants of the various empires transshipped to the Mediterranean world the spices, condiments, luxury commodities, and other goods of southern Asia and eastern Africa (along with those commodities over which the Yemenis exercised a substantial degree of monopoly control—*e.g.,* frankincense, myrrh, and indigo). This trade produced huge profits, enabling the ancient empires to construct the many cities, temples, and monuments whose remnants are visible throughout Yemen today. In the ancient world, it was the Romans who first formidably challenged the Yemeni trade monopoly. Much later, in the 16th century, the Portuguese set out to replace the Yemeni merchant fleets with their own. This effort succeeded in redirecting Europe's trade with Asia around the continent of Africa, which turned the Red Sea region, and especially Yemen, into an economic backwater.

In more recent times, the construction of the Suez Canal (in 1869) revitalized the Red Sea route between Asia and Europe, proving the British decision to take Aden (in 1839) to have been a prescient one. Aden's deep-water berths, as well as its sophisticated and extensive port facilities (which the British constructed over the years), not to mention the extensive military installation located nearby (in Khor Maksar), made it one of the world's preeminent ports. Until 1961, about three-quarters of (North) Yemen's international trade passed through Aden. Following the revolution of 1962, however, the new government, in a move calculated to demonstrate its displeasure with the British authorities there, redirected trade through the port of Al-Ḥudaydah, which was expanded and modernized with major financial assistance from the Soviet Union. This trade was, however, modest until the economic boom of the 1970s; even then, the value of Yemeni exports (primarily coffee, cotton goods, and hides and skins) amounted to only about 1 percent of that of imports, which comprised foodstuffs of all types, manufactured goods (consumer as well as industrial), machinery, transportation equipment, chemicals, and petroleum products—the basic goods demanded by a population formerly isolated from the modern consumer economy.

Exports and imports

The long, undemarcated frontier with Saudi Arabia, as well as the fluid political situation along those portions of the frontier that are demarcated (*e.g.,* near Najrān), has made smuggling—and thus the loss of much-needed import duties—a chronic problem. Yemen conducts all but an infinitesimal portion of its export trade with its regional neighbours.

Transportation. Until the 1960s, there was no modern transportation infrastructure anywhere in Yemen except in the city of Aden. In the last years of the imamate, the first all-weather roads were built in the north, primarily by the People's Republic of China, the United States, and the Soviet Union as part of foreign-aid packages. These first roads—*i.e.,* the one from Al-Ḥudaydah to Ṣanʿāʾ and the one from Mocha (Al-Mukhā) to Ṣanʿāʾ via Taʿizz—represented major feats of engineering. They cut the transportation time between the cities involved from days to hours and set off an explosion of intrastate traffic and trade. Since then, many of the formerly rudimentary roads in the north and south have been paved, and demands for similar improvements have been raised by numerous isolated villages seeking both a convenient outlet for locally produced goods and easier access to consumer products. Although all the major towns and cities are now served by all-weather roads, there are thousands of miles of tracks that are barely passable by all-terrain vehicles. In both the north and the south, the former capital cities of Aden and Ṣanʿāʾ remain the transportation hubs, and communication among lesser towns and cities is not possible except through these centres.

The last few years have seen the development of an extensive and rather sophisticated public transportation system of buses and taxis with regular schedules. The distribution of goods is almost solely handled by modern trucks, some of immense size; these trucks are often overloaded, and the accident rate on Yemeni roads is disproportionately high.

The ports of Aden and Al-Ḥudaydah handle Yemen's sea traffic. The importance of Al-Ḥudaydah dates from the postrevolutionary period in the north; although the port is well-equipped, it is often congested. Aden's extensive facilities were underutilized during the communist period. It is anticipated that most international trade will in the future be directed through Aden, which has good road connections to Taʿizz and beyond. The older ports, most notably Mocha, have silted in and are now used only by small craft, smugglers, and coastal traffic. There is, however, a Yemen Navigation Company, which operates cargo and passenger service to other ports in the Red Sea region, including those on the east coast of Africa.

Prior to unification, North and South Yemen each had its own international airline; these have now been amalgamated. Yemen Airways operates regular service to a large number of cities in the Red Sea region and other Arab states, as well as to a number of European transportation hubs.

Administration and social conditions. *Government.* The former states of North Yemen and South Yemen, which merged in 1990, had sharply contrasting political systems. North Yemen was a republic, governed under a provisional constitution dating from the early 1970s. Although a succession of bodies (the Consultative Assembly, the Consultative Council, the People's Constituent Assembly, and the General People's Congress) carried out some of the functions of a legislature, they exercised little real power until the 1980s. Until that time, policy making remained in the hands of a technocratic elite that worked closely with a relatively progressive military elite. South Yemen, on the other hand, had an avowedly Marxist government, and the political system and economy reflected many of the goals and principles of Marxism. The Yemen Socialist Party (YSP), the only legal political organization, determined government policy.

Unified political system

The unified political system created in 1990 represented a pronounced departure from either of the previous ones. The most important change was the decision to establish—in the course of a 30-month transition period—a multiparty representative democracy. By the midpoint of the transition, the official political organizations of the respective predecessor states—the General People's Congress and the Yemeni Socialist Party—had become just two of more than 30 political parties representing virtually every shade of the political spectrum. Elections to the new parliament were scheduled to take place in the winter of 1992–93.

One issue designated to be addressed during the transition phase was that of territorial and administrative subdivisions. In the north, the provinces had corresponded to more or less obvious topographical regions. Each province was subdivided into *qaḍāʾ* (district) and *nāḥiyah* (tract) levels, largely representing distinctions within the population (*e.g.,* tribal affiliations).

In the south, under the British, there had been a major distinction regarding administrative autonomy and political influence between the city of Aden (governed directly from London via the colonial office) and the hinterland (divided into more than 20 "statelets," many of which were clearly associated with ancient tribal groupings of one form or another). In order to break down the old tribal affiliations, and the associated economic and political factionalism, the postindependence government abolished these traditional units and reorganized the country into numbered "governorates." Later this numbering system was also abolished, and the governorates were given names in order to encourage some degree of regional identity. The brief civil war of January 1986, however, indicated that these administrative changes had not succeeded in completely eliminating the older loyalties, affiliations, and ethnic associations.

In their own ways, however, both north and south had moved to greater public participation in policy making by the 1980s. In the north, the various institutions that the government introduced during this period allowed an ever-increasing percentage of the population to participate in elections for both local office and the national "legislature." In the south, the determinedly modernizing YSP had undertaken various measures to mobilize the population, including extensive programs of education and support designed to improve the economic, political, and social status of women. The more radical of these programs were among the objects of negotiation during the 1990–92 transition.

The justice system. The two parts of the new state had markedly contrasting legal traditions. In the north, two separate legal systems operated: (1) a religious one, applying the principles and precedents of the Sharīʿah (the Islāmic legal code; since the content of the Sharīʿah varies according to sect, in effect there were two religious codes, the Zaydī and the Shāfiʿī), and (2) a tribal one (*ʿurf*), comprising the complex principles, including precedent, used by the tribes in regulating their civil and criminal disputes.

In the south, although the Shāfiʿī version of the Sharīʿah obtained in matters of personal status, there was a long history of applying essentially British commercial law, as well as the common law in many civil and criminal disputes. The Marxist government overlaid these principles with some significant modifications concerning economic and social affairs. The rural areas, on the other hand, continued to employ both the Sharīʿah and the *ʿurf* in local disputes. The accommodation of these separate legal traditions was another of the many challenges posed by the reunification process.

Armed forces. The respective military sectors of the former states brought to the combined system extensive inventories supplied by the former Eastern bloc. The structure of the united military, as well as its perception of its constitutional role, were major issues of the transition period. In the north, the military played the dominant role in the political system following the overthrow of the civilian government by Colonel Ibrāhīm al-Ḥamdī in 1974. In the south, as was usual in Marxist-communist states, the military was subordinate to the ruling political party, the YSP.

Role of the military

Education. In the north, education in the recent past was largely provided by traditional Qurʾānic schools—*i.e.,* small facilities associated with the local mosque. A modern school system, providing free primary, intermediate, and secondary programs, was instituted immediately after the 1962 revolution. For a variety of social and cultural reasons, certain subgroups of the school-age population—most notably girls—remain underrepresented in the system. The lack of adequately qualified Yemeni teachers has been a major problem; Egyptian expatriates have largely filled this void.

In the south, a complete system of secular education was introduced in Aden after World War II; in the protectorate states, however, the limited educational opportunities were comparable to those available in the imamic regime of the north. Like most Marxist states, the south placed great emphas is on education and was determinedly egalitarian in providing access to all levels of the three-stage system.

The overall literacy rate remains relatively low—around two-thirds in the urban centres and near 20 percent in rural areas—though it is steadily rising. There is also a large disparity between the rates for males and females.

Both North and South Yemen established universities in the 1970s; the University of Ṣanʿāʾ was founded in 1970, largely with grants from Kuwait. It is coeducational and comprises a variety of specialized colleges—*e.g.,* those of agriculture, medicine, commerce, and law. The University of Aden, founded in 1975, offers a similar array of specialties. These two remain the only general institutions of higher learning in the country. As was the case in prerevolutionary North Yemen and preindependence South

Yemen, many families still elect to have their offspring educated abroad. Ironically, a significant portion of the student body and faculty at the domestic institutions is foreign. There are also now several small colleges as well as vocational and polytechnic institutes that provide training in such varied fields as aviation and telecommunications. These are located in the larger urban agglomerations. Both of the major Islāmic sects also operate theological institutes for the preparation of judges and other religious personnel (though this often requires additional study at such well-known institutions as al-Azhar University in Cairo).

Health and welfare. Despite the generally agreeable climate of the Yemeni highlands, where most of the population live, the standard of public health remains relatively low. Contributing factors include: (1) unsanitary water supplies, (2) numerous cultural patterns that compromise both personal and group hygiene, (3) the presence of numerous diseases at endemic rates (*e.g.,* malaria in the coastal belt and gastroenteritis in the highlands), and (4) insufficient personnel and financial resources to undertake any massive program of public health improvement, though there are various programs operated by foreign donors (*e.g.,* China and Saudi Arabia). Ṣanʿāʾ and Aden have numerous hospitals, many under foreign ownership and operation, though few meet Western standards of sanitation and medical practice.

Factors contributing to public health problems

Cultural life. Yemen is a part of the Islāmic world and as such reflects many of the contemporary trends in Islām. At the same time, the Yemenis are intensely proud of their pre-Islāmic heritage. The national museum in Ṣanʿāʾ and the archaeological museum in Aden house important treasures from this period. In their extensive networks of overland and maritime trade, the ancient Yemenis encountered myriad cultures and civilizations. There is ample evidence of Greek, Roman, Indian, Indonesian, and Chinese influence on various aspects of both traditional and contemporary Yemeni culture. Similarities have been drawn, for example, between marriage institutions in India and Yemen and between religious music in Yemen and Byzantine masses.

Dances, performed with or without musical accompaniment, are a feature of weddings and other social occasions; these are performed by men and women separately. The male dances are often performed with traditional weapons—*e.g.,* the *jambīyah* dagger. Some characteristics of Yemeni instruments and music remain unique.

No doubt the best-known characteristic of Yemeni culture is its architecture, which dates back more than 2,000 years. In the mountainous interior, buildings are constructed of stone blocks to a height of four to six stories, with highly decorated windows and other features designed to beautify them and emphasize their height. In the desert regions, the buildings are usually made of adobe, with the various layers emphasized and often tinted.

Architecture

Among the more traditional crafts (*e.g.,* silver and gold filigree work and jewelry, textiles, metalwork, and stonecutting) in which Yemen developed a reputation for fine craftsmanship, few artisans remain. The markets are, sadly, filled with foreign imports of less interest and lower quality but bearing much lower prices.

The most widespread and traditional cultural outlet is oral, in the form of proverbs, popular stories, and especially poetry that deal with timeless themes (such as love and death) as well as with Yemeni history, biography, Islāmic themes and traditions, and so forth. Today, with modern communications and publishing and distribution networks, Yemen forms an integral part of contemporary Arab trends in literature, essays, and historical and political writings.

Through its control of the media, education, and trade, the Marxist government of the south severely restricted the participation of its population in both regional and global cultural trends during its most ascetic period (the late 1970s and early 1980s). The northern government correspondingly exercised certain restrictions in order to protect itself from the influence of the south.

These conditions changed drastically with the merger in 1990. Since that time more than 85 newspapers and journals, representing political, social, economic, and cultural organizations, have come into being. The national television and radio network, although still operated by the government, has been substantially freed of governmental control over its programming.

HISTORY

The pre-Islāmic period. In the millennia prior to the arrival of Islām, Yemen was the home of a series of powerful and wealthy city-states and empires whose wealth was largely based upon their control over the production of frankincense and myrrh, two of the most highly prized commodities of the ancient world, and their exclusive access to such non-Yemeni luxury commodities as various spices and condiments from southern Asia and ostrich plumes and ivory from eastern Africa. The three most famous and largest of these empires were the Minaean, the Sabaean (the Biblical Sheba), and the Himyarite (called Homeritae by the Romans), all of which were known throughout the ancient Mediterranean world; their periods of ascendancy overlap somewhat, extending from roughly 1200 BC to AD 525.

The Romans began expanding their power and influence into the Red Sea in the 1st century AD and soon learned the secret of the Yemeni traders: how to exploit the monsoon winds to traffic between the Red Sea and southern Asia. It was then only a matter of time before Yemeni prestige began to dwindle, since they could not effectively compete against imperial Rome. The resulting economic decline made it impossible for the Yemeni states to maintain their extensive cities and attendant facilities; the most famous instance was the failure to maintain the Great Dam at Ma'rib—the heart of a monumental irrigation project and one of the engineering marvels of the ancient world. Its rupture in AD 525 constitutes the symbolic end to the ascendancy of the Yemeni empires.

Decline of economic activity

Dhū Nuwās (Yūsuf As'ar Yath'ar; 6th century AD), the last Himyarite king, was a convert to Judaism, who carried out a major massacre of the Christian population of Yemen (there was once a major cathedral in Ṣanʿāʾ). The survivors called upon the Byzantine emperor to avenge them, and he arranged to have the Christian Aksumites (Ethiopians) punish Dhū Nuwās. The Aksumite leader Abraha called for a massacre of Jews and subsequently ruled Yemen, attempting to add the Hejaz (the area around Mecca and Medina in modern Saudi Arabia) to his realm (this effort is reported in the Qur'ān). The Himyarites, however, resented the Ethiopian usurpers and called in the Persians to expel them. By obliging, the Persians added the satrapy of Yemen to their domains. The last Persian governor of Yemen converted to Islām in AD 628.

The advent of Islām. The new faith of Islām spread readily and quickly in Yemen, no doubt at least in part because of the atrocious behaviour of both Jews and Christians in the preceding centuries. The Prophet Muḥammad sent his son-in-law as governor, and two of Yemen's most famous mosques—the one in Janadīyah (near Taʿizz) and the Great Mosque in Ṣanʿāʾ (said to have incorporated some materials from earlier Jewish and Christian structures)—are thought to be among the earliest examples of Islāmic architecture.

Despite the fact that Muḥammad's first successor, the caliph Abū Bakr (served 632–634), managed to unify the Arabian Peninsula, it was not long before Yemen once again demonstrated its fractious nature. Often when the caliph sent a representative to put down rebellions or other uprisings, the representative would establish his own dynasty (as was the case with Muḥammad ibn Ziyād, who early in the 9th century founded the city of Zabīd as his capital).

For the history of Yemen, however, the most important event after the triumph of Islām was the introduction in the 9th century of the Zaydī sect from Iraq—a group of Shīʿites who accepted Zayd ibn ʿAlī, Muḥammad's great-grandson, as the last legitimate successor to the Prophet. Much of Yemeni culture and civilization for the next 1,000 years was to bear the stamp of Zaydī Islām. Succeeding centuries present a confusing series of factional, dynastic, local, and imperial rulers contesting for control of Yemen—among them the Ṣulayḥids, the Fāṭimids, the

Ayyūbids, and the Rasūlids, some of whom were Ismāʿīlīs, some of whom were Sunnites, and some of whom were Zaydīs.

Yemen next appeared on the world stage when (according to one account) Sheikh ʿAlī ibn ʿUmar of the Shādhilīyah order discovered the distinctive properties of coffee as a beverage, probably about the beginning of the 15th century. As a result, Yemen and the Red Sea became an arena of conflict between the Egyptians, the Ottomans, and later, various European powers seeking control over both the long-standing trade in Indian condiments and spices and the emerging market for *Coffea arabica*. This conflict occupied most of the 16th and 17th centuries; by the beginning of the 18th century, with the route to Europe around Africa having become the standard one (owing to the endeavours of such European powers as the Portuguese), the world once again lost interest in Yemen. In the meantime, the coffee plant had been smuggled out of Yemen and transplanted into a great variety of new locales, from Asia to the New World. The effect of the redirection of trade was dramatic: cities such as Aden and Mocha, which had burgeoned with populations in excess of 10,000, shrank to villages barely supporting 500.

The age of imperialism. Developments in the 19th century precipitated great change. The determination of various European powers to establish a presence in the Middle East elicited an equally firm determination in others to thwart such goals. The most important participants in the drama as far as Yemen was concerned were the British, who took over Aden in 1839, and the Ottoman Empire, which at mid-century moved back into (North) Yemen, from which it had been driven two centuries earlier. The interests and activities of these two powers in the Red Sea basin and Yemen were substantially intensified by the opening of the Suez Canal and the reemergence of the Red Sea route as the preferred passage between Europe and the Far East. As the Ottomans expanded eastward (inland toward Ṣanʿāʾ) from the coast, the British expanded north and east from Aden, more in the interest of protecting Aden's hinterland from the territorial pretensions and military incursions of the imams than of adding the various entities there to the empire. By the early 20th century, the confrontations between the British and the Ottomans required a border agreement; in 1904 a border commission surveyed the area, and a treaty established the frontier between (Ottoman) Yemen and the British possessions in (South) Yemen. Later, of course, both Yemens considered the treaty an egregious instance of non-Arab interference in Arab affairs. The lack of clearly demarcated borders mentioned above has also led to more recent friction, specifically between Saudi Arabia and Yemen over ownership of territories east of Ma'rib that contain extensive oil and natural gas deposits.

British and Ottoman conflict

The north became independent at the end of World War I with the departure of the Ottoman forces; the imam (a religio-political figure) of the Zaydīs, Yaḥyā ibn Muḥammad, became the de facto ruler by virtue of his lengthy campaign against the Ottoman presence in Yemen. Yemeni independence allowed the imam to resuscitate Zaydī claims to "historic Yemen," which included all of what the British considered the protectorates and Aden, as well as the Saudi province of Asir and some important areas around the Najrān oasis. The imam, of course, did not recognize the standing Anglo-Ottoman border agreement.

The British, on the other hand, retained control over the south, which they considered strategically and economically important to their empire. Friction between the two Yemens characterized the entire interwar period, as Imam Yaḥyā sought to include the south in the united Yemen that he perceived to be his patrimony. The imam also brought about conflict with his neighbour to the north, Saudi Arabia, over the status and ownership of Asir and the Najrān oasis.

Eventually, in the early 1930s, Imam Yaḥyā had to sign agreements concerning the borders of Yemen with both Saudi Arabia and Britain. The British, in the meantime, were consolidating their presence in the south; the most important change was the incorporation of the Ḥaḍramawt valley into the protectorates—the result of the labours of Harold Ingrams, who negotiated the famous "Ingrams' Peace" among the more than 1,400 tribes and clans that had been feuding in that district for longer than they themselves could remember.

Dynasty of Imam Yaḥyā

In the north, Imam Yaḥyā had consolidated his own hold on the country: he had succeeded in bringing the Shāfiʿī areas under his administrative jurisdiction and had subdued much of the intertribal feuding. In an effort to enhance the effectiveness of his campaigns against the tribes and other fractious elements, the imam sent a group of Yemeni youths abroad (to Iraq) to learn modern weaponry and techniques. These students were eventually to become the kernel of domestic opposition to the imam's policies.

By the end of World War II, dissatisfaction had spread to a rather wide segment of Yemeni society, including secular reformers, Muslim reformers, other elements of the traditional elite, and even the *ʿulamāʾ* (religious scholars). This tide of dissent culminated early in 1948 in the assassination of Imam Yaḥyā and a coup d'état by the reformers. Much to the consternation of the various reform elements, however, Imam Yaḥyā's son, Aḥmad, succeeded in bringing together many of the tribal elements of the north, overthrowing the new government, and installing himself as imam. Although Aḥmad had indicated that he supported many of the popular political, economic, and social demands (*e.g.*, creation of a cabinet with real responsibilities, abandonment of the principle of economic autarky, and the establishment of free public education), his own government soon resembled his father's in nearly all respects. An attempt on Aḥmad's life in 1955 only brought about increased repression; in fact, his paranoia concerning the loyalty of the tribal elements prompted a number of irrational acts that eventually cost his son the support of the tribes against the revolution of 1962.

In the south, in the interim, the policies of the imams had backfired: although the imams had the advantage of offering an indigenous Muslim regime as an alternative to secular British rule, their aggressive policies had alarmed many of the ruling families. The latter now believed, probably correctly, that if their statelet were to be taken over by the imam, their perquisites and status would be curtailed, if not eliminated. Consequently, most deemed it advantageous to cooperate more closely with Britain, which after all paid them a subsidy and implied a role for them in future arrangements. By the late 1950s, an earlier proposal to federate some of the smaller statelets had grown into a much broader scheme to include all of the principalities and sheikhdoms into a larger political entity that would eventually achieve independence.

Britain's insistence that Aden be a part of the new entity created the anomaly that eventually killed the plan. The sophisticated business community, the activist trade unions, and other similarly modern political and social organizations in Aden feared for their future at the hands of what they perceived to be a group of largely illiterate and parochial tribal leaders from the rural areas of the protectorates. The tribal leaders, on the other hand, feared at worst their overthrow, or at best a degree of political and economic participation severely limited by an Adeni population that included many non-Muslims and non-Arabs.

The British continued to insist upon their chosen course of action, and by 1965, all but four of the 21 protectorate states had joined the "federation." Shortly thereafter, Britain announced that independence would ensue no later than 1968. This announcement unleashed the violent political conflict that prevailed in Aden and the protectorates for the next two years as sundry organizations fought for control of the destiny of South Yemen.

In the north, meanwhile, Imam Aḥmad died (of natural causes) in late September 1962, and his son, Muḥammad al-Badr, became imam. Within a week, however, elements of the military, supported by a variety of political organizations (and quite possibly some foreign powers), attempted to assassinate the new imam and declared the foundation of the Yemen Arab Republic. The imam escaped into the northern highlands and began the traditional process of rallying the tribes to his cause. The new republic called upon Egypt for assistance; Egyptian troops and equipment

Establishment of the Yemen Arab Republic

arrived almost immediately to defend the new regime of ʿAbd Allāh as-Sallal.

The establishment of a republic in North Yemen provided a tremendous incentive to the elements in the south that sought to eliminate the British presence there. Furthermore, the Egyptians agreed to provide support for some of the organizations campaigning for southern independence—*e.g.,* the Front for the Liberation of South Yemen (FLOSY). However, not all elements in either of the two Yemens were sympathetic to Egyptian policies, much less to the dominant role that Egypt had begun to play in southwestern Arabia. An emergent alternative movement, the National Liberation Front (NLF), drew its support primarily from indigenous sources. As the time for independence drew near, the conflict between the various groups, and especially the NLF and FLOSY, escalated into open warfare for the right to govern the state after British withdrawal. By late 1967, the NLF clearly had the upper hand; the British finally accepted the inevitable and arranged the transfer of sovereignty to the NLF on Nov. 30, 1967.

In North Yemen, the conflict between the imam's royalist forces and the republicans had escalated into civil war. Participation, however, was not limited to the Yemenis: Saudi Arabia, Iran, and Jordan supported the royalists, whereas Egypt and the Soviet Union and other communist-bloc states supported the republicans. Britain and the United States, as well as the United Nations, also eventually became major players, even if only at the diplomatic level. By the late 1960s, however, the Yemenis decided that the only logical outcome of the conflict was a compromise, which would have as its most important side effect the departure of the various foreign forces. Accordingly, with the blessing of the two major foreign participants—Egypt and Saudi Arabia—the northern Yemenis agreed upon the Compromise of 1970, which established a republican government in which some major positions were assigned to members of the royalist faction. It was, nevertheless, agreed that the imam and his family were not to play any role whatsoever in the new state; accordingly, the imam went into exile in Britain.

The compromise government immediately embarked upon a program of political and economic development; with few resources and even fewer skilled personnel to implement the desired changes, the military (and some tribal elements) became impatient and, in 1974, dismissed the civilian cabinet and replaced it with a military-led cabinet of technocrats. The government slowly but surely began the development of a complete set of institutions—at the local as well as the national level. Not all sectors of the population, however, accepted the government's new powers and influence over traditional political, economic, and social relationships; a clear indication of this discontent was the assassination of two presidents in succession (Ibrāhīm al-Ḥamdī in 1977 and Aḥmad al-Ghashmī in 1978). The Constituent Assembly, which had been created somewhat earlier, selected Colonel ʿAlī ʿAbd Allāh Ṣāliḥ as al-Ghashmī's successor. Ṣāliḥ managed, despite early public skepticism, to conciliate all factions, to improve relations with Yemen's neighbours, and to resume various programs of economic and political development and institutionalization.

Two independent Yemeni states

Now that the two Yemeni states were independent, expectations rose that there would be some form of amalgamation, especially since both states publicly claimed to support the idea; such a move was not, however, forthcoming, the primary reason being the drastic divergence of political orientation that developed after the departure of all the various foreign elements from both states. Whereas the north elected to remain a market economy and retain ties with the Western states, as well as with Saudi Arabia, the south began to move rapidly in a socialist direction under the leadership of the more radical elements of the NLF.

The new southern government changed the name of the country to the People's Republic of South Yemen. Short of resources and unable to obtain any significant amounts of aid either from the Western states or from most of the Arab ones, it began to drift toward the Soviet Union, which had no Arab state in the "socialist camp" and was therefore eager to provide economic and technical assistance. By the early 1970s, South Yemen had become an avowedly Marxist state and had inaugurated a radical nationalization and "communization" of the economy and society, renaming itself the People's Democratic Republic of Yemen (PDRY). The differences over all manner of policies led to a brief war between the two Yemens in 1972; despite efforts by others to resolve these disputes and promote some measure of accommodation, the basic conflicts appeared irreconcilable. In fact, South Yemen helped to instigate and fund a broad-based opposition movement in the north, the National Democratic Front. The South Yemenis perceived their cause—that of Marxist transformation of the Arab political, economic, and social systems—to be in desperate need of direct action; accordingly, elements of the leadership sanctioned the assassination of the North Yemeni president in 1978. At the same time, they supported other revolutionary organizations in the region, such as the Popular Front for the Liberation of Oman (PFLO). The continuing friction thus engendered led to another brief war, in 1979, which was followed by new efforts on the part of other Arab states to effect a reconciliation (in order to avert intervention by the Great Powers). All the while, however, significant fissures—both ideological and practical—were opening within the Yemen Socialist Party (YSP). ʿAbd al-Fattāḥ Ismāʿīl was the major ideologue of the NLF and was the driving force behind the organization's move toward the Soviet Union as well; he succeeded the president who had been held responsible (and executed) for the 1978 assassination, Sālim ʿAlī Rubayyī.

Ultimately, Ismāʿīl was found to be too dogmatic and rigid—in his analyses, policies, and methods of implementation—and was deposed in 1980. His successor, ʿAlī Nāṣir Muḥammad, instituted a far less dogmatic political and economic order. In January 1986, the various personal and ideological differences surfaced briefly in a violent civil war that left Ismāʿīl and many of his supporters dead, resulted in the exile of ʿAlī Nāsir Muḥammad, and brought to power a group of moderate technocrats led by Ḥaydar Abū Bakr al-ʿAṭṭas. It was this element of the YSP that undertook the negotiations that brought about the unity of the two Yemens.

Unification

Two factors made the unity agreement of 1990 possible: (1) the discovery of oil and natural gas in both countries at roughly the same time and in roughly the same geographic region (from Ma'rib to Shabwah), some of which was in dispute between them (clearly, it would not have been in the best interest of either country to engage in a costly conflict over such important resources; it made far more sense to unite and share the profits to be gained from a rational exploitation of the deposits), and (2) the decision by Mikhail Gorbachev, then president of the Soviet Union, to abandon that country's support of the governments and policies of a number of eastern European states, some of which were the PDRY's principal sources of financial, technical, and personnel assistance. Once the communist bloc gave way to popular democratic movements, it was only a matter of time before the isolated South Yemeni regime would crumble. The rational option for the YSP—and the one it chose—was to enter into negotiations with North Yemen while still in power.

Discussions between the two states began in 1989 and reached a successful conclusion earlier than anyone had anticipated (in light of their previous relations). The official merger conducted in May 1990 commenced a 30-month transition period, during which details of the political, economic, and social integration of the two recently hostile states were to be negotiated. An all-Yemen parliamentary election was scheduled to follow. (M.W.W.)

For later developments in the history of Yemen, see the *Britannica Book of the Year* section in the BRITANNICA WORLD DATA ANNUAL.

BIBLIOGRAPHY

General works. Introductions to the area include SHEILA A. SCOVILLE (ed.), *Gazetteer of Arabia: A Geographical and Tribal History of the Arabian Peninsula,* vol. 1 (1979); ROBERT W. STOOKEY (ed.), *The Arabian Peninsula: Zone of Ferment*

(1984); HASSAN S. HADDAD and BASHEER K. NIJIM (eds.), *The Arab World: A Handbook* (1978); ALOIS MUSIL, *Northern Negd* (1928, reprinted 1978), on the Najd region of Saudi Arabia; and DEREK HOPWOOD (ed.), *The Arabian Peninsula: Society and Politics* (1972). See also M.W. DEMPSEY (comp.), *Atlas of the Arab World* (1983). Early explorations are chronicled in ROBIN BIDWELL, *Travellers in Arabia* (1976); and ZAHRA FREETH and H.V.F. WINSTONE, *Explorers of Arabia: From Renaissance to the End of the Victorian Era* (1978). The people of the peninsula are described in PETER MANSFIELD, *The New Arabians* (1981); H.R.P. DICKSON, *The Arab of the Desert,* 3rd ed. rev. and abridged by ROBERT WILSON and ZAHRA FREETH (1983); MAX FREIHERR VON OPPENHEIM, *Die Beduinen,* 2 vol. (1939, reprinted 1983); and WALTER DOSTAL, *Die Beduinen in Südarabien* (1967). Religious life and history are detailed in GONZAGUE RYCKMANS, *Les Religions arabes préislamiques,* 2nd ed. (1951); J. SPENCER TRIMINGHAM, *Christianity Among the Arabs in Pre-Islamic Times* (1979); and A.J. ARBERRY (ed.), *Religion in the Middle East,* vol. 2, *Islam* (1969, reprinted 1976). Articles on the geography, history, and religion of the Arabian Peninsula may be found in *The Encyclopaedia of Islam,* 4 vol. and a suppl. (1913–36), with a new edition in progress, beginning in 1960; and *The Shorter Encyclopaedia of Islam* (1953, reprinted 1974), with articles taken from the larger work. Periodicals include *Arabian Studies* (annual); *The Middle East and North Africa* (annual); *The Middle East Journal* (quarterly); and *Proceedings of the Seminar for Arabian Studies* (annual).

Comparative coverage of the five Persian Gulf states—Bahrain, Kuwait, Oman, Qatar, and the United Arab Emirates—is provided by RICHARD F. NYROP (ed.), *Persian Gulf States: Country Studies,* 2nd ed. (1985); JOHN BULLOCH, *The Persian Gulf Unveiled* (also published as *The Gulf,* 1984); and ALVIN J. COTTRELL (ed.), *The Persian Gulf States: A General Survey* (1980). Discussions of early history include JUAN R.I. COLE, "Rival Empires of Trade and Imami Shiʿism in Eastern Arabia, 1300–1800," *International Journal of Middle East Studies,* 19:177–203 (May 1987); AHMAD MUSTAFA ABU-HAKIMA, *History of Eastern Arabia, 1750–1800: The Rise and Development of Bahrain and Kuwait* (1965); and J.B. KELLY, *Britain and the Persian Gulf, 1795–1880* (1968). Politics, economics, and strategic significance are considered in ANTHONY H. CORDESMAN, *The Gulf and the Search for Strategic Stability: Saudi Arabia, the Military Balance in the Gulf, and Trends in the Arab-Israeli Military Balance* (1984), an assessment of military conditions; MUHAMMAD RUMAIHI (MUḤAMAD GHĀNIM RUMAYḤI), *Beyond Oil: Unity and Development in the Gulf* (1986); THOMAS L. MCNAUGHER, *Arms and Oil: U.S. Military Strategy and the Persian Gulf* (1985); J.E. PETERSON, *Defending Arabia* (1986); and HUSAIN M. ALBAHARNA, *The Arabian Gulf States: Their Legal and Political Status and Their International Problems,* 2nd rev. ed. (1975).

History and cultural development. Archaeology and early history are described in RICHARD LE BARON BOWEN, JR., and FRANK P. ALBRIGHT, *Archaeological Discoveries in South Arabia* (1958); G. LANKESTER HARDING, *Archaeology in the Aden Protectorates* (1964); F.V. WINNETT and W.L. REED, *Ancient Records from North Arabia* (1970); and BRIAN DOE, *Southern Arabia* (1971). General historical studies include J. WELLHAUSEN, *The Arab Kingdom and Its Fall* (1927, reprinted 1973; originally published in German, 1902), covering the Islāmic empire, AD 622–750, still useful though some views are now disputed; and HERMANN V. WISSMANN, *Zur Geschichte und Landeskunde von Alt-Südarabien* (1964). The study of more recent history should begin with the brilliant but controversial analysis of KHALDOUN HASAN AL-NAQEEB, *Society and State in the Gulf and Arab Peninsula: A Different Perspective* (1990; originally published in Arabic, 1987). Useful surveys also include R.B. SERJEANT, *Studies in Arabian History and Civilisation* (1981); and IAN RICHARD NETTON (ed.), *Arabia and the Gulf: From Traditional Society to Modern States* (1986). More specialized works are NIGEL GROOM, *Frankincense and Myrrh: A Study of the Arabian Incense Trade* (1981); M.J. KISTER, *Studies in Jāhiliyya and Early Islam* (1980); R.B. SERJEANT, *The Portuguese off the South Arabian Coast: Hadrami Chronicles, with Yemeni and European Accounts of Dutch Pirates off Mocha in the Seventeenth Century* (1963, reprinted 1974); ZĀMIL MUḤAMMAD AL-RASHĪD, *Suʿūdī Relations with Eastern Arabia and ʿUmān, 1800–1870* (1981); WILLIAM OCHSENWALD, *Religion, Society, and the State in Arabia: The Hijaz Under Ottoman Control, 1840–1908* (1984); and JOHN C. WILKINSON, *Arabia's Frontiers: The Story of Britain's Boundary Drawing in the Desert* (1991).

The countries of Arabia. *Bahrain:* Good general accounts include JOHN WHELAN (ed.), *Bahrain* (1983); ANGELA CLARKE, *The Islands of Bahrain: An Illustrated Guide to Their Heritage* (1981); and JAMES H.D. BELGRAVE, *Welcome to Bahrain,* 9th ed. (1975), a detailed guidebook that includes the geography, history, and customs of Bahrain, together with a bibliography of works in Arabic, English, and French. The islands' history is surveyed in CURTIS E. LARSEN, *Life and Land Use on the Bahrain Islands: The Geoarcheology of an Ancient Society* (1983); ABBAS FAROUGHY, *The Bahrein Islands, 750–1951: A Contribution to the Study of Power Politics in the Persian Gulf: An Historical, Economic, and Geographical Survey* (1951); and M.G. RUMAIHI, *Bahrain: Social and Political Change Since the First World War* (1976). Economic, political, and social conditions are addressed in JEFFREY B. NUGENT and THEODORE THOMAS (eds.), *Bahrain and the Gulf: Past Perspectives and Alternative Futures* (1985), which has a good account of resources and economic development; FUAD I. KHURI, *Tribe and State in Bahrain: The Transformation of Social and Political Authority in an Arab State* (1980); and MAHDI ABDALLA AL-TAJIR, *Bahrain, 1920–1945: Britain, the Shaikh, and the Administration* (1987). Further bibliographic information can be found in P.T.H. UNWIN (comp.), *Bahrain* (1984). (C.G.S.)

Kuwait: JILL CRYSTAL, *Kuwait: The Transformation of an Oil State* (1992), provides a general and timely overview of the country. AHMAD MUSTAFA ABU-HAKIMA, *The Modern History of Kuwait, 1750–1965* (1982), offers a historical introduction. JACQUELINE S. ISMAEL, *Kuwait: Social Change in Historical Perspective* (1982), is a sociological treatment. SHAFEEQ N. GHABRA, *Palestinians in Kuwait: The Family and the Politics of Survival* (1987), examines one important expatriate community; on expatriates in general, see ABDULRASOOL AL-MOOSA (ʿABD AL-RASŪL ʿALĪ MŪSĀ) and KEITH MCLACHLAN, *Immigrant Labour in Kuwait* (1985). The role of women is addressed in S.M. AL-SABAH, *Development Planning in an Oil Economy and the Role of the Woman: The Case of Kuwait* (1983). Works on the economy include RAGAEI EL MALLAKH and JACOB K. ATTA, *The Absorptive Capacity of Kuwait: Domestic and International Perspectives* (1981); and Y.S.F. AL-SABAH, *The Oil Economy of Kuwait* (1980); and on politics, ALAN RUSH, *Al-Sabah: Genealogy and History of Kuwait's Ruling Family, 1752–1987* (1987); and JILL CRYSTAL, *Oil and Politics in the Gulf: Rulers and Merchants in Kuwait and Qatar* (1990). (J.C.)

Oman: General works include DONALD HAWLEY, *Oman & Its Renaissance,* 4th ed. (1987); B.R. PRIDHAM (ed.), *Oman: Economic, Social, and Strategic Development* (1987); LIESL GRAZ, *The Omanis: Sentinels of the Gulf* (1982); JOHN DUKE ANTHONY, JOHN PETERSON, and DONALD SEAN ABELSON, *Historical and Cultural Dictionary of the Sultanate of Oman and the Emirates of Eastern Arabia* (1976); and S.B. MILES, *The Countries and Tribes of the Persian Gulf,* 2 vol. (1919, reissued in 1 vol., 1966) which focuses on Oman. Anthropological studies include JÖRG JANZEN, *Nomads in the Sultanate of Oman: Tradition and Development in Dhofar* (1986; originally published in German, 1980); and FREDRICK BARTH, *Sohar: Culture and Society in an Omani Town* (1983). The role of women is the subject of CHRISTINE EICKELMAN, *Women and Community in Oman* (1984); and UNNI WIKAN, *Behind the Veil in Arabia: Women in Oman* (1982). PATRICIA RISSO, *Oman & Muscat: An Early Modern History* (1986); and ROBERT GERAN LANDEN, *Oman Since 1856: Disruptive Modernization in a Traditional Arab Society* (1967), are scholarly treatments of the first and second halves of the 19th century, respectively. J.E. PETERSON, *Oman in the Twentieth Century: Political Foundations of an Emerging State* (1978), gives a political history of the sultanate; and JOHN C. WILKINSON, *The Imamate Tradition of Oman* (1987), outlines the background of the events leading to the demise of the Ibāḍī imamate in the 1950s. The period before the 1970 coup d'état is described in IAN SKEET, *Muscat and Oman: The End of an Era* (1974, reprinted 1985); while JOHN TOWNSEND, *Oman: The Making of a Modern State* (1977), gives a general assessment of the challenges facing the state after the coup. Further information may be found in FRANK A. CLEMENTS (comp.), *Oman* (1981), an annotated bibliography.

Qatar: JILL CRYSTAL, *Oil and Politics in the Gulf: Rulers and Merchants in Kuwait and Qatar* (1990), provides a general introduction and a political history; while ROSEMARIE SAID ZAHLAN, *The Creation of Qatar* (1979), is a historical introduction. Surveys of the country's culture are JOHN WHELAN (ed.), *Qatar* (1983); HELGA GRAHAM, *Arabian Time Machine: Self-Portrait of an Oil State* (1978); and LEVON H. MELIKIAN, *Jassim: A Study in the Psychosocial Development of a Young Man in Qatar* (1981). Economic studies include RAGAEI EL MALLAKH, *Qatar: Energy and Development* (1985); ZUHAIR AHMED NAFI, *Economic and Social Development in Qatar* (1983); and NASSER AL-OTHMAN (NĀṢIR MUḤAMMAD ʿUTHMĀN), *With Their Bare Hands: The Story of the Oil Industry in Qatar* (1984; originally published in Arabic, 1980). (J.C.)

Saudi Arabia: Overviews are provided by NORMAN ANDERSON *et al., The Kingdom of Saudi Arabia,* 7th ed. rev. (1987); MIDDLE EAST RESEARCH INSTITUTE, *MERI Report: Saudi Arabia* (1985); RICHARD F. NYROP (ed.), *Saudi Arabia: A Country Study,* 4th ed. (1984); TREVOR MOSTYN (comp.), *Saudi Arabia,* 2nd ed. (1983); and ISMAIL I. NAWWAB, PETER C. SPEERS, and PAUL F.

HOYE (eds.), *Aramco and Its World: Arabia and the Middle East* (1980). HUSSEIN HAMZA BINDAGJI, *Atlas of Saudi Arabia* (1978), includes thematic, regional, and city maps. Two major cities are the subject of GERALD DE GAURY, *Rulers of Mecca* (1951, reissued 1980); and ANGELO PESCE, *Jiddah: Portrait of an Arabian City*, rev. ed. (1977). Sociological studies include SORAYA ALTORKI, *Women in Saudi Arabia: Ideology and Behavior Among the Elite* (1986); and WILLIAM LANCASTER, *The Rwala Bedouin Today* (1981), a case study. See also G.R.D. KING, *The Historical Mosques of Saudi Arabia* (1986), a study of mosque architecture; and SAFEYA BINZAGR, *Saudi Arabia: An Artist's View of the Past* (1979), a pictorial perspective of Saudi Arabia's culture and people. The economy is examined in ALI D. JOHANY, MICHEL BERNE, and J. WILSON MIXON, JR., *The Saudi Arabian Economy* (1986); ADNAN M. ABDEEN and DALE N. SHOOK, *The Saudi Financial System, in the Context of Western and Islamic Finance* (1984); A. REZA S. ISLAMI and ROSTAM MEHRABAN KAYOUSSI, *The Political Economy of Saudi Arabia* (1984); JOHN R. PRESLEY, *A Guide to the Saudi Arabian Economy* (1984); ARTHUR N. YOUNG, *Saudi Arabia: The Making of a Financial Giant* (1983), a historical survey of the impact of oil; TIM NIBLOCK (ed.), *State, Society, and Economy in Saudi Arabia* (1982); FOUAD AL-FARSY, *Saudi Arabia: A Case Study in Development*, 2nd ed. rev. (1980); and DONALD M. MOLIVER and PAUL J. ABBONDANTE, *The Economy of Saudi Arabia* (1980). Policy studies are found in RAGAEI EL MALLAKH, *Saudi Arabia, Rush to Development: Profile of an Energy Economy and Investment* (1982); HASSAN HAMZA HAJRAH, *Public Land Distribution in Saudi Arabia* (1982), on transformation of land ownership; ROBERT E. LOONEY, *Saudi Arabia's Development Potential: Application of an Islamic Growth Model* (1982); WILLIAM B. QUANDT, *Saudi Arabia in the 1980s: Foreign Policy, Security, and Oil* (1981), a diplomatic study; and ROBERT D. CRANE, *Planning the Future of Saudi Arabia: A Model for Achieving National Priorities* (1978), with a summary of the five-year plans. Further bibliographic information can be found in HANS-JÜRGEN PHILIPP, *Saudi Arabia: Bibliography on Society, Politics, Economics* (1984), in English and German; and FRANK A. CLEMENTS, *Saudi Arabia*, rev. and expanded ed. (1988).

The most important historical works include KAMAL SALIBI, *A History of Arabia* (1980); ABDELGADIR MAHMOUD ABDALLA, SAMI AL-SAKKAR, and RICHARD T. MORTEL, *Sources for the History of Arabia*, 2 vol. (1979), symposium proceedings; and H.ST.J.B. PHILBY, *Sa'ūdi Arabia* (1955, reprinted 1972). For a more interpretive discussion, see JOSEPH KOSTINER, "Tracing the Curves of Modern Saudi History," *Asian and African Studies*, 19(2):219–244 (July 1985). R. BAYLY WINDER, *Saudi Arabia in the Nineteenth Century* (1965, reprinted 1980), remains the definitive work on that period. The life of Ibn Sa'ūd, the founder of the modern Saudi state, is discussed in a sympathetic fashion in MOHAMMED ALMANA, *Arabia Unified: A Portrait of Ibn Saud* (1982); DAVID HOLDEN and RICHARD JOHNS, *The House of Saud* (1981), a detailed history of the years 1902–80; HAFIZ WAHBA, *Arabian Days* (1964); and AMEEN RIHANI, *Ibn Sa'oud of Arabia: His People and His Land* (1928, reprinted 1983). The work of CHRISTINE MOSS HELMS, *The Cohesion of Saudi Arabia: Evolution of Political Identity* (1981), combines political geography, history, and diplomacy for the early 20th century. Works covering the same time include JOHN S. HABIB, *Ibn Sa'ud's Warriors of Islam: The Ikhwan of Najd and Their Role in the Creation of the Sa'udi Kingdom, 1910–1930* (1978); MADAWI AL-RASHEED, *Politics in an Arabian Oasis: The Rashidi Tribal Dynasty* (1991); and CLIVE LEATHERDALE, *Britain and Saudi Arabia, 1925–1939: The Imperial Oasis* (1983). Histories of Aramco and U.S.-Saudi foreign policy include IRVINE H. ANDERSON, *Aramco, the United States, and Saudi Arabia: A Study of the Dynamics of Foreign Oil Policy, 1933–1950* (1981); and AARON DAVID MILLER, *Search for Security: Saudi Arabian Oil and American Foreign Policy, 1939–1949* (1980). Two important internal issues in the post-World War II period are analyzed in AYMAN AL-YASSINI, *Religion and State in the Kingdom of Saudi Arabia* (1985); and ALEXANDER BLIGH, *From Prince to King: Royal Succession in the House of Saud in the Twentieth Century* (1984). See also MORDECHAI ABIR, *Saudi Arabia in the Oil Era: Regime and Elites: Conflict and Collaboration* (1988). (W.L.O./B.K.M.)

United Arab Emirates: For general works, see MALCOLM C. PECK, *The United Arab Emirates: A Venture in Unity* (1986); TREVOR MOSTYN (ed.), *UAE* (1982); ALI MOHAMMED KHALIFA, *The United Arab Emirates: Unity in Fragmentation* (1979); and MICHAEL TOMKINSON, *The United Arab Emirates* (1975). LINDA USRA SOFFAN, *The Women of the United Arab Emirates* (1980), discusses changes in the status of women. See also RAGAEI EL MALLAKH, *The Economic Development of the United Arab Emirates* (1981). Historical works include FRAUKE HEARD-BEY, *From Trucial States to United Arab Emirates: A Society in Transition* (1982); MUHAMMAD MORSY ABDULLAH, *The United Arab Emirates: A Modern History* (1978); and CLARENCE MANN, *Abu Dhabi: Birth of an Oil Sheikhdom*, 2nd ed. (1969). (J.D.An./Ed.)

Yemen: Introductions are given in MANFRED W. WENNER, *The Yemen Arab Republic: Development and Change in an Ancient Land* (1991); TAREQ Y. ISMAEL and JACQUELINE S. ISMAEL, *The People's Democratic Republic of Yemen: Politics, Economics, and Society* (1986); ROBERT W. STOOKEY, *South Yemen, a Marxist Republic in Arabia* (1982), and *Yemen: The Politics of the Yemen Arab Republic* (1978); B.R. PRIDHAM (ed.), *Economy, Society, & Culture in Contemporary Yemen* (1985), and *Contemporary Yemen: Politics and Historical Background* (1984); RICHARD F. NYROP (ed.), *The Yemens: Country Studies*, 2nd ed. (1986); and WERNER DAUM (ed.), *Yemen: 3000 Years of Art and Civilisation in Arabia Felix* (1987). Sociological and anthropological information may be found in PAUL BONNENFANT (ed.), *La Péninsule arabique d'aujourd'hui*, 2 vol. (1982); and JOSEPH CHELHOD *et al.*, *L'Arabie du sud: histoire et civilisation*, 3 vol. (1984–85). *Qāt* is discussed by JOHN G. KENNEDY, *The Flower of Paradise* (1987); and SHELAGH WEIR, *Qat in Yemen: Consumption and Social Change* (1985). CHARLES F. SWAGMAN, *Development and Change in Highland Yemen* (1988); and THOMAS B. STEVENSON, *Social Change in a Yemeni Highlands Town* (1985), chronicle the impact of the changes of the past two decades. The background and the nature of Yemeni migration are addressed in JON C. SWANSON, *Emigration and Economic Development: The Case of the Yemen Arab Republic* (1979); and JONATHAN FRIEDLANDER and RON KELLEY (eds.), *Sojourners and Settlers: The Yemeni Immigrant Experience* (1988). Economic characteristics are outlined in *People's Democratic Republic of Yemen: A Review of Economic and Social Development* (1979), a study published by the World Bank; and RAGAEI EL MALLAKH, *The Economic Development of the Yemen Arab Republic* (1986). FRED HALLIDAY, *Revolution and Foreign Policy: The Case of South Yemen, 1967–1987* (1990); STEPHEN PAGE, *The Soviet Union and the Yemens: Influence on Asymmetrical Relationships* (1985); and MARK N. KATZ, *Russia & Arabia* (1986), examine the PDRY's development and its relationship with the former USSR and other countries.

Works on the history of the past four centuries are ERIC MACRO, *Yemen and the Western World, Since 1571* (1968); HUSAYN B. ʿABDULLAH AL-ʿAMRI (ḤUSAYN ʿABD ALLĀH ʿAMRĪ), *The Yemen in the 18th & 19th Centuries: A Political and Intellectual History* (1985); ROBIN BIDWELL, *The Two Yemens* (1983); and MANFRED W. WENNER, *Modern Yemen, 1918–1966* (1967). (M.W.W.)

Arachnids

The class Arachnida, part of the invertebrate phylum Arthropoda, includes forms such as spiders (Araneida), harvestmen (daddy longlegs; Opiliones), scorpions (Scorpionida), mites and ticks (Acari), and a few lesser known groups. Only a few species are of economic importance, including the acarids that transmit diseases to humans, other animals, and plants.

For coverage of related topics in the *Macropædia* and *Micropædia,* see the *Propædia,* section 313.

This article is divided into the following sections:

Arachnids 853
- General features 853
  - Size range and diversity of structure
  - Distribution and abundance
  - Importance
- Natural history 854
  - Reproduction and life cycle
  - Ecology and habitats
  - Locomotion
  - Food and feeding
  - Associations
- Form and function 855
  - General features
  - External features
  - Internal features
- Evolution and paleontology 856
- Classification 857
  - Distinguishing taxonomic features
  - Annotated classification
  - Critical appraisal

Major arachnid orders 858
- Scorpions 858
- Acarids (mites and ticks) 862
- Spiders 865

Bibliography 871

ARACHNIDS

GENERAL FEATURES

Size range and diversity of structure. Arachnids range in size from mites that measure 0.08 millimetre (0.003 inch) to the enormous scorpion *Hadogenes troglodytes* of Africa, which may be 21 centimetres (eight inches) or more in length. In appearance, they vary from the small rounded mites to the long-legged opilionids and the crablike spiders.

Like all arthropods, the arachnids have a segmented body, a tough exoskeleton, and jointed appendages. Most are carnivorous. Arachnids lack jaws and, with only a few exceptions, inject digestive fluids into their prey before sucking the liquefied remains into their mouths. Except among the acarids (mites and ticks), in which the entire body forms a single region, the arachnid body is divided into two distinct parts: the cephalothorax, or prosoma, and the abdomen, or opisthosoma. The sternites (ventral plates) of the lower surface of the body show more variation than those of the upper surface. The arachnids have simple eyes.

The cephalothorax is covered dorsally with a rigid cover (the carapace) and contains six pairs of appendages, the first of which are the chelicerae; these are the only appendages that are preoral in position; and in many forms they are chelate, or pincerlike, and are used to hold and crush prey. Among spiders the chelicerae contain venom sacs, and the second segment, the fang, can inject venom. The second pair of appendages are the pedipalps, or palps, which in arachnids function as an organ of touch. In spiders and harvestmen the pedipalps are elongated structures; in scorpions they are large, chelate, prehensile organs. Among spiders the pedipalps are highly modified as sexual intromittent organs. The basal segment is frequently modified for crushing or cutting food. The remaining four pairs of appendages are walking legs, though the first of these pairs serves as tactile organs among the amblypygids, or tailless whip scorpions, while it is the second of these pairs that functions as such among the opilionids. Among the ricinuleids special copulatory organs are located on the third pair of legs. Some mites, particularly the immature individuals, have only two or three pairs of legs.

Pedipalps

In many arachnids the cephalothorax and abdomen are broadly joined, while in others (such as spiders) they are joined by a narrow, stalklike pedicel. The abdomen is composed of a maximum of 13 segments. The first of these may be present only in the embryo and absent in the adult. In some orders a mesosoma consisting of seven segments and metasoma of five may be distinguished; in others a few posterior segments may form a pygidium, or postabdomen. In general, except for the spinnerets of the spiders, the opisthosoma has no appendages. In some groups the abdomen is elongated with free tergites; in others it may be shortened with indistinct segmentation. Postanal structures vary in both appearance and function. The scorpions have a short stinger with a swollen base enclosing a poison gland; the orders Uropygi (whip scorpions) and Palpigradi (palpigrades) have long whiplike structures of unknown functions.

Distribution and abundance. With the exception of a few groups that have secondarily become aquatic, the arachnids are terrestrial predators. Spiders, harvestmen, false scorpions (order Pseudoscorpiones), and mites and ticks are nearly worldwide in distribution. Scorpions, solpugids (wind scorpions, including sun spiders; order Solpugida), tailless whip scorpions (order Amblypygi), and vinegarroons, or whip scorpions (order Uropygi), are widespread within the tropical and subtropical areas of the world, only occasionally being encountered in northern areas. Of more sporadic distribution, but more common in tropical areas, are the palpigrades, or microwhip scorpions (order Palpigradi), the schizomids (Schizomida), and the ricinuleids (Ricinulei). In northern areas mature spiders and harvestmen are particularly conspicuous during the early autumn, though they are abundant throughout the year. Most, however, are seldom observed, for they inhabit leaf mold or soil and form an important part of the cryptozoic fauna. Most abundant of the arachnids are the acarids found in soil, in fresh and marine waters, and as parasites of animals and humans.

Terrestrial predators

Importance. The numbers and predaceous habits of arachnids make them important to humans. Free-living mites play an important role in the conversion of leaf mold to humus. Many mites are parasitic. Many ticks are intermediate hosts for organisms that cause serious diseases. Though all spiders possess poison that can be utilized for catching prey, only a few have a poison sufficiently powerful to affect humans. A bite of the black widow spider (*Latrodectus mactans*) may result in discomfort or serious illness; that of the brown recluse spider (*Loxosceles reclusa*) may result in a severe local reaction. The sting of some species of scorpions may cause a severe reaction and even death in humans.

Parasitic mites

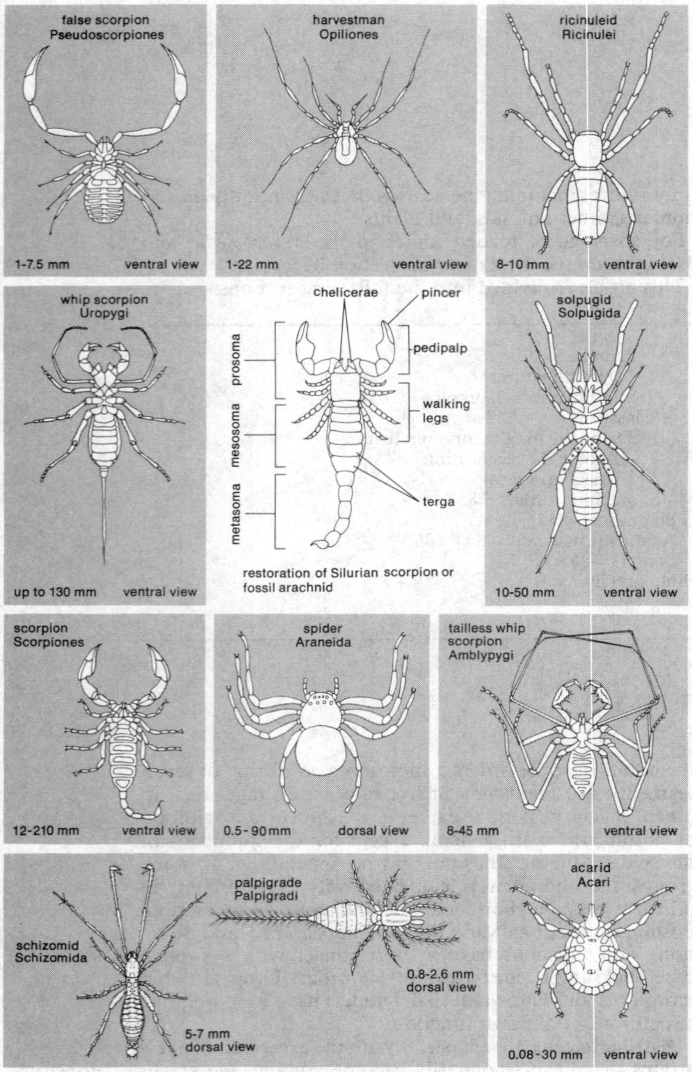

Figure 1: Diversity of arachnids.

From (restoration) R.R. Shrock and W.H. Twenhofel, *Principles of Invertebrate Paleontology*, copyright 1953, used with permission of McGraw-Hill Book Company; (Araneida) *Invertebrate Identification Manual* by Richard A. Pimentel, © 1967 by Litton Educational Publishing, Inc., reprinted by permission of Van Nostrand Reinhold Company; (Ricinulei, Uropygi, Solpugida, Scorpiones, Amblypygi) *Transactions of the Connecticut Academy of Arts and Sciences*, vol. XXXI (1933); (Schizomida) after *American Museum Novitates*, The American Museum of Natural History, New York City (1957), in A. Kaestner, *Invertebrate Zoology*, John Wiley & Sons, Inc.

NATURAL HISTORY

Reproduction and life cycle. In most cases the male does not transfer the spermatozoa directly to the female but rather initiates courtship rituals in which the female is induced to accept the gelatinous sperm capsule (spermatophore). During mating the sperm are transferred to a sac within the female reproductive system, the spermatheca. The eggs are fertilized as they are laid. Mating in solpugids is more active, occurring at dusk or during the night; during courting the male seizes the female, lays her on her side, massages her undersurface, opens her genital orifice, and forces a mass of sperm into her spermatheca. Reproductive behaviour in mites is highly variable; sperm usually are produced in a spermatophore and transferred to the female either by the chelicerae or by the third pair of legs of the male. In the ricinuleids the third legs rather than the pedipalps are modified for the transfer of sperm into the female genital opening.

Spermatophore

The harvestmen appear to be the only arachnids in which sperm transfer is direct. There is little or no courtship among the members of this class; rather, mating occurs whenever a male and female encounter one another. The male has a chitinized penis that is inserted into the genital opening of the female as the partners face one another.

Care for eggs

Many arachnids simply deposit their eggs in the soil or in a protected site, and no further care is given to them; others, particularly tropical species, guard the eggs by remaining with them during the period of development. Some spiders place their eggs in cocoons, and the eggs of some tailless whip scorpions, schizomids, whip scorpions, and false scorpions are attached beneath the abdomen.

Among scorpions the fertilized eggs develop inside the mother, and the young are born alive. In scorpions whose eggs contain much yolk, the eggs develop within the oviduct; in those with little yolk, the eggs remain in place and each embryo lies in a diverticulum (hollow outpouching) with a tubular extension through which nutrient fluids pass from the wall of the maternal intestine. When the young are sufficiently developed, they are expelled and carried about on the mother's back until after the first molt. False scorpions carry their eggs in a brood sac attached to the genitalia. The embryos develop and grow within this brood sac and are nourished by the female.

Details of early development are not known for all forms, but that of egg-laying spiders is considered typical. The two major divisions of the body (the cephalothorax and the abdomen) appear at an early stage, and the appendages first appear as knobs. In many arachnids the organism is wrapped around the yolk, a situation altered by a process termed inversion or reversion, after which hatching usually occurs.

Molting

Growth occurs by molting, or ecdysis. In many, the first molt occurs while the animal is still within the egg. The newly hatched arachnid is small and the exoskeleton less sclerotized (hardened) than the adult. With the exception of the acarids and ricinuleids, which have three pairs of legs when hatched, the hatchlings have four pairs of legs. The number of molts required to attain maturity varies; some spiders, for example, have 12. Before molting, arachnids seek protected sites; spiders, false scorpions, and some mites produce a cocoon to protect themselves.

Mites differ in both development and growth. In the life cycle of the mite, unlike other arachnids, an egg hatches into the six-legged, or hexapod, larva, which passes through one or several immature (nymphal) stages before becoming an adult. Most mites lay eggs, though some are ovoviviparous; *i.e.,* the eggs develop within the body of the female and hatch within or immediately after extrusion. Acarids are also able to reproduce from unfertilized eggs (parthenogenesis). The life cycle of ticks is similar to that of mites.

Life span

The life span of arachnids in temperate areas is usually a single season; they rely upon their eggs to perpetuate the species. In warm regions some groups (*e.g.,* whip scorpions, tailless whip scorpions, scorpions, solpugids, and tarantulas) appear to live more than a single year.

Ecology and habitats. Although most arachnids are inconspicuous free-living terrestrial forms, some acarids are parasitic, a few spiders live on or near water, and some mites are aquatic. Most arachnids lead solitary lives, coming together only briefly for mating. Even though they possess a chitinous exoskeleton, most arachnids are subject to damage by desiccation. Many arachnids, especially small, little-known forms, (ricinuleids, for example), are found only in well-protected niches. The favourable environment of the relatively constant, moisture-containing microclimate provided by soil litter, burrows, or caves is the reason these species constitute a high proportion of the cryptozoic fauna. Cave-dwelling species often have special adaptations—for example long extremities, light colour, and no eyes. Most arachnids, even those adapted to desert areas, avoid excessive heat by adopting a cryptozoic habitat and by being active only during the cooler parts of the day.

A few arachnids (*e.g.,* some scorpions, solpugids, spiders, and harvestmen) are capable of producing rasping sounds by rubbing together horny ridges or other special sound-producing structures. Sound may be used in general to warn predators or by males during courtship. Preening is common among arachnids. This consists of cleaning the legs by passing them through the chelicerae. A method of protection and escape from predatory enemies consists of the quick dropping of a captured limb.

Locomotion. Locomotion among arachnids involves a sequence of movements of the legs: the first and third legs of one side and the second and fourth legs of the other side are brought forward nearly simultaneously. Most arachnids are not great travelers. Those that do travel long distances rely upon methods other than walking or running; for example, a spider about to migrate scales a vertical object, releases a strand of silk, and relies upon the wind to carry it away (ballooning). Pseudoscorpions often rely on an activity termed phoresy, in which they cling to the legs of more mobile animals, such as flies or harvestmen, and are carried about. Mites may use phoresy or gusts of air to carry them to new sites.

Phoresy

Food and feeding. As carnivores, most arachnids feed chiefly upon smaller arthropods; exceptions are among parasitic acarids and plant-feeding harvestmen. Acarids are nourished principally by fluids obtained either from living animal or plant material or from decaying organic matter. Parasitic forms have mouthparts modified for sucking blood or juice. Harvestmen appear to be the only arachnids capable of ingesting small particles. More commonly the prey is torn into small pieces as digestive fluids flow over it—or a hole is made in the body of the prey, and digestive fluids are injected—and the digested contents are sucked up.

While many arachnids actively seek their prey, the more common method is that of lying in wait. Active arachnids, such as the solpugids, use both tactile and visual responses in prey recognition as they run at random. The American whip scorpion (*Mastigoproctus giganteus*) hunts mostly at night, moving slowly with pedipalps extended and touching objects with the extended first leg. Harvestmen run rapidly over bushes, herbs, and other vegetation in pursuit of prey.

Associations. Though most arachnids are solitary animals, some spiders live in enormous communal webs housing males, females, and spiderlings. Most of the individuals live in the central part of the web, with the outer part providing snare space for prey shared by all of the inhabitants. In some cool and dry areas harvestmen often gather in enormous numbers, probably protecting themselves against extremes of temperature or desiccation. Mimicry is seen among some spiders that are found in ant colonies. These spiders resemble the ants in appearance and habit, are tolerated by the ants, and actually feed upon the ant pupae.

Communal spiders

FORM AND FUNCTION

General features. Though arachnids are easily recognized by the division of the body into two parts (the cephalothorax and abdomen) and their possession of six pairs of appendages, they are extremely diverse in form. The dorsal region of the prosoma has a solid covering, the carapace, and the underside has one or more sternal plates or the coxal segments of the six pairs of appendages. The opisthosomal segments do not bear appendages. The soft body is protected by an exoskeleton composed of chitin, and the somites are united by a soft membrane. Eyes, if present, are simple, and their number varies with the species. Sexes are always separate, but it is often difficult to distinguish between them. At times, however, either males or females, but especially males, may develop special structures, brighter colour, larger spines, or larger size.

External features. There are many modifications of the cephalothorax and abdomen. Among the scorpions the abdomen is subdivided into the mesosoma, or preabdomen, and the metasoma, or postabdomen; the latter is mobile and more slender. Similar arrangements are found among whip scorpions, schizomids, and ricinuleids. Among the harvestmen the division between the two parts is only partial, and among most acarids the body is rounded and shows no segmentation. Spiders exhibit the greatest variation in body shape.

The form and function of the six pairs of appendages is variable. The first pair, the chelicerae, often have claws. They transport spermatophore (solpugids, some acarids), produce sounds (solpugids, some spiders), cut strands of silk (web-dwelling spiders), and produce silk (pseudoscorpions). The pedipalps, the second pair, likewise are often highly modified. Among the scorpions and pseudoscorpions the pedipalps are large; among the tailless whip

Function of chelicerae

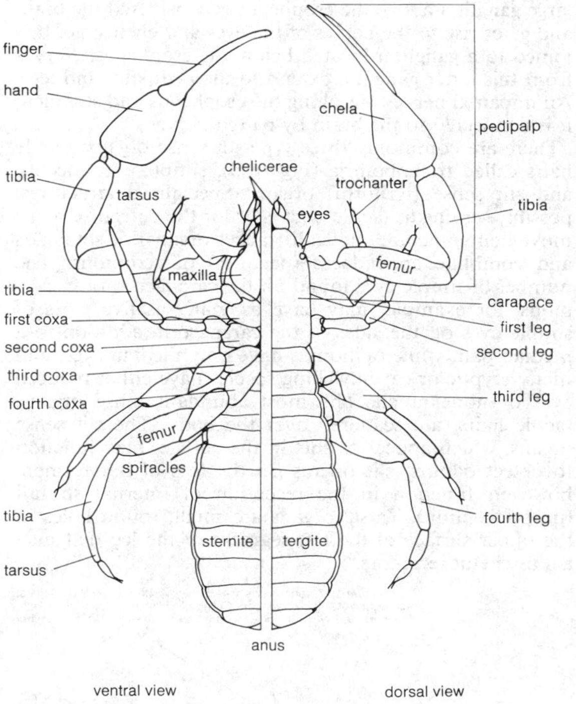

Figure 2: Anatomy of a pseudoscorpion.

From A. Petrunkevitch, *Treatise on Invertebrate Paleontology*, part P (1955), courtesy of the Geological Society of America and the University of Kansas Press

scorpions and some harvestmen they are elongated and equipped with many heavy spines. Among some arachnids they are prehensile, serving both to capture and hold prey. In spiders they serve to transfer sperm, and for the scorpions, pseudoscorpions, and tailless whip scorpions they play an important role during courtship.

There are typically four pairs of walking legs, each of which usually has seven segments of variable lengths, with the last segment often bearing claws. The legs serve chiefly for locomotion but may be modified to serve as tactile organs (harvestmen), for capturing and immobilizing prey (running spiders), and for producing sound (harvestmen, spiders, solpugids, and scorpions).

Internal features. *Support, skeleton, and exoskeleton.* The arachnid exoskeleton is formed of chitin, a nitrogen-containing carbohydrate associated with a protein. This complex is tough but pliable. The exoskeleton consists of two parts: the thin outer epicuticle, which is usually a wax and is impermeable to water, and the thicker endocuticle. Membranes, flexible portions of the cuticle, are present wherever there are movable articulations.

Growth can occur only by shedding the old skeleton, a process termed molting, or ecdysis. This process is under hormonal control and involves the secretion of a new cuticle below the old one. Sclerotization, or hardening, may be accompanied by pigmentation.

While the exoskeleton provides both support and protection, the arachnids have an endoskeleton, the endosternite, which provides a surface for muscle attachment.

Tissues and muscles. The muscles of the cephalothorax are well developed, while those of the abdomen are reduced. The muscles are striated, similar to those of vertebrates; those of the legs have their origin either on the endosternite or on the body wall and extend to the basal segments of the appendages. Muscles within the appendages make possible the movements of the individual segments. Within the opisthosoma, muscles consist primarily of bundles that connect the various segments. Most of the space between the digestive tract and the body wall, the hemocoel, is filled with blood.

Striated muscles

Nervous system and organs of sensation. The arachnid nervous system is similar to that of other arthropods in that it consists of a brain and a chain of paired ganglia. The nervous system has been highly modified by ganglionic fusion and migration forward toward the head region. The large ganglion above the esophagus is considered the brain and gives rise to the nerves of the eyes and chelicerae. It is joined to a ganglion located below the esophagus. Nerves from this latter ganglion extend to the pedipalpi and legs. An unpaired nerve runs along the esophagus and stomach; it is connected to the brain by paired nerves.

There are commonly three types of sense organs: tactile hairs called trichobothria (Figure 3), simple eyes (ocelli), and slit sense (lyriform) organs. Specialized structures, possibly serving as tactile organs or for the detection of air movements, include malleoli (racket organs) of solpugids and comblike appendages (pectines) of scorpions. The number of simple eyes found on the carapace varies; scorpions, for example, may have as many as five pairs of simple eyes on the sides of the carapace in addition to a median pair, while opilionids have only median eyes, and many cryptic or cave-dwelling species have either reduced eyes or none at all. The most abundant sense organs, tactile hairs, are scattered over the body. The slit sense organs, which appear as slits in the cuticle, may function to detect odours; slit organs on the legs of harvestmen, however, function in the reception of internal stimuli (proprioception). Tarsal organs are small, round holes in the upper surface of the last segment of the leg that may act as chemoreceptors.

Figure 13-7 from *Invertebrate Zoology*, 4th ed., by R.D. Barnes, copyright © 1980 by Saunders College Publishing, a division of Holt, Rinehart, and Winston, Inc., reprinted by permission of the publisher

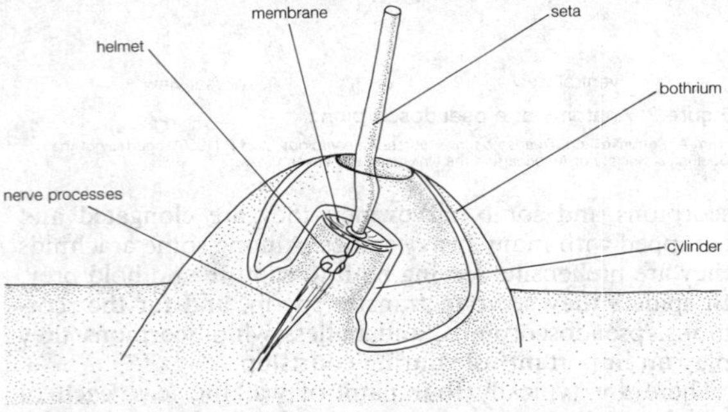

Figure 3: Trichobothrium of a spider with only the lower part of the hair showing.

Digestion and nutrition. With the exception of some harvestmen and mites, arachnids are predators, relying upon smaller arthropods for their food. The harvestmen may be the only arachnids capable of ingesting food particles; most species partially digest their prey as it is held in the chelicerae. The digestive system is a tube that begins with the mouth situated below the chelicerae, leading into the pharynx, then into the esophagus, and from there into the sucking stomach, which has heavy muscles and serves to pump the partially digested food into the midgut, where special enzymes digest the food. The absorptive surface of the midgut is increased by a series of blind sacs. Fecal material accumulates in the hindgut and is voided through the anus.

Excretion. Two main types of excretory organs occur in arachnids: coxal glands and Malpighian tubules. The coxal glands consist of three parts: a large excretory sac lying opposite the coxal segment of the first pair of legs; a long coiled tubule; and a short exit tube that opens to the exterior through orifices behind the first and third coxal leg segments. The nitrogen-containing waste material usually is the organic compound guanine.

Respiration. Two types of respiratory organs are found among arachnids: book lungs and tracheae. Book lungs are found in hardened pockets; diffusion of gases occurs between the blood circulating within thin leaflike structures (lamellae) stacked like pages in a book and the air in spaces between these thin structures (Figure 4). The tracheal system consists of a number of tubes that open to the exterior by paired respiratory pores (spiracles) and is similar to that of insects; diffusion of gases occurs within small fluid-filled tubes that ramify over the internal organs. Scorpions, the tailless whip scorpions, and the whip scorpions rely upon book lungs; the pseudoscorpions, solpugids, ricinuleids, harvestmen, and acarids have only tracheae;

Book lungs and tracheae

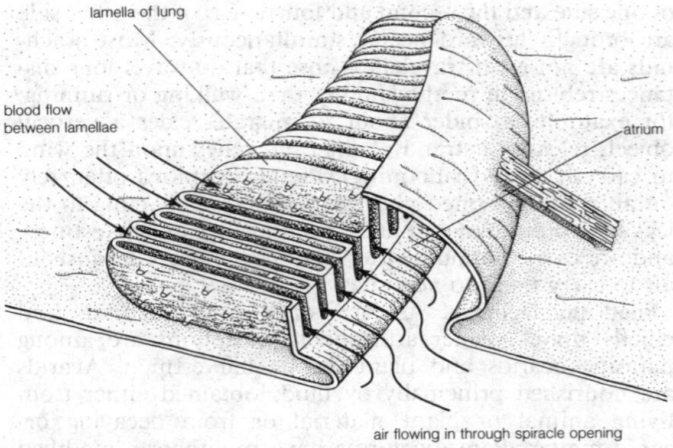

Figure 4: Diagrammatic section through a book lung.
From R.D. Barnes, *Invertebrate Zoology*, 4th ed., (1980), Saunders College, Philadelphia

most spiders have both; and the small palpigrades and acarids have only cutaneous respiration.

Circulatory system. The circulatory system of the arachnids is an open system; that is, blood circulates in tissue sinuses. Special venous channels conduct blood from the tissues to the heart, from which it is pumped through a series of blood vessels back to the sinuses. The respiratory pigment usually is hemocyanin and is in solution in the hemolymph; cells are present but do not carry oxygen.

Reproductive system. There is considerable variation in the number and appearance of both ovaries and testes. In general, the ovaries are associated with oviducts; and the testes have vasa deferentia. The genital orifice of both sexes (except mites) is on the undersurface of the second abdominal segment; in mites it may be dorsal. Sperm are usually transferred to a special structure of the female, the spermatheca.

Glands and hormones. The glands of arachnids are usually peculiar to individual orders. In spiders, silk is stored as a viscous liquid in the silk glands, which are found at the end of the abdomen; the number of spinnerets is variable. The viscous liquid, a protein, passes through minute tubes at the tips of the spinnerets; the change from liquid to solid thread occurs by a structural rearrangement of the protein molecules after the silk is drawn from a silk droplet. The silk of the pseudoscorpions is produced by a spinneret located on a movable finger of the chelicera; the few mites that produce silk have glands in the area of the mouth.

Toxic substances

Toxic substances are secreted by special glands found in the chelicerae of spiders, in the pedipalps of false scorpions, and in the poison glands of scorpions. The poisonous substances (and their effects) differ even within species of the same order. The strongly alkaline poison of spiders is much less poisonous to mammals than to arthropods; bites of spiders of the genera *Loxosceles* (brown recluse) and *Latrodectus* (black widow) may cause human discomfort; those of the latter may cause serious illness. The venom of most scorpions, sufficiently toxic to kill most invertebrates, usually is not dangerous to humans; the venoms of some genera (*Androctonus* and *Buthus* of Africa, various species of *Centruroides* of Mexico, Arizona, and New Mexico), however, are highly toxic nerve poisons. The toxicity of the venom of the pseudoscorpions is not known. The paired glands of whip scorpions located near the anus secrete specific acids (formic, acetic) that serve as irritants and apparently are used for defense. The openings of paired odoriferous glands are found on the cephalothorax of harvestmen; when irritated these animals secrete a fluid containing cyanic acid that probably serves to repel predators.

EVOLUTION AND PALEONTOLOGY

While arachnid fossils are abundant, it is extremely difficult to trace the evolution of individual groups. The earliest forms recognizable as arachnids include a scorpion that dates from the Silurian Period (about 430,000,000–395,000,000 years ago) and an acarid from the Devonian Period (about 395,000,000 to 345,000,000 years ago). Spiders with segmented abdomens and presumably four pairs of spinnerets are known to have existed during the Carboniferous Period (345,000,000 years ago). Palpigrades have been described as fossils only from the Jurassic Period (190,000,000 years ago) in Europe, and the schizomids are known from the late Cenozoic Era in Arizona (about 7,000,000 years ago). The Mesozoic Era (about 225,000,000–65,000,000 years ago) is poor in arachnid fossils; while the Cenozoic Era (from about 65,000,000 years ago to the present) is rich in them. A. Petrunkevitch (1953) concluded that all orders of arachnids were either already extant or in the process of evolving by the Silurian Period. Since the Silurian scorpion closely resembled modern forms, the hypothetical arachnid ancestor must antedate any known fossil forms. The stem group of the chelicerates is believed to be among the members of the trilobite-like Olenellinae. These date from the Cambrian Period (about 570,000,000 years ago). During Paleozoic times the eurypterida, large animals resembling modern scorpions, were abundant, and both groups can be traced to a common ancestor.

It is impossible to reconstruct an exact phylogeny of the arthropods, but possibly they arose from some simple segmented worm prior to the Cambrian Period. Two divergent lines (other than the trilobites) appeared early among the marine forms; one group remained aquatic, the other gave rise to the terrestrial arachnids.

Invasion of land

The invasion of the land probably started in moist habitats, such as under leaf-litterlike material. Many changes in anatomy and reproductive behaviour had to occur before the arthropods were successful in their transfer to terrestrial life.

A major characteristic of arachnid evolution is that segments were fused or lost. The five posterior segments of the scorpions were retained as a tail. Among the spiders, primitive families had abdomens composed of 12 distinct segments, which were reduced to five or six in other families and completely fused in adults. Among the acarids, abdominal segmentation was lost and the body showed no external segmentation. In general, scorpions have the largest number of primitive arachnid features, and spiders and mites are the most highly evolved.

CLASSIFICATION

Distinguishing taxonomic features. In classifying arachnids, taxonomists rely mostly upon external structures, including such features as general body form, the degree of visible external segmentation, structural modifications of prosoma and opisthosoma, characteristics of appendages, and special structures involved in sperm transfer. Internal anatomical features, developmental traits, and serological characteristics are used to a limited extent; conceivably, however, as information becomes available, traits such as these could play a more important role in arachnid classification.

Annotated classification. The following classification of arachnids is based chiefly on work by L. Störmer (1944) and by A. Petrunkevitch (1949). In the classification below, the groups marked with a dagger (†) are wholly extinct and known only from fossils.

CLASS ARACHNIDA (arachnids)
Chelicerate arthropods with adult body composed of 18 somites, divided into anterior prosoma (6 somites) and posterior opisthosoma (12 somites); prosoma with 6 pairs of appendages, 1st pair preoral, last 2 pairs secondarily lost in some mites; genital opening in both sexes on 2nd abdominal somite (except some mites); heart usually in abdomen; respiration by means of book lungs, tracheal tubes, a combination of the two, or cutaneous (some cryptozoic forms); excretion by coxal glands and/or Malpighian tubules; digestive system with a pumping foregut, midgut with blind sacs, and a short hindgut opening with an anus on ventral side of opisthosoma; nervous system with a tendency to fuse; not more than 12 simple eyes (ocelli); sexes dimorphic; courtship frequent before sperm transfer; usually terrestrial, carnivorous, nocturnal, and cryptozoic; social organization rare; instinctive behaviour highly developed; distribution variable; about 70,000 species described.

Order Scorpiones (or *Scorpionida;* scorpions). Prosoma compact, opisthosoma subdivided, taillike portion ending in stinger; chelicerae chelate (pincerlike), 3-jointed; size 14–210 mm; ovoviviparous; earliest fossil records from Silurian; widespread in tropical and subtropical regions; about 1,200 to 1,300 species described.

Order Pseudoscorpiones (or *Pseudoscorpionida;* false or book scorpions). Length 1–7.5 mm; carapace entire, abdominal somites often subdivided dorsally; chelicerae chelate, movable finger with spinneret; oviparous; worldwide distribution; about 2,000 species described.

Order Opiliones (harvestmen or daddy longlegs). Size 1–22 mm; 3 to 8 opisthosomatic dorsal regions of segments (tergites) fused with carapace, remainder free; single pair of eyes, usually on median tubercle; oviparous; worldwide distribution; about 4,500 species described.

†*Order Architarbi.* Fossil forms with segmented opisthosoma; carapace complete, with 2 to 6 eyes; chelicerae chelate; Upper Carboniferous of Europe, Pennsylvanian of North America.

†*Order Haptopoda.* Fossil forms with carapace complete; chelicerae 3-jointed, chelate, from Upper Carboniferous, England.

†*Order Anthracomarti.* Fossil forms with complete carapace; abdomen with 10 segments; from Upper Carboniferous of Europe, Pennsylvanian of North America.

†*Order Trigonotarbi.* Fossil forms with complete carapace, chelicerae 2-jointed, pedipalps leglike, arrangement of coxae as in spiders; from Devonian of Scotland, Upper Carboniferous of Europe, Pennsylvanian of North America.

Order Palpigradi (palpigrades). Size 0.8–2.6 mm; carapace subdivided into 3 parts; eyes absent; coxae movable; chelicerae chelate; 3-jointed pedipalps leglike; telson a many-segmented flagellum; no book lungs or tracheae; sporadic distribution; about 60 species described.

Order Uropygi (whip scorpions or vinegarroons). Size to 130 mm; carapace complete; coxae movable, pedipalps predatory; 1st tarsus tactile; long, whiplike telson; order coextensive with 1 family, Thelyphonidae; fossils nearly identical with living forms; known from Carboniferous of Illinois, Czechoslovakia, and England; widespread in tropical and subtropical regions; about 85 species described.

Order Schizomida (schizomids). Size 2–15 mm; prosoma with segmented carapace; chelicerae 2-segmented; telson short; sporadic distribution; about 80 species described.

†*Order Kustarachnae.* Fossil forms known only from Pennsylvanian of North America; sternum small, coxae radiate from it.

Order Amblypygi (tailless whip scorpions). Size 8–45 mm; prosoma broader than long, covered with carapace; 8 eyes; chelicerae not chelate; pedipalps very long, strong; 1st pair of legs tactile; members widespread in tropical and subtropical regions; about 70 species described.

Order Araneida (*Araneae;* spiders). Size 0.5–90 mm; carapace complete; chelicerae 2-jointed, with ducts of poison glands; pedipalps leglike in males, with special copulatory apparatus; opisthosoma nonsegmented, bearing spinnerets; group large and variable in appearance and habits; worldwide distribution; about 34,000 species described.

Order Solpugida (*Solifugae;* solpugids [wind scorpions]). Size 10–50 mm; anterior part of 3-part prosoma swollen into head; chelicerae powerful; opisthosoma 10 or 11 segments; widespread in tropical and subtropical regions; about 900 species described.

Order Ricinulei (ricinuleids). Size 8–10 mm; carapace complete, with cucullus; abdomen of 9 segments, last 3 forming caudal region pygidium, development with a 6-legged larval form; of sporadic distribution; about 33 species described.

Subclass Acari (Acarina or Acarida; mites and ticks)
Size from 0.08 to 30 mm in some fully engorged ticks; prosoma and opisthosoma fused, somites not apparent; mouthparts adapted to piercing, sucking, biting, grating, or sawing; highly variable in appearance; many parasitic and economically important forms; worldwide distribution; about 30,000 species described.

Order Opilioacariformes (or *Opilioacarida*). Body divided into hairy anterior portion bearing 2 to 3 pairs of simple eyes and nude posterior portion, with 4 pairs of stigmata and 12 secondarily developed segments; terminal palpal apotele a pair of claws; terrestrial; 1 family; 12 species.

Order Parasitiformes (mites and ticks). Small to large in size; usually heavily sclerotized mites; 1 to 4 pairs of stigmata on posterior portion of body; peritremes, or grooves, present or absent; palpal apotele present or absent; tarsi of first pair of legs with sensory organs.

Order Acariformes (mites). Weakly sclerotized with few plates; eyes present or absent; stigmata, when present, at or between bases of chelicerae or on anterior portion of body; chelicerae styletlike, chelate (pincerlike), or reduced; habitats from aquatic to terrestrial, predatory to parasitic.

Critical appraisal. Many schemes for the classification of the Arachnida have been proposed. The system used here recognizes the name Arachnida as that of a terrestrial class of the subphylum Chelicerata. Members of this class differ from those of the aquatic class Merostomata (the horseshoe crabs) in the absence of gill books and compound eyes, while resembling them in possession of six pairs of prosomatic appendages. This definition of Arachnida results in the exclusion of the pycnogonids from the class (consequently establishing them in their own chelicerate class, the Pycnogonida) and is in accord with taxonomic practices of subdividing and separating groups in order to clarify relationships.

A systematization of arachnids based upon the work of P. Weygoldt and H.F. Paulus (1979) reflects the phylogeny of the group and is known as cladistic. This systematization is the result of a careful comparative study of structures of ancient origin (*i.e.,* segmentation) as well as the modifications occurring on more recently inherited structures. Thus, a well-constructed cladogram will indicate not only the phylogeny of the group but also its relationships to other forms. (M.L.Go.)

MAJOR ARACHNID ORDERS

Scorpions

Scorpions (order Scorpiones) often play the role of evildoers in fables and legends; Greek respect for scorpions prompted the naming of the constellation Scorpio, a sign of the zodiac. A long, curved tail tipped with a venomous stinger and grasping, fingerlike first appendages are typical scorpion features.

GENERAL FEATURES

Size range and diversity of structure. Scorpions are relatively large arachnids, with an average size of about six centimetres (about 2½ inches). Only some spiders and myriapods and a few insects rival the size of larger scorpions. Larger scorpion species are larger than almost all terrestrial invertebrates and 33 to 50 percent of all terrestrial vertebrate species (*e.g.,* frogs, lizards, rodents). Giants among scorpions include the black species from tropical Africa—*Pandinus imperator* of Guinea attains a body length of about 18 centimetres and a mass of 60 grams. The length of the smallest scorpion, the Caribbean *Microtityus fundorai,* is 12 millimetres. Although many were of average size, a few precursors of modern scorpions were comparative giants; some early scorpions (*Gigantoscorpio willsi, Brontoscorpio anglicus*) measured 35 centimetres to one metre or more; an undescribed species is estimated to have been 90 centimetres. Most species from deserts and other arid regions are yellowish or light brown in colour; those scorpions that are found in moist or mountain habitats, however, are brown or black.

Distribution and abundance. Modern scorpions live on all major landmasses except Greenland and Antarctica (they were accidently introduced into New Zealand and England). They range from Canada and central Europe to the tips of South America and Africa. Scorpions have radiated into all non-boreal habitats, including deserts, savannas, grasslands, and temperate, tropical, and rain forests.

Greatest concentration

The most diverse scorpion faunas occurs in temperate and subtropical deserts. Scorpions live at altitudes that range from sea level to 2,000 metres (6,000 feet) in the Alps, 3,000 metres in the mountains of southwestern North America, and 4,000 to 5,000 metres in the Andes. Only 14 species are reported in all of the Soviet Union, while more than 40 species occur in California and 62 in Baja California. In North America only one species occurs as far north as southern Canada (*Paruroctonus boreus*) and one as far south as Tierra del Fuego (*Bothriurus burmeister*). In Europe one species of scorpion is known as far north as southern Germany, but none is found in Scandinavia. Diversity at one location in the tropics ranges from five to seven species in Trinidad and Venezuela to three species in Brazil.

NATURAL HISTORY

Reproduction and life cycle. Scorpions exhibit few sexual differences, although males usually are more slender and have longer tails than females. In order to survive on land, scorpions evolved mating behaviours that prevent eggs and spermatozoa from drying out.

The breeding season almost always occurs during the warm months (late spring through early fall). At this time males become vagrant and may travel hundreds of metres to find receptive females. It appears that males find females by localizing a pheromone that the female emits from the end of her metasoma. Mating in scorpions is preceded by a complicated and characteristic courtship; it is initiated by the male, who faces and grasps the female by appendages called pedipalps. The pair, directed by the male, moves sideways and backward in a dancelike motion called *promenade à deux.* Many of these actions actually result from the efforts of the pair to find a smooth surface on which the male can extrude and attach the spermatophore by its stalk. The spermatophore bears spermatozoa at the tip of the stalk. His maneuvers also serve to bring the spermatophore near the open genital opercula of the female. Once the female is positioned over the spermatophore, physical contact with it causes spermatozoa to be ejected into the genital opening (gonopore) of the female. Males that remain near females after mating sometimes are killed and eaten by them.

Courtship rituals

Males can mate more than once with a certain amount of time between matings (probably the period necessary to produce a new spermatophore). Females also mate repeatedly. Some females in the family Buthidae mate even while carrying newborn scorpions. Some female buthids produce multiple (two to seven) litters from a single insemination. At least two species are parthenogenetic. Scorpion reproduction is uncharacteristic of terrestrial arthropods.

The mother invests a great amount of time and energy in her offspring. Further, unlike almost all other animals except mammals, scorpions are viviparous, with embryos nourished in utero by the mother. Once fertilized, eggs are retained in the female's body for periods varying from several months to a year before the young are born alive. Birth lasts several hours to several days. Temperate species usually give birth in spring and summer. Tropical species, as a group, give birth throughout the year, although many restrict parturition to a few months. Litter size averages 25, with a range of one to 105.

Each young scorpion, white in colour, is still enveloped in a membrane, or chorion, at birth; after freeing itself, the immature scorpion crawls onto the mother's back, where it remains for a period ranging from one to 50 days. During this time the young scorpions are defenseless, receive water transpired through the mother's cuticle and taken up through their own, and utilize food reserves in their bodies. Newborns then molt their soft embryonic cuticle for one that is fully functional when they assume independence. This early mother–young association is obligatory for newborns; without it, they do not molt successfully and usually die. The young usually leave the mother soon after this first molt.

Mother–young interaction

As in all arthropods, growth is accompanied by ecdysis (molting). Scorpions molt an average of five times, with a range of four to nine times, before reaching maturity. The number in some species is variable; in others, males reach maturity after a different number of molts. For example, in some *Centruroides* small males mature after four molts and large males after five. There are no reports of molting occurring after reproductive maturity has been reached.

Food and feeding. Scorpions are opportunistic predators that eat any small animal they can capture. Common prey include insects, and spiders and other arachnids. Scorpions often prey on other scorpions. Less common, but regular, prey include terrestrial isopods, snails, and small vertebrates (lizards, snakes, rodents). The only known

Common prey

specialist scorpion is the Australian *Isometroides vescus,* which feeds solely on burrowing spiders.

Scorpions are largely nocturnal and hide during the day in the confines of their burrows, in natural cracks, or under rocks or bark. Individuals become active at the beginning of the night and cease activity some time before dawn.

Most scorpions are sit-and-wait predators that remain motionless until a suitable prey moves into an ambush zone. Airborne vibrations of flying prey are detected. Scorpions also sense substrate vibrations of prey walking on the surface. These behaviours are sophisticated enough that scorpions can determine the precise distance and direction of their prey. Once the prey is detected, the scorpion orients, runs to the prey, and seizes it. The prey is stung if it is relatively large, aggressive, or active; otherwise, it is simply held in the pedipalps while it is eaten.

Many buthids, however, actively search for prey. These species usually have long, slender bodies and chelae. Many have powerful venoms to offset their small chelae.

Scorpions lack conventional jaws, and their feeding habits are unusual; a pair of toothed pincerlike appendages (chelicerae) and sharp edges of adjacent jawlike structures (maxillae and coxae) macerate the prey, as quantities of digestive fluids secreted from the small intestine pour over it. The victim's soft parts are broken down, liquefied, and sucked into the scorpion's stomach by a pumping action. The victim is gradually reduced to a ball of indigestible material, which is cast aside. Eating is a slow process, often taking many hours. (W.J.G./G.A.Po.)

Ecology and habitats. Because scorpions fluoresce under ultraviolet light, biologists can study their natural behaviour and ecology. Portable camping lights equipped with black light bulbs are used to detect scorpions at night. On a moonless night, scorpions can be seen at distances of 10 metres.

Scorpions' habitats range from the intertidal zone to snow-covered mountains. Several species live in caves, with one species, *Alacran tartarus,* found at depths more than 800 metres below the surface.

Specificity to habitat

Some species are specific in habitat and substrate requirements. For example, psammophilic species exhibit a morphology that both adapts and restricts them to sand. Setae form combs on the legs that increase the surface area and allow them to walk on sand without sinking or losing traction. Lithophilic species occur only on rocks. They possess stout, spinelike setae that operate in conjunction with highly curved claws to provide the legs with a strong grip on rock surfaces. The longest scorpion in the world, *Hadogenes troglodytes,* in which a South African female averages 210 millimetres, is a lithophile that can move rapidly on any spatial plane, even upside down.

Other species show adaptability in habitat use. The European *Euscorpius carpathicus* occurs in caves, above ground, and in the intertidal zone. *Scorpio maurus* occurs from sea level in Israel to above 3,000 metres in the Atlas Mountains thousands of kilometres to the west.

In some habitats scorpions are one of the most successful and important predators in terms of density, diversity, population biomass, and role in community energetics and structure. Many species occur locally at densities up to one or more individuals per square metre. *Vaejovis littoralis,* an intertidal scorpion from Baja California, exhibits the highest density, two to more than 12 per square metre along the high-tide mark. Since adult scorpions commonly weigh from 0.5 to five grams, the population biomass of the denser species is high. In some desert areas the population biomass of scorpions exceeds that of all other animals except termites and ants.

Adaptability

Several factors contribute to scorpions' success. Although they are morphologically conservative, scorpions are quite adaptable in terms of ecology, behaviour, physiology, and life history. They continue to thrive in extreme environmental conditions. Some species can be supercooled below the freezing point for weeks, yet return within hours to normal levels of activity. Others survive total immersion under water for as long as one to two days. Desert scorpions can withstand warm temperatures (45°–47° C), several degrees higher than the lethal temperatures for other desert arthropods.

Associations. Scorpions are a valuable prey because many are relatively large and quite dense. Vertebrate predators include birds (mostly owls), lizards, a few small snakes, mammals (some rodents and carnivores), and frogs and toads. Some vertebrates specialize on scorpions, at least seasonally. Scorpions are a major predator on other scorpions as well; both cannibalism and predation on other species is frequent. Such predation can be a major mortality factor and may limit the abundance and distribution of some species. A few large arthropods (spiders, solpugids, centipedes) also eat scorpions.

Antipredator adaptations

Scorpions exhibit several antipredator adaptations. The most obvious are the stinger and venom. Venom has a dual function: one of its chemical components is directed at arthropods (prey capture) and one at vertebrates (predator deterrence). An injection of potent neurotoxin is an overkill for most insects. Nocturnal activity and the low levels of surface activity may have evolved to avoid predation (most species are active only a few hours on 20 to 50 percent of all nights in the year).

Many predators exhibit typical behaviours that enable them to handle scorpions safely. Most vertebrate predators bite or break off the scorpion's tail and stinger. Some vertebrates and arthropods are immune to scorpion venom, even from those species that are lethal to humans.

The vast majority of scorpions are nonsocial, solitary animals that interact only at birth, courtship, or cannibalism. They are often aggressive and are usually considered "inveterate cannibals." A few, however, exhibit social behaviour. Some form overwintering aggregations with individuals of their own species, usually under bark or in fallen trees. A few extend the mother–offspring association for weeks to months or even years. In some cases (*e.g., Pandinus imperator*) offspring may remain with the family group even as adults, and some family groups cooperate in prey capture.

FORM AND FUNCTION

General features. The anatomy of scorpions has changed little from the Paleozoic Era. Consequently, their

From I.W. Sherman and V.G. Sherman, *Invertebrates: Function and Form,* 2nd ed. (1976), Macmillan Publishing Company, New York City

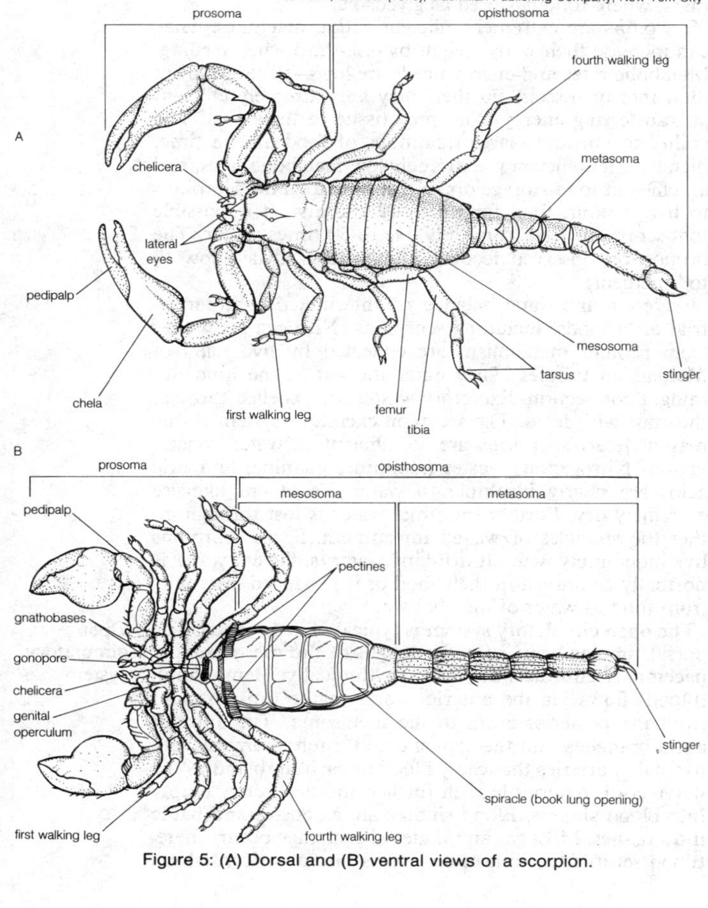

Figure 5: (A) Dorsal and (B) ventral views of a scorpion.

body plan is relatively primitive. Segments and associated structures were lost or fused during evolution from ancestral arthropods and arachnids to more highly evolved descendants. Scorpions have more segments (18) than any other arachnids and are strongly segmented in the design of the heart and nervous system. The possession of book lungs, rather than a trachea, for respiration is also primitive.

Major body regions

External features. The three major regions that form the body are the anterior prosoma, the medial mesosoma, and the posterior metasoma. The mesosoma and the metasoma form the opisthosoma. The prosoma has six segments, each with a pair of appendages. The three-segmented chelicerae that arise from the first segment are chelate (pincerlike) and serve to masticate food. The pedipalps originate in the second segment and terminate in chelate pincers (chelae). Pedipalps are used for a variety of purposes, including prey capture, defense, courtship, and burrow excavation. Four pairs of legs arise from segments three through six. The pedipalps and legs are composed of segments: (basal) coxa, trochanter, femur, patella, tibia, basitarsus, and tarsus. Legs end in tarsal claws used to grasp the surface during walking. The coxae of the pedipalps and the first two pairs of legs are expanded ventrally to form a gnathobase that encloses a preoral cavity where food is masticated, squeezed, and transferred from the chelicerae to the mouth. One medial and from zero to five lateral pairs of eyes are set into the dorsal carapace that covers the prosoma.

The mesosoma has seven segments: the first (pregenital) segment is reduced and bears the sternum; the second (genital) bears the ventral gonopore covered by a pair of small genital opercula. The unique comblike pectines arise from the genital segment. Four pairs of book lungs are on the ventral side of mesosomal segments three through six. The seventh mesosomal segment marks the end of the "body." The mesosoma is covered dorsally by seven tergites and ventrally by five sternites; these plates are separated from each other and laterally by a flexible pleural membrane. The tail is composed of the five-segmented cylindrical metasoma and a posterior telson bearing the stinger. The anus exits at the end of the fifth metasomal segment.

Process of molting

The exoskeleton is composed of chitinous cuticle overlain by impermeable epicuticular waxes. Growth is accompanied by ecdysis. Scorpions increase in weight until the exoskeleton becomes too small to allow further growth and a new exoskeleton is secreted by the epidermis under the old. During this process, some materials are resorbed from the old cuticle. Scorpions, like other arachnids, probably increase blood pressure just before molting. The cuticle ruptures at the side and front margins of the carapace. The chelicerae, pedipalps, legs and body are withdrawn from the old cuticle over a period of 12 hours. Scorpions then probably change blood pressure to expand body volume temporarily while the new cuticle hardens. This allows room for future growth in mass. As the cuticle tans, it hardens, darkens, and gradually acquires the ability to fluoresce under ultraviolet light.

Internal features. Muscles attach to the inner cuticle. Scorpion muscles are striated with individual fibres innervated by several neurons. A single neuron can attach to several muscle fibres. The strength of muscular contraction is a function of the rate of impulse delivery rather than of the number of fibres contracting (as is the case in vertebrates). The neuromuscular system has fast (phasic) neurons that produce rapid movement and slow (tonic) neurons that produce the prolonged contractions necessary in posture or slow movement.

The central nervous system consists of a brain and ventral nerve cord. The brain is composed of two large ganglia that surround the esophagus. The supraesophageal ganglion is bilobed: the protocerebrum processes optic information and is the origin of complex behaviours; the tritocerebrum mainly controls the normal body functions. The subesophageal ganglion innervates the chelicerae. Locomotion is controlled by both ganglia. A pair of circumesophageal connectives links the two ganglia. The nerve cord, which runs posteriorly along the length of the animal, consists of seven ganglia connected by pairs of fibres.

Scorpions perceive the world through visual, tactile, and chemical sense organs. Their eyes cannot form sharp images; however, their medial eyes are among the most sensitive to light in the animal kingdom. Evidently they can navigate at night using shadows cast by starlight. Lateral ocelli sense only changes in light intensity and are used to entrain circadian cycles. Light receptors occur in the tail in some species.

Trichobothria

Scorpions interpret vibrations transmitted through the air and substrate. Long, thin trichobothria are deflected best by air vibrations originating perpendicular to one plane. These hairs are situated on the pedipalps along different planes, thus allowing scorpions to detect the direction of air movement—*e.g.,* to catch aerial prey, detect predators, and navigate using prevailing winds. Tarsal slit sense organs are used by some species to detect substrate vibrations produced by prey, potential predators, and mates. These thin areas in the cuticle are deformed by mechanical energy transmitted up the leg from the substrate.

Chemoreceptors are located in the oral cavity (for taste) and the pectines. Receptors in the pectines are used by some species to locate some prey. Males use their pectines to detect pheromones produced by receptive females. Pectines are sexually dimorphic in that males have larger pectines with more and larger teeth.

Preoral digestion

Digestion by all arachnids, including scorpions, begins outside the mouth. The preoral cavity is supplied with digestive juices from the gut that semi-digest the food before it enters the mouth. Setae in the preoral cavity filter undigestible material such as prey exoskeleton. These particles are matted together and expelled. Food passes from the mouth to the pharynx to the esophagus to the midgut to the hindgut and is expelled through the anus. The muscular pharynx acts as a pumping organ drawing food into the body. Several pairs of cecal glands arise in the hepatopancreas and enter the midgut. These glands produce the amylases, proteases, and lipases used to digest food in the midgut and preoral cavity. Absorption occurs in the midgut and hindgut. The hepatopancreas is a large organ constituting about 20 percent of the total body mass, where food is stored as glycogen.

Scorpions are extremely efficient eating machines. They can increase their body weight by one-third when feeding. Metabolic rates and energy needs are low—10 times lower than that of insects. Further, they are extremely efficient at transferring energy from prey tissue to their own. The ability to consume large quantities of food at one time, high transfer efficiency, extremely low metabolic rates, and an efficient food-storage organ combine to allow scorpions to live without food for up to 12 months. It is possible that scorpions feed from only five to 50 times a year. The proportion observed feeding in nature is always low (2 to 7 percent).

Excretion and water balance are interlinked in all terrestrial arthropods, including scorpions. Nitrogenous wastes from protein metabolism are collected by two pairs of Malpighian tubules. They enter the gut at the hindgut–midgut connection. Excretory wastes are expelled through the anus with feces. The scorpion excretory system is one reason desert scorpions are so efficient at water conservation. Nitrogenous wastes (xanthine, guanine, and uric acid) are nearly insoluble to water. Feces are likewise extremely dry. Further, minimal water is lost through either the spiracles or waxed integument. Some scorpions live indefinitely without drinking water; sufficient water is normally contained in their food or is produced internally from food as water of metabolism.

Open circulatory system

The open circulatory system is typical of arthropods. The dorsal tubular heart runs the length of the mesosoma. A pacemaker contracts the heart rhythmically. Hemolymph (blood) flows via the anterior aorta to the prosoma and from the posterior aorta to the metasoma. The anterior aorta branches into the cephalic and cerebral arteries and to smaller arteries that carry blood to each limb and to the nerve cord. Arteries branch further and eventually empty into blood sinuses. Blood sinuses are extensive and bathe most tissues. Most gas and material exchange occurs there. Blood returns via sinuses and veins into a pericardial sac surrounding the heart, entering the heart through seven pairs of slitlike ostia. Blood is a colourless fluid containing proteins and salts. There are no blood cells.

Book lungs consist of a cavity and internal parallel leaves (lamellae) of thin cuticle across which gas exchange occurs. A sinus surrounds the book lungs, and blood is pumped in and out indirectly by the heart; the cardiac pulse is transmitted by ligaments attached to the sinus. Ventilation occurs passively when individuals move.

The paired gonads are a network of tubules that superficially appear similar in both sexes. Males possess seminal vesicles, and large paraxial organs produce the spermatophore. The spermatophore is produced in two parts that fuse during extrusion. Sperm enters the female's gonopore, and fertilization is internal. Eggs (from ovarian follicles within the ovariuterus) undergo two types of embryologic development. Apoikogenic scorpions have ova with various amounts of yolk; katoikogenic scorpions have smaller, yolkless ova. Both are viviparous but differ in the amount of nutrition derived directly from the mother. Apoikogenic embryos primarily use yolk and receive only some nourishment from the mother, possibly by diffusion across embryonic membranes. Katoikogenic embryos are nourished via a specialized oral feeding apparatus that develops early. They use their chelicerae to grip the nipple of a specialized, stalked diverticulum that branches from the mother's ovariuterus. This "teat" receives and transports nutrients from the hepatopancreas to the embryo, which uses its pharyngeal musculature to pump nutrients into its body.

Hazards to humans

Venoms. About 25 species in eight genera possess potent venoms capable of killing humans. With the exception of snakes and bees, scorpions cause more deaths than any other nonparasitic group of animals. More than 5,000 people are thought to die each year from scorpion stings. In Mexico alone, five species of *Centruroides* caused an average of 1,696 deaths per year during the 1950s.

Scorpions are major health hazards in parts of India (*Buthotus tamulus*), North Africa and the Middle East (*Androctonus, Buthus occitanus, Buthotus minax, Leiurus quinquestriatus*), South America and the West Indies (*Tityus, Rhopolarus*), and South Africa (*Parabuthus*). All these species are members of the family Buthidae. Buthids produce a complex neurotoxin that causes local and systemic effects. Severe convulsions, paralysis, and cardiac irregularities precede death. Death can be avoided if antivenoms are administered (now available against most lethal species).

The venoms of more than 1,200 other species are not deadly. These species produce hemotoxins that cause mild to strong local effects, including edema, discoloration, and pain. (The sting is often far less painful than that of a bee.) Victims fully recover in minutes or in a matter of days.

EVOLUTION AND PALEONTOLOGY

Scorpions first appeared in the Silurian Period (430,000,000 to 395,000,000 years ago). Some believe that they almost certainly evolved from the Eurypterida (water scorpions). Paleozoic scorpions and eurypterids share several features: external book gills, flaplike abdominal appendages, large compound eyes, and similar chewing structures on the coxae of the first legs.

Earliest scorpions

Like many of the modern crabs, early scorpions were marine or amphibious. The earliest scorpions not only apparently possessed gills but also had legs adapted to a benthic (bottom-dwelling) existence. The fact that many of the earliest scorpions were relatively large also strongly suggests that these species needed water for support. Finally, the earliest fossils are associated with marine organisms.

Marine and amphibious scorpions probably persisted well into the Carboniferous Period (345,000,000 to 280,000,000 years ago). The first decidedly terrestrial scorpions probably appeared during the Upper Devonian or Lower Carboniferous periods (350,000,000 to 325,000,000 years ago). The evolution of enclosed book lungs in place of external book gills was the major change associated with the transition from water to land. Although the arrangement of early scorpions into categories is uncertain, they radiated into several extinct families and superfamilies.

Several other terrestrial arthropods were on land before scorpions appeared. Fossils of other arachnids, myriapods, and possibly even insects occur in the Devonian Period (380,000,000 years ago). Thus, land was colonized repeatedly by arthropods, and scorpions were probably not the first arthropods to establish successfully.

The presence of these fossils along with differing interpretations of embryologic and morphological data have produced a controversy over the origin of the arachnids and the relationship of scorpions to other arachnids. One view considers that scorpions are a group in the phylum Arachnida and may even be the ancestor of other arachnids. The alternate view contends that scorpions are not arachnids at all but modern, terrestrial merostomes: the horseshoe crab *Limulus* is the closest living relative, and the Merostomata, including scorpions, are a group distinct from the arachnids. Whatever their exact taxonomic relationship, it is clear that scorpions form a distinct group consistently separated by taxonomists from other arachnids.

Except for changes in locomotion and respiration necessitated by the migration to land, the basic scorpion body plan is similar to that of scorpions that lived 430,000,000 years ago. The earliest scorpions possessed a segmented opisthosoma with the mesosoma and metasoma clearly differentiated, well-formed chelate pedipalps and chelicerae, eight walking legs, pectines, and a terminal stinger. This body plan was a particularly successful one; no great architectural revolution in external morphology accompanied the taxonomic diversification of scorpions, and there has not been extensive modification during radiation into different habitats. Although some species show ecomorphological adaptation to different substrates, similarities among scorpions far overshadow morphological differences. (G.A.Po.)

CLASSIFICATION

Distinguishing taxonomic features. Eight extant families and about two dozen subfamilies are identified by the structure of the sternum, gnathobase, legs, cheliceral dentation, venom gland, and number and distribution of lateral eyes and pedipalpal trichobothria. Embryologic patterns and the anatomy of the reproductive system are also important diagnostic traits.

Annotated classification.

ORDER SCORPIONES (or **SCORPIONIDA**; scorpions)
Chelicerate arachnids with single carapace over cephalothorax; pair of 3-jointed chelicerae; large chelate pedipalps; 4 pairs of walking legs; comblike pectines; 4 pairs of book lungs; tropics to warm temperate zone; about 1,200–1,300 species described.

Family Buthidae (buthids)
Oldest living family; in tropics to warm temperate zones; triangular sternum; often with spine under stinger; worldwide distribution; about 600 species, including those most dangerously venomous.

Family Scorpionidae (scorpionids)
Mostly in tropics and subtropics of Eastern Hemisphere; pentagonal sternum; single spur at base of tarsus; worldwide except North America; includes the largest scorpions (*Pandinus* and *Hadogenes*); about 175 species.

Family Diplocentridae (diplocentrids)
Warm regions of Middle East, Mexico, and the Antilles; pentagonal sternum, single tarsal spur, and tubercular spine under stinger; about 50 species.

Family Chactidae (chactids)
Tropical to warm temperate zones, mostly in South America; a few species in Australia, Mexico, and Mediterranean region; pentagonal sternum and 2 lateral eyes on each side; about 75 species.

Family Vaejovidae (vejovids)
Mostly in warm temperate region of western North and South America, Middle East to eastern Asia; sternum with nearly parallel sides; 3 lateral eyes; about 125 species.

Family Bothriuridae (bothriurids)
Tropical and subtropical South America; 1 Australian genus; broad, inconspicuous sternum consists of 2 narrow, transverse plates; 3 lateral eyes on each side; about 80 species.

Family Chaerilidae (chaerilids)
Pedipalpal femur with 9 trichobothria; gnathobases expanded to broad lobes anteriorly; female reproductive system including an ovariuterus, with yolk-rich ova developing in the lumen; moist habitats in the Malay Peninsula; 15 species.

Family Iuridae (iurids)
Pedipalpal femur with 3 trichobothria; female reproductive system including an ovariuterus, with yolk-poor ova developing in the lumen; arid regions of the Americas and the Aegean region of Europe; *Hadrurus* the largest in the United States; 20 species.

(W.J.G./G.A.Po.)

Acarids (mites and ticks)

Mites and ticks, close relatives of spiders, scorpions, and harvestmen, constitute the subclass Acari (Acarina, Acarida), which is part of the arthropod class Arachnida. The acarids may be separated into three orders, Opilioacariformes, Parasitiformes, and Acariformes, consisting of six suborders and about 428 families.

GENERAL FEATURES

Size range and diversity of structure. Some mites are 0.1 millimetre in length; the largest ticks are slightly more than 30 millimetres. Nymphs and adults generally have four pairs of legs, the larvae three. Members of some families have a dense covering of stiff hairs, or setae, while others are almost nude. Soft-bodied mites and ticks have only a few hardened plates, or shields; others that are strongly sclerotized have numerous hardened plates. Acarids range in shape from minute, soft-bodied, elongated or circular individuals to large, hard-bodied, spiderlike ones. Some are flattened; others assume grotesque body shapes as they become engorged with food or filled with eggs.

By courtesy of (B) G.W. Wharton, *Science*, 167: 1382 (1970); (C, bottom) from G.O. Evans, J.G. Sheals, and D. Macfarlane, *The Terrestrial Acari of the British Isles*, vol. 1, p. 139, figure 160, Trustees of the British Museum (Natural History); (others) E.W. Baker and G.W. Wharton, *An Introduction to Acarology*

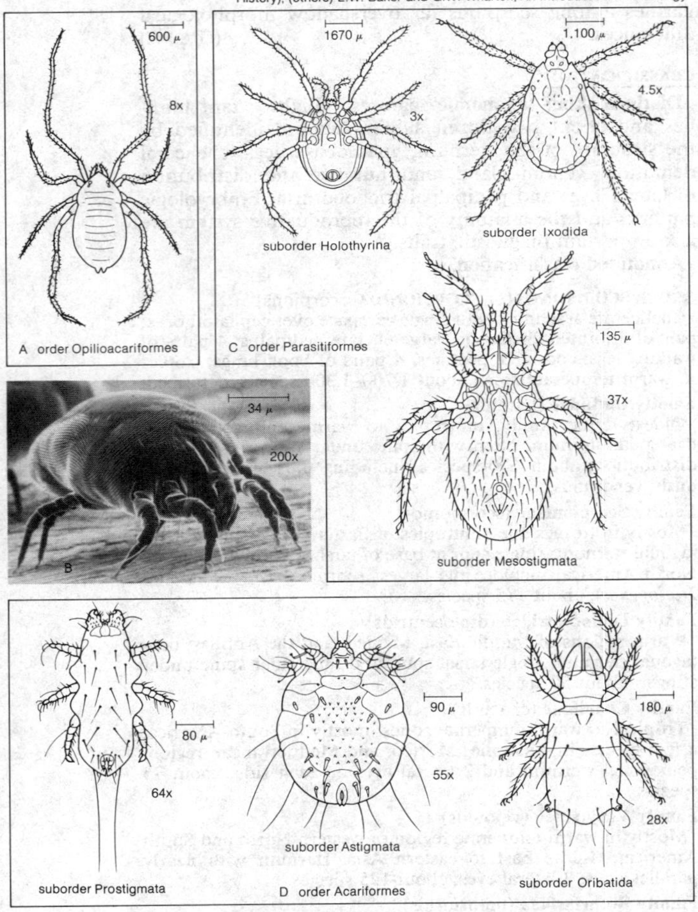

Figure 6: *Diversity of Acari.*
(A) *Opilioacarus segmentatus*, female, dorsal view.
(B) Protonymph of the North American house-dust mite (*Dermatophagoides farinae*). (C, left) *Holothyrus nitidissimus*, male, ventral view; (C, right) *Dermacentor variabilis*, female, dorsal view; (C, bottom) *Ornithonyssus bacoti*, female, ventral view. (D, left) *Myobia musculi*, female, dorsal view; (D, centre) *Sarcoptes scabiei*, female, dorsal view; (D, right) *Parhypochthonius aphidinus*, female, dorsal view.

Distribution and abundance. Mites and ticks are distributed throughout the world in almost every conceivable habitat and frequently occur in large numbers. They are recorded as high as 5,000 metres on the slopes of Mount Everest and as deep as 5,200 metres in the northern Pacific Ocean. More than 50 terrestrial species are known from the Antarctic. A few mites have been found drifting high in the atmosphere.

Acarids have been found in diverse habitats that include hot springs, caves, harsh deserts, and tundras. Although many of the approximately 35,000 species described are free-living, some are parasites of animals. The total number of species of mites and ticks has been estimated at more than 500,000.

Importance. The Acari are an economically important arachnid group; the ticks (suborder Ixodida), for example, surpass all other arthropods (except mosquitoes) in the number of diseases they transmit to humans. Many mites also are intermediate hosts of diseases transmissible to humans, domesticated animals, and crops. Others are pests as a result of their biting or feeding habits or the damage they cause to food and related products.

Carriers of disease

In the mite suborder Holothyrina (order Parasitiformes), one species of *Holothyrus* is known to secrete an irritant substance that is toxic to fowl and humans. The house-mouse mite (*Liponyssoides sanguineus*) transmits rickettsialpox to humans. Widespread species such as the tropical fowl mite (*Ornithonyssus bursa*), northern fowl mite (*O. sylviarum*), and chicken mite (*Dermanyssus gallinae*) also are pests of poultry and humans.

Eriophyid and tetranychid mites (Prostigmata), widespread plant-feeding species, frequently seriously injure or kill the host plant; the former are the only phytophagous Acari known to transmit plant viruses. The mange, itch, or scab mites (Astigmata) occur on many different animals including humans. House-dust allergy is caused by species of *Dermatophagoides,* a common arthropod.

The beetle mites (Oribatida), among the most numerous soil arthropods, are important in the development of soil fertility and also act as intermediate hosts for important tapeworm parasites of domestic animals.

Lyme disease of humans and some animals is caused by a spirochete transmitted by *Ixodes dammini* or related species. Rocky Mountain spotted fever, a rickettsial disease that occurs in the United States, is transmitted to humans by the bite of several species of hard ticks (Ixodidae), especially the Rocky Mountain wood tick (*Dermacentor andersoni*) and the American dog tick (*D. variabilis*). Relapsing fever, an important bacterial disease throughout the world, is transmitted to humans by certain species of soft ticks (Argasidae) of the genus *Ornithodoros.* Texas cattle fever is a widespread protozoan disease transmitted by cattle ticks (*Boophilus*); the disease, no longer prevalent in the United States because the tick has been eliminated, remains important in many tropical and subtropical countries. Various other diseases transmitted to animals by ticks include anaplasmosis, tularemia, Q fever, Colorado tick fever, hemorrhagic fever, and tick-borne encephalitis.

The chiggers (Prostigmata), important pests of humans, also transmit scrub typhus (tsutsugamushi disease), a rickettsial disease occurring in the Asiatic-Pacific region.

NATURAL HISTORY

Reproduction and life cycle. The sexes occur separately in acarids; *i.e.,* there are both males and females. Most species lay eggs (oviparity), but in some parasitic ones the eggs hatch within the female, and the young are born alive. Many species also can reproduce by parthenogenesis; *i.e.,* by the development of unfertilized eggs.

Fertilization

The actual process of sperm transfer occurs directly or in packets called spermatophores. The male spermatozoa may be introduced by the male copulatory structure (aedeagus) directly into the female genital opening or, as in some Astigmata, into a special female copulatory structure called a bursa copulatrix. The males of species that use the latter method may have special copulatory structures (*e.g.,* suckers, spurs, or enlarged legs) for grasping the female. Some males produce a sealed packet containing spermatozoa (spermatophore) that is transferred to the female genital opening, either directly by the mouthparts of the male or indirectly by deposition on a surface, after which the female places it in her genital opening. Eggs begin to develop after mating and fertilization; although only a few eggs develop simultaneously in many acarids, large numbers develop at the same time in ticks and some mites. Eggs are deposited haphazardly on food material by many plant- and grain-feeding species and are hidden in the soil by predatory soil-inhabiting species. One predatory mite, *Cheyletus eruditus,* broods her small cluster of eggs and drives other arthropods from them.

The primitive life cycle among species that lay eggs has four active immature stages—hexapod larva, protonymph, deutonymph, and tritonymph. There are many deviations from this primitive type of life cycle, which is found only in the Oribatida and some Prostigmata. The hexapod larva, characterized by three pairs of legs, is common to all families of acarids except Eriophyidae (Prostigmata), whose members have only two pairs of legs in all active stages. Among the Parasitiformes the Mesostigmata lack the tritonymphal stage; the Ixodida may have only one nymphal stage (Ixodidae) or as many as eight (Argasidae). Some Prostigmata (Podapolipidae) develop directly from egg to larviform adults; others have from one to three nymphal stages. Many Astigmata (order Acariformes) have a nonfeeding, or hypopal, stage between the protonymphal and tritonymphal stages; it frequently occurs during adverse environmental conditions.

Free-living acarids

Ecology. The free-living acarids include species from all of the suborders except Ixodida (ticks). The beetle mites (Oribatida), largely fungal feeders, are extremely numerous in the surface layers of soil; it is estimated that as many as 6,000,000 members of one species occur in an acre of pasture soil.

Some families of free-living mites have specialized stylet-like feeding organs (chelicerae), which can pierce plant cells and are used to suck out their contents; feeding by members of the family Eriophyidae (Prostigmata), for example, causes the formation of galls, dwarfing of shoots, and malformation of fruits and leaves. The family Tetranychidae (Prostigmata) contains the spider mites, which are foliage feeders; several species capable of producing silk spin a light web over plant leaves.

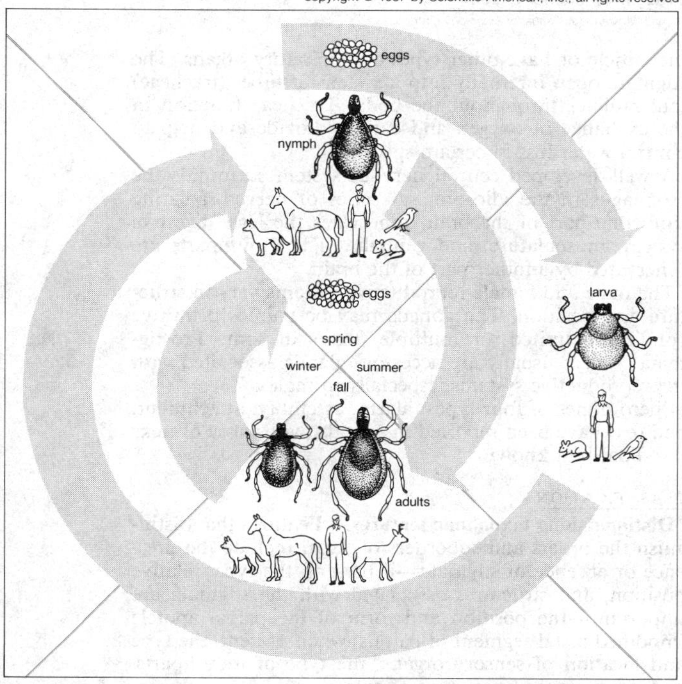

Figure 7: *Life cycle of a hard tick* (*Ixodes dammini*). The cycle requires two years for completion. Eggs are deposited in the spring and larvae emerge several weeks later and feed once during summer, usually on the blood of small mammals. Larvae molt the following spring into eight-legged nymphs and feed once during the summer on mammals before molting into adults in the fall. Adults attach to a host, where they mate; the male dies but the female continues to feed until she lays her eggs and dies. The cycle is then repeated.

The families Acaridae and Glycyphagidae (Astigmata), pests of stored grain and cereal products, have blunt, toothed chelicerae that enable them to scrape and gouge their food material; certain species of these two families frequently increase to tremendous numbers in foodstuffs, causing "grocers' itch" or "copra itch" in humans. A large group of free-living predatory mites lives in soil, humus, other organic matter, and water; these mites prey on small arthropods, their eggs, and other small invertebrates.

Many free-living mites utilize insects or other arthropods to disperse themselves; this nonparasitic association is known as phoresy. Adults of the genus *Dinogamasus* (Laelapidae), for example, live in a special mite pouch on an abdominal segment of certain carpenter bees.

Parasitic acarids

Parasitic species are known in all acarid groups except Opilioacariformes, Holothyrina, and Oribatida. The majority are external parasites, including those most important to humans and domesticated animals. A few species are internal parasites of animals. One ecological group contains families found only on the skin surface or feathers of the host. Psoroptidae (Astigmata), or scab mites, for example, attack the skin surface of mammals and feed on skin scales; the continuous abrasion of the skin causes a lesion over which a protective scab eventually forms. A second ecological group contains several families of mites that burrow into skin, hair follicles, or quills of the host and feed on fatty secretions, lymph material, or, occasionally, blood. The families Sarcoptidae (Astigmata) and Psorergatidae (Prostigmata), for example, contain species that burrow just beneath the skin of a mammalian host, causing mange or itch. A third ecological group contains species that pierce the skin and suck up tissue fluid or blood without actually invading the tissues. These species may spend either short or long intervals on the host.

The larvae of Trombiculidae (Prostigmata), the chiggers, parasitize many vertebrates and a few invertebrates, feeding on host tissues; chigger nymphs and adults, however, are free-living and predatory. Species of Dermanyssidae, Macronyssidae, and many Laelapidae (Mesostigmata) feed on blood or tissue secretions of mammals, birds, and reptiles. Some species, which spend much of their time off the host and in the nest, frequently are referred to as nest parasites, or nidicolous species. The protonymph of one species of Macronyssidae, found in the mouth of a long-nosed bat, causes destruction of tissues; and a species of Spinturnicidae (Mesostigmata) is found in the anal opening of certain species of cave-dwelling bats. Most members of the tick families Argasidae and Ixodidae (Ixodida) are obligate blood-sucking parasites of vertebrates; most Argasidae nymphs and adults feed on the host for only a few minutes, but Ixodidae in most stages in the life cycle remain attached to the host for several days.

A few families of mites are found in additional parasitic associations with vertebrates. Rhinonyssidae, Entonyssidae, and Halarchnidae (Mesostigmata), for example, are respiratory parasites of birds, snakes, and mammals, respectively. Several families of mites have established a parasitic relationship with invertebrates. Larvae of Trombidiidae and Erythraeidae (Prostigmata) and other families, for example, are parasitic on insects; in later stages the mites are free-living. In contrast, in the aquatic family Unionicolidae (Prostigmata), nymphs and adults parasitize mollusks and sponges, and larvae are free-living.

FORM AND FUNCTION

External features. The subclass Acari is distinguished by the lack of body segmentation (secondarily developed in a few families), a characteristic shared only with the spiders among the arachnids. An anterior region called the gnathosoma contains the mouth, specialized feeding appendages (chelicerae), and segmented structures called palps, or pedipalps. The mouth or buccal cavity joins the pharynx internally; paired salivary glands may discharge into the mouth or in front of its opening. The chelicerae

Major body regions

are basically three-segmented pincerlike appendages; as a result of the diverse feeding habits of some mites, however, chelicerae sometimes are modified as piercing organs or stylets. The pedipalps, which may be simple sensory structures or predatory organs modified for grasping or piercing, usually have five free segments—trochanter, femur, genu, tibia, tarsus; frequently there also is a clawlike apotele (modified sixth distal segment of appendage).

Behind the gnathosoma is a large region (idiosoma) that bears the legs, the genital and anal openings, and an assortment of tactile and sensory structures; respiratory pores (stigmata) and sclerotized shields of various shapes and sizes usually are present. The functions of the idiosoma parallel those of the abdomen, thorax, and portions of the head of insects. Although nymphs and adults commonly have four pairs of legs, some Prostigmata (Eriophyidae, Podapolipidae, Tenuipalpidae) and Astigmata (Evansacaridae, Teinocoptidae) have one to three pairs. Legs have the same basic segmentation as pedipalps plus a basal coxa; fusion or division of segments frequently occurs. The tarsus may be terminated either by several sensory hairs (setae) or by a clawlike or suckerlike apotele. The legs, which frequently bear ridges and spurs, always have tactile and sensory setae that follow a fixed pattern in position and number; the arrangement of leg setae is helpful in establishing systematic relationships. The first pair of legs usually functions in locomotion but sometimes is modified as a sensory or predatory structure.

The genital opening, usually located on the underside between the legs, frequently is protected by one or more shields or flaps and has two or three pairs of disks; in some Prostigmata (Cloacaridae, Demodicidae, Myobiidae, Ophioptidae, Podapolipidae), however, the male genitalia (aedeagus) is located on the dorsal side. The anal opening, also generally on the underside, is surrounded by a shield in the Mesostigmata and is always closed by a pair of valves; in some Prostigmata (Penthaleidae) and Astigmata (Chirorhynchobiidae, Knemidocoptidae) the anal opening is located on the dorsal side. As in all arthropods, the cuticle of acarids is secreted by an outer cell layer called the epidermis, which contains numerous pore canals. The cuticle of many acarids absorbs water from the air, enabling them to avoid desiccation.

Sensory receptors

There are many different types of sensory receptors, most of which are setal. The setae, of many shapes and sizes, may be hollow chemoreceptors or solid, tactile structures. Other specialized setae, known as trichobothria, pseudostigmatic organs, eupathidia, or famuli, occur only in the Acariformes. A sensory pit called Haller's organ contains sensory setae and is found on the tarsal segment of the first pair of legs of all ticks (Ixodida). One to three pairs of eyes are present on the anterior of the idiosoma in Opilioacariformes, a few Astigmata, and many Ixodida and Prostigmata. A single median eye also may be present in some Prostigmata.

Internal features. The digestive system consists of an anterior muscular pharynx, long narrow esophagus, ventriculus (stomach), short intestine, hindgut, and posterior rectal cavity. The ventriculus may have several paired gastric cecae (blind sacs), which function partly as food-storage organs and enable some acarids to go for long periods without feeding. One or two pairs of excretory organs (Malpighian tubules), which may open into the hindgut, absorb waste material from the body cavity and transform it into an organic compound called guanine, which passes into the hindgut, is mixed with other residues, and eventually is excreted from the anal orifice. Some Ixodida and Prostigmata have no connection between the ventriculus and hindgut, and the latter serves as an excretory organ.

The idiosomal body cavity contains various organ systems bathed in blood, or hemolymph. Circulation of blood carrying the products of digestion and excretion may be by the movement of muscles or by a heart, which is present in some suborders. The blood of some soft ticks (Argasidae) differs from that of other acarids biochemically, although similar morphologically.

One to four pairs of stigmata are present in the idiosomal region of all acarid orders except Astigmata and some Prostigmata and Oribatida, which respire through

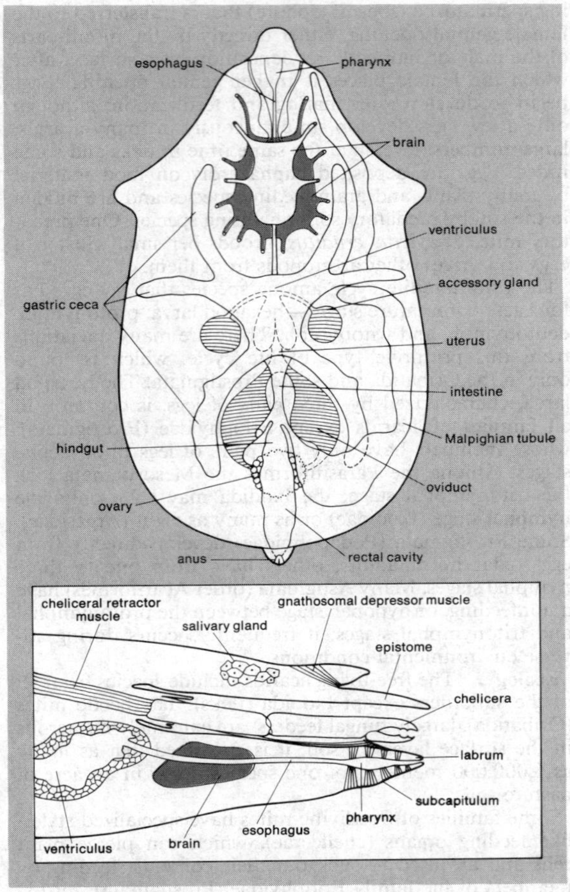

Figure 8: *Internal features of a mite.*
(Top) Dorsal internal aspect. (Bottom) Midsagittal section through the anterior region.
From G.W. Krantz, *A Manual of Acarology*, 2nd ed.

the cuticle or have other types of respiratory organs. The stigmata open internally into a system of tubes (tracheae) that radiates throughout the body. Tracheae function in the exchange of oxygen and carbon dioxide and help to control water loss in certain species.

A well-developed central nervous system surrounds the esophagus in the idiosoma. A series of nerves radiating from one part of the brain innervates the legs, digestive system, musculature, and genitalia. The mouthparts are innervated by another part of the brain.

The male and female reproductive systems vary in structure and position. The gonads may be paired (primitive condition), united, or multiple (testes in some Prostigmata). There usually are accessory glands associated with the reproductive systems, especially in males.

Pheromones of four types (alarm, assembly, attachment, and sex) have been reported in acarids, with those of ticks (Ixodida) best known.

CLASSIFICATION

Distinguishing taxonomic features. Features that distinguish the orders and suborders of Acari include the presence or absence of stigmata—if present, the type, relative position, and structures associated with the stigmata are important—the position and form of the palpal apotele (modified distal segment of palpus) when present, the type and location of sensory organs, the type of mouthparts, and the presence or absence of eyes.

Annotated classification. The ordinal classification presented here is after Donald E. Johnston in Sybil P. Parker (1982). The process of evolution in mites and ticks has resulted in a degree of specialization and morphological diversity not found in any other group of arachnids. Acarids, believed to be derived from two lines of descent, have a long, though meagre, fossil history dating from the Devonian Period (about 395,000,000 years ago).

SUBCLASS ACARI (ACARINA, ACARIDA; mites and ticks)
Arachnids usually without visible segmentation; mostly minute in size; larvae usually with 3 pairs of legs, adults usually with 4 pairs; diverse habitats include plants, soil, animals, stored foods, fresh and marine water; parasitic forms may transmit diseases; worldwide distribution; about 35,000 described species.

Order Opilioacariformes (mites)
Weakly sclerotized mites superficially resembling members of arachnid subclass Opiliones; 1–2.5 mm in size; body divided into hairy anterior portion bearing 2 or 3 pairs of simple eyes and nude posterior portion with over 200 pores, 4 pairs of stigmata, and 12 secondarily developed segments; terminal palpal apotele a pair of claws; rutellae (hypertrophied setae) present; all coxae of legs movable; first 2 pairs of legs with 6 segments, last 2 with divided trochanter, 7 segments; tritosternum paired base divided; terrestrial, under stones and other debris in semiarid habitats; recorded from southwestern United States, Puerto Rico, South America, Central Asia, Africa, and the Mediterranean region; carnivorous and possibly omnivorous; of no economic importance; 1 family and about 12 species.

Order Parasitiformes (mites and ticks)
Small to large in size; usually heavily sclerotized mites; 1 to 4 pairs of stigmata on posterior portion of body; peritremes, or grooves, present or absent; palpal apotele present or absent; tarsi of 1st pair of legs with sensory organs.

Suborder Mesostigmata
Generally with a number of sclerotized plates; 0.2–2 mm in size; eyes absent; pair of stigmata between coxae of 2nd, 3rd, or 4th pair of legs; usually associated with elongated peritremes; palpal apotele present; tritosternum usually well developed but reduced to absent in some parasitic families; majority free-living in soil or decaying organic matter; many parasites of vertebrates (except amphibians and fishes) and invertebrates; some economically important; cosmopolitan; about 76 families, and 5,050 species.

Suborder Holothyrina
Heavily sclerotized; 2–7 mm in size; eyes absent; pair of coxal glands opening at base of coxae of 1st pair of legs; pair of stigmata behind coxae of 3rd and 4th pair of legs, peritremes present; palpal apotele present; tritosternum absent; terrestrial, under stones and decaying vegetation; recorded from Indo-Pacific region, southeastern United States; carnivorous; of minor economic importance; 3 families and about 13 species.

Suborder Ixodida (ticks)
Largest Acari; adults 2–30 mm in size, eyes present or absent; pair of lateral stigmata enclosed in stigmatal plate (modified peritreme) anterior or behind coxae of 4th pair of legs; palpal apotele and tritosternum absent; sensory organ on tarsus of 1st pair of legs a pit (Haller's organ); mouthparts modified to form hypostome (holdfast organ) with teeth turned backward; active stages mostly external parasites (some nonfeeders), feeding primarily on blood of vertebrates (except fishes); many members economically important as disease carriers; cosmopolitan; 3 families and about 825 species.

Order Acariformes (mites)
Small to large in size; generally weakly sclerotized mites (except most Oribatida); palpal apotele and posterior body stigmata absent; anterior portion of body with or without sensory organs that are specialized setae.

Suborder Prostigmata
Most heterogeneous order includes chiggers; 0.1–16 mm in size; weakly sclerotized with few plates; eyes present or absent; stigmata, when present, at or between bases of chelicerae or on anterior portion of body; chelicerae styletlike, chelate (pincerlike), or reduced; diverse in habitat and habits—terrestrial, aquatic, marine, parasitic, predatory, phytophagous; many species economically important; cosmopolitan; about 135 families and 14,100 species.

Suborder Oribatida (oribatid or beetle mites)
Usually strongly sclerotized and slow moving, 0.2–1.5 mm in size; eyes and stigmata absent; pseudostigmata generally present, palps without claws, 3–5 segments; chelicerae usually chelate; rutella present; tarsi with 1–3 claws; ventrally with various shields; majority terrestrial in forest humus and soil, a few aquatic; feed on algae, fungi, or decaying material; of some economic importance; cosmopolitan; about 145 families and 8,500 species.

Suborder Astigmata
Homogeneous group includes mange, itch, or scab mites; weakly sclerotized and slow moving; 0.2–1.5 mm in size; eyes rarely present, stigmata absent; palps single segmented (sometimes with 2 false segments); chelicerae chelate; true claws absent; rodlike sensory setae on tarsus of 1st pair of legs; wide range of terrestrial habitats; parasitic, predatory, or feed on decaying material; some species economically important; cosmopolitan; about 65 families and 6,500 species.

Critical appraisal. Acarologists are not in total agreement as to the classification of mites and ticks. Much of the disagreement concerns the levels at which taxonomic divisions should be made and the use of ordinal names; consequently, seemingly different classifications are actually more alike than they may initially appear to be. Knowledge of Acari systematics is so incomplete that any classification proposed below the ordinal level is difficult and may quickly become obsolete.

Three major classifications, including that used above, have been proposed since 1978 for the mites and ticks. The suborders listed above are treated as orders in other classifications, with the choice of ordinal names differing in some cases. (N.A.W.)

Spiders

Spiders (order Araneida) are common terrestrial members of the invertebrate arthropod class Arachnida. They differ from the insects, another arthropod group, in having eight legs rather than six and in having the body divided into two parts rather than three. The use of silk is highly developed among spiders. About 34,000 species of spiders have been described; the world's spider fauna outside of northern Europe, Japan, and North America, however, has not been thoroughly collected and studied.

Spiders are predators, feeding almost entirely on other arthropods, especially insects. Many spiders that are active hunters and overpower their prey have a well-developed sense of touch or sight. Others construct silk snares, or webs, to capture prey, sometimes in larger numbers than can be consumed; webs, constructed instinctively, effectively trap flying insects. Many spiders are able to inject venom into their prey to kill it; others use silk to overpower prey.

GENERAL FEATURES

Size range. Spiders range in body length from 0.5 to about 90 millimetres (0.02–3.5 inches). The largest spiders, hairy mygalomorphs (tarantulas), are found in warm climates and are most abundant in the Americas; the largest, *Theraphosa leblondi,* is found in Guyana. The smallest spiders belong to several families found in the tropics, and information about them became known only in the 1980s.

Distribution. Spiders are found on all continents except Antarctica (though spider fragments have been reported there) and at elevations as high as 5,000 metres (16,400 feet) in the Himalayan ranges. Many more species occur in the tropics than in temperate regions. Though most spiders are terrestrial, one Eurasian species is aquatic and lives in slow-moving fresh water; a few species live along shores or on the surface of fresh water or saltwater.

Small spiders and the young of many larger species secrete long silk strands that catch the wind and can carry the spiders great distances. This ballooning behaviour occurs in many families and expedites distribution. Ballooning spiders drift through the air at heights that range from three metres or less to more than 800 metres.

Importance. Spiders are predators and because of their abundance are the most important predators of insects. The impact of spider predation is difficult to assess. One reason for this is that the web of a spider may catch many more insects than the spider can use as food. Spiders have been used to control insects in apple orchards in Israel and rice fields in China. Spiders also have been observed feeding on insects in South American rice fields and in fields of various North American crops. Modern pest management uses insecticides that do the least damage to natural predators of insect pests.

Pest control

Some spiders attract their insect prey by secreting substances that mimic the odour attractants (pheromones) of female insects. A male moth in search of a female, for example, is attracted to the spider and is caught by a sticky globule on a silk line thrown by the spider. If synthesized commercially, the odoriferous substances might have importance in pest control.

Spiders harmful to humans

A few spiders are toxic to humans. The venom of the black widow spider and others of the *Latrodectus* genus acts as a painful nerve poison. The bite of the brown recluse and others of the *Loxosceles* genus may cause localized tissue death. Other venomous spiders include the mygalomorph funnel weaver (*Atrax*) of southeastern Australia and some members of the family Theraphosidae (tarantulas) of Africa and South America. In North America *Cheiracanthium mildei,* a small, pale, clubionid spider introduced from the Mediterranean, enters houses in late fall and is responsible for some bites; rarely, the site of the bite becomes necrotic. Some American theraphosids, or tarantulas, throw off abdominal hairs as a defense against predators. The hairs have tiny barbs that penetrate skin and mucous membranes and may cause temporary itching and allergic reactions.

NATURAL HISTORY

Reproduction and life cycle. *Courtship.* In male spiders the second pair of appendages (pedipalps) is modified to form a complex structure for holding sperm; the enlarged tips of the pedipalps form copulatory organs. When the time for mating approaches, the male constructs a special web, called the sperm web. The silk comes from silk glands and emerges from the spinnerets; epigastric silk glands also supply silk, which emerges from spigots in the epigastric area (between the book lungs). A drop of fluid containing sperm is deposited onto the sperm web through an opening (the gonopore) located on the underside of the abdomen. The male draws the sperm into his pedipalps; the process of charging the pedipalps, known as sperm induction, may require minutes or hours for completion. Sperm induction may occur before a male seeks a mate or after the mate is found; if more than one mating occurs, the male charges his pedipalps between copulations.

Charging the pedipalps

The way in which a male finds a female varies among species. The males of many species wander more extensively than the females, and males of the relatively sedentary web weavers generally have longer legs than females. The wandering males of some species follow silk threads; some may recognize both the threads produced by a female of his own species and the female's condition—*i.e.,* whether she is mature and receptive. Pheromones are involved. Other species (*e.g.,* jumping spiders) also use visual senses to recognize mates.

Males in a few species locate a female and then unceremoniously run to her and mate. In most species, however, elaborate courtship patterns have evolved, probably to protect the male from being mistaken for prey. The male web spider courts by rhythmically plucking the threads of a web; after the female approaches, he pats and strokes her before mating. When male wolf spiders or jumping spiders see a female, they wave the pedipalps, conveying a visual message characteristic of the species; an appropriate response from a female encourages the approach of the male. Some male wolf spiders tap dry leaves, perhaps to attract a female; an aggregation of tapping males produces sound that can be heard some distance away. A crab spider male quickly and expertly wraps his intended mate with silk. Although the female is able to escape, she does not do so until mating is completed. After the male of the European nursery web spider locates a suitable mate, he captures a fly, wraps it in silk, and presents it to the female; while the female is occupied with eating the fly, the male mates with her. If no fly is available, the male may wrap a pebble. Some male spiders use specialized jaws or legs to immobilize the jaws of the female during mating.

Mating. After a male has successfully approached a female and mounted her, in most groups he inserts his left pedipalp into the left opening of her genital structure and the right pedipalp into her right opening.

The female genital structure, or epigynum (epigyne), is a hardened plate on the underside of the abdomen anterior to the gonopore. After the sperm are transferred into the epigynum, they move into receptacles (spermathecae) that connect to the oviducts; eggs are fertilized as they pass through the oviducts and out through the gonopore. In some primitive spiders (*e.g.,* haplogynes, mygalomorphs) and some Tetragnathidae lacking an epigynum, the male inserts both pedipalps simultaneously into the female's genital slit, the left pedipalp on her right side and the right pedipalp on her left side.

Fertilization

The force that causes the injection of sperm from the pedipalp of the male into the receptacle of the female has not been established with certainty but may involve blood pressure. Increases in blood pressure expand a soft vascular tissue (hematodocha) between the hard plates of pedipalps, causing a bulbous structure containing a duct to twist and to hook into the epigynum of the female.

Mating may require seconds in some species, hours in others. Some males recharge their pedipalps and mate again with the same female. After mating, the males of some species smear secretion over the epigynum; called an epigynal plug, the secretion prevents the female from mating a second time. Male spiders usually die soon after, or even during, the mating process. The female of one European orb weaver species bites into the abdomen of the male and holds on during mating. Although some females eat the male after mating, the practice is not common. The male of the black widow, *Latrodectus mactans,* for example, usually dies days after mating; occasionally he is so weak after mating that he is captured and eaten by the female.

Epigynal plug

Females of some species mate only once; others accept several males, one after another. The long-lived females of mygalomorph spiders must mate repeatedly because they shed their skins once or twice a year, including the lining of the sperm receptacles.

Eggs and egg sacs. Female spiders produce either one egg sac containing several to a thousand eggs or several egg sacs with successively fewer eggs. Females of some species die after producing the last egg sac or after the young have been taken care of; these females live one or, at most, two years. On the other hand, the females of the mygalomorph spiders may live up to 25 years, and those of the primitive haplogyne spiders, 10.

National Audubon Society Collection/Photo Researchers, (top) Robert C. Hermes, (bottom) Cesco Clapanna

Figure 9: *Eggs of spiders are enclosed in silk sacs.* (Top) Female wolf spider with her portable egg sac attached to spinnerets; (bottom) cave orb weaver (*Meta menardii*) with egg sac suspended from ceiling.

The protective egg sac surrounding the eggs of most spiders is made of silk. Although a few spiders tie their eggs together with several strands of silk, most construct elaborate sacs of numerous layers of thick silk; the colour of the silk may vary. Eggs, which often have the appearance of a drop of fluid, first are deposited on silk and then wrapped in silk and covered, so that the finished egg sac is spherical or disk-shaped. The females of many species place the egg sac on a stalk, attach it to a stone, or cover it with smooth silk before abandoning it. Other females guard the egg sac or carry it either in their jaws or attached to the spinnerets. If a female loses an egg sac, she makes searching movements and may pick up a pebble or a piece of paper and attach it to the spinnerets. The European cobweb spider, *Achaearanea saxatile,* lowers its egg sac from a protective thimble-shaped structure or pulls it inside, depending on the temperature. Female wolf spiders carry their egg sacs attached to the spinnerets and instinctively bite the egg sac to permit the young to emerge after a certain length of time has elapsed.

Fate of the egg sac

Maturation. After hatching, young wolf spiderlings, usually numbering from 20 to 100, climb onto the back of their mother and remain there about 10 days before dispersing. If they fall off, they climb back up again, seeking contact with bristlelike structures (setae) or something similar in texture. Some female spiders feed their young; the female of one European species dies at the time the young are ready to feed, and they eat her carcass. When food has been sufficiently liquefied by females of other species (in spiders, digestion occurs outside the mouth), the young also feed on their mother's prey. The mother of one web spider species plucks threads of the web to call her young, both to food sources and to warn them of danger. The young of many species are independent when they emerge from the egg sac.

Molting

Young spiderlings, except for size and undeveloped reproductive organs, resemble adults. They shed their skins (molt) as they increase in size. The number of molts varies among species, within a species, and also among related young of the same sex. Males have fewer molts than females and mature earlier; females may molt six to 12 times, males two to eight. Males of some species may emerge mature from the egg sac, one or two molts having occurred before emergence. Some spiders mature a few weeks after hatching, but many overwinter in an immature stage. Mygalomorph spiders require three to four years (some authorities claim nine years) to become sexually mature in warm climates.

Before molting, many spiderlings hang by the claws in some inconspicuous place; mygalomorph spiders turn on their side or back. The carapace surrounding the cephalothorax breaks below the eyes or the opposite end, and the spider laboriously extracts its legs from their casings as the old abdominal cuticle (skin) shrinks. The cast-off cuticle, or exuviae, remains hanging, and the newly emerged spider dangles on a thread, helplessly soft. Molting is hazardous for spiderlings: they may dry out before emerging from the old cuticle or fall victim to a predator while defenseless. Even a small injury during a molting period usually is fatal. Emergence from the exuviae is accompanied by wide fluctuations of blood pressure; these raise and lower the setae and gradually force the legs free. The first break around the carapace edge also is caused by increased blood pressure. Growth and molting are believed to be under the control of hormones; some spiderlings fail to molt, others undergo delayed molts, perhaps because of faulty hormone balance, and may die. Many spiderlings eventually disperse by ballooning, usually in the fall.

Feeding behaviour. *Stalking prey.* Most hunting spiders locate prey by searching randomly or by responding to vibrations; wolf spiders and jumping spiders have keen eyesight. The latter stalk their prey within five to 10 centimetres (two to four inches), then pounce when it moves. Many crab spiders wait for prey on flowers similar in colour to their own; they use their legs to grasp an unsuspecting insect and then give it a lethal bite.

Spitting spiders

Unique among the hunters are the spitting spiders (family Scytodidae). When these spiders encounter an insect, they touch it, back off, and shoot a zigzag stream of sticky material over it. The sticky material, produced by modified venom glands in the cephalothorax, emerges from pores near the tips of the fangs, which are located on the chelicerae; as the victim struggles, the spider approaches cautiously and bites the entangled insect.

Trapping prey. Spiders that use silk to capture prey utilize various techniques. Ground-dwelling trap-door spiders construct silk-lined tubes, sometimes with silk trapdoors, from which they dart out to capture passing insects. Other tube-dwelling spiders place silk trip threads around the mouth of the tube and trip insects; vibrations of the threads inform the spider of a victim's presence. Funnel-weaving spiders live in silk tubes with a narrow end that extends into vegetation or into a crevice and an expanded sheetlike end that vibrates when an insect walks across it. Many web spiders construct silk sheets in vegetation, sometimes one above the other, and often add anchor threads, which trip unsuspecting insects. The irregular three-dimensional web of cobweb spiders (Theridiidae) has anchoring threads of sticky silk. An insect caught in the web or touching an anchor line becomes entangled, increasingly so if it struggles; if a thread breaks, the force of elasticity in it pulls the insect toward the centre of the web.

Web construction

The most elaborate webs (orb webs), which are conspicuous on mornings with dew, are constructed by several spider families, suggesting that they are efficient traps, covering the largest area with the least possible silk. The web acts as an air filter, trapping weak-flying insects that cannot see the fine silk. The orb web is usually rebuilt every day. The web may be up only during the day or only at night. A web is damaged during capture of prey, and most spiders construct new web-parts frequently. The ways by which spiders keep from becoming entangled in

National Audubon Society Collection/Photo Researchers, (left) Lynwood M. Chace, (right) Richard B. Hoit

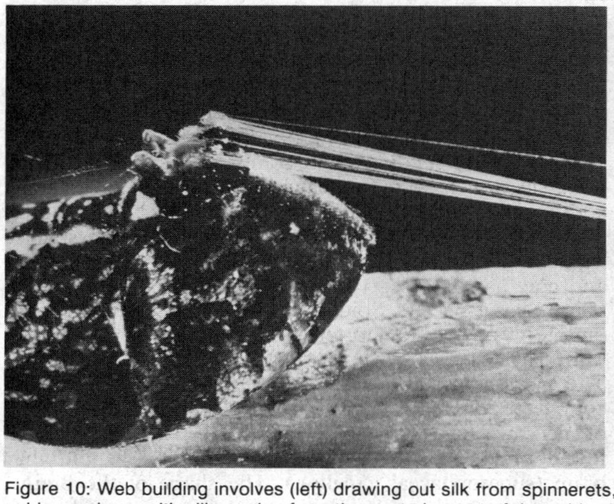

Figure 10: Web building involves (left) drawing out silk from spinnerets, as is shown for the golden argiope, with silk coming from the posterior part of the spider (the animal is on its back) and (right) weaving strands into geometric traps like the orb of the silver argiope spider.

their own webs are not completely understood nor is their mechanism for cutting the extremely elastic silk threads used in web construction.

To begin orb web construction the spider releases a silk thread that is carried by wind. If the free end does not become attached to an object, the spider may pull it back and feed on it; if it becomes firmly attached—for example, to a twig—the spider secures the thread and crosses the newly formed bridge, reinforcing it with additional threads. The spider then descends from the centre of the bridge, securing a thread on the ground or on a twig. The centre, or hub, of the web is established when the spider returns to the bridge with a thread, carrying it part way across the bridge before securing it; this thread is the first radius, or spoke. After all of the spokes are in place, the spider returns to the hub and constructs a few temporary spirals of dry silk toward the outside of the web. The spider then reverses direction, deposits ensnaring silk, and removes the spiral. The ensnaring threads form a dense spiral. Some species attach a signal thread from the hub to a retreat in a leaf so that they are informed (by vibrations) of trapped insects; others remain head down in the centre of the web, locating prey by sensing tensions or vibrations in individual spokes. To build radii and orb takes only about an hour. Webs of the family Uloboridae have a woolly (cribellate) ensnaring silk; those of the families Araneidae and Tetragnathidae have spirals constructed of a sticky material that dries after several days and must be rebuilt.

Wrapping the prey

Spiders usually cover a captured insect in silk and turn it efficiently, as on a spit, before biting it and carrying it either to a retreat or to the hub of the web for feeding or storage. Although the scales on butterfly and moth wings facilitate their escape from the web, spiders have evolved a counterstrategy: they bite the moths before wrapping them, rather than afterward.

The webs of uloborid spiders of the genus *Hyptiotes* consist of only three sections of the orb web. The spider, attached by a thread to vegetation, holds one thread from the tip of the hub until an insect brushes the web; then the spider alternately relaxes and tightens the thread, and the struggling victim becomes completely entangled. Tiny theridiosomatid spiders also control web tension. Ogre-faced spiders of the family Deinopidae build small flat webs during the evening hours and then cut the attachments and spread the web among their four long anterior legs. During the night the web is thrown over a passing insect. The spider abandons or eats the web in the morning and passes the day resting on a branch before constructing a new web. The bolas spider, *Mastophora,* releases a single thread with a sticky droplet at the end (bolas) and holds it with one leg; some species swing the bolas, and others throw it when a moth approaches. Only male moths are attracted to the spider by emanations of odours that mimic those of female moths. Many other examples of web specializations have been described.

Communal spiders

Some tropical species of spiders are social and live in large communal webs containing hundreds of individuals, most of them female. They cooperate to build and repair the web. A pack of spiders overpowers and kills insects that have been caught in the communal web. Feeding is communal.

FORM AND FUNCTION

External features. The bodies of spiders, like those of other arachnids, are divided into two parts, the cephalothorax (prosoma) and the abdomen (opisthosoma). The legs are attached to the cephalothorax, which contains the stomach and brain. The top of the cephalothorax is covered by a protective structure, the carapace; the underside is covered by a structure called the sternum, which has an anterior projection, the labium. The abdomen contains the gut, the heart, the reproductive organs, and the silk glands. Spiders (except the primitive suborder Mesothelae) differ from other arachnids in lacking external segmentation of the abdomen and in having the abdomen attached to the cephalothorax by a narrow stalk, the pedicel. The gut, the nerve cord, the blood vessels, and sometimes the respiratory tubules (tracheae) pass through the narrow pedicel,

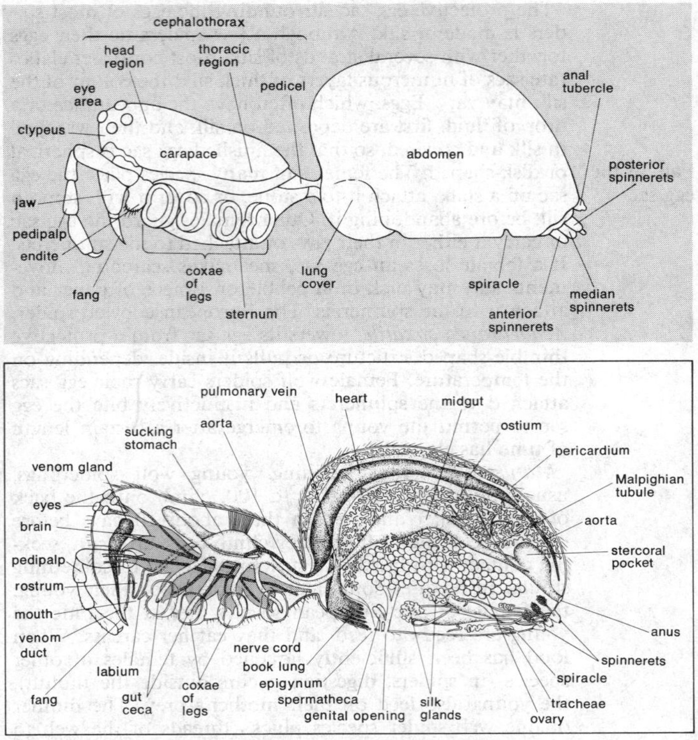

Figure 11: (Top) External and (bottom) internal organization of a spider.

(Top) After P.A. Meglitsch, *Invertebrate Zoology*, copyright © 1967 by Oxford University Press, Inc., reprinted by permission; (bottom) from *General Zoology* by T.I. Storer and R.L. Usinger, copyright © 1957 by the McGraw-Hill Book Company, Inc., used with the permission of McGraw-Hill Book Company

which allows the body movements necessary for efficient use of the spinnerets during web construction. Among arachnids other than spiders, the tailless whip scorpions (order Amblypygi) have a pedicel but lack spinnerets. Spiders, like other arthropods, have an outer skeleton; inside the cephalothorax is the endosternite, to which some jaw and leg muscles are attached.

Spiders have six pairs of appendages. The first pair, the jaws, or chelicerae, have a fang containing the opening of a poison gland near the tip. The chelicerae move forward and down in the orthognathans (mygalomorph spiders), sideways and together in the labidognathans (araneomorph spiders). The venom ducts pass through the chelicerae, which sometimes also contain the venom glands. The second pair of appendages, the pedipalps, are modified in the males of all adult spiders to carry sperm (see above *Reproduction and life cycle*). In females and immature males, however, the leglike pedipalps are used to handle food and also function as sense organs. The pedipalpal proximal segment (coxa) attached to the cephalothorax usually is modified to form a structure (endite) that is used in feeding.

The pedipalps are followed by four pairs of walking legs. Each leg consists of eight segments—the coxa, attached to the cephalothorax; a small trochanter; a long, strong femur; a short patella; a long tibia; a metatarsus; a tarsus, which may be subdivided in some species; and a small pretarsus, which bears two claws in running spiders and an additional median claw in web-building ones. The young of two-clawed running spiders often have three claws. The legs, covered by setae, contain several types of sense organs and may have accessory claws. A few species use the first pair of legs as feelers. Spiders can amputate their own legs (autotomy); new but shorter legs appear at the next molt.

Internal features. *Nervous system and sense organs.* The nervous system, unlike that of other arachnids, is completely concentrated in the cephalothorax. The masses of nervous tissue (ganglia) are fused with a ganglion found under the esophagus and below and behind the brain (subesophageal ganglion). The shape of the brain, or epipharyngeal ganglion, somewhat reflects the habits of the spider; *i.e.,* in the web weavers, which are sensitive to touch, the posterior part of the brain is larger than in spiders that hunt with vision.

Eyes

The simple eyes of spiders, which number eight or less, consist of two groups, the main or direct eyes (called the anterior medians) and the secondary eyes, which include anterior laterals, posterior laterals, and posterior medians. The rhabdoms, which receive light rays, face the lenses in the main eyes; in the other eyes the rhabdoms turn inward. Both the structure of the secondary eyes and eye arrangement are characteristic for each family.

Other sense organs are long fine hairs (trichobothria) on the legs, which are sensitive to air currents and vibrations. Slit sense organs are minute slits, or several parallel slits, located either near the leg articulations (or hinges) or scattered over the body. The slit is closed toward the outside by a thin membrane and on the other side by a delicate membrane that may be penetrated by a nerve. Slit sense organs are sensitive to stresses on the cuticle; others act as vibration receptors or hearing organs. Internal receptors (proprioceptors) provide information about body movement and position. Olfactory organs of spiders are specialized hollow hairs found at the tips of pedipalps and legs.

Digestion and excretion. The mouth leads into a narrow passage, the pharynx, which leads to a stomach. The midgut has a variable number (usually four pairs) of blind extensions, or ceca, that extend into the coxae. Additional ceca and a branched digestive gland are located at the front of the abdomen. At the end of the gut a cecum (stercoral pocket, or cloaca) connects with the hindgut before opening through the anus.

Ceca

Food is digested outside the mouth (preorally). Some spiders chew their prey as they cover it with enzymes secreted by the digestive tract; others bite the prey and pump digestive enzymes into it before sucking up the nutrient liquid.

The excretory system includes large cells in the prosoma that concentrate nitrogen-containing wastes (nephrocytes); a pigment-storing layer (hypodermis); the ends of the abdominal gut ceca, which are filled with a white excretory pigment (guanine); coxal glands; and tubular glands (Malpighian tubules) in the abdomen. The excretory compounds include various nitrogen-containing compounds—*e.g.,* guanine, adenine, hypoxanthine, and uric acid. Silk may have evolved from an excretory product.

Respiration. The respiratory system, located in the abdomen, consists of book lungs and tracheae. Book lungs are paired respiratory organs composed of 10 to 80 hollow leaves that hang into a blood sinus, are separated by small hardened columns, and open into chambers (atria), which open to the outside through one or several slits (spiracles). Book lungs frequently transform into tracheae, which are tubes that conduct air to various tissues. The two respiratory organs at the very front end of the abdomen usually are book lungs; the posterior two are tracheae; in some groups, however, both pairs are book lungs (orthognathans—mygalomorph spiders) or tracheae (some minute araneomorph spiders). Because book lung covers, which are hardened plates, may be present in species in which the book lungs have transformed into tracheae, it is impossible to determine from surface structure whether a spider has lungs, tracheae, or both.

Circulation. The circulatory system is best developed in spiders with book lungs and is least developed in spiders with bundles of tracheae going to various parts of the body. The abdomen of all spiders contains a tube-shaped heart, which usually has a variable number of openings (ostia) along its sides and one artery to carry blood forward and one to carry it backward when the heart contracts. The ostia close during contraction. The forward-flowing artery, which goes into the cephalothorax, is branched in spiders with book lungs; the blood eventually empties into spaces, flows into the lung sinus, and travels into a cavity (pericardial cavity) from which it enters the heart through ostia. The blood, or hemolymph, contains various kinds of blood cells and a respiratory pigment, hemocyanin. Changes in blood pressure function to extend the legs and break the skin at molting time.

Heart

Reproductive system. The sex organs (gonads) of male and female spiders are in the abdomen. The eggs are fertilized as they pass through the oviduct to the outside from sperm stored in the seminal receptacles after mating. The fertilized egg (zygote) develops in the manner typical of arthropod eggs rich in yolk.

Specialized features. *Venom.* Venom glands, present in most spiders but absent in the family Uloboridae, are located either in the chelicerae or under the carapace; venom ducts cross the chelicerae and open near the tips of their fangs. A muscle layer covers the venom glands in *Latrodectus.* Venom glands probably originated as accessory digestive glands whose secretions aided in the external digestion of prey. Although the secretions of some spiders may consist entirely of digestive enzymes, those of many species effectively subdue prey, and venoms of a few species are effective against predators, including vertebrates. The spitting spiders (*Scytodes,* Scytodidae) secrete a sticky substance that glues potential prey to a surface. The high and domed carapace of the spitting spiders is modified as a result of the large glands it contains.

Characteristics of the venom of widow spiders, especially the black widow, have been determined. The various protein components of the venom affect specific organisms; *i.e.,* different components affect mammals and insects. Widows exhibit a warning coloration in the red hourglass-shaped mark on the underside of the abdomen and often have a red stripe; because the spider hangs upside down in its web, the hourglass mark is turned conspicuously upward. The venom, a nerve toxin, causes severe pain in humans, especially in the abdominal region, but is usually not fatal. There are widow spiders in most parts of the world, except central Europe and northern Eurasia. Some areas have several species. Although all appear superficially similar, each species has its own habits.

Spider bites

In southeastern Australia the funnel weaver, *Atrax* (family Hexathelidae), a mygalomorph spider, is considered dangerous to humans. There are also venomous theraphosid spiders (tarantulas) in Africa and South America.

The bite of the brown recluse (*Loxosceles reclusa*) results in a localized region of dead tissue (necrotic lesion) that heals slowly; the larger *Loxosceles laeta* of South America causes a more severe lesion in humans. The bites of several other species belonging to different families may occasionally cause necrotic lesions; *e.g., Lycosa raptoria, Mastophora, Phidippus formosus, P. sicarius, Cheiracanthium mildei,* and other species of *Cheiracanthium.* Knowledge of the effects of spider bites on humans is limited because the bite is not noticed at the time it occurs or because the spider is never identified.

Silk. Although silk is produced by some insects, centipedes, and millipedes, and a similar substance is produced by mites, pseudoscorpions, and some crustaceans (ostracods and amphipods), only the spiders are true silk specialists. Spider silks that have been studied are proteins called fibroin, which has chemical characteristics similar to those of insect silk. The silk is produced by more than seven different types of glands in the abdomen. Ducts from the glands traverse structures called spinnerets, which open to the outside through spigots. Abdominal pressure forces the silk to flow outward; the rate of flow is controlled by muscular valves in the ducts. The primitive Mesothelae have only two types of silk glands, but orb weavers have at least seven, each of which produces a different kind of silk; *e.g.,* aciniform glands produce silk for wrapping prey, ampullate glands produce the draglines and frame threads, and cylindrical glands produce parts of the egg sac. Epigastric silk glands of male spiders produce silk that emerges through spigots in the abdomen between the book lung covers; silk from these glands provides a surface for the sperm drop in sperm induction.

Silk glands

Threads of *Nephila* silk have a high tensile strength and great elasticity. Silk probably changes to a solid in the spigot, or as a result of tension forces. Strands usually are flat or cylindrical as they emerge and are of surprisingly uniform diameter. The glob of silk that binds or anchors strands emerges from the spigot as a liquid.

The movable spinnerets, which consist of telescoping articles, are modified appendages; two pairs are from the 10th body segment, two pairs from the 11th. *Liphistius,* of the suborder Mesothelae, is the only spider with a full complement of four pairs of spinnerets in the adult. Most spiders have three pairs; usually the anterior median pair is lost or reduced either to a nonfunctional cone, called the colulus, or to a flat plate, the cribellum, through which open thousands of minute spigots. Spiders with a cribellum also have a comb, the calamistrum, on the metatarsus of the fourth leg. The calamistrum combs the silk that flows from the cribellum, producing a characteristically woolly (cribellate) silk.

CLASSIFICATION

Distinguishing taxonomic features. The Araneida are separated into three suborders—Mesothelae, Orthognatha (mygalomorph spiders), and Labidognatha (araneomorph spiders)—on the basis of the type of movement of the two jaws; *i.e.,* movement forward and down is orthognath (paraxial), movement sideways and together is labidognath (diaxial). Other features that distinguish suborders include the structure of the male pedipalps, presence or absence of an epigynum in the female, presence and number of book lungs, number of small openings (ostia) in the heart, and extent of fusion of nerve ganglia in the prosoma. Families are distinguished on the basis of such characteristics as number and spacing of simple eyes, number of tarsal claws, number of spinnerets, habits, structure of chelicerae, and specialized (apomorph) characters such as glands, setae, and teeth and peculiarities of the external genitalia. Species and also genera of areneomorph spiders are usually separated by specializations in their external genitalic morphology, that of the female epigynum and male pedipalp.

Annotated classification. Of the numerous classification schemes published in the 1930s, most of them in response to one of Alexander Petrunkevitch, none is acceptable and up-to-date. All classifications have relied heavily on the work of Eugène Simon, who published in France in the late 19th century. Although newer tools, such as scanning electron microscopy, molecular methods, and cladistics, remain little tried for spiders, they have changed traditional classification schemes. In addition, many new spiders have been found in the Southern Hemisphere that do not readily fit into established families, prompting the proposal of new ones, but without the overall view for a new system. Less than 30 percent of the large neotropical spiders are known (and probably less of the small neotropical spiders), while in north and central Europe, northern North America, Korea, and Japan 80 percent or more of the species are known. The known species are placed into about 90 families, only the most important of which are discussed below.

ORDER ARANEIDA (or **ARANEAE**; spiders)
Members of the class Arachnida; unsegmented abdomen (opisthosoma) attached to cephalothorax (prosoma) by pedicel; prosoma with poison glands whose ducts open through large chelicerae with a movable fang, no pincers; leglike pedipalps usually with modifications (endites) on coxae to aid in feeding, modified as copulatory organs in males; abdomen usually with 2 pairs of respiratory organs, anterior book lungs and posterior tracheae; spinnerets at posterior end of abdomen; 4 pairs of walking legs; 1 or 2 pairs of coxal glands; about 34,000 species described; worldwide distribution.

Suborder Mesothelae
Abdomen clearly segmented dorsally from 7th segment (pedicel) to 18th; 8 spinnerets at middle of abdomen; chelicerae orthognath (paraxial), attached in front of carapace; pedipalpal coxae without endites; male pedipalps relatively complicated; epigynum absent in females; 18 ganglia in prosoma more distinctly separated than those in other suborders; heart with 5 pairs of ostia in segments 8 to 13; 2 pairs of book lungs; a few species from Japan to Southeast Asia; inhabit trapdoor tubes in ground; family Liphistiidae.

Suborder Orthognatha (mygalomorph spiders)
Chelicerae orthognath (paraxial), attached in front of carapace; pedipalpal coxae without endites (except in Atypidae); 2 pairs of book lungs; heart with 4, rarely 3, ostia; bulb of male pedipalps simple; female without epigynum; 13th through 18th ganglia lost, others fused; most species large and long-lived in warm climates; about 2,000 to 3,000 species.

Family Ctenizidae (ctenizid trap-door spiders). Chelicerae with structure (rake or rastellum) used to dig; 3 tarsal claws; labium and sternum separate; eyes closely grouped; most species at least 3 cm or more in length; inhabit silk-lined tubes in ground, with entrances covered by hinged silk lids.

Family Dipluridae (diplurid funnel-web mygalomorphs). No cheliceral rastellum; 3 tarsal claws; 4 to 6 spinnerets, posterior (lateral) pair very long; body hairy; web similar to funnel webs of Agelenidae.

Family Hexathelidae. Arched, glabrous carapace differentiates it from Dipluridae. *Atrax* found in southeastern Australia is venomous.

Family Atypidae (purseweb spiders). No cheliceral rake; 3 tarsal claws; pedipalpal coxae with endites; 6 spinnerets; less than 3 cm long; live in closed silk tubes partly below ground; bite prey through tube and pull it in; found in Europe, North America, Japan, Burma, and Java.

Family Theraphosidae (hairy mygalomorphs, "tarantulas" of North America; monkey spiders of South Africa; bird-eating spiders of Australia). No cheliceral rake; 2 tarsal claws; labium not fused to sternum; large, hairy, nonsocial, nocturnal; some burrow, others inhabit trees; mostly tropical; *Aphonopelma hentzi* in south-central United States; *Theraphosa* of Amazon River Basin up to 9 cm long with 28 cm leg spread; about 800 species.

Suborder Labidognatha (araneomorph spiders)
Chelicerae labidognath (diaxial), attached below carapace; pedipalpal coxae with endites; usually 1 pair of book lungs, sometimes replaced by tracheae; heart with 3, sometimes 2, ostia; 13th through 18th ganglia lost, others fused; 31,000 to 32,000 species.

Family Dysderidae. Respiratory tracheae with 4 spiracles (openings) in 2 pairs, one behind the other.

Family Scytodidae (spitting spiders). Six eyes arranged in 3 groups; high, domed carapace, slopes anteriorly; catch prey with well-aimed squirt of saliva; mostly in tropical and subtropical regions; about 200 species.

Family Loxoscelidae (brown spiders). Six eyes arranged in 3 groups; carapace low; overpower web-entangled prey; *Loxosceles reclusa* (brown recluse) and *Loxosceles laeta* venomous to humans; about 20 other species found in North and South America and Mediterranean region.

Family Sicariidae (6-eyed crab spiders). Large, six eyes, low carapace; legs extended toward sides; burrow in sand in deserts of Southern Hemisphere; about 40 species.

Family Pholcidae (harvestmen). Tarsi of legs with many false articulations; no tracheae; web loose and tangled; *Pholcus* of Europe and America; about 500 species.

Family Uloboridae (uloborids). Cribellum; lack poison glands; 3 tarsal claws; eyes in 3 rows; anal tubercle large; make orb webs; *Hyptiotes,* triangle spiders; about 300 species; worldwide.

Family Deinopidae (ogre-faced spiders). Cribellum; three tarsal claws; eyes in 3 rows; anal tubercle large; *Dinopis,* huge anterior eyes, holds web, throws it over prey; about 60 species, found throughout tropics.

Family Tetragnathidae (long-jawed orb weavers). Males with long chelicerae; epigynum often secondarily lost; worldwide; about 500 to 700 species.

Family Araneidae (orb weavers). Legs with strong setae; chelicerae strong, truncated proximally, with 6 to 8 teeth; colulus always present; paracymbium fused to cymbium of male pedipalp; usually construct orb webs; *Araneus* widespread; *Mastophora,* the bolas spider, probably venomous to humans; many species make no webs; wait for prey to stumble into them; more than 3,000 species; worldwide.

Family Theridiosomatidae (ray spiders). Globular abdomen; high clypeus (area below eyes); chelicerae lack boss; orb webs; about 50 species.

Family Theridiidae (cobweb weavers or comb-footed spiders). Has comb on each 4th leg, used to throw silk over prey (attack wrap); chelicerae pointed on proximal end under carapace, few teeth; male pedipalp with accessory arm (paracymbium) absent or present as a small hook on side of cuplike modification of tarsus (cymbium); no stridulating (sound-producing) structures on side of chelicerae; web irregular; sometimes hunt on ground; *Latrodectus* (widows) poisonous to mammals; more than 2,500 species; worldwide.

Family Linyphiidae (sheet-web weavers and dwarf spiders). Chelicerae with many teeth, blunt on proximal end, often with stridulating file on side; legs with many strong setae; colulus always present; paracymbium a separate sclerite in male pedipalp; about 3,500 species; worldwide.

Family Dictynidae (dictynids). Cribellum; three tarsal claws; tarsi lack trichobothria and brush of setae; small in size; make irregular webs under leaves or in branches of herbs; common in temperate areas; about 500 species.

Family Amaurobiidae (amaurobiids). Cribellum, three tarsal claws without brush of setae; tarsi with dorsal row of trichobothria; resemble Agelenidae; make an irregular funnel web between stones; common; about 350 species; worldwide.

Family Agelenidae (funnel weavers). Eyes in 2 rows; anterior (lateral) spinnerets long; most make funnel web (flat web in vegetation with a tube-shaped retreat at the side); *Argyroneta,* the Eurasian water spider, constructs an air bell beneath surface of slow-moving waters; in its own family but related to agelenids; about 1,000 species; worldwide.

Family Lycosidae (wolf spiders). Eyes in 3 rows; anterior row with 4 eyes; hunting spiders; females carry egg sac attached to spinnerets and carry young on abdomen; may dig tubes in soil; numerous species in the Arctic and on high mountains; true tarantula, *Lycosa tarentula* of southern Europe, probably not poisonous to humans; about 2,500 species throughout world.

Family Ctenidae (wandering spiders). Eyes in 3 rows; median eyes face same direction, form a trapezoid wider behind than in front; eyes of posterior row largest, anterior laterals smallest; 1st 2 legs armed with strong ventral setae; some adults with only 2 tarsal claws; aggressive *Phoneutria fera* of South America venomous to humans; mainly large tropical spiders; about 400 species.

*Family Gnaphosidae (*gnaphosids). Anterior (lateral) spinnerets cylindrical and separated; posterior median eyes often oval and diagonal; nocturnal hunters; common and widespread; about 2,000 species.

Family Clubionidae (sac spiders). Anterior pair of spinnerets conical and touching; *Cheiracanthium* species may be venomous to humans; common and widespread hunting spiders; about 2,000 species.

Family Oxyopidae (lynx spiders). Eyes arranged in a hexagon; hunt on vegetation, pounce on prey; worldwide; about 500 species.

Family Sparassidae (*Heteropodidae*) (huntsman spiders, tarantulas in Australia). Eyes in 2 rows; legs extended sideways; large, slightly flattened body; found in most tropical regions; about 1,000 species.

Family Thomisidae (crab spiders). May sit on flowers awaiting insects; some change colour; some live on or under bark; many species; common; worldwide; about 3,000 species.

Family Salticidae (jumping spiders). Hunt during daylight hours by stalking and jumping on prey; best vision of all spiders; more than 4,000 species; mostly tropical, but many species also found in northern and Arctic regions; the largest family.

(H.W.L./L.R.L.)

BIBLIOGRAPHY. The arachnids as a whole are discussed in VICKI PEARSE *et al., Living Vertebrates* (1987), ch. 22, "Chelicerates," pp. 529–564, an introduction; ROBERT D. BARNES, *Invertebrate Zoology,* 5th ed. (1987), with a particularly good discussion of arachnids in ch. 13, "The Chelicerates," pp. 492–553; ALFRED KAESTNER, *Invertebrate Zoology,* vol. 2, trans. and adapted by HERBERT W. and LORNA R. LEVI (1968; originally published in German, 1965), an expanded textbook of arachnology and myriapodology; J.L. CLOUDSLEY-THOMPSON, *Spiders, Scorpions, Centipedes, and Mites,* new ed. (1968), a general account of natural history and ecology; and P. WEYGOLDT and H.F. PAULUS, "Untersuchungen zur Morphologie, Taxonomie und Phylogenie der Chelicerata," *Zeitschrift für zoologische Systematik und Evolutionsforschung,* 17 (2):85–116 (June 1979), a discussion, in German, of the phylogeny of the arachnids. Detailed higher classifications, with brief summaries of each group, are provided in SYBIL P. PARKER (ed.), *Synopsis and Classification of Living Organisms*, vol. 2 (1982).

(M.L.Go.)

The scorpions are treated in the zoology works above and in ERIK N. KJELLESVIG-WAERING, *A Restudy of the Fossil Scorpionida of the World* (1986), the best work on fossil scorpions, with comments on the modern fauna. (G.A.Po.)

The acarids (mites and ticks) are examined in TYLER A. WOOLLEY, *Acarology: Mites and Human Welfare* (1988), a comprehensive treatment of the entire field; G.W. KRANTZ, *A Manual of Acarology,* 2nd ed. (1978), a systematic arrangement; BURRUS MCDANIEL, *How to Know the Mites and Ticks* (1979), a comprehensively illustrated work of U.S. mites and ticks; W. HELLE and M.W. SABELIS (eds.), *Spider Mites: Their Biology, Natural Enemies, and Control,* 2 vol. (1986); ASHER E. TREAT, *Mites of Moths and Butterflies* (1975), presenting almost 100 species classified as scavengers, hitchhikers, or parasites and discussed on a global basis; FREDERICK D. OBENCHAIN and RACHEL GALUN (eds.), *Physiology of Ticks* (1982), a collection of review articles; and JOHN R. SAUER and J. ALEXANDER HAIR (eds.), *Morphology, Physiology, and Behavioral Biology of Ticks* (1986).

(N.A.W.)

Works focusing on the spiders include FRIEDRICH G. BARTH (ed.), *Neurobiology of Arachnids* (1985); PIERRE BONNET, *Bibliographia Araneorum*, 3 vol. in 7 (1945–61), an indispensable work, listing all references to spiders and spider species up to 1938; PAOLO M. BRIGNOLI, *A Catalogue of the Araneae Described Between 1940 and 1981* (1983); RAINER F. FOELIX, *Biology of Spiders* (1982; originally published in German, 1979), the best introduction to morphology and physiology; R.R. FORSTER and L.M. FORSTER, *New Zealand Spiders: An Introduction* (1973), beautifully illustrated; WILLIS J. GERTSCH, *American Spiders,* 2nd ed. (1979), a natural history of American spiders; B.J. KASTON, *How to Know the Spiders,* 3rd ed. (1978), with keys to identifying North American spiders; HERBERT W. LEVI and LORNA R. LEVI, *A Guide to Spiders and Their Kin* (1968, reprinted with title *Spiders and Their Kin,* 1987), coloured illustrations of spider families; WOLFGANG NENTWIG (ed.), *Ecophysiology of Spiders* (1987), summaries of research by more than 30 specialists; VINCENT D. ROTH, *Spider Genera of North America: With Keys to Families and Genera and a Guide to Literature* (1985); WILLIAM A. SHEAR (ed.), *Spiders—Webs, Behavior, and Evolution* (1986), in which specialists report on the results of recent research; EUGÈNE SIMON, *Histoire Naturelle des Araignées,* 2nd ed., 2 vol. (1892–97), one basis for the classification system used in this article; and PETER N. WITT, CHARLES F. REED, and DAVID B. PEAKALL, *A Spider's Web: Problems in Regulatory Biology* (1968), an excellent introduction to orb-web-building spiders. (H.W.L./L.R.L.)

Archimedes

Archimedes, the most famous ancient Greek mathematician and inventor, was born *c.* 290–280 BC in Syracuse, the principal city-state in Sicily. He probably spent some time in Egypt early in his career, but he resided for most of his life in Syracuse, where he was on intimate terms with its king, Hieron II. Archimedes published his works in the form of correspondence with the principal mathematicians of his time, including the Alexandrian scholars Conon of Samos and Eratosthenes of Cyrene. He played an important role in the defense of Syracuse against the siege laid by the Romans in 213 BC by constructing war machines so effective that they long delayed the capture of the city. But Syracuse was eventually captured by the Roman general Marcus Claudius Marcellus in the autumn of 212 or spring of 211 BC, and Archimedes was killed in the sack of the city.

The Archimedes screw

Far more details survive about the life of Archimedes than about any other ancient scientist, but they are largely anecdotal, reflecting the impression that his mechanical genius made on the popular imagination. Thus, he is credited with inventing the Archimedes screw, a device for raising water, and he is supposed to have made two "spheres" that Marcellus took back to Rome—one a star globe and the other a device (the details of which are uncertain) for mechanically representing the motions of the Sun, Moon, and planets. The story that he determined the proportion of gold and silver in a wreath made for Hieron by weighing it in water is probably true, but the version that has him leaping from the bath in which he supposedly got the idea and running naked through the streets shouting "Heurēka!" ("I have found it!") is popular embellishment. Equally apocryphal are the stories that he used a huge array of mirrors to burn the Roman ships besieging Syracuse; that he said, "Give me a place to stand and I will move the Earth"; and that a Roman soldier killed him because he refused to leave his mathematical diagrams—although all are popular reflections of his real interest in catoptrics (the branch of optics dealing with the reflection of light from mirrors, plane or curved), mechanics, and pure mathematics.

According to Plutarch, Archimedes had so low an opinion of the kind of practical invention at which he excelled and to which he owed his contemporary fame that he left no written work on such subjects. While it is true that—apart from a dubious reference to a treatise, "On Sphere-Making"—all of his known works were of a theoretical character, nevertheless his interest in mechanics deeply influenced his mathematical thinking. Not only did he write works on theoretical mechanics and hydrostatics, but his treatise *Method Concerning Mechanical Theorems* shows that he used mechanical reasoning as a heuristic device for the discovery of new mathematical theorems.

Extant works

His works. There are nine extant treatises by Archimedes in Greek. The principal results in *On the Sphere and Cylinder* (in two books) are that the surface area of any sphere is four times that of its greatest circle (in modern notation, $S = 4 \pi r^2$) and that the volume of a sphere is two-thirds that of the cylinder in which it is inscribed (leading immediately to the formula for the volume, $V = \frac{4}{3} \pi r^3$). Archimedes was proud enough of the latter discovery to leave instructions for his tomb to be marked with a sphere inscribed in a cylinder. Cicero found the tomb, overgrown with vegetation, a century and a half after Archimedes' death.

Measurement of the Circle is a short work in which π (pi), the ratio of the circumference to the diameter of a circle, is shown to lie between the limits of $3\frac{1}{7}$ and $3\frac{10}{71}$. The approach to this problem devised by Archimedes, which consists of inscribing and circumscribing regular polygons with large numbers of sides, was the one followed by all those who subsequently dealt with the problem of determining π until the development of series expansions in the late 17th century. This work also contains accurate approximations (expressed as ratios of integers) to the square roots of 3 and several large numbers.

On Conoids and Spheroids deals with determining the volumes of the segments of solids formed by the revolution of a conic section (circle, ellipse, parabola, or hyperbola) about its axis. In modern terms, these are problems of integration. *On Spirals* develops many properties of tangents to the spiral of Archimedes—*i.e.,* the locus of a point moving with uniform speed along a straight line that itself is rotating with uniform speed about a fixed point.

On the Equilibrium of Planes (or *Centres of Gravity of Planes;* in two books) is mainly concerned with establishing the centres of gravity of various rectilinear plane figures and segments of conics. The first book purports to establish the "law of the lever" (magnitudes balance at distances from the fulcrum in inverse ratio to their weights), and it is mainly on the basis of this treatise that Archimedes has been called the founder of theoretical mechanics. Much of this book, however, is undoubtedly not authentic, consisting as it does of inept later additions or reworking, and it seems likely that the basic principle of the law of the lever and—possibly—the concept of centre of gravity were established on a mathematical basis by scholars earlier than Archimedes. His contribution was rather to extend these concepts to conic sections.

Quadrature of the Parabola demonstrates, first by "mechanical" means (as in *Method,* below) and then by conventional geometrical methods, that the area of any segment of a parabola is $4/3$ of the area of the triangle having the same base and height as that segment. This is, again, a problem in integration.

The Sand-Reckoner is a small treatise that is a *jeu d'esprit* written for the layman—it is addressed to Gelon, son of Hieron—that nevertheless contains some profoundly original mathematics. Its object is to remedy the inadequacies of the Greek numerical notation system by showing how to express a huge number—the number of grains of sand that it would take to fill the whole of the universe. What Archimedes does, in effect, is to create a place-value system of notation, with a base of 100,000,000. (This was apparently a completely original idea, since he had no knowledge of the contemporary Babylonian place-value system with base 60.) The work is also of interest because it gives the most detailed surviving description of the heliocentric system of Aristarchus of Samos and because it contains an account of an ingenious procedure that Archimedes used to determine the Sun's apparent diameter by observation with an instrument.

Method Concerning Mechanical Theorems describes the process of discovery in mathematics. It is the sole surviving work from antiquity and one of the few from any period that deals with this topic. In it Archimedes recounts how he used a "mechanical" method to arrive at some of his key discoveries, including the area of a parabolic segment and the surface area and volume of a sphere. The technique consists of dividing each of two figures, one bounded by straight lines and the other by a curve, into an infinite but equal number of infinitesimally thin strips, then "weighing" each corresponding pair of these strips against each other on a notional balance, and summing them to find the ratio of the two whole figures. Archimedes emphasizes that, though useful as a heuristic method, this procedure does not constitute a rigorous proof.

On Floating Bodies (in two books) survives only partly in Greek, the rest in medieval Latin translation from the Greek. It is the first known work in hydrostatics, of which Archimedes is recognized as the founder. Its purpose is to determine the positions that various solids will assume when floating in a fluid, according to their form and the variation in their specific gravities. In the first book various general principles are established, notably (in Proposition 7) what has come to be known as Archimedes' principle, which is that a solid denser than a fluid will, when immersed in that fluid, be lighter by the weight of the fluid it displaces. The second book is a mathematical tour de force unmatched in antiquity and rarely equalled since. In it Archimedes determines the different positions of stability that a right paraboloid of revolution assumes when floating in a fluid of greater specific gravity, according to geometric and hydrostatic variations.

Archimedes' principle

Archimedes is known, from references of later authors, to have written a number of other works that have not come down to us. Of particular interest are treatises on catoptrics, in which he discussed, among other things, the phenomenon of refraction; on the 13 semiregular (Archimedean) polyhedra (those bodies bounded by regular polygons, not all of the same type, that can be inscribed in a sphere); and the "Cattle Problem" (preserved in a Greek epigram), which poses a problem in indeterminate analysis, with eight unknowns. In addition to these, there survive several works in Arabic translation ascribed to Archimedes but that cannot have been composed by him in their present form, although they may contain "Archimedean" elements. These include a work on inscribing the regular heptagon in a circle; a collection of lemmas (propositions assumed to be true that are used to prove a theorem) and a book, "On Touching Circles," both having to do with elementary plane geometry; and the "Stomachion" (parts of which also survive in Greek), dealing with a square divided into 14 pieces for a game or puzzle.

Archimedes' mathematical proofs and presentation exhibit great boldness and originality of thought on the one hand and extreme rigour on the other, meeting the highest standards of contemporary geometry. While *Method* shows that he arrived at the formulas for the surface area and volume of a sphere by "mechanical" reasoning involving infinitesimals, in his actual proofs of the results in *Sphere and Cylinder* he uses only the rigorous methods of passage to the limit that had been invented by Eudoxus of Cnidus in the 4th century BC. These methods, of which Archimedes was a master, are the standard procedure in all his works on higher geometry that deal with problems of integration. Their mathematical rigour stands in strong contrast to the "proofs" of the first practitioners of integral calculus in the 17th century, when infinitesimals were reintroduced into mathematics. Yet Archimedes' results are no less impressive than theirs. The same freedom from conventional ways of thinking is apparent in the arithmetical field in *Sand-Reckoner*, which shows an understanding of the nature of the numerical system unparalleled before the modern era.

Archimedes as astronomer

In antiquity Archimedes was also known as an outstanding astronomer: his observations of solstices were used by Hipparchus, the foremost ancient astronomer. Very little is known of this side of Archimedes' activity, although *Sand-Reckoner* reveals his keen astronomical interest and practical observational ability. But there has been handed down a set of numbers attributed to him giving the distances of the various heavenly bodies from Earth, which has been shown to be based not on observed astronomical data but on a "Pythagorean" theory associating the spatial intervals between the planets with musical intervals. Surprising though it is to find these metaphysical speculations in the work of a practicing astronomer, there is good reason to believe that their attribution to Archimedes is correct.

His influence. Given the magnitude and originality of Archimedes' achievement, the influence of his mathematics in antiquity was rather small. Those of his results that could be simply expressed—such as the formulas for the surface area and volume of a sphere—became mathematical commonplaces, and one of the bounds he established for π, $^{22}/_{7}$, was adopted as the usual approximation to it in antiquity and the Middle Ages. But his mathematical work was not continued or developed, as far as is known, in any important way in ancient times, despite his hope expressed in *Method* that its publication would enable others to make new discoveries. It was not until some of his mathematical treatises were translated into Arabic in the late 8th or 9th century that attempts were made to extend his results, particularly in the determination of the volumes of solids of revolution. Several meritorious works by Arabic mathematicians of the early medieval period were inspired by their study of Archimedes.

But the greatest effect of his work on that of later mathematicians came in the 16th and 17th centuries with the printing of texts derived from the Greek, and eventually of the Greek text itself, the *editio princeps*, in Basel in 1544. The Latin translation of many of Archimedes' works by Federico Commandino in 1558 contributed greatly to the spread of knowledge of them, which was reflected in the work of the foremost mathematicians and physicists of the time, including Johannes Kepler and Galileo. David Rivault's edition and Latin translation (1615) of the complete works, including the ancient commentaries, was enormously influential in the work of some of the best mathematicians of the 17th century, notably René Descartes and Pierre de Fermat. Without the background of the rediscovered ancient mathematicians, amongst whom Archimedes was paramount, the development of mathematics in Europe in the century between 1550 and 1650 is inconceivable. It is unfortunate that *Method* remained unknown to both Arabic and Renaissance mathematicians (it was only rediscovered in the late 19th century), for they might have fulfilled Archimedes' hope that it would prove of use to his successors in discovering theorems. (G.J.T.)

BIBLIOGRAPHY. The standard edition, in Greek and Latin, of the works of Archimedes, with the ancient commentaries, is that of JOHAN LUDVIG HEIBERG (ed.), *Archimedis Opera Omnia cum Commentariis Eutocii*, 3 vol. (1910–15, reprinted 1972). To the reprint was added *Über einander berührende Kreise* (1975), a translation into German by YVONNE DOLD-SAMPLONIUS, HEINRICH HERMELINK and MATTHIAS SCHRAMM of the Arabic text "On Touching Circles." An English translation is THOMAS L. HEATH (ed.), *The Works of Archimedes* (1897), with a supplement, *The Method of Archimedes* (1912; both reprinted in 1 vol., 1953). Unfortunately Heath, by paraphrasing Archimedes' mathematics in modern notation, misrepresents him. For those wishing to get the flavour of the original, a much better translation is the French one by PAUL VER EECKE, *Les Oeuvres complètes d'Archimède* (1921). The best detailed discussion of the contents of Archimedes' work is EDWARD J. DIJKSTERHUIS, *Archimedes* (1956), which also assembles most of the biographical data. Valuable too is the article "Archimedes" by MARSHALL CLAGETT, in the *Dictionary of Scientific Biography*, vol. 1 (1970), particularly for its bibliography and discussion of the influence of Archimedes. On the textual tradition and knowledge of Archimedes in Europe in the Middle Ages and early Renaissance, an indispensable work is MARSHALL CLAGETT (ed.), *Archimedes in the Middle Ages*, 4 vol. in 8 (1964–80). A particularly useful guide to the modern literature is IVO SCHNEIDER, *Archimedes* (1979), in German. The basis of Archimedes' numbers for the planetary distances was explained satisfactorily for the first time by CATHERINE OSBORNE in "Archimedes on the Dimension of the Cosmos," *Isis*, vol. 74, no. 272, pp. 234–242 (June 1983).

The Art of Architecture

Architecture is the art and the technique of building, employed to fulfill the practical and expressive requirements of civilized people. Almost every settled society that possesses the techniques for building produces architecture. It is necessary in all but the simplest cultures; without it, man is confined to a primitive struggle with the elements; with it, he has not only a defense against the natural environment but also the benefits of a human environment, a prerequisite for and a symbol of the development of civilized institutions.

The characteristics that distinguish a work of architecture from other man-made structures are (1) the suitability of the work to use by human beings in general and the adaptability of it to particular human activities; (2) the stability and permanence of the work's construction; and (3) the communication of experience and ideas through its form.

All these conditions must be met in architecture. The second is a constant, while the first and third vary in relative importance according to the social function of buildings. If the function is chiefly utilitarian, as in a factory, communication is of less importance. If the function is chiefly expressive, as in a monumental tomb, utility is a minor concern. In some buildings, such as churches and city halls, utility and communication may be of equal importance.

The present article treats primarily the forms, elements, methods, and theory of architecture. For treatment of the architecture of particular cultures and regions, see, for example, AFRICAN ARTS; ARCHITECTURE, THE HISTORY OF WESTERN; EAST ASIAN ARTS; and SOUTHEAST ASIAN ARTS.

For coverage of related topics in the *Macropædia* and *Micropædia,* see the *Propædia,* section 626, and the *Index.*

This article is divided into the following sections:

Use 874
- Architectural types 874
  - Domestic architecture
  - Religious architecture
  - Governmental architecture
  - Recreational architecture
  - Architecture of welfare and education
  - Commercial and industrial architecture
- Architectural planning 879
  - Planning the environment
  - Planning for use
  - Economic planning

Techniques 880
- Materials 881
  - Stone
  - Brick
  - Wood
  - Iron and steel
  - Concrete
- Methods 882
  - Wall
  - Post-and-lintel
  - Arch
  - Vault
  - Dome
  - Truss
  - Framed structures

Expression 887
- Content 887
  - Symbols of function
  - Expression of technique
- Form 889
  - Space and mass
  - Composition
  - Scale
  - Light
  - Texture
  - Colour
  - Environment
- Ornament 893
  - Mimetic ornament
  - Applied ornament
  - Organic ornament

Theory of architecture 895
- Distinction between the history and theory of architecture 895
- Distinction between the theory of architecture and the theory of art 896
- Functionalism 896
- The art of building 896
- "Commodity, firmness, and delight": the ultimate synthesis 897
  - Venustas
  - Utilitas
  - Firmitas

Bibliography 899

Use

The types of architecture are established not by architects but by society, according to the needs of its different institutions. Society sets the goals and assigns to the architect the job of finding the means of achieving them. This section of the article is concerned with architectural typology, with the role of society in determining the kinds of architecture, and with planning—the role of the architect in adapting designs to particular uses and to the general physical needs of human beings.

ARCHITECTURAL TYPES

Architecture is created only to fulfill the specifications of an individual or group. Economic law prevents architects from emulating their fellow artists in producing works for which the demand is nonexistent or only potential. So the types of architecture depend upon social formations and may be classified according to the role of the patron in the community. The types that will be discussed here—domestic, religious, governmental, recreational, welfare and educational, and commercial and industrial—represent the simplest classification; a scientific typology of architecture would require a more detailed analysis.

Domestic architecture. Domestic architecture is produced for the social unit: the individual, family, or clan and their dependents, human and animal. It provides shelter and security for the basic physical functions of life and at times also for commercial, industrial, or agricultural activities that involve the family unit rather than the community. The basic requirements of domestic architecture are simple: a place to sleep, prepare food, eat, and perhaps work; a place that has some light and is protected from the weather. A single room with sturdy walls and roof, a door, a window, and a hearth are the necessities; all else is luxury.

The essential components of a domestic building

"Vernacular" architecture. In much of the world today, even where institutions have been in a continuous process of change, dwelling types of ancient or prehistoric origin are in use. In the industrialized United States, for instance, barns are being built according to a design employed in Europe in the 1st millennium BC. The forces that produce a dynamic evolution of architectural style in communal building are usually inactive in the home and farm. The life of the average person may be unaltered by the most fundamental changes in his institutions. He can be successively a slave, the subject of a monarchy, and a voting citizen, without having the means or the desire to change

Palace of Versailles, France, built chiefly by Louis Le Vau and Jules Hardouin-Mansart during the last half of the 17th century.
Aerofilms, Ltd., London

his customs, techniques, or surroundings. Economic pressure is the major factor that causes the average individual to restrict his demands to a level far below that which the technology of his time is capable of maintaining. Frequently he builds new structures with old techniques because experiment and innovation are more costly than repetition. But in wealthy cultures economy permits and customs encourage architecture to provide conveniences such as sanitation, lighting, and heating, as well as separate areas for distinct functions, and these may come to be regarded as necessities. The same causes tend to replace the conservatism of the home with the aspirations of institutional architecture and to emphasize the expressive as well as the utilitarian function.

"Power" architecture. As wealth and expressive functions increase, a special type of domestic building can be distinguished that may be called power architecture. In almost every civilization the pattern of society gives to a few of its members the power to utilize the resources of the community in the construction of their homes, palaces, villas, gardens, and places of recreation. These few, whose advantages usually arise from economic, religious, or class distinctions, are able to enjoy an infinite variety of domestic activities connected with the mores of their position. These can include even communal functions: the palace of the Flavian emperors in ancient Rome incorporated the activities of the state and the judicial system; the palace of Versailles, a whole city in itself, provided the necessities and luxuries of life for several thousand persons of all classes and was the centre of government for the empire of Louis XIV. Power architecture may have a complex expressive function, too, since the symbolizing of power by elegance or display is a responsibility or a necessity (and often a fault) of the powerful. Since this function usually is sought not so much to delight the patron as to demonstrate his social position to others, power architecture becomes communal as well as domestic. In democracies such as ancient Greece and in the 20th-century Western world, this show of power may be more reserved, but it is still distinguishable.

Group housing. A third type of domestic architecture accommodates the group rather than the unit and is therefore public as well as private. It is familiar through the widespread development of mass housing in the modern world, in which individuals or families find living space either in multiple dwellings or in single units produced in quantity. Group housing is produced by many kinds of cultures: by communal states to equalize living standards, by tyrants to assure a docile labour force, and by feudal or caste systems to bring together members of a class. The apartment house was developed independently by the imperial Romans of antiquity to suit urban conditions and by the American Indians to suit agricultural conditions. Group architecture may be power architecture as well, particularly when land values are too high to permit even the wealthy to build privately, as in the 17th-century Place des Vosges in Paris, where aristocratic mansions were designed uniformly around a square, or in the 18th-century flats in English towns and spas. Although most domestic architecture of the 20th century employs the style and techniques of the past, the exceptions are more numerous and more important for the development of architecture than ever before. This is because the distribution of wealth and power is widespread in parts of the world where architecture is vital and because the modern state has assumed responsibility for much high-quality housing.

Cultures in which group housing has been produced

Religious architecture. The history of architecture is concerned more with religious buildings than with any other type, because in most past cultures the universal and exalted appeal of religion made the church or temple the most expressive, the most permanent, and the most influential building in any community.

The typology of religious architecture is complex, because no basic requirements such as those that characterize domestic architecture are common to all religions and because the functions of any one religion involve many

Mayan ruins at Tikal, with Temple of the Giant Jaguar (right); central Petén department, Guatemala, *c.* AD 300–900.
George Holton—Photo Researchers, Inc.

different kinds of activity, all of which change with the evolution of cultural patterns.

Design related to the demands of the ritual

The temple or church. Temples or churches serve as places of worship and as shelters for the images, relics, and holy areas of the cult. In the older religions, the temple was not always designed for communal use. In ancient Egypt and India it was considered the residence of the deity, and entrance into the sanctum was prohibited or reserved for priests; in ancient Greece it contained an accessible cult image, but services were held outside the main facade; and in the ancient Near East and in the Mayan and Aztec architecture of ancient Mexico, where the temple was erected at the summit of pyramidal mounds, only privileged members of the community were allowed to approach. Few existing religions are so exclusive. Beliefs as dissimilar as Christianity, Buddhism, Judaism, and Islām are based on communal participation in rites held inside the temple or church. The buildings have even evolved into similar plans, because of a common requirement that the maximum number of worshippers be able to face the focal point of the service (the mosque's "point" is the wall facing the direction of Mecca, the city of Muḥammad's birth and therefore the most sacred of all Islāmic religious sites). Consequently, the Muslims were able to adopt the Byzantine church tradition, modern synagogues are often scarcely distinguishable from churches, and early Protestantism absorbed Catholic architecture with only minor revision (elimination of subsidiary chapels and altars, repositories of relics, and some symbolic decoration).

Shelter is not always required for worship. Primitive rites are often practiced outdoors with some monument as a focus, while the altar of Pergamum and the Ara Pacis Augustae (Augustan Altar of Peace) in Rome are evidences of the open-air religious observances of the classical world. The atrium of early Christian architecture and the cloister were isolated areas for prayer.

The complex programs of later religions made the place of worship the focus for varied activities demanding architectural solutions; for example, the baptistery, bell towers, and chapter houses of Christian architecture, the minarets of the Muslims, and the holy gates of Buddhism. Most modern sects demand space for religious education adjoining the community church or temple. Catholicism and the religions of Asia have produced monasteries, convents, and abbeys—connected to places of worship—that accommodate the organized practice of religion, adding domestic and often industrial, agricultural, and scholarly functions to the religious.

Shrines and memoria. Shrines consecrate a holy place for its miraculous character or for its association with the life of the founder, gods, or saints of a cult. Since the importance of such structures is usually proportionate to the antiquity of their tradition and associations with cult origins, they have had little importance in later architectural history. The major commemorative buildings of Christianity are those connected with the life of Jesus Christ (Church of the Nativity in Bethlehem) and the apostles or early Church Fathers (St. Peter's in Rome) or with the medieval cult of relics (Santiago de Compostela in Spain). No single formal design characterizes this type, but the theme of the domed or central-plan structure (round, square, polygon, Greek cross, etc.) connects the *memoria* of Asia (the Indian stupa, Chinese pagoda), pagan antiquity (the Pantheon in Rome), and Christianity (the Church of the Holy Sepulchre in Jerusalem). The significance of the form is discussed below under *Content.*

Funerary art. Expressing man's relationship to the afterlife, funerary art is not always architectural, since it may be purely symbolic and therefore suitable to sculptural treatment, as in the classic Greek, medieval, and modern tomb. Funerary architecture is produced by societies whose belief in the afterlife is materialistic and by individuals who want to perpetuate and symbolize their temporal importance. Monumental tombs have been produced in ancient Egypt (pyramids), Hellenistic Greece (tomb of Mausolus at Halicarnassus, which is the source of the word mausoleum), ancient Rome (tomb of Hadrian), Renaissance Europe (Michelangelo's Medici Chapel, Florence), and Asia (Tāj Mahal, Āgra, Uttar Pradesh, India). Modern tomb design has lost vitality, though it remains as elaborate (Monument to Victor Emmanuel II, Rome) or as meaningful in terms of power (Lenin Mausoleum, Moscow) as before. The exceptional examples are partly sculptural in character (*e.g.,* Louis Sullivan's Wainwright

Variety of architectural types

Säynätsalo town hall group, Finland, designed by Alvar Aalto, 1950–52: governmental architecture in which indigenous building traditions and materials are combined with modern design and building technology.

The Tāj Mahal at Āgra, India, built by Shāh Jahān for his wife, Mumtāz Maḥal, *c.* 1632–*c.* 1649: marble mausoleum, with formal gardens.

Place des Vosges, Paris, built by the French king, Henry IV, 1605–12: group housing with a residential square and an arcaded walking area.

Alcázar at Segovia, Spain, built by Henry IV of Castile, 15th century: combination of military and residential architecture that uses siting functionally, as well as for psychological and aesthetic effect.

Auditorium of the Auditorium Building, Chicago, by Dankmar Adler and Louis Sullivan, 1889, renovated 1967–68: horseshoe-planned theatre with boxes and sloping galleries engineered for acoustical perfection and advantageous sight lines.

Plate 1: (Top left) GEKS, (top right) C.A. Peterson—Publix, (centre left) © Interphototheque Doc. Francaise. SODEL. Mr. Brigaud, (bottom left) Erwitt—Magnum, (bottom right) Gerald Clyde—FPG/EB Inc.

Interior of the TWA terminal, John F. Kennedy International Airport, New York, by Eero Saarinen, 1956–62: imaginative sculptural use of reinforced concrete.

Borgund Stave church, Norway, *c.* 1163: rich visual texture and colour created by wood.

Diverse kinds of building materials and architectural surface effects

The Seagram Building, New York City, by Ludwig Mies van der Rohe and Philip Johnson, 1956–58: elegance of design expressed in steel frame and curtain wall construction.

Contemporary vernacular architecture in Zaria, Nigeria: clay houses decorated with low relief ornament and vibrantly coloured designs.

"Fallingwater," Mill Run, Pennsylvania, residence by Frank Lloyd Wright, 1936–38: sensitivity to the environment expressed by site orientation and use of natural as well as man-made materials.

Plate 2: By courtesy of (bottom right) the Western Pennsylvania Conservancy, Pittsburgh; photographs, (top left) Marvin B. Winter—Photo Researchers, Inc., (top right) C.A. Peterson—Publix, (centre right) Frank Willett, (bottom left) Photo Media, Ltd.

Base of the Marble Pagoda with the Jade Pagoda in the background, Jade Fountain Hill, west of Peking, 18th century (Ch'ing dynasty).
Fritz Henle—Publix

Tomb, St. Louis, Missouri; Walter Gropius' war memorial, Weimar, Germany).

Since the 18th century much of religious architecture has lost individuality and importance through the weakening of liturgical traditions. But today, as in the past, outstanding architects have met new demands of use and expression with superior solutions.

Governmental architecture. The basic functions of government, to an even greater extent than those of religion, are similar in all societies: administration, legislation, and the dispensing of justice. But the architectural needs differ according to the nature of the relationship between the governing and the governed. Where governmental functions are centralized in the hands of a single individual, they are simple and may be exercised in the ruler's residence; where the functions are shared by many and established as specialized activities, they become complex and demand distinct structures. There are, however, no basic formal solutions for governmental architecture, since the practical needs of government may be met in any sheltered area that has convenient space for deliberation and administration. A distinct type is created rather by expressive functions arising from the ideology of the different systems of political organization (monarchy, theocracy, democracy, etc.) and from the traditions of the various offices of government (law courts, assembly houses, city halls, etc.). Governments that exercise power by force rather than by consent tend to employ the expressive functions of architecture to emphasize their power; they tend to produce buildings of a monumentality disproportionate to their service to the community. Those in which the ruler is given divine attributes bring religious symbolism into architecture. Democratic governments have the responsibility of expressing in their architecture the aims of the community itself, a difficult task in the modern world, when the community may be neither small enough to express itself easily nor homogeneous enough to agree on how to do so.

Relation of political ideology to expressive function

The simple democratic processes of the Greek city-states and the medieval free towns produced governmental architecture on a domestic scale, while the Roman Empire and later monarchies seldom made important distinctions between the palace and the seat of state functions. The widespread growth of representative government and the increase in the size and functions of the state in the 19th century created a great variety of buildings, some for entirely new uses. Some examples are: first, capitols, courthouses, parliament buildings, printing offices, and mints and, later, post offices, embassies, archives, secretariats, and even laboratories, when the work, the increased personnel, and the complexity of mechanical aids demanded specialized architectural solutions. Bureaucracy, for better or for worse, has made governmental architecture more important than at any time in history.

In the first rapid expansion from about 1780 to 1840, Neoclassical architects found impressive solutions to the new problems, but afterward governmental architecture lapsed into a century of conservatism, following at a safe distance behind private building. After World War II, governmental architecture showed new vitality. Outstanding are Le Corbusier's work at Chandīgarh, Punjab, India, the United Nations Educational, Scientific and Cultural Organization headquarters in Paris, and the program of the U.S. Department of State for building American embassies.

Military architecture is closer to the governmental type than to others, but its expressive function is so much subordinated to the practical that it is usually regarded as a class of engineering (see WAR, TECHNOLOGY OF: *Fortifications*).

Recreational architecture. Few recreations require architecture until they become institutionalized and must provide for both active and passive participation (athletic events, dramatic, musical performances, etc.) or for communal participation in essentially private luxuries (baths, museums, libraries). Throughout history, recreational architecture has been the most consistent in form of any type. Diversions may change, but, as in domestic architecture, the physical makeup of the human being provides consistency. If his participation is passive he must be able to hear and to see in comfort. If his participation is active, he must be given spaces suited to the chosen activity. In most cultures, recreational institutions have their origins in religious rites, but they easily gain independence, and religious expression is reduced or eliminated in their architecture.

Historical consistency of building types

Theatres. Theatres originated in ancient Greece with the rites of the god Dionysus, first as temporary installations and later as outdoor architecture using the natural slope and curves of hillsides to bring the spectator close to the stage and to avoid the need for substructures. The Greek theatre was monumentalized and modified by the Romans, whose arches and vaults allowed construction of sloping seats from level foundations. In the Middle Ages churches and temporary structures were used for dramatic purposes, and in the Renaissance the form of the Roman theatre was occasionally revived (Andrea Palladio's Teatro Olimpico in Vicenza, Italy). The 17th-century development of opera, drama, and ballet in Europe brought about a revival of theatre building but in a new form conceived to satisfy class and economic distinctions (*e.g.,* the Teatro Farnese in Parma, Italy; Residenztheater, in Munich). A flat or inclined pit accommodated standing patrons, tiers of boxes rose vertically above in a horseshoe plan, and permanent covering (for both acoustics and comfort) made artificial lighting an important feature in theatrical performances. While the modern theatre has been greatly improved in efficiency by new acoustical methods and materials, it also has kept much of the Baroque form. However, it provides seating throughout and usually substitutes sloping galleries (into which the unprivileged have been moved) for boxes. The motion picture has had little effect on theatre design (see THEATRICAL PRODUCTION).

Auditoriums. The auditorium is distinguished by the absence of stage machinery and by its greater size. The development of large symphony orchestras and choirs and of the institution of lectures and mass meetings combined with growing urban populations to produce this modification of the theatre.

Athletic facilities. Sport arenas, racetracks, and public swimming pools of the present day owe their origin to the ancient Romans (though certain precedents can be found in Crete and Greece). Although the classical tradition of

Importance of Roman prototypes

sports was broken from the early Middle Ages to the 19th century, even the design of arenas and tracks has been scarcely altered from the Colosseum and Circus Maximus, though the construction of large grandstands has inspired magnificent designs in reinforced concrete (stadiums at Florence, Helsinki, and the Universidad Nacional Autónoma de México). Sports that have no precedents in antiquity, such as baseball, have required modifications in design but have not been important for architecture.

Museums and libraries. Museum and library architecture was also an innovation of classical antiquity (library architecture appears independently in ancient China and Japan). Early examples are found on the acropolis of Hellenistic Pergamum and in Roman Ephesus. Museums were not cultivated in the Middle Ages, and libraries were incorporated into monasteries. In the Renaissance and Baroque periods, library construction like Johann Bernhard Fischer von Erlach's Hofbibliothek in the Hofburg, Vienna, was rare, but important civic buildings were designed within religious institutions (Michelangelo's Biblioteca Laurenziana in Florence) and universities (Sir Christopher Wren's Trinity College Library, Cambridge; James Gibbs' Radcliffe Camera, Oxford). This type of architecture became truly communal for the first time in the 19th century, when the size of library collections and the number of visitors inspired some of the finest architecture of the modern period (Michael Gottlieb Bindesbøll's Thorvaldsen Museum, Copenhagen; Sir Robert Smirke's British Museum in London; Henri Labrouste's Bibliothèque Sainte-Geneviève in Paris; Alvar Aalto's library in Viipuri, Finland; Frank Lloyd Wright's Solomon R. Guggenheim Museum in New York City). (See MUSEUMS; LIBRARIES AND LIBRARY SCIENCE.)

Architecture of welfare and education. The principal institutions of public welfare are those that provide facilities for education, health, public security, and utilities. Some of these functions are performed by the church and the state, but, since their character is not essentially religious or political, they may require independent architectural solutions, particularly in urban environments. A consistent typology of this architecture, however, cannot be established throughout history, because the acceptance of responsibility for the welfare of the community differs in degree in every social system.

Buildings for the specific purposes of public welfare were seldom considered necessary in antiquity, in most of Eastern architecture, or in the early Middle Ages. But in ancient Greece health facilities were included in precincts of Asclepius, the god of healing, and in the East within Buddhist precincts. The Romans produced a highly developed system of water supply and sewerage, of which their monumental aqueducts are an impressive survival.

In the later Middle Ages consistent forms began to emerge. With the separation of the university from a purely religious context, a concept of planning developed (particularly at Oxford, Cambridge, and Paris) that still influences educational architecture. Hospitals designed as large halls were established as adjuncts to churches, convents, and monasteries (Hôtel-Dieu, Beaune, France) and gained architectural independence in the Renaissance (Ospedale degli Innocenti, Florence). Ancient and medieval prisons and guardhouses were occasionally isolated from military architecture (*e.g.,* Tower of London; Bargello in Florence), but the prison did not become an important architectural type until the late 18th and 19th centuries (*e.g.,* George Dance's Newgate Prison, London; Henry Hobson Richardson's Allegheny County Jail, Pittsburgh).

The expansion of education and health facilities beginning in the 19th century created a widespread and consistently growing need for specialized architectural solutions. Schools, from the nursery to the university, now demand not only particular solutions at all levels but structures for a variety of purposes within each level; advanced education demands buildings for scientific research, training for trades and professions, recreation, health, housing, religious institutions, and other purposes. Most of the countries of the Western world have produced educational architecture of the highest quality; this architectural type is more important than in any past age.

Specialized solutions demanded since the 19th century

By courtesy of the Solomon R. Guggenheim Museum, New York

Interior of the Solomon R. Guggenheim Museum, New York, by Frank Lloyd Wright; opened 1959.

Commercial and industrial architecture. Buildings for exchange, transportation, communication, manufacturing, and power production meet the principal needs of commerce and industry. In the past these needs were mostly unspecialized. They were met either within domestic architecture or in buildings distinguished from domestic types chiefly by their size. Stores, banks, hostelries, guildhalls, and factories required only space for more persons and things than houses could accommodate. Bridges, warehouses, and other structures not used for sheltering people were, of course, specialized from the beginning and survived the Industrial Revolution without basic changes. The Industrial Revolution profoundly affected the typology as well as the techniques of architecture. Through the introduction of the machine and mass production, economic life moved out of the domestic environment into an area dominated by devices and processes rather than by individuals, creating the need for buildings more specialized and more numerous than the total accumulation of types throughout history. All the types cannot be discussed here, but a categorical listing into which they can be fitted will illustrate their importance for architecture: exchange (office buildings, stores, markets, banks, exchanges, warehouses, exhibition halls); transportation (roads, bridges, tunnels; stations for rail, sea, and air transport and the dispensing of fuel; garages, hangars, and other storage facilities; hotels); communication (structures for the transmission and reception of telephone, telegraph, radio, television, and radar communication; for the printing and distribution of newspapers, magazines, books, and other reading matter; for motion-picture production; and for advertising functions); production (mines, factories, laboratories, food-processing plants); power (dams, generating plants; fuel storage, processing, and distribution installations). (See PUBLIC WORKS.)

Effect of the Industrial Revolution

Each of these functions demands its own architectural

solution, but in general they may be divided into two classes according to whether the plan must give greater attention to the size and movement of machinery or of persons. Wherever human activity is the chief concern, there has been less departure from traditional expression; banks in the form of Roman temples are an obvious example. The demands of machines have no tradition and have encouraged a search for greater, simpler, and more flexible spaces; but frequently the practical function has entirely eliminated the expressive, so that with some distinguished exceptions (*e.g.,* Frank Lloyd Wright's S.C. Johnson & Sons, Inc., building, Racine, Wisconsin; Eero Saarinen's General Motors Technical Center, Warren, Michigan), most modern factories are not architecture. Where both men and machines must be given equal attention, as in railroad stations, architecture of the 19th and 20th centuries has vacillated between creating new forms and grasping for irrelevant traditions.

Difference between man- or machine-centred buildings

ARCHITECTURAL PLANNING

The architect usually begins to work when the site and the type and cost of a building have been determined.

The site involves the varying behaviour of the natural environment that must be adjusted to the unvarying physical needs of human beings; the type is the generalized form established by society that must be adjusted to the special use for which the building is required; the cost implies the economics of land, labour, and materials that must be adjusted to suit a particular sum.

Thus, planning is the process of particularizing and, ultimately, of harmonizing the demands of environment, use, and economy. This process has a cultural as well as a utilitarian value, for in creating a plan for any social activity the architect inevitably influences the way in which that activity is performed.

Planning the environment. The natural environment is at once a hindrance and a help, and the architect seeks both to invite its aid and to repel its attacks. To make buildings habitable and comfortable, he must control the effects of heat, cold, light, air, moisture, and dryness and foresee destructive potentialities such as fire, earthquake, flood, and disease.

The methods of controlling the environment considered here are only the practical aspects of planning. They are treated by the architect within the context of the expressive aspects. The placement and form of buildings in relation to their sites, the distribution of spaces within buildings, and other planning devices discussed below are fundamental elements in the aesthetics of architecture.

Importance of determining a building's axis

Orientation. The arrangement of the axes of buildings and their parts is a device for controlling the effects of sun, wind, and rainfall. The sun is regular in its course; it favours the southern and neglects the northern exposures of buildings in the Northern Hemisphere, so that it may be captured for heat or evaded for coolness by turning the axis of a plan toward or away from it. Within buildings, the axis and placement of each space determines the amount of sun it receives. Orientation may control air for circulation and reduce the disadvantages of wind, rain, and snow, since in most climates the prevailing currents can be foreseen. The characteristics of the immediate environment also influence orientation: trees, land formations, and other buildings create shade and reduce or intensify wind, while bodies of water produce moisture and reflect the sun.

Architectural forms. Planning may control the environment by the design of architectural forms that may modify the effects of natural forces. For example, overhanging eaves, moldings, projections, courts, and porches give shade and protection from rain. Roofs are designed to shed snow and to drain or preserve water. Walls control the amount of heat lost to the exterior or retained in the interior by their thickness and by the structural and insulating materials used in making them. Walls, when properly sealed and protected, are the chief defense against wind and moisture. Windows are the principal means of controlling natural light; its amount, distribution, intensity, direction, and quality are conditioned by their number, size, shape, and placement and by the characteristics of translucent materials (*e.g.,* thickness, transparency, texture, colour). But the planning of fenestration is influenced by other factors, such as ventilation and heating. Since most translucent materials conduct heat more readily than the average wall, windows are used sparingly in extreme climates. Finally, since transparent windows are the medium of visual contact between the interior and exterior, their design is conditioned by aesthetic and practical demands.

The role of fenestration

Colour. Colour has a practical planning function as well as an expressive quality because of the range of its reflection and its absorption of solar rays. Since light colours reflect heat and dark colours absorb it, the choice of materials and pigments is an effective tool of environmental control.

Materials and techniques. The choice of materials is conditioned by their own ability to withstand the environment as well as by properties that make them useful to human beings. One of the architect's jobs is to find a successful solution to both conditions; to balance the physical and economic advantages of wood against the possibility of fire, termites, and mold, the weather resistance of glass and light metals against their high thermal conductivity, and many similar conflicts. The more violent natural manifestations, such as heavy snow loads, earthquakes, high winds, and tornadoes, are controlled by special technical devices in regions where they are prevalent.

Any number of these controls may be out of reach of the planner for various reasons. The urban environment, for example, restricts freedom of orientation and design of architectural forms and creates new control problems of its own: smoke, dirt, noise, and odours.

Interior control. The control of the environment through the design of the plan and the outer shell of a building cannot be complete, since extremes of heat and cold, light, and sounds penetrate into the interior, where they can be further modified by the planning of spaces and by special conditioning devices.

Temperature, light and sound are all subject to control by the size and shape of interior spaces, the way in which the spaces are connected, and the materials employed for floors, walls, ceilings, and furnishings. Hot air may be retained or released by the adjustment of ceiling heights and sources of ventilation. Light reflects in relation to the colour and texture of surfaces and may be reduced by dark, rough walls and increased by light, smooth ones. Sounds are transmitted by some materials and absorbed by others and may be controlled by the form of interiors and by the use of structural or applied materials that by their density, thickness, and texture amplify or restrict sound waves.

Conditioning devices played only a small part in architecture before the introduction of mechanical and electrical systems in the 19th century. The fireplace was almost the only method of temperature control (though the ancient Romans anticipated the modern water system for radiant heating); fuel lamps and candles had to be movable and were rather in the sphere of furnishings than of architecture; the same is true of the tapestries and hangings used for acoustical purposes and to block drafts.

Early temperature conditioning devices

Today, heating, insulation, air conditioning, lighting, and acoustical methods have become basic parts of the architectural program. These defenses and comforts of industrialization control the environment so efficiently that the contemporary architect is free to use or to discard many of the traditional approaches to site and interior planning.

Planning for use. While environmental planning produces comfort for the senses (sight, feeling, hearing) and reflexes (respiration), planning for use or function is concerned with convenience of movement and rest. All activities that demand architectural attention require unique planning solutions to facilitate them. These solutions are found by differentiating spaces for distinct functions, by providing circulation among these spaces, and by designing them to facilitate the actions of the human body.

Differentiation. The number of functions requiring distinct kinds of space within a building depends not only upon the type of building but also upon the requirements of the culture and the habits and activities of the individual patrons. A primitive house has a single room with a hearth area, and a modern one has separate areas for cooking, eating, sleeping, washing, storage, and recreation. A meetinghouse with a single hall is sufficient for Quaker religious services, while a Roman Catholic cathedral may require a nave, aisles, choir, apse, chapels, crypt, sacristy, and ambulatory.

The planning of differentiated spaces involves as a guide to their design (placement, size, shape, environmental conditions, sequence, etc.) the analysis of use (number of uses and character, duration, time of day, frequency, variability, etc., of each), users (number, behaviour, age, sex, physical condition, etc.), and furniture or equipment required.

Circulation. Communication among differentiated spaces and between the exterior and the interior may be achieved by openings alone in the simplest plans, but most buildings require distinct spaces allotted to horizontal and vertical circulation (corridors, lobbies, stairs, ramps, elevators, etc.). These are designed by the procedure of analysis employed for differentiating uses. Since their function is usually limited to simplifying the movement of persons and things toward a particular goal, their efficiency depends on making the goal evident and the movement direct and easy to execute.

Facilitation. The convenience of movement, like the comfort of environment, can be increased both by planning and by devices. Planning methods are based on analysis of the body measurements, movements, and muscular power of human beings of different ages and sexes, which results in the establishment of standards for the measurements of ceilings, doorways, windows, storage shelves, working surfaces, steps, and the like and for the weight of architectural elements that must be moved, such as doors, gates, and windows. These standards also include allowances for the movement of whatever furnishings, equipment, or machinery are required for the use of any building. Devices for facilitating movement within buildings replace or simplify the labours of daily life: the traditional pumps, plumbing, and sewerage systems and the innumerable modern machines for circulation, food preparation and preservation, industrial processing, and other purposes.

Thomas Airviews

Rockefeller Center, New York, by Reinhard & Hofmeister, Corbett, Harrison & MacMurray, and Hood & Fouilhoux, 1929–40; an example of urban planning using skyscrapers.

Economic planning. Major expenses in building are for land, materials, and labour. In each case they are high when the commodity is scarce and low when it is abundant, and they influence planning more directly when they become restrictive.

Cost of land, materials, and labour as planning factors

The effect of high land values is to limit the amount of space occupied by any building as well as the amount of expenditure that can be reserved for construction. When land coverage is limited, it is usually necessary to design in height the space that otherwise would be planned in breadth and depth, as in the ancient Roman *insula* (apartment houses) or the modern skyscraper. When the choice of materials is influenced by cost, all phases of architectural design are affected, since the planning procedure, the technique, and the form of buildings are dependent on materials. High labour costs influence the choice of techniques and, consequently, of materials. They encourage simplification in construction and the replacement of craftsmanship by standardization. The development in the 19th and 20th centuries of light wood-frame construction and methods of prefabrication were largely the result of the rising cost of labour.

Planning involves not only the control of cost in each area but also the proportioning of expenditures among land, materials, and labour in order to produce the most effective solution to an architectural problem.

Techniques

The techniques of architecture in the sense that they will be considered here are simply the methods by which structures are formed from particular materials. These methods are influenced not only by the availability and character of materials but also by the total technological development of society, for architecture depends on an organized labour force and upon the existence of the tools and skills necessary to secure, manufacture, transport, and work durable materials.

The influence of economic and expressive forces in the development of technique

The evolution of techniques is conditioned by two forces. One is economic—the search for a maximum of stability and durability in building with a minimum of materials and labour. The other is expressive—the desire to produce meaningful form. Techniques evolve rapidly when economic requirements suggest new expressive forms or when the conception of new forms demands new procedures. But they remain static when architects avoid the risk of pioneering with untried and possibly unsuccessful methods and depend instead on proved procedures or when the need for the observance of tradition, for the communication of ideas, or for elegance and display is best fulfilled by familiar forms.

The ultimate purpose of building techniques is to create a stable structure. In mechanical terms, structures are stable when all their parts are in a state of equilibrium, or rest. Walls and roofs can buckle, crack, or collapse if they are not properly designed. These movements are caused by forces that tend to push or pull bodies in a given direction. Forces acting on any member (part) of a building are, first, its own weight and, second, the loads it carries, principally from other members but also from persons, furnishings, wind, etc. Their action encounters a reaction in opposing forces that hold the member in place by resisting at its joints. These forces may be active in all directions, and they must be balanced for stability. They tend to crush, pull apart, and bend the member—in other words, to change its size and shape.

Within the member itself there are forces, too, that tend to resist any deformation. They are called stresses, and they vary according to the strength of materials and the form of the member. The kinds of stress under consideration are compression, which resists crushing; tension, which resists pulling apart; and bending, which occurs when one part of a member is in compression and the other is in tension. A column is put into compression by the loads it carries; in a trussed roof the piece that forms the base of the triangle is put into tension by the outward-pushing forces in the sides; and a lintel or beam (the member that spans a space) is put into bending by loads and forces that push down on its top and encounter a reacting force at its ends. Some materials are strong only in compression (*e.g.,* stone, brick, cast iron, concrete) and others in tension as well (*e.g.,* wood, steel, reinforced concrete), so the latter are more efficient in resisting bending forces.

Finally, the stability of the total structure whose single members are all in equilibrium is achieved by diverting the loads from all of them downward so that they may be resisted by the upward-supporting forces of the ground.

Techniques will be discussed in terms of the characteristics of building materials and the methods by which they are used in architecture (see BUILDING CONSTRUCTION).

MATERIALS

Stone. In most areas where stone is available, it has been favoured over other materials for the construction of monumental architecture. Its advantages are durability, adaptability to sculptural treatment, and the fact that it can be used in modest structures in its natural state. But it is difficult to quarry, transport, and cut, and its weakness in tension limits its use for beams, lintels, and floor supports.

The simplest and cheapest stonework is rubble; *i.e.,* roughly broken stones of any shape bounded in mortar. The strongest and most suitable stonework for monumental architecture is ashlar masonry, which consists of regularly cut blocks (usually rectangular). Because of its weight and the precision with which it can be shaped, stone masonry (in contrast with brick) does not depend on strong bonding for stability where it supports only direct downward loads. The entablatures (the upper sections of a classical order that rest on the capital of a column) of an ancient Greek temple, for example, were bonded by small bronze dowels. But the weight creates problems of stability when loads push at an angle; stone vaults and arches require more support and buttressing than equivalent forms in other materials.

The best stone (and brick) bonding is that in which blocks are placed so that the vertical joints in one course are not above the joints in the courses above and below, since the stone resists deformation better than any bonding material. Many stones are strong enough to provide monolithic supports (columns and piers) and beams (lintels); and in some styles stone slabs are employed even for roofing (ancient Egyptian temples, early Christian basilicas in Syria). But this roofing requires so many columns that unvaulted masonry buildings are almost always combined with floors and covering in wood. Stone has been consistently used for building since the Stone Age, as exemplified by Stonehenge, in England. Although it has generally been replaced as a structural material by cheaper and more efficient manufactured products, it is still widely used as a surface veneer for its practical and expressive qualities.

Durability of stone

Brick. Brick compares favourably with stone as a structural material for its fire- and weather-resisting qualities and for the ease of production, transportation, and laying. The size of bricks is limited by the need for efficient drying, firing, and handling, but shapes, along with the techniques of bricklaying, have varied widely throughout history. Special shapes can be produced by molding to meet particular structural or expressive requirements (for example, wedge-shaped bricks are sometimes employed in arch construction and bricks with rounded faces in columns). Bricks may be used in construction only in conjunction with mortar, since the unit is too small, too light, and too irregular to be stabilized by weight. Each course must be laid on an ample mortar bed with mortar filling the vertical joints. The commonest ancient Roman bricks were cut into triangles and laid with the base out and the apex set into a concrete filling that provided additional strength. Rectangular bricks are bonded either as headers (short side out) or stretchers (long side out). Standard modern types provide a ratio of width to length of slightly less than 1:2 to permit a wide variety of bonding patterns within a consistent module, or standard of measurement. Brick, which has been used since the 4th millennium BC, was the chief building material in the ancient Near East. The versatility of the medium was expanded in ancient Rome by improvements in the manufacture of both bricks and mortar and by new techniques of laying and bonding. Employed throughout the Middle Ages, brick gained greater popularity from the 16th century on, particularly in northern Europe. It is widely used in the 20th century, often for nonbearing walls in steel frame construction.

Wood. Wood is easier to acquire, transport, and work than other natural materials. All parts of a building can be efficiently constructed of wood except foundations; its disadvantage is susceptibility to fire, mold, and termites. The strength of wood in both tension and compression arises from its organic nature, which gives it an internal structure of longitudinal and radial fibres that is not impaired by cutting or long exposure. But like all organisms it contains moisture and is not uniformly strong, so it must be carefully selected and seasoned to prevent warping, splitting, and failure under loads. Wood is used in building both solid and skeletal structures. The principal solid system, called log construction, is employed when only primitive cutting tools are available. Four walls must be built up together in horizontal layers of single hewn or uncut logs and jointed at the corners. The stability of the log building depends entirely on the mutual support of the walls, and the method is suitable only for simple structures of limited size. The skeletal system requires precise cutting and shaping of lumber. It provides a rigid framework of jointed or nailed members independent of the walls, which are attached to the exterior and interior surfaces after completion.

Organic nature of wood structures

Almost all masonry buildings of the past had wood floors and coverings, since wood is the lightest, the most practical, and the most inexpensive material for spanning spaces.

The monumental architecture of the West has typically employed materials rarer than wood for expressive purposes, but the history of wood construction can be traced consistently in China, Korea, and Japan and in the domestic architecture of northern Europe and North America. Wood continues to be used in a growing number of techniques and products: heavy framing systems with compound beams and girders, interior and exterior facing with plywood and other composite panels, and arch and truss systems with laminated members that can be designed to meet particular structural demands (see FORESTRY AND WOOD PRODUCTION).

Iron and steel. The development of construction methods in iron and steel was the most important innovation in architecture since ancient times. These methods provide far stronger and taller structures with less expenditure of material than stone, brick, or wood and can produce greater unsupported spans over openings and interior or exterior spaces. The evolution of steel frame construction in the 20th century entirely changed the concept of the wall and the support.

In architecture before 1800, metals played an auxiliary role. They were used for bonding masonry (dowels and clamps), for tension members (chains strengthening domes, tie rods across arches to reinforce the vaults), and for roofing, doors, windows, and decoration. Cast iron, the first metal that could be substituted for traditional structural materials, was used in bridge building as early as 1779. Its ability to bear loads and to be produced in an endless variety of forms, in addition to its resistance to fire and corrosion, quickly encouraged architectural adaptations, first as columns and arches and afterward in skeletal structures. Because cast iron has much more compressive than tensile strength (for example, it works better as a small column than as a beam), it was largely replaced in the late 19th century by steel, which is more uniformly strong, elastic, and workable, and its high resistance in all stresses can be closely calculated.

Advantages of steel construction

Steel structural members are rolled in a variety of shapes, the commonest of which are plates, angles, I beams, and U-shaped channels. These members may be joined by steel bolts or rivets, and the development of welding in the 20th century made it possible to produce fused joints with less labour and materials. The result is a rigid, continuous structure in which the joint is as firm as the member and which distributes stresses between beams and columns. This is a fundamental change in architectural technique, the effect of which cannot yet be estimated.

Normally, steel must be protected against corrosion by surface coverings, but alloys such as stainless steel have been developed for exposed surfaces. Aluminum and other light metal alloys have come to be favoured for exterior construction because of their weather resistance.

Concrete. Concrete is a manufactured mixture of cement and water, with aggregates of sand and stones, which hardens rapidly by chemical combination to a stonelike, water- and fire-resisting solid of great compressive (but low tensile) strength. Because it can be poured into forms while liquid to produce a great variety of structural elements, it provides an economical substitute for traditional materials, and it has the advantages of continuity (absence of joints) and of fusing with other materials.

Concrete was employed in ancient Egypt and was highly developed by the ancient Romans, whose concrete made with volcanic-ash cement (pozzolana) permitted a great expansion of architectural methods, particularly the development of domes and vaults (often reinforced by brick ribbing) to cover large areas, of foundations, and of structures such as bridges and sewerage systems where waterproofing was essential. The technique of manufacture declined in the Middle Ages and was regained in the 18th century, but concrete had only a limited importance for architecture until the invention of reinforced concrete in the 1860s.

Development of reinforced concrete

Reinforced concrete was developed to add the tensile strength of steel to the compressive strength of mass concrete. The metal is embedded by being set as a mesh into the forms before pouring, and in the hardened material the two act uniformly. The combination is much more versatile than either product; it serves not only for constructing rigid frames but also for foundations, columns, walls, floors, and a limitless variety of coverings, and it does not require the addition of other structural materials. Although the making of forms is a slow and costly process, the technique competes economically with steel frame construction because the mesh, composed of thin, bendable metal rods or metal fabric, employs far less steel, and concrete is itself inexpensive.

The steel reinforcement is employed to take full advantage of the plastic, or sculptural, character of concrete. It can be jointed or bent to unify supporting members with the floors and the coverings they carry. Furthermore, stresses produced in floors, domes, and vaults may be distributed within the slabs themselves to reduce load, and the diminished load may be concentrated at desired points so that the number and size of supports is greatly reduced.

Three 20th-century developments in production are destined to have a radical effect on architecture. The first, concrete-shell construction, permits the erection of vast vaults and domes with a concrete and steel content so reduced that the thickness is comparatively less than that of an eggshell. The second development, precast-concrete construction, employs bricks, slabs, and supports made under optimal factory conditions to increase waterproofing and solidity, to decrease time and cost in erection, and to reduce expansion and contraction. Finally, prestressed concrete provides bearing members into which reinforcement is set under tension to produce a live force to resist a particular load. Since the member acts like a spring, it can carry a greater load than an unstressed member of the same size.

Concrete shells, precast concrete, and prestressed concrete

METHODS

Wall. The two types of wall are load bearing, which supports the weight of floors and roofs, and nonbearing, which at most supports its own weight.

Load-bearing wall. The load-bearing wall of masonry is thickened in proportion to the forces it has to resist: its own load, the load of floors, roofs, persons, etc., and the lateral forces of arches, vaults, wind, etc., that may cause it to crack or buckle. Its thickness often can be reduced at the top, because loads accumulate toward the base; in high buildings this is done by interior or exterior setbacks at the floor level of upper stories. Walls that must resist lateral forces are thickened either along the whole length or at particular points where the force is concentrated. The latter method is called buttressing. Doors and windows weaken the resistance of the wall and divert the forces above them to the parts on either side, which must be thickened in proportion to the width of the opening. In multistory buildings, windows—unless they are very small—must be placed one above the other so as to leave uninterrupted vertical masses of wall between them to transfer loads directly to the ground. The number of openings that can be used depends on the strength of the masonry and the stresses in the wall. Walls in light, wood-framed structures and in reinforced-concrete construction may have a bearing function also. But the nature of the material admits other means of resisting forces than the increase of mass.

The placement of walls is determined by the type of support for floors and roofs. The commonest support is the beam, which must be jointed to walls at both ends; consequently, its maximum permissible length establishes the distance between bearing walls. All floors and coverings are most easily supported on straight, parallel walls except the dome (see below *Dome*).

Nonbearing wall. Excluding the independent garden variety, the nonbearing wall appears only where loads are carried by other members, as in heavy timber and other skeletal structures. Modern steel and reinforced-concrete frames require exterior walls only for shelter and sometimes dispense with them on the ground floor to permit easier access. Since the wall rests or hangs upon members of the frame, it becomes a curtain or screen and admits treatment in any durable, weather-resisting material. Traditional materials are often used, but light walls of glass, plastic, metal alloys, wood products, etc., can be equally efficient. This freedom of choice extends also to the form of walls and offers greatly expanded opportunities for creative expression.

Curtain walls

Post-and-lintel. The simplest illustration of load and support in construction is the post-and-lintel system, in which two upright members (posts, columns, piers) hold

Toni Schneiders

Post-and-lintel system of support, temple of Poseidon, Cape Soúnion, southeast of Athens, *c.* 430 BC.

up a third member (lintel, beam, girder, rafter) laid horizontally across their top surfaces. This is the basis for the evolution of all openings. But, in its pure form, the post-and-lintel is seen only in colonnades and in framed structures, since the posts of doors, windows, ceilings, and roofs are part of the wall.

The job of the lintel is to bear the loads that rest on it (and its own load) without deforming or breaking. Failure occurs only when the material is too weak or the lintel is too long. Lintels composed of materials that are weak in bending, such as stone, must be short, while lintels in materials that are strong in bending, such as steel, may span far greater openings. Masonry lintels are inefficient because they must depend on the cohesiveness of mortar, which is weaker than the blocks it bonds; so, in masonry construction, lintels of monolithic (single-slab) stone, wood, and stronger materials are employed.

Lintel materials

The job of the post is to support the lintel and its loads without crushing or buckling. Failure occurs, as in lintels, from excessive weakness or length, but the difference is that the material must be especially strong in compression. Stone, which has this property, is more versatile as a post than as a lintel; under heavy loads it is superior to wood but not to iron, steel, or reinforced concrete. Masonry posts, including those of brick, may be highly efficient, since the loads compress the joints and add to their cohesiveness. Although monolithic stone columns are used, they are extravagant to produce for large structures, and columns are usually built up of a series of cylindrical blocks called drums.

From prehistoric times to the Roman Empire, the post-and-lintel system was the root of architectural design. The interiors of Egyptian temples and the exteriors of Greek temples are delineated by columns covered by stone lintels. The Greeks opened their interior spaces by substituting wooden beams for stone, since the wood required fewer supports. The development of the arch and vault challenged the system but could not diminish its importance either in masonry construction or in wood framing, by its nature dependent on posts and beams.

Ancient uses of the post-and-lintel were refined but not fundamentally altered until the production of cast-iron columns, which, offering greater strength and smaller circumference, greatly reduced the mass and weight of buildings. Much construction in modern materials is based on the post-and-lintel system of the past. Steel and concrete skeletons restore to modern architecture the formal simplicity of the oldest structures known. But, because they are rigid frames, they abandon the fundamental concept of the duality of post-and-lintel by fusing them into a unit throughout which stresses are distributed. The "mushroom" column is a further departure, since the unit can be extended into a covering slab and becomes a ceiling as well as a support.

"Mushroom" column with fountain, supporting a cantilever, Museo Nacional de Antropología, Mexico City, by Pedro Ramírez Vázquez and Rafael Mijares, 1964.

Victor Englebert—De Wys, Inc.

Arch. The arch can be called a curved lintel. Early masonry builders could span only narrow openings because of the necessary shortness and weight of monolithic stone lintels. With the invention of the arch, two problems were solved: (1) wide openings could be spanned with small, light blocks, in brick as well as stone, which were easy to transport and to handle; and (2) the arch was bent upward to resist and to conduct into its supports the loads that tended to bend the lintel downward. Because the arch is curved, the upper edge has a greater circumference than the lower, so that each of its blocks must be cut in wedge shapes that press firmly against the whole surface of neighbouring blocks and conduct loads uniformly. This form creates problems of equilibrium that do not exist in

Problems of equilibrium in the arch

George Holton—Photo Researchers, Inc.

Pont du Gard, Roman aqueduct, Nîmes, France, by Marcus Vipsanius Agrippa, during the Augustan period.

Two types of vaulting used in the medieval period.
(Left) Barrel-vaulted nave of Saint-Savin-sur-Gartempe, France, early 12th century. (Right) Rib-vaulted nave of the Bourges cathedral, France, begun *c.* 1195.
(Left) Jean Roubier; (right) Archives Photographiques

lintels. The stresses in the arch tend to squeeze the blocks outward radially, and loads divert these outward forces downward to exert a resultant diagonal force, called thrust, which will cause the arch to collapse if it is not properly buttressed. So an arch cannot replace a lintel on two free-standing posts unless the posts are massive enough to buttress the thrust and to conduct it into the foundations (as in ancient Roman triumphal arches). Arches may rest on light supports, however, where they occur in a row, because the thrust of one arch counteracts the thrust of its neighbours, and the system will remain stable as long as the arches at either end of the row are buttressed by walls, piers, or earth.

The size of arches is limited only by economy; large arches exert large thrusts, and they are hard to buttress and to build. The form may be varied to meet specific problems; the most efficient forms in masonry are semicircular, segmental (segment of a circle), and pointed (two intersecting arcs of a circle), but noncircular curves can be used successfully.

Arches were known in Egypt and Greece but were considered unsuitable for monumental architecture. In Roman times the arch was fully exploited in bridges, aqueducts, and large-scale architecture. New forms and uses were found in medieval and particularly Gothic architecture (flying buttress, pointed arch), and Baroque architects developed a vocabulary of noncircular forms for expressive reasons. Steel, concrete, and laminated-wood arches of the 20th century have changed the concept and the mechanics of arches. Their components are completely different from wedge-shaped blocks; they may be made entirely rigid so as to require only vertical support; they may be of hinged intersections that work independently, or they may be thin slabs or members (in reinforced concrete) in which stresses are so distributed that they add the advantages of lintels to those of arches, requiring only light supports. These innovations provide a great freedom of design and a means of covering great spans without a massive substructure.

Vaults in antiquity and the Middle Ages

Vault. The evolution of the vault begins with the discovery of the arch, because the basic "barrel" form, which appeared first in ancient Egypt and the Near East, is simply a deep, or three-dimensional, arch. Since the barrel vault exerts thrust as the arch does, it must be buttressed along its entire length by heavy walls in which openings must be limited in size and number. This is a disadvantage, since it inhibits light and circulation.

But Roman builders discovered that openings could be made by building two barrel vaults that intersected at right angles to form the groin vault, which is square in plan and may be repeated in series to span rectangular areas of unlimited length. This vault has the additional advantage that its thrusts are concentrated at the four corners, so that the supporting walls need not be uniformly massive but may be buttressed where they support the vault.

Two disadvantages of the groin vault encouraged Gothic builders to develop a modification known as the rib vault. First, to build a groin vault, a form must be made to pour or lay the entire vault, and this requires complex scaffolding from the ground up; second, the groin vault must be more or less square, and a single vault cannot span extended rectangular areas. The rib vault provided a skeleton of arches or ribs along the sides of the area and crossing it diagonally; on these the masonry of the vault could be laid; a simple centring sufficed for the ribs. To cover the rectangular areas, the medieval mason used pointed arches, which, unlike round arches, can be raised as high over a short span as over a long one. Thus, the vault could be composed of the intersection of two vaults of different widths but the same height.

To reduce further the thickness of the wall (to the point

of substituting large areas of glass for masonry), Gothic builders developed the flying buttress, which counteracts vault thrust not by continuous wall mass and weight but by counterthrust created by exterior half-arches placed at the height of the vaults at the points of greatest stress. These buttresses conduct stresses to heavier wall buttresses below the window level.

The next important development in vaults, as in arches, came with 19th-century materials. Great iron skeleton vaults were constructed as a framework for light materials such as glass (Crystal Palace, London). The elimination of weight and excessive thrust, the freedom in the use of materials, and the absence of centring problems favoured the simple barrel vault and made more complex types obsolete. But in many of the modern frame systems the vault itself loses its structural function and becomes a thin skin laid over a series of arches.

Modern methods of vaulting

While the arch is supplanting the vault in one area of technique, the vault has abandoned the arch principle in another. The reinforced-concrete shell vault, based on the principle of the bent or molded slab, is one of the most important innovations in the history of architecture. It has all the advantages of load distribution of the concrete floor slab, plus the resistance to bending provided by its curved form. The shell is reinforced in such a way that it exerts no lateral thrust and may be supported as if it were a beam or truss; hence, the form no longer necessitates the conducting of loads into the wall, and the vault may be designed with great freedom.

Dome. Domes appeared first on round huts and tombs in the ancient Near East, India, and the Mediterranean region but only as solid mounds or in techniques adaptable only to the smallest buildings. They became technically significant with the introduction of the large-scale masonry hemispheres by the Romans. Domes, like vaults, evolved from the arch, for in their simplest form they may be thought of as a continuous series of arches, with the same centre. Therefore, the dome exerts thrusts all around its perimeter, and the earliest monumental examples required heavy walls. Since the walls permitted few openings and had to be round or polygonal to give continuous support, early domes were difficult to incorporate into complex structures, especially when adjacent spaces were vaulted.

Byzantine architects perfected a way of raising domes on piers instead of walls (like groin vaults), which permitted lighting and communication from four directions. The transition from a cubic plan to the hemisphere was achieved by four inverted spherical triangles called pendentives—masses of masonry curved both horizontally and vertically. Their apexes rested on the four piers, to which they conducted the forces of the dome; their sides joined to form arches over openings in four faces of the cube; and their bases met in a complete circle to form the dome foundation. The pendentive dome could rest directly on this foundation or upon a cylindrical wall, called a drum, inserted between the two to increase height.

Development of pendentives

The dome was unsuited to the lightness and verticality of late-medieval styles but was widely used in the Renaissance and Baroque periods. Renaissance builders adapted the Gothic rib system to dome construction and found

Interior showing dome on pendentives, Hagia Sophia, Istanbul, by Anthemius of Tralles and Isidore of Miletus, completed 537.
Hirmer Fotoarchiv, Munich

Buckminster Fuller

Climatron, geodesic dome, Missouri Botanical Garden, St. Louis, by R. Buckminster Fuller, opened 1960.

new means to reduce loads and thrust (concentric chains, etc.) that permitted high drums and variations in the curvature of the dome. The awkward, tunnellike effect produced on the interior by high domes was often hidden by an internal shell built on the same foundations (as at Florence Cathedral and St. Paul's Cathedral, London).

The effort and ingenuity devoted to doming rectangular buildings can be explained principally by the symbolic character of the form, since vaulting is a simpler alternative. So it was chiefly the desire to observe tradition that preserved the dome in the early era of iron and steel construction, and, with rare exceptions (Halle aux Blés, Paris; the Coal Exchange, London), 19th-century examples retained masonry forms without exploiting the advantages of metal.

Modern techniques of vault construction

Newer techniques, however, have added practically to the expressive advantages of domes. The reinforced-concrete slab used in vaulting can be curved in length as well as width (like an inflated handkerchief or a parachute). And in this development the distinction between vaults and domes loses significance, being based on nothing but the type of curvature in the slab. Geodesic domes, developed in the 20th century by R. Buckminster Fuller, are spherical forms in which triangular or polygonal facets composed of light skeletal struts or flat planes replace the arch principle and distribute stresses within the structure itself, as in a truss. Geodesic domes can be supported by light walls and are the only large domes that can be set directly on the ground as complete structures.

Truss. By far the commonest covering throughout history is the trussed roof, constructed upon a frame composed of triangular sections spaced crosswise at intervals and made rigid in length by beams. Trusses formerly were principally of wood and were used to cover masonry as well as framed structures, even when these were vaulted. The variety of trusses is so great that only the general principle of the form can be given here.

The truss is based on the geometric law that a triangle is the only figure that cannot be changed in shape without a change in the length of its sides; thus, a triangular frame of strong pieces firmly fastened at the angles cannot be deformed by its own load or by external forces such as wind pressure. These forces, which in a vault thrust outward against the walls, are contained within the truss itself, because the piece (chord) at the base of the triangle resists by tension the tendency of the two sides to behave like a vault. With its forces in equilibrium, the truss exerts only a direct downward pressure on the walls, so that they need not be thickened or buttressed. This explains why most roofs are triangular in cross section.

Alinari—Art Resource/EB Inc.

Nave with view toward the apse and crypt, showing roof trusses, S. Miniato al Monte, Florence, 11th century.

In trusses that are too large to be constructed of three members of moderate size, a complex system of small triangles within the frame replaces the simple triangle.

Not all peaked roofs are trusses, for in primitive building, in ancient Greece, and in much Chinese and Japanese wood architecture the chord is omitted and the sides exert thrust. Nor are all trusses triangular, since the principle may be modified (as in modern steel and heavy timber construction) to apply to arches and vaults if chords of sufficient strength can be found.

Framed structures. A framed structure in any material is one that is made stable by a skeleton that is able to stand by itself as a rigid structure without depending on floors or walls to resist deformation. Materials such as wood, steel, and reinforced concrete, which are strong in both tension and compression, make the best members for framing. Masonry skeletons, which cannot be made rigid without walls, are not frames. The heavy timber frame, in which large posts, spaced relatively far apart, support thick floor and roof beams, was the commonest type of construction in eastern Asia and northern Europe from prehistoric times to the mid-19th century. It was supplanted by the American light wood frame (balloon frame), composed of many small and closely spaced members that could be handled easily and assembled quickly by nailing instead of by the slow joinery and dowelling of the past. Construction is similar in the two systems, since they are both based on the post-and-lintel principle. Posts must rest on a level, waterproof foundation, usually composed of masonry or concrete, on which the sill (base member) is attached. Each upper story is laid on crossbeams that are supported on the exterior wall by horizontal members. Interior walls give additional beam support.

The American balloon frame

In the heavy-timber system, the beams are strong enough to allow the upper story and roof to project beyond the plane of the ground-floor posts, increasing the space and weather protection. The members are usually exposed on the exterior. In China, Korea, and Japan, spaces between are enclosed by light screen walls and in northern Europe partly by thinner bracing members and partly by boards, panels, or (in half-timbered construction) bricks or earth.

The light frame, however, is sheathed with vertical or horizontal boarding or shingling, which is jointed or overlapped for weather protection. Sheathing helps to brace as well as to protect the frame, so the frame is not structurally independent as in steel frame construction. The light-frame system has not been significantly improved since its introduction, and it lags behind other modern techniques. Prefabricated panels designed to reduce the growing cost of construction have not been widely adopted. Modern heavy-timber and laminated-wood techniques, however, provide means of building up compound members for trusses and arches that challenge steel construction for certain large-scale projects in areas where wood is plentiful.

Steel frame structures

Steel framing is based on the same principles but is much simplified by the far greater strength of the material, which provides more rigidity with fewer members. The load-bearing capacity of steel is adequate for buildings many times higher than those made of other materials. Because the column and beam are fused by riveting or welding, stresses are distributed between them, and both can be longer and lighter than in structures in which they work independently as post-and-lintel. Thus, large cubic spaces can be spanned by four columns and four beams, and buildings of almost any size can be produced by joining cubes in height and width. Since structural steel must be protected from corrosion, the skeleton is either covered by curtain walls or surfaced in concrete or, more rarely, painted. The steel frame is used also in single-story buildings where large spans are required. The simple cube then can be abandoned for covering systems employing arches,

Miniature showing heavy timber frame construction, from the "Bedford Book of Hours," British Museum, Add. 18850, Folio 15 v., French, 15th century.
By courtesy of the trustees of the British Museum

trusses, and other elements in a limitless variety of forms in order to suit the functions of the building.

Differences between reinforced-concrete and steel framing are discussed in the section on materials. The greater rigidity and continuity of concrete frames give them more versatility, but steel is favoured for very tall structures for reasons of economy in construction and space. An example is the system called box frame construction, in which each unit is composed of two walls bearing a slab (the other two walls enclosing the unit are nonbearing curtain walls); this type of construction extends the post-and-lintel principle into three dimensions. Here, again, concrete crosses the barriers that separated traditional methods of construction.

Expression

Expression in architecture is the communication of quality and meaning. The functions and the techniques of building are interpreted and transformed by expression into art, as sounds are made into music and words into literature.

The nature of expression varies with the character of culture in different places and in different times, forming distinct modes or languages of expression that are called styles. Style communicates the outlook of a culture and the concepts of its architects. The boundaries of a style may be national and geographical (*e.g.,* Japanese, Mayan) or religious (*e.g.,* Islāmic) and intellectual (*e.g.,* Renaissance), embracing distinct linguistic, racial, and national units, and different expressions within each of these boundaries are produced by the particular style of regions, towns, groups, architects, or craftsmen. The lifespan of styles may be long (ancient Egyptian, over 3,000 years) or short (Baroque, less than 200 years) according to the changeability of cultural patterns. The principal forces in the creation of a style are tradition, the experience of earlier architecture; influence, the contribution of contemporary expressions outside the immediate cultural environment; and innovation, the creative contribution of the culture and the architect. These forces operate to produce an evolution within every style and ultimately to generate new styles that tend to supplant their predecessors.

The components of expression, which communicate the particular values of style, are content and form. Since content can be communicated only through form, the two are organically united, but here they will be discussed separately in order to distinguish the specific and concrete meaning (content) from the abstract expression of qualities (form).

CONTENT

Content is the subject matter of architecture, the element in architectural expression that communicates specific meanings that interpret to society the functions and techniques of buildings.

Symbols of function. Society requires that architecture not only communicate the aspirations of its institutions but also fulfill their practical needs. Differences in expres-

Wayne Andrews

West facade with dome of cast-iron construction, U.S. Capitol building, Washington, D.C., dome begun by Thomas Ustick Walter, 1851.

sion, apart from differences in planning, distinguish the forms of architectural types (the house from the church, etc.), the kinds of use (the Catholic from the Protestant church), and the traditions and customs of users (the English from the Swiss Protestant church). When architectural forms become the vehicles of content—in plan, elevation, and decoration—they are symbolic. Their symbolism can be understood consciously or unconsciously, by association (*e.g.,* spire = church) to a building one has seen before and by the fact that it suggests certain universal experiences (*e.g.,* vertical forms "rise"; low roofs "envelop"). One comprehends the meaning of symbols that are new, as well as those that are known, by association, because the laws of statics restrain builders from putting them into forms so completely unfamiliar that they do not suggest some tradition, just as the structure of language permits endless new meanings but retains a fairly constant vocabulary. The meaning of architectural symbols—or of words—may even change, but the process must be both logical and gradual, for, if the change is irrational, the purpose—communication—is lost.

Expressive identity through symbolic form

The architectural plan, when used symbolically, communicates through its shape. From prehistoric times and in many cultures, the circle, with its suggestion of the planets and other manifestations of nature, gained a symbolic, mystical significance and was used in the plans of houses, tombs, and religious structures. By slow processes it came to be employed for *memoria* and shrines and for hero cults in both the East and the West. When building techniques permitted, its symbolism often merged with that of the dome. In Hindu temples, the square (and the cross plans developed from it) expressed celestial harmony. The central-plan Christian church (circle, polygon, Greek cross, ellipse) fascinated the architects of the Renaissance by its symbolic and traditional values, and it is found in their drawings and treatises to the virtual exclusion of the more practical longitudinal basilicas that the architects were often commissioned to build.

Plan symbolism remained almost exclusively in the sphere of religion after antiquity, and its traditions gradually disappeared in the course of the 19th century. The modern plan is determined by problems of form (space-mass relationships, etc.) and by the practical demands of use rather than by symbolic communication.

Symbolic forms in elevation

In elevation the most consistent symbolic forms have been the dome, the tower, the stairway, the portal, and the colonnade. Domes imply the meanings of the circle and more, since a dome is a covering. Long before masonry domes could be built, the hemisphere was associated with the heavens as a "cosmic canopy," and throughout history domes have been decorated with stars and astrological symbols.

In ancient Rome and among Christians and Indian Buddhists the dome came to mean universal power. During the Renaissance it spread from religious structures to palaces and government buildings, retaining some of its implications of power. In the United States the national capitol is domed and there are few state capitols without domes; the symbol has survived the loss of its original meanings.

The tower, with origins in primitive nature rites, has consistently symbolized power. The Chinese pagoda extends central-plan symbolism into towers; many towers and spires rose from the northern European Gothic cathedral and the medieval Italian city was a forest of towers erected by nobles in constant competition to express their supremacy. This meaning survives in modern skyscrapers; their height is more frequently boasted of than their efficiency or beauty.

Functional architectural elements as symbols

Architectural elements conceived to facilitate the use of buildings may also take on symbolic significance. The stairway, employed in the past to give "monumentality" to important buildings, frequently became more expressive than convenient, especially in Baroque palaces. Portals, from the time of ancient Egyptian temple pylons and Babylonian city gates, became monuments in themselves, used to communicate a heightened significance to what lay behind them. In the Gothic cathedral they became the richest element of the facade—a translation of biblical doctrine into stone. Since the classic development of the ancient Greek temple, the colonnade on the exterior of buildings has borne similar implications.

Baroque staircase, Residenz (1719–44), Würzburg, West Germany, by Balthasar Neumann.
Erich Muller

Such symbols have become archaic in modern culture and appear as a sign of resistance to new forms. This resistance is especially evident in the popular symbolism of domestic architecture, where the atmosphere of the home is often expressed by cottage-like roofs, shutters, trellises, mullioned windows, grilles, and other associations with a more peaceful past.

Decoration, the most easily recognized medium of content, communicates meaning either through architectural elements or through the figural arts (sculpture, painting, mosaic, stained glass, etc.). The architectural elements used decoratively, such as the classical orders, usually originate in technique and in time lose their structural significance to become symbols. In Rome and from the Renaissance to the 20th century, the formal Grecian orders were applied to buildings of many different techniques as expressions of the continuing influence of Greek institutions. Similarly, the new vocabulary of Gothic architecture, developed with new building techniques (the pointed arch, the flying buttress, etc.), became in later periods a source for religious and romantic symbolism. The Art Nouveau of the turn of the 20th century, a system of ornament based on floral and other organic forms, survived for only two decades, perhaps because its symbols were neither drawn from a tradition nor derived from a structural system. (The role of architectural ornament will be further treated below).

The role of the figural arts

The function of the figural arts in conveying content is a subject outside the scope of this article, but its importance for architecture must be mentioned. The figural arts not only offer the means of expressing more specific ideas than any architectural symbols, but in many architectural styles they define the character of mass and space. The sculptures of the Hindu temple, the mosaics of the Byzan-

The Studio Elvira, 1897–98, Munich, by August Endell; an example of Art Nouveau ornament.
Foto Marburg

tine church, and the stuccoes of Moorish palaces are not ornamental applications; they determine the form of the building itself.

The virtual absence of traditional symbols in modern architecture is evidence of the failure of these symbols to express the cultural patterns of the 20th century. In these times, architecture, like painting, sculpture, and other arts, has tended to be abstract, to emphasize qualities of form rather than the communication of familiar ideas through symbols.

Expression of technique. The second aspect of content is the communication of the structural significance of materials and methods. Its purpose is to interpret the way in which architecture is put together. The characteristics of materials that are important in expressing design techniques are the properties of their composition (*e.g.*, structure, weight, durability) and the way they are used in structure. Their properties may be expressed and interpreted by the treatment of the surface, and their use may be expressed by emphasis on the dimensions and joining of the building units into which they are formed.

The hardness, weight, and crystalline composition of stone masonry traditionally have been emphasized by devices not necessarily connected with structural methods: rustication (finishing in rough, uneven surfaces), drafting (more refined, linear cutting), and polishing. Niches and other indentations, projecting courses, or frames around openings suggest massiveness. In nonbearing walls, a smooth, unbroken surface implies thinness. The use of stone or brick masonry in construction is emphasized by clarifying the limits of each block and by the amount of mortar used and by distinguishing lintels, arches, and other specific members from the construction of the wall. The properties of wood are suggested by revealing and emphasizing its texture in load-bearing members and by treating the sheathing of light wood frames in patterns (of shingling or boarding) that communicate thinness. The plasticity of concrete is shown by freedom in modelling and its use in construction by emphasizing the impressions of the wooden forms in which it is cast. The sections of light metal curtain walls are frequently stamped into geometric patterns to illustrate their nonbearing character. Materials that must be covered for protection, such as unfired brick and the steel used in framing, are not adaptable to this type of communication.

Interpretive expression of structural method

At times building methods are demonstrated simply by exposing the structure, as in the heavy timber frame, but in many styles the functions of structural systems have been interpreted by designing their members in forms that often are more explanatory than efficient. The Greek column, which is narrower at its summit than at its base, is diminished by a curve beginning slightly below the midpoint, giving it an effect of an almost muscular power to resist loads. The expression is more explicit in the caryatid, a human figure that replaces the column, and in the burdened animals and dwarfs that support the columns of Romanesque portals. Many elements in the Gothic cathedral serve as diagrams of structure: the supporting piers are clusters of shafts, each of which extends upward without interruption to become the rib of the vault, and the ribs themselves are an elucidation of technique; the flying buttress and the window tracery are elegant interpretations of their functions. In the modern steel-frame building, the hidden forms of the skeleton are often repeated on the facade to enable one to "see through" to the technique, but the system also permits the alternative of expressing the lightness and independence of the curtain wall by sheer surfaces of glass and other materials. The work of the concrete slab is made explicit by projecting indications of the placement of reinforcement or of the distribution of stresses.

The expression of technique is characteristic not of all architectural styles but only of those such as the Gothic and modern, in which new techniques excite a search for the interpretive design of their materials and methods. More often than not, both materials and methods have been disguised by decorative forms or surfacing such as veneers, stucco, or paint, because of emphasis on the expression of content or of form. Most early stone architecture in Egypt, Greece, and India retained as decoration the forms developed in wooden forerunners. The precious marble of Greek temples was disguised under painted stucco; Roman brickwork was hidden by slabs of coloured marble; and 19th-century cast-iron columns were molded into classic or Gothic forms. The history of domes is filled with examples of the successful disguising of method, of giving the ponderous mass the effect of rising from the exterior and of floating from within.

Disguised methods and materials

Technical content has been one of the foundation stones of 20th-century architectural theory, particularly in its early phases, and has represented a reaction against 19th-century symbolic content. It is essential for the understanding of modern architecture that the expression of technique be seen as an art—a creative interpretation that heightens awareness of the nature of architecture.

FORM

In the sphere of function and technique, the architect is responsible to the patterns of his culture on one hand and to the patterns of technology on the other; but, in the expression of form, he is free to communicate his own personality and concepts. Not every architect has the

Nave toward the apse, S. Giorgio Maggiore, Venice, designed by Andrea Palladio, 1566; an example of Renaissance space.

Osvaldo Bohm—EB Inc.

gift to exercise this prerogative to the fullest. As in other arts and sciences, a few individuals generate new styles, and others follow, interpreting these styles in original and personal ways. But the majority accepts styles as given and perpetuates them without leaving its mark. The architect's principal responsibility in the formation of style is to create meaningful form. When form is spoken of in the arts, not only the physical shape, size, and mass of a work are meant but also all the elements that contribute to the work's aesthetic structure and composition. Many of these may be without a fixed form of their own—a rest in music, a line in painting, a space in architecture—and gain significance only as they are organized into the finished product. The basic formal elements of architecture in this sense are space and mass. The process of organizing these elements into an ordered form is called composition, and the principal means by which they are given expressive quality are scale, light, texture, and colour.

Space and mass. Space, that immaterial essence that the painter suggests and the sculptor fills, the architect envelops, creating a wholly human and finite environment within the infinite environment of nature. The concept that space can have a quality other than emptiness is difficult to grasp. When a building is entered, floor, supports, walls, and a ceiling are seen, all of which can be studied and perhaps enjoyed, while the space, in the sense that one is accustomed to think of it, is void: the absence of mass, filled by air.

Experiencing space

But spatial experiences that express something are common to everyone, though they are not always consciously grasped. One feels insecure in a low cave or a narrow defile, exhilarated and powerful on a hilltop; these are psychological and motor reactions that result from measuring one's potential for movement against the surrounding spaces, and the same reactions take root even in language ("confining" circumstances and "elevating" experiences are spoken of). An infinite variety of such reactions may be summoned by the architect, because he controls the limits above, below, and on all sides of the observer. As a person enters the architect's space he measures it in terms of the degree and the quality of his potential for movement. The concept of potentiality is important, first, because the observer can anticipate where he may move merely looking about him and, second, because he can conceive movements that he cannot execute. Thus, in the nave of a Gothic cathedral the high walls closely confining the observer on two sides restrict his possible movements, suggesting advance along the free space of the nave toward the altar; or their compression forces him to look upward to the vaults and the light far overhead, there to feel a sense of physical release, though he is earthbound. The experience of Gothic space is called uplifting because it urges one to rise.

Alinari—Art Resource

St. Peter's, Vatican City, colonnade and piazza designed by Gian Lorenzo Bernini, begun 1656.

Renaissance space, on the other hand, attempts to balance its suggestion of movement, to draw the observer to a focal point at which he can sense an equilibrium of movement in all directions, a resolution of the conflict of compression and release. At this point one feels physically at rest, at the opposite extreme from the elevating sensation of the cathedral.

Of course, one does not use his eyes alone to feel spatial quality, because only the simplest spaces—a cubic room, for example—can be wholly experienced from one standpoint. In a complex of spaces, such as that of the cathedral, the observer walks about, gaining new sensations, seeing new potentials for movement at every step. Most modern architecture, in its free organization of space sequences, demands mobility; its techniques have made it possible to remove the heavy walls and supports of the past, reducing the sense of compression. Walls become membranes to be arranged at will for spatial experience, and some are transparent and so extend one's potential for movement into the limitless out-of-doors.

Spatial experience is not restricted to the interiors of buildings. The sensations one has in nature's open spaces may be re-created by art. City squares and streets, even gardens, achieve a variety of expression comparable with that of interiors. The Baroque piazza of St. Peter's in Rome, which directs the observer along its great embracing arcs toward the entrance, is at least as moving as the church interior.

The exterior of a single building, particularly one that is isolated from other architecture, does not create a space. It occupies the space of nature. Thus, it may be experienced as sculpture, in terms of the play of masses in a void. The aesthetics of masses, like that of spaces, is rooted in one's psychology. When a tall tree or a mountain is called majestic and a rocky cliff menacing, human attributes are being projected. Man inevitably humanizes inert matter and so gives the architect the opportunity to arouse predictable patterns of experience.

Appreciating mass

The appreciation of mass, like that of space, depends on movement, but this movement must be physical. It cannot be experienced in anticipation, because, no matter where one stands to observe even the simplest building, part of it is out of sight. The mass of a complex building is differently composed from every point of view. The 20th-century art critic Sigfried Giedion, emphasizing the need for movement in experiencing modern architecture, suggested that architecture may be four-dimensional, since time (for movement) is as meaningful as the spatial dimensions.

Some architecture depends much more on mass expression than on space expression. The Egyptian pyramid, the Indian stupa, and the dagoba of Sri Lanka have no meaningful interior spaces; they are architectural in function and technique, sculptural in expression. The interior of a Greek temple is of little interest compared with the wonderful play of forms on its colonnaded exterior, while early Christian and Byzantine architecture reverse the emphasis, making the simple exterior a shell for a splendid and mystical space. Gothic architecture balances the two, partly in order to express a dual content: earthly power over the world outside, spiritual power inside. Modern techniques permit a reduction of the contrast between space and mass expressions by reducing the mass of walls and the size and number of supports and by allowing the interpenetration of interior and exterior space.

Composition. Space and mass are the raw materials of architectural form; from them the architect creates an ordered expression through the process of composition. Composition is the organization of the whole out of its parts—the conception of single elements, the interrelating of these elements, and the relating of them to the total form.

The simplest architectural element is a plane, the flat, two-dimensional surface that limits masses and spaces. The simplest plane is a rectangular one without openings or decoration—the wall of a room, for example. This wall is given quality solely by the proportion of its width to its height. Now a door is put into the wall; the door itself has a certain proportion, and a third element is injected, the relation of two proportions. A window is added, and the composition becomes more complex; then a row of windows, and sequence becomes a factor in addition to the elements of proportion and relation. Sequence again involves the concept of motion; the row of windows is said "to run along" the facade or is "rhythmically" designed.

Finally, this wall may gain rich subtleties of composition within its proportions and rhythms. It can be modelled—into a complex of planes or irregular or curved surfaces—to provide the dimension of depth to its proportions; or symbols of use or of technique can become part of its expressive form.

No architectural planes stand alone, of course; they always intersect other planes. The room wall meets two other walls, the floor, and the ceiling, and a facade wall

Paul Popper Ltd.—Publix

The Ruanveli dagoba at Anurādhapura, Sri Lanka, 2nd century.

meets the ground, the roof, and two other walls. So the total composition of a wall must be harmonized with the composition of other planes in a three-dimensional whole.

Systems of proportions

The means of achieving this harmony differ in every style. Greek architects developed a system of proportions based on the lower diameter of the temple column, from which spatial intervals and the measurement of masses were derived by multiplication and division. Medieval architects first used arithmetical modules based on the measurements of areas in the cathedral plan and, in the Gothic period, changed to a geometric system that employed chiefly the equilateral triangle and the square, figures that had symbolic and mystical values. In Renaissance theory, proportions and harmonies were developed from systems of musical composition, since architects believed that relationships in all the arts depended on an all-pervading celestial harmony. Several modular and proportional systems have been evolved by modern architects (*e.g.,* Le Corbusier's "Modulor"), but none has been widely adopted.

Behind these changing theoretical methods, however, there seems to be a constant human reaction to spatial relationships that distinguishes harmony from cacophony, that makes one bored with a perfectly cubic room or prefer certain rectangular forms to others. This psychological response to form probably is connected to one's mechanisms of balance, movements, and stature—in short, to one's own composition—but the scientific analysis of the process is still at an early stage of development.

By courtesy of the National Gallery of Art, Washington, D.C., Samuel H. Kress Collection

"The Interior of the Pantheon," oil painting by Gian Paolo Pannini (1691/92–1765). In the National Gallery of Art, Washington, D.C.

Some buildings have only a single, simple interior space (the Pantheon in Rome) or exterior mass (the pyramids of Egypt) and are not less expressive on this account. But composition carries on into a richer dimension as soon as two or more spaces or masses are organized into the whole. Such a complex composition must give a coordinated form to connecting spaces and masses, each of them in itself a unique harmony. The observer must be made to feel, in moving through the spaces and around the masses, not only that each is related to the one that precedes and follows it but that each one is contributing to a concept of the whole: a form that is greater than the sum of its parts. In the Gothic cathedral, the nave, the aisles alongside it, the transept that crosses it toward one end, the choir, and apse beyond may each be experienced separately for its own quality. But the experience gains its full meaning only when the form of the total expression is realized: the low aisles giving grandeur to the high nave, the three together leading to the confluence of the two transept arms at the crossing in a vast climax that prepares for the resolution or finale at the altar. In the same way, the significance of a total mass composition unfolds as one moves about its separate parts. At St. Peter's in Rome, the three projecting apses are gathered into a unity by the undulating walls; they prepare for the cylindrical drum, the drum for the dome, the form of which leads to the culminating lantern, which is harmonized with the drum. Toward the facade, two little domes frame and prophesy the great one, as the cathedral aisles do the nave. While these particular examples from the past illustrate symmetrical compositions with a climax, other buildings that are of equal quality might be chosen to show irregular unity that is no less expressive (*e.g.,* the Erechtheum in Athens; the abbey of Mont Saint-Michel in France).

Perception of both the whole and its parts

In modern architecture, as in modern painting, Renaissance laws of composition, which emphasized the symmetry and balance of semi-independent units, have been supplanted by principles that imply the continuity of the whole and remove distinctions between parts. The biological term organic is sometimes used to describe a process of composition that seeks to develop interdependent spaces and masses that function expressively as members of an organism.

If composition were merely a matter of organizing a certain number of relationships, the process would be mechanical, not creative, and all architecture would be equally good or, more likely, bad. The purpose of composition is to express particular concepts and experiences, and it is successful only when these are fully communicated to the observer.

Scale. When the proportions of architectural composition are applied to a particular building, the two-termed relationship of the parts to the whole must be harmonized with a third term—the observer. He not only sees the proportions of a door and their relationship to those of a wall (as he would in a drawing of the building), but he measures them against his own dimensions. This three-termed relationship is called scale.

A well-scaled building such as a Greek temple will serve for illustration. If it were to be magnified to the size of St. Peter's in Rome, with its proportions remaining unchanged in their own relationships, the temple would be out of scale, and the result would appear monstrous. If the columns were to be doubled in width while the temple remained the same size, they would be out of scale and out of proportion with the whole. The proportions of the temple are satisfactory as they are because they are based on certain aesthetic principles established by the Greeks, principles that are partly rooted in human psychological makeup and partly accepted by custom (*e.g.,* as are musical consonances). It is difficult to understand, however, why the scale of these temples is so successful within a certain range of size, for neither the ancient Greeks nor anyone else established laws to relate scale to size. They found their solution by experiment and subjective judgment.

Comprehension of proportions

It may be that the success of scale depends upon man's ability to comprehend proportions in relation to some unit or module that is roughly human sized and close enough to a person in a building to permit him to measure it against himself. The Greeks, in employing the base of the column as a module for all the proportions of a temple, found a unit of a size that can be grasped easily and one that is close to eye level as a person approaches the temple. This module is a key to relationships among elements too far away to measure. This can be done in much larger buildings, too, where the elements close to the observer are too massive to be measured easily. Roman and Renaissance architecture retained the ancient Greek orders as decoration partly for this reason, using them to break up huge masses into more comprehensible parts. In entirely different styles of architecture, such as the Gothic, where the expressive function requires immeasurable proportions, there is still a measurable module given in the base of the pier. But piers and columns are not always a source of the module. In masonry construction, the single block can serve the same purpose. In frame construction, the bay (distance between floors or columns) or doors and windows may make a better key. The most successful modern skyscrapers retain a comprehensible scale, in spite of their size, by the repetition of some such module, and this is one reason why the skeleton is so often expressed on the exterior even when it is hidden behind walls.

Light. Light is a necessity for sight and, in architecture, a utility. But light is also a powerful, though ephemeral, vehicle of expression. Because it moves, changes character, and comes and goes with its source, light has the power to give to the inert mass of architecture the living quality of nature. The architect, though he does not quite control it, can predict its behaviour well enough to catch its movements meaningfully. He channels it through openings into his spaces and molds it on the surfaces of his masses by changes of plane, making it enliven his forms by contrast with shadow (see LIGHTING AND LIGHTING DEVICES).

Attempts to control light for expressive effect

The sunlight that falls on the exteriors of buildings cannot be directed or changed in quality, but it can be reflected or absorbed in a wide range of modulation by the relief and texture of surfaces. The planes and decoration of a facade, therefore, are not just the lines the architect makes on his working drawings but receptacles of light and shadow that change in character, even in form, as the Earth moves about the Sun.

Because of this link between nature and art, an important part in the formation of local architectural styles is played by the variation in the quality and intensity of light in different climatic regions.

The architect controls interior light better than exterior light, since he can select the position, size, and shape of its source. With glass and other transparent materials he transforms even its colour and intensity and so gives light a meaning independent of that which it imparts to the structure. One realizes this most powerfully in the Gothic cathedral, where the stained-glass windows transform the rays of the sun into a mystical diffusion that descends from above like a supernatural vision.

Furthermore, light may be illusory, dissolving rather than clarifying form. When it comes out of darkness in great intensity it seems to spread outward from its architectural channel. This illusion may be employed to express meanings, as at Hagia Sophia in Istanbul, where the light from the base of the dome hides the supports, giving the impression that the canopy floats on air.

Texture. Texture plays a dual role in architecture: it expresses something of the quality of materials, and it gives a particular quality to light. Although one absorbs both qualities simultaneously by eye, the first has tactile, the second visual associations.

Specific tactile textures are peculiar to every material by virtue of its manufacture or natural composition, but they may be altered to produce a variety of expressive qualities. Any stone may be used in its natural, irregular state, or it may be chiselled in a rough or smooth texture or highly polished to convey a range of meanings from vigour to refinement.

Visual textures are produced by the patterns given to the lighting of the surface both through the way the materials are worked (*e.g.,* vertical or horizontal chiselling of stone) and through the way they are employed in building (*e.g.,* vertical or horizontal boarding, projection and recession of courses of brick). Like all patterns, visual textures create associations of movement, giving rhythm to the surface.

A single texture is rarely employed in building. The variety of materials and treatments typically produces a complex of textures that must be composed and harmonized like the forms and spaces of architecture into a consistent expressive whole.

Colour. Since colour is a characteristic of all building materials, it is a constant feature of architecture. But building materials are selected primarily for their structural value, and their colours are not always suited to expressive requirements; thus, other materials chosen for their colour are frequently added to the surface. These include pigments, which usually preserve the texture of the original surface, and veneers of stone, wood, and a variety of manufactured products that entirely alter the surface character.

But colour, regardless of how it is produced, is the most impermanent element in architecture. It changes with the weathering and staining of materials (the white Gothic cathedrals are now deep gray), or, if it is superficial, it can easily be altered or removed (as the coloured stucco veneers of ancient Greek temples or the bright marble facing on Roman brickwork).

The values that are associated with colour (yellow and red, for instance, are called "gay," black and deep blue "sombre") are independent of materials and forms, and they give the architect a range of expression not provided by other means at his disposal. A different expressive device is provided by the great range of light reflection in the colour scale. Colours that reflect light brilliantly appear to advance toward the viewer, and those that absorb light appear to recede; the degree of projection and recession of architectural forms may be altered, emphasized, or subdued by the colours of their surfaces.

Environment. Architecture, unlike most of the other arts, is not often conceived independently of particular surroundings. The problems of design extend beyond the organizing of space and mass complexes to include the relating of the total form to its natural and architectural environment.

In site planning, a primary function of architectural design, the architect aims to create harmonies with preexisting elements in the landscape and "townscape."

But the province of the architect is not limited to the conception of single structures in harmony with a given setting. Throughout history, architects have been employed in giving a new form to the environment itself: planning the natural surroundings by the design of parks, roadways, waterways, etc.; designing complexes of related buildings; and organizing the urban environment into areas of residence, recreation, assembly, commerce, etc., both to increase their utility and to give them unique expressive qualities through the interrelationship of groups of buildings to the open areas about them. (J.S.Ac.)

ORNAMENT

Although it would be difficult to cover in any single definition all conceptions, past and present, of what constitutes ornament in architecture, three basic and fairly distinct categories may be recognized: mimetic, or imitative, ornament, the forms of which have certain definite meanings or symbolic significance; applied ornament, intended to add beauty to a structure but extrinsic to it; and organic ornament, inherent in the building's function or materials.

Mimetic ornament. Although it is still found in the 20th century, mimetic ornament is by far the commonest type of architectural ornament in primitive cultures, in Asian civilizations, and generally throughout antiquity. It grows out of what seems to be a universal human reaction to technological change: the tendency to reproduce in new materials and techniques shapes and qualities familiar from past usage, regardless of appropriateness. This tendency may be called the principle of mimesis. Most common building types in antiquity, both East and West (*e.g.,* tombs, pyramids, temples, towers), began as imitations of primeval house and shrine forms. An obvious example is the dome, which developed as a permanent wooden or stone reproduction of a revered form originally built of pliable materials. In the mature stages of early civilizations, building types tended to evolve beyond primitive prototypes; their ornament, however, usually remained based on such models. Decorative motifs derived from earlier structural and symbolic forms are innumerable and universal. In developed Indian and Chinese architecture, domical and other originally structural forms occur often

Traditional nature of mimetic ornament

and lavishly as ornament. In ancient Egypt, architectural details continued to preserve faithfully the appearance of bundled papyrus shafts and similar early building forms. In ancient Mesopotamia, brick walls long imitated the effect of primitive mud-and-reed construction. In the carved-stone details of the Greco-Roman orders (*e.g.,* capitals, entablatures, moldings), the precedent of archaic construction in wood was always clearly discernible.

The prevalence of mimetic ornament in architecture may be explained in two ways. Some (perhaps most in primitive cultures) is religious in origin. Certain forms and shapes, through long association with religious rites, became sacred and were preserved and reproduced for their symbolic value. These forms continued to be understood even though they were often stylized into abstract or geometric patterns, unrecognizably removed from their naturalistic models. Much mimetic ornament, however, even in early times, can be ascribed simply to inertia or conservatism. People have generally tended to resist change; they find it reassuring to be surrounded by known and familiar forms. Reproducing them as ornament on newly introduced forms is a common reaction to the vague feeling of uneasiness that rapid social and technological change induces; it provides a satisfying sense of continuity between the past and the present. This resistance was a factor in the 19th- and early-20th-century practice of disguising new techniques of construction in metal and glass by an overload of ornament imitating earlier styles.

Applied ornament. Architectural ornament in the 19th century exemplified the common tendency for mimetic ornament, in all times and places, to turn into mere applied decoration, lacking either symbolic meaning or reference to the structure on which it is placed. By the 5th century BC in Greece, the details of the orders had largely lost whatever conscious symbolic or structural significance they may have had; they became simply decorative elements extrinsic to the structure. The Doric frieze is a good case: its origin (*i.e.,* an imitation of the effect of alternating beam ends and shuttered openings in archaic wood construction) remained evident, but it came to be treated as a decorative sheath without reference to the actual structural forms behind. In losing their mimetic character, the details of the Greek orders acquired a new function; they served to articulate or unify the building visually, organizing it into a series of coordinated visual units that could be comprehended as an integrated whole, rather than as a collection of isolated units. This concept of applied decoration was passed on through the Greco-Roman period. The triumphal arch of Rome, with its system of decorative columns and entablature articulating what is essentially one massive shape, is a particularly good illustration; the Colosseum is another. Most of the great architecture of the Renaissance and Baroque periods depends on it; to a large extent, the difference between these styles is the difference in decoration. The characteristic serenity and balance of Filippo Brunelleschi's architecture in the 15th century, for example, is very largely effected by his treatment of pilasters (rectangular ornamental columns with bases and capitals) and entablatures applied to them, whereas, in 16th-century wall-surface designs such as Michelangelo's Medici chapel or the dome of St. Peter's, the same elements are used in different combinations to create a quite opposite effect of tension and release.

Function as an element to achieve organization

Judicious and intelligent use of applied ornament remained characteristic of most Western architecture until the 19th century, when the rationale of applied ornament frequently broke down, and an often indiscriminate and inappropriate use of decoration became characteristic. The reasons for this development are complex. In part it was a reaction to an overly rapid pace of social change during the period; partly, also, it was a logical outgrowth of the increasingly lavish decoration of late Baroque and Rococo architecture in the 18th century. Also, there was an overemphasis on the purely literary and associative values attached to the ornament characteristic of historical architectural styles. But compounding all these factors was the development of machinery, such as multiple lathes and jigs, which provided builders with cheap prefabricated ornament to give their often shoddy and ill-proportioned structures an illusion of elegance. Architectural ornament and architectural forms proper tended to part company and to be designed quite independently of each other.

Organic ornament. By the early 20th century a preoccupation with the proper function of architectural ornament was characteristic of all advanced architectural thinkers; by the mid-20th century a concept of architectural ornament had been formulated that has been called organic ornament. This concept, however, is by no means peculiar to the 20th century. Its essential principle is that ornament in architecture should derive directly from and be a function of the nature of the building and the materials used. This principle is characteristic of both Christian and Islāmic religious architecture of the medieval period. In the architectural ornament of Muslim India or Persia, as in early Christian and Byzantine work, there is a strong mimetic element. The proscription of representational forms in the Qur'ān and the tendency of both Muslim and early Christian artists to borrow and adapt their formal vocabulary from preceding cultures led inevitably to their transforming what had been meaningful forms into systems of abstract ornament. But basically this ornament was neither mimetic nor applied. Throughout the Middle Ages, church buildings were conceived primarily as tangible symbols of heaven. Their architectural ornament, no matter how various or lavish, was consistently designed to promote this symbolism; whether by gilt, intricacy, or multiplicity, it all contributed to an overall effect of glory and so was integral to the architectural form.

Relation of ornament to nature, function, and structure

Twentieth-century concepts of the function of architectural ornament, generally speaking, began with an understanding of this medieval usage that grew out of the 19th-century writings of the English art critic John Ruskin and the French Gothic Revival architect Viollet-le-Duc, as well as through the interpretations and applications of the British designer William Morris. The immediate influence of these men proved rather unfortunate. The first result of Viollet-le-Duc's disciplined and scholarly investigations into the principles of medieval architecture was a school of slick archaeological architects, capable of decorating all manner of collegiate, civic, and domestic buildings with frigidly correct reproductions of the details of medieval cathedrals and châteaus. Out of Ruskin's demonstration of the origins of medieval decoration in natural forms there grew the so-called Art Nouveau movement toward exaggerated floral and curvilinear ornament; and out of Morris' insistence on handicrafts, inspired by infatuation with the medieval guild system, developed the Arts and Crafts movement.

As early as the 1870s the U.S. architect H.H. Richardson adopted the Romanesque style, less for its historical associations than for the opportunities it afforded him to express the nature and texture of stone. In mature examples of his architecture from the mid-1880s, ornament in the older, applied sense had virtually disappeared, and his buildings depend for their aesthetic effect mainly on the inherent qualities of their materials. The generation following Richardson saw a further international development of this principle.

In Great Britain Sir Edwin Lutyens and Charles Rennie Mackintosh, in The Netherlands Hendrick Petrus Berlage, and in the United States Louis Sullivan were among many architects who contributed to the new ornamental expression. It was largely based on intrinsic texture and pattern but with interspersed bands and patches of naturalistic ornament, applied with studied discipline. With the general reaction against 19th-century eclectic principles of ornamentation after World War I, however, leading designers rejected even this kind of applied ornament and relied for ornamental effect on building materials alone. The so-called International Style, in which the German architect Walter Gropius and the Swiss-French architect Le Corbusier were the chief figures, dominated advanced design during the late 1920s and 1930s. The barrenness that resulted from their reliance on such materials as concrete and glass, however, along with other factors, resulted in a reaction in the 1940s in favour of the neglected precedent set by the U.S. architect Frank Lloyd Wright in his early-20th-century work, which emphasized more visually in-

20th-century usage of ornament

teresting materials, intricate textural patterns, and natural settings as the proper basis of architectural ornament. This trend continued in later decades; the style known as the New Brutalism was related to it. (Al.Go.)

Theory of architecture

The term theory of architecture was originally simply the accepted translation of the Latin term *ratiocinatio* as used by Vitruvius, a Roman architect-engineer of the 1st century AD, to differentiate intellectual from practical knowledge in architectural education; but it has come to signify the total basis for judging the merits of buildings or building projects. Such reasoned judgments are an essential part of the architectural creative process. A building can be designed only by a continuous creative, intellectual dialectic between imagination and reason in the mind of each creator.

A variety of interpretations has been given to the term architectural theory by those who have written or spoken on the topic in the past. Before 1750 every comprehensive treatise or published lecture course on architecture could appropriately be described as a textbook on architectural theory. But, after the changes associated with the Industrial Revolution, the amount of architectural knowledge that could be acquired only by academic study increased to the point where a complete synthesis became virtually impossible in a single volume.

The historical evolution of architectural theory is assessable mainly from manuscripts and published treatises, from critical essays and commentaries, and from the surviving buildings of every epoch. It is thus in no way a type of historical study that can reflect accurately the spirit of each age and in this respect is similar to the history of philosophy itself. Some architectural treatises were intended to publicize novel concepts rather than to state widely accepted ideals. The most idiosyncratic theories could (and often did) exert a wide and sometimes beneficial influence; but the value of these influences is not necessarily related to the extent of this acceptance.

Analysis of historical buildings

The analysis of surviving buildings provides guidance that requires great caution, since, apart from the impossibility of determining whether or not any particular group of buildings (intact or in ruins) constitutes a reliable sample of the era, any such analyses will usually depend on preliminary evaluations of merit and will be useless unless the extent to which the function, the structure, and the detailing envisaged by the original builders can be correctly re-established. Many erudite studies of antique theories are misleading because they rest on the assumption that the original character and appearance of fragmentary ancient Greek and Hellenistic architectural environments can be adequately deduced from verbal or graphic "reconstructions." Even when buildings constructed before 1500 remain intact, the many textbooks dealing with antique and medieval theories of architecture seldom make qualitative distinctions and generally imply that all surviving antique and medieval buildings were good, if not absolutely perfect.

Nevertheless, the study of the history of architectural philosophy, like that of the history of general philosophy, not only teaches what past generations thought but can help the individual decide how he himself should act and judge. For those desirous of establishing a viable theory of architecture for their own era, it is generally agreed that great stimulus can be found in studying historical evidence and in speculating on the ideals and achievements of those who created this evidence.

DISTINCTION BETWEEN THE HISTORY AND THEORY OF ARCHITECTURE

Emergence of two disciplines in the 18th century

The distinction between the history and theory of architecture did not emerge until the mid-18th century; indeed, the establishment of two separate academic disciplines was not even nominal until 1818, when separate professorships with these titles were established at the École des Beaux-Arts in Paris. Even then, however, the distinction was seldom scrupulously maintained by either specialist. It is impossible to discuss meaningfully the buildings of the immediate past without discussing the ideals of those who built them, just as it is impossible to discuss the ideals of bygone architects without reference to the structures they designed. Nevertheless, since any two disciplines that are inseparably complementary can at the same time be logically distinguishable, it may be asserted that this particular distinction first became manifest in *Les Ruines des plus beaux monuments de la Grèce* ("The Ruins of the Most Beautiful Monuments of Greece"), written in 1758 by a French architecture student, Julien-David LeRoy. Faced with the problem of discussing Athenian buildings constructed in the time of Vitruvius, he decided to discuss them twice, by treating them separately under two different headings. Before this date, "history" was of architectural importance only as a means of justifying, by reference to classical mythology, the use of certain otherwise irrational elements, such as caryatids. Even Jacques-François Blondel, who in 1750 was probably the first architectural teacher to devote a separate section of his lecture courses to "history," envisaged the subject mainly as an account of the literary references to architecture found in antique manuscripts—an attitude already developed by the 15th-century Renaissance architect Leon Battista Alberti.

The modern concept of architectural history

The modern concept of architectural history was in fact simply part of a larger trend stimulated by the leading writers of the French Enlightenment, an 18th-century intellectual movement that developed from interrelated conceptions of reason, nature, and man. As a result of discussing constitutional law in terms of its evolution, every branch of knowledge (especially the natural and social sciences) was eventually seen as a historical sequence. In the philosophy of architecture, as in all other kinds of philosophy, the introduction of the historical method not only facilitated the teaching of these subjects but also militated against the elaboration of theoretical speculation. Just as those charged with the responsibility of lecturing on ethics found it very much easier to lecture on the history of ethics, rather than to discuss how a person should or should not act in specific contemporary circumstances, so those who lectured on architectural theory found it easier to recite detailed accounts of what had been done in the past, rather than to recommend practical methods of dealing with current problems.

Moreover, the system of the Paris École des Beaux-Arts (which provided virtually the only organized system of architectural education at the beginning of the 19th century) was radically different from that of the prerevolutionary Académie Royale d'Architecture. Quatremère de Quincy, an Italophile archaeologist who had been trained as a sculptor, united the school of architecture with that of painting and sculpture to form a single organization, so that, although architectural students were ultimately given their own professor of theory, the whole theoretical background of their studies was assimilated to the other two fine arts by lecture courses and textbooks such as Hippolyte Taine's *Philosophie de l'art,* Charles Blanc's *Grammaire des arts du dessin,* and Eugène Guillaume's *Essais sur la théorie du dessin.*

Similarly, whereas before 1750 the uniformity of doctrine (the basic premises of which were ostensibly unchanged since the Renaissance) allowed the professor of architecture to discuss antique and 16th-century buildings as examples of architectural theory and to ignore medieval buildings completely, the mid-19th-century controversy between "medievalists" and "classicists" (the "Battle of the Styles") and the ensuing faith in Eclecticism turned the studies of architectural history into courses on archaeology.

Importance of visual analysis in the 20th century

Thus, the attitudes of those scholars who, during the 19th and early 20th centuries, wished to expound a theory of architecture that was neither a philosophy of art nor a history of architecture tended to become highly personal, if not idiosyncratic. By 1950 most theoretical writings concentrated almost exclusively on visual aspects of architecture, thereby identifying the theory of architecture with what, before 1750, would have been regarded as simply that aspect that Vitruvius called *venustas* (*i.e.,* "beauty"). This approach did not necessarily invalidate the conclusions reached; but many valuable ideas then put forward as theories of architecture were only partial theories, in which it was taken for granted that theoretical concepts concerning construction and planning were dealt with in other texts.

DISTINCTION BETWEEN THE THEORY OF ARCHITECTURE AND THE THEORY OF ART

Before embarking on any discussion as to the nature of the philosophy of architecture, it is essential to distinguish between two mutually exclusive theories that affect the whole course of any such speculation. The first theory regards the philosophy of architecture as the application of a general philosophy of art to a particular type of art. The second, on the contrary, regards the philosophy of architecture as a separate study that, though it may well have many characteristics common to the theories of other arts, is generically distinct.

The first notion (*i.e.,* that there exists a generic theory of art of which the theory of architecture is a specific extension) has been widely held since the mid-16th century, when the artist and writer Giorgio Vasari published in his *Le vite de' più eccellenti pittori, scultori ed architettori italiani . . .* (*The Lives of the Most Eminent Italian Painters, Sculptors and Architects . . .*) his assertion that painting, sculpture, and architecture are all of common ancestry in that all depend on the ability to draw. This idea became particularly prevalent among English-speaking theorists, since the word design is used to translate both *disegno* ("a drawing") and *concetto* ("a mental plan"). But its main influence on Western thought was due to Italophile Frenchmen, after Louis XIV had been induced to establish in Rome a French Academy modelled on Italian art academies.

As a result of the widespread influence of French culture in the 17th and 18th centuries, the concept of the *beaux arts* (literally "beautiful arts" but usually translated into English as "fine arts") was accepted by Anglo-Saxon theorists as denoting a philosophical entity, to the point where it was generally forgotten that in France itself the architectural profession remained totally aloof from the Académie Royale de Peinture et de Sculpture until they were forced to amalgamate after the French Revolution.

This theory of fine art might not have been so widely adopted but for the development of aesthetics, elaborated after 1750. Thus, when academies of fine art were being established successively in Denmark, Russia, and England on the model of the French Academy in Rome, German philosophers were gradually asserting (1) that it was possible to elaborate a theory of beauty without reference to function (*Zweck*); (2) that any theory of beauty should be applicable to all sensory perceptions, whether visual or auditory; and (3) that the notion of beauty was only one aspect of a much larger concept of life-enhancing sensory stimuli.

The alternative theory (*i.e.,* that a philosophy of architecture is unique and can therefore be evolved only by specific reference to the art of building) will be dealt with below with reference to the traditional triad usually cited in the formula coined, by the English theorist Sir Henry Wotton, in his book *The Elements of Architecture,* namely "commodity, firmness, and delight."

Theorists' reluctance to use specific buildings as examples

Generally speaking, writers on aesthetics have been noticeably reluctant to use architectural examples in support of speculations as to the nature of their general theories; but references to buildings have been used in most "philosophies of art" ever since the German philosophers Immanuel Kant and G.W.F. Hegel first popularized the philosophical discipline. Kant, in his *Kritik der Urteilskraft* (1790; Eng. trans., *Critique of Judgment,* 1951), distinguished between what he termed free beauty (*pulchritudo vaga*) and dependent beauty (*pulchritudo adhaerens*). He classified architecture as dependent beauty, saying that in a thing that is possible only by means of design (*Absicht*)—a building or even an animal—the regularity consisting in symmetry must express the unity of the intuition that accompanies the concept of purpose (*Zweck*), and this regularity belongs to cognition. Nevertheless, he claimed that a flower should be classified as free beauty (where the judgment of taste is "pure") "because hardly anyone but a botanist knows what sort of thing a flower ought to be; and even he, though recognizing in the flower the reproductive organ of the plant, pays no regard to this natural purpose if he is passing judgment on the flower by taste." What Kant's reaction would have been to a modern plastic imitation flower is impossible to guess; but it will readily be perceived (1) why those who, in the 19th century, accepted the notion that beauty in architecture is *pulchritudo adhaerens* felt such antipathy toward "shams," (2) how the distinction between "pure art" and "functional art" (*Zweckkunst*) became confused, and (3) why there arose a tendency to pursue definitions of "pure beauty" or "pure art" without specifically referring to the function and structure of any particular class of beautiful or artistic objects, such as buildings.

This latter tendency was reinforced when the French philosopher Victor Cousin, writing in 1835, classified the history of philosophy under three distinct headings: the true, the beautiful, and the good. The ensuing acceptance of the idea that beauty was to be studied independently of truth and goodness produced a tendency not merely to regard beauty as something added to a building (rather than conceptually inseparable from the truth and goodness of its structure and function) but to regard beauty as limited to visual and emotional qualities.

Influence of aesthetics in 20th-century theory

In the first half of the 20th century, philosophers grew less dogmatic about aesthetics. But its influence on theories of architecture became stronger because of the popular view that sculpture was essentially nonrepresentational. Thus, although the assertion that "aesthetically, architecture is the creation of sculpture big enough to walk about inside" is meaningful in the 20th century, it would have seemed nonsensical to any architectural theorist living before 1900, when sculpture was invariably thought of either as representational or as a carved refinement of load-bearing wood or stone.

FUNCTIONALISM

The notion of functional art, most actively promoted by German writers and termed by them *Zweckkunst,* is most appropriately related to architectural theory under three headings, namely (1) the idea that no building is beautiful unless it properly fulfills its function, (2) the idea that if a building fulfills its function it is ipso facto beautiful, and (3) the idea that, since form relates to function, all artifacts, including buildings, are a species of industrial, or applied, art (known in German as *Kunstgewerbe*).

The first proposition will be dealt with later under the heading *utilitas.* The second proposition, though widely popularized through the publication of the French architect Jean-Nicholas-Louis Durand's lectures delivered during the economic depression of the beginning of the 19th century, has had little influence except during similar periods of economic depression. The third proposition has, however, had a wide influence, since, unlike the second proposition, it is closely akin to (rather than antagonistic toward) the theory of aesthetics, in that it regards all the visual arts as generically related.

This last theory seems to have been popularized, if not originated, by Gottfried Semper, an architect from Dresden who, after finding political asylum in England (where he then helped to organize the Great Exhibition of 1851), published a book in German on arts and crafts that seems to have been influential not only in Germany but also in areas of the United States heavily populated by German-speaking immigrants, such as Chicago. Later, in 20th-century Germany, the Bauhaus (officially Hochschule für Gestaltung; Academy for Form Giving) was ostensibly intended to train students in separate creative disciplines, but its didactic method was based on the assumption—implied by the general introductory courses—that, if one could design anything, one could design everything. In the explanatory words of its founder, the architect Walter Gropius, "The approach to any kind of design—a chair, a building, a whole town or a regional plan—should be essentially identical."

Bauhaus functionalism

THE ART OF BUILDING

The notion that architecture is the art of building was implied by Alberti in the first published treatise on the theory of architecture, *De re aedificatoria* (1485; Eng. trans., *Ten Books on Architecture,* 1955); for, although he was a layman writing for other lay scholars, he rejected, by his title, the idea that architecture was simply applied mathematics, as had been claimed by Vitruvius. The specific denotation of architecture as "the art of building," however, seems to be a French tradition, deriving perhaps from the medieval status of master masons, as understood by the 16th-century architect Philibert Delorme. This definition occurs in most French treatises published before 1750; and, although the humanistic and antiquarian aspects of fine building were rarely questioned after the Renaissance, the distinction between "architecture" and "building" never had any appreciable significance before Renaissance ideas succumbed to the combined assault of "aesthetics" and the Gothic Revival movement.

Before the 18th century it was generally accepted that the theory of architecture was concerned mainly with important private or civic buildings such as palaces, mansions, churches, and monasteries. Buildings such as these required the superior skill that only book learning could provide, and so relatively little attention was given, in theoretical writings, to simple and straightforward buildings that could be competently built in accordance with local traditions by unlettered craftsmen. But, with the expansion of the architectural profession, with the perversion of the idea that social prestige was symbolized by ornamentation, with the wider distribution of wealth, and with the growing urge toward individualism in an increasingly egalitarian society, the real distinction between these two kinds of buildings was obscured, and in its place was substituted an antithesis. Henceforth, "building" was associated with the notion of cheapness, whereas "architecture" was associated with what John Ruskin would have called "sacrifice" (but which his antagonists would have called conspicuous waste). A distinction was made between the respective attitudes of "art architects" and practical-minded civil engineers. This distinction persisted because of the different methods of training candidates for the two professions. Whereas a fledgling engineering student is seldom asked to design a whole structure (such as a bridge), architectural students begin by designing whole structures and proceed with structures of increasing size and complexity, either graphically or by means of small-scale models.

Differentiation between "building" and "architecture"

It was doubtless the difference in educational methods that prompted Le Corbusier to state:

> The engineer, inspired by the law of economy and led by mathematical calculation, puts us in accord with the laws of the universe. He achieves harmony. The architect, by his arrangement of forms, achieves an order which is a pure creation of his spirit . . . it is then that we experience beauty.

Yet some 80 years previously the English critic James Fergusson had felt obliged to qualify, with a comparable distinction, his enthusiasm for the new architecture of the Crystal Palace, by observing that "it has not a sufficient amount of decoration about its parts to take it entirely out of the category of first-class engineering and to make it entirely an object of fine art." The distinction between architecture and "mere building" was stated by Nikolaus Pevsner in the opening paragraph of his *Outline of European Architecture* (1942): "a bicycle shed is a building; Lincoln Cathedral is a piece of architecture . . . the term architecture applies only to buildings designed with a view to aesthetic appeal." Whatever the justification for such assertions, it must nevertheless be recognized that neither of these authors suggests that aesthetic appeal or art are synonyms for superfluity. Although adjustment in proportions or refinement of profiles may increase the thickness of short-span structural members beyond the structural analytical minima, this does not necessarily imply any radical decrease in real economy but simply indicates a concept of economy that takes into account the assembly and amenity of spatial enclosures and admits that there is value in environmental harmony. It is thus as misleading to imply (as Fergusson implied) that architecture is civil engineering plus ornament as it is to imply (as Le Corbusier did) that the status of the two professions is to be distinguished by the relative superiority of beauty over harmony.

It is important to insist that the theory of architecture is concerned primarily with the attainment of certain environmental ideals rather than with their cost; for these two problems are philosophically distinct, as is clear if one considers such a concept as, for example, that of standardization. The financial saving made by standardizing rolled-steel sections or by casting concrete in reusable formwork is so obvious that it requires no elaboration with respect to Vitruvius' demand for *oeconomia.* But such standardization also fulfills Vitruvius' concurrent demand for order, arrangement, eurythmy, symmetry, and propriety.

Standardization as a concept

The Place Vendôme in Paris is adorned with over 100 identical pilasters and half columns, all carved with the same Corinthian capitals under the supervision of a member of the Académie Royale de Peinture et de Sculpture. Whether or not the resultant uniformity was or still is both pleasing and desirable is certainly open to discussion; but it will be perceived that any argument about architectural standardization must primarily be a question of value, rather than of cost, and it is with values that architectural theory has always been predominantly concerned.

"COMMODITY, FIRMNESS, AND DELIGHT": THE ULTIMATE SYNTHESIS

It has been generally assumed that a complete theory of architecture is always concerned essentially in some way or another with these three interrelated terms, which, in Vitruvius' Latin text, are given as *firmitas, utilitas,* and *venustas* (*i.e.,* structural stability, appropriate spatial accommodation, and attractive appearance). Nevertheless, a number of influential theorists after 1750 sought to make modifications to this traditional triad (1) by giving its components a radically different equilibrium (such as the primacy given by the 18th-century French architect Étienne-Louis Boullée to the effects of geometric forms in light or the claim made by J.N.L. Durand that the fulfillment of function was the sole essence of architectural beauty), (2) by adding ethical values (such as Ruskin's "sacrifice" and "obedience"), or (3) by introducing new scientific concepts (such as Giedion's "space-time").

Furthermore, it has been argued that the traditional concept of *firmitas, utilitas,* and *venustas* ceased to have any real value after 1800, when engineers began creating structures that seemed so ostentatiously to defy the stonemasons' laws of gravity, when scientific studies were creating more and more doubts as to the economical, sociological, psychological, acoustical, thermal, or optical determinants of appropriate spatial accommodation and when beauty was "altogether in the eye of the beholder."

Clearly, one must be wary of attributing too much importance to the sequence, since a slight variation occurs in the writings of even the most traditional theorists. Vitruvius gives these terms in the sequence *firmitas, utilitas, venustas,* whereas both Alberti and, following him, the 16th-century Venetian architect and theorist Andrea Palladio reverse the order of the first two. Thus, Sir Henry Wotton's sequence (which is normally used in English-language texts) does not, as so often stated, derive directly from the Latin text of Vitruvius but from the Italian text of Palladio's *I quattro libri dell' architettura* (*i.e., comodità, perpetuità, bellezza*). But it does seem worth noting that *venustas* generally comes last, implying that *firmitas* and *utilitas* are to be regarded as essential logical prerequisites of architectural beauty.

On the other hand, the practical advantages, in academic treatises, of giving priority to *venustas* are evident. Jacques-François Blondel, in his nine-volume *Cours d'architecture* (1771–77) used this sequence because he observed that considerations of "decoration" are almost entirely within the domain of the theory of architecture, whereas neither distribution (*utilitas*) nor construction (*firmitas*) can be explained properly without practical experience. The growing emphasis on aesthetics, combined with developments in psychology and the influence of art-historical methods, added weight to this argument, while the corresponding independence of scientific techniques of structural and spatial analysis led many teachers of architecture to consider *utilitas* and *firmitas* as totally separate academic disciplines. Important exceptions can be found to this gen-

Modern concepts of teaching archi-tectural theory

eralization. At the end of the 19th century, Julien Guadet, in reaction against the creation of a chair of aesthetics at the Paris École des Beaux-Arts, considered it his duty, as professor of architectural theory, to devote his lectures to the study of architectural planning, and this method, which achieved prestige as a result of his keen mind and wide historical knowledge, was pursued by many later scholars. But Guadet's approach became unfashionable, and since the 1960s the predominant methods of teaching architectural theory have ranged from a return to the synthesis of structural, spatial, and formal values espoused by Robert Venturi to the exploration of the architectural implications of general theories of linguistics advanced by Christian Norberg-Schulz.

Venustas. This Latin term for "beauty" (literally, the salient qualities possessed by the goddess Venus) clearly implied a visual quality in architecture that would arouse the emotion of love; but it is of interest to note that one of the crucial aspects of this problem was already anticipated by Alberti in the 15th century, as is made clear by his substitution of the word *amoenitas* ("pleasure") for Vitruvius' more anthropomorphic term *venustas.* Alberti not only avoids the erotic implications of the term *venustas* but, by subdividing *amoenitas* into *pulchritudo* and *ornamentum,* gives far more precise indications as to the type of visual satisfaction that architecture should provide. *Pulchritudo,* he asserts, is derived from harmonious proportions that are comparable to those that exist in music and are the essence of the pleasure created by architecture. *Ornamentum,* he claims, is only an "auxiliary brightness," the quality and extent of which will depend essentially on what is appropriate and seemly. Both *pulchritudo* and *ornamentum* were thus related to function and environment in that, ideally, they were governed by a sense of decorum; and, since the etymological roots of both "decoration" and "decorum" are the same, it will be understood why, before 1750, the term decoration had in both English and French a far less superficial architectural implication than it often does today.

After the German philosopher and educator Alexander Gottlieb Baumgarten had introduced the neologism aesthetics in about 1750, the visual merits of all artifacts tended to be assessed more subjectively than objectively; and, in the criticism of all those sensory stimuli that, for want of a better term, critics somewhat indiscriminately lumped together as the fine arts, the visual criteria were extended to include not only beauty but also sublimity, picturesqueness, and even ugliness. Now it is clear that, once ugliness is equated with beauty, both terms (being contradictory) become virtually meaningless. But ugliness, after the mid-19th century, was not only one of the most important themes of many popular dramas and novels; ugliness was also often considered the most appropriate architectural expression for all sorts of virtues—especially those of manliness, sincerity, and so on.

Before 1750, architects had expressed these qualities more subtly (*e.g.,* by slight modifications of proportions or by unobtrusive ornament). In later years, when the value of proportion and ornament became highly controversial, architectural theorists tended to avoid committing themselves to any criteria that might be subsumed under the heading *venustas.* In the last resort, however, some concept of beauty must be essential to any theory of architecture; and, whether one considers Le Corbusier's buildings beautiful or not, his most stabilizing contribution toward the theory of modern architecture was undoubtedly his constant reiteration of this term and his insistence on the traditional view that beauty in architecture is essentially based on harmonious proportions, mathematically conceived.

20th-century response to Alberti's theory

In the 20th century the main obstacle to an acceptance of Alberti's notions of *pulchritudo* and *ornamentum* resulted from the influence of nonrepresentational sculpture after 1918, whereby ornament was no longer conceived as an enrichment of proportioned structure but as an integral, all-pervading part of each building's totality. This ideal of the fusion between good proportions and "auxiliary brightness" was expressed by Walter Gropius in *The New Architecture and the Bauhaus* when he wrote in 1935:

> Our ultimate goal, therefore, was the composite but inseparable work of art, the great building, in which the old dividing-line between monumental and decorative elements would have disappeared for ever.

The idea was accepted in most schools of architecture by the mid-20th century; but one may question whether it fully justified the expectations of its protagonists, once it had been exemplified and proliferated in so many urban environments. It is by no means certain that Gropius' concept of the fundamental interdependence of architectural proportion and architectural ornament was irrevocably established by the Bauhaus theorists or that future architectural theorists need only concentrate on such minor modifications to the concept as may be required by sociological and technological developments.

Utilitas. The notion that a building is defective unless the spaces provided are adequate and appropriate for their intended usage would seem obvious. Yet the statement itself has been a source of controversy since the 1960s. The main reasons for the controversy are: first, whereas there are seldom exact statistical means of computing spatial adequacy or appropriateness, there are many building types or building elements for which one cannot even establish the optimum forms and dimensions with any confidence that they will be generally accepted. Second, edifices are frequently used for purposes other than those for which they were originally planned. Furthermore, there is some doubt as to whether "form follows function" or "function follows form," since, although, in general, it can reasonably be assumed that an architect's task is to construct specific spaces for the fulfillment of predetermined functions, there is plenty of historical evidence to suggest that many important social institutions have resulted from spaces already built. No better example could be found than the evolution of parliamentary systems. The British system, based on the concept of legislatures in which the sovereign's government and the sovereign's opposition confront each other, originated in the fact that the earliest parliaments met in the medieval palace chapel. The French system, created concurrently with the Greek and Roman revivals, was based on the concept of legislatures addressed by orators, and its environment was that of an antique theatre. In the former system the seating was designed in accordance with the liturgical requirements of a Christian church; in the latter, with the evolution of Greek drama. Neither had anything to do with preconceived notions regarding the most effective environment for parliamentary debate, yet both have had divergent influences on constitutional procedures, thereby deeply affecting the whole theory of government.

The issue of a building fulfilling its function

Third, the exact significance of what is meant by "adequate appropriate spaces" becomes far more complex in buildings requiring a large number of interrelated spaces than it is in single-cell buildings. The emotional effect of transitions from spacious to constricted volumes and vice versa transcends in architectural importance the statistical evaluation of floor areas; a fact which explains the attractiveness of theories that have tacitly adopted places of worship as spatial paradigms and bolstered their arguments by historical reference to temples and churches. This bias is perceptible not only in the most influential theories enunciated before 1900 (when the prototypes were either primeval, antique, or medieval) but also in the most influential ideas promulgated by such great architectural leaders of the 20th century as Frank Lloyd Wright and Ludwig Mies van der Rohe.

The idealization of monumental single-cell spaces is sometimes justified, but the difficulty of evolving theories of planning by the use of historical prototypes should be emphasized. It is in this branch of architectural theory that the influences of historicism have been most insidious, precisely because they are less obvious here than in systems of construction, of proportions, and of ornamentation. Such influences persist mainly because of art-historical indifference to the essential distinction between building types, since such distinction conflicts with the chronological sequence of particular architects' stylistic evolution; but it is for this reason that Julien Guadet's greatest contribution to the theory of architecture may well have been his decision to evolve a history of architecture in which all buildings were classified solely in accordance with their function.

Firmitas. Two plausible reasons can be given for according logical primacy in the Vitruvian triad to *firmitas.* The first is the notion that architecture is essentially the "art of building." The second is that, since the uses or functions of a building tend to change, the structures serving such functions may be considered as taking logical precedence over them. This idea was expressed with characteristic lapidary vigour by the 20th-century French architect Auguste Perret when he asserted that

> architecture is the art of organizing space; but it is by construction that it expresses itself... Functions, customs, and building regulations and fashions impose conditions which are only transitory.

Some later architectural theorists have become so concerned with the rapid obsolescence of modern buildings that they have envisaged edifices that express the temporary nature of these transitory qualities and are therefore built in such a way as to enable the structures themselves to be discarded completely after a few years. On the other hand (since the economic feasibility of this technique is questionable), there are still many architects who believe in the inevitability of permanent buildings and who therefore hold views more compatible with this belief.

The issue of revealing the structural system to the observer

From the time of the Renaissance to the mid-18th century—as also before the decline of the ancient Roman Empire on which the culture of this era was modelled—little concern seems to have been given to the idea that there was any virtue in manifesting the actual structural system of a building. Alberti recommended a distinctive articulation of the skeleton frame in conformity with the antique concept of trabeation, or the post-and-lintel system (and hence the independence of the "infilling" elements, such as arches or solid walling); but the more commonly accepted notion seems to have been that, provided a trabeated system was expressed externally, the relationship of this visual expression to the actual system of construction was relatively unimportant. Theoretical pronouncements on this matter depended of course on the architectural traditions of each country. In Italy (where the traditional technique of building had, even during the Middle Ages, assumed that structure was independent of appearance and where it was common to complete a building in brick before adding its marble facades) the idea that there could be any theoretical dilemma regarding the unison between these two elements was virtually inconceivable. Palladio and his generation seem to have generally accepted the idea that, in regions where masonry was scarce, the use of stuccoed, painted, or veneered brickwork, with plastered timber beams, was architecturally as "genuine" as the use of stone, provided it was all of one colour. But in the Île-de-France region around Paris, on the contrary, the medieval traditions of French masonry construction, combined with the abundance of good freestone, caused theorists from the Renaissance to the time of the French Revolution to favour a less tenuous relationship between the external appearance of a building and the system by which it was constructed. Nevertheless, it is probably fair to say that in all European countries before the end of the 18th century, as well as in their American colonies, the only problem concerned with *firmitas* (other than technical problems) was the problem of the relationship between "real and apparent stability"; and, when theorists pronounced on this problem, it was usually to assert that a building should not only be structurally stable but should also appear to be so.

A violent assault upon this point of view was launched by the Gothic Revivalists, who, in the mid-19th century, contended that the breathtaking counterpoise of a cathedral's flying buttresses was far more dramatically expressive of *firmitas* than the ponderous massiveness of its sturdy western towers. It was in this era that the term daring (which Ruskin had frequently used with reference to the paintings of the English Romantic artist Joseph Mallord William Turner) became popular as a laudatory epithet, thereby indicating an ideal of structural expression that was to be increasingly exploited when steel and reinforced concrete permitted higher buildings with fewer and more slender supports.

The concept of truthful architecture

But the most controversial issue concerning *firmitas* in the 19th century—which also arose through the influence of the Gothic Revival movement—concerned the extent to which a building should manifest its structural system and the materials used. The attraction of this particular interpretation of the concept of truthful architecture was probably due to the popularity of new attitudes toward experimental science and to the disrepute into which mythology had been cast by the philosophers of the Enlightenment. Presumably, truth was no less prized in the 17th or 18th centuries than in the 19th century (though shams may have been less rife), while hypocrisy was regarded with as much contempt. Moreover, although the 19th century was a period of growing realism in literature, it was also a period of growing expressiveness in painting and music. Whatever the reason for this change of attitude, the 19th century saw a general acceptance of the notion that buildings were "true" only insofar as their structural form and appearance corresponded to the structural systems and materials employed, and this dogma was developed by means of many elaborate biological and mechanical analogies.

This particular doctrine had a highly beneficial influence on architectural evolution during the 20th century, since it helped to demonstrate why the radical changes in building technology rendered earlier concepts of architectural form (based on load-bearing masonry construction) theoretically untenable. For, while it may readily be admitted that a building can express many other things besides its function and structure, failure to express the latter in some manner, however remote, must always lead to arbitrariness. This would not only be harmful to the evolution of architectural form but would inevitably result in a somewhat cynical concept of building as "pure form"—a concept that only those who regard architecture as nothing more than large-scale packaging or abstract sculpture could accept. (Pe.C.)

BIBLIOGRAPHY

General: JOHN FLEMING, HUGH HONOUR, and NIKOLAUS PEVSNER, *The Penguin Dictionary of Architecture* (1966), a general reference work of architectural terminology and biography; PAUL FRANKL, *Die Entwicklungsphasen der neueren Baukunst* (1914: Eng. trans., *Principles of Architectural History,* 1914, reprinted 1968), a classic analysis of architectural form, 1400–1850; SIGFRIED GIEDION, *Space, Time and Architecture,* 5th ed. (1967), a stimulating survey and justification of modern architecture and its antecedents; STEEN E. RASMUSSEN, *Experiencing Architecture,* 2nd ed. (1962), a beginner's guide to architectural appreciation; JULIUS SCHLOSSER, *Die Kunstliteratur* (1924; Italian trans., *La letteratura artistica,* 2nd ed., 1956), a bibliography of theoretical writing up to 1800; selected titles in the "Pelican History of Art Series," general surveys of significant periods; MICHAEL RAGBURN (ed.), *Architecture of the Western World* (1980), an excellent survey.

Use: JEFFREY ARONIN, *Climate and Architecture* (1953), on the influence of physical environment on planning; SIGFRIED GIEDION, *Mechanization Takes Command* (1948, reprinted 1969), on the impact of machinery on 19th- and 20th-century building; LEWIS MUMFORD, *The Culture of Cities* (1938, reprinted 1970), the growth of modern cities seen from a historical and humanitarian viewpoint; AMOS RAPOPORT, *House Form and Culture* (1969), an analysis of basic domestic forms in the light of cultural anthropology.

Techniques: LEWIS MUMFORD, *Technics and Civilization* (1934, reprinted 1962), a general view of the cultural role of technology; DEPARTMENT OF SCIENTIFIC AND INDUSTRIAL RESEARCH (London), *Principles of Modern Building,* 3rd ed., 2 vol. (1959–61), a study of building techniques and materials; CHARLES RAMSEY and HAROLD SLEEPER, *Architectural Graphic Standards,* 6th ed. (1970), the practicing designer's handbook of standards and equipment; MARIO SALVADORI and ROBERT HELLER, *Structure in Architecture* (1963), a clear, well-illustrated explanation of structural principles.

Expression and theory: (*Sources*): JOHN RUSKIN, *The Seven Lamps of Architecture* (1849, reprinted 1956), an aesthetic of architecture of the Romantic era allied to ethics; EUGENE VIOLLET-LE-DUC, *Entretiens sur l'architecture,* 2 pt. (1862–72; Eng. trans., *Discourses on Architecture,* 1875), a premodern architectural theory based on rational construction; VITRUVIUS, *Ten Books on Architecture* (Eng. trans. 1914), the only architectural treatise to survive from antiquity—exerted great influence on Renaissance and later design. (*Modern*): CHRISTOPHER ALEXANDER, *Notes on the Synthesis of Form* (1964), design calculations for the cybernetic age; LE CORBUSIER, *Vers une architecture* (1925; Eng. trans., *Towards a New Architecture,* 1927); WALTER GROPIUS, *Scope of Total Architecture* (1955); and FRANK LLOYD WRIGHT, *Modern Architecture* (1931), the credos of the three most influential modern architects. (*Surveys*): PETER COLLINS, *Changing Ideals in Modern Architecture, 1750–1950* (1965), a survey of architectural principles; PAUL FRANKL, *The Gothic* (1960), a medieval style and its survivals through the centuries; GEOFFREY SCOTT, *The Architecture of Humanism,* 2nd ed. (1924, reprinted 1969), combines a critique of 19th-century theory with a psychologically based defense of Baroque design; JOHN SUMMERSON, *The Classical Language of Architecture* (1963), on the use of the classical repertory of motives through the ages; RUDOLF WITTKOWER, *Architectural Principles in the Age of Humanism,* 3rd ed. (1962), architectural thought in the Renaissance; ALDO ROSSI, *The Architecture of the City* (1982), architectural and urban theory.

Ornament: A useful general survey of ornamental forms and designs is JOAN EVANS, *Pattern: A Study of Ornament in Western Europe from 1180 to 1900,* 2 vol. (1931). For an account of mimetic ornament and design, the works of E. BALDWIN SMITH are recommended: *Egyptian Architecture As Cultural Expression* (1938, reprinted 1968), *The Dome* (1950), and *Architectural Symbolism of Imperial Rome and the Middle Ages* (1956). For a theory of ornament as social function, identifying use and humanizing artifacts, see ALAN GOWANS, "The Unchanging Arts of Beautification: Commercial Design and Decoration," in *The Unchanging Arts* (1971); CAROLE RIFKIND, *A Field Guide to American Architecture* (1980), covers styles, building types, ornamentation, elements of construction.

Theory and criticism: LEONE BATTISTA ALBERTI, *De re aedificatoria* (1485), the first printed book on the theory of architecture—numerous English translations are available; REYNER BANHAM, *Theory and Design in the First Machine Age* (1960), an authoritative study of the theories of architecture developed in the second quarter of the present century; PETER COLLINS, *Architectural Judgement* (1971), a comparative study of decision making in architecture and law; CHRISTIAN NORBERG-SCHULZ, *Intentions in Architecture* (1963), an influential study of architectural theory based on linguistics; HOWARD ROBERTSON, *The Principles of Architectural Composition* (1924), a characteristic textbook of the first quarter of the present century; ROBERT VENTURI, *Complexity and Contradiction in Architecture* (1966), a proposal for a new theory of architecture based on recent art-historical interpretations of Mannerism and Baroque architecture; EDWARD DE ZURKO, *Origins of Functionalist Theory* (1957), a compendious historical analysis of the relationship between form and function, as conceived by philosophers and architectural theorists.

The History of Western Architecture

Architecture, the art of building, is perhaps the best example of the partnership and basic identity of a fine and a useful art, beauty and utility, form and function. A building—whether a temple, church, factory, office complex, exhibition hall, or domestic dwelling—must demonstrate the solution of the practical problems associated with its purpose. In addition, the building must show the careful manipulation of structural and ornamental materials, used to express aesthetic, cultural, or symbolic ideas.

The primary concern of the architect is the definition and articulation of exterior space and the spanning and enclosure of interior space. The moment a square or circle has been described on the ground, one area has been physically and intellectually separated from another and the architectural process has begun. As the architect spans the space—on the ground as with a wall or road or in the air as with an arch or bridge—he encounters not only the complex technical problems of the craft but aesthetic factors as well. Materials must be molded with an eye for the proportions of masses and voids; for the interaction of qualities, textures, colours, and capacities of these materials; for the harmonious relationship of open windows and doors to closed wall space; for the control and flow of lighting; and above all for architecture in action—that is, for the shelter, comfort, and movement of the people who will be living, working, and carrying on their various activities within the building.

The history of architecture may be read in the progressive changes in the solution of structural problems. The transition from the most primitive shed roof and simple truss construction to the vertical posts, or columns, supporting horizontal beams, or lintels, covers the period from the beginning of civilization through ancient Greek culture. Greek architecture also formalized many structural and decorative elements into three of the classical orders—Ionic, Doric, and Corinthian—which, to a greater or lesser extent, have influenced architectural style since that time. The Romans exploited the arch, vault, and dome and made broader use of the load-bearing masonry wall; and in the late medieval period the pointed arch, ribbing, and pier systems gradually emerged. At this point all the problems of brick and stone masonry construction had been solved, and little innovation except in decoration was achieved until the Industrial Revolution. Not until the 19th century, with the advent of cast-iron and steel construction, did a new architectural age dawn and higher, broader, and lighter buildings become possible. With the advances of 20th century technology, new structural methods such as cantilevering received more extensive use.

Building materials evolved in much the same way from simple, often perishable materials such as primitive grass thatch, stick frame, and wattle and daub to more durable materials such as clay, adobe, brick, stone, and cement. The modern use of reinforced and pre-stressed ferroconcrete and of various metals, including steel, copper, and aluminum, as well as of glass and structural fabrics and plastics, has led not only to more daring structural innovations but also to much beauty through the realization of the inherent qualities of such materials and their use in novel decorative schemes.

In postmodern architecture the classical orders have been reintroduced as one of a number of contrasting design methods, so that late 20th-century architecture attempted to include historical references in its design approach and was characterized by a new aesthetic pluralism.

(Wm.F./D.J.Wa./Ed.)

This article considers the history of architecture in the West from about 2000 BC. For a discussion of the architecture of ancient Egypt, see EGYPTIAN ARTS AND ARCHITECTURE, ANCIENT.

For coverage of related topics in the *Macropædia* and *Micropædia,* see the *Propædia,* section 626, and the *Index.*

The article is divided into the following sections:

European Metal Age cultures 902
Aegean and Eastern Mediterranean 902
Minoan Crete
Mycenaean Greece
Western Mediterranean 903
Bronze Age cultures
Iron Age cultures
Ancient Greek 905
The early periods 905
The Orientalizing period
The Archaic period (*c.* 750–500 BC)
The Classical period 906
Early Classical (*c.* 500–450 BC)
High Classical (*c.* 450–400 BC)
Late Classical (*c.* 400–323 BC)
Hellenistic period 908
Roman and early Christian 908
Republic and empire 908
Early Christian 914
Eastern Christian 917
The early Byzantine period (330–726) 917
The Iconoclastic Age (726–843) 919
The middle Byzantine period (843–1204) 919
The late Byzantine period (1204–1453) 920
Kievan Rus and Russia 921
Western Christian 923
Early Medieval 923
Migratory period
Merovingian period
Carolingian period
Ottonian period
Prelude to Romanesque in the north
Romanesque 926
Burgundy
Normandy
Aquitaine, Languedoc, and Auvergne
Provence
Germany and the Low Countries
Iberia
Italy
Norman Italy and Sicily
Palestine
Gothic 932
Early Gothic
High Gothic
Italian Gothic (*c.* 1200–1400)
Late Gothic
The end of Gothic
The Renaissance 937
Early Renaissance in Italy (1401–95) 938
High Renaissance in Italy (1495–1520) 941
Italian Mannerism or late Renaissance (1520–1600) 943
The Renaissance outside Italy 947
France
Spain and Spanish America
Portugal
Germany
Flanders and Holland
England
Eastern Europe
Baroque and Rococo 954
Origins and development in Rome 955
National and regional variations 956
Italy
Spain
Flanders
Holland
France
England
Central Europe
Russia

Colonial architecture in the Americas
Urban design 962
17th century
18th century
Classicism, 1750–1830 963
Origins and development 963
National and regional variations 964
Great Britain
France
Italy
Spain and Portugal
Germany
Scandinavia and Finland
Poland
Russia
United States
Spanish America and Brazil
Gothic Revival, *c.* 1730–*c.* 1930 971
Origins and development 971
National and regional variations 971
Great Britain
France
Germany and central Europe
The Low Countries
Scandinavia
Italy
Spain and Portugal
United States
Classicism, 1830–1930 980
Continuing development 980
National and regional variations 980
France
Great Britain
Italy
Germany and Austria
Scandinavia and Greece
United States
Late 19th-century developments 982
19th-century construction in iron and glass 982
Art Nouveau 984
20th-century architecture 985
The Modern movement 985
Before World War II
After World War II
Postmodernism 993
Bibliography 995

European Metal Age cultures

AEGEAN AND EASTERN MEDITERRANEAN

The islands of the eastern Mediterranean and the Aegean Sea form a natural link between the landmasses of the Middle East and Europe. A westward expansion from the civilizations of western Asia and Egypt began about 3000 BC and led to settlements in Crete, the Cyclades, and mainland Greece. The fundamental difference between these and the earlier, Neolithic cultures is that stone tools and weapons were replaced by those made of copper and, later, bronze. The Chalcolithic (Copper-Stone) Age, lasting in the Aegean area from the early 3rd millennium BC to the beginning of the 2nd, is usually considered a part of the greater Bronze Age, which was superseded by the Iron Age from about 1200 BC.

The hallmark of the Aegean civilizations was the facility with which Asiatic motifs and techniques were adapted to form original local styles. In architecture, by far the most important achievements were those of the civilizations of Minoan Crete and Mycenaean Greece.

Minoan Crete. The great maritime civilization of Crete crystallized around palaces such as those at Knossos, Phaestus, Ayía Triáda, Mallia, and Tylissos. The immensely important Palace of Minos at Knossos, excavated and reconstructed early in the 20th century by Sir Arthur Evans, offers evidence of unbroken architectural and artistic development from Neolithic beginnings, culminating in a brilliant display of building activity during the third phase of the Middle Minoan period (1700–1580 BC) and continuing until the invasion of the Achaeans in the 12th century. The palace, however, is essentially a structure of the late two Middle Minoan periods (1800–1580 BC). It no doubt rivaled Middle Eastern and Egyptian palaces in monumentality. As in these, a quadrangular complex of rooms and corridors is grouped around a great central court, at Knossos roughly 175 × 100 feet (50 × 30 metres). At the northern end, toward the sea, a grand portico of 12 pilasters gave access to the central court. At this end, also, is situated the grand theatrical area, a rectangular open-air theatre perhaps used for ritual performances. The east wing of the palace is divided into two parts by a long corridor running on an east–west axis; originally it rose four or five stories above the slope of the valley. The southeast portion of the palace contains domestic apartments, elaborately supplied with plumbing and flushing facilities, as well as a sanctuary. A wide stairway led to an upper story, which no longer exists. The northeast portion of the palace is occupied by offices and storerooms. The west portion is again divided by a main corridor, more than 200 feet long, running north and south. Behind this corridor, along the western side, was discovered a series of long narrow storerooms containing great numbers of pithoi, or human-size storage vessels for oil. On the other side of the corridor, facing toward the central court, are the rooms of state, including the throne room with its unique gypsum throne and world-famous griffin frescoes.

Palace of Minos

Light was supplied from above by an ingenious system of light wells, and several colonnaded porticoes provided ventilation during the hot Cretan summers. Brilliantly hued frescoes played an important part in both the interior and the exterior decoration of the palace.

The development of the other Minoan palaces (Phaestus, Mallia, Ayía Triáda, Tylissos) roughly parallels that of Knossos. Each has its special interest, and Phaestus is particularly fascinating, due to extensive Italian excavations. Maritime hegemony enabled the Cretan sea kings to build these palaces in low and unprotected places; consequently there is a conspicuous absence of fortification walls, as contrasted to the great walls of Mesopotamian palaces. Since Cretan worship seems to have been conducted largely in the open air, there are no real temples as in the Middle East. Yet, the disposition of the various parts of the palace around the central court and the avoidance of outside windows as much as possible are characteristics that seem to indicate an early contact with the Middle East. A taste for long, straight palace corridors, as well as a highly developed water-supply system, may also have been inherited from older civilizations to the east. The column made its first European appearance in the Cretan palace, where it is often employed individually to divide an entranceway.

The development of funerary architecture in Crete proceeds from the old chamber ossuaries of the Early Minoan period (2750–2000 BC) to the developed tholoi, or beehive tombs, of the Mesara plain and the elaborate temple-tombs of Knossos that appeared at the end of the Middle Minoan period.

On the crest of Minoan prosperity came the great crash. An invasion from the mainland about 1400 BC destroyed the palaces and resulted in the removal of power to Mycenaean Greece. Architectural remains in Crete of structures that are pre-Greek in design and yet were built subsequent to this catastrophe are very rare. Several country shrines belong to this post-destruction period, and at Prinias a unique temple building may date from as late as 700 BC. The doorway of this temple, now in the Archaeological Museum at Iráklion, has low reliefs on its architectural members. The opening above the lintel is flanked by seated figures, while the lintel itself is carved on its underside with figures of a goddess and of animals. That the Minoan tradition was not entirely extinct is indicated by the column that seems to have stood in the middle of this doorway, as at the Palace of Minos.

Mycenaean Greece. The sudden architectural awakening of the Mycenaean Greek mainland is intimately connected with the zenith and decline of Minoan Crete and can only be understood against the background of a long Cretan development. Unlike Minoan Knossos, the archaeological remains on the mainland are fragmentary.

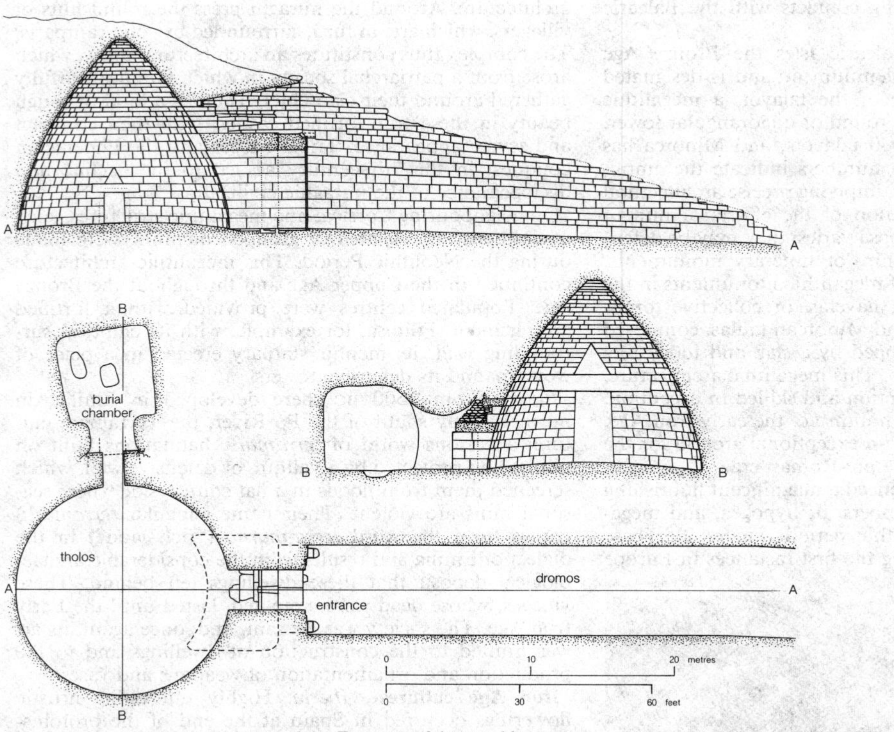

Figure 1: Cross sections and plan of the Treasury of Atreus, Mycenae.

Redrawn after Fig. 5 in Alan J.B. Wace, *Mycenae: An Archaeological History and Guide* (copyright 1949 by Princeton University Press). Reprinted by permission of Princeton University Press

Knowledge of at least three sites, Mycenae, Tiryns, and Pylos, suggests a picture of Mycenaean architecture. The important architectural monuments visible today date largely from Late Helladic times (1580 to *c.* 1100 BC), and little earlier architecture is preserved.

Fortification. The tremendous building activity of the 14th century BC reflects an age of warfare, when powerful Greek-speaking kings built fortresses in key defensive positions on the mainland. The cyclopean walls (*i.e.,* walls in which great blocks of irregular untrimmed stone fitted together without mortar were employed) of Mycenae and Tiryns and the strategically placed Lion Gate at Mycenae were constructed in this period. The latter consists of two colossal doorjambs that support a monolithic lintel. The wall above the gate is so constructed as to form a relieving triangle over the lintel, and this space is blocked with the famous relief panel of two heraldic lions, which has given the gate its name. This method of construction provides an ingenious substitute for the arch, which was unknown to the Mycenaeans.

Lion Gate

Also justly famed are the concealed galleries of Tiryns, where the primitive corbel vault (constructed of rows of masonry placed so that each row projects slightly beyond the one below, the two opposite walls meeting at the top) makes its first appearance in mainland Europe.

Palaces. Mycenaean palaces have been unearthed at Mycenae, Tiryns, Pylos, Gla, and Phylakopi (Cyclades). The palace at Pylos is a typical mainland palace of the Heroic Age as described in the poetry of Homer. The characteristic plan comprises four elements: (1) a narrow court on which the structure fronts; (2) a double-columned entrance portico; (3) a vestibule (*prodomos*); and (4) the richly frescoed *domos,* or hall proper. The latter had a fixed throne at one end and a central fixed hearth between four wooden columns that supported an open towerlike structure rising above the roof for light and ventilation. Archives, comparable to those of the Hittite kings at Boğazköy, were associated with this palace. Private houses, such as have been discovered at Mycenae, exhibit similar features as well as the basement storage magazines mentioned by Homer.

Tombs. The earliest royal burials known from Mycenae are those of the two grave circles, the first discovered by Heinrich Schliemann in 1876 and the second by Alan J.B. Wace in 1951. These grave circles have no architectural character, consisting essentially of vertical shafts cut into the bedrock.

More important architecturally are the tholoi. The evolution of these family sepulchres began in Minoan Crete but culminated in the so-called Treasury of Atreus at Mycenae, now believed to have been constructed as late as about 1250 BC (Figure 1). This most impressive monument of the Mycenaean world is a pointed dome built up of overhanging (*i.e.,* corbeled) blocks of conglomerate masonry cut and polished to give the impression of a true vault. The diameter of this tomb is almost 50 feet; its height is slightly less. The enormous monolithic lintel of the doorway weighs 120 tons and is 29½ feet long, 16½ feet deep, and three feet high. It is surmounted by a relieving triangle similar to that over the Lion Gate and decorated with relief plaques carved in a variety of coloured stones. A small side chamber hewn out of the living rock contained the burials, whereas the main chamber was probably reserved for ritual use. Two engaged half columns (*i.e.,* attached to the wall and projecting from it for about half their diameter) of Cretan type (now in the British Museum, London) were secured to the facade, which was approached by a dromos, or ceremonial passageway, revetted with cyclopean blocks of masonry and open to the sky. Other tholoi, not as well preserved, exist at Mycenae and Orchomenos. (H.Hn./Ed.)

WESTERN MEDITERRANEAN

Bronze Age cultures. Metalworking improved and promoted the progress of the western Mediterranean lands, which developed maritime relations joining them to one another and binding them to the eastern Mediterranean. Several great centres displayed considerable architectural activity, of which some splendid evidence remains.

Iberia. The Bronze Age was a brilliant stage of culture in the Iberian Peninsula and was designated El Argar, honouring the name of a great site of southeastern Spain. El Argar, which stood well fortified on a plateau about 1,000 feet long and about 330 feet wide, enjoyed, from 1700 BC, several centuries of prosperity and exerted an influence that spread over the eastern coasts of Spain and over southern Portugal. A necropolis of about 1,000 burials has yielded goods of quality from the graves. The El

El Argar culture

Argar culture had continuing contacts with the Balearic Isles, Malta, and Sardinia.

Balearic Isles. In the Balearic Isles the Bronze Age corresponds to the 2nd millennium BC and is designated "talayotic" from the name of the talayot, a megalithic monument in the form of a round or quadrangular tower. Majorca still has about 1,000 talayots, and Minorca has more than 300. These high numbers indicate the amplitude of construction activity, implying precise architectural planning and the coordination of the efforts of human groups. Their intended purpose varies: they may be defensive towers, places of worship, or funerary monuments. There are also other types of megalithic monuments in the Balearic Isles; for example, navetas, or collective tombs built in the form of ships, and Minorcan taulas, composed of a monolithic column topped by a slab and today recognized as places of worship. This megalithic architecture, which is imposing in conception and skilled in execution, continued into the 1st millennium BC, the early Iron Age, and made the Balearic Isles an exceptional ground for the study of the structures of the pre-Roman era.

Malta. Malta had experienced a magnificent flourishing of underground burial chambers, or hypogea, and megalithic temples in the Neolithic period (Figure 2). These Neolithic temples are among the first instances in Europe of buildings erected for a particular functional purpose. They have a trefoil plan and a roof construction of corbelled stone that is the earliest known example of its kind. The arrival of Cycladic and Cretan influences in Malta stimulated the birth of a stone and terra-cotta statuary representing the deities and their worshipers. This continued brilliantly in the Copper Age, but the beginning of the 2nd millennium witnessed the appearance of a new people who conquered and destroyed, which is well known from the cremation burial ground of Tarxien. Small terra-cotta female idols recall contemporary figurines of Cyprus, but the culture was rapidly impoverished.

H. Roger-Viollet

Figure 2: One of the chambers of a megalithic temple at Tarxien, Malta, Late Neolithic (2300–1900 BC).

Sardinia and Corsica. It is necessary to go farther north—Sardinia and Corsica—to find an original and prosperous Bronze Age, the creations of which continue to pose certain problems of interpretation. The Sardinian bronze civilization is characterized by the nuraghi, round towers that may occur alone or form the centre of complex fortified arrangements. About 7,000 of them, dating from about 1500 to 1100 BC, have been discovered on different parts of the island. They are efficiently and skillfully constructed defensive fortresses, the interior arrangements of which give evidence of an art developed out of military architecture. Around the nuraghi press the round huts of villagers, which are, in turn, surrounded by solid ramparts. The complex thus constitutes an architectural unity, which arose from a patriarchal society in which families fearfully gathered around their clan chief. There is a kind of rough beauty in these true fortified castles, with their compact and severe appearance. Tribal battles and the Phoenician conquest in the 7th century BC led to the decline and disappearance of the nuraghic civilization.

Nuraghic civilization

On neighbouring Corsica, fine megalithic structures, such as dolmens and isolated or grouped menhirs, were made during the Neolithic Period. This megalithic architecture continued in the Copper Age and throughout the Bronze Age. Populated centres were provided with a fortified arrangement; Filitosa, for example, with its elliptical surrounding wall, its menhir statuary erected in a place of worship, and its defensive towers.

Italy. From 1500 BC there developed in Emilia, in northern Italy south of the Po River, the Terramare culture, a curious world of *terramare*, habitations built on pilings and protected by a vallum, or defensive wall, which screened them from floods in a flat countryside where seasonal rains are violent. Their name (singular *terramara*) comes from the word *terra-marna* ("rich land") in the dialect of Emilia and results from the considerable archaeological deposit that these dwellings left behind. These villages, whose dead were cremated, lasted until the Early Iron Age. The society was peasant, and, once again, its art was limited to the construction of dwellings and to the production and ornamentation of weapons and vases.

Iron Age cultures. *Iberia.* Highly interesting artistic flowerings occurred in Spain at the end of the protohistoric era. First, in the southwest of the peninsula, near the town of Cadiz, there developed at the extreme end of the 2nd millennium BC a civilization, still poorly understood, that tradition attributes to the semi-historic, semilegendary state of Tartessus. Archaeology has not yet revealed the splendour ascribed by the ancients to the Tartessian culture, which was strongly influenced by early Phoenician commercial contacts from the southern coast of Spain. Along the coasts of the Levant and penetrating deeply into the interior of the peninsula, an indigenous population, the Iberians, developed a truly original art under combined Grecian, Carthaginian, and Phoenician influences.

Iberian dwelling sites

Many Iberian dwelling sites have been discovered on the eastern coasts of Spain, where they were established on such high places as steep-sloped plateaus and protected by surrounding walls with round and square towers and doors. The street network does not seem to follow a regular plan. Great temples such as those of Castellar de Santisteban and Despeñaperros in the Sierra Morena have sacred storerooms where a great number (about 6,000 for the two sites) of votive statuettes have been discovered.

Italy. The fate and art of the Etruscan people—who made their appearance in the heart of Italy between the Arno and Tiber rivers about 700 BC and vanished, under the legions' blows, in the last centuries of the Roman Republic—must be mentioned here because in the early years of their existence they were deeply involved in Italic protohistory. In antiquity the Etruscans were regarded as skillful architects and excellent builders. Precise ritual rules of town planning made it possible for them to construct cities on regular plans, the most beautiful remains of which are those of Marzabotto, near Bologna, and of Capua, in Campania. Nothing much remains of the Tuscan cities, which were, nevertheless, very splendid. On the other hand, there remain thousands of tombs that reveal the structure of the vanished houses. The tomb was the dwelling of the dead and simulated the appearance of one or several rooms, constructed in bedrock and built of stone. Thus well protected, Etruscan grave goods and artistic creations were preserved. (R.Bl./D.J.Wa.)

What little remains of Etruscan stonework has survived by virtue of its massiveness. Foundations of city walls survive at Volterra, Volsinii, and Cortona, but those of Perugia are more complete and have surviving vaulted gates. The tombs, themselves replicas of house interiors, show something of moldings, arches, and vaults. True vaulting and arching were known, and these enabled buildings larger than those of Greece to be constructed. Wood was the chief building material for domestic purposes and for temples, from which the terra-cotta decorations alone survive. Blocks of houses in carefully paved streets are known only from Marzabotto, although the layout of the tombs with paved streets in the Banditaccia at Caere and the Cuccumella at Vetulonia makes them veritable cities of the dead. The Latian hut urns show that houses of the Villanovan period (8th century BC) were circular in plan with conical roofs, but a stone urn from Clusium is modeled in the form of a rectangular Etruscan house erected on a tall, stepped platform. The roof is a hipped gable and has a gabled gallery over it. In this connection it is interesting that the Romans attributed to the Etruscans the construction of the atrium house. Temples were rectangular in plan and divided into three cellae (chambers); ground plans and nothing more are known from Rome and Bolsena. Etruscan temples, such as those of which remains survive at Bolsena and Orvieto, were built of wood and brick upon high platforms of dressed stone and were consequently more perishable than their Greek equivalents. They were crowned and decorated by brightly painted statues and revetments of terra-cotta, many of which have survived. (W.Cu./D.J.Wa.)

Ancient Greek

The increased wealth of Greece in the 7th century BC had been promoted by overseas trade and by colonizing activity in Italy and Sicily that had opened new markets and resources. Athens did not send out colonists and did not engage in vigorous trade, and it declined as a cultural and artistic centre. Corinth, Sparta, the islands, the cities of eastern Greece, and Crete came to the fore with their diverse artistic interests and means of expression. At no other time were there such strongly differentiated regional schools of art in the Greek world. The cities demonstrated their wealth and power, particularly in temple building, which was to foster new architectural forms, and also in the decoration of the temples and of the national sanctuaries. These architectural arts in turn encouraged imaginative and ambitious forms in sculpture and painting.

THE EARLY PERIODS

Throughout the history of Greek art, the architect's main role was to design cult buildings, and until the Classical period it was virtually his only concern. The focus of worship in Greek religion was the altar, which for a long time was a simple block and only much later evolved into a monumental form. It stood in the open air, and if there was a temple, generally the altar was positioned to the east of it. The temple was basically a house (*oikos*) for the deity, who was represented there by his cult statue. Temple plans, then, were house plans—one-room buildings with columnar porches (Figure 3). To distinguish the divine house from a mortal one, the early temple was given an elongated plan, with the cult statue placed at the back, viewed distantly beyond a row of central pillar supports. The exterior came to be embellished by a peristyle, an outer colonnade of posts supporting extended eaves. This colonnade provided a covered ambulatory (roofed walkway), and it was also a device to distinguish the building

Standard Greek temple plan

Phaidon Press, Inc.

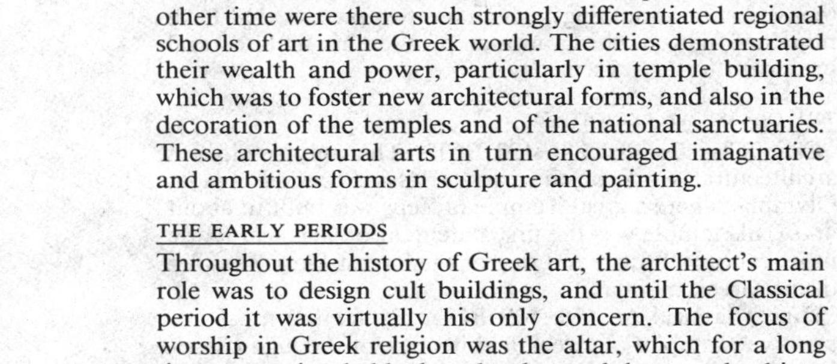

Figure 3: Plan of typical Greek temple with pronaos (inner portico), opisthodomus (rear chamber), peristyle, and two rows of columns in the cella, illustrated by the Temple of Zeus at Olympia, *c.* 460 BC.

from purely secular architecture. This plan can be seen in buildings on Samos and at Thermum in central Greece. The construction remained simple: well-laid rubble and mud brick, with timbering and a thatched or flat clay roof. By about 700 BC, fired-clay roof tiles made possible a lower pitched roof, and by the mid-7th century, fired- and painted-clay facings were being made to decorate and protect the vulnerable wooden upperworks of buildings. As yet, nothing had been constructed in finished stone.

The Orientalizing period. From about 650 on, the Greeks began to visit Egypt regularly, and their observation of the monumental stone buildings there was the genesis of the ultimate development of monumental architecture and sculpture in Greece. The first step in architecture was simply the replacement of wooden pillars with stone ones and the translation of the carpentry and brick structural forms into stone equivalents. This provided an opportunity for the expression of proportion and pattern, an expression that eventually took the form of the invention or evolution of the stone "orders" of architecture. These orders, or arrangements of specific types of columns supporting an upper section called an entablature, defined the pattern of the columnar facades and upperworks that formed the basic decorative shell of the Greek temple building.

Influence of Egyptian monumental architecture

The Doric order was invented in the second half of the 7th century, perhaps in Corinth. Its parts—the simple, baseless columns, the spreading capitals, and the triglyph-metope (alternating vertically ridged and plain blocks) frieze above the columns—constitute an aesthetic development in stone incorporating variants on themes used functionally in earlier wood and brick construction. Doric long remained the favourite order of the Greek mainland and western colonies, and it changed little throughout its history. Early examples, such as the temple at Thermum, were not wholly of stone but still used much timber and fired clay.

The Ionic order evolved later, in eastern Greece. About 600 BC, at Smyrna, the first intimation of the style appeared in stone columns with capitals elaborately carved in floral hoops—an Orientalizing pattern familiar mainly on smaller objects and furniture and enlarged for architecture. This pattern was to be the determining factor in the full development of the Ionic order in the 6th century.

The Archaic period (c. 750–500 BC). About 750 BC there began a period of consolidation of the diverse influences that had been entering Greek art at a rapid rate over the previous 100 years; it is known as the Archaic period. It was an age of preoccupation with domestic troubles brought on by the new prosperity rather than an age of reaching out to other cultures. It was also the age of the tyrant, whose individual rule was often supported by arms and by the allegiance of the merchant classes. The courts of these tyrants became the significant cultural centres, and there was an increase in the demand for art of all kinds; demonstration of the rulers' wealth and power took the form of temple building more ambitious than in almost any other period of Greek art, while in sculpture there was a growing use of expensive and elaborate statuary for dedication and for marking tombs. In contrast to the previous relation of Greece to the outside world in art, there developed for the first time a substantial production of bronzes and pottery for export; sometimes styles or motifs were even deliberately conceived with the foreign customer in view.

Age of the tyrant

During this period the arts of sculpture, vase painting, and bronze working reached a level of technical mastery and imaginative freedom that brought narrative action and even emotion under the command of figural representation. Simultaneously, out of extensive experimentation with the architectural innovations of the later 7th century, the Classical Doric and Ionic orders were fully established and largely standardized.

In the 6th century the western Greek colonies claimed a position of importance in the history of Greek art. The colonies in southern Italy and Sicily had grown as strong and rich as many cities in the motherland and had made similar demonstrations of wealth by the dedication of treasuries in the national sanctuaries and by lavish temple building at home. The temples were generally in the Doric

Figure 4: Temple of Hera II, Paestum, Italy, *c.* 460 BC.
Hirmer

style, but they often bore Ionic details. In their sculpture and architecture the colonies were handicapped by the lack of local sources for fine white marble, and they relied more on painted and stuccoed limestone; the lack of marble, however, stimulated their production of major sculptural works in fired clay to a degree not matched at home. The colonial art centres seem to have been Syracuse, Selinus, and Acragas in Sicily and Poseidonia, or Paestum (Figure 4), Sybaris, and Tarentum in Italy. Although the Greek colonies seem to have attracted artists from the homeland, all their art tends to a largeness of scale and of detail that often contrasts with popular notions of Greek monumental art. For example, the most striking ancient building on Sicily is the colossal Doric temple of Olympian Zeus at Acragas, begun in about 500 BC and left unfinished a century later. To carry the weight of the massive entablature, the outer columns were not freestanding but were half-columns engaged against (that is, partially attached to) a continuous solid wall. An earlier Sicilian variant of this use of the plastically molded wall mass with the orders applied decoratively can be seen in the columnar curtain walls of Temple F at Selinus, begun about 560 BC. The engaged columns of Acragas were echoed in the late 5th century by the architect Ictinus in the cella of the Temple of Apollo at Bassae and half a century later by the sculptor Scopas in the Temple of Athena at Tegea. All these buildings suggest that the 18th-century Enlightenment idea of Greek architecture as a system based solely on post-and-lintel construction, in which the columns carried the load, was erroneous.

Because temples constructed entirely of stone were expensive, they were not replaced without a compelling reason; in many central and southern Greek cities, therefore, the robust Archaic forms of the Doric temples dominated the townscape through the Classical and later periods. The forms were heavy, with plump columns and capitals and brightly coloured upperworks. Although little change was made in the basic order in the 6th century, there was a gradual refinement of detail and proportion approaching the Classical form of the order (Figure 5). At this time also the place of sculpture in Doric architecture was once and for all established.

Maturing of the Ionic order

The more exotic Ionic order of eastern Greece was slower to determine its forms; the order developed through the so-called Aeolic capital with vertically springing volutes, or spiral ornaments, to the familiar Ionic capital, the volutes of which spread horizontally from the centre and curl downward. There were also several distinctive local methods of treating bases or entire plans. The order was always fussier and more ornate, less stereotyped than Doric, yet it was still limited to monumental plans, and the Ionic temples of the 6th century exceed in size and decoration even the most ambitious of their Classical successors. Such were the temples of Artemis at Ephesus in Asia Minor and the successive temples of Hera on the island of Samos, all of which were more than 300 feet long and set with forests of more than 100 columns standing in double and triple rows around the central rectangular room (cella), where the cult image stood. At the same time, masons developed and refined the carved cyma (double curve) and ovolo (convex curve) moldings, which are two profiles that have remained part of the grammar of Western architectural ornament to the present day.

THE CLASSICAL PERIOD

Early Classical (c. 500–450 BC). The only significant architectural work of the early Classical period was at Olympia, where a great Temple of Zeus was built in about 460. This temple was the first statement of Classical Doric in its canonical form and one of the largest Doric temples of the Greek mainland.

High Classical (c. 450–400 BC). By far the most impressive examples of Greek architecture of the high Classi-

From *Praeger Picture Encyclopaedia of Art*

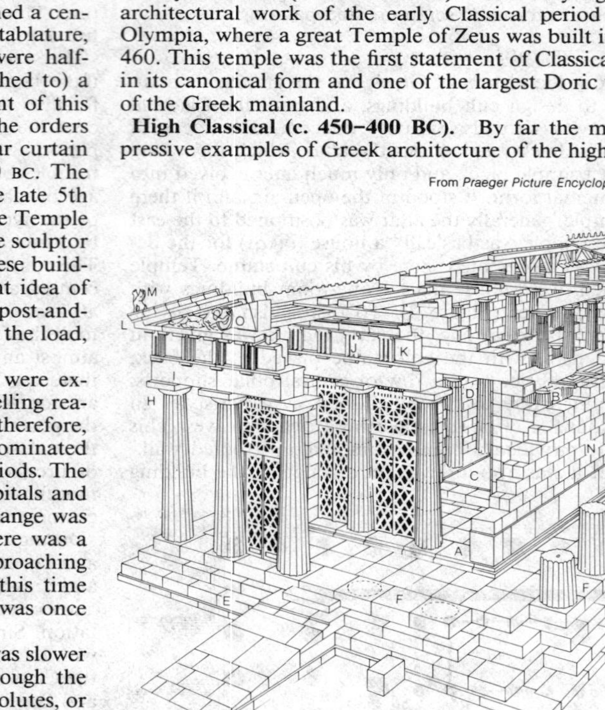

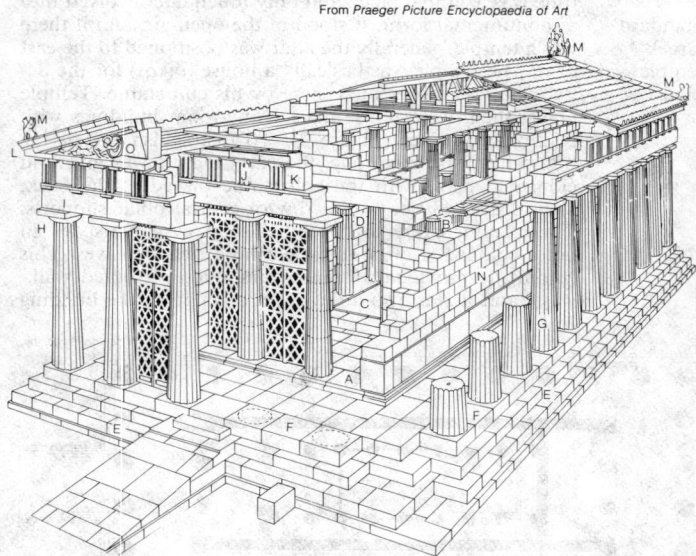

Figure 5: *Typical Archaic period Doric temple.*
Restored sectional view of Temple of Aphaea in Aegina.
(A) Pronaos; (B,C,D) naos, or cella; (E) crepidoma, or crepis; (F) stylobate; (G) Doric columns; (H) Doric capital, consisting of the echinus and abacus; (I) epistyle, or architrave; (J) triglyph; (K) metope; (L) geison, or cornice; (M) acroterion; (N) exterior wall of cella; (O) sculptured gable.

cal period were the buildings constructed under Pericles for the Athenian Acropolis. The Acropolis architecture, which is in several ways a clear display of civic pride, also exhibits considerable subtlety of design in the use of the Doric and Ionic orders. The ensemble of the major buildings—the Parthenon, a temple to Athena; the Erechtheum, a temple housing several cults; and the monumental gateway to the Acropolis, the Propylaea—shows the orders used in deliberate contrast: the Erechtheum provides a decorative Ionic counterpart to the severe Doric of the Parthenon, which itself has an Ionic frieze; and in the Propylaea, columns of both orders complement each other.

The buildings of the Acropolis

The Parthenon, designed by the architect Ictinus, is a broader, more stately building than most Doric temples, with an eight-column facade instead of the usual six. With the four-square Doric style there had always been the possibility of giving an impression of dull immobility, a danger that in the Archaic period was partially avoided through the use of bulging columns and capitals. In the Classical period—and best observed in the Parthenon—a subtle deviation from strict linearity accomplishes the same correction. The Parthenon was the display place for a great statue of Athena by the sculptor Phidias, a statue that honoured the city goddess but not the oldest cult of Athena, which was housed in the Erechtheum. The obvious implications of civic pride are enhanced by the unparalleled portrayal of a contemporary event on the frieze of the building: the procession of citizens in the yearly festival in honour of Athena. The Erechtheum was a more complicated building than the Parthenon; built on an awkward site, it also had to serve different cults, which meant that its architect had to design a building with three porches and three different floor levels. Its Caryatid porch, with figures of women for columns, makes use of an old Oriental motif that had appeared earlier, in Archaic treasuries at Delphi. The Propylaea was designed by Mnesicles, who had to adapt the rigid conventions of colonnade construction to a steeply rising site. In the precision and finish of their execution, which complements the brilliant innovation of their design, these three buildings had no rival in the Greek world.

Other architecture of the high Classical period

By this time use of the orders was no longer confined to temple buildings. The marketplace at Athens was adorned with various public buildings in which the orders were applied to structures of different plans: the colonnade stoa, or portico, a council house, and even a circular clubhouse for state officials. The stage buildings of theatres began to receive monumental treatment as well, although the action still took place on the flat circular orchestra and the seats were for the most part still wooden (or were missing—the audience sitting upon the bare hillside that was usually chosen for theatre sites) rather than stone. Several new Doric temples were also built in the lower city of Athens and in the Attic countryside. The Ionic order was used only for the smaller temples, as for the Temple of Athena Nike on the Acropolis; but even though the Ionic was never to be used as the exterior order for major buildings on the Greek mainland, Athens did contribute new forms of column base to the order.

At Bassae in remote Arcadia in the mountains of the Peloponnese, a Doric temple was built for Apollo incorporating unusual variants on the Ionic column in the interior and a new type of capital, which had two rows of acanthus leaves curling below the volutes—the first recorded Corinthian capital. This type was reputedly invented by the sculptor-architect Callimachus to provide an alternative for the Ionic order that could be viewed from any side and so placed at corners or in interiors. It was difficult to carve, however, and slow to win favour in Greece.

Late Classical (c. 400–323 BC). With growth now concentrated in outlying areas, there was understandably less temple building in mainland Greece in this period than there had been in the 5th century, but the Doric temples at Tegea and Nemea in the Peloponnese were important, the former for admitting Corinthian capitals to columns engaged on its interior walls. In eastern Greece, on the other hand, there began a series of new temple constructions rivaling those of the Archaic period but consciously copying the Archaic in their plan and elaboration of detail. Some are simply replacements, such as that at Ephesus replacing an earlier temple destroyed by fire, or the rather later one at Didyma. Similarly, the town of Priene in Ionia, although built on a new foundation after the mid-4th century, was laid out as a grid of streets on a principle developed by the 5th-century architect Hippodamus, who had applied the same scheme to his home city, Miletus, and to the port of Athens, Piraeus. The new Athena Temple at Priene is the best example of classic Ionic known, with no eccentricity of plan or detail. The eastern Greeks had long worked for their neighbours in the Persian towns of Lycia and Caria, supplying monumental tombs of native pattern decorated with sculpture in Greek style. At Xanthus, the capital of Lycia, a tomb resembling a Greek temple raised high on a platform had been built by the end of the 5th century; and similar structures were made there in the 4th century, culminating in the great tomb built in mid-century at Halicarnassus for King Mausolus of Caria, a king who has given his name to all such monumental mausoleums. The fine architectural detail and the sculpture (British Museum, London) executed by Greek artists of the first rank show a total Hellenization of local taste and exemplify the high quality that Greek art in foreign lands had attained at this time.

Major temple building in Ionia

The 4th century saw much greater diversity of architectural forms than ever before. Theatres received marble seats and elaborate stage buildings. Circular temples (tholoi) appeared in mainland Greek sanctuaries—Doric in style but with the new Corinthian columns within. A small-scale tholos with Corinthian columns was also used for the choragic monument of Lysicrates in Athens (Figure 6). The two-storied stoa became an essential element in the planning of marketplaces or administrative areas. Architects were at pains to adapt the rigid orders to architectural forms and needs more complicated than those of the basic Greek temple plan.

Diversification of architectural forms

Figure 6: Choragic monument of Lysicrates, Athens, 335/334 BC.

HELLENISTIC PERIOD

The successors to Alexander's empire split the new Greek world, which now ran to the borders of India in the east and the Sudan in the south, into separate kingdoms. The generals who ruled them established dynastic control and created a court life that provided a type of stimulus to the arts that had not been experienced in Greece since the Bronze Age. The Attalids, who had become the rulers of Pergamum in northwest Asia Minor, constructed there a new capital city in which influential schools of sculpture and architecture flourished. The Seleucids ruled the Eastern world as far as Persia, and under them the art of architecture in particular evolved in near-Baroque forms that were to have their effect on Roman architecture. In Egypt the Ptolemies, at the new capital city that bore Alexander's name and was founded by him, built the famous lighthouse and library; and there another important sculptural school developed. In the Aegean world, Rhodes proved an important centre and so, of course, did the Macedonian homeland in the north. By comparison, the great cities of central Greece declined in importance; but Athens in particular had a hold on the imagination of Greeks everywhere for its former role against the Persians and the achievements of the Classical period, and as a result it benefited from the gifts of the new kingdoms, especially in building.

Alexander's aspirations and closer knowledge of Eastern and Egyptian ways led the new rulers to take more seriously their roles of near divinity. This gave considerable impetus to the art of portraiture, since these rulers thus deserved commemoration as much as any god; in fact, even private citizens aspired now to some heroic status after death, so that portrait monuments for tombs and honorific statues became more common. Except for this growth of portraiture, however, the mood in the arts during the Hellenistic period was to intensify and elaborate styles developed by Classical Greece. Palatial architecture aimed at effects never contemplated hitherto; and even domestic architecture for the first time had palatial pretensions. Trade and the newly acquired resources of the East opened up new possibilities for the artist, in both materials and inspiration; the results, however, generally tended to elaboration and grandeur such that the finer qualities of balance and precision characteristic of earlier periods are often difficult to discern in later works.

The Classical form of the Doric temple was out of favour in the new age, and the few that were built are elaborate in plan and detail, impairing the sober quality of the order. This age appreciated the Ionic and the more flamboyant Corinthian forms, and at any rate most new temple building was done in the new eastern areas of the Greek world, where Ionic had been the usual idiom. The 3rd-century architect Hermogenes of Priene codified the Ionic order in his books, and his buildings popularized new features in plan, notably the broad flanking colonnades ("pseudo-dipteral"), where the earlier Ionic temples of eastern Greece had set ranks of columns. For the first time the Corinthian order was used for temple exteriors, and work was resumed on the great Temple of Olympian Zeus at Athens, financed by an Eastern king, Antiochus IV Epiphanes. The two-storied stoa became an architectural form of importance, serving as hotel, emporium, or office block, and the design of central market and administrative areas depended largely on the disposition of such buildings. An Attalid king paid for a fine stoa for Athens' marketplace, recently restored; and his city of Pergamum seems to have been important in developing stoa design.

First major use of the Corinthian order

Monumental tombs were naturally still required for ruling families, but nobles and the nouveaux riches could also aspire to them now, designing some as minor sanctuaries for the heroized dead. The finest Macedonian tombs of the period displayed a painted architectural facade below ground, leading to a painted and elaborately furnished vaulted underground chamber. The variety of administrative and court requirements for buildings led to original designs that broke still more decisively with the colonnade orders of Classical temples. A few important examples of particularly original designs are the famous lighthouse (Pharos) of Alexandria with its tiers of masonry 440 feet high; the library of Alexandria; the clock house Tower of the Winds at Athens; monumental fountains and assembly halls; and a new elaboration of stage architecture for theatres, in which for the first time the acting took place on a raised stage. To the established decorative repertory of moldings and carved ornament was added a variety of floral and animal forms that enriched the surface decoration of buildings. In the East especially these forms were combined in original ways that, together with compositions that defied the logic of the Classical orders, tended to a style that in many respects anticipates the Baroque. Slowly, too, the advantages of arch and vault, avoided hitherto by Greek architects, were exploited; but architecture was still basically that of mass on mass, and it was left to Rome to make significant progress in construction methods. (Jo.Bo./D.J.Wa.)

Roman and early Christian

Rome before the Etruscan advent was a small conglomeration of villages. It was under the new masters that, according to tradition, the first public works such as the walls of the Capitoline Hill and the Cloaca Maxima were constructed. Considerable evidence of the Etruscan period in Rome's history has come to light in the region of the Capitol. That there were rich tombs in Rome itself cannot be doubted—tombs similar to those in the Latin town of Praeneste. Meanwhile, by the beginning of the 6th century BC the Etruscans had included Fiesole and Volterra in their northern limits and at the same time began to push southward into Campania. Capua became the chief Etruscan settlement in this region and Nola a second; a necropolis has been found in the Salerno region and Etruscan objects in low levels at Herculaneum and Pompeii. The coastal region was still, however, in Greek hands. (W.Cu.)

REPUBLIC AND EMPIRE

Roman architecture was almost as complex as the Roman Empire itself; it was influenced by a multitude of geographic, climatic, political, economic, social, and cultural factors. The cohesive factor through all the differences was the Roman character, which possessed the talent and felt the necessity to organize in large and complex terms, politically, architecturally, or otherwise.

Sources of modern knowledge about Roman architecture

Modern knowledge of Roman architecture derives primarily from extant remains scattered throughout the area of the empire. Some are well preserved, and others are known only in fragments and by theoretical restoration. Another source of information is a vast store of records, including dedicatory and other inscriptions on public works. Especially important is a book on architecture by the architect Vitruvius, who lived about the time of Christ. His book *De architectura* (*c.* 27 BC) is a handbook for Roman architects and covers almost every aspect of architecture, but it is limited because it was based on Greek models and was written at the beginning of a more creative phase of Roman architecture, in the period of the empire.

Building materials. The material employed in the earliest buildings constructed around Rome was tuff, a volcanic rock of varying hardnesses, some soft enough to be worked with bronze tools. Later, other harder volcanic stones were used, such as peperino and albani stone from the nearby Alban hills. Under the later republic and the empire the most important stone for building was travertine, a limestone quarried mainly at Tivoli. An example of the use of travertine is the exterior of the Colosseum in Rome. The use made by the Romans of marble was mainly decorative. It was set in cement and applied in slabs to brick and concrete walls. It was used for pavements either in slabs cut and arranged in patterns or as mosaic. Under the empire a great demand arose for coloured marbles and such stones as porphyry, granite, and alabaster, which were imported from various parts of the empire. The abundant use of these marbles is well illustrated by the remains of the Flavian palace on the Palatine Hill in Rome and of Hadrian's Villa at Tivoli.

Unburned bricks faced with stucco were used especially for private houses during the republic. Of these, naturally, very few remain. Under the empire, kiln-baked bricks and tiles were the most common facing for concrete. They were never used to build a whole wall in the modern manner but merely as a protective skin. These bricks or tiles were almost always used in triangular shapes. Large tiles about two feet square called bipedales were also employed.

Use of stucco and concrete

The use of stucco over unbaked brick and over coarse stone was prevalent from the earliest times in Greece, Sicily, and Italy. It served as a protection against the weather and also as a finish. Later it was used over brick and concrete. It was often made of lime, sand, and fine marble dust, and some forms would take a high polish or fine molding. Thus, it became the usual ground for decoration especially in the interiors of houses, examples of which abound at Pompeii and Rome. Bronze was another material primarily used in a decorative manner; doors, grilles, panels of ceilings, and other details were made of it.

For their concrete the Romans used pozzolana, of which there are extensive beds at Pozzuoli, near Naples, and around Rome. It is a fine, chocolate-red volcanic earth, which when mixed with hydrated lime forms an excellent cement that will set well even under water. With this cement was mixed an aggregate of broken tuff, travertine, brick, or even marble, with pumice stone being used in vaults after the 1st century AD to lighten the weight of the structure. Concrete was used in all great imperial buildings (for example, the Pantheon, Baths of Caracalla, and Basilica of Maxentius in Rome). New forms of architecture that were developed by the use of this material spread throughout the Roman Empire, although in the provinces other, often weaker, kinds of concrete were used.

Construction. Walls were built of ordinary masonry or of concrete (faced or unfaced). There are several examples of early stone walling without courses (continuous layers), especially in such Italian towns as Norba and Praeneste. Most of the stone walls existing, however, were built of fairly large squared blocks laid in regular courses as headers (stone or brick laid with its end toward the face of the wall) and stretchers (stone or brick laid with its length parallel to the face of the wall). This type of masonry was called *opus quadratum.*

Concrete walls, except below ground, were always faced. They are divided into types according to the kind of facing used. (1) *Opus quadratum*—that is, ordinary stone walling—was used as a facing especially for important public buildings under the earlier empire (for example, the exterior of the Colosseum). (2) *Opus incertum* was the most common facing for ordinary concrete walls of the 2nd and 1st centuries BC. The face of the concrete was studded with three- to four-inch irregularly shaped pieces of stone, usually tuff. (3) *Opus reticulatum* came into vogue in the 1st century BC and remained until the time of Hadrian (AD 117). The construction was like that of *opus incertum* but the pieces of stone were pyramid-shaped with square bases set diagonally in rows and wedged into the concrete walls. (4) Brick- and tile-faced concrete (so-called *opus testaceum*) was by far the most common material for walling during the empire. Triangular tiles were used with their points turned into the concrete and their long sides showing, thus giving the appearance of a wall built of thin bricks. Bonding courses of bipedales were employed at intervals of two or three feet. (5) Mixed brick and stone facing, called *opus mixtum,* was popular under the later empire and especially under Diocletian (AD 284–305).

Kinds of facing for concrete

Other kinds of supports included columns and piers. Columns were usually of stone and often monolithic; occasionally, small columns were of brick covered with stucco. Piers (solid blocks of masonry supporting either an arch or a lintel) were often of stone, but those serving as primary support for large vaults were usually of concrete.

Arches occurred in gates, bridges, and aqueducts, as well as in colonnades and doors. Not only round but also segmental (part of a circle but less than a semicircle) and flat arches were used freely. The discovery of concrete enormously facilitated the spread of arch construction. Concrete arches were faced with wedge-shaped stones or tiles called voussoirs.

Vaults and domes

The vaults used by the Romans were simple geometric forms: the barrel vault (semicircular in shape), the intersecting (groined) barrel vault, and the segmental vault. By the 1st century BC, extensive systems of barrel vaulting were employed. The surfaces of the vaults were tile-faced or covered with stucco. A fine example of Roman vaulting is the Basilica of Maxentius in Rome. The construction of the dome naturally follows that of the vault. Characteristic of imperial Roman design was the elaboration of complex forms of domes to fit multilobed ground plans.

Most monumental buildings were erected for public use, and income, if any, from rents or fees went to the public treasury. Many of these buildings, however, were erected by wealthy individuals and given to the community in a form of voluntary income tax. Construction was done by state agencies or private contractors, employing slave or free labour. Techniques and crafts were highly developed, though machines were simple and powered by men or animals.

Design. The pervasive Roman predilection was for spatial composition—the organization of lines, surfaces, masses, and volumes in space. In this the Romans differed from their predecessors in the ancient Mediterranean world, and, however freely they used the elements of earlier styles, in Rome or in the provinces they recast them according to their own taste.

The Roman architectural orders

Their most conspicuous inheritance was the order. These were taken directly from Greek tradition, with little alteration of their major form, although the Romans did use them with little attention to their internal logic. There were five orders of Roman architecture: Doric, Ionic, Corinthian, Tuscan, and Composite. Tuscan and Composite were modifications of the Greek Doric and Corinthian orders, respectively. In general, the proportion of the Roman order was slenderer than that of the corresponding Greek order, and there was a tendency toward greater elaboration. Columns were often unfluted, but the faces of the entablature, left plain in Greek work, were covered with decoration.

Unlike the Greek Doric, the Roman Doric order almost invariably had a base molding that was probably taken from the Etruscan Doric or Tuscan column. Examples of Roman Doric are to be found in the Tabularium (78 BC), Rome, and in the lowest order of the Colosseum (AD 80), where it was used in conjunction with the arch. The Temple of Hercules at Cori, Italy (*c.* 80 BC), is one of the few known Roman Doric temples.

The Ionic order was used in some temples and public buildings, and the number of isolated capitals found suggests that it had a certain vogue in private homes. Notable examples of this order are the Temple of Fortuna Virilis and Trajan's Forum at Rome.

Because of its richness, the Corinthian order was by far the most popular with the Roman builder. Columns removed by the conquering Roman general Sulla in about 86 BC from the Temple of Olympian Zeus at Athens were the model, but the whole order became progressively elaborated in detail and showed a tendency toward sharp contrasts of light and shadow. Examples of this order are seen at the temples of Mars Ultor and of Castor and Pollux in Rome and the Temple of Vesta at Tivoli.

The Composite capital is formed from a Corinthian capital and an Ionic volute (spiral, scroll-shaped ornament) at each of the four corners. Examples of this capital are found in Rome on the triumphal arches of Titus and Septimius Severus and in the Baths of Diocletian.

Comparison of Greek and Roman use of the orders

Although the orders were taken bodily from the Greeks, in Roman architecture columns carried arches as well as entablatures, permitting more varied linear patterns, wider intercolumniations, and greater freedom in articulating spatial forms. Moreover, as a development of Greek practice in temples at Acragas, Selinus, Bassae, and Tegea, columns were used not only as primary supports but also decoratively as detached columns and pilasters (flattened columns), together with other projecting elements and recessed niches of all kinds, so as to modulate the sheer face of a wall or pier into a composition of mass and volume in depth, supplementing the larger forms of the main volumes. Realistic or fanciful architectural compositions were even painted on some walls to give an illusion of the same effect.

In terms of primary architectural forms, Roman design from its first emergence from Italic and Etruscan traditions favoured temples with spacious porches, like the Temple of Apollo at Pompeii. In imperial architecture the design of the temple precinct, forum, thermae (baths), and other public buildings was normally conceived as a complex of variously formed spaces related to variously formed masses. Even landscaping was incorporated, as at the imperial Roman villas at Tivoli and Capri. Interiors of smaller houses as well as of grand structures were designed around vistas through variously shaped rooms of varying qualities of illumination. There was a powerful, even rigid, final dominant of axial symmetry, but against this was exploited richly every kind of spatial form in a highly developed system of organization.

Characteristics of the Roman temple

Types of public buildings. Roman temples differed in many important respects from those of the Greeks. For a comparatively low stylobate (the foundation on which a colonnade rests) with three steps all around the structure, the Romans substituted a high platform or podium with a flight of steps on the entrance facade. Greek temples were isolated from other buildings and almost always faced east and west; those of the Romans were turned to all points of the compass, their orientation governed by their relation to other buildings. This resulted in the entrance facade being emphasized and the entrance portico being deepened. The cella was wider, and the colonnade that surrounded the Greek temple was often reduced to a row of engaged, or applied, columns or pilasters along the cella walls, except on the entrance facade. In some cases the cella was vaulted in concrete and might have an apsidal (semicircular) end, such as in the so-called Baths of Diana at Nîmes, France, and especially the double Temple of Venus and Rome in Rome. The best preserved example of a Roman temple now existing is that known as the Maison-Carrée at Nîmes. Among the most important temples of which remains exist are those of Fortuna Virilis, Mars Ultor, Castor and Pollux, Concord and Antoninus, and Faustina in Rome; in Italy, the Temple of Minerva at Assisi and the temples at Pompeii; and in Syria, the Temple of Bacchus at Baalbek (now in Lebanon) and the Temple of the Sun at Palmyra.

Circular temples

The Romans built many circular temples. Among the most important remaining examples of these are the temples of Vesta and Mater Matuta in Rome, Vesta at Tivoli, and Venus at Baalbek (Figure 7). The greatest surviving circular temple of antiquity, and in many respects the most important Roman building, is the Pantheon in Rome. It consists of a rotunda about 142 feet in diameter surrounded by concrete walls 20 feet thick, in which are alternate circular and rectangular niches. Light is admitted through a central opening, or oculus, about 28 feet across, at the crown of the dome. In front is a porch with an inscription commemorating an earlier building of Marcus Agrippa (12 BC–AD 14) but built with the existing rotunda (AD 120–124) under the emperor Hadrian. The rotunda and dome are among the finest examples of Roman concrete work. The interior was lined with precious marbles, the coffers (decorative recessed panels) of the dome were ornamented with bronze rosettes, and the dome itself once was covered externally with bronze plates.

The large Roman tomb consisted of an earth mound or tumulus, surrounded by a ring of masonry rising usually to a considerable height. Few of the type now exist, the most notable being the Tomb of Caecilia Metella on the Via Appia and Hadrian's Tomb, now Castel Sant'Angelo. Smaller tombs, in particular those of the columbarium type (a structure of vaults with recesses for cinerary urns) are usually underground, though there is sometimes an upper story built of brick, from which steps lead down to the tomb proper. There is a line of such tombs just outside Rome along the Via Appia and also along the Via Latina, and such a cemetery has been found under St. Peter's in Rome. Examples of Roman funeral monuments of various kinds exist along the Street of Tombs at Pompeii and in the provinces (for example, at Jerusalem; Palmyra, Syria; and Petra, Jordan).

The basilica was a large covered hall used as a court of justice and for banking and other commercial transactions.

Figure 7: Temple of Venus at Baalbek, 3rd century AD.
Fototeca Unione, Rome

The Roman basilica

In the Forum at Rome are the Basilica Julia on the south side and the Basilica Aemilia on the north side, both of which had a central hall and side aisles. The Basilica Ulpia in Trajan's Forum was similar in plan but had at either end semicircular halls (apses), which served as law courts. The fourth and greatest of the basilicas was that begun by Maxentius (AD 306–312) and finished by Constantine about AD 313. This huge building covered 63,000 square feet (5,850 square metres) and followed in construction and plan the great hall of the Roman baths (Figure 8). Vaults over the bays on the north side are still overhanging without support, a striking testimony to the marvelous cohesion and enduring strength of Roman concrete (Figure 9). A hall at Pompeii is an example of the simpler type of basilica generally constructed in the provinces.

By the end of the republic, baths (*balneae*) had become a recognized feature of Roman life. Under the empire

After Huelsen in H.W. Janson, *History of Art*

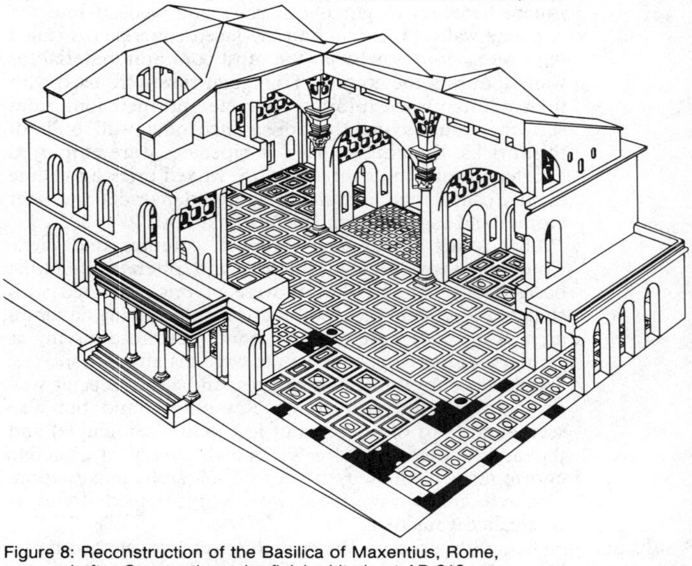

Figure 8: Reconstruction of the Basilica of Maxentius, Rome, renamed after Constantine, who finished it about AD 313.

Figure 9: Detail of the Basilica of Constantine, Rome (see Figure 8).
GEKS

their numbers increased, until at the beginning of the 4th century AD they numbered 1,000 in Rome alone. Like the 20th-century Turkish baths, Roman steam baths had rooms heated to different temperatures. Remains of these establishments are common throughout the empire. The Stabian Baths at Pompeii are the best preserved of such structures.

Imperial thermae were more than baths. They were immense establishments of great magnificence, with facilities for every gymnastic exercise and halls in which philosophers, poets, rhetoricians, and those who wished to hear them gathered. The earliest of these thermae were those built in Rome by Agrippa about 21 BC. Others were built by Nero, Titus, Trajan, Caracalla, Diocletian, and Constantine. The best preserved are the Baths of Caracalla (begun *c.* AD 217), which covered an area about 1,000 feet square, and those of Diocletian (*c.* AD 298–306), with accommodation for 3,200 bathers. Parts of the latter are now occupied by the church of Santa Maria degli Angeli and by the Roman National Museum.

Theatres, amphitheatres, and circuses

Roman theatres differed in several respects from those of the Greeks. The auditorium was not excavated and the walls surrounding stage and seating were continuous, entrance to the orchestra being by vaulted passages. As the chorus played no part in the Roman theatre, the orchestra or dancing space became part of the auditorium. The facade behind the stage was elaborately adorned with architectural fantasies.

The only theatre in Rome of which any remains exist is that of Marcellus, built by Augustus (*c.* 11–10 BC), but there are numerous examples throughout the Roman Empire, especially in Asia Minor. The theatre at Orange, Fr., and Leptis Magna (near Tripoli, Libya) are among the best-preserved examples. The Odeum of Agrippa in Athens is a good example of a completely enclosed music hall.

Amphitheatres were arenas in which spectacles were held. The largest and most important amphitheatre of Rome was the Colosseum, built by the emperors Vespasian, Titus, and Domitian in about AD 70/72–82 (Figure 10). Covering six acres (2.4 hectares), it had seating for about 50,000 spectators, and its 80 entrances were so arranged that the building could be cleared quickly. The whole is built of concrete, the exterior faced with travertine and the interior with precious marbles that have long since disappeared. Other important amphitheatres are those at Verona, Italy; Pula, Yugos.; and Arles, Fr.

The circus was essentially a racecourse, lined, ideally, with tiers of seats along each side and curving around one end, with the opposite end squared off and provided with arrangements for chariots to enter and draw up for the start. Down the middle ran a barrier, on which judges and referees might perform their functions. Since it was the largest facility for watching a function, the circus was also used for spectacles other than racing, such as, traditionally, the burning of the Christians by Nero. There are remains of one of these circuses at Perga, near the southern coast of Turkey.

Triumphal arches and city gates

Triumphal arches were sometimes erected to commemorate an important event or campaign. They were often isolated rather than built to span a roadway. The triumphal arch was usually decorated with columns and bas-reliefs of the chief events it commemorated and was frequently surmounted by sculpture. The most important of these arches are the Arch of Titus (*c.* AD 81), commemorating the capture of Jerusalem (Figure 11), and the arches of Septimius Severus (*c.* AD 203) and Constantine (*c.* AD 315) all in Rome, and Trajan's arches at Benevento and Ancona. There are several other triumphal arches in the provinces, notably those of Tiberius at Orange, of Augustus at Susa, and Caracalla at Tébessa.

A monumental city gate, while sometimes serving a commemorative purpose, differs from an arch in being part of the defenses of the city. Of these gates the most famous are the Porta Nigra at Trier in Germany and the gate from Miletus in Turkey (Pergamon Museum, East Berlin).

The bridges and aqueducts of the Romans rank among their greatest monuments. The most famous surviving examples of Roman aqueducts are the Pont du Gard at Nîmes and the aqueduct at Segovia in Spain.

There are not many of the larger Roman bridges now remaining. The best preserved is that built by Augustus and Tiberius at Rimini, and perhaps the finest is that across the Tagus River at Alcántara in Spain.

Residential architecture. Private houses, even palaces, were usually of the style that emphasized interior courts and gardens rather than external facade; this tradition was even maintained so far as possible in Roman settlements in northern Europe and Britain, where elaborate arrangements for heating had to be added. In the native Mediterranean climate, however, construction tended to be light and open rather than compact and imposing.

Even the palaces of the Caesars in Rome consisted essentially of series of gardens and, considering their purpose, relatively unmonumental buildings, spread somewhat casually over the Palatine Hill. Augustus himself bought and enlarged the house known as the House of Livia, which still exists. Tiberius built a palace on the northwest side of the hill. Another palace was built on the southeast corner of the hill by Claudius or Nero. The central space

Figure 10: Ruins of a wall of the Colosseum, Rome, built by the emperors Vespasian, Titus, and Domitian, *c.* AD 72–80.

J. Allan Cash

was covered by the palace of the Flavians, Domitian with his architect Rabirius being responsible for a magnificent suite of state apartments and for the sunken garden called the *hippodromus.* Hadrian extended the palace toward the Forum, and Septimius Severus raised a huge structure overlooking the Circus Maximus. Very little remains of the famous Golden House of Nero, which originally occupied an area of more than 300 acres on the site now covered by the Baths of Titus, the Colosseum, and the Basilica of Maxentius.

Hadrian's Villa at Tivoli, begun about AD 123, was a sumptuous residence with parks and gardens on a large scale. The unevenness of the site necessitated large terraces and flights of steps. There are remains of great brick and concrete structures. All the buildings are Roman in style and method of construction, though with Greek names.

The Palace of Diocletian at Spalato (Split) in Yugoslavia, to which he retired on his abdication in AD 305, combined a palace with a fortress. It consisted of an immense rectangle surrounded on three sides with walls guarded by towers; on the fourth it was protected by the sea. The palace itself was on the south side with a great gallery 520 feet long with 51 windows overlooking the sea.

The Latin word *villa* pertained to an estate, complete with house, grounds, and subsidiary buildings. Relatively modest villas were found around Pompeii; descriptions in literature, such as that of Pliny the Younger of his villa at Laurentum, and remains of the palatial residence of the 4th century at Piazza Armerina in Sicily, might represent the most opulent class. Hadrian's Villa at Tivoli is too elaborate and extensive to be taken as typical (Figure 12).

The domus and the insula

In Roman architecture there were two types of houses, the domus and the insula. The domus consisted of suites of rooms grouped around a central hall, or atrium, to which were often added further suites at the rear, grouped around a colonnaded court, or peristyle. The atrium, a rectangular room with an opening in the roof to the sky, and its adjoining rooms were peculiarly Roman elements; the peristyle was Greek or Middle Eastern. There were few windows on the street, light being obtained from the atrium or peristyle. The domus, as exemplified by those remaining at Pompeii and Herculaneum, has long been regarded as the typical Roman house. In Rome itself, however, very few remains of the domus have come to light, the chief examples being the House of the Vestals in the Forum and that of Livia on the Palatine Hill.

From Latin writers it has long been known that there were in Rome great blocks of flats or tenements to which the term insulae was applied. Excavations at Ostia, Italy, have revealed the design of these blocks. Planned on three or four floors with strict regard to economy of space, they depended on light from the exterior as well as from a central court. Independent apartments had separate entrances with direct access to the street. Since Ostia was a typical town of the 1st and 2nd centuries AD and was almost a suburb of Rome itself, it is supposed that insulae at Rome would have similar features. Shops might line the street front of either domus or insula.

Town planning. Vitruvius clearly indicated that the Romans were keenly aware of the fundamentals of town planning. When a new town was established, such considerations as its function, climate, and geographic environment were examined.

A characteristic Roman plan, either inherited from early Italic towns or developed in the discipline of army camp engineering, was used. The overall plan was square, with main avenues bisecting the sides and intersecting at the centre. The rest of the streets were in checkerboard grid.

At or near the centre of the Roman town was the forum, the principal focus of Roman life. This was a space in which important business might be conducted. Gradually buildings were built on the periphery for particular civic, commercial, and religious activities, as at Pompeii or in the Forum in Rome. In late republican or imperial times a forum might be laid out as a single comprehensive architectural design including all the facilities, as in the Imperial Forums at Rome. In a very large and old city, such as Rome itself, there might be several forums, some devoted primarily to administrative, legal, or financial affairs, others to trade in particular commodities, including meat and vegetables. For the latter kind of commerce, however, structures architecturally distinct from the forum though superficially similar were developed. One is the *macellum,* which was not essentially an open square but a market building consisting of shops around a colonnaded court. Great warehouses, called *horrea,* served in wholesale commerce.

Importance of the forum

Long-established communities, which had developed by accretion rather than by plan, were often gradually brought, under Roman influence, within some approximation of this scheme, sometimes with considerable subtlety. Often, however, as in Rome itself, the scale and topography prevented the achievement of any fully logical order. In general, colonnades lined the important streets;

Figure 11: *Details of reliefs from the Arch of Titus, Rome, AD 81.*
(Left) Titus standing in a quadriga (four-horsed chariot), led by Roma, while Victory crowns him. (Right) Triumphal parade in Rome of Jewish vessels (a seven-branched candlestick, table for the shewbread, and the sacred trumpets) removed after the sack of Jerusalem (AD 70).
Alinari—Art Resource/EB Inc.

water was conveyed to spectacular ornamental fountains or to practical neighbourhood basins from reservoirs fed by aqueducts (in some climates cisterns were necessary); many large sewers collected waste water from the street, if not from private homes; and building codes were devised and enforced.

The layout of a whole town can be most easily seen in some of the towns in North Africa (for example, Timgad, Tébessa, Thuburbo Majus), where there has been little or no subsequent building to modify the original lines of the plan.

Stylistic development. Roman monumental architecture emerged about the 6th century BC as an Italic style, closely related to that of the Etruscans. The Temple of Jupiter Capitolinus in Rome, built about this time, resembled Etruscan buildings in central Italy—at Signia, Orvieto, Veii, and elsewhere—in its podium (base or platform on which it rests), its triple cella, its broad low Etruscan porch, and its characteristic terra-cotta adornment. The Capitolium Temple at Cosa, a Roman foundation located northeast of Rome, was similarly conceived in the 3rd century BC. The forms, sculptural and spatial, had evolved locally in a tradition of wood and terra-cotta, though even at this time there was a slight Greek influence.

Republican period

From about 200 BC to about AD 50, the rise of republican Rome and the increasing contacts with Greece resulted in a Greek influence strong enough to control the sculptural forms and even to modify the spatial effects. A temple at Gabii, perhaps of the 3rd century, and the Temple of Apollo at Pompeii, of about 120 BC, had approximately the Greek single-cella, peripheral (having a single row of columns surrounding the building) plan; the latter retained the Italic podium and open porch, and it had pronounced modifications of the Greek Ionic order. Buildings such as the temple under the present church of San Nicola in Carcere (*c.* 31 BC) and the Temple of Fortuna Virilis (*c.* 40 BC), both in Rome, show the height of Hellenistic influence. But the slightly later Augustan temples of Concord, Castor and Pollux in the Roman Forum, and Mars Ultor in the Forum of Augustus in Rome had a native freedom of arrangement of space and highly elaborated moldings, particularly in the entablature, where new forms, mostly floral, were lavishly displayed in finely worked, full masses, and consoles (projecting ornamental brackets) became increasingly important.

During this period the more peculiarly Roman concepts developed chiefly in secular architecture. The Stabian Baths at Pompeii, built perhaps as early as 120 BC, were already composed of vaulted spaces, though quite compactly and with little of the later freedom and spaciousness. In some buildings—such as the Carcer and Tullianum (prisonlike structures of about 100 BC or earlier) and the Tabularium of about 78 BC, all just west of the Forum in Rome—arches and concrete were basic, though orders influenced by Hellenistic architecture were used for ornament. The Theatre of Marcellus (*c.* 11–10 BC) was built with a high exterior facade where orders and arches blended—a type of theatrical design that became standard.

The beginning of Roman influence outside Italy is evident in theatres and amphitheatres at Arles and Nîmes (perhaps as early as 30 BC), in a temple built about 12 BC at Nîmes called the Maison-Carrée (Figure 13), and in small buildings in Greece and Syria built shortly thereafter.

Imperial architecture

About the middle of the 1st century AD there was a surge of development of spatial composition. The orders and other ornament inherited from Greece were increasingly modified and elaborated in nonfunctional perspective effects, and other kinds of ornament and spatial configurations gained importance. Buildings such as the Colosseum (AD 80) in Rome preserved a more conservative character, but with the baths and palaces of Nero began the series of imperial compositions of grand, elaborate spaces. The movement came to a climax under Trajan and Hadrian (*c.* 98–138), with Trajan's Forum at Rome, the great complex of buildings at Baalbek in Syria, the Pantheon in Rome, and Hadrian's Villa at Tivoli.

Through the 2nd and 3rd centuries countless buildings were erected in cities and towns throughout the empire, in part under imperial patronage and in part by local enterprise. Provincial buildings had great individuality, but the more ambitious usually followed the influence of the capital. Forms evolved by about AD 140 were followed conventionally for the next 50 years (and longer), but from about AD 200 to the age of Constantine, there was a growing trend toward increased majesty and less emphasis on the material substance or appearance of a building. Even before the end of the 2nd century, deep cutting with sharply contrasting light and shadow had begun to detract from the impression of the solid forms in carved ornament. In the arches of Septimius Severus (*c.* AD 200), for instance, light and shadow alone formed the design—not the masses of the forms of the motifs. Especially in Africa, illogical composition of the elements of entablatures robbed them of structural significance. In the Palace of Diocletian (*c.* AD 300), extensive use of arched colonnades emphasized movement rather than mass. The sheer faces of some wall surfaces, like those of towers flanking the gates, became austere geometric forms. Experimentation and elaboration in vaulting, as in the so-called Temple of Minerva Medica (*c.* AD 260) at Rome, was directed toward making the supports lighter structurally and aesthetically. Compared with the Baths of Caracalla (*c.* AD 217), the Basilica of Maxentius (*c.* AD 310–320) was simpler in design and more concentrated, increasing its sense of elemental vastness and permanence, whereas in contrast to the Pantheon its shape and ornament are less tangible.

Finally, evolving into the early Christian art to come, the

Figure 12: The Canopus Canal in Hadrian's Villa at Tivoli, Italy, begun *c.* AD 123.
Bernard G. Silverstein from Rapho/Photo Researchers—EB Inc.

Constantinian mausoleum of Santa Costanza (Figure 15), with its dome resting on a drum supported on arches on a circle of pairs of slender columns, already was striving to suggest the independence of roof and space from material support. (R.L.S./D.J.Wa.)

EARLY CHRISTIAN

Early in the 20th century it was thought that Christian art and architecture began after the death of Christ or, at least, in the second half of the 1st century AD. But later discoveries and studies showed that a truly Christian style did not exist before the end of the 2nd or beginning of the 3rd century. The terminal date of this period is even more difficult to establish; it may be placed in the 4th, 5th, or 6th century. Early Christian architecture penetrated all the provinces of the Roman Empire, adapting itself to existing pagan architecture. It subsequently created its own forms, which varied according to local stylistic evolution. The new capital at Constantinople (ancient Byzantium), founded by the emperor Constantine the Great (306–337), was to be an important centre. The art and architecture of this city henceforth became known as Byzantine and extended throughout the entire Christian East. It is customary to distinguish early Christian architecture of the West, or Latin part of the Roman Empire, from the Christian architecture of regions dominated by the Greek language and to consider the latter as proto-Byzantine, while acknowledging, however, a certain latitude in the initial date of this separation: 330, the foundation of Constantinople; 395, the separation of the Greek part of the empire from its Latin sector; or, finally, the reign of Justinian (527–565). For the purposes of this article, monuments shall be treated as early Christian mainly on the basis of their style, as distinct from the genuine Byzantine style of Constantinople; since the transition from the earlier to the later architecture discussed in the next section took place at different times in different locations, this section has no precise chronological boundary. Only after Justinian's reign did many Eastern regions submit to the ascendancy of Constantinople, following until the 6th and even the 7th century the paths traced by Christian architecture in its beginnings. In the West the end of early Christian architecture is easier to determine. Closely tied to Roman architecture, it finished with the collapse of the empire at the end of the 5th century. Then, transformed into a multitude of regional styles, it assimilated various influences from the East and from the barbaric peoples who superseded their Roman masters.

Early Christian architecture is divided into two periods, quite unequal in length and in importance. During the first—which preceded the Edict of Milan, by which Constantine the Great in 313 decreed official tolerance of open practice of the Christian religion—Christianity was often persecuted, while in the second it soon became the state religion. The monuments of the first period were modest and few in number, those of the second phase were numerous and splendid.

First period, to AD 313. Little is known about Christian places of worship before 313. By bringing together the relevant texts and the results of excavations, one can, however, succeed in forming an idea of them. These *domus ecclesiae* ("meeting houses"; *ecclesia,* "assembly, meeting") were private homes placed at the disposal of communities by well-to-do members. A spacious room, already existing or fitted out for the occasion, served as chamber of worship, while others were allotted for various activities of the community: charity work, study, funeral services, and living quarters for the clergy. This was the arrangement of the only extant *domus ecclesiae* from the 3rd century, that in the Syrian caravan city of Doura-Europus, on the west bank of the Euphrates. A Syrian home of the common type, it contained a longitudinal sanctuary, a baptistery, and four smaller rooms grouped around an interior courtyard. The sanctuary, stripped of decoration, was distinguished only by a small dais at the western end, probably the seat of the bishop, and by a small cupola, the use of which is unknown, set in the ground near this platform. The general character of these meeting houses seems to have been the same everywhere. They must have been rather numerous; the *tituli* ("titles") of the 25 Christian basilicas in Rome today are, in fact, the names of the private houses in which these congregations were first established.

First Christian church: the *domus ecclesiae*

The double Church of Bishop Theodore of Aquileia marks a step toward the creation of a monumental edifice of the Christian religion. Standing within the enclosure of a Roman villa, it occupied all the space of the earlier building and more. Two sanctuaries of considerable size, 121 by 66 feet and 121 by 56 feet, were rectangular rooms subdivided by pillars into three longitudinal aisles that outlined the naves of the standard Christian basilica plan.

Second period, after AD 313. It was this kind of plan that architects adopted when Constantine officially recognized the church in 313 and was converted to Christianity. Whether in Rome or in other cities of the empire, his architects took their inspiration not from pagan temples,

Figure 13: Maison-Carrée, Nîmes, Fr., *c.* 12 BC.
Wayne Andrews

old-fashioned in the 4th century, but, rather, from a secular building type of utilitarian character, the basilica, which had served as a hall of assembly, commerce, reception, or law-making. Of Hellenistic origin both in form and in name (*stoa basileōs,* or "royal room"), the basilica under the Romans varied in plan and size according to use and to the importance of the social group to which it belonged. It could be either a simple hall or one divided by columns into three longitudinal aisles, or surrounded on three sides by one- or two-story arcades with a dais on a short or long side.

The first Christian basilicas, built in Rome, were variations of secular basilicas adapted to the new cult. St. John Lateran, superficially transformed in the 17th and 19th centuries, is the oldest, begun about 313. It was followed by St. Peter's (replaced in the 16th century by the present church) in the last years of the reign of Constantine and his sons (Figure 14). San Clemente, Santa Pudenziana, St. Paul's Outside the Walls, San Sebastiano, Santa Sabina, and others belong to the late 4th and to the 5th century.

The Christian basilica plan

These were, in most cases, halls with five longitudinal aisles, the central one raised and lit directly by windows piercing the high walls. A semicircular protrusion of the wall, or apse, on the short side opposite the entrance, first on the west side but later on the east side, was covered over with a half-dome vault, while the so-called hall itself usually had a wooden frame roof. The side aisles were separated from the central nave by rows of columns. These supported a rectilinear entablature, or solid horizontal section; later this entablature was replaced by a series of arches resting on capitals (San Clemente, 360; St. Paul's Outside the Walls, 385; Santa Sabina, 422–432), but at Santa Maria Maggiore, still intact under its 17th-century Baroque facing, Pope Sixtus III (432–440) returned to the classical form of the straight entablature.

Whereas St. John Lateran and San Clemente were used entirely for the eucharistic service, St. Peter's and St. Paul's Outside the Walls were also martyria, buildings commemorating the martyrdom of their titular saints. This commemorative function influenced the plan: in front of the apse a large transept, sheltering the site of the relics, facilitated the presentation of the liturgy and the circulation of the faithful around the sacred place.

The churches built under Constantine at Constantinople and in Palestine were more complex in plan and structure. The destroyed Church of the Holy Apostles at Constantinople, known only through a description by Eusebius of Caesarea, was begun in 333 and completed by Constantius II (337–361). It was cross-shaped, and a drum (*i.e.,* a cylindrical or polygonal wall that usually supports a dome) rose above the crossing, probably covered by a conical wooden roof. The sarcophagus of Constantine stood in the centre, surrounded by memorials to the 12 Apostles. It was less a church than a mausoleum in honour of the first Christian emperor, who was made to appear in that church as the 13th Apostle. In the sanctuaries in Jerusalem and in the church of Bethlehem, the commemorative building and the hall of worship (basilica) were united. At Jerusalem several structures combine to form the Church of the Holy Sepulchre. The Anastasis (the Resurrection), a rotunda approximately 131 feet in diameter whose foundations and remains of the walls have been discovered under later additions, was built about 340 on the "tomb" of Christ, the funeral place hewn into the rock and surmounted by a small temple. Two levels of galleries surrounded the rotunda, and the whole was covered by a wooden cupola. The site of Golgotha, open to the sky, was preceded toward the east by a martyrium, a five-aisled basilica with tribunes, or raised platforms, intended for gatherings of the faithful. It probably terminated at the west with a rotunda, open to the nave and surrounded by 12 columns marking the place where it was thought that Helena, mother of Constantine, had found Christ's cross. The Church of the Holy Sepulchre and the court of Golgotha were surrounded by porches aligned along the exterior aisles of the basilica (martyrium) and on the galleries of an atrium (forecourt), which preceded the martyrium. The Constantinian basilica at Bethlehem, still partly intact, having five aisles without tribunes, the central aisle raised, was preceded on the west by an atrium and terminated in the east by an octagon built above the Grotto of the Nativity. Justinian had it replaced by a triconch (three-apsed building), which still stands.

Prototypes of the standard Byzantine church

The considerable dimensions of all these complexes (657 by 230 feet including the atrium in the case of St. Peter's, the largest) and the richness of their decoration (marble columns and inlay; mosaics on the vaults; *opus sectile,* or inlaid stone, in the pavements; and sometimes gold coffered ceilings, as at the Martyrium in Jerusalem) lent to these structures a sumptuousness that made them the equals in scale and splendour of the imperial palaces. Moreover, the liturgical ceremony became progressively

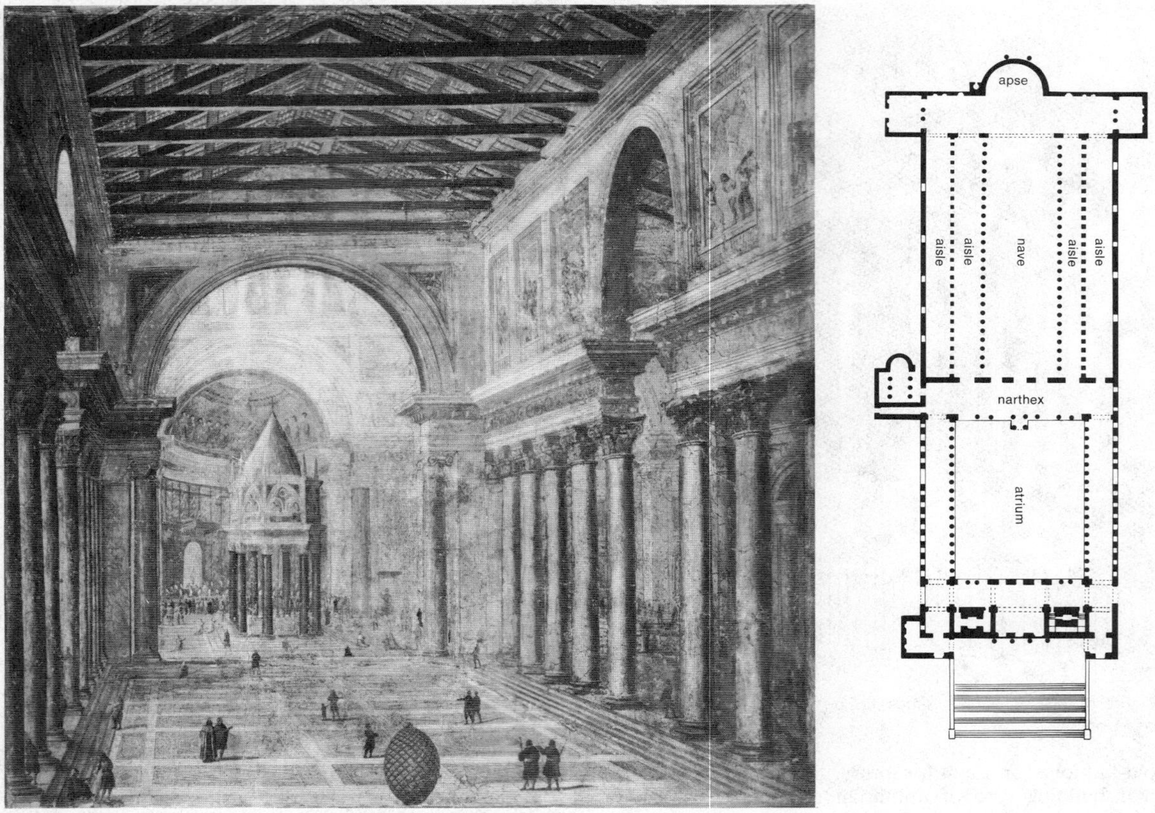

Figure 14: *Old St. Peter's Rome, second quarter of the 4th century.*
(Left) Interior, from a portion of a Renaissance fresco in San Martino ai Monti, Rome.
(Right) Plan.

(Left) Alinari—Art Resource/EB Inc.; (right) from H.W. Janson, *Key Monuments of the History of Art*

assimilated with that of the court; the image of Christ standing or enthroned in the apses of the basilicas evoked the emperor presiding over reception ceremonies in his palace.

Centralized Greek church plan

The differences of plan between the Greek and the Latin Constantinian churches have been a subject of controversy. One hypothesis explains them on the grounds of the Greek traditions—differing from those of the Romans—of the cult of heroes and of the dead. Since the churches of Palestine commemorate the earthly appearances of Christ, his Birth, and his Resurrection, they are comparable in function to the Greek *hērōa,* which are commemorative temples. In the West, however, the churches enclose actual graves, the focus of a funerary cult, completely different from the cult of the Greek heroes.

The central-plan building, round, polygonal, or cruciform in design, gathered considerable momentum in the West as well as in the East in the course of the 4th and 5th centuries. The deconsecrated church of Santa Costanza in Rome, built between 337 and 350 for members of the imperial family, was a rotunda with ambulatory or circular walkway separated from the central area by columns (Figure 15); the mausoleum of Centcelles (Tarragona) in Spain, likewise a rotunda, was probably the burial place of Constans, son of Constantine, assassinated in 350. Both are somewhat related in type to the Tomb of Diocletian (*c.* 300) at Split in Yugoslavia.

Milan, which had been the imperial residence several times since 350 and seat of the bishop St. Ambrose since 374, has preserved the remains of some centrally planned churches of the 4th century. San Lorenzo Maggiore, begun about 370, is a quadrifoil room with four niches and ambulatory; an octagon adjoining it (today Sant'Aquilino) was formerly an imperial mausoleum or baptistery. The Church of the Holy Apostles, the present San Nazaro Maggiore (begun in 382), is cruciform in plan with an apse in the east, built in imitation of the church of the same name at Constantinople. At Cologne, the oval plan of St. Gereon (built about 380) is enriched by eight smaller apses (apsidioles), an apse in the east, and a narthex, or large rectangular room placed before the west entrance. At Antioch in Syria an octagonal structure, called the Golden House because of its gilded roofing, was begun as early as 327 by Constantine. Near this city at Kaussich are preserved the foundations of a cruciform church, built between 378 and the end of the 4th century; it served both the normal cult and the commemoration of three martyrs whose sarcophagi were found in the transept.

Since most of these churches were not consecrated to the cult of a martyr, the mausoleum could not be the only source of inspiration for their plans. Imperial reception rooms may have been models. The octagonal church at Antioch and that of San Lorenzo in Milan were probably palace churches, and the transfer of plan from one to the other seems perfectly plausible.

From H.W. Janson, *Key Monuments of the History of Art*

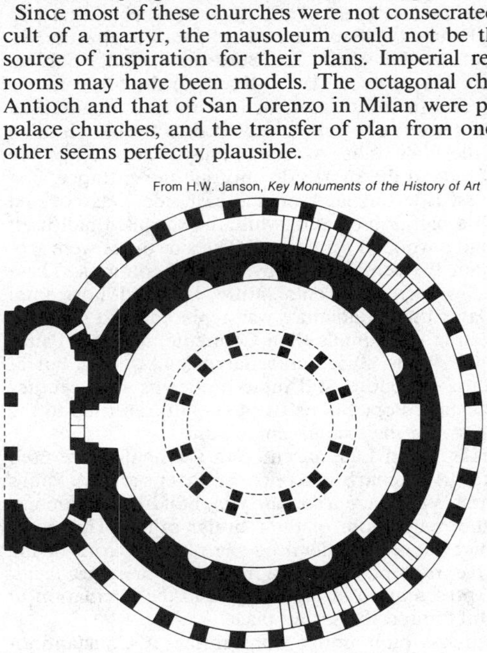

Figure 15: Plan of Santa Costanza, Rome, early 4th century.

In the 5th century, as local schools formed, the unity of Christian architecture with that of the empire ceased to exist. In Italy, although basilicas of the classical type continued to be built, they assimilated Eastern influences. North Africa modified the basilica plan only by multiplying the number of side aisles (Damous-el-Karita in Carthage has eight) or by adding apses.

Ecclesiastical architecture of the East

The ecclesiastical architecture of the East is more varied, partly as a result of differences in the liturgies. The ruins of St. John Studios in Constantinople (463) and the Church of the Acheiropoietos at Thessalonica (470) were basilicas with tribunes and narthexes, which, in their proportions, approached those of centrally planned structures. The large central aisle, inaccessible to the faithful, was reserved for the service of the eucharist, the side aisles for the men, the tribunes for the women, and the narthex for those who for some reason could not participate in the communion. Later, this form of basilica spread into the Greek countries and gave birth to an essentially Byzantine type of church, the "domed basilica." Nevertheless, the ordinary basilica plan, of three or five aisles with an apse in the east, remained no less popular in Greece, on the islands, in the Balkans (Stobi in Serbia), and in the Middle East. In Asia Minor the Church of St. John of Ephesus (450), later replaced by a building of Justinian, was cruciform in plan, inspired by the Church of the Holy Apostles in Constantinople. Extending from the square ciborium (a canopy over the altar supported by columns) placed at the crossing were four wings, the eastern one having an apse and five aisles, the others having three aisles.

In Syria, Israel, and Jordan a particularly large number of 5th-, 6th-, and 7th-century churches are preserved. The triple influence of the Greek countries, Constantinople, and the imperial sanctuaries of the Holy Land resulted in many plans, whereas the materials and construction methods remained in the tradition of the region. At Qalʿat as-Simʿān near Aleppo, Syria (Figure 16), lies the ruin of a martyrium built about 470 around the column on which the ascetic St. Simeon Stylites spent the last years of his life. The precious relic was enclosed by a central octagon of considerable dimensions, adjoined by four arms of a cross in the form of basilicas. At Jarash in Jordan the Church of the Apostles and Martyrs (465) is a cross inscribed in a square, heralding a typically Byzantine plan of later centuries. Also at Jarash, the triple church dedicated to Saints Cosmas and Damian, to St. John the Baptist, and to St. George consists of two basilicas flanking a rotunda with an ambulatory (528–533) and an apse in the east. Other rotundas are at Buṣrā ash-Shām and Izraʿ in Syria, as well as the octagonal Church of the Theotokos (484) on Mount Gerizim (now in the occupied West Bank territory). The sanctuaries of Egypt were also influenced by those of Constantinople, the Greek countries, and Italy. The cathedral of Hermopolis (al-Ashmūnayn), built about 430–440 in southern Egypt, and the martyrium-church of St. Menas, nearer the coast (first half of the 5th century), combine the influences of Constantinople and Italy in the three-lobed sanctuary, the transept, and the long basilica room with three aisles. The ties between the Latin West and the Greek East, particularly strong in the 4th and 5th centuries, relaxed in the 6th. Beginning with the reign of Justinian, a true Byzantine architecture developed from the new capital. In the western Mediterranean, the end of the ancient world and of early Christian architecture came with the fall of the Roman Empire in 476. (He.S.)

Eastern Christian

THE EARLY BYZANTINE PERIOD (330–726)

When Constantine began to build his new capital on the Bosporus, a mass of artisans was assembled for the purpose. The majority of them were drawn from Rome, so that, at first, official art was early Christian in style and was, in fact, virtually Roman art: the classical basilica was adopted as the usual type of Christian church; portrait statues of emperors were set up as in pagan times, and sarcophagi were elaborately sculptured; floor mosaics of classical character were widely used; and works in ivory and metal retained a basically Roman character. Change was in the air, however, even before the capital had been moved from Rome. In architecture the post-and-lintel style in stone, which had been taken over from the Greeks, was already giving place to an architecture of arches, vaults, and domes in brick, whereas sculptural ornament was becoming more formal and less naturalistic. These changes were accelerated at Constantinople partly because of the proximity of the city to Asia Minor and Syria, both fertile centres of new artistic ideas that had developed independently of Rome. Indeed, church architecture in those areas progressed considerably between the 4th and the 6th centuries, while in the visual arts a style that favoured formality and expression rather than the idealized naturalism of classical art had begun to find approval at an early date.

Constantine's new capital was carefully laid out and boasted an important series of secular buildings—walls, hippodrome, forums, public buildings, arcaded streets, and an imperial palace—all of great magnificence. The religious structures he set up were of two principal types: longitudinal basilicas and centralized churches. The former, usually with three aisles, were intended for congregational worship; the latter, which were circular, square, or even octagonal, were for burial or commemorative usage. Both types were to be found over a very wide area, though there were, of course, numerous local variations. It was through a subtle combination of the two types that the characteristic Byzantine church emerged, thanks to some experiments made in the eastern Mediterranean area in the 5th century. The progress cannot be followed exactly because so much has been destroyed, but the earliest sur-

Development of the characteristic Byzantine church

George H. Forsyth, Kelsey Museum, Ann Arbor, Michigan

Figure 16: South facade of the martyrium at Qalʿat as-Simʿān near Aleppo, Syria, *c.* 470.

viving church in Constantinople, that of St. John of the Studium (Mosque of İmrahor), shows that this process had already gone quite far by the year it was built, 463. It is a basilica in that it has an eastern apse and three aisles, but in plan it approaches a centralized building, for it is nearly square, in contrast to the long basilicas in vogue in Rome. A similar change characterizes the sculptures that adorn its facade, for they are in low relief, in contrast with typical Roman high-relief sculpture, and the motifs are treated formally, as pieces of pattern, rather than as depictions of natural forms.

The process of development that can be seen here in embryo had greatly advanced by the end of the century, as recently discovered remains of the Church of St. Polyeuktos show. The church was founded by the princess Juliana Anicia (granddaughter of Valentinian III), whose name is known from an illuminated manuscript dated 512. The change was advanced still further some 30 years later, thanks to the patronage of the emperor Justinian, one of the greatest builders of all time. He was responsible for four major churches in Constantinople: SS. Sergius and Bacchus, a centralized building; the Church of St. Eirene (Irene), a basilica roofed by two domes in echelon (*i.e.,* parallel-stepped arrangement); the Church of the Holy

(Top) GEKS, (centre) R.L. Van Nice, *Saint Sophia in Istanbul,* (bottom) RIBA, London and University of London

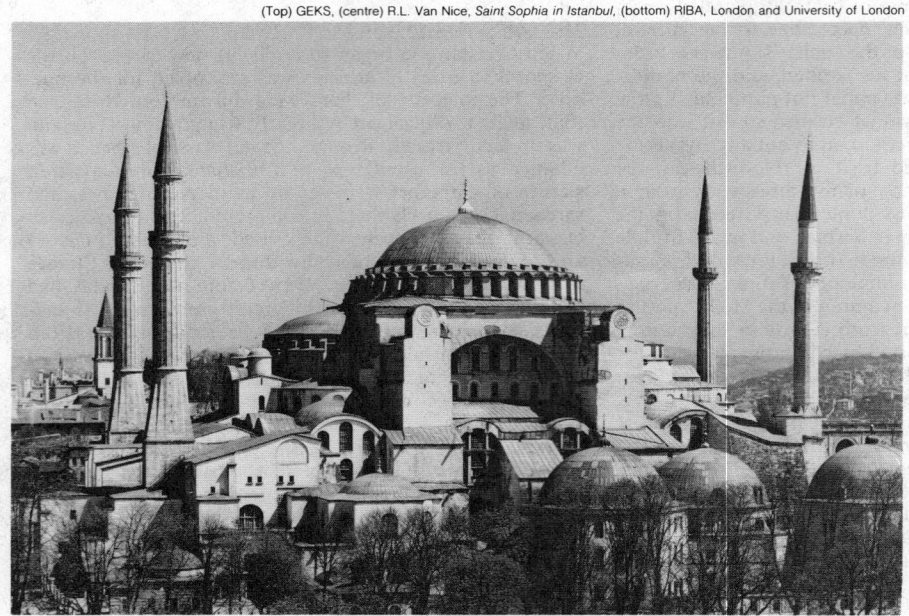

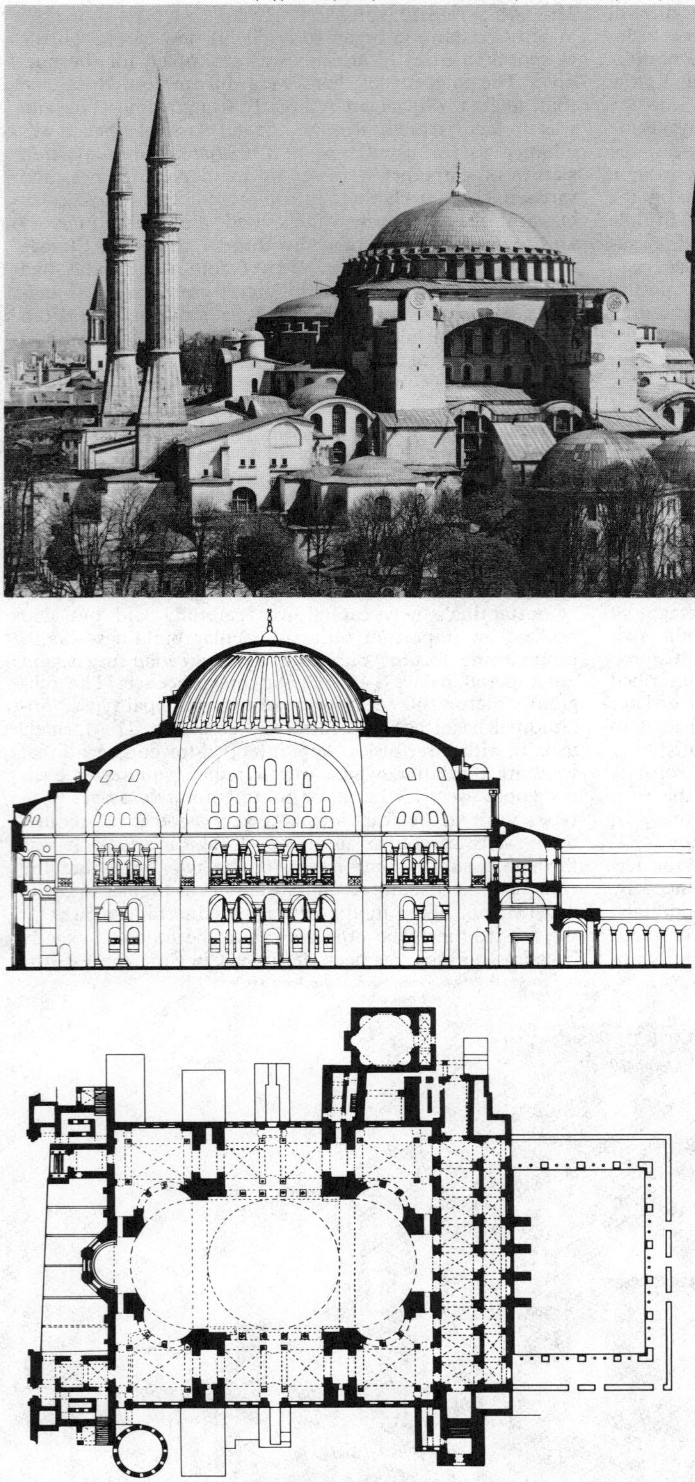

Figure 17: Hagia Sophia, Istanbul, designed by Anthemius of Tralles and Isidorus of Miletus, 532–537. (Top) Exterior, (centre) cross section, (bottom) plan.

Apostles, which was cruciform, with a dome at the crossing and another on each of the arms of the cross; and, finally, the great cathedral of Hagia Sophia, where the ideas of longitudinal basilica and centralized building were combined in a wholly original manner (Figure 17). The distinctive feature of all these structures was the form of roof, the dome. In SS. Sergius and Bacchus it stood on an octagonal base, so that no great problems were involved in converting the angular ground plan to a circle on which the dome could rest. But in the others the dome stands above a square, and the transition from the one to the other was complicated. Two separate processes of doing this had evolved: the squinch, a niche or arch in the corner of the square, which transformed it into an octagon, over which the dome could be placed without great difficulty; and the pendentive, a spherical triangle fitted into the corners of the square, its vertical sides corresponding to the curves of the arches supporting the dome and its upper side corresponding to the circular base of the drum. This served to brace and support the weight and to transfer it downward to the ground at the same time. The squinch served its purpose well enough and continued in use for many centuries, but it had certain weaknesses; the pendentive was one of the great architectural inventions of all time, transforming what had been mere building, where stress was counteracted by mass, into organic architecture, where thrust was compensated by thrust and strength depended on balance. So far as is known, the squinch was first used in Persia and the pendentive in Syria.

Hagia Sophia

Though Justinian's domed basilicas are the models from which Byzantine architecture developed, Hagia Sophia remained unique, and no attempt was thereafter made by Byzantine builders to emulate it. In plan it is almost square, but looked at from within, it appears to be rectangular, for there is a great semidome at east and west above that prolongs the effect of the roof, while on the ground there are three aisles, separated by columns with galleries above. At either end, however, great piers rise up through the galleries to support the dome. Above the galleries are curtain walls (non-load-bearing exterior walls) at either side, pierced by windows, and there are more windows at the base of the dome. The columns are of finest marble, selected for their colour and variety, while the lower parts of the walls are covered with marble slabs. Like the elaborately carved cornices and capitals, these survive, but the rest of the original decoration, including most of the mosaics that adorned the upper parts of the walls and the roof, have perished. They were all described in the most glowing terms by early writers. But enough does survive to warrant the inclusion of Hagia Sophia in the list of the world's greatest buildings. It was built as the result of the destruction in a riot of its predecessor, the basilica begun by Constantine, and the work of rebuilding was completed in the amazingly short period of five years, 10 months, and four days, under the direction of two architects from Asia Minor, Anthemius of Tralles and Isidorus of Miletus, in the year 537.

Early secular architecture

From the little known it would seem that similar changes were taking place in secular architecture. The walls of the city, which still in greater part survive, were set up under Theodosius II (408–450) early in the 5th century, and already the method of construction (where a number of courses of brick alternate with those of stone) and the forms of vaulting used to support the floors in the numerous towers show several innovations. The walls themselves, a triple line of defense, with 192 towers at alternate intervals in the inner and middle wall, were far in advance of anything erected previously; they were, indeed, so well conceived that they served to protect the city against every assault until the Turks, supported by cannon, attacked with vastly superior odds in 1453. Also distinctive were the underground cisterns, of which more than 30 are known in Constantinople today. They all took on the same character, with strong outer walls and roofs of small domes supported on tall columns. Some are of great size, some comparatively small. In some, like the great cistern near Hagia Sophia called by the Turks the Yerebatan (Underground) Palace, old material was reused; in others, like the even more impressive Binbirdirek (Thousand and One Columns) cistern, new columns of unusually tall and slender proportions and new capitals of cubic form were designed specially. These cisterns assured an adequate supply of water even when the aqueducts that fed the city were cut by an attacking enemy. Many of them were still in use at the end of the 19th century. Contemporary texts show that the houses were often large and elaborate and had at least two stories, while the imperial palace was built on enormous terraces of masonry on the slopes bordering the upper shores of the Sea of Marmara. The palace was founded by Constantine, but practically every subsequent emperor added to it, and it eventually became a vast conglomeration of buildings extending over more than 100 acres. Many of the buildings were of a very original character, if the descriptions that survive are to be believed; unfortunately, nearly all have been destroyed in the course of time.

THE ICONOCLASTIC AGE (726–843)

In spite of the ban on the representation of saintly or divine personages, and the reduced prosperity of the state during this period, churches continued to be built, including the Church of the Assumption at Nicaea and Hagia Sophia at Salonika. The emperors were not necessarily opposed to all building and art, however. It is known from texts that Theophilus (829–842) was responsible for numerous additions to the Great Palace.

THE MIDDLE BYZANTINE PERIOD (843–1204)

The most understanding of the emperors in the years immediately succeeding iconoclasm was Basil I (867–886). Like many of his predecessors, he built in the area of the Great Palace, his most interesting contributions being two churches, the New Church and the Church of the Theotokos of the Pharos. These set a fashion in church building and decoration that was to exercise an influence for many centuries. Neither survives, but something is known of them from written descriptions, and it would seem that both were typical of what was to be the mid-Byzantine style. Broadly speaking, the churches of this age conform to a single type, usually termed the cross-in-square. It is made up of three aisles, each one terminating in an apsidal chapel at the east, with a transverse nave, known as the exonarthex, at the west. Invariably, there was a dome over the central aisle, supported on four columns, with four vaults radiating from it to roof the central aisle to the west, the sanctuary to the east, and the central portions of the side aisles to the north and south. These vaults rose above the roofs of the other portions of the building, so that the church was cruciform at roof level. Excluding the exonarthex, the churches were usu-

The mid-Byzantine church type

After K.J. Conant, *A Brief Commentary on Early Mediaeval Church Architecture;* The Johns Hopkins University Press

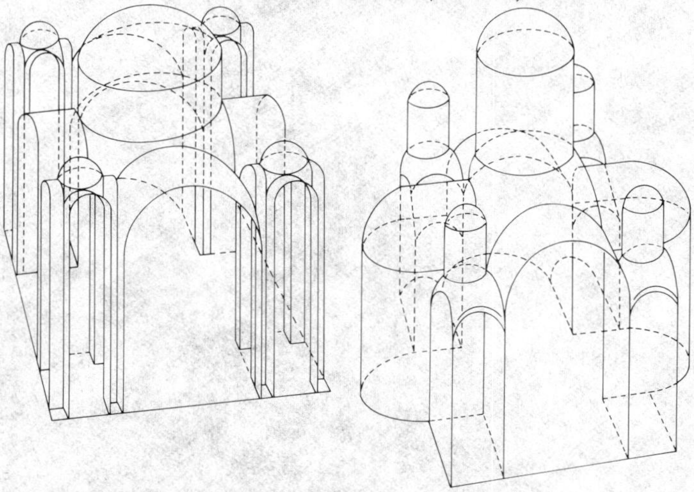

Figure 18: *Types of Byzantine quincunx churches.*
(Left) "Five-spot" or quincunx church, a church type of the second Golden Age based on the domed cross element.
(Right) Trefoil quincunx church, a church type of the Byzantine Renaissance.

Figure 19: Interior of the church at St. Luke's Monastery looking toward the apse, near Delphi, Greece, *c.* 1050.
Holle Bildarchiv, Baden-Baden

ally almost as broad as they were long, making the basic plan virtually a square. Occasionally, additional columns were used to extend the nave westward, producing a type known as the domed basilica; sometimes the walls separating the eastern ends of the side aisles from the central presbytery were extended westward as substitutes for the two eastern columns upholding the dome, but the essentials of the plan were always retained. Subsidiary domes were sometimes added, either in place of the vaults on the arms of the cross, producing a true five-domed type, like St. Mark's Cathedral at Venice, or placed above the eastern and western extremities of the side aisles, producing a type called the quincunx (Figure 18). These domes were usually comparatively small and were set on drums, which tended to become narrower and taller with the progress of time. The eastern extremities of the side aisles formed chapels which played an important part in the liturgy, that to the north being termed the prothesis and that to the south the diakonikon. Both the chapels and the main sanctuary were separated from the body of the church by a screen, which also became taller and heavier until it developed into the massive iconostasis that constitutes such a characteristic feature of Orthodox churches today. As in earlier periods, the lower portions of the walls were, in the richer churches, covered with marble slabs; and there were elaborately carved cornices and capitals, though ornament was always rather formal and in low relief. The main church at the monastery of St. Luke near Delphi, in Greece (*c.* 1050), is the most complete surviving example of the type (Figure 19).

The quincunx type

THE LATE BYZANTINE PERIOD (1204–1453)

Quite a number of buildings from the late Byzantine period survive in Constantinople, Salonika, and throughout Greece and the Balkans (Figure 20). In general they are on a small scale and follow the plan of those of the middle Byzantine period. But their appearance changed quite considerably, the domes becoming smaller and higher, while the wall surfaces of the exterior were usually elaborately decorated, either with intricate patterns in brickwork or by setting glazed pottery vessels into the wall to form friezes similar to work in tile. In Constantinople elaborate blank arcading also played an important role, as, for example, in the Church of the Pammakaristos Virgin (Mosque of Fethiye; *c.* 1315). The building material varied with the locality, though generally brick was preferred to stone. In the details of planning and in the handling there was considerable regional variation, and numerous local styles may be distinguished. Grandeur was generally lacking—except perhaps in the churches set up for the Comnene emperors of Trebizond, a state on the south side of the Black Sea, ruled by Greeks (1204–1461)—but all the buildings have considerable charm and deserve fuller consideration than they have sometimes received. Good work was done even after the Turkish conquests, especially on Mount Athos, Greece, and in the Romanian region of Moldavia (Figure 21), where the large-scale painted churches, which mostly date from the 16th and 17th centuries, are often both magnificent and very beautiful.

Smaller scale of buildings with elaborate brickwork

Even at this period, little is known of secular architecture,

J. Powell, Rome

Figure 20: Church of St. John the Baptist, Gracanica, Serbia, *c.* 1320.

Figure 21: Frescoed monastery church, Voronet, Rom., 1488–1547.
Holle Bildarchiv, Baden-Baden

but a portion of the Blachernae Palace at Constantinople may be noted (Figure 22), as well as the monasteries, particularly those on Mount Athos; though they have been much restored or even wholly rebuilt, the general layout of most follows a Byzantine scheme. (D.T.R.)

KIEVAN RUS AND RUSSIA

Kievan Rus was converted to Christianity in 988, and in Kiev, its dominant political and cultural centre, mosaics, which date from about 1045, were the work of Byzantine craftsmen. Other Byzantine artists and artisans worked intermittently in the area from that time onward, so that Russian art as a whole was founded on a Byzantine basis. Architecture and icon painting grew up as important independent arts, both having their beginnings during this period.

From Kiev the Byzantine style of architecture soon spread throughout the principalities of Novgorod and Vladimir-Suzdal. The emphasis of the Byzantine church on the physical splendour of its edifices was a cardinal factor

THA—Keystone

Figure 22: Wall of the Blachernae Palace, the so-called Tekfur Sarayı, Istanbul, *c.* 1300.

Figure 23: Cathedral of St. Sophia, Novgorod, U.S.S.R., portions of which date from 1045–52.
Novosti Press Agency

in determining the characteristics of Russian ecclesiastical architecture. Everything connected with the design and decoration of the new churches followed the Byzantine pattern; and the standard scheme of the Greek church—the cross inscribed in a rectangle and the dome supported on piers or on pendentives—became the accepted type for Orthodox churches. The design and support of the central dome or cupola, together with the number and disposition of the subsidiary cupolas, remained for a long time the principal theme of Russian architecture.

The main monuments of Kiev were the Church of the Tithes (989–996), the Cathedral of St. Sophia (1037), and the Church of the Assumption in the Monastery of the Caves (1073–78). All of these churches were built in the Byzantine tradition, though certain influences from Bulgaria, Georgia, and Armenia can be discerned. The Cathedral of St. Sophia is the only structure of this period that still stands and retains, at least in the interior, something of its original form. The central part of the cathedral was in the form of a Greek cross. The nave and four aisles terminated in semicircular apses, and it had 13 cupolas (symbolizing Christ and his Apostles). It was reconstructed and enlarged at the end of the 17th century, and it was later obscured by additional bays and stories to its lateral galleries, a new tower, and many bizarre Baroque cupolas. Only five apses and the central interior portion survive from the 11th century.

Novgorod was the centre of a unique and quite original art that lived on long after the political death of the city in the 16th century; it was there that the fundamental features of later Russian architecture were developed. The ecclesiastical architectural history of Novgorod began with the Cathedral of St. Sophia (Figure 23). It was built in 1045–52, replacing a wooden, 13-dome church of the same name. The new cathedral followed its Kievan namesake in plan, but the divergences from the Byzantine pattern are quite apparent; it has double aisles but only three apses. Externally, the church differs even more from its southern prototype; it has only five cupolas, its walls are austere, the buttresses are flat and bare, and the windows are small and narrow. There is something unmistakably Russian in the silhouette of its helmeted cupolas and in the vigour and verticality of its solid masses.

Development of the Novgorod church type

The churches of the 12th century resemble St. Sophia, Novgorod, only in the general tendency toward simplicity and verticality; they were small, cubic in form, and modest in decoration. The severe climate and heavy snowfalls of the north necessitated various modifications of the Byzantine architectural forms. In the course of time windows were narrowed and deeply splayed; roofs became steeper; and flat-dome profiles assumed the bulbous form, which, in different varieties, eventually became the most notable feature of Russian church architecture.

The churches of Pskov in northwest Russia were relatively tiny and squat and usually had three low apses. The cupolas, roofs, and decorative elements were similar to those of Novgorod. Because these churches were too small to contain interior columns for the support of the cupola, the Pskov builders developed the structural device of recessive rows of corbel arches (*i.e.,* stepped archlike structures built out from the walls) for the support of cupola drums and cupolas. This feature—the *kokoshniki*—was to become a favourite Russian structural and decorative element. The church porches, the exterior walled-in galleries, and the arcaded bell towers were Pskov's other outstanding contributions to Russian architecture.

Stylistic fusion in the Vladimir-Suzdal region

The region of Vladimir-Suzdal (also in northwest Russia), as another centre of early Russian culture, was a factor in a creative fusion of Byzantine, Romanesque, and Caucasian influences—the Romanesque being seen in the style that was growing up in western Europe and the Caucasian influence appearing in the churches to the south. The 12th- and early-13th-century structures were a further modification of the earlier Byzantine style, leading toward the innovations at Moscow in the 15th century.

Among the outstanding monuments of Vladimir-Suzdal are the Church of the Assumption (1158–89), which was to serve as a model for its namesake in the Moscow Kremlin; the Church of the Intercession of the Virgin on the Nerl, one of the loveliest creations of medieval Russia (1165); and the Church of St. Dmitri (1194–97). These churches as a group represent the continuation of the Kievo-Byzantine tradition in their ground plan, but the old scheme was given a new interpretation. From Byzantium the Suzdalians adopted the general features of the square plan with semicircular apses and the four columns supporting a cupola with its circular drum. Instead of brick, so characteristic of Byzantine and Kievan ecclesiastical architecture, they used cut stone, and instead of polychrome wall facings they used carved-stone embroideries. The treatment and decoration of the walls and the deeply splayed portals and windows suggest the Romanesque architecture of Western Christendom; the character of the carved ornament is analogous to the intricate decoration of the Caucasus; but the organization and arrangement of the forms and patterns is definitely Russian.

After Constantinople fell to the Turks in 1453, Russia continued for several centuries to develop a national art that had grown out of the middle Byzantine period. During the 10th–15th centuries, Russian art had begun to show marked local variation from the Byzantine model, and after the fall of Constantinople it continued along these distinctive lines of development. This period of Russian art, which lasted until the adoption of western European culture in the 18th century, is also known as the Moscow or National period.

After the hegemony in the world of Orthodox Christianity shifted to Muscovite Russia, Moscow, having become the new city of Constantine—the "third Rome"—and aspiring to rival the older centres of culture, launched a building program commensurate with its international importance. The Kremlin and two of its important churches were rebuilt by Italian architects between 1475 and 1510. These churches, the Assumption (Uspensky) Cathedral and the Cathedral of St. Michael the Archangel, were largely modeled after the churches of Vladimir. The Italians were required to incorporate the basic features of Byzantine planning and design into the new cathedrals; it was only in the exterior decoration of St. Michael the Archangel

Figure 24: Church of the Ascension, Kolomenskoye, 1532.
S.C.R., London

that they succeeded in introducing Italian decorative motifs. A third church, the modest Annunciation Cathedral (1484–89), with its warm beauty, was the work of Pskov architects. There the *kokoshniki* were introduced in the treatment of the roof. This element, similar in outline to the popular Russian *bochka* roof (pointed on top, with the sides forming a continuous double curve, concave above and convex below), foreshadowed a tendency to replace the forms of the Byzantine arch by more elongated silhouettes. Ecclesiastical architecture began to lose the special features associated with the Byzantine heritage, becoming more national in character and increasingly permeated with the taste and thought of the people. The most important change in Russian church design of the 16th century was the introduction of the tiered tower and the tent-shaped roof first developed in wood by Russia's carpenters. Next was the substitution of the bulb-shaped spire for the traditional Byzantine cupola. This affected the design of masonry architecture by transforming its proportions and decoration and even its structural methods. The buildings acquired a dynamic, exteriorized articulation and specifically Russian national characteristics.

Changes in church design

The boldest departures from Byzantine architecture were the churches of the Ascension at Kolomenskoye (1532; Figure 24) and the Decapitation of St. John the Baptist at Dyakovo (*c.* 1532) and, above all, the Cathedral of St. Basil (Vasily) the Blessed (the Pokrovsky Cathedral) in Red Square in Moscow (1554–60). In St. Basil the western academic architectural concepts, based on rational, manifest harmony, were ignored; the structure, with no easily readable design and a profusion of disparate colourful exterior decoration, is uniquely medieval Russian in content and form, in technique, decoration, and feeling. St. Basil, like its predecessors the churches at Kolomenskoye and Dyakovo, embodies the characteristic features of the wood churches of northern Russia, translated into masonry (Figure 25). An effective finishing touch was given to the ensemble of the Kremlin's Cathedral Square by the erection of the imposing Belfry of Ivan II the Great, begun in 1542. The colossal white stone "column of fame," with its golden cupola gleaming above the Kremlin hill, was the definite expression of an era, reflecting the tastes and grandiose political ambitions of the rising Russian state.

The basic types and structural forms of the Russian multicolumned and tented churches were fully developed in the 16th century. It remained for the next century to concentrate its efforts on the refinement of those forms and on the embellishment of the facades. The tent spires degenerated into mere decoration; they were used as exterior ornamental features set loosely in numbers over gabled roofs and on top of roof vaulting (Church of the Nativity in Putinki in Moscow, 1649–52). This decorative use of the formerly functional element was combined with the liberal employment of the *kokoshnik*. The latter, in converging and ascending tiers and in diversified shapes and arrangements, was used as a decorative screen for the drumlike bases of the spires and sometimes as parapets over the cornices. At the same time the formerly large expanses of unbroken wall surfaces (of the Novgorod-Pskov architectural traditions) were replaced by rich decorative paneling. Polychromy asserted itself: coloured and glazed tile and carved stone ornament, used in combination with brick patterns, were employed extensively. This was especially evidenced in a large group of Yaroslavl churches.

Refinement and embellishment in the 17th century

(A.Vo.)

Western Christian

EARLY MEDIEVAL

Migratory period. The migration of European peoples, which was one of the consequences of the decline and ultimate fall of the Roman Empire, had its prelude in the transmigration of the Goths, who, about AD 200, had crossed from Sweden to the region around the mouth of the Vistula River, thence eventually reaching southern Russia. There they came into contact with an ancient artistic tradition that they largely succeeded in grafting onto decorative styles brought over from Scandinavia. When, in 375, the Huns invaded Russia, the Goths demanded and obtained permission to settle within the borders of the Roman Empire. This westward movement was the beginning of the great migration of peoples. In this way, too, new forms of art, soon to be amalgamated with influences from other tribes, also reached western and southern Europe.

When the Ostrogoths under Theodoric came into contact with the late classical and Byzantine cultures, their

K. Scholz/H. Armstrong Roberts, Inc.

Figure 25: Cathedral of St. Basil the Blessed in Red Square, Moscow, 1554–60.

art was influenced by these civilizations. This is evident from the Mausoleum of Theodoric in Ravenna (built *c.* 520), which generally reflects the classical and Byzantine traditions but in its abstract ornamentation is linked with the art of the migration period. It is likely that the mausoleum also reflects influences that had lived on from prehistoric megalithic graves, which were piled up from solid blocks of stone.

Merovingian architecture

Merovingian period. *France.* Of the architecture of this period, little has survived. In the south of France there are still a few baptisteries (Fréjus, Riez, Venasque) that reveal a distinct affinity to similar structures in Italy. The Poitiers baptistery, in its present form dating from the 8th century, is on the threshold of the Carolingian epoch, but it contains much more ancient wall work. Most of the major church buildings are known only from descriptions by early medieval writers or from research work undertaken through excavation of the foundation ruins. According to Apollinaris Sidonius, the naves of the cathedral of Lyon (founded about 470) were separated from each other by a forest of columns and were covered by gilded, paneled ceilings. Gregory of Tours relates that the church of Bishop Namatius of Clermont (built *c.* 450) boasted 70 columns, 42 windows, and eight portals. The same author also praises the church of Saint-Martin at Tours, which was begun by Bishop Perpetuus in the latter half of the 5th century. Also 5th-century in their original form were the chapel of Saint-Maurice-d'Agaune and the church of Saint-Germain at Auxerre. Excavations have revealed the shape of such churches as those of Saint-Martin at Autun (built 590) and the church of Jouarre (*c.* 680). The Merovingian kings were great builders; about 510 Clovis founded a church on the tomb of Sainte-Geneviève in Paris, and Childebert built Sainte-Croix-et-Saint-Vincent (today Saint-Germain-des-Prés). Both churches were decorated with marble and mosaic and roofed with bronze tiles—as was the church of Notre-Dame-de-la-Daurade in Toulouse, which probably dates from the end of the 6th century and was demolished only as late as 1761.

Ireland. Of the earliest Irish architecture very little is known. There are some ruins of monasteries found, for example, at Skellig Michael (on the east coast of Ireland), at Nendrum (County Down), and, in England, at Tintagel (Cornwall).

England. The oldest churches in Kent and Essex (including those at Canterbury, Lyminge, Reculver, and Rochester) consist of a rectangular nave with an apse. Most of these churches were later enlarged by the addition of two smaller spaces flanking the nave and connected by narrow passageways. The outside walls are lined with pilasters, or columns projecting about one-third of their widths from the walls. In some of the churches the choir is separated from the nave by an arcade, as at St. Pancras in Canterbury and Bradwell-on-Sea in Essex.

Spain. In the second half of the 5th century, the Visigoths penetrated into Spain and, as early as 470, ruled practically the entire country. Toulouse remained their capital until 507, when Clovis I pushed them back beyond the Pyrenees. In 554 Byzantine troops invaded Spain but were driven back in the last quarter of the 6th century; nevertheless, contact with the Byzantines left an indelible impression on Visigothic art. The influence was short-lived, however, ending when the Arabs conquered almost the whole of Spain in 711. The only surviving Visigothic structure is the church of San Juan Bautista at Baños de Cerrato, consecrated in 661; it is a small structure, originally planned as a three-aisled basilica, in which the horseshoe-shaped arch is predominant.

Carolingian period. In contrast to Merovingian architecture, a comparatively large number of Carolingian buildings have survived. The most renowned edifice is the Palatine Chapel of Charlemagne at Aachen (consecrated 805), the core of the present-day cathedral (Figure 26). Built in the shape of an octagon with two superimposed galleries, this structure resembles San Vitale in Ravenna, and the ground-floor section of the interior recalls the mausoleum of Theodoric. The building was enriched with classical columns brought from Ravenna and Rome, and the bronze railings and door wings were presumably fashioned by artisans from Lombardy. Above the octagonal chapel rises a dome, which is 101.5 feet high on the inside with a diameter of 46.7 feet. This desire for loftiness is neither classical nor Byzantine but Germanic, and it continued into the Romanesque and Gothic styles. Central architecture also found favour elsewhere; Bishop Theodulf of Orléans, for example, built a chapel in the vicinity of the abbey of Fleury (afterward Saint-Benoît-sur-Loire), a chapel that, unfortunately, has been greatly altered by 19th-century restoration. As in Charlemagne's chapel, the highest part is the square central section, from which four branches extend, forming a Greek cross; in the corners of the cross are four lower chapels, and at the ends are apses shaped somewhat like horseshoes. The arches are also slightly horseshoe-shaped—possibly a Visigothic influence from Spain. Unlike the cathedral at Aachen, which in the 18th century lost all mosaic decoration, this church has preserved its Carolingian apse mosaic.

Palatine Chapel of Charlemagne

In addition to central architecture, the T-shaped basilica form was frequently employed; fairly well-preserved examples of this can be found at Steinbach and at Seligenstadt in Germany. The walls of the nave at Steinbach (821–827) rest on square masonry pillars. On the east side there are two transept chapels, which are lower in height than the nave but higher than the aisles; like the nave, they end in semicircular apses. The church had a tripartite narthex no longer in existence. In the church of SS. Marcellinus and Peter at Seligenstadt (830–840) only the three-aisle nave on pillars is original. In the style of the great basilicas of Rome, this church had a hall-shaped, wide transept with a semicircular apse adjoining it. Some churches, such as Centula (Saint-Riquier, Fr.), which is known only through pictures, had a second choir on the west side (Figure 27). A fairly well-preserved west choir, forerunner of the later Romanesque westwork, is to be found in the church of Corvey, in Germany (873–885). Notable also is the gatehouse of the monastery of Lorsch (Figure 28), near Worms, Ger. (founded *c.* 760–764). This edifice borrowed its three arch-shaped passageways and its sectioning by means of classically influenced half-columns from ancient triumphal arches. On the other hand, Teutonic influence is evident in the upper section of the blind arcade, which

Bildarchiv Foto Marburg—Art Resource/EB Inc.

Figure 26: Palatine Chapel of Charlemagne at Aachen, Ger., 790–805.

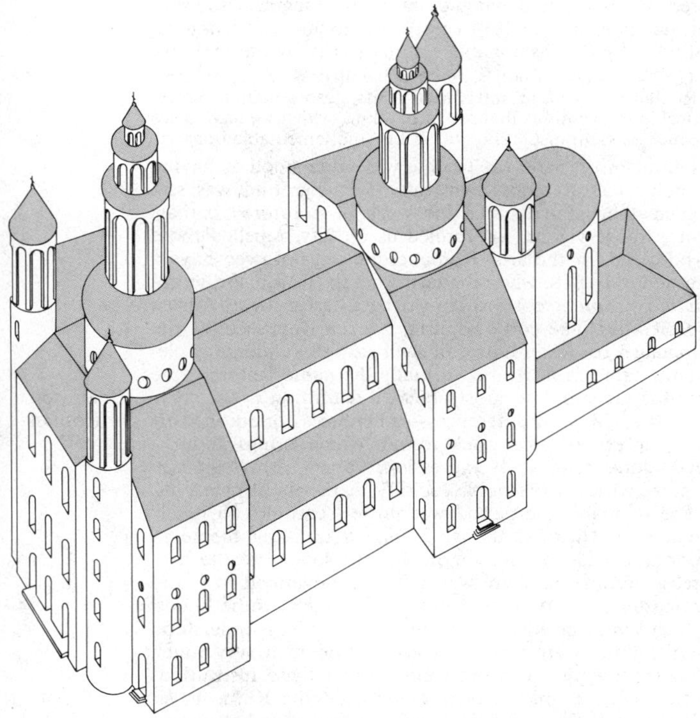

Figure 27: Reconstruction of the abbey church, Centula, Fr., 790–799.

From N. Pevsner, *An Outline of European Architecture* (Figure 27 in the seventh edition). Copyright © Nikolaus Pevsner, 1943; Penguin Books Ltd.

consists of baseless triangles, and in the multicoloured decoration of the masonry.

Ottonian period. Ottonian art is the official art of the realm in the epoch of the Saxon, or Ottonian, emperors and of their first successors from the Salic house (950–1050). Its centre was Saxony, birthplace of the Ottonians, but its influence extended over the whole realm, with the exception of Italy. Ottonian art was shaped by the Carolingian tradition, by early Christian art, and—because Otto III's wife, Theophano, was a Byzantine princess—by contemporary Byzantine art.

It was architecture especially that followed early Christian and specifically Roman examples, while at the same time remaining true to the Carolingian style (the west choir, for example). In Saxony, the art-loving bishop Bernward, who had seen the great basilicas in Rome and had come into contact with classical art, was the great builder; about 1001 he founded the abbey church of St. Michael in his episcopal city of Hildesheim (Figure 29). At an earlier date (961) the margrave Gero had had the Church of St. Cyriacus built at Gernrode. The two churches have wooden-roofed, three-aisle naves; but, in contrast to the Carolingian pillar basilicas, alternating pillars and columns have been used, and at Gernrode the side aisles are crowned by galleries. The two churches have both an east and a west choir and transept arms as high as the nave. At Hildesheim both choirs have a transept with a square dome over the crossing, flanked by staircase towers. Gernrode has crypts underneath both choirs whereas Hildesheim has them only beneath the west choir. The harmony and clarity that characterize both the interior and the exterior of the church at Hildesheim make it the finest example of Ottonian architecture. On the alternating pillars and columns (that is, a pair of columns between each pillar), one encounters for the first time the cubical, or cushion, capital that was later to become such a characteristic feature of the Romanesque style.

Church at Hildesheim

Few of the innumerable major churches built about the year 1000 have survived in a good state of preservation; others have completely disappeared. Some of the outstanding ones are, or were, the cathedrals of Magdeburg, Merseburg, Paderborn, Liège, Mainz, Worms, Strasbourg, Verdun, Basel, Metz, Eichstätt, Bamberg, Regensburg, Augsburg, Lausanne, and Dijon. The surviving ground plans show that frequently they were wooden-roofed basilicas with east and west choirs. Of the basilicas on columns, which are rare, there is Oberzell, in the south, on the island of Reichenau, and, in the north, St. Peter's at Utrecht (The Netherlands). Churches with a nave are also rare; notable examples are the original St. Pantaleon at Cologne and St. Patroclus' Church at Soest, Germany. The Aachen chapel's octagon was fairly widely imitated; the best preserved examples are in Ottmarsheim (France) and Nijmegen (The Netherlands), both dating from the early 11th century. The west choir of the Minster at Essen is remarkable in that it imitates the forms of the chapel at Aachen on a ground plan of a semihexagon.

Prelude to Romanesque in the north. Northern construction of wood in pre-Romanesque times is well represented by the "long hall" or palace at Lojsta (built *c.* 1000) on the island of Gotland. Judging from the remains of the building, the superstructure must have consisted of tall, triangular frames stiffened by timbers that mark out a supporting square in the lower half of the triangle. There was a smoke hole above the hearth. This type of construction, originating on the Continent, spread throughout Scandinavia. It has been traced by excavation in Greenland (Gardar) and in Newfoundland (La Baie aux Meadows, near Cape Race); and actual modern examples of the traditional mode exist in Iceland (Vidhmýri). In fine medieval examples, the timbers were richly carved and painted.

"Long halls"

By the time churches were being built, the sloping exterior bank of a longhouse, or long dwelling of wood, was often replaced by vertical timbers and plank walls. In the more ambitious buildings there might be four files of interior supports, instead of two, under the steep two-slope roof. The churches were distinguished by having the aisles carried entirely around the central space, which projected above them in order to permit small windows. The sanctuary was a small, shedlike projection with a pinnacle, and the belfry took the form of a small shed perched on the roof, with a pinnacle above it. These churches are called stave (wooden-plank) churches or, more properly, mast churches, because of the novel way in which the inner

Bildarchiv Foto Marburg—Art Resource/EB Inc.

Figure 28: Gatehouse of the monastery at Lorsch, Ger., *c.* 760.

Figure 29: Nave, Church of St. Michael, Hildesheim, W.Ger., *c.* 1001–33.
Marburg—Art Resource/EB Inc.

middle part is supported by masts, or vertical posts, on its periphery; the masts themselves are supported on a stout chassis the timbers of which extend outward to sustain the aisles and porches. It is probable that this formula was achieved by the year 1000, when Christianity began to dominate in Scandinavia. The churches are extraordinarily picturesque, in contrast to the longhouses or palaces near which they were often placed as palace chapels—their special form suggested, perhaps, by reliquaries or manuscript drawings of churches. The more elaborate churches had wonderfully energetic carvings, in particular the panels of interlaced lacertine, or lizard-like, creatures (as at Urnes in Norway, *c.* 1100). They were replaced by simple Romanesque buildings of English and German inspiration when the congregations outgrew the mast churches, which are necessarily rather small.

When towns and cities came to be built, improved versions of the longhouses, with several stories, were placed side by side. A reminder of this persists in the many-gabled street frontages not only in Scandinavia but also in The Netherlands and along the south Baltic littoral—regions that are heavily timbered. In Russia, walls were built of horizontal timbers sometimes as much as three feet square in cross section. In Scandinavia the ancestors of the American frontier log cabin were built in this way. In the Germanic area, however, half-timber and palisade construction were preferred. A survivor of the latter type is the old part of the Saxon church (1013) at Greenstead, Essex, Eng.

ROMANESQUE

Romanesque is the name given to the architectural and artistic style current in Europe from about the mid-11th century until the advent of Gothic.

Romanesque is a less familiar term than classical, Gothic, or Renaissance because of the historical circumstances under which it entered artistic terminology. The classical and the Renaissance were clearly defined by men who considered their canons inevitable and who thought of the medieval styles as fanciful (if not objectionable) aberrations. Blinded by the fashionable canon, a critic wrote in 1750:

> The Goths and Vandals, having demolished the Greek and Roman architecture, introduced in its stead a certain fantastical and incentious manner of building, which we have since called modern or Gothic, full of fret and lamentable imagery.

Half a century later the Gothic was understood as having a noble canon of its own, but its background was still veiled—considered to be the work of untutored barbarians, whose vigour, interpreted as crudity, repelled those who cared for the arts. Romanesque did not even have a name until 1818, when the term roman (Romanesque, *romanico, romanisch*) was coined by Charles-Alexis-Adrien de Gerville. The corresponding term is Romance for the languages based on Latin; in each case the underlying elements came from Rome. Actually the name Romanesque itself is the simplest, most practical definition of the style. It is Roman, with differences—differences conditioned by a complex historical background, which brings about a marvelous richness of expression, varied from region to region, with a truly noble lucidity in the finest creations.

Definition of Romanesque

The Romanesque period was no less complex in its art than in its history, though it had a unifying theme in monasticism. To compensate for the loss of stable central governments, there was a strong movement to found monasteries from about 650 to 1200. Such brotherhoods, which lived the ideal Christian life as it was understood at the time, were islands of civilization in a very much disturbed world. The most effective of these institutions were in the Frankish territory between the Rhine River on the east, the Loire River on the south, and the coast on the north and west.

Records of lost buildings show how much of the later architectural development was envisaged in the time of Charlemagne. As a basis for monastic unity he chose the Rule of St. Benedict. On his estate at Aniane a later Benedict—of Aniane—with Charlemagne's encouragement, built a monastery where all the arts were brought into play (782) and later constructed a model monastery at Cornelimünster (Inden, near Aachen). Meanwhile, a monastic holy city had been built at Centula, where the monastic church of 799, with its cloister and chapels, was the centre of all. Around it, the wards and various guild quarters of the city were laid out in regular fashion; at some distance there were seven satellite villages bound to the monastery by periodical ceremonial visits in the form of processions. For better exploitation of the imperial estates everywhere, a type of villa was evolved; with the passage of time and the retreat of the gentry to their castles, many of these became ecclesiastical possessions—then priories, or even monasteries, as in the case of Cluny (910). By 820 the typical monastic layout had been fully studied (as at Inden and St. Gall). This later site, the Insula Felix in Lake Constance, was a stopping place for the imperial journeys, and it developed as a powerful monastic and missionary centre—one of the many that enlarged the boundaries of Christendom as Charlemagne's dominions expanded to the north and east.

In the Middle Ages the population of Europe had diminished by half since Roman times. Communication and transport, either by land or by sea, might be difficult or hazardous, and this tended naturally to divide the country into neighbourhoods. Under these conditions, a great monastery, like a city, could serve a considerable surrounding area as an administrative, intellectual, and spiritual centre and as a workshop, granary, and refuge. With increasing prosperity the monastic building complexes were progressively better organized, better built, and more impressive. Showing the way for cathedral and domestic architecture, the great patrons of the age were the abbots, though not to the exclusion of the bishops and magnates.

The Romans had not solved the problem of the fireproof basilican church—a problem that became pressing with the frequent conflagrations in timber-built towns and, not less, the incendiarism that was a lamentable consequence of endemic local wars and the incursions of organized marauders. By AD 1000 the monastic builders had begun

Improvements upon Roman construction

to solve this problem by vaulting. Moreover, they had improved upon the Roman attempts at systematic plans for the monasteries themselves, which might accommodate 1,000 persons—monks, brethren, craftsmen, servants, slaves, and guests—with provision for their multiple activities and also suitable storage facilities.

The solution, well exemplified in the plan of 820 for the monastery at St. Gall, was a quadrangular court, or cloister, provided with arcaded walks, or "alleys," and placed beside the nave of the church. Typically, the east walk had an entrance into the church near the sanctuary; and the members of the community, entering processionally, would turn into their choir enclosure in the nave, while the celebrants would occupy their posts in the sanctuary. Important rooms bordered the east walk: the chapter house, where the community met as a corporation; the parlour, where speaking was allowed for the transaction of business; and the camera, or workroom. The walk parallel to the church gave access to the calefactory (in early times often the only heated room) for fellowship, the refectory, the pantries, and the kitchens. The cellars stretched along the west walk between the kitchens and a porter's lodge adjoining the church. The door at the porter's lodge was the principal entrance to the cloister. The scriptorium and library were typically in the walk beside the church; the dormitory was usually located directly above the buildings of the east walk.

This plan was very flexible, for in a large monastery there would be several cloisters or courts with suitable independent arrangements for archives, administration, guests, wayfarers, servants, artisans, shops, and folds; special quarters were provided by such courts for retired or sick monks and for novices. Special chapels were provided, where necessary, in these subsidiary parts of the establishment.

The several cloisters or courts of a large monastery carried on the tradition established by the greater Germanic households of the pagan time; they too were composed of "proliferating quadrangles." The basic unit, as has been learned from excavation, was a wide, framed, compartmented longhouse with a steep, thatched roof. By Charlemagne's time longhouses of this type were sometimes adapted as churches.

The Roman heritage

Though Rome could no longer present fresh models for universal emulation or exercise unifying control, its architectural monuments were still numerous in many regions and could not be ignored. The Roman heritage is particularly apparent in conservative southern regions, where Roman massiveness and horizontality persist and are perceptible to some degree even in the Gothic architecture of the area. In the regions where the Roman population had been large, commonplace buildings continued for a long time to be built in much the same way as before, with increasing emphasis—especially in the north—on the use of timber construction in small or utilitarian structures. In the wet northern climates steeper roofs were necessary, particularly where thatch was used. New importance accrued to the fact that the various regions had differing materials and aesthetic ideals. The artists had a wider choice among sources of inspiration than the Romans, but the choices that were made by responsible architects varied from region to region. This explains the origin of "schools" of Romanesque—families of designs inspired by successful buildings in a local context. These were usually churches, often of novel design, and situated at the centre of an important region that, in modern parlance, gives its name to the school.

The forward-looking Romanesque artists were aware of and could synthesize ideas and practices from Rome, Byzantium, the Islāmic world, Scandinavia, and the Teutonic regions. The number of options was fairly large, offering a great many possibilities of variety; moreover,

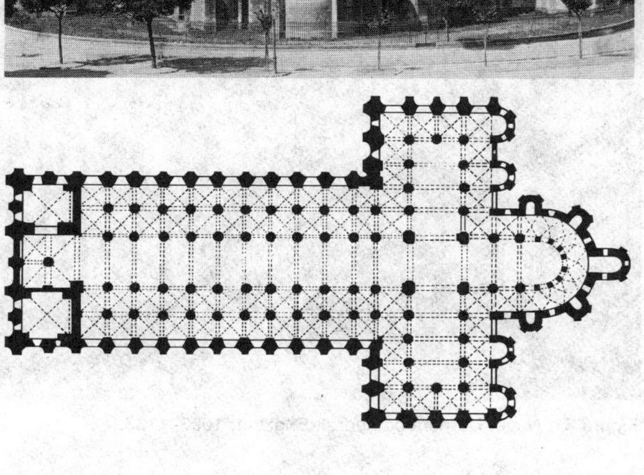

Figure 30: Saint-Sernin, Toulouse, Fr., 1077 or 1082–1118. (Top left) Chevet, east end; (top right) nave; (bottom) plan.

(Top left) Giraudon—Art Resource/EB Inc., (top right) H. Roger-Viollet, (bottom) after Conant in H.W. Janson, *History of Art*

the importance given to certain features varied from one school to the next.

Elements of Roman origin might involve one or several important Roman types of fabric and material, plan, vaulting, decorative elements, and, in the south, the Roman canon of proportion. Early Christian works offered a choice of plans, with or without towers and porches. Elements of Eastern origin might be structural or decorative, and they might be derived from Iberian, African, or Asiatic examples. From the north came not only imaginative timber construction but also various lively decorative systems and verve in their application.

Perhaps even more important was the northern love of aspiring and intersecting forms, powerfully composed, which affected almost the entire Romanesque area, stretching from Portugal to the Holy Land, including Scandinavia and the Holy Roman Empire. The greater buildings were most often churches, which stood out boldly above the ordinary constructions but had an organic relationship to them. The resulting silhouette, so much in contrast with placid classical design, quite transformed the idea of what a city or church group should look like, either from within or from a distance as an ensemble. This dynamic mode was bequeathed to Gothic, Renaissance, and modern times.

After 950 the excellent construction, the grand scale, the assured design, the increasingly capable use of masonry vaulting, and the increasingly rich and appropriate use of foliate and figural sculpture showed that the initial period was over and that a noble, new Romanesque style had come into existence (fully, by 1050). The greatest works in the Romanesque style date from 1075 to 1125, the classic age of Romanesque, so to speak; after this, in some regions, the style entered a florid "baroque" phase that lasted a generation and then was revivified as Gothic.

The coming eclipse of Romanesque may first be sensed in new structural developments that began about 1090. Sophisticated but unsatisfactory attempts to vault the great basilican naves safely, with elements of Roman, Byzantine, or Eastern origin, impelled progressive Romanesque engineers, from about 1090 onward, to invent a new type of ribbed groin-vaulted unit bay, using pointed arches to distribute thrust and improve the shape of the geometric surfaces. Fifty years of experimentation produced vaulting that was light, strong, open, versatile, and applicable everywhere—in short, Gothic vaulting. A whole new aesthetic, with a new decorative system—the Gothic—was being evolved as early as 1145. The spatial forms of the new buildings sometimes caused acoustic difficulties, which may help to account for the concomitant development of the new polyphonic music that supplemented the traditional Romanesque plainsong. Romanesque architecture became old-fashioned, but its heavy forms pleased the Cistercian monks and, likewise, other conservative patrons in Germany, Poland, Hungary, Italy, Spain, and Portugal. Thus, buildings that were essentially Romanesque in spirit continued to be built, even when such extraordinary Gothic works as the Amiens cathedral were under construction (begun 1220).

Effect of architecture on music

The development of proto-Romanesque in the Ottonian period culminated in the true Romanesque style represented by five magnificent churches on the international pilgrimage routes leading from central France to the reputed tomb of St. James at Santiago de Compostela in Spain: Saint-Martin at Tours (a huge once wooden-roofed basilica that was rebuilt on the new model beginning about 1050), Sainte-Foy at Conques (*c.* 1052–1130), Saint-Martial at Limoges (*c.* 1062–95), Saint-Sernin at Toulouse (1077 or 1082–1118; Figure 30), and the new cathedral at Santiago de Compostela itself (*c.* 1075–1211). This was a real family of buildings; each one had a splendid apse with ambulatory (a sheltered place to walk) and radiating chapels, a transept and nave with aisles and galleries, an imposing tower system, and beautiful sculptures. Each one was entirely vaulted, typically, with barrel vaults over the nave, quadrant vaults (four-part vaults, formed by two intersecting arches) over the galleries, and groin-vaulted aisles. A little later, at the Cluniac priory of Saint-Étienne (Nevers, Fr.), such a church was boldly built with clerestory (part of the nave, choir, and transept walls above the aisle roofs) windows under the high vault.

Burgundy. Since the monasteries had done so much to create the new Europe now bursting into architectural flower, it is appropriate that there are two families of churches that express the greatness of Burgundian federative monasticism: Cluny and Cîteaux. Cluny ultimately had about 1,400 dependencies under centralized rule, of which about 200 were important establishments. The Cistercians had a ramified system that ultimately included 742 monasteries and about 900 nunneries.

Rebuilding of Cluny

It was Cluny that, after an impressive rebuilding of the monastery buildings (1077–85), undertook the Maior Ecclesia, or Cluny III (1088–1130 and later). Until it was largely demolished in the early 19th century, it was the largest monastic church, the largest Romanesque church, and the largest French church. It had many features that prepared the way for Gothic: tall proportions, grouped piers, pointed arches, specialized wall and vault construction. It had carvings of great beauty in the apse (where one of the first medieval sculptural allegories was placed by 1095) and at the portals of the nave (where the first really grand ensemble of monumental carved and painted west portals was placed, about 1108). Cluny III inspired only a few great buildings (including, however, Paray-le-Monial, La Charité-sur-Loire, and Autun cathedral) because of its special, advanced character and the fact that the design was soon attacked in an unfortunate Cistercian polemic (1124). It may be that certain architects at Cluny itself considered the design too bold, for they built at the priory of Vézelay (1104–32) a groin-vaulted nave nearly as wide but only two-thirds as high as that of Cluny III. In the narthex at Vézelay there was one groin vault that had ribs, and buttresses resembling flying buttresses were concealed under roofs of the galleries. A pair of towers flanking a carved portal were planned for the facade.

Thus, between these features of Vézelay and the pointed arches composed in tall proportions at Cluny III, the ingredients of the Gothic style were at hand in Burgundy by 1135, awaiting the creative Gothic spark of Saint-Denis (near Paris). The rich portals of Saint-Denis show the influence of the great Burgundian carving. Account must

By courtesy of the National Monuments Record, London

Figure 31: Nave, Durham cathedral, England, 1093–1133.

be taken, however, of another episode—the development of consistent ribbed vaulting in the Norman dominions. Probably the high-ranking Lombard ecclesiastics who undertook the reform and development of the Norman church brought with them some knowledge of ribbed vault construction, which then passed to England. The cathedral abbey church of Durham (1093–1133) was a very early demonstration of the dramatic potentialities of this type of construction (Figure 31). Lombard experiments may have been as early as 1080, but the dating is uncertain; in any event, the development of this structural unit into the admirable Gothic type of ribbed groin vault is due to the skill of French and Anglo-French engineers.

Cistercian architects

Returning to another great family of Burgundian monastic builders, it should be noted that the Cistercian Order was founded as an austere reform institute in 1098 and that it spread rapidly. The Cistercian architects were commanded to build well but without bravura of any kind. They accepted the pointed arch but built ponderously within it a style that might be called half-Gothic, because it has the general appearance but not the special structural characteristics of Gothic. Cistercian constructions were for a long time massive, like the Romanesque. Fontenay Abbey (1139 and later) represented the personal preference of St. Bernard, and it is almost Roman, with its very simple and substantial scheme of pointed barrel vaulting. In general, however, the Cistercian churches came more and more to approximate Gothic designs. In the ground floors of their monastery buildings they early introduced the idea of using ribbed groin vaulting in repetitive square bays (a Gothic scheme). To the east, the south, the west, and the northwest of Europe, the first buildings resembling Gothic were erected by the Cistercians: Pontigny, 1140–1210 (Burgundy); Alcobaça, 1158–1223 (Portugal); Fossanova, 1187–1208 (Italy); Maulbronn, 1146–78 (Germany); Fountains, 1135–50 (England); Vreta, about 1100–62 (Sweden); Kercz, 1202 (Hungary); and Beirut, about 1150 (Lebanon)—all of these give an idea of the power and extension of their effort.

The Cistercian establishments were located in remote places, but the husbandry of the communities was superb and benefited the whole of Europe. Their monasteries were so uniform in conception that a monk coming from a Cistercian house anywhere would feel quite at home in one of these monasteries anywhere else. The basic plan was traditional, but the western court (where visitors were usually received) was reduced to a mere corridor. The Cistercians did not encourage visitors; they were not provided with space in guesthouses within the enclosures or even in the churches. Cistercian refectories were regularly placed at right angles opposite the church, rather than parallel, as in early plans. The monks chose well-watered sites and used waterpower. Ideally, the brotherhoods were able to supply all of their own needs.

Normandy. Another great architectural family was Norman: Rouen cathedral (*c.* 1037–63), followed by Westminster Abbey (1050–65) and the splendid abbeys built in Caen by Duke William and his duchess, Matilda. She built La Trinité, beginning in 1062, and was buried as queen in its sanctuary (1083). William's church, Saint-Étienne, was begun in 1067 and dedicated in 1081 (Figure 32). The Norman series was continued in England by the foundation and endowment of magnificent Benedictine abbeys after the Conquest, as royal policy—to gain the favour of the church, to improve the exploitation of the land, and to pacify the country. Many of the church buildings still exist, and they are very impressive indeed. Typically, they have, or have had, long, wooden-roofed naves with vaulted aisles and wooden-roofed galleries, embellished, stage by stage, with bold, rich interior arcading. The churches have spacious transepts and deep sanctuaries, the apses being arranged in echelon or with ambulatories. It gives one a sense of the builder's means to know that a very large part of the beautiful limestone used in facing the walls was transported across the Channel from the famous quarries of Caen. Though the walls and piers are beautiful, the mortar was not good, and only great thickness made the masonry strong. The Norman parish churches that survive are neither numerous nor striking. Among the more ambi-

Benedictine abbeys

Figure 32: West facade, Saint-Étienne, Caen, Fr., begun in 1067 and dedicated in 1081.
Jean Roubier

tious naves originally roofed in wood but now closed with Gothic vaults are those of the cathedrals at Winchester (1079), Gloucester (1089), and Norwich (1096). Peterborough cathedral (1118) still possesses its old ceiling, painted in lozenge-shaped panels. In many of the churches a large number of additions have been made in the Gothic style without impairing the dignity of the Norman construction. But Durham cathedral, with its Romanesque ribbed groin vault, remains by far the finest example of the Norman style.

Aquitaine, Languedoc, and Auvergne. Long united to the English crown after 1152, Aquitaine has a quite separate church architecture. To achieve free interior space, masonry domes of special construction were used, often four in line, as at Saint-Étienne-de-la-Cité, Périgueux (*c.* 1100–50), and the cathedral of Saint-Pierre at Angoulême (1105–28 and later), with a richly sculptured facade.

In Poitou, elaborately arcaded facades formed somewhat illogical frontispieces for spacious "three-naved" churches, with windowed aisles almost as tall as the central windowless naves. There are beautiful paintings in such churches (as at Saint-Savin-sur-Gartempe). This region has several Romanesque castles, in the usual form (as at Loches, about 1100) of a great square tower, the donjon or keep, with guard and residential rooms on several levels, and appropriate outworks.

Romanesque castles

The churches of Languedoc have bold massing and beautiful sculpture, the tradition of which goes back to the formative period (Saint-Genis-des-Fontaines, 1020). Saint-Sernin at Toulouse, in the pilgrimage style, has beautiful carvings, and many churches in the region are related to it.

In Auvergne, a long tradition (Clermont cathedral, 946) developed, more or less in the manner of the pilgrimage churches. The high "lantern transepts" are characteristic (for example, Notre-Dame-du-Port at Clermont-Ferrand, 1150). The cathedral of Le Puy-en-Velay (11th and 12th centuries), with zebra work in the masonry and a file of domes, represents reflex influence from Spain; Muslim motifs were brought in via the pilgrimage road. Such influence is perceptible also in Burgundy and perhaps in the west of France.

Figure 33: Northeast view of Speyer cathedral, W.Ger., 1030–65, remade *c.* 1082–1137.

Marburg—Art Resource/EB Inc.

Provence. Turning eastward to Provence, the old Provincia Romana, one finds that there Romanesque architecture is most Roman in feeling: grand, simple, spacious bulks were built, usually in fine ashlar (squared stone blocks) masonry, as at Avignon cathedral (about 1140–1200), and often with fine sculpture, as at the cathedral of Arles (Saint-Trophime, 1150 and later) and Saint-Gilles-du-Gard (1116 and later, to about 1170). Some of the portals, especially, seem very Roman.

Germany and the Low Countries. By contrast with the fresh activity in France, the imperial lands, which had done so much to further the development of Romanesque architecture, remained conservative. The period of the mature Romanesque was prosperous in Germany; new buildings were larger and more numerous but technically less interesting. The embellishment and vaulting of the cathedrals in the Rhine country date from this time: Mainz (1036–1137), Speyer (1030–65, remade *c.* 1082–1137; Figure 33), and Worms (12th and 13th centuries). A prime example is the abbey church of Maria Laach (1130–56). Elsewhere, there is a spectacular church design with five towers at Tournai (*c.* 1110–1200), and there are ponderous but handsome palaces with fine upper rooms at Goslar (*c.* 1050, rebuilt after 1132) and Eisenach (the Wartburg, 12th century).

Romanesque architecture in the Low Countries is generally divided into four stylistic classifications: the style of Meuseland, the Scheldt district style, the style of the bishopric of Utrecht, and the style prevalent in the provinces of Groningen and Friesland. The Meuseland churches are characterized by their use of the Carolingian basilica plan. Among the most outstanding examples are St. Servatius at Maastricht; Saint-Denis, Saint-Barthélemy, Saint-Jean, and Sainte-Gertrude at Nivelles. At the end of the 12th century, Rhenish influences were evident in Meuseland, such as in the apse of St. Servatius at Maastricht. In the Scheldt district a pronounced Norman influence is apparent, as in the cathedral of Tournai and the Church of St. Vincent at Soifnies. A blending of Ottonian, Rhenish, and Meuseland styles characterizes Romanesque churches in the bishopric of Utrecht as St. Peters at Utrecht, Grote Kerk at Deventer, and St. Martin at Emmerich. Groningen and Friesland possess a great number of Romanesque village churches that were founded by abbeys in the region. Stylistically, they are related to monastic churches in Meuseland and parts of northern France.

Iberia. The pre-Romanesque types of building in the peninsula were insufficient to satisfy the needs and ambitions of the Spaniards as the Christian states increased in population by immigration and expanded southward by the reconquest in Romanesque times. The architecture clearly testifies to the great influx of men and ideas, particularly from Burgundy, Poitou, and Languedoc (as at Santiago de Compostela cathedral). Cistercian half-Gothic

J. Allan Cash from Rapho/Photo Researchers—EB Inc.

Figure 34: Piazza del Duomo with the baptistery, cathedral, and Leaning Tower, Pisa, 1063–13th century.

Figure 35: Cathedral of Monreale, Sicily, 1174.
Anderson—Alinari from Art Resource/EB Inc.

became important (*e.g.,* Poblet, 1180–96). Catalonia long remained faithful to the Lombard style. Everywhere there are Muslim reminiscences, sometimes obvious, sometimes very subtle.

The walls of Ávila (1090 and later) are among the finest of Romanesque military constructions, and Loarre in Aragon, with its beautiful chapel, is perhaps the finest Romanesque castle.

Romanesque style in Lombardy

Italy. Lombardy was an area in which the proto-Romanesque style was transformed into the true Romanesque, particularly because of the development of ribbed groin vaulting. Decorative arcading, in enriched form, was used and brick was widely employed in later work. Romanesque forms continued in use long after the coming of Cistercian half-Gothic. The Lombard cities built tremendous cathedrals, simple in plan, during the 12th century; examples are Modena (1099–1184), Parma (1117–32), and Cremona (1129–1342). Parma and Cremona have large freestanding baptisteries, unusual at the time. A very handsome type of belfry tower was brought to perfection by the Lombards, and impressive town halls were built with Romanesque inspiration but at Gothic dates. Turbulence in the city streets caused the construction of private fortifications in the form of taller houses: Bologna, for example, had 180, and Lucca "rose like a forest."

Tuscany retained strong early Christian traditions, exemplified in the octagonal Baptistery of Florence (restored in 1059) and the common use of basilican church forms. In the Romanesque period, marble was used extensively, often in panels and zebra work (for example, the cathedral group at Pisa; cathedral 1063–13th century, baptistery 1152–1278, and the Camposanto 1278; Figure 34).

Central Italy was still more conservative; the early Chris-

Giraudon—Art Resource/EB Inc.

Figure 36: Southeast view of the Cathedral of Notre-Dame, Paris, begun 1163.

Figure 37: Laon cathedral, begun *c.* 1165. (Left) West facade, *c.* 1190. (Right) Nave, after *c.* 1165.
(Left) Marburg—Art Resource/EB Inc., (right) Jean Roubier

tian style survived there with little change except degeneration. The region about Monte Cassino was more inventive; the famous abbey built the typical church of the region, basilican in form (1066–71). A school of painters developed there, under Byzantine influence, which was drawn on by the Cluniacs in their work.

Norman Italy and Sicily. Buildings basically Lombard, Tuscan, Muslim, Byzantine, or early Christian were built as the realm became prosperous. Nuances of design and a strange mingling of influences give them strong local feeling. Examples are San Nicola, Bari (1087), where St. Nicholas is buried; the cathedral of Monreale (1174), with wonderful mosaics and a poetic, half-Oriental cloister (1172–89; Figure 35); and San Cataldo at Palermo (1161), a former synagogue in the Muslim domed style. These Sicilian buildings are actually more exotic than the structures built by the crusaders in Palestine (1099–1244).

Architecture of the crusaders

Palestine. The crusaders built extensively in the Latin Kingdom of Jerusalem. The buildings are southern French or Burgundian Romanesque or Burgundian half-Gothic in style (for example, new constructions at the Church of the Holy Sepulchre, 1099–1147, and the cathedral of Tortosa, or Tartūs, late 12th century). Many remarkable castles were built before and after 1200, incorporating Byzantine and Muslim innovations in military architecture, as at the Krak des Chevaliers or at Margat, "whose bastions seemed to sustain the sky; only eagles and vultures could approach its battlements"—striking witness, in so remote a place, to Romanesque faith and power. (J.J.M.T.)

GOTHIC

Throughout this period, the central corridor of Europe running northwest from Lombardy to England, between Cologne and Paris, retains an exceptional importance. Much of the significant art—especially architecture—was produced within this geographic area, because it appears to have been an extraordinarily wealthy area, with enough funds to attract good artists and to pay for expensive materials and buildings. Paris—for much of this period the home of a powerful and artistically enlightened court—played an especially important role in the history of Gothic art.

The role of Paris in Gothic art

Early Gothic. At the technical level Gothic architecture is characterized by the ribbed vault (a vault in which stone ribs carry the vaulted surface), the pointed arch, and the flying buttress (normally a half arch carrying the thrust of a roof or vault across an aisle to an outer pier or buttress). These features were all present in a number of earlier, Romanesque buildings, and one of the major 12th- and early 13th-century achievements was to use this engineering expertise to create major buildings that became, in succession, broader and taller. How their visual appearance changed is easy to see if one compares, for instance, the early 13th-century Reims cathedral, in France, with the late 11th-century Durham cathedral, in England. A broad comparison of this sort also brings out the artistic ends to which the new engineering means were applied. Skilled use of the pointed arch and the ribbed vault made it possible to cover far more elaborate and complicated ground plans than hitherto. Skilled use of buttressing, especially of flying buttresses, made it possible both to build taller buildings and to open up the intervening wall spaces to create larger windows. In the 12th century larger windows produced novel lighting effects, not lighter churches. The stained glass of the period was heavily coloured and remained so—for example, at Chartres cathedral—well into the 13th century.

One of the earliest buildings in which these techniques were introduced in a highly sophisticated architectural plan was the abbey of Saint-Denis, Paris. The east end was rebuilt about 1135–44, and, although the upper parts of the choir and apse were later changed, the ambulatory and chapels belong to this phase. The proportions are not large, but the skill and precision with which the vaulting is managed and the subjective effect of the undulating chain windows around the perimeter have given the abbey its traditional claim to the title "first Gothic building." The driving figure was Suger, the abbot of Saint-Denis, who wrote two accounts of his abbey that are infused with his personal aesthetic of light as a reflection of the infinite light of God. Something similar to what he intended at Saint-Denis was attempted soon after at Notre-Dame, Paris, begun in 1163 (the east end was subsequently altered; Figure 36), and Laon cathedral, begun about 1165 (the east end was rebuilt in the early 13th century; Figure 37). Perhaps because of liturgical inconvenience, it later became more common to keep firm the architectural divisions between the peripheral eastern chapels, as at Reims (rebuilt after a fire destroyed the original cathedral in 1210) and Amiens (begun 1220) cathedrals, for example. This particular feature of Saint-Denis did not, therefore, have a very long subsequent history.

It is not known what the original 12th-century interior elevation of Saint-Denis was like. Elsewhere, though, the problems that followed in the wake of the increasing ability to build gigantic buildings are easily seen. Possibly the most important one concerns the disposition of the main interior elevation. The chief elements are the arcade, the tribune (upper gallery set over the aisle and normally opening into the church) or triforium galleries (arcaded wall passages set above the main arcade) or both, and the clerestory. These may be given equivalent treatment, or one may be stressed at the expense of the others. Precedents for almost every conceivable combination existed in Romanesque architecture. In a building such as Sens cathedral (begun *c.* 1140), the arcade is given prominence, but in Noyon (begun *c.* 1150) and Laon cathedrals the four elements mentioned above are all used, with the result that the arcade is comparatively small. Subsequently, the arcade came back into prominence with Bourges cathedral (begun *c.* 1195). But one of the most influential buildings was Chartres cathedral (present church mainly built after 1194). There, the architect abandoned entirely the use of the tribune gallery, but, instead of increasing the size of the arcade, he managed, by a highly individual type of flying buttress, to increase the size of the clerestory. This idea was followed in a number of important buildings, such as the 13th-century Reims and Amiens cathedrals. The conception that the content of a great church should be dominated by large areas of glazing set in the upper parts was influential in the 13th century.

The decorative features of these great churches were, on the whole, simple. In the second half of the 12th century it became fashionable, as at Laon cathedral, to "bind" the interior elevation together by series of colonettes, or small columns, set vertically in clusters. Again, as at Laon, much of the elaborate figured carving of Romanesque buildings was abandoned in favour of a highly simplified version of the classical Corinthian capital—usually called a "crocket" capital. Under the influence of Chartres cathedral, window tracery (decorative ribwork subdividing the window opening) was gradually evolved.

Cistercian churches

There is one group of churches, built for houses of the Cistercian order, that requires separate consideration. They tend to be similar, but it is often a similarity of general simplicity as much as of architectural detail. The Cistercian order was bound to ideas of austerity laid down by St. Bernard of Clairvaux. During his lifetime these ideals were maintained largely through the degree of centralized control exercised from the head house at Cîteaux (Burgundy). Thus, many of the Cistercian churches built in England, Italy, or Germany seem to have had characteristics in common with French Cistercian churches. A good French example survives at Fontenay (begun 1139). These buildings probably encouraged the early dissemination of the pointed arch. That they did much more than this is doubtful.

If one examines the architecture outside north and northeastern France, one finds, first, that buildings in what might be called a Romanesque style continued up to the end of the 12th and into the 13th century and, second, that the appreciation of the developments in France was often partial and haphazard. In England the most influential building in the new fashion was the choir of Canterbury cathedral (1175–84), which has many of the features of Laon cathedral. It is the decorative effects of Laon that are used rather than its overall architectural plan, however. There is only a rather depressed tribune gallery, and the building retains a passage at clerestory level—an Anglo-Norman feature that remained standard in English architecture well into the 13th century. Both in the shape of the piers and in the multiplicity of attached colonettes, Canterbury resembles Laon. Colonettes became extremely popular with English architects, particularly because of the large supplies of purbeck marble, which gave any elevation a special coloristic character. This is obvious at Salisbury cathedral (begun 1220), but one of the richest examples of the effect is in the nave of Lincoln cathedral (begun *c.* 1225).

The early stages of architectural development in the Gothic period are untidy and have a strong regional flavour. During this period in Germany, large buildings showing northern French characteristics are few. The Church of Our Lady at Trier (begun *c.* 1235) and the Church of St. Elizabeth at Marburg (begun 1235) both have features, such as window tracery, dependent on northern French example; but the church at Trier is highly unusual in its centralized plan, and St. Elizabeth is a "hall church" (that is, the nave is virtually the same height as the aisles), which places it outside the canon of contemporary French building.

In Spain the two most important early Gothic buildings were Burgos (begun 1222) and Toledo (begun 1221) cathedrals. Their architects probably knew Reims and Amiens; but their models were undoubtedly Bourges and Le Mans (begun 1217), since the main internal architectural feature is a giant arcade rather than an extended clerestory. By contrast, Scandinavian architects seem to have been influenced, to begin with, by English buildings. Certainly there is a strong English flavour in the 13th-century Trondheim cathedral (Norway).

High Gothic. During the period from about 1250 to

(Top) After Dehio and Bezold, (bottom) RIBA, London and University of London

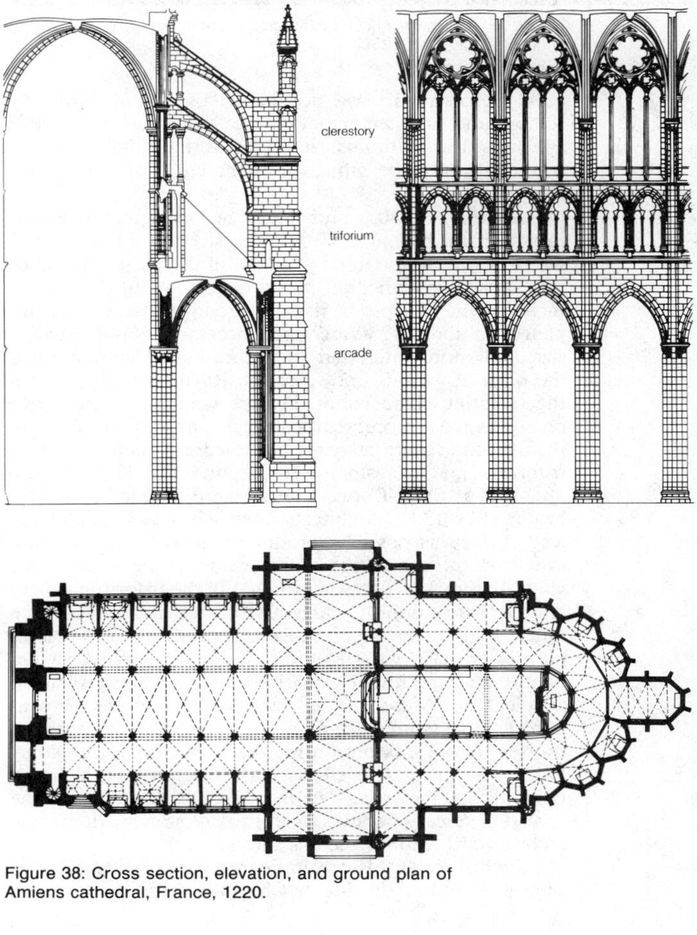

Figure 38: Cross section, elevation, and ground plan of Amiens cathedral, France, 1220.

Figure 39: Interior of Amiens cathedral, France, begun 1220, choir probably after 1236.
Giraudon/Art Resource, New York City

1300 European art was dominated for the first time by the art and architecture of France. The reasons for this are not clear, although it seems certain that they are connected with the influence of the court of King Louis IX (1226–70).

By about 1220–30 it must have been clear that engineering expertise had pushed building sizes to limits beyond which it was unsafe to go. The last of these gigantic buildings, Beauvais cathedral, had a disastrous history, which included the collapse of its vaults, and it was never completed. In about 1230 architects became less interested in size and more interested in decoration. The result was the birth of what is known as the Rayonnant style (from the radiating character of the rose windows, which were one of its most prominent features). The earliest moves in this direction were at Amiens cathedral, where the choir triforium and clerestory were begun after 1236 (Figure 38), and at Saint-Denis, where transepts and nave were begun after 1231. Architects opened up as much of the wall surface as possible, producing areas of glazing that ran from the top of the main arcade to the apex of the vault (Figure 39). The combination of the triforium gallery and clerestory into one large glazed area had, of course, a unifying effect on the elevations. It produced an intricate play of tracery patterns and instantly unleashed an era of intense experiment into the form that these patterns should take. Many of the achievements of the Rayonnant architects are extremely fine—for instance, the two transept facades, begun during the 1250s, of Notre-Dame, Paris. The decorative effect of this architecture depends not only on the tracery of the windows but also on the spread of tracery patterns over areas of stonework and on architectural features such as gables.

Rayonnant style

In the history of this development, one building deserves special mention, the Sainte-Chapelle, Paris (consecrated 1248). This was Louis IX's palace chapel, built to house an imposing collection of relics. It is a Rayonnant building in that it has enormous areas of glazing. Its form was extremely influential, and there were a number of subsequent "saintes-chapelles"—for instance, at Aachen and Riom—that were clearly modeled on the Parisian one. The interior of the Parisian Sainte-Chapelle is extraordinarily sumptuous (Figure 40). Although the sumptuosity itself set new standards, its characteristics belonged, curiously, to a past age. The glass is heavily coloured, the masonry heavily painted, and there is much carved detail. One of the characteristics of the second half of the 13th century is that glass became lighter, painting decreased, and the amount of carved decoration dwindled. Thus, in its chronological context, the Sainte-Chapelle is a Janus-like building—Rayonnant in its architecture but, in some ways, old-fashioned in its decoration.

Of the many smaller Rayonnant monuments that exist in France, one of the most complete is Saint-Urbain, Troyes (founded 1262). There, one can see the virtuosity practiced by the architects in playing with layers of tracery, setting off one "skin" of tracery against another.

In a sense, the Rayonnant style was technically a simple one. Depending, as it did, not primarily on engineering expertise or on sensitivity in the handling of architectural volumes and masses but on the manipulation of geometric shapes normally in two dimensions, the main prerequisites were a drawing board and an office.

Most countries produced versions of the Rayonnant style. In the Rhineland the Germans began one of the largest Rayonnant buildings, Cologne cathedral, which was not completed until the late 19th century. The German masons carried the application of tracery patterns much further than did the French. One of the most complicated essays is the west front of Strasbourg cathedral (planned originally in 1277 but subsequently altered and modified). One feature of Strasbourg and of German Rayonnant architecture in general was the application of tracery to spires—at Freiburg im Breisgau (spire begun *c.* 1330), for example, and the spire of Strasbourg that was begun about 1399. Few such medieval spires survive (though often they were completed in the 19th century).

Application of tracery to spires

Of all the European buildings of this period, the most

A.F. Kersting

Figure 40: Interior of Sainte-Chapelle, Paris, consecrated 1248.

important is probably the cathedral of Prague (founded in 1344). The plan was devised according to routine French principles by the first master mason, Mathieu d'Arras. When he died in 1352, his place was taken (1353–99) by Petr Parléř, the most influential mason in Prague and a member of a family of masons active in south Germany and the Rhineland. Parléř's building included the start of a south tower and spire that clearly continued the traditions of the Rhineland. His originality lay in his experiments with vault designs, from which stem much of the virtuoso achievement of German masons in the 15th century.

London, too, has Rayonnant monuments. Westminster Abbey was rebuilt after 1245 by Henry III's order, and in 1258 the remodeling of the east end of St. Paul's Cathedral began. King Henry was doubtless inspired by the work carried out by his brother-in-law, King Louis IX of France, at the Sainte-Chapelle and elsewhere. Westminster Abbey, however, lacks the clear lines of a Rayonnant church, mainly because, like the Sainte-Chapelle, it was heavily decorated with carved stonework and with colour.

In fact, English architects for a long time retained a liking for heavy surface decoration; thus, when Rayonnant tracery designs were imported, they were combined with the existing repertoire of colonettes, attached shafts, and vault ribs. The result, which could be extraordinarily dense—for instance, in the east (or Angel) choir (begun 1256) at Lincoln cathedral (Figure 41) and at Exeter cathedral (begun before 1280)—has been called the English Decorated style, a term that is in many ways an oversimplification. The interim architectural effects achieved (notably the retrochair of Wells cathedral or the choir of St. Augustine, Bristol) were more inventive generally than those of contemporary continental buildings. The inventive virtuosity of the masons of Decorated style also produced experiments in tracery and vault design that anticipated by 50 years or more similar developments in the Continent.

English Decorated was, however, never really a court style. Already by the end of the 13th century, a style of architecture was evolving that ultimately developed into the true English equivalent of Rayonnant, generally known as Perpendicular. The first major surviving statement of the Perpendicular style is probably the choir of Gloucester cathedral (begun soon after 1330). Other major monuments were St. Stephen's Chapel, Westminster (begun 1292 but now mostly destroyed) and York Minster nave (begun 1291).

A.F. Kersting

Figure 41: Angel Choir, Lincoln cathedral, England, begun 1256.

Figure 42: Nave of Santa Croce, Florence, begun 1294.
Alinari—Art Resource/EB Inc.

Spain also produced Rayonnant buildings: León cathedral (begun *c.* 1255) and the nave and transepts of Toledo cathedral, both of which have, or had, characteristics similar to the French buildings. But, since the Spanish partiality for giant arcades (already seen in the earlier parts of Toledo and at Burgos) persisted, one can hardly classify as French the three major cathedrals of this period: Gerona (begun *c.* 1292), Barcelona (begun 1298), and Palma-de-Mallorca (begun *c.* 1300). They are, in fact, so individual that it is difficult to classify them at all, although peculiarities in the planning and buttressing of the outer walls gives them some similarity to the French cathedral of Albi (begun 1281).

Toward the end of the century, the influence of French ideas spread northward to Scandinavia, and in 1287 French architects were summoned to Sweden to rebuild Uppsala cathedral.

Italian Gothic (c. 1200–1400). In its development of a Gothic style, Italy stood curiously apart from the rest of Europe. For one thing, the more obvious developments of the Italian Gothic style occurred comparatively late—in the 13th century. For another, whereas in most European countries artists imitated with reasonable faithfulness architectural styles that were derived ultimately from northern France, they seldom did so in Italy. This was in part because of geographic and geologic factors. In the figurative arts the combined influences of Byzantine Constantinople and classical antiquity continued to play a far more important role in Italy than in countries north of the Alps. Furthermore, Italian architectural style was decisively affected by the fact that brick—not stone—was the most common building material and marble the most common decorative material.

The distinctiveness of Italian art emerges as soon as one studies the architecture. Twelfth-century buildings such as Laon, Chartres, or Saint-Denis, which appear to have been so important in the north, had virtually no imitators in Italy. Indeed, buildings with Romanesque characteristics, such as Orvieto cathedral (begun 1290), were still being built at the end of the 13th century. The Italians, however, were not unaware of what, by French standards, a great church ought to look like. There is a sprinkling of churches belonging to the first third of the century that have northern characteristics, such as attached (partially recessed in the wall) shafts or columns, crocket capitals, pointed arches, and ribbed vaults. Some of these were Cistercian (Fossanova, consecrated 1208), others were secular (Sant'Andrea, Vercelli; founded 1219). The chief common feature of the larger Italian 13th-century churches, such as Orvieto cathedral and Santa Croce in Florence (begun 1294), was the size of their arcades, which gives the interiors a spacious feeling (Figure 42). Yet in detail the churches vary from the French pattern in a highly individual way.

Italian version of French Rayonnant style

To the extent that Rayonnant architecture is particularly concerned with the manipulation of two-dimensional patterns, the Italian masons produced their own version of the style. In these terms, the facade of Orvieto cathedral (begun 1310), for example, is Rayonnant; the front of Siena cathedral was planned as a Rayonnant facade (Figure 43), and the Campanile, or freestanding bell tower, of Florence cathedral (founded 1334) is Rayonnant to the extent that its entire effect depends on marble patterning (which is traditionally ascribed to the painter Giotto). Finally, it is perhaps legitimate to see Filippo Brunelleschi's 15th-century architecture as a continuation of this tendency—a kind of Florentine equivalent, perhaps, to English Perpendicular. But before the 15th century, Italian architectural development never appears to have the logic or purpose of northern architecture.

Though the rebuilt Milan cathedral is, in plan and general character, Italianate, its decorative character is mainly derived from the north, probably Germany. The exterior is covered with tracery, which makes Milan cathedral more like a Rayonnant building than any other large church in Italy.

Late Gothic. During the 15th century much of the most elaborate architectural experiment took place in southern Germany and Austria. German masons specialized in vault designs; and, in order to get the largest possible expanse of ceiling space, they built mainly hall churches (a type that had been popular throughout the 14th century). Important hall churches exist at Landshut (St. Martin's and the Spitalkirche, *c.* 1400), and Munich (Church of Our Lady, 1468–88). The vault patterns are created out of predominantly straight lines. Toward the end of the 15th century, however, this kind of design gave way to curvilinear patterns set in two distinct layers. The new style developed particularly in the eastern areas of Europe: at Annaberg (St. Anne's, begun 1499) and Kuttenberg (St. Barbara's, 1512).

Figure 44: The interior of Gloucester cathedral cloisters, England, begun 1337.
A.F. Kersting

SCALA/Art Resource, New York City

Figure 43: Facade of the cathedral of Siena, Italy, 1285–1377.

Such virtuosity had no rival elsewhere in Europe. Nevertheless, other areas developed distinctive characteristics. The Perpendicular style is a phase of late Gothic unique to England. Its characteristic feature is the fan vault, which seems to have begun as an interesting extension of the Rayonnant idea in the cloisters of Gloucester cathedral (begun 1337), where tracery panels were inserted into the vault (Figure 44). Another major monument is the nave of Canterbury cathedral, which was begun in the late 1370s, but the style continued to evolve, the application of tracery panels tending to become denser. St. George's Chapel, Windsor (*c.* 1475–1500), is an interesting prelude to the ornateness of Henry VII's Chapel, Westminster Abbey (Figure 45). Some of the best late Gothic achievements are bell towers, such as the crossing tower of Canterbury cathedral (*c.* 1500).

Flamboyant style

In France the local style of late Gothic is usually called Flamboyant, from the flamelike shapes often assumed by the tracery. The style did not significantly increase the range of architectural opportunities. Late Gothic vaults, for instance, are not normally very elaborate (one of the exceptions is Saint-Pierre in Caen [1518–45], which has pendant bosses). But the development of window tracery continued and, with it, the development of elaborate facades. Most of the important examples are in northern France—for example, Saint-Maclou in Rouen (*c.* 1500–14; Figure 46) and Notre-Dame in Alençon (*c.* 1500). France also produced a number of striking 16th-century towers (Rouen and Chartres cathedrals).

The most notable feature of the great churches of Spain is the persistence of the influence of Bourges and the partiality for giant interior arcades. This is still clear in one of the last of the large Gothic churches to be built—the New Cathedral of Salamanca (begun 1510). By this time, Spanish architects were already developing their own intricate forms of vaulting with curvilinear patterns. The Capilla del Condestable in Burgos cathedral (1482–94) provides an elaborate example of Spanish Flamboyant, as does—on a larger scale—Segovia cathedral (begun 1525).

There was a final flowering of Gothic architecture in Portugal under King Manuel the Fortunate (1495–1521). The fantastic nature of much late Gothic Iberian architecture has won for it the name Plateresque, meaning that it is like silversmith's work. The decorative elements used were extremely heterogeneous, and Arabic or Mudéjar forms emanating from the south were popular. Ultimately, during the 16th century, antique elements were added, facilitating the development of a Renaissance style. These curious hybrid effects were transplanted to the New World, where they appear in the earliest European architecture in Central America.

The end of Gothic. The change from late Gothic to Renaissance was superficially far less cataclysmic than the change from Romanesque to Gothic. In the figurative arts, it was not the great shift from symbolism to realistic representation but a change from one sort of realism to another.

Architecturally, as well, the initial changes involved decorative material. For this reason, the early stages of Renaissance art outside Italy are hard to disentangle from late Gothic. Monuments like the huge Franche-Comté chantry chapel at Brou (1513–32) may have intermittent Italian motifs, but the general effect intended was not very different from that of Henry VII's Chapel at Westminster. The Shrine of St. Sebaldus at Nürnberg (1508–19) has the general shape of a Gothic tomb with canopy, although much of the detail is Italianate. In fact, throughout Europe the "Italian Renaissance" meant, for artists between about 1500 and 1530, the *enjolivement,* or embellishment, of an already rich decorative repertoire with shapes, motifs, and figures adapted from another canon of taste. The history of the northern artistic Renaissance is in part the story of the process by which artists gradually realized that classicism represented another canon of taste and treated it accordingly.

But it is possible to suggest a more profound character to the change. Late Gothic has a peculiar aura of finality about it. From about 1470 to 1520, one gets the impression that the combination of decorative richness and realistic detail was being worked virtually to death. Classical antiquity at least provided an alternative form of art. It is arguable that change would have come in the north anyway and that adoption of Renaissance forms was a matter of coincidence and convenience. They were there at hand, for experiment.

A.F. Kersting

Figure 45: Interior of Henry VII's Chapel, Westminster Abbey, London, early 16th century.

Figure 46: West facade of Saint-Maclou, Rouen, Fr., c. 1500–14.
Archives Photographiques

The "rightness" of classical antiquity

The use of Renaissance forms was certainly encouraged, however, by the general admiration for classical antiquity. They had a claim to "rightness" that led ultimately to the abandonment of all Gothic forms as being barbarous. This development belongs to the history of the Italian Renaissance, but the phenomenon emphasizes one aspect of medieval art. Through all the changes of Romanesque and Gothic, no body of critical literature appeared in which people tried to evaluate the art and distinguish old from new, good from bad. The development of such a literature was part of the Renaissance and, as such, was intimately related to the defense of classical art. This meant that Gothic art was left in an intellectually defenseless state. All the praise went to ancient art, most of the blame to the art of the more recent past. Insofar as Gothic art had no critical literature by which a part of it, at least, could be justified, it was, to that extent, inarticulate.

(A.Ma./D.J.Wa.)

The Renaissance

The concept of the Renaissance, whose goal was the rebirth or re-creation of ancient classical culture, originated in Florence in the early 15th century and thence spread throughout most of the Italian peninsula; by the end of the 16th century the new style pervaded almost all of Europe, gradually replacing the Gothic style of the late Middle Ages. It encouraged a revival of naturalism, seen in Italian 15th-century painting and sculpture, and of classical forms and ornament in architecture, such as the column and round arch, the tunnel vault, and the dome.

Knowledge of the classical style in architecture was derived during the Renaissance from two sources: the ruins of ancient classical buildings, particularly in Italy but also in France and Spain, and the treatise *De architectura* by the Roman architect Vitruvius. For classical antiquity and, therefore, for the Renaissance, the basic element of architectural design was the order, which was a system of traditional architectural units. During the Renaissance five orders were used, the Tuscan, Doric, Ionic, Corinthian, and Composite, with various ones prevalent in different periods. For example, the ornate, decorative quality of the Corinthian order was embraced during the early Renaissance, while the masculine simplicity and strength of the Doric was preferred during the Italian High Renaissance. Following ancient Roman practice (*e.g.,* the Colosseum or the Theatre of Marcellus), Renaissance architects often superimposed the order—that is, used a different order for each of the several stories of a building—commencing with the heavier, stronger Tuscan or Doric order below and then rising through the lighter, more decorative Ionic, Corinthian, and Composite.

Importance of proportion

For the Renaissance, proportion was the most important predetermining factor of beauty. The great Italian humanist and architect Leon Battista Alberti defined beauty in architecture as

> a Harmony of all the Parts in whatsoever Subject it appears, fitted together with such Proportion and Connection, that nothing could be added, diminished or altered, but for the Worse. (*Ten Books on Architecture,* trans. by J. Leoni, book vi, ch. 2, 1755.)

On the authority of Vitruvius, the Renaissance architects found a harmony between the proportions of the human body and those of their architecture. There was even a relationship between architectural proportions and the Renaissance pictorial device of perspective; the Italian painter Piero della Francesca said that perspective represented objects seen from afar "in proportion according to their respective distance." In fact, it was an Italian Renaissance architect, Filippo Brunelleschi, who was the first to formulate perspective. The concern of these architects for proportion caused that clear, measured expression and definition of architectural space and mass that differentiates the Renaissance style from the Gothic and encourages in the spectator an immediate and full comprehension of the building.

The Renaissance was the great moment in the history of architecture for the expression of architectural theory. Inspired by the rediscovery or reevaluation of the treatise by Vitruvius, many architects recorded their theories of architecture; some were preserved in manuscript (*e.g.,* those of the 15th-century Italian architects Francesco di Giorgio and Antonio Filarete), but most were published. Alberti's treatise *De re aedificatoria* (*Ten Books on Architecture*), modeled on Vitruvius, was written in the middle of the 15th century and published in 1485. But it was during the last three-quarters of the 16th century that architectural theory flourished. The Italians Sebastiano Serlio, Giacomo da Vignola, and Andrea Palladio published famous books on architecture at that time. Elsewhere, works were published by the Frenchmen Jacques Androuet du Cerceau, Philibert Delorme, and Jean Bullant; the Fleming Vredeman de Vries; the German Wendel Dietterlin; and John Shute in England.

EARLY RENAISSANCE IN ITALY (1401–95)

The Renaissance began in Italy, where there was always a residue of classical feeling in architecture. A Gothic building such as the Loggia dei Lanzi in Florence continued to use the large round arch instead of the usual Gothic pointed arch and preserved the simplicity and monumentality of classical architecture. The Renaissance might have been expected to appear first in Rome, where there was the greatest quantity of ancient Roman ruins; but during the 14th and early 15th centuries, when the Italians were impelled to renew classicism, the political situation in Rome was very unfavourable for artistic endeavour. Florence, however, under the leadership of the Medici family, was economically prosperous and politically stable.

In 1401 a competition was held among sculptors and goldsmiths to design a pair of doors for the old baptistery at Florence. The sculptor Lorenzo Ghiberti won, and a losing goldsmith, Filippo Brunelleschi, resolving to be the leader in one of the arts, then turned to the study of architecture. Brunelleschi spent the period between 1402 and

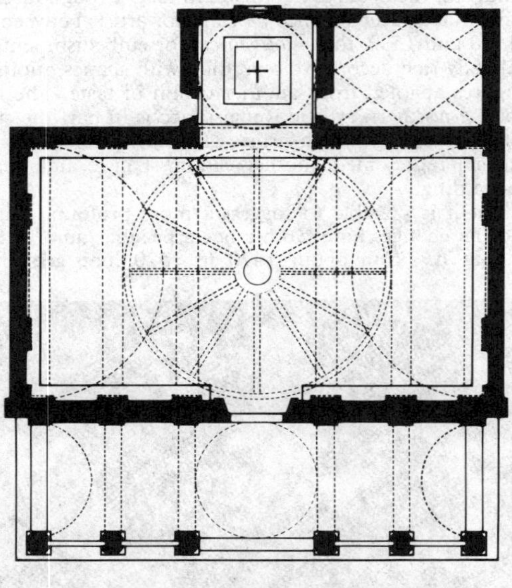

Figure 47: Pazzi Chapel, in the medieval cloister of Santa Croce, Florence, by Filippo Brunelleschi, 1429–60. (Left) Exterior; (top right) plan; (bottom right) interior view.
(Top right) From H.W. Janson, *History of Art,* reproduced by permission of Prentice-Hall, Inc.; photographs, Alinari—Art Resource/EB Inc.

1418 alternately in Florence and Rome. During this time he studied mathematics intensively and formulated linear perspective, which was to become a basic element of Renaissance art. At the same time, Brunelleschi investigated ancient Roman architecture and acquired the knowledge of classical architecture and ornament that he used as a foundation for Renaissance architecture. He was also influenced by the local Florentine tradition, which had flowered in the 11th and 12th centuries in the so-called Tuscan proto-Renaissance style found in churches such as San Miniato al Monte. Brunelleschi's great opportunity came in 1418 with the competition for the completion of the duomo, or cathedral, of Florence. The medieval architects had intended a great dome over the crossing of the cathedral, but it had never been created, and no one knew how to accomplish it. Winning the competition, Brunelleschi began the great dome in 1420 (the finishing touches were not applied until 1467, after his death).

The Florentine dome still belongs within the Gothic tradition, as it was built with rib construction and a pointed arch form, but the introduction of a drum, which made the dome more prominent, was to become characteristic of the Renaissance dome.

First Renaissance building

Brunelleschi also produced in Florence other notable examples of the Renaissance style. The loggia of the Ospedale degli Innocenti (1419–51) was the first building in the Renaissance manner; a very graceful arcade was designed with Composite columns, and windows with classical pediments were regularly spaced above each of the arches. This style was more fully exploited in the church of San Lorenzo (*c.* 1421 to *c.* 1460). Using the traditional basilica plan, the plan and elevations were organized on a system of proportions with the height of the nave equal to twice its width. All the ornament is classical, with Corinthian columns, pilasters, and classical moldings. Brunelleschi used almost exclusively the Corinthian order. All the moldings, door and window frames, and orders are of a soft blue-gray stone (*piètra serena*) contrasted against a light stucco wall. The ornamental features have very little projection, being rather lines on a surface. Colour was used in Florentine architecture to stress the linear relationship rather than for overall patternistic uses (as in northern Italian architecture).

The traditional plan for medieval churches was the Latin cross plan, as at San Lorenzo; the longer arm of the cross formed the nave of the church. During the Middle Ages this plan was considered a symbolic reference to the cross of Christ. During the Renaissance the ideal church plan tended to be centralized; that is, it was symmetrical about a central point, as is a circle, a square, or a Greek cross (which has four equal arms). Many Renaissance architects came to believe that the circle was the most perfect geometric form and, therefore, most appropriate in dedication to a perfect God. Brunelleschi also worked with the central plan. In the Pazzi Chapel (1429–60), constructed in the medieval cloister of Santa Croce at Florence, the plan approaches the central type. On the inside it is actually a rectangle, slightly wider than it is deep; at its rear is a square bay for the sanctuary, and at the front is a porch. There are three domes, a large one over the centre of the chapel and small ones over the sanctuary and over the centre of the porch on the exterior. Its plan, but not its interior space, resembles a Greek cross. On the exterior the large dome is covered by a conical roof with a lantern at the top. The porch has a horizontal entablature supported by six Corinthian columns but broken in the centre by a semicircular arch that centralizes the composition, repeats the shape of the dome in the porch behind it, and gives a lift to the horizontal facade (Figure 47).

Soon after the commencement of the Pazzi Chapel, Brunelleschi began a central-plan church, that of Santa Maria degli Angeli (begun 1434) at Florence, which was never completed. It was very important because it was the first central-plan church of the Renaissance, the type of plan which dominates Renaissance thinking. The plan is an octagon on the interior and 16-sided on the exterior, with a domical vault probably intended to cover the centre.

Early residential architecture

An outstanding example of secular architecture was the Medici Palace (1444–59; now called the Palazzo Medici-Riccardi) at Florence by Michelozzo, a follower of Brunelleschi (Figure 48, left). Created for Cosimo de' Medici, a great political leader and art patron of Florence,

Brogi—Alinari from Art Resource/EB Inc.

Figure 48: *Early Renaissance palaces in Florence.*
(Left) Facade of Palazzo Medici-Riccardi, by Michelozzo, 1444–59. (Right) Palazzo Rucellai, designed by Leon Battista Alberti, 1452?–1470?

the palace was arranged around a central court, the traditional Florentine palace plan.

Medieval Florentine palaces were built of great rusticated blocks of stone, as if they had just been hacked out of the quarry, giving the impression of fortification. With the Renaissance, some fundamental changes appeared. Michelozzo crowned his palace with a massive horizontal cornice in the classical style and regularized the window and entrance openings. Even the rustication of the stonework was differentiated in each of the three stories. The ground floor has the usual heavy rustication; the second story is marked by drafted stonework with smooth blocks outlined by incised lines; and the third story has ashlar stonework with no indications of the blocks. Unlike medieval patternistic rustication, that of the Renaissance, which carefully distinguished between the stories, set up a logical relationship among them.

Further development of the palace facade

This Renaissance treatment of a palace facade was carried further in the Palazzo Rucellai (1452?–1470?) at Florence, following the design of the great architect Alberti (Figure 48, right). Classical orders were applied to the palace elevation by Alberti, using pilasters of the different orders superimposed on the three stories, so that there was another relationship established among the differentiated stories, from the short, strong Tuscan pilaster on the ground floor to the tall, decorative Corinthian at the top. For Alberti the beauty of architecture consisted of a harmonious relationship among the parts, with ornament, including the classical orders, being auxiliary to the proportional relationships.

The culmination of Alberti's style is seen at Mantua in the church of Sant'Andrea (begun 1472, completed in the 18th century), an early Renaissance masterpiece that was to exert much influence on later religious architecture. It is important as a brilliant application of the ancient Roman triumphal arch motif both to the facade of a church and to its interior articulation. The plan, as completed, is a Latin cross with one long arm for the nave flanked by side chapels, but the crossing at the sanctuary end was treated as a central plan with the nave added to it. It is unknown whether this plan corresponds to Alberti's intention, for only the nave portion was erected in the 15th century. The facade is of square proportion, with a wide bay at the centre twice the width of each of the side bays. The interior elevation was organized on this same alternating system, the so-called rhythmic bay that was to be popularized in the early 16th century by Bramante. As a result of this system, there is a close correspondence between the interior and exterior composition of Sant'Andrea (Figure 49).

From Florence the early Renaissance style spread gradually over Italy, becoming prevalent in the second half of the 15th century. In the architecture of northern Italy there was a greater interest in pattern and colour. Colour was emphasized by the use of variegated marble inlays, as in the facade of the church of the Certosa di Pavia (begun 1491) or in most Venetian architecture. The favourite building material of northern Italy was brick with terra-cotta trim and decoration, a combination by means of which a pattern of light and dark was created over the entire building. On occasions when stone was used, as at the Palazzo Bevilacqua in Bologna (*c.* 1479–84), the blocks were cut with facets forming a diamond pattern on the facade. This was actually a decorative treatment of rustication. Even the classical orders were affected by this decorative approach. Classical pilasters often had panels of candelabra and arabesque decoration in delicate relief on the surfaces of their shafts; the lower third of a column was frequently carved with relief sculpture.

Pattern and colour in northern Italian architecture

Florentine artists, such as Filarete with his project for the Ospedale Maggiore at Milan (begun 1457), brought classical decoration and a slight knowledge of Renaissance architecture to the region of Lombardy. The style was transferred to Venice by such Lombard architects as Pietro Lombardo and Mauro Coducci. The church of Santa Maria dei Miracoli (1481–89) at Venice, with its facade faced with coloured marble, is typical of Lombardo's work (Figure 50).

The Venetian palace, as exemplified by the Palazzo Corner-Spinelli (late 15th century) and the Palazzo Vendramin-Calergi (*c.* 1500–09), both of which are the work of Coducci and both with large and numerous windows, was more open than the palaces found in central Italy (Figure 51).

Roman palaces

In Rome in the second half of the 15th century, there were several notable Renaissance palaces, principally derived from the style of Alberti, who spent extensive periods in Rome as a member of the papal court. The Palazzo Venezia (1455–1503) has a rather medieval exterior, but set within the palace is a characteristically Renaissance court (1468–71), of which only two sides forming an angle were completed. It has been suggested without definite proof that Alberti may have furnished the design for this court; it at least reveals his influence in its full understanding of the classical style. The court consists of two stories of semicircular arches supported by piers, on which are attached superimposed classical half columns, Tuscan below and Ionic above. The model for this arcade is the ancient Colosseum of Rome. The sense of mass created by the heavy piers contrasted with the lighter effect of the early Renaissance court typical of Florence, which has arches supported on columns. The Palazzo della Cancelleria (1495) shows its dependence upon Alberti's style in its facade, which resembles in part his Palazzo Rucellai in

(Left) Alinari—Art Resource/EB Inc., (right) RIBA, London and University of London

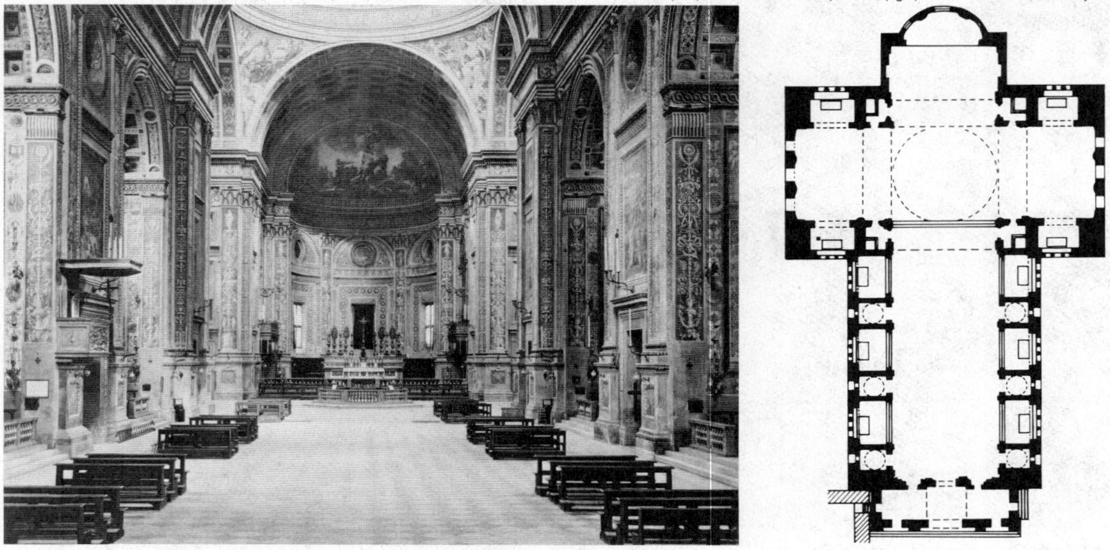

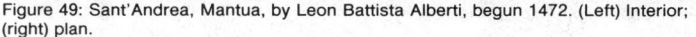

Figure 49: Sant'Andrea, Mantua, by Leon Battista Alberti, begun 1472. (Left) Interior; (right) plan.

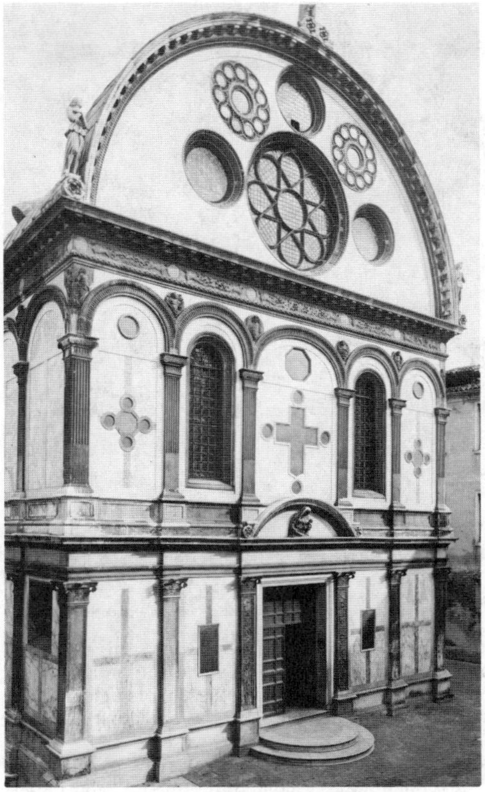

Figure 50: Santa Maria dei Miracoli, Venice, by Pietro Lombardo, 1481–89.
Alinari—Art Resource/EB Inc.

Florence. The lower story simply has drafted or leveled and squared stonework, but the two upper stories have rather flat Corinthian pilasters as well as the drafted stone. Unlike the Rucellai palace, the bays composed by the pilasters alternate wide and narrow, but this alternation had been used by Alberti already in Sant'Andrea at Mantua. Alberti's influence is also visible in the facades of the churches of Sant'Agostino (1479–83) and Santa Maria del Popolo (rebuilt 1472–77) in Rome.

These examples of the early Renaissance in Rome were rapidly approaching the simplicity, monumentality, and massiveness of the High Renaissance of the early 16th century. Donato Bramante, who was to create this new style, was active in Lombardy in northern Italy, but his work in Milan, as at Santa Maria presso San Satiro (about 1480–86), was still in the Lombard early Renaissance manner. He was in contact at this time, however, with the great Florentine Leonardo da Vinci, who was active at the Milanese court. Leonardo was then considering the concept of the central-plan church and filling his notebooks with sketches of such plans, which Bramante must have studied. When Bramante moved to Rome at the very end of the 15th century, his study of ancient ruins—combined with the ideas of Leonardo and the growing classicism of Roman early Renaissance architecture—resulted in the flourishing of the High Renaissance.

HIGH RENAISSANCE IN ITALY (1495–1520)

High Renaissance architecture first appeared at Rome in the work of Bramante at the beginning of the 16th century. The period was a very brief one, centred almost exclusively in the city of Rome; it ended with the political and religious tensions that shook Europe during the third decade of the century, culminating in the disastrous sack of Rome in 1527 and the siege of Florence in 1529. The High Renaissance was a period of harmony and balance in all the arts, perhaps the most classic moment in this respect since the 5th century BC in Greece.

Political and cultural leadership shifted from Florence to Rome particularly because of a succession of powerful popes who wanted to develop the papacy as a secular power. The greatest of all was Julius II (1503–13), who was likewise a fabulous patron of the arts. Almost all the leading Italian artists were attracted to Rome. With the exception of Giulio Romano, none of the important artists active in Rome at this time was Roman by birth.

Rome as the new artistic centre

Bramante, the leader of this new manner, had already acquired an architectural reputation at Milan. Almost immediately after his arrival in Rome, in 1499, there was an amazing change in Bramante's work, as he became the exemplar of the High Renaissance style and lost his Lombard early Renaissance qualities. The Tempietto (1502), or small chapel, next to San Pietro in Montorio, typifies the new style. Erected on the supposed site of the martyrdom of St. Peter, the Tempietto is circular in plan, with a colonnade of 16 columns surrounding a small cella, or enclosed interior sanctuary. The chapel was meant to stand in the centre of a circular court, which was likewise to be surrounded by a colonnade, so that the whole structure was to be self-contained and centralized. The enclosing

Alinari—Art Resource/EB Inc.

Figure 51: Palazzo Vendramin-Calergi, Venice, by Mauro Coducci, *c.* 1500–09.

circular court was never erected. The ultimate inspiration of the Tempietto was a Roman circular temple, like the temples of Vesta at Rome or Tivoli, but so many notable changes were made that the Renaissance chapel was an original creation. On the exterior it was organized in two stories, the Doric colonnade forming the first story. Above is a semicircular dome raised high on a drum. The present large finial, or crowning ornament, on the dome is of a later date and destroys some of the simplicity of the massing. Niches cut into the wall of the drum help to emphasize the solidity and strength of the whole, as does the heavy Doric order that Bramante was so fond of—in contrast to Brunelleschi, who had a predilection for the ornate Corinthian. The monument is very simple, harmonious, and comprehensible.

Several churches present the same qualities as the Tempietto on a larger physical scale. The church of Santa Maria della Consolazione (1504–1617) at Todi, probably by Bramante, is likewise centralized in plan, being square with a semicircular or polygonal apse opening off each side. The mass is built up of simple geometric forms capped by the cylinder of a drum and a slightly pointed dome. On the interior the outstanding quality is a sense of quiet, harmonious spaciousness. The Florentine architect Antonio da Sangallo the Elder, influenced by Bramante, created his church of San Biagio at Montepulciano (1518–29) on a Greek cross plan. On the facade in the two recesses of the arms of the cross were to rise two towers, the right one never completed. Otherwise the massing is similar to that of Todi, with dome and drum above. All the moldings and ornamental elements were carved with strong projection, so that on the interior heavy Roman arches, with deep coffers containing rosettes, define the tunnel vaults rising over the arms of the church. The churches at Todi and Montepulciano are pilgrimage churches or shrines and thus have the centralized planning characteristic of the martyrium or church built over the tomb of a martyr or saint.

Rebuilding of St. Peter's

Sangallo's church at Montepulciano reflects Bramante's greatest undertaking, the rebuilding of St. Peter's in Rome. Early in 1505 Pope Julius II began to consider the question of a tomb for himself that would be appropriate to his idea of the power and nobility of his position. The sculptor Michelangelo soon presented a great project for a freestanding tomb, but such a monument required a proper setting. The Renaissance artist and biographer Giorgio Vasari claimed that the question of an appropriate location for this projected tomb brought to the Pope's mind the idea of rebuilding St. Peter's, which was in very poor condition. Bramante, therefore, prepared plans for a monumental church late in 1505, and in April 1506 the foundation stone was laid (Figure 52). Bramante's first design was a Greek cross in plan, with towers at the four corners and a tremendous dome over the crossing, inspired by that of the ancient Roman Pantheon but in this case raised on a drum. The Greek cross plan being unacceptable, Bramante finally planned to lengthen one arm

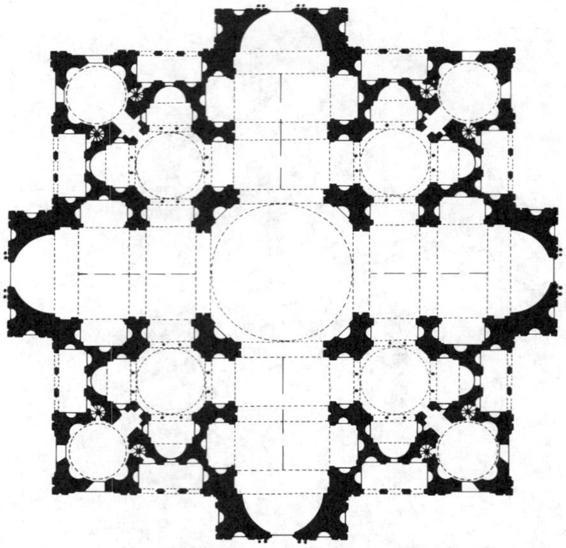

Figure 52: Plan for the Basilica of St. Peter's, Rome, 1505, by Donato Bramante.

From *Art Through the Ages* by Helen Gardner, Fifth Edition, edited by Horst de la Croix and Richard G. Tansey, © 1970 by Harcourt Brace Jovanovich, Inc. and reproduced with their permission

to form a nave with a centralized crossing. At his death in 1514 Bramante had completed only the four main piers that were to support the dome, but these piers determined the manner in which later architects attempted the completion of the church.

As important as the central-plan churches of this period were several notable secular buildings. At the papal palace of the Vatican, next to St. Peter's, Bramante added two important features. The great Belvedere court (begun 1505) was planned to bring together the two disparate elements of the older palace attached to the church and the Belvedere villa of Innocent VIII on the hill above the palace. Bramante gave the new court a neo-antique flavour recalling the imperial palaces on the hills of Rome and the *hippodromus* on the Palatine. Terraced up the hillside on three levels joined by monumental stairs, it was enclosed on the two long sides by arcaded loggias with superimposed orders. This large court was completed in the later 16th century with some minor changes, but in 1587 the whole concept was destroyed by the building of the present Vatican Library across the centre of the court. Just before his death, Bramante also began a series of superimposed loggias attached to the face of the old Vatican Palace looking out over the city and river. As completed by Raphael, there are two superimposed arcades with Tuscan and Ionic orders and a colonnade with Composite columns.

The Palazzo Farnese

The largest palace of the High Renaissance is the Palazzo Farnese (1517–89) at Rome, designed and commenced by

(Left) Anderson—Alinari from Art Resource/EB Inc., (right) Alinari—Art Resource/EB Inc.

Figure 53: Palazzo Farnese, Rome, by Antonio da Sangallo the Younger and Michelangelo, 1517–89. (Left) Facade; (right) courtyard.

a follower of Bramante, Antonio da Sangallo the Younger, nephew of the older Sangallo. At Sangallo's death, in 1546, Michelangelo carried the palace toward completion, making important changes in the third story. On the exterior Sangallo gave up the use of the classical orders as a means of dividing the facade into a number of equal bays; he used instead a facade more like those of the Florentines, but with quoins, or rough-cut blocks of stone at the edges of the building, to confine the composition in a High Renaissance fashion. The facade is composed in proportions as a double square. On the interior the central square court is more classical, using superimposed orders. Based on the ancient Roman Theatre of Marcellus or the Colosseum, the two first floors have an arcade supported by rectangular piers against which are half columns. On the third story Michelangelo eliminated the arcade and used pilasters flanked by half pilasters, which destroyed the High Renaissance idea of the careful separation and definition of parts (Figure 53).

Villa architecture

One of the most charming buildings of the period is the Villa Farnesina (1509–11) at Rome by Baldassarre Peruzzi from Siena. Designed for the fabulously wealthy Sienese banker Agostino Chigi, the villa was the scene of numerous elaborate banquets for the pope and cardinals. A suburban villa, the Farnesina was planned in relation to the gardens around it with two small wings projecting from the central block to flank the entrance loggia. Originally, another loggia opened at the side upon the gardens stretching to the bank of the Tiber, but this loggia was later walled in. The elevation appears as two stories comparted into equal bays by Tuscan pilasters. The neat, reserved quality of the present building was originally lightened by painted fresco decoration over all the exterior wall surfaces. Other important buildings were designed by the painter Raphael, such as the Villa Madama (begun 1518) at Rome or the Palazzo Pandolfini (begun *c.* 1516) at Florence.

(D.R.C./D.J.Wa.)

ITALIAN MANNERISM OR LATE RENAISSANCE (1520–1600)

Mannerism is the term applied to certain aspects of artistic style, mainly Italian, in the period between the High Renaissance of the early 16th century and the beginnings of Baroque art in the early 17th. From the third decade of the 16th century, political and religious tensions erupted violently in Italy, particularly in Rome, which was sacked in 1527 by the imperial troops of Charles V. The school of Bramante and Raphael, which had produced the High Renaissance style, was dispersed throughout Italy as the artists fled from devastated Rome. Mannerism appeared and prevailed in some regions until the end of the 16th century, when the Baroque style developed. Mannerism was antithetical to many of the principles of the High Renaissance. In place of harmony, clarity, and repose it was characterized by extreme sophistication, complexity, and novelty. Mannerist architects were no less interested in ancient classical architecture than were their predecessors, but they found other qualities in ancient Roman architecture to exploit. In fact, they often displayed an even greater knowledge of antiquity than did earlier artists.

For Vasari, as a practicing Mannerist architect, the same criteria of stylishness in design could be applied to a building as to a work of painting or sculpture. Vasari designed and built for an educated elite, one that would appreciate both his understanding of the rules of Roman architecture and the ingenious liberties that he took with these rules. Florentine and Roman 16th-century architecture is characterized by a secular cleverness—a building was judged on elegance, ingenuity, and variety of form.

The change in style between the High Renaissance and Mannerism can be seen in the work of Baldassarre Peruzzi, who was active in both periods. Unlike his High Renaissance Villa Farnesina, Peruzzi's design for the Palazzo Massimo alle Colonne (about 1535) in Rome shows indications of Mannerism (Figure 54). The facade of the palace was curved to fit the site on which it was erected; instead of remaining the passive form it had been in the earlier phases of Renaissance architecture, the wall surface was beginning to assert itself. The classical order is limited to the ground floor of the palace; the upper three stories have imitation drafted stonework made of brick covered with stucco, inscribed to feign stone coursing. Under these three stories in the centre of the facade is a loggia or colonnade, which seems of questionable adequacy as a support for the apparent load. The second story has rectangular windows crowned by Peruzzi's usual neat lintel supported on volutes, but the windows of the upper two stories are set horizontally with rather elaborate curvilinear moldings about them. There is, therefore, no longer a harmonious balance among the various stories. The architecture shows a greater emphasis on decorative qualities than on the expression of structural relationships.

The two directions of Mannerist development

After the resolved classical order and measured harmony of Bramante's High Renaissance buildings, two main, though interwoven, directions of Mannerist development become apparent. One of these, emanating largely from Peruzzi, relied upon a detailed study of antique decorative motifs—grotesques, classical gems, coins, and the like—which were used in a pictorial fashion to decorate the plane

Alinari—Art Resource/EB Inc.

Figure 54: Palazzo Massimo alle Colonne, Rome, by Baldassarre Peruzzi, *c.* 1535.

of the facade. This tendency was crystallized in Raphael's Palazzo Branconio dell'Aquila (destroyed) at Rome, where the regular logic of a Bramante facade was abandoned in favour of complex, out-of-step rhythms and encrusted surface decorations of medallions and swags. The detailed archaizing elements of this manner were taken up later by Pirro Ligorio, by the architects of the Palazzo Spada in Rome, and by Giovanni Antonio Dosio.

The second trend exploited the calculated breaking of rules, the taking of sophisticated liberties with classical architectural vocabulary. Two very different buildings of the 1520s were responsible for initiating this taste, Michelangelo's Laurentian Library in Florence (Figure 55) and the

Alinari—Art Resource/EB Inc.

Figure 55: Staircase of the Laurentian Library, Florence, by Michelangelo, 1524–71.

Palazzo del Te by Giulio Romano in Mantua (Figure 56). Michelangelo's composition relies upon a novel reassembly of classical motifs for plastically expressive purposes, while Giulio's weird distortion of classical forms is of a more consciously bizarre and entertaining kind. The various exterior aspects of the Palazzo del Te provide a succession of changing moods, which are contrived so as to retain the surprised attention of the spectator rather than to present him with a building that can be comprehended at a glance. In the courtyard the oddly fractured cornice sections create an air of ponderous tension, whereas the loggia is lightly elegant. Similarly, the illusionistic decoration of the interior runs the full gamut from heavy (if self-parodying) tragedy to pretty delicacy. Giulio also created a series of contrived vistas, through arches and doors, much like that later projected by Michelangelo for the Palazzo Farnese in Rome. Such management of scenic effects became one of the hallmarks of later Mannerist architecture.

Complexes of architecture, sculpture, and gardens

Increasingly, architecture, sculpture, and walled gardens came to be regarded as part of a complex (but not unified) whole. In the Villa Giulia (*c.* 1550–55), the most significant secular project of its time, Vasari appears to have been in charge of the scenic integration of the various elements; Giacomo da Vignola designed part of the actual building, while the Mannerist sculptor Bartolommeo Ammanati was largely responsible for the sculptural decoration. In spite of the continuous stepped vista, the building makes its impact through a succession of diverse effects rather than by mounting up to a unified climax. There, and in Vasari's design for the Uffizi Palace (1560), the vista seems to have been based upon the supposed style of antique stage sets, as interpreted by Peruzzi (Figure 57). It is not surprising that the Venetian architect Andrea Palladio came closest to achieving a fully Mannerist style in his Teatro Olimpico at Vicenza, where the receding vistas and rich sculptural details create an effect of extraordinary complexity. Similarly, it is not surprising that the greatest of the later Mannerist architects in Florence, Bernardo Buontalenti, should have been an acknowledged master of stage design. He was employed at the Medici court as a designer of grandly fantastic ephemera—mock river battles and stage intermezzi (interval entertainments) in which elaborate stage machinery effected miraculous transformations, figures descending from the clouds to slay dragons that spouted realistic blood, followed by music and dance *all'antica.* As a garden designer, Buontalenti enriched the traditional formal schemes with entertaining diversions, in which water often played a prominent role—either in fountains or in wetting booby traps for the strolling visitor. Buontalenti's buildings possess much of this capricious spirit in addition to his brilliantly inventive command of fluently plastic detailing.

In their treatment of detail, 16th-century Florentine architects inevitably looked toward Michelangelo as their example of innovative genius. Michelangelo's Medici Chapel in San Lorenzo (Figure 58) was executed, in Vasari's opinion, "in a style more varied and novel than that of any other master," and "thus all artists are under a great and eternal obligation to Michelangelo, seeing that he broke the fetters and chains that had earlier confined them to the creation of traditional forms." By Vasari's time the Mannerist quest for novelty had reached a thoroughly self-conscious level.

Michelangelo's design for St. Peter's

Michelangelo's later architecture in Rome was more restrained than his Florentine works. In 1546 he was commissioned to complete St. Peter's Basilica in Rome, succeeding Antonio da Sangallo the Younger. During the next 18 years he was able to complete most of his design for the church, except the facade and great dome above. In plan he returned to a central-plan church reminiscent of Bramante's first project but with fewer parts (Figure 59). Michelangelo's elevation, still visible at the rear or sides of the church, is composed of gigantic pilasters and a rather

James Austin

Figure 56: Palazzo del Te, Mantua, by Giulio Romano, 1525/26–1535.

Figure 57: Uffizi Palace Court, Florence, by Giorgio Vasari, 1560.
Alinari—Art Resource/EB Inc.

high attic story. Between the pilasters are several stories of windows or niches. Unlike the harmonious orders and openings of the High Renaissance, these are constricted by the pilasters so that a tension is created in the wall surface. Michelangelo planned a tremendous semicircular dome on a drum as the climax of the composition. Engravings of his original project suggest that this dome would have been overwhelming in relation to the rest of the design (Figure 60). The great central dome was executed toward the end of the 16th century by Michelangelo's follower, Giacomo della Porta, who gave a more vertical expression to the dome by raising it about 25 feet higher than a semicircle. In the early 17th century, the Baroque architect Carlo Maderno added a large nave and facade to the front of the church, converting it into a Latin cross plan and destroying the dominating quality of the dome, at least from the exterior front.

Early Mannerism in northern Italy

Early Mannerism in northern Italy developed out of the dissolution of the school of Bramante after 1527. Giulio Romano, the chief assistant of Raphael, became court artist and architect in the city of Mantua. With the works of Galeazzo Alessi of Genoa, Leone Leoni of Milan, and Sebastiano Serlio of Bologna, Mannerist architecture gained a firm hold. In 1537 Serlio began to publish his series of books on architecture, in which antiquity was examined through Mannerist eyes and a series of pattern-book Mannerist designs was provided. Three years later, Serlio joined the Italian Mannerist painter Francesco Primaticcio at Fontainebleau, where he helped to consolidate the early acceptance of Mannerist ideals in France. In the work of Alessandro Vittoria, the influence of central Italy was pronounced. His heavy ceiling moldings are composed of classical motifs and bold strapwork. The north's taste for bizarre fancies—such as Vittoria's fireplace for the Palazzo Thiene—was often in advance of that in Rome and Florence.

Even Venice proved to be quickly susceptible to the clever tricks of Mannerist license. Michele Sanmicheli, a pupil of Bramante and Antonio da Sangallo the Younger, returned after the sack of Rome to his native town of

SCALA—Art Resource/EB Inc.

Figure 58: The Medici Chapel, the New Sacristy of the church of San Lorenzo, Florence, by Michelangelo, 1520–34.

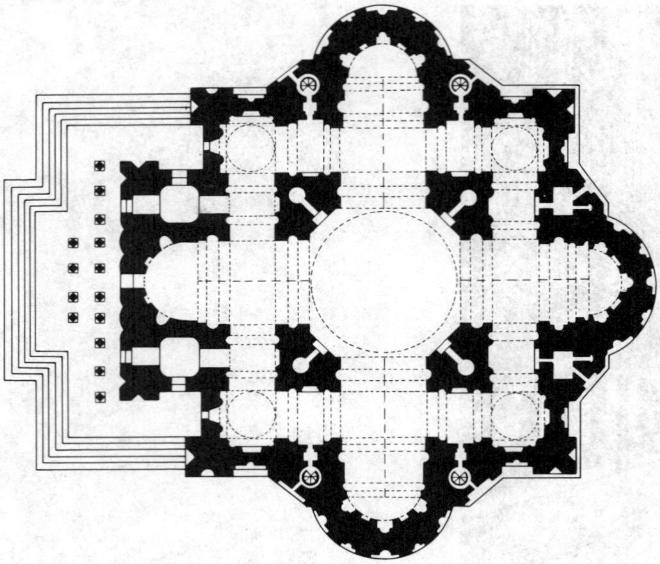

Figure 59: Plan for the Basilica of St. Peter's, Rome, by Michelangelo.

From *Art Through the Ages* by Helen Gardner, Fifth Edition, edited by Horst de la Croix and Richard G. Tansey, © 1970 by Harcourt Brace Jovanovich, Inc. and reproduced with their permission

Verona and later went to Venice, where his architecture shows a clear awareness of Giulio Romano's Mantuan experiments. Another prominent architect in Venice was the Florentine sculptor Jacopo Sansovino, who also had fled to the north from Rome after the sack. Sansovino's architecture, as represented by the Loggetta (1537–40) at the foot of St. Mark's campanile or by the Old Library of St. Mark's (Libreria Vecchia [1536–88]), is rich in surface decorative qualities. The library has two stories of arcades; it has no basement but merely three low steps, so as to match the Gothic Palazzo Ducale opposite it. The upper entablature is extremely heavy, equaling half the height of the Ionic columns on which it rests. The rich application of relief sculpture with no unadorned wall surfaces creates this decorative quality, which has only superficial affinities with Florentine Mannerism.

This period of free and decorative Mannerism was followed by a more restrained classical architecture seen to perfection in the work of one of the greatest architects of the Renaissance, Andrea Palladio. The city of Vicenza, not far from Venice, was almost completely rebuilt with edifices after his design, including the basilica or town hall (1549) and the Loggia del Capitaniato (1571), as well as many private palaces. In the varied design of these buildings and in numerous villas in the Venetian mainland around Vicenza, Palladio brilliantly demonstrated the versatility of a range of neo-antique formulas. The Villa Capra or Rotonda (1550–51; with later changes) is magnificent in its simplicity and massing. In the centre of a cubelike block (typical of most Palladian villas) is a circular hall, and on all four sides are projecting classical temple fronts as porticoes, resulting in an absolute classical symmetry in the plan. In Venice, Palladio built several churches, all with the Latin-cross plan and rather similar facades (Figure 61). San Giorgio Maggiore (1566–1610) has a Roman temple front, on four giant half columns, applied to the centre of the facade; abutting the sides are two half temple fronts with smaller coupled pilasters. The resulting composition suggests the interpenetration of two complete temple fronts in a Mannerist way, since the elements of the composition are less independent than they would be in High Renaissance architecture (Figure 62). Also typical of Mannerism is the way in which the interior space, instead of being classically confined, is permitted to escape through a colonnaded screen behind the sanctuary into a large choir at the rear. Palladio's greatest fame rests on his treatise *I quattro libri dell'architettura* (1570; *Four Books on Architecture*).

Palladio's classical Mannerism

The most important architect of this period in Rome is Giacomo da Vignola, who wrote a treatise, *Regola delli cinque ordini d'architettura* (1562; "Rule of the Five Orders of Architecture"), devoted solely to a consideration of the architectural orders and their proportions. Like Palladio's book, Vignola's *Regola* became a textbook for later classical architecture.

Of his many buildings the project for the church of Il Gesù (1568) at Rome, the central church of the Jesuit Order, was very influential on the later history of architecture (Figure 63). The plan is a Latin cross with side chapels flanking the nave, but the eastern end is a central plan, capped by a dome. Il Gesù's plan was imitated throughout Europe, but especially in Italy, during the early Baroque period of the 17th century. Vignola built the church except for its facade, which was executed by Giacomo della Porta. Della Porta, inspired by Vignola's original design,

Influence of Il Gesù

By courtesy of the Metropolitan Museum of Art, New York City, Harris Brisbane Dick Fund, 1941

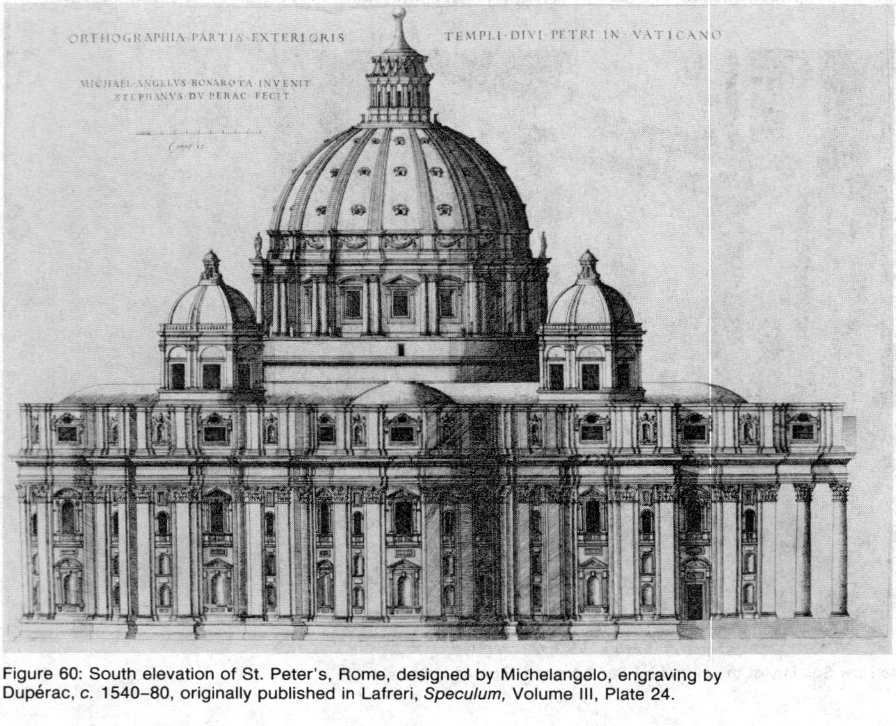

Figure 60: South elevation of St. Peter's, Rome, designed by Michelangelo, engraving by Dupérac, *c.* 1540–80, originally published in Lafreri, *Speculum,* Volume III, Plate 24.

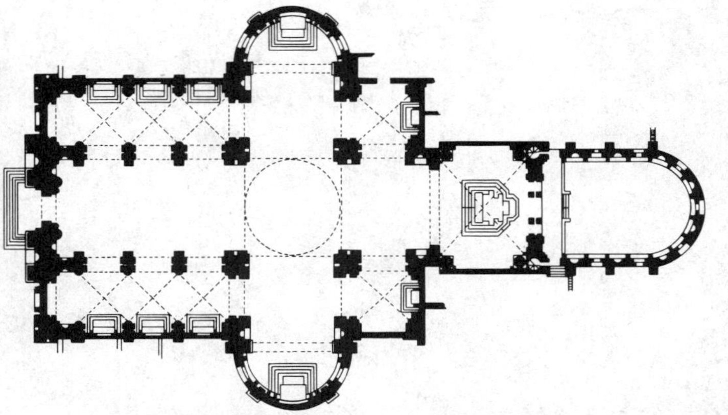

Figure 61: Plan of San Giorgio Maggiore, Venice, designed 1565, by Andrea Palladio.

From H.W. Janson, *Key Monuments of the History of Art*

created a facade concentrated toward its centre, which, like the plan, was the prototype for most early Baroque facades of the late 16th and 17th century.

(D.R.C./M.J.Ke./D.J.Wa.)

THE RENAISSANCE OUTSIDE ITALY

France. The Renaissance style of architecture appeared in France at the very end of the 15th century and flourished until the end of the 16th century. As in other northern European countries and in the Iberian Peninsula, the new Renaissance manner did not completely supplant the older Gothic style, which survived in many parts of France throughout the 16th century. French Renaissance architecture is divided into two periods: the early Renaissance, from the end of the 15th century until about 1530, and Mannerism, dating from about 1530 to the end of the 16th century.

Early Renaissance. The many invasions of Italy from 1494 until 1525 by French armies acquainted the French kings and nobles with the charms of Renaissance art. During the reigns of Louis XII and Francis I, the French possessed the city of Milan for the first 25 years of the 16th century. It was in Lombardy, therefore, that contact was made between French art and the Renaissance, and it was the Lombard Renaissance style that appeared in France during its early Renaissance.

The new style had a certain prestige since it was imported by the nobility and aristocracy, while the middle-class burghers continued to support their native Gothic style. This social difference also applied to the artists themselves. The French aristocracy imported Italian architects and artists who had been influenced by the Italian Renaissance, in which artists were considered to have a higher social standing than artisans. The French builders and craftsmen who executed the designs of the Italians still belonged to the social level of medieval artisans. This created a friction between the two groups, which was furthered by French resentment of imported foreign artists.

Social aspects of the French Renaissance style

With the exception of a few brief outcroppings of classicism in such centres as Marseille and Gaillon, French early Renaissance architecture was centred in the Loire Valley since the capital of France was at nearby Tours during the reign of Louis XII and the early part of the reign of Francis I. Most of the new architecture was secular, such as the château, which was an offshoot of the medieval feudal castle combined with the idea of an Italian villa. A characteristic example is the château at Blois, where two wings in the early Renaissance manner replaced parts of the 13th-century château. The first wing, erected (1498–1503) for Louis XII, is almost completely in the late Gothic Flamboyant style, with high roofs, an asymmetrical elevation, and pointed, depressed, and ogee arches. The only hint of the Renaissance is the occasional use of a bit of classical decoration, such as egg and dart molding, mingled with the Gothic. The second wing, built (1515–24) by Francis I, is more nearly in the Renaissance style. The structure remained Gothic with a high roof and dormers and the irregular spacing of the vertical windows, but all the ornament was in the classical mode, although its handling was often non-classical. Classical pilasters were used to divide the elevation into bays, but there is no consistency in the proportions of the pilasters. The most notable feature of the interior elevation of the wing of Francis I is a great octagonal open staircase, five sides of which project into the court. Within is a spiral staircase set on a continuous tunnel vault that is supported by radiating piers. On the surface of the piers are panels in low relief of arabesque decoration, of a type that is found often in Lombard Renaissance architecture. The richness of the Lombard style blends very well with Flamboyant Gothic, which had always been characterized by intricate and rich decoration. The exterior elevation of the wing of Francis I consists of a series of open loggias—the two lower ones arched, the upper one with a straight entablature—reminiscent of the famous series of loggias just completed by Bramante and Raphael at the Vatican Palace in Rome. Yet the Italian High Renaissance concept was expressed in France in early Renaissance terms with squat pilasters, irregularly spaced bays, and somewhat depressed arches.

By courtesy of the Giorgio Cini Foundation, Venice

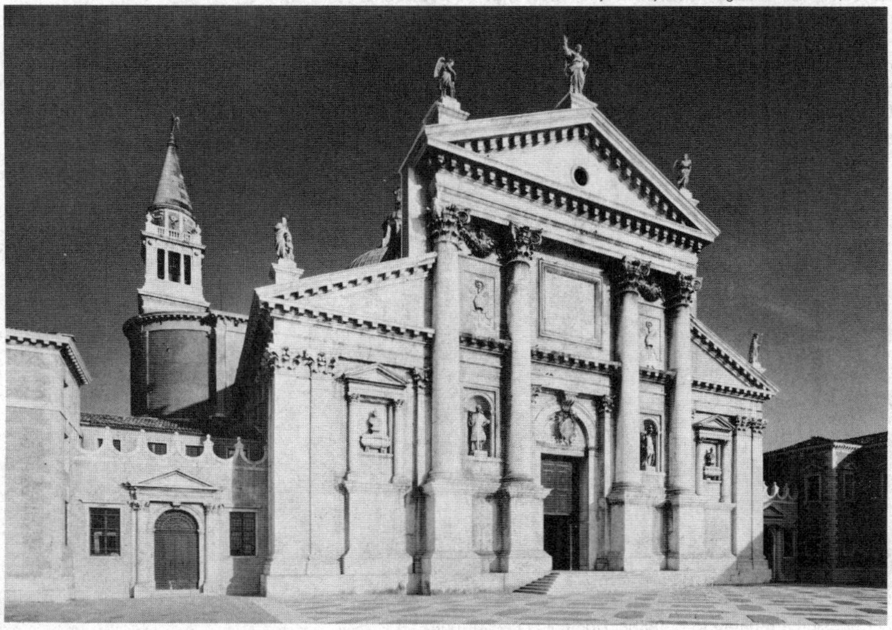

Figure 62: San Giorgio Maggiore, Venice, by Andrea Palladio, 1566–1610.

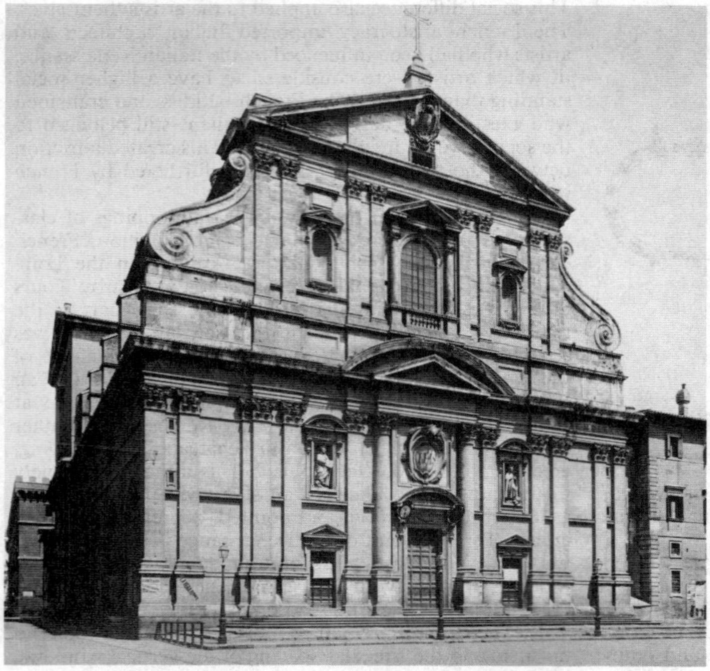

Figure 63: Facade of the church of Il Gesù, Rome, designed by Giacomo della Porta and Giacomo da Vignola, c. 1568–84.

Anderson—Alinari from Art Resource/EB Inc.

The finest example of the early Renaissance style is the château, or hunting lodge, erected between 1519 and 1547 for Francis I at Chambord (Figure 64). The Italian architect Bernabei Domenico da Cortona presumably made the basic model for the château, but the designs of Italian architects were usually executed by French builders (in this case Pierre Nepveu), often with many changes. Chambord is a tremendous structure, about 500 feet wide, with a plan showing the gradual breakdown of the old castle plan. There is a rectangular court surrounded by walls with round towers at the corners, but on three sides of the court there are only low walls serving as screens. The old donjon, or massive chief tower of medieval castles, developed into the château proper as a blocklike building with round towers at each corner. The flat passageways over the screen walls and on top of the central block were intended to form galleries from which the ladies of the court could observe the hunt. The plan of the main block of the château reveals Italian influence in its symmetrical organization on cross axes with a double spiral staircase at the centre. In the four corners left by the cross axes are four identical apartments, each of which consists of three basic rooms (chamber, antechamber, and cabinet); this form of apartment was from then on the favourite unit of French domestic planning.

Chambord

Typically for this period, the silhouette and structure remained Gothic in elevation with strip windows, a multiplicity of elements, and a general vertical expression. Ornament, however, is in the classical vocabulary of pilasters, round arches, and at times a geometric decoration consisting of slate panels set in the cream-coloured stone.

Mannerism. From about 1530, Francis I imported numerous Italian artists, such as Rosso Fiorentino (Giovanni Battista di Jacopo Rosso), Primaticcio, Serlio, Vignola, and Benvenuto Cellini. Most of these artists were followers of Michelangelo or Raphael, so that the new period of French architecture partook of Italian Mannerism. The style that resulted lasted until about 1590 and is sometimes known as the style of Henry II, although it actually was produced under five different kings, beginning late in the reign of Francis I.

Italian influence at Fontainebleau

The full influence of the new Italian style can best be seen in the château at Fontainebleau. In 1528 Francis I began to make revisions and additions to this medieval château, the exterior architecture being carried out by French builders under Gilles Le Breton. The Italian

Archives Photographiques, Paris

Figure 64: Château at Chambord, Fr., design attributed to Bernabei Domenico da Cortona, executed by Pierre Nepveu, 1519–47.

painter Rosso Fiorentino was placed in charge of the interior decoration of the Gallery of Francis I (*c.* 1533–45). The gallery is a long, narrow room covered by a wooden ceiling. On each side of the room is a high dado (*i.e.*, the lower section of a wall) of carved walnut with rich decoration above of stucco relief sculpture and painting. As Rosso was a Mannerist painter, France went directly from the early Renaissance style of the Loire châteaus to Mannerism. Rosso, who died in 1540, was succeeded by another Italian, Primaticcio, who decorated the ballroom, or gallery (1548–56), of Henry II and added the wing called the Aile de la Belle Cheminée (1568).

The most important Italian architect to build in France was Serlio, who arrived in 1541 to take Rosso's place as court architect. Serlio prepared plans for the rebuilding of the royal palace of the Louvre at Paris, but his ideas seem to have been too grandiose for Francis I. He did manage to build two châteaus, the casino of the Cardinal of Ferrara at Fontainebleau (1544–46), now destroyed, and the château of Ancy-le-Franc (begun 1546) in Burgundy. Serlio devoted most of his time to an architectural treatise that he had begun in Italy. Various books of the treatise were published during his lifetime from 1537 on, but the collected work was published after his death with the title *Tutte l'opere d'architettura, et prospetiva* (1619; "Complete Works of Architecture and Perspective"). It was influential in spreading the Renaissance style in France, England, and the Low Countries.

The influx of Italian artists soon compelled the French architects to adopt Renaissance principles of design as well as Renaissance ornamental details. Many French architects began to study the theory of design and often went to Italy as the source of the Renaissance style.

Rebuilding of the Louvre

After Serlio's failure with the palace of the Louvre in Paris, a French gentleman of the court, Pierre Lescot, was ordered to design and build a Renaissance palace to replace the medieval castle. Lescot, in collaboration with the sculptor Jean Goujon, designed a palace set around a square court about 175 feet wide. Only two sides, the west and south, of Lescot's court were built (1546–51). The execution and amplification of this design extended to the middle of the 19th century. The small section carried out under Lescot, the Gallery of Francis I, reveals a thorough understanding of the principles of Italian design but is expressed in French terms. The classical elements are used as low-relief surface decoration with little emphasis on mass (Figure 65).

The two leading architects of the second half of the 16th century, Philibert Delorme and Jean Bullant, studied in Rome. Delorme was trained as a builder before going to Rome and, therefore, was always interested in the constructive side of architecture as well as in the theory of design. About 1547 Delorme was commissioned by the mistress of Henry II, Diane de Poitiers, to design her château at Anet. The original château (about 1547–52) formed three sides of a court closed at the front by a screen wall and entrance gateway. Much of the château has been destroyed; only the left wing of the house, the screen wall, and the chapel that formed part of the right wing survive. The entrance gateway, which originally contained Cellini's bronze relief of Diana (now in the Louvre), is very Mannerist with a complicated superstructure, a semicircular arch with raised bands cutting across the moldings, and, at the top, a bronze group of a stag that strikes the hour with its hoof as the accompanying hounds bay mechanically. The chapel at Anet has a centralized Greek-cross plan with a large circle capped by a dome at the crossing. The exterior of the chapel is Mannerist, with the windows cutting through the entablature and half pediments abutting the main block. Delorme commenced in 1564 a large palace called the Tuileries, since it was situated on the site of tileworks in front of the Louvre. Again, elements of Mannerism were visible. On the first story Delorme used his own so-called French order, consisting of Ionic half columns and pilasters with decorative bands across the shafts, but this order was actually an Italian Mannerist treatment of the classical order.

Delorme's French order

Bullant's architecture was rather like that of Vignola in that it was very classical in details but often Mannerist in relationships. His early and best-preserved works were for Anne, duc de Montmorency and constable of France: part of the Château d'Ecouen (about 1555) and the chatelet (about 1560) at the Château de Chantilly. The architect Jacques Androuet du Cerceau the Elder prepared a two-volume set of engravings, *Les plus excellents bastiments de France* (1576–79), which depict the new Renaissance 16th-century buildings of France, many of which have been destroyed or drastically altered. The Mannerist style died out in the early 17th century as slight hints of the Baroque style blended with a renewed classicism to form gradually the Academic style prevalent in the 17th century.

Spain and Spanish America. Italian Renaissance decorative elements first appeared in Spanish architecture at about the time of the unification of Spain and the expulsion of the Moors in 1492. There were three phases of Spanish Renaissance architecture: (1) the early Renaissance, or Plateresque, from the late 15th century until about 1560; (2) a brief classical period, coexistent with the

Giraudon—Art Resource/EB Inc.

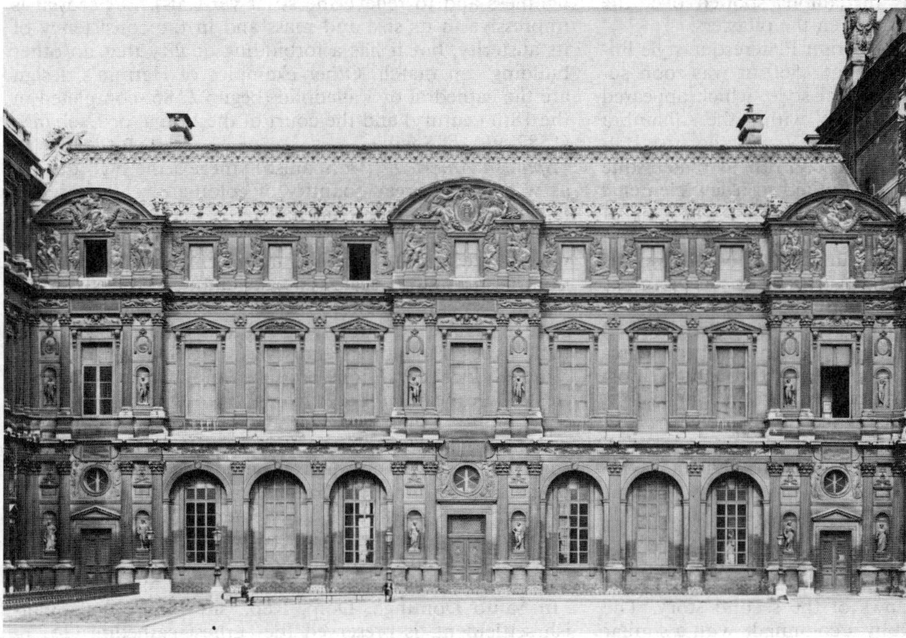

Figure 65: Square court of the Louvre, Paris, by Pierre Lescot, 1546–51.

Plateresque from about 1525 to 1560; and (3) the Herreran style from 1560 until the end of the 16th century.

Plateresque. The earliest phase of Renaissance architecture in Spain is usually called the Plateresque (from *platero,* "silversmith") because its rich ornament resembles silversmith's work. There has always been a long tradition in Spain of elaborate decoration, explained in part as an influence from Moorish art. The Moors possessed almost all of Spain during the Middle Ages and left this decorative heritage to the Spaniards. During the early 16th century, minor northern Italian sculptors and artisans, particularly from Lombardy and Genoa, were imported into Spain to execute tombs and altars for the Spanish nobles and ecclesiastics. These artisans introduced the northern Italian Renaissance vocabulary of classical decoration, such as the pilaster paneled with arabesques or the candelabrum shaft. Spanish architects picked up these elements and applied them to their buildings.

Tradition of elaborate ornamentation

The Renaissance Plateresque style is purely one of architectural ornament. There was no change in structure; heavy walls were used with either Gothic ribbed vaults or intricately carved wooden ceilings (*artesando*) that indicated Moorish influence. Many of the elements of decoration also preserved the influence of Gothic and Moorish art, such as the Flamboyant Gothic pinnacle and pierced balustrade or coats of arms and bits of heraldry used as ornamental motifs. Richly coloured tiles created decorative patterns on the walls as in Moorish art. The richness of the classical decoration imported from northern Italy blended effectively with the elements of the Moorish and Flamboyant Gothic styles to form the new Plateresque style. The luxuriance of its ornament was a fitting expression of the splendour-loving culture that Spain developed as the wealth of the Americas began to pour in during the early 16th century.

In most cases the new Plateresque decoration was confined to rich spots or panels of ornament around the portals and windows of the buildings. These ornamental areas were relieved by large expanses of bare wall, as in the facade of the Royal Hospital at Santiago de Compostela (1501–11) by Enrique de Egas or his Santa Cruz Hospital at Toledo (1504–14).

The greatest centre of the Plateresque style was the town of Salamanca, with buildings such as the university (about 1516–29) and the Monterey Palace (1539). Perhaps the most outstanding example of the style is the Ayuntamiento, or town hall, of Seville (begun 1527) by Diego de Riaño, with Lombard paneled pilasters on the ground floor and half columns completely covered with relief sculpture on the second floor. Also in the Lombard manner are the numerous medallions spotted over the wall under the windows or between the pilasters.

Classical. Although the exuberant Plateresque style lingered in some regions until about 1560, it was soon superseded by a much more classical style, which appeared in 1526 in the Palace of Charles V within the Alhambra at Granada. The Palace of Charles V was the first Italian classical building in Spain, in contrast to Plateresque buildings whose classicism was limited to a few elements of Italian Renaissance decoration. Charles V, as king of Spain and Holy Roman emperor, was the most powerful political figure in Europe, dominating Italy, as well as Spain, the Low Countries, and Austria. His palace in the Alhambra reflected the increasing contact with Italy. Designed by the Spaniard Pedro Machuca, who had studied in Italy, the Palace of Charles V has never been completed, although work on it continued throughout most of the 16th century. The palace is square in plan with a huge central circular court (100 feet in diameter), which was intended for bullfights and tournaments. The plan is, therefore, fully Renaissance, being centralized and symmetrical; it is organized on cross-axes formed by the four entrances, one in the centre of each side. The facade shows a full understanding of the principles of Italian Renaissance design in its superimposition of orders and in the alternating rhythm of the triangular and segmental pediments above the windows of the second story. The interior court is surrounded by a colonnade with a similar superimposition of Doric and Ionic.

The Palace of Charles V

Herreran. The classicism of the Palace of Charles V was succeeded by an extremely austere and cold style named after the greatest Spanish architect of the 16th century, Juan de Herrera. Perhaps more important than the architect was the social and cultural atmosphere in which the Herreran style developed, from about 1560 to the end of the 16th century. Charles V had been a true Renaissance prince; his only son, Philip II, who came to the throne in 1556, was one of the most typical representatives of the age of Mannerism as it was manifested in Spain. Philip II was morbid and melancholic, a religious fanatic against whose strict rule the Low Countries soon rose in revolt, beginning the difficulties that gradually dispelled Spanish political and cultural power in Europe.

El Escorial

The finest example of the Herreran style illustrates clearly the change in cultural atmosphere under Philip II. This is the palace-monastery of El Escorial (1563–84), which Philip II had built as a retreat outside Madrid. It is a great contrast to the worldly Palace of Charles V with its tournament court set in the luxurious, sensuous Alhambra. El Escorial was more than a royal palace, as it also contained provisions for a monastery and college. A city in itself, El Escorial was planned as a tremendous rectangle (675 by 525 feet), with a large church at the centre.

El Escorial was begun by the architect Juan Bautista de Toledo, who may be responsible for the planning, but the execution and architectural style were that of his assistant and successor, Herrera. Philip II himself reviewed the drawings for the palace, removing anything ornamental or ostentatious. On the exterior the architecture is very simple, a plain wall with a monotonous series of unadorned windows expressing the general monastic character of the whole. The only segment of the classical Renaissance style on the exterior is at the central portal with two stories of giant Doric half columns supporting a triangular pediment. The church, at the centre of the complex, has two bell towers and a great dome set on a drum, which surmount the whole. The austerity is enhanced by the cold, gray granite of which El Escorial was built (Figure 66, left). On the interior a similar severity of manner is indicated by the lack of decoration. Except for the classical Doric order, which is the least ornamental of the orders, there is no architectural decoration. Plain arches of stone were used under the vaults without any coffering. Occasional raised panels on the wall surface suggest where Plateresque ornament would normally be located, but instead of relief sculpture, there are only starkly smooth panels (Figure 66, right). Even the Doric order was handled severely; the pilasters on the interior show no entasis (*i.e.,* an upward taper of the width of the pilaster to give a sense of lightness and to relieve the strict verticals). El Escorial is impressive in its size and mass and in the consistency of its austerity, but it has a forbidding quality that no other building can match. Other examples of Herrera's design are the cathedral of Valladolid (begun 1585, completed in the 18th century) and the court of the Lonja, or Exchange (1582–99), of Seville. (D.R.C./D.J.Wa.)

Spanish America. In Spanish America the high quality as well as the great quantity of colonial architecture establish it as a major contribution of the New World to civilization. The zeal and power of the Spanish church were abetted by the wealth of the colonies in the construction of sumptuous ecclesiastical buildings. Skilled Indian labour also contributed to the early development of large-scale programs in both religious and domestic architecture. Types of buildings and styles were Spanish in origin, although local conditions produced modifications. In centres of European culture, such as Santo Domingo, Mexico City, Quito, Lima, and Cuzco, architectural styles were contemporary with those in Spain. Medieval traditions survived, however, especially in monastic structures; even in the 17th century, late Gothic ribs persisted in the vaults of churches. Spanish-Moorish elements (Mudéjar), such as wooden ceilings in geometric patterns, coloured tiles, the rectangular frame of an arch (*alfiz*), and the trefoil arch, were popular throughout Spanish-American architecture.

In Santo Domingo, Dom. Rep., site of the first Spanish settlement, is preserved the earliest cathedral (1523–37), which has a superb Renaissance facade and a Gothic

Figure 66: El Escorial, near Madrid, by Juan de Herrera, 1563–84. (Left) Exterior; (right) interior.
Archivo Mas, Barcelona

interior. In Mexico large building campaigns (*c.* 1550–1600) were carried out by Franciscan, Augustinian, and Dominican friars. Their monasteries generally have a huge vaulted church, cloister, and monastic buildings, all based upon Spanish prototypes. The large atrium yard and the open chapel (*capilla abierta*) for outdoor religious services are special features developed in America to accommodate crowds of Indians, as at Acolman, Cuernavaca, and Huejotzingo. Portals display a wide variety of styles, including medieval and Renaissance elements and occasional Indian influences. The largest Mexican cathedrals, those of Mexico City (begun 1563) and Puebla (1575–1690), have the rectangular basilican plan and other features of the Andalusian Renaissance.

Important early monuments of Peru were destroyed by earthquakes; the surviving structures, of modest character, are found in Ayacucho, on the shores of Lake Titicaca, and in Sucre, Bol. Vaulted churches were virtually unknown in South America until the 17th century. In Quito, Ecuador, the Franciscan and Dominican monasteries are notable for their cloisters and Mudéjar ceilings, and the cathedral (1562–72) is an example of Andalusian Gothic-Mudéjar construction. (H.E.W.)

Portugal. The architecture of Portugal tends to parallel the development of Spanish architecture. The Manueline style of the late 15th and early 16th centuries, like the Plateresque of Spain, is a very decorative mode in which small motifs of classical ornament are introduced into a local late Gothic style. After the middle of the 16th century, a fully Italianate classical style is visible in the architecture of Diogo de Torralva. His cloister in the Cristo Monastery (1557–62) at Tomar is composed of the rhythmic bay of alternating arches and coupled Classical orders made popular by Bramante in Italy. The full projection of the superimposed Doric and Ionic columns suggests the stolidity of the Italian High Renaissance. During the last two decades of the century the work of the Bolognese architect Filippo Terzi presents that austere planarity, seen in the church of São Vincente de Flora, Lisbon (1582–1605), reminiscent of Herrera.

Germany. The burgeoning of Italian Renaissance architectural forms in Germany was even slower than in other northern European countries. Only by the middle of the 16th century was the Renaissance style manifestly important, generally in those regions in closest contact with Italy, such as southern Germany or the trade route along the Rhine River leading from the south to the Low Countries. The style lingered in Germany until about the middle of the 17th century. The few hints of classicism in Germany prior to the mid-16th century can be considered the early Renaissance phase. They were limited to minor architectural monuments, such as the Fugger Chapel in St. Anne's Church at Augsburg (1509–18), which was the first Renaissance building in Germany, or they consisted of bits of Renaissance decoration attached to Gothic structures. An example of the latter is Hartenfels Castle (*c.* 1532–44) at Torgau by Konrad Krebs, which is completely medieval in design but has occasional fragments of classical ornament applied to the surface. The rear portion of the Residence (*c.* 1537–43) at Landshut is exceptional in that its architecture and decoration are fully Italianate, but this is explained by the visit in 1536 of Duke Ludwig X of Munich to Mantua, where Giulio Romano had just completed the Palazzo del Te.

Use of Italian Mannerist ornamentation

After 1550 Renaissance style architecture in Germany often had Mannerist details derived from Italian ornamental engravings. German architecture of this period was abundant with medallions, herms (*i.e.,* architectural elements topped by human busts), and caryatids and atlantes (*i.e.,* human figures used as columns or pilasters). The German treatise on the five orders by Wendel Dietterlin, entitled *Architectura* (1598), is filled with such Mannerist ornament. An architectural example is the Otto-Heinrichsbau added to the Gothic castle at Heidelberg (burned by the French in 1689). The three tall stories presented the usual verticality of northern architecture, but there was an understanding of the classical superimposition of the orders with Corinthian above Ionic. Nevertheless, there was a certain freedom in the treatment of the orders, for a Doric frieze was supported by the Ionic pilasters. From Italian Mannerism came the rustication of the lower order, the use of herms as window mullions, and the caryatids flanking the portal. Other examples of the German Renaissance are the porch of the Rathaus, or Town Hall (1569–73), at Cologne by the Dutchman Wilhelm Vernuiken (Figure 67) and the Friedrichsbau (1601–07), which was added to the castle at Heidelberg by Johannes Schoch.

Flanders and Holland. In the Low Countries, Flanders, because of trade and finance, was in close communication with Italy from the 15th century. As a result, there are slight hints of the Renaissance style in the Flemish architecture of the early 16th century, as in the palace of Margaret of Austria, now the Palais de Justice (1507–25), at Mechelen (Malines), completed by Rombout Keldermans.

The most important building of the Flemish Renaissance style was the Stadhuis, or Town Hall (1561–65), at Antwerp, designed by Loys du Foys and Nicolo Scarini and executed by Cornelis II Floris (originally de Vriendt [1514–75]). It was decided to replace Antwerp's small medieval town hall with a large structure, 300 feet long, in the new style, as a reflection of Antwerp's prosperity as the leading northern port of the 16th century. As with many northern buildings, there is a lack of monumentality, for its physical hugeness is not expressed in the details. There is a low basement with a rusticated arcade, which was originally used by traders during fairs. Above are two principal stories with superimposition of Doric and Ionic pilasters, between which large windows almost completely open each bay (Figure 68).

The advent of the Baroque style early in the 17th century replaced the Renaissance in Flanders much sooner than it did in Germany. Among the few examples of the 16th-century Renaissance style in Holland were the town hall (1597) at Leiden and the town hall (*c.* 1564) at The Hague.

England. The Renaissance style of architecture made a very timid appearance in England during the first half of the 16th century, and it was only from about 1550 that it became a positive style with local qualities. In fact, the Gothic style continued in many parts of England throughout most of the 16th century, and English Renaissance architecture was a very original fusion of the Tudor Gothic and classical styles. This style flourished until the early 17th century when Inigo Jones created a much more Italianate style that gradually replaced the English Renaissance style.

During the reign of Henry VIII (1509–47), some elements of Italian Renaissance decoration were imported by England through a few minor Italian artists, such as Pietro Torrigiani, who executed the tomb (1512–18) of Henry VII in Westminster Abbey. At the great palace of Hampton Court, begun by Cardinal Wolsey in 1515 and continued by Henry VIII until 1540, a few bits of Italian Renaissance decoration have been added, although the structure is completely in the Tudor manner. On the gateways are several terra-cotta medallions by the Italian Giovanni da Maiano, and there is a symmetry and regularity in the plan of the palace that hints of the Renaissance.

The Renaissance style really begins in England in the middle of the 16th century in architecture built for the circle of the Lord Protector Somerset, who served as regent after Henry VIII's death. During the 16th century the patron played a much greater role in the development of English Renaissance architecture than did the architect; there were almost no professional architects who were trained as the Italians were in the theory of design and building. Most of the building was executed by mason or carpenter designers. A typical example of the role of the patron in introducing the Renaissance style of England is to be found in the quadrangle that John Caius added to Gonville Hall (now Gonville and Caius) at Cambridge. Caius had spent a long time in Italy as well as elsewhere in Europe. The architecture of the new court was basically Tudor Gothic, but Caius planned three gateways in connection with the court, two of which were in the Italian style. The three gates were to mark the progress of the student through the university. At the entrance was the Gate of Humility (1565), a modest doorway, now in the Master's garden. The Gate of Virtue (after 1565), opening into the new quadrangle, is a fine classical portal with Ionic pilasters, but with a Tudor Gothic many-centred arch for the opening. Finally, the Gate of Honour (1573) is a separate tiny triumphal arch leading out toward the schools for the final disputation and degree. Caius probably designed these gates with the aid of the Flemish 16th-century architect Theodore de Have.

Role of patrons in the creation of the English Renaissance style

There was little religious architecture created in England during the 16th century, in part because of the break of Henry VIII with Rome. It is in the great country houses of the nobility that the Renaissance style is visible. Sir John Thynne, steward to the Lord Protector Somerset, designed several notable examples. The finest of these was his own house, Longleat (1568–*c.* 1580), on which he had the assistance of the mason Robert Smythson, who was to be the leading architect of the late 16th century. Except for the symmetry of the plan, arranged around two courts, there was little new in planning at Longleat, for the Tudor house was usually organized about a court. The typical English great hall at Longleat was an element derived from the hall of the medieval castle and retained in English architecture through the 16th century. The main entrance of the house opens directly into one end of the great hall, but a low screen at the end of the hall, topped by a musicians' gallery, forms a passageway. In elevation Longleat is a long, horizontal building with a wealth of windows; it is one of the most open secular buildings in Europe of the 16th century. There is a rectangular quality about the

Foto Marburg—Art Resource/EB Inc.

Figure 67: Porch of the Rathaus (Town Hall), Cologne, by Wilhelm Vernuiken, 1569–73.

Figure 68: Stadhuis (Town Hall), Antwerp, designed by Loys du Foys and Nicolo Scarini and executed by Cornelis II Floris, 1561–65.
Fotowerken Frans Claes, Antwerp, © Sabam-Brussels

whole exterior that is characteristic of English architecture; it is augmented by the repeated use of the bay window unit. There are now three stories on the exterior, with the correct classical superimposition of the Doric order on the ground floor and Ionic and Corinthian orders above, but the third story was probably added after Thynne's death, replacing a pitched roof and dormers (Figure 69, right).

Wollaton Hall

Robert Smythson, who aided Thynne at Longleat, later designed and built several notable houses, the finest being Wollaton Hall (1580–88) near Nottingham. Wollaton has a magnificent site on a small hill overlooking a large park. The plan of the house is a square with four square corner towers, resembling a plan in the treatise on architecture by Serlio, whose book was influential in English Renaissance architecture. The great hall is in the centre of the square; it rises an extra story above the whole building. The house has a low basement story that contained the kitchens and service rooms; it is one of the first buildings to use this arrangement, which became common in the history of later English and American architecture. On the exterior the massing is that of a rectangular block the rectilinear quality of which is further emphasized by the numerous many-mullioned rectangular windows (Figure 69, left). The decoration is completely classical, with superimposed pilasters, round-arched niches, and classical balustrades, but it shows touches of Italian Mannerism, which came into England primarily from Flanders. The pilasters and half columns have raised bands across their middles, and the gables crowning the corner towers are decorated with Flemish strapwork (*i.e.,* bands raised in relief assuming curvilinear forms suggestive of leather straps). Other examples of this style are Hardwick Hall (1590–97) in Derbyshire, probably by Smythson; Kirby Hall (about 1570–78) in Northamptonshire, perhaps by the mason Thomas Thorpe; and Montacute House (1588–1601) in Somerset.

Eastern Europe. Because of the unstable political situation in eastern Europe, the appearance there of the Renaissance style of architecture is very sporadic and usually closely dependent upon the ruling personalities. The election in 1458 of Matthias Corvinus as king of Hungary marks the first serious interest in this region in the new architectural style. Matthias had translations prepared of the contemporary Italian architectural treatises of Filarete and Alberti and in 1467 invited to Hungary briefly the Bolognese architect and engineer Aristotele Fioravanti. The buildings designed for Matthias, such as his hunting lodge of Nyek, have been destroyed. The Bakócz Chapel (1507) erected by Cardinal Tamás Bakócz as his sepulchral chapel at the Cathedral of Esztergom is completely Italianate. Built on a Greek-cross plan surmounted by a dome, the chapel resembles late 15th-century Florentine chapels. Turkish occupation, however, soon delayed the adoption of the classical architectural style until the 18th century.

The patronage of Matthias Corvinus

In Russia during the reign of Ivan III the Great (1462–1505), as Tatar pressure lessened and Moscow gradually assumed importance, there was a brief interest in Western cultural developments. Thus, in 1475 Fioravanti, who had

A.F. Kersting

Figure 69: *Renaissance architecture in England.*
(Left) Wollaton Hall, near Nottingham, by Robert Smythson, 1580–88. (Right) Longleat, Wiltshire, probably designed by Sir John Thynne and Robert Smythson, 1568–*c.* 1580.

Figure 70: Letohrádek, or garden belvedere (summerhouse), Prague, 1538–63.
By courtesy of the Ministry of Culture, Prague; photograph, Vladimir Fyman

been in Hungary earlier, was brought to Moscow. Soon Tsar Ivan resolved to rebuild the Kremlin, most of which was still of wood. From 1485 to 1516 the Italian architects Antonio Solario and Marco Ruffo enclosed the Kremlin with brick walls and erected within them the Granovitaya Palace (1487–91). This was a two-story blocklike palace with a rusticated exterior, as its name (*granovitaya,* "faceted") indicates, in the manner of early Renaissance palaces of Bologna and Ferrara. Cultural contacts with the West then diminished under the impact of rising nationalism until the reign of Peter the Great in the early 18th century.

The Renaissance architectural style appears in Poland under the late Jagiellon dynasty, and especially in the reign of Sigismund I (1506–48), whose wife came from the Sforza family of Lombardy. The rebuilding of his Wawel Castle (1507–36) in Kraków was begun by the Italian Francesco della Lore and continued by Bartolommeo Berecci of Florence. It presents a blend of local Gothic and 15th-century Italian architecture. The great courtyard has three stories of loggias; the two lower ones, with semicircular arches on squat Ionic columns, suggest the new style, but the much taller upper story, with the steep roof supported by excessively slender posts, betrays a medieval wooden tradition. The mortuary chapel (1517–33) for Sigismund attached to the Wawel Cathedral in Kraków, also after the design of Berecci, represents one of the richest examples of the Italian Renaissance style in central Europe. Square in plan, each wall is divided by elaborately carved pilasters into a wide central bay for the tombs or altar, flanked by narrower bays with statue niches. Above, a coffered, semicircular dome rests on a drum with great circular windows. Unlike the other central European countries, in Poland Renaissance architecture continued to flourish throughout the remainder of the 16th century. In 1578 Jan Zamoyski, chancellor of Poland, commissioned the Venetian architect Bernardo Morando to design the fortified town of Zamość following the latest Italian ideas. The resultant town with street arcades resembles those of northern Italy.

Polish Renaissance buildings

The shift from the Gothic style to the Renaissance in Bohemia is visible in the architecture of the leading late 15th-century architect in Prague, Benedikt Ried. The interior of his Vladislav Hall, Prague (1493–1510), with its intertwining ribbon vaults, represents the climax of the late Gothic; but as the work on the exterior continued, the ornamental features of windows and portals are classical. Religious architecture continued in the Gothic mode, and most secular architecture was local in style with only a slight influence from the Italianate Renaissance. A few minor royal commissions were more classical, such as the Letohrádek (1538–63), or garden belvedere (summerhouse), at Prague for Queen Anne, wife of Ferdinand I, with its delicate exterior arcade (Figure 70). The nearby tennis court (1565–68), designed by Bonifaz Wolmut, is in a heavier classicism expressed by the alternation of engaged Ionic half columns with deeply recessed arched openings. Several castles or large houses like that at Opočno (1560–67) or of Bučovice (1566–87), designed by the Italian Pietro Ferrabosco, had spacious courtyards with arcades on classical columns. (D.R.C./D.J.Wa.)

The Renaissance style in Bohemia

Baroque and Rococo

Baroque and late Baroque, or Rococo, are loosely defined terms, applied by common consent to European art of the period from the early 17th century to the mid-18th century.

Baroque was at first an undisguised term of abuse, probably derived from the Italian word *barocco,* which was a term used by philosophers during the Middle Ages to describe an obstacle in schematic logic. Subsequently, this became a description for any contorted idea or involuted process of thought. Another possible source is the Portuguese word *barroco,* with its Spanish form *barrueco,* used to describe an irregular or imperfectly shaped pearl; this usage still survives in the jeweler's term baroque pearl.

Origin of the terms Baroque and Rococo

The derivation of the word Rococo is equally uncertain, though its source is most probably to be found in the French word *rocaille,* used to describe shell and pebble decorations in the 16th century. In the 18th century, however, the scope of the word was increased when it came to be used to describe the mainstream of French art of the first half of the century; Neoclassical artists used it as a derogatory term. Fundamentally a style of decoration, Rococo is much more a facet of late Baroque art than an autonomous style, and the relationship between the two presents interesting parallels to that between High Renaissance and Mannerist art. (P.C.-B./D.J.Wa.)

During the Baroque period (*c.* 1600–1750), architecture, painting, and sculpture were integrated into decorative ensembles. Architecture and sculpture became pictorial, and painting became illusionistic. Baroque art was essentially concerned with the dramatic and the illusory, with vivid colours, hidden light sources, luxurious materials, and elaborate, contrasting surface textures, used to heighten immediacy and sensual delight. Ceilings of Baroque churches, dissolved in painted scenes, presented vivid views of the infinite to the worshiper and directed him through his senses toward heavenly concerns. Sev-

The aesthetic of Baroque art

enteenth-century Baroque architects made architecture a means of propagating faith in the church and in the state. Baroque palaces expanded to command the infinite and to display the power and order of the state. Baroque space, with directionality, movement, and positive molding, contrasted markedly with the static, stable, and defined space of the High Renaissance and with the frustrating conflict of unbalanced spaces of the preceding Mannerist period. Baroque space invited participation and provided multiple changing views. Renaissance space was passive and invited contemplation of its precise symmetry. While a Renaissance statue was meant to be seen in the round, a Baroque statue either had a principal view with a preferred angle or was definitely enclosed by a niche or frame. A Renaissance building was to be seen equally from all sides, while a Baroque building had a main axis or viewpoint as well as subsidiary viewpoints. Attention was focused on the entrance axis or on the central pavilion, and its symmetry was emphasized by the central culmination. A Baroque building expanded in its effect to include the square facing it, and often the ensemble included all the buildings on the square as well as the approaching streets and the surrounding landscape. Baroque buildings dominated their environment; Renaissance buildings separated themselves from it.

The Baroque rapidly developed into two separate forms: the strongly Roman Catholic countries (Italy, Spain, Portugal, Flanders, Bohemia, southern Germany, Austria, and Poland) tended toward freer and more active architectural forms and surfaces; in Protestant regions (England, the Netherlands, and the remainder of northern Europe) architecture was more restrained and developed a sober, quiet monumentality impressive in its refinement. In the Protestant countries and France, which sought the spirit through the mind, architecture was more geometric, formal, and precise—an appeal to the intellect. In the Roman Catholic south, buildings were more complex, freer, and done with greater artistic license—an appeal to the spirit made through the senses.

Architectural treatises

Treatises on the orders and on civil and military architecture provided a theoretical basis for Baroque architects. While many 16th-century architects published treatises on architecture or prepared them for publication, major 17th-century architects published very little. Two fragmentary volumes by Francesco Borromini appeared years after his death, and Guarino Guarini's major contribution (though he brought out two volumes on architecture before he died) did not appear until well into the 18th century. Other Italian publications tended to be repetitions of earlier ideas with the exception of a tardily published manuscript of Teofilo Gallaccini, whose treatise on the errors of Mannerist and early Baroque architects became a point of departure for later theoreticians.

In France, François Blondel and Augustin d'Aviler published notes for lectures given at the Academy of Architecture, but the most important publications were those of Fréart de Chambray and Claude Perrault. Perrault attacked established Italian theory. Other notable French works included writings by René Ouvard, André Félibien, Pierre Le Muet, and Julien Mauclerc. In England, Sir Henry Wotton's book was an adaptation of Vitruvius, and Balthazar Gerbier's was a compendium of advice for builders. Among the notable 17th-century German publications were books by Georg Boeckler, Josef Furttenbach, and Joachim von Sandrart.

Definition of the Rococo style

During the period of the Enlightenment (about 1700 to 1780), various currents of post-Baroque art and architecture evolved. A principal current, generally known as Rococo, refined the robust architecture of the 17th century to suit elegant 18th-century tastes. Vivid colours were replaced by pastel shades; diffuse light flooded the building volume; and violent surface relief was replaced by smooth flowing masses with emphasis only at isolated points. Churches and palaces still exhibited an integration of the three arts, but the building structure was lightened to render interiors graceful and ethereal. Interior and exterior space retained none of the bravado and dominance of the Baroque but entertained and captured the imagination by intricacy and subtlety.

In Rococo architecture, decorative sculpture and painting are inseparable from the structure. Simple dramatic spatial sequences or the complex interweaving of spaces of 17th-century churches gave way to a new spatial concept. By progressively modifying the Renaissance-Baroque horizontal separation into discrete parts, Rococo architects obtained unified spaces, emphasized structural elements, created continuous decorative schemes, and reduced column sizes to a minimum. In churches, the ceilings of side aisles were raised to the height of the nave ceiling to unify the space from wall to wall (Church of the Carmine, Turin, Italy, 1732, by Filippo Juvarra; Pilgrimage Church, Steinhausen, near Biberach, Ger., 1728, by Dominikus Zimmermann; Saint-Jacques, Luneville, Fr., 1730, by Germain Boffrand). To obtain a vertical unification of structure and space, the vertical line of a supporting column might be carried up from the floor to the dome (*e.g.,* church of San Luis, Seville, Spain, begun 1699, by Leonardo de Figueroa). The entire building was often lighted by numerous windows placed to give dramatic effect (Schloss Brühl, near Cologne, Balthasar Neumann, 1740) or to flood the space with a cool diffuse light (Pilgrimage Church, Wies, Ger., Zimmermann, 1745).

Concept of Rococo space

ORIGINS AND DEVELOPMENT IN ROME

The work of Carlo Maderno in Rome represented the first pure statement of the principles that became the basis of most of the architecture of the Western world in the 17th century. A northern Italian, Maderno worked most of his life in Rome where, about 1597, he designed the revolutionary facade of the church of Santa Susanna (Figure 71). Roman church facades in the late 16th century tended to be either precise, elegant, and papery thin or disjointed, equivocal, and awkwardly massive. Maderno's Santa Susanna facade is an integrated design in which each element contributes to the central culminating feature. Precision and elegance were relinquished to gain vitality and movement. Disjointed and ambiguous features were suppressed to achieve unity and harmony. A towering massiveness obtained by an increased surface relief

Alinari—Art Resource/EB Inc.

Figure 71: Facade of Santa Susanna, Rome, by Carlo Maderno, *c.* 1597.

and quickened rhythm of architectural members toward the centre replaced the papery-thin walls and hesitant massiveness of the 16th century. Vertical unification was achieved by breaking the entablature at similar places on both stories and by repeating pilasters and columns at both levels. Maderno also conceived the facade as part of an integrated unit, including the two-story church and one-story associated areas to either side, and thereby gave form to the Baroque desire to associate buildings, street facades, and squares in a continuous whole.

Aesthetic principles of early Baroque architecture

The basic premises of the early Baroque as reaffirmed by Maderno in the facade and nave of St. Peter's, Rome (1607), were: (1) subordination of the parts to the whole to achieve unity and directionality; (2) progressive alteration of pilaster rhythm and wall relief to emphasize massiveness, movement, axiality, and activity; and (3) directional emphasis in interiors through diagonal views and culminating light and spatial sequences (Figure 72).

The three great masters of the Baroque in Rome were Gian Lorenzo Bernini, Francesco Borromini, and Pietro da Cortona. Bernini, also a brilliant sculptor, designed both the baldachin (an ornamental canopy-like structure) with bronze spiral columns over the grave of St. Peter (1624–33) and the vast enclosing colonnade (begun 1656) that forms the piazza of St Peter's. He was responsible also for the facade of the Palazzo Chigi-Odescalchi (1664), a model for later urban palaces, and the exquisite oval church of Sant'Andrea al Quirinale (1658–70), the epitome of richly coloured marble-encrusted church interiors.

In contrast to Bernini, Borromini preferred monochromatic interiors. The buildings of Borromini, who came from northern Italy, are characterized by their inventive transformations of the established vocabulary of space,

Robert Harding Picture Library

Figure 72: St. Peter's, Vatican City, Rome, by Carlo Maderno, 1607.

Figure 73: San Carlo alle Quattro Fontane, Rome, by Francesco Borromini, 1634–41.

Alinari—Art Resource/EB Inc.

light, and architectural elements in order to increase the content of their work. Borromini's works, composed of fluid and active concave and convex masses and surfaces (San Carlo alle Quattro Fontane, 1634–41; Figure 73), contain spaces that are intricate, geometrically derived irregular ovals, octagons, or hexagons (Sant'Ivo della Sapienza, 1642–60). His late palace facade for the College of the Propagation of the Faith (1646–67) was a bold and vigorous essay that became a major source for Rococo architects in the early years of the 18th century.

Pietro da Cortona's early design for the Villa del Pigneto, near Rome (before 1630), was derived from the ancient Roman temple complex at Palestrina, Italy, and decisively altered villa design; his San Luca e Santa Martina, Rome (1635), was the first church to exhibit fully developed high Baroque characteristics in which the movement toward plasticity, continuity, and dramatic emphasis, begun by Maderno, achieved fruition. Pietro's reworking of a small square in Rome to include his facade of Santa Maria della Pace (1656–59) as an almost theatrical element is a cogent example of the Baroque insistence on the participation of a work in its environment.

In the early years of the 18th century in Rome, parallel to the development of Rococo in France, renewed interest in the work of Borromini was shown by Alessandro Specchi in his Ripetta Gate (1704), and by Filippo Juvarra, a gifted, if unorthodox, pupil of Carlo Fontana, in his early architectural projects and scene designs. Italian Rococo developed out of this new interest in Borromini. In Rome the Rococo developed further with the so-called Spanish Steps (1723) by Francesco de Sanctis; the facade of Santa Maria della Quercia (begun 1727) and Piazza Sant'Ignazio (1727) by Filippo Raguzzini; and, in Piedmont, Santa Caterina, Casale Monferrato (1718) by Giovanni Battista Scapitta.

NATIONAL AND REGIONAL VARIATIONS

Italy. Architects in northern Italy, notably Guarino Guarini, Filippo Juvarra, and Bernardo Vittone, developed a Baroque style of great structural audacity. Guarini's San Lorenzo (1668–80) and Palazzo Carignano (1679), both in Turin, have swelling curvilinear forms, terra-cotta construction, exposed structural members, and intricate spatial compositions that show his relation to Borromini and also represent significant developments in the relationship between structure and light. Juvarra's Palazzo Madama, Turin (1718–21), has one of the most spectacular of all Baroque staircases, but the true heir to Guarini was Vittone. To increase the vertical effect and the unification of space in churches such as Santa Chiara, Brà (1742), Vittone raised the main arches, eliminated the drum, and designed a double dome in which one could look through spherical openings puncturing the inner dome and see the outer shell painted with images of saints and angels: a glimpse of heaven.

Emphasis on surface and decoration

Spain. Spanish Baroque was similar to Italian Baroque but with a greater emphasis on surface decorations. Alonso Cano, in his facade of the Granada cathedral (1667), and Eufrasio López de Rojas, with the facade of the cathedral of Jaén (1667), show Spain's absorption of the concepts of the Baroque at the same time that it maintained a local tradition. The greatest of the Spanish masters was José Benito Churriguera, whose work shows most fully the Spanish Baroque interest in surface texture and decorative detail (Figure 74). His lush ornamentation attracted many followers, and Spanish architecture of the late 17th century and early 18th century has been labeled Churrigueresque. Narciso and Diego Tomé, in the University of Valladolid (1715), and Pedro de Ribera, in the facade of the San Fernando Hospital (now the Municipal Museum) in Madrid (1722), proved themselves to be the chief inheritors of Churriguera.

The outstanding figure of 18th-century Spanish architecture was Ventura Rodríguez, who, in his designs for the Chapel of Our Lady of Pilar in the cathedral of Saragossa (1750), showed himself to be a master of the developed Rococo in its altered Spanish form; but it was a Fleming, Jaime Borty Miliá, who brought Rococo to Spain when he built the west front of the cathedral of Murcia in 1733.

Robert Frerck/Odyssey Productions

Figure 74: Facade of the church of San Esteban, Salamanca, by José Benito Churriguera, 1693.

Flanders. Roman Catholicism, political opposition to Spain, and the painter Peter Paul Rubens were all responsible for the astonishing full-bodied character of Flemish Baroque. Rubens' friends Jacques Francart and Pieter Huyssens created an influential northern centre for vigorous expansive Baroque architecture to which France, England, and Germany turned. Francart's Béguinage Church (1629) at Mechelen (Malines) and Huyssens' St. Charles Borromeo (1615) at Antwerp set the stage for the more fully developed Baroque at St. Michel (1650) at Louvain, by Willem Hesius, as well as at the Abbey of Averbode (1664), by Jan van den Eynde.

Holland. Seventeenth-century architecture in Holland, in contrast, is marked by sobriety and restraint. Pieter Post, noted for the Huis ten Bosch (1645) at The Hague and the Town Hall of Maastricht (*c.* 1658), and Jacob van Campen, who built the Amsterdam Old Town Hall (1648; now the Royal Palace), were the principal Dutch architects of the 17th century. After the middle of the century, Dutch architecture exerted influence on architecture in France and England. Dutch colonial architecture was especially evident in the 17th and 18th centuries in the Hudson River Valley of North America and the Dutch West Indies (notably Willemstad on the island of Curaçao).

France. Salomon de Brosse's Luxembourg Palace (1615) in Paris and Château de Blérancourt (1614), northeast of Paris between Coucy and Noyon, were the bases from which François Mansart and Louis Le Vau developed their succession of superb country houses.

Mansart and Le Vau

Mansart was the more accomplished of the two architects, and his Orléans wing of the Château de Blois (1635) in the Loire Valley and Maisons-Laffitte, near Paris (1642), are renowned for their high degree of refinement, subtlety, and elegance. Mansart's church of Val-de-Grâce (1645) in Paris and his designs for the Bourbon mausoleum (1665) established the full Baroque in France; it was a rich, subtle Baroque that was quiet in its strength and restrained in its vigour.

Le Vau was Mansart's only serious competitor, and in 1657, with his Château de Vaux-le-Vicomte, near Paris, he fired the imagination of Louis XIV and of his finance minister Jean-Baptiste Colbert. Vaux, though exhibiting certain Dutch influences, is noted for its integration of Le Vau's architecture with the decorative ensembles of the painter and designer Charles Le Brun and the garden designs of landscape architect André Le Nôtre. By serving as a model for Louis XIV's Palace of Versailles, the complex at Vaux was perhaps the most important mid-century European palace. Le Vau showed a sensitivity to Italian Baroque architecture that was unusual in a French architect, and his College of Four Nations (1662; now the Institute of France) in Paris owes much to the Roman churches of Santa Maria della Pace by Pietro da Cortona and Sant'Agnese in Agone (1652–55) in the Piazza Navona by Borromini and Carlo Rainaldi. Le Vau, Le Nôtre, and Le Brun began working at Versailles within a few years of their success at Vaux, but the major expansion of the palace did not occur until after the end of the Queen's War (1668). At Versailles, Le Vau showed his ability to deal with a building of imposing size. The simplicity of his forms and the rich, yet restrained, articulation of the garden facade mark Versailles as his most accomplished building. Le Nôtre's inventive disposition of ground, plant, and water forms created a wide range of vistas, terraces, gardens, and wooded areas that integrated palace and landscape into an environment emphasizing the delights of continuity and separation, of the infinite and the intimate. Upon Le Vau's death, Jules Hardouin-Mansart, grandnephew of François, succeeded him and proved himself equal to Louis XIV's desires by more than trebling the size of the palace (1678–1708). Versailles became the palatial ideal and model throughout Europe and the Americas until the end of the 18th century. A succession of grand palaces was built, including the following: Castle Howard and Blenheim Palace by Sir John Vanbrugh in England; the Residenz of Würzburg, Ger. (1719), by Neumann; the Zwinger in Dresden, Ger. (1711), by Matthäus Daniel Pöppelmann; the Belvedere, Vienna (1714), by Johann Lukas von Hildebrandt; the

Versailles as a model for Baroque palaces

Figure 75: Dôme des Invalides, Paris, by Jules Hardouin-Mansart, *c.* 1675.
Leo de Wys Inc./J. Messerschmidt

Royal Palace at Caserta, Italy (1752), by Luigi Vanvitelli; and the Royal Palace (National Palace) at Madrid (1736), by Giovanni Battista Sacchetti.

Hardouin-Mansart's Dôme des Invalides, Paris (*c.* 1675), is generally agreed to be the finest church of the last half of the 17th century in France (Figure 75). The correctness and precision of its form, the harmony and balance of its spaces, and the soaring vigour of its dome make it a landmark not only of the Paris skyline but also of European Baroque architecture.

After Nicolas Pineau returned to France from Russia, he, with Gilles-Marie Oppenordt and Juste-Aurèle Meissonier, with their increasing concern for asymmetry, created the full Rococo. Meissonier and Oppenordt should be noted too for their exquisite, imaginative architectural designs, unfortunately never built (*e.g.,* facade of Saint-Sulpice, Paris, 1726, by Meissonier).

Origins of the Rococo style

The early years of the 18th century saw the artistic centre of Europe shift from Rome to Paris. Pierre Lepautre, working under Hardouin-Mansart on the interiors of the Château de Marly (1679), invented new decorative ideas that became the Rococo. Lepautre changed the typical late 17th-century flat arabesque, which filled a geometrically constructed panel, to a linear pattern in relief, which was enclosed by a frame that determined its own shape. White- and gold-painted 17th-century interiors (the central salon of the palace at Versailles) were replaced by varnished natural-wood surfaces (Château de Meudon, Cabinet à la Capucine) or by painted pale greens, blues, and creams (Cabinet Vert, Versailles, 1735). The resulting delicate asymmetry in relief and elegant freedom revolutionized interior decoration and within a generation exerted a profound effect on architecture. Architects rejected the massive heavy relief of the Baroque in favour of a light and delicate, but still active, surface. Strong, active, and robust interior spaces gave way to intricate, elegant but restrained spatial sequences.

England. The late designs of Inigo Jones for Whitehall Palace (1638) and Queen's Chapel (1623) in London introduced English patrons to the prevailing architectural ideas of northern Italy in the late 16th century. Although he was influenced heavily by 16th-century architects such as Palladio, Serlio, and Vincenzo Scamozzi, Jones approached the Baroque spirit in his late works by unifying them with a refined compositional vigour. Sir Christopher Wren presented English Baroque in its characteristic restrained but intricate form in St. Stephen's, Walbrook, London (1672), with its multiple changing views and spatial and structural complexity. Wren's greatest achievement, St. Paul's Cathedral, London (1675–1711), owes much to French and Italian examples of the Baroque period; but the plan shows a remarkable adaptation of the traditional English cathedral plan to Baroque spatial uses (Figure 76). Wren is notable for his large building complexes (Hampton Court Palace, 1689, and Greenwich Hospital, 1696), which, in continuing the tradition of Inigo Jones, paved the way for the future successes of Sir John Vanbrugh. Vanbrugh's Castle Howard in Yorkshire (1699) and Blenheim Palace in Oxfordshire (1705) mark the culmination of the Baroque style in England.

Wren as a Baroque architect

Even in England, reflections of an interest in continuous curvilinear form inspired by Borromini and Bernini may be seen in isolated examples such as St. Philip, Birmingham (1710), by Thomas Archer.

Central Europe. A stable political situation in central Europe and the vision of Rudolf II in Prague in the late 16th and early 17th centuries created an intellectual climate that encouraged the adoption of new Baroque ideas. The Thirty Years' War and the defense against the encroachments of the expanding French and Ottoman

Perfecta Publications Ltd.; photograph, Sydney W. Newbery

Figure 76: West facade of St. Paul's Cathedral, London, by Sir Christopher Wren, 1675–1711.

Figure 77: Interior of the church of the Benedictine abbey at Ottobeuren, Ger., by Johann Michael Fischer, begun 1744.
Angelo Hornak

empires, however, absorbed all of the energies of central Europe. The fully developed Baroque style appeared in Germany, Austria, Bohemia, and Poland after 1680 but flourished only after the end of the debilitating War of the Spanish Succession (1714). In the late 17th and early 18th centuries, Germany and Austria turned for their models principally to Italy, where Guarini and Borromini exerted an influence on Johann Bernhard Fischer von Erlach and Johann Lucas von Hildebrandt. The third Austrian master, Jakob Prandtauer, on the other hand, came from a local stonemason tradition and worked primarily for monastic orders. Fischer von Erlach's University Church in Salzburg (1696) is particularly noteworthy and shows direct Italian inspiration, while the Karlskirche, Vienna (1715), demonstrates his original, mature phase. Hildebrandt's Belvedere palace in Vienna and Prandtauer's superbly sited Abbey of Melk overlooking the Danube (1702) are among their most notable works.

In Bohemia the developed, or high, Baroque was heralded by the work of a French architect, Jean-Baptiste Mathey, who carried both Roman and French ideas to Prague from Rome in 1675. The Bavarian Christoph Dientzenhofer, however, transformed architecture in Prague and Bohemia with his boldly conceived buildings in the high Baroque style (Prague, nave of St. Nicholas, 1703, and Břevnov, Benedictine church, 1708).

German and Austrian Rococo

The spectacular Rococo of central Europe, Germany, and Austria, which by 1720 had begun to influence Italian architecture, grew out of a fusion of Italian Baroque and French Rococo. Its chief monuments are to be found in the Roman Catholic regions. Johann Michael Fischer, Balthasar Neumann, the brothers Cosmas Damian and Egid Quirim Asam, and Dominikus Zimmermann were the most accomplished of the native architects, while the Frenchmen François de Cuvilliés, Philippe de La Guêpière, and Nicolas de Pigage made the most important foreign contributions to mid-century architecture in Germany.

Fischer's austere, dignified facade of the church at Diessen (1732) and his masterpiece of integrated painting, decorative stucco, sculpture, and architecture, the Benedictine abbey of Ottobeuren (1744), are landmarks of the Bavarian Rococo (Figure 77). Neumann's joyous, airy Rococo Pilgrimage Church at Vierzehnheiligen (1743) and his later, more restrained Benedictine abbey at Neresheim (1745) characterize the increasing influence of classicism in Germany. In the north, in Berlin, Georg Wenzeslaus von Knobelsdorff alternated between Rococo (Potsdam, Sanssouci, 1745) and neo-Palladian classicism (Berlin, Opera House, 1741). Two influential country houses, La Guêpière's Solitude, near Stuttgart (1763), and Cuvilliés's Amalienburg, Munich (1734), exquisitely graceful and refined, are examples of French influence in Württemberg and Bavaria. (H.A.M./D.J.Wa.)

Russia. The Baroque appeared in Russia toward the end of the 17th century. The Russians imaginatively transformed its modes into a clearly expressed national style that became known as the Naryshkin Baroque, a delightful example of which is the Church of the Intercession of the Virgin at Fili (1693) on the estate of Boyarin Naryshkin, whose name had become identified with this phase of the Russian Baroque.

Western Europeans brought the prevailing Baroque styles characteristic of their own countries, but the very different artistic and physical setting of St. Petersburg produced a new expression, embodying Russia's peculiar sense of form, scale, colour, and choice of materials. The transformed Baroque eventually spread all over Russia and,

K. Scholz/H. Armstrong Roberts, Inc.

Figure 78: Smolny Cathedral, Leningrad, by Bartolomeo Rastrelli, 1748–55.

with its vast register of variations, developed many regional idioms.

Russian Rococo in St. Petersburg

A French architect, Nicolas Pineau, went to Russia in 1716 and introduced the Rococo style to the newly founded city of St. Petersburg (*e.g.*, Peter's study in Peterhof, before 1721). The Rococo in Russia flourished in St. Petersburg under the protection of Peter I and Elizabeth. Peter's principal architect, Gaetano Chiaveri, who drew heavily on northern Italian models, is most noted for the library of the Academy of Sciences (1725) and the royal churches of Warsaw and Dresden. Bartolomeo Rastrelli was responsible for all large building projects under the reign of Elizabeth, and among his most accomplished designs in St. Petersburg (now Leningrad) are the Smolny Cathedral (Figure 78) and the turquoise and white Winter Palace. (A.Vo./H.A.M.)

Colonial architecture in the Americas. *North America.* The colonial architecture of the United States and Canada was as diverse as the peoples who settled there: English, Dutch, French, Swedish, Spanish, German, Scots-Irish. Each group carried with it the style and building customs of the mother country, adapting them as best it could to the materials and conditions of a new land. Thus, there were several colonial styles. The earliest buildings of all but the Spanish colonists were medieval in style: not the elaborate Gothic of the great European cathedrals and manor houses but the simple late Gothic of village houses and barns. These practical structures were well adapted to the pioneer conditions that prevailed in the colonies until about 1700, and few changes were needed to adapt them to the more severe climate. The styles were frank expressions of functional and structural requirements, with only an occasional bit of ornament. So far as is known, no single new structural technique or architectural form was invented in the North American colonies.

There were seven reasonably distinct regional colonial styles: (1) the New England colonial, visible in almost 100 surviving 17th-century houses, was predominantly of wood construction with hand-hewn oak frames and clapboard siding; its prototypes are to be found chiefly in the southeastern counties of England. (2) The Dutch colonial, centring in the Hudson River Valley, western Long Island, and in northern New Jersey, made more use of stone and brick or a combination of these with wood; its prototypes were in Holland and Flanders. The style persisted in this region until after the American Revolution. (3) The Swedish colonial settlement, established in 1638 along the lower Delaware River, was of short duration but contributed the log cabin (in the sense of a structure with round logs, notched at the corners and with protruding ends) to American architecture. (4) The Pennsylvania colonial style was late in origin (the colony was not founded until 1681) and rapidly developed into a sophisticated Georgian mode, based on English precedents. A local variant, often called Pennsylvania Dutch, evolved in the southeastern counties where Germans settled in large numbers after 1710. (5) The Southern colonial flourished in Maryland, Virginia, and the Carolinas. Story-and-a-half brick houses, sometimes with large projecting end chimneys and decorative brick masonry, prevailed. (6) The French colonial, stemming from medieval French sources, evolved in Canada in the Maritime Provinces and the St. Lawrence Valley. The earliest impressive structure was the Habitation of the French explorer Samuel de Champlain, built at Port Royal, N.S., in 1604. Most of the surviving early houses of New France are to be found in the province of Quebec. The French settled the Great Lakes and Mississippi regions by the late 17th century and introduced the Quebec style. Far to the south, Louisiana was established as a colony in 1699, and New Orleans became the capital in 1718. There grew up a distinctive regional style in the close-packed streets of the Vieux Carré of New Orleans and in the quiet plantations of the bayou country. (7) The Spanish colonial style in the United States extended geographically and chronologically from St. Augustine in 1565 to San Francisco in 1848. The five great mission fields were in Florida, New Mexico (from 1598), Texas, Arizona (both from 1690), and California (from 1769). Unlike other colonial styles, which were essentially medieval, the Spanish colonial followed the Renaissance and Baroque styles of Spain and Mexico.

Georgian architecture in Anglo-America

The architectural style of the 18th century in England and in the English colonies in America was called Georgian. There are slight differences in usages of the term in the two countries. In England, Georgian refers to the mode in architecture and the allied arts of the reigns of George I, II, and III, extending from 1714 to 1820. In America, Georgian refers to the architectural style of the English colonies from about 1700 to the American Revolution in the late 1770s. Formal and aristocratic in spirit, it was at first based on the Baroque work of Sir Christopher Wren and his English followers; but after 1750 it became more severely Palladian. Typically, houses were of red brick with white-painted wood trim. Interiors had central halls, elaborately turned stair balustrades, paneled walls painted in warm colours and white plaster ceilings. All of these features were new to the colonies in 1700. Some of the earliest Georgian buildings were at Williamsburg, capital of Virginia from 1699 to 1780 (Figure 79); other notable examples are Independence Hall, Philadelphia (1745), and King's Chapel, Boston (1750). The style was followed by the Federal style, 1780–1820. (Hu.M.)

By courtesy of Colonial Williamsburg, Williamsburg, Virginia

Figure 79: Carter's Grove, near Williamsburg, Va., attributed to Richard Taliafero, *c.* 1750–55.

Spanish South America. The architecture of the first half of the 17th century in Spanish America preserves the late classical style of Juan de Herrera, the 16th-century Spanish architect of El Escorial. Herreran austerity, for example, also characterizes San Agustín and Santo Domingo in Puebla, Mex., as well as the facade of the cathedral.

Most impressive is the cathedral (1598–1654) of Cuzco, Peru, rectangular in plan and Herreran in its sobriety except for the early Baroque portal. The Jesuit church in Cuzco, whose handsome facade was designed in 1664 by Diego Martínez de Oviedo, constituted the first late Baroque architecture in the Americas. The city abounds in handsome churches and palaces, built of Andean stone in the second half of the 17th century, and it is in many respects unrivaled in America. At Lima, the rebuilding of the monastery of San Francisco (1657–*c.* 1673) brought a new wave of Mudéjar influence in the geometric designs of the plasterwork. The main portal (1674) of the church inaugurated in that city the late Baroque type of facade, closely resembling a carved altarpiece.

Mudéjar influence

In Bolivia the chief architectural centre was Sucre, where Gothic vaults persisted; but otherwise both religious and domestic buildings adhered to simple classical designs. The Jesuit church of St. Ignatius (*c.* 1625–50) in Bogotá, Colom., owes its Italianate classicism to an Italian architect, the Jesuit priest Father Coluccini. The greatest masterpiece of Jesuit architecture in North and South America is, however, the church La Compañía, in Quito. There the Mudéjar patterns, which stand out in gold against a red background, make the interior (1605–89) of the church unforgettably sumptuous. More provincial though extremely colourful Mudéjar interiors are characteristic of the monastic churches of Tunja, Colom. Due to the splendid designs of its monastic buildings, Quito stands with Cuzco as one of the major schools of architecture in South America.

The first stage of Baroque architecture in Spanish America is generally distinguished by richly sculptured facades, whereas the interiors often remain sober settings for resplendently carved and gilded altarpieces. The late Baroque altar of spiral columns (Salomonica) was imported from Spain about 1650–60. Its translation into stone on the facade of a church first occurred (1697–1704) in South America in Our Lady of La Merced at Lima, to be followed by San Agustín there and by three churches in Cajamarca, Peru.

In this period there appeared in southern Peru and Bolivia a school of architectural decoration characterized by native Indian contributions in the primitive manner of carving and in the introduction of non-European ornament. The crossbred style is known as mestizo because it, like the people, is compounded of European and native Indian stock. Evidences of Indian contribution are also found in Mexico throughout the colonial period, and there exist parallel phenomena in Central America. The first examples of the independent Peruvian-Bolivian style are preserved in Arequipa, Peru, where the facade (1698) of the Jesuit church La Compañía is carved like a stone tapestry. Other examples of mestizo style are the church of Santiago at Pomata, Peru (*c.* 1690–1722), San Lorenzo (1728–44), and the Jesuit church La Compañía (1700–07) at Potosí, Bol., and San Francisco (1753–72) at La Paz, Bol.

Mestizo style

Argentina lay in the outer periphery of the Spanish colonies, and its early architecture consisted of provincial chapels of rubble and adobe, with the exception of the Jesuit monastery La Compañía (1654–71) at Córdoba. In the 18th century, two Italian Jesuit architects, Blanco and Primoli, established the spacious style of the Italian Baroque in the Jesuit estates of Alta Gracia and Santa Catalina near Córdoba and in the church of Our Lady of Pilar at Buenos Aires.

Baroque architecture reached its climax in Mexico with lavishly carved facades in which the tapering pilaster (*estípite*) was a distinguishing feature. Introduced in Mexico City in the Metropolitan Sacristy facade (1749–68) under the architect Lorenzo Rodríguez (Figure 80), it spread rapidly and appeared in La Santísima, in the Jesuit seminary at Tepotzotlán, in the churches of Guanajuato, and elsewhere. The school of Puebla maintained independence in producing an extraordinary array of brilliantly coloured exteriors of glazed tiles, both in churches and in countless palaces. The varied geometric contours of doorways, windows, and roof levels created picturesque effects in Mexican buildings of this period.

Throughout Spanish America, cities were designed and built on a gridiron plan, with a rectangular plaza in the centre and the covered sidewalks (*portales*) of Mediterranean tradition. Houses, large or small, were arranged about a central patio. Handsome domestic buildings exist throughout the region; notable were those in Mexico City and Puebla; in South America at Tunja, Potosí, Lima, and Cuzco. Many remarkable civil edifices, such as the customhouse and viceregal palace, survive in Mexico City, whereas elsewhere only the royal mint at Potosí, Bol. (1753–73), and the government palace (1764) in Antigua, Guat., are comparable in architectural importance. Spanish colonial architecture came to an abrupt end with the triumph of Neoclassicism (1800).

Brazil. The architecture, language, and culture of Portugal were transplanted to Brazil, which was the only major area of non-Spanish origin throughout Latin Amer-

Archivo Mas, Barcelona

Figure 80: Facade of the Metropolitan Sacristy, Mexico City, by Lorenzo Rodríguez, 1749–68.

ica. Unlike the unified Spanish settlements, the first cities were built upon hills in medieval style. Little of importance survives from the 16th century, when buildings were mostly of wattle and palm thatch.

The Jesuit style

The Jesuits carried to Brazil the first significant ecclesiastical style, a severe and undecorated architecture (Olinda, 1592). With variations, it persisted in Brazil until 1750. Plans are rectangular with square sanctuary and sacristy directly behind, and basilican structures are few. Long lateral chapels parallel with the nave are an unusual feature, derived from Portugal. Vaults and domes are rare, and decoration is limited to the occasional use of imported blue glazed tiles.

Salvador, the viceregal capital until 1763, had the closest ties with Lisbon; and its architecture reflected contemporary Portuguese models. A former Jesuit church, now the cathedral of São Salvador (1657–72), has a late Mannerist facade of stone in two principal stories, decorated with Doric pilasters and topped by a large attic story. The prominent windows in the second story are typical of Portuguese and Brazilian ecclesiastical and domestic design.

The more exotic Brazilian church facades began to make their appearance in the 18th century; great volutes over the centres between square towers created extraordinarily ingenious effects. This development can be traced in the facades at São Salvador, Deodoro, Penedo, Olinda, João Pessoa, and elsewhere, in a series of Franciscan churches that feature arched open porticos, three windows in the second story, and fantastic volutes crowning the top.

In the last period of Brazilian colonial architecture (1750–1822) the court style of Lisbon took hold in Belém and the new viceregal capital (1763) at Rio de Janeiro. The neo-Palladian church of the Candelaria (1775) there is the most important monument in the early Neoclassical style. The Rococo was, however, still well entrenched, and in the mining country of Minas Gerais it found its most original expression after 1750. There the great sanctuary of the Bom Jesús de Matozinhas at Congonhas do Campo is approached by terraces, a provincial version of the shrines at Braga and Lamego in Portugal (Figure 81). The oval and octagonal plans, which earlier had been introduced at Rio and Recife, reached a new development in São Pedro dos Clérigos at Mariana and in the double oval plan of the Rosario at Ouro Prêto (1785), where they are combined with round towers and curving facades. Curving exteriors in various forms in the Franciscan churches at Ouro Prêto (1766) and São João del Rei, designed by Aleijadinho (Antonío Francisco Lisboa), and in other monuments established the keynote of this late period.

Extreme decorative luxuriance characterized the altars and church furnishings in the 18th century, and often the walls of chapels and churches were overlaid with carved ornament. Rio, Salvador, and Minas Gerais became the chief centres of interiors in which gilding, spiral columns, late Baroque ornament, and illusionistic painting combined to create extraordinary decorative ensembles. An equal flowering of late Rococo ornament distinguished portals, windows, and profiles of both ecclesiastical and domestic buildings. (H.E.W.)

URBAN DESIGN

17th century. The basic rational principles of Renaissance urban design—geometric order, gridiron or single focus radial plans, primary and dispersed activity centres, and restricted and unlimited vistas—as stated early in the Renaissance by the 15th-century Italian architects Filarete, Alberti, and Francesco di Giorgio, remained basic to 17th-century thought. Only in the New World—in the Utopian religious settlements that were founded by dissident sects in the American colonies—were there new cities planned as agrarian communities composed of closely spaced but freestanding houses that seemed to reject both medieval and Renaissance urban-design theories.

By the middle of the 17th century, new organizational principles, developed in France by Le Nôtre in garden design (Vaux-le-Vicomte and Versailles), replaced the diffuseness of Renaissance urban design with a more highly integrated radial axial scheme, with multiple subordinate radial focuses at locations of significant activities that gave overall coherent form to an entire city. A city form that disclosed the hierarchical interrelationship of functions and portions of a city reinforced prevailing concepts of hierarchical social and political order. The fusion of form and content had the effect of transforming the concept of a city and continues to be felt to the present day.

In the late 16th century in Rome the major street pattern was largely the creation of Domenico Fontana, who, under Pope Sixtus V in the years just before 1600, imposed an avenue plan that linked all the major pilgrimage churches. The avenues were laid out over the most direct routes, regardless of the terrain; and at the focal points (*i.e.,* piazzas in front of the major monuments) obelisks were erected. Fontana's emphasis on communication routes and gathering spaces became the model for most later large-scale urban designs or renovations, such as Wren's plan for London, submitted after the Great Fire of 1666. This unexecuted proposal showed a series of avenues linking the major religious and commercial centres superimposed on a rational gridiron plan.

The residential square

The regularized residential city square received its greatest development in France with the planning of the royal squares. The Parisian Place des Vosges (1605), with its

From *Brazil Builds* by Goodwin and Kidder Smith

Figure 81: Statues of the 12 prophets, soapstone sculpture by Aleijadinho, 1800–05, on the terraces of the sanctuary of Bom Jesús de Matozinhas (attributed to Aleijadinho, 1780), Congonhas do Campo, Braz.

well-proportioned facades, shadowed arcades, and balanced colour scheme, was the beginning of a series that culminated with the circular Place des Victoires (1685) and the Place Vendôme (1698), both in Paris. Italian city squares tended to be either open, grand, and monumental (St. Peter's Square, Rome) or intimate, formally provocative, and spatially exciting (Santa Maria della Pace, Rome).

18th century. Urban design in the 18th century placed greater emphasis on unity and direction through the subordination of lesser parts to the whole. Entire cities were laid out on regularized multiaxial schemes (*e.g.,* Washington, D.C., 1792, by Pierre L'Enfant); the spaces between the radiating avenues were subdivided either geometrically or on a gridiron pattern. New principles calling for a sequence of different spatial experiences were also introduced, as in the plan for Nancy, Fr. (1752–55), by Emmanuel Héré de Corny. In Italy outstanding examples of the new style are the splendid oval Piazza Sant'Ignazio, Rome (1727), by Filippo Raguzzini; and the grand military quarter of Turin (1716), by Juvarra. Notable among the many English examples of planned urban development in this period are St. James's Square, London (1726), and the Circus (1754) and the Royal Crescent (begun 1767), Bath, by John Wood the Elder and the Younger. In Reims, Fr., the solemn Place Royale (1756) by the engineer J.G. Legendre is notable, but the finest example of an 18th-century large, urban pedestrian square may be the Place Louis XV (now the Place de la Concorde), Paris (1755), by Jacques-Ange Gabriel. On the banks of the Seine, in its original design, it served as a focal point for the gardens of the Louvre, for the street which led to the Church of the Madeleine, and for three radiating streets of the Champs-Élysées.

(H.A.M.)

Classicism, 1750–1830

ORIGINS AND DEVELOPMENT

The classicism that flourished in the period 1750–1830 is often known as Neoclassicism, in order to distinguish it, perhaps unnecessarily, from the classical architecture of ancient Rome or of the Renaissance. In the 18th century, modern classicism was described as the "true style," the word Neoclassical being then unknown. The search for intellectual and architectural truth characterized the period. Stylistically this began with an onslaught on Baroque architecture, which—with its emphasis on illusion and applied ornament—was felt to be manifestly untruthful. As early as the 1680s the French architect Claude Perrault had undermined the Renaissance concept of the absolute right of the orders. According to Perrault, the proportions of the orders had no basis in absolute truth but were the result of fancy and association. The consequent attempt to discover a new basis for architectural reality took many forms, from archaeology to theory.

Characteristics of the Neoclassical movement

Essentially representing a new taste for classical serenity and archaeologically correct forms, 18th-century classicism manifested itself in all the arts. It corresponded to a new attitude toward the past that began to be perceptible about 1750. In Europe it represented a reaction against the last phase of the Baroque and was symptomatic of a new philosophical outlook. As the Baroque was the style of absolutism, so Neoclassicism corresponded loosely with the Enlightenment and the Age of Reason. Coincidental with the rise of Neoclassicism and exerting a formative and profound influence on the movement at all stages was a new and more scientific interest in classical antiquity. The discovery, exploration, and archaeological investigation of classical sites in Italy, Greece, and Asia Minor were crucial to the emergence of Neoclassicism.

Neoclassicism, in its nostalgia for past civilizations and its attempt to re-create order and reason through the adoption of classical forms, was, paradoxically, also a Romantic movement. Prompted by feeling as well as by reason, architects interested themselves as much in the picturesque aspects of nature and objects in nature (such as ruins) as in rational procedures. While superficially opposite, Neoclassicism and Romanticism share the same roots. Two movements as different as the Greek Revival and the Gothic Revival were essentially alike, sharing, at least in their earlier phases, similar motivations and even compositional expressions and equally reflecting the mood of the age that created them.

The term Romantic Classicism has been used by some 20th-century art historians to describe certain aspects of Neoclassical architecture. This widening of the term admits non-Greco-Roman forms and the many attempts to imitate Chinese, Moorish, Indian, Egyptian, and, of course, Gothic buildings.

The role of classical archaeology

The emergence of the science of archaeology was indicative of a new attitude to the past in which separate and distinct chronological periods could be distinguished. This sense of a plurality of valid styles replaced the older conception of classical Rome as the unique object of veneration. An important architectural corollary of this idea, which was to spring into prominence in the 19th century, was the notion of a modern style of building. Just as the past could now be interpreted and re-created by the study of a diverse range of monuments, each now seeming to be uniquely characteristic of its own particular moment in time, so it was thought possible that a mode of building reflecting the present, a mode recognizable by future archaeologists as uniquely representative of their own time, might be created.

Numerous events beginning in the second decade of the 18th century, when English tourists began to visit Italy to experience, explore, and collect fragments of its antique past, herald this new and increasing interest in archaeology. As early as 1719, Bernard de Montfaucon, a French antiquarian, began to publish his 10-volume *Antiquité expliquée.* It was an immediate success. Excavations at the newly discovered ancient cities of Pompeii and Herculaneum (discovered in 1719) began in 1748 and 1738, respectively. The publication of the Comte de Caylus's *Recueil d'antiquités,* which began to appear in 1752, was another landmark. Influential plates of Roman antiquities drawn by Giovanni Battista Piranesi first appeared in 1743, the year of publication of the *Prima parte di architettura.* A steady stream of similar works followed from Piranesi's workshop, among them the *Antichità romane* (1748), the *Carceri* (*c.* 1745), *Della magnificenza ed architettura de' Romani* (1761), and the *Parere su l'architettura* (1764). The first of a long and significant list of publications of measured drawings and picturesque views of Roman and Greek antiquities was Robert Wood's *Ruins of Palmyra* (1753), which was followed in 1757 by the same author's *Ruins of Balbec* and by the *Ruins of the Palace of the Emperor Diocletian at Spalatro in Dalmatia,* written in 1764 by the English Neoclassical architect and designer Robert Adam.

At the same time a significant interest in Greek antiquities was emerging along with a growing belief in the superiority of Greek over Roman that was to result in a Greek Revival in architecture. At about this time the 6th-century Greek ruins at Paestum in southern Italy and in Sicily began to attract the attention of visitors. The Paestum sites were first described by the Italian artist Domenico Antonini in 1745. In 1750 the French architect Jacques-Gabriel Soufflot visited Paestum. The following year Giuseppe Maria Pancrazi's *Antichità siciliane* appeared, and in 1769 the architect Gabriel-Pierre-Martin Dumont's *Ruines de Paestum* was published. The picturesque qualities of these Greek temples, with their heavy baseless columns broken and overgrown with romantic vegetation, prompted those interested in architecture to venture farther afield and to explore the Greek mainland and Asia Minor. The first book with detailed illustrations of Greek monuments to be published was the Frenchman Julien-David LeRoy's *Ruines des plus beaux monuments de la Grèce* (1758). This was followed by *The Antiquities of Athens* by two English architects, James Stuart and Nicholas Revett, which appeared in three parts in 1762, 1789, and 1795.

Rationalism in architecture

The pursuit of Greek architecture had as one incentive the pursuit of primitive truth and thus of an inherent rationalism. This line of thought had been developed early in the 18th century and was popularized by a French Jesuit, Marc-Antoine Laugier, whose *Essai sur l'architecture* appeared in French in 1753 and in English in 1755. Advocating a return to rationalism and simplicity in building and taking the primitive hut as his example of the fundamental expression of human needs, Laugier was both reacting against the excesses of the Rococo period and laying the theoretical groundwork for Neoclassicism. He did not advocate copying Greek forms, with which he was probably unacquainted, but argued that all forms not having a structural or functional purpose should be eliminated. The actual imitation of Greek architecture developed slowly, though the idea of the superiority of Greek over Roman architecture was established by Johann Joachim Winckelmann's *Gedanken über die Nachahmung der griechischen Werke in der Malerei und Bildhauerkunst* (1755; *Reflections on the Painting and Sculpture of the Greeks*).

The centre of international Neoclassicism was Rome, a gathering place, from the 1740s on, for talented young artists from all over Europe. Virtually every figure who was to play a significant role in the movement passed through that city. Piranesi arrived in 1740, Anton Raphael Mengs in 1741, Robert Adam in 1754, Winckelmann in 1755, the French painter Jacques-Louis David in 1755, and the Italian sculptor Antonio Canova in 1779. Although it was Rome, the cradle of Italian antiquities, that provided the stage, the leading actors in the Neoclassical drama were French, German, or English; very little was contributed by Italians to this new movement. The centre of activity was the French Academy, where winners of the academy's coveted Prix de Rome went to study the monuments firsthand and to be exposed to the artistic life of the Italian capital. The projects produced by French Prix de Rome winners are characterized by their grandeur of scale; strict geometric organization; simplicity of geometric forms; Greek or Roman detail; dramatic use of columns, particularly to articulate interior spaces and create urban landscapes; and a preference for blank walls and the contrast of formal volumes and textures. The same qualities describe Neoclassical architecture as it was to emerge throughout Europe and in America.

NATIONAL AND REGIONAL VARIATIONS

Great Britain. In England the Palladianism of architects such as Lord Burlington, Colen Campbell, and their followers, beginning in the 1720s, had already marked a turning away from the Baroque style of Wren's successors Vanbrugh and Nicholas Hawksmoor and the adoption of a simpler and more restrained style. As early as 1715 the new spirit was discernible in Campbell's introduction to the first volume of his *Vitruvius Britannicus.* Advocating the judgment "truly of the Merit of Things by the Strength of Reason," his heroes were Vitruvius, Palladio, and Inigo Jones; his villains, the architects of the Italian Baroque: "The Italians can no more now relish the Antique Simplicity." The works of Bernini and Carlo Fontana are "affected and licentious"; for Borromini, "who has endeavoured to debauch Mankind with his odd and chimerical beauties," he feels only disgust. By 1731 Burlington's Assembly Rooms at York, based on Palladio's reconstruction of an Egyptian hall, was fully Neoclassical. Similarly, William Kent's entrance hall at Holkham Hall, Norfolk, begun in 1734 and reminiscent of a Roman basilica, would not in a European context seem out of date 50 years later. Despite these early essays by Burlington and his circle, the next generation of English designers remained conservatively in the Palladian mold and showed little interest in the architecture of Greece and Rome.

Birth of English Neoclassicism

By mid-century the atmosphere was beginning to change, and two events of 1758 marked the birth of English Neoclassical architecture: the erection of a Greek Doric garden temple in the grounds of Hagley Park, Worcestershire, by James ("Athenian") Stuart and the return to England of the 30-year-old Robert Adam.

Adam, the son of a leading Scottish Baroque architect, William Adam, arrived in London fresh from four years in Italy, his head full of Roman ruins and Renaissance arabesques, his style of drawing and composition bearing the telling marks of his friendship with Piranesi and the French draftsman Charles-Louis Clérisseau. Essential to the Adam style, that mode of decoration and planning that was to effect a revolution in English taste, was the notion of freedom. Absorbing a variety of influences ranging from the Palladianism of the Burlington–Campbell school and the decorative elements and spirit of France to the archaeology of Italy, Greece, and Asia Minor, Adam re-created and recombined the elements of architecture in a way that was wholly new—and wholly Neoclassical. His executed works consisted mainly of the remodeling of existing houses, the most important of which were Osterley Park, Middlesex (1761–80); Syon House, Middlesex (1762–69); and Kenwood House, Hampstead, London (1767–69). At Kedleston Hall, Derbyshire (*c.* 1765–70), he completed James Paine's plan and added a garden front in which the central portion (centrepiece) is clearly derived from an ancient Roman triumphal arch, the first use of this form in domestic architecture. This use of antique forms in a new context is a recurring characteristic of Neoclassical architecture. Adam's planning, to which he devoted considerable attention, was based on a variety of contrasting room shapes, each geometric in itself and contained within an overall geometric plan yet creating a sense of movement, variety, and surprise. Such play with shapes and spaces was to characterize Neoclassical planning, particularly in France.

Adam's style of planning

But the Adam revolution was over by 1780, and a new mood, one closer to that exemplified by Stuart's small Doric temple at Hagley, was taking its place. Now it was "noble simplicity" and "antique grandeur" that were sought after, and Horace Walpole, that weather vane of fashion, was writing how sick he was of "gingerbread" and "snippets of embroidery."

Of the next generation the leading architects were George Dance the Younger, Henry Holland, and James Wyatt. Dance's Newgate Prison, London (1769; demolished 1902), was among the most original English buildings of the century, a grim, rusticated complex combining the romantic drama of Piranesi with the discipline of Palladio and the Mannerist details of Giulio Romano in an imaginative paradigm of Neoclassicism. Holland was architect to the Prince of Wales and his most important work in this capacity was the extensive remodeling of Carlton House begun in 1783, a refined and elegant whole with a joint debt to Adam and to France and a simplicity that pleased Walpole. Wyatt, tremendously successful and busy, was equally at home in his own classical idiom, a stripped derivative of the Adam style, as in Gothic. There was no contradiction, for Wyatt's Gothic, like that of Adam before him, was classical in all but its details with cloisters substituted for arcades and battlements for balustrades.

By 1800 nearly all English architecture reflected the Neoclassical spirit. Sir John Soane, pupil of the younger Dance and architect to the Bank of England, developed a highly personal style characterized by a stripping down and linear abstraction of the classical elements, use of archaeological detailing such as the Greek key pattern, and the creation of dramatic interior space by toplighting. Totally original, his work invites comparison with the projects of Boullée and Ledoux in France.

Increased interest in Greek models

After 1800 the interest in revival of Greek forms intensified and the stream of buildings based either wholly or in part on Greek models continued well into the 19th century. One of the earliest was William Wilkins' Downing College, Cambridge (1806–11), with details closely copied from the Erechtheum on the Acropolis at Athens. Following this were Sir Robert Smirke's Covent Garden Theatre (1809), London's first Greek Doric building; Wilkins' Grange Park, Hampshire (1809), a monumental attempt to cram an English country house into the form of a Greek temple; Smirke's vast Ionic British Museum (1824–47); and St. Pancras Church (1819–22) by William and Henry William Inwood, with a portico and two caryatid porches based on the Erechtheum and an octagonal tower based on the ancient Athenian Tower of the Winds. The design of Regent Street and Regent's Park (with its palatial terraces) by John Nash in the second decade of the 19th century exemplifies the kind of town planning associated with the mood of Neoclassicism, a combination of formal elements with the picturesque (Figure 82).

Both Ireland and Scotland produced significant Neoclassical buildings. In Dublin, James Gandon's Four Courts

Figure 82: Cumberland Terrace, Regent's Park, London, by John Nash, 1826–27.
A.F. Kersting

(1786–96), with its shallow saucer dome raised on a high columnar drum with echoes of Wren's St. Paul's Cathedral, and his Custom House (1781–91) owe joint allegiance to the Palladianism of Sir William Chambers and contemporary French Neoclassicism. Edinburgh, the "Athens of the North," experienced a particularly tenacious Greek Revival. Among its monuments are the Royal High School (begun 1825) by Thomas Hamilton and the Royal Institution (now the Royal Scottish Academy) by William Henry Playfair. David Hamilton built the Royal Exchange (now Stirling's Library), Glasgow (1829–30), in a style showing the Greek influence, and the revival in that city remained strong well into the 19th century, culminating in the work of Alexander ("Greek") Thomson, whose Caledonia Road Free Church (1856–57) is among the finest monuments of Neoclassical architecture in Scotland.

Reaction against the Rococo style

France. In France a reaction against the Rococo style began in the 1740s. Never very satisfactory for exterior architecture, the Rococo nevertheless had considerable appeal as a decorative program, reaching its height in the work of Meissonier and Oppenordt. A dogmatic classicism in architecture had been a serious consideration in France as early as 1671 when Louis XIV's Royal Academy of Architecture was formed. The style, produced for Louis XIV, adopted the richness and grandeur of the Roman Baroque while modifying its more dramatic excesses by a rational application of *le bon goût* ("good taste"). A cornerstone of rationalism already had been laid in 1714 with the publication of the French theorist the Abbé de Cordemoy's *Nouveau traité de toute l'architecture* (1714; "New Treatise on All Architecture"). Reaction against the Rococo crystallized in the writings of Charles-Nicolas Cochin and in the lectures of the Comte de Caylus at the Royal Academy of Painting and Sculpture in 1747. Along with the return to nature and reason, the twisting curvilinear forms of the Rococo were seen to work against nature. The same desire for truth to nature accounted for the growing preference in France for the informal landscape gardens of the English.

The *Essai sur l'architecture* of Laugier provided a rational alternative to the Rococo and formed the theoretical basis for Neoclassicism in France and in the rest of Europe. Already by mid-century a new interest in archaeology, Rome, and antiquity had been established.

A significant architectural event marking a reaction against the Baroque was the design of a new facade for the important Paris church of Saint-Sulpice in 1733 by Giovanni Nicolò Servandoni, who manifested a new taste for sobriety. His project for Saint-Sulpice represented a break with the Roman Baroque tradition of church facades deriving from Giacomo da Vignola's Gesù church, Rome (1568), and still being used in Paris at Saint-Roche (by Robert de Cotte) in 1735. Servandoni's design derived inspiration from Roman basilicas, from Perrault's Louvre colonnade, and from Wren's St. Paul's. In execution the design lost its central pediment and arches. Superimposed open colonnades were substituted and the two lateral towers were built to different designs, the north one being completed only in 1777 by Jean-François-Thérèse Chalgrin. Nevertheless, the new restraint and classicism that pervades Servandoni's facade was a portent of what was to come.

The work of Jacques-Ange Gabriel, director of the Academy of Architecture from 1735, is a successful compromise between the new rationalism of the 18th century and the French classical tradition of the 17th century. In 1757 he began the Place de la Concorde in Paris, with its twin palaces (Hôtel de Crillon and the Admiralty) that boast columnar facades inspired by Perrault's great east front of the Louvre (begun 1667). Despite his many major public works, Gabriel is probably best known for his enchanting Petit Trianon, built at Versailles in 1761–64 for Louis XV and Madame de Pompadour (Figure 83). Classically restrained and elegant, this subtle cubic composition achieves a timeless gravity that seems beyond the compass of stylistic terms such as Baroque or Neoclassical.

Importance of Soufflot

The leading Neoclassical architect was Jacques-Germain Soufflot, who was in Italy in the 1750s and was the first French architect to study the Greek ruins at Paestum. Soufflot's great building was the church of Sainte-Geneviève (now the Panthéon), Paris (1757–90), a domed cruciform edifice combining the new taste for antique grandeur and simplicity with a structural rationalism, the offspring of the marriage of a Roman temple and a Gothic cathedral. A crucial Neoclassical building that owes nothing to the Baroque, Soufflot's church nevertheless is not purely antique in character, as its dome is derived from Wren's St. Paul's and it has a Roman rather than a Greek temple front.

A second Parisian church already fully Neoclassical in feeling is Chalgrin's Saint-Philippe-du-Roule of 1768–84. Saint-Philippe, inspired by early Christian basilicas, is remarkably pure, with an Ionic colonnade separating nave from aisles. The nave terminates in a semicircular apse and is covered with a coffered Roman barrel vault. The exterior is a model of simplicity in the antique taste with

Figure 83: Le Petit Trianon, Versailles, Fr., by Jacques-Ange Gabriel, 1762.
Giraudon—Art Resource/EB Inc.

a Roman Doric portico framed against the cubic mass of the wall. Similar and of about the same date (1764–70) is Louis-François Trouard's church of Saint-Symphorien at Versailles, again basilical with a Roman Doric portico.

Boullée's originality of design

A most remarkable and original architect of the Revolutionary period was Étienne-Louis Boullée, whose work before 1780 was in the style of his contemporaries but who after that date produced a number of curious and revolutionary projects. Of his several Paris townhouses, or *hôtels,* the Hôtel de Monville of about 1770 and the Hôtel de Brunoy of 1772 deserve mention. The former has a central facade featuring giant Ionic pilasters divided by sculptured panels and the latter a giant Ionic colonnade flanked by arcaded wings forming the three-sided court (*cour d'honneur*). Boullée's project for a cenotaph to Sir Isaac Newton based on a pure spherical form (*c.* 1780) is an example of that formalistic aspect of Neoclassicism that sought pure geometry and simplicity.

Other Neoclassical architects of the pre-Revolutionary period were Marie-Joseph Peyre, whose *Livre d'architecture* of 1765 was influential in publicizing the type of work being produced by French students in Rome; Charles de Wailly, who was an important teacher and, with Peyre, was the architect of the Paris Odéon; Jacques Gondoin, architect of the School of Medicine (1769–76), which, with its Corinthian temple portico and Roman-inspired amphitheatre covered by a coffered half dome and lit from a half oculus (a round opening in the top of a dome), was one of the most advanced interiors of its date anywhere; Jacques-Denis Antoine, winner of the competition for the new Mint (Hôtel des Monnaies); and Victor Louis, whose theatre at Bordeaux (1772–80) with its Roman colonnade and vaults set the model for Neoclassical theatres. All had studied in Rome.

Innovative Neoclassicism of Ledoux

The boldest innovator in the world of French Neoclassical architecture was Claude-Nicolas Ledoux. Like Boullée he designed a number of buildings between 1765 and 1780 in which he attempted to reconcile the traditional elements of French classicism with the new spirit of the antique. Among these were the Château de Benouville, Calvados (1768–75), and the Hôtel de Montmorency, Paris (*c.* 1770–72), both of which feature Ionic colonnades with straight entablatures and are somewhat English in feeling. More original were the Pavilion at Louveciennes of 1771 for Madame du Barry, which again invited comparison with contemporary English villas and with the Petit Trianon, and the Hôtel Guimard of 1772. The theatre at Besançon, with its cubic exterior and interior range of baseless columns stylistically derived from those at Paestum, dates from 1775–84.

But it is for later projects, such as the royal saltworks at Arc-et-Senans (1775–79), with their simplified forms, and the highly original series of *barrières* (tollgates) for Paris (1784–89), that ensure to Ledoux his central role in the evolution of Neoclassical and, indeed, of modern architecture. The Barrière de la Villette, consisting of a tall cylinder rising out of a low square block with porticoes of heavy, square Doric piers, exhibits all the essentials of the style: megalomania, geometry, simplicity, antique detail, formalism, and stylophily (use of many columns). Even more influential were the unexecuted projects by Ledoux published in his *Architecture considérée sous le rapport de l'art, des moeurs et de la législation* ("Architecture Considered with Respect to Art, Customs, and Legislation") in 1804, which contains his ideal city of Chaux, a plan for a whole city with buildings in which symbolism and abstraction are carried to new heights (Figure 84).

The revolutionary Neoclassicism of Ledoux resulted in few monuments. It was the Paris of Napoleon that saw the erection of the most conspicuous examples of the style, intended to symbolize in stone the grandeur of the Emperor. The two architects associated with this transformation of Paris were Charles Percier and Pierre-François Fontaine, who were responsible for the extensive planning scheme at the beginning of the 19th century that included the rue de Castiglione, the rue and Place des Pyramides, and the rue de Rivoli. The Arc du Carrousel was built to their designs in 1806–08 and the grander Arc de Triomphe by Chalgrin and Jean-Armand Raymond in 1806–35 (Figure 85). Conspicuous in Napoleonic Paris was an imposing

By courtesy of the Institute for the Arts, Rice University, Houston

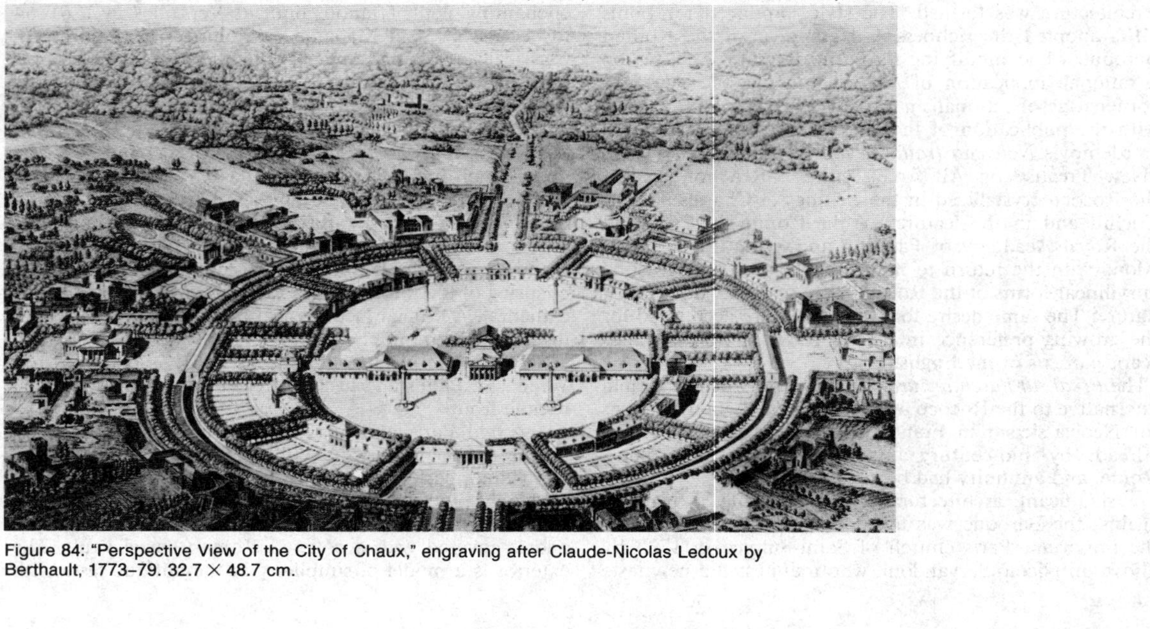

Figure 84: "Perspective View of the City of Chaux," engraving after Claude-Nicolas Ledoux by Berthault, 1773–79. 32.7 × 48.7 cm.

Figure 85: Arc de Triomphe, Paris, by Jean-François-Thérèse Chalgrin and Jean-Armand Raymond, 1806–35.
EDI Studio, Barcelona

Corinthian temple, the Church of the Madeleine, begun in 1806 by Pierre-Alexandre Vignon and completed in 1842 (Figure 86). Similar in scale and effect were the Paris Bourse (1808–15) by Alexandre-Théodore Brongniart and the Chamber of Deputies of 1806–51 by Bernard Poyet (now the National Assembly).

Italy. Italy was the centre from which Neoclassicism emanated in the sense that Neoclassicism would be unimaginable without Rome. The remains of antiquity on Italian soil, many of which were by the 18th century romantically overgrown and half buried, inspired all artists and architects. Yet Italian architects were followers rather than initiators of international Neoclassicism. One of the most important formative influences on the movement was Piranesi, whose etchings of Roman ruins transformed those antique fragments into sublime romantic compositions. Piranesi was in the forefront of Roman activity, and through his acquaintance with the foreign architects and patrons who visited the Italian capital he helped to crystallize the growing taste for Neoclassicism. Juvarra's designs for a tomb for the King of France (1715?) served as a source for Piranesi in his design for the Piazza of the Knights of Malta in Rome (*c.* 1765). In the church of Santa Maria del Priorato, Piranesi incorporated classical references that were to greatly influence the succeeding generation of architects.

Lodoli's theories of functionalism

In the field of pure theory a Venetian, Carlo Lodoli, was an important early advocate of functionalism whose ideas are known through the writings of Francesco Algarotti, the *Saggio sopra l'architettura* (1753) and *Lettere sopra l'architettura* (beginning 1742). Lodoli's theories were similar to those of Laugier, requiring that every part of a building derive from necessity and that architecture be true to the nature of materials, and tolerating no useless ornament. The theories of Francesco Milizia contained in his *Principi d'architettura civile* of 1785 were similar.

The tradition of the Baroque was of course strong in Italy and lingered on throughout the 18th century in many parts of what was still an agglomeration of independent states. Early tendencies toward Neoclassicism appear in the late work of Luigi Vanvitelli; for example, the Castelluccio Reale (1774) in the park at Caserta, an octagonal structure with a round superstructure. Other barometers of the new taste were the Villa Albani, Rome (completed *c.* 1760), built by Carlo Marchionni to house a collection of ancient marbles formed by Cardinal Alessandro Albani; and the new Pio-Clementino Museum at the Vatican (1776–81), the work of Michelangelo Simonetti.

Palladian revival

Early in the 18th century Italy had experienced a fertile Palladian revival, and a number of buildings based on the Pantheon model were built, among them Tommaso Temanza's church of Santa Maria Maddalena in Venice in 1748. Palladianism was a significant element in much Italian Neoclassical architecture.

Giacomo Quarenghi, who was to work in Russia for Catherine II, built the monastery of Santa Scolastica, Subiaco (1774–77), with a barrel-vaulted nave characteristic of the new taste. In 1787 the first baseless Greek Doric columns in Italy appeared in the Chiesetta di Piazza di Siena in the gardens of the Villa Borghese, Rome, designed by Mario Asprucci, 20 years after Stuart's temple at Hagley. Also Greek was the Gymnasium, in the Botanic Garden, Palermo (1789–92), built by Léon Dufourny, who had been a pupil of LeRoy and Peyre.

Neoclassical buildings after 1800 were more numerous, and a few examples illustrate the character and range of the movement. Peter von Nobile's Sant'Antonio, Trieste (1826–49); Luigi Cagnola's Rotunda, Ghisalba (1834); and Giovanni Antonio Selva's Canova Temple, Possagno (1819–33), all took the Pantheon as their starting point. Cagnola also built the Ionic Ticinese Gate, Milan (1801–14), and the Arch of Sempione, Milan (1806–38), a Roman triumphal arch similar to the contemporary Parisian Arc du Carrousel. Luigi Canina's Greek propylea, or gateway, at the entrance to the Villa Borghese (1827–29); Carlo Barabino's Doric Teatro Carlo Felice, Genoa (1826–28); and Giuseppe Japelli's meat market at Padua (1821) using the unfluted Paestum order, all exemplify the continuing taste for Greek forms. Japelli was also the architect of the Pedrocchi Café, Padua (1816–42), which, with its Doric and Gothic exteriors and equally eclectic interiors is a remarkable extravaganza.

The greatest achievement in urban planning of the period was the design of the Piazza del Popolo in Rome (1813–31) by Giuseppe Valadier, a great open space with three diagonal avenues leading off it.

Spain and Portugal. In Spain the leading Neoclassical architect was Juan de Villanueva, who studied in Rome and returned to Spain in 1705 with a style similar to that evolved by the leading contemporary French and English architects. His buildings include three villas; the Casita de Arriba (1773) and the Casita de Abajo (1773), both at El Escorial, and the Casita del Principe at El Prado (1784). His major building was the Prado, Madrid (1785–87). In Portugal the destruction of Lisbon by earthquake in 1755 necessitated rebuilding, most of which was carried out by military engineers. The Ajuda Palace (begun 1802) by the Italian Manuel Fabri is Neoclassical; and in Oporto, the Hospital of Santo Antonio with a vast Doric portico was designed by the English architect John Carr.

Figure 86: The Church of the Madeleine, Paris, begun in 1806 by Pierre-Alexandre Vignon, completed 1842.
Giraudon—Art Resource/EB Inc.

Germany. The Louis XVI style of mid-18th century France was taken to Germany by the many French architects who worked there, such as Philippe de La Guêpière (Mon Repos, near Ludwigsburg, 1760–64, and La Solitude, Stuttgart, 1763–67). Many German patrons were also Anglophiles, including Prince Franz of Anhalt-Dessau, for whom the talented architect Friedrich Wilhelm von Erdmannsdorff created the schloss and park at Wörlitz, near Dessau (1766–90). Schloss Wörlitz was directly inspired by English Palladian country houses such as Claremont, Surrey; and Erdmannsdorff laid out the park with a range of exotic garden buildings around a lake, recalling contemporary English gardens such as Stourhead and Stowe. The association of such naturalistic gardens with ideals of political liberty is underlined by the presence at Wörlitz of the remarkable Rousseau Island, which was planted with poplars in 1782 in imitation of the island on which Rousseau was buried in the celebrated landscaped garden at Ermenonville in France.

King Frederick William II of Prussia (reigned 1786–97) decided to make Berlin a cultural centre dominated by German artists. Among the architects he called to Berlin were Carl Gotthard Langhans and David Gilly, who, with Heinrich Gentz, created a severe but inventive style in the 1790s that was indebted to Ledoux as well as to Winckelmann's call for a return to the spirit of ancient Greek architecture. The great early monument of the Berlin school was the Brandenburg Gate (1789–93) by Langhans. Distantly inspired by the propylaea on the Acropolis in Athens, it was the first of the ceremonial Doric gateways to rise in modern Europe. The Greek Revival in Germany was linked with the growth of Prussian nationalism and imbued with the supposed moral virtues of the Doric order. Key buildings in this stern geometric style include the Berlin Mint (1798), by Gentz, and the Vieweg House, Brunswick (1800–07), by David Gilly. Gilly also founded a school of architecture in Berlin, where both Karl Friedrich Schinkel and Leo von Klenze received formative training. The apogee of German Neoclassical architecture can be traced in the work of three brilliant designers: David Gilly's son, Friedrich, and the latter's disciples, Schinkel and Klenze.

Friedrich Gilly built little, dying in 1800, but left some remarkable designs that justify his central place in German Neoclassicism. His project for a monument to Frederick the Great (1797) consisted of a raised Greek Doric temple on a geometric substructure surrounded by obelisks and set in a vast open space (Figure 87). This caught the imagination of German architects as a symbol of Prussian nationhood during the humiliating occupation of Berlin by Napoleon in 1806–13. It was in those years that Gilly's pupil Schinkel was active as a designer of theatre sets and as a Romantic painter. Schinkel, who was named state architect in 1815 by Frederick William III, transformed Berlin with a series of monuments in a rationalist Greek style, beginning with the New Royal Guardhouse (1816–18). His Schauspielhaus (theatre and concert hall) of 1818–26 is essentially a grid of trabeated elements framing glazed openings. The modern flavour of this construction, which, according to Schinkel, derived from the Choragic Monument of Thrasyllus in Athens, has contributed to Schinkel's popularity as an architect in the 20th century.

Schinkel's next major work in Berlin, the Old (Altes) Museum (1823–33), is important as an early example of a national museum built in order to educate the public. With its long but undemonstrative Ionic colonnade, it is comparable to Smirke's contemporary British Museum. Indeed, in 1826 Schinkel made an important tour of France and, more particularly, of Britain to collect information on the display of paintings. The detailed diary he kept on his tour shows that what interested him most was the architecture and technology of the Industrial Revolution in Britain. On his return to Berlin he designed a number of buildings in which he incorporated the new methods of fireproof construction he had seen in England. The most important of these was the School of Architecture (1831), with walls of red brick ornamented with glazed violet tiles, windows of unpainted terra-cotta, and internal construction of iron beams and brick cap vaults. For Schinkel, who was not a pure functionalist, the poetry of architecture was as important as it was for Soane in England. Thus the facades of the School of Architecture were ornamented with carved terra-cotta panels depicting the history and symbolism of architecture.

As part of his concern for poetry in architecture, Schinkel was also keenly aware of the need to relate buildings to their settings. He gave beautiful expression to this in the 1820s in a number of asymmetrical but classical villas—for example, Schloss Charlottenhof at Sanssouci, for Crown Prince Frederick William, and Schloss Glienicke, near Potsdam, for his younger brother, Prince Charles. Schinkel developed this theme on a more extravagant scale in two unexecuted palaces of the 1830s, one on the Acropolis in Athens for the King of Greece and one at Orianda on the Black Sea for the Empress of Russia. The coloured lithographs that he subsequently published of these gorgeous polychromatic dream-palaces are among the greatest products of the 19th-century Romantic imagination.

Klenze, who had studied in Paris with Durand and Percier and had visited Italy, developed Munich into a monumental souvenir of the Grand Tour for his patron, Ludwig I of Bavaria. The result was an extraordinarily successful transformation of a minor court city into a great cultural capital that was intended to be the Florence of the 19th century. Klenze laid out a wide new street, the Ludwigstrasse, which he lined with palaces and public

Figure 87: Project for a monument to Frederick the Great by Friedrich Gilly, 1797.
Dr. Franz Stoedtner

buildings. The program was widely adopted in the expansion of European capitals, notably Vienna, later in the 19th century.

More eclectic than Schinkel, Klenze created a living museum of styles in Munich, including his noble Sculpture Gallery (Glyptothek, 1816–30), with its Greek Ionic portico; his Leuchtenberg Palace (1816), modeled on the Palazzo Farnese in Rome; and his Königsbau (1826–35) at the Residenz, which was an echo of the Pitti Palace in Florence. Klenze's Sculpture Gallery, commissioned by the future Ludwig I, has some claim to be regarded as the first public museum ever erected solely for the display of sculpture. With no examples to follow, Klenze produced a novel plan with galleries around the four sides of a square courtyard. In accordance with the desire of both patron and architect to make the building a total work of art, its interiors were decorated with (now destroyed) stuccowork and frescoes that were stylistically related to the exhibits they contained. This decoration mounted in richness from the first rooms, which contained Egyptian sculpture, to the final gallery, which exhibited Roman sculpture.

Scandinavia and Finland. Neoclassical taste was introduced into Denmark and Sweden between 1750 and 1790 by French designers such as Louis Le Lorrain, Nicolas-Henri Jardin, and Louis-Jean Desprez. In Denmark, Jardin's pupil Caspar Frederik Harsdorff built the austere royal mortuary chapel of Frederick V in Roskilde cathedral (1774–79), while in Sweden Desprez was responsible for the Botanical Institute, Uppsala (1791–1807), with a Greek Doric portico. The Danish architect Christian Frederik Hansen, a pupil of Harsdorff, turned the medieval and Baroque city of Copenhagen into a Neoclassical capital. He built the town hall, court house, and prison (1803–16) and the Church of Our Lady (1810–29), with its Boullée-inspired interior. Schinkel's example in Berlin was followed by Hansen's pupil Heinrich Grosch, who provided Christiania (Oslo), the new capital of Norway, with a series of Greek Revival public buildings. Perhaps the finest example of this classical urban planning is in Helsinki, established as capital of Finland in 1812. Beginning in 1818, Johan Ehrenström and Carl Engel created a monumental group of the Lutheran Cathedral flanked by the Senate, University, and University Library.

Poland. Stanisław II August Poniatowski, king of Poland from 1764 to 1795, brought the Louis XVI style of contemporary France to the Royal Castle in Warsaw in a series of interiors designed by Dominik Merlini and Jan Chrystian Kamsetzer in 1776–85. Merlini also designed the Łazienki Palace at Ujazdów near Warsaw (1775–93) for the King, while Szymon Bogumił Zug brought Neoclassicism to ecclesiastical architecture in his Lutheran Church, Warsaw (1777–81), modeled on the Pantheon. Zug also designed Arkadia (1777–98), one of the many Picturesque gardens in Poland. Laid out on the Radziwiłł family estate of Nieborow, the garden contains numerous romantic buildings. After 1815, Warsaw was rebuilt as a model Neoclassical city with major public buildings by Merlini's pupil Jakub Kubicki and the Italian architect Antonio Corazzi.

The patronage of Catherine II

Russia. The leading role played by Russia in the production of early Neoclassical architecture was almost entirely due to Catherine II. Under her aegis St. Petersburg was transformed into an unparalleled museum of Neoclassical buildings as advanced as contemporary French and English work. As in other countries, the new taste for antique simplicity represented a reaction against the excesses of the Rococo, which in Russia had its apotheosis in the work of Bartolomeo Francesco Rastrelli.

Two foreign architects played important roles: a Scotsman, Charles Cameron, whose most extensive work was at Tsarskoye Selo in the style invented by Robert Adam and who was responsible for introducing the first correct Greek Doric column and entablature in Russia in the circular Temple of Friendship at Pavlovsk (1780); and an Italian, Giacomo Quarenghi, who arrived in Russia in 1780 and built for Catherine the Palladian English Palace at Peterhof (1781–89).

The two leading Russian architects were Vasily Ivanovich

J. Allan Cash

Figure 88: Main gate to the Admiralty, St. Petersburg (now Leningrad), by Andreyan Dmitriyevich Zakharov, 1806–15.

Bazhenov and Ivan Yegorovich Starov, both of whom studied in Paris under de Wailly in the 1760s, bringing back to Russia the most advanced Neoclassical ideas. Bazhenov designed the new Arsenal in St. Petersburg (1765) and prepared unexecuted designs for the Kamenni Ostrov Palace (1765–75) and for a new Kremlin. Starov designed a country house for Prince Gagarin at Nikolskoye (1774–76), the new cathedral of the Trinity, St. Petersburg (1776), and the influential prototype of Russian country houses, the Tauride Palace (1783–88), for Grigory Potemkin, Catherine's lover. The Tauride Palace consisted of a central-domed and porticoed central block connected by narrow galleries to large wings.

Under Catherine's grandson, Alexander I (reigned 1801–25), the Russian version of the Empire style flourished. The great monument of this later period was the St. Petersburg Bourse (1804–16) by Thomas de Thomon, a vast peripteral (surrounded by a row of columns) edifice. Andrey Nikiforovich Voronikhin, also a pupil of de Wailly, was architect of the Kazan Cathedral, St. Petersburg (1801–11), and Andreyan Dmitriyevich Zakharov built the Admiralty (1806–15) in the same city (Figure 88).

United States. Neoclassical architecture thrived in the United States throughout the 19th century, and examples of it exist in nearly every major city. The analogy with imperial Rome and later (after the War of Greek Independence, 1821–32, in particular) with the grandeur and political ideals of Periclean Athens strengthened the case for the adoption of Roman and Greek architectural models in the United States. In 1785 Thomas Jefferson planned the Virginia State Capitol with the Frenchman Charles-Louis Clérisseau, taking as his model the ancient Roman Maison-Carrée at Nîmes. It was to be the first public building in the modern world directly based on an antique temple. Jefferson's own house at Monticello, in Virginia, featured a central-domed space and was indebted to ancient Roman villas as well as to Palladianism and to modern French and English domestic design (Figure 89). If Monticello echoed the private agrarian retreat of classical statesmen, as described in the writings of Cicero and the younger Pliny, the University of Virginia at Charlottesville (1817–26) was an example of Jefferson's effort to educate the public of the new United States. He conceived the campus as an academic village of extraordinary charm and novelty in which a central Pantheon-like rotunda, containing a library, stands at the head of a grassy open space flanked by two lines of small templelike pavilions, which are linked by colonnades.

Relation of architectural style to political philosophy

In Boston, the Massachusetts State House, designed 1787–88 and built 1795–98 by Charles Bulfinch, derived from English Neoclassical models. By far the most gifted architect working in the United States in these years was Benjamin Latrobe. Latrobe was born in England, where he was trained by the innovative architect Samuel Pepys Cockerell. He evidently became familiar with the radical work of Dance, Soane, and Ledoux and of engineers such as John Smeaton. In 1796 he went to the United States, where he worked as the first fully professional architect and eventually became known as the father of the American architectural profession. A characteristic early building is his Bank of Pennsylvania (1798–1800), in Philadelphia, which was then the largest American city and was, indeed, the U.S. capital from 1790 to 1800. The bank is a novel reinterpretation of ancient temple architecture, with a Greek Ionic portico at each end but no classical order on its long side walls. It was also fireproof, being the first American building to be vaulted in masonry throughout. The shallow top-lit saucer dome in the central banking hall recalls the work of Soane, as does Latrobe's Roman Catholic Cathedral at Baltimore (1805–18). Drawing on the Pantheon and on Soufflot's Sainte-Geneviève, the cathedral contains a dome resting on segmental arches perhaps inspired by Soane's interiors at the Bank of England. Latrobe's most poetic and inventive work is a series of interiors at the Capitol in Washington, D.C., which he executed in his capacity as surveyor of public works, a position to which Jefferson appointed him in 1803. The Supreme Court Chamber (1815–17), with its strange lobed vault resting on stunted Doric columns, suggests a search for a new architecture, as do the capitals of corn (maize) and tobacco leaves that he invented for use in other parts of the building. Jefferson responded warmly to Latrobe's attempt to symbolize in architecture the values of the newly founded republic. (S.Mi./D.J.Wa.)

Spanish America and Brazil. In the Caribbean, Neoclassical influences are evident in the Post Office of 1770–92 and the Government House of 1776–92 in Havana, Cuba, both attributed to the architects Pedro de Medina of Cadiz and Fernández Trevejos of Havana.

From about 1780 Neoclassicism began to replace the ornamental Churrigueresque style in Mexico. The leading Neoclassical architects were the Spaniard Manuel Tolsá and two Creoles, Eduardo Tresguerras and José Damián Ortiz de Castro. Among the most distinguished Mexican examples of Neoclassicism are the School of Mines (1797–1813) in Mexico City by Tolsá and the church of El Carmen at Celaya (1803–07) by Tresguerras. Many of the Mexican missions in California were designed with Neoclassical features.

Neoclassical architecture was built throughout South America, but especially in Brazil, Argentina, Uruguay, and Chile, where initially many of the most important Neoclassicists were French: Prosper Catelin in Buenos Aires, Auguste-Henri-Victor Grandjean de Montigny in Rio de

De Wys, Inc.

Figure 89: Monticello, Charlottesville, Va., by Thomas Jefferson, 1770–1809.

Janeiro, and François Brunet de Baines in Santiago. The Palace of the Mint (1788–99) in Santiago, one of the finest Neoclassical buildings in South America, was conceived, not by an architect designing in the French tradition, but by an Italian, Joaquín Toesca, who had worked in Madrid with Francisco Sabatini, an Italian whose architecture was stylistically transitional between the Baroque and Neoclassicism. (Ed.)

Gothic revival, c. 1730–c. 1930

ORIGINS AND DEVELOPMENT

The architectural movement most commonly associated with Romanticism is the Gothic Revival, a term first used in England in the mid-19th century to describe buildings being erected in the style of the Middle Ages and later expanded to embrace the entire Neo-Gothic movement. The date of its beginning is not easy to pinpoint, for, even when there was no particular liking for Gothic, conservatism and local building practices had conditioned its use as the style for churches and collegiate buildings. In its earliest phase, therefore, Gothic Revival is not easily distinguished from Gothic survival.

The first clearly self-conscious imitation of Gothic architecture for reasons of nostalgia appeared in England in the early 18th century. Buildings erected at that time in the Gothic manner were for the most part frivolous and decorative garden ornaments, actually more Rococo than Gothic in spirit. But, with the rebuilding beginning in 1747 of the country house Strawberry Hill by the English writer Horace Walpole, a new and significant aspect of the revived style was given convincing form; and, by the beginning of the 19th century, picturesque planning and grouping provided the basis for experimentation in architecture. Gothic was especially suited to this aim. Scores of houses with battlements and turrets in the style of a castle were built in England during the last years of the 18th century.

Archaeological revivalism

With developing archaeological interest, a new and more earnest turn was given to the movement—a turn that coincided with the religious revivals of the early 19th century and that manifested itself in a spate of church building in the Gothic style. Only toward the middle of the century were the seriousness and moral purpose that underlay this movement formulated as a doctrine and presented to architects as a challenge to the intellect. Augustus Charles Pugin, in England, was the first to codify the principles of the Gothic Revival. Far more persuasive and influential exponents, however, were Eugène-Emmanuel Viollet-le-Duc in France and John Ruskin in England, who gave to the movement a moral and intellectual purpose. The second half of the 19th century saw the active and highly productive period of the Gothic Revival. By then, the mere imitation of Gothic forms and details was its least important aspect; architects were intent on creating original works based on the principles underlying Gothic architecture and deeply infused with its spirit.

Another contribution that the Gothic Revival made to architecture was the encouragement of freedom and honesty of structural arrangement. Structural elements could be provided as and where they were needed. There was no need for dissimulation. French architects, in particular Viollet-le-Duc, who restored a range of buildings from the Sainte-Chapelle and Notre-Dame in Paris to the whole town of Carcassonne, were the first to appreciate the applicability of the Gothic skeleton structure, with its light infilling, to a modern age, and the analogy was not lost on subsequent architects at a time when the steel frame was emerging as an important element of structural engineering. Functionalism and structural honesty as ideals in the Modern movement were a legacy of the Gothic Revival.

Structural freedom and expression

Not surprisingly, the Gothic Revival was felt with most force in those countries in which Gothic architecture itself was most in evidence—England, France, and Germany. Each conceived it as a national style, and each gave to it a strong and characteristic twist of its own.

NATIONAL AND REGIONAL VARIATIONS

Great Britain. A Gothic Revival was in a sense initiated early in England during the late 16th century under the influence of Elizabethan and Jacobean notions of chivalry and again between 1620 and 1630 under the impetus of William Laud's Anglicanism; but it is in the Gothic experimentalism of the late 17th century, particularly that of Wren's circle, in which seeds of a Gothic Revival can be discerned. Although buildings erected at these times imitated Gothic forms, none of them were revivalist in spirit. The Gothic Revival was largely conditioned by literary theory and practice. Although it had antecedents, the so-called "revolution of taste" in the mid-18th century was most clearly marked by publication of Richard Hurd's *Letters on Chivalry and Romance* (1762) and Thomas Percy's *Reliques of Ancient English Poetry* (1765). Thomas Gray, especially in his poems of the 1750s and, later, in his letters, was the first major poet to seek inspiration in a "Gothic" past—not only medieval but Celtic and Icelandic. Thomas Warton, poet and critic, acquired his interest in the Middle Ages from architecture and, in his work on medieval English cathedrals and churches, connected the literary aspect of the Gothic Revival with the work that was begun by a group of antiquaries in the late 17th century and that was continued into the 18th.

The transition from a survival to a revival phase of Gothic architecture took place almost imperceptibly. Curiously enough, it was Vanbrugh, England's great exponent of the Baroque spirit, who made the first successful attempt to evoke sensations of the medieval past. In 1717 he built a house for himself at Greenwich, near London, that was intended to conjure up a "castle air." It is a simple, robust, brick building that relies for its effect on slender proportion rather than detail. But it is an isolated work of its kind.

Only toward the end of the 18th century did "picturesque" take on a precise meaning, affecting the planning and the forms of English architecture, but, from the late 17th century onward, isolated gardens and estates were

A.F. Kersting

Figure 90: Strawberry Hill, Twickenham, Middlesex, Eng., by Horace Walpole with William Robinson and others, 1749.

laid out to take advantage of the irregularity of landscape, resulting in compositions that approximated those in the paintings of such 17th- and 18th-century artists as Claude Lorrain, Salvator Rosa, and Gaspard Poussin—hence, the denomination of the style as Picturesque. It was William Kent, in response to the literary ideal of "naturalness" of such writers as Sir William Temple, Joseph Addison, and Alexander Pope, who was first acclaimed for fashioning the Picturesque landscape that was to be made famous in the 18th century by Lancelot ("Capability") Brown and who introduced occasional buildings into it, often in a Gothic style, to serve as a focus of interest. There were, however, other precursors, notably Vanbrugh and Charles Bridgeman.

Kent first used the fanciful Rococo Gothick that was to become characteristic of the 18th century in 1732, on a gateway in the Clock Tower at Hampton Court. He also reconstructed the Tudor buildings of Esher Lodge between 1729 and 1733, introducing ogee arches and quatrefoil openings. These he used again in the late 1730s in the Temple of the Mill at Rousham, Oxfordshire, where he laid out one of the first irregular gardens. The ornamental character of the Gothic Revival was thus established from the start, and it was popularized as such within a few years by Batty Langley, author of *Gothic Architecture Improved by Rules and Proportions* (1742). Pretensions to archaeological accuracy appear in two churches built in 1753 by Henry Keene—that at Shobdon, Herefordshire, and a charming, though now derelict, octagonal church at Hartwell, Buckinghamshire. An ardent admirer of Gothic, Keene had begun Gothicizing Arbury Hall, Warwickshire, as early as 1748. It was to the amateurs Sanderson Miller and Horace Walpole, however, that the credit for a full-scale domestic Gothic Revival was due.

Miller, a Warwickshire squire, began about 1744 by inserting pointed arches in the south front of his Tudor house at Radway, Warwickshire. Later, he put up a garden ornament in the form of a mock Gothic castle at nearby Edgehill, the idea of which became fashionable and made a reputation for him as a designer of Gothic extravaganzas. His most significant work was Lacock Abbey, Wiltshire, the symmetrical, flattened facade of which is thinly decorated with Gothic motifs. Walpole's Gothic, though apparently as lighthearted, was more serious in intent.

Strawberry Hill

When, in 1747, he decided to rebuild his house, Strawberry Hill, Twickenham, Middlesex (Figure 90), he proposed to reflect faithfully in its architecture his tastes for topography, history, and heraldry. He formed a "committee on taste" to advise him on the design. Among the members were the amateur archaeologists Richard Bentley and John Chute, both of whom provided designs. The architect responsible for the execution of most of the work was William Robinson. During the early phase of building, alterations and interior decorations were made in a pretty, decorative style, with a freedom unhampered by any serious archaeological study. Nor was there any real feeling for medieval composition in the massing of the elements. But in 1761, when a vast circular tower was added to the southwest corner of the house, Walpole gave evidence of a deliberate attempt to achieve an asymmetrical, picturesque composition. The west of the house was more freely grouped. Finally, in 1776, James Essex, probably the most earnest Gothicist of the period, inserted the Beauclerc Tower between the west end and the round tower, making the whole the first and most determined example of a large-scale Picturesque composition.

The fortuitous appearance and the deliberate irregularity of Strawberry Hill were exploited in many late 18th-century buildings. The most extravagant and sensational

Fonthill Abbey

of all Gothic Revival buildings was Fonthill Abbey (1796–1806), Wiltshire, designed by James Wyatt primarily as a landscape feature for the arch-Romantic William Beckford (Figure 91). The great central tower collapsed in 1807, and most of the building has today disappeared; but, in John Rutter's *Delineations of Fonthill* (1823), it is still possible to perceive something of the grotesquely spectacular quality that made this building, for a short time, notorious.

Although many classical architects, including Sir William Chambers and Robert Adam, applied Gothic details to

Figure 91: Fonthill Abbey, Wiltshire, Eng., designed by James Wyatt, 1796–1807. Engraving by T. Higham, 1823, from *Delineations of Fonthill* by John Rutter.

J.R. Freeman & Co. Ltd.

the exterior of their country houses (and Adam was even employed at Strawberry Hill), they displayed no great interest in the style and always retained strict symmetry of composition. George Dance used it more thoughtfully and originally in his occasional Gothic buildings—the facade of the Guildhall (1789), London; Cole Orton Hall (1804–08), Leicestershire; Ashburnham Place (1813–17), Sussex; and the churches of St. Bartholomew-the-Less (1789), London, and Micheldever (1808), Hampshire.

Publication of the theory of the Picturesque

Walpole's innovation assumed real significance only toward the end of the century, after the theory of the Picturesque was evolved and publicized by Richard Payne Knight and Uvedale Price. Already Knight had given architectural form to his ideas of rugged, irregular, and apparently "natural" composition in Downton Castle, Herefordshire, near Ludlow (1774–78). This was the first irregularly planned castellated (castle-style) building with a classical interior. It inspired a vast range of such buildings. John Nash is the best known and most proficient exponent of the style. Starting with his own house, East Cowes Castle, on the Isle of Wight, in about 1798, he exploited the deliberate irregularity of plan and silhouette afforded by the castellated style; from Caerhayes (1808), Cornwall, in the south, to Ravensworth Castle (1808), Durham, in the north, Nash dotted England (and also Ireland) with Picturesque castles, houses, and ornamental cottages all of vaguely Gothic or Italianate inspiration.

Sir John Soane attempted the Gothic style on at least three occasions—at Port Eliot (1804–06), Cornwall, at Ramsey Abbey (1804–06), Huntingdonshire, and for the library at Stowe (1805–07), Buckinghamshire—but, like his master Dance, strongly influenced by the French Neoclassical theorists Cordemoy and Laugier, he attempted to distill the effects of Gothic rather than to imitate the style. His suspended arches and his clustered ribs rising sheer from the floor and continuing around the vault are, ultimately, of Gothic inspiration.

The influence of antiquarianism

The great change that occurred at the beginning of the 19th century, when the Gothic Revival moved from a phase of sentimental and picturesque attraction to one of greater archaeological exactitude, was determined largely by the research and publications of antiquarians. In the *Itinerarium Curiosum* of 1725 William Stukeley first introduced plans, in addition to topographical views, of Gothic buildings; but it was not until 1753, with the publication of Francis Price's *Salisbury,* that sectional drawings were included. Knowledge was but slowly accumulated, and active, enterprising scholars appeared only toward the end of the 18th century. Foremost of these was John Carter, author of *The Ancient Architecture of England* (1795 and 1807), in which Gothic details were more faithfully and accurately recorded than in any earlier publication. Thomas Rickman designated the various styles of medieval architecture in *An Attempt to Discriminate the Styles of English Architecture* (1817), and the French refugee Augustus Charles Pugin, who was first employed by Nash, produced a series of meticulously measured details in *Specimens of Gothic Architecture* (1821–23). The great popularizer of Gothic archaeology was John Britton, who diffused a knowledge of the medieval buildings of Great Britain with two series of books, *The Architectural Antiquities of Great Britain* (1807–26) and *The History and Antiquities of the Cathedral (Churches of England)* (1814–35).

For many years architecture, however, lagged far behind scholarship. Buildings continued to be put up in an effete, decorative, and unconvincing Gothic style. Dozens of castellated houses were built during the first decades of the century. The first successes of Smirke—Lowther Castle (1806–11), Westmorland, and Eastnor Castle (*c.* 1810–15), Herefordshire—were in this style. The most spectacular was Windsor Castle, by James Wyatt's nephew, Sir Jeffry Wyatville, who began the remodeling in 1824. Gothic was also employed in collegiate work. William Wilkins built the screen and hall at King's College, Cambridge, between 1824 and 1827, and Rickman and Henry Hutchinson added New Court to St. John's College, Cambridge, between 1827 and 1831. But Gothic was to be most widely used—and even exploited—for church architecture, not because it was thought more appropriate than classical architecture but because it was cheaper.

Commissioner's churches

The Church Building Act of 1818, providing for the expenditure of £1,000,000 on churches, emphasized once more Gothic as the ecclesiastical style. It was the discovery by the commissioners responsible for the spending of this money (together with an additional £500,000 voted in 1824) that a Gothic church cost less to build than a Neoclassical one with its requisite stone portico that determined the widespread utilization of the Gothic style. The first significant church to which the commissioners contributed, St. Luke's (1820–24), Chelsea, London, by James Savage, was splendidly vaulted in Bath stone, but meanness as well as meagreness progressively controlled the design of their churches. Of the 612 churches built for the commissioners, more than 550 were Gothic or some related style.

Gothic was established as a national style when, in 1836, the commissioners for the rebuilding of the Palace of Westminster (Houses of Parliament) accepted a Gothic design by Sir Charles Barry. This was to be the first public building of any consequence in the style. Barry had already experimented with Gothic in no less than nine churches—the best known being St. Peter's (1824–26), Brighton—and had built King Edward's Grammar School (1833–37) in Birmingham in the Gothic style. His great and elaborate Palace of Westminster, however, is not a convincing essay in Gothic composition. The plan is formal, the facade to the river altogether symmetrical, and the detail repetitive. But it derives a Picturesque effect from the placing and proportioning of its two towers, St. Stephen's (Big Ben), halfway along the north face, and the squatter Victoria tower, in the west facade. In England the Palace of Westminster was not imitated—though in Budapest it was formally commemorated in Imre Steindl's Parliament House (1883–1902). Work at Westminster was completed slowly and was finished only after Barry's death. By then the Gothic Revival had been put on an altogether different footing, paradoxically, by the man who was responsible for all the Gothic details of both the King Edward's Grammar School and the Palace of Westminster, Augustus Welby Northmore Pugin, son of the author of *Specimens of Gothic Architecture.*

Pugin's use of Gothic to express the spirit of Catholicism

A Roman Catholic convert, the younger Pugin was intent to show that Gothic was an expression of the Catholic spirit and thus the only form of architecture properly suited to its ritual. In his book *Contrasts* (1836) he also sought to show that architecture reflects the state of the society by which it is built: The society of the Middle Ages was good; therefore, Gothic architecture was good. In *The True Principles of Pointed or Christian Architecture* (1841) he first laid down firm principles for the Victorian Gothic Revival. Architecture, he held, should be honest in its expression. Every feature of a building should be essential to its proper functioning and construction, and every feature of this construction should be frankly expressed. Architecture was to be judged by the highest standards of morality. Such concepts are a part of Pugin's French heritage; they were commonplace in 18th-century France, but Pugin's ideals came as a revelation to British architects and gave to the Gothic Revival a wholly new seriousness of purpose.

Most of the buildings in which Pugin attempted to give form to his ideas were built between 1837 and 1844. His first church of any consequence was St. Mary's (1837–39), Derby; his most influential were St. Wilfrid's (1839–42), Hulme, Manchester, and St. Oswald's (1840–42), Old Swan, Liverpool. But all three—like most of his other buildings and even his own favourite, St. Augustine's (1845–51), built near his house at Ramsgate, Kent—though solid and broadly proportioned and far more convincingly imbued with the Gothic spirit than earlier buildings, are not successful as works of architecture. Pugin was too much concerned with the minutiae of medieval detail. When incomplete in their detail and furnishing, his churches are grim; fully and expensively finished, as at St. Giles's (1841–46), Cheadle, Cheshire, they appear overexquisite.

Pugin's doctrines were taken up by the Anglican reformers, the Tractarians of Oxford and the Camdenians of Cambridge. The Ecclesiological Society, into which the Camden Society was transformed in 1845, so successfully aroused the liturgical enthusiasm of the clergy that most architects employed by the established Church of England in the years that followed were subject to the most doctrinaire of disciplines. Numerous architects were castigated by the critics of the *Ecclesiologist,* though Richard Cromwell Carpenter—who in 1838 had applied Neo-Tudor details to Lonsdale Square in Islington, London—was consistently upheld for the "correctness" of his work, as were those far more original and competent architects William Butterfield and John Loughborough Pearson. Pearson's masterpiece was St. Augustine's (1870–80), Kilburn Park Road, London.

A.F. Kersting

Figure 92: All Saints' Church, Margaret Street, London, by William Butterfield, 1849–59.

Butterfield is remembered today chiefly for the polychromy of his collegiate work at Keble College (1866–86), Oxford, and Rugby School (1868–86), but he was responsible for a range of simple, though no less rigorous and emphatic, country parsonages and churches in Yorkshire, culminating in the group at Baldersby St. James (1855–61), and those bold, ruthless, and highly idiosyncratic churches, St. Matthias' (1849–58), Stoke Newington, London; St. Alban's (1859–63), off Holborn, also in London; St. Augustine's (1864–66), Penarth, near Cardiff, and All Saints' (1865–74), Babbacombe, Devon. Butterfield brought a new vigour to the Gothic Revival. The building that first gave evidence of his power and originality was All Saints', Margaret Street, London, designed in 1849 and largely completed by 1852 (Figure 92). This church was sponsored by the Ecclesiological Society. But it is not its liturgical correctness that makes it so important in the history of the Gothic Revival. From the pavement to the top of the tower, the church was built in bands of black and red brickwork, setting a fashion for "structural polychromy." Internally, marbles and tiles were used to cover all surfaces, giving them a rich coloration. Butterfield became famous for his polychromy.

This taste for polychromatic decoration was initiated, encouraged, and sustained by the greatest apologist of the Gothic Revival, the critic John Ruskin. In 1849 he published *The Seven Lamps of Architecture* in time to influence Butterfield at All Saints', Margaret Street. Ruskin's *Stones of Venice* appeared between 1851 and 1853; and within a few years architects throughout England were adapting the details and colour combinations of Italian, especially Venetian Gothic, architecture for myriad clients who had been enraptured by Ruskin's mellifluous descriptions and high-sounding sanctions for a Gothic Revival. Like Pugin and the Camdenians, he judged Gothic to be a style with a firm moral basis.

By the middle of the 1850s, Gothic had become the established mode for church architecture in Great Britain, but it was also considered appropriate to many other types of architecture. In the prodigiously productive decades that followed, the style was applied by a host of industrious and competent architects to many buildings that had no medieval precedents. The most active practitioners of Gothic were Sir George Gilbert Scott and George Edmund Street. Both were busy restorers of medieval cathedrals and churches, but they found time to build a great number of new buildings in the Gothic style. Scott designed no less than 800. His first success was the Martyrs' Memorial (1841) in Oxford; others included the Albert Memorial (1862–72), Hyde Park, London; Glasgow University (1866–71); and the vast and picturesque Midland Hotel (1867–74) at St. Pancras Station, London (Figure 93, left). He firmly established the supremacy of England as arbiter in the Gothic Revival by winning a competition in 1844 for the Church of St. Nicholas (1844–63), Hamburg. Street, who was trained by Scott, designed about 260 original buildings, starting with a number of small churches and schools in Cornwall, an outcrop of churches in Oxfordshire, Buckinghamshire, and Berkshire, and another in Yorkshire. His churches vary in style, from the elaborate, decorative polychromy of St. James-the-Less (1858–61), Thorndike Street, London, through the more forcefully detailed style of St. Philip and St. James's (1860–62), Oxford, to the bare barn of St. George's (1861), Oakengates, Shropshire. His most famous and probably his noblest work was a secular building, the Law Courts, London, competed for in 1866 but not begun until 1874 and completed only after his death in 1882 (Figure 93, right). His influence was exerted through both his architecture and his famous publication *Brick and Marble in the Middle Ages* (1855).

High Victorian Gothic

The other great secular work of the Gothic Revival, Manchester Town Hall, was won in competition in the same year as the Law Courts, 1866, and begun in 1869. The designer was Alfred Waterhouse, an architect almost as active as Street but one who was responsible for very few churches. Waterhouse demonstrated conclusively that, because of its flexibility, Gothic was not only suit-

Figure 93: *English secular architecture in the Gothic Revival style.* (Left) Midland Hotel at St. Pancras Station, London, by Sir George Gilbert Scott, 1867–74. (Right) Law Courts, London, by George Edmund Street, 1874–82.

By courtesy of (left) *The Architectural Review*; photographs, (left) De Burgh Galwey, (right) J. Allan Cash from Rapho/Photo Researchers—EB Inc.

able but was virtually the only revival style applicable to the design of the large and complex buildings required by Victorian administration and institutions. A master planner, he first achieved fame as a result of a competition for the Manchester Assize Court (1859–64); then followed the ingenious Town Hall (1869–77) and later Owens College (1870–98), also in Manchester. For Oxford he designed Balliol College (1867–69); for Cambridge, the Union (1865–67), Gonville and Caius Colleges, started in 1870, and buildings at Pembroke College (1871–72). His vast London buildings include the Natural History Museum (1873–81), the Prudential Assurance building (1879, 1899–1903), and University College Hospital (1897–1906).

Though Scott, Street, and Waterhouse dominated the mature phase of the Gothic Revival, they were not always responsible for the most interesting and experimental work of the period. William Burges (1827–81) designed St. Finbar's Church of Ireland Cathedral in Cork (1863–76) in a curious 12th-century French style. In 1865, at Cardiff Castle in Wales, he began to interpret medieval architecture with merry and decorative freedom. The interiors of this building and of Castell Coch, built 10 years later, are a riot of decoration. His friend Edward William Godwin, on the other hand, was more restrained; he built two small, neat town halls in the Gothic style, one at Northampton (1861–64), the other at Congleton (1864–67), Cheshire. Other notable Gothicists were George F. Bodley, who often employed the artist William Morris and his associates, including the painters Ford Madox Brown and Sir Edward Burne-Jones, to decorate his churches; and Philip Webb, who had himself been a pupil with Morris in the office of Street and was to build for Morris the Red House (1859–60) at Bexleyheath near London. Little in this building is overtly Gothic—rather, it is intended to evoke the solidity and sound craftsmanship of medieval architecture, an ideal he had adopted from a greatly neglected architect, William White, and one that was to be taken up later by Richard Norman Shaw.

20th-century British Gothic

The Gothic Revival survived into the 20th century, though largely for ecclesiastical architecture. Truro Cathedral, Cornwall, was built in 1880–1910 from designs by J.L. Pearson. After his death in 1897, it was completed by his son, Frank Loughborough Pearson, as was his last work, Brisbane Cathedral, Australia, the construction of which did not begin until 1901. Similarly, Sir Giles Gilbert Scott, the grandson of Sir George Gilbert Scott, maintained the family tradition by designing a cathedral for Liverpool in 1903 in a Gothic style; this magnificent building was completed in 1978. Stephen Dykes-Bower made extensive additions in a late Gothic style to Bury St. Edmunds cathedral (1960–70).

Scott, Butterfield, and Carpenter all supplied designs for churches in the British Commonwealth, but their designs were often modified and slowly executed: Butterfield's Anglican cathedral, St. Paul's, in Melbourne, Australia, although designed in 1847 and begun in 1850, was not finished until 1934. The direct influence of the English leaders on colonial Gothic was thus small, and numerous churches built in the British dominions during the second half of the 19th century were mostly in a meagre, uninspired Gothic mode.

France. In France a taste for medieval legend survived into the 16th century in aristocratic circles and was nurtured not only by the literary works of the Italian Renaissance poets Ludovico Ariosto and Torquato Tasso but also by books on heraldry and blazonry by humanist scholars. More remarkable as evidence of conscious, widespread, and continuing popular interest in the Middle Ages—and especially in Gothic building—were topographical studies and guidebooks published from the middle of the 16th century onward. The Gothic tradition of building continued, especially in ecclesiastical circles, far into the 18th century. But it was largely survival rather than revival. French admirers of Gothic architecture regarded it primarily as a challenge to the intellect. The architects Delorme in the 16th century and Derand in the 17th analyzed the construction of the Gothic vault. They were quick to appreciate it as a highly efficient and economical framework of columns and ribs, supporting the webs of the vaults (which they regarded as no more than infilling panels carrying no thrust) and counterbalanced by buttresses and flying buttresses—as something, indeed, of a structural scaffold. It was this structural elegance that early 18th-century enthusiasts of Gothic, such as Cordemoy, sought to infuse into contemporary architecture. In the *Nouveau Traité de toute l'architecture* (1706) Cordemoy proposed that a new, honest, and economical architecture might be arrived at by abstracting the principles of Gothic construction and applying them in a perfectly regular classical way. There was no question of reviving the Gothic style; interest in Gothic was to be altogether transmuted into classical terms. The building of the church of Sainte-Geneviève (now known as the Panthéon) in Paris, designed in a style confirming the Neoclassical ideal but on principles derived from Gothic architecture, gave a new impetus to the study of Gothic construction. French architects were imbued with a rational appreciation of Gothic that was without parallel.

Although there was a native French vogue in the 18th century for the medieval literature of the troubadours, it was the intrusion of English ideas that prompted more authentic representations of the medieval world in stage settings and history paintings after 1772. Certainly, the Gothic taste in architecture was conditioned by the introduction of the informal landscape garden. By 1781 there were a number of English gardens in France with mock-Gothic pavilions, and, during the last two decades of the century, many more were built. But the frivolous, lighthearted "Gothick" of 18th-century England never took hold in France; the French made virtually no attempt to imitate, let alone rival, the splendours of Strawberry Hill and Fonthill Abbey.

To the Revolutionaries at the end of the 18th century, Gothic architecture seemed a symbol of the vested power of the aristocracy and the church, and many buildings were wantonly destroyed. Yet, popular interest in the picturesque charms of Gothic architecture was sustained and even intensified by such men as Alexandre Lenoir, who in 1795 turned the largest of the Paris depots for plundered works of art, the Petits-Augustins (now the École des Beaux-Arts), into the Museum of French Monuments. Here, by clever juxtaposition and subtle lighting, the Middle Ages seemed to be endowed with an aura of magic. By suggesting a relationship between a chivalric past and the actual forms of Gothic sculpture and architecture, Lenoir coloured the imagination of a whole generation of Romantics. The great Romantic writer François-René, vicomte de Chateaubriand, was fascinated by Lenoir's collection. Indeed, a celebrated chapter on Gothic architecture in Chateaubriand's *Le Génie du christianisme* (1802; "The Genius of Christianity"), in which Gothic is not only taken as the symbol for the old French Catholic spirit but also is traced beyond, through the forests of Gaul, to nature itself, was directly inspired by Lenoir's work. Inevitably, a Romantic Gothic image was popularized in the years that followed; Romantic playwrights, novelists, and painters were seduced by the charms of Gothic. Even antiquarians succumbed to the Romantic myth, and from 1810 onward a spate of popular guidebooks and studies of Gothic architecture was published.

Gothic as a symbol of the old French Catholic spirit

In spite of a few Gothic-inspired fantasies and an archaeological interest in medieval architecture that found expression in the Neo-Romanesque church of Saint-Paul (1835) at Nîmes by Charles-Auguste Questel, architecture remained a virtually impregnable stronghold until after 1840, when a hard core of Gothic Revivalists began to emerge. This was composed of consistent medievalists who were stirred primarily by archaeological pretensions. Stimulated by the activity of English scholars in Normandy, they patiently studied the medieval remains of that region and slowly forged the science of French Gothic archaeology. An equally important aspect of the Gothic Revival was inaugurated by the great Romantic author Victor Hugo, when he published in 1831 *Notre-Dame de Paris,* the explicit purpose of which was the glorification of Gothic as a national and Catholic style of architecture. But it was the Protestant statesman François Guizot who first gave real impetus to those ideas promoted by Hugo.

In 1830 he inaugurated the organization that seven years later became the Commission on Historical Monuments.

All the serious, acceptable architects of the Gothic Revival were amateur archaeologists, and they acknowledged an archaeological standard of taste. They designed from the first in the 13th-century style, and nearly all had restored at least one Gothic building before they undertook to build anything new. The patronage of the Commission on Historical Monuments and later of the Diocesan Buildings Service (formed in 1848), for which thousands of medieval buildings were restored and enlarged, was thus of enormous importance in furthering the aims and the technical skill of the Gothic Revivalists. The men who sustained the Gothic Revival were almost all taught by the commission's leading architects, Jean-Baptiste Lassus and Viollet-le-Duc. Lassus trained Viollet-le-Duc first on the restorations in Paris of Saint-Germain-l'Auxerrois (1838) and the Sainte-Chapelle (1842). In 1844 they were both appointed to restore Notre-Dame de Paris and to build a new sacristy in the Gothic style; this was regarded as an official sanction for the Gothic Revival. But, although a picturesque revival of Gothic had already been initiated in the provinces, official sanction for a full-scale revival was not easily accorded. The members of the French Academy, faithful to Neoclassical ideals, were firmly against it.

Official sanction of the Gothic Revival

In 1844 the north tower of the abbey church of Saint-Denis, begun under Suger in 1135, was found to be in danger of collapse. All Gothic Revivalists were aghast. Adolphe-Napoléon Didron, editor of the *Annales archéologiques* and propagandist for the Gothic Revival, tactlessly accused the Council of Civil Buildings, which was charged with the approval of all building plans in France, of irresponsibility. Its members, mainly academicians, retaliated by arbitrarily stopping the construction of three churches in the Gothic style that Didron had acclaimed in his journal. Didron then launched a counteroffensive; he demanded a public inquiry into the restoration of Saint-Denis. Under threat of this inquiry, which was powerfully supported by the prefect of the Seine district, Barthelot Rambuteau, the council was forced to approve the plans for Sainte-Clotilde in Paris by Franz Christian Gau, plans that they had held up for more than four years. It became a cause célèbre. A furious pamphlet war followed, from which the Gothic Revivalists emerged triumphant, and in 1852 Didron estimated that 200 neo-Gothic churches had been built or were in the process of construction. But the victory was short-lived. Sainte-Clotilde, as completed by Gau and his successor Théodore Ballu in 1857, was an anomalous expression of revivalist ideals. Didron disliked it intensely, and the dispute caused many admirers of Gothic architecture to reflect seriously on the merits of a Gothic Revival.

Lassus went on to build Saint-Nicolas (1848) at Moulins, Saint-Pierre at Dijon (1852), and Saint-Jean-Baptiste-de-Belleville (1854) in Paris. Viollet-le-Duc constructed Saint-Gimer (1853–57) at Carcassonne, the church of Nouvelle Aude (1855) and Saint-Denys-de l'Estrée (1860–67) at Saint-Denis; he restored the Château de Pierrefonds (1858–70) to a state of colourful medieval splendour for Louis-Napoleon; and, in his *Dictionnaire raisonné de l'architecture française* (1854–68; "Analytical Dictionary of French Architecture") and the *Dictionnaire raisonné du mobilier française* (1858–75; "Analytical Dictionary of French Furniture"), together running into 16 volumes, he provided the vital visual and intellectual inspiration required to sustain the Gothic movement. But he was by no means a convinced revivalist. All but one of his secular works are in an uneasy Renaissance mode. He determined to think his way beyond the Romantic attractions of the Gothic style. Pursuing the inquiries of 18th-century theorists, he envisaged an architecture of the 19th century that would be based on the rational system of construction and composition that he recognized to be embodied in Gothic but would in no way imitate its forms and details. Architecture, he thought, should be the clear expression in 19th-century materials of 19th-century structural and functional needs. He was unable to accept the challenge of his own ideas. Both he and his disciples—Paul Abadie, Émile Boeswillwald, Eugène-Louis Millet, Maurice Ouradou, Anatole de Baudot, Édouard Corroyer, Félix Narjoux, and Edmond Duthoit—continued to design buildings (primarily churches) in a weak Gothic style. There were many less thoughtful and determined men who put up imitations of Gothic architecture in the late 19th century, but the Gothic Revival was never a full-blooded affair. Some of the finest buildings designed after the medieval manner—Saint-Pierre-de-Montrouge (1864–72) in Paris, by Joseph-Auguste-Émile Vaudremer, is one—were isolated works by architects who worked outside the orbit of the Gothic Revivalists and who had no qualms about the intellectual honesty of their chosen mode of expression.

Gothic rational construction and composition as the basis of a new architecture

Germany and central Europe. As in France, German interest in medieval legend, history, art, and architecture was sustained throughout the Renaissance both by the general public and by scholars and antiquarians. Interest was focused, in particular, on the cathedrals of Strasbourg and Cologne, buildings that were to assume an almost symbolic significance in the history of the Gothic Revival on the Continent. In his *Rerum Germanicarum Epitome* (1505; "Epitome of Things German") the humanist Jakob Wimpheling extolled Strasbourg cathedral as the rarest and most excellent of buildings, and Oseas Schadaeus' guide to the cathedral, *Summum Argentoratensium Templum* (1617; "Strasbourg's Finest Church") was the first illustrated guidebook ever devoted to a single medieval building and, in spite of its Latin title, was written in German. Other 17th- and early 18th-century histories and guides—and there were many—give ample evidence of a respectful appreciation of Gothic, despite the jibes of fashionable leaders. Appreciation of Gothic was a traditional and emotional affair, far removed from the studied and analytical interest of the French. Not surprisingly, English Gothic sentiments permeated Germany with the mid-18th-century taste for things English. *Conjectures on Original Composition* (1759) by the English poet Edward Young enjoyed a vogue in Germany that it never aspired to in England. English attitudes and ideas provided the German Gothic Revival with its peculiarly impassioned character.

The Sturm und Drang ("Storm and Stress") conception of the late 18th century invested Gothic with extraordinary and unparalleled qualities; it seemed to such philosophers as Johann Gottfried von Herder (and, under his inspiration, to the genius and writer Goethe) to be of the most sublime and exalted inspiration—an expression at once of all nature, all things divine and infinite. Goethe's paean to the cathedral at Strasbourg—and to its builder Erwin von Steinbach—was a 16-page pamphlet, *Von deutscher Baukunst* (1772; "On German Architecture"), that was an inspiration to all future revivalists. Goethe epitomized Gothic as the expression of the German spirit. Gothic became a German architecture, and it was to remain such in the estimate of all Germans, even German scholars, for 50 years and more. Goethe's passion for Gothic was not long sustained, but his enthusiasm was shared by other contemporaries, notably, the author and statesman Friedrich von Schlegel, who saw Gothic not only as an expression of the German spirit but specifically of a German Catholic spirit. This belief he shared with the brothers Sulpiz and Melchoir Boisserée, by whom he was largely inspired.

Influence of Sturm und Drang

Sulpiz Boisserée was the most active and enthusiastic of early Gothic Revivalists. His great preoccupation was the cathedral of Cologne, which he measured minutely, starting in 1808 but continuing up to the publication of *Ansichten, Risse und einzelne Theile des Doms von Köln* ("Elevations, Sections, and Details of the Cathedral of Cologne"), issued between 1823 and 1831, and an accompanying text, *Geschichte und Beschreibung des Doms von Köln* ("History and Description of the Cathedral of Cologne"), of 1823. The purpose of this study was the restoration and completion of the unfinished cathedral. He enlisted the moral support even of Goethe and the financial support of King Frederick William III, who in 1824 ordered the preservation of the building. This work of conservation was carried out by Friedrich Ahlert, under the guidance of Schinkel, and after his death by the most gifted of Schinkel's pupils, Ernst Friedrich Zwirner. The task of completion was started in 1842, at the command of King Frederick William IV, and was carried through after Zwirner's death by Richard Voigtel, who finished the work only in 1880. The building of the Cologne cathedral was an expression of German nationalism and marked the beginning of the Gothic Revival proper in Germany.

Influence of English architectural fashions

Earlier expressions of the Gothic Revival in architecture were of a Rococo or Picturesque nature and were much influenced by contemporary fashions in England. Between 1725 and 1728, Joseph Effner, gardener to the elector Maximilian II Emanuel of Bavaria, built the Gothic-inspired Magdalene Chapel on the grounds of the Nymphenburg Palace in Munich. In 1755 Frederick II the Great of Prussia himself designed the Nauener Gate in Potsdam, and in 1768 Prince Franz of Anhalt-Dessau laid out his park in the Picturesque manner and scattered it, in the years that followed, with Gothic hermitages and ruins. Other 18th-century German gardens were similarly embellished: the New Garden in Potsdam, laid out in the 1780s for Frederick William II by Langhans, or the more spectacular ruined Ritterburg (1793–98), in the park of the landgrave William IX of Hesse at Wilhelmshöhe. There were even odd or idiosyncratic interpretations of Gothic—the tower of Mainz cathedral (1767–74) by Franz Ignaz Neumann or the Laugier-inspired remodeling of the St. Nikolai Church in Leipzig (1784–97) by Johann Friedrich Carl Dauthe. In the latter church, the Gothic ribs of the vault were transformed into palm fronds.

The first architect of any distinction to take an active interest in Gothic was Karl Friedrich Schinkel. He was inspired by Friedrich Gilly's engravings of the castle of Marienburg in East Prussia (1799) to paint, between 1810 and 1815, a number of visionary studies of Gothic buildings in the manner of the German Romantic painter Caspar David Friedrich. He also designed several stage sets in the Gothic style. Schinkel's first serious architectural composition was a Gothic mausoleum designed in 1810 for Queen Louisa of Prussia. He did other equally Romantic designs in Gothic, the most spectacular being that for a cathedral in the Leipzig Square, Berlin. But none of his ambitious Gothic projects was executed; those that were built are of little consequence.

Other prominent Neoclassicists who experimented with Gothic were Friedrich von Gärtner, designer of the Ludwigskirche (1829–44) in Munich, and Gottfried Semper, who provided the plans for the Cholera Fountain in Dresden (1843). But their handling of Gothic forms was stiff and awkward, as was that of most German architects of the period, whose works were adulterated and unconvincing essays into the style.

Gothic Revival architecture in Vienna

The first significant church of the Gothic Revival was the Votive Church (1856–79) in Vienna by Heinrich von Ferstel (Figure 94). Indeed, Vienna was the centre of the most active and intriguing adaptations of Gothic. Friedrich Schmidt, who had worked under Zwirner at Cologne, was the leading revivalist. He built no less than eight churches in Vienna, ranging in date from the Church of the Lazarists (1860–62) to St. Severinus Church (1877–78). The most ambitious is the Fünfhaus parish church (1868–75) outside Vienna. He was the architect also of the Academische Gymnasium on Beethoven Square (1863–66) and the town hall (1872–83).

Along the Rhine, several great castles were restored and dramatized with spiky Gothic trimmings. In Dresden there was a minor outburst of revivalism, but these works cannot be said to have contributed much to the course of architectural history. The Gothic Revival in Germany was not a concerted movement, and there is no specific term in German to describe it. One of the rare buildings that may be considered as characteristic of a specifically German revival and exuberantly Gothic is the Munich Town Hall (1867–74, enlarged 1899–1909), by Georg Joseph von Hauberisser.

The Low Countries. The Gothic style continued strong in the Low Countries throughout the 16th, 17th, and 18th centuries, inflecting the revived classical architecture to so great an extent that it retained a peculiar, hybrid quality. But no significant contribution was made to the Gothic movement until the Dutch architect Petrus Josephus Hubertus Cuypers, an ardent and painstaking interpreter of the ideas of Viollet-le-Duc, began work. The career of Cuypers was, indeed, parallel to that of Viollet-le-Duc; he restored numerous Gothic churches and built many new ones in that style, mainly of brick, the Vondel Church of 1870 and the Church of Mary Magdalene of 1887, both in Amsterdam, being the most impressive. For his great secular buildings in that city, the Rijksmuseum (1876–85) and the Central Station (1881–89), he chose a Gothic that passes rather into the Renaissance style.

Figure 94: Votive Church, Vienna, by Heinrich von Ferstel, 1856–79.

By courtesy of the Osterreichische Nationalbibliothek; photograph, A. Obermayer

In Belgium the work of Cuypers finds its counterpart in that of Jozef Schadde, architect of the Antwerp stock exchange (1858–80) and the station in Brugge.

Scandinavia. The emergence of National Romanticism in the 1880s gave rise to buildings such as Martin Nyrop's Copenhagen Town Hall (1892–1902), which combined Northern Renaissance features with a crenellated Gothic skyline. Its fine craftsmanship and delicate eclecticism were echoed in the celebrated Town Hall at Stockholm, designed in 1908 by Ragnar Östberg and executed in 1911–23. In Finland, Lars Sonck worked in a powerful Arts and Crafts Gothic style reminiscent of the work of H.H. Richardson in the United States: for example, his Tampere Cathedral (1902–07) and Telephone Exchange, Helsinki (1905).

Italy. The Gothic Revival never really took hold in Italy. The Pedrocchi Cafè (1837), with its Venetian Gothic wing erected in Padua by Giuseppe Japelli, and Pelagio Palagi's pavilion La Margheria (1834–39), at Racconigi, are isolated examples. The revival was confined in the main to the completion of church facades, starting with that of the cathedral in Milan (1806–13) by Carlo Amati and Giuseppe Zanoia. It included Giorgio Morandi's fanciful addition to the front of the cathedral at Biella (*c.* 1825) and the facades of Santa Croce (1857–63) in Florence, by Niccolò Matas; the cathedral of Florence (1867–87) by Emilio de Fabris; and the cathedral of Naples (1876–1907) by Enrico Alvino, Niccolò Breglia, and Giuseppe Pisanti.

Spain and Portugal. There was virtually nothing in the way of revived Gothic architecture in Spain before the middle of the 19th century, when Juan Martorell and a group of his disciples in Catalonia took up the idea of evolving a national style based on medieval precedent. The source of their inspiration was the work of Viollet-le-Duc. But it was not until Antoni Gaudí i Cornet, the most idiosyncratic of all Catalan architects, started designing in the 1870s that anything of more than marginal interest was built. His first independent work, the house of Don Manuel Vicens in Barcelona (1878–80), was, however, Mudéjar rather than Gothic in style, as were such later works as the Episcopal Palace at Astorga (1887–93) and the College of Santa Teresa de Jesús (1889–94) in Barcelona. His Gothic sympathies were evident in the crypt of the church of the Holy Family in Barcelona, which he completed from 1884 to 1887, to the design of his master Francesc de Paula del Villar i Carmona. Gaudí also restored the Gothic cathedral of Palma, on the island of Mallorca, between 1901 and 1914. The Gothic element is implicit rather than overt, however, in most of his intensely personal mature works.

United States. The Gothic Revival in the United States was inevitably a stylistic import; it was not the outcome of deeply felt original sentiments of either a Romantic or moral nature. At first, it was regarded only as a facet of architectural historicism. Architects later adopted the aspirations and ideals of Pugin, the Camdenians, and even of Viollet-le-Duc and attempted to use the Gothic style in conformity with the principles that they had laid down; but few were consistent (the Episcopalians alone adhered to the doctrines of the Ecclesiologists), and fewer still had sufficient first-hand knowledge of the style to interpret it with any conviction.

Early examples of Gothic design in the United States

Drawings exist for Gothic garden pavilions for Monticello, Thomas Jefferson's plantation near Charlottesville, Va.; but the first recorded building in the Gothic style was Sedgeley, a mansion erected outside Philadelphia in 1798 to the design of Benjamin Latrobe. The thin, etiolated Gothic of this house was repeated in other of his designs—an unexecuted project for Baltimore cathedral (1805); the Bank of Philadelphia (1807–08); Christ Church (1808), Washington, D.C.; and St. Paul's at Alexandria, Va. (1817)—but he was essentially a Neoclassical architect. The same could be said of other early practitioners of Gothic—William Strickland, who built the Masonic Hall (1809–11) and St. Stephen's (1822–23), both in Philadelphia, and Charles Bulfinch, architect of the Federal Street Church, Boston (1809).

The first Gothic Revival church of any consequence, St. Mary's Seminary in Baltimore (1807), was designed by a Frenchman, Maximilien Godefroy. Others were built in the early decades of the 19th century—*e.g.,* St. Luke's at Rochester, N.Y. (1824–26)—but not before the 1830s was a series of churches put up in and around Boston that gives evidence of a consistent Gothic Revival movement—Solomon Willard's Bowdoin Street Church (1830) and the First Methodist Episcopal Church in Temple Street, both in Boston, and St. Peter's (1833) and the First Unitarian Church (1936–37) in Salem, Mass., are examples. Most of these churches are constructed of granite and consequently are plain and simple in detail. In sharp contrast are the light timber churches with intricate and fanciful Gothic details put up at the same period, in particular St. Peter's at Waterford, Pa. (1831), by Bishop John Hopkins, author of an *Essay on Gothic Architecture* (1836).

The second phase of the U.S. Gothic Revival

The active, enterprising architect of the next phase of the Gothic Revival was Richard Upjohn. In 1835 he built a somewhat thin and vitiated Gothic mansion, Oaklands, at Gardiner, Maine. He achieved fame, however, as a builder of churches. St. John's (1836), Bangor, Maine, was his first Gothic church; but it was Trinity Church (1839–46) at New York City, in a flat, harsh Gothic style, that established his reputation (Figure 95). This was built for the Episcopalians and was rigidly "correct" in the ecclesiological sense. During the next 30 years he designed no fewer than 40 Gothic churches, mostly for the Episcopalians. Externally, they appear as brittle, uninspired adaptations of English models, but in his internal work and especially in such buildings as the First Parish Church (1845–46), Brunswick, Maine, he showed himself to be an extraordinary and unparalleled manipulator of timber arcading and trussing. Equally important as exemplars of intrinsically American interpretations of the Gothic Revival theme are his churches built entirely of timber—wooden framed and sheathed with vertical boarding and battening—such as St. Paul's at Brunswick, Maine, of 1845, or St. Thomas', Hamilton, N.Y., of 1847.

Figure 95: Trinity Church, New York City, by Richard Upjohn, 1839–46.
Wayne Andrews

The timber tradition (or "carpenter's Gothic") was in no way limited to ecclesiastical work. *Upjohn's Rural Architecture* (1852) applied the same method of design to the construction of timber houses and cottages. Decorated with details deriving from Gothic sources, this domestic architecture was, in sheer quantity, the chief expression of the Gothic Revival during the middle years of the century. Powerful support for the movement came also from Andrew Jackson Downing, landscape gardener and architectural critic, who was a close friend of the architect Alexander Jackson Davis. In 1845 Davis designed the first plantation mansion in the Gothic style (Belmead, Powhatan County, Va.) and, more significantly, Ericstan (1855), the John J. Herrick house in Tarrytown, N.Y., which introduced castellated Gothic into the Hudson River Valley, and did Gothic cottage designs like the home of William H. Drake at Hartford, Conn. (Figure 96). Downing leaned heavily on the theorists of the English Picturesque style—his major work, *A Treatise on the Theory and Practice of Landscape Gardening Adapted to North America* (1841), is, indeed, a paraphrase of their arguments—but, in his pattern books *Cottage Residences* (1842) and *The Architecture of Country Houses* (1850), he provided an inherently American variant on the "stick style," with its use of board-and-batten finish to imitate half-timbering, that was soon diffused widely as the "bracketed cottage style."

About 1860 the Gothic movement entered a new and de-

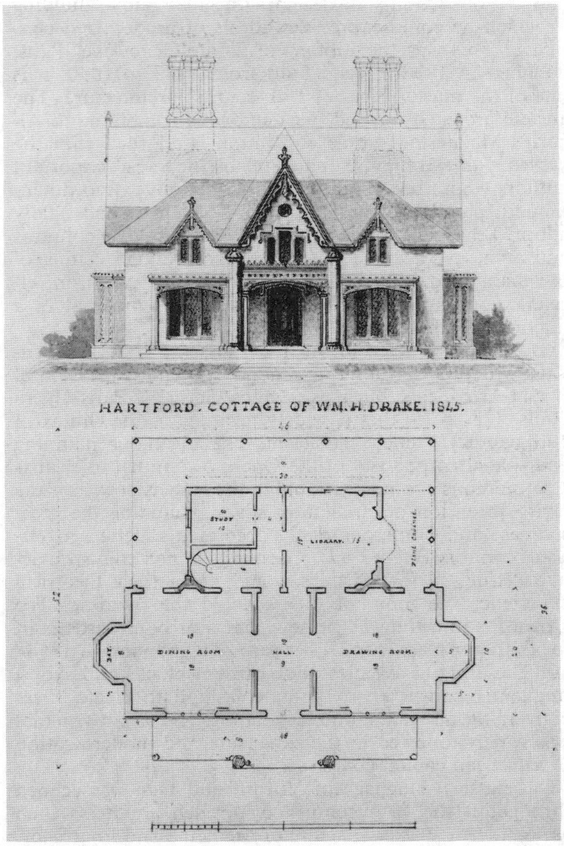

Figure 96: William H. Drake Cottage, Hartford, Conn., drawing by Alexander Jackson Davis, 1845. (Top) Exterior; (bottom) plan. In the Metropolitan Museum of Art, New York City.

By courtesy of the Metropolitan Museum of Art, New York, Harris Brisbane Dick Fund, 1924

terminedly serious phase. James Renwick (1818–95), who in 1848 had designed the Smithsonian Institution in Washington, D.C., in a Neo-Norman style, used continental models again in 1859 when building St. Patrick's Roman Catholic Cathedral in New York City. Most architects of the period, however, sought inspiration from England and acclaimed the writings of Ruskin. The first building to give expression to his teachings was perhaps the Alumni Hall, Union College, Schenectady, N.Y., designed in 1858 and completed in 1875, by Edward T. Potter, a pupil of Upjohn. The banded and pointed arches of this building at once suggest the influence of Ruskin. More successful—and controversial—as an exponent of the Ruskinian aesthetic was Peter B. Wight, architect of the National Academy of Design, New York City (1863–65). There the Venetian Gothic mode came into its own. Wight and Potter—and, later, Potter's brother William Appleton—were responsible for a number of collegiate and public buildings in this harsh, polychrome Gothic style, but it was William Robert Ware and his partner Henry Van Brunt who were to become its most fashionable exponents. In 1859 Ware built St. John's Chapel at the Episcopal Theological Seminary on Brattle Street in Cambridge, Mass.; six years later he and his partner started the First Church (Unitarian) in Boston, and in 1870 they began Memorial Hall at Harvard, a conspicuous, if not altogether polished, exemplar of the style. Other purveyors of "collegiate Gothic" were Richard Morris Hunt, architect of the Yale Divinity School (1869), and Russell Sturgis, a partner of Wight, who designed several of the halls at Yale University between 1869 and 1885.

Influence of Ruskin in the United States

John H. Sturgis and Charles Brigham, architects of the Museum of Fine Arts on Copley Square (1876) and the Church of the Advent (1878), both in Boston, attempted to give to this tough, uneasy Gothic style something of monumental grandeur in their competition design of 1872 for the Connecticut State Capitol Building in Hartford. Their design was reminiscent of that submitted by William Burges in 1866 for the Royal Courts of Justice in London. The competition, however, was won by Richard M. Upjohn, son of the church builder, who provided a Gothic project that was equally grandiose if more equivocal in expression. Within a few years Hartford was to possess an authentic Burges building, Trinity College. Only a small part of Burges' magnificent design of 1873 was, however, executed.

The most original architects to emerge from the late Gothic Revival movement were Frank Furness, known for his vigorous handling of Gothic motifs on the Pennsylvania Academy of Fine Arts (1872–76) and a series of banks in Philadelphia—the most extraordinary of which was the Provident Institution on Chestnut Street (1879)—and Henry Hobson Richardson, who used characteristics of the Gothic and Romanesque as a point of departure for the creation of a distinctive and altogether personal style. Richardson started his Gothic career with the Unity Church (1866–69), Springfield, Mass. During the following years he developed a robust, broadly proportioned style in a series of churches—Grace Episcopal Church, West Medford, Mass. (1867–68); Brattle Square Church, Boston (1870–72); and the North Congregational Church, Springfield, Mass. (1872–73)—culminating in Trinity Church on Copley Square, Boston (*c.* 1872–77). Overt Gothic influence is evident in most of Richardson's early works, but later the Gothic style was to be superseded by the introduction of Romanesque paradigms, to which he gave so strong an imprint of his own distinct sense of style that they are rarely disquieting.

In the 20th century the most ardent exponents of Gothic were Ralph Adams Cram and his partners, Bertram G. Goodhue and Frank W. Ferguson, who regarded it as particularly suitable for educational establishments. The Graduate College (1913) and University Chapel (1929) at Princeton University are among their finest achievements. Other powerful Gothic buildings include their Cadet Chapel, United States Military Academy, West

20th-century Gothic

Giraudon/Art Resource, New York City

Figure 97: Grand staircase of the Opera House, Paris, by Charles Garnier, completed 1875.

Point, N.Y. (1910), and James Gamble Rogers' Memorial Quadrangle and Harkness Tower, Yale University, New Haven, Conn. (1916–33). Goodhue's most arresting building is his State Capitol, Lincoln, Neb. (1921–32), with a soaring tower that has a Gothic flavour though its design is fundamentally abstract. Gothic elements are also responsible for the medieval-tower aspect of many of the early skyscrapers, the most notable example being Cass Gilbert's Woolworth Building, New York City (1910–13), which has a steel frame clad in fireproof, lightweight terra-cotta, richly carved with Gothic detail and dramatically illuminated at night. (R.D.Mi./D.J.Wa.)

Classicism, 1830–1930

CONTINUING DEVELOPMENT

Until recently conventional histories of architecture treated the 19th century as an unfortunate period in which historicist architects needlessly obstructed the path to a new functionalist architecture based on technology and engineering. The importance of the 20th century, according to this view, consisted in the establishment of the Modern movement as the final victory of functionalism—in which buildings are designed so as to avoid all historical reference and are even constructed of "new" materials.

Today, however, a new interpretation has arisen, for two reasons: first, the growth of serious study of the historical architecture of the 19th century led to its reappraisal as an independent architectural movement of high quality; second, the arrival of postmodernism in the 1970s led to a realization that the Modern movement was not a permanent plateau to which the whole of the 19th and 20th centuries had been leading but was simply another historical period. With the withdrawal of the privileged status that had been for so long granted to the Modern movement, it became possible to take a broader look at the period from 1830 to 1930. From the conventional histories, for example, one would scarcely be aware that most buildings erected up to the 1930s were designed in a range of classical and traditional styles.

NATIONAL AND REGIONAL VARIATIONS

École des Beaux-Arts

France. The École des Beaux-Arts (School of Fine Arts) in Paris was the most important centre of architectural education in the Western world in the 19th century. Founded in 1819 as the successor to the Royal Academy of Architecture, the École drew students not only from France but also from throughout Europe and, after 1850, from North America. At the École, architecture was seen as a public service involving the representation in stone of national and civic dignity, and teaching thus centred on the problems of designing monumental public buildings in the classical style. Jacques-Ignace Hittorff was typical of those architects who combined the practice of modern classicism with archaeological investigation into Greek and Roman architecture. His Gare du Nord, Paris (1861–65), showed brilliantly how a language ultimately inspired by the triumphal arches of ancient Rome could lend an appropriate monumental emphasis to a major metropolitan railway terminus. In Saint-Vincent-de-Paul, Paris (1830–46), a church with a giant portico leading to an aisled basilican interior, Hittorff incorporated polychromatic decoration inspired by his discoveries that Greek temples had been systematically painted in strong colours. His publications on this subject between 1827 and 1851 were important because the gaudy and essentially ephemeral character of polychromatic decoration was incompatible with the image of timeless purity with which Greek art had been invested by Winckelmann.

Henri Labrouste, a more inventive architect than Hittorff, pursued similar research into Greek architecture with the ambition of making it seem human rather than divine or unapproachable; for example, he argued that what is now known as the Temple of Hera I at Paestum was not a temple but a civil assembly hall. His drawings showing the building in use, with transitory adornments such as trophies, inscriptions, paintings, and even graffiti, shocked the members of the Academy of Fine Arts to whom he submitted them in 1828. Ten years later he had the opportunity of designing a great public building in which he could express his ideals of modernized classicism. This was the Library of Sainte-Geneviève, Paris, designed in 1838–39 and built from 1843 to 1850; it is one of the masterpieces of 19th-century architecture. The austere arcuated (arched) facade, owing something to Alberti's Malatesta Temple at Rimini, is adorned with the carved names of more than 800 of the most important authors whose books are housed within: an extraordinary modern parallel to the graffiti with which he had boldly adorned the walls of the basilica at Paestum. The columns and arches supporting the huge barrel-vaulted ceiling of the main reading room are constructed of cast iron, elegantly ornamented—an early use of this material in a major public building.

Louis Duc's Palace of Justice, Paris (1857–68), articulated with a powerful Doric order, is a major expression of Beaux-Arts ideals, but it is Charles Garnier's Paris Opera House (1862–75) that is widely regarded as the climax of 19th-century French classicism. The ingenious planning and spatial complexity of the Opera owe much to Beaux-Arts methods of organization, but the scale is new, as is the lavish provision of circulation space, including the great staircase and numerous richly decorated galleries, foyers, and corridors (Figure 97). Garnier planned this spectacular setting so that visitors would begin their theatrical experience the moment they entered the building. The Opera fits into the web of new streets or boulevards built for Emperor Napoleon III by Baron Haussmann in 1854–70. These broad avenues of apartment blocks and shops, frequently contrived in Baroque fashion to create vistas converging on major public buildings, set a pattern that was widely followed in the expansion and modernization of European capital cities.

Haussmann's boulevards

The classical language of Hittorff and Duc was echoed throughout the 19th century by French architects such as Jean-Louis Pascal (Faculty of Medicine and Pharmacy, Bordeaux; 1880–88) and Henri-Paul Nénot (New Sorbonne, Paris; 1885–1901), both of whom were influential teachers at the École des Beaux-Arts. A high point was reached with the Paris Exposition of 1889, for which Henri Deglane and Victor Laloux erected, respectively, the Grand Palais and the Gare d'Orsay (renovated as the Orsay Museum, 1979–86). These monumental buildings are in a frothy Baroque style, though they incorporate much glass and iron. Reaction to this exuberance was expressed in the work of Auguste Perret, who attempted to apply the newly developed technique of reinforced-concrete construction to buildings designed in a trabeated (post-and-lintel) style that was ultimately classical: for example, his Theatre of the Champs-Élysées, Paris (1911–12), and the much drier Museum of Public Works, Paris (1936), now the headquarters of the Economic and Social Council. At the International Exposition of 1937, or Paris World's Fair, pavilions in a range of styles were dominated by the Chaillot Palace, built from designs by Jacques Carlu, Louis-Hippolyte Boileau, and Léon Azéma. This is a striking example of the austere trabeated classicism that was the most popular style for public buildings in the 1930s in many parts of the United States and Europe, including the Soviet Union. It is often known as stripped classicism because features such as columns and pilasters were reduced to a grid and deprived of their customary mouldings.

Great Britain. Britain in 1830 was still in the middle of a building boom that had begun at the end of the Napoleonic Wars in 1815. Towns were expanded with buildings in the international Greek Revival manner such as William Wilkins' Yorkshire Museum, York (1827–30). The architect Charles Robert Cockerell, despite being a distinguished classical archaeologist, regarded this rigid Greek formula as stylistically restricting. He felt that he belonged to a continuing classical tradition that linked Ictinus with Borromini. In his masterpiece, the Ashmolean Museum and Taylorian Institution, Oxford (1841–45), he produced a type of Grecian mannerism in which elements from Greek, Roman, Renaissance, and Baroque architecture were united in a rich sculptural weave of powerful originality. He was also important for bringing the same high quality of design and materials to the field of commercial architecture, as in his Bank of England, Liverpool (1844–47).

Despite the high regard in which the allusive classical buildings of this learned and sensitive architect were held, the immediate future for British architecture did not lie with Cockerell. The Gothic Revival attracted the most thoughtful minds and the most gifted architects between about 1840 and 1870. From the 1870s, however, Richard Norman Shaw and William Eden Nesfield led a move away from the Gothic Revival, with its strongly ecclesiastical flavour, to the more domestic charms of the so-called Queen Anne Revival. In prominent buildings such as his red-brick mansion for Frederick White at No. 170, Queen's Gate, London (1888–90), and Parr's (now National Westminster) Bank, Liverpool (1898–1901), Shaw demonstrated the virtues of the simple astylar (columnless) classical tradition of English 17th- and 18th-century architecture.

English domestic architecture

Among the many who were profoundly influenced by the brilliance and diversity of Shaw in the field of domestic and commercial architecture, none was more important than Sir Edwin Lutyens. In early houses such as Deanery Garden, Sonning, Berkshire (1901), he adopted local vernacular styles but was nonetheless able to display his characteristic geometric massing on the exteriors and his love of complex spatial flow in the interiors. These qualities make such houses an interesting parallel to the domestic work of Lutyens' contemporary Frank Lloyd Wright. The same play with volume and space governs the design of Lutyens' masterpieces such as Viceroy's House (now the Presidential Palace), New Delhi (1912–30), and the Memorial to the Missing of the Somme, Thiepval, Fr. (1928–30), in which he reduced the language of the classical orders to an almost abstract synthesis.

Italy. The Neoclassical town planning of the years around 1815 was succeeded in Italy, as elsewhere in Europe, by a Renaissance Revival of which an ambitious example is the Palace of Justice, Rome (1888–1910), by Guglielmo Calderini. This revival was appropriate in a country that was home to the Renaissance. It thus blended well with the growth of Italian nationalism, of which the most conspicuous architectural expression is Giuseppe Sacconi's Monument to Victor Emmanuel II, Rome (1885–1911). This amazingly confident, if generally unloved, re-creation of imperial Roman grandeur commemorates the king under whom Italian unity had been achieved in 1861.

Italy's ancient Roman past was recalled once more in the 1920s and '30s as a consequence of Mussolini's attempt to legitimate his political regime. In Rome during the 1930s Marcello Piacentini and Vittorio Ballio Mopurgo created, respectively, the Via della Conciliazione and the Piazza Augusto Imperiale. Though monumental in scale, these were in a dull and simplified classical style and involved the destruction of substantial parts of the historic centre of the city. More attractive were the new towns, such as Littoria (now Latina) and Aprilia, created south of Rome in 1932–39, whose architects drew on the recent archaeological discoveries at the ancient Roman town of Ostia.

Germany and Austria. Schinkel set the pattern for the transformation of 18th-century royal cities into modern urban centres with numerous Neoclassical public buildings built in Berlin between 1815 and 1835. His many successors in Berlin included Friedrich Stüler and Johann Strack, who designed the National Gallery (1865–69), but architects such as Paul Wallot adopted an increasingly turgid neo-Renaissance manner, as in the Reichstag Building (1884–94). In the mid-19th century Munich was transformed for King Ludwig I of Bavaria by Leo von Klenze and Friedrich von Gärtner into a major cultural capital. Their twin models were Periclean Athens and Renaissance Florence, the former providing the inspiration for Klenze's Greek Doric Ruhmeshalle (1843–54) and Propylaeon (1846–60) and the latter for Gärtner's Bavarian State Library (1832–43). The most poetic product of a Winckelmannesque identification of the spirit of modern Germany with that of ancient Greece was the Walhalla above the Danube River near Regensburg. This great Greek temple was built in 1830–42 for Ludwig I from designs by Klenze as a monument to pan-German unity.

Ancient Greek influences in Germany

Vienna was also transformed from 1858 by the construction of the Ringstrasse, a great boulevard on the site of the old city walls. In the 1870s and '80s it was lined with monumental public buildings in a variety of styles thought historically appropriate for their functions: the Danish architect Theophilus Hansen's neo-Greek Parliament House, Gottfried Semper's and Karl von Hasenauer's neo-Baroque Burgtheater, and Friedrich von Schmidt's neo-Gothic Town Hall.

About 1900 the search for a more indigenous German classicism encouraged Alfred Messel in Berlin to study the austere Neoclassicism of Gentz and Gilly of a century earlier, hence the Greek Revival flavour of Messel's offices for the AEG (formerly the Allgemeine Elektricitäts-Gesellschaft) and his National Bank, both built in Berlin in 1905–07. Messel was succeeded as architect to the AEG by Peter Behrens, who worked in many styles, of which the most influential was the neo-Schinkelesque stripped classicism of his German Embassy in St. Petersburg (1911–12). This style was popular between the world wars when it was regarded as so essentially Germanic that it was adopted for the design of key monuments of the Third Reich, such as Paul Ludwig Troost's House of German Art, Munich (1933–37), and Albert Speer's New Chancellery, Berlin (1938–39).

Scandinavia and Greece. The key building in the development of Scandinavian classicism in the period 1830–1930 is the Thorvaldsen Museum in Copenhagen, erected in 1839–48 from designs by Michael Gottlieb Bindesbøll. It was built to house the collection of sculpture that the celebrated Danish Neoclassical sculptor Bertel Thorvaldsen presented to his native country in 1837. The opportunity was taken of providing a major cultural monument to strengthen national consciousness at a time of political crisis and to symbolize the new constitutional democracy that was established in 1849. The exterior walls of Bindesbøll's grave Schinkelesque courtyard were enlivened with polychromatic decoration and painted with appropriate narrative scenes. This system of ornament was inspired by his knowledge of the recent archaeological discoveries in Greece and Sicily. He had visited Athens in 1835–36, and it was in this city, appropriately, that the Greek Revival was given perhaps its most fitting civic expression: Hans Christian Hansen, a friend of Bindesbøll, excavated and restored the ancient Greek monuments on the Acropolis and built the University (1839–50). This crisp Ionic building eventually formed a group with the National Library and the Academy of Science, which were added from designs by Hans Christian and his brother Theophilus between 1859 and 1892.

The buildings of Bindesbøll and the Hansen brothers were a potent influence on the Scandinavian classicists of the early 20th century such as Carl Petersen (Fåborg Museum, Denmark, 1912–15) and Hack Kampmann (Police Headquarters, Copenhagen, 1919–24). Other notable expressions of this cool and austere language in Stockholm are Ivar Tengbom's Concert House (1920–26) and two masterpieces by Gunnar Asplund, the City Library (1920–28) and Woodland Crematorium (1935–40). (D.J.Wa.)

United States. The followers of Latrobe lacked his inventive genius but adapted the more conventional aspects of his Greek Revival work to create a public style that symbolized the dignity of the new democracy. The Greek Revival in the United States had as its leading exponents William Strickland, Robert Mills, Thomas Walter, and Ithiel Town. Strickland was the architect of the Merchants' Exchange, Philadelphia (1832–34), which featured a soaring lantern reminiscent of the Choragic Monument of Lysicrates in Athens. Mills built many government buildings in Washington, D.C., including the Treasury (1836–42) and the Patent Office (begun 1836), He also designed the Washington Monument in Baltimore (1815–29), a giant Doric column, the first such monument in the United States. Walter worked on the U.S. Capitol building and in Philadelphia, where he designed Girard College (1833–47) in the form of an elegant Corinthian temple. Countless state houses and public buildings throughout the United States continued to be built from Greco-Roman models into the 20th century. Alexander Jackson Davis was one of the leading architects of the Greek-temple house, of which the Bowers House, Northampton, Mass. (1825–26), is an example. Such Greek houses were particularly numerous in the South, fine examples being Berry Hill, Halifax County, Va. (1835–40), and Belle Meade, near Nashville, Tenn. (1853). (S.Mi./D.J.Wa.)

These Neoclassical buildings were ultimately of English derivation, but the pattern of architecture in the United States shifted in 1846 when Richard Morris Hunt became the first American to enroll as an architectural student at the École des Beaux-Arts in Paris. Hunt specialized in mansions for the new commercial aristocracy of America: for example, The Breakers, Newport, R.I., built in 1892–95 in an opulent neo-Renaissance style for Cornelius Vanderbilt II (Figure 98). In 1859–62 Henry Hobson Richardson trained at the École, and on his return to the United States he specialized in a rock-faced Romanesque style probably inspired by the work of Viollet-le-Duc's rationalist follower, Vaudremer. Richardson's most celebrated buildings in this vein are the Allegheny County Court House and Jail, Pittsburgh (1883–88), and the Marshall Field and Company Wholesale Store, Chicago (1885–87; demolished in 1930; Figure 99).

Hunt and Richardson

Richardson's pupil Charles Follen McKim, who had been trained at the École in 1867–70, set up a partnership with William Rutherford Mead and Stanford White that was to change the course of American architecture. Following their early domestic masterpieces in the vernacular, or Shingle, style, such as the Low House, Bristol, R.I. (1887; demolished in 1962; Figure 100), McKim, Mead, and White produced a chain of classical buildings that were more consistently monumental than anything seen since the days of the Roman Empire. These include the Boston Public Library (1887–95), the Rhode Island State Capitol (1891–93), Columbia University, New York City (1894–98), and Pennsylvania Station, New York City (1902–11; demolished in 1963); the last is a mighty adaptation of the Baths of Caracalla and a reminder that the Roman baths exercised a powerful influence on the imagination of architects from at least the time of Bramante.

The World's Columbian Exposition at Chicago in 1893, which included buildings by McKim, Mead, and White, commemorated the 400th anniversary of the discovery of the New World and also helped modern Americans rediscover the value of classical planning in civic design. The dazzling spectacle of monumental classical architecture on the fair's Midway caught the fancy of Americans who saw in its great axes, lagoons, sculpture, white buildings, and large plazas an answer to the dreary urban environments of their hometowns. Similar schemes were supported in other cities; some of these were designed by the fair's principal planner, Daniel Burnham, who brought the "great white city" to Cleveland, Washington, D.C., New York City, and San Francisco. The best parts of many American cities are spacious because of the planners of the City-Beautiful movement.

Three of the many architects who continued this classical tradition after World War I were John Russell Pope (Jefferson Memorial, 1934–43, and National Gallery of Art, 1937–41, both in Washington, D.C.), Paul Philippe Cret (Hartford County Building, Connecticut, 1926), and Philip Trammell Shutze (Temple of the Hebrew Benevolent Congregation, Atlanta, Ga., 1931–32). Despite this classical strain, the keynote of 1930s architecture was stylistic pluralism. The Gothic Revival continued, especially in university buildings, whereas domestic architecture in the suburbs could be neo-Tudor or neo-Georgian. With the aid of technology, buildings in the style of Spanish estates were built in Florida, French farmhouses in Philadelphia, Georgian and colonial houses in New England, and pueblos in the Southwest. Georgia revived its antebellum architecture, and Santa Barbara, Calif., which was destroyed by an earthquake in 1925, was quickly rebuilt in the style of a Spanish mission. (D.J.Wa.)

Late 19th-century developments

19TH-CENTURY CONSTRUCTION IN IRON AND GLASS

The Industrial Revolution in Britain introduced new building types and new methods of construction. Marshall, Benyou, and Bage's flour mill (now Allied Breweries) at Ditherington, Shropshire (1796–97), is one of the first iron-frame buildings, though brick walls still carry part of the load and there are no longitudinal beams. The cloth mill at King's Stanley, Gloucestershire (1812–13), is more convincing as an iron-frame building. Fully fireproof and avoiding the use of timber, it is clad in an attractive red-brick skin with Venetian windows and angle quoins. Leading Regency architects even used cast-iron construction members in major public buildings in the classical style: Smirke incorporated concealed cast-iron beams in the British Museum (1823–46), while Nash openly displayed cast-iron Doric columns at Buckingham Palace (1825–30).

Iron was frequently combined with glass in the construction of conservatories; early surviving examples include the conservatory (1827–30) at Syon House, Middlesex, by Charles Fowler and the Palm House (1845–47) at Kew Gardens, Surrey, by Decimus Burton. These led naturally to the Crystal Palace, the climax of early Victorian technology. In the design of the Crystal Palace, built for the Great Exhibition held at London in 1851, Sir Joseph Paxton, a botanist, employed timber, cast iron, wrought iron, and glass in a ridge-and-furrow system he had developed for greenhouses at Chatsworth in 1837. Paxton was partly inspired by the organic structure of the Amazonian lily *Victoria regia,* which he successfully cultivated. The

By courtesy of The Preservation Society of Newport County, Rhode Island

Figure 98: The Breakers, Newport, R.I., by Richard Morris Hunt, 1892–95.

Figure 99: Marshall Field and Company Wholesale Store, Chicago, by H.H. Richardson, 1885–87; demolished 1930.

Chicago Architectural Photo Company

The importance of the Crystal Palace

Crystal Palace contained important innovations in mass production of standardized materials and rapid assembly of parts, but its chief architectural merit lay in its cadence of colossal spaces. French designers recognized its magic, and a series of buildings for universal exhibitions held at Paris in 1855, 1867, and 1878 showed its influence.

The emancipation of markets and stores was no less impressive. Designers erected iron and glass umbrellas, such as Victor Baltard's Halles Centrales, Paris (1853–70; demolished 1971). An especially beautiful example of iron-and-glass construction is Labrouste's nine-domed reading room at the Bibliothèque Nationale, Paris (1859–67; Figure 101).

Closer to the English tradition are the billowing Laeken glass houses, Brussels (1868–76), by Alphonse Balat. Visitors were admitted to the Coal Exchange in London (1846–49, J.B. Bunning) through a round towered classical porch at the corner of two Renaissance palaces to a magnificent rotunda hall, which was surrounded by three tiers of ornamental iron balconies and roofed by a lace-like dome of iron and glass. In Paris, Alexandre-Gustave Eiffel, together with the architect Louis-Auguste Boileau, gave the retail shop a new and exciting setting in the Bon Marché (1876), where merchandise was displayed around the perimeters of skylighted, interior courts. The United States saw nothing comparable, but cast-iron columns and arches appeared during the 1850s in commercial buildings such as the Harper Brothers Building at New York City (1849) by John B. Corlies and James Bogardus. Stores were given cast-iron faces, as in the pioneering Stewart's Department Store (later Wanamaker's) by John Kellum in New York City (1859–62). Iron was frequently intended to simulate stone, and it was admired for its economy of maintenance as well as such neglected qualities as precision, standardization, and efficient strength. British parallels to these American examples include Gardner's Warehouse, Glasgow (1855–56), by John Baird and Oriel Chambers, Liverpool (1864), by Peter Ellis.

The Eiffel Tower (1887–89), the most important emblem of the Paris exhibition of 1889, was designed by Alexandre-Gustave Eiffel, an engineer who had done outstanding work in the Paris Exposition of 1878 and in steel structures such as the trussed parabolic arches in the viaduct at Garabit, Fr. (1880–84). In the Palais des Machines (at the 1889 exhibition) by Ferdinand Dutert and Victor Contamin, a series of three-hinged trussed arches sprang from small points across a huge space, 385 feet long and 150 feet high. Similar spaces had already been created in railway stations in England such as St. Pancras, London (1864–68, by William H. Barlow), where the wrought-iron arches have a span of 243 feet and rise to a height of 100 feet.

The inception of the Chicago School

In the United States a major effort took place in one of the most important new building types, the large office building. This building type was made necessary by the concentration of markets, banks, railroad terminals, and warehouses in small sections of growing cities, and it pushed skyward as a result of the attempt to get maximum income from expensive urban properties, the desire for the commercial prestige of tall emblems, and the need of businesses for mutual proximity in the days before rapid electronic communication. The safe, fast elevator removed the major prejudice against height. Designed by traditionalist architects, the tall buildings stretched masonry construction to its limits; they frequently resembled towers composed of smaller buildings stacked one on another, as in Hunt's Tribune Building at New York City (1874).

Metal frame construction

The structural problem was solved at Chicago in 1884–85, when an engineer, William Le Baron Jenney, developed in the Home Insurance Company Building a metal skeleton of cast-iron columns—sheathed in masonry—and wrought-iron beams, carrying the masonry walls and windows at each floor level. Technically innovative, the building retained masonry sidewalls, and its elevations were disunified and inept.

Inspired by the architectural rationalism of Viollet-le-Duc, Chicago architects sought a better aesthetic expression of the metal frame, but even the talented John Wellborn Root, working with Daniel Burnham, failed to achieve it in the Ashland Block (completed 1892). Lesser designers, such as William Holabird and Martin Roche in the Tacoma Building (1887–89), also missed their chance. Even the great Louis Sullivan was not successful in his early buildings, such as the Ryerson (1884). Covering them with gross, somewhat Art Nouveau ornament, he accentuated first the vertical columns and then the horizontal beams in a covert admission of failure. At his best, as in

Wayne Andrews

Figure 100: W.G. Low House, Bristol, R.I., by McKim, Mead, and White, 1887; destroyed 1962.

Figure 101: Reading room of the Bibliothèque Nationale, Paris, by Henri Labrouste, 1854–68.
W. Rawlings/Robert Harding Picture Library

his Auditorium Building, Sullivan trod Richardson's path toward unified Romanesque forms. The Marshall Field Wholesale Store showed Sullivan the way toward a theme for the skyscraper, which he first stated with assurance in the Wainwright Building at St. Louis (1890–91). Brick piers mark each steel column and half module to create a rhythm of tall, narrow bays punctuated by recessed spandrels (the spaces above and below each window), terminating at the roofline. Jenney's Leiter Building II (1891; later Sears, Roebuck and Company's main retail store) and Burnham and Root's Monadnock Building (1891), both in Chicago, went beyond the Wainwright Building and were the first modern commercial buildings to demonstrate in their designs formal simplicity and ornamental abstinence, resulting from a new form of harmony between the demands of artistic expression, function, and technology.

Chicago as the centre of architectural innovation

The ferment in Chicago was neither halted nor marred by classicism's transcontinental popularity. Burnham's firm went on to produce Chicago's Reliance Building (1890–95), an excellent office building with logically ordered spaces enclosed by faceted walls of glass and a steel skeleton covered by terra-cotta panels (Figure 102). Sullivan found his best expression of the skyscraper in the Prudential Building, Buffalo (1894–95), and developed the theory for it in an essay published in *Lippincott's Magazine* (1896). That theory received even more dramatic expression in the Schlesinger-Mayer Department Store (later Carson Pirie Scott) in Chicago (1899–1904), in which the towered corner marked the climax of the logic of the steel frame and the entrance was made inviting with rich, naturalistic ornament (Figure 103). At the very end of the 19th century, the important emblem of modern commerce thus received an appropriate form: its structure was made of steel, its spaces were planned efficiently, its elevations were expressive of the skeleton, and its scale was marked by the fenestration and ornament. (A.B.-B./D.J.Wa.)

ART NOUVEAU

Although known as Jugendstil in Germany, Sezessionstil in Austria, Modernista in Spain, and Stile Liberty or Stile Floreale in Italy, Art Nouveau has become the general term applied to a highly varied movement that was European-centred but internationally current at the end of the century. Art Nouveau architects gave idiosyncratic expression to many of the themes that had preoccupied the 19th century, ranging from Viollet-le-Duc's call for structural honesty to Sullivan's call for an organic architecture. The extensive use of iron and glass in Art Nouveau buildings was also rooted in 19th-century practice. In France bizarre forms appeared in iron, masonry, and concrete, such as the structures of Hector Guimard for the Paris Métro (*c.* 1900), the Montmartre church of Saint-Jean L'Évangéliste (1894–1904) by Anatole de Baudot, Xavier Schollkopf's house for the actress Yvette Guilbert at Paris (1900), and the Samaritaine Department Store (1905) near the Pont Neuf in Paris, by Frantz Jourdain (1847–1935). The Art Nouveau architect's preference for the curvilinear is es-

Chicago Architectural Photo Company

Figure 102: Reliance Building, Chicago, by D.H. Burnham and Company, 1890–95. Photograph, *c.* 1905.

Figure 103: Carson Pirie Scott Store, Chicago, by Louis Sullivan, 1899–1904, addition by Daniel H. Burnham and Company, 1906.
Chicago Architectural Photo Company

pecially evident in the Brussels buildings of the Belgian Victor Horta. In the Hôtel Tassel (1892–93) he used floral, tendrilous ornaments (Figure 104), while his Maison du Peuple (1896–99) exhibits undulating enclosures of space. Decorative exploitation of the architectural surface with flexible, S-shaped linear ornament, commonly called whiplash or eel styles, was indulged in by the Jugendstil and Sezessionstil architects. The Studio Elvira at Munich (1897–98) by August Endell and Otto Wagner's Majolika Haus at Vienna (*c.* 1898) are two of the more significant examples of this German and Austrian use of line.

Wagner continued to combine academic geometry with classical modified Art Nouveau decoration in his Karlsplatz Stadtbahn Station (1899–1901) and in the Postal Savings Bank (1904–06), both in Vienna. Wagner's pupils broke free of his classicism and formed the Secessionists. Joseph Olbrich joined the art colony at Darmstadt, Germany, where his houses and exhibition gallery of about 1905 were boxlike, severe buildings. Josef Hoffmann left Wagner to found the Wiener Werksätte, an Austrian equivalent of the English Arts and Crafts Movement; his best work, the Stoclet House at Brussels (1905), was an asymmetrical composition in which white planes were defined at the edges by gilt lines and decorated by formalized Art Nouveau motifs reminiscent of Wagner's ornament. Josef Pečnik, a talented pupil of Wagner, began his career in 1903–05 with the office and residence of Johannes Zacherl in Vienna. This was in a Wagner-inspired style that Pečnik developed in the 1930s in a fascinating series of buildings, especially in his native city of Ljubljana, Yugos.

Viennese Secessionists

In Finland Eliel Saarinen brought an Art Nouveau flavour to the National Romanticism current in the years around 1900. His Helsinki Railway Station (1906–14) is close to the work of Olbrich and the Viennese Secessionists. Close links existed between Art Nouveau designers in Vienna and in Glasgow, where Charles Rennie Mackintosh's School of Art (1896–1909), with its rationalist yet poetic aesthetic, is one of the most inventive and personal of all Art Nouveau buildings. In The Netherlands, Hendrik Petrus Berlage also created a sternly fundamentalist language of marked individuality that is best appreciated in his masterpiece, the Amsterdam Exchange (1897–1903). The exterior is in a rugged and deliberately unpicturesque vernacular, while the even more ruthless interior deploys brick, iron, and glass in a manner that owes much to the rationalist aesthetic of Viollet-le-Duc.

In the United States the Art Nouveau movement arrived with Louis Comfort Tiffany and was especially influential on ornamental rather than spatial design, particularly upon Sullivan's decorative schemes and, for a time, those of Frank Lloyd Wright. Decorative exuberance and the formally picturesque were elements of Stile Floreale buildings by the Italian Raimondo D'Aronco, such as the main building for the Applied Art Exhibition held at Turin, Italy, in 1902. These qualities, along with dynamic spatial innovations, were manifested in the works of perhaps the most singular Art Nouveau architect, the Spaniard Antonio Gaudí. His highly imaginative and dramatic experiments with space, form, structure, and ornament fascinate the visitor to Barcelona. With their peculiar organicism, the Casa Milá apartment house (1905–10; Figure 105), the residence of the Batlló family (1904–06), Gaudí's unfinished lifetime projects of the surrealistic Güell Park and the enigmatic Church of the Holy Family were amazingly personal statements. Their effect, like that of most Art Nouveau architecture, was gained through bizarre form and ornament.

20th-century architecture

THE MODERN MOVEMENT

Before World War II. The Modern movement was an attempt to create a nonhistorical architecture of functionalism in which a new sense of space would be created with the help of modern materials. A reaction against the stylistic pluralism of the 19th century, the Modern movement was also coloured by the belief that the 20th century had given birth to "modern man," who would need a radically new kind of architecture.

Austria and Germany

The Viennese architect Adolf Loos opposed the use of any ornament at all and designed purist compositions of bald, functional blocks such as the Steiner House at Vienna (1910), one of the first private houses of reinforced concrete. Peter Behrens, having had contact with Olbrich at Darmstadt and with Hoffmann at Vienna, was in 1907

By courtesy of the Museum of Modern Art, New York

Figure 104: Hôtel Tassel, Brussels, by Victor Horta, 1892–93.

Figure 105: Casa Milá, Barcelona, by Antonio Gaudí, 1905–10.
Archivo Mas, Barcelona

appointed artistic adviser in charge of the AEG (Allgemeine Elektricitäts Gesellschaft), for which he designed a turbine factory (1909) at Berlin. Behrens strongly affected three great architects who worked in his office: Walter Gropius, Le Corbusier, and Ludwig Mies van der Rohe.

In Germany, Gropius followed a mechanistic direction. His Fagus Works factory at Alfeld-an-der-Leine in Germany (1911) and the Werkbund exposition building at the Cologne exhibition (1914) had been models of industrial architecture in which vigorous forms were enclosed by masonry and glass; the effect of these buildings was gained by the use of steel frames, strong silhouette, and the logic of their plans (Figure 106). There were no historical influences or expressions of local landscape, traditions, or materials. The beauty of the buildings derived from adapting form to a technological culture.

Gropius succeeded van de Velde as director of the ducal Arts and Crafts School at Weimar in 1919. Later called the Bauhaus, it became the most important centre of modern design until the Nazis closed it in 1933. While he was at Weimar, Gropius developed a firm philosophy about architecture and education, which he announced in 1923. The aim of the visual arts, he said, is to create a complete, homogeneous physical environment in which all the arts have their place. Architects, sculptors, furniture makers, and painters must learn practical crafts and obtain knowledge of tools, materials, and forms; they must become acquainted with the machine and attempt to use it in solving the social problems of an industrial society. At the Bauhaus, aesthetic investigations into space, colour, construction, and elementary forms were flavoured by Cubism and Constructivism. Moving the school to Dessau in 1925, Gropius designed the pioneering new Bauhaus (1925–26) in which steel frames and glass walls provided workshops within severely Cubistic buildings. Gropius assembled a staff of modern teachers, including the artists László Moholy-Nagy, Wassily Kandinsky, Paul Klee, Marcel Breuer, and Adolf Meyer, whose projects, such as the 116 experimental standardized housing units of the Törten Estate at Dessau, Ger. (1926–28), bore a highly machined, depersonalized appearance.

The mechanistic philosophy of Gropius

By courtesy of Walter Gropius/Bauhaus Archive

Figure 106: Fagus Works, Alfeld-an-der-Leine, Ger., by Walter Gropius, 1911.

In France, Tony Garnier caught the modern currents in materials, structure, and composition when he evolved his masterful plan for a *Cité industrielle* (1901–04), published in 1917, in which reinforced concrete was to be used to create a modern city of modern buildings. With insight, Garnier developed a comprehensive scheme for residential neighbourhoods, transportation terminals, schools, and industrial centres, and his plan became a major influential scheme for 20th-century urban design. Garnier received no mandate to build such a city, but his town hall at Boulogne-Billancourt (1931–34) recalled the promise he had shown, though it was not so innovative and masterful as might have been expected.

The Futurist movement counted among its members another early 20th-century urban planner, the Italian architect Antonio Sant'Elia. Influenced by American industrial cities and the Viennese architects Wagner and Loos, he designed a grandiose futuristic city, entitled "Città nuova" ("New City"), the drawings for which were exhibited at Milan in 1914. He conceived of the city as a symbol of the new technological age. It was an affirmative environment for the future, however, in opposition to the negating inhuman Expressionistic city of the future conceived by Fritz Lang in the 1926 film classic *Metropolis*.

Centred in Germany between 1910 and 1925, Expressionist architects, like the painters who were part of the

Figure 107: Centenary Hall, Breslau, Ger. (now Wrocław, Pol.), by Max Berg, 1912–13.

Dyckerhoff & Widmann

Expressionism in Germany

Brücke and Blaue Reiter groups, sought peculiarly personal and often bizarre visual forms and effects. Among the earliest manifestations of an Expressionistic building style were the highly individual early works of Hans Poelzig, such as the Luban Chemical Factory (1911–12) and the municipal water tower (1911) of Posen, Ger. (now Poznan, Pol.), which led to his monumental, visionary "space caves," such as the project for the Salzburg Festival Theatre (1920–21) and the Grosses Schauspielhaus, built in Berlin (1919) for Max Reinhardt's Expressionistic theatre. These later works by Poelzig show the influence of the structural audacity of Max Berg's Centenary Hall at Breslau, Ger. (now Wrocław, Pol.; 1912–13), with its gigantic reinforced concrete dome measuring 213 feet in diameter (Figure 107). The second generation of Expressionists centred their activities in postwar Germany and The Netherlands. Distinctly personal architectural statements were given form in such dynamically sculptured structures as the Einstein Observatory in Potsdam (1920), by Erich Mendelsohn (Figure 108); the anthroposophically based design by Rudolf Steiner for the Goetheanum in Dornach, Switz. (1925–28); the Eigen Haard Estates (housing development) at Amsterdam (1921), by Michel de Klerk; and Fritz Höger's (1877–1949) Chilehaus office building in Hamburg (1922–23), with its imperative thrust of mass and acute angularity.

As Germany was the centre of Expressionism, Paris was the stronghold of the advocates of a new vision of space, Cubism, which Georges Braque and Pablo Picasso developed in 1906. Forms were dismembered into their faceted components; angular forms, interpenetrated planes, transparencies, and diverse impressions were recorded as though seen simultaneously. Soon architectural reflections of the Cubist aesthetic appeared internationally. Interior spaces were defined by thin, discontinuous planes and glass walls; supports were reduced to slender metal columns, machine finished and without ornamentation; and Cubistic voids and masses were arranged programmatically in asymmetric compositions.

The Dutch de Stijl movement was influenced by Cubism, although it sought a greater abstract purity in its geometric formalism. Organized in Leiden in 1917, the painters Piet Mondrian and Theo van Doesburg and the architects Jacobus Johannes Oud and Gerrit Thomas Rietveld were counted among its members. Their Neoplastic aesthetic advocated severe precision of line and shape, austerely pristine surfaces, a Spartan economy of form, and purity of colour. Rietveld's Schroeder House, built in 1924 at Utrecht, was a three-dimensional parallel to Mondrian's paintings of the period (Figure 109). Van Doesburg's work for the Bauhaus art school at Weimar brought the influence of Dutch Neoplasticism to bear upon Gropius and Mies, whose plans for houses at times markedly resembled van Doesburg's paintings. Meanwhile Oud collaborated with van Doesburg for a time and vigorously proclaimed the new style in housing developments he built at Rotterdam (after 1918), Hook of Holland (1924–27), and Stuttgart, Ger. (1927).

Cubism and the related movements of Futurism, Constructivism, Suprematism, and Neoplasticism, like any artistic styles, might have faltered and fallen into a merely decorative cliché, as at the Paris Exposition of 1925, but for Gropius, Mies van der Rohe, and Le Corbusier.

Mies van der Rohe's contribution

Gropius was succeeded at the Bauhaus in 1930 by Mies van der Rohe, whose training as a mason was supplemented by the engineering experience he had gained from 1908 to 1911 in the office of Behrens; both of these elements of his education were synthesized in his project for the Kröller House in The Hague (1912). Influenced by van Doesburg's de Stijl, Mies's natural elegance and precise orderliness soon revealed themselves in unrealized projects for a brick country house, a steel and glass skyscraper, and a glazed, cantilevered concrete-slab office building (1920–22). He directed the Weissenhof estate project of the Werkbund Exposition at Stuttgart (1927), contributing the design for an apartment house. Such practical problems failed to show his talent, which was not fully known until he designed the German pavilion for the International Exposition at Barcelona in 1929. The continuous spaces partitioned with thin marble planes and the chromed steel columns drew international applause. His Tugendhat House at Brno, Czech. (1930), along with Le Corbusier's Savoye House, epitomized the Modern domestic setting at its best.

The Swiss-French architect Charles-Édouard Jeanneret, known as Le Corbusier, gave the new architecture, sometimes referred to as the International Style, a firm foundation by writing the strong theoretical statement, *Vers une*

By courtesy of Sonnenobservatorium Einsteinturm, Potsdam

Figure 108: Einstein Observatory, Potsdam, E.Ger., by Erich Mendelsohn, 1920.

Figure 109: Schroeder House, Utrecht, Neth., by Gerrit T. Rietveld, 1924.
Dr. Franz Stoedtner

architecture (*Towards a New Architecture*), published in 1923. It revealed a world of new forms—not classical capitals and Gothic arches but ships, turbines, grain elevators, airplanes, and machine products, which Le Corbusier said were indexes to 20th-century imagination. His love of machines was combined with a belief in communal authority as the best means of accomplishing social reforms, and Le Corbusier directed his attention toward the problems of housing and urban patterns. An architectural attack, using standardized building components and mass production, was required. His sociological and formal ideas appeared in a Cubist project for Domino housing (1916), and his aesthetic preferences led him, after World War I, to develop an extreme version of Cubist painting that he and the painter Amedée Ozenfant called Purism. Returning to architecture in 1921, he designed a villa at Vaucresson, Fr. (1922), the abstract planes and strip windows of which revealed his desire to "arrive at the house machine," that is, standardized houses with standardized furniture. In 1922 he also brought forth his project for a skyscraper city of 3,000,000 people, in which tall office and apartment buildings would stand in broad open plazas and parks with the Cubist spaces between them defined by low row housing.

Le Corbusier's support of the International Style

Much of his work thereafter—his Voisin city plan, his Pavilion of the New Spirit at the Paris Exposition of 1925, his exhibit of workers' apartments at the Werkbund Exposition at Stuttgart (1927), and his influential but unexecuted submittal to the League of Nations competition—was a footnote to that dream of a new city. The villa, Les Terrasses, at Garches, Fr. (1927), was a lively play of spatial parallelepipeds (six-sided solid geometric forms the faces of which are parallelograms) ruled by horizontal planes, but his style seemed to culminate in the most famous of his houses, the Savoye House at Poissy, Fr. (1929–30). The building's principal block was raised one story above the ground on pilotis (heavy reinforced-concrete columns); floors were cantilevered to permit long strip windows; and space was molded plastically and made to flow horizontally, vertically, and diagonally until, on the topmost terrace, the whole composition ended in a cadenza of rounded, terminating spaces. Gaining greater facility in manipulating flowing spaces, Le Corbusier designed the dormitory for Swiss students at the Cité Universitaire (1931–32) in Paris.

Early Soviet architecture

In the period after the Revolution the Soviet Union at first encouraged modern art, and several architects, notably the German Bruno Taut, looked to the new government for a sociological program. The Constructivist project for a monument to the Third International (1920) by Vladimir Tatlin was a machine in which the various sections (comprising legislative houses and offices) would rotate within an exposed steel armature. A workers' club in Moscow (1929) had a plan resembling half a gear, and the Ministry of Central Economic Planning (1928–32), designed by Le Corbusier, was intended to be a glass-filled slab but, because of Stalin's dislike of modern architecture, was never completed. Its foundation later was used for an outdoor swimming pool.

Modern European styles of architecture were subjected to official disfavour in the Soviet Union in the 1930s, as Stalin's government adopted classical monuments—such as Boris Mikhaylovich Iofan's winning design for the Palace of the Soviets (1931), which was intended to pile classical colonnades to a height of 1,365 feet and have a colossal statue of Lenin at its summit. With its gigantic Corinthian columns, the building for the Central Committee of the Communist Party at Kiev (1937) showed an overbearing scale.

After 1930 the Modern movement spread through Europe. In Switzerland Robert Maillart's experiments with reinforced concrete attained great grace in his Salginatobel Bridge (1930). Finland's Alvar Aalto won a competition for the Municipal Library at Viipuri (now Vyborg, U.S.S.R.) in 1927 with a building of glass walls, flat roof, and round skylights (completed 1935; destroyed 1943); but he retained the traditional Scandinavian sympathy for wood and picturesque planning that were evident in his Villa Mairea at Noormarkku (1938–39), the factory and housing at Sunila (1936–39, completed 1951–54), and his later civic centre at Säynätsalo (1950–52). Aalto and other Scandinavians gained a following among those repelled by severe German modernism. Sweden's Erik Gunnar Asplund and Denmark's Kay Fisker, Christian Frederick Møller, and Arne Jacobsen also brought regional character into their modern work. In The Netherlands, Johannes Andreas Brinkman and Lodewijk Cornelis van der Vlugt, at the Van Nelle Tobacco Factory in Rotterdam (1929–30), aimed at more mechanistic, universal form. In England, refugees from Germany and other countries, alone or with English designers, inaugurated a radical modernism—for example, the apartment block known as Highpoint I, Highgate, London (by Berthold Lubetkin and the Tecton group, 1935).

The locus for creative architecture in the United States remained the Middle West, although Californians such as the brothers Charles Sumner Greene and Henry Mather Greene struck occasional regional and modern notes, as in the Gamble House at Pasadena, Calif. (1908–09). The second generation of architects of the Chicago school, such as William G. Purcell, G.G. Elmslie, and William Drummond, disseminated Middle Western modern architecture throughout the United States.

The greatest of all these new Chicago architects was Frank Lloyd Wright. His "prairie architecture" expressed its site,

The "prairie style" of Frank Lloyd Wright

region, structure, and materials and avoided all historical reminiscences; beginning with its plan and a distinctive spatial theme, each building burgeoned to its exterior sculptural form. Starting from Richardson's rustic, shingle houses and making free use of Beaux-Arts composition during the 1880s and 1890s, Wright hinted at his prairie house idiom with the Winslow House at River Forest, Ill. (1893), elaborated it in the Coonley House at Riverside, Ill. (1908), and, ultimately, realized it in 1909 in the flowing volumes of space defined by sculptural masses and horizontal planes of his Robie House at Chicago (Figure 110). Meanwhile, he scored a triumph with his administration building for the Larkin Company at Buffalo in 1904 (destroyed 1950), which grouped offices around a central skylighted court, sealed them hermetically against their smoky environs, and offered amenities in circulation, air conditioning, fire protection, and plumbing. In its blocky fire towers, sequences of piers and recessed spandrels were coupled together in a powerful composition. Wright was, however, ignored by all except a select following. The buildings of the single figure who gave international distinction to early 20th-century American architecture remained the cherished property of personal clients, such as Aline Barnsdall, for whom Wright designed the Hollyhock House at Los Angeles (1918–20).

Organic architecture in the United States

Wright's *Autobiography* (1943) recorded his frustrations in gaining acceptance for organic architecture. The first edition summarized the chief features of that architecture: the reduction to a minimum in the number of rooms and the definition of them by point supports; the close association of buildings to their sites by means of extended and emphasized planes parallel to the ground; the free flow of space, unencumbered by boxlike enclosures; harmony of all openings with each other and with human scale; the exploitation of the nature of a material, in both its surface manifestations and its structure; the incorporation of mechanical equipment and furniture as organic parts of structure; and the elimination of applied decoration. There were also four new properties: transparency, which was obtained through the use of glass; tenuity, or plasticity of mass achieved through the use of steel in tension, as in reinforced concrete; naturalism, or the expression of materials; and integration, in which all ornamental features were natural by-products of manufacture and assembly.

The Millard House at Pasadena, Calif. (1923), exemplified many of these principles; its concrete-block walls were cast with decorative patterns. Taliesin East, Wright's house near Spring Green, Wisc., went through a series of major rebuildings (1911, 1914, 1915, and 1925), and each fitted the site beautifully; local stone, gabled roofs, and outdoor gardens reflected the themes of the countryside. A period of withdrawal at Taliesin afforded Wright several years of intensive reflection, from which he emerged with fabulous drawings for the Doheny ranch in California (1921), a skyscraper for the National Life Insurance Company at Chicago (1920–25), and St. Mark's Tower, New York City (1929). The last was to have been an 18-story apartment house comprising a concrete stem from which four arms branched outward to form the sidewalls of apartments cantilevered from the stem to an exterior glass wall. Unexecuted like most of Wright's most exciting projects, St. Mark's Tower testified to his revolutionary thinking about skyscraper architecture. His ideas gained a wide hearing in 1931 when he published the Kahn lectures he had delivered at Princeton in 1930. In keeping with the needs of the United States during the Depression, Wright turned his attention to the low-cost house, designing a "Usonian house" for Herbert Jacobs near Madison, Wisc. (1937), and a quadruple house, "the Sun houses," at Ardmore, Pa. (1939). These exemplified the residences he intended for his ideal communities, such as rural, decentralized Broadacre City (1936), which was Wright's answer to European schemes for skyscraper cities.

At about the same time, Wright produced four masterpieces: Fallingwater, Bear Run, Pa. (1936), the daringly cantilevered weekend house of Edgar Kaufmann; the administration building of S.C. Johnson & Son, in which brick cylinders and planes develop a series of echoing spaces, culminating in the forest of graceful "mushroom" columns in the main hall, and the Johnson House (1937), aptly called Wingspread, both at Racine, Wisc.; and Taliesin West at Paradise Valley, near Phoenix, Ariz. (begun 1938), where rough, angular walls and roofs echo the desert valley and surrounding mountains. With increasing sensitivity to local terrain and native forms and materials, Wright stated more complex spatial and structural themes than European modernists, who seldom attempted either extreme programmatic plans or organic adaptation of form to a particular environment. Eventually, Wright himself developed a more universal geometry, as he revealed in the sculptural Solomon R. Guggenheim Museum at New York City (1956–59).

The emblem of business, the office building, continued to suffer from demands for unique, distinctive towers. Harvey Wiley Corbett, a New York architect, admitted that publicity was the ruling motivation. Sometimes a business with nationwide suboffices developed a corporate iconography; Sears, Roebuck and Company, Bell Telephone, Howard Johnson, A & P, and the various gasoline companies were recognizable instantly. The Gothic skyscraper, popularized by Gilbert's Woolworth Building, was the style used by Raymond Hood for his winning entry in the *Chicago Tribune* competition (1922). Some buildings gained attention through their classical ornament; others were Renaissance palaces. About 1920 some architects developed simple cubical forms, and the stepped ziggurat was popularized by renderers, notably Hugh Ferriss, and such painters as Georgia O'Keeffe, John Marin, and Charles Sheeler. This soaring and jagged form received legal support from the New York City zoning law of 1916 and economic justification from the fact that, in order to obtain rentable, peripheral office space in the upper floors, where the banks of elevators diminished, whole increments of office space had to be omitted. These cubical envelopes were not without ornament at their crests, as in Hood's American Radiator Building in New York City

Hedrich-Blessing photo

Figure 110: Robie House, Chicago, by Frank Lloyd Wright, 1909.

(1924–25), suitably described as "one huge cinder incandescent at the top." Such decoration might be chic, as in New York City's Barclay–Vesey (telephone company) Building, where Ralph Walker re-created the Art Deco interiors of the Paris Exposition of 1925. In San Francisco, Miller, Pflueger, & Cantin used Chinese ornament to enliven their telephone building (1926). Paradoxically, one archaeological find led to simpler buildings when, about 1930, Mayan pyramids inspired Timothy Pflueger in his work on the 450 Sutter building in San Francisco. Clifflike blocks arose in Chicago, the Daily News and Palmolive buildings (1929) being the best examples; New York City acquired a straightforward expression of tall vertical piers and setback cubical masses in the Daily News Building (1930), by the versatile Hood, who had run the course from Gothic to modern form (Figure 111). The bank and office building of the Philadelphia Savings Fund Society (1931–32) by George Howe and William Lescaze, a Swiss architect, gave the skyscraper its first thoroughly 20th-century form, and Hood, again, produced a counterpart in New York City, the McGraw-Hill Building (1931). Few of these, including the Empire State Building (1931), did anything to solve urban density and transportation problems; indeed, they intensified them. Rockefeller Center, however, begun in 1929, was, with its space for pedestrians within a complex of slablike skyscrapers, outstanding and too seldom copied.

American industry showed some inclination to respect function, materials, and engineering between the world wars, as was evident in Joseph Leland's glazed, skeletal buildings for the Pressed Steel Company at Worcester, Mass. (1930). Occasionally, a traditional architect had produced an innovation, such as Willis Polk's (1867–1924) Hallidie Building at San Francisco (1918). With the aid of Ernest Wilby, the engineering firm of Albert Kahn created a work of architectural merit in Detroit's Continental Motors Factory (about 1918). The National Cash Register, United States Shoe Company, National Biscuit, Sears, Roebuck and Company and various automobile companies, such as Ford, sponsored Functional architecture.

By courtesy of New York News Inc.

Figure 111: The Daily News Building, New York City, by Raymond Hood, 1930.

Rockefeller Center indicated that by 1930 there was a move toward simple form, which was presaged by the architecture of the TVA (Tennessee Valley Authority). European modernism gained a firm following in the United States as some of its best practitioners emigrated there. Eliel Saarinen, who won second prize in the *Chicago Tribune* competition, gained the acclaim of Sullivan and other architects. He settled in Bloomfield Hills, Mich., a Detroit suburb, where he established a school of architecture at the Cranbrook Academy. Saarinen designed its new buildings, gradually freeing himself from historical reminiscences of his native Scandinavia. He remained sensitive to the role of art in architecture, best revealed by his use of the sculpture of the Swede Carl Milles. The Austrian architect Richard Neutra established a practice in California, notable products of which were the Lovell House at Los Angeles (1927–28) and the Kaufmann Desert House at Palm Springs (1946–47).

The United States as the centre of the International Style

A modern architecture exhibit in the Museum of Modern Art, New York City, in 1932, recorded by the architectural historian Henry-Russell Hitchcock and the architect Philip Johnson in the book *International Style; Architecture Since 1922,* familiarized Americans with the International Style. After 1933, as modernists fled the Soviet Union, Germany, and Italy, the United States received Gropius, Breuer, and Mies. Gropius joined the architectural school of Harvard University and established an educational focus recalling the Bauhaus.

After World War II. Initially, the leading interwar architects of modernism, Gropius, Mies van der Rohe, Le Corbusier, Wright, and Aalto, continued to dominate the scene. In the United States, Gropius, with Breuer, introduced modern houses to Lincoln, Mass., a Boston suburb, and formed a group, The Architects Collaborative, the members of which designed the thoroughly modern Harvard Graduate Center (1949–50). Mies became dean of the department of architecture at the Illinois Institute of Technology at Chicago in 1938 and designed its new campus. Crown Hall (1952–56) marked the apogee of this quarter-century project (Figure 112).

Not all the immigrants remained in the United States. Aalto, whose work first appeared on the American scene in the Finnish pavilion at the New York World's Fair and again in the Massachusetts Institute of Technology's Baker Dormitory (1947–49), returned to Finland. The European who might have contributed most was Le Corbusier. The United Nations buildings at New York City, for which he was a member of a 10-man commission headed by New York architect Wallace Harrison, is a token of the new forms he might have suggested for American cities. His plan for rebuilding Saint-Dié, Fr. (1945), was the inspiration for many city-planning proposals made after mid-century.

Beginning with private houses by Hood, Lescaze, Edward Stone, Neutra, Gropius, and Breuer during the 1930s, American Modernism gradually supplanted the historical styles in a range of building types, including schools and churches; for example, Eliel Saarinen's simple, brick Christ Lutheran Church (1949–50) at Minneapolis, Minn.

Architecture as a commercial and industrial symbol

After World War II, big industry turned to Modern architects for distinctive emblems of prestige. The Connecticut General Life Insurance Company hired one of the largest modern firms, Skidmore, Owings, and Merrill, to design their new decentralized headquarters outside Hartford, Conn. (1955–57). Lever Brothers turned to the same firm for New York City's Lever House (1952), in which the parklike plaza, glass-curtain walls, and thin aluminum mullions realized the dreams of Mies and others in the 1920s of freestanding crystalline shafts (Figure 113). Designed by Eliel Saarinen's son Eero, the General Motors Technical Center (1948–56) at Warren, Mich., was compared with Versailles in its extent, grandeur, and rigorous conformity to an austere, geometric aesthetic of Miesian forms. The Harrison and Abramovitz's tower for

Figure 112: Crown Hall, Illinois Institute of Technology, Chicago, by Mies van der Rohe, 1952–56.
Hedrich-Blessing photo

the Aluminum Company of America at Pittsburgh (1954) advertised its own product, as did Skidmore, Owings, and Merrill's Inland Steel Building at Chicago (1955–57). Perhaps the most chaste of all was the Seagram Building (1954–58) at New York City, designed by Mies and Philip Johnson. Wright alone avoided the rectilinear geometry of these office buildings. In 1955 he saw his Price Tower rise at Bartlesville, Okla., a richly faceted, concrete and copper fulfillment of the St. Mark's Tower he had designed more than 25 years earlier.

Advent of Formalism

About 1952 there was a significant shift within Modernism from what had come to be called Functionalism, or the International Style, toward a monumental Formalism. There was increasing interest in highly sculptural masses and spaces, as well as in the decorative qualities of diverse building materials and exposed structural systems. Wright's Guggenheim Museum is a manifestation of this aesthetic. Those who had focused their attention on the rectilinear portions of Le Corbusier's Savoye House and Unité d'Habitation apartments at Marseille (1946–52), tended to ignore the plastic sculpture on the roofs of those buildings; to such people, Le Corbusier's highly individual buildings at Chandīgarh, India (begun 1950), and the cavernous space in the lyrical church of Notre-Dame-du-Haut at Ronchamp, Fr., seemed to be examples of personal whimsy (Figure 114). Pier Luigi Nervi in Italy gave structural integrity to the complex curves and geometry of reinforced-concrete structures, such as the Orbetello aircraft hangar (begun 1938) and Turin's exposition hall (1948–50). The Spaniard Eduardo Torroja, his pupil Felix Candela, and the American Frederick Severud followed his lead. Essentially, each attempted to create an umbrella roof the interior space of which could be subdivided as required, such as Torroja's grandstand for the Zarzuela racetrack in Madrid (1935). Mies constructed rectilinear versions of such a space in Crown Hall and in his Farnsworth House at Plano, Ill. (1946–50), while Philip Johnson allowed a single functional unit, the brick-cylinder utility stack, to protrude from his precise glass house at New Canaan, Conn. (1949). Other designers used curvilinear structural geometry, best indicated by Matthew Nowicki's (1910–49) sports arena at Raleigh, N.C. (1952–53), in which two tilted parabolic arches, supported by columns, and a stretched-skin roof enclose a colossal space devoid of interior supports. In 1949 Nowicki had challenged Louis Sullivan's precept, form follows function, with another, form follows form, a dictum that freed architecture from programmatic expression. Hugh Stubbins' congress hall, at Berlin (1957), and Eero Saarinen's Trans World Airlines terminal at John F. Kennedy International Airport, New York City (1956–62), were outstanding examples of these dynamically monumental, single-form buildings the geometric shapes and silhouettes of which were derived from mathematical computation and technological innovation. International competitions for the opera house at Sydney (1957) and a government centre at Toronto (1958) were won by the Dane Jørn Utzon and the Finn Viljo Revell, respectively. Both architects were exponents of the new monumentalism.

These designs posed problems in structural engineering and in scale, but many architects, such as the American Minoru Yamasaki in the McGregor Building for Wayne State University at Detroit (1958), attempted to make structure become decorative, while the decorative screen, as used by Edward Durell Stone at the U.S. embassy in New Delhi (1957–59), offered a device for wrapping

Ben Schnall

Figure 113: Lever House, New York City, by Skidmore, Owings, and Merrill, 1952.

Figure 114: Church of Notre-Dame-du-Haut, Ronchamp, Fr., by Le Corbusier, 1950–55.
George Holton—Photo Researchers/EB Inc.

programmatic interiors within a rich pattern of sculptured walls.

Latin-American developments

Mexico and South America broke their bonds to French, Spanish, and Portuguese academic design during the 1930s. Le Corbusier's influence became partially strong in Brazil, where the Brazilian Oscar Niemeyer and other architects designed the Corbusier-inspired Ministry of Education and Public Health at Rio de Janeiro (1937–42). Brazil's Lúcio Costa, Affonso Reidy, and Niemeyer; Mexico's Felix Candela, Juan O'Gorman, José Villagran Garcia, and Luis Barragán; and Venezuela's Carlos Raúl Villanueva were the vanguard of Latin-American architectural modernism. Whole communities such as Caracas and São Paulo essentially were rebuilt during the 1950s, and new cities, such as Brasília, the capital of Brazil, and "university cities," such as those of Mexico and Venezuela, were conceived and erected. In Mexico there was avid support for modern design in buildings such as the Presidente Juárez housing at Mexico City (1950) by Mario Pani and Salvador Ortega. In Colombia, after World War II, enormous strides were made in thin-shelled reinforced-concrete construction. In Brazil, dramatic complexes were erected from concrete by Reidy, such as the school and gymnasium at Pedregulho housing at Rio de Janeiro (1953) and Rio's Museum of Modern Art (1960–67).

After 1959, office buildings for administrative headquarters of large corporations followed the 1955–57 suburban-campus model of Skidmore, Owings, and Merrill's Connecticut General Life Insurance Company or, if urban, the towerlike form, often with strong structural expression (Torre Velasca, Milan, by Belgiojoso, Peressutti, and Rogers, 1959) or the slab form, usually emphasizing glazed walls (Mannesmann Building, Düsseldorf, by Paul Schneider-Esleben, 1959), but they rarely achieved an urban composition such as the 1962 Place Ville-Marie, built at Montreal by the Chinese-born American architect I.M. Pei.

Air transportation, trade exhibitions, and spectator sports summoned the often awesome spatial resources of modern technology. The stadiums for the 1964 Olympics at Tokyo by Tange Kenzō, Rome's Pallazzi dello Sport done by Nervi (1960), Eero Saarinen's Dulles International Airport at Chantilly, Va. (1958–62), and Chicago's exposition hall, McCormick Place, by C.F. Murphy and Associates (1971) are examples of the colossal spaces achieved in reinforced concrete or steel and glass. International exhibitions seldom offered comparable architecture. At the New York World's Fair (1964) the Spanish pavilion by Javier Carvajal and the Japanese pavilion by Maekawa Kunio were buildings of merit. There were also several notable examples at Montreal's Expo 67: the West German pavilion by Frei Otto, the U.S. pavilion by R. Buckminster Fuller, and the startling Constructivist apartment house, Habitat 67, by the Israeli Moshe Safdie, in association with David, Barott, and Boulva, whose 158 precast-concrete apartment units were hoisted into place and post-tensioned to permit dramatic cantilevers and terraces.

World's fair architecture

World's fairs continued to provide a setting for occasionally distinguished examples of modern structures that demonstrated innovations in building technology.

The architecture of South and Southeast Asia as well as of Japan has been decisively influenced by Western architects, particularly Le Corbusier. The leading figure in Japan was Tange Kenzō, whose many powerful buildings of rough concrete include the Peace Centre, Hiroshima (1949–55), and St. Mary's Roman Catholic Cathedral at Tokyo (1965). His disciples included the so-called Metabolism Group, led by Kikutake Kiyonori, Maki Fumihiko, and Otaka Masato. Their work, characterized by a dynamic science-fiction quality expressive of fluidity and change, culminated in the Osaka Expo 1970, with constructions such as Tange's giant space frame, known as the Theme Pavilion, and Kikutake's Landmark Tower.

Educational architecture

Much significant architecture in the postwar period was sponsored by cultural centres and educational institutions, such as Berlin's philharmonic hall (1963) by Hans Scharoun. Louis I. Kahn, in his design for the Richards Medical Research Building (1960), gave the University of Pennsylvania in Philadelphia a linear programmatic composition of laboratories, each served by vertical systems for circulating gases, liquids, and electricity. Paul Rudolph's art and architecture building (1963) at Yale University in New Haven, Conn., gathered its studios, galleries, classrooms, and light wells on 36 interpenetrating levels distributed over six stories. The Morse and Stiles colleges (1962), also at Yale, were designed by Eero Saarinen and set a new standard for multiple-entry urban dormitories. Even the traditionalist campuses of New England preparatory schools gained modern architecture, such as the art building and science building at Phillips Academy in Andover, Mass., by Benjamin A. Thomson (1963) and the dormitories at St. Paul's School in Concord, N.H., by Edward Larrabee Barnes (1965).

The innovations in educational architecture were international. In England, distinctive educational architecture arrived at Hunstanton Secondary School, Norfolk (1949–54), by Peter and Alison Smithson. An example of what became known as the New Brutalism, this building was influenced by Mies van der Rohe. Most New Brutalist buildings, however, owed more to Le Corbusier's late work—for example, the gray concrete masses of Denys Lasdun's University of East Anglia, Norfolk (1962–68)—while James Stirling's History Faculty, Cambridge (1964–67), brought a neo-Constructivist element to the Brutalist tradition. Canada gained the Central Technical School Arts Center by Robert Fairfield Associates (1964) and Scarborough College by John Andrews, with Page and Steele (1966), both at Toronto. Italian innovative educational architecture is exemplified in Milan's Instituto Marchiondi (1959) by Vittoriano Viganò. Led by disciples of Le Corbusier, the Japanese built Waseda University (1964), which was designed by Katsuo Ardo, and Maekawa Kunio's Gakushuin University (1964), both in Tokyo.

Some of the new educational settings proposed solutions to what was undoubtedly the mid-20th century's greatest problem, its urban environment. The high-rise, dense campus at Boston University by José Luis Sert and the skyscraper towers of MIT's earth-sciences building (1964) by I.M. Pei, as well as Harvard's behavioral sciences building (1964) by Minoru Yamasaki, were imaginative single buildings responding to urban circumstances. The Air Force Academy at Colorado Springs, Colo., and the Chicago Circle Campus of the University of Illinois (1965), both by the firm of Skidmore, Owings, and Merrill with Walter A. Netsch as the principal designer (1956), and the Salk Institute for Biological Studies at La Jolla, Calif., by Louis I. Kahn (1966), all offered intimations of a new city built around a cultural, educational centre.

New cities

No comparable concentration of intensive, harmonious urban architecture was achieved for cities, even though, after 1955, the building of new cities produced some remarkable examples such as Vällingby, Swed.; Brasília, the new capital of Brazil; Cumbernauld, in Scotland; and Chandīgarh, in India; and some remarkable renovations of old cities, as in Eastwicks in Philadelphia (Reynolds Metals Co.; plans by Constantinos Doxiadis, 1960) and Constitution Plaza in Hartford, Conn. (Charles DuBose, with Sasaki, Walker & Associates 1964), and New York's Lincoln Center for the Performing Arts (1962). By this time, however, it was beginning to be felt that the application of Modern movement principles had caused visual damage to historic cities and had also failed to create a humane environment in new cities. It was at this moment that the postmodernist era began. (A.B.-B./D.J.Wa.)

POSTMODERNISM

The 1960s saw the rise of dissatisfaction with consequences of the Modern movement, especially in North America, where its failings were exposed in two influential books, Jane Jacobs' *The Death and Life of Great American Cities* (1961) and Robert Venturi's *Complexity and Contradiction in Architecture* (1966). Jacobs highlighted the destruction of urban coherence wrought by the utopian iconoclasm of the Modern movement, whereas Venturi implied that Modern buildings were without meaning because they were designed in a simplistic and puritan way that lacked the irony and complexity which enrich historical architecture. This dissatisfaction was translated into direct action in 1972 with the demolition of several 14-story slab blocks that had been built only 20 years earlier from designs by Yamasaki as part of the award-winning Pruitt-Igoe housing development in St. Louis, Mo. Similar apartment blocks in Europe and North America were demolished in the following decades, but it was at St. Louis that the postmodernist era was begun.

Venturi's *Learning from Las Vegas* (with Denise Scott Brown and Steven Izenour) was also published in 1972. In seeking to rehumanize architecture by ridding it of the restricting purism of the Modern movement, the authors pointed for guidance to the playful commercial architecture and billboards of the Las Vegas highways. Venturi and his partner John Rauch reintroduced to architectural design elements of wit, humanity, and historical reference in buildings such as the Tucker House, Katonah, N.Y. (1975), and the Brant-Johnson House, Vail, Colo. (1976). These owed something to Lutyens, who, as a master of paradox and complexity, exercised a deep appeal for Venturi and for his followers, such as Charles Moore and Michael Graves. Graves's Portland Public Service Building, Portland, Ore. (1980–82; Figure 115), and Humana Tower, Louisville, Ky. (1986), have the bulk of the modern skyscraper yet incorporate historical souvenirs such as the colonnade, belvedere, keystone, and swag. Like Moore's

Wit and historical reference in buildings

Figure 115: Portland Public Service Building, Oregon, by Michael Graves, 1980–82.
Peter Aaron/ESTO

Piazza d'Italia, New Orleans (1975–80), and Alumni Center, University of California at Irvine (1983–85), these confident and colourful buildings are intended to reassure the public that it need no longer feel that its cultural identity is threatened by modern architecture. That mood was encapsulated in Venice in 1980 when a varied group of American and European architects, including Venturi, Moore, Paolo Portoghesi, Aldo Rossi, Hans Hollein, Ricardo Bofill, and Léon Krier, provided designs for an exhibition organized by the Venice Biennale under the title, "The Presence of the Past." These key architects of postmodernism represented several different outlooks but shared the ambition of banishing the fear of memory from modern architectural design.

The many American architects in the 1970s and '80s who adopted a populist language scattered with classical souvenirs included Philip Johnson and his partner John Burgee and the prolific Robert Stern. Johnson and Burgee designed the AT&T Building, New York City (1978–84), a skyscraper with a Chippendale skyline. Their School of Architecture Building, University of Houston (1982–85), is inspired by Ledoux's project for a House of Education at Chaux (1773–79). Stern's Observatory Hill Dining Hall, University of Virginia, Charlottesville (1982–84), is in a cheerful Jeffersonian classicism, while his Prospect Point Office Building, La Jolla, Calif. (1983–85), incorporates Spanish Colonial references. Many postmodernist architects were either trained by or began their careers as modernists, and many elements of Modernism carried over into postmodernism, especially in the work of architects such as Graves, Venturi, and Richard Meier.

Rejecting the playful elements in such buildings as kitsch, some architects, notably Allan Greenberg and John Blatteau, chose a more historically faithful classical style, as in their official reception rooms of the U.S. Department of State in Washington, D.C. (1984–85). The most complete instance of historical accuracy is probably the J. Paul Getty Museum, Malibu, Calif. (1970–75), an essay in Neoclassicism designed by the Los Angeles partnership of Langdon and Wilson, who relied on archaeological advice to achieve the authentic character of a Roman villa at Herculaneum.

A similar duality existed in this period in Britain, where the populist style of Graves was paralleled in the work of

Figure 116: Interior of the Clore Gallery at the Tate Gallery, London, by James Stirling, 1980–87.
Angelo Hornak

Terry Farrell (TV-am Studios, Camden Town, London, 1983), and of James Stirling (Clore Gallery at the Tate Gallery, London, 1980–87; Figure 116), while undeviating classicism was pursued by Quinlan Terry (Riverside Development, Richmond, Surrey, 1986–88), Julian Bicknell (Henbury Rotunda, Cheshire, 1984–86), and John Simpson (Ashfold House, Sussex, 1985–87). The spirit of classical urban renewal was represented in France by Christian Langlois's Senate Building, rue de Vaugirard, Paris (1975), and the Regional Council Building in Orléans (1979–81). Urban preoccupations have been more dramatically expressed in France by Ricardo Bofill's vast housing developments, such as Les Espaces d'Abraxas, Marne-la-Vallée, near Paris (1978–83; Figure 117). The gargantuan scale of this columnar architecture of prefabricated concrete pushes the language of classicism to its limits and beyond.

Neorationalism

A third branch of postmodernism was represented by a neorationalist or elementalist approach that echoes the stripped classicism of the 19th and early 20th century. This movement was again in part a reaction to changes in the urban environment by the combination of commercial pressure and Modern movement ideology. Neorationalism originated in Italy where the architect Aldo Rossi published an influential book, *L'architettura della città* (1966; *The Architecture of the City*), Rossi's Modena Cemetery (1971–77) exhibits both his austerely fundamental classicism and his concern for contextualism, since it echoes features of the local farms and factories of Lombardy.

Neorationalist ideals have also been realized in the Italian-speaking Swiss canton of Ticino: for example, in the work of Mario Campi (Casa Maggi, Arosio, 1980); Mario Botta; and Bruno Reichlin and Fabio Reinhardt, whose Casa Tonino, Torricella (1972–74), is a pristine stripped Palladian essay in white concrete. Close to this work is a group of buildings in the Basque region, including the School at Ikastola (1974–78) by Miguel Garay and José-Ignacio Linazasoro; Casa Mendiola at Andoian (1977–78) by Garay; and the Rural Centre at Cordobilla (1981) by Manuel Iniguez and Alberto Ustarroz. The projects of the German architect Oswald Matthias Ungers—for example, his Stadtloggia in the Hildesheim marketplace (1980)—promoted the same kind of rationalist contextualism in Germany. They have been influential on the design of infill buildings in other historic towns in West Germany, Italy, and France. The Viennese architect Hans Hollein also contributed to this vein of radical eclecticism, as in his sophisticated interiors in the Austrian Travel Bureau, Vienna (1978), which distantly recall the city of Otto Wagner and Josef Hoffmann. The urban work of the Belgian architect Rob Krier has been related to this movement, as can be seen in his housing in the Ritterbergstrasse, West Berlin (1978–80). His brother, Léon Krier, has been influential in both the United States and Britain for his iconlike drawings of city planning schemes in a ruthlessly simple classical style and for his polemical attacks on what he sees as the destruction by modern technology of civic order and human dignity.

The 1920s revivalist element in the neorationalist move-

Pupkewitz/Rapho

Figure 117: Les Espaces d'Abraxas, Marne-la-Vallée, by Ricardo Bofill, 1978–83.

ment is demonstrated in the United States in the work of Richard Meier, for example in his Smith House, Darien, Conn. (1965–67), inspired by Le Corbusier's Citrohan and Domino houses, and his more complex High Museum, Atlanta (1980–83). Helmut Jahn's Bank of the South West, Houston (1982), recalls the Art Deco glass skyscraper, while the prolific Kevin Roche, originally a minimalist trained in the 1950s by Eero Saarinen, returned to the heroic formalism of the early skyscrapers for his Morgan Bank headquarters, New York City (1983–87), a 48-story skyscraper resting on a 70-foot-high entrance loggia of coupled granite columns.

Western influences in Asian architecture

In Japan, Isozaki Arata and Yamashita Kazumasa led the move away from Brutalism and Metabolism toward a postmodernism inspired by Charles Moore—for example, Isozaki's Tsukuba Centre building, Tsukuba Science City, Ibaraki (1983), and Yamashita's Japan Folk Arts Museum, Tokyo (1982). In India, Charles Correa led a parallel shift away from high-rise mass-housing of the Le Corbusier type. In the 1950s he worked in the International style, as in his hotel of white concrete at Ahmadabad, but in later low-rise housing and in his book, *The New Landscape* (1985), he demonstrated the virtues of a return to the more indigenous building types of the Third World.

The spirit of technology is, by contrast, celebrated in the Centre Pompidou, Paris (1971–77), by Renzo Piano and Richard Rogers. With its services and structure exposed externally and painted in primary colours, this exhibition centre can be seen as an outrageous joke in the historic centre of Paris. Though defiantly "modern," it has a postmodernist flavour as a playful statement of the modernist belief, going back at least to Viollet-le-Duc, in the truthful exposure of the structural bones of a building. Rogers repeated the theme in his Lloyd's Building, London (1984–86), but Stirling's addition to the Staatsgalerie, Stuttgart, W.Ger. (1977–82), is a key postmodernist building in the Venturi sense: that is, it makes ironic references to the language of Schinkel without accepting the fundamental principles of classicism. (D.J.Wa.)

BIBLIOGRAPHY

General works: *Sir Banister Fletcher's A History of Architecture,* 19th ed., edited by JOHN MUSGROVE (1987), provides a comprehensive standard survey of Western architecture; as do DAVID WATKIN, *A History of Western Architecture* (1986); SPIRO KOSTOF, *A History of Architecture: Settings and Rituals* (1985); and NIKOLAUS PEVSNER, *An Outline of European Architecture,* 7th ed. (1963, reprinted 1974). Standard reference works include ULRICH THIEME and FELIX BECKER (eds.), *Allgemeines Lexikon der bildenden Künstler von der Antike bis zur Gegenwart,* 37 vol. (1907–50, reprinted 1978); continued by HANS VOLLMER (ed.), *Allgemeines Lexikon der bildenden Künstler des XX. Jahrhunderts,* 6 vol. (1953–62); *Encyclopedia of World Art,* 16 vol. (1959–83); and ADOLF K. PLACZEK (ed.), *Macmillan Encyclopedia of Architects,* 4 vol. (1982). See also ALEXANDER TZONIS and LIANE LEFAIVRE, *Classical Architecture: The Poetics of Order* (1986; originally published in Dutch, 1983); and ROGER SCRUTON, *The Aesthetics of Architecture* (1979).

Bronze Age: Introductions to the architecture of the period are found in EMILY VERMEULE, *Greece in the Bronze Age* (1972); and JOHN BOARDMAN, *Pre-Classical: From Crete to Archaic Greece* (1967, reprinted 1978). SIR ARTHUR EVANS, *The Palace of Minos: A Comparative Account of the Successive Stages of the Early Cretan Civilization as Illustrated by the Discoveries at Knossos,* 4 vol. in 6 (1921–35, reissued 1964), is a classic on Minoan architecture; it is in part superseded by RICHARD W. HUTCHINSON, *Prehistoric Crete* (1962); and SINCLAIR HOOD, *The Minoans: The Story of Bronze Age Crete* (1971). For Helladic art, see GEORGE E. MYLONAS, *Mycenae and the Mycenaean Age* (1966); and LORD WILLIAM TAYLOUR, *The Mycenaeans,* rev. ed. (1983). For Cyprus, see VASSOS KARAGEORGHIS, *Cyprus, from the Stone Age to the Romans,* new ed. (1982), with a useful bibliography; and for the western Mediterranean, ANTONIO ARRIBAS, *The Iberians* (1964); DAVID TRUMP, *Central and Southern Italy Before Rome* (1966); and MARIO MORETTI and GUGLIELMO MAETZKE, *The Art of the Etruscans* (1970; originally published in Italian, 1969).

Classical Greek and Hellenistic: Major surveys are offered in WILLIAM B. DINSMOOR, *The Architecture of Ancient Greece: An Account of Its Historic Development,* 3rd rev. ed. (1950, reprinted 1975); D.S. ROBERTSON, *Greek and Roman Architecture,* 2nd ed. (1943, reprinted 1969); A.W. LAWRENCE, *Greek Architecture,* 4th ed., rev. by R.A. TOMLINSON (1983); J.J. COULTON, *Greek Architects at Work: Problems of Structure and Design* (1977, reprinted 1982); RHYS CARPENTER, *The Architects of the Parthenon* (1970); BERNARD ASHMOLE, *Architect and Sculptor in Classical Greece* (1972); JOHN TRAVLOS, *Pictorial Dictionary of Ancient Athens,* trans. from Greek (1971); and J.J. POLLITT, *The Art of Greece, 1400–31 B.C.: Sources and Documents* (1965), and *Art in the Hellenistic Age* (1986).

Roman: The basic source is VITRUVIUS, *The Ten Books on Architecture,* trans. from Latin by MORRIS HICKY MORGAN (1914, reprinted 1960), the only complete treatise to survive from antiquity. Authoritative surveys with informative bibliographies are AXEL BOËTHIUS, *Etruscan and Early Roman Architecture,* 2nd rev. ed. by ROGER LING and TOM RASMUSSEN (1978); and J.B. WARD-PERKINS, *Roman Imperial Architecture* (1981). See also WILLIAM L. MACDONALD, *The Architecture of the Roman Empire,* rev. ed., 2 vol. (1982–86); and MARGARET LYTTELTON, *Baroque Architecture in Classical Antiquity* (1974); MARION E. BLAKE, *Ancient Roman Construction in Italy from the Prehistoric Period to Augustus* (1947, reprinted 1968) and *Roman Construction in Italy from Tiberius Through the Flavians* (1959, reprinted 1968); MARION E. BLAKE and DORIS TAYLOR BISHOP, *Roman Construction in Italy from Nerva Through the Antonines* (1973); J.J. POLLITT, *The Art of Rome, c. 733 B.C.–337 A.D.: Sources and Documents* (1966, reprinted 1983); and ERNEST NASH, *Pictorial Dictionary of Ancient Rome,* 2nd rev. ed., 2 vol. (1968, reissued 1981).

Early Christian and Byzantine: RICHARD KRAUTHEIMER, *Early Christian and Byzantine Architecture,* 4th ed., rev. by RICHARD KRAUTHEIMER and SLOBODAN ĆURČIĆ (1986), and *Rome, Profile of a City, 312–1308* (1980), are major studies. See also E. BALDWIN SMITH, *Architectural Symbolism of Imperial Rome and the Middle Ages* (1956, reprinted 1978); WILLIAM L. MACDONALD, *Early Christian & Byzantine Architecture* (1962); and STEVEN RUNCIMAN, *Byzantine Style and Civilization* (1975). On Constantinople (Istanbul), see THOMAS F. MATHEWS, *The Byzantine Churches of Istanbul: A Photographic Survey* (1976); and DAVID TALBOT RICE (ed.), *The Great Palace of the Byzantine Emperors* (1958). HUBERT FAENSEN and VLADIMIR IVANOV, *Early Russian Architecture* (1975; originally published in German, 1972), is a useful introduction.

Early Medieval and Romanesque: The fundamental study is KENNETH JOHN CONANT, *Carolingian and Romanesque Architecture, 800 to 1200,* 3rd ed. (1973). HARALD BUSCH and BERND LOHSE (eds.), *Romanesque Europe* (1960; originally published in German, 1959), is a good photographic survey. See also A.W. CLAPHAM, *Romanesque Architecture in Western Europe* (1936, reprinted 1967); JOAN EVANS, *The Romanesque Architecture of the Order of Cluny* (1938, reprinted 1972); and WALTER HORN and ERNEST BORN, *The Plan of St. Gall: A Study of Architecture & Economy of Life in a Paradigmatic Carolingian Monastery,* 3 vol. (1979). On England, see H.M. TAYLOR and JOAN TAYLOR, *Anglo-Saxon Architecture,* 3 vol. (1965–78); A.W. CLAPHAM, *English Romanesque Architecture Before the Conquest* (1930), and *English Romanesque Architecture After the Conquest* (1934), reprinted as *English Romanesque Architecture,* 2 vol. (1969); and ERIC FERNIE, *The Architecture of the Anglo-Saxons* (1983).

Gothic: PAUL FRANKL, *Gothic Architecture,* trans. from German (1962), provides a full scholarly survey; while LOUIS GRODECKI, *Gothic Architecture,* trans. from French (1977, reissued 1985), offers a well-illustrated summary. Earlier classics include JOHN FITCHEN, *The Construction of Gothic Cathedrals: A Study of Medieval Vault Erection* (1961, reissued 1981); OTTO VON SIMSON, *The Gothic Cathedral: Origins of Gothic Architecture and the Medieval Concept of Order,* 3rd expanded ed. (1988); and ERWIN PANOFSKY, *Gothic Architecture and Scholasticism* (1951, reissued 1976); while later scholarship is represented in JEAN BONY, *The English Decorated Style: Gothic Architecture Transformed, 1250–1350* (1979), and *French Gothic Architecture of the 12th and 13th Centuries* (1983). See also TERESA G. FRISCH, *Gothic Art 1140–c. 1450: Sources and Documents* (1971, reissued 1987).

Renaissance: The best general survey of Italian Renaissance architecture is LUDWIG H. HEYDENREICH and WOLFGANG LOTZ, *Architecture in Italy, 1400 to 1600,* trans. from German (1974). PETER MURRAY, *The Architecture of the Italian Renaissance,* new ed. (1969, reprinted 1986), is a useful account. RUDOLF WITTKOWER, *Architectural Principles in the Age of Humanism,* 4th ed. (1973), a scholarly study, may be read in conjunction with historical treatises, especially LEON BATTISTA ALBERTI, *The Ten Books of Architecture,* trans. from Latin (1755, reprinted 1986); and ANDREA PALLADIO, *The Four Books of Architecture* (1738, reprinted 1977; originally published in Italian, 1570). On Rome, see PAOLO PORTOGHESI, *Rome of the Renaissance* (1972; originally published in Italian, 1971); and DAVID R. COFFIN, *The Villa in the Life of Renaissance Rome* (1979).

For Renaissance architecture outside of Italy see ANTHONY BLUNT, *Art and Architecture in France, 1500 to 1700,* 4th ed.

(1980); GEORGE KUBLER and MARTIN SORIA, *Art and Architecture in Spain and Portugal and Their American Dominions, 1500 to 1800* (1959); JOHN SUMMERSON, *Architecture in Britain, 1530–1830,* 7th rev. ed. (1983); HOWARD COLVIN, *A Biographical Dictionary of British Architects, 1600–1840* (1980); HENRY-RUSSELL HITCHCOCK, *German Renaissance Architecture* (1981); BRIAN KNOX, *Bohemia and Moravia, an Architectural Companion* (1962); HELENA KOZAKIEWICZOWA and STEFAN KOZAKIEWICZ, *The Renaissance in Poland* (1976; originally published in Polish, 1976); and GEORGE HEARD HAMILTON, *The Art and Architecture of Russia,* 3rd ed. (1983).

Baroque and Rococo: Important general studies include ANTHONY BLUNT (ed.), *Baroque & Rococo: Architecture and Decoration* (1978); VICTOR L. TAPIÉ, *The Age of Grandeur: Baroque Art and Architecture,* 2nd ed. (1966; originally published in French, 1957); and FISKE KIMBALL, *The Creation of the Rococo* (1943; reprinted as *The Creation of the Rococo Decorative Style,* 1980). The classic study on Italian Baroque is RUDOLF WITTKOWER, *Art and Architecture in Italy, 1600 to 1750,* 3rd rev. ed. (1973, reprinted with corrections, 1980). On Rome, see ANTHONY BLUNT, *Guide to Baroque Rome* (1982); and RICHARD KRAUTHEIMER, *The Rome of Alexander VII, 1655–1667* (1985); and for other parts of Italy, see ANTHONY BLUNT, *Sicilian Baroque* (1968), and *Neapolitan Baroque & Rococo Architecture* (1975); and RICHARD POMMER, *Eighteenth-Century Architecture in Piedmont: The Open Structures of Juvarra, Alfieri & Vittone* (1967). See also EBERHARD HEMPEL, *Baroque Art and Architecture in Central Europe: Germany, Austria, Switzerland, Hungary, Czechoslovakia, Poland,* trans. from German (1965); JOHN BOURKE, *Baroque Churches of Central Europe,* 2nd rev. ed. (1962, reprinted 1978); HENRY-RUSSELL HITCHCOCK, *Rococo Architecture in Southern Germany* (1968); NICHOLAS POWELL, *From Baroque to Rococo: An Introduction to Austrian and German Architecture from 1580 to 1790* (1959); KARSTEN HARRIES, *The Bavarian Rococo Church: Between Faith and Aestheticism* (1983); HAROLD E. WETHEY, *Colonial Architecture and Sculpture in Peru* (1949, reprinted 1971); PÁL KELEMEN, *Baroque and Rococo in Latin America,* 2 vol., 2nd ed. (1967; reprinted in 1 vol., 1977); ANTHONY BLUNT, *Art and Architecture in France, 1500 to 1700,* 4th ed. (1980); JACOB ROSENBERG, SEYMOUR SLIVE, and E.H. TER KUILE, *Dutch Art and Architecture: 1600–1800,* 3rd ed. (1977); W. KUYPER, *Dutch Classicist Architecture: A Survey of Dutch Architecture, Gardens, and Anglo-Dutch Architectural Relations from 1625 to 1700* (1980); PETER THORNTON, *Seventeenth-Century Interior Decoration in England, France, and Holland* (1978); KERRY DOWNES, *English Baroque Architecture* (1966); and JUDITH HOOK, *The Baroque Age in England* (1976).

Classicism, 1750–1830: Stimulating general studies include JOSEPH RYKWERT, *The First Moderns: The Architects of the Eighteenth Century* (1980), and *On Adam's House in Paradise: The Idea of the Primitive Hut in Architectural History,* 2nd ed. (1981); EMIL KAUFMANN, *Architecture in the Age of Reason: Baroque and Postbaroque in England, Italy, and France* (1955, reprinted 1968); and ROBIN MIDDLETON and DAVID WATKIN, *Neoclassical and 19th Century Architecture* (1980, reissued in 2 vol., 1987). Special subjects are covered in ALLAN BRAHAM, *The Architecture of the French Enlightenment* (1980); WEND GRAF KALNEIN and MICHAEL LEVEY, *Art and Architecture of the Eighteenth Century in France* (1972); SVEND ERIKSEN, *Early Neo-Classicism in France: The Creation of the Louis Seize Style in Architectural Decoration, Furniture and Ormolu, Gold and Silver, and Sevres Porcelain in the Mid-Eighteenth Century,* trans. from Danish (1974); WOLFGANG HERRMANN, *Laugier and Eighteenth Century French Theory* (1962, reprinted 1985); DORA WIEBENSON, *The Picturesque Garden in France* (1978); J. MORDAUNT CROOK, *The Greek Revival: Neo-Classical Attitudes in British Architecture, 1760–1870* (1972); DAVID WATKIN and TILMAN MELLINGHOFF, *German Architecture and the Classical Ideal* (1987), a well-illustrated survey with a full bibliography; HERMANN G. PUNDT, *Schinkel's Berlin: A Study in Environmental Planning* (1972); BRIAN KNOX, *The Architecture of Poland* (1971); GEORGE HEARD HAMILTON, *op.cit.;* and MIKHAIL A. IL'IN, *Moscow Monuments of Architecture, 18th–the First Third of the Nineteenth Century,* parallel Russian and English texts, 2 vol. (1975); WILLIAM H. PIERSON, JR., *American Buildings and Their Architects: The Colonial and Neo-Classical Styles* (1970, reprinted 1986), which largely supersedes the pioneering study by TALBOT HAMLIN, *Greek Revival Architecture in America* (1944, reprinted 1964). See also HUGH MORRISON, *Early American Architecture: From the First Colonial Settlements to the National Period* (1952, reissued 1987), a well-illustrated account; CARL W. CONDIT, *American Buildings: Materials and Techniques from the First Colonial Settlements to the Present,* 2nd ed. (1982); and MARCUS WHIFFEN and FREDERICK KOEPER, *American Architecture, 1607–1976* (1981).

Gothic Revival: PAUL FRANKL, *The Gothic: Literary Sources and Interpretations Through Eight Centuries* (1960), is a fundamental study. GEORG GERMANN, *Gothic Revival in Europe and Britain: Sources, Influences, and Ideas,* trans. from German (1972), has an unusually broad perspective. For Britain, see CHARLES L. EASTLAKE, *A History of the Gothic Revival,* 2nd ed., edited by J. MORDAUNT CROOK (1978), a basic text first published in 1872; later analyses include KENNETH CLARK, *The Gothic Revival: An Essay in the History of Taste,* 3rd ed. (1962, reprinted 1974); STEFAN MUTHESIUS, *The High Victorian Movement in Architecture, 1850–1870* (1972); and GEORGE L. HERSEY, *High Victorian Gothic: A Study in Associationism* (1972). Comprehensive information for Germany is found in W.D. ROBSON-SCOTT, *The Literary Background of the Gothic Revival in Germany: A Chapter in the History of Taste* (1965); and for the United States, PHOEBE B. STANTON, *The Gothic Revival & American Church Architecture: An Episode in Taste, 1840–1856* (1968); and WILLIAM H. PIERSON, JR., *Technology and the Picturesque: The Corporate and the Early Gothic Styles* (1978).

Classicism, 1830–1930: The standard general study is HENRY-RUSSELL HITCHCOCK, *Architecture, Nineteenth and Twentieth Centuries,* 4th ed. (1977). PETER COLLINS, *Changing Ideals in Modern Architecture, 1750–1950* (1965, reissued 1975), offers a challenging interpretative approach. See also ARTHUR DREXLER (ed.), *The Architecture of the École des Beaux-Arts* (1977, reprinted 1984); ROBIN MIDDLETON (ed.), *The Beaux-Arts and Nineteenth-Century French Architecture* (1982); NORMA EVENSON, *Paris: A Century of Change, 1878–1978* (1979); HENRY-RUSSELL HITCHCOCK, *Early Victorian Architecture in Britain,* 2 vol. (1954, reissued 1972); ALBERT E. RICHARDSON, *Monumental Classic Architecture in Great Britain and Ireland,* new ed. (1982); CARROLL L.V. MEEKS, *Italian Architecture, 1750–1914* (1966); SPIRO KOSTOF, *The Third Rome, 1870–1950: Traffic and Glory* (1973); TILMANN BUDDENSIEG, *Industriekultur: Peter Behrens and the AEG, 1907–1914* (1984; originally published in German, 1981); BARBARA MILLER LANE, *Architecture and Politics in Germany, 1918–1945* (1968, reprinted 1985); SIMO PAAVILAINEN (ed.), *Nordic Classicism, 1910–1930* (1982); E. KIRICHENKO, *Moscow Architectural Monuments of the 1830–1910s,* parallel English and Russian text (1977); JOHN W. REPS, *Monumental Washington: The Planning and Development of the Capital Center* (1967); DAVID F. BURG, *Chicago's White City of 1893* (1976); and WILLIAM H. JORDY, *American Buildings and Their Architects: Progressive and Academic Ideals at the Turn of the Twentieth Century* (1972).

20th century: (*Iron and glass*): FRANÇOIS LOYER, *Architecture of the Industrial Age, 1789–1914* (1983; originally published in French, 1983); SIGFRIED GIEDION, *Mechanization Takes Command: A Contribution to Anonymous History* (1948, reprinted 1969); CARROLL L.V. MEEKS, *The Railroad Station: An Architectural History* (1956, reissued 1978); and CARL W. CONDIT, *American Building Art: The Twentieth Century* (1961). (*Art Nouveau*): A comprehensive survey is provided in FRANK RUSSELL (ed.), *Art Nouveau Architecture* (1979, reprinted 1986); ROBERT SCHMUTZLER, *Art Nouveau,* trans. from German (1962, reissued 1978); and S. TSCHUDI MADSEN, *Art Nouveau,* trans. from Norwegian (1967, reprinted 1976).

(*Modern movement*): Early classic studies include HENRY-RUSSELL HITCHCOCK and PHILIP JOHNSON, *The International Style: Architecture Since 1922* (1932, reprinted 1966); NIKOLAUS PEVSNER, *Pioneers of Modern Design: From William Morris to Walter Gropius,* rev. ed. (1975, reprinted 1986); SIGFRIED GIEDION, *Space, Time, and Architecture: The Growth of a New Tradition,* 5th rev. ed. (1967, reprinted 1982); and REYNER BANHAM, *Theory and Design in the First Machine Age,* 2nd ed. (1967). For broader explorations, see KENNETH FRAMPTON, *Modern Architecture: A Critical History,* rev. ed. (1985); and ARTHUR DREXLER, *Transformations in Modern Architecture* (1979). Modern American architecture is discussed in WILLIAM H. JORDY, *American Buildings and Their Architects: The Impact of European Modernism in the Mid-Twentieth Century* (1972, reissued 1986); JANE JACOBS, *The Death and Life of Great American Cities* (1961, reissued 1984); and CARL W. CONDIT, *American Building Art: The Twentieth Century* (1961). (*Postmodernism*): Postmodernism has been surveyed in PAOLO PORTOGHESI, *Postmodern: The Architecture of the Post-Industrial Society* (1983; originally published in Italian, 1982); and CHARLES A. JENCKS, *The Language of Post-Modern Architecture,* 4th rev. ed. (1984), and *Post-Modernism: The New Classicism in Art and Architecture* (1987).

(D.J.Wa.)